PRAISE FOR *THE MOODY BIBLE COMMENTARY*

This commentary is concise. It takes into account the latest scholarship and is directed to all who are interested in the meaning of the text. It helps all of us understand the practical application of Scripture. This will be a commentary that stays on my desk and is used often.

Erwin W. Lutzer
Senior Pastor, The Moody Church, Chicago

The Moody Bible Institute has been my proudest association for more than four decades, and *The Moody Bible Commentary* is one more reason why. This is the perfect resource for a layperson like me, and I expect it to inform my study, my devotions, and my writing for years to come.

Jerry B. Jenkins
Novelist and chairman of the Board of Trustees, Moody Bible Institute

I'm thrilled that *The Moody Bible Commentary* is available. What a tremendous resource for everyone who loves studying the Bible and values teaching the "whole counsel of God." This remarkable work provides verse by verse exposition of both the Old and New Testaments by solid, trusted evangelical scholars who believe deeply in the inerrancy of the Scriptures and power of the Word to transform lives. It is quickly becoming an invaluable part of my reference library. I highly recommend that you add it to yours.

Joel C. Rosenberg
New York Times best-selling author and Bible teacher

What a great addition to the library of anyone who seeks to probe the riches of God's Word—for application, edification, and transformation. Who better to write it than the faculty of Moody Bible Institute! I add my enthusiastic endorsement to the many others who will find this to be a valued companion in the study of God's Word.

Joseph M. Stowell
President, Cornerstone University, Grand Rapids, MI

For so many people, the name "Moody" is synonymous with the word "trust." Having a Bible commentary that is written by the faculty of Moody Bible Institute means you can trust what you are reading to be accurate as well as edifying. This commentary is a "must-have" in the Parshall library.

Janet Parshall
Nationally syndicated talk-show host

Once again, Moody Publishers, the name you can trust, has provided Bible students and teachers alike a comprehensive biblical resource that will help them to understand and communicate biblical truths effectively. It is a must-read tool for every Christian's library.

Tony Evans
President, The Urban Alternative
Senior Pastor, Oak Cliff Bible Fellowship, Dallas

The Moody Bible Commentary is a very readable resource, helpful to the layman, Bible study teacher, and serious student alike. The introductory material to each book provides excellent information, and the actual commentary offers a verse-by-verse explanation of the text and deals with the important words. *The Moody Bible Commentary* enables the reader to come to a clear understanding of Scripture that will be helpful for personal knowledge, spiritual growth, and ministry.

PAUL ENNS
Professor and Director, Tampa Extension
Southeastern Baptist Theological Seminary

The Moody Bible Commentary offers a user-friendly way to understand God's Word. Christians everywhere will find it an indispensable resource for unlocking the meaning of the text. This volume is destined to become a modern classic.

RAY PRITCHARD
President, Keep Believing Ministries
Author, *An Anchor for the Soul*

Here in one volume is skillful theological wisdom and commentary from God's library of sixty-six books. This is a gift for laypeople who serve Jesus without having had the privilege of formal biblical training.

JILL P. BRISCOE
Author and speaker

The Moody Bible Commentary is a dependable, dynamic, understandable, verse-by-verse study of the entire Bible. The contributors are teaching scholars who have given their lives to accurately teach God's Word. I can't wait to order my personal copy and learn from it.

GEORGE SWEETING
Chancellor Emeritus, Moody Bible Institute

Moody Bible is a name you can trust and this *Moody Commentary* is a book you can trust. It's concise, biblically solid, deals with current theological issues, and provides quality scholarship in understandable language. I highly recommend it!

CHIP INGRAM
CEO and Teaching Pastor, Living on the Edge

The Moody Bible Commentary provides the reader with a great reference, an overview, a synthesis, an outline, and detailed notes that address difficult or thorny passages. You don't have to be a scholar to benefit from this resource. One can (almost) never have too many commentaries, so add this volume to your library. It will serve you for years to come.

MICHAEL EASLEY
Teaching Pastor, Fellowship Bible Church, Nashville, TN

THE MOODY BIBLE COMMENTARY

MICHAEL RYDELNIK AND
MICHAEL VANLANINGHAM
GENERAL EDITORS

MOODY PUBLISHERS
CHICAGO

The commentary on Daniel by Michael Rydelnik is adapted and expanded from the previously published study notes on Daniel by Michael Rydelnik in the *HCSB Study Bible*, edited by Edwin A. Blum and Jeremy Royal Howard (Nashville: Holman Bible Publishers, 2010), pp. 1429–58. Used with permission.

Managing Editor: Allan Sholes
Editors: Christopher Reese, Paul Brinkerhoff, Philip Rawley, Jim Vincent
Interior Design: The Livingstone Corporation
Cover Design: Smartt Guys design

Produced with the assistance of The Livingstone Corporation (www.LivingstoneCorp.com).

ISBN: 978-0-8024-2867-7

Originally delivered by fleets of horse-drawn wagons, the affordable paperbacks from D. L. Moody's publishing house resourced the church and served everyday people. Now, after more than 125 years of publishing and ministry, Moody Publishers' mission remains the same—even if our delivery systems have changed a bit. For more information on other books (and resources) created from a biblical perspective, go to www.moodypublishers.com or write to:

Moody Publishers
820 N. LaSalle Boulevard
Chicago, IL 60610

9 10

Printed in the United States of America

CONTENTS

Dedicated to the students of Moody Bible Institute,
who have committed to studying God's Word
and given us, the general editors and contributors,
the honor and privilege of teaching it to them
and then watching them go out to teach it to
others around the world.

••••

Be diligent to present yourself approved to God as a workman who does not need to be ashamed, accurately handling the word of truth.

2 Timothy 2:15

Theme Verse of the Moody Bible Institute

FOREWORD

The Bible is the most important book you or I will ever read. It is the bestselling book of all-time with an estimated five billion copies sold. The complete Bible has been translated into 717 languages, giving 5.75 billion people access to Scripture. This book is not simply historically significant and hugely popular—it is the inspired, inerrant Word of God!

The Bible contains sixty-six books written by forty authors over a period of 1,500 years, yet it delivers one cohesive, powerful, life-changing message. This is not a dry, dusty text, but God-breathed and alive and relevant for us today. It goes without question then that the study of God's Word must be a high priority for any Jesus follower.

At Moody Bible Institute, we have a Bible verse engraved on the stone wall of the school's entrance: 2 Timothy 2:15, "Be diligent to present yourself approved to God as a workman who does not need to be ashamed, accurately handling the word of truth." As many have said, "Bible" is our middle name, and the study and teaching of God's Word is central to everything we say or do. So with this commentary, we want to help every man and woman become devoted students of God's Word.

My own time spent studying God's Word has had a profound and lasting effect on me. It guided me, shaped me, molded me, and corrected me. It has been an anchor in difficult times, and a light when my way was dark. It speaks truth that I need to hear and guides me as I follow Jesus.

We hope that the contents of this Bible commentary will be a useful tool as you spend time in God's Word, not just reading, but spending in-depth time on each book and letting the truth of Scripture seep into your heart and mind. Our founder, evangelist D. L. Moody, once said, "Read the Bible, my friends, as if you were seeking for something of value. It is a good deal better to take a single chapter, and spend a month on it, than to read the Bible at random for a month."

I want to assure you that this is a commentary you can trust. It has been authored and edited by faculty members of the Moody Bible Institute, scholars devoted to the study and teaching of God's Word. In this volume you'll find a high level of biblical scholarship presented in a way that is clear and easy to understand. The commentary in this volume takes the Bible in the plain sense of the language. The authors have remained true to the original meaning of the biblical text, avoiding current trends or personal conjecture. Finally, those familiar with Moody Bible Institute will find that the commentary aligns with the teachings of the Institute. Since its founding in 1886, Moody has always stood for sound Bible doctrine, and this commentary fulfills that tradition.

We hope this becomes not just another book on your shelf, but a daily companion, wise teacher, and helpful guide as you learn and grow from God's Word. Together, we can "accurately handle the word of truth," the living, breathing Word of our almighty God.

Mark Jobe
President, Moody Bible Institute

CONTRIBUTORS

To maintain the coherency and consistency of *The Moody Bible Commentary*, the individual commentaries have gone through multiple levels of editorial review and revision. The commentaries as they now appear occasionally include content or views that differ from those originally submitted by the contributors. The general editors were collaborators on each of the commentaries and are ultimately responsible for their contents.

Louis A. Barbieri Professor Emeritus of Theology, Moody Bible Institute, *Mark, 1 and 2 Peter, Jude*
BA, Westmont College; ThM, ThD, Dallas Theological Seminary

Michael J. Boyle Associate Professor of Pastoral Studies, Moody Bible Institute, *Nahum*
BS, University of North Dakota; ThM, Dallas Theological Seminary; DMin, Gordon-Conwell Theological Seminary

James F. Coakley Professor of Bible, Moody Theological Seminary, *Numbers, Deuteronomy*
BA, Calvary Bible College; MDiv, ThM, Grace Theological Seminary; DMin, Covenant Theological Seminary; ABD, University of Stellenbosch

Charles H. Dyer Professor-at-Large of Bible, Moody Bible Institute, *Jeremiah, Lamentations, Ezekiel*
BA, Washington Bible College; ThM, PhD, Dallas Theological Seminary; Graduate Study, Institute of Holy Land Studies, Jerusalem

David Finkbeiner Chair and Professor of Theology, Moody Bible Institute, *Proverbs, Ecclesiastes*
BA, Bob Jones University; MA, MDiv, Biblical Theological Seminary; PhD, Trinity International University

John K. Goodrich Assistant Professor of Bible, Moody Bible Institute, *Hosea*
BA, Moody Bible Institute; MDiv, ThM, Talbot School of Theology; PhD, Durham University

Daniel D. Green Professor of Pastoral Studies, Moody Theological Seminary, *Micah, Revelation*
BA, Michigan State University; ThM, Dallas Theological Seminary; DMin, Trinity Evangelical Divinity School

John F. Hart Professor of Bible, Moody Bible Institute, *John, James*
BS, West Chester University; ThM, Dallas Theological Seminary; ThD, Grace Theological Seminary

John A. Jelinek Vice President and Dean, Professor of Theology, Moody Theological Seminary, *Leviticus, Amos*
BREd, William Tyndale College; ThM, Dallas Theological Seminary; ThD, Grace Theological Seminary

John M. Koessler Professor of Pastoral Studies, Moody Bible Institute, *1 and 2 Timothy, Titus*
BA, Wayne State University; MA, MDiv, Biblical Seminary; DMin, Trinity International University

John T. McMath Professor of Bible, Moody Bible Institute–Spokane, *Judges*
BA, Whitworth College; MDiv, Western Conservative Baptist Seminary; STM, Dallas Theological Seminary; DMin, Western Conservative Baptist Seminary

William H. Marty Professor of Bible, Moody Bible Institute, *Acts*
BA, Biola University; MDiv, Denver Seminary; STM, ThD, Dallas Theological Seminary

Eugene J. Mayhew Professor of Old Testament and Semitic Languages, Moody Theological Seminary, *Job*
BREd, Detroit Bible College; ThM, Dallas Theological Seminary; ThD, Grace Theological Seminary

Winfred Neely Professor of Preaching and Pastoral Studies, Moody Bible Institute, *1 and 2 Samuel*
BA, Trinity College; MA, Wheaton College Graduate School; DMin, Trinity Evangelical Divinity School

Bryan O'Neal Professor of Theology, Moody Bible Institute, *Nehemiah*
BA, Moody Bible Institute; MA, Purdue University; PhD, Purdue University

Gerald W. Peterman Professor of Bible, Moody Bible Institute, *Galatians, Ephesians, Philippians, Colossians*
BDes, University of Florida; MDiv, MA, Trinity Evangelical Divinity School; PhD, King's College, University of London

Michael A. Rydelnik Professor of Jewish Studies, Moody Bible Institute, *Song of Solomon, Isaiah, Daniel, Joel, Habakkuk, Haggai, Zechariah, Malachi*
Diploma, Moody Bible Institute; BA, Azusa Pacific University; ThM, Dallas Theological Seminary; DMiss, Trinity Evangelical Divinity School

Steven H. Sanchez Professor of Bible, Moody Bible Institute,, *Obadiah*
BA, Columbia University; ThM, PhD, Dallas Theological Seminary

Ronald Sauer Professor of Bible, Moody Bible Institute, *Hebrews, 1, 2 and 3 John*
BA, Mississippi College; ThM, Dallas Theological Seminary; PhD, University of Manchester, England

Harry E. Shields Adjunct Professor of Pastoral Studies, Moody Theological Seminary, *1 and 2 Kings*
BA, Indiana University of Pennsylvania; ThM, Dallas Theological Seminary; DMin, Trinity Evangelical Divinity School

Tim M. Sigler Professor of Bible, Moody Bible Institute, *Song of Solomon*
BA, Faith Baptist Bible College; MA, MDiv, Faith Baptist Theological Seminary; PhD, Trinity International University

James Spencer Vice President and Dean of Distance Learning, Moody Bible Institute, *Isaiah*
BS, University of Illinois at Chicago; MA, Wheaton College Graduate School; MDiv, Moody Theological Seminary; PhD, Trinity Evangelical Divinity School

William D. Thrasher Professor of Bible and Theology, Moody Theological Seminary, *Jonah*
BS, Auburn University; ThM, ThD, Dallas Theological Seminary

J. Brian Tucker Associate Professor of New Testament, Moody Theological Seminary, *Ezra*
BS, Lee College; MA, Liberty University; MDiv, DMin, Michigan Theological Seminary; PhD, University of Wales, Lampeter

Michael G. Vanlaningham Professor of Bible, Moody Bible Institute, *Matthew, Romans, 1 Corinthians*
BA, Nebraska Wesleyan University; MDiv, Talbot Theological Seminary; PhD Trinity Evangelical Divinity School

Gerald D. Vreeland Professor of Bible, Moody Bible Institute–Spokane, *Joshua*
BA, Oregon State University; MDiv, ThM, Western Conservative Baptist Seminary; PhD, Trinity International University

Michael G. Wechsler Professor of Bible, Moody Bible Institute, *Ruth*
BS, Rutgers University; MA, Trinity International University; PhD, University of Chicago

Walter White, Jr. Former Alumni Director and faculty member, Moody Bible Institute, *Zephaniah*
Diploma, Moody Bible Institute; BA, University of Illinois; ThM, Dallas Theological Seminary

David L. Woodall Professor of New Testament and Greek, Moody Theological Seminary, *2 Corinthians*
BA, Cedarville College; MDiv, ThM, Grand Rapids Baptist Seminary; PhD, Trinity Evangelical Divinity School

Kevin D. Zuber Professor of Theology, Moody Bible Institute, *Exodus, 1 and 2 Chronicles, Luke, 1 and 2 Thessalonians*
BA, Grace College; MDiv, ThM, Grace Theological Seminary; PhD, Trinity Evangelical Divinity School

ACKNOWLEDGMENTS

Any project as extensive as *The Moody Bible Commentary* requires the talents and efforts of many people to bring it to print. As general editors we are greatly indebted to every contributor who wrote, reviewed, rewrote, and produced excellent commentaries on all the books of the Bible. It is a rare honor and privilege for us to serve the Lord Jesus together with these fine scholars at Moody Bible Institute—and now to have co-labored with them to provide this resource for God's people. Also, we are indebted to Greg Thornton, senior vice president of media at Moody Bible Institute, whose vision, wisdom, encouragement, patience, and guidance helped make this commentary not just a dream but a reality.

Thanks also go to Allan Sholes, MA, managing editor of this commentary. His diligence and editorial skill have been instrumental in bringing this work to publication.

We also want to recognize these talented editors for their splendid assistance: Christopher Reese, MA; Jim Vincent, MA; Paul Brinkerhoff, MDiv; and the late Roy Zuck, ThD. Our special thanks go to Eva Rydelnik, MA, and Philip Rawley, ThM, for their writing talents and extensive editorial work. Elizabeth Newenhuyse provided oversight of this project as editorial director, and we are so grateful for her contribution. Our thanks also go to Ryan Lloyd, production director at Moody Publishers, for his oversight of the typesetting and printing. We wish to express our appreciation, as well, to Miss Sarah Goldman for her secretarial assistance.

Words cannot fully express our immense thankfulness for our wives, Eva and Sue. With much patience they have endured our many days and hours of work on this project, as well as our perpetually distracted minds even when not working on this project, and always did so with kindness, grace, and encouragement.

Finally and most importantly, we give our greatest thanks to God our Father and the Lord Jesus our Messiah, who gave us the Bible, called all of us to study it, and by His Spirit, enabled us to produce this commentary. Blessed are You, O Lord our God, King of the universe, who has granted us life, sustained us, and allowed us to reach this day. Amen.

LIST OF ABBREVIATIONS

SCRIPTURE ABBREVIATIONS

Old Testament

Gn	Genesis	Ec	Ecclesiastes
Ex	Exodus	Sg	Song of Solomon
Lv	Leviticus	Is	Isaiah
Nm	Numbers	Jr	Jeremiah
Dt	Deuteronomy	Lm	Lamentations
Jos	Joshua	Ezk	Ezekiel
Jdg	Judges	Dn	Daniel
Ru	Ruth	Hs	Hosea
1Sm	1 Samuel	Jl	Joel
2Sm	2 Samuel	Am	Amos
1Kg	1 Kings	Ob	Obadiah
2Kg	2 Kings	Jnh	Jonah
1Ch	1 Chronicles	Mc	Micah
2Ch	2 Chronicles	Nah	Nahum
Ezr	Ezra	Hab	Habakkuk
Neh	Nehemiah	Zph	Zephaniah
Est	Esther	Hg	Haggai
Jb	Job	Zch	Zechariah
Ps(s)	Psalms	Mal	Malachi
Pr	Proverbs		

New Testament

Mt	Matthew	1Tm	1 Timothy
Mk	Mark	2Tm	2 Timothy
Lk	Luke	Ti	Titus
Jn	John	Phm	Philemon
Ac	Acts	Heb	Hebrews
Rm	Romans	Jms	James
1Co	1 Corinthians	1Pt	1 Peter
2Co	2 Corinthians	2Pt	2 Peter
Gl	Galatians	1Jn	1 John
Eph	Ephesians	2Jn	2 John
Php	Philippians	3Jn	3 John
Col	Colossians	Jd	Jude
1Th	1 Thessalonians	Rv	Revelation
2Th	2 Thessalonians		

ABBREVIATIONS OF BIBLE TRANSLATIONS

ESV	English Standard Version
HCSB	Holman Christian Standard Bible
NKJV	New King James Version
KJV	King James Version
NABRE	New American Bible Revised Edition
NIV	New International Version
NASB	New American Standard Bible
NET	New English Translation
NLT	New Living Translation
NLTse	New Living Translation 2nd edition
RSV	Revised Standard Version
TNIV	Today's New International Version

GENERAL ABBREVIATIONS

AD	in the year of our Lord
ANE	ancient Near Eastern
Aram.	Aramaic
BC	before Christ
c.	circa
cf.	compare or consult
chap (s).	chapter or chapters
DSS	Dead Sea Scrolls
e.g.,	for example
Eng.	English
esp.	especially
ET	English translation
et al.	and others
etc.	and so forth
ff.	and the following
Gk.	Greek
Hb.	Hebrew
i.e.,	that is
Lat.	Latin
lit.,	literally
LXX	Septuagint
MT	Masoretic Text
ms(s)	manuscript(s)
NT	New Testament
OT	Old Testament
p (pp).	page(s)
par.	parallel
pl.	plural
sg.	singular
v(v).	verse(s)
viz.	namely
vol(s).	volume(s)

ABBREVIATIONS OF ANCIENT SOURCES

Ant.	*Jewish Antiquities*
ANET[3]	*Ancient Near Eastern Texts Relating to the Old Testament*, 3rd ed.
Apoc. Mos.	*Apocalypse of Moses*
2 Apoc. Bar.	*2 Baruch (Syriac Apocalypse)*
b. Ketub.	*Babylonian Talmud, tractate Ketubbot*
b. San.	*Babylonian Talmud, tractate Sanhedrin*
b. Yeb.	*Babylonian Talmud, tractate Yebamot*
CD	Cairo Genizah copy of Damascus Document
Exod R	*Exodus Rabbah* (Midrash)
Gen R.	*Genesis Rabbah* (Midrash)
Hist. Eccl.	*Church History* (Eusebius)
Jub	Jubilees
m. 'Abot	*Mishnah 'Abot* (Talmud)
m. Tamid	*Mishnah Tamid* (Talmud)
m. Yoma	*Mishnah Yoma* (Talmud)
PsSol	Psalms of Solomon
QH	Qumran Hebrew
1QIsa[a]	Isaiah[a]
1QS	Rule of the Community
QH	Qumran Hebrew
Sam	Samaritan Pentateuch
Seqal.	Seqalim
SibOr	Sibylline Oracles
Sir	Sirach/Ecclesiasticus
Sukk.	Sukkah
Sym	Symmachus
Syr	Syriac
Theod	Theodotian
TJud	Testament of Judah
TLev	Testament of Levi
Vg	Vulgate

ABBREVIATIONS OF MODERN SOURCES

AB	*Anchor Bible Commentaries*
AYB	(*Anchor Yale Bible Commentaries)*
BAGD	(Bauer, W., W. F. Arndt, F. W. Gingrich, and F. W. Danker. *A Greek-English Lexicon of the New Testament and Other Early Christian Literature.* 2d ed. Chicago:University of Chicago Press, 1979)
BAR	*Biblical Archaeological Review*
BCB	Baker Commentary on the Bible
BDB	*Hebrew and English Lexicon of the Old Testament*
BDAG	Frederick W. Danker, ed., and Walter Bauer. *A Greek-English Lexicon of the New Testament and Other Early Christian Literature.* 3rd ed. Chicago: University of Chicago Press, 2001.
BDB	Brown-Driver-Briggs Hebrew and English Lexicon
BECNT	Baker Exegetical Commentary on the New Testament
BibSac	*Bibliotheca Sacra*
BKCNT	The Bible Knowledge Commentary, New Testament

BKCOT	The Bible Knowledge Commentary, Old Testament
BSE	The BE Series Commentary
BST	The Bible Speaks Today
BTCB	Brazos Theological Commentary on the Bible
CBC	The Cambridge Bible Commentary
COT	Commentary on the Old Testament
CCSOT	The Communicator's Commentary Series: Old Testament
EBC	The Expositor's Bible Commentary
HALOT	Koehler, Ludwig; Walter Baumgartner, and Johann Jacob Stamm. *The Hebrew and Aramaic Lexicon of the Old Testament.* 4 vols. Leiden: E. J. Brill, 1994–1999.
Hermenia	Hermenia: A Critical and Historical Commentary on the Bible
HNTC	Harper's New Testament Commentaries
ICC	International Critical Commentary
IVPNTC	InterVarsity Press New Testament Commentary
JETS	*Journal of the Evangelical Theological Society*
JPS	Jewish Publication Society
L&N	Louw, J. P. and E. A. Nida, Greek-English Lexicon of the New Testament: Based on Semantic Domains
LSJ	Liddell, Henry G, Robert Scott, and Henry S. Jones. *A Greek-English Lexicon.* 9th ed. Oxford, 1996.
MNTC	MacArthur New Testament Commentary
NAC	New American Commentary
NEAEHL	New Encyclopedia of Archaeological Excavations in the Holy Land
NIBC	New International Bible Commentary
NICNT	New International Commentary on the New Testament
NICOT	New International Commentary on the Old Testament
NIGTC	New International Greek Testament Commentary
NIVAC	NIV Application Commentary
NSBT	New Studies in Biblical Theology
NTC	New Testament Commentary
Pillar	Pillar New Testament Commentary
SBEC	Studies in the Bible and Early Christianity
SNTMS	Society for New Testament Studies Monograph Series
TOTC	Tyndale Old Testament Commentaries
TWOT	*Theological Wordbook of the Old Testament.* Edited by R. Laird Harris, Gleason L. Archer, Jr., and Bruce K. Waltke. 2 vols. Chicago: Moody, 1980.
WBC	Word Biblical Commentary
WEC	Wycliffe Exegetical Commentary
WTJ	*Westminster Theological Journal*

INTRODUCTION

"In order to understand the Bible, you must read it." This is an axiom that we both firmly believe. A secondary principle to which we both hold is, "If you didn't understand it the first time, read it again." More than anything else, the understanding of the Bible requires reading it, and then reading it some more. For many generations, committed believers held to the principle of the clarity of Scripture. Among other things, this simply means that if followers of Jesus the Messiah read the Bible, they can understand it. Nevertheless, there are some qualifications for this general principle:

1. Understanding the Bible requires effort—we need to work at studying the Scriptures.
2. Understanding the Bible will take time—we won't get it all immediately.
3. Understanding the Bible requires that the Holy Spirit open our hearts and minds to the Scriptures.
4. Understanding the Bible will happen only if we are willing to obey it.
5. Understanding the Bible will never be complete—we can always learn more.

Having said this, we all need some help from time to time to understand the Scriptures. A person may be reading the Bible for his or her own personal time in the Word and run across a phrase or a word, and wonder, *"What does that mean?"* Or a Sunday school teacher or small group leader might be preparing a Bible Study and wonder, *"How does this passage fit with the paragraph that went before it?"* Or pastors or teachers might encounter people confused by a particular verse and might need some help clarifying its meaning. It is for these reasons, and many more, that all of the contributors for this resource have worked so hard to produce *The Moody Bible Commentary.* We want to help that reader, Sunday school teacher, home group leader or pastor have a better understanding of the Bible. Of course, there are many good commentaries to which the Bible student could turn. What makes this commentary distinctive?

***The Moody Bible Commentary* is trustworthy.** For generations Moody Publishers has had the slogan, "The Name You Can Trust." That derives from being the publishing house of the Moody Bible Institute, an institution that has maintained its commitment to the truth of the Word of God since 1886. Since the founding of Moody Bible Institute, there have been countless attacks on the veracity of Scripture, innumerable attempts to undermine its teaching, and significant challenges to its authority. Nevertheless, in all that time, the administrators and professors at Moody Bible Institute have maintained a commitment to the inerrancy and inspiration of the Bible as the very Word of God. This high view of Scripture, along with a determination to practice first-rate biblical scholarship, has made Moody the name you can trust. Thirty faculty members of the Moody Bible Institute have worked together to produce *The Moody Bible Commentary* with explanations that are reliable.

***The Moody Bible Commentary* is understandable.** The authors and editors have striven to explain the Scriptures in a simple and clear way. They defined theological terms, clarified the meaning of difficult biblical words, identified ancient sources with which readers might be unfamiliar, and gave the geographical locations of ancient biblical cities and towns. Although the writers engaged in excellent scholarly research, they made sure that readers would not need a commentary to help them understand this commentary.

***The Moody Bible Commentary* shows the logic of biblical books.** Too often people read the Bible without regard for its literary context or structure. But the writers of Scripture, under the superintending work of the Holy Spirit, wrote inspired text with great literary artistry. Therefore, all biblical books have literary structure and strategies. One distinctive feature of this commentary is that it follows the structures that are inherent in the biblical books themselves. The commentary on each biblical book has an outline in its introduction. The body of the commentary follows that same outline so a reader can follow the structure throughout that specific book. Moreover, the commentary itself traces the flow of thought, showing how each individual section fits in the overall argument of the biblical book. In essence, *The Moody Bible Commentary* will provide a road map through each book of the Bible.

***The Moody Bible Commentary* deals with difficult verses.** Sometimes the most frustrating aspect of using a commentary is that it complicates the explanation of difficult or disputed verses and fails to offer help precisely where it is most needed. The authors and editors worked hard to be alert to the possible difficulties in a text and its interpretation, and to address those issues clearly. Of course, every reader finds different questions and sees different difficulties. Nevertheless, this commentary hopes to answer the more perplexing questions. For example, does a particular Bible passage seem to contradict another? Not if it is the inspired Word of God. Also, readers of Scripture are often perplexed by biblical prophecies, wondering when and how these were or will be fulfilled. When these apparent contradictions or perplexing difficulties present themselves, this commentary will address those issues. After all, if a commentary does not address the hard or unclear verses, then it really is not much help at all.

***The Moody Bible Commentary* uses a literal interpretive method and applies it consistently.** By "literal" we mean that the method that governs this commentary understands the words of the text in a normal way. Unless there is a good reason to think otherwise, the phrases and expressions of Scripture are interpreted according to what appears to be their plain sense. If there is a figure of speech or symbol, then it is interpreted with sensitivity to that figurative expression. However, even in the case of figurative language, there is always some spiritual or physical reality the biblical author is conveying through the figure of speech. For example, Jesus is not a literal door (see Jn 10:9), but this metaphor describes Him literally, as the only way for a person to enter a forgiven relationship with God.

Virtually all biblical interpreters agree with this "literal" approach. However, all do not apply it consistently, particularly in prophetic passages. A distinctive feature of this commentary is that it understands much of prophecy in its literal sense and even prophetic symbols are recognized as referring to a genuine reality. As a result, this approach to interpretation will affect how the commentary understands Israel, the Church, and the end of days. In our view, this method of interpretation is the least subjective and easiest way to understand the Bible.

***The Moody Bible Commentary* sees the Old Testament as a messianic text.** The Lord Jesus taught His disciples about "all things which are written about Me in the Law of Moses and the Prophets and the Psalms" (Lk 24:44). In commenting on this passage, A. T. Robertson once remarked, "Jesus found himself in the Old Testament, a thing that some modern scholars do not seem to be able to do" (*Word Pictures in the New Testament,* vol. 2 [Nashville: Broadman, 1930], 294). Even though much of contemporary scholarship does not believe in direct predictive Old Testament prophecies of the Messiah, this commentary does. It presumes that God could and did reveal the messianic hope to the writers of the Hebrew Bible. Moreover, it consistently shows how these prophecies make sense in their literary context, pointing to the coming of the future Redeemer. Additionally, this commentary shows how the New Testament refers to Jesus of Nazareth as the fulfillment of these predictions, identifying Him as the Messiah of Israel and the Savior of the world.

***The Moody Bible Commentary* is based on the original languages of Scripture.** The commentary uses the *New American Standard Bible* as its English language Bible text. When you see quotations from the biblical text in the commentary, they are in bold and taken from the NASB. We chose this translation for the commentary because it is, at the same time, among the more literal and readable translations of the Bible available. However, the commentary authors did not rely on the translation of the NASB. Rather, in their research and study, they used the Hebrew, Aramaic, and Greek texts of the Bible. As a result, there are places where a commentary might point out a more favorable translation of a word or phrase. The authors explain why this particular translation is preferred and often show how a different English version may understand it in the same way or, if necessary, include their own translations of that phrase or word. As a result, this commentary provides a fresh exposition of the biblical text based on the original languages of Scripture.

***The Moody Bible Commentary* is user-friendly.** A variety of elements make this commentary easy to use. Besides using understandable language, it is a one-volume commentary. By limiting it to just one volume, the commentary can be the one book on your shelf to which you can turn when you need help understanding the Bible. Of course there are times when readers will want to study a particular passage in greater detail. Therefore, the contributors included in-text citations, directing readers to works they can use for deeper study. Also, for those who would like greater depth in their study, there is a list of recommended works at the end of each individual commentary. Other helpful elements include an introduction to each book of the Bible, dealing with key features, such as author, date, recipients, historical setting, theological issues, place in the canon, and an outline. There are also maps of the Bible lands as they relate to the Scriptures and helpful charts that clarify the biblical text.

Other aids are included to help with your own personal study and deeper application. Of course, there are subject and Scripture indexes to help readers locate or return to key themes and issues as needed. At various points throughout, there are cross references to key Bible passages that discuss related issues (typically shown with cf. and the Bible verses). Also included are notes directing the reader to other parts of the commentary for further discussion of the same issue if it is discussed elsewhere. In addition, each chapter in the commentary includes some points of application for today's reader, reflecting the Scripture's teaching that it remains a light to guide our paths (Ps 119:105) and is useful in daily life "for teaching, for reproof, for correction, for training in righteousness" (2Tm 3:16). Overall, this commentary wants to give you an accessible resource that will readily open the Bible for you, making simple what some might think is overly complex.

Most of all, we want to encourage you never to substitute reading this commentary for actually reading the Bible. All of us, editors and contributors alike, want to support your reading of the Bible by helping you understand it. But it is the actual reading of the Bible that will transform our lives. We concur with the wisdom of Proverbs: "He who gives attention to the word will find good, and blessed is he who trusts in the LORD" (Pr 16:20).

MICHAEL A. RYDELNIK
MICHAEL G. VANLANINGHAM
GENERAL EDITORS

●●●●

THE OLD TESTAMENT

GENESIS

MULTIPLE FACULTY CONTRIBUTORS

INTRODUCTION

Author—Traditional View. Jewish and Christian traditions consistently affirm that Moses was the writer of the Pentateuch, the first five books of the Bible.

Moses is identified—either explicitly or implicitly—as the writer of the Pentateuch more often than any other writer is identified with any other biblical book(s). Mosaic authorship can be supported with several lines of evidence. (1) The Pentateuch claims this for itself (Ex 17:14; 24:4, 7; 34:27; Nm 33:1-2; Dt 31:9). (2) Other OT books claim Mosaic authorship (see, e.g., Jos 1:7-8; 8:32, 34; 22:5; 23:6; 1Kg 2:3; 2Kg 14:6; 21:8; Ezr 6:18; 2Ch 25:4; Dn 9:11-13; Mal 4:4). (3) Mosaic authorship is also the view of the NT (Mk 12:26; Lk 24:27; Jn 5:46; 2Co 3:15). (4) The details included in the Pentateuch point to an eyewitness author (Ex 15:27; Nm 2:1-31; 11:7-8), not an author writing centuries later. (5) The author was knowledgeable about Egyptian names, words, customs, and geography. Such knowledge indicates a writer from Egypt (Gn 13:10; 16:1-3; 33:18; 41:43), as Moses was, not an author or editor from Israel many centuries later. (6) Above all, the Lord Jesus Christ identified Moses as the author of the Torah. He stated (Jn 7:22) that Moses "gave" the Israelites *the account of* circumcision (Gn 17), whereas the rite itself was given to and handed down from "the fathers," that is, the patriarchs, Abraham, Isaac, and Jacob. This shows that the Lord Jesus did indeed recognize Mosaic authorship.

Author—Documentary Hypothesis. The Pentateuch was one of the first portions of the Bible in the post-Enlightenment period to be seriously reexamined by humanist-inclined scholars. The starting point for these scholars' research was the conviction that the Bible is a purely (or primarily) human literary product, representing a collection of various ancient Near Eastern sources, both historical and mythological, which were collected, systematized, edited, and refashioned over centuries of time.

The application to the Pentateuch (and thus to Genesis) of this less-than-traditional approach was consolidated toward the beginning of the 19th century under the rubric of what has come to be known as the "documentary" or "JEDP" theory of the Pentateuch's origins. According to this theory the Pentateuch is comprised of at least four different sources (Jahwistic, Elohistic, Deuteronomic, and Priestly), each of which is characterized by certain distinct features and emphases.

The ideological starting point of this view and its attendant methodology is, necessarily, that Moses did not write (or, at the very least, *may* not have written) the Pentateuch. A review of some of the "proofs" of this assertion illustrates the tenuousness, and even the circular logic through which the data are sifted:

1. *The Different Names for God.* In the Torah, different names for God are used in different passages, so advocates of the documentary hypothesis claim that this indicates different sources. For example, God is called Elohim in Gn 1:1–2:3 but called Yahweh Elohim (the LORD God) in Gn 2:4–3:24. This, however, does not derive from two separate sources but rather two distinct emphases. Elohim is the name for God as the Almighty Creator of the universe, while Yahweh is the relational, covenant name for God. It makes sense therefore, that the passage that describes the creation of the world would use Elohim, but the passage that describes the creation of humanity would use His relational name. Moreover, multiple names for God appear in other literature, such as Homer's epics

and the Quran, without requiring different sources.

2. *The Presence of Duplications.* In the Torah, there are several accounts that some claim are repetitions of the same event. For example, it is claimed that there are two creation accounts (1:1–2:3; 2:4-25), two covenant accounts (chaps. 15, 17); two banishments of Hagar (chaps. 16, 21); two name changes for Jacob (32:28; 35:10); two times Abraham claims Sarah as his sister, as does Isaac once (12:11-13; 20:11-13; 26:7); two complaints about food resolved by manna and quail (Ex 16:1-21; Nm 11:4-35); and two times water came from the rock (Ex 17:1-7; Nm 20:8-13). However, several possible reasons exist for these repetitions that do not require multiple sources. These events happened repeatedly, and the author included them for emphasis, or to show patterns of behavior, or to complement one another. In each case, there are good literary reasons for these repetitions.

3. *The Presence of Anachronisms.* It is claimed that when the text notes that "the Canaanite was then in the land" (Gn 12:6; 13:7) it reflects authorship at a time long after Moses when the Canaanites no longer were the dominant people in the land. Hence, the author was informing the audience of a prior state of affairs. However, the statements may simply imply that Moses, writing to the generation about to enter the land, sought to remind them that the Canaanites were also there in the days of the patriarchs. Another alleged anachronism is that the ancient city of Laish is called Dan (Gn 14:14), a name only given to that city after the conquest of Canaan (Jos 19:47; Jdg 18:29). However, calling the city Dan in the account of Abraham may be a result of a later scribe, when copying the Torah before the close of the OT canon, updating the city name, so that later generations would be able to identify the city under discussion. Another alleged anachronism is the statement that certain kings reigned in Edom "before any king reigned over the sons of Israel" (Gn 36:31), implying that this was written many years after Moses when there was kingship in Israel. But this could merely be Moses anticipating that Israel would one day have a king (cf. Dt 17:14-20) or even an editorial comment by a later scribe, copying the text before the close of the OT canon, and reflecting that Israel did indeed have kings later.

Clearly, these and other alleged anachronisms are easily resolved by recognizing that later scribes, writing before the close of the OT canon, would bring place names and circumstances up to date so that the readers could better understand the text.

4. *The Characterization of Moses.* This claim is that the Torah speaks of Moses as if he were a character in the narrative and not the author. For example, in the Torah, Moses is spoken of in the third person. This claim *presupposes* that the early Israelites were either unacquainted with or literarily too unsophisticated to employ the technique of third-person self-reference. However, this technique is attested in many instances throughout the OT (as in Ezra, Nehemiah, and most of the prophetic books) as well as in the NT and early postbiblical Hebrew literature. Another example is that the Torah reports that Moses "was very humble, more than every human on the face of the earth" (Nm 12:3). It is difficult to picture the humblest man on earth writing these words. However, this is a problem only if the concept of humility is understood as "marked by meekness or modesty," "low in rank," or "deferential." But the Hebrew term *'anav* conveys the fundamental idea of "unworthiness," "needy," or even "afflicted" (see, e.g., Pss 10:16; 34:3; Is 29:19; 61:1). One other example is that the Torah includes an account of Moses' death (Dt 34). However, all that this indicates is that Moses did not write the last part of Dt and that God used a later prophet to add these words.

Date. Moses probably wrote the Pentateuch during the Israelites' 40-year sojourn in the wilderness (c. 1446–1406 BC), completing the literary work shortly before his death (see Dt 33:1). The dating of the Pentateuch is derived from dates mentioned in 1Kg 6:1. There it says that Solomon began construction of the temple in "the fourth year" of his reign, approximately 967/966 BC, also stating that it was 480 years after the exodus. This would make the date of the exodus 1447/1446 BC. With a 40-year wilderness wandering, the date of the Pentateuch's completion would be approximately 1406 BC.

Additionally, the text of the Pentateuch was copied repeatedly between the time of composition by Moses and the close of the Hebrew canon (in approximately 400 BC). As such, these scribes frequently included inspired updates, making historical comments, changing the names of cities to more contemporary names, and even adding sections, such as the account of the death of Moses, likely added by Ezra or one of his contemporaries (see comments on Dt 34:1-12).

Purpose. Genesis, like the rest of the Pentateuch, is both a sophisticated piece of literature as well as a thematically and theologically multilayered revelation. It therefore has not just one but several purposes.

As expressed by Christ, quoting from Dt 6:5, the greatest commandment requires a person's all-consuming love for God (Mt 22:37). Fulfilling this commandment occurs when one loves other humans, those who are made in God's image. Jesus then quoted from Lv 19:18 the complementary commandment, "You shall love your neighbor as yourself." These commandments are really two sides of the same coin, and in fulfilling the first, a person fulfills the other. And in effect he is fulfilling "the whole Law and the Prophets" (Mt 22:40), a first-century Jewish way of referring to the entire Scriptures. Thus, the purpose of Scripture (including Genesis) is to direct people toward worshiping and loving God.

The *secondary* purposes of Genesis are reflected in (1) 1:1–11:9, a record not simply of early human history, but more specifically of *humanity's overarching depravity and therefore their need for a saving Messiah*, Jesus of Nazareth according to the NT writers; and in (2) 11:10-50:26, which is a record not simply of Israel's patriarchal history, but specifically of *the path through which humanity's need for the Messiah can be met.*

Other purposes show *humanity's need* for the Messiah by (1) establishing that humanity was not meant for sin (1:1–2:25); (2) showing how sin entered the world; (3) highlighting the negative consequences of sin; and (4) emphasizing that sin is an ongoing problem endemic to human nature, which people are incapable of resolving apart from God. In the larger part of Genesis, the path by which this need would be met becomes the focus—specifically, God's work in laying the foundation for that nation through which Jesus would come. The Abrahamic covenant (12:1-3) consists of three essential elements: a defined location (the land of Israel 12:1); a distinct people (12:2); and an authoritative moral standard (12:3). The rest of Genesis shows how these three elements were realized and refined, so that "in the fullness of time" (Gl 4:4) would come the one through whom man's need is fully met, "Jesus the Messiah, the son of David, the son of Abraham" (Mt 1:1).

Christology. For the Christian who affirms the inspiration of Scripture and its divine authorship there can be no question that Genesis—as every part of the Hebrew Bible—has much to say about the Messiah. This was affirmed by Jesus Himself, who, when appearing unrecognized to those two disciples on the road to Emmaus, "explained to them the things concerning Himself in all the Scriptures" beginning "with Moses and with all the prophets" (Lk 24:27). Christ may have begun with Genesis, the first book of "Moses" (here intended as a metonymy for the Pentateuch).

The Christology of Genesis accordingly may be divided into two general categories: direct Christology and indirect Christology. Direct Christology comprises those passages in which direct verbal reference (i.e., a predictive utterance) is made to the person and work of the Messiah, such as Gn 3:15 on the Messiah's victory over Satan. Also belonging to this category is the culminating Abrahamic promise in 12:3 of blessing for "all the families of the earth" (this "blessing" being salvation in Abraham's seed, Christ), as well as Jacob's statement in 49:10, in which he referred to a future ruler to come from Judah, to whom "shall be the obedience of the peoples."

To the category of indirect Christology belong those *symbolic* portents of the person and work of Christ otherwise described in the NT by the term "type" (*typos*) or "shadow" (*skia*) (both terms are applied to the temple and its sacrificial ritual in Heb 8:5). Among those indirect representations of Christ and His work in Genesis are Adam, "a type of Him who was to come" (Rm 5:14), and Isaac, whom Abraham "received . . . back as a type" (Heb 11:19).

A third category is by far the most extensive, though it does not pertain to Christology proper. "Christology," whether direct or indirect, concerns the person and work of Christ, which began with His incarnation by conception in Mary. In Genesis, however, as throughout the OT, the Son of God appears (usually in the form of a man) in various situations that are not connected to his future role as Christ. These preincarnational appearances of the Son, otherwise termed "theophanies" (meaning "appearances of God"), or more precisely "Christophanies" (i.e., "appearances of the Christ"), are of great significance. That the many appearances of God throughout the OT are indeed always appearances *of the Son* is made clear by John's pointed statement at the beginning of his gospel (Jn 1:18), that "no one has seen God at any time;

the only begotten God who is in the bosom of the Father, He has explained Him." John's point is that the triune God is made known to man—whether in the past, present, or future—always and only by the manifestation of the Son.

Patterns and Themes. Genesis, by virtue not only of its place in the canon but also in the time line of biblical and revelatory history, is filled with events and concepts that are intended both logically and *theo*logically to be viewed as patterns, or paradigms. These paradigms are for understanding those same or similar events and concepts whenever they appear later on, both in Scripture as well as in history generally. In this vein Paul wrote that some of the experiences that befell Israel "happened to them as an example, and they were written for our instruction" (1Co 10:11). By studying the details of the biblical record, in other words, one can better understand the details and patterns of behavior, both positive and negative, divine and human, as seen time and time again in both biblical and post-biblical history, within Israel as well as within the church. The following are some of the significant patterns and concepts established in Genesis.

Blessing. Blessing is the bestowal or experiencing of something favorable, whether material or immaterial. Considering the blessings at the outset of the two thematic sections of Genesis (e.g., in chaps. 1 and 12), readers can see that blessing has to do with the expansion of life. The expansion of spiritual life, however, was inhibited by Adam's sin. Therefore, though all men possess a "living soul" (Gn 2:7), the full and "expanded" life of that soul is realized only when reconnected to the divine by grace through faith (Eph 2:8). Thus "blessing" is the *expansion,* that is, the full realization, of spiritual life that God intended when He established the path of man's redemption in His initial expression of the Abrahamic promise— that in Abraham's seed "all the families of the earth will be blessed" (Gn 12:3; cf. 22:18; Gl 3:16-17.).

Temptation. Genesis 3 not only tells of the past event of humanity's first encounter with temptation, but it also gives a present paradigm by which to understand the process of temptation. Though the forms of temptation may change over time, the fundamental lure of every temptation remains the same—specifically, as delineated in Gn 3:6, the lure will be to improperly "satisfy" one or more of the following three "needs" fundamental to humanity: our physical need ("good for food"), our intellectual-emotional need ("pleasing to the eye"), and our spiritual need ("desirable for gaining wisdom"). These three "needs" or "categories" encompass all temptation in the world a person in any place or time will ever face. The apostle John affirmed this in 1Jn 2:16, and Jesus experienced victory over the same three categories of temptation (Lk 4:1-13).

Death. The typical understanding of death as the "cessation" or "termination of life" contrasts with the overall biblical data on this topic. God told Adam that "in the day that you eat from it [the tree of the knowledge of good and evil] you will surely die" (Gn 2:17). Of course when Adam and Eve ate the forbidden fruit, they did not cease to live physically. The fundamental idea of death is not cessation, but separation. In death the soul is separated from the body, and for the unredeemed, from God.

God's paternal mercy. God responded to the first sin not with anger but with gentle patience and loving mercy. Knowing what they had done, "the LORD God" entered into the garden, in the form of a man, "walking" among the trees (3:8). He asked gentle, leading questions intended to draw the first couple out of the dark seclusion prompted by their awareness of having sinned and into the light of confession to their Father. After they confessed, God chastised them and forgave them. This shows how He will respond to the sins of all those who are likewise His children.

Forgiveness/atonement. After responding to the first sin with gentleness and merciful chastisement, God undertook a profound act of forgiveness which clearly set the pattern for the way in which all future sin is to be properly forgiven. In Gn 3:21, three indispensable elements of the atonement process (e.g., forgiveness conclusively realized on a divine level) are presented. (1) Atonement requires a blood sacrifice (cf. Heb 9:22: "without the shedding of blood there is no forgiveness"). (2) Providing the sacrifice is ultimately God's work alone (the subject of both the verbs "made" and "clothed" is God alone). (3) God's work of atonement, once achieved, is durable (e.g., *permanent*) as born out by the clear contrast between the fig leaves with which the couple attempted to cover their shame and the leather garments (animal skins) God applied. For more details on this, see the comments on 3:21.

Human depravity. Gn 3:22–4:26 describes three consequences of the fall epitomizing characteristics of the overall human experience—both throughout the Bible as well as in human history generally, up to the present day. These three are (1) exile for disobedience (as would later happen to Israel for disobedience to the Torah (3:22-24), indicating communal depravity; (2) first-degree murder (4:1-18), expressing personal depravity; and (3) wrongful execution (4:19-26), signifying legal depravity.

God's grace in election. In Gn 2, immediately after creating Adam, and before Adam did or said anything (hence underscoring the absence of *merit*), God proceeded to "set him at rest" (lit., v. 15), an expression that throughout the Bible denotes the granting of spiritual rest, through faith and God's grace (cf. Ps 95:11; Heb 4:1-11). In Gn 12:1-3 God chose Abram to be both the recipient of personal blessing (material and spiritual) as well as the means through whom that same blessing will be extended to "all the families of the earth" (v. 3). Nothing that Abram did or said prior to God's choosing him indicates he merited that choice.

The Days of Creation. Few other interpretive issues in Genesis have received more attention or been more debated in modern times than the meaning of "day" in Gn 1 and its consequent bearing on the chronology and nature of the creative process described therein. Several facts need to be noted regarding the "days" of creation.

- That the Bible is a literary and theological work does not preclude its being scientifically accurate.
- The words of the biblical text in describing the creative process are to be understood in a manner consistent with the use of those words (both in meaning as well as syntax) attested elsewhere in the OT.
- Where the meaning of the biblical text runs (or seems to run) contrary to the theories or conclusions of contemporary science, precedence should be given to the biblical text.

When considering the "days" of creation in a manner consistent with these principles, the inevitable conclusion is that these days are to be understood as "24-hour" days. While acknowledging that the term "day" (*yom*) may signify an indeterminate period of time, such as in the expression "day of the Lord," or in Gn 2:4, where *yom* does indeed appear as a period of time (in that case, the six days of creation are called a "day"), it seems likely that *yom* in Gn 1 refers to a 24-hour day for the following five reasons:

(1) Each of the six days of creation is specifically defined by the terms "evening" and "morning," both of which are consistently employed throughout the OT to denote those two parts of a literal ("24-hour") day (e.g. Ex 16:8; 18:13). The few exceptions are in poetic passages, which Gn 1 is not.

(2) The immediate and complete creation of the various parts of the world is consistent with the immediate and complete creation of man and woman. The creation of humans is not presented as a gradual process, nor were they created as children whose physical and intellectual capacities still needed to develop. Adam and Eve were created as physically and mentally mature individuals with a fully developed capacity to physically and intellectually enjoy the home into which they were placed. Given that the world was created specifically *for* humanity (cf. Gn 1:28), there would be no reason for God to draw out its creation over billions of years. The modern scientific consensus of what constitutes evidence of "age" is founded on a presuppositional analysis of the geologic data that precludes the testimony of Scripture. It is just as logically valid for Christians to view these geologic and other such data as evidence of *maturity* rather than of age. Just as God immediately created man with the full and mature capacity to enjoy his world, so too did He immediately create that world at a full and mature state to be enjoyed.

(3) The coupling of the word "day" (*yom*) with an ordinal number (e.g., "second day," "third day," etc.) is consistently employed throughout the history of the Hebrew Bible as the conventional way to designate a literal day in a literal seven-day week (e.g. Gn 7:4; 17:12).

(4) The fourth of the Ten Commandments logically implies that all six days of creation, as well as the seventh (Sabbath) day of rest, were literal 24-hour days. In Ex 20:9-11 the Israelites were told to work for "six days" and rest on "the seventh day" in commemoration of God having done precisely the same thing. He worked for "six days" and rested on "the seventh day." Also, the verbal expression "the LORD "rested" in Ex 20:11 is a completed action/past tense verb, which disallows the notion, sometimes put forth by "day-age" proponents, that the seventh day (and hence the previous six) was/is an "age," and that in fact we are still in it (for then God would *still be* resting).

(5) An "age" of time for each day is irreconcilable with the specific genealogy of Adam and his descendants presented in Gn 5. According to that

genealogy Adam's *third* son, Seth, was begotten when Adam was 130 years old. In other words, no more than 130 years (hardly an "age"!) had passed from Adam's creation early on the sixth day to a point well after the seventh day when Seth was begotten. The genealogy in chap. 5 cannot be dismissed as "abridged," since (a) this runs counter to the references to each person's age when he "became the father of" his son, and (b) the expression "he became the father of," which is used throughout this genealogy, is always used in connection with one's immediate children (i.e., the generation immediately following the father).

Background. Genesis is volume one of a five-part work known as the Pentateuch in English and the *Torah* (law) in Hebrew. Despite the division into five parts, the Torah was intended to be read as a single book by one author. The Hebrew Bible always views it as one book (Jos 1:8; 23:6; 2Ch 25:4; 35:12; Ezr 6:18; Neh 13:1) as does the NT (e.g. Mk 12:26) and the Apocrypha (*Ecclesiasticus*, Prologue; *The Letter of Aristeas* 15). As such, Genesis functions as a prologue to the entire Pentateuch.

Structurally, the opening of Genesis focuses on an extended period of time, covering all of primeval history in just 11 chapters, followed by the patriarchal history of Israel, covering four generations in 39 chapters. Following the emphasis of the author (the law of proportion), Genesis should be viewed more as the book of the beginnings of Israel rather than the beginning of the world.

Additionally, Genesis uses the Hebrew word *toledoth* (commonly translated as "generations") as a structural marker. Although some have mistakenly thought of this word as a summary of the previous material, rather it functions as a forward marker. Hence, the phrase "these are the generations of . . ." (KJV; "this is the account of . . ." NASB) would best be paraphrased, "this is what became of. . . ." Thus, after the opening account of creation (1:1–2:3) and beginning in 2:4, the author stated 10 times, "this is what became of" the heavens and the earth (2:4), Adam (5:1), Noah (6:9), the sons of Noah (10:1), Shem (11:10), Terah (11:27), Ishmael (25:12), Isaac (25:19), Esau (36:1, 9), Jacob (37:2). In each case, the text proceeds with the story of what follows. So for example, the Abraham narrative follows the statement "this is what became of Terah" (11:27–25:11), the Jacob story comes after "this is what became of Isaac" (25:19–35:29), and the Joseph narrative follows "this is what became of Jacob" (37:2–50:26).

The first three chapters of Genesis introduce all the major concepts that are developed in the rest of the Bible: God's nature, man's purpose, the divine image, divine mercy, divine grace, temptation, human depravity, atonement, blessing, the future Messiah, etc. Thus more commentary space is devoted here on these three chapters. Where these concepts and paradigms appear later, therefore, readers should refer back to the more substantive comments in these opening chapters.

OUTLINE

- I. Primeval History: Establishing the Need for Redemption (1:1–11:26)
  - A. Perfect Creation: The Absence of Sin (1:1–2:25)
    - 1. An Overview of Perfection (1:2–2:3)
      - a. Inanimate Perfection (1:1-19)
      - b. Animate (Animal) Perfection (1:20-25)
      - c. Human Perfection (1:26–2:3)
    - 2. A Close-Up on the Human Ideal (2:4-25)
      - a. The Ideal Creation of Man (2:4-7)
      - b. The Ideal Place of Man (2:8-14)
      - c. The Ideal Responsibility of Man (2:15-25)
  - B. Fallen Humanity: The Advent of Sin (3:1-21)
    - 1. The Lead-up to Sin (3:1-6)
      - a. Step One: Wrongly Recalling God's Word (3:1-3)
      - b. Step Two: Wrongly Assessing God's Purpose (3:4-5)
      - c. Step Three: Wrongly Approving What Seems "Good" (3:6)
    - 2. Humanity's Response to Sin (3:7-8)

a. Conviction (3:7a)
b. Division from Each Other (3:7b)
c. Division from God (3:8)
3. God's Response to Sin (3:9-21)
a. Gentle Confrontation (3:9-13)
b. Merciful Chastisement (3:14-20)
c. Gracious Forgiveness (3:21)
C. Dire Consequences: The Aftermath of Sin (3:22–4:26)
1. Exile: The Communal Aftermath of Sin (3:22-24)
a. The Problem (3:22)
b. God's Gracious Solution (3:23)
c. The "Eastward" Paradigm (3:24)
2. Murder: The Personal Aftermath of Sin (4:1-22)
a. The Priority of Heart Attitude (4:1-8)
b. God's Mercy, Again (4:9-12)
c. Cain's Repentance and God's Grace (4:13-22)
3. Injustice: The Legal Aftermath of Sin (4:23-26)
a. Injustice as a Result of Ignoring God's Example (4:23-24)
b. Injustice Not Preclusive of God's Blessing (4:25)
c. Injustice as a Catalyst for Turning People to God (4:26)
D. Fallen World: The Attachment of Sin (5:1–11:26)
1. Break in the Prosecution: God's Blessing Despite Depravity (5:1–6:8)
a. Hope of Redemption (5:1-32)
b. God's Gracious "Cap" on Depravity (6:1-4)
c. Measure of True "Spirituality" (6:5-8)
2. The Flood: Humanity's Chance to "Come Clean" of Depravity (6:9–9:29)
a. Prelude: A Righteous Remnant in a Depraved World (6:9-10)
b. Corruption of the Land (6:11-12)
c. God's Covenant with Noah (6:13-20)
d. God's Provision for Life (6:21-22)
e. Entering the Ark (7:1-9)
f. Prevailing of the Flood (7:10-24)
g. Subsiding of the Flood (8:1-14)
h. Exiting the Ark (8:15-22)
i. God's Provision for Life (9:1-7)
j. God's Covenant with Noah and All Life (9:8-17)
k. Corruption of the Land (9:18-19)
l. Postlude: A Righteous Remnant in a Depraved World (9:20-29)
3. The Depth of Depravity in Post-Flood Humanity (10:1–11:26)
a. Setting the Stage for Universal Rebellion (10:1-32)
b. Rebellion Expressed: The Rise and Fall of Universal Human Pride (11:1-9)
c. Transition to Pardon (11:10-26)
II. Patriarchal History: Delineating the Path of Redemption (11:27–50:26)
A. Descendants of Terah: God Making His Own Name for Man (11:27–25:11)
1. The Abrahamic Covenant: God's Promise for Israel and the Nations (11:27–12:20)
a. God's Sovereign Choice: Abram's Passivity (11:27-32)
b. God's Gracious Promises: Resetting Abram's Direction (12:1-9)
c. God's Unshakable Hold: Abram's Deep Depravity (12:10-20)
2. Living in the Land: God's Affirmation of the Covenant (13:1–14:24)
a. Affirming Abram's Right to the Land (13:1-18)
b. Affirming Abram's Might and Prosperity (14:1-16)
c. Affirming Abram's Blessing and Status (14:17-24)
3. Ratifying the Covenant: God's Compromise with Weak Faith (15:1-21)
a. Answering Abram's Doubt about the Son (15:1-5)

- b. Affirming Abram's Imperfect Faith (15:6)
- c. Answering Abram's Doubt about the Land (15:7-21)

4. Doubting God: The Fall Reprised (16:1-16)
   - a. The Temptation (16:1-4a)
   - b. The Human Consequences (16:4b-6)
   - c. The Divine Response (16:7-16)
5. Circumcision: The Sign of the Covenant (17:1-16)
   - a. The Effected Covenant as the Basis of the Rite (17:1-8)
   - b. Content of the Rite (17:9-16)
   - c. Abram's Response to the Rite (17:17-27)
6. An Expression of Divine Fellowship (18:1-33)
   - a. God Affirming His Empathy with Abraham (18:1-8)
   - b. God Affirming His Grace toward Abraham (18:9-15)
   - c. God Affirming His Justice to Abraham (18:16-33)
7. A Paradigm of Corporate Judgment (19:1-29)
   - a. Cause of Judgment (19:1-11)
   - b. Distinction of Judgment (19:12-22)
   - c. Purpose of Judgment (19:23-29)
8. Persistence of Sin (19:30–20:18)
   - a. Struggles of Lot's Household (19:30-38)
   - b. Struggles of Abraham's Household (20:1-16)
   - c. God's Faithfulness and Grace in Sanctification (20:17-18)
9. Sovereignty of God in Blessing (21:1-34)
   - a. God's Sovereignty in Blessing Abraham and Sarah (21:1-8)
   - b. God's Sovereignty in Blessing Hagar and Sarah (21:9-21)
   - c. God's Sovereignty in Blessing Abimelech and His People (21:22-34)
10. The Pinnacle of Abraham's Faith (22:1-19)
    - a. God's Call to Faith (22:1-2)
    - b. Abraham's Expression of Faith (22:3-9)
    - c. The Angel's Affirmation of Faith (22:10-19)
11. Family Matters (22:20–23:20)
    - a. Keeping Up with the Relatives (22:20-24)
    - b. Mourning Sarah (23:1-2)
    - c. Purchasing the Family Burial Plot (23:3-20)
12. Finding Rebekah in Mesopotamia (24:1-67)
    - a. Abraham's Petition (24:1-9)
    - b. God's Answer (24:10-49)
    - c. The People's Response (24:50-67)
13. Transferring the Torch to Isaac (25:1-11)
    - a. Abraham's Affirmation of Isaac (25:1-6)
    - b. Isaac and Ishmael's Burial of Abraham (25:7-10)
    - c. God's Affirmation of Isaac (25:11)

B. Descendants of Ishmael: A Locus of Conflict with God's People (25:12-18)

C. Descendants of Isaac: Learning to Wait on God (25:19–35:29)

1. Jacob and Esau: The Sons of Isaac (25:19-34)
   - a. Barrenness of Rebekah (25:19-21a)
   - b. Birth of Jacob and Esau (25:21b-26)
   - c. Sale of Esau's Birthright (25:27-34)
2. Isaac: Struggles of a Patriarch (26:1-33)
   - a. Struggling to Trust in God's Promises: Isaac Lies about Rebekah (26:1-17)
   - b. Struggling to Live with Sinful Men: Isaac Quarrels with the Men of Gerar (26:18-25)
   - c. Struggling to Recognize the Sovereignty of God: Isaac Makes a Covenant with Abimelech (26:26-33)

3. Jacob: Successor of Isaac (26:34–35:29)
   a. In the Land: Striving with Esau (26:34–28:9)
      (1) Prologue: Esau Marries Foreign Women (26:34-35)
      (2) Body: Jacob Strives for a Blessing (27:1–28:5)
      (3) Epilogue: Esau Marries Foreign Women (28:6-9)
   b. Outside the Land: Striving with Laban (28:10–31:55)
      (1) Jacob's Journey (28:10-22)
      (2) Jacob's Marriages (29:1-30)
      (3) Jacob's Children (29:31–30:24)
      (4) Jacob's Prosperity (30:25-43)
      (5) Jacob's Flight (31:1–32:2)
   c. Return to the Land: Striving Resolved with People and God (32:3–35:29)
      (1) The Restoration of Jacob and Esau (32:3–33:20)
         (a) Jacob's Fear of Esau (32:3-23)
         (b) Jacob's Fight with God (32:24-32)
         (c) Jacob's Restoration with Esau (33:1-17)
         (d) Jacob's Restoration to the Land (33:18-20)
      (2) The Rape of Dinah (34:1-31)
      (3) The Close of the Jacob Story (35:1-29)

D. Descendants of Esau: Another Locus of Conflict with God's People (36:1–37:1)

E. Descendants of Jacob: God's Providence over Joseph and Israel (37:2–50:26)

1. Joseph in the Pit (37:2–40:23)
   a. Joseph Is Sold into Slavery by His Brothers (37:2-36)
   b. Judah Receives a Male Heir by Deception (38:1-30)
   c. Joseph Is Falsely Accused by Potiphar's Wife (39:1-23)
   d. Joseph Is Forgotten by the Cupbearer (40:1-23)
2. Joseph as Prime Minister (41:1–50:26)
   a. Joseph Becomes Prime Minister (41:1-57)
   b. Joseph Tests His Brothers (42:1–44:34)
      (1) The Conscience Test (42:1-38)
      (2) The Character Test (43:1-34)
      (3) The Compassion Test (44:1-34)
   c. Joseph Reconciles with His Brothers (45:1-28)
   d. Joseph Cares for All Egypt (46:1–47:26)
      (1) Joseph Provides for the Family of Israel (46:1–47:12)
      (2) Joseph Provides for the People of Egypt (47:13-19)
      (3) Joseph Provides for Pharaoh (47:20-26)
   e. Joseph Receives the Blessing for His Sons (47:27–48:22)
   f. Jacob Blesses the Twelve Tribes (49:1-33)
   g. Joseph Believes God to the End (50:1-26)

COMMENTARY ON GENESIS

I. Primeval History: Establishing the Need for Redemption (1:1–11:26)

As discussed in the introduction, Genesis is thematically-theologically divisible into two major sections. In this first section God established man's *need* for redemption. He did this by presenting not a "comprehensive" and "objective" history of humanity from creation to Abram, but rather a careful selection of specific events, viewed from a specifically biblical-theological perspective, and logically sequenced so as to provide a clear explanation of this section's central thesis (i.e., *why* humanity needs divine redemption). This section may be characterized as a divine "prosecution" of depraved humanity, opening with an account of all the best that God gave to humanity, both materially and spiritually, and ending with the account of humanity's willful, corporate rejection of God at Babel. Genesis 1:1–11:26 is divided into four discrete "trial parts," each one of which makes a specific point (or answers a specific "objection" that mankind might raise). By the end of the fourth "trial part" God rested His case concerning human depravity.

A. Perfect Creation: The Absence of Sin (1:1–2:25)

In these opening two chapters God established the point most fundamental to His prosecution of human depravity, namely that humanity was meant for something better. Were humanity *meant* to be depraved, like Satan and the evil angels, there would be no need for redemption—just as there is none for Satan and the evil angels. In response therefore to man's first potential objection—"Why is redemption necessary if this (i.e., depraved) is what we are?"—God's answer in these two chapters carries with it the seeds of hope: that people *were* meant for something better—for complete and unbroken communion with God in the "tabernacle" of an incorruptible and untainted creation.

1. An Overview of Perfection (1:1–2:3)

This opening section does not present a comprehensive survey of *all* that God created, but rather, in keeping with the theme of 1:11–11:26, with those aspects of creation that are specifically relevant to the good of man. This is underscored by the repetition of the statement "And God saw that it was good" after each creative act that bears specifically on the need of man, as is consistent with the use of this same expression throughout the rest of the OT. Therefore certain aspects of the creative process are left out entirely because they are not directly relevant to the need or good of man (e.g., the creation of the angels, of space/black matter, of the "raw material" of planet earth and its waters). This enhances the theological value of the creation account by emphasizing, both by *what* it presents as well as how it presents it, that God's motivation and focus throughout the creative process was ultimately on humanity and providing what is best for people. In other words the motivation for God's work of creation and the "plumb line" that guides all that He does in the process is His love for humankind.

On a literary level the idea of "perfection" in this section is underscored in a sophisticated manner by the repeated use of the number seven into the structure of the narrative itself. Although it is possible to "overdo" the interpretive significance of numbers in the Bible, in this instance the evidence and import of the number seven is undeniable. Umberto Cassuto (*A Commentary on the Book of Genesis* [Jerusalem: Magnes, 1996] 1: 13-15) notes the following. (1) This section is divided into *seven* paragraphs (one for each day). (2) Each of the three "foundational" nouns in this section—"God" (*elohim*), "land" (*eres*), and "sky" (*shamayim*)—occurs a multiple of *seven* times. (3) The expression "And God saw (that) it was good" occurs *seven* times. (4) There are *seven* "acts" of creation preceding the crowning event of humanity's creation, and each of these seven acts is initiated by the expression "Let (there) be." The creation of man is the only creative "act" that God does not verbalize, but in fact performs physically. (5) There are seven words in the Hebrew text of v. 1. (6) There are 14 words in the Hebrew text of v. 2. (7) The words "light" (*or*) and "day" (*yom*) occur altogether seven times in the first paragraph. (8) The expression "the waters" occurs altogether seven times in paragraphs 2 and 3. (9) The expression "living creature" (*hayya*) occurs altogether seven times in paragraphs 5 and 6. (10) The three "center" sentences of the seventh paragraph (2:2-3a) contain seven words each. (11) The total number of words in the seventh paragraph is 35 (five times). The point of all this structural emphasis on the number seven is clearly to highlight the *perfection* and *completeness* of the home God made for humanity.

On the first three days God created and/or separated (i.e., lit., "isolates") the "realms" to be occupied, and on the next three days He created the living things that are to occupy those realms. Both the third and sixth days, moreover, contain two acts of creation.

a. Inanimate Perfection (1:1-19)

1:1-3. Throughout the history of English Bible translation these opening three verses have typically been rendered as three independent sentences: (1) the first act of *ex nihilo* ("out of nothing") creation, specifically, the creation of **the earth** and the surrounding universe/empty space (**the heavens**) (v. 1); (2) the earth was in an unfinished state, though **waters** are already in place, with creative power of the Holy Spirit **moving** (or hovering) at the ready (v. 2); (3) in another act of creation God called **light** into existence and separated it from the darkness (v. 4).

The Days of Creation

Day One (1:1-5)	Day Two (1:6-8)	Day Three (1:9-13)	Day Four (1:14-19)	Day Five (1:20-23)	Day Six (1:24-31)
Light created and isolated from darkness ("space"/dark matter)	Waters separated and sky created between them	Land separated out from the lower waters; plants created	Luminaries (suns and planets) created and placed into space	Water animals and flying animals created in one act	Land animals created; man and woman (not termed "animal") created

However, how can something that was just created—thus implying both form and substance—have at the same time *neither* form *nor* substance (this being the plain meaning of the expression **formless and void**)? Moreover, the idea that v. 2 presents the earth in an "unfinished" or "semi-finished" state runs contrary to the way in which God created everything else in this chapter, namely, immediately and completely, without any suggestion of a "pause" during which the creative act remains an unfinished or incomplete creation.

The terms **heaven** (or **heavens**) and **earth** that are employed in most English translations of v. 1, though not strictly wrong, are inaccurate in light of how these English words are commonly defined. The word translated **heaven** can indeed denote "space" (i.e., the universe), yet always as an extension of the *sky* as perceived by men. On the other hand many times in the Hebrew Bible the term *shamayim* refers *only* to the sky. Therefore to determine whether the reference is to the sky or to the sky plus the space beyond it, one must consider how the word is used elsewhere in the same context. In v. 8, *shamayim* refers to "the expanse in the midst of the waters," that is the *sky alone* (without extending to the rest of "space").

The translation of the Hebrew word *ereṣ* by the English word **earth** is similarly misleading, since the former is regularly used throughout the Hebrew Bible to designate some or all of the 25 percent of the planet humanity lives on, that is, *dry land* (as opposed to the *oceans* and the land underneath them), which is exactly how God applied the term in v. 10 ("and God called the dry land *ereṣ*"). The term *ereṣ*, therefore, does not refer here to the entire planet (though this is the typical idea conveyed by the English word "earth").

How, therefore, should v. 1 be understood and what is its relationship to what follows? And, if the reference here is specifically to the *sky* and the *dry land*, when *was* the actual planet created along with its raw material of submerged land and covering **waters**? And when did God create the **darkness**, the existence of which as *something* (as opposed to *nothing*) is implied by the light being separated "from" it (v. 4; see also the explicit reference to God "creating" darkness in Is 45:7)?

The answer to all these questions has to do with the *specific perspective* by which the creative acts in this chapter are presented, coinciding with God's specific motivation for undertaking these creative acts in the first place, namely, *to demonstrate His love for humanity by providing humanity with what is best.* God's purpose here in Genesis was not to fill in *all* the blanks in one's knowledge of history, science, or even theology, but rather to reveal those things that relate specifically to His love and plan for man. Thus the creation account begins in 1:1 *not* with the very first act of *creatio ex nihilo* ("creation out of nothing," for which one can refer to any number of other passages, such as Is 44:24a; Jn 1:3; Heb 11:3), but rather at that point when, with the "raw materials" of creation already in place, that is, darkness (space/black matter [?]), the planet with its land and overlaying waters—and the angelic host standing ready to sing God's praise (Jb 38:4-7)—He undertook the first creative act *that bears specifically on the good of man* (hence the recurring assessment, "And He saw ... that it was good").

This reading of the first three verses has long been recognized by Jewish interpreters. Verses 1-3 constitute one complex sentence, the first two being composed of dependent clauses and v. 3 composing the main clause (i.e., describing the "event" itself). These three verses thus read: "In the beginning of God's creating the sky and the (dry) land—while the land was (still) uninhabitable and unproductive, and darkness was over the surface of the deep, and the Spirit of God was hovering over the surface of the waters—God said, 'Let there be light.' And there was light."

In v. 2 the Hebrew expression (*tohu va-vohu*) is usually translated "formless and void." But this is not satisfactory because the land—though it has not yet "appeared" as "dry land" (v. 9)—is nonetheless *there*, under **the waters**, and hence had a certain form (as opposed to "formless") and mass (as opposed to "void"). In fact in its only other biblical occurrence, Jr 4:23, this expression is applied to land that has both form and substance—the land of Israel—but which is characterized at that point as being uninhabited (vv. 25-26: "there was no man . . . all its cities were pulled down") and unproductive (v. 26: "the fruitful land was a wilderness"). Verse 2 states that **the Spirit of God was** hovering (ESV, HCSB, NASB). The word here translated **Spirit** (*ruah*) may also denote "wind." But "Spirit" is intended because "hovering" is not the action of wind. This verb, which may also be translated "poised," implies the Spirit's readiness to "empower" the first act of creation specifically intended for the "good" (v. 4) of humanity. (On the Holy Spirit's empowering role in creation see Jb 33:4). This picture of God "hovering," or "poised," to lovingly supply the need and ensure the welfare of His people is also seen in Dt 32:11.

Since vv. 1-3 pertain to the same "stage" in the creative process, it is impossible to infer any historical "gap" between any of the clauses in these three verses. Some interpreters infer such a historical "gap," claiming that *billions* of years elapsed between the end of v. 1 and the beginning of v. 2. According to this "gap theory," in which its proponents seek to reconcile the Bible to the current scientific opinion concerning the earth's age, the creation of the world and all life was originally completed before v. 2, and yet a catastrophe of some sort took place and "the earth became formless and void." However, v. 2 has the word **was** not "became." Moreover, v. 2 indicates a *contemporaneous* situation, not a *subsequent* one (as required by the "gap theory").

1:4-5. The **light** God created and that "separates" from **the darkness** is not the light of the sun, but simply light, employed by God to enforce the distinction between **night** and **day** until that "task" is relegated to the sun (i.e., "the greater light") that He clearly *created* on the fourth day. The existence of light (i.e., photons) as *distinct* from the solar source that produces it (such as the sun) is a well-recognized fact, but in fact the existence of light in the absence of the sun is here *theologically consistent* with the description of creation restored to its ideal at the end of the Bible, in Rv 22:5 (humanity "shall not have need of the light of a lamp nor the light of the sun, because the Lord God shall illumine them"; see also Rv 21:23).

The statement **God saw that the light was good** underscores the human focus of all that God did in this chapter. The verb **saw** may also convey the meaning "provide" (similar to the English idiom "to see to it"). This same verb is used in Gn 16:13-14, where Hagar described God as the One "who sees" because He provided for her need, and in Gn 22:8, 14, where this verb is translated "will provide." The reference to God's "seeing" in Gn 1 suggests the specific assessment of the *good,* that is, the *benefit,* of that creative act for man.

God's naming the light **day** and the darkness **night** underscores His dominion over these fundamental "parts" of creation. The act of naming conveys the idea of "dominion," e.g., man's naming the animals (2:19); and God's naming of individuals, such as Abraham/Abram (17:5), Isaac (17:19, before his conception), and Jacob/Israel (35:9), John (Lk 1:13, before his conception) and Simon/Peter (Jn 1:42).

In 1:5, the **evening** is reckoned first no doubt because **the darkness** was created before **the light,** and therefore in the Bible and Jewish tradition, days are reckoned from sunset to sunset. The complete **day**, as presented at the end of v. 5 and comprising both **evening** and **morning** is unquestionably to be understood as a literal (i.e., 24-hour) day (for further discussion see "The Days of Creation" in the Introduction).

1:6-8. The **expanse** that God created and called **heaven**, employing the same word used in v. 1, is clearly the *sky*, since it divides **the waters which were below** (i.e., the worldwide ocean) . . . **from the waters which were above** (i.e., the clouds and water vapor of the troposphere). Whether this **expanse**, or "firmament" (NASB), is just the peplosphere (the lowest layer of the atmosphere) or more (perhaps including all the layers of the atmosphere) is unclear. The creation of the expanse is concisely represented from a human (i.e., earthbound) perspective, and is no more indicative of a "primitive" or "inaccurate" understanding of the natural world than the statement of a modern climatologist who refers to the sunrise or sunset. To the contrary, the Hebrew word translated **expanse** (*raqia'*) is elsewhere used to describe a thin layer of gold that completely encompasses an idol (Is 40:19), the implication being that the **expanse** completely encompasses the planet, which therefore suggests that the planet is conceptualized as a sphere. And when one looks at satellite images of the earth, the atmosphere clearly is seen as an unbroken halo enveloping the earth.

The statement, **God made** (v. 7) is not another creative act, but rather a *reiteration* of the single creative act on the day described in v. 6. The purpose of this is to emphasize that the sky is a part of creation, and therefore not something to be worshiped (vv. 16, 21). The relevance of this point becomes evident when considering that in the ancient world the sky was viewed as a deity that could withhold or release rain along with other meteorological phenomena. God wanted the Israelites to know that He controls all aspects of the weather, and does so in a way that is consistent with His revealed character and purposes.

1:9-13. On the third day God formed the **dry land** and filled it with **vegetation** (*flora* in the broad sense), and both actions were paralleled on the sixth day by His acts of creating the land animals and creating man. This clear balance in the structure and relationship of God's creative acts in this chapter is not evidence of the purely "literary" origin of the creation account, but rather a reflection of the process itself. **The dry land** here was not called *into being*, but rather called *out from under* the worldwide ocean, thus affirming what has been said above about this chapter picking up at that point in the creative process where the raw materials of space (dark matter?) and planet Earth, with its waters and submerged land mass, are already in place. The stage is set for God to begin working *with* and *within* this "raw setting" to prepare a home specifically designed for the "good" of humankind. The *anthropocentric* perspective of the creation account is especially evident in the way the second creative act on this day is described: after describing the creation of *flora* generally (**Let the earth sprout vegetation**), reference is made to two specific groups, namely, **plants yielding seed** (i.e., cultivatable plants consumable by man) and **fruit trees**. These are the same two groups of *flora* mentioned in v. 29 as being for food for humanity. Yet v. 30 refers to a *third* group of flora, the "green plant," intended for the food of animals. This third group is not mentioned in this description of the third-day events, *not* because that group (the "green plants") was not created, but rather because it was not relevant to the "good" of humankind. The green plants are mentioned only in connection with man's charge to rule over the animals once they have been created.

Verse 9 refers to God's removal of the barrier of water from a land that is brought to a state of floral (agricultural) maturity for the good of His people before they were brought into it.

1:14-19. On the fourth day God filled the darkness, that is, the void of space extending from **the expanse**—with stars (i.e., suns and planets), referred to here as **lights**. All these stars, including the sun (**the greater light**) and the moon (**the lesser light**) are here (v. 14) called into being—not, as some interpreters claim, being "placed" in their fixed positions or orbits (having been created with the "light" on the first day). This is clear from the observation that the word **lights** in v. 14 lacks the definite article "the" which, as a grammatical rule, is normally required when referring to defined nouns that have already been noted (implicitly or explicitly) in a narrative.

More significant is the purpose assigned by God to the stars. In addition to marking the passage of **days and years**, God indicated that they are primarily intended **for signs and for seasons** (not "as signs for [marking] seasons," etc.). The Hebrew word translated **signs** (*otot*) is commonly employed in Scripture to denote miracles, that is, to testify to God's active involvement in human history, usually in connection with a redemptive purpose (as in Ex 4:8-9 and Dt 34:11). The word translated **seasons** (*mo'adim*) is typically employed to denote the "appointed times" or "holy days" of Israel (Lv 23:2-3). These are also intended to serve as testimonies to God's redemptive activity in human history, specifically with respect to God's plan of messianic redemption, as Paul wrote in Col 2:16-17. In other words knowing full well that man would sin and be in need of redemption, God graciously and lovingly wove into the fabric of creation itself—even before humans were created—those elements that would serve as postfall "signposts" of redemption, the festivals of Israel, intending to point humanity back into "relationship" with the Creator-Father through the redemptive work of the Messiah.

The statement in v. 16 (**God made**) is not an additional act of creation, but a reiteration, as in v. 7, of what God already had made, the purpose of which was to dissuade man from worshiping these parts of creation (a problem relating to the sun and moon in the ancient world) rather than the Creator Himself. With respect to **the stars** (e.g., planets and suns), from humanity's perspective the number of "stars" visible to the naked eye (as noted already by the time of Ptolemy in the second century AD) in the solar system is *seven* (the sun, moon, Mercury, Venus, Mars, Jupiter, and Saturn), which, consistent with the significance of this number elsewhere (especially throughout the creation account), seems to be another divinely intended memorial to the perfection of prefall creation. Even with the advent of modern telescopy this number has been maintained, for while Neptune and Uranus are now included in the number of the solar system's planets, the sun and moon have been excluded from this category in view of their distinguishing characteristics.

b. Animate (Animal) Perfection (1:20-25)

1:20-23. Parallel to God's single act on the second day of creating the sky and isolating the lower waters, on the fifth day He created, likewise in a single act, the animal life whose activity occurs in those realms: birds and water life (not just "fish"). In v. 21 God reiterated that among the **living creature**[s] He created in v. 20 were **the great sea monsters** lit., "the great reptiles," perhaps referring to *marine dinosaurs* like the plesiosaur. The point is that these awe-inspiring creatures, like the sky in v. 7 and the sun and moon in v. 16, as mere parts of creation are not to be worshiped in place of or in addition to the Creator Himself. The need for this warning is underscored by the observation that Leviathan, who was clearly one of these "great reptiles" (his description in Jb 41 closely fits that of a plesiosaur), was well known to the ancient peoples. The Leviathan is mentioned again in Is 27:1 and Pss 74:14 and 104:26. Recent archeological evidence has also shown that among the people of ancient Ugarit, a coastal city just north of biblical Canaan that flourished during the time of the Israelite conquest (c. 1450–1200 BC), Leviathan (in Ugaritic pronounced "Lotan" or "Litan") was viewed and revered as the god of the sea. In ancient Egypt the smaller species of *tannin* (crocodiles) were objects of worship in the "crocodile god" Sobek.

The first reference to blessing is in v. 22. From this first occurrence, and as borne out by its following application to humanity, it may be reasonably deduced that the fundamental idea or purpose of blessing in Genesis and the Pentateuch is the expansion of life.

1:24-25. Parallel to the two third-day acts of drawing out the dry land and filling it with vegetation, God completed creation on the sixth day with the two acts of creating the animate life for which the dry land and its vegetation were intended. The first act presented in these two verses is that of creating *animal* life, from which humanity is excluded (contrary to the method of modern scientific classification). The land animals, moreover, are divided into three groups: **cattle**, **creeping things**, and **beasts of the earth**. The first of these, **cattle** (or livestock, HCSB) denote domesticated animals. In other words—and again contrary to modern scientific theory— a certain number of animal species have *always* been "tame" and of a nature given to husbandry by man. This further underscores the human-focused nature of creation in this chapter.

c. Human Perfection (1:26–2:3)

1:26-27. These verses present the final and crowning act of God's creation. As the *seventh* creative act in this chapter, God's creative work is finished. This point is underscored by the fifth and final repetition of the phrase, "And God saw that it was good" (1:25). The presentation of humanity's creation in v. 27 as a single collective event (**God created man . . . male and female He created them**) does not contradict the more specific description of the two-stage process in chap. 2, but is rather intended to emphasize here that the **image** of God imparted to humanity is equally presented in both sexes.

As to identifying the meaning of that **image**, it relates to plural language used here (**Let Us make man in Our image**). This phrase has been interpreted in a variety of ways. First, some believe this is merely a plural of majesty, i.e. God speaking in royal "We." A second view held is to understand the plurals as reflecting God's deliberation, as if He were talking to Himself. A third approach is to understand the plurals here as God's statements to the heavenly court, i.e. the angels. This is least likely since humanity is clearly made in the image of God and not of the angels. Although the first two options seem possible, the most contextually and grammatically tenable explanation of the plural language is that it is an expression of the plural nature of the one true God. That is not to say that this passage is giving a fully expressed statement of the Trinity. Rather, it seems to be saying that even as God is one, He also has a mysterious plural aspect to His essence. And thus, "the singular 'human being' is created as a plurality, 'male and female.' In a similar way, the one God created humanity through an expression of his plurality." (John H. Sailhamer, *The Pentateuch as Narrative* [Grand Rapids, MI: Zondervan, 1992], 95). Thus, the divine plurality anticipates "the human plurality of the man and the woman as a reflection of God's own personal relationship within Himself" (John H. Sailhamer, *NIV Compact Bible Commentary* [Grand Rapids, MI: Zondervan, 1994], 13).

The **image** of God in humanity pertains to the capacity for spiritual relationship. Just as God has the capacity for relationship, so humanity, male and female, have been made to reflect that image and enter into a relationship with their creator. This is also seen in the use of the word the *soul*. The soul most distinguishes humanity from the rest of created life, for only into man did God breathe in a "living soul" (2:7), and it is only human individuals, regardless of their mental capacity, physical ability, or material circumstances, who by virtue of having a soul can experience spiritual communion or "relationship" with God.

1:28-31. The image of God in humanity also includes human beings created to represent God on earth and rule as His regents under Him. Of all created living beings, only humanity has been given dominion over God's creation, and it extends over all other living beings, whether in the sky, sea, or land animals (v. 28; Sailhamer, *The Pentateuch as Narrative*, 95).

God's blessing of humankind, like His blessing on the animals in v. 22, is fundamentally concerned with the expansion of life. Further, God then charges both the man and the woman (**God said to them**) to **subdue** the land and **rule over** its animal life. The same command to **subdue** the land, moreover, was given by God to the Israelites with reference to the land of Canaan.

The picture of this day closes with God instructing the couple on what they are to eat (a pattern repeated after God's "resetting" of the world in chap. 9). They are to eat of the same two groups of vegetation (**plant[s] yielding** [lit., "sowing"] **seed** [i.e., "crop" plants] and **fruit** trees) mentioned in vv. 11-12 that were created on the third day. Verse 30 also refers to a *third* group of vegetation, the **green plant**, mentioned here for the first time not because it was here created, but because it is only now *relevant for man*. The chapter concludes for the seventh time (and for the first time with the intensifying adverb "very"), **And God saw . . . that it was very good**. The addition to this utterance of the adverb **very** is equivalent to what one might otherwise express in English as, "It was the *very best* that it could possibly be." The divine work of special creation (i.e., fashioning the raw material of creation into a home specifically good for humanity) was brought to a close—though one crucial point yet remained to be made.

2:1-3. That God **rested** on the seventh day does not reflect "primitive" theology, in which God needed rest from the physical exertion of His creative work. The Hebrew verb here (*vay-yishbot*) does not mean to rest in the sense of recuperation from physical exertion. It means "to cease," "to abstain," or "to not work." It denotes the absence or cessation of "work" or "labor."

God **blessed** the seventh day and **sanctified** it. Blessing, as already noted, concerns the expansion of life, whereas *sanctification* (lit., "making holy") concerns the sovereign granting by God of that quality that most distinguishes Him from all creation and that, when granted to human individuals, is what fundamentally enables people to commune (or "relate" or "connect") with God. Some have argued that rest on the seventh day is a creation ordinance and as such should be observed, even by contemporary believers. However, God's rest described here became a model for Israel to remember when they received the command to observe the Sabbath, upon leaving Egypt (Ex 16:23-26; 20:8-11; 31:12-17). Thus, Sabbath observance is not a creation ordinance for all, but a command given to Israel to commemorate God's creative acts and rest on the seventh day. It is also a reminder for believers to enter the spiritual rest God has provided through the Messiah Jesus. As stated in Heb 4:10, "The one who has entered His rest (is the one who) has himself also rested from his works, as God did from His" (see comments on Heb 4:1-16).

2. A Close-Up on the Human Ideal (2:4-25)

This section is not, as thought by some, an alternative presentation of general creation in which, contrary to the previous section, everything is created on one day—and in a different order (heaven and earth, then Adam, then vegetation, then animals, then Eve). Rather, this is a "backtracking" to the last and crowning event of creation on the sixth day—the creation of man. This begins the first section of the narrative proper, concerning Adam and Eve and the first generations that came from them (2:4–4:26). This perspective, in fact, is clearly established in 2:4 by the use of the formula **This is the account of**.... This phrase is regularly used throughout Genesis to introduce new major narrative sections (5:1; 6:9; 10:1; 11:10, 27; 25:12, 19; 36:1; 37:2), and in which the word **account** (lit., "generations," *toledot*) always refers, *not* to the history of that which is named in the title, but rather to the human generation(s) that *come from* what is named in the title. Hence, a good paraphrase of this recurring phrase is "this is what became of..." In v. 4 regarding **the heavens and the earth**, the phrase refers to what came from it: in this case Adam—who came from the land—and Eve, as well as their own children.

a. The Ideal Creation of Man (2:4-7)

2:4-6. The second half of v. 4 begins the narrative proper and introduces a series of dependent ("background") clauses intended to "set up" the main event—in this case the creation of "man" in v. 7. The purpose of these "background" clauses comprising vv. 4-6 is to underscore the perfection of the environment into which God was about to place humanity, not by reiterating what was *included* in prefall creation (which is clearly presented in chap. 1), but by telling from the opposite perspective what was *excluded* from prefall creation.

Some interpreters go astray in claiming that this is a contradictory account, taking the word **day** in v. 4 as the **day** on which **the heavens and the earth** and all else in this chapter were created (contra the six days of chap. 1), and taking the phrases **shrub of the field** and **plant of the field** in v. 5 as a reference to vegetation generally, hence implying that man (and woman) was created before the plants (again, contrary to the picture in chap. 1). However, the word **day** in v. 4 could just as well mean "when" and can refer to all six days of creation. It can function as a summary of chap. 1 and a transition to chap. 2, focusing on the sixth day of creation alone. What follows is what became of that creation, beginning with the creation of humanity.

The **shrub of the field** properly refers not to plants in general, but specifically to "troublesome" plants, such as thorns and thistles. The **plant of the field** refers to cultivated grain, unlike the vegetation created on the third day, which replanted themselves with their own seed (cf. 1:11-12). The "troublesome" plants entered creation only *after* the fall, as did the need for man to plant crops to grow. Hence, after Adam and Eve sinned, Adam was told he would now have to cope with thorns and thistles while also cultivating the plants of the field (3:18). That the "good" vegetation created on the third day in 1:11-12 was indeed already present in 2:4-5 is also evident from the reference to the **mist** in 2:6 that would **water the whole surface of the ground.** This would make little sense if there were no plants to be watered.

Likewise indicative of what was excluded from prefall creation are the remaining two statements in v. 5: (1) that **the LORD God had not sent rain upon the earth**, because it was only the sixth day and it had yet to rain, and (2) that **there was no man to cultivate the ground**, connoting that man had not yet been created on the sixth day and that humanity had not yet fallen, so the need to cultivate the soil had not yet arisen. Cultivation of the soil was a specifically postfall consequence of depravity. This is further evident in that the next time this precise expression is used (3:23), it clearly refers to the "toil" and hard labor that came with the punishment for humanity's sin.

2:7. Whereas vv. 1:26-27 refer generally to God's creation of humankind and underscore the distinctive gift of God's "image" that He granted them, this verse presents a detailed description of the *process* by which He did so. Two facts here are of significance: (1) the *proximity of God* to what He was here creating, and (2) the imparting of a "soul" to man *from God's own self*. The first point is emphasized in this verse by the use of the verb **formed** (*vay-yiṣer*, from *yaṣar*), which, when not applied to God's creation of man (cf. Is 49:5; Zch 12:1), is typically employed, especially as a verbal adjective (*yoṣer*), to describe the role and work of a potter—which, perhaps more so than any other human activity, requires the careful and gentle use of the potter's own hands. Since God could have created humanity in any other way He chose, such as by simply calling a man into being (as He did for everything else), the question naturally arises, "Why did He create humanity in *this* way?" And the answer is, "To demonstrate His special care (love) for man and His desire to relate to him in an intimate way."

As to the second point, concerning the imparting of a *soul* to man—it is this that constitutes the "image" of God and that allows us, uniquely among God's living creations, to commune or "relate" to God at a level that *transcends material creation*. In other words, as far as the evidence of Scripture itself, it was only into humanity that God breathed what derives exclusively from Himself—not simply "breath," but in fact the *soul*. Of its 24 occurrences in the OT, this term is applied only to God and people. Hence it describes what humanity and the Creator uniquely share, namely, the *capacity for spiritual relationship*. That capacity is fulfilled when a person ceases from his or her own attempts to find spiritual "rest" and instead enters that permanent rest provided in Jesus Christ (Heb 4:10).

b. The Ideal Place of Man (2:8-14)

2:8-9. In the phrase **a garden . . . in Eden, Eden** (which means "delight") refers to the larger area within which the garden was **planted**. At the center of the garden was **the tree of life**, indicating that humanity was not created immortal but needed this tree to live. Also there was **the tree of the knowledge of good and evil**, whose fruit provided the ability to make moral distinctions, a sense of ethical awareness. **Knowledge of good and evil** is a merism for full moral knowledge, appropriate for God alone since He alone is omniscient.

Both of these trees were sourced in God. It was in the garden, in the proximity of trees, that God later manifested Himself in order to "stroll" with the first couple and instead found them hiding behind the trees (3:8). The garden was planted **toward the east**, (lit., "from the east"). Thus, the entrance to the garden was "toward" the east, and so to go *into* the garden one would walk in from the east (i.e., heading west) whereas to leave one would walk out from the west (i.e., heading east, as in Gn 3:24). This establishes a pattern of distinguishing between east and west in the early chapters of Genesis. Generally, the west is viewed positively (11:31–12:5) while the east is negative (3:24; 4:16; 11:2).

2:10-14. This description of the garden is not given for the purpose of finding the garden. The post-flood topography of the Middle East at the time of the Israelites was fundamentally no different from what it is today. The identifications of the **Pishon** and **Gihon** are unknown, although the **Gihon** is described as being in **Cush**, in Africa, south of Egypt. The **Tigris** and **Euphrates** rivers are in Mesopotamia. Thus, although it is not clear where the garden of Eden was precisely located, plainly it sat between Mesopotamia and Egypt, indicating that its logical location would be Israel. Additionally, the book of Revelation emphasizes the parallel between the garden and the new Jerusalem. These four rivers symbolize life and abundance. In the new Jerusalem, the waters of the river of life will flow out "from the throne of God," flanked on either side by the overspreading branches of the tree of life (Rv 22:1-2). Additionally, the emphasis on **gold** and precious jewels (v. 12) is also found in John's depiction of the new Jerusalem (Rv 21:18).

These associations between the garden of Eden and the new Jerusalem function as an *inclusio*, highlighting the purpose of redemption history between the fall and the final creation. Humanity will return fully to what was lost—intimate access to God's presence. The new Jerusalem will take the place of Eden, and God the Son will be at its "center" in place of the temple. This unrestricted access will not be just for some people for a short time (such as the Levites, and in particular the high priest, during their term of service according to the OT), but for each one of God's children, forever.

c. The Ideal Responsibility of Man (2:15-25)

2:15. This verse includes the only purpose statement in chaps. 1–2. They set forth the answer to the most fundamental question of theology and philosophy, "Why do I exist?" That answer, however, is not to serve as a gardener, as the traditional reading "to cultivate it and keep it" (the "it" being the garden) suggests. Indeed, this verse also presents a prime—though unfortunate—example of how giving attention both to context and the canonical meaning of Hebrew words is critically important for the proper understanding of this or any passage in the Hebrew Scriptures. The phrase **put him** in the first part of v. 15 (**Then the Lord God took the man and put him into the garden of Eden**) requires a closer look. Though apparently a repetition of the same action described in v. 8, the verb used in v. 15 is different. Of course, this might simply represent stylistic variation. Yet considering how the verb in v. 15 is used elsewhere with God as the subject, a different idea emerges. The verb in question is lit., "and He set him at rest" (*vay-yannihehu*, from *nuh*). When *God* is the subject, as He is here, this verb is typically intended to denote the *rest* God promised to give His people when they were in the land ("I/He will give you rest"; cf. Dt 3:20; 12:10; 25:19; 2Sm 7:11). Moreover, as clarified in Heb 3–4 (following David in Ps 95), this divine promise of "rest" refers not merely to physical rest and the cessation of warfare, but ultimately to the all-encompassing *rest of faith*, that is, the spiritual rest, or salvation, that comes from accepting by faith what God has provided (Heb 4:3-10). Therefore the point being made in the first half of this verse is that, *after* creating man and placing him in the garden (v. 8), God immediately placed him in that state for which man was originally intended, the state of being in full relationship with God, the state of being at spiritual rest in and with Him.

From this state of spiritual rest man is to live out his intended purpose as described in the second part of v. 15. Because of the markedly spiritual tone set by the first part of v. 15, the second part should also be understood in a spiritual sense—and not in a physical sense, as suggested by the usual translation **to cultivate it and keep it**. This usual translation betrays a crippling grammatical and translational error, revealed when three points are noted. First, "it" is mistakenly understood as an ending attached to verbs that functions like a pronoun, but it is probably not such an ending in this verse. However, if it *were* a pronoun ending, by its form attached to the two infinitives here it would be *feminine* (and better translated "her" than "it") and would not have "garden," which is *masculine*, as its antecedent. It is unlikely that a feminine pronoun would refer to a masculine noun. Second, and related to the first point, the ending that only looks like a "her" or "it" pronoun ending is actually nothing more than a common ending for Hebrew infinitives without actually being a pronoun ending. It is simply part of the Hebrew infinitive, not an affixed pronoun. In this case "it" (or more properly "her") does not belong in the translation. Third, the infinitives would be translated better as *to worship* (or "to serve") and *to obey* (or "to keep charge"). These translations are preferable because whenever the two verbs here translated **cultivate** (*'avad*) and **keep** (*shamar*) are used together elsewhere in the Hebrew Bible, they are always intended in the sense of *worshiping/serving* (God) and *obeying* Him (Nm 3:7-8; Dt 10:12-13, 28:45-47; Jos 22:5; Cassuto, *Genesis*, I:122-23).

Thus the proper translation of the second part of v. 15, and the purpose for which man was fundamentally created, is to worship and to obey God. This obedience in worshiping and obeying God (v. 15) is expressed by keeping His command (v. 16). This is consistent with the purpose of man as taught in the rest of Scripture, such as in Dt 10:12-13, where Moses asks rhetorically: "What does the LORD your God require from you, but . . . to serve the LORD your God with all your heart and with all your soul, and to keep the LORD's commandments?" and in Ec 12:13, where the only thing man can do that will have any lasting value is "to fear [a biblical synonym for "worship"] God and keep His commandments."

2:16-17. Significantly, after stating that humanity was to worship and obey God, the next verse begins with **the LORD God commanded the man**. God's command is not, as commonly thought, that man was not to eat **from the tree of the knowledge of good and evil**—this statement in v. 17 represents the latter (and lesser) part of God's command, which in fact begins in v. 16. Reflective of God's character as a loving and generous Father who desires what is "good" for His children, He began His command with the positive statement, **From any tree of the garden you may eat freely**! However, the words "you may eat freely" should be translated "you shall certainly eat." This is grammatically parallel to the emphatic expression at the end of v. 17, **you will surely die** (*mot tamut*). The tendency to translate the first part of the command in v. 16 as a mere suggestion is no doubt caused by the perception that people would hardly need to be commanded to eat from all the good fruit trees that were permitted to him. Yet it is precisely this point that God was seeking to make here, namely, that obeying His command should *not* be difficult. Indeed it should be "second" nature, absolutely consistent with man's *sinless* (prefall) created nature. This is the same point Jesus made when He told the Jewish people who were weighed down by the unbearably heavy burden of the Mosaic law and rabbinic law combined: "Take My yoke upon you ["yoke" was a rabbinic metaphor for law] . . . for My yoke is easy and My burden is light" (see comments on Mt 11:28-30).

2:18. This is the first and only time in prefall creation that God assessed something as being **not good**. This does not mean, of course, that the creation of Adam resulted in a situation God did not foresee. God waited to meet that need—and in so doing to bring His creative work to completion—by showing Adam the animal kingdom so that he would realize he had a need that only God, in His love and wisdom, could meet. Then when this need was eventually met, Adam would have a greater sense of gratitude (and hence more glory) to God as well as a greater appreciation of the woman herself.

2:19-20. In v. 20, Adam named three types of animals: **cattle**... **birds of the sky**, and **every beast of the field**. Yet v. 19 mentions only the latter two—that is, those animals that were *not tame* and which man can handle only by hunting or trapping them. Thus in order to serve the main purpose of demonstrating to Adam his need for a female mate, God here created some specific representatives of the bird and wild land-animal categories to be named along with the tame animals. The argument that this naming of the animals would have taken more than a single day is not valid. The primary purpose of bringing these animals before Adam was not to give them names, but rather to highlight his need for woman—which a relatively small number of animal pairs would suffice to establish. Indeed, the Hebrew word **names** (*shemot*) is perfectly consistent with the understanding that Adam simply gave general designations to each general category or class of animal (e.g., "equine," "serpentine," "canine," etc.) rather than precise labels such as "*Equus ferus caballus*," "*Crotalus horridus*," "*Canis lupus familiaris*," let alone "Spot" or "Rex."

And so Adam came to perceive what God always knew—that he stood in need of a female **helper suitable for him** (v. 20). In this description of woman, which occurs in the Bible only here and in v. 18, there are two key ideas. First, concerning the woman's role, the word **helper** (*'ezer*) according to its usage is not a demeaning term as it is used elsewhere in Scripture of God (Pss 33:20; 70:5; 115:9). In Ps 121:1-2, when used of God, it indicates one who gives both material and spiritual assistance. Hence, the woman was to assist the man in accomplishing the task God gave him to worship and obey Him. Second, concerning the woman's *value* or *worth*, the expression **suitable for him** (*ke-negdo*, lit., "facing him," as one might describe his image in a mirror) underscores that woman is intrinsically all that man is, yet in the feminine, and hence she is of equal worth. This second part of the description serves to avoid any potential misunderstanding of the first part, namely, the idea that the woman's role as assistant implies any differing value or worth. In God's eyes men and women are equally valued, and are judged according to the same standard of how faithfully they fulfill the roles that they have been given. Still, from creation, God intends them to have distinct but harmonizing roles. For how this influences the role of men and women in the church, see comments on 1Co 11:2-9 and 1Tm 2:12-15.

2:21-23. The **deep sleep** into which God placed the man is not "divine anesthesia." In three other instances in the Hebrew Bible God placed people into a **deep sleep** (Gn 15:12; 1Sm 26:12; Is 29:10, in each instance employing the same Hb. expression, *tardema*). And in each case the point is to underscore the people's need for complete dependence on God and God's ability to meet that need in the proper way. In this instance, therefore, God excluded Adam from even a visual participation in the process of creating Eve, so that when he awoke he would immediately perceive that his need had been completely met by God.

By creating the woman from one of Adam's **ribs** God further underscored the equal worth of the woman, since she is made, lit., of the same "stuff" as the man. The rib, in particular, offers a neutral symbol that cannot be used either to devalue the woman (as if she had been taken from Adam's foot) or to overvalue her at the expense of man (as if she had been taken from man's head). At the same time, however, the woman is distinguished in her creation from that of man by the specific use (here for the first time) of the verb **fashioned** (*vay-yiven*, from *bana*). The verb "formed" in 2:7 is often used of a potter. But the verb **fashioned**, which may also be translated "built," is applied to the making of more complex constructions.

That God **brought her to the man** is a semi-formal expression that is used elsewhere in Scripture to describe the action of a father when bringing his daughter in marriage to the bridegroom (Gn 29:23); and indeed God's bringing Adam and Eve is described as a marriage in Gn 2:24. The verb **brought** was also used in 2:19 for God bringing animals to Adam for him to name them, indicating, among other things, Adam's authority over them. By implication, the bringing of Eve to Adam, and his naming her (see the verb "call" in both 2:19 and 23), also is an indication of God's intention that he would provide leadership for her.

In v. 23, presenting the first recorded words of humanity, Adam expressed a clear awareness of the woman's intrinsic equality as well as her feminine distinctiveness. He did this by means of an adept wordplay, describing his mate by the term *ishsha*, which is typically translated **woman**. From the *sound* of it, this word is the feminine form of the Hebrew word for **man**, *ish* (*-a* being the typical feminine noun suffix in Hb.). This is also implied by the statement in which the two words are used: **she shall be called *Woman*** [*ishsha*], **because she was taken out of *Man*** [*ish*], italics added. This underscores the woman's intrinsic equality with the man: all that he is in essence, "beneath" his masculine packaging as a **man** (*ish*), so too is she "beneath" her feminine packaging as a **woman** (*ishsha*). The *spelling* of the word *ishsha*, however, shows that the feminine ending (*-a*) has *not* been added to the Hebrew word for **man** (*ish*), but in fact to the Hebrew root meaning "soft" or "delicate" (*'-n-sh*, from which is derived the name "Enosh" in Gn 4:26). Therefore Adam was affirming both the **woman**'s equal value to **man** (by the *sound* of the word) as well as her distinctiveness (by the *spelling* of the word) as "a delicate vessel" (1 Pt 3:7, in which the term typically translated "weaker" [*asthenestero*] can—and *should* in view of the present passage—be translated "delicate" or even "tender").

2:24-25. Marriage is described as consisting of three essential *actions* (reflecting the three clauses in the Hebrew text), all of which, if not always perfectly realized in a marriage, are nonetheless intended as life-long ideals for which a married couple is to strive unceasingly. The first action, represented by the statement **a man shall leave his father and his mother**, is that of clearly shifting one's primary human loyalty to his spouse. The *man* is the subject of the verb (the "doer" of the action), suggesting not that the leaving is to be done only by the man, but that the degree of relational "severance" will typically be greater for him than he should expect it to be for his wife.

The second essential action is noted in the clause **and** he shall **be joined to his wife** (or "cleave to" KJV), in which "be joined to" (*davaq*) refers *not* to the sexual union of the couple, but rather to an intentional and unbreakable commitment, with the *best* interest of the other party being both the motivation and the goal of the one making that commitment. This verb is often used to describe the ideal of Israel's (or an individual's) covenant relationship with God, as in Jos 23:8: "But you are to cling (*tidbaqu*) to the Lord your God, as you have done to this day" (cf. Dt 30:20; 2Kg 18:6; Ps 63:8; Jr 13:11). The word is also used to describe Ruth's commitment to Naomi, "Orpah kissed her mother-in-law, but Ruth clung [*daveqa*] to her" (Ru 1:14). Ruth clarified this commitment in her following statement: "Where you go, I will go, and where you lodge, I will lodge. Your people shall be my people, and your God, my God" (v. 16). These sentiments expressed by Ruth are intended to characterize the "cleaving" within marriage. Genesis 2:24 presents the *man* as the subject (i.e., the one "doing" the cleaving) perhaps because men frequently have greater difficulty with marital commitment.

The third action is expressed by the statement, **and they shall become one flesh**. This refers not merely to the sexual union within marriage, but in fact to the uniting of two people into one. It refers to two people sharing of all of life in common so as to be like one person. Sexual union is a way to express this exclusive unity and a reason the Bible limits sexual relations to married couples.

On entering into the marriage union both the man and the woman are obligated to meet the physical needs of the other, just as they would hope for those same needs to be met in themselves. Paul made this point in Eph 5:28-30: "So husbands ought also to love their own wives as their own bodies. He who loves his own wife loves himself; for no one ever hated his own flesh, but nourishes and cherishes it, just as Christ also does the church, because we are members of His body." As a result of the first couple experiencing marriage in this perfect setting, they are described as being **naked and were not ashamed**, indicating the lovely innocence and intimacy available in marriage.

B. Fallen Humanity: The Advent of Sin (3:1-21)

In this second part of His "prosecution" of depraved humanity God built His case by showing that the "fall" from the ideal of perfection and unbroken "rest" (i.e., relationship) with God was because of man's choice, via Adam, to disobey the divine prohibition and to seek to determine for themselves what is "good." In addition to bringing man's culpability into focus, these 21 verses also introduce, in masterful fashion, the foundational concepts of temptation, guilt, mercy, grace, death, curse, chastisement, forgiveness, and substitutionary atonement.

1. The Lead-up to Sin (3:1-6)

This detailed account of the temptation that confronted the first couple gives a detailed blueprint of how temptation "works" in people's lives today as well. And by comparing Adam's failure with the parallel temptation experience of Christ, believers are given a blueprint for success over the same temptations that confront them.

a. Step One: Wrongly Recalling God's Word (3:1-3)

3:1-3. That the serpent was described as **more crafty than any beast of the field** indicates that it was a real animal and not a mere symbol. Nevertheless, that the serpent here is under Satan's control is beyond question, inasmuch as serpents cannot talk. Moreover, the apostle John clearly identified him as "the serpent of old" (Rv 12:9; 20:2) and also the clear intention of Christ's statement in Jn 8:44: "He was a murderer from the beginning"—referring to Satan's deceptive role in inciting the first couple to sin and thus experience death. The text never states why Satan chose to use a serpent in his temptation of humanity. In seeking to incite the couple to sin Satan focused his efforts on the woman, since her basis for obedience was potentially less stable, being dependent on Adam's communication of the command as well as for his guidance in resolving any questions or doubt about it. Since the couple at this point was inseparable (Adam was "with her;" v. 6), Satan did not overtly "corner" or isolate the woman, which would undoubtedly have raised Adam's ire and more quickly prompted him to defend his wife. Rather, Satan spoke to them both—as underscored by the fact that all of the "you" pronouns in this exchange are plural, yet he addressed the woman (v. 1, **he said to the woman**), and in doing so he subtly marginalizes her husband. Nor did Satan state an outright lie; rather, he recalled (or, better, *rephrased)* God's precise words in 2:16-17 in such as a way that he distorted both the focus of the command and the character of the God who gave it. God had presented the command by emphasizing that much more comprehensive part of it that reflects His parental love and grace, that is, they *were* to eat from every tree (v. 16) and then He added the single and comparatively minor restriction (v. 17). Satan rephrased the command in such a way that the *whole* of it was focused on and colored by the single restriction. To her credit, however, Eve responded by reiterating the command as properly intended, beginning with emphasis on the greater and easier part reflective of God's grace and generosity.

Some interpreters, however, have criticized Eve's (or Adam's) adding to the command the words **or touch it.** They claim that this is an example of the unfortunate human tendency to unnecessarily encumber God's Word. However, such criticism here is unjustified, because before eating from the tree they were not depraved and therefore were not sinners. Their sin is identified with eating from the tree, not with a supposedly wrongful addition to God's command. And even where such "additions" *are* later condemned, this is only where such additions are either contrary to God's Law or intended in a truly *legalistic* sense.

b. Step Two: Wrongly Assessing God's Purpose (3:4-5)

3:4-5. Since Eve clearly was not caught by Satan's rephrasing of God's command, Satan adopted an alternate plan: calling into question God's purpose or motive for giving them the command. God intended the restriction for the benefit of man—to serve as a privileged opportunity for their obedience as well as to ensure their dependence on God as the only source of the knowledge of good and evil. But Satan suggested that God's intention was petty, for He was unwilling to share His divine position with man who, by eating from the tree, would be equally as qualified to be called God (hence, **like God**, or "as gods," as the phrase may also be translated). Ultimately therefore God's character as a loving and gracious Father, with the best interest of His children at heart, was being called into question.

c. Step Three: Wrongly Approving What Seems "Good" (3:6)

3:6. Significantly the initial "formula" used here to describe Eve's assessment—she **saw that the tree was good**—is identical to the "formula" that up to this point has been used exclusively in connection with *God's* assessment of what is good for man, from the initial creation of light (1:4) to the final act of creating the woman, whose absence from Adam's life was "not good" (2:18). The point inevitably emerges that people, on their own, are not able to assess accurately what is truly **good**—or, more specifically, that man's assessment of what *is* good must be guided by the parameters established by God's Word.

Eve assessed the "good," or appeal, of eating the fruit in three distinct ways: it was practical, being useful for food, it was aesthetically beautiful, and it had the possibility for wisdom. These three areas preyed upon the woman's physical, emotional, and spiritual desires. Some have seen these same three "categories" of temptation reflected in "the lust of the flesh and the lust of the eyes and the boastful pride of life" (1Jn 2:16).

The strongest appeal to the woman was that of wisdom, which in Scripture is both "mental and spiritual acumen" (Allen P. Ross, *Creation and Blessing*, [Grand Rapids, MI: Baker, 1988], 136). As a result, the temptation is not presented as flagrant rebellion but rather "a quest for wisdom and 'the good' apart from God's provision" (Sailhamer, *The Pentateuch as Narrative,* 104). Therefore, the woman took the fruit and ate and **gave also to her husband with her**.

Since both the man and the woman ate, why is the man deemed more culpable than the woman? Perhaps because he had heard the prohibition against eating directly from God but also he had experienced firsthand, in a way that Eve had not, the paternal love and grace of God in receiving from His hand, especially in God providing Eve herself. Tragically, however, Adam kept silent during the temptation, and in so doing he gave a certain degree of "tacit approval" to the validity of Satan's alternative and improper characterization of God's motive. For this reason, the text emphasizes that the woman was deceived (3:13, cf. 1Tm 2:14, "the woman being deceived"). Although Eve should have known better, she sinned without fully realizing that her sin was inconsistent with the true character of God. Adam, on the other hand, fully understood, and is therefore ascribed a far greater culpability, as is evident from God prefacing Adam's chastisement (but not Eve's) with explicit reference to his intentional disobedience (3:17). In Nm 30:6-12, a husband is held responsible for his wife's vows. In fact, if he hears his wife make a vow but does not speak up, he is responsible for her vow (Nm 30:9-11). Similarly, Adam was responsible to speak his disapproval during the temptation and since he failed, is considered more culpable. Not only did the man fail to speak and stop the woman, but joining her folly, he also took the fruit, and **he ate**.

2. Humanity's Response to Sin (3:7-8)

These two verses show that the death about which God had warned Adam in 2:17 would take place "in the day" that he ate was not an empty threat, as Satan had deceived Eve into thinking. The death that they experienced, however, was not that of immediate physical cessation, nor was it that of becoming "subject" to death (i.e., mortal), since this was already the case before they ate (see 2:9). Rather death here was separation. Just as death is a separation of the spirit from the body (Jms 2:26), spiritual death is a separation of the person from God. Here it was a spiritual and *experiential* separation, a separation or "break" in the ideal experience of their relationship with God and with each other. In this respect the narrative presents a vivid paradigm for understanding (and hence avoiding) the consequences of sin in life.

a. Conviction (3:7a)

3:7a. The reference to **the eyes** of the couple being **opened** is an idiom that expresses their acquisition not of new visual information but of new knowledge, that is full wisdom, the developed understanding of what is good and what is evil. Such knowledge or wisdom is of course a good thing, and its attainment was just as much an intended goal for Adam and Eve as it is for people today. Yet God had intended for them to attain this understanding of good and evil by dependence on Him, through the process of taking continual recourse to Him and instruction from Him. Because they did not, ironically their immediate acquisition of this full knowledge (i.e., their "open eyes") also enabled them to realize that since the manner in which they acquired this knowledge (by breaking God's command) was "evil," they were guilty and deserving of punishment from God. Thus, in the following phrase **and they knew that they were naked**, the word "naked" (*'erummim*) does not signify merely the state of being unclothed (this is denoted by a *different* Hebrew word, *'arummim,* translated "naked" in 2:25), but also their state of shameful and guilty nakedness resulting from sin, specifically in connection with God's punishment for sin (cf. Dt 28:48; Ezk 16:22, 39; 23:29). The sense of this statement therefore is that their newly acquired knowledge of what constitutes good and evil "opened their eyes" to see that what they had done was evil and had justly left them "naked," that is, *exposed*, to God's impending punishment.

b. Division from Each Other (3:7b)

3:7b. The **loin coverings** the couple made from **fig leaves** should be understood not only as an attempt to cover their physical nakedness, but also, in light of the previous comment, as an attempt to assuage their sense of "exposure" to the impending punishment that they know their sin justly deserved. In addition the "donning" of these loincloths highlights the typical impact of sin on our human relationships (especially when that sin is jointly committed), namely, division and disruption. This is consistent with the fundamental concept of "death" as noted in

2:17, as separation rather than cessation. In this case the "death" or "disjunction" was not in the *fact* of their relationship (the couple was still "married"), but in the ideally intended *experience* of that relationship, outwardly reflected in the barriers they set up between those parts of themselves that are most representative of physical intimacy.

c. Division from God (3:8)

3:8. The impact of the couple's sin on their relationship with God— the "death" that He warned would occur "in the day" that they ate (2:17)—is here borne out by a "break" or "separation" in the experience of that relationship. This consequence is presented with especially tragic emphasis by the depiction of **the Lord God walking in the garden in the cool of the day**. Since the verb "walking" logically implies the use of feet, it must be concluded that God had at this point taken human form—and if so, as in 2:7 and based on the theological consideration that only God the Son can be seen walking about (Jn 1:18), it was *the Son* specifically who is in view here. The verb here translated **walking** is a relatively infrequent form of the verb that indicates not a walking from point A to point B, with a specific endpoint in view, but rather a "strolling," "meandering," or a circular type of walking. In other words though the Son knew what the couple had done, He wanted them to know that His ideal intention was to enjoy fellowship with His human children to the fullest capacity of their created nature, which is physical as well as spiritual. There is perhaps no more universally poignant picture of such holistic relationship than that of God seeking to stroll with man in the garden toward the evening time of day. The tragedy in this passage is that God's first children were pushing away this privileged experience of fellowship by using those very things that their divine Father gave them for their good (the trees of the garden) as a barrier to His presence.

3. God's Response to Sin (3:9-21)

God's response to the sin of Adam and Eve is not merely that of a Creator, nor even that of a Judge who is *just*; rather it is the response of a God who desires to be—and be seen as—a Father in every ideal sense of the word. In this respect the detailed description of how God responded to the couple's sin "sets the course" for the way in which people today are to anticipate and assess God's response to the sins of His children.

a. Gentle Confrontation (3:9-13)

3:9-13. Unexpectedly to Adam and Eve, since they were anticipating God's immediate (and just) response to their sin, the Son (see comments at 3:8) did not call out to them in wrath, but in a tone of gentle and patient questioning. These questions are not, as some interpreters claim, reflections of an "immature" early Israelite theology in which the concept of God's omniscience is not yet fully developed. Instead these questions are not being asked to give Him information He did not have, but for the benefit of the ones being questioned. Rather than overwhelming them with judgment because *His* honor was offended, God responded in a way reflective of concern for their welfare and betterment. He wanted them to understand why what they did was so bad, so that it would serve as a deterrent to future sin. Thus the first question **Where are you?** was intended to have the couple leave behind the barriers (the trees) and distance they placed between themselves and God because of their shame. And by the second question—**Who told you that you were naked?**—God's intention for them was to understand *how* they ended up at this less-than-ideal distance from God.

God's paternal and even *gentle* mercy (i.e., *not* giving them the punishment they deserved) is further evident in the second question God asked, supplying the content of their confession (**Have you eaten from the tree of which I commanded you not to eat?**). In response the man need only say, "Yes" or "I ate" to acknowledge his sin. And Adam did say this, but only *after* seeking to mitigate his guilt by shifting much of the blame to the woman and in a sense to God Himself (**whom You gave to be with me**). Nonetheless, God played along and His similar question to Eve "What is this you have done?" showed that His personal interest in the woman's welfare was just as keen. She gave essentially the same response, with much of the blame being shifted to the Serpent. That these questions were indeed intended to draw the couple to confession is underscored by God asking no question of the Tempter—the questions had no application to him, for Satan is not God's child.

Another significant observation with respect to God's questions here is that once the man and the woman say **I ate** (vv. 12-13) God ceased His questioning and moved on. If the purpose of these questions was to draw each of them to confess, one may reasonably conclude that God's purpose had been satisfied. This conclusion is established as a certainty by v. 21, where God expresses toward the couple one of the most vivid and visual examples of forgiveness to be found anywhere in the OT. Therefore the implication emerges that *God is satisfied with less than perfect confession.* In His paternal mercy and perfect love, God fervently desired to express forgiveness toward His children (and what good parent would not?). The theological-thematic emphasis of this episode therefore is on God's *mercy* rather than on the couple's *merit.* The challenge in all this is clear: since the goal of any child of God is to strive to be like his heavenly Father (Mt 5:48), believers should follow God's lead and strive to forgive those who have sinned against them, even when their apology or confession is less than what one would like.

b. Merciful Chastisement (3:14-20)

Though one may describe God as "punishing" all three (Adam, Eve, and Satan), God's words to Satan are characteristic of *judgment* (which always proceeds from condemnation), whereas His words to Adam and Eve are characteristic of *chastisement* (which always proceeds from love, never condemnation which, according to Rm 8:1, is never the experience of God's children).

3:14-15. God's words are first addressed to the serpent (v.14), the literal animal used by Satan. The judgment of crawling on his belly is not to be taken as meaning the serpent at one time had legs and now would lose them. Just as there were rainbows before the flood and circumcision existed before the Abrahamic covenant, so crawling on the belly and eating dust are conditions previously descriptive of the serpent but now given symbolic significance. These actions will now represent *complete defeat* (**dust you will eat** in Mc 7:17,) and *absolute diminution of life.* Moreover, the serpent is more cursed (v. 14) than the rest of the animal kingdom. This is so in that the whole creation was cursed because of the fall, however that curse will be lifted from the rest of the animal kingdom in the Messianic kingdom but will not be lifted from the serpent (see Is 65:25).

In v. 15 God addressed the power behind the serpent, Satan, further underscoring the difference between His treatment of Satan and that of the couple by indicating that Satan's final defeat will be brought about by one of the couple's own descendants—yet one who is at the same time *more* than a mere descendant. This pronouncement in fact represents the first direct specific prediction concerning the work of the Messiah, and has appropriately been regarded from the earliest period of Christian interpretation as the *Protevangelium* (lit., "the first gospel"). Even before the NT was written, the messianic import of this verse was recognized by Jewish interpreters (as evident in the translation of the LXX), and it continued to be affirmed within the Jewish community for several centuries after the birth of Christianity (in the early Aramaic paraphrastic translations, known as the *targumim Pseudo-Jonathan, Neofiti,* and *Onqelos* as well as the rabbinic commentary *Genesis Rabbah 23:5*). This shows how entrenched this view was, and clearly this is the most "natural" and logical understanding of the passage. This passage bears out not only a reference to the final victory of Messiah, but also to His death in that He will be bruised **on the heel**. His divine nature may be implied by the use of **He**, the "seed" of the woman, who is portrayed as issuing the final "death blow" to Satan (**He shall bruise you on the head**), which is something that only God can and will do. God the Son will do this, as stated in Ps 110:6b (lit., "He will crush [the] head"); Rm 16:20; 1Jn 3:8; Rv 20:10 (where Satan is thrown into the lake of fire under the authority—if not directly by—the enthroned Christ).

3:16. God's chastisement of the woman consists of two parts: the first is that He would **greatly multiply** her **pain** (lit., "hard labor") **in childbirth** (v. 16a). The second part of the woman's chastisement is that her **desire will be for** her **husband**—the "desire" here being not the emotional desire that was unquestionably present in their prefall relationship, but rather the psychological desire to *dominate and control* her husband. This is clear from the contrast with the following clause (v. 16b being an antithetic parallelism), **and he will rule over you**. The man will seek to exercise mastery and control over the woman; the *ideal,* however, was they were to rule together, with final authority and responsibility resting with the man. Also the word for "desire" (*teshuqa*) is used again in chap. 4 (the only other occurrence of this word in the Pentateuch) where it is *again* followed by a contrastive clause and paralleled by the *same* verbal root for "rule" (*mashal*) as in 3:16. God warned Cain, "[Sin's] desire [*teshuqa*] is for you, but you must master [*yimshol*] it" (4:7). The man's leadership of the woman is not a result of the fall. It was in place before it, as evident in man's authority to name (2:20) and his explicit naming of the woman (2:23). Rather, the fall brought with it the woman's tendency to dominate her husband, and male leadership became vexing for the woman for the first time.

3:17-19. God spoke **to Adam**, suggesting that He held Adam most culpable for the sin. This point is also underscored by the order in which God responded to the sinning parties, moving back up the true "chain of blame" (from Adam to Eve to Satan) though the sinning parties were Satan, then Eve, followed by Adam. Yet Adam's chastisement was essentially *identical* to that of Eve, consisting of both a *psychological* component (the specific desire to "master" the other, v. 16) and a *physical* component (the specific experience of **toil**, the same word used in v. 16 to describe the increased "pain" of the woman's childbirth).

The physical death to which God referred in the last line of v. 19—**and to dust you shall return**—does not represent an additional chastisement that Adam was made mortal. Since "immortality" was not part of Adam and Eve's created nature, God was simply indicating the *end point* of man's life of hard toil, that is, physical death, the inevitable consequence of being restricted from the tree of life.

3:20. Prior to this point the woman had been referred to as "Eve," but in v. 20 Adam actually gives her name to her. This does not contradict 2:23 in which Adam called her "woman," since this latter is a noun intended to designate her sex, whereas the name **Eve** is her individual designation (as is "Adam" for the man). This represents her unique role as **the mother of all the living**, that is, the first mother from whom the rest of human life would descend. Nor is this verse "misplaced," interrupting the flow of God's continuing punishment from v. 19 to the couple's exile in vv. 22-24. To the contrary, God's chastisement of the couple is completed by the end of v. 19, with v. 20 representing the immediate realization of one aspect of that chastisement, namely, the man's assertion of "rule" or "mastery" over the woman (v. 16), represented by the act of naming Eve.

c. Gracious Forgiveness (3:21)

3:21. Having responded to their sin with paternal gentleness and merciful chastisement, God sealed His response with a vivid act of forgiveness, and in so doing He established the pattern by which sin is thereafter properly atoned for (i.e., divinely forgiven). This picture of atonement/divine forgiveness in v. 21, and not that of the exile from the garden in vv. 22-24, is the proper "conclusion" to the episode of the couple's sin. The exile is more consistent with the events of the next chapter in reflecting the inevitable aftermath of human sin. Also in Jewish liturgy v. 22 marks the beginning of the next Sabbath reading section, with v. 21 serving as the conclusion to the previous section that began in 2:4.

In 3:21 three indispensable elements of true atonement/divine forgiveness may be discerned. First, it requires a *blood sacrifice* (cf. Heb 9:22, "Without shedding of blood there is no forgiveness"), as implied by the guilty parties being clothed with garments made from animal **skin**, logically requiring the death of an animal. Second, the work of providing the sacrifice is, ultimately, *God's work*, for He alone is the subject of the two verbs **made** and **clothed** (underscoring, by contrast, the complete passivity in this process of Adam and Eve). Third, God's work of atonement, once achieved, is *durable*, that is, *permanent*, as borne out by the contrast between the fig leaves with which the couple attempted to cover their shame and the **skin** (leather) garments that God provided.

C. Dire Consequences: The Aftermath of Sin (3:22–4:26)

In view of God's expression of forgiveness in v. 21, one may be tempted to conclude that the consequences of the first couple's sin extended no further than their own lifelong experience of God's chastisement. However, in this section God further built his case (that *humanity* is completely depraved and in dire need of divine redemption) by making clear that the consequences of that first sin did indeed extend beyond the first parents.

1. Exile: The Communal Aftermath of Sin (3:22-24)

While the experience of exile throughout human history is almost always the direct result of human depravity (i.e., the desire by some to master others and take what belongs to them), such was not the case here. The first couple's exile from the garden, though a consequence of their sin, is in this instance enforced directly by God—not as an extra element of punishment but as a necessary step in ensuring that they ultimately receive what is *best* (of which the *good*—in this case, staying in the garden—is often the enemy).

a. The Problem (3:22)

3:22. Though God had forgiven the couple, a fundamental problem still remained, as expressed by God Himself: they had **become like**

one of Us, knowing good and evil. The point of this is not simply that they, like God, were fully able to distinguish evil from good, which is hardly a problem as such. Instead, the problem was that, unlike God, they were unable (because of depravity) to live according to that knowledge. God alone in his omniscience knows how to effect that which is good and to avoid that which is evil (see 2:9). Humanity's moral discernment though now present was limited and could not bring about that which is good. Were they therefore to **eat** at that point from the tree of life, they would **live forever** in a less than ideal state. They would be forgiven by God, but would nevertheless possess a fallen nature and fallen bodies as a consequence of the fall. Knowing God's righteous requirements, because of depravity they would be incapable of observing those requirements, and would thus lack the kind of intimacy with God for which He created them. God, therefore, in His mercy, keeps them from eating from **the tree of life** and excludes them from Eden.

The ironic outcome of this episode is that humanity began like God, having been created in His image. However, now, having pursued their desire to become like God, and somewhat inadequately attained that status, the man and woman will be expelled from God's presence. Hence, they are "like God" but not with God.

Humanity's expulsion from the garden would serve as a foreshadowing and warning to Israel. As the nation was about to enter the land of milk and honey, it would be warned that obedience to God's commands would bring blessing in the land (Dt 28:1-14) and disobedience would bring discipline (Dt 29:15-68), specifically expulsion from the land (Dt 28:64-68).

b. God's Gracious Solution (3:23)

3:23. God's solution of expelling man from the garden, though certainly a "bad" thing in the short run, is ultimately a "very good" (i.e., the *best*) thing in the long run, and from this perspective it was an act of divine grace. Once restricted from the tree of life, every child of God must die, yet in so doing he must undergo the renewal of being made as man was meant to be—physically immortal, but also spiritually incorruptible and pure (1Co 15:50). In this state the child of God will one day eat from the tree of life, in the garden of the new Jerusalem and in the presence of the Lord (Rv 22:1-2).

c. The "Eastward" Paradigm (3:24)

3:24. Here begins another significant paradigm: that of man moving east, corresponding to an increasing "distance" from God. Because of their sin, Adam and Eve, though forgiven, were no longer able to experience that ideal of intended intimacy with God in the garden, from which they were sent out toward **the east**; so too was Cain sent eastward as a consequence of his sin (4:16); and so too did mankind move farther east before building the tower of Babel (11:2). Abram's father, Terah, was the first one in Scripture to reverse this eastward direction when he set out toward Canaan (11:31), indicating a desire on his part to draw closer to God. And Christ Himself, at His second advent, will finally reverse this eastward direction, when "the glory of God" will return to the temple "from the way of the east" (Ezk 43:2). There, God (the Son) will establish His throne and "dwell" for all eternity (43:7). This is all the more significant when one bears in mind that the temple itself was intended as a symbolic "recasting" of the prefall "Eden-garden" arrangement. The point of Ezekiel's prophecy therefore is that the Son at His second advent will vanquish not only His human enemies, but also sin's very dominion over man.

2. Murder: The Personal Aftermath of Sin (4:1-22)

The tragic presence and outworking of depravity is emphatically driven home in this section by the vivid description of humanity's first murder. Today this would be legally classified as first-degree murder, and in most societies it would justify the harshest of penalties. The focus of the chapter is not on the criminal act as such, described in v. 8, but on the pivotal factors involved in both the *lead-up* as well as the *follow-up* to that act. Careful attention to the latter, in fact, is crucial for a proper appreciation of the value of this episode and its challenge to believers.

a. The Priority of Heart Attitude (4:1-8)

4:1. By commencing this episode with reference to the births of **Cain** and **Abel**, the dark cloud attending the overall theme of this section (i.e., the "attachment" of sin) is briefly dispersed first, by the simple fact of the births themselves (showing that God's fundamental blessing expressed in 1:28 has not been dramatically affected by the advent of sin and depravity), and second, by Eve's statement about her firstborn son Cain, which hearkens back to the messianic hope of God's promise in 3:15. Eve's statement is to be translated, "I have acquired a male, the LORD." Eve's expectation about Cain is that he was none other than the promised "seed" of 3:15, who, as the coming Seed, would restore humanity to its prefall ideal by "crushing" Satan's head and ending the reign of sin over creation. Such an expectation on Eve's part is reasonable in the absence of those much more specific limitations on the time, place, identity, and work of the promised Seed as subsequently revealed in Scripture. These later limitations may have prompted many translators to "interpret" the second part of Eve's statement in a grammatically abnormal sense, **with the help of the LORD**. This reading goes back to the LXX and the Vulgate. Notably, however, the more straightforward, messianic reading given above is precisely attested in the oldest translation of the entire Bible (i.e., OT and NT), the Peshitta, or Eastern Aramaic (Syriac) version.

4:2-5. When they grew up, Cain and Abel adopted the respective "professions" of farming and shepherding, neither of which is morally preferable to the other, since both flora and fauna have been equally affected by the "corruption" resulting from man's sin (Rm 8:20-22). In their desire to worship, therefore, the brothers quite naturally present **to the LORD** what is theirs to give—namely, a **fruit** offering and a **flock** offering. Cain's offering was not rejected because it was a non-animal offering (this distinction is made only later on in the law of Moses, and even then fruit and grain offerings were legitimate offerings, see Lv 2:1-16), but rather because Cain's heart, or attitude, was not consistent with the act of worship. This is evident by comparing the description of Cain's offering as **of the fruit of the ground** to the description of Abel's offering as **of the firstlings of his flock and of their fat portions**. Abel, whose heart was fully devoted to worship, gave not just "of the flock," but also *the best* of the flock, the specific sense of the Hebrew word for "firstlings." Not coincidentally a corresponding term from the same Hebrew root designates the best of a cereal/fruit offering (i.e., "firstfruits" in Lv 2:14). Thus its omission from the description of Cain's offering implies that Cain did not offer the firstfruits, the choicest produce, because his heart was not in the "right place" for worship. Not only therefore does this focus on the nature of the brothers' offerings help readers understand the spiritual cause of the ensuing conflict, but it also serves as an important "prelude" to the detailed sacrificial ritual presented later on in the Mosaic law.

4:6-7. God graciously and gently confronted Cain while anger was still simmering in his heart, and exhorted him to **master it**, to bring it completely under his control (the same expression is also in 3:16; see comments there). Contrary to what is often thought, Cain is to be regarded as a believer (see comments on 4:9-12 and 4:13-22), and hence one to whom the believing reader of this episode can relate. This episode enables the reader to understand the "activity" of temptation, sin, chastisement, and divine grace.

4:8. Cain's anger did not immediately vent itself in murder. Instead it moved from the stage of inner enmity to verbal dispute. This is implied by the reference in this verse to Cain "speaking" with Abel. However, the translation of this word "to say" makes little sense. Thus various renderings of the verb are "talked with" (KJV), "told" (NASB), "spoke" (ESV), or with the addition of the words, "Let us go out to the field" (RSV, NIV). But the word may have been the less-common sense of "disputed" (like the English idiom, "to have words with"). This same verb is used in the same way in Est 1:18. In any event, the relationship of anger to verbal abuse/dispute and murder is the pattern Jesus addressed in Mt 5:21-22. Strife between brothers (family members), as seen here between Cain and Abel, becomes a common theme throughout Genesis. Other examples are Noah's sons (Gn 9:20-27), Abraham and Lot (Gn 13:7-12), Isaac and Ishmael (Gn 21:9), Jacob and Esau (Gn 25–28; 32–33), Jacob and Laban (Gn 29–31), Joseph and his brothers (Gn 37, 39–50).

b. God's Mercy, Again (4:9-12)

4:9-12. God's response to Cain's sin parallels His response to the sin of Cain's parents in the previous chapter. This underscores by implication the point noted above (on vv. 6-7) that God viewed Cain as His *child* (i.e., as a believer) who was in need of correction (i.e., chastisement) so that he might attain the *best* that His divine Father intended for him. Just as with Cain's parents, God commenced His response with specific **Where**? and **What**? questions (vv. 9-10), designed to bring the sinning child face to face with his sin and hopefully to the point of confession. At this point, however, a notable difference emerged. Whereas Cain's parents did confess, though in an imperfect manner, Cain did not. Yet this is not evidence that Cain was a "lost cause," that is, an example of one who is "beyond redemption." God's reaction to Cain's absence of confession was *not* to condemn

Cain to death, which was in fact the required penalty for murder under the Mosaic law and even under the more general punitive principle revealed by God to Noah in 9:6. Instead God consigned Cain to the life of a nomad [the connotation of idleness in the oft-used **vagrant** is misplaced here] **and a wanderer** (vv. 12, 14). In effect, his punishment was to deter him from further sin by his taking the profession of his brother Abel and becoming a shepherd, which by definition entails a nomadic life (thus Cain's descendants become the "fathers" of nomadic shepherding; 4:20). God showed Cain preemptive mercy by withholding from him, despite his lack of remorse, the full penalty his sin deserved. This is precisely what it took to crack Cain's hardened shell of unrepentance and to bring him to his knees, pouring out one of the most heart-rending expressions of remorse and confession in Scripture. (In this respect it is important to note that the negative NT references to Cain [Heb 11:4; 1Jn 3:12; Jd 11] apply specifically to his depravity as described in vv. 3-12, *not* explicitly to the portion thereafter, let alone to his life as a whole).

c. Cain's Repentance and God's Grace (4:13-22)

4:13-14. Any sense of confession would seem to be quite far from Cain's statement in v. 13 as typically translated: **My punishment is too great to bear!** (NASB) or, "My punishment is greater than I can bear!" (RSV). The Hebrew word typically translated "punishment" (*'avon*) normally means "iniquity" or "evil," and when used as the object of the verb "bear" it usually has the idiomatic sense of "bearing away (that is, *forgiving*) sin" (Cassuto, *Genesis*, I:122). David used these same two words in Ps 32:5 in praise of God's forgiveness, "You forgave [*naśa'ta*, from *neśo'*] the guilt [*'avon*, "iniquity, evil"] of my sin." Cain was expressing deep remorse and confession when he said, "My iniquity/evil is too great to forgive!" If v. 13 is an expression of remorse over the recognition of a sin so wicked that God's great mercy seems unacceptable, v. 14 makes perfect sense as an expression of the despair rightly caused by sin, with the wish that he would just die, or that someone might execute him, even if God did not slay him due to His mercy. Viewed in this way, the latter part of v. 14 should therefore be translated, "And may it come about that whoever finds me will kill me!" What an encouragement to the stumbling believer that he can never transcend the reach of God's mercy! And what a challenge to the offended believer to preemptively forgive the one who has offended him and so to "be perfect" as their "Father in Heaven is perfect" (Mt 5:48).

4:15. As with his parents, so also with Cain, God piled grace on top of mercy, bestowing on His chastised and forgiven child what he did not deserve—the very definition of grace (whereas mercy entails the withholding of the full punishment that one *does* deserve). Specifically in response to Cain's remorseful recognition of guilt (v. 13) and yearning for immediate, full punishment (v. 14) God, with the parental foresight of his child's *best* in view, gracefully appointed **a sign for Cain**. This sign would indicate that Cain was under divine protection, and it would prevent any one from enacting the full punishment from which God Himself mercifully refrained. In popular culture, however, this "mark of Cain," is taken to mean exactly the opposite, namely, to denote anything considered a sign of infamy. Actually this sign was a supernatural indication of God's grace and parental care for Cain. The word here for "sign" (*ot*), is the same one used in 1:14, to denote a miracle—testimonies to God's active involvement in human history, usually in connection with a *redemptive* (and by definition therefore *gracious*) purpose.

4:16-22. The farsighted aspect of God's gracious purpose for Cain is borne out in these verses by the reference to his marrying and begetting a flourishing line of descendants. The Bible gives no indication that this line of descendants is to be viewed negatively, being somehow more depraved than the rest of humanity. Cain's descendants developed and established the fundamental elements of human culture as grounded in God's imperatives in 1:28b—to be "ruling" over the animals, which is established by **Jabal . . . the father of those who dwell in tents and have livestock** (farming in its broadest sense), and "subduing" the land (i.e., creatively using the land's resources for human benefit), which is established by **Jubal . . . the father of all those who play the lyre and pipe** (the fine arts), and **Tubal-cain, the forger of all implements of bronze and iron** (technology). These same three fundamental elements of human culture established by Cain's descendants (farming, fine arts, and technology) are present in later prophetic descriptions of redeemed humanity in the messianic kingdom (cf. Gn 49:11; Is 2:4; Jr 31:4; 33:12-13; Ob 14). As expressed, therefore, toward both the sinner as well as his descendants, the picture of God's grace (and man's obligation to respond in worship) is all the more profound.

3. Injustice: The Legal Aftermath of Sin (4:23-26)

The third and last expression of sin's aftermath in this section centers on the unjust (i.e., excessive) punishment for wrongdoing imposed by Lamech. This is a striking contrast to the punishment imposed by God on Cain earlier in this same chapter.

a. Injustice as a Result of Ignoring God's Example (4:23-24)

4:23-24. In this second episode of "crime and punishment" the crime consists of a young man causing an unspecified physical injury, described by **Lamech** in his poetic declaration as a strike and a wound. Though these were not life-threatening injuries, Lamech responded with his own act of judgment by killing the offender, an excessive penalty, far more than the crime deserved. By comparison with the previous episode involving Cain, the contrast that emerged and the conclusion to draw is clear: God's response to sin, consistent with His nature, is characterized by the fullest possible expression of *mercy*, by definition, less than the sin deserves (the just penalty for Cain's sin being "life for life"; cf. Lv 24:17). On the other hand man's response to sin, consistent with his nature (here exemplified by Lamech), is characterized by severe injustice, by definition, *more* than the sin deserves (the just penalty for the young man's sin being literally "bruise for bruise;" cf. Ex 21:25). Thus the *lex talionis* (the "equal measure" principle of "life for life") is not God's ideal (i.e., what He Himself would do), but rather a compromise that God graciously legislated to ensure that depraved humanity would not exceed the bare standard of the requirements of justice. That God desires humanity to show mercy restricts Him from legislating mercy as man's response to sin—for in legislating mercy the response would cease to be mercy, but would simply be the imposing of the legal standard. For mercy to truly be mercy it must be a willing decision by the victim or judge to impose on the offender less than the legal standard requires. Thus, this chapter is an important prologue to the later Mosaic law, indicating by example that the *lex talionis* ("eye for eye," etc.) rule is not the required penalty, but is in fact the "limit" that man is not to exceed. The real challenge, whether for the Israelites who first received this or for believers today, is to take up this example of the *imitatio Dei* (the obligation to imitate God; cf. Lv 19:2; Eph 5:1) and in reacting to those who have offended them, to "be merciful just as your Father is merciful" (Lk 6:36).

b. Injustice Not Preclusive of God's Blessing (4:25)

4:25. As was borne out by the births of Cain and Abel at the beginning of this chapter, so too it is further emphasized here, that human depravity does not nullify God's fundamental blessing in 1:28 that humans "be fruitful and multiply." This further underscores God's universal grace, that is, His grace in permitting all people, not just those who are His specific children, to beget children, who "are a gift of the LORD" (Ps 127:3). The expectation of creation's imminent restoration to the ideal (i.e., prefall) state at the hands of the promised Seed (3:15), so hopefully expressed by Eve at the birth of her first son (4:1), is now somewhat diminished. Eve declared that **God . . . appointed . . . another offspring . . . Seth** to her as a replacement for Abel but he was not the divine Redeemer whom she had expected (cf. 4:1).

c. Injustice as a Catalyst for Turning People to God (4:26)

4:26. Though the specific genealogical details of **Enosh** are given in 5:6-11, the brief mention here of his being **born** to **Seth** serves (1) to provide an apt literary segue to the extended genealogy commencing in 5:1, and (2) to set up the important concluding thought of this section as expressed in the second part of the verse. It shows that as children continue to be born and the population consequently increases, so too does the presence, realization, and aftermath of depravity, with the result that **the name of the LORD** (a synecdoche for the Lord Himself) is increasingly invoked. The purpose of this invoking or "calling on" "the name of the LORD" would therefore be to seek His aid in deliverance from death or distress, as is consistent with the use of this expression elsewhere in Scripture (cf. 2Kg 5:11; Ps 116:4; Jl 3:5). Also invoking "the name of the LORD" as an act of worship in response to His acts of deliverance and sovereign self-revelation (cf. 1Kg 18:39; Ps 105:1; Zph 3:9). The use of this expression thus serves to bring this section to thematic-theological closure, implying not only the increasing depravity of humanity—consistent with the overall theme of 1:1–11:26—but also on the positive side God's continuing concern for the welfare of humankind and His increasing glorification by means of the worshipful response of those who receive and recognize His attentive care.

D. Fallen World: The Attachment of Sin (5:1–11:26)

This section represents the last facet of God's prosecution of depraved humanity. As in the previous two "trials" addressing the advent and aftermath of sin, so too in this trial there are brief allusions and references to the hope of redemption, though the main point of this section is that human depravity is here to stay, for it is endemic to the human condition. This is emphasized by the two grand episodes in this section—the flood and the building of Babel/Babylon. Both episodes make clear that depravity (i.e., the predilection to sin) is not the result of environment or circumstance (though this may certainly exacerbate the expression of depravity), but rather is the result of human *nature*, and that is found in every individual. These two events encompass all of humanity.

1. A Break in the Prosecution: God's Blessing Despite Depravity (5:1–6:8)

This opening section of the fourth part of God's prosecution resumes the positive note on which the otherwise tragic strain of the previous part ended. Despite the tragic *aftermath* of sin and even its inseparable *attachment* (apart from God's gracious intervention) to human nature, God's fundamental blessing expressed in 1:28 (that mankind "be fruitful and multiply") has not been nullified. Moreover, the ideal of man's relationship with the Creator-Father, as intended prior to the fall, remains both a *present possibility* as well as a *future certainty*. That God's final and just emphasis on human depravity should be prefaced by this brief, albeit bright, ray of hope serves to crystallize all the more His undiminished attributes of mercy, grace, and love, and further establishes a paradigm replayed throughout the OT.

a. Hope of Redemption (5:1-32)

5:1-2. These opening verses reiterate the central idea set forth in 1:26-28: mankind (both males and females equally) was **created**—uniquely among all living creatures—**in the likeness of God**. By repeating this point here after humankind's fall from perfection, this fundamental divine "likeness" remains intact, though it is marred by the fall. So too by implication does humanity retain pride of place as the crowning recipient of God's blessing, both materially, as the administrators and prime benefactors of creation, and spiritually, as those who have been uniquely privileged with the potential of experiencing spiritual "wholeness" (i.e., unbroken and complete relationship with the Creator-Father). Added to this is that God **named** humanity **in the day when** He **created** them. The point of this is twofold: (1) to underscore God's continuing *dominion* over humanity (now despite the advent of depravity); and, (2) to underscore God's continuing paternal role as the Father of humanity. (Throughout the Bible, generally a father names his son.)

5:3-5. The formula in vv. 3-5 is repeated throughout the genealogy that follows: An individual was a certain number of years old, he became a father of a son, the father lived a certain number of years after the son was born, and then the father died. This is repeated throughout the entire chapter, with only two exceptions, Enoch and Noah, neither of whom are said to have died in this genealogy. It appears then that the greatest purpose of this genealogy is to draw attention to those that broke the pattern. What makes these two distinctive is that Enoch and Noah walked with God (4:24; 6:9) and they did not die, Enoch being taken by the Lord and Noah escaping the flood. Noah would die only after becoming drunk and guilty (9:20-29). Thus the message is clear: walking with God is the key to life. Hence, later in Genesis, Abraham is told to "walk with God and be blameless" even as Israel is later told to walk in God's ways so that thereby they may have life (Dt 30:15-16).

In addition to genealogical pattern, each successive event of begetting reinforces the crucial link between Adam and Noah and his three sons, from whom "the whole earth was populated" (9:19). Since every ethnic group that has ever existed after the flood has come from Noah, all humanity is thus linked to or implicated in the disease of depravity contracted by Adam.

5:4-24. That there is a cure available *now* for this disease of depravity is indicated by the example of **Enoch**, who **walked with God** (v. 22). The verb used here (*(vay) yithallekh*) is the same infrequent form of the verb used in 3:8 (the *hitpa'el* form used in 64 of 1,549 occurrences of the verbal root *halakh*, "to walk"). Here as in its previous occurrences, it properly denotes a repeated activity that may be more precisely translated as "walked about" or even "strolled." In the present context, as in later uses of the idiom "to walk with/before God" (cf. Gn 6:9; 24:40; 48:15; 2Ch 27:6), the intended idea is that of *relating to God* by *living a godly life*. This sense of "walking" is thus also carried over into the NT, as in Gl 5:16; Col 3:7; 1Jn 1:6-7; 3 Jn 3. And juxtaposing the second rare occurrence of this form of the verb with its first occurrence in 3:8, the point clearly emerges that, although sin prevented Adam and Eve from experiencing the prefall ideal of "strolling" (*mithallekh*) in most intimate *physical* proximity to God, the possibility still remains open for human beings to experience that more fundamental *spiritual* proximity to God.

5:25-32. The hope of experiencing this prefall ideal *completely* by spiritual and physical interaction with God (i.e., "walking" with Him in unrestricted proximity) is further highlighted in connection with **Noah**, whose father, Lamech (not the same as in 4:23), bases his son's name in the expectation that Noah **will give us rest... from the ground which the LORD has cursed**. The possible messianic tenor of this statement is derived both from the name **Noah** (*Noah*), which derives from the root *nuah*, meaning "to give rest" and used to describe humanity's initial state in 2:15, as well as from the specific reference to **the ground** that God **cursed**. Just as Eve thought the Redeemer had come when her first child was born (see comments at 4:1), so it appears that Noah's father thought the same—that this child would bring rest from the problem of sin. Though the reason for this expectation concerning Noah is unstated (and hence not essential to the point of the narrative), the "messianic" hope at this point is still imminent.

b. God's Gracious "Cap" on Depravity (6:1-4)

6:1-4. Few places in the Bible have engendered as much discussion and debate among interpreters as these four verses, with the debate centering primarily on the identity of **the sons of God** and **the daughters of men**. Several different views have been set forth. (1) **The sons of God** are angels (as the expression is also used in Jb 1:6; 2:1), described in 6:4 as **Nephilim** (which derives from the root meaning "to fall," hence "fallen" angels), and sinned by taking human women (**the daughters of men**) and begetting children by them. (2) **The sons of God** are the male descendants of Seth, and **the daughters of men** are the female descendants of Cain, the sin therefore being that the righteous line of Seth was "corrupted" by intermingling with the "wicked" line of Cain. (3) **The sons of God** are early rulers, or kings, who established dynasties via polygamous (and thus sinful) marriages to **the daughters of men**.

Though long-standing and popular, the view that these **sons of God** in v. 2 are angels who sinned by marrying human women is to be dismissed since it makes no contextual sense—whether in the immediate context of v. 3, in which God's reaction is exclusively toward man, the slightly larger context of what precedes and follows this episode (i.e., Adam's genealogy and the flood, both focused on man, not the angels), or the broader thematic context of Genesis, this first "half" of which (chaps. 1-11) represents God's prosecution of *human*, not angelic, depravity. Also, the one other occurrence of the term **Nephilim**, in Nm 13:33, refers to men of large stature (like Goliath), not angels. Nor is there any evidence in Scripture that angels can in fact produce children (see Mt 22:30).

The view that the **sons of God** are righteous "Sethites" who sinned by marrying wicked "Cainite" women is likewise unsubstantiated by context, for there is no indication that Seth or his descendants were more righteous than anyone else, just as there is no indication that the descendants of Cain were more wicked than anyone else. Neither the expression "sons of God" nor "daughters of man" is used anywhere else in the OT to designate an individual's spiritual state or orientation. One must also wonder how truly righteous the Sethite line was if they collectively committed such a grave sin as marrying wicked women *en masse*.

The third view is that **the sons of God** were early rulers who entered into polygamous relationships and established royal dynasties. This is inconsistent with both God's reaction in v. 3 to *all* of mankind as well as the larger theme of chaps. 1-11 concerning the depravity of humanity—not just a certain group of men. Nor is there any linguistic evidence, either from antiquity or from the Bible itself, that any group of early rulers or kings were ever called "the sons of God."

A fourth view, consistent with both the context and language of the passage, views men (**the sons of God**) as "taking" women (**the daughters of men**) in marriage (for which the expression "to take a wife/woman" is normally used; Gn 28:6; 34:9, 16; etc.). The expression "sons of God" should thus be understood, simply, as an idiomatic designation for *men*, reflecting the creation of man first by God, just as the expression "daughters of men" is clearly intended as an idiomatic designation for *women* (as in Gn 24:13, where the same expression refers to women generally, not wicked women). Likewise consistent with both this contextual understanding as well as its use in Nm 13:33 to denote *men* of large stature (such as Goliath), the term **Nephilim** in v. 4 should be understood as an alternative designation of the same group described in the next clause as **mighty men** (*gibborim*, lit., "proven warriors"), that is, men who because of their stature and military prowess were objects of infamy (*anshe ha-shem*, otherwise translated "men of renown") and of great moment when they "fell" in battle (or caused others to do so). Furthermore, this view is consistent with the following statement expressed by God in response to the activity of vv. 1-2, that **My Spirit shall not strive with man forever**. Though there is some debate about the meaning of the verb "strive," the Hebrew has "abide (*yadon*). "Abide" is supported by the LXX (*katameine*), the Vulgate (*permanebit*), and the Arabic translation of the Saadia ben Joseph Gaon (*yanghamidu*)—as well as by the similar semantic use of the same Hebrew root in 1Ch 21:27, in the noun "sheath" (i.e., that in which the sword "abides"). Whichever view one assigns to the verb, the point of the verse *in context* is essentially the same. That is, in response to the expanding human population, God dramatically limited the duration that the "breath" (Hb. *ruah*, otherwise translated here as "spirit") which He breathed into man (see 2:7) would abide or remain within him in his depraved state. In other words, as an expression of His mercy and love—*not* judgment—God here (as in His "expulsion" of man from the garden) acted to *limit* the potential expression of human depravity (and hence to limit His potential judgment) by reducing the human lifespan from the multiple centuries attested in chap. 5 to about 120 years. There is no indication, moreover, that this reduction in lifespan was to be immediate—a steady decline in lifespan is evident throughout Genesis (205 for Terah, 175 for Abraham, 180 for Isaac, 130 for Jacob), ending with the death of Joseph at 110 years (50:22).

c. The Measure of True "Spirituality" (6:5-8)

6:5-8. God also stated that **every intent** (lit., "impulse") **of the thoughts of** man's **heart was only evil continually**. This verse establishes the principle of human depravity, that humanity not only has the *potential* of sinning through wicked *deeds*, but also that everyone already is a sinner postfall because of wicked *thoughts*. Verse 5 makes clear that God's assessment of people is based on what they *think*, as opposed only to what they *do*. This principle, not surprisingly, is reiterated time and again throughout the Bible as the unchanging ideal, both for Israelites who would faithfully follow the law of Moses (cf. Dt 30:6; Pr 23:7a) as well as for Christians who would faithfully follow "the law of Christ" (Mt 5:22, 28; Mk 7:20-23).

The NASB translates the opening clause of v. 6 as **the LORD was sorry that He had made man on the earth.** The expression "was sorry" (Hb., [*va*-]*yinnahem*) should not be understood in the sense of "regretted" but rather in the sense of "was pained" or "was sorrowful, grieved, or sad." God was not "second-guessing" His decision to create humanity, for His decisions and actions are always perfect and exactly as they should be (Nm 23:19; Rm 11:29). God was demonstrating His undiminished concern for humankind. What people do—and even what they *think*—affects the heart of the One who created them, and He continues to take an active, loving interest in peoples' lives. From this perspective, the content of vv. 7-8 must be understood: God determined to **blot out man . . . from the face of the land**, not merely because he had offended God's righteous standard, but because such action was necessary for *the welfare of man himself*, to preserve man from the full effects of his unmitigated depravity. Much as when one severs a gangrenous limb, so will a "stump" of humanity—although imperfect—remain embodied in the family of **Noah** who, uniquely among the people of his day, **found favor in the eyes of the LORD**.

2. The Flood: Humanity's Chance to "Come Clean" of Depravity (6:9–9:29)

In this narrative of the flood God made clear that the cause of human depravity is not *nurture* (environment) but rather *nature* (who people are as a result of Adam's sin). For this reason God's judgment of humanity was executed by means of a flood and not, for example, through disease (2Sm 24:15), war (2Kg 24:10-14), sudden death (Is 37:36), famine, or wild beasts (Ezk 5:17). By wiping out the majority of depraved humanity with a deluge of the extent described in Gn 6-9, God was also "washing away" all evidence of human depravity from the land—from the bloodshed in murder by which the land was polluted (cf. Gn 4:10 and the use of "corrupt" [lit., "polluted"] in 6:11-12) to the use of the land's resources (wood, stone, and metal) for the fashioning of idols and detracting from the worship of the One true God. The increasing and then decreasing expression of divine judgment is further driven home by the presentation of the flood narrative in the form of a chiasm (see below) in which the points and themes in the "rising" of the flood waters are mirrored—and thus further reinforced—in the "subsiding" part of the narrative. The function of this chiasm is to shift from the story's emphasis on judgment to the focal point of the story—that God remembered Noah—to grace. Hence the flood narrative focuses on God's grace in the midst of judgment as opposed to judgment without grace whatsoever, as shown in a distinctive chiasm (see below).

Chiasm in the Flood Narrative

Chiasm in the Flood Narrative

7 Days of Waiting (7:4)
7 Days of Waiting (7:7-10)
40 Days of Flood (7:17a)
150 Days of Flood (7:24)
BUT GOD REMEMBERED NOAH (8:1)
150 Days of Water Waning (8:3)
40 Days of Waiting (8:6)
7 Days of Waiting (8:10)
7 Days of Waiting (8:12)

Noah and the flood are referred to four other times in the Bible (Is 54:9; Ezk 14:14; Mt 24:38; 1Pt 3:20), thus showing that this structure reflects the inherent order in the event itself as superintended by God.

a. Prelude: A Righteous Remnant in a Depraved World (6:9-10)

6:9-10. God always has a remnant of those who strive to remain faithful to the Him, represented here by Noah and his immediate family. Through Noah, God sought to give humanity a "second chance" at living the ideal. The likelihood that humanity would succeed this time seems more likely, since Noah, unlike Adam, already had a proven record of living righteously (and hence overcoming temptation) during an extended exposure of 600 years to an extremely wicked world. No one except for the Messiah Himself is described in more glowingly positive terms in the Hebrew Bible than Noah. Any *one* of the three expressions applied to Noah in v. 9 would suffice to identify him with a select group of saints that included Abraham, who like Noah is described as **a righteous man** (Gn 15:6); Job, who like Noah is described as **blameless** (Jb 1:1; 12:4); and Enoch, who like Noah **walked with God** (Gn 5:22). Humanity's depravity, however, was not overcome through Noah, despite the "resetting" of humankind's environment. Thus, in this last "trial part," God's essential point is evident—that ever since Adam's sin, depravity is part of humankind's nature, and cannot be removed except through the sovereign act of God in washing and cleansing the heart, and not by changing humanity's environment (cf. Ezk 36:25-26; 1Co 6:11; Heb 10:22).

b. Corruption of the Land (6:11-12)

6:11-12. Because the problem of depravity and sin does not lie in the environment, the emphasis of the text is on **the earth** (lit., "the land," not the planet, but the "dry ground" on which humanity lives). This term is employed four times in these two verses. Similarly, the term **corrupt**—various forms of which are employed three times in these two verses (*tishahet, nishhata, hishhit*)—denotes the "corruption" or "pollution" caused by sin, such as the "pollution" of blood shed in murder (as of Abel in 4:10) or the use of the earth's resources to make idols that "pollute" the land (as in 1Sm 6:5, which employs the same wording to describe the effect of the Philistines' idols on the land). That the "corruption" of the land is the result of man's wicked actions is further emphasized by the reference to the land being **filled with violence**. The word **violence** (*hamas*) is employed throughout the OT to denote violence motivated by wicked intent, as opposed to violence intended as chastisement for sin or restraint or defense against wicked deeds.

c. God's Covenant with Noah (6:13-20)

6:13-20. God informed Noah of His plan **to destroy** humanity as judgment for their sin. Here, as He often does, God informed those whom He "knows" (i.e., those who are justified by faith and regarded by Him as His children) of His future plans—whether for the deliverance and/or chastisement of believers, or for the judgment of unbelievers. This same principle underlies the prophetic revelation of specific future events throughout Scripture, the knowledge of which is ultimately intended for the edification and encouragement of believers, those to whom "it has been granted" (Mt 13:11).

Though some claim that the flood was a localized event restricted to the ancient Near East, the text makes it clear that this was as a worldwide event. Three times in this passage the words **all flesh** (*kol baśar*, vv. 13, 17, 19) appear, the phrase occurring 33 times elsewhere in the Hebrew Bible, each time referring to all living creatures, both human and animal (e.g., Jb 34:15; Jr 25:31; Ezk 21:5). The universal scope of the flood is further emphasized by the later reference to the water covering "*all* the high mountains *everywhere* under the heavens" (7:19, italics added) as well as God's promise to "never again destroy *every living thing*" with a flood (8:21, italics added).

God's concern for animal life was borne out by His statement to Noah in vv. 19-20 about their preservation by their boarding **the ark** in representative pairs of **male and female**. This statement is intended to inform Noah of the content of the ark, not as a directive for him to find and assemble these pairs himself, which would be an impractical if not impossible human feat. God told Noah that these animal pairs **will come to** him of their own accord (i.e., by God's leading).

d. God's Provision for Life (6:21-22)

6:21-22. Verse 21 shows a shift in emphasis from God's statement about the preservation of life generally to specific instructions about the nourishment required to maintain that life. If Noah was dependent on God to bring the proper number of animal pairs into the ark, he was also dependent on God to give him specific information about the type and amount of plant **food** to gather and bring into the ark.

Significantly, **Noah did; according to all that God commanded him**—repeated again in 7:5—because Noah said nothing throughout the entire course of the flood narrative proper. Indeed Noah is the only major figure involved in an extended biblical event to whom no words are attributed in the course of that event. The point is that his obedience was expressed by his action. Peter referred to Noah as a "preacher of righteousness" (2Pt 2:5), and yet, as far as the text records, he never said a word! And the writer of Hebrews emphasized the evangelistic ministry of Noah as extending from his actions: "in reverence [Noah] prepared an ark . . . by which he condemned the world" (Heb 11:7). Similarly believers today need to follow up their words of evangelism with actions.

e. Entering the Ark (7:1-9)

7:1-9. After the ark was completed God again referred to the animal pairs that were to enter with **Noah** and his **household**. The purpose of this repetition was to teach Noah the distinction between **clean animal[s]** and **animals that are not clean**. Of the former, Noah was told, seven pairs were to enter the ark, whereas only one pair of each unclean animal, was to enter. The reason for this distinction and greater number of clean animals was not to identify and ensure an ample supply of food for Noah's family in the ark. Rather, this distinction was intended to ensure a proper supply of animals that were fit for sacrifice in humanity's expression of divine worship. Thus as soon as Noah left the ark, his first action was to build an altar and offer one "of every clean animal and of every clean bird" (8:20). This set forth the way to "frame" the understanding of the later distinction between "clean" and "unclean" animals in the Mosaic food laws. This distinction was intended to reinforce symbolically the necessity and spiritual benefit of maintaining the same distinction in sacrificial worship.

Another reason for God's repeated reference to the animals in this section is to indicate their specific "place" in the order of events about to ensue, now that the flood was at hand. This order (in vv. 1-4) is as follows: (1) Noah and his family were to enter the ark; (2) the clean and unclean animals would then enter; (3) **after seven more days** God would begin to **send rain on the earth**; and (4) the rain would endure continuously for **forty days and forty nights** until **every living thing** on **the face of the land** was dead. The events unfolded in this order as related in vv. 6-12.

In this order of events are two theologically significant numerical paradigms. First is the period of **seven days**, which establishes the expectation of a sevenfold period during which special emphasis is placed on (the possibility of) repentance before final judgment. The peaceful coexistence of Noah's family and the animals in the ark served as a striking testimony to Noah's generation of God's true involvement in the event, and hence of His impending judgment should the people fail to repent. God later granted the Israelites a period of 490 years (70 x 7) during which, through continual prophetic revelation and unmistakable miracles, God called them to national repentance for their collective sin (epitomized by their failure to give the land its seventh-year [sabbatical] rests) until he judged them by the Babylonian conquest and 70-year exile that was intended to make up those missed rests (see 2Ch 36:21). Also the prophets spoke of a seven-year period (otherwise known as "the Tribulation") of intense supernatural activity during which humankind—and especially the Jewish people—will be given a final opportunity to repent and be saved before the Messiah Jesus returns to destroy all of wicked humanity (Dn 9:27; Mt 24:36-51; Rv 11:2; 12:6).

The seven-day period in the present narrative emphasizes the depth of Noah's obedience, for he remained in the ark for the entire week, during which nothing was happening outside, in strict adherence to God's command to **enter** (v. 1). Implicit in this is the more refined point—and much more challenging example—that doing **all that the LORD had commanded** (v. 5) included *not* doing anything that would run contrary those commands unless the Lord had said to do so. This point, in keeping with the symmetry of the chiasm (see above) is further driven home in the section on Noah's exiting from the ark.

The second significant numerical paradigm is the period of **forty days**, which establishes the expectation of a 40-fold period of "spiritual preparation" in transition from one stage or state of affairs to another. Thus the Israelites sojourned in the wilderness for 40 years, when they were instructed in God's law and so prepared for life in the promised land. And so too Christ, the ideal Israelite, sojourned and fasted for 40 days in the wilderness, immediately following His baptism, in spiritual preparation for His temptation and His ensuing ministry.

f. Prevailing of the Flood (7:10-24)

7:10-24. The repetition in vv. 13-17a of information that has already been presented in the previous verses (i.e., the entrance into the ark of Noah's family and the animals and the flood for 40 days) has led some to conclude that another, different version of the "flood legend" from some other ancient culture has here been interwoven with the previous one. Such analysis, however, is unnecessarily simplistic (in addition to presupposing the absence or minimization of inspiration). Another example of the literary sophistication of the writer of Genesis is his recourse here to narrative "flashback" or "retrogression," that is, the repetition of previously given information (along with new details), usually for the sake of emphasis. Not only is this emphasis justified by the nature and scope of the event (i.e., the destruction of humanity in judgment for their sin), but also to strengthen identification with that preserved remnant who were saved because of Noah's obedience and righteousness. This purpose in the use of repetition/flashback would have been especially relevant in the religious culture of Israel, wherein Scripture was typically "experienced" through oral recitation (as it still is to this day in Jewish synagogues).

The significance of Noah and his household, as symbolic of the remnant, is explicitly made in 1Pt 3:20-21. There Peter wrote that the people in the ark who were "saved (*diesothesan*) through water" (HCSB) found their "antitype" (*antitypos*)—their superior NT counterpart and "fulfillment"—in those who were saved through spiritual "baptism" into (i.e., union with) Christ. See comments on 1Pt 3:18-21 for the nature of the parallel between Noah, the flood, and Christian baptism.

The divinely superintended order within the flood event is further borne out by the various periods of days mentioned throughout the course of this and the following section: **seven days** of waiting (7:10), **forty days** of rain after the door of the ark was "closed" (7:12, 17), **one hundred and fifty days** of the water "prevailing" (7:24), one hundred and fifty days of the water receding (8:3), "forty days" before the window of the ark was "opened" (8:6), and "seven days" of waiting before the dove was sent out the second time (8:10). As the waters of the flood rose, peaked, and subsided, so did God's judgment on humanity rise, peak, and subside.

g. Subsiding of the Flood (8:1-14)

8:1-14. In this section, which represents the first stage in the "reverse arm" of the chiasm (see above) inversion, several clear parallels, both thematic and linguistic, emerge to link the new world of Noah and his family with, on the one hand, the prefall world of Adam and Eve and, on the other hand, the exodus-generation of Israelites and the promised land. The point of these parallels is to underscore God's unchanging ideal for humanity as well as humanity's inability to attain that ideal apart from the sovereign intervention of God (see comments on 2:8-14). Two of these parallels are attested in the opening verse, beginning with the statement **God remembered Noah**. This expression is clearly an anthropomorphism (the figurative attribution of human characteristics to God).

Here the idea is that God has humanity specifically and centrally in mind. This is a direct parallel to God's central focus on humanity throughout the creative process as described in chap. 1, and this precise figure of speech ("and God remembered") is likewise employed at the outset of the exodus to signal that the process of the Israelites' deliverance had begun (Ex 2:24).

The second parallel appears in the second part of v. 1, which states that **God caused a wind** [*ruah*] **to pass over the earth** [*ha-areṣ*]. Since the Hebrew word translated "wind" here can also be translated "spirit," and the word translated "earth" is the same as what is elsewhere translated "land," here is a clear parallel to the creation event, in which God's "Spirit" (*ruah*) was actively present as He prepared to draw back the water that stood as a barrier to the new "land" (*ereṣ*) onto which He would set man (see 1:2, 9-10). Hence what God was doing for Noah was a kind of "second creation." The wind passing over the earth also points to the Exodus event, in which God sent a strong "wind" (*ruah*) to force back the water that stood as a barrier to the Israelites' entrance into the new land (*ereṣ*) of Canaan (Ex 14:21). The rescue of Noah thus functions as a precursor to God leading people out of an oppressive situation, whether the sinfulness of Noah's world or the toil of Egypt.

Two more parallels are evident toward the end of this section, in vv. 13-14. The first of these (v. 13), is centered in the reference to **the surface of the ground** being dry of all flood water **in the six hundred and first year, in the first month, on the first of the month**—the threefold emphasis on "first" being to recast this day as the truly new *first* day of the new creation (and humanity's "second chance"), parallel to the "first day" of prefall creation. Looking forward to the exodus, was to be "the beginning of months" for the Israelites (Ex 12:2), and hence the festival commemorating that event (Passover), the first of their festivals (cf. Lv 23:5).

The specific dating of the year as **the six hundred and first** refers to the onset of the flood from the birth of Noah. He is the most prominent personage in the account and, in the immediate post-flood world he was the leading patriarch of humanity.

The next parallel is centered in the concluding statement of v. 14, which states that 56 days *after* the flood water had completely dried up from the surface of the ground, **the earth was** just as **dry** as before the flood and awaiting man's occupation. The same Hebrew root used here to describe the ready state of **the earth** (*ha-ares*) for human (and animal) occupation as **dry** (*yabesha*) was likewise employed in the creation account to describe the "stuff" that God drew out from the water that is, the "dry land" (*yabbasha*; 1:9-10)—which He then called "land" (*ereṣ*) and granted humanity to "fill and subdue it" (1:28). And so too, in the exodus, the land from which God drew back the water and across which He led the Israelites to their new home was "dry land" (*yabbasha*; Ex 14:22).

Several scholars see a contradiction between the statement in v. 4 that **the ark rested upon the mountains of Ararat** (Ararat being a region—not a single mountain—in the general area of eastern Turkey) and the statement in v. 5 that about two and a half months later **the tops of the mountains became visible.** However, there is no reason that these verses should be regarded as anything but confluent. A ship of the size and weight of the ark would unquestionably have had quite a bit of the lower hull submerged, and thus v. 4 is indicating that a portion of this submerged lower hull was "caught" on some still-covered mountaintops, whereas v. 5 states that subsequently the water receded to a point that these mountaintops became visible.

h. Exiting the Ark (8:15-22)

8:15-22. In this section, as in its thematic counterpart, "Entering the Ark" (7:1-9), Noah's obedience is emphasized by virtue of what he does *not* do. He does not leave the ark, even though he has been in it for 320 days (313 days [7:11, 8:13 and assuming the usual biblical lunar year] plus the initial seven days of waiting [7:4, 10]). The ground was perfectly dry and ready for occupation (8:13-14), but not until 56 days later, on the 27th of the second month, did God command him, **Go out of the ark** (v. 15). This is truly a profound example of "waiting on the Lord"! The reason God has Noah and his family wait 56 *more* days until they set foot onto the new/renewed land underscores that humanity is truly being given a "second chance" to attain the original, prefall ideal.

After leaving the ark Noah expressed his devotion by building **an altar** and offering one **of every clean animal** to the Lord (v. 20). This anticipated the use of clean animals in the sacrificial worship of the Israelites, and thus further reinforced the link between the Israelites, Noah, and prefall humanity. Significantly God then affirmed that the purpose of the flood had been achieved: not that humanity had attained the ideal, but rather that it had not. Humanity was, even at this point, no fundamentally different from how it was before the flood, repeating the phrase **for the intent of man's heart is evil from his youth** (v. 21 parallel to 6:5). Though this statement may seem out of place in light of Noah's unblemished record of obedience, its purpose was to remind that the fundamental definition of a person is not derived from behavior but from thought and even the very **intent** (lit., "impulse" [*yeser*]) by which those thoughts are produced. The tense of this statement, moreover, is unmistakable: it is not an assessment of what *will be*, but a maxim describing what *is*. Although God had achieved His purpose in the flood, humanity had not fundamentally changed but remained with evil intent. In this light God's assertion that He will **never again destroy every living thing** in the same manner (i.e., by a flood, this being the sense of **as I have done**) is yet another expression of divine *mercy*, i.e., requiting "us less than our iniquities deserve" (Ezr 9:13).

i. God's Provision for Life (9:1-7)

9:1-7. Here, as in 6:21, God focused on the provision required to maintain human life. In 6:21, however, that focus was on the food that would sustain Noah's family (and the animals) through the flood, whereas in the present section, consistent with the developing theme of humanity's "second chance" at life in a "perfect" world, God focused more broadly on providing all those essential elements that will enable Noah and his family to live in the new world into which they have been placed. The link between these two "beginnings" is underscored by the use of similar or even identical terminology in the presentation of these essential elements, which may be represented as seen in the chart below.

God's specific restriction on eating **blood** parallels His specific restriction against eating from the tree of the knowledge of good and evil (2:17). It also establishes a principle that stands at the very core of the redemptive process as later expounded in the Mosaic laws of sacrifice and reiterated continually throughout Scripture, namely, that the **blood** of man—as of any living creature—represents **its life**, and thus God, the giver of life, justly holds man's life (his **lifeblood**, v. 5) in debt, of which one may be forgiven *only* when that debt is supplied/paid in equal measure by the life ("lifeblood") of another. This is precisely God's point in stating at the outset of v. 5, **I will require your lifeblood**, which is better translated **I will require your** "blood for (i.e., in payment for) your souls." For this reason God later legislated that whereas the flesh of certain sacrifices could be eaten by the priests (Lv 6:26), the blood of that sacrifice must always be poured out on the altar, "for the life of the flesh is in the blood, and I have given it to you on the altar to make atonement for your souls; for it is the blood by reason of the life that makes atonement" (Lv 17:11). Verse 12 then states the prohibition against eating blood expressed in wording similar to Gn 9:4. In the NT this principle is concisely reiterated in Heb 9:22—"without shedding of blood there is no forgiveness." This leads to the culminating thesis

God's Provision for Life

God's Provision (The Essential Element)	Adam and Eve	Noah and His Family
Fecundity (reproductive blessing)	"Be fruitful and multiply" (1:28).	"Be fruitful and multiply" (9:1, 7, an inclusio).
Dominion (rule over the animal world)	"Rule over the fish . . . and over the birds . . . and over every living thing that moves on the earth" (1:28).	"The fear of you . . . will be on every beast . . . every bird . . . and all the fish . . . into your hand they are given" (9:2).
Nourishment (a defined category of food)	"Every plant yielding seed . . . and every tree which has fruit . . . shall be food for you" (1:29).	"Every moving thing that is alive shall be food for you" (9:3).
Morality (behavioral standards, including restriction and punishment)	"From the tree of the knowledge of good and evil you shall not eat, for in the day that you eat from it you will surely die" (2:17).	"You shall not eat flesh with its life, that is, its blood" (9:4); "Whoever sheds man's blood, by man his blood shall be shed" (9:6).

of biblical soteriology, namely, that Christ shed and poured out "His own" blood (Heb 9:12)—the only blood that could ever fully compensate for that of unbelievers (Heb 10:4)—on the heavenly altar "once for all . . . for sins for all time" (Heb 9:23–10:14).

The reference in v. 6 to the **image of God**—the first reference to this image in the *postfall* world (previously mentioned only in 1:26-27)—is also significant for it establishes beyond any doubt not only that the image of God is still present in humanity, but that that image is present in *every individual.* Concluding the thought of v. 5, God referred to **the life of man** (*nefesh ha-adam*), (lit., "the human soul") that He will **require** of **every** *individual* **man** (*ish*) for his (mal) treatment of his **brother** (i.e., his fellowman). This further supports the principle of Lv 19:18 and Mt 22:39). God then referred in v. 6 to the *epitome* of individual/personal depravity (as already established in 4:1-22), that is, murder, and its requisite penalty (the individual murderer's **blood shall be shed**) and the reason for its prohibition (the murdered individual was characterized by **the image of God** in which **He made man**).

j. God's Covenant with Noah and All Life (9:8-17)

9:8-17. Continuing the theme of His provision for humanity in the new (post-flood) world, God now established a **covenant** with mankind (v. 9) and all the animals that were represented in the ark (v. 10) never again to bring worldwide destruction **by the water of the flood** (v. 11; see also v. 15). This does not, of course, preclude God's final judgment and destruction of wicked humanity, or His consequent restoration of creation to its ideal (prefall) state, both events being clearly established throughout the Scriptures. God's purpose in bringing the flood, however, has been achieved, and need not be repeated. The depravity of humanity is an "internal" disorder, endemic to the postfall leaning of humankind's heart (cf. 8:21), and no amount of environmental resetting can cure it.

The positive nuance of God's present **covenant**, entailing the preservation of life from destruction by another worldwide **flood**, has a clear parallel to God's previous covenant with Noah made before the flood promising to preserve the lives of ("keep alive," 6:19) Noah's family and the animal representatives. This previous covenant He introduced with the words, "Behold, I, even I [*va-ani hineni*] am bringing the flood . . . but I will establish My covenant with you" (6:17-18). Now in 9:9-11 God introduced His covenant with the words, **Now behold, I Myself** [*va-ani hineni*] **do establish My covenant . . . I establish My covenant** (*va-haqimoti et beriti*) **with you**. God then indicated that the **sign** (*ot*) of this **covenant** is His **bow** (i.e., the rainbow), which is not only apropos as a regularly repeating **sign** (i.e., reminder), but also a prime example of how otherwise *natural* phenomena and God's *supernatural* purposes can intersect. In other words, God's involvement in human history—His expressions of righteous judgment as well as His expressions of mercy and love for man—is not only manifest through awe-inspiring, albeit brief-lived miracles, but also through such naturally occurring phenomena as the rainbow. Whether one can perceive the divine (and ultimately therefore *supernatural*) testimony of such "natural" phenomena depends, ultimately, on the nature and basis of one's faith (Rm 1:18-21)—as does one's acceptance even of truly "rule-bending" miracles (cf. Lk 16:31; Jn 10:25).

This designation of the rainbow as the **sign** (*ot*) of God's covenant also links this covenant together with God's future covenants involving the preservation/giving of life. Thus for the Abrahamic covenant (Gn 12:1-3) God established the "sign" (*ot*) of circumcision (17:11); for the Mosaic covenant He established the "sign" (*ot*) of the Sabbath (Ex 31:17); and for the new covenant He established the sign of baptism (Mt 28:19).

k. Corruption of the Land (9:18-19)

9:18-19. Though the abiding presence of depravity in post-flood humanity has already been noted in 8:21, its potential *severity* is here specifically highlighted by the reference to **Canaan** in v. 18. This reference cannot be simply for the sake of filling out Ham's genealogy, for then Canaan's three older brothers (per 10:6) should also have been included; nor can it be to indicate the recommencement of the divine imperative in 9:1 ("Be fruitful and multiply"), for then the proper reference would have been to Ham's firstborn son Cush. The reason, rather, must be to hint at Canaan's role in the first post-flood *expression* of depravity—which was indeed quite perverse—in the immediately following section (vv. 20-29).

This implication of depravity's continued post-flood expression is pushed even further in scope in v. 19, which states that **from these** (i.e., the three sons of Noah) **the whole earth was populated**. Though at first sight this is a seemingly positive reference to repopulation, the Hebrew verb used (for the first time) here (*nafeṣa*) is in fact quite ominous, for it is the same verb used to describe God's judgment of mankind at Babel in 11:9, where it is typically translated as "scattered" or "dispersed," as also in many other biblical depictions of God's judgment or chastisement for grave sin (Dt 28:64; Neh 1:8; Jb 40:11; Ps 68:1; Jr 13:24; Ezk 36:19). The present verse, moreover, is the only biblical instance (out of 64 total occurrences of the verbal root) in which the "recipient" of the verb's action is the *land itself*, rather than, as is usually the case, the gravely sinning people of the land. The text, it would seem, is going out of its way to conclude the flood narrative on precisely the same note with which it began—the negative impact on **the earth** (lit., "the land," *ha-ares*) resulting from man's sin (6:11-12). In this instance, **the whole earth was populated** (lit., "the entire land was divided"), referring to the *division* of the land into separate geopolitical entities of *us* and *them* (i.e., countries, city states, tribal regions, etc.) resulting from the linguistic (and hence ultimately ethnic) dispersion occasioned by man's sin at Babel (11:9).

l. Postlude: A Righteous Remnant in a Depraved World (9:20-29)

9:20-29. The inability of the flood to resolve or diminish the "attachment" of depravity to mankind is further underscored here by several additional parallels to the circumstances of Adam and Eve in the garden: (1) the planting of a specially cultivated area—in this case **a vineyard** (cf. 2:8); (2) partaking of the fruit of that specially cultivated area—in this case **wine** from the grapes of the vineyard (cf. 3:6); (3) with an explicit reference to resulting **nakedness** (cf. 3:7); (4) a depiction of that nakedness being **covered** (cf. 3:21); and (5) a pronouncement of curse—in this case against **Canaan** (cf. 3:14). This also bears out the implicit reason for the reference to **Canaan** in v. 18 (as again in v. 22), for it is in him that the first significant post-flood *expression* of depravity is centered.

Ham has often been viewed as the main culprit in this episode, his sin being that he publicized—and perhaps even gloated over—**the nakedness of his father**. As punishment Noah cursed Ham's son **Canaan**, consistent with the principle voiced in Dt 5:9 ("I . . . am a jealous God, visiting the iniquity of the fathers on the children, and on the third and fourth generations of those who hate Me"). Yet the reasoning in support of this view is less than satisfactory, for the expression **and [he] told** in v. 22 is not inherently negative and does not normally mean "to publicize" (cf. Est 1:20; 3:14). Nor does the principle in Dt 5:9 indicate that "punishment" will be visited on the sons *instead* of the fathers, but rather that God will maintain the adverse consequence(s) of the father's "iniquity" (*'avon* in Dt 5:9 denoting sin and its negative impact, not specifically "punishment") on his progeny. That is, He will not extend the additional mercy of *restricting* the adverse impact of a father's sin(s) on his children when that father and his progeny "hate" Him.

The following considerations, on the other hand, clearly support the view that Canaan was the culprit. Noah himself identified the culprit as **his youngest son** (v. 24), and whereas Ham was Noah's middle son (5:32; 6:10; 7:13; 9:18; 10:1; 1Ch 1:14), Canaan was his youngest grandson (10:6; 1Ch 1:8). Whether Canaan was the youngest of all Noah's grandchildren, he was the youngest so far mentioned (Gn 9:18, 22) and hence the only person with whom the **youngest son** in v. 24 can be identified. **Canaan** was the one **cursed**, and the biblical pattern, already established in 3:14, is that the *actual culprit* is cursed (cf. Dt 27:15-16; 1Sm 26:19; Jr 48:10). Also the sin involved something that the culprit had physically **done** (*'asa*, which typically denotes physical, not merely verbal, activity) **to** Noah in his nakedness (note that Lv 18 uses the expression "to uncover the nakedness" of a relative to refer to inappropriate sexual relations). The phrase about seeing **the nakedness of his father** (v. 22) seems to imply that a homosexual sin was committed, which is consistent with the same specific perversity by which Canaan's descendants are characterized a few chapters later (namely, the Sodomites in 19:4-7, whose "exceeding wickedness" is already noted in 13:13; on their explicit descent from Canaan, see 10:19). For these reasons Canaan's identity as the culprit has long been recognized in Jewish interpretive tradition.

If Ham was guilty of anything, it was his not maintaining better oversight toward his son. As soon as Noah realized what had been done to him, he at once connected it with his grandson Canaan. This possible failing of Ham to restrain his son may be the reason Ham is omitted from Noah's oracle in vv. 26-27. This silence regarding Ham may constitute a mild rebuke. To read anything more into this omission would be unjustified, especially since these were not Noah's "death-bed" words (as were Jacob's in chap. 49) and hence not preclusive of Ham from a part in his father's inheritance. On the other hand Noah's statement here does affirm the preeminence of his eldest son **Shem**, as well as establish the canonical basis for the Canaanites' subservience to and conquest by Shem's descendants, the Israelites (Dt 7:1-5). The strife between relatives in this passage reflects a common theme in Genesis (see comments at 4:8).

3. The Depth of Depravity in Post-Flood Humanity (10:1–11:26)

In this section God concluded His "prosecution" of depraved humanity by presenting a concise description of the first and greatest collective expression of human depravity in the post-flood period. The point is that sin—even more fundamentally, indeed, the impulse to sin (i.e., depravity)—is here to stay. At the same time, however, this section also introduces the complementary idea—taken up and developed in the next thematic "half" of Genesis (11:27–50:26)—that a pardon from sin is available to humanity and that humankind's attainment of the prefall ideal is both the active and inevitable goal of human history.

a. Setting the Stage for Universal Rebellion (10:1-32)

Several purposes are served by the genealogies of Shem, Ham, and Japheth as presented in this chapter. First, they bear out the ongoing fulfillment of God's blessing, "Be fruitful and multiply," applied in 9:1 to post-flood humanity (i.e., "Noah and his sons"). This also reinforces the positive paradigm (and expression of God's grace) clearly established within pre-flood humanity by the genealogies in chaps. 4 and 5, that neither the presence of depravity nor even its manifestation in grave sin has negated the realization of God's blessing of man in *fertility* and *rest*.

Second, with respect to the immediately preceding pericope, the genealogies indicate the fulfillment of Noah's declarative statement in 9:25-27 that the Shemites would subjugate the Canaanites as related in 14:1-12. This in turn reinforces both the divine imperative as well as the historical precedent for the Israelites—likewise descendants of Shem—to do the same. And third, with respect to the *immediately following* pericope, the historical notes contained in the genealogy provide relevance to the upcoming building project "in the land of Shinar" (10:10; 11:2). For example, Nimrod's exploits are described, and then Babel is identified as one of his cities (10:8-10).

The usual custom of presenting sons in descending birth order is reversed in the presentation of the genealogies of Noah's sons. That of Japheth, the youngest, is recorded first, and that of Shem, the oldest, is recorded last. This structure allows for Shem's genealogies to frame and thereby contrast the rebellious events at the building of Babel.

10:1-5. As borne out later on in Scripture, several of the names of Japheth's descendants mentioned here became the names of the *regions* (not always "countries" in the sense of strictly defined geopolitical entities) these individuals occupied. Thus **Gomer** is later applied to the people (probably Cimmerians, an ancient Indo-European people living north of the Caucasus and the Sea of Azov as early as the 14th century BC) allied with **Togarmah** "in the uttermost parts of the north" against Israel (Ezk 38:6). **Magog** is also later applied to a people at odds with Israel (Ezk 38:2; 39:6) and located apparently at some point north of the latter (various identifications include the Scythians, Commagene, an Armenian people of the Hellenistic age, and the Goths). **Madai** is later applied to the people of Media (located in the midwestern region of present-day Iran), successors of the Babylonians (cf. Jr 51:11; Dn 9:1) and allies of the Persians (Dn 8:20; Est 1:3). **Javan** is later the designation of Ionia (in the western Anatolian region of present-day Turkey) or the Greeks in general (cf. Ezk 27:13; Dn 8:21; 10:20; 11:2); and **Tubal** and **Meshech** are also later applied together to territories/peoples in Asia Minor (Ezk 27:13; 32:26), in the general area of which the descendants of **Tiras**—mentioned only here and in the parallel genealogy of 1Ch 1:5—are probably also to be located (a common identification of **Tiras** in fact being with the Etruscans). Consistent with this ethno-geographical identification of Japheth's sons, his seven grandsons that are here mentioned (i.e., **Ashkenaz**, **Riphath**, **Togarmah**, **Elishah**, **Tarshish**, **Kittim**, and **Dodanim**) are typically identified with peoples in the lands (and islands) along the northern Mediterranean basin.

10:6-20. As to the later ethno-geographical association of the names of Ham's sons, **Cush** is applied to the region of northeast Africa, including Ethiopia and Nubia (cf. Est 1:1). This excludes Egypt, a country designated in Hebrew by the name of Ham's second son, **Mizraim** (cf. Ex 1:1, as well as Egypt's pairing with adjacent **Cush** in Is 20:3-4; 45:14; Nah. 3:9). **Put**, though its later application is not quite clear, may designate the region and people of Libya (cf. its pairing with **Cush**, in Jr 46:9; Ezk 30:5; 38:5). **Canaan** is the name later applied to the region inhabited by the collected ethnic groups, tribes, and city-states of what is otherwise known as the promised land, from "the river of Egypt" in the south to "the great river . . . Euphrates" in the northeast (Gn 15:18; Nm 34:1-12), encompassing not only present-day Israel, but also parts of Egypt, Jordan, Syria, and Lebanon. Consistent with this ethno-geographical identification of Ham's sons, his 24 grandsons are mentioned here: **Seba**, **Havilah**, **Sabtah**, **Raamah**, **Sabteca**, **Nimrod** (vv. 7-8); **Ludim**, **Anamim**, **Lehabim**, **Naphtuhim**, **Pathrusim**, **Casluhim**, **Caphtorim** (vv. 13-14); and **Sidon**, **Heth**, and the progenitors of the **Jebusite** (i.e., Jebus; Jdg. 19:10, **Amorite**, **Girgashite**, **Hivite**, **Arkite**, **Sinite**, **Arvadite**, **Zemarite**, and **Hamathite** (vv. 15-18). These are later identified with places and peoples from lands along the Mediterranean basin (including Asia Minor), through the Sinai Peninsula, to the coast of the Red Sea.

Some scholars have found it surprising, even inconsistent, that **Canaan** is linked genealogically to Ham rather than Shem, since Canaan's descendants spoke a dialect of Hebrew, belonging to the family of Semitic languages otherwise spoken by the descendants of Shem (hence the term "Semitic," i.e., "Shemitic"), such as Arabic (spoken by the Ishmaelites), Aramaic (spoken the Arameans), and Akkadian (spoken by the Babylonians and Assyrians). Some assume that the term "Semitic" as a linguistic category must be accurate—i.e., that it accurately describes the languages spoken only by Shem's descendants. Yet this is not so, for the term "Semitic," though derived from the biblical name Shem, was introduced into modern linguistics toward the end of the 18th century in disregard of the further biblical data that the advent of different languages occurred several generations *after* Shem, at Babel (which occurred 101 years after the flood, when Peleg was born in the fourth generation from Shem; 10:25; 11:10-18). There is no reason to assume that the distribution of languages was determined by descent from one of Noah's three sons. Therefore, it is illogical to cite this assumed distribution as a basis for critiquing the descent of later generations as presented in chap. 10. Also the term "Semitic" does not refer simply to the language of Canaan's descendants that is classified as "Semitic," but also that of the Ethiopians (i.e., Ge'ez, now replaced by Amharic, Tigre, and Tigrinya), descendants of Ham's oldest son **Cush**.

Canaan's place in this genealogy establishes a solid link between Noah's curse of Canaan in 9:25-27 ("a servant of servants he shall be to his brothers") and its fulfillment in the biblical-historical record in 14:1-12. Specifically four of the five communities that were conquered and enslaved by the eastern alliance led by Chedorlaomer, the Shemite king of Elam (see 10:22), are identified in chap. 10 as specifically Canaanite communities: **Sodom**, **Gomorrah**, **Admah**, and **Zeboiim.**

Also of special significance is **Nimrod**, of whom more is said in this genealogy than anyone else (vv. 8-10). This is not because of any positive contribution he made. In Hebrew "Nimrod" means "We will rebel." Nimrod was the first individual in Scripture to whom a **kingdom** (v. 10) was attributed. Nimrod was the leader of a corporate human rebellion against God, the primary authority figure until his time. This implication is strengthened by the immediately following statement that **the beginning of** Nimrod's **kingdom was Babel . . . in the land of Shinar**, which clearly anticipates and sets the theological "tone" for the next narrative event and epitome of human depravity, namely, the building of the tower and surrounding city called "Babel" (11:9), located in "a plain in the land of Shinar" (11:2). Not surprisingly, this negative association of **Babel** in its first biblical appearance is retained throughout its many later biblical appearances as the land of Israel's enemies and eventual exile (i.e., the Hb. word *bavel* is the same for "Babel" in Gn 10–11 as it is for "Babylon" elsewhere). In its last biblical appearance in Rv 18:21, Babel/Babylon will be in rebellion against God. And it will be the object of His judgment, after which Babel/Babylon "will not be found any longer." The references to Nimrod as **a mighty one** (v. 8) and **a mighty hunter before the LORD** (v. 9), when linked with the meaning of his name ("We will rebel") and the tie to the corrupt but mighty men of Gn 6:4, are to be taken as negative (as consistently recognized in traditional Jewish and many early Christian sources). The term translated **mighty** (*gibbor*), which normally denotes a man possessed of proven killing ability in battle (a *warrior*, like Goliath in 1Sm 17:51), is also negatively intended in its first occurrence in Gn 6:4. Not only that, these mighty men, as warriors, were killing *members of their own family,* those who spoke the same language and lived in the same place (11:1), and who were under the same governing authority, God. These uses of the word "mighty" (6:4 and 10:8-9) show human depravity and divine judgment (by the flood and Babel). In turn, they further drive home the point of this last "trial part" concerning the depth and attachment of sin.

10:21-32. Regarding the later ethno-geographical association of the names of Shem's sons, **Elam** is applied to the region between Persia and Mesopotamia (modern Khuzistan in southwestern Iran) in which the capital city of Susa is located (Dn 8:2). **Asshur** is the Hebrew name for Assyria, in northern Mesopotamia; **Arpachshad**, which name does not appear later in the Bible as an ethno-geographical term, has been tenuously identified with the southern Mesopotamian locations of Chaldea or Arrapkha (Kirkuk). **Lud** is later mentioned in association with regions in Asia Minor and northeastern Africa (Is 66:19; Ezk 30:5), though its precise application is unclear. **Aram** is later applied to the peoples and region of Aramea, spanning the Fertile Crescent from the area east of the Jordan River, through present-day Syria and the Tigris-Euphrates basin, to the Persian Gulf in southeastern Iraq. Consistent with this ethno-geographical identification of Ham's sons, his five grandsons here mentioned (**Uz**, **Hul**, **Gether**, **Mash**, **Shelah**, vv. 23-24a)—as also his later descendants from **Shelah** (vv. 24b-30)—were located throughout the Arabian Peninsula and Mesopotamia.

Presenting Shem's genealogy last, though contrary to the biblical convention of giving the firstborn "pride of place," highlighted the central point of both the first thematic "half" of Genesis (1:1–11:26: God's prosecution of depraved humanity), as well as the second thematic "half" of Genesis (11:27–50:26: God's redemption of depraved humanity). In the line of Shem, Noah's firstborn, God's promise was established and its blessing—both material and spiritual—first applied.

b. Rebellion Expressed: The Rise and Fall of Universal Human Pride (11:1-9)

This narrative concerning Babel, just like the flood narrative, is structured in the form of a chiasm in which the points and themes in the "upward" part of the narrative are mirrored—and thus reinforced—in the "downward" part of the narrative. This identical structuring of the flood and Babel narratives links them together and thus reinforces the concluding point of both, namely, that depravity is as "attached" to man as it can be (and its impending judgment as inevitable)—as much so after the flood as before it. The structure of this brief narrative may be diagramed as follows:

11:1-4. Just as at the beginning of the flood narrative (6:11-12), the present narrative begins with a reference to **the whole earth** (lit., "the land," *ha-areṣ*), referring to *the people* living on the land. This also serves to anticipate the negative impact of humanity's sin on the land itself as described at the end of this narrative, as at the end of the flood narrative. In both instances the people are scattered, and the land is divided (9:19; 11:8-9). As in the flood narrative, the present account also represents an indictment of *all* humanity, not just a portion thereof. That all humanity was *willingly* involved in the Babel rebellion is underscored by their use of **the same language**, sharing "identical ideas" (**the same words**).

The negative event to ensue is already implied by the reference both to **Shinar** (v. 2), previously mentioned in connection with the rebel Nimrod (10:10), as well as man's journeying (from the land of Ararat; 8:4) and settling in the **east** (see comments at 3:24). Humanity's great sin is, in any event, explicitly indicated in v. 4, centered in their collective desire—expressed with one "voice" (**Come, let us**)—to **build for ourselves a city, and a tower . . . and . . . make for ourselves a name.** In other words the building project itself did not represent man's sin. Instead the sin was in *the purpose* for which the building project was undertaken, to "make for ourselves a name."

The term "name," as commonly used elsewhere, refers to *reputation* or *memorial.* Thus the sin was that by building the great city with a tower, humanity was seeking to establish a memorial or testimony to themselves *in exclusion from God.* (God is neither mentioned nor alluded to anywhere in this human-focused passage.) Interestingly this relates to the previous chapter that ends with the genealogy of Shem, whose name actually means "name" (or "reputation"). This is, in essence, the first expression of secular humanism (i.e., the promotion of human values and achievement to the exclusion of theological ones). In contrast, God promises Abram that as part of the promised blessing, God would make his name great.

The city and tower could not have been a ziggurat, as some scholars claim, since ziggurats were specifically constructed for religious purposes in the worship of various gods (hardly reconcilable with the expression "for ourselves").

11:5-9. Just as the emphasis in the "upward" part of the inversion is on *man's activity to the exclusion of God*, the emphasis in this "downward" arm is on *God's activity to the exclusion of man*—the *only* activity that man "undertakes" in this section was that of "ceasing" to build (v. 8). The statement that **the LORD came down** should be understood as a literary-theological device emphasizing the actual futility of man's goal and the essential "distance" between him and God. At the same time this "distance" between man and God is immediately "bridged" by God's *goal* in "coming down," namely, **to see** what man had done. This verb **to see** often denotes God's keen interest in the affairs of men (as opposed to a disinterested "looking" or "observing").

Consistent therefore with this well-established pattern, God's act of "confusing" (i.e., differentiating) the language of man (v. 7) was intended not only as an act of punishment, but also as an act of *grace.* Concerned for what is *best* for man, God "assessed" their building activity, as represented by the statement, **this is what they began to do, and now nothing which they purpose to do will be impossible for them** (v. 6). God was not affirming that man is capable of undertaking *any* conceivable activity, but rather that they would inevitably achieve their present purpose by completing the city *just as they already completed the tower* (that the tower was completed is indicated by the past tense verb **had built** [*banu*] in v. 5).

God's concern here did not reflect some jealousy of humans as potential creative rivals. Instead His concern reflected His perfect love for people and His consequent desire that they *not* succeed in establishing a memorial to their *collective* rejection of God. Indeed, the present narrative serves as one of the most vivid "counterpoints" by which Scripture later sharpens the imagery and anticipation of humanity finally attaining this ideal of what is *best.* For what happens then will be the reverse of what happened at Babel, and yet the motivating character of God's role will remain the same. Just as He graciously prevented humanity from expressing their collective rejection of Him by "confusing" their language and causing them to scatter, so He will graciously enable them to one day express their collective worship of Him by "restoring" to them a clarified speech to serve Him in one accord (Zph 3:9). A foretaste of this was given at Pentecost, on the day the church was born, when the language of the people was clarified and the gospel was heard by all (Ac 2:5-6).

c. Transition to Pardon (11:10-26)

11:10-26. Much like the genealogies in chaps. 4, 5, and 10, so the genealogy here follows immediately after a brief narrative describing the commission of grave sin (4:1-15 [the murder of Cain]; 4:23-26 [unjust capital punishment]; 9:20-29 [sexual perversion]; and 11:1-9 [collective rejection of God]). Thus this "moderates" the negative tone of the previous episode by demonstrating that God's fundamental blessing of humanity in 1:28 remains intact, and if intact in its physical aspect, then also, *potentially*, in its spiritual aspect. The present genealogy, moreover, being that of Shem, also serves as an adept literary-theological transition to the next thematic "half" of Genesis. The expectation is thus laid that the present genealogy of Shem will likewise be followed by a narrative episode involving the making of a *shem* ("name") for a man. And indeed it is, for in 12:2 God declared to Abraham, "I will . . . make your name [*shem*] great."

II. Patriarchal History: Delineating the Path of Redemption (11:27–50:26)

Having established in the previous section (1:1–11:26) that humanity is depraved and stands in need of redemption, God focused in the rest of Genesis on delineating the "path" by which that need will be met. Since Gn 3:15 shows that man's need for redemption will be solved by the divine-human "seed" of the woman, the present section is concerned with establishing the ethnic and familial parameters of that seed, commencing with the prophetic promise of His descent from Abraham (12:3) and concluding with the prediction of His descent from the tribe of Judah (49:10).

A. Descendants of Terah: God Making His Own Name for Man (11:27–25:11)

This entire section involving key episodes in the life of Abraham is subsumed under **the generations of Terah** (11:27), which bears out the important principle that the action of one's male descendant(s) reflects to a certain degree on the reputation (the "name") of the father. In this Terah set the direction, both spiritually and geographically, for Abraham and his own descendants in the line of promise.

1. The Abrahamic Covenant: God's Promise for Israel and the Nations (11:27–12:20)

The thematic focus on the "path of redemption" begins in this section with God's unconditional promise to Abraham—later known as the Abrahamic covenant. This placement is significant, for the Abrahamic covenant entails blessing not only for Abraham and his own descendants, but also for **all the families of the earth** (12:3; cf. 22:18). This underscores the preeminence of God's love for humanity among the factors that motivated Him to lay out the path of redemption culminating in the sacrifice of the Messiah Jesus.

Many scholars argue that the Abrahamic covenant is a conditional covenant, dependent upon Abraham's obedience to be fulfilled. In response to this interpretation, see below the comments on Gn 17:1-8. Seeing the Abrahamic covenant as unconditional is of great importance for understanding God's character and the nature of His salvation of humanity in *any* age. This unconditionality is implied not only by the absence of any conditional ("if-then") statement in God's declaration of the covenant in 12:1-3 (hence Paul's designation of this covenant as a "promise" in Gl 3:17), but also by the structural arrangement of the biblical narrative surrounding that declaration. Both in the preceding episode where Abraham is "taken" by his father (11:27-32) and in the following episode on the sojourn in Egypt (12:10-20), Abraham's lack of merit—even *demerit*—as a covenantee is clearly evident. As with all God's redemptive covenants (i.e., promises), the causative factor is God's grace, not human merit.

a. God's Sovereign Choice: Abram's Passivity (11:27-32)

11:27-32. Terah, not Abram, is presented as the one taking the lead to set out toward Canaan. This is clear from v. 31a, which portrays Terah as the one who **took** Abram, Lot, and Sarai. This passive portrayal of Abram is extremely significant, for it disallows the conclusion that the promise was given to Abraham as a result of anything especially meritorious that he did.

This view of Terah as the leader of the journey does not contradict Stephen's statement in Ac 7:2, in which he indicated that Abram received his call from God "when he was in Mesopotamia, before he lived in Haran." Having received this call, Abram would have sought, quite naturally, to consult with the family patriarch. Terah, though a pagan (as made clear in Jos 24:2-3) affirmed the validity of the call and took it upon himself, as patriarch, to take the lead. This shows that Terah explicitly intended **to enter the land of Canaan**. This *westward* move was significant in view of the general trend of human migration up to this point was *eastward* and was associated with rebellion, its consequences, and further "distancing" from God (Gn 3:24; 4:16; 10:10-12; 11:2). Thus for a Mesopotamian who desired to "bridge" that distance and so draw as close as possible *toward* God, Canaan was a perfectly logical destination, being at the end of a direct line westward from Mesopotamia.

b. God's Gracious Promises: Resetting Abram's Direction (12:1-9)

12:1-3. This opening paragraph constitutes the first expression of God's great promise to Abraham, what is known as the Abrahamic covenant. This covenant consists of three provisions: (1) **land** (v. 1b), at this point generally identified as "the land of Canaan" (11:31; 12:5), the content and borders of which are increasingly specified throughout the Pentateuch, culminating in the detailed description in Nm 34:1-12; (2) **a great nation** (v. 2a), in which the word translated **nation** (*goy*) is typically applied to the Gentile nations and only rarely to Israel (typically the term *'am* [people] is used for Israel), thus hinting at God's broader, *human*-centered purpose in bestowing this covenant; and (3) **blessing** (vv. 2b-3), given the most space in God's declaration, thereby bearing out its preeminence among the provisions. To emphasize the importance of the blessing, the phrase **And I will bless you** occurs in the exact middle of God's utterance (the 14th of 27 words) as well as in the various circumstances in which that blessing will be applied. These circumstances are threefold and increasingly expansive: to Abraham, his descendants (cf. Ps 105:8-10), and **all the families of the earth**. The term **families** generally denotes extended families (a living patriarch and all the members of his household by blood or marriage). God's love is seeking to "push" His blessing as far as His justice will allow.

12:4-9. In response (not as a prerequisite) to God's promises **Abram . . . departed from Haran** and continued on to Canaan with **Sarai his wife and Lot his nephew**. This statement, together with the reference in 11:32 to their halting in Haran (most likely because of ailment or infirmity on the part of Terah), suggests that the declaration in 12:1-3 was in fact God's second, given to Abram in Haran, and not the first declaration given to him in Mesopotamia (see Ac 7:2-3). The implication for Abram's faith at this point is hardly flattering, for this would suggest that he was contemplating a return to his home city following Terah's death. Thus God repeated His call and exhorted Abram to continue the journey his father had begun. On a theological level, however, this is perfectly consistent with the manner in which the Abrahamic covenant is introduced—as a promise that is actively and sovereignly made by God to a passive and undeserving recipient. At the same time Abram responded to God's promise with commendable obedience, completing the journey to Canaan and building **an altar** to the Lord at **Shechem** (a city in the hill country of Ephraim about 40 miles [65 km] north of Jerusalem).

c. God's Unshakable Hold: Abram's Deep Depravity (12:10-20)

12:10-20. However, Abram's initial obedience was short-lived. When faced with **a famine in the land** he took matters in his own hands, rather than trusting that God would bless and provide for him in the midst of the famine (as He did for Isaac, Gn 26:1-3) or seeking guidance through sacrifice and prayer (as Jacob did during the famine in his day, 46:1-4). Abram adopted a course of "situational ethics." First, he demonstrated a lack of faith in God's provision, prompting him to leave Canaan and go to Egypt. Then he demonstrated a lack of faith in God's protection, prompting him to lie—and to ask Sarai to lie as well—about their marital relationship. Rather than loving his wife as himself (see Eph 5:33; Lv 19:18), considering her welfare, and guarding her honor, Abram was concerned with only his own welfare—**that it may go well with me** (Gn 12:13). In his self-interest and weak faith Abram remains silent not only when Sarai was taken to the palace, but also when she was taken as Pharaoh's **wife**. In this way Abram was the cause of the additional sin of *adultery* on the part of Sarai and Pharaoh. Though some translations attempt to soften the situation by paraphrasing Pharaoh's words in v. 19 in a way that suggests he had not yet married her, the Hebrew text is quite clear. Pharaoh employed the typical verbal idiom for marriage, "to take so-and-so to oneself as a wife" in a form signifying completed (past) action. When confronted with his misbehavior, Abram said nothing. He simply took Sarai and departed. Though admittedly an inference, a lack of repentance indeed appears to be Abram's last—and most depraved—sin in this episode. This is supported by the observation that, when confronted for this same sin committed later against Abimelech (in chap. 20), Abram responds by excusing himself and denying any guilt in misrepresenting the truth, for Sarai, he points out, "actually is my sister, the daughter of my father, but not . . . of my mother" (20:12). This indicates that Abraham's lie was justified in his mind since it was partially true.

The purpose of this episode is not to single out Abram as *more* depraved than anyone else, for in the end he is merely symptomatic of the human condition and the virus of depravity endemic to all humanity. Rather, by presenting this episode immediately after God's declaration of the Abrahamic covenant, Scripture is making clear that God gave the promise in the presence of demerit (indeed, God "justifies the ungodly," Rm 4:5; Abram was without merit). And since this was true of Abram, it is also true of present-day beneficiaries of that covenant.

As to this episode's significance in the patriarchal narrative, this is the first time (but certainly not the last) that God's promise to Abraham was placed in jeopardy. By allowing his wife to become part of Pharaoh's harem, Abram nearly obstructed God's promise of a great nation coming from him, specifically because Abraham's promised line would only be through Sarai as God would make clear later (Gn 17:15-22). Other episodes that place the promise in jeopardy are Abram's peace offer to Lot, which threatened the land promise (13:1-13); Sarai's manipulative attempt to obtain a child by giving her maid-servant Hagar to Abraham, jeopardizing the seed promise (16:1-6); Abraham's deceit in calling

Sarah his sister and allowing her to become part of Abimelech's harem, once again threatening the promised line (20:1-18); and the ultimate example, when God seemingly placed the promise in jeopardy by calling on Abraham to sacrifice his son Isaac, thereby threatening the seed promise (22:1-19). In each case it appears that God's promise would be thwarted only to have God intervene and assure the certain outcome of His promises.

A common aspect of narratives in Genesis is that they frequently foreshadow future events that will occur later in the Pentateuch. Here are examples: Abram's Egyptian sojourn foreshadows Israel's experience in the exodus. Abram went to Egypt because of a famine (12:10); so did Israel (see the entire Joseph narrative but particularly Gn 41:54 and 45:11). Both Abram and Israel sojourned in Egypt and were threatened with death (Gn 12:13; Ex 1:16). Abram acquired wealth from Pharaoh (Gn 12:16); so the Israelites received wealth in Egypt (Gn 47:27). In the same way that the Lord sent **plagues** upon Pharaoh to deliver Abram (Gn 12:17), so He sent plagues upon Egypt to deliver Israel (Ex 9:14; 11:1); In Genesis, Pharaoh sends Abram out of Egypt (Gn 12:19-20), while in Exodus Pharaoh sends the Israelites out from Egypt (Ex 12:32-33). Finally, Abram went out to the Negev with Lot; was rich in livestock, silver, and gold; and worshipped the Lord (Gn 13:1-4). Likewise, Israel left Egypt and went to the Negev with a mixed multitude; was rich in livestock, silver, and gold; and worshipped by celebrating the Passover (Ex 12:35-42). For these and other parallels, see Sailhamer, *The Pentateuch as Narrative*, 142. Sailhamer astutely explains the author's purpose for shaping these narratives in parallel fashion: "[T]he author permits the reader to see the implications of God's past deeds with his chosen people. The past is not allowed to remain in the past. Its lessons are drawn for the future. Behind the pattern stands a faithful, loving God. What he has done with Abraham, he will do for his people today and tomorrow" (142).

2. Living in the Land: God's Affirmation of the Covenant (13:1–14:24)

Having declared what He would do for Abram, God was now bound by His attributes of truth and justice to fulfill His word (the ratification ceremony of chap. 15 will serve to more firmly "establish" the covenant in the mind of Abram), and the rest of the Abrahamic narrative will focus on the outworking of the three provisions of that promise for Abram. At the end of the previous section, despite Abram's lack of faith and multiple sins, God already began to fulfill the material aspect of the blessing He promised Abram by moving Pharaoh to allow Abram to keep the vast wealth he had received (12:16). This is another indication that the covenant does not depend on obedience. At this point in the narrative that material wealth provided the basis for focusing on the provision of the *land*, specifically establishing Abram's "hold" on and reputation in Canaan, the land of promise.

a. Affirming Abram's Right to the Land (13:1-18)

13:1-18. Canaan was a fruitful land and hence in high demand in Abram's day (as today). The Canaanites, as already noted (see comment on 10:6-20; cf. Gn 10:15-19), were in fact a collection of sociopolitical and ethnic groups situated throughout the land and always therefore in the background as potential competitors wherever Abram went. That Abram's descendants eventually became the dominant force throughout all that land is thus powerful testimony of God's sovereign involvement in fulfilling His promise. To highlight this point to a reader living during this later period of Israelite dominance—when the Canaanites had all but vanished from the land—God prompted a later writer (prophet) to add to the Mosaic text the statement in v. 7b: **Now the Canaanite and the Perizzite were dwelling then in the land** (cf. 12:6). The competition for this fruitful land was fierce, all the more so because of the increased wealth in livestock and servants Abram had acquired in Egypt from Pharaoh (12:16). And that was in addition to the large entourage Abram had already brought with him from Mesopotamia (conservatively numbering at least 500 people and their necessary provisions; see 14:14). As Lot also had his own large entourage, **strife between . . . the herdsmen** was inevitable. So Abram called on Lot to **separate** (i.e., distance himself) **from** him, giving his nephew the first choice of location. The strife between relatives in this passage reflects a common theme in Genesis (see comments on 4:8).

It may seem surprising to read that (1) such fierce competition existed in this region of the **Negev**, which is primarily a desert, and (2) that Lot, when given first choice, chose not only to stay in that general area, but, in particular, to relocate to the especially inhospitable region along the southern shore of what is today the Dead Sea (the general area where most contemporary scholars locate **Sodom and Gomorrah**). That the land Lot chose **was well watered everywhere** (v. 10) contrasts with the situation familiar to the Israelites and to people today. The answer is that all of this took place **before the LORD destroyed Sodom and Gomorrah**. In other words, the inhospitable, barren state of that portion of the upper Negev and lower Jordan Valley (i.e., the "Dead Sea") region is the direct result of the manner by which God judged the sins of the Canaanites who lived there. This stands in direct contrast to the theory that the formation of the Dead Sea and barrenness of the surrounding area resulted from millions of years of interrelated geologic processes. The sudden transformation of this region that was **well watered** and filled with life **like the garden of the LORD** to a region whose land and water are all but *dead* serves as a reminder of the consequence of sin (2Pt 2:6).

Christians and Jews sometimes cite Gn 13 as a paradigm for peace in the Middle East today. "If Abram gave away land for peace," it is claimed, "should not his descendants, the Jewish people, be willing to do the same?" This chapter, however, nowhere indicates that Abram "gave" any land to Lot. And God affirmed twice toward the end of this chapter (v. 17) that the land was given to Abram (the only two times that the verb **give** [*natan*] is used in this chapter)—and not only to Abram, but also to his **descendants** in the line of promise (i.e., Israel; cf. Ps 105:10-11) **forever** (v. 15). Though peace is unquestionably an important goal, Christians must support it by means consistent with God's revealed truth, and certainly not by advocating giving away to a non-Jewish national entity land that was divinely deeded to the people of Israel as an eternal possession.

b. Affirming Abram's Might and Prosperity (14:1-16)

14:1-16. This passage concerning the conquest of the **five** Canaanite **kings** by the **four kings** of the east, though at first sight seemingly tangential in nature, serves the following three significant purposes. *First*, the narrative presents the first explicit evidence of the truly prophetic nature of Noah's statement in 9:25-26, according to which (the descendants of) Canaan would be subordinated/enslaved to (the descendants of) his siblings and uncles (this being the general sense of *achim*, "brothers"). The conquering quartet was led by the **king of Elam**, and the Elamites were descendants of Shem (10:22). This historical precedent would also have served as further encouragement for the Israelites, likewise descended from Shem, in their divinely ordained conquest of the Canaanites. *Second*, the message gives an extremely vivid example of God's military concern for Abram, who succeeded in rescuing **Lot** (who was taken captive with the people living in Sodom) by defeating the four kings from the east. This would have served as a historical precedent of military success for the Israelites, Abram's descendants in the line of promise, both in their initial conquest of Canaan as well as in their ensuing battles to maintain control of the land (cf. 2Sm 5:24-25). *Third*, the passage sets up the immediately following episode in which Abram gave "a tithe of all" the spoil (i.e., the spoil he had taken from the four eastern kings, who had themselves taken it from the five Canaanite kings) to Melchizedek. This is one of the most theologically important encounters in the Bible.

c. Affirming Abram's Blessing and Status (14:17-24)

14:17-24. Other than the present passage, the figure of **Melchizedek** is mentioned in the OT only in Ps 110:4. Both of these passages are cited in Heb 7 as the basis for one of the most important topics in Christian theology, namely, the eternal efficacy of Christ's high priestly work. In the general priestly economy of God, the nature of the priest inevitably determines the nature of his priestly work (cf. Heb 7:26-28). Therefore the discussion of Melchizedek in Heb 7 commences with an explicit discussion of his titles/names. **Melchizedek** (Hb. *malki-tsedeq*) means "King of Righteousness," and **King of Salem** (Hb. *melek shalem*) means "King of Peace." Since "righteousness" and "peace" are qualities centered in and administered by God, the implication is that Melchizedek is none other than God Himself—yet another example of the many theophanies (preincarnational appearances of the Son of God) in the OT (though for the alternative view that Melchizedek was a type of the Messiah, see comments on Heb 7:1-10). These two titles/names are not employed for any other individual—king, priest, or otherwise—in Israel, and the two names are prophetically applied to the Messiah in His eschatological role of eternal Priest-King: "the LORD our righteousness" (*'adonay* [*yhvh*] *tsidqenu*) in Jr 23:6 and "Prince of Peace" (*shar-shalom*) in Is 9:6.

This identification of Melchizedek with God explains why Abram immediately recognized and submitted to Melchizedek's superiority—not simply out of social respect, but as an expression of faith and worship. Abram allowed himself to be **blessed** (though typically "the lesser is blessed by the greater," cf. Heb 7:7) and responded by giving Melchizedek a **tenth of all** (tithe), portrayed throughout the OT as a specific act of worship. The implication of Melchizedek's deity is further seen in Heb 7 by (1) the contrast in Heb 7:8 between the receiving of tithes by the Levites, who are "mortal men," and the receiving of tithes by Melchizedek, who "lives on" (i.e., who is immortal); and (2) the statement in Heb 7:3 that "he" (Melchizedek) "remains a priest perpetually." If Jesus "continues [lit., abides] forever" (Hb 7:24) as high priest "according to the order of Melchizedek" (Gn 7:17)—and there can be only one high priest—how can Melchizedek of Gn 14, who we are told "remains (or abides, Gk. *menei*, present tense) a priest perpetually" (Hb 7:3), be anyone but Christ, the believer's great high priest?

A small number of Jewish people, prior to the first advent of Christ and based on the Hebrew Scriptures, did in fact believe that Melchizedek was none other than God Himself, in the form of a man, who not only atones for the remnant of His people Israel, but is also the One who will execute final judgment on the wicked at the end of this age before the establishment of God's kingdom on earth. This belief is attested by one of the DSS, dated to c. the first century BC, known as 11Q13, or 11QMelch, and referred to as *Melchizedek* (see Michael O. Wise, Martin Abegg, Jr., and Edward Cook, trans., *The Dead Sea Scrolls: A New Translation*, rev. ed. [San Francisco: HarperSanFrancisco, 2005].

3. Ratifying the Covenant: God's Compromise with Weak Faith (15:1-21)

In this chapter God affirmed, clarified, and "ratified" His promise of 12:1-3. The concept of "ratification" is an inherent part of postfall (i.e., depraved) human culture, since by definition it assumes that the word alone of the one(s) making the promise/covenant is insufficient. In ratifying the Abrahamic covenant God is not "activating" it, but rather establishing the certainty of its fulfillment in the mind of Abram. Moreover, it is designed to give further assurance to those Israelites who originally received the Torah at the end of their wilderness wanderings and were then about to embark on the conquest, that God had surely given them this land. Here, as continually throughout the history of redemption, God condescended to "meet" people in their lack of faith by doing more (or less, depending on one's perspective) than that required by the ideal since the depraved with whom He interacts are so far from that ideal.

a. Answering Abram's Doubt about the Son (15:1-5)

15:1-5. As in the initial expression of God's promise in Gn 12, so too here the scene commenced immediately with God's active expression of what *He* will do *for* Abram (and his descendants in the line of promise). And so too here, as in the latter part of chap. 12, God's declaration of promise is followed by a clear expression of doubt on the part of Abram. In the present instance this doubt is represented by Abram's questioning response, **O Lord God, what will You give me, since I am childless, and the heir of my house is Eliezer of Damascus?** By this question, Abram was, *at best*, seeking to "force" God's "hand" into specifying and fulfilling His previous statement, "I will make you a great nation" (12:2). *At worst* he was denying that God could give him the son that he so desired, since Sarai was barren (11:30) and postmenopausal (18:13). Thus Abram's statement in 15:2 could be understood as the despondent statement of an old man of little faith anticipating his death: "O Lord God, what *can* You give me, since I am childless, and the heir of my house is Eliezer of Damascus?" (italics added). As in chap. 12, however, God responded not with judgment, but with patience and grace, thus emphasizing the unconditional nature of His promise. Condescending to meet Abram in his lack of faith, God declared outright what His words in 12:2 logically implied, namely, that **one who will come forth from your own body** [lit., "inner parts"], **he shall be your heir** and thence Abram's descendants would expand into a mighty nation, which God illustrated by the panoply of stars illuminating the night sky (v. 5).

b. Affirming Abram's Imperfect Faith (15:6)

15:6. God **reckoned** Abram's faith **as righteousness**. The Hebrew grammar indicates this verse is parenthetical—background information that Abram had previously believed God. This harmonizes with Heb 11:8, which depicts Abraham expressing saving faith previous to Gn 15, in response to God's call to emigrate to Canaan (Gn 12:1). Abram's faith in Gn 15 reflects his growth of faith since that call. This verse presents three facts about justification. (1) *Justification is based on faith*, not works, since there is nothing that Abram had ever done to earn it. This was *precisely* Paul's point when he cited Gn 15:6 in Rm 4:3-5 as an example of one "who does not work, but believes in Him who justifies the ungodly." (2) *The faith on which justification is based need not be perfect*, since Abram's faith in God's promise of a genetic heir is also the very thing he continued to doubt (see, e.g., Gn 17:17). One can appreciate the value of this for all believers, for who can claim his faith is truly perfect? (3) *Justification is not a matter of being "made" actually and practically righteous, but of being "declared" righteous.* Genesis 15:6 does not say God "made him righteous," but rather God **reckoned it to him as righteousness**. The expression "reckoned it" may also be translated "considered it" or "credited it." While believers are still sinful, through justification, God has imputed righteousness to them. It is through sanctification that, by God's grace, believers can overcome their sinful inclinations and grow in righteousness, a process not addressed in Gn 15:6 (for sanctification see comments on Rm 5–8, esp. Rm 6:21-23; 8:12-17).

c. Answering Abram's Doubt about the Land (15:7-21)

15:7-21. Having assured to Abram the promise of an heir, God next affirmed His promise that Abram would possess **this land** (i.e., Canaan). Not unexpectedly, this prompted a new expression of doubt on the part of Abram, who responded to God's affirmation by asking, **How may I know that I will possess it?** Again God responded with patience and grace. In this instance, however, since the provision in view is abstract (the right of possession/ownership) rather than material (such as an heir and descendants), God affirmed His promise and assuaged Abram's doubt by condescending to participate in the human convention of covenant "ratification" (i.e., establishing a "binding" agreement). In this act the covenantee was "bound" to the conditions of the agreement by the blood of a sacrifice—either by walking between the bloody parts, as here, or being sprinkled by the blood, as in Ex 24:6-8, where both Israel and God (represented by the altar) were sprinkled with the sacrificial blood. In this instance, however, though God adopted the generally accepted form of ratification, He altered it slightly to conform to the unconditional nature of His promise to Abram. Thus, while Abram was waiting for God, as the superior party, to pass between the pieces, he fell into **a deep sleep** (induced by God), during which God **passed between these pieces** in the form of **a smoking oven and a flaming torch** (v. 17), thereby ensuring that the pieces were completely burned up in the process. When Abram awoke, he would have perceived (1) that God had passed between the pieces, and (2) that He had done so in such a way as to prevent Abram from doing so afterward. Thus the only one to whom the covenant was "bound" for its fulfillment is God, that is, the covenant was *unconditional*. This is also Paul's point in his comment on this event in Gl 3:17, in which he stated that the Abrahamic covenant was "ratified by God" alone, hence justifying his designation of it as a "promise" (an unconditional covenant) rather than "the Law" (a conditional covenant).

4. Doubting God: The Fall Reprised (16:1-16)

In this section Abram's doubt in God's promise of an heir resurfaced, prompting the sin with Hagar. The specific pattern surrounding the temptation, sin, consequences, and divine response to Abram parallels Adam's sin in Gn 3. This reinforces that God's ideal purpose for humanity is refocused in Abram, and God will sovereignly ensure the success of this purpose despite Abram being tainted by depravity.

a. The Temptation (16:1-4a)

16:1-4a. Like Adam, Abram was the leader of his family. God had communicated His word directly to Abram, and therefore Abram was responsible for properly communicating this word to his family and leading them to obey it. Here as in chap. 3, the temptation to doubt and disobey God's word was subtly set before the husband through the mediation of his wife, to whom Abram, like Adam, gave in and did what he knew was wrong. The sinfulness of Abram's action is underscored in v. 2b by the words **And Abram listened to the voice of Sarai** in describing his action. God said a similar thing in His comments to Adam in 3:17, "Because you have listened to the voice of your wife."

b. The Human Consequences (16:4b-6)

16:4b-6. As in the garden, the immediate consequence of the sin was personal enmity. This enmity between Adam and Eve was expressed in their covering/hiding from each other those parts of themselves that physically reflect their deepest intimacy. In the present instance the marital enmity is expressed in v. 5, where Sarai accosted Abram for impregnating Hagar. This resulted in Sarai being **despised in her** [Hagar's]

sight. As in the case of Adam and Eve, the enmity resulting from sin was carried over into the relationship of the couple's children. This also reinforces that sexual sin invariably results in personal enmity at some level.

c. The Divine Response (16:7-16)

16:7-16. As a result of the enmity between Sarai and Hagar, Sarai, who was still in the socially superior position as first wife, **treated** Hagar **harshly**, causing Hagar to flee **from her presence** (v. 6). Then, as in the garden following the fall, the Son of God appeared, here described for the first time as **the angel** [lit., "messenger"] **of the Lord**. He responded with patient, gentle grace, first by asking questions (**Where have you come from and where are you going?** v. 8) and then by issuing a pronouncement that both affirmed the consequence of sin but also established the promise of great blessing. In chap. 3 that promise of blessing is centered in the male "seed" of the woman (3:15), who will ultimately defeat the instigator of the fall and restore creation to its ideal. In chap. 16 the promise of blessing is likewise centered in the male seed (as it is lit., in v. 10, though often translated **descendants**) of the woman (Hagar), whom God promised to **greatly multiply**... **so that they will be too many to count** (see also 17:20).This employed the same language of blessing applied to Isaac and Israel (cf. 22:17).

The angel of the Lord said that her son **Ishmael**... **will be a wild donkey of a man** (v. 12; i.e., uncontrollable and fractious), with especial animosity (such being the sense of **to the east**—i.e., in rebellion/enmity) toward **his brothers** in the line of promise, namely, Israel (v. 12). Throughout the Bible, the Ishmaelites are represented as being in continual opposition to Israel and their assertion of ownership and dominion of the land of Israel (cf. Ps 83:2-6; Jdg 8:24).

5. Circumcision: The Sign of the Covenant (17:1-16)

In this chapter, wherein Abram still struggled with believing God's promise of an heir from him and Sarai, God affirmed His unconditional covenant yet again, at the same time also underscoring its eternality (see vv. 7-8). He also decreed circumcision as the "sign" of this covenant, as an outward marker of those to whom the covenant is applied, and a symbol of the submission to God for which they are to strive.

a. The Effected Covenant as the Basis of the Rite (17:1-8)

17:1-8. God prefaced His establishment of the rite of circumcision by affirming again His already active and unconditional **covenant** with Abram. As often represented in translation, however, it would seem that God is in fact here *conditioning* His covenant on Abram's obedience, for immediately after commanding him to **walk before Me, and be blameless** (v. 1) God stated, **I will establish My covenant between Me and you** (v. 2). This translation in v. 2 (as again in v. 7) in the future tense implies a sequential relationship to His previous command (**walk before Me**, etc.). This, in turn, leads to the deduction that establishment of the covenant depended on obedience to the previous command. Yet this future-tense translation in both vv. 2 and 7 is not the only grammatical one possible. In Hebrew this verbal form can be used to denote either present or future tenses. In light of the context, a future-tense translation clearly contradicts God's statement in v. 4 that **My covenant *is* with you** (italics added). A future-tense translation also contradicts previous passages in Genesis that indicate that the covenant was already established, active, and ratified. In fact it was ratified and then sealed, for once a covenant "has been ratified, no one... adds conditions to it" (Gl 3:15). Furthermore, the verb rendered **establish** may also be translated "uphold" or "maintain." Thus, God's statement in vv. 2 and 7 would be better translated, "I am upholding My covenant." Hence God's previous command to **walk before Me, and be blameless** (v. 1) should not be viewed a *condition* to ensure that the covenant *will be* made, but rather as a *response* to the covenant *having already been* made.

b. Content of the Rite (17:9-16)

17:9-16. Part of the reason the Abrahamic covenant is viewed by some as conditional is the conditional language surrounding the use of the word "covenant" (*berit*) here in vv. 9-16 (**you shall keep My covenant**; **he has broken My covenant**. Biblical Hebrew, however, is an extremely efficient language, and so the same word can be used in different passages in somewhat different senses, determined as always by the word's use in *context*. Since the unconditionality of the Abrahamic covenant has already been established, the word "covenant" in this section signifies an individual *rite* or *obligation*. This is clarified further in v. 11, in which circumcision is called **the sign of the covenant** that already existed between Him and His people Israel (cf. 12:1-9; 15:18-21). In this respect circumcision anticipates and parallels baptism, which as a sign of the new covenant is likewise a follow-up rite of obedience, not a precondition of entrance.

c. Abram's Response to the Rite (17:17-27)

17:17-27. After establishing the rite of circumcision, God changed Sarai's name to **Sarah** (the former possibly meaning "striver," foreshadowing her difficulties with Hagar [16:1-6; 21:9-14], to the latter meaning "princess," reflecting the promise that kings of peoples will come from her, vv. 15-16), even as He had earlier changed Abram's to **Abraham** ("exalted father" to what sounds like "father of a multitude," v. 5). Following this, God once again affirmed His promise to give Abraham a son by her, in response to which **Abraham fell on his face** (as He did in v. 3). But instead of worshiping God he **laughed** (v. 17, *vayitschaq*), asking instead that **Ishmael** be confirmed as his heir and inheritor of the promise. To this God responded with gentle patience and unflappable grace (a perfect Father!), declaring that it will not be Ishmael with whom He **will establish** (better, "maintain") His **covenant** (vv. 19, 21), but rather with the son **whom Sarah will bear to** Abraham the following **year** (v. 21). God also told Abraham to name that son **Isaac** (v. 19, *yitschaq*), meaning "he laughs," thus serving as a continual reminder to the parents, from the moment of Isaac's birth, of their faithless response (Sarah laughed also in 18:12) to the promise that God faithfully fulfilled (the negative nuance of the laughter is also given a positive twist in 21:6). In light of these specifics, Abraham's doubt, as in 15:4-5, is again quelled—this time more substantially since no further expression of doubt is attributed to him. For this reason, Paul wrote that Abraham did not waver but was strengthened in his faith (see Ro 4:19-20 and comments there). In marked obedience he proceeded to circumcise **all the men of his household, who were born in the house or bought with money** (v. 23-27).

6. An Expression of Divine Fellowship (18:1-33)

This chapter presents a beautiful picture of divine fellowship with humanity—one that shows that God's interaction with humanity during this postfall period of corruption and sin is not only about accomplishing tasks. He goes beyond tasks such as giving revelation, making covenants, enacting judgment, but also emphasizes experiencing relationship, taking the time to *relate* to man even during the "downtime" or more "mundane" periods of life.

a. God Affirming His Empathy with Abraham (18:1-8)

18:1-8. One of the most frequent venues of "mundane" human life is mealtime. God's visit in this instance is a half-day affair, beginning with His arrival when the Middle Eastern sun was at its hottest—this being the sense of the expression **in the heat of the day** (v. 1)—and continuing until the evening (as the process of preparing the **choice calf**, v. 7, would require), when the two angels then left and headed toward nearby Sodom (see 18:22 and 19:1). That Abraham immediately recognized that God Himself had come in human form to visit him is clear from his greeting in v. 3, in which he addressed him with the specific form of the Hebrew word **lord** reserved exclusively for God: *'adonay* (as opposed to *'adonay*, ending with a short vowel). Also the verbs and possessive pronouns are sg. rather than pl. (as they would be if Abraham were addressing all three visitors).

b. God Affirming His Grace toward Abraham (18:9-15)

18:9-15. While sitting over the meal (or after it) God reiterated His promise of 17:21 that He would grant Abraham **a son** by his wife **Sarah** in a year's time (v. 10). Notably Abraham received this reiteration of God's promise without any expression of doubt; apparently his faith was growing in concert with the anticipation of its near realization. Sarah, on the other hand, who heard this from God for the first time while **listening at the tent door**, responded as Abraham did in the previous chapter—with laughter (v. 12). In Sarah's case, however, the laughter was **to herself** (lit., "within herself"), that is, it was internalized laughter, accompanied by the disbelief that she might still **have pleasure**, both she and her husband **being old** (lit., past childbearing, postmenopausal). In God's response to Sarah's disbelief, notably, He was just as gentle and patient as He was toward Abraham. As He did with Eve, so with Sarah; God was concerned foremost with her spiritual welfare and with having her confront her sin squarely. So He rephrased her faithless thought in more direct fashion: **Shall I indeed bear a child, when I am so old?** (v. 13). That God intended to perform a miracle by permitting Sarah to become pregnant from Abraham is evident from his following statement, **Is anything too difficult for the LORD?** (v. 14). The word translated **difficult** which means "wonderful," is applied to God (Jdg 13:18; Is 9:6) and the divine and/or miraculous actions He performs (Ps 139:14; Is 29:14).

c. God Affirming His Justice to Abraham (18:16-33)

18:16-33. The two angels rose up and directed their attention **toward Sodom** (v. 16), as they prepared for their redemptive task of warning Lot and his family to flee the city before its destruction by the Lord. God then deliberated—for the benefit of the reader—whether to inform Abraham of His impending plan for Sodom, which He then did (because **I have chosen him** (v. 19). By this statement God was reinforcing a profound fact that likewise applies to every believer, for the verb here translated **chosen** literally signifies "knowing." Hence "I have come *to know* him." Throughout the OT this verb denotes the deepest or most "intimate" possible knowledge of the object in view. It usually refers to one of three types: (1) knowledge of information, usually acquired by experience; (2) one person's thorough knowledge of another person acquired by sexual intercourse (or sodomy; cf. 19:5); and (3) God's thorough knowledge of human individuals acquired by union with the Holy Spirit—in Jn 10:27 Jesus intended this third type of knowledge when He said, "My sheep hear My voice, and *I know them*, and they follow Me" (italics added). By contrast, not to be known by God leads ultimately to "perishing" (Ps 1:6) or the "second death" (Rv 20:6)—that is, being severed eternally from the experience of His love.

Continuing this theme of the difference between how God treats those whom He knows and those whom He does not, Abraham stated that **the LORD** will not **sweep away . . . the righteous** (v. 23; i.e., those who are *reckoned* righteous) of Sodom along **with the wicked** (v. 23), and that as **Judge of all the earth** He is expected to **deal justly** (v. 25). In his theological naivete Abraham was in fact merging two distinct expectations: (1) that God acts *justly* by treating the (reckoned) righteous differently from the wicked and (2) that He acts *mercifully* by not executing Sodom's just punishment in consideration of the few righteous ones in the city. In adhering to perfect justice God is not obligated to spare the righteous from the consequences of life in a corrupt and fallen world. But He is obligated to mete out *justice* when *judgment* is to be passed, at the resurrection of the dead, when some (the reckoned righteous) will be acquitted and experience "everlasting life" and others (the wicked) will be condemned and experience "everlasting contempt" (Dn 12:2; Rv 20:4-15). However, because Abraham was still little more than an "infant" in faith, God demonstrated His justice (in combination with mercy) prior to the point of proper final judgment so as to visibly instruct Abraham in these essential divine attributes.

7. A Paradigm of Corporate Judgment (19:1-29)

a. Cause of Judgment (19:1-11)

19:1-11. When **the two angels** arrived in **Sodom** (v. 1), they were immediately spotted by **Lot**, who was **sitting in the gate of** the city. He graciously invited them to **spend the night** as guests in his **house** (v. 2). In contrast to Lot's hospitality, when the other **men of the city . . . both young and old** hear of the strangers' arrival, they **surrounded** Lot's **house** and demanded that he **bring them out** so that they might **have relations with them** (vv. 4-5) (lit., "that we might know them," referring to *sexual* knowledge). From this incident derives the term *sodomy*.

Some modern proponents of homosexuality have argued that the word "know" as used here means "getting acquainted," as in Middle Eastern hospitality, or in the sense of interrogating the angels to see if they were spies. Thus, they argue this is not a reference to homosexual behavior and the sin of Sodom was merely inhospitality. However, although the word "know" could mean "get acquainted," in this context it is clearly a reference to sexual behavior. First, the word "know" is frequently used in Genesis for sexual behavior (4:1, 17, 25; 24:16; 38:26). Second, the context indicates that this is sexual behavior or else Lot would not have offered his daughters as an alternative. Furthermore, Lot describes them as not yet having "known a man" (lit., Hb. translation, v. 8), clearly using the word with a sexual meaning. Finally, in the NT, Jdg 7 says that the sin of Sodom was "gross immorality" and pursuing "strange flesh," demonstrating that the sin was sexual, not a lack of hospitality.

This concerted, perverse desire on the part of the Sodomites clearly bears out why God decided to destroy them. In somewhat perplexing fashion, however, Lot sought to protect his two guests by offering his **two** virgin **daughters** instead to the rapacious mob (v. 8)!

All the more astonishing in light of this offer is Peter's reference in 2Pt 2:7-8 to "*righteous* Lot . . ." who "felt his *righteous* soul tormented day after day by their [i.e., the Sodomites'] lawless deeds" (italics added). As with Abraham in 15:6 the emphasis is on Lot's being *reckoned righteous*—that is, the righteousness that God credited to him by virtue of his faith aside from any works, imperfect though that faith and his consequent behavior may have been. Abraham's "reckoned" righteousness was both preceded (chap. 12) and followed (chap. 20) by his own intentional "handing over" of a female family member (his wife Sarai/Sarah) for what inevitably resulted in the commission of sexual sin.

b. Distinction of Judgment (19:12-22)

19:12-22. The two angels carried out their mission by warning **Lot** to flee the city and **bring out** with him his **son-in-law**, **sons**, **daughters**, and **whomever** else was part of his household (vv. 12-16). The term **sons-in-law** (v. 14) is applied here to the men living in Sodom **who were to marry** Lot's two **daughters**, that is, the men who were betrothed to his daughters, for whom the marriage was yet to be completed. This reflects an approach to marriage consistently applied within Israel throughout the biblical period and even up to the present day in many strictly traditional Jewish societies, specifically that the marriage "begins" with the betrothal and is "completed" a year later with the ceremony and consummation. Hence, the marriage effectively begins with the betrothal, the process—even if not yet consummated—and can only be annulled by a writ of divorce. This shows why Joseph thought of "divorcing" Mary even though they were still in their betrothal period (see comments on Mt 1:18-20). In any event, all the males connected with Lot's household rejected his appeal, thinking he was **jesting**. However, Lot's **wife** and his **two daughters** fled with him. This was not necessarily because they believed him or desired to leave Sodom any more than the men did, but because in His **compassion** the **Lord** had the two angels seize them by their **hands** and force them out of the city.

c. Purpose of Judgment (19:23-29)

19:23-29. When exhorting Lot and his family to leave Sodom, the two angels had specifically stated that they were not to **look behind** them (v. 17), yet this is precisely what Lot's wife did. As a result **she became a pillar of salt**. Why this happened was not simply because of her action of looking, but rather (consistent with the principle already established in 4:3-5 and 6:5) because of the heart attitude and spiritual allegiance that prompted her to "look back." The Hebrew verb employed by the angels in their warning and in the statement afterward that Lot's wife **looked back** (*vathabbet*) is not the usual verb employed to denote the *action* of looking or seeing, but is a less frequent verb that carries the specific idea of looking at something *with desire, approval, or confidence* (Ps 119:6; Is 66:2; Am 5:22; Zch 12:10). Abraham himself **looked** at the destruction, yet he did not become a pillar of salt (v. 28). Here the more common verb was used, the verb that indicates that the "looking" was no more than an action (although prompted, no doubt, by concern for Lot and his family), not the type of "looking" expressed by Lot's wife. On the significance of both the permanent nature of God's judgment (i.e., by **brimstone**) as well as its broad scope (i.e., **all the valley . . . and what grew on the ground**, v. 25), see 13:10 and comments on 13:1-18.

8. Persistence of Sin (19:30–20:18)

a. Struggles of Lot's Household (19:30-38)

19:30-38. This passage vividly—and tragically—illustrates the potential danger of surrounding oneself with wicked society. Lot's **two daughters** had been born and reared in Sodom, as may be inferred from the fact that they were marriageable virgins (19:8, 14), which in the Bible typically applies to women in their early teens, whereas Lot had by this point been living in Sodom for about 25 years. Lot had moved there when Abram was about 75 years old (12:4; 13:10), whereas Abraham was now 99 (17:1, 21; 18:10). Of course, simply living *in* a wicked society does not inevitably mean that one's children will turn out "bad." Isaac, for example, who grew up in a land filled with Canaanites, turned out quite good. The problem lies in the degree to which the family unit itself, the parents in particular, assimilates to the surrounding culture, which will impact the children's spiritual and moral development. In this instance it is borne out by the logical implication that Lot's wife, the mother of their daughters, was herself from Sodom. This would explain not only why she is mentioned in this chapter for the first time, but also why she "looked back" toward Sodom (v. 26), longing for what she did not want to leave. Also, since their husbands-to-be were destroyed along with Sodom, and in the absence of any other prospects, Lot's daughters—being "children" of Sodom in the moral-spiritual as well as natal-cultural sense—**made their father drink wine** (i.e., they got him drunk) and **lay with** him (vv. 33-35) The resulting conceptions and births of the sons **Moab** and **Ben-ammi** continue the tragic paradigm begun with Hagar and Ishmael, namely, the commission of sexual sin in the patriarchal family, which ultimately resulted in the existence of another ethnic group at enmity with Israel, in this case **the Moabites** and **the sons of Ammon** (the Ammonites; vv. 37-38). Later, Moab sought to have Balaam curse Israel (Nm 22–24), and the Ammonites were at war with Israel at various times during the period of the judges and the monarchy (Jdg 3:12-30; 10:6-18; 1Ch 19).

b. Struggles of Abraham's Household (20:1-16)

20:1-16. During his sojourn in the land of **Gerar**, located in the **Negev** of southern Israel, Abraham embarked on the same "chain of sin" previously described in 12:10-20 during his sojourn in Egypt. In contrast to this previous episode, however, in which the text occupies four vv. on Abraham's sinful motives (fear of famine, fear of death), in the present instance **Abraham** simply **said of Sarah his wife, She is my sister** (v. 2). Though the same lack of faith was undoubtedly motivating Abraham to lie again about his relationship, the narrative focuses in this instance on the *response* to Abraham's sin—and inevitably therefore on the contrast between Abraham's response and that of **Abimelech**. This then underscores God's grace and faithfulness in upholding His covenant with Abraham (whereas the focus on Abraham's depraved motives in chap. 12 underscores God's grace in *establishing* His covenant). **Abimelech**, king of the Philistines (see 26:1), conducted himself throughout this episode in **blameless** fashion, as he explicitly affirms to God who came **to** him **in a dream** and revealed to him that Sarah was **married** (v. 3). Indeed, as a result of Abimelech's **integrity** and **innocence** in this matter God **kept** him **from sinning**, that is, from going through with the marriage and thus unwittingly committing the sin of adultery. Although a pagan, Abimelech would likely have included the God of Abraham in his panoply of gods. Moreover, like the pagan sailors in the story of Jonah (Jnh 1:10-16), in this instance he demonstrated more righteous behavior than the follower of the one true God.

In a clear demonstration of both subservience to and respect for the God of Abraham, Abimelech arose **early** the next **morning**, taking the first opportunity to "right" the situation by summoning **Abraham** and confronting him with his sin (v. 9-10). In contrast to Abimelech's behavior Abraham refused to acknowledge his lie, seeking instead to excuse himself for two reasons that are (at best) only "half-truths" themselves, namely: (1) **because** he **thought** . . . **there** was **no fear of God** among the Philistines of Gerar (v. 11)—which Abimelech's behavior had clearly disproven; and (2) because Sarah **actually** was Abraham's **sister** (i.e., half sister) by the same **father** (v. 12) (However, this can hardly be claimed as a justifiable interpretation of a man introducing his wife as his "sister"!). To Abimelech's credit—and as an undoubted example to the reader—he did not press the matter, but rather, having done his part in confronting the sinner with his sin, he left the hoped-for conviction and repentance of Abraham as something to be worked about between the sojourner and his God. In fact Abimelech even went beyond what anyone could justly ask of him and freely gave **a thousand pieces of silver** to Abraham as a public **vindication** of Sarah's purity (v. 16). And who can blame Abimelech for giving vent to a slight bit of sarcasm when he told Sarah that he gave this money not to her husband but to her **brother**!

c. God's Faithfulness and Grace in Sanctification (20:17-18)

20:17-18. Notwithstanding Abraham's lack of repentance and generally unfaithful behavior, God demonstrated His own abiding and undiminished faithfulness by affirming His relationship with Abraham and underscoring the latter's role as "a prophet" (v. 7), a spokesman to God on behalf of others (even in the midst of his sin!). As a prophet he prayed for Abimelech's healing and the opening of **all the wombs** of the women of his **household**. The unconditional nature of God's covenant with Abraham is vividly borne out by God afflicting Abimelech and closing the wombs of his women in the first place, all for a sin that they had unwittingly (almost) committed against the object of God's parental love! For better or for worse God had made His commitment and would adhere to it, protecting and preserving His children for the sake of both His name as well as their ultimate recognition of His love (Dn 9:18-19; Mal 1:5).

9. Sovereignty of God in Blessing (21:1-34)

a. God's Sovereignty in Blessing Abraham and Sarah (21:1-8)

21:1-8. Despite the relative absence of any merit on Abraham's part, God **did for Sarah as He had promised** (v. 1; see 17:16, 21; 18:10, 14) and miraculously (since she was postmenopausal; see 18:11) enabled her to conceive and bear **a son**. As God had commanded him in 17:19, Abraham named his son **Isaac** (*yitschaq*), meaning "he laughs/will laugh," thus serving as a continual reminder to his parents of *their faithless reaction* to God's (ultimately) faithfully fulfilled promise (see 17:17; 18:12). At the same time—illustrating how God is able to "turn to good account" anything that sin or doubt has corrupted (cf. Rom 8:28)—Sarah highlighted the newly realized significance of Isaac's name as direct testimony to the experience of God's blessing by declaring, in a clearly intentional play on the name "Isaac" (*yitschaq*), **everyone who hears will laugh** [*yitschaq*] **with me** (v. 6), that is, they will laugh out of joy with her at the miracle of Isaac's birth.

b. God's Sovereignty in Blessing Hagar and Sarah (21:9-21)

21:9-14. Following Isaac's weaning (v. 8), when he would have begun to "step out" from under the direct supervision of his mother, the enmity that God had declared would exist between the promised son and Ishmael (see 16:12) inevitably began to materialize. Thus Ishmael would have been around 16 or 17 years old at this point. He was 13 a year before Isaac's birth (17:21, 27), with the weaning lasting for two or three years (1Sm 1:22-24; 2:11; 2 Macc 7:27; and in the Talmud in *b. Ketub.* 60b; *b. Yebam.* 43a). Ishmael acted in a **mocking** manner toward his younger brother. The word **mocking** is a deliberate example of wordplay, being identical to the name Isaac ("laughter") but used here in the negative sense of mockery. Furthermore, some ancient rabbis noted something more sinister than mere sibling teasing, rather identifying a variety of evil actions. The ancient Jewish commentary, called the Midrash (cf. Gen. Rab. 53:11) notes that in addition to mockery (Pr 22:18), the word was associated with sexual immorality (Gn 39:17), idolatry (Ex 32:6), and attempted murder (2Sm 2:14). Although no conclusive meaning is offered, the Midrash does accurately demonstrate that Ishmael was likely not engaged in innocent play. The strife between brothers in this passage reflects a common theme in Genesis (see comments on 4:8).

The matter, once known, brought distress to everyone in the family (another reminder of the consequences of sin and not waiting on God): to Isaac, as the object of Ishmael's mocking; to Sarah, who observed and fretted over Isaac's maltreatment; to Abraham, in whose eyes **the matter distressed** him **greatly**; and to Hagar and Ishmael, who were ultimately **sent . . . away** from Abraham's household for good and **wandered about in the wilderness of Beersheba** (v. 14). The expulsion of Ishmael distressed Abraham in particular because he loved Ishmael as was evident in his desire for him to be the heir of the promise (Gn 18:18) and his continuing desire to protect Ishmael as his son (21:11). Thus, it is a true act of sacrifice for Abraham to expel Hagar and Ishmael. Nevertheless, in comforting Abraham God assured him that He would act according to His own sovereignty—in determining that Isaac would be the heir to the Abrahamic promise and that Ishmael would become the father of a great nation (21:12-13).

21:15-21. When **the water** of Hagar and her son was **used up** and they resigned themselves to death in the desert, God sovereignly and graciously (being under no covenant obligation to them) attended to their needs by providing **a well of water** and reiterating His unconditional blessing to **make a great nation of** Ishmael (vv. 15-19; see 16:10). There is no textual indication as to whether **the angel of God** who **called to Hagar** was a theophany (as in 18:1-8). Significantly, the word for **God** is *Elohim*, reflecting His power but not His covenantal, relational name *Yahweh*. As with Isaac in the previous section, God's blessing in this instance is also underscored by a play on the son's name. The Hebrew for Ishmael is *yishma'el*, which introduces God's active involvement in v. 17, that is, **And God heard** (*vayishma' 'elohim*)—while at the same time hearkening back to God's earlier, identical provision for Hagar and Ishmael in 16:7-11.

c. God's Sovereignty in Blessing Abimelech and His People (21:22-34)

21:22-34. In anticipation—and as a reminder—of His ultimate goal of extending blessing (i.e., the blessing of *knowing* Him) more broadly among the Gentiles (12:3), God here prompted **Abimelech**, along with **Phicol, the commander of his army**, to make an oath of peace with Abraham on behalf of their people (the Philistines; vv. 22-24; cf. 26:1). This is especially significant when one considers that Abraham himself perversely misrepresented how a believer in the one true God should behave toward others, having gravely offended and sinned against Abimelech in the previous chapter. Yet contrary to human expectation Abimelech was drawn—not to Abraham—but to the **God** of Abraham, whom he affirmed was **with** Abraham **in all that** he did (v. 22). This affirmation indicates the beginning process of *evangelism*, that is, a budding awareness on the part of the Gentile king that Abraham's God, Yahweh, is indeed the one and only true God to whom he was obligated to submit. This is seen when comparing the statement of Abimelech and Phicol in v. 22 to their statement to Isaac in 26:28, in which they employed the *covenant name* of God. The oath of peace between Abimelech (and his people) and Abraham was then sealed by the transfer to Abimelech of **sheep and oxen** (v. 27). The Hebrew is not clear as to whether the **seven ewe lambs** (v. 28) were part of the gift mentioned in v. 27 or an additional gift. The significance of seven in Hebrew thought was completion—hence indicating the "completion," or "sealing," of the oath. The Hebrew word for "seven" and "oath," in fact, is the same (*sheva'*), as reflected in the name of the **well** (and eventually the town) over which the oath was made—i.e., **Beersheba** (*be'er sheva'*), which bears the complementary (not contradictory) meanings, "Well of the Oath" and "Well of the Seven." That Abraham alone gave gifts and not Abimelech suggests that Abraham was the supplicant in this treaty. Moreover, the entire narrative portrays Abraham as dwelling in Philistine land and therefore still awaiting the fulfillment of God's promises. The writer of Hebrews reflects this perspective, writing that Abraham "lived as an alien in the land of promise, as in a foreign land . . ." even as "strangers and exiles on the earth" (Heb 11:8-13).

10. The Pinnacle of Abraham's Faith (22:1-19)

The significance of this chapter is twofold. On the one hand, it gives an exemplary paradigm of faith—both Isaac's faith as well as Abraham's—at its strongest, and shows how the strength of true faith will inevitably find expression in outer *action*. On the other hand, the chapter presents one of the most vivid *types* (prophetic-symbol patterns) of the Messiah to be found anywhere in the OT. In fact this is the *only* episode identified in the NT as a type of Christ in both His death and resurrection (Heb 11:17-19). Even in long-standing Jewish tradition—which precludes any specifically Christological significance—the general spiritual-redemptive symbolism of this chapter is reflected in the practice of reading this chapter on the second day of Rosh Hashanah (the New Year festival), which commences the ten-day period of "awe and repentance," culminating in the Day of Atonement. The reason is that, in Jewish thought, Abraham's binding of Isaac became the supreme example of faithful obedience and self-sacrifice to God. Thus, Abraham's sacrifice is recalled in the *Remembrance* prayers of the Rosh Hashanah liturgy, asking God to "consider the binding with which Abraham our father bound his son Isaac on the altar, how he suppressed his compassion in order to perform Thy will with a perfect heart. So may Thy compassion overbear Thine anger against us; in Thy great goodness may Thy great wrath turn aside from Thy people" (Louis Jacobs, "Akedah" in *Encyclopaedia Judaica*, ed. Cecil Roth [Jerusalem: Keter Publishing, 1971], 2:480–81).

a. God's Call to Faith (22:1-2)

22:1-2. In response to God's call Abraham stated simply, **Here I am** (v. 1), indicating not simply that he was *present*, but more importantly that he was *available*, ready and willing to undertake whatever task God might assign to him. Others too affirmed their unconditional obedience, in each case expressed by the same simple statement, "Here I am" or "Here am I. Send me!" These include Jacob (46:2), Moses (Ex 3:4), Samuel (1Sm 3:4), and Isaiah (Is 6:8). And in each case the content of God's call or commission was revealed only *after* the individual had expressed his readiness to serve. Though this might seem a sharp change in Abraham's spiritual "fiber" as otherwise attested in the fiasco of chap. 20, we should recall that at least 13 years had passed between the present episode and the birth of Isaac in the previous chapter. During this period Abraham had ample time to reflect on God's omnipotence, faithfulness, and grace—all turning on His fulfillment of the pivotal promise of an heir—with the result that he now moved substantially forward in aligning his thoughts and actions with the righteousness that was long ago already reckoned as his (Gn 15:6).

The typology of this chapter, though culminating in the binding and imminent sacrifice of Isaac, begins in v. 2, and is centered in the epithets applied to Isaac, each one of which is likewise applied to Christ. Thus Jesus, like Isaac, is described as a **son**, and the Father willingly sacrificed him (Is 53:10; Jn 3:16; Ac 2:23). Isaac is described as Abraham's **only son**, but the Hebrew *yachid* should be translated "unique." (Also "only" is not a suitable translation because Ishmael also was a son of Abraham.) Similarly the Messiah is called the *monogenes* Son (Jn 1:14, 18; 3:16, 18; 1Jn 4:9). Though incorrectly translated as "only begotten," this word too has the sense of "unique" when applied to the Messiah. Just as Isaac was the object of his father's love, so too Jesus is described as the object of His Father's **love** (Mt 3:17; Lk 3:22). Also the name **Isaac**, like the name Jesus, was chosen by God and not the parents (Gn 17:19; Mt 1:21). This too was an extremely rare occurrence in Scripture. Thus, the collective force of these parallels establishes the typological link between Isaac and the Messiah.

b. Abraham's Expression of Faith (22:3-9)

22:3-5. Abraham arrived at the place of sacrifice **on the third day** (v. 4), the messianic significance being that this was not only the day on which he prepared to offer Isaac as a sacrifice but also the day on which "he also received him back as a type" (Heb 11:19), that is, as a type of the One who was likewise received back "on the third day" (Ac 10:40) as "the first fruits of those who are asleep" (1Co 15:20). Abraham's strong faith is noted in Heb 11:19 in that "he considered that God is able to raise [Isaac] even from the dead." So Abraham told **his young men** (i.e., servants, v. 5) that he and Isaac would **go** up the mountain to **worship and** then **return** (both verbs in Hb. are pl.). For this to happen, God had to be able not only to resurrect Isaac from the dead, but also to reconstitute him from the ashes of being offered as a **burnt offering**. The basis for Abraham's faith was God's unconditional promise in the immediately preceding chapter that "through Isaac your descendants shall be named" (21:12; cf. Heb 11:18). Since Isaac was not yet married, this could not happen if he remained dead.

22:6-9. Isaac had not yet been told what would happen, as is evident from his question, **Behold, the fire and the wood, but where is the lamb . . . ?** (v. 7). How difficult it must have been for Abraham to talk about (let alone undertake) what God had asked of him. Yet in response to Isaac's question Abraham stated with confident faith **God will provide for Himself the lamb for the burnt offering, my son** (v. 8). However, this translation contradicts the expectation that God would resurrect Isaac, which later is clearly the correct expectation in view of God's command that Isaac be offered "as a burnt offering" (v. 2), as well as the interpretation of this event given in Heb 11:19. The alternative explanation that Abraham is simply telling a "white lie" to Isaac, in order not to make him anxious, is also insufficient, since (1) lying is lying, and such a sin in the context of the present narrative exemplar of strong faith is incongruent, and (2) if this was what Abraham meant (and what Isaac understood), it is certainly surprising that Isaac did not ask where the lamb was when he was being tied to the altar. Actually Abraham was not referring to the future provision of a lamb at all. Keeping in mind that the same Hebrew verb form is used for the present as well as future tenses (see comments on 17:1-8), Abraham's answer may be literally rendered, "God is providing the lamb." This translation resolves any contradiction, for it is therefore to Isaac that Abraham was referring, that is, Isaac was the "lamb" God was providing. This understanding of Abraham's response further underscores the typological significance of this event by presenting yet another linkage between Isaac and Jesus, namely, the description of both as a **lamb** specifically provided by God (Jn 1:29; 1Co 5:7). Also of significance is that Isaac, like Jesus, was not forced to be a sacrifice. Just as Isaac was a willing sacrifice, so the Lord Jesus willingly undertook this role as placed on Him by His Father (Mk 10:45; Jn 10:18). Isaac was strong enough to carry the necessary amount of **wood** that would be used to consume him as a **burnt offering** (another typological connection to the wooden cross borne by Jesus), so he was strong enough to refuse being bound if he were so inclined. Also the verb translated **provide** in vv. 8 and 14 is the same verb meaning "to see" (*r-'-h*) that typically denotes God's assessment and/or provision of what is always *best*.

c. The Angel's Affirmation of Faith (22:10-19)

22:10-12. Having taken **the knife** in hand **to slay his son** (v. 10), and thus having psychologically passed the test of obeying God's command (this is the point of Heb 11:17-19), **the angel of the Lord** (i.e., a preincarnate appearance of the Son of God) called out to Abraham to stop. This affirmed his mature faith (**I know that you fear God, since you have not withheld your son . . . from Me**, vv. 11-12). That is not to say that the omniscient God did not know that Abraham feared Him. Rather, God's foreknowledge became actualized. As the medieval rabbinic theologian Nachmanides said, "At the beginning Abraham's fear of God was latent; it had not become actualized through such a great deed, but now it was known [by God] in actuality . . ." (Ramban–Nachmanides, "Bereishis, Genesis Part 1" in *Commentary on the Torah*, vol. 1, ed. R. Yaakov Blinder [Brooklyn, NY: Mesorah Publications, 2004], 503).

22:13-14. And the angel then provided **a ram** to be sacrificed **in the place of his son** (v. 13). As a result Abraham named that place **The Lord Will Provide** (v. 14). This phrase, for the same reason noted in the previous section, should properly be translated in the present tense, as a proverbial statement of general truth: "The Lord Provides" (lit., "The Lord sees"). This refers not just to what God will do but also to what He has just done and what He does generally. In the second part of v. 14 a later biblical editor, writing under the superintendence of the Holy Spirit before the close of the OT canon, inserted the comment **it is said to this day, In the mount of the LORD it will be** [or, is] **provided**. "The mount of the LORD" is Mount Moriah and this very mountain, where these events occurred, would later become the temple mount (22:2; 2Ch 3:1; Is 2:2). The offering on Mount Moriah is a vivid "shadow" of God the Father's "provision" of the one and only sacrifice that could ever take away sin: the sacrifice of His Son, Jesus the Messiah, the "seed" of Abraham (v. 18), who offered His blood on the heavenly altar, "one sacrifice for sins for all time" (Heb 10:12).

22:15-19. As a result of Abraham's faith, God reaffirmed the Abrahamic covenant, promising to **bless** Abraham and **greatly multiply [his] seed** (v. 17a). In this sentence, Abraham's seed is obviously to be taken in a collective sense, since they will be as numerous **as the stars of the heavens and as the sand . . . on the seashore**. Then, God promised that Abraham's **seed shall possess the gate of their** [lit., "his"] **enemies**, and in that **seed all the nations of the earth shall be blessed** (vv. 17b-18). This usage of "seed" appears to refer to an individual who will bless the whole world. This is evident in that the pronoun referring back to that seed is singular (lit., "shall possess the gate of *his* enemies," italics added). T. D. Alexander has correctly proposed that this reflects an oscillation from a collective use of the word "seed" in v. 17a to an individual sense in vv. 17b-18. His point is that although 22:17a uses "seed" in the collective sense, a new sentence begins in 22:17b (without a *vav consecutive*, typically used in Hebrew for a continuation of thought but instead here with a simple imperfect verb indicating the beginning of a completely new thought). This new sentence makes it likely that the word "seed" is being used in a new, individual sense. The significance of this is that this oracle looks forward to one particular descendant of Abraham who will rule over His enemies and bless the world. (T. Desmond Alexander, "Further Observations on the Term 'Seed' in Genesis," *Tyndale Bulletin* 48, no. 2 [1997]: 363-67). Paul recognized that this individual seed was a reference to the Messiah and fulfilled by Jesus of Nazareth (Gl 3:8, 16).

11. Family Matters (22:20–23:20)

a. Keeping Up with the Relatives (22:20-24)

22:20-24. This brief record of what **was told** to **Abraham** about the children born to his **brother Nahor**, and specifically the reference to Nahor's granddaughter **Rebekah**, serves as a link between the previous Abrahamic narratives and what follows. Thematically, since Rebekah was the only female descendant mentioned in this brief genealogy, it anticipated the death of Sarah in the next chapter and ensures a "gapless" transition to the next matriarch and thus the continuation of the descendants of Abraham and the safeguarding of the continued viability of the Abrahamic covenant. Theologically it anticipates Abraham's righteous desire not to find a wife for Isaac from among "the daughters of the Canaanites" (24:3; see v. 4), which in turn establishes the principle of not being spiritually "unequally yoked" as legislated in the Mosaic law (Dt 7:3-4; and see Ezr 9:1-2; Neh 13:27) and reiterated in the NT (1Co 7:39; 1Pt 3:7; cf. 2Co 6:14).

b. Mourning Sarah (23:1-2)

23:1-2. After living **one hundred and twenty-seven years . . . Sarah died in** the city of **Kiriath-arba**, so-named after Arba, the father of Anak (Jos 14:15; 21:11). To clarify the location of this city, which is about 19 miles (30.5 km) southwest of Jerusalem, a later editor has inserted the clarification, **that is, Hebron**, the name by which the city was generally known to the Israelites. This is also the burial site of Abraham (25:9), so this city has special significance for the Jewish people. It is also the burial site of Sarah (23:19), Isaac (39:29), Rebekah, Leah, and Jacob (49:31; 50:13; Ac 7:16), and is also the city from which David ruled for seven and a half years over Judah before being recognized as king by all twelve tribes (see 2Sm 5:3-5).

c. Purchasing the Family Burial Plot (23:3-20)

23:3-20. The rest of this chapter is devoted to a detailed—and at points even quite legally worded (esp. vv. 16-20)—description of the transaction by which Abraham purchased the **cave of Machpelah** (as **a burial site** for Sarah) and the surrounding **field** from **Ephron the Hittite** (vv. 9-10, 20). Why the narrative devotes almost an entire chapter to this transaction may seem puzzling since God had *already* deeded over to Abraham and his descendants the entire land of Canaan, including specifically the land of "the Hittite" (15:20). Considering Abraham's military prowess (see 14:14-16 and the comments on 14:1-16), he could simply (and justly) have taken the land by force. Had he done this, however, the sanctity and integrity of Sarah's burial site would almost certainly *not* have been respected by the other inhabitants of the land. In this chapter Abraham is thus an example of a believer living among and interacting with unbelievers who, by definition, do not share his faith presuppositions or worldview. Because Abraham realized that the Hittites did not recognize his divine right to the land, he did what was necessary to ensure that his possession of the land would be respected by going through the culturally accepted process of **commercial** transaction.

12. Finding Rebekah in Mesopotamia (24:1-67)

a. Abraham's Petition (24:1-9)

24:1-9. True to His promise of 12:2, **the LORD had blessed Abraham in every way** (v. 1). So, as Abraham drew nearer to the end of his life, he focused on accomplishing the one remaining task to ensure that the patriarchal "torch" would be passed on: finding **a wife** for Isaac. He charged **his servant** (in all likelihood his personal servant Eliezer of Damascus; see 15:2) **not [to] take a wife for** Isaac **from the daughters of the Canaanites** (v. 3), but rather from a family he knew had some predilection for the one true God, that is, his father's house in Mesopotamia (v. 4). Abraham's faith in the Lord is also seen in his statement to his servant that the choice of a proper wife did not depend on him, but rather on God who **will send His angel before** the servant (v. 7). In contrast to his spiritually immature leaving of the promised land to go to Egypt (12:10), Abraham here refused either to leave the land himself or to allow Isaac to leave. His reason was that **the LORD . . . took** him **from the land of** his **birth** to bring him into **this land** which was his and his **descendants**' by divine right. To leave Canaan would be to express a lack of faith in God's ability to provide. The servant **swore** to keep the charge of his master by **plac[ing] his hand under the thigh of his master** (v. 9). This was likely an ancient Near Eastern method of oath taking, similar to today's practice of raising the right hand.

b. God's Answer (24:10-49)

24:10-49. When the servant arrived at **the well of water** just outside **the city of Nahor** (v. 10), where Abraham's relatives lived, he asked the Lord to **grant** him **success** in finding the right wife for Isaac. The servant proposed a rather specific "test," that the **appointed** woman be the one who responded to his request for water by offering not only to give him a **drink**, but also of her own accord to **water** his **camels**. The servant had with him ten camels (v. 10), and the typical one-humped camel (*Camelus dromedarius*) found throughout the Middle East can drink between 25 and 40 gallons (100-150 liters) in one drink! After the servant turned directly to the Lord for help, the chosen woman made her appearance even **before he had finished speaking** (v. 15). This vividly illustrates the crucial point that God "knows what you need before you ask Him" (Mt 6:8). While **Rebekah**, described as a **girl** (v. 17; *na'arah* generally denotes an adolescent), **ran back** and forth with **her jar** from **the well** to **the trough** as she **drew** water **for all his camels** (Gn 24:19-20) . . . **the man was gazing at her in silence, to know whether the LORD had made his journey successful or not** (v. 21). Apparently the answer to his prayer had come so quickly, he needed a little time to process what was happening. Eventually, of course, he did perceive the clear answer to his prayer, and he responded in proper fashion with deep thanksgiving: **then the man bowed low and worshiped the LORD** (vv. 26-27). Rebekah then **ran** home and **told** her family **about these things**. Rebekah's **brother Laban** then **ran** back to the **spring** and took the servant to their **house**, where the **servant** related everything to **Laban** and her father **Bethuel**, emphasizing the sovereign role of **the LORD, the God of** his **master Abraham** throughout the matter (vv. 33-49).

c. The People's Response (24:50-67)

24:50-67. Laban and Bethuel['s] response to the servant's account of his mission (**The matter comes from the LORD; so we cannot speak to you bad or good** [v. 50]) was noncommittal. One must be careful not to infer from their affirmation of Yahweh's existence (**The matter comes from the LORD**) and even involvement in the matter that they are committed to Him as *their* God. The recognition of other peoples' god(s) was common throughout the Bible. Were He truly *their* God, they would certainly have spoken "good"—i.e., responded in the affirmative that Rebekah was God's choice. As it was, Laban and Bethuel were not opposed to the marriage (Isaac was, after all, a rather wealthy relative), and they initially acquiesced to the marriage, telling the servant to **take her and go** (v. 51). They apparently had second thoughts, however (vv. 55-56), and—probably hoping to reverse their acquiescence in "face-saving" fashion—they undertook the rather unusual move of summoning Rebekah to **consult her wishes** in the matter (vv. 57-58). She again demonstrated her exemplary character (and the propriety of God's choice) by stating simply, **I will go** (v. 58). This response indicates not just a willingness to recommit socially and geographically, but also theologically (to belief in Yahweh), as borne out both by her later actions (25:22) and that the very phrase **I will go** (*'elek*) likewise later expressed the recommitment of Ruth (Ru 1:16) to Naomi and her God. The servant then took her back to Isaac (vv. 61-66), who **took** her as **his wife, and he loved her** (v. 67).

The author records the blessing of Rebekah as a continuation of the theme of the "seed" begun in Gn 3:15. Just as the seed of the woman will crush the head of the serpent (3:15), so the seed of Abraham will rule over the gate of his enemies and bless all nations (22:17b-18). Here Rebekah's "seed" (mistranslated in v. 60 by the NASB as **descendants**) will one day **possess the gate of those who hate** Him (the Hb. uses the singular pronoun "Him," mistranslated as **them** in the NASB). Genesis deliberately shows the progress of that one special offspring, the Messiah, who will have dominion over His enemies and bless the world.

13. Transferring the Torch to Isaac (25:1-11)

a. Abraham's Affirmation of Isaac (25:1-6)

25:1-6. After Sarah's death Abraham **took another wife, whose name was Keturah** (v. 1), by whom he had six sons (vv. 2-4)—among them the ancestor of another future nation inimical to Israel, namely, **Midian** (cf. Nm 31 and Jdg 6). Though Abraham undoubtedly loved all these sons—as also **the sons of his concubines**—and **gave** them **gifts** (v. 6), he affirmed that **Isaac** was the heir of **all that he had** (v. 5).

b. Isaac and Ishmael's Burial of Abraham (25:7-10)

25:7-10. When Abraham died at the age of **one hundred and seventy-five . . . Isaac and Ishmael**, though estranged (16:12; 21:21; 25:18), came together in peace to bury their father alongside Sarah **in the cave of Machpelah**. This demonstrates that, at certain times, Ishmael acted contrary to his character (see 16:12). Moreover, it appears that Ishmael ultimately was able to reconcile himself to Isaac's status as heir to Abraham.

c. God's Affirmation of Isaac (25:11)

25:11. Isaac's assumption of the patriarchal role—not only as the leader of his father's household, but also as the mediator of God's unconditional promise (the Abrahamic covenant)—is here (as expected) affirmed by God, as indicated by the statement that **after the death of Abraham . . . God blessed his son Isaac**. This covenantal allusion to the language of 12:2 and 24:1 is further crystallized in 26:3-4, where God explicitly affirmed the application to Isaac (and his descendants in the line of promise) of all three provisions of the covenant (*land*—a defined location, the land of Israel, 12:1; *seed*—a distinct people, 12:2; and *blessing*—an authoritative moral standard, 12:3) as first expressed to Abraham in 12:1-3. The delineation of the promise through Isaac is also explicitly highlighted in several other Bible books (e.g., 1Ch 16:16; Ps 105:9; Rm 9:7; and Heb 11:18).

B. Descendants of Ishmael: A Locus of Conflict with God's People (25:12-18)

25:12-18. Although the Abrahamic promise—and hence the central narrative focus on the "path of redemption"—continues through Isaac, this brief presentation of the genealogy of Ishmael serves several important purposes. (1) It bears out the fulfillment of God's blessing of Ishmael, in which God had promised to make him the father of **twelve princes** (v. 16), to "multiply him exceedingly" and "make him a great nation" (cf. 17:20; see also 16:10; 21:13). (2) The concluding statement that Ishmael **settled in defiance of all his relatives** (v. 18) shows that despite uniting with Isaac to bury their father, the enmity that God had decreed would be instigated and perpetuated *by* Ishmael and his descendants toward "everyone" generally and "his brothers" in particular (see comments on 16:12) did indeed come to pass. (3) Perhaps this genealogy of Ishmael establishes the connection between Ishmael and his twelve sons with the Arabs of later biblical and postbiblical history. Some scholars have denied this connection, noting that Genesis includes nothing to link Ishmael to the Arab peoples and that it is the Qur'an that makes this association—not the Bible. However, possible biblical evidence for associating Ishmael with the Arabs is that Ishmael's second eldest son **Kedar** is identified with "Arabia" in Is 21:13-17 and Ezk 27:21. Other evidence to associate Ishmael with the Arab peoples is historical, with "Geshem the Arab" of Neh 6:1 being possibly mentioned in a fifth-century BC inscription as "king of Kedar," linking the Arabs with the second eldest son of Ishmael. Also Arabs, since the rise of Islam in the seventh century (2,700 years after Abraham) have maintained their descent from Ishmael, and Jewish and Christian tradition has generally accepted this.

C. Descendants of Isaac: Learning to Wait on God (25:19–35:29)

A new narrative "cycle" is introduced in 25:19, like every major narrative section in Genesis (except the first, the beginning of which is obvious), by the expression **these are . . . the generations of** (e.g., 5:1; 6:9; 10:1; 11:27; 25:19; 37:2) with the focus of attention being given not to the person named in the title (i.e., Isaac), but rather to that son in the next generation through whom the Abrahamic covenant is channeled (i.e., Jacob). Just as the previous narrative cycle focusing on Abraham and Isaac was followed by a brief genealogical "epilogue" devoted to Ishmael, the elder son who was not chosen as the covenant mediator, so too the present narrative cycle focuses on Jacob followed by a brief genealogical epilogue devoted to Esau (36:1–37:1). The focus in this narrative is primarily on the patriarchal growth process of *learning to wait on the Lord* (i.e., to do things in His way and in His time) in light of what He has already promised and accomplished. Jacob is another vivid example (like Adam and Eve, Cain, and Abraham) of a *believer* struggling to overcome his abiding depravity and live as he truly *is*: as the child of a perfect and loving Father who delights to interact with His children "face to face" (32:30).

1. Jacob and Esau: The Sons of Isaac (25:19-34)

a. Barrenness of Rebekah (25:19-21a)

25:19-21a. When **Isaac** married Rebekah he **was forty years old**, a relatively late age for a man during the biblical period to enter into his first marriage. The norm was to marry as teenagers—the early teens for women and the late teens for men (cf., e.g., the expression "wife of [one's] youth" [Pr 5:18; Is 54:6; Mal 2:14-15], in which the term "youth" [*ne'urim*] primarily denotes the teenage years; and in one of the earliest rabbinic statements on the subject, a man's preferred marriage age is explicitly set at 18 [*m. 'Abot* 5.21]). Nevertheless one may deduce from the example of Isaac that it is more important to marry the right person than to marry early—especially when one finds oneself, like Isaac, surrounded by a culture that is overwhelmingly "unfit" for one's self in the preeminent matter of faith. Like Sarai (11:30), Rebekah too **was barren**, though the response of the patriarch in each case—reflecting their spiritual maturity—is different. Abraham did nothing (at least nothing is stated in Scripture), whereas **Isaac prayed to the Lord . . . and the Lord answered him and Rebekah his wife conceived** (v. 21). God's answer was not immediate, for Rebekah gave birth 20 years after their marriage, when Isaac was 60 (v. 26). This further bears out, in any event, the important biblical principle already clearly set forth in 4:25; 20:17-18; and 21:1-2 that the Lord alone ultimately enables a woman to conceive (or who "opens" and "closes" the womb), for "children are a gift of the Lord" (Ps 127:3).

b. Birth of Jacob and Esau (25:21b-26)

25:21b-26. Not knowing that she was pregnant with twins, and concerned by the movement that she felt **within her**, Rebekah **went to inquire of the Lord** (v. 22). In response God indicated not only that there were **two nations** (i.e., twin *sons* from whom will arise two peoples) **in** her **womb**, but also that **the older shall serve the younger** (v. 23). By this statement God was declaring that by His own sovereign will—and in contrast to the convention of recognizing the eldest son as preeminent—Jacob and all his descendants (i.e., the "nation" that Jacob/Israel would later become) will be privileged to be the benefactors and mediators of the Abrahamic covenant. The preference of the younger for the older is a common theme in Genesis. Some additional examples are that Abel was preferred over Cain (Gn 4:1-8), Isaac over Ishmael (Gn 21:1-21), Rachel over Leah (Gn 29:30-31), Joseph over all his brothers (Gn 37:4), Perez over Zerah (Gn 38:29-30), and Ephraim over Manasseh (Gn 48:13-20). To make the point that God's choices are based on His own sovereign will and not on human merit Paul cited this divine response in Rm 9:11-12: "though the twins were not yet born and had not done anything good or bad." God's response to Rebekah was not merely *prophetic* (i.e., looking forward to the national ascendancy of Israel over Edom) but rather *declarative* (i.e., His decision for the twins as of that moment). Paul emphasized that God spoke with respect to *the twins* before they were even born or had done anything. Hence, the sole explanation for this is God's sovereign election. God made the same point in His statement through Malachi, "I have loved Jacob; but I have hated Esau" (Mal 1:2-3; see comments on Rm 9:6-13 and Mal 1:2-3). This refers not to God's *emotional* attitude toward the two, but rather to His simple, sovereign *choice* of one and rejection of the other (see also Gn 29:30-31; with respect to His *emotional* orientation, God loves everyone; see Jn 3:16).

c. Sale of Esau's Birthright (25:27-34)

25:27-34. Though spiritually mature and of commendable character, Isaac was not perfect.

Here he fell into the common parental trap of favoring one child with whom he had more in common over another. This pattern was carried over by his son Jacob, both toward his own children (preferring Joseph and Benjamin over the other ten) as well as in his marital relationships (favoring Rachel over Leah). Thus, **Isaac loved** (i.e., preferred) **Esau** (v. 28), who was **a skillful hunter . . . because he [Isaac] had a taste for game**. But **Rebekah**, falling into the same parental trap, **loved** (i.e., preferred) her more **peaceful**, tent-dwelling son **Jacob**. This parental split favoritism no doubt later encouraged that "distance" between Jacob and Esau that prompted the former to solicit the latter's **birthright** (v. 31) for a bowl of **stew**. The strife between brothers that begins in this passage continues throughout the Jacob narrative and reflects a common theme in Genesis (see comments on 4:8).The birthright under dispute is distinct from the paternal *blessing*; see 27:30-46 and 49:8-12. Esau, of course, was also at fault for having **despised** (not having valued) **his birthright** (v. 34), and in infamous commemoration of his selling it for a bowl of **red** (*'adom*) **lentil stew**, his descendants are identified ever afterward by the label **Edom** (*'edom*, "red [people]", v. 30).

2. Isaac: Struggles of a Patriarch (26:1-33)

This chapter presents Isaac in the role of patriarchal head and trustee of God's promise. Carrying out this responsibility leads to a variety of struggles in Isaac's life. He must confront his lack of faith in God's protection as he feared identifying Rebekah as his wife to Abimelech, deal with quarrels over wells of water with locals in the land of promise, and make a covenant with Abimelech, king of the Philistines.

a. Struggling to Trust in God's Promises: Isaac Lies about Rebekah (26:1-17)

26:1-17. As soon as Isaac adopts his role as patriarchal head and trustee of God's promise, he reprises the failures of his father Abraham, who misrepresented his relationship with Sarah on two occasions (12:10-20; 20:1-18). This account exhibits several striking parallels to the first major episode involving Abraham in the same role (in chap. 12). (1) Each was confronted at the outset with **a famine in the land** (v. 1; cf. 12:10a), which, when occurring in the promised land, was always a test of faith. (2) Each responded to the famine by moving south, with a view to going **down to Egypt** (v. 2, cf. 12:10b). (3) God sovereignly affirmed His covenant with each man, referring explicitly to the three provisions of **land**, seed (**descendants**), and blessing—for the patriarch personally as well as ultimately for **all the nations of the earth** (vv. 3-4; cf. 12:1-3). (4) Following God's affirmation of His covenant, each patriarch falsely said of his wife, **She is my sister**, out of fear that the local men would **kill** him on account of her beauty (v. 7; cf. 12:11-13, 19). (5) The **king** of that place deduced the lie and responded—quite to the contrary of the patriarch's fearful expectation—by affirming their marriage, rebuking the patriarch for lying about it, and issuing a royal "charge" to ensure their protection (and, in Abram's case, safe departure from Egypt) (vv. 10-11; cf. 12:19-20). The point of these parallels, centering on the patriarchs' less-than-perfect faith and expressed sin, is to highlight that Isaac did not merit being the covenant recipient. It thus emphasizes the unconditional nature of the covenant as well as the faithfulness and sovereignty of God in maintaining it.

Of special significance is God's statement in v. 5 that **Abraham . . . kept My charge, My commandments, My statutes and My laws**. Though God did command Abraham to do a *few* things, such as immigrating to Canaan (12:1), adopting circumcision (17:10), and sacrificing Isaac (22:2), such actions would hardly seem to square with this emphatic "piling up" of specifically legal terminology. Indeed, this is the first time in Scripture that any one of these four specific terms (whether pl. or sg.) is used, and after this they are applied almost exclusively to the Mosaic law, especially when they are used together (cf. Dt 11:1). This Mosaic legal terminology in God's statement is intended to teach the reader that by his faith Abraham was credited with the righteousness of perfect law-keeping. It is precisely this point, in fact, that Paul the apostle made in Rm 3:31, as an introduction to his extended discussion of Abraham's righteousness: "Do we then nullify the [Mosaic] Law through faith? May it never be! On the contrary, we establish the Law [i.e., we prove what the law teaches]."

b. Struggling to Live with Sinful Men: Isaac Quarrels with the Men of Gerar (26:18-25)

26:18-25. The patriarchal parallels continue. Abram's "chain of sin" in 12:10-20 was followed in chap. 13 by the depiction of strife between Abram's herdsmen and Lot's herdsmen over the land's resources. So too in this passage **the herdsmen of Gerar quarreled with the herdsmen of Isaac** (v. 20) over water, a preciously rare Middle Eastern commodity. To his credit, though Isaac's entourage undoubtedly outnumbered and overpowered the Canaanite herdsmen (since he would have inherited the formidable fighting force of Abram; described in 14:14-15), he patiently moved on from each disputed site until finding a location that the herdsmen **did not quarrel over** (vv. 21-22). God subsequently affirmed His covenant protection and provision for Isaac (v. 24) just as He had done for Abram (13:14-17; 15:1). In response the patriarch Isaac **built an altar . . . and called upon the name of the LORD** (v. 25).

c. Struggling to Recognize the Sovereignty of God: Isaac Makes a Covenant with Abimelech (26:26-33)

26:26-33. Again, just as Abimelech initiated a covenant with Abraham in chap. 20, despite having been gravely offended by the patriarch, so too in this section **Abimelech** initiated a covenant with Isaac (vv. 26-31). This was despite Isaac offending the king in precisely the same way (i.e., by almost allowing Abimelech to be unknowingly drawn into the sin of adultery with the patriarch's wife, 20:3-4)!

The present episode took place at least 75 years after the events in chap. 20, so this **Abimelech** may be different from the one who interacted with Abraham. The name "Abimelech" (meaning "father of [the] king" or "Melech is a father") may be intended as a Philistine throne name, like "pharaoh" for the king of Egypt (also in the heading of Ps 34 where the Philistine king Achish is called "Abimelech"). On the other hand, this may be the same **Abimelech** who interacted with Abraham, as suggested by the following observations: (1) **Phicol**, the name of **the commander of his army**, is the same in both accounts (v. 26; see 21:22); (2) the life span of man at this point was in the 200-year range (Terah died at age 205, Abraham at 175, and Isaac at 180), which is consistent with a reign of 80-plus years; and (3) the initiative and wording of Abimelech's **covenant** with Isaac (vv. 28-29) is similar—at points even identical—to that expressed by Abimelech to Abraham in 21:22-23.

More importantly this passage stands as a testimony to God's absolute, gracious sovereignty in fulfilling the mission of God to bless even the Gentiles, for here, as in chap. 21, the patriarch failed to exhibit the confident trust and righteous behavior of a believer in the one true God—even common human decency, doing what most people in general know "ought not to be done" (see 20:9). And yet in both instances Abimelech, the one most directly sinned *against*, affirmed not only a covenant of peace with Isaac who, by his irresponsible actions, hindered the extension of God's blessings to the Gentiles, but also the supreme sovereignty and gracious character of Isaac's God! Indeed, the possibility that Abimelech's appreciation of, and perhaps *faith in*, the one true God had been deepening since his encounter with Abraham is suggested by his use of the general term for "God" (*'elohim*) in his encounter with Abraham (21:22-23). But here Abimelech referred to God by His covenant name "Yahweh" (*yhwh*) in his encounter with Isaac (26:28-29).

In terms of blessing the nations through Abraham's "seed" today (Gn 12:1-3; 22:18; 26:4-5), God calls believers to share the good news of salvation in Jesus primarily for their own sakes, giving them the privilege of showing their love and gratitude to the Lord as the Church fulfills its redemptive mandate (Mt 28:18-20). Yet the work of salvation is His alone, and regardless of what one does or does not do, God's purposes *will* be accomplished, and each one who has "been predestined according to His purpose" (Eph 1:11) will ultimately be drawn to Him (cf. Jer 31:3; Jn 6:44, 65).

3. Jacob: Successor of Isaac (26:34–35:29)

The Jacob narrative is told in three narrative sections, determined by Jacob's presence or absence from the land of promise. The first shows Jacob in the promised land, striving with his brother Esau (26:34–28:9). The second depicts Jacob outside the land of promise, striving with his uncle Laban (28:10–31:55). The third part of the Jacob narrative records Jacob's return to the promised land, when his striving with both Esau and God will finally be resolved (32:1–35:29). The purpose of these three narratives is to emphasize the sovereign choice of God in granting His promise to Jacob.

a. In the Land: Striving with Esau (26:34–28:9)

The first part of the Jacob narrative, when he is in the land, striving for the blessing with his brother Esau, has three sections. It begins with a prologue about Esau's marriages to foreign women, is followed by the body of the story, depicting the strife about the blessing, and concludes with an epilogue, returning to Esau's further marriages to foreign women.

(1) Prologue: Esau Marries Foreign Women (26:34-35)

26:34-35. The story of Jacob's deception of Isaac resulting in Jacob being blessed instead of Esau opens with a prologue about the two marriages of Esau. In both cases, Esau married pagan Hittite women, rather than returning to Mesopotamia to find a bride from among his relatives. These marriages **brought grief to Isaac and Rebekah**. The story of Jacob's deception of Isaac also concludes with an epilogue about Esau's additional marriages (28:8-9), forming a frame around this narrative. For the significance of this narrative framing, see 28:8-9 and comments on 28:6-9.

(2) Body: Jacob Strives for a Blessing (27:1–28:5)

27:1-46. The story of Isaac blessing Jacob emphasizes the transference of the patriarchal blessing. This single narrative section (26:34–28:9) uses the word "blessing" in either a noun or verb form 28 times in the NASB. As a background to this present narrative, it begins with Esau selling his birthright to Jacob for a bowl of stew (25:29-34). The birthright appears to have included the blessing of the firstborn. For this reason, Heb 12:16-17 correctly equates the birthright with the blessing.

Now that Isaac had grown **old** (at least 100, since Esau was born when Isaac was 60 [see 25:26] and was married prior to this at 40 [26:34]) and **his eyes** were **too dim to see**, he decided that it was to time to pass on the patriarchal blessing **before** he died (27:4). Although Isaac lived on for many more decades, seeing all 12 of his grandsons by Jacob (see 35:22b-27), this was now the crucial moment when the "path of redemption"—the genealogical line that would carry on the Abrahamic covenant—was decided, since preeminence in the covenant was bound up with the patriarchal blessing (see also 49:8-12). Since Isaac intended to bless Esau, it may be that Rebekah had not yet revealed to her husband God's birth oracle, indicating His choice of "the younger" son over "the older" (25:23). Rebekah's silence is consistent with the two parents each favoring different sons. However, it is more likely that Isaac knew of the birth oracle and of Esau's sale of the birthright but was choosing to ignore these facts in granting the blessing.

So Rebekah, rather than trusting God to accomplish His purposes, when overhearing Isaac's intention, initiated a plot to deceive her husband into blessing her favored son Jacob instead (27:5-13). At Rebekah's direction, Jacob succeeded in stealing the blessing by presenting himself as Esau to the touch and smell of his blind father. He used the deceptive stratagem of wearing Esau's clothes and counterfeiting Esau's hairy arms by wearing goat skins (27:15-17). When his brother found this out, he pointed out that **Jacob** (whose name means "he supplants" had again lived up to his name, **for he has supplanted me these two times** (referring to Jacob trading red lentil stew for Esau's birthright [25:29-34] and then to deceiving Isaac into granting the patriarchal blessing, v. 36). When Esau's plan to avenge himself on Jacob by **kill[ing]** him was **reported to Rebekah** (v. 42), she urged her favored son to take refuge with her **brother Laban** until Esau's **fury** would subside (v. 44).

Readers often see this story through the eyes of Esau—emphasizing Jacob's culpability in deceiving his father and stealing the blessing. Nevertheless, the narrator wants to emphasize that all four parties to this story are guilty. Isaac and Esau are guilty of deliberately overlooking God's intended recipient of the blessing. Isaac chose to ignore Esau's sale of the birthright and the birth oracle. Esau chose to ignore that he willingly sold his birthright. Rebekah and Jacob are guilty of deliberately deceiving to achieve their goal of blessing. Rebekah deceived her beloved husband by preparing savory food and using clothing and hairy goat skins to present Jacob as a counterfeit Esau to blind Isaac. Jacob somewhat begrudgingly went along with his mother's scheming to achieve his goal of being blessed. Jacob's deception was wrong not because he stole the blessing—it was rightfully his because he had already purchased it. Rather, his deception was wrong because it lacked faith in God to accomplish His will without Jacob's human deceit and manipulation. Thus, God, who had sovereignly decreed that "the older shall serve the younger" (25:23), accomplished His sovereign purpose despite human failings. Once again, the blessing of God was unmerited but still given an act of divine grace and election.

Though Rebekah's deception of Isaac was clearly condemnable, she was not a completely ill-natured person, and—no doubt feeling guilty over what she had done—her words and actions in vv. 45-46 evince a tender concern for her ailing husband. Rather than informing Isaac of his favored son's intention to kill his brother, which would undoubtedly have caused the patriarch great distress (by the phrase **you both** [v. 45] she is probably referring to Jacob and his frail father, not Esau), she exhorted him to send Jacob away for the single purpose (not *pretense*, since the goal is valid—even spiritually requisite) of finding a wife among their relatives back in Mesopotamia.

Although the narrator never explicitly condemned Jacob's deceitfulness, the events of Jacob's life show that, by manipulating his father instead of trusting God, he brought suffering to himself and others. First, Jacob, a homebody, now had to flee his home. Second, as the favorite son of Rebekah, he never saw his beloved mother again. Third, Jacob would be exploited by his uncle Laban even as he had taken advantage of Esau. Fourth, even as his father's blindness was a veil to enable Jacob to deceive, so Laban used a veil over Leah's face to deceive Jacob (note how both Isaac and Jacob say they were deceived, 27:35; 29:25). Fifth, just as Jacob deceived his father using Esau's garments, so his sons would deceive him using Joseph's garments (37:32). Sixth, Jacob was miserable at the end of his life (47:9) in contrast to both Abraham (25:8) and Isaac (35:28-29) who both appeared to have been satisfied with life when they died.

28:1-5. In response to Rebekah's urging, and no doubt out of similar concern on his part, Isaac **charged** Jacob to go to **Paddan-aram** (Upper Mesopotamia, southeastern modern Turkey), **to the house of** his maternal grandfather **Bethuel**, and **take to** himself **a wife from the daughters of Laban**, his uncle. The reason Isaac gave is the same as that given by Abraham in 24:3, namely, that he **not take a wife from the daughters of Canaan** (28:6; i.e., that he not be unequally "yoked" in faith; cf. 2Co 6:14 and see comments on 22:20-24).

(3) Epilogue: Esau Marries Foreign Women (28:6-9)

28:6-9. The story of the deception of Isaac began with a prologue about Esau marrying pagan women and bringing grief to his parents (26:34-35). Here, the narrative of the deception concludes with an epilogue about Esau's additional marriages. It says that when Esau saw the displeasure his parents had with his first foreign wives, rather than repent, he **went to Ishmael, and married** other pagan wives, in order to further annoy his father. The point of framing the deception narrative with Esau's pagan marriages is to show that despite Jacob receiving the blessing by deception, Esau was distinctly unworthy of the blessing in his unwillingness to maintain the purity of the seed.

b. Outside the Land: Striving with Laban (28:10-31:55)

The second part of the Jacob narrative depicts Jacob outside the land and striving with his uncle Laban. This section demonstrates how God cared for Jacob despite the deceitful and dishonest actions of Laban. In a sense, the narrative here shows how God taught Jacob a lesson for his own disreputable behavior. If Jacob was guilty of deceitful behavior, now by the hand of Laban he would learn what it was like to be at the other end of trickery and dishonesty.

(1) Jacob's Journey (28:10-22)

28:10-15. The Jacob/Laban story begins with Jacob's journey to Mesopotamia and God's assurance that His promise would be the guiding principle of the entire story. On his way to Paddan-aram via **Haran**, Jacob camped for the night at **a certain place** known by the Canaanites as **Luz** (see v. 19), which he called **Bethel**, about 10.5 miles (17 km) north of Jerusalem. As he leaves the land of Israel, Jacob dreamed that he saw **a ladder** bridging **the earth** and **heaven**, with **angels of God** (not "*the* angels of God") **ascending and descending on it** (v. 12), representing the ongoing activity of the angels on Jacob's behalf. Likely, the ascending angels represent those of the land of Israel, who had protected Jacob while he was in the land, and the descending angels represent those who operate outside the land, and will protect Jacob in his travels. The **Lord**, who was standing **above** the ladder, affirmed to Jacob all three provisions of the promise (Abrahamic covenant): **the *land*** (of Canaan), ***descendants*** who will **be like the dust of the earth**, and *blessing* of **all the families of the earth** through his **descendants** (lit., "seed," vv. 13-14, emphasis added).

28:16-22. In response to the dream, when he **awoke from his sleep**, Jacob affirmed God's presence in that **place**. Therefore he marked it as a sacred place by anointing his **stone** pillow with **oil**. He concluded with a **vow** (vv. 20-22) that **if God** (1) would **be with** him and **keep** him safe **on** his **journey**, (2) **give** him **food to eat**, (3) **give** him **garments to wear**, and (4) bring him back **to** his **father's house in safety, then the Lord** (Yahweh, the covenant God) would **be** his **God** (v. 21). From this point forward until his return from Paddan-aram, Jacob never calls Yahweh his God but always identifies Him as the God of Abraham and/or Isaac (this suggests that Jacob had not yet come to saving faith in the Lord, showing that God's choices do not depend on human understanding or merit).

(2) Jacob's Marriages (29:1-30)

29:1-14. The second part of the Jacob/Laban story is about Jacob's marriages and Laban's deceitful behavior toward him. Jacob eventually arrived at his destination of Paddan-aram (see 28:2), where he encountered **three flocks of sheep** and their shepherds by **a well** (29:2). After greeting the shepherds and learning they were from **Haran**, the city of his uncle **Laban**, Jacob issued them a mild rebuke for allowing their flocks to lie around (v. 7) when they should still be grazing (though likely there would be little to graze in the environs of the well). Since the shepherds had also told Jacob that Laban's daughter **Rachel** was on her way to the well **with her father's** (i.e., Laban's) **sheep**, his rebuke of the shepherds and urging that they **water the sheep, and go, pasture them** was likely motivated by a desire to make it easier for his cousin to get through to the well with her own flock. When **Rachel** arrived, **Jacob** rolled **the stone from the mouth of the well and** watered her sheep. Jacob's own mother Rebekah had industriously watered the camels of Abraham's servant when he was sent to find a bride from the same family for Isaac (24:20). As an appropriate greeting for his **relative**, **Jacob** also **kissed** (but did not embrace) **Rachel** (v. 11), just as he subsequently **embraced** . . . **kissed** his uncle Laban (v. 13).

29:15-30. After staying with Laban for a month (v. 14), Jacob fell in love with Rachel, and Laban agreed to **give her to** him as his wife in return for **seven years** of service. When this **time is completed**, however, Laban deceived Jacob by giving him **Leah**, whom Jacob did not recognize because it was **evening** (v. 23) and because she would have been veiled. This is an example of retributive justice since Jacob had previously deceived his blind father (27:1-29). Nevertheless, Laban is not thereby exonerated since he deliberately and unfairly deceived Jacob. The strife between relatives Jacob and Laban, continuing throughout the narrative, is a common theme in Genesis (see comments on 4:8). After working another **week** (seven years) Jacob was then given **Rachel**, whom **he loved . . . more than Leah** (lit., "preferred over Leah"). This section demonstrates that God would indeed discipline Jacob for his scheming but still fulfill all His promises. The discipline is evident in the fair retribution Jacob experiences, living with his even more deceitful uncle. But the promise is also evident, as Leah, the unwanted wife, actually becomes the primary matriarch of Israel.

(3) Jacob's Children (29:31–30:24)

29:31–30:24. The third part of the Jacob/Laban story pertains to the birth of Jacob's children while working for Laban. It begins with the expression **the Lord saw** (see comments on 1:4-5) setting up the expectation that God was about to do something for the benefit of the one whom God has seen. In this case the Lord saw **Leah**, who in most translations is described as being **unloved** (29:31). The translation of v. 30, **he loved Rachel more than Leah**, sets up a contradiction, for Leah's being loved less is not the same as her being "unloved." In the Hebrew text, however, there is no contradiction, for the adjective describing Leah in v. 31 can also mean "unpreferred" (*shenu'ah* from *sh-n-'*), just as its antonym used in v. 30 can also mean "preferred" (*ye'ehav* from *'-h-b*). These words "unpreferred" and "preferred" are the only ones that make sense in the present context. Thus v. 30 says Jacob *preferred* Rachel over Leah, whereas v. 31 says Leah was *unpreferred*. Therefore, God graciously acted for the benefit of Leah and opened **her womb**, after which she bore Jacob's first four sons (vv. 31-35)—the fourth of whom, **Judah**, would be the one through whom the greatest provision of the Abrahamic covenant was mediated (49:8-12). Of Jacob's other eight sons, two more were born by Leah (**Issachar** and **Zebulun**, 30:18, 20), and two each by **Leah's maid Zilpah** (**Gad** and **Asher**, 30:11, 13), Rachel (**Joseph**, 30:24 and, in 35:18, Benjamin), and **Rachel's maid Bilhah** (**Dan** and **Naphtali**, 30:6, 8).

Besides recounting how the 12 sons of Jacob were born, the purpose of this story is to show that the promise of God would be obtained through God's gracious gift, not human scheming. In this story, Rachel has what Leah yearns for—Jacob's love. Leah has what Rachel longs for—children. As a result, all sorts of human manipulations, schemes, and tensions ensue to obtain that which is desired. Yet, whatever is received, is of grace. Hence, the story culminates with the words **God gave heed to Leah** (30:17) and **God remembered Rachel** (30:22), indicating God's blessing comes from grace, not human machinations. This foreshadows God's gracious election of the nation of Israel, whom God chose and loved "not . . . because you were more in number than any of the peoples . . . but because the Lord loved you and kept the oath which He swore to your forefathers" (Dt 7:7-8).

(4) Jacob's Prosperity (30:25-43)

30:25-26. The fourth part of the Jacob/Laban story reveals how the Lord gave Jacob prosperity despite Laban's efforts to cheat him. After the birth of **Joseph**, **Jacob** informed his uncle **Laban** of his desire to return to his **own country** (Canaan, v. 25). Laban, however, urged Jacob to stay, observing that the LORD had blessed him on Jacob's account (v. 27)—providing yet another example of God fulfilling His promise to "bless those who bless" Abraham and his descendants in the line of promise (12:3). Although Laban had not treated Jacob with honesty, it was merely by his association with Jacob in his household that caused God's blessing to "spill over" onto Laban.

30:27-30. Laban's recognition that the Lord had blessed him was based not on personal faith in the one true God, but rather on divination. Laban's words **I have divined** do not merely refer to "discovering" something "by intuition or insight," as the English verb *to divine* is often used, but in fact to the pagan religious practice of "reading" livers, observing the flight of birds, and so forth. This is later specifically condemned by God in the law given to Israel through Moses (Lv 19:26; Dt 18:10; cf. 2Kg 17:17). However, God's blessing of those who bless His covenant family does not depend on the nature of their faith. This reflection of God's grace and the unconditional nature of His covenant are evident all the more in His blessing of the covenant family itself.

30:31-36. The patriarch Jacob agreed to stay on the condition that his wages be culled from all **the speckled and spotted** among Laban's goats and sheep, as well as **every black lamb among** Laban's flock (v. 32). Since these colorings would normally represent a minority of the flock, Laban readily accepted Jacob's terms. Not satisfied with the unlikelihood that Jacob would then receive many sheep, Laban unscrupulously removed the speckled and spotted animals and transported them **three days journey** away from Jacob (vv. 35-36). This would make it far less likely for the remaining animals to give birth to speckled, spotted, and black ones.

30:37-43. Jacob responded with an elaborate process of intermittently placing freshly peeled **rods of poplar and almond and plane trees** before the animals while they mated. This was based on the commonly held but completely false view that whatever an animal sees while mating will cause its offspring to look similarly. Jacob was still not trusting completely in the sufficiency of God's covenant provision and continued his behavioral pattern of seeking to better his circumstances through his own maneuverings. Jacob's behavior shows the degree of his human striving to attain what God had otherwise promised to bestow in His own sovereign power and grace. Nevertheless, the process seemingly worked because, having looked at the striped bark while mating, **the flocks brought forth striped, speckled, and spotted** animals (v. 39). Ultimately, Jacob does not credit his own manipulation for the success but attributes it to God, saying "God has taken away your father's livestock and given them to me" (31:9).

God granted prosperity to Jacob, even as He did for Abraham (12:16) and Isaac (26:12-14). Thus, the passage demonstrates God's faithfulness to His promises despite the scheming and opposition of Laban. This account foreshadows Israel's experience in Egypt. Just as Jacob wanted to return to his land (30:25), so would Israel (Ex 3:7). Even as Laban was reluctant to let him go because Jacob's service was useful to him (Gn 30:26), so Pharaoh would be reluctant to allow Israel to leave (Ex 1:14). Furthermore, just as Jacob's abundance literally "teemed" (Gn 30:43, translated as **became exceedingly prosperous**), so Israel would also "teem" with people (Ex 1:12, translated "spread out"). Hence, the promise of God to His people, personified in Jacob, would succeed despite opposition.

(5) Jacob's Flight (31:1–32:2)

31:1-16. The fifth and final part of the Jacob/Laban story recounts Jacob's flight from his uncle's house (31:1-55). This section of the narrative begins with why Jacob fled (31:1-16). The relationship between Jacob and Laban had deteriorated because the expected minority of stripped, speckled, and spotted sheep and goats, as well as black lambs, turned out to be the vast majority of new animals born to Laban's flocks. This greatly enhanced Jacob's wealth at the expense of Laban's. Though this may seem to contradict Laban's affirmation in the previous chapter that God had blessed him on Jacob's account (30:27), this new turn of circumstances was completely consistent with (and an early example of) God's accompanying covenant promise to curse "the one who curses [lit., 'slights'] you" (12:3); for as Jacob told his wives Rachel and Leah, **Your father has cheated me and changed my wages ten times** (31:7). This refers to the time following their agreement of 30:31-34, according to which Jacob was to have *all* the striped, speckled, and spotted sheep and goats, as well as black lambs. Then becoming dissatisfied with this arrangement, Laban went back on his word and told Jacob that only **the speckled** would **be** his **wages**; and **then**, when **all the flock brought forth speckled**, Laban changed again and told Jacob that only **the striped** would **be** his **wages** (31:8). In this way Jacob observed, **God has taken away** Laban's **livestock and given them to me**. This bears out not only the covenant paradigm of "cursing for slighting," but also raises the expectation that He will curse the one who curses in much the same way as he sought to curse the covenant family. Jacob's eyes were being slowly opened to the true character and covenant love of the Lord, for he affirmed that **the God of** his **father has been with** him (v. 5) and protected him from being **hurt** economically (v. 7). Despite his elaborate undertaking at animal husbandry, Jacob did not attribute the accumulation of **striped, speckled, and mottled** livestock to anything but the activity of God (vv. 11-12). Thus in obedience to God's command to him **in a dream** and because of the enmity between him and Laban, Jacob and his household prepared to return to the land of Canaan (vv. 13-16).

31:17-30. The next section describes Jacob's actual flight. The cycle of deception—contrasted with God's unmitigated blessing—continued as Jacob led **away all his livestock** and departed from **Paddan-aram** with his household **to go to the land of Canaan**, when **Laban** was distracted with the need **to shear his flock** (vv. 17-19). A key verb that underscores, both explicitly and implicitly, the theological immaturity and sin of the three major figures in this episode (Jacob, Rachel, and Laban) is the verb "to steal" (*ganab* from the root *g-n-b*), employed here eight times (vv. 19, 20, 26, 27, 30, 32, 39 [twice]). This is the same verb God used in the eighth commandment against stealing (see Ex 20:15). **Rachel stole** Laban's **household idols** (v. 19), and in v. 20 **Jacob** stole the heart of Laban (lit., marg. reading, which is often paraphrased as **deceived**, including NASB). There is a subtle irony here, for in the immediately following statement that **Jacob deceived Laban . . . by not telling him that he was fleeing**, one might assume that the "stealing" of Laban's "heart" centered in the surreptitious removal of his **daughters** (Rachel and Leah) and grandchildren. Laban himself seems to have suggested this in vv. 26-27. However the parallelism between this reference to "stealing" Laban's "heart" (v. 20) with the reference to "stealing" Laban's "idols" (v. 19b) suggests that his heart was more attached to his idols than his own flesh and blood! And indeed Laban was clearly preoccupied with recovering his idols. Laban ultimately **caught up with Jacob** (v. 25) and made four specific accusations. First, he accused Jacob of stealing his heart (**deceiving me**, v. 26 NASB) in fleeing secretly. Second, he charged that Jacob, by taking his **daughters** away **like captives** (v. 26), was in a sense stealing them. Third, he accused Jacob of stealing away **secretly** and not allowing Laban to say farewell to his grandchildren (vv. 27-28). Finally, he charged Jacob with the theft of his **gods** (idols) (v. 30). In some respects these were all unfair accusations. First, Jacob had good cause to flee secretly since God had seen Laban's mistreatment and told him to leave (vv. 11-13). Second, Jacob's wives had agreed to go with him because they felt mistreated by their father (vv. 14-16). Third, telling Laban of his departure might have endangered Jacob and his family as seen in Laban's acknowledgment that it was **in** his **power to do [Jacob] harm** (v. 29), but **God** had warned him against it in a dream (vv. 24, 29). Finally, **Jacob did not know that Rachel had stolen** the idols (v. 32).

31:31-42. Not only was Laban deceived, but so too was Jacob, since he did **not know that Rachel** has **stolen** her father's idols. Had he known that he would not have vowed to Laban that **the one with whom you find your gods** [idols] **shall not live** (v. 32). The idols were not found because Rachel **put them in the camel's saddle, and she sat on them** (v. 34), excusing herself from moving by saying that **the manner of women** (i.e., her menses) was **upon** her (v. 35). Despite the potential volatility of the situation—fomented by Laban's ire over the stealing of his "gods" (vv. 30, 32, 35b) and Jacob's anger at being accused of such (vv. 36-37)—God extended his blessing to *both* sides by warning Laban, who had the power to do Jacob harm, not to injure him (vv. 29, 42).

Jacob responded to Laban by reminding him that his uncle had falsely accused him (vv. 36-37) and mistreated him for **twenty years** despite his hard work (vv. 38-41). In this way God's covenant protection of Jacob was upheld, and Laban was spared the inevitable curse of God that would follow from injuring the patriarch in His promised line (v. 42). In anger, Jacob recognized the Lord's covenant protection, noting that it was **the God of [his] father, the God of Abraham, and the fear of Isaac**, who had provided justice for him. Years before, when Jacob fled Canaan, he had vowed that if God brought him back to Canaan safely, only then would the Lord be his God (28:20-21). Even now, having escaped from Laban but not yet having made it all the way back to Canaan safely, true to his vow, Jacob recognized that the LORD was the God of his fathers, but not yet his own God. In describing the LORD, he used the unique name, **the fear of Isaac**, meaning the God whom Isaac feared (31:42, cf. 31:53).

31:43-55. The two men then **[made] a covenant** of peace (v. 44), and they established **a witness** to it by making a mound of **stones** that Laban called in Aramaic (his native tongue) **Jegar-sahadutha** and Jacob in Hebrew (his native tongue) called **Galeed** (meaning "a witness mound" in both languages) and additionally **Mizpah** (meaning "watchtower"). The mound of stones was to establish a boundary between the two relatives, thereby establishing a cold peace between them. As a polytheist, Laban swore his oath of peace by **the God of Abraham and the God of Nahor**, while Jacob swore by the one true God, **the fear of his father Isaac**, the One whom Isaac feared. This section then ends with the positive statement that **Laban . . . kissed his sons and his daughters** and grandchildren **and blessed them**. This ending demonstrates the break with Paddan-aram (Upper Mesopotamia) for the sons of Israel. There would be no returning to the land of their fathers for wives or any other reason.

32:1-2. As a postlude to the separation from Laban and his return to the promised land, Jacob had a vision of **the angels of God**. Jacob **named that place Mahanaim**, meaning "Two Camps," indicating that there were two camps aligned with each other in this place, God's camp with these angels and Jacob's camp with his wives, children, and flocks. This vision of angels is clearly tied to Jacob's dream 20 years earlier with "angels of God . . . ascending and descending" on a ladder as he left the land of promise (28:11-13). This deliberate linkage is evident in that the phrase **angels of God** can be found only in these two passages in the entire OT. Thus, as Jacob returns to land, he is once again reminded of God's protection, just as he was shown when he departed the land. Knowing that God would continue to protect Jacob with His angels would be a great encouragement to him as he prepared to encounter his brother Esau.

The purpose of this entire section of the narrative describing the final break between Jacob and Laban was to show God's protection and provision for Jacob (despite the human machinations, Rachel's theft of household idols, and Laban's animosity). Despite Laban's animosity, evident in his changed attitude toward Jacob (31:5), his cheating of Jacob (v. 6-7), and his changing of Jacob's wages (vv. 8-9), the Lord was with him (v. 5), protected him (v. 7), and gave him flocks (v. 9). Not only had God protected Jacob but provided for him as well, giving him great wealth (vv. 9, 16, 42), even as He had done for Abraham (12:16; 20:14) and Isaac (26:13-14). This would serve as a reminder to Israel centuries later as they entered the promised land, that God would indeed protect and provide for the nation despite the mistreatment by the Egyptians. Believers today can also be encouraged that the Lord will indeed protect and provide for His own, despite mistreatment by unscrupulous people: "If God is for us, who is against us?" (Rm 8:31).

c. Return to the Land: Striving Resolved with People and God (32:3–35:29)

The third part of the Jacob narrative depicts his exploits back in the land of promise. Its purpose is to show how Jacob finally resolved his striving and experienced peace with both his brother Esau and his God.

(1) The Restoration of Jacob and Esau (32:3–33:20)

The narrative of Jacob's struggles continues as he enters the land, depicting his fear of Esau (32:1-23), his fight with God (32:24-32), and ultimately his restoration with Esau (33:1-17).

(a) Jacob's Fear of Esau (32:3-23)

32:3-8. The story begins with a description of Jacob's fear of Esau. As Jacob returned to Canaan, he drew closer to the dwelling place of **his brother Esau in the land of Seir**, a mountainous region in **the country of Edom** (see 36:21) southeast of the Dead Sea. He sent **messengers before him** to request that he **find favor in** his brother's **sight** (vv. 4-5; since the main reason Jacob departed was Esau's plan to kill him; 27:42). In response **Esau** set out **to meet** his brother with **four hundred men**, causing Jacob to believe this to be a war party and therefore he was **greatly afraid and distressed** (v. 7). These latter two verbs imply Jacob's immaturity or even complete lack of true faith in the Lord and His covenant promises. The same two verbs are elsewhere used in the Hebrew OT (as in Jdg 10:9; 2Kg 25:26; etc.) to describe, among other things, the Israelites' lack of faith in God's covenant protection as well as in commands not to "be afraid . . . [or] be discouraged" because He "goes before [them] and will be with" them and "will never leave [them] nor forsake" them (Dt 31:8). God's command not to fear or be afraid is one of the most frequent given in Scripture (e.g., Is 44:8; Lk 12:32; Ac 27:24; Rv 1:17), and the Lord's promise to be with His people and never to leave them nor forsake them is likewise reiterated by Jesus (Mt 28:20b; Jn 14:16-18), who Himself was called Immanuel, which means "God with us" (Mt 1:23; cf. Jn 1:14).

32:9-23. Jacob thus implored the **LORD** (Yahweh) to **deliver** him **from the hand of** his **brother** (vv. 9-12), noting that God *must* do so if He is to uphold His promise to **prosper** him (Jacob) **and make** his **descendants as the sand of the sea** (vv. 11-12). Yet, consistent with his pattern of behavior up to this point, although he invoked God's covenant name, Jacob prayed to the **God of . . . Abraham and God of . . . Isaac**, not recognizing the Lord as his own God yet (vv. 9-10). Additionally, Jacob jumped ahead with his own plan, not content to wait on God, having already (before his prayer!) divided his household into two companies (v. 7), apparently coming upon this idea because of his experience at Mahanaim (32:12) in which he saw two companies, the angelic camp and his own. His logic was that "if Esau . . . attacks" one, the other "might escape" (31:8). Further, in an effort to mollify Esau, Jacob sent out a peace offering (vv. 13-21) of 550 animals (vv. 14-15). This section of the narrative demonstrates that Jacob is still at his old scheming ways; he is including God but not fully depending on Him. This would serve as a reminder for Israel when they entered the land of promise, not to follow Jacob's scheming or to offer tribute to the Canaanites but to trust and obey the Lord for the conquest of the land.

(b) Jacob's Fight with God (32:24-32)

32:24-25. Jacob's spiritual struggle is here epitomized as well as brought to a climactic resolution by God when **a man** appeared and **wrestled with him until daybreak**. This struggle is not to be seen as an isolated event but a synopsis of Jacob's entire life, constantly striving with both God and people. That this "man" was in fact God Himself in human form (specifically, a preincarnate appearance of the Son of God) is evident from the following facts. (1) **Jacob's thigh was dislocated** just by the man's having **touched** it (vv. 25, 32). (2) The man changed Jacob's **name** (v. 28) to one better suited to his *covenant* position: **Israel**, meaning "God strives" (i.e., on behalf of Jacob), *not* "he has striven with God." The former over the latter rendering is supported by (a) the imperfect (i.e., ongoing) Hebrew tense, (b) the normative presentation of *God* as the verbal subject in theophoric names, and (c) the ongoing covenant reality of Jacob's position as intended by God, the Namer. This final item of support hearkens back to the same reason God changed Jacob's grandfather's name from "Abram" to "Abraham" in 17:5 (and, more generally, with Christ's changing of the names of those who submit to Him in faith). (3) The man's reference to Jacob having **striven with God**—which, while reflecting the overall trajectory of Jacob's life to this point, also clearly referred to the present struggle or wrestling match between Jacob and the man Himself (v. 28). (4) Jacob named the site of the wrestling match "Peniel," meaning "The face (or "presence") of God," for as Jacob himself explained, "I have seen God face to face" (v. 30). Although Ex 33:20 says that no one can see God and live, that text likely refers to God the Father (cf. Jn 6:46; 1Tm 6:16; 1Jn 4:12). The Son of God is the visible God (Col 1:15), making preincarnate appearances as the Angel of the Lord (as He appears to be doing in this narrative; cf. Jdg 6:11-16; Is 6:1-5; Dn 10:5-6) and after the incarnation in the person of the God-man, Jesus (Lk 2:25-32; Jn 1:18; 17:1-8; 2Co 4:6; Php 2:6; Heb 1:3; Rv 1:12-18).

32:26-32. Jacob continued to struggle, holding on to the mysterious man, even with his dislocated thigh, until He blessed him. Ultimately, the Angel of the Lord acquiesced and changed the patriarch's name, because he had **striven with God and with men and [had] prevailed** (v. 28). The word **prevailed** does not mean that Jacob won the wrestling match by overpowering the man. Instead, it means that Jacob, having in the end been forcibly subdued by God, prevailed in receiving the blessing. That is, he was not just a benefactor of the material promises of the Abrahamic covenant, but also of its more selective spiritual promise of the blessing of saving faith. Paradoxically, he **prevailed** (received the blessing) through submission. This is precisely Jacob's point at the end of v. 30, in which he said, **Yet my life has been preserved**. However, this is better translated, "and my soul has been rescued (or, 'saved')." This is the picture of a man who was brought to God (*by God*) "kicking and screaming." As a result, Jacob was transformed from being a schemer to a triumphant receiver of God's blessing. Thus, the original readers—the people of Israel entering the promised land—would learn that their victory was not to come only through striving with others but also through God's blessing.

(c) Jacob's Restoration with Esau (33:1-17)

33:1-4. Having received the blessing from God, Jacob still anticipated difficulties with Esau. As he saw Esau arriving with what appeared to be a war party (v. 1), Jacob next acted nobly, placing his wives and children behind him so that he could meet Esau first. After he **passed on ahead of them** and approached his brother, he **bowed down to the ground seven times** before Esau (vv. 2-3). In a totally unexpected act, **Esau ran to meet him and embraced him, and fell on his neck and kissed him, and they wept** (v. 4). After years of bitterness and even threats of murder (27:41), Esau was reconciled to his brother. This was the result of God's work in his heart and not of any manipulation by Jacob.

33:5-17. After introducing his family to Esau (vv. 5-7), Jacob gave Esau gifts and insisted that his brother take them (vv. 8-11). Jacob also declined Esau's offer of an escort back to the land out of concern for his own **children** and his **flocks and herds** at their slower **pace** (vv. 12-15) and perhaps in part out of fear, lest Esau experience a change of heart. Thus, Jacob returned to the promised land, settling temporarily in booths in a place named **Succoth** (booths), east of the Jordan River and north of the Jabbok River (v. 17), in the opposite direction of **Seir**, where Esau had gone (v. 16).

This story of the reconciliation of Esau and Jacob was designed to identify the transformations of both Esau and Jacob as works of God. Esau was changed from threatening to murder his brother to a desire to be at peace and even provide protection for him. This was clearly the work of God in answer to Jacob's prayer in 32:9-10. Jacob was also changed from a schemer to a follower of the Lord. This is evident in his bravery, going before his family to meet Esau (33:3), his humility, bowing before Esau (33:3) and his generosity, insisting that Esau take his gifts even though it was apparent that Jacob was no longer in danger (33:10-11). Jacob's behavior became the model for Israel—like Jacob, they would be able to conquer and settle in the land of promise only if they were to rely on the Lord for the victory.

(d) Jacob's Restoration to the Land (33:18-20)

33:18-20. In a brief epilogue to the story of his reconciliation with Esau, Jacob is depicted as settled back in **Canaan**, the land of promise. He settled in the **city of Shechem**, about 20 miles (32 km) west of the Jabbok River, and there purchased land from **the sons of Hamor** just as his grandfather Abraham had purchased land near Hebron from the sons of Heth (23:1-20). Most significantly, Jacob built **an altar and called it El-Elohe-Israel** (v. 20), meaning "El (is) the God of Israel." "Israel" at this point refers specifically to Jacob (as opposed to the later nation). This act of worship emphasized Jacob's spiritual transformation. When Jacob left the land, he vowed that if God kept His promise and brought him back, then He the God of his fathers would be his God (28:21). Throughout the Jacob narrative following that vow made 20 years earlier, Jacob always referred to the Lord as the God of Abraham and the God of Isaac but never as his own God. Now, with God having kept His promise and returned him in safety, Jacob, in naming the altar, finally identified the Lord as his own God. Jacob's spiritual transformation is now complete—he is not perfect and will still have his struggles, but he is clearly now a man of God and a follower of the God of Israel.

(2) The Rape of Dinah (34:1-31)

Now that Jacob had returned to Canaan, it might be thought that at this point God would fulfill the Abrahamic covenant and grant this land to Jacob and his twelve sons. To clarify that the conquest of the land was not to take place at this point, the story shows the difficulties Jacob had as a guest, living in the land God promised to him and his descendants.

34:1-12. Jacob and his family were now encamped on the outskirts of the city of Shechem. When **Shechem**, the **prince** named for the city, saw Jacob's daughter **Dinah** (whose birth was mentioned previously as a prelude to this passage, 30:21), he **lay with her by force** (v. 2, lit., "humiliated her," i.e., raped her). Jacob was surprisingly indifferent to the rape of his daughter (v. 5), perhaps because of fear of the Shechemites or because she was the daughter of the less loved Leah, or both. Through **his father Hamor**, Shechem petitioned Jacob to be given Dinah as his **wife** (vv. 3-12). The petition was made in the presence of Jacob's sons, who rightly considered rape **a disgraceful thing** (v. 7).

34:13-24. The brothers, though grieved and angry over the crime, agreed to the marriage **on** the **condition** that **every male** among Shechem's people **be circumcised** and thus **become one people** with the family of Israel (vv. 15-16). All parties in this deal, except for Jacob, appear to be acting **with deceit** (v. 13). Jacob's sons were specifically described as deceiving the Shechemites and thus also their father (v. 13), much like Jacob had deceived his father. The Shechemites also were acting deceitfully because implicit in this arrangement, since they were uniting with Israel *on Israel's terms*, was submission to the God of Israel (i.e., conversion) and hence inclusion in the Abrahamic covenant of which circumcision is the outward sign (see 17:11 and comments on 17:1-16). Yet, Hamor convinced the men of Shechem to accept circumcision in order **to become one people** with Israel (v. 22) and thereby confiscate the wealth (**their livestock and their property**, v. 23) of Israel.

34:25-31. The ensuing crime of Simeon and Levi was even more grave, for as the Shechemite men were recovering **in pain** from their circumcision (v. 25)—with Dinah having already been taken to **Shechem's house** (thus married, v. 26)—the two brothers went throughout **the city** and **killed every male**. When the news of the sons' deceit was brought to Jacob, who was sincere in his consent to the marriage, he angrily pointed out that when the other tribes of the land heard of the affair **they** would gather together against him **and attack** him, thus destroying him and his **household** (v. 30). To this Dinah's brothers (note that Simeon and Levi and Dinah were full siblings whose mother was Leah) simply said, **Should he treat our sister as a harlot?** (v. 31).

This story served a variety of purposes in the account of the life of Jacob. First, it showed that the conquest of the land was not to occur at this time but at a much later time (as God had told Abraham, Gn 15:13-16). Second, although the behavior of Jacob's sons seemed to jeopardize the covenant/promise, God in His grace would still give the land to Israel. For this reason, everywhere they went, the terror of God surrounded and protected them (Gn 35:5), contrary to what Jacob anticipated (v. 30). Third, the narrative functioned as a warning to Israel not to make treaties or to intermarry with the Canaanites when centuries later they would eventually enter and settle in the land. The final function of this story was to explain that Simeon and Levi, as the instigators of this treachery, would be disqualified as the royal tribe in Israel (cf. Gn 49:5-7).

(3) The Close of the Jacob Story (35:1-29)

Although Jacob appears later in the Genesis narratives, this chapter closes the section in which he is the main character. As such, it demonstrates God's faithfulness to the promises that He made to Abraham, Isaac, and Jacob.

35:1-15. Despite the treacherous behavior of his sons, Jacob knew that God, in keeping with His covenant promises, would not let his family be destroyed. So he exhorted **his household** to **purify** themselves and, with him, to turn **to God, who answered** (lit., "answers") him **in the day of** his **distress and [had] been with** him **wherever** he had **gone** (v. 3). Notwithstanding their many imperfections, therefore, Jacob's family was preserved, and the patriarch's faith affirmed, by **a great terror** that God caused to fall **upon the cities which were around them** (v. 5). The connection of this denouement to the Abrahamic covenant—and God's faithfulness in unconditionally upholding it—is underscored by the explicit reference to the covenant and its main provisions: i.e., *blessing* (v. 9, **and He blessed him**); descendant *nationhood* (v. 11, **a nation . . . shall come from you**); and *land* (v. 12, **the land . . . I will give . . . to you, and . . . to your descendants**). Additionally, there was a promise that **kings shall come forth from you** (v. 11), a promise fulfilled in the line of Judah, through whom the ultimate messianic king would come (Gn 49:8-12).

35:16-22a. As Jacob and his household **journeyed from Bethel**, about 10 miles (17 km) north of Jerusalem, **to Ephrath** (the early name of **Bethlehem**), about 5 miles (8 km) to Jerusalem's south, **Rachel** began **to give birth, and suffered severe labor**, eventually resulting in her death. Yet the baby—a **son**—was born, and as she was dying, Rachel named him **Ben-oni**, meaning "son of my suffering." Jacob, however, seeking to give the event a more positive memorial, renamed his 12th and last son **Benjamin**, meaning "son of (my) right (hand)." Rachel was then **buried** in the vicinity of **Ephrath (that is, Bethlehem)**, where her tomb still stands. Not long after this, Jacob's oldest son, Reuben, committed a grave personal offense against his father (thus disqualifying him from receiving the covenant blessing; 49:4) by laying **with Bilhah his father's concubine** (v. 22). This was incest, since a concubine was considered one's wife, which is how Bilhah is described in 30:4. This brief narrative was not irrelevant but was included to explain why Reuben, as firstborn, would not be named as the leader of the tribes of Israel. Jacob bypassed Reuben (49:3-4) and Simeon and Levi (49:5-7, cf. 34:25-30) because of their sins, instead identifying Judah as father of the royal line and the one through whom the future messianic King of Israel would come (49:8-12).

35:22b-29. The "records of the generations of Isaac" (25:19) ends here with a summary look at God's overall blessing of **Isaac**. God's material blessing of Isaac (and Jacob) is evident in his "full quiver" (to employ the terminology of Ps 127:4-5) of sons—that is, in addition to Jacob and Esau, his **twelve** grand**sons** from whom the promised nation (see Gn 12:2) would descend. God's blessing of Isaac is further indicated by the reference to him dying as **an old man of ripe age** (35:29), or translated literally, "satisfied of (i.e., with his) days." This phrase also hints at God's spiritual blessing of Isaac (that he knew God and was known by God). In addition to Isaac, the other four occurrences of the terms "ripe" age and full of "days" in Scripture all describe men who died as believers, mature in faith: Job (Jb 42:17), Abraham (Gn 25:8), David (1Ch 23:1; 29:28); and Jehoiada (2Ch 24:15). Isaac's two sons, formerly at odds with each other but having reconciled (Gn 33:1-17), came together in peace to bury their father.

D. Descendants of Esau: Another Locus of Conflict with God's People (36:1–37:1)

36:1–37:1. A record of the descendants of Ishmael, the older brother, was given in 25:12-18. So too here a record of **the generations of Esau** is given, the older brother whom God excluded from the Abrahamic covenant. One of the purposes for this record is to show that in the fulfillment of God's word, Esau's descendants would likewise constitute a nation. However, an important difference is to be noted. Whereas Ishmael was blessed by God and promised to become a great nation (17:20), Esau was simply declared to become a "nation" (25:23), without any explicit connection to divine blessing. In fact Esau's descendants, the nation of **Edom** (36:8), was eventually wiped out as a distinct people because of their opposition to the Lord and His people (see Mal 1:3-4).

Also, Esau's list of "generations" is roughly six times longer than that of Ishmael because of the nature of two additional purposes unique to the genealogy of Esau. The first of these concerns **the sons of Seir the Horite** presented in vv. 20-30. Though Seir was not a descendant in the Abrahamic line, his descendants became interlinked with those of Esau through intermarriage with Esau's descendants. Among the descendants common to both was **Amalek**, the son of **Esau's son Eliphaz**, and Seir's daughter **Timna** (vv. 12, 22). Because the descendants of Esau (the Edomites; see vv. 9, 19, 43) became more numerous and prominent than the descendants of Seir, the entire region, which included the dwelling place of **the sons of Seir**, was designated after the former, that is, **the land of Edom** (v. 21). Also its inhabitants, though not all linked to Esau, were known generally as **Edomites**, and in particular "Amalekites" (Ex 17:8; Nm 24:20; Dt 25:17; Jdg 3:13, etc.) since these later became the predominant tribe among the Edomites (analogous to the eventual use of the term "Judahite" [hence, "Jew" from "Judah"] for a descendant of any of the 12 tribes). **Amalek**, however, was one of the few tribes cursed by God with complete annihilation (at the hand of Israel) because of their extreme perversity and opposition to His people (see Ex 17:14). Yet had the specific details of Amalek's descent, together with those of Seir, not been presented here, the Israelites would inevitably have killed *all* those people known after the predominant tribe as "Amalekites" who were not in fact related to the Amalekites at all (Gn 14:7). These details thus prevented the Israelites from the sin (committed in ignorance) of shedding "innocent blood" (cf. Dt 19:10; 21:7-9) and exemplified God's discriminating application of justice (as earlier affirmed by Abraham in 18:23).

The second purpose unique to Esau's genealogy concerns **the kings who reigned in the land of Edom**, presented in vv. 31-39. The eight kings here enumerated (**Bela**, **Jobab**, **Husham**, **Hadad**, **Samlah**, **Shaul**, **Baal-hanan**, and **Hadar**) contrast sharply with the monarchy later established in Israel. Each of these kings of Edom epitomizes enthronement by human effort, since each one of them is explicitly associated with a different city, thereby discounting genealogical succession. But the later monarchy of Israel epitomizes enthronement *by divine effort*, since it was founded, maintained, and in the end personally upheld by God alone (cf. 2Sm 7:12-16). This contrast is even more vividly borne out by the explicit statement that these *eight* Edomite kings reigned well **before any king reigned over the sons of Israel** (v. 31). Yet already by the *eighth* king in the true Israelite (Judean) monarchy, that is, Jehoshaphat, "there was no [longer any] king in Edom" (1Kg 22:47).

E. Descendants of Jacob: God's Providence over Joseph and Israel (37:2–50:26)

In this final section of Genesis, the biblical framework of the "path of redemption" is completed, with emphasis being given not only to

God's sovereignty in the process of establishing (and hence maintaining) that path, but also to its ultimate end point in a descendant of Judah in whom will center the perfect and eternal administration of the three key provisions of the Abrahamic covenant: the *land*, the *people*, and the *blessing*. In terms of space, of course, Joseph is the most prominent of Jacob's 12 sons. Yet this should not obscure the importance of Judah, as the second most prominent brother in this section, and in a respect, the most prominent brother of all because of his messianic significance (49:8-12). Whereas the paths of the two brothers Joseph and Judah diverge with the selling of Joseph in 37:28 (in which Judah took the lead), Judah, unlike the other ten brothers, was kept at literary "arm's length" (hence chap. 38), with his path merging back again with that of Joseph later in Egypt.

1. Joseph in the Pit (37:2–40:23)

The "records of the generations of Jacob" (v. 2) focus attention not on Jacob, but rather on that son in the next generation through whom the Abrahamic covenant is channeled (i.e., Joseph; see comments on 25:19–35:29 and 38:1-30) until the emphasis in the narrative begins to shift from Joseph to Judah (see 43:8-9 and 44:18-34 and related comments below). Thus begins the Joseph cycle now that the subsequent narrative cycles for Abraham, Isaac, and Jacob have come to their respective conclusions.

a. Joseph Is Sold into Slavery by His Brothers (37:2-36)

37:2-17. The account of **Joseph**, around whom the majority of this last major section in Genesis revolves, presents a pattern that is employed by God throughout later history as one among several means of displaying His concern for Israel. This pattern features the elevation of a Jewish person to the upper echelons of governmental power, resulting in an elevation of the Jewish sociopolitical standing, and often also the improvement of their material welfare. Other examples from the biblical period include Moses (the adopted son of Pharaoh; Ex 2:10), David (commander and bodyguard of the Philistine king Achish; 1Sm 28:2), Daniel (adviser to the Babylonian and Persian king from Nebuchadnezzar until Cyrus; Dn 1:21), Esther (queen of the Persian king Ahasuerus [or Xerxes]; Est 2:17), her relative Mordecai (first chamberlain of Ahasuerus, then second to the king himself; Est 2:21; 10:3), and Nehemiah (cupbearer to the Persian king Artaxerxes; Neh 1:11).

Jacob, though having come to a place of true dependence on God, was not perfect. Not surprisingly he fell into the same pattern of sin expressed by his parents, namely, showing clear favoritism for one among several siblings. Just as Isaac's preference for Esau and Rebekah's preference for Jacob fueled the fraternal enmity that eventually prompted Esau to plot his brother's murder (27:42), so too did Jacob's preference for Joseph—whom his **father loved . . . more than all his brothers** (v. 4). This was the first factor that fueled an outright hatred of **him** on the part of his brothers that culminated in their plotting "to put him to death" (v. 18). The strife between Joseph and his brothers that begins in this passage reflects a common theme in Genesis (see comments on 4:8).

An important tidbit of parental instruction is here, for though any parent with several children may be inclined to favor one of them, the true hatred of Joseph's brothers was fanned into life only after their father's natural inclination toward Joseph as **the son of his old age** was outwardly displayed by his giving him **a varicolored tunic** (v. 3). This was a continual visual reminder to the brothers of Joseph's favored status. Moreover, the strife between brothers was exacerbated by a second factor—Joseph's own pride. This was evident when he told **his brothers** about **his** two **dreams**—both of which clearly symbolized his family **bowing down to** him (in submission, not worship)—and **they hated him even more** (vv. 5-11). For **the sun and the moon and eleven stars**, see comments on Rv 12:1-6. The fulfillment of these dreams becomes evident later in the narrative, when the family must go down to Egypt for food and had to bow before Joseph (Gn 42:9). Yet a third factor in the strife-developing hatred was Joseph's brothers' envy of him. They **saw that their father loved him more than all his brothers** (v. 4) and resented his dreams so much that the **brothers were jealous of him** (v. 11).

37:18-36. Thus the brothers decided to **kill** Joseph **and throw** his body **into one of the pits** in the wilderness (v. 20). Yet the oldest brother **Reuben**, in an act of compassion—or at the very least out of respect to his father—persuaded them, for the moment (cf. v. 26), **not** to **lay hands on** (i.e., kill) their brother, but rather to **throw him** into a **pit** so that he (Reuben) **might** later **rescue** Joseph and **restore him to his father** (v. 22). Sadly, Reuben's good intentions were a fourth factor in Joseph's descent to slavery—rather than forthrightly defend his brother, his scheme failed to protect his younger brother. The fifth factor causing Joseph to be sold into slavery was his brother Judah's greed. Without Reuben's knowledge, Judah then took the lead, perhaps showing some compassion (**for he is our brother, our own flesh**, v. 27) but mainly displaying a greedy attitude. He wondered aloud about the **profit** in murdering their brother (v. 26) and instead proposed selling Joseph to **Ishmaelite** traders **on their way . . . down to Egypt** (vv. 26-27). Already this revealed the enmity God declared in 16:12 would arise between Ishmael's offspring and Isaac's. Since Ishmael was Joseph's great-uncle, these **Ishmaelites** would have been Joseph's second cousins, no more than two or three times removed). The sixth and final factor in the strife between family members is the deception by the brothers caused by dipping **Joseph's tunic** in **the blood** of a **goat** and bringing **it to their father** (vv. 31-32). Jacob concluded that a **wild beast** had **devoured** Joseph, for whom he then **mourned for . . . many days** and **refused to be comforted** (vv. 33-34). Many years earlier Jacob had deceived his own father using his brother Esau's garments (27:1-46); now his sons deceived him using Joseph's torn and blood-stained garments (37:33-35).

There are three results for the sad events described in this chapter. First, Joseph will now live in slavery (cf. 39:1-6). Second, Jacob is to live the next 22 years in sorrow, grieving for his favorite son (37:35). Third, Joseph's brothers will continue to live in guilt, always seeing the sin against their brother as the source of all their woes (cf. 42:21-22; 44:16).

b. Judah Receives a Male Heir by Deception (38:1-30)

That this chapter is about Judah and makes no mention of Joseph has led critical interpreters of the Bible to consider it an "intrusion" or "interruption" to the Joseph narrative. This determination, however, presumes that the purpose of this last section of Genesis (i.e., the "generations of Jacob," from 37:2 to 50:26) is *solely* to present the story of Joseph. Yet a significant purpose of this last section is to continue to trace the progressive fulfillment of the seed of redemption, first promised in Eden (3:15), also promised to Abraham (22:18), and culminating with the coming of the rightful king from the line of Judah (49:10). In keeping with this purpose, the present chapter is in fact quite integral, for by its *focus* on Judah it anticipates or "sets up" the essential place that Judah will come to occupy (even greater than that of Joseph!) in providing that seed.

In addition to keeping the focus on the "seed," Gn 38 includes several other narrative links to the Joseph story. First, the Judah/Tamar story creates narrative suspense. The Joseph story concludes in the previous chapter with his being sold into slavery (37:36), and this chapter changes the scene and returns to events in Canaan. This is classic storytelling, allowing curiosity to build by letting the reader wonder what became of Joseph.

Second, the Judah/Tamar narrative gives time for the Joseph story to develop. According to the time markers in the text, 22 years pass from the time Joseph was sold into slavery until his brothers in their time of need finally appear before him (see chart, "Joseph's Progression in Status and Age," in comments on 41:38-57). Hence, there is plenty of time for Judah's family to grow up, to marry, and to raise children.

Third, the Judah/Tamar narrative provides textual links with the previous story. Robert Alter has demonstrated a variety of verbal and thematic links between chap. 38 and the rest of the Joseph narrative. For example, Joseph's brothers use the words "please examine" (*haker-na*) when showing Joseph's blood stained coat to Jacob (37:32), and Tamar uses the exact same words, "please examine" (*haker-na*) when showing Judah the items she took as a pledge from him (38:25). Also, in both stories, deception occurs through the use of a goat: the brothers deceive Jacob with goat's blood on Joseph's coat (37:31), and Tamar deceives Judah with the contrivance of taking his pledge while waiting for a young goat (38:17-18). Additionally, there is the contrast between Judah's sexual impurity (38:15-16) and Joseph's commitment to sexual purity (39:10-12; Robert Alter, *The Art of Biblical Narrative* [New York: Basic Books, 1981], 3-12 esp. 10).

Fourth, the Judah/Tamar narrative is linked to the wider themes of Genesis. For example, there is the problem of childlessness, previously experienced by Sarah and Rachel and here experienced by Tamar. Also, in this narrative Judah is deceived as were the other patriarchs (Isaac by Jacob, Jacob by Laban, and Jacob by his sons). This story also shows the covenant/promise in jeopardy once again, this time from the line of Judah coming dangerously close to not having an heir. And at the end of the story, the younger son Perez is preferred over the older Zerah, as is the pattern throughout Genesis. Clearly, the Judah/Tamar story fits within the narrative of Genesis and is not an unnecessary or random interpolation.

38:1-13. The specific episode of chap. 38 reveals the spiritual "turning point" in Judah's life. This in fact explains the dramatic moral reversal in his attitude and behavior toward his father's new favorite son, Benjamin (since Joseph is assumed dead) in 44:18-34, where Judah shows great compassion both for his youngest brother's welfare and for his father's feelings, in contrast to his blameworthy participation in the betrayal of Joseph. The way to this "turning point" for Judah was set up by his own sin and less-than-ideal behavior with Tamar (as is often the case with such spiritual turning points). At the outset, he did not do what **duty** required, that is, giving **Tamar**, the widow of his two older sons (**Er** and then **Onan**), to his surviving son **Shelah as** his **wife** (vv. 6-11, 14). This custom of marrying the sonless widow of one's closest relative was intended as an important expression of maternal honor (to ensure that one's mother would be provided for in old age; see Ru 4:15) as well as of familial honor (to ensure that the "name" of the deceased husband is maintained through a male heir; see Ru 4:5). Eventually this custom was legally codified by God in the Mosaic law (Dt 25:5-6), though His approval of the custom even here is evident from the statement that **Onan**'s refusal to give a **seed** (i.e., male heir) **to his** deceased **brother**, Er, **was displeasing in the sight of the Lord** (v. 8-10).

38:14-26. Tamar therefore undertook to deceive Judah, following the pattern of one's mischief returning "upon his own head" (Ps 7:16). As Judah took the lead in deceiving Jacob by lying about Joseph being killed by a wild beast, so now was he himself deceived. She disguised herself so that **Judah** . . . **thought she was a harlot** (v. 15) . . . **and** he **went in to her, and she conceived** (v. 18). **Three months later**, when her pregnancy became noticeable, Judah accused her of **harlotry** (*zenunim*, lit., "illicit [i.e., extramarital] sex") and commanded that she **be burned** (v. 24). Judah's "turning point" then came when she revealed that he was in fact the father, whereupon Judah was resolutely (and very publicly!) confronted with his sins: (1) his failure to show compassion and do his "duty" toward Tamar (as well as his son Er) by giving her to Shelah as his wife; (2) his engaging in illicit sex with a harlot (as he thought Tamar to be); and (3) his hypocrisy in mercilessly calling for the execution of Tamar (and her baby) for the very same sin that he had committed—*with her*, as he now realized. Expressive of his contrition, Judah declared, Tamar **is more righteous than I** (v. 26). True, Tamar was *more* upright than Judah in the drama of this chapter, but certainly not perfectly righteous, for though the conception of a son from Judah's line was her right, the way in which she went about ensuring that conception was still sinful. However, the declaration of righteousness is not really a statement about her better morals than Judah's. Rather it is derived from the overarching purpose of this chapter, namely, to explain the preservation of the line of Judah, which will ultimately produce the Messianic king (49:8-12). Hence, it is evil to be unconcerned with preserving the promised line as evident in the behavior of Onan, who refused to raise up seed for his brother, and Judah, who also refused to give his youngest son as a husband to Tamar to raise up seed for his line. In contrast, Tamar demonstrated that she was indeed righteous, not by practicing deception or harlotry, but by being concerned with the preservation of the promised line, through which the messianic king would come.

The transformation of Judah plays a significant role in the Genesis narrative in that he becomes the progenitor of the royal and messianic line in Israel (49:8-12). The narrative reveals the change in Judah's role and standing through subtle clues. For example, early in Genesis, Judah appears to be greedy, calling for Joseph to be sold rather than killed, in order to get monetary benefit from the betrayal of his brother (37:26-27). In this chapter, Judah appears callous and cruel in regard to his daughter-in-law. Moreover, he was indifferent toward his need to maintain the purity of his line (he married a Canaanite woman, 38:2) or even his responsibility to continue his line. However, after his "turn around" recorded here, the narrative begins to elevate Judah. For example, afterwards Jacob ignores Reuben's request to return to Egypt (42:37-38) but listens to Judah (43:8-11). Once the brothers return to Egypt for food, Judah is plainly seen as their leader (44:14; 46:28). Moreover, afterwards Judah demonstrates compassion for his brother Benjamin and his father (44:30-34). This transformation sets the stage for Jacob's oracle that Judah's line would be ascendant and the source of the future Messiah (49:8-12).

38:27-30. So Tamar gave birth to twin sons, **Perez** and **Zerah**, continuing Judah's line. Zerah

put out a hand . . . **first**, indicating that he would be the firstborn only to draw it **back**. Then Perez was born. So once again in Genesis, the younger son becomes the preferred one and the perpetuator of the Abrahamic promise. This emphasizes the sovereignty of God in providing the seed for the promised line (see comments on 25:21b-26). Significantly, Jesus the Messiah would descend from Perez (Mt 1:3), being the culmination of the path of redemption here being laid.

c. Joseph Is Falsely Accused by Potiphar's Wife (39:1-23)

The already tragic story of Joseph gets worse, going from a pit to slavery and by the end of this chapter, to prison. This chapter clearly establishes the historical (yet unpopular and often unrecognized) principle of righteous living specifically, that "all who desire to live godly . . . will be persecuted" (2Tm 3:12). Through such persecution, however, that the greatest "training in righteousness" (2Tm 3:16) often occurs, as the believer learns what it is to truly depend on God in the process. In the present chapter, accordingly, we see God complementing Joseph's effort at godly living by causing him to "find favor" in the sight of key individuals (an important phrase denoting God's "behind-the-scenes" activity, vv. 4, 21) and blessing the results of His work in a way that ultimately benefits the welfare of Israel, God's covenant people.

39:1-6a. Thus **Joseph found favor** (v. 4) in the sight of **Potiphar,** . . . **the captain of** Pharaoh's **bodyguard**, who **bought him from the Ishmaelites** to whom his brothers had sold him (v. 1). The source of Joseph's ensuing success is revealed immediately with the surprising words, **the LORD was with Joseph** (vv. 2-3). It would appear that if the Lord were indeed with Joseph, he would not have been sold into slavery. Yet the presence of God in one's life and the extent of success is not to be measured by the absence of adversity but a faithful attitude in the midst of adversity. On this score, Joseph was a great success. While some might attribute Joseph's success in Potiphar's household to his diligence at work, it was truly because **the LORD caused all that he did to prosper** (v. 3). As a result, Joseph was made **overseer in** Potiphar's **house** and **the LORD's blessing** continued on **all that he owned** (v. 5).

39:6b-23. Just when it appeared that Joseph had found a satisfactory situation, even in slavery, the narrator prepares the way for Joseph's spiraling descent into greater difficulty by describing him as **handsome in form and appearance** (v. 6). His youthful good looks led to the repeated adulterous advances of his master's wife (vv. 7, 10). Joseph's strength in refusing these advances were fueled by his loyalty to his master (vv. 8-9) and even more significantly, his recognition that the Lord was indeed with him. Thus, he asks, **How then could I do this great evil and sin against God?** After one particularly tempting situation, Joseph wisely **fled** from her presence (v. 12; see Paul's admonition to Timothy in 2Tm 2:22; also 1Co 6:18), which prompted Potiphar's wife to falsely accuse Joseph when **his master**, her husband, returned **home**. As a result, **Joseph's master took him and put him into the jail . . . where the king's prisoners were confined** (v. 20). Joseph now had experienced both betrayal and false accusation, had descended from the status of favored son to slave to prisoner, and the narrator surprisingly reminds the reader **the LORD was with Joseph** (v. 21). In prison, once again God—whose plan continued to unfold undiminished—**gave him favor**, this time **in the sight of the chief jailer**, who placed him in **charge** of **all** of **the prisoners** . . . **in the jail** (vv. 21-22). Too often adversity is considered a sign of God's abandonment. Yet, in the life of Joseph, despite his difficulties, the Lord was present in his life, granting favor and success. Plainly the story is establishing the providence of God in achieving God's good purposes despite Joseph's adverse circumstances.

d. Joseph Is Forgotten by the Cupbearer (40:1-23)

40:1-15. God's hand in the affair now became more explicit as He prepared the way for Joseph's elevation—and thus Israel's preservation—by the dreams He gave to **two** newly arrived prisoners from Pharaoh's court, **the chief cupbearer and the chief baker** (v. 2). The dreams were both given on **the same night**. Though they did not understand the dreams' meanings—both officials were clearly **dejected** the next **morning** (vv. 5-6). Though these men were strangers, Joseph displays clear compassion toward them by asking **why** their **faces** were **so sad**. And when they told him he sought to resolve their dilemma by offering to interpret their dreams, affirming that the **interpretations** of all dreams **belong to God** (vv. 7-8).

40:16-23. The dream of the chief cupbearer Joseph interpreted **favorably** (v. 16), indicating that **within three more days Pharaoh** would **restore** him **to** his **office**, and he would continue to serve Pharaoh **according to** his **former custom** (v. 13). The dream of the chief baker, however, was interpreted unfavorably, for **within** the same **three days** Pharaoh would **hang** him **on a tree** (v. 19). And so the events unfolded **just as Joseph had interpreted** (v. 22), yet despite Joseph's request that he do him a kindness and mention his unjust imprisonment to Pharaoh (v. 14), **the chief cupbearer . . . forgot Joseph** (v. 23). In this Joseph was undoubtedly continuing to learn what it means to wait on the Lord (the cupbearer neglected his word to Joseph for "two full years," 41:1) as He continued to prepare the present path of deliverance and maneuver "the king's heart . . . like channels of water in [His] hand" (Pr 21:1). A notable parallel, moreover, which is clearly intended to bear out the same theological principle, may be found in failure of King Ahasuerus to remember to reward Mordecai's deed (likewise concerning two of the king's officials) until that time when it was most effectively suited to the deliverance of Israel (and not just the elevation of Mordecai; see comments on Est 6).

2. Joseph as Prime Minister (41:1–50:26)

a. Joseph Becomes Prime Minister (41:1-57)

41:1-13. God did not resolve Joseph's personal situation—which was, after all, only one thread in a much larger tapestry depicting His care for His *people*—until **the end of two full years** (v. 1), at which time **Pharaoh** had two dreams that caused **his spirit** to be **troubled** (v. 8). Since Pharaoh could find no one to interpret these dreams—in the first of which **seven . . . gaunt . . . cows ate up seven . . . fat cows**, and in the second of which **seven . . . thin ears** of grain **swallowed up the seven . . . full ears** (vv. 2-7)—**the chief cupbearer** (implicitly prompted by God) recalled Joseph and told Pharaoh of his ability to **interpret . . . dreams** accurately (vv. 9-13).

41:14-37. Significantly when Pharaoh summoned Joseph and asked if he could truly interpret dreams, Joseph's response—his first recorded words in two years—was, **It is not in me** (v. 16), which may be more literally translated, "[It is] apart from me," that is, "It has nothing to do with me." Joseph had not grown bitter after spending thirteen years (unjustly) as a slave and then prisoner, but his focus was in fact set squarely on God and His glory—a focus that was undoubtedly essential to staving off despair during those years. At the first opportunity Joseph unabashedly emphasized the sovereignty (and hence glory) of God to Pharaoh himself, for he told him **God will give Pharaoh a favorable answer** (v. 16). This clause, however, should be rendered "God will respond to Pharaoh's situation." The word translated "situation" is the Hebrew word *shalom* (generally signifying "peace" or "completeness"), and is here intended in the sense of "situation" or "welfare." Pharaoh then told Joseph his dreams, which Joseph interpreted as both signifying the same thing: **seven years of great abundance** will come to **Egypt**, and **after them seven years of famine**, which will be **very severe** (vv. 29-31). Joseph then advised Pharaoh to find a **man discerning and wise** who can implement the specific steps he described to prepare for this famine. In contrast to his successor 400 years later "who did not know Joseph" (Ex 1:8), the present Pharaoh responded enthusiastically by affirming the truth of what Joseph's God had informed him (Gn 41:38).

41:38-57. Pharaoh realized that Joseph was himself the very **discerning and wise** man needed for the task (v. 39). Pharaoh then made Joseph second in authority only to himself (anticipating the same redemptive "positioning" of, Esther and Mordecai, among others, at the opposite end of Israel's biblical history; Est 8:2; 10:3) and declared that **without your permission no one shall raise his hand or foot in all the land of Egypt** (v. 44). Joseph prepared for the famine by storing **up grain in great abundance** (v. 49), and he also took a wife who bore him **two sons** (v. 50). The names of his sons further reflect Joseph's selfless, *theocentric* perspective in the narrative, focusing not on his 13 years of ignominy and affliction (he was 17 when sold and 30 when promoted by Pharaoh; 37:2; 41:46, see chart, "Joseph's Progression in Status and Age," below), but rather on the grace and blessing that God had shown him according His own time and plan: **Manasseh** (meaning "He causes to forget"), **for . . . God has made me forget all my trouble** (v. 51) and **Ephraim** (meaning either "fruitful land" or "double fruitfulness") **for . . . God has made me fruitful in the land of my affliction** (v. 52).

Some might consider Joseph's ascendency to the prime minister's office in Egypt to be the climax of the Joseph narrative. Nevertheless, this part of the story is but a means to an end. The climax will be Joseph's restoration with his brothers and the recognition that all his painful experiences were part of God's plan to deliver the sons of Israel.

Joseph's Progression in Status and Age

Age	Joseph's Status	Reference
17	Sold into slavery	Gn 37:2
28	Forgotten in prison	Gn 41:1; 41:46
30	Made prime minister	Gn 41:46
39	Revealed to his brothers	Gn 45:6
56	Present at his father Jacob's death	Gn 47:28
110	Died in Egypt	Gn 50:22

b. Joseph Tests His Brothers (42:1–44:34)

In the next three chapters, although it might seem as if Joseph toyed with his brothers, in reality he was testing them. These interactions were designed to evaluate their consciences, their character, and their compassion, all traits sorely lacking when they sold him into slavery.

(1) The Conscience Test (42:1-38)

42:1-24. In chaps. 42–45 God "tied together" the various strands of circumstance that were spun in the previous five chaps. (from 37:2 onward), bringing the brothers face to face with their sin, for the purpose of reconciliation and *refinement* in godliness as He continued to mold them into the ideal covenant people that they would one day be in the prophetic future (cf. Dt 10:12-22; Is 1:25-26; Mal 1:5). This denouement commenced when, as a result of the famine—which extended even to the land of Canaan (see 41:57)—Jacob sent the **ten brothers of Joseph . . . to buy grain from Egypt** (v. 3). When they arrived, though **Joseph . . . recognized his brothers, . . . they did not recognize him** (vv. 7-8). Joseph wisely exploited this situation, not to torture his brothers or to gain vengeance but to test them in several ways, in order to determine whether their collective character had improved and they had moved beyond their predilection to deceitfulness. Joseph began with a test of their collective consciences, to see if they were penitent about the evil they had done to him, their own flesh and blood.

Joseph first sought to test their consciences by making circumstances difficult for them, accusing them of being **spies** (v. 14). Joseph knew this was untrue and the brothers of course denied it, whereupon Joseph set a condition to determine whether the **truth** was really **in** them (v. 16). Though initially this condition was that **one of** them would return to bring their younger brother, Benjamin (v. 34), while the other nine **remain confined** (held as prisoners), Joseph compassionately mitigated this condition (he would not do to them, even for a much shorter period, what they did to him) and confined only one of then, **Simeon** (v. 24). It is at this point that Joseph, overhearing their discussion in Hebrew, understood that they did indeed feel guilt and regret for their behavior toward Joseph. They did not realize **Joseph understood** their words (v. 23) when they said, **Truly we are guilty concerning our brother** (v. 21), and Reuben declared, **Now comes the reckoning for his blood** (v. 22).

42:25-38. Then, while Simeon remained behind and the other nine returned **to their father Jacob in the land of Canaan** (v. 29), Joseph continued to test their consciences, but now with kindness. Next **Joseph gave orders to fill their bags with grain and to restore every man's money . . . and to give them provisions for the journey** (v. 25). Their response upon discovering this generous gift was not to bless God for His kind provision but instead to become distraught, asking, **What is this that God has done to us?** (v. 28), declaring their guilt once again for their treatment of Joseph. Plainly, more than 20 years later, Joseph's brothers were no longer the callous and heartless men they had been before. God was indeed bringing discipline to them by the hand of Joseph all these many years after their sin. However, when they returned home and told their father what had happened, Jacob refused to let Benjamin return to Egypt with them, lest **harm should befall him** and Jacob would thus go **down to Sheol in sorrow** (i.e., die of heartbreak; v. 38).

(2) The Character Test (43:1-34)

43:1-15. With the need to return to Egypt, the brothers demonstrate that they have passed yet another test, this time pertaining to character. **The famine** remained **severe**, and **when** the family of Israel finished **eating the grain**

which they had brought from Egypt (vv. 1-2), they were forced to return to Joseph to buy some more, and thus also to take Benjamin with them. Thus, the first aspect of the character test becomes apparent even while still in Jacob's house—they prove responsible (43:1-15), particularly when Judah promised his father that he would be **responsible for** Benjamin (vv. 8-9). At this point Judah's role began to expand and theologically overshadow that of Joseph, for to ensure the safety of Benjamin, Judah took the positive initiative (just as he took the negative initiative to sell Joseph), declaring to his father that he would **be surety for** his brother (v. 9). The expression used here (i.e., *'e'erennu*) is significant, for it is from the same root (*'-r-b*) used previously—and certainly not coincidentally!—by Judah in 38:17-18 to describe the "surety" or "pledge" (*'erabon*) that Tamar took from him and that served as the catalyst for his own spiritual "turning point." The use of the same root here thus serves as an unmistakable, though subtle, link between the two episodes that underscores Judah's moral-behavioral shift in the latter of the two. Thus, in obedience to Joseph's demand, the brothers returned to Egypt with Benjamin in hand **and stood before Joseph** (v. 15).

43:16-23. The second aspect of their test of character becomes evident when they are at Joseph's door, where they prove themselves to be honest men. Rather than greedily keeping their unexpected benefit of returned payment and in contrast to their greedy behavior in selling Joseph, they immediately offered to return the money they had found in their sacks (vv. 20-22). Much to their surprise, Joseph told them that he had received their money and that their **God** . . . had **given** them **treasure in** their **sacks** (v. 23).

43:24-34. Yet a third aspect of their character test became clear at Joseph's table, where he had a banquet prepared for them. The literary tension mounts as the expectation of Joseph's self-revelation to his brothers grows stronger, as indicated by the statement that he had them seated **according to** . . . **birthright** and **youth** (v. 33), that is, according to their age or birth order. A stranger would logically have been unaware of this. Another strange aspect of this feast was that the **Egyptians** sat separately **by themselves**, as did **Joseph** . . . **by himself**, as well as the eleven brothers **by themselves** (v. 32). This was because Joseph was observing the Egyptian caste system in which foreigners, and particularly shepherds, were considered uncultured and vulgar. Joseph's brothers did not sit with him because they were shepherds. But Joseph sat separately from the other Egyptians, a first sign to the brothers that the prime minister of Egypt was a foreigner as well. Then, as a test, Joseph gave food **from his own table** to his brothers but gave his full brother Benjamin **five times as much** (v. 34). Nevertheless, they all **feasted** and were content, not exhibiting any of the jealousy they had previously shown toward Joseph.

(3) The Compassion Test (44:1-34)

Joseph's final test of his brothers was to see if they had been transformed from the callous indifference they had shown previously to being compassionate and caring.

44:1-34. The setting for this test came when Joseph's brothers set off on their way back to Canaan. Joseph's **house steward** overtook them and found his master's silver cup **in Benjamin's sack** (where the steward had planted it per his master's instructions). The penalty for this alleged wrongdoing required that Benjamin become Joseph's **slave** (vv. 1-13). The brothers returned **to Joseph's house**, where Judah (whose preeminent role is anticipated by the statement **Judah and his brothers**, v. 14) stepped forward to intercede for the life of his brother (v. 18). After summarizing the entire situation (from 42:13), Judah drew his plea to a conclusion in 44:32 by telling Joseph that he had become **surety for** Benjamin—again employing (as in 43:9) the verbal form (i.e., *'arab*) of the same root used in a noun in 38:17-18 to denote Judah's "surety" or "pledge" (*'erabon*). In chap. 38 the "surety" consisted of certain possessions (Judah's seal, cord, and staff), but in chap. 44 it consisted of the person of Judah himself. The messianic significance of this term is expressed in the OT in the Lord's eschatological declaration through Jeremiah (Jr 30:21) that the Messiah will one day reconcile His people Israel to Himself because "their leader [who] shall be one of them . . . will give Himself in surety" for them (lit., translation).

The brothers, and particularly Judah as their leader, demonstrated that they did indeed pass the compassion test. Previously they were indifferent to the suffering of their own brother, contemplating his murder, casting him into a pit, and then selling him into slavery (37:18-28). Moreover, they had been callous toward the grief of their own father, by deception leading him to believe that wild beasts had killed his favorite son

(37:31-35). Now, however, besides Judah being willing to take the punishment in the place of Benjamin (44:33), he expressed his grave concern for his father should Benjamin not return: **For how shall I go up to my father if the lad is not with me—for fear that I see the evil that would overtake my father?** (v. 34). No longer were they the cruel, jealous, deceitful, and callous perpetrators of a crime against their brother and their father. Now they were sorrowful men of integrity with concern for their youngest brother and compassion for their aged father.

c. Joseph Reconciles with His Brothers (45:1-28)

45:1-15. Seeing that his brothers were changed and overcome with emotion, Joseph revealed his true identity to his brothers, declaring **I am Joseph!** (vv. 1-3). In response, the brothers were naturally **dismayed** (v. 3, lit., "dumbfounded") at this news and were afraid that Joseph might seek vengeance. Up to this point, Joseph's brothers had experienced a general sense of guilt, seeing their difficulties with this powerful Egyptian as just recompense for their sin in selling Joseph (42:22; 44:16). But out of concern for his brothers, Joseph sought to comfort them with kind words, which provide a theologically mature reflection on God's all-encompassing goodness and sovereignty. Despite his brothers' sinful intention in selling him as a slave to the Egypt-bound traders, Joseph realized a greater good: **God sent me before you to preserve life** (45:5; see also 50:20). Seeing the providence of God is the key to Joseph's reconciliation with his brothers, as is true for reconciliation between all estranged and hurt people. Although Joseph stated one time that they had **sold** him as a slave **into Egypt** (45:4), three times he clarified that in reality it was **God** who **sent** him to Egypt (vv. 5, 7, 8) as an act of concern to preserve the family of Israel. In other words, all Joseph's sufferings during his 13 years as a slave and later as a prisoner was a result, ultimately, not only of the sinful will and actions of his brothers, but ultimately of the perfect will and behind-the-scenes work of God Himself. The verb **sent** (v. 5) is an active-voice verb and indicates God's providence over the sinful actions of Joseph's brothers. The verb **sold**, used for the sinful actions of the brothers, also is an active-voice verb (vv. 4-5). This is one of the key texts in the Bible indicating that God is sovereign over free human actions and that these two seemingly polar dynamics are nevertheless compatible in Scripture. Of course, this did not exonerate his brothers from the sinful part they played, though in response to their obvious repentance Joseph's declaration of this profound theological insight provided his brothers significant comfort and conciliation. For a brief discussion of the interplay between God's sovereignty (over sin and evil) and human responsibility, see comments on Rm 9:17-23. The genuineness of the full reconciliation of Joseph and his brothers is evident in Joseph's behavior toward them in providing a place for them to live (v. 10), food for them to endure the last five years of the famine (v. 11), and encouragement for them to **bring [his] father down** to Egypt (v. 13). True reconciliation shows genuine fruit and betrays no vengeance or bitterness.

45:16-28. Hearing **the news** that **Joseph's brothers had come**, Pharaoh—in whose eyes God had granted Joseph enduring favor—graciously told Joseph to invite his entire family to **come** down to the land of Egypt, where he would **give** them **the best of the land** (v. 18). The 11 brothers returned **to the land of Canaan to their father Jacob** (v. 25), loaded with **provisions** and gifts from Pharaoh and Joseph, and they relayed Pharaoh's gracious invitation, as well as the news that **Joseph is still alive and . . . ruler over all the land of Egypt** (v. 26).

d. Joseph Cares for All Egypt (46:1–47:26)

The next section of the Joseph story shows the outworking of the God's providence in the lives of many people, especially Joseph's brothers and father Jacob. Joseph had told his brothers that God had sent him to Egypt "to preserve life" (45:5). Similarly, the story that follows shows how God used Joseph to care for the life of the family of Israel (Jacob), the people of Egypt, and even Pharaoh.

(1) Joseph Provides for the Family of Israel (46:1–47:12)

46:1-34. In clear contrast to Abram, whose spiritual immaturity was expressed (among other things) by his immediate forsaking of Canaan for Egypt when the former was struck by famine (12:10), Jacob went first to **Beersheba** (46:1) on his way **to Egypt** (vv. 5-6). Beersheba was a significant place because there Jacob's grandfather Abraham "called on the name of the LORD" (Gn 21:33). Furthermore, in Beersheba God appeared to Jacob's father Isaac and reiterated the Abrahamic promises to him (Gn 26:23-24). In response, Isaac "built an altar there and called upon the name of the LORD" (v. 25).

Thus, Jacob **offered sacrifices to . . . God**, calling on His name and proceeding no further until the Lord assured him he could do so (46:1-7). The total number of family members whom Jacob brought with him **to Egypt** was **sixty-six** (v. 26). This number excludes the wives (per genealogical convention in antiquity), as well as Jacob and Joseph with his two sons, Ephraim and Manasseh (who were already in Egypt), whereas including these latter four males brings the total number of persons **of the house of Jacob** in **Egypt** to **seventy** (v. 27). Stephen gave the total persons as 75 (Ac 7:14), which was most likely caused by his inclusion of Joseph's three grandsons and two great-grandsons (Gn 50:23 with Nm 26:29, 35-36, that is, *all* the children of Jacob in Egypt mentioned in Genesis, prior to the exodus). To ensure a minimum of social contact with (and hence potential molestation by) the Egyptians, Joseph instructed his family to emphasize (*not* to lie about) their role as **shepherds**, since, according to the Egyptian caste system (see comments on 43:24-34) **every shepherd is loathsome to the Egyptians** (46:34).

47:1-12. The sojourn to Egypt enabled Jacob and his family to be physically reunited with Joseph and his family. But it also provided the ideal venue within which the family of Jacob could grow into the "great people/nation" God had promised to make them (see 12:2; 15:5; 17:2; 22:17; 26:4, 24; 28:14; 35:11). In the land of Canaan the patriarchal family was one among a plethora of tribes and peoples (most of them stronger and more numerous) constantly contending for land and resources (cf. 13:7; 15:19-21; 21:25; 26:18-21; 47:4), but in Egypt they were given, at Pharaoh's order, a privileged place **in the best of the land . . . in the land of Goshen** (47:6). Goshen is not mentioned in Egyptian literature, but it was later called the district of **Rameses** (v. 11). Its fertility and proximity to Joseph makes it likely that Goshen was a fertile area in the Nile Delta. Here they had the room to expand and grow, free from harassment or famine. Thus, Joseph fulfilled God's providential purpose in sending him to Egypt, in that he **provided his father and his brothers and all his father's household with food** (v. 12), Moreover, after 400 years had passed they had "increased greatly, and multiplied, and became exceedingly mighty, so that the land was filled with them" (Ex 1:7). The people were then numerous enough to spread throughout and fill the land of Canaan, their divine inheritance.

(2) Joseph Provides for the People of Egypt (47:13-19)

47:13-14. Besides bringing Joseph to Egypt to provide for his own family, God also was concerned for the lives of all Egypt and Canaan. Indeed, **there was no food in all the land**, so that **Egypt and . . . Canaan languished because of the famine** (v. 13). Therefore, the plan that God gave Joseph to store up food during the seven years of plenty not only saved his own family but all the people of Egypt and those that lived in Canaan as well (cf. 45:5, 7; 50:20).

47:15-19. Joseph accepted money and then livestock and finally land in payment for food. When that ran out, the Egyptians willingly sold themselves into a relatively benign form of slavery to Pharaoh. In return, Joseph not only gave them food but seed to grow food on the land from which Pharaoh would receive 20 percent of the produce. In essence, the people could work their own land and receive their own produce with a tax rate of 20 percent to Pharaoh. This narrative indicates a deliberate ironic literary strategy: Even as Joseph was sold into Egyptian slavery for 20 shekels of silver (Gn 37:28; cf. 39:17), now Joseph sold the whole land of Egypt into slavery, taking all the **money** (lit., silver) of the land (vv. 14, 18). In a sense, this was retributive justice upon all the Egyptians for buying a Hebrew slave (12:3). Nevertheless, the Egyptians saw their slavery as a means of deliverance and declared to Joseph, "You have saved our lives!" (v. 25).

(3) Joseph Provides for Pharaoh (47:20-26)

47:20-26. God brought Joseph to Egypt not only to save the family of Israel and the people of Egypt but also to provide great wealth for Pharaoh. Thus, through Joseph's shrewd dealings with the people, their wealth, their livestock, and their land, even the people themselves became the property of Pharaoh (except for the priests, vv. 22, 26). As a result, Pharaoh, who blessed Jacob and his family and welcomed them to Egypt and provided them with food, good land, and safety, experienced blessing as well, in fulfillment of the Abrahamic covenant, receiving blessing for blessing (12:3).

e. Joseph Receives the Blessing for His Sons (47:27–48:22)

After describing Joseph's providential role in saving the entire land of Egypt, with distinct emphasis on the deliverance of the family of Israel, the narrative now turns to emphasize the blessing of Joseph as the firstborn.

47:27. The story now transitions away from

the deliverance of Egypt to the blessing of Israel. As such, it describes Israel's sojourn **in the land of Egypt** as prosperous in that they **were fruitful and became very numerous** (v. 27) The text here uses the same Hebrew words ("be fruitful and multiply") spoken to Adam and Eve in the garden (1:22, 28), but spoken even more significantly to Jacob when he returned to Canaan and was blessed by God (35:11). Just as the Lord directed Jacob, so He had now made it possible, with His own providential care, for Jacob to obey that command. The "incubational" aspect of Israel's stay in Goshen is vividly underscored in v. 27, in which the writer skillfully transitioned from a reference to Israel *the person* (**Now Israel lived in the land of Egypt, in Goshen** [v. 27], in which the verb **lived** is sg.)—to the first biblical reference to Israel *the people* (**and they acquired property in it and were fruitful and became very numerous** in which the verbs are all pl.). The wording of this latter statement recalls God's promise to Abraham in 17:6: "I will make you exceedingly fruitful," thus connecting this future state of affairs to the important theme of God's covenant faithfulness.

47:28-31. As a prelude to Jacob giving his blessing to Joseph, the narrative shifts to a new time frame. It is now **seventeen years** after Jacob had moved to Egypt, and the famine is long over (v. 28). Jacob is 147 years old. Anticipating his own death, Jacob asks Joseph to be sure to bury him in the promised land. Central to the patriarchal promises was that God would give this land to their descendants. Jacob anticipates the ultimate fulfillment of the land promise and longs to be part of it, when the dry bones once again come to life, and Joseph and Judah become one nation under the greater son of "David" their King (Ezk 37:22-24, see comments there).

48:1-22. As Jacob drew near to the end of his life (as he was fully aware; 48:21), he turned his attention to bestowing the patriarchal blessings on his male children. Thus when Joseph heard that his **father** was **sick** and went to visit him with his two sons, **Manasseh and Ephraim** (v. 1), Jacob exhorted Joseph to **bring them** closer so **that** he **may bless them** (vv. 8-16). In blessing his two grandsons—whom he in fact elevated to the status of sons begotten by himself (see v. 5)—Jacob intentionally granted the preeminent blessing to the younger rather than to the older, as has been the pattern throughout Genesis (see comments on 25:21b-26). This highlights the sovereignty of God in election (cf. Rm 9:10-16), but it also anticipates the similar "unconventional" election of Jacob's fourth-oldest son (Judah) as the recipient of the messianic blessing in the next generation (49:8-12). Moreover, before turning to his final pronouncements over his 12 sons, Jacob granted to Joseph **one portion more than** his **brothers** (48:22). In other words, the inheritance would be divided 13 ways between the 12 sons, and Joseph would receive two thirteenths of it, but the rest one thirteenth. This signifies that although the preeminent (messianic) blessing would go to Judah (see comments on 49:8-12), the birthright (i.e., double the amount of the material inheritance the other brothers would receive, here denoted by the "one portion more") would go to Joseph (as affirmed in 1Ch 5:2; cf. also the distinction between the blessing and the birthright in Gn 27:36).

f. Jacob Blesses the Twelve Tribes (49:1-33)

49:1-2. To underscore not only the importance but also the *prophetic* nature of his final words of blessing (which are in a few instances mixed with rebuke), Jacob exhorted his sons to **assemble** themselves so **that** he **may tell** them **what will** happen to them **in the days to come** (lit., "in the end of days," v. 1). Consistent with its usage elsewhere in the Hebrew Bible (including its three other occurrences in the Pentateuch: Nm 24:14; Dt 4:30; 31:29), this phrase ("in the end of days") refers specifically to that future period toward the end of redemption history, culminating in the final advent of the messianic King and His restoration of Israel, both *spiritually* as well as *physically* (cf. Is 2:2; Jr 23:20; Ezk 38:16; Dn 10:14). The expectation is thus laid for an expression of the Abrahamic blessing that specifically depicts the promised seed in this eschatological ruling role. This fits with an overall theme of Genesis, that God will restore the blessing lost in the garden through the messianic King, the ultimate seed of Abraham.

49:3-7. In selecting the son on whom to bestow this blessing, Jacob followed the conventional order of birth. The first three sons, however, were disqualified from receiving the messianic blessing because of their previous commission of sins that directly (and severely) violated their father's honor. In the case of **Reuben**, he violated Jacob's concubine Bilhah (35:22; alluded to in 49:4), and in the case of **Simeon and Levi**, they violated their agreement with the Shechemites (34:11-17, 30; alluded to in 49:5-6).

49:8-12. The messianic blessing thus fell to **Judah**; the central focus of Jacob's pronouncement was on the *preeminence* of the messianic King who would descend from Judah. Specifically four aspects of Judah's/the Messiah's preeminence are depicted, beginning with his *preeminence over his brothers*, indicated by **your brothers shall praise you** and, even more significantly, by the parallel clause **your father's sons shall bow down to you**. This statement uses the same wording that was originally applied to Joseph in 37:10. The point is that, though the family of Israel would bow down to Joseph in the near future, in the far-term they would all bow down to Judah, represented by his descendant, the messianic King, on his eternal throne (cf. 2Sm 7:16).

The future king will also have *preeminence in power*, with the image of a **lion** ready to pounce upon his prey, indicating the victorious power of the future king (cf. Nm 24:9 where the words are virtually identical). This prediction of victorious power is the source of the messianic title in Rv 5:5, "the Lion that is from the tribe of Judah, the Root of David, has overcome."

Jacob next depicted the future king's *preeminence over royalty*, first by indicating that he would transcend all the kings of Judah (i.e., the Davidic line) in the *duration* of his rule. Hence, the office of ruler—represented by the terms **scepter** and **staff** (Gn 49:10)—would be successively handed down only **until** that final king would come to take up the royal scepter and staff forever (such being the natural implication of **shall not depart . . . until**). Second, the ruler's preeminence is such that he would transcend all rulers in his very *nature* as the true and rightful king. According to the NASB, the future king's title is **Shiloh** and has been interpreted in a variety of ways: (1) Shiloh can be a proper name (as in the NASB and in the Talmud in *b. Sanh.* 98b), meaning "peacemaker," but this cannot be confirmed lexically or by the analogy of Scripture. (2) The word can be derived from a place name, the city of Shiloh, but the Hebrew Bible, despite containing various spellings of the city name, never spells the city name as it does in Gn 49:10. Additionally, the biblical convention is for city names to be derived from those of individuals, not vice versa. (3) The word could be revocalized as *sheloh* and would mean "to whom tribute will be brought." Support for this reading is derived from the seemingly parallel next phrase, **the obedience of the peoples**, so those who obey will bring tribute. But this translation requires changing the verb form from the active **comes** to the passive "be brought" making possible revocalization unlikely. (4) The word could be a contracted Hebrew word, meaning "to whom it belongs." The primary objection to this interpretation is that it is only found in a minority of MT manuscripts. However, Walter Kaiser contends that there is indeed significant textual support for it, with 38 Masoretic manuscripts holding to this reading. Further, it is the source of the LXX's translation, "to whom it belongs." This interpretive view is also supported by Targum Onkelos, Aquila, Symmachus, and Theodotion and seems to have an inner-biblical reference in Ezk 21:25-27, making this the likely interpretation (Walter C. Kaiser, *The Messiah in the Old Testament* [Grand Rapids, MI: Zondervan, 1995], 51-52). Hence, the descendant of Judah will be the ultimate and true King of Israel, the One to whom rightful kingship belongs.

The King will also surpass all the future kings from Judah in the *extent* of his rule, for **to him shall be the obedience of the peoples** (Gn 49:10). The term for **peoples** (*'ammim*) is regularly employed in the singular (*'am*) to denote the entire nation of Israel. So, since it is used in the pl. here, it denotes more than just Israel but the nations of the world obeying the future king.

Jacob then depicted the future king as having *preeminence in wealth*, that is, the ideal abundance of both natural and cultivated provision that will characterize the land under his reign. One will be able to tie **his foal** or **donkey's colt to the choice vine** (v. 11) without worrying whether the animal will damage it or eat its grapes, for the land will be filled with such vines. Moreover, the amount of choice **wine** these vines produce will be such that one can use it instead of water to wash **his garments** without feeling the slightest shade of loss! These images are of course hyperboles that to underscore the all-pervasive fruitfulness of the Messiah's kingdom, as also depicted, for example, in Jl 3:18: "And in that day the mountains will drip with sweet wine, and the hills will flow with milk." The peoples' physical health during that time will naturally also be ideal, as emphasized by the picture of the King Himself, whose **eyes are dull from** (lit., "darker than") **wine** (i.e., the darkness of his Semitic irises is set off by his healthy eye-whites), **and** whose **teeth** are **white from** (lit., "whiter than") **milk**. This picture stands in contrast to the jaundiced yellowing of the whites of one's eyes often present in those suffering from famine and/or malnutrition, along with the attendant yellowing of the teeth that also results from, among other things, a poor diet and old age.

49:13-27. Jacob's final blessing over the rest of his sons are for the most part brief, cryptic, future oriented, and generally related to a wordplay derived from each name. They each depict a time of future blessing and abundance, indicating that these prophecies are all about the end of days (49:1-2), when Judah's messianic descendant rules over the world (49:8-12). **Zebulun['s]** borders will extend, at the end of days, to **Sidon** in Lebanon (v. 13). **Issachar** will labor as a **strong donkey** with the hope of ultimate settlement in the land of rest (vv. 14-15). **Dan** (Hb. "judge") will **judge his people** (v. 16), a phrase likely fulfilled by Samson's judgeship (Jdg 13–16). The cryptic phrase about **a serpent** that will **bite the horse's heels** (Gn 49:17) is unclear in its meaning, but based on Jacob's exclamation (**For your salvation I wait, O Lord**, v. 18) it points to end-of-days deliverance by the Lion of Judah. The prophecy for **Gad** is filled with wordplay, as four of the six Hebrew words contain the same letters as those in Gad's name. It looks to the end-of-days victory when Gad will **raid** the **heels** of Israel's enemies (v. 19). **Asher** is promised prosperity (v. 20), and he will obtain it when the messianic King brings prosperity to Israel (49:11). The enigmatic prophecy of **Naphtali** (v. 21) depicts freedom and pleasantness, conditions that will be experienced under the messianic King. The prophecy of Joseph (vv. 22-26), as would be expected, is more expansive than the words to the other brothers (except Judah). While recounting the story of Joseph with poetic images (vv. 22-24), Jacob emphasized the future blessing of Joseph's descendants through repetition of the word **blessings** (vv. 25-26). The oracle for Benjamin recalls the promise to Judah, as both tribes are depicted as predators (Judah as a lion, 49:9; Benjamin as a **wolf**, v. 27). Benjamin is promised a military victory that will be won when the Lion of Judah takes His throne (49:10).

49:28-33. The paragraph that follows these words of prophecy provides a transition from Jacob's blessing of the tribes to the end of the Joseph story. It begins by emphasizing Jacob's blessing of the tribes (v. 28), three times using the word **blessing** in some form. These blessings will be realized when the One to whom kingship belongs (49:10) takes His throne and paradise will be regained. The purpose of Moses' inclusion of Jacob's blessing was to point Israel, as they entered the land of promise, to the hope that peace and prosperity would be theirs when their ultimate rightful king would come. As a final request, Jacob once again asks his sons to bring his body back to Canaan (vv. 29-33, cf. 47:29-30) in far more specific fashion than previously. This is designed to remind the reader of the land promise and to show that Jacob remained confident that God would indeed fulfill this promise to Israel. Fittingly, at this point, Jacob died **and was gathered to his people**, an expression that occurs only in the Pentateuch (Gn 25:8; Nm 31:2; Dt 32:50).

g. Joseph Believes God to the End (50:1-26)

This chapter functions as both the close of the Joseph narrative and the book of Genesis. It is designed to show Joseph's faith in God and trust in the promises God made to his fathers to the very end of his life.

50:1-14. Joseph's faith is evident in his request made to Pharaoh to personally bury his father **in the land of Canaan** in accord with Jacob's wishes (v. 5). With Pharaoh's assent, **Joseph and his brothers** then **carried** Jacob's body **to the land of Canaan and buried him in the cave of the field of Machpelah** (vv. 7-12), where Abraham and Sarah, Isaac and Rebekah, and Leah were buried (49:31). In Canaan, Jacob's family mourned him for a period of **seven days** (50:10), which, together with the similar reference in 1Sm 31:13, underlies the contemporary Jewish practice of *shivah* (setting aside seven days for the purpose of mourning over a deceased family member). This extended narrative about Joseph's burial of his father, including the record of the large procession of Egyptians and the tribes of Israel (Gn 50:7) that went back to the land of Canaan is designed to show Joseph's faith in the land promise. His trust that God would indeed keep His promise to return the family of Israel to the promised land (15:13-16) prompted this significant funeral so far from Egypt.

50:15-21. Joseph's trust in God is also evident in his relationship with his brothers now that their father Jacob had died. Thinking that perhaps Joseph had stayed his hand of vengeance against them in deference to their father, the brothers now feared that perhaps Joseph would finally punish them (v. 15). As a result they once again apologized for the wrong they did to Joseph (vv. 16-18). At this point, Joseph's faith in God becomes evident and served to remind his brothers that he forgave them, not for his human father's sake, but because he saw God's hand working in his own life. Thus, Joseph reiterates the ultimate point of the entire narrative about his life (cf. 45:7), reminding them that it was God who arranged for him to go to Egypt **to preserve many people alive**. Joseph's words remind them of the providence of God: **You meant evil against me, but God meant it for good** (v. 20). It was trust in God's good plan that enabled Joseph to forgive his brothers.

50:22-26. Joseph's faith in God becomes apparent once again with the request he made of the sons of Israel. Although Jacob's family returned to their privileged place in Goshen in the land of Egypt, Joseph continued the focus on returning to the promised land, as he bound **the sons of Israel** with the charge that **God will surely take care of** [lit., visit] **you, and you shall carry my bones up from here** (v. 25). The key words here are "visit" (the verb *yiphqod*, from the root *p-q-d*, when used of God, implies an active interest on behalf of His people, plus the infinitive absolute here, *paqod yiphqod* [twice in vv. 24-25], is the strongest way to say that the action will occur, "God will surely visit / take care of you") and "carry up" (*veha'alitem*, a verb from the root *'-l-h*, when used directionally, refers to movement toward the promised land, and when used within the promised land, to Jerusalem, and when in Jerusalem, to the temple; hence, "to go up" is to move closer to the presence of the Lord). Joseph faithfully trusted that God would indeed return the people of Israel to the promised land, and he wanted to participate when God finally brought it to pass.

Thus Genesis comes to a close by anticipating the return not only of Israel to the ideal of the promised land, but also therefore of "all families of the earth" (12:3, etc.) to the ideal of creation as it was in the prefall garden, when all of God's servants "will see His face" and as coheirs with the Son will "reign forever and ever" (Rm 8:17; Rv 22:4-5).

BIBLIOGRAPHY

Alexander, T. Desmond. "Further Observations on the Term 'Seed' in Genesis." *Tyndale Bulletin* 48, no. 2 (1997): 363–67.

Allis, O. T. *God Spake by Moses*. Nutley, NJ: Presbyterian and Reformed, 1958.

Alter, Robert. *The Art of Biblical Narrative*. New York: Basic Books, 1981.

______. *Genesis: Translation and Commentary*. New York: W. W. Norton & Co, 1996.

Atkinson, David. *The Message of Genesis 1–11*. Downers Grove, IL: InterVarsity, 1990.

Baldwin, Joyce. *The Message of Genesis 12–50*. Downers Grove, IL: InterVarsity, 1986.

Cassuto, Umberto. *A Commentary on the Book of Genesis*, vol 1. Jerusalem: Magnes Press, 1961.

______. *The Documentary Hypothesis and the Composition of the Pentateuch*, trans. Israel Abrahams. Jerusalem and New York: Shalem, 2008.

Davis, John J. *Paradise to Prison*. Grand Rapids, MI: Baker, 1975.

Garrett, Duane. *Rethinking Genesis*. Grand Rapids, MI: Baker, 1991

Hamilton, Victor. *The Book of Genesis*, 2 vols. New International Commentary on the Old Testament. Grand Rapids, MI: Eerdmans, 1990–95.

Hertz, J. H. *The Pentateuch and Haftorahs*. London: Soncino Press, 1950.

Jacob, Benno. *The First Book of the Bible: Genesis*. New York, NY: Ktav, 1974.

Jacobs, Louis. "Akedah." In *Encyclopaedia Judaica*, vol. 2. Edited by Cecil Roth, 480–81. Jerusalem: Keter Publishing, 1971.

Morris, Henry M. *The Genesis Record*. Grand Rapids, MI: Baker, 1976.

Ramban–Nachmanides. "Bereishis, Genesis Part 1." In *Commentary on the Torah*. Vol. 1. Edited by R. Yaakov Blinder. Brooklyn, NY: Mesorah Publications, 2004.

Ross, Allen P. *Creation and Blessing: A Guide to the Study and Exposition of Genesis*. Grand Rapids, MI: Baker, 1981.

Sailhamer, John H. *Genesis*. The Expositor's Bible Commentary. Grand Rapids, MI: Zondervan, 1990.

______. *The Pentateuch as Narrative*. Grand Rapids, MI: Zondervan, 1992.

Sarna, Nahum. *Genesis*. The JPS Torah Commentary. Philadelphia: Jewish Publication Society, 1989.

______. *Understanding Genesis*. New York: Schocken Books, 1966.

Waltke, Bruce K. *Genesis: A Commentary*. Grand Rapids, MI: Zondervan, 2001.

Wenham, Gordon. *Genesis*, 2 vols. Word Biblical Commentary. Waco, TX: Word, 1987–1994.

Wise, Michael O., Martin Abegg, Jr., and Edward Cook, trans. *The Dead Sea Scrolls: A New Translation*. Rev. ed. San Francisco: HarperSanFrancisco, 2005.

Youngblood, Ronald, ed. *The Genesis Debate*. Nashville: Thomas Nelson, 1986.

EXODUS

KEVIN D. ZUBER

INTRODUCTION

The title of Exodus in Hebrew (*w'elleh semot*) is taken from the first few words of 1:1, "Now these are the names." This phrase, which also appears in Gn 46:8, introduces the list of the persons who "came to Egypt with Jacob." Since the book begins with an adverb of time, "Now," as well as this unmistakable connection with Genesis, it is evident that Exodus was meant to be a continuation of the narrative of Genesis. Furthermore, the subject matter of the tabernacle (the last major portion of Exodus) and the subject of the functions of the Levitical priests who served in the tabernacle (the first chapters of Leviticus) tie the second and third books of the Torah (Law) or Pentateuch (five books) together. Plainly the Torah was intended to be read as one book with five volumes, not five separate books.

The title of the book in the English Bible is derived from the Septuagint (the ancient Gk. version of the OT) through the Latin (*exodus* is the Lat. of the Gk. *exodos* which means "going out"). This title is, of course based on the major theme of the first part of the book, the "exodus," the departure of the nation of Israel from bondage in Egypt. This departure was the first vital step on a journey to the land of promise (cf. 3:8, 17; 13:5; 32:13; 33:1; 34:11-12). That journey, which began with the exodus, is taken up again in the book of Numbers (cf. Nm 15:2) only to be delayed by fear and unbelief (see commentary on Nm 13, 14). When the story of that journey is taken up once more in Deuteronomy (cf. Dt 1:6-8), it ties together the narrative of the nation's promise from the Lord (Gn 12–50), deliverance by the Lord (Exodus), provision, preservation, and protection from the Lord (Exodus–Numbers), and preparation (for entering the land, Deuteronomy). Viewed in this way "Exodus forms the heart of the Torah" (Walter C. Kaiser Jr., "Exodus," in vol. 2 *Expositor's Bible Commentary*, ed. Frank E. Gaebelein [Grand Rapids, MI: Zondervan, 1990], 287).

Author. The liberal and critical view that the Pentateuch is a late (c. 550 BC) compilation of earlier materials from a variety of somewhat incommensurate sources (i.e., the JEDP theory; see Bill T. Arnold, "Pentateuchal Criticism, History of," in *Dictionary of the Old Testament Pentateuch*, ed. T. Desmond Alexander and David W. Baker [Downers Grove, IL: InterVarsity, 2003], 622–31; see also Kaiser, "Exodus," 288, and John J. Davis, *Moses and the Gods of Egypt* [Winona Lake, IN: BMH Books, 1986], 45) stands in stark contrast to the view indicated in the text itself that Moses himself was the author of the Pentateuch. Kitchen simply states, "The basic fact is that there is *no* objective, independent evidence for any of these four compositions (or any variant of them) anywhere outside the pages of our existing Hebrew Bible" (Kenneth A. Kitchen, *On the Reliability of the Old Testament* [Grand Rapids, MI: Eerdmans, 2003], 492).

Several lines of evidence support Mosaic authorship of Exodus. First, internal evidence can be found in Exodus in passages where Moses is instructed to write things down (17:14; 34:4, 27-29) and where the text records that "Moses wrote down all the words of the LORD" (24:4; cf. Nm 33:1-2; Dt 31:9). Second, "the great abundance of details reflecting an eyewitness account would seem to support" Mosaic authorship (Davis, *Moses and the Gods*, 46; note especially the account of Moses' call [chaps. 3 and 4] when only he and the Lord were present; no one but Moses could know the details of this conversation). Third, other OT books indicate Mosaic authorship of Exodus and the

Pentateuch (cf. Jos 1:7; 8:31-32; 1Ki 2:3; 2Ki 14:6; Ezr 6:18; Neh 13:1; Dn 9:1-13; Mal 4:4). Fourth, the NT also clearly affirms Mosaic authorship. "Mark 12:26 locates Exodus 3:6 in 'the Book of Moses,' [cf. Mk 7:10] while Luke 2:22-23 assigns Exodus 13:2 to both 'the Law of Moses' and 'the Law of the Lord'" (Kaiser, "Exodus," 288). John likewise confirms Moses' authorship of the Law (Jn 7:19; cf. 5:46-47; Ac 3:22; Rm 10:5).

Finally, it is eminently plausible that Moses wrote the books attributed to him, for he "was educated in all the learning of the Egyptians and he was a man of power in words and deeds" (Ac 7:22).

Date. The contemporary debate on the date of the exodus itself is a question mainly reserved "for those who take the biblical record seriously" (John H. Walton, "Exodus, Date of," *Dictionary of the Old Testament Pentateuch*, ed. T. Desmond Alexander and David W. Baker [Downers Grove, IL: InterVarsity, 2003], 258–72). Broadly speaking, the issue has come down to two possible dates: an early date at the time of the later pharaohs of the 18th Dynasty (c. 1580–1321 BC) or a late date at the time of the 19th Dynasty (c. 1321–1205 BC) (cf. Kaiser, "Exodus," 289).

Advocates of the late date point to the identity of the storage cities identified in 1:11 as Pithom and Raamses and identify the latter with Raamses II of the Nineteenth Dynasty. Late date advocates also point to certain strands of archaeological data to bolster their view (cf. Walton, "Exodus, Date of," 263; Kaiser, "Exodus," 289).

On the other hand, the early date is supported by two texts of Scripture. One is found in Jdg 11:26, which indicates that three hundred years had passed between entrance of the nation into the land (the conquest of the land) and Jephthah's rule as judge. The second text is 1Ki 6:1; this verse states clearly that the exodus happened 480 before the fourth year of Solomon. If the latter is dated as 966/5 BC (cf. Davis, *Moses and the Gods*, 34; see commentary on 1Ki 6:1) then the exodus itself took place 1446/5 BC, a date much in line with the time indicated in Jdg 11:26 (when one adds the years between the exodus itself and the start of the conquest; cf. Nm 14:34). As for the city being named after Raamses II, the city could have been built earlier by Israelite slaves and renamed after Raamses II came to power. Then later copyists may have updated the names (even as they did with Laish, substituting Dan, Gn 14:14; see "The Presence of Anachronisms" in the section on the Documentary Hypothesis in the introduction to Genesis).

The matter of the date of the exodus is related to the question of the identity of the different kings and pharaohs in the narrative of Exodus. Since the entire time of bondage was over four hundred years (cf. Gn 15:13; Ex 12:40; Ac 7:6), it is obvious that the king who began the oppression is not the one who was alive at the time of the exodus itself. The "new king" (1:8) was probably one of the Hyksos (c. 1730–1570 BC), a Semitic people who conquered Egypt briefly in the era before the 18th Dynasty (cf. Davis, *Moses and the Gods*, 40, 53; Ronald F. Youngblood, *Exodus*: *Everyman's Bible Commentary* [Chicago: Moody, 1983], 23; cf. Kaiser, "Exodus," 305n8). The early date of the exodus places that event late in the 18th Dynasty (which ran from c. 1580–1321 BC), thus the "Egyptians" mentioned in 1:13 were those (probably pharaohs Kamose and Ahmose I, first rulers of the 18th Dynasty) who expelled the Hyksos, but persisted in the oppression of the Hebrews. The king who "spoke to the Hebrew midwives" (1:15) was most likely Thutmose I, during whose reign Moses was born (1525 BC). After Thutmose died his son Thutmose II ruled only briefly and was followed by Queen Hatshepsut. Her stepson was Thutmose III and he was the pharaoh from whom Moses fled (forty years before the exodus; 2:15) and the one whose death was noted in 4:19. His son Amenhotep II was the pharaoh at the time of the exodus itself (cf. Davis, *Moses and the Gods*, 42–43; Youngblood, *Exodus*, 24–25).

Purpose. Obviously the book of Exodus supplies a crucial link in the historical narrative of the nation. Even as the Lord made an unconditional promise to Abram and his descendants (see Gn 15), He informed Abraham that his descendants would be "strangers in a land that is not theirs" and that they would be "enslaved and oppressed" but ultimately they would "return here"—to the land of promise (see Gn 15:13-16). Exodus provided the details of the nation's bondage and deliverance to impress upon the generation that experienced the exodus (and subsequent generations) that the enslavement and the great deliverance they had experienced was in accord with the sovereign and gracious plan and purposes of God.

Furthermore, the book was meant to impress upon the nation the privilege and importance of the presence of God among them. The tabernacle (along with the instructions for the priests in

Leviticus) was a tangible reminder of the importance of careful, serious, and solemn worship; one could hardly be flippant about approaching God in a venue like the tabernacle. And of course Exodus contains the first writing of the Decalogue—the Ten Commandments—which was the gracious gift from the Lord to encourage the people to live in such a way that they might enjoy the blessings of His sovereign plan for them and His awesome presence with them.

In the light of the failure of that exodus generation to enter the land of promise, the second generation, that of the conquest (see Joshua), would have read this part of the Pentateuch (Exodus) as both encouragement (the Lord keeps His promises, specifically to live in the land of promise) and warning (the Lord is to be trusted and obeyed for any generation to know and enjoy His promises) (see Dt 28).

Themes. No incident in the history of the nation is referred to more frequently by the rest of the OT than is the exodus. The theme of deliverance from bondage—redemption—is central to the theology and history of the OT, and this theme is at the heart of the first part of the book of Exodus. The second major theme in Exodus is worship. This theme is highlighted by instructions about and construction of the tabernacle. The details of the construction and furnishings of the tabernacle testify to the central role worship was to play in the life of God's people.

Overall, the major theme of the book of Exodus is theology proper, the study of God. Few other books can rival the breadth of theology, teaching about God, revealed in this book, including the revelation of the person, attributes, and perfections of God. The theology of Exodus is foundational for understanding the person and program of the Lord God in the remainder of the OT and indeed the whole Bible. In Exodus the Lord is shown to be the God who keeps His covenant promise to the nation. He is the God who calls, empowers, and employs unlikely but submissive servants; He is I AM (cf. 3:14). He is revealed as the One who demonstrates His sovereign power and authority (while idols and false gods are proven impotent). He is the holy God who desires His people to live before Him in holiness (and to that end He gave them the Ten Commandments). His very character is revealed in the law; "the law is something of a transcript of the nature of God" (Millard J. Erickson, *Christian Theology* [Grand Rapids, MI: Baker, 1998], 820). He is displayed as the longsuffering and faithful God who cares for, provides for, and protects His people. He is revealed as the awesome and holy God who nevertheless desires to dwell in the presence of His people (in the tabernacle); He is the worthy God who demands true worship.

OUTLINE

I. Redemption: The Lord Delivered the People of Israel from Bondage in Egypt (1:1–18:27)
  A. How the Bondage Began (1:1-22)
    1. Opening Genealogy (1:1-7)
    2. The Oppression Begins (1:8-14)
    3. The Oppression Continues (1:15-22)
  B. Moses: Early Life and Calling (2:1-22)
    1. Moses' Mother Endeavors to Save Her Son (2:1-4)
    2. Moses' Life Is Preserved by Pharaoh's Daughter (2:5-10)
    3. Moses' Failure (2:11-15a)
    4. Moses' Sojourn in Midian (2:15b-22)
  C. The Call of Moses: Reluctance and Compulsion (2:23–4:26)
    1. The Nation's Bondage Recalled (2:23-25)
    2. Moses Called to the Burning Bush (3:1-9)
    3. Moses Commissioned by "I AM WHO I AM" (3:10–4:17)
      a. Moses' First Objection (3:10-12)
      b. Moses' Second Objection (3:13-17)
      c. A Preview of Coming Events (3:18-22)
      d. Three Signs and One Spokesman for Moses (4:1-17)
    4. Transitions (4:18-26)

D. The Return of Moses: Failure and (Re-)Confirmation (4:27–7:7)
   1. Reunion of Moses and Aaron and Reception by the Nation (4:27-31)
   2. Rejection by Pharaoh (5:1-23)
   3. A Patient Reminder of the Lord's Promises (6:1-8)
   4. Reassurance and Preparation (6:9–7:7)

E. The Judgment of the Plagues (7:8–10:29)
   1. Initial Confrontation (7:8-13)
   2. The Nine Judgments or Plagues (7:14–10:29)

F. Free at Last (11:1–15:21)
   1. The Last Judgment or Plague (11:1-10)
   2. Deliverance from Death and Preservation by Passover (12:1-30)
      a. The Preparation of the People for the Passover (12:1-13)
      b. The Instructions for the Feast of Unleavened Bread (12:14-20)
      c. The Passover Executed (12:21–22, 28)
      d. The Promise of the Passover and the Promise to the Nation (12:23-27)
      e. The Last Judgment Executed: The Death of the Firstborn (12:29-30)
   3. The Exodus Itself (12:31-39)
      a. Pharaoh Relented in Sorrow (12:31-32)
      b. The Nation Departed in Haste (12:33-39)
   4. Summary: The Years of Bondage (12:40-41)
   5. Instructions Regarding the Foreigner and Sojourner and the Passover (12:42-51)
   6. The Consecration of the Firstborn (13:1-16)
   7. Deliverance through the Sea (13:17–14:31)
      a. Phase One: The Lord Led the People (13:17-22)
      b. Phase Two: Pharaoh Chased the People (14:1-12)
      c. Phase Three: The Lord Preserved the People (14:13-31)
   8. Praise for Deliverance and Preservation: The Song of Moses (15:1-21)

G. The Journey from the Sea to Sinai, Part One (15:22–17:7)

H. The Journey from the Sea to Sinai, Part Two (17:8–18:27)
   1. War with Amalek (17:8-16)
   2. Reunion with and Advice from Jethro (18:1-27)

II. The Law and the Tabernacle (19:1–40:38)

A. Preparation of the People to Receive the Law (19:1-25)
   1. The People Accept and Commit to the Covenant (19:1-8)
   2. The People Demonstrate Consecration (19:9-25)
      a. The Place of the Lord (19:9)
      b. The Place of the People (19:10-15)
      c. The Place of the Priests (19:22)
      d. The Appearance of the Lord (19:16-20)
      e. The Warning of the Lord (19:21, 23-25)

B. Presentation of the Decalogue to the People (20:1-17)
   1. Preamble (20:1-2)
   2. The First Tablet Commanded the People to Honor the Lord (20:3-11)
      a. No Other Gods (20:3)
      b. No Idols (20:4-6)
      c. No Swearing (20:7)
      d. Sabbath Observance (20:8-11)
   3. The Second Tablet Commanded the People to Honor Others (20:12-17)
      a. Honor Parents (20:12)
      b. Do Not Murder (20:13)
      c. Do Not Commit Adultery (20:14)
      d. Do Not Steal (20:15)
      e. Do Not Lie (20:16)
      f. Do Not Covet (20:17)

C. The People Respond with Devotion, Fear, and Worship (20:18-26)
D. Application of the Law: Living the Life of Faithfulness (21:1–23:19)
  1. Laws Pertaining to Slavery (21:1-11)
    a. Male Slaves (21:1-6)
    b. Regarding Female Slaves (21:7-11)
  2. Laws Pertaining to Personal Injury (21:12-36)
  3. Laws Pertaining to Personal Property (22:1-15)
  4. Laws Pertaining to Personal Integrity (22:16–23:9)
  5. Laws Pertaining to Worship (23:10-19)
E. Plans for the Conquest of the Land (23:20-33)
F. The Ratification of the Covenant (24:1-18)
  1. The Approach to the Lord (24:1-11)
  2. Moses on the Mountain (24:12-18)
G. Intructions on The Tabernacle, Its Builders, and the Priests (25:1–27:31:18; 35:1–38:31)
      Excursus: Introduction to the Tabernacle
      Focal Point for the Nation
      Theories of Origin
      Terms to Designate the Tabernacle
      Purposes of the Tabernacle
  1. The Initial Instructions (25:1-9)
    a. The Contributions (25:1-8; 30:11-16; 35:4-9; 38:21–39:1)
    b. The Lord's Pattern (25:9)
  2. The Ark of the Covenant: Symbol the Lord's Holy Presence (25:10-16; 26:34; 37:1-5)
  3. The Mercy Seat: Symbol of Propitiation (25:17-22; 37:6-9)
  4. The Table of Showbread: Symbol of Physical Provision (25:23-30; 26:25; 37:10-15)
  5. The Golden Lampstand: Symbol of Spiritual Provision (25:31-40; 26:35; 37:17-24)
  6. The Tabernacle Itself: Symbol of God's Personal Presence (26:1-30)
  7. The Veil and Screen: Symbol of God's "Hiddenness" (26:31-37)
  8. The Bronze Altar: Symbol of the Need for a Sacrifice for Sin (27:1-8; 38:1-7)
  9. The Court: Symbol of Separation (27:9-20; 38:9-20)
  10. The Priests of the Tabernacle (27:21–29:46)
    a. Priestly Functions (27:21–28:1)
    b. Priestly Garments (28:2-43; 39:1-31)
    c. The Consecration of the Priests (29:1-46)
  11. The Altar of Incense: Symbol of Prayer and Intercession (30:1-10; 37:25-29)
  12. The Census (30:11-16)
  13. The Bronze Laver: Symbol of Cleansing (30:17-21; 38:8; 40:30-32)
  14. The Anointing Oil and Incense: Symbol of Consecration (30:22-38)
  15. The Builders of the Tabernacle (31:1-11; 35:30-35; 36:1-2)
  16. Sabbath Reminder (31:12-18; 35:1-3)
H. Apostasy and Aftermath (32:1–34:35)
  1. The Golden Calf (32:1-29)
    a. The Folly of Aaron and the People (32:1-6)
    b. Anger and Intercession (32:7-14)
    c. Confrontation: Moses Against Aaron and the People (32:15-29)
      (1) A "Heavy" Descent (32:15-18)
      (2) A "Hot" Confrontation (32:19-20)
      (3) A "Heated" Conversation, Moses vs. Aaron (32:21-24)
      (4) A Harsh Division (32:25-29)
  2. Five Scenes of Intercession and Intimacy, Moses and the Lord (32:30–33:23)
    a. Scene One: A Selfless Offer (32:30-35)
    b. Scene Two: A Hopeful and Sorrowful Word (33:1-6)
    c. Scene Three: A Separate Arrangement (33:7-11)

COMMENTARY ON EXODUS

I. Redemption: The Lord Delivered the People of Israel from Bondage in Egypt (1:1–18:27)

The narrative begins with the account of how God provided Israel with deliverance/liberation from bondage in Egypt, preservation/protection in the exodus from Egypt, and guidance/provision on the journey to Sinai.

A. How the Bondage Began (1:1-22)

The explanation of how the children of Israel came to be in bondage in Egypt is brief and to the point. This section reveals how the nation came to need deliverance.

1. Opening Genealogy (1:1-7)

1:1-7. In the brief opening paragraph of Exodus the author has tied the narrative of Genesis to the narrative of Exodus with a genealogy of the sons of Jacob (cf. Gn 46:8-27), highlighting the special status of Joseph. He is mentioned last in the list and his death is singled out. The Lord's providence was evident in His preservation of Joseph personally and was the means of the preservation of the family of Jacob and thus of the nation of Israel (see Gn 37; 39–47; 50:20). That family that came to Egypt amounted to just over seventy persons (cf. Gn 46:27; Dt 10:22; Ac 7:14; seventy came to Egypt with Jacob, and Joseph's family was already there). That family had, in fulfillment of the promises of the Lord to Abraham (Gn 15:5, 13; 17:6) and Jacob (35:11-12) become a nation. They had **increased greatly, and multiplied** in number (1:7; see Nm 1:46) and potentially in power. These few verses summarize a period of over four hundred years.

2. The Oppression Begins (1:8-14)

1:8-14. After so many years the memory of, and gratitude for, the ministry of Joseph and his service to Egypt was lost. A **new king** (probably a ruler in the Hyksos period; see Introduction: Date) **arose over Egypt** (1:8). The expression **arose over** may be meant to convey something more like "arose against," thus indicating that this was not the normal succession but a takeover by a hostile power (cf. Davis, *Moses and the Gods*, 53). This king recognized that the remarkable growth and prosperity of the children of Israel (no longer a mere family but now a nation) was an internal threat to his administration of Egypt and/or a potential ally of any invading army. His response, to diminish the threat, was to initiate a program of oppression and affliction by enslaving the children of Israel. Perhaps he intended to deplete the population of Israel or simply meant to keep their growth in check while keeping them as subjects and slaves. The policy failed, however, because the more they were afflicted, the faster the population of Israel increased and the further they spread out. Still, the pharaoh pursued his shortsighted and oppressive policy with increased vigor.

Since the bondage lasted over four hundred years (12:40; cf. Gn 15:13; Ac 7:6) it is obvious that there was a gap of time between the initial bondage of the **new king** and the continued systematic oppression indicated in 1:13. Here it is **the Egyptians** (see Introduction: Date) who devised the manner of oppression by means of brickmaking and **labors in the field** (1:14).

3. The Oppression Continues (1:15-22)

1:15-22. When the policy of oppression failed to reduce the numbers of the sons of Israel or to diminish the perceived threat against them, the Egyptians initiated a policy of genocide (and not for the last time would the descendants of Israel face such a horror). Essentially the king of Egypt (probably Thutmose I, see Introduction: Date) instructed the Hebrew midwives **Shiphrah** and **Puah** to murder all the male children born to the Hebrew women. These two women were probably the acknowledged, if unofficial, authorities over the vocation of midwifery, and all the Hebrew midwives were to carry out the king's orders. These brave and faithful women are said to have **feared God**, and no doubt they believed that children were the gift of God (Ps 127:3) and the killing of such was simply murder. They knew the principle that when the laws of man are in conflict with the commandments and will of God the faithful must obey God rather than men (Ac 5:29). And so these godly women defied the king's orders, and the children of Israel continued to thrive and multiply.

When asked for an explanation for the ongoing male births, the midwives told the king that the Hebrew women were **vigorous** and gave birth without their intervention, which may have been the case but highly unlikely. It is possible that the midwives were blessed, not for their less-than-forthright answer to the king's inquiry but because they **feared God**. Another possibility is that they chose the greater good (life-saving over truth-telling), and were thus exempt from the requirement of telling the truth. This would be similar to a surgeon performing life-saving surgery being exempt from laws forbidding cutting someone with a sharp instrument, or the exemption for traffic laws that an ambulance driver receives when rushing a coronary victim through a red light in order to get him to the hospital. In this case, the midwives were blessed for their lifesaving and their less-than-forthright answer.

In frustration the king simply ordered **all his people** (1:22) to take an active role to ensure the death of the newborn male children of the Hebrews.

B. Moses: Early Life and Calling (2:1-22)

The narrative proceeds to tell how Moses came to be God's instrument to deliver the children of Israel from bondage in Egypt: this section chronicles the life of the instrument of Israel's deliverance.

1. Moses' Mother Endeavors to Save Her Son (2:1-4)

2:1-4. The narrative quickly moves from the menace of Pharaoh's command to the nation as a whole to the peril it posed for one Levite couple (Amram and Jochebed, cf. Ex 6:20) and their newborn son. The description that the child **was beautiful** indicates that even in infancy this child was recognized as exceptional (cf. Ac 7:20; Heb 11:23). The tenderness of a mother's love led to desperate measures to preserve Moses' life. In terms reminiscent of the ark of Noah (which preserved life), Moses was placed in a papyrus basket covered with **tar and pitch** (cf. Gn 6:14) and set afloat on the Nile (in literal, if not intentional, obedience to Pharaoh's command; cf. 1:22). This ark was placed out of the current of the river (**among the reeds**) and watched over by his sister (Miriam, cf. Ex 15:20; Nm 26:59).

2. Moses' Life Is Preserved by Pharaoh's Daughter (2:5-10)

2:5-10. Either by the design of Moses' mother or simply God's providence, the ark was placed near the spot where a royal princess **came down to bathe at the Nile** (2:5). In short order, the ark and child were discovered and the crying infant elicited the princess' pity, even though she recognized that this baby was **one of the Hebrews' children**. Sensing the princess' intention to preserve this child, Moses' sister stepped forward with a bold proposal to find a wet-nurse to care for the infant, a proposal that was quickly accepted. By this unlikely means Moses' life was spared and he was reunited with his birth mother (who was paid for the privilege to nurse him).

As the son of the Egyptian princess, he received a royal upbringing (and likely a high level Egyptian education, Ac 7:22) but being cared for by his birth-mother, he would also have understood his heritage as a Hebrew. His name, **Moses**, perhaps related to contemporary Egyptian names (Ahmose, Thutmose), was a pun drawn from his being "drawn out" (the meaning of a Hb. verb *mashah*) of the water. It is unlikely that an Egyptian princess would have made a pun using a Hebrew verb; the name was likely given or suggested by Moses' birth mother. God's providential care was clearly evident. Just as God was faithful in protecting Moses, this episode would encourage the Israelite readers of Moses' book that He would be faithful to them as they would fight to enter and subdue the promised land in the years to come.

3. Moses' Failure (2:11-15a)

2:11-15a. Moses' first attempt to deliver and preserve **his brethren** was inept and an utter failure. Many years (about forty, Ac 7:23) passed and the narrative moves to Moses the man. Apparently, while still living in the privileged position as the son of an Egyptian princess, he was nevertheless aware of his Hebrew lineage and knew them as **his brethren** (2:11; noted twice in the text). No doubt their **hard labors**, in contrast to his life of relative privilege, aroused an acute sense for injustice in Moses (cf. Heb 11:25). On one occasion, Moses saw an Egyptian abusing a Hebrew and his sense of injustice was provoked. This incited a misguided and rash act—Moses killed the Egyptian. That he had looked around to assure himself that he would not be seen and that he **hid** the body **in the sand** (2:12) shows that Moses himself knew this act was wrong. If Moses expected that his brethren would applaud his act and protect his identity he was mistaken. On **the next day** Moses witnessed **two Hebrews** fighting and sought to intervene, only to be rebuffed and threatened with exposure. The offenders' comment (**as you killed the Egyptian**, 2:14) was a not-so-subtle threat letting Moses know **the matter has become known**; and indeed when Pharaoh heard of the offense **he tried to kill Moses** (2:15).

4. Moses' Sojourn in Midian (2:15b-22)

2:15b-22. Once again the narrative moves quickly through the story of Moses' sojourn and subsequent marriage. God's providential plan for preparing Moses to guide the people of Israel led to an extended sojourn (of about forty years, cf. Ac 7:29-30) in the desert region of **Midian**. There, his sense for injustice once again led him to intervene in a dispute between the daughters of **the priest of Midian** (Reuel, Jethro, Ex 3:1) and some shepherds at the well for watering livestock (2:17). This act of chivalry led to his marriage (to Zipporah), a family (son, Gershom), and a life as a shepherd. "The long years in the desert were not wasted but times of further maturity and reflection in the things of God (cf. Ac 7:29ff.)" (Davis, *Moses and the Gods*, 57).

C. The Call of Moses: Reluctance and Compulsion (2:23–4:26)

1. The Nation's Bondage Recalled (2:23-25)

2:23-25. While the sons of Israel continued to suffer in bondage, Moses was being prepared; even with a change of regime in Egypt, the need for his service grew even more acute. The bondage of the nation was severe; but God heard Israel's cries and He **remembered His covenant** (2:24) with the patriarchs. When He **took notice of them** (2:25), He would soon send them a man to liberate and lead them. The point of this brief note in 2:23-25 is to place Israel's need to be freed from bondage in the context of Moses' call. While the nation suffered the Lord was preparing for their deliverance. They were completely unaware that, in an unknown place in an unimaginable way, the Lord was calling an unexpected man to be their deliverer. God's providence in the preparation of Moses may have served as an encouragement for Moses' readers. During the oppression in Egypt, the Jewish people could not have anticipated how God would work to prepare a leader for them, but He was working. In the same way, He would undertake for them in equally surprising ways to conquer the land when they would enter it.

2. Moses Called to the Burning Bush (3:1-9)

3:1-6. God called Moses while Moses was engaged in the mundane business of tending his father-in-law's flock, probably in a location he had been to many times before during these forty years away from Egypt (see Ac 7:23 and Ex 7:7). It was at **Horeb** (3:1; another name for Sinai; cf. Ex 19:11), the **mountain of God**, that the Lord called Moses, and it was a calling as unexpected to Moses as it was inescapable in God's eternal purposes. Here a brilliant manifestation of God appeared (cf. Gn 15:17; Ex 13:21; 40:34; 1Ki 8:11), the burning bush, to signify that the Lord (here in the form of **the angel of the Lord**) was present (3:2). The expression **angel of the LORD** may also be translated "messenger of the Lord" leading some to conclude that this is a supernatural being ("a special divine messenger from the court of heaven . . . representing the Lord" [Youngblood, *Exodus*, 32]) but not the Lord Himself. Others argue, however, that the entity here "is unlikely to be a supernatural being distinct from God" (Victor P. Hamilton, *Exodus: An Exegetical Commentary* [Grand Rapids, MI: Baker, 2011], 46). The "angel/messenger" of the Lord appears in a number of biblical narratives (cf. Gn 16:7, 9, 11; 22:11, 15; 31:11; 48:16; Jdg 6:11; 13:13, 15, 16), and a number of "these references speak of angel/God/Lord as if interchangeable and undistinguishable, reinforcing the idea that the Lord himself is the angel and the angel is the Lord himself" (Hamilton, *Exodus*, 46). Some have gone further and suggested that the "angel of the Lord" is a pre-incarnate manifestation of Jesus Christ. Since "no man has seen God at any time" and since Jesus Christ is the Revealer of the Father (cf. Jn 1:18; 12:45; 14:9), they argue, the theophanies (visible manifestations of God) in the OT are actually manifestations of the pre-incarnate Christ. (See comments on Gn 32:24-25).

The angel established the solemnity and sacredness of the setting and of the moment by a solemn address, **Moses, Moses**, and a stern command to remove his sandals (being filthy) because the place was made holy by the presence of the Lord (3:5). The Lord's self-identification as the God of the patriarchs signified that Moses' calling was to be in service to the Lord's promise (cf. Gn 12:1-3; 15:13-16). What began as mere curiosity (3:3) was turned to reverential fear (3:6b) by the awesome encounter with God.

3:7-9. Immediately the Lord turned Moses' attention to the **affliction of My people who are in Egypt** (3:7). God informed Moses that He was well aware of their misery (cf. 2:24-25), **their cry** caused by **their sufferings**. Moreover, He was about to fulfill His promise to Abraham and bring them up from Egypt to the land of promise, the land of blessing, **flowing with milk and honey** (3:8). The land was clearly demarcated in the promise He had made to Abraham in Gn 15. A comparison of the list of Canaanite names here with those in Gn 15:19-21 demonstrates the continuity of this narrative with that of Genesis and the abiding validity of the promise God made to Abraham.

Here in Exodus as there in Genesis the intent of the list of these names is to specify the actual geography—the land, the "dirt"—where the promise to Abraham was to be fulfilled. Since both Abraham and Moses would have been thinking of an actual physical land as God reiterated His promise, it is obvious that nothing less than the actual physical land could be or will be the fulfillment of this promise. It should also be noted that the list in both contexts ends with the **Jebusites** (cf. 3:17; 13:5; 23:23), the Canaanite tribe that David later displaced in order to establish his capital at Jerusalem (cf. 2Sm 5:6ff.). The defeat of the Jebusites and the establishment of Jerusalem as the nation's (everlasting) capital is foreshadowed in this seemingly pedantic list of Canaanite names. By reiterating this list to Moses—first given to Abraham and looking forward to David—the Lord tied together several stages of the history of His promise-people.

Lastly, the oppression of the nation by the Egyptians was noted again, not simply to say the Lord was aware but to indicate that it was about to come to an end.

3. Moses Commissioned by "I AM WHO I AM" (3:10–4:17)

In the light of the cry of Israel and the intense oppression by the Egyptians, Moses was told that he was chosen to be the human instrument to accomplish God's deliverance of the nation (**My people**). Immediately Moses objected to this call and in the course of this encounter he offered several more objections. The Lord answered each objection consecutively, until Moses reluctantly and humbly accepted the task to which God was calling him.

a. Moses' First Objection (3:10-12)

3:10-12. In this first objection Moses feigns personal insignificance and inadequacy; he displayed a false humility (3:11). God's answer essentially accepted his argument, Moses was, in and of himself, insignificant and inadequate; but with the Lord's presence—**I will be with you**—His power, and His purpose, Moses could not fail. Moses would be sufficient and adequate for the call with a sufficiency and adequacy supplied by God Himself. Only by obeying the call and seeing **the sign** of an accomplished work, when a redeemed nation will be gathered for worship on this very mountain (3:12) could Moses accomplish the monumental task the Lord set before him. God unfolded to Moses what would come about, and the role Moses would play in it. Since these events did transpire as God predicted, the original audience, Israelites who were about to enter the land, would do battle to take the land. They would be encouraged that God not only knew what would happen, but promised that they would succeed, just as He did for Moses.

b. Moses' Second Objection (3:13-17)

3:13-17. This objection is rather odd: the Lord had identified Himself to Moses as the God of the patriarchs (cf. 3:6), the fathers. Here Moses seems to be suggesting that if he returned and told the **sons of Israel** that this God had authorized him they would ask for His name. Moses was implying that if he could not supply them with a name this would somehow undermine his authority with them. In the majestic and awesome response, God gave one of the most important expressions of His self-revelation recorded in Scripture. He identified Himself as **I AM WHO I AM** and informed Moses that he should simply say to the people **I AM has sent me to you** (3:14).

The name **I AM** is a literal translation of first person singular of the Hebrew verb *'ehyeh* ("I am"); the third person singular of this verb is transliterated *yehweh* ("he is"). This latter term is taken as the name of God ("Yahweh") and is rendered in most English translations as "LORD"; the combination of these four letters (in Hb. *YHWH*) is called the "tetragrammaton" (the four letter name of God). This name is dense with implications about the nature and being of God—He is self-existent, affirming that God is uncaused and depends on no other source for His existence—and rich with theological meaning —as the **memorial-name** this name becomes the name identifying God as the deity who makes covenant promises and keeps them **to all generations** (3:15). But the immediate significance for Moses and the nation was readily apparent. This name declared that the God who IS (exists), the God who IS God (the living God, the real God), the God upon whose existence all that exists depends (cf. Jn 1:1-2; Col 1:17) is none other than the God who spoke to and made promises to the patriarchs (3:15).

In short, His name and His association with the patriarchs would mean to the nation that their God was the only God, the true God (cf. Is 44:6-8), and He had the power and authority as God and the interest and commitment to them as the God of the fathers (the patriarchs, Abraham, Isaac, and Jacob) to bring about their deliverance from bondage. God's explanation to Moses reiterated that His concern for them was not merely because of their sufferings but that He intended to fulfill His promise concerning the land, a promise that may have provided considerable encouragement for the people as they were preparing to enter the land. In terms reminiscent of the covenant promise to Abram in Gn 15, the Lord specified the location (based on the tribal identities of the Canaanite tribes) and fruitfulness of **the land** (3:17) to which He would deliver the nation.

c. A Preview of Coming Events (3:18-22)

3:18-22. God took this moment to provide Moses with a brief overview of the events of the exodus that were soon to unfold. He assured Moses that while the **elders of Israel** would **pay heed** to Moses' words, the **king of Egypt** would not (3:19). Even a modest request for the opportunity to worship and sacrifice to the Lord, **the God of the Hebrews**, would be rejected. Thus, only by force, **under compulsion** and by the miracle power of **My hand**, **My miracles** (the coming plagues), will the king of Egypt let them go. And in the process the people will **not go empty-handed** from Egypt but the Egyptians themselves will provide every household (**every woman**) with wealth and provisions (perhaps like a bride) to have them leave after the devastation of the plagues; thus they would **plunder the Egyptians** (3:22). Abraham's sojourn in Egypt foreshadowed the events described here (see comments at Gn 12:10-20). This overview was given to encourage Moses, and later the nation, that the Lord's plan will unfold exactly as He had foretold. As they saw His previous promises fulfilled as He said, they could trust Him to fulfill His promises to enable them to conquer the land.

d. Three Signs and a Spokesman for Moses (4:1-17)

4:1-9. Moses was still not ready to commit himself to God's calling. His third objection was that he lacked the credentials necessary to authenticate that the Lord had indeed appeared to him (4:1). To overcome this objection, Moses was given three signs (cf. Dt 13:1-3). First, his own shepherd's staff would be enabled to become a serpent and then a staff again (4:2-5). That this was not a mere illusion of a snake but a real snake is proven by the note that when Moses first performed this sign even he **fled from it** (4:3). Also, Moses picked the serpent up by the tail (4:4; the usual manner is to pick up dangerous snakes is by the neck to avoid the fangs) to demonstrate total mastery over the creature. The symbolism here is fairly clear. The serpent had been an instrument of Satan (cf. Gn 3:1, 14), hence an emblem of evil and was used often in Egyptian iconography and religion. Moses' mastery over the serpent indicated the Lord's mastery over Satan and the gods of Egypt. This point will be made even more clearly in the coming judgments on the Egyptians; cf. chaps. 7–12.

For the second sign, Moses' hand could be turned leprous and then restored (4:6-7). Kaiser notes that "leprosy," or Hansen's disease, was known in antiquity. But leprosy in the Bible apparently covered cases of psoriasis, vitiligo, ringworm and other skin ailments (Kaiser, "Exodus," 326). For the purposes of the sign the disease had to be advanced and then instantly cured. Living in the dry and insect-infested environment they did, the Egyptians were constantly afflicted with skin ailments and they were scrupulous about skin hygiene. This sign would have at first horrified them and then intrigued them. This kind of power spoke directly to the existential realities of their daily lives.

In the third sign Moses was to take water from the Nile which when poured out on dry ground was turned to blood (4:8-9). This sign proved the power of the Lord over one of the most sacred elements of Egyptian religion and obviously had the potential to affect the most vital aspect of Egyptian daily life, water from the Nile River.

The overall point of these particular signs was obviously the supernatural power they demonstrated. These wonders were beyond the power of a mere man and verified that the message Moses spoke was, like these wonders, from the Lord (cf. 1Ki 17:24). Beyond that they demonstrated the power of God over elements that the Egyptians held sacred and over things they considered were under the authority of their gods. And just as God would overcome Moses' reluctance to confront the Egyptians with His promises and power, so also the narrative might encourage any of the Jewish people who were reluctant in the face of the daunting prospects of subduing the promised land.

4:10-17. Even after these amazing signs are given to him, Moses had two more objections. In the fourth of his objections he protested that he had **never been eloquent** and that he was **slow of speech and slow of tongue** (4:10). God responded that since He made **man's mouth** and gave men the abilities of their senses (4:11) He could overcome any deficiencies in His chosen messenger. In a final objection Moses bluntly asked God to send someone else (4:13). With His patience at an end, **the anger of the Lord burned** (4:14a). However, He was still gracious to His chosen servant, and the Lord answered the fourth objection by giving Moses a spokesman, Aaron, his brother, to speak for him (4:15-16). In His providence Aaron was already on his way to meet Moses (4:14c). Thus, Moses was to take his hand, his staff, the signs, and himself and "Go!"

4. Transitions (4:18-26)

4:18-23. Between Moses' call and his first confrontation with Pharaoh a series of transitional events occurred. Moses needed to transition from his temporal obligations and prepare for the climatic confrontation with Pharaoh. Moses had not been simply sitting around waiting for the Lord's call. He had an active home life and obligations that needed to be addressed before he was ready to devote himself to God's calling. First, in an act of deference and respect, Moses took leave of his father-in-law, Jethro (v. 18). The Lord then reassured him that those who sought his life were now dead. Then he packed up his family, **his wife and his sons** (Gershom, cf. 2:22; Eliezer, cf. 18:5), **on a donkey** (indicating that he was traveling light), took the symbol of his calling, **the staff of God in his hand** (for reassurance), and left for Egypt. Once again the Lord warned Moses that he should be prepared to use all the signs given to him but that Pharaoh would be obstinate (on the meaning of **harden his heart**, see 7:3) and refuse to comply with the demand to let the people go. Here the Lord called Israel His **firstborn** son (4:22), an indication of priority and preferred status. Because Pharaoh had afflicted the Lord's firstborn he would suffer the death of his firstborn, foreshadowing the last plague on Egypt.

4:24-26. Then a curious event took place that involved Moses' son. The man of God cannot be less than dutiful and thorough in his obedience to the Lord in all things and apparently, Moses had failed to circumcise one of his sons. For this, the Lord disciplined him, and **sought to put him** (Moses) **to death** (4:24). The death threat was probably some life-threatening illness but the exact nature is not clear. It seems that Zipporah then took it upon herself to perform the rite, even though she found the act repulsive, likely because of her non-Israelite origins. She flung the baby's foreskin **at Moses' feet** (possibly a euphemism for genitals but not necessarily) and called him **a bridegroom of blood**. In saying this, Zipporah is declaring that Moses is now her bridegroom for a second time. Umberto Cassuto explains that she was saying, "I have delivered you from death, and your return to life makes you my bridegroom a second time, this time my blood bridegroom, a bridegroom acquired through blood" (Umberto Cassuto, *A Commentary on the Book of Exodus,* 3rd ed. [Jerusalem: Magnes Press, 1967], 60).

The significance of this passage is twofold. First, it demonstrated that if Moses was to be the spokesman for the covenant-keeping God of Abraham, he needed to keep the provisions of the covenant (Gn 17:9-22). Second, it foreshadowed the requirement that those participating in the Passover were required to be circumcised (Ex 12:43-48). It may have been at this time that Moses' family returned to Midian (see comment on 18:2).

D. The Return of Moses: Failure and (Re-) Confirmation (4:27-7:7)

While the reunion of Moses and Aaron brought them joy, and their initial report brought the nation joy, the first encounter with Pharaoh brought the nation increased hardship and affliction. Already the Lord would have to reassure a discouraged and distracted leader.

1. Reunion of Moses and Aaron and Reception by the Nation (4:27-31)

4:27-31. Aaron had been sent by the Lord to meet Moses (cf. 4:14), and the two brothers were reunited **at the mountain of God** (4:27). After relating to Aaron all that God had told him, Moses proceeded with Aaron to Egypt and assembled **all the elders** and **sons of Israel** and showed them the signs and informed them of God's intention to free them from their affliction. They **believed** and **worshiped** (4:31).

2. Rejection by Pharaoh (5:1-23)

5:1-23. The hardhearted resistance of Pharaoh soon dissipated the initial joy of the people over the news of God's intention to free the nation from bondage. Moses' initial request to Pharaoh was instantly and harshly rebuffed. When Pharaoh said, **I do not know the LORD** (5:2), he probably did not mean he had no knowledge of Israel's God but that their God was not one he acknowledged, worshiped, or served. Moses and Aaron made a milder request and asked to be released merely for a respite to worship. Perhaps Moses and Aaron were testing Pharaoh or attempting to gauge how far he would be willing to negotiate. Perhaps they intended to "work up" from this mild request to the bolder demand to let the people go. They argued that they made this plea in fear of divine judgment, **otherwise He will fall upon us** (5:3).

This was an odd argument because the Lord had said nothing like this in any of His previous instructions to Moses. In any case, Pharaoh rebuffed even this milder request. The exchange here seems to indicate that Moses and Aaron were negotiating with Pharaoh rather than forthrightly speaking exactly what God had commanded them (cf. 7:2). Nor did Moses perform the sign that had been given to him as the Lord had directed him (cf. 4:21; 7:10).

Pharaoh then accused Moses of catering to the laziness of the people (5:4; cf. 5:8, 17), and he even increased the intensity of their labors and the severity of their treatment by the **taskmasters** (5:6-9). Straw served as a binding and strengthening agent for the clay used to make the bricks, and was apparently provided for them. But at this point the responsibility for gathering the straw was forced upon them. Yet the quota of bricks was to remain the same as before. In order to fulfill this demand the people were forced to spend more time and effort gathering **stubble for straw**, that is, the remnants of the stalks left in the fields after the harvest. To compel compliance for this increased labor, even the **foremen of the sons of Israel** (5:15a) (probably Israelite man who served as "lead men" or level of foremen under the taskmasters and foremen of the Egyptians) **were beaten** (5:14). Perhaps thinking that the taskmasters were exceeding their authority and that they were being unreasonable, the Israelite foremen appealed to Pharaoh, **Why do you deal this way with your servants?** (5:15b). Pharaoh's response was an even more direct accusation that they were lazy and a reiteration of the directive that they were to produce their quota of bricks (5:17-18) while also gathering straw. This left the foreman despondent and upon meeting Moses and Aaron they accused them of bringing this trouble upon them; **you have made us odious** ("you have made us stink") and you have **put a sword into their hand** ("you have made it even easier for them to destroy us") (5:20-21).

Moses himself succumbed to this despondency and complained, **Oh Lord, why?** (Why this? Why me?) (5:22). Evidently, Moses had forgotten the Lord had told him to expect this reaction from Pharaoh (cf. 4:21).

3. A Patient Reminder of the Lord's Promises (6:1-8)

6:1-8. For Moses and the people, Pharaoh's rejection of Moses' request was a disheartening setback. The people's quick reversal of attitude, from the joy of Moses' revelation of God's intent to deliver them (cf. 4:31) to the dejection of the foremen, led to a despondent Moses. So God once again patiently reassured him. In a passage of rich theological importance, He reminded Moses **I am the Lord** (6:2, 6), the God who makes promises and keeps them (cf. 3:14-15). He reminded Moses that this deliverance was something He would do (**I will**; 6:1, 6 [3x], 7 [2x], 8 [2x]). He reminded Moses of the covenant promise made to the patriarchs (6:4, 5, 8). He reminded Moses of His compassion and concern over their **burdens** and **bondage** (6:7, 9). When the Lord said that the patriarchs knew Him as **God Almighty** but that by the name **Lord** He had **not made [Himself] known to them** (6:3), He could not have meant that they had never heard or learned of that name, for they surely had (cf. Gn 4:26; 9:26; 12:8; 22:14; 24:12).

The idea here is the patriarchs knew of the God who *made* the promise (of a great nation) but this generation, Moses' generation and the generation that conducted the conquest, would know Him as the God who *keeps* the promise (of making them a great nation and leading them out of bondage, cf. Gn 15:13-14). The patriarchs knew Him as a promise-making God. Moses's people will know Him as a promise-keeping God and they will say He is: **the Lord your God, who brought [us] out** of bondage (6:7). And this God would fulfill the promise by giving this people the land of promise (6:4 [2x]; 8).

4. Reassurance and Preparation (6:9–7:7)

6:9–7:7. Such was the disappointment over the initial failure to move Pharaoh to release the nation that the people were not reassured even by what the Lord had told Moses (6:9), and Moses again expressed his lack of confidence in his speaking ability (6:12b, 30). Two arguments are given for reassurance that Moses was indeed the man for the job: first, a selective genealogy is given that records Moses' and Aaron's hereditary and familial background. "The Hebrew method of identification was to give a genealogy" (Alan R. Cole, *Exodus*, TOTC [Downers Grove, IL: InterVarsity, 1973], 93). As the ones who are called by God to confront Pharaoh with the demand for release of the nation, Moses and Aaron had to be legitimate spokesmen for the nation—and for that they had to be part of the nation—as this genealogy attests. The charge to Moses and Aaron (6:13, and 6:28-29) brackets the genealogy.

Second, God simply and firmly reminded Moses and Aaron of three facts. First, they have been called by God for this task and all they were required to do was **speak all that I command** you (7:2). Second, the resistance of Pharaoh was not only to be expected but was in fact a part of the plan. And third, the aim of all this was to demonstrate that **I am the Lord** (6:29; 7:5). The use of weak (and aged, 7:7) instruments (i.e., Moses and Aaron) and the resistance of the most powerful monarch on earth at the time would make it clear to all that the deliverance to come would be accomplished not by Moses' persuasive ability or by the nation's own might or as the result of the weakness of the king but by the compassion and awesome power of God in fulfillment of His promises. So it would be when the weak instrument consisting of the wilderness generation would face its opponents when entering the land.

The matter of the hardening of Pharaoh's heart (7:3) is a question that has been debated at length (see the commentary on Rm 9:17-18), and often comes down to a debate over the sovereignty of God and the question of human free will. It should be noted that the author of Exodus makes no attempt to reconcile the issue. It is true that God hardened Pharaoh's heart (4:21; 7:3; 9:12; 10:1, 20, 27; 11:10; 14:4, 8, 17) and it is true that Pharaoh hardened his own heart (7:13, 14, 22; 8:15, 19, 32; 9:7, 34, 35; 13:15). Some have tried to resolve the issue by suggesting that Pharaoh is responsible for hardening his own heart, and God simply determined what He (fore-)knew Pharaoh would do of his own free will. But this will not do since it is clear from 4:21 and here in 7:3 that the hardening was initially and principally the Lord's doing for His purposes.

This is a classic case of compatibilism, which simply means that the determined plan, purpose, or action of God is compatible with the free act of an agent (in this case Pharaoh). The Lord had determined that Pharaoh's heart would be hardened—God is sovereign—but Pharaoh, in the act of hardening his own heart, was still free because he was not forced to do something he did not want to do, something that was contrary to his will. As John Feinberg explains, "an action is free even if causally determined so long as the causes are nonconstraining" (John Feinberg, "God Ordains All Things," in *Predestination and Free Will: Four Views of Divine Sovereignty and Human Freedom*, ed. David Basinger and Randall Basinger [Downers Grove, IL: InterVarsity, 1986], 24).

That is, even though God determined (sovereignly made it happen in such a way that it might legitimately be said that He caused it to happen) that Pharaoh would exhibit a hardened heart, since there were no constraining causes (that is, Pharaoh was not forced to act against what he wanted to do anyway) he was free and thus he is responsible for his own hard heart. Pharaoh freely chose to do exactly what God determined he would do.

The immediate point to be made here in this context is that the Lord Himself makes it clear He is the one behind the hardening and this was for the purpose of manifesting His power, **My signs and My wonders in the land of Egypt** (7:3b).

E. The Judgment of the Plagues (7:8–10:29)

The narrative proceeds to relate how the children of Israel were finally freed from bondage in Egypt. This section and the next describe the process of Israel's deliverance by means of the ten judgments. A series of miracles, the "signs and wonders" of which the Lord spoke (7:3), take place. These miracles authorize the Lord's spokesmen, demonstrate the Lord's power, humble the Egyptians and Pharaoh, and are directly aimed at the false deities of the pagan Egyptian religion to discredit them, and to unmask them for the false gods they are.

1. Initial Confrontation (7:8-13)

7:8-13. Once again the Lord directed His servants to confront Pharaoh. Here the sign of the rod that became a serpent (cf. 4:2-5), which had been used to authorize Moses and Aaron to the nation (4:30), was employed again in response to Pharaoh's request to **work a miracle** (lit., "to show a wonder"). In contrast to the first encounter with Pharaoh (cf. 5:1-3), Moses and Aaron **did just as the LORD commanded** (cf. 7:6, 10), and Aaron threw down his staff and it became a serpent. Pharaoh attempted to deflect this display of divine authority and power when he called on his **wise men**, **sorcerers**, and **magicians** (officials and practitioners of Egyptian religion; cf. 2Ti 3:8) to employ their **secret arts** (that is, occultic and demonically empowered practices; cf. Rv 16:14) to mimic the sign either by sleight of hand, by illusion such as the physical manipulation of an actual snake, or by an actual supernatural event empowered by Satan and demons (cf. 2Co 11:13-14; 1Ti 4:1). However, the superior power of the Lord was quickly revealed when Aaron's staff/serpent **swallowed up** the staffs/serpents of the Egyptian sorcerers.

In spite of the obviously superior power of the Lord and the preeminence of His servants, Pharaoh's heart was adamant and he remained implacable. Apparently, Moses and Aaron were not discouraged and despondent at this apparent failure as they had been after the first encounter; perhaps this is because this time they remembered that this had happened just **as the LORD had said** it would (7:13).

2. The Nine Judgments or Plagues (7:14–10:29)

7:14–10:29. The next encounter with Pharaoh set up the dramatic series of events often referred to as the "ten plagues." A few preliminary points are in order before giving a summary view of the overall flow of these events. First, it seems best to consider the first nine judgments as a unit unto themselves and the final judgment—the death of the firstborn—as the single culminating event, with the Passover, that precipitates the exodus proper. As will be noted, there is a pattern to the first nine events that is not seen in the last event; and the presentation of the last event is much more detailed, indicating that it is distinct from the first nine. Second, the typical designation for these events is "plagues"; but the English term "plague" (as something pertaining to communicable diseases or epidemics) does not fit in that sense with all of these events. The term "judgments" is more descriptive of all of the events and it conveys the divine intent behind them as well. Third, when considering these judgments, especially the first nine, many commentators have attempted to explain them as instances of natural occurrences with perhaps divinely guided timing (cf. 8:23), divinely directed locating (9:4, 6, 26), and in divinely produced proportions. However, it seems best in the light of the timing (viz. Moses' pronouncements), extent (some were limited to the Egyptians; cf. 8:22; 9:4, 6, 26; 11:7) and evident intent (as attacks on the Egyptian pantheon; see comments below) to take them as genuine miracles (cf. 7:3), manifestations of supernatural divine power that only the Lord God could have accomplished.

This leads to the observation that, fourth, there is an unmistakable theological intent in these events that should not be missed but often is by those who focus more on naturalistic explanations rather than seeing the very point they were originally meant to make: the Lord is the only true God (cf. 40:17). This leads to two final observations: fifth, there was a gradual intensification about these judgments from serious inconvenience to life-threatening disaster; and sixth, though not explicitly indicated, it is clear these judgments were attacks on key features of Egyptian religion and in effect are contests with Egyptian deities (cf. Nm 33:4), designed to prove their impotence and unreality (see the notes under the fourth point below). These tests also are intended to show Pharaoh and his people that the God of the Hebrews, the Lord YHWH, is God.

It is clear that there is a general pattern to these events: First, there was God's instruction to Moses and Aaron (**Then the LORD said to Moses and Aaron**: 7:14; 8:1, 16, 20; 9:1, 8, 13; 10:1, 21). Here, at last, Moses and Aaron learned to say and do exactly what God had told them to say and do and thus, in spite of Pharaoh's recalcitrance, they remained bold, resolute, and determined throughout the unfolding process of these judgments.

Second, in several instances, God, through Moses, made a demand, **Let My people go** (7:16; 8:1, 20; 9:1, 13; 10:3). This demand is missing in the third, sixth, and ninth events.

Third, in several instances God through Moses gave a warning (7:17-18; 8:2-4, 21; 9:2-3, 14-16; 10:4). Again this warning was missing in the third, sixth, and ninth events. That the demands and warnings were sometimes given indicates that, on the one hand, the Lord was gracious to make His will clear; He wanted Pharaoh to know that His people must be released from bondage and there would be consequences if Pharaoh refused. He did not simply send the judgments and leave Pharaoh wondering why these calamities were happening. In one instance, the Lord even made it clear that the disaster could be avoided if the Egyptians would only seek shelter (cf. 9:18-21). But, on the other hand, in those instances when there was no prior demand and no warning before the judgment fell, the Lord was warning Pharaoh not to be presumptuous. God's gracious warning was not to be treated lightly or interpreted as a lack of divine resolve. From this it is clear that people should never be presumptuous and expect God will give them time to prepare for the calamity of His judgment (cf. Lk 12:20).

Fourth, often the judgment would be at the expense of a revered god of the Egyptians. Prior to one looming judgment, God described the event: water was to be turned to blood (7:17-18). This was an attack on the god of the Nile, perhaps the river itself, which was considered a deity, or against Hapi, the god of the Nile, or Khnum, god of water and life. The attack could have been to humble Osiris, for whom, in one myth, the Nile was his bloodstream. In 8:3-4 frogs were to invade the land. This was an attack on the god or goddess Heket—or Heqt, wife of Khnum, who was usually represented as a frog. This goddess was in charge of childbirth. In 8:16b gnats (the term is unclear, perhaps "mosquitos") were to cover man, beast, and the land. This was an attack on Geb, god of the land, the dirt itself. In 8:21 flies (lit., "swarms"; the LXX has *kynomuia*, a type of blood-sucking "dog-fly") were to swarm over the land. This was in effect an attack on all the gods of the land.

In 9:3 the judgment fell upon the livestock; these would die across the land. This was an attack on Apis, a male god of fertility, often represented as a bull, or Hathor, a goddess of the sky who was symbolized in the form of a cow. In 9:9 boils were to break out on man and beast. This was an attack on Qadshu, goddess of sex, indicating the boils were likely sores on the genitals. The irony here is that ash, or **soot from a kiln** (9:8), was often used by the Egyptians to make soap to keep one clean from such infections, but now would cause them under God's providence.

Likewise the judgments by hail, locusts, and darkness all were attacks on Egyptian gods. In 9:18-19 fiery hail was to fall on the land. This was an attack on Seth, god of wind and storms. In 10:4-6 locusts were to descend on the land. This was an attack on Serapis, the god of protection of the land; or Isis, the goddess of life associated with flax and making clothes; or Min, a god of fertility and vegetation, who was supposed to be a protector of crops. When darkness overtook the land (10:21-23), several major deities associated with the sun were humbled: Re, Ra, and Amon-Re, and also Aten, Atum, and Horus. These attacks on the Egyptian pantheon would be much more obvious and pointed for the Egyptians living at the time. In effect these were attacks on their entire worldview. Everything that helped them to make sense of the world would crumble around them.

Fifth, a gesture of judgment was performed: for the first (7:20), second (8:6), third (8:17), seventh (9:22), eighth (10:13), and ninth (10:22) judgments this gesture was either Aaron or Moses raising the staff, or both hands, one holding the staff, or just raising one hand. This would not only lend a solemnity to the event but it would make clear that these judgments did not just happen. They descended at the bidding of the spokesmen of the Lord.

Sixth, a description of the event often revealed its impact. The description variously concerned (1) the *extent of the judgment* (e.g., **all the water . . . was turned to blood,** 7:20; **through all the land**, 7:21; frogs will be everywhere **into your bedroom and on your bed . . . into your kneading bowls**, 8:3; **all the dust of the earth became gnats through all the land of Egypt**, 8:17; **insects in all the land of Egypt**, 8:24; **all the livestock of Egypt died**, 9:6; **sores on man and beast through all the land of Egypt**, 9:9; **the hail struck . . . all the land of Egypt**, 9:25; **the locusts came up over all the land of Egypt**, 10:14; **thick darkness in all the land of Egypt**, 10:22), (2) *the timing of the judgment* (e.g., for **seven days**, 7:25; **tomorrow**, 8:10; **tomorrow this sign will occur**, 8:23; **a definite time**, 9:5; **about this time tomorrow,** 9:18; **for three days**, 10:22); and/or (3) *the effect of the judgment* (e.g., **so that the Egyptians could not drink water from the Nile**, 7:21; **the land was laid waste because of the swarms of insects**, 8:24; **all the livestock of Egypt died**, 9:6; **the hail struck every plant of the field and shattered every tree . . . Now the flax and the barley were ruined**, 9:25, 31; the locusts **ate every plant of the land and all the fruit of the trees . . . Thus nothing green was left**, 10:15; **a darkness** that could **be felt** so **they did not see one another, nor did anyone rise from his place for three days**, 10:21, 22) In some instances the description noted the protection granted by the Lord to the Hebrews: the flies did not invade Goshen where **My people** lived, 8:22-23; the cattle of Israel did not die of the pestilence 9:4, 6, 7; **in the land of Goshen, where the sons of Israel were, there was no hail**, 9:26; **but all the sons of Israel had light in their dwellings**, 10:23. Those exemptions would have been disconcerting and galling to the proud Egyptians.

Seventh, there was the reaction of the Egyptians to the judgment, beginning with the reaction of Pharaoh. At first Pharaoh was indifferent (**with no concern**, 7:23), but as the judgments continued to fall and became increasingly severe he was forced to call and re-call Moses and Aaron (e.g., 8:8, 25; 9:27; 10:8, 16, 24) to seek a mitigation of the suffering. Second, there was the reaction of the Egyptian magicians. They were able to reproduce the wonders at first (7:22; 8:7), but then became unable to do so (8:18-19, even confessing that the judgments were **the finger of God**, 8:19), and finally becoming victims of the judgments themselves (specifically the boils, 9:11). Third, there was the reaction of the **servants** (likely a reference to the general population); after eight judgments they call upon Pharaoh to comply with Moses' demands and **Let the men go** (10:7).

Eighth, as noted, Pharaoh was forced to call Moses and Aaron, and in several instances the king seemed ready to concede. There were instances of Pharaoh (1) asking for Moses' and Aaron's intercession (e.g., **Entreat the Lord**, 8:8; **Make supplication for me**, 8:28; 9:28; 10:17) and (2) beginning negotiation (e.g. 8:25ff.; 10:8ff.; 10:24ff.). In each of these it is clear the Pharaoh was not bargaining in good faith and even apparent instances of (3) repentance (e.g., 9:27; 10:16). Instead Pharaoh's repentance was disingenuous at best.

Ninth, there were instances of Moses and Aaron interceding for Pharaoh and Egypt, followed by a mitigation of the judgment granted by the Lord (e.g., 8:12, 30; 9:33; 10:18). This demonstrated the patience and longsuffering of God, and that note should always be added to any discussion of the hardening of Pharaoh's heart. While it is obvious the Lord is in control and He is inexorably moving Pharaoh to resist and oppose His demand (see the themes below), it is also true the Lord graciously gives opportunity for, and in a genuine sense desires, true repentance (cf. Ezk 33:11; Mt 23:37).

Tenth, the pattern concludes in each case with the note concerning the reneging of Pharaoh, going back on his promise to let the people go, and the hardening of his heart (7:22; 8:15, 19, 32; 9:7, 12, 34-35; 10:20, 27).

Several themes run through the narrative of the first nine judgments. There is the theme of God's watch-care over His own. As noted, in several of these judgments the Lord made it clear that He would protect His people from the judgments inflicted on Egypt (cf. 8:22-23a; 9:26; 10:23b). Of course, the best protection would come when the people were taken out of Egypt altogether (similar to what will happen to the Church when it is raptured and escapes the wrath of God during the great tribulation; cf. the comments on 1Th 4:13, 5:11 and Rv 3:10).

A second theme is resistance to the will of the Lord is futile. Pharaoh is made to confront the fundamental reality that the Lord's will is irresistible. A sub-theme here is that partial repentance and temporary or insincere sorrow for one's sins against the Lord are unavailing. Only sincere submission is acceptable. Only utter humility before God is appropriate (cf. 10:3).

And that leads to a third, but actually the primary, theme of this narrative, and it is summed up in the majestic declaration: **By this you shall know that I am the LORD** (7:17a). These events prove that God is sovereign; He is utterly unique (**there is no one like the LORD our God**, 8:10; **there is no one like Me in all the earth**, 9:14b); He is active in His creation (**I am in the midst of the land**, 8:22b); He desires the worship of His people (**that they may serve Me**, 7:16; 8:1, 20; 9:1, 13; 10:3); He demands the compliance and obedience of all creatures (e.g., every command made to Pharaoh in the narrative).

In the heart of the narrative are two important and revealing passages relating the very words of the Lord to Moses and Aaron. In the first passage in 9:14-16, in words directed to Pharaoh, the Lord explained why He was going about this piecemeal process of delivering the nation from bondage. It was **so that you may know that there is no one like Me in all the earth** (9:14). Again, this is a direct attack on the paganism and false religion practiced by Pharaoh and the Egyptians. All their gods are impotent and false but these judgments prove that He, **the LORD, the God of the Hebrews** (9:13) is the only true God. Furthermore, the Lord explained, in effect (9:15) He could have wiped Pharaoh out (**cut off from the earth**) instantly but He says, **I have allowed you to remain** (9:16a), it is by divine permission, and grace, and patience, **in order** [note the divine purpose clause] **to show My power and in order to proclaim My Name through all the earth** (9:16b; cf. also the comments on Rm 9:17-18). This magnificent purpose is still being fulfilled as the people of God read this account and over thirty-five-hundred years after these events, are still proclaiming to the world His power and His name on account of this amazing demonstration of His grace and power.

In a second key passage, 10:1-2, the Lord revealed specifically that this series of events was to be told to the succeeding generations of the nation so that they would **know that I am the LORD** (10:2c). Whereas the word to Pharaoh was meant to reveal a God sovereign over **all the earth**, this word to the nation was meant to reveal that this Lord was God to them in a special sense; He was acting and had acted in their behalf. That word would be especially significant to the next generation reading the account as they stood on the cusp of protracted warfare in order to subdue and conquer the land God promised to them. In effect, while they had not been there in Egypt as the Lord performed these judgments, these judgments were just as much existentially "for them" and for their encouragement as they had been for the people who experienced them firsthand.

The whole of the narrative arrives at a denouement in 10:28-29. Pharaoh speaks better than he knows when in his frustration and humiliation he orders Moses, **Get away from me! Beware, do not see my face again**. In other words, "This is the last time we will meet." Moses acknowledges that he has spoken truly, but obviously not in the way he, Pharaoh, meant it. While it was Pharaoh who made the "death threat," it is Moses who will survive the final confrontation to come.

F. Free at Last (11:1–15:21)

The narrative carefully describes how it was that the children of Israel left Egypt and survived Pharaoh's last attack: this section narrates Israel's deliverance accomplished and Israel's preservation from a pursuing enemy. Moses may have intended this section to encourage the people of Israel as they were getting ready to enter the land to possess it, a process that would require the displacement of a number of tribes who were living there. God would deliver Israel from her enemies during the conquest and preserve them from those who would pursue her to destroy her.

1. The Last Judgment or Plague (11:1-10)

11:1-8. The nature of last plague, the death of the firstborn, was revealed to Moses in simple but compelling terms. God probably revealed to Moses the information given in 11:1-3 during the three days of darkness, and Moses probably delivered it to Pharaoh at the same time as that in 10:29, immediately after Pharaoh's death threat. God informed Moses that the protracted rounds of judgments were about to end. Moreover, not only would Pharaoh "let the people go" he would, in fact, **drive you out** (11:1). Furthermore, the Lord told Moses to instruct the people to **ask** for **articles of silver** and **gold** from the Egyptians. The nation could expect the Egyptian people to be generous to the Hebrews, for He would **give the people favor in the sight of the Egyptians** and Moses himself would be **greatly esteemed in the land of Egypt**. This was not only a remarkable reversal of fortunes, it also had a practical purpose—the nation would need that wealth to facilitate their journey and provide the wealth for the construction of the tabernacle (cf. 25:2-7; 35:20-29; 38:21-31). Also (11:3) this description of Moses as **greatly esteemed** by both Egyptians and the people of Israel would clarify why the Egyptians were willing to give up their wealth and to let the people of Israel go.

Moses delivered to Pharaoh a most chilling, and righteously indignant (11:8c), description of the coming judgment. In the dead of night (**about midnight**) death would visit the land of Egypt in an unprecedented way—**all the firstborn in the land of Egypt shall die**. The **firstborn** in a family was an especially significant position in Egypt as well as Israel, and in many other ancient patriarchal societies. The firstborn in any family was the main heir of the family fortune and the symbol of the ongoing social position of the family; much was invested in his well-being. The firstborn of the king or pharaoh was to inherit the throne, and with him rested, literally and symbolically, the fortunes and future of the dynasty and the nation. The death of the firstborn was a religious, social, and dynastic as well as personal/familial cataclysm. The extent of the catastrophe reached from Pharaoh's throne to the most humble dwelling of slaves and even to the stables and barnyards of that nation. Literally every home, every house, every barn would know a death in Egypt that night (cf. 12:30b), and the devastation would produce **a great cry** (11:6), a singular national lamentation, of extraordinary and unequaled proportions. In one night it would have incapacitated this nation for a generation or more.

To make the injury even more poignant for the Egyptians, the **sons of Israel** would be spared even the insult of a barking dog, that is, no one would utter a word of protest against the nation. This was to show that God **makes a distinction** between His own and those who oppose Him. Pharaoh is even told that this catastrophe would cause his people to come to Moses, not to him, and demand that Moses **Go out, you and all the people who follow you.**

11:9-10. The summary verses (11:9-10) are intended to recall the entire previous narrative and add justification for the drastic calamity of the final judgment. The wonders that should have produced humility, repentance, and submission to the word of the Lord yielded a hard heart and culminated in a final, terrible retribution.

2. Deliverance from Death and Preservation by Passover (12:1-30)

a. The Preparation of the People for the Passover (12:1-13)

12:1-10. Preparation for the Passover consisted of several sets of instructions about pertinent topics. These instructions were probably also given during the days of darkness and were for all the **congregation** (*'eda*) of Israel (12:3), and for **the whole assembly** (12:6). This is the first use of the term *'eda*—a term that appears over one-hundred times in the Exodus–Joshua narrative. It has the basic meaning of "community" or "congregation." Up to now the people have been identified as "Hebrews" or "sons of Israel," but from now on they are constituents of a unique assembly; they will be exclusively bound together by this Passover experience into the *'eda*. Furthermore, "whenever the text explicitly states that Moses addresses 'the entire congregation of Israel,' one can be sure that what will follow will be of extreme importance" (see Ex 35:1; Nm 1:2, 8; 26:2) (Hamilton, *Exodus*, 180). The Lord began with instructions regarding a new calendar (12:1-2). To emphasize the significance of the event at hand, the exodus itself, the Lord instructed Moses to reorient the Hebrew calendar so that the month of the exodus (**this month**), the month of Abib (cf. Ex 13:4; 23:15; 34:18; Dt 16:1; March/April), was the first month of the religious year. After the Babylonian captivity there was another re-orientation of the religious calendar; Abib was changed to Nisan (cf. Neh 2;1; Est 3:7) so, in effect, by the time of Christ, there were two calendars, one religious, one civil (secular) and the first month of the one was in the seventh month of the other.

This was followed by instructions dealing with the timing for Passover. A lamb (or kid goat) was to be selected on the tenth of Abib (12:3a) and kept (that is, observed and examined for suitability, as well as separated from the rest of the flock) until the fourteenth (12:6a); on that night **at twilight** (12:6b lit., "between the two evenings"; cf. Dt 16:6 "at sunset") it was to be slain (cf. Hamilton, *Exodus*, 180).

The instructions about the lamb itself were specific: the lamb was to be of sufficient size for a household (12:3b); if one's household was too small, he was to share that of a neighbor (12:4a); the lamb was to be **an unblemished male a year old** (12:5a); if a suitable lamb was not found, a kid goat with the same qualities could be used (12:5b). Then there were specific instructions about the eating of the Passover: the animal was to be killed, and roasted, not boiled (cf. Dt 16:7, "cooked") or **raw** (12: 9a); "The command not to eat the meat raw was significant because many of the surrounding pagan peoples often ate raw flesh at their sacrificial meals" (Davis, *Moses and the Gods*, 148). The animal was to be prepared whole, **its head and its legs** (12:9b; and its legs were not to be broken, cf. 12:46); it was to be fully consumed that night (12:10a) and leftovers were to be burned up, nothing was to be left behind (12:10b).

In addition the lamb was to be eaten along with **unleavened bread and bitter herbs** (12:8b; cf. Nm 9:11). The **bitter herbs** ("such as endive, chicory and other plants with a bitter taste [which were] native to Egypt" [Youngblood, *Exodus*, 60]) were to remind the nation of the bitterness of their bondage (cf. Ex 1:14). The **unleavened bread** was bread made without yeast and in such haste that the bread had no time to rise. The exact etymology of *matzot* is uncertain: it may have the idea of "squeezed, or pressed (flat) bread" or it may be related to terms in cognate Semitic languages that indicate common types of bread (cf. Kaiser, "Exodus," 375). Also the participants were to eat this meal fully clothed, as if ready to depart **in haste** (12:11a). Following this were instructions about manipulating the blood of the Passover: the blood of this Passover lamb was to be handled in a most unusual fashion: it was to be applied to **the two doorposts and on the lintel** of any home where this meal was being eaten in the prescribed manner (12:7; on the significance of this see comments on 12:21-22 below).

12:11-13. Then came the summary explanation (12:11-13) of the purpose of the death in the Passover and the manipulation of the blood. Emphatically this was called **the LORD's Passover** (12:11b). He was the One who conceived of this Passover; in effect He provided for it, and He was the One who actually "passed over" upon seeing this blood. All of this presumed that He had the right to judge: **I will execute judgments, I am the LORD** (12:12). And yet it proved that He was a gracious God: **when I see the blood I will pass over you** (12:13b). The Lord also made it clear that the judgment of the tenth plague would be **against all the gods of Egypt** (12:12). Those gods would once and for all be proven (as they had already been proven) to be impotent and empty. Yet, while sin brought judgment, there was grace, a provision—salvation was made possible by the shedding of blood. "Salvation always comes through judgment. Everyone who gets saved is saved through judgment" (cf. James M. Hamilton Jr., *God's Glory of Salvation Through Judgment* [Wheaton, IL: Crossway, 2010], 57, 58). The nation of Israel was saved, delivered through and from judgment (on Egypt) by the death and shedding of the blood of the lamb. "Redemption, including the forgiveness of sin, takes place only when the blood of an innocent offering is shed (Heb. 9:22); 1 John 1:7). The 'Passover lamb' (12:21) typifies [pointed to and illustrates the cross work of] Jesus as 'the lamb of God'" (Youngblood, *Exodus*, 60).

The apostle John applied this aspect of the Passover to Jesus Christ and the salvation He accomplished when he declared of Jesus of Nazareth "Behold the Lamb of God who takes away the sin of the world" (Jn 1:29; see the comments there). And the apostle Paul also tied the Passover ceremony to the sacrificial work of Jesus Christ when he affirmed "Christ our Passover also has been sacrificed" (1Co 5:7; see the comments there). As the nation was saved from the judgment (on Egypt), so believers in Jesus Christ are saved through and from judgment by the death/blood of The Lamb.

b. The Instructions for the Feast of Unleavened Bread (12:14-20)

12:14-20. This meal was clearly and definitely connected to the Passover (cf. Ex 23:15; Lv 23:5-8; Dt 16:1-8), so the Passover and the Feast of Unleavened Bread were "for all practical purposes combined as one feast; see Mark 14:1, 12" (Youngblood, *Exodus*, 61). First the nature of the Feast was noted: it was to be a **memorial**, a celebration (12:14) and a **permanent ordinance** (12:17). These notes made the point that this whole experience (the entire Egyptian bondage and the trauma of the last plague) had been a hard lesson for all involved and it was to be remembered so (1) the lesson would not have to be repeated and so (2) subsequent generations would know that they had much to be thankful for from the Lord. "Passover would forever commemorate their deliverance from Egypt and Unleavened Bread would remind them of the hardships of their hurried flight" (Youngblood, *Exodus*, 61).

The feast was to last **seven days** (12:15, 18, 19), and so it would have brought all mundane activity to a halt. The dedication to the Lord was to be conscientious and conspicuous. It required concerted thought and planning—it would have interrupted their daily routine to plan, to prepare, to think about their actions and the reasons for performing them.

Next the instructions for the preparations for the feast were given. They began with the removal of all leaven (v. 15). In passages such as Lv 2:11 and 1Co 5:7-8 leaven is understood as "a symbol of corruption" (Davis, *Moses and the Gods*, 150), but it does not always signify this (see the comments on Mt 13:33). So "the whole household needed to be pure and clean of heart; therefore all yeast was to be removed from the entire house (12:19)" (Kaiser, "Exodus," 374). The physical and actual removal of leaven from the house was to indicate a spiritual and inward removal of impurity from their hearts.

Then there were instructions about the assemblies (12:16a); these were to occur at the beginning and at the end of the seven days of celebration. Both of these assemblies were called **holy** (12:16a) indicating they were to be celebrations separated and dedicated to the things of the Lord. In other words, this entire celebration was meant to help subsequent generations focus their minds and hearts in order to recall the work of God on behalf of the nation at this first Passover in fulfillment of His promises.

The Lord also revealed several stipulations for celebrating the feast: no work was to be done (12:16b), this was to be a time devoted to the Lord; and **whoever eats what is unleavened . . . shall be cut off** (12:15, 19), that is, removed from the blessing and protection of the community. These stipulations were meant to protect the purpose and value of the celebration. If someone disregarded the feast in these ways it diminished its significance for the entire community. The sanction in v. 19 applied to **an alien or a native of the land**, which indicates that "Gentiles may be celebrants along with Israel even as was contemplated in the Abrahamic covenant of Genesis 12:3" (Kaiser, "Exodus," 374).

The significance of this feast was twofold: the nation was to remember that the Lord had delivered the people from Egypt in haste (12:17b): **for on this very day I brought your hosts out of the land of Egypt**. But they were also to know that He had delivered them to be a separate people. The purging of leaven from their houses was meant to reinforce both of those themes. The nature of leavening involves infiltration (of the yeast fungus) and the pervasiveness and the spread of the yeast. It also speaks to an influence or a permeating effect of something. It is that feature of leaven to which later biblical passages refer (e.g., the spread of the kingdom in Mt 13:33; Lk 13:20-21; the spreading influence of the teaching of the Pharisees in Mt 16:6; Mk 8:15; Lk 12:21; the old leaven of malice and wickedness in 1Co 5:6-8; cf. Gl 5:9). So here it would seem that the point of purging leaven for the seven day feast was conscientiously to keep out the unspiritual influences of the life, worldview, and values of the culture (here of the Egyptians) around them. They were to purge the worldliness that seeks to infiltrate and influence their thinking away from living for and devotion to the Lord.

c. The Passover Executed (12:21-22, 28)

12:21-22, 28. In simple but moving terms these verses record that **just as the LORD had commanded Moses and Aaron, so they did** (12:28). The **lintel** is the beam across the top of a doorway and the **doorposts** are the two sides framing the doorway (12:22). It was assumed (and this was typical) that there was only one way in or out of the dwelling. Hyssop (12:21) is a plant from the mint family that is itself rather pungent and fragrant and has "masses of tiny white flowers" and a surface of hairy filaments "good for dipping and sprinkling" (cf. Davis, *Moses and the Gods*, 151; cf. Lv 14:49-52; Nm 19:18-19). Sprinkling sacrificial blood with hyssop was an act of consecration and cleansing (cf. Lv 16:14-15). Actually, any sprinkling blood usually implied atonement, specifically substitutionary atonement. Placing the blood on the doorposts and lintel was not an act of superstition but indicated that the occupants had faith that the atonement had been made that now provided for their protection. "The act of slaying the lamb and sprinkling the blood on the door, which represented the entry and protection of the house, had great significance. It immediately pointed out the great price of redemption [death, shedding of blood, sacrifice, payment, ransom] and symbolically it pointed to the death of Jesus Christ (cf. 1 Pet 1:2; Rom 5:8-9; Heb 9:13-14; 13:12)" (Davis, *Moses and the Gods*, 147). What that lamb was for them, Jesus Christ is for believers today. See commentary on Jn 1:19; 1Co 5:7.

d. The Promise of the Passover and the Promise to the Nation (12:23-27)

12:23. The immediate promise of protection from **the destroyer** (12:23) was linked to the promise of the land (12:25). The **destroyer** "was not a demonic power that rivaled God but probably an angel of the Lord who expedited his will" (Kaiser, "Exodus," 376). It may even be that this was *the* Angel of the Lord (cf. 2Sm 24:16; Is 37:36), that is, a theophany, an appearance in angelic form of God Himself. Whether by His direct or mediated (cf. Ps 78:49) action this was the Lord's doing, **the LORD will pass through to smite** (cf. Heb 11:28), yet He would **pass over the door** that had the blood on the lintel and doorposts.

12:24-27. The focus shifts seamlessly from the promise to those who experienced the actual Passover to the generations to come (12:24) and specifically to those who will enter the land (12:25). They too were to observe this feast; this **ordinance** was to be observed perpetually (**forever**) and it was the responsibility of parents to involve and instruct their **children** (12:24, 26) in its significance. Specifically they were to perform this ceremony in the land, **when you enter the land** (12:25). As the children of Israel read this immediately prior to entering the land to subdue it, they would be reminded of God's power exhibited so dramatically at the exodus and would take heart at the prospect of the daunting task awaiting them in the conquest. The exodus, though indeed grand and glorious, was not an end in itself but the means to an end. These people were meant for **the land**, they were redeemed *from* bondage in Egypt *to receive* what **He has promised** (v. 25).

This was a key component in the covenant promises made to Abraham (cf. Gn 15:13-16; 17:7, 8). Sadly, the nation was wildly inconsistent in observing this feast until after the Babylonian exile. It is recorded as being observed only three times between entering the promised land and the Babylonian captivity: by Solomon (2Ch 8:13), by Hezekiah (2Ch 30), and by Josiah (2Ch 35). Perhaps it was observed at other times, but these later texts do indicate that the practice had been neglected and was being revived.

e. The Last Judgment Executed: The Death of the Firstborn (12:29-30)

12:29-30. Just as He had said it would happen, **the LORD struck all the firstborn in the land of Egypt** (12:29) and **there was a great cry in Egypt**. Not a single home was exempt: **there was no home where there was not someone dead** (12:30). Of course, the point here is that every *Egyptian* home knew a death that night, but it was also true in a more absolute sense *every home* knew a death! It was either the death of the firstborn or the death of the Passover lamb. The only thing that averted the judgment of God was a bloody, substitutionary sacrifice.

3. The Exodus Itself (12:31-39)

a. Pharaoh Relented in Sorrow (12:31-32)

12:31-32. The event of the actual exodus came in dramatic fashion. After the death of the firstborn of Egypt and pointedly after the death of **the firstborn of Pharaoh** (cf. 12:29), Pharaoh relented. Without waiting until daybreak (**at night**), he summoned Moses and Aaron. His words **Rise up, get out** (12:31) were still defiant but were unequivocal. Previously he had offered (disingenuously) to allow them some limited freedom to worship (see 8:25; 10:8, 24), but here his concession was absolute.

Not only did they have permission to go; they were ordered to go (just as God had predicted to Moses, cf. 11:1). "No qualifications, no concessions were part of his response; in fact, the departure was to take place on Moses' terms (12:32)" (Davis, *Moses and the Gods*, 153). Even when he said **bless me also** (12:32c) it was insincere; "Pharaoh desires a blessing, but repenting for his disgraceful, arrogant behavior never crosses his mind" (Hamilton, *Exodus*, 193).

b. The Nation Departed in Haste (12:33-39)

12:33-39. The sons of Israel left Egypt in such haste that the bread had no time to rise (**before it was leavened**) and their utensils were hastily bound up in sacks of clothing (12:34). The Egyptians were anxious to see them gone (12:33), so anxious apparently that they did not balk at giving the Israelites many gifts as a means to hasten their departure (the Jewish people would not have to be as painstaking in gathering supplies for their journey if the Egyptians just gave them many things; 12:36). Apparently (and this was foretold as caused by the Lord's favor, cf. 11:2-3), all they had to do was ask. The Egyptian motives here were probably not good will or guilt. Perhaps this reflected a desire to win favor with the Hebrews' God, a desire to be rid of the Jewish people because of the grief brought upon Egypt because of them (see 12:33), or it may be that the Egyptians simply had no use for the silver and gold trinkets, idols, precious objects of devotion for their now defeated and discredited gods. In any case, it was the Lord who moved the Egyptians to this show of generosity, for **the LORD had given the people favor in the eyes of the Egyptians** (12:36); and this was in fulfillment of the promise to Abraham (cf. Gn 15:14).

The nation moved out quickly, moving **from Rameses to Succoth**; while the precise locations are uncertain it is likely that this was a move away from the place where the Egyptians had subjugated them (cf. Ex 1:11) to a border town "in the eastern delta of the Nile, south and a bit east of Raamses. About a day's journey [sic]" (Hamilton, *Exodus*, 193). The word **Succoth** (v. 37) is the Hebrew term *sukkot* which means "booth," and may indicate that **Succoth** was nothing much more than a caravan stop, a place of mere booths.

The note that there were **six hundred thousand men on foot** would mean that the entire population ranged from two to two-and-a-half million persons. While a number of scholars have denied the accuracy of this number and have declared it to be impossible, others have offered several arguments for its viability (see Davis, *Moses and the Gods*, 154–56; Hamilton, *Exodus*, 194; Kaiser, "Exodus," 379). For instance, the number 600,000 "reappears consistently in the biblical record: Ex 38:26; Num 1:46; 2:32 (603,550); 11:21 (600,000)" (Hamilton, *Exodus*, 194) and this argues against scribal error or misunderstanding of the Hebrew numbering system. Also, the reference to a more specific number as in Nm 2:32 (cf. above) mitigates against a non-literal interpretation or a misreading in the texts that use the round number of **six hundred thousand**. And it may be noted that the number had to be large enough for Pharaoh to say "the people of the sons of Israel are more and mightier than we" (cf. 1:9); a contingent of 600 families (as some critics take the number) would hardly elicit such apprehension.

In many instances the attempt to reduce the number to something "more reasonable" has been dictated by nothing more than what seems reasonable to the critical scholar despite the clear testimony of the text. However, such a hermeneutic is much too subjective and has led to serious misreading (and outright denials) of the biblical/historical accounts. Given the time (four-hundred-plus years) of the sojourn in Egypt it is not unreasonable to suppose that the nation had grown to over two-and-a-half million persons and given the second generation was numbered at 601,730 families (Nm 26:51), it seems most reasonable to accept the accuracy of the number given here.

Along with the people of Israel was a **mixed multitude** (*'ereb rab*). This was probably a collection of other enslaved peoples as well as Egyptians who "were impressed by the power of the God of the Hebrews" (Davis, *Moses and the Gods*, 156). Some may have been genuine converts to the faith of Israel but many were not and later they were the source of problems for Moses and the nation (cf. Nm 11:4).

4. Summary: The Years of Bondage (12:40-41)

12:40-41. The number of the years of the sojourn in Egypt was noted as four hundred and thirty (12:41). Some have suggested a contradiction between this and the number given in Gn 15:13 in the promise and prophecy to Abram, where an even four hundred years is mentioned. Most likely the time noted in Gn 15:13 is a round-number approximation (Abram hardly needed a more precise number for the point being made there), and this (Ex 12:41) is the historically accurate number (which might be expected here in the summary accounting at the end of the actual time of Egyptian bondage).

5. Instructions Regarding the Foreigner and Sojourner and the Passover (12:42-51)

12:42-51. These instructions deal with a circumstance that might have been anticipated given the contest between the true Lord God and the false gods of Egypt, namely what should happen with any non-Israelite who is either attached to an Israelite household or who wished to sojourn with them (i.e., an Egyptian who wanted to escape the devastation and participate in the Passover and go with the nation of Israel). These instructions stipulated that such persons needed to be circumcised and be made **like a native of the land** (12:48). While the whole Passover ceremony indicated that the deliverance, the protection, and the salvation are only for those who have come under the blood of the Passover lamb, it also affirmed that any who will come and believe, and submit, and obey will be welcomed and they too would be saved. This was true not only for the generation that participated in the exodus, but for the generation that read Exodus, that would conquer the holy land and subsequently live in it.

6. The Consecration of the Firstborn (13:1-16)

13:1-16. These instructions were given to the nation (for this and future generations) so that the nation would remember the event of the exodus and the Passover (13:3b-4). God spoke to Moses, and Moses instructed the people (13:3) to **remember**. Moses probably gave these instructions at the same time he gave the instructions about the Passover (chap. 12). This memorial was to take place once the nation was in **the land** (13:5), again making the point that the exodus was a means to an end—that the nation might possess the land of promise (cf. 3:8, 17; Gn 15:13-21). The memorial was to take place at the appointed time, **this day in the month of Abib** (13:4) and **at its appointed time every year** (13:10). It was to be a family memorial (13:8, 14).

Further, Moses explained how they would remember. There were to be three means (essentially three mnemonic devices) given for this remembering: First, they were to dedicate (**sanctify to Me**, v. 2; **devote to the Lord**, 13:12) the firstborn. This could be accomplished by either sacrifice or the firstborn could be given over to the service of the Lord as appropriate (13:13). Obviously, this was meant to recall the last judgment on Egypt (death of the firstborn) and thus the preservation of the firstborn by the God (via the Passover lamb). Also, it was meant to be a way to show that every son and daughter (indeed, every person), every life (every animal)—they all really belonged to the Lord. The priority of the firstborn was an indication of the priority of devotion to the Lord (see Davis, *Moses and the Gods*, 161).

Second, there were more instructions about the unleavened bread (13:3, 6-7) and once again this was to remind them of the dedication that was to guide their lives and they were to demonstrate to others. The idea behind the metaphor of the leaven is that of pervasive influence. As the leaven pervades and affects the whole loaf, so the leaven of ungodly influences must be eliminated if the people were to be wholly dedicated to the Lord.

Third, the remembering was to be facilitated by the wearing of **a sign** on the hand and **a reminder** on the forehead (lit., "between your eyes"). Some take this as a figurative wearing (see Pr 3:3; 6:21) but the Jewish people took this literally and introduced the use of *phylacteries* (the term means something like "frontlet bands," in effect forehead bands; indeed, that seems to be what 13:16 is indicating). These were small leather boxes with bits of Scripture on parchments that were held on heads and arms by leather bands to remind them of these events and their significance, parallel to the current idea of "tying a string around one's finger" in order to remember to do something important.

Finally, Moses noted what they were to remember, **for with a powerful hand the Lord brought you/us out of Egypt** (13:9, 16). In a sense this deliverance was not just for the generation that experienced it but it was for every Israelite of every generation of the nation afterward. In a way their very existence as a nation and people was made possible by this great deliverance.

7. Deliverance through the Sea (13:17–14:31)

This dramatic section describes three phases of this deliverance.

a. Phase One: The Lord Led the People (13:17-22)

13:17-20. The narrative explains that the Lord did not lead the people **by the way of . . . the Philistines**, that is, along the coastal road (this northeast route would have been apparently the most direct) because the Philistines (or pre-Philistine "sea-peoples") were there and it would have required an intense and prolonged military campaign (13:17). They marched along **in martial array** (13:18b). This probably simply means with weapons and perhaps in a military-like formation (cf. Jos 1:14; 4:12; Jdg 7:11; cf. Davis, *Moses and the Gods*, 164). But in spite of appearances they were not ready to engage in a military conflict. It was not that they lacked the weapons. Rather, they did not have the heart. That is, they lacked the settled convictions and unwavering confidence in the Lord required to do battle. Before they took on the conquest, this people needed to see what the Lord was about to do and they needed the commitment and cohesiveness that only the law could give them. At that point in their history, they were still only a loose band of former slaves. They needed to be a nation before they could engage in the serious battles to come.

So the Lord led them **around by the way of the wilderness to the Red Sea** (13:18a) and He took them to **Succoth and camped in Etham on the edge of the wilderness** (13:20). The precise location of these places is unknown (Kaiser lists several suggestions but concludes "Everyone is guessing!"; cf. Kaiser, "Exodus," 385; see Kitchen, *Reliability of the OT*, 256–60), but the general sense is that the route was south-southeast and mostly into the desert regions on the eastern border of Egypt.

It is clear the author of this record knew where these places were and by recording them in such detail he gave a testimony to the historicity of the record (cf. Davis, *Moses and the Gods*, 168). The **Red Sea** (*yam-suph*) could be rendered "Reed Sea," designating a papyrus marsh. Kitchen notes that in "extended usage"

Four Possible Routes of The Exodus from Egypt

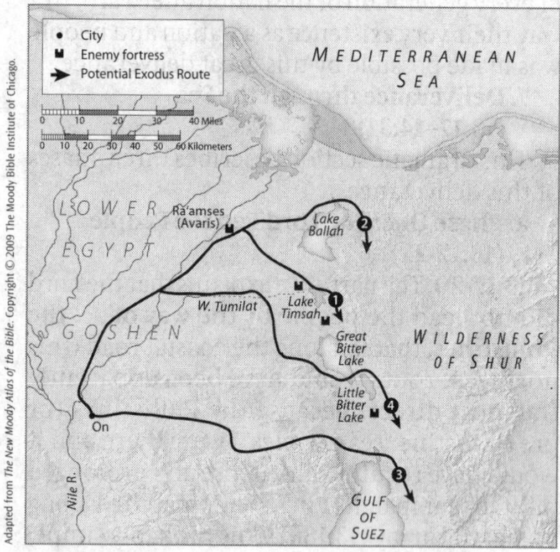

the term is even "applied to the Gulf of Suez and the Gulf of Aqaba" which may render *yam suph* less a specific location and merely a reference the general area "from north to south" which featured "a series of stretches of often salty water" that ended at the Gulf of Suez (cf. Kitchen, *Reliability of the OT*, 262–63).

As to the exact location of the crossing, Davis notes four views: One view places the crossing near "Lake Timsah or the southern extension of the present Lake Menzaleh" (Davis, *Moses and the Gods*, 176; this view is based on references to these bodies in Egypt writings as *yam suph*). However, as noted, *yam suph* was used for several marshy waterways. Another view puts the crossing through the northeastern areas of the Nile delta but these would have been the forbidden **way of the land of the . . . Philistines** (13:17) and was actually in the wrong direction from Marah, a known location where the Israelites went (see 15:22, 23). A third view suggests the crossing was much farther south, at the northern end of the Gulf of Suez. But this crossing would not place them in the Wilderness of Shur (which was on the northwest section of the Sinai Peninsula, where the Israelites clearly went; see 15:22) when they reached the other side. A fourth view is that the crossing took place in the so-called Bitter Lakes region, a location that could appropriately be called a *yam suph* since it was a marshy area and which was located directly across from the Wilderness of Shur. A crossing at this location would have put them easily within three days' journey of Marah (15:22-23).

Of course, critical scholars hold a fifth view: the event never happened, and it should be read as a mythological story of divine deliverance. However, the overall sense of the text and the precision of names and locales argue that the author wanted his reader to know that this was historical narrative. And as Oswalt argues, if these events are not historical and did not happen as the author has recorded them, "we are hard-pressed to explain why Israel chose to create this unique historical fiction to tell its story" (John N. Oswalt, *The Bible Among the Myths* [Grand Rapids, MI: Zondervan, 2009], 150).

In sum, while the precise locations are debated, *Yam Suph* could well be referring to a portion of the **Red Sea**; at least "nothing prevents our linking *Yam Suph* with the Red Sea" (Kaiser, "Exodus," 384); hence either the first or third views seem the most viable.

The comment about **the bones of Joseph** (13:19) recalls Joseph's request (cf. Gn 50:24-25), a testimony to Joseph's faith in God's promise. Joseph knew that even in death God would give the nation that land! The reading of this episode by the Israelites as they prepared to take the land would have been a model for them of the kind of faith they should have in the Lord—the kind of faith exemplified by Joseph long before. He had great confidence in what God would do in the future. They needed their own confidence bolstered as well.

13:21-22. In this journey the Lord led the people with a unique manifestation, **a pillar of cloud by day** . . . and **a pillar of fire by night** (13:21-22). For the hundreds of thousands following Moses in the wilderness, this would have been impressive, encouraging, and very practical. Later it became clear this was a manifestation of God (cf. 14:19; 23:20-23; such brilliant manifestations are typical for depicting the presence of God (e.g., the Shekinah glory). The sight would remind the people that God was always present with them. It would have been inspiring to them and an assurance that He was providing for their security and guidance. Perhaps this was why no one questioned the unexpected direction of their exodus from Egypt.

b. Phase Two: Pharaoh Chased the People (14:1-12)

14:1-4. In brief compass the Lord laid out the whole series of events about to unfold (14:1-4); . . . **you shall camp** . . . **Pharaoh will say** . . . **I will**

harden . . . he will chase . . . I will be honored . . . Egyptians will know. Once again the precise locations of **Pi-hahiroth** and **Migdol** (lit., "tower") are unknown, but the inference of this being **between Migdol and the sea** (14:2) is reasonable. This camp would leave them with no escape since they were pinned against the sea, and from a logistical point of view it was not a defensible place. To Pharaoh it appeared that their wanderings had been aimless and had left them trapped, **shut them in** (14:3). But while the people might have appeared to be trapped, the Lord was setting the stage to ensnare Pharaoh. The hard-hearted (see commentary on 7:3) and arrogant king would pursue the people only to be destroyed by the Lord. Thus God would be **honored through Pharaoh** (14:4a), for after his defeat all would know that **I am the LORD** (14:4b; see also the comments on Rm 9:17-18, 23).

14:5-9. At some point after the shock of the last judgment had worn off, Pharaoh and his servants (virtually the whole population of Egypt) had **a change of heart** (14:5). They expressed regret at allowing their slaves to escape and made plans to chase them down with chariots (15:5b-6, 9). The number of chariots employed by Pharaoh—**six hundred select chariots, and all the other chariots of Egypt with officers over all of them**—was an indication of his intention to have a complete victory. The chariots were the seemingly invincible weapon of ancient times and were the symbol of Egyptian might and power. They are highlighted here in order to set up the contrast between God's power and Pharaoh's. In short order this massive mighty military force was to be wiped out by the Lord's forces, their resources consisting, ironically, of nothing but the simple elements of wind and water.

14:10-12. At first the **sons of Israel** "were going out boldly" (lit., "with a high hand" 14:8), triumphantly and confidently. But **as Pharaoh drew near** they became **very frightened and** they **cried out to the LORD** (14:10). This reaction might be understandable, but what they said next betrayed their immaturity and lack of faith. With "bitter sarcasm and irony" (Davis, *Moses and the Gods*, 169) they lamented, **Were there no graves in Egypt**? Which was to say, "If you meant to kill us, it would have been easier to do that in Egypt because there certainly were plenty of graves there!" In other words, they were assuming they were about to die in the wilderness and they even wished themselves back in bondage to Pharaoh as a condition preferable to being slaughtered by Pharaoh in the wilderness (14:11-12). Apparently, the terror of the moment had caused them to forget the great manifestations of the power of God they had so recently witnessed, and they lost heart. They were estimating the outcome of events based on their external circumstances (which were admittedly bad from a human perspective) and their own resources (which were certainly weak).

c. Phase Three: The Lord Preserved the People (14:13-31)

14:13-15. Moses' response showed that at least he had been changed, not by the events but by his knowledge of the Lord. He did not rehearse all the events, judgments, and demonstrations of power they have recently experienced. He simply commanded the people, **Do not fear** (14:13a). They were not told to get ready to fight but to **stand by** (lit., "take your stand") **and see** (14:13b). And they were to stop talking (14:14b). This was perhaps in part to stifle the panic their talking had fueled. It may be recalled that the last time the people became discouraged (cf. 5:20-21) Moses followed them into despondency (cf. 5:22-23). But this time he took his eyes off Pharaoh and recalled the words of the Lord. Moses told the people, **the LORD will fight for you** (14:14) and that they would see His salvation and that they would not see any more Egyptians after that day (14:13c). This did not mean they were to remain inactive. They needed to **go forward** (14:15b) but that the battle was the Lord's.

14:16-20. These dramatic events, briefly expressed in the text, would have taken some time to unfold. First, Moses was commanded to do something seemingly incongruous and unexpected. He was to raise his staff **over the sea and divide it** (14:16a) thus providing a completely unexpected way of escape for the people **through the midst of the sea on dry land** (14:16b). Again, the Lord reiterated His plan and purpose for the Egyptians (14:17-18; cf. 3:4). In the meantime the **angel of God**, in the form of the **pillar of cloud** (i.e., smoke and fire, cf. 13:21-22) performed a rear guard action to keep the Egyptians back so that the people would have sufficient time to make their escape through the sea (14:19-20).

14:21-29. And then, in dramatic action, Moses **stretched out his hand . . . and the LORD swept** (lit., "caused to go") **the sea back by a strong east wind** and **the sea turned to dry land** and **the waters were like a wall** (14:21-22, 29; cf. Ps 78:13).

The entire event itself is best understood as a supernatural occurrence, not, as skeptics often argue, a sudden drainage of a lake, not a natural wind, not a frozen or congealed surface of the waters (cf. Davis, *Moses and the Gods*, 171–75).

When the Egyptians attempted a pursuit (14:23) the God sent **confusion** (v. 24; the time was **the morning watch**, the last night watch just before sunrise) to the Egyptian army such that their best and most powerful weapons, their chariots, were rendered utterly ineffective (14:25a). At that point the Egyptians become discouraged and they acknowledged **the LORD is fighting for them** (14:25). Although they intended to retreat, it was too late and the process that made Israel's deliverance possible was reversed. **At daybreak** Moses raised his staff to return the waters to their basin (14:27a) and the Egyptian army was utterly destroyed (14:27b-28). If, as many critical scholars argue, the Israelites escaped through knee-deep water without any real miracle, then it was miraculous that the Egyptian soldiers drowned in such shallows.

14:30-31. The summary verses (14:30-31) are in sharp contrast to the fear and complaints that the people had expressed just before the great event unfolded. The emphasis in these verses is on **Israel**. Whereas they came to this place as "a people" delivered from bondage, now they stood as a cohesive nation observing an utterly defeated enemy. They no longer had to fear Pharaoh, but the people rightly **feared the LORD, and they believed in the LORD** (14:31).

8. Praise for Deliverance and Preservation: The Song of Moses (15:1-21)

15:1-21. Inserted into the narrative of Exodus, the so-called "Song of Moses" is a psalm of praise to commemorate and celebrate the great event of the deliverance of the nation through the sea. It is a poetic retelling of the historical account related in the previous chapter, and it was probably composed much later in Moses' lifetime and placed here in a late edition of the book (likely by Moses himself). The references to Edom and Moab in v. 15 indicate this, for those nations did not enter the story or experience of the nation until much later (cf. Nm 20:14ff.; 22:1; 26:3). Davis notes that this song "sets the spiritual and theological standard for all subsequent praise" (Davis, *Moses and the Gods*, 183).

This psalm contains four major themes: (1) praise to the Lord for His victory over the Egyptians, 15:1-3, 6-8, 11-13, 21; (2) joy over the defeat of the Egyptians by the Lord, 15:4-5, 9-10; (3) warning to the nations, 15:14-16a, b; and (4) expectation of the fulfillment of the Lord's promise to the nation, 15:16c, d-17. The psalm speaks of the enemies of the Lord and the attributes of the Lord. Each of these four themes would be relevant for the readers of Exodus as they prepared to enter the land and fight to possess it.

The contents of the song describes the Lord's enemies, attributes, and deliverance. First the song speaks about the enemies of the Lord. They actually were powerful (15:4) because they had chariots and officers. But in their presumption (15:9a) they were sure they would prevail. Instead the Egyptian soldiers were (and all such enemies will be) utterly defeated (15:5b, 10b). They sank like a stone and were destroyed (15:9b). As a result, God's enemies should fear (15:14-16a, b) and yet they do not fear and this will result in their own eventual destruction.

Second, the song speaks of God's attributes. He is "transcendent." The rhetorical question **Who is like You among the gods, O LORD?** (15:11a) leads to the obvious answer, "No one is like Him!" He is holy (15:11b). Indeed He is **majestic in holiness**. He is all powerful, including over enemies, over elements, over circumstances, and with that power He fights for His people (15:3, 6, 8a; 15:10a, 12).

He is a "relational" God (15:2) and the psalmist can say with confidence, **The LORD is my strength and song, And He has become my salvation; This is my God, and I will praise Him; My father's God, and I will extol Him**. The first person singular pronoun here should be understood as applying to or speaking for the nation as a whole. And yet this is something each individual could say, for God is personally active in the lives of His own (15:13). He is a promise-keeping God (15:17), He is Lord, and He **will reign forever and ever** (v. 18; see Ps 10:16; 29:10; 146:10; Rv 11:15). The final, ultimate victory is yet to come in the last days!

Finally, the song speaks of the Lord's deliverance of Israel. A summary description of the exodus (in effect the third retelling; 15:19) follows. There is a description of celebration featuring Miriam **the prophetess** (15:20-21; cf. Nm 12:2). Miriam was the first woman ever given this title in the Bible (cf. Deborah, Jdg 4:4; Huldah, 2Ki 22:14; Anna, Lk 2:36; Philip's daughters, Ac 21:9). Contrary to the culture of that day, women in Israel were accorded high privileges and duties and given great honor for their devotion and service to the Lord.

Together with the song of Moses this scene depicts "the affairs of a community" in which "both men and women take essential parts. When the community joins together for the common songs and celebration there is a strong senses of solidarity. In the leadership of these two [Moses and Miriam]... mutual complementarity functions as a key model for the unity and efficiency of the entire community" (Hamilton, *Exodus*, 235). It is remarkable to note that she had to be near ninety years old and yet she was dancing and playing **timbrels** (probably small finger cymbals).

G. The Journey from the Sea to Sinai, Part One (15:22–17:7)

The journey from the sea to the Sinai centers on the grumbling of the people and the provision of God: The people grumbled about water (15:22-27). They grumbled about food (16:1-12). Then they grumbled about water again (17:1-7).

15:22-27. They first grumbled just three days after the passage through the sea (15:22), and those grumblings were about water, a serious problem for a large number of people living in the desert. They did find water at **Marah** (Hb. "bitter") but it was undrinkable (15:23), probably because of high mineral content or simply uncleanness. In answer to Moses' prayer (15:25a) God provided a special tree to make the water drinkable. No known tree has the quality to turn impure water pure or to filter out the mineral content. This is to be seen for what it appears to be—a miracle of the Lord's provision.

When the people set out into the wilderness the issue of provisions, especially the need for water, should not have been unexpected by the nation. It certainly was not something unforeseen by the Lord. He intended to make it an object lesson and a test for the people, **and there He tested them** (15:25c). The word for "test" here has the idea of "to prove the worth" of something, "to verify the quality" of something. The Lord was not trying to cause them to fail Rather, as an exercise in training and testing, the need for provisions gave the people an opportunity to verify their faith. In effect, this was to remind them that, after delivering them from the plagues and dividing the sea, God would be the One to provide for their everyday needs (something for which at the commencement of the conquest, Moses' readers would need reassurance as well). And yet He wanted to provide those daily needs in such a way that they would be reminded to **give earnest heed to the voice of the LORD your God, and do what is right in His sight** (15:26a). The *unusual* manner of God's provisions was intended to remind the people of their *usual* obligation to **keep all His statutes** (15:26b). Soon after this they came to a place (**Elim**, present day Wadi Garandel, an oasis some 60 miles southeast of Suez) where the water was abundant (15:27).

16:1-12. The next incident of grumbling happened less than a month after the passage through the sea, (16:1) and this time the issue was food (16:3). Again, God explained to Moses that this was a test, **that I may test them** (16:4). The daily provision of manna was meant, as with the water, to remind them that He, the Lord, the same Lord who **brought** them **out of the land of Egypt** (16:6), was the One doing the providing (cf. 16:7, **you will see** and 16:12, **you shall know that I am the LORD your God**). At the same time the Lord sent **meat** (lit., "flesh") (16:12-13) in the form of quails (16:13; cf. Ps 78:27, where it says He "rained meat" upon them). This was not the only food they had. In 12:32, 38 (cf. 17:3) it was noted that they took their flocks and herds, so they would have had plenty of food; but of course if they ate all their livestock they would have had nothing with which to re-stock the promised land once they had settled there.

This food came each day—a regular provision by unusual means to remind them **to do what is right** (cf. 15:26), to **walk in My instruction** (16:4). These provisions were gracious but they were also a "test" (15:25; 16:4) for the people. Each day as they gathered these food supplies they would either gratefully and humbly acknowledge the Lord's provision as such or thoughtlessly and selfishly consume them. If one daily acknowledged the Lord's provision it should naturally lead that one to acknowledge and submit to the Lord's commandments and statutes. However, if one was unmindful of the source of these provisions one would likely be unmindful of the Lord's command to **walk in My instruction**. In spite of the continued grumblings of the people (16:2, 7) the Lord was gracious and provided for the needs of His people.

16:13-36. In the middle of these grumbling accounts is an extended section about the manna. Regardless of many attempts, all naturalistic explanations of the manna fail. The quantity and qualities of the substance described here are nothing like the lichen (fungus-like organisms) that grow on rocks and trees, or like the bark, twigs, leaves, or sap of any known flora (e.g., tamarisk bushes) of the region. "The very fact that so much space is devoted to [explaining] this phenomenon referred to so many times in the Old Testament is an indication of its supernatural quality" (Davis, *Moses and the Gods*, 192). "Manna must be regarded as a peculiar substance, miraculously created for a special purpose" (Kaiser, "Exodus," 403).

Several features regarding this manna are noteworthy. First, Moses recorded the discovery and provided a description of manna (16:13-15, 31). The manna appeared with the early-morning dew and it was there after the dew dried. It was **a fine flake-like thing** ... **it was like coriander seed, white, and its taste was like wafers with honey**. In short it had a familiar taste but was not exactly like anything they were used to eating. Appropriately they asked, **What is it?** In Hebrew this question is *man hu*, forming a wordplay with *man* (the Hb. word transliterated into Eng. as *manna*). The Greek OT [LXX] has *ti esti touto* or "what is this?" So the actual name of this substance is literally "What is it?" Both their question and the lack of an answer indicates that this was not a natural food.

Next Moses described the process for gathering the manna (16:16-21). Again, the supernatural nature of the substance was made even clearer when they gathered it. Everyone was to pick up an **omer** (about two quarts; cf. 16:36) per person. But no matter how much they gathered, everyone had just enough—not too much, not too little. Furthermore, no one could gather enough in one day to last two days because it would spoil overnight. Everyone had to gather it day-by-day. Of course, some of them tried to gather extra anyway but they found out that that was not wise because **it bred worms and became foul** (16:20). The note that Moses was **angry with them** (16:20b) reflects the frustration he felt in dealing with a people who refused to follow even such simple instructions. This suggests that God intended to teach Israel daily reliance upon Him—just as Jesus taught His followers to pray, "Give us this day our daily bread" (Mt 6:11).

There were also special instructions pertaining to the Sabbath and the manna (16:22-30). On the sixth day they were to gather twice the usual amount so that it would not be necessary to gather it on the Sabbath (16:22a, 25-26). Moses informed the leaders (16:22b-23a) that everything for the Sabbath was to be prepared on the sixth day (16:23). Unlike the extra manna gathered on other days, the manna collected on the sixth day was perfectly fine on the seventh, the Sabbath (16:24). Once again some tried to go out on the Sabbath and gather some manna but they were disappointed to find it was not there (16:27). This time it was the Lord who expressed frustration when the people failed to follow instructions, and He reiterated the importance and privilege of the Sabbath (16:28-30).

The final verses of this excursus (16:32-36) record the memorial of the manna. This paragraph demonstrates that Moses completed writing the Pentateuch just prior to the conquest since it mentions the forty years of wanderings (16:35). A portion of this manna was preserved to remind the nation of the provision of the Lord. Later it was placed in the ark, **before the Testimony** (16:34). This was to remind succeeding generations that manna was not just a provision of food for those who ate it. Without manna, the exodus generation would not have survived. Had that generation not survived the later generations who only saw the manna would not have existed either. They were to realize that "What is it?" had made the lives of succeeding generations possible as well—the manna was the means the Lord chose to preserve the people so that He could fulfill His promises to them, not only to meet their needs.

17:1-7. The third instance of grumbling was once again over water. Here the situation was a bit different, for it seems now the people were testing the Lord (see 17:2c, 7, **because they tested the Lord**). Here the idea is a test in the sense of a challenge. They were challenging God to provide, and they were challenging the leadership of Moses to the point that he was actually afraid for his life (17:4). While the Lord did provide, and He did vindicate Moses' leadership, the sorry event was memorialized in two names imposed on this the location, **Massah and Meribah** (lit., "testing" and "quarreling"), to remind the people that their behavior was inappropriate and proved that they had a long way to go before they passed His test. It may be noted that here Moses was instructed to **strike the rock** (17:6) in contrast to Nm 20:8 (see commentary on that text).

H. The Journey from the Sea to Sinai, Part Two (17:8–18:27)

1. War with Amalek (17:8-16)

17:8-16. Exactly who the Amalekites were (apart from the fact that they were descendants of Esau; cf. Gn 36:12) and why they opposed the nation of Israel at this point is not clear. They would appear several more times in Israel's history (cf. Dt 25:17-18; Nm 14:43-45; 1Sm 15:2-9; 30:1-20.) This is the first mention of Joshua, the man who becomes the nation's general (17:9) and Moses' personal aide (cf. Ex 24:13; 32:17; 33:11; Jos 1:1). It should be noticed that Moses gave him orders (17:9) and **Joshua did as Moses told him** (17:10), an example of obedience that stands in contrast to the people as a whole. This battle is most remarkable because the ebb and flow of the battle seemed to be more dependent on Moses, who was literally above it all, than it was with the men who were actually engaged in the fighting. Of course, the act of Moses holding up his hands (17:11) was not merely encouraging to the combatants nor was it simply a matter of Moses' personal intercession. This action symbolized that the success of the army was dependent on the constancy of the Lord, for after the victory the memorial altar was called **The Lord** [not "Moses' Arms"] **is My Banner** (17:15 *YHWH–Nissi*; meaning "the standard," "the flag," or "the emblem"). The Lord was the source of courage and strength, and hence the Author of this victory.

2. Reunion with and Advice from Jethro (18:1-27)

18:1-12. This chapter begins with a reunion with Moses' wife and sons. The names of Moses' sons reflect Moses' spiritual experiences, "Gershom means 'banishment' and Eliezer literally means 'my God is help'" (Davis, *Moses and the Gods*, 197). This is followed by a reunion of Moses with his father-in-law (18:5-12). Moses clearly held Jethro in high esteem and probably regarded him as a priest (perhaps like Melchizedek in Gn 14; or Job) of the true God. Apparently, Moses' story served to confirm Jethro's faith (18:11).

18:13-23. As he observed Moses' routine, Jethro saw a problem. Moses was trying to serve as the main priest (intercessor) and magistrate (judge) for the whole nation. The people went to Moses with spiritual matters (**to inquire of God**, 18:15) and for mundane matters (to settle **a dispute**, v. 16). This was far too demanding on Moses and the people (v. 18a). Jethro's rebuke was blunt: **you cannot do it alone** (18:18b), but he did offer a solution (18:19-23). He first advised Moses to be **the people's representative before God** (18:19a). This would mean intercession *for them* before God (18:19b) and instruction about God *to them* (18:20). Then Moses was to **select... able men**, men with some serious qualifications for service (18:21), and he was to subdivide the workload of judging among these men (18:22-23). Thus if there were major issues or disputes, Moses could handle them, but all minor matters these men and the parties involved could work out for themselves under the direction of these men (18:22). Not only did this advice provide Moses with some excellent management principles, but as the spiritual leader, Moses was freed up for spiritual service (cf. Ac 6).

18:24-27. Moses fully accepted the advice of Jethro: **Moses listened to his father-in-law and did all he said**. Apparently the program instituted by Moses worked well and Jethro departed **into his own land** (v. 27b).

II. The Law and the Tabernacle (19:1–40:38)

The children of Israel, having been delivered from bondage, were given the Sinai covenant, which was to be a blessing to them in three areas: life in a relationship with God, life in kinship with the people of God, life centered on true worship of God.

A. Preparation of the People to Receive the Law (19:1-25)

1. The People Accept and Commit to the Covenant (19:1-8)

19:1-2. The arrival at Sinai is recorded in simple terms without fanfare. It had taken three months for the nation to go from Egypt to Sinai (19:1). By comparing 19:1 and Nm 10:11 it seems the nation began an eleven-month stay at Sinai. "Everything that happens in Exodus 19:1-40:38 + Leviticus 1:1-27:34 + Numbers 1:1-10:10 transpires while God's people are resting at this holy site" (Hamilton, *Exodus*, 291). This "was for Moses a return to familiar surroundings"; he had returned to a location that was "majestic and inspiring" (Davis, *Moses and the Gods*, 202, 203). The term **wilderness** is repeated to emphasize that the great event of the giving of the law happened in the wilderness, a place where there were no distractions, no other associations, and nothing of the world. There was really nothing here but the Lord Himself. All other associations were set aside so that the people could focus on the covenant, the relationship about to be established. This is "one of the high points in Hebrew history" (Davis, *Moses and the Gods*, 202).

19:3-8. These verses reveal the covenant itself and reflect the provisions of a standard ANE suzerain treaty (that is a treaty between an underling and an overlord; see J. W. Marshall, "Decalogue," in Dictionary of the Old Testament Pentateuch, ed. T. Desmond Alexander and David W. Baker [Downers Grove, IL: InterVarsity: 2003], 173ff.). There was a standard pattern or formula to such treaties: *preamble* ("Hear ye, hear ye"; 19:3); *history* of relations between the vassals and their master ("This is how we have arrived at this stage in our relationship"; 19:4); *stipulations* ("This is what you [underling] will do"; 19:5a); *promises/blessings* ("This is what I [overlord] will give you"; 19:5b-6a); *formal presentation* (19:6b-7); and *formal acceptance* (19:8). A covenant such as this was meant to elevate and formalize an already extant relationship (see Hamilton, *Exodus*, 301). Here the relationship with the nation was based on the Lord's promises to the patriarchs (cf. 6:8; 13:5) and on His sovereign and gracious deliverance of them from bondage: **bore you on eagles' wings and brought you to Myself** (19:4).

The stipulations **obey My voice and keep My covenant** (19:5) were thus not the means to earn the promises (as noted above, those promises had been given to the patriarchs Abraham [Gn 12:1-3; chaps. 15, 17], Isaac [Gn 26:24], and Jacob [Gn 28:13-15; 35:11-12), but the way to live so as to enjoy the promises. The idea is "If you obey and keep the commandments you will *prove to be* **My own possession** . . ." (19:5). They already *were* His people (see Hamilton, *Exodus*, 301). God gave Israel the law to ensure that *Israel would be able to fulfill the Abrahamic covenant by avoiding sin and therefore, the consequences of experiencing the temporal discipline of God.*

If God disciplined them, the nation would be driven from the land (Dt 28:64-65) and they would not be able to experience His glory and blessings. A further result would be that the Abrahamic covenant could not be fulfilled in its entirety. Eventually, of course, Moses anticipated Israel's inability to keep the law (Dt 31:29) and predicted that God would make the fulfillment of the promises possible for Israel through receiving the circumcised hearts of the new covenant (Dt 30:6). Thus, God gave these laws to Israel because only by living as He commanded and according to His standards by His own nature could they expect to enjoy His blessings. "In essence, the Sinaiatic covenant spells out the type of nation that Yahweh intends Israel to be . . . . Israel, the patriarch's promised descendants, could enjoy the divine-human relationship anticipated in Genesis 17:7-8 only by maintaining the ethical distinctiveness enshrined in God's instructions to Abraham ('Walk before Me and be blameless,' Gen 17:1)" (P. R. Williamson, "Covenant," in *Dictionary of the Old Testament: Pentateuch* [Downers Grove, IL: IVP Academic, 2002], 150).

The blessings were summarized in three "titles": they would prove to be **My own possession** ("unique treasure," a "chosen and special status"; Dt 7:6; 14:2; 26:18; Ps 135:4; Mal 3:17), they would be **a kingdom of priests**, and they would be **a holy nation** (19:5-6; cf. 1Pt 2:9). These titles indicate that as a new nation (in the truest sense "under God") they had a unique relationship with the Lord, they had a unique responsibility to the rest of humanity, and they had a unique standing in the world of nations—a new name and privilege, a new responsibility, and a new character. These titles speak of the nation's royal (kingly), priestly, and prophetic standing before God and before the world, **among all the peoples, for all the earth is Mine** (19:5). This has been called the "Great Commission" of the OT (cf. Youngblood, *Exodus*, 90).

In sum, to enjoy their promise-based relationship with God they had to accept it. Then they had to commit to it; that is, they had to commit to *live by* the stipulations and *live up to* the blessings. The people were enthusiastic at this point, answering, **All that the Lord has spoken we will do!** (19:8). Sadly this commendable sentiment was not always matched with consistent action.

2. The People Demonstrate Consecration (19:9-25)

a. The Place of the Lord (19:9)

19:9. God informed Moses that He would speak to the people from **a thick cloud** (19:9). This manifestation was meant to convey two truths: He was immanent (near them) and yet He was transcendent (above and beyond them). These two truths had to be acknowledged and kept in theological and existential balance. Too much immanence and He would be too familiar and the people might be flippant about this relationship. But then too much transcendence and He might seem too distant and even unknowable. As noted later, the tabernacle was designed to keep these two qualities in balance. He was near—He was to dwell with them –but He was hidden, covered by the walls and veils to be approached only by sacrifice. He was in the

thick cloud but He could be heard, **so that the people may hear when I speak.**

b. The Place of the People (19:10-15)

19:10-15. The Lord told Moses that he must first **consecrate them** (19:10a). The basic idea of this consecration is that they be set apart, purified, and cleansed in preparation to meet the Lord. The procedures for this consecration and cleansing followed several steps: first, they were to have their garments washed (19:10b, 14); this was an obvious symbol of cleansing. Second, they were to dedicate three days for preparation (19:11, cf. 19:15a). This in effect took putting aside all the regular activities of daily life and apparently the people were to use that time to prepare for the presence and words of the Lord (19:11b). Third, they were to observe the boundaries of the mountain since it was "holy" (19:12a; cf. 3:5, this is "holy ground"). These boundaries were to be taken seriously since to violate them would mean death (19:12b). A person who violated the boundaries was to be considered so unclean he was not to be touched even in his execution. He was to be killed by stoning or **shot through** (apparently with arrows) (19:13). Fourth they were to wait for the proper sound, a blast through **a ram's horn**, before they could begin to approach the mountain (19:13c). In the Hebrew, it states that at the blast of the ram's horn, **they shall come up . . . the mountain.** So after keeping away from the mountain for three days, on the third day, the entire nation was to ascend the mountain. And fifth they were to abstain from sexual relations (19:15b; see Lv 15:16).

These external preparations (of the body, the wearing clean clothes, standing at a respectful distance) were to demonstrate the inward preparations of heart and mind. All of this was meant to make them consider carefully, worshipfully, the One they were about to meet.

c. The Place of the Priests (19:22)

19:22. In addition there were special instructions for the priests at this meeting. The priests were to **consecrate themselves** (19:22). These were not yet the official priests (the Levitical priesthood had not yet been established; cf. Nm 3:45) but were most likely the family heads, or perhaps the firstborn who had been dedicated to the Lord (cf. 13:2). This was another layer of protection against mindlessness and against any casual flippancy in their approach to the Lord.

d. The Appearance of the Lord (19:16-20)

19:16-20. The Lord's appearance was accompanied by dramatic and amazing manifestations: thunder, lightning, **a thick cloud**, **a very loud trumpet sound** (19:16), smoke, fire, quaking, and **the trumpet** sound growing **louder and louder** (19:18-19). Naturalistic explanations of these manifestations are inadequate and unnecessary. This was no volcano nor was it a mere thunderstorm. It was a decidedly supernatural and awe-inspiring display meant to convey the awesome presence of the Lord, and it was appropriately "frightening and fascinating" (Hamilton, *Exodus*, 307; even for Moses, cf. Heb 12:21). It was meant "to impress upon the people the majestic power of this sovereign God" so that the commitment they had made (19:8) would not "be taken lightly" (Davis, *Moses and the Gods*, 206). "A deep moral impression was made on the people, for they were in the presence of the glorious majesty of the Holy God who was about to reveal his person and character in his law" (Kaiser, "Exodus," 418).

It seemingly terrified them to such an extent, that the people refused to ascend the mountain (19:17) as they had been commanded (cf. comments at 19:13). Therefore, instead of God giving His covenant to the entire nation, He gave it to their mediator, Moses. As a result, the nation would not be a nation of priests (cf. 19:5), but a nation with priests (mediators) (John H. Sailhamer, *The Pentateuch as Narrative* [Grand Rapids, MI: Zondervan, 1992], 53–57).

e. The Warning of the Lord (19:21, 23-25)

19:21, 23-25. The instructions about boundaries given in preparation are likely not repeated here. Rather, only after refusing to come up the mountain (cf. 19:13, 17; 20:18-21), God now gave them a powerful warning that they were no longer to attempt to come to the top of the mountain. This was the consequence of becoming a nation with priests. Therefore, God commanded **that they do not break through . . . to gaze** (19:21) or **to come up to the LORD** (19:24). They needed to keep their place if they wanted to keep their lives. To clarify that God's expectation of the people had changed, the Lord gave this new command (19:24). Therefore, Moses **went down . . . and told them** (19:25). This once again indicated that the God with whom they had to do was not One to take lightly or approach flippantly. To enjoy this relationship with God required that they know, respect, and observe His place and their place.

B. Presentation of the Decalogue to the People (20:1-17)

1. Preamble (20:1-2)

20:1-2. The opening words of the Decalogue proclaim three great theological truths: The Lord is the God who speaks (in **words**), He is self-revealing, the God who relates: **I am the Lord *your God*** (emphasis added). The Lord is the God who acts, He is the God who redeems, **who brought you out**. "The lawgiver places His law in the environment of grace, for it was His gracious act of redemption and deliverance from Egypt that revealed His name Yahweh" (Lord). Many scholars have noted the parallel between this "historical prologue" and "the great suzerain-vassal treaties of the ancient Near East" (Kaiser, "Exodus," 422). The Lord probably revealed the law to Moses in this form so that Moses and the people would be familiar with its structure and have some understanding of how they related to it.

There were two tablets of the law: tablet one contained commandments one through four and these set down the obligation of men and women to God as creatures to honor their Creator; tablet two set down the obligations of men and women toward one another in their various relationships, family, and society.

2. The First Tablet Commanded the People to Honor the Lord (20:3-11)

a. No Other Gods (20:3)

20:3. The Lord is God, the only God (20:3)! The expression **before Me** probably has the sense of "in addition to Me." One was not allowed to worship the one true God as if He were a part of a pantheon of gods. This expression is not suggesting that there actually are other gods. It prohibits the honoring of any other entity, real or imaginary, as God. Nothing else, no other gods (money [cf. Mt 6:24], pleasure, power, fame, even one's self) can have the priority in one's thoughts, words, or deeds. God's people and indeed all living creatures, owe ultimate allegiance to Him and Him alone.

b. No Idols (20:4-6)

20:4-6. Idolatry is unacceptable because any attempt to depict or represent God (especially for the ostensible purpose of worship) not only falls short of the truth about God but inevitably distorts the worshipers' understanding of God. "God is Spirit" (Jn 4:24). Thus any physical representation will misrepresent Him and lead to false notions about Him. All idols are thus false gods, and even an idol meant to depict or represent the true God by some carving, statue, or any other physical representation is deforming of the truth about God. The prohibition extends to **any likeness** of creatures heavenly, earthly, or of the sea (**water under the earth**). The three tiers of existence—heaven (that is the atmospheric heaven, not the "spiritual" place), earth, and water—were the mythological locations of those Egyptian gods that had been defeated in the plagues (see Rm 1:22-25). Two reasons were given to reinforce this prohibition. First God revealed that He is a **jealous God**, that is, He has a consuming love for His people and thus He will brook no rebellion from them. The consequences of His chastisement will extend for three or four generations. This is not to mean that God brings generational curses for sin or even that the Lord judges the children for the parents' sins (Dt 24:16; Ezk 18:20). Rather, it means that the consequences of sin and rebellion (idolatry) and the judgment that befalls such will extend to several generations. One of the consequences of such rebellion is that the children frequently follow in the parents' ways and become rebels and practice idolatry themselves, thus extending the judgment.

Second, the Lord revealed that He is a loving God, that is, His blessings for obedience will extend for many generations **to those who love Me and keep My commandments**. Clearly, the imbalance of the consequence for obedience, blessings for **thousands**, as opposed to consequences for rebellion to three or four generations, shows that the Lord is not a vengeful God but He practices lovingkindness, being merciful and gracious. He loves His people and desires their best, and He is their best.

c. No Swearing (20:7)

20:7. In Scripture the name of a person was not merely a label but was shorthand for the total character of the person, "a revelation of his true nature." Thus, "the name of God is the revelation of the nature of God" (G. F. Hawthorne, "Name," vol. 3, *International Standard Bible Encyclopedia* [Grand Rapids, MI: Eerdmans, 1986], 481–82). God's name is to be respected because He, His person, is to be respected. Thus to use the Lord's name in a flippant or disrespectful manner, **in vain** (lit., "to no purpose"), whether in an informal oath (i.e., cursing) or in a formal oath (i.e., swearing an oath *before* God in a court of law but without any serious thought *about* God), was forbidden. This does not rule out legitimate oaths but the idea is this: when one utters the name of the Lord one should do so with reverence, respect, and the conscious acknowledgment that He is the true Lord God. The mindless invoking of the name of the Lord is not merely disrespectful but an implicit denial and trivializing of His majestic personhood and ultimate governance of all life.

d. Sabbath Observance (20:8-11)

20:8-11. The Sabbath was to be observed as an acknowledgment that the Lord deserved complete loyalty, including not only singular and absolute devotion and worship but also the entirety of His people's individual lives. This is indicated by the Lord's demand on time. The basic thrust of the fourth Commandment is that Israel was to devote one day in seven to the Lord as a token of a lifetime devoted to Him. The basic idea of the term *Sabbath* means "rest" (cf. Kaiser, "Exodus," 423). The pattern of six days of work and one of rest was meant for all mankind (cf. Gn 2:1-3; Mk 2:27; cf. Dt 5:13-15) and the Sabbath also had special significance for the nation of slaves, who could seldom rest, delivered from bondage in Egypt (cf. Dt 5:15). "Israel observed the Sabbath to remember God's work of Creation and the Exodus" (Kaiser, "Exodus," 424). Davis observes, "The Sabbath became a foundation for all the festival times and observances of the Israelites since they culminated in a Sabbath rest" (Davis, *Moses and the Gods*, 214). The command concerning the Sabbath (as such) is not repeated in the NT, and while there are applicable principles (one day in seven for rest and worship), the command was given in a unique sense to the nation of Israel as a sign between the Lord and the sons of Israel (cf. Ex 31:13-17) and thus it is not applicable to the Church in the same way as it was to Israel (cf. Col 2:16-17). (See Thomas R. Schreiner, *40 Questions About Christians and Biblical Law* [Grand Rapids, MI: Kregel Academic, 2010], 209ff.).

4. The Second Tablet Commanded the People to Honor Others (20:12-17)

a. Honor Parents (20:12)

20:12. "To honor" means "to prize highly" (cf. Pr 4:8), "to care for" (cf. Ps 9:15), "to show respect for" (cf. Lv 19:3) (cf. Youngblood, *Exodus*, 98). Since all authority belongs to the Lord and since He instituted the family and established all human authority structures into human social relationships, all such authority structures are to be respected. Rebellion and insubordination to parents, governments (cf. Rm 13), teachers, and others, ultimately is rebellion and insubordination to God. The commandment is not just applicable to minor children but teaches that adult children are to have respect and to care for their aged parents. "The fifth commandment provides the key to real social stability" (Davis, *Moses and the Gods*, 216). The promise attached to this commandment had primary applicability to the nation of Israel living in the land, but the principle "a stable family-life leads to a stable-society" allows for a broader application (cf. Eph 6:1-3).

b. Do Not Murder (20:13)

20:13. If any of the seven terms for killing in the OT prohibits premeditated and intentional killing, it is the term *murder* (cf. Kaiser, "Exodus," 424–5). All life belongs to the Lord, since He is the Creator of life, especially human life. Murder is not only an attack on another human being but since every person is made in the image of God (cf. Gn 1:26-27; 9:6) it is an attack on God. All life is therefore sacred; that is, it is set apart to and belongs to the Lord and should be devoted to Him. Thus it is His and His alone to give or to take. This commandment prohibits murder and all taking of innocent life as well as taking of one's own life but does not prohibit one from self-defense, national-defense or capital punishment. Indeed, the OT itself recognizes there are times when killing in self-defense is not culpable (Ex 22:2; cf. Est 9:1-5), when war is necessary (Ex 17:9), and capital punishment is the appropriate punishment (Gn 9:6).

c. Do Not Commit Adultery (20:14)

20:14. God created marriage and the family and it must be honored for His sake. This commandment says in effect that any form of sexual expression (by either man or woman) outside of the bonds of marriage is a perversion (in both the most basic and the fullest sense of that term) and is prohibited (cf. Mt 5:27-28; cf. Lv 20:10).

d. Do Not Steal (20:15)

20:15. The "right of private property is an important principle for the stability of any society" (Davis, *Moses and the Gods*, 218). This commandment forbids the taking of any goods or valuables of another without due compensation and any form of dishonest profit or gain at the expense of another.

e. Do Not Lie (20:16)

20:16. The Lord is a God of truth, He loves truth (because He loves Himself) and He "hates every false way" (cf. Ps 119:104, 128). Lying is a denial that truth is always right. It is a denial of God's character and of His attributes. Without truth-telling the whole social structure will fail. This command prohibits blatant lies, any conscious deceptions, and unsubstantiated assertions (i.e., gossip and rumor).

f. Do Not Covet (20:17)

20:17. "This commandment is a staunch prohibition against all lustful desire" (Davis, *Moses and the Gods,* 220). A person cannot be said to live by these words if he or she keeps them only in an external way. These commandments must be kept in one's heart as well as in one's actions. Jesus taught this when He taught that hate was in effect murder, and lust was in effect adultery (see the comments on Mt 5:21-30). The corruption of sin is in the heart before it is in the actions. "Covetousness has a psychologically degrading effect upon an individual" (Davis, *Moses and the Gods,* 220). It takes away contentment (cf. Php 4:11-12; 1Tm 6:6-8) and rivets one's attention on acquiring earthly and temporal toys rather than the heavenly and eternal treasures (cf. Mt 6:20, 33).

C. The People Respond with Devotion, Fear, and Worship (20:18-26)

20:18-21. This narrative retells the story of Ex 19:13-16 and actually took place before Moses descended the mountain and gave the Ten Commandments. The previous narrative (19:13-16) told the story of the people's fear of God and failure to ascend the mountain from a divine perspective. Here (20:18-21) it recounts the story from the people's perspective (Sailhamer, *The Pentateuch as Narrative,* 56). In this telling, Moses sought to encourage the people to **not be afraid** (20:20a). He explained: **for God has come . . . in order that the fear of Him may remain with you, so that you may not sin** (20:20b). The point was, "Do not be so fearful that you run from Him or fail to come up the mountain, but in your fear you must stand and listen and obey" (20:20b). Nevertheless, the people refused to ascend the mountain and afterwards, were prohibited from doing so (cf. 19:24). As a result, God gave Moses, Israel's mediator, even more laws for them to obey, a section of the law known as the "Covenant Code" (20:22–31:18).

20:22-26. The people responded to the Ten Commandments with worship. Keeping in mind the stipulations just revealed, namely, they were to embrace no other gods and no idols (20:22-23), the people were instructed to make an altar (20:24) for sacrifice. Even though **the sons of Israel** had plenty of gold and silver (see 12:35-36), the Lord instructed them that He wanted only an earthen altar (20:24) or one made of natural (uncut, un-worked) stones (20:25). It seems these instructions were intended to distance Israelite worship from that of the pagans around them. Apparently somehow the use of tools would **profane it** (20:25), but why that would be the case is not clearly indicated; perhaps this was meant to restrict any image or representation from being chiseled into the stone. In any case great care was to be taken to avoid any form of idolatry as well as to distance the acts of worship on this altar from those of the pagans (20:26). The altar was to be erected to the Lord **in every place where I cause my name to be remembered** (20:24c) and not to the "local deities" the nation would encounter. The altar of the tabernacle would have, when completed, obviated the need for these altars.

D. Application of the Law: Living the Life of Faithfulness (21:1–23:19)

After the "Ten Words" and the instructions for proper worship, Moses received instructions from the Lord, **ordinances which you are to set before them** (21:1) that amounted to principles for living faithfully in the community of God's people. These laws were of both the casuistic form (i.e., case-law, recognized by the common "If . . . then" structure, providing examples or cases as guides for community living and resolving disputes) and the apodictic form (i.e., commands and precepts laid down, the "do's and don'ts"). There are basically two purposes for such laws: one, to promote faithfulness in living in the community and two, for fostering faithfulness in devotion to the Lord. This section, encompassing chaps. 21 through 23, is called the "book of the Covenant" (see 24:7).

Some have suggested that the "law codes" of the OT "borrowed" from other ANE law codes (e.g., Sumerian codes, Urnammu and Lipit-Ishtar; Babylonian codes, Hammurabi and Eshnunna, Hittite law codes) (See Davis, *Moses and the Gods*, 223–26; Hamilton, *Exodus*, 359). However, it is more likely that the similarities are the result of simply living in similar socioeconomic conditions and cultures (which would generate the same sorts of issues and problems, e.g., unruly animals). On the other hand, the differences are striking and basic (e.g., the way slaves were to be treated, the care and concern for "the widow, the orphan, the poor, the defenseless" [Youngblood, *Exodus*, 102]). The Lord gave the "book of the Covenant" to Moses but in none of these other ANE law codes does a deity speak. There are parts of this "book of the Covenant" that only fit in the story and narrative of Promise, Exodus, Conquest, Kingdom that is recorded in the OT (see Hamilton, *Exodus*, 360).

1. Laws Pertaining to Slavery (21:1-11)

Slavery was a fact of life (as it has been for more cultures and societies in history than not). In that culture generally and in Israelite culture specifically it was not the same institution as the forced servitude and racially demarcated bondage familiar to many today. Nevertheless, the Hebrew word *'ebed* meant more than mere "servant." In that society when people fell into bad economic circumstances they might adopt "indentured servitude," becoming the slave of another in exchange for the basic necessities of life. Since elimination of the institution was not feasible, its regulation was necessary. One might become a slave for a variety of reasons: a captive of war (cf. Nm 31:26; Dt 20:10ff.); a foreigner acquired by purchase (Lv 22:11; 25:44-45); a child sold by parents in hard times (Neh 5:5; cf. possibly Am 2:6; 8:6); at times, even someone selling himself (Lv 25:39). This would be a form of "indentured servitude." The slave in view here was most likely a "debt-slave," a person who had to become a slave because they had "fallen on hard times," or they were required to serve a term of slavery as restitution for a crime (22:3c; cf. Hamilton, *Exodus*, 373, 395).

a. Male Slaves (21:1-6)

21:1-6. The law set down several stipulations regarding males slaves. The first demand limited the length of servitude to six years (21:2) This was a unique feature of the institution of slavery in Israelite society. The second stipulation dealt with the complication of marital status. While the man had a right to keep his wife (21:3), the master had the right to keep his slave(s) (21:4). Exactly how this would have been worked out is not fully explained, allowing for the latitude necessary for particular cases to be worked out equitably. The key point was that there had to be a balance between the personal rights of the slave and the economic and property rights of the owner. The third condition dealt with the case of a slave who wished to remain with his master (21:5-6). That such cases were frequent enough to require this formal recognition would seem to indicate that the institution in view was not the harsh bondage normally associated with pre-Civil War American slavery; it was "slavery," but it was often a congenial arrangement. In order to formalize this relationship there had to be a public "testimony" and "permanent sign" that is for the life of the individual so marked (see the HCSB "for life.") There is a question here about the "witnesses" (21:6). The term is *ha'elohim* and could be "God" [NASB] or "the judges" [KJV]. Since this was to be a formal and solemn and public ceremony it seems best to take the term as referring to the human judges as "witnesses before God."

b. Regarding Female Slaves (21:7-11)

21:7-11. The law also set down several regulations regarding female slaves. The parallel text in Dt 15:17b seems to suggest that there could be female slaves who fall into the arrangement indicated in vv. 2-6, that is, those laws might pertain to female as well as male slaves. However, the arrangement in view here appears to be somewhat different. The first stipulation dealt with an arrangement wherein apparently a father does not himself enter into "debt-slavery" but puts his daughter up (presumably in payment of his debt) instead. This arrangement was not so easily dissolved (21:7) since (it may be supposed) this was matrimonial in nature. However, the second regulation indicated the steps to be taken if the arrangement failed, and so different scenarios are described. If she had been **designated** for the master he could not resell her but she could be redeemed by her family (21:8a). Emphatically the law stated she *could not* be sold to a foreigner or non-Israelite (21:8b). If she had been designated for a son she was to be treated as a daughter with full familial rights (21:9), and she retained her status even if other wives were brought into the family (21:10). Finally, if her rights and status were not maintained she was free to leave this family, without payment, and more than likely she would return to her own family. At that point she would then be free to be attached or designated to another (21:11).

The point of these laws was to ensure that the rights of the individual were respected, but at the same time taking the rights of the master into account. Perpetual slavery was unacceptable (21:2). Even a female servant had rights, a remarkable point of law in that culture. If she had been purchased for marriage or concubinage she could not simply be thrown out (21:7) and within the family she had rights, even rights to her own personal possessions (21:10).

All of this shows that God cares about individual rights and personal dignity. In any economy there may be (will be) "haves and have nots" but the individual's personal dignity and rights, under God, before others, must be respected. In short, people are to be treated as people, not things, objects, or possessions.

2. Laws Pertaining to Personal Injury (21:12-36)

In a series of "case laws" the pattern of a protasis ("What if there is . . . ?" clause) is followed by an apodosis ("Then," or "In that case . . .") to stipulate laws that provide for equity and justice in the life of the community. First is a series of cases where someone inflicts an injury on another (more or less) directly (21:12-27).

21:12, 14. What if there was a blow—one man struck another with malice aforethought (premeditation), and death followed (21:12a, 14a)? In that case there must be a payment in kind, namely a death (21:12b, 14b). The Bible is not unclear or equivocal about clear cases of "murder" or "homicide." Life, especially human life (cf. Gn 9:6), belongs to God. Any such murder is a usurping of His prerogative and is actually and ultimately an attack upon Him. It is also an attack on the whole society (of humanity). And it is an attack on the deceased's family. It usurps a personal right (the person's very life), a divine right (the devotion and service to God that life should have been allowed to perform), a social right (the contribution that life could/should have made for the whole society), and a family right (the provisions/roles that life were to have fulfilled for the well-being and prosperity and happiness of his/her family). Murder undermines more of what holds a culture and a society together than any other single crime. It violates *both* tablets of the law at once by usurping God's role in life and death and in harming one's neighbor. If life itself is not respected and protected there can be no secure social structure. No sanctuary is to be given for such a murderer (21:14).

21:13. What if there was a blow where one man struck another in an act of "un-premeditated" manner or in a spontaneous act of vengeance and there was a death? In such a case the perpetrator had the option to flee to refuge (later revealed as the six cities of refuge; cf. Nm 35:6-24; Dt 19:1-13). In such a case it was presumed that God had allowed it. Providence was seen as a mitigating circumstance.

21:15, 17. What if there was a blow to, or even a curse directed at, a parent? Once again the penalty was death. The son or daughter **who strikes** may carry out an actual physical attack or a metaphorical assault (such as a son who undermines his father's authority; e.g., Absalom). The one **who curses** may engage in a verbal attack or, more likely, a "sin of omission" (e.g., a man does not take care of his aged and dependent parents; cf. Hamilton, *Exodus*, 378–79). This might seem severe to modern ears but again, the message was that such an act was tantamount to undermining the authority of the Lord and the basic societal institution of the family. Those values had to be taken seriously.

21:16. What if there was a kidnapping? Once again the penalty was death (cf. Dt 24:7). The motive for such an act in those days was probably not to gain a ransom but to enslave, resulting in a deprivation of personal rights for the person and his/her family.

It may be noted that four times the text has said the perpetrator **shall surely be put to death** (vv. 12, 15-17), but it does not say who is to perform the execution or how. That seems to make this law more of a moral standard than a civil prescription. Hamilton points out that the expression **shall surely be put to death** is *mot yumat* and may be translated either "*must* be put to death" or "*may* be put to death." ("The Hebrew imperfect does not distinguish between 'must' and 'may'" [Hamilton, *Exodus*, 378].) Furthermore, there is a curious lack of interest in how or who should do the executing, which leads Hamilton to suggest that "the main intent of these capital offenses is less legal than moral," and so "death injunctions or death threats alert to the gravity of transgression" but may not prescribe the legal necessity of actual execution in every case. In other words, perhaps these sins are worthy of death in God's eyes but that is a moral judgment more than a specific legal command to carry out such executions (cf. Hamilton, *Exodus*, 378). Therefore, the law in these cases may not actually have been as harsh, or strictly applied, as it first appears.

21:18-19. What if there was a blow that resulted in a serious injury but not in death? Then the perpetrator was required to pay all the expenses of the injured until he was completely healed. If he died, of course, then the stipulations of 21:12 would be in effect. The point here is obvious; God's people are required to take personal responsibility for their actions. The injured person should, in the end, after his recovery, be in a position as if nothing happened; all the "loss" should be incurred by the perpetrator. The detail that the blow was delivered with **a stone or fist** would indicate that it happened in the context of an all-out brawl or a spontaneous act in a fit of anger.

21:20-21, 26-27. What if the blow was to a slave? Here several scenarios are envisioned. If the slave died then the perpetrator would **be punished** (21:20; lit., "suffer vengeance," which could be death for the perpetrator since even slave life is still human life). If the slave survived, for even a day or two, there would be no punishment. Perhaps the situation in view here is that of a particularly difficult slave who has required multiple and increasingly harsh beatings. Here the law is attempting to balance the need of the master for respect and service while protecting the slave from overly harsh, even fatal, treatment. In a case where the slave loses an eye or tooth from the discipline, the result was freedom for the slave (21:26-27). In short, the master had rights as the slave owner but at a basic level the slave had personal rights that superseded those of the master.

21:22-25. What if the blow was to a pregnant woman? Again, different scenarios are envisioned. First if there was no injury (presumably to the woman herself) but the wife **gives birth prematurely**, a fine would be levied. The woman's husband would **demand** [a certain] **amount** but the **judges** [would] **decide** to preserve true equity. However, if there was an injury to the woman herself then there had to be "equivalent punishment," a "retaliatory injury" to the perpetrator (21:23-25).

Some Bible versions incorrectly translate 21:22 "that she has a miscarriage." Consequently, some have contended that, since only a fine is levied and not capital punishment, a pre-born child has less value than other humans, thereby legitimizing abortion. The Hebrew literally reads "that her children come out," indicating a premature birth. Moreover, the assault in this circumstance does not cause **further injury**. The word for **injury** means "serious or fatal injury" The *Mekhilta* (an ancient rabbinic commentary on Exodus) understood it to mean "death" (*Mekhilta Mishpatim N'zik. S. 8*). Therefore, this is describing an assault on a woman that causes a premature birth but there is no fatality, either to the woman or her children. Thus, this verse does not indicate that the life of the fetus is in any way less than fully human; any suggestion to that effect is quite beyond the intent or implication of this text.

The well-known stipulation of **eye for eye, tooth for tooth**, etc., is called "The Law of Retaliation"—*Lex Talionis* (cf. Mt 5:38-41). This principle has been ridiculed as barbaric and mocked as unworkable and "lacking social sophistication" (cf. Davis, *Moses and the Gods*, 236). And yet it simply means "the punishment must fit the crime." It was never meant to be taken in as literal a manner as some seem to think but was to be applied "in principle." In fact, it was far from barbaric but actually limited vengeance. For example, if someone lost an eye in a mishap, they could not insist on killing someone in response. "The goal of *talion* laws was a simple one: to see that full justice was done" (Douglas K. Stuart, *Exodus*, NAC [Nashville, TN: Broadman & Holman, 2006], 492-94).

21:28-32. Next the law set forth some cases where the injury was inflicted more or less inadvertently either by an animal or through personal carelessness. In the case where one's ox gored a person (21:28-32) various dispositions are envisioned. If this was a one-time goring that resulted in a human death the animal was to be killed and disposed of but the owner was not liable (21:28). If the animal was known to be aggressive (with other animals presumably) and the owner should have known, and that animal kills someone, the owner was liable, even to the death penalty (21:29). However he was given the option to pay a redemption price instead (21:30), and that may be whatever the aggrieved family decided, except for slaves and that price was set at thirty shekels (21:32).

21:33-36. The next law considered the case of one who owned an open pit. Open pits were common mostly as cisterns for water reclamation. The owner of such a pit was to take care to cover it to prevent animals (and humans) from becoming stuck (and usually drowned) (21:33). If an owner was negligent and an animal died, the pit owner in effect "just bought himself a dead ox" and had to **make restitution** to the animal's owner (21:34). In the case where one's ox gored another animal (21:35-36) two scenarios were envisioned. A first time goring that resulted in one dead animal left the live one to be sold and the price divided and the dead animal is divided (21:35) between the respective owners. Where an animal was known to be a repeat offender (**in the habit of goring**) and was allowed to "gore again" the owners were to trade animals, the dead one for live one (21:36).

The enduring principles of these laws reveal that God is the author of life, all life is His, and He cares about all life; that people are more important than animals; and that God's people are to "Take [personal] responsibility for what is yours" (Hamilton, *Exodus*, 393).

3. Laws Pertaining to Personal Property (22:1-15)

22:1-15. In that culture owning livestock meant more than just having personal property. It was both an indication of social standing and at the same time provided for basic necessities of daily life. If a man stole another man's livestock he was not taking a mere status symbol but likely another's means of livelihood. In such cases when he was caught he was required to make restitution (22:1).

In cases of theft involving breaking and entering, several scenarios are envisioned. If a thief was killed in the course of his attempt, no guilt would be attributed to the homeowner (22:2). If the thief survived the attempt (or was caught), he was required to make restitution (22:3-4). However, the restitution was not merely a matter of returning the stolen items but a penalty was exacted as well.

In cases of carelessness with one's own or another's property, several scenarios are envisioned. If an owner allowed his livestock to over graze his own ground and then let his livestock graze in another's field, he was required to make restitution (22:5). If one was careless with fire and it caused damages, the fire-starter was required make restitution (22:6). If someone acted as trustee for another's goods and the goods were stolen or mishandled, he was required make restitution (22:7-13). However, if the thief was caught he was required to make restitution (22:7, 12). If someone borrowed another's property he was considered to be responsible for it (22:14), unless it was a case of hiring the original owner along with the item in question (22:15).

The operative word in each of these scenarios is "restitution"; the perpetrator was to "make it good," "pay it back," "just compensation," and "restore the item or make the equivalent in payment." "Restitution is at the heart of every penalty for theft. Even forgiveness does not cancel the need for making amends" (Hamilton, *Exodus*, 395). The Lord intended that His people have and own "personal property" and that an individual's personal property had to be respected by others.

4. Laws Pertaining to Personal Integrity (22:16–23:9)

22:16-17. To provide for a functioning society the law addressed matters of personal behavior. A seducer of a virgin was required to pay the dowry price of the woman he seduced regardless of whether he married the girl or not. This of course was not meant to make allowances for such behavior but to provide for a just outcome when such inappropriate behavior occurred. To be clear, this text is not addressing rape, but a seduction of an unmarried woman leading to her consent to sexual relations. The result of this unholy relationship would be that she would be unable to marry someone else. Therefore, this law was designed to protect the woman afterwards. The seducer could not discard her but needed to make provision for her as a wife.

22:18-20. The practices of sorcery (22:18), bestiality (22:19), and idolatry (22:20) were punishable by death. Besides being morally offensive (contrary to the nature of God) in their own right, such practices were destructive to the social structure of the community. All of these practices were typical of the pagan and cultic behaviors of the surrounding culture and as such were avoided by God's people.

22:21-24. The exploitation of aliens (**strangers**), widows, or orphans was prohibited. To do so would arouse the Lord's anger and bring severe punishment (22:23-24). The note of the Lord's personal concern in this matter stands in stark contrast to most of the other ANE law codes where this matter was not even addressed. The alien (stranger) and the foreigner in most ANE societies had no rights and were often oppressed and enslaved. They were among the most vulnerable in that society, as were orphans and widows who were vulnerable in obvious ways. Among the Lord's people the oppressed, the unnoticed and uncared-for, and the defenseless had to be protected.

22:25-27. Several laws pertaining to the use of money were established: usury was prohibited (22:25) and the demand for unjust collateral is prohibited (22:26-27). The poor were another "abused and vulnerable" class. They were easily exploited and used. This is not calling for "no interest loans" for everybody but for fairness and deference when the loan is made to the poor.

22:28-30. Several laws that spoke to the need for singular devotion to God were established. One was not to curse God (22:28) but rather honor God with the firstborn (22:29-30; cf. 13:2, 12). This was another reminder of where their "first devotion" in life belonged. Another was not to eat the flesh of animals discovered already dead, that is, carrion (22:31). This may seem an odd law in this context, but it was meant to remind the people of the need for purity.

23:1-9. Several laws were given that seemed to reiterate some of the laws previously established. Lying (**a false report**) was prohibited (23:1). So also was participating in a false testimony (**join your hand**) (23:1). One was not to join in a mob-like action (23:2) for this often leads to more injustices. Nor is one to be **partial to the poor** in a legal or criminal matter simply because he is poor; the principle of "fairness" was to be upheld above all (23:3). One was enjoined to care for the property of others (23:4-5); the principle of the right and value of personal property was just as much a concern as the need to care for the vulnerable and needy. Justice (as in a court of law) was to be maintained—no false witness was to be given, no bribe was to be taken, no oppression (advantage taken) of strangers (23:6-9) was permitted.

Some of these laws appear to be fairly obvious as to their intent and purpose. They teach that there must be equity and evenhandedness in social relationships. Furthermore they teach that these behaviors are simply incompatible with the mind, heart, and will of God. These actions, such as immorality, impurity, injustice, inconsideration of others, and lies, are simply contrary to His nature. Devotion to God will mean living and serving and worship in ways quite distinct from the surrounding culture. The Lord is a God of truth and justice and His people must be the people of truth and justice.

5. Laws Pertaining to Worship (23:10-19)

23:10-13. A series of laws were given that pertained to the nation's worship and life before the Lord. The law of Sabbath rest for the land (23:10-11) stipulated that there should be six years of sowing and reaping and then one year for the land to lie fallow. This requirement for a sabbatical "seventh year seems to have been unique with Israel" (Davis, *Moses and the Gods*, 244). In part this was a provision for the poor, **so that the needy of your people may eat**; presumably they could harvest the residual crop that grows up on fallow ground. This was also for **the beast of the field**, presumably to give wild animals some suitable habitation. The nation failed notoriously to observe the land sabbatical and was in part the reason for the seventy-year captivity (cf. 2Ch 36:17-21). "All Sabbaths were reminders of the sovereignty of God in His exercise of power in creative acts. The Sabbath year was a reminder that the land belonged to God and man merely possessed it in trust under God (Lv 25:23)" (Davis, *Moses and the Gods*, 244). In addition there was to be a Sabbath rest for the domestic animals and the domestic servants (23:12). Thus there were times for work and times for rest; there was to be rest personally, for animals, and for slaves.

23:14-19. The law at this point included a brief summary of the laws regarding the three feasts set aside for national worship. This is the first of five "Festival Calendars" in the writings of Moses (cf. Ex 34:18-26; Lv 23; Nm 28–29; Dt 16:1-17). The text at this point is only a brief notice; the parallel texts give the detailed instructions and explanations of these festivals. The Feast of Unleavened Bread was a memorial of the exodus; The Feast of the Harvest (or of First Fruits, 34:22 [of Weeks]) was a celebration of the Lord's provision of grain; The Feast of Ingathering (or of Tabernacles/Booths, Lv 23:33-36) was a celebration of the Lord's bounty of the rest of the agricultural produce. Although the Feast of Trumpets and the Day of Atonement are not mentioned, they likely were included as part of the fall festivals. When Israelites would appear before the Lord for Booths, they would likely come earlier and participate in these others. It was specified that on the three feasts no one was to attend **empty-handed** (23:15c).

If the point of these festivals was to celebrate what the Lord had provided, it would be a contradiction to appear with nothing (cf. 23:19a). Requiring all males (and presumably their wives and families with them; cf. Dt 31:10-12; 1Sm 1:3-5; Neh 8:13ff.) to attend the feasts **three times a year** (23:17) would foster unity and devotion in the nation grounded in their mutual faith in the Lord, national and theological unity.

Finally, the care one must take for proper worship is noted: there was to be no idolatry (23:13) but there were to be appropriate sacrifices (23:18-19a). Some have thought that the prohibition against boiling a **young goat** in the **milk of its mother** (23:19b) referred to some pagan ritual or practice (cf. Davis, *Moses and the Gods*, 246). Neither pagan-like incantations (23:13) nor pagan-inspired practices (such as the use of the "blood" and the "fat"; 23:18) were to be a part of the true worship of God. It is more likely that "boiling a kid in its mother's milk" meant not that milk and meat cannot be eaten together, the common Jewish understanding, but that a young animal was not to be taken away from its mother and cooked (boiled) while still suckling (**in the milk of its mother**). Doing so would cause considerable trauma to the mother.

The enduring principles found in these verses teach the overarching precept, "He is the Lord of your property and your time" (Hamilton, *Exodus*, 426). So devotion to the Lord must be a concern daily, weekly, annually, and continually. Keeping the feasts was meant not only to unite the nation in a common worship but further to remind them annually of the blessings of the covenant-keeping Lord. The devotion owed to Him was to be woven into the calendar, the ebb and flow, of life. The worship of God must be according to His ways and not a mixture of societal ways and forms of worship, that is, ways and forms familiar to and with associations meaningful to pagans. The Lord cares about such matters, even the apparently mundane aspects of life (respecting it, preserving it) and property (oxen); and He cares about fairness, justice, and common concern for others.

E. Plans for the Conquest of the Land (23:20-33)

This section of Ex 23 is often considered the epilogue to the book of the Covenant; but in some respects this final portion is distinct from the rest of the book of the Covenant. As one commentator notes, "A natural question that might arise from this material is 'What is it doing here?' After all, this [23:20-33] is a passage of promise and warning, so how does it fit with this legal material?" (Stuart, *Exodus*, 541). Three reasons may be suggested: one, this reiterated to the nation that the land promise had not been forgotten (cf. Gn 12:1; 15:18-21). Second, in some cases it is obvious that the land was important to the fulfillment and application of some parts of the book of the Covenant just revealed. That is, several stipulations assume possession of the land (e.g., the Sabbath rest for the land, 23:10ff.) because it was in their own land that they were to live out these laws and to celebrate these feasts (23:14-19). Third, mostly the "land" was meant to be somewhere "separate" from the rest of the "world." The law separated the Jewish people from the "world." The land also was to be a place "separate" from the world. The nation was to have its own place to *live as* the people of God, a place where the people could worship and serve the Lord separated, and more precisely, distinct from the world around them. If they were going to be the nation and people He was calling them to be, if they were to really keep the covenant, they needed their own land, a place that itself looked and was different and distinct! If they were to be different and distinct in the *way they lived*, they needed to be different and distinct in *where they lived*.

23:20-26. In this section God revealed four promises to facilitate the conquest. First there was the promise of the warrior angel. Some suggest this is a "special-agent angel" charged with a unique, one-time mission, i.e., pre-conquest terror delivered to the inhabitants of the land. Others are confident that this is *The* Angel of the Lord, a theophany of the pre-incarnate Christ (cf. Davis, *Moses and the Gods*, 247). The key to the identity of this angel is the phrase **since My name is in him** (23:21c). This could simply mean "He carries My authority" (and it surely does mean at least that); or it could mean "My character and nature is His character and nature" (since in the OT one's "name" was that which reflected one's character and nature). So to say this angel comes in the name of the Lord is to say he comes with the Lord's authority, with His power, and with His promise.

This brief section has a longer parallel in Dt 7; there it is clear that it is the Lord Himself who "brings [them] into the land" (Dt 7:1) and who defeats the enemy nations (7:2). In short, this angel is the Lord (cf. Gn 18:2, 16-17; 19:1) appearing as a theophany.

What will this angel do? First, the angel will be sent to **guard** them **along the way** (23:20a) and to guide (**bring**) the nation into the land, **the place which I have prepared** (23:20b, 23a). This nation was not to rely on itself to find its own way nor to "look for its own place." This nation was to look to the angel! God was protecting and guiding this nation and by His angel, He would ultimately lead it to the place chosen and "prepared" by Him. Second: the angel will "take on" the enemies and adversaries of the nation and destroy them (23:22b, 23b). This, of course, did not mean they did not have to fight at all, but that the victories would ultimately be not because of them but because God's power and promise.

Then there was the promise of provision and good health (23:24-26), prefaced with a twofold admonition. On the one hand, there was a prohibition against syncretistic devotion (23:24a) and an injunction for the utter destruction of pagan worship (23:24b). Nothing short of complete separation from and destruction of pagan and Canaanite religion would be acceptable.

There was to be absolutely no allowance for pagan religion and absolutely no opportunity given for the vile Canaanite religions to mix with or influence the worship and life of the nation.

On the other hand, they were to show absolute devotion to the Lord (23:25a). The simple phrase **serve the LORD** has the idea not only of serving in worship (in the sense of observing the feasts, 23:14-19), but (in the context of the "book of the Covenant") they were to "serve the Lord" by living this way, by observing the law just revealed to them. For heeding this admonition and living out this devotion, God promised the people a fourfold blessing: basic provisions, (**bread and . . . water**, 23:25b), general good health, no **sickness** (23:25c), healthy pregnancies, no miscarrying or barrenness (23:26a), and longevity (23:26b). These particular blessings were important blessings for a growing, thriving nation. (See Dt 7:12ff.)

23:27-30. Next came the promise of successful conquest (23:27-30). The Lord told the nation that the conquest would be accomplished by a series of probably supernatural but severe events (23:27-28). The **terror** and even the **hornets** (cf. Dt 7:20) are probably to be understood in a figurative or metaphorical way; that is, in some fashion the Lord sent "fear and panic" ahead of the nation to cause **confusion** and create dismay and despondency to undercut morale among the occupants of the land, thus facilitating the actual conquest. Whatever this was, it worked as Rahab told the spies "the terror of you [Israel] has fallen on us," such that "all the inhabitants of the land have melted away before you" (Jos 2:9). Furthermore, God informed them that the conquest would be accomplished in a controlled manner (23:29-30; cf. Dt 7:22ff.). This was a "practical" point. Without people in the land, the land would become overgrown and need to be re-cleared for agriculture, and the wild animals would take over, posing a danger to human life. God's program was to remove the Canaanites gradually so as to make Israel's occupation easier.

23:31-33. Finally came the promise of secure borders. The final promise reiterated the dimensions of the land (23:31a; to the west, the **sea of the Philistines** refers to the Mediterranean [so called because of their domination of that coastline, cf. Ex 13:17]; to the south, **the wilderness** is the desert areas south and east of the Dead Sea; and to the north, **the River** is the Euphrates in Babylon or modern Iraq). The description here is of the "western border and the eastern border." However, secure borders (to keep enemies out) would mean little if there remained "enemies within." Thus the Lord commanded that the Canaanites be defeated and driven out. There was to be no treaty with them (cf. Dt 7:2) and none were to be allowed **to live in your land** (23:31b-33a). The reason for this apparently severe requirement was clear: unless they were eliminated they would be **a snare**, a temptation to **make you sin** (23:33b). For a discussion of the morality of God's requirement, see the "Excursus: Canaanite Genocide—Killing the Seemingly Innocent" at Jos 6:21.

F. The Ratification of the Covenant (24:1-18)

1. The Approach to the Lord (24:1-11)

24:1-2. The actual ratification of the covenant took place in three steps: First the principals approached the Lord. While Aaron and his sons Nadab and Abihu with the seventy elders were invited with Moses to **Come up to the LORD** (v. 1a) only Moses was invited to **come near to the LORD**, and the others were to **worship at a distance**; the people were to stay even further back. Utter reverence is due the Lord, so approach to Him is limited and access denied except to the few. This is in contrast to what believers enjoy today (cf. Heb 2:17-18; 4:16). Texts like this should make believers in Jesus Christ more appreciative of the warm invitation they have to come freely with their worship and to have their needs met by their merciful Father (Heb 2:17-18; 4:16).

24:3-8. Second, the people gave their approval. Their consent took place in two phases: One, Moses spoke (**recounted**) to the people **all the words of the LORD**, and they responded in affirmation(24:3). Then (two) Moses **wrote down all those words of the LORD** (24:4a). This was the "book of the Covenant" (24:7) provided in the previous section (chaps. 20–23). An altar was built with a symbolic design: the twelve pillars represented the twelve tribes (24:4). The sacrifices presented also were symbolic: the young men were probably representative of the "firstborn," as were the young bulls. The sacrifices, the manipulation of blood were the common elements in "covenant making" (cf. the comments on Gn 15). These were **peace offerings** (24:5; cf. Lv 3:1ff.), that is, offerings that celebrated, as opposed to establishing, the peace and fellowship the nation and worshiper enjoyed with God. The blood was sanctifying, cleansing, and consecrating and so it was **sprinkled on the altar** to purify and sanctify it (24:6) and it was **sprinkled . . . on the people** who had affirmed their commitment to this covenant (24:8) to sanctify and set them apart. It was a solemn service to remind them of their solemn oath.

24:9-11. Third, the Lord appeared. After this solemn service came one of the most mysterious events in the OT. In some fashion not altogether clear, the leaders then acted on the earlier invitation (24:1-2) and they went up the mountain part way (but still "at a distance," 24:1b), and there **they saw the God of Israel** (24:10a). In this context there are two different terms translated "saw"; *ra'a*, "see" (24:10a), has the idea more of a glance, and *haza*, "behold" (24:11b), has the idea more of a sustained gaze. In some fashion (again, not altogether clear) the men both "saw" and "beheld" Him in a time of fellowship. Perhaps this was like the experience of Abraham (Gn 18) or Manoah (Jdg 13).

Adding to the wonder is the description of what was **under His feet . . . a pavement of sapphire** (24:10b), no doubt giving the setting an "other worldly" sense. The note that **He did not stretch out His hand against** them (24:11a) is made in light of Ex 33:20, which says "no man can see God and live" apparently unless God permits it. Moreover, it is likely that they saw only God's glory or a vision of God, and not God Himself. Finally, the whole scene ends with the note that **they ate and drank** (v. 11c). Eating and drinking is a common element within worship. For example, Abraham worshiped with Melchizedek (Gn 14:18); believers today worship with food and drink when celebrating the Lord's table (1Co 11:23-26); in the future, there will be a great celebration of worship with food and drink at the marriage supper of the Lamb (Rv 19:7-10); in the messianic kingdom, the nations will gather for the great messianic banquet (Is 25:6). Clearly, this scene in Exodus was meant to show that the covenant commitment of the people was accepted by the Lord, for here was a "covenant ratification meal," and now there was genuine fellowship with God and the nation, indicated by His personal fellowship with these leaders.

2. Moses on the Mountain (24:12-18)

24:12. The final part of this section records that Moses was called up to receive the tablets (24:12). This is the first mention of the **stone tablets**. No doubt the choice of stone had to do with durability and permanency, representing those qualities of the law itself. These stone tablets would also have been impressive and weighty, again indicating, metaphorically, that those same qualities were inherent in the law. The imagery is clear: the **law and commandments** were to have the same qualities as the "stone" they were written on.

24:13-18. Moses was called up alone. Even with the good men around him, Moses was a leader and he would be the mediator of the law (cf. Jn 1:17). Once on the mountain Moses was surrounded by glory (24:15-18). This manifested the presence of the Lord, a bright, brilliant, fiery cloud. See the intentional and typological parallels with Mt 17:1-8 and the transfiguration, which was meant to confirm who Jesus Christ was—the One who has the glory of the Lord. Not only did Moses receive the stone tablets, but during his **forty days and forty nights** (24:18) on the mountain he no doubt received the details about the tabernacle. It was an awesome display during a glorious revelation about an awe-inspiring structure.

G. The Tabernacle (25:1–27:21; 30:1-21; 35:1–38:31)

Excursus: Introduction to the Tabernacle

Focal Point for the Nation

The tabernacle was to be the focal point for the nation, both in a physical/literal sense and in a figurative/spiritual sense. The directives for the tabernacle came from the Lord Himself (25:1; 30:11, 22, 34; 31:1, 12). This was meant to drive home the significance of this structure for (1) the relationship between the nation and the Lord, (2) the proper and acceptable worship of the Lord, and (3) the nation's overall devotion to the Lord. "Exodus devotes approximately two chapters to narrating the [actual] exodus from Egypt, [only] two-thirds of one chapter to the Decalogue, but thirteen [chapters] to the tabernacle . . . That is about one-third of the entire book" (Hamilton, *Exodus*, 449). This indicates that God desired the nation's priorities to center on worship and devotion to Him. Starting with 25:1 (through 30:10), this section records the longest sustained speech of the Lord in Exodus (Hamilton, *Exodus*, 455).

Theories of Origin

Several theories have been proposed for the origin of the tabernacle. Some view the tabernacle as (1) *an idealized (and anachronistic) reimaging of the temple* projected back onto a fictional narrative of the nation's early history, "a projection backward of the temple into Israel's nomadic past" (e.g., this was the critical view of the Wellhausen school of thought). Thus, the "weight of modern [critical] scholarship is opposed to the historicity of the Tabernacle" (see the key points and counter points in Charles L. Feinberg, "Tabernacle," vol. 5, *Zondervan Pictorial Encyclopedia of the Bible* [Grand Rapids, MI: Zondervan, 1976], 578–81; Kaiser, "Exodus," 451). "However, contrary to the claims of the hypothetical source theory, the text presents Exodus 25, 40 as being historical" (Kitchen, *Reliability of the OT*, 275ff., 495).

Some suggest the tabernacle was (2) *a reproduction or version of other portable shrines* found in the surrounding ANE cultures. That there were such portable shrines is not in question, but the tabernacle has several distinctive features that distinguish it from the examples suggested by the critics (which will be identified in the commentary).

Of course, some see the tabernacle as (3) *a unique structure whose plan and purpose was revealed by God*. "The only really adequate explanation for the magnificent tabernacle structure is that it originated not in the fertile mind of Moses but as a revelation from God" (Davis, *Moses and the Gods*, 253; see 251–53). Repeatedly the text notes that **The LORD spoke to Moses . . . According to all that I am going to show you . . . after the pattern which was shown you on the mountain** (25:1, 9, 40; also 26:30; 27:8b; cf. Ac 7:44; cf. Heb 8:5; 9:23-24). "Scripture makes it perfectly clear that the origin of the tabernacle was found in God and given to Moses by special revelation" (Davis, *Moses and the Gods*, 253).

Terms to Designate the Tabernacle

At least five different terms were used to designate the tabernacle (see Davis, *Moses and the Gods*, 254; cf. Feinberg, "Tabernacle," 572–73). (1) In 25:8 the term is "sanctuary" (*miqdash*). This indicated that this place was a holy (*qadahs; qodesh*) place, set apart and holy to the Lord. This marked the tabernacle out as a place apart so that it was distinct. It was sacred, and so the profane and unclean were to be kept out. Everything about it and in it was devoted to the worship of the Lord, and it was to be used for nothing else. (See Richard E. Averbeck, "Sanctuary," *miqdas*, vol. 2, *New International Dictionary of Old Testament Theology and Exegesis* [Grand Rapids, MI: Zondervan, 1997], 1078–87). (2) In 25:9 the term is "tabernacle" (*miskan*), which comes from the term *sakan* "to dwell" or "to abide"; this was a place for God to dwell among His people. (3) In 26:36 the term is "tent" (*'ohel*), and which simply means it was a temporary and portable structure. (4) In 29:42 the term is "tent of meeting" (*'ohel mo'ed*) and comes from the term for "meeting" and carries the idea of a solemn meeting at an appointed place. This meeting was actually for worship. (5) In 38:21 the term or phrase is "tabernacle of the testimony" (*miskan ha'edut*) (cf. Nm 17:7 and 23). The name "tent of testimony" indicates that this place was to serve as a "testimony" to the Lord's power, promise, and provision for relationship; it was meant to foster the nation's faith and commitment. The tablets of the Ten Words were themselves called the "testimony" (40:20, 21); hence this was the place that housed those tablets.

Purposes of the Tabernacle

The tabernacle served the nation of Israel in several ways. "The wilderness tabernacle brought three dynamics to the worshiping community"; it was established to give "order to the worship of God." Further, it provided a "tangible sense of God's presence." And it provided "a point of stability" and a "location" for the nation; even in the wilderness there was "the place to be" (see Hamilton, *Exodus*, 449). Also, it would foster national unity (which is often accomplished through shared symbols such as a flag or national monuments). It would provide a sense of social cohesion (the activities of the community literally revolved around this structure). And the tabernacle would offer a focal point for/of civic pride, since they all contributed to its construction, *they* "brought it to fruition," together they worked on it and watched it being built.

But mostly the tabernacle acted as a symbol of "the basic concept . . . that underlay the theocracy itself: the Lord dwelling in visible glory in His sanctuary among His people. . . . God dwelling with man is the dominant theme of the symphony of the tabernacle" (Feinberg, "Tabernacle," 583).

The basic theological purposes of the tabernacle may be summed up under three headings: Relationship/Worship/Typology (see Davis, *Moses and the Gods*, 255–56). The nation was to have fellowship with the Lord (in a restricted but real sense) and each other through the services of the tabernacle. Besides the sacrifices for atonement, other offerings, grain offerings (cf. Lv 2:1-16) and peace offerings (cf. Lv 3:1-7) provided people a means to express devotion, for the sake of "fellowship."

Of course, the nation was to worship at the tabernacle. Thus "the sanctuary provided a visible center for the worship of the one true God and thus provided a bulwark against the worship of the many gods of the heathen. This [tabernacle], like the law [itself] was a protection against idolatry (Ex 29:43, 45; Nm 35:34)" (Davis, *Moses and the Gods*, 255).

Finally, the tabernacle served the purpose of typology (illustration) of the atoning work of Jesus Christ on the cross. "The tabernacle also provided a prophetic pre-figurement of the redemptive program of God as focused in Jesus Christ. It is clear from the book of Hebrews that the earthly tabernacle was only a pattern of the heavenly, but was designed to point to the ministry and the deity of our Lord Jesus Christ" (Davis, *Moses and the Gods*, 255). Davis notes the word "dwelt" in Jn 1:14 is literally "to tabernacle"; Jesus was indeed "God with us!" And He was *the* atoning sacrifice for sin. And immediately after *His* death "the veil of the temple was torn in two from top to bottom" (Mt 27:51) symbolizing that now believers can "draw near with confidence to the throne of grace" (Heb 4:16; 10:19). Furthermore, knowing that He, Jesus Christ, is in the "heavenly sanctuary" where "He always lives to make intercession" for them (Heb 7:25).

"The tabernacle of Moses' day was a remarkable picture of both the high priestly work of Christ here on earth and His eternal work in the heavens" (cf. Heb 7:26-27) (Davis, *Moses and the Gods*, 255–56). However, attempts to find typological significance in every element of the tabernacle (the number and materials, the length of the poles, the size of the sockets, the length of the curtains, etc.) are unwarranted and diminish the significance of the tabernacle in its original setting.

A few scholars have suggested that there are "a number of parallels between the Garden of Eden account in Genesis 2–3 and the tabernacle" (Richard E. Averbeck, "Tabernacle," *Dictionary of the Old Testament Pentateuch* [Downers Grove, IL; InterVarsity, 2003], 817; Gordon J. Wenham, "Sanctuary Symbolism in the Garden of Eden Story," in *"I Studied Inscriptions From Before the Flood": Ancient Near Eastern Literary Approaches to Genesis 1–11*, ed. Richard S. Hess and David Toshio Tsumura [Winona Lake, IN: Eisenbrauns, 1994]. If such parallels are granted, then it seems the tabernacle could be viewed as copy in miniature of the heavenly throne room and the place where human beings may have fellowship with God. See the chart "The Creation and the Tabernacle."

1. The Initial Instructions (25:1-9)

a. The Contributions (25:1-8; 30:11-16; 35:4-9; 38:21–39:1)

25:1-7; cf. 35:20-29. God had blessed the nation "exceedingly abundantly" (cf. Eph 3:20-21) with the plunder from Egypt (cf. Ex 12:35-36) so when the **sons of Israel** were called upon to supply the materials to furnish the tabernacle they responded with generous contributions of precious metals, **gold, silver and bronze**, as well as other rare materials and money. Critical scholars have questioned the accounting of the precious metals used in the tabernacle. However, the precise numbers recorded would indicate that a careful accounting was taken and dutifully recorded (cf. 38:21-31). Stuart notes that "various equivalencies" between modern weights and measures have been proposed but "we cannot know for sure what exact weights and measures were employed at any given ancient time and place" (Stuart, *Exodus*, 772 n. 300). Many assume that one talent is about seventy-five pounds and one shekel is between two-fifths and one-half an ounce. Roughly speaking, then, the total amount of gold used was between 2,000 and 2,200 pounds; the silver would amount to about 7,500 pounds and the bronze about 5,300 pounds. The silver alone, according to 38:26, worked out to half a shekel's worth for each of the 605,550 men who were at least twenty years old.

25:3-7. Fourteen component materials are mentioned, but it is not necessary to think this list is exhaustive. Minor components may have been too common to mention.

A rather obvious question is: "Where did all this come from?" And the equally obvious answer is: "mostly from Egypt." This was the plunder from the Egyptians (cf. Ex 12:35-36). Also, they would have had some plunder from the defeat of the Amalekites (cf. 17:8-16). Furthermore, they may have had opportunities for trade with the Midianites and caravans that passed through the region.

The basic materials were both organic and non-organic. The former included animal skins that were readily available (goats were obviously plentiful, as were rams). The reference to **porpoise**

The Creation and the Tabernacle

Creation	Tabernacle
Seven Acts/Marked by Divine Speech "And God said . . ." Gn 1:3, 6, 9,14, 20, 24, 26	Seven Acts/Marked by Divine Speech "And the Lord said . . ." Ex 25:1; 30:11, 17, 22, 34; 31:1, 12
The Spirit of God was moving over the surface of the waters Gn 1:2	I have filled him (Bezalel) with the Spirit of God Ex 31:3; 35:31
God saw everything and it was very good Gn 1:31	Moses saw all the work . . . so had they done it Ex 39:43
The heavens and the earth were finished Gn 2:1	All the work of the tabernacle was finished Ex 39:32
God finished His work Gn 2:2	Moses finished the work Ex 40:33
So God blessed the seventh day Gn 2:3	And Moses blessed them Ex 39:33
God rested on the seventh day and sanctified it Gn 2:2-3	God commanded Israel to rest on the seventh day and to sanctify it Ex 31:12-18
The garden of Eden had pure gold and precious jewels Gn 2:12a	The tabernacle had pure gold and precious jewels Ex 25:3, 18
The garden of Eden had the tree of knowledge of good and evil in the midst of it Gn 2:9; 3:6	The tabernacle had the law in the holy of holies Ex 25:16; Dt 31:26; Pr 3:18
The Lord walked about the garden Gn 3:8	The Lord walked in the midst of the tent Lv 26:12; Dt 23:14
Humanity was "to worship and obey" God in the garden Gn 2:15	Levites to "serve" (worship) and "heed" (obey) in the tabernacle Nm 3:7-8; 18:5-6
The fall—Humanity broke God's command regarding the Tree Gn 3:1-7	The fall—Israel broke God's command regarding idolatry Ex 32
Cherubim guard the garden Gn 3:24	Cherubim guard the mercy seat Ex 25:18

(25:5; 26:14) translates a term that is obscure but probably refers to some type of a marine animal. Textiles were mostly linen (common in Egypt) made from flax or animal hair (woven or spun) fabrics; the dyes used to decorate and color these items may have been homemade (from shellfish, plants, minerals) or acquired by trade (from the Phoenicians, who traded all across the Mediterranean basin). Acacia wood came from a kind of "thorn tree" or bush. It was plentiful in that region, and could grow up to twenty-five feet high. The wood was orange-colored, hard, durable, and highly insect resistant. The trunks and the branches made excellent "poles." "Consumable" materials would have to be replenished: oil for lighting the lamps (25:6) and oil (mixed with aromatic spices; cf. Kaiser, "Exodus," 453) for anointing, as well as incense (25:6; see 30:22-38).

The nonorganic materials required various levels of refinement. Semiprecious stones would be cut or shaped to be used as decoration sewn in or on in some fashion; metals like gold, silver, and bronze would have to be refined and worked; the technology, though rudimentary, was fairly common. The tabernacle itself contained a symbolic gradation of the metals, from the least precious, bronze, mostly used in the court (the altar and laver), to the silver and gold in the building itself, to the most extensive use of gold in the holy of holies on the ark and mercy seat.

25:8; cf. 35:4-9. God instructed Moses to ask for the contributions before He gave them the plans, and with only one motivation, **that I may dwell among them** (25:8). The Lord made it clear to Moses that He desired only those gifts that were given willingly, **whoever is of a willing heart** (35:4-9), and not merely out of grudging obligation (cf. 2Co 8:4-5; 9:7). Those who gave did so because their hearts were "stirred" and "moved" (35:21, 22, 29). It is evident from 35:21-29 and 36:3-7 that the people did respond, out of joyful hearts, so much so that they had to be "restrained from bringing" any more (36:3-7). "A similar spirit was witnessed in David's time when preparations for construction of the Temple were undertaken (cf. 1Ch 29:1-9)" (Davis, *Moses and the Gods*, 261).

30:11-16. In addition to these voluntary offerings for the construction of the tabernacle, the Lord instituted a tax for the upkeep and continuing operations of the tabernacle. This was called **atonement money** and was to be used **for the service of the tent of meeting** (30:16). This tax was calculated by a **census of the sons of Israel** (30:11), and it was determined that the tax should be one-half shekel for everyone **who is numbered, from twenty years old and over** (30:14). The tax was spread evenly over the population, and there was no distinction between rich and poor. All paid the same (30:15). As the **atonement money** (30:16), the tax was **to make atonement** (30:15, 16) and called a **ransom** (30:12). This tax was to be taken seriously; failure to pay it put them in danger of judgment, a **plague** (30:12). Apparently, the point is that this money was necessary for the ongoing work of the tabernacle, which was necessary for the accomplishment of atonement. Any failure to pay the tax was tantamount to failure to regard seriously the need for atonement.

b. The Lord's Pattern (25:9)

25:9. The **pattern of the tabernacle** (25:9b) as given by the Lord Himself to Moses was to be followed carefully, **just so you shall construct it** (25:9c). The tabernacle was both a court (a self-contained compound) and a building (the tabernacle proper) within the court and compound. The tabernacle was apparently a rectangle, placed inside an oblong compound (of two perfect squares; 27:9-12, 18). There was only one opening on the east end. The structure was always set up with the entrance on the east and the holy of holies in the western end of the compound, probably so the ark was at the center of the western half (square) and the bronze altar at the center of the eastern half (square). From the entrance one would see the bronze altar; the laver was next (and may have been placed to one side); next came the tabernacle proper, with its two chambers: the holy place and the holy of holies (cf. 26:33).

2. The Ark of the Covenant: Symbol of the Lord's Holy Presence (25:10-16; 26:34; 37:1-5)

25:10-16; 26:34; 37:1-5. The center (both in a literal and figurative/spiritual sense) of the tabernacle was the ark of the covenant, "clearly the most sacred of all the pieces of furniture in the tabernacle" (Hamilton, *Exodus*, 459). Kaiser notes the ark "is mentioned 180 times, thereby stressing its importance" ("Exodus," 454). Actually, this was merely an oblong wooden box, (*'aron*, "chest"), albeit overlaid in gold, but it had "transcendent significance!" With the lid, the mercy seat, it was the only object in the holy of holies. It was two and a half cubits (about 3 feet 9 inches) long, one and a half cubits (about 2 feet 3 inches) wide, and one and a half cubits (about 2 feet 3 inches) high. It had four **feet** or

Tabernacle

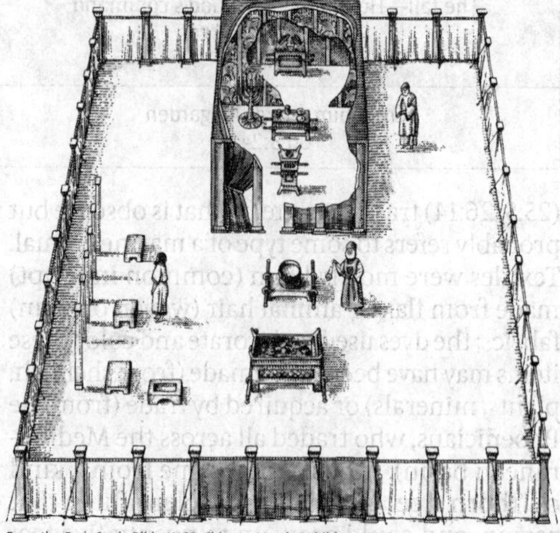

From the *Ryrie Study Bible*, NASB. Chicago: Moody Publishers, 2012.

posts, one on each corner, and rings on each of the feet, through which poles, also of acacia wood overlaid with gold, were installed to carry the object; in the case of the ark (unlike other furniture with rings and poles) these poles were never to be removed (25:15).

The ark was to serve as the depository of the two stone tablets (25:16, 21; 40:20) referred to as **the testimony** (cf. Dt 10:1-5, "tablets," "Ten Commandments"). Later the ark contained the manna and Aaron's rod (cf. Heb 9:4-5). Numbers 4:5-6 reveals that the ark was to be covered when being transported; no doubt this was for protection from the elements but also to prevent it from being seen.

3. The Mercy Seat: Symbol of Propitiation (25:17-22; 37:6-9)

25:17-22; 37:6-9. Kaiser notes that "[William] Tyndale was the first to render this word [the term *kapporet* ('atonement cover')] as 'mercy seat' followed in 1534 by Luther's translation" (Kaiser, "Exodus," 454). Indeed, "atonement cover" is an appropriate title for this object since "atonement" is a central rationale for the entire tabernacle and sacrificial system, and this object is a focal point of the tabernacle. This lid of the ark was solid gold; the description **pure gold** (here and in reference to other items, e.g., the lampstand) should probably be understood as "solid gold" since the technology of the day was unable to make "pure gold" as this is understood today.

The mercy seat featured two cherubim, one at each end, facing each other, wings extended and touching. The cherubim were a class of angels and were associated with the transcendent, glorious presence of God (Ezk 10:1-22). Images of these creatures were also woven into the decorations of the curtains in the holy place (cf. 26:1, 31). The term "mercy seat" comes from a Hebrew term "to cover," and conveys the idea of "atonement"; it is the focal point of the Day of Atonement ceremony (cf. Lv 16), on the only day of the year when the high priest was allowed to enter the holy of holies. On that day the blood of a sacrifice was sprinkled on the mercy seat and accomplished the "covering of sin" for the nation for one year. The symbolism was clear: above was the Shekinah glory of God (cf. 40:34ff.), in the ark was the law (the "testimony") and between on the mercy seat, was the atoning blood.

"The ark of the covenant with the mercy seat was quite clearly the most important object in the tabernacle proper" (Davis, *Moses and the Gods*, 264) No one saw it, but they knew it was there and that this was where He was: **There I will meet with you; and from above the mercy seat,** (cf. 1Sm 4:4) **from between the two cherubim** (25:22). The central meaning of human existence on planet earth was to have a relationship with God that brings Him glory; this tabernacle was a symbol of how that relationship might be made viable. It brought God near: it provided for propitiation (the Gk. word often translated "propitiation" in Rm 3:25 refers to Jesus as the "mercy-seat"; see the comments there), it offered atonement for the sinner and it made the nation's worship acceptable.

4. The Table of Showbread: Symbol of Physical Provision (25:23-30; 26:25; 37:10-15)

25:23-30; 26:25; 37:10-15. The table was also made of acacia wood and overlaid with gold and decorated with gold. It was a rather narrow table, as tall as the ark but shorter and not as wide (i.e., two cubits long, one cubit wide and one and a half cubits high). This table was to be placed on the north side of the holy place inside the tabernacle. The details concerning the border and the relatively wide rim (a **handbreadth** 25:25) indicate this was to be not only a beautiful work of the craftsman's art but a functional table. The rim, obviously, was meant to keep things from falling off easily. The table was supplied with rings and poles (similar to the ark) to facilitate transporting it and the appropriate "tableware" (**pans, jars, bowls**) to be used for the various offerings presented there.

The main use of the table was as a display for **the bread of the Presence** (25:30). This bread, which was to be placed on the table each week on the Sabbath (a new batch of twelve loaves each week; see Lv 24:5-8), was not a "meal for God" (as such offerings were often meant in pagan shrines). It was not to be eaten by anyone other than the priests (who were permitted to use it for their own food, Lv 24:9). The twelve loaves were symbolic of the participation of the twelve tribes in the table fellowship with the Lord; this tabernacle made this "fellowship" possible, the bread was in His **Presence** and the tribes were there by proxy in the persons of the priests. The bread was no doubt symbolic as well of the physical provision the Lord gave to the nation; "The bread itself perhaps represents the Lord's provision of the basic necessities of life for His people (see Mt 6:11; Lk 11:3)"

(Youngblood, *Exodus*, 120). Davis notes, "The loaves furthermore point toward Jesus Christ who was the bread of life (John 6:32, 35). As the bread of the table supplied the priests, so Jesus Christ meets the needs of His" own (Davis, *Moses and the Gods*, 265).

5. The Golden Lampstand: Symbol of Spiritual Provision (25:31-40; 26:35; 37:17-24)

25:31-40; 26:35; 37:17-24. The solid gold lampstand (*menorah*) stood on the south side of the holy place opposite the table of showbread. This lampstand was not built to burn candles (because candles were not invented until Roman times) but oil. It weighed one talent (about seventy-five pounds; 25:39), crafted from one piece of gold (29:36). Its base supported a shaft (25:31) that held **six branches**, three on each side (25:32-33), with one lamp atop each branch and one atop the shaft, for a total of seven **lamps**. Made themselves of gold, the lamps were shaped into **cups**, **bulbs** (technically a "calyx", the cup-like structure of petals forming a small flower), and **flowers** designed to resemble the flowers of an **almond** tree. Although the exact appearance of the lampstand is unclear, the purpose and basic design is plain. In some fashion oil was poured into a reservoir on each branch and in turn each reservoir fed another cup that held the burning oil. The oil used was to be **clear oil of beaten** (crushed) **olives** (27:20).

Each morning and evening someone serviced the lamps (30:7-8; Lv 24:3-4); "trimming" is not the right word for this service since these were not candles. The term **trims** (30:8) means "to cause to ascend," indicating that perhaps the oil reservoir was below the cup and oil was somehow fed up to it. These lamps were to be kept burning continually (27:21).

The lampstand had a practical purpose, providing light in the windowless and shrouded inner tabernacle. It also had a symbolic purpose, signifying the "illumination" the Lord gave by His presence, since His presence was "revelatory." Also, the lampstand had typical significance pointing to "Jesus Christ who is the True Light (John 1:6-9; 8:12)" (Davis, *Moses and the Gods*, 267).

6. The Tabernacle Itself: Symbol of God's Personal Presence (26:1-30)

26:1-30. The overall construction of the area comprising the holy place and the holy of holies (26:33) formed a trellis-like structure with a framework covered with several layers of curtains. The first layers consisted of linen curtains dyed **blue and purple and scarlet** (26:1) and cut to precise lengths. These curtains were decorated with **cherubim** (26:1), and suspended in a series of **loops** (26:4-5), probably alternating the colors, with golden clasps (26:6). Over these layers were laid eleven layers of **goats' hair** curtains (26:7; no doubt shutting out all outside light) and then layers of rams and porpoise skins (26:14; perhaps for soundproofing and no doubt for waterproofing).

Underneath all of these layers was that trellis-like structure itself made of acacia wood **boards** (26:15ff.; more than likely these were not "planks" but "frames," "ladder like" objects) that acted as the "uprights" of the trellis. "There were forty-eight frames in all, twenty each for the north and south sides, six for the west side, and two at the rear corners, most likely for added support ([26:]18, 20, 22, 23)" (Hamilton, *Exodus*, 471–72). It could be that the description **they shall be double beneath . . . complete to its top** (26:24) means these frames were wide at the bottom and tied together at the top forming an A-frame, another reason to have two on each corner. The bars (26:26ff.) were the "cross-ties" and there were fifteen of them, five to each side (26:26-27). Finally there was one central cross bar (26:28). These **boards** (or frames) and **bars** were to be assembled with a "tenons and sockets" system that made the structure sturdy when erected but easy to disassemble and reassemble. Like the court, the tabernacle itself opened to the east.

7. The Veil and Screen: Symbol of God's "Hiddenness" (26:31-37)

26:31-37. Two curtains featured prominently in the holy place. One curtain or **screen** (26:36) covered the opening on the east (court side); this was made of linen and dyed in the same colors as the linen layers that were over the tabernacle itself, **blue and purple and scarlet** (26:36; cf. 26:1). It was suspended on **five pillars of acacia** and held on by golden **hooks** (26:37). Another curtain (**a veil**, 26:1) hung between the holy place (which held the altar of incense, the table of showbread and the lampstand) and the holy of holies (which contained the ark and mercy seat). Only the high priest could open this second curtain (Lv 16:11-12), and only once each year (Lv 16:2, 34) during the Day of Atonement ceremony (Lv 16:29-30).

These items "hide" God even though He is "near." Although He was "with them," He was still the "transcendent God." In the temple of Herod's day this inner curtain was no mere linen veil (see Alfred Edersheim, *The Life and Times of Jesus the Messiah*, vol. II, [London: Longmans, Green and Co., 1900], 609), yet Mt 27:51 records that upon Jesus' death "the veil of the temple was torn from top to bottom"; see the comments there. This was meant to convey two truths: the death of Christ opened the way into the presence of the Holy God as no other sacrifice could (cf. Heb 4:16; 10:19) and also that it was God alone, "top to bottom", who made this access into "the throne of grace" possible.)

8. The Bronze Altar: Symbol of the Need for a Sacrifice for Sin (27:1-8; 38:1-7)

27:1-8; 38:1-7. This altar was a large box; at five cubits by five cubits by three cubits high (or approximately seven and a half feet by seven and a half feet by four and a half feet) it was the largest piece of furniture in the tabernacle. Made of acacia wood and overlaid with bronze (27:1), its center was hollow except for a grating (27:4); there the coals would be placed to burn the sacrifices. (It was called "the altar of burnt offering" in Lv 4:7, 10, 18.) The inside of the box probably was lined with earth when the fire was burning (to keep the box itself from igniting); workers could remove the earth for easy transport when necessary. Craftsmen created bronze implements for removing the ashes of a sacrifice (**shovels**, **basins**, **forks**, **firepans**, 27:3).

Four **horns** adorned the altar, one on each corner; these were essentially vertical corner extensions probably stylized to resemble the horns of an animal. The horns were used to tie up and suspend the sacrifice over the fire (27:2; cf. Ps 118:27). The horns themselves would be smeared with the blood of the sacrifice (Ex 29:12; Lv 8:15; 9:9; 16:18) to sanctify it to receive the sacrifice. The altar was fitted with rings through which poles, also of wood covered with bronze, could be installed to facilitate carrying the altar.

As noted, the altar was the first object a worshiper would see on entering the court; it was a powerful reminder that sin separates one from God and that sin means death. It spoke of the absolute necessity for atonement if one were to approach the Lord. "The slaughter of animals on this altar was a very vivid reminder to Israel that sin indeed requires a high price. It was not a pleasant thing to see an innocent animal slaughtered and burned, but then sin is an ugly thing and the sacrifice here, as well as at Calvary, should be a vivid reminder to everyone of the hideousness of sin and its price" (Davis, *Moses and the Gods*, 272).

9. The Court: Symbol of Separation (27:9-20; 38:9-20)

27:9-20; 38:9-20. A series of bronze pillars marked off the court/courtyard/compound. Between the pillars curtains were suspended, attached with silver hooks (27:10). Made of **fine twisted linen** (27:9) **five cubits high** (27:18) or approximately seven and a half feet high, the curtains kept "casual eyes" from observing what was happening in the tabernacle area; activities inside the courtyard were solemn and serious and were not to be viewed nonchalantly. The curtains of the entrance were unlike the rest of the curtains that made up the court (27:16), identifying the only way in to the court and tabernacle.

10. The Priests of the Tabernacle (27:21–29:46)

a. Priestly Functions (27:21–28:1)

27:21–28:1. The priests oversaw the ongoing operation of the tabernacle, and the whole nation needed to recognize the priests' position (authority and duties). The priests were consecrated for their duties, which needed to be clearly articulated or else this effort to build the tabernacle would be in vain. How unlike the times before Moses: "In pre-Mosaic times the office of priest was occupied by the father of a family (cf. Jb 1:5) or the head of a tribe . . ., for example Abraham, Isaac, and Jacob built altars and offered sacrifices (Gn 12:7; 13:18; 26:25; 33:20; 35:1, 2). Other pre-Mosaic priests included Melchizedek, Genesis 14 and Jethro, Ex 2:16; 3:1)" (cf. Davis, *Moses and the Gods*, 278). However, the role of the priest in service to the tabernacle was unique.

The most detailed set of instructions concerning the priests is given in Leviticus chaps. 1–8. (See commentary on Lv 1–8). The priest's primary role was as a mediator between God and man (standing before God on behalf of others), and his basic functions were sacrifice and intercession (prayer). The priest's duties took place **in** the tabernacle (27:21a; **in the tent of meeting**) and **before the Lord** (27:21b). Davis notes, "The idea of a priesthood naturally implies a consciousness of sin and the need for mediatorial representation" (Davis, *Moses and the Gods*, 278).

The priest's work alternated between the maintenance work in and on the tabernacle (cf. 30:7-8) and the spiritual work of a mediator (cf. 29:38-44; Lv 9:22; Nm 6:23-27).

"The priests were not self-appointed mystics or cultists that rose [to prominence and position] by their own power in Israel. They were selected by God and had to be descendants of Aaron" (Davis, *Moses and the Gods*, 278). Exodus 27:21 simply identifies **Aaron and his sons** as the authorized persons to perform functions in the tabernacle (this is the first verse in the OT to explicitly tie Aaron and his sons to the priestly service), and 28:1 identifies Aaron and his sons, **Aaron**, **Nadab**, **Abihu**, **Eleazar**, and **Ithamar**, as priests. The Lord said explicitly that these men are called **to minister as priest to Me**; that phrase is repeated twice more (28:3, 4), making it emphatic. This office was not one a man could aspire to or assume on his own authority; it was not an office intended to elevate the man but to meditate between God and Israel. Everything about the priests, their clothes, their duties, their role, was designed to focus on the office and the function of the man. The quality and character of the man under the clothes counted, but only so far as the man's character did not defile the clothes or demean the office. In his person he did not contribute to the value and vitality of the position, He could detract from it but it was all about the office and it was all about the mediatorial function.

b. Priestly Garments (28:2-43; 39:1-31)

28:2-5; 39:1. God describes the garments of the priests as **holy garments . . . for glory and for beauty** (28:2). They were designed to impress. (This was much like a case in which "the clothes made the man.") They were unique, unlike the daily wear of the common person. This was for an obvious reason: The priests performed unique duties so unlike those of the common person. In addition their clothes, sometimes referred to as vestments (clothing that indicates an office or position of authority) reflected the dignity and magnificence of the tabernacle itself. And in some instances these garments were to be functional in the sense that in some cases the very elements of the garments themselves were to be used by the priest to perform his functions and accomplish his duties.

"The priestly office was intentionally elevated in the eyes of the people. The apparel would serve to distinguish the priests as a class by themselves and in a certain sense above the rest of the nation. The distinctiveness of their garments would be a constant reminder to the priests themselves of their holy station and its demand for consecrated living" (Davis, *Moses and the Gods*, 283). For these reasons the work on these garments demanded especially skillful persons (28:3; cf. 28:8, 15).

The complete list and general description of the garments is given first (28:4-5; cf. 39:1) and then the descriptive details are furnished. The garments listed are the **breastpiece**, **ephod**, **robe**, **tunic**, **turban** and **sash**. The descriptive details do not follow the order of that list (although there does not seem to be any particular reason for the difference).

28:6-14; 39:2-7. The **ephod** was similar to an apron or coverall, yet made of the same beautiful materials and in the same colors as the curtains in the tabernacle itself (cf. 26:1). As the primary symbol of the priestly office (cf. 1Sm 2:18; 28; 14:3; 22:18), the ephod had a front and a back, made of linen, probably sleeveless, with (real) gold threads **woven** into the fabric (39:3-3). The two parts joined at each shoulder by a clasp or strap of gold (28:13-14); a **band** (28:8) secured the waist. The most striking features of the ephod were the **two onyx stones** atop each shoulder in a setting on the clasp or strap. Each of these stones bore the engraved names of six of the twelve tribes of Israel (28:9-12). The significance was clear: the priest was representing the whole nation every time he put the ephod on. These stones were **memorial stones for the sons of Israel** (39:7).

28:15-30; 39:8-21. The instructions concerning **breastpiece** exceeded those for any other item, thereby highlighting its importance. Made of the same material as the ephod and attached with gold cords and rings (28:24-28; 39:15-21) to the front of the ephod, the breastpiece was **folded double** to be made in a square (28:16) of about nine inches (a **span**). In all likelihood this was a pouch of some sort and it was worn over the high priest's heart (28:29). Mounted on this were **four rows** of precious stones (28:17-20; 39:13), three in each row, that again, represented the twelve tribes since the names of the tribes were to be engraved on the these stones (28:21; 39:14). Thus every time the high priest entered the holy place he carried the nation with him (28:29).

Among the more notable (and mysterious) parts of the breastpiece were the **Urim** and **Thummim** (v. 30); the terms mean respectively "lights" and "perfection." They apparently helped the high priest to determine the will of God (cf. Nm 27:21) in a manner not clearly understood today. Some have suggested that they were used as sacred lots (something like modern dice) to gain yes and no answers to specific questions. However, it might be that these objects were only symbolic of the high priest's special authority as the Lord's spokesman; in other words, when the priest was wearing these stones he was speaking for God (cf. Davis, *Moses and the Gods*, 286; Kaiser, "Exodus," 467).

28:31-35; 39:22-26. The **robe** of the high priest was worn under the ephod. The blue robe was slightly longer than the ephod, reaching to the knees. This seamless, one-piece covering "had slits for the arms and a hole for the head to pass through" (Kaiser, "Exodus," 467). Blue, purple and scarlet bits that looked like **pomegranates** adorned the hem,. These "pomegranates" alternated with a row of golden bells **all around on the hem of the robe** (28:34). The bright colors and **pomegranates** would have made the high priest stand out, and the golden bells would have made him sound off. The sound of the tinkling bells as the high priest moved within told those outside the holy place that the unseen priest remained alive in his godly duties, obeying and pleasing God.

28:36-38; 39:30-31. The **turban** or miter was the headdress of the high priest and was both literally and figuratively the crowning feature of the high priest's regalia. This turban probably consisted of folded fabric around the head, the sort of thing made familiar in pictures of men from the Middle East and Islamic countries today. On its front hung **a plate of pure gold** attached with a **blue cord** (28:37). The plate had a most significant engraving: **Holy to the Lord** (28:36). (It should be noted that the description of this item started with this plate.) This plate was more than likely the first item people would have looked at when seeing the high priest, and they would have noticed it repeatedly when the high priest was in view, appropriately dominating the whole outfit. And it should have, because it "indicated the very essence of Israel's worship" (Davis, *Moses and the Gods*, 287). The high priest had to be **Holy to the Lord** (28:38) because the entire venue was a testimony to the "Holiness of the Lord," and the whole process was to make the worshiper "holy to the Lord."

Wearing this turban and this plate with this inscription qualified the high priest (as one who bore the sanctifying presence of the Lord into the holy place) **to take away** (lit., "bear") **the iniquity of the holy things**, that is, to sanctify fully all the **holy gifts** that made up this tabernacle and made them **accepted before the Lord** (28:38).

28:39-43; 39:27-29. The rest of the items of clothing mentioned were to be worn by all the priests. The **tunic** (28:39) was a long white linen garment worn over the underwear, the **linen breeches** (28:42), but under the blue ephod; modesty was the point of this item (28:43). The **tunics**, **caps**, and **sashes** of the ordinary priests (28:40-43; 39:27-29) were simple yet intended to display the same **glory** and **beauty** (28:40) as the rest of the features in the tabernacle.

Summary. The details with which the garments of the priests are described and the care that was taken to make them **just as the Lord had commanded Moses** (39:1, 5, 7, 21, 26, 29, 31) reinforces once again the major lesson from these chapters: the Lord cared about how He was to be worshiped. All of this was designed to make the people aware of what was going on and to think carefully about what was happening. "Conscious faith is central to religious ritual. . . . In other words, a person's belief about what he or she is doing in a religious act is essential to the validity of that act" (Stuart, *Exodus*, 615). All of this was to make individual worshipers realize: "I am worshiping a holy God here" and to reorient their minds and hearts toward God.

c. The Consecration of the Priests (29:1-46)

29:1-46. Once the garments of the priests were ready, the appropriate individuals and Moses clothed themselves in order to **consecrate them**[selves] **that they may serve** the Lord **as priests** (28:41). Consecrating the priests simply meant setting them apart to **minister as priests to** the Lord(29:1a).

The service for consecrating the priests (29:2-9; cf. Lv 8) began with sacrifices (29:1b) and offerings (29:2-3). The animals were to be **without blemish** (29:1). This would have indicated to the worshiper that the sacrifice had to be pure and acceptable to God. Also, there was cleansing with water (29:4), again highlighting the need for purity and sanctification of the priests to make the sacrifices and offerings acceptable. The service then continued with a solemn ceremony of investiture, that is, actually providing the high priest with the regalia and the garments appropriate to his office (29:5-6). Then the priest would be anointed with oil (29:7) and finally, all the priests were provided with **tunics**, **sashes**, and **caps** appropriate to their calling (29:8-9).

After giving the summary of the service, Ex 29 describes the sacrifices in greater detail. Davis summarizes, "The sacrifices consisted of one young bullock for a sin offering, one ram for a burnt offering and the ram of consecration" (Davis, *Moses and the Gods*, 289). Three times the priests were to lay hands on the sacrificial animals (29:10, 15, 19). The priest laying hands on the animal symbolized the transfer of guilt (imputation) from the guilty to the innocent. This was a key feature of the entire sacrificial system (cf. Lv 16:21-22; cf. 1Pt 2:24; Is 53). The concepts of transfer and imputation point to a system and theology of substitution. Combined with the act of slaying the animal, the entire scene pictured penal substitution.

In the consecration ceremony, the priests killed the animals and applied the blood: with the bull's blood the altar was cleansed (29:11-14); with the ram's blood propitiation (appeasing God's wrath) was accomplished (29:16-18); with blood from the other ram the priests were cleansed and consecrated (29:20-21). The entrails and the bread and cakes were used for wave or heave offerings (29:24, 28). These offerings were obviously so named for the action of the priest waving and holding up the sacrifice symbolically before the Lord ("See this!" See Lv 7:30-32). The significance of such offerings is indicted by the terms **peace offering** (29:28). A peace offering (cf. Lv 7) was in a sense celebratory, a joyful act symbolizing the peace now enjoyed (after the sin and guilt offerings had been made and accepted by the Lord) between the worshiper and God. (For a much fuller treatment of all this, see commentary on Lv 1–8.)

The final paragraphs of this chapter (Ex 29) provided further regulations for the priests and their duties. The high priest's garments were to be passed down to succeeding generations. They were to be reused, not remade (29:29-30); this allowed continuity across generations. The offerings became food for the priests, but laymen were expressly forbidden to consume the flesh of a sacrifice or eat the bread that had been a part of the offerings (29:31-34); this prevented the sacrifices from becoming a mere commodity. The ordination ceremony was to last for seven days (29:35-37); this made it a memorable event. Some details were given concerning the daily sacrifices and how they were to distinguish between morning and evening sacrifices (29:38-41; cf. Nm 28:3-8); this would give order and symmetry to the daily activity of the priests.

Finally, the continual burnt offering (29:42) was to be a reminder and promise of the Lord's intention to **meet with** the nation in this **tent of meeting** (29:42-44) and to do so through the mediatorial work of the priests (29:44). This tabernacle was the culmination of what had been God's intention through and since the actual exodus itself—it was that **I might dwell among them**, because **I am the Lord their God** (29:45).

11. The Altar of Incense: Symbol of Prayer and Intercession (30:1-10; 37:25-29)

30:1-10; 37:25-29. In addition to the golden lampstand and table of showbread, the third piece of furniture in the holy place was the altar of incense. Like the other pieces, the altar was made of acacia wood and overlaid with gold (30:1, 3). It was one cubit in length and width and two cubits tall (30:2). Apparently, this was a smaller version, in gold, of the bronze altar in the court, complete with the **horns** on each corner. Like the other items, it was fitted with rings and supplied with poles to be inserted through the rings when the item was being transported. The altar of incense stood on the west side of the holy place just **in front of the veil** and so, in effect, just **in front of the mercy seat** (30:6).

As with the lamps so with the incense, the priest was to service the altar every day (30:7) and this practice was to be perpetual (30:8). No other incense (**strange incense**; see 30:34-38 and the discussion below on the sacred incense) and no other offering was to be placed on this altar except the atonement blood on the Day of Atonement (30:9, 10). The solemn pronouncement **It is most holy to the Lord** (30:10) was meant to reiterate the care and reverence the nation was to maintain in worship and devotion to God. This altar was symbolic of the nation's prayers and praise; like this pleasing incense, the prayers of the people were to ascend continually to a glorious and gracious Lord God (cf. Ps 141:2; Rv 5:8; 8:3-4).

12. The Census (30:11-16)

See comments on 25:1-9.

13. The Bronze Laver: Symbol of Cleansing (30:17-21; 38:8; 40:30-32)

30:17-21; 38:8; 40:30-32. The bronze laver was essentially a washbasin made of bronze mirrors donated by the women who were serving the worshipers at the entrance (38:8). The laver may have been made in two parts, the main reservoir and under it another basin to be used for the actual washing; thus the priest would draw some water from the main bowl and pour it into the **base of bronze, for washing** (30:18). Significantly the laver was to be used by the priests not *after* the sacrifices were made but *before* they were made (30:20). It was another vivid reminder that God expected "clean hands and a pure heart" (Ps 24:3-4) from those who served and worshiped Him. The priest needed to be cleansed from the "defilement of the world" before he could serve the Lord (cf. Eph 5:25-26).

14. The Anointing Oil and Incense: Symbol of Consecration (30:22-38)

30:22-38. Moses was given special instructions (note the insertion of the phrase **the LORD spoke to Moses**; 30:22, 34) about the anointing oil (30:22-33) and the sacred incense (30:34-38). The **holy anointing oil** (30:25) was to be made from a precise recipe using **the finest of spices** (30:23), the most expensive ingredients. **Myrrh** is mentioned frequently in the Bible; perhaps the best known instance being as one of the gifts of the magi to the infant Jesus (Mt 2:11). Made from the gum or resin from the tree of the same name, myrrh had many uses. A second spice, cinnamon, can come from both the oil of the crushed nut produced by the blossom of the tree by the same name and the shavings of the bark from that tree. Cassia is the oil of the blossom of the cinnamon tree. Cane was probably the pith from the root a reed plant. Olive oil made up the base of the mixture.

This special oil was used extensively to **anoint** the structure of the tabernacle, the furniture, the furnishings, and the utensils (30:26-28). The purpose was to mark and distinguish these items so that that they would be considered **most holy** (30:29), separated for sacred use. In addition, this oil was to be used to anoint the priests to **consecrate them** (30:30). This oil, in this formula, was to be reserved for this use and not reproduced for any other or common use, for to do so would undermine its value for identifying that which is to be considered "sacred" and "consecrated." Anyone caught violating this restriction would be **cut off from his people** (30:33). Hamilton notes, "'Cutting off' a person is a metaphor borrowed from the felling of trees"; cf. Jr 11:19) (Hamilton, *Exodus*, 516). It was a euphemism for execution.

Likewise the sacred incense was to be made from a precise formula of expensive spices (30:34), processed with great care (30:35), and used in the tabernacle and nowhere else. It too was to be considered **most holy to you** (30:36, 37). Again, the Lord expressed the singular significance He attached to even this minor aspect of the tabernacle system and His worship by decreeing the death penalty for any who would violate this injunction and use this perfume for a common purpose.

15. The Builders of the Tabernacle (31:1-11; 35:30-35; 36:1-2)

31:1-11; 35:30-35; 36:1-2. Several texts indicate the vital importance of the skilled craftsmen. The Lord's insistence for **skill** and **skillful** workers (31:6) and **skill to perform every work** (35:35) necessary for the tabernacle is woven throughout Moses' instructions (cf. 26:1, 31; 28:3, 6, 8, 15, 27; 29:5). Of the many skilled craftsmen who worked on the tabernacle, the passage names only two: Bezalel (whose name means "in the shadow of God," indicating "protection"; note 31:2; 35:30; 36:1-2) and Oholiab (whose name means "the father [God] is my tent"; see 31:6; 35:34; 36:1-2). These two men probably served like foremen, leaders in some capacity over the other skilled men (and women; cf. 35:25-26).

While all the craftsmen were filled with **skill** (the Hb. word is lit., "wisdom") (31:6; 36:1), only Bezalel was said to be "filled with the Spirit of God" (31:3; 35:31, **in wisdom, in understanding and in all knowledge and in all . . . craftsmanship**). This likely means he was provided with a spiritual giftedness that enabled him to use his "technical skills" (either natural or acquired) in exactly the way the Lord wanted them used and this project required them to be used. ("In fact, 'being filled with the Spirit' is a biblical idiom for 'having from God the ability to do and say exactly what God wants done or said'"; Stuart, *Exodus*, 650–52.) Thus, it would seem that the "skillful" were already capable craftsmen who were given increased facility in their area of expertise in order to work on the tabernacle. Not only did they execute the necessary works of skilled craftsmanship but they taught others how to perform the work as well (35:34). Hamilton notes, "It is of some interest that the first 'Spirit-filled' individual in the Bible" is not a patriarch or prophet or priest but "a construction foreman, Bezalel. The Bible sanctifies the work and craftsmanship of the laborer as much as it does of the work of the patriarch or prophet or priest. What one does with one's hands [can be] as sacred as what one does with one's mind" (Hamilton, *Exodus*, 483).

The work of building the tabernacle required a wide variety of technical skills—metallurgy, carpentry, molding, wood-carving, metal engraving, sewing, embroidering, weaving, perfumery and overall design and more (cf. 35:10-19). The work occupied **every skillful man** (35:10). It would have been a singular privilege to work on the tabernacle, but it was a privilege enjoyed by many; and it was a merit-based privilege—any who had the skill were employed; anyone could work on the tabernacle without regard to his or her social position. In the Lord's work all who were willing and able were welcomed.

16. Sabbath Reminder (31:12-17; 35:1-3)

31:12-18; 35:1-3. Inserted into His directives concerning the tabernacle, the Lord gave Moses a reminder about the Sabbath (31:12-17) and Moses later repeated that reminder (35:1-3). These reminders probably were given to reiterate the priorities of the Lord even in the context and process of tabernacle construction. The craftsmen were to understand that the Sabbath requirement still pertained even as they worked on the tabernacle. As Youngblood suggests, "The Sabbath passages in Ex 31 and 35 are obviously meant to warn Israel not to work on the construction of the tabernacle or its furnishings on the Sabbath day" (Youngblood, *Exodus*, 113).

The Lord made three points regarding this Sabbath observance. First, the purpose of Sabbath observance was to impress upon the nation that God is the One who **sanctifies you** (31:13); this was to be a day when one's life was to be centered on the Lord. They were to "do" no work but they were to **celebrate** [lit., that term means simply "do"] **the sabbath** (31:16). Second, the penalty for violating the Sabbath was death (31:14, 15; 35:2). While this might seem to be a harsh penalty by modern standards, it impressed upon the nation the importance of that day and its purposes (rest, cf. 31:15, 17; 35:2, and devotion). Third, this Sabbath observance was meant to give the nation a transgenerational sense of national identity centered on the covenantal relationship that the Lord Himself had accomplished for them (v. 16). It was a **perpetual covenant** and the regular (perpetual) observance of the Sabbath was meant to be a reminder of that fact; it was **a sign between Me and the sons of Israel forever** (31:16-17). Just as the Noahic covenant had an outward sign (the rainbow, Gn 9:12-17) as did the Abrahamic covenant (circumcision, Gn 17:9-22), so the sign of the Sinai covenant was the Sabbath.

H. Apostasy and Aftermath (32:1–34:35)

These three chapters come between God's instructions for the tabernacle (25:1–31:18) and the record of the actual construction of the tabernacle (35:1–39:31). They record a devastating act of apostasy on the part of the nation and an amazing act of grace on the part of the Lord. They are placed here to emphasize the need for the tabernacle, which at that point was still under construction. Without the constant lessons provided by the tabernacle itself and the service of the tabernacle, the people would follow the patterns of worship from the world in which they lived. If they did not have a divinely, graciously provided pattern for fellowship with God, they would invent one of their own making. But the Lord accepts only the way to God and true worship that He has shown and graciously provided.

1. The Golden Calf (32:1-29)

a. The Folly of Aaron and the People (32:1-6)

32:1-6. The account of idol worship begins after **Moses** had been **delayed**; this caused the people to fear that he was lost (32:1a). The people were foolishly impatient and fickle. Rather than allow Moses the time to receive the law from the Lord, they wanted events to happen in a time of their own choosing. This led to a god of their own making. Kaiser notes, "Without proper visible leadership, people fail" (Kaiser, "Exodus," 478). This is true but in reality it was not Moses' leadership that the people were missing. That they viewed Moses as **the man who brought us up from the land of Egypt** indicates that the people did not understand that the Lord Himself was their true "leader." When Moses was around they had a leader, they concluded; but when he was absent they assumed they had no "leader." Although the people could not see Moses while he was on the mountain, the people had never "seen" the Lord either, the One who really brought them up from the land of Egypt. Especially here, at the foot of Sinai, they should have "walked by faith and not by sight." But without Moses in view, they wavered in their faith.

Furthermore, they had seen the manifestations of God's power and majesty (cf. 19:18; so much for those who think seeing miracles are the key to engendering faith), and they knew that the Lord had called Moses up (cf. 19:21; 24:1). They knew their representatives had seen God (including seventy elders; cf. 24:9-11), and they had committed themselves to the Lord, to be obedient (24:3, 7). Their eyes should have been *on*, and their trust should have been *in* the Lord.

Their impatience and fear led to a foolish request (32:1b), **Come, make us a god**. The people were religious, they were spiritual, and they wanted to worship, but they had an inadequate theology.

The term **god** (*'elohim*) is plural, and this has generated several views. Some have suggested this was indicative that the people held to a form of polytheism. Others have proposed that this is simply a "plural of majesty." Still others have offered that this is simply a grammatical necessity since the verb **will go** in the phrase **who will go before us** is plural; however, Davis notes, "Normally when *'elohim* is used of the true God a singular verb is employed" (Davis, *Moses and the Gods*, 293). In other words, the use of *'elohim* does not by itself indicate that the people had reverted to polytheism.

As the scene develops, it seems that the issue here is simple idolatry—they were not attempting to add another god to a pantheon, but they were attempting to worship the God who had delivered them from bondage (32:4) in this idolatrous form. In short it was not a matter of the people wanting more or newer gods but a case of trying to worship the true God by means of a "graven image." Thus the golden calf was not merely a false god. Rather (as v. 4 seems to suggest) it was an attempt to depict the true God in a false way.

Acceding to the demands of the people, Aaron encouraged them to make a foolish contribution (32:2-3). They gave up their **gold rings**. This was a bad transaction. The people had contributed generously to the construction of the tabernacle (cf. 25:2-7; 35:21-24) but now they took their most precious personal possessions to be used to make a golden idol.

Aaron's actions are described deliberately: **He took**, he **fashioned**, he **made** (32:4a). This emphasizes that while the decision to make this idol was rash, the action was deliberate. This took time, time that should have given Aaron pause to think about his actions. "Sometimes even the holiest of men, as Aaron, can be persuaded to do things contrary to their testimony" (Kaiser, "Exodus," 478). This "thing" was probably not "solid gold" but a "cheap wooden knock-off" of some Egyptian god covered with the gold from the rings of the people. A **molten calf** meant it was made of "molten (melted and recast) metal," here gold. The calf was probably chosen because it was common object of worship in Egypt and elsewhere; it was a symbol of virility and power. This was a blatant example of religious syncretism, taking parts of the (pagan) culture and trying to make them fit with what the Lord had revealed. This sort of idol was familiar to them and so it seemed right—it was what they were used to seeing in Egypt. Therefore, they thought they could use it to worship the Lord. That is how syncretism works.

Aaron's declaration betrayed a foolish theology. **This is your god, O Israel** (32:4b). Again, this was not an attempt to change their faith because Aaron went on to say this was the one **who brought you up from the land of Egypt**. In other words, Aaron did not think of this as a change of gods but an improvement of the worship of the true God. (See 1Kg 12:28, where Jeroboam made the same claim when he set up the idolatrous shires in Israel. Jeroboam's motive seems to have been political as well. He wanted to keep his people from going to Jerusalem because it might tend to prompt them to honor the king of Judah, undermining his claim to the regency in Israel.) This is nothing short of blasphemy.

Aaron then made a foolish proclamation and promoted an idolatrous worship (vv. 5-6). In effect Aaron attempted to introduce a new holy-day and provided the people with an altar and offerings and a new way to celebrate it. This act was not merely foolish—it was degrading. The last line in v. 6, **and rose up to play**, implies some rather unsavory connotations; this was carnal, fleshly, sensual, and immoral play, "drunken orgies and sexual play" (Kaiser, "Exodus," 478). This sort of behavior was fairly typical in conjunction with idolatry; cf. Gl 5:19-21; 1Pt 4:3.

Here was worship designed to meet the personal wishes of the worshipers. It was selfish (man-centered, it was something *they* liked), it was syncretistic (it took parts of the culture, the surrounding cultures' religious practices, and tried to make them fit them with the worship of the Lord; it was something the world would have understood) and it was sensual (it had "sex appeal"). But it was blasphemous toward God and corrupting for the people.

b. Anger and Intercession (32:7-14)

32:7-10. Before Moses even knew what had happened in the camp below him, he faced the anger of the Lord up on the mountain. The

Lord's words must have been something of a shock to Moses, **Go down at once**. In contrast to the inviting and personal words He had previously spoken (cf. 24:1, 12), here the Lord's words were "abrupt and detached" (Kaiser, "Exodus," 478). Speaking to Moses, instead of "My people" (cf. 3:7), He called them **your people**. Instead of affirming that it had been His purpose to bring the people "out from under the bondage of the Egyptians" (cf. 6:6ff.), God identified the people as those **whom *you*** (emphasis added) **brought up from the land of Egypt** (32:7a). The Lord had verbally disowned them. Even before the sad events were explained to Moses, God's indictment was pronounced: **they have corrupted themselves** (32:7b). This "renders the same verb found in Genesis 6:12 for the apostasy and corruption in Noah's day. It means 'to go to ruin or destruction' (cf. Dt 9:6; 10:16; Ps 75:5; Jr 17:23; Ac 7:51)" (Kaiser, "Exodus," 478). They had not just erred, this was not merely a "mistake in judgment" but they had **quickly turned aside**, they had rapidly and rashly fallen into iniquity and transgression. They had failed to walk in **the way which I commanded them**; they had missed the mark and fallen short (32:8a). Taking the definition of "sin" as "any want of conformity unto, or transgression of, the law of God" (*Westminster Shorter Catechism*, Question 38), the people had failed on both counts.

In His explanation to Moses (32:8b) the Lord related the information that was just recorded in the previous verses (32:1-6). As Moses was hearing it from the mouth of the Lord, it made for chilling and stunning news. The Lord related the actions of the people in something like verbal thrusts: **they have made** . . . they **have worshiped** . . . they **have sacrificed** (32:8). These thrusts culminated in a testimonial that must have been especially troubling to the Lord. The people were assured, **This is your god, O Israel, who brought you up from the land of Egypt** (32:8c). To hear His people profess devotion to a stupid, impotent idol and then give to that grotesque monstrosity the praise due to the one true God must have been particularly distressing and provoking to Him. Thus God's anger began to rise. **I have seen these people** (32:9a) is a summary statement to indicate "I have watched them, I have answered their fears, I have supplied their needs, I have blessed them, I have preserved them and *now* I have seen them do *this*! All I have done for them and *this* is the thanks I get?!"

His indictment is, **They are an obstinate** (32:9b; lit., "stiff-necked") **people**. The expression "stiff-necked" was used to describe the people with distressing frequency in succeeding narratives of the nation (cf. 33:3, 5; 34:5; Dt 9:6; 10:16; 2Ch 30:8; 36:13; Ps 75:5; Jr 17:23; Ac 7:51). The picture is that of a horse that refused to turn its head when the reins were pulled one direction or another by a rider; the nation often refused to heed the Lord's direction. Ironically, they willingly bowed before an inert, stupid, lifeless idol but they stubbornly refused to bend before the living, sovereign Lord.

The Lord's impatient response, **let Me alone** (32:10a), was meant to express to Moses the depth of God's disappointment. To convey the depth of His sentiment, He spoke of His **anger** and even suggested that He **may destroy them** and start over with Moses alone (32:10b). This is an instance of anthropopathism, expressions describing a truth about the Lord using human (*anthropos*, Gk. for "man") terms to describe God's emotions. The emotions and feelings of the Lord are higher and holier than those of fallen human beings, but they are no less real and genuine. In this case the anthropopathic description reveals the pain or distress of God when His own people sin egregiously to their own destruction.

These words amounted to something of a test for Moses (e.g., Kaiser, "Exodus," 479; Davis, *Moses and the Gods*, 296). Would Moses selfishly accept the offer to **make of** him a **great nation**, in effect a new Abraham (cf. Gn 12:2), or would he keep his faith in God's promises? Would Moses trust the Lord, prove to be a faithful mediator, and intercede for the people? Moses "chooses the role of intercessor over that of patriarch" (Hamilton, *Exodus*, 538).

32:11-14. Moses recognized the seriousness of the situation and lost no time in beseeching and imploring (he **entreated**) the Lord (32:11a). Moses offered four reasons for the Lord to relent, to turn from, to not do what He said He would do . . . what He "felt like doing." First, he recalled how God Himself had delivered these people from bondage in Egypt. In effect Moses was saying, "Remember Lord, these people, who have just aroused Your anger were the same ones who had aroused Your compassion when they were in bondage" (32:11b; cf. Ex 2:23-25; 3:7, 9). God had just (speaking to Moses) called the people "your people" but Moses returns to the covenantal language the Lord had previously used and referred to them as "Your people." Moses was appealing to the Lord's previous expressions of love and concern for the people.

Second, he reminded the Lord of the **great power** He had displayed and the demonstration of His **mighty hand** in delivering them (32:11c). That work would prove to be futile if the Lord gave up on them now. In effect, "You provided an astonishing deliverance for them; it would be a shame for all that to be for naught." Third, Moses pointed out that the Egyptians would be watching; if the Lord destroyed this nation it would give the Egyptians an opportunity to gloat over God (32:12a). The Egyptians might conclude that He was foolish to deliver such a people from bondage. Or worse, perhaps they might think that He was really an evil deity and that the deliverance was a nasty trick to get them to a place where He could destroy them. The great testimony to God's justice and compassion in delivering His people from bondage would be lost. Fourth, Moses recalled the covenant promises to the fathers, **Abraham, Isaac, and Jacob** (32:13a). These men are identified as **Your servants** and the promises of many descendants and **all this land** are recalled (32:13). These promises were sovereignly decreed (**You swore . . . I will . . . I will**) and intended to be everlasting (**forever**) (32:13b). Moses directly pleads with God: **Turn from Your burning anger and change Your mind** (32:12b). In a way, he was asking God to "keep His word," to "hold on to His original intention" to bless this nation as He had promised and abandon any thought of terminating them.

In response to Moses' intercession, God **changed His mind** (32:14) away from the threatened destruction and *back to* His first plan, namely the fulfillment of His covenant promises. In effect, this "repentance" was not really a change of mind. It was an expression of His intention to remain who He is, constant and faithful. The term "repent" (KJV) is "a translation of the Hebrew word *naham* meaning 'to be sorry, move to pity, have compassion.' This word is used thirty times in reference to God and in each case He changes His mind or intention in accord with His righteous purposes and takes action commensurate with that purpose" (Davis, *Moses and the Gods*, 297).

This repentance does not mean that God has literally "changed His mind" about what He intended to do. Rather, "when God is said to repent, it indicates 1) his awareness that the human situation has altered and 2) his desire to act in a way fitting to this changed situation." (Bruce A. Ware, *God's Lesser Glory: The Diminished God of Open Theism* [Wheaton, IL: Crossway Books, 2000], 90) Thus the "change of mind" is not the Lord's but the people's, and in the light of that He returns to, or rather remains committed to His original purpose—namely to bless this people. "The grounds for the Lord's repenting are three: (1) intercession (cf. Am 7:1-6); (2) repentance of the people (Jer 18:3-11; Jonah 3:9-10); and (3) compassion (Dt 32:36; Jdg 2:18; 2 Sam 24:16)" (Kaiser, "Exodus," 479).

c. Confrontation: Moses Against Aaron and the People (32:15-29)

Having averted the disaster of God's anger, Moses now returned to the people to deal with this calamity. From his heartfelt intercession before the Lord he turned to heated confrontation with the people and Aaron.

(1) A "Heavy" Descent (32:15-18)

32:15-18. Moses not only had to carry the **two** stone **tablets of the testimony** but he also, no doubt, had to carry a heavy heart as he considered the words of the Lord and what he had to face after he descended the mountain and returned to the people. "This is the only passage that informs us that the 'two tablets of the Testimony' were inscribed 'on both sides' (32:15)" (Kaiser, "Exodus," 479). The text here says that the tablets were **God's work** and **the writing was God's writing** (32:16) and yet 34:28 says that Moses "wrote on the tablets." This is not a contradiction but an affirmation of "verbal plenary inspiration" (meaning that the inspiration of Scripture extends to the individual words and included all of Scripture, cf. Charles C. Ryrie, *Basic Theology* [Chicago: Moody, 1999], 76–82). When Joshua heard the noise from below the mountain he presumed that it must have been caused by a battle of some sort in the camp. Joshua's reaction to the tumult showed he had a good heart. His first thought was the people were being attacked and he apparently did not suspect that the people were capable of such sinful behavior and gross idolatry. Moses poetically corrected him (32:18 is in poetic verse) and he sang a short song about the singing below. It was not, as Joshua assumed, a war cry but singing, and it was not a joyful noise unto the Lord but the cacophony of pagan-like worship.

(2) A "Hot" Confrontation (32:19-20)

32:19-20. As Moses approached the camp and saw the calf and the dancing, his reaction was swift and violent. The expression **Moses' anger burned** does not sufficiently express the depth of his fury. The popular expressions "he exploded" or "he was infuriated" are accurate renderings of the level of his ire. He smashed the tablets, **shattered them** at the base **of the mountain** (32:19). This may have been a hasty act but it was also symbolic one: the people had shattered the law by this idolatry and debauched worship, so Moses shattered the tablets! Moses then reduced the idol to ashes and cast the ashes on the water and made the people drink the water. This would not be difficult to do since (as noted above) this was probably a mostly wooden idol overlaid with gold so it would have burned easily. The strange and dramatic act of making them "drink the ashes" was a way to humiliate them (cf. Is 44:20, where the idolater is said to "feed on ashes"). It was a shameful punishment for a shameful act of infidelity to the Lord (cf. 2Ki 23:15).

(3) A "Heated" Conversation, Moses vs. Aaron (32:21-24)

32:21-24. Moses then turned to Aaron. The conversation was in many ways predictable. First Moses accused Aaron of bringing a **great sin** upon the nation (32:21b). There is a subtle indication that Moses considered Aaron's actions even more egregious than that of the people: **What did this people do to you that you have** done this to them? (32:21a; in effect, Moses said, "Aaron, you could not have done more harm to the people if you meant to do it!"). Aaron's response was threefold (and again predictable). To start with he blamed the people (32:22-23a), claiming that they were the ones who demanded a god be made. In fact, the specific charges Aaron made about the people, that they were **prone to evil** (32:22c) and that they were making unrighteous demands (32:23a), should have been the exact reasons for Aaron *not* to give them what they were asking for. Second, Aaron suggested that the cause of the people's angst was Moses' delay (32:23b), thereby subtly suggesting that in a sense it was Moses' fault. Finally, he offered the preposterous suggestion that the idol was self-generated and therefore, miraculous—the spontaneous result from tossing the gold he had collected into the fire (**I threw it into the fire and out came this calf**, 32:24). So he was saying in effect, "I didn't make it! It made itself!" (One wonders if such reasoning by a youthful Aaron had worked with his mother Jochebed?)

These rationalizations are so transparently bad and implausible that Moses did not even bother to refute them. Aaron stood condemned by his own foolish excuses. He is a profile in failed leadership, for a leader fails when he blames others and suggests events are just out of his control.

(4) A Harsh Division (32:25-29)

32:25-29. Moses then acted to separate the true infidels from those who had merely been "led astray." At this point the situation was completely chaotic (32:25); the people had cast off all restraint and they were **out of control** (32:25; the term [*pr*'] is used twice). This term has the idea of "loosening" or "uncovering." This chaos would have been a cause for ridicule had the enemies of Israel witnessed it (32:25c). Moses called out from **the gate of the camp**, a place where he could make himself heard and seen: **Whoever is for the LORD, come to me** (32:26a; lit., simply "to me!"). This would have stunned the whole camp and brought the celebration to a halt. This would then have given a chance to those who were mere bystanders to the debauchery an opportunity to separate themselves from it. Given the chance to make a "clean break" from the folly, idolatry, and immorality, the **sons of Levi gathered together** (32:26b). Moses' instructions (32:27) to the Levites might seem to some to be rather harsh, even extreme: **Every man of you put his sword upon his thigh . . . and kill every man his brother, and every man his friend, and every man his neighbor**. However, it would seem (considering the actual number struck down was **about three thousand**, 32:28b) that only those who persisted in the idolatry and debauchery were executed. The punishment was severe indeed, but not overly harsh given the crime and the real danger it posed to the fledgling nation. This blatant instance of unfaithfulness and idolatry required swift and definite punishment for the sake of the nation's purity before the Lord and its future devotion to the Lord. And yet, even though it was just and necessary, it would have been difficult for the Levites to carry out, for these were fellow Israelites, not enemies. They were brothers and friends (32:27b).

Nevertheless, they knew it had to be done. In this work, in this clash between truth and error, there was no neutrality; there could be no halfway covenant. Idolatry, especially of such a brazen nature, simply could not be tolerated. Idolaters had to be cut off (cf. Ex 22:20; Dt 7) to preserve the nation as the people of God, separate and distinct. The action was no doubt bloody and heartbreaking; it took "dedicated men" (32:29a) and yet it yielded a **blessing** for those men who undertook it (32:29b).

Summary. There is no doubt that the incident of the golden calf drove a wedge between the nation and the Lord. Such unfaithfulness is bound to have a lasting impact; the loss of trust, the pain of a broken promise, the sense of emotional distance that inevitably comes with infidelity and unfaithfulness was now a part of God's relationship with these people. How could the Lord keep to His intention to dwell with such people? He could not be close to them when they were so prone to be fickle toward Him (cf. 33:5). As He had done before (e.g., Enoch, Noah, Abraham) and would do again (e.g., Samuel, David, Solomon, Hezekiah, Josiah), God narrowed His focus to one man. His purpose to dwell with them that they may dwell with Him must be accomplished without violation to His righteous holiness and without the need for harsh measures whenever they prove unfaithful by dwelling in intimate communion with one man, Moses.

In the next section of the exodus experience, we can see Moses taking on two roles. He became the intercessor for Israel, and at the same time the intimate companion of the Lord.

2. Five Scenes of Intercession and Intimacy, Moses and the Lord (32:30–33:23)

a. Scene One: A Selfless Offer (32:30-35)

32:30-35. In this scene Moses offered himself for the sins of the people; but the Lord informed him that people must suffer for their own sins. This is one of the most selfless prayers ever uttered (cf. Rm 9:1-3). "So moved was Moses in his appeal to God that he did not complete the conditional sentence recorded in v. 32" (Davis, *Moses and the Gods*, 301). In effect he prayed, "If You will forgive their sin, then . . . I would be content. But if You do not then . . . ." Moses' distress is so great he asks God to **blot me out from Your book which You have written** (v. 32b). This book referred to here may be the same as that referred to in Ps 69:28, the "book of life." It apparently refers to a book or record in heaven ("a celestial book," Hamilton, *Exodus*, 555) that identifies those who are recipients of the Lord's favor (cf. Is 34:16; Dn 12:1; Mal 3:16; cf. Php 4:3; Rv 3:5; 20:12, 15; 21:27). In a display of utter selflessness and self-sacrifice Moses offered to give up his place in this book, including the promise of blessing, in exchange for God's favor for the people (cf. Rm 9:3). But the Lord refused and reaffirmed the principle, "the person who sins is accountable for his own sin (Deut 24:16; Ezek 18:4, 13, 17)" (Kaiser, "Exodus," 481).

b. Scene Two: A Hopeful and Sorrowful Word (33:1-6)

33:1-6. This scene depicts a classic good news/bad news revelation from the Lord. In the good news God reaffirmed His intention to keep His promise to the patriarchs. The land would be theirs (33:1-3a). However, the bad news was He would not be with them on this journey in the way they had envisioned (33:3b, 5a). The reason given was that if He were present with them and they lapsed once again He would be forced to **destroy** them (33:5a). This bad news was indeed depressing (33:4a). They were instructed to remove (**put off**) their **ornaments** (33:5b-6). Perhaps after they had stripped off their gold rings for the folly of the golden calf they had made other ornaments to hide that they had given up their precious personal possessions. Now they would become bare-fingered and vacant-eared (no finger rings, no earrings). The absence of these items would be a sad reminder of what they had lost, not merely physically but more importantly, spiritually—of their relative lack of the presence of God.

c. Scene Three: A Separate Arrangement (33:7-11)

33:7-11. This scene describes how Moses and the Lord conducted their intimate conversations, no doubt before the arrangement before the tabernacle was complete. The tent of meeting in these verses should be distinguished from the tabernacle itself. While the phrase *tent of meeting* is used later for the tabernacle, this **tent of meeting** was a temporary tent **outside the camp** (33:7) used only by Moses (whereas the tabernacle was to be used by Aaron and the Aaronic priests). The cloud of God's presence came to and departed from this tent depending on Moses' presence in the tent (whereas the presence of God in the tabernacle, once established, was constant). It seems this was a provisional and temporary **tent of meeting** set up to assure the necessary communication between the Lord and the nation until the tabernacle was completed.

This arrangement made it possible for the Lord to be present enough to continue to guide the nation while He was not in their midst (cf.

33:3). A dramatic sign made it evident when the Lord was talking to Moses: when Moses went to the tent the pillar of cloud would **descend and stand at the entrance of the tent** (33:9); this meant that God and Moses were speaking with one another. At such times the people would stand at attention, each at their own individual tents, and **worship** (33:8 and 10). The statement **the Lord used to speak to Moses face to face** (33:11) should not be taken literally since the Lord God is a spirit (cf. Jn 4:24) and has no body, much less a face (see 33:20 below). This is anthropomorphic language, language that communicates some truth about God in His relation to His creatures using human terms. "The fact that the Lord spoke to Moses 'face to face, as a man speaketh to a friend' (33:11a) indicated the warm communication that Moses had with his God. The expression denotes familiar conversation" (Davis, *Moses and the Gods*, 303). This likely refers to *direct* revelation as opposed to dreams and visions (cf. Nm 12:6-8). Significantly, at the close of the Pentateuch, it states that there had not yet been a prophet like Moses with whom the Lord spoke face to face indicating that Israel was to keep looking for such a prophet (see Dt 34:10-12 and comments there). After these sessions **Joshua . . . would not depart from the tent** (33:11b). This may mean that Joshua would attend to Moses in Moses' tent and not leave while Moses needed him.

d. Scene Four: An Intimate Conversation (33:12-17)

33:12-17. This scene features one of the conversations (perhaps representative of many) between Moses and God. "The words of Moses do not reflect arrogant boldness or lack of godly reverence. On the contrary, they represent a confidence in prayer which is only achieved when one is earnestly searching the heart of God" (Davis, *Moses and the Gods*, 304). As Moses considered the task of leading the people he had some concerns to lay before God (33:12a). Moses needed the Lord to reassure him that he, Moses, was truly the man chosen to lead the people. At first Moses appeared to ask the Lord for a helper, **whom You will send with me** (33:12b). God's answer to this was simply **My presence shall go with you** (33:15a). Moses then needed to be reassured that he had the Lord's **favor** (grace). The phrase "found favor in Your sight" (and equivalents) is repeated several times in this exchange (33:12b; 13 [2 times]; 16; 17) and is clearly Moses' main concern. Moses knew that this **favor** (grace) was necessary to know God's name (33:12b), to know God's ways (33:13a), and to be reassured of God's unique relationship with His people (33:16b). Moses asked that this favor be assured to him by a pledge from the Lord that He would grant His **presence** in the impending journey (33:14-15). This the Lord graciously promised to Moses (33:17).

e. Scene Five: A Glorious Encounter (33:18-23)

33:18-23. Moses made the boldest request in all of his intimate conversations with God in this final scene: **I pray You, show me Your glory!** (33:18). God's response showed His willingness to grant Moses' desire, although He tempered it by acknowledging the reality of the distance, metaphysically and morally, between them.

The Lord began by explaining what would happen. Moses would be allowed to see His **goodness**, he would hear a proclamation of **the name of the Lord**, and he would have a demonstration of the Lord's graciousness and compassion (33:19). Also, Moses was informed about what could not happen: **You cannot see My face . . . and live** (33:20). Finally, the Lord explained how Moses would receive this revelation: first Moses was to be given a place of protection in the **cleft of the rock** and covered by the Lord, **My hand** (33:22). Again, this is an example of anthropomorphic language. Precisely what mechanism the Lord used to accomplish this act is not specified. Then the Lord promised that He would pass by with/in His glory: **while My glory is passing by** (33:22). Thus Moses was to be allowed to see the Lord "from behind" (**My back**), but would not be allowed to view Him from the front (**My face shall not be seen**, 33:23). The clear statement of 33:20, **no man can see Me and live** (cf. Jn 1:18; 6:46; 1Tm 1:16-17), seems to be in conflict with other OT instances where individuals are said to have seen God's face or at least seen God (e.g., Hagar, Gn 16:13; Jacob, Gn 32:30; Manoah, Jdg 13; Isaiah, Is 6:1ff.; etc). In many of those instances the appearance is likely a theophany or visible manifestation of God in a form or manner perceptible by human senses. In other instances the expression is meant to convey not physical sight per se but a genuine encounter or relationship with God.

It seems that Moses' encounter transcended those other types of seeing or meeting the Lord, but precisely how is not indicated. Although it might be that Moses saw only the Shekinah glory of God and not the Lord Himself, any speculation as to what really happened is just that, speculation. "What really occurred on Mount Sinai between Moses and God on this occasion will never be fully known. Undoubtedly Moses saw things which the human tongue would be incapable of uttering" (Davis, *Moses and the Gods*, 305; cf. 2Co 12:4).

3. Restoration and Renewal (34:1-35)

Exodus 34 is a bittersweet chapter of restoration and covenant renewal. It is *bitter*-sweet because it was sin in the life of the nation that required this act of restoration and made this ceremony covenant renewal necessary. But it is bitter-*sweet* because the grace of God, His longsuffering, His unwavering commitment to His promises, and His perfections (esp. 34:6-7) are so marvelously evident in these events.

a. Restoration of the Two Tablets (34:1-9)

34:1-9. The restoration process began when the Lord gave His instructions to Moses (34:1-3). Moses had shattered the original two tablets upon his return to the camp when he saw the golden calf (34:1; cf. 32:19). If the relationship between the Lord and His people was to be restored these tablets had to be restored. There is much grace behind the simple words **Now the LORD said to Moses** (34:1a). That the Lord was willing to begin again with these people was itself an act of incalculable grace and mercy. He Himself offered to **write on the tablets the words that were on the former tablets** (34:1b). Significantly, God did not add words or jettison words from the original tablets; the law did not need to be edited in the light of Israel's failure. Rather they needed to be reiterated, to be heard and this time heeded. Once again, Moses was to come up the mountain alone. However, unlike the first time (24:1-18), there is no mention of Aaron, his sons, or the other elders. Once again, reflecting the changed relationship with the people (cf. 33:3-5), God was no longer dealing with the nation through their several representatives but through His one representative—He is dealing with Moses alone.

Dutifully Moses complied and the solemn descent (cf. 32:15-16) was reversed; Moses ascended the mountain once more (34:4; cf. 24:12-15). While that first ascent had been full of joyful anticipation, this ascent must have been full of sad contrition. And yet the word from the Lord was rich with mercy and grace. The record of the Lord giving His revelation to Moses is one of the most amazing paragraphs in Exodus (34:5-7), and several points are noteworthy.

First, the condescension (in the best sense of that term) of the Lord is seen, literally and figuratively, when He comes to stand with Moses **as he called upon the name of the LORD** (34:5c). The Lord had said "Let Me alone" (cf. 32:10), but now He has called Moses to **come up** to Him (v. 2) and now He actually **stood there with him** (34:5), because Moses had called upon Him. Then the Lord **passed by in front of him** (34:6a) to indicate that He was prepared to give Moses a revelation. That revelation consisted of His Name and His attributes: the Name, **The LORD, the LORD God** was meant to remind Moses and the nation of His "memorial" and covenant name (cf. 3:14, 15). This was the Lord—the God who makes promises and keeps them.

The attributes and perfections—being benevolent, **compassionate and gracious, slow to anger and abounding in lovingkindness** [*chesed*, "permanent, covenantal love"] **and truth** (34:6b)—all were attributes vital to the blessing and preservation of this nation. "Everything the Lord says autobiographically is something God is or does for the benefit of others, especially His chosen people" (Hamilton, *Exodus*, 576). The attributes of His justice and righteousness, **lovingkindness**, forgiveness, and judgment (34:7) are meant to reassure and warn the people. He shows His lovingkindness to thousands, but **He will by no means leave the guilty unpunished** (34:7b). This refers to His distributive justice, that is, His dispensing of both rewards and punishments (cf. Is 3:10; Rm 2:6; 1Pt 1:17; cf. Paul Enns, *Moody Handbook of Theology*, rev. ed. [Chicago: Moody] 200) as well as His retributive justice, that is, the "expression of Divine wrath in which God punishes the wicked" (Enns, *Handbook of Theology*, 200; cf. Gn 2:17; Dt 27:26; Gl 3:10; Rm 6:23). These attributes reflect the balance of justice and benevolence; He is a God of justice but He is also very much a God of compassion. Going forward God's people were not to presume on the latter by being reminded of the former. They should not think lightly of His wrath but they should not expect anything less than lovingkindness (cf. 20:5, 6). For Paul's use of this episode, see the comments on Rm 9:14-16.

The only appropriate response to this revelation is worship; Moses worshiped (34:8) and interceded (34:9). Again, it is Moses who is the single representative of the people; as such his request is personal: **If now I have found favor in Your sight** (v. 9a). The people are not deserving, but for the sake of God's servant, Moses asks for three blessings. He asks for the Lord's presence **in our midst**, for **pardon** for their **iniquity** and **sin**, and that He might again take the people for His **own possession** (34:9b).

b. Renewal of the Covenant (34:10-26)

34:10-26. The Lord now spoke directly to the people and in such a way to show that He answered Moses' prayer. He began by revealing His intention to make or renew the covenant (34:10a).

Two concerns relative to the conquest of the land were noted. First, the Lord promised to **perform miracles** designed to amaze the inhabitants of the land; these miracles would be unusual (**which have not been produced in all the earth**), they would be widely visible (**all the people . . . will see**), and they would produce dread (**it is a fearful thing**) (34:10). Second, the Lord promised to **drive out** the nations that inhabit the land (34:11). He admonished and warned the people concerning several matters: they were **to make no covenant** (treaty) **with the inhabitants of the land**. Rather, they were **to tear down their altars and smash their sacred pillars** (34:11-13). No compromise with the inhabitants was to be considered or allowed. And moreover they were not to **worship any other god** (34:11-14a). The reason for this last admonition is given: the Lord's name is **Jealous** (34:14b). This was an unusual self-designation by the Lord. Of course, no negative connotations of "overly possessive selfishness" are to be attached to this. To say He is **a jealous God** means He is "justly protective of both His own honor and the proper and fitting devotion of His people." Total separation from the inhabitants is commanded to prevent assimilation to their pagan ways of behavior and thinking. A **covenant** with the inhabitants would lead to participation in their worship (**play the harlot . . . sacrifice to their gods**) which in turn would lead to intermarriage (34:15-16). The syncretism that led to the golden calf must be avoided totally (34:17).

The Lord's covenant stipulations (34:18-26) are somewhat repetitive and are intended to be a summary of the previous stipulations in the book of the Covenant (cf. chaps. 21 through 23). However, this "shorter list" is not meant to indicate that a "reduced" version of the stipulations has replaced the book of the Covenant; it was a summary way of saying that all of those stipulations are still in force. It may be significant that there is no mention of the people making a profession of obedience (cf. 24:3, 7); this time the covenant is all of the Lord.

c. Summary and Transition (34:27-28)

34:27-28. Once again, (cf. 24:4) Moses was commanded to record the words of the covenant (34:27); these words were not to be forgotten or ignored but lived. Verse 28 is a transitional verse noting the time, conditions, and purpose of Moses' sojourn on the mountain.

d. Epilogue: Moses' Face Shines (34:29-35)

34:29-35. After Moses had spent another forty-day and forty-night sojourn on the mountain re-receiving the tablets and the stipulations of the covenant, he returned to the sons of Israel. Apparently, Moses was unaware that his face was shining because he had been in the glorious presence of the Lord **speaking with Him** (v. 29). "The radiance of Moses' face was a reflection of divine glory (2Co 3:7)" (Davis, *Moses and the Gods*, 308). This otherworldly manifestation frightened **Aaron and all the sons of Israel** and they were afraid to approach him (34:30). After he called to them (and no doubt reassured them that all was well with him), he **commanded them to do everything the LORD had spoken to him on Mount Sinai** (vv. 31-32). This manifestation could have been distracting to some people and disconcerting to others. Some may have found it intimidating; others may have found it perplexing that the glory faded after some time. Thus Moses chose to wear a veil that he would don on all occasions except "when he was alone with God either in the temporary tent of meeting or in the tabernacle" or "when he had a message for the people from God" (Davis, *Moses and the Gods*, 308). See the application of this manifestation by the apostle Paul in 2Co 3:13.

I. The Instructions for the Tabernacle Are Repeated (35:1–39:43)

These five chapters repeat the Lord's instructions to Moses. Here Moses told the **congregation** to perform the work just as God had commanded: **These are the things the LORD has commanded you to do** (35:1). Several reasons or purposes may be suggested for this repetition. For one thing, the repetition is not exact. In chaps. 25–31 the text emphasizes the word of the Lord. He is personally giving the instructions and the emphasis is on the planning. However, in chaps. 35–40 the text emphasizes the accomplishment of the people and workers. And the record of the actual construction (36:8; 39:31) placed the emphasis on not just *what* was to be done but that it *was indeed* done—complete and finished— and on the ones (artisans and builders) who did it. In these verses the words **he made** (and similar terms) are repeated over and over in order to make the point that the items did not just "appear out of thin air"; they were made by skilled dedicated workers.

Also, the repetition "draws attention to the faithfulness of Moses in transmitting accurately the message God gave him to deliver to his people" (Hamilton, *Exodus*, 611). The action is put into the past tense. The work that had been envisioned by the Lord and revealed to Moses was being done, and was actually completed. Beginning in 39:1 the point was driven home that the construction was completed and the structure erected **just as the LORD had commanded Moses** (39:1, 5, 7, 21, 26, 29, 31, 32, 42, 43; 40:19, 21, 23, 25, 27, 29, 32).

Of course, another major point to be made by the repetition is that the debacle of the golden calf (chaps. 32–34) did not ultimately put an end to the grand project of the tabernacle.

1. The Sabbath Reminder (35:1-3)

See comments on 31:12-17.

2. The Contributions (35:4-9)

See comments on 25:1ff.

3. The Workmen and Their Work (35:10-19)

See comments on 26:1-30 and 31:1-11.

4. The Workmen and the Contributions (35:20–36:7)

Once again the emphasis is on the willingness of the people to give and labor for the work, **everyone whose heart stirred and everyone whose spirit moved him** (35:21; cf. 35:22, 29). See comments on 25:1-9.

5. The Construction Continued (36:8–37:29)

See comments on 26:1-30, 31-37.

a. The Curtains, the Boards, the Veil and Screen (36:8-38)

See comments on 26:1-37.

b. The Ark, the Mercy Seat, the Table, the Lampstand, the Altar of Incense (37:1-29)

See comments on 25:10-40; 30:1-10.

6. The Bronze Altar, the Laver, the Courtyard (38:1-20)

See comments on 27:1-20; 30:1-17.

7. The Inventory (38:21–39:1)

See comments on 25:1ff.

8. The Priestly Garments: Ephod, Breastpiece, Robe, Tunics, Turban (39:2-31)

See comments on 28:2-43.

9. Summary: Tabernacle Completed (39:32-43)

39:32-43. Kaiser suggests that this final statement, **all the work of the tabernacle of the tent of meeting was completed** (39:32), "is reminiscent of Genesis 2:1-2, the concluding words of the creation account" (Kaiser, "Exodus," 495). This again emphasizes that the tabernacle was a "finished project." Furthermore, the summary list of the parts was intended to emphasize that it was indeed complete. No parts were missing. And again, it is emphasized that the work was done just as **the Lord had commanded Moses** (39:32, 42, 43).

J. The Construction and Erection of the Tabernacle (40:1-33)

40:1-33. The tabernacle was completed and erected **in the first month of the second year, on the first day of the month** (40:17). This was about one year from the time the nation had arrived at Sinai. All that time they had devoted themselves to this project. The tent was set up (40:18-19); the ark was brought in, the mercy seat was installed (40:20-21); the furniture was put in place (40:22-30). All the now familiar items are mentioned here, as a summary, as a final checklist. Quite literally everything was falling into place; then Moses and Aaron and the priests washed (40:31-32), and they looked around and it was all there and it was finished (40:33). Moses had finished the tabernacle, a vehicle to show the value of having "atonement." By contrast, Jesus actually provided atonement (Jn 19:30).

K. The Occupation of the Tabernacle (40:34-38)

40:34-38. The grand culmination of the work is reached when the cloud of the glory of the Lord **covered** then **settled on** the tent and finally **filled the tabernacle**. This would have been a thrilling climax and a deeply satisfying moment for the leaders, the skilled workers, and all the people who had made contributions. The work was not only complete but by this manifestation it was clear that God was pleased with the final product. Hamilton observes that in a way the tabernacle "relocates the Mount of Sinai experience. The God whose presence has shrouded the top of Mount Sinai, far away from the Israelites at the base, will now dwell in the midst of His people, at the center of their encampment. The transcendent One becomes the incarnate One [and yet] He remains, to use something of an oxymoron, an out-of-sight Immanuel" (Hamilton, *Exodus*, 451).

The intensity of the phenomenon is evident in that even **Moses was not able to enter the tent of meeting** (40:35).

This phenomenon became the means to let the people know it was time to move, **whenever the cloud was taken up** (40:36; cf. Nm 10:11) and conversely was the sign that He desired the people to remain where they were. This phenomenon followed the pattern of the previous manifestation of the divine presence and protection, the pillar of cloud and fire (13:21). It was not literal fire that the people saw inside the tabernacle (40:38) but the brilliance of the glory of the Lord.

The book ends looking forward. The tabernacle is finished but it was designed to move and this nation needed to be on its way to the land of promise.

BIBLIOGRAPHY

Cole, R. Alan. *Exodus*. Tyndale Old Testament Commentaries. Downers Grove, IL: InterVarsity, 1973.

Davis, John J. *Moses and the Gods of Egypt: Studies In Exodus*. Winona Lake, IN: BMH Books, 1986.

Hamilton, Victor P. *Exodus: An Exegetical Commentary*. Grand Rapids, MI: Baker, 2011.

Kaiser, Jr., Walter C. *Exodus*. Vol. 2 of The Expositors Bible Commentary, ed. by Frank E. Gaebelein, 287–497. Grand Rapids, MI: Zondervan, 1990.

Motyer, Alec. *The Message of Exodus*. The Bible Speaks Today. Downers Grove, IL: InterVarsity, 2005.

Sailhamer, John H. *The Pentateuch as Narrative*. Grand Rapids, MI: Zondervan, 1992.

Stuart, Douglas K. *Exodus*. The New American Commentary. Nashville: Broadman & Holman, 2006.

Youngblood, Ronald F. *Exodus*. Everyman Bible Commentary. Chicago: Moody, 1983.

LEVITICUS

JOHN JELINEK

INTRODUCTION

Author. Since general questions about the authorship of the Pentateuch are addressed elsewhere in this volume (see the introduction to Genesis), this section addresses corollary supporting information found in Leviticus itself. The substance of the book is the direct speech of God with Moses ("the LORD called to Moses," 1:1), revealed over some span within the forty days (cf. Ex 40:17 with Nm 1:1) when the people were near Mount Sinai. The book repeatedly designates Moses as the recipient of the Lord's words (e.g., 1:1; 4:1; 6:1, 8, 19, 24; 7:22, 28; 8:1). If there were a red-letter edition of the Bible in which God's speech in the OT directed to an individual or individuals was highlighted, nearly all of Leviticus would be in red. In this sense God is the Author of Leviticus and Moses recorded the inspired revelation as he received it from the Lord.

Date. With the exception of Jerome and later Ibn Ezra (12th century) and Andreas Carlstadt (Luther's rival), few challenged the Mosaic authorship of the Pentateuch before the 19th century (for examples, see G. Herbert Livingstone, *The Pentateuch in its Cultural Environment* [Grand Rapids, MI: Baker, 1974], 220–21). Arguments for the documentary hypothesis and its atomistic and evolutionary approach to texts that arose in the 19th century are not justified in an impartial reading of the books. As Allen Ross has observed,

> Whatever one thinks about the formation of the Pentateuch, it is clear that Leviticus cannot be isolated from its present setting in the Pentateuch. Its teachings assume the reality of the sanctuary with all of its furnishings (recorded in Ex 25–31) and the existence of that sanctuary assumes the reality of the covenant itself. That covenant was made with promises to the fathers. . . . All the legal and cultic instructions that follow form the content of the covenant, providing the details for the worship and service of the covenant people (*Holiness to the Lord: A Guide to the Exposition of Leviticus* [Grand Rapids, MI: Baker, 2002], 19).

The content of Leviticus with the rituals and purity rites fits with what is known of other cultures in the same period. Julius Wellhausen advocated that the language in Leviticus is later than that of Exodus. But linguistic analysis and intertextual studies have raised doubts as to the validity of this theory (A. Hurvitz, "Linguistic Criteria for Dating Problematic Biblical Texts," *Hebrew Abstracts* 14 [1973], 74–79, and Mark Rooker, *Biblical Hebrew in Transition: The Language of the Book of Ezekiel* [New York: Continuum, 1990], 54–64). In sum, there are compelling reasons to consider Moses as the author of Leviticus as well as the entire Pentateuch, and therefore to date the composition 1440–1420 BC (see the introduction to Genesis for a discussion of the Documentary Hypothesis).

Purpose. Soon after God delivered His people from Egypt He gave Moses numerous instructions for Israel, including many details on how they could access His presence for fellowship and worship. Leviticus explains the role of worship in the nation of Israel. When Moses told Pharaoh that God required His people to sacrifice to Him and thus acknowledge His higher authority over them (cf. Ex 3:18; 5:3), God had these prescriptions for worship in mind. Whereas many read the book as a litany of outdated rituals pertaining to an alien and bygone era, when properly interpreted, it is vitally instructive on how to approach God in worship.

Some might wrongly conclude that nothing of value can be derived from the outdated rituals of the emerging nation of Israel. Does not Jesus' death on the cross eliminate the need for animal sacrifices? Is not Leviticus outdated with its bloody rituals that have no bearing on the present day? Yet Paul wrote that all Scripture is profitable (2Tm 3:16-17). After all, Leviticus was written in the context of the struggling nation of Israel and its departure from Egypt. It had relevance then, as now, in that God's law was given to address the kinds of daily situations the people would encounter en route to and within the promised land.

Contribution. Why is this book here? What relevance does it have to anyone reading it today? Leviticus gives a deepened understanding of the holiness of God to a people who were not fully acquainted with His character. One should study Leviticus for these five reasons.

First, proper interpretation of the book will deepen one's understanding of the nature of sin as an offense before the holy God. The book deals repeatedly with the obstacle of man's sin and fallen condition. Sin is presented as affecting man's experience in several ways.

First, sin excludes man from nearness to God (sacred space is to be maintained in order to accommodate the distance sin creates between men and God). Leviticus thus assists in rounding out the revelation of the nature of God that He personally revealed to the patriarchs in Genesis, to Moses, and to the nation in Exodus (showing the extent and excellencies of His holiness in liberating them from bondage in keeping with His promises to Abraham). Also, the tabernacle was the observable display of the Lord among His people. The establishment of His covenant with them at Mount Sinai had marked that spot as holy—a place where the Israelites had encountered the divine. But the mountain was not the permanent residence of God's people. How then could they retain the holiness and the sanctity of this location after they left? The layout and rituals assigned to the tabernacle answer this problem (James K. Hoffmeier, *Ancient Israel in Sinai* [New York: Oxford University Press, 2005], 201–2). Though small in comparison to Mount Sinai, the tabernacle was portable and, more importantly, it was designed by the Lord Himself. There the encounter with the divine could take place on a regular basis. It would house, as it were, the holiness of the Mount Sinai experience and the very presence of the Lord as Israel traveled to the promised land.

Second, sin excludes humanity from having a true knowledge of God (it prevents proper perceptions and application of truth that honors God).

Third, sin excludes humanity from communion or fellowship with God, the Creator. God's relationship with sinners is assumed throughout the book, including their need for reconciliation to Him.

Second, exploring atonement symbolism will expand one's understanding of the nature of the redemption God provides for sinners. The way to redemption is highlighted wherever there is substitution in the worship rituals. One life or one thing is presented in place of another. Substitution implies humanity's guilt, the need for atonement, and the need for propitiation (satisfaction of the divine wrath against sin). Further, in God's plan for redemption there is imputation, the transference of guilt from the guilty party to another through substitution. Then there is death. Sacrifice requires the death of the substitute (i.e., unblemished animals). The redemption God has provided is based on His righteousness and the satisfaction of that righteousness, not His pity. God's redemption is possible only through the blood of innocent victims (cf. Heb 9:22). Redemption is intended to produce holiness. God's redemption does not excuse people from the need to be holy and distinct in their behavior.

The animal and grain sacrifices of the OT were symbolic of the way the Lord extended His justice tempered by His mercy to sinful people. When Israel was enslaved in Egypt, their God distinguished Himself from the Egyptian gods as the God of redemption. The God who revealed these rituals for His people is the same God with whom people are to relate today. Learning about the rituals points to the character of the God behind them. He is a redeeming God who, though unseen by human eyes, desires interaction between Himself and His people. Involvement with the God of Israel focuses on sacrificial prayer, praise, and giving. These same relational and redemptive elements are found in Israel's legislation and its symbolism. The God who brought Israel out of bondage to slavery still redeems His chosen ones from slavery. Believers today hear His call to be a "holy nation" (1Pt 2:9, though the Church is not the new Israel) and will be brought into His dwelling place at the end (Rv 21:3).

Third, one will grasp more deeply God's desire to dwell in holiness with a holy people and grow in appreciation of the incarnation of Christ. One of the things humanity learns about God in reading the Pentateuch is that the world is in the state it is in because people are out of fellowship with the holy God. God created humanity for fellowship with Him and even created a place, Eden, where humanity could live in fellowship with Him. Eden was a "sacred space," as John Walton has called it (*Old Testament Today: A Journey from Original Meaning to Contemporary Significance* [Grand Rapids, MI: Zondervan, 2004], 122–24). Leviticus gives a glimpse not only of what was lost when Adam sinned, but also a sense of the measures that must be taken to restore a temporal, earthly sacred space. As such, it is vitally instructive for one's attempts to worship God today. Further, it foreshadows the act of Messiah taking on human flesh to tabernacle among mankind (cf. Jn 1:14).

Fourth, comprehending the sacrificial system can assist in evangelism, for it portends the Messiah's ultimate and final sacrifice for sin. The sacrifices serve as illustrations or life lessons that depict the richness of the ultimate sacrifice of Jesus Christ. No singular sacrifice prefigures all that was accomplished at the death of Jesus, but collectively there is a richness and a fullness that point distinctly forward to that event. Someone reading a textbook on the anatomy and physiology of sharks, but who has never seen a shark, has a wholly different appreciation of sharks than the one who has seen sharks at an aquarium. The one who has not only seen sharks, but has swum with sharks, has an even greater appreciation than one who merely casually observes them from a distance at an aquarium. The textbook presents the "shadows" of shark existence, but an encounter with a shark is the "substance." Similarly, one can appreciate salvation without reading all of Leviticus, but to understand Jesus Christ's sacrifice in its fullness one must understand what the Father did in bringing His Son to that moment on the cross that effected our salvation. The picture of God as found in Leviticus prepares believers for a fuller understanding of the final sacrifice of Jesus, and it can help explain why the death of Christ was needed to expiate (remove the guilt of) sin and propitiate (turn away) God's just anger against sin.

Fifth, through Leviticus readers gain a deeper understanding of the meaning of certain Old and New Testament passages (particularly in Romans and Hebrews). Leviticus provides a framework for understanding the millennial sacrifices (Ezk 40–48). Many NT texts are better understood against the background that Leviticus provides (e.g., Paul being "poured out as a drink offering," Php 2:17). The finality of the offering of Christ as presented in Hebrews assumes a knowledge of Leviticus (cf. Heb 7:26-28; 9:12, 26, 28).

The Lord's desire to maintain His presence in the midst of His people prompted the record that is known as Leviticus. What that record teaches about His character is still relevant and instructional today.

Background. The events of the book of Leviticus occurred during Israel's exodus from Egypt to Canaan in an approximately one-month period between Ex 40:17 and Nm 1:1. Exodus 40 states that God's instructions for erecting the tabernacle in the wilderness were completed "and the glory of the LORD filled the tabernacle" (v. 34). On a larger scale the whole of Leviticus is encompassed by the narrative of the treaty between God and His people at Mount Sinai, extending from Ex 19 through Nm 10 (see David A. Dorsey, *The Literary Structure of the Old Testament* [Grand Rapids, MI: Baker, 1999], 72). In this broader setting the holiness of God forms the theological basis (Ex 19–20) on which the liturgy for worship was built. Leviticus communicated to God's people the steps necessary to ensure His presence in their midst as they set out for Canaan.

Leviticus records the historical fulfillment of commandments given by God in Ex 29 (the legislation to ordain priests) and Ex 40:1-16 (the command to ordain the tabernacle as a center of worship with its priesthood). Leviticus expands on Ex 40:17-38, which records the partial record of that fulfillment. Leviticus gave the nation of Israel a guide on how to maintain the place where God dwelt with His people and how they would be holy before Him.

As has been noted above, many portions of the Bible make sense only in light of God's instruction in this book. The death of Christ and all that is implied and explicit in the atonement of our Lord finds its origin in the Levitical portrait of the holy God.

In some ways Leviticus can be classified as legal literature with its apodictic (prescribing) and casuistic (if . . . then) elements. Apart from the brief narrative section in chap. 10, the book presents the legislation of Israel's manner of approach to God. Legal literature, however, may seem daunting to the average person, as seen, for example, in an attorney's office with its volumes of technical court cases. The legal literature of Leviticus, however, involves the practical aspect of worship of the one true God. Most contemporary believers do not think of prescriptions for the order of worship because the NT does not prescribe a specific worship form or liturgy. Compared to the freedom and spontaneity with which believers today worship the Lord, the rituals in Leviticus may seem like empty repetition. Yet in Leviticus, the priest, when properly exercising his duties, was looking for far more than just external obedience on the part of worshipers. Without a clear and sustained vision of God's holiness, any act of worship could quickly degenerate into an irreverent routine.

Structure. A popular, two-part approach to Leviticus considers the means by which believers can approach God, and the means by which their approach can be maintained before God. In this light the book may be viewed as having two major parts:

Part 1: The Means of Access to God: Sacrifice (chaps. 1–10).

Part 2: The Walk before God: Sanctification (chaps. 11–27).

However, the book may be more appropriately divided along the lines of chaps. 1–16 and 17–27. If God was to dwell among His people according to His revealed purpose at Sinai (cf. Ex 25:8; 33:17) and in keeping with Moses' petition for the Lord's very presence to accompany the nation (cf. Ex 33:15-16), then "sacred space" must first be created (establishment of the tabernacle, Ex 40:1-33; Lv 1–16) and a national holiness and purity must be maintained (Lv 17–27) (Richard Averbeck, "Sacred Space and Sacred Community in the Old Testament and the New Testament," paper read at the Evangelical Theological Society Annual Meeting, Danvers, MA, November 18, 1999.)

Leviticus 16 is the theological center of the book. On the Day of Atonement, the holiness of the tabernacle *and* the holiness of the nation are central. Thirteen times in chap. 16 the word "atonement" is used in referring to the result of the five varied sacrifices performed on that day. Two blood atonements were made on behalf of the priests and the people (vv. 3, 5); a scapegoat offering was made on behalf of the entire congregation (vv. 20-22); and two burnt offerings were presented for the priests and the people (vv. 23-24). The point is clear: atonement for sin is required in order to maintain a "space" in which God may dwell with His people. These rituals not only cleansed the tabernacle of God's dwelling with blood (vv. 32-33, referring back to vv. 11-19), but they also cleansed the people (vv. 29-31), making them fit for His inhabitation as well.

OUTLINE

I. Divine Instruction Ensuring a Sanctified Dwelling Prepared for the Lord's Presence among His People (1:1–16:34)
 A. God's Holiness Must Be Maintained by Those Who Secure His Dwelling through Presentation of Appropriate Sacrifices and Offerings (1:1–7:38)
  1. The Law of the Whole Burnt Offering: an Offering Conveying God's Wrath against Sin and a Worshiper's Acceptance by God (1:1-17)
  2. The Law of the Grain Offering: an Offering Conveying a Believer's Recognition of the True Source of His Life as Found in God (2:1-16)
  3. The Law of the Peace Offering: a Community Celebration of a Believer's Peace with God and the Communion Available between God and Man (3:1-17)
  4. The Law of the Sin Offering: an Offering Presented for an Individual's Unintentional Sin (4:1–5:13)
   a. Rituals to Atone for Unintentional Sin (4:1-35)
    (1) The Purification Offering for the High Priest (4:3-12)
    (2) The Purification Offering for the Congregation (4:13-21)
    (3) The Purification Offerings for Leaders and Commoners (4:22-35)
   b. Illustrations of Offenses Requiring the Sin Offering (5:1-6)
   c. Concessions for the Poor in the Sin Offering (5:7-13)
  5. The Law of the Reparation Offering: an Offering Presented When Making Amends for Unwittingly Defrauding God or Man (5:14–6:7)
   a. Abusing the Lord's Property Unwittingly (5:14-19)

- b. Abusing Man's Property and the Lord's Name (6:1-7)
- 6. Additional Priestly Administrative Instructions Pertaining to the Sacrifices (6:8–7:38)
  - a. In the Ritual of the Whole Burnt Offering, the Priest's Actions and Dress Convey the Availability of Access to an Ever-Present God through an Ever-Available Atonement (6:8-13)
  - b. In the Ritual of the Grain Offering of the Common Person, the Priest's Actions Should Express God's Acceptance of Offerings Presented in Faith (6:14-18)
  - c. In the Ritual of the Grain Offering of the Priest, the Priest Was Expected to Demonstrate His Own Devotion to the Lord (6:19-23)
  - d. In the Ritual of the Sin Offering of the Priest, the Priest Was Expected to Demonstrate His Awareness of the Seriousness of Sin before God (6:24-30)
  - e. In the Ritual of the Reparation Offering, the Priest Reinforced Confession and Repentance of Sin (7:1-10)
  - f. In the Administration of the Peace Offering and Its Variant Forms, the Priest Ensured the Integrity of the Offering by Instructing Laypersons concerning the Proper Consumption of the Offerings (7:11-21)
  - g. The Priests Ensured the Layperson's Knowledge of the Lord's Right to the Fat and the Blood (7:22-27)
  - h. Through Proper Handling and Consumption of Dedicated Portions of the Peace Offering the Priests Conveyed Reverence for God (7:28-38)
- B. Those Ordained to Present Offerings, and the Land and People They Represent, Must Demonstrate the Holiness of the Lord in Their Midst by Ensuring That All That Enters the Lord's Presence Is Itself Holy (8:1–16:34)
  - 1. God's Holiness Must Be Maintained by Those Who Secure His Dwelling through the Consecration and Presentation of Themselves in Unique Holiness (8:1–10:20)
    - a. The Consecration of the Levitical Priests (8:1-36)
    - b. The Inauguration of the Tabernacle Worship (9:1-24)
    - c. Violation of God's Holiness and the Resultant Statutes Pertaining to Priestly Tabernacle Duties: Nadab and Abihu Offer Strange Fire (10:1-20)
  - 2. God's Holiness Must Be Maintained by His People in Their Presentation of Themselves and All That They Own and Do in Unique Holiness (11:1–15:33)
    - a. God's People Distinguish Themselves as His People in What They Regard as Clean and Unclean, Consuming Only That Which God Has Prescribed (11:1-47)
    - b. God's People Distinguish Themselves as His among All People by Virtue of Their Respect for Blood That Enters His Holy Presence (12:1-8)
    - c. God's People Distinguish Themselves as His Unique People in the Ways in Which They Deal with Disease and Contamination (13:1–14:57)
    - d. God's People Distinguish Themselves as His Unique People in the Ways in Which They Seek to Honor God with Their Stewardship of Their Bodies (15:1-33)
  - 3. God's Holiness Requires a Particular Day of Atonement on the Part of His People and Priests (16:1-34)
- II. Divine Instruction Ensuring the Preservation of a Holy Land and a Holy People Declaring the Lord's Presence (17:1–27:34)
  - A. Reminders on Sacrificial Offerings: Sacrifice to God Alone, Treat the Blood as Holy, and Approach God in Purity (17:1-16)
  - B. Exhortations toward Community Holiness: God Is To Be Honored in the Sexual, Social, and Ethical Lives of His People, and in His Exclusive Right to Their Worship (18:1–20:27)
    - 1. God Is To Be Honored by a Sanctified Sexuality among His People (18:1-30)
    - 2. God Is To Be Honored by the Sanctified Social and Ethical Practices of His People, and Is To See His Holiness Reflected in Their Lives (19:1-37)

3. God Is To Be Honored by the Exclusive Nature of the Sanctified Worship and Family Practices of His People (20:1-27)

C. Things or Persons That Are Holy (Set Apart) with Instruction to Maintain Their Holiness (21:1–27:34)
   1. Matters Related to the Defilement or Disqualifications of the Priests or the Holy Offerings (21:1–22:33)
      a. Priestly and High Priestly Qualifications (21:1-24)
      b. Rules to Preserve the Holiness of Offerings to the Lord (22:1-33)
   2. Calendric Convocations: Stipulations Ensuring That Israel Sanctifies Time to the Lord (23:1-44)
   3. Things To Be Treated as Holy in the Service of God: Bread, Oil, and the Sanctity of the Divine Name (24:1-23)
   4. The Land As Holy in the Service of God: Regulations for the Sabbath Year and the Year of Jubilee (25:1-55)
   5. The Land as Holy in the Service of God: Experiencing Conditional Covenantal Blessings in the Land and the Consequences of Disobedience to the Lord (26:1-46)
   6. The Holiness of Gifts Offered at the Sanctuary of God and the Regulations That Ensure Proper Dedication to the Lord (27:1-34)

COMMENTARY ON LEVITICUS

I. Divine Instruction Ensuring a Sanctified Dwelling Prepared for the Lord's Presence among His People (1:1–16:34)

The average Israelite who followed Moses out of Egypt may not have had a clear understanding of the nature of the God of Abraham, Isaac, and Jacob. The years of enslavement in Egypt with exposure to the Egyptian pantheon of gods and religious rituals no doubt left many in Israel without a distinct sense of their relationship to God. Israel may not have lacked a monotheistic perspective, but they may have been deficient in their understanding of God and how to approach Him. These deficiencies needed to be corrected by a clear word from God.

The first 16 chapters of Leviticus, therefore, focus on the rituals and circumstances that ensure that God would accompany His people in the wilderness experience and abide with them in the land. God's divine name Yahweh had been revealed to Moses in his mission (cf. Ex 3:14). As Moses reintroduced Israel to her God, the symbolism and theology of access were vital in helping the nation form a concrete and distinct identity from the pagan nations that would surround her in her land. The regulations and rituals of Leviticus codify and thus prescribe the liturgy of the nation's relationship to God. Further, they helped solidify Israel's national identity. What the rituals taught Israel about the nature of God and man is still instructive for believers today. Worship is to be less about what people want than it is about a focus on the worthiness of God. Worship is to be directed to God and it is for Him. Unfortunately, much of worship is based on the assumption that what pleases the worshiper (aesthetically or culturally) must be pleasing to Him. But worship that focuses solely on what people enjoy misses the point as surely as worship that focuses only on traditional and approved forms. Worship should focus on the centrality of God's holiness and on man's need for atonement in order to approach Him and to maintain fellowship with other worshipers. Although worship today may take a variety of forms, one's attitude in worship is basic.

At the center of OT worship are the sacrifices described in Lv 1–7. Of course, this was not the beginning of God's sacrificial system. Adam knew of sacrifice (Gn 3:21), as did Cain and Abel (4:3-4), and Noah (8:20-21). In these sacrifices the worshiper expressed his inferiority to God and unworthiness to approach Him without due recognition of his sin. The sacrifices also acknowledge God's gracious provision for giving worshipers access to Him. By the sincere expression of these rites the worshiper was accepted by God, union with Him was achieved, and guilt was removed. These rites were not displays of magic, as pagans in their contemporary rituals believed. The external action was effective (efficacious) only if the inner convictions and attitudes of the worshiper were right. In other words, the believer's salvation was by grace through faith in God's provision. Without faith it has never been possible to please God, and these rituals reinforced that very teaching.

A. God's Holiness Must Be Maintained by Those Who Secure His Dwelling through Presentation of Appropriate Sacrifices and Offerings (1:1–7:38)

1. The Law of the Whole Burnt Offering: an Offering Conveying God's Wrath against Sin and a Worshiper's Acceptance by God (1:1-17)

The Hebrew name for the book can be translated from the first word, "And He [the Lord] called" (1:1). Leviticus is part of the historical narrative found in Exodus and Numbers (Ex 19:1–Nm 10:10). God's law was given in the context of Israel's encounters with Him. The contents of Leviticus were revealed to Moses during the thirty days between the completion of the tabernacle (one year after the exodus from Egypt, Ex 40) and the first day of the second month of that second year (Nm 1:1). As noted above, Leviticus should be read in close proximity to Ex 34–40. At the outset, Leviticus contains God's requirements for the various sacrificial offerings given to Israel, as seen in the chart below.

1:1-9. God called to Moses (1:1) in this context. The burnt offering was to be a voluntary offering made by a believer as an expression of communion or fellowship with God. This offering was not a private worship act like personal prayer, or the observance of the Passover in which celebrations could be conducted within groups or families. The burnt offering was to be a dedicatory, public witness and testimony that God could be approached (v. 3). As an act of worship made in communion with God, it was instructional to all who observed and participated. The presence of a sinner in

The Laws of Sacrifice

Name	Sacrifice	Procedure	Meaning	Application
Burnt 1:1-17	Cattle, Sheep, Goats, Birds	Offerer—lay on hand and kill animal Priest—sprinkle blood on side of altar, put on fire. Entirely burned	Complete consecration "Offer up in smoke all of it"	Present ourselves as living sacrifices Rm 12:1
Grain 2:1-16	Raw Flour, Cooked Cakes, Roasted New Grain	Flour—labor Oil—anointing Incense—soothing aroma	Acceptable service to God	All our labor should be offered to God as acceptable service Col 3:17
Peace 3:1-17	Cattle, Sheep, Goats	Blood on sides of altar Fat portions burned Meat shared by priests and offerers	Celebration meal (Gratitude/Free Will)	We should celebrate the Lord's Table 1Co 10:16-18
Sin 4:1–5:13	Cattle, Sheep, Goats, Birds	Substitution Identification Death Exchange of Life	Forgiveness by faith in a substitutionary sacrifice	We must receive forgiveness by faith in the substitutionary sacrifice of the Messiah
Guilt 5:14–6:7	Rams	Blood around altar Fat burned	Make restitution to God (5:15-16) or to people (6:4-5)	Be reconciled and make restitution for wrong done Mt 5:23-24

God's sanctuary (and thus the holy presence of God) was possible only on the basis of a substitutionary atonement by blood sacrifice. The book of Leviticus began with a sacrifice that brought together two disparate thoughts: (1) Sin separates man from the holy God, and (2) communion with God is possible only for those who approach Him through an appropriate sacrifice.

That the entire animal was consumed indicated that it was completely received by God (it ascended **in smoke**, v. 9), and it portrayed God's burning wrath against sin. The offering thus symbolized the complete surrender to God by the offerer and God's complete acceptance of the offerer. The animal offered could have no defects at all (vv. 2-3). A male without defects was a costly animal for the worshiper who either raised the animal for himself, or purchased it from a farmer or shepherd. The ability of the offerer to give could affect the type of animal given (vv. 10, 14), but the worshiper must only bring an acceptable animal as his gift. This requirement suggests to NT believers that the Lord desires gifts from them that are costly and call for sacrifice. God desires complete dedication to Him by living sacrifices (Rm 12:1-2).

Having selected an animal according to his means, the worshiper brought it to the tabernacle and laid one **hand on the head of the burnt offering** (v. 4). Laying a hand on the animal symbolized the worshiper's identification with the sacrifice and his transfer of guilt to the animal (cf. 8:14; 16:21; Nm 27:18-20). An Israelite presenting his sacrifice held the animal with one hand and slit its throat with the other. The animal died at his own hands, thereby dramatizing that the spilt blood should have been his own. The expiation or purgation of sin through sacrifice resulted in God's wrath being turned away (cf. Lv 16:16-19). As atonement was made, the relationship between God and man was restored.

God's provision for forgiveness and atonement has always required the shedding of blood (cf. Gn 4:4; Nm 17:11; Heb 9:22). The sacrifices in Leviticus were repetitive, bloody, and in many ways, troubling. Moderns are not used to reading such details about blood. Most people today never see where their meat comes from; it is already packaged and sanitized by the time people purchase it. But animals were the basis of the economy for ancient people, and thus the idea of animal sacrifices was relevant to their spiritual lives.

Messiah is the antitype (fulfillment) of these offerings, as the NT authors make clear. Like the burnt offerings, the death of Christ was complete (cf. Heb 10:5-7). In His final sacrifice there was the complete exhaustion and satisfaction of God's wrath. The emphasis on the unblemished, perfect sacrifice portrays Christ's flawless sacrifice. By this same offering He presents His church spotless (cf. Eph 5:27), a sweet savor to the Father (Lv 1:9). The offering in this way typifies the effectual work of Christ. Those who worship God must still approach Him on the basis of a substitutionary sacrifice.

In Leviticus the Lord made it clear that the offering was not to be made just anywhere, but **before the Lord** (v. 3) at **the tent of meeting** (vv. 3, 5; cf. Dt 12:13-14). To be accepted by God the sacrifice was given publicly. The priests who supervised the offering collected the blood from each sacrificed animal and sprinkled it **on the altar** (v. 5). The blood belonged to God exclusively and was the divine provision for forgiveness. The blood cried out to God that punishment had been exacted through death (cf. Heb 12:24).

The priest was allowed to keep the skin as a source of clothing and income (Lv 7:8). God has always provided for the basic needs of His people in the exercise of individual and corporate worship. Offerings to the Lord through the church today in support of those who minister accomplish this same sacred ministry.

The burnt offering was arranged **on the altar** (1:7) to be completely consumed **by fire** (1:9), thus signifying the complete acceptance of the offering before the Lord. This is the only posture to assume in presenting oneself before God; one must sacrifice to God all he is and has.

The burnt offering was **to make atonement** (1:4). This term for sacrifice means "to appease" or "to ransom" (removing the guilt and thus the need for punishment; cf. Gn 32:20; 2Sm 21:3-4). The rendering of "atone" in Is 6:7 is "taken away." The idea is that to atone means to "remove iniquity." So the purpose of this sacrifice is to "turn away" or "appease" God's judgment on sin. In Ps 78:38 the word is translated "forgive." The point is that no worshiper can approach God without first having his sin and defilement atoned for, turned away, forgiven.

In the burnt offering an unblemished life was taken in the place of the blemished or sinful worshiper. The ritual for this substitution involved the blood of the animal being offered (vv. 5, 11). The lesson is at least threefold. First, to provide God's forgiveness a sacrifice had to include the offering of blood. Second, the blood signifies life (cf. Lv 17:11). The blood (i.e., the life) belonged to God exclusively. It was God's provision for forgiveness. Third, Jesus, as the only way to God, had to offer Himself as a spotless offering with His blood shed (cf. Heb 12:24).

The priest collected the blood from the sacrificed animal in a basin and sprinkled it **around on the altar** (1:5, 11). (For a bird, where the blood would be less, the blood would be allowed to run down the side of the altar.) The offerer then skinned the animal and **cut it into its pieces** (v. 6). The priest put the parts on the altar—the cut-up parts, head, and fat (v. 8)—and the **entrails** and **legs** were washed and then put on the altar (v. 9). Any unclean elements had to be removed before an animal could be used as a spotless substitute. The offering was followed by a meal offering and a drink offering (cf. Nm 6:13-17 [the Nazirite vow]; Nm 15:22-24; also during Pentecost, cf. Lv 23:18).

The overall point made in the imagery of the offering is that God accepted the offering completely as a **soothing aroma** (v. 9), and thus the offerer was accepted as well (provided the sacrifice was given in faith). Jesus Christ fulfills the typology of these sacrifices in that He too was "unblemished" (cf. Heb 7:25-27).

1:10-17. Verse 10 refers to other animals—a **sheep** or one **of the goats**—that could be offered in place of a bull from the herd. This is a common feature in the book. At times the differences in animals accommodate the poor, and at other times the reasons for the differences are not stated.

God allowed worshipers to offer according to their means. If they could not afford an animal from their herd or flock, they could offer a bird (a turtledove or pigeon, v. 14). No one would be unable to approach God because of his poverty. God does not show favoritism in worship to the rich, and neither should believers (cf. Jms 2:5). Even Joseph brought a turtledove offering (cf. Lk 2:24). The birds to be offered were common and could have been snared or otherwise secured by the worshiper. The bird's **crop** and **feathers** were removed (v. 16), and the bird was split by pulling on **its wings** to show its helplessness (v. 17).

Even in the offering of smaller animals God intended a lesson for the Israelites: God allows a substitutionary sacrifice to expiate the distance between Himself and His worshipers (vv. 3, 10, 14). Every worshiper must bring an *acceptable* substitute for sacrifice. To be acceptable it had to be an animal without a blemish. A sacrificial animal could have no defects at all. A bull, sheep, or goat without defect could be a costly, prized animal, one that was hard to give up.

Also, every worshiper must present his offering in unqualified obedience. The sacrifice was a gift, one that was to be completely burned up. The sacrifice was called the *'ola* (one that ascends in smoke, i.e., a whole burnt offering), and the noun *qorban* identified it as a gift. The animal could not be a wild animal. According to Dt 14:5, wild game could be eaten, but not offered in sacrifice because it would be an offering to the Lord that cost nothing, and this was not complete obedience.

The **soothing aroma to the Lord** (v. 13) is an anthropomorphism of an olfactory sensation (v. 13). God did not "smell" the offering, but He was pleased with it. In "smelling" the burning flesh, God wanted the worshiper to know that the aroma signified His acceptance of the gift. Similarly, the death of Christ is called "a sacrifice to God as a fragrant aroma" (Eph 5:2). God was well pleased with Christ's offering.

The whole burnt offering typified the effectual work of Christ that makes the believer acceptable before God. The faith of the believer is pictured by the offerer laying his hand on the sacrifice, an act of identification and appropriation. With the blood being shed, the life was taken away, and so sin was expiated. The worshiper deserves death in the presence of the holy God, but His holiness has been satisfied in the pouring out of His wrath on Christ.

2. The Law of the Grain Offering: an Offering Conveying a Believer's Recognition of the True Source of His Life as Found in God (2:1-16)

Leviticus 2 describes how the meal or grain offering (the only bloodless offering) was to be carefully prepared and then given to the priest for consecration to God. The grain offering could be offered publicly or privately. If it were done publicly, it might be presented in the form of twelve loaves of showbread in the tabernacle, or the sheaf on the day of Pentecost, or the two wave loaves presented at the festivals of Harvest (cf. Lv 23:9-14) and Pentecost (cf. Lv 23:15-22). If privately, the offering could be brought to the tabernacle at any time except with the sin or trespass offerings.

2:1-8. The chapter begins with *nephesh*, the Hebrew word for "life." In the grain offering, as in any offering a believer might present, the believer gave back to God a token of his life to show that he recognized that God was the source of his life. No Israelite believed that he was somehow sustaining God symbolically or physically with his offering. That some OT offerings were called "food offerings" in some translations reflects the human standpoint of the offering.

When these commands were given, the Israelites were in the desert. Grain could not be grown there, and it could be purchased only at some expense and that with difficulty. Thus, the sacrifice of grain was either impossible to do until the nation reached Canaan, or was very difficult. This offering was also a way of relating the seasonal cycles and their productivity (or lack thereof) to the direct hand of the Lord once Israel entered the land. Now that they were no longer to be nomadic shepherds but landholders, their offerings would reflect this change in status under God's blessing. A believer may demonstrate his dedication to the Lord by giving Him a portion of the best of his material goods. The symbolism inherent in the grain offering demonstrated both the worshiper's dedication to God and his gratitude for the Lord's provision. In the same way, God is pleased today when His people demonstrate their dedication to Him by offering a portion of their life goods.

A worshiper at the tabernacle would declare his dedication to the Lord by giving a pure grain offering to the priest that the Lord accepted as a **soothing aroma** (v. 2). Truly dedicated gifts to God were free from impurity so as to reflect personal loyalty to God and His covenants with Israel. Normally the dedication offering consisted of a mixture of grain (grits) or **fine flour**, olive **oil**, and **frankincense** (not just incense). It could be uncooked (v. 2) or cooked grain (vv. 4-7). If baked into loaves, these were either ring-shaped or perforated. Oil in the OT frequently symbolized things set apart for the Lord (e.g., the anointing of the priests; cf. 8:30). Dedication to the Lord and His work required that only the best elements were to be used.

The provision for the priests in the grain offering was made, at least in part, because they were not entitled to land rights in Israel on which to grow grain (v. 3, cf. Nm 8 and 1Co 9:13-14). A grain offering might accompany the burnt or peace offerings, as part of a believer's food gift to the Lord. Just as the priest served as a mediator between the offerer and God, so today Jesus is the mediator through whom God is pleased to accept a believer's offerings (cf. Heb 5:5-10).

But why did the grain offering need to be **unleavened**? Some have suggested that leaven was to be excluded because impurities could arise from fermentation. But why then was wine required in some offerings (e.g., 23:13)? Perhaps it was because leaven was popular in Canaanite sacrificial rites (Am 4:4-5).

2:9-16. The **memorial portion** (v. 9) that was burned by the priest on the altar showed the worshiper that God had accepted his offering (vv. 2, 9). God accepts the offerings of those who are in fellowship with Him. The remainder of the grain offering was for the needs of the priest (cf. 6:14-23). The presence of **salt** (v. 13) in the grain offering may have been symbolic of the covenant relationship between the worshiper and God. Numbers 18:19 and 2Ch 13:5 refer to a "covenant of salt." Although salt (like leaven) appears in judgment contexts (cf. Gn 19:26), it also appears as a positive image in the NT (e.g., "Let your speech always be . . . seasoned with salt," Col 4:6). While leaven is often portrayed as corrupting (e.g., Mt 16:6), salt preserves and purifies. In Ezk 43:24, God said that salt was to be thrown on the millennial burnt offerings. Salt was used symbolically in other covenants of that day in the ancient Near East. Salt then spoke not only of purity, but even more importantly of longevity. Adding salt to the grain offering reminded Israel that the covenant God had made with them was an enduring covenant.

3. The Law of the Peace Offering: a Community Celebration of a Believer's Peace with God and the Communion Available between God and Man (3:1-17)

The **peace** (or fellowship) offering was a voluntarily shared meal in which the offerer celebrated with others that he was at peace with God. (The kinds of peace offerings that could be made are explained in chap. 7.) Then, as now, a believer's celebration of peace with God is based on the shed blood of the substitutionary sacrifice. This was a thank offering for the Lord's deliverance.

3:1-5. Any unblemished, flawless animal from the **herd, whether male or female** (v. 1), or **the flock** (v. 6), or **a goat** (v. 12), could be presented to the priest at the door to the tabernacle. The peace offering served as an OT equivalent to the Lord's Supper, though the communal meal is not mentioned here. Whenever several offerings were made, the peace offering was the final in the sequence to convey that all was well between God and man.

As in the burnt offering (cf. Lv 1:4), the worshiper laid **his hand on the head** of the animal as an act of identification (v. 2). Although no sin or guilt was dealt with in this offering, the person who desired to commune with God identified himself with the sacrificial victim in an act of self-surrender. This is consistent with any approach to the holy God requiring the presence of blood. Also, **the fat** of the offering was specially designated as belonging to the Lord (v. 3). The fat portions (considered the choice portions) of each animal were to be burned in an act of dedication to God.

3:6-11. Once again, the animal being offered for sacrifice had to be without any blemish, and it died at the hands of the offerer (vv. 6-8). The fatty **tail** (v. 9) of certain broad-tailed ancient sheep in Israel could weigh up to 90 pounds. Ancient peoples also prized both the liver and the kidneys (v. 4) as culinary delicacies and regarded them as centers of the emotional life. Some Near Eastern peoples employed the **entrails** (v. 9) of animals or the lobe of the liver in seeking to "divine" the will of the gods, but this sort of paganism was forbidden in Israel. The Israelites, it seems, regarded the liver as the primary seat of life. If an arrow pierced one's liver (cf. Pr 7:23), death would result.

The point of this offering was to signify to the worshiper and everyone present that the best portion of life belongs to God. Such costly sacrifice is worth the price, for pleasing God is the highest value and always the believer's highest good. Those who would celebrate being at peace with God should be surrendered to Him in all that He requires. Worship should signify that kind of surrender not only in words but also in deeds.

3:12-17. Whether the animal came from the herd (cattle, vv. 1-5) or the flock (sheep or goats, vv. 6, 12), God was specific in stating that the animal was to be without defect (3:1) and was to be presented **before the LORD** (vv. 1, 7, 12). No Israelite was allowed to worship God in any way he preferred. He was to follow God's instructions. So today believers are to be obedient to God's revealed will in their worship.

Verse 17 summarizes the chapter. The **perpetual** nature of the command meant that God desired that His people focus on Him exclusively as they celebrated being at peace with Him. Believers today also celebrate the peace they have with God because of Jesus' shed blood. All the **fat** belonged to the Lord, with no exceptions (v. 16). Whereas no concessions were made for the poor to give a bird as in the burnt offering, they would be allowed and even expected to share in the generosity of the fellowship meal.

4. The Law of the Sin Offering: an Offering Presented for an Individual's Unintentional Sin (4:1–5:13)

a. Rituals to Atone for Unintentional Sin (4:1-35)

4:1-2. Once again **the LORD spoke to Moses**, this time in an extended way. God's regulations for the sin offering extend to 5:13 as one long saying from the Lord. John Calvin once wrote that man does not know one one-hundredth of the sin that cleaves to his soul. These verses emphasize that point. Small imperfections, like cavities in teeth, can cause significant problems. Similarly, sin creates problems for humanity that we do not often realize. Because of God's holiness even unintentional sins (sins committed without the person knowing these actions are contrary to God's standards) are sinful and a serious affront to Him. Should the priest (v. 3), the congregation (v. 13), a leader (v. 22), or a common Israelite (v. 27) sin **unintentionally**, he was to make restitution. The sins referred to here were committed unwittingly (lit., "not with a high hand"; cf. Nm 15:27-31).

This offering is traditionally called a "sin offering," but it is actually a purification *from* sin. The purpose of this offering was to purify the place of worship, making it holy to the Lord (R. K. Harrison, *Leviticus: An Introduction and Commentary* [Downers Grove, IL: InterVarsity, 1990], 61). God graciously provides for the sins of His people, even their unintentional sins. The impression created by this situation is that the sin offering was to be presented immediately after an unintentional sin was known. If even unknown sins create a gulf between man and God, then sin obviously must be addressed.

Emphasis in this context was placed upon the sins of Israel's leaders (vv. 3, 22). Sin that arises in leaders often proves pernicious and produces sin in the lives of followers. Early on, God established His pattern of requiring much from those who lead.

The phrase "a soothing aroma to the LORD" occurs frequently in the first three offerings (1:9, 13, 17; 2:2, 9, 12; 3:5, 16), but is rare in the sin offering (only in 4:31). However, the term "atonement" is found only in 1:4 in the first three offerings of Leviticus, but eight times in the verses on the sin offering.

Four individuals or groups are addressed in chap. 4: the anointed (high) priest (vv. 3-12); the congregation of Israel as a whole (vv. 13-21); a leader (vv. 22-26); and a common person (vv. 27-35). The offerer was to lay his hand on the head of the animal as an act of identification and acknowledgement (vv. 4, 15, 24, 29). Sin was to be acknowledged to God before the transgression could be imputed to the substitute. Only then could atonement be made (4:20, 26, 31, 35; 5:6, 10, 13). God forgave the sinner who appealed to Him for atonement on the basis of the blood of a sacrifice that is pleasing to Him. This principle is applied to the death of Christ in 2Co 5:21.

(1) The Purification Offering for the High Priest (4:3-12)

4:3-12. Since the high **priest** served as the people's representative to God, his own guilt from an unintentional sin extended guilt to the people he represented (v. 3). Blood from the sacrificial **bull** was brought into the sanctuary and sprinkled **seven times . . . in front of** the curtain (v. 6) and applied to **the horns of the altar** (v. 7) in the holy place. The fatty portion (v. 8) was offered up **on the altar of burnt offering** (v. 10) in a manner parallel to the peace offering. The carcass of the animal was then burned in a ritually **clean place outside the camp** (v. 12). Portions of the animal that would normally have been given to the priest would now not be his because of his involvement in the offense. By commanding the priest to sprinkle the blood and discard the rest of the animal, God was indicating that blood alone could atone for Israel's sin. Only the blood could cleanse the tabernacle, the priests, the people, and the land from the defilement caused by sin. In the words of the writer to the Hebrews, "without shedding of blood there is no forgiveness" (Heb 9:22).

(2) The Purification Offering for the Congregation (4:13-21)

4:13-21. The ritual sin offering for the congregation as a whole paralleled the ritual for the priest. The sins referred to here were sins of ignorance, carelessness (cf. 5:4), or sin without defiance (lit., "without a high hand"). A young **bull of the herd** (v. 14; "young bull," NIV) was offered rather than its full-grown counterpart, and the elders identified with the bull on behalf of the people (4:15-16). The result was **atonement** and forgiveness of sins (v. 20).

(3) The Purification Offerings for Leaders and Commoners (4:22-35)

4:22-26. In the case of the sin of **a leader** (v. 22), a flawless **male goat** (v. 24) was to be offered. The blood was applied to **the horns of the altar of burnt offering . . . and the rest of its blood** was poured out at the altar's **base**.

4:27-35. The ritual was the same for a common person of the land, though he or she might offer a spotless female goat. All of these rituals reminded God's people that the holy God desired to dwell among a holy people in a holy place.

Sin is offensive to God, requiring death. God requires a pure and costly offering to atone for the sin. All who approach God must have their sin completely removed by means of a substitutionary sacrifice. Unlike the grain offering, no oil or frankincense was included in the sin offering because they were symbols of joy. Truly repentant worshipers acknowledge their sin with remorse rather than joy.

Jesus suffered "outside the camp" both in fulfillment of this lesser purification offering and also in fulfillment of the Day of Atonement offering (Lv 16:27; Heb 13:11).

b. Illustrations of Offenses Requiring the Sin Offering (5:1-6)

In Lv 5:1-13 the topic is still that of the sin offering, but the approach to the topic changes.

5:1-6. These verses cite some examples of intentional and unintentional sins. Verse 1 gives an example of an intentional sin. One who gave false testimony under oath did so in a premeditated fashion. And if he withheld evidence, he violated the law. Thus he must **bear his guilt**. Verses 2-3 suggest how a person might unknowingly come into contact with something **unclean**, and thus become guilty and in need of a sin offering. Specific ways in which a person could become unclean are given in Lv 12–22. Physical cleanliness in the OT was a symbol of spiritual cleanliness. Israel was set apart from her pagan neighbors by keeping God's specifications regarding cleanliness.

Verse 4 includes a case of inadvertent sin in one's speech. Yet minor sins are still sins. Just because they become evident later does not negate their reality. Persons who are irresponsible in their speech are guilty of sin. Anyone who carelessly made an oath brought guilt on himself. Moses was eventually denied entrance into the promised land for his rash speech arising from unbelief (cf. Nm 20:12; Ps 106:32-33).

The illustrations conclude with a reiteration of the kind of offering already cited in chap. 4 as appropriate for those bearing unintentional guilt. Confession of sin was more than mere recognition of facts. It was an acknowledgement of both the character of the sin and the character of God who was offended by that sin. Confession of sin and obedience to the Lord restore fellowship with Him (cf. 1Jn 1:9).

c. Concessions for the Poor in the Sin Offering (5:7-13)

5:7-13. God's grace extends even to the poorest of believers. These verses make explicit God's gracious provision of an exception for those who are poor. The one who could not afford to sacrifice a **lamb** as a sin offering was allowed to sacrifice **two turtledoves or two young pigeons**. But if in his poverty he could not afford even these birds, he could offer a small quantity of flour (v. 11). It may be objected that this was not a blood sacrifice and therefore conclude that God did not require a blood sacrifice for sin in every case. Yet the priest was to take the flour and **offer it up in smoke ... with the offerings of the LORD** (v. 12), thereby uniting the flour to previous animal sacrifices. Thus, the grain offering became part of a blood offering. Hence, although not everyone could afford a peace offering, everyone could afford a sin offering. The priest received a portion of the **sin offering** for his use (v. 13). Presumably a priest would not accept an offering from a non-contrite worshiper. As the priest received the offering, he communicated to the penitent worshiper that God had accepted his offering and **forgiven** the sin.

5. The Law of the Reparation Offering: an Offering Presented When Making Amends for Unwittingly Defrauding God or Man (5:14–6:7)

a. Abusing the Lord's Property Unwittingly (5:14-19)

5:14-19. God is pleased when believers acknowledge their failure to treat Him as holy. When the faithful recognize wrongs committed in ignorance and do what is necessary to make amends, His name is honored. Making restitution, or putting right what is wrong, thus shows genuine repentance. Because sin usually involves the defrauding of God or man, when sin is confessed, the injury must be made right. All of 5:14–6:7 involves violations of the law that render a person guilty and require a reparation offering. Here reparation was required, whereas in the previous section (4:1–5:13) it was not. The traditional term "guilt offering" may wrongly imply that the earlier sin offering was not intended to expunge guilt. The intent here was to remove the evil that blocked fellowship with God.

Sinning **against the LORD's holy things** (5:15) refers to abuse or misuse of the exclusive property of the tabernacle (and later the temple). A thing becomes "holy" when it is dedicated to the Lord and remains holy until such time as it is properly disposed of. The guilt offering would be **a ram without defect** (v. 15). Temple tradition may suggest that the value of the ram be at least two shekels of silver. In addition, one-fifth of the value of the Lord's holy things was to be paid by the violator (v. 16). All of this indicates that God's view of sin differs from the human view. Many times believers offend the Lord when they are not even aware of it. Forgiveness may be needed in areas they are not even aware of.

b. Abusing Man's Property and the Lord's Name (6:1-7)

Unfaithfulness to the Lord can be expressed in one's relationships with other people. When a person defrauds someone, the Lord Himself is offended.

6:1-7. Blatant and deliberate sins such as those mentioned in vv. 2-3 required restitution of the stolen property, plus a penalty of one-fifth the value of the property. Examples of how one might cheat or defraud one's neighbor are spelled out here. One might cheat by deceiving someone about a deposit, failure to return vouchsafed properties, robbing someone, extorting goods or wealth, holding on to property that should have been returned to its original owner, or swearing falsely about any of these matters. Such sins were viewed as unfaithful **acts ... against the LORD** (v. 2). The restitution offered by Zaccheus in the NT is illustrative of the attitude required (cf. Lk 19:2-10). The **ram** (v. 6) was for the expiation of the sin, and the one-fifth fine was for restitution over and above the sin. God is pleased when people acknowledge their guilt before Him and seek to make amends with those who have been injured. When a sin has been committed, reparations should be made whenever and wherever possible. A right standing with people demonstrates a right standing with God (cf. Mc 6:8).

Christ is the final guilt offering. In His death He provided for restitution, compensation, and expiation. When He gave His life as a ransom for many (cf. Mk 10:45), the fullest satisfaction possible was made to God. Nevertheless, a believer today, while trusting Christ for atonement, must make restitution when confessing a sin against another (Mt 5:23-24).

6. Additional Priestly Administrative Instructions Pertaining to the Sacrifices (6:8–7:38)

The same five offerings presented in the previous chapters are presented here in their administrative order with additional details for the priests to carry out. One difference is that the peace offering is discussed (7:11-35) in greater detail. This reflects the relative frequency of the offerings and something of the divine perspective on the offerings. Some details of the offerings relate to the priest's handling of his own portions.

a. In the Ritual of the Whole Burnt Offering, the Priest's Actions and Dress Convey the Availability of Access to an Ever-Present God through an Ever-Available Atonement (6:8-13)

6:8-13. The priest was to ensure that the fire **kept burning** continually (vv. 9, 12-13). Even the ashes and their fatty residue were to be removed to a ceremonially **clean place** (v. 11). A constantly burning fire ensured that the burnt offering was offered completely to God. The perpetual fire also indicated that God's offer of atonement was always accessible, and that God was dwelling in the midst of His people for the purpose of such access. Unlike the pagan sacrificial rituals in which sexual exhibition and even intercourse were often involved, the conduct of the Israelite priest was to be modest. He was to put on his linen robe and fresh undergarments to take up the ashes, thus symbolizing God's holiness. Those who would minister for God must be holy in all their tasks. Leaders who make provisions for others to approach God must themselves exhibit holiness in their demeanor. Today, all believers in Messiah Jesus are priests (cf. 1Pt 2:5), and should be concerned that their actions portray God's holiness.

b. In the Ritual of the Grain Offering of the Common Person, the Priest's Actions Should Express God's Acceptance of Offerings Presented in Faith (6:14-18)

6:14-18. When a common Israelite brought his **grain offering** to the Lord, the priest was to ensure him that God accepted such faithful acts of devotion. Hence, each regulation prescribed by God must be followed with care, lest the worshiper gain the wrong impression about God. By burning a **memorial** part of the **offering** with fire (v. 15), the priest signified God's acceptance of the offering. By himself eating a part of the offering (v. 16), the priest also demonstrated God's acceptance of the gift in that the priest would not eat anything that might defile or profane his sanctified status (v. 18).

c. In the Ritual of the Grain Offering of the Priest, the Priest Was Expected to Demonstrate His Own Devotion to the Lord (6:19-23)

6:19-23. The high priest was to present a **regular** (i.e., daily, morning and evening, v. 20; cf. Heb 7:27) **grain offering** for himself and for the priesthood in general. The amount was about a day's ration of grain (v. 20), or 2.3 liters. Unlike the common person's offering, the priest had no portion to consume (v. 23); the offering was totally consumed by fire. Besides *receiving* offerings from God's people, the priests themselves were to be models of faithful giving and devotion. The daily act would also serve to remind him of his consecration to the priestly role because the priest had offered such a sacrifice at his consecration. The section ends by stressing the permanence of the command (v. 22), reinforcing God's desire that His people lead by example.

d. In the Ritual of the Sin Offering of the Priest, the Priest Was Expected to Demonstrate His Awareness of the Seriousness of Sin before God (6:24-30)

6:24-30. The sin offering was to be offered any time there was a violation of the commandments by ignorance (cf. Lv 4) as well as on these occasions: at the festival of the new moon, each day of the Passover, each day of the Feast of Weeks, the Feast of Trumpets, each day of the Feast of Booths, the Day of Atonement, at the consecration of the priests (cf. Ex 29:10-14), at purification rites from various types of defilement (e.g., childbirth, cf. Lv 12:6, 8; and leprosy, Lv 14:31), and when purification waters for ritual use were prepared (cf. Nm 19:1-10). The frequency of the offering may have contributed to familiarity that led to carelessness or impropriety. For this reason vv. 24-26 emphasize that the offering was to be **before the LORD**. The sin offering was a reminder that people sin against God every day.

The focus in this section remains on the leaders of the rituals, the priests. Each priest was required to conform to higher standards of holiness than were the common people. The emphasis on presenting and eating the offering in prescribed locations served to remind the worshipers and the priest that forgiveness came from God. The sin offering was to be eaten in God's presence, **in the court of the tent of meeting** (v. 26). Priests had to go to great lengths to ensure that the ritual remained pure (vv. 27-28). Any contact with the unclean was to be avoided at all costs. Similarly, those who lead in worshiping God today must prevent defilement from entering His presence through unrepentant attitudes or unconfessed sin.

Earthenware vessels used to boil the meat eaten by the priest were to be destroyed, and **bronze** vessels were to be thoroughly scoured and rinsed out (v. 28). The priest was to eat the sacrifice (v. 29), but not if its blood had been **brought into** the tabernacle **to make atonement** (v. 30).

e. In the Ritual of the Reparation Offering, the Priest Reinforced Confession and Repentance of Sin (7:1-10)

7:1-5. The reparation (or guilt) offering was the gift purportedly made by only the most dedicated and spiritual of the Israelites who learned of unintended violations of God's law and sought to make amends (cf. 5:14-19). For this reason, one may assume that it was offered less frequently than many others. One role of the priest was to convey to the worshiper that God had dealt with his sin. In this system God provided for regular confession and repentance of even unknown sin.

7:6-10. The priest who administrated this offering, as with many offerings, received some of his pay from it. God takes care of those who minister through the giving of His worshipers. This has always been God's way (cf. Dt 25:4; 1Co 9:7-11). When offerings were scarce, as was often the case, this made obedience to His calling difficult. The Lord graciously reminded His servant that the offering is **holy** (cf 7:1) and must be handled properly. In faithful days the sheer number of animal skins made available from such sacrifices would enable the Levites to engage in various forms of trade to sustain their livelihood. The words **every male** (v. 6) refer only to the priestly community itself and not the members of their immediate families.

f. In the Administration of the Peace Offering and Its Variant Forms, the Priest Ensured the Integrity of the Offering by Instructing Laypersons concerning the Proper Consumption of the Offerings (7:11-21)

7:11-15. Here the focus changed from the sacrifices in which the priests ate a portion to the sacrifices that allowed laypersons as well as priests to consume a portion of the offering (vv. 11-36). Foremost among the common offerings are the **peace offerings** (vv. 11-21). Though these verses occur in the section where the priests are addressed (6:8–7:36), the instruction for laypersons was given to the priests to ensure compliance by the laity. These verses supplement Lv 3:1-17. A contribution to the Lord was required of those who celebrated being at peace with God. In addition to the sacrificial animal, the worshiper was to bring grain cakes and wafers (vv. 12-14). True worship always involves a cost. Believers should never receive from God without giving back to Him. God does not give so that believers can hoard their resources. The peace offering could be presented as a thanksgiving offering or as a freewill offering, but if it were a thanksgiving offering, it had to be consumed **on the day** it was offered (v. 15).

7:16-21. A **votive or a freewill offering** could be eaten that same day and the next day (v. 16), but anything that remained had to be **burned on the third day** (v. 17). Possibly the animal was to be consumed the same day it was offered in order to stress the need to recognize the benefits of God while they were still fresh in the believer's mind. Ritual purification was essential in this offering. Nothing defiled was to come into contact with an offering to be consumed by those in covenant (v. 19). By merely touching the food, anything unclean would transfer ceremonial uncleanness. In this way the worshiper who wanted to celebrate his peace with God was reminded to maintain purity from worldly defilements (v. 21). The failure to do what was required was met with strict punishment. To be **cut off from** one's **people** (vv. 20-21) was to be excluded from the worship rituals and perhaps even judged by death. Those who celebrate peace with God must do so openly and without hypocrisy.

g. The Priests Ensured the Layperson's Knowledge of the Lord's Right to the Fat and the Blood (7:22-27)

7:22-27. The fat of animals that died by means other than for sacrifice was not to be eaten (vv. 23-25). God also forbade anyone from eating the **fat** or the **blood** of a sacrificial animal, under penalty of death (vv. 25-27). To take either the fat or the blood was to plunder what was holy. The command not to eat an animal's blood goes back to the Noahic era (cf. Gn 9:3-4). God requires worshipers to concede that the best of what they own belongs to Him. The fat represented the best a worshiper could offer, but the blood was accepted as a substitute for the worshiper's life. To offer the blood was to offer one's very life (cf. 17:11).

h. Through Proper Handling and Consumption of Dedicated Portions of the Peace Offering the Priests Conveyed Reverence for God (7:28-38)

7:28-34. This section designates the parts of the peace offering that belonged to the Lord and to the priests, and how each one was to be presented, manipulated, and consumed. The offerer was to bring his **offerings (the fat with** the animal's **breast**) to the priest for its proper presentation (vv. 28-30). The raised (often called **wave offering** from Hb. *tenupah*) offering (the **breast** of the animal) was placed in the offerer's **hands** (v. 30). Then, according to Jewish tradition, the priest would place his hands behind the worshiper's hands and heave them upward (toward God) and downward and backward and forward to symbolize consecrating the gift publicly. In addition to the wave offering, a "heave offering" (KJV) was made (from the **right thigh** of the animal, vv. 32-34). The animal breast went to the priesthood, to be generally distributed among the serving priests (v. 31), and the thigh went to the priest officiating the offering (v. 32).

7:35-38. The portions for the priests increased over the centuries. An indication of this is evident in Samuel's day, when Eli's sons, who were priests, coveted more of the sacrifice than was due to them. Deuteronomy 18:3 states that the priest eventually received the animal's two cheeks and stomach in addition to the shoulder.

B. Those Ordained to Present Offerings, and the Land and People They Represent, Must Demonstrate the Holiness of the Lord in Their Midst by Ensuring That All That Enters the Lord's Presence Is Itself Holy (8:1–16:34)

1. God's Holiness Must Be Maintained by Those Who Secure His Dwelling through the Consecration and Presentation of Themselves in Unique Holiness (8:1–10:20)

Basic to the idea of the priesthood is the revelation that the nation of Israel was a kingdom of priests (cf. Ex 19:5-6). Even before the nation was formed, others, such as Job, Noah, and Abraham functioned as priests on behalf of their families. The Israelite priests appointed here had a specialized function and specific tasks and roles, as outlined above. The command from the Lord for their appointment called for the material, participants, and congregation to be assembled prior to the actual consecration (8:1-5). This was followed by the preparation by washing, anointing, and robing of the priests (vv. 6-13). The offerings of consecration (vv. 14-29) were finalized by Moses **anointing** Aaron and his sons (v. 30). This was followed by a waiting period of seven days with specific instructions from the Lord (vv. 31-36). The strict obedience of Aaron and the people to the Lord's commands was emphasized in the repeated refrain, **[he] did just as the LORD commanded** (cf. 8:4, 5, 9, 13, 17, 21, 29, 34, 36; 9:6, 7, 10, 21; 10:7, 13, 15).

a. The Consecration of the Levitical Priests (8:1-36)

8:1-5. The priestly consecration was a public ceremony as prescribed by divine revelation. When the appropriate materials were gathered (v. 2), **Aaron and his sons** were taken to **the tent of meeting** and **the congregation** assembled **at the doorway** (v. 3). To this day, consecrating a servant of the Lord to ministry is celebrated as a community event by the people of God. Moses made a public announcement that all that was about to transpire was by the Lord's directive. The community of believers was to know that the consecration of the Lord's servants originated from the words of the Lord Himself (vv. 4-5).

8:6-13. The consecration ceremony began with the washing of **Aaron and his sons** (v. 6). The washing here is literal but has symbolic implications. It symbolically restored a person who had become soiled with the evils of life, reminding everyone that the Lord's minister must be purified from worldly corruption.

The robing of Aaron and his sons (v. 7) was an investiture (cf. Ex 28:2). The ornate garments served as a visible reminder of the glory and honor of the invisible Lord. Wearing these clothes impressed on the priest the awesome nature of the God he served. Spiritual leaders are to reflect God's distinctive nature even in their dress. The **robe** or cape worn by the high priest was a stately garment made of blue material woven in one piece and, like **the tunic**, it reached to the knees or slightly past them. Its hem was adorned with pomegranates made from blue, purple, and scarlet yarn, with bells between them.

Over the high priest's robe was **the ephod** (v. 7, described in Ex 28:5-14), which supported the

breastpiece, the most impressive of the high priest's garments. The breastpiece represented the high priest's mediatorial role between the people and God. Each of its twelve precious jewels represented a tribe in Israel (along with the name of each tribe inscribed on the breastplate). The **Urim and the Thummim** (v. 8) were objects located in the breastpiece (see comments at Ex 28:15-30). Whatever they were, they served as a means of making inquiry of God for matters beyond human comprehension.

8:14-21. In the ancient Near East, a visitor would be anointed as a sign of welcome into one's house (cf. Ex 30:30-33; Ps 23:5). Symbolically, Aaron's anointing (and the priestly anointing in general) signified God's acceptance of Aaron and his welcome into "His house" and the priestly ministry. This anointing also signified Aaron's identification with God. Since oil is associated with the Holy Spirit (e.g., Is 61:1), it is possible that the anointing also symbolized the presence of the Spirit for empowerment in his life (cf. 2Co 1:21; Lk 4:18; Jn 2:20). The oil primarily served in a consecrating function, for it was sprinkled "on the altar" and "utensils . . . seven times" (v. 11) to set them apart for service.

The point of vv. 14-21 is to indicate that though anointing oil may consecrate, it is insufficient of itself. Sin and burnt offerings were required of those who would represent God to the people. No one could serve as priest whose life had not been sanctified by the **blood** of the substitutionary sacrifice (vv. 14-17), and whose life had not been consecrated to His service (vv. 22-28). This first sacrifice (a **sin offering**) was for cleansing from sin (cf. Lv 4). Those who would lead must be cleansed from their sin as surely as any followers must be cleansed. The second sacrifice was a burnt offering (v. 18); no part of this sacrifice would be enjoyed by the priest. Because it was on the priest's behalf, it was dedicated totally to the Lord. Its presence in the ceremony reminded the priest of his need to be in a constant state of fellowship with God in order to approach Him.

8:22-30. The third sacrifice was known as **the ram of ordination** (v. 22), which celebrated the purpose to which the priest was called. The blood of the ordination offering was applied to the priest's **right ear** lobe, the right **thumb**, and the right **big toe** (vv. 23-24). These bodily areas of hearing, doing, and walking were thus consecrated to the Lord's use. Today, the consecrated believer yields these areas of his life to the Spirit's control and use. This passage contributes to understanding Heb 5:8-9. Jesus was "made perfect" in the sense that by His offering He was fully consecrated and dedicated to God to become the perfect High Priest, to which purpose He was called. The portions of the offering were presented as **a wave offering** (vv. 27-29), but they were not consumed, again, because they were made on behalf of the priests.

8:31-36. The last few verses of the chapter explain that **Aaron** and **his sons** were to remain at the tent for **seven days**, repeating the sacrifices to complete their ordination. Perhaps this weeklong stay was to impress on the priests the significance of their future ministry. Aaron was obedient in all this, a promising beginning to the priesthood. In spite of later failures of the priesthood in general (and Aaron and his sons in particular; cf. chap. 10), spiritual leaders were instructed not to cut corners in this ceremony. Those who lead must be obedient to all that the Lord commands. Members of the "royal priesthood" (1Pt 2:9) have no justification for selective obedience to the Lord.

b. The Inauguration of the Tabernacle Worship (9:1-24)

9:1-7. After one week of ordination service (thus **on the eighth day** of the priestly consecration), the community as a whole was to begin its worship. Verse 2 enjoined **Aaron** to prepare the sacrifices, and v. 3 called on the community as a whole to prepare according to the word of the Lord. Twice Moses expressed his confidence that the Lord Himself would **appear** to ratify the priestly ministry (vv. 4, 6). **The glory of the Lord** (vv. 6, 23) was the visible presence of the Lord among His people (cf. Ex 24:16-17; 40:34-38). Apart from the presence of the Lord, any ritual is meaningless. God makes His presence known only to obedient people. God is not satisfied when people go through the motions of worship without acknowledging the reality of His presence.

Moses mediated the inaugural ritual. The Lord required the Israelites to establish communion with Him by means of mediated substitutionary sacrifice. The priests were required to "buffer" the people from God in that they took the sacrifices **before the Lord** (lit., "to the face of the Lord," vv. 3-5). No brash approach to God was allowed.

9:8-21. Sacrifices were offered first on behalf of the priests for the **sin** or purification **offering** (the bull **calf**, vv. 8-11) and for a **burnt offering**

(vv. 12-14). In the priestly purification offering (vv. 8-9), Aaron applied some of the **blood** of the bull **calf** to the **horns of the** great **altar** (not the same ritual as in 4:5-7, where blood was applied to the altar of incense). Again intercession for atonement always preceded communion with God. After the burnt-offering animals for the priests were killed (vv. 12-14), Aaron splashed **the blood** on all sides of **the altar** (v. 12) to purify it and to set it apart. Next, sacrifices were made on behalf of the community as a whole, including a sin or purification offering (a male **goat**, v. 15), a **burnt offering** (v. 16), a **grain offering** (v. 17) and a **peace** offering (an **ox** and a **ram**, vv. 18-21).

9:22-24. The chapter concludes with the glorious appearance of the Lord and His consuming fire to consume the sacrifices and thus validate the Aaronic priesthood. The details of the rituals have been covered earlier (see comments at 1:2–6:7), so they are not repeated here. The order of the rituals, however, is important. The sin offering preceded the others. A purity offering followed for the priests, because purity is a precondition for a mediatorial capacity before God. The culmination in the peace offering (vv. 18-21) taught Israel that fellowship with the God who condescends to dwell among them was conditioned on the full consecration of one's person to Him through the propitiation of the sin offering. Total dedication of all of life and its substances (hence the grain offering with oil) is the only reasonable response in light of this truth. Believers continue to celebrate being at peace with God (cf. Rm 5:1). The manner or mode of the celebration may differ, but such peace has always been obtained at great cost.

Aaron raised **his hands** and **blessed** the people (v. 22) as their mediating priest. Raised hands indicated the focus of one's attention on God. David raised hands toward the most holy place, where God dwelt, while praising in the sanctuary (cf. Ps 28:2). Believers continue to have access to God through the mediation of Jesus Christ, their High Priest (cf. Heb 4:11-16). As God's **glory** appeared (v. 23), believers found assurance of their faith in this clear evidence of God's presence. His glory indicated His approval: this was the place where God could be seen and heard. As believers today approach God through Jesus Christ, who shed His blood for them, they may also be assured of God's presence with them.

Contrasts between Aaron's Ministry as Priest and the Messiah's Ministry as Priest

Aaron's Priesthood		Messiah's Priesthood	
Perishing sinners offered sacrifices for their own sins	Lv 4:3-12; 9:1-11; 16:6ff.; Heb 8:4	Sinless, resurrected Son; no sacrifice needed for sin since He did not sin	Heb 4:15; 7:27
Offered substitutes to die for their own sin and the sin of others	Heb 5:1-3	Died as the Substitute for the sins of others	Is 52–53; Heb 9:26; 2Co 5:21
Offered recurrent sacrifices to inaugurate, maintain, or restore a sacred space for fellowship with God	Nm 28–29; Heb 9:6	Offered one sacrifice to provide access to fellowship with God (entering the holy place once)	Heb 9:12, 26 (inaugural sacrifice: Jr 31:34; Heb 10:20).
Provided no expiation for sins "with a high hand" (i.e., rebellious, intentional sins)	Nm 15:31	Provides expiation and a clean conscience	Ac 13:39; Heb 9:14
Offered incense to protect themselves in the presence of the Lord	Lv 16:2, 13	Is face-to-face with God and at the right hand of the Father, having accomplished cleansing for sins	Jn 1:1; Heb 1:3

c. Violation of God's Holiness and the Resultant Statutes Pertaining to Priestly Tabernacle Duties: Nadab and Abihu Offer Strange Fire (10:1-20)

Moses narrated events about Aaron's sons Nadab and Abihu that occurred soon after the establishment of the tabernacle worship. Moses had prepared his readers for the events of this chapter and its prescriptions by the repeated refrain in chaps. 8 and 9, "just as the LORD had commanded Moses." The priests were required to fulfill the command of the Lord without variation. Relating this incident of the sin of Nadab and Abihu shows that God is to be treated as holy by all who draw near Him.

In addition, the placement of this event here serves a structural purpose in the book. Leviticus 11–15 is the largest canonical segment on laws about what is "clean" or "unclean," and these chapters are preceded by this account of the death of Aaron's two sons for improperly approaching the sanctuary. Significantly, this section is followed by the Day of Atonement ritual (cf. Lv 16) where Moses referred again to the death of Aaron's sons as part of a warning against casual entrance into the sanctuary (cf. 16:1-2). God then issued a command to conduct a sacrificial ritual to cleanse the priest first, and then to remove sin and uncleanness from both the sanctuary and the people (vv. 3-19). The point was clear: uncleanness brought peril on the whole assembly.

10:1-3. Aaron's sons **Nadab and Abihu** offered **strange fire** (v. 1). The text is clear: **which He had not commanded them**. What is the nature of this strange fire and the offense of these priests? Some see a reference to a violation of the timing of the incense offering and point to Ex 30:7-8. Another view is that they made their offerings while intoxicated because in the section immediately following priests are forbidden **wine or strong drink . . . so that [they] may not die** (10:9). A third interpretation is that they brought fire from a source other than the sacred source (cf. Lv 16:12). This view focuses on the use of the word **strange**, which is used in other contexts of outside peoples (Dt 25:5) or those outside the priesthood ("layman," Lv 22:12; Nm 16:40). Thus, it was outside fire and is best rendered as "strange" in the sense of "unauthorized." They may have thought they had good reason for doing what they did, but God did not deem it so. As the sons of the high priest, Nadab and Abihu should have known what God required. But they did not obey, and they were consumed by a **fire** whose source was God Himself (possibly from the altar, v. 2). God's servants must hold themselves to God's standards or risk direct discipline from Him (they died **before the LORD**). When God prescribes obedience, a substitute or surrogate will not do. Those who would carry out God's revealed will should differentiate between what is holy and what is profane.

10:4-7. The consequences of Nadab and Abihu's sin extended to the manner of the disposal of their corpses and the mourning that followed (vv. 4-6). Moses prohibited **Aaron** and his sons from mourning for the dead, but he allowed the kinsmen to **bewail the burning**. Here is a most vivid picture of the truth that God does not show favoritism when it comes to sin. Aaron was not allowed to publicly mourn (vv. 6-7), even though these were his sons. Even the mourning of God's priest was a consecrated endeavor.

10:8-11. Although it is not recorded that Aaron's sons were drunk when they sinned, the priests were now warned against using inebriating drink when worshiping the Lord (vv. 8-9). Drunk priests could make mistakes when carrying out the rituals (v. 10) and in teaching about God's law (v. 11). Those with an undiminished capacity to distinguish between the holy and the profane are in a better position to instruct God's people. God's people needed to see reverence for Him by example, so the priests were to avoid anything that could diminish their ability to carry out God's will. Moreover, those who worship God must not wonder whether the priest is dispensing God's work in a way he thinks best (cf. Mal 2:7-8).

10:12-15. Moses specifically instructed Aaron's **surviving sons, Eleazar and Ithamar,** to carry out the ritual of the **grain** and **wave** offerings and to eat their portions in the designated areas, **as the LORD [had] commanded**. The statutes given here on priestly portions (vv. 12-15) may seem like an insertion, but including them reminded the priests that God had not rejected them along with Nadab and Abihu.

10:16-20. Aaron and his remaining sons refrained from eating the **sin offering**, and for good reason. They were mourning the loss of their kin, and also apparently they did not want to bring further shame on the Lord's name. Moses accepted Aaron's explanation (v. 20). The underlying motivation behind difficult choices in life should always be the pleasure of God. The primary focus of the priests, despite the day's events, was on self-denial and exalting God in their efforts.

2. God's Holiness Must Be Maintained by His People in Their Presentation of Themselves and All That They Own and Do in Unique Holiness (11:1–15:33)

God is concerned that the practical, everyday, and mundane matters of people's lives reflect His holiness. These chapters detail God's instructions that were to govern ritual purity, that which allows or disallows access to the encampment where God had taken up His "residence." The dietary system in Israel (Lv 11) served God's purpose in making Israel distinct from other nations by identifying pure and impure animals. The holy God differentiates between the clean and the unclean in the daily activities of His people as well as their diet. Chapters 12–15 identify human sources of impurity, their diagnosis, and ritual cleansings. The concept of clean and unclean first appears in Gn 8, where God made this distinction between the animals Noah brought on the ark. Noah also understood enough to sacrifice clean animals after the flood.

Care should be exercised in interpreting these texts, for not everything that is unclean is by nature sinful, and yet everything sinful is unclean in the sense of being unfit for entrance into the holy presence of God. In other contexts, however, uncleanness refers specifically to acts of sin (e.g., Lv 18:20, 23).

The Hebrew word for "unclean" is *tame'* ("abnormal, unnatural, weak, ill") and the word for "clean" is *taher* ("normal, clean, pure, whole"). Uncleanness is a dominant subject in Leviticus. The word "unclean" occurs 182 times in the OT, and two-thirds of these are in Leviticus. The word "clean" occurs 92 times in the OT, and half of those are in Leviticus. Certain animals, if consumed or touched, could render a worshiper unfit to enter God's presence. And mere contact with the corpse of an animal would render a person unfit to enter the Lord's presence. In Lv 11 cleanness and uncleanness are discussed in relation to food. Cleanness or uncleanness that is the result of contact with a dead animal is also mentioned, but it seems that the reason the dead animal is called unclean is because one could not eat it and remain ritually pure. Even a clean animal, one allowed for consumption, could not be eaten if it were not killed in a sacrificially prescribed way. Even a ceremonially clean person, like a priest, needed to be elevated to holiness through sacrificial ritual in order to enter the Lord's presence.

For something or someone to be clean meant that it or he was free from the abnormalities that could not by nature enter the presence of the Lord (and this included imperfection, weakness, illness, and the like). Also, certain animals were precluded from Israel's diet and rituals. Why certain animals were considered clean and others were not is debatable. Answers include that these animals were used in pagan rituals, concern for health and hygiene, symbolic representations, and the like. However, dogmatic assertions about the reasons behind excluding certain animals and including others should be avoided. It is simply that the Lord revealed them to be "clean" or "unclean," thereby providing yet another way for Israel to be separate and distinct from the nations (Lv 11:44-45).

a. God's People Distinguish Themselves as His People in What They Regard as Clean and Unclean, Consuming Only That Which God Has Prescribed (11:1-47)

11:1-19. Believers are commanded to be holy (Lv 11:44-45; cf. 19:2; 20:26; 1Pt 1:16), and in the OT that holiness extended even to what they ate. It may seem strange that God cares about an issue so basic as what His people eat. However, to this day in some cultures of the Middle East, people can be identified by their diet. What a Muslim may eat and what a Christian may eat can keep them from eating together at the same table. The Egyptians regarded shepherds as objectionable (cf. Gn 46:34) and would not eat with them, perhaps because of the sacred nature of some animals in their diet. In prescribing the Israelites' diet in this way, perhaps God was also protecting His people from undesirable influences that marked pagan cultures that would surround them in Israel. Under the new covenant, Jesus declared all foods clean (cf. Mk 7:19; cf. Ac 10:10-16). As Paul reminded the Corinthians much later, everything is to be done to the glory of God, even eating and drinking (1Co 10:31).

The concept of uncleanness in Lv 11 refers to something that does not function according to its normal or expected behavior. For land animals (vv. 1-8), normal characteristics included cloven hooves (split into two sections) and cud chewing or rumination (v. 3). For aquatic animals the standard was fins and scales (v. 9). Such uncleanness should not be considered sinful as such, but unclean in the sense of physical irregularities that rendered the animals unacceptable for Israel. The **camel**, the **shaphan** (rock badger or hyrax) (v. 5), and the **rabbit** were declared **unclean** because they do not have cloven hooves (vv. 4-6; the standard of the other animals mentioned in Dt 14:4-5). The use of the definite article in Hebrew in association with these animals indicates that this refers to a class of animals. The camel was employed by many Arabic peoples as a sacrifice and its meat was eaten throughout the Middle East.

The pig . . . divides the hoof (v. 7), but does not chew the cud and was therefore unclean. Pigs may have been raised in Egypt during the Old Kingdom period (2700–2200 BC; cf. Harrison, *Leviticus*, 121–22). They were valued by settlers not only for their flesh, but also for their proclivity to root up soil in search of edibles (seeds, roots, etc.). Although they were employed for sacrifice in Canaanite worship (18th to 16th centuries BC at Tel el-Far'ah), this does not necessarily explain the prohibition here. Other animals employed in pagan worship were used in Hebrew rituals. Some have drawn parallels between the animals used in sacrifice by the Israelites and their diet. In fact, God limited what was appropriate for sacrifice, so the dietary prohibitions may follow a similar pattern.

The forward motion of fish vv. (9-12) is normally by means of **fins and scales**. Some marine animals do not move through the water by these "normal" means, therefore they were considered unclean. God had a strong word for the required Israelite response to such unclean aquatic animals: they were to regard them as **detestable** or **abhorrent** (both used to translate the Hb. word *sheqetz* used of detestable things in the sense of ceremonially unclean and therefore abominable). **Birds** of prey (vv. 13-19) were prohibited from the Hebrew diet because they eat flesh with its blood still in it.

11:20-23. Insects that darted about on all **fours** were also called **detestable** (vv. 20-23) but no reason was given for this. Perhaps it was because of their erratic, haphazard motion. By contrast, the **locust**, **cricket**, and **grasshopper** (which move by means of jumping hind **legs**) were permitted. Such insects were clean and formed a regular part of John the Baptist's diet (cf. Mt 3:4).

11:24-28. Here the focus moved from living animals to dead ones. **Carcasses** of animals were to be considered unclean, the exception being animals appropriately slaughtered in ritual sacrifice (with the blood also properly handled). Believers who came into contact with the defilement dead animals created had to be cleansed before they could approach the holy God. All corpses pollute and contaminate because death is not natural to the presence of God. Washing and a period of isolation (**until evening**) were required.

11:29-38. Small animals (moles, mice, lizards, and others) situated close to the ground that swarm in hordes were also considered unclean. Pollution accompanied such **swarming** and affected any **article**, **clothing**, or **vessel** that came into contact with these creatures. This transmitted temporary uncleanness that affected persons and things, lasting **until evening**.

11:39-40. Even carcasses of clean animals were defiling if they died of natural causes (v. 39). The person who touched the carcass of a food animal, or ate part of the carcass, was also **unclean until evening** (v. 40).

11:41-47. The command to refrain from eating or touching unclean animals is stated again in vv. 41-43, followed by the reason: the Lord is **holy**. The believer should be holy because the God who delivered him from eternal destruction is holy. The only restriction on NT believers concerning food is love for one's brother (cf. Rm 14:15; 1Co 8, 10). God's redeemed people are to imitate His holiness. Verse 45 gives three reasons for avoiding unclean things: (1) God redeemed His people **from Egypt**—that is, they are uniquely His, (2) He is their **God**, and (3) He is **holy**.

b. God's People Distinguish Themselves as His among All People by Virtue of Their Respect for Blood That Enters His Holy Presence (12:1-8)

12:1-5. Just as an issue as simple as food made a difference in one's ability to approach God, matters other than food (fungi, disease, bodily discharges, etc.) could render a person unfit to approach the tabernacle. The flow of blood present after the birth of a child meant the woman was ceremonially unclean and was not to **enter the sanctuary** (v. 4). It required an interval of **purification** followed by sacrifice to restore her full participation in the sanctuary. This was not because the act of childbearing was sinful—far from it. God had commanded Adam and Eve to be fruitful (Gn 1:28), and had consecrated the act of bearing children within marriage. Instead, the blood that accompanied childbirth could not be brought near the sanctuary; only sacrificial blood could be brought near, and that only in definite ways by prescribed persons. Contact with blood apart from the ritual sacrifices made a person unclean (not sinful). Just as touching a corpse made a person unfit to approach God, childbirth required a purification ritual, as this chapter relates.

On the eighth day after a male child was born, he was to be circumcised, and his mother was to be ceremonially impure for **seven days**. Through circumcision God reminded His people that they were set apart to Him solely by His gracious provision of election (cf. Gn 17:10-14; 21:4). In spite of human weakness, God provided continual reminders of His grace and faithfulness to believers. The birth of a **female child** doubled the period of impurity for the mother (v. 5). No explanation for this is given, though some speculate that the female child would someday be subject to ceremonial uncleanness through menstruation and childbirth. Whatever the case, the Lord used His sovereign right to mark this distinction between the sexes from birth.

12:6-8. Whether a mother gave birth to a boy or a girl, she was to offer a yearling **lamb** as a symbol of her dedication to God. Such a sacrifice underscored her status in the covenant community. Like any male, she too could relate to God personally and find acceptance in His presence. Modern readers may find such limitations for access into God's presence unfathomable. Revelation 21:27, however, states that the unclean and impure will not enter God's presence in the future. This seems to reflect those passages in Leviticus where God revealed what His holiness requires.

c. God's People Distinguish Themselves as His Unique People in the Ways in Which They Deal with Disease and Contamination (13:1–14:57)

Certain skin conditions and contaminations were barriers to the camp and the place of offering. Bodily diseases were symptoms of the state of uncleanness in the human race. Translated **leprosy** (*tsara'at*, from a verb meaning "to strike") in the NASB, the scaly or reddish skin diseases listed here (vv. 2, 6, 10, 18, 30, 39) include various kinds of skin infirmities. They are not the modern medical diagnosis of leprosy (or Hansen's disease). The translation "leprosy" derives from the third-century BC Greek Septuagint mistranslation of the Hebrew text. For the word *tsara'at*, the translators erroneously used the word *leprosum*, the adjectival form of the Greek word *lepra*, leading to the English mistranslation "leprosy" instead of the correct "skin disease."

All disease and sickness is symptomatic of advance toward death; they are proof of the corruption that is in the world as a result of the fall of man. The text addresses both the diagnosis and isolation of skin conditions (13:1-46), and then does the same for molds and mildews and the physical decay they create (13:47-59). The ritual of restoration for skin conditions (14:1-32) is followed by the ritual of restoration for molds and mildews (14:33-57).

13:1-46. The **priest** was to inspect each affliction (13:2). If a skin affliction was only suspected but not certain, the priest imposed a seven-day quarantine. At the end of this period the afflicted was examined again, and if no further degeneration was apparent he was isolated for another week, after which he could be pronounced healed (v. 17). The priest, however, did nothing to promote the cure. His rituals were performed only after the disease had passed. Later, Dt 24:8-9 charged the people to follow the authority of the priests in all matters dealing with "skin diseases" (of which leprosy would be but one form), citing the case of Miriam (Nm 12:11-15), who challenged the authority of Moses. In Miriam's case, however, healing did not come through her brother Aaron, who was a party to the offense, but through the prophet Moses and his prayer. Healing comes from God directly (cf. Ex 15:24-26) or through his prophets (e.g., Moses, cf. Ex 15:25; Elisha, 2Kg 2:19-22; 20:7-9).

Bodily diseases separated the worshiper from the presence of God and the practice of prescribed worship (cf. Nm 13:45-46). He was considered ceremonially unclean, though not necessarily sinful. It would be wrong to conclude that such diseases were indicative of God's punishment for sin in an individual's life. They are, however, incompatible with the presence and glory of God. They serve in this way as a "picture" of sin. Israelites could worship while sick, but could not enter God's presence in a state that was not whole. For the chronically ill, their hope lay in their future resurrected body, which would not undergo corruption. Similarly, believers today await the time when God will make their corruptible flesh incorruptible and the mortal will put on immortality (cf. 1Co 15:53-54). The healing God grants today is a token of the promise that He will ultimately heal believers' bodies forever.

13:47-59. When a **greenish or reddish** fungus growth appeared on any woolen, linen, or **leather . . . garment**, it was to **be shown to the priest** for his analysis (13:47-49). After seven days of observation, if the growth had spread, the **garment** was to be burned (v. 52). This showed that God's concern for His people extended to the very things that touched their lives, such as their clothing. If the fungal **mark** had **not spread** after seven days, the priest ordered it to be **washed**. If it had **not changed** after a week, it was to be burned (v. 55). But if the mark had **faded**, it was to be torn **out of the garment** (v. 56); then if it appeared elsewhere, the garment was to be burned. If the mark was gone, the garment was to be **washed a second time** and declared **clean** (v. 58).

Physical decay is an outward sign of the spiritual corruption that is rampant in this fallen world. Decay, like death, was not part of God's original purpose for His creation, and these requirements reminded the common and the great that God was still concerned about the fallen nature of His creation.

14:1-9. Chapter 14 records the rites of restoration the priests were to carry out for a person who was healed of a skin infirmity. The ritual was a public testimony of the person's belief that God had brought about the healing. Following the priestly examination **outside of the camp** to verify that the **infection** was **healed** (vv. 1-3), **the priest** was to get **two clean** living **birds**, a **cedar** rod, **scarlet string** (actually a scrap of fabric made red from the eggs of the *coccus illicus* worm; cf. Ex 25:4), and **hyssop**. The red of the cedar and the fabric presumably depicted the blood of the life being restored. **One bird** was to be killed in **an earthenware vessel over running water** (v. 5). The living bird with the **cedar**, fabric, and **hyssop** was to be dipped in the blood of the dead bird. The priest would then sprinkle the recovered leper **seven times**, and release the living **bird** (v. 7). This ritual bears similarities to the later scapegoat ritual (cf. Lv 16), but there the release of the animal signified the departure of the affliction (through death) and the restored access to God that was then possible.

At this point the unclean person was pronounced clean, but more was required of him. He had to wash his clothes, shave, bathe, and stay away from **his tent for seven days** (vv. 8-9). The appearance of one following this ritual would have been a dramatic pronouncement that his life was made new.

14:10-20. These ablutions and the shaving were repeated, and then, on **the eighth day** the person was to offer at the tabernacle a **grain offering**, a **guilt** offering, a **wave offering**, a **burnt offering,** and a **sin offering** (vv. 10-13). The ritual included an anointing of oil on the **right** earlobe, **thumb**, and **big toe** of the restored worshiper in a manner not unlike that of the priestly anointing (vv. 15-18; cf. 8:24-27). The blood anointing (v. 14) consecrated the worshiper to his renewed tasks of serving as such, and the oil anointing served as a form of welcome back into the fellowship of the house of the Lord.

14:21-32. The alternative offerings for the poor followed the same essential ritual, while instructing the Israelites that God in His grace does not discriminate against the poor or the rich. Later rabbis taught that curing a leper was as difficult as raising a person from the dead, and that actual healings were rare. The cleansing of lepers, however, was expected as one of the signs of the messianic age as indicated in the gospels. When John the Baptist sent messengers to ask Jesus if He was the "Expected One," Jesus replied, "Go and report to John what you hear and see: the BLIND RECEIVE SIGHT and the lame walk, the lepers are cleansed and the deaf hear, the dead are raised up, and the POOR HAVE THE GOSPEL PREACHED TO THEM" (Mt 11:4-5).

14:33-57. The final section of this chapter details the extent to which holiness was to extend into the lives of Israelites. Even buildings, garments, and vessels had to be cleansed. Often what people may consider mundane and unimportant has great importance to God. Sin is the source of all contamination and disease in the world. The ritual related to the cleansing of a house pointed to the holiness of the God who owns all that a believer calls his own.

That the priest performed the inspection, and saw to the removal of the afflicted stones or plaster (vv. 39-42) visually reinforced the instruction that believers should sanctify their possessions in order to please God. If the contamination occurred in the house again (vv. 43-47), the Israelite was to pull down the house and remove it from the city. Though this would have been costly and inconvenient, believers would learn that only such obedience preceded all proper sanctification. A final purification ceremony (mirroring that of the cleansing of the leper) was prescribed in order to ensure that God could come to dwell among His people (vv. 48-53). God expects believers to be pure from worldly contamination, completely honoring to Him.

d. God's People Distinguish Themselves as His Unique People in the Ways in Which They Seek to Honor God with Their Stewardship of Their Bodies (15:1-33)

15:1-12. Leviticus 15 relates God's prescription for separation and for sanctification in the event of unclean bodily "discharges" (from a word meaning "to flow"), whether voluntary (semen) or involuntary (menstruation). God ordained the act of procreation, and He also prescribed the circumstances under which it is appropriate. Specifically, this chapter provided guidelines for those who were ritually unclean in relation to human sexual organs, thus demonstrating that God's concern for holiness includes all areas of human sexuality. The sexual act in marriage is not considered sinful. Some ritually impure genital emissions or ejaculations are healthy and normal during intercourse within marriage or menstruation. Only the association of the sexual act with the worship of God was forbidden.

The priests were to instruct Israelites to keep any aspect of intercourse or disease from entering God's presence. Such instruction served as a polemic against the surrounding nations with their abuse of this gift of God in fertility rituals. **Uncleanness** was clearly viewed as contagious and could be transmitted to items touched by the **unclean** person (vv. 4-11). Anything that came close to the source of the unclean discharge was automatically rendered unclean (whether the unclean person sat or lay on the item). This included such things as beds (v. 4), furniture (v. 6), clay vessels touched by the unclean person (v. 12), and even saddles on which the person had ridden (v. 9).

15:13-33. The text also addresses the ritual of restoration of the worshiper to the divine presence for the male (vv. 13-18; first the man whose issue is abnormal, and then the normal) and then for the female (vv. 19-30, first the female whose issue is normal, and then the abnormal), before summarizing the purity regulations for bodily discharges (vv. 31-33). The aim of these regulations on ritual purity was for both health and cleansing. In contrast to other forms of uncleanness that must be inspected by the priest (Lv 13–14), individuals were required to make the necessary determinations for themselves and then to follow through with the prescribed ceremonial remedies of washing and separation from the worship site (vv. 13, 16, 21, 22, 27). Their cleansing also required the burnt and sin offerings of **turtledoves** or **pigeons** (vv. 14, 29). The sacrifice, identical in substance to the woman's postpartum offering (cf. 12:8), removed any remaining ritual impurity. Of course, God in no way was saying that marital intercourse is impure (cf. Heb 13:4). He was simply emphasizing again the need for purity before Him.

3. God's Holiness Requires a Particular Day of Atonement on the Part of His People and Priests (16:1-34)

At the center of the priestly manual of Leviticus, in the middle of the Torah, was the festival of *Yom Kippur*, the Day of Atonement. The ceremonies described here were unique among the priestly rituals. The day was a reminder that the nation's ritual uncleanness imperiled the whole nation before God. Uncleanness defiled the Lord's tabernacle, God's dwelling place in their midst (cf. Lv 16:16; Nm 19:13, 20), as well as the land itself (cf. Lv 18:27). Impurity could make God's continued dwelling in their midst impossible (cf. Ezk 9:7; 43:7). If unpurged, uncleanness could lead to an outbreak of divine wrath and ultimately the expulsion of the land's inhabitants (cf. Lv 18:25), which in fact happened to Judah in the Babylonian exile. So various sacrifices were needed to purge uncleanness caused by sin and ceremonial impurity from the tabernacle.

16:1-19. God's instructions to Aaron concerning the Day of Atonement began with a reminder of the death of his two sons, as recorded in Lv 10. This serves as a sequential clue. The commandments given here may have come shortly after the death of Aaron's sons. Also, there is a logical connection. Aaron's sons died while they were burning incense in the tabernacle. Aaron too would offer incense on this occasion (v. 12) for his own protection and in a meticulously prescribed manner. Obedience is everything in this ritual.

God made provision for a proper entry into His very presence. The preparation of the high priest was meticulous. He had to come at the proper time and bring the appropriate sacrifices for himself and the other priests (vv. 3, 6). Whereas regular priests were to rinse their hands and feet with water drawn from the holy basin (cf. Ex 30:18-21), the high priest was to bathe his entire body in preparation for this event (v. 4). After bathing, he was to wear the proper vestments reserved for this occasion and oversee the selection process of the proper animals (vv. 5, 7-10).

The fate of the two goats pictures both atonement and expiation (vv. 8-10). The high priest cast lots to determine the fate of each (v. 8). One was brought for a sin offering (v. 5). The atonement consisted, however, not only in the shed blood of the first goat (in the ritual of the purification offering [v. 9]), but also in the removal of sin and guilt by the second goat that was sent away (picturing the removal of sins; see vv. 20-22).

Impurities (vv. 16, 19) referred to deviations of morality. This day became the holiest of the year for Israelites, for on that day all the sins of the nation of Israel were atoned for by vicarious blood sacrifice. Similarly, the heart of NT worship centers on the death of Christ, the great high priest, who bore the sins of the entire human race. In a sense the Day of Atonement was the OT version of Good Friday.

Though the priest cast lots to determine the fate of the goats, the determination belonged to the Lord (lit., "which the lot has gone up on it for the Lord," v. 9). The direction given to Aaron (and later to other high priests) is that the first sacrifice is a sin offering for himself (stressed twice in v. 11) and for his **household** members. This was followed by placing a censer in the most holy place to create a **cloud of incense** smoke (vv. 12-13). Presumably the purpose of the cloud was to protect Aaron from death in the presence of God's glory by covering the mercy seat, the lid above the ark of the covenant, that contained the Ten Commandments (cf. Ex 25:22). Then he was to bring the **blood of the bull** and sprinkle it once upon the **side** of the **mercy seat** and seven times **in front of the mercy seat** (v. 14). Aaron was then to **slaughter the goat** on behalf of the nation (v. 15) and apply the blood in a similar manner. He was to begin the sin or purification offering of the goat before completing the offering of the bull.

The purpose of the blood in this sevenfold manner was to purge the holy place from the impurities of the nation and to remove transgressions and sins from the holy of holies, which represented God's presence. The sin or purification offering, including the special sin offering on the Day of Atonement, served to cleanse from both sin and ritual impurities (vv. 16–22). The priest was then to go to **the tent of meeting**, or outer sanctuary, and cleanse it with blood in a similar manner, by applying the blood of the bull and the goat to the incense altar (16:16; cf.

The High Priests' Ministries and the Great High Priest's Ministry

High Priest	Great High Priest
Festivals, new moons and Sabbath days are but shadows (Col 2:17a).	Christ is the substance (or reality) behind the shadows (Col 2:17b).
The high priest mediates access to God through the law (Lv 8–10).	Christ is the fulfillment and end (*telos*) of the law (Heb 3:1-3; 4:14; 7:17-21; 9:15).
Sin offerings required repetitious death and sacrifice (Lv 4:1-35).	Christ is the final Sin Offering (Rm 3:25; Heb 7:27; 9:26-28) and therefore the perfect sacrifice.
Sacrifices presented brought a cleansing to the high priest and his family (Lv 16:6, 17), to the people of Israel (16:17), and to the earthly tabernacle (16:16, 20, 33).	Christ's sacrifice cleansed the heavenly "things" of the heavenly tabernacle (Heb 9:23-5; defiled by Satan's rebellion?) and the consciences of those who approach in faith. No cleansing offering was required for Christ Himself!
The high priest did not glorify himself by taking on this role, but was chosen (Heb 5:4).	What is true of the Levitical high priests is also true of the greater high priest, Christ, who was chosen by God (Heb 5:5-6).
After the pattern of Aaron (Heb 5:4; 7:23)	After the pattern of Melchizedek (Heb 7:17; 7:23-25)
Took office without an oath (Heb 7:21)	Took priestly position by the Lord's oath (Heb 7:20-28)

Ex 30:9-10). All of these actions were the activity of the high priest with no others present (v. 17). As he exited the courtyard, Aaron was to daub the blood of the bull and goat on **the horns** of the sacrificial **altar** (v. 18), re-consecrating it since the nation and its priests had brought both their sins and impurities before it all year (v. 19). The remaining carcasses of the slain bull and goat were to be burned outside the camp (v. 27), thus removing the ritual impurities of the people.

16:20-34. The ceremony of the release of the live goat (vv. 20-22) symbolized the removal of the moral faults of the community. In this ritual the high priest, Aaron in this case, represented the nation as a whole. He was to place **both of his hands on the head of the live goat, and confess** all the transgressions of the Israelites (vv. 20-21). How long might Aaron's confession for the people's sins have taken? One could imagine him confessing for hours. The confession of Moses (cf. Ex 32–34) gives an idea of what Aaron's prayer might have included. This was the only ritual that required placing both hands on the animal, and only here did the priest confess sin at the same time. This action may depict a transfer of sin rather than identification with the goat. The word for **scapegoat** (v. 8) is *Azaz'el* (meaning "the goat that departs" or "the wilderness goat" or, as some suggest, the name of a demon). In that the goat is said to be "for" or "to" *Azaz'el*, some have seen this as a reference to a wilderness dwelling demon (cf. *Azaz'el* in later Jewish literature, *Enoch* 8:1; 9:6). In this case, the sins were sent back to their author, the prince of demons. But nowhere does the Bible commend that homage or offerings are due to demons and Lv 17:7 portrays such actions as heinous and not to be continued. Alternately, the term *Azaz'el* can be rendered "complete destruction." A Second Temple tradition (*m. Yoma* 6:6) suggests that the beast was pushed over a cliff (another meaning for *Azaz'el* is "rocky precipice"), or led to a mountain where it was destroyed so as to prevent its return. In this case the high priest then sent the goat **away into the wilderness**, taking the sins with it (vv. 21-22). This seems the best interpretation as the public nature of the event left no doubt that sin had been carried away.

Aaron then returned to **the tent of meeting** and removed his clothes for a second ritual bathing (vv. 23-24). Perhaps the defilement of his encounter with the scapegoat left him unfit for the remainder of his duties, and so another washing was required. This would fit with the requirement of ritual washing for the man who led the scapegoat away (v. 26). Whatever the case, after bathing a second time, the priest completed the sin offering (v. 25).

This perpetual **statute** (v. 29a) included a **sabbath of solemn rest** (v. 31). Two vital functions of life (eating and working) ceased in order to compel the worshipers to focus on the spiritual realities of life. On this one day the worshipers were to remove their thoughts from the cares and concerns of the physical world and focus on what God had provided for their spiritual lives. The animating force behind the Day of Atonement was the penitent heart of the worshiper. Atonement, which consists of the sacrifice of shed blood and the removal of sin, provides the only way for repentant sinners to approach God. Contrition was expected of those who approached God on that day, which was a day of national mourning and repentance.

Since this was also a Sabbath-day observance, it meant that no work could be done (cf. 23:26-32). Anyone who did not observe this Sabbath was to be cut off from his people (23:29). Also, this was a day when the people were to **humble** their **souls** (Lv 16:31; 23:27; cf. Nm 29:7), which possibly included fasting. This would thus be the only holy day characterized by mourning, fasting, and repentance. The chapter concluded with this call for the observance of an additional **sabbath** and reviewed the day as a whole (vv. 29-34). As public and impressive as these ceremonies were, they were insufficient to address sin fully (Heb 10:4). Some see the Day of Atonement, *Yom Kippur*, as covering even intentional sins, that for which no other sacrifice in Leviticus provided. It seems better, however, to view this as a "day of purgation" that removed from the camp and the sanctuary all ritual impurities and moral faults that had accumulated at the sanctuary and among the people in the previous year. In this sense, sins were *expiated*, but not *propitiated*. The propitiation awaited the final sacrifice of Messiah who could offer himself without blemish as High Priest and sacrifice (Heb 9:11-14). It is in this sense that the blood of bulls and goats could never fully deal with the human sin issue. If they could, Messiah would not have had to die.

Both of Israel's goats for her sin offering symbolized the death of Messiah, Jesus Christ, in the years to come. The dying goat signified the death Christ died. The goat that was driven away from the camp into the wilderness never to return symbolized the Messiah's even greater agony of separation from the Father as He bore the sins of the world (Heb 13:11-13). This OT sacrifice reflects one of the most gruesome aspects of the Lord's atoning work as the sinner's substitute.

The NT, particularly the book of Hebrews, stresses the superiority of the death of Jesus in contrast to the OT sacrifices. Jesus Christ is vastly superior to Aaron and to every high priest in Israel. Aaron was a sinner, but Jesus is sinless; He did not need to make an offering for Himself (cf. Heb 7:26-28). Aaron died, but Christ lives forever (cf. Heb 7:15-25).

II. Divine Instruction Ensuring the Preservation of a Holy Land and a Holy People Declaring the Lord's Presence (17:1–27:34)

A. Reminders on Sacrificial Offerings: Sacrifice to God Alone, Treat the Blood as Holy, and Approach God in Purity (17:1-16)

Chapters 1–16 focused on God's prescriptions for sin and ritual impurity that separated Israel from him, but chaps. 17–27 focus on commandments that have no remedies for those who violate them. Chapter 17 bridges the gap between the priestly instructions on ritual and the expected behavior on the part of Israel. The chapter presents three warnings to those who would violate God's precepts set forth in previous chapters. First, bring all sacrifices to the Lord and no other (vv. 1-9). Second, do not eat the blood that God has assigned to specific functions (vv. 10-14). Third, do not neglect to purify yourself (vv. 15-16).

17:1-9. First, the sanctity of the sacrificial blood is set forth, as God warned the Israelites about false worship and disregard for the blood (vv. 1-4). God's people were expected to treat the blood with reverence (as a symbol of both life and redemption). Similarly, believers today who fail to treat Christ's blood as holy also face a stern rebuke (cf. Heb 10:19-27). Only sacrifices that are offered exclusively to the one true, living God are acceptable. God's people must present their offerings to God alone. All slaughtering (for offerings) was to be done at the tabernacle in order to prevent sacrifice to the false gods (an act of idolatry in violation of the first Commandment). Violators were to be cut off from the community (cf. 7:20-21). The purpose behind the bringing of the offerings to the tabernacle was to put a halt to sacrificing to any god but the Lord. Here there was an association with false gods described as **goat demons** (v. 7). Eventually, with the establishment of the temple, the site of slaughtering was focused on Jerusalem when prescribed festivals were in view. Additional regulations (cf. Dt 12:15-16, 20-28) allowed the Israelites to eat the meat of animals in a non-sacrificial manner in their cities. But sacrificial animals had to be slaughtered in Jerusalem.

17:10-14. The life of the flesh is in the blood (v. 11), and the Lord has given blood the function of ransoming the lives of offerers who present it at the altar. Believers recognize that only God has the right to the life of all flesh. The blood, as a symbol of life and redemption, must be treated as holy by the people of God. This meant Israelites had to drain the blood of an animal that was killed in hunting. Every time blood was shed from animals, it was a reminder of God's right to the life of all flesh. The loyal worshiper of the living God would present his offering to God alone, recognizing that life belongs to Him. The penalty for failure to observe these requirements was to be **cut off** (vv. 10, 14). The passage again points to Christ's atonement. Since Christ gave His life a ransom (life for life) for many (cf. Mk 10:45), one must not trample underfoot the blood of Christ by worshiping something or someone other than the true God. Even the blood of game was not to be eaten (v. 13). God reserves for Himself the unchanging and exclusive rights to the allegiance of His people in all areas of their lives.

17:15-16. An animal that had died naturally or as the result of another animal's predation could be eaten, but apparently not by a priest (cf. 22:8). An individual eating such meat, however, would be rendered (ceremonially) unclean.

B. Exhortations toward Community Holiness: God Is To Be Honored in the Sexual, Social, and Ethical Lives of His People, and in His Exclusive Right to Their Worship (18:1–20:27)

1. God Is To Be Honored by a Sanctified Sexuality among His People (18:1-30)

18:1-5. The Lord told Moses to warn the Israelites against the practices of the Egyptians and the Canaanites as a matter of covenant loyalty. Just as God would judge the Canaanites for their sins in this regard, Israelites who broke God's covenant could expect the same. Because God's people belong to the Lord, they must distinguish themselves from the pagan world by their loyalty to His commands.

God's people must refrain from practicing the corrupt and degrading abominations of the world. This command extended to sexual practices as well as ritualistic worship. Sexual laws were to solidify Israel's identity among her neighbors. If an alien was admitted into Israel, this would only be allowed on the condition that they not violate these established commands (cf. Lv 18:26; 20:2). Penalties for violations included death (cf. Lv 20:2, 9-16) and national forfeiture of the land (cf. Lv 18:25).

18:6-18. These verses present warnings about sexual practices that mirror the vices of the Canaanites and Egyptians (v. 3), all descendants of Ham. Sacred prostitution, incest, homosexuality, and various orgiastic rites were common in the lives of these peoples. The gods that were worshiped in Canaan were particularly debased, being devoid of moral character. Child sacrifice, snake worship, and sacred prostitution (both male and female) took place in Canaan on a scale unknown by other peoples. Israel later failed to heed these warnings and became corrupted from within.

The prohibitions are specific (more specific than many modern incest laws) and apodictic in character (**You shall not**...). Verse 6 begins the prohibitions with a general statement that is applied to specific situations in vv. 7-18. **To uncover nakedness** is a euphemism for intercourse. Close relatives are those who are literally "flesh of his flesh," that is, within one's family boundaries. The prohibitions are straightforward and include one's own birth mother (v. 7), stepmother (v. 8), sisters, either by birth or stepsisters (vv. 9, 11), grandchildren from either sons or daughters (v. 10), uncles or spouses of uncles (v. 14), daughters-in-law (v. 15), or sister-in-law (v. 16), and a mother and her daughter or grandchildren (v. 17). These relations are summarily described as **lewdness** (indecent or shameful).

18:19-23. Some have suggested (e.g., Roy Gane, *Leviticus, Numbers*, NIVAC [Grand Rapids, MI: Zondervan, 2004], 320–21) that the cases in vv. 19-23 are five laws grouped according to the commonality of the misuse of one's seed (semen). Intercourse with a menstruating woman rendered a man unclean. The list expanded outward to prohibit approaching a woman who is a **neighbor's wife** (v. 20) for the same reason. Such an action was a violation of Ex 20:14, and was also a misuse of the stewardship of one's body within the covenant of marriage. This prohibition is surprisingly placed alongside a prohibition against giving one's **offspring... to Molech** (v. 21) for purposes of child sacrifice. Homosexuality and bestiality are explicitly condemned in vv. 22-23. Later, Lv 20:13, 15-16 repeats these commands and adds the death penalty. Gane puts it well: "Our task here is to understand what the Bible says, not to rewrite it. Whether we like it or not, the Bible is simply not bound by modern Western constraints of political correctness" (p. 321). The condemnation extended to the morality of the action itself—not merely its association with pagan worship.

18:24-30. God's people must remember that the holiness of God requires that He impart judgment on the base practices of the pagans. Those who live abominable lives will be held responsible for their actions by God. Likewise, God's people today must remain loyal to their covenant God and not become involved in the practices of the world, or they will suffer discipline for their sins. In OT theology the sins of the people fell not only on the persons themselves, but also had ramifications for the land (v. 27). Since the land itself was God's holy property (cf. Ex 19:5; Lv 25:23), profane actions on that land had profound implications. The land itself would **spew** them **out** (v. 28) and the violators would be **cut off from** God's covenant **people** (v. 29).

The Jerusalem Council in Ac 15 followed the course of Levitical instruction in these chapters in highlighting areas of offense that Gentile Christians were to avoid. That list included eating things offered to demons (cf. Lv 17:3-9), eating blood in improperly killed meats (Lv 17:10-14), and sexual immorality in general (Lv 18). There seems to be no good reason to suggest that Christians are exempt from these stipulations, though they are free from the power of sin inherent in them through Christ (cf. Rm 6).

2. God Is To Be Honored by the Sanctified Social and Ethical Practices of His People, and Is To See His Holiness Reflected in Their Lives (19:1-37)

19:1-4. Again, the instructions **to Moses** from **the LORD** were for all of the assembly of **Israel** (v. 2). Bound up in the nature of these laws is the nature of the God who gave them, and in keeping them Israel would reflect her Lord. God called for Israel to emulate Him in **holy** (set apart, consecrated) practices that distinguished them as bearing His family likeness (v. 2). The people of Israel were to lead righteous lives, not merely observe rituals and sacrifices. One might wrongly assume from the extent of the rituals that sacrifice alone sufficed to relate to a holy God. Leviticus 19 highlights many seemingly isolated laws related to this truth. The Decalogue is summarized in a threefold set of commands: *Keep the law*: Revere your parents, keep the Sabbath, make no idols (vv. 1-4). *Celebrate God's goodness in worship*: Offer peace offerings (v. 5). *Care for the needy*: Make provision for the poor in gleaning (vv. 9-10).

God is intrinsically separate from evil, so God's people must conform to His holiness and keep His commandments that lead away from evil. A faithful believer recognizes and respects the rightful place of authority granted to his parents by God's own authority (v. 3a). The command to **keep My Sabbaths** (v. 3b) meant observing them according to commands governing this special day. Doing so demonstrated loyalty to God who established the covenant that included a Sabbath provision for man (cf. Ex 20:8-11). And since God was the one true God and Israel's Lord, it was wrong to cast **molten gods** as idols.

19:5-8. The ritual for the **peace** offering, which was given in detail in Lv 3:1-17 and 7:11-21, is mentioned here as a reminder to the believers that even peace with God must be celebrated in holiness and with attention to God's explicit commandments. If some of the offering was not eaten till **the third day**, the offerer would be **cut off from his people** (v. 8).

19:9-18. Believers exhibit Godlike social behavior when they provide for the needs of those less fortunate than themselves (vv. 9-10). The extent of a person's generosity could be seen in the amount of grain he left in his fields for gleaning for the needy and the stranger. Similarly, one's priorities today can be seen in the entries in one's checkbook.

Believers deal with one another in good faith. They do **not steal** (v. 11; cf. Ex 20:15). They are honest and fair in their business and personal ethics (vv. 11-16) because God is just and His character shapes their daily decisions. Swearing **falsely** does not characterize their words (v. 12; cf. Ex 20:16). God is not a companion to fraudulent oaths. Believers do not extort and withhold wages that are due (v. 13). Similar prohibitions against extortion are in Dt 24:14-15 and Pr 22:16. Believers do not presume on others' possessions willfully or by violent force. Everyone is to be treated fairly by believers. One should never take advantage of anyone. Believers are also to respect the **deaf** and **blind** (v. 14).

Believers also do not exercise partiality in their judgments (v. 15). A person's status in society was not a basis for favoritism (whether poor or rich). Righteousness requires impartiality toward everyone and the avoidance of tale-bearing. Loving others means that believers do not bear personal grudges and hatreds (vv. 17-18). These laws reinforced the underlying principles of the Ten Commandments, but they went further by extending them to situations beyond the context of Ex 20.

19:19. Why this verse groups together a number of seemingly unrelated commands is not clear. Verse 19 prohibits breeding **two kinds** of plow animals, **two kinds of seed**, and disparate cloths like wool and linen. Perhaps the reason for these commands was to remind God's people that they were separated to Him. They were to conform to God's holiness by keeping the distinctions that God made. Similarly, Israel was prohibited from mixing oils and incenses like those used in the tabernacle (cf. Ex 30:32-38).

19:20-22. If a man lay with a female **slave**, his sin could be expiated through a **guilt offering** of a **ram**.

19:23-25. After the Hebrews entered the land and planted fruit **trees**, they were to refrain from eating the fruit for three years, dedicate the fruit of the fourth year **to the Lord**, and then eat from the trees in **the fifth year**. The **fourth** year's fruit was especially dedicated to the Lord as a form of a firstfruits offering. This recalls God's words to Adam and Eve not to eat of the tree of the knowledge of good and evil (cf. Gn 2:17). Believers who recognize God's ownership of everything are willing to worship Him no matter what He may require of them.

19:26-31. This section likely refers to practices of religious cults of the dead (cf. Dt 14:1-2; Jr 16:6; Am 8:10). Literally the Hebrew of v. 26 reads, "You shall not eat on the blood." This may not be a repetition of the prohibition against eating blood, or it may be a warning against being involved in some aspect of pagan worship. Pagan practices, such as cutting one's hair and beard (Jr 9:25-26; 25:23), or making **tattoo marks** on one's body (v. 28), were an abomination to the Lord. Prostitution (v. 29), **divination** (vv. 26, 31), and consulting **mediums** (v. 31; cf. Lv 20:6) were also forbidden. It is important to separate oneself from pagan practices and thus to maintain the distinction of being God's child.

19:32-37. Believers are expected to conform to God's holiness by demonstrating kindness and justice to others. This includes treating **the aged** with dignity and those less fortunate (such as resident aliens) with kindness (vv. 32-34), and dealing ethically in business matters (vv. 35-37). Though weights and measures are not at the forefront of business ethics today, packaging smaller portions of products in grocery stores offers less to the consumer for the same price. The problem is not in offering less, but in presenting it as though it were of the same value.

Thus, in Lv 19 God's people were to demonstrate conformity to His holiness by keeping His commandments (the letter of the law), by relating to others in love (the spirit of the law), by living according to His standards of separation from the world (the requirement of the law), and by demonstrating His kindness and justice to others (the heart-application of the law).

3. God Is To Be Honored by the Exclusive Nature of the Sanctified Worship and Family Practices of His People (20:1-27)

This chapter details punitive prescriptions for Israel in dealing with pagan religious (idolatrous) sins and sexual (incestuous, bestiality) sins uncovered in the covenant community. Chapter 18 identified and prohibited certain dangerous actions that brought defilement to the land, and chap. 20 identifies the penalties for such actions. There were penalties for offenses committed against the Lord (vv. 1-8), and for offenses among the Israelite family (vv. 9-21). The order of the prohibitions, though at first puzzling, is according to the punishments prescribed. Verses 9-16 list actions meriting the death penalty, vv. 17-19 list offenses meriting being cut off, and vv. 20-21 mention offenses that result in barrenness or childlessness.

20:1-8. Grave sins were to receive the death penalty (e.g., by stoning, v. 2), a measure designed to render such practices inoperative. Those who worshiped **Molech** did so through presenting their children (cf. 18:21) to him either sacrificially or sexually (vv. 2, 4). Molech was the god of the Ammonites who lived in the Transjordan (cf. 2Kg 23:10; Jr 32:35). Those who were involved in such acts showed utter disregard for the stewardship of the precious life God entrusted to parents. Further, such actions defiled the tabernacle (God's **sanctuary**) and God's own reputation (**name**, v. 3).

This chapter also enumerated the many sinful practices that emanated from false worship including spiritism, disrespect for parents shown through cursing (invoking the "gods" to bring evil on one's parents), adultery (the destruction of an Israelite home), incest, homosexuality, and bestiality (common in the ancient Near East). Even today, too many ministers treat the symptoms of unbelief (a pagan lifestyle) with a series of lists (legalistic prescriptions), when they should be confronting the root of the problem, namely, that false worship leads to false conduct.

Religions of the ancient Near East were rife with magic and superstition, including necromancy and veneration of various demons (vv. 2-6). These verses warn against false worship of **Molech**, in which child sacrifice was performed, and spiritism. Believers must refuse pagan beliefs if they are to develop a life of holiness to the Lord. One should recognize throughout this chapter the repeated refrain/promise of divine judgment for moral failures: **I will cut him off from among his people** (vv. 3, 5-6). One should also recognize the repeated incentives of the Lord's identity (**I am the Lord your God;** vv. 7, 24) and His holy character (vv. 8, 26).

Necromancy (v. 6) involved conjuration for the purposes of magically revealing the future or influencing the course of future events (cf. 1Sm 28:7). Such practices were compared to prostitution, a violation of covenant. Those who provided such services were sentenced to capital punishment. The basis for the commandments in this section, as for the section as a whole (beginning in chap. 18), was reinforced through a reminder of the Lord's holiness (vv. 7-8). God's exhortations to keep His laws have been stated frequently (cf. 18:4-5, 26; 19:37).

Here, however, is the first instance in Leviticus where God is identified as the one who sanctified Israel (**I am the Lord who sanctifies you**, v. 8). As the Israelites observed His statutes, He sanctified them. With this reminder of God's call to be holy, believers must shun both pagan beliefs and practices if they are to lead a life of holiness to the Lord. Worship and service will eventually affect the lifestyle of those practicing it. If one believes and worships like a pagan, eventually one will live like a pagan. The solution is not to merely stop living like a pagan; that deals only with the surface issue. The solution is to worship the Lord in spirit and in truth (cf. Jn 4:24).

20:9. Cursing one's parents was prohibited under penalty of death. This followed the law on holiness because of the place of honoring one's parents given in the fifth Commandment (cf. 19:2-3). Such cursing meant more than uttering a word in anger. "To curse" was the opposite of "to honor." To honor meant investing one's parents with the weight of authority and attention that was due to them. To curse meant making light of their authority or treating them as despicable. In the process, one might invoke the "gods" to afflict one's parents. Cursing one's parents was a capital crime (cf. Ex 21:17; Pr 20:20; Mt 15:4), though rabbinic custom indicates that it was seldom, if ever, enforced. God designed His laws so that exhortations to obey Him follow verses that refer to familial relationships. If one honors one's parents, many of the violations noted here will not take place.

20:10-21. The sins listed in vv. 10-21 are essentially the same sins elaborated in chap. 18. Here the emphasis is on the penalties prescribed for such offenses. Capital crimes included **adultery** (v. 10), incest between a man and **his father's wife** (v. 11), incest between a man and **his daughter-in-law** (v. 12), male homosexuality (v. 13), and bestiality (vv. 15-16). Though these sins are private, they are an offense to the Lord.

Capital punishment for man and beast was prescribed both for male and female acts of bestiality (vv. 15-16). God created the world with order (Gn 1–2), and these activities were violations of God's intent when He created sex. All the violations of near relatives (vv. 17-21) in uncovering their nakedness were outside of God's design and blessing. Though approaching a woman in her menses has been noted before (cf. 15:24; 18:19), this was the first time punishment (being cut off from Israel) for that act was mentioned.

20:22-27. The final section of this chapter highlights the relationship of the Lord to His sanctified **land**, and His expectation that His people distinguish themselves from other nations. God's "sacred space" was not only in the tabernacle, but also in the land He had reserved for His tabernacle. Israel's privileged position within the land was contingent on their obeying the Lord's statutes. He had separated them for this purpose (v. 26), and His expectation and demand was that they act as though they belonged to Him, for indeed they did.

C. Things or Persons That Are Holy (Set Apart) with Instruction to Maintain Their Holiness (21:1–27:34)

1. Matters Related to the Defilement or Disqualifications of the Priests or the Holy Offerings (21:1–22:33)

a. Priestly and High Priestly Qualifications (21:1-24)

Thus far in the instructions from the Lord, the exhortations to holiness have been directed to the people as a whole (cf. 17:2; 18:2; 19:2; 20:26). Chapters 21–22 are concerned with three matters related to the defilement or disqualification of the priests and the qualities needed in animals for sacrifice.

The structure of these chapters reinforces the central point driven home for the priests in 22:1-16 that God's holy sanctuary must not be desecrated:

A. Qualifications rendering priests eligible for service (21:1-15)
B. Defects rendering priests ineligible for service (21:16-24)
C. Preserving the sacred space from desecration (22:1-16)
B'. Defects rendering animals ineligible for sacrifice (22:17-25)
A'. Qualifications rendering animals eligible for sacrifice (22:26-33)

The force of this structure focused on the central section (C), emphasizing the priestly requirement to keep the sacred space in the tabernacle free from desecration. This compelled the priests to maintain vigilance in their enforcement of standards for maintaining the sacred space in which God was approached. The lesson extended to the whole of the encampment: If God is present with sinful man, only divinely appointed conditions make this possible.

21:1-15. In the priests' relationship to other Israelites, particularly in marriage, the potential for defilement needed to be addressed. A priest could incur defilement by contact with death (vv. 1-3), by means of self-mutilation or shaving the head (v. 5), by means of unsanctioned marriage (vv. 4, 7-8), or by physical imperfections (vv. 16-24). Those who minister in God's presence have been given a higher standard than others. God's servants must lead lives that can be fully commended to the conscience of others.

For purposes of ministry, their contact with death (v. 11) was limited because death, as the final curse for human sin, was defiling and prevented one from entering the Lord's presence (cf. Nm 19:11-22). The priest was to perpetuate hope and purity in the eyes of the people of God by holding himself aloof from the ritual defilement that came by mourning and death. As a priest he must stand ready to mediate at all times. His fellowship with the Lord was his highest intimacy, transcending even his relationship to near kin. Shaving the head, mutilating the beard, and fleshly mutilation were aspects of Canaanite mourning rituals forbidden to the priests (cf. Jr 9:26; 25:23; Ezk 5:1).

The priest must exemplify the purity of the Lord's covenant in his marriage (vv. 7-9, 13-15). The priest could not marry a prostitute, a divorced woman (v. 7), or a non-virgin, or even a widow (vv. 13-14). The reputation of a priest's wife must not detract from her husband's fitness to minister in holy matters. He was to be pure and blameless, exemplifying the ideal marriage for the people. In fact, in an important sense all Israelites were priests (the nation was to mediate the blessing of Abraham to the world), and yet God set a higher standard for the tabernacle priests. Similarly, the NT includes passages that demand higher standards for elders and church leaders (cf. 1Tm 3:1-13). Those who lead in corporate worship, teach people the Word of God, and serve as God's representatives must lead lives that are exemplary in every way.

The same was true of the priests' families. They were to meet higher standards in their conduct. If a priest's daughter was found to have engaged in **harlotry** (false worship), she was to be burned as an indication of the desire of Israel to purge the nation of the evil associated with false worship (v. 9).

In vv. 10-12 the focus shifted from the priest to the high priest while applying the same principles. He had already been distinguished from his fellow priests by means of his anointing and his garments. The high priest was required to hold to a higher standard: unkempt hair or an uncovered head might communicate that his head did not belong to God, in contrast with the significance of the anointing oil (v. 10). No acts of devotion, even toward a deceased mother or father (v. 11), were allowed. He was required to marry a virgin of his own people lest he **profane his** descendants (v. 15) and disqualify them from office. All these external indicators were intended to show that his allegiance was to the Lord alone. Of course, the heart of the priest was supposed to reflect that same desire, but selfish desires negate any external actions. Only Jesus, the great high priest who entered the sanctuary and offered a sacrifice once for all time (Heb 10:14), demonstrated a fervor to the Lord that fulfilled this imagery.

21:16-24. The man of God had to be fully qualified to perform his duties, reflecting the perfections of the Lord Himself. The priests themselves had to be without physical imperfections or blemishes (vv. 16-23). This qualification is identical to that of the sacrifices and offerings in Lv 22:17-25. Just as the animals for sacrifice were to be without defect (22:17), so the priest was to be of perfect heart (wholehearted and sincere). Deformities do not reflect the original perfection of God's creation. God's mediators were required to be examples to the people. He could not demand purification from defilement and disease if he was in defilement himself.

Such imperfections, while preventing priestly service, did not prevent the descendants of Aaron from consuming their allotted portions (vv. 22-23). Can religious leaders call for obedience and purity in their followers if they themselves are living below that standard? The OT requirement dealt with physical features because the ritual laws required physical wholeness for tabernacle/temple worship. In the church we are concerned about the proper gifts and moral character of those who lead the worshipers. For this reason many ought to be disqualified even if they desire or seek such positions of authority.

The issues in chaps. 21–22 that mark the highest obstacle to holiness relate to one's family relations. This remains true for believers today. Jesus taught that they should be willing to leave father and mother and take up their cross and follow Him (cf. Mt 10:37-38).

b. Rules to Preserve the Holiness of Offerings to the Lord (22:1-33)

22:1-16. God's ministers must remain clean if they are to participate in spiritual service. Moses issued a warning that priests ought not eat the bread of sacrifice if it was defiled by some uncleanness. The priests' proximity to holy things made them the most likely perpetrators of the offense. A spiritual leader who is not spiritual himself (because of sins, unworthy eating, or the like) ought not lead other people spiritually (cf. Lk 6:39-42). Part of the holy things was given to the priests as their stipend (vv. 1-2; cf. 6:14-18; 7:6, 35-36). The priests were responsible to ensure that the holy things entrusted to them were properly used. Only those who were truly dependent on a priest (e.g., a slave or widowed daughter, vv. 11, 13) were allowed to eat the holy things—no alien, hired man, or sojourner was allowed, lest the holy be mixed with the common. In God's economy, leaders will be held accountable for their stewardship. That includes their personal cleanliness (vv. 4-6). The penalty for failing to follow the instruction was death (v. 9).

If a person such as a guest of any priest (v. 10) somehow inadvertently ate of the sacred foods, he was required to restore the sacred food plus 20 percent (v. 14). The priest's family members benefited from the priest's portion (v. 11), but they disqualified themselves from this portion by marrying outside the priestly line (v. 12). Every bite of food provided for the priests was treated as a holy trust. God's ministers must not squander or misappropriate gifts from God's people (cf. 1Tm 6:7-11).

22:17-33. The instructions given in 22:17-30 address not only the priests, but also the Israelites who were selecting appropriate sacrifices to bring to the sanctuary. One can only imagine how tempting it was at times to offer less than what the Lord required. The standards for safeguarding the holiness of the sacrifice during the ritual of worship for the burnt offering (vv. 17-29) and peace offering (vv. 21-30) were prescribed for the priests as well as for the congregation. The requirements for the animal in an acceptable sacrifice were detailed; these were reminders to the priests and people that God is to be approached only by those who offer their best. To offer any less is to misrepresent God's character.

Obedient worshipers still approach God with a pleasing sacrifice (cf. Rm 12:1-2). What folly to act in pious hypocrisy and to give God something worthless! An astute person might figure that he could take a business loss on a deformed animal and give it to the Lord in an act of spiritual beneficence. The apparent reason for the reiteration of the rules pertaining to these sacrifices here was to reinforce that the imperfect cannot be presented when God requires what is perfect. The sacrifices must reflect the condition of the offerers' hearts, and the priest was charged with ensuring and reinforcing this condition.

Faithful worshipers were to comply with the requirements of the holy God who sanctified them (vv. 29-33). Those who wish to worship the redeeming, sanctifying Lord God must make acceptable offerings to Him. Only the truly excellent should be brought to God (2Co 8–9; Php 4:10-20; 1Pt 2:5; Eph 5:2; Heb 13:15-16). The standards for a perfect sacrifice anticipate the final and ultimate sacrifice made by Jesus Christ. He was completely free from any sin (cf. Heb 9:14), a Lamb without blemish or spot (cf. 1Pt 1:19; Jn 1:29; Rv 5:6; 7:9; 12:11; 13:8; 15:3; 17:14; 19:9; 21:22). The last verses (vv. 31-33) were a plea to honor the Lord's name, since He is the one who sanctified the nation.

2. Calendric Convocations: Stipulations Ensuring That Israel Sanctifies Time to the Lord (23:1-44)

This section is one of five festal calendars in the Torah (cf. Ex 23:14-17; 34:18-26; Nm 28–29; Dt 16:1-7; but cf. Ezk 45:18-25). The calendars in Leviticus and Numbers clarify the duration of each festival and pinpoint their starting points. Leviticus 23 identifies seven appointed meeting times, beginning with the Passover and ending with the Feast of Booths. The first three feasts of Passover, Unleavened Bread, and Firstfruits occurred in rapid succession in the spring of the year over a period of eight days. These later came to be referred to collectively as "Passover." The fourth feast, Harvest, occurred fifty days later at the beginning of the summer. By NT times this feast had come to be known by its Greek name, Pentecost, a word meaning "fifty" (cf. Ac 2). The last three feasts—Trumpets, Atonement, and Tabernacles—extended over a period of 21 days in the fall of the year (the seventh month). They came to be known collectively as "Tabernacles."

23:1-3. In the institution of the Sabbath law, God's people were encouraged to esteem and worship their Creator by imitating His rest in creation. In honoring the Sabbath, God's people proclaimed His sovereignty over their lives (cf. Ex 20:3). Some kinds of work not permitted on the Sabbath were detailed in the Torah. They included food preparation (cf. Ex 16:23), plowing and harvesting (cf. Ex 34:21), and making a fire or gathering wood (cf. Ex 35:3; Nm 15:32-36). In this way the Israelites avoided being preoccupied with worldly affairs. Here God was willing to meet with man where he was (**in all your dwellings**, v. 3), rather than at the sanctuary. For believers today, Christ is their ultimate rest (cf. Heb 4:3-11).

Based on this passage and others in the OT, the Israelites came together on the Sabbath (Saturday), ceased their work, and worshiped God. Of the ten commandments listed in Ex

20:1-17, only nine of them were reinstituted in the NT. (Matthew 19:18-19 repeats murder, adultery, stealing, false witness, honoring parents, and, implicitly, worshiping God; Rm 13:9 cites coveting.) Worshiping God properly covers the first three commandments. The one commandment that was not reaffirmed was the Sabbath. Instead, Jesus said that He is the Lord of the Sabbath (Mt 12:8).

Following His creative work, God rested on the seventh day. The all-powerful God does not get tired or need to take a break and rest. He ceased from labor for the simple reason Jesus cited in Mk 2:27: "The Sabbath was made for man, and not man for the Sabbath." God established the Sabbath as a rest for His people who are mortal and need a time to focus on God. In this, human spirits and bodies are both renewed. The OT law required keeping the Sabbath as part of the moral, legal, and sacrificial system by which the Israelites satisfied God's requirements for behavior, government, and access to God. The Sabbath was part of the law in that sense. In order to "remain" in favor with God, one kept the Sabbath. If it was not kept, then the person was in sin and faced possible punishment (cf. Ex 31:15; Nm 15:32-36).

With Messiah's atonement, and justification by faith (Rm 5:1), Christians no longer are required to keep the law and hence the Sabbath, which was only a shadow of things to come (Col 2:16-17). Believers in Christ are not under law, but grace (Rm 6:14-15). The Sabbath is fulfilled in Jesus because in Him there is rest (Mt 11:28). New covenant believers are not under obligation to keep the law and this goes for the Sabbath as well. Nevertheless, the wisdom of a weekly day of rest and spiritual rejuvenation remains appropriate. It no longer need be on the seventh day (Rm 14:5), but it would be wise to include a rest and worship day on a weekly basis.

23:4-8. In the Passover and Unleavened Bread, God's people were to recall His acts of mighty deliverance on their behalf by remembering their Egyptian bondage and the exodus. Recalling the faithfulness of God on behalf of believers in specific historical celebrations is thus a commended practice. The Israelites were to eat unleavened bread for a week, cease from ordinary work, and (a requirement not stated in Ex 12:15-16) present a burnt offering to the Lord (v. 8). The presentation of an offering that was totally burned symbolized the obliteration of one's own self-centered nature. Believers today should consider that Christ, as their Passover Lamb (cf. 1Co 5:7), has been sacrificed for a similar purpose for them (cf. Rm 6:6).

23:9-14. In the offering of the first fruit sheaf, God's people were to recognize His provision and offer praise from their material goods. Here the first grain sheaf was presented as a **wave** offering (v. 11; cf. Lv 7:30). The waving of the sheaf signified the acceptance of the worshiper, but also since it was presented on the eighth day it signified a new beginning. Presented on the first day of the week, it pointed worshipers to the total dedication of the year's produce to the Lord.

23:15-22. The Feast of Weeks or Pentecost was a time of thanksgiving for God's provision. Believers gave to Him a token of their best and shared their abundance with the needy. This offering came seven weeks after the Firstfruits offering (v. 16). In this firstfruits offering they brought what the grain offering had made possible: **loaves of bread** (v. 17). The church began on the day of Pentecost, fifty days after Jesus' resurrection (cf. Ac 2:1). God gave the Holy Spirit to signify the fulfillment of Christ's work and the beginning of the Church Age. The addition of the peace offering (v. 19) to the ritual stressed the fellowship between God and the redeemed.

23:23-25. For the Israelites, the **blowing of trumpets** represented God calling to His people (cf. Nm 10:1-10) to prepare for a holy assembly. God regularly calls His children away from their labor and into His holy assembly where they may worship Him. The **first** day of **the seventh month** (*Tishri*), *Rosh Hashana* (head of the year), was a day of particular preparation (v. 24) for the coming feasts of Atonement and Booths. The people were to abstain from **work** and **present an offering . . . to the Lord** (v. 25). Some say the trumpet of this feast depicts the trumpet that will signal the rapture of the Church (cf. 1Th 4:16; 1Co 15:52). Others see it as a reference to the end-time regathering of dispersed Israel.

23:26-32. On **the day** of Purgation or Atonement, God obligated His people to convene in His presence to find spiritual renewal by humbling themselves, refraining from work, and entreating Him on the basis of the efficacious atoning sacrifice . The Day of Atonement was to be celebrated on **the tenth day of** the **seventh month** (v. 27). The day actually began on the **evening** of the **ninth** day **of the month** and extended to the evening of the tenth day (v. 32). Later rabbinic tradition carried this timing to all special days.

23:33-44. The people, once in the land, must never forget the hardships of their temporary dwellings in the wilderness (vv. 42-43). In the wilderness they experienced God's guidance. Living in **booths** for a week was also a reminder of the selfishness and self-indulgence that too often characterized the nation in its Egyptian bondage. Several prophets borrowed imagery from this feast to relate it to the coming reign of the Lord (cf. Is 52:7-13; Mc 5:1-4). This feast will be celebrated during the millennium (cf. Zch 14:16), presumably as a remembrance of God's deliverance through the Messiah. Remembering God's dealings in the past encourages believers to trust Him in the present.

3. Things To Be Treated as Holy in the Service of God: Bread, Oil, and the Sanctity of the Divine Name (24:1-23)

24:1-16. Along with holy times, Israel was to maintain holy objects in the presence of the Lord. These included **oil** for the lamps in the sanctuary and the bread to be placed on the **table** there. Bread as food and oil for light, as essential reminders of God's grace toward man, were maintained in the daily service of the tabernacle.

The rituals pertaining to the bread and oil served as reminders to the priests and to all who approached that a divine King was in residence at the tabernacle (cf. Nm 23:21). The tabernacle, and later the temple, were places of worship, but they also signified the residence of the Lord among His people (Solomon later recognized this, cf. 1Ki 8:27-29). Tending lamps, burning incense, and giving grain offerings paralleled the kinds of services performed for earthly kings. Though the Lord did not consume the bread, it was there to remind His people that He was the source of their livelihood.

The sons of Israel brought the oil to supply the **lampstand** (cf. Ex 27:20-21). The perpetual presence of the oil (beaten, not crushed, for purer quality) reminded believers that devoted service to the Lord ensures that the way of access to Him is forever open.

The bread is called "showbread" in the KJV. The NASB has "bread of the Presence" in Nm 4:7, which is literally "bread of the face." This may have reminded the priests that God's people could enjoy continual communion with their Lord. Regular meals were a time of communion and fellowship. Fresh unleavened bread was placed on the table each Sabbath (vv. 8-9). The priests' partaking of this bread may have symbolized that all members of the twelve tribes were in fellowship with their God. Though it was God's "food" in the sense that it was devoted to Him, it was not considered divine sustenance.

Alongside the holy objects, an account is given of a person who **blasphemed** the **Name** of the Lord (v. 11). This is the second of two narrations in the book (cf. Lv 10:1-20). This story served to reinforce the theme of holy matters. When the son of an **Israelite** mother and an **Egyptian** father **blasphemed** the name of the Lord (a violation of Ex 20:7; cf. Ex 22:28), that person was to be stoned. God's desire to dwell among His people required that they be vigilant about the sanctity of the divine name. The "name" of the Lord is far more than an identification label. It refers to His nature, His person. This Israelite should have known better than to use God's name in a curse. God's justice demanded that the blasphemer be judged. As a result he was stoned to death **outside the camp** by **the congregation**.

How should believers treat the name of the Lord? The words "Hallowed be Your name" (Mt 6:9) mean "May Your name be holy." Believers must speak and live with concern for God's reputation. All that many people will ever know of God is what they hear and see in believers' lives.

24:17-23. Chapter 24 closes with penalties for various violent actions. The penalty for murder is death (v. 17). God had made a distinction in Ex 21:12-14 between murder and manslaughter. Those who engaged in violent acts were liable to find themselves facing violent punishment (an **eye for eye**, v. 20). Although these retributive laws are often seen as cruel and unusual, their purpose was to preserve justice and limit vengeance. The point was to have the punishment fit the crime rather than meting out the death penalty in response to an injury. Whether native born or alien (v. 22), each was to take care to honor the name of the Lord.

4. The Land as Holy in the Service of God: Regulations for the Sabbath Year and the Year of Jubilee (25:1-55)

This chapter again considers holy times, not from the abbreviated schedule of the feasts of chap. 23, but from the standpoint of the consecration of an entire year (once in six years and once in fifty years). The Lord spoke to Moses again and addressed the Israelites on the sanctity of the land He had promised them. Chapter 25 addresses the Sabbath and Jubilee regulations, and chap. 26 states that the penalty for failure to obey was exile from the land.

25:1-7. The Sabbath year was to be celebrated commencing with Israel's conquest of Canaan (vv. 2-3). Every **seventh year** was to be reserved by the Israelites to acknowledge the Lord's provision in a Sabbath rest for the land in which the land was to revert to its natural state. All agricultural processes were to be suspended and the land was to lie fallow. Whatever grew was to be shared by all. God encouraged the people to share His bounty with one another as they exhibited their strict dependence on Him in this act of obedience (v. 6). Like the manna in the wilderness, the unharvested bounty served as a reminder of their need for the Lord's daily provisions (see vv. 20-21). Sadly, the nonobservance of this command led in subsequent years to Israel's captivity, in which the land observed its Sabbaths without the presence of the people of the covenant (2Ch 36:21; Jr 25:11).

25:8-19. Stipulations for the Year of Jubilee (**fiftieth year**) are set forth in vv. 8-19. The admonitions set forth here related to the impoverished Israelite and the expectation that others in the nation would provide for his need. Verses 8-12 consider the accounting for the Year of Jubilee. Proceeding by sevens in terms of years, the fiftieth year (the Year of Jubilee) coincided with the first year of the next cycle of seven years. In other words, there was a two-year Sabbath rest for the land required at that time. Five years of normal agricultural work followed the Year of Jubilee, and then another Sabbatical Year.

In the celebration of the Jubilee year, all property was to be returned to its original owners (v. 13). This related to situations where Israelites might need to sell their land because of poverty. The guiding principle is stated in vv. 14 and 17: **you shall not wrong one another**. The value of the payment in receiving the use of the land was calculated on the basis of the proximity of the Year of Jubilee (vv. 15-16). The text makes it clear that the land was to remain with its owner; what was being sold was the value of the **crops** (vv. 16, 23). This made the failure to comply with this command even more egregious: it was stealing land that belonged to another. Further, every Israelite slave had the option of being released this year from his servitude (v. 10, **each of you shall return to his family**; cf. Ex 21:2). Debts due from one Israelite to another were remitted, but not those that foreigners owed to Israelites (cf. Dt 15:1-3).

This passage is addressing the moral requirement to repay one's debt in the context of the centrality of the land in God's promises to His people. Of course, the principle taught here was subject to abuse, as certain Israelites may have gauged their willingness to loan money based on the nearness of an approaching Sabbatical Year. God's intent was to expand upon a practical problem addressed in Dt 15:13-14. There, masters were to provide their slaves with gifts upon their release. Here the emphasis is on the land to which the Israelite returned to make his living. Losing one's land to a lender had its limits (six years), but this was not a short wait for one making a living from that land.

25:20-22. These laws ensured that God's people set aside times to acknowledge that the bounty of the earth they share is a gift from the sovereign Creator. Obedience is met with divine blessing. God would see to it that compliance with His commandments would result in His bounty for His people. A threefold increase in the sixth year of reaping (v. 21) ensured that property owners would benefit sufficiently as a result of their stewardship of the land.

25:23-54. Moreover, the law provided that a fellow Israelite or near kinsman was to redeem persons or property on behalf of kin (v. 25). This is the first of a series of four instances, extending through v. 54, in which fellow Israelites became impoverished. Verses 29-34 impose rules on redemption for houses in cities and villages, and grant a **permanent right of redemption** for Levites. Verses 35-38 clarify that loans must be made without interest or usury in order to honor God, who seeks justice for the poor, aliens, and sojourners in His land. Verses 39-43 applied to situations where an Israelite became a **slave** to pay a debt. Israelites were to be treated as hired men, not slaves, for their true service was to the divine Master (vv. 42, 55), not to any earthly lord. Less lenience was granted toward slaves from other countries (vv. 44-46), but in these circumstances too God was concerned with just treatment (cf. 19:33-34). Israelites conscripted into the service of a foreigner (vv. 47-54) were justly redeemed from such situations by their near kinsmen as a matter of high priority.

Some have objected that it is morally offensive that the law treats slavery as acceptable and normal, especially the laws related to foreign slaves as chattel or property (vv. 44-46). With regard to Israelite slaves, they were actually indentured servants and would obtain their freedom upon paying their debt or at the Sabbatical Year (v. 40; Dt 15:12). As for foreign slaves, the law did not treat them as chattel in a technical sense. Throughout history, chattel slaves had no rights of kinship or marriage, of physical protection, of freedom of movement, or of opportunity to obtain freedom. Although the law did permit Israelite slave owners to leave foreign slaves to their heirs, there were limits on the way they could treat them that was distinct from normal chattel slavery in the ancient Near East.

Walter C. Kaiser Jr. notes some of the distinctions of biblical laws pertaining to foreign slaves, stating that Israelite masters did not have

> absolute power of life and death over the slaves. According to biblical law, a master could lose his life if he killed his slave. If he merely inflicted bodily injury on his slave, such as knocking out a tooth or injuring an eye, the slave immediately won his full emancipation (Exod. 21:20, 26). The foreign slave, along with the Hebrew household also had a day of rest each week (Exod. 20:10; Deut. 5:14).

Kaiser continues,

> A female captive who was married by her captor could not be sold again as a slave, and if her master, now her husband, grew to hate her, she too had to be liberated and was a free person (Deut. 21:14). Even marriage between slaves was recognized as sacred as that between free persons and any violation of that covenant by another man, free or not, even while that slave was only engaged to another, was a sin requiring a guilt offering (Walter C. Kaiser Jr, *Toward Old Testament Ethics* [Grand Rapids, MI: Zondervan, 1983], 289).

Despite these helpful distinctions that demonstrate that the law did not treat foreign slaves as the rest of the ancient Near Eastern world did, it still seems ethically questionable that this form of foreign slavery was permitted at all. Although there is no perfect answer to this ethical question, the following should mitigate the problem to a degree: First, there was no racial component to this sort of slavery. It is not as though non-Israelites were considered non-persons or even inferior persons as was the case in European and North American slavery. Second, Israelites were permitted to buy—not capture—(the word **acquire** in Lv 25:44 lit., means "buy") foreign slaves from remote nations. This would make the incidence of this sort of slavery quite rare. In fact, it was most likely limited to royalty and the upper echelons of society. These slaves likely had special skills such as reading, writing, or translating, making them valuable assets who were treated well. Some of the purchased foreign slaves were outsiders living within the midst of Israel. Their circumstances would be much like those of Israelite indentured servants, albeit without the ability to leave every seventh year. Third, the purchase of a slave was likely not from a foreign master or slave trader but from the slave himself. Thus, this was more like the Israelite institution wherein a Hebrew slave could sell himself to a master and even decide to make his slave status permanent (Ex 21:5-6). Fourth, masters were not permitted to abuse or treat their foreign slaves with brutality (Lv 19:34; Dt 10:19). Finally, if a foreign slave became a follower of the one, true God of Israel, he would no longer be considered a foreigner and would have the same rights and privileges of a Hebrew slave.

25:55. The chapter ends with an affirmation of the theological justification for all these laws: God is the Master of all Israelites. Unless this dictum was understood and taken to heart by all within Israel, obedience to any of these specific laws would be unlikely. Unfortunately, later prophets like Amos (Am 2:6-10; 4:1-2) exposed how Israel's self-serving interests often superseded their just treatment of others, even their own people. Every provision was made for assisting the poor out of their situation. Slave labor was not allowed; rather, individuals were consigned to work as hired laborers and were to be afforded the dignity that came with that status.

5. The Land as Holy in the Service of God: Experiencing Conditional Covenantal Blessings in the Land and the Consequences of Disobedience to the Lord (26:1-46)

26:1-13. This chapter is reminiscent of a treaty between a sovereign king and his vassals. The King (the Lord) lays out the stipulations of loyalty to be shown by those who are in covenant with Him (Israel, His vassal). The Lord advised and admonished His people regarding their covenant obligations. The Israelites must keep the law, especially the essential elements of avoiding idols and sanctifying both the Sabbath and God's sanctuary (vv. 1-2). Prostrating oneself before a **stone** or dishonoring God's Sabbaths were examples of covenant disloyalty. The Lord rewards those who live obediently (vv. 4-10). Obedience before Him will bring agricultural fertility (vv. 4-5), **peace** and protection in the land (v. 6), and victory in battles (vv. 7-8). The Lord's own presence among His people is the guarantee of the rewards for obedience (vv. 11-13).

26:14-39. These verses spell out the consequences of disobedience, calling down the curses that fall on the disobedient in the sovereign-vassal relationship of the covenant. If Israel refused to repent of its disobedience, God would bring down curses on the nation, cited here in five stages of increasing severity. Stage 1: **Terror, consumption and fever** and defeat in battle (vv. 14-17); Stage 2: famine and drought (vv. 18-20); Stage 3: wild beasts (vv. 21-22); Stage 4: war, pestilence, and rationed food (vv. 23-26); and Stage 5: cannibalism and exile from the land (vv. 27-38). The land in which God would dwell with His people must be holy. When the disobedient people were exiled as a result of their failures, the land would enjoy its rest.

The message of these verses is clear: Disobedience to God will bring discipline, and continued, persistent disobedience will bring more severe forms of discipline from the hand of the Lord. That the section of curses is longer than the statement of blessings is also instructive. "If" (vv. 14, 15 [twice], 18, 21, 23, 27, 40) Israel should prove unfaithful, God would prove faithful to His holy nature and not to their sinful interests. Overt manifestations of covenant-breaking disloyalty (v. 15) would result in military defeat (v. 17). And **pride** in earthly **power** would result in an infertile earth (vv. 19-20). Hostility toward the Lord would result in His sending plagues and wild **beasts** to devour both man and **cattle** (vv. 21-22). Further hostility would be met with a sevenfold punishment (vv. 24, 28) for sin in the form of pestilence and famine (vv. 23-26). Unrepentant and continued hostility would be met with situations forcing cannibalism of one's own family (vv. 27-29), the demolition of idolatrous centers (v. 30), the decimation of cities (vv. 31-32), and ultimately exile (vv. 33-39).

Repentance, however, brings hope (vv. 40-46). Forsaking egocentric endeavors and returning to God while forsaking disobedience will bring forgiveness and blessing. The principle here is clear—believers are to obey God, humble themselves, repent, and confess their sins (vv. 40-41). God will then act in accord with His gracious nature to forgive and reinstate the blessings of their forefathers **Jacob** (who experienced his season away from God and returned), **Isaac**, and **Abraham**.

26:40-46. Chapter 26 concludes with the expectation of grace extended by God for a repentant people who will have violated the commandments concerning the land in which He dwells (vv. 40-46). Moreover, it emphasizes the unconditional nature of God's covenant with Israel. Despite His discipline of the nation, including dispersion, God promises that He **will not reject them, nor will [He] so abhor them as to destroy them, breaking [His] covenant with them; for I am the Lord their God** (v. 44). Thus, even Israel's disobedience will not make God ever forget His covenant with Israel nor will He ever remove the land grant He gave to Israel.

Chapter 27 will specify the transactions that occur when holy things or persons (as defined in chaps. 25–26) are redeemed from the Lord.

6. The Holiness of Gifts Offered at the Sanctuary of God and the Regulations That Ensure Proper Dedication to the Lord (27:1-34)

27:1-34. To curb the abuse of vows (and to specify alternate reimbursement on ones made without restraint), God allowed specific fiscal equivalents to be exchanged for people who were the objects of or parties to a vow (vv. 2-8). Of significance is that a book that begins and proceeds as the speech of God to Moses ends by asking Israel to consider how seriously God views the words one speaks. The chapter begins with vows involving persons (vv. 2-8) and then mentions vows involving animals (vv. 9-13), dedication of houses and properties (vv. 14-25), dedication of firstborn animals (vv. 26-27), certain banned or "devoted" items (vv. 28-29), and tithes (vv. 30-33).

God allowed one to buy back specified possessions or persons at a higher penalty price, but He declined to provide redemption on possessions such as sacrificial animals (vv. 9-10) and firstborn animals (since they already belonged to Him, v. 26). When a person makes a pledge to God, He stipulates that the person be faithful to that pledge. God requires believers to be faithful in doing all that they promise so that they might reflect His faithfulness and be discouraged from making rash promises (Mt 6:33-37; Eph 4:25). Illustrative of this is that an acceptable animal presented to God could not be redeemed by a more acceptable animal; both became God's possession in such attempts (v. 10).

Redemption of a field or property required a 20 percent addition to its value, which was determined by its proximity to the nearest Year of Jubilee (vv. 16-25). If someone failed to **redeem** a field, then it became the property of the **priest** at the Year of jubilee (v. 21). The **firstborn among** all **animals** already belonged **to the LORD** (v. 26; cf. Ex 13:2, 12), and so they could not be presented as dedicatory offerings. Others who could not be redeemed included persons placed under a ban (vv. 28-29; cf. Achan in Jos 7).

The book concludes (vv. 30-34) with instructions about tithes. One might assume that a book so concentrated on the worship of God might begin here. Instead, the tithe is the culmination of this worship setting. Giving ten percent is not a command reiterated in the NT since contemporary believers are not under law but under grace. Obedient, Spirit-led believers, however, should be intentional about the stewardship of all their God-given resources and be generous toward God's purposes (Ac 20:35; see comments at 2Co 8–9). Of all that the land produced, whether seeds or fruit, one tenth was reserved for the **LORD** (v. 30). If an Israelite wanted to **redeem** a portion of his tithe with money, he was to present the amount along with the usual 20 percent addition (v. 31). Such a practice discouraged people from feeling entitlement in reference to the benefits of the Lord. Because it is through the sweat of one's brow that crops are produced or animals are raised, some might draw the mistaken conclusion that the resultant blessings of ownership did not originate with the Lord. God's worshipers today should avoid a similar mistake. God gave these commands to the Israelites through Moses **at Mount Sinai** (v. 34) so that they might dwell at peace with Him in the land. One must never think that God's blessings are rewards for one's labors, as something to which one is entitled. Reserving a portion (a **tenth**) in praise to the Lord demonstrates that awareness. It also militates against the selfishness that human beings are naturally prone to.

C. S. Lewis observed in *The Lion, the Witch and the Wardrobe* that the lion "Aslan [God] is not safe, but He *is* good." Israel certainly understood, upon leaving Egypt, that the God who called them back into fellowship with Him was not "safe." He had wreaked havoc upon the Egyptians through the plagues. Yahweh was not One to be trifled with. In this setting, the book of Leviticus reveals that out of God's love for humanity He has provided redemption for sinners and access into His presence with opportunities for fellowship and worship. At its heart, Leviticus is a book explaining the costs of worship to the nation of Israel. When Moses told Pharaoh that God required His people to sacrifice to him and thus acknowledge His higher authority over them (Ex 3:18; 5:3), God ultimately had these prescriptions for worship in mind. Whereas many read the book as a litany of outdated rituals pertaining to an unfamiliar and bygone era, the book is, when properly interpreted, vitally instructive about approaching the Holy God in worship. It becomes evident from Leviticus that without a clear understanding of God's holiness, what one might call worship can quickly degenerate into a predictable or even irreverent routine.

BIBLIOGRAPHY

Bailey, Lloyd R. *Leviticus–Numbers*. Smythy & Helwys Bible Commentary. Macon, GA: Smith & Helwys, 2005.

Boyce, Richard N. *Leviticus and Numbers*. Westminster Bible Companion. Louisville, KY: Westminster John Knox, 2008.

Dorsey, David A. *The Literary Structure of the Old Testament*. Grand Rapids, MI: Baker, 1999.

Douglas, Mary. *Leviticus as Literature*. Oxford: Oxford University Press, 1999.

Gane, Roy. *Leviticus, Numbers*. The NIV Application Commentary. Grand Rapids, MI: Zondervan, 2004.

Goldberg, Louis. *Leviticus: Bible Study Commentary*. Grand Rapids, MI: Zondervan, 1980.

Harrison, R. K. *Leviticus: An Introduction and Commentary*. Downers Grove, IL: InterVarsity, 1990.

Hoffmeier, James K. *Ancient Israel in Sinai*. New York: Oxford University Press, 2005.

Kiuchi, Nobuyoshi. *Leviticus*. Apollos Old Testament Commentary. Downers Grove, IL: InterVarsity, 2007.

Livingstone, G. Herbert. *The Pentateuch in Its Cultural Environment*. Grand Rapids, MI: Baker, 1974.

Rooker, Mark. *Leviticus: An Exegetical and Theological Exposition of Holy Scripture*. New American Commentary. Nashville: Broadman & Holman, 2000.

Ross, Allan. *Holiness to the Lord: A Guide to the Exposition of Leviticus*. Grand Rapids, MI: Baker, 2002.

Sailhamer, John H. *The Pentateuch as Narrative*. Grand Rapids, MI: Zondervan, 1992.

Sawyer, John F. A., ed. *Reading Leviticus: A Conversation with Mary Douglas*. Sheffield: Sheffield Academic Press, 1996.

Wenham, Gordon J. *The Book of Leviticus*. The New International Commentary on the Old Testament. Grand Rapids, MI: Eerdmans, 1979.

NUMBERS

JAMES COAKLEY

INTRODUCTION

The English title for the book comes from the Greek Septuagint (LXX) name, *Arithmoi*, "Numbers." That is because several numbered lists appear in the book, including censuses. The Jewish title for the book is *Bemidbar* ("in the wilderness") and is derived from the fifth Hebrew word of the first verse. This title relates to the geographical location so central to the book.

The historical background of the book of Numbers is the wilderness wandering of the nation of Israel after the exodus from Egypt (1445 BC) and before the crossing of the Jordan River into the promised land (1405 BC).

Author. Numbers is traditionally held to be authored by Moses. There is strong association of this book with the fivefold "book of the law/ book of Moses," attributed to Moses in both the OT and the NT (Jos 23:6; Neh 8:1; Mk 12:26). Numbers 33:2 states that Moses recorded events in Israel's wilderness journey, so he had the skills to keep and write records.

Some scholars doubt Mosaic authorship and view this book as coming from various sources that editors later compiled into the present book. According to the "documentary hypothesis," the book is comprised mainly from P (Priestly) sources (1:1–10:28 and chaps. 15, 17–19, 26–31, 33–36), while the other chapters are a mixture of J and E sources. For a critique of the "Documentary Hypothesis, see Genesis, Introduction.

Date. This book, as part of the singular book of the law, was probably penned in the final year of Moses' life. It ends with the Israelites camped on the east side of the Jordan River opposite Jericho. Deuteronomy was written in the 11th month of the 40th year after the exodus (Dt 1:3). Therefore the book of Numbers would have been written just prior to Deuteronomy, in the year 1405 BC.

Theme and Purpose. The book of Numbers compares and contrasts two generations of Israelites as counted in the two censuses within the book (in chaps. 1 and 26). The first generation was sentenced to die in the wilderness as a result of their rebellion. The second generation faithfully prepared to enter the promised land. Their story is bracketed by narratives regarding Zelophehad's daughters and the promise of land inheritance (27:1-11; 36:1-12). Suspense is naturally created as to whether the second generation will follow the errors of the first generation. The book is structured so that each subsequent reader/listener of the book can place himself in the place of the second generation to see which of the generations he or she will emulate.

The book is a combination of multiple genres, the main ones being historical narrative (10:11–14:45) and poetry (chaps. 21–24). Other genres are law (chaps. 5–6), lists (chaps. 1–4), and travel itineraries (chap. 33)

The book of Numbers is notoriously difficult to outline. There are several time references within the book, but it is hard to outline the book chronologically (cf. 1:1 with 9:1), so those markers are not all that helpful in structuring the book.

A common way to outline the book is by the geographic movements within the book.

I. Sinai (1:1–10:10)
II. Kadesh-barnea (10:11–20:13)
III. Moab (20:14–36:13)

Dennis Olson has suggested that the book be divided according to the two generations and their censuses (Dennis T. Olson, *The Death of the Old and the Birth of the New: The Framework of the Book of Numbers and the Pentateuch* [Chico, CA: Scholars Press, 1975], 120–23). Thus, chaps.

1–25 deal with the first generation of God's people out of Egypt on the march in the wilderness. Then, chaps. 26–36 cover the second generation of God's people out of Egypt as they prepare to enter the promised land. The outline in this commentary will follow his suggestion.

OUTLINE

I. History of the First Generation in the Wilderness (1:1–25:18)
  A. Preparations of the First Generation for Entering the Promised Land (1:1–10:36)
    1. First Census and Arrangement of the Tribes (1:1–2:34)
    2. Levites and Their Duties (3:1–4:49)
    3. Purity and the Law of Jealousy (5:1-31)
    4. The Nazirite Vow and the Aaronic Benediction (6:1-27)
    5. Dedicating the Tabernacle (7:1-89)
    6. Dedicating the Levites (8:1-26)
    7. Celebrating Passover (9:1-23)
    8. Departure from Sinai (10:1-36)
  B. Rebellion of the First Generation (11:1–25:18)
    1. Rebellion in the Camp (11:1-35)
    2. Rebellion of Aaron and Miriam (12:1-16)
    3. Rebellion at Kadesh (13:1–14:45)
    4. Additional Instructions Regarding Offerings (15:1-41)
    5. Rebellion of Korah (16:1-50)
    6. Vindication of Aaron (17:1-13)
    7. Additional Instructions for the Levites (18:1-32)
    8. Waters of Purification (19:1-22)
    9. The Sin of Moses and the Death of Aaron (20:1-29)
    10. The Bronze Serpent (21:1-35)
    11. The Prophet Balaam (22:1–25:18)
      a. Balaam's Meeting with Balak (22:1-41)
      b. Balaam's Oracles (23:1–24:25)
      c. Balaam's Perversion of Israel (25:1-18)
II. Hope for the Second Generation as They Enter the Promised Land (26:1–36:13)
  A. Preparations of the Second Generation for Entering the Promised Land (26:1–32:42)
    1. The Second Census (26:1-65)
    2. Instructions for the Second Generation (27:1–30:16)
    3. War against Midian and the Settlement of the Transjordanian Tribes (31:1–32:42)
  B. Encouragement for the Second Generation for Entering the Promised Land (33:1–36:13)
    1. Review of Israel's Journey (33:1-56)
    2. Boundaries of the Promised Land (34:1-29)
    3. Levitical Cities (35:1-34)
    4. Inheritance of Women (36:1-13)

COMMENTARY ON NUMBERS

I. History of the First Generation in the Wilderness (1:1–25:18)

Numbers continues the history of Israel one year after the exodus from Egypt and continues to chronicle their experiences until they are ready to cross the Jordan River.

A. Preparations of the First Generation for Entering the Promised Land (1:1–10:36)

1. First Census and Arrangement of the Tribes (1:1–2:34)

1:1. The clause **the LORD spoke to Moses** occurs over 45 times in this book, emphasizing the divine origin of its contents. The setting for this book is **in the wilderness of Sinai**. This geographical location was inhospitable and sparsely populated. The wilderness as a place of testing is a theme that appears at numerous junctures in the Bible (Dt 8:1-2; Ps 95:8-9; Mt 4), and here early in the book it introduces the reader to a major theme of the book. **The tent of meeting** is one of two designations of the tabernacle in the book (the other is "tent of the testimony," 17:8). The book begins **on the first of the second month** (April/May) in the **second year** after the exodus. This is exactly one month after the anointing of the tabernacle (Ex 40:17; Nm 7:1). Numbers does not follow a strict chronological chain of events. This shows that Moses was not focusing on establishing a timeline but rather an account concerned primarily with thematic and theological lessons within their history.

1:2-46. The Lord instructed Moses to **take a census** of all the males over 20 years old of all the tribes except Levi, whose tribe would be addressed later. This census is framed in a military context (**whoever is able to go out to war**, v. 3) in order to make necessary preparations for the conquest. One head from each tribe was selected to assist Moses.

The total (603,550) equals the same number given in Ex 38:26 (rounded down to 600,000 in Ex 12:37 and Nm 11:21). It is not clear here why Gad is listed 11th when the heads are selected (1:14) but listed third (vv. 24-25) when the actual census numbers are given. This may be because Gad marched alongside Reuben and Simeon (according to 2:10-16). These figures may have been rounded up or down slightly, since it would appear that these numbers occur only in multiples of fifties or hundreds. All of these heads are mentioned again in Nm 2 and 7 when the camp locations were assigned and when offerings were presented, but the leaders were listed in a different order.

Attempts to adjust the total figures to a much lower number by taking the Hebrew word *'eleph* to mean "clan" or "chief" instead of "thousand" cannot be reconciled with the total number given in 1:26. In such an attempt, the total number of digits before *'eleph* from each tribe do not add up to 603 (i.e., 46 + 59 + 45 + 74 +54 +57 + 40 + 32 + 35 + 62 + 41 + 53 = 598, not 603) and the digits after the *'eleph* add up to 5,550. It is best to take the numbers at face value even though there are challenges to the logistics of having over 2 million people (once the wives and children are factored in) in a geographical location not conducive for such a large company. Certainly God had shown Himself miraculous in the plagues and the exodus event, and there is no reason to think that He would not continue to provide supernaturally for the nation, as is clearly indicated in such verses as Dt 29:5, "I have led you forty years in the wilderness; your clothes have not worn out on you, and your sandal has not worn out on your foot."

1:47-54. The tribe of Levi was not to be included in the census. Since the census of the other tribes was primarily for military purposes, the tribe of Levi was not numbered. Their primary function was to officiate over the tabernacle. This section focuses on the organizing of the Levites for their responsibilities for all things related to the tabernacle. They were tasked with the oversight of the tabernacle furnishings, including transporting, setting up, dismantling, and guarding over the entire process, lest any non-Levite come near and die. When the camp was set up for the nation, the Levites were to camp in ring-like fashion around the tabernacle complex, thereby serving as a buffer zone for all of the other tribal camps and as a defense against encroachment by foreign enemies.

2:1-33. Numbers 1 listed the large population of Israel at the time of the exodus for military purposes. Here the book focuses on the logistics of such a large group moving through the wilderness period. The camp was arranged by tribal groupings, reflecting some measure of status. So Judah was given the preeminent position on the east side of the camp, just as Moses and Aaron and his sons were located on the east side near the doorway of the tent of meeting. While the direction east has ominous overtones in the earlier parts of Genesis (the east is often viewed negatively because movement in that direction appears in the context of disobedience, i.e., Gn 3:24; 4:16; 11:2), it may be the direction from which redemption would ultimately come. Each tribal unit was identified by family banners and was situated symmetrically around every side of the tent of meeting, presumably to demonstrate order as well as provide a military guard. There are no details given as to the size, shape, and colors of these standards and banners. Jewish tradition has it that they were based on the colors of the stones on the high priest's breastplate (Ex 39:14). (Numbers 2 does not state the order of the tribes on each side of the camp; i.e., it is uncertain whether Judah was in the center as the lead tribe or at one of the corners.)

Arrangement of the Camp

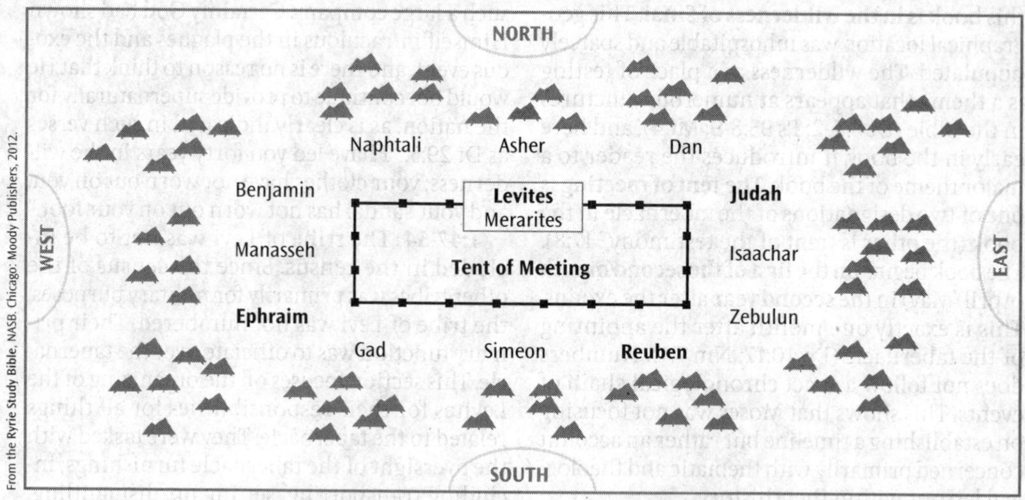

Rachel's sons were located together on the west side of the tabernacle. Leah's offspring were on the east and south side of the tabernacle with one exception—Gad (the oldest son of Zilpah, Leah's handmaid) was in the open slot with Leah's two oldest sons, Reuben and Simeon, on the south side. The rest of the handmaids' sons were together on the north side of the encampment.

When the tribes set out, the tent of meeting was to be positioned between the second and third contingent of tribal groupings. Being in that position would place it in a safer location in case of enemy attack.

2:34. The posture of the people presented at this point is one of order and obedience. Here there was universal harmony and submission to both the Lord and Moses. This early obedience contrasts, however, with the people's later rebellions.

2. Levites and Their Duties (3:1–4:49)

3:1-13. Now the attention is on the tribe of Levi and specifically the sons of Aaron. The expression **these are the records of** is the same expression used 11 times in the book of Genesis as a structuring device (Hb. *toledoth*). This phrase ties Numbers with Genesis by the use of that Hebrew word, especially since both books focus on lists and genealogies. The four sons of Aaron are listed in birth order: Nadab, Abihu, Eleazar, and Ithamar.

Nadab and **Abihu**'s deaths are mentioned (v. 4). Since they had no children when they died, they had no heirs to continue their priestly line. The account of their deaths in Lv 9–10 was close in time to the census of Nm 1 since only one month had passed (cf. Ex 40:17 with Nm 1:1). This is the first recollection of an act of previous disobedience in the book of Numbers. Sadly this theme will play a major role later on in the book. Interestingly, this first failure was from the priests, not the people. Those being led often take their lead from those in authority over them. **Eleazar and Ithamar**, Aaron's other sons, **served as priests** under **their father Aaron**, the high priest.

The rest of the Levites were to serve as assistants to the priests by servicing the tabernacle. Any nonsanctioned individuals who approached the tent of meeting were to be **put to death**. This regulation again emphasized the complete sanctity of the tabernacle and its objects.

The tribe of Levi functioned as the **firstborn** for all the tribes. Instead of having each tribe commissioning their firstborn to be conscripted as priests, the entire tribe of Levi served as proxy substitutes for the entire nation. Every **firstborn**, whether man or beast, belonged to the Lord as a result of His striking the firstborn of Egypt in the plagues account. This is an example of the important theme of substitution.

3:14-39. The tribe of Levi was not **numbered** in the military census (1: 47), but now they were counted from the age of one **month . . . and upward** so that they could be registered in preparation for their duties and encampment.

They were divided according to Levi's three **sons**: **Gershon . . . Kohath and Merari** (often labeled Gershonites, Kohathites, and Merarites).

Numbers and Responsibilities of the Levites

Clan	Gershonites	Kohathites	Merarites	Moses & Aaron Aaron's sons: Ithamar & Eleazar
Total Males (above 1 month old)	7,500	8,600	6,200	
Head	Eliasaph	Elizaphan	Zuriel	Aaron
Overseer	Ithamar	Eleazar	Ithamar	
Responsibilities	Tabernacle and tent, including coverings, screen, hangings, doorway, cords	Ark, table, lampstand, altars, utensils, screen of incense, related articles, and veil	Frames, bars, posts, pillars, sockets, and cords	Served as priests; packed up and unpacked the tabernacle vessels on moving days
Workforce (30 to 50 years of age)	2,630	2,750	3,200	

The Kohathites were the most favored clan of the tribe of Levi because of their responsibility to care for the objects of the holy place. Because both Moses and Aaron descended from that clan, the Lord gave Moses and Aaron and his sons a campsite on the favored east side of the **tabernacle, toward the sunrise**.

The number of Kohathites in v. 28 is listed at **8,600**. To harmonize this with the total number of Levites (3:22, 28, 34) listed in v. 39 at 22,000, some Greek LXX manuscripts have the total number of Kohathites as 8,300, indicating a possible copyist error (the addition of one Hebrew letter changes the six to a three). Another solution offered to address this discrepancy is that this is a round number, but that is unlikely since the number of firstborn males in v. 43 (22,273) is not rounded off. The simplest solution is that the additional 300 were excluded from consideration because they were themselves firstborn of the Levites and thus were not eligible to redeem the firstborn of Israel. All of the Levites over a month in age were tallied, and the count was 22,000.

3:40-51. Instead of all the males above age 20 being counted in a military census as in chap. 1, all the **firstborn . . . sons** of all the tribes were tallied. This was to see if there was an even correspondence between them and the number of Levites, since they served as substitutes for the other tribe's firstborn sons. The total number of non-Levitical firstborn was 22,273. This figure raises several issues. (1) This is the first number that does not end in a 100 or 50 in the book. All of the other numbers given so far might possibly be rounded up or down, but this number is exact. (2) The ratio of this number to the total fighting force listed at 603,550 (1:46) is small (only 1 out of every 27 males within the nation would be firstborn). One possible explanation may be that only the firstborn males born since the first Passover were tallied, but the text does not specifically state that.

Since there were 273 more non-Levite firstborn, the Lord set a **ransom** price of **five shekels** for the overage, for a total of 1,365 shekels (34 pounds). Once again the theme of substitution is prominent in this passage. It is not understood who specifically paid this ransom or what it was used for after it was given to **Aaron and to his sons**. Another emphasis in this section is the statement **I am the LORD,** occurring twice (vv. 41, 45) and functioning as a small chiasm:

A. Take the Levites for Me, I am the LORD . . . firstborn . . . cattle (3:41)
  B. Moses numbered all the firstborn (3:42a)
    C. just as the LORD commanded him (3:42b)
  B.' firstborn . . . numbered men (3:43)
A.' Take the Levites . . . firstborn . . . cattle . . . Levites shall be Mine; I am the LORD (3:45)

The focus of chiastic structures is the center pivot. In this case it stresses Moses' obedience in numbering the firstborn (v. 42; cf. v. 51). This is another example of stressing the theme of obedience by both Moses and the Israelites.

4:1-3. The focus now turns to the three Levitical families and their responsibilities. The clans are listed, not by their birth order, but by the sanctity of the objects they oversaw. The many details here stress that God wanted to emphasize the holiness and sacredness of the contents of the sanctuary. Only men from ages 30 to 50 were qualified to serve in the tent of meeting. These men were in the prime of life and had the maturity to carefully execute their duties exactly as the Lord commanded. Moses and Aaron were in charge of overseeing the census and assigning roles for each of the Levitical clans.

Descendants of Levi

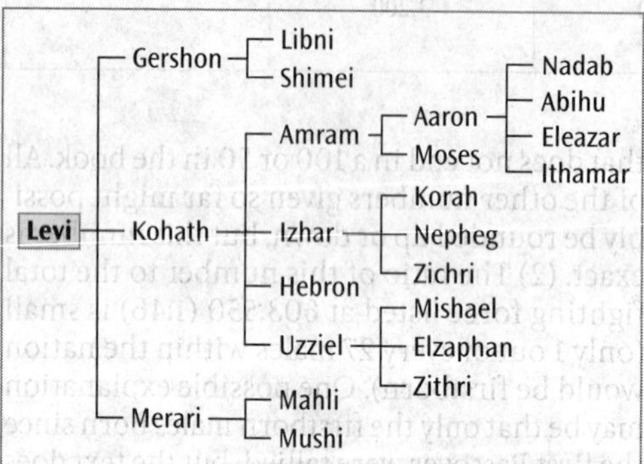

4:4-20. Since the Kohathites were the clan of Moses and Aaron and because they took care of the most holy things, they are listed first, even though Kohath was not the firstborn. Only the priests were allowed to handle the sanctuary furniture, including the **ark of the testimony**. The phrase "the ark of the testimony" was used earlier in Exodus to refer to what is commonly understood as the ark of the covenant. In the early part of Numbers it is still referred to by that name, and then in 10:33 and following the phrase "the ark of the covenant" is used. The word "testimony" was used of the Ten Commandments (Ex 31:18) so it makes sense to call the structure that housed the two tablets the ark of the testimony. But since the term is more general it began gradually to be known more by the more specific title "ark of the covenant." There were specific instructions on how to dismantle the holy place, how to prepare the objects for travel, and even how to transport them with poles or frames. Aaron and his sons were to cover each piece in animal **skin**, and **blue**, **scarlet**, or **purple cloth**, depending on the object. These colors are often associated with a royal setting (Est 1:6). This would prevent the Kohathites (who were tasked with carrying these items) from touching or even seeing these objects. To stress the holiness of these items, the penalty for touching a sacred object was death (Nm 4:15, 20), and there are examples of violation of this command in 1Sm 6 and 2Sm 6. **Eleazer** was specifically tasked with oversight of the **oil . . . incense**, and flour used for the **grain offering**.

4:21-28. The Gershonites were assigned to transport the **curtains** and outer **coverings** and the equipment associated with them. These were items not associated with the holy place but with the tabernacle enclosure in general. All their work was performed under the direction of the priests supervised by **Ithamar**.

4:29-33. The Merarites were assigned to transport all the framing objects for the **tent of meeting** under the supervision of Ithamar. The movement from assigning the most important objects to the least important was now complete. Even specific instructions were given regarding the handling of these lesser items to emphasize that even those objects were to be transported according the Lord's word. While the Kohathites were assigned the holiest objects, every Levitical clan was needed and aided in setting up, tearing down, and transporting the tent of meeting.

4:34-49. The number of Levites from the ages of 30 to 50 who assisted in attending to the needs of transporting the sanctuary was 8,580 (2,750 Kohathites, 2,630 Gershonites, 3,200 Merarites). This represented 39 percent of the total number of Levites above one month in age (22,000) for service in the tent of meeting (3:39). Four times this section states that the Levites were counted **according to the commandment of the Lord** (4:37, 41, 45, 49). This continues the theme that has been stressed so far in this book that Moses obeyed God's instructions precisely. Also the focus has narrowed in that the text has proceeded from numbering all the tribes, to the tribe of Levi, and then to the clans of Levi. The core focus on this narrowing is the worship of the Lord in relation to the tent of meeting.

3. Purity and the Law of Jealousy (5:1-31)

5:1-4. The Lord ordered Moses to send away anyone who was ceremonially **unclean** to live **outside the camp** during that time. This was because the Lord was dwelling in their midst (v. 3) and did not want anyone unclean to defile that area. The emphasis here is on purity, not discrimination, or personal status. This heightened focus on purity indicates that the Lord was not only concerned about the uncleanness of individuals but also the effects that their impurity would have on the sacred space of the camp. If He was to **dwell in their midst** both the people and the space had to be pure. Sin and impurity negatively affect the individual, the nation, and the sanctuary, so holiness in all domains must be preserved at all costs. That the Israelites obeyed this instruction is another example of the strict obedience to the Lord's commands that has been a theme thus far in the book.

5:5-10. Here the attention was on interpersonal relationships within the camp, specifically when there was an offense between individuals. The emphasis moved from visible physical uncleanness to inward personal uncleanness. Any offense within the community was viewed as unfaithfulness **against the LORD**, and so confession and restitution were required. **Restitution** demanded not only a return of whatever the damages were but also a surcharge of 20 percent. If the offended party or a relative of the offended party was not available to receive restitution, then the restitution was to be given to the **priest**, along with a **ram** for sacrifice. Priestly involvement in the restitution process between individuals indicates that holiness is not just affected by the external doings of the camp but also the inner aspects that will affect the whole community. Just as the unclean had to be removed from the camp, the cause of interpersonal conflict had to be dealt with equitably to maintain not just the outward purity of the camp but also the inward purity of the people.

5:11-28. Continuing the focus of movement to more and more personal hidden sin, the attention in this section is on the purity of the husband-wife relationship. Like ceremonial uncleanness and personal offenses, marital infidelity was viewed not only as a serious breach of the marriage relationship but also an act of unfaithfulness to the Lord. If a husband suspected his wife of adultery and he had no proof, he was to take his wife to the priest, along with an offering of barley, to have her undergo an ordeal.

The procedure began when the priest brought the wife to stand **before the LORD** (v. 16). This was probably done at the entrance of the tent of meeting, since dust from the tabernacle floor was needed for this ritual, and since the altar for the grain offering was nearby and the grain from it would be needed for part of the procedure. Once she was in position the priest would take **some . . . dust** from the tabernacle **floor** and mix it with holy water in a clay jar (5:17). He would then loosen her hair, and she would hold the barley grain offering (just over two quarts) in her hands, the text specifically calling it a memorial offering and a grain offering of jealousy.

The priest then would place her under oath, stating that this **water of bitterness** would not harm her if she had not defiled herself. However, if she had **defiled** herself she would bring a **curse** on herself that would cause her abdomen to swell and her thigh to waste away. The suspected wife would then reply **Amen**. The priest would write a curse on a scroll and then wash the ink off into the jar of bitter water, meaning that the woman would be eating the words of the curse. The grain offering would then be waved before the **LORD** and offered on the altar, and then the woman would drink the concoction of holy water, dust, and ink. The timetable for when the results would become visible is not stated, but if she had defiled herself she would experience suffering and visible physical symptoms. If she was not guilty she would not suffer any consequences. She would be cleared of any guilt and would still have the opportunity to bear children in the future.

This passage includes several interpretive challenges:

Patriarchal perspective. This ordeal is followed whenever a husband suspects his wife of adultery. Nothing is said about what the process should be if a wife suspected her husband of adultery or what the status of the relationship would be if a wife was suspected of infidelity but was later found to be innocent of the charges. If any wife or husband were ever caught in the act of adultery the punishment would be death (Lv 20:10), so this ritual would apply only in cases without direct physical evidence or witnesses. Mercy is shown here because even if adultery had been committed, the wife would receive a sentence of a curse, public derision, and infertility. Since the judgment was not death, it could be viewed as a gracious act. This act also offers a measure of protection for the wife, for if her husband continuously accused her of unfaithfulness she could undergo this ordeal and remove all doubt. Her husband might even suffer humiliation if she were innocent, since this was a public ordeal.

Spirit of jealousy. What initiated this jealousy on the part of the husband toward his wife is not stated. One possible explanation is that this may have occurred because a man's wife was pregnant and he suspected he was not the father of the child. What happened as a result of this ordeal is that she would suffer a miscarriage and would no longer be able to bear children in the future.

Barley. The normal grain used for offerings was wheat, ground into fine flour. Barley was not as expensive as wheat (2Kg 7:1) and was often used by the poor as food (Ru 2:17) and as fodder for animals (1Kg 5:8). Philo (the first-century Jewish philosopher from Alexandria) thought it was an appropriate product for this ritual, because of the association of barley with irrational animals and people in unhappy circumstances.

Hair loosened. The hair of a wife was probably usually bound up. So for it to be loosed in this location before the Lord suggests a loss of reputation, a symbol of mourning, a sign of her possible uncleanness, or a picture of her vulnerability and openness.

Use of "magic." Israel was expressly forbidden to cast spells (Dt 18:11), but this trial by ordeal might be considered a magical procedure. However, this trial was done expressly by the Lord's instructions, and He superintended the results. The overt symbolism embedded in it demonstrates that this ritual should not be viewed as magical.

Natural or supernatural results. Some see a natural punishment after the drinking of the "water of bitterness" by a physiological reaction to the dust in the water, coupled with an emotional response of guilt. However, the text implies a supernatural punishment imposed on the wife if she is guilty. The Lord's role in this ordeal is emphasized (vv. 16, 21, 25) to demonstrate that this is not a magical incantation or physiological guilt detector.

Nature of the punishment. The punishment fell on the part of the woman's body that was used in the adulterous activity. "Thigh" was sometimes used as a euphemism for the genital area (Gn 24:2, 9) and the wasting away (lit., "fall") may even suggest a miscarriage or prolapsed uterus. Also the swollen abdomen could signify the typical bodily response if a pregnancy did occur; but in this case it would be used as an outward manifestation of her guilt instead of her joy at conception. Whatever the exact physical nature of this punishment was, the result was that this woman would not be able to bear children in the future. There are echoes of the fall in Gn 3 with similar concepts and words such as "eating dust," "curse," "belly/abdomen," "childbirth," etc.

5:29-31. An epilogue to this ritual summarizes the ordeal and states that the husband would not bring guilt on himself by asking his wife to perform this test of sexual fidelity. Purity in the home is just as important as purity in the tent of meeting. The Lord was committing Himself to respond in this case, thereby demonstrating that even hidden sin would not be tolerated among His people.

4. The Nazirite Vow and the Aaronic Benediction (6:1-27)

6:1-21. The focus so far has been on purity issues, but now the attention is on anyone in the nation, not just the priests and Levites, who wished to be consecrated. Any man or woman who wished to **make a special vow** of **separation** to God had the opportunity to do so for a designated period of time.

This text addresses the process for a man, and Nm 30 goes into more detail for women who wish to make a vow. Parents apparently could also initiate this vow on their sons as was done with Samuel (1Sm 1:11). For men this vow is called "the **Nazirite** vow," and in order to fulfill that vow there were strict requirements.

First, he was not to partake of anything associated with the **grape vine** (no wine, juice, raisons, seeds or even the **skin** of grapes). Foregoing any grape products would certainly demonstrate self-restraint, especially in the Mediterranean world where these were dietary staples. While the fruit of the vine was often seen as a blessing, it had its negative side, as seen in the life of Noah, Lot, and the Israelites at the golden calf incident. Alcohol has the tendency to cloud judgment (Lv 10:8-10) for priests, and since the Nazirite vow functions as a "priest-like" state for laypeople, it is easy to see why wine was forbidden in this vow.

Second, he was not to shave any hair on his **head**. The reason for this focus on the hair as the object of consecration was that it could become "defiled" and it was offered up as a sacrifice. The hair could represent the strength of an individual as it did with Samson, but in this vow the symbolic function of the hair is not clear. Since hair is a constantly, visibly growing and living part of the human body, it may be an embodiment of the life of the person.

Third, he was not to go near any dead bodies, even those of close family members. Contact with dead bodies caused defilement.

Following contact with a corpse, a person would be unclean for seven days (Nm 19:1-2). The guidelines were even stricter for a Nazirite, who would become defiled if someone **suddenly** died in his proximity, even if there was no physical contact with the corpse. After defilement he would shave his head on the seventh day. This would virtually guarantee that all hair that was defiled would be shaven off since it had another week to grow. On the eighth day he would offer two doves or two young pigeons, one as a sin offering and one as a burnt offering. He also must offer a one-year-old lamb as a sin offering and a one-year-old ram as a peace offering. He was to consecrate his head and resume the vow period of time from the beginning.

If the period of time established was without violation, then at the completion of the vow he was to offer a series of burnt, sin, peace, grain, drink, and unleavened bread offerings. He could then **shave** his . . . **head** and offer the hair on the altar where **peace offerings** were made. The worshiper would eat a portion of the peace offering, and another portion would be given to the priest for his services.

Even though the Nazirite was not a priest, he in effect functioned as one. Complete holiness was not restricted only to the Levites, as any man or woman could consecrate himself or herself in full devotion to God.

6:22-27. A blessing was then pronounced on the Israelites. To **bless** someone means to pronounce the favor of God upon the person. It is in the form of a wish or desire from a benefactor to a human recipient. Blessings in the OT vary widely in their construction and contents—from God blessing mankind (Gn 1:22, 28) to a father blessing his sons (Gn 27:27-29; 49:1-28). The Lord instructed Moses exactly what to tell Aaron **to say**. The express purpose for this blessing is stated in v. 27, in order that the Lord would place his **name** on them. The placement of this blessing here in the book stresses that a primary role of the priesthood was to bless the people. This blessing is at the end of a long legislative segment of the Pentateuch that began in Ex 20. This strategic position implies that if the people listen to and follow the instructions of the Lord, as they have so far in the book of Numbers, they could expect divine blessing and favor.

The structure of the blessing itself is threefold in nature, each with two clauses, in typical poetic fashion. Each part gets more specific and emphatic. The first blessing is general in nature, asking for God's blessing and protection. The second blessing more specifically asks the Lord in an anthropomorphic way to direct His **face** toward the recipient in a gracious manner. The last blessing is even more specific, asking that the Lord's **face** focus attention on the worshiper in such a way that the individual experiences **peace** (Hb. *shalom*, wholeness) in a powerful way. The image of God's face as light shining upon someone is used elsewhere in the Bible (Ps 44:3; 80:3). When God's face shines He looks to invoke benefits, but when He hides His face He is angry (Dt 31:17-18; Ps. 30:7; 104:29). This **peace** is a sense of rightness in the relationship with the Lord, coupled with tangible blessing.

5. Dedicating the Tabernacle (7:1-89)

The narrative of Nm 1–4 resumes here. Numbers 5–6 provided a somewhat parenthetical discussion about a variety of matters such as ceremonial uncleanness, restitution for transgressions, a ritual to determine infidelity, and the Nazirite vow. The narrative now refers to an earlier event (the consecration of the tabernacle). As was pointed out earlier in Nm 1:1, a strict chronology of events is not followed in these chapters, as seen in the table on the following page.

Moses was not concerned about presenting events in chronological order in the book of Numbers. Instead, he seemed intent on presenting a picture of obedience (both on his part and in the nation of Israel). For literary and thematic reasons, he placed the account of the tabernacle dedication at this particular place in the text.

This chapter (the second longest in the Bible) lays out a detailed, repetitive description of offerings presented by the **leaders** of the 12 tribes at the dedication of the tabernacle on 12 successive days.

7:1. The anointing of the **tabernacle**, with specific attention to the **altar**, is described.

7:2-88. The **leaders** who were mentioned earlier as the ones in charge of the census were now to oversee their tribe's dedication **offering**. According to the timeline above, the dedication offerings were given first (second year, first month, first day), whereas the census did not start until one month later (1:1). Rather than start with the more celebratory dedicatory presentations from these leaders, Moses chose

Events in the First Two Months of the Second Year after the Exodus

Date (Day in second year after exodus)	Event	Scripture
Day 1, first month	Erection of tabernacle	Ex 40:2, 17; Nm 7:1
	Instructions regarding offerings begin	Lv 1:1
	Offerings for dedication begin (12 days total)	Nm 7:3
	Ordination of priests begins	Lv 8:1-36
Day 8, first month	Ordination of priests completed	Lv 9:1-7
Day 12, first month	Offerings for dedication completed	Nm 7:84
	Appointment of Levites	Nm 8:5
Day 14, first month	Second Passover	Nm 9:2
Day 1, second month	Census begins	Nm 1:1
Day 14, second month	Passover for those unclean	Nm 9:11
Day 20, second month	The cloud moves, the camp starts out	Nm 10:11

to tell of their faithful, yet perhaps mundane, assistance in the census first and then to focus on their role as worshipers bringing offerings.

These dedication offerings were also combined with **carts** and **oxen** to assist the Levitical clans in their transportation of the tabernacle structure. In addition to these carts and oxen, each leader presented silver dishes and bowls filled with grain offerings, a gold pan filled with incense, and sacrificial animals for burnt, sin, and peace offerings. These offerings no doubt came from the items the people requested from the Egyptians just before the exodus (Ex 12:35-36). The total amount of **silver** was **2,400 shekels** (about 60 pounds), and the **gold 120 shekels** (about three pounds).

This chapter presents much repetition with little variation. The repetitive nature of the account of each tribe's offering stresses the unity of the tribes and their common participation in this religious ceremony. While this account may seem overly repetitive to modern-day readers, ancient readers would have processed this positively and celebrated each tribe's participation. The only variation is the different ordering of the leaders from that given in Nm 1.

In this order Judah is given the prominent role as the first to present (v. 12), whereas in the census-taking, the firstborn Reuben is listed first.

7:89. This verse functions as a brief aside on **Moses** receiving direct revelation from God whenever he **went into the tent of meeting**. Even though Moses was not the high priest, he must have had access to the holy of holies because the place of this revelation was the mercy seat atop the **ark of the testimony, from between the two cherubim**. Even though Aaron was the current high priest, Moses must have retained privilege to access the holy of holies, since he functioned as high priest before Aaron received that title. This verse implies that after appropriate offerings and the celebration of the Lord's presence in their midst the Lord delighted to reveal Himself to the nation.

6. Dedicating the Levites (8:1-26)

8:1-4. The Lord told Aaron where to set up and direct the **light** from the **lampstand**. Verse 4 refers back to the construction of the lampstand, again stressing that it was crafted exactly according to the specifications the **Lord had showed Moses**. According to Ex 25:31-40, it was fashioned from one talent of gold (about seven pounds). While there are clear instructions regarding its form, no clear dimensions are given for its height and width. The seven individual lamps of the lampstand were to be located in such a way that they cast light forward toward the north. Moses had been shown the blueprint, and it was followed exactly. The lampstand was shaped in the form of a tree with branches. Along with the other pieces of furniture, it may have been reflecting back on the garden of Eden with its trees and guardian cherubim.

8:5-13. This section details the purification of the **Levites** for their assigned responsibilities with the tent of meeting. The tribe of Levi is clearly a focal point of the book of Numbers.

They previously had been counted (chap. 3), had been given their camp location (chap. 2), and given tabernacle assignments according to their different clans (chap. 4). Next they were being set apart and commissioned to their assigned duties. According to Lv 8–9, the process of priestly ordination (for Aaron and his sons) had begun on the first day of the first month and was completed seven days later. Since this passage follows the 12 days of dedication offering presented by the tribal leaders (chap. 7) and precedes the Passover (chap. 9) celebrated on the 14th of the first month, there is only a short window of time for this dedication to take place between the 12th and 14th days of the first month. These instructions were not for the Levitical priests (who were already set apart) but for the entire tribe of Levi. The priests were ordained in Lv 8, and while there were some similarities there were also a number of differences between the two ceremonies.

The setting apart of the Levitical tribe consisted of several steps. First, the **purifying water** was sprinkled on them. This is the only place in the Bible where this exact phrase is used, and the text does not state how this water was prepared for this purpose. It may have been produced by adding the ashes of the red heifer to water and was later used as a means of removing impurities (Nm 19:9). The next requirement was for the Levites to shave their **whole** bodies. This would indicate a complete cleansing, but it is not clear why the priests did not have to shave when they were being consecrated. Possibly the verb used for "shave" means to "trim." Instead of shaving off all hair, the instructions may have been to trim their existing hair so as to make themselves more presentable to the Lord. This correlates with the next step of washing their clothes.

Two bulls were used in the ceremony, one for a burnt offering, and one for a sin offering. The entire tribe of Levi, presumably all the males since they were the ones counted in the census, was then assembled in front of the tent of meeting. The rest of the Israelites were to lay their hands on the Levites as a sign of identifying them as their representatives. Then Aaron presented the Levites as a group as a wave offering to the Lord. This functioned as a sort of living sacrifice of the Levites as a tribe by the nation before the Lord.

The Levites were then to **lay their hands** on the two **bulls** that were offered as a burnt and sin offering. Next the Levites were assembled once again as a group and were presented a second time as a **wave offering** to the **LORD**, this time by Aaron and his sons.

8:14-19. After they had been purified, the Levites became ready to do their assigned tasks at the **tent of meeting**. This section stands between a prescriptive (vv. 3-13) and a descriptive (vv. 20-22) section of the same event, and thus this information discusses some of the main theological purposes for purifying the Levites. The Levites are specifically stated as being set apart as the Lord's possession. This notion is repeated in vv. 14, 16, 17, and 18, so this is clearly the main focus of this passage.

The Levites were the Lord's exclusive possession in that they were the substitutes for all the tribes of Israel's **firstborn**. Instead of each firstborn being the Lord's possession from all the tribes' offspring, the entire tribe of Levi served as their proxy. This claim is related to the plague narrative of Exodus, when the Lord struck down all the firstborn of Egypt. Once His divine claim on all the Levites was established, the Lord gave them as gifts back to Aaron and his sons so that they had help in all the duties associated with the tent of meeting. Since the Levites were sanctioned by the Lord to assist in the care of the tabernacle, the rest of the Israelite nation was not in physical danger when they approached the sanctuary.

8:20-22. This section is the descriptive account of what was prescribed earlier (vv. 5-13) in relation to the purifying of the Levitical tribe in assisting Aaron and his sons in the work of the tabernacle. This section emphasizes that all the instructions the Lord gave were followed completely (vv. 20, 22). This is another example thus far in the book that stresses total obedience on the part of the nation's leaders as well as individuals. No example of disobedience on the part of the people has been noted in the text up to this point (although Nadab and Abihu's earlier disobedience in Lv 10 was alluded to in Nm 3:4).

8:23-26. The Levites who were qualified had to be between the ages of 25 and 50. After 50 they were to retire, but they could still serve as assistants to the qualified Levites. Much of the work was physical in nature, so this stipulation guaranteed that the Levitical workers were both mature and physically fit in handling the sacred objects. In Nm 4:3 the starting age for Kohathites is given as 30. One possible explanation for the difference is that for the first five years Levitical workers served as apprentices until they reached the age of 30. Later in David's reign Levites were able to begin service in the temple at the age of 20 (1Ch 23:24-25). There the explanation is given that this was because the Levites no longer had to transport the tabernacle and its sacred objects.

7. Celebrating Passover (9:1-23)

9:1-5. Events in the book of Numbers began in the second month of the second year after the exodus (1:1), but now the text refers back to an earlier event that happened in the first month of the second year, namely, the giving of instructions regarding **Passover**. One possible explanation for this chronological rearrangement is that the book is narrowing the subject matter to items that have more spiritual weight. The book starts with descriptions of census numbers and camp locations, moves to a description of the tabernacle assignments of the Levitical clans, and then narrows in on the Passover celebration. The Passover was to be celebrated on the 14th day of the first month (Abib), corresponding to March/April. Another statement of the tacit obedience of the Israelites appears in v. 5.

9:6-14. These verses discuss the problem of being ceremonially **unclean** on the Passover and thus unable to celebrate it on that exact date. Some Israelites had been rendered unclean because of contact with a **dead** body. They wished to fulfill Passover obligations at the same time as everyone else without having to wait a year until the next Passover. Moses did not give an immediate answer to their concern. He asked for a delay until he could find out what the Lord's instructions were on this matter. Numbers 7:89 noted that he had opportunity to speak to the Lord whenever he entered the tent of meeting. This mention here of Moses seeking to ask for the Lord's clear guidance shows his dependence on the Lord and his desire to disseminate God's instructions, not his own wisdom. Honored by such dependence, the Lord gave Moses the instructions he sought.

Whenever there was involuntary uncleanness or an individual was away from home on a **journey** he was permitted to celebrate the Passover one month later. If, however, there was willful neglect in observing the Passover, that individual was to be **cut off** and to suffer consequences. If an **alien** wished to celebrate the Passover, he was to observe it on the day the Israelites observed it. Exodus 12:48 previously stated that such a worshiper, however, must be circumcised in order to partake. Based on Jos 5:10, possibly Israel did not observe another Passover until after they entered the promised land, since no uncircumcised male could observe Passover and the men were not circumcised until they got to Gilgal after they crossed the Jordan. The stipulation that whoever partook of the Passover meal must not **break** any of the bones while cooking or eating the lamb (Nm 9:12) is mentioned in Jn 19:36 in reference to the death of Christ as a fulfillment of this Scripture.

9:15-23. This section describes the phenomenon of the **cloud** that appeared over the **tabernacle** and how it guided the Israelites during their wilderness journey. This section is not chronological in its presentation because it describes the routine of this guidance system even before the Israelites actually set out. It introduces future information from the entirety of the wilderness-wandering period and places it here. The repetitive nature and rhythmic quality of this section make it unique in comparison to the sections around it. In 9:1-14 the Israelites celebrated the Passover, a tangible reminder of God's redemptive power in the past. Now in speech that rises almost to that of poetry, Moses described in heightened words a different visible tangible symbol. The Passover lamb could be seen as an object lesson of the Lord's power in the past, and the cloud could represent a visual manifestation of the Lord's commitment to the nation's present and future guidance.

This phenomenon is often called the "Shekinah glory" from Ex 40:35, but the text in Numbers never refers to it by that name. Instead it is consistently called **the cloud**.

On the first day the tabernacle was erected, a cloud covered it, and it was continuous and had the **appearance of fire**. The cloud **lifted** whenever the nation was to set out to a new location. This was a tangible, visual sign. It could lift anytime day or night, and it could lift up again after **two days** or even a **year**. Several statements of the Israelites' obedience are given again in vv. 19 and 23. The Israelites moved in response to the Lord's instructions, and the Lord was the nation's true leader (v. 23).

8. Departure from Sinai (10:1-36)

10:1-10. Silver **trumpets** were blown to notify the camp of different events. When two were blown together, the tribes were to move out. When one was blown the leaders of the various clans were to gather together. The tribes on the east were the first to move out, and then the south tribes were to move out at the next blast. The other two compass points are not mentioned (west and north), but surely the tribes from those positions would be the next to march. Since the moving of the cloud was a visible reminder to the entire nation that they were about to break camp, the trumpet blasts served as a more specific time marker and helped maintain order and discipline when they were on the move.

While on the subject of trumpet blasts, Moses described other instances when the trumpets were to be used and who would blow them. The **sons of Aaron** were to be the only ones to make the signals. They were to blow them not only when the nation broke camp but also as a way of signaling going into **war**, as well as announcing appointed **feasts** and **offerings**. The use of the trumpet as a battle cry invoked God to rise up and defeat Israel's enemies. Trumpets were also blown to celebrate God's presence in their midst at these occasions.

10:11-13. This section marks a major division geographically in the book and in the Pentateuch. Ever since Ex 19 the nation had been at Sinai, and now for the first time in about a year they began to move out. They began their journey on the 20th day of the second month in the second year after the exodus from Egypt. The expectation was that they would be in the promised land in just a few short months. Deuteronomy 1:3 gives the ending time of the wilderness wanderings as "the fortieth year on the first day of the eleventh month." So the total span of the period in the wilderness after starting out was 38 years, 8 months, 11 days. Numbers 10:13 is the last clear mention of obedience, before Moses stressed the disobedience that began to characterize the nation for the rest of the wilderness-wandering period. Once they set out, they headed for the **wilderness of Paran**, about 100 miles southwest of the Dead Sea. The mention of the wilderness of Paran here echoes the story of Hagar in Gn 21. Several parallels can be seen between Hagar's experience and that of the Israelites in the book of Numbers. Both the Israelites and Hagar left their homes and wandered in the wilderness, including the wilderness of Paran; they encountered shortages of water and experienced God's provision of water.

10:14-28. The various leaders of the tribes mentioned here are the same ones listed in chaps. 2, 3, and 7. So for the fourth time these 12 names are specifically mentioned as leaders of their respective tribes. The tribes marched out in the same order as was given in Nm 2, but there is a discrepancy as to where the Levitical clans marched. According to 2:16-17 the tent of meeting and the camp of the Levites all were to set out after the second grouping of tribes (headed by Reuben). Yet 10:17 states that both the Gershonite and Merarite clans actually marched behind the first group of tribes (headed by **Judah**), and the **Kohathites** are the only clan (v. 21) to follow the second group of tribes (headed by **Reuben**) as was stipulated in 2:16-17. This may simply be a clarification of what was said in 2:16-17, or this may be a subtle hint that Israel did not completely obey what the Lord had commanded. Numbers 10 and 11 mark the transition from full and complete obedience to partial obedience and then outright rebellion. The only uncertainty pertains to the exact time when the shift from obedience to disobedience occurred.

10:29-32. What happened here could be considered another example in Israel's transition from obedience to disobedience, or it could be viewed as a brief conversation between **Moses** and **Hobab** that demonstrates good common sense. Many take this account of the discussion between Moses and Hobab, his brother-in-law, as an example of Moses seeking good counsel to assist him and the nation as they embarked on this journey to the promised land. Moses asked Hobab to be his **eyes** while in the wilderness, and he promised that Hobab would gain materially if he agreed to be their guide. While that may sound like a good practical move on the part of Moses, there may be some contextual hints within the book of Numbers that cast suspicion on this request by Moses.

Perhaps then this should not be viewed as a neutral or even a positive proposition. First, the Israelites clearly had the cloud (9:15-23) to tell them when to set out and where. Second, Moses had direct access to the Lord (7:89) and could get any specific input he needed from Him (as was demonstrated in the case of those who missed the Passover because of being ceremonially unclean, 9:8-13). Third, the Midianites as a group would become a major negative moral influence on Israel as seen in Nm 25 and 31. Moses' invitation may have been to a virtual "Trojan horse" that resulted in moral harm to Israel.

This request by Moses could be viewed as his "Plan B." If the cloud was not a dependable guide, he had a backup plan or at least a viable second opinion. Even if Hobab knew possible routes and food sources, the size of the nation at this time would seem to neutralize any tactical wisdom Hobab could offer. Looking at the way Moses framed the request may also offer some subtle hints as to his motivation. Even though his original offer was rebuffed, he came back with an even more urgent appeal. He asked for Hobab's physical presence: **do not leave us**. The next appeal sounds as though he was dependent on Hobab's knowledge: **you know where we should camp**. Also Moses seems to have wanted Hobab's insight and direction: **you can be our eyes**. Moses may have been asking Hobab to function as the surrogate "Lord" or the "cloud."

This account may be intimating that a seed of doubt and disbelief could be sprouting in Moses. This doubt sprouted later when he struck the rock and the Lord clearly stated that he did it because he "did not believe" (20:12). If the switch in the order of where the Levitical clans marched (10:17-21; cf. 2:16-17) can be seen as even a slight departure from the Lord's command by the Levitical clans, there is some evidence that Moses may have dropped a subtle hint that even he as a leader of the nation began to let disbelief in the Lord's instructions creep into his heart. By the next chapter (11:1) it is clear that entire nation had allowed rebellion and discontent to become public in their relationship to the Lord. The progression from a tiny deviation of the Lord's commands (by the Levitical clans) to doubt (by Moses) to outright rebellion (by the nation) is a pattern that was apparent even in the garden of Eden (Gn 3).

10:33-36. The text now returns to the account of the Israelites setting out from Sinai. The initial journey lasted three days, and the **ark of the covenant** went before them. This is the first time the term "the ark of the covenant" is used in Scripture. Since the ark was to be covered (4:5-6) during transport, it is doubtful that the nation saw the ark out in front of them. The ark along with the cloud seem to have been involved in guiding the nation about where they should stop on their journey.

Moses had a musical refrain recited (vv. 35-36) every time the ark set out that has strong military language **Rise up, O LORD! And let Your enemies be scattered, And let those who hate You flee before You.** This refrain invoked the Lord to protect Israel from its foes, and it asked (v. 36) for His presence among His people.

B. Rebellion of the First Generation (11:1–25:18)

1. Rebellion in the Camp (11:1-35)

11:1-3. The text so far (at least through Nm 10:13) has continually stressed the complete obedience of Moses, the Levites, and the entire nation of Israel. Now, in just a short period of time, that behavior waned. After 10 chapters that described the preparations for the journey, the people were shown on the move. But all was not well. The people began to **complain** about their adversities, and the Lord's **anger was kindled** against them. The nation had complained soon after the Red Sea deliverance about the lack of food and water (Ex 15:22-27; 16; 17), but this is the first time in the book of Numbers that complaints were voiced. This complaint also came after a period of three days (Ex 15:22-27; cf. Nm 10:33). A connection between Israel's complaints and the Lord's anger is introduced here in the book and repeated thereafter. **Fire** came out from the Lord and struck some of those at the outskirts of the camp. This fire **consumed** them, but their bodies were not totally burned. (This was also true of Nadab and Abihu whose bodies, consumed by fire [Lv 10:2], were carried outside the camp.) The corpses would be a tangible sign of God's displeasure. The people entreated Moses, **Moses prayed** on their behalf, and the fire died down. This introduces another theme in the book: Moses' intercession for the people. The place was called **Taberah**, based on the Hebrew verb "to burn." Place names in Numbers are often based on an event that took place in that location (cf. Nm 11:34-35).

The purpose of these parallels is to show not only the cyclical pattern of Israel's sinfulness and God's faithfulness during this wilderness period, but also to show moral and spiritual

Similarities and Differences between Exodus and Numbers

Exodus	Numbers
People grumble, 14:2, 27	People grumble, 11:1-3
Manna provided, 16:13-16	Manna provided, 11:7-9
Quail provided, 16:13	Quail provided, 11:31
Leaders appointed to assist Moses, 18:17-26	Leaders appointed to assist Moses, 11:25
Miriam rejoices, 15:20-21	Miriam rebels, 12:1
Amalek defeated, 17:8-16	Amalek victorious, 14:39-45

decline. This bad behavior manifested by the nation and their leaders in these downward cycles had negative consequences on them.

11:4-9. Even after the fire died down, the **rabble** began to voice another complaint, this time about food. This is the only time that "rabble" is used in the OT. The phrase used in reference to this group earlier was "mixed multitude" (Ex 12:38). These were non-Israelites, who were also Semites, living in Egypt at the exodus, or perhaps even Egyptians themselves. The rabble was not satisfied with the provision of manna and began to crave **meat** and a diet that had various flavors. The demand for meat is unusual since the nation was said to be rich in flocks (Ex 12:38; Nm 32:1), and "meat" is not specifically mentioned as something they consumed while slaves in Egypt. While they were certainly exaggerating the types of foods they enjoyed in Egypt, they may not have wanted to consume from their own flocks since their livestock were a main part of their economic holdings. Therefore, they were probably looking for sources of meat other than their own animals.

Manna was **like coriander** with olive oil. Exodus 16:31 previously stated that it tasted like wafers made with honey, so the people described it in various ways. Manna could be prepared in a number of ways after it was gathered and ground. Depending on personal preference, it could be cooked in a **pot** or baked as **cakes**. Suggestions of naturalistic explanations for manna (i.e., plant secretions) do not fit the supernatural qualities detailed in the text. If there was no supernatural power at work, no natural substance could make a daily appearance in sufficient quantity for the entire nation for 38 years and not be available to be gathered on Saturdays.

11:10-15. The complaints of the people were so massive that Moses heard all the people **weeping** at the doorways of their tents. Once again the Lord's **anger** was kindled because of their ingratitude for His providing them food. Instead of seeing the manna and quail as gracious provisions from the loving God, they disdained not only the daily food but also the Lord Himself. Moses himself was displeased with their response. Instead of asking the Lord how he should personally respond, he too complained to God about having to lead an ungrateful people alone. Moses bombarded the Lord with several rhetorical questions to which he already knew the answers. One of Moses' weaknesses was anger, as revealed in his first account as an adult when he struck and killed an Egyptian who was beating a Hebrew (Ex 2:11). In Moses' eyes the weight of leading the people was too burdensome, and if the Lord would not relieve him of it then he wished for death.

11:16-17. Earlier Jethro had recommended that Moses appoint judges to assist him in dealing with all the judicial cases brought before him (Ex 18:13-26). Now, to release Moses from carrying all the spiritual load of caring for the nation, the Lord told Moses to select 70 of Israel's elders so that the Lord could take some of the Spirit that Moses had and redistribute it to them.

11:18-23. Two separate story lines are intertwined in this chapter. One deals with the request for meat, and the other deals with Moses' complaint about being overburdened. This section gives the next sequence of events regarding meat that was started in vv. 4-9. The people were instructed to **consecrate** themselves because the Lord would provide meat not just for one day but also **for a whole month**. In fact it would come out their **nostrils** (v. 20). This is interesting because the word for "anger" (v. 1) and the word for "nostril" are spelled the same in Hebrew (*ap*). The seat of anger was associated with nostrils (i.e., nostrils flaring when one is angry). When the Lord's "nose" is angered, the consequences will be felt in the "nose" of those being judged.

Moses expressed disbelief at the Lord's abilities to provide such a large quantity of meat, and the Lord rebuked Moses by asking him, **Is the Lord's power limited?** Verse 23 gives the essence of the problem behind these complaints and the divine solution to it. This lesson is for both the nation and its leaders. The fundamental problem is disbelief and doubt of God's power, and the solution to doubt and disbelief is to believe that His **word** is **true**.

11:24-30. After the **seventy . . . elders** were gathered at the entrance of the tabernacle the Lord fulfilled what He said He would do in v. 17. He caused the Spirit that was on Moses to rest on the **seventy** as clear evidence of their spiritual authority. They began to prophesy in a way that was not repeated again in the future. Two men, **Eldad** and **Medad**, were selected to be among the **seventy**, but for some reason they were not with the other elders. These two began to prophesy where they were located in the camp, and a report of their activities was relayed to Moses. **Joshua**, Moses' longtime aide, with a desire to protect his master's status, asked him to have them stop **prophesying**. Moses was not threatened by this visible display of the Spirit's power and wished that all the **LORD's people** could enjoy the Spirit's special gift demonstrated here. This display of humility by Moses reflects a key aspect of his character and provides a fitting backdrop to the unjustified challenge to his leadership in the next chapter.

11:31-35. This section connects with the previous passage by a wordplay with the Hebrew word *ruah*, meaning "spirit" or "wind." The Spirit of the Lord had just blessed the seventy elders with prophetic gifts, and now the **wind** of the Lord would bless the people with **quail**. These quail either flew in a three-foot thick flight pattern or they hovered at a height of three feet off the ground, meaning they could easily be captured. For about 36 hours they flew by so that each individual in the camp was able to gather more than 60 bushels. It must have been quite a feat to store that much meat in the midst of the camp. God's provision of quail was a mixed blessing in that while they were given the opportunity to partake of meat in abundance, it demonstrated the nation's gluttonous appetite, so much so that it provoked the Lord's anger. Before the quail could even be consumed, the Lord sent a severe plague and many died. The place was called Kibroth-hattaavah meaning, graves of **greediness**.

2. Rebellion of Aaron and Miriam (12:1-16)

12:1-8. After the nation set up camp at Hazeroth (11:35), **Miriam** and **Aaron spoke against Moses**. Though Miriam and Aaron are paired together, the Hebrew verb is in the feminine form, indicating that Miriam was the instigator in this challenge against Moses' leadership and explaining the reason she suffered the consequences. The combination of Aaron and Miriam, however, was a serious threat, not just because they were siblings, but also because he was the high priest and she was a prophetess (Ex 15:20). The explanation for this defiance was his marriage to **a Cushite woman**. It is not clear whether this is referring to Zipporah (since Midian and Cush/Cushan are perhaps related, as seen in Hab 3:7) or to a second wife from the area today known as either Nubia or Ethiopia. Even though the nationality of this woman is not transparent, what is clear is that Moses' siblings raised an ethnic objection.

While ethnic purity in Israel was an issue, foreigners were allowed to participate in the spiritual community (9:14). Though ethnicity was the issue Miriam raised, her underlying concern was jealousy and possibly concern over losing some of her spiritual status to this woman. Perhaps Moses' wife was viewed as a threat to Miriam's position as the most influential woman in Israel. Considering the newly elevated spiritual authority of the 70 elders (11:25), perhaps Miriam thought her spiritual authority was dwindling. Or perhaps she thought that by challenging Moses she could reclaim some of her former spiritual status. These concerns were clearly a repudiation of the Lord's choice of Moses as Israel's supreme human leader.

The next statement about Moses' humility (12:3) is a parenthetical thought and seems to be one of the few places in the Pentateuch where a later inspired editor gave a simple statement about God's perspective on Moses' character. Moses' humility was revealed in the previous chapter (11:29), and so a reference to it here makes Miriam's charges seem all the more egregious. In response to this challenge the **LORD** summoned **Moses . . . Aaron . . . and Miriam . . . to the tent of meeting** and reconfirmed Moses' authority and status. The Lord directly addressed them from within the **cloud** in a poetic form and verbally defended Moses' special relationship. When the Lord revealed Himself, He did so, He said, through visions and dreams, but He addressed Moses **mouth to mouth**, that is, face to face. Moses even saw the **form** of the **LORD** that no one else has had the privilege of seeing (v. 8). With all these special privileges, Moses' siblings were asked why they were **not afraid to speak against** him as God's servant. This affirmation established Moses' uniqueness as a prophet—he alone received direct revelation from God. This became significant later when the Lord promised Israel a messianic prophet like Moses (Dt 18:15-19). This future prophet, the Messiah, would not be like all the other prophets of Israel, but like Moses He would engage in direct communication with God without dreams or visions.

12:9-16. Then the Lord in anger struck Miriam with leprosy, making her ceremonially unclean and an outcast within the community. Aaron pleaded with his brother and intervened on her behalf. He said Miriam's physical condition was like that of a stillborn child **whose flesh is half eaten**. Moses without hesitation interceded on his sister's behalf and asked the Lord to **heal** her. Yet, she was not immediately healed. Since her offense was so serious she was like someone whose father spat in her face. Such a person would have to remain **outside the camp** for seven days. Spitting was an extreme act of contempt (Dt 25:9) and left one unclean for obvious reasons. The public nature of her challenge caused her to suffer public humiliation. Her sin delayed the movement of the camp until she was able to return from her weeklong exile. After she **was received** back, the nation moved **out** from **Hazeroth** to the **wilderness of Paran**.

3. Rebellion at Kadesh (13:1–14:45)

13:1-16. The Lord now instructed Moses to **send out . . . men** to explore the land. The location of the Israelite base camp gets increasingly more specific throughout this section. First, they were in the general region of the Wilderness of Paran (12:16, about 100 miles southwest of the Dead Sea), then in the more distinct section known as the Wilderness of Zin (13:21, about 25 miles southwest of the Dead Sea), and then at a specific location at Kadesh (13:26, about 60 miles southwest of the Dead Sea). Moses later stated that it was from here that the Israelites were commanded to "go up and take possession" (Dt 1:21). Before they went forth, they asked Moses to send men to search out routes and report back on the cities (Dt 1:22). While their motivation for this sounds good, it does not demonstrate stepping out in faith in response to the Lord's word to simply "go" and "take." Nevertheless the Lord graciously heard that request and told Moses to select the men to send (v. 1). These men were to be selected from the **leaders of each of their fathers' tribes**. The individuals selected were not the same tribal representatives mentioned previously as leading in the census and bringing tribute (chaps. 1, 2, 7, 10). Probably the previously-mentioned leaders were elderly statesmen, and this mission called for men who would be perhaps more physically fit to handle the reconnaissance mission. They were not officially labeled as "spies" like the ones Joshua later sent to survey Jericho (Jos 2:1), but they were to be individuals of good standing who could easily sway the people with their opinion. That they were individually named in an official list along with their tribal associations demonstrates their importance and standing within the nation. They could be trusted to give an honest report of what they saw, and their recommendations would be weighty. Two of the men selected played more prominent roles in the future: **Hoshea . . . from the tribe of Ephraim**, whom Moses renamed Joshua (13:16), and **Caleb . . . from the tribe of Judah**.

13:17-33. Moses gave clear and explicit instructions, yet their report had mixed results (as seen in the chart "Instructions to the Twelve Spies" on the following page).

In the past Moses had shown the Israelites' obedience to God's instructions by either giving a detailed report of those instructions being followed (i.e., the instructions for the tabernacle were given in Ex 26–30 and then they were followed, as seen in Ex 36-40), or he stated that what was done was "according to all which the Lord had commanded" (Nm 1:54). In this account Moses gave clear instructions and questions for the men to answer on their return. But there is no statement that they did what was asked, nor did the men address all the questions Moses posed. The account they gave was reported in a different order from what Moses gave them, and they often gave additional information on items they were not asked to research.

Even though Joshua and Caleb were among these spies they were not culpable since they followed the Lord fully (Nm 14:24). The rest of the spies left out content that might have influenced the people positively. For instance they visited Hebron on their trip but failed to mention that in their report. Hebron was a place clearly associated with the patriarch Abraham and would have invoked in the mind of the Israelites the land promises given to him, since Abraham was buried there. The statement about Hebron being built seven years before Zoan in Egypt (13:22) is a curious parenthetical thought. Zoan is associated with the city of Tanis in the north Nile delta and was to become a political capital for Egypt around the time of King David. That Hebron predates this Egyptian city certainly underscores Hebron's importance.

The route the men took began in the south at the Wilderness of Zin (v. 21) and went as far north as Rehob, near Lebo-hamath (beyond the city of Damascus). On the way back they stopped at the valley of Eshcol (lit., "cluster"), near Hebron, and brought back produce from that area, including a single cluster of grapes (so large that it had to be **carried . . . on a pole**) along with pomegranates and figs. These items would be clear examples of the agricultural fertility of the land to which the Lord was sending them. The entire expedition took 40 days, and they returned to the camp, now specifically mentioned

Instructions to the Twelve Spies and the Report of the Ten

Instructions	Order of Instructions Once They Arrive	Order in Report	Report	Completed Yes or No
v. 17—Go up there into the Negev; then go up into the hill country.			v. 21—They went up and spied out the land from the wilderness of Zin as far as Rehob, at Lebo-hamath. v. 22—When they had gone up into the Negev, they came to Hebron.	Yes, but went to additional places
v. 18—See what the land is like, and whether the people who live in it are strong or weak.	1	3	v. 28—The people who live in the land are strong. v. 32—All the people whom we saw in it are men of great size.	Yes, but added size of inhabitants
v. 18b—Whether they are few or many.	2	n/a		No
v. 19a—How is the land in which they live, is it good or bad?	3	1a	v. 27—It certainly does flow with milk and honey.	Yes, but they did not use the word "good"
v. 19b—And how are the cities in which they live, are they like open camps or with fortifications?	4	4	v. 28—The cities are fortified and very large; and moreover, we saw the descendants of Anak there.	Yes, but they mentioned the size and names of inhabitants
v. 20a—How is the land, is it fat or lean?	5	1b	v. 27—It certainly does flow with milk and honey.	Yes, but they do not use same words
v. 20b—Are there trees in it or not?	6	n/a		No
v. 20c—Make an effort then to get some of the fruit of the land.	7	2	v. 23—Then they came to the valley of Eshcol and from there cut down a branch with a single cluster of grapes; and they carried it on a pole between two men, with some of the pomegranates and the figs.	Yes

as being located at Kadesh (v. 26, about 60 miles southwest of the Dead Sea).

The report started out positively by stating that the land **does flow with milk and honey**, a common phrase emphasizing the fruitfulness of the promised land (e.g., Ex 3:8, 17). The exact meaning of the expression is not readily discernible. The word for milk (Hb. *chalab*) has the same consonants as the word for fat (*cheleb*), but the by-product of flocks is probably more in mind here than "fat." Honey refers to what wild bees produce, or the sap of trees, or the syrup by-product of figs or other fruit. The image of a land filled with flocks (milk) and fruit (honey) is a graphic metaphor. Whatever these words mean, it is clear that they evoked the bountiful and sweet provisions of the land they just visited. For a people who were used to eating manna day-in and day-out, this must have seemed extremely attractive.

Even though their report started in a positive manner, there is a subtle shift in their opening statement. The **nevertheless** (v. 28) qualifies their introduction and reveals the group's faulty attitude. They quickly moved from answering Moses' earlier questions to inserting their own opinion as to whether Israel should proceed with entering the land, and their doubts about being able to overpower the inhabitants of the land. Caleb spoke up against what the 10 men were saying and gave his motivational challenge to take possession of what God had promised. He said they could **take possession** of the land. The 10 men were mainly concerned about the size of the people who lived in Canaan and their strongly **fortified** cities. They cited the descendants of **Anak** (v. 28) and the **Nephilim** (v. 33) so as to elicit the most amount of fear in those hearing the report. The Anak were a group living near Hebron (Jos 11:21-22) and were very tall (Dt 2:10). Nephilim were previously mentioned as a pre-flood people (Gn 6:4).

The question has arisen as to how there could be Nephilim if their line did not survive Noah's flood. Since the spies were giving a false report regarding the challenges the nation would face in conquering the land, they may have exaggerated the large people they encountered and mistakenly believed them to be the Nephilim. Another explanation is that these Nephilim may simply have been a different people with the same name but with the same qualities of height and arrogance that the original Nephilim displayed in Gn 6. The spies reported that **all the people** (v. 32) were of **great size**, and they belittled themselves as small **like grasshoppers** (v. 33). They saw themselves as prey, not as victors.

14:1-4. The Israelites were swayed by the negative report of the 10 spies, and their displeasure was audibly heard throughout the camp. They directed their complaint at Moses and Aaron, saying they longed to be put out of their misery and wished they had **died** when they were in **Egypt** or now in the **wilderness**. The Israelites longed to die in the wilderness, and, ironically, God did eventually grant this generation that request (14:29). Women and children were often taken away as spoil after battle so it was true that they and their families were vulnerable in this location. But instead of expressing fear and rebellion they should have trusted the Lord for protection from their enemies and for power to go up and possess the land. They had many clear and tangible expressions of the Lord's presence in their midst, and He had miraculously protected them from enemies in their recent past. Yet in their minds it would be better for them to go back in submission to their oppressors in Egypt than to go forward and trust the Lord for their future. They quickly forgot the toils of their bondage while they were in Egypt (Ex 2:23-24), and they sought to select a new leader to guide them back to Egypt.

14:5-10. Moses and Aaron then **fell** prostrate on the ground in front of the whole camp in a display of self-humiliation. They let their body language speak before opening their mouths. This so moved Joshua and Caleb that as an act of solidarity with Moses and Aaron they **tore their clothes** as a sign of mourning and deep grief (Gn 37:29). At this juncture Joshua and Caleb implored the people to remember that the land was **an exceedingly good land**. This was the first time Joshua was vocal in the book of Numbers, even though he was one of the men selected to explore the promised land. Being the personal attendant of Moses (Ex 24:13) probably caused Joshua not to speak up earlier (Nm 13:30) along with Caleb. Since he was closely associated with Moses, the people would naturally expect him to support Moses, his mentor. Now, however, he boldly joined with Caleb in addressing the folly of the nation in rebelling against the Lord. He emphasized that they need **not fear the people**, for they would fall before them because the Lord was on their side. The people pleaded for a leader (14:4) and ultimately Joshua became their new leader. But he would not take them back to Egypt as they requested; instead he would lead them into the promised land. Joshua and Caleb's passionate plea did not convince the people, who rallied to **stone them**. To prevent them from proceeding, the **glory of the Lord** appeared, graciously protecting His servants and warning the people.

14:11-19. The Lord addressed Moses and rhetorically asked him several questions. Essentially He was asking Moses how much longer He should tolerate the nation's rejection and unbelief in the face of all the supernatural visible and tangible signs that were performed in their midst. The Lord proposed to **smite them with pestilence**, as He did to get Egypt to let His people go. He also sought to start the nation all over again by starting afresh with Moses. But Moses pleaded again with the Lord as he did earlier (Ex 32:11-13) not to go forth with that plan because it would mar His testimony and reputation with the Egyptians. And all the other nations who heard about the Lord's doings with this nation would mock His inability to fulfill His promises. Appealing to God's attributes, Moses prayed that the Lord would display His great power, patience, and **lovingkindness**, and that He would forgive the **iniquity** of this people. Moses' made a lawyer-like argument: if the Lord wiped out the nation, it would reflect more on His character than on the character of rebellious Israel. His inability to fulfill His promise to bring this people into the promised land would negatively impact His reputation if He carried out His plan to destroy the nation.

Moses, however, knew that the Lord could not let this rebellion go unpunished. He wanted the Lord to rethink His plan to start all over again with him. Moses mentioned that the Lord would visit the **iniquity of the fathers on the children to the third and the fourth generations**. This phrase is repeated elsewhere in the Pentateuch (Ex 20:5; Dt 5:9), and heightens the consequences of remaining unrepentant (and thus unforgiven) of sin. Elsewhere Moses stated that individuals die for their own sins and not for their father's sins (Dt 24:16). So this particular phrase may simply be communicating that patterns of sin often get repeated in the next generation. The next generation begins where the last generation left off, and the sin continues to compound. It may also indicate that sin brings natural negative consequences that often continue to affect later generations. Without biblical support, some today blame every sin and problem on some sort of generational curse. They confuse God's warning of the consequences for sin with deliberate cursing by God from generation to generation. Moses boldly concluded his intercession by asking that the Lord forgive this people out of the abundance of His mercy.

14:20-38. On the basis of Moses' argument and prayer the Lord graciously pardoned the people and did not wipe them out. But there would be consequences for their rebellious actions. The punishment meted out, as well as this act of forgiveness, would assist in filling **the earth . . . with the glory of the Lord** (v. 21). The sentence God imposed on the nation was that anyone over the age of 20 who grumbled against the Lord would die in the wilderness. This sentence was so harsh because, having seen the Lord's glory and His supernatural signs, they still put the Lord to the test 10 times. The 10 tests may not necessarily be literal but could be a literary device to mean a great many times (cf. Jb 19:3). Nevertheless there are at least 10 times the people put the Lord to the test that can be documented: Ex 14:11-12; 15:23-24; 16:2-3, 20, 27; 17:1; 32:1-10; Nm 11:1, 4; 14:1-3.

The number "ten" (Nm 14:22) is significant in that it is the number of the plagues the Lord sent against Egypt (Ex 7–11). The 10 plagues demonstrated God's power, and the 10 tests of Israel similarly taxed God's patience. **Caleb** was exempt (v. 24) from this sentence because he **had a different spirit** and **followed** the Lord without reservation (Joshua was mentioned later, v. 30).

Instead of leaving Kadesh and going directly toward the promised land through the **valleys** where the **Amalekites and Canaanites** dwelled, the people were now to set out the next day by a longer and circuitous route toward the **Red Sea** (most likely the Gulf of Aqaba, about 120 miles south of the Dead Sea, and about 80 southeast of Kadesh—or basically in the opposite direction of the Holy Land).

The Lord now instructed Moses and Aaron to explain to the people what their disciplinary sentence would be. Earlier the people had wished for death **in the wilderness** (v. 2), and now the Lord would grant that request. The adage "be careful what you wish for" was never so true as in this incident. Their **children**, whom they earlier thought would be prey to the enemy (v. 3), would instead be the ones to enter the promised land, along with **Joshua** and **Caleb**. The nation's sin may have been forgiven (v. 20), but the consequences of their actions meant that their children would have to suffer for their unfaithfulness until those over 20 died in the wilderness. Ezekiel 18:13-18 argued that children are not responsible for the moral guilt of their parents' individual sin, but it does not preclude them from suffering the consequences of their parents' sin. The specific punishment was a year for every one of the days the men were on the spying expedition. Since the expedition lasted **forty days** (Nm 13:25) they were to spend **forty years** in the wilderness before going up into the promised land. The people had already spent just over a year in the wilderness since leaving Egypt (9:1; cf. 1:1), and a short period of time transpired since Nm 1:1, so the actual punishment period was just over 38 years. To underscore the heinousness of their unbelief and rebellion, the Lord judged the men who tried to convince the nation not to take possession of the land by sentencing them to die by a **plague** (v. 37).

14:39-45. After the sentence was meted out and the people saw the ten spies die by plague, the nation **mourned**, but the next day they resolved to take the land by way of the **hill country**. They acknowledged their sin and were now ready to go up into the land the Lord had promised. Moses warned them against doing so and stated that they would be unsuccessful because

The Israelites' Wilderness Wanderings

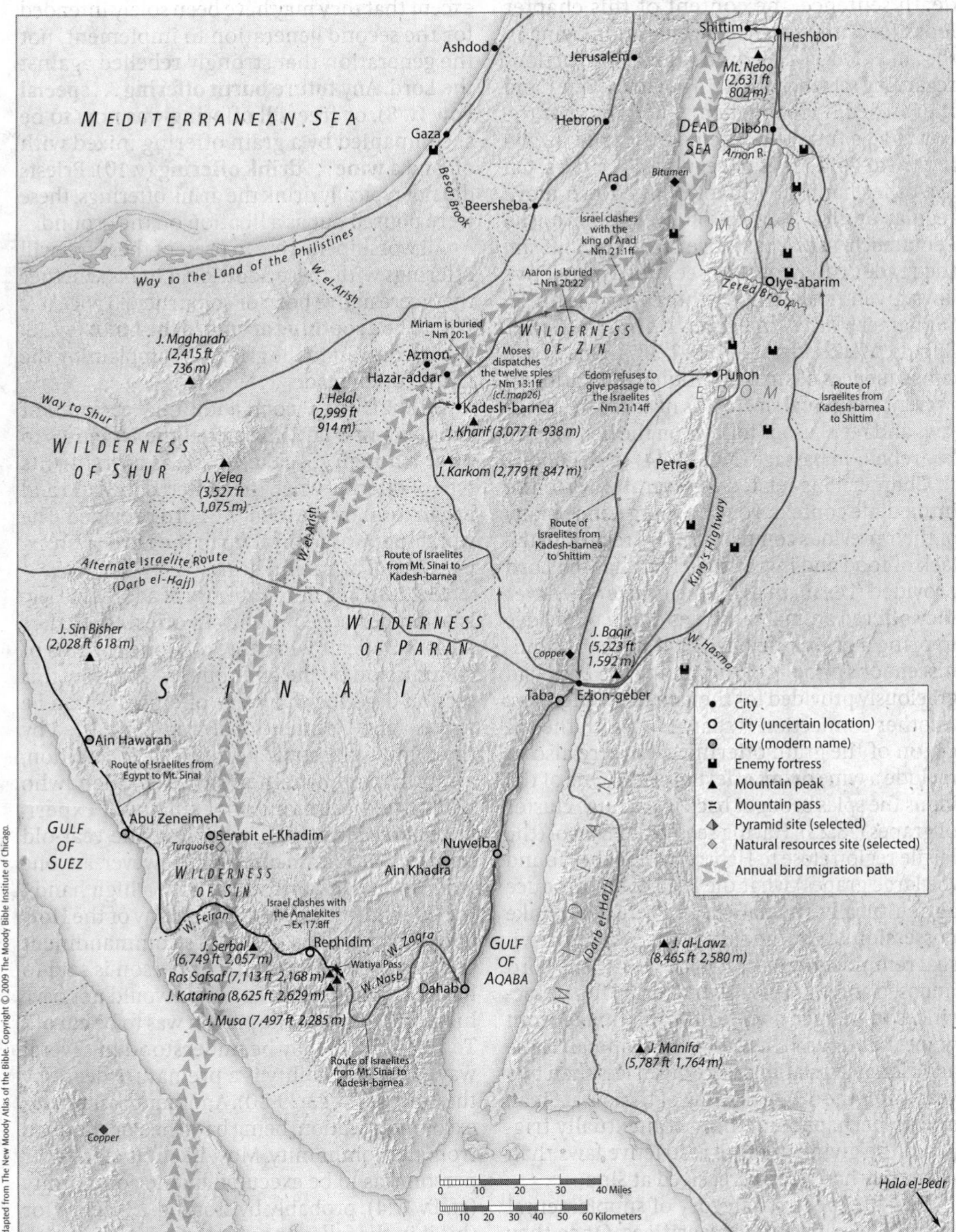

the Lord's presence would not be with them. Again in another act of defiance they acted on their own without **Moses** or the **ark of the covenant**. They were struck down handily and driven back by **the Amalekites and the Canaanites**.

4. Additional Instructions Regarding Offerings (15:1-41)

This chapter includes four categories of supplemental law, broken up by a short narrative account about a Sabbath-breaker. Even though the first generation had just been handed a death sentence, the content of this chapter looks forward to the next generation being in the land. God gave them additional instructions regarding sacrificial offerings. On the one hand it provided hope for them, knowing that the Lord had a future for them in the land by giving them guidelines to regulate sacrifices. On the other hand this chapter lays down more regulations for them to follow. Whenever the Pentateuch gives a narrative account about sin, the reader can expect to see more restrictive laws given immediately thereafter (John H. Sailhamer, *The Pentateuch as Narrative* [Grand Rapids, MI: Zondervan, 1992], 387). One of the consequences of sin is additional legislation to prevent additional sin. In this instance this set of laws and regulations follows on the heels of the key rebellion passage (Nm 13–14) in the book.

Chapter 15 is related in several ways to the immediate context. For one thing, since many of their previous complaints were related to the lack of food and ingratitude for what the Lord provided (i.e., manna), in the future whenever they offered animal sacrifices they would have to bring a **grain offering** (15:4) perhaps reminiscent or symbolic of the manna the Lord had graciously provided for them in the wilderness. Another connection is that along with the addition of the grain offering they were also to include a wine **drink offering** (15:5). One of the items the spies brought back was a huge cluster of grapes (13:23). Having seen from Eshcol (the fertile region close to Hebron where they found the large grapes) what the land could produce agriculturally, the nation still refused to take possession of the land. Perhaps as a future visual reminder of rejecting that "fruit," the Lord imposed additional legislation on all future sacrifices to include a wine offering (made from grapes) along with the designated animal. These additional legislations were given less than two years after the original giving of the law at Sinai, and so perhaps something contextually triggered the giving of more restrictive laws than what they had already received at Sinai.

15:1-16. The first category of supplemental laws deals with animal sacrifices. Once they entered the land, worshipers were instructed to present supplemental offerings along with their usual animal sacrifices. These additional stipulations did not apply to sin or guilt offerings, but only to freewill-type offerings. Why these supplemental laws were not to go into effect immediately in the wilderness is not clear, except that they may have been solely intended for the second generation to implement, not the generation that strongly rebelled against the Lord. Any future **burnt offering . . . special vow** (v. 8), or freewill offering was now to be accompanied by a grain offering mixed with oil and a **wine . . . drink offering** (v. 10). Priests did not typically drink the drink offerings; these were poured out as a libation on the ground.

All worshipers were to present these freewill offerings with these additional items whether they were native born or sojourners. Twice it is said to be **a soothing aroma to the Lord** (vv. 13, 14), in contrast to the grievous complaining the nation often made.

15:17-21. The second additional category of supplemental law instructed the Israelites to offer a **dough . . . cake** (v. 20) as a first fruits type of offering when they entered the land and began to enjoy the food the Lord provided. The worshiper was to lift it up to the Lord as an expression of a grateful heart.

15:22-31. The third category of additional legislation pertained to the **sin offering**. Earlier Lv 4:13-21 dealt with how to atone for sins of commission by the community, and now this section describes how sins of omission can be made right. Unintentional sins committed by the community could be forgiven. In addition, an individual, whether native or alien, who committed unintentional sin could experience atonement if he brought a one-year-old **female goat** as a **sin offering**. However, anyone who sinned **defiantly** (lit., "with a high hand," the OT equivalent to the blasphemy of the Holy Spirit) had broken the Lord's commandment and despised His word. That person is said to have blasphemed the Lord and would not have his guilt removed. The person was to be **cut off**. To be "cut off" may be understood in several ways. One possibility is a premature death by the Lord (cf. Lv 23:29-30). Another possibility is excommunication, being banished or shunned from the community. Most likely, it means the person was to be executed by the community (cf. Lv 17:4), probably by stoning. Evidence for this is in the following verses (vv. 32-36), which give an example of what it meant to be "cut off" for violating the Sabbath (cf. Ex 31:14-15). There, the transgressor was **stoned . . . to death** for a defiant sin.

15:32-36. At this point the text switches from law back to narrative and relates the account of a man who was found gathering wood on the Sabbath day. The first and second of the Ten Commandments (Ex 20) were clearly violated by the nation in the book of Exodus when they worshiped the golden calf (Ex 32). The book of Leviticus then follows with a description of a clear violation of the third Commandment when a blasphemer was stoned (Lv 24:10-14, 23). Now the next book in the Pentateuch (Numbers) contains a clear violation of the fourth Commandment in this account of the Sabbath-breaker. This pattern of clear sequential violations of the Ten Commandments since Sinai does not bode well for the nation's ability to keep the law. In Ex 31:14-15 the punishment for violating the Sabbath was death, so it is not clear here why that sentence was not handed out immediately. Perhaps it was because this individual had violated the Sabbath "unintentionally" (Nm 15:27). Other possibilities could be that Moses and the people were not sure if **gathering wood** violated the "no-work" stipulation of the Sabbath law, or they did not know what means of capital punishment to use, or they may have been reticent to carry out the death penalty. Whatever the case, the violator was placed in custody until a clear verdict could be given by the Lord through Moses. The Lord pronounced him guilty of a capital sin, and he was to be stoned **outside the camp**. In a brief respite from their usual rebellious behavior the people obeyed **just as the Lord had commanded Moses**. This does provide a glimmer of hope in that it reminds the reader that the people were capable of obeying the Lord.

15:37-41. The fourth category of new legislation pertained to the placement of blue **tassels** on **garments**. Once again this section follows a narrative passage that highlighted disobedience (specifically breaking the Sabbath, but also the recent rejection of the promised land). If the people were forgetful about keeping the basic laws such as keeping the Sabbath, then an additional law would be added to their legislative code. In this case the additional supplemental law fit the transgression. God would now require them to wear visual symbols (tassels) to remind them to keep the previous laws He had already given them. The fundamental problem is articulated in v. 39. They were following their **own heart and . . . eyes**, and thus they needed an object lesson on every garment in their possession. The color blue, often representing royalty, was also used in the priest's wardrobe (Ex 28). The tassels would also be a subtle reminder that all the people were in a sense priest-like, even though not from the tribe of Levi. These tassels depicted their unique status as God's chosen people.

5. Rebellion of Korah (16:1-50)

16:1-11. The focus now shifts back to a narrative depicting a rebellion led by the Levite **Korah**. An earlier challenge against Moses' leadership was led by Aaron and Miriam (Nm 12). Now this attack came from a coalition of some individuals from the Kohath clan of the Levites as well as some from the tribe of **Reuben**. The Kohathites were given privileged responsibilities in handling the most sacred objects of the tabernacle (4:1-20). Yet for Korah that authority was not enough, so he led the coalition. He was joined by some Reubenites who may have been jealous of the privileged role of Judah in the camp placement, especially since their forefather was the firstborn son of Jacob, while Judah was Jacob's fourth son. Thus this challenge was not just a religious dispute. It also incorporated political overtones since it included more than just the priestly Levitical tribe—250 Israelite community leaders who had great sway in the nation joined the instigators. This was no small challenge. Their ire was not just with Moses but with Aaron the high priest as well.

Their vexation was based on the notion that there should be a more democratic spiritual authority structure, because **all the congregation** was **holy** and experienced the Lord's presence just as much as Moses and Aaron did. They disliked that Moses and Aaron seemed to place themselves as the sole authorities in governing the nation of Israel. The rebels failed to take into account that the Lord had appointed Moses and Aaron. Thus, their insurrection was not just against their human leaders but also against the Lord Himself.

Hearing this, Moses fell on his face just as he did in 14:5. In the face of such a challenge Moses recommended a trial by ordeal to settle their dispute. On the next morning the Lord would visibly demonstrate **who is holy**, and He would **bring . . . near** to Him (v. 5) the one who was divinely appointed to lead. Moses instructed them to bring censers so that they could burn incense in them before the **presence of the Lord**. Just as Korah had thought that Moses and Aaron had "gone far enough" (Nm 16:3), Moses now used the exact same phrase (v. 7) in saying that it was they who had in fact **gone far**

enough. Chiding the Levites, Moses reminded them that they already had a favored position with the Lord in their duties at the tabernacle. He reprimanded them for wanting to be priests as well. He argued that the root of their defiance was directed not against Aaron but against the **LORD** Himself.

16:12-15. Indignant against Moses for setting the terms, **Dathan** and **Abiram** refused to participate in the ordeal. It is not clear why they and not Korah were singled out here. As Reubenites their complaint may have been more political than spiritual in nature, and perhaps they felt Moses had only thus far addressed the concerns of the Kohathites. They exclaimed that instead of leading the nation into a land flowing with milk and honey, Moses had done the opposite. He brought them out of a rich, prosperous land to let them die in the wilderness. That Korah and his followers had the audacity to use the phrase **flowing with milk and honey** of Egypt, the same phrase the Lord had previously used of the promised land (Ex 3:8), shows the depths of their arrogance. They stated sarcastically that Moses would have **to put out** the people's eyes (v. 14) so that they would not see what Moses' failed leadership skills had brought to the people thus far. Moses became angry and entreated the Lord not to accept **their offering** (most likely referring to their incense offering they were to bring the next morning). He also defended his motives by saying that he had not personally benefited or sought any special privileges as the nation's leader. Moreover, he gave evidence of his integrity by stating that he had not previously **done harm** to any of them and thus had no personal vendetta against these men.

16:16-27. Moses instructed Korah and his 250 followers to be prepared to appear with Aaron **before the LORD** the next morning and to come with a **censer** of **incense**. The next day they gathered at the entrance of the tent of meeting ready for the trial by ordeal. The purpose was that the Lord could visibly demonstrate who would be His representatives. The glory of the Lord then appeared, and the Lord asked Moses and Aaron to **separate** themselves from the rest of those gathered so that he might **consume them instantly**. Moses and Aaron both fell on their faces and appealed to God to spare the rebels. They invoked the title **O God, God of the spirits of all flesh** (v. 22), a phrase used in only one other place in the Scriptures (27:16). This means that God knows a person's inner motives.

Since Moses and Aaron believed that only one man (Korah) instigated this rebellion and that God would be able to discern that, they felt that the Lord should not punish the **congregation**. Without addressing Moses' plea, the Lord stated that Moses and Aaron should get away from these rebels and that the entire nation should separate themselves from the three main dissenters. Since Dathan and Abiram had refused to participate (v. 12), Moses and the elders went to where their tents were located and announced that nothing of these men should be touched because they and what belonged to them would receive the Lord's wrath. The families of Dathan and Abiram came out of their tents and stood there while the rest of the congregation backed away.

16:28-40. Moses then issued an ultimatum. He stated that if the rebels died of natural causes, then Moses was not the divinely selected leader. But if the earth opened up and swallowed them **alive**, it would prove that they had spurned the Lord. Immediately after Moses finished saying this, the ground **opened its mouth and swallowed . . . up** (vv. 31-32) those who had followed Korah, along with their possessions, and then closed back on top of them. Those swallowed up **went down alive into Sheol**. In this instance "Sheol" probably means "the grave" and not "the netherworld" (the realm of disembodied souls after death). Since the Kohathites camped on the southern side of the tabernacle complex close to the tribe of Reuben, this was a geographically isolated event. All the people, however, panicked. They thought the earth would swallow them up too, so they **fled**. While they were panicking, **fire** came out **from the LORD** and **consumed** the 250 men who held the censers.

The Lord instructed Moses to have Eleazar take the censers from the charred remains because they were made **holy** (set apart) and then gather the burning coals left on the censers and scatter them. The censers were then to be hammered into **plating** for the **altar**. This was a permanent reminder that only descendants from Aaron should ever offer **incense** (serve as priests) before the Lord.

16:41-50. Even after a clear display of the Lord's discipline the people **grumbled** the next day and blamed Moses and Aaron for the deaths of the rebels. The congregation did not call them rebels but instead referred to them as **the LORD's people**, apparently showing some solidarity with those recipients of God's wrath. As the congregation assembled at the tent of meeting, **the cloud covered it and the glory of the LORD appeared**. Moses and Aaron came to the front, and then the Lord told them to separate themselves from the rest of the people so that He might consume them instantly just as He did with Korah and the rebels the previous day.

Moses and Aaron again **fell on their faces**. Moses acted quickly, and instead of pleading with the Lord to relent, he instructed Aaron to get his censer and put incense in it along with fire from the altar to **make atonement** for the people. Aaron quickly sprang into action, got the censer, incense, and fire, and ran out into the midst of the assembly, even though the **plague** had already started to break out.

Some have suggested that **incense** was an alternative means of atonement, other than animal sacrifice. However, according to the Torah, atonement for sin is possible only by a blood sacrifice (Lv 17:11). Here in Nm 16:46-47, the issue is not atonement for sin but stopping a **plague**. Although the verb *kipper* usually means "to make atonement or to expiate," in vv. 46-47, Jacob Milgrom correctly asserts that "in this context, [it] carries the connotation of 'make appeasement.'" According to him, incense served "to appease and sooth divine wrath" (Jacob Milgrom, *JPS Torah Commentary: Numbers* [Philadelphia: Jewish Publication Society, 1989], 142). Hence, this passage is not offering an alternative means of atonement for sin apart from animal sacrifice but describing incense as a means of appeasing God and stopping the plague. Furthermore, incense carries the notion of prayer (Ex 30:8; Ps 141:2), and so instead of intercessory prayer the smoke of the incense rising up functioned as prayer to stop God's wrath from breaking out further. This was a powerful confirmation of Aaron as high priest and proof that not everyone could stand before the Lord as priests as Korah had assumed (16:3). Most of the people were spared because of Aaron's quick response. But **14,700** people were not spared, and so they added to the death count of those who died the day before.

6. Vindication of Aaron (17:1-13)

17:1-13. The placement of this next account right after Aaron's quick action in the previous chapter (16:47) demonstrates that the Lord clearly approved of Aaron as the high priest over against any who sought to challenge him (e.g., Korah). The Lord once again vindicated Aaron against those who resisted his selection and authority.

The Lord told Moses to get **twelve rods**, one from each tribal leader to represent the tribe as a whole and the authority of its owner. The word for **rod** (Hb. *matteh*) is the same Hebrew word used for "tribe" (cf. 1:4). In this interesting play on words only the rod/tribe of Levi was selected to be the Lord's representative. The "rod" chosen by the Lord would symbolize the "tribe" He divinely appointed. The rod served multiple functions among the ancient Jewish people: as a walking stick, as a shepherd's tool (Ex 4:2), and as a family insignia and symbol of authority (Gn 38:18; Ps 110:2).

Each leader was instructed to **write** his **name** on his rod, and Aaron was specifically named to do so as the representative head of the tribe of Levi. Moses placed all the rods in the tent of meeting in front of the **testimony**. The word "testimony" refers to the Ten Commandments as in the phrase "two tablets of the testimony" (Ex 31:18). This meant that the rods were placed before the ark of the covenant (40:20). The rods would be safe there because of restricted access and because they would be **before the LORD** (Nm 17:7). The rod God selected would sprout, and it would not only identify God's choice but it would also reduce the **grumblings** against Moses and Aaron. The tabernacle is referred to here as the **tent of the testimony** instead of the "tent of meeting," as Numbers usually labels it, and dovetails with the name given for the ark of the covenant (i.e., "testimony") given in v. 4.

The next day, when Moses went to retrieve the rods, he saw that Aaron's rod **sprouted** and had also budded, blossomed, and **produced . . . ripe almonds**. For a dead hardened piece of almond wood to bud, blossom, and bear fruit was clearly a supernatural sign. The cups of the lampstand in the tabernacle were shaped like almond blossoms (Ex 25:33-36), so this allusion to an item closely connected to the tabernacle heightens the Lord's selection of Aaron who served there. Aaron's rod was now placed back in the ark as a future warning to any **rebels** who would grumble against the Lord and to note His choice of Aaron as high priest. Aaron's rod was placed with the tablets of the Ten Commandments (Ex 25:16) and the bowl of manna (Ex 16:33-34) in the ark. Whereas the nation before had thought anyone could be the Lord's representatives (Nm 16:3) and offer incense before Him, now they overreacted and believed that they **all** would **die** because they were near the tabernacle. Instead of humble submission to the Lord's appointed servants and a repudiation of their grumbling, they cowered in fear. Their focus was still on themselves instead of on the Lord's gracious acts.

7. Additional Instructions for the Levites (18:1-32)

18:1-7. This passage follows the pattern of more laws being given after a narrative passage that chronicled sin. After the rebellion against Aaron as priest (chap. 16) and the nation's fear about coming near to the tabernacle (17:12-13), old laws were now reviewed and additional new laws were given to confirm Aaron and his sons as priests. In addition, laws described who was responsible for protecting the sanctuary complex from encroachment.

Usually divine instructions were given first to Moses, but in this case the Lord addressed Aaron directly, since he and his sons and extended family were now spiritually liable for any transgressions against the sanctuary and/or committed by the priests. Because the priests were ordained to handle the holy objects and they were responsible to maintain the sanctity of the priesthood, they were to use every precaution in carrying out their duties. The broader Levitical family, not the Kohathites, but rather the ones not responsible for the holy objects, were instructed not to approach the furnishings or the altar; otherwise they and the Kohathites would **die**. The transgressors would die for their own sin, and Aaron and his sons would die for failing to prevent that encroachment. Aaron was told that his fellow Levites were given directly to him as a **gift** from the Lord so that they could assist in all the nonpriestly duties pertaining to the tabernacle. Only he and his sons were ever to perform priestly duties, and any outsider who came near was to be executed.

18:8-11. Aaron and his sons were to receive a share of their support from the **offerings** that were brought to the tabernacle. This included portions from the grain, sin, and guilt offerings. In addition, portions of the wave offerings could be consumed by Aaron's extended family (including the women) so long as they were ceremonially **clean**.

18:12-19. Aaron and his sons were also to receive as a gift from the Lord the **best of the**... **oil**... **wine**... **grain**, and **first fruits** offerings, since they were not offered as a burnt sacrifice. In fact **every**... **thing** that was **devoted** to the Lord was to be used for their support. The **firstborn** of man and animal was set apart for the priest's use, and in lieu of receiving the actual offspring a worshiper could keep the offspring for himself for five shekels of silver. This redemption, however, was not possible for clean animals since they were to be offered as sacrifices to the Lord. The blood of firstborn clean animals was to be sprinkled before the altar and its fat burned up, but the meat was allocated to the priests for their support. All these provisions were evidences of God's blessings to Aaron and his children.

That Aaron specifically pleased the Lord by his actions in 16:47 resulted in these additional regulations that benefited his family. Obedience was rewarded with tangible blessings in Aaron's life. In fact the Lord established these provisions as an everlasting **covenant of salt**. Salt often suggested inviolability or permanence, thereby indicating an unbreakable covenant. A **covenant of salt** can also be taken as an idiomatic expression expressing loyalty or agreement. The notion is that if a person shares "salt" (in a meal) with someone, that one is a recipient of the host's hospitality, and the guest was to look after his gracious host's interests (cf. Ezr 4:14).

18:20-24. Instead of receiving a tribal **inheritance** of **land**, Aaron (and implicitly the priesthood) was to have the **Lord** personally as an inheritance, and all the Levites would receive the **tithe** as their portion. Their income would come from the offerings presented by the other tribes as compensation for fulfilling their duties in the tabernacle. No other Israelite could **come near the tent of meeting**, under penalty of death, so the Levites would have to represent the nation there as their substitute. The Levites were totally dependent on the offerings from the other tribes since they had no other means of financial support.

18:25-32. Now the Lord addressed Moses instead of Aaron (vv. 1, 8, 20) and instructed him to tell the Levites to present to the Lord their own **tithe** from the tithe they received from their fellow Israelites. Moses may have been addressed instead of Aaron because he functioned more than just a priest. He also seems to have fulfilled the office of prophet and ruler (functioning as a king, though not anointed as king, cf. Dt 33:5). This tithe came from the proceeds of the grain and wine offerings that were given to them as their portion. They were also to present offerings themselves from what they received as Levites, and it was to be from the best portions given to them. A portion of this offering would go directly to **Aaron**, and then the rest could be eaten **anywhere** by any other Levite, since it was part of their overall compensation for serving in the tabernacle. This was the Lord's means of providing for the Levites. If they did so in proper fashion, they would bear no sin, but if they did **profane the sacred gifts**, they would die.

8. Waters of Purification (19:1-22)

Since the first generation would die off in the wilderness because of their rebellion and refusal to take the land the Lord had promised them, they would constantly be exposed to dead bodies during the next 38 years. The ritual of the **red heifer** was another means for removing uncleanness. Uncleanness could be removed in two ways, as spelled out in Leviticus. (1) If one came in contact with a dead animal or the blood of menstruation, the uncleanness could be removed by washing with water and then waiting **until evening** (Lv 11:27-28, 39-40; 15:25-27). (2) In more complex situations the individual who became unclean would need to wait **seven days** and then offer animal sacrifices (Lv 15:28-30). Numbers 9:6-8 had addressed those who could not eat the Passover because of contact with a dead body (there was a one-month waiting period until they could enjoy the Passover meal, v. 11). Since there would now be many corpses during their wilderness journey (let alone the expense of offering animal sacrifices because of uncleanness from contact with a dead body), the Lord graciously provided an alternative method. The people could cleanse themselves by means of a water-based mixture made from ashes and other agents. In this way the tabernacle could be kept pure and free from contamination.

19:1-10. The Lord gave Moses and Aaron instruction on how to prepare **water to remove impurity** (v. 9). A red-skinned female cow was to be brought to Eleazar, and it must not have any defect or blemish. Most translations render this animal as a **heifer**, but technically a heifer is a female cow before she has had her first calf. Yet the text here stresses only that it be a female cow that had never been yoked. Instead of this animal being sacrificed inside the tent of meeting, it was to be **brought outside the camp** and slaughtered in the presence of **Eleazar**. Presumably Eleazar was selected to be sure that the procedure was performed just as the Lord commanded and to protect Aaron's status as high priest because of the potential for contamination. It was to be a red heifer because the color red symbolizes blood. Eleazar was then to take some of the blood and sprinkle it toward the front of the tabernacle seven times.

Two views are held on the purpose of this sprinkling. One view is that it consecrated the heifer itself as a suitable acceptable sacrifice. Since the blood was consecrated by the act of sprinkling it in the direction of the tabernacle, by extension so was the red heifer itself consecrated as a purification offering. A more likely view is that the blood was sprinkled toward the tabernacle in order to purify the tent and protect it from contamination. The focus in this section of Numbers has been on maintaining a pure tabernacle (Nm 18:1). Since the location of the tabernacle is the direction toward which this blood is sprinkled, that makes this view more likely. The notion of the tabernacle as "sacred space" that must be kept holy is a key theme in Leviticus (cf. Lv 16).

In this procedure the entire heifer was to be **burned** up, including parts normally left out of the traditional animal sacrifices. Also this was the only sacrifice in which the **blood** of the animal was to be burned up. While the animal was being reduced to ashes, a priest was to cast **cedar wood . . . hyssop and scarlet material** into the fire. These three additional elements were also part of another "outside-the-camp" purification ritual when a leper had been cleansed from his disease (Lv 14). There is clearly a focus on red objects all throughout this ritual. Cedar wood (having a red hue) and scarlet material continue to reinforce the "redness" theme. **Scarlet material** could be rendered "scarlet worm," referring to an insect used to produce a red dye. Regarding **hyssop**, some have suggested it is a plant called "marjoram" or a similar type herb, but it is difficult to determine precisely which plant is meant. This plant was used to sprinkle blood (Ex 12:22), so it does have associations with blood. The word translated "hyssop" (Hb. *'zb*) is also close in spelling to the word for "cedar" (Hb. *'rz*). So it is entirely possible that this plant may have been red in color or at least closely associated with red like the other two objects. The combination all of these elements probably symbolized blood and the cleansing it could provide.

Three men were needed to perform this ritual. Eleazar was needed to supervise, another was needed to burn the animal, and another to collect the ashes. All three were rendered **unclean until evening**. The one who actually used the ashes at a future time in a ritual was also unclean until evening (v. 21). This procedure was done to produce ashes, which were then gathered and stored outside the camp in a clean place. The ashes were mixed with water to be used as **water to remove impurity**, that is, to symbolically purify from sin. The purification properties of this red bloodlike solution was reconstituted whenever water was added to these ashes and other agents, thus making a "ready-made" mixture suitable for sprinkling purposes in this purification ritual.

19:11-13. When a person touched a **corpse**, he was to be sprinkled with the potion on the third and seventh days. As mentioned earlier, this ritual was a gracious response on God's part. Otherwise the unclean person would have to offer a costly animal sacrifice. Failure to follow these instructions resulted in the person remaining unclean, and then he would have to be **cut off from Israel** (executed; cf. 15:31). The **tabernacle** was sacred space because God dwelt there, and it was not to be **defiled** by anyone unclean.

19:14-22. These verses discuss situations when an individual became unclean because of being around someone who died. Anyone who was in a tent or came into the **tent** when someone died was to be sprinkled with the **water for impurity** (vv. 20, 21). Any open vessel that was not securely covered was also considered unclean. The impurity of death could be transferred to inanimate objects, which also had to be purified. Anyone who happened upon a dead body in a **field** who was killed by a sword or who died of natural causes or who happened to touch a **grave** or human **bone** was also rendered unclean for seven days (v. 16).

The procedure for applying the "water to remove impurity" was as follows. First, an individual was to take some of the ashes and mix it together with flowing (fresh) water . . . in a **vessel**. Then a clean person was to **take hyssop**, dip it into the mixture, and sprinkle it on the tent and all that was in it and on all the people who were in the tent around the time of death. This was also to be done for anyone who touched a dead body in the field or a grave or a human bone. This ritual was performed on the third and seventh days, and the one who applied it was to wash himself in water and be unclean until evening. The text stresses again that anyone who did not undergo this ritual would be unclean and would defile the sanctuary of the Lord. This ritual provided a cost-effective, ready-made means to deal with those who had become unclean by contact with a dead body.

9. The Sin of Moses and the Death of Aaron (20:1-29)

A long period of time passed between 19:22 and 20:1. All the previous events took place in the second year after the exodus (Nm 9:1). Now the text states that this account was **in the first month**. The verse does not state the year, but since Aaron died (Nm 20:28) during this time and a later verse (33:38) specifically states that Aaron died on the first day of the fifth month of the 40th year after coming out of Egypt, it is assumed that Miriam died in the first month of the 40th year after the exodus. The last clearly stated camp movement was in 14:25 when the Israelites set out toward the desert by way of the Red Sea, evidently from Kadesh (13:26). Now 38 years later they returned to Kadesh, the place where they last rebelled. Thirty-eight years passed by in the narrative world of the text with little or no narrative about what transpired. Clearly Moses was focusing on the events of the beginning and ending of the wilderness pattern. The large block of time in the middle, devoid of any information, is a graphic reminder of the consequences of their rebellion.

This passage starts with the death of Miriam and concludes with the death of Aaron and focuses on Moses' sin of unbelief in the middle. Three main journeys are depicted in the Torah, Red Sea to Sinai (Ex 13:17–19:25, 32), Sinai to Kadesh (Nm 10:11–12:16), and Kadesh to Moab (Nm 20:1–22:1). While there are some key differences among them, these travel narratives also have much in common, including battles against enemies, songs of victory, complaints about God's provision of food and water, prayers by Moses, and episodes about Miriam.

As Wenham notes, this last cycle (from Kadesh to Moab) inverts the patterns found in the earlier two. Whereas they recount triumphs that turned into tragedy, this tells of tragedy that ended in triumph and a reawakened hope of entry into the promised land (Gordon J. Wenham, *Numbers: An Introduction and Commentary*, TOTC [Downers Grove, IL: InterVarsity, 1981], 148).

20:1 Miriam died and was buried at Kadesh. Her death is a reminder that all of the old generation would share this same punishment (14:26-30), even though she would live until the last year of the wilderness wanderings period. The same was also true of Aaron and Moses. Miriam was the most significant female of the nation, yet this account gives no detail of the circumstances surrounding her death. Even though the text does not state that Miriam's death outside the promised land was a result of her rebellion, it may imply it since Aaron also dies in this chapter and his death is attributed to rebellion (20:24, 28).

20:2-13. This section describes yet another complaint by the congregation over a lack of food and water. Miriam has had a close association with water in her past (Ex 2:1-7; 15:20-21). Now, after her death is reported, intriguingly the text mentions there was no water (v. 2). The nation directed their anger against Moses and Aaron once again and wished that they had **perished** along with their brothers in previous judgments. The brothers they referred to all died rather instantaneous deaths (11:33; 14:29, 36-37; 16:32, 35, 49) early in the wilderness period, but these who complained in 20:2-5 lived for 38 more years, knowing that they would die in this last year of the wilderness wandering. They probably felt they had nothing else to lose since they were going to die anyway, and so they felt emboldened to grumble once again. These complainers were still as stiff-necked as they were previously, and the 38 years of wandering did nothing to correct their bad attitude.

Moses and Aaron responded as they had done previously (14:5, 10; 16:4, 19, 22) by falling **on their faces** at the doorway of the tent of meeting, waiting for the Lord to respond. Once again the **glory of the LORD appeared** and spoke to them (v. 6; see also the comments on 1Co 10:1-5). The Lord instructed them to **take the rod** and to **speak to the rock** in front of the congregation. Since the rod was retrieved **from before the LORD**, it most likely refers to Aaron's rod that budded (17:10) and was placed near the ark as a sign to stop their grumblings. The mere sight of this particular rod should have been enough to stop their complaints and move them to repentance. Moses and Aaron gathered the nation before the rock and instead of speaking to the rock he addressed the assembly as **rebels**, sternly rebuked the people, and then **struck the rock twice** with the staff. The Lord graciously supplied water for the nation even though His instructions were not followed. The Lord then addressed Moses and Aaron and punished them ("you" is pl. in v. 12) by not allowing either of them to lead the people into the promised land. It is commonly held that Moses and Aaron were not allowed into the promised land because Moses struck the rock twice (v. 10a) rather than speaking to it, or that he was punished because of his anger of speaking harshly to the people (v. 10b) or that he was attempting to take credit ("shall we bring forth," v. 10c). The stated reason in the text is not due to their disobedience but their lack of faith (**because you have not believed Me, to treat Me as holy in the sight of the sons of Israel**, v. 12). The form of the verb "believe" here involves acknowledging what someone says as true, but it also has the added meaning of acting in response to what is heard with trust or obedience.

The Lord stressed that their unbelief led to the people's premature death in the wilderness. Their sin was wholly a lack of faith and trust in the Lord. Certainly Moses, Aaron, and the Israelites disobeyed the Lord, but that was the fruit of their unbelief, not the root cause of their punishment. It was not a failure to keep the law that led to their death in the wilderness. Instead, just as the people had failed to believe God and trust Him in chap. 14, so also Moses and Aaron were lacking in faith (Sailhamer, *The Pentateuch as Narrative*, 397). The name **Meribah** ("place of strife") was associated with this incident. Psalm 95:8 later referred to this incident as a reminder not to harden one's heart. Since they were probably encamped at Kadesh (Nm 20:1, 14), the name **Meribah** may be more associated with the event and not necessarily the geographical location. In any case the Lord proved Himself holy among them.

20:14-21. Now the nation encountered strife in dealing with the nation **Edom**. Edom was a distant relative of Israel (through Jacob's brother Esau, Gn 36:8), and Moses sought to establish an amicable relationship with them so that they might have permission to travel through their land. Moses gave a short account of their history since they went down to Egypt in order to build sympathy for allowing them to **pass through**. Moses added that as they passed they would stay on the road (the **king's highway**), and they would **not . . . drink water** from any of their wells. Edom, however, still refused to give Israel passage and even **came out against** them with a strong show of **force**. (For the area of the King's Highway, see map "The Israelites' Wilderness Wanderings" with comments on Nm 14:20-38.)

Perhaps Edom's hostile response was an attempt to exact revenge for the earlier conflict between Esau and Jacob (Gn 27–28). Just as Israel experienced strife from a foreign nation

(Amalekites; 14:42-45) in a failed attempt to get to the promised land quickly after their major episode of unbelief (Nm 14), so now Moses' unbelief (20:9-12) led to strife with another foreign nation (Edom; 20:14-21) and a short-circuited effort to reach the promised land via the most direct route. Edom and Israel continued to experience strife throughout their history (Ob 10-14). Instead of taking a more direct route, the whole congregation was rerouted to **Mount Hor** (location not clearly known). The Israelites were forced to take a detour around Edom.

20:23-29. After they arrived at Mount Hor the Lord addressed Moses and Aaron and informed them that **Aaron** was about to die for his participation in the unbelief at **Meribah**. Moses was to escort Aaron and Eleazar up Mount Hor, where he took the clothes (high priestly garments) off of Aaron and put them on Eleazar. Moses did as he was instructed, and **Aaron died** . . . **on the mountain top** after his clothes were removed and placed **on his son Eleazar**. Moses and Eleazar came down, and the Israelites mourned for Aaron **thirty days.** Aaron died in the 40th year after the exodus at the age of 123 (33:38-39). Aaron's death was another reminder that all of the older generation would die before they reached the promised land. There was a glimmer of hope in that the new generation represented by Eleazar was beginning to assume leadership.

10. The Bronze Serpent (21:1-35)

21:1-3. This next brief account describes the new generation's first victory and sets a tone of hope for the nation's future. While in the region of Mount Hor, a **Canaanite** . . . **king** from **Arad**, who lived in the southern Negev, came and attacked the Israelites because he heard that Israel was planning to travel by the way of Atharim (location unknown). Arad is about 20 miles south of Hebron. Since some of their population was taken **captive** by this king, the Israelites vowed that if the Lord delivered them then the Canaanite cities involved would be **utterly destroyed**. The Lord granted that request, and the Canaanites were defeated and destroyed. They named the place **Hormah**. Earlier they experienced defeat in this region (14:45), but now it was associated with victory.

21:4-9. Though Israel had just experienced a taste of victory, the people resorted to complaining when **they set out** . . . **to go around the land of Edom**. They expressed their impatience once again about the lack of **food** and **water**, and this time they complained about the quality of food (**miserable**) they received from the Lord's gracious hand. In response to their rebellion **the LORD sent fiery serpents** among the people, and **many people** . . . **died** after being bitten. Instead of being emboldened, the people repented of their rebellion and asked Moses to **intercede** to ask the Lord to **remove** the serpents. Moses began to pray, and the Lord heard that prayer and instructed Moses to make an image of a fiery serpent and place it on a **standard**, so that those who were bitten simply needed to **look at** the image to be healed and **live**. Jesus referred to this account to describe the manner of His execution (see the comments on Jn 3:13-14). By focusing their gaze upon Jesus on the cross, lifted up and dying for sin, believers are able to contemplate the depths of their sin and the greatness of His mercy. This **bronze serpent** later became a stumbling block in Hezekiah's day because it had become an object of worship and had to be destroyed (see the comments on 2Kg 18:1-6).

21:10-20. The text resumes a travel itinerary that began at **Oboth** (location unknown) and proceeded to **Moab**. The nation traveled on the east side of Edom and avoided the King's Highway since Edom refused them passage (20:21). They proceeded on the east side of Moab until they reached the other side of the **Arnon**, a river that separated Moab from the **Amorites** (it flows from east to west into the central shore of the east side of the Dead Sea). It served as a natural **border** because of its steep slopes. The rugged and steep terrain is poetically remembered and recorded in a book entitled **the Book of the Wars of the LORD**. This book is similar to the "Book of Jashar" (Jos 10:13; 2Sm 1:18) but is not extant. These extrabiblical sources are not inspired but contain information that biblical writers used when composing their inspired texts, similar to what Luke did when he consulted material in the crafting of his gospel (Lk 1:1-4).

After they crossed the Arnon, they **continued** north **to Beer** where the Lord miraculously provided a **well** to give the people **water** (21:16). A song was crafted honoring this incident, lyrically telling the tale of how nobles (and not skilled well-diggers) seemingly scratched the surface with their staffs to provide abundant water. These musical interludes at the end of their wilderness journey seem to form a bracket with the song sung in 10:35-36, at the beginning of their march toward the promised land. The nation then proceeded through several stops until they reached **Pisgah**.

21:21-35. The defeat of **Sihon** of Heshbon and **Og** of Bashan are another foretaste of victory for the Israelites as they looked forward to conquering the land of Canaan. These victories were recalled later as examples of the Lord's ability to come to the aid of His people (Dt 2:24; 3:7; Pss 135:10-12; 136:17-21). The exact movements of the people are not clear. Possibly what transpired here is a flashback to their movement just before they arrived at Pisgah (Nm 21:20), as the Amorites and the region of Bashan were to the north of Moab. In other words they may have proceeded north to defeat Sihon and Og after crossing the Arnon River, and then looped back to the plains of Moab. What is not stated is why they traveled north in the Transjordan before crossing over into the promised land. Perhaps the Lord wanted the nation to taste victory before they crossed into Canaan.

Just as they had done with Edom (20:14-18), they requested permission from the Amorites to pass through their land, and once again they were denied passage. **Sihon gathered . . . his people** to prevent them access and **fought against Israel** (v. 23). Israel defeated the Amorites and took possession of their land. An Amorite proverb written in honor of King Sihon to scorn Moab was then recited as a taunt by the Israelites against the Amorites themselves (vv. 27-30). Since Sihon had boasted about his victory over Moab, Israel must be the greater victor since they defeated Sihon and the Amorites.

After the defeat they occupied the Amorite territory and even sent out spies and captured **Jazer**, about 20 miles northeast of the Dead Sea, another Amorite city. Then they proceeded northward and battled against **Og the king of Bashan . . . at Edrei** (about 15 miles southeast of the Sea of Galilee) and defeated him and his people. The Lord encouraged the Israelites that just as Sihon was defeated so would Og be conquered. After their victory at Edrei the Israelites also occupied the land of Bashan, the region to the east of the Sea of Galilee. A fuller account of this victory is given by Moses in Dt 3:1-11.

11. The Prophet Balaam (22:1–25:18)

This new section details the interaction of **Balaam** and **Balak** with the nation of Israel. These chapters seem to be an independent unit. Still they are related to the wilderness travel itinerary in that Moab is another one of the nations located in the Transjordan that Israel had to confront en route to the promised land. While it has comical elements, a serious message is communicated here in relation to the Abrahamic covenant (Gn 12:2-3). God's promises to Israel are still intact, despite major rebellion on their part.

a. Balaam's Meeting with Balak (22:1-41)

22:1. The Israelites returned south to **the plains of Moab**, which became their staging area in the beginning of their conquest of Canaan. The mention of the camp being **beyond the Jordan opposite Jericho** (v. 1) noted their location, but it also foreshadowed the challenges that lay ahead, that of crossing the Jordan and conquering Jericho. The Israelites would be in this location until Jos 3:1. It is specifically called Shittim in Nm 25:1.

22:2-6. The nation of Moab was fearful of having such a large Israelite presence in their midst, especially after the Israelites defeated the **Amorites**. **Balak**, the king of Moab, is mentioned several times in the Scriptures (Jos 24:9; Jdg 11:25; Mc 6:5; Rv 2:14). The Moabites had just recently been under the control of King Sihon of the Amorites (Nm 21:26), and after Sihon had been defeated by the Israelites (21:23-26) Moab was able to regain their independence. Balak of course would have wanted Moab to retain that status, and hence there is clear motivation for his subsequent actions.

This concern about the Israelite presence was also of great concern to the Midianites, who were contacted by the Moabites. The Midianites were descendants of Abraham through Keturah (Gn 25:1-2), and Moses was married to a Midianite woman (Ex 2:16, 21). Whereas Moses had previously experienced good relations with the Midianites (Nm 10:29), this incident was the beginning of conflict between Israel and the Midianites (25:6, 14-18; 31:2-10; Jdg 6:1-8:28).

The Moabites had nothing to fear, because God never intended for the Israelites to possess the land of Moab (Dt 2:9). The Moabites compared Israel to an **ox**, an image that was later attributed to God in Nm 24:8. Israel's larger numbers and recent victories in the area caused Balak to hire Balaam to **curse** Israel as an alternative warfare strategy.

Where Balaam was from is uncertain. There are several geographical and ethnic designations associated with Balaam: **Pethor . . . near the River** (v. 5, often taken to mean the Euphrates), **land of the sons of his people** (22:5, or "land of the sons of Amaw," some versions read

"Ammon"), Aram (23:7), "mountains of the East" (23:7) and Mesopotamia (Dt 23:4, lit., "Aram Naharaim"). Most scholars claim he was from Mesopotamia (modern-day Iraq), although it is challenging to assume that several 400-mile one-way trips were undertaken to secure Balaam's services in this account's time frame. Alternatively, he may have been from the Transjordan area (Syria), placing him much closer to Moab. At Deir Alla, in modern-day Jordan, an inscription (from around 850 BC) was found in 1967 that specifically mentioned a "Balaam, son of Beor," so there is a strong association with Balaam in the Transjordan region.

22:7-14. Balak sent messengers and **elders** from both Moab and Midian to bring Balaam to hire him to **curse** Israel. Balak sought to secure him because he believed that those whom he blessed were blessed and those he cursed were cursed (22:6), ascribing to Balaam what had been divinely promised to Abraham in Gn 12:3. When the messengers relayed what Balak had requested, Balaam asked them to **spend the night** there so he could consult the Lord. In each of the scenes the Balaam narrative mentions divine instructions to Balaam about what he should say and references to divine encounters between Balaam and the Lord. These repetitions serve to unify the entire section of Nm 22–24.

Confusion exists regarding Balaam's spiritual status. Some assume he was a true believer since he used the personal name for the God of Israel ("Yahweh," 22:8), and he sought to carry out what the Lord told him to do. On the other hand he was a diviner (Jos 13:22), an office expressly forbidden in the law (Dt 18:10), and he is negatively portrayed in the NT (2Pt 2:15; Jd 11; Rv 2:14). While Balaam's character is not explicitly commented on in Nm 22–24, he is later shown to be a completely negative character, causing Israel "to play the harlot with the daughters of Moab" (Nm 25:1-9; 31:16). He even died as a result of his wickedness (31:8). His negative character was not noted in Nm 22–24 because he had an important role in blessing the Israelites. The literary or thematic purposes of this section would not have been served if his negative traits were highlighted before the Lord used him as an agent of blessing.

During the night God came to Balaam and asked him a rhetorical question about who sent the men to hire him. Several threefold repetitions in the Balaam account seem to be a clear literary device to heighten the absurdity of Balaam's overall behavior: Balaam had three divine encounters (22:10, 20, 22-35); a donkey avoided an angel three times (22:23, 25, 27); and Balaam participated in three sets of sacrifices (23:1, 14, 29).

There is a shift in the use of the names for God in this section of Numbers. Balaam stated that he needed to have contact with the Lord (22:8), and yet the text states that God met him. This may provide a clue as to how Moses portrayed Balaam. Balaam claimed to have direct contact with the Lord of Israel, but in reality this pagan diviner was far from having a personal relationship with the Lord. The words of Balak from vv. 5-6 are summarized, but there are a few differences (primarily the Hb. words for **curse** are different). Either the messengers changed the words slightly or Balaam did in reciting the instructions back to God. God graciously communicated with Balaam (as He did with other pagan authorities; Gn 20:6-7), and warned him **not** to **go with them** or to **curse** Israel. In the morning Balaam's refusal to go back with the messengers was conveyed to Balak.

22:15-21. Balak **sent** a larger retinue with more prestigious members and the promise of great reward to entice Balaam to agree to curse Israel. At first Balaam stated that financial incentives alone could not get him to go against the Lord's command. Still, he asked them to **stay** the night while he enquired once again of the Lord, likely desiring to hear that God changed His mind. After Balaam consulted with the Lord he was permitted to go with them so long as he communicated **only** what God told him to **speak**. So **in the morning** Balaam left on his **donkey** . . . with **the leaders of Moab**. Suspense grows in the account, as the first prohibition stated earlier to Balaam in v. 12 ("Do not go") has been rescinded. Now what about the second prohibition (Do "not curse," v. 12)? Could that possibly be reversed as well? Since the Lord had not been pleased with the Israelites' behavior and attitude throughout most of the wilderness-wandering period, Moses was certainly raising the tension of the story by allowing the reader to think that God could possibly allow Balaam to curse Israel.

22:22-30. God was angry with Balaam for **going**, so He sent **the angel of the Lord** to impede Balaam's progress. Sometimes the angel of the Lord is a Christophany (a preincarnate appearance of the second member of the Trinity i.e., Ex 3:2-5). It is not clear whether or not this is the case here because in v. 31 the Lord and the angel appear to be two separate entities, not the same person.

A tension exists here in that God had given him permission to go with the leaders of Moab (v. 20), and now He was angry with him for doing what He gave him permission to do. Some believe that God's anger was directed not at Balaam's actions but at his unvoiced intention, since he obviously loved the "wages of unrighteousness" (2Pt 2:15). Yet the text clearly states that God was angry **because he was going** (v. 22, although it is possible to translate the phrase temporally "while he was going"). Jewish tradition believes that Balaam's quick acquiescence here indicates his eagerness to curse Israel, and therefore he incurred God's wrath. The text clearly portrays Balaam in a comical way. For instance it is ironic that this "diviner" cannot "divine" a supernatural angel in his path, and this "seer" could not "see" this adversary in the way. Balaam wrongly assumed that God would yet allow him to curse Israel so he could reap a financial reward. Hence the Lord was angry.

This is another instance of God meeting (even sometimes in anger) with someone on a journey (see accompanying chart). These accounts all serve as a reminder that God is still in control of human movement and that individuals need to be careful to do the Lord's bidding.

While Balaam was on the way, **the donkey saw the angel of the LORD** and **went** off the path **into a field**. Balaam struck the donkey to get back on the road. Further on down the way in a vineyard the donkey leaned into one of the walls that lined each side of the path crushing Balaam's foot. Again Balaam struck the donkey. When

God's Meeting with Individuals on a Journey, Particularly at a Border

#	Scripture	Individual and Location
1	Gn 28:10-22	Jacob at Bethel en route to Paddan-aram
2	Gn 32:22-32	Jacob at the Jabbok en route to Canaan
3	Gn 46:1-5	Jacob at Beersheba en route to Egypt
4	Ex 4:24-26	Moses in the desert en route to Egypt
5	Nm 22:21-35	Balaam en route to Moab

they started moving again, the angel of the Lord stood in a place where the donkey could not maneuver, so the donkey **lay down** right on the path. In anger **Balaam struck the donkey with his stick**. Then **the LORD opened the mouth of the donkey** and she asked Balaam why he had struck her three times. Balaam did not seem fazed by what had just transpired. He continued on with the conversation as if this was a normal everyday occurrence. In his anger the diviner stated that because he was humiliated he wished that he had a **sword** to kill the beast. The donkey politely responded that she was not in the habit of such behavior and that there must be some other explanation for her actions.

That a donkey could speak plays an important narrative preparation for Balaam's oracles (Nm 23–24). Israel might wonder how they could accept the words of this false seer who would later be responsible for leading Israel astray. Therefore this narrative is included to show that just as God could open the mouth of a donkey, so God could speak truth through Balaam.

22:31-35. The Lord **opened the eyes** of the "seer" Balaam so that he could see the **angel of the LORD** standing there with a drawn **sword**. Balaam **bowed** . . . reverently to the ground. Acting like a donkey, Balaam assumed the same prostrate position his beast of burden assumed earlier. This time the **angel of the LORD** spoke and asked Balaam **why** he had **struck** the donkey . . . **three times**. All the donkey was doing was trying to protect him from being killed. Balaam confessed his sin and volunteered to turn back.

The **angel of the LORD** responded that Balaam could go with the men from Moab, but he was to **speak only** what the Lord revealed to him. This was to make him clearly understand that without the Lord's revelation he, a seer, could not begin to "see" anything. Even a stubborn donkey was able to see what the supposedly skilled seer could not perceive. The account of Balaam and his donkey foreshadows how Balak will treat Balaam. What happened here will be reenacted in Nm 23–24. Just as the donkey was caught between a rock and a hard place three times—between a sword-wielding angel and a stick-wielding blind seer—so Balaam, who now sees that the Lord's will for him is to bless Israel, will soon be trapped in three ever-tighter situations. Balaam will soon switch roles with the donkey. He will see divine displeasure and have his mouth opened by the Lord in spite of Balak's enticements.

22:36-41. Balak went out of his way to greet Balaam at the Moabite **border** and reprimanded him for not coming sooner. He perceived that maybe Balaam thought that he did not have the means to properly compensate the diviner for his services. Balaam sarcastically replied that he was there now and that he was able to **speak the word that God** placed in his **mouth**. The two then proceeded to Kiriath-huzoth (unknown location), where ritual preparations were made. Balak was king, but he also was directly involved in sacrificing oxen and sheep. The animals were slain as a combination of sacrifice and communal meal, and it is likely that other rituals such as extispicy (reading the lobes of the liver or other organs for omens) were also performed. After these preparation rituals, the next **morning** . . . **Balak took Balaam** . . . **to the high places of Baal**, from where they could see a portion of the Israelite camp. The notion of seeing only a small part of the Israelite population assumed that the object of the curse must be within visual range for it to be effective. Balak may have been afraid of showing Balaam the entire panorama of the Israelite camp because the massive numbers may have frightened Balaam.

b. Balaam's Oracles (23:1–24:25)

23:1-6. Balaam asked Balak to **build seven altars** and to prepare a bull and ram offering for each altar. Throughout the ancient Near East "seven" was a sacred number, so it is not uncommon for that number to be associated with pagan rituals as here. Each sacrifice was a **burnt offering** (v. 6). While there was a Levitical sacrifice (Lv 1) by that name, that does not mean that Balaam and Balak were worshiping the God of Israel, since whole animal offerings were offered up by other nations. After the offerings were sacrificed, Balaam **went to a bare hill**, presumably to be by himself to hear a response from God. God met with Balaam and gave him a message to tell Balak and all the leaders of Moab.

23:7-12. What follows is the first of four oracles Balaam relayed to the Moabites. Balaam began by stating the place from where he came and the reason he was brought here. His words were cast in heightened speech that rises to the level of poetry. The first line exhibits synonymous parallelism, as do many of the lines in this oracle (**Aram** refers to the mountains of the East, and **Balak** was Moab's king). Balaam came from a region normally understood to be northern Mesopotamia, but it could also refer to an area closer in Syria (see discussion on 22:2). He was summoned by Balak to curse Israel, and Balaam pondered how he could perform such a task when God Himself would not curse that nation. As the seer gazed at a distance on God's people, he stated that Israel was not . . . **reckoned among the nations** (v. 9). This refers to her divinely conferred status as being set apart from all other peoples. The Israelites were as plentiful as dust particles (v. 10) and even **the fourth part** (probably the quarter of the camp closest to him) could not be numbered. Balak was angry at Balaam's response because he had assumed that Balaam could manipulate the gods to his intended outcome. The diviner responded that he could recite only what the Lord put in his mouth. This first oracle reveals that the Lord would not go back on His covenant faithfulness to the nation of Israel.

23:13-26. Balak hoped that by changing the vantage point he could change the result. Balak was being just as stubborn and persistent as Balaam was with the donkey (Nm 22). The exact location (the field of **Zophim**) is not clear, but **Pisgah** (v. 14) is part of a range that overlooks the plains of Moab. Another seven altars were built, and more bulls and rams were sacrificed on each one. Balaam once again separated from Balak so he could convene with the Lord, and once again the Lord revealed to Balaam what he was to say to Balak. After he received the oracle, Balaam returned to Balak, who then inquired about what the Lord revealed.

The second poetic oracle begins with a clear theological statement about God's immutability (v. 19) and that He had already given a clear, irrevocable command to bless Israel. The exodus is recalled with the words **God brings them out of Egypt**, demonstrating God's commitment to His people (v. 22). They had also experienced great fortune and the Lord's personal presence. The phrase **the shout of a king is among them** (v. 21) demonstrates the "Divine Warrior" motif, an image of God's military power spoken on behalf of Israel (Ps 47:5). A God with such might, who will protect Israel as with **the horns of a wild ox**, is able to thwart any omen or divination placed on Israel. God's people will be like a **lion**, devouring any who would seek to threaten her.

This time Balak entreated Balaam not to curse Israel nor bless Israel because he was not getting the results for which he intended to pay handsomely. Balaam simply reminded Balak what he had stated previously, that he was powerless to speak anything but what the Lord directed.

23:27-30. Balak sought for the third time to set up a location whereby he could launch a **curse** on Israel. Balak naively thought that another change of venue would get him the result he desired, so he took Balaam to **the top of Peor** and once again built seven altars and sacrificed a bull and a ram on each one.

24:1-2. Previously Balaam had consulted with the Lord (23:3, 15), but this time he did not practice divination. Instead he received revelation directly from the **Spirit of God** when he looked out on the entire camp of Israel. That **the Spirit of God came upon him** does not necessarily indicate that he put his faith in the God of Israel. It simply means he was especially endued to deliver this specific message. The phrase "falling down" (vv. 4, 16) may refer to a prophetic trance he was experiencing at the time of delivering this message.

24:3-9. Balaam's third poetic oracle begins with awareness that his eyes have been opened to **the vision** of the Almighty and he has now clearly heard the **words of God** concerning Israel. The introduction to this oracle clearly communicated to Balak that God had inspired him to say these words. As Balaam surveyed the Israelite camp, he used descriptive language from the geographical domain (valleys and gardens) and the botanical domain (aloes and cedars) to vividly portray Israel's fruitfulness. The reference to **water** flowing **from his buckets** pictures a man carrying two containers, and as he is walking the water is recklessly sloshing out. This is another graphic illustration of God's abundant blessings, especially in this arid region. The mention of **seed** also connects this oracle to God's promise in the Abrahamic blessing, stating He would greatly multiply his seed (Gn 22:17).

Agag (v. 7) is not the individual in Saul's day (1Sm 15:32-33). Agag may have been a dynastic royal name (as Pharaoh was for Egypt) among the Amalekites, an early enemy of Israel (Ex 17:8-13) whose defeat is predicted in Nm 24:20. In the Septuagint and the Samaritan Pentateuch, the text is emended to read instead of **higher than Agag** to "greater than Gog" (cf. Ezk 38–39), the end-time enemy of Israel. If the emended reading is followed it strengthens the messianic message of the third oracle since it would highlight that this Messiah will have an exalted kingdom superior to Gog (Michael Rydelnik, *The Messianic Hope: Is the Hebrew Bible Really Messianic?* [Nashville, TN: Broadman & Holman, 2012], 102). The emphasis is Israel's king and kingdom being a force to be reckoned with (Gn 17:16).

Numbers 24:7-9 repeats much of what was already communicated in the second oracle (23:21-24) but with a subtle difference. There is a shift in pronouns from third-person plural to third-person singular ("God brings *them* out of Egypt," 23:22 versus **God brings *him* out of Egypt**, 24:8). The shift is from talking about Israel's past history to talking about Israel's future king. The messianic implications of these oracles are evident. Moses viewed "the reign of the future king in terms taken from God's great acts of salvation in the past.... What God did for Israel in the past is seen as a type of what he will do for them in the future when he sends his promised king" (Sailhamer, *The Pentateuch as Narrative*, 408). This prophecy about a future king was also foretold in previous passages in the Pentateuch (Gn 17:6; 35:11; 49:10; see the comments there). This future **king**, Balaam continued, will be like a **lion** which one dare not arouse (cf. Gn 49:9). He then concluded this third oracle by repeating a key statement from the Abrahamic covenant: **Blessed is everyone who blesses you, And cursed is everyone who curses you** (Nm 24:9; cf. Gn 12:3). Even though Balaam was a pagan diviner, his oracles made full use of concepts found in the OT (e.g., Gn 12:3; 49:8-10). He may have known these Scriptures ahead of time, or the Spirit of God may have used him to refer to these verses unknowingly through these oracles.

24:10-14. Balak finally realized his futility in trying to hire Balaam to curse Israel, so he sent him away without remuneration for his services. Balaam reminded Balak that he had told him earlier that he could not speak anything **contrary** to the **command of the Lord** (22:18). Balak could not pay Balaam any amount of money to get him to undo what the Lord declared. Balaam wanted to return home, but before he did he had one more unsolicited oracle from God to deliver to Balak, the Moabites, and other neighboring nations. The form he used (v. 14) is one used elsewhere in the Pentateuch whenever a key messianic prophecy is given of the future. In each passage the central character (Jacob, Balaam, Moses) called together (with an imperative form) an audience and proclaimed what would happen in the days to come (Gn 49:1; Nm 24:14; Dt 31:29). In each instance a long narrative account is followed by a poetic lyrical interlude that introduces a key messianic concept (Sailhamer, *The Pentateuch as Narrative*, 36). The accompanying chart gives an overview of these messianic prophecies.

Messianic Prophecies in the Pentateuch

4 NARRATIVES				4 POETIC SECTIONS
Genesis 49	**Exodus 15**	**Num 22–24**	**Deuteronomy 32**	**Deuteronomy 33**
CANAAN — POEM	EGYPT — POEM	WILDERNESS — POEM	TRANSJORDAN — POEM	POEM
Gen 49:1 Then Jacob summoned his sons and said, "Assemble yourselves that I may tell you what will befall you in the days to come." **Gen 49:10** "the scepter shall not depart from Judah . . ."	**Ex 15:17-18** "You will bring them and plant them in the mountain of Your inheritance, The place, O LORD, which You have made for Your dwelling, The sanctuary, O Lord, which Your hands have established. "The LORD shall reign forever and ever."	**Num 24:14** "And now, behold, I am going to my people; come, and I will advise you what this people will do to your people in the days to come." **Num 24:17** "I see him, but not now; I behold him, but not near; A star shall come forth from Jacob, A scepter shall rise from Israel,. . ."	**Deut. 31:28-29** "Assemble to me all the elders of your tribes and your officers, that I may speak these words in their hearing and call the heavens and the earth to witness against them. For I know that after my death you will act corruptly and turn from the way which I have commanded you; and evil will befall you in the latter days, for you will do that which is evil in the sight of the LORD, provoking Him to anger with the work of your hands."	

24:15-19. Balaam's fourth poetic oracle opens as the third one did—with an acknowledgment that this message came from one whose eyes were opened by **the Almighty** God. It foretold defeat for many of Israel's enemies and predicted a royal figure who would become a major factor in vanquishing Israel's foes. What Balaam declared is one of the clearest messianic statements in all the Pentateuch.

Balaam the seer began to describe an individual whom he saw (**I see him**, v. 17), yet there would be both chronological (**not now**) and spatial (**not near**) distance until this individual's arrival. Balaam envisioned this individual as a **star** and a **scepter**. A **star** was often mentioned in conjunction with royal figures (Is 14:12; Mt 2:2), and the **scepter** designated power and authority (Gn 49:10; Ps 45:6). While King David foreshadowed many of the predictions here, these images were clearly fulfilled in Christ (Mt 2:2; Heb 1:8; 2Pt 1:19; Rv 22:16). That this ruler would **crush** . . . **the forehead of Moab** foreshadowed David's future victories over the Moabites (2Sm 8:2), but it also alluded to the messianic overtone of Gn 3:15.

The **sons of Sheth** (v. 17) are variously identified as ancient Sutu or a reference to **Seir** (Edomites). Yet since this is cast in synonymous parallelism, it may simply refer to a Moabite royal line heretofore unknown or to a general term used for the Moabites as a whole. **Edom** (v. 18) is also prophesied as suffering defeat and subjugation at the hands of this messianic royal figure. The **city** (v. 19) is most likely Sela (later known as Petra).

24:20-25. Amalek is also addressed in this final oracle. The Amalekites had attacked Israel right after the exodus (Ex 17:8-16). Even though they were one of the first nations (they are traced back to Esau in Gn 36:16), they would experience destruction in the end.

Balaam, moving his gaze toward the **Kenite** people (Nm 24:21), predicted that, even though they had seemingly impregnable homes in the cliffs, they would be taken **captive** by **Asshur** (Assyria). Assyria was developing as a nation at that time and later rose to prominence in the ninth to sixth centuries BC. The Kenites and the Midianites are related, and perhaps are the same (10:29; cf. Jdg 1:16).

Balaam again saw far into the future and spoke of **ships** (v. 24) that would come from the coast of **Kittim** that would destroy **Asshur** and **Eber**. It is likely that Kittim refers not to Cyprus but to the extended Mediterranean region that includes Greece and Rome (Jr 2:10; Ezk 27:6; Dn 11:30). This is a powerful example of predictive prophecy in that Asshur lies in the area of Mesopotamia (Assyria and Babylon) and Persia, and in that Eber is a name closely associated with the Hebrews (Gn 11:14-17). Greece and Rome did conquer and control both of these areas while building their empires. Once Balaam completed this oracle he **arose** and **returned to his place**. The place is not clearly identified. Many assume it to be Pethor (Nm 22:5), yet later in the book (31:8), he was living among the Midianites. This is perhaps another indication that Balaam's home was closer to Syria than in distant Mesopotamia.

What is the overall point of the Balaam narratives? At a key transitional time in Israel's history, with Aaron the high priest dead (20:28) and Moses the prophet basically sidelined because of his lack of faith at Meribah (20:9-12), God raised up a pagan seer by the name of Balaam to serve as a pseudo-surrogate, prophet-priest figure for Israel. God was keeping His covenant with Israel even when their leaders failed them. The Abrahamic covenant (Gn 12:3) was still intact because God blessed Israel from an unlikely source, and curses fell on those who were cursing this nation.

c. Balaam's Perversion of Israel (25:1-18)

25:1-5. Although Balaam's attempts to curse Israel did not work, he did have an influential role in seducing Israel to worship false gods and commit immorality. During Israel's stay at **Shittim** (about eight miles northeast of the Dead Sea), the men began to engage in fornication with Moabite women, who in turn induced them to sacrifice and bow down to **Baal of Peor**. Baal of Peor was one of the main gods of the Moabites, Midianites, and Ammonites, similar to the Canaanite Baal and Moloch, who were often associated with sexual fertility rites. There is an additional association with eating sacrifices of the dead (Ps 106:28) with this god. Baal-peor is also spoken of as a place where Israel worshiped false gods (Hs 9:10). The Lord responded in anger and instructed Moses to **execute** (v. 4) the perpetrators in a public forum, to reverse His anger. Moses ordered the judges of Israel to kill any of the men under their jurisdiction who participated in worshiping **Baal**. A number of parallels exist (see accompanying chart) between what happened at Mount Sinai and what happened here on the plains of Moab.

These similarities demonstrate that the second generation needed to remember the negative lessons from the first generation before they began their conquest of the promised land and to remember that the Lord responded the same way in each account.

25:6-9. At the time Moses was giving the order to execute the violators, an individual (Zimri, v. 14) dared to bring a Midianite (who was aligned with the Moabites) woman (Cozbi, v. 15) in plain view of the entire camp into his tent for sexual relations. Phinehas, the son of Eleazar, the son of Aaron, instantly took a spear, went into the tent, and thrust it through both of their bodies. This quick response suspended the plague, but not before 24,000 people died (Paul mentioned that in one day 23,000 died in 1Co 10:8. The simplest reason for the alleged

Parallels between Mount Sinai and the Plains of Moab

Similarity	Mount Sinai	Plains of Moab
Revelation followed by rebellion	Ex 20–31/Ex 32	Nm 23–24/Nm 25
Worship of false god	Golden calf, Ex 32:8	Baal of Peor, Nm 25:3
God's anger stopped by an immediate execution of those guilty	Ex 32:26-28	Nm 25:7-8
Response resulting in priesthood	Tribe of Levi, Ex 32:29	Phinehas, Nm 25:11-13
Census	Ex 30:12	Nm 26:2-4
Laws regarding sacrifice	Ex 34:25	Nm 28:1-8
Laws regarding festivals	Ex 34:18-24	Nm 28:11-31
Inheritance	Ex 32:13	Nm 27:1-11
Joshua	Ex 32:17	Nm 27:18-23
Sabbath	Ex 35:1-3	Nm 28:9-10

discrepancy may be that Paul was highlighting that 23,000 died in one day, and this passage includes a count of 1,000 more who died in the days following; see additional discussion there). It is possible that this plague primarily, and the deaths caused by Korah's rebellion earlier, drastically affected the tribes on the south side of the tent of meeting (Reuben, Simeon, and Gad) since the population of the three tribes,camped was reduced by 45,020 (about 30 percent) between the two censuses.

25:10-13. The Lord told Moses that because of Phinehas's zealous bold action He did not totally destroy the nation. That quick response caused Phinehas to receive a **covenant of peace**, that is, a perpetual priesthood. Aaron's sons were earlier said to be a "perpetual priesthood" (Ex 29:9), but now the priesthood was narrowed down specifically to Aaron's grandson Phinehas. His actions here modeled God's just and holy character.

25:14-18. While the names of the individuals who started the outbreak of the plague were not named earlier, they were now identified as **Zimri** (a Simeonite) and **Cozbi**, the daughter of a Midianite official. Even though this event took place on Moabite soil, the Lord instructed Moses to be antagonistic against the Midianites, who were allied with the Moabites.

II. Hope for the Second Generation as They Enter the Promised Land (26:1–36:13)

A. Preparations of the Second Generation for Entering the Promised Land (26:1–32:42)

1. The Second Census (26:1-65)

26:1-51. The rest of the first generation apparently died in the plague of chap. 25 (14:29; 26:65), and now the Lord instructed Moses and Eleazar (since Aaron had died) to conduct another **census**. The purpose of this census had military overtones (v. 2) since hostilities against the Midianites were just announced (25:17) and the nation needed to make logistical preparations as well for the conquest. This census would also aid in deciding how much land allotment (26:53) each tribe would need after possessing the promised land.

The totals for this census provide a basis for comparison with the earlier one from Nm 1.

With the numbers given in this chapter, it is possible to calculate approximately on average how many of the first generation died per day during the wilderness-wandering period. Massive deaths occurred at the Korah rebellion and the plague of Baal-peor, but an average of 90 funerals a day would have had to be conducted during this period.

Just as the Levites were not numbered in the census, they may have been exempt from this judgment. **Eleazar . . . son of Aaron** was most likely older than 30 (4:47) when he began to serve in the tent of meeting (4:16). Since he was older than 30 before the spies were sent (Nm 13–14) and since he served as a priest succeeding his father Aaron and was alive during the conquest (Jos 14:1), he was probably alive at the time of the first census, just as were Joshua and Caleb. Perhaps some women may also have been excluded from this judgment, since the focus seems to be on males over age 20 who were able to go to war.

This census mirrors the one in Nm 1 except that the order of Manasseh and Ephraim is reversed. This may be because of Ephraim's more serious decline in population and the desire to place Manasseh in the coveted seventh position in the list, focusing on the daughters of Zelophehad, who played an important role in Nm (see the comments on chaps. 27; 36).

The other major difference between the two censuses is that this second one not only states the totals of each tribe but also lists the families or clans that comprise each tribe. The mention of these additional tribal family names highlights the Abrahamic covenant, promising that Abraham's descendants would become a mighty nation (Gn 12:2; 26:24; 46:3). These family names can be traced back to Gn 46:8-27. There are a few omissions of names from Gn 46, but that probably means that some grandsons of Jacob's line died off (e.g., Ohad of Simeon, Becher and Ard of Benjamin, Ishvah of Asher) either in Egypt or in one of the plagues. Note the several variations in the spellings of names (e.g., Jemuel to Nemeul of Simeon). Over the course of some 400 years, spelling variations of family clans were bound to have happened.

Scattered throughout the census are mentions of those whom the Lord judged: Dathan and Abriam (v. 9), and Er and Onan (v. 19). These references are to specifically remind the Israelites of their propensity to sin. Interesting are the expansive discussion of the Manasseh clans, compared with discussion of only one clan for the populous tribe of Dan (**Shuham**, v. 42), and the citation of **Serah**, (v. 46), the only granddaughter of Jacob specifically named in the census ("Jochebed," another granddaughter, is mentioned in v. 59).

This census, minus the tribe of Levi, totaled 601,730. During the wilderness-wandering period the Lord had prospered the second generation so that in essence its military force was about the same size as it was at the time of the exodus.

26:52-56. Now that the census was complete the Lord instructed Moses to give the larger tribes a larger inheritance and to determine their allotments by lot. The larger tribes should receive certain territories, and yet the territories themselves were assigned by lot. How, at the same time, could it be determined that a larger tribe should have a larger territory and have that allotment of territory be determined by casting lots? The easiest solution is probably to envision that the general territory allotments were determined by lot, and then based on the tribe's size the actual boundaries would be expanded for the larger tribes and lessened for the smaller tribes.

26:57-65. The tribe of Levi is also numbered by their family clan and with an emphasis on **Amram**, a Kohathite. Amram married **Jochebed** (Levi's granddaughter and his father's sister; Ex 6:20), the mother of Aaron, Moses, and Miriam. This makes Moses the great-grandson of Levi, a possibility that is difficult to reconcile with the 430 years that Israel was to sojourn in Egypt (Ex 12:40-41). There are only four generations identified between Levi and Moses (in another family tree there are only six generations given between Joseph and Zelophehad). Possible explanations include (1) that there are two Amrams in Levi's lineage spaced several hundred years apart, (2) that there are gaps in the genealogy not listed, or (3) that the 400-year sojourn is an idealized number to denote several generations.

The view that there are gaps in the genealogy is probably the best solution. In 1Ch 7:20-29 up to ten generations are listed between Ephraim and Joshua, so there could be gaps in the Levitical line, which has only four generations between Levi and Moses. In any case, the point here is that the tribe of Levi increased in size by 1,000 during the wilderness wandering, even though they were not counted in the military census of the other tribes. Furthermore they were not included because they were to receive no land inheritance in the promised land.

The census is summarized as being accomplished by **Moses and Eleazar**, and it highlights that not one of those counted in the earlier census remained alive **except Caleb . . . and Joshua**. This stresses the faithfulness of God to keep His promises to those loyal to Him and to punish those who are unfaithful to His covenant. This new census also foreshadows a spirit of hope for the new generation as they look forward to inheriting the land God promised them.

2. Instructions for the Second Generation (27:1–30:16)

27:1-11. The narrative concerning the **daughters of Zelophehad** is central to the structure of book of Numbers, as it frames the account of the new generation (chaps. 27 and 36). Zelophehad's lack of any male offspring became the basis of a case law that was created after Sinai. These five daughters were from the tribe of Manasseh and were concerned enough about their future inheritance that they approached the **tent of meeting** and presented their case before **Moses** and **Eleazar**.

Their father had **died**, but not because he had sided with **Korah** in his rebellion. He died like all of the first generation for his unbelief after the spies' report. These women were asking for an exception to the patrilineal transfer of land in the situation where a father had daughters and no sons. They were making an appeal for property rights equal to that of male sons. Moses **brought their case before the Lord**, and the Lord ruled in favor of Zelophehad's daughters and granted them full property rights in their father's inheritance. Precedent was then set for the rest of the nation. When a man died without a **son**, the inheritance was to be transferred to his **daughter**(s). If there were no daughters, then it would pass to the man's brothers, and if no brothers were living then the inheritance was to be transferred to his uncles, and if no uncles were alive then the inheritance was to be passed to the nearest relative in the family.

This account is important in Numbers for two reasons. First is its placement both here and at the very end of the book (Nm 36). As mentioned earlier, it bookends the account of the second generation, so it helps identify a break in the structure of the content. Second is the timing of this request. Even before they had entered the land these daughters presented their request. So before any of the land was conquered, they expressed concern about inheritance rights. This request by the daughters models what the author of Numbers wanted to highlight, namely, great faith. These daughters so trusted the Lord that they were confident of receiving an **inheritance** of their father's estate. They took the effort to deal with the issue of property rights before any property in the promised land was actually parceled out. Earlier they expressed concern that they did not want their father's **name** to **be withdrawn** from among his family (v. 4) so they seem to have believed in the Lord who established the Abrahamic covenantal blessing, and they did not want their father's household to miss out on the legacy that covenant provided. In spite of the murmuring and rebellion of the nation in the wilderness, these daughters exemplified great faith in God's promises to Israel, and they wanted to lay hold of them. They provide a role model as to how this new generation should respond to God's promises.

27:12-23. Besides inheritance rights, another pressing issue faced the nation. Who would succeed Moses as the leader to bring the Israelites into the promised land? This section confirms that **Joshua** would be chosen as Moses' successor. Miriam had died (20:1) and so had Aaron (20:28); now it was time for Moses to prepare for his death.

Because of his rebellion at **Meribah** . . . **in the wilderness of Zin**, Moses was prevented from entering the promised land. But God allowed Moses an opportunity to **see the land** from a distance on top of one of the mountains of the Abarim range (later described as Nebo; Dt 32:49, the traditional site being about seven miles east of the north end of the Dead Sea). Moses, displaying great leadership, expressed concern to the Lord and entreated Him to appoint a leader who would **shepherd** the people in his absence. Moses called the Lord **the God of the spirits of all flesh** (also used in 16:22), highlighting God's ability to ascertain man's motives. The Lord instructed Moses to **lay** his **hand** on **Joshua** . . . **a man in whom is the Spirit**, and **commission him** before Eleazar and the congregation.

The word "spirit" (*ruah*) can refer to his natural leadership capacity. But it is more likely the word **Spirit** is a distinct reference to the Holy Spirit. This phrase means that Joshua was Spirit-endowed as the leader of the people (Dt 34:9). Many leaders (i.e., David, Ps 51:11; Zechariah, 2Ch 24:20) and key individuals (Bezalel, Ex 35:30-31) in the OT were given special measures of the Spirit to be able to carry out specific duties. By this act of commissioning, Moses would place some of his authority on Joshua so that the Israelites would submit to his leadership. Joshua had proven himself as a faithful aide to Moses (Ex 33:11) and as a faithful, believing spy (Nm 14:6, 30). Just as Aaron assisted Moses, Eleazar was to assist Joshua. Eleazar would inquire for him before the Lord with the aid of the **Urim**.

The Urim was a revelatory device designed by God to reveal His will. It may have been a lot or colored stones that signaled God's intentions. Since believers today have God's completed revelation in the complete canon and the indwelling Holy Spirit, it is no longer necessary to use lots to determine God's will. Moses carried out the Lord's commands just as they were given. This twofold statement of obedience (27:22-23) is another positive sign for Moses and the people of Israel. In the early part of Numbers the people's obedience to the Lord's command was often repeated (1:19; 2:33; 4:49; 5:4; 8:22) and now that obedience is again stated repeatedly (Nm 31:7, 31, 41, 47, 36:10). There was much hope for this new generation if they would continue in the path of obedience.

Instructions regarding the sacrificial system are given in various places in the Pentateuch (Ex 29:38-46; Lv 1:7; 16; 23; Nm 15), but on the threshold of entering the promised land, the Lord gave a descriptive summary of the regular required offerings. This list is not entirely exhaustive because the Feast of First Fruits (Lv 23:9-14) is not included in this summary.

The purpose of this summary at this point in Numbers is not identified. But since it follows close after the second census, it serves as a clear reminder for this second generation of their spiritual duties. The nation was soon to be in the land the Lord promised, and these directions prepared them for the type of pastoral life they soon would be experiencing in Canaan. Also these instructions were given before the Israelites acquired great herds of animals when they conquered the Midianites (Nm 31). These regular sacrifices would be a constant reminder of the Lord's provision for this generation. The arrangement of the offerings is by their frequency: daily, weekly, monthly, and then annual religious holy days. The daily offerings would be offered besides any of the additional sacrifices described.

Not including the Day of Atonement sacrifices or other feast day sacrifices addressed elsewhere (e.g., First Fruits; Lv 23), the burnt sacrifices here included 113 bulls, 37 rams, and 1,093 lambs annually, as well as 30 goats for sin offerings.

28:1-15. The instructions began with a description of the daily offerings (vv. 1-8) followed by the **sabbath day** sacrifices (vv. 9-10) and the first-day-of-each-month offerings (vv. 11-15). The **strong drink** (v. 7) was most likely beer because distilled liquor would not be invented for thousands of years. The strong drink here was made from grain (barley or wheat), as compared to wine, a drink made from fruit. The daily offerings were brought twice each day, one in the morning, and one at twilight. The sabbath day offerings were added on top of the daily sacrifices as well as all of the other offerings in this section (Nm 28–29). **At the beginning** of every **month** (the first day), offerings not only included burnt, grain, and drink offerings, but also added a sin offering of a male goat (28:15). Instructions regarding the blowing of trumpets (10:10) had been given on this new moon holiday.

28:16-31. Instructions regarding **Passover** were given earlier (Ex 12; Lv 23:5-8), but this section elaborates on the Feast of **Unleavened Bread**, for it continued for seven days immediately after Passover (these feasts are held in March/April on a modern calendar). Each day was to include sacrifices, and the last day was considered a **holy convocation** (v. 18), a day on which no work was to be done. Next the **Feast of Weeks** offerings were listed (vv. 26-31). This holiday celebrated the end of the barley harvest and the beginning of the wheat harvest in the early summer months.

29:1-6. All throughout the religious calendar the number seven is celebrated (i.e., Sabbath offerings were presented in sevens or multiples of seven). Here **on the first day** of the **seventh month** (September on a modern calendar) a special convocation marked by the **blowing** of **trumpets** was called for with its requisite offerings.

29:7-11. The tenth day of the seventh month was to be a **holy convocation** as well (elsewhere known as the Day of Atonement; Lv 16; 23:27). This special day was marked by the inclusion of a **goat for a sin offering** in addition to the scapegoat ritual described in Lv 16.

29:12-38. The Feast of Booths began on the **fifteenth** of the **seventh month** and lasted for eight days (v. 35). This festival was both a memorial and an agricultural festival. As a memorial, the Israelites were to live in booths to recall that the Lord had them live in booths when they wandered in the wilderness (Lv 23:42-43). With regard to agriculture, the Lord required the greatest number of sacrifices, compared to all the festivals, as a token of appreciation of the yearly harvest provided by the Lord. Each day was marked by multiple sacrifices and a decrease of one bull offering, each successive day starting with **thirteen bulls** and descending to **seven** on the seventh day and then finally on the last day (a Sabbath day) only one bull, one ram, seven lambs, and one sin offering of a goat were to be sacrificed.

29:39-40. This section concludes with a challenge to present these calendar-related offerings to the Lord at their **appointed times** but also to remember to bring other non-calendar-related offerings (**votive** and **freewill offerings**). Moses fulfilled his responsibility by faithfully relaying all this information to the nation.

30:1-16. The mention of "votive offerings" in 29:39 leads to an extended discussion on the establishment of **vows**. Vows took the form of a promise to do something or a pledge to abstain from an activity. Leviticus 27 gave instructions about the setting of vows but did not address how to **annul** them. Since vows were taken seriously, Moses now gave instructions from the Lord regarding when and where they could be **annulled**. Several case law scenarios are presented to illustrate when vows could be overturned. These situations follow an overall pattern (two groupings of three). The instructions state that whenever a **man** or **widow** or **divorced woman** made a vow, it was unbreakable. Whenever a daughter or wife made a vow, if the father or husband wanted to annul it, he could do so without guilt. This allowed the male figure to maintain authority in cases where the daughter or wife may have made either a rash vow or one that was at odds with his headship. The nation was to maintain authority structures not only in spiritual matters but also in the home.

Another example of that headship occurred when a woman was pledged to be married. If her future husband wanted to annul her vow, he could do so if he desired. A husband had the opportunity to later annul a vow that his wife had made. But if he originally let it stand and then sought to annul it later, he would bear the guilt of her not keeping the vow. The possibility of incurring that guilt probably kept him from annulling an active vow. Or if he wanted to **annul** a vow his wife made, he must do so immediately on hearing it.

3. War against Midian and the Settlement of the Transjordan Tribes (31:1–32:42)

This account picks up where Nm 25 ended, that is at the rebellion relating to Baal of Peor instigated by the Moabites and Midianites. The Lord specifically commanded Moses to strike the Midianites (25:17), and this narrative fulfills that order. The conquest of the Midianites here was to infuse hope into the new generation and to remind them that the conquest of the promised land was certainly possible with the Lord's power. The allotment of spoils to the Levites from the battle foreshadowed the Lord's provision for their needs as well (giving cities of refuge and pasture lands; Nm 35).

31:1-6. The Lord instructed Moses to **take full vengeance . . . on the Midianites** and then he would **be gathered to** his **people**. This is a clear reminder that his days were numbered as a result of his sin at Meribah. Of course the content of the book of Deuteronomy is yet to be delivered, but since that book is mainly his farewell speeches, his imminent death was merely days away. Moses' first wife (Zipporah) was a Midianite, and yet this marriage and linkage to the Midianites during a 40-year stay did not excuse him from carrying out this directive. Moses instructed the people to take **a thousand men from each tribe** (minus Levi) to execute the Lord's vengeance on the Midianites. That they were led by **Phinehas** demonstrates that this was viewed as "holy war" (also attested by the presence of **holy** objects from the tabernacle and the signal **trumpets**).

31:7-12. The war was so successful that they were able to kill **every** Midianite **male** as well as the **five kings**. **Balaam**, who was now associated closely with the Midianites, was also put to death by the **sword**. The account does not address the logistics or even where these battles took the place. Rather, the focus is on the Israelites' obedience to the Lord's command to wage holy war and on the spoil the nation was able to capture. Though the Midianites suffered a severe blow militarily here, they were able to regroup and to be a threat to the Israelites in the time of the Judges (Jdg 6–8). The Midianites were a nomadic type people and it would have been difficult to kill every single one. Nevertheless all their cities and campsites were **burned** with fire, but the plunder (**spoil—cattle . . . flocks . . . goods**) was confiscated along with the women and children. All the spoils of war were brought to Moses and Eleazar at the Israelite **camp** on the **plains of Moab**. That the camp was by the Jordan **opposite Jericho** was mentioned previously in Nm 22:1 and will be repeated several more times in the book (33:48, 50; 34:15; 35:1, 13). The reference to Jericho right on the heels of the Midianite victory would be an ominous reminder of what would be their first major obstacle when they crossed the Jordan. The Lord, who gave them victory over their enemies in the Transjordan, would give them victory over their enemies when they entered the land.

31:13-18. Moses and Eleazar and the leaders of the people went out to meet the soldiers outside the camp. Moses **was angry** with the military leaders for sparing the lives of the women. He painfully reminded them that Midianite women were a major cause in the downfall of the nation at Peor when they were counseled by Balaam to trespass against the Lord. Moses ordered all the male children and all the women who had ever had sexual relations to be executed. One may wonder why such a command was issued to execute women and children, but several points should be noted. (1) The Midianites were true enemies of Israel, and their involvement at Baal-peor so angered the Lord that He brought down vengeance on the entire nation. (2) Since the Midianite women were directly involved in the Baal-peor incident, any sexually experienced woman could not be trusted (the penalty for adultery was death; Lv 20:10). (3) The Midianite women had earlier used sexual relations to entice the Israelites to worship false gods, so the blending of immorality and idolatry could not be treated delicately. (4) The execution of the male children would prevent any future rebellion against the nation. The execution of the Midianites was a theological matter, not just a military matter. The Abrahamic covenant stated that those who curse Israel will be cursed (Gn 12:3) and so God was fulfilling His promise to Abraham's descendants.

31:19-24. Since the soldiers were in contact with dead bodies in executing the Midianites, they and any objects they **touched** were ceremonially unclean. Therefore, they were all in need of ritual purification (Nm 19) on the third and seventh days. Any metals confiscated as spoil that could **stand . . . fire** were heated up or melted down and then sprinkled with the water for impurity (cf. 19:17-21). Any object that could not stand fire was to be sprinkled. After these soldiers waited seven days and washed their clothes they could return to camp.

31:25-47. All the spoils and virgin women were apportioned according to a formula. The soldiers were given **half** of the spoils (minus a portion given to Eleazar), and the other half was divided among the rest of the nation (minus a portion given to the Levites).

Of the virgin women, 320 were given to the Levites, who evidently served as servants to the priests before the tent of meeting (31:35, 40; cf. Ex 38:8).

31:48-54. The officers of the soldiers told Moses that since not one of their 12,000 soldiers died in the war against the Midianites, they were bringing a freewill offering of gold objects. Their said their intention was **to make atonement for ourselves before the Lord** (31:50). According to the Torah, blood sacrifices were the only way to atone for sin (Lv 17:11) so how could gold function as an alternative means of atonement, i.e., atonement money? The answer is that the Hebrew word *kopher* used in 31:50 has the same root as the word for atonement but it does not carry the same nuance of "atonement or expiation for sin." Instead, it means "to pay a ransom for your lives" (cf. Ex 21:29-30; 30:12). The word *kopher* is used 14 times in the Hebrew Bible and never does it refer to atonement for sin but rather it denotes "a ransom, bribe, or payoff" (e.g., Is 43:3; 1Sm 12:3; Pr 6:35; Am 5:12). Hence, this passage should state that the soldiers were offering the gold "to pay a ransom for ourselves before the Lord." These men were giving the Lord a ransom for sparing their lives, not making atonement for sin. The total tribute brought was **16,750 shekels** (over 400 pounds) of gold. Moses and Eleazar brought the gift to the tabernacle as a memorial.

32:1-5. The conquest of the Transjordan was recorded in Nm 21:21-35, but since chap. 22 the focus has been on threats against Israel with which the nation dealt. Next, attention shifts toward settlement. After the victory over the Midianites (Nm 31) the tribes of Reuben and Gad made an appeal to settle in the Transjordan in the region of Jazer and Gilead.

The tribes of **Reuben** and **Gad** had much **livestock** (but then again so did everyone else; 31:42-46). When they gazed on the region of **Jazer** and **Gilead**, they asked Moses and Eleazar if that land could be their inheritance since it was good grazing ground. Gilead was in the northern Transjordan region, and Jazer was probably located south of Gilead. They made their request in a way seeming to suggest that they wanted Moses to get a hint so that he would recommend that these two tribes be given land for their vast livestock in the Transjordan area. They mentioned a list of captured cities (v. 3) and then stressed their animal holdings (v. 4), but the direct request did not come until after the text states that **they said** (v. 5) a second time (cf. 32:2), indicating there may have been a pause between verses 4 and 5. They seem to have been operating out of selfish motivation (concern about their livestock) rather than a lack of desire to inherit God's original promise (by requesting land in the Transjordan).

32:6-15. Moses responded harshly to the Gadites and Reubenites, saying that their actions would be **discouraging** to the rest of the Israelites—while most of the nation would be fighting they would be living comfortably. He directly compared their actions to the spy incident at **Kadesh-barnea** (Nm 13–14). In both instances there was a lack of interest in settling the promised land. Would this new generation repeat the failure of the first generation in not laying hold of the land the Lord promised them, and would they be doomed to further wandering outside the land? Moses forthrightly declared that God was greatly angered (vv. 10, 13, 14) at the first generation. He stated that those making this request were like them and in danger of experiencing the same punishment (wandering and death).

32:16-32. Gad and Reuben then responded that they would not forsake their brothers in the conquest. However, they wanted to **build sheepfolds** for their livestock and **cities** for their little ones for their protection while they assisted in conquering the promised land. They would not return home until the conquest was finished, and they would not receive an **inheritance** on the other side since the Transjordan would be their possession.

There are several concerns about their request. (1) While ultimately the Transjordan was part of the land promised in the Abrahamic covenant, the Lord's purpose was for the nation to dispossess the Canaanites as a nation and then divide the inheritance according to tribal size. Gad and Reuben were asking prematurely for a possession before God's purpose could be implemented. (2) Their original request was motivated by selfishness, not by faith in the Lord's promises. They only seemed to assent to joining in the military conquest of Canaan. (3) Their request could foster disunity among the tribes and lack of proximity and closeness to their brothers.

Nevertheless Moses agreed to their plan, but only if they submitted to the stipulation that all their fighting men had to help in the conquest until the Lord had driven out His enemies in the promised land. Once the land was subdued they would return to the Transjordan to receive it as a **possession** before the Lord. If they failed to do so, they would be sinning against the Lord and their sin would be appropriately punished. The tribes of Gad and Reuben agreed to this stipulation, and Moses conveyed this agreement to Eleazar since Moses would not be around to see this fulfilled.

32:33-42. Moses then **gave** Gad, Reuben, and the half-tribe of Manasseh the territory conquered from the kingdoms of Sihon and Og. The **half-tribe of Manasseh** is mentioned first as recipients of some of the Transjordan territory as a possession. They may have entered the negotiation once Gad and Reuben's request seemed that it might be granted, or it may be that since Zelophehad's daughters were from the tribe of Manasseh (Nm 27) there was already a concern about land inheritance for members of that tribe (specifically from the family of **Machir**; cf. 27:1; 32:39-40). The Transjordanian tribes then built up various cities around the region.

B. Encouragement for the Second Generation for Entering the Promised Land (33:1–36:13)

1. Review of Israel's Journey (33:1-56)

This section chronicles the itinerary of Israel from Egypt to the plains of Moab. Many of the campsites mentioned in this chapter cannot be identified with modern sites. Such a detailed itinerary may have been given at this point in the book of Numbers for several reasons: (1) Since Moses was about to be "gathered to his people" (31:2), the chronicling of all these place names where Moses led them may serve as a geographical eulogy to his leadership. One of Moses' qualities once again being stressed here is that he often listened to **the command of the Lord** (33:2). (2) The record of the nation's **journeys** also serves as a key theological lesson for the new generation. Since God faithfully led and provided for them for more than 40 different stops along the way, He could be trusted to continue to lead them in the conquest of Canaan.

33:1-49. Moses recorded the starting places of their journeys beginning with **Rameses** in Egypt. The Israelites left Egypt confidently the **day after the Passover** while the Egyptians were burying their firstborn who were struck down in the 10th plague. In striking down Egypt, God provided a powerful polemic against their impotent gods. (See map "The Israelites' Wilderness Wanderings" with comments on Nm 14:20-38.)

33:50-56. Here the Lord gave Moses instructions about the conquest. Since a major purpose of Numbers is to prepare the nation (especially the new generation) for settlement in the promised land, this last section of the book focuses on laws dealing with the conquest of **Canaan**. As in other places in the Pentateuch, whenever there is a narrative account that describes sin or rebellion on the part of the Israelites, a series of laws immediately follows. Whenever there was sin, more laws were given. Several examples will suffice.

Israel's fear and disobedience by not going up the mountain to worship the Lord after hearing the ram's horn (Ex 3:12; 19:9-25) is immediately followed by the Ten Commandments and the "book of the Covenant" (Ex 20–23). The narrative describing the sin of the golden calf (Ex 32) is followed by a lengthy series of laws (Ex 34ff.). The narrative describing the sin of the 10 spies (Nm 13–15) is followed immediately by a section of more laws (Nm 15). The laws here deal with the conquest that followed soon after Reuben and Gad's premature request (Nm 32) to inherit their possession before the conquest of Canaan had even started. The Lord commanded the Israelites to **drive out** the **inhabitants** of **Canaan** and **destroy** their idolatrous figures and molten images, as well as their religious shrines on **high places**. Once the conquest was finished, they were to assign **by lot** each tribe's **inheritance** according to their size. Failure to drive out the inhabitants would result in their being troublesome **pricks in** Israel's **eyes** and **thorns in** Israel's **sides**. If Israel would not fully drive out the Canaanites, the Lord would drive Israel out for disobedience.

2. Boundaries of the Promised Land (34:1-29)

The Lord continued to give Moses instructions, this time regarding the boundaries of the land of Canaan. The locations are not always easily identified, but a general idea can be ascertained regarding the borders.

34:1-6. The **southern** border began at the southern end of the Salt Sea (Dead Sea) and extended eastward south of the ascent of Akrabbim (lit., "Scorpion Pass") to Zin, continuing on south of Kadesh-barnea, then in the direction of the brook of Egypt and terminating at the sea (the Mediterranean). The **western border** was easy to identify since it was the coastline of the Great Sea (the Mediterranean).

34:7-15. The **north border** began at the Great Sea near Mount Hor (not the one where Aaron died), through Lebo-hamath, Zedad, and Ziphron, and ended at Hazar-enan. The **eastern border** started at Hazar-enan, through Shepham and Riblah, then continued down to the slope on the east side of the Sea of Chinnereth (Sea of Galilee). Then it followed the Jordan River southward down to the Salt Sea (Dead Sea).

The Tribal Distribution of the Land

The land now defined was to be the possession of the nine and a half tribes since Reuben, Gad, and the half-tribe of Manasseh had already been assigned their **possession** in the Transjordan.

34:16-29. The Lord instructed Moses to have Eleazar and Joshua oversee the apportioning of the land. Each of the 10 tribes that had **inheritance** in Canaan was to have a **leader** to assist in the process. **Caleb**, representing the tribe of Judah, is the only leader mentioned elsewhere in the Scriptures.

3. Levitical Cities (35:1-34)

As elsewhere in the book of Numbers, so here instructions regarding the Levites follow instructions given for the other tribes (Nm 1:47-54/1:1-46; 3:1-49/2:1-34; 26:57-62/26:1-56).

35:1-5. There has been a variety of explanations of the difficulty of determining the dimensions of these Levitical cities. The challenge is how to harmonize vv. 4 and 5 in determining the precise layout for the **cities** and their **pasture lands** (the Hebrew text reads 1,000 cubits in v. 4 and 2,000 in v. 5, while the LXX reads 2,000 cubits in both verses). The inner city dimensions (which are not stated) had to be very small to accommodate the dimensions given, or the **pasture lands** were either geometrically interlocked or viewed as frontage lots on each side (see possible explanations in the layouts in the accompanying chart).

Whatever the layout entailed, the main point is that the Lord provided for the Levites and their livestock.

Possible Layouts of Levitical Cities

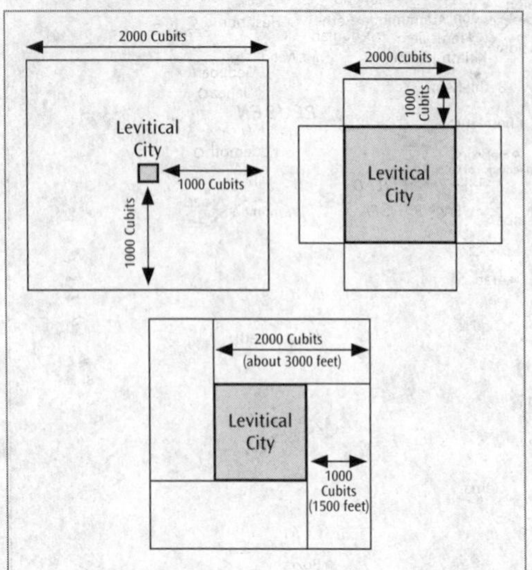

35:6-15. The Levites were assigned **forty-eight cities**, of which six were designated as **cities of refuge**. These cities were geographically allocated proportionately among the other tribal inheritances. The names of these cities are given in Jos 21. Since Canaan was the Lord's possession, Israel was to keep it holy by protecting it from becoming impure by the shedding of human blood (Nm 35:33). Therefore cities of refuge were established to deal with bloodguilt. Murder and the resulting blood that was shed was such a powerful pollutant on the land that it had to be rectified because the Lord dwelt there in the land (v. 34). As "sacred space," the promised land was not to be contaminated by improperly shed blood. Murder was typically dealt with by capital punishment (Gn 9:5-6; Ex 21:12-14). But if an accidental homicide occurred, the laws of the cities of refuge provided a mechanism for the **manslayer** to **flee** in order to stand trial. Anyone accused of murder could receive sanctuary among the Levites.

35:16-21. When someone committed premeditated murder, that person was to be executed. Weapons made of **iron**... **stone** or **wood** that were used to kill someone were proof of murderous intent. Such a killer could not flee to a city of refuge. Instead he was to be killed by a **blood avenger** (a relative of the one killed). Any previous hostility between individuals resulting in death of any sort meant that the perpetrator was to be put to death by the blood avenger. Compared to modern legal procedure where a trial before a judge and jury is conducted to determine guilt or innocence this may seem like a case of barbaric personal vengeance. However this practice of blood avenger was initially set forth after the flood (Gn 9:5-6). It is intimately connected to fact that humanity is made in the image of God. The shedding of human blood is a serious matter that can only be accounted for by the blood of the one who shed it.

35:22-29. If, however, an individual was killed by accident, or if there had not been any previous **enmity** between the one killed and the manslayer, then the manslayer could flee to a city of refuge to await trial. A trial would be conducted by the **congregation**, most likely a group of citizens. This trial may have even been held where the death occurred, since v. 25 speaks of restoring the one who fled back **to his city of refuge** afterward. The congregation's task was to adjudicate the matter and determine the outcome. If a manslayer was not found guilty of murder, then he was allowed to return to the city of refuge and was to remain there **until the death of the high priest**. If the avenger of blood ever found the individual outside the city limits and killed him, then the avenger would not be guilty of murder. But why would the death of the high priest result in the release of the manslayer? The death of the high priest may have been regarded as a substitute for the death of the manslayer himself. Or more likely, the high priest's death simply marked the end of a legal period of limitation (statute of limitations) similar to the Year of Jubilee.

35:30-34. Whenever there was an intentional homicide, there could be an execution only if there was more than one witness. Anyone convicted of murder could not pay a ransom (fine) in lieu of execution, nor could a manslayer who had received sanctuary at a city of refuge ransom himself with monetary compensation. Since the shedding of human blood polluted the land, the only way it could be expiated was through **the blood** of the perpetrator. God dwelt in the land and did not want to take up residence in a land defiled by blood.

4. Inheritance of Women (36:1-13)

36:1-13. Previously, the five daughters of Zelophehad from the tribe of Manasseh had requested and been granted full property rights equal to that of sons (27:1-11). They were concerned that their father's name would vanish. Since he did not have any sons, his share of the inheritance would be deeded to other members of the family. Now the implications of that decision are discussed and are presented by the elders of the tribe of **Manasseh** to Moses. Whenever a daughter married, the inheritance to which she was entitled would pass on to her husband's family. If her husband was from another tribe, then that would create an imbalance in the land allocations prescribed in Nm 33:50–34:29. A further complication would be that when **the jubilee** (Lv 25:10) would be celebrated every 50 years, that particular land inheritance would be permanently allocated to another tribe. So Moses issued a new commandment that the daughters of Zelophehad **marry within the family . . . tribe**. This would prevent land inheritances from transferring to another tribe. Each tribe would then continue to possess the inheritance of their fathers. Zelophehad's daughters **married their uncles' sons** (cousins) and thus obeyed Moses' instructions.

The book of Numbers ends with this case law narrative regarding Zelophehad's daughters. It thus highlights two themes that are important to the book and to the nation, as they were soon to enter the promised land. (1) The daughters were obedient. If Israel were to experience God's blessing, they would have to be obedient just as those daughters were. Just as the book began by stressing obedience to doing "just as the LORD had commanded" (1:19), the book closes with an account where obedience is highlighted. There was hope for this second generation if they continued that practice. (2) They exhibited great faith in the land promise. If the nation wanted to please the Lord, they had to trust in the promises of God just as these women did. They did not want their father's family to miss the land inheritance given by God, so they beseeched Moses about this land inheritance even before the nation crossed over the Jordan.

The focus of the last few chapters of Numbers has been on "land" (Nm 34–36)—its allocation, boundaries, and purity. The whole book has focused on progress and movement toward the promised land. This last section stresses that each tribe shall **hold to the inheritance of the tribe of his fathers** (v. 7). As the book closes, there is an unanswered question: Will this new generation lay hold of God's promises (Gn 17:8) and possess the land as their inheritance? The last line of the book summarizes that **these are the commandments and the ordinances . . .** the Lord gave to Moses on the plains of Moab opposite Jericho. The enemy lay just on the other side of the Jordan, but the nation had the opportunity to believe God and see Him fulfill His word.

BIBLIOGRAPHY

Allen, Ronald B. "Numbers." In *Genesis–Numbers*. Vol. 2 of The Expositor's Bible Commentary, edited by Frank E. Gaebelein. Grand Rapids, MI: Zondervan, 1990.

Ashley, Timothy R. *The Book of Numbers*. New International Commentary on the Old Testament. Grand Rapids, MI: Eerdmans, 1993.

Cole, R. Dennis. *Numbers*. The New American Commentary. Nashville, TN: Broadman & Holman, 2000.

Harrison, R. K. *Numbers*. Wycliffe Exegetical Commentary. Chicago: Moody, 1990.

Merrill, Eugene H. "Numbers." In *The Bible Knowledge Commentary: Old Testament*, edited by John F. Walvoord and Roy B. Zuck. Wheaton, IL: Victor Books, 1985. Reprint, Colorado Springs: Cook Communications, 1996.

Olson, Dennis T. *The Death of the Old and the Birth of the New: The Framework of the Book of Numbers and the Pentateuch*. Chico, CA: Scholars Press, 1975.

Rydelnik, Michael. *The Messianic Hope: Is the Hebrew Bible Really Messianic?* Nashville, TN: Broadman & Holman, 2010.

Sailhamer, John H. *The Pentateuch as Narrative*. Grand Rapids, MI: Zondervan, 1992.

Wenham, Gordon J. *Numbers: An Introduction and Commentary*. Tyndale Old Testament Commentary. Downers Grove, IL: InterVarsity, 1981.

● ● ● ●

DEUTERONOMY

JAMES COAKLEY

INTRODUCTION

The English title for the fifth book of Moses comes from the Greek Septuagint (LXX) name *Deuteronomion,* meaning "second law." The LXX derived this from the phrase "copy of this law" from Dt 17:18, erroneously understanding the book as a repetition of the book of Exodus. The Jewish title for the book is *elleh haddebarim,* the first Hebrew words of the book, meaning "these are the words." This is a more accurate reflection of Deuteronomy since the bulk of it consists of the speeches Moses gave to the nation Israel just before they entered the promised land. Also, this title reflects the sermonic element of this material, rather than focusing on the legislative quality of the book.

Author. Internally the book is clearly attributed to the hand of Moses (31:9, 24), and there are several references to Moses "speaking" the content of this book (1:9; 5:1; 29:2; 31:30). No other OT book is as clearly attributed to a human author as this one, so to suggest otherwise means that the burden of proof clearly lies with those do not hold to a Mosaic authorship of the book. Some editorial additions have been inserted (e.g., 34:5-12), but the core of this book is attributed to Mosaic composition as Joshua (Jos 1:7-8), Ezra (Ezr 3:2), and Jesus Himself attest (Jn 5:45-47). For most critics of the Pentateuch, Deuteronomy is the "D" portion of the JEDP documentary hypothesis identified with the "book of the law" found in the temple in 2Kg 22:8-11 and is a unified whole edited by a single writer who lived in the seventh century BC. For a critique of the documentary hypothesis see the Introduction to the book of Genesis.

Date. The historical background of the book is the period of the nation Israel just before they crossed the Jordan River into the promised land (c. 1405 BC).

Covenantal in form, this book resembles the format of ancient Near Eastern treaties, specifically the suzerain-vassal treaty texts as advanced by Meredith Kline (*Treaty of the Great King: The Covenant Structure of Deuteronomy: Studies and Commentary* [Grand Rapids, MI: Eerdmans, 1963]), but the overall style and genre of Deuteronomy is hortatory and homiletical. Moses was exhorting the readers/listeners to certain behavior by using motivation clauses and directives. While the book does include some laws, it is not entirely a book of laws since it also contains narrative and poetry. In addition, while it does use treaty language, the word "covenant" (Hb. *berith*) is not used in the book to describe its overall nature. It is best to view the book, as Olson does (D. T. Olson, *Deuteronomy and the Death of Moses,* [Minneapolis: Fortress Press, 1994], 10-12), mainly as a catechetical type book that distills the essential traditions and theology of Israel. The book includes the core of the faith-based education that was to be passed down from generation to generation. Deuteronomy is the closest that the OT comes to a systematic theology. Deuteronomy should not be viewed as a self-standing, independent book but as one part of a unified book, the Torah, which includes all five books of the Pentateuch.

Theme and Purpose. Since it is primarily a teaching book, its purpose is to call Israel to covenant loyalty and obedience. Each subsequent generation of readers is, as it were, on the plains of Moab being reminded to love the Lord wholeheartedly and not to forget the God who graciously fulfills promises and longs for a personal relationship with His children. Israel was to prepare to claim God's promises by being rooted in God's Word and by abounding in love for Him and others.

Structure. Deuteronomy has three overlapping structures:

First it mirrors the form of ancient Near Eastern treaties, which highlights the book's covenantal emphasis:

I. Preamble (1:1-5)
II. Historical Prologue: Covenant History (1:6–4:49)
III. Stipulations (5–26)
IV. Blessings and Cursings (27–30)
V. Witnesses (30:19; 31:19; 32:1-43)

Second, Deuteronomy is also organized in a chiastic structure, which pivots on the central body of legislation in chaps. 12–26.

A Historical Look Backward (chaps. 1–3)
  B Exhortation to Keep the Covenant (chaps. 4–11)
    C The Center: The Stipulations of the Covenant (chaps. 12–26)
  B' Ceremony to Memorialize the Covenant (chaps. 27–30)
A' Prophetic Look Forward (chaps. 31–34)

Third, various superscriptions are used to introduce the different portions of the book, which serves the book's internal organization as a teaching book:

1:1. "These are the words"—The Past (chaps. 1–4)
4:44. "This is the law"—The Ten Commandments (chap. 5)
6:1. "This is the commandment, the statues and the judgments"—Laws for the Present (chaps. 6–28)
29:1. "These are the words of the covenant"—The Future Covenant Renewal (chaps. 29–32)
33:1. "This is the blessing"—Blessing for the Future (chaps. 33–34)

Background. The presence and influence of Deuteronomy is evident throughout the Bible. It provides orientation for what happens in the rest of the OT and even influences the NT. Seven facts may be noted in this connection.

First, Deuteronomy explains the success of Joshua and the failure of the period of the judges. To have success, Joshua was instructed (Jos 1:8) to meditate and keep "this book of the law" (i.e., Deuteronomy). Joshua faithfully executed the teaching of this book, even to the point of conducting a covenant renewal ceremony at the end of his life. He certainly impressed the Word on his children, because at the end of his life he boldly proclaimed, "As for me and my house, we will serve the LORD" (Jos 24:15). Joshua was successful because he knew and lived Deuteronomy. The complete opposite happened in the period of the judges. It was a chaotic period, full of flawed leaders when "everyone did what was right in his own eyes" (Jdg 21:25). In that time period Israel was not doing what was right according to "the book of the law," and so it experienced failure.

Second, Deuteronomy explains the success and failure of the Israelite kings (Dt 17:14-20). Each king was to handwrite his own personal copy of the "book of the law" (a phrase which might refer only to Deuteronomy since it is the only book in the Torah to use it (29:21; 30:10; 31:26).). That way he could not feign ignorance of God's commands. King David most likely followed this injunction (Ps 1, 19, 119), whereas his son Solomon did not (cf. Dt 17:16-17 with 1Kg 10–11). Jeroboam clearly violated the commands of Deuteronomy in 1Kg 12, and this was later true of other evil kings (1Kg 15:34; 16:26).

Third, Deuteronomy explains the existence of many prophets in the eighth to sixth centuries BC. Israel's spiritual decline caused God in His grace to send prophets, who in essence said: "Read and heed Deuteronomy." The nation needed to hear the message that if they listened and lived by Deuteronomy God would bless them and forestall His judgment against them. If they responded correctly, they would receive the blessings of Dt 28, and if not they would reap the curses of Dt 28. In essence the prophets' repeated message was the book of Deuteronomy. All the prophets, especially Hosea, Jeremiah, and Daniel, all beat with the same heartbeat of Deuteronomy. For readers to understand the prophets they must understand the message of Deuteronomy.

Fourth, Deuteronomy explains the reason for the Babylonian exile (Dt 28:36): "The LORD will bring you and your king, whom you set over you, to a nation which neither you nor your fathers have known, and there you shall serve other gods, [gods of] wood and stone." In summary the exile of 586 BC happened because no one heeded Deuteronomy.

Fifth, Deuteronomy greatly influenced the NT. Deuteronomy is one of the four books most frequently quoted in the NT (Psalms, Genesis, and Isaiah are the others). Paul's epistles are loaded with quotations from and allusions to this book.

Sixth, Deuteronomy was an integral part of the "Bible" Jesus read and lived. Jesus astounded the teachers at the temple with His knowledge of the law at the age of 12 (Lk 2:46-47). After He was baptized, He was driven by the Spirit into the Judean wilderness to be tempted by the devil, where in Mt 4 (vv. 4, 7, 10) He quoted three times from Deuteronomy. The first Adam fell to temptation in a garden by doubting God's Word, and the Last Adam resisted temptation in a desert by reciting what God said in Deuteronomy. This shows that Jesus is the ideal perfect King, for He "knows" Deuteronomy (cf. Dt 17:18-20).

Seventh, Deuteronomy summarizes the first great commandment. When Jesus was asked "Which is the great commandment in the Law?" He replied: "You shall love the LORD your God with all your heart, and with all your soul, and with all your mind" (Mt 22:36-37; Dt 6:5). Deuteronomy is the first book in the OT to command believers to love God, and it mentions this repeatedly. "Love the LORD your God" (Dt 11:1; 30:16).

OUTLINE

I. Introduction (1:1-5)
II. Moses' First Address: Historical Prologue (1:6–4:43)
- A. Historical Review of God's Gracious Acts from Horeb and Beth Peor (1:6–3:29)
- B. An Exhortation to Obey the Law Faithfully (4:1-40)
- C. Additional Cities of Refuge (4:41-43)

III. Moses' Second Address: The Stipulations (4:44–26:19)
- A. The Essence of the Law and Its Fulfillment (4:44–11:23)
- B. Exposition of Selected Covenant Laws (12:1–25:19)
- C. Ceremonial Fulfillment of the Law (26:1-19)

IV. Moses' Third Address: Blessings and Curses (27:1–28:68)
- A. Renewal of the Covenant Commanded (27:1-26)
- B. Blessings and Curses (28:1-68)

V. Moses' Fourth Address: Exhortation to Obedience (29:1–30:20)
- A. An Appeal for Covenant Faithfulness (29:1-29)
- B. The Call to Decision: Life and Blessing or Death and Cursing (30:1-20)

VI. Conclusion (31:1–34:12)
- A. Deposition of the Law and the Appointment of Joshua (31:1-29)
- B. Song of Moses (31:30–32:43)
- C. Preparation for Moses' Death (32:44-52)
- D. The Blessing of Moses on the Tribes (33:1-29)
- E. Death of Moses (34:1-12)

COMMENTARY ON DEUTERONOMY

I. Introduction (1:1-5)

1:1-5. While the book of Deuteronomy takes its shape from the covenant treaty format, the opening words state that this book is a series of addresses (**words**) from the mouth of **Moses** to the entire nation of **Israel** located **across the Jordan in the wilderness**. The words **all Israel** often occur at key section breaks in the book (5:1; 29:2; 31:1; 32:45) and are used as bookends in the last verses of the book (1:1; 34:12). For Moses, the unity of the nation is a key element in his theology, introduced early on in the Pentateuch in the Cain and Abel account, stressing that they should be their "brother's keeper" (Gn 4:9).

The Israelites camped in desolate surroundings **in the wilderness, in the Arabah**. The Arabah is the rift valley that begins in the north near the Sea of Galilee and proceeds southward to the Gulf of Aqaba. The location is further specified with geographical place names that are not easy to identify. While the bulk of the book of Deuteronomy is composed of the words of Moses, the opening verses (1:1-5) seem to be an introduction written by someone else (possibly Joshua or whoever included the epilogue at the end of Deuteronomy) residing at the time in the land of Israel (which Moses never entered). Moses spoke to Israel while they were **across the Jordan in the wilderness** (v. 1), which would not be the geographical point of view of Moses if he penned this exact introduction. The conclusion of Deuteronomy (chap. 34) includes information about the death of Moses, so probably another person superintended by God to write inspired text framed the book with Moses' words in the introduction and conclusion. The book is placed both geographically and chronologically (vv. 2-3). The Israelites' location was said to be an **eleven days' journey from Horeb**, which is about 150 miles distance. **Horeb** is another name for Mount Sinai. Horeb is mentioned nine times in Deuteronomy and Sinai only once (33:2). The mention of "eleven days' journey" contrasts starkly with the Israelites' earlier movement of that same span that took 40 years. This is a clear reminder of the Israelites' lack of faith and disobedience after God brought them out of Egypt. At this time (the 40th year) Moses spoke all **that the Lord had commanded him to give to them**. The historical setting is further identified as taking place after the defeat of two kings, Sihon and Og (Nm 21:21-35), and the geographical setting is repeated (Dt 1:1, 5) as being **across the Jordan** (v. 5).

These opening words set up the introduction of the book of Deuteronomy as given by Moses, and they also present a proper perspective for all future readers. Every generation, as it were, can be seen to be "across the Jordan," not having fully inherited the promises of God. Each subsequent generation, not just the first one, needs to be reminded of the consequences of disobedience (40 years instead of 11 days) and also of God's grace (defeat of Sihon and Og)—and of the importance of listening to "all that the Lord commanded" by the mouth of Moses. This introduction masterfully presents the book's historical setting, and also its theological importance, to all who read this book.

II. Moses' First Address: Historical Prologue (1:6–4:43)

A. Historical Review of God's Gracious Acts from Horeb and Beth Peor (1:6–3:29)

1:6-8. Moses' first speech begins by stating that it is **the LORD our God** who **spoke**. That phrase occurs over 20 times in the book, including the Shema passage (6:4). It stresses the relational and communal aspects of the relationship the Israelites enjoyed with the Lord. In retelling the history of their journey, Moses began by quoting the Lord's detailed instructions about the lands they were to possess. After a year at Horeb (Nm 10:11) the Lord commanded them to leave and begin to claim the land He promised to the patriarchs. By stating these specific words of the Lord first, Moses was stressing the gift of the promised land and God's promise-keeping ability. The Israelites' responsibility was simply to see and possess (v. 8). They merely needed to see God's gift with their eyes and then lay hold of it.

1:9-18. While Moses was stressing God's promise-keeping ability, he was also highlighting his own inadequacies in leading the nation alone (v. 9). As he did at God's initial calling of him in Ex 3–4, Moses revealed his character trait of inadequacy, stating his inability to do alone what the Lord asked him to do. So he requested the aid of others to fulfill the task. Now, instead of having Aaron assisting him (Ex 4:14-16), he rehearsed how tribal leaders were selected to assist him in solving legal disputes (Ex 18:13-27). He felt he could no longer manage the growing Israelite population nor could he properly respond attitudinally to their strife (v. 12). The Israelites were increasing like the stars of heaven as a result of God's fulfilling the Abrahamic covenant (Gn 15:5). It appeared as though the nation would only get larger, so Moses was open about his need for help to govern.

Another one of his character traits revealed early in his life was his anger (Ex 2:12). Anger is also one of the reasons he was forbidden to enter the promised land (Nm 20:10-11). So Moses in his opening words transparently revealed two of his own flaws: feelings of inadequacy and anger in the midst of strife. Even though Jethro is not mentioned here, he was the one who specifically suggested to Moses that he appoint judges to adjudicate the small cases and that Moses handle only the "hard" cases (Ex 18:14-15). The judges were to be wise and discerning, with experience and reputations above reproach. The division of the judges in ever-larger circles of authority speaks of military-like precision in the handling of personal and civil matters. These judges were to be impartial and not influenced by a person's origin, wealth, or status.

This emphasis on justice and righteousness early in the book suggests these are key themes and purposes of the book. Of all the possible narratives about the wilderness wanderings to focus on in this opening section of Deuteronomy, Moses selected the account that stressed judges be impartial in their rendering of judgments. This is an important matter to keep in mind for whoever would seek to apply the laws found later in this book.

1:19-21. Moses continued his survey of the experiences in the exodus. After they set out from Horeb, Israel passed through the great and terrible wilderness until they arrived at Kadesh-barnea. The barrenness of the wilderness contrasted starkly with the fruitful land the Lord promised them. In such inhospitable territory God would show His faithfulness by providing for them. This land was currently under the control of the Amorites, meaning that Israel would need to uproot them if they were to possess the land. Verse 21 in essence repeats v. 8, stressing not only the gift of the land but also the importance of obediently taking possession of it without fear or discouragement of the mission now before them.

1:22-33. After arriving at Kadesh, Moses agreed to the people's request to send men to search out the land to map out a battle strategy. So twelve representatives, one from each tribe, spied out the land. They brought back fruit as a proof of the land's fertility, and they verbally attested to its overall goodness and suitability as a homeland. Moses did not stress the role of the ten men (Nm 13:31-33) in tainting the report. Instead he placed the blame for failure to take possession of the land on the entire nation, who rebelled against the Lord's command. Not only did they fear the size and strength of the Amorites (by exaggerating their fortifications Dt 28), but they also questioned God's goodness and motives, thinking that He hated them and was out to destroy them. The words **the sons of the Anakim** (v. 28) were used to evoke fear in those who heard them. The words are used often as the epitome of a formidable enemy (2:10, 21; 9:2; Nm 13:33). Moses sought to calm their fears by reminding them of the Lord's presence and protection in their escape from Egypt. He also used a tender familial metaphor (**as a man carries his son**, v. 31) to portray God's compassionate care for the nation while they were in the wilderness. Yet in spite of the Lord's presence, protection, and compassion, the people failed to trust the LORD, who acted as a military scout to guide them every step of the way during their journeys in the desert.

1:34-40. In response to their rebellion and grumbling, the Lord was angry and took an oath saying that none of the men from that evil generation would see or enter the land, except for Caleb and Joshua. Even Moses was not allowed to enter the land because the Lord **was angry** against him for his rebellion and lack of belief (Nm 20:12). The rebellious generation feared that their children would be devoured by the inhabitants of Canaan, but it was those children who would actually inherit and possess the land. The Lord then sentenced them to turn around and head back into the wilderness.

1:41-46. Even though the people acknowledged their sin and sought to follow the Lord's previous command to go up and fight, Moses relayed the Lord's message, stating that they should not attempt to take the land by force or else they would be defeated. Again the people failed to obey and presumptuously attacked the Amorites in the hill country. The enemy crushed their attempt and chased them back to Hormah (most likely in the Negev; cf. Jos 15:30). The nation wept over their behavior, but the Lord did not reverse His sentence and allow them to enter the land. Instead they remained in the wilderness at Kadesh many days.

2:1-8. Even though the nation rebelled there were times of obedience as here when they **set out for the wilderness . . . as the LORD spoke** (v. 1). However, instead of heading directly to the promised land they headed south toward the Red Sea. The phrase **many days** (repeated from 1:46) evokes an image of futility, further heightened by the innumerable times they circled Mount Seir, located in a mountain range on the border of Edom south of the Dead Sea. The Lord addressed Moses during this wandering and gave the nation clearance to head northward, passing through the territory of the sons of Esau (Edomites). They are familially referred to as "your brothers," but the Jewish people lived in fear of them. So Israel was to not do anything to provoke them as they passed through their territory and to compensate them for any food or water they consumed. As the Lord had graciously provided for the Israelites during the 40 years in the wilderness, they were in turn to remunerate the Edomites so that they would not be deprived at Israel's expense. The Israelites were not the only people group given a possession, as the Lord had allocated the region of Mount Seir as a gift to the sons of Esau. Even with this stipulation the Edomites refused to allow Israel passage (Nm 20:14-21), and so the nation had to pass beyond them to the east by way of the wilderness of Moab, the region immediately east of the Dead Sea.

2:9-15. Just as they were not to provoke Edom, the Israelites were forbidden the same with Moab. The Lord gave Ar (a city or region in Moab about seven miles east of the Dead Sea, perhaps close to the Arnon River; 2:18) to the sons of Lot as a possession, just as Seir had been given to the sons of Esau (v. 5). Verses 10-12 give parenthetical background information about the Emim and how the Edomites came to possess Seir. These verses may have been inserted by a later inspired author to give additional clarifying information and historical backdrop. The clause **just as Israel did to the land of their possession** (v. 12) seems to refer to some time after the conquest of Joshua. The Emim were the previous occupiers of Moab. They were similar in size and strength to the Anakim and were known as Rephaim. These multiple aliases for tall people (along with the Nephilim [Nm 13:32-33] and the Zamzummin [Dt 2:20]) and a concern to describe their history and territory demonstrate that any information about them was of great interest to the original readers. There was both a fascination and a fear of them, so much so, that information about them would be inserted into multiple accounts in the Scriptures.

That Moab was able to drive out these great, numerous, and tall foes should have strengthened the Israelites' faith to do the same with the Anakim in Canaan, but instead their hearts melted in their presence (Dt 1:28). This parenthetical insertion functions as an "illustration." If the Moabites could vanquish the Emim and claim their land and the Edomites could do the same with the Horites, then Israel should have no trouble claiming the promised land no matter who currently lived there, especially since they had the **Lord** to fight with them. After the parenthetical information (vv. 10-12) Moses continued the account by referencing the Lord's command to cross over **the brook Zered** (at the southern boundary of Moab, near the southeastern tip of the Dead Sea), which the Israelites did.

2:14-23. The time it took to go from Kadesh-barnea (1:19) to crossing the brook Zered was **thirty-eight years**. It took that long for all the fighting men of Israel to die as punishment for their unbelief (1:35). As they crossed **the border of Moab** at **Ar** and passed into Ammonite territory, the Israelites were not to provoke them either (just as they were not to provoke Edom or Moab) since the Lord had not given them their territory as a possession. Another parenthetical insertion similar to vv. 10-12 appears in vv. 20-23. These verses give information similar to the earlier insertion, but this time they refer to Ammon and whom the Ammonites dispossessed (the Rephaim or Zamzummin) with the Lord's help in order to live there. A further illustration of a people group who uprooted the previous occupants were the **Caphtorim** (Philistines) from **Caphtor** (Crete?) who drove out the Avvim and settled **as far as Gaza** (on the southeast coast of the Mediterranean Sea). The purpose of this insertion about people groups being displaced was meant to encourage the Israelites that they too, with the Lord's help, could uproot the original occupants of the land of Canaan.

2:24-31. Picking up from v. 19, Moses then chronicled the next stage of the journey after crossing through Ammon. Instead of peaceful interaction as was the policy with Edom, Moab, and Ammon, the Israelites were now to begin to take possession of Amorite territory east and north of the Dead Sea, then under the control of **Sihon, king of Heshbon**, a city about 12 miles east and slightly north of the northern tip of the Dead Sea. The Lord began to place the dread and fear of the Israelites within the hearts of all other nations (cf. Ex 15:14-16). At first Sihon was given an opportunity to allow peaceful passage for Israel and to be compensated for any food and water consumed along the way. This was the same policy that was offered to both Edom and Moab.

Sihon refused those terms because **the Lord . . . hardened his spirit and . . . heart** so that he might be delivered into the Israelites' hand (v. 30). Previously the Lord had hardened the heart of Pharaoh, (Ex 4:21) another foreign ruler, who was also reluctant to grant Israel leave to travel.

This does not mean that Sihon had no free will in this, for he was predisposed on his own (Nm 21:23) not to give them passage, whether because of fear or confidence in his own military strength. The Amorites were not related to the Israelites like the Edomites, Moabites, and Ammonites, and there is no statement that the Amorites were given a possession of land by the Lord as these others were (Dt 2:5, 9, 19). In fact the Lord clearly stated that He is the one who would deliver Sihon and his land over to the Israelites as a possession (v. 31).

2:32-37. The Israelites battled against **Sihon . . . at Jahaz** (unknown location). The Lord gave them a definitive victory over the Amorites, by their killing Sihon and his heirs, capturing all their cities, and leaving no survivors. They did allocate the animals and material possessions for themselves as **booty**. The phrase **utterly destroyed** (Hb. *charam,* v. 34) invokes "holy war" terminology and is used several times in the book (3:6; 7:2; 13:16; 20:17). (See the discussion at chap. 7 regarding the ethics of killing noncombatants.) All the Amorite territory from Aroer in the south to Gilead in the north was now under Israelite control. The clause **there was no city that was too high for us** (v. 36) referred to their city walls. This was a rebuke to the earlier notion that Israel would not be able to conquer the Canaanites because their walls were "fortified to heaven" (1:28). Israel was obedient in that they did not encroach on Ammonite territory (related to Israel via Lot, Gn 19) and went only wherever the Lord commanded them.

3:1-7. After the Amorites were defeated, the next foe to be dealt with was **Og, king of Bashan**, roughly the region east of the Sea of Galilee. Og gathered his forces to do battle with Israel at **Edrei** (southern border of Bashan). The Lord told Moses that the Israelites were not to fear him, for just as they defeated Sihon and possessed his land they would do the same with Og and his territory. The Lord did deliver Og and his people into their hands and captured 60 fortified cities and many unwalled towns. Just like Sihon and his people (2:34) all the people of Bashan (also called "Argob") were utterly destroyed, but their animals and possessions were taken as spoils of war. (See discussion at chap. 7 regarding the ethics of killing noncombatants.)

3:8-11. This section summarizes the capturing of the Transjordanian region (**beyond the Jordan**) ruled by the Amorite kings Sihon and Og. These victories were momentous events meant to strengthen the Israelites' resolve to do the same in the land of Canaan. This was large territory to control from the valley of **Arnon** (south) to **Mount Hermon** (north). Hermon was a natural boundary marker because of its height (9,230 feet) and location. Other nations in the area named it Sirion or Senir. Israel now possessed all the formerly Amorite cities in Gilead and Bashan. Og was the last of the Rephaim (2:11), so he probably ruled over the Amorites because of his lineage and tall stature. His height is confirmed by the dimensions of his bed, which was nine by four cubits (i.e., 13 and a half feet by 6 feet). His iron "bed" may actually be his sarcophagus (coffin), placed after his death on display in Rabbah as a trophy by the Ammonites.

Israel's Occupation of Transjordan

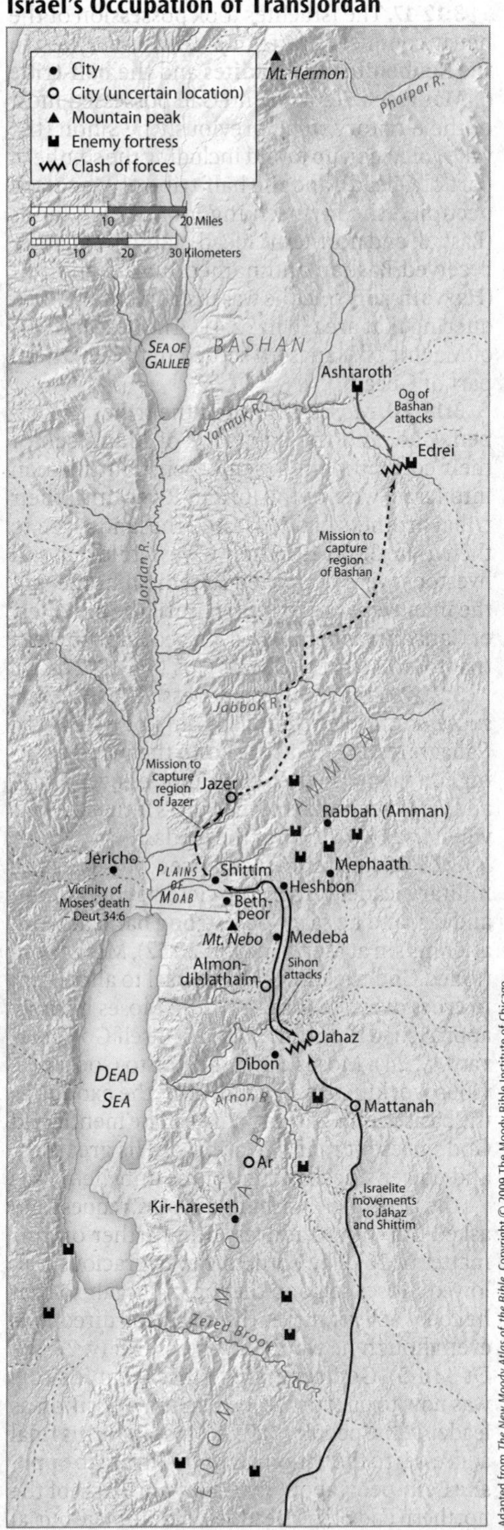

3:12-17. The Israelites took possession of the newly conquered territory, which was given to the **Reubenites** and **Gadites** and the **half-tribe of Manasseh**. Reuben and Gad possessed most of the territory ruled previously by Sihon (the valley of Arnon up to and including the southern part of Gilead), and the half-tribe of Manasseh occupied the former kingdom of Og's lands (Bashan and northern Gilead). **Jair** of Manasseh received Bashan and named it after himself (**Havvoth-jair**) since he was instrumental in conquering that area (Nm 32:41). The descendants of Machir of Manasseh settled in the northern part of Gilead.

3:18-20. Moses reminded the tribes of Reuben, Gad, and the half-tribe of Manasseh of their commitment to send their fighting men into Israel west of the Jordan River until their tribal brothers had possessed the land given to them (Nm 32:16-19). Their wives, children, and livestock were permitted to remain home, but the men were not to return until the conquest of Canaan was completed, an accomplishment that took at least five years (Jos 14:6-15; 22:1-4).

3:21-22. Moses then addressed **Joshua**, his successor, and encouraged him not to fear the Canaanites, for it was the **LORD** their **God fighting** for them. He used the victories over Sihon and Og as reminders of the Lord's future actions when they would cross the Jordan.

3:23-29. Since the Lord used Moses as the military leader during the victories over Sihon and Og, and he saw God's **strong hand** at work after his sin at Meribah (Nm 20:12), Moses petitioned God to rethink His refusal to allow him to **cross over** the **Jordan** (v. 25). Moses humbly approached the Lord, calling himself God's **servant** (v. 24). Moses did not refer to God's previous workings in Egypt during the exodus as the basis for his entreaty; instead he mentioned God's present manifestation of His greatness and power since the time of his unbelief.

The Lord angrily rebuffed Moses' request and asked him not to address him further on this matter (v. 26). The Lord, however, graciously allowed Moses to go to the top of Pisgah so that he could at least survey the land in all directions even though he would never enter it (v. 27; see Dt 34:1-5). God reminded Moses that his role was now to encourage Joshua in his position as leader of the people (31:7-8). Moses gave his final addresses to the nation in a **valley** in Moab **opposite Beth-peor**, about five miles northeast of the northern end of the Dead Sea, his ultimate burial place (34:6). The reference to Peor (3:29) alludes to two incidents recorded in Numbers: the place where Balaam prophesied (Nm 23:28) and the rebellion at Shittim, where they worshiped the Baal of Peor (25:1-3). Moses' final words are spoken against the backdrop of the nation of Israel's most recent act of serious rebellion.

Moses' question **what god is there?** (Dt 3:24), does not imply that he thought that other deities exist. This was a rhetorical device stressing the Lord's matchless nature and power.

B. An Exhortation to Obey the Law Faithfully (4:1-40)

This chapter reflects much of the form of an ancient Near Eastern treaty, especially second-millennium BC Hittite treaties. While it is not an overt treaty format, there are many similarities. These similarities heighten that this is a deeply relational book, so much so that formalized wording is used.

4:1-2. Up to this point Moses had been chronicling God's dealing with Israel for the previous 40 years. Now he moved into a more sermonic mode. All of Israel's history had been chronicled with an eye to motivate the nation as they were getting ready for the conquest of the land. Moses stated his first command in the book—they were to **listen** (Hb. *shema,* as in 6:4) to **the statutes and the judgments** he was teaching them. The Lord's faithfulness to Israel in the recent past would obligate the nation to obey Him. **Statutes** may refer to decreed law (apodictic, general commands), and **judgments** may refer to case law (casuistic, "if-then" commands) and the decisions of appointed judges. The motive clause **so that you may live and go in and take possession of the land** reflects that God's blessing and the acquisition of the promised land is dependent on obedience. God's commands (the verb and the noun are used three times in v. 2) are not to be altered in any way.

Similarities of Deuteronomy 4 to Ancient Treaties

Commonality	Reference in Dt
Parties are mentioned	Dt 4:1-2
Historical prologue and acts	Dt 1:1–3:29; 4:10-12
Call to obey	Dt 4:1
No alterations	Dt 4:2
Proclamation/transmission	Dt 4:10
Witnesses	Dt 4:26

4:3-4. By recounting the incident at **Baal-peor**, Moses gave a clear illustration of the effects of sin and disobedience. There they engaged in Moabite idolatry and immorality (see Nm 25:1-9), so that God clearly manifested His judgment by destroying those who participated in the sin but preserving those **who held fast to the LORD**. Moses personalized the issue by stating that those who were directly hearing these words understood God's delivering grace because they experienced that situation firsthand.

4:5-8. Moses gave himself as an example of obedience by stressing that he had been faithful to proclaim the **statutes and judgments** (v. 5), and so he urged them to **keep and do them**. Obedience to God's laws is the path to wisdom and understanding. The law was given to enable Israel to avoid God's judgment and remain in the promised land. Thus, the nation could fulfill its role as an instrument to glorify God among the nations. But the law was never given, nor intended by God, to be the means whereby Israel would find eternal salvation. When Israel submitted to God's authority, other nations, when exposed to these laws, would concur that Israel's laws are of special quality and would thereby acknowledge Israel's unique status in the world. Moses elaborated that point by stating that no other nation enjoyed as intimate a relationship with their deity as Israel did and that no other nation had a law code as righteous as the one they were receiving. Israel's God is superior to all other gods because of His personal intimacy and the **righteous** nature of His law.

4:9-14. The words **give heed to yourself** (v. 9) occur frequently in the book (6:12; 8:11; 12:13, 19, 30; 15:9), and stress the personal applicational nature of Moses' instructions. The nation was not to forget what their own eyes saw. Since they did not "see" God directly or worship a representation of Him, their memory of these events had to be embedded in their minds and hearts. In addition to internalizing the teachings within their own hearts, the people were instructed to make them known to their **sons... and grandsons**. This begins a key aspect of the book of Deuteronomy in that it was to function somewhat as a catechism for the nation, to be passed down from generation to generation.

Moses illustrated the importance of this task by reminding the people of their commitment at Horeb (Mount Sinai) to fear the **LORD** all of their lives and to teach their children (v. 10; see also 6:20). God's **words** in v. 10 would later be identified as the **Ten Commandments** (v. 13). The focus here is on the nation's initial experience to laws given at Horeb, hence the restricted reference here to the "Ten Commandments" as compared to all the other injunctions the Lord gave to Israel in the wilderness—yet it also serves to heighten their importance. The Lord's speaking out of the fire is reminiscent of His initial calling of Moses out of the burning bush (Ex 3:2). The imagery of fire, darkness, and clouds heightens the omnipotence of the Lord. It also shows that since God had no distinct form, no one could fashion an image or statue (an idol) that would represent Him. The Israelites were to focus their attention on the voice that emanated from the fire and the words that were spoken. In Dt 4:13 the term **covenant** (Hb. *berith*) is used for the first of 27 times in the book of Deuteronomy, and the phrase **the Ten Commandments** (lit., "ten words") is also mentioned for the first time.

The commandments were written on two tablets of stone. Perhaps each tablet had the ten words engraved on it rather than some on one tablet and some on the other. The notion would be that each party to this covenant would have their own copy and they would be kept and stored together in the most sacred location in Israel (the ark of the covenant in the holy of holies). Besides being the one through whom the Ten Commandments were delivered, Moses was to teach the Israelites **statutes and judgments**, to guide the people in properly applying God's commands once they arrived in the promised land.

4:15-20. Having mentioned that the Israelites saw no form when the **LORD** spoke (v. 12), Moses expanded upon that and expressly forbade the making of any physical representation of the Lord. All the surrounding pagan nations had idols representing their gods, but the Israelites were not to **act corruptly** and make any image, whether a male or female figure, or any animal or bird or any insect or fish. The language used in vv. 16-18 echoes the wording used in Gn 1 to describe all the creatures God had created. Since they were merely creatures and not the Creator, it would be inappropriate for them to be worshiped. Also the Israelites were not to worship any of the heavenly bodies either. The **sun... moon and... stars** were worshiped by other ancient Near Eastern peoples, but the Israelites were not to be enticed by their practices and serve astronomical bodies. The **host of heaven** were **allotted to all** peoples, presumably for calendar purposes as well as simply to provide light on the earth (Gn 1:14-15); they were not to be objects of worship.

Moses reminded the people that they had been taken and brought out of Egypt, the dominant superpower of that day, to be **His own possession**. Israel was God's inheritance, so He placed special demands on them. Egypt was likened to an **iron furnace**, used to remove impurities from metal. That is, the Lord used their time in Egypt as a means of purification so they would be fit to enter the promised land.

4:21-24. The importance of purity raised by the furnace imagery in v. 20 is stressed by an example from Moses' own life. Moses' act of unbelief when he struck the rock (Nm 20:12) provoked God's anger, so that Moses was not to **enter the good land which the LORD** gave Israel **as an inheritance** (v. 21). This was the third time Moses mentioned his disqualifying sin (Dt 1:37; 3:26), and each time he mentioned that he was missing out on a **good land** (1:35; 3:25; 4:21-22). Moses again told the people to be watchful (cf. v. 15), lest they **forget the covenant** and make graven images (v. 23). Worshiping idols was the clearest identifier that the nation had forgotten the covenant. Picking up the fire imagery from vv. 15 and 20, Moses stressed that the **LORD . . . is a consuming fire** and **a jealous God** (v. 24). The Lord demands total loyalty and will not tolerate idolatry in any fashion (a point Moses emphasized in vv. 25-28).

4:25-31. The injunction against idolatry was important not only for Moses' immediate audience but also for future generations. If any Israelites acted **corruptly** by making **an idol**, that would provoke God to anger (v. 25). **Heaven and earth** would **witness** to their guilt, and the Israelites would be expelled from the land. Israel would dwindle in size and be scattered **among the peoples** (vv. 26-27). In a punishment that would fit the crime they would be forced to serve the blind and deaf gods of **wood and stone** in foreign lands (v. 28). However, exile and punishment would not negate the covenant, for if they sought the **LORD** wholeheartedly while under God's judgment, He would respond and restore them (vv. 29-31). This is not merely a hypothetical promise. Rather it is a prediction of **the latter days** when Israel will return to the Lord and put their trust in Jesus their Messiah (see comments at Hs 3:5; Zch 12:10-14; Mt 23:37-39; and Rm 11:26).

The **LORD** is a **compassionate God,** faithful to His promises, who will not utterly destroy them and who will never forget the covenant He established with their forefathers. Verse 29 is sometimes cited in support of the possibility that someone might respond correctly to the light of God found in creation and seek God in such a way that God might save that person even without the gospel (for a critique of this idea, see the comments on Rm 1:18-32). But the verse is spoken to Israel, is based upon God's specially-revealed covenant promises (not "natural revelation" in creation), is a prophecy about what will happen in the future, and cannot be applied to an individual or a people group outside of His covenant people.

4:32-34. Switching from the future (v. 25), to the past, Moses now asked his audience to reflect all the way back to creation to try to find any situation similar to their experience in the exodus and Sinai events. Israel alone could claim direct revelation of which everyone was a part, not just the priests. No other nation was forged by having been redeemed from another nation as Israel was out of Egypt. Nor had any other nation seen their gods work with such miraculous signs and wonders as the Lord did in redeeming Israel out of Egypt with the plagues, the Red Sea crossing, and the provision of manna in the wilderness. The Lord's **mighty hand** and **outstretched arm** were visible **before** the **eyes** of all the people, not just a select few.

4:35-40. The Lord revealed Himself in history so that Israel would learn **that the Lord . . . is God** and **there is no other besides Him** (v. 35). The Israelites needed to understand God's supremacy and uniqueness and trust in Him before proceeding any further. As Moses had said, God was not seen at Horeb. But His voice was heard out of the heavens, and the tangible expression of His presence was manifested by a **great fire** (v. 36). God revealed Himself in order to teach Israel His love, sovereignty, and superiority. God loved this generation's forefathers, particularly the patriarchs, so much so that **He chose their descendants after them**, and He was personally involved in bringing the nation out of **Egypt** (v. 37). God's love is not just an emotion; it is a covenantal relational love that works on behalf of its recipients. Like a sovereign military king, God assisted in the process of driving out foes from the promised land and then distributed that property to His vassal state, Israel, as **an inheritance** (v. 38). With the repetition of the word **today** (vv. 38, 39) Moses stressed the immediacy of personally internalizing that their God is God alone and **there is no other**. Thus Moses' focus was on God's nature, leading to His expectation that the Israelites **keep His statutes and His commandments** (v. 40). If they were obedient they could expect to enjoy prosperity in the land for many generations.

C. Additional Cities of Refuge (4:41-43)

4:41-43. The reference here to the **three cities** of refuge on the **east** side of the Jordan may seem awkward. Why would details about these cities be given right after Moses' address in 1:6–4:40? Moses discussed the cities of refuge in more detail later (see the comments on 19:1-14 for more detail). But here Moses is referred to in the third person (his last specific reference by name was in 1:5), which signals a transition of content. This interlude serves a structural purpose by separating Moses' passionate plea to keep God's commandments (4:40) from the statement of the laws and commandments that begins in v. 44.

The insertion here is appropriate because Moses understood that a long, prosperous stay in the land (v. 40) must include this practice of having cities of refuge for a manslayer. Before giving a lengthy account of individual laws and commandments in 4:44–26:19, Moses described this merciful practice that demonstrates due process for offenders who would violate these laws and commandments. While God does demand full obedience, He also is loving and merciful in including protection against extreme punishment of an innocent manslayer. The manslayer is innocent in that he accidentally committed a homicide rather than committing murder with premeditation (cf. Nm 35:31). Inclusion of the cities of refuge laws here provides a qualification for the absolute command in the next chapter (Dt 5:17) "you shall not murder" (John H. Sailhamer, *The Pentateuch As Narrative* [Grand Rapids, MI: Zondervan, 1992], 435). The practice of naming the individual cities of refuge in the promised land was to wait until the Israelites crossed the Jordan (Nm 35:9-28), but since they were at that time on the east side of the Jordan, Moses was able to name three cities in territory they had already conquered: **Bezer** for the **Reubenites, Ramoth** . . . **for the Gadites,** and **Golan** . . . **for the Manassites.** The other three cities would be named after the conquest (Jos 20:7).

III. Moses' Second Address: The Stipulations (4:44–26:19)

A. The Essence of the Law and Its Fulfillment (4:44–11:23)

4:44-49. Having reviewed God's provisions in the past, Moses moved toward instructions for the present audience by reiterating the law to prepare them for the future in the land. This paragraph begins the next major section of the book. Verse 44 is one of the key superscriptions that help divide the major sections of the text (1:1; 4:44; 6:1; 12:1; 29:1; 33:1). This is the law (Hb. *torah*) that **Moses set before the sons of Israel.** "Law" is best understood not just as legislative material but also as instruction or teaching. "Law" is further classified as testimonies, statutes, and ordinances. These are not different from the law given at Mount Sinai, and are recorded here for the generation of Israelites about to enter the promised land. A historical summary highlighting the key military victories (over Sihon and Og) is restated, as well as the boundaries of the land already in their possession. These victories served as a precursor of what was about to happen once they crossed the Jordan. They are reviewed here yet again to encourage Israel for the future by reminding them of divine successes in the past.

5:1-3. After setting a geographical and historical introduction (4:44-49), Moses moved to his second major speech in the book (chaps. 5–12). As he did earlier (1:1), he **summoned all Israel** to give their attention to a reiteration of the Ten Commandments as well as additional statutes and ordinances. He began with the command **Hear,** a frequently used imperative in this section of the book (4:1; 6:4; 9:1). Israel was to do more than listen passively to these laws; they were to **learn them and observe them carefully** (v. 1). Moses' goal for Israel was to obey these laws as a reflection of their wisdom and righteousness (4:6-8). The laws were a mixture of "religious laws" and regulations that affected their community and justice. Moses stressed that **the LORD . . . made a covenant** with Israel at **Horeb** (v. 2), not with previous generations but **with all those of us alive here today** (v. 3). The adult population present at Horeb, nearly 40 years earlier, would have all died because of the sin of rebellion at Kadesh-barnea (Nm 14:1-4), with the exception of Joshua and Caleb. So Moses was probably addressing the children of the first generation of the exodus. These children would have been present at Mount Sinai, but were not sentenced to die in the wilderness (see Dt 1:39-40) as were their parents who lacked faith and obedience. They were "the second generation." Moses, intriguingly, mentioned the third and fourth generations (Dt 4:9), so he definitely was concerned about future generations while mainly addressing the second generation.

5:4-5. Moses further elaborated on the first-hand experience of his listeners as they witnessed God's establishing of the covenant with Israel. Moses stated that the **LORD** spoke to them **face to face** at the mountain from the midst of the fire (v. 4). There is some question as to what was to happen when the nation approached Mount Sinai. In Ex 3:12 God told Moses at the burning bush, "Certainly I will be with you, and this shall be the sign to you [the "you" is singular] that it is I who have sent you: when you have brought the people out of Egypt, you [plural] shall worship God at [lit., "on"] this mountain." Apparently God's intent was for the entire nation, not just Moses, to go up the mountain. When they ultimately arrived at the mountain, the LORD instructed Moses to tell the people that "when the ram's horn sounds a long blast, they shall come up to [lit., "on"] the mountain" (Ex 19:13). The trumpet sounded, and instead of going up the mountain to worship God they "trembled" (Ex 19:16), obviously experiencing fear, but allowing their fear to lead them to disobey by not going up onto the mountain. So only Moses went up the mountain and the rest of the nation, because of their fear and unbelief, lost the opportunity to worship God on the mountain as He intended. In Dt 5:5, Moses stressed his role as a mediator standing **between the LORD and you**. But he also stated that you [plural] **were afraid because of the fire and did not go up** [lit., "on"] **the mountain**. This reflects the same reason given in Ex 19:16. As a result of this disobedience the nation lost the opportunity to worship God collectively and now could only approach through mediators. Sadly they could have become a "kingdom of priests" (Ex 19:6) but now would only become a nation "with priests." At this point in the timeline (at Sinai), the Aaronic Levitical priesthood had not yet been established (it is started later (Ex 28:1-4).

5:6-21. Moses restated the Ten Commandments of Ex 20. (See comments there for a more thorough discussion of each one of the Ten Commandments.) By comparing the two accounts, some variations can be detected. (1) Regarding the Sabbath, in Deuteronomy Moses used the verb "observe" (v. 12) instead of "remember" (Ex 20:8). (2) In Ex 20:11 keeping the Sabbath is related to the creation week, whereas in Dt 5:15 the Israelites were to keep the Sabbath in remembrance of their status as slaves in Egypt. (3) In Deuteronomy, the words **as the LORD your God commanded you** (Dt 5:12, 15, 16) are not in the Ex 20 account. (4) In Deuteronomy, the order of **you shall not covet your neighbor's wife** and . . . **your neighbor's house** (Dt 5:21) is reversed from the order in Ex 20:17. The only variations mentioned so far that bear any significance are the ones concerning the Sabbath. Moses strengthened the injunction from Ex 20:8 to not just "remember" but "observe" (v. 12) the Sabbath. He also drew upon their recent experience as slaves in Egypt rather than upon the more distant creation week. (5) Various traditions differ in their numbering of the Ten Commandments, as seen in the chart below.

The Ten Commandments (Decalogue) seem to begin with the more prominent commandments. The Decalogue is given priority in the book of Deuteronomy as it is the first important piece of legislation Moses gave. It is the core of the theological message of the book, and many scholars see it as a basic outline for the content of chaps. 12–26 (John Walton, *"Deuteronomy: An Exposition of the Spirit of Law," Grace Theological Journal* 8.2 [1987], 213-25). The Ten Commandments have traditionally been divided into two categories: those that govern one's vertical relationship with God (1-4) and those that govern one's horizontal relationship in community with others (5-10).

5:6-7. The First Commandment: The foundation of the Ten Commandments is based on God's salvific event—the exodus from Egypt. As the most significant deliverance event in the OT, the exodus functions as the theological core of the first testament much as the death and resurrection of Jesus do in the NT. On the basis of God's personal involvement in bringing them out of slavery **out of the land of Egypt**, He commanded that they have **no other gods before Me**. This does not necessarily assume the existence of other pagan gods. It is stressing that no Israelite was to worship any deity whether believed to be real or not. Even if other nations assumed the existence of deities, Israel was not to worship them or acknowledge their presence. God was to be the exclusive, sole focus of their worship and service and was not to be rivaled by anyone or anything.

5:8-10. The Second Commandment: Related to the first commandment, Israel was forbidden to make into an idol any physical representation of God of any kind. Since God created everything, no created likeness of any object in the sky, on earth, or in water should ever be the focus of worship. This command also extended to forbidding the making of any tangible

Numbering of the Ten Commandments

	Jewish View	Catholic and Some Lutherans' View	Protestant View
1	I am the Lord your God, who brought you out of the land of Egypt.	I am the Lord your God, who brought you out of the land of Egypt, out of the house of slavery. You shall have no other gods before Me.	You shall have no other gods before Me.
2	You shall have no other gods before Me.	You shall not take the name of the Lord your God in vain.	You shall not make for yourself an idol.
3	You shall not take the name of the Lord your God in vain.	Observe the Sabbath day to keep it holy.	You shall not take the name of the Lord your God in vain.
4	Observe the Sabbath day to keep it holy.	Honor your father and your mother.	Observe the Sabbath day to keep it holy.
5	Honor your father and your mother.	You shall not murder.	Honor your father and your mother.
6	You shall not murder.	You shall not commit adultery.	You shall not murder.
7	You shall not commit adultery.	You shall not steal.	You shall not commit adultery.
8	You shall not steal.	You shall not bear false witness against your neighbor.	You shall not steal.
9	You shall not bear false witness against your neighbor.	You shall not covet your neighbor's wife.	You shall not bear false witness against your neighbor.
10	You shall not covet your neighbor's wife, and you shall not desire your neighbor's house, his field or his male servant or his female servant, his ox or his donkey, or anything that belongs to your neighbor.	You shall not desire your neighbor's house, his field or his male servant or his female servant, his ox or his donkey, or anything that belongs to your neighbor.	You shall not covet your neighbor's wife, and you shall not desire your neighbor's house, his field or his male servant or his female servant, his ox or his donkey, or anything that belongs to your neighbor.

representation of the invisible Lord God of Israel. The reason for this prohibition is that the Lord is a **jealous God**, a repeated theme in the book (4:24; 6:14-15). This emotion befits a call to exclusivity in a covenant relationship, which Israel had with their God. If Israel attached her affections spiritually to some other divine being, God's jealousy would lead Him to punish the nation. A warning is attached to violation of this commandment: God will visit **the iniquity of the fathers on the children, and on the third and the fourth generations of those who hate Me**. Idolatry is equated with hating God, and parents who engage in idolatry will influence their children and grandchildren negatively. Yet for those parents who love the Lord and keep His commandments, there is a spiritual legacy that extends multigenerationally. Hence, the reference to multiple generations has nothing to do with "generational curses" but rather normal consequences. An outward keeping of the commands was inadequate; God wanted them to **love** Him as they kept His commandments.

5:11. The Third Commandment: The command not to take the Lord's name in vain is more than refusing to use any of His various appellatives in profanity. The word "vain" is also used in v. 20 in the context of "false" testimony, so its primary usage here would narrow this prohibition against using the Lord's name in giving false witness. It would extend to any deceptive use of His name in any verbal speech act, such as oaths and promises. His name is an extension of His person and should be respectfully appropriated in all conversations.

5:12-15. The Fourth Commandment: The injunction to observe the Sabbath day is the first of two positively stated commands. The verb **observe** is used here instead of the verb "remember" (Ex 20:8), implying a more active physical response than merely recalling something in one's mind. This command, more than any other, shows the most variation in wording from the Exodus account and demonstrates that additional significance had been attached to Sabbath-day observance compared with 40 years earlier. Deuteronomy does not repeat the teaching of Exodus but expands on the exposition originally given at Sinai. This command has no explicit connection to the creation week as in Ex 20. Here the focus is on relating the observance of Sabbath as a memorial of the exodus event. The seventh day was set apart from the others as a day to remember God's act of creation, but now it is fused with His work of redemption. This command is very specific as to who should observe it: **you or your son or your daughter or your male servant or your female servant or your ox or your donkey or any of your cattle or your sojourner who stays with you**. The Sabbath was to be observed by members of the covenant community but also by foreigners (whether visiting or employed as servants), and it also extended to animals. God's act of deliverance was to be marked by a day each week when all work ceased and even household servants and animals could enjoy a mini "deliverance" themselves in honor of God's redemptive work of Israel. This is the only command in this list that is not repeated in the NT. It is important for NT believers to set aside time to reflect upon God's goodness and grace, but a day where no physical labor is even attempted does not have NT biblical authority. The apostle Paul clearly stated there that no one is to act as your judge in respect to observing a Sabbath day (Col 2:16).

5:16. The Fifth Commandment: The charge to **honor your father and your mother** is the first of the horizontal commandments and the second in a string of positive injunctions (cf. Lv 19:3). This commandment addresses the first and primary relationship among humans. The command probably focuses on the attitude of adults toward their aging parents, since the Decalogue is not elsewhere specifically addressed to the young (cf. v. 14). Moreover, Jesus understood this commandment as applying to adult children (cf. Mt 15:4-6). However, the young are not excluded, as Paul noted in Eph 6:1-2. This command includes a promise of long life and a prosperous stay in the land.

5:17. The Sixth Commandment: The word **murder** can refer to both premeditated and unintentional killing. Special consideration will be given later to unintentional manslaughter (19:1-13), so the primary focus in this context is on premeditated murder. This commandment cannot be applied to soldiers fighting in a war or to executions of criminals sentenced to capital punishment since those actions are mandated elsewhere (Gn 9:6; Nm 31:7).

5:18. The Seventh Commandment: The prohibition against **adultery** highlights the importance of yet another human relationship (cf. 5:16-17). While other sexual sins are forbidden elsewhere, the sexual faithfulness in a marriage relationship is emphasized here because it speaks of a covenantal relationship. Faithfulness to a spouse pictures faithfulness to God.

5:19. The Eighth Commandment: While stealing is wrong (cf. Ex 22:1-13), the juxtaposition of this prohibition with other commands dealing with horizontal human relationships seems to narrow this command more against kidnapping and manstealing than stealing someone's physical property, though such pilfering is not excluded here. Kidnapping violates a covenant relationship by removing someone from his family for financial gain.

5:20. The Ninth Commandment: The command to not **bear false witness against your neighbor** deals with how one treats people in a legal environment and once again speaks of faithfulness within the covenant community. Integrity and truthfulness are to characterize God's people.

5:21. The Tenth Commandment: The last prohibition in the Decalogue is the only command that is not clearly visible in outward behavior. Coveting is a sin of the heart and is the basis of all the other sins addressed in the Ten Commandments. The order of "wife" and "house" is reversed from the Exodus account, and "field" is added. This may reflect the rising status of women's rights in conjunction with the matter of inheritance laws granted to Zelophehad's daughters (Nm 36).

5:22-26. The sacredness of the Ten Commandments is highlighted because of the unforgettable backdrop of their original setting **from the midst of the fire, of the cloud and of the thick gloom, with a great voice** and because **He added no more** commands. While the people were afraid of what they were experiencing, they sent all the tribal heads and **elders** to act as mediators. A popular notion (Jdg 13:22) was that if anyone saw God he or she would immediately die (although it was not the case with Jacob in Gn 32:30 and later with Moses in Ex 33:11). The nation saw that Moses was still alive after his encounter with God. Still they were not convinced that they would survive seeing God, so they volunteered Moses to be the intermediary, promising that they would obey whatever he received from God.

5:27–6:3. The Lord was pleased with the people's response to **hear** and obey (**do**) His word, and He hoped that this same attitude of reverence and submission would always be characteristic of them (vv. 28-29). After they were dismissed to their tents, Moses was to remain with God and receive additional legislation for the people to **observe . . . in the land** (v. 31). With a rhetorical flourish, Moses associated the nation's obedience with a long prosperous stay in the land they were to possess.

The subject matter at the end of chap. 5 dovetails with the beginning of chap. 6 as shown in the chiasm to follow. All pivot on the injunction in v. 32, **you shall not turn aside to the right or to the left**, summarizing the nation's need for strict obedience to God's commandments.

Moses' purpose of structuring this passage in this way is to clearly define these verses as a unit (in this case it crosses a chapter division!) and to focus on the outside verbal injunction (to "hear/listen" 5:27/6:3) and the pivot in the middle where the nation was **not** to **turn aside to the right or to the left** (5:32).

To live long in the land (5:31, 33) the nation was to listen to (**hear**, 5:27; 6:3) God's commandments (5:29; 6:1) by fearing (reverencing; 5:29; 6:2) Him and not deviating (5:32) in their obedience.

Structure of Deuteronomy 5:27–6:3

A hear (Hb. *shema*) . . . speaks (Hb. *dabar*) to you (5:27)
 B fear . . . keep all My commandments . . . sons (5:29)
  C commandments and the statutes and the judgments . . . teach (5:31)
   D land which I give them to possess (5:31)
    E you shall observe to do just as the LORD your God has commanded you (5:32)
     F you shall not turn aside to the right or to the left (5:32)
    E' You shall walk in the way which the LORD your God has commanded you (5:33)
   D' land which you will possess (5:33)
  C' commandment, the statutes and the judgments . . . teach (6:1)
 B' son . . . fear . . . keep . . . His commandments (6:2)
A' listen (Hb. *shema*) . . . promised (Hb. *dabar*) you (6:3)

6:4. This is one of the key verses in the entire OT. It has been designated, "The *Shema*," which comes from the Hebrew word **Hear**. The summons for Israel to hear is stated here for the second time in the book (5:1) and clearly is meant to cause the nation to pay strict attention and obey the instructions of this passage. This verse is the core credo statement of Judaism. Yet it is challenging to translate because of the number of ways in which the Hebrew can be understood. The first words can be interpreted as either a predicated statement, **The LORD is our God** (supplying a helping verb), or as a nominal phrase ("The **LORD** our God"). The predicated statement is unlikely here since the clause "The Lord is our God" is not likely to be understood that way in any of the 21 uses in the book (cf. 1:6,20; 6:20, 24). The real crux is whether the last word in the verse is to be translated as an adjective "one" (**The LORD is one**) or as an adverb "alone" ("the **LORD** alone"). Either translation is possible, and perhaps this is a rare instance of intentional ambiguity to allow for both notions. The wording, however it is translated, would imply monotheism, and other passages in Deuteronomy (e.g., 32:39) support that notion as well. If it is an adjective ("one"), then this would allow for the doctrine of the Trinity since elsewhere in the Pentateuch the Hebrew word *'ehad* can designate a compound unity as in the case of two people (Adam and Eve) being "one" (*'ehad*) flesh (Gn 2:24). In light of the immediate context in Dt 6, it may be better to take the last word as an adverb. The Ten Commandments clearly call for the worship of God *alone* ("no other gods before Me," 5:7), and verses in the immediate context (5:13-15) elaborate further on worshiping Him exclusively for His uniqueness. Although the doctrine of the Trinity is an important truth, it does not seem to be the focus in this verse.

6:5. The faith statement of the *Shema* is followed up by the charge to **love the LORD your God**, implying complete devotion to Him and not just emotional attraction. Moses' sense of love is to express loyalty to Him **with all your heart and with all your soul and with all your might**. The whole person is to express this loyal devotion to God. The **heart** was generally associated in Hebrew thinking with the mind, the **soul** denoted the innermost being or emotions, and **might** refers to doing the previous two injunctions exceedingly (lit., "very, very much"). The repetition of the word "all" shows that Israel's commitment to the Lord was to be undivided and complete.

6:6-9. Moses stated that these divine instructions were to **be on your heart**. Since "heart" refers more to the mind and intellect than to one's emotions, the Israelites were to meditate and reflect on these commandments, as Jos 1:8 stressed later. These were to be taught diligently to their children, not in the sense of a formalized education, but throughout the everyday common experiences of life: **when you sit in your house and when you walk by the way and when you lie down and when you rise up**. The command to **bind them as a sign on your hand and . . . as frontals on your forehead** (v. 8) designates that God's instructions were to be constant reminders to guide all their actions (suggested by "hand") as well as how they viewed the world (suggested by "forehead"). They were also to be written **on the doorposts of your house and on your gates**, meaning that God's laws were to be obeyed in the home ("doorposts") and in the greater community ("gates"). Although later Judaism later took these commands literally in the use of phylacteries (Mt 23:5) and mezuzoth (Dt 6:4-9 and 11:13-21 written on miniature scrolls, placed in small cases, and affixed to a home's doorposts), it is better to understand these injunctions as to be taken figuratively.

6:10-15. These verses contain a warning against Israel being too complacent after they entered the land and were enjoying the bounty and prosperity of its provisions. The Israelites would enjoy the fruit of others' labors and in which they did not personally invest (vv. 10-11). But in partaking of those wondrous blessings there was the danger of not being watchful and forgetting **the Lord** who brought them out of **Egypt . . . the house of slavery** (v. 12) This thought is later echoed in Pr 30:7-9. Prosperity has a way of causing forgetfulness. The way to prevent spiritual amnesia is to **fear only the Lord** and **worship** only **Him** (v. 13) When Satan tempted Jesus, offering Him all the kingdoms of the earth if Jesus would only bow down to him, Jesus cited this verse (Dt 6:13) to rebuke him (see the comments on Mt 4:10).

Moses then expanded on the topic of the Lord's uniqueness and exclusivity. They were **not** to **follow** after **other gods**, specifically those of the neighboring nations for the **Lord your God . . . is a jealous God**. God wanted their complete devotion and loyalty; if they forgot Him He would wipe them off the **face of the earth**. This does not mean that God would potentially break His promise to Abraham (Gn 12:1-8; 15:1-21; 17:1-22), but rather that disobedience might cause Him to destroy a generation completely and start Israel anew.

6:16-19. The Israelites were further instructed not to put **the Lord your God to the test, as you tested Him at Massah** (Ex 17:7). There they lacked water, and instead of trusting God to meet their needs they grumbled against Him. Jesus cited Dt 6:16 when rejecting the Devil's temptation to jump from the pinnacle of the temple and let His angels rescue Him (see the comments on Mt 4:5-7). For the nation to have success and longevity in the land they needed to adhere diligently to God's commands.

6:20-25. Here Moses returned to the subject of teaching children, begun in 6:7. He instructed parents to have a ready response when their offspring asked them the meaning of all these laws (v. 20). They were to rehearse the history of their slavery in Egypt and also to tell of the Lord's miraculous deliverance, bringing them out of **Egypt** and into the **land which He had sworn to our fathers** (vv. 21-23). As a result of God's work on their behalf they were to obediently **observe all these statutes, to fear the Lord [their] God for [their] good always and for [their] survival** (v. 24). Obedience would result in **righteousness** (v. 25). This may have several possible meanings. It could refer to (1) physical deliverance (Is 46:13), (2) saving acts accomplished on their behalf by God (Jdg 5:11), or (3) a right relationship with the Lord as in the case of Abraham (Gn 15:6). But in this context it seems best to understand it in the sense of enjoying the covenant blessings (prosperity and longevity in the land, cf. Ps 24:5, where righteousness is synonymously paired with blessing), since keeping the law is not the basis for righteousness but is instead the outward demonstration of covenant loyalty.

7:1. In keeping with the concept that the book of Deuteronomy is loosely based structurally on expounding the Ten Commandments (see discussion on Dt 5:6-21), chap. 7 expands on the first commandment, which states that Israel was to worship no other gods. By annihilating the current occupants and by tearing down any vestiges of their worship, Israel would be more apt to live in obedience to the first commandment.

This verse lists seven nations, which connotes the totality of the population of the Canaanite people groups. Amalek is another group of people living in the land of Canaan (Ex 17:8-16; Nm 13:29) not mentioned in this list, so the list was not meant to be exhaustive. These Canaanite nations were collectively **greater and stronger** than

Israel. Many of the nations listed are not readily identifiable. The **Hittites** had a clear presence in Canaan already (Gn 23:10; 27:46) but are historically most associated with Asia Minor. The **Girgashites**, who descended from Noah's son Ham (Gn 10:15-16) were possibly located in Asia Minor or the Transjordan. The **Amorites** had an established connection with Canaan (Gn 14:13). This nation denoted the Canaanite nations in general (Gn 15:16) and occupied territory in Canaan (1:19-20) as well as the Transjordan (Nm 21:13). The **Canaanites**, who descended from Noah's grandson Canaan (Gn 10:6), were seen as the ancestor of many of the nations in the region and had far-reaching territorial boundaries "from Sidon as you go toward Gerar, as far as Gaza; as you go toward Sodom and Gomorrah and Admah and Zeboiim, as far as Lasha" (Gn 10:19). The **Perizzites** are often combined with the Canaanites (Gn 13:7; 34:30) as an entity that stands for a larger grouping of nations. They were elsewhere located in the hill country of Canaan (Jos 11:3). The **Hivites** descended from Ham (Gn 10:17). They were generally located in the central part of Israel from Gibeon (Jos 9:7; 11:19) to Shechem (Gn 34:2). The **Jebusites** descended from Ham's son Canaan (Gn 10:16). They were in the hill country of Canaan (Nm 13:29) and were the original inhabitants of Jerusalem (Jos 15:63).

7:2-6. God's call to exterminate all the people groups currently occupying the land has been thought of as unloving and severe. Several factors may help explain the reasons such a command was given. First, all people are sinners and are under God's judgment. Only by God's mercy are any people groups allowed to live. Second, the context (7:10) implies that these nations hated the Lord, so they were not neutral toward the God of Israel. Third, Gn 15:13 states that God had been patient with these nations for hundreds of years and had delayed their punishment until this exact point in history. God was giving the Canaanites as much time as was needed to become as wildly corrupt as possible. God's command to annihilate them is tied to this circumstance alone and should not be used as justification for any genocide. Fourth, if Israel let these nations live in their land, their pagan practices would be propagated and emulated by the people of God (Dt 20:17-18). Fifth, the command to exterminate the Canaanite nations is mitigated somewhat by God's allowing individual non-Jewish women like Rahab and Ruth to enter into the messianic line. God always had a plan that included the nations (Gn 12:2-3), but He promised Israel they would occupy this land as gift from Him. Israel was actually to offer peace with any nation outside her borders (Dt 20:10-18), but to exterminate any pagan nation within its borders. Even though not specifically mentioned here, extending annihilation to Canaanite children is an affront to modern sensibilities. The totality of this destruction is connected in this text (v. 3) to the prohibition of assimilation to other nations. If these children were allowed to live they would become a snare for Israel. The killing of all Canaanites, including the children, served as a preventative measure against assimilating with the Canaanite way of life and as a stark reminder that Israel was to be set apart exclusively for God.

A major concern in these verses is that there was not to be any intermarriage with people of other nations in the land, lest they turn their **sons away from following Me to serve other gods** (v. 4). Any vestige of their religious practices like their **altars . . . sacred pillars** (male fertility objects), **Asherim** (female consorts of Baal), and **images** was to be torn down or burned (v. 5). The reason for this extermination policy was that Israel was **a holy people to the Lord** (v. 6). He had chosen them to be **a people for His own possession out of all the peoples who are on the face of the earth** (v. 7). The initiative was God's, and He wanted them be His exclusive representative nation.

7:7-11. These verses give the grounds for God's selection of the nation. The **Lord did not set His love** on them because they were vast in number, for they **were the fewest of all peoples** (v. 7). God's sovereign covenantal love was set in motion on one man Abraham (Gn 12:1-2), whose family then grew in size to 70 (Dt 10:22) and then ultimately to the size it was at this point in their history. The Lord kept His oath with their forefathers and redeemed Israel by bringing them out with **a mighty hand** from **slavery** in Egypt (v. 8). By doing so He was demonstrating that they truly were "His own possession" and retained this status (v. 6). This status was another outgrowth of the first of the Ten Commandments—that they were to have no other gods before Him. The nation was not to worship any other possible god because the *Lord* chose them, redeemed them, loved them, and kept His promise to them; therefore they were exclusively His. Israel was to reflect on the nature of their God, remembering that He is **faithful**, so faithful in fact that He continues **His lovingkindness to a thousandth generation with those who love Him and keep His commandments** (v. 9) This expression signifies that He will be faithful in His covenant-love to them forever. However, those who hate (reject) Him will be repaid without delay (v. 10). While His faithfulness is sure and long, His judgment will be direct and swift. Moses concluded this section with another reminder to **keep the commandment and the statutes and the judgments** (v. 11). These multiple designations of the law often serve as division markers within the text (4:1, 40; 6:1, 20; 8:11; 10:13; 11:1, 32; 12:1; 26:16; 30:16).

7:12-16. When the Israelites would give attention to and obey these laws, the Lord would honor His side of the covenant and bestow His lovingkindness on them (v. 12). These blessings would flow out of His love and result in their increased fertility, not only in the number of offspring but also in abundant harvests and flocks (vv. 13-14). This blessing would be evident to all because there would be no barrenness throughout the land and no illness would befall them. In addition, their military conquests would be successful. In the process they should not be tempted to show mercy to the Canaanites because their negative influence could lead them astray (v. 16). Moses again emphasized the first of the Ten Commandments by enjoining them not to **serve their gods, for that would be a snare to you** (v. 16).

7:17-26. Moses now addressed Israel's potential fears in carrying out these injunctions to wipe out the Canaanites from the land. If they thought they did not have the strength to dispossess them, then Israel should think of what the Lord had done for them in the exodus event (vv. 17-19). In addition the **LORD** would **send the hornet against them** to deal with any who would try to escape (v. 20). The **hornet** may refer to literal insects that would come alongside Israel's soldiers to assist them. Or the **hornet** may refer to some sort of foreign military force that "softened up" the Canaanites before the Israelite conquest. Or metaphorically it may mean that the Canaanites would respond in panic to their arrival as if they were being attacked by a swarm of hornets. Exodus 23:27-28 uses this word in tandem with the word "terror," so the metaphorical view is the more likely. Whatever the hornet was, the Israelites were not to fear the enemy because God was in their midst and He would help **clear away these nations** (v. 22). This conquest would take place gradually (**little by little**). Otherwise the land would too quickly be void of those who could keep the population of wild beasts from growing too quickly. The Lord would throw the nations into great confusion and would deliver their kings over to them for execution so that their exploits and their legacy in the land would be forgotten (vv. 23-24). During the conquest the graven images were to be totally burned up, even if they were made of precious metals that could be extracted. No religious objects were to be taken as spoil and brought into any of their houses, regardless of monetary value (vv. 25-26).

8:1. Moses reiterated that the Israelites needed to be careful to obey all that he was commanding them so that they **may live . . . multiply, and . . . possess the land . . . the LORD** promised to give them. Moses' repeated use of the word **today** in the book of Deuteronomy (2:18; 9:3; 11:32) highlights the need of that generation to respond appropriately to the covenant, but it also adds a sense of immediacy for all subsequent readers to respond appropriately to God's commands as well.

8:2-10. Remembering the Lord's past guidance during their 40 years in the wilderness gave motivation for Israel to keep the Lord's commandments in the future. God allowed their time spent in the wilderness to **humble** them and to see if they would obey the covenant (v. 2). God was **testing** them, not because He was ignorant, but so that Israel's commitment or lack thereof could be disclosed. The Lord ordained that they experience physical hunger, and then He supernaturally gave them **manna**. He did this to provide what their physical bodies needed and to emphasize that man does not live by physical **bread alone**, but also by spiritual food (commandments and teaching) that **proceeds out** of His **mouth** (v. 3). This mention of food echoes back to the first temptation in the garden of Eden—which pertained to food. Jesus cited this (Dt 8:3) in resisting the Devil's temptation for Him to turn stones into bread (see the comments on Mt 4:4).

Besides giving Israel nourishment in the wilderness, God also did not allow their clothes to wear out. Nor did any of them suffer from swollen feet (v. 4), though they were walking on hot, rough terrain. His treatment of them during the wilderness period was based on His desire to discipline them for their good (v. 5), not out of any vindictiveness on His part. In keeping with the theme of discipline, Moses again reminded the Israelites to **keep the commandments of the LORD your God, to walk in His ways and**

to fear Him (v. 6). He disciplined them so that they would be prepared to enter and receive the **good land**. This land had an abundant supply of different water sources (**brooks . . . fountains and springs**) as well as fields, vineyards, and orchards, all yielding abundant produce and even rich minerals for mining (vv. 7-9). All these gracious provisions were to be enjoyed and were reminders to bless the **LORD** for the good land He benevolently furnished for them (v. 10).

8:11-20. Moses warned Israel **not** to **forget the LORD . . . by not keeping His commandments**. Moses cautioned them ahead of time not to let pride creep into their hearts, nor to forget that everything they enjoyed came directly from the Lord. If they did **forget the LORD . . . and go after other gods and serve them and worship them** (v. 19), the consequences would be severe, and they would perish. They would experience destruction as Sihon and Og encountered (Nm 21:33-34; Dt 1:4; 3:3), and it would be because of their own disobedience to the **voice of the LORD**.

9:1-6. Moses reminded his audience of the enormity of the task before them in having to uproot nations, greater and mightier than their own—nations that were great, tall, and living in **fortified** cities (vv. 1-2). This same information caused them to be afraid after the spies' report in Nm 14, so Moses was resurfacing this data to caution them against repeating that incident of unbelief. Since the Lord would go before them as a **consuming fire**, all they needed to do was follow after Him and **drive them out and destroy them quickly** (v. 3).

Earlier (in 8:17), Moses said the Israelites might be tempted to think that their physical ability allowed them to prosper in the promised land. Here he spoke against another potential temptation: to attribute their success in the land to their own **righteousness** (vv. 5-6). Moses stressed that their success in driving out the nations dwelling in the promised land would be because of the Canaanites' **wickedness**, not the Israelites' goodness. In addition the Lord would be fulfilling an oath to Israel's forefathers rather than rewarding them for good behavior. In truth, the **good land** was being given to them as a gracious gift despite Israel being a **stubborn people** (v. 6), as Moses would soon attest in the examples given later in this chapter.

9:7-14. Next Moses presented a clear illustration of their stubbornness by recalling the incident of the golden calf (Ex 32). Continuing his exposition of the Ten Commandments, Moses stressed that the Lord alone was their God and that they were not to make any idols (v. 7; see Dt 5:8). The premier example of idol-making **at Horeb** happened at the very time Moses was up on the mountain for **forty days and nights**, so he did not want them to forget such an egregious sin of provocation. While Moses was fasting in preparation for receiving the two stone tablets written by the finger of God, the nation was feasting and was forging a **molten image** (v. 12). The imagery of fire is a repeated theme in this section: God is "a consuming fire" (9:3), the Lord spoke out of the **midst of the fire** (v. 10), and the mountain **was burning with fire** (v. 15). In contrast to fire surrounding God's presence, the people were using fire of their own in making a molten calf (9:12, 16).

Verses 6-13 form a chiasm, with the pivot (v. 10) focusing on the **two tablets of stone written by the finger of God** containing the Ten Commandments. The structure is bookended by the statements about Israel's stubbornness (vv. 6, 13).

Structure of Deuteronomy 9:6-13

A a stubborn people (9:6)
 B left the land of Egypt (9:7)
  C I went up (9:9)
   D tablets of the covenant (9:9)
    E forty days and nights (9:9)
     F The LORD gave . . . the two tablets of stone written by the finger of God (9:10)
    E' forty days and nights (9:11)
   D' tablets of the covenant (9:11)
  C' Arise, go down (9:12)
 B' you brought out of Egypt (9:12)
A' a stubborn people (9:13)

By use of this structure, Moses was stressing the nation's stubbornness (the initial bookended item) and also highlighting the center element where the Lord's grace provided a handwritten copy of the Ten Commandments. As a result of their rebellion God sought to **destroy them and blot out their name under heaven** and start a new nation with Moses (v. 14).

9:15-21. This section records Moses' reaction to the golden-calf incident, giving his perspective as he came down from the mountain and personally witnessed their sin of making an idol (vv. 15-16). His response to their rebellion was to smash the two tablets to demonstrate his disgust at their sin and to provide a visual reminder that the nation had violated the covenant (v. 17). In his role as mediator Moses fell down before the

Lord for another 40-day period without eating or drinking, to intercede for the nation on behalf of their sin (v. 18). The Lord listened to Moses' prayers (vv. 26-29) for both the nation and his brother Aaron, who was instrumental in making the golden-calf idol (vv. 19-20). Moses **burned** the idol and then crushed it, ground it into fine powder, and threw it into their drinking supply (v. 21; see also Ex 32:20).

9:22-24. Moses described four more examples to prove that they were a rebellious nation (vv. 6, 13). The locations of these offenses were at **Taberah** (Nm 11:1-3), **Massah** (Ex 17:1-7), **Kibroth-hattaavah** (Nm 11:31-34), and **Kadesh-barnea** (Nm 13-14). Taberah was located three days north of Mt Sinai (Nm 10:33) and was named for the fire that God sent there as judgment (Nm 11:3). Kibroth-hattaavah was located somewhere between Mt. Sinai and Hazeroth, but its exact site is not known. The name means "graves of greed" and is connected to the account of quails (Nm 11:34). Kadesh-barnea is an oasis in northeast Sinai on the southern border of the wilderness of Zin (Jos 15:3), about 85 miles southeast of Jerusalem. The sin of the people was disobedience to the Lord's commands—and also unbelief. Their rebellious ways were characteristic of them from the beginning.

9:25-29. Moses resumed talking about his prayer (vv. 18-19) and recorded the content of his intercessory petition, which lasted **forty days and nights** (v. 25). This prayer actually resulted from the golden-calf incident (and not the additional rebellions listed in vv. 22-23), but the litany of these additional rebellions underscores the importance of Moses' intercessory prayer. The Lord wanted to **destroy** the people, but Moses reminded the Lord of His promises to Abraham, Isaac, and Jacob, which would have been nullified if He had started over with Moses (vv. 26-27). Moses argued on the basis of maintaining the Lord's testimony before other nations, lest they say that **the LORD was not able to bring them into the land which He had promised them and because He hated them He has brought them out to slay them in the wilderness** (v. 28). Moses urged God to be mindful that Israel was still His **inheritance**, as rebellious as they were.

10:1-5. Moses' prayer was effective in preserving the nation because the Lord instructed him to **cut . . . two tablets of stone like the former ones, and come up to Me on the mountain** (v. 1). This meant that the covenant with Israel was still in effect. In addition Moses was instructed to make an ark (a chest) of wood to contain the tablets (cf. Ex 34:1). This ark was most likely the precursor to the ark of the covenant, which Bezalel later artistically fashioned (Ex 37:1-9). After Moses went up the mountain, the Lord **wrote . . . the Ten Commandments** on the two tablets (v. 4). Each of the two tablets most likely contained a full set of all the commandments, representing a copy for each party to this covenant, which would then be safeguarded in the ark.

10:6-11. These verses are a historical parenthesis on matters that are not necessarily chronological, but thematic, tying together a number of elements Moses had been addressing. The last geographical location mentioned was Horeb, where Moses received the Ten Commandments, but now the wilderness-wandering period is fast-forwarded to their departure from **Beeroth Bene-jaakan to Moserah**, much later than their departure from Mt. Horeb (cf. Nm 33:31). Beeroth Bene-jaakan is an unknown site near the border of Edom and means "well of Jaakan's sons." The exact location of Moserah is also uncertain, but it was near Mt. Hor on Edom's border (cf. Nm 20:25-26). These names place the events near the end of the wandering period when **Aaron** died (Nm 20:28). The Lord had told Moses (Ex 32:10) that he could start a new nation with him (Moses was from the tribe of Levi). Even though Moses did not actually become an Abraham-like founder of a new Israelite nation, there was still a special place for the tribe of Levi (even with Aaron gone) in the future of Israel. The Levites received the honor of being **set apart . . . to carry the ark of the covenant** and **to stand before the LORD** serving and blessing Him (v. 8). The tribe of Levi received no land allotment, but the LORD Himself was their inheritance (v. 9). Inheritance generally referred to the plot of land assigned to each tribe. Since the tribe of Levi was not apportioned any land, the Levites' support came from their work as priests. The Lord blessed the tribe of Levi, seemingly because of Moses' intercessory mediatorial act on behalf of the rebellious nation at Horeb. At the end of the second 40-day time frame the **LORD listened** to Moses and did not **destroy** the people.

10:12-22. Moses signaled a conclusion to this address by the words **Now, Israel** (cf. 4:1). He summarized the message by asking the rhetorical question, **what does the LORD your God require from you**? (v. 12). The definitive answer is to **fear the LORD your God, to walk in all His ways and love Him, and to serve the LORD your God with all**

your heart and with all your soul, and to keep the LORD's commandments and His statutes which I am commanding you today for your good. This is an appropriate way to summarize his message which began in 4:44 and ends at 11:32. Many of the key verbs are repeated from this larger section (i.e. "fear" 5:29; 6:13, "walk" 5:33; 8:6, "love" 6:5; 7:9, "serve" 5:9; 8:19, "keep" 6:2; 8:6).

Moses sought to foster total commitment to the Lord, not only because of His sovereignty, since to Him **belong heaven** and **earth** (v. 14), but also because God was continuing to demonstrate His love for the descendants of their **fathers**, whom He intentionally **chose** (v. 15). The intended result was that the people were to **circumcise** their **heart** (mind and emotions) and **stiffen** their necks (their wills) no longer (v. 16). Circumcision was an outward sign of conformity to the covenant, but Moses here was saying that an inner conformity of the heart to the LORD was more important. Another purpose Moses had in mind for this message was to encourage the people to execute justice to those less fortunate in their midst (vv. 17-19). The **awesome God . . . does not show partiality** or take bribes, so neither should the Israelites as they interacted with the **orphan . . . widow** and **alien** in their midst. Micah later captured the embodiment of this section (Mc 6:8). To elicit praise for God, Moses reminded them of the **great and awesome things** God did for them which were visibly demonstrated before their own eyes (v. 21). Another proof of His love is that Israel, starting with only **seventy persons** had now multiplied in size **as numerous as the stars of heaven** (v. 22).

11:1-7. This section continues the conclusion Moses began in 10:12 and repeats the call to **love the LORD** and **keep** . . . His **commandments.** The sermonic style of Moses' speech is evident with the use of such phrases as **know this day** (v. 2), heightening the rhetorical effect not only for the original audience but also for all subsequent readers. Note whom Moses was addressing here. He was not addressing the original adult generation (those over 20) who came out of Egypt, rebelled at Kadesh-barnea, and were sentenced to die in the wilderness.

At this point in the timeline Moses was addressing the second generation (those under 20 at the time of the exodus), just before they were about to enter the promised land. That first generation (except for Joshua and Caleb) had already died in the wilderness. Moses was focusing his attention on the second generation, since they were the ones who would actually enter the land. Moses here emphasized that he was not speaking to the offspring of that second generation (i.e., third generation) since they neither experienced the exodus nor observed the main disciplinary judgment that God executed on the first generation in the wilderness (such as when Dathan and Abiram were swallowed up by the earth, v. 6; see Nm 16:31-33). The second generation lived through these events, but they were not held accountable because they were under 20.The injunction to love the Lord (Dt 11:1) was based on their having seen with their own eyes their deliverance from Egypt (v. 7).

11:8-17. The word **therefore** underscores that the call to covenant loyalty, once they went in to **possess the land**, was based on what the Lord did for them in Egypt (vv. 8-10). The primary theme in this section is the land and that the covenant enjoyment of the land depended on their faithfulness, especially to the first two injunctions of the Ten Commandments. Covenant fidelity on their part would ensure prolonged days in the land, described by the oft-repeated proverbial phrase **flowing with milk and honey** (i.e., Ex 3:8; Dt 6:3, etc.). As bountiful as the food production was in Egypt, it still required human-engineered effort by the Egyptians to govern the irrigation process whenever the Nile River would overflow its banks. By contrast the land of Israel received the **rain of heaven** without any human effort (v. 11). It also was under the watchful **eyes of the LORD** (v. 12). The regularity of the **early and late rain** was conditioned on their being obedient to **love the LORD your God and to serve Him with all your heart and all your soul** (vv. 13-15). If they were deceived into serving or worshiping **other gods**, then the Lord's **anger** . . . would **be kindled**, and He would **shut up the heavens** so that there would be no rain or crops, and people would **perish quickly** in the land (vv. 16-17).

11:18-21. The offspring of the second generation did not see God's mighty hand at work in Egypt and in the wilderness (11:2) so these second-generation parents were to impress the Lord's words first on their own **heart** and **soul** (v. 18; cf. 6:5). This is symbolically pictured as binding them on their hands and foreheads to show that God's **words** were to be lived out in all they did (hands) and in how they viewed the world (foreheads; cf. the comments on 6:8). As the word was implanted in their own lives, then they would be able to **teach** their children, creating teachable moments all throughout the day

(v. 19; cf. 6:7). God's words were also to be written on the **doorposts** of each house and on the city **gates**, reflecting that God's word was to be lived out in the home and in the greater community at large (v. 20). As God's laws were lived privately at home and publicly in their cities, the Lord would multiply the days of their offspring in the land sworn to them for **as long as the heavens remain above the earth**—in perpetuity.

11:22-25. The Lord's promise to **drive out** the nations from the land was contingent on the Israelites being careful to keep His commandments and to **love the LORD your God, to walk in all His ways and hold fast to Him**, echoing again the need for covenant loyalty. The success of the conquest was based not on military prowess but on fidelity to the Lord. The borders were to be **from the wilderness** (the Negev in the far south) **to Lebanon, and from the river, the river Euphrates, as far as the western** (Mediterranean) **sea**. This is similar to other boundary descriptions (Gn 15:18; Ex 23:31; Nm 34:2-10; Dt 1:7-8).

11:26-32. As this speech of Moses drew to a close, it focused on the blessing and cursing stipulations, a common element of most covenant treaties of that time. This section bookends the next discourse of Moses (chaps. 12–26) with another blessing and cursing section in chaps. 27–28. The covenant renewal ceremony was to take place at another mountainous area (Mount Gerizim and Mount Ebal, located about 30 miles north of Jerusalem and just south and north, respectively, of the town of Shechem v. 29), similar to where the covenant was first established at Horeb (Mount Sinai). It was to take place in the midst of the Canaanite territory **opposite Gilgal, beside the oaks of Moreh** (v. 30). This Gilgal is not the one of Joshua's time (Jos 5:9) but a different place located 18 miles north of Jerusalem. The oaks of Moreh were a grove of trees near Shechem (Gn 12:6). The deliberate mention of the **oaks of Moreh** recalls the place where Abraham first built an altar (Gn 12:6-7) when he entered the land of Canaan. This raised the importance of Abraham and the covenant God established with him as well as the spiritual significance of the area (near Shechem, 30 miles north of Jerusalem) for worshiping God in the midst of Canaanites. Here Jacob buried under an oak tree all the foreign gods his family had accumulated while in Paddan-aram (Gn 35:4). If the nation was obedient, they would receive the blessings that would be recited on **Mount Gerizim**. But if they should **turn aside** and follow **other gods,** then they would receive the curse that was to be recited on **Mount Ebal** (v. 29). Moses finished this address with another reminder to be **careful to** observe **all the statutes and the judgments** (v. 32) God had given.

B. An Exposition of Selected Covenant Laws (12:1–25:19)

This longest section of Deuteronomy is a law code, but it is still presented in the hortatory style that has characterized chaps. 6–11. Even though a new section begins with chap. 12, a small chiastic seam stitches it together with the previous discourse, as can be seen in the next column.

In a structure like this the focus is on the initial bookended item (here the gift of land) and the center pivot, which stresses the immediacy of obeying the statutes and the judgments today.

Structure of Deuteronomy 11:31–12:1

A land (Hb. *eretz*) (11:31)
  B giving you, and you shall possess (11:31)
    C careful to do (11:32)
      D the statutes and the judgments (11:32)
        E which I am setting before you today (11:32)
      D' the statutes and the judgments (12:1)
    C' carefully observe (12:1)
  B' given you to possess (12:1)
A' earth (Hb. *eretz*) (12:1)

12:1. This is a superscription that begins this major block of material and is similar to the others used to structure the book (1:1; 4:44; 6:1; 12:1; 29:1; 33:1). The terms used to identify the type of law code found here are **statutes and the judgments.** These two Hebrew words are often paired together (4:1; 5:31; 6:1) and essentially mean much the same (like "rules and regulations"). The usage here has the effect of narrowing from general stipulations (Dt 5–11) to more specific commands.

12:2-3. Repeating what was commanded earlier (7:5), Moses told the people to **destroy** all the worship centers in the land, especially the ones associated with mountains and trees. Mountains were often the locations of cultic centers, and pagan worship was often carried on in groves of trees. Forests were not only important for providing timber for building projects in the ancient Near East but were also considered important symbols of fertility and hence readily associated with pagan practices (cf. Gn 12:6 where the "oak of Moreh" is juxtaposed next to "the Canaanite"). Abraham often erected altars by trees (e.g., Gn

13:18; cf. Dt 11:30), perhaps to counter the Canaanite practices associated with trees. Any objects related to worship were to be torn down or burned. The Israelites were to leave no trace and were to **obliterate their name from that place**.

12:4-14. For the first time in Deuteronomy, Moses developed the theme of a central sanctuary. "Central sanctuary" is a term scholars use to designate the place the Lord chose as the one center of worship for Israel. The Canaanites worshiped on hills and high mountains and by trees, but the Israelites were not to **act like this toward the LORD your God** (v. 4). Instead they were to **seek the LORD at the place which the LORD your God will choose** (v. 5). At one single place He would **establish His name** (v. 6). Establishing the Lord's name at this place is a repeated theme throughout the book (12:11, 21; 14:23-24; 16:2, 6, 11; 26:2). This could be wherever God instructed the tabernacle to be set up until it ultimately was centered at Jerusalem, but the focus was on only one designated national worship center, not multiple sites. At this one site they were to bring their **burnt offerings . . . sacrifices**, and **tithes** as well as other offerings. At only one place could grateful worshipers share a sacred communal meal **before the LORD** (v. 7). In the wilderness wandering period every man was doing **whatever** was **right in his own eyes** (v. 8), since they had not **as yet come to the resting place and the inheritance which the LORD your God** would give them (v. 9). However, when they did cross the Jordan and lived in the land, then they were obligated to worship and **rejoice before the LORD** there (vv. 10-12). They were forbidden to offer any **burnt offerings** at any cultic place they came across; they were to offer sacrifices only in the **place in which the LORD your God will choose** (v. 11).

12:15-28. With all animal sacrifices to be offered at one designated location (vv. 11, 14), Moses elaborated on the killing of animals, whether for food or worship. Animals, whether wild game or domesticated, could be slaughtered for meat within any of their communities without any regard for who could eat it. The people were forbidden to **eat the blood** for it was to be poured out **on the ground** instead (v. 16). Since blood represents life (Lv 17:10-12) it was to be considered sacred and not consumed, and it should be properly disposed of whenever an animal was killed intentionally. They were also prohibited from eating anything at home (**within your gates**, v. 17) that was to be offered as a sacrifice, because the only designated place to **eat** those offerings **before the LORD** was in the central sanctuary.

Since Levites were not granted tribal allotment, Moses instructed the people not to **forsake** them as long as they would **live in [their] land** (v. 19) Presumably in this discussion about food, Moses wanted to be sure the rest of the nation provided food for the Levites. Placing instructions about Levites between two almost identical sections on the eating of meat was perhaps intentional to highlight the need to focus on their well-being and not just on their performance as religious figures in the tabernacle. Whatever the case, the Lord clearly allowed for the consumption of meat and did not restrict its use for personal dietary preference. This was particularly the case for those who lived a great distance from the central sanctuary and does not contradict the injunction to bring sacrifices only to the tabernacle/temple. Moses repeated most of the instructions here (vv. 20-28; cf. vv. 15-18) regarding the killing and eating of animals. For the original audience who most likely heard it orally, this repetition would aid in their comprehending these instructions. Moses repeated his warning to **be careful to listen to all these words which I command you** (v. 28), as he had done earlier in this section (vv. 13, 19, 28). This assumes that the people were stubborn and in need of constant admonition to do **what is good and right in the sight of the LORD**.

12:29-32. In keeping with the theme of destroying all vestiges of Canaanite worship practices (v. 2), Moses stated again that in addition to tearing down and burning all their religious symbols, the people were not to engage in the religious practices of the Canaanites, even out of curiosity. They chanced becoming **ensnared** in following after these gods and even incorporating some of their abhorrent pagan rituals into their worship practices. The reason for not emulating any of their cultic practices is that the Canaanites performed **every abominable act which the LORD hates**, even to the point where they were burning **their sons and daughters in the fire to their gods**. Israel was to follow meticulously the Lord's commands without adding or taking away from them. This last verse in chap. 12 (v. 32) best fits as the introduction to the next section as it does in the Hebrew Masoretic text.

13:1-5. This section describes three cases where the nation might be tempted to go after other gods. The nation could be drawn away by a false prophet, a close family member, or even an entire city that had apostatized. The focus of placing these instructions here would be to expand on the second commandment (have no other gods before me, Dt 5:7) since that is certainly what these false prophets would be calling the people to do. A prophet here is one who speaks on behalf of another. One can be a "prophet" for another person (as Aaron was for Moses, Ex 7:1) or for a deity. Moses does not stipulate that these particular prophets are "false prophets," but that is what he intends by the term in this passage.

A real danger was present **if a prophet or a dreamer of dreams** arose from within the nation who would then give a **sign or a wonder** that ultimately came to fruition (vv. 1-2). Based on the accuracy of that one prophecy, the false prophet might entice others to **go after other gods** and **serve them** (v. 2). Prophets were respected people in the ancient Near East, so the threat would be a serious one if a false prophet was able to predict events correctly or perform wonders. If that prophet or dreamer did successfully get individuals to worship anyone but the Lord, the solution was simple: that prophet should be **put to death** because he **counseled rebellion** and seduced them **from the way** (v. 5). Although Jesus was put to death it does not necessarily mean that He was a false prophet since other true prophets were also put to death (2Ch 24:20-22; Mt 23:30). Even though some opponents of Christianity may appeal to this passage to justify their rejection of Jesus as Messiah (since He performed signs and wonders, v. 1, and then supposedly seduced people from the way, v. 5), Jesus clearly possessed all the qualities of a true prophet and brought people to a right understanding of the law. The Lord may actually ordain such a false prophet to arise to see if the nation truly does **love the Lord** with all their **heart** and **soul** (v. 3). Later Israel did not apply capital punishment to false prophets except in rare situations (1Kg 18:40). The solution was for the nation to **follow the Lord . . . fear Him . . . keep His commandments, listen to His voice, serve Him, and cling to Him** (v. 4), all injunctions that again envision covenant loyalty and faithfulness.

13:6-11. Even more threatening than a false prophet were cases in which a close family member enticed someone to serve other gods. One would be inclined not to tell that a loved one was guilty of this sin for fear of losing him or her to stoning. The clause **whom neither you nor your fathers have known** (v. 6) does not imply that they had never heard of these gods but rather that they had not been involved in worshiping them. The first step was not to **yield** or **listen** to such family members at all (v. 8), and the next step was not to **pity** them or attempt to **conceal** what they did. The family member who reported their wayward loved one was to be the first to be involved in the stoning (v. 9), and then other members of the community were to join in putting that enticer to death. The result would be that **all Israel** would **hear and be afraid** (v. 11) and others would be deterred from following in their path. Again Moses was stressing the importance of following the first commandment—not to have any other gods before Him.

13:12-18. A third example of people being enticed to follow after other gods was when an entire city had been taken over by some **worthless men** who in turn had introduced idolatry on a wide-scale basis in a local area. Instead of taking action based on hearsay, a thorough investigation was to be launched to determine the veracity of such a takeover (vv. 12-14). If it was found to be true, then the entire city should be struck with the **edge of the sword**, and the city and all its livestock should then be destroyed as well (v. 15). Anything valuable was to be collected and deposited in a heap in the middle of the town square and then offered to the Lord as **a . . . burnt offering** (v. 16). In addition the charred remains were to be left and the city was never again to be rebuilt, as a testimony to its unfaithfulness. Even though there was potential value in the booty, nothing **under the ban** was to be appropriated for personal use (v. 17). Such drastic measures and even financial losses were to be incurred so that the Lord's burning anger (against the city) would not come on the nation. Instead He would **show mercy** and **compassion** and make them prosperous, thereby making up for any financial shortfall experienced by not benefiting from their possessions. Moses concluded this section by again admonishing them with a passionate appeal to **listen to the voice of the Lord**, to keep **all His commandments**, and to continue **doing what is right in the sight of the Lord** (v. 18).

14:1-2. Moses moved from a rejection of Canaanite gods (via false prophets) to a rejection of individual Canaanite practices. This section deals with several matters of personal holiness, and the first concern pertains to mourning the dead. This is the first time the Israelites were called **sons of the Lord your God**, which speaks of their special familial relationship to God. In light of that intimate relationship the nation was not to **cut** themselves or **shave [their] forehead for the sake of the dead**. Cutting or gashing oneself was practiced even among later Hebrews (Jr 16:6) as a form of grief, but here it is expressly forbidden. Egyptians were known for their desire to be clean-shaven (Gn 41:14), and God's people were not to emulate that ritual when someone died. The nation was to be a **holy people to the LORD**, to be **His own possession**; therefore it was not appropriate to mimic mourning practices that did not convey an intimate relationship with the Lord.

14:3-21. Another concern related to personal holiness was the eating of food and the laws of kosher (as they became known in post-biblical Judaism). The nation was to eat no **detestable thing**. The types of foods the Israelites ate were an important matter to the Lord because they are related not just to diet but also to theology. While it is not always clear what specific animal is being mentioned in these verses, the animals were grouped according to the domain in which they lived. These included land animals, water creatures, and those whose domain is in the air. Land animals included domesticated animals such as oxen, sheep, and goats, and wild game animals such as deer, gazelles, wild goats, and others. These were to have divided hooves and to chew the cud (v. 6). Animals that do not meet these two criteria were forbidden to be eaten: these included camels, rabbits, the hyrax (a small rodent resembling a woodchuck, called in the NASB a **shaphan**), and pigs (vv. 6-8). No reason is given why these characteristics were determiners.

Holiness is a major focus in this passage (cf. they were to be "a holy people," 14:2), and it encompasses a wide variety of domains: spiritual, ritual, symbolic, and physical. The emphasis here is on the outward display of an internal condition in that what the Israelites ate was to reflect a clear fixed picture of external holiness. Clean animals were expected to meet a fixed standard (in this case animals that split the hoof and chew the cud). So any creature that did not meet that standard was considered unclean and therefore not emblematic of holiness. The same explanation would relate to the next category, describing creatures from the domain of water. Anything with **fins and scales** was permitted to be eaten, but all other creatures that live in the water were forbidden (vv. 9-10). Fish that were permitted were to picture the purity and holiness that the Israelites were to reflect even in their diet.

The third domain included creatures that occupy the sky. Clean birds were permitted to be eaten, but in this passage no example of clean birds is given. The list of unclean birds, however, includes the **eagle**, **vulture**, **buzzard**, **kite**, **raven**, **ostrich**, **owl**, **sea gull, hawk**, **pelican**, **stork**, **heron,** and **bat** (vv. 12-18). This may be because they are birds of prey that eat their catch without properly draining blood, or eat carrion, like vultures, also mentioned in the list.

Other miscellaneous food restrictions were given. The first is that the people were **not** to **eat anything which dies of itself** (v. 21). Aliens living in the community were permitted to eat it, or it could even be sold to foreigners for a profit. But if the cause of death for that animal could not be determined, or if that animal did not have its blood properly drained, then Israelites were not to eat it. The next command, **You shall not boil a young goat in its mother's milk** (v. 21, cf. Ex 23:19; 34:26) is puzzling. The typical explanation is that such an injunction reflects a Canaanite fertility practice. The scant evidence supporting this interpretation is based on a likely incorrect reconstruction of a thirteenth-century Ugaritic inscription that never mentions boiling the kid in the milk (Jacob Milgrom, "You Shall Not Boil a Kid in its Mother's Milk," *Bible Review* 1 [October 1985]: 48-55). This view, however, would fit the context here with its emphasis on purity and abstaining from practices associated with pagans. Another possible interpretation is to render the sentence, "You shall not boil a young goat *on* its mother's milk." In other words a baby kid was not to be eaten while still nursing. Respect for young animals is reflected elsewhere in the Pentateuch (Lv 22:27-28; Dt 22:6), so that is a possibility here. Possibly also the command expresses concern for the mother of the animal whose distress at the slaughter of her baby would be intolerable. But this does not seem to fit the subject of purity. Another interpretation, which goes back as far as Philo (*De Virtute* 143), is that this is a prohibition against mingling life with death: "You shall not take a goat and season it after its death with what brought it life." Just as other "separations" have been noted in this section (clean and unclean) here is another distinction that ought not to be crossed (life and death). In 14:1 Israelites were forbidden to show any symbol of death on their bodies while they were alive, so this view seems to fit the context and is the preferred view. The injunction is probably not related to the avoidance of eating milk with meat, a common Jewish understanding of the verse.

14:22-29. Moses moved to the topic of the tithe, but it too is related to the immediate context of food (13:3-21) in that it focuses on that portion of the tithe that can be eaten in the Lord's presence (14:23, 26). Moses instructed the people to **tithe all the produce from what you sow, which comes out of the field every year**, whether it be of grain, wine, oil, or of the firstborn of the flock (v. 22). This was so that they **may learn to fear the LORD** their God always (v. 23). If the distance would be too far from wherever the central sanctuary was located, they were permitted to **exchange it for money** and then repurchase whatever their **heart desires** and then **rejoice**, along with their household, **in the presence of the LORD** (vv. 23-26). The option of purchasing **wine** or **strong drink** and then consuming it in a communal fellowship meal does not encourage intoxication. Instead these were beverages valued as a part of celebration. The next legislation reminded each family to donate a portion of their tithe to the Levites since they had **no portion or inheritance** (v. 27). The word "tithe" comes from the Old English word *tenth* and was an early custom in the OT (cf. Gn. 14:20; 28:22). Tithing had two main features. It first represented a mandatory token repayment gift to God (14:22), recognizing that all produce and livestock came from Him. It also was the means to fund the court (1Sm 8:17), as well as priests and the needy. At the end of every third year a second tithe of the people's produce was to be deposited, not at the sanctuary, but in their hometown (v. 28). It was then to be distributed among the Levites (Nm 18:26-32), aliens, orphans, and widows so that they might **eat and be satisfied** and so that the Lord would continue to bless the work of their hands (v. 29). Thus a paradox was revealed: in order for the Israelites to receive more they had to give a tenth of it back to the Lord and to give a portion of their produce on a triennial basis to care for the underprivileged.

15:1-6. Continuing the theme of caring for the underprivileged (14:28-29), Moses gave instructions regarding the Sabbath year. The Sabbath year was earlier mentioned (Ex 23:10-11; Lv 25:1-22), whereby Israel was not to cultivate the land every seventh year. This may be an expanded exposition of the fourth commandment. *At the* **end of every seven years** every creditor **shall grant a remission of debts** that their fellow Israelites had incurred (v. 1). While the practice of debt remission may seem unfair to the lender (especially if he were to lend out money close to the Sabbath year), several points can be made in defense of the practice. The overall theme of this passage focuses on God's blessing the people, so it seems inevitable that God would richly bless the lender for his obedience, even if it made no financial sense to forgive a loan made so close to the Sabbath year. These verses also focus on the moral (not financial) principle behind the command to forgive loans. They were, in essence, debtors to God and morally responsible to likewise forgive debts to others. Debts, however, were still to be paid for any loans granted to a **foreigner** (v. 3). Mercy was to be extended to any Israelite who for whatever reason had taken out a loan (v. 2). As a result of complete obedience to the Lord and His commandments there would be **no poor among** them, since the Lord would **bless** them **in the land** and there would be more than enough for everyone (vv. 4-5). In fact there would be so much abundance that they would be able to **rule over many nations** and make loans to them instead of the other way around (v. 6).

15:7-11. Moses then discussed a different situation. If **a poor man** was with them **in any of** their **towns** then they were not to harden their hearts toward him (v. 7). Instead they were to be generous, lending him whatever amount he needed (v. 8). Also, lenders were not to withhold loans simply because little time was left before the next seven-year release (v. 9). If loans were not made, the poor person **may cry to the LORD against** the Israelite, and his failure to grant a loan would be a **sin**. Loans were not to be given with resentment, for the Lord would bless the creditors, making up for whatever financial losses they might incur. If they were completely loyal to the covenant, there would not be any poor in Israel (15:4). Moses realistically stated that there will always be poor . . . in the land because of unfaithfulness. But that did not free them from opening their hands to underprivileged Israelites in their midst.

15:12-18. Moses addressed the matter of indentured servants for those who had sold themselves into slavery to pay any debts. The word **kinsman** is the Hebrew word often translated "brother," and it is the seventh time that word has been used in this passage (15:2, 3, 7 [twice], 9, 11, 12). Interestingly this is the same number of times the word is used in the Cain and Abel account (in Gn 4). The repeated use of the term "brother" surfaces a key theme in Dt 15: the Israelites are responsible to care for their brothers just as Cain was for Abel. If an Israelite bought slaves, whether male or female, they were to serve only **six years** and then to be released in the **seventh** (v. 12). When slaves were released, they were to be given something material or financial so that they would not be going away **empty-handed** (v. 13). They should be given proceeds from the owner's flocks, crops, and wine vats (v. 14). The slaves had given of themselves in labor for six years and therefore should receive some benefit related to the tasks performed on behalf of their owners.

Since the entire nation had been enslaved to the Egyptians and was subsequently redeemed, so indentured Israelite servants should also be released from their servitude (v. 15). However, if a servant wished to remain as a slave because **he loves** his owner and **fares well** under his roof, then the owner **shall take an awl and pierce it through his ear into the door** as a sign of his commitment to his master (vv. 16-17). When the ear of the servant was pierced with an awl to the door of the master's house, the servant was stating lifelong loyalty to his owner. The pierced earlobe would testify to others that the servant had relinquished his personal rights. This is also the situation for female servants. To help soften the blow of releasing a servant in the seventh year, Moses reminded owners that they had been able to reap more than twice what it would have cost if they had hired day laborers to do what the servant had been doing for six whole years.

15:19-23. Why these instructions about consecrating **firstborn males** of animals are placed here is not entirely clear. One explanation is that these instructions fit with the other legislation in this chapter. That is, when there is a release of either debts or servants after six years, some may think of the economic loss that may also occur with the consecration of the firstborn. There was to be no economic benefit in the use of the firstborn animal (**you shall not work with** the animal, v. 19) for a firstborn animal must be taken every year to the central sanctuary for sacrifice and then eaten by the family in a communal meal **before the Lord** (v. 20). However, no firstborn male animal with any sort of defect could be sacrificed. Such an animal could be eaten at home much as one would eat wild game, but the blood had to be properly poured **out on the ground like water** (vv. 21-23; see also 12:16, 23, 24).

16:1-8. While on the topic of bringing firstborn male animals to the central sanctuary, Moses discussed the major religious holidays (16:1-17) when they would be brought there. The first holiday was **Passover** . . . in the **month of Abib** (from mid-March to mid-April), for it was in that month that the Lord brought them out of Egypt (v. 1). New information in this passage is that the Passover animal must be sacrificed at the central sanctuary, whereas earlier (Lv 23:4-8; Nm 28:16-25) the place was not specified because it was observed in private homes (v. 2). Along with the Passover, the Israelites were instructed to eat **unleavened bread** for **seven days** as a reminder that they had to leave Egypt **in haste** and did not have the normal time to cook leavened bread (v. 3). For that weeklong period no leaven was to be stored anywhere they dwelt, and none of the meat left over from the Passover meal was to be kept overnight for consumption at a later time (v. 4). In Egypt they were expected to leave in haste the next morning so there was no time to prepare the leftover meat or to cook leavened bread before they had to flee. Moses emphasized again that the Passover was to be observed only at the central sanctuary and not in their communities (v. 5). They were to cook and eat it at night (sundown the night before, v. 6) and then **in the morning** to return to their temporary quarters near the central sanctuary (v. 7). Since this section expanded on the fourth commandment related to the Sabbath, Moses stressed that on the seventh day of the festival they were to **do no work** (v. 8)

16:9-12. The second festival that required a pilgrimage to the central sanctuary was the **Feast of Weeks**. Elsewhere it is called the Feast of the Harvest (Ex 23:16) or "the day of the first fruits" (Nm 28:26). Its date was calculated **seven weeks** after a **sickle** was first used on the **standing grain**, signaling the beginning of harvest in March/April and so was celebrated in May/June, 50 days after Passover. The focal point of this festival was to celebrate the bountiful crops of that year. Regardless of economic or social status, all were to celebrate **before the Lord** joyously while presenting a **freewill offering**. The reminder that they were once slaves in Egypt was enjoined again (Dt 5:15; 15:15), so that they would be more grateful.

16:13-15. The third pilgrimage festival to the central sanctuary was the **Feast of Booths** (Tabernacles). This was another seven-day festival and was held seven days after the grain and grape harvests in September/October. The earlier festival (Feast of Weeks) was celebrated after the wheat harvest, and the Feast of Booths was celebrated after most of the other grains were harvested and the orchards ripened. Again (cf.

16:11) this was to be observed by all within the community, not just the landowners.

16:16-17. Moses stated that **three times . . . a year all . . . males** were to appear before the LORD at the central sanctuary for the three annual festivals just mentioned. Males were required to attend, but women and children were invited to participate if they were able (vv. 11, 14). All three celebrations involved bringing tribute, whether firstborn animals or freewill offerings. Each person was to give as he was able, in accord with God's blessings on him for that year.

16:18-20. This is the beginning of a new section that continues until 18:22. Moses had just appealed for compassion toward those in need and for worship of the LORD with rejoicing. Here he returned to the theme of chap. 13, which focused on the conduct of national and spiritual leaders. This passage deals with job descriptions for different officials within Israel. Having discussed commands dealing with covenant loyalty, Moses transitioned to human leaders who would have political and spiritual administrative responsibilities. The first officials to be discussed, because of their importance in maintaining justice, were the judges. Since Deuteronomy is a law code, it is fitting that Moses began with those who would arbitrate on legal matters. After the nation settled in the land, **judges and officers** were to be appointed for judging the **people with righteous judgment**. Earlier (1:9-18) Moses addressed the need for impartial judges to assist in administration, and here he gave additional instructions. Theses judges were in no way to **distort justice**, **be partial**, or **take a bribe**. Bribes were especially forbidden since they blind **the eyes of the wise**. Their main task was to pursue justice, because when justice characterized Israel they would remain alive and continue to **possess the land . . . the LORD** was **giving** them.

16:21-22. This section may seem out of place in an overall discussion of justice. Yet Moses may have been using the case of not setting up idols (16:1-2) and not sacrificing blemished animals (17:1) as a matter that judges (16:18-20) would need to watch over so that justice prevailed in the land. Besides overseeing civil matters judges were also tasked with supervising theological and religious issues and maintaining the Ten Commandments, especially the first two. Here the specific instruction was that no **Asherah** or **any kind of tree** was to be planted **beside the altar of the LORD** in the central sanctuary, or a **sacred pillar** anywhere. These were objects the Lord vehemently hated because they were associated with Canaanite fertility rites and were expressly forbidden by the first and second commandments.

17:1. This command prohibits the sacrificing of any defective or blemished animal. This could be seen as a further exposition of the third commandment, which prohibits taking the name of the Lord in vain. Sacrificing flawed animals would be seen as despising Him by offering Him unworthy gifts. Even though priests performed the sacrifices, it can be assumed, based on the context, that judges maintained authority to make sure there were no violations even over spiritual matters.

17:2-7. Judges were now commissioned to mete out capital punishment for covenant violators without distinction of gender (v. 2). Any **man or . . . woman** who does what is evil in the sight of the LORD was to be stoned, but only after the matter had been **thoroughly** investigated (v. 4) and only on the evidence of two or more witnesses (v. 6). One witness would not be enough to convict someone (19:15) because of the possibility of personal vendettas. To preserve the integrity of their statements in court, if the witnesses' statements were enough to sentence someone to death, then the witnesses themselves were to be the first to pick up stones in the execution (v. 7). This was a preventive measure, for if a witness lied, that would have been a grave matter. But to then go further and commit murder would, it was hoped, give them pause against making a false accusation in the first place. The bottom line is that purity was to be maintained, even if it meant implementing capital punishment to **purge the evil** from their midst (v. 7).

17:8-13. If local courts could not render a decision because the **case** was **too difficult**, such as determining **one kind of homicide or another**, then the case was to be brought to either the Levitical priest or an appointed judge there (perhaps both in conjunction) who would adjudicate the case (vv. 8-9). The officials deciding the case were to give the reasons for their decision and thus **teach** those present in the law (v. 11). Anyone who did not abide by his or her decision was to be put to death because the person was acting presumptuously (v. 12). The death sentence applied in these cases would **purge the evil** from the land, and it would also serve as a deterrent for anyone else rebelling against the authority of the priests and judges. For 17:10, see the comments on Mt 23:3.

17:14-20. In these verses Moses addressed the guidelines for a future king (v. 14). In the ancient Near East kings were granted almost unlimited power and authority. But such was not the case with Israel. A king's authority was severely regulated compared to neighbor nations. The Lord anticipated the nation's request for a king so that they could be **like all the nations** . . . around them, so He gave explicit instructions regarding their conduct. Several qualifications needed to be in place even before a king was to begin ruling. First, he must be one **whom the LORD your God chooses** (v. 15a, b), not one selected by the people or appointed by someone else. Second, he must not be a **foreigner** (v. 15c); the king must be a native Israelite. Third, he must **not multiply horses for himself** (v. 16). Horses were considered a military asset, and the king must not seek to amass a mighty military arsenal. Acquiring horses meant that the king would have to form trade alliances to secure them, and Moses prohibited the king from going to others, especially **Egypt, to multiply horses** since the **LORD has said . . . You shall never again return that way** (v. 16). Fourth, the king must **not multiply wives** (v. 17). Marriages were often entered into to secure political alliances, so the Israelite king was not to seek to consolidate power by forming alliances. Another danger in having multiple wives is that they could turn the king's **heart** away from the Lord, either because of their pagan religious background or because he was focused on meeting his own family needs over those of the nation. Fifth, the king must not multiply **silver and gold** for himself. The source of the nation's power was their relationship with God, not its treasuries. One of the major reasons for Solomon's later downfall was his failure to abide by these injunctions (1 Kg 10:14-15, 23, 26-28; 11:1-6).

Now that the kings' background (Dt 17:15) and behavior (vv. 16-17) were noted, Moses addressed the king's training. When any king came on the throne, he was to **write for himself a copy of this law on a scroll** (v. 18). His mind was to be filled with the content of this law (either the entire book of Deuteronomy or a subsection such as Dt 5–26). After having written a copy for himself, he was to keep it **with him** and **read it all the days of his life** (v. 19) so that these regulations would guide every decision he made. In the process he would **learn to fear the LORD his God**, and he would not be lifted up with pride **above his countrymen** (v. 20). If he observed all these stipulations without deviation, he and his sons would enjoy long, prosperous reigns.

18:1-8. Having discussed the political roles of the judges and the kings, Moses then focused on the spiritual duties of priests. Since the tribe of Levi had no tribal land allotment as did the other 11 tribes (v. 1), they were to receive provisions from the fire **offerings** brought to the Lord. The portions of the animal mentioned here (v. 3) differ somewhat from the legislation in Leviticus and Numbers (Lv 7:28-36; Nm 18:8-9). The previous legislation set aside the breast and the right thigh, whereas here the **shoulder . . . two cheeks** and . . . **stomach** were set aside. The difference may have been that the earlier passages dealt specifically with the peace offerings and other Levitical offerings, whereas Deuteronomy was dealing with other "freewill" or festival offerings. Also some modifications were made, and the overall thrust of this legislation was that Israel would adequately care for the Levitical tribe out of proceeds from the overall sacrificial system. The priests and Levites were also given a portion of the first fruits offerings of **grain . . . wine** . . . and **oil** as well as the **first shearing of . . . sheep** (v. 4). These provisions were to be granted to the Levites because **the LORD your God has chosen him and his sons from all your tribes, to stand and serve in the name of the LORD forever** (v. 5). Most of the Levitical priests would live near the sanctuary, but some Levites lived scattered throughout the nation (v. 6) in what would later become the Levitical cities (Jos 21). Such priests had equal standing with those who served at the central sanctuary and would receive equal portions, except that they could keep the proceeds from their fathers' inheritance for themselves (vv. 7-8).

18:9-14. To maintain their spiritual uniqueness, the Israelites, on entering the land, were not to **imitate the detestable things of those nations** (v. 9). High on the list of forbidden practices was child sacrifice, in which children were made to **pass through the fire** (v. 10). This practice was probably done for determining or discerning the will of the gods. Moses also forbade the practice of divination of any kind, whether it be by **witchcraft . . . omens**, sorcery, spells, mediums, spiritists, or **one who calls up the dead** (vv. 10-11). These are **detestable** practices, which show no reliance on the Lord. So the Lord Himself **will drive them out before** them (v. 12). Under no circumstances would the Lord allow them to resort to any such divination practices, and by avoiding them they would be **blameless before the Lord** (vv. 13-14).

18:15-22. Instead of relying on diviners, the people could receive spiritual guidance from **a prophet like** Moses whom the **Lord** would **raise up from** their **countrymen** (v. 15). Some consider this to be a prediction of a future order of prophets (just as the previous sections established orders of priest/judges and kings, 17:8-20). Others understand this to be a progressive prophecy, beginning with the order of prophets and culminating in the final prophet, the Messiah. In both of these interpretations, the word "prophet" (*nabi'*) must be understood as a collective noun. However, Delitzsch notes that generally, if *nabi'* is intended to be understood with a collective sense, it is common to interchange singular and plural forms within the passage, but this passage only uses the singular sense (F. Delitzsch, *Messianic Prophecies in Historical Succession,* trans. S. I. Curtis [Edinburgh: T&T Clark, 1891], 61).

A more likely interpretation is that Dt 18 is predicting a future eschatological and messianic prophet (Sailhamer, *The Pentateuch as Narrative,* 456). The primary objection to this interpretation is that the discussion of the presumptuous prophet (18:20-22) is speaking generically and not of one particular false prophet. Hence, this contrast assumes that the prophet like Moses must also be a generic prophet and not one in particular. In response to this, first, the conjunction **but** (Hb. *'ak*, 18:20) is a mild adversative, short of a full antithesis. What is actually being contrasted is that the prophet like Moses will indeed speak in God's name, while the presumptuous prophet will only presume to do so. Second, in vv. 15-19 the word "prophet," when speaking of the one like Moses, does not have the definite article, but it does have the article when used of the presumptuous prophet. When used without the article (vv. 15-19) it is a simple singular defined by being "like Moses." But when used with the article (vv. 20-22), it is a generic use of the article, referring to any false prophet. By this slight change of form, the text clearly distinguishes the two uses of prophet: there will a particular prophet one day, who is defined by being like Moses; there will also be generic prophets who speak in their own name and should be disregarded.

Two other passages in the Torah clarify the meaning of the prophet like Moses. First, Nm 12:6-8 indicates that Moses is unique among all prophets, speaking to God directly ("mouth to mouth"). Thus, a true prophet like Moses will practice direct communication with the Lord. Second, Dt 34:10, written much later and likely near the close of the canon (see comments there), states that "no prophet has risen in Israel like Moses, whom the Lord knew face to face." This indicates that at the close of the Hebrew canon, the prediction of Dt 18:15-19 remained as yet unfulfilled and directed the reader to keep looking for that messianic Prophet like Moses. (For a full discussion of this messianic prediction, see Michael Rydelnik, *The Messianic Hope: Is the Hebrew Bible Messianic?* [Nashville: Broadman & Holman, 2010], 56-64). Likely, this is the reason Ac 3:22-23 refers to Jesus as the direct fulfillment of this prophecy.

This is important contextually in that the nation was not to rely on divination of any sort (18:10). The nation was to execute any prophet who spoke **presumptuously** what the Lord had not revealed to him or who spoke **in the name of other gods** (v. 20). To speak presumptuously was to speak without authorization or to claim rights that are not legitimately possessed. In this passage it refers to a false prophet who espouses an attitude or behavior that rejects God's authority. To determine whether a prophet spoke in the name of the Lord, people were to see if the prophet's words came true. If they did not, then that prophet had spoken presumptuously, and the people were not to be afraid of what he predicted (vv. 21-22).

19:1-3. Previously Moses had designated three cities of refuge in the Transjordan area (4:31-43), and now he gave instructions regarding **three cities** of refuge in the land of Canaan in conjunction with earlier legislation (Nm 35:6-34). After the nation entered the land and dispossessed the nations there and they settled **in their cities and in their houses**, then they were to set aside three designated cities. The cities were to be accessible by good roads and evenly spaced out so that **any manslayer** could get to them readily. A manslayer was anyone who took someone's life, whether intentionally or not. After the conquest under Joshua, the three cities were officially assigned (Jos 20:7-9).

19:4-7. If someone accidentally killed **his friend** (e.g., if an **iron** axe head slips **off the handle** and **strikes his friend**) and there was no malice between them beforehand, then the manslayer **may flee** to one of the designated cities **and live**. The cities of refuge offered protection to the manslayer. Otherwise the **avenger of blood**, typically a family member, could pursue the manslayer, catch up to him, and then kill him before the manslayer could reach one of the designated cities (even though the two had no previous animosity).

19:8-9. Moses gave further instructions about the possibility of needing to designate three additional cities of refuge if the Lord ever enlarged their **territory** and allowed them to occupy the full boundaries of what the Lord promised to give their forefathers. Additional cities would need to be established only if the nation practiced covenant loyalty by carefully walking in obedience to the commandments. Sadly, the nation was never completely faithful, and so three additional cities were never designated. Theoretically they could still be established when the Messiah sets up His kingdom on earth. For more discussion about the cities of refuge see the discussion at Nm 35.

19:10-13. Bloodshed was an important matter, and every case in which someone was killed had to be handled properly lest innocent blood be shed and bloodguilt applied to the nation. This explains the rationale for the next case study. Earlier (in vv. 4-7) Moses discussed a situation in which someone unintentionally killed a friend. But now Moses addressed the intentional killing of a fellow human being. If someone lay in wait for someone and struck **him so that he die[d]** and then ran to one of the cities of refuge for protection, the elders (presumably after an investigation with multiple witnesses; cf. vv. 15) were to send for him out of the city of refuge and hand him over to the avenger of blood for execution. No mercy was to be shown to that individual because the killing of an innocent life required that atonement would be made for the bloodguilt (v. 10) for the sake of the entire nation. Since the nation has been contaminated by death of an innocent individual, executing the murderer was required to purge the entire nation of that innocent blood.

19:14. This verse is connected to the previous context through the linkage of land and the respect of others. Not only were their neighbors' lives important, but also their neighbors' property. Boundary stones were often used to designate the corners of one's legal land holdings. No one was to move them intentionally to gain more property for themselves. This verse is an example of a violation of the tenth commandment of coveting against a neighbor. Later a curse would be placed on all who violated this injunction (27:17).

19:15-21. These verses expand on the ninth commandment not to bear witness against one's neighbor (5:20). Earlier, capital punishment cases were to be meted out only when there was more than one witness (17:6). Now that same principle is applied to any criminal case (v. 15). The new legislation here pertains to someone who intentionally bore false witness in a malicious manner. When that happened, both parties were to **stand before the Lord** (v. 17), presumably at the central sanctuary where the appointed priest and/or judge would investigate and adjudicate the matter (v. 18). If false malicious testimony was given, then the guilty one would be sentenced with the penalty he was seeking to have ruled against the other party (v. 19). In this way **evil** would be purged from the land, and this would deter others from bearing false witness in criminal matters (v. 20). Again no mercy (v. 13) was to be shown to the false accuser. Perjury was subject to the law of *lex talionis*: **life for life, eye for eye, tooth for tooth, hand for hand, foot for foot** (v. 21). In other words the penalty had to fit the crime and not be excessive. These principles were to be implemented for the sake of the community within the promised land and thus were seen as judicial, not personal, punishment. Jesus later communicated that this principle need not be followed in interpersonal relationships (Mt 5:38-42).

20:1-9. This chapter includes the only legislation on the conduct of war. The chapter follows after instructions regarding homicide (chap. 19), so it relates to the subject of when it *is* appropriate to take a human life. This section also seeks to clarify further the sixth commandment ("you shall not kill" or "murder"). This passage does not provide any information regarding the circumstances that justify when war should be waged on foreign soil. The verses only provide some general guidelines to govern it when it does occur. Elsewhere the OT does acknowledge that there is "a time to kill" (Ec 3:3), and throughout their nation's history, God commanded the Israelites to attack their enemies (i.e. 1Sm 23:4; 2Ch 20:15). Yet it was always with the recognition that peace (vv. 10-12) is the goal to be desired.

Moses began by stating that Israel was never to be **afraid** when doing **battle**, even if her enemies had more numbers and superior weaponry (v. 1). Since war was not just a military issue but also a religious and theological one, priests had a major part in preparing the people for war. Priests were employed to encourage the troops just before battle by strengthening their will to fight, reminding them that the **LORD** would come alongside to **fight** against Israel's enemies and provide deliverance from them (vv. 2-4). The priest stood as a tangible reminder to the troops that the Lord was with them and that they could trust Him for a favorable outcome in battle.

To achieve high morale among the troops, officers were to inquire among the soldiers before battle if any of them had **built a new house** or **planted a vineyard** or had become **engaged** but were not yet married. If any of those situations applied, then those soldiers were dismissed so that they could enjoy for a little while those special events of life, and this practice would also help stabilize family units as well as the economy (vv. 5-7). The officers were also to inquire whether any soldiers experienced excessive fear to the point where it would affect the morale of those around them. If that was the case and the priest's prior encouragement did not strengthen their resolve, then they too were to be sent home (v. 8). After it was determined that there was a faithful army, then the officers were to **appoint commanders** to lead the troops in actual battle (v. 9).

20:10-15. This section deals with wars on foreign soil because Israel was to eliminate any nation in the land of Canaan. So with any city that was **very far from** them, the Israelites were to offer them terms of peace (i.e., they were given the chance to become a vassal state). If that was agreeable then the people of that city would perform forced labor on their behalf (vv. 10-11). If a city did not abide by the terms of peace, then it was to be besieged so that **when the LORD your God gives it into your hand**, the entire male population was to be executed (vv. 12-15). The **women**, the **children**, the **animals**, and the **spoil** could all be appropriated as plunder.

20:16-18. However, within the boundaries of the promised land, as the conquest of the land progressed and the battles were fought with those who occupied the land, the Jewish people were to leave nothing **alive** (see discussion at 7:2-6 for an explanation as to why children would be included). The various nations within the land of Canaan (7:1) were all to be utterly destroyed in compliance with the Lord's command. Complete eradication was necessary so that they would not have opportunity to **teach you to do according to all their detestable things**. If the nations were left alive, then they would have the ability to influence the Israelites to participate in idolatry, which would be a **sin against the LORD your God**.

20:19-20. Here Moses gave additional information about the rules of engagement when Israel was besieging a city, presumably whether inside or outside the promised land. Often armies were ruthless in seeking to conquer resistant cities, so that the entire area was laid waste. This was not to be the case with Israelite warfare. They were not to cut down any fruit trees when besieging a city. They could be a source of food for the soldiers during that time, and also it was considered too cruel and vindictive. The value of fruit trees is heightened by Moses' question, **for is the tree of the field a man, that it should be besieged by you?** This may seem hypocritical for God to command that fruit trees be spared and children and infants be exterminated, but Moses earlier had raised the concern about assimilation (7:3) with the Canaanites, hence the need for total annihilation (men, women, and children) of these nations. However, with trees there is no danger of assimilation or cultural transference, so they can and should be spared. Respect for God's creation was to be maintained even in a time of war. However, in times of war, non-fruit-bearing trees could legitimately be cut down and used as **siegeworks**.

21:1-9. Moses expanded his exposition of the sixth commandment, "You shall not murder," by covering a number of issues meant to maintain order. These verses discuss a specific case law regarding an unsolved murder. **If a slain person is found lying in the open country** and it is not **known** who killed him, then **elders and . . . judges** are to arrive at the scene of the crime and determine which city is the closest to the scene (vv. 1-2). The **elders of that city** are then to be notified, and they are to take over by bringing an unbroken (never plowed or sown) **heifer down to a valley with running water** (vv. 3-4). Apparently the valley did not have to be adjacent to the crime scene because running water was necessary for the following ritual. In the valley the elders were to break the neck of the heifer (perhaps with an ax). This was not a sacrificial act because the blood was not to be poured out on the ground or manipulated in any way. Breaking the neck of the heifer symbolized that a capital crime had occurred and the guilty one, even though unknown at that time, was worthy of death. The priests, the Lord's representatives in this matter, were to be summoned to the valley where they would wash their hands (with the running water nearby as a symbol of purity; v. 4) over the dead heifer and publicly announce,

Our hands did not shed this blood, nor did our eyes see it. Forgive Your people Israel whom You have redeemed, O Lord, and do not place the guilt of innocent blood in the midst of Your people Israel (vv. 7-9). This ritual signifies the need for Israel to deal with all bloodguilt matters, even in cases where the perpetrator was not known. The land was to remain undefiled, and this ritual was the prescribed means of removing bloodguilt in unsolved murder cases.

21:10-14. Moses legislated a number of family related laws, the first dealing with regulations regarding **captive** women. Earlier the law stated (20:14) that women and children from captured cities were to be spared. The possibility arose, as described here, that one of the soldiers might find one of the captive woman attractive enough for marriage. Caution was in order here because intermarriage was expressly forbidden with women from the Canaanite nations (7:3) and should not have been even possible if all the inhabitants, including the women, were put to death as the Lord had instructed. The background for this situation (although not explicitly stated) is that some of the captive women might wish to associate themselves with the God of Israel (like Rahab), and now the possibility of an Israelite marrying one of these women was an option. Several stipulations, however, were in order. She was to **shave her head and trim her nails** and get rid of her wardrobe (vv. 12-13). The purpose of these acts is not clear. Some think that if the only reason the woman was desirable in the first place was that she was physically **beautiful**, the removal of adornments would mean she would be less attractive. The most likely reason is that these acts demonstrate that she needed to remove anything pertaining to her former life and embrace life within the Israelite community. This would also remind her husband that he is no longer to treat her as an alien but as a wife. She was also given a full month to mourn her parents. Presumably her **father and mother** would be dead after the city was captured, so she would need time to grieve those losses. If those stipulations were met, then the soldier would be free to marry her, but if he was ever displeased with her, she was to be released from the marriage and she could **go wherever she wishes** (v. 14). Even though she was a foreigner, she had certain rights and was not to be sold **for money** or mistreated in anyway because she had been humbled (as a result of the divorce, and so he may not humiliate her further). While some of these regulations may affront modern sensibilities, these regulations were a far cry from the common way war captives were treated throughout other ancient Near Eastern nations of the time.

21:15-17. Genesis 2:22-24 states that monogamy is the standard for marriage, but this current stipulation seeks to regulate polygamy when it does occur in order to protect the family rights of the firstborn. The placement here after vv. 10-14 may suggest that she is the unfavored wife in a polygamous marriage. In a polygamous marriage, if each wife had **borne . . . sons**, then regardless of which wife was the more favored by the husband, the firstborn son was to receive a double portion of the father's estate. Family order was to be maintained and was not to be manipulated to achieve a different outcome from what was clearly mandated. Polygamy (like divorce), although not ever expressly sanctioned by God, was practiced. It was typically entered into by men of wealth or power (Abraham, Elkaneh, David) and not by the common man. It was done either as a means of status or in some cases altruistically to benefit women who had no other means to support themselves. Even though it is mentioned as a practice within the OT it is best to follow the original mandate of one man and one woman (Gn 2:22-24) since polygamy often leads to difficult cases such as this one.

21:18-21. The case law in these verses expands the fifth commandment regarding honoring one's parents. If a man had a **stubborn and rebellious son** who was grossly disobedient to his parents and did not respond to disciplinary measures, then his parents were to take him to the **elders** at their city gate. This situation applied when the son was completely incorrigible and willfully rebellious against any authority structure in his life. The parents were to attest to his rebelliousness and give specific examples of his behavior. In this case the parents attested that their son was **a glutton and a drunkard**. The former speaks of his lack of control regarding food and the latter of his inability to moderate consumption of alcohol. The parents did not have unilateral authority to assign the death penalty to their son, but if the elders were in agreement with the parents then the men of the city were to **stone** the son **to death**. The morality of individual families affects the moral and spiritual fabric of the nation. For this reason insubordination was an **evil** to be purged from the community.

21:22-23. Several times throughout

Deuteronomy capital punishment was set forth for certain behavior (13:10; 17:5; 21:21), but no instructions were given in those passages regarding the disposition of the criminal's **corpse** after execution. Here Moses presented a case study of what was to be done in those situations. If someone was executed and hung **on a tree**, the body was to be removed and buried before sundown **on the same day** as his execution. Hanging on a tree was not the means of execution (stoning was the typical means), but often the bodies of executed criminals were hoisted up on a stake as a demonstration of their death as well a deterrent for any who sought to emulate their behavior. The executed criminal was considered cursed by God, not because he was hung on a tree but because of the behavior that brought about his punishment. While there is a clear object lesson in these situations to warn people about the consequences of their behavior, the body of the criminal was still to be treated in such a way that Israelites did not **defile** their **land**. In Gl 3:13 Paul quoted this passage, stating that Christ's death enabled believers to be redeemed from "the curse of the Law."

Chapter 22 seems like disparate material, but subtle clues indicate that it is a unit. Repeated words (such as ox [vv. 1, 4, 10], donkey [vv. 3, 10], garment/clothing [vv. 3, 5, 12], and house [vv. 2, 8]) stitch these laws together. This section also transitions from the taking of life (21:18–22:8) to purity, including sexual purity (22:9-30).

22:1-4. The injunction here relates to lost property and the care and return of it. To demonstrate love to their neighbor and respect for life in general, the Israelites were to maintain high ethical standards in regard to other people's possessions. Moses wrote of straying oxen or sheep and commanded that they be returned to their owner (vv. 1-2). This was then expanded to include all other possessions that could be lost or misplaced. Animals, especially oxen, were valuable pieces of property because of the work they performed. So returning them to their owner was the right thing to do, and it also allowed the owner to maintain a standard of living. This courtesy is to be extended to the owner to assist him in retrieving property, but it is also to be extended the animals themselves. If someone saw an animal in distress, he was to come to its aid.

22:5. Next, a law prohibiting cross-dressing and transvestite practices may seem out of place in the context, but Moses was slowly transitioning to purity laws and taboo mixtures or mixed messages. Some have suggested that cross-dressing was sometimes used in pagan fertility rituals, and the Israelites were to maintain their separateness from pagan practices at all times. Others see this legislation as seeking to discourage homosexuality. Whatever the background, the theme of purity and expected norms stands out. Wearing clothing of the opposite sex sends a mixed message, and thus is prohibited.

22:6-7. Scholars differ on the reason Moses gave this prohibition not to take the mother bird and her young or eggs at the same time. Most scholars see it as a tangible way for the Israelites to be taught reverence for life, especially in the animal kingdom, but since the life of the young is taken that seems unlikely. This may simply be a means of preserving the food source so as to secure a supply of food for the future. This was the same principle at work earlier when fruit trees were not to be cut down when besieging a city (20:19-20). Obedience to this injunction results in prosperity and prolonged days.

22:8. As another tangible expression of love toward a neighbor, parapets (or fences) were to be built around one's roof deck. Since roofs were used as living space and a place for hospitality, it was a common courtesy to build safety measures for their guests' protection while entertaining them. Human life was to be valued, and any means implemented to preserve and protect life was to be used to prevent bloodguilt.

22:9-11. Moses now listed injunctions against the mixing of different materials. Israelites were prohibited from mixing **two kinds of seed** while sowing, or plowing with two different kinds of animals, or wearing garments with mixed fabrics. There is nothing physically harmful in any of those mixtures, but since the outward demonstration of purity in these matters symbolized an internal spiritual purity that was to characterize the Israelites, anything that did not conform to a high standard of purity was forbidden.

22:12. Tassels were to be placed **on the four corners** of their garments, and while the explanation or reason is not stated here, it was earlier (Nm 15:37-41). The tassels were to serve as object lessons to help the Israelites remember the Lord's commandments wherever they went.

22:13-21. The family was an important building block of the Israelite community, so it was important to maintain the highest sexual standards to maintain its purity. Moses now gave further exposition of the seventh commandment.

The first case study involves a husband who

charges his wife **with shameful deeds and publicly defames her** because he claims she was not a virgin when he married her (vv. 13-14). First, Moses addressed what to do if it was a false charge, and then what to do if it was a valid accusation. In either case the parents of the wife were to bring **evidence of the girl's virginity to the elders** (v. 15), announce the accusation, and present the evidence for inspection. The evidence of her virginity was the bloodstain on the bedsheet from the breaking of the hymen after the marriage was consummated. If the elders found the evidence compelling, then the husband was chastised (whipped) and fined 100 shekels **of silver** to be paid to the father (vv. 18-19). The penalty was twice the normal bride price (v. 29) that a groom paid the father. The husband was thus punished for **publicly** defaming **a virgin**, and he was unable to divorce her afterward (v. 19). The high fine and the public humiliation were measures to protect the wife from false accusations. But if she were not a virgin at the time of the marriage, then she was to be executed by stoning at the doorway of her father's house (vv. 20-21). This was mandated because the parents did not help maintain their daughter's virginity or were perhaps even complicit in making her appear to be a virgin to her potential husband when she was not.

22:22. Moses then set forth a clear injunction against adultery (the seventh commandment), specifying that the penalty was death for any man or woman caught **lying** with someone who was married. In this case there had to be clear proof of the infidelity and the manner of execution was presumably stoning (cf. vv. 21, 24).

22:23-27. A virgin engaged to a man was legally equivalent to a married woman, and so if she engaged in sex with another man while within the city, both she and the man were to be stoned to death (vv. 23-24). If she alleged that she was raped, but she **did not cry** out to prevent it from happening, she was judged as engaging in consensual sex and she was still to be executed for immorality. However, if the sexual act occurred in a **field** (away from people nearby), then only the man should be executed because it was presumed to be an act of rape. The girl was not to be punished because she did nothing wrong. This was a criminal act against her (vv. 25-27).

22:28-29. In another scenario **if a man . . . seizes** a virgin who was not yet engaged **and lies with her**, then the man shall pay the **father fifty shekels of silver**, and she shall become his wife and he will be unable to **divorce her all his days** (vv. 28-29). Some object to a law forcing a woman to marry the man who raped her. However, for several reasons, it is more likely that the verb "seized" (*taphas*) does not refer to rape but seduction leading to consensual premarital sex, rather than rape. (1) In the parallel law found in Ex 22:16-17, the verb used is not "seizes" (*taphas*) but "entice" (*pathah*) and then results in consensual sex. (2) The verb "seizes" (*taphas*), used here, is distinguished from the word "forces" (22:25, from the root *chazak*, meaning "overpower") in the previous paragraph, referring to rape. (3) The verb "seizes" (*taphas*), while literally referring to physical capture, can also have a metaphorical sense, much like "to capture one's heart" (cf. Ezk 14:5), and much more in keeping with seduction. Hence, this law is dealing with a man who seduces a young virgin with words of love so that she **lies** with him. Afterward, this "seducer of an unbetrothed virgin was obliged to take her as wife, paying the customary bride price and forfeiting the right of divorce" (Meredith Kline, *Treaty of the Great King*, 111). While marrying a seducer may be an affront to modern sensibilities, there is some rationale behind this legislation. It was a means of protecting a woman's honor. Also if a child were conceived from this illicit relationship, then the child would have a source of financial support. This law may have also provided a strong deterrent against seduction and premarital sex since divorce was not an option. The stability of the family unit and sexual purity were values held in high esteem over feelings in that culture.

22:30. A situation that could not be technically construed as adultery but was nevertheless prohibited was when a man married his stepmother after his father's death. Such an act uncovered **his father's skirt** (a euphemistic idiom describing the invasion of the privacy of sanctioned sexual relationships). This act violated the sanctity of his father's marriage and was considered incestuous.

23:1-8. This section pertains to limiting those who had access to the **assembly of the Lord** (v. 1). That "assembly" is not explained, but the most prevalent view is that it was the central sanctuary. Again the notion of purity and symbolism is evident here, and this regulation was not necessarily making a moral judgment about those excluded. The first exclusion goes to individuals who were **emasculated** or had their **male organ cut off**. Now this emasculation could be due to genetics or an accident or intentional, but no matter the cause the result is still the same—they could not enter the assembly. This injunction was probably aimed at men who had been emasculated in dedication to foreign deities (and by extension to those who had official positions under foreign governments). "Wholeness" was important in the Israelite worship system, so anything that did not conform to the "perfect" template (in this case a complete male body) was excluded. With something missing from his body he was no longer representative of a man made fully in God's image (Gn 1:27).

Another person who was excluded is **one of illegitimate birth** (v. 2). The word **illegitimate** is rare, and so it may refer to all who are illegitimate. But that is unlikely since unmarried individuals who had sexual intercourse were either put to death (22:20-22), or required to get married (22:28-29). It more likely refers to children of forbidden cross-cultural marriages or to children born to cult prostitutes who had been associated with pagan rituals. The prohibition of not being able to enter, even to the tenth generation, is an idiom meaning forever; it probably does not mean that a person of the eleventh generation could be included.

Ammonites or Moabites were excluded from the assembly (vv. 3-6) because they did not show hospitality to the Israelites after the exodus from Egypt and they attempted to curse the nation by hiring Balaam. They also may have been barred because they were the offspring of an incestuous relationship between Lot and his daughters (Gn 19:3-38). However, Balaam's **curse** ultimately turned into a **blessing . . . because the LORD** loved Israel (Gn 12:3). The nation was never to **seek their peace** by ever entering into a peace agreement with them or to seek **their prosperity** by entering into trade agreements.

Edomites and Egyptians were to be treated differently from the Moabites and Ammonites (vv. 7-8). Edomites were considered brothers because they descended from Jacob's brother Esau. Egyptians were not to be detested since the Israelites were aliens in their land and received hospitality, at least initially, when they sojourned there. The offspring of these two nations could enter into the Israelite assembly after the **third generation**. In other words, their grandchildren were granted full rights into Israel's religious ceremonial worship system.

While these are the stated standards, what about obvious exceptions such as David, who descended from Ruth the Moabitess? The exclusion may be focused more on Moabite men than Israelites taking Moabite wives. However Ezra later interpreted it in an absolute way as forbidding all such intermarriage (Ezr 9:1-2). This also may be a statement that no *unbelieving* foreigner may participate in the ceremonial worship at the assembly, fitting the theme of purity. The simplest view is that we have here an example of "faith" trumping "law." Ruth demonstrated great faith in the God of Israel, especially during the dark period of the judges, and was graciously allowed to be included into the Israelite community as well as the messianic line.

23:9-14. While vv. 1-8 deal with purity concerns for the assembly, vv. 9-14 deal with purity issues for the army as soldiers went to war. Soldiers were to keep themselves from **every evil thing** (v. 9). Specifically, if any man had a **nocturnal emission**, then he must leave **the camp**, wait until evening, **bathe himself** and then he may reenter the camp at **sundown** (vv. 10-11). Nothing is morally wrong here, but since he was ceremonially unclean (because his semen was not spilt in the "normative" way—that is in conjunction with sexual intercourse with one's wife) and since war was seen as something theological (since God was a warrior in their midst), this was not just a military event. The same goes for the command to bury one's excrement outside the camp (vv. 12-14). Since God is a warrior along with the Israelite troops, no impurity was to be anywhere in the camp. The camp was to **be holy**.

23:15-16. Runaway slaves from foreign nations were not to be returned to their masters. Instead they were to be allowed to live among the Israelites wherever they chose and without being harassed. This policy was vastly different from what was practiced throughout the ancient Near East. Slaves were often legally required to be extradited, and often a reward was paid to the one who returned the slave. Israel, however, was to be seen as a refuge where others could flee and find sanctuary. How this law fits the context of purity is not clear, but the same Hebrew word is used in both v. 14 ("deliver") and v. 15 ("escaped"), so verbal linkage unites this material.

23:17-18. On the theme of purity no Israelite **daughters** or **sons** were to be employed as a **cult prostitute**, and no proceeds from prostitution were to be presented as a **votive offering** to the Lord. A **dog** is a pejorative term for a male prostitute. These practices associated with pagan fertility rites were an **abomination to the LORD**.

23:19-20. While on the topic of money, Moses

wrote that no Israelite was ever to **charge interest** on a loan or any other legal borrowing agreement made to a fellow Israelite, but interest could be charged to a foreigner. Since the Lord was going to richly **bless** His obedient people in the land, plenty of funding would be available to assist each other. This also prevented the strong from preying on the weak in order to prosper.

23:21-23. Also on the topic of money, the next law demanded that worshipers not delay in paying their vows. **A vow** was an agreement with the **LORD**, so the worshiper was responsible to follow through on what he was verbally committed to do. This could be seen as an exposition of the third commandment not to take the Lord's name in vain. It was better not to vow at all than to make a promise and not be able to follow through on it.

23:24-25. The law stated here protected the poor and allowed for brotherly love. People were allowed to **eat grapes** or **grain** from anyone's vineyard or field so long as they ate it immediately and did not store any for later consumption. Again this allowance assumed that the Lord would abundantly bless His obedient people in the land and that such a provision would not interfere with the people's overall prosperity.

Chapter 24 includes a number of laws on issues dealing primarily with purity, justice, and compassion for the poor. All these themes have been discussed earlier in the book.

24:1-4. (For this section, see also the comments on Mt 19:3-9.) Legislation concerning grounds for a divorce is not something overtly discussed in the law. Earlier in the book, divorce is assumed to happen in some situations except when it is clearly prohibited (22:19, 29). The situation described here has several conditions, so that it cannot be used as the basis for an overarching policy for divorce. The law here sought to regulate what had presumably already been happening in the nation. If a married man found **no favor** in his wife because of **some indecency in her**, then he could write **her a certificate of divorce** and send her away. Then if she became the wife of another man, who then subsequently wrote her **a certificate of divorce** or died, the woman was not free to remarry the first husband. Views differ on the meaning of the **indecency** that the first husband found in his wife. It probably does not refer to adultery or premarital unfaithfulness since the punishment for those was death (22:20-22). Perhaps the indecency was some other sexual impurity, but its real meaning is unknown. The important issue here is that remarriage to a spouse after an intervening marriage was not permissible because of defilement. Nor is it clear what caused the defilement. Perhaps this was because the first husband disgraced her when he sent her away. While this may not make much sense to modern-day readers, the issues of purity, expected norms, and the protection of the weak are paramount and guide many OT laws. In any case this law seeks to regulate divorce and perhaps even discourage its implementation within Israelite society. See the discussion at Ezr 9 for more information on divorce.

24:5. A very family-friendly law is instituted here that allows for a one-year military exemption for anyone who has just married. This not only allows the couple the opportunity to enjoy the experience of marriage but also the possibility of starting to raise up heirs for the next generation.

24:6. Since millstones were used every day to prepare food, it was unlawful to use them as collateral for loans because it would take away the means to sustain **life** or to earn money to pay back the debt.

24:7. This is an exposition of the eighth commandment or more particularly of manstealing. **Kidnapping** was often done in the ancient Near East not so much to secure a ransom but as a means to take someone and sell him as a slave for profit. Although the captured person did not die, he would be deprived of his freedom and as good as dead, especially if he was sold abroad and unable to participate in the covenant community and blessings. The penalty for kidnapping was capital punishment.

24:8-9. These verses show clear dependence on Lv 13–14 (see the comments there), where Moses had earlier instructed the priests on ways to deal with **leprosy**. He now resurfaced that information, urging the nation to be diligent to **observe** the leprosy laws. The mention of **Miriam** and what happened to her (Nm 12:9-16) serves as a graphic reminder to encourage strict obedience of the leprosy laws. It also serves as a warning of what the Lord can do to His covenant people if they fail to observe His commandments.

24:10-13. The issue of pledges had already been mentioned (v. 6), but now the topic is expanded, especially in relation to treating debtors with dignity. Creditors were prohibited from entering a debtor's **house**, thus maintaining dignity and the privacy of his own home. If the debtor is destitute, the creditor must not take as collateral anything the debtor needs to secure a good night's sleep. For instance a cloak, an outer garment used not only by day but also as a covering at night from the chilly air, could not be used as a **pledge**. If Israel was obedient in the land, then the Lord would bless creditors with **righteousness** because of their compassion on the poor.

24:14-15. Similar to the previous legislation, employers were to pay laborers each day before the workers went home. This way the **poor** had funds necessary to provide for their families who were living hand-to-mouth. If employers did not implement this policy, then the workers could cry out to the **Lord**, who would reckon the employer's merciless action as **sin**.

24:16. Many previous law violations stipulated capital punishment. This particular legislation seeks to provide further guidance for its implementation. The law made no provision for voluntary substitutionary death for criminal acts. **Fathers** were not to **be put to death** for their sons' behavior, and vice versa. This does not negate what was said earlier (5:9). There the context was dealing with a father's sinful actions in the spiritual realm (not criminal realm) that had long-range consequences for his offspring. Contextually, this law in 24:16 is centrally located in this section and helps heighten the importance of individual responsibility.

24:17-18. Aliens, orphans, and widows were often easy targets for judicial and economic abuse and mistreatment. Israelites were not to **pervert . . . justice** at their expense or to use as collateral what little the underprivileged had and needed. The basis for compassionate behavior toward them was that Israel knew what it was like to be in that situation while they were enslaved in **Egypt**.

24:19-22. In continuing legislation that relates to the poor, further laws were stipulated about gleaning and reaping. Landowners were to leave some grain, olives, and grapes during the harvest for the **alien**, **orphan**, and **widow** (v. 19) to glean. This gave them direct involvement in a dignified way of providing for the poor. An example of this law in practice is in Ru 2. By following these laws for the poor they were modeling God's gracious acts toward them while they were enslaved in Egypt (cf. Dt 24:18).

25:1-3. This legislation deals with corporal punishment, and it places limits on its use. Dignity is a theme that runs throughout many of the laws in this book, and another example is seen here. A guilty man was due his punishment, but it was not to be excessive, nor was it to degrade and insult him in the process. In this situation anyone who was to be **beaten** (flogged) could not be struck more than **forty times**. To avoid going over this amount, Jewish law later limited this punishment to only 39 stripes, lest the flogging inadvertently go over the limit (2 Co 11:24).

25:4. This next law is specific: **You shall not muzzle the ox while he is threshing**. In other words kindness must be shown to animals while they work for the farmers. Since few people owned oxen (because of their expense), it was common to borrow or rent someone else's ox to help with threshing one's harvest. In this case a person could not muzzle his own or someone else's rented ox, while it was threshing his own grain, in order to maximize his profits. This would not be "neighborly" and could cause harm to the animal. Paul used this verse twice (1Co 9:9; 1 Tm 5:18) to illustrate that ministers should benefit materially from those to whom they minister.

25:5-10. Here is an example where values could be in tension, and so a law was needed to provide clarity as to how to handle the situation. One value was the desire for a husband to have male heirs to pass on his family name, and another value was to maintain high standards of sexual purity. If a husband died having not yet produced a male heir, how could an heir be provided in a legitimate fashion? A brother was not permitted to sleep with his sister-in-law (Lv 18:16), but here is an exception to that law if specific requirements were met. If **brothers live together** and one of them married but then passed away without producing an heir, then one of his brothers was allowed to take the deceased brother's wife as his own wife to produce an heir who would assume the name of **his** dead brother. This is often called a Levirate marriage (vv. 5-6).

A brother had the option of not agreeing to this, but in that case he would have to go through a humiliating ceremony to get out of it. The dead brother's wife would go before the elders of the city and remove the surviving brother's **sandal** and then **spit in his face** (vv. 7-9). From then on he would be known as **The house of him whose sandal is removed** (v. 10). The symbolism behind removing the sandal is not clear, but it certainly demonstrated that he had relinquished any claim to his dead brother's estate, as happened in the account of Ruth (Ru 4:7). Spitting in his face would mean that he would be ceremonially unclean for at least seven days (Nm 12:14). Strong social pressure ensured compliance in this situation because it was important for each clan of each tribe to continue having offspring to inherit all of God's promises to Israel.

25:11-12. The concern about the ability to raise up offspring seems to be behind the rationale for this next law. If two men are in a physical struggle and one of the wives seized the other man by his **genitals** to assist **her husband** in the struggle, then her hand was to be cut off with no mercy or **pity** shown. Two values were at play here. One is an overall concern for modesty, but the stronger value here, especially coming right after another law dealing with posterity, is that the woman by her act may be putting the attacker's virility in jeopardy by her actions. This is the only example in the law code of physical mutilation as a punishment for violating a law.

25:13-16. Moving to laws regarding commerce, Moses commanded that Israelites were to be completely honest in their business transactions. They must not have two sets of measuring standards to manipulate trade in their favor. Integrity in this area ensures a long prosperous stay **in the** promised **land**, for the people's obedience would enable them to avoid God's judgment.

25:17-19. The Amalekites are singled out in the Pentateuch as the Canaanite archenemy of Israel. Two earlier battles with them had been mentioned earlier (Ex 17:8-16; Nm 14:39-45), but here Moses revealed even more information about their actions against Israel. During Israel's exodus from Egypt the Amalekites purposely killed the weak and the stragglers at the rear of the Israelite march (cf. 1Sm 15:2). This is especially egregious not just because they killed Israelites but because they killed the **faint and weary**. Care for the weak is an important theme in Deuteronomy, and the Amalekites intentionally violated a value that is dear to God's heart. As a result the Israelites were to **blot out the memory of Amalek from under heaven** after they successfully occupied and settled in the promised land. Sadly they were not able to do so, as the Amalekites were still a force to be reckoned with later (2Sm 1:1; cf. 1Sm 15:20).

C. Ceremonial Fulfillment of the Law (26:1-19)

26:1-11. Moses here closed off an extended exposition on specific legislation that began in chap. 12. Chapter 26 also serves as a transition to the next major section of the book, which begins in chap. 27. This chapter forms a bracket with Dt 12, the beginning of the major section of "statutes and judgments" (12:1) in the book. Deuteronomy 12:6 anticipated the bringing of special offerings after the nation possessed the promised land, and Moses closed this section (in chap. 26) with instructions regarding special tithes and offerings.

The focus on the opening and closing passages of this key section of Deuteronomy has been on injunctions regarding appropriate worship—a key theological message of the book. This may explain why the first fruits offering was not mentioned in the list of holidays in Dt 16, in order to heighten its role here in this section of Deuteronomy. This offering in 26:1-11 and the special tithe mentioned next (vv. 12-15) were to be presented soon after they entered the land. This provided a smooth transition to another act of worship at Mount Ebal and Mount Gerizim (chaps. 27–28), to be performed after they entered the land. They were to take some of the **first of all the produce of the ground . . . in a basket** and take it to the central sanctuary (v. 2). Apparently this was a one-time offering for the first generation, since much of the wording here would apply only to the special audience Moses was addressing on the plains of Moab. When the worshiper arrived at the central sanctuary, he was to make a public statement to the priest proclaiming, **I declare this day to the Lord my God that I have entered the land which the Lord swore to our fathers to give us** (v. 3). Then the priest was to take the basket of produce and set it before the altar (v. 4).

Then a second longer credo-like statement was to be said in rehearsing the nation's pilgrimage and the Lord's faithfulness. In this second declaration the worshiper was to say, **My father was a wandering Aramean** (v. 5). The father is Jacob since he was the one who **went down to Egypt . . . few in number** but came out a mighty nation. The word **wandering** refers to the unsettled nomadic nature of Jacob's family. **Aramean** surfaces the geographical association of Jacob with northern Mesopotamia (Paddan-aram, 400 miles northeast of Jerusalem, Gn 24:4, 10; 25:20). This confession frequently mentions the Lord's faithfulness in delivering them out of Egypt and in providing a fruitful land inheritance (vv. 6-9). This is the only time in the book where the worshiper spoke. By bringing this first fruit offering to the Lord at the central sanctuary, the worshiper was offering thanksgiving to the Lord, which is a catalyst for him, the Levites, and the foreigners living in their midst to **rejoice** in the Lord's goodness.

26:12-15. This special **tithe** offering, like the one before it (vv. 1-11), was to be presented in the **third** full year after the nation entered the land. It was not to be presented at the central sanctuary but was to be distributed to the Levites, strangers, orphans, and widows in their towns so that **they may eat** and **be satisfied**. Each individual worshiper was to share God's blessings with the wider community. This tithe was to be accompanied by a public statement that this tithe was being presented in direct obedience to God's specific guidelines. The worshiper also entreated the Lord to bless both the people of Israel, and the land given to them as a bountiful gift. **Heaven** is declared here for the first time to be God's specific dwelling place (**habitation**).

26:16-19. Moses concluded this major section that began in 12:1 with an appeal to obey all these **statutes and ordinances** . . . **with all** their **heart and** . . . **soul**. The immediacy of this appeal is heightened for this first generation entering the land by the use of the words **this day** and **today**. Moses' statement that they had **declared the Lord** to be their God and that they **would walk in His ways and keep His statutes, His commandments and His ordinances, and listen to His voice** functioned as a formal ratification of this Moab edition of the Sinai covenant. By agreeing to these laws, the **Lord** had declared Israel to be **His people, a treasured possession**. They would be an exalted nation in terms of **praise, fame, and honor** and a people **consecrated** (holy) to the Lord. Consecrated is the Hebrew word normally translated "holy" (*qados*) and in this passage means "set apart" or sanctified for the Lord's purposes.

IV. Moses' Third Address: Blessings and Curses (27:1–28:68)

A. Renewal of the Covenant Commanded (27:1-26)

27:1-8. Moses now appeared with the elders of Israel to motivate the people to **keep all the commandments** (v. 1) in preparation for a covenant ratification ceremony. The elders served to verify that Moses had been faithful as God's mediator in giving God's law. Also the elders began to function in this role of providing spiritual and national leadership for the nation, since Moses would soon die and they would be the ones to facilitate the blessing and cursing ceremony. This chapter is part of a structural bookend surrounding the main body of laws in the book (Dt 12–26) as shown in the chiasm below.

Structure of Deuteronomy 11:26–28:15

- A Blessings or curses are a choice (11:26)
  - B Promised blessings recited at Gerizim; Promised curses recited at Ebal (11:29)
    - C Obey the commands (11:32)
      - D The commands to be obeyed (chaps. 12–26)
    - C' Obey the commands (26:16)
  - B' Promised blessings recited at Gerizim; Promised curses recited at Ebal (27:12-13)
- A' Blessings or curses are a choice (28:2, 15)

The overall effect of this structure is to bracket the middle section containing the body of legal material (i.e., "the statutes and the judgments" 12:1) in the context of blessing, worship, and obedience.

After arriving in the land the nation was to erect on Mount Ebal **large stones and** to **coat them with lime** (v. 2). This was so that these stones would have a proper surface on which to write **all the words of this law** (v. 3). Scholars debate what constitutes "the words of this law." Because of the length of the entire Pentateuch or even the book of Deuteronomy some have suggested that it refers to the book of the covenant, that is, Dt 12–26, or even just the Ten Commandments (Dt 5:7-21). If these stones were erected out of doors, the intention may have been for this inscription to be used solely for this ceremony, since rain and other weather elements would quickly wash the plaster away. This inscription was to be a graphic reminder of the nation's need to live by God's laws. In addition to the plastered inscribed stones, the Israelites were to build an altar of uncut stones for making burnt and peace offerings (vv. 5-8). The stones were to be uncut, either to emphasize that the Israelites were not to depend on the technology of pagan craftsmen in building such an altar, or simply because the use of any tool would profane an altar dedicated to the Lord (Ex 20:25-26). Possibly the Mount Ebal/Mount Gerizim area (near Shechem) was to be considered the central sanctuary. But since what is described here is a one-time ceremony, it is better to assume that Jerusalem was the ultimate intended central sanctuary, because in later passages God's name is said repeatedly to dwell there.

27:9-10. As Moses stood earlier with the elders (v. 1) he now stood with the Levitical priests who would also be instrumental in maintaining the nation spiritually after his death. By his public association with them Moses was transferring his authority to the elders and the priests. The priests also repeated the injunction to the nation for them to **obey the LORD** their God and to obey **His commandments**. Thus the priests immediately exercised spiritual authority over the Israelites.

27:11-14. After the stones were inscribed and the altar built, the nation was to be divided into two groups with six tribes standing on Mount Gerizim to pronounce God's blessings upon the people and six tribes standing on Mount Ebal pronouncing the curses. No reasons are given as to why certain tribes announced the blessings and others recited the curses. The tribes that represent the blessings were all born of Leah and Rachel (Ephraim and Manasseh being combined under Joseph), and the tribes announcing the curses were born of the handmaids, in addition to Reuben and Zebulun, sons of Leah. Reuben, though the eldest, was probably selected to announce the curses because of his having defiled his father's bed by sleeping with Bilhah (Gn 35:22; 49:3-4). Zebulun was listed with the tribes that pronounced the curses probably because he was the youngest of the sons of Leah and six tribes were needed for each grouping. Although certain tribes announced the curses does not mean that God had cursed their tribe. The Levites of v. 14 were probably Levitical priests (cf. Jos 8:33) since the rest of the tribe of Levi was standing on Mount Gerizim.

27:15-26. Of the twelve curses, as many as eight can be traced specifically to a violation of one of the Ten Commandments, as can be seen in the chart below.

After the Levites recited each of the curses, the people on both slopes would respond with **Amen**, signifying their assent to each curse and agreement to what was stipulated. Many of these violations could be done in secret (vv. 15, 24), and thus even if there were no witnesses the violations would bring a curse on the one committing the act. The curses relate to various domains: those that relate to God (v. 15), to family (v. 16), to neighbors (v. 17, 24), to those less fortunate (v. 25), to sexual violations (vv. 20, 22, 23), and to murder (i.e. premeditated killing of a neighbor). The last violation: **cursed is he who does not confirm the words of this law by doing them** (v. 26) is unlike the others in that it is not a violation of a specific commandment but a general catchall violation of the entire body of laws contained in Deuteronomy. While the curses are listed in chap. 27, the formalized recitation of the blessings is not stated. Explanations for their absence could include: (1) it was expected that Israel as a nation would not be obedient to the covenant and hence would not receive the blessings; or (2) this could simply be a structural device on Moses' part since the next chapter (Dt 28) begins with a listing of

The Warnings about Curses Delivered on Mount Ebal and the Ten Commandments

Curse	Curse Injunction	Ten Commandments
1	v. 15 man who makes an idol	1st/2nd (5:8-10)
2	v. 16 he who dishonors his father or mother	5th (5:16)
3	v. 17 he who moves his neighbor's boundary mark	8th (5:19)
6	v. 20 he who lies with his father's wife	7th (5:18)
8	v. 22 he who lies with his sister	7th (5:18)
9	v. 23 he who lies with his mother-in-law	7th (5:18)
10	v. 24 he who strikes his neighbor in secret	6th (5:17)
11	v. 25 he who accepts a bribe to strike down an innocent person	6th (5:17)

blessings, and they serve as the literary counterpoint to the curses.

B. Blessings and Curses (28:1-68)

28:1-14. Moses addressed the nation and linked additional information about blessings and curses after the instructions for the ceremony to be performed on Mount Ebal and Mount Gerizim (Dt 27). Blessing and cursing go all the way back to the opening chapters of the Pentateuch (Gn 1:22; 3:17), and the mentions there and here of those topics serve as bookends for the entire book of Moses (from Genesis to Deuteronomy). The conditional element of this covenant is evident here in that the blessings depend on Israel's diligent and careful obedience to the Lord's commandments. If followed, these commands would result in Israel being exalted **above all the nations of the earth** (v. 1). These blessings extend to all areas of their lives in the land, whether in the home or in times of war. Merchants in the city as well as farmers in the country would all experience material prosperity. Verses 3-6 sound as if they could have been used as part of the communal blessing ceremony at Shechem (27:9-26), since the blessings part of the ceremony is absent there.

In 28:7-14 Moses expanded on those blessings of vv. 3-6 by giving greater detail. The blessings pertain to three domains: (1) All their military endeavors would be victorious (v. 7). (2) All their families would experience material prosperity (v. 8), in terms of flocks and crops (vv. 11-12). (3) Their standing among the nations would be exalted, with Israel being **the head and not the tail** if they listened **to the commandments** and carefully observed them without deviation (vv. 13-14). Note that while these blessings include the promise of prosperity for God's people, they are written to Israel and accrue to the people as they obey the Mosaic covenant. Christians cannot claim these because they are not under the Mosaic covenant (see the comments on Rm 6:14; 7:1-4; Gl 3:23–4:7).

28:15-19. Obedience would result in blessing, but disobedience would result in experiencing the curses. The curses are much more expansive than the blessings, indicating that Israel would struggle to keep her end of the covenant and needed the warnings about the curses to be much more explicit. The four curses in vv. 16-19 are the exact opposite of the four blessings in vv. 3-6, but not in the same order since numbers two and three are reversed. This may signal that the consequences of disobedience may not always be predicted since one of the results of the curse is confusion (v. 20).

28:20-24. Just as Moses expanded on the blessings in vv. 7-14, so here he expounded on the implications of the curses. When Israel forsook the Lord and committed evil deeds, the nation would experience painful physical maladies until they perished, and nothing they attempted to do would succeed. The Lord would send drought so that nothing could grow.

28:25-37. Not only would the curses affect their bodies and the land; in addition, any military undertaking would result in defeat so horrendous that no one would be left to bury the slain, and their **carcasses** would be **food to all birds . . . and to the beasts** (vv. 25-26). The nation would be under God's judgment, so much so that He would inflict on Israel the **boils** He inflicted on Egypt during the ten plagues (v. 27; see Ex 9:8-12). Mentally and physically they would be so afflicted that they would not be able to accomplish anything they set out to do (vv. 28-29). Instead they would be the victims of various oppressors. Even the common celebrations of life, such as marriage and enjoying a newly built home and harvesting a vineyard's first crops, would elude them (v. 30). They would not be able to eat meat from their own flock, and their own children would be taken away as slaves because they would have no power to stop their enemies from plundering them (vv. 31-33). All of this hopelessness, despair, and disease would drive them mad (v. 34). Ultimately the nation along with their **king** would be taken away in exile to be employed in the service of **gods** of **wood and stone**. Instead of being exalted among the nations (v. 36; see Dt 28:10, 13), they would be the source of ridicule wherever they were exiled (v. 37).

28:38-48. A significant area where the curse will be evident is in agriculture. The yield of their crops, vineyards, and orchards will either wither or be consumed by locusts, worms, or crickets (vv. 38-40; 42). The next generation will be led by foreigners in their midst because their own sons and daughters will be led away in captivity (v. 41). They will be victimized by predatory lenders and lose stature (v. 43). Moses assumed that the nation would experience these curses, as indicated by his statement **all these curses shall come on you and pursue you and overtake you until you are destroyed** (v. 45). The judgment that was to ensue would be a legendary reminder for future descendants (v. 46) and directly attributable to their failure to **obey the Lord** or **serve** Him with **joy**

and a glad heart (v. 47). Instead of blessings they would endure **hunger . . . thirst** and **nakedness** and be under an **iron yoke** of their enemies (v. 48).

28:49-57. Moses painted a graphic picture of a military siege, one of the severe consequences of disobedience. Foreign nations would swoop down on Israel (v. 49) and show contempt for the normal cultural values such as **respect** for the elderly (v. 50). All their **produce** would be utterly consumed by the enemy (v. 51), and all of their city defenses would be torn down (v.52). It would be so dire during sieges that even dignified men and refined women would be hostile toward other family members so that they would even eat their own offspring or the afterbirth in secret without having to share (vv. 53-57). Historical examples of this are found in later Israelite history (2Kg 6:24-29; Lm 2:20; 4:10). Moses was predicting the depth of depravity to which they would sink as a result of their disobedience to the law. These prophecies came true, especially in connection with the Babylonian exile.

28:58-68. Moses warned the people once again to be careful **to observe all the words of this law** and to fear the Lord's **honored and awesome name** (v. 58), for if they did not, the nation would suffer extraordinary plagues and diseases like the ones God had inflicted on Egypt (vv. 59-61). Whatever blessings God planned for them would be completely reversed. Instead of being **as numerous as the stars of heaven** (Gn 22:17), they will be **few in number** (v. 62). Whereas the Lord delighted to prosper them, their disobedience would cause Him to delight in destroying them (v. 63). The notion that God delights in destroying them is troubling to many. Yet when His people intentionally disobey and spurn God's grace, the same passion that delights when His people obey will be turned against them in their disobedience. Instead of peace and rest in the land they will experience fear, **despair**, **doubt**, and **dread** (vv. 64-66). They will long each morning for it to be evening, and they will long, when evening begins, for it to already be the next morning (v. 67)—a stark picture of hopelessness because no relief is forthcoming. There will be a reverse exodus, but with a bizarre twist (v. 68). They will willingly offer themselves as slaves to the Egyptians, who will not even be willing to purchase them for slave labor. Moses was saying that there is something even worse than enslavement: sinking so low that those willing to be sold into slavery will find no one willing to pay the low purchase price.

V. Moses' Fourth Address: Exhortation to Obedience (29:1–30:20)

A. An Appeal for Covenant Faithfulness (29:1-29)

29:1. The superscription here, **these are the words of the covenant**, signals another major section of the book, just as it did earlier in the book (1:1; 4:44; 6:1; 12:1). This superscription actually functions here as a fitting conclusion to the legal core of the book that began in 12:1. But it also is a transition to Moses' focus on his present audience and what he needed to say to them before he passed off the scene. Moses had effectively blended the covenant that the Lord made with the nation's first generation **at Horeb** with the words of this covenant, which Moses gave to the second generation **in the land of Moab.**

29:2-8. Like an effective speaker, Moses reviewed the main historical events that led them to this point, mainly the exodus from Egypt, accompanied by **great signs and wonders** (v. 3), as well as God's guidance and provision for the nation during their **forty years in the wilderness** (v. 5). Moses also recounted the victories over **Sihon** (Nm 21:23-26 and Og (Nm 21:33-35) and the parceling out of their land to the tribes of Reuben, Gad, and the half-tribe of Manasseh (Nm 32:33). Despite these benefits, Moses surprisingly warns, **yet to this day the LORD has not given you a heart to know, nor eyes to see, nor ears to hear**. This may seem to be stating that the Israelites simply lacked insight because of their constant refusal to trust God, as evidenced at Kadesh (9:22-24). But it is more likely that the Lord was responsible for the nation's faithlessness because He did not grant them spiritual perception to His ways (see discussion at Rm 9). Whatever the case, still Moses seemed to be laying out hope for the nation. The words **yet to this day** at the beginning of v. 4 imply that things were about to change. Moses was laying the groundwork for a future work by God when He would circumcise their hearts and allow them to love Him with all their hearts (30:6). This indicates that God had to do a work first in their hearts so that they would have the capacity for faith and love for God as they should. Paul referred to this passage in Rm 11:8 in the context of the need for God's grace for salvation (see the comments there and on Rm 9:6-23). Israel needed grace to appropriately respond to God just as NT believers do.

29:9-15. Prosperity for the nation depended on the nation keeping **the words of this covenant**

(v. 9). Moses was stressing the present with the repetition of words like **today** (vv. 10, 12, 13, 15) and the need for all the groups standing before the **LORD** from the **chiefs** (v. 10) down to the lowest of servants, to engage in a formalized commitment ceremony. The Lord was keeping His promises to Abraham, Isaac, and Jacob (v. 13) by renewing this covenant not just with those standing before Moses but also with those not present at that time (v. 15), that is, all future Israelites.

29:16-21. Moses reminded the nation once again of the importance of abstaining from idolatry as they saw it being practiced by the Egyptians. They had been mostly isolated from idolatry during the wilderness wandering, and they could easily become susceptible to following the idolatrous ways of the Canaanites as they entered the land of Canaan. So this warning was particularly pertinent. Israel must not allow even one person to serve any pagan god lest a **root** (v. 18) take hold and spread into greater apostasy. Such an idolater would never be forgiven by the **LORD**. Instead he would incur all the curses previously mentioned in this book, and his name would be blotted out from under heaven (v. 20).

29:22-28. Continuing his perspective on the future, Moses addressed the consequences that disobedience would have on the physical properties of the land. Future offspring and even foreigners would attest to the devastation the Lord was to inflict on the land (v. 22). This is graphically illustrated with an allusion to the destruction of **Sodom and Gomorrah** (v. 23; cf. Gn 19). The desolation and destruction will be attributed to the Israelites forsaking the covenant (v. 25) and following idolatrous ways. The land will be cursed, and the Lord will uproot the people and **cast** them away into exile because of His **great wrath** (v. 28).

29:29. This final statement (**the secret things belong to the LORD . . . the things revealed belong to us . . .**) can be taken in a number of ways. Some maintain that the **secret things** (v. 29) are the hidden sins of individuals. In this case, the verse is saying that God will punish a person's private sins, but the nation was responsible for rooting out the **things revealed** (i.e., open, observable sins) so that the nation could faithfully observe the law. A better view is that the "secret things" refer to God's knowledge and future plans that He has intentionally not revealed to Israel. This better fits the context because it is more in line with the corporate national focus of this passage than the behavior of private individuals. Israel was not to concern itself with trying to ascertain all the mysteries of God's ways. Instead they were to concentrate on adhering to the great body of material He had already revealed to them (e.g., "the words of the covenant," v. 1 and "this book," v. 27). Obedience would lead to God's continued blessings, but to try to determine His ways was not a privilege He would grant them.

B. The Call to Decision: Life and Blessing or Death and Cursing (30:1-20)

30:1-10. Moses anticipated a time when the nation would fall into disobedience and experience exile as part of the curses of the covenant. Apostasy would be inevitable. Yet he also injected hope: while they were banished they would have the opportunity to repent and return to the **LORD** and subsequently be restored from captivity back into the land (v. 3). Their repentance while in exile would trigger God's compassion so that He would then actively bring the outcasts (v. 4) back into the land and prosper them even more than He did with previous generations. The **LORD** (v. 6) would even circumcise their hearts (cf. 10:16), enabling them to love the **LORD** their God wholeheartedly. This is the foundation for Jeremiah's and Ezekiel's concept of a new covenant (Jr 31:31-34; Ezk 36:24-32).

As a result of their future repentance, the Lord would once again uphold a core element of the Abrahamic covenant (Gn 12:3) in that He **will inflict . . . curses . . . on** those who **hate** and **who persecuted** Israel (v. 7). All the blessings that would have been withheld because of disobedience would be reinstated. Still, once again these future blessings would depend on Israel's obedience to the Lord and their relating to Him with their whole **heart and soul** (v. 10).

30:11-14. Moses stated that the Israelites could comprehend and attain the commandments, and that no one has to **go up to heaven** (v. 12) or **cross the sea** (v. 13) to retrieve them because the commands are already nearby. They are so close to them that they could speak of them (**in your mouth**) and internalize them deeply (**in your heart**, v. 14). Paul quoted vv. 12-14 in Rm 10:6-8 (see the comments there). The Jewish people could not say that the law was too obtuse or inaccessible to them in Moses' day and thereafter. God made every provision to make it readily available to them. Paul's point in citing this text was to draw a parallel with the gospel of Jesus Christ. God, through Paul and the other apostles, had made the gospel available and accessible. The problem was not that God had not done enough;

the problem was (and remains) the refusal of people to embrace Jesus as their Messiah.

30:15-20. Moses presented a choice, in stark contrast, before the people. They could either choose **life and prosperity** or **death and adversity** (v. 15). To enjoy their relationship with God, Moses reminded them of their fundamental responsibilities: **to love the LORD your God, to walk in His ways and to keep His commandments and His statutes and His judgments** (v. 16). If they followed those injunctions, then they would **live and multiply**. But if they would **not obey**, then they would **surely perish** (v. 18) and their days would be short in the land. Moses summoned **heaven and earth** as witnesses (v. 19) to the choice set before them, and he urged them to **choose life** so that they and their descendants would prosper under the blessing of God. Parents who lovingly and obediently dedicated themselves to the Lord, as Moses urged them to do, would have a long-lasting impact on future generations.

VI. Conclusion (31:1–34:12)

A. Deposition of the Law and Appointment of Joshua (31:1-29)

31:1-8. To prepare for his approaching death, Moses had previously associated himself in public settings with the elders (27:1) and the priests (27:9), and now he would confer the leadership on Joshua. Moses reminded the people that he was 120 years old and **no longer able to come and go** (v. 2). At the time of his death, "his eye was not dim, nor his vigor abated" (34:7). So even at his advanced age he still had full use of his faculties—although he did not have the physical stamina to lead the people in the military conquest of Canaan. In addition, because of his unbelief (Nm 20:12) the Lord forbade him from crossing over the **Jordan** (v. 2). As important as a human leader was, the **LORD** would be the one who would **cross ahead** (v. 3) of them to **destroy** the nations. Nevertheless, Joshua was the human figure God approved as their leader (cf. 3:28) in the conquest. The Lord would vanquish their enemies in Canaan just as He did with Sihon and Og (Nm 32:33; Dt 1:4), but the Israelites were responsible to follow the rules of engagement set forth earlier (7:1-5). Moses charged the people to be **strong and courageous** (vv. 6-7), for the Lord was with them (v. 8), and He would be faithful so that they need not **be afraid**. Moses then gave the same message to Joshua. The Lord later repeated these same words Himself to Joshua, just before the nation crossed the Jordan River (Jos 1:6-9).

31:9-13. To ensure its continuity, Moses wrote down this law and safeguarded it with the priests, who carried the ark of the covenant, the sacred possession of the Israelites. **This law** (v. 9) refers either to the entire book of Deuteronomy or to the body of laws in chaps. 6–28. Moses gave instructions that this law was to be read publicly **every seven years . . . at the Feast of Booths** (v. 10) at the central sanctuary. This public reading of Deuteronomy was not just for the men but also for the women and children, as well as any foreigners in their midst (v. 12). All people were to have access to this law so that they might not only hear it but also learn through it to fear the Lord and carefully observe God's law.

31:14-22. Since the death of Moses was now imminent, God told him to appear privately at the **tent of meeting** along with Joshua, so that the Lord could **commission** his replacement (v. 14). This is the only mention of the tent of meeting in the entire book of Deuteronomy. The Lord's presence was signaled by the appearance of the **pillar of cloud . . . at the doorway of the tent** (v. 15). Moses had earlier anticipated the nation's future apostasy (30:1), but now God told him directly that the Israelites **will arise and play the harlot** (v. 16) with strange gods, thereby forsaking the Lord and His covenant. Their disobedience would unleash the Lord's anger, and He would then forsake them. As a result, **many evils and troubles** (v. 17) would come upon them so that they would be forced to acknowledge publicly that their calamity was tied to **God . . . not** being **among** them. Moses was now instructed to **write** a **song** and **teach** it (v. 19) to the nation so that it would be a constant witness and reminder of the consequences of disobedience. If they would not remember the commandments, they would remember the words of this song **for it shall not be forgotten from the lips of their descendants** (v. 21). The Lord already knew of their intent not to obey Him even before He brought them into the promised land. So Moses wrote this song (Dt 32) that very day and began to teach it to the Israelites (v. 22).

31:23-29. Moses and Joshua were earlier summoned to the tent of meeting for Joshua's commissioning (v. 14), and now it officially took place. The commissioning of Joshua is a structural bookend around a section (31:16-22) that stressed Israel's future apostasy. As Moses was unable to prevent the nation from becoming disobedient, Joshua also would not be successful in keeping the nation from going astray. Nevertheless Joshua was to be **strong and courageous** (v. 23) since God's presence would be with him as he led the conquest of Canaan.

When Moses finished writing out the words of this law, he commanded that his copy be placed **beside the ark of the covenant** (v. 26) so that **it may remain there as a witness**. The Sinai covenant was memorialized by the placing of the two stone tablets of the Ten Commandments inside the ark of the covenant. And now the covenant, as reiterated here in the region of Moab, was memorialized by the placing of a copy of the book of Deuteronomy beside the ark of the covenant. Moses' words here to the priests reflected his assessment of their **rebellion** and **stubbornness**. He predicted that the priests would only increase their disobedience after his death (v. 27). He then called for the **elders** and **officers** to **assemble** (v. 28) to hear his negative assessment of their future prospects after his death. Then Moses widened the circle even more by speaking to the entire nation the words of this song (chap. 32).

Several witnesses were being summoned here. The copy of Deuteronomy beside the ark (v. 26) was a witness against the priests. **The heavens and the earth** would witness against the elders and officers (v. 28), and now the Song of Moses would be a witness against the entire nation (v. 21). Moses mustered these three witnesses to testify against the future apostasy of the nation: a book, nature itself, and a song. That is what Moses would leave with them after he was gone. What Moses was saying in vv. 28-29 had a forward-looking emphasis as it related to the latter days. Moses used similar language to introduce all the major poetical material in the Pentateuch. Major poems that contain key messianic prophecies are included after long narrative sections, and they shape the overall structure of the books of Moses. (See the chart "Pentateuch" in "Numbers," p. 250, which looks at four poetic sections and four narratives.)

Moses used the major poems of the Pentateuch (Gn 49; Ex 15; Nm 22–24; Dt 32–33) not only to summarize long narratives but also to stop, pause, and insert key information about the coming Messiah within those songs. Moses crafted the Pentateuch with these forward-looking poetic pieces to provide an emphasis on the future Messiah (whom he also hinted at in Dt 18:15, "God will raise up for you a prophet like me"). Deuteronomy adds to this emphasis by actually concluding the Pentateuch with not just one major poem, but with two (i.e., "The Song of Moses," chap. 32 and "The Blessing of Moses," chap. 33).

B. The Song of Moses (31:30–32:43)

31:30–32:4. The book of Deuteronomy concludes with two songs: the Song of Moses (chap. 32) and the Blessing of Moses (chap. 33). Moses in psalm-like fashion poetically crafted the words as a memorial to Israel's future generations. He invoked heaven and earth (v. 1) to pay attention to what was being communicated because they would be eyewitnesses to verify what they saw Israel do while in the land. Moses desired that his lyrics would be like refreshing **rain** on **fresh grass** (v. 2). With these words Moses proclaimed the Lord's name and His greatness. For the first time in the Scriptures the Lord is described as a **Rock** (v. 4), suggesting His constancy and permanence. His actions are **perfect** and **just**, compared to the often-capricious actions of other ancient Near Eastern deities. He is faithful and treats everyone **without injustice**.

32:5-14. In sharp contrast to the Lord's righteousness, the nation of Israel acted **corruptly toward Him** (v. 5). They bore no likeness to their father but instead were **a perverse and crooked generation** (v. 5). Sadly, the nation responded foolishly and unwisely to their Creator (v. 6). Their fathers and elders could testify of the Lord's gracious actions when He **separated** (elected) them out as **His inheritance** (vv. 8-9). The elders could also testify of God's great deliverance in the exodus when He protected them like an eagle that **hovers over its young** and He **carried them on His pinions** (v. 11). The **Lord . . . guided** them through the wilderness where in the Transjordan they enjoyed the finest of produce of the field and flock (vv. 13-14).

32:15-18. In spite of all that prosperity the nation grew **fat** and **forsook God** who created them and **scorned the Rock** who delivered them (v. 15). Israel is ironically referred to as Jeshurun (cf. 33:5, 26), meaning "upright one," even though they were anything but righteous. Their apostasy extended to worshiping idols and sacrificing to strange gods (v. 16). They were so perverse that they were involved in sacrificing to demons (v. 17; cf. Lv 17:7). They preferred new deities to the One who actually **begot** them (v. 18). God is portrayed both as the One who fathered them and the mother who gave them birth (v. 18).

32:19-27. The Lord then responded to their **provocation** by spurning them (v. 19). He would withdraw from them and see how they fared (v. 20). Since they had made Him angry by their idolatry, He would likewise provoke them to anger by using foreign nations (v. 21). God's fierce anger knows no limits, extending even to the depths **of Sheol**, referring here to the grave (v. 22). The Lord would heap all sorts of misfortunes on them so that they would be laid waste and consumed (v. 23). They would be destroyed by big beasts as well as by tiny bugs (v. 24). Outside their homes the sword would bereave them of their loved ones, and terror would reign inside their hearts (v. 25). The effects of this destruction would be felt by those in their prime as well as those very young and very old. Their future was in serious jeopardy, to the point that the **memory of them** could have been eradicated from the earth (v. 26). The only reason God did not totally **cut them to pieces** is that if He had done so, Israel's enemies would have misjudged the Lord's power and assumed in their pride that Israel's destruction was their own doing (v. 27).

32:28-33. What made matters worse for the nation was that Israel lacked perspective on what God was doing, as if they were unable to discern that all of this destruction was sent by God to get their attention. They failed to perceive God's discipline because **there** was **no understanding in them** (vv. 28-29). They should have been able to conclude that one enemy soldier could not **chase a thousand** of them away unless their God (the Rock) had caused it (v. 30). Even enemy troops would not be able to explain their success because it was so uncharacteristic of their gods to grant such ability (v. 31). These enemies would be worse than **Sodom and . . . Gomorrah** (v. 32), yet God unhesitatingly would use the poison of vile nations to discipline His wayward children (v. 33).

32:34-43. The tone now changed drastically to one of hope. Though God would use enemies to judge Israel, He would let them go only so far before He turned the tables and held them accountable for their actions. The **LORD** would once again **vindicate** His people and express **compassion** on Israel once **He** saw **that their strength** was **gone** (v. 36). In other words, He would come to their aid only when they had exhausted their own efforts and when they renounced the gods in whom they **sought refuge** (v. 37).

God's discipline was never intended to destroy the nation but only to get them to recognize that there is **no god besides** Him (v. 39). He alone has the power to **put to death** and to **give life**. The Lord wounded them, but He also desired now to **heal** them. Once Israel recognized this, God would then take **vengeance** on Israel's **adversaries** (v. 41). This was to be a cause for rejoicing not just among His people but also among all **nations** because the Lord will execute justice on the earth and **will atone for His land and His people** (v. 43). Even though the song of Moses contains a negative warning about the consequences of apostasy, it ends on a positive note extolling God's justice and atoning ability.

C. Preparation for Moses' Death (32:44-52)

32:44-47. After Moses and Joshua taught the song (v. 44), Moses again challenged the nation to take to heart **all the words** of his **warning** and to command their children to observe **all the words of this law** carefully (v. 46). These lyrics could be preventive medicine if they would only heed its message. These were not just **idle** words; they were the source of life to Israel, and by observing them the people would **prolong [their] days** in the land (v. 47).

32:48-52. The very day the Song of Moses was composed (v. 48), Moses was summoned (v. 49) to ascend **Mount Nebo . . . in the land of Moab** (a mountain situated eight miles east of the Jordan River at the northeast corner of the Dead Sea) and from **a distance** (v. 52), to take one last look at the land of Canaan that the Lord was giving to the Israelites. Then Moses would **die** there and **be gathered to** his **people**, just as happened to Aaron on Mount Hor. The Lord said again that Moses was not permitted to enter the promised land because he **broke faith** (v. 51) with the Lord in the midst of the people at Meribah-kadesh and did not treat the Lord **as holy** (see comments at Nm 20:1-13). There are two different locations named **Meribah**. This one is near Kadesh-barnea, about 90 miles southeast of Jerusalem. God would permit Moses a panoramic view of the land from a distance, but Moses had relinquished his authority to lead the people personally into the promised land.

D. The Blessing of Moses on the Tribes (33:1-29)

33:1-5. The Song of Moses (chap. 32) is followed by the Blessing of Moses. The Pentateuch comes to an end with a twofold poetic flourish. Within the books of Moses poetic pieces often close out major sections (Gn 49; Ex 15; Nm 22–24; Dt 32–33). This poem was obviously added to the Pentateuch sometime later because the introduction to it states that Moses would bless the nation with these words **before his death**.

Hence, this begins the section of Deuteronomy that was added after Moses died and continues to the end of chap. 34.

The blessing here is a kind of last will and testament of Moses similar to the one Jacob made at the end of his life that bestowed a blessing on each of the tribes. The structural constraint of keeping the listing of tribes at 12 meant that one of the tribes would be left out. In this passage Levi is included and Simeon is left out. Why Simeon was left out is not clear. Later on in Joshua's day the tribal allotment of Simeon was totally included in the territory of Judah (Jos 19:1-9) and eventually was absorbed into the tribe of Judah. So the lack of mention of Simeon in Dt 33 may be a foreshadowing of decline for that tribe.

Moses began with an introduction that extolled the Lord as a divine warrior, having come from Sinai, since that is where He visibly met with Israel to give them the law. The Lord loves the people, and the holy ones (angels) were escorting him on this occasion when God revealed Himself through words. Moses was the human mediator in delivering the law and was called the king in Jeshurun.

These last two chapters of Deuteronomy present an interesting portrayal of Moses. He pronounced a **blessing** on the tribes similar to what a priest would do (33:1), he was called **king in Jeshurun** (33:5; cf. 32:15) because he exercised royal-like power over Israel, and the next chapter states that no prophet had risen in Israel like Moses (34:10). The NASB capitalizes the pronoun "He" in v. 5, signaling that the translators of that version take the pronoun to refer to God and not to Moses. It is better to take the pronoun as a reference to Moses since he is the closest antecedent (v. 4). The phrase in v. 26 "God of Jeshurun" would appear to rule out that God is one and the same with Jeshurun. So embodied in the person of Moses were the offices of priest, king, and prophet, that Moses was a pattern of the coming Messiah.

33:6-25. Now Moses began to give a blessing for the 12 tribes of Israel. His desire for **Reuben** (v. 6), the firstborn son of Jacob, was that his offspring would **not die** out. The next line, **Nor his men be few**, could be translated "Let his men be few," matching the negative assessment Jacob had of Reuben in Gn 49:3-4. That there are no other negative statements of any other tribe in this blessing, coupled with the Septuagint understanding it in a positive sense, weighs in favor of the notion that this is a prayer that Reuben's numbers not dwindle. **Judah** (v. 7) was the prominent tribe and the first to set out whenever the nation moved. So Moses desired that they enjoy God's help in military battles in that initial position.

With **Levi** (v. 8) Moses specifically mentioned the Thummim and Urim as the possessions of the priestly tribe. Evidently these were some type of precious stones used in the casting of lots to determine God's will. No description explains them, but they may have been stones or lights that when consulted revealed responses to yes-or-no-type questions. Moses desired that they remain under the control of godly men who were devoted fully to God. The word Urim means "lights" and provides a clue as to how these precious stones might have functioned. They may have supernaturally glowed when used as God intended. In a time before the completed canon God implemented such a device to reveal His clear will. Since we now have the full revelation of God's Word there is no need for believers to possess such a device. The specific historical reference to which Moses alluded demonstrates that tribe's loyalty to God in that they were willing to kill their own countrymen who had committed idolatry in the golden calf incident (Ex 32:25-29). The Levites received the important role of teachers of the law for the nation. Moses prayed that their tasks be blessed and that any of their adversaries be thwarted.

Benjamin (v. 12) was to receive peace and security and be shielded between the Lord's shoulders as His beloved. The phrase **between His shoulders** is unclear. It can mean that Benjamin lay safely between the shoulders (arms) of the Lord or that Benjamin was carried on the Lord's shoulders as a father might carry his son—an image used earlier in Deuteronomy (1:31). It most likely is not referring to where Benjamin dwelt but to where the Lord dwells—that is among the "shoulders" (i.e., hills) of the tribe of Benjamin. The verb "dwell" was used earlier (12:11) in reference to the sanctuary—ultimately this will become Jerusalem. In the book of Joshua, the sanctuary was regarded as being located within the tribal allotment of Benjamin (Jos 15:8; 18:28). **Joseph** (v. 13), representative of both Ephraim and Manasseh, received the longest blessing of all the tribes. They were to receive great material prosperity by receiving the choicest of goods as well as military strength (represented by the **ox**). Even though Manasseh was the oldest son, Ephraim is credited with more numbers (**ten thousands**), as Jacob foretold (Gn 48:17-20).

Zebulun and **Issachar** (v. 18) are paired as they were in Jacob's blessing (Gn 49:13-15). They were to rejoice in their daily activities and in what they would draw out of the **abundance of the seas**. **Gad** (v. 20) was blessed with a large territory in the Transjordan and was pictured as a ferocious lion in executing the justice of the Lord, presumably in the conquest of Canaan.

Dan (v. 22) is said to be a **lion's whelp**, which was earlier said of Judah (Gn 49:9). Dan had the strength of a young lion and prowess to leap into action. **Naphtali** (v. 23) was full of the **blessing of the LORD** and was to **take possession of the sea** (probably the Sea of Galilee). **Asher** (v. 24) was to be **favored** more than the other tribes and to enjoy material prosperity, symbolized by his dipping his feet in olive oil.

33:26-29. The mention of Jeshurun (v. 26) here bookends the blessing of Moses (v. 5), and this section mirrors the theme of vv. 1-5. The incomparable divine warrior image is used to portray God as One who **rides the heavens** to come to their aid. God is eternal and a dwelling place, and the nation would be secure from whatever foes were against them because the everlasting arms were underneath them, bearing them up. Just as God is incomparable (v. 26), Israel was incomparable in terms of receiving God's blessings. Israel would be victorious before their enemies only because the Lord had been their **shield** (v. 29) to protect them defensively and their **sword** to fight for them offensively.

E. Death of Moses (34:1-12)

34:1-12. Now that Moses had written the words of the book of the law (31:24), taught them the Song of Moses (32:24), and pronounced his blessing on the tribes of Israel (33:1), he ascended **Mount Nebo** (v. 1) as he was previously instructed to do (32:48-50). The LORD supernaturally showed him a panoramic view of the promised land starting in the north and proceeding to the south. The western sea (the Mediterranean Sea) was not visible from Mount Nebo unless the Lord specifically opened his eyes to see it. The Lord's promises to Abraham, Isaac, and Jacob are mentioned (v. 4) to demonstrate God's faithfulness to His word to the patriarchs. The reason Moses was not able to cross over into the promised land is not stated here, as it was earlier in the book (32:51-52). Yet because Moses was a faithful servant of the Lord, he was granted a gracious view of the land. Moses then **died . . . in the land of Moab** (v. 5), and was buried in an unmarked grave, presumably by the Lord Himself (Jd 9) in a valley **opposite Beth-peor**.

Clear support exists for the view that the human author of the entire Pentateuch was Moses. But several clues indicate that this specific account of Moses' death was added later by someone other than Moses. First, Moses would have had to write down details prophetically regarding his burial spot even before he died. Another clue is that the mention of Dan (34:1) in the northern part of Israel would signal at least an editorial updating sometime after the tribe of Dan migrated northward to Laish (Jdg 18). The last clue is the phrase "to this day" (34:6), signaling that some time had passed between the time of Moses' actual death and the time when that comment was added to the account. Moses' eyes were **not dim** nor was his **vigor** (v. 7) (physical or possibly even sexual potency) abated, so the cause of death was not the result of any physical weakness or disease.

The nation mourned for Moses 30 days (v. 8), much longer than the usual seven-day period (Gn 50:10). Joshua was then **filled with the spirit of wisdom** (v. 9), attributed to the laying-on-of-hands ceremony that Moses performed earlier (Nm 27:23; cf. Dt 31:23). Joshua was now the established leader of the nation, and the **sons of Israel listened to him**.

Some debate surrounds the statement, **Since that time no prophet has risen in Israel like Moses, whom the LORD knew face to face**. Although many suggest that Joshua was the author of the final section of Deuteronomy (chaps. 33–34), for several reasons, it is more likely that it was added significantly later, near the close of the Hebrew canon. First, in Dt 33:1, Moses is called "the man of God," whereas throughout the rest of the Pentateuch he was called "the servant of the LORD." The phrase "man of God" is not used anywhere else in the Pentateuch but is an exilic term for a prophet of God. Second, no one remembered where Moses was buried (34:5-6), indicating that a great deal of time had elapsed. Third, the clause **no prophet has risen in Israel like Moses** assumes that the time of prophecy in Israel had ceased. Therefore, it seems likely that Dt 33–34 serve as a postexilic inspired appendix to the original Mosaic composition (See Michael Rydelnik, *The Messianic Hope: Is the Hebrew Bible Really Messianic?*, 62–63).

The significance of this postexilic addition to the Pentateuch is that at the time of Ezra, when the words **no prophet has risen in Israel like Moses** were added, the writer would have been able to look back at all the OT prophets and not find one as great as Moses. Therefore, the prediction of a prophet like Moses (Dt 18:15-19) remained unfulfilled, and the reader was being reminded to keep looking for its future fulfillment in the Messiah.

Thus the book of Deuteronomy and the entire Pentateuch concludes with the prediction that at some point in the future (cf. 18:15-19) a prophet (the Messiah) would arise in Israel to rival Moses. Moses experienced an intimate **face to face** (v. 10) relationship with the Lord, unique among all prophets (Nm 12:6-8), that was never matched in the entire OT period. Furthermore, no nation had ever seen, nor had any prophet performed, such mighty signs and wonders as Moses did. Consequently, the Pentateuch ends with a hopeful expectation that someday the messianic prophet, greater in word and deed than Moses, would arise on behalf of the nation of Israel. The Pentateuch closes with this look forward, and the NT writers rightly see Jesus of Nazareth as the fulfillment of this prophecy (see the comments on Dt 18:15-19; Ac 3:22; 7:37).

BIBLIOGRAPHY

Craigie, Peter C. *The Book of Deuteronomy.* The New International Commentary on the Old Testament. Grand Rapids, MI: Eerdmans, 1976.

Deere, Jack S. "Deuteronomy." In *The Bible Knowledge Commentary: Old Testament*, edited by John F. Walvoord and Roy B. Zuck, 259-324. Wheaton, IL: Victor Books, 1985; reprint, Colorado Springs: David C. Cook, 1996.

Kline, Meredith G. *Treaty of the Great King: The Covenant Structure of Deuteronomy: Studies and Commentary.* Grand Rapids, MI: Eerdmans, 1963.

McConville, J. G. *Deuteronomy*. Apollos Old Testament Commentary. Leicester: Apollos, 2002.

Merrill, Eugene H. *Deuteronomy*. The New American Commentary, vol. 4. Nashville: Broadman & Holman, 1994.

Merrill, Eugene H. "Deuteronomy." In *Cornerstone Biblical Commentary*, vol. 2, edited by Philip W. Comfort, 445-679. Carol Stream, IL: Tyndale, 2009.

Olson, D.T. *Deuteronomy and the Death of Moses: A Theological Reading*. Minneapolis: Fortress Press, 1994.

Sailhamer, John H. *The Pentateuch as Narrative.* Grand Rapids, MI: Zondervan, 1992.

Thompson, J. A. *Deuteronomy: An Introduction and Commentary.* The Tyndale Old Testament Commentaries. Downers Grove, IL: InterVarsity, 1974.

● ● ● ●

JOSHUA

GERALD D. VREELAND

INTRODUCTION

Author. The book is anonymous. The title "Joshua" is taken from the principal figure. It is possible that Joshua also wrote this book. This theory of authorship becomes difficult in light of the book including the death of Joshua (24:29-33). However someone else could have added these appendices (cf. Dt 34:5-12), perhaps Eleazar or one of the elders who outlived Joshua. Joshua could have written most of the book himself as hinted by the first person plural in the narrative (5:1 NASB footnote indicating "other mss. read we," 6).

Date. Two dates for the book are ably defended by scholars. Some defend a date parallel with the 19th Dynasty of Egypt (1300s BC). The events, however, may be safely dated in the late 15th and early 14th century BC. In 1 Kg 6:1, readers are told, "In the four hundred and eightieth year after the sons of Israel came out of the land of Egypt, in the fourth year of Solomon's reign over Israel, in the month of Ziv which is the second month, . . . he began to build the house of the LORD." This date for the beginning of the temple construction would be spring of 966 BC. Counting backward 480 years to the exodus from Egypt and then adding 40 years for the wilderness wandering, one arrives at the date of 1405/6 for entrance into the land. This also fits the 300 years later indicated by Jephthah (Jdg 11:26).

From the standpoint of secular history, the Merneptah Stela should be considered. Merneptah reigned 1236–1223 BC. Merneptah was the pharaoh after Raamses II, the pharaoh of the exodus by adherents of the later exodus theory (for these matters, see the introduction to the commentary on Exodus). The monument mentions Israel as already in the land (*ANET*[3], 376–78). Thus the exodus would be dated at about 1230 BC. The stela does not regard Israel as emerging; it views her as an indigenous enemy. At the time of the Merneptah Stela, Israel occupied a prominent place regionally and a distinct position culturally. Recent studies on the Berlin Pedestal, the base of a recently rediscovered monument with hieroglyphic writing on it naming Israel, indicate that Israel was an enemy of Egypt in the late 18th Dynasty, perhaps in the early 1300s BC. Again, it shows Israel as an indigenous enemy.

The events of the book cover 25 to 30 years. The three initial campaigns took about seven years (Jos 14:7, 10). If Joshua was 79 at the time of the invasion and 110 at death, the total period covered is about 31 years. This makes it likely that the events of the book of Joshua span about 1406 BC to approximately 1375 BC.

Theme and Purpose. For OT theologians who view the center of their theology as promise/fulfillment, this book represents the fulfillment of centuries of prophetic promise and historical movement. Thus the narrative has a twofold emphasis: the destruction of an idolatrous people and the progress and victory of faith in the one true God. The theme is "the venture and victory of faith." As an historical account, the book of Joshua demonstrates the faithfulness of God, despite the inconsistent nature of the faith of God's people. It shows Him as the covenant-keeping God (Jos 1:26). The purpose is to strengthen faith in and commitment to the Lord by giving a history of the conquest of Canaan and the distribution of the land among the tribes.

Contribution. It is impossible to think through the Bible without including Joshua. The bare fact of "Israel in the land" presupposes the people getting there. Many of the cities mentioned in the conquest are revisited in the drama of biblical narrative. Soon enough the story will spiral into the despair engendered in the epoch of the Judges; but for now, at the outset, Joshua presents the conquest of the land with Joshua and Israel just as God had promised Abraham.

Joshua sets a context for what follows in the OT. Judges would be a theological whiplash (how something begun so well could proceed so poorly!) without the words, world, and themes of Joshua. Readers would know less that obedience leads to blessing had that truth not first appeared in Joshua.

Furthermore, the events recorded in Joshua are referenced in significant ways in the Old and New Testaments. After the Babylonian captivity, the reader is told that Israel had not celebrated the Festival of Booths since the days of Joshua (Neh 8:17). Also, Stephen mentions the tabernacle crossing the Jordan with Joshua (Ac 7:44-45). There is, finally, the contrast between the "rest" that Joshua gave Israel from war and the "rest" believers have in Christ (Heb 4:8).

Background. The biblical book of Joshua opens with Israel on the eastern bank of the Jordan River. The memory of Egyptian bondage is four decades old. The people of Israel are younger: those over 20 after the exodus perished in the wilderness. Moses has just passed away, and the mourning for the great legislator of Israel has drawn to a close as Joshua assumes leadership of the nation. The reader joins Israel as the people prepare to enter the land and take possession as God had promised Abraham four centuries earlier (Gn 13:14-18).

Prior to the death of Moses, the great leader affirmed the request of two and a half of the tribes (Reuben, Gad, and half of Manasseh [Nm 32:1-5, 20-33]) to settle their wives, families, and livestock in the Transjordan area. Forty thousand of their men, however, would participate in the invasion of Canaan (Jos 4:13). The entire population of Israel may have numbered two million people. Though the people mourned greatly the death of Moses (Dt 34:5-8), eventually they would be in high spirits after their Transjordanian victories over the Amorites, and they were in support of Joshua (1:15-18).

Joshua is assumed to have been about the same age as Caleb, who was 40 years old at the time when they spied the land (Nm 13). He would thus be about 79 at the time of the crossing of the Jordan River. Joshua was from the tribe of Ephraim and had distinguished himself as a lieutenant of Moses (Ex 17:9-13). He served as Moses' servant at the giving of the law (Ex 24:33). Caleb and Joshua were the only spies who had the faith that God would help them take the land of Canaan. Thus they, and perhaps the two sons of Aaron, Eleazar and Ithamar (Jos 14:1), were the only ones of that generation to enter Canaan. Following a special commissioning by the Lord, Joshua became a fearless warrior and general, superintending a cyclonic campaign in Canaan. He would die at age 110 (Jos 24:29).

"Canaan" designated the western strip from Sidon in the north to Gaza and Sodom in the south (Gn 10:19). The original meaning of "Canaan," if related to the Hebrew word, was "trader" or "merchant." It was, however always known as the "land of purple," from its manufacturing of purple dyes. The valley cities were more impenetrable for Israelite forces because their armies were equipped with iron chariots (Jdg 1:19).

Canaan was populated by many tribal groups, but predominantly by the Hittites, Amorites, Canaanites, Perizzites, Hivites, Jebusites, and Girgashites (Gn 15:19-21; Jos 9:1). Of these, the Canaanites and Jebusites appear to be indigenous groups. The Hittites were from Asia Minor in the north; the Amorites were from the East; and the Hivites were probably from across the Dead Sea in the mountains of Seir (Gn 36:20), and originally from Mesopotamia. Of the Perizzites, nothing is known, and the Girgashites' exact location in Canaan is unknown.

The religions of Canaan were the basest of fertility cults. El was the chief god; Baal was his preeminent son who was the paramour of Ashtoreth (or Anath). Baal was the god of rain, sun, and vegetation and his consort was the personification of sexual love and fertility. These deities had no discernible moral character and the worship of these entailed some of the most degenerate practices in history. Their worship and lore fostered brutality and the most decadent immorality. The culture was due for extinction (Lv 18:21-30; Dt 12:30-32).

OUTLINE

COMMENTARY ON JOSHUA

I. Introduction: Preparations for the Conquest of the Land (1:1–5:15)

A. Joshua's Commission and Commanding (1:1-18)

1:1-4. The book opens with Joshua standing with Israel on the verge of the Jordan gazing westward. After apportioning the land to the two and a half tribes, Moses the great legislator of Israel has died (Dt 34:4-8). Who would be in charge and by what authority? What were Israel's ties to the past and directions for the future? The first verse answers these questions, linking to the final episodes of Deuteronomy. The vocabulary indicates the exalted status of Moses as **the servant of the Lord**, while Joshua was only **Moses' servant**. The final epitaph on Joshua's life will be "servant of YHWH" (Jos 24:29); but the process would have to be vindicated in 24 brief chapters.

The people had been invited to the commissioning of Joshua (Dt 31:7, 23). Now the Lord would commission Joshua directly to cross the Jordan River and take the land (Jos 1:3). This language mirrors the statement made by Moses (Dt 11:24) and is prefigured in God's invitation to Abram (Gn 13:14-17). The land promise to Abraham is on the verge of fulfillment. The borders, painted in broad brush strokes, will be refined later (chaps. 13–21).

1:5-7. Great promises were given here: no enemy would stand before Joshua for the rest of his life. God promised that the relationship He would share with Joshua was like that with Moses. Finally, Joshua was told: **I will not fail you or forsake you**, a promise later made to all true believers (Mt 28:20).

Joshua was then commanded to **be strong and courageous**. The idea of being strong need not mean physically strong— though for warfare, that would not hurt. The root idea is holding firmly to something. It means "to be in firm control of one's faculties." Far from the absence of fear, courage holds the energy of fear under control and channels it toward positive ends. Joshua would apportion the land. The same guarantee had been extended to twelve administrators (Nm 24:16-29). All these would survive the wars of Canaan.

In the second challenge, Joshua was commanded to obey the Torah of Moses, **so that you may have success wherever you go**. This is not necessarily a means to material prosperity—though neither is it necessarily precluded. However, in a spiritual context the faithful should expect success.

1:8-9. "This book of instruction must not depart from your mouth; you are to recite it day and night . . ." (HCSB). The HCSB translators have chosen the word "instruction" for the Hebrew word "torah," which is the Hebrew word for the Pentateuch —the five books of Moses. It is a word more related to teaching, instruction, or doctrine than to law. (Torah is much more: it has statute and case law; but it also contains narrative, prophecy, poetry, and exposition.) This instruction is to be recited. A Westerner might think of meditation as something silent in the mind. A growing consensus of Hebrew scholars considers meditation musing out loud. Unlike the repetition of a mantra as in Eastern thought, it is the recitation of propositional revelation. The purpose is **so that you may be careful to do according to all that is written in it**. Obedience is in view, motivated by the promise of success (cf. Ps 1). The whole section on success is bracketed by imperatives to **be strong and courageous** (1:6, 9). Joshua was motivated by the land promise, the promise of success, and the promise of God's presence.

1:10-11. Joshua first **commanded the officers** to go through the camp and have the people prepare **provisions**. The word "officers" is related to the Akkadian word meaning "to write." It was used for officers caught between the demands of Pharaoh and the difficulties of the people (Ex 5:6-19). The word appears elsewhere as "administrators." The mention of crossing the Jordan **within three days** would turn into seven days because of the delayed return of the spies from Jericho. Joshua's commission on "what" was clear; but "when" may have been delayed.

1:12-15. Joshua reminded the east Jordanian tribes of their obligation to participate in the conquest of Canaan (Nm 32:16-32; Dt 3:18-20). The two and a half tribes reaffirmed what they had said to Moses.

1:16-18. The first statement from these tribe members is clear: They promised to be obedient. However, the sentence: **Just as we obeyed Moses in all things, so we will obey you**, is ironic! A whole generation had died off in the wilderness because of disobedience. Even this generation could not claim a clean slate (cf. Nm 25:1-9). The second phrase in v. 17—**only may the Lord your God be with you as He was with Moses**— is not a wish or a prayer. It should be stated more strongly: "(Certainly) the Lord *will* be with you as He was with Moses." The verb is a future indicative rather than a wish (a modal or jussive verb). Some of these oath takers would perish in the coming conflict. For the believer, a vow to spouse, family, church, or country is often costly. When one obligates himself before God, God is watching to see if the promise is kept – despite the difficulties of life (Ps 15:4).

B. Spies Infiltrate Jericho (2:1-24)

The story of Rahab's faithfulness assumes the shape of a quest. Note the chiastic arrangement in the following diagram:

Rahab's Quest

A Commission of the Two Spies by Joshua (v. 1a)
- B Ingress/Tension: Protection of the Spies (vv. 2-7)
  - C. Rahab's Stunning Confession of Faith (vv. 8-14)
- B' Egress/Tension: Protection of Rehab's Family (vv. 15-21)

A' Completion of Reconnaissance, Report to Joshua (vv. 22-24)

The symmetry places the central focus on Rahab's confession.

2:1a. Joshua commissioned two agents **secretly** (related to a word that means "to be deaf; to keep silent") to gather information for the upcoming campaign into Canaan. Joshua had good reasons for secrecy. First, the spies were less likely to be intercepted. Second, they would report back directly to Joshua before going before the congregation with potentially alarming news. This had happened some 38 years previously (Nm 13:25-33) at Kadesh. What followed their report was widespread disobedience and lack of faith that resulted in the death of an entire generation while they wandered in the wilderness. Joshua, a key player in the earlier mission, now demanded discretion.

2:1b. When the spies arrived in Jericho, they **came into the house of . . . a harlot**. The text is clear: the spies engaged in no illicit behavior.

The text is equally clear: Rahab was an immoral woman. From the first-century historian Josephus to the present, there have been attempts to make her an innkeeper and her house a hostel; none is compelling. The Hebrew word **harlot** (*zona*) means either "an immoral woman" (usually for hire, cf. Gn 38:24), or refers to someone prostituting himself to paganism from faith in Israel's God ("playing the harlot after other gods"; cf. Lv 20:5; Ezk 6:9). To force another meaning here would be special pleading.

Some sense the need to rescue this member of the "Faith Hall of Fame" (Heb 11). Perhaps it seems odd that such a pronouncement of faith should come from one with such a checkered past. But that is exactly what the believer's redeeming God does: His ineffable grace makes human wreckage beautiful and serviceable. They went to a house of prostitution because it would have been a good place to gain information.

2:2-4a. Soon discovered, the spies were reported, and so the king sent agents to apprehend them whose plans go awry. Verse 4 begins, **But the woman had taken** [better, "took," reflecting the *qal* stem and the urgency and suddenness of Rahab's action] **the two men and hidden them**. Rahab acted swiftly to get the spies hidden before discovery by the king's agents.

2:4b-5. Rahab lied to the king's emissaries. She claimed that she did not know where the spies were from and that they had already left. She claimed she had no idea where they were going but then admonished the king's agents to chase after them in the false hope that they might be caught. Despite the ruse, God wished them to go chasing after phantoms of Rahab's imagination. Frequently we run up against these ethical conundrums in the Bible. It does not seem that the NT lauds Rahab so much for her personal righteousness in word and action as it does for her faith in God's program and her part in it (cf. Heb 11:31; Jms 2:24).

2:6-7. Most **flax** came from Egypt. However, perhaps Rahab was industrious enough to go gather some of it growing wild in the area. Perhaps she was able to buy some to dry and have woven into linen later. Nonetheless, it made a good hiding place for expatriate spies. The scene in v. 7 cuts to the fool's errand of the king's agents.

2:8-11. Rahab first approached the spies, confirming their hopes: she knew the Lord had given them the country. Second, she confessed that everyone was terrified: hearts **melted** like wax. Her historical memory was long (Ex 14:27-31) and recent (Nm 21:21-35). Rahab's word for **utterly destroyed** is related to the noun "being placed under the ban." In Jericho everything alive was to be killed, everything combustible burned, everything precious devoted to God. Third, Rahab shared her own fears: **When we heard it, our hearts melted** (Jos 2:11a). And then she offered this stunning credo: **for the LORD your God, He is God in heaven above and on earth beneath** (Jos 2:11b). Perhaps this statement is the logical result of her despair, but it is not without some rather remarkable antecedents. The Ten Commandments include, "Do not make an idol for yourself, whether in the shape of anything *in the heavens above or on the earth below* or in the waters under the earth" (Ex 20:4; cf. Dt 4:39; 5:8). This has the ring of a basic creed that Rahab could have known only by reason or direct revelation.

2:12-13. Next, Rahab negotiated for her family's life. The word **kindly** (v. 12) is the Hebrew word *chesed*. "Kindness" is too weak for this word. When it pertains to God and His favor upon His people, it means "everlasting loving-kindness." When it is used in reference to people, it means "loyalty." In effect she is saying, "Since I have proven my loyalty to you, show your loyalty to me and save my family." Sparing someone condemned to death makes "kindness" an understatement; it is undeserved and ineffable mercy. She asked for a sure sign and seemed satisfied with their word (vv. 13-14).

2:14-21. The spies spoke. They vowed loyalty with three caveats: First, Rahab was not to betray their meeting. Second, she was told to tie a scarlet cord in the window. Third, those to be preserved alive were to be with Rahab when Israel attacked. Repeating the terms, she agreed to them as the spies fled into the darkness.

2:22. There are cliffs some 1,500 yards west of Jericho (Tel es-Sultan). Likely, the two spies stayed in a cave there for the three days it took for the trackers to return to Jericho. Eventually, they forded the Jordan and returned.

2:23-24. The men **related to him** [Joshua] **all that had happened to them**. That hair-raising story sealed the leader's resolve (Jos 2:24). There was no fear, as voiced by the 10 spies at Kadesh 38 years previously. There was no hesitation (cf. Nm 14:8), only bold faith in God. In regard to the people of the land, the men reiterated Rahab's words "to melt like wax." There were no misgivings, as the story was disseminated among the

Israelites. The next day everyone rose early and readied themselves to cross the Jordan—where impending conflict awaited.

Rahab is immortalized in several ways: she appears in genealogies as the grand-matriarch of David and Jesus (Mt 1:5). She is also recalled for her deeds—not necessarily her words—in both Hebrews (11:31) and James (2:25). There is no need to save Rahab from her reputation: God is in the business of saving the most inveterate liars, cheats, thieves, and even prostitutes. No wall can be built between God and His intended child. Neither should readers be astonished at such magnificats as those of Mary (Lk 1:46-55), Hannah (1Sm 2:1-10), or Rahab (Jos 2:9-11). Rahab, an outlander, reminds believers that "the LORD your God, He is God in heaven above and on earth beneath."

As one reads the book of Ruth, remember that Rahab was Boaz's mother. Rahab probably never lived to welcome her daughter-in-law Ruth into the family; but Boaz's understanding of an outlander's loyalty (*chesed*) to Israel's God was nothing new to him. He learned it from his mother. Neither was the acceptance of such an outlander new. He learned it from Salmon, his father. This enabled him to see past an instinctive nationalism, bringing a "woman of excellence" (Ru 3:11) into his home.

C. Israel Crosses the Jordan (3:1-17)

Israel was about to cross the Jordan; however, several events needed to occur first. These verses proceed in stately cadence, giving a ritualistic feel to the narrative. Other rituals will follow, but now Israel approaches the river.

3:1-2. Israel rose early and camped on the east bank of the river. Perhaps the **three days** were additional if Joshua was wrong in his original assessment, delayed by the late return of the spies; or it could be that the spies had been sent out prior to the command to the officers (1:10).

3:3-4. The people were to wait until they saw the ark of the covenant and then follow; but they were to keep a respectful distance of about a thousand yards.

3:5. The people were commanded: **Consecrate yourselves**! "Consecrate" from *qadash*, means to "be separate." It also signifies a readiness for service. Jeremiah spoke of God's anger against Jerusalem and said that He had set apart or "consecrated" destroyers against her (Jr 22:7). Babylon's army cannot be said to be "sanctified" in any real sense. The word means God was "readying" Babylon for disciplinary action against Judah. Here "consecration" means separate *from* sin, separate *from* the entanglements of life and separate *to* the Lord's mission and ready to go take the land.

The writer provides the motivation for their consecration: because **tomorrow the LORD will do wonders among you**. "Wonders" is the closest word the OT has for "miracle." Israel was being prepared for exodus-like events.

3:6-7. The priests, ordered to pick up the ark, moved ahead of the people. The ceremony-like cadence mirrors their obedience. Speaking to Joshua directly, the Lord told him his reputation would be advanced in Israel's sight and he would be compared with Moses. God reaffirmed the promise that He would be with Joshua.

3:8-13. The priests carrying the ark were instructed to stop at river's edge. Then the people were given further orders and told what to expect: God would be with them and they would be victorious over the Canaanites (v. 10). The **waters of the Jordan will be cut off**, as the Red Sea had been at the exodus (v. 13). For reasons to be given later, the people were to select tribal representatives.

The lists of nations to be dispossessed vary; however, these are "the usual suspects." See the introduction for peoples and origins. "The Jebusite" is the only people group represented as a city-state. "Jebus," the older name for Jerusalem, was difficult for the Jewish people to subdue until David's time (2Sm 24). It was also represented in the Amarna Letters, where, for instance, one viceroy, Abdu-Heba, complained to the pharaoh about Egypt's apparent disinterest in the plight of Jebus and that the other city states are not helping (*ANET*[3], 487–89).

3:14-16. The narrative advances with Israel breaking camp, the priests moving the ark ahead of the people. The verbs change to progressive action to give the reader a real-time experience: **the priests [were] *carrying* the ark** . . . **before the people**; and as those *carrying* the ark *were approaching* the Jordan; and the feet of the priests carrying the ark *were dipped* in the edge of the water . . . the waters going down from above *stood* in one heap . . ." (vv. 14-16, author's translation and emphasis). Not until the waters *stood* is finality described by the historical tense. It is as though the author was saying, "Do you see how wonderful our God is? Would you like to know more about Him?"

3:17. The water stood far upstream from the ark, perhaps so that Israel could remain at a respectful distance. Observe the details of the miracle: the waters were cut off at flood stage, long enough for Israel to cross over; the priests stood on, and Israel crossed over on dry ground. This stoppage was not the Jordan alone—all tributaries below Adam and Zarethan had to be stopped as well; the event took place exactly as God had predicted.

In correspondence with the exodus story, the water was separated, dry ground crossed, God was glorified, and God's servant honored (Ex 14:29-31). Believers understand that if God wishes to deliver them by miracles, He certainly can do so. They should, however, trust Him even with the "river" ahead of them.

D. Israelite Men Set Up Memorials (4:1-24)

Joshua 3 and 4 are best read as a single unit. An emphasis on perspective is helpful: there is a difference between "crossing over" the river (e.g., v. 11) and "coming up out of" the river (e.g., vv. 16-18). That is, in the former, participants are in Transjordan crossing over to the land; whereas in the latter, participants are in the promised land watching movement toward themselves. The last verse of Jos 4 concludes: "that all the peoples of the earth may know and so that you may fear the LORD," ending the Jordan crossing episode; so, 5:1 functions as a "hinge" between two episodes.

4:1-10. The command to select 12 men (3:12) was reissued—this time to collect **twelve stones . . . out of the middle of the Jordan** (v. 3) as memorial stones. The men, each representing one of the 12 tribes, brought the stones to the west side of the river; then **Joshua set** [them] **up at Gilgal** (v. 20; about 7 miles northwest of the Dead Sea adjacent to Jericho; see v. 8). These were to be **a sign** (v. 6), so that inquisitive children might be told of the Lord's miraculous power in bringing Israel across the river on dry ground at flood stage.

Oddly, Joshua also set up his own memorial—in the middle of the river (v. 9)! Large enough boulders might be visible at low water. Although Joshua's purpose is difficult to know, the purpose of any monument is pedagogical, and perhaps his stone monument was less visible so that it would never eclipse the greatness of Israel's God. The reader is only left with the parting: **They are there to this day**, from the date of the final words of the book (24:29-33). Finally, everyone hurriedly did as commanded.

4:11-13. When all the people had finished crossing, the ark of the LORD and the priests crossed before the people. Everything has a ritualistic feel; but the discipline of the nation is also evident. As commanded by Moses, the east Jordan tribes moved across ahead of the rest, having left their families and livestock on the east side. They presented a formidable fighting force in case of initial resistance to Israel's advance.

4:14. Joshua's exaltation was then celebrated in several highlights: The Lord **exalted Joshua in the sight of all Israel**; his high station was a lifelong appointment, and he was venerated as Moses had been. When the Lord elevates someone, others will notice and barring the need for humiliation, it may be a lifelong station.

4:15-18. The change in perspective from "go across" to come up out of the river" indicates a new section. The Lord commanded Joshua to direct the priests carrying the ark of the testimony to **come up from the Jordan**; he issued the command, the priests complied, and as soon as their feet touched the **dry ground . . . the waters of the Jordan returned to their place, and went over all its banks as before.**

Again paralleling the exodus account, notice the repetition of the words **come up from the Jordan**. Aspects of the ark are repeated: **the ark of the testimony** and **the ark of the covenant**. The ark was a special container containing a jar of manna, Aaron's budding almond rod, and the plaques of the Ten Commandments—the covenant. It was characterized as the place of testimonial (cf. Ex 25:16).

4:19-23. When the people had come up out of the water on the western bank, an additional parallel with the exodus became apparent. They had crossed the River Jordan during Passover, **the tenth** day **of the first month** (= Abib, March–April), just as they had crossed the Red Sea during the Passover. Thus here was the final culmination of the exodus: The people are finally in their homeland. The people then moved west and camped at the extremity of Jericho's territory, about two miles away. The memorial stones were then either laid in a circle or heaped. Both ideas fit if the event is somehow related to the name Gilgal, as discussed in 5:9. (This would represent an etiology, the naming of a place to commemorate an event.) The didactic purpose of the memorial stones is explained to the people. They are to tell their sons and daughters who would ask about the stones, **the LORD your God dried up the waters . . . before you until you had crossed, just as the**

Lord . . . had done to the Red Sea. As the Lord was with Moses and the first generation, He was with Joshua and the second generation, leading them into the promised land.

4:24. At this point the text is summed up with two purpose clauses. First, God delivered the people through the Jordan **that all the peoples of the earth may know that the hand of the Lord is mighty**. The reasons for Israel's existence had always been to glorify the Lord and to draw others to Him. Second, this was **so that** they **may fear the Lord** their **God always**. Israel was always to love (Dt 6:5) and fear God. It is difficult to love and fear a God who is a consuming fire (Heb 12:29) and into whose hands it is a terrifying thing to fall (Heb 10:31); but He is the same loving heavenly Father that sent His Son to be our Savior, the Father who retrieves the lost sheep and welcomes the prodigal son.

E. Israel Is Consecrated and Lives in the Land (5:1-12)

The key to this chapter is holiness. The nation's men must receive the sign of the covenant, circumcision; then the nation's people celebrated the Passover; and finally, the nation's leader met with the supreme commander of God's forces. Two important changes occurred: Israel began to live off the land and the manna was no longer provided. This also reflected the exodus events. As noted in the "Parallels" chart, some events are repeated sequentially and some mirror (by chiasm) earlier events.

5:1. Israel's enemies were paralyzed with fear. Seemingly it would have been a good time to go on the offensive, but three elements were lacking: circumcision (5:1-9), an observance of the Passover (5:10), and the meeting with the Lord's Captain (5:13-15). The first, circumcision, had to do with Israel's condition with respect to the covenant. The sign of the covenant was circumcision, a practice that should have been practiced by every Israelite male (cf. Gn 17). It was the entrance rite into the community of Israel.

5:2-3. Joshua was commanded by God to make **flint** [or obsidian] **knives** to **circumcise again the sons of Israel**. This does not mean that each individual was to be circumcised a second time, as the following verses explain. Meanwhile, Joshua complied.

5:4-5. The parents had not practiced circumcision as prescribed (Gn 17:9-14; Lv 12:3). Young men had grown up, raised by the unfaithful generation that refused to circumcise their infant sons on the eighth day. Ironically, the parents of the faithless generation (even the slaves and foreigners) had circumcised them (Ex 12:42-51).

5:6. The text now reflects upon the extermination of the faithless generation: they **walked forty years in the wilderness, until all the nation . . . perished**. The Lord did not allow those who shirked their initial opportunity to enter and take the land. Perhaps the author indicates his presence in the change to the pronoun **us**. This does not necessitate Joshua's authorship, but it certainly

Parallels between Events of Exodus and Joshua

Exodus	Joshua
God meets with His leader, Moses (2–3)	God meets with His leader, Joshua (1:3-5; 5:13-15)
Passover celebrated (11–12)	
Exodus from Egypt (12–14)	
Israel crosses the Red Sea (14:13-31)	Israel crosses the Jordan (3–4)
Egyptians destroyed (14–15)	
Circumcision (12:44, 48 re: Passover); every male at eight days (Lv 12:3)	Circumcision of new generation (5:1-9)
	Passover celebrated (5:10)
Supplies from Egypt consumed; manna provided (Ex 16)	Supply of manna ceases (5:12)
Affirmation of the covenant with God (19–24)	Reaffirmation of the covenant at Mt. Ebal/Gerizim (8:30-35)
Wilderness wandering, disobedient generation dies off (Nm 14–Dt 34)	Jericho destroyed (6)

indicates that the writer acknowledged the blessing of the land that God was now granting them.

5:7-8. The Lord raised up a subsequent generation that believed and was obedient. Since they had not been circumcised, it was imperative that they have this procedure. During their recovery time they would be vulnerable to attack (cf. Gn 34). The reason Israel's enemies were frozen in fear (v. 1) was that God was protecting His people at this risky time.

5:9. Israel had long borne reproach. It had been more than 400 years since God promised the land to the patriarchs; much of that time was spent in Egypt. Many years of the Egyptian sojourn were in slavery. Upon leaving Egypt, it appeared that Israel was poised to enter the land and begin the conquest; however, they refused the opportunity and spent 38 years wandering in the wilderness after the rebellion at Kadesh. The faithless generation was left behind in the wilderness, having perished there. Now a more obedient and faithful generation was ready to inaugurate the reception of the promise.

The name "Gilgal" is a wordplay on God's words: **Today I have rolled away the reproach of Egypt from you**. The Hebrew word *galal*, "to roll," is similar in sound to the word "Gilgal," and may be related to it etymologically. This may be a new reason for the name of the place or a renaming of it. The place was known by Moses and Joshua (Dt 11:30; Jos 4:19, 20). Sometimes places retained the same name but were infused with new meaning, as was Beersheba (Gn 21:31; 26:33). Perhaps Gilgal was already named but gained new significance, as it became associated with God rolling away the reproach of Egypt, a connotation it did not have previously. Henceforth, Gilgal would be a frequent reference point as a base or operations.

5:10. It was necessary to circumcise the nation before Passover (Ex 12:42-51). They had crossed the Jordan on the tenth of the first month (Abib), the day the Passover lamb was to be set aside; the men were circumcised as a symbol of covenant fidelity; then Passover was celebrated on the 14th. Whenever Passover is celebrated, it is a memorial of the birth of the nation of Israel. As with circumcision, the first Passover was a defining event; it was a national event, and every celebration a commemoration.

5:11-12. Two more significant events happened: The Israelites began to forage off the land and the supply of manna ended. There would be no more need for this provision.

F. The Supreme Commander Meets with Joshua (5:13-15)

5:13-14. In this confrontation with a divine being, **the captain of the host of the LORD**, one wonders if Joshua bared his own blade. Apparently, this visitor was not much alarmed by Joshua. Joshua asked: **Are you for us or for our adversaries?** The visitor gave no direct answer.

He answered, literally: "No, because I am the Captain of the army of YHWH; now I have come." Joshua then prostrated himself. Joshua recognized his visitor as a divine being. It was not a matter of whose side the visitor was on; it was a matter of whose side Joshua was on. The text reads, literally, "Joshua fell to his face to the ground and he prostrated himself." The word translated **bowed down** by the NASB is translated in the HCSB by "worship," suggesting that the HCSB translators view this being as a theophany (manifestation of God) or a Christophany (appearance of the pre-incarnate Christ), the more likely possibility here. He was the captain of an army belonging to another: Christ the Lord Himself.

5:15. Joshua's second question (v. 14) was followed by what was probably to Joshua an unexpected answer: **Remove your sandals from your feet, for the place where you are standing is holy**. This language is similar to that of the call of Moses (Ex 3:5): the word "ground" is missing. There would be no need for "holy ground" when Joshua was prostrate in the Holy Land. In a sense, the whole area is holy ground.

By the parallel with the story of the Moses' commission, Joshua has filled the sandals of Moses. From this point forward, Moses will receive less frequent mention excepting his written legacy, the Torah. Joshua has become the new Moses. He will lead his people in government and military, and he will empower the priesthood to do its work.

For believers, there are times when a leader will apply the authoritative Word of God to a new situation, and others will follow cooperatively. But sometimes a new leader arises with a new direction for the Word to be applied, and the people of God might resist. In both situations, the leaders and the people must be careful to maintain close communion with the Lord in order for Him to accomplish great things. Believers are called to be holy if they would have these times of close communion with the Lord and would recognize His direction through others.

II. Conquest of the Land in Three Major Theaters of Engagement (6:1–12:24)

Israel had entered the promised land with the door closed behind her; thé people's only path was forward. Jericho, at nearly the lowest point on earth, had to be conquered. The conquest of the land after Jericho was both literally and metaphorically all uphill from there.

A. Jericho and the Central Campaign (6:1–8:35)

The first fortification encountered after crossing the Jordan was Jericho. It had to be subdued to gain access to the highlands because it guarded the fords of the Jordan and sat astride a major east-west road.

6:1. The author signals the start of a new episode by repeating a phrase used earlier in reference to a city or its gates being "shut" or secured (cf. 2:5, 7). The city was shut tight, indicative not only of the terror of the inhabitants, but also their vigilance. The camp of Israel was visible in smoke by day and ominous campfire glow by night. Were anyone to wander out, there were 40,000 Israelites from east of the Jordan to confront (cf. Jos 4:12-13).

6:2. God speaks of the conquest as an accomplished fact: **I have given Jericho into your hand**. Older commentaries refer to this verb as a "prophetic perfect." The action is certainly viewed as if it were completed in the past with its results continuing to the present from God's standpoint. It was worded this way to give Joshua confidence.

6:3-5. The approach to the "coming assault" is perhaps counterintuitive. It may appear "senseless" (Donald H. Madvig, "Joshua." Vol. 3 of EBC, ed. Frank E. Gaebelein [Grand Rapids, MI: Zondervan, 1992], 278); but God's program sometimes may appear silly when it is the perfect plan. The Canaanite people were paralyzed in terror (2:9, 11; 5:1), and Jericho was no exception (6:1). It must have been unnerving for the people of this small fortress to see tens of thousands of Israelites parading just out of bowshot. God's plan, as always, was brilliant. On the final day they were to rise early, march around the city seven times and at the last blast of the trumpets, the warriors were to shout.

6:6-14. In the progression of the first two days, the front guard (possibly the Israelite warriors from the tribes that settled east of the Jordan, Jos 1:14) was followed by the priests, some carrying the ark, others blowing trumpets. They, in turn, were followed by the rear guard. The guard was not God's protection from enemies; He needs none! The guards were sanctified soldiers to keep a hedge between chance defilements and the ark, the priests, and God Himself. Again, if this repeated circuit has the feel of a holy convocation, it very likely was intended.

These seven days correspond to those of the Feast of Unleavened Bread following Passover. Although there is no evidence of magical numbers in the Bible, the number "seven" is repeated often in this chapter: four times in v. 4 and 14 times total throughout the chapter. "Seven" may indicate "totality, completion, and perfection" (David M. Howard, Jr., *Joshua*. Vol. 5 of NAC, ed. E. Ray Clendenen [Nashville, TN: Broadman & Holman, 2002], 169). When God overthrows this city, He will do it in totality, completely and with unmatched perfection.

6:15-20. The number of events were increased and complicated on the seventh day. The armed men and the priests rose early in the morning in order to complete seven circuits. This sounds like a staggering amount of ground to cover for the Israelite soldiers, but Jericho was only about 350 yards long north to south, and about 180 yards wide east to west. At the final circumnavigation, Joshua commanded them: **Shout! For the Lord has given you the city**. In v. 20, the trumpets blasted, the warriors shouted and the "wall fell down under it" (author's rendering, cf. v. 5). The HCSB has "collapse"; it likely indicates that the walls fell outward and down the slope. In Garstang's archaeological records (excavated from 1930–36), more recently vindicated by Bryant Wood (see bibliography at the end of this chapter), there is evidence for such a collapse. Perhaps vv. 17-19 reflect commands given earlier to leaders and passed down through the ranks.

The city was to be destroyed and burned. All the people and livestock were to be killed. Gold, silver, bronze, and iron, were to be devoted to the Lord and placed in the tabernacle treasury. This destruction had been ordered by God (Dt 7:2; 20:16-18) because He wanted these people eradicated: indigenous pagan survivors would bring compromise and syncretism to Israel. These people were unredeemable, exterminated for their wickedness. God had told Abraham four hundred years earlier that "the sin of the Amorite was not yet complete" (Gn 15:16). Now it was. Besides their horrific religious practices including ritual prostitution and child-sacrifice, these people were involved in wickedness in their day to day lives. If Lv 18 reflects Canaanites practices, they were regularly involved in incest, adultery, child-sacrifice, sodomy, and bestiality (Lv 18:6-23). God calls these practices the most heinous sin. It cannot be demonstrated that these practices contribute anything positive to society. Israel was not to do any of these practices (Lv 18:24-30). They were to kill or to drive the Canaanites into exile (Dt 20:16-18).

Amidst the chaos of battle, God's grace came to one believer and her family. Rahab was spared along with anyone wise enough to separate from their countrymen and join with Israel. The walls fell down and the city was easily captured. A short battle narrative does not mean there were no casualties. No matter how certain the engagement, there will be the happenstances of war.

6:21. Most of the words here translated "destruction" are from the *charam* word group. It is an act of obedient worship, a "dedicated destruction" for God's glory. The warriors tore down every building and killed every living thing.

Excursus: Canaanite Genocide – Killing the Seemingly Innocent (6:21)

It is often said that a God who condoned, much less commissioned, the slaughter of "innocents" during the Canaan conquest is unworthy of worship. If such a thing is commanded by God, then a certain exercise in theodicy (discussion of God's justice) necessarily follows. Before such a discussion, consider a few brief propositions: (1) It is impossible to know the fate of the "innocents." God is both good and just; but the destiny of a person is between that person and his or her God. (2) Jesus was far more interested in one's eternal destiny than in the person's earthly existence and departure. In the context of living the life of a virtuous disciple, He says: "Do not fear those who kill the body, but are unable to kill the soul; but rather fear Him who is able to destroy both soul and body in hell" (Mt 10:28). (3) The worst possible scenario for a war survivor may not be death—we simply cannot know what the sorts of horrors are to which any particular "innocent" war survivor might have been exposed. Every now and again, glimpsing the atrocities into which the little ones suffer at the hands of their fellow human beings makes it possible to conclude that there are times when the dead are more to be congratulated than the living (Ec 4:2; Rv 14:13).

Apart from these ideas, there are several reasons for God's command to destroy the Canaanites. First, the sin of the Amorite was now complete (cf. Gn 15:16). The point of God's words to Abram was that He was going to give the Canaanites over to the lusts of their hearts and to impurity (Rm 1:24-32). He let them go as far from Him as they desired. As a result, now, like Sodom and Gomorrah, they were ripe for destruction.

Second, the interpreter must interface with the "curse on Canaan" from earlier in Genesis (Gn 9:24-27). The behavior of the Canaanites had finally spiraled so far out of control that the best outcome for the Canaanites was annihilation. Even this was not without precedent: Cain was cursed for killing his own brother (Gn 4:11), with the result that the whole family line would die out in the flood (Gn 6). This still does not address the question of the children. Why was there nothing redeemable about them?

Third, the taking of slaves, much less prisoners, would have been impossible in the constant movements involved in a war of this scope. Children prisoner/slaves would have been an added encumbrance and would likely have been the victims of further atrocities.

Fourth, the command and its fulfillment are couched in history. This was a one-time affair to be fulfilled only in the conquest. No philosophy, theology or *modus operandi* should be deduced from this.

Still, the unique nature of this command is not going to make anyone feel better. So why there, why then? A fifth reason to destroy Jericho and other Canaanites may be that God felt that it was necessary to start the new nation upon its land with an absolutely clean slate; the only way to do that was to kill every living thing in Jericho and elsewhere.

Sixth, there is the sacerdotal argument: complete destruction, *herem*, was required for the conditions of such a holy God. If the sin of the Amorite is complete, then the affront to the holiness of a perfect God is also complete.

Sixth, in "Yahweh War" as Eugene Merrill has called this (Eugene H. Merrill, "The Case for Moderate Discontinuity" in Stanley N. Gundry, ed., *Show Them No Mercy: Four Views on God and Canaanite Genocide* [Grand Rapids, MI: Zondervan, 2003], 63–94), there is (as with Pharaoh) a hardness of heart that is irremediable (cf. Jos 11:20). Considering that a civilization's decline and renaissance are rare, there is no reason to suspect that, in the case of such a degenerate society as that of Canaan, any subsequent generation would be an improvement, humanly speaking. It is not just a cultural spiral—it runs deep within a people's sinful nature, and only God has the right to make the determination as to who is ripe for such a harvest.

Seventh, it seems that in most cases of "Yahweh War" and at least in Israel's conquests, God opened some unusual odd channels of grace before, during, and after hearts were finally hardened. Only consider Rahab and her family and the Gibeonites. Also, what of those who survived the wars of Canaan by merely outlasting them and then also survived long enough to be absorbed into Israel? Grace is indeed evident, even for the Canaanites.

Israel needed to be redeemed from her servitude in Egypt, needed a place to go, and was commissioned by God to eradicate the Canaanites and take their land. More importantly, this gives no license for any concept of a "holy war" in any age other than the age of the conquest.

6:22-23. Joshua commissioned the two spies (chap. 2) to protect Rahab and her family, who were then settled outside the regular encampment. This served as a period of spiritual quarantine (cf. Nm 12:10, 14-16). Rahab would soon be absorbed into the tribe of Judah.

6:24. The final disgrace of this Canaanite city is conflagration. Her precious metals were purified in the fire, collected and placed in the treasury of the tabernacle (most of them; cf. Jos 7:20-21).

6:25. The reason for Rahab's deliverance was because **she hid the messengers whom Joshua sent to spy out Jericho**. In the NT, her heroic action is regarded as a reflection of her faith (Jms 2:25; Heb 11:31). Living in Israel **to this day** represents the day of the composition of the text, sometime in the generation after Joshua (Jos 24:31). Rahab is immortalized as a trophy of God's ineffable grace and mercy. A woman of faith, she proved herself faithful to the servants of Israel's God. She would live on in history: her son Boaz would marry the Moabitess Ruth, who would become the great grandmother of David, and thus two of the distant grandmothers of Jesus (Ru 4:20-22; Mt 1:4-17).

6:26. Joshua then made Israel take an oath to curse anyone who dared rebuild the city. Any would-be rebuilder would do so at the cost of his sons. Centuries later when this actually happened (see 1 Kg 16:34), the writer of 1 Kings knew that this was "according to the word of the Lord, which He spoke through Joshua the son of Nun."

6:27. As the smoke of Jericho rose, the text says that **the LORD was with Joshua, and his fame was in all the land**. This answers Joshua's question ("Are you for us or for our adversaries?") to the Lord's captain, the angelic being who appeared to him previously (5:13). At that moment the captain sensed no compulsion to dignify the question with an answer. But at the end of the siege of Jericho, the author does. One consequence of a successful action is that, in winning big in a limited engagement, it is easier to go with confidence to the next battle. The nations were immobilized in dread of Israel. Now the reason is known: Canaan's terror is at the prospect of total annihilation at the hands of Joshua and the God of Israel. So his personal fame now extended beyond the ethnic lines of Israel as its people began to carve out a homeland.

Chapters 6–8 were to be read as a single episode; chap. 7 is the chapter of "trouble." Much of modern criminal justice is based upon the principle that "a crime against one of us is a crime against all of us." The story of Achan's crime, apprehension, trial, and punishment corresponds to that principle. "The whole nation could be devoted to destruction through the actions of a single person . . . the sin of an individual has consequences for the family and the community" (Madvig, "Joshua," 281). When someone does something wrong, anyone in community with them will experience collateral damage.

7:1. Even though the deed was done by one man, Achan, the crime is viewed as unfaithfulness of **the sons of Israel**. This may be troubling to a modern individualist. Yet the danger here was that hidden and unresolved sin would, like leaven, spread to all Israel. As a result, Achan's sin needed to be addressed collectively and seriously.

7:2. There is a subtle distinction in the depiction of the reconnaissance of Ai here: the wording used for spying out the region more resembles that of the catastrophic failure a generation ago (Nm 13:2) than it does that of the successful espionage of Jericho (Jos 2:1). Literarily, the reading in Numbers foreshadows the calamity that is about to happen to Israel.

7:3-4. One of the consequences of Achan's sin was that Israel was presumptuous about the military success at Jericho. **Do not make all the people toil up there, for they are few**, the spies counseled Joshua. Yet without God, they could not win.

7:5. Casualties are first numbered at Ai, although possibly human losses occurred during the Jericho victory that were not recorded. The number **thirty-six** was not large but it signifies far more: Israel had, in one brief engagement, lost all its momentum. They no longer appeared invincible. The terror the surrounding peoples felt would melt away as their courage had melted before (cf. 2:11, 24). Conversely, Israel's hearts **melted** away **and became as water**.

7:6-9. Joshua's reaction, along with that of the elders, may seem melodramatic. However, mourning is more expressive in some cultures. The similarities with some of the difficulties Moses and Aaron faced are apparent. Questions about crossing the river and leaving the Transjordan mirror those of crossing the Red Sea and leaving Egypt. Joshua feared destruction and appealed to God based on His reputation as Moses often had (e.g., Ex 32:11-13; Nm 14:15-16).

7:10-12. God answered Joshua abruptly. In short, the only reasons Israel *could* lose a battle were presumption and sin. God commanded Joshua to action based on the fact that Israel had sinned. Verse 1 states that something very bad has been done. Now the narrator gradually reveals how God will unveil not only the crime, but also the culprit to Joshua. When items dedicated to God are taken, He views that as theft, and the wrong must be rectified. Israel, beaten back in a limited engagement, has traded places with the *herem*, that which had been devoted to destruction, and has now become devoted to destruction. God told them He would no longer be with them unless they **destroy the things under the ban**.

7:13-15. Joshua was told to **consecrate the people**. God was about to pass judgment on the offender, and the people had to be ready for His visitation. Their preparation involved being clean, changing clothes, and abstaining from sexual expression. On numerous occasions a culprit would be found out through God's providence over the casting of lots (cf. 1Sm 10: 20-21; 14:29, 39-42). The culprit and his family would be killed by stoning first (cf. 7:25); then their bodies burned. Fire purified everything. The word translated **disgraceful thing** is more often translated "stupidity," or by extension "willful sin" (*HALOT*, 664). In short, Achan knew it was wrong and stupidly, defiantly, did it anyway.

7:16-18. Joshua arose early in the morning (3:1; 6:12; 7:18), indicating his preparation to meet God and cooperate with Him in the judgment process. Apparently using lots (see v. 14), Joshua, with God's help, narrowed the search for the offender to the specific tribe (Judah), then the specific clan (Zerah), then the extended family (the family of Zabdi), and finally settling on the head of a household, Achan. Likely, God led Joshua through this process in order to make a public display of His displeasure over Achan's crime.

7:19. Joshua commanded Achan to give glory to God by confessing what he had done. Achan waited to confess, as the concentric rings inexorably tightened. There may be a "law of first offense" wherein the first crime of a type or a period is punished severely indicating exactly what God thinks of it (possibly Adam and Eve; the flood generation; the exodus generation; Achan stealing from God; King Saul; and Ananias and Sapphira with whom Achan is often compared). If God punished everyone who sinned in this way, there would be fewer people and those left would obey, not out of devotion, but out of fear of reprisal.

7:20-21. Achan admitted his guilt; but when he described his action, he spoke using words used to describe Eve's infraction: "I **saw** . . . I **coveted** . . . I **took** . . ." (cf. Gn 3:6). An observant biblical reader should recall the original offense in the Eden narrative and recognize the similarities in the crimes. The volume and value of what Achan had taken was high. This is important considering the severity and scope of punishment.

7:22-23. Messengers found everything as Achan had described and **they poured them out before the Lord**. The words "poured out" are used of "pouring out" a drink offering before the Lord. This has the feel of ritualistic purification.

7:24-26. There are several uses of the term **trouble** before the naming of the place is formalized. Joshua and the people of Israel brought Achan **and all that belonged to him** to the "valley of trouble." They probably killed him and his family by stoning, then burned them and raised a heap of stones as a monument to this trespass against God's holiness. Then **the Lord turned from the fierceness of His anger** and the place was named "the Valley of Trouble."

Why were Achan's sons and daughters killed? Scripture says: "Fathers shall not be put to death because of their children, nor shall children be put to death because of their fathers. Each one shall be put to death for his own sin" (Dt 24:16 ESV). Perhaps these adult children were complicit in Achan's crimes. With regard to the words "all that belongs to him" (v. 15), perhaps Joshua interpreted them to mean livestock and inanimate possessions as well as family. God had not, however, specified *anyone* other than the culprit. In the first six chapters Joshua was listening carefully to God. But in chap. 7, he was not seeking the Lord's counsel until forward momentum had been lost. God rebuked him (7:10-15) and sent him to apprehend the culprit. Joshua did not ask the specifics of the sentencing. The traditional solution is that the children were accessories to the crime and that Joshua complied with the Lord's directive completely (7:12-15, 24-26). As a result of this punishment, God's anger was assuaged in the specifics; but He will "feel" more distant throughout most of the remainder of the book.

Another ethical problem affects individualists. Often they are told, "Nobody else was hurt" when a sin is committed. Sin, in modern Western thinking, is supposedly a matter affecting an individual's conscience and life. In the case of Achan, God was displeased and did not help Israel in what should have been an easy victory. "Israel" was blamed for the infraction. "Israel" lost the battle. Thirty-six warriors lost their lives. The nation lost its momentum and became demoralized. Valuable time was expended in finding the perpetrator. The punishment was capital, affecting Achan, his sons, daughters, and livestock. The nation had to restart a campaign that should have been well under way. Every damaged relationship and every questionable acquisition have negative consequences. Sin, crime, and immorality all negatively affect the family, community, and nation.

As the narrator comes to chap. 8, everything from the taking of Jericho (chap. 2) through the initial defeat and subsequent conquest of Ai were to be read as a single episode. The covenant renewal section in 8:30-35 then presents a major break in the narrative.

8:1. The Lord had promised Joshua His presence in the upcoming engagement with Ai. The previous loss to Ai woke Israel up so that this time she would not be so presumptuous (7:3-4), there would be so many warriors engaged that allied cities would be less likely to leave the safety of their fortresses, and Ai could be lulled into Israel's trap.

8:2. Ai and its king would be like Jericho and its king. Israel could now enjoy the spoils of war for themselves. If only Achan had waited! God told Joshua: **Set an ambush for the city behind it**. God commanded His general to use a battle plan including deception. The main force was to do a feint maneuver to draw people away into the field.

8:3-8. The ambush involved three fighting forces for Israel, all strategically placed. The majority of Joshua's military force was called **all the people of war** (vv. 3 and 11). From this group **Joshua chose 30,000** . . . **valiant warriors** (also v. 3). Later Joshua selected from all the people of war **about 5,000** soldiers (vv. 11-12). Precisely where the 30,000 (v. 3) and 5,000 (v. 12) Israelite warriors from among the larger group were placed is difficult to determine. Ai was oriented toward a road to the north. Thus the word **behind** (v. 2) may not refer to the west but rather to the south (*meachareyha*, 8:2, usually means "after" or "behind," but here probably refers to the south), the side opposite of the city's "front door" by that road to the north.

The Lord's initial commands for ambush were broadly fulfilled. The 30,000 valiant warriors were sent up the hill from Gilgal to spend the night in a secret location close behind the city (south or southwest). The main force ("all the people of war") was to approach from the east. There would be a feint to draw the army of Ai away. Joshua then anticipated their reactions. The soldiers of Ai will say, **They are fleeing before us as at the first**. As they were drawn away from the city (8:16-17), the 30,000 Israelite warriors in hiding were to take the city, put it to the torch, and then form the hammer to crush Ai as Israel, the anvil, turned to face them.

Thirty thousand warriors are a lot to hide; perhaps they spread out to the southwest, forming part of the buffer between Ai and Bethel, located about two miles northwest of Ai. Waiting in ambush were the 5,000 stationed between Ai and Bethel to the "west" (*miyyam* 8:12). Their job was to keep Bethel from having an influence on the battle. "All the people of war" (the bulk of the Israelite forces) were in the valley across the road to the "north" (8:13). But those Ai soldiers had no idea how large Israel's army to the east and north actually was, having fought only 3,000 men during the first attack on Ai (see 7:4).

8:9-17. The battle joined, Israel adopted the posture of defeat and fled toward the east. The people from Ai chased them, unaware of events behind them. A portion of the 30,000 Jewish soldiers waiting in ambush struck and burned the city, while the 5,000 soldiers to the west neutralized Bethel. Bethel came out (8:17) to fight, but would not be a factor. (In the king/city list of Jos 12, Bethel is not mentioned with Ai [v. 9], but at end of the southern campaign [v. 16].)

8:18-23. The Master of strategy and timing told Joshua, **Stretch out the javelin that is in your hand toward Ai, for I will give it into**

your hand. God's words are similar to those at the Red Sea crossing, when Moses stretched out his hand over the sea and Pharaoh's army was destroyed (Ex 14:26-27). Joshua used this prearranged gesture to turn around the largest group of his soldiers, "all the people of war." **All Israel** ceased their flight to the east, **turned back** to the west, and caught the soldiers of Ai between them and some of the 30,000 now pursuing from the west. The hammer of some of the 30,000 **valiant warriors** and the anvil of Israel's largest group (**all the people of war**) began to crush the army of Ai. The city became an inferno (8:19), the people of Ai were killed, the plunder and the king taken.

8:24-29. When everyone in the field had been killed, the women (8:5) and most likely the children were killed. This is the only conquest battle where a tally is given for the enemy. A few days before, 36 from Israel had been killed (7:5); this day some 12,000 adults from Ai were killed. The king was impaled upon a pike (cf. *ANET*[3], 288), and then entombed in a heap of rocks visible "to this day" (cf. 7:25-26). Ai was allowed to burn and would remain a ruin to the time of the writing of the book of Joshua. So the evil king and his town mirror the treasonous Achan and his family, executed by the judgment of God and immortalized in a pile of rocks.

8:30-35. This "floating pericope" is found in three positions: A DSS fragment has it between 5:1 and 5:2; in LXX it is found after notice of the formation of the Canaanite coalition at 9:2; and it appears here at 8:30ff. However, there is no reason to follow anything other than the universal Hebrew reading, which places it at the end of chap. 8. There is no action against the people of Shechem. Shechem is not mentioned as one of 31 cities and kings in chap. 12. Perhaps they were overthrown without comment, or they may have made peace with Israel. There was an ancient history between them: Abraham passed through on his way into the land (Gn 12:6; 34). And there was the negative event of the sons of Jacob deceiving the Shechemites (Gn 34; cf. 48:22). The text does indicate the presence of **strangers**, perhaps Shechemites (8:33, 35).

With so many armed people, Israel traveled unmolested. The people built an altar upon Mt. Ebal of uncut stones (Ex 20:25; Dt 27:5-6). The whole-burnt offerings were for atonement, the peace offerings a fellowship offering shared by the laity. This may be compared to the time during the monarchy when the ark of the covenant was in Jerusalem and yet Solomon met God at Gibeon because the faith had not yet been entirely centralized (defacto) in Jerusalem (1Kg 3:4).

Everything was done just as commanded (8:31, 33, 35; cf. Dt 27:11-14). Joshua wrote a copy of the law, much as the future king would be required to do (Dt 17:18-20). He did this not because he viewed himself as their king but because he was functioning as their spiritual leader. Half of the people stood either in front of or on top of Mt. Ebal and the rest correspondingly at Mt. Gerizim. Shechem is about 27 miles north of Jerusalem. Mt. Ebal is less than two miles to the north of Shechem's ancient city center, whereas Mt. Gerizim is less than a mile to the southwest. They probably chanted antiphonally the blessings and the curses of the covenant. Most importantly, Joshua **read all the words of the law, the blessing and the curse, according to all that is written in the book of the law**.

Israel was a mixed multitude, consisting of the descendants of Abraham, Isaac, and Jacob and resident aliens (8:33, 35). Rahab and her family were present, absorbed as true Israelites. Achan and his family were absent, executed as rebels against God's monarchy, in a sense no better than the Canaanites. Anyone who confessed Israel's God, as Rahab had, **stranger** or native, was welcome.

B. The Southern Campaign (9:1–10:43)

Earlier, hearing about Israel's strength created paralysis among the surrounding nations (2:9-11; 5:1). Here Israel's opponents are provoked to action. The difference was the failure at the initial encounter with Ai. Israel no longer appeared invincible. They attempted to form one coalition and formed two, divided in half to Israel's advantage (cf. Jos 9:1; 10:1 and 11:1-3). The list of nations parallels that of the commission (Dt 20:17). Verse 3 indicates strong disjunction: "*Now* the inhabitants of Gibeon . . ." (author's translation and emphasis). The text almost self-consciously resumes the overarching scenario of the southern coalition fighting against Israel (10:1-2), with statements about their fear, Israel's victories, and four Hivite cities added as allies.

Disappointment may have lingered among the people over the theft of Achan and the failure at Ai; however, God made it turn out better than expected (cf. Rm 8:28). Unless God intended to destroy each city as He had Jericho, siege warfare would have slowed the conquest and decimated Israel's resources. So the Canaanites were provoked into offensive action, enabling Israel to beat them in the field, destroy their armies, and capture virtually undefended cities. This is also the reason archaeology has yielded little evidence of burned cities from the time of the conquest. (Hazor, about eight miles northwest of the Sea of Galilee, is a notable exception, showing evidence of being burned at the time of the conquest.)

9:1-2. The attempt at an alliance would produce only a divided one (10:1-2; 11:1-3). This order of presentation for the nations is the same as that of Dt 20:17, and hence the careful reader would have recalled this certainly at the level of foreshadowing if not of prophecy fulfilled.

9:3-5. The Gibeonites needed to act deceptively or face extermination. Perhaps they had had spies at Mt. Ebal when the law was read and realized that they were next. The Gibeonites prepared for the ruse with undesirable provisions and worn-out clothing.

9:6-7. The Gibeonites knew the treaty regulations for those living far away (Dt 20:10-15). Their call for a covenant aroused suspicions: **Perhaps you are living within our land; how then shall we make a covenant with you?** Building tension, the author intimates the people of Gibeon were Hivites: they should have been annihilated.

9:8. The Gibeonites sidestepped the question by merely stating: **We are your servants** (cf. v. 11). Joshua asked again to ascertain their ethnicity and origin.

9:9-10. The Gibeonites repeated their tale and then magnified the reputation of the Lord. The story was crafted so as to recall events distant enough in time not to betray their proximity: the exodus and the Transjordanian wars, but not the miraculous crossing, the fall of Jericho or the rout of Ai, because that would betray their location. Their statements parallel Rahab's (2:9-11), but their knowledge of God's power does not parallel Rahab's genuine faith.

9:11. Perhaps the Hivites were not under the rule of a monarch but under elder rule, indicating a correspondence with Israelite culture. There are two statements on servanthood and treaty (cf. vv. 6, 8).

9:12-13. The Gibeonites continued by talking about their provisions and clothing as having been in good condition upon departure. Their story's tensions approached the breaking point. The word **crumbled** is the word "spotted" for goats and sheep (Gn 30:39). "Moldy" may be a better translation.

9:14-15. The Israelites examined their food to ascertain its age; however, Israel **did not ask for the counsel of the Lord**. This was where they had gone wrong at Ai. Now Joshua and the leaders made a treaty with the Gibeonites without truly knowing their origin. These people would be integrated into Israelite society, but it was a violation of an order from God (Dt 20:17).

9:16-17. In **three days**, the Israelites discovered the Gibeonites were neighbors. Perhaps another reconnaissance mission revealed the truth. The Gibeonites were allied with four other cities, mostly to the west of them.

9:18-19. The people of Israel were irritated with their leadership. The people were ready to destroy the Hivites, but the leadership would not allow a breach of treaty. As with the spies and Rahab, an oath in the Lord's name sometimes seemed stronger to the leadership than Moses' edict to "utterly destroy" the enemy. On the part of the Gibeonites, one wonders if the lie should have nullified the oath.

9:20-23. The covenant probably looked more like an alliance of equals to the people. So the leadership decided that the Gibeonites were to serve the community, specifically the tabernacle. Joshua's curse does seem to carry some weight. Later King Saul would attempt an ethnic purge (2Sm 21:1-9).

9:24-27. The Gibeonites made the decision that, whatever the outcome, the end of avoiding extermination justified the means of deception. So they deferred to Joshua. Because **good and right** was turned upside down by the oath, they were shielded from annihilation. The people must have still been angry because Joshua had to deliver the Gibeonites from them.

A people group was preserved alive; those with a Judeo-Christian heritage would likely side with the Gibeonites. The Gibeonites became the closest non-Israelites to the tabernacle. They cut wood for sacrifices and drew water for ritual washings. No other outlander had such a proximate view of the nature of atonement. They lived under the threat of violence (cf. 2Sm 21), but would not cease to be under God's watch-care (cf. Neh 3:7; 7:25). One can point to God's superintending grace in such a case: it seems that even though Joshua was careless, neither he nor the people were directly punished for this failure to consult the Lord; however, it shows God's grace to the Gibeonites in that, unlike the rest of the Amorites, we might infer that their sin was not yet complete.

The Canaanites formed a coalition against the Gibeonites for having made a treaty with Israel. Mere "hearing" about Israel's strength and the paralysis related to it now shifts into action because the nations were no longer stymied by fear, and this made Israel's work easier. The various kingdoms, emboldened by the defeat at Ai, came out to meet Israel in battle. Joshua 10 contains some of that initial offensive action against Israel, including the siege of Gibeon by the Canaanite coalition, Joshua's mission to rescue Gibeon, the unusual meteorological and astronomical phenomena, and the southern campaign.

10:1-5. Reports of the fate of Jericho's and Ai's kings circulated throughout the region, but the paralysis these victories once caused now goaded the enemies into offensive action. Gibeon was a fortress city somewhat like Gezer (see map "The Central and Southern Campaigns") and its warriors men of note. The king of Jerusalem summoned the kings and armies of Hebron (about 20 miles south of Jerusalem), Jarmuth (about 15 miles west-southwest of Jerusalem), Lachish (about 28 miles southwest of Jerusalem), and Eglon (about 28 miles south-southwest of Jerusalem). He requested their help to regain the central plateau from the Israelite-Hivite alliance. Thus **the five kings of the Amorites** joined in besieging Gibeon.

10:6-9. The Gibeonites sent messengers to Joshua at Gilgal (in the vicinity of Jericho) announcing their plight: **All the kings of the Amorites that live in the hill country have assembled against us.** The Israel army quickly mobilized, perhaps already poised to intercept another force (cf. 9:1-2). Joshua conducted a forced night march (v. 9; cf. 8:3). The **valiant warriors** in this passage were not just an elite force, but the entire army. Trained for war, they were all deployed in the forthcoming action. God promised His presence and overwhelming victory (cf. 1:5; 3:7; 6:2; 8:1).

10:10. Israel's army was in pursuit and **the LORD confounded them**, giving God the credit for the victory. Already the battlefield was littered with slain Canaanites, but now God continued their demise.

10:11. Terror is a great motivator, and when the Canaanite army fled west they were going downhill. The space between became a killing zone as **the LORD threw large stones from heaven on them**. The Scripture specifies these were **hailstones**, indicating a meteorological event rather than a meteorite shower. Joshua's shock-attack was horrible, but **more . . . died from the hailstones than those whom the sons of Israel killed with the sword**.

10:12-14. The challenge of these verses has to do with their startling nature and several certainties: The Amorites were defeated; Joshua

The Central and Southern Campaigns

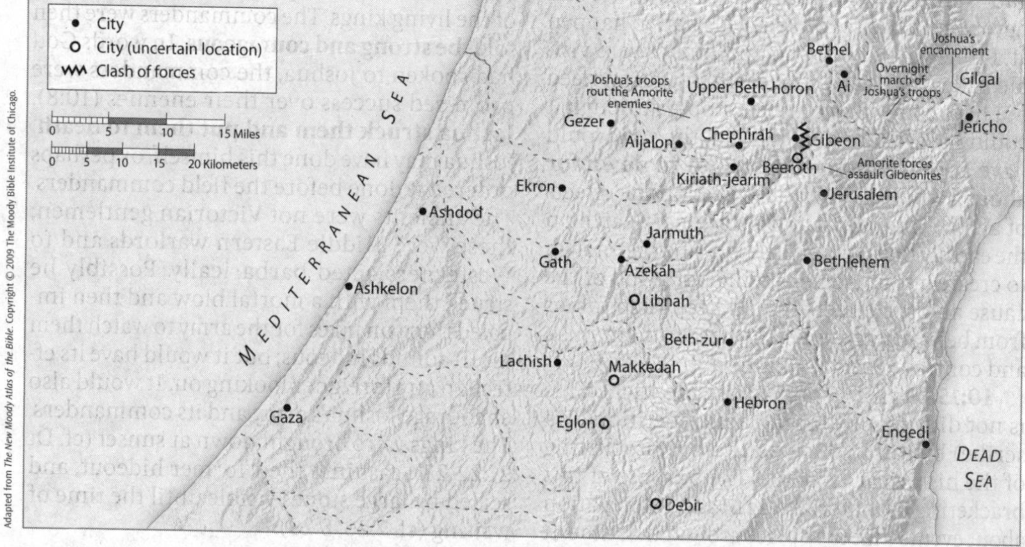

spoke to the Lord; the daylight was extended as **the sun . . . did not hasten to go down** and the moon **stopped**; the nation was avenged; the book of Jashar was mentioned; **there was no day like** this; and God listened and fought for Israel.

Critical scholarship employs a mythological and figurative (non-literal) approach to the events depicted in the text. If the text can be laid out in poetic format, then it is either mythological writing or the high imagery renders the words hyperbole. But art can still reflect reality, so no problem is really solved. Another approach presupposes phenomenal language. That is, circumstances only seem to be the way they appear: reality must be sought elsewhere. For instance, the army of Israel was able to inflict so much damage that it *seemed* as if the sun stood still in the sky, that it *seemed* like an incessant day during which they accomplished more than would seem possible on a typical day. A third approach sees a meteorological event creating conditions causing light to be refracted longer at dusk. Perhaps some astronomical event caused this. A fourth explanation evaluates the positioning of the sun and moon that day: a full moon illuminating Joshua's march of eight to ten hours (10:9) could make the shock attack and aftermath seem like a double day.

The words, however, should be allowed to mean what they say. According to the simplest reading of the text, there is a reference to the slowing of the earth's rotation. Phenomenal language need not be "pre-scientific": even today meteorologists refer to the time of a "sunrise" and "sunset," even though technically the sun never actually rises or sets. This had to happen at a time when both sun and moon were visible, at least initially. The earth's rotation need not have come to a complete stop—although it could have. Had it just slowed, the sun would have appeared to **not hasten to go down for about a whole day**. Critics question the effects of an orbiting moon and a stationary earth on the earthly tides. Nevertheless, a God big enough to create our universe—being both God of the cause and the effect—could keep such forces from being cataclysmic; the Lord can diminish and control the tidal action.

10:15. Verses 15 and 43 are identical. This is not dittography (accidental repetition by a scribe) but an inclusio (a literary bracketing of the historical account). The purpose of this bracketing of material was to add information about events that took place around that time. It suggests the army advanced successively on the defenses at Makkedah, Libna, Lashish, Eglon, Hebron, Debir, and Negev after the execution of the five kings, achieving with God's help several days of victory before returning to Gilgal.

10:16-18. The report of the five defeated kings taking refuge in a cave inspired Joshua to order them temporarily sealed and guarded. The record of this event draws a connection with the "piles of rocks" placed over the fallen opponents of God and Israel (cf. 7:26; 8:29; 10:27).

10:19-21. The soldiers of Israel were commanded to pursue their enemies. The enemies were not allowed to reenter their fortifications because it would have necessitated lengthy sieges, costly for the offensive strategy of Joshua's army. A fortress might be defended against ten-to-one odds, reducing the effectiveness of Joshua's fighting force considerably with much of the conquest yet to go. Perhaps there was a forward base of operations at Makkedah (possibly a site 25 miles southwest of Jerusalem), or the laying of the first siege. Although the armies were rendered inert, a few stragglers had made it back to their fortifications. **No one uttered a word against any of the sons of Israel** (v. 21) is literally "no man sharpened his tongue at the sons of Israel." Sheer terror and dejection held their words in check.

10:22-27. The five kings were brought out. The cadence of v. 23 is as a death sentence: place names were mentioned, signifying armies commanded and aggression against Israel. In ancient Near Eastern fashion, the field commanders were told to put their feet on the necks of the living kings. The commanders were then told, **be strong and courageous**. In words God had spoken to Joshua, the commanders were promised success over their enemies (10:8). **Joshua struck them and put them to death**. Joshua may have done this himself, or perhaps ordered it done before the field commanders. The ancients were not Victorian gentlemen; these were Middle Eastern warlords and to Westerners acted barbarically. Possibly he struck them with a mortal blow and then impaled them on pikes for the army to watch them die. It sounds hideous; but it would have its effect on any foreigner looking on. It would also encourage Joshua's army and its commanders. The kings were brought down at sunset (cf. Dt 21:22-23), cast into their former hideout, and sealed by large stones visible until the time of writing (cf. 7:26; 8:29).

10:28. The story is bracketed by the successful siege of Makkedah. The people were exterminated and its king treated as Jericho's king (cf. 8:29; 10:1). The southern campaign was in motion.

10:29-39. After this success, the nation of Israel captured seven cities in southern Canaan (see Howard, *Joshua*, 257; and Richard S. Hess, *Joshua: An Introduction and Commentary*. TOTC, ed. D. J. Wisémen [Downers Grove, IL: InterVarsity, 1996], 203), and the parallels are clear in the following chart.

The symmetry demonstrates enough variation that it cannot be a formulaic caricature; but it also demonstrates that the author intended to present the events systematically.

Jerusalem was not taken at this time (cf. 2Sm 5:8-10). Gezer was not taken at this time (cf. 1Kg 9:16). Even though Hebron's and Eglon's kings had already been killed at the cave near Makkedah, succession is often rapid after a monarch's death; the text describes their appointed successors who suffered the same outcome when Joshua's army besieged their towns. The second half of this chapter presents Israel's military movements as a rapid set of victories, but it is impossible to determine the length of the campaign.

The seven southern cities were taken in an arc to the west (see map "The Central and Southern Campaigns"), then south along the low hills known as the *shephelah*, and then back inland to the east. According to chap. 12, there were additional cities taken in the Negev, the arid region in Israel's near south.

10:40-42. The scope of the southern conquest included the highlands (**hill country**), the southlands (**Negev**), the foothills (*shephelah*, **lowland**) and the ascents (**slopes**). Joshua **left no survivor, but he utterly destroyed all who breathed**, as commanded. The data about Gezer precludes the possibility of the annihilation of every living being there (Jos 16:10). This apparent contradiction is resolved by examining the commands for war in Dt 20:10-18. There it states that more distant nations (like Gezer) were to be offered terms of peace. Those that refused were to have the leadership destroyed and people subjugated, just as happened with Gezer. Joshua defeated Gezer's king and army because they joined the battle to aid Lachish (Jos 10:33), but he only subjugated the actual city (Jos 16:10).

Thus, Israel's obedience was complete. From Kadesh-barnea and Gaza in the south, to Gibeon in the central plateau, all was secured. Theologically, with God victory was assured when fought according to His rules. The words, **the Lord, the God of Israel, fought for Israel**, mirror those of Jos 10:14, 42).

10:43. With the southern campaign ended, Israel returned to Gilgal. Although the time lapse between the two campaigns cannot be known, the northern coalition against Israel was likely forming while the southern campaign was in progress.

C. The Northern Campaign (11:1-15)

When the central and southern regions were subdued and the army of Israel was at Gilgal, the northern coalition rose against Israel. Only two kings were mentioned by name: Jabin and Jobab. Jabin summoned four cities and an immense region to battle. The size of Jabin's legions cannot be known. Josephus wrote, "the number of the whole army was three hundred thousand armed footmen, and ten thousand horsemen, and twenty thousand chariots" (*Ant.*: 5, 1, 18). Josephus read fear among the Jewish people between the lines and sensed that "God upbraided them" for their lack of faith. There is irrational dread and there is realistic apprehensiveness; God would tell them, lit., "cease fearing them." (v. 6).

The Conquest of Southern Canaan

City	Victims	Weapon	Clause Comparison
Makkedah	king, city, people	sword	like Jericho
Libnah	king, city, people.	sword	like Jericho
Lachish	king, city, people	sword	like Libnah
Gezer	king, people	—	—
Eglon	king, city, people	sword	like Lachish
Hebron	king, its cities, people	sword	like Eglon
Debir	king, its cities, people	sword	like Hebron, Libnah

11:1-5. When Jabin the **king . . . heard**, he knew that Israel had silenced the southern coalition. The people summoned were from a huge region: from Mt. Hermon in the far north to the Mediterranean, Transjordan, Edom (southeast of the Dead Sea), and remains of the southern coalition (e.g., Jebusites from the region associated with Jerusalem). They were summoned to **the waters of Merom, to fight against Israel**. This encampment was likely several miles northwest of the Sea of Galilee, near the Horns of Hittin (Hess, *Joshua*, 211), where chariots could maneuver.

11:6. In times of dread, the Lord spoke with His leader, who then encouraged the people. The words **tomorrow at this time** probably astonished Joshua. Slaughtering and putting to flight myriads of well-equipped warriors would certainly be extreme providence.

The hamstringing of horses seems cruel, but there were important reasons for doing this. In Dt 17:16, the leadership is commanded not to multiply horses, symbolic of affluence and power. Also, a hamstrung horse would be no longer militarily useful. (Unable to run, its only remaining use might be for food for sojourners.) Israel's land was defensible by infantry, but cavalry was considered an offensive force.

11:7-9. God's promise of victory was followed by rapid deployment (cf. 8:1-2; 10:7-9). While the Canaanites were planning tactics, Israel was upon them! The quick deployment and brilliant maneuvering by Israel contributed, but the Lord's work was in focus: **The Lord delivered them into the hand of Israel**. The slaughter at the camp caused the enemies to flee. Israel chased the enemy as far as Sidon to the far northwest Mediterranean coast and Mt. Hermon to the northeast. Joshua obeyed in hamstringing the horses and burning the chariots.

11:10-11. The phrase **at that time** serves to differentiate actions rather than to mark time. They **turned back** from pursuit and focused on the center of the coalition, Hazor (about eight miles north of the Sea of Galilee), which they conquered, killing everyone, taking what plunder was left and burning everything else. Hazor was, with Jericho and Ai, the third foul zone purified by fire.

11:12-15. The other city fortifications were breached, the kings captured and killed. Any ability for resistance was destroyed. The burning of Hazor is reemphasized and the plundering of the towns noted. **But they struck every man with the edge of the sword, until they had destroyed them. They left no one who breathed** (v. 14). Such statements are grave: Where Joshua's armies went, there was complete destruction; where they neglected to go, people survived. Waging "total war" was because the sin of the Amorite was irremediable (cf. Gn 15:16). God's only solution, as in Sodom and Gomorrah, was to rid the world of these people (see v. 20). Joshua did everything that Moses had commanded in general and everything that the Lord commanded in particular.

D. Victory in Review: Regions and Rest (11:16-23)

11:16-18. Thus Joshua took all that land. This synopsis includes lands taken in all campaigns. The first hill country is most likely the Galilean highlands. The Negev is the Judean desert in the south with Beersheba as central. The land of Goshen is in the southwest. The plains included the coastal plain (**the lowland**) as well as the Esdraelon plain (encompassing a flat fertile region generally about 20 miles southwest of the Sea of Galilee). The second hill country is the central highlands of Judea, Ephraim, and Manasseh. **The hill country and its lowland** (*shephelah*) is the low hills to the west of Jerusalem and Hebron. In v. 17, the regions that are listed encompass Edom (southwest of the Dead Sea), Lebanon (in the far north), and Syria (in the far northeast). In all these locations Joshua conquered towns and killed leaders. What is presented in the narrative seems to have transpired in a short amount of time. But narrative features and temporal distance should not be confused. Although the accounts are brief, **Joshua waged war a long time with all these kings** (v. 18). Based upon statements by Caleb (14:7-11), the conquest took seven years.

11:19-20. Only **Gibeon** (the cities of Chephirah, Beeroth, and Kiriath-jearim were part of the Gibeon alliance) made peace (see Jos 9). These Hivites, although temple-slaves, were left alive by God's grace, as Rahab and her family had been. The other peoples who lived around them, however, were to die, including women and children.

Theology and theological history are in view: **For it was of the Lord to harden their hearts, to meet Israel in battle in order that he might utterly destroy them, that they might receive no mercy** (v. 20). This may be compared with the hardening of Pharaoh's heart (Ex 4:21; see the comments there and in Rm 9:17-18). The author of Joshua ascribes the downfall of the various kingdoms during the conquest to God's sovereignty, the intentions of the leaders of those realms being under His divine supervision. Apart from a work of grace, neither Pharaoh nor the Canaanites could operate contrary to their nature. And so when God hardened the Canaanites to meet Israel in battle, their choices were ordained by God, who intended to destroy these people—and He had known it would come about for over 400 years (Gn 15:16). There was no benevolent grace extended to them, other than to Rahab and her family and the Gibeonites. For a season God allowed them to engage in their desires, and then He had the Canaanites destroyed according to the judgment of God because of their unparalleled debauchery (cf. Rm 1:18-28); even in the NT era, people's destinies are sealed before death (1Pt 2:8; see the comments on Rm 9:13-23). As alarming as this sounds, it appears to be the plain meaning of Jos 11:20. Time was up. They forfeited their lives. Condemnation was inevitable, all in keeping with God's sovereign plans.

11:21-22. The second occurrence of the phrase **at that time** (see 11:10 for the first) changes the scene to the extermination of the Anakim. These two verses form a necessary conclusion to the conquest. The **Anakim** had been the reason for the evaporation of Israel's courage at Kadesh (Nm 13:32-33; cf. Dt 1:28; 9:2). Moses describes the giant Anakim and the Rephaim together as "numerous and tall" (Dt 2:10-11, 20-21) and reveals that Og, the king of Bashan, part of the last remnant of the Rephaim, slept in a bed measuring 13½ feet long by 6 feet wide (Dt 3:11).

The spies said that they had seen "the Nephilim" (cf. Gn 6:4). The parenthetical statement "The sons of Anak are part of the Nephilim" (Nm 13:33) could be either the author's comment or part of the quote from the men who spied out the land. The NASB has it as a parenthesis, but leaves it within the quotation marks. The report by the spies about the Nephilim was inaccurate in several ways. First, the spies were exaggerating. Second, the Nephilim were wiped out in the flood. Third, Moses gave no credence to their opinion (cf. Dt 1:28; 9:2). Although the Anakim were clearly large and threatening, these giants had been killed or run out of the highlands of what would become Judah. The only place where these people still existed at the time of writing was in what would become the Philistine coastal plain (cf. 1Sm 17; 2Sm 21:16-22; 1Ch 20:4-8).

11:23. Joshua took the whole land. Israel was now the possessor of the land. Everyone else henceforth was considered a foreigner. Joshua's obedience to the Lord was complete. The first half of the verse looks back upon the conquest of Canaan, whereas the next looks forward to the events of chap. 13 and following. Finally, **the land had rest from war**. From now on, battles will be regional and tribal. The land was now at peace, and the division of the land could begin. **Rest from war** is fleeting, life being often thus unsettled. And even within the book of Joshua, the rest was not comprehensive (see 17:12-13). The NT mentions this: "For if Joshua had given them rest, He would not have spoken of another day after that" (Heb 4:8). There is land resting from war and there is the believer resting in the Lord. Augustine's statement is germane: "Thou hast formed us for Thyself, and our hearts are restless till they find rest in Thee" (*Confessions* 1:1).

E. Victory in Review: Cities and Kings (12:1-24)

The pedagogical value to repetition of the basic themes is that the more they are repeated, the more they will be remembered. The cadence in chap. 12 has the feel of a formal, holy convocation, a stately march through the fraternal graveyard of deceased kings sharing alike in a failed attempt to thwart God's purposes.

Of the three sections, the first and third (vv. 1-6 and 9-24) share a similar length but differ in content and genre (narrative vs. list). Verses 1-6 are a reprise of the conquest east of the Jordan River; vv. 7 and 8 a synopsis of the regions and peoples conquered, and vv. 9-24 the list of the cities defeated and kings killed. The differences between vv. 1 and 7 include directions and the insertion of Joshua's name.

12:1-6. This section recalls the events of the conquest of the Transjordan (Nm 21:21-35) and land distribution (Nm 32:1-42). Sihon and Og ruled over large regions, but the 31 kings who ruled west of the Jordan River were mostly city-state warlords, ruling over their immediate surroundings. The land conquered while Moses was alive included land from modern southwest Syria to modern central Jordan.

12:7-8. These verses outline the regions and peoples conquered: on the east side the border followed an arc from the base of Mt. Hermon in the far north, south to the territory of Edom (southeast of the Dead Sea). The western lands included the central highlands, the low hills (*shephelah*), the plains (coastal and Esdraelon), the *Arabah* valley, and the south (*negev*). For these locations, see the comments on 11:16-18. The groups conquered compare to those of the original commission by Moses (Dt 20:17) and the original coalition (9:1).

12:9-24. The Hebrew text is laid out as lists with the name of the king's town at the right and the adjective "one" to the left. At v. 24, on the right it reads literally, "Group of kings *was* thirty and one" (author's trans.).

The list reflects the general progress of the conquest in chaps. 6-11. Perhaps Bethel was not initially conquered in chap. 8, but was subdued later (cf. 12:9 and 12:16). According to 8:17, the army of Bethel participated in the battle of Ai, but the account indicates nothing in regard to army or king (cf. Jdg 1:22-26). Although Jerusalem and Gezer would not be conquered for centuries (2Sm 5:6-9; 1Kg 9:16), their armies were defeated in the field and their kings killed. **Hormah** and **Arad** (v. 14) are mentioned at this point (cf. Nm 21:1-3). Though they had been destroyed under Moses, they apparently were subdued again under Joshua. Perhaps people filtered into the ruins and rebuilt the city between the days of Moses and Joshua.

In the section indicating "land yet to be taken" (17:12; cf. Jdg 1:27), the Israelites defeated armies in the field and killed the kings, but could not breach the great fortresses. So when Israel was strong, the Canaanites were subjugated; when the Canaanites were strong, Israel was oppressed (Jdg 1:27-36). This oppression was based upon spiritual defection and idolatry (see commentary on Judges in this volume, for the theology of the "cycles" of defection and repentance).

The land had "rest from war" (11:23), the kings and their armies being pacified beyond resistance. The third major phase, the land distribution, began with a notice that the conquest has taken its toll: **now Joshua was old and advanced in years** (13:1; cf. 23:1-2). God fought for Israel; but occasional misfortunes would cause wounds that would disable, and deaths that would add to the widows and orphans among the Israelites. Necessary familial readjustments followed with the absorption of children into extended families. But having "rest from war" also meant that the survivors could now receive land.

III. Distribution of the Land (13:1–21:51)

A. Land Distribution: Command and Transjordan Review (13:1-33)

Joshua had been told that he would both lead Israel in victories and distribute the land (1:6). What follows leaves the impression that the book of Joshua is a book of the Levites, by the Levites, and for the Levites (with apologies to Abraham Lincoln). It often appears that the prime real estate was given to the Levites. In addition, the land closest to protection (the city walls) was also given to the Levites. In several cases cities hard won by Israel become "cities of refuge" (cf. Jos 20), or Levitical cities (cf. Jos 21).

Chapter 13 includes a catalog of the land remaining to be taken (13:1-7), the Transjordanian holdings (13:9-13), and the places given to Reuben (13:16-23), to Gad (13:24-28), and to East Manasseh (see discussion under 13:29-31). The author comments on the finalizing of the allotment to the Transjordanian tribes (13:32) and states the "inheritance" of the Levites (13:33). For the specifics of regions and cities, see the map "The Tribal Distribution of the Land" in the commentary on Numbers, p. 259.

While the record of the lands, cities, and boundaries parceled out to the various tribes is tedious to the modern reader, it is important to remember that God intended Israel's economy to be strictly agrarian. The Lord's blessing meant a fruitful land (Lv 26:4; Dt 11:14). His plan was to put them in the land and have them depend on Him to provide through blessing the land (Lv 26:3-4; Dt 7:13; 8:11-18; 28:1-8). For that reason, the land was not to be sold to others outside one's clan and tribe (Lv 25:25), and land that did pass into an outsider's possession was to be returned to the original owners during the Year of Jubilee (Lv 25:10-13, 23). Their dependence upon God, and God's provision for them, would become a beacon to the rest of the world of His goodness and power (Dt 15:6; 28:10). This theme also reflects the expression of God's judgment when He chooses to remove them from the land when they forsake Him (Dt 28:63; 29:25-28; 30:17-18). The precision and detail with which each tribe was allotted land reflects His design to tie their well-being to the land and thus to Himself. So the land is important.

13:1-7. Joshua's advanced age is mentioned (cf. 23:1-2). He is likely Caleb's age (14:7-10), so about 85 years old. The southwest coastal plain, later Philistia, was not firmly in Israel's grasp. The conquest was around 1400 BC. The sea peoples who settled on Israel's southwestern coast arrived en masse probably from the Aegean region about 1375 BC. Proto-Philistines are evident from texts such as Gn 26:1 (cf. 20:1-2), but were culturally Canaanite. Phoenicia (the region from Mt. Carmel north, including Sidon and Tyre) was also not taken; but the land Israel held was apportioned by Joshua (Jos 13:7).

13:8-13. The bequest to the Transjordanian tribes reaffirmed the words of Moses (13:8). This land later became a point of contention with Ammon (cf. Jdg 11). In v. 12, the Geshurites and Maacathites were conquered, but not displaced. David's son, Absalom, was the troubled son of a Geshurite princess (2Sm 15–18).

13:14. The Levites were given no larger territory because **the offerings by fire to the LORD, the God of Israel, are their inheritance**. It is possible that this means that because they would often have dual residence between a Levitical city and the worship center, there would be less need to raise crops and livestock because of the participation in the meals of the offerings.

13:15-23. The southernmost of the Transjordanian tribes was Reuben, whose cities ran from the Arnon Valley (about half-way down the eastern side of the Dead Sea) as far north as Rabbah (near modern day Amman, about 25 miles northeast of the Dead Sea). There was a ravine about 30 miles north of the Dead Sea between them and Gad to their north that served as a boundary.

13:24-28. To the north, Gad's territory was a triangle from the ravine that flows into the Jordan mentioned above, including the River Jabbok, extending to the southern tip of the Sea of Galilee, as far east as Rabbah.

13:29-32. Northernmost, **the sons of Machir the son of Manasseh**—and one of the two major clans of Manasseh—claimed East Manasseh's lands (13:31). This was among the largest allotments. Their borders ran southeast from the south end of the Sea of Galilee as far as Ramoth Gilead (about 30 miles southeast of the Sea of Galilee), arcing northeast across the desert to Mt. Hermon (about 25 miles northeast of the Sea of Galilee), then south along the upper Jordan (north of the Sea of Galilee) and the eastern shore of the Sea of Galilee being the western border.

13:33. The chapter concludes with another statement on the heritage of the Levites: **The LORD, the God of Israel, is their inheritance**. The Levites were set aside for the Lord's service. They were religious officials (cf. v. 14), but were also responsible for pastoral, educational, legal, and medical functions.

These three tribes were the first to be taken into captivity when the Assyrian king set his sights on the south (1Ch 5:26). The Transjordanian steppe was good pastureland, but as a wide-open steppe it lacked a defensible high ground. The Transjordanian Levites may have migrated to Judah after the fall of Samaria in 722 BC (2Ch. 30:10-11).

B. Land Distribution: Land for the Faithful Hero Caleb (14:1-15)

Chapter 14 divides into two sections: land to be distributed (vv. 1-4), and Caleb's request and conquest of Hebron (vv. 6-14a). Each section is followed by a comment (14:5, 14b) indicating faithfulness. There is a concluding comment on Hebron (14:15). This appears to be something of a hinge chapter; that is, it balances the conquest narratives with the land-grant narratives. Part of the author's strategy appears to be to show the primacy of Judah in the taking of the land. In view of Hebron later becoming a Levitical city, it also shows the primacy of Levi and the priesthood.

14:1. Bracketing the land grant narrative is the notice that Eleazar and Joshua were the chief officials (14:1; 19:51). **The heads of the households of the tribes** were involved. They are most likely the same men as in Numbers (Nm 34:17-29). God wanted these twelve men to survive the war.

14:2. The territories were assigned **by the lot of their inheritance**. The "lot" was prescribed by God (Nm 26:55). The "casting of lots" was the only sanctioned means of divination; it was to be performed before the high priest. It may be related to the *Urim* and *Thummim* controlled by the priest. Judah was drawn first, his territory rivaled only by East Manasseh. The last biblical example of casting lots for decision-making appears in Ac 1:26. Apparently, after the giving of the Holy Spirit (Ac 2:1-13), this sort of guidance from God was no longer used.

14:3-5. These verses review the Transjordanian tribes, Manasseh and Ephraim and the Levites. The eastern tribes had received their lands but the Levites received no major lands. Following Jacob's "blessing" (Gn 49:5-7), Simeon would be swallowed up by Judah and virtually disappear. Levi would be dispersed throughout

Israel. Joseph's first two sons doubled his share. This introduction to the land grant closes with the notice of Israel's faithfulness in apportioning the land.

14:6-7. Caleb will make a request after reminding Joshua of Moses' words and Caleb's faith. There is irony, poetic justice, and closure in the request (cf. v. 12) and subsequent commission of the octogenarian Caleb to lead a raid against the Anakim, so terrifying to the previous generation (Nm 13–14). This raid must be included in what finally drove the Anakim onto the Philistine coastal plain (Jos 11:21-22). Caleb was a Kenizzite. He may have been descended from the Kenizzites (cf. Gn 15:19), and so considered part of Judah by the time of Moses (Nm 13:6). Perhaps he was an outlander who joined Israel, absorbed into the tribe with which he most closely aligned. Another solution is etymological: the Gentile designation, "Kenizzite," may be derived from the name "Kenaz," thus becoming a clan designation: Caleb's brother Othniel is called "the son of Kenaz" (Jos. 15:17; cf. Jdg 1:13). In either case, outlanders were commended for valor as they joined with Israel.

In the **word . . . the Lord spoke to Moses**, notice the use of pronouns for emphasis. The Hebrew finite verb contains the person and number of the subject (the performer) of the verb, so that separate nouns or pronouns are not needed to convey the subject who enacts the verb. But when a separate pronoun *is* added, it makes the subject emphatic and may be translated with a reflexive pronoun: "You *yourself* know the word that YHWH spoke . . . concerning you [Joshua] and me [Caleb] at Kadesh-barnea" (author's trans. and emphasis). God had said, "Surely you shall not come into the land in which I swore to settle you, except Caleb the son of Jephunneh and Joshua the son of Nun" (Nm 14:30).

In v. 7 Caleb recounted events from Nm 13–14. He said that he was 40 years of age when he left Kadesh to spy the promised land. He **brought back to** Moses **as it was in my heart**, lit., "what was in my heart." That included both fortifications and giants, but also included faith that God would give them land.

14:8. Ten spies of the older generation **made the heart of the people melt with fear**, Caleb recalled (cf. Jos 2:9, 11, 24; 5:1). Again using an emphatic pronoun, Caleb said, "**but I [myself] followed the Lord my God fully**."

14:9. There is no reference to Moses making a vow to Caleb in Dt 1:36. Moses simply relayed to Caleb what God had forecast for him. Perhaps Caleb knew something the readers did not know. But whether God simply makes a promise (as in Dt 1:36) or even makes a vow, He speaks on no greater authority than His own (Heb 6:13) and He can be counted on to keep His word.

14:10. Using emphatic language Caleb expressed his astonishment: **Now behold, the Lord has let me live, just as He spoke, these forty-five years**. Then he said, **And now behold, I am eighty-five years old today**. Caleb's elation at having survived so as to see the fulfillment of God's promises is evident. Moreover, his faith is demonstrated by his silence throughout the 40 plus years of the wilderness experience and the conquest period. From this, the seven-year duration of the conquest may be inferred.

14:11. Caleb said he was physically as powerful as he had been 45 years previously at Kadesh. Caleb's **strength . . . for war** indicates military activity. The phrase **going out and coming in** denotes returning unscathed after conflict.

14:12. Now Caleb made his request: **Give me this hill country**. He did so knowing the risks: **for you** [yourself] **heard on that day that Anakim were there, with great fortified cities**. His plea was without arrogance; but with faith that **perhaps the Lord will be with me, and I will drive them out**.

14:13. Joshua's blessing naturally followed. The important Hebrew concept of conferring and receiving a blessing was used when the people of Israel were standing upon Mt. Ebal and Joshua blessed them (Jos 8:33). This blessing included the material blessings of an important place: Hebron, a city important to David's reign (cf. 2Sm 2).

14:14-15. Places named according to the events surrounding them are often signaled by the phrase **until this day**. The phrase flags Hebron as the possession of Caleb and his descendants **because he followed the Lord God of Israel fully**. The city's name had been Kiriath-arba. Arba was the greatest of the Anakim. Considered giants (cf. Dt 1:28; 9:2), this is probably a reference to size and ferocity. Nevertheless, the overall theme is that victory follows faithfulness.

The promise of God had been issued to Caleb 45 years previously, a long time to watch friends and family pass away. Occasionally physical and mental abilities go beyond the normal. It is not impossible that an octogenarian stormed a fortress—unusual, but not impossible, and the reader would do well to remember that Caleb did not act single-handedly. What is astonishing is that a man would silently carry the torch of faith, opposed and alone, for 45 years, and then live to see the fulfillment of God's promise. Believers should likewise "follow fully after the Lord" no matter the weight of opposition, discouragement, or span of time. Caleb is also a model for those who retire with good health and financial resources today. In his old age he remained ambitious and active for the Lord, as should we. This is preferable to sitting by a pool sipping sodas in the sun. There are still strongholds to be taken for the Lord.

C. Land Distribution: The Tribes West of the Jordan and Joshua (15:1–19:51)

In peacetime (cf. Jos 14:15), the land was apportioned to the remaining tribes. The "lot" fell first to Judah, both by expediency and prophecy: from the census Judah remained the largest (Nm 26). Judah's priority was predicted: "The scepter shall not depart from Judah" (Gn 49:10). Prime central land was theirs, nearly the largest land grant, necessary because of another prophecy: "I will disperse them in Jacob, and scatter them in Israel" (Gn 49:5-7). Simeon, absorbed into Judah, would eventually lose its visibility. For locations of these cities, see map "The Tribal Distribution of the Land" on p. 259.

15:1-12. Two of Judah's boundaries are easier to trace than the others: The eastern border was the Dead Sea (lit., "the Sea of Salt"), the western border the Mediterranean (lit., the Great Sea), from the **brook of Egypt** (Wadi el-'Arish), south of modern day Gaza to Jabneel (near the Mediterranean coast about 35 miles northeast of Jerusalem). From there it followed a watercourse northwest, which began east of Ekron. From the Mediterranean, the northern boundary went into the hill country and passed south of Jerusalem, perhaps winding down the Wadi Kelt, passing south of Jericho to the Dead Sea. The southern boundary arced from the southern tip of the Dead Sea to the west of the Arabah (Rift Valley), and followed the watercourse of the **brook of Egypt** to the sea. How far south the "arc" extended is unknown. In the monarchy, landholdings included the shore of the Gulf of Aqaba (Ezion Geber).

15:13-19. This is the second of the conquest narratives inserted in the land-grant texts. In chap. 14 Caleb's forces have conquered Hebron; now a detail is added. Caleb readied an assault on Kiriath-sepher, later named Debir (about 30 miles northeast of the Dead Sea). He announced, **the one who attacks Kiriath-sepher and captures it** would receive Caleb's daughter Achsah as a wife. Othniel, Caleb's younger brother captured the town and married Achsah. Achsah requested a special blessing. Arable land requires water, so Achsah wisely asked for the upper and lower springs.

Caleb was 85 years old and yet had a daughter of marriageable age. Perhaps he remarried and had this daughter. Women are mentioned less frequently in the OT, but when they are, it is correct to pay special attention. Achsah is immortalized as a woman of wisdom and courage in vv. 16-19 and Jdg 1:12-15, as she persuades her husband to ask for a field and receives her father's blessing, as he adds **the upper springs and the lower springs**. Debir became a Levitical city, Hebron a city of refuge. Hebron would be where David returned from exile and was first crowned king (2Sm 2:1-4).

15:20. In Jos 15:20-62, the descriptions of towns distributed to the tribe of Judah move counterclockwise and divide into five "districts" following Hebrew terms or units. The LXX adds a sixth, giving the proper count of towns and introducing Bethlehem. But the absence of Bethlehem from this list in the Hebrew version is what it means in Mc 5:2: "But as for you, Bethlehem Ephrathah, too little to be [listed] among the clans of Judah . . . ."

15:21-32. District one was in the south (*negev*). It included Ziph, later betraying David (1Sm 23:19); Beersheba, land of the patriarchs (Gn 21:32-33; 26:23-33); and Ziklag, apportioned also to Simeon (Jos 19:5); never successfully occupied, Philistine Achish gave Ziklag to David and Judah (1Sm 27:6).

15:33-44. District two was in the western foothills (*shephelah*). It included Eshtaol and Zorah, later belonging to Benjamin and featured in the Samson story, and ceded back to Judah (Jdg 13:2; 18:1-31); Adullam, where David hid fleeing Saul (1Sm 22:1); Azekah and Socoh, where David defeated Goliath (1Sm 17); Lachish, featured in Jeremiah (Jr 34:7), and in the history of the Assyrian and Babylonian conquests (*ANET*^{3}, 288, 321–322, 488–490); and Keilah, where David relieved a Philistine siege (1Sm 23).

15:45-47. District three was associated with Philistia (*philistim*). The Philistines occupied mostly Judah's land. Three towns near the Mediterranean coast bordered Philistia: Ekron to the northeast, Ashdod to the northwest, and Gaza to the southwest. (All three are shown on the accompanying map "Tribal Distribution of the Land," p. 259. They will reappear in the Samson cycle (Jdg 13–16), and the ark narrative (1Sm 4–6).

15:48-60. District four was in the hill country of Judah. This district included several notable cities: Debir, re-conquered by Othniel, became a Levitical city. Hebron, re-conquered by Caleb, was to become a city of refuge. It would become the first royal seat of the house of David (2Sm 2) and the place from which Absalom would launch his insurrection (2Sm 15:7-12). Maon and Carmel feature in the triangle among David, Nabal, and Abigail (1Sm 25). When David fled Saul, he took another wife by the name of Ahinoam from Jezreel (1Sm 25:43). In addition, Kiriath-baal, renamed Kiriath-jearim, was a landmark in the story of the Danite migration (Jdg 18:12); it was also a place where the ark of the covenant returned home after its circuit of death among the Philistines (1Sm 6:21-7:2; cf. 2Sm 6:1).

The LXX offers a sixth district including Bethlehem, the hometown of David and his nephews, Joab, Abishai, and Asahel; it would become the birthplace of the Messiah (Mc 5:2).

15:61-62. District five was the desert. The town of **Engedi**, located on the northwestern shore of the Dead Sea, would be a refuge for David after leaving Keilah (1Sm 23:29; 24:1). In the end times the waters will be desalinated: there will be good fishing there (Ezk 47:10).

15:63. This is the first "conquest lacuna," or seeming gap in the conquest account. Even though Jerusalem was allotted to Benjamin (Jos 18:21–27), Joshua writes: **as for the Jebusites, the inhabitants of Jerusalem, the sons of Judah could not drive them out**. Perhaps Judah's boundary included the southern part of Jerusalem. Compare the depiction in Judges: "Then the sons of Judah fought against Jerusalem and captured it and struck it with the edge of the sword and set the city on fire" (Jdg 1:8). Joshua 15:63 may refer to the initial campaign (Jos 10). However, the truth of ownership is also shown: "But the sons of Benjamin did not drive out the Jebusites who lived in Jerusalem; so the Jebusites have lived with the sons of Benjamin in Jerusalem to this day" (Jdg 1:21; note the parallel with Jos 15:63). Both statements were true: neither Benjamin nor Judah could dispossess the Jebusites: they lived in their midst to the day of writing. Technically, the land would be in Benjamin; but the royal seat of David would be there as well.

David's unfortunate census would reveal the ongoing presence of the Jebusites, as the sacrifice was performed on the threshing floor of Araunah the Jebusite (2Sm 24:18-25). The entire area cost 600 gold shekels (1Ch 21:25), perhaps 150 ounces of gold. Araunah's property became the site of Israel's temples, and is venerated by Jews, Christians, and Muslims. In early medieval times, the Mosque of Omar (the Dome of the Rock) and the Al-Aqsa Mosque were built in the vicinity of the temple.

Chapter 16 gives the impression that something has been lost. The southern boundary matches the northern border of Benjamin and Dan. The northern border is confusing, the corresponding city list missing. The source of this ambiguity is not immediately clear. It is unlikely, though, that this is a manuscript corruption. Maybe there was an understanding among the tribes involved, and precision was not the intent of the author or requirement of the parties. Nevertheless, Ephraim and West Manasseh received one huge allotment in the central highlands (see map "The Tribal Distribution of the Land"). It appears that the lands of Ephraim, Manasseh, and Benjamin joined just north of the Dead Sea.

16:1. The boundary for the **sons of Joseph** started at **the waters of Jericho**. Possibly Jericho became the property of both Benjamin and Ephraim. More likely, Ephraim's line skirted the city on the north. It then ascended toward Bethel.

16:2. The text makes a distinction between **Bethel** and **Luz**, but elsewhere they refer to the exact same place (e.g., Gn 28:19; cf. Jos 18:13). Perhaps one district retained the older name. Ataroth is not the same city as that of the same name mentioned in 16:7. It will, however, be mentioned as part of Benjamin's boundary or allotment (16:5; 18:13). The **Archites** were not entirely dislodged. Hushai the Archite was David's friend, showing courage and wisdom in undercutting Ahithophel's counsel during Absalom's insurrection (2Sm 15:31-37; 17:5-16).

16:3-4. As the boundary descended to Lower Beth Horon, it passed through the country of the otherwise unknown Japhletites. The boundary went toward the Mediterranean, passing Gezer (see v. 10). Chapter 17 fills in details about Manasseh; henceforth, chap. 16 is about Ephraim.

16:5-7. Beginning east of Upper Beth Horon, at Ataroth-Addar, the border of Ephraim swept past Michmethath (cf. 17:7). Janoah reappears in

2Kg 15:29 in a list of cities captured by Assyrian King Tiglath-pileser. The boundary then went past Jericho to the Jordan.

16:8-9. On the west, the boundary left Tappuah and followed the Kanah ravine to the Mediterranean. Some cities are mentioned but there is no listing as in other allotments.

16:10. Verse 10 contains another omission of information regarding the conquest related to the town of Gezer. The subdued people of Gezer (10:33) either returned and rebuilt the damaged fortress, or were never dislodged. They would be overthrown by Pharaoh and the territory given as a dowry to his daughter, Solomon's wife (1Kg 9:16). Until then, **the Canaanites live in the midst of Ephraim to this day, and they became forced laborers.**

The Israelites were to eradicate the Canaanites (Dt 20:16-18). Their failure may have been from battle fatigue (Jos 11:23; 14:15) or flagging faith. Yet, "when Israel became strong . . . they put the Canaanites to forced labor" (Jdg 1:28; cf. v. 35). Had Israel completely killed or exiled the indigenous population, her history might have been quite different. Israel would have been less tempted to adopt pagan customs.

Chapter 17 has five sections: (1) the allotment given to West Manasseh (17:1-2); (2) a reminder of the legacy of Zelophehad's daughters in Transjordan (17:3-6); (3) a boundary description (17:7-11); (4) Manasseh's inability to remove the Canaanites of the Jezreel Valley (17:12-13); and (5) a complaint by the Joseph tribes about the difficulty in subduing the land (17:14-18).

17:1-2. Manasseh's reason for taking land east of the Jordan was that the tribe owned much livestock (Nm 32:1-2, 33-42); however, v. 1 adds the detail that it was because of their prowess in war. There are six clan names given. Hepher, the father of Zelophehad and grandfather of some famous women of Scripture appears in the next section.

17:3-6. In these verses Hepher's granddaughters receive the spotlight. They made a land request based on two truths: their father had no sons and they had not participated in rebellion (Nm 27). They were granted land. The second issue was: if the girls married into another tribe the land would be withdrawn from Manasseh. So the girls—always named in the same order—were told to marry within their extended family (Nm 36). Hepher's lineage went through Zelophehad to his five daughters, multiplying his inheritance fivefold. In this way these five daughters maintained the name and heritage of their father and established inheritance rights for women in Israel. Their actions demonstrated both ingenuity and courage.

17:7-11. West Manasseh's east boundary was the Jordan River nearly from the Dead Sea to the Sea of Galilee. Their western border was the Mediterranean Sea. The northern border touched the territories of Issachar, Zebulun and Asher. On the north, Manasseh included Beth-shean and cities at the base of the Carmel Ridge: Ibleam, Taanach, Megiddo and Jokneam. The southern border included Shechem and then proceeded west-southwest joining the Yarkon River below Aphek, ending at the Mediterranean north of Joppa (see map "The Tribal Distribution of the Land", p. 259).

The inhabitants of Dor are third in the list, and some think "Napheth" is another name for Dor. Napheth could refer to "the heights" or "the heights of Dor" with only a slight change in vocalization (cf. Jos 11:2; 12:23; 1Kg 4:11).

17:12-13. The hardened cities (v. 11) were indomitable. Beth-shean, Ibleam, Taanach, and Megiddo all had land defensible by chariotry. When Israel was strong, the Canaanites were subject to them (cf. Jdg 1:21, 27-36). If conquered, Taanach would become a Levitical city.

17:14-18. This fourth land grant narrative (cf. 14:6-15; 15:18-19; 17:3-6; 17:14-18; 21:1-3) contrasts with Caleb's humility and courage. The Joseph tribes complained about how small their land was and how difficult it was to control. Noting God's blessing upon their population, the Joseph tribes complained of only getting one lot (cf. 17:1; cf. 16:1). Joshua's response showed dignity and diplomacy. He told them to clear the highland forest: Perizzite and Rephaim lands. The Rephaim were reputed to be giants (cf. Dt 3:11). Unlike in Caleb's war with the Anakim, the sons of Joseph were intimidated by the Rephaim.

Unsatisfied, the representatives of Joseph complained that the highlands were insufficient and that they were unable to approach the valleys because of the Canaanites' chariots (cf. Jdg 4–5; Heb 11:32). Encouraging them, Joshua noted that their numbers and strength were great, and so they should have another lot. They would also do as commanded (v. 15): clear the forest and live there. They were to drive out the Canaanites despite their chariots. These chariots probably had wooden framework and iron fittings, hardening them for battle.

Contrasted to Caleb, Achsah, and Zelophehad's daughters, the case of the Joseph tribes is unsatisfying. The former were people of integrity, ingenuity, and courage, while this case depicts people that cannot solve problems and lacked faith. The previous three are immortalized by name; in this case, however, there is only a general complaint made by those who remain unnamed and uncertain resolution.

Joshua 18 is the record of the land distribution to the first of the remaining seven tribes. In boundary drawing, it is among the most spartan; in named cities, it is the most detailed (see map "The Tribal Distribution of the Land"). There are few textual and geographical problems, with everything in Hebrew lining up with the LXX, and every location but Kiriath-jearim aligns with other lists (Jos 9:17; 15:9, 60).

Benjamin was the son of Rachel, Jacob's favorite wife. She died in childbirth (Gn 35:18). The tribe of Benjamin, the first lot of the seven, was located safely between Judah, from which tribe would come the future king and Messiah, and Ephraim, the bearer of the birthright blessing (after it passed from Reuben to Joseph's sons Ephraim and Manasseh; 1Ch 5:1-2; cf. Gn 48:17-19). Benjamin's geography included Jerusalem, and its legacy would include Saul, the first king of Israel. Many of these 26 towns are recognized from biblical history. The chapter divides into three sections: vv. 1-10 include a rebuke and reconnaissance; vv. 11-20, Benjamin's boundaries; and vv. 21-28, city lists.

18:1-3. Israel and the tabernacle moved from Gilgal to Shiloh in the geographical center of the nation. This became the religious and administrative center of Israel for several centuries. It would remain there until the Philistine invasion (1Sm 4:2-11). Joshua began with a rhetorical question addressed to the nation: **How long will you put off entering to take possession of the land . . . ?** The question feels like a rebuke, as though they were willing to continue a nomadic existence. The promise to the patriarchs that the Holy Land would be theirs should have been sufficient motivation for these seven remaining tribes to begin to act.

18:4-10. After the rebuke, Joshua commissioned **three men from each tribe** for a land survey. In his instructions for this vital reconnaissance of the land, Joshua emphasized certain key words: "arise" (v. 4), "go/walk" (vv. 4, 8 [4x], 9, "write/describe" (vv. 4, 6, 8 [2x], 9) and "return/came [back]" (vv. 4, 8, 9). The repetition accentuates the urgency of the task.

Judah had already taken possession of its land to the south; Ephraim its land to the north. The third aspect of the Levitical inheritance is presented (cf. 13:14, 33); now the reader is granted the larger perspective of **the priesthood of the Lord** (18:7). Not merely the slaughtering of animals, the priesthood involved deeper responsibilities, namely the religious functions, diagnosis of diseases, education, counseling, and criminal justice.

18:11-20. The boundary lines followed those of Ephraim on the north (16:1-4, 5) and Judah on the south (15:5-11).

The northwest and southwest points of the territory form the boundary between Benjamin and Dan. On the north was Beth Horon, on the south was Kiriath-jearim (18:14). Kiriath-jearim was one of three Hivite cities allied with Gibeon (cf. 9:17). It appears as a possession of Judah (cf. 15:9, 60). For 20 years it would become the place of residence for the ark on its return from Philistia (1Sm 7:1-2; 1Ch 13:6; cf. 2Ch 1:4). Kiriath-jearim, a town of Benjamin, became **a city of the sons of Judah** (v. 14). The Jebusites (cf. chap. 15) were a problem that neither Benjamin nor Judah could solve until the time of David almost 400 years later (2Sm 5:6-9; cf. 2Sm 24:16, 18-25). The boundary line skirted the problem in that it **went down to the valley of Hinnom, to the slope of the Jebusite southward, and went down to En-rogel** (v. 16).

18:21-28. Many of these cities are immortalized in biblical history, with only 10 of them passing into obscurity. **Jericho** would be rebuilt and, in fulfillment of the imprecation of Joshua (Jos 6:26), two of the builder's sons would perish in the undertaking (6:26; 1Kg 16:34). **Bethel**, mentioned in the history of the patriarchs (Gn 28:10-22; 35:1-15), was an embarrassment for Joshua and Israel. The **Avvim** were a wide ranging group, rather than a town (v. 23; cf. Dt 2:23; Jos 13:3; 1Kg 17:31). The important Philistine town of **Geba** (1Sm 13:3, 16) would be liberated by Jonathan (1Sm 14:5-15). **Gibeon**, a problem because of the treaty (Jos 9:3-21), would be a problem even for David (2Sm 21:1-9). **Chephirah** was one of the four towns in the Gibeonite league (Jos 9:17). **Ramah** would become the hometown of Samuel (1Sm 1:1, 19; 2:11; 7:17; 8:4). **Jerusalem**, of course, would become the most central city to all biblical literature.

Benjamin was now safe between Judah and Ephraim, surrounding Jerusalem, with natural boundaries to the east. Benjamin, with Judah, would comprise the southern kingdom after the split (cf. 1Kg 12). They survived the eighth century BC Assyrian expedition. Benjamin occupies a significant role in Israel. Although the king would come from Judah and the priests from the tribe of Levi, Benjamin had Jerusalem.

Six lots remained to be cast, as described in Jos 19. But the situation would go from certain to tenable to complete failure. Dan, unable to maintain possession in west central Israel, would move to the far north. Asher would do little better. Many locations unknown and some of the major sites would be kept by the Phoenicians (e.g., Tyre and Sidon), and others would be ceded to Tyre, Phoenicia in a bargain between Solomon and Hiram (1Kg 9:11-13).

19:1-9. In fulfillment of prophecy (Gn 49:5-7), Simeon was to have spots of land within the larger territory of Judah. The stated reason was that **the share of the sons of Judah was too large for them** (v. 9). Simeon helped in Judah's efforts to control the land (Jdg 1:3). Most of these cities were named in Judah's list, but only a few would be remembered. Beersheba was known from the patriarchal period (e.g., Gn 46:1); but the slogan, "from Dan to Beersheba" (e.g., Jdg 20:1; 1Sm 3:20; 1Kg 12:29-30) would signify the whole nation. **Beersheba** was a southern garrison against marauding Edomites and Amalekites. **Hormah** was defeated before Israel entered the land (Nm 21:3). **Ziklag**, later under control of Philistine King Achish, was granted to David and thereafter ceded to Judah (1Sm 27:6).

When the kingdom split under the heavy hand of Rehoboam, Solomon's son (see 1Kg 12), ten tribes in the north seceded from the two (Judah and Benjamin) in the south. Benjamin stayed with Judah because Jerusalem was in the south; perhaps many of the Levites left the north and east and came to Judah. Simeon either went north (2Ch 15:9; 34:6) or was absorbed into Judah. The geography of the tribes is one factor in how biblical history played out in later periods.

19:10-16. The third allotment fell to **Zebulun**, occupying a place with Manasseh on the south, Asher on the west, Issachar on the east, and Naphtali on the north. The last two joined boundaries with Zebulun upon **Aznoth-tabor** (19:34). These cities determined Zebulun's location in the Jezreel and the Bet Netofa valleys. History remembered **Shimron**, part of the northern Canaanite coalition (11:1), and **Bethlehem** in Zebulun where Ibzan was from (Jdg 12:8-10). Zebulun sided with the northern rebellion against Rehoboam and was little remembered afterward.

19:17-23. The next lot fell to **Issachar**, providing a town list extensive enough to delineate borders. It occupied land in the Beth-shean plain and eastern Lower Galilee, touching the outlet of the Sea of Galilee. The towns are listed by location: the first four in the Jezreel Valley, the next five in "the basalt heights," and the last four at the cliff edges.

Shunem was the place where Elisha would have a benefactress (2Kg 4:8-37); **Kishion** and **En-gannim** appear as Levitical cities (Jos 21:28-29), Mt. **Tabor** would be immortalized as the beginning point in Barak's victory (Jdg 4); and Beth-shean's walls would be where the Philistines hung the bodies of Saul and his sons (1Sm 31). **Issachar** sided with the north when it broke away (1Kg 12), passing from significance.

19:24-31. The fifth lot fell to the tribe of... Asher, the Carmel Ridge being its southern boundary. Its eastern boundary was Naphtali and Zebulun. Most of the western boundary was the Mediterranean Sea. Its northern boundary perhaps was the Litani River. It occupied the place where the Kishon flowed into the Mediterranean, and the western slopes of the Galilean highlands.

Phoenician domination has caused most of the Levitical cities to remain unknown. The conquest of Tyre and Sidon would be difficult. Asher was never able to remove the Canaanites from Acco, Sidon and five others including the Levitical city, Rehob (cf. Jdg 1:31-32). Their land holdings increasingly diminished. Though not taken in battle, the "worthless" land of *Cabul* would be ceded to the Phoenicians by Solomon (1Kg 9:10-14). Asher was to diminish in significance after the united monarchy, having sided with Jeroboam; however, even in NT times there was a testimonial to its continued existence in a prophetess by the name of Anna (Lk 2:36-38).

19:32-39. The sixth lot fell to... Naphtali whose land hosted much of Jesus' Galilean ministry. This had been prophesied: "the land of Zebulun and the land of Naphtali... the way of the sea,... Galilee of the Gentiles. The people who walk in darkness will see a great light" (Is 9:1-2). Perhaps the advent of Messiah was the "beautiful words" Jacob once ascribed to Naphtali (Gn 49:21).

Naphtali's lands included the eastern slopes of the Galilean highlands with Asher and Zebulun on the west and Issachar on the south. Naphtali's eastern border ran from the southern tip of the Sea of Galilee to the headwaters of the Jordan, including Dan southwest of Mt. Hermon and perhaps Ijon farther to the north. The northern boundary may also have been the Litani River.

Naphtali's cities alone are called **the fortified cities**: **Chinnereth** was on the Magdalan plain; **Hazor**, burned by Joshua (Jos 11:11), would later head a coalition defeated by Barak's small force (Jdg 4). Barak's hometown was **Kedesh**, the northernmost of the cities of refuge. Nearly half these cities never reappear in Scripture.

19:40-48. The least desirable location fell to **Dan**. Sandwiched between Ephraim on the north and Judah on the south, it touched the Mediterranean on the west and Benjamin on the east between Kiriath-jearim and Beth-horon.

Zorah and **Eshtaol** reappear in the Samson story (Jdg 13:1, 25; 16:31), both towns mentioned as the starting point for the reconnaissance of the Danites when they go to obtain new land in the far north (Jdg 18:2, 8, 11). Dan's allotment had been the property of the Amorites (Jdg 1:34). **Timnah** was the home of the Philistine girl Samson wanted for a wife (Jdg 14:1). Although **Ekron** was supposed to belong to Dan, it became part of the Philistine pentapolis (cf. 2Sm 5:17-25). **Me-jarkon** may refer to the springs beginning at Apheq flowing to the Mediterranean. This land was absorbed by Judah before the Assyrian incursions. Dan's inability to hold the land motivated them to conquer Leshem or Laish in the north by Mt. Hermon, to which they moved their people, renaming it Dan (Jdg 18).

19:49-50. The land grant started with Caleb in chap. 14 and now ended with Joshua. The two faithful warriors were promised victory and land (cf. Nm 14:30). Joshua took his place last. Neither does he take the best: **Timnath-serah** (cf. Jdg 2:9), about 20 miles northwest of Jerusalem, was hilly and rocky. Having been an administrator, a general, and Moses' servant, he would end his days as a builder.

19:51. The concluding statement is from **the doorway of the tent of meeting** at Shiloh, where the ark would rest for centuries. The job was nearly complete. Two details remained: a home for the Levites and place for the cities of refuge.

The nomadic lifestyle was giving way to an agrarian-based society. The people of Israel were to become farmers, beginning the settled life God had planned for them. Several details punctuate this idyllic conclusion and some warnings cast shadows over these great victories.

D. Land Distribution: Cities of Refuge and Levitical Cities (20:1–21:45)

In chap. 20, there is a reminder of the Torah and the Transjordanian cities, and an introduction to the three cities west of the Jordan. Both Jos 20 and 21 feel Levitical. The veneer over the reallocation of these prime cities is that of legal exigencies—the cities of refuge. Chapter 20 shows the advantage: these cities would form district courts.

The Ten Commandments appear in Ex 20 (cf. Dt 5), and the city of refuge regulations soon after (see Ex 21:12-13 and the comments there). There would be at least six cities of refuge (Nm 35:9-15), guaranteeing protection of the individual until justice could be served. Moses named the three cities east of the Jordan (Dt 4:41-43). This chapter fills in the blanks for the others.

20:1-6. The people were told to select the cities west of the Jordan, reaffirming Moses' statements. There was no directive for specific cities in the west: the only limitation was expediency. The city had to be within reasonable proximity to the district it was to serve. The rule was, in contrast to murder, one who had committed manslaughter (for instance, accidental death in which **he struck his neighbor without premeditation** [v. 5]) would quickly flee to one of these cities. There, at the city gate, the refugee would **state his case in the hearing of the elders**, after which they would decide whether to protect him or release him to the avenger (cf. Dt 19:11-12). This may be jolting to the modern reader. In the ancient Near East, the death of an individual was avenged either by the government or by the individual, and the system of refuge cities regulated abuses (e.g., an escalating vendetta). If the refugee's case was legitimate, he was granted asylum.

The word **beforehand** (v. 5) is the Hebrew colloquialism that means literally "yesterday" or "the day before." The NASB's translation, **did not hate him beforehand**, is rendered in the NIV as "without malice aforethought." This is certainly the sense, although it is modern legal language. From ancient times murder and manslaughter have been treated differently.

The delay until **the death of the . . . high priest**, perhaps established a cooling off period for the blood avenger who pursued the slayer to a city of refuge, and a kind of statute of limitations, restricting movement of the slayer. He stayed there **until he** stood **before the congregation for judgment**; his confinement was complete at the high priest's death.

20:7-8. The three cities designated to be cities of refuge west of the Jordan included **Kedesh** of Naphtali in upper Galilee, centrally located **Shechem** in Ephraim, and **Hebron** in central Judah (see accompanying map "The Levitical Cities and Cities of Refuge"). The cities of refuge east of the Jordan were then reiterated. The land grant to the two and a half tribes east of the Jordan was larger, so each received one city. They

The Levitical Cities and Cities of Refuge

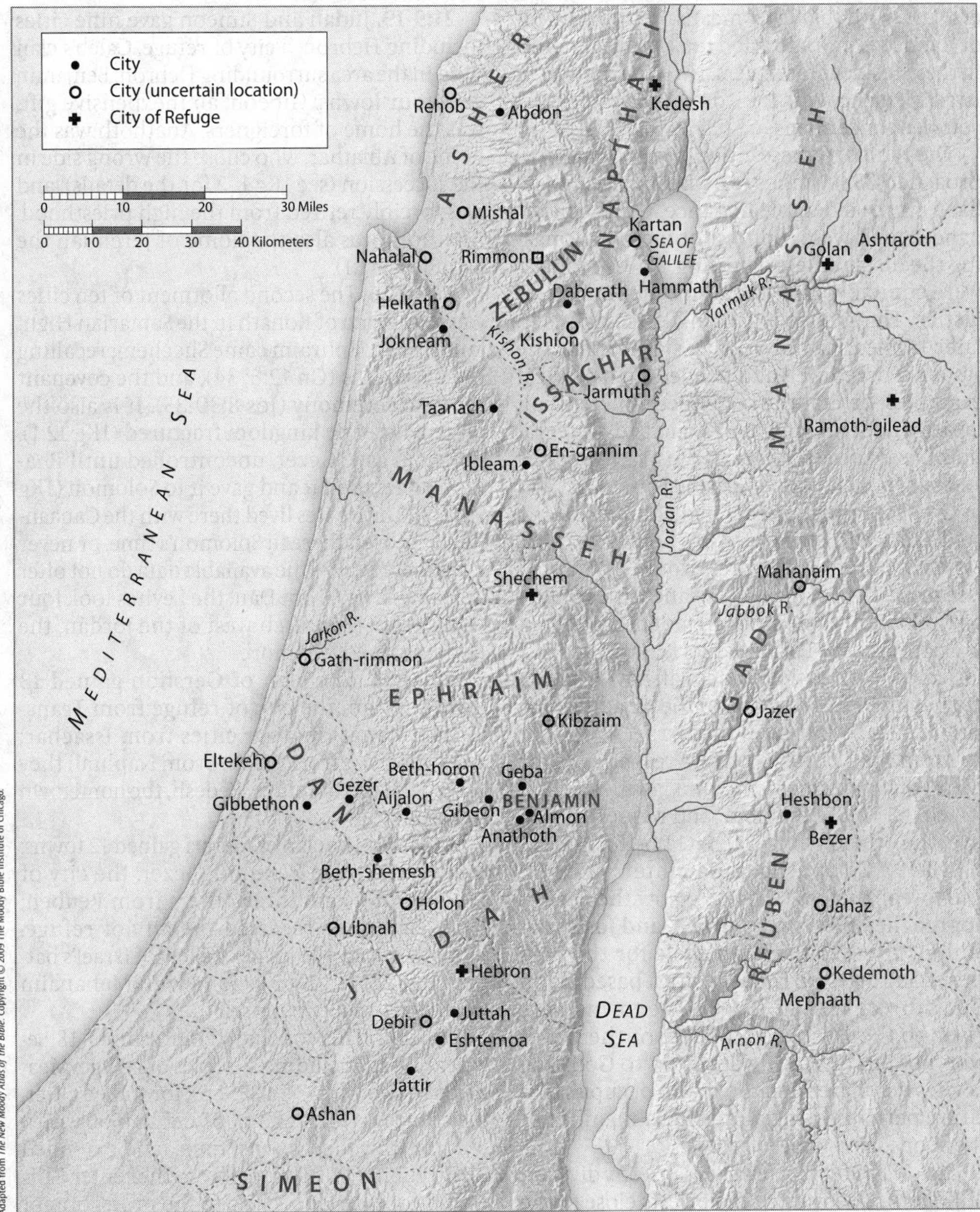

were **Bezer** in Reuben, **Ramoth** in the region of Gilead in the land provided for the tribe of Gad, and **Golan** in the territory of Bashan belonging to the tribe of Manasseh east of the Jordan. The location of Bezer is disputed.

20:9. In these designated cities the law would (1) govern unpremeditated death; (2) protect a witness; (3) mitigate unbridled revenge; and (4) guarantee a legitimate trial. The law also addressed the protection and fair trial of foreigners. The word *sojourner* means "resident alien" or "landed expatriate." God took special interest in these resident foreigners. He often motivated Israel's leniency with the words, "remember that you were once aliens . . ." (cf. Dt 5:12-15).

The radius to these cities in some cases approached 35-40 miles (e.g., Beersheba to Hebron), a considerable distance. On the other hand, people were running for their lives, making the distance less daunting. These "courts" were equitably distributed for facilitation of justice. The silence regarding these places in later biblical narrative may signify that the system worked well and needed no historical examples, or that the system completely collapsed under the weight of societal disintegration. Nevertheless, it was an illustration of fair and speedy justice and jurisdiction.

God had fought, Israel had conquered, the land had been distributed. Now homes for God's closest servants, the Levites, would be granted (see map "The Levitical Cities and Cities of Refuge"). Some of these cities are not named again in Scripture. The Levites largely controlled historical writing, so their cities will have a longer memory. The distribution of the 42 additional cities in Jos 21 indicates that Israel was never far from the Levites who were responsible for their education, medicine, and law.

21:1-3. This is the final land request narrative, the others being Caleb (14:6-15), Achsah (15:13-19), Zelophehad's daughters (17:3-6), and Joseph's tribes (17:14-18). Now **the Levites approached Eleazar the priest, and Joshua** at Shiloh, home to the tabernacle for the next three centuries, to request cities based upon God's directive (Nm 35:1-8). The towns were given to the Levites by the rest of the tribes whether out of duty or devotion to God. The Levites may have been too few to occupy some cities, perhaps living alongside a member of the sponsoring tribe.

21:4-8. The first lot fell to the priestly division of Kohath. God wanted the priests close to the tabernacle. They received 13 cities from Judah, Simeon, and Benjamin; every city given by Simeon had originally been claimed by Judah (cf. 15:21-62; 19:1-9). The remaining Kohathites received 10 cities from Ephraim, West Manasseh, and Dan. The Gershonites received 13 cities to the north in Asher, Naphtali, and East Manasseh. The Merarites received 12 cities from Reuben and Gad in Transjordan and from Zebulun in the Esdraelon Plain.

21:9-19. Judah and Simeon gave nine cities including Hebron, a city of refuge. Caleb's clan lived in the area surrounding Hebron. Benjamin gave four towns: Gibeon, an inexpensive gift, was the home of foreigners. Anathoth was the home of Abiathar, who chose the wrong side in the succession (see 1Kg 1–2 for the details), and was forcibly retired from the high priesthood. Anathoth was also the home of Jeremiah the prophet (Jr 1:1).

21:20-26. The second allotment of ten cities was to the clan of Kohath in the Samarian Highlands. From Ephraim came Shechem, recalling the patriarchs (Gn 12:6; 34), and the covenant renewal ceremony (Jos 8:30-35). It is also the place where the kingdom fractured (1Kg 12:1). Ephraim gave Gezer, uncontrolled until Pharaoh conquered it and gave it to Solomon (1Kg 9:15-17). The Levites lived there with the Canaanites, or moved there in Solomon's time, or never lived there at all—the available data do not offer a clear answer. From Dan, the Levites took four cities; from Manasseh west of the Jordan, the Levites gained two more.

21:27-33. The clan of Gershon gained 13 towns: Golan, the city of refuge from Transjordan Manasseh; four cities from Issachar; and four cities from Asher. From Naphtali they gained the city of refuge, Kedesh, the hometown of Barak (Jdg 4).

21:34-40. The clan of Merari gained 12 towns: four towns from Zebulun, Bezer, the city of refuge (20:8), and three others from Reuben; from Gad, they received the city of refuge, Ramoth-gilead, the scene of a few of Israel's battles (1Kg 22; cf. 2Kg 9), along with Mahanaim (cf. Gn 32), and two more.

21:41-42. This concluded the grant of 48 Levitical cities, including six cities of refuge. Measured in two ways (Nm 35: 4-5), for walled cities, their land was to extend 1,000 cubits (500 yards) out; for unwalled towns, their land extended 2,000 cubits (1,000 yards) from the center. This would provide land, close to the protection of the city walls or group defense, upon which the Levites could raise crops and livestock.

21:43-45. The inaugural efforts in the fulfillment of the land promise are now complete. **The LORD gave them rest on every side, according to all that He had sworn to their fathers** (cf. 11:23; 14:15). Militarily, **no one of all their enemies stood before them; the LORD gave all their enemies into their hand** (cf. 13:1-5). **Not one of the good promises which the LORD had made to the house of Israel failed; all came to pass.** Yes, the Philistines soon would invade the Judean lowlands; but there would be peace as long as Israel served the Lord. This now opened future possibilities for national Israel, which will ultimately be fulfilled only at the advent of the millennial kingdom of Messiah.

IV. Epilogue: Last Farewells (22:1–24:33)

Chapter 22 contains the dismissal of the warriors whose tribes settled east of the Jordan River. Chapter 23 relates Joshua's first farewell address. Chapter 24 recounts his second and more well-known farewell address, and is followed by notices of the deaths of Joshua and Eleazar.

A. Joshua Dismisses the Transjordanian Tribes (22:1-34)

The soldiers from the tribes that settled east of the Jordan had not all been away from their families for seven years, but many had. Some were promoted to leadership roles or retired, or sent home wounded. Those boys became men, joining the army in the field. There was constant movement as supply lines were used and strengthened. An army of this magnitude could not live entirely from scavenging. No further engagements were planned; so the easterners could return home across the Jordan River.

22:1-8. Joshua **summoned the Reubenites and the Gadites and the half-tribe of Manasseh** (i.e., East Manasseh)—the men from the tribes that settled east of the Jordan—and announced that their vow to fight with their brothers was fulfilled. He commended them and then reminded them, **Be very careful to observe the commandment and the law which Moses the servant of the LORD commanded you.** Some elements of v. 5 recall the *Shema'* (Dt 5:4-6), but almost all of Joshua's injunction comes from Dt 10:12-13. He ordered them to keep the commandments and the law, love the Lord their God, walk in all His ways, obey His commands, and to **hold fast to Him and serve Him with all** their **heart and . . . soul.**

Joshua then blessed them and sent them away. The two and a half tribes were returning with much more material wealth: livestock, metal, and clothing (vv. 7-8, cf. Nm 32:1). They were to share with those at home.

22:9. The sons of Reuben and the sons of Gad and the half-tribe of Manasseh returned home and departed from the sons of Israel at Shiloh. Locations and directions are meaningful. There are geographical, personal, and directional oppositions. There is the opposition of the three eastern tribes with Israel, Shiloh/Canaan with Gilead/their own land, Joshua with Moses, and whether to stay in Canaan.

Distances not only separate people geographically, they can also separate people socially. They will not see each other regularly, and in the interval, misunderstandings can occur. When the warriors of the tribes of Reuben, Gad, and the half-tribe of Manasseh left Shiloh and returned to their families across the Jordan, the barrier could become more than a river; misperceptions could ensue. And that is exactly what happened. The rest of the chapter recounts the fears and misunderstanding of the tribes in the west toward those in the east after the returning soldiers of Reuben, Gad, and East Manasseh completed a small but unusual building project.

22:10-20. The Transjordanians departed, but before crossing the Jordan, they built a stone structure. Literally, they "built there an altar by the Jordan, an altar great in appearance" (v. 10) on the west bank of the lower Jordan. Depending upon the location of the fords, they traveled from central Ephraim, northeast through West Manasseh. The altar would have been on West Manasseh's land opposite Gad's territory. To someone not understanding the motivation, it would look like theocratic treason because of the perceived syncretism and what would look like the decentralization of Israel's worship and sacrificial system.

A report went quickly to Shiloh (v. 11), apparently innocently, without intention to slander the east Jordan tribes. But the ten tribes west of the Jordan were alarmed. There followed complete mobilization of the Israelite army for war against the members of the tribes of **Reuben . . . Gad**, and **the half-tribe of Manasseh** (vv. 12-13). First, ten chiefs, one from each tribe, were selected to accompany Phinehas on a fact-finding mission. Phinehas was likely selected because of his demonstrated zeal in matters of theological purity (see vv. 17, 20), and in dealing with apostasy (Nm 25:6-8).

The indictment included East Manasseh (22:11), but one of the 10 delegates represented West Manasseh. Perhaps Phinehas represented the Levites. Their trip was all the way to Gilead, a journey of perhaps 55 miles (v. 15).

The perceived treachery of the two and one-half tribes was breaking national unity by the appearance of covenant infidelity (v. 16). If they offered sacrifice to other gods at this altar, it amounted to theological adultery or apostasy. If they offered sacrifice to the Lord in a location other than Shiloh without the priests, it amounted to theological compromise or divisiveness.

The unknown speaker of v. 16 mentioned the incident of Baal Peor, recalling Phinehas (cf. Nm 25:1-18). The national memory ran deep: **which we have not cleansed ourselves to this day, although a plague came on the congregation of the Lord**. Either Israel was still tempted by that form of Baalism or still reeling from losses in the plague. The emissaries thought that God might judge all Israel for the supposed sin of the tribes east of the Jordan.

To modern Western readers, the idea of a pure versus an **unclean** land seems odd (v. 19). Perhaps this is ethnocentric language, only land west of the Jordan being deemed pure by the majority of Israel. More likely it is a matter of perspective. It is as though the Israelites who lived west of the Jordan River were saying, "If, to your way of thinking, the land east of the Jordan is ceremonially unclean, move your families and livestock west."

The indictment expressed by the western tribes shifted from rebellion against God to rebellion against the community (v. 20). They referred to the Achan episode in which he took items devoted to the Lord (Jos 7), something that had been expressly forbidden. Their point is **that** Achan **did not perish alone in his iniquity**. Several warriors died in the first battle with Ai, and Achan's family and livestock were killed with him after the battle. If the tribes east of the Jordan built an altar that was an act of sin, then perhaps all Israel would suffer the consequences.

22:21-23. The indicted tribes from the east of the Jordan denied the charges. After their exclamation to **"The Mighty One, God, the Lord, the Mighty One, God, the Lord!** (v. 21), they called for an imprecation on themselves—requesting that the Israelites not spare them if proven guilty, or that God Himself hold them accountable should the Israelites decide the issue not worth pursuing (22:23). They claimed that they neither turned away from the Lord, nor had they even used the altar at all.

22:24-25. The building of an altar looked suspicious. Somebody could use it wrongly, either apostate Israelites or pagan Canaanites. But the Israelites from east of the Jordan claimed to have done this from theocratic concerns. They feared being considered outcasts from the covenant community (v. 24). They noted the barrier of the Jordan River between them (v. 25). The aspect they singled out was gradual exclusion from the community of the western tribes; they feared the physical and social separation would cause the eastern tribes to cease fearing the Lord, "that **your sons** [those west of the river] **may make our sons stop fearing the Lord**."

22:26-29. Using the word **copy** (v. 28, or "model," "reproduction of"), the spokesman for the eastern tribes explained the altar was intended only as a memorial of the one true altar in the tabernacle, housed in Shiloh at this time. Rather than being **for burnt offering or for sacrifice . . . it is a witness between us and you**, and a reminder to their sons and future generations to sacrifice only to the true God and only at **His tabernacle** (vv. 27, 29).

22:30-31. Phinehas and the leaders were satisfied with the integrity of the members of the eastern tribes. As the spokesman, Phinehas withdrew the charges.

22:32-33. The delegation returned to the west with good news. Israel, satisfied with the intent of the Transjordanians, demobilized their army.

22:34. The tribesmen from east of the Jordan, breathing a sigh of relief, named the altar **Witness**. The naming may extend to the clause **witness between us that the Lord is God**. This fits the story well but requires an anomaly in translation. The story concluded safely. Confrontation occurred, yet integrity was discovered and civil war was averted.

Practical lessons from Jos 22 include the need to care enough to confront a brother or sister who appears to be straying into sin, gathering as many facts as possible before confronting, reporting those facts accurately, acknowledging misunderstanding when it exists, and celebrating when one suspected of wrongdoing is exonerated.

The Canaanites not yet removed from the land might have hoped for civil war among the various tribes of Israel. They might then conquer a weakened Israel and reclaim the land. Similarly, when Christians are not diplomatic toward other believers with whom they have sharp differences, then faultfinders in our society love it and use it to smear the church and its Savior.

B. Joshua's First Farewell Address (23:1-16)

Chapter 22 records the last major crisis in the conquest narrative. With that, the transition to chap. 23 seems abrupt. But peace has come, and Joshua expressed the passage of time as follows: "Now it came about after many days, when the LORD had given rest to Israel from all their enemies on every side. . . ."

Joshua would begin by reaffirming his seniority (v. 2; cf. 13:1). From chap. 13 to the present some 25 years have passed. If Caleb and Joshua are approximately the same age (about 85 years old) during the land distribution (see 14:10), and if Joshua died at the age of 110 (24:29), and this is one of the last events in Joshua's life, then the narrative refers to events that transpire 25 years after the land distribution. So peace and quiet have covered the new land for more than two decades—time for the next generation to become adults.

In his first farewell speech, Joshua would expand upon a theme from the previous chapter (21:5). He spoke of fearing and loving the Lord and keeping and obeying the law. He was positive, claiming the widespread fulfillment of God's promises, but he was also realistic, observing that there was still much of the land to be taken. If not for some of the memorable words in chaps. 1 and 24, this would be the best address of the book. It draws together threads from early in the book, as Joshua tells Israel to "be very firm" (cf. Jos 1:6; 10:25), and ends with fair warning. Disobedience on the part of Israel, and covenantal defection, will result in judgment.

23:1-2. Knowing his time of departure was near, Joshua called together **all Israel, . . . their elders and their heads and their judges and their officers.**

23:3-5. The picture is both positive and realistic. In v. 3, Joshua noted that God had fought for them, fulfilling the promises. Nevertheless, some of the land was only marginally subdued. Joshua apportioned it so the tribes could finally get mastery of it. The enemies were largely defeated; most of their men were killed, yet the survivors would in a generation produce other armies. In v. 5, Joshua spoke optimistically, indicating that God would continue to force these aliens back.

23:6-7. Joshua admonished them to **be very strong** (v. 6 HCSB), echoing his words of the southern campaign decades earlier (10:25). He wanted Israel to be resolutely devoted to the law, part of which involved not becoming spiritually or socially entangled with the remaining Canaanites. It might be thought that intermarriage would make the Canaanites become Israelites. However, parents communicate culture and religion, and they would turn their children to pagan practices (cf. Ex 34: 12-16; Dt 20:16).

23:8-11. Instead of assimilating Canaanites into their communities, or themselves into Canaanite life, Israel was to remain faithful to the Lord and believe that the Lord would continue the process begun several decades before (v. 9). Joshua reminded them of the overwhelming odds they had already faced: **One of you routed a thousand, because the LORD your God was fighting for you, as He promised** (v. 10 HCSB; cf. 1Sm 4-6). Joshua admonished Israel: "Be very diligent to love the LORD your God for your own well-being" (v. 11 HCSB; cf. Dt 6:5). The true path to spiritual victory and the joy it brings is through dependence upon, and obedience to, the Lord who loves His people.

23:12-13. Joshua gave fair warning. If Israel defected from the covenant and intermarried with the remaining pagans, forward motion in securing the land would cease and God would stop fighting for Israel (v. 13). Lack of vigilance on the part of Israel would mean that **they** [the Canaanites and others] **will be a snare and a trap to you, and a whip on your sides and thorns in your eyes**, until the "thorns" take over the land and Israel succumbs.

23:14. Joshua punctuated his speech with another notice of his mortality, grabbing their attention as at the reading of a will. He reminded Israel of God's faithfulness. The promises were from God, they were good, and they did not fail. Every word from God was ultimately to be fulfilled. Not one promise would fall void.

23:15-16. If God fulfilled the good promises, He would certainly fulfill the negative ones in the event of Israel's covenantal defection. God's anger would blaze in the event of a broken covenant and Israel would be removed from the good land quickly. **When you transgress the covenant of the LORD your God. . . , and go and serve other gods and bow down to them, then**

the anger of the Lord will burn against you, and you will perish quickly from off the good land. The land was given by God and it was His to take away. Gentile Christians have no specific land promises. Christians will inherit the world, within which redeemed Israel will inherit the land, from the Nile River of Egypt to the Euphrates. However, Israel has no guarantee that she will remain in the land should she prove faithless; in fact Moses prophesied that God would judge them for their unfaithfulness by removing them from the land (see Dt 28:63; 29:25-28; 30:17-18). The privilege of possessing and enjoying the good land was contingent not upon God's whimsy, but upon Israel's dependence on Him and obedience to the covenant (being **very firm**, v. 6).

Joshua's admonitions to the tribes east of the Jordan (22:5) and to Israel (chap. 23) indicate contact points for today. Whether in the theocracy of old or in faith communities today, individuals and communities of faith should always recall what God has done (vv. 3, 9-10) and trust God when suffering and conflict arises because of life in this fallen world. The people of God, whether in Joshua's day or today, must guard against allowing those outside the community of faith to influence them in their spiritual lives and values (v. 7). Believers must be wary to "love the Lord [their] God with all [their] heart, with all [their] soul and with all [their] mind" (Dt 6:5). In so doing, the object of their affections becomes the source of all their blessings and benefits (Jos 13:11).

Conversely, when believers turn cold in respect to the Lord (v. 12), they can expect spiritual progress in their lives to be severely hampered (v. 13). God has kept His promises and will continue to do so (v. 14). And as God's beneficent promises have been fulfilled, so will His punitive ones (v. 15). Even those who have truly trusted Christ for salvation may experience severe chastisement from God if they insist on living in ways that put themselves at cross purposes with God's revealed will found in Scripture. The nation of Israel under Joshua could not afford to be presumptuous about their relationship with God, and neither should contemporary believers.

C. Joshua's Final Farewell Address (24:1-28)

Recalling Hebrew history, the location at Shechem provides an appropriate setting to conclude the narrative. When Abram arrived in Canaan, the first location noted was Shechem, where God promised him the land (Gn 12:5-9). Shechem was the reentry point for Jacob when, returning from Mesopotamia, he celebrated by building a commemorative altar to the Lord (Gn 33:18-20). He returned with a large family that would become the 12 tribes. As Jacob was leaving there, he appealed to his family and servants to get rid of their idols (Gn 35:2-4). Shechem also was the location of the covenant renewal ceremony (Jos 8:30-35).

In his final address, Joshua expressed himself using repetitions and triads. Three times various approaches to paganism would be mentioned (24:2, 14, 15). Twice Joshua ordered them to put away their gods (24:14, 23; cf. Gn 35:2-4). Twice the people affirmed that they would serve the Lord (Jos 24:16-18, 21-24). The word "witnesses" is repeated as part of the oath formula (Jos 24:22), as is Joshua's statement about the memorial stone as a "witness" against them in the event of covenant breach (v. 27). The structure and contents of chap. 24 have the form of an ancient treaty. However, as David Howard, Jr., writes, "Joshua 24 does not claim to be the text of a treaty or covenant but rather a report of a covenant-renewal ceremony" (*Joshua*, 428). The format of the chapter can be outlined as follows:

I. Preamble (vv. 1-2)
II. Historical Prologue (vv. 2-13)
III. Stipulations (vv. 14-15; 16-25)
IV. Preservation and Legacy (v. 26)
  A. Archiving in Tabernacle/Temple
  B. Provision for Public Reading
V. Witnesses (vv. 22, 27)
VI. Benefits/Consequences (implied vv. 19-20)

24:1. As in chap. 23, this assembly in Shechem included all of Israel along with the same four groups of officers: **the elders of Israel and . . . their heads and their judges and their officers** (cf. 23:2). Even though the aged Joshua convened the meeting, they were all gathered **before God**.

24:2-13. Joshua reminded Israel of Abraham's history (Gn 11:26-12:3). Their geographical location had moved from Mesopotamia to the promised land, along with allegiance from the worship of idols to the Lord alone. Joshua then rehearsed the patriarchal period ending with the Egyptian sojourn (vv. 3-4). Collapsing four hundred years into the word **then** (v. 5), Joshua condensed many of the events of the exodus into two verses: Egypt suffered plagues; Israel departed and was pinned against the shore of the Red Sea. Virtually none of those present participated with Joshua in those events. Joshua reminded Israel that when their ancestors cried out to God, they passed through the Red Sea whereas the pursuing Egyptians were drowned. Joshua emphasized the darkness separating the two nations keeping Israel safe in flight from the Egyptians (cf. Jos 3:15-17; 4:18, 23).

And you lived in the wilderness for a long time (v. 7). The people listening to Joshua knew well that their parents and grandparents had been left in graves along the way. They circumnavigated Edom, Ammon, and Moab and risked open hostilities with the Amorites east of the Jordan River. The theological point is that God was the author of their victories (v. 8). Then Joshua recounted the conspiracy between the king of Moab, Balak; and the soothsayer, Balaam. In antiquity, an imprecation (curse) was considered effectual. It cannot work, however, against that which God has determined to bless. Modernity tends to view curses as powerless, but there is at least a psychological effect in a curse. God said that He would not listen to Balaam. Instead, he "repeatedly blessed" Israel, and God delivered them (v. 10). Some think that this is emphatic rather than repetitive, but Balaam's repeated blessings of Israel (Nm 23–24) and the grammar require the repetition. The intention is to show that repeated efforts of cursing what God has blessed are futile.

After the memorial of the crossing of the Jordan (4:5-9, 20-24), Joshua told Israel that they had staked their claim on foreign territory. The mention of the seven nations in v. 11 recalls Jos 3:10. God **sent the hornet before** them. The word **hornet** is singular and not plural, but it may be a collective noun that could refer either to one nasty hornet or a whole hive of them (cf. Ex 23:28; Dt 7:20).

The theological point is: It was **not by your sword or your bow**. Whether by landslides, earthquakes, astronomical phenomena, or crazed hornets, God had orchestrated everything and Israel's victories were to His credit. Lands and cities were theirs though, from a purely human perspective, such success should have been impossible for a nomadic people without fortresses or formal military training. Moses had prophesied this success at God's hand (Dt 6:10-12).

24:14-15. Joshua used the historical review as a motivation for a series of commands. God's character and actions since the time of Abraham caused Joshua to (1) direct Israel to fear the Lord and worship Him loyally. They were to (2) rid themselves of the gods of Egypt and Mesopotamia. They were to (3) choose between the useless pagan gods or the Lord who had proved powerful and faithful. Joshua ended by utilizing himself as an example with the well-known words: **As for me and my house, we will serve the LORD**. Joshua has indicated by history, command, and example which way the people should go.

24:16-18. The people said they would remain faithful. They rehearsed their own abbreviated history, in which they focused on the slavery of Egypt and the miracles and providence in travel (v. 17). They affirmed that it was the Lord who had provided them with the promised land and reiterated that they would continue to worship the Lord.

24:19-20. Joshua responded that God was too high for them to serve. He is holy and jealous and may at times appear to be unforgiving. The tone is a bit morbid. The Hebrew construction is most naturally, "Because you will abandon the Lord and you will worship foreign gods [to the end that] He will turn against you, He will harm you and He will completely destroy you, after [despite the fact that] He has been good to you." Moses had uttered similar warnings (Dt 28:15-68). Perhaps Joshua sensed insincerity in their reply and so used stronger language. History would prove his warnings valid. However, this and the subsequent generation would remain basically faithful (24:31).

24:21-24. The people reiterated their faithfulness to the Lord, and so Joshua called them to testify against themselves. He told them that they were **witnesses** to these facts, and they reaffirmed that they would be **witnesses** (v. 22). Joshua suspected that Israel had kept idols throughout history, and so he bracketed his discussion from v. 14 with the command to put away their foreign gods (v. 23). The word **incline** entails a complete reorientation from the hedonistic materialism of paganism to the pursuit of holiness inherent in Yahwism (v. 24). So the people reaffirmed that they would **serve the LORD our God and . . . obey His voice**.

24:25-28. In some of his last known acts, Joshua formalized the covenant with that generation of Israelites. These events were recorded (v. 26), perhaps as an appendix to the Torah.

Joshua set up a memorial stone next to the sanctuary, which was likely a temporary sacred space set up for the present festivities. The tree in Shechem is reminiscent of the tree where Jacob's family buried their idols (Gn 35:4). Joshua then called them to account, saying that this sacred memorial pillar was a **witness** and had **heard** and would hold them accountable to God (Jos 24:27).

Joshua's final known act was to send the people home. They had sworn to be true to God. There was no designated successor to Joshua. Leadership would be in the hands of the priesthood now. Phinehas was to be the next generation's leader, along with a Levitical team to adjudicate cases, diagnose disease, and provide instruction in the Torah.

D. Appendices: Joshua's Death, Israel's Faithfulness, Joseph's Bones, Eleazar's Death (24:29-33)

The final time marker, "after these things," introduces three events marked by geographical notations recalling key events from Genesis and Exodus. They have to do with several parallels between Shechem in Genesis and in the book of Joshua, one important parallel between the patriarch Joseph and Joshua, and Eleazar. Verses 29-33 indicate the fulfillment of many promises God made in the book of Genesis. The promise that the descendants of Abraham, Isaac, and Jacob would possess the land was inaugurated and at least partially fulfilled. The points of contact between Genesis and the book of Joshua, whether the importance of Shechem in both books, Joseph and Joshua both living to be 110 years old, or Joseph's remains, all serve to remind the reader that God is faithful to His promises.

24:29-32. This section serves as an obituary of Joshua as well as offering parallels to one of the great patriarchs, Joseph. Joshua passed away, finally being called **the servant of the LORD** as Moses had been.

The first parallel between Joshua and Joseph is that Joshua is said to have died at the age of 110 years; Joseph died at the same age (Gn 50:22, 26). In Egypt, where each man spent part of his life, 110 was considered the perfect age. Vizier Ptah-Hotep (2450 BC), an adviser to a fifth dynasty pharaoh, wrote some advice to instruct his son. In it he said: "What I have done on earth is not inconsiderable. I attained one hundred and ten years of life . . . through doing right for the king up to the point of veneration" (*ANET*[3], 414).

Joshua was buried in the hill country of Ephraim, in his adopted town of Timnath-serah (Jos 19:50; cf. Jdg 2:9). Joshua's legacy included influence that went well beyond his own lifetime, much like the enduring influence of Joseph.

Joseph's burial land would be in the same Holy Land area as Joshua's. Joseph had told his surviving relatives that God would one day return the people and his remains to the land of Canaan (Gn 50:24). The patriarchs had been buried in Canaan and so, by faith, Joseph made his sons swear they would eventually bring remains to Canaan (Gn 50:25). At the exodus, Moses took Joseph's bones (Ex 13:19), transporting them for over forty years! Nevertheless, they finally came to rest less than 20 miles from Joshua's resting place, at Shechem (where Jacob had purchased land hundreds of years before [Gn 33:18-19]). Though born in Paddan-aram, Joseph's journey was now complete.

And so, we have come full circle: the promises made to Abraham in the land, the Egyptian sojourn, the exodus and wilderness wandering, and now the conquest and inhabiting the land —so with the cycle of Joseph being taken to Egypt and his bones being brought back, Israel descended to Egypt as an extended family and has now returned as a nation to dwell peacefully in her homeland.

24:33. Phinehas had long been groomed for the office of high priest; but now his father, Eleazar, Aaron's son, has died (Jos 24:33). The location of this **Gibeah** (the words in Hb. are lit. *gib'ath pinechas* and could be rendered "the hill or mountain of Phinehas") is uncertain. Gibeah is considered to be part of Benjamin rather than Ephraim, although the borders were somewhat fluid. Perhaps it is best to consider this an unknown site in Ephraim.

As noted, vv. 29-33 indicate that God closed the loop on His promise to the patriarchs that the people of Israel would possess the land. The details of this brief section, and indeed, the entire book of Joshua, all serve to remind that God is faithful to His promises. But it is incumbent upon each generation, including our own, to "choose . . . today whom you will serve" . . . and to agree with Joshua of old: "As for me and my house, we will serve the LORD" (Jos 24:15).

BIBLIOGRAPHY

Abegg Jr., Martin, Peter Flint, and Eugene Ulrich. *The Dead Sea Scrolls Bible: The Oldest Known Bible Translated for the First Time into English.* San Francisco: Harper, 1999.

Beitzel, Barry J. *The New Moody Atlas of the Bible.* Chicago: Moody, 2009.

Gundry, Stanley N. ed., *Show Them No Mercy: Four Views on God and Canaanite Genocide.* Grand Rapids, MI: Zondervan, 2003.

Bimson, John J. and David Livingston. "Redating the Exodus," *Biblical Archaeological Review* 13 (September–October 1987): 40–53, 66–8.

Boice, James Montgomery. *Joshua.* Grand Rapids, MI: Baker, 1989.

Butler, Trent C. "Joshua." *Word Biblical Commentary.* vol. 7. Waco, TX: Word, 1983.

Campbell, Donald K. "Joshua" in *The Bible Knowledge Commentary,* Old Testament. Colorado Springs, CO: Victor, 1985. 325–71.

Davis, John J. *Conquest and Crisis.* Grand Rapids, MI: Baker, 1969.

Garrett, Duane A. *Proverbs, Ecclesiastes, Song of Songs.* Vol. 14. The New American Commentary. Ed. E. Ray Clendenen. Nashville: Broadman & Holman, 1993.

Hess, Richard S. *Joshua: An Introduction and Commentary,* Tyndale Old Testament Commentaries, ed. D. J. Wiseman. Downers Grove, IL: InterVarsity, 1996.

Howard Jr., David M. *Joshua.* The New American Commentary. Vol. 5. ed. E. Ray Clendenen. Nashville: Broadman & Holman, 2002.

Jensen, Irving L. "Joshua: Rest-Land Won." *Everyman's Bible Commentary.* Chicago: Moody, 1966.

Kitchen, K. A. *On the Reliability of the Old Testament.* Grand Rapids, MI: Eerdmans, 2003.

Madvig, Donald H. "Joshua." *The Expositor's Bible Commentary.* Vol. 3. ed. Frank E. Gaebelein. Grand Rapids, MI: Zondervan, 1992. 239–371.

Merrill, Eugene H. "The Case for Moderate Discontinuity" in Stanley N. Gundry, ed., *Show Them No Mercy: Four Views on God and Canaanite Genocide* (Grand Rapids, MI: Zondervan, 2003), 63–94.

______. *Kingdom of Priests: A History of Old Testament Israel.* Grand Rapids, MI: Baker, 1989.

Pritchard, James B., ed. *Ancient Near Eastern Texts: Relating to the Old Testament* ANET. Princeton: Princeton University Press, 1969.

Wood, Bryant G. "Did the Israelites Conquer Jericho: A New Look at the Archaeological Evidence," *Biblical Archaeological Review* 16 (March–April, 1990): 44–58.

______. "Notes and News: Khirbet el-Maqatir, 1995–1998," *Israel Exploration Journal,* 50 (2000): 123–130.

Wood, Leon J. *A Survey of Israel's History.* Revised by David O'Brien. Grand Rapids, MI: Zondervan, 1970, 86.

Woudstra, Marten H. "The Book of Joshua." *The New International Commentary on the Old Testament.* Grand Rapids, MI: Eerdmans, 1981.

JUDGES

JOHN MCMATH

INTRODUCTION

The book of Judges continues the historical narrative of the people of Israel in the land after the death of Joshua to the beginning of the united kingdom under the ministry of Samuel.

The book is called *shophetim* in Hebrew, *Kritai* in the LXX, and *Liber Iudicum* in the Latin Vulgate. In all three languages these words mean "judges." The English "Judges" follows this tradition.

Although the judges did sometimes decide civil disputes (e.g., Deborah), their major function was political and military leadership.

The Hebrew root *sh-ph-t* for "judge" probably derives from a Semitic term with a semantic range including "ruling and controlling," as well as "correcting," "putting in order," or "making just." The book of Judges also emphasizes the empowerment of the Spirit of God. This "filling" of the Spirit has led many commentators to note that the judges reveal God's work of specially gifting people for God's work. While there are parallels to the political functions of the judges in Mesopotamia and in Carthage, and even in ancient Ebla, the divinely empowered status of the Israelite judges appears to be unique in history.

Author. Who wrote Judges is unknown. Critics have pointed to the obvious three-part structure of the book (see the outline) as evidence for a complicated tradition history. But such a hypothesis is unnecessary. The central point of the book, that even divinely empowered human leaders cannot lead Israel to spiritual triumph, is well served by the structure of the book. The commentary will assume that the book is the work of a single author.

The author of Judges used sources, as all historians do. The story of the wars of occupation (1:1–2:5) may have been a parallel account to the Joshua story (with some significant differences of emphasis). The appendix (chaps. 17–21) may have come from other hands. Certainly the Song of Deborah (chap. 5) was ancient by the time the final author included it in the book. The stories of the individual judges may have come from separate sources. However, a single author put the material into its canonical form under the inspiration of the Holy Spirit.

The Talmud attributes the authorship of Judges to Samuel. The major argument against this view, however, is that the book seems to be an argument for a king, whereas Samuel seems to have opposed the idea. Those who favor Samuel's authorship of Judges say that he opposed, not so much the idea of a king, as the Israelites' motivation for seeking a king. The people saw a king as a solution to their immediate political and military problems, and Samuel saw a godly king as a representative of the King of kings. Samuel may have written the book as a polemic against mere human kingship, since even the divinely empowered leaders failed. Ultimately, the work was designed to be anonymous and should be read that way.

Date. Several clues point to the conclusion that the author of Judges wrote during the early years of the monarchy. First, the hectic days of the judges appear to be viewed from a more stable and secure position. Second, Jdg 1:21 points to a time before David's capture of Jerusalem when the "Jebusites . . . lived with the sons of Benjamin . . . to this day." Third, 1:29 reports Canaanite control of Gezer, a major site about 20 miles west and slightly north of Jerusalem on the international trade route at the entrance to the Aijalon Valley. Not until later (in 970 BC) did Gezer come under Israelite control.

The note of 18:30, that the idolatrous priests of Micah continued to serve "until the captivity of the land" has led some critics to insist on a postexilic date for the writing of Judges. However, it is unlikely that such a dreadful situation would have been allowed during the years of David and Solomon. E. J. Young's suggestion (in *An Introduction to the Old Testament* [Grand Rapids, MI: Eerdmans, 1949]) that "land" should read "ark" (so that the verse refers to the Philistine capture of the ark of the covenant in about 1075 BC), makes good sense, and requires only a minor change of the consonants (*'arets* to *'aron*). However, there is no manuscript support for this, and modern scholars have generally not accepted that idea.

Themes. The key to understanding the work of the judges appears in 2:16: "The LORD raised up judges who delivered them from the hands of those who plundered them." "Delivered" is the common verb meaning "to save." This is ironic, for Moses was sent to deliver the people from Egypt, and ended up presiding over funerals in the wilderness for 38 years. Joshua, whose name means "Deliverer" or "Savior," succeeded only partially in delivering the people. The apparent motivation for the writing of the book of Judges is the recurring failure of the judges to deliver the people. This theme occurs twice in the book: "In those days there was no king in Israel; every man did what was right in his own eyes" (17:6; 21:25). That even divinely empowered human leaders could not lead Israel to spiritual triumph points to the need for a great King beyond even Saul and David. The term "great King" is a Near Eastern concept, first applied by the Hittites, of a "king above the kings," or leader of an empire. In the context of Israel in the time of the judges, the term "great King" refers to the messianic leader who alone can fulfill the needs of mankind.

Purpose. The book of Judges continues the history of Israel, bridging the years between the conquest and the rise of the monarchy.

But, in addition, the author was building a case for the need for a great King. In doing so he demonstrated the downward trend of the spiritual condition of Israel over the centuries of the judges, arguing that temporary and local leaders could not provide a solution for the underlying problems the people of Israel faced. Genuinely impressive victories under Deborah and Barak and then Gideon were followed by the nation's collapse again into sin and idolatry. The later judges Samson and Jephthah gave only limited respite from anarchy. Chapters 17–21 show a period of history in which the people of Israel increasingly slid into apostasy. The location of these chapters in the book may not be chronological, but the intention is clear: to give the reader a bad portrait of Israel without God as their King.

Background. Judges is included in the larger corpus of material often called the "Primary History"—Pentateuch, Joshua, Judges, Samuel, Kings, Ezra-Nehemiah—all probably written by prophets, and distinguished from the chronicler's history. This constitutes a well-planned metanarrative behind the entire history of Israel, written by multiple authors who used a wide variety of literary sources from about 1500 to 400 BC.

In this larger historical framework the story of heroes and prophets, deliverers and judges, kings and conquerors is one of frequent tragedy. Moses, the man of God, was unable to enter the promised land. Joshua, the conqueror, was unable to lead the people to nearly complete victory over the land of Canaan. Judges, one after another, staved off defeat for decreasing periods of time. Saul was a failure. David committed adultery with Bathsheba and had her husband Uriah murdered. Solomon acquired numerous wives and horses, and slid into idolatry. Many of the kings of Israel and Judah were a rogues' gallery with occasional bright moments on the way to the increasingly predictable destruction of the kingdom.

The metanarrative, then, tells a broader story, of which Judges is merely a part. Biblical theologians speak of the "center" or "theme" of biblical theology. From Genesis to Revelation the Bible is designed to reveal God in His glory. For this overarching glory of God, two great parallel themes develop: the kingdom program and the redemption program, intertwined from Gn 3:15 (the "protoevangelium"; see the comments there) to eternity.

The author of Judges despaired of the possibility of a mere earthly kingdom providing the foundation for lasting godliness. God knew that no earthly king could ever solve Israel's problems. The massive sin problem of mankind demands a King who is also the Redeemer.

For this reason it is best to see the metanarrative of the primary history as a messianic prelude. The messianic "seed" predicted in Gn 3:15 and followed through the kingly line is picked up by the prophets as the great King who would suffer for sin and ultimately rule on the earth and in heaven for all eternity.

The King who was "not in Israel" (Jdg 18:1) in the time of the judges was not merely a temporal head of state. The great King is Messiah the Prince, Jesus Christ. Judges is then part of an overall biblical narrative with a trajectory pointing to Christ and eternity. Jesus, whose name is the Greek equivalent of the Hebrew "Joshua," is the great "Deliverer."

The period from the death of Joshua to the establishment of the monarchy was roughly 300 years. Judges recounts the turmoil of the tribes during the years following the failure to occupy the land completely. The surrounding world was also in turmoil. Significantly, the Egyptians were in disarray during the Amarna Age (15th century BC), followed by the resurgence of the Nineteenth Dynasty pharaohs Ramses II and Mernepthah. The Hittites were in mortal confrontation with the Mesopotamian Mitanni, and minor regional powers jockeyed for position. The Philistines, part of a larger Aegean people group sometimes called "Sea-Peoples," were migrating into the region during this period, and posed a threat to Israel.

The years of the judges' rulership and the years of rest, when added together, comes to a total of between 410 and 490 years. Most interpreters allow for an overlapping of judgeships to account for this chronological problem. Samson and Jephthah, for example, were possibly contemporaries, with Samson in the West and Jephthah in the East.

Most conservative scholars believe the exodus occurred in 1446 BC, and the conquest under Joshua was from 1405 to 1400. In Jdg 11:26 Jephthah indicated that Israel had occupied the region of Heshbon and Aroer for 300 years. Since Jephthah (and Samson) were at the end of the line of judges, this means the period of the judges extended from about 1400 to at least 1100. The period may have extended another 49 or 50 years (for a total of 349 or 350) because Saul began his reign in 1051. Or more likely, the period of the judges may have begun in 1351 and ended 300 years later in 1051.

The book of Judges is a story of warfare, assassinations, treachery, and general mayhem. Ehud's secretive stabbing of Eglon, Jael's tent-peg exploit, and Gideon's execution of the kings all may seem somewhat less than ethical today. In many ways the treatment of these issues is like that of the imprecatory psalms (e.g., 109:6-13) in which the enemies of Israel are viewed as the enemies of God, and their cruel punishment is a means of glorifying God.

Chronology of the Judges

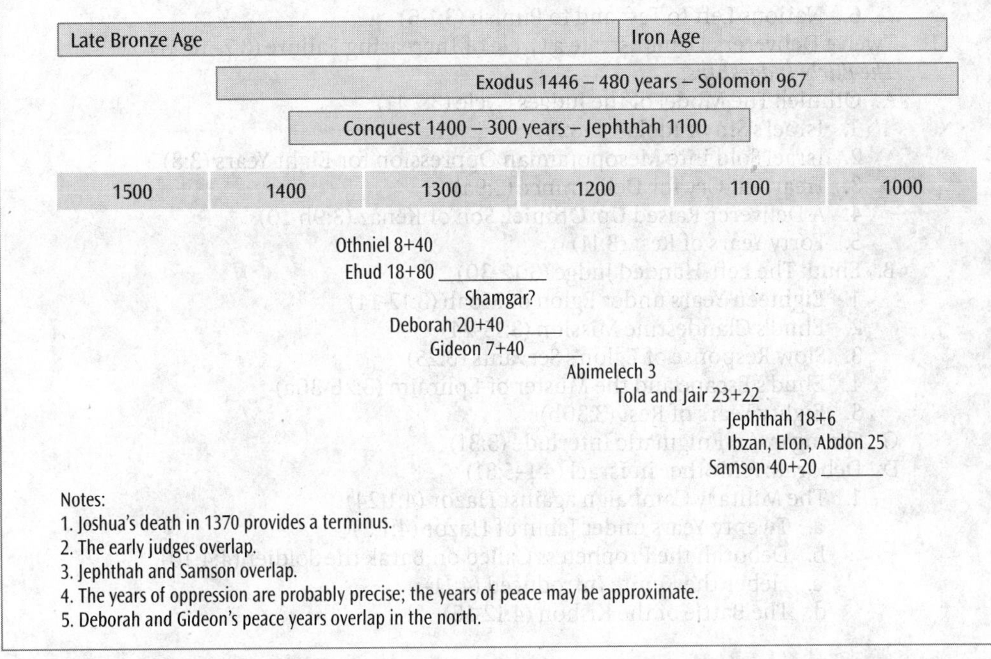

Some of the judges, however, are particularly distasteful. Samson and Jephthah raise the question, "How can a good God use evil men?" The answer is that God's judgment is often carried out in political and military movements. In this way the Babylonian invasion was explained to Habakkuk and the coming of Cyrus, king of the Persian totalitarian empire, was extolled as God's servant in Is 44–45.

Perhaps these ethical shortcomings are a part of the argument that human deliverers will always fall short of the perfection that people expect and desperately need.

The following outline of Judges assumes that a single author used his literary art to put existing historical materials into a coherent frame. The dual prologue is matched by a parallel pair of epilogues framing 12 stories of deliverers. The prologues explain the historical failure and theological basis of the period. The list of judges is divided into two parts; the early judges were generally helpful, and the later ones were much less sympathetic. The epilogues graphically portray the tenor of an age when every man did what was right in his own eyes.

OUTLINE

I. Two Prologues: Israel's Partial Obedience after Joshua's Death Leads to a Cycle of Sin and Grace (1:1–3:6)
  A. An Account of Obedience and Failure (1:1–2:5)
    1. Stage Setting (1:1)
    2. Faithful Judah (1:2-21)
    3. Failure of the Northern Tribes (1:22-36)
    4. Israel's Lament (2:1-5)
  B. The Theology of Sin and Grace (2:6–3:6)
    1. Account of the Death of Joshua and the Aftermath (2:6-10)
    2. Account of the Idolatry of Israel (2:11-13)
    3. God's Anger Displayed in the Rise of Oppressors (2:14-15)
    4. The Judges Raised Up as a Respite from Oppression (2:16-19)
    5. God's Anger at Covenant Transgression Resulted in Pagan Nations that Could Not Be Driven Out (2:20-23)
    6. Nations Left to Test and to Punish (3:1-6)

II. Twelve Deliverers Demonstrate a Cycle of Increasing Failure (3:7–16:31)
  The Early Judgeships:
  A. Othniel: The Model of the Judges Cycle (3:7-11)
    1. Israel's Sin of Idolatry (3:7)
    2. Israel Sold into Mesopotamian Oppression for Eight Years (3:8)
    3. Heartfelt Cry for Deliverance (3:9a)
    4. A Deliverer Raised Up: Othniel, Son of Kenaz (3:9b-10)
    5. Forty Years of Rest (3:11)
  B. Ehud: The Left-Handed Judge (3:12-30)
    1. Eighteen Years under Eglon of Moab (3:12-14)
    2. Ehud's Clandestine Mission (3:15-24)
    3. Slow Response of Eglon's Servants (3:25)
    4. Ehud's Escape and the Muster of Ephraim (3:26-30a)
    5. Eighty Years of Rest (3:30b)
  C. Shamgar: An Enigmatic Interlude (3:31)
  D. Deborah: A Mother in Israel (4:1–5:31)
    1. The Military Campaign against Hazor (4:1-24)
      a. Twenty Years under Jabin of Hazor (4:1-3)
      b. Deborah the Prophetess Called on Barak the Soldier (4:4-10)
      c. Heber the Kenite Introduced (4:11)
      d. The Battle of the Kishon (4:12-16)

- e. Sisera Meets Jael (4:17-22)
- f. The Long Campaign against Jabin (4:23-24)

2. The Song of Deborah (5:1-31)
   - a. Call to Praise the Lord (5:1-5)
   - b. Deborah's Motivation, as a Mother in Israel (5:6-11)
   - c. The Muster of the Tribes (5:12-18)
   - d. The Battle at the Kishon (5:19-23)
   - e. Jael: Most Blessed of Women (5:24-27)
   - f. Lament of Sisera's Mother (5:28-31a)
3. Forty Years of Rest (5:31b)

E. Gideon: A Lesser Son of a Lesser Son (6:1–9:57)

1. Introduction to the Gideon Episode (6:1-10)
   - a. Seven Years of Oppression by Midian (6:1-6)
   - b. The Covenant Message of a Prophet (6:7-10)
2. Gideon's Call to Deliver Israel (6:11-40)
   - a. Gideon Called by the Angel of the Lord (6:11-18)
   - b. Gideon's Presentation and Fear (6:19-24)
   - c. Hacking the Altar and Asherah (6:25-27)
   - d. Confrontation with Joash (6:28-32)
   - e. Muster of the Northern Tribes (6:33-35)
   - f. Sign of the Fleece (6:36-40)
3. The Defeat of Midian (7:1-25)
   - a. The Camp at Harod (7:1)
   - b. The Selection of the Fearless (7:2-3)
   - c. The Selection of the Unobservant (7:4-8)
   - d. Gideon Overheard a Dream (7:9-14)
   - e. Preparation for the Battle (7:15-18)
   - f. The Battle on the Plains of Esdraelon (7:19-23)
   - g. The Muster of Ephraim (7:24-25)
4. Aftermath of the Battle (8:1-27)
   - a. Appeasement of Ephraim (8:1-3)
   - b. No Help from Succoth and Penuel (8:4-9)
   - c. Capture of Kings; Routing of Midian (8:10-12)
   - d. Punishment of Succoth and Penuel (8:13-17)
   - e. Execution of Zebah and Zalmunna (8:18-21)
   - f. Gideon Offered the Kingdom (8:22-27)
5. The Era of Gideon's Rest (8:28-35)
   - a. Forty Years of Rest (8:28)
   - b. Gideon's Later Life and Descendants (8:29-32)
   - c. Israel Forgets the Lord (8:33-35)
6. Abimelech and the Fall of Shechem (9:1-57)
   - a. Abimelech's Treachery and Jotham's Response (9:1-21)
     - (1) Abimelech Conspired to Become King of Shechem by Treachery (9:1-6)
     - (2) Jotham's Fable (9:7-15)
     - (3) Jotham's Challenge and Escape (9:16-21)
   - b. The Fall of Shechem and Abimelech (9:22-55)
     - (1) Three Turbulent Years of Rule (9:22-25)
     - (2) Gaal, the Challenger (9:26-29)
     - (3) Zebul, the Lieutenant, Warned of Treachery (9:30-33)
     - (4) The Defeat of Gaal (9:34-41)
     - (5) The Capture of Shechem (9:42-45)
     - (6) Burning the Tower of Shechem (9:46-49)
     - (7) Death of Abimelech at Thebez (9:50-55)
   - c. Fulfillment of the Curse of Jotham (9:56-57)

The Later Judgeships:

F. Tola and Jair: Two Minor Administrators (10:1-5)
  1. Tola: Twenty-Three Years of Stability (10:1-2)
  2. Jair: Twenty-Two Years of Prosperity (10:3-5)

G. Jephthah: Outcast Deliverer (10:6–12:7)
  1. Gilead and the Challenge of Ammon (10:6-18)
    a. Sin and Affliction for 18 Years (10:6-9)
    b. Supplication until God Could Not Bear It (10:10-16)
    c. The Muster of Ammon and Gilead (10:17-18)
  2. Jephthah Called to Face Ammon (11:1-11)
    a. Jephthah Introduced (11:1-3)
    b. Jephthah Agreed to Lead Gilead (11:4-11)
  3. The Battle of Ammon (11:12-40)
    a. Jephthah's Diplomacy (11:12-28)
    b. Jephthah's Foolish Vow (11:29-33)
    c. Jephthah's Daughter (11:34-40)
  4. Civil War with Ephraim (12:1-6)
  5. Six Years of Rest (12:7)

H. Ibzan, Elon, and Abdon: Three Minor Administrators (12:8-15)
  1. Ibzan: Seven Years a Family Man (12:8-10)
  2. Elon: Ten Years in Zebulun (12:11-12)
  3. Abdon: Eight Years with Donkeys (12:13-15)

I. Samson: A Deeply Flawed Deliverer (13:1–16:31)
  1. Forty Years of Philistine Oppression (13:1)
  2. Conception and Birth of a Remarkable Boy: Samson Introduced (13:2-25)
    a. The Angel of the Lord Appeared to Manoah's Wife (13:2-7)
    b. Manoah Spoke with God (13:8-14)
    c. Sacrifice before the Angel of the Lord (13:15-20)
    d. Common Sense of Manoah's Wife (13:21-23)
    e. Samson's Birth and Divine Empowerment (13:24-25)
  3. Samson's Marriage at Timnah (14:1–15:20)
    a. Samson Chose a Wife from the Philistines (14:1-4)
    b. Samson Took His Parents to Meet the Girl (14:5-9)
    c. Samson's Wedding Debacle (14:10-20)
      (1) The Feast (14:10-11)
      (2) Samson's Riddle (14:12-14)
      (3) Treachery on Treachery (14:15-20)
    d. Samson's Destruction of Philistine Crops (15:1-8)
    e. Samson Submitted to the Men of Judah (15:9-13)
    f. The Battle of Lehi (15:14-19)
    g. Twenty Years of Samson's Leadership (15:20)
  4. Samson's Lust and Death (16:1-31)
    a. Samson and the Harlot of Gaza (16:1-3)
    b. Samson and Delilah (16:4-22)
      (1) Delilah Introduced (16:4-6)
      (2) Three Tests of Strength (16:7-14)
      (3) Delilah Extracted the Secret of Samson's Strength (16:15-17)
      (4) Samson Captured by the Philistines (16:18-22)
    c. Samson's Humiliation and Vengeance (16:23-31)
      (1) Samson's Humiliation (16:23-27)
      (2) Samson's Vengeance (16:28-31)

III. Two Epilogues: The Abominable Spiritual Condition of Israel Called for a Great King to Stabilize and Lead the Nation (17:1–21:25)

A. The Idolatry of Dan (17:1–18:31)

1. Idolatry in Ephraim (17:1-13)
   a. Micah and His Mother (17:1-6)
   b. A Levite for a Priest (17:7-13)
2. Danites on the Move (18:1-31)
   a. Danite Patrol Meets the Priest of Micah (18:1-6)
   b. Danites Find a New Place to Settle (18:7-10)
   c. Journey of the Six Hundred to Ephraim (18:11-13)
   d. Subversion of Micah's Priest (18:14-20)
   e. Confrontation with Micah (18:21-26)
   f. Establishment of Idolatry in Dan (Laish) (18:27-31)

B. The Perversion of Benjamin (19:1–21:25)
1. Degrading Murder of a Levite's Concubine (19:1-30)
   a. A Levite Fetched His Concubine in Bethlehem (19:1-9)
   b. Journey to Gibeah (19:10-15)
   c. Kindness of a Stranger in Gibeah (19:16-21)
   d. Perversion of the Men of Gibeah Leads to Rape and Murder (19:22-26)
   e. Grisly Summoning of the Tribes (19:27-30)
2. Resolution to Punish the Guilty (20:1-17)
   a. Muster of the Tribes at Mizpah (20:1-7)
   b. Agreement to Punish Benjamin (20:8-11)
   c. Deployment of Benjamin and All Israel (20:12-17)
3. Civil War and Benjamin's Defeat (20:18-48)
   a. Inquiring of the Lord (20:18)
   b. First Failed Attack (20:19-23)
   c. Second Failed Attack (20:24-28)
   d. Third Attack and Success by Ambush (20:29-48)
4. Reconstitution of a Lost Tribe (21:1-24)
   a. Dilemma for the Tribes of Israel (21:1-7)
   b. Destruction of Jabesh-Gilead (21:8-12)
   c. Gift of Wives to Benjamin (21:13-15)
   d. More Wives from Shiloh (21:16-24)
5. The Refrain: No King in Israel (21:25)

COMMENTARY ON JUDGES

I. Two Prologues: Israel's Partial Obedience after Joshua's Death Leads to a Cycle of Sin and Grace (1:1–3:6)

The prologues illustrate the historical failure of the tribes, even with the best of intentions, to capitalize on the efforts of Joshua. The reasons for this failure are ethical and theological. The people of Israel forgot the Lord and began to live as though He does not exist. The only real solution to the sin principle in the nation is the grace of God.

A. An Account of Obedience and Failure (1:1–2:5)

This first prologue includes details that parallel portions of the book of Joshua, thus building a context for the spiritual failure recounted in the second prologue. That the Canaanite population was allowed to remain in significant enclaves led to the downfall of the nation.

1. Stage Setting (1:1)

1:1. The phrase **after the death of Joshua** forms the context for the entire book. The people asked the Lord who should be **first** to go up and fight **against the Canaanites** who were still living in the land. The miracle-marked leadership of Moses and Joshua was over, and no clear leadership had yet arisen. No God-ordained and empowered leadership of the nation was in sight. Joshua's death is reported again at the beginning of the second prologue (2:8; cf. Jos 24:29).

2. Faithful Judah (1:2-21)

The listing of tribes in this prologue is not exhaustive, but moves generally from south to north, beginning with Judah.

1:2. God responded to Israel's inquiry that **Judah** should **go up** first against the Canaanites. Judah's alliance with Simeon is reported in these verses as the beginning of continued efforts to rid the land of the Canaanites. These events are to some extent paralleled by the account in Jos 15–17.

1:3-5. The **Canaanites** generally represent all the native people of the land. The word **Perizzites** is related to "village life" (Hb. *perazon* in 5:7). Thus the Perizzites were the village dwellers, that is, peasants living in unwalled settlements in the hill country, and the Canaanites were occupants of the cities.

Ten thousand men were defeated. A continuing problem in OT studies is the large numbers often reported. Most scholars agree that the population and army deployment sizes, as well as the numbers killed in various encounters, are improbably large. Expositors have suggested a variety of explanations, but none solves all the problems. The best solution involves attempts to understand the Hebrew *eleph*, traditionally translated "thousand." If an *eleph* is understood as a "company," "clan," or "army unit," some problems are eased, but others are made worse. It is better not to be dogmatic about the numbers.

1:6-7. The defeat of **Adoni-bezek** ("Lord of Bezek") is difficult to locate geographically. Bezek is also mentioned in 1Sm 11:8 as the place where Saul assembled an army. The ruin of Khirbet Bezqu northeast of Gezer, which is about 20 miles northwest of Jerusalem, may preserve the name.

The severing of thumbs and big toes was a means of humiliating the severely defeated kings. Adoni-bezek admitted that he had done the same to his own foes, so he deserved no mercy. The humiliation and mutilation of royal prisoners was not unusual in ancient Near Eastern warfare. While no example of the severing of thumbs and toes is evident in ancient monuments, many reliefs show prisoners bound, kneeling, and mutilated. Also heaps of hands are common in the Egyptian monuments.

1:8. Jerusalem does not refer to the Jebusite fortress in the tribal allotment of Benjamin, which the Benjamites could not take (v. 21). Instead this is the unfortified western hill, known today as Mount Zion, outside the wall that now contains the Jewish and Armenian quarters of the modern old city Jerusalem. Few remains in this area can be dated to the Late Bronze Age except for a few potsherds.

1:9-15. Judah defeated the Canaanites **in the Negev** in **Hebron** and **Kiriath-sepher**. The **Negev** is the southern arid region of Israel. **Hebron** is about 20 miles south of Jerusalem, and **Kiriath-sepher**, also called "Debir," is about 10 miles southwest of Hebron.

1:16-17. Moses' father-in-law, Jethro, was a **Kenite** and a priest of Midian (Ex 18:1). His priesthood was related to the general revelation priesthood of Melchizedek (see the comments on Gn 14). The Kenites were apparently a nomadic Semitic people living in the Sinai area. Their transplantation to the Negev indicates a uniting of spirit with Israel. Apparently a monotheistic tradition among nomadic people existed in the desert from the earliest times. The exact locations of **Arad**, **Hormah**, and **Zephath** are difficult to know. Hormah means "ruin" and could easily be a commemoration of Israel's destruction of the place. Zephath probably means "lookout" and may originally have been associated with a high spot nearby.

1:18. The men of Judah took three Philistine cities: **Gaza . . . Ashkelon . . . and Ekron**. This makes some sense only if the Hebrews' conquest and settlement of the land was taking place during the Late Bronze II Age (1400–1200 BC). If the Judges period came later, during the time of Philistine dominance in the region, this note would be ludicrous. The coastal plain, from Gaza to Dor, was occupied strongly by the Philistines from at least 1158, according to archaeological data from Lachish, near Gath. Only an early reference to the cities of the coastal plain in Israel's hands makes sense. Since all three of these cities were along the coastal strip and were stations along the international trade route, Judah was probably not able to hold them for any length of time. The Philistines, when they finally arrived on the scene, apparently fought the Egyptians for control of the area before ever running into Israel.

1:19-20. Judah could not drive out the Canaanites in **the valley because they had iron** reinforced **chariots**. This may seem to contradict v. 18, but apparently a partial success is in view. Caleb was given **Hebron . . . as Moses had promised** (cf. Jos 15:13).

1:21. The **Jebusites** living in Jerusalem are included among the Amorites in Jos 10, but they may have had a mixed ancestry. Ezk 16:3 suggests Jerusalem's background was Canaanite, Amorite, and Hittite. The owner of the threshing floor David purchased later for the temple was Araunah the Jebusite. His name is probably the Hurrian word *ewrine* ("lord") and not a personal name at all.

3. Failure of the Northern Tribes (1:22-36)

1:22-25. The house of Joseph spied out Bethel. These spies were probably an "armed reconnaissance patrol," distinguishing it from the mission of the two undercover agents sent by Joshua to Rahab (Jos 2). The word **spied** is from the verb "to observe." The deliverance of the young man who betrayed the city is a simple parallel to the Rahab story. **Kindly** is *chesed*, the common word for God's loyal, covenant-based love.

1:26. The man and his family who helped the Joseph tribes capture the city were allowed to escape to the north **into the land of the Hittites**, roughly equivalent to Syria today. The Hittites at that time controlled the region roughly north of the Litanni River, about 30 miles northwest of the Sea of Galilee.

1:27-36. This passage parallels Jos 13, adding detail but making no changes in the situation. Many of the tribes had difficulty driving the Canaanites out of their areas.

Manasseh included several key cities of the Jezreel Valley. **Beth-shean** controlled a strategic crossing of the Jordan River and remained in Canaanite and Egyptian hands. Later the Philistines took over the place and hung King Saul's body from the wall (1Sm 31:2, 8-10).

4. Israel's Lament (2:1-5)

2:1-5. Israel's lack of an appropriate countermeasure for Canaanite iron chariots was not their biggest problem. Their lack of genuine commitment to the Lord resulted in Israel's failure, and that set the stage for the era of the judges, a period of cyclical failure in the face of internal and external enemies. Since the Israelites did not obey the Lord by tearing **down** the **altars** of the Canaanites, they would become **thorns in** their **sides and their gods** would become **a snare**. Israel did not drive out the Canaanites, so their pagan culture continued to exist—and in some places to thrive—well into the Iron Age (beginning around 1200 BC). Likely, the Philistines of Iron Age I, rather than Israel, expelled the Canaanites.

B. The Theology of Sin and Grace (2:6–3:6)

This second prologue introduces the theological context of the period of the judges. Here is the account of another full generation that grew up knowing neither the Lord nor His doings. This unfortunate failure of the people over time to educate their own children contributed to many of the moral and spiritual breakdowns of Israel during this era.

The contrast between those who **served the Lord** (2:7) and those who **served the Baals** (2:11) is striking. The essence of godliness is a willingness to submit to *the* King, that is, the Lord of Israel, but the essence of sinfulness is a growing willingness to submit to the gods of the nations. Israel, surrounded by an ungodly culture, slowly took on the characteristic worldview of that culture and began to serve and worship the "Baals." The text here accounts for the distinction between the received religion of Canaan, found in the myths and legends represented in the Canaanite city of Ugarit, versus the folk religion of the region, which included individual Baals on every mountaintop and sacrifice place. Canaanite religious practice emphasized the fertility of land, animals, and man, through the imitative magic of prostitution and orgiastic feasting. This religious system was attractive to many Israelites.

The answer to the sin problem in Israel is not given all at once. In the progress of revelation, God chose at this time to reveal to Israel that sin is a corrosive problem that cannot be solved without His grace. Even the divinely empowered temporal solutions—the judges themselves—would not be the answer to the underlying sin problem. On the deepest level this is an object lesson about the need for Messiah, the great King.

1. Account of the Death of Joshua and the Aftermath (2:6-10)

2:6. The sons of Israel went each to his inheritance to possess the land. This is the ideal outcome of God's instruction to the people to conquer the land. This passage follows chronologically from Jos 24:28.

2:7. In the phrase **the people served the Lord**, the word "serve" is *`ewed*, also used in v. 11 of the worship of the Baals. The point is not so much a syncretism as a contrast. That service, which should belong only to God, was given illicitly to the Baals. **The elders . . . had seen all the great work of the Lord** (lit., "the great doings of Yahweh"). The word "work" or "doings" normally refers to God's miracles in the exodus and the conquest. These mighty acts of miraculous power were foundational to Israel's history, but they stopped at the end of Joshua's ministry. Not until hundreds of years later were the prophetic ministries of Elijah and Elisha authenticated with miracles. Other authenticating miracles occurred in the NT times, and then died out with the end of the apostolic era (Eph 2:20; Heb 2:3-4).

2:8-10. In the phrase **another generation . . . who did not know the Lord**, the word "know" (*yada'*) implies a personal, experiential knowledge, not merely an intellectual acquaintance.

That a generation could grow up without this vital relationship speaks volumes about the parents, and about the importance of the Dt 6 imperative to teach from personal passion.

2. Account of the Idolatry of Israel (2:11-13)

Next the narrator introduced the schematic called the "Judges cycles." Each of the cycles included the following elements in this approximate order: *sin* (the Jewish people fell into idolatry); *subjugation* (foreign powers vanquished and ruled Israel); *supplication* (the Jewish people cried out to the Lord); and *salvation* (God raised up judges to liberate Israel from foreign domination).

2:11. The term translated **evil** is *hara'* (lit., "the evil" or "the evil thing"). *Ra'* is the common term for evil in the OT, and is almost always indefinite, emphasizing the abstract quality of evil. With the definite article, as here, the author specified a particular evil, namely, their serving **the Baals**.

Some scholars have suggested their evil was the sin of taking foreign wives. More likely, however, the often-repeated phrase **Israel did evil in the sight of the LORD** refers to Israel's debauched practice of Canaanite religion, complete with its pervasive sensuality (see the comments under "B. The Theology of Sin and Grace [2:6–3:6]" above for information regarding Baal worship). The failure to drive the Canaanite population out of the promised land resulted in a cultural context for spreading depravity. The second generation of Israelites in the land had been effectively compromised.

The words **the sons of Israel did evil** occur in 2:11; 3:7, 12; 4:1; 6:1; 9:23; 10:6; and 13:1, each time at the introductions to the accounts of the major oppressions by foreign powers. The statement serves as a refrain, marking the progression of the evil in Israel.

Why is **Baals** in the plural, whereas the singular **Baal** occurs in v. 13? The myths of Baal, Yam, and Asherah speak of only one Baal. According to their beliefs, the great God El was an aloof and detached overlord who was said to be living far away on a mountain. Under him Baal was the god of fertility who made sure the rains came in season. His conflicts with the chaos monster, *Yam* ("the Sea"), and with *Mot* ("Death") form the core of Canaanite religion. With the prostitute goddesses Anat and Asherah, Baal was the model for Canaanite debauchery. In their theology, Baal engaged in sexual relations with these goddesses and thereby brought fertility to the earth. Their worshipers could generate their favor by also engaging in cultic sexual acts done in their name. Baal would then cause his worshipers' crops and herds and procreative abilities to be fertile.

The plural "Baals" refers to various portrayals of Baal on hilltop shrines called *bamot*. Unfortunately, many of the Israelites simply adopted the seemingly attractive local religious traditions.

2:12-13. That Israel worshiped **other gods** refers again to the polytheistic nature of the Canaanite religion. Other peoples, including the Phoenicians, Moabites, Philistines, and others, worshiped a wide variety of gods and goddesses, most of whom fit the general fertility cult pattern. Yet many of them also had unique elements of evil or sensuality associated with them. Many stone and metal images of these gods have been found in the ruins of Canaanite and Israelite settlements.

3. God's Anger Displayed in the Rise of Oppressors (2:14-15)

2:14-15. When God gave the people up to their **plunderers**, they were helpless to rise in their own defense. **Wherever they went, the hand of the LORD was against them for evil.** This contrasts strongly with God's promise to Joshua in Jos 1:5: "No man will be able to stand before you all the days of your life." Had Israel lived in sincere obedience to God's law, the Lord would have given them success. Their turmoil, however, was an indication of God's judgment against them for their disobedience.

4. The Judges Raised Up as a Respite from Oppression (2:16-19)

2:16. Judges are introduced as deliverers raised up by the **LORD**. These judges stood in opposition to the oppressors, whom the Lord had raised up. God used oppressors and judges alike to teach Israel the principles of godliness.

2:17. Israel, however, failed to follow the Lord. The reason for their failure is made clear in this analysis: (1) **They did not listen to their judges**, that is, they refused to obey them. (2) **They played the harlot** and **bowed . . . down** to other gods. To "bow down" is to worship, in the sense of a wholehearted submission of life to a god. Here it is likened to spiritual unfaithfulness or harlotry. (3) **They turned aside quickly from the way** of **their fathers** who obeyed **the LORD**. (4) **They did not do as their fathers** had done.

2:18-19. The Lord had **pity** on the people because they were **oppressed** by their enemies. So he used **judges** to deliver them. But the success of any given deliverer was short-lived. The deliverance lasted until the death of the judge. Here is a powerful demonstration that deliverance available through even the greatest human leaders will always be deficient. A deliverer who could truly solve the deepest human problems must be infinite, not only in power, but even in being able to produce transformation in the lives of people. All others will eventually fall short.

5. God's Anger at Covenant Transgression Resulted in Pagan Nations that Could Not Be Driven Out (2:20-23)

2:20-21. Israel had repeatedly **transgressed** God's **covenant**, causing His **anger** to burn against them. Israel was not merely a people group sharing ancestors and culture. They were a nation explicitly chosen by God and created for His purposes. They were to exist in covenant relationship with Him forever—with the primary obligation to listen to and obey His **voice**.

2:22-23. God's purpose in leaving the Canaanites and other nations was to **test Israel**. "Test" here, of course, does not mean that God was in doubt as to the outcome. It is clear that God, who knows the end from the beginning, knew that Israel would fail (Dt 31:29). The point was to demonstrate that fact through experience, and thus further demonstrate Israel's need for a saving relationship with the Lord.

6. Nations Left to Test and to Punish (3:1-6)

3:1-2. That various **nations** were still in the land was a **test** for **Israel**. This meant **that** . . . **generations of the sons of Israel** would **be taught war**. But 2:22 states that God's purpose in testing Israel was to see if they would obey Him (cf. 3:4). The ideal would have been universal godliness and obedience, as a result of which God would have established them peacefully and securely in the land. But the reality, because of sin, was growing ungodliness accompanied by intermittent wars. Every generation of Israel would experience threats and violence until the second coming of the Prince of Peace. The presence of Canaanite nations then fulfilled two purposes expressed here: to demonstrate, by failure, Israel's need for the Messiah; and to chastise Israel for that failure by constant violence and warfare.

3:3. Some scholars question the reference to the **five lords of the Philistines** as if it were anachronistic. Of course there were Philistines in the land from as early as the time of Abraham who met with King Abimelech of Gerar, who was a Philistine (Gn 21–22). Possibly the Philistines were a relatively small people group along the coast, perhaps working as vassals of the Egyptians, until the large migrations began around the turn of the Iron Age (around 1200 BC). It is also possible, since the editing of Judges did not take place until the beginning of the monarchy (around 1000 BC), that this note about five Philistine kings was a name for the region from that era.

3:4-6. Again the nations in the land of Canaan were there to test Israel (cf. the comments at v. 1) to see if they **would obey** Him. Unfortunately the Israelites intermarried with the daughters of these unconquered nations **and served their gods**, thus failing the test.

II. Twelve Deliverers Demonstrate a Cycle of Increasing Failure (3:7–16:31)

The Early Judgeships:

Though 12 judges are often cited, there were actually only six major judges. Also, Shamgar was not, properly speaking, a judge. And Abimelech was a usurper and is not counted among the judges. Five minor judges appear by name only, without any account given regarding their oppressors or their wars, if any.

The first set of major judges, Othniel, Ehud, Deborah, and Gideon is presented in chaps. 3–10. They are generally sympathetic characters who served local constituencies and perhaps had overlapping terms of office. The moral tone of their stories is relatively high, but with a slow downward progression. The second set of judges includes only Jephthah and Samson (along with the five minor judges). The two are generally conceded to be late in the period (perhaps near 1100 BC), and to be overlapping in time, with Samson on the west of the Jordan and Jephthah on the east. There is little to admire in Jephthah and Samson. Jephthah may have sacrificed his daughter (Jdg 11:31 and 39), and he precipitated a deadly civil war (Jdg 12:1-6). Samson was an unmitigated scoundrel who killed many Philistines but ultimately failed to break their power over Israel.

The repeated statement that Israel did evil (2:11; 3:7, 12 [two times]; 4:1; 6:1; 10:6; 13:1) pointed out the need for a genuinely godly leader. In time, of course, even the kings themselves demonstrated their inability to maintain godly leadership.

A. Othniel: The Model of the Judges Cycle (3:7-11)

Othniel is given a brief discussion. His judgeship serves merely to demonstrate the pattern of the cycle.

1. Israel's Sin of Idolatry (3:7)

3:7. Israel did what was evil (lit., "the evil thing"), explained by two statements: they **forgot the LORD their God** and they **served the Baals and the Asheroth**. The sin of transgressing

General Location of Major Judges and Adversaries

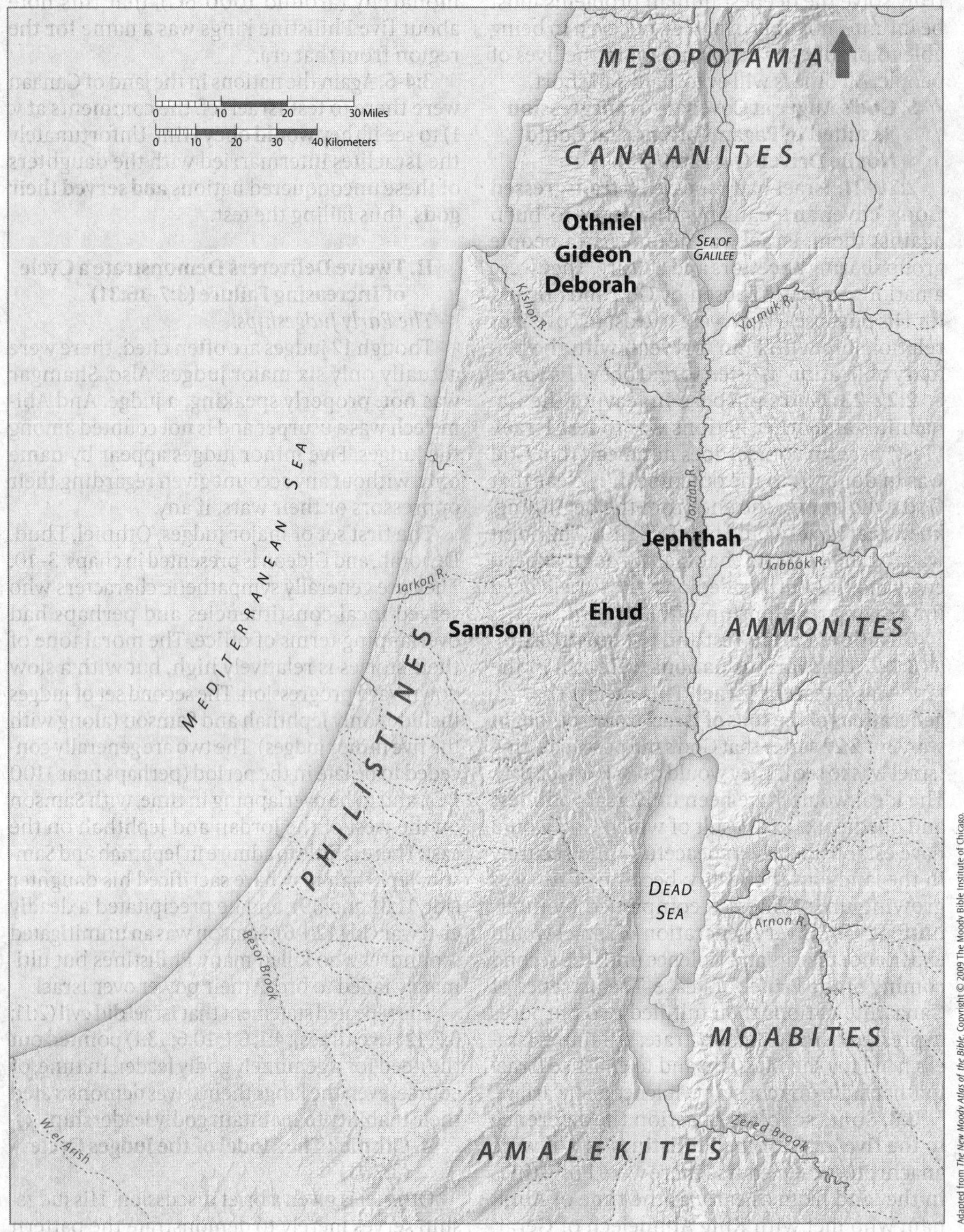

the covenant began with forgetting the truth of the basic relationship. Israel had forgotten who they were and who the Lord was, and as a result they began to behave like the nations that surrounded them.

2. Israel Sold into Mesopotamian Oppression for Eight Years (3:8)

3:8. Subjection to a Mesopotamian power is the first of many such oppressions, and this is the only instance where the power was some distance away. All the later oppressors were close by. Little is known of **Cushan-rishathaim** ("Cushan of double evil," an epithet that may have been given him by the Israelites). The oppressor here is **Mesopotamia** (Hb. Aram-Nahariyim, lit., "Aram of the Two Rivers") referring more specifically to the Aramean or Syrian region at the northwestern corner of the Mesopotamian alluvial plain.

None of the history of the great powers of that time (Egypt, Mitanni, Hittites) is represented in this brief passage. Cushan must have been a warlord-sized king who was too small to be noticed by his major contemporaries.

3. Heartfelt Cry for Deliverance (3:9a)

3:9a. When Israel was truly contrite, the nation **cried to the Lord**. Then He **raised up a deliverer**. A **deliverer** (judge) was one who rescued a people whose situation was otherwise hopeless. The Bible is clear about the need of sinners for a Savior, not merely a coach or even a physician. People are not simply sick in sin, nor are they merely untrained in righteousness. Mankind is "dead in [their] trespasses and sins" (Eph 2:1) and in need of God's grace for deliverance.

4. A Deliverer Raised Up: Othniel, Son of Kenaz (3:9b-10)

3:9b-10. Othniel, a **brother** of Caleb (Jos 15:13-19), and thus a younger contemporary of Joshua himself, prevailed over Cushan-rishathaim by the power of God. The fighting probably took place in the north, although Othniel was of the tribe of Judah.

5. Forty Years of Rest (3:11)

3:11. After noting the land's 40 years of rest (perhaps the length of time is approximate), the passage ends with the note that **Othniel . . . died**. The rest from oppression lasted only for the life of this judge.

B. Ehud: The Left-Handed Judge (3:12-30)

Ehud was the next of the "major" judges—major in the sense that much detail is given of his work. Ehud was confronted apparently by a coalition of raiders led by the king of Moab, who set up his headquarters in the City of the Palms, that is, Jericho.

1. Eighteen Years under Eglon of Moab (3:12-14)

3:12. Moab was the desert kingdom directly east of the Dead Sea, from the Arnon River at the midpoint of the Dead Sea north to south, to the Zered River at the southern tip of the Dead Sea. During the Late Bronze Age, this area was sparsely populated. Archaeologist Nelson Glueck found the ruins of approximately 22 towns or villages in this area dated to the time of this account.

3:13-14. Ammon was the kingdom on the plateau from the Arnon River to the Jabbok River, north of Moab, and the Amalekites were semi-nomadic peoples who inhabited much of the region. **The city of the palm trees** (Jericho) had been destroyed by Joshua and was in ruins at this time. Eglon must have built his summer palace in the fertile flat lands to the east of Jericho.

2. Ehud's Clandestine Mission (3:15-24)

Ehud's action here is what modern military leaders would call a "special operation." He went in under the false pretenses of diplomatic cover to carry out an assassination. Ehud planned his operation carefully, choosing a weapon and the setting for the greatest advantage. The cover, approach, execution, and retreat were all well planned, with the intention of summoning the tribes afterward. Ehud's act is a finely detailed act of war. Significantly, that war had been imposed by Eglon, the invader and oppressor. So there is no inherent ethical problem in the Ehud cycle.

3:15. Ehud was **left-handed.** Through much of history and literature left-handed people have suffered bad press. Archaeology demonstrates that the left-handed were not considered a serious military threat. Figures on monuments in victorious military poses are almost always right-handed. For example, in the famous chariot scene from the chest of Egyptian King Tut, the king is drawing his arrow with the right hand. And on the Egyptian Narmer Palette King Narmer raises his mace with his right hand to smite an Asiatic prisoner. The gates leading into walled cities were approached by ramps that put right-handed soldiers at a disadvantage, with the shield arm on the wrong side. Various languages, in their handling of the vocabulary of left and right, put the lefty in a bad light. In Latin, for example, the right hand is "*rectus*" or "*dextra*," and left is "*sinister*."

This seemingly innate (and unreasonable) prejudice proved the undoing of evil King Eglon. He and his keepers simply could not believe that a left-handed man was a threat. This incident is particularly ironic in light of Ehud's heritage; he was a Benjamite, lit., a "son of the right hand."

3:16. Ehud's double-edged sword, hidden where it would not be found on the right hip, is an object of some interest. During the Late Bronze Age, most weapons were made of bronze, which was cast in a variety of heavy shapes. Bronze tended to be brittle, and thin blades were simply not durable enough for use. Most of the swords shown in the monuments of this period are the so-called "sickle" swords, shaped a bit like a sickle, with the single axe-like smiting edge on the outside. But Ehud's sword must have been more like a dagger, with two sharp edges and small enough to be easily hidden in the folds of his garment. He made it himself, and it was about a cubit (18 inches) long, including the handle. Since it was probably made of bronze, it is unlikely it would have survived long in battle. It was a one-time-use weapon, specifically formed for this mission.

3:17-18. Warlords who could hold territory by force collected protection money (euphemistically called "tribute") from the villages in their area. No government services of any sort were provided for the people in such regions. Eglon certainly had no sense of empire. He was in business merely to extract money from his victims.

3:19. Whether Hebrew *pesilim*, from *psl,* "to hew or cut," is to be translated **idols** (NASB and most translations) or "stone quarries" (NIV), this place was clearly a well-known landmark near **Gilgal**. The Gilgal in question was probably not the better known Gilgal to the east of Jericho, but rather a town on the border of Benjamin and Judah north of the pass of Adummim, about 15 miles northeast of Jerusalem. From this landmark Ehud **turned back** and carried on his fatal conversation with the king.

3:20. Ehud went to Eglon **while he was sitting alone in his cool roof chamber**. In this upper room the rare breezes might be caught.

3:21-24. Ehud **thrust** his sword into Eglon's **belly**. The stealthy treachery is emphatic, and is clearly portrayed as a heroic action. Ehud left the sword in the king's stomach and fled. **Relieving himself** (v. 24) is literally "covering his feet" (cf. 1Sm 24:3).

3. Slow Response of Eglon's Servants (3:25)

3:25. Ehud had locked the **roof chamber** when he left, so that Eglon's men needed to use a **key** to enter. Keys in the ancient world were relatively unusual. Several examples have been found and are on display in the Israel Museum and elsewhere. Such keys were large items designed to reach through a door and interface with a heavy bolt on the far side.

4. Ehud's Escape and the Muster of Ephraim (3:26-30a)

3:26-30a. Departing from Eglon, Ehud called for help by blowing a horn (*shophar*) to summon the tribe of Ephraim. Fighting men arrived quickly to block the fords of the Jordan, where **ten thousand Moabites, all robust and valiant men** were struck down (v. 29; cf. the comments on 1:4).

5. Eighty Years of Rest (3:30b)

3:30b. Eighty years takes the chronology down to the early to mid-thirteenth century, depending on the overlap with Othniel. This provides the earliest point in the chronology for Shamgar, who came after him (i.e., after Ehud).

C. Shamgar: An Enigmatic Interlude (3:31)

3:31. Some expositors call **Shamgar** a minor judge, but more likely he was not related to Israel at all, except that he was in the right place at the right time. Virtually every detail in this verse is a linguistic or archaeological problem.

Shamgar's name is the first problem. It is not Hebrew. Various suggestions have been made. The Canaanite hypothesis is probably best, taking the name as a *shin* prefix participle on the Semitic verb *mgr*. *Shin* prefixes are unknown in Hebrew, but are found in Ugaritic and perhaps other NW Semitic languages, and they correlate to the Hebrew *mem* prefix found on some participles. *Mgr* is the common verb "to farm." That would yield the translation "farmer," which fits the **oxgoad** nicely.

Son of Anath may refer to his heritage from the village of Anath. Several such places have been identified. Or it may refer to a well-known Canaanite goddess of love and war. Perhaps Shamgar gained this label after his exploits recorded here.

At first thought the **oxgoad** may seem a strange weapon. The Hebrew is *malamad*, which is echoed in the name and shape of the Hebrew letter *l* (*lamed*). The oxgoad likely was a long stick with a point at one end for poking the ox and a shovel at the other for doing necessary work around the ox. Sharpening either or both ends would produce a formidable weapon in the hands of a stout peasant warrior.

Shamgar's **Philistines** are a problem because of their timing. Rameses III defeated the great wave of Sea Peoples around 1190 BC. Israeli archaeologist David Ussishkin (who led the excavation at Lachish in the Judean Shephelah) insists that the Canaanite cities of the plain did not fall until roughly 30 years after that time (cf.

New Encyclopedia of Archaeological Excavations in the Holy Land [Jerusalem: Israel Exploration Society], 904, and other references in the literature). Shamgar's timing is difficult to pin down. He is said to have done his work after Ehud. He is also said to have been a contemporary of Jael and Deborah (5:6), putting him in the late thirteenth century. As stated earlier, the Philistines may refer to a regiment-sized force of Philistines that raided the coast of Canaan some 50 years before their great migration.

The closing note in this verse announces that Shamgar **also saved Israel**. The Hebrew *yasha'* is the same term used of deliverance by the other judges, and so this has led some to classify Shamgar as a judge.

D. Deborah: A Mother in Israel (4:1–5:31)

Deborah, the third of the judges, and the only woman in the sequence, appeared about the same time as Shamgar, mentioned in 5:6. Her gender, the ineffectiveness of Barak, and even her husband Lappidoth (4:4) contribute to the feeling that strong male leadership was lacking at that time in Israel.

1. The Military Campaign against Hazor (4:1-24)

This chapter recounts a second battle of Hazor (following Joshua's initial burning of the site in Jos 11). This cannot be a duplicate report, for the details are different, except for the name of the king.

a. Twenty Years under Jabin of Hazor (4:1-3)

4:1-2. Joshua 11 also records the fall of **Hazor**, which Joshua burned. Its king at that time was also called **Jabin**. The Canaanite population seems to have continued until the beginning of Iron Age I (c. 1200 BC). Jabin may have been the king's name, or it may have been his title, in much the same way the terms Pharaoh, Czar, Caesar, and others are used as titles.

4:3. Sisera, Jabins' commander, **had nine hundred iron chariots**. This is a huge chariot army, but not unparalleled in the ancient world. The Egyptian pharaoh Thutmose III spoke of capturing over 900 chariots at Megiddo (c. 1470 BC). A chariot army required substantial state resources. One could compare the development and deployment of a chariot army to the building of a modern aircraft-carrier battle group. The same resource commitment, technology research and development, personnel training and support, and logistic infrastructure went into fielding such an army. Chariot soldiers could not be militia or conscripts, but had to have been professionals who devoted their full time to training and preparations. In the feudal structure of Canaan these men would have been land-owning nobility with servants to care for their properties.

Chariot horses were specially bred and trained for combat. Most horses will not voluntarily proceed into the kinds of situations pictured on monuments. They must be trained to charge, trample, and obey commands under noisy, frightening circumstances. Such horses would have been quite expensive and would have required large pastureland and training areas.

Hazor's lower city, nearly a square mile in area, was once believed to consist mostly of the Canaanite chariot camp. However, Israeli archaeologist Yagael Yadin's excavations have shown the lower city to have been a relatively densely populated area during the Late Bronze Age (NEAEHL, 597). The horses and chariots may have been housed in the surrounding countryside. Certainly the professional troops for such an army could not have all lived in Hazor.

b. Deborah the Prophetess Called on Barak the Soldier (4:4-10)

4:4-5. Deborah, who was **judging Israel at that time**, may have been a "seer"-type prophet, whose visions under the **palm tree** provided inspiration for the people. The culture of the era would not normally have supported a woman in military and political leadership, so the situation speaks of the probable lack of qualified men. She is an "exception that proves the rule"—that is, the rule being God's intention that men provide spiritual leadership (Gn 2:20, 23; 1Tm 2:11-15). The extraordinary circumstances around her serving as a judge in Israel indicate just how unusual it was for a woman to exercise this kind of leadership. Deborah's palm tree must have been a well-known landmark, but of course it is impossible to identify it today. Palm trees of various kinds are common throughout Israel.

4:6-10. Deborah's involvement with leaders from Naphtali and Zebulun (v. 6) indicates the national scope of the Canaanite problem at this point. Barak's home was **Kedesh** of Naphtali, overlooking the Hula Valley in the Lebanon range, about 16 miles north of the north end of the Sea of Galilee. The **Kedesh** in vv. 9-10, which was used as a meeting place, cannot reasonably be the same place. This Kedesh is probably near the south end of the Sea of Galilee and the slopes of Mount Tabor. From the northern slopes of

Tabor one could see **ten thousand men** gathered for battle, but they would be hidden from the Canaanite forces in Jezreel to the south.

c. Heber the Kenite Introduced (4:11)

4:11. Heber the Kenite is introduced here in anticipation of the exploit of Jael, his wife (v. 17). **The oak in Zaanannim** is probably near the lower Galilee Kedesh and was mentioned in Jos 19:33 as a landmark on the border of Naphtali.

d. The Battle of the Kishon (4:12-16)

The climax of this confrontation took place on ground apparently of Deborah's choosing, since no self-respecting chariot captain would willingly deploy his chariots in a swamp.

4:12-13. Mount Tabor is the volcanic dome that dominates the central Jezreel Valley and is the primary landmark along the international trade route in this region. The gathering of a major force at Mount Tabor had obvious military significance to those who needed to keep the trade route open. **Sisera** deployed his forces—some **nine hundred iron chariots** and the foot soldiers with them—from **Harosheth-hagoyim** (perhaps in the western Jezreel Valley area) to the **river Kishon**, a swampy area near Megiddo that drains through the pass of Beth Shearim into Haifa Bay. This location would have seemed preferable since it was quite broad, with room to deploy chariots and associated infantry. An observer from a high spot near Nazareth would think this land was ideal for fighting, when in fact it can turn into a quagmire in the rain.

4:14-16. Barak defeated **Sisera**, killing every soldier in his army.

e. Sisera Meets Jael (4:17-22)

4:17-22. In a serious breach of hospitality, **Jael the wife of Heber the Kenite** killed Sisera by pounding a tent peg through his head into the floor while he slept. Barak found him there, killed by a woman. The irony of Jael's deadly action, in the larger context of Deborah's leadership, points to a failure of the classic biblical pattern of male leadership. As Adam was first created, and then Eve, the Bible shows ontological male-female equality (Gn 1:27) with a pattern of male functional leadership (Gn 2:20, 23; 1Tm 2:11-15). Hence, the actions of Deborah and Jael provide the exception that proves the rule—that men are expected by God to be godly leaders. Moreover, it emphasizes the sorry state of Israel's male leadership in the period of the Judges, being so problematic that women were required to lead in this military situation.

f. The Long Campaign against Jabin (4:23-24)

4:23-24. Apparently the struggle against Jabin did not end on the day of the battle of the Kishon. Instead Jabin was not **destroyed** until some time later. The text does not suggest that Hazor was burned or even occupied.

2. The Song of Deborah (5:1-31)

This song, one of the earliest Hebrew songs, bears most of the earmarks of Hebrew poetry, including the parallelism and meter. This chapter provides a number of insights into the life of Israel in the settlement period.

a. Call to Praise the Lord (5:1-5)

5:1-2. The words **the leaders led in Israel** are parallel to the words **the people volunteered**. The enigmatic term *pera* (**leaders**, NASB) must be translated as something to do with leadership—in contrast to the people who volunteered. Ugaritic suggests a leadership function.

5:3-5. The song challenges **kings** to **hear** and **rulers** to **give ear**. **Sing** (*shir*) and **sing praise** (*zāmar*) are technical terms also found in the Psalms (e.g., 49:1, "hear," "give ear"; 30:4, 12, "sing"—the participle *mizmor* is generally translated "psalm"). The attitude toward the kings of the earth establishes an anticipatory pattern: that is, the author is looking forward to the day when the nations and their kings will bow and worship the King of kings (Ps 2:8; 110:1).

b. Deborah's Motivation, as a Mother in Israel (5:6-11)

5:6-7. In the days of Shamgar and **Jael, the highways were deserted**. The instability of life in Israel at the end of the Late Bronze Age is poignantly illustrated in this passage. The roads could not be protected and made secure because there was no longer any central government to do the job. For most of the Late Bronze II era (c. 1400–1200 BC) the Egyptians had given up on their pretensions to empire. Israel was certainly not a central power in any sense of the word, and had little overall influence on the situation. Village life consisted of the families who lived on the land, namely, subsistence farmers and stockkeepers who provided food for marketplaces in larger cities. A secure village life was essential for the stability of the overall economy.

The last major Asiatic campaign of the Egyptian Empire was the expedition of Pharaoh Mernepthah (c. 1230 BC), recorded in the famous Israel stele (which celebrates Mernepthah's victory over the Libyans). Deborah's description of life in Israel at the end of the Late Bronze Age is a good explanation for the need Mernepthah found to make his expedition in the first place.

5:8-9. Archaeologists have long held that no walls datable to the Late Bronze Age existed in the land of Israel, and so they question the statement in v. 8 that **war was in the gates**. However, even a cursory examination of the Egyptian monuments dating to that period show the major cities of Israel/Canaan, secure behind their massive walls, falling to the armed technology of Pharaoh. Many of these walls certainly were built in the Middle Bronze Age, and many of them continue to stand today! There is no reason that the walls, even in time of peace and expansion, could not have continued to serve their intended purpose during the Late Bronze Age.

Deborah clearly had in mind here (and in v. 11) the **gates** of the regional commercial cities. When trade and agriculture are disrupted by bandits, a nation is in deplorable condition. These cities, like the Canaanite centers, were fortified, at least in a rudimentary way, especially as chaos again swept over the land.

In v. 8 the Hebrew word for **Then** is *'az*, a common temporal particle used to introduce the military moves mentioned in vv. 8b, 11b, 13a, 19, and 22. Both **commanders** and **volunteers** (v. 9) responded in times of warfare.

5:10-11. The mention of **the sound of those who . . . recount the righteous deeds of the LORD** may provide a glimpse into Israel's most important communication device: word of mouth. Much of the history and lore of Israel was committed to poetry and song for dissemination to the whole culture. The rich (those **who ride on white donkeys** and **sit on rich carpets**) and travelers were challenged to sing of the Lord's victory.

c. The Muster of the Tribes (5:12-18)

5:12-13. The nobles and the **warriors** were those who came to Deborah for help in the midst of the trouble with the northern Canaanites. The word "nobles" is the Hebrew *'adirim*, from *'adar*, "to be prominent or powerful," and "warriors" translates the more common word *gibborim*, used of men of substance who were also prepared to go to war. David's "mighty men" are called *gibborim* in 2Sm 23:8-39. Boaz, the husband of Ruth, is called a *gibbor*, referring to his substantial place in the community.

The Hebrew word translated **survivors** (Jdg 5:13) is *sarid*. But a surviving remnant (as from a defeat) seems out of place here. N. Na'aman has suggested that this Hebrew word refers to the town of Sarid (c. six miles south of Taanach, about 25 miles southwest of the Sea of Galilee, and a likely mustering spot for the Canaanites, see *VT* 40 [1990]: 423–26). That would yield the translation, "Then down to Sarid he marched to the nobles; the people of the Lord came down to me as warriors." This is the preferred view, since it smoothes the interpretation.

5:14-18. Verses 14-18 give the poetic account of Deborah and Barak's summons to battle. **Ephraim** and **Benjamin**, two southern tribes, are mentioned first, perhaps because of their association with Deborah. Why Ephraim is associated with **Amalek** is difficult to know, but perhaps it is because some of Ephraim's territory lay in formerly Amalekite lands. **The staff of office** refers to a "commander's staff," held by leaders of military units. The staff may have been a ceremonial emblem or a practical weapon. The commander would be called on to dispatch the leaders of a defeated enemy, and might do that with the mace or axe he carried for that purpose. In some contexts this staff seems to be the tool of a scribe, so some have suggested that this staff was an administrator's emblem; but that seems unlikely here in the midst of battle.

Machir usually refers to the half tribe of Manasseh that stayed east of the Jordan in the Golan, the far north region of Israel. But here it refers to Manasseh itself, since the fighting took place on Manasseh's western territory in the Jezreel Valley. **Zebulun** and **Naphtali** (v. 18) are singled out for special praise, presumably because they were the first to respond to the call to duty. Their unique position across the international trade route made them a difficult and urgent problem for the Canaanites.

Other tribes, farther removed from the trouble, did not participate, and are mentioned in anger. **Reuben**, on the border with Moab, was the farthest away, and chose to stay in relative tranquility beside the campfires, listening to the whistling or playing small flute-like instruments to call the flocks of sheep. For Gad, Deborah uses instead the name **Gilead**, usually the pastoral region north and east of the Dead Sea between the Yarmuk and the Jabbok rivers shared by Gad and Manasseh. Gad was probably in mind here to round out the Transjordan tribes.

The mention of **Dan** who chose to **stay in ships** indicates that Dan was not engaged in the battle because they were occupied with

Canaanites and Philistines to the west. This verse probably dates to a time before Dan had migrated to Laish in the far north. The reference to **ships** implies that Dan occupied at least some of the Mediterranean seacoast. The river Yarkon, on the northern border (now in the northern suburbs of Tel Aviv), would have provided an anchorage for small vessels, as would the promontory at Joppa.

Asher was overrun with Phoenicians by this time. Most of the coastline, from Carmel to Tyre, seems to have stayed in Canaanite and Phoenician hands. There is little evidence of early Israelite occupation here until the time of Solomon.

d. The Battle at the Kishon (5:19-23)

5:19-22. The battle took place **at Taanach near the waters of Megiddo**. **Taanach** is *Tel Ta'anak* on the southern edge of the Jezreel Valley, about 25 miles southwest of the Sea of Galilee. The **Kishon** River runs through the swampy lowlands to the north of the city. The reference to the fighting **stars** is probably part of Deborah's poetic license. Most likely she was referring to the sudden downpour of rain from the heavens, which God sent just in time to defeat the Canaanite chariots. Nothing impedes a chariot maneuver like too much soft ground. **The dashing of his valiant steeds** is almost certainly sarcasm, for the horses were up to their haunches in mud.

5:23. Deborah pronounced a **curse** on **Meroz**, a village whose location is not known but was probably in the vicinity of Mount Tabor and the battlefield, apparently because its **inhabitants** did not come to the Israelites' aid in the battle or in apprehending Sisera when he fled.

e. Jael: Most Blessed of Women (5:24-27)

5:24-27. This extended account of Jael's heroic act spells out in poetic style what was recorded in prosaic style in 4:17-21.

f. Lament of Sisera's Mother (5:28-31a)

5:28-31a. This poetic description of Sisera's mother is not a statement of sympathy for her but rather is a sardonic evaluation of her false expectations. She anticipated that Sisera should have already returned in victory and wondered at his **delay in coming**. Her princesses incorrectly encouraged her to believe that Sisera and his warriors were delayed by **dividing the spoil**, ravaging **two maidens for every warrior**, and gathering spoils of expensive **dyed work of double embroidery** (likely to be received by her). The writer implies she would experience great sorrow and disappointment when discovering the truth of Sisera's end and is mocking all such arrogance toward the Lord. She calls on the Lord, therefore, asking that **all [His] enemies perish** in the way of Sisera and that **those who love** the Lord grow stronger **like the rising of the sun in its might**.

3. Forty Years of Rest (5:31b)

5:31b. This note takes the chronology to about 1200 BC, or the end of the Late Bronze Age II in Canaan.

E. Gideon: A Lesser Son of a Lesser Son (6:1–9:57)

The Gideon cycle represents the largest portion of the book of Judges. It has 100 verses. Compared with the Samson episode, which has 71 verses, Gideon's victory was of major importance to the entire nation, since the Midianites and their allies raided wherever they pleased throughout the land. Chapter 9 should probably be included in the cycle, since it recounts the misadventures of Gideon's son, Abimelech.

Gideon appeared on the scene as an unlikely deliverer. While he was a relatively godly man, he was immature and timid. Many scholars have tried to demonstrate the steady decline of Israelite morals and leadership in a downward spiral. It is better to see the first set of judges, which ends with Gideon's story, as good but incomplete heroes. But lasting deliverance was yet to come.

1. Introduction to the Gideon Episode (6:1-10)

This portion introduces the Midianites and their allies, along with the hero of the story, Gideon. The story is set in the north, in the Jezreel Valley of Manasseh, near Gideon's town of Ophrah. This town should probably be identified with ruins found in the modern town of Afula, conveniently near Mount Moreh, the Jezreel Valley, and En Harod (all about 15 miles south of the Sea of Galilee), sites that figure in the narrative.

a. Seven Years of Oppression by Midian (6:1-6)

6:1-6. The **Midianites** were the offspring of Abraham, through his handmaid Keturah (Gn 25:2). They were camel caravaneers in the Joseph narrative (Gn 37), close allies and relatives of Moses in the wilderness (Ex 2:15-25), and objects of an Israelite attack and plundering (Nm 31:1-24). The Midianites were probably a broad collection of related tribes, led by separate "kings" or "princes," without a common political focus. The transportation for Midianite aggression was the camel, which gave them both range and speed, allowing the raiders to do their damage and get away before effective counterforce could be mounted. **The Midianites** with **the Amalekites** and **the sons of the east** destroyed Israel's troops, attacking **like locusts** in **number**. The Amalekites, descendants of Esau (Gn 36:12) had been enemies of Israel before (in Nm 14:45 and afterward). The **sons of the east** (*bene qedem*) are nomadic peoples in general, perhaps other descendants of Esau not otherwise specified.

b. The Covenant Message of a Prophet (6:7-10)

6:7-10. The sending of a prophet was a new development. Previously the people had cried out and had been rewarded with deliverance by the Lord in the form of a judge. This time a prophet, otherwise unknown, was sent to encourage them not to fear **the gods of the Amorites** and to deliver the rebuke, **you have not obeyed Me**.

2. Gideon's Call to Deliver Israel (6:11-40)

This extended account of Gideon's call to the work puts him in a different class from other judges, who simply appeared on the scene or were given brief histories. Gideon was not a nobleman, even though his father **Joash** was apparently the headman of the district. His family is of little importance outside the region. That seems to be the point of the passage, as God demonstrated His willingness to work through the most humble and the most poorly equipped if they will walk in faith. Gideon's growth in faith and courage is a theme in this passage.

a. Gideon Called by the Angel of the Lord (6:11-18)

6:11. The angel of the LORD spoke to Gideon when he was **beating out wheat in** a **wine press**. Wheat was normally threshed on a wide, flat beaten area called a threshing floor. The best ones were on high ground in the midst of the fields. The idea was to dislodge the grain from the stalks by marching oxen and people over them. Next came winnowing, tossing wheat and chaff in the air to allow the wheat, which is heavier than the stalks and chaff, to fall to the threshing floor while wind blew away its chaff. This process was normally a time of communal celebration and was easily visible to anyone passing by. But the Midianite threat made any such event impossible. The wine press, on the other hand, was a square or round vessel, often cut out of the rock, in which grapes could be trodden. The juice from this process ran through a conduit to a lower and smaller wine vat from which the juice was collected in jars for fermentation. Such presses are normally found in the midst of gardens and vineyards, out of sight of passersby. Gideon was so fearful of the Midianites that he prepared this grain in a secluded wine press. He no doubt hoped to be able to thresh enough grain for a meal or two. This speaks of the desperation of the people under the oppression of the Midianite raiders.

6:12-14. The angel of the LORD appeared to him at the wine press. Scholars continue to argue about the identity of **the angel of the LORD** in this passage and throughout the OT. Since this angel has the authority of God Himself and was actually willing to accept worship, it seems likely that this is a theophany, a visible manifestation of God on earth. This is the extent that the text reveals. Nevertheless, since the Scriptures affirm that "No one has seen God at any time" and it is "the only begotten God . . . [who] has explained Him" (Jn 1:18), this visible manifestation was likely a preincarnate appearance of Christ (or a Christophany). When Gideon questioned why the Midianites oppressed Israel, the angel told him that Gideon was being sent by God to deliver Israel.

6:15. How shall I deliver Israel? Gideon's humility is not feigned. He was really an insignificant son in an unimportant family. In a society in which clan pecking order was paramount (cf. the dispute with Ephraim later) Gideon was simply being realistic about his chances of gaining a following.

6:16-18. God's answer to Gideon, **Surely I will be with you**, is reminiscent of God's call of Moses. In answer to Moses' complaint, "Who am I?" God replied, "I AM" the One who is sending you to Pharaoh (Ex 3:14). The point is clear: a person's social status is insignificant when compared to walking with God. The power and the strength are in God Himself.

b. Gideon's Presentation and Fear (6:19-24)

6:19-24. The presentation of an offering to the angel of God demonstrates Gideon's understanding that he was in the presence of God. The offering was accepted by the angel in the classic way—by a consuming fire. In the early biblical period all sacrifices were accepted by fire that issued from the presence of God (Lv 10:1-2; 1Kg 18:38).

Gideon's fear in the presence of the angel is only reasonable if this was a divine manifestation. The angel's reassurance was a means of building Gideon's faith.

The altar Gideon built was another step of faith. The statement about the altar's continued existence (**To this day it is still in Ophrah of the Abiezrites**) indicates that the book was either written or had a final editing a significant time after the events described.

c. Hacking the Altar and Asherah (6:25-27)

6:25-27. Following Gideon's call by the angel of the Lord, he was commanded to demonstrate (and stretch) his faith by destroying his father's altar to Baal and the Asherah pole nearby. The altar was a structure of cut stones where sacrifices were made to Baal. The Asherah pole was a sacred tree or carved pole set in the ground representing the Asherah consort of Baal. Together the two elements formed the Canaanite high place, scene of the debauched worship of the Baal cult, often involving immoral acts by the worshipers in order to curry the favor from Baal to grant fertility to one's endeavors. This format was adopted by Israelites, and was opposed only by the godliest of the kings of Judah.

Gideon's destruction of the high place was a severe blow to his entire community. Much as a synagogue, church, or mosque would be to later towns, the high place was a focus of the investment of resources, both financial and emotional. Its destruction made a clear statement.

d. Confrontation with Joash (6:28-32)

6:28-30. The destruction of the **altar of Baal** and the **Asherah** pole was a blow to the entire structure of that community. A death sentence for Gideon seems outlandish to modern ears, but would have made perfect sense in the ancient world. When **the men of the city** learned that Gideon was responsible, they wanted to kill him.

6:31-32. But **Joash**, Gideon's father, said, **let him** [Baal] **contend for himself**. This statement was a challenge to the worldview of the people of Ophrah. If Baal were who he claimed to be, he could certainly take care of himself. In fact baalism focused on the ability of Baal to defeat the chaos monster and even death itself, bringing order and life to the people of the world. If any of this were actually true, it would be no small matter for Baal to destroy Gideon on the spot. But when this did not happen—and no doubt many there must have expected such a reaction from Baal—this was a powerful testimony to the helplessness of the Canaanite god. This statement by Gideon's father is witness to the underlying but dormant faith in the God of reality that continued to smolder in the hearts of Israel.

e. Muster of the Northern Tribes (6:33-35)

6:33-35. The eastern peoples again came across the Jordan and camped in Jezreel. **So the Spirit of the Lord came upon Gideon; and he blew a trumpet**. The words "came upon" translate the Hebrew *labash*, "to clothe," or "to put on clothing." This is a more picturesque image than the simple statement in 3:10 that the Spirit of the Lord "came upon" Othniel.

f. Sign of the Fleece (6:36-40)

6:36-40. Gideon's immature faith is pictured in this two-phase testing of the Lord's authority. That the Lord cooperated in this action and did not rebuke Gideon is hardly a ringing endorsement of the practice. Modern-day Christians who are tempted to use "the fleece" should be aware that no promise of miraculous guidance applies to the present day. In addition, there is nothing in the Gideon narrative that indicates that the divine or human author intended Gideon's actions to serve as a model for how God's people should make decisions.

3. The Defeat of Midian (7:1-25)

This massive battle resulted in the defeat of Midian. This in turn kept the nomadic nation at arm's length from Israel for many generations. Isaiah 9:4 refers to this battle as a great moment in Israel's history.

a. The Camp at Harod (7:1)

7:1. The likely location of **the spring of Harod** and **the hill of Moreh** is in the western reaches of the foothills of Gilboa, on the south side of the Harod Valley (which has nothing to do with Herod the Great at the time of Christ) opposite Mount **Moreh**, about 25 miles south of the Sea of Galilee. The springs form the headwaters of the Harod River, which drains past Beth Shean into the Jordan. The likely position of the Midianite camp was across the valley to the north, less than two miles away, at the foot of Mount Moreh.

b. The Selection of the Fearless (7:2-3)

7:2-3. A large number of men from the tribes of Manasseh, Asher, Zebulun, and Naphtali (6:35), with the strange absence of Issachar on whose boundaries the events took place, arrived on the scene to take part in the battle. Rather than congratulating Gideon on his successful recruitment job, God informed Gideon that he would have to reduce the number. Those who were fearful accounted for the first 22,000; these were allowed to go home.

c. The Selection of the Unobservant (7:4-8)

7:4-6. To make the army even smaller, God told Gideon to separate between those who lapped **the water with his tongue as a dog laps** and those who knelt **to drink**. This description is somewhat ambiguous. Likely each of the 300 men in the first group scooped the water in one hand, held his weapon in the other, and drank by lapping from his palm as a dog laps, while the others knelt, putting their faces to the water, and then drank. Some have suggested that, in this way, the 300 showed that they were more alert for battle and therefore better soldiers. On the other hand, Josephus wrote that the 300 were actually less watchful than the others, and thus God's power was more evident (*Antiquities of the Jews*, 5.6.3, lines 216-217). According to this view, God reduced Gideon's army to 300 careless and carefree men.

7:7-8. An alternative and more likely proposal is that this test was purely random and arbitrary, designed to reduce the number of warriors, so that Israel would be small enough to give God the glory for the victory rather than take credit in their own military strength. The point of the passage is to demonstrate to Israel that God wins battles by His own might and not by the strength of His people. That is why the Lord told Gideon, **I will deliver you** (7:7). The 300 chosen do not necessarily reflect a more alert group or a less battle-ready army, as if God chose them on the basis of their military savvy. Such an understanding plays against the whole theme of the episode, which focuses on *God's* power to deliver. If ever God did something arbitrarily, the selection of these 300 would be a prime example, done by Him to demonstrate His astounding power. It did not matter which 300 were chosen. This is all about God, not Gideon and his men.

d. Gideon Overheard a Dream (7:9-14)

7:9-14. Gideon still needed some support for his faith, however, and that night the Lord sent him into the Midianite camp with his servant Purah to overhear a Midianite dream. The dream of a barley loaf that devastated a tent demonstrated for Gideon the extent of the demoralization of the enemy camp.

e. Preparation for the Battle (7:15-18)

7:15-18. Gideon divided the 300 men into **three companies** of 100 men each, and gave them **trumpets . . . pitchers**, and **torches**. These three commonplace objects, one for each soldier, became the basis of Gideon's defeat of the Midianites. The **trumpets** were ram's horn *shofars*. These were not musical instruments, as anyone who has heard a *shofar* blown knows. Only the leader of a military unit ordinarily had access to such a noise-making device. So from the sound of 300 *shofars* the Midianite soldiers would have inferred the existence of an enormous body of soldiers. The **pitchers** would have been common earthen pots, of the sort made in a few moments by a potter, large enough to carry some provisions, and later to hide the torches. **Torches** would have appeared to the Midianites as the fires of the 300 Israelite soldiers.

f. The Battle on the Plains of Esdraelon (7:19-23)

7:19-23. At the beginning of the middle watch (about 10:00 p.m.) Gideon's men **blew** their **trumpets** and **smashed** their **pitchers**, and **held** up **the torches**. These sounds and sights, along with 300 men shouting, **A sword for the LORD and for Gideon!** led to Midian being routed. **Naphtali**, **Asher**, and **Manasseh** were summoned for the chase.

g. The Muster of Ephraim (7:24-25)

7:24-25. Ephraim was called up in this maneuver to cut off a retreat. **Oreb** and **Zeeb**, Midianite field commanders, were captured and killed by Ephraim.

A few statistics are in order to indicate the miracle involved with this victory. The Midianite army numbered about 135,000 soldiers (see 8:10 for the 15,000 Midianite survivors plus the 120,000 killed in the battle). The army of Gideon numbered 300. That yields a ratio of 450 Midianite soldiers to each Jewish soldier. Who else but God could receive the credit for such a victory? And this is precisely the point of the narrative. It is God, *not Gideon*, who is the hero in this and every story!

4. Aftermath of the Battle (8:1-27)

a. Appeasement of Ephraim (8:1-3)

8:1-3. The leaders of Ephraim rebuked Gideon for not asking them earlier to be involved in the battle. Yet God had deliberately limited the size of the army. Gideon certainly had the right to rebuke them, but he wisely appeased the Ephraimites, downplaying his own role while exalting theirs.

b. No Help from Succoth and Penuel (8:4-9)

8:4-9. After the men of Ephraim had dealt with Oreb and Zeeb at the fords of the Jordan, Gideon went after the two kings of the enterprise, **Zebah** and **Zalmunna**. The relationship of these kings and commanders may have been similar to that of General Sisera and Jabin of Hazor.

Gideon, still with only his original 300, in spite of Ephraim's pride, pursued the enemy past Succoth and Penuel, stopping to ask for food. When their request was refused by village leaders who were reasonably apprehensive about the chances of Gideon's little band to rout the Midianites, Gideon responded with a harsh promise of retribution.

c. Capture of Kings; Routing of Midian (8:10-12)

8:10-12. Gideon crossed the river with his men at the fords of Succoth, just north of the Jabbok River. He then followed a route up the Jabbok watercourse to the desert. This must be **the way of those who lived in tents**. Penuel and Succoth dominated this route.

The Midianites by this time had arrived in **Karkor** (perhaps located in the Wadi Sirhan east of the Dead Sea) and thought themselves out of range of pursuit. However, Gideon, still pursuing them, went through **Nobah** and **Jogbehah**, about seven miles northwest of Amman (which is northeast of Jericho), and surprised the unsuspecting and demoralized enemy, routing them again.

d. Punishment of Succoth and Penuel (8:13-17)

8:13. Gideon returned from battle by the **ascent of Heres** (lit., "the pass of the Sun"). This place is unknown, but was probably in the Jabbok region east of Penuel, which is about 22 miles northeast of Jericho.

8:14-16. That Gideon **captured a youth** and had him write down the names of 77 **princes** and **elders** of **Succoth** attests to fairly widespread literacy in this era. The Hebrew language was written with an alphabet that could be easily learned. The writing here was probably scratching on a potsherd. When the **men of Succoth** refused to give bread to Gideon, he disciplined them by striking them with a switch made of **thorns** and **briers**.

8:17. As he had vowed (v. 9), Gideon demolished **the tower of Penuel**, the symbol of its power and perhaps a religious symbol as well. It was probably a citadel guarding an approach to the city.

e. Execution of Zebah and Zalmunna (8:18-21)

8:18-21. After killing Zebah and Zalmunna, the kings of Midian, and the murderers of his actual brothers (in Gideon's words, **the sons of my mother**, v. 19), Gideon took the crescent-shaped ornaments from the camels' necks.

f. Gideon Offered the Kingdom (8:22-27)

8:22-27. The grateful people of Israel offered hereditary kingship to victorious Gideon. Many of the people may have thought that a unified nation would be better able to stand against outside oppressors. This method of choosing a king was not unusual in the ancient world. Tribal and city-state-sized groups often chose a king who had demonstrated prowess in battle, frequently by defeating the previous king. The hereditary right of a king lasted only until another king could successfully challenge the son or grandson. After Israel in the north seceded from Judah in the south following the death of Solomon in 931 BC, the northern kingdom of Israel followed this pattern of cyclical coups.

It is to Gideon's credit that he refused this offer. Yet he took to himself a number of the prerogatives of a king. He amassed a fortune (v. 26), acquired royal robes (v. 26), made an ephod to consult the Lord (v. 27), and established a harem (v. 30). He even named his son Abimelech (lit., my father is king, v. 31).

From **the gold earrings** ... **ornaments** ... **pendants** and camels' **neck bands**, Gideon made **an ephod**, which later proved to be a snare. It was probably intended as a means of communication with God. The ephod was a kind of jeweled vest or chest piece and was the most elaborate of the Aaronic priestly garments, used in some unknown way to ascertain the will of God. The amount of gold on the ephod itself indicates that it had an idolatrous image on it. Gideon's taking the gold earrings to make the ephod is a reminder of Aaron's use of gold earrings to make the golden calf (Ex 32:2-4). Gideon used this to establish a worship system devoted to him, even as done by the Canaanite kings. This led to spiritual disaster for Israel who **played the harlot with** the ephod.

5. The Era of Gideon's Rest (8:28-35)

a. Forty Years of Rest (8:28)

8:28. This rest period probably overlapped with Deborah's rest, and takes the story line to about 1160 BC.

b. Gideon's Later Life and Descendants (8:29-32)

8:29-32. Gideon had **seventy sons**, including Abimelech by a **concubine** ... **in Shechem**. One of Gideon's worst characteristics was his penchant for wives and concubines. The presence of many wives normally had two purposes: to demonstrate vast wealth (for it was quite expensive to support them all) and to demonstrate political power (most wives were the result of alliances with foreign rulers). While several of Israel's kings later took multiple wives, Gideon was the first Israelite leader to do this. The hatred and murder that plagued Gideon's family are typical of OT polygamous marriages.

c. Israel Forgets the Lord (8:33-35)

8:33-35. As soon as Gideon died, the people went back to worshiping the **Baals**. The words, **the sons of Israel again played the harlot**, are literally, "the sons of Israel returned to the practice of fornication." This was true both spiritually, in that they practiced idolatry, but also physically, since fornication was a key element in Canaanite worship and culture. This evaluation is presented four times in the book of Judges (2:17; 8:27, 33; 19:2) Also the people forgot **the Lord** and were unkind to Gideon's family. The temple mentioned here belongs to Baal-berith (only here and 9:4), literally, "lord of the covenant," referring to the patron deity of Shechem. Israel forgot the true **God, who had delivered them from... their enemies**. Ironically, they did so in Shechem, the very place where Israel had recommitted themselves to the Lord and swore never to worship the Canaanite gods (cf. Jos 24).

6. Abimelech and the Fall of Shechem (9:1-57)

Abimelech is not called a judge, and God did not raise him up to save Israel. This chapter is thus a break in the cyclical action, functioning as an epilogue to the Gideon narrative. In a polygamous society, when jealousy and warfare break out between half-brothers, the refugees would flee to their mother's relatives for help. This is what seems to have happened at Shechem. The purpose of the author is to emphasize the anarchy that results when anyone but the Lord is the leader of Israel.

Shechem had been important in the biblical narrative since the time of the patriarchs. Jacob's sons captured Shechem, and Joseph was buried there. Joshua did not conquer it, but apparently the city cooperated with him. Nevertheless ties to the Canaanite past continued. Gaal, son of Ebed, stood against Abimelech and appealed to the townsmen's loyalty to the men of Hamor, the Canaanite founder of the city (v. 28).

a. Abimelech's Treachery and Jotham's Response (9:1-21)

The story of Gideon could easily have ended in 8:28. That the narrative continues with the account of Gideon's many concubines and sons, including Abimelech, argues for a continuing story line with a more dismal point. Gideon may have delivered Israel in the short term, but he was a failure as a father and ultimately as a leader of Israel.

(1) Abimelech Conspired to Become King of Shechem by Treachery (9:1-6)

9:1-2. Gideon may have officially rejected the offer of kingship but his son Abimelech (lit., my father is king) had no compunctions against pursuing kingship. He went to **the whole clan** of his mother's father and claimed authority to rule over Shechem because he was their kinsman. He said, **Remember that I am your bone and your flesh**. This was not an unimportant consideration in antiquity.

9:3. Abimelech's mother's relatives **were inclined to follow Abimelech** (lit., "their hearts leaned toward Abimelech"). As is often the case in politics, emotion trumped reason.

9:4-5. Abimelech then **hired worthless and reckless fellows**. Like David after him, Abimelech started out with a motley crew of worthless men (cf. 1Sm 22:1-2). But unlike David, Abimelech failed to develop their character or skills. As noted above, the era of the judges was one of instability in the region. Outlaws, even whole tribes of fringe people, were like scavengers around the edges of society, waiting for openings to move in and obtain an advantage. Abimelech then killed all of his brothers except one, **Jotham**, Gideon's youngest, who **hid**. He killed them on **one stone** implying a similarity to sacrifice on a stone altar, indicating that they were not killed in battle but by formal execution. This note foreshadows the fable to come and signals a complication in the forthcoming plot.

9:6. Beth-millo (lit., "house of the fill") may refer to the massive Middle Bronze II structure in Tell Balata, known as the *Migdol* or "Fortress Temple." It is a large temple built on the remains of a Middle Bronze fortress within the walls of Shechem. It would have served admirably as a defensive citadel. The **pillar** may well be the sacred stone (*masseba*) set up in front of that temple. Abimelech was crowned king here, although his "reign" probably never reached beyond a small area of Manasseh.

(2) Jotham's Fable (9:7-15)

9:7-15. The lecture of Jotham to the elders of Shechem is the finest biblical example of a fable, a short prose or poetic morality lesson in which animals or plants behave like people. The stylized account of the trees searching for a king among the plants, only to settle on the bramble, is classic satire in fable form. The bramble, a noxious bush, represents Abimelech in the fable. The other trees, that would have been more qualified, were simply not willing to serve such a miserable constituency. So the story is a backhanded swipe at Shechem itself. In detail there are enough disjunctions between the fable and the surrounding story to make some scholars wonder if the fable was composed earlier and was part of the local culture. Possibly Jotham knew the fable from his childhood and repeated it here for polemic effect.

(3) Jotham's Challenge and Escape (9:16-21)

9:16-21. By beginning and ending the challenge with the same phrase, **If you have dealt in truth and integrity** (vv. 16, 19), Jotham emphasized (with this literary device called an *inclusio*) the main point of his criticism. His tone was ironic, as he leveled his critique at the truthfulness and moral integrity of the elders of Shechem.

b. The Fall of Shechem and Abimelech (9:22-55)

(1) Three Turbulent Years of Rule (9:22-25)

9:22. Although Abimelech was acclaimed king by the men of Shechem, the narrator refused to grant him that honor, saying only that **Abimelech ruled over Israel three years**. The Hebrew word for "ruled" is *yasar*, "to govern, to be a captain" and does not indicate kingship.

9:23-25. The men of Shechem dealt treacherously with Abimelech in revenge for his slaughter of Gideon's **sons**. The **evil spirit** mentioned here might just as well be called "bad blood"; certainly no demonic spirit is in view. The opponents of Abimelech sought to make his reign more difficult by ambushing the caravans that came through Shechem. This would have the effect of drastically reducing commerce. During the Amarna Age (early 14th century BC), Labayu of Shechem was accused of the same tactics by the king of Megiddo. This is a likely story, since Shechem was in an ideal location for such an ambush. The phrase **that the violence . . . might come** probably refers to the principle of vengeance. The men of Shechem likely believed that an evil deed would be repaid somehow, and they justified their own evil deeds as a way of hastening the vengeance.

(2) Gaal, the Challenger (9:26-29)

9:26-29. Gaal was an elder of Shechem who presumably had not supported Abimelech. When he arrived in the city, he was welcomed with a wild party and an emotional denunciation of Abimelech. Gaal challenged the people to follow him, and he challenged Abimelech to oppose him. The hand of God in judgment governs this entire story, in fulfillment of the curse of Jotham (v. 20).

(3) Zebul, the Lieutenant, Warned of Treachery (9:30-33)

9:30-33. Zebul, Abimelech's second-in-command, apparently witnessed the party in Shechem, and so he warned his master of the treachery, advising him to mount an attack at sunrise, the traditional best time for a surprise attack.

(4) The Defeat of Gaal (9:34-41)

9:34-41. Abimelech responded to the challenge, and he drove **Gaal** and his relatives out of **Shechem**. **The diviners' oak** (v. 37), a terebinth or oak, marked a sacred spot well known to the men of Shechem, but it cannot be identified today.

(5) The Capture of Shechem (9:42-45)

9:42-45. Abimelech and his soldiers then slaughtered many of the inhabitants of Shechem who emerged from the city and those who **were in the field**. In his foolish vindictiveness Abimelech destroyed and dismantled the main city of his realm, sowing salt over it as a symbol of total defeat. This use of salt is documented much later in the Roman destruction of Carthage, and perhaps represents a curse: "May the land be forever useless," since salt in significant amounts would make agriculture difficult. The city was not mentioned again as being rebuilt until the time of Jeroboam I, two centuries later (1Kg 12:25).

(6) Burning the Tower of Shechem (9:46-49)

9:46. The **tower** mentioned here is the same as Beth-millo, mentioned in v. 6. For its significance, see the comments there.

9:47-49. Abimelech and his men cut branches **from . . . trees**, placed them in the tower's **inner chamber**, and set them on fire, thus killing **about a thousand men and women**. This vicious behavior is included as further evidence of Abimelech's excessive vindictiveness and cruelty.

(7) Death of Abimelech at Thebez (9:50-55)

9:50-55. When Abimelech attacked **Thebez** (about 10 miles northeast of Shechem, a strategic fortress at the convergence of the roads to the Jezreel valley at Dothan, and at the northern border of Abimelech's domain) people fled to **the roof of the tower**. A woman threw an **upper millstone** against Abimelech. This was a large, cylindrical stone used to grind grain against a lower, fixed stone. It could be carried, and when dropped from an upper story by a woman it served as humiliation to Abimelech at his death.

c. Fulfillment of the Curse of Jotham (9:56-57)

9:56-57. In these verses all the elements of Jotham's curse have been fulfilled. For the first time in the book God is seen clearly acting with the law of retribution in mind. The people of Shechem received the king they deserved, and the king received the subjects he deserved. The principle is that God is just in working out the consequences of people's sins.

The Later Judgeships:

Several minor judges are mentioned in passing between the major judges of this later period, Jephthah and Samson. While neither Jephthah nor Samson was particularly praiseworthy, together they served to outline the geopolitical situation of the era. Both men operated during the end of the twelfth century (1100 BC). Jephthah faced the Ammonites in the east, and Samson fought the Philistines in the west. These twin threats, from opposite sides of the central hill country, served as the stimulus that ultimately led Israel to call for a king.

F. Tola and Jair: Two Minor Administrators (10:1-5)

Little is known of these minor judges. Archaeology provides little help in identifying their towns or the oppressors who gave them reason to rise to power.

1. Tola: Twenty-Three Years of Stability (10:1-2)

10:1-2. The location of **Shamir**, a common name, is probably someplace in the hill country of Ephraim.

2. Jair: Twenty-Two Years of Prosperity (10:3-5)

10:3-5. Jair's **thirty cities in . . . Gilead** are called **Havvoth-jair** (lit., "tent-settlements of Jair"). The dates for these two judges are not known, but they were likely contemporaries on opposite sides of the Jordan River.

G. Jephthah: Outcast Deliverer (10:6–12:7)

In this passage the author again took opportunity to give details of the cycle of sin and judgment that characterized the judges era. In this case the sin of the nation had increased so badly that God Himself refused—at least the first time asked—to save them from their enemies.

1. Gilead and the Challenge of Ammon (10:6-18)

While Israel dealt with the minor powers of Ammon and Philistia, the great powers were apparently on the sidelines. During the later period of the judges, the great world powers of Asia Minor, Mesopotamia, and Egypt did not interfere, thus giving Israel about 150 years to develop as an independent nation. The Mittani of Mesopotamia, known from the Amarna correspondence, had years before been neutralized by the Hittites. In turn, Egypt and the Hittites fought to a draw at Kedesh on the Orontes River (near the NT town of Syrian Antioch) in 1290 BC. The Sea Peoples, moving into the region, apparently destroyed the Hittite Empire around 1200 BC before fighting Egypt to a standstill along the coast of Palestine. All this mutually destructive activity left the great powers exhausted. They simply did not care what happened in the former lands of the empire, including Israel.

a. Sin and Affliction for 18 Years (10:6-9)

10:6-9. A long list of foreign gods is presented in v. 6, including, for the first time, the gods of the Ammonites and of the Philistines. The Israelites were quick learners when it came to sin. Though these various gods were similar in many ways—all were part of the fertility pantheon—they were distinctive as well. Dagon of the Philistines was probably not a fish god, as has sometimes been thought. The name *Dagan* is the common Semitic word for "grain," suggesting that *Dagan/Dagon* may have been a West Semitic fertility god. In fact, he is included in the literature of Mesopotamia. The Ammonites' god was Milcom (corruption of Molech), who delighted in child sacrifice, and Moab served Chemosh, who also accepted human sacrifice. Both of these are represented by ugly metal statues in the literature and may well be gods of the underworld. God was angry at Israel because His people were so engaged in the idolatrous worship of these nations, and so for **eighteen years** the **Philistines** and Ammonites fought against Israel on both sides of **the Jordan** (v. 8).

b. Supplication until God Could Not Bear It (10:10-16)

10:10-16. This passage is the most striking confrontation between God and Israel in the book. Israel's confession of sin in v. 10 is clear and concise. God's response in vv. 11-14 is a detailed catalog of His mighty works up to that point (deliverance from Egypt, Ex 12; Amorites, Nm 21:21-25; Ammonites, Jdg 3:13; Philistines are mentioned in Jdg 3:3, but not elsewhere until chap. 15; Sidonians are mentioned also in Jdg 3; Amalekites are mentioned in Numbers and Judges as a constant threat; Maon is obscure—perhaps the LXX is correct in translating this Midian, Jdg 7). God's response was also a reminder that Israel had turned away, choosing to serve other gods. More significantly, the seven nations from whom God had delivered Israel correlated with the number of false gods they had worshiped (10:6). Israel's reply of contrition in v. 15 is pathetic. Verse 16b states that God **could bear the misery of Israel no longer**, meaning that He could no longer stand by and allow Israel to be oppressed. Some have suggested that this phrase should read, "His soul was short with the misery," suggesting that God had run out of patience with Israel's repeated attempts at insincere repentance. Nevertheless, since God did empower Jephthah to deliver Israel (Jdg 11:29, 33), it seems better to understand the phrase as referring to God's compassion for Israel.

c. The Muster of Ammon and Gilead (10:17-18)

10:17-18. This passage speaks volumes on ancient warfare customs. The Ammonites and Gileadites mustered for battle (v. 17) before Gilead had chosen a general. The call of Jephthah to be both general and political leader (v. 18) is almost an afterthought. **Mizpah**, where the Israelite army gathered, is a common name, meaning "watchtower," and is not otherwise identified.

2. Jephthah Called to Face Ammon (11:1-11)

a. Jephthah Introduced (11:1-3)

The Jephthah story is notable for God's use of an unlikely person. As Israel continued its decline in this era, the Lord had to turn to one of dubious background and character to defend His people. Nevertheless, this does give encouragement to those who would serve the Lord that it is not human pedigree but divine empowerment that brings success. If only Jephthah had ended as well as he began.

11:1-2. Jephthah is called a **valiant warrior** (*gibbor hayil)*, a term that normally speaks of a man of status in the community because of property ownership, pedigree, and/or war-fighting skill. Jephthah probably was called this because of his fighting ability and not because of community status. He was the son of a man named "Gilead" by a prostitute, likely a Canaanite, who is not named. His brothers refused him his inheritance because of that disgrace. Jephthah was forced into the life of an outcast.

11:3. Taking to himself a group of **worthless fellows** (cf. 9:4), he built for himself a small private army, apparently becoming the only significant force in the area. When the Ammonites decided to capitalize on Israel's weakness in the region after almost 300 years, Jephthah was the only leader with the experience to help. So it was that the men of Gilead turned to who could best be described as a local gang leader to come to their aid. Jephthah's victories led this unlikely leader to be identified in the biblical roll call of faith (Heb 11:32).

b. Jephthah Agreed to Lead Gilead (11:4-11)

11:4-11. These negotiations between Jephthah and the men of the region revealed their desperation and Jephthah's own wariness. When Jephthah repeated all these words of the negotiated settlement before the Lord, he was solemnizing the contract before God (v. 11).

3. The Battle of Ammon (11:12-40)

This battle took place c. 1100 BC, and although God granted Jephthah victory, this was not the end of conflict with the Ammonites. They were not finally subdued until the time of David, 100 years later (2Sm 12:31).

a. Jephthah's Diplomacy (11:12-28)

11:12-28. This passage provides details that are not available elsewhere about Ammon's territory and Israel's length of time in the region. The most prominent geographical feature of the region is the Wadi Jabbok, which begins in a series of springs northwest of Amman, Jordan, runs northward as far as modern Zerqa, then westward to the Jordan, dropping some 2,500 feet in the process through a spectacular rocky gorge.

The Ammonites, probably allied with the Moabites, saw an opportunity for territorial expansion. In this extended historical-geographical description Jephthah presented Israel's argument for ownership of the land on which Reuben and Gad lived. While at Kadesh, Moses asked permission to **pass through** (v. 17) the territory of Edom and Moab, and was refused (Nm 20). These two peoples, along with Ammon, descended from the same family as Israel, and God had given them inheritances in the plateau (Dt 2:5, 9, 19). No such relationship existed with the Amorite **Sihon** (v. 19), however, and Moses wasted little time liquidating that kingdom along the Arnon River (on the east side of the Dead Sea, at its mid-point north to south, Nm 21).

The Israelites **possessed** the Amorite territory **from the Arnon as far as the Jabbok, and from the wilderness as far as the Jordan** (v. 22). One could wish that the text had been a bit more specific in describing the eastern boundary. Certainly the Ammonites occupied the area around Amman itself, and probably to the edge of the plateau, along a line roughly from Jogbehah (25 miles northeast of the Dead Sea) to Heshbon (14 miles east of the north end of the Dead Sea). Reuben probably occupied most of the Medeba plateau from Bezer (about eight miles east of the north end of the Dead Sea) to the Arnon, and Gad stretched along the rolling hills east of the Jordan. The exact boundary under dispute here is open to question.

The mention of **three hundred years** of occupation (v. 26) is the key to understanding the dating of the Judges period. Though this is certainly a round number, it is inherently plausible and easily fits a conquest date of c. 1400 BC, putting Jephthah c. 1100 BC, near the end of the period of the Judges. Jephthah's argument in this passage was simply that each nation had received its inheritance from the hand of God. He referred to the honorable behavior of **Israel**, and requested similar honorable acts from **Ammon**. Although he did say that the Ammonites could **possess what Chemosh . . . gives you to possess**, he was not necessarily acknowledging Chemosh as a true god. He was merely negotiating with the Ammonites, with some irony, based on what the Ammonites themselves believed.

b. Jephthah's Foolish Vow (11:29-33)

11:29-33. In the process of destroying **twenty cities** of Ammon from **Aroer to . . . Minnith** (v. 33), Jephthah committed an act that has earned him a large amount of scholarly examination. His vow to sacrifice as a burnt offering **whatever** (or whoever) first came out his front door showed his lack of faith as he approached battle. It was a mistake common in Israel—thinking that one could negotiate with God and thereby win His favor.

While it is true that human sacrifice was prohibited by Moses (Lv 18:21; Dt 12:31), it is not at all clear that Jephthah had the training and background in the Lord to know that. The surrounding nations—the most important being Ammon and Moab—practiced the sacrifice of children. The slaughter of the crown prince of Moab in 2Kg 3:27 was an example of such an atrocity. Jephthah may well have been influenced by these pagan practices in his misguided devotion to the Lord. However, it is possible that Jephthah's daughter was not killed. One way of reading the Hebrew conjunction "and" in the phrase **it shall be the LORD's, *and* I will offer it up as a burnt offering** is as a "disjunctive"—(*or*), thus giving Jephthah a choice (11:31).

c. Jephthah's Daughter (11:34-40)

11:34-40. Although this passage has historically been interpreted that Jephthah did indeed offer his daughter as a human sacrifice, this is unlikely for several reasons. First, his daughter took the news of her fate with surprising calm, saying **you have given your word to the LORD; do to me as you have said**. It is unlikely that she would be so placid if she were facing death. Second, she asked that she be given time to **weep because of [her] virginity**, not for her life, implying that she was not to be a burnt offering but more likely confined as a virgin servant in the tabernacle precincts. Psalm 68:25 uses similar language to speak of virgin tambourine players serving in the tabernacle and dancing in procession. Although this would be wonderful for a worshiper of the Lord, she would have considered this sorrowful because Jephthah had no other children, and being kept a virgin would mean the end of his line. Third, at the end of her mourning period, the text says her father kept his vow **and she had no relations with a man**, not that he killed her as a human sacrifice. Therefore, it is best to assume that Jephthah did not make a burnt offering of his daughter, but instead sacrificed her to serve in the tabernacle. In any case, Jephthah's foolish vow is emblematic of the period and had serious implications for his family.

4. Civil War with Ephraim (12:1-6)

12:1-6. The story now shifts from Jephthah's foolishness to Ephraim's arrogance. The large tribe of Ephraim again complained of missing out, as they had done with Gideon some years before (8:1). Jephthah reminded them that he had asked for their assistance but they had not responded. At this point, Jephthah apparently ran out of patience for diplomacy, and his discussion with the leaders of Ephraim resulted in civil war. Part of the reason for the civil strife was that the Ephraimites had called the Gileadites **fugitives . . . in the midst of Ephraim and in the midst of Manasseh**, a taunt that called these descendants of Joseph traitors for having settled across the Jordan. After the battle, the defeated Ephraimites tried to escape across the Jordan at the fords. As the Ephraimites fled to cross the Jordan, it was not readily apparent to the Gileadite followers of Jephthah who they were, since many non-Ephraimites crossed the Jordan often as well. So the Gileadites devised a test to catch the Ephraimites. The test for Ephraimites—pronouncing the word "Shibboleth"—is of interest to linguists, who explain that the sibilants in the Semitic languages are notorious for dialectic shift. In the 300 years of separation of the tribes, small variations of pronunciation probably occurred. This also argues for a more lengthy period of the Judges than critics are willing to allow.

5. Six Years of Rest (12:7)

12:7. This brief period of peace, having come only after a brutal civil war caused by mutual affronts, suggests the overall declining situation in Israel.

H. Ibzan, Elon, and Abdon: Three Minor Administrators (12:8-15)

Before launching into a detailed description of Samson's exploits, the author mentioned three minor judges, who had no apparent military function but served as regional administrators.

1. Ibzan: Seven Years a Family Man (12:8-10)

12:8-10. Ibzan ruled from Bethlehem, which is probably the less well-known site in Zebulun (about seven miles east of Mt. Carmel in the north), since the southern Bethlehem is normally called "Bethlehem in Judah." His marriage practices and his habit of going outside the clan for mates for his children indicate an effort on his part to unify Israel after the tragic civil war.

2. Elon: Ten Years in Zebulun (12:11-12)

12:11-12. Elon is virtually unknown. His town may be related to the more famous town in the Aijalon Valley, but this is unlikely.

3. Abdon: Eight Years with Donkeys (12:13-15)

12:13-15. Abdon lived in Pirathon about six miles south of Shechem, on the border of Manasseh and Ephraim. His wealth is indicated by his many children. He had **sons and . . . grandsons who rode on . . . donkeys**, a sign they considered themselves nobility since this was a mark of high rank (10:4).

I. Samson: A Deeply Flawed Deliverer (13:1–16:31)

The Samson cycle is one of the most fascinating in the Bible. Most readers find themselves at once attracted and repelled by this amoral hero. His insatiable lust and sinful pride led him to self-destruction. Yet he too was used by God to deliver Israel.

1. Forty Years of Philistine Oppression (13:1)

13:1. The mention of a forty-year oppression by the Philistines supports the assertion that Samson was a contemporary of Jephthah. If the Philistines arrived in force to attempt a takeover of the land around 1154 BC, as suggested by archaeologists, 40 years of oppression and some time for Samson to grow to maturity would put these events shortly after 1100 BC.

2. Conception and Birth of a Remarkable Boy: Samson Introduced (13:2-25)

In contrast to Jephthah, Samson was divinely appointed and empowered, surrounded by signs of divine selection.

a. The Angel of the Lord Appeared to Manoah's Wife (13:2-7)

13:2-3. These events took place in the twelfth century BC, about 100 years after the **Danites** had migrated north (see the chronological explanation at Jdg 17:1). As such, it appears that Manoah and his wife remained in the ancestral area of Dan, indicating that their families had not migrated north with the bulk of the tribe. **Zorah**, about 15 miles west of Jerusalem, is one of the critical guard cities on the western approaches to Jerusalem. It sits across the Sorek Valley (to the north about two miles from Beth Shemesh) on an impressive natural hill. As the Philistines began to mount their offensive drives into the hill country, Zorah would have been on the front line.

Manoah's **wife was barren**, but Ps 113:9 cites the classic image of God blessing "barren women" who became "joyful mothers." This miraculous conception and birth echos Isaac and prefigures the Messiah, with the point that life always comes from the Lord.

13:4-7. The instructions about no **wine** and **strong drink** and **no razor** relate to the unusual requirement that Samson be a Nazirite from birth. The Nazirite vow (Nm 6) was generally a temporary vow related to special spiritual discipline or work. Samson was the only perpetual Nazirite mentioned in Scripture.

b. Manoah Spoke with God (13:8-14)

13:8-14. Manoah was understandably hesitant to take his wife's word for such a momentous announcement. He wanted to hear it from the angel himself. **The angel of God** (vv. 6, 9) is also called **the angel of the LORD** (vv. 3, 13). The definite article "the" suggests that this angel, like Gideon's angel, was a theophany (see comments on 6:12-14 above).

c. Sacrifice before the Angel of the Lord (13:15-20)

13:15-20. This remarkably detailed passage reinforces the divine power of the **angel of the LORD**. He refused a meal, suggesting a lack of fellowship between the nation and their God. He asked instead for a sacrifice, and he helped to point Manoah toward a correct understanding of his visitor. When asked his name, he responded **it is wonderful**. The Hebrew *pel'* suggests something that is beyond understanding and is a word associated with the wondrous acts of God (cf. Is 9:6).

The sacrifice, a whole burnt offering, is accepted in a miraculous way, with fire coming from the Lord to consume it. It also included a further a miraculous aspect: **the angel . . . ascended in the flame of the altar**. Then, Manoah and his wife **fell on their faces to the ground**, in the classic attitude of worship.

d. Common Sense of Manoah's Wife (13:21-23)

13:21-23. Having seen **the angel of the LORD**, Manoah said, **We will surely die**. This reflects Manoah's traditional understanding of the consequence of seeing God (Ex 33:20). His wife, on the other hand, put the whole event in context, realizing that something truly marvelous had happened and that they were not likely to die. Manoah, though a good man, is shown to be spiritually obtuse, but at least his wife had common sense.

e. Samson's Birth and Divine Empowerment (13:24-25)

13:24. Samson's birth and growth are noted briefly. As he grew, **the LORD blessed him**. Samson's name is the diminutive of *shemesh*, "sun," and perhaps reflects his sunny disposition. A more troubling possibility is that Samson was named for the pagan sun god Shamash. Such names were common in the ancient world.

13:25. Eshtaol is probably Tel Eshtaol located several miles farther north up the Sorek Valley (about 12 miles west of Jerusalem) from **Zorah**. **Eshtaol** is always mentioned with **Zorah**. Between the two was located the **Mahaneh-dan** ("Camp of Dan") where Samson first felt the stirring of God's Spirit. Later he was buried there (17:31). The major site in the region, Beth Shemesh (about 17 miles west and slightly south of Jerusalem), must certainly have been within the region known as the "Camp of Dan." This tel commands the entrance to the Sorek Valley from the west.

3. Samson's Marriage at Timnah (14:1–15:20)

These chapters give a first look at the central tragedy in Samson's life, namely, his uncontrollable lust. His parents, despite their godly outlook, simply could not reign in this strong-willed son.

a. Samson Chose a Wife from the Philistines (14:1-4)

14:1-3. Samson saw a Philistine woman in **Timnah**, which is Tel Batash, about four miles west of Beth Shemesh and Zorah in the Sorek Valley. The border between Philistine and Israelite territory must have run roughly north and south between the two settlement areas. Standing on Beth Shemesh, it is possible to trace the strategic situation, as the two Danite cities of Beth Shemesh and Zorah presented a strong defensive position toward the west, where the Sorek Valley widens to connect with the Aijalon Valley just to its north. Philistine chariots roamed freely on that plain, hesitating only as they approached the narrow confines of the upper Sorek Valley.

When Samson asked his parents to get this Philistine woman as his wife, they questioned the wisdom of that suggestion. But he liked her appearance.

14:4. In Samson's request **the Lord . . . was seeking an occasion against the Philistines**. This is the key to the entire Samson narrative: in spite of Samson's lack of godliness, the Lord was accomplishing His own agenda through the life of Samson.

b. Samson Took His Parents to Meet the Girl (14:5-9)

14:5-9. The trip to Timnah took the family through the vineyards of Timnah, where Samson first received **the Spirit of the LORD**, and **tore [a young lion] as one tears a young goat**. This seemingly irrelevant exploit is the prelude to Samson's riddle of v. 14. The lion was a part of God's plan for dealing with the Philistines, as will be seen in Samson's wedding banquet and interplay with his companions, resulting in the death of 30 Philistines!

c. Samson's Wedding Debacle (14:10-20)

The customs mentioned here are virtually the same as customs attested elsewhere in the Scriptures. The wedding process was divided into two phases: betrothal and the marriage. Betrothal was nearly as binding as the marriage itself, and was normally arranged by the parents. It was not uncommon for the couple involved to hardly know one another before the betrothal. The marriage feast involved both families, all their friends, and the entire community of the bride. Wedding ceremonies must have been simple, an exchange of agreements between parents and then between the couple in the presence of witnesses. The wedding feast was the more significant event. Samson's marriage is strange in that the bride continued to live in her father's house. Normally the bride joined the young man in his parent's home. When the Philistines fought with

Samson and the girl was given to another, she continued to live in her father's house and the bridegroom visited her there.

(1) The Feast (14:10-11)

14:10-11. This feast, a bachelor party consisting of Samson and 30 young Philistine male companions, provided the context for the riddle game.

(2) Samson's Riddle (14:12-14)

14:12-14. Middle-Easterners loved the challenge of logical conundrums, and these are found or hinted at regularly in their literature. Samson's confrontation with the Philistines over a riddle could have been a similar serious game. If they could solve his riddle, he would give them **thirty linen wraps and thirty changes of clothes**. If not, they would give him the same.

(3) Treachery on Treachery (14:15-20)

14:15-20. This passage suggests interlocking treachery on the part of the Philistines, Samson's wife, and Samson himself. When threatened by the Philistines if she did not find out from Samson the meaning of the riddle, she pressed Samson for it. She told the Philistines the answer to the riddle, and they relayed it to Samson. Samson accused them of taking advantage of his wife, remarking that if they **had not plowed with [his] heifer** they could not have succeeded. The use of the term heifer to describe his wife is likely a reference to her rebellious stubborn spirit (Jr 50:11; Hs 4:16). That **the Spirit of the LORD came upon him mightily** is a testimony to God's desire to punish the Philistines, not to Samson's virtue (on Jdg 14:20, see 15:2).

Ashkelon, situated on the Mediterranean and protected by the rest of the Philistine pentapolis, was the natural center of Philistine higher culture. There Samson in anger killed 30 otherwise uninvolved Philistines. It might appear that this was an act of personal vengeance. Yet, the Spirit of God motivated it. Therefore, while Samson may have been seeking revenge for what was done to him, he seems to have unwittingly become an instrument of God in fulfilling his role as judge and defeating the enemies of Israel.

d. Samson's Destruction of Philistine Crops (15:1-8)

15:1-8. In retaliation for the loss of his wife, Samson tied the tails of **three hundred foxes** together, set them on fire, and released the foxes into the **standing grain** and **vineyards and groves**. As noted above, the region around Timnah is excellent for agriculture. Adequate rainfall makes it possible to grow many crops without irrigation. In the flat alluvial valley, grain of all kinds will grow nicely, separated into fields by windrows of stones and hedges. The rolling hills are a fine location for olive trees and vineyards. In the summer, as the grain is ripening in the sun, a fire could easily be spread in the manner suggested here. The Philistines then burned Samson's wife **and her father** (v. 6). Then Samson took revenge by slaughtering many Philistines. All of this, as vindictive as it clearly was, can be seen in the larger narrative as a part of God's plan to punish the Philistines through Samson's judgeship.

He then went to live **in the cleft of the rock of Etam**. This could be virtually anywhere in the hill country, where limestone outcroppings are abundant, and caves make a convenient hiding place.

e. Samson Submitted to the Men of Judah (15:9-13)

15:9. Lehi in Judah (about 12 miles southwest of Jerusalem), where **the Philistines . . . camped** means "jawbone." This was the name given to the place in Judah after the battle described here.

15:10-13. The conversation between the Philistines and the men of Judah here gives insight into their relationship. The Philistines are called **rulers** of Israel, a term that implies dominion or sovereignty. As part of the prediction of blessing for godly obedience in Dt 15:6, Israel was promised that they would "rule" nations, but the nations would not "rule" over them. The corollary, that disobedience will result in foreign rulers, is made clear in Israel's history. The men of Judah were willing to obey Philistine orders, and Samson, apparently unwilling to resist the efforts of the men of Judah, went quietly with them, bound with new ropes. When Samson saw the Philistines and heard them shouting, the Spirit of God empowered him yet again and the battle was on.

f. The Battle of Lehi (15:14-19)

15:14-19. In this battle against the Philistines Samson killed **a thousand men** with a **jawbone**. A jawbone found at Tel Qasile in the northern portion of the Philistine Plain illustrates this striking story. It is fitted with flint teeth, making it a sickle for cutting grain. A fresh jawbone, one still moist from a recently dead donkey, would be the best weapon, for it would not be as likely to break under stress. Later God opened a hollow in the region to provide water for Samson, who named it **En-hakkore**. Although this location cannot be identified, the author's point in including this story is to show that God not only empowered Samson by His Spirit (15:14), but also physically sustained him with water, so that Samson would accomplish God's purposes as judge.

g. Twenty Years of Samson's Leadership (15:20)

15:20. This brief note covers **twenty years** of Samson's life. He is called a judge here over Israel.

4. Samson's Lust and Death (16:1-31)

It is fitting that Samson should die as he lived, in a confusion of passion and blood.

a. Samson and the Harlot of Gaza (16:1-3)

16:1-3. This brief episode provides insight into Samson's character as both morally weak and physically strong. As for his moral weakness, he made a habit of frequenting the Philistine city of Gaza and other cities, looking for sensual entertainment. On this occasion he went to Gaza and visited **a harlot there**, resulting in an attack plot by the local Philistines. Samson outsmarted them by getting up in the middle of the night, ripping out the city gates (posts, bar, and all), and carrying them to Hebron, a distance of 40 miles (although some consider this to be a hill just outside of Gaza in the direction of Hebron). The author includes this demonstration of amazing strength and prowess not merely to show Samson's ability to destroy a defensive feature of the enemy. Rather, he is contrasting Samson's moral weakness with his enormous physical strength. Imagine the sort of judge Samson could have been if his moral might was comparable to his physical power.

b. Samson and Delilah (16:4-22)

(1) Delilah Introduced (16:4-6)

16:4-6. In the **valley of Sorek** Samson fell in love with **Delilah**. As noted above, the Sorek Valley provides one of three western approaches to Jerusalem and the hill country, though it is the least accessible of the three. The word **Sorek** derives from a word meaning "bright red," which apparently refers to the quality of the grapes. Samson's Nazirite vow was certainly in jeopardy on this account.

The passage records a simple intelligence operation on the part of the Philistine leaders who proposed a substantial bribe to Delilah.

(2) Three Tests of Strength (16:7-14)

16:7-14. Samson told her he would be **weak** like anyone else if she bound him with **seven fresh cords**. These **cords** (*yetharim*) were actually made from animal intestines and may have been used as bowstrings. **Fresh cords**, like fresh donkey jaws, may have been tougher than the seasoned variety. But Samson was playing a dangerous game. Next, **new ropes** were proposed, and Samson snapped them easily. **Tow** translates a rare Hebrew word (*ne'oret*) found only here and in Is 1:31, where it is translated "tinder." Ugaritic evidence suggests the material may be produced by combing flax.

Samson suggested she weave **seven locks of** his **hair** with a **web** (probably a horizontal loom, with lines pinned to four corners on the floor, since Samson was asleep during the weaving process). The Hebrew text (MT) of 16:13-14a was shortened through a mistaken scribal omission, and has generally been restored (by NASB, NIV, ESV) according to the LXX reading, adding elements of the story pattern that are present in the other three Delilah sections.

(3) Delilah Extracted the Secret of Samson's Strength (16:15-17)

16:15-17. Then Samson told her that if his hair was **shaved** with **a razor** he would **become weak**. The best ancient razors were made of flint or obsidian. The hard, glass-like igneous rock has sharp edges. Of course Samson's hair did not give him his strength. Instead God's Spirit gave him strength (as found in 14:19 and elsewhere in the Samson narrative). But Delilah's razor-wielding was as much a symbol of Samson's spiritual bankruptcy as a cause of his downfall.

(4) Samson Captured by the Philistines (16:18-22)

16:18-21. The basis of Samson's strength was not primarily his own physical prowess (which must have been substantial) neither was it his long hair, which was merely an external symbol of his Nazirite vow. The Nazirite vow was designed by God (Nm 6:1-2) as a way for Israelite men to set themselves apart for special service or prayer. God had honored Samson's Nazirite status in using him for the special task of defeating Israel's enemies. When his hair was cut it was only an outward symbol that **the LORD had departed from him**, the real reason for his utter defeat. Cutting Samson's hair indicated that he had broken his vow by foolishly telling Delilah about it. What happened to Samson could not happen to a believer today because in the OT it was normative for the Spirit to come upon people temporarily for special service and then to leave. It is only after the birth of the Church in Ac 2, that the Lord Jesus' promise of the Holy Spirit's universal and permanent indwelling of believers was fulfilled (Jn 14:16-17). As a result of Samson's defeat, he was made physically blind to represent his foolish spiritual blindness and made to grind grain, the hardest and lowest kind of slave labor possible.

16:22. After Samson's hair was shaved, time passed, and it **began to grow again**. There was no magic in the hair, of course, but rather it represented the restoration of Samson's Nazirite vow. The word "began" is a literary foreshadowing of the work of the Spirit in Samson's life (see 13:5, 25 where it was used of the Lord beginning to use Samson). Here it suggests that God was not done with him, but would yet again use him, and that he would have his opportunity for vengeance on the Philistines.

c. Samson's Humiliation and Vengeance (16:23-31)

(1) Samson's Humiliation (16:23-27)

16:23-27. To add insult to tragedy, the Philistine leaders chose to exhibit Samson in the temple of **Dagon**, including coercing him to entertain them.

(2) Samson's Vengeance (16:28-31)

16:28-31. Philistine temples, such as those found superimposed at Tel Qasile on the Yarkon River (on the north side of modern Tel Aviv), are not large at all. The pillars of these temples were probably not massive. They may have been about a yard in diameter and perhaps six to seven yards tall.

The structure at Qasile was held up by two pillars about two yards apart. The roof, made of large wooden rafters supported by a central wood or stone beam, would certainly have collapsed if the pillars were forced apart. About **3,000** Philistines who were on **the roof** were killed.

Samson's life ended in tragedy. Yet God used him to accomplish the deliverance of Israel, for a time, from the Philistines.

III. Two Epilogues: The Abominable Spiritual Condition of Israel Called for a Great King to Stabilize and Lead the Nation (17:1–21:25)

The incidents described in chaps. 17–21 do not follow chap. 16 chronologically. Rather they are events from the earliest period of the judges. This is evident in 18:30 where Jonathan, the Levite who became the Danite pagan priest, is identified as the grandson of Moses (see comments there). This puts the story within 100 years of the conquest under Joshua. The author's purpose in using these stories here was to identify them as archetypical events, indicating the rampant apostasy and degradation that occurred when there was no king and each man did what was right in his own eyes (17:6; 21:25).

The author deliberately framed these narratives to resemble stories previously recorded in Scripture. For example, the story of the Levite and his concubine (19:1-26) deliberately calls to mind the account of Sodom in Gn 19, indicating that Israel in the period of the Judges was as sinful as Sodom. Also, the story of the battle with the Benjamites (Jdg 20:1-48) reminds readers of Israel's failures in Ai (Jos 7–8). Thus, the author shows Israel's unwillingness to obey the Lord, thereby repeating the sins of their fathers. This portion of the book serves to characterize the judges period as a time of spiritual decline and political chaos, the lack of a king being directly related to the spiritual problem. Although some think this is merely a defense of David and his dynasty, the narratives in the books of Samuel and Kings demonstrate that neither David nor his sons met Israel's need. Hence, the book points ultimately to the Messianic descendant of David who would fulfill the promise of kingship in Israel.

A. The Idolatry of Dan (17:1–18:31)

1. Idolatry in Ephraim (17:1-13)

This disgusting episode of a thieving Ephraimite named Micah and his mother demonstrates the depths into which Israel had sunk. Micah was a thief, and his mother was a fool. The two made the silver into idols and consecrated a family member to be a priest! Eleven hundred shekels of silver probably represented the old woman's life savings. There being no banks or mutual funds, it was kept in and around the house in the form of silver, gold, or precious stones.

a. Micah and His Mother (17:1-6)

17:1-4. Micah admitted **to his mother** that he stole **eleven hundred pieces of silver** from her, but that he was returning them to her. She then **took two hundred pieces** to have them made into idols. The OT uses no fewer than 10 words to speak of idols. Most of them have to do with the method in which the idol was made. In this passage (v. 4) the terms *pesel* and *massekah* are used. The first may be translated "carved [**graven**] image," the second "cast [**molten**] image." Many examples of such idols are extant, and descriptions of them are available in archaeological literature. The earlier example of Laban and his household gods (the *teraphim,* "household idols" of Gn 31:19; see the comments there) demonstrates the value placed on such objects. Probably a set of household gods represented the wealth of the household, as well as a family's inheritance that would be passed along.

17:5. To go along with his new collection of idols (or perhaps just one idol) Micah turned a portion of his home into a **shrine**, probably building a niche in one wall, an architectural feature regularly found in sacred buildings in Israel. He then formally consecrated one of his sons to be a **priest**, thereby perverting the true intentions of the Aaronic priesthood, which was to be a continuous picture of the work of Christ in the tabernacle and temple service.

17:6. The refrain **there was no king in Israel; every man did what was right in his own eyes** is repeated, reminding readers of the spiritual decline that results from the lack of a king, and particularly, the lack of the Messiah (see introductory remarks after III. Two Epilogues, above).

b. A Levite for a Priest (17:7-13)

17:7-13. The young Levite who later became Micah's priest obviously had no better grasp of the principles of the worship of the Lord than Micah did. He was from Bethlehem, which was not one of the Levitical cities, suggesting that by this time the Levites had probably been scattered because of lack of support, and sought any sort of living they could find. Micah assumed that having the Levite living in his house meant that **the LORD** would **prosper** him. The idea of the Levite as a "good luck charm" is clearly far away from the biblical pattern of the Levite as servant of the Lord in the tabernacle. Micah's arrangement betrays a misunderstanding of the purpose of the priesthood altogether.

2. Danites on the Move (18:1-31)

a. Danite Patrol Meets the Priest of Micah (18:1-6)

18:1-6. That the Danites had a difficult region to settle is unquestionable. The Philistines were able to operate in most of Dan's territory without fear of opposition, since their chariots could easily control the plains and rolling Shephelah country in the area west and south of Jerusalem. Their failure, however, was because of spiritual shortcomings rather than military weaknesses. This episode at Micah's house demonstrates the character of these men more than any technical description. The Danites lacked the faith to follow through on God's commands to take the land, and their idolatry is the outward evidence of that lack of commitment to the living God.

That **an inheritance had not been allotted** to the tribe of Dan (v. 1) probably reflects their pessimistic view of their situation. Joshua had allotted a tribal territory to Dan (see Jos 19:40-48), but the territory had hardly been handed over to them. It was their responsibility to secure it, and this they failed to do. Because the Philistines were such a constant threat to them, they began to scout out other places to live, to which they could relocate. So a patrol of five men was sent **to spy out the land**. This parallels Jos 2:1, the story of the spies at Rahab's house, in a perverse way. When the five men went to Micah's house, they recognized the voice of the Levite. So they asked him to ask God if their journey would **be prosperous**.

b. Danites Find a New Place to Settle (18:7-10)

18:7. When the five scouts went **to Laish**, they were impressed that the people there were **living in security**. On the advice of the spies the tribe moved to Laish, about 100 miles north. A Canaanite civilization had existed at the headwaters of the Jordan for at least a millennium and a half by the time the Danites got there. Laish was founded in the upper Jordan valley at the same time as many urban centers in the ancient East. The location is an obvious one, a hill near a luxuriant spring surrounded by fertile farmland next to the international trade route. Not surprisingly the site has been almost continuously inhabited.

18:8-10. The spring that made Laish desirable flows from the base of Mount Hermon, itself a vast pile of porous limestone. Water runoff from Hermon's snow seeps through the limestone and is conducted through springs and rivers to the whole area throughout the entire year and makes life possible in this otherwise relatively arid region. A massive fortification system gave the people of Laish a sense of security. Here indeed was a city that was **quiet and secure** (v. 7), in contrast to the tribe of Dan's assigned location in the region of the Philistines (see Jos 19:40-48).

c. Journey of the Six Hundred to Ephraim (18:11-13)

18:11-13. Six hundred men armed with weapons of war . . . camped at Kiriath-jearim several miles northwest of Jerusalem, and then went to Micah's house in **Ephraim**. Six hundred is the approximate size of a British regiment. The Danites probably did not have such a sophisticated organization, but the number (like the number that Shamgar slew, 3:31) is suggestive of careful military planning.

d. Subversion of Micah's Priest (18:14-20)

18:14-20. The 600 Danites **took the graven image and the ephod and household idols** (*teraphim*) and the molten image from Micah's house and encouraged the priest to go with them and be the **priest** for their **tribe**. This theft betrays an underlying relationship between idolatry and mere avarice: the idols represented pagan deities; they also represented monetary wealth. That wealth provided a kind of security that could also be sought in a relationship to the gods.

e. Confrontation with Micah (18:21-26)

18:21-26. When **Micah** confronted the 600 **sons of Dan** for taking his idols, he realized he was outnumbered, and so he returned home. The 600 operated with the threat of raw military strength. No one seemed to be operating from the standpoint of spiritual appropriateness.

f. Establishment of Idolatry in Dan (Laish) (18:27-31)

18:27-31. The 600 **burned the city** of Laish **with fire**, but then the city was **rebuilt**, and named **Dan**. Recent archaeology at Dan has confirmed a burn layer dating c. 1200–1150 BC, fitting the biblical pattern nicely. Self-appointed **priests** ministered there.

Verse 30 represents several difficulties. First, a textual problem has been introduced by the Masoretes, who inserted an additional Hebrew letter ("nun," equivalent to an English "n") elevated between consonants in the name "Moses" to make it **Manasseh** as found in some English translations. Since neither the versions nor other manuscript evidence supports this addition, it is best to assume that the idolatrous priest was in fact a descendant of Moses through Gershom. The purpose of the Masoretic addition was likely to preserve the honor of Moses the lawgiver. Second, the text indicates that the pagan priesthood that began with the Danite migration continued until **the captivity of the land** (*gelot ha'aretz*). This whole phrase is not found elsewhere, although the term *gelot* is often used of the exile of Israel. Young, Keil, and Delitszch and others have suggested a textual emendation (from *ha'aretz* = the land to *ha'aron* = the ark, and associated the time frame with the battle of Aphek (1Sm 3:15ff.). But there is neither manuscript nor version evidence in support of this suggestion. Thus it more likely refers to the exile of the northern kingdom of Israel in 722 BC or the southern kingdom of Judah in 586 BC. This would point to the book of Judges being written at a significantly later date than the events described within it or perhaps further copying and editing of the book after one of those later dates. This would have been an important reminder to Israel that, once again, after the exile, they were without a king, and therefore not to fall into the same sin of doing what was right in their own eyes.

B. The Perversion of Benjamin (19:1-21:25)

1. Degrading Murder of a Levite's Concubine (19:1-30)

This story paints a grim picture of the period. Morals had died. The family unit was breaking down as society deteriorated. No chronology is given, and none is possible, but the story itself sounds like an indictment of modern Western culture. Almost all the characters are anonymous, suggesting that they serve as pictures of the entire nation at a time when "every man did what was right in his own eyes" (17:6; 21:25).

a. A Levite Fetched His Concubine in Bethlehem (19:1-9)

19:1-9. A certain Levite . . . of Ephraim . . . took a concubine for himself from Bethlehem (v. 1). Probably a number of Levites left the Levitical cities designated for them in Joshua 20–21 because of lack of support from their society at large. This particular Levite seems to have no particular ethical persuasion, disregarding his responsibility of being holy as a servant of the Lord. He arranged for a concubine from Bethlehem, who left him out of anger. Although the NASB translation states that she **played the harlot**, the Hebrew root *zanah* is more likely related to the Akkadian "to be angry; to hate." None of this was morally acceptable. He went to the concubine's father to persuade her to return, but the father-in-law, following normative Middle Eastern hospitality, kept urging the Levite to stay day after day for five days. The reader perhaps is expected to assume that the father is quite devoted to his child.

The father-in-law seems not to have known how to take the whole matter. His background was clearly simple, as his speech abounded with nomadic metaphors (in v. 8 the word **afternoon** is lit., "the pitching"; in v. 9 the clause "the day has drawn to a close" is "the camping of the day"; and in v. 9 the Levite's **home** is lit., his "tent").

b. Journey to Gibeah (19:10-15)

19:10-15. The Levite, his concubine, and his servant were near Jebus at the end of the day, but rather than staying there, they went on to **Gibeah**.

c. Kindness of a Stranger in Gibeah (19:16-21)

19:16-21. The city square or a town was always just inside the main entrance to a city, inside the gate if there was one. The square was used as a primary meeting place, political forum, business locale, and resting place. The Levite's willingness to spend the night in the square was not unusual. The danger of the square came as a surprise here for the simple reason that this should have been the safest place to be: inside the gate, in a public place, where everyone would pass by. The danger of the place is one more indication of the deterioration of Israel. In typical ancient Near Eastern hospitality **an old man** took the Levite into his home overnight.

d. Perversion of the Men of Gibeah Leads to Rape and Murder (19:22-26)

19:22-26. This passage is a strong reflection of Gn 19 and the story of Lot's visitors in Sodom. In the same way Sodom was exceedingly evil and in peril of judgment, so the Benjamites here were in danger of judgment. The literary parallel is meant to underline the moral vacuum of a nation which has rejected living by the law of the Lord and did whatever it thought was right in its own eyes. The men of Gibeah are described in much the same manner as the men of Sodom, and their brutality is straightforwardly exposed. This is the only mention of any homosexuality among the Israelites, although it was common (and religiously sanctioned) among the Canaanites. The practice is forbidden in Lv 18 and 20. The old man refused to give his guest over to the **worthless fellows** of the city. Strangely, he then offered them his own **virgin daughter**, and his guest gave them his concubine, and they **raped . . . and abused her all night**. The behavior here is terribly shocking, and reminiscent of Lot's offer of his virgin daughters to the men of Sodom (Gn 19:8). Nevertheless, it is reported here, not merely for shock value, but to demonstrate God's basis for the judgment that is about to fall, just as it fell on Sodom. The devastation of Benjamin is the sad but necessary justice of God, wielded in the hands of the rest of Israel, who are scarcely better than their brothers.

e. Grisly Summoning of the Tribes (19:27-30)

19:27-30. Strangely, the guest/Levite, finding his concubine dead in **the doorway . . . with her hands on the threshold** (v. 27), then took her home and dismembered her. She is anonymous in death even as she was in life. Her desecrated corpse, cut into **twelve pieces**, served to summon the tribes to civil war.

2. Resolution to Punish the Guilty (20:1-17)

a. Muster of the Tribes at Mizpah (20:1-7)

20:1-7. The disgusting climax of the previous episode led to an attack by the rest of the tribes of Israel on the men of Benjamin. When the tribal muster arrived, the Levite explained his situation, with the ironic conclusion, **they have committed a lewd and disgraceful act in Israel**.

b. Agreement to Punish Benjamin (20:8-11)

20:8-11. One-tenth of the men were chosen **to supply food** for the rest of **the people**. For the first time in the book, the statement occurs that **all the men of Israel were . . . united as one man**. They were determined to attack Gibeah in return for the rape of the Levite's concubine in Gibeah.

c. Deployment of Benjamin and All Israel (20:12-17)

20:12-17. When the Benjamites were given opportunity to give up the evildoers (lit., "sons of Belial"), they chose not to betray their brothers. Even their left-handed slingers came out to battle, numbering 700. The 26,700 Benjamites fought **400,000** men of the other tribes.

3. Civil War and Benjamin's Defeat (20:18-48)

The tragedy of civil war underlines the failure of the leaders of Israel in this intermediate period before the kings of Israel. Neither judges nor clan leaders seem to have been able to stabilize Israelite society. This state of affairs lays the foundation for the call for a king in 1 Samuel. Ultimately, the OT demonstrates that no merely human king can bring peace to the earth. Ultimately, only the Messiah, the ideal King, can do that. The OT uniformly looks forward to the work of the Messiah.

a. Inquiring of the Lord (20:18)

20:18. The inquiry at Bethel may mean they asked the priests to consult the Urim and Thummim.

b. First Failed Attack (20:19-23)

20:19-23. Battle lines were drawn for an assault on Gibeah. Israel lost **22,000** of its 400,000 on the first day of the campaign. This loss was a disaster, as is often the case in an infantry attack on a hardened position. The leaders inquired of the Lord, who ordered a second attempt.

c. Second Failed Attack (20:24-28)

20:24-28. A second attack was organized in much the same way as the first, and resulted in the predictable second disaster with a loss of **18,000**. Praying and fasting all day and the intervention by Phinehas the priest led to a promise from God that they would be successful the next day.

d. Third Attack and Success by Ambush (20:29-48)

20:29-48. The tactical situation here is reminiscent of Jos 7–8 and the battle of Ai. The main attack must have come from the north, near Rahmallah and along the ridge route. The ambush, when it finally came from the west, may have been hidden in the rocky wadi of Nahal Atarot, which eventually drains into Aijalon Valley. Even the burning of Gibeah is similar to Ai. Benjamin suffered the loss of all but 600 of their men.

4. Reconstitution of a Lost Tribe (21:1-24)

a. Dilemma for the Tribes of Israel (21:1-7)

21:1-7. When the horror of what had just happened became clear to the men of Israel, they despaired at the loss of the tribe of Benjamin from the ancestral 12 tribes. Since all the towns of Benjamin had been destroyed (20:48) and virtually everyone killed, and since the men of Israel had vowed to give the surviving Benjamites none of their daughters, they had a difficulty.

b. Destruction of Jabesh-Gilead (21:8-12)

21:8-12. They solved this problem by noting that the city of **Jabesh-gilead** (in Manasseh, about 60 miles northeast of Jerusalem, east of the Jordan River) was not represented in the camp. A quick decision was made to kill everyone in that town except the young **virgins**, who were then given to the men of Benjamin. Jabesh-gilead turns up a number of times in the OT (1Sm 11:1 rescued by King Saul and 2Sm 21, where they retrieved Saul's bones).

c. Gift of Wives to Benjamin (21:13-15)

21:13-15. The survivors of Benjamin at the rock of Rimmon were willing to accept peace and young wives, but there were not enough wives.

d. More Wives from Shiloh (21:16-24)

21:16-24. An additional supply of wives was requisitioned from the annual dances at Shiloh. Because no family could voluntarily give their daughters to Benjamin since they vowed they would not do so (21:1), the survivors were told to *ambush* the girls they needed from Shiloh, where the people of every tribe went to worship at the tabernacle, thus absolving the Israelite parents of responsibility for voluntarily *giving* the girls in marriage. This highly unorthodox method of reconstituting a tribe apparently worked, for Benjamin continued in existence until the Assyrian deportation in 722 BC. This appalling episode points to the central theme: without a great King, the people of God can have no stability.

5. The Refrain: No King in Israel (21:25)

21:25. The book of Judges closes with the refrain, **In those days there was no king in Israel; everyone did what was right in his own eyes** (cf. 17:6). This serves as the end of the inclusio (literary parenthesis) begun in 17:6, designed to surround the stories of the epilogue. The epilogue began with this same statement as an opening parenthesis, followed by the horrific stories of Israel's self-willed behavior, and concludes with a restatement of this theme as a closing parenthesis. This epilogue captured the problem of the time of the Judges. Without a king, **everyone did what was right in his own eyes**, ignoring the law of the Lord. As such, it points to that future day, when a righteous King would come and lead Israel into the fear of the Lord.

Together, the books of Joshua and Judges provide the historical transition between Moses and the monarchy. They set forth the foundations of history and geography that form the framework for the rest of the OT. These books are indispensable for an understanding of that history. In addition they lay the foundation for the claim that Israel needed a king. In the larger sense, though, the failure of Joshua and then the judges to deliver Israel pointed to the need of the nation and of everyone for the great King, the Messiah, who will come to deliver and set up His kingdom for all time.

BIBLIOGRAPHY

Bimson, John. *Redating the Exodus and Conquest.* Sheffield, England: Almond Press, 1981.

Biran, A. *Biblical Dan.* Jerusalem: Israel Exploration Society, 1994.

Block, Daniel I. *Judges, Ruth.* New American Commentary. Nashville: Broadman & Holman, 1999.

Cundall, Arthur. *Judges.* Tyndale Old Testament Commentary. Downers Grove, IL: InterVarsity, 1968.

Finkelstein, Israel. *The Archaeology of the Israelite Settlement.* Jerusalem: Israel Exploration Society, 1988.

Garstang, John. *Joshua–Judges.* Grand Rapids, MI: Kregel Publications, 1935, 1978.

Gordon, Cyrus H. *Before the Bible: The Common Background of Greek and Hebrew Civilizations*. New York: Harper and Row, 1962.

Lindsey, F. Duane. "Judges." In *The Bible Knowledge Commentary, Old Testament*, edited by John F. Walvoord and Roy B. Zuck. Wheaton, IL: Victor Books, 1985; reprint, Colorado Springs: David C. Cook, 1996.

Mazar, Amihai. *Excavations at Tell Qasile*, Part 1. Jerusalem: Hebrew University, 1980.

———. *Excavations at Tell Qasile*, Part 2. Jerusalem: Hebrew University, 1985.

Wolf, Herbert. "Judges." Vol. 3 of The Expositor's Bible Commentary, edited by Frank Gaebelein. Grand Rapids, MI: Zondervan, 1992.

Wood. Leon. *Distressing Days of the Judges*. Grand Rapids, MI: Zondervan, 1975.

● ● ● ●

RUTH

MICHAEL G. WECHSLER

INTRODUCTION

Author and Date. As with several of the books in the biblical canon, the writer of Ruth is not identified in the book itself. According to long-standing Jewish (and hence Christian) tradition it was written by Samuel. One of the oldest strata of the Babylonian Talmud (*Bava' Batra'* 14b) records: "Samuel wrote down his own book [i.e., Samuel, up to 1Sm 24:22], Judges, and Ruth." There is no reason to doubt this tradition, as the scribal/recording role of the early Jewish prophets—and Samuel in particular—is attested elsewhere (1Ch 29:29; 1Sm 10:25). Moreover, as recognized by scholars specializing in historical Hebrew linguistics, the style and phraseology of the Hebrew in Ruth are indeed that of the early biblical period, being similar to that attested in Judges, Samuel, and the earlier parts of Kings. As the writer, therefore, Samuel would most likely have written Ruth sometime toward the end of the 11th century BC, after the enthronement of David recorded in 2Sm 5:3 (or, at the earliest, after his anointing in 1Sm 16).

Purpose. The purpose of the book of Ruth is not simply to provide us with information concerning the genealogy of David (and hence of the messianic "Son of David," Jesus; see Mt 1). For that the last five verses of the book alone would suffice—and even they are not essential, as the same information is given in a fuller genealogical context in 1Ch 2:3-15. Rather, the purpose of Ruth is to present *within* the genealogy of David a positive case study of what may be termed an "anatomy" of faith in the present world. It encompasses *the breadth of faith's operation*—i.e., those crucial moments when faith is tested, the much longer period of perseverance in faith, and the rewards for such that God may extend in this life. Moreover, with the exemplar of faith in this case being Ruth the Moabitess, the book also addresses *the extent of faith's application*—i.e., that this operation of true faith and the blessing that attends it potentially applies to those who are not ethnic Israelites (descendants of Jacob).

Indeed, it is this latter point in particular that helps explain why this example of faith is presented within the genealogy of David. Her association with one of the most respected figures in Jewish history who is also, together with Abraham, the recipient of God's most prominent messianic promises (see 2Sm 7), ensures that her Moabite (i.e., pagan) genealogy is *not* ultimately held against her (even though the kinsman closer than Boaz does hold it against her; see comment on Ru 4:6).

Rather, her Gentile status is in fact *highlighted* as a reminder of God's divine intent in choosing Israel and establishing the Davidic-messianic dynasty in the first place: to bring the blessing of faith in the true God to "all families of the earth" (see Gn 12:3 and comments there). It is this same point, no doubt, that Matthew intended at the outset of his Gospel (Mt 1:3-5). There he explicitly, and very unconventionally, mentioned Ruth *as the third* of three Gentile women in the genealogy of David, and hence of Jesus. (The previous two were Tamar and Rahab, who was Boaz's mother!) Thus, he underscores the universal scope of the Messiah's ministry and the motivating breadth and depth of the Father's love in commissioning Him.

Background. In Christian Bibles Ruth appears among the "Historical Books," the second of four divisions into which the Old Testament is divided. This follows the older ordering of books adopted by Hellenistic Jewry (i.e., Greek-speaking Jews living outside the land of Israel). This ordering is attested in the Septuagint (a Gk. translation of the Hb. Bible begun

c. 280–60 BC), which reflects primarily a *genre-based* (i.e., stylistic) division and organization of the biblical books.

In the enduring Jewish tradition, on the other hand, Ruth appears among the books collectively known as the *Ketuvim* (lit., "Writings"). The Writings are the third and last division of the Hebrew Bible according to the tradition of the Jews living in the land of Israel (sometimes referred to as the "Palestinian" tradition). This tradition reflects primarily a *thematic* (and to a lesser extent liturgical) division and organization of the biblical books.

Within the Writings, moreover, Ruth is part of the smaller collection known as the "Five Scrolls" (*hamesh megillot*), comprising five small books that are traditionally read in the synagogue during one of the yearly Jewish holidays. As attested by the oldest complete and most authoritative manuscripts of the Hebrew Bible, Ruth is the first of these Five Scrolls and follows the book of Proverbs. It is read on the Feast of Weeks, known per Hellenistic tradition as Pentecost (see further in "Purpose"). The thematic—even homiletical—concern underlying this organization becomes evident when one considers that Proverbs closes with an ideal description of the "woman of valor" (*eshet hayil*; Pr 31:10). This expression occurs outside of Proverbs only in Ru 3:11, with reference to Ruth herself (see further *"The Woman of Valor"* below).

Themes. Several themes appear in the book of Ruth and figure in its interpretation.

(1) The Kinsman Redeemer. The book provides the only clear biblical enactment of the Mosaic law concerning the "kinsman redeemer"—or, as the process is otherwise designated, "levirate marriage"—described in Dt 25:5-6 (where "brothers" probably signifies the closest male relations). According to this law, the closest male relative (yet in post-biblical practice only actual *paternal brothers*) of a woman's dead husband is obligated to marry that widow if she has no son (yet in post-biblical practice *no child*, so that if she has a daughter the law does not apply). The practice of levirate marriage is well attested and legislatively expanded among post-biblical (including contemporary religious) Jewry. This law represents God's compassionate codification and refinement of the pre-Mosaic custom attested in Gn 38:6-14, 26 (hence the comparison in Ru 4:12). It was intended to ensure that (1) the woman's needs would be supplied in a proper way by a male provider, and (2) the "name" (i.e., reputation and inheritance; see comments on Gn 11:1-4, 10-26) of the deceased husband would endure (i.e., "not be blotted out from Israel," per Dt 25:6).

This law and its exemplification by Boaz is also significant as a further enhancement of the biblical image of God as "Redeemer," since the legal term for "kinsman-redeemer" (*go'el*)—and hence the term applied to Boaz (in Ru 2:20; 3:9, 12; 4:14)—is also applied in the Bible to God. This occurs especially in the book of Isaiah with reference to His complete (i.e., spiritual *and* material) work of redemption, as in Is 49:6-7: "'It is too small a thing that you should be My Servant to raise up the tribes of Jacob and to restore the preserved ones of Israel; I will also make you a light of the nations so that My salvation may reach to the end of the earth.' Thus says the LORD, the Redeemer [*go'el*] of Israel and its Holy One . . ." (cf. also Is 44:24; 47:4; 48:17; 49:26; 54:5-8; 59:20; 60:16; 63:16; Jb 19:25; Ps 19:15; Jr 50:34).

(2) The "Woman of Valor". As noted above, in the predominant Jewish tradition of biblical organization (following the early tradition of Jews living in the land of Israel), the book of Ruth immediately follows Proverbs, thus highlighting the canonical-thematic link between the last pericope in Proverbs describing the ideal "woman of valor" (*ēshet hayil*; Pr 31:10) and Ruth. She is the only real biblical woman to whom that expression is applied (Ru 3:11).

As therefore might be expected, the various positive qualities and actions that characterize the "woman of valor" in Pr 31 are associated with Ruth at various points throughout the narrative, in some instances even employing the same terminology. Thus the woman of valor rises early in the morning to set about her work (31:5), as does Ruth (2:7; 3:14); the woman of valor works with dogged industriousness (31:27), as does Ruth (2:7, 17); the woman of valor is not dissuaded from difficult tasks, but rather "girds herself with strength" (31:17), as does Ruth (2:17-18, see comments); the woman of valor always takes thought to supply her family's needs (31:15), as does Ruth (2:14, 18); the woman of valor is characterized by "the teaching" (i.e., the *exemplary doing*) of *hesed* ("lovingkindness"; 31:26), as is Ruth (1:8; 3:10); the woman of valor is blessed by her husband (31:28), as is Ruth (by her husband-to-be; 3:10); and because of her works the woman of valor is praised "in the gates" (i.e., by the city; 31:31), as is Ruth (3:11).

Considering Ruth's background, moreover, the practical challenge of this canonical link and unique distinction is clear: If Ruth could achieve this status in the face of her many disadvantages (raised outside the community of faith, a new convert, a widow, and beset by poverty), how much more so should the Israelite (or Christian) woman behave who is not beset by these cumulative disadvantages?

(3) The Doing of Chesed. One of the key words in the book of Ruth is the Hebrew term *chesed*, which may be variously translated/understood as "lovingkindness," "kindness," "favor," or "grace." Perhaps it is best described by the preeminent medieval Jewish scholar Maimonides (late 12th century): "the doing of good to one who is not entitled to it from you at all . . . [or] the doing of more good to one than that to which he is entitled . . . for which reason every good thing deriving from the Exalted One is designated *chesed*" (*Guide of the Perplexed*, ed. Qafih, §iii.53).

Significantly, of its three occurrences in the book of Ruth, Ruth herself is the doer and/or recipient of the *chesed*. Thus, in 1:8 Ruth and Orpah are presented as the past doers and potential recipients of divine *chesed* in Naomi's statement, "May the LORD treat you with *chesed* just as you have treated those who are (now) dead and me." Also, in 2:20 Ruth and Naomi (i.e., "the living," which is plural); as well as Elimelech and Ruth's husband Mahlon ("the dead," likewise plural) are identified as the recipients of divine *chesed* in Naomi's statement, "May he [i.e., Boaz] be blessed of the LORD who has not withdrawn his [*chesed*] to the living and to the dead." Further, in 3:10 Ruth is presented as the doer of *chesed* in Boaz's declaration, "You have shown your last [*chesed*] to be better than the first . . ." This consistent presentation of Ruth as the doer and/or recipient of *chesed* is both rooted in and reflective of the larger purpose of the book: to emphasize the extent of application (i.e., for Gentiles as well as Jews) of true faith and the blessing that attends it (see above).

OUTLINE

- I. The Test of Faith (1:1-18)
  - A. Testing the Judaean Men (1:1-5a)
  - B. Testing the Judaean Woman (1:5b-7)
  - C. Testing the Moabite Women (1:8-18)
- II. The Perseverance of Faith (1:19–4:12)
  - A. The Persevering of Ruth (1:19–2:18)
  - B. The Persevering of Naomi (2:19–3:4)
  - C. The Persevering of Boaz (3:5–4:12)
- III. The Reward of Faith (4:13-22)
  - A. The Rewarding of Ruth (4:13)
  - B. The Rewarding of Naomi (4:14-17)
  - C. The Rewarding of Boaz (4:18-22)

COMMENTARY ON RUTH

I. The Test of Faith (1:1-18)

A. Testing the Judaean Men (1:1-5a)

1:1-5a. The events narrated in this book are set within **the days when the judges governed**. This phrase serves to further set this book apart (and hence to justify its presentation as a separate book rather than another "episode" within the book of Judges) from the cycle of immature faith that characterized the Israelites of that period. A hint of this immature faith is, nonetheless, implied here at the outset when the patriarchal head of the family, **Elimelech**, responded to the onset of **a famine in the** promised **land** by taking his family from their hometown of **Bethlehem in Judah** ("in Judah" distinguishes it from the identically named town in Zebulun; see Jos 19:15) **to sojourn in the land of Moab**.

The onset of a famine in the promised land was always a test of faith, as well as, on occasion, an expression of divine chastisement. The proper response to such a test would be to stay in the land *in dependence on God*, as did the majority of the residents of Bethlehem. (See also Jacob's specific appeal to God about leaving

Canaan even when invited by his son to do so during famine in Gn 46:3 and the comments there.) It is against this theological backdrop that the death of Elimelech should be viewed. It was the "ultimate" divine chastisement of a believer (cf. 1Co 5:5) for the sin of leaving the land (which God never gives His people warrant to do without first consulting Him) and having **remained** in Moab (v. 2). These actions underscored his entrenched unwillingness to repent and correct his sin (see comments on 1:21).

Elimelech's spiritual immaturity was likewise reflected in the decision of **his two sons**... **Mahlon and Chilion**, to "take **for themselves**" (the standard biblical idiom for the act of marriage) **Moabite women as** their **wives**. Though **Ruth**, of course, eventually became a believer of the highest caliber, the act itself was a clear violation of the Mosaic commandment in Dt 7:3 not to "intermarry with them" (i.e., the pagan residents of the land, which included Moabites per Dt 23:3). From God's perspective, the means can *never* be justified by the ends (cf., *among others*, Php 2:14-16; 2Tm 3:10-12; 1Pt 2:13-20; 5:9-10). It is against this backdrop as well that the "premature" deaths of Mahlon and Chilion should be viewed, as chastisement for their egregious and public violation of God's law.

B. Testing the Judaean Woman (1:5b-7)

1:5b-7. With the death of the men, who were the direction-setters and final decision-makers of the family, Naomi was left as the default leader of her diminished family unit, then comprised of her and **her** two Moabite **daughters-in-law**. Her first decision in this role—and one that stood in marked contrast to that of her husband's—was to arise and **return from the land of Moab**. Note the narrator's—and hence the reader's intended—perspective from *within* the promised land. Though the following causal statement, **for she had heard... that the LORD had visited His people in giving them food**, would appear to diminish from the spiritual motivation of Naomi's decision, more should not be read into this statement than is warranted. The text does not state that this was the only reason for her decision. Considering that her daughters-in-law and their families would unquestionably have provided for Naomi in Moab, she evinced a clear preference for being in Israel. Indeed, any disparagement of Naomi's spiritual maturity at this point would not only be premature, but would also be unjustified in view of her obvious sensitivity to the will and solicitude of God (who is mentioned for the first time in v. 6). This sensitivity is borne out in the ensuing narrative—beginning with her profound concern for the spiritual welfare of her **two** Moabite **daughters-in-law** who had apparently decided to return to Judah **with her**.

C. Testing the Moabite Women (1:8-18)

1:8-18. Though many scholars have considered Naomi's statements in this section to be expressions of spiritually immature complaining and unjustified bitterness, a careful reading reveals in fact just the opposite. Rather, Naomi had a keen perception of and concern with spiritual matters—specifically, a focus on the will and work of God *as well as* the spiritual welfare of her daughters-in-law. This was borne out, perhaps most significantly, by Naomi's culminating challenge at the end of each of her three rhetorical addresses to her daughters-in-law (vv. 8-9a; 11-13, and 15).

In the first instance she expressed her hope that **the LORD** would grant them **rest, each in the house of her husband**. The challenge centers on the term **rest** (*menuha*), which is employed elsewhere in the Bible to describe the *spiritual rest* (relationship with God) that one experiences through faith in the True God (cf. Ps 95:11 with Heb 4:3, as well as our comment on Gn 2:15, in which the same Hb. root is used). Such rest was therefore hardly to be found in the house of a pagan husband. In the second instance she challenged them by observing that **the hand of the LORD has gone forth against** her. That is to say, living with her will not be easy, since she was experiencing the bitter consequences of the sinful decisions of her husband and two sons. In the third instance, when Orpah had already "thrown in the towel," Naomi presented her third and most direct "challenge" to Ruth: **Behold, your sister-in-law has gone back to her people and her gods; return after your sister-in-law**—which is to say, "return to your gods"!

It is only when Ruth decisively answered this challenge and affirmed her commitment to Naomi (**where you go, I will go**...), to her people (**your people shall be my people**), and to her God (**your God, my God**), that Naomi **said no more to her** on this topic. Naomi's three appeals are thus to be understood as carefully worded expressions of *evangelistic warning*, in which—contrary to the method often practiced today—she was seeking *not* to "smooth out" the hardships entailed by conversion, but in fact to highlight them in all of their potentially unappealing detail. In this, Naomi was in quite good company, for Jesus Himself adheres to the same method, never paving the way to "easy" faith, but always making sure that the potential disciple understands the true and potentially painful cost of following Him (cf., e.g., Mt 8:18-22; Mk 13:9-13; Lk 18:18-30; Jn 10:24-26).

In this respect Ruth and Orpah also provide a vivid real-life example of two of the "seeds" of faith described by Jesus in Lk 8:4-15. The seed that "fell on rocky soil," represented by Orpah, was "those who, when they hear, receive the word [of God] with joy; and these have no firm root; they believe for a while, and in time of temptation [*peirasmou*, which is synonymous with Hb. *massa* ("test(ing)"); cf., e.g., the LXX Ex 17:7] fall away." The seed that fell into the "good soil," represented by Ruth, was "the ones who have heard the word in an honest and good heart, and hold it fast, and bear fruit with perseverance."

II. The Perseverance of Faith (1:19–4:12)

A. The Persevering of Ruth (1:19–2:18)

1:19-22. When Naomi and Ruth arrived in **Bethlehem** the **women** of the city were **stirred** up **because of them**, no doubt glad to receive Naomi back and interested as well to learn about her family's ill-motivated sojourn in Moab. After all, these women who were asking about her did not leave. The implication of Naomi's response is that the sojourn in Moab was indeed ill motivated—which is to say, that it was not just a poor decision, but also a *sin*. By this, she affirmed those women, and especially their husbands, who remained in Bethlehem. Thus Naomi's leaving the promised land (though in fact initiated by her husband Elimelech) is presented as an exclusively *human* action, i.e., ***I* went out full** (emphasis added). The exclusion of God from this decision is underscored by contrast with Naomi's reference to her bitter return, in which she presented herself as the passive recipient of an exclusively *divine* action, i.e., **but *the LORD* has brought me back empty** (emphasis added). In her mind, clearly, the "emptiness" of her return—the absence, due to death, of her husband and sons—was the result of divine chastisement for their sinful decision to leave and sojourn in **the land of Moab**.

It is unusual that **Ruth the Moabitess** should be described as having "**returned**" **from the land of Moab.** Grammatically there is no question that this expression is referring to Ruth. The same expression is also used in 2:6. The reason may well be that the same verb which here denotes a physical-locational "return" is elsewhere commonly employed to denote a spiritual "return"—which may otherwise be rendered by the English verb "(to) repent" (e.g., Is 19:22; see further Even-Shoshan, *A New Concordance*, s.v. *sh-w-b*, meaning "d"). This verb use is all the more apropos here by association with **the land of Moab**. Considering the close association in the Hebrew Bible between ethnicity/geography and religion (as in 1:15) saying that she "returned from" Moab is the same as saying she repented of *her faith in the gods of* Moab. This maintains the focus on Ruth's spiritual commitment as the basis of her perseverance in upright conduct (i.e., her "valor" as a "woman of excellence" [3:11]) as described in following verses.

2:1-18. Ruth's valor and commitment to Naomi are immediately borne out by her expressed initiative to **go to the field and glean among the ears of grain** (v. 2) so that both she and Naomi might have something to eat (cf. 2:18). This indicates Ruth's awareness (no doubt informed by Naomi) of the Mosaic commandment that the Israelites leave the gleanings of their harvest "for the needy and for the stranger" ... "for the orphan, and for the widow" (Lv 19:9-10; 23:22; Dt 24:19). This was a practical guideline for applying that "law of love" which has always stood at the heart of the law and its fulfillment (see Mt 22:39; Rm 13:8-10). Moreover, while Naomi was already an "old" woman (see 1:12; 4:15), Ruth was probably still in her early twenties, as implied by the reference to her as a **young woman** (*na'ara*) in 2:5 (and again in 4:12). The term typically denotes a woman between adolescence and her mid-twenties at the latest. That is also consistent with her having been married, per the usual custom at that time, at 12 or 13, with 10 years then passing (per 1:4) until the death of Mahlon and the commencement of the present narrative.

By apparent "coincidence," Ruth **happened to come to the portion of the field belonging to Boaz, who was of the family of Elimelech**. The significance of this is hidden from Ruth until revealed to her by Naomi in 2:20. Of course, in view of the biblical concept of divine sovereignty, this is no "coincidence" at all, for God "causes all things to work together for good to those who love God, to those who are called according to His purpose" (Rm 8:28). Divine activity is also suggested in that the same verb here translated **happened** (*vay-yiqer*, from the root *q-r-h*), which is relatively infrequent in the Bible (used 23 times), appears earlier in a clearly causative sense regarding God's active solicitude (see Gn 24:12; 27:20). Further emphasis on Ruth's persevering valor is borne out by her day-long, tireless gleaning (v. 7: **she came and has remained from** [lit., "been on her feet since"] **the morning** . . . [and] **she has been sitting** [i.e., taken her rest] **in the house for a little while**; v. 17: **So she gleaned . . . until evening**), her humble gratitude for Boaz's unmerited favor; (v. 13: **I have found favor in your sight, my lord . . . though I am not like one of your maidservants**), and her conscientiousness in setting aside some of *her own* food for Naomi (v. 14: **she ate and was satisfied and** set some aside [*not*, as this grammatically *active* expression is sometimes translated: "and had some left over"]).

B. The Persevering of Naomi (2:19–3:4)

2:19-23. Naomi kept a persevering focus on the will and ongoing work of God, *despite* her suffering brought into her life through the chastening of her husband and her sons (see comment on 1:1-5a). This focus is evident from her immediate reaction when Ruth told her that **the name of the man** in whose field she **worked** was **Boaz**. Naomi declared in worship, **May he be blessed of the Lord, who has not withdrawn his kindness** [Hb. *chesed*, see Introduction] **to the living and to the dead**. She then explained to Ruth: **the man is our relative, he is one of our closest relatives** [lit., kinsman-redeemers]. Naomi could only mean by this that God specifically and providentially directed Ruth to the field of Boaz so that Boaz might get to know her and ultimately marry her as her kinsman-redeemer. God's provision of this marriage would thus be His *chesed* **to the living**, meaning Ruth and Naomi, by ensuring the two women would be cared for by Boaz for the rest of their lives, **and to the dead**, meaning Elimelech and Mahlon, by ensuring that, per the law of the kinsman-redeemer (i.e., "levirate" marriage; see Dt 25:5-6), the "name" (i.e., reputation and inheritance) of Mahlon (and hence Elimelech) would endure in the couple's first-born son (see Introduction).

3:1-4. In dogged allegiance to God's will, and realizing that Boaz may need some encouragement, Naomi counseled Ruth about the best way, consistent with righteousness, of making known to Boaz her desire that he marry her. Boaz was either a widower himself or—as seems more likely—never married. He may have been waiting for a righteous woman in an age when unrighteousness among God's people was rampant. Thus she told Ruth to **wash** herself (since she had been working in the field all day), **anoint** herself (i.e., to perfume herself), **and put on** her **best clothes. Then** Boaz would understand immediately what Ruth intended and, taking her lead, would **tell** her **what** she should **do**. Naomi's counsel, it should be pointed out, makes clear that the apostle Peter's exhortation in 1Pt 3:3-5 is against the unbalanced *prioritization* of such things, not their complete exclusion, especially since Peter would unquestionably have counted Ruth among "the holy women" of "former times" whom he cited as examples.

C. The Persevering of Boaz (3:5–4:12)

3:5-18. Ruth obediently prepared herself **according to all that her mother-in-law had commanded her**. After Boaz **had eaten** and found a quiet, isolated spot by **the heap of grain** in which to lie down and sleep, **she** came **secretly** (i.e., with *discretion*, not deception, to avoid giving fodder for slander to anyone who might see her and misconstrue her intentions—and perhaps those of Boaz. She **uncovered his feet** (v. 7), which was intended as a gentle way of waking him up. As the night breeze blew over his exposed feet he "shivered and twisted" (as the verbs in v. 8 are literally rendered, rather than the NASB: **was startled and bent forward**). Although some have claimed that uncovering Boaz's feet was a sexual act, there was no hint of immorality here. Boaz greeted her in the name of **the Lord** (3:10), called her **a woman of excellence** (or "virtue," i.e., godly character; 3:11), protected her through the night (3:13), and guarded her reputation in the morning (3:14).

When Boaz awoke Ruth immediately identified herself and made her intentions clear with the simple, direct plea: **Spread your covering** (lit., "wing," on which see below) **over your maid, for you are a** kinsman-redeemer (*go'el*, not simply **close relative**, as in some translations; see Introduction.) While Ruth's godly character was already well established in the narrative, here it was explicitly affirmed by Boaz: **all my people in the city know that you are a woman of excellence**. This is the same expression used to introduce the ideal *godly* woman in Pr 31:10 (see Introduction).

Her simple plea seems to have considered the all-pervasive male (and husbandly!) desire for respect (Eph 5:33; 1Pt 3:2; Est 1:20): (1) She employed the same phraseology that Boaz employed in his previous affirmation of her spiritual commitment (see 2:12, finding refuge under "the wing of"; and the same image employed by their great-grandson David in Pss. 36:7 [Heb 8] and 91:4), thus showing that she was thoughtfully attentive to what he would say. (2) Though she was in fact the initiator, she expressed her plea in such a way as to emphasize Boaz as the subject (i.e., the "doer" of the action) and herself as the object (i.e., the "receiver" of the action). For his part, Boaz immediately took Ruth's lead and, just as Naomi said would happen, he told her exactly what to do: wait until dawn and then return to Naomi while he sought to bring the matter to its conclusion in the **morning**.

4:1-12. Just as he said he would, and as anticipated by Naomi in 3:18, Boaz doggedly pursued the matter of Ruth's marriage. On the following day, Boaz went **to the gate** of the city, where most matters of civic and juridical importance were conducted (cf. Gn 23:10; 34:20; Dt 21:19; Jos 20:4). There he gathered together the "kinsman-redeemer" (*go'el*, again, not simply "close relative") who was "closer" than Boaz (and hence had first right to marry Ruth; see 3:12) and the minimum of **ten men of the elders of the city** to witness and affirm the "transaction" officially. It is from this key passage, among others (i.e., Gn 18:32, the ten "righteous men" petitioned by Abraham; Gn 42:3, the ten brothers who go down to Egypt; Nm 14:27, concerning the ten "grumbling" spies), that the Jewish rule of the *minyan* ("quorum") is derived. That rule requires a minimum of ten men for congregational prayer and other important religious ceremonies (cf. Joseph b. Judah ibn Aqnin [d. 1226], *Sefer ha-musar*, on *Abot* chap. 5; *Yalqut shi moni ad loc.*; etc.).

Boaz then presented the matter by referring first to Elimelech's (and now Naomi's) **piece of land** to be redeemed (v. 3-4a), and *secondarily* to the necessary redemption of Ruth that this would entail. At first sight this may seem unusual, since this emphasis on the acquisition of land was clearly attractive to the other man, which is why he initially responded, **I will redeem it** (v. 4b). In this, Boaz—as an expression of his spiritual maturity and godliness—was doing *in principle* the same thing that Naomi did with her daughters-in-law in chap. 1. He was expressing himself in a way that, though contrary to his own desire, reflected a greater concern *for the welfare of his neighbor* than himself. Naomi, who undoubtedly desired to have both of her beloved daughters-in-law continually with her, sought to dissuade them from returning with her so as to ensure that their commitment would be solid and true (see comment on 1:5b-7). So too Boaz, who clearly desired to marry Ruth himself, was presenting his offer in such a way that the offer of redemption would be more attractive. Following the other man's initial acceptance, it would be harder for him to withdraw. To forfeit his right to Ruth and the land would not just be to the man's material and marital detriment, but also to his social and spiritual detriment; see consequence of such forfeiture in Dt 25:7-10. Nonetheless, when this other kinsman-redeemer learned that he would also be required to redeem (i.e., marry) Ruth along with the land, he withdrew his acceptance and forfeited his right of redemption to Boaz.

Though some commentators seek to excuse this other man's rejection by claiming that he was already married and was seeking to avoid strife between multiple wives and/or heirs, nowhere does the text say that the man was in fact married. Indeed, his explicit reason for rejecting the marriage to Ruth was that he did not want to **jeopardize** his **own inheritance** (v. 6). The word **jeopardize** (*ashhit*, from the root *sh-h-t*) means literally "(to) *corrupt* or *pollute*" (often in connection with sin, as in Gn 6:12; Dt 31:29). His point was that to marry and have children by Ruth would be to "pollute" his seed and their inheritance by ethnic association with a Moabite. His position reflected, perhaps, an ill-motivated interpretation according to the *letter*, not the *intent* (which was to prevent spiritual contamination), of God's command in Dt 7:3-4. This man, in other words, was holding Ruth's ethnic heritage over her proven commitment to the LORD and His people (which he, as one of all the people in the city [3:11], was undoubtedly familiar with)—an example of true racism! It is for this reason, his refusal to perform the Mosaic duty of a kinsman-redeemer and **raise up the name of the deceased on his inheritance** (v. 5), that this man's own name has been forever omitted from the record of this event in Scripture.

III. The Reward of Faith (4:13-22)

A. The Rewarding of Ruth (4:13)

4:13. As a result of her spiritual commitment and perseverance in godliness, including her obedience to Naomi's counsel in 3:3-4, Ruth experienced three additional blessings: (1) She was taken as the **wife** of a godly man. In 2:1 Boaz, was described as a *gibbor hayil*, representing the masculine counterpart of the expression *eshet hayil* ["woman of valor"] applied to Ruth in 3:11 (see comment there). He would ensure not only that her (and Naomi's) physical needs were supplied, but also her spiritual needs by instructing and nurturing her in righteousness (cf. 1Co 14:35; Eph 5:26). (2) Once married to Boaz, she was **enabled** by God **to conceive** (lit., "the LORD granted her conception"), in contrast with her inability to conceive (i.e., God withholding conception) during her 10 years of marriage to Mahlon (see 1:4; on children as a divine "gift/inheritance" see Ps 127:3). (3) Her conception, specifically of **a son**, was of especial importance in biblical culture since it was the son(s) who would sustain the parents in their old age, as explicitly noted in v. 15.

B. The Rewarding of Naomi (4:14-17)

4:14-17. As a result of her persevering focus on the will and work of God, and her attendant counsel to Ruth in 3:3-4, Naomi enjoyed the blessing of having a **daughter-in-law who love[d]** her and was **better to [her] than seven sons**. She was further blessed by the birth of a grandson who would **be to** her **a restorer of life** (lit., "restorer of soul" [*meshiv nefesh*], the same expression David used in Pss 19:7; 23:3; 35:17) and her **sustainer** in **old age**. Even more, she **became** the boy's **nurse** (*omenet*)—a term that could indicate that Naomi nursed the child by actual lactation (possible even in post-menopausal women), but better construed here in the sense of "guardian/rearer" (like the equivalent masculine term, *omen*, applied to Mordecai in Est 2:7). This is still the case with grandparents in many (especially Eastern) cultures to this day. Therefore, Naomi played a central role, together with the parents, in the daily upbringing of her grandchild. The child's name **Obed** (Hb. *'Oved*), which means "Servant," is in all likelihood a shorter form of the name Obadiah (Hb. *'Ovadya[hu]*), meaning "Servant of Yah" or "the LORD."

C. The Rewarding of Boaz (4:18-22)

4:18-22. The blessings Boaz experienced paralleled those Ruth experienced: (1) receiving a godly woman (*eshet hayil*) for his wife, (2) having Ruth bear him a child, and (3) that child being a son. This last blessing entailed the further distinction for Boaz of ensuring him an enduring "name" in the genealogy (typically delineated through the male ancestors) of **David** (v. 17; the link to whom is clearly specified in vv. 18-22) and ultimately therefore of the Messiah Himself. This distinction is also borne out more subtly by the phrase that introduces this brief genealogy, including Boaz: "these are the generations of" (*elleh toledot*). This is the 12th occurrence and the *only* occurrence outside of the Pentateuch. There, this phrase applies primarily to those "generations" on which God's promises and plan of messianic redemption are focused (i.e., those of Adam, Gn 5:1; Noah, Gn 6:9; Shem, Gn 11:10; Terah, Gn 11:27; Isaac, Gn 25:19; Jacob, Gn 37:2; Moses and Aaron, Nm 3:1).

The conclusion with a genealogy is not an authorial afterthought but rather a significant point. It establishes the lineage of David, the ideal king of Israel, and provides the foundation for the Messianic line. It is a reminder that although Ruth, Naomi, and Boaz anticipated the birth of Obed with joy and expectation, Israel would have to wait for the Son of David, Israel's ultimate Redeemer, foreshadowed by Boaz, to bring redemption for the nation.

BIBLIOGRAPHY

Atkinson, David. *The Message of Ruth: The Wings of Refuge*. The Bible Speaks Today. Edited by J. A. Motyer. Downers Grove, IL: InterVarsity, 1985.

Block, Daniel I. *Judges, Ruth*. New American Commentary. Nashville: Broadman & Holman, 1999.

Bush, Frederic W. *Ruth, Esther*. Vol. 9 of Word Biblical Commentary. Dallas: Word Books, 1996.

Duguid, Iain. *Esther & Ruth*. Reformed Expository Commentary. Phillipsburg, NJ: P&R Publishing, 2005.

Franke, John R., ed. *Joshua, Judges, Ruth, 1–2 Samuel*. Vol. 4 of Ancient Christian Commentary on Scripture: Old Testament. Downers Grove, IL: InterVarsity, 2005.

Hubbard, Robert L. *The Book of Ruth*. New International Commentary on the Old Testament. Grand Rapids, MI: Eerdmans, 1988.

Huey, F. B. "[Commentary on] Ruth." Vol. 3 of The Expositor's Bible Commentary. Edited by Frank E. Gaebelein, et al., 509–549. Grand Rapids, MI: Zondervan, 1992.

Keil, C. F. and F. Delitzsch. *Joshua, Judges, Ruth*. Vol. 4 of Biblical Commentary on the Old Testament. Trans. by James Martin. Edinburgh: T & T Clark, 1865. Reprint. Grand Rapids, MI: Eerdmans, 1956.

Lewis, Arthur. *Judges and Ruth*. Everyman's Bible Commentary. Chicago: Moody, 1979.

Reed, John W. "Ruth." Vol. 1 of The Bible Knowledge Commentary, Edited by John F. Walvoord and Roy B. Zuck, 415–429. Wheaton, IL: Victor Books, 1985.

Younger, K. Lawson, Jr. *Judges and Ruth*. NIV Application Commentary. Grand Rapids, MI: Zondervan, 2002.

1 SAMUEL

WINFRED O. NEELY

INTRODUCTION TO 1 AND 2 SAMUEL

In the Hebrew Bible the title of 1 and 2 Samuel is simply "Samuel." This one book was named "Samuel" because he was the dominant person in the early chapters, and he anointed the first two kings of Israel, Saul and David. When the OT was first translated into Greek, the scrolls available at the time did not have enough space to include the contents of all of Samuel. Therefore the book was divided into two books in our English Bibles. Of course, the present division is not a problem; in no way does it affect the divine inspiration of these accounts. Still, one should keep in mind that these two books are one account, and they should be read and studied as such.

Author. Even though the title of the book is "Samuel," Samuel was not the author. The human author is unknown. Evidence from Samuel implies that the account was written not long after Israel was divided into the northern kingdom of Israel and the southern kingdom of Judah (cf. 1Kg 12; 1Sm 6:18, 9:9, 27:6).

Apparently the Holy Spirit led the author/narrator to consult sources such as the Book of Jashar (2Sm 1:18), and those described as "the acts of King David, from first to last . . . written in the chronicles of Samuel the seer, in the chronicles of Nathan the prophet and in the chronicles of Gad the seer" (cf. 1Ch. 29:29). Although the books are anonymous and therefore the human author of 1 and 2 Samuel is unknown, it is known that the divine author is the Lord.

Date. The date of the writing of 1 and 2 Samuel cannot be fixed with absolute certainty. The Talmud incorrectly identifies Samuel as the author of the books that bear his name. This, along with "eyewitness" accounts and "general antiquity of linguistic features" have caused the unlikely suggestion that the material was written either "during David's day or shortly thereafter (c. 1025–900 BC)" (J. Carl Laney, *First and Second Samuel* [Chicago: Moody, 1982], 8). But the reference in 1Sm 27:6 to the kings of Judah suggests that it was written after the division of the kingdom (about 930 BC). Further, the author did not mention the fall of the northern kingdom of Israel to Assyria in 722 BC, which he surely would not have ignored in his writing, which makes it likely that the books were written before that date. Thus, "some [date] the books' composition between 930 and 723/22 BC" (David M. Howard, Jr., *An Introduction to the Old Testament Historical Books* [Chicago: Moody, 1993], 145).

Purpose. These books were written to encourage people living in Judah at the time of the divided kingdom to walk with the Lord in bold faith and to honor Him in all circumstances. The narrator's objective was to see them shun and reject evil choices, the choices of unbelief and disobedience, bad choices that leave devastating consequences in their wake. To see this purpose achieved, the narrator regarded the lives of people such as Hannah, Samuel, Saul, Jonathan, David, and others.

His purpose however, was not merely to share information but to see more Samuels, Davids, Hannahs, Abigails, and mighty men and women raised up in Israel as a result of their faith. Laney says: "The biblical record of Israel's beginnings as a political nation are masterfully recorded to give us not only an accurate historical document, but also to present significant spiritual lessons concerning the effects of sin, the workings of the Holy Spirit, and the sovereignty of God" (Laney, *First and Second Samuel*, 7).

The most significant purpose of 1 and 2 Samuel is to point to the ultimate Son of David, the

Messiah, using David as the central character. The story of Samuel was included since he was the prophet who anointed kings. Saul's story was included as a foil, an example of a king not after the heart of God, unlike David. David's story is central to both books, showing him develop from shepherd boy, to warrior, to fugitive, to king, to failure, to exile, to restoration as king. He is depicted as the ideal king. Central to his entire story is that God promised to give Him a descendant with an eternal house, kingdom, and throne (2Sm 7:12-16). This promise, called the Davidic covenant, is essential to the book, because it is the Messiah who will reign as the eternal king.

Background. The historical setting of 1 and 2 Samuel is the sunset of the judges period embodied in Samuel and the dawn of the theocratic monarchy embodied in Saul and David. Samuel, one of the greatest prophets since Moses, served as the last of the judges and facilitated the transition from the judgeship to the monarchy. The period of time covered in 1 and 2 Samuel cannot be stated with precision, but it covers approximately 150 years. If one estimates the time of the events of Hannah's experiences in 1Sm 1 to be about 10 years, and notes that Samuel was old (1Sm 8:1) when he anointed Saul as king (60–65 years of age?), and takes into consideration the 40-year reigns of Saul and David, David's reign ending with his death in 970 BC, one has an estimated time span of 150 years from about 1120 BC to 970 BC.

The genre of 1 and 2 Samuel is historical narrative, that is, a recounting of historical facts from the Lord's perspective, related and relived in the form of a story for the purpose of instruction. The books belong to the part of the canon designated as the historical books. Baldwin states: "The books of Samuel are the product of highly developed literary art . . . purposefully selective . . . intending to engage the reader in an active relationship with the text" (Joyce G. Baldwin, *1 and 2 Samuel*, TOTC, edited by D. J. Wiseman [Downers Grove, IL: InterVarsity, 1988], 16].

The narrator recounted the history from God's point of view. Since the Lord is the ultimate author of the account, the narrator's perspective is the perspective of the Lord Himself.

The narrator is a skilled storyteller. One can hardly overestimate the incredible literary skill and subtlety of the narrator/storyteller of 1 and 2 Samuel. His skillful use of irony, humor, flashback, and dramatic tension and resolution is astounding.

The narrative demands our imaginative participation in the events themselves, thus helping us see how our own story by God's grace can fit into and is a part of the big story of redemption.

Unforgettable characters, real people, dot the narrative landscape. The narrator devotes many chapters to David. Next to Moses, no other person captured Israel's imagination like David, Israel's greatest king, the measure by whom all subsequent kings were evaluated. He was a man after God's own heart, and yet the Spirit of God did not hide his terrible sin recounted in 2Sm 11. More than anyone else, the Lord is met in 1 and 2 Samuel by the reader. First and 2 Samuel are truly His story, as is all of Scripture.

OUTLINE

I. Samuel: The Son of Hannah's Vows (1:1–7:17)
  A. The Lord Grants Hannah's Request (1:1–2:11)
    1. Hannah's Prayer and Vow (1:1-28)
    2. Hannah's Joyful Prayer of Praise and Celebration (2:1-11)
  B. Eli's Sons and Samuel (2:12-36)
    1. The Great Sin of Eli's Sons (2:12-17)
    2. Eli's Sons in Contrast to Samuel (2:18-36)
  C. The Boy Who Became the Prophet (3:1-21)
    1. The Lord Called Samuel (3:1-9)
    2. The Lord Spoke to Samuel (3:10-14)
    3. Samuel Makes Known the Lord's Word to Eli (3:15-18)
    4. The Growth of Samuel (3:19-21)
  D. The Danger of Trying to Manipulate God (4:1-22)
    1. The Misuse of the Ark in Battle (4:1-4)

a. The Lord Looks at the Heart (16:1-13)
b. David Serves in the Court of Saul (16:14-23)
2. David's Victory over Goliath (17:1-58)
a. Forty Days of Defiance (17:1-11)
b. David's Visit to the Battlefront (17:12-19)
c. David Answers Goliath's Challenge (17:20-30)
d. David Kills Goliath (17:31-58)
3. Responses to David's Godly Success (18:1-30)
a. Godly Covenant Friendship and Love (18:1-5)
b. Saul's Murderous Envy and Suspicion (18:6-9)
c. Demonic Influence on Saul (18:10-11)
d. Fear and Manipulation (18:12-19)
e. A Grisly Dowry (18:20-30)
4. Four Examples of David's Divine Protection (19:1-24)
a. The Lord Uses Jonathan to Protect David (19:1-7)
b. The Lord Uses Saul's Miss to Protect David (19:8-10)
c. The Lord Uses Michal to Protect David (19:11-17)
d. The Lord Uses His Own Spirit to Protect David (19:18-24)
5. Covenant Friendship Put to the Test (20:1-42)
a. One Step between Life and Death (20:1-11)
b. The Covenant in the Field (20:12-17)
c. The Coded Message in the Arrows (20:18-23)
d. Missed at the King's Table (20:24-29)
e. The Unveiling of True Intentions (20:30-34)
f. The Parting of Friends (20:35-42)
B. David, a Fugitive from Saul's Court (21:1–31:13)
1. A Hungry, Weaponless, and Scared Fugitive (21:1-15)
a. Eating the Consecrated Bread (21:1-7)
b. David Receives Goliath's Sword (21:8-9)
c. David's Convincing Performance (21:10-15)
2. The Cave of Adullam and the Priests of Nob (22:1-23)
a. Joining David at the Cave of Adullam (22:1-2)
b. Protection for David's Parents in Mizpah of Moab (22:3-4)
c. Leaving the Stronghold for the Forest of Hereth (22:5)
d. Saul's Complaints under the Tamarisk Tree (22:6-10)
e. Saul's Revenge on the Priests of the Lord (22:11-23)
3. The Faithful God and Unfaithful People (23:1-28)
a. David's Deliverance of Keilah (23:1-5)
b. The Unfaithful People of Keilah (23:6-14)
c. Encouragement from a Friend (23:15-18)
d. The Rock of Escape (23:19-28)
4. David Compassionately Spares Saul (23:29–24:22)
a. David Cuts off a Corner of Saul's Garment (23:29–24:7)
b. David Presents Evidence of Compassion (24:8-15)
c. Saul Responds to David's Mercy (24:16-22)
5. Listening to the Wisdom of a Wise Woman (25:1-44)
a. Samuel Dies (25:1)
b. The Introduction of Nabal and Abigail (25:2-3)
c. Nabal Shows Contempt for David and His Men (25:4-13)
d. Abigail Wisely Intervenes (25:14-35)
e. The Lord Strikes Nabal (25:36-38)
f. David Marries Abigail (25:39-44)
6. David Spares Saul Again (26:1-25)
a. Saul Pursues David Again (26:1-5)

b. David Finds Saul Sound Asleep (26:6-12)
c. David Calls to the King's Men (26:13-16)
d. David Addresses Saul (26:17-20)
e. David Displays the King's Spear (26:21-25)

7. David Takes Refuge among the Philistines (27:1-12)
a. David Crosses over to Achish Again (27:1-4)
b. David Spends 16 Months in Gath (27:5-7)
c. David Undertakes Covert Operations (27:8-12)

8. Saul and the Medium of En-dor (28:1-25)
a. David's Dilemma (28:1-2)
b. Saul's Dilemma (28:3)
c. A New Low in Saul's Life (28:4-25)

9. The Providential Philistine Rescue of David (29:1-11)
a. The Philistines' Mistrust of David (29:1-5)
b. An Honorable Discharge (29:6-11)

10. David Strengthens Himself in the Lord (30:1-31)
a. The Amalekites Raid Ziklag (30:1-10)
b. An Unexpected Source of Information (30:11-15)
c. David Recovers All that Was Taken (30:16-20)
d. David Shares the Spoils (30:21-31)

11. Saul and His Sons are Slain (31:1-13)
a. Saul Commits Suicide (31:1-7)
b. The Philistines Find Saul and His Sons (31:8-10)
c. The Men of Jabesh-gilead Show Courage and Gratitude (31:11-13)

COMMENTARY ON 1 SAMUEL

I. Samuel: The Son of Hannah's Vows (1:1–7:17)

Samuel is the principal figure in the first eight chapters of 1 Samuel. His mother, Hannah, asked for a son in prayer, and the Lord's answer was Samuel. Most commentators agree that David was the central character in the books of Samuel. Still, the events of these opening chapters, especially Hannah's request for a son, may have been included, as Baldwin suggests, because Hannah's request "was in line with the overarching will of God, who was preparing to bring into the world a man who would be his faithful representative and mouthpiece" (Baldwin, *1 and 2 Samuel*, 50). It also may have been important to demonstrate Samuel's Levitical descent (1:1), since he served as a priest as well as prophet and judge (Laney, *First and Second Samuel*, 16). Samuel's priestly function was clear in his instructions to Saul: "And you shall go down before me to Gilgal; and behold, I will come down to you to offer burnt offerings and sacrifice peace offerings" (1Sm 10:8). The narrative about Samuel's birth established his credential to anoint kings, specifically Saul (who failed as king) and then David (who became the ideal king).

A. The Lord Grants Hannah's Request (1:1–2:11)

1. Hannah's Prayer and Vow (1:1-28)

1:1-2. Elkanah, whose name means "God created," is mentioned first. **Ramathaim-zophim** is a longer form of **Ramah** (cf. 1:19; 2:11; 7:17). Ramah means "height" or "elevation"; Ramathaim means "two heights." In ancient Israel people built cities on hills for protection and security. The city of Ramah, about seven miles northeast of Jerusalem, was built on two adjacent heights or hills. Since it was one city, it was called Ramah; since the city was built on two adjacent hills, it was called **Ramathaim** (1:1).

Elkanah had two wives, **Hannah** ("grace") and **Peninnah** ("pearl"). The order of mention suggests that Hannah was his first wife and Peninnah the second. Hannah, the first wife, had a respectable prominence that Peninnah did not share.

Hannah, however, had experienced maternal tragedy; she could not have children. In the ancient world a woman's ability to have children, especially to provide her husband with a male heir to continue his name, was considered an expression of God's blessing (cf. Gn 16:1-16; 21:1-8; Ps 127:3-5). The narrator did not give the reason for the second marriage, but Elkanah probably did it to be sure he had a male heir.

In the OT the Lord permitted bigamy and polygamy, but these practices never received His sanction. Merrill says that Elkanah's bigamy was "one indication of how lawless were the times in which Samuel was born" (Eugene H. Merrill, "1 Samuel," *BKCOT* [Wheaton, IL: Victor Books, 1985], 433). Some commentators say a second marriage was allowed in the case of a childless first marriage—which was Elkanah's situation—but bigamy and polygamy were still clear violations of God's standard for marriage, which is one man and one woman for life (cf. Gn 2:18-25). Youngblood notes, "although polygamy is never explicitly condemned in Scripture, its complications and unsavory results are everywhere apparent" (Ronald F. Youngblood, "1, 2 Samuel" in *EBC*, rev. ed., edited by Tremper Longman, III and David E. Garland [Grand Rapids, MI: Zondervan, 2009], 45).

1:3. Even though he had two wives, Elkanah feared the Lord. Every year he went to Shiloh (about 25 miles northwest of the Dead Sea) to worship and sacrifice to the Lord. Males in Israel were required to go up to the place the Lord had chosen (whether at the tabernacle in Shiloh or later at the temple in Jerusalem) to participate in three annual feasts: the Feast of Unleavened Bread, the Feast of Weeks, and the Feast of Booths (cf. Ex 23:14-17, 34:23; Dt 16:16-17). Perhaps Elkanah's annual pilgrimage was in connection with one of the annual feasts. At that time, the central sanctuary for worship (the tabernacle) and the annual celebrations were in Shiloh.

1:4-5. Elkanah's family accompanied him to Shiloh. The annual worship was a time of celebration before the Lord. The worshiper offered his sacrifices to the Lord and shared in the peace offering along with his family. As the head of his family, Elkanah distributed portions of the offering to Peninnah and her children, but he gave Hannah a double portion of the sacrifice, showing his love and his sensitivity to her maternal plight: **the Lord had closed her womb** (v. 5). Hannah's infertility was not merely a biological weakness; it was also the direct result of God's sovereignty.

1:6. Elkanah valued Peninnah because of her fertility, but he loved Hannah. And as might be expected in a bigamous household, Peninnah envied Hannah. As her rival, she troubled Hannah. Every year Peninnah took advantage of the annual family worship celebration to provoke Hannah, slinging the mud of her barrenness in her face.

1:7-8. Hannah endured emotional trouble in her family for years. On this last occasion she wept and refused to eat. Refusing to eat on the occasion of the annual feast was like someone refusing to eat Thanksgiving dinner with the family. Elkanah attempted to comfort Hannah, but Hannah's pain was beyond his sympathetic reach.

1:9-10. Eli the priest was sitting on a seat by the temple's doorpost when Hannah came to pray for a child. A seat was a place of honor and authority in a society where most people sat on the ground. In the ancient world a temple was the residence of a king. In Israel the temple was the Lord's earthly residence. The temple in Jerusalem was built during Solomon's reign, but **temple** here was applied to the tabernacle and the temporary structures built up around it. The words **greatly distressed** literally mean "bitter of soul." Bitterness of soul is mental and emotional anguish due to suffering and pain. Hannah's soul bitterness drove her to prayer.

1:11. Distressed Hannah prayed, making a **vow**. A vow is a promise made to the Lord as an act of worship. Vowing is not compulsory in worship. The making of a vow, however, is a serious matter. Once a person makes a vow, the Lord demands that the vow be honored (cf. Dt 23:21-23; Ps 50:14; Pr 31:2; Ac 18:18). Hannah is the only woman in the Bible who is said to have made a vow to the Lord.

Hannah addressed God as the **Lord of hosts**. The first time God is called by this particular title in Scripture is in 1Sm 1:3. It is a declaration of the Lord's power; the NIV translates the term **hosts** as "Almighty." The **hosts** are armies consisting of angels, the stars, and redeemed people. The title implies that God has resources of infinite power that can never be exhausted. Hannah's prayer demonstrates her understanding of God's ability to open her womb and give her a child. The Lord of hosts was concerned about her, an obscure, afflicted woman. Hannah identified herself as the Lord's **maidservant**, an expression of her humility before the Lord, and then she asked God to **remember** her. God remembering a person means that He will act in a special way on that person's behalf. If her request for a son was granted, she promised to dedicate him to the Lord all the days of his life.

Hannah's words **a razor shall never come on his head** bring to mind the Nazirite vow (cf. Nm 6:1-21). The phrase **all the days of his life** suggests that Samuel was to be a lifelong Nazirite (Robert D. Bergen, *1, 2 Samuel*, NAC [Nashville: Broadman & Holman, 1996], 69), although Tsumura notes that the Nazirite vow was normally temporary (David Toshio Tsumura, *The First Book of Samuel*, NICOT [Grand Rapids, MI: Eerdmans, 2007], 118).

When a person made a Nazirite vow, during the time stipulated in the vow he did not cut his hair. As Baldwin notes, the Nazirite's uncut hair would be a sign to all that he was consecrated, set apart, to the Lord (Baldwin, *1 and 2 Samuel*, 52). Then when the time period stipulated in the vow ended, the person cut his hair. Yet Hannah promised to give her son to the Lord, not for a specified period of time, but for all his life. The razor never coming on his head symbolized lifelong consecration. Hannah understood that walking with God means receiving from Him and giving back to Him as well.

1:12-16. As Hannah was pouring out her soul to the Lord, Eli sat, observing her. Hannah's prayer was not audible, but as Eli saw her lips silently forming her prayer, he incorrectly concluded that she was drunk.

1:17-18. Eli offered her a word of encouragement: **May the God of Israel grant your petition that you have asked of Him**. Then she ate and she was no longer sad. Her circumstances were the same, but her discouragement evaporated. Hannah's joy transformed her face.

1:19-20. Elkanah had sexual relations with Hannah **and the Lord remembered her**. In the biblical world names were more than simply a way of identifying a person. They were summary statements of a person's character or summary statements of God's work in a person's life, a means of pointing to some aspect of God's person or saving work. Hannah named her son **Samuel**, saying, **because I have asked him of the Lord**. The context implies that his name means "asked of God" (cf. vv. 17, 20, 27-28).

1:21-23. The following year Elkanah went up to Shiloh to worship, but Hannah did not go. She wanted to wean Samuel first before she left him in Shiloh. In those days mothers did not have resources such as baby formula to feed their babies. Therefore, breast-feeding was common, sometimes until their children were five years old.

1:24-28. The moment of promise-keeping arrived. Hannah took Samuel to Shiloh, leaving him in Eli's care. Hannah used the oath formula **As your soul lives, my lord**, to underscore that she was the woman who prayed in Eli's presence several years before. Samuel was the son of Hannah's prayers and vows. The boy was given to the Lord, not to Eli. The parting must have been a painful experience for Hannah, but she honored her commitment. The text does not specify who worshiped at the end of v. 28. Laney suggests that **he** refers to Elkanah (*First and Second Samuel*, 19), who was present at Samuel's presentation to Eli. The worshiper may also have been Samuel himself, even though he was probably no more than three years old. He was clearly an unusual child, and the text says the boy ministered to the Lord (2:11; cf. 2:21; 3:1).

2. Hannah's Joyful Prayer of Praise and Celebration (2:1-11)

2:1. Verses 1-10 move from prose to poetry. Some emotions and thoughts require the elevated language of poetry for adequate expression. This is the first poem in the book. It serves as an opening poetic bracket of 1 and 2 Samuel, and the closing poetic bracket is in 2Sm 22–23. Hannah's prayer may have been made as her personal testimony to God's power in hearing and answering her petition, (Laney, *First and Second Samuel*, 19-20). If so, her testimony would fit with the author/narrator's purpose of encouraging the people of the divided kingdom to walk with the Lord in bold faith and trust Him in all circumstances (see the discussion in the introduction). Mary also quoted from Hannah's prayer in her *Magnificat* (cf. Lk 1:46-55).

Reflecting on the Lord's goodness to her, **Hannah prayed**. Verses 2-10 are the content of her prayer. Hannah's prayer is a wonderful example of prayer as praise and celebration. Her gratitude was personal—**my heart . . . my horn . . . my mouth** (v. 1). The Lord, not Samuel, was the supreme source of her joy. **Horn** symbolizes God's strength and dignity (cf. Pss 18:2; 92:10). She was delivered from disgrace and elevated to a place of honor. Delighting in the Lord's salvation, Hannah spoke against her enemies. They were also God's enemies because they attacked her trust in the Lord (v. 2).

2:2-3. Hannah twice stated **there is no one** and added **nor is there any** to stress the Lord's incomparable holiness (cf. Ex. 15:11; Lv 11:44-45), uniqueness (cf. Ex 15:11), and unrivalled strength as His people's rock (cf. Dt 32:4). The rock metaphor is common in the OT, picturing God as His people's refuge and protection (which a rock fortress would provide), and stability (as a solid foundation for a building) (cf. Dt 32:15, 18; 2Sm 22:47). Arrogant human boasting is out of place in the presence of the incomparable God because He is omniscient, and He sees man's heart and motivations and weighs actions in the scales of infinite justice.

2:4-5. The Lord reverses circumstances. The climax of reversal is exactly what Hannah herself had experienced: **Even the barren gives birth to seven**. Hannah eventually gave birth to six children, but seven is the number of completeness, signifying her life's complete reversal. Peninnah had many children, but she disappeared from history.

2:6-9. Baldwin calls v. 6 "the most surprising couplet of all" because it "envisages the Lord bringing people back to life from the realm of the dead" (*1 and 2 Samuel*, 57). The word **Sheol** is often translated "the grave," but it can also refer to the realm of the dead, the abode of departed spirits (Youngblood, "1, 2 Samuel," 58). As Laney points out, "Sheol can also be used in a more technical sense of the place of punishment for the wicked dead awaiting resurrection and final judgment (cf. Nm 16:33; Jb 24:19; Ps 30:9; Is 38:18). In this latter sense it would be the equivalent of 'Hades' in the New Testament" (*First and Second Samuel*, 20).

Hannah also spoke of God lifting **the needy from the ash heap** (v. 8). In the ancient Near East the **ash heap** was the garbage dump outside the city gates. There people disposed of garbage, refuse, and animal wastes. It was the haunt of dogs, and people with incurable maladies. Sitting at a garbage dump was a sign of distress, pain, shame, and deep need (cf. Jb 2:7-8; Lm 4:5). Hannah also rejoiced because the Lord is able to lift the needy from the ash heap to **a seat of honor** when that is His sovereign choice. God can do this because the earth's pillars belong to Him. A pillar is a metaphor for stability and support. The Lord stabilizes the earth. The word for **godly ones** (Hb. *hasidim*) means "one who is in covenant relationship with God" and is an object of the Lord's covenant love (Hb. *chesed*). In contrast the wicked are reduced to silence in the darkness of a lost eternity. Victory in life is not the product of human strength.

2:10-11. Hannah's song ends on a prophetic note. At this time in Israel's history they did not have a king. But Hannah had insight into God's purpose. God will **exalt the horn of His anointed**. This is the first time **His anointed** (Messiah; Hb. *meshiach*) is mentioned in the Bible in connection with the king. Hannah's words point prophetically not merely to the Davidic dynasty, but to David's greatest son, the Lord Jesus the Messiah. She likely knew the prophecies of Gn 49:10 or Nm 24:17, both of which prophesy the coming of the messianic King in Israel. Moreover, the coming of this King is central to the message of the books of Samuel (2Sm 7:12-16). This same expectation of the Messiah continued to thrive in the exilic and postexilic periods (Dn 7:13-14; 9:24-27; Hg 2:20-23; Zch 6:11-15; 9:9; 12:10; Mal 4:4-5). The poem ends with a reference to **the horn** and begins with a reference to "My horn" (v. 1). With her song ended, Hannah went home with Elkanah (v. 11).

B. Eli's Sons and Samuel (2:12-36)

1. The Great Sin of Eli's Sons (2:12-17)

2:12-17. "Eli's family stands in striking contrast to Elkanah's. The pious and tender considerations of 1:21ff. are completely absent" (Laurence E. Porter, "1 and 2 Samuel," in NIBC, edited by F. F. Bruce [Grand Rapids, MI: Zondervan, 1979], 355). Eli's sons (Hophni and Phinehas, cf. 1:3) in particular formed a stark contrast to Samuel, and their unfaithfulness also served to illustrate the spiritual crisis Israel was in at the time of Samuel's birth.

Hophni and Phinehas were **worthless men**, (lit., "sons of Belial," v. 12). To say a person is "a son of faith" or "a son of Belial" is a biblical way of characterizing a person. The narrator used the word "Belial" nine times in 1 and 2 Samuel (cf. 1:16; 2:12; 10:27; 25:17, 25; 30:22; 2Sm 16:7; 20:1; 23:6). The term does not appear to have any reference to a particular being in the OT, although in later Jewish writings Belial came to be personified as a demon. The word was also used as a designation for the devil, as in 2Co 6:15 (C. L. Feinberg, "Belial," in *The Zondervan Pictorial Encyclopedia of the Bible*, vol. 1, edited by Merrill C. Tenney [Grand Rapids, MI: Zondervan, 1975], 513).

"Belial" means "wicked," "worthless," "without use or profit," "destructive", "good-for-nothings" (Ralph W. Klein, *1 Samuel*, 2nd ed., WBC [Nashville: Thomas Nelson, 1983], 25). As sons of Belial, Eli's sons were wicked, worthless in character, utterly destructive men. They did not know the Lord, nor did they have regard for the priest's responsibilities as they related to how offerings were to be made or consumed (cf. Lv 7:28-36; Dt 18:3). Hophni and Phinehas took whatever portion of meat their three-pronged fork brought up, thus mocking divine providence. God was to receive His portion, all the animal fat, first (cf. Lv 3:16; 4:8-10, 26, 30-31; 7:28-31; 17:6). But the priests took their portions unlawfully before the Lord received His portion, even using effort to get it. Thus their sin was **very great** in the Lord's sight (v. 17).

2. Eli's Sons in Contrast to Samuel (2:18-36)

2:18-21. In contrast to Eli's sons, Samuel as a boy ministered before the Lord. The narrator alternated between scenes of Samuel's growth in godliness and the moral decadence of Eli's sons, perhaps to heighten this contrast between Samuel's spiritual sensitivity and regard for the Lord, even as a small child, and the utter lack of both on the part of Eli's adult sons.

The **ephod** Samuel wore was a priestly garment (Ex 28:4-9; 1Sm 22:18)—a close-fitting, apron-like, sleeveless linen tunic extending to the hips (G. L. Archer, "Ephod," in *The Zondervan Pictorial Encyclopedia of the Bible*, Vol. 2, edited by Merrill C. Tenney [Grand Rapids, MI: Zondervan, 1975], 332-33). His mother made him a robe every year because he was a growing boy. The robe was probably the robe of the ephod, underscoring Samuel's place as an apprentice priest. The Lord visited Hannah, giving her five more children. The Lord gave Hannah much more than she gave Him.

2:22-26. Women had a place of service at the doorway of the tent of meeting (cf. Ex 38:8). The nature of that service is not specified. Eli's sons perverted and reduced the service of these women to cultic prostitution. The sin of Eli's sons spread among the people, causing them too to disobey the Lord. Eli rebuked his sons, but **they would not listen**. Because they crossed a moral point of no return, the Lord's judgment of death was inevitable.

2:27-36. An unnamed man of God addressed Eli, using the prophetic formula, **Thus says the Lord**. This expression is used 293 times in the Hebrew Bible. Even in the dark times of the judges, the Lord had His spokespersons. Through the man of God, the Lord asked Eli a series of questions to show him that what he had done was stupid in light of God's blessing. **My sacrifice** and **My offering** (v. 29) summarize the entire sacrificial system. Eli honored his sons above the Lord by tolerating their sinful behavior and not insisting they show appropriate deference to the Lord. The following sums up the Lord's response: **those who honor Me I will honor** (lit., make heavy, have weight, be noteworthy), **and those who despise Me will be lightly esteemed** (lit., "made light") (v. 30). To **break your strength and the strength of your father's house** is literally, "to break your arm and the arm of your father's house." Eli would see distress in God's dwelling, that is, in the tabernacle. This took place when the Philistines took the ark of God, and there was a tragic loss of life among God's people (cf. 4:2, 10-11). Eli's descendants included no one with experience, wisdom, and influence (cf. 22:14-20).

Saul later massacred the priests at Nob (cf. 1Sm 22:6-23). Only one of Eli's descendants, Abiathar, escaped. But Solomon removed Abiathar from the priesthood, and transferred the priesthood to the family of Zadok, "to fulfill the word of the Lord, which He had spoken concerning the house of Eli at Shiloh" (cf. 1Kg 2:26-27; 4:2). The deaths of Hophni and Phinehas on the same day (cf. 2:34; 4:11) would show Eli that judgment on his posterity would be fulfilled. But the Lord would raise up **a faithful priest** to do His will (v. 35). Most commentators agree that this prophecy was realized initially in Zadok (although it may also refer to Samuel), and completely fulfilled in the Lord Jesus Christ (cf. Heb 2:17-18). Eli's descendants would be reduced to poverty, begging for bread and pleading to do menial tasks at the sanctuary.

C. The Boy Who Became the Prophet (3:1-21)

1. The Lord Called Samuel (3:1-9)

3:1-9. The Lord's word was rare (i.e., God seldom spoke to His people), and visions were infrequent **in those days**, in the days of the judges. A vision is God's word revealed to a prophet in a way that may certainly include physical sight, although the emphasis is on what is seen through other than the physical eyes, such as a vision in a dream or a state of ecstasy (J. M. Lower, "Vision," *The Zondervan Pictorial Encyclopedia of the Bible*, Vol. 5, edited by Merrill C. Tenney [Grand Rapids, MI: Zondervan, 1975], 889–90). The prophet then communicated that vision to people in words. The few visions the prophets did receive in Samuel's day were limited in impact because of the blindness of Israel's people and leaders. God Himself was silent for the most part (cf. Pr 29:18; Am 8:11). Because of old age most of Eli's eyesight was gone, and later he was blind (cf. 1Sm 4:15). The priest was responsible to assure that the lamps of the golden lampstand (menorah) were lit at twilight and stayed lit until dawn (cf. Ex 25:31-37; 27:20-21; Lv 24:1-4).

Samuel slept in the tabernacle complex, which apparently included both the tabernacle and auxiliary permanent buildings that had a doorpost and gates (Youngblood, "1, 2 Samuel," 47), near where **the ark of God was** (v. 3). The ark represented God's presence. The statement that **the lamp of God had not yet gone out** (cf. 1Sm 3:3) suggests that the following episode took place sometime before dawn. When the Lord called Samuel, Samuel thought Eli was calling him. Samuel responded to the voice as a prophet responds to the Lord's call: **Here I am** (as also in Gn 22:1, 11; Ex 3:4). Samuel misunderstood because **Samuel did not yet know the Lord, nor had the word of the Lord yet been revealed to him** (v. 7). Samuel's lack of experience in matters pertaining to God was twofold: (1) he did not know God in his personal experience; and (2) the Lord had never spoken directly to Samuel before. Eli discerned that the Lord was calling Samuel. So he gave Samuel some instructions on how to respond to the Lord's call.

2. The Lord Spoke to Samuel (3:10-14)

3:10-14. Then the Lord appeared to Samuel, calling him by name twice. Several other "double calls" are recorded in Scripture (cf. Gn 22:11; Ex 3:4; Lk 10:41; Ac 9:4), each occurring at momentous times in a person's life. The first message Samuel received from the Lord was a message of judgment on Eli's family, who were like family to him.

3. Samuel Made Known the Lord's Word to Eli (3:15-18)

3:15-18. Samuel experienced his first test as the Lord's messenger—fear to communicate a message of judgment to someone close to him. Eli spoke tenderly to Samuel, but he also called down a curse on Samuel if he did not tell him the entire message. After hearing Samuel's message, Eli's attitude is commendable: **It is the Lord; let Him do what seems good to Him** (v. 18).

4. The Growth of Samuel (3:19-21)

3:19-21. These verses summarize Samuel's physical growth and devotional progress. The expression **from Dan even to Beersheba** means the northern extremity of Israel in Dan to the southernmost extremity in Beersheba. As **a prophet of the Lord**, Samuel was a divinely chosen, authorized spokesperson for God. He was the first named prophet in Israel since Moses.

D. The Danger of Trying to Manipulate God (4:1-22)

1. The Misuse of the Ark in Battle (4:1-4)

4:1-4. Israel met the Philistines in battle without seeking God's mind through Samuel, no doubt a further indication of the people's spiritual lethargy. This battle is also significant because it records the beginning of the fulfillment of God's judgment on the house of Eli (Laney, *First and Second Samuel*, 24), The Philistines were a pagan, uncircumcised people who migrated to the Mediterranean coastal region from the Aegean Islands and Asia Minor in the twelfth century BC (Laney, *First and Second Samuel*, 24). The Philistines were "inveterate enemies of Israel during the latter half of the period of the judges and in the early years of the Israelite monarchy" (Youngblood, "1, 2 Samuel," 70). Youngblood also notes that the Philistines are mentioned almost 150 times in 1 and 2 Samuel. The Philistine threat was pervasive in 1 Samuel. Here is the first recorded battle between Israel and their longtime enemies.

Ebenezer (about 40 miles northwest of the Dead Sea and about eight miles from the Mediterranean coast) means "stone of help." The meaning of the place's name is ironic in this chapter. Presumptuous Israel would not experience the Lord's help.

When the Philistines defeated Israel near Aphek, Israel's elders decided to take into battle the ark of God, thinking that it would save them from the Philistines. Trusting the ark and not God, the **elders** treated the ark like a fetish, an object they hoped would bring good luck.

2. A Profound Misunderstanding (4:5-9)

4:5-9. However, the ark's presence in the camp did not mean that the Lord was obligated to grant Israel victory. Two miles away, when the Philistines heard Israel shouting with excitement about the presence of the ark, they began to fight even more strenuously, being motivated by fear of what the ark's presence might mean for them.

3. The Loss of the Ark to the Philistines (4:10-11)

4:10-11. Then the unthinkable occurred: The Philistines captured **the ark of God**. Six times this chapter states that the ark was taken (vv. 3, 11, 17, 19, 21-22), indicating that the author intended his readers to understand what a self-induced tragedy this was for Israel. Israel suffered devastating consequences for using the ark as a fetish instead of seeking God's will.

4. The Death of Eli (4:12-18)

4:12-18. A man from the tribe of Benjamin ran uphill for about 20 miles from the scene of the battle to Shiloh. The dust on his head and his torn clothes were symbols of grief. Eli heard the commotion, but he could not see the messenger whose clothing and hair spoke so loudly of tragedy. Eli therefore inquired. The bad news included the defeat of many Israelites, the death of Eli's two sons, and the capture of the ark. **When he mentioned the ark of God . . . Eli fell off the seat backward beside the gate, and his neck was broken and he died, for he was old and heavy** (v. 18). The capture of the ark was too much for Eli. His death marked the end of an era.

5. The Departure of Israel's Glory (4:19-22)

4:19-22. Eli's **daughter-in-law, Phinehas' wife**, was pregnant. The tragic news of that day pushed her into premature labor. Dying in childbirth, she named the baby **Ichabod**, which means "No glory." This reflected the circumstances surrounding his birth: **The glory has departed from Israel, because the ark of God was taken** (v. 22). The "glory" was the visible manifestation of God's presence dwelling among His people in the tabernacle. One of Israel's privileges was to enjoy God's glory, that is, His manifest presence in the tabernacle (cf. Rm 9:2-5). God was not taken away, but the capture of the ark signaled the tragic reality that the evidence of God's glory had left His people. They would not permanently have the evidence of His divine presence with them again.

E. God's Heavy Hand on the Philistines (5:1-12)

1. The Ark in the Philistines' Hands (5:1-5)

5:1-2. The Philistines took the ark of God **from Ebenezer to Ashdod** (a trip of about 30 miles southwest; **Ashdod** was near the coast, about 35 miles west of Jerusalem), treating it like a trophy of war and wrongly assuming its capture represented a victory of their god over the Lord Himself. Ashdod was one of the city-states in the Philistine Pentapolis, the five cities united in a confederation, each one under the leadership of a lord, hence the expression "the five lords of the Philistines" (cf. 6:16). The five cities were Gaza (the southernmost of the five cities, about 20 miles south of Ashdod), Ashkelon (about 10 miles south of Ashdod), Ashdod, Gath (about 10 miles southeast of Ashdod), and Ekron (the northernmost of the five cities, about 10 miles northeast of Ashdod). Dagon was the national Philistine deity, thought to be Baal's father, and the god of fertility and grain. The Philistines dedicated temples in his honor in Gaza (cf. Jdg 16:23-31), in Beth-shan (cf. 1Sm 31:10; 1Ch 10:8-10), and in Ashdod. The Philistines placed the ark in Dagon's temple in Ashdod as a symbol of the Lord's defeat.

5:3-5. The next day, when the Ashdodites arose, they found Dagon **fallen on his face** in his own house before the ark. Fallen on his face is a posture of humiliation (and possibly worship). This showed that Dagon was an impotent god; probably being knocked over by the Lord, he could not even pick himself up.

The next morning the Ashdodites found Dagon on his face again humiliated before the Lord. This time his **head** was cut off along with **both the palms of his hands**. Youngblood notes, "In the ancient world severed heads . . . and hands . . . were battlefield trophies. The Lord had therefore vanquished Dagon" (Youngblood, "1, 2 Samuel," 77). The Lord showed His power and superiority over Dagon by knocking him down into a posture of humility and executing him in his own temple. Thus the Lord maintained His own glory. The Philistines were so shaken by this that when they saw Dagon's head and palms on the temple's threshold, they made the **threshold** of Dagon's temple off limits, probably out of fear that something like what happened to Dagon would happen to the person who walked on the threshold.

2. Tumors, Confusion, and Death (5:6-12)

5:6-12. God's hand is mentioned four times in this episode (vv. 6-7, 9, 11), for His hand **was heavy on the Ashdodites**. They experienced His judgment in the outbreak of tumors (vv. 6, 9, 12), a Hebrew word that can mean any type of swelling, or perhaps boils (Laney, *First and Second Samuel*, 28). There was also emotional and mental confusion (vv. 9-11), and for some death (v. 12). The Lord demonstrated His superiority by toppling Dagon in his own house, and by plaguing the Philistines to the extent that they cried out to Him!

F. The Philistines Return the Ark to Israel (6:1–7:1)

1. The Philistine Mode of Transporting the Ark (6:1-18)

6:1-9. After the ark was in Philistine hands for seven months (v. 1), they consulted their pagan religious authorities: the priests and the diviners. Diviners engaged in occult practices. The specifics of their practices are not identified.

According to the Mosaic law a guilt offering required a ram without spot (cf. Lv 5:15). But the Philistine priests were advised by their diviners to use golden tumors and golden mice. Mice were unclean in God's eyes (cf. Lv 11:29). Also the ark was never to be transported on a cart (cf. Nm 4:5-15), as the Israelites would later learn in a tragic episode (cf. 2Sm 6:1-7).

Still, the Lord used the pagans' ignorance to accomplish His purpose. Returning the ark to Israel was an admission of defeat. The **golden tumors** represented the physical affliction itself; the **five golden mice** represented the mice ravishing the land, which were possibly the source of the tumors. Rats carry bubonic plague. This may have been the plague the Philistines were experiencing (Laney, *First and Second Samuel*, 28). The religious leaders explained to them how to know if the plagues came from God or not. They were to use **milch cows** that had never borne **a yoke** to lead the cart with the ark. But these cows were not trained to walk in a straight path. And since they had calves, their instinct would be to return to their young. However, if the cows disregarded their natural instincts, going instead to Beth-shemesh, the Philistines would know that the Lord had sent the plagues.

6:10-18. Against their maternal instincts, the cows went directly to Beth-shemesh (about 18 miles east of Ashdod and 15 miles west of Jerusalem), showing the Philistines that the Lord was the source of their plagues.

2. Treating the Ark with Irreverence (6:19–7:1)

6:19–7:1. The men of Beth-shemesh disrespected **the ark of the Lord** by opening it and looking inside—a clear violation of the Mosaic law that only the Levites could handle the ark, and even then not touch it directly lest they die (Merrill, "1 Samuel" 437). So the Lord struck down **50,070 men**, a figure which seems high for a small town. The NIV and several Hebrew manuscripts have 70 people put to death. According to Laney, "the 50,070 is doubted even by conservative scholars and probably represents a scribal error in transmission" (*First and Second Samuel*, 29). The significance of this story is that Israel was not to take God's grace for granted. It was of grace that He was present with the nation through the holy ark, and they needed to treat the ark as holy. The men of Beth-shemesh did not treat the Lord as holy and were disciplined for it.

G. The Lord Delivers Israel from the Philistines (7:2-17)

1. Twenty Years of Mourning (7:2-4)

7:2-4. For two decades the ark remained at Kiriath-jearim. Perhaps because of the ark's "reduced status" in not being housed in the tabernacle (Youngblood, "1, 2 Samuel," 86), and no doubt because of the consequences of the people's bad choices in worshiping idols, the nation of Israel was mourning and longing **after the Lord**. Samuel encouraged the people to **return to the Lord**. The word **return** means "turning from sin and idolatry and turning to the Lord." And their return was to be sincere, **with all your heart**. The **Ashtaroth** were idol goddesses, Baal's female consorts, representing fertility and sex appeal and called holy "in a perverted moral sense" (Merrill F. Unger, *The New Unger's Bible Dictionary,* edited by R. K. Harrison [Chicago: Moody, 1988], 484). To serve the Lord alone meant to devote oneself completely and exclusively to Him. This was necessary if Israel was to experience divine deliverance from Philistine superior might and oppression.

Baal was the idol god of fertility, one of the chief male gods of the Canaanites, according to Unger. Baal's domain was the sky; idolaters thought the sound of thunder was Baal's voice. Removing the Baals involved destroying the images, breaking them, and burning them. Removing the **Ashtaroth** involved destroying the images and refusing to engage in the lewd idolatrous practices associated with the worship of Baal and Ashtaroth.

2. A Day of Fasting (7:5-6)

7:5-6. Samuel summoned all Israel to Mizpah (about six miles north of Jerusalem) for a prayer meeting. Mizpah was already a gathering place for Israel (cf. Jdg 20:1) and was on Samuel's regular ministry circuit (1Sm 7:16). After the fall of Jerusalem, Mizpah even became the nation's capital (2Kg 25:23) (Baldwin, *1 and 2 Samuel*, 79). There the people drew water from a well and **poured it out**, symbolizing the pouring out of their souls in repentance before the Lord (cf. 1Sm 1:15; Pss 42:4; 62:8; Lm 2:19). They confessed their fundamental problem: **We have sinned against the Lord**. At Mizpah Samuel became Israel's judge—in fact, Israel's last judge.

3. A Plea for Samuel's Intercession (7:7-11)

7:7. When the Philistines heard that the sons of Israel had gathered at Mizpah, they decided to attack. The Philistines may have reasoned that having all the Israelites in one place would be a good time to strike. Laney (*First and Second Samuel*, 31) notes that Israel had been defeated twice before near this site (cf. 1Sm 4:1-2; 5:1), suggesting that the Philistines might have been confident of another victory.

7:8-11. Israel begged Samuel to intercede for their deliverance. So Samuel took two steps: he offered a lamb as a burnt offering to the Lord, and he prayed for the people. While Samuel was in the process of making his offering, the Philistine army was right outside the city wall. **But the Lord thundered . . . against the Philistines**. The sound of thunder was the voice of God Himself (cf. Ps 29:3). The powerful thunder threw the Philistines into panic and confusion.

4. Erecting the Ebenezer (7:12-14)

7:12-14. The use of stones as memorials of significant events in Israel already had a long history by this time. Jacob and his father-in-law Laban piled up a heap of stones to commemorate their agreement (cf. Gn 31:46-49). Joshua commanded Israel to make a memorial of 12 stones from the Jordan when Israel crossed over into the promised land (Jos 4). Samuel placed the stone between Mizpah and Shen, calling it **Ebenezer**, meaning "stone of help." The stone memorialized the Lord's help up to this point in Israel's history.

5. A Summary of Samuel's Ministry (7:15-17)

7:15-17. These verses summarize Samuel's ministry in Israel. In his hometown, **Ramah**, he built an altar to the Lord, worshiping the Lord and expressing his dependence on Him.

H. The People Reject the Lord as Their King (8:1-22)

1. The Problem of Samuel's Sons (8:1-3)

8:1-3. The mention of Samuel's ministry as a "circuit riding" judge served to introduce the reader "to the need—however ambiguous and contradictory—for a king" (Youngblood, "1, 2 Samuel," 88). It was now almost 1051 BC, the year that Saul became king. Many years had passed, and Samuel was an old man, perhaps 65-70 years old (Merrill, "1 Samuel," 439). Recognizing his advanced age, Samuel did something that only God should have done (cf. Jdg 2:16, 18; 3:9, 15). He appointed his sons, **Joel** and **Abijah**, to be judges over Israel. Joel means "Yahweh is God"; Abijah means "My Father is Yahweh." However, Samuel's sons did not live up to their names; they **took bribes and perverted justice**, using their judgeship for financial gain. As serious as the ungodly character of Samuel's sons was, that is not the most disturbing concern in this episode.

2. The Demand for a King (8:4-9)

8:4-9. The intolerable situation of Samuel's ungodly sons brought action on the part of Israel's elders, older men who were the heads of tribes, clans, and families, and thus were invested with leadership in the nation (Unger, *The New Unger's Bible Dictionary*, 343). Speaking on behalf of the people (they were **the voice of the people**, v. 7), the elders had a solution for the negative leadership of Samuel's sons. They asked for a king. But the elders' solution would be worse than the problem. The Lord told Samuel to do what the people asked, even though their request for a king in place of the Lord meant that Israel was rejecting the Lord Himself. This was the disturbing element in the people's request. Israel already had a perfect King, the only true God. Not only did their request involve rejection of the Lord's rulership; it also was made for perhaps the worst of reasons. Israel wanted to be **like all the nations** around them. The people's behavior was tragic, but all too typical. The Lord, however, instructed Samuel to tell them what kind of king would **reign over them** (v. 9).

3. Warning about a King (8:10-18)

8:10-18. The Lord specified how the king would treat the people, using memorable language to anchor His words in their minds. The conclusion was sobering: **You will cry out in that day because of your king whom you have chosen for yourselves, but the Lord will not answer you in that day** (v. 18).

4. The People's Refusal to Listen (8:19-22)

8:19-22. Nevertheless, the people refused to listen to Samuel, demanding a king. God granted them their request. Much later in Israel's history, the Lord made known His sentiments about the people's demand: "I gave you a king in My anger and took him away in My wrath" (cf. Hs 13:11). When God grants His people their fleshly demands, it spells disaster and pain for the recipients and is a manifestation of His displeasure. The old adage, "Be careful what you wish for," was true for Israel. **That our king may judge us and go out before us and fight our battles** (v. 20) indicates their hope for a king included military victory. Yet when Saul encountered Goliath (cf. 1Sm 17), Saul failed to fulfill his obligations to lead Israel into battle. When David succeeded, he demonstrated that he was qualified to be king, not Saul.

Thus the first section of 1 Samuel ends with the people rejecting the Lord as their king. This was a staggering and ultimately harmful turning point in the nation's history, one that God warned the people they would regret. Laney's summary is helpful here. He notes that although prophecies dating back to Moses indicate it was God's sovereign will for Israel to have a king, they went about it at the wrong time with the wrong attitude, which was not God's prescriptive will. However, God allowed the choice to go forward in His permissive will (Laney, *First and Second Samuel*, 36).

II. Saul, the People's King (9:1–15:35)

In chaps. 9–15, Saul, Israel's first king, dominated the narrative. The narrator also introduced Jonathan, Saul's firstborn son and crown prince of Israel. Saul and Jonathan are in contrast. Chapter 15 closes section two of 1 Samuel with God rejecting Saul as Israel's king.

A. The Secret Anointing of Saul (9:1–10:16)

A chapter division divides this episode, but a close reading of 9:1–10:16 suggests that this is one episode.

1. Saul, the Tallest and Most Handsome Man in Israel (9:1-2)

9:1-2. Saul's father was **Kish**, from the tribe of Benjamin. Kish was **a mighty man of valor**. Three other people in the OT are described in this way: Boaz (cf. Ru 2:1, "a man of great wealth"), Jephthah (cf. Jdg 11:1, "a valiant warrior"), and David (cf. 1Sm 16:18, "a mighty man of valor"). Kish's genealogy points to a prominent family in the tribe of Benjamin. Saul "was outstandingly well endowed" (Baldwin, *1 and 2 Samuel*, 87), which is ironic since Saul later proved to be a weak leader and a coward in refusing to face Goliath. Saul's name, which means "asked," is ironic, because in choosing Saul to be their king, the people received from the Lord what they asked. Saul looked like a king, but the narrative (especially related to the episode involving Goliath) revealed that he was not qualified for that role.

2. The Decision to Consult the Seer (9:3-14)

9:3-5. When Kish's donkeys **were lost**, Saul searched for them in four places but was unsuccessful (v. 4; one of the places was **Shalishah**, also known as Baal-shalishah, about 27 miles northwest of Jerusalem). Saul was ready to call off the search for fear his father would be worried about his safety. As insignificant as this discussion appears, it seems that Saul wanted to quit searching for his father's donkeys. In contrast, David later would be presented as one who never gave up on caring for his father's sheep, whether they were the animals that belonged to Jesse, or the sheep (people) of Israel who belonged to his heavenly Father. This is one way in which Saul demonstrated himself to be unqualified for his role as king.

9:6-12. Saul's servant encouraged him to consult the man of God at Zuph (probably a family name for a region occupied by the tribe of Benjamin north of Jerusalem) so that **perhaps he can tell us about our journey**. Saul was reluctant to consult the man of God because he did not have a gift to give him. But the servant happened to have **a fourth of a shekel of silver**, so he suggested Saul give that to the man of God. An explanation of a former practice in Israel interrupts the narrative flow in v. 9. To **inquire of God** meant to seek the Lord's wisdom and guidance about a particular problem (cf. Gn 25:22-23, 1Kg 22:5-8; 2Kg 3:11). The difference between a prophet and a seer was that the prophet was the Lord's spokesperson, whereas the seer was one who received a message through visions. Merrill says that a seer's ministry was primarily involved with receiving divine revelation, whereas the prophets were primarily declarers of divine revelation, although he adds that prophets were also seers ("1 Samuel," 440-41). Perhaps this is why Laney states that while there may have at one time been a distinction between the two terms, it was not so at the time of the writer of 1 Samuel (*First and Second Samuel*, 38). The parenthetical statement (v. 9) also prepares the reader for the use of "seer" instead of "prophet" (vv. 11, 19) in the narrative.

The difference between a village and a city in the ancient Near East was the presence or absence of a surrounding wall. Villages did not have walls, but cities were clusters of homes and buildings surrounded by a wall. People built cities near water sources. Usually the water source was at the foot of the elevation. It was necessary to draw water from a well or spring and carry the water back up to the city. Women were generally the water carriers, a task they usually performed in the evenings (cf. Gn 24:11). Going up the city's slope, Saul and his servant encountered some **young women** going down to fetch some water (v. 11). The young women spoke to Saul with a sense of urgency as they informed Saul about Samuel's whereabouts. **Hurry now . . . he must bless the sacrifice . . . go**

up for you will find him at once. The words **bless the sacrifice** are used only here in Scripture and mean "to give thanks to God for the sacrifice before it is eaten" as an expression of worship (cf. Lk 9:16; Jn 6:11).

9:13-14. The high place was outside the city, at a higher elevation. A high place was a place of worship. Generally they were associated with pagan worship. After the building of Solomon's temple, in only one instance was this not the case. Worshiping the Lord at the high place was acceptable during Samuel's time because Shiloh had been destroyed about 1050 BC, presumably by the Philistines, when the ark was taken (cf. 1Sm 4; Unger, *The New Unger's Bible Dictionary*, 1183), and the temple that would be built by Solomon had not yet been constructed (cf. 1Kg 3:1-5, 2Ch 1:2-3). The high place in this episode is devoted to the worship of the Lord. There was a building there that could hold at least 30 people (1Sm 9:22).

3. Providential Activity Woven into the Ordinary (9:15-21)

9:15-17. The Lord Himself worked in the ordinary activities of Saul's searching for donkeys, in his decision-making, in the information he received from the young women, working out His own purpose, and sending Saul to Samuel. The day before Saul arrived, the Lord told Samuel that he would send to him a man from the tribe of Benjamin. God told Samuel to **anoint** him leader over the Lord's people. To "anoint" means "to consecrate or to set apart for a divine purpose." The act of pouring oil on the head of the anointed person also "symbolized the coming of the Holy Spirit in power" (Youngblood, "1, 2 Samuel," 101). In the OT, prophets, priests, and kings were anointed. God used people like Samuel to anoint others, but ultimately God anointed and authorized a person to exercise the ministry in question. And the word "anointed" conveys the ideas of the presence of God's Spirit and power (cf. 10:9-10; 16:13), responsibility (cf. 15:17; 2Sm 12:7), and honor (cf. 1Sm 24:6; 26:10-11; 2Sm 1:14). The Lord expressed His compassion for His people, saying that the king **will deliver My people from the hand of the Philistines. For I have regarded My people, because their cry has come to Me** (vv. 16-17). Because Israel belongs to the Lord, it is not surprising that He referred to them as "My people" four times in vv. 16 and 17.

9:18-19. The action resumed in v. 18. **In the gate** is literally "in the middle of the gate." The city gate in the ancient Near East was more than an entrance to a city; it was the hub of the city's social, political, and economic life. The city streets were narrow, but the open area in front of the gate gave people space to congregate for various purposes: buying and selling (cf. 2Kg 7:2), holding court to settle legal matters (cf. Ru 4:1-2), discussion (cf. Ps 69:12), and public worship and the hearing of God's Word (cf. 2Ch 32:6; Neh 8:1-8).

9:20-21. Samuel said to Saul, **For whom is all that is desirable in Israel? Is it not for you and for all your father's household?** The statement was both encouraging and troubling. Israel was waiting with anticipation for God's rule. But Saul was their choice of a king, and not the Lord's choice (cf. 12:1). Saul was not the first person to have a sense of inadequacy about God's call on his life (cf. Ex 3:11; 4:10; Jdg 6:15; 2Sm 7:18; Jr 1:4-6).

4. Celebration in the Hall and Counsel on the Roof (9:22-27)

9:22-27. Samuel understood the Lord's call on Saul's life. So he disregarded Saul's concerns about the smallness of his tribe and clan. Samuel took Saul and his servant **into the hall** on the high place and gave them a place of honor at the head of those invited. As a further expression of honor, a special part of the meal was set aside just for Saul. The roof of a home in the ancient Near East was typically flat, surrounded by a wall to prevent people from falling. It was an important part of a house. It was a place of protection (cf. Jos 2:6, 8), and people had private devotions (cf. Ac 10:9) and private conversations there (cf. 1Sm 9:25). Guests could sleep on the roof, enjoying the night's cool air (v. 26). The narrator did not record the conversation between Samuel and Saul, but perhaps they discussed the kingdom and kingdom responsibilities.

5. The Three Signs of Confirmation (10:1-8)

10:1. Samuel privately anointed Saul, and **kissed** Saul out of respect. Later, the Lord anointed Saul leader over His inheritance.

10:2-8. Three signs confirmed the Lord's call on Saul's life. The first sign occurred near **Rachel's tomb** (probably in the vicinity of Bethlehem, a few miles south of Jerusalem, though the location is disputed), where two men informed Saul that his father's donkeys were found. The second sign occurred at the **oak of Tabor**, "a landmark on the road to Bethel" (Baldwin, *1 and 2 Samuel*, 91), where three men gave Saul **two loaves of bread**. The bread was a sign of God's provision for Saul.

The third sign occurred at the **hill of God** where the Philistine garrison was located. Baldwin says the Hebrew term *gibeathelohim* may refer to Gibeah, Saul's city, and also that the mention of the Philistines was a reminder of the threat Saul was to remove, for which he needed divine power (Baldwin, 1 and 2 Samuel, 91) Saul received that power in an unusual way when he met a procession of prophets coming down from the high place. Encountering this group, the spirit of God came on Saul, giving him the power he needed to carry out his ministry.

6. The Last Sign and the Return Home (10:9-16)

10:9-16. God did a work in Saul's heart before he met the prophets. In vv. 10-13 the narrator focused on incidents associated with the third sign. When Saul met the musical procession of prophets, **the Spirit of God came upon him mightily, so that he prophesied among them**. Those who witnessed the occasion thought it strange that Saul was among the prophets. This did not mean that Saul became a prophet, but that only at this one time he exercised a prophetic gift. It was surprising but also a persuasive and powerful sign of God's presence in Saul's life.

B. Samuel Recognizes Saul as King in Public at Mizpah (10:17-27)

10:17-19. Previously Saul was privately selected by Samuel as king. Now the people publicly chose Saul as their king. Samuel opened his message with the prophetic introduction, **Thus says the LORD**. Samuel declared that in response to the Lord's ongoing care, love, and protection, Israel nevertheless rejected God, who delivered her from all her calamities and distresses, and insisted on having a human king in the place of God. This rebuke was a reminder that the people's insistence on having a human king was not God's plan for them. Indeed, no king would be able to deliver Israel from slavery, as the Lord did in Egypt, and from all their **calamities** and **distresses**. But since the people were determined to have a king, Samuel said, in effect, "Let's get on with it," and began the process of identifying the king whose name was unknown to everyone but him.

10:20-24. So the Israelites presented themselves before the Lord by their **tribes** and **clans** in a process of elimination that would bring them to Saul. The tribe was the first and largest organizational division in Israel, and the clan was the next subdivision. Clans were subdivided into families. **The tribe of Benjamin** was chosen **by lot**. Casting a lot was a means of ascertaining God's mind about various concerns (cf. Nm 26:55; 33:54; Jos 7:14-26; 1Ch 24:5; Pr 18:33; Lk 1:9; Ac 1:24-26). Though people cast the lot, the Lord determined the result (cf. Pr 16:33). Therefore the decision was not questioned. The casting of lots is no longer a valid practice for Christians today to determine God's will. There is no verse that commands Christians to engage in this practice to ascertain God's specific will. Instead, since the giving of the Holy Spirit at Pentecost (Ac 2), He enlightens the believer's mind to see how Scripture bears on one's decisions. The lot is no longer needed.

Saul was identified as the king. But ironically the people had to inquire of God about the whereabouts of their chosen. Saul was hiding among the **baggage**, strange behavior for the new king. Saul was the tallest man in Israel, standing head and **shoulders** over every one in Israel. He looked like a king, but the real issue was whether he was above everyone in his devotion and commitment to the **LORD**.

10:25-27. Though the people had rejected the Lord, He was gracious with them. He touched the hearts of some **valiant men**, who supported Saul. In contrast, some **worthless men** (lit., "sons of Belial"), **despised** Saul, apparently contemptuous of his ability to lead the people and **deliver** Israel from her enemies. Saul, however, wisely refused to respond to his detractors' ungodly words and attitude at that moment, "in order not to provoke the situation" (Laney, *First and Second Samuel*, 41).

C. Saul's Spirit-Empowered Victory over the Ammonites (11:1-15)

1. The Siege of Jabesh-gilead (11:1-4)

11:1-4. The siege of Jabesh-gilead by the Ammonites, and Saul's deliverance of the city, gave the new king an important opportunity to establish his administration in several ways. First, his victory and deliverance of Jabesh-gilead won Saul the loyalty of another portion of his kingdom. He also proved his detractors wrong in their accusation, "How can this one deliver us?" (10:27), by delivering his people from their oppressors (Baldwin, *1 and 2 Samuel*, 96). Also, Saul was likely connected to the people of Jabesh-gilead by ancestry, since they too were Benjamites (Merrill, "1 Samuel," 442).

Nahash, the king of Ammon, was called **the Ammonite** to distinguish him from David's father Jesse, who also bore the name Nahash (cf. 2Sm 17:25). The Ammonites descended from

Ben-ammi, Lot's son whom he fathered by his own daughter (cf. Gn 19:30-38). Jabesh-gilead was a town of Gilead, on the east side of the Jordan River, over 20 miles southeast of the Sea of Galilee. Nahash engaged in a campaign that threatened them, so the men of Jabesh said to Nahash, **Make a covenant with us**. Nahash was willing, but his conditions were cold and cruel. The gouging out of the right eye was designed to incapacitate the men of war and bring reproach and shame on the nation. The men of Jabesh-gilead were concerned not with divine deliverance, but with trust in a human leader: **Let us alone for seven days, that we may send messengers throughout the territory of Israel. Then, if there is no one to deliver us, we will come out to you**. Confident of victory, and sure that no help would come for the city, Nahash allowed the men of Jabesh seven days to go over to the other side of Jordan to seek help.

The messenger arrived in **Gibeah of Saul**, three miles north of Jerusalem (Youngblood, "1, 2 Samuel," 117). Its name distinguished it from other places with the same name (cf. Jos 15:57; Jdg 24:33). Gibeah of Saul and Gibeah of Benjamin were the same place. Gibeah of Saul was Saul's birthplace and residence (cf. 1Sm 9:26; 15:34). The men of Jabesh-gilead had a close family relationship with the tribe of Benjamin (cf. Jdg 21:1-15). The people in Gibeah **lifted up their voices and wept**, expressing pain and grief over the plight of the men of Jabesh-gilead.

2. The Spirit of God Comes Mightily on Saul (11:5-13)

11:5-13. Saul providentially showed up at that moment (v. 5). Apparently during the monarchy's early days Saul was still engaged in activities such as farming. **The Spirit of God** coming on Saul in power is the crucial and central moment in the story and was the key to Saul's victory over the Ammonites (v. 6). God's people are successful in war and ministry to the extent that they are under the power and energy of the Holy Spirit (cf. Zch 4:6).

Everything Saul did from this point on to v. 13 resulted from the Spirit's work in him. The cutting up of oxen and distributing the pieces throughout the land was a call to battle with a threat: **Whoever does not come out after Saul and after Samuel, so shall it be done to his oxen** (v. 7). Mentioning Samuel gave more weight to the summons.

The people responded in unison to Saul's summons. They had a sense of God's holy dread and reverence in connection with his summons. For the first time in Scripture **the dread of the Lord** was said to be on His people. In all other cases God's dread was on the enemies of the Lord's people (cf. 2Ch 20:29).

Bezek was on the west side of the Jordan River, about 10 or so miles west of Jabesh-gilead. Because of the proximity of Bezek to Jabesh-gilead, it was a good rallying point for the troops. There Saul counted them—a substantial number of **300,000** from Israel, and **30,000** from Judah (v. 8). The distinction made between Israel and Judah in v. 8 may be evidence of a later authorship after the actual division of the two kingdoms in 931 BC, or possibly a recognition that the division was already "incipient" at this time (Laney, *First and Second Samuel*, 43; Youngblood, "1, 2 Samuel," 118).

God's assurance of victory did not eliminate cunning as part of military strategy. The men of Jabesh-gilead gave overconfident Nahash the impression that they would surrender the next day (v. 10).

The **next morning** (v. 11), Saul under the Holy Spirit's guidance employed good military strategy. He divided the company into three units and used the element of surprise, attacking the Ammonite camp during the morning watch. In ancient Israel, nighttime was divided into three watches: (1) the beginning watch, sunset to 10:00 p.m. (cf. Lm 2:19); (2) the middle watch, 10:00 p.m. to 2:00 a.m. (cf. Jdg 7:19); and (3) the morning watch, 2:00 a.m. to 6:00 a.m. or sunrise (cf. Ex 14:24).

After victory, the people wanted to put to death those who questioned Saul's selection as king at Mizpah (cf. 1Sm 10:27). But Saul responded **not a man shall be put to death this day**, attributing their victory to the Lord.

3. The Renewing of the Kingdom (11:14-15)

11:14-15. Samuel discerned that it was a good time for the people to **go to Gilgal** to **renew the kingdom** before the Lord. Gilgal, a city in the Jordan Valley not far from Jericho, was full of historical and theological significance for Israel (cf. Jos 4:1-24; 5:1-9; 1Sm 7:16). It was there that the Israelites first camped after crossing the Jordan under Joshua. Samuel also judged there, and king Agag was put to death there (Unger, *The New Unger's Bible Dictionary*, 477). The verb "renew" implies that the people had departed from the Lord and needed to be restored. The kingdom had to be renewed because Israel had rejected the Lord as king. Renewing the kingdom was a recommitment to the Lord Himself in view of the new theocracy under Saul.

Samuel installed Saul as Israel's king before the Lord at Gilgal. Israel offered **peace offerings**. In the peace offering the worshiper gave the best part of the sacrifice to the Lord first before eating his portion (cf. Lv 3:1-16; 7:15). Then the worshiper ate his portion of the peace offering and gave the priest his portion as well (cf. Lv 7:11-18, 28-34). The sacrifice of the peace offering was a symbol of peace and fellowship with God based on the shed blood of an unblemished sacrifice. At this point, Saul was at the zenith of his ministry as king.

D. Samuel Addresses the Nation (12:1-25)

1. Samuel's Moral Authority (12:1-5)

12:1-5. Samuel began his message to Israel by saying in essence, "I have given you what you asked for—a king." He then said he had **walked before** the people, which means he lived a life before them that could be observed and evaluated. Israel had observed Samuel's life, noting that he was a man of character and integrity whose leadership was above reproach. He had not used his place in Israel to take advantage of people, nor did he enrich himself through corrupt practices. Israel attested to Samuel's integrity before the Lord.

2. The Lord's Righteous Acts (12:6-18)

12:6-8. Launching into the second part of his message, Samuel noted that **Moses and Aaron** were not human appointments. This was an implied rebuke because the people chose Saul instead of looking to the Lord in faith. Samuel then spoke of **all the righteous acts of the LORD which He did for you and your fathers** (v. 7). Israel was challenged to take her stand and to remember God's great acts on her behalf. Verse 8 is a concise recounting of Jacob's going down to **Egypt**, the exodus, and the conquest of the land.

12:9-11. Even though the Lord had worked in powerful and righteous ways on their behalf, **they forgot the LORD their God**. To forget the Lord is not a lapse of memory like forgetting one's keys. Forgetting God in Scripture is a conscious choice to disobey God (cf. Dt 8:11), a choice to follow idols (cf. Dt 8:19). First Samuel 12:9-11 summarizes the cycle of the book of Judges up to the time of Samuel: departure from God, the Lord selling them to their enemies, the cry for help, and the divine raising up of judges. The metaphor of "selling" (v. 9) suggests the image of slaves being sold in the marketplace.

Conscious of the Lord's call on his life, Samuel associated himself with Moses, Aaron, **Jerubbaal** (another name for Gideon), **Bedan** (i.e., Barak), and **Jephthah**. Verse 11 states the result of Israel turning from idolatry and trusting in the Lord: **you lived in security**.

12:12-18. Samuel placed Israel's recent actions in the context of redemptive history. In addition to the corruption of Samuel's sons, the Philistine threat on the east and the threat of **Nahash** from the west were reasons Israel demanded a king. But historically, they had no basis for this action. God had always defended them in the past, and would do so in their future if they depended on Him and walked with Him. What motivated them to seek a king was unbelief. But instead of judging His people, God demonstrated His "gracious, permissive will" by granting the people their request; v. 13 makes it clear that it was the Lord who **has set a king over you** (Youngblood, "1, 2 Samuel," 127).

Now Israel had what it asked for—**a king**. This was the central statement in Samuel's message. But God was still gracious with His people. If they walked with Him, all would go well with them. But if they rebelled against Him (v. 15), **then the hand of the LORD will be against you, as it was against your fathers**.

Still, Israel needed to understand the gravity of their sin in asking for a king. To bring this home, Samuel challenged Israel for the second time to **see this great thing which the LORD will do before your eyes**. He then prayed for unseasonable rain and thunder (v. 17), which came as a visual, auditory, and tactile teaching tool, helping Israel realize that their wickedness in asking for a king was great. This was the time of **the wheat harvest**, which took place between May and June. It did not rain during this season; therefore **thunder and rain** on this occasion was a sign of God's displeasure with Israel's choosing a human king over having Him as their King.

3. The People's Response to the Message (12:19-25)

12:19-25. The people sensed their alienation from God and pending death. To their long list of disobedience they had now added another one, the request for a king. Samuel then expressed the words that the Lord said so many times to His people: **Do not fear**. Samuel did not ignore their sin, but he told them the way forward. **You have committed all this evil, yet do not turn aside from following the LORD, but serve the LORD with all your heart**. He warned them of the utter stupidity of turning away from God (v. 21).

Samuel assured the people that the Lord was committed to them for His own glory. Samuel said he would **pray** for them; in fact he considered it a **sin against the LORD** not to pray for them. Although the leadership of the nation was being given to Saul, Samuel still had a role to play as pastoral prophet. He would instruct the people **in the good and right way**.

Samuel also challenged the people to **fear** and **serve** the Lord. Then he concluded with a warning, using a powerful metaphor. **But if you still do wickedly, both you and your king will be swept away**. Much as trash is swept into a pile and then swept away from the floor, so Israel and her king would be swept way with God's judgment.

Samuel's address was an important message spoken to Israel at a pivotal moment in her history.

E. The Divine Rejection of Saul's Dynasty (13:1-23)

13:1. This episode opens with a statement of Saul's age and the number of years he reigned over Israel. The seemingly simple statement of Saul's age and the length of his reign have been troubling for scholars. The source of the trouble is the lack of information concerning Saul's age at the beginning of his reign, and the short duration of his reign stated in the Hebrew text. The NASB says **Saul was *thirty* years old** when he began to reign, and **he reigned *forty* two years**. The numbers "thirty" and "forty" are in italics, meaning they are not in the Hebrew text. According to Baldwin, "It seems likely that that information was missing from the start, or that it was misunderstood by later scribes who thought the numbers given could not be correct" (*1 and 2 Samuel*, 102-3).

In an attempt to make sense of the apparent lack of information in the Hebrew text, some translators have followed the Septuagint manuscripts and have supplied the number "thirty" for Saul's age, and "forty" for the length of his reign. But the Hebrew text does not state Saul's age when he began to reign. The Hebrew text says Saul reigned for two years, seeming to contradict Ac 13:21, which says Saul reigned over Israel for "forty years." Is there a contradiction between the two statements? No. Saul's two-year reign is from God's perspective. Saul reigned legitimately before the Lord for two years. From the perspective of the people he reigned 40 years, but for 38 of those years, he reigned in open defiance of the Lord. Others scholars share this point of view: "Thus, from God's point of view Saul has been king only for a short period, and the exact age of Saul's accession did not matter to the narrator, since he was already rejected by his God" (Tsumura, *The First Book of Samuel*, 333).

1. Israel Becomes Odious to the Philistines (13:2-7)

13:2-7. Michmash was a town in the land of Benjamin about seven miles northeast of Jerusalem. For the first time the narrator mentioned **Jonathan**, Saul's son. He had a military victory over the Philistine garrison **in Geba**, a city in Benjamin about five miles north of Jerusalem. The garrison was a military outpost including the soldiers in it. Jonathan's defeat of the Geba garrison made Israel **odious to the Philistines**. The translation "odious" is not as strong as the Hebrew term, which means "a strong and disgusting stench." In addition to his **3,000** troops, Saul summoned the volunteers he had sent home (v. 2b) to **Gilgal**. He needed more men.

The Philistines assembled for battle in force. They had **30,000 chariots**. Since Israel did not have chariots, the Philistines had a military advantage. The Philistines were **like the sand which is on the seashore in abundance** (v. 5). Saul and his **2,000** men were at Michmash, but when they saw the Philistine military presence they panicked and left for Gilgal. And instead of preparing for battle through prayer, Saul's army collapsed emotionally and went into hiding **in caves, in thickets, in cliffs, in cellars** [cisterns], **and in pits** (v. 6).

2. Saul's Foolish Sacrifice (13:8-18)

13:8-9. Matters then reached a new low. After waiting **seven** tension-filled **days** (v. 8), the people remaining with Saul began to leave him. So Saul took matters into his own hands and offered a **burnt offering** (v. 9). But only consecrated priests were qualified to offer sacrifices to the Lord (cf. Ex 29:38-46; Lv 1:5, 7). As soon as Saul finished offering the sacrifice, **behold, Samuel came** (v. 10), and as a priest he could have made the offering legitimately. If only Saul would have waited a little longer in faith.

13:10-13. Samuel asked Saul, **what have you done?** (v. 11). Saul tried to justify his actions. But Samuel was blunt, for he said to Saul, **you have acted foolishly** (v. 13). To "act foolishly" means "to be deficient in moral or spiritual capacity." Usually it is used in contexts where one acts sinfully out of fear and lack of trust in the Lord (cf. Gn 31:28; 1Sm 26:21; 2Sm 24:10; 1Ch 16:9-10; 21:8). When a child of God faces an overwhelming situation and compromises his standards, sinning in the process, and tries to "rescue" himself, disaster is the outcome.

13:14. As a result of Saul's disobedience, his kingdom would not endure. Saul would not have a dynasty. God **has sought out for Himself a man after His own heart, and the LORD has appointed him as ruler over His people** (v. 14). According to Youngblood, **a man after [God's] own heart** is a man "chosen by God . . . and therefore a man who has God's interests at heart" ("1, 2 Samuel," 137). Baldwin agrees, saying such a person is "prepared to let the Lord's will, as spoken by his prophet, be the guide of his life" (*1 and 2 Samuel*, 105). He is a man who is concerned for God's glory and agenda. God had already chosen Saul's replacement.

13:15-18. Saul's troops had been reduced to **six hundred men** (v. 15). In the meantime, a part of the Philistine military plan was to send three companies of raiders to different places from their camp in **Michmash** (v. 16). They went in three directions from Michmash: one group took the road north to **Ophrah**, another went west to **Beth-horon**, and another took the road east toward **Zeboim** (vv. 17-18), following a common military practice of the day which allowed for more options and mobility (cf. 1Sm 11:11). Gideon did the same in Jdg 7:16 (Youngblood, "1, 2 Samuel," 139).

3. Military Advantages and Economic Exploitation (13:19-23)

13:19-23. A blacksmith was a worker in iron. At this time the Philistines knew how to smelt iron. They intentionally did not allow Israel to acquire skill in iron-smelting for strategic military reasons, thinking, **otherwise the Hebrews will make swords or spears** (v. 19). Iron swords and spears were stronger and more deadly than bronze ones, not to mention wooden spears and arrows. Skill in smelting gave the Philistines another advantage over Israel. The only iron implements in Israel's possession were farming tools. But to maintain these implements they had to go to the Philistines. For this service the Philistines charged **two-thirds of a shekel** (v. 21), about one-fourth of an ounce, or eighty grams. No doubt this was an inflated fee.

The Philistines secured their base in Michmash by placing a garrison of troops at the pass that led to Michmash, but the Israelites had no weapons, except for **Saul and his son Jonathan** (v. 22). These parenthetical verses are important because they show that, humanly speaking, Israel was outmatched! This prepares the reader for the revelation that Israel's upcoming victory over the better-armed Philistines was the Lord's deliverance (cf. 14:23). That Jonathan had a sword also sets the stage for the story of his courageous attack in the following chapter. The narrator was preparing to remind his readers again that one man with the Lord was a "one-man army," for as Jonathan himself would say, "the LORD is not restrained to save by many or by few" (14:6).

F. The Lord Saves Israel (14:1-52)

1. The Faith and Godly Courage of Jonathan (14:1-15)

14:1-3. Jonathan is identified for the first time as Saul's son. In faith Jonathan said to his armor bearer, **Come and let us cross over to the Philistines' garrison that is on the other side** (v. 1). The Philistine garrison was on the pass to Michmash, on the other side of the pass, south of where Jonathan and his armor bearer were. Any armor bearer who carried the armor of a high-ranking soldier had to be a man of courage himself, and a skilled warrior. He was with the soldier as he fought in battle, protected the soldier, and if necessary gave his life for him. Meanwhile, Saul was under a **pomegranate tree** in **Migron** (v. 2, which means "precipice"). **Ahijah**, Eli's great grandson, was the priest with Saul. In principle he was there to give Saul guidance from the Lord.

14:4-5. To reach the Philistine garrison, Jonathan would have to pass through two sharp, rocky, treacherous cliffs named **Bozez** and **Seneh, on the north** and **south** slopes of the pass at **Michmash**. Bozez means "slippery" or "shining," and Seneh means "thorny." Bozez reflected the sunlight, making it difficult to see, and was slippery, making one's step unsure and difficult. Seneh was thorny, perhaps because of thorn bushes or other plants with thorns, making climbing difficult. The jagged cliffs rose up like towering pillars. The topography shows the courage Jonathan exercised in passing through these cliffs to reach the Philistine garrison.

14:6-10. Jonathan then said to his armor bearer, **Come and let us cross over to the garrison of these uncircumcised; perhaps the LORD will work for us** (v. 6). Jonathan added that the Lord could save **by many or by few**. The armor bearer responded, **Here I am with you**

according to your desire (v. 7; lit., "according to your heart"). Jonathan's armor bearer was committed to Jonathan's faith commitments.

14:11-15. The Philistines mocked them saying, **Behold, Hebrews are coming out of the holes where they have hidden themselves** (v. 11). Overconfident, the Philistines invited Jonathan and his armor bearer to come up, not realizing that God would give them into Jonathan's hand. The garrison was on a steep hill, requiring Jonathan to climb on his hands and feet. After passing through the dangerous crags, Jonathan and his armor bearer scaled the steep incline leading to the garrison. When they reached the garrison, Jonathan and his armor bearer killed **about twenty men within about half a furrow in an acre of land** (v. 14). The NIV renders this phrase as **an area of about half an acre**, that is, a small plot of land.

In 13:7 the men following Saul were "trembling." Now the Philistines were **trembling in the camp, in the field, and among all the people** (v. 15). Even a great earthquake caused **a great trembling** (v. 15b; lit., "trembling of God").

2. Great Confusion among the Philistines (14:16-23)

14:16-19. Seeing what happened in the Philistine camp, Saul's watchmen in Gibeah said **the multitude melted away** (v. 16). Knowing something had happened, Saul demanded to know who was missing from the Israelite camp. The report that the missing men were **Jonathan and his armor bearer** (v. 17) was ominous in light of Saul's curse that same day (cf. 14:23-24). While Saul was talking, the commotion in the Philistine camp continued to increase, so Saul told the priest Abijah, who had come to pray and consult God for the troops (cf. 14:3), **withdraw your hand** (v. 19). Saul's order was a serious breach of the biblical rules of engagement in a battle. According to the Lord's word (cf. Dt 20:1-4), before Israel engaged in battle the priest was instructed to pray for the people and offer words of encouragement with the challenge to trust the Lord. Yet Saul stopped Abijah in the middle of his required task because he thought he would lose the strategic military moment. Saul led as if the Lord was not a part of the equation.

14:20-23. Ironically, the Lord used the many swords of the Philistine military against them. The battle went so well for Israel that two groups who had refused to fight now joined in the attack. These included some **Hebrews** who had defected to the side of the Philistines, probably deserters who wanted to save their own skins (v. 21). And as the news of victory reached the Israelites, those **who had hidden themselves in the hill country of Ephraim** (v. 22) also pursued the Philistines in battle. Even these two groups of cowardly soldiers joined those with Saul and Jonathan (v. 21). The narrator attributed the deliverance that day to **the Lord** (v. 23).

3. Saul's Foolish Vow (14:24-35)

14:24-30. Now the men of Israel were hard-pressed on that day (v. 24). On the very day of one of the greatest deliverances in Israel's history, instead of rejoicing, singing, and dancing as their fathers and mothers did after the deliverance at the Red Sea (cf. Ex 15:20, Jdg 5:1-31), the people were hard-pressed (cf. 13:6) because Saul put the people under a "foolish oath" (Tsumura, *The First Book of Samuel,* 368), cursing anyone who ate food until the evening (v. 24). Men in battle need the physical strength that food provides. Saul's oath was rash and unnecessary, made because of his desire for revenge on his enemies. It also caused the people to commit a grievous error that night when the famished troops ate several animals with the blood (cf. v. 32). Though hungry, **no man put his hand to his mouth, for the people feared the oath** (v. 26). Unaware of his father's oath, Jonathan ate some of the honey, and he was strengthened (**his eyes brightened**). An unnamed person told Jonathan about the oath: **Cursed be the man who eats food today** (v. 28). Jonathan responded, **My father has troubled the land** (v. 29). Jonathan was wise, using himself as an example of the benefits of eating a little of the honey. Had the people been allowed to eat of the spoil of their enemies, the victory over the Philistines would have been even greater.

14:31-35. The narrator reported that **the people were very weary** (v. 31) in addition to being hungry. The weariness and hunger of the people explain the ravenous consumption of the spoil, and the eating of the meat with the blood in direct violation of Scripture (cf. Lv 3:17; 17:10-13). Hearing about the people sinning against the Lord by eating meat with the blood, Saul took measures to stop them (vv. 33-34). So for the first time **Saul built an altar to the Lord**. Saul seemingly did so out of expediency instead of heartfelt devotion, although some commentators say he was being "scrupulously pious" (Walter Brueggemann, *First and Second Samuel*, Interpretation: A Bible Commentary for Teaching and Preaching [Louisville, KY: John Knox Press,

1990], 105) and his offering was "a propitiatory sacrifice to the Lord" (Merrill, "1 Samuel," 446).

4. The Lottery that Identified Jonathan (14:36-46)

14:36-44. Saul took some initiative in battle, desiring to go down after the Philistines at night. Saul inquired of God, but God **did not answer him on that day** (v. 37). On the great day of the Lord's deliverance, He did not speak to Saul, because Saul's relationship with the Lord was not as it should have been. Saul thought the Lord was silent because of someone's hidden sin. Hence, he called for an investigation to identify the culprit, who was Saul himself (v. 38). Ironically Saul did something rash again, declaring that even if the culprit were his son Jonathan, he would **surely die** (v. 39). The lot pointed to Jonathan, and Saul pronounced the death penalty on his courageous son (vv. 40-44).

14:45-46. Jonathan was a victim of his own father's poor leadership. The people, however, came to Jonathan's rescue. They refused to bow to the king's wishes, saying, **as the Lord lives, there shall not one hair of his head fall to the ground** (v. 45). The great victory the Lord accomplished through Jonathan would have been even greater had Saul used wisdom and sound judgment. Like Saul, carnal and incompetent leaders can make foolish decisions, thereby reducing divine impact.

5. Summary of the Good Years of Saul's Reign (14:47-52)

14:47-52. These verses give the impression that in spite of some major bumps in the road such as the rejection of Saul's dynasty, Saul was destined to have a great reign. But it was not to be so—in the very next chapter he would lose his status as the Lord's chosen leader. According to Bergen, the probable explanation for the "puzzling" inclusion of this summary of Saul's career at this point (vv. 47-48) is that, in the narrator's view, Saul was no longer God's anointed leader (Bergen, *1, 2 Samuel*, 162). Thus, his career was summarized as if he were deceased. This same reason is possibly the explanation for listing Saul's family members (vv. 49-51).

G. The Lord Rejects Saul as King (15:1-35)

1. Saul Disobeys the Word of the Lord (15:1-9)

15:1-2. Samuel reminded Saul that his purpose as king over Israel was to **listen to the words of the Lord** (v. 1). This meant to listen with the intent to obey. The Amalekites were the descendants of Esau (cf. Gn 36:12). The tension between them and Israel was not because of ethnic differences, but because of the Amalekites' satanically charged animosity against the Lord and His people (cf. Nm 24:20; Dt 25:17-19). Saul's mission was to execute the Lord's wrath on the Amalekites for their vicious attack on Israel centuries earlier when Israel came out of Egypt (cf. Ex 17:8-16; Dt 25:17-19). Their attack was actually against the Lord and His reign (cf. Ex 17:16).

15:3-5. Samuel told Saul to **utterly destroy** all that the Amalekites had. The verb "destroy" (Hb. *herem)* means "to completely turn something over to the Lord" in judgment, in this case, the belongings of enemies. The Hebrews were not to keep these spoils, but to destroy them completely. This verb occurs several times in this chapter (vv. 3, 8, 9, 15, 18, 20). Verse 21 uses the noun *zeram,* **devoted to destruction**. Saul was not to spare any of the Amalekites, not even children and infants. Though this command is difficult to comprehend, the severity of *herem* underscores how serious sin is in the Lord's eyes. "The command came from a perfectly just God and was the just execution of judgment on sin" (Laney, *First and Second Samuel*, 51). What God commanded turned Saul and his army into instruments of God's wrath. This practice was restricted to the OT theocracy; it is not to be practiced today. Israel was uniquely the people and the chosen nation of God, set apart to bear His name and His witness to the world. It was vital that the Israelites not be exposed to the influence of sinful, pagan peoples who would lead them into compromise and syncretism in the worship of God (for further discussion, see Excursus: Canaanite Genocide – Killing the Seemingly Innocent at Jos 6:21).

15:6-9. The Kenites, whom Saul encouraged to leave the scene of battle for safety, were descendants of Moses' father-in-law Jethro (cf. Ex 2:16-22; 3:1; 18:1-27; Jdg 1:16; 4:11). Unlike the Amalekites, the Kenites had treated Israel "with loyalty on their march up from Egypt" (Klein, *1 Samuel*, 150). Saul defeated the Amalekites, but his obedience was partial, for he spared **Agag**, the Amalekite king.

2. The Lord Regrets that He Made Saul King over Israel (15:10-35)

15:10-12. According to Marvin R. Wilson, to **regret** (v. 11) indicates that God relents or changes His dealings with people according to His sovereign purposes (cf. Gn 6:6-7: Ex 32:14; Jdg 2:18; 1Sm 15:11). Wilson writes, "On the surface, such language seems inconsistent, if not contradictory, with certain passages which affirm God's immutability . . . (1 Sam 15:29 contra v. 11 . . . Ps 110:4). When [regret] is used of God, however, the expression is anthropopathic and there is not ultimate tension. From man's earthly, limited, finite perspective it only appears that God's purposes have changed. Thus the OT states that God 'repented' of the judgments or 'evil' which he had planned to carry out (1 Chr 21:15; Jr 18:8; 26:3, 19; Amos 7:3, 6; Jon 3:10)" (Marvin Wilson, "regret," in TWOT, edited by R. Laird Harris, Gleason L. Archer, Bruce K. Waltke (Chicago: Moody, 1980], 570–71). Saul's disobedience brought sorrow to the heart of God. The next day Samuel learned that Saul was setting up **a monument for himself** in Gilgal (v. 12). People erected monuments in honor of the Lord, but never in honor of a human.

15:13-16. Saul's statement that he **carried out the command of the LORD** (v. 13) was untrue and inaccurate. In 15:1, Samuel told Saul to "listen (from the verb *shama*) to the words (lit., "voice," *qol*) of the LORD." Ironically, in v. 14, Samuel asked, **what then is this bleating** [lit., "voice," *qol*] **of the sheep in my ears, and the lowing** [also *qol*] **of the oxen which I hear?** ("hear" is also from the verb *shama*, as in 15:1). By this ironic word play, the author clearly indicated that Saul had failed to do what Samuel and the Lord required, in spite of Saul's insistence to the contrary. Saul attempted to deflect his disobedience by piously declaring that **the people spared the best of the sheep and oxen, to sacrifice to the LORD your God; but the rest we utterly destroyed** (v. 15).

15:17-19. In light of everything that the Lord had done for Saul, his disobedience was foolish and inexcusable. Saul himself was in a greedy, lustful frenzy. Samuel asked him, **Why then did you not obey the voice of the LORD, but rushed upon the spoil?** (v. 19). Saul rushed on the spoil like a predatory animal seizes its victim. The verbs "rushed" and "did" in v. 19 are in the second person singular, indicating that Samuel was singling out Saul himself as the guilty party.

15:20-23. Saul blamed the people for the partial disobedience. He said, **the people took . . . the choicest of the things devoted to destruction** [*herem*]. But the narrator wrote in v. 9, "Saul and the people spared Agag." Then Samuel uttered an unforgettable statement to communicate to Saul the error of his way. Samuel began with a question to probe Saul's thinking: **Has the LORD as much delight in burnt offerings and sacrifices as in obeying the voice of the LORD?** (v. 22). The question implied that the Lord delights in obedience to His Word far more than sacrifices. Samuel then said, **Behold, to obey is better than sacrifice, and to heed better than the fat of rams**. Samuel then identified the nature of Saul's sin. **Rebellion is as the sin of divination, and insubordination is as iniquity and idolatry** (v. 23a). Divination was the sin of consulting mediums and witches (which Saul later did [cf. 1Sm 28:3-25], even though he had removed them!). Iniquity was the twisting of sin, and idolatry involved replacing God with false gods as objects of worship. Saul's sins of rebellion, willful disobedience, and insubordination bore similarities to these other sins in that they removed God from His rightful place in a person's life (Bergen, *1, 2 Samuel*, 172-73). Saul's disobedience had serious consequences. **Because you have rejected the word of the LORD, He has also rejected you from being king** (v. 23b). Not only would Saul not have a dynasty, but the Lord also had rejected Saul himself as king. In God's eyes Saul's reign ended when Samuel spoke these words to him.

15:24-31. Saul admitted, **I have sinned**. Then he stated that fear was the source of his disobedience. Instead of listening to the voice of God, he had listened to the voice of the people. Because Saul rejected God's words, God would reject him from being king. Rejection is mentioned twice in v. 23 and twice in v. 26. When Saul took hold of Samuel's robe and **tore** it (v. 27), Samuel used the tearing action as a disturbing object lesson for Saul. Samuel said, **The LORD has torn the kingdom of Israel from you today** (v. 28).

Samuel used a striking term for God in v. 29, calling Him **the Glory** [or Eminence] **of Israel**. He is immutable and His plans do not change. The rejection of Saul and the giving of the kingdom to his neighbor were as fixed as God's unchangeable nature. Image control was the only reason Saul wanted Samuel to return with him (vv. 30-31).

15:32-35. Samuel then executed God's judgment on Agag, the Amalekite king. Agag thought, **Surely the bitterness of death is past**. But Samuel's words to Agag showed that because Agag was an evil man, he would suffer the same fate as his many victims. The narrator wrote that Saul's disobedience **grieved** Samuel, just as God

regretted making **Saul king** (v. 35; cf. 1Sm 16:11). These two statements (vv. 11 and 35) form an *inclusio*, bracketing the action of vv. 11 through 35, showing that both the Lord and Samuel were grieved over Saul's rebellion (Laney, *First and Second Samuel*, 52). Rebellion against the Lord's voice grieves Him, resulting in disastrous consequences for the disobedient. Saul's rejection opened a new period in the history of the monarchy in Israel.

III. David, a Man after God's Own Heart (16:1–31:13)

Chapter 16 begins one of the most engaging sections of the Old Testament. The author focused attention primarily on David, the main subject of the books of Samuel, until the end of 2 Samuel. In essence, the stories of Samuel and Saul were included as prologue to the story of David. Next to Moses, no one captured Israel's imagination like David.

A. David Prospers in Saul's Court (16:1–20:42)

Although rejected, Saul did not relinquish the throne; he held on to power for years until the day he committed suicide on Mount Gilboa. The Lord, however, prepared David to be the next king of Israel, using the demonically influenced Saul to shape David. Years would pass before David reached the throne over all Israel, but in the process David learned to trust the Lord in times of despair, fear, and pain. David's experiences under Saul are some of the most moving and instructive accounts in the OT.

1. The Divine Choice of David (16:1-23)

a. The Lord Looks at the Heart (16:1-13)

16:1-3. Although Samuel continued to grieve over Saul's disobedience, God was ready to do something new. This is a momentous point in the narrative, bringing onto the scene the central character of the rest of 1 Samuel and all of 2 Samuel. Saul did not have God's will, interests, and glory at heart, so God selected a person who did—a shepherd boy who became the shepherd of all of Israel (cf. 2Sm 5:2, Brueggemann, *First and Second Samuel*, 119). God selected as king the youngest son of Jesse of Bethlehem, called **Jesse the Bethlehemite** (v. 1). When Samuel expressed his apprehension to the Lord about doing what God had just told him to do, the Lord did not dismiss Samuel's fears. He told Samuel how to proceed.

16:4-5. The elders were a group of older and experienced men who were responsible for the leadership of the city. Consecrating oneself meant "to set oneself apart to God." Consecration involved ceremonial cleansing and abstaining from certain foods and sex with their wives. Consecration was necessary because of the solemnity of the occasion before the Lord. Samuel invited two groups of people to the sacrifice: the elders of Bethlehem and Jesse and his sons.

16:6-7. Observing Eliab, Jesse's eldest son (cf. 1Ch 2:13), Samuel concluded, **Surely the Lord's anointed is before Him**. Samuel may have thought of Saul's impressive physical appearance, but that is not what the Lord was seeing. He was looking at the heart. He chooses His servants based on their inner lives, not on how they look.

16:8-10. All seven of Jesse's sons passed before Samuel from the oldest to the youngest, but the Lord had not chosen any of them.

16:11-13. This posed a problem for Samuel, so he asked, **Are these all the children?** Jesse responded that he had one more son, **the youngest** in the family. He was **tending the sheep**, and his father did not even mention his name. So David was sent for, and he was God's choice. David was ruddy, that is, he was tan from working and living outdoors, and he was **handsome**. How much David's family understood about what happened is not important. Samuel anointed David as king and then went home **to Ramah**.

b. David Serves in the Court of Saul (16:14-23)

16:14. In contrast to the Spirit of God coming on David (v. 13), **the Spirit** of God **departed from Saul** (v. 14). The Spirit of God did not indwell believers in the OT era the way He does today. When a person today receives Christ as his Lord and Savior, the Spirit of God comes to indwell that person forever (cf. Jn 14:16-17; 1Co 12:13). But there was more evidence that the Lord had rejected Saul from being king. **An evil spirit from the Lord terrorized him**. Rather than suggesting that the Lord's Spirit could at times be evil, the Hebrew phrase is better translated, "a spirit of evilness (or disaster)," in this case probably a spirit whose mission is judgment upon Saul (Tsumura, *The First Book of Samuel*, 427). The terror brought upon Saul was not just fright, but of partial incapacitation. This raises questions about God's morality and sovereignty. The Bible teaches here and elsewhere (see for example Jb 1–2) that God governs even the powers of darkness through His providence without being morally culpable for their actions (a profound mystery indeed). God's sovereignty over such a spirit served two purposes. First, it was surely an act of judgment against Saul for his rebellion against God. Second, David's music would provide relief for Saul from the spirit's torment. This would also lead Saul to retain David, resulting in David gaining important experience in how to lead as a king by being exposed to Saul.

16:15-18. Saul's servants knew the source of his problem, so they proposed music as a solution. Providentially, one of Saul's servants knew about David, who already had a good reputation. He was described as a **skillful musician, a mighty man of valor, a warrior, one prudent in speech, and a handsome man; and the LORD is with him** (v. 18). The presence of God in David's life was observable.

16:19-23. The way Saul asked for David suggests that Saul knew of young David's occupation. So he said to Jesse, **Send me your son David who is with the flock**. Thus David **attended** (lit., "stood before" in order to serve) Saul. Saul admired David, but it was short-lived. For the time being, however, David became Saul's armor bearer. An armor bearer was a special assistant to a king or a prominent military person. His main task was to carry the king's armor. In times of danger and battle, the armor bearer stood with the king or prince; the armor bearer was available to carry out the king's orders and wishes. Being close to the king, David would gain some insight into what was involved in being a king. Unknown to Saul, God in His providence placed David—God's choice for king—in his presence as his musician and his armor bearer. It is likely that David learned a considerable amount about what it meant to function as king during this time.

The plan of Saul's servants worked for the moment. When David played, **the evil spirit would depart** from Saul (v. 23).

2. David's Victory over Goliath (17:1-58)

The account of David and Goliath is one of the longest and best-known Bible stories. Its inclusion here is to answer the question raised in the previous chapter at the anointing of David, where it says, "Man looks at the outward appearance, but the LORD looks at the heart" (16:7). What did the Lord see in David that was not present in his brothers or in Saul? The answer to that question is in the story of David and Goliath.

a. Forty Days of Defiance (17:1-11)

17:1. Preparing for battle against Israel, the Philistines camped on the south side of "the valley of Elah" a few miles southwest of Jerusalem (Merrill, "1 Samuel," 448) in **Ephes-dammin** (which means "boundary of blood" because of blood spilled there in battles).

17:2-4. Saul and his men assembled on the north side of **the valley of Elah**. The valley's plain was between the two armies.

A Philistine **champion** named Goliath appeared on the scene (v. 4). The word "champion" means "a man between two," that is, between two armies. Sometimes a champion from each army would fight, and the war's outcome was decided by which champion won the battle. This approach minimized bloodshed. Goliath was **six cubits and a span** in height. A cubit was approximately 18 inches, and a span was half a cubit. So Goliath was nine feet, nine inches in height. The Lucian recension of the LXX from the third century AD, a Dead Sea Scroll version of 1 Samuel (called 4QSama) and Josephus (*Ant.* 6.171) all predate the Hebrew Masoretic Text, providing an ancient witness to Goliath being "*four* cubits and a span" in height, or about six feet nine inches tall.

If this is the preferred reading (and there is much evidence to suggest that it is), then Saul although shorter than the giant, was closer in size, standing a head taller than the rest of the Israelites (1Sm 9:2), perhaps six-feet-five-inches. (The height of the average Israelite male at this time was no more than five-feet six-inches tall.) Clearly it would be more logical that Saul should have been the one to fight the Philistine. He also was one of the few Israelite soldiers to have bronze armor similar to Goliath's (cf. 17:38-39) since bronze was rare in those days. By any measure, Saul was the obvious choice to fight the Philistine.

In addition, the people believed Saul's job as king was to "go out before us and fight our battles" (8:20). His failure to engage Goliath—his apparent cowardice in running away from him with the other soldiers (cf. 17:24)—is included by the writer to prove that Saul was unfit for duty as Israel's king, and that David was (see the comments below). For this understanding of the Goliath episode, see J. Daniel Hays, "Reconsidering the Height of Goliath," *JETS* 48 (December 2005): 713-14. This story is more about David vs. *Saul* than David vs. *Goliath*!

17:5-7. Armor covered a warrior's chest and abdomen. Goliath's bronze armor **weighed five thousand shekels of bronze**, that is, about 126 pounds. Goliath's shin guards were **bronze**. Between his shoulders, meaning on his back, was a **bronze javelin**. A javelin was like a spear, but was shorter and lighter. Goliath had a spear shaped **like a weaver's beam**, which suggests that it was thick and easily handled. The head or point of the spear **weighed six hundred shekels of iron**, or about 15 pounds of iron. Goliath had a **shield-carrier** walk in front of him. Shields were large enough to protect a warrior, so Goliath's shield was about nine feet in height. Goliath also had a sword in his sheath (cf. v. 45). Viewing this giant must have been terrifying to the Israelites.

17:8-11. Goliath challenged Israel to battle twice a day for **forty days** (v. 16). The events of chap. 17 cover a period of almost one and a half months. When Saul and all Israel heard Goliath's challenge, terror seized them—**they were dismayed and greatly afraid**. Their fear demonstrated a serious lack of trust in God and His covenant promises.

b. David's Visit to the Battlefront (17:12-19)

17:12. Jesse, David's father, is identified here as an **Ephrathite** from **Bethlehem** (cf. 16:1). Ephrath was the ancient name of Bethlehem (cf. Gn 35:19; 48:7), and so an Ephrathite was an inhabitant of Bethlehem.

17:13-16. The three eldest sons of Jesse are mentioned again as they were in chap. 16. These men were old enough to engage in battle (cf. Nm 1:3). Their failure to engage Goliath shows the reason the Lord did not select one of them to be king. David served in Saul's court, but Saul permitted him to go **back and forth** (v. 15) between the court and David's home to look after his father's sheep.

17:17-19. Jesse sent David to the front line to learn of the welfare of his brothers and to take them some food. Jesse's words that **Saul . . . and all the men of Israel are in the valley of Elah, fighting with the Philistines** (v. 19) are ironic, because Saul and his army were in a standoff that would reach 40 days by the time David arrived on the scene of the battle.

c. David Answers Goliath's Challenge (17:20-30)

17:20-23. About the time David arrived at the camp, providentially Goliath approached with his taunt against God's people. He repeated what he said earlier, and this time **David heard** the giant's words.

17:24-25. During the previous 40 days, Saul gave incentives for someone to answer Goliath's challenge. To be **free in Israel** meant that a person did not have to pay taxes and was exempt from military service. These are hefty incentives even by 21st century standards!

17:26-30. David asked, **Who is this uncircumcised Philistine, that he should taunt the armies of the living God?** Calling him **uncircumcised** was not merely addressing a physical characteristic but indicated that Goliath was a pagan and, unlike Israel, did not have any covenant promises upon which to rely. David understood the spiritual heart of the matter: Goliath's taunt was not merely about Israel, but the God of Israel. **Eliab**, David's oldest brother, became angry at David's words. Perhaps Eliab was upset that his little brother had more faith and courage than he did.

d. David Kills Goliath (17:31-58)

17:31-33. The word that someone in Israel's camp had challenged Goliath reached Saul's ears, so he sent for David. Saul was not impressed with David's youth and lack of military training, thinking the youthful David was no match for Goliath who had been trained in the art of combat since he was a **youth**.

17:34-37. David's response to Saul was admirable. David, the teenaged shepherd, had had some major private victories in his life. In David's day fierce animals such as lions and bears roamed the countryside. But when a lion attacked David's flock and took a lamb, David pursued it. Most people would just take a loss instead of going after a lion, but not David. He attacked the lion and rescued the sheep from its mouth. If the lion decided to fight back, David would grab it by its **beard** (its mane, v. 35) and kill it. Unlike Saul, who was introduced as one who was reluctant to expend the effort to find his father's donkeys (cf. 1Sm 9:5), David was portrayed as ferociously protective, steadfast, and courageous in caring for his father's sheep—a detail included to indicate David's suitability for being Israel's "shepherd" rather than Saul. David considered the Philistine as posing a similar threat as the predatory beasts he encountered. The Lord had delivered David from the lion and the bear, and He would deliver David from Goliath.

17:38-39. Saul tried to prepare David for battle by outfitting him with his own armor. However, David had not used Saul's armor in battle, so he took the armor off. David would trust in God, not human devices, to accomplish the task.

17:40. David selected **five smooth stones from the brook** and put them in his shepherd's bag. Since the text gives no reason for David taking five stones, it is speculation to try to determine the significance of his choice; perhaps he took extra stones in case he missed. Then he held a **sling . . . in his hand**. This was not a child's slingshot, but a deadly weapon that was used by ancient armies, consisting of a pouch or pocket attached at each side to two long cords (Klein, *1 Samuel*, 179). A master slinger could sling a tennis-ball sized stone that traveled at the speed of well over one hundred miles an hour, faster than most professional baseball pitchers can throw a fastball today. David then **approached the Philistine**.

17:41-42. Looking at David, Goliath drew the wrong conclusion about him. The giant believed he could easily kill this **youth . . . he disdained** David.

17:43-47. In antiquity warriors talked to each other before they fought, lacing their speeches with curses and expletives. Goliath threatened to feed David to the vultures and wild **beasts** (v. 44). But David's response was different. He battled in God's name. David's goal was the glory of God, **that all the earth may know that there is a God in Israel** (v. 46).

David's miraculous victory over Goliath would point the nations to God and serve an evangelistic purpose. David's purpose was also to help God's people see that human weaponry alone was not the means of deliverance, because **the battle is the LORD's** (v. 47). Goliath was not fighting against David; he was defying God. Since the battle belonged to the Lord, He would **give** Goliath into David's **hands**.

17:48-54. Suddenly, the talking stopped. **David ran quickly toward the battle line** (v. 48) in contrast to Saul and the others running away (cf. v. 24). **David put his hand into his bag and took from it a stone and slung it, and struck the Philistine on his forehead. And the stone sank into his forehead** (v. 49). Goliath was defeated in a matter of a few seconds.

Goliath was out cold, but he was not dead. So David took Goliath's own **sword** and **cut off** Goliath's **head** (v. 51). Seeing Goliath dead, the Philistines fled. Israel decisively defeated the Philistines on this day. After chasing the Philistines, the Israelites went through their camps and **plundered** them, taking useful goods and animals (v. 53). David took Goliath's **head . . . to Jerusalem**.

17:55-58. The narrator went back to an earlier part of the story when David was going out to face Goliath. Saul questioned Abner, the commander of his army, about David's father. Saul's questioning seems strange in light of Saul having earlier asked Jesse's permission to keep David at his court. After the battle Abner took David to Saul. The chapter ends with Saul questioning David about who his father was. A likely explanation for this scene is that because Saul did not ask David for his name, but the name of his father, he wanted to make sure of David's family so he could properly reward Jesse (cf. v. 25; Laney, *First and Second Samuel*, 50). Merrill suggests another possibility, that Saul's questioning may reflect that David's earlier service had been intermittent, and it may have been several years since Saul had last seen him (Merrill, "1 Samuel," 448-49). Whatever the case, the Lord used David instead of Saul because David learned lessons from past victories (vv. 34-36), understood the nature of the threat (v. 26), and recognized that each battle is the Lord's (v. 47).

The dramatic narrative shows why the Lord had David anointed: the youth had a distinct quality that made him more suitable to be king than either Saul or his brothers. This quality was that David cared more for the honor of God than his own safety or security. When applying this passage today, it is best not to allegorize it with discussions of how to overcome the giants in life. Rather it is appropriate to ask, what kind of people does God choose to use? The answer, of course is, people who care more about honoring the Lord than preserving their own safety and security.

3. Responses to David's Godly Success (18:1-30)

A number of scenarios unfolded in this chapter. David was divinely moved closer to the throne he would occupy when Saul made him a permanent member of his court. But according to Chisholm, the hatred and jealousy of Saul show that the road to the throne would not be easy for David; it "will consume the story until Saul's death and even then will not be completely resolved" (Robert Chisholm, *1 & 2 Samuel* [Grand Rapids, MI: Baker, 2013], 122). Yet, Chisholm continues, this posed no conflict for the narrator, whose description of events showed that everyone else loved David—even Saul's own son and daughter (Chisholm, *1 & 2 Samuel*, 122).

a. Godly Covenant Friendship and Love (18:1-5)

18:1-5. Jonathan, Saul's son, admired David, having observed his courageous faith. Saul no longer allowed David to return home to care for his father's sheep (cf. 16:19; 17:15), probably because David was now old enough to serve in the army. Saul had earlier made David his armor bearer (cf. 16:21), and now Saul put David in command of the army (v. 5). **Then Jonathan made a covenant with David** (v. 3). A covenant in Scripture was a solemn promise that bound the parties to its provisions. So strongly did Jonathan love David that merely expressing his friendship was not enough. Jonathan also recognized that David, not he, was the true heir to Israel's throne. Evidently these two realities led Jonathan to make this covenant of friendship, a friendship that demanded loyalty. The friendship between these two godly men lasted for the rest of their lives. Jonathan gave David his **robe** . . . **armor** . . . **sword** . . . **bow** . . . and **belt** (v. 4), symbolic gestures of respect and friendship. Saul set David over his soldiers, and David's promotion pleased everyone. The shepherd boy's courageous faith fired the entire nation's imagination.

b. Saul's Murderous Envy and Suspicion (18:6-9)

18:6-9. The women from all Israel's cities sang and danced in the streets with **tambourines** as they welcomed their men home. Centuries earlier, the same kind of celebration occurred after the miraculous crossing of the Red Sea (cf. Ex 15:20-21). Tsumura states, "Women in Israel celebrated a victory with singing and dancing and instruments," and adds Jdg 11:34 as an example (Tsumura, *The First Book of Samuel*, 476). The women sang that Saul had **slain his thousands** (v. 7a). However, Saul had not actually killed thousands in battle; this was poetic liberty. Then the women sang their second line: **And David his ten thousands** (v. 7b). Hearing that, **Saul became very angry, for this saying displeased him; and he said** [thought], **they have ascribed to David ten thousands, but to me they have ascribed thousands. Now what more can he have but the kingdom?** (v. 8). From now on Saul would view David through the lens of envy, jealously, and **suspicion** (v. 9), and with good reason. Saul had failed miserably in his role as king, namely, to lead his warriors in battle (cf. 8:20). Where he failed, David succeeded, and even at this early stage there was a widespread recognition of his abilities. David, who was the true, anointed king (cf. 16:13), could have begun to exercise his kingly role at this point and the people would have welcomed it—and Saul knew it. Thus his reaction was not simply one of envy. It included fear of being displaced as king.

c. Demonic Influence on Saul (18:10-11)

18:10-11. Saul yielded to this fear and jealousy. As in 16:14, 23, **an evil spirit from God** afflicted Saul yet again (for the theology of this, see the comments on 16:14). Saul tried to kill David twice, but he was not successful.

d. Fear and Manipulation (18:12-19)

18:12-16. Saul feared David because **the LORD was with** David but had departed from the king. Fearful of David, Saul demoted him, assigning him military leadership over **a thousand** (v. 13), thereby regularly putting David's life at risk. In spite of his demotion, David prospered in all his ways because **the LORD was with him** (v. 14).

18:17-19. Saul should have given his **older daughter Merab** to David after he slew Goliath (cf. 17:25), but Saul did not keep his word. Instead he offered **Merab** in marriage to David, provided David fought **the LORD's battles**. Saul used the cloak of marriage and zeal for the Lord to hide his dark purpose to set David up to be killed in battle by God's enemies. A date was set for the marriage, but when the time came the marriage was cancelled. Then Saul gave Merab to **Adriel the Meholathite** as his **wife**. Even though David was humble, not feeling worthy to become the king's son-in-law, Saul's behavior was inexcusable. Merab and Adriel had five sons.

Years later, in a severe act of judgment on "Saul and his bloody house" (cf. 2Sm 21:1), seven of his descendants were hanged by the Gibeonites (cf. 2Sm 21:7-9). Saul had sinned by putting some of the Gibeonites to death in his zeal to rid Israel of pagans, even though Israel had a long-standing treaty with the Gibeonites (cf. Jos 9:3-27). Five of those who died were the sons of Merab and Adriel (Laney, *First and Second Samuel*, 123-24). All five were executed by hanging (cf. 2Sm 21:7-9). They were executed "before the Lord" (2Sm 21:9), indicating that the judgment was ultimately His.

e. A Grisly Dowry (18:20-30)

18:20-22. The name **Michal**, which means "who is like God?" is the feminine form of "Michael." When Saul heard about Michal's love for David, he was pleased. However, he was pleased not for his daughter and David, but because he designed to use his daughter's love as a snare to David. Saul hid his true thoughts and feelings about David in words of praise and with an invitation to become his **son-in-law**.

18:23-27. David could not afford Michal's dowry, the amount of money a man gave to the parents of his bride when he married her. Saul, however, was willing to be "flexible" by accepting the grisly dowry of one **hundred** Philistine **foreskins** (v. 25). When victors defeated enemy soldiers in battle, sometimes they cut off their heads, taking them as victory trophies. Saul's request for foreskins instead of heads or other body parts may have something to do with the Philistines being uncircumcised, and were often called by that "title" (cf. 1Sm 14:6; 17:26; Tsumura, *The First Book of Samuel*, 486). In any case, Saul was hoping that with the danger involved in David's seeking to secure the grisly dowry, the Philistines would kill David in the process. David had an allotted time to secure the foreskins, but before the time was up, David and his men killed not only one hundred Philistines but **two hundred** (v. 27). David walked into the king's chamber with his dowry, so Saul had no choice but to give his daughter Michal to David in marriage.

18:28-30. Saul became even more afraid of David when he realized the Lord was with David (repeated three times in this chapter, vv. 12, 14, 28), and that his daughter loved David. The very actions Saul plotted against David contributed to his success because the Lord was with David.

4. Four Examples of David's Divine Protection (19:1-24)

a. The Lord Uses Jonathan to Protect David (19:1-7)

19:1-7. If there was any lingering doubt that David was God's choice as Israel's next king, and thus enjoyed divine protection, chap. 19 would lay that doubt to rest. Saul's fear of David grew to a new level of homicidal intent when, "dropping all ruses, Saul now explicitly ordered Jonathan and all his servants to 'kill David'" (Bergen, *1, 2 Samuel*, 206). Saul wanted Jonathan involved in the vicious plot to murder David because Saul knew his son was close to David. However, Jonathan's attitude toward David contrasted with his father's. For the first time David learned from Jonathan himself about Saul's intentions to have David killed. Jonathan reasoned with his father Saul, urging him not to kill him. Listening to Jonathan, Saul vowed in the Lord's name that David **shall not be put to death** (v. 6). Thus, the Lord protected David through Jonathan's intervention.

b. The Lord Uses Saul's Miss to Protect David (19:8-10)

19:8-10. While David was playing his harp to soothe Saul, the king hurled his spear at David in another attempt to kill him, but he missed. The Lord protected David through Saul's miss and through David's skill in escaping Saul's presence. Saul failed to keep his vow (v. 6). (Regarding the **evil spirit from the Lord**, see the comments on 16:14.)

c. The Lord Uses Michal to Protect David (19:11-17)

19:11-17. David's house was a part of the city's wall complex. Escape through the window put him outside the city, out of the messengers' immediate sight and reach. The Hebrew word for **household idol** (v. 13) is *teraphim*. These were idols kept in a home, and used for divination purposes and misguided worship. Possessing them was thought to promote fertility. The OT denounced the use of *teraphim* (cf. 2Kg 23:24; Ezk 21:21; Zch 10:1-2). Michal used these idols to mislead her father's men to think David was in bed. She **put a quilt of goats' hair at its head** to look like David's hair, and **covered it with clothes**, presumably David's (v. 13). When Saul sent a second group to take David, Michal told them that David was **sick** (v. 14). Saul then sent a third group to David's house, demanding that they bring David on his sickbed so Saul could execute him. In humor the narrator wrote that when the messengers entered the house, they found the **household idol was on the bed with the quilt of goats' hair at its head** (v. 16). When Michal claimed she helped David because he threatened her life (the sense of v. 17), she lied again in order to protect herself from Saul. The Lord protected David through the warning, deception, lying, and slick behavior of Michal. In response to this event David composed Ps 59 (see the comments on the heading for the psalm there).

d. The Lord Uses His Own Spirit to Protect David (19:18-24)

19:18-23. The narrator emphasized David's escape (vv. 10, 12, 17-18) and constant flight (vv. 10, 12, 18; cf. 20:1). He and Samuel **stayed** in **Naioth**, near Ramah (v. 18, cf. 20:1). It is uncertain as to whether **Naioth** is a proper name or a common noun. It may refer to the compound in Ramah where Samuel's company of the prophets (cf. 20) lived (Youngblood, "1, 2 Samuel," 201). If so, it would seem to have been a safe place for David to hide from Saul. Three times Saul sent messengers to take David (vv. 20, 21 [twice]). But then the unexpected happened: The Spirit of God came on all three groups of Saul's emissaries. Then when Saul himself went to apprehend David, God's Spirit came on him.

19:24. Saul then **stripped off his** royal **clothes** (v. 24). This bizarre incident, in which Saul lay incapacitated by the Holy Spirit for 24 hours, may have been to keep him from committing "some dreadful crime" against David (Baldwin, *1 and 2 Samuel*, 133), or the result of God's Spirit working in Saul to bring him to repentance (Laney, *First and Second Samuel*, 43-44), or both. Bergen says that Saul's removal of his royal clothes in the presence of God's Spirit was a powerful image of God's rejection of him as king (Bergen, *1, 2 Samuel*, 211). The word **naked** (v. 24) does not necessarily mean that Saul removed all of his clothes, but just his outer garments (Tsumura, *The First Book of Samuel*, 499). God protected David by His Spirit coming on Saul's men and on Saul himself, showing that the Lord uses different ways and means to protect His servants.

5. Covenant Friendship Put to the Test (20:1-42)

a. One Step between Life and Death (20:1-11)

20:1-4. Leaving **Naioth**, David asked Jonathan, **What have I done? What is my iniquity? And what is my sin before your father, that he is seeking my life?** According to vv. 2-3, Jonathan was unaware of the events recorded in chap. 19. David's oath, **as the Lord lives and as your soul lives**, voiced words that captured the sentiments of people who felt death's razor edge: **there is hardly a step between me and death** (v. 3). If Saul was trying to kill him, this meant David would need to leave Saul's court, his wife, and the comfort of home and become a fugitive.

20:5-6. David and Jonathan used the occasion of **the new moon** to ascertain Saul's true intentions. David would be expected to accept the king's invitation to the celebration, so his absence would give Saul the opportunity either to accept David's reason gladly and excuse him, or fly into a rage at the snub, revealing to Jonathan the true depth of Saul's intent to do David harm—and Saul's past actions gave a clue as to his response (Brueggemann, *First and Second Samuel*, 147). When the new moon appeared, people celebrated the beginning of a new month by worshiping the Lord. On such an occasion David was expected **to eat with the king**. But since David did not feel safe with Saul, he wanted to hide himself **until the third evening**, perhaps meaning that David wanted to wait until he was sure the observance was over, since in some months the new moon festivities lasted for two nights (Tsumura, *The First Book of Samuel*, 505). In any case, David felt matters would be made clear by then. The pretext for David's absence was his family's annual celebration that took place at this particular new moon.

20:7-9. As stated above, Saul's reaction to David's three-day absence would reveal Saul's intention. Saul's anger would confirm David's statements about Saul's intent to do him harm. David asked Jonathan to deal kindly with him because Jonathan had made a covenant of friendship with David (cf. 18:3). To **deal kindly** meant "to show covenant fidelity, loyalty" in the context of a covenant agreement. David expressed humility, referring to himself as Jonathan's **servant**. The covenant of friendship between Jonathan and David had a vertical dimension as well as a covenant before the Lord. Jonathan's actions in the next section of the chapter exemplify the loyalty of his and David's covenant friendship before the Lord. On the nature of covenanted friendship, see the comments on 18:1-5.

20:10-11. Jonathan and David developed a plan so that if Saul's intentions were as David asserted, Jonathan could communicate Saul's evil plans to David.

b. The Covenant in the Field (20:12-17)

20:12-13. Jonathan emphasized his commitment to inform David if Saul planned to harm him. The formula Jonathan employed was used when a person called down on himself or others a curse or other dire consequences from God for failure to do something specific. **And may the Lord be with you as He has been with my father.** Jonathan realized that David would be king, and he desired that the Lord be with David as king. He departed from the present tense (is) for his father's kingship because he also realized that the Lord was no longer with his father as king.

20:14-15. Jonathan asked David to show **the lovingkindness** (*chesed,* loyal love, love based on covenant fidelity) **of the Lord** to him so that he would **not die**. The practice of a new king killing all potential rivals to the throne was a way of securing power (cf. Jdg 9:5-7; 1Kg 2:19-25, 28-34, 36-49; 15:28-30; 16:10-11; 2Kg 11:1-3). He asked David not to take his life when he came into power. Jonathan said to David, **You shall not cut off your lovingkindness from my house forever, not even when the Lord cuts off every one of the enemies of David from the face of the earth**.

20:16-17. The narrator summarized what occurred between Jonathan and David. If the stipulations of the covenant were not carried out, then instead of saying, "May the LORD require it of David," Jonathan said, **May the LORD require it at the hands of David's enemies**. Jonathan was so concerned for David that he distanced from David the notion of God's judgment.

c. The Coded Message in the Arrows (20:18-23)

20:18-23. The new moon began the next day. After hiding **for three days**, David was to remain **by the stone Ezel**. This prominent stone was a location marker. Baldwin cites the Targum as saying that Ezel, which means "stone of departure," was a "sign stone," and adds that it was an "unmistakable place" (Baldwin, *1 and 2 Samuel*, 136). Jonathan said he would shoot three arrows, and if they went to David's side, that would mean David was safe and he could return to Saul's court. However, if Jonathan told the lad, **the arrows are beyond you** (v. 22), that would mean David must flee.

d. Missed at the King's Table (20:24-29)

20:24-29. Saul noticed David's absence, but he did not say anything. He reasoned that David was not present because of ritual uncleanness (v. 26). The meal was a sacrificial meal and required consecration such as the washing of clothes, physical cleansing, and abstinence from sexual activity between husband and wife. For the first of many times Saul referred to David as **the son of Jesse**, using the designation in a pejorative sense (v. 27, cf. vv. 30-31, 22:7, 8, 13, 28-29). Jonathan explained, lying, that David's family invited him home to Bethlehem to join in a sacrifice.

e. The Unveiling of True Intentions (20:30-34)

20:30-31. Saul used vulgar language to show disrespect to Jonathan and his mother. In his anger Saul attacked his own son, calling him a traitor for siding with David, thereby bringing shame on himself and on his mother. The Lord had rejected Saul from being king; yet he tried to poison Jonathan's mind with the thirst for power, trying to convince him that David was a threat to his future reign.

20:32-34. Saul tried to murder his own son with **his spear** just as he had tried to murder David (cf. 19:8-10). Jonathan **did not** even **eat food on the second day of the new moon**. Not eating on such an occasion was a sign of grief and sorrow over something painful in one's life.

f. The Parting of Friends (20:35-42)

20:35-38. The next morning, when Jonathan shot some arrows past a lad (as he and David had planned, see above on 20:18-23), Jonathan said, **Is not the arrow beyond you?** (v. 37). This meant that Saul planned to murder David. Then when Jonathan told the lad, **Hurry, be quick, do not stay!** this meant David must flee.

20:39-42. In one of the most moving scenes in the Bible David fell on the ground and **bowed three times**, and he and Jonathan **kissed each other**, not indicating any sexual encounter but as the common cultural expression of deep friendship between men (cf. Rm 16:16; 1Co 16:20; 2Co 13:12; 1Th 5:26; 1Pt 5:14). God's young warriors wept, but the narrator adds, **but David wept the more** (v. 41). David would see Jonathan briefly only once more (cf. 1Sm 23:16-18) before Jonathan's death on Mount Gilboa (cf. 1Sm 31:2). Michal, David's wife of his youth, would be given to another man, and David did not see her and reclaim her until some years later (cf. 2Sm 3:12-16).

B. David, a Fugitive from Saul's Court (21:1–31:13)

This section is not random but is included to demonstrate David's training to be the ideal king. Being a fugitive, or living his life on the run, was designed to teach David how to sit on the throne. Hence, such difficult times taught him the lessons of kingship.

1. A Hungry, Weaponless, and Scared Fugitive (21:1-15)

a. Eating the Consecrated Bread (21:1-7)

21:1-2. Nob was "the city of the priests" (cf. 1Sm 22:19) in Benjamin, about two miles east of Jerusalem. The tabernacle, the house of God, was there. Nob may have replaced Shiloh as the central place of worship. This explains why David stopped there first. Ahimelech means "the king's brother." David was alone in that he was not surrounded by high-ranking people from Saul's court. Someone of David's stature usually traveled with a royal entourage, including bodyguards.

21:3-4. David lied to Ahimelech about his presence in Nob. One commentator finds "attractive" the explanation that David was referring to the Lord as **the king** (v. 2) not Saul (Youngblood, "1, 2 Samuel," 213), and thus he spoke truly. But there is nothing in the text to commend that view. Others point out that David was probably unsure if he could trust Ahimelech, who was the brother of Saul's spiritual adviser, Ahijah (cf. 1Sm 14:3; 22:9) (Tsumura, *The First Book of Samuel*, 529; Baldwin, *1 and 2 Samuel*, 137). But again, this is conjecture, and hardly justification anyway for David's lie, which would lead to the slaughter of the priests (cf. 22:6-23). Some young men were with David. **Consecrated bread**, or bread of the Presence (cf. v. 6), was bread baked specifically for use in the tabernacle. Twelve loaves were baked and replaced each Sabbath, and the bread removed from the table was to be eaten only by the priests (cf. Lv 24:5-9). Consecrated bread was available for consumption at that time because the priest had recently removed it from the golden table, replacing it with fresh bread. But since David was in need, the priest made an exception, and gave some of the bread to David and his young men. The Lord Jesus agreed with Ahimelech's decision to act for the greater good (cf. Mt 12:1-7).

21:5-6. David asserted that he and his men met the ceremonial requirements necessary to eat **the bread of the Presence**.

21:7. One of Saul's servants, **Doeg the Edomite**, was detained at Nob that day. Edomites were Esau's descendants (Gn 25:19-23; 36:9). Given the history of Edomite opposition to the Lord and His people (Nm 20:14-21; 24:18, Ob 1), the mention of Doeg "introduces a note of villainy into the narrative" (Eugene H. Peterson, *First and Second Samuel* [Louisville, KY: Westminster John Knox, 1999], 111).

b. David Receives Goliath's Sword (21:8-9)

21:8-9. David lied again about why he did not have a sword. The only sword available was the **sword of Goliath**, whom David slew **in the valley of Elah**. What a reminder to David of the Lord's power to bring victory against incredible odds!

David's visit to Ahimelech the priest taught him a lesson about the need for integrity and honesty, albeit in a grave fashion. Although at first it seems as if his lie (21:2) brought him personal safety, afterward it led to the slaughter of the priests in the city of Nob (22:9-19). Upon seeing the deadly damage he had caused, David expressed regret for what he had done and took responsibility for it (22:22-23).

c. David's Convincing Performance (21:10-15)

21:10-15. Saul did not pursue David in Philistine territory, so David went there for a respite. But in Gath, the hometown of the slain Goliath whose location is uncertain (Unger, *The New Unger's Bible Dictionary,* 459), David feigned loyalty to King Achish. Achish's **servants**, however, recognized David (v. 11). Realizing that Achish's officials knew who he was, David was fearful of his life. To get himself out of this predicament, he pretended to be insane. His strategy worked. Verse 15 implies that David may have talked to some people and convinced them to take him to Achish. They did not know who David was. In connection with his experience at Gath, David composed Pss 34 and 56. The lesson David learned is that he could depend on the Lord's faithfulness in protecting him even when he behaved in a fearful and desperate manner.

2. The Cave of Adullam and the Priests of Nob (22:1-23)

a. Joining David at the Cave of Adullam (22:1-2)

22:1-2. Adullam was a town about 25 miles southwest of Jerusalem. The Judean wilderness was a part of the region. **The cave of Adullam** ("refuge") became David's hiding place. This cave experience may have prompted David to compose Ps 47. In light of the practice of murdering all potential rivals to one's throne, the lives of David's entire family were now in jeopardy, so they joined David at Adullam. In addition to his father's household, more people join David. These were **in distress . . . in debt**, and **discontented** (v. 2). The word **distress** means "to suffer overwhelming external pressure," often brought on by enemies (cf. Is 51:13). The men who came to David were distressed by the circumstances of life, stemming perhaps from Saul's oppression or other circumstances.

Debt means "having a creditor." A creditor in the OT was a person who loaned money to the poor and charged interest on the loan for financial gain. Creditors took advantage of God's people with financial difficulties. Interest on the loan meant the creditor might take the person's home, vineyard, olive groves, and so forth (cf. Neh 5:1-13). This was a violation of God's Word for a person in Israel to charge interest on a loan to one of God's people (cf. Ex 22:25; Lv 25:35-38; Ezk 18:7). Furthermore, at the end of every seven years the remission of all debts was to be granted in Israel to all of God's people who owed a lender (cf. Dt 15:1-11; Neh 10:31). This was the Lord's safety net for those who became poor through financial setbacks (cf. Lv 25:35-38). Creditors took advantage of these men, charging them exorbitant interest, making heartless demands on them, refusing to grant forgiveness of debts in the seventh year, and perhaps even trying to force them and their children into slavery, driving them to even more financial ruin and heartache.

Some of the disenfranchised poor joined David. **Discontented** is literally "bitter of soul," and "bitter" here means "the emotional response to a destructive, heart-crushing situation" (Hamilton, "Bitter," TWOT, 528). Life had hurt them deeply under Saul's reign and they needed the Lord's intervention. David became the leader of the distressed, the indebted, and the discontented. Some of these troubled people became leaders in David's administration, and some of them became his mighty men. The transformation of this group was a credit to David's leadership under God, and a reminder to the Church today that under godly leadership the Lord can transform marginalized people of the world to become mighty men and women of God.

b. Protection for David's Parents in Mizpah of Moab (22:3-4)

22:3-4. Apparently David and his family had relatives in **Moab**, because Ruth the Moabitess was David's great-grandmother (cf. Ru 4:18-22). Therefore, it made sense for David to go to Moab to seek protection for his parents from Saul. **Mizpah** (about six miles north of Jerusalem) may have been the royal residence of Moab's king. David then went to a place called **the stronghold**. The Hebrew word for "stronghold" is *metsuda*, from which the English word "Masada" is loosely transliterated. The location of the stronghold is not specified, but it is quite likely identified with the site in Israel known today as Masada, not far from the western shore of the Dead Sea on the top of a rock plateau that rises steeply 1,200 feet above the surrounding desert. A narrow, snake-like path traverses the eastern side of the fortress up to the summit. From the plateau a person can see in every direction for miles. It was and is a suitable stronghold.

c. Leaving the Stronghold for the Forest of Hereth (22:5)

22:5. Having joined David, the **prophet Gad** told him to go to Judah. **Hereth**, a group of forested mountains in Judah, was a good place for David and his men to hide.

d. Saul's Complaints under the Tamarisk Tree (22:6-10)

22:6-8. Saul was sitting under a **tamarisk** tree when word came to him that David was in Judah. This deciduous tree could grow to 30 feet in height, and its leaves gave shade. Saul appealed to his officials' baser instincts, calling them **Benjamites**, underscoring tribal loyalty to him since he too was a Benjamite. He told them **the son of Jesse** would not give them **fields** or **vineyards**, that is, economic power, nor would he make them **commanders of thousands and commanders of hundreds**, that is, men with military influence (v. 7). Saul even suspected his own men, accusing them of being in conspiracy against him.

22:9-10. Doeg exploited Saul's paranoia to gain some favor with him. Doeg reported that he had seen David with **Ahimelech** the priest, who **inquired** of God for David. But Doeg left out that David lied to Ahimelech.

e. Saul's Revenge on the Priests of the Lord (22:11-23)

22:11-17. Saul misconstrued Ahimelech's aid to David as treason, and the king was further angered when Ahimelech spoke up in defense of David (vv. 14-15). Saul ordered the execution of the Lord's priests, but Saul's servants refused to put them to death.

22:18-19. Saul therefore ordered **Doeg the Edomite** to kill **the priests**. Doeg killed 85 priests, and even murdered everyone in Nob, including **women, children and infants** (v. 19). Doeg's slaughter of the priests is one of the most disturbing massacres in the OT.

22:20-23. Abiathar, one of Ahimelech's sons, escaped and informed David about Saul's massacre of the priests. Even though Doeg was the actual murderer, Saul was the one who gave the order. David understood the damage he had done with his lie and took responsibility for the massacre (v. 22). The Lord's prophet Gad was with David, and now the Lord's priest Abiathar was with him (cf. 23:9-10; 30:7; 1Ch 15:11-15). David would compose Ps 52 about Doeg's treachery.

3. The Faithful God and Unfaithful People (23:1-28)

a. David's Deliverance of Keilah (23:1-5)

23:1. Though David was a fugitive, people still looked to him for godly leadership and help. **Keilah**, a walled city with double gates and bars (v. 7) located about 18 miles southwest of Jerusalem, would be difficult for an enemy to capture. Siege warfare would be necessary. However, the threshing floors were outside the city, making them difficult to protect them. So the Philistines began **plundering the threshing floors**, stealing the wheat and killing the workers.

23:2-5. David asked God if he should **attack** the Philistines to **deliver Keilah** and the Lord said "Yes." Making sure about the Lord's direction, David asked the Lord again, and He assured David of victory over the Philistines. David's men were with him, but it was David who led the charge.

b. The Unfaithful People of Keilah (23:6-14)

23:6-12. Learning that David was in Keilah, Saul assumed that God had **delivered him into** his **hand** (v. 7). So he and his men went down to the city to besiege it, hoping to trap David and his men. Aware of Saul's plan, David sought God's mind through the use of Abiathar's **ephod,** a garment that had attached to it a pouch containing the Urim and Thummim (Bergen, *1, 2 Samuel*, 232), which would be consulted to ascertain the mind and will of God (see comments on Ex 28:30).

David was concerned that another city might be destroyed on his account (v. 10; cf. 22:14-19). God then informed David that Saul would come down to attack the city (v. 11). This information was important for David because there were about six hundred men with him (v. 13); he needed assurance that leaving Keilah was justified. Though the Lord used David to save Keilah, God told him the unappreciative citizens of Keilah planned to turn David and his men over to Saul (v. 12). Herein, David learned another significant lesson of leadership: leaders trust God alone for deliverance and not the people who they have served.

23:13-14. David and his men were on the run again, hiding from Saul. Saul gave up the pursuit momentarily, not knowing where David went. Ziph (about 22 miles south of Jerusalem) was an elevated town surrounded by part of the Judean desert. **Saul sought** David **every day, but God did not deliver him into his hand**. From the time Saul looked at David with suspicion until the day of Saul's death, God's protection of David is one of the major themes of 1 Samuel.

c. Encouragement from a Friend (23:15-18)

23:15-18. Providentially, David's best friend, Jonathan, arrived and **encouraged him in God**. "Encouraged him" is literally "strengthened his hand." David was fearful. But Jonathan encouraged David, saying, **Do not be afraid** (v. 17). Jonathan knew that the kingdom belonged to David. Jonathan would not be king; he assumed he would be second in command. Jonathan then made a third **covenant** with David, a covenant that pertained to Jonathan's place in David's kingdom. This once again confirmed David's rightful kingship, even at the hand of the heir of Saul.

d. The Rock of Escape (23:19-28)

23:19-23. Some **Ziphites** told Saul that David was hiding near **Jeshimon**, a stretch of desert leading to the Dead Sea on the east side of the Judean mountains. These mountains were filled with caves, and other elevated rock formations, suitable as hiding places. Saul used pious language to hide his murderous envy of David (v. 21).

23:24-28. David was in Maon, an elevated town seven miles south of Hebron, surrounded by another section of the Judean desert in the **Arabah**. The Arabah is an arid valley that runs about 120 miles south from the Dead Sea to the Gulf of Aqabah on the Red Sea. Saul and his men caught up with David and his men in the Arabah. As Saul and his men were about to capture David and his men, a messenger reported to Saul that **the Philistines** had attacked Israel (v. 27). This report caused Saul to stop pursuing David. Thus, the Lord, in His providence, brought about a Philistine attack to deliver David from Saul's hand. In memorial, David and his men named the place where they were almost killed **the Rock of Escape**, that is, the place where they escaped from Saul (v. 28).

4. David Compassionately Spares Saul (23:29–24:22)

The theme of revenge connects chaps. 24–26. In chaps. 24 and 26, David spared Saul instead of avenging himself. These incidents not only show David's respect for the Lord and "the Lord's anointed" (24:6), they also reveal that although David was God's choice as Israel's next king, "he was not a usurper who took the life of the preceding king" (Laney, *First and Second Samuel*, 70). Between these two episodes is an account about David being kept from taking vengeance on an unsavory character, Nabal. Under the pressure of losing his life, feeling the sting of contempt, David learned on three different occasions the important lesson of forgoing revenge, even when the subjects (Saul and Nabal) deserved to feel his wrath. By so doing, David kept his hands unstained from shedding their blood, and allowed God the opportunity to deal with his enemies (cf. 25:26). In the words of Rm 12:19, David learned, "Never take your own revenge . . . but leave room for the wrath of God, for it is written, 'Vengeance is Mine, I will repay,' says the Lord."

a. David Cuts off a Corner of Saul's Garment (23:29–24:7)

23:29–24:3. Engedi was a desert town about 30 miles southeast of Jerusalem on the western shore of the Dead Sea. The region had hills and mountains full of rocks and caves, inhabited by wild goats. A spring of water was there. Hence it was named Engedi, "fountain of the wild goats." In David's day Engedi was uninhabited. Pursuing David, Saul came to **sheepfolds**, pens where sheep were kept and protected (24:3). Nearby was a cave where **Saul went in to relieve himself**. "To relieve himself" is literally, "to cover his feet" (with a garment), a euphemism for eliminating bodily wastes. Saul was alone in the cave, needing privacy.

24:4-5. David's men saw this as a divine opportunity for him to take Saul's life. But instead of taking Saul's life, David cut **off the edge of Saul's robe secretly**. Evidently Saul had laid his robe aside while he was relieving himself. Then David's **conscience bothered him**, (lit., "David's heart struck him"), that is, he felt guilty for cutting off a piece of Saul's clothing.

24:6-7. Respecting Saul's position, David was not willing to kill Saul, though his men were. But David showed strong leadership in the cave, persuading his men not to harm Saul. In view of all that Saul had done to David, it is amazing that David resisted the temptation to take Saul's life. In some respects entrusting vengeance to God, instead of taking matters into his own hands, required a greater act of faith than slaying Goliath! Unaware of what had transpired, Saul left the cave.

b. David Presents Evidence of Compassion (24:8-15)

24:8-10. David then acted in a way that must have shocked his men. Leaving the protection of the cave, David called to Saul, and **prostrated himself** before the king as an expression of humility. David was gracious. The idea to kill David did not result from someone convincing Saul that David was seeking to harm him. When David said that he **had pity** on Saul (v. 10), he was speaking of a compassionate feeling expressed toward a person who is in trouble. Saying he would **not stretch out [his] hand against . . . the LORD's anointed** indicated that David recognized that God had placed Saul on the throne. Therefore, David would trust the Lord to make him king and not strike Saul, taking matters into his own hands.

24:11-12. David had visible evidence to prove to Saul that he had compassionately spared the king's life. David held **the edge** of Saul's garment for Saul to see. David wanted to convince Saul of three truths: there was no evil in David's hands, David was not rebelling against Saul and his kingdom, and David had not **sinned against** Saul (v. 11; cf. 20:1), even though Saul was on the hunt to take David's life.

24:13. David uttered a proverb, a short and concise saying that had been in circulation in Israel a long time: Evil comes from evil persons. David's actions indicated that he was not an evil person. If his heart were evil, he would have taken Saul's life in the cave.

24:14-15. David used two metaphors to highlight his lack of worth even to be pursued by Saul. He referred to himself as **a dead dog** and then as **a single flea**. So David committed himself to the Lord to judge his case and deliver him from Saul.

c. Saul Responds to David's Mercy (24:16-22)

24:16-22. Unlike other times, Saul now addressed David as **my son David**, not as "the son of Jesse." David was the king's son-in-law. Even Saul in his alienation from God understood that a man does not send his enemy away unharmed. Saul admitted that he knew David would be Israel's king and the kingdom would be established in his hand (v. 20). Sometimes when a new regime came to power, the more heartless kings would execute the sons and other claimants to the throne from the old regime. Saul asked David to promise that he would **not cut off** Saul's **descendants** (v. 21), and David took that oath. Later, however, three of Saul's sons fell to the Philistines (cf. 31:2), the remaining son, Ish-bosheth, was executed by others in his own camp (cf. 2Sm 4:5-12), and seven of Saul's grandsons were executed in an act of judgment from the Lord (2Sm 21:1-9; see comments on 1Sm 18:17-19). But David showed great kindness to Saul's crippled grandson Mephibosheth (cf. 2Sm 9:1-13).

5. Listening to the Wisdom of a Wise Woman (25:1-44)

a. Samuel Dies (25:1)

25:1. Samuel, the greatest prophet in Israel since Moses, died and **all Israel . . . mourned**. His death marked the end of an era. Then David went to **the wilderness of Paran**, in the east-central region of the Sinai Peninsula (Gn 21:20-21). The location of David's stay is disputed. The Hebrew text reads "Paran," while the NIV follows the LXX and says it was in the "Desert of Maon" (Laney, *First and Second Samuel*, 72). Bergen favors the Paran reading, stating that the narrator was deliberately presenting David's life as a parallel to the history of Israel. Thus David's stay in Paran is reminiscent of Israel's journey in the region five centuries earlier (cf. Nm. 10:12; 12:16; Bergen *1, 2 Samuel*, 243).

b. The Introduction of Nabal and Abigail (25:2-3)

25:2-3. One of the inhabitants of Maon, seven miles south of Hebron, was a businessperson whose business was in Carmel ("God's vineyard"). Carmel was a region in Judah, to be distinguished from Mount Carmel, the range of mountains in the northwest of Israel along the Mediterranean coast. In Israel's agricultural society wealth was measured in livestock and land. This man had **three thousand** sheep and **one thousand** goats. Sheep-shearing occurred annually between April and May. Wool was a valuable commodity, used to make clothes among other items. Sheep-shearing was a festive time, a time of rejoicing and celebration.

The man's name was Nabal ("fool," in Scripture this word means godless, morally contemptible, cf. Ps 14:1; a fitting name for this character). Nabal had a wife named Abigail, which means "the joy of her father." She was **intelligent** (literally, "*good* of understanding," contrasting her goodness with Nabal's evil) and **beautiful**. Beauty and brains mixed well in Abigail. Her husband, on the other hand, was **harsh and evil in his dealings**. Nabal was a Calebite, part of a clan in Judah, from the same tribe as David. As a descendant of Caleb, Nabal certainly did not reflect his noble ancestry.

c. Nabal Shows Contempt for David and His Men (25:4-13)

25:4-8. The wilderness was a dangerous place: robbers roamed the wilderness, engaging in sheep stealing and murdering of shepherds. David and his men provided security for Nabal's shepherds, who **have been with us** (v. 7); his men had protected the shepherds and Nabal's sheep from robbers and wild animals. At this festive moment, David asked for a token of appreciation for his labor. So he sent **ten young men** (v. 5) to ask Nabal to give them goods that Nabal had on hand. David was not operating a protection racket. Rather, when Nabal's men accepted the protection that David had provided, they made him contractually obligated to provide for David and his men.

25:9-13. In response, Nabal referred to David as **the son of Jesse** (v. 10), the pejorative term Saul used for David. He accused David indirectly of **breaking away** from Saul, **his master**. Obsessed with his possessions, Nabal referred to his own goods as **my bread** . . . **my water** . . . **my meat that I have slaughtered for my shearers** (v. 11). Treating David's men with contempt, Nabal refused to give them provisions to fulfill his contractual obligation for their protection of his property. David and 400 angry men prepared to execute vengeance on Nabal and his household while 200 remained **with the baggage**. The Hebrew word translated **baggage** (v. 13) means tools, farm implements, armor, containers, and other equipment necessary to live in the wilderness.

d. Abigail Wisely Intervenes (25:14-35)

25:14-17. One of the young men told Abigail how Nabal had scorned David's men. He used a meaningful metaphor to communicate to her how David's men protected them: **they were a wall to us both by night and by day** (v. 16). The young man called Nabal **a worthless man** (lit., "a son of Belial"; see the comments on 2:12).

25:18-22. Abigail sprang into action and prepared food to take to David and his men. She did not tell her husband what she was going to do because Nabal was obstinate and unreasonable. It would have been a waste of time to talk to him. David was angry because Nabal had exploited him, so he called down God's judgment on his enemies (v. 22). It can be argued here that David was responding in undue anger. Tsumura says David had "lost control" of his feelings and needed "God's gracious intervention" to keep him from violence (Tsumura, *The First Book of Samuel*, 585). Baldwin concurs, saying that although David spared Saul, in the case of Nabal he had "no second thought about incurring blood-guilt" (Baldwin, *1 and 2 Samuel*, 150).

25:23-25. Abigail met David in one of the Bible's great male-female encounters. Before David opened his mouth, the smart and beautiful woman had dismounted her donkey and fell on her face at his feet. The first words she spoke were, **On me alone, my lord, be the blame** (v. 24). Then she wisely asked for permission to speak. Her words are some of the wisest words in Scripture. Her words in vv. 24-31 are the longest recorded speech by a woman in the OT (though see the song of Deborah and Barak in Jdg 5). She explained to David that her husband's name summed up who he was. Nabal ("fool") was his name, and folly was in him (v. 25).

25:26-31. Abigail reminded David of the Lord's providential work in his life, noting that the Lord had restrained him **from shedding blood**. She was probably referring to David's having spared Saul's life in the cave. She reminded him that vengeance is the Lord's (v. 26), a lesson David learned in chap. 24, one that would be reinforced in chap. 26, and one that he was in the process of learning under different circumstances in this chapter. Not to take vengeance on the king is one thing, but it is altogether another test of godly resolve not to take vengeance on a fool who has held one in contempt.

Abigail asked that the gift (lit., "blessing"), she brought **be given to the young men who accompany my lord** (v. 27; lit., "who walk at the feet of my lord"). She then asked David for forgiveness of her **transgression** even though her husband was in the wrong. She based her request on several facts. (1) The Lord will make for David **an enduring house**, that is, a dynasty (v. 28). Abigail spoke prophetically of David life; years would pass before God would promise a dynasty to David (cf. 2Sm 7:8-17). (2) David was fighting the Lord's **battles**. (3) No **evil** would be found in David all his days. This statement could have been a subtle warning to David not to commit an evil against Nabal, rather than a prophecy (Youngblood, "1, 2 Samuel," 248), since David did commit evil later in the case of Bathsheba. (4) The Lord will protect David. (5) The Lord will destroy David's enemies (v. 29). She explained that this destruction of the Lord would be like His using a sling against them. This imagery would have resonated with David, who slew Goliath with a stone and a sling. (6) Taking vengeance against Nabal and his innocent household would be a guilty load on David's conscience after he became king. Abigail ended her reasoned request for forgiveness with a request: **When the LORD shall deal well with my lord,** [i.e., "when you become king,"] **then remember your maidservant** (v. 31). "To remember" means "to act in a special way on a person's behalf."

25:32-35. David recognized that the Lord providentially sent Abigail to keep him from avenging himself. Of credit to David is that he listened to Abigail and granted her request. Her intervention demonstrated that she was a wise woman.

e. The Lord Strikes Nabal (25:36-38)

25:36-38. When Abigail returned home, Nabal was intoxicated. Abigail did not talk with him until the next morning, when she told sober Nabal what happened. The news was so shocking that **his heart died within him so that he became as a stone**. He may have had a massive heart attack or stroke. Then ten days later the Lord struck Nabal and he died.

f. David Marries Abigail (25:39-44)

25:39-42. David blessed the Lord for pleading his cause and for preventing him from taking vengeance into his own hands. David asked Abigail to marry him. While polygamy was not God's ideal for marriage (David already had Ahinoam as his wife, v. 43; see comments on 1:1-2 for a discussion of polygamy), Abigail married a man she could respect.

25:43-44. Saul had given Michal, his daughter and David's first wife, to another man, Palti. Legally Michal was still David's wife, and so years later, David got Michal back.

The kingship lesson David learned in his encounter with Nabal and Abigail is that, as king, he was not to carry out personal vengeance but to trust the Lord to defend him. He was to fight the Lord's battles (v. 28), while also allowing the Lord to fight his battles.

6. David Spares Saul Again (26:1-25)

This second account of David sparing Saul's life shows once again that David would not take by force what was to be his inevitable victory in his struggle with Saul. Interestingly, the roles were reversed here, with David stalking Saul (Brueggemann, *First and Second Samuel*, 182).

a. Saul Pursues David Again (26:1-5)

26:1-5. The Ziphites informed Saul again (cf. 23:19-20) about David's whereabouts. They told Saul that David was **hiding on the hill of Hachilah** (v. 1), some 15 miles southeast of Hebron and overlooking the desert surrounding the Dead Sea. David, a wise military leader like Moses and Joshua, sent out scouts to see if Saul was approaching.

b. David Finds Saul Sound Asleep (26:6-12)

26:6-8. Two people were with David: **Ahimelech the Hittite** and **Abishai the son of Zeruiah, Joab's brother**. More than one person in the OT was named Ahimelech. Ethnically this Ahimelech was a Hittite, though his name was Semitic. Some Gentiles had identified with God's people, embracing the Lord and His word.

At night David and Abishai, his nephew, passed around a number of Saul's soldiers who were in **a sound asleep from the LORD** (v. 12) and arrived at the very center of the camp where Saul was asleep, along with Abner (v. 7). Saul's spear is mentioned six times in this episode (vv. 7-8, 11-12, 16, 22), which is significant because it was no doubt the same spear Saul had hurled at

David twice before in an attempt to kill him (cf. 18:10-11; 19:10). Taking Saul's spear also demonstrated David's refusal to kill the king and gain the throne by murder (Laney, *First and Second Samuel*, 75).

Again Saul was in a vulnerable position. In fact Abishai interpreted the occasion as the Lord delivering Saul into David's hand (v. 8). Abishai was willing to take Saul's life with one blow. He said a second strike would not be required because the first one would be fatal.

26:9-11. But David restrained Abishai from striking Saul, because Saul was the **LORD's anointed**. David was confident that the Lord would deal with Saul as He dealt with Nabal.

26:12. David spared Saul's life for the second time. The reason no one saw David is that God had sent **a sound sleep** on them.

c. David Calls to the King's Men (26:13-16)

26:13-16. At a safe distance David called out to Abner and the people. David mocked Abner and his men for their failure to protect Saul when his life was in jeopardy. Then David presented evidence that he had been in their camp. He showed him Saul's **spear** and his water **jug**, both of which were at Saul's head (v. 16).

d. David Addresses Saul (26:17-20)

26:17-19. David pleaded with Saul as he did in chap. 24, raising essentially the same questions. **Why then is my lord pursuing his servant? For what have I done? Or what evil is in my hand?** (v. 18). If the Lord had moved Saul against David, David was ready to make an offering so that forgiveness and reconciliation could occur. But if the pursuit was simply man's doing, they were **cursed . . . before the LORD**, David said, because they **have driven me out** of the land and from among God's people, **the inheritance of the LORD** (v. 19). Further, they were encouraging him to turn to idolatry (by **saying, Go, serve other gods**), which was a sin against the Lord.

26:20. David reminded Saul of the incongruity of the king of Israel pursuing him. David spoke of himself as if Saul were pursuing a **flea**, and he compared Saul's search for him as being like hunting **a partridge in the mountains**, not an activity befitting a king.

e. David Displays the King's Spear (26:21-25)

26:21. For the third time Saul admitted, **I have sinned** (cf. 15:24, 30), but this was not a heart confession. Saul's next request was stunning: **Return, my son David, for I will not harm you again because my life was precious in your sight this day**. Saul also admitted, **Behold, I have played the fool**. Likely Saul was sincere in his penitence. But he was so erratic and paranoid, that after each episode of repentance, he would revert to his hatred and desire to kill David.

26:22. Unimpressed, David simply said, **Behold the spear of the king!** and then invited one of Saul's men to come and reclaim it. Apparently David did not return the water jug, a valuable item for anyone living in the desert as Saul and David were.

26:23-25. Even though the Lord had delivered Saul into David's hand, David refused to lift up his hand against **the LORD's anointed**. Saul admitted that David would accomplish much and would succeed. This is the last time Saul would speak with David.

This completes the trilogy of stories in which David learned that a king is not to exact vengeance on his foes. It appears that David was always clear in not seeking revenge against **the LORD's anointed** but needed to learn that vengeance was also inappropriate for a king when dealing with evil fools like Nabal. When he became king, David was notable in his graciousness toward those who opposed him.

7. David Takes Refuge among the Philistines (27:1-12)

a. David Crosses over to Achish Again (27:1-4)

27:1. In spite of God's providential work on his behalf, David was fearful. He was under more pressure than when he first fled from Saul (chap. 20). He had his wives to think about and the wives and children of his men. They could not go on indefinitely moving from place to place under the threat of death in the desert. As long as David was in the land, Saul would continue to pursue him.

27:2-4. This time when David went **to Achish . . . king of Gath**, he was not alone (cf. 21:10). He had six hundred men with him. Counting their wives and children, the number of people with David may have been well over 1,000. When Saul learned that David had fled to Gath, **he no longer searched for him**, perhaps reasoning that the Philistines would kill him.

b. David Spends 16 Months in Gath (27:5-7)

27:5-6. The narrator did not explain Achish's reason for being open to receiving David and his people. Perhaps Achish thought that David was now willing to join the Philistines. Achish's offer of asylum to David obligated David and his men to be available to go to war against the

Philistine's enemies. David asked Achish to grant him a place in one of the cities in the country. As a king of a city-state, Achish had the authority to grant land to whomever he chose, so he gave the city of **Ziklag** to David. Ziklag was part of the tribal allotment of Judah (cf. Jos 15:31), and is thought to be about 22 miles south of Gath (though there is a lack of certainty on its precise location). This was one of the cities in the tribal inheritance the Lord had granted to Judah centuries earlier (cf. Jos 15:31). The narrator noted, **Ziklag has belonged to the kings of Judah to this day**.

27:7. Unknown to David, his time as a fugitive was coming to an end. After his **year-and-four-month** stay in the land of the Philistines, David would become the king of Judah. Still, David would learn some valuable lessons of kingship during his stay among the Philistines.

c. David Undertakes Covert Operations (27:8-12)

27:8-10. David and his men raided three different groups of people, all of whom were enemies of God and His people. When David attacked them, he killed them all and **took away** their **sheep . . . cattle . . . donkeys . . . camels, and the clothing** (v. 9). From time to time David gave reports to Achish. David lied to Achish, leading him to think that he was raiding places in Israel—**the Negev** (south country) **of Judah**, and **the Negev of the Jerahmeelites, and . . . the Negev of the Kenites**. Raiding these places was acceptable to Achish because He considered these Israelite peoples his enemies. The text makes no statement about David's lies to Achish. Bergen says that while lying is wrong, David's "conscious use of deceit" was "the lesser of two evils" because it saved Israelite lives and fulfilled military assignments to put these people to death that had been left undone since the days of Moses (Bergen, *1, 2 Samuel*, 262). Moreover, David may have felt justified in lying because he was acting in a time of war against a pagan enemy of Israel.

27:11-12. David did not leave anyone **alive** among the groups he attacked because survivors might tell Achish about David's covert actions. This would have resulted in devastating consequences for David and those with him. While this seems to be a self-serving motive for such extensive massacres, the complete destruction of Canaanite peoples was likely justified in that David was completing God's command to Joshua that Israel had never completed (for further discussion, see *Excursus: Canaanite Genocide—Killing the Seemingly Innocent* at Jos 6:21). Achish remained unaware of David's covert operations. David was shrewd, fighting the Lord's battle under the cover of loyalty to the Philistines.

In a sense, David's time in Gath prepared him for a significant part of his role as king, namely, to be the military leader of Israel. Fighting with his band of mighty men developed his leadership and military skills.

8. Saul and the Medium of En-dor (28:1-25)

Chapters 28 and 31 deal with Saul, and chaps. 29 and 30 deal with David. Saul reached a new low when he consulted the medium of En-dor because he was afraid of going into battle against the Philistines (chap. 28), while David was providentially delivered from going to war with the Philistines (chap. 29). And when David did go to war, he defeated the Amalekites and recovered everything that was taken (chap. 30). Meanwhile, Saul and his sons died in a battle on Mount Gilboa, and Saul committed suicide (chap. 31).

These concluding chapters of 1 Samuel show that a life of disobedience to the Lord leads to ruin, and a life of faith and obedience to the Lord leads to blessing.

a. David's Dilemma (28:1-2)

28:1-2. With misguided confidence in David, Achish informed David that he and his men should join the Philistines in battle against Israel. This put David in a dilemma because he did not intend to fight against his own people, Israel. The narrative will revisit David's dilemma later, in chap. 29.

b. Saul's Dilemma (28:3)

28:3. On the eve of a battle between Saul and the Philistines two significant events were underway. (1) The nation mourned for Samuel. If Saul wanted Samuel's counsel about how to proceed in the battle, such counsel was no longer available. (2) Instead of executing the Lord's mandated death penalty on the mediums and spiritists in Israel, Saul had expelled them from the land. The **mediums and spiritists** were those who tried to communicate with and consult the dead about issues and problems faced by the living. The Lord had condemned these people and strictly forbade His people from engaging in such occult practices (cf. Lv 19:31; 20:6, 27; Dt 18:10-11, Is 8:19).

c. A New Low in Saul's Life (28:4-25)

28:4-5. The Philistine armies set up camp in Shunem (about 15 miles southwest of the

Sea of Galilee) in the valley of Jezreel, on the southwestern slopes of the hill of Moreh. And Saul's men **camped in Gilboa** (a string of foothills called "Mount Gilboa"), six miles south of Moreh. Looking down into the valley of Jezreel from Mount Gilboa, Saul and his men were able to see the Philistine army's camp, size, equipment, chariots, and movements. The sight of the Philistine army filled Saul with fear.

28:6. Terrified, Saul sought God's mind for counsel about the battle. Saul sought God through several valid means of communication—**dreams**, **Urim**, and **prophets**. But the Lord did not speak to him through any of these means.

28:7. Isolated by heaven's silence, a fearful Saul decided to consult a medium. Since he had driven all mediums out of the land, Saul asked his servant where he could find one. The servant had a ready answer: **Behold, there is a woman who is a medium at En-dor**. En-dor means the "fountain of Dor." En-dor was north of the Philistine camp, which meant that Saul had to cross enemy lines several miles to consult with the medium.

28:8. Passing through enemy lines, disguised, and under the cover of darkness, Saul reached the medium's house and told the woman to **conjure up for me . . . and bring up for me whom I shall name to you.**

28:9-14. Ironically, the medium herself related that Saul had expelled the mediums from the land, indicating that she thought she was being trapped. Saul vowed that the woman would not be punished.

When Saul asked the woman to **bring up Samuel** (v. 11), the unexpected happened. She actually saw Samuel. The mediums and spiritists were not actually consulting the dead. Their work was a demonic sham, and they knew it. This event, however, was a special occasion in which God Himself allowed Samuel actually to appear. The medium cried out when this happened, indicating that she had not anticipated it, and that Samuel himself actually appeared (v. 12). Realizing that it was Samuel, the woman understood that she had been deceived, and that the inquirer was Saul himself. The woman described to Saul what she saw, and Saul knew it was Samuel (v. 14).

28:15-18. Samuel said to Saul, **Why have you disturbed me by bringing me up?** Saul rationalized his actions to Samuel. (1) He was **greatly distressed**. (2) **The Philistines** were fighting against him. (3) God had **departed from** him. (4) God would not answer him. Then Samuel asked Saul why he consulted him when the Lord had **departed** from him and had **become** his enemy (v. 16). The Lord would not answer Saul because of his disobedience years before in not destroying the Amalekites (cf. 1Sm 15).

28:19-23. So Samuel announced that in judgment the Lord would give Saul, his sons, and the army into the Philistines' hands. God would not protect them. Fearful and weak, Saul **fell** to **the ground** (v. 20). Then in stunning irony, the medium spoke encouraging words to Saul and encouraged him to eat (v. 22).

The narrative places emphasis on the word **listen** (cf. vv. 21-23). Though Saul failed to listen to the Lord, he did listen to the voice of his men and of the medium.

28:24-25. The description of the medium's preparation of a meal for Saul and his servants was ironic. It was like a ceremonial royal meal for a king who had just learned his kingship was lost (Klein, *1 Samuel*, 273).

9. The Providential Philistine Rescue of David (29:1-11)

a. The Philistines' Mistrust of David (29:1-5)

29:1-3. On the eve of a major battle with the Israelites, the Philistine **lords** wanted no part of David and his men. These commanders no doubt knew of David's prowess, and they may have remembered an earlier incident in which the **Hebrews** who had gone over to the Philistines turned on them in battle and started fighting for Israel (cf. 14:21). The Philistine leaders referred to them in a pejorative manner, as **these Hebrews** (v. 3). Brueggemann suggests that the term on Philistine lips referred to scavengers, down-and-outers who are a menace to society (Brueggemann, *First and Second Samuel*, 197). The leaders questioned King Achish about the presence of the Hebrews with their troops on the eve of battle. Achish trusted David, but David did not support Achish at all. Instead, he had been raiding and exterminating people sympathetic to the Philistine cause.

29:4-5. But the Philistine **commanders** considered David a threat. To make their point, they even quoted the lyrics of the song that galled Saul. For the third time, these lyrics are quoted in 1 Samuel (cf. 18:7; 21:11). The Philistine commanders may have quoted this verse to remind Achish that David was so skilled at killing Philistines that his deeds were "celebrated in both song and dance among the Israelites" (Bergen, *1, 2 Samuel*, 271). These leaders may also have quoted the verse as evidence to Achish that David and Saul were linked in solidarity, thus making it unlikely that David would fight against Saul (Brueggemann, *First and Second Samuel*, 198). From the narrator's standpoint, this threefold repetition may also serve as a reminder of David's fitness for kingship as opposed to Saul's, and of God's blessing on David's life and exploits.

b. An Honorable Discharge (29:6-11)

29:6-7. Possibly Achish had an interest in the God of Israel, because he used God's name in his oath, **as the LORD lives**. Still, Achish's oath indicated how well David deceived him.

29:8. David's response is an enigma. Was David mocking Achish without Achish being aware of it? He asked Achish, **What have I done?** David knew that Achish had not found out anything that would prevent David from fighting, because David had killed all those who could have passed on information about his covert operations. Perhaps David was "acting" again.

29:9-11. Providentially working through the distrust of the Philistine leaders, the Lord delivered David from his dilemma, in which he would have to fight against God's people, Israel. The Lord providentially arranged these events in David's life so that he and his men were able to respond to the ensuing crisis in chap. 30.

10. David Strengthens Himself in the Lord (30:1-31)

a. The Amalekites Raid Ziklag (30:1-10)

30:1-2. David and his men marched about 80 miles south from the Jezreel Valley close to the Sea of Galilee to the Philistine city of Ziklag, where they had left their goods and families. In the three days it took them to get there, the Amalekites had raided the city and carried off everyone. Ziklag's relative isolation made it vulnerable to such raids. As David and his men approached their home away from home, they saw it had been **burned** to the ground. The Amalekites also took their wives and children. But the narrative includes a comforting detail, **without killing anyone** (v. 2). David and his men, however, were not aware of this fact.

This account reminds the reader that even though David had been providentially delivered from having to fight against Israel, plenty of enemies still opposed him (Peterson, *First and Second Samuel*, 130). Peterson points out a contrast in leadership. Both David and Saul knew their lives were on the line. But at about the same time that Saul was consulting with a witch, David was praying to God and consulting the "biblically sanctioned ephod" (Peterson, *First and Second Samuel*, 130) see comments on the ephod on 30:7-8).

30:3-6. David and his men wept until they were so tired they could no longer cry. David's two wives were taken captive and his pressure increased, because for the first time his own men **spoke of stoning him** (v. 6). David's next act was an example of godly courage. With nothing visible in Ziklag to encourage him, **David strengthened himself in the LORD his God**, meaning that David drew strength from knowing that he was doing God's will and obeying God's Word.

30:7-8. In contrast to Saul, David had access to the ephod (see description at 2:18-21 and 23:6-12). And in contrast to Saul, the Lord answered David. The Lord told David to **pursue** the enemy, assuring David that he would rescue everyone.

30:9-10. David and his **six hundred** men traveled 16 miles south from Ziklag to **the brook Besor**. The Hebrew word translated here as "brook" actually means "a wadi," a dry stream or riverbed that has water only during the rainy season. At the wadi **Besor**, **two hundred** of David's men were so exhausted they could not continue.

b. An Unexpected Source of Information (30:11-15)

30:11-14. David and his men "happened" to find a half-dead, abandoned **Egyptian** servant **in the field**. After feeding the man, David interrogated him. The Egyptian gave David valuable information about the Amalekite raiders (vv. 13-14).

30:15. The man agreed to take David to the place where the Amalekites were, provided David swore to spare his life and not to return him to his **master**. Apparently David agreed with these terms. The Lord providentially brought about the meeting with the abandoned sick man to advance His purpose.

c. David Recovers All that Was Taken (30:16-20)

30:16-17. The Amalekites were spread out, celebrating their victory by drinking and dancing. David slaughtered all the Amalekites except 400 men who escaped on camels.

30:18-20. David recovered everything including his two wives, just as the Lord had said (cf.

v. 8). Since David was the leader who expressed his trust in the Lord to bring about this recovery, David's men gave the spoil a name: **This is David's spoil** (v. 20).

d. David Shares the Spoils (30:21-31)

30:21-25. Some **wicked and worthless men** in David's band did not want to share the spoils with the 200 men who stayed behind and guarded the baggage (v. 22). David responded that spoils must be shared with the 200 because the Lord had granted all of them the victory, not just the combatants. This incident was the origin of a statute in Israel concerning spoils of victory (vv. 24-25), which the narrator noted was still in force. This indicates that the account was written many years after David had become king; but the point here is that David was "performing the judicial functions of a king" (Klein, *1 Samuel*, 284), even though he had not yet ascended to the throne. David's strong and godly leadership influenced Israel even before his official coronation as king.

30:26-31. David remembered those who helped him when he was a fugitive from Saul. He shared some of the spoils with the people of more than a dozen towns in Judah where the people assisted him.

The leadership lesson David had learned was how to lead even when no one was following. A godly king was to find strength in God even when others would no longer support him. Moreover, he was to not allow the selfish motives of wicked men to have influence but to care for all his flock.

11. Saul and His Sons Are Slain (31:1-13)

a. Saul Commits Suicide (31:1-7)

31:1-2. The battle recorded in chap. 31 was going on at the same time as the events recorded in chap. 30. The men of Israel fled from the battlefield at the floor of the Jezreel Valley to their previous camp on **Mount Gilboa** (about 20 miles southwest of the Sea of Galilee), but they did not make it. The Philistines slew them on the eastern slopes of Mount Gilboa. Then the Philistines **overtook Saul and his sons**, and killed Saul's three sons—**Jonathan** (David's best friend), **Abinadab**, and **Malchi-shua**.

31:3-6. The piercing power of an arrowhead wounded Saul badly. Fearing abuse and torture from the Philistines, Saul asked his armor bearer to kill him. But the armor bearer refused to execute Saul's dying orders (v. 4). Therefore, Saul took his own life. Saul's armor bearer followed Saul in his final act, committing suicide as well (v. 6). This was a devastating loss of the Israelite leaders and soldiers to the Philistines.

31:7. After this defeat, two groups of Israelites panic. Both groups abandoned their cities—those who lived near the scene of the battle and those on the other side of **the Jordan** River. **The Philistines** came and moved into those abandoned cities, an indication of the impressive nature of their victory (Youngblood, "1, 2 Samuel," 290).

b. The Philistines Find Saul and His Sons (31:8-10)

31:8. Stripping the defeated slain of whatever valuables they had was a common practice in ancient war. In the process of stripping the slain, the Philistines found the greatest spoils in their victory—the dead bodies of **Saul and his three sons**.

31:9-10. The Philistines beheaded Saul and took his weapons. They sent them throughout the land of the Philistines to celebrate the victory in their idolatrous houses of worship and among the Philistine populace. In the ancient world victory in war was thought to be a result of the work of the victors' god(s). The Philistines fastened Saul's desecrated and disgraced body **to the wall of Beth-shan** (v. 10) for everyone to see, to complete his humiliation.

c. The Men of Jabesh-gilead Show Courage and Gratitude (31:11-13)

31:11-13. At great risk to themselves, the valiant men of Jabesh-gilead (a city located about 21 miles southeast of the Sea of Galilee and east of the Jordan River) **walked all night** (about 12 miles one way) and **took the** bodies of **Saul and . . . his sons from the wall of Beth-shan** (v. 12). The Philistines probably mutilated their corpses so badly that in an effort to honor Saul and his sons in death, the men of Jabesh-gilead **burned** their bodies. But they did it in a way that their bones were not reduced to ashes. They **buried** their bones **under the tamarisk tree at Jabesh** (v. 13). The men of Jabesh-gilead were motivated by gratitude for Saul's previous deliverance of that city in his first act as king (cf. 11:1-11). They gave Saul and his sons a respectful burial, an important need in Israel. Even in the midst of Saul's tragic influence, there was still some godly courage and respectful gratitude in Israel.

BIBLIOGRAPHY FOR 1 AND 2 SAMUEL

Anderson, A. A. *2 Samuel.* Word Biblical Commentary. Nashville: Thomas Nelson, 1989.

Archer, G. L. "Ephod." In *The Zondervan Pictorial Encyclopedia of the Bible.* Vol. 2, edited by Merrill C. Tenney. Grand Rapids, MI: Zondervan, 1975.

Baldwin, Joyce G. *1 and 2 Samuel.* Tyndale Old Testament Commentaries. Edited by D. J. Wiseman. Downers Grove, IL: InterVarsity, 1988.

Bergen, Robert D. *1, 2 Samuel.* The New American Commentary. Nashville: Broadman & Holman, 1996.

Brueggemann, Walter. *First and Second Samuel.* Interpretation: A Bible Commentary for Teaching and Preaching. Louisville, KY: John Knox Press, 1990.

Davis, Dale Ralph. *1 Samuel.* Focus on the Bible. Ross-Shire, UK: Christian Focus Publications, 2000.

__________. *2 Samuel.* Focus on the Bible. Ross-Shire, UK: Christian Focus Publications, 2007.

Feinberg, C. L. "Belial." *The Zondervan Pictorial Encyclopedia of the Bible.* Vol. 1, edited by Merrill C. Tenney. Grand Rapids, MI: Zondervan, 1975.

Fokkelman, J. P. *Narrative Art and Poetry in the Books of Samuel.* Vol. 1. Assen, Netherlands: Van Gorcum, 1981.

Harris, R. Laird, Gleason L. Archer, Jr., and Bruce K. Waltke. *Theological Wordbook of the Old Testament.* Chicago: Moody, 1980.

Howard, David M., Jr. *An Introduction to the Old Testament Historical Books.* Chicago: Moody, 1993.

Klein, Ralph W. *1 Samuel.* Word Biblical Commentary. Nashville: Thomas Nelson, 1983.

Lower, J. M. "Vision." *The Zondervan Pictorial Encyclopedia of the Bible.* Vol. 5, edited by Merrill C. Tenney. Grand Rapids, MI: Zondervan, 1975.

Merrill, Eugene H. "1 Samuel." In The Bible Knowledge Commentary, Old Testament. pp. 431–455. Edited by John F. Walvoord and Roy B. Zuck. Wheaton, IL: Victor Books, 1987.

__________. "2 Samuel." In The Bible Knowledge Commentary, Old Testament. pp. 457–482. Edited by John F. Walvoord and Roy B. Zuck. Wheaton, IL: Victor Books, 1987.

Peterson, Eugene H. *First and Second Samuel.* Louisville, KY: Westminster John Knox Press, 1999.

Porter, Laurence E. "1 and 2 Samuel." *New International Bible Commentary.* Edited by F. F. Bruce. Grand Rapids, MI: Zondervan, 1979.

Tsumura, David Toshio. *The First Book of Samuel.* The New International Commentary on the Old Testament. Grand Rapids, MI: Eerdmans, 2007.

Unger, Merrill F. *The New Unger's Bible Dictionary.* Edited by R. K. Harrison. Chicago: Moody, 1988.

Woodhouse, John. *1 Samuel.* Preaching the Word. Wheaton, IL: Crossway, 2008.

Youngblood, Ronald F. "1, 2 Samuel." *The Expositor's Bible Commentary.* Vol. 3, edited by Tremper Longman, III and David E. Garland, 13–614. Grand Rapids, MI: Zondervan, 1992.

2 SAMUEL

WINFRED O. NEELY

INTRODUCTION

See the Introduction to 1 and 2 Samuel at the beginning of 1 Samuel on p. 375.

OUTLINE

I. The Rise and Conquest of King David (1:1–10:19)
   A. David's Response to the News of Saul's Death (1:1-27)
      1. David Learns of Saul's Death (1:1-10)
      2. David Grieves the Death of Saul and Jonathan (1:11-16)
      3. How Have the Mighty Fallen! (1:17-27)
   B. David the King vs. the House of Saul (2:1-32)
      1. David Is Anointed King over Judah (2:1-4a)
      2. The Lord's Anointed King Reaches out to Jabesh-gilead (2:4b-7)
      3. General Abner Makes Ish-bosheth King over Israel (2:8-11)
      4. A Battle Spreads between the Houses of David and Saul (2:12-32)
   C. The Growth of the House of David (3:1-39)
      1. David's House Increases as Saul's Declines (3:1)
      2. David's Family Increases (3:2-5)
      3. Abner Grows Stronger in the House of Saul (3:6-11)
      4. Abner Makes a Covenant with David (3:12-25)
      5. Joab Murders Abner (3:26-30)
      6. David Mourns the Death of Abner (3:31-39)
   D. The Murder of Ish-bosheth (4:1-12)
      1. Ish-bosheth Loses Courage (4:1-3)
      2. Mephibosheth Crippled in an Accident (4:4)
      3. David Responds to Rechab and Baanah's Treachery (4:5-12)
   E. The Crowning and Conquest of David, the King of Israel (5:1-25)
      1. David Becomes King over All Israel (5:1-5)
      2. The King Captures Jerusalem (5:6-10)
      3. Hiram Builds David a House (5:11-12)
      4. David Enlarges His Already Large Family (5:13-16)
      5. David Battles the Philistines (5:17-25)
   F. Bringing the Ark to Jerusalem (6:1-23)
      1. Israel Returns the Ark in the Wrong Way (6:1-11)
      2. Israel Returns the Ark in the Biblical Way (6:12-15)
      3. Michal Despises David (6:16-23)
   G. The Lord Will Build David an Eternal House (7:1-29)
      1. David Desires to Build the Lord a House (7:1-3)
      2. The Lord Sends Nathan to David with a Message (7:4-17)

3. David Responds to God's Promise (7:18-29)
H. David's Victories and Righteous Rule (8:1-18)
1. David Triumphs over Many Enemies (8:1-14)
2. David Rules with Righteousness and Justice (8:15-18)
I. The Kindness of the King (9:1-13)
1. David Summons Mephibosheth (9:1-8)
2. Mephibosheth Eats Bread at the King's Table (9:9-13)
J. Hanun Spurns the Kindness of the King (10:1-19)
1. David's Servants Are Shamed (10:1-5)
2. Ammon Becomes a Stench to David (10:6-8)
3. Two Brothers Lead the Battle (10:9-14)
4. David Finds Victory over the Arameans (10:15-19)
II. Great Sin, Great Grace, Terrible Consequences (11:1–12:31)
A. War and Great Sin (11:1-27)
1. The King Is Intimate with Bathsheba (11:1-5)
2. David Tries to Deceive Uriah (11:6-13)
3. David Writes a Chilling Letter (11:14-21)
4. Uriah the Hittite Dies in Battle (11:22-25)
5. The Lord Views David's Acts as Evil (11:26-27)
B. Great Grace, Terrible Consequences, and War (12:1-31)
1. The Lord Sends Nathan to David (12:1-15a)
2. David's Baby Dies (12:15b-23)
3. David and Bathsheba Have Solomon (12:24-25)
4. David's Army Wins More Victories (12:26-31)
III. More Fallout from David's Sin in His Own Family (13:1–20:26)
A. Rape, Vengeance, and Murder in the Family (13:1-39)
1. Amnon Desires His Sister (13:1-3)
2. Amnon Rapes His Own Sister (13:4-19)
3. Absalom Comforts His Sister and Hates His Brother (13:20-22)
4. Absalom Takes Revenge (13:23-36)
5. Absalom Flees to His Grandfather's House (13:37-39)
B. David Restores Absalom to His Court (14:1-33)
1. Joab Enacts a Shrewd Plan on Absalom's Behalf (14:1-3)
2. The Shrewd Woman Fabricates a Story (14:4-20)
3. David Recalls Absalom to Jerusalem (14:21-33)
C. The Flight and Return of King David (15:1–20:26)
1. Absalom Dethrones David (15:1-37)
a. Absalom Steals the Hearts of the People of Israel (15:1-6)
b. Absalom Conspires against the King (15:7-12)
c. King David Flees Jerusalem (15:13-18)
d. David Receives Unexpected Loyalty: Ittai and Hushai (15:19-37)
2. Ziba, Shimei, and More Sexual Abuse (16:1-23)
a. The Opportunistic Ziba (16:1-4)
b. Shimei Curses David (16:5-14)
c. Absalom Takes David's Throne and Concubines (16:15-23)
3. Hushai, Ahithophel, and Three Other Men (17:1-29)
a. Ahithophel Advises a Small Attack (17:1-4)
b. Hushai Offers a Different Plan (17:5-14)
c. Hushai Sends Word to David through the Spy Connection (17:15-22)
d. Ahithophel Commits Suicide (17:23)
e. The Lord Provides through Three Men (17:24-29)
4. Defeat, Victory, and Guilty Grief (18:1-33)
a. David Assembles His Troops for Battle (18:1-5)
b. David's Servants Fight Israel; Absalom Murdered (18:6-18)

COMMENTARY ON 2 SAMUEL

I. The Rise and Conquest of King David (1:1–10:19)

A. David's Response to the News of Saul's Death (1:1-27)

1. David Learns of Saul's Death (1:1-10)

1:1. In the Hebrew Bible there is no break between 1 and 2 Samuel. The opening words of 2 Samuel, however, indicate the beginning of a new era in David's life: **Now it came about after the death of Saul.** From now on, the narrative would include events relating to David himself. Second Samuel 1 is a transitional chapter that fills in the details of Saul's demise and David's rise to the throne. As Peterson points out, the reader should be prepared to cheer for the death of Saul and the rise of David. But the story will not permit it, because even though David's archenemy was dead, he did not rejoice (Peterson, *First and Second Samuel*, 39–41). The king of Israel was dead, and David was wracked with grief.

1:2-3. After David slaughtered **the Amalekites**, David had returned to Ziklag (see the comments on 1Sm 27:5-6 for its location). Three days later he received a visitor from Mount Gilboa, Saul's camp. This visitor traveled about 85 miles southwest to Ziklag. With all the trapping of grief, he attempted to get David's approval by falling down to the ground and paying homage to David. David was unaware of the outcome of the battle between Israel and the Philistines.

1:4-10. The young man explained to David how he knew of Saul's and Jonathan's deaths (v. 4). An Amalekite (and thus a member of Israel's enemy, v. 8), the young man came across Saul on the battlefield and saw that Saul's attempted suicide did not work. Therefore at Saul's behest, the Amalekite assisted Saul with his last wishes. As evidence of his claim the Amalekite showed David Saul's crown and bracelet (v. 10).

However, the Amalekite's account contradicted the narrative account in 1Sm 31. The text is indicating that the Amalekite was lying. True, he took Saul's crown and waistband to prove his story. But he lied about having killed Saul in an attempt to win David's favor. Other commentators believe the Amalekite was telling the truth because of the believability of his conversation with Saul, his eyewitness account, and that he had Saul's personal items (see Bergen, *1, 2 Samuel*, 287, for a cogent discussion of this view). In Bergen's view, "Saul had been ordered to kill the Amalekites [cf. 1Sm 15:3]—now he ordered an Amalekite to kill him" (Bergen, *1, 2 Samuel*, 287). Nevertheless, it is unlikely that the omniscient narrator was mistaken in recording the details of Saul's death (1Sm 31). More likely, this Amalekite, in his attempt to curry favor with David, did not anticipate David's gracious heart toward Saul and was unaware of David's commitment that no one was ever to raise a hand against the Lord's anointed. Hence, the Amalekite lied and would pay for it with his life.

2. David Grieves the Death of Saul and Jonathan (1:11-16)

1:11-12. David and his men did not rejoice when they learned of Saul's death. Instead, they tore their **clothes**, a sign of grief and pain, and **mourned and wept and fasted**. David's grief was an expression of his godly character.

1:13-16. When David asked the Amalekite, **Where are you from?** he said he was **the son of an alien**, that is, he was the son of a foreigner living in Israel. Thus he should have had an appreciation for Saul, although Brueggemann says the man was ignorant of Saul's "religious legitimacy" (Brueggemann, *First and Second Samuel*, 212). But in David's mind, no excuse justified the Amalekite's actions. He should have known better than to kill the Lord's anointed, as David had steadfastly refused to do. Despite the untruthfulness of his account, his own lips condemned him, and so David had him executed (vv. 15-16).

3. How Have the Mighty Fallen! (1:17-27)

1:17-18. David responded to the deaths of Saul and Jonathan by chanting a **lament** (lit., "lamenting this lament"). A lament was a bereavement poem, a poetic and structured expression of sorrow using thoughtfully chosen words composed for mourning at a person's funeral, or because of tragic events (cf. Lm 1–5), or at the anniversary of a person's death (cf. 2Ch 35:25-26). David instructed his men **to teach the sons of Judah the song of the bow**. Perhaps he gave the lament this title because an archer had gravely wounded Saul on Mount Gilboa. **The book of Jashar** was a book/scroll that contained the record of events in the life of Israel (cf. Jos 10:13). The book of Jashur is not extant, but it was in existence at the time of the writing of 1 and 2 Samuel and may have been one of the sources the narrator used under the superintending of the Holy Spirit. David's lament is the second poem in Samuel. The first one was Hannah's song, composed in joy (cf. 1Sm 2:1-10); the second is David's lament, composed in sorrow.

1:19. Verses 19-27 are the lyrics of the lament itself. The theme is **how have the mighty fallen!** This refrain occurs twice, at the beginning and ending of the lament (vv. 19, 27). David used the word **mighty** five times and the verb form of **mighty** once (**stronger**, v. 23). The refrain is enlarged in v. 25 to the words **How have the mighty fallen in the midst of the battle!** in relation to Jonathan. David mentioned both **Saul** and **Jonathan** four times in the poem (Saul in vv. 21d, 22c, 23a, 24a; and Jonathan in 22b, 23a, 25b, 26a). Verse 19 is the introduction and v. 27 is the conclusion. The body of the poem has five stanzas: stanza 1 (v. 20); stanza 2 (v. 21); stanza 3 (vv. 22-23); stanza 4 (v. 24); and stanza 5 (vv. 25-26). David opened the lament by referring to Saul and Jonathan as the **beauty** of Israel.

1:20. Gath and **Ashkelon** were Philistine

cities, representing the whole land of the Philistines. No one in Israel should utter a word in Gath or Ashkelon about the deaths of Saul and Jonathan.

1:21. In stanza 2, David addressed Mount **Gilboa**. Since Saul and Jonathan's blood was spilled on her, David called down a poetic curse on the mountain: **Let not dew or rain be on you**.

1:22-23. Stanza 3 is the poem's central stanza. Here David eulogized the courage of Saul and Jonathan in battle and their commitment to each other in life and in death.

1:24. In the fourth stanza David addressed the **daughters of Israel**, charging them **to weep** for **Saul**. Weeping over loss was appropriate.

1:25-26. In v. 26 of the fifth stanza, David addressed **Jonathan** himself. He felt deeply the loss of his friend. Some people today misconstrue the following words of David about Jonathan: **Your love to me was more wonderful than the love of women**. David's words do not imply a homosexual relationship between himself and Jonathan. Homosexual practice was condemned in the strongest terms in the OT. Since David was a man after the Lord's own heart, homosexual practice between two godly men like David and Jonathan is inconceivable, and cannot be justified biblically. The love that David mentioned was the love of covenant friendship. In the ancient world a man's closest confidants were other men, but this does not indicate any kind of sexual relationship.

1:27. In a powerful metaphor David spoke of Saul and Jonathan as **weapons of war**. In spite of Saul's many attempts to kill David, David did not mention any of that in his lament. David's lament shows the need not to be vindictive in the loss of an enemy but to be reflective and thoughtful about grief when one of God's anointed, even a failed one, dies.

B. David the King vs. the House of Saul (2:1-32)

1. David Is Anointed King over Judah (2:1-4a)

2:1-2. David sought the **Lord** Himself about his next steps. God told David to go to **Judah**, but He did not specify where in Judah, so David asked God for specifics. David is an example of a believer being specific in his prayer life. The Lord directed David to leave Ziklag and go northeast to **Hebron**. Hebron was a city in Judah's hill country 20 miles south of Jerusalem, about three thousand feet in elevation, a city of great historical significance in Israel (cf. Gn 23:19; 25:9-10; 49:29-33; 49:31-33; Nm 35:6; Jos 21:7-9; Jdg 1:20). According to Baldwin, "Hebron, with its importance in the Abraham narratives and its associations as the burial-place of the patriarchs, was the most distinguished of Judah's cities" (Baldwin, *1 and 2 Samuel*, 183), a fitting place for David's second anointing as king of Israel. The name Hebron signifies "community, fellowship."

2:3-4a. David's men and their households (i.e., their wives and children) may have numbered well over a thousand. They settled in the villages surrounding **Hebron**, which became the seat of David's government over Judah. David was a theocratic king, ruling as the Lord's representative.

2. The Lord's Anointed King Reaches out to Jabesh-gilead (2:4b-7)

2:4b-5. David sent messengers to **the men of Jabesh-gilead** (for its location, see 1Sm 11:1-4), commending them for the kindness they had shown to Saul. When they risked their own lives to retrieve Saul's body, treated his corpse with respect, and provided him with a decent burial, they showed covenant fidelity and commitment as well as gratitude for Saul's previous deliverance of their city.

2:6-7. Truth in v. 6 means "faithfulness," "reliability," "trustworthy behavior" in the context of covenant obligations. The Lord is trustworthy and faithful, and so David wanted the Lord to show lovingkindness and truth to the men of Jabesh-gilead for having buried Saul. **Lovingkindness** (*chesed*) and **truth** (*emet*) are the twin virtues of the OT (cf. Pss 40:11; 57:3; 61:7), much like grace and truth in the NT. David challenged the men of Jabesh to be **strong** and **valiant** (lit., be "sons of valor") for two reasons: Saul, their master, was **dead** and **Judah** had **anointed** David **king over** Judah. Strength was required to deal with the loss of Saul, and to adjust to the new divinely selected royal administration in Judah in the hands of David.

3. General Abner Makes Ish-bosheth King over Israel (2:8-11)

2:8-9. Abner was first introduced in the narrative as the captain, or **commander**, of Saul's army (1Sm 14:50), and his status is repeated in v. 8. Merrill says that with the death of Saul, Abner was the true "power behind the throne" and David's real rival in the north (Merrill, "2 Samuel," 458). Abner was in charge of what remained of Saul's regime. Apparently **Ish-bosheth**, one of Saul's sons, did not participate in the battle of

Gilboa. Since he did not lose his life in that battle, Abner made him king. There was no prayer here; no inquiring after the Lord. The name "Ish-bosheth" means "man of shame." Abner took this "man of shame" and made him king. Sinful and rebellious decisions are not only morally wrong; they are stupid. Abner's quest was an attempt to hold on to power God did not intend him to have, and it was an act of rebellion against the Lord.

2:10-11. The **two years** of Ish-bosheth's reign may have coincided with the last two years of David's reign in Hebron over Judah, which lasted for seven-and-a-half years. For reasons that the text does not state, the Lord did not grant David the entire kingdom of Israel immediately. It is evident that there was still some loyalty to Saul in the north, and perhaps this delay in receiving the entire kingdom was another preparation of David for his later reign as king over all of Israel.

4. A Battle Spreads between the Houses of David and Saul (2:12-32)

2:12-15. Civil war soon began between David's men and Saul's men. **The pool of Gibeon** (v. 13) was a well known pool in the region. Abner suggested that **young men** engage in **a contest**, with 12 from each side (v. 15). The purpose of limiting the battle to 12 men was in the interest of reducing bloodshed in a battle that determined who would rule over Israel and Judah. Joab, however, did not have the authority to make such a decision, but he accepted Abner's challenge.

2:16-17. The outcome of the contest was inconclusive, which made a full battle inevitable. The place was given a name for what happened there, **Helkath-hazzurim**, meaning "the field of sword edges." Instead of reducing casualties, the twenty-four-man contest became a fierce full-scale battle, which Abner and his men lost.

2:18. David's sister Zeruiah (cf. 1Ch 2:16) had three sons, **Joab and Abishai and Asahel**. Asahel **was as swift-footed as one of the gazelles which is in the field**. Gazelles were known for their incredible speed, especially when fleeing predators. Asahel had a sprinter's speed combined with a distance runner's endurance.

2:19-22. Abner, Saul's army commander, retreated, running for safety after his defeat by Joab and the army of David (v. 19). **Asahel**, however, **pursued Abner**, hoping that by executing him he could end the conflict between David and the house of Saul, and David would become king over all Israel. Asahel was a sprinter, but he was no match for the experienced Abner in close combat. Knowing he could defeat Asahel, Abner used four imperatives to convince Asahel to pursue someone he could handle in a fight: **turn** . . . **take hold of one of the young men** . . . **take for yourself**, and **turn aside** (vv. 20-21). Abner did not want to have Asahel's shed blood to be between him and Joab.

2:23. But Asahel did not listen. Abner's use of his spear's butt suggests that he was running away from Asahel. When Abner suddenly stopped, Asahel did not have time to slow down so he ran right into the spear. The use of Asahel's own speed, combined with Abner's skillful thrust, resulted in the spear piercing Asahel and coming out through **his back**.

2:24. Even though they did not have the speed of their slain brother, **Joab and Abishai pursued Abner**. As **the sun was going down**, they reached **the hill of Ammah**, near **Gibeon**, about five miles northeast of Jerusalem.

2:25-26. In a show of support, **the sons of Benjamin gathered together behind Abner**. From his position of superior strength, Abner asked Joab three questions designed to get him to call off the pursuit.

2:27-29. Joab basically said to Abner, "You started this fight. Had you not given us a challenge at the pool of Gibeon, none of today's events would have occurred." Then **Joab blew** his **trumpet**, signaling that it was time to end the fighting. The words **nor did they continue to fight anymore** (v. 28) do not mean hostilities between David and Saul's family ended. War continued for some time between them (cf. 3:1), but they did not fight any more on this occasion. Abner and his men crossed over to the east side of the **Jordan** River. In great physical condition, they marched **all** . . . **night** and **all morning** of the next day (v. 29). It was safer to march at night under the cloak of darkness.

2:30-32. Nineteen of David's men had died, but 360 of **Abner's men** died in this conflict. **Asahel** was **buried** . . . **in Bethlehem**, his ancestral home.

C. The Growth of David's House (3:1-39)

1. David's House Increases as Saul's Declines (3:1)

3:1. The two years of Ish-bosheth's reign do not seem to fit the description of the war as **long**. The war in all likelihood was going on before Abner made Ish-bosheth king over Israel. Still, David was becoming **stronger** and Saul's house became **weaker**.

2. David's Family Increases (3:2-5)

3:2-5. David's first six sons were born in Hebron. They are listed by name and birth order along with their mothers' identification. This record may be included here to show David's involvement in marriage alliances with foreign powers (Laney, *First and Second Samuel*, 90). In addition, the birth of so many sons was a way of demonstrating the statement that **the house of David . . . grew steadily stronger** (v. 1). David's second son **Chileab** is only mentioned here. He may have died fairly young because he is not mentioned at all during the tumultuous times in David's family in chaps. 13–19. One of David's wives, Absalom's mother, was **Maacah, the daughter of Talmai, king of Geshur**. Since she was a Gentile, this marriage was probably political. Her relationship to the Lord is not mentioned, but it is unlikely that David married an idolater.

3. Abner Grows Stronger in the House of Saul (3:6-11)

3:6. David's growth resulted from the Lord's blessing, but Abner's growth was because of his own efforts. **Abner** was the most powerful man in Israel outside of Judah. Hence, the next few verses explain what he did.

3:7-8. Rizpah was Saul's **concubine**. A concubine did not have the same status as a wife, but she did have some rights. The relationship was legally binding. (Rizpah is mentioned again in 21:8-11.) Ish-bosheth accused Abner of having sexual relations with Saul's concubine, an accusation that the text does not deny or affirm (Bergen, *1, 2 Samuel*, 307). It was a serious charge, because to have a sexual relationship with a king's concubine was a back-door claim to the throne. When Ish-bosheth accused Abner of treason, the accusation angered Abner. He questioned Ish-bosheth, employing a biting metaphor, **Am I a dog's head that belongs to Judah?** Laney renders the question as, "Am I a contemptible traitor?" (Laney, *First and Second Samuel*, 91), which is plausible given the heated rivalry between Israel in the north and Judah in the south. Dogs were despised in Israel and considered unclean. To refer to a person as a dog's head was a stinging insult. In accusing Abner, Ish-bosheth was making the unfounded charge that Abner was a treacherous dog from Judah.

3:9-11. Motivated by his anger toward Ish-bosheth, Abner, the most powerful man in Saul's house, said he would take steps **to establish** David's **throne** over all Israel, **from** the northern extremity, **Dan**, **to** the southern extremity, **Beersheba**.

4. Abner Makes a Covenant with David (3:12-25)

3:12-13. Abner sent word **to David** to make a **covenant** with him. David agreed to do so, provided Abner brought with him David's wife, **Michal**. This gesture restored David's lawful wife to him and signified Abner's sincerity of effort to transfer the kingdom of all Israel to David.

3:14. David sent messengers to Ish-bosheth, demanding his wife's return, reminding Ish-bosheth of the dowry he gave to his father Saul for her. Saul had asked for one **hundred** Philistine **foreskins,** but David gave him two hundred (cf. 1Sm 18:25-27).

3:15-16. Michal had remarried, but her union with **Paltiel** came to a tragic end. Paltiel did not have the power to resist Abner, and Michal had no say in the matter. Her husband Paltiel accompanied her part of the way, **weeping**. This painful situation was the result of another of Saul's bad decisions.

3:17-19. Wisely, **Abner** consulted Israel's **elders** before he went to meet David in Hebron with Michal. Abner indicated that at some time in the past, at least a faction in Israel wanted David to be their king. Anderson suggests this may have been after Saul's death, and David was wanted because of his military exploits (A. A. Anderson, *2 Samuel*, WBC [Nashville: Thomas Nelson, 1989], 59-60). Abner presented his counsel as the plan of God, not just a good political move (Anderson, *2 Samuel*, 59–60).

3:20-21. In ancient Israel **a feast** in connection with a covenant was prepared for honored guests. Preparing the feast and participating in the meal were expressions of covenant commitments and goodwill on the part of the participants. Under the circumstances of peaceful reconciliation, **David sent Abner away**.

3:22-25. Returning from a **raid**, Joab voiced his disapproval of Abner's visit to David, fearing that Abner was using the occasion to spy on David. David did not answer Joab's accusation of spying by Abner, but Joab took matters into his own hands.

5. Joab Murders Abner (3:26-30)

3:26-27. The **well of Sirah** was near Hebron. Unknown to David, Joab called Abner back, so Abner returned to **Hebron**. Since reconciliation and peace had been established between Abner and David, Abner was not expecting violence. In the **gate** complex Joab stabbed Abner **in the**

belly, similar to how Abner killed Joab's brother, Asahel (cf. 2:23). Joab did this **on account of the blood of Asahel his brother**. In violation of God's Word, Joab murdered Abner in Hebron, which had been designated as a city of refuge in Joshua's day (cf. Jos 21:13). A city of refuge was a place where a person in Israel who killed someone without malicious intent was able to flee and be safe from revenge by the dead person's family. Joab ignored this law by killing Abner to avenge the death of his brother Asahel. Asahel was killed in battle, and should not have been avenged in the first place.

3:28. Hearing of Joab's murder of Abner, David declared that he and his **kingdom** were **innocent before the Lord** of Abner's **blood**. The words **the blood of Abner** signify that Abner's life was violently taken. Without David's knowledge, much less his approval, Joab murdered Abner.

3:29. Then David called down a curse of retribution on the head of Joab and his descendants. David was speaking as the agent of God's righteous judgment on Joab for his guilt, not in personal anger of petty vengeance. Brueggemann believes the narrator was "at great pains" with this matter because "bloodguilt" had now come close to David (Brueggemann, *First and Second Samuel*, 229). The curse included affliction with infectious skin diseases, needing crutches because of severe weakness, death in battle for many of Joab's house, and intense poverty (**lacks bread**).

3:30. Joab's brother, **Abishai**, is mentioned in this verse because he was involved with Joab in Abner's murder, although Joab bore the main responsibility.

6. David Mourns the Death of Abner (3:31-39)

3:31-39. David commanded Joab and his men to mourn for Abner: to **tear** their **clothes**, to wear **sackcloth, and** to **lament. David walked behind the bier** (v. 31), a hand-carried cart for transporting a dead body to a burial site. In ancient Israel when a person died, he was buried almost immediately, usually the same day. Natural openings in rocks served as graves. The king took the lead role in Abner's funeral; he **walked behind the bier** in the procession to the gravesite, he **wept** at Abner's **grave** (v. 32), he composed **a lament** for the occasion (v. 33), and called down a curse on himself if he ate anything before sundown (v. 35). The people observed David's grief and correctly concluded that David was not involved in Abner's murder (vv. 36-37).

D. The Murder of Ish-bosheth (4:1-12)

1. Ish-bosheth Loses Courage (4:1-3)

4:1-3. The news of Abner's death reached Ish-bosheth and **he lost courage** (lit., "his hands fell" or "dropped"). This physical gesture showed his loss of courage. Without a leader, all Israel was alarmed. Ish-bosheth knew he could not maintain his position without Abner, the narrator showed how quickly any remaining opposition to David's reign faded away (Baldwin, *1 and 2 Samuel*, 192). At some point in their history, **the Beerothites fled to Gittaim** (v. 3). The flight may have occurred earlier, or it may have resulted from David's determination to avenge the murder of Ish-bosheth (vv. 9-12). This parenthetical note may have been included to underscore the treachery of the assassins, who were from Saul's tribe of Benjamin and would be expected to be loyal to his house (Youngblood, "1, 2 Samuel," 337).

2. Mephibosheth Crippled in an Accident (4:4)

4:4. A **nurse** was someone who provided care for young children when their parents were deceased or unavailable. Sometimes the service was rendered for the parents. Since the nurse was a woman, it is likely that she also breast-fed him. Hearing of Saul's death, his nurse picked the boy up to run, and in her haste she dropped him and he became crippled in both feet so that he could never walk again. The boy's **name was Mephibosheth**, which means "exterminator, dispeller of shame." By inserting this parenthetical detail, the author provided information on Mephibosheth that would be needed later (Peterson, *First and Second Samuel*, 154).

3. David Responds to Rechab and Baanah's Treachery (4:5-12)

4:5-6. Rechab and Baanah entered Ish-bosheth's house, pretending **to get wheat**. They went there **in the heat of the day**, that is, when the sun was at its zenith, the hottest part of the day (v. 5) when they apparently knew Ish-bosheth would be taking his **midday rest** (v. 5). This statement also had cultural implications, for unless it was an emergency it was inappropriate to disturb someone during these hours—especially someone purported to be king. They murdered Ish-bosheth, stabbing him **in the belly** (v. 6; Asahel and Abner died of the same wound), a blow which, combined with decapitation (v. 7), was designed to bring about a quick and certain death (Bergen, *1, 2 Samuel*, 316).

4:7. More details were given on how the assassination was accomplished; Ish-bosheth was **on his bed**, completely unsuspecting and off-guard. The assassins then carried his head to David, hoping—like the Amalekite in chap. 1—to receive a handsome reward.

4:8-12. The assassins showed David Ish-bosheth's head and voiced words that must have angered David greatly: **thus the LORD has given my lord the king vengeance this day on Saul and his descendants** (v. 8). But they were unprepared for what he said and did next. These two brothers misunderstood David's heart for God. In addition, David had made a covenant with Saul that he would not cut off his descendants when he came to power. David prefaced what he said with the oath formula, **As the LORD lives** (v. 9).

David's ordering the death of these men was not personal vengeance, but capital punishment for two opportunistic, cold-blooded murderers. After their execution David's men cut off the murderers' **hands and feet** (v. 12), the body parts employed in carrying out the murder. Cutting off a dead person's hands and feet and then hanging them up for all to see was the height of disgrace in death, serving as a stern warning to anyone who contemplated a similar act. David, however, treated Ish-bosheth's **head** with respect, burying it in Abner's **grave**.

E. The Crowning and Conquest of David, the King of Israel (5:1-25)

1. David Becomes King over All Israel (5:1-5)

5:1-2. The people wanted David to be their king for three reasons: (1) David was one of their own, an Israelite; (2) David was an able leader; and (3) the Lord called David to lead and shepherd His people.

5:3-4. David made a covenant with Israel's **elders** in the Lord's presence at **Hebron**. The covenant stipulated that David was **king over Israel**. For the third time David was anointed, now as the widely-recognized king over all Israel. What a day of rejoicing and relief this must have been for David and his family and for all Israel! David **reigned** for **forty years**, that is, until he was 70 years old.

5:5. Beginning with David's enlarged reign, Jerusalem loomed large in the rest of OT history. He had reigned in **Hebron** over **Judah** for **seven years and six months**, so now as he began his reign over all Israel and Judah he was 37 years old.

2. The King Captures Jerusalem (5:6-10)

5:6. David's first action as king of all Israel was his march against **Jerusalem**, where the **Jebusites** were living. The Jebusites were one of the Canaanite people groups in the land (cf. Gn 10:16; Nm 13:29; Jos 11:1-3; 15:63). In the conquest under Joshua, Benjamin's sons could not drive the Jebusites from Jerusalem (cf. Jdg 1:21); so at the beginning of David's reign over all Israel, they were fortified in Jerusalem. They lived there for centuries in a fortified stronghold on Mt. Zion's southern hill. Humanly speaking, the stronghold was invincible. So, the Jebusites mockingly told David that he was no match for even their **blind and lame**. They were so confident because they thought, **David cannot enter here**.

5:7-8. In an amazing military feat David captured Zion's **stronghold**. Water flowed from the spring of Gihon outside the city walls through a **tunnel** (an open vertical shaft in the rock) into the city. Some archaeologists have maintained that "Warren's Shaft," discovered in the city of David by explorer Charles Warren, is the same tunnel through which David and his men conquered the city. Other archaeologists vehemently oppose this view. The evidence is inconclusive; therefore, it is best to accept the biblical account without identifying precisely which tunnel was used. Going through any subterranean water shaft would be challenging, but once through it, capturing the city was not difficult. Using their own words to mock them, David referred to all the Jebusites in the stronghold as **the lame and the blind**. A proverb developed in Israel from this event: **The blind or the lame shall not come into the house** (v. 8). The proverb was a mocking jab at pagans who try to conquer the Lord's people.

5:9-10. David renamed **the stronghold and called it the city of David** (v. 9), referring to the city where David reigned, not to be confused with Bethlehem, which was called "the city of David" as the city of his birth (Lk 2:4, 11). The word **Millo**, a fortified area, is a transliteration of the Hebrew word. David filled in areas and enlarged the city of Jerusalem, making it suitable as the nation's capital and the seat of his government.

3. Hiram Builds David a House (5:11-12)

5:11-12. Hiram king of Tyre sent **cedar trees** and workmen to build **a house for David**. David perceived in Hiram's gesture that **the LORD had established him as king**, not for his **sake**, but for the good and blessing of **His people Israel**.

4. David Enlarges His Already Large Family (5:13-16)

5:13-16. Settled in Jerusalem, **David took more concubines and wives**, who bore him 11 sons, including **Solomon**. But by taking on more wives David was disobeying the law (cf. Dt 17:17). Youngblood notes that by listing David's concubines first, "the narrator is perhaps deploring David's proclivity for the trappings of a typical Near Eastern monarch, including a harem" (Youngblood, "1, 2 Samuel," 355). God did not rebuke David for this, although, as Merrill points out, David's actions here brought him great sorrow later on (Merrill, "2 Samuel," 461).

5. David Battles the Philistines (5:17-25)

5:17-19. The Philistines considered King **David** a threat and pursued him. In response, David went to **the stronghold** (v. 17), but not the stronghold of Zion. It was one of the strongholds where David and his men lived when they were fugitives from Saul, indicating that these events took place prior to the capture of Jebus.

The Philistines ... spread ... out in the valley of Rephaim, "the valley of the giants" (v. 18). Probably the place name reminded David of the victory the Lord granted him over the giant Goliath years earlier. The valley was not far from Bethlehem (cf. 2Sm 23:13-15).

As usual, David asked the Lord for guidance, and He assured David of victory. Victory was because of God's power, not David's military skill.

5:20-21. David used a simile in describing the Lord's victory in the battle: **The LORD has broken through my enemies before me like the breakthrough of waters.** David then **named** the site of their victory **Baal-perazim**, meaning "the master of the breakthrough." The Lord was the master of the breakthrough. The Philistines recognized that **their idols** were powerless, so they abandoned them (cf. Is 2:20-21).

5:22-25. The Philistines amassed **again** for battle against Israel in the same place. Again David asked the Lord for guidance, and this time He gave David a new battle plan. He was to attack them from the rear instead of using a direct frontal attack (vv. 23-24). **The sound of** the **marching in the tops of the balsam trees** was a divine sign that David was to go out to battle because God Himself would have gone out before David to strike the army of the Philistines. **David** obeyed God and **struck down the Philistines from Geba as far as Gezer**. The distance between these two locations is substantial, about 25 miles, underscoring the extent of David's victory.

F. Bringing the Ark to Jerusalem (6:1-23)

1. Israel Returns the Ark in the Wrong Way (6:1-11)

6:1. As Laney points out, David was always "intensely interested in the worship of Yahweh," in contrast to Saul (*First and Second Samuel*, 95). David now demonstrated again that he was "a man after [God's] own heart" (1Sm 13:14) by bringing the ark of the covenant to Jerusalem. It had been neglected during the reign of Saul, another evidence of Saul's spiritual indifference (Laney, *First and Second Samuel*, 95).

Chosen men were men trained and skilled as warriors. These valiant men were usually used in major military offensives. But David called on these men to bring the ark of God from Baale-judah (a Gibeonite town [cf. Jos 9:17] that was assigned first to Judah (cf. Jos 15:60), then to Benjamin (cf. Jos 18:28) (Unger, *The New Unger's Bible Dictionary*, 743), to Jerusalem. This town was also known as Kiriath-jearim, and was located about nine miles northeast of Jerusalem. In case the Philistines attempted to attack Israel during this procession, David had **thirty thousand** men on hand ready for battle.

6:2. The ark had been at **Baale-judah** since the days of Samuel, before the birth of the monarchy (cf. 1Sm 7:1), for approximately 70 years. The ark symbolized God's presence; it was like His earthly throne. David wanted to show by moving the ark that the presence and worship of the Lord were central to Israel and to his reign.

6:3. As the Philistines had placed the ark on a new cart (cf. 1Sm 6:7), so now God's people **placed the ark of God on a new cart**. Actually, the ark was never to be placed on any cart. The Levites were to carry it in order to insure that it was treated with reverence (cf. Nm 4:15; Dt 10:8).

6:4-5. The procession was a joyful one, with music being played on several kinds of musical instruments: **instruments made of fir wood**, and **lyres, harps, tambourines, castanets and cymbals**.

6:6-7. When the oxen leading the ark stumbled and nearly upset it, **Uzzah reached out** to steady the ark. But God in anger struck him down. The reason given was for **his** [lit., "the"] **irreverence**. Touching the ark was not a helpful gesture; it was the essence of a monumentally irreverent act resulting from the disobedience of placing the ark on a cart rather than carrying it with poles.

6:8-9. David became angry perhaps **because** he felt the Lord overreacted in light of the sincerity of what they were trying to do. The words **the LORD's outburst** literally means "the LORD broke through a breakthrough." There was a breakthrough earlier against the Philistines, but now the Lord broke through in discipline. The Philistine approach to handling holy items, which the Israelites emulated here, was disastrous for God's people. David accordingly named the place **Perez-uzzah**, which means "the breakthrough of Uzzah."

David's emotions moved from anger to fear. He was **afraid** of God in the sense of being awe-struck at how holy and dreadful the Lord is.

6:10-11. This experience sobered David; he now had a deeper reverence for the Lord. He also did not want to take any further risks in trying to transport the ark (Anderson, *2 Samuel*, 104). So instead of taking the ark to Jerusalem, David took it **to the house of Obed-edom the Gittite**.

2. Israel Returns the Ark in the Biblical Way (6:12-15)

6:12. That the Lord visibly **blessed the house of Obed-edom** because of the ark encouraged David to bring the ark to Jerusalem, which he did **with gladness** (v. 12).

6:13. This time the Levites carried the ark as directed in the Mosaic law, rather than having oxen pull it on a cart. After they took only **six paces** or steps, David **sacrificed an ox and a fatling**, that is, a fatted calf. Saying that David **sacrificed** does not mean that David acted as a priest, but rather that he gave the animals which were then offered through the mediation of a Levitical priest.

6:14. David danced **with all his might** before the Lord, that is, he invested all of his physical strength in the dance, demonstrating the full engagement of his whole being in this act of worship. And he did so **before the LORD**, that is, in His presence. **Wearing a linen ephod**, part of the priestly garment, David was not usurping priestly authority. He was expressing heartfelt worship of the Lord.

6:15. The celebration was loud! The people brought the ark with **shouting** and blowing of the **trumpet**. David may have composed Ps 24 for this occasion. The presence of the Lord, the King of glory, accompanied the ark into the city of David, Jerusalem, the very place that had been an unconquerable Jebusite stronghold for centuries.

3. Michal Despises David (6:16-23)

6:16. When the ark entered **the city of David**, **Michal** observed the scene from a window. This is the first time Michal is mentioned since chap. 3. The ark's coming to David's city was a stupendous event in Israel's history, but this did not impress her. Instead she noticed her husband, King David, **leaping** (another physical expression of David's joy) **and dancing**. In her mind David's expressive worship was beneath the king's dignity. So she **despised** him, that is, she held him in contempt and scorn, just as the giant Goliath had despised and ridiculed young David (cf. 1Sm 17:42). But her sentiments were not in harmony with the wonder of the moment.

6:17. David pitched a **tent** in Jerusalem for the ark and in worship he offered **burnt offerings** (symbolizing full devotion and commitment to the Lord) and **peace offering**s (symbolizing peace and fellowship with the Lord and with one another). About David as priest, see comments at 6:13.

6:18-19. In a pastoral manner (cf. Nm 6:22-27), David spoke words of blessing to the people in the Lord's name. And he gave each person **a cake of bread**, a cake of **dates**, and a cake of **raisins**. No doubt the people returned home with joy in their hearts, tangible tokens of God's blessing in their hands, with God's blessing pronounced over them, and rejoicing that the ark of God was now present in David's city.

6:20-22. After blessing the people, David **returned** home **to bless his household**. But before one word of blessing fell from his lips, **Michal** met him and insulted him, calling him **foolish** (v. 20). David replied that his actions were **before the LORD** (see vv. 5, 14, 16, 17). He reminded Michal that **the LORD . . . chose** him instead of her father and his house and made him leader **over Israel** (v. 21). Even if he was humble in his own eyes, the slave girls whom Michal disparaged would honor David, which Michal should have done. In this chapter Michal is called **the daughter of Saul** (vv. 16, 20, 23), not David's wife.

6:23. In the ancient world infertility was a major calamity for a married woman. Michal experienced the tragedy of infertility as an expression of God's judgment on her because of her scornful attitude toward David, the Lord's anointed.

G. The Lord Will Build David an Eternal House (7:1-29)

1. David Desires to Build the Lord a House (7:1-3)

7:1-3. After many years of suffering and struggle, life settled down for King David. David **lived in his house**, and he had **rest on every side from all his enemies**. "House" is a key word in chap. 7 (vv. 1, 2, 5, 6-7, 13, 16, 18, 19, 25-26, 29). The Lord took the image of a house, and David's desire to build the Lord a house/temple, to instruct him in other matters. The prophet **Nathan** (v. 3), mentioned here for the first time in 1 and 2 Samuel, played a strategic role in David's life. David mused about his living conditions being better than the ark of God. Nathan discerned in David's words his intentions to build a house/temple for the Lord and he encouraged him to do so (v. 3).

2. The Lord Sends Nathan to David with a Message (7:4-17)

7:4-5. That **night**, the Lord said to Nathan, **Go and say to My servant David**. For the first time in Scripture the Lord referred directly to David as His servant, placing him in the company of Moses (cf. Nm 12:2; Dt 34:4), Joshua (cf. Jos 24:19), and Job (cf. Jb 1:8; 2:3; 42:7-8). David's intentions were good, but King Solomon, David's successor, would build the temple, not David. The reason is given in 1Ch 22:8—David had shed too much blood. But more than that, the Lord was saying to David, in the expressive words of Peterson, "You want to build me a house? Forget it. I'm building you a house. The kingdom that I'm shaping here is not what you do for me but what I do for you" (*First and Second Samuel*, 167).

7:6-7. Up to the present point in Israel's history, the Lord manifested Himself in portable tents. He never asked anyone to build Him a house of cedar like the one that David was living in.

7:8-9. God continued to speak to Nathan by beginning with the words **thus you shall say to My servant David**. The Lord plucked David out of obscurity to make him king over Israel. God promised David **a great name** (v. 9), similar to His promise to Abraham. David was great in his day, but the greatness here was because of David's name enduring forever.

7:10-11. The Lord will make a house [dynasty] **for you** (v. 11) is the central covenant promise to David. The narrator did not use the word "covenant" in chap. 7 to describe the Lord's words to David, but the term is used in other places to define the nature of God's message to David (cf. 2Sm 23:5; 2Ch 13:5; Ps 89:3). Here is the origin of the promise of the Davidic dynasty, which is one of the great mountain peaks of biblical revelation, and a significant advance in the progress of biblical revelation about the majestic seed of David, the Messiah. The Messiah is the seed of the woman (cf. Gn 3:15), the seed of Abraham (cf. Gn 12:3), and the seed of David (cf. Rm 1:3; lit., "born from the seed of David").

God's covenant begins by promising David that God would provide a secure place for the people of Israel. God will **plant them** in the land of Israel and they will be given **rest from all [their] enemies** (v. 11). This is not referring to peace in the days of David or Solomon, but peace under the future Son of David, the Messiah.

7:12-17. Besides promising David a secure place for his people, the Lord also promised David a special Seed, translated **descendant** here (v. 12). There are four aspects to the covenantal promise of the Seed of David. First, God will grant the Seed a secure kingdom (**I will establish His kingdom**, v. 12). The Seed's kingdom is secure in that it is eternal. Second, the Lord promised that David's descendant/Seed would build **a house** for God (v. 13). This is a reference to David's special offspring who will build a temple for the Lord. Third, the descendant will have a Father/Son relationship with God (v. 14). Fourth, this promise is unconditional—God's **lovingkindness shall not depart from him** (v. 15) no matter what—the descendant will never lose the promise (v. 15).

Finally, the Lord summarizes the essence of this eternal and unconditional covenant with David. The Lord has granted David an eternal **house** (dynasty), **kingdom** (nation), and **throne** (sovereignty). All of these **shall be established forever** (v. 16).

Obviously the question that must be answered is, "Who is the Seed of David in the covenant?" On a surface level, it appears that perhaps Solomon is in view. He certainly built the temple for the Lord. Also, within the narrative, none of David's other sons survived the conflicts, intrigues, and tensions of David's royal house. Moreover, Solomon seems to believe that the Davidic covenant was fulfilled in him (cf. 1Kg 8:20).

However, Solomon's viewpoint is not necessarily the perspective of the author of the book of 2 Samuel. The story of David continues, from this book into the books of the Kings, detailing what became of David's descendants. There, the author, using dramatic literary artistry, seems to build up Solomon as the potential fulfillment of the covenant, only to prove that Solomon was unfaithful, marrying foreign women and following foreign gods (cf. 1Kg 11:1-2). Therefore, the covenant was not fulfilled in him (cf. 1Kg 11:9-12). Nevertheless, the author is careful to include that Solomon's failure did not negate the promise to David, saying that God would still give one tribe to the Davidic house "for the sake of My servant David" (1Kg 11:13). Thereafter in the narrative in the books of Kings, each Davidic king is viewed as a possible fulfillment to the covenant, yet each one ends in failure. Hence the book of 2 Kings ends with Israel going to captivity and the promise unfulfilled. Therefore, the point of the narrative is to have the reader keep looking for a future Seed of David, the Messiah, who will have an eternal house, kingdom, and throne.

It is not only the writer of the Kings who reads the Davidic covenant as messianic. In v. 19, in David's response to the Lord's statement of the Davidic covenant, David marvels that this covenant is concerning the distant future (v. 19), demonstrating that the author of Samuel did not view it as fulfilled in Solomon but in the end of days. Later OT writers and prophets always interpreted the covenant as finding its fulfillment in the messianic King, the eschatological Son of David (cf. Ps 89:51; 132:17-18; Is 9:6-7; 11:1,10; 16:5; 42:1, 6; 55:3-4; Jr 23:5; 30:9; 33:15-17; Ezk 34:23-24; 37:24-28; Hs 3:4-5; Am 9:11-15). Much as the Hebrew Bible read the Davidic covenant as messianic, so does the NT (cf. Lk 1:31-33; Ac 2:30-36; Rm 1:3; 2Tm 2:8).

Two possible objections to the messianic interpretation of 2Sm 7 are (1) the seeming expectation that the Seed of David would commit iniquity (**when he commits iniquity, I will correct him with the rod of men**, v. 14) and (2) Solomon did indeed build the temple as the covenant stipulated he would.

As to the first objection, it would be better to translate the Hebrew word for **when** (*asher*) as "if," as in "if he commits iniquity." The same word is translated this way in other passages (cf. Dt 11:27; Jos 4:21). In fact, the second-century BC Greek translation of the OT, the Septuagint, also translates 2Sm 7:14 with the word "if" (*ean*). Thus, the prediction of being the Seed is potentially true of each of the descendants of David. Each one is potentially the fulfillment of the covenant but *if* he commits iniquity, he is disqualified. Nevertheless, the covenant is secure, and will be fulfilled in a later descendant, namely, the Messiah, the Son of David.

With regard to the second objection, although Solomon did build the first temple, he certainly did not have an eternal kingdom (**He shall build a house for My name, and I will establish the throne of his kingdom forever**, v. 13). Nor did Zerubbabel, who built the second temple, ever become king, let alone have an eternal kingdom. For this reason, the prophets always foretold that when the Messiah, the Son of David comes, He would build a temple for the Lord (cf. Zch 6:11-15; Ezk 40–48). Neither Solomon's temple nor the second temple ever fulfilled the promise here (v. 13). But when the Messiah comes to establish His eternal kingdom, then He will build the messianic temple of the Lord, in fulfillment of this passage. Thus, when Jesus the Messiah takes His seat on the throne of His father David (Is 9:7), David's dynasty will exist **forever** (v. 16); it will never end.

3. David Responds to God's Promise (7:18-29)

7:18. David the king went in and sat before the LORD. The sitting posture was one of humility. Even though he was a king, David humbled himself before the Lord. The idea of being before the Lord expressed in 6:14, 16, 21, now appears in chap. 7. David humbly prayed and praised the Lord, expressing to the Lord a healthy sense of inadequacy about himself and his house in light of His mercy and grace toward him.

7:19-20. The Lord's work in David's life was small in comparison to the Lord's promises that would reach beyond his own lifetime and beyond the next generation. In fact, David recognized that the fulfillment of God's promises would be in **the distant future** (v. 19). David was overwhelmed that God would make of his house an eternal dynasty! Then he added, **And this is the custom of man, O Lord GOD** (v. 19). This is a problematic passage, specifically because the word translated **custom** (*torah*) is generally translated "law" or "instruction."

This is resolved in the HCSB, which has David saying of God's statement of the Davidic covenant, "this is a [or your] *revelation* for mankind" (emphasis added), a far more appropriate translation of the word *torah*. Therefore, David is exclaiming that the fulfillment of God's revelation of the Davidic covenant will be in **the distant future** and that its benefits have been revealed not just for his own life and family but for all of humanity too.

7:21-22. People's recorded prayers are one of Scripture's outstanding features. Here David extolled God's **greatness** and uniqueness (**there is none like You**). The Lord is unparalleled in His person and glory. In this prayer, David calls God by the exceptional name **Lord God** (Adonai Yahweh) six times (vv. 18, 19, 20, 22, 28, 29), using the very name that God used when granting the Abrahamic covenant (cf. Gn 15:2, 8). This is no accident but a deliberate attempt to link the Davidic covenant to the Abrahamic.

7:23-29. The Lord's people **Israel** were unique as well. Besides David's dynasty enduring forever, **Israel** will be the Lord's **own people forever** (v. 24). In a posture of worship, David called on the Lord to confirm His pledged word not for the benefit of his family alone, but also so that the **name** of the Lord would **be magnified forever** (v. 26). Nine times in his prayer David described himself as the Lord's **servant** (vv. 19, 20, 25, 26, 27 [twice], 28, 29 [twice]). While the word "servant" underscores David's humility, David considered it a high honor to identify himself in this way. Describing God's **words** as **truth**, David called the divine promise of a dynasty a **good thing** (v. 28). The Lord's blessing on David's house was the sole guarantee of its eternal duration.

H. David's Victories and Righteous Rule (8:1-18)

1. David Triumphs over Many Enemies (8:1-14)

8:1-14. By the Lord's grace David's life was on an upward trajectory. Chapter 8 records one of the summits in David's reign. The Lord had just made tremendous promises to David, and the writer was showing that these promises would be fulfilled (Bergen, *1, 2 Samuel*, 346). The Lord now granted David victory in every geographical direction: over the **Philistines** in the west (v. 1), **Moab** in the east (v. 2), **Hadadezer** and **the Arameans of Damascus** on the north (vv. 3-8), and **Edom** in the south (v. 14). The Lord's promise to Abraham was being realized (cf. Gn 13:14). These victories were a continuation of the conquest begun centuries earlier under the leadership of Joshua (cf. Jos 1:7, 9). And the major factor in David's exploits was that **The Lord helped [him] wherever he went** (v. 14, cf. v. 6).

2. David Rules with Righteousness and Justice (8:15-18)

8:15-18. This section of 2 Samuel closes with a summary of the quality of David's reign, and the names of the administrators who occupied key posts in his government. Merrill says the inclusion of this list shows that the expansion of David's kingdom required a "bureaucracy" to administer it ("2 Samuel," 465). David also served in a judicial capacity, administering **justice and righteousness for all** the **people** (v. 15). He was neither partial in administering justice, nor did he tolerate the oppression and exploitation of people in his kingdom. In spite of David's work in administering justice, Absalom would later exploit an apparent weakness in it for his own political advantage (cf. 15:1-6). **Jehoshaphat** was the royal **recorder** (v. 16); his role is not clear, but perhaps he was responsible for preserving the memory of significant events in the nation's life. He would be responsible for overseeing the writing of the documents in which those memorable events are recorded. He may also have been responsible to remind the king of important affairs of state that needed to be addressed. The recorder is mentioned second in the list of David officials, suggesting that his role was important in David's administration.

Seraiah was the royal **secretary** (v. 17), whose function involved writing down important decrees and other documents on scrolls. But there were other administrative and diplomatic responsibilities that carried with them great authority (cf. 2Kg 12:10-16; Is 22:15-23; 36:1-3). **Benaiah . . . was over the Cherethites and the Pelethites** (v. 18). These were a group of elite warriors who served as David's royal bodyguard (cf. 2Sm 15:18; 20:23; 1Kg 1:38, 44). Although Philistine in background (cf. Ezk 25:16; Zph 2:45), this group of elite soldiers, being under David, were probably committed to the Lord.

I. The Kindness of the King (9:1-13)

1. David Summons Mephibosheth (9:1-8)

9:1. Chapters 9 and 10 highlight David's kindness. The growth of royal power did not conflict with the commitment David made to Jonathan and Saul's house years earlier, and he intended to carry out that promise. What else would one expect of a king who administered justice and righteousness for all his people (8:15)? The narrator opened the story with David asking a question: **Is there yet anyone left of the house of Saul, that I may show him kindness for Jonathan's sake?** The word "kindness" (*chesed*) is love, commitment, and loyalty pledged in the context of covenant agreements. David honored his covenant commitments.

9:2-4. Ziba was a man of high social standing, having 15 sons and 20 servants (cf. v. 10). He was responsible to care for Saul's estate. David asked him basically the same question he voiced in v. 1: **Is there not yet anyone of the house of Saul to whom I may show the kindness of God?** (v. 3). Ziba informed the king that there was one, Jonathan's **son**. He was lame **in both feet**. He was living with **Machir**, who evidently supported the house of Saul and who may have provided for Mephibosheth and his family. He must have been wealthy (Anderson, *2 Samuel*, 141). Later Machir was a great help to David also (17:27-29).

9:5. Learning of Jonathan's son, David sent for Mephibosheth and had him brought from Lo-debar (about 25 miles northwest of Jerusalem) to Jerusalem. Without doubt, the disabled man thought David would execute him. Even though Mephibosheth was disabled, he was a male descendent of Saul, and one of Saul's sons could become a claimant to David's throne. Brueggemann says the mention of Mephibosheth's disability may have been added to show that he was not a military or political threat to David (Brueggemann, *First and Second Samuel*, 267).

9:6. Mephibosheth was not mentioned by name until here in v. 6. Years had gone by since the tragic events of 4:4. Mephibosheth was now an adult. He was married, and he had a son, who could have become a potential rival to David's throne.

Mephibosheth fell on his face before David, terrified. Humanly speaking, he had every reason to be afraid, especially since the events of 2Sm 21:1-14, the execution of seven of Saul's male descendants by the Gibeonites, may have transpired at this time.

9:7. David eased his fears, promising Mephibosheth all of Saul's land. Saul's possessions became the royal possession of David (cf. 12:8). To return Saul's land to Mephibosheth was a risky move on David's part. But David did not stop there. He granted Mephibosheth a privilege reserved for his sons and other key officials in his administration. **And you shall eat** [lit., "eat bread"] **at my table regularly**. The expression "to sit at the king's table" (mentioned three times in this chapter in various ways: vv. 7, 10, 13) is an idiom for participating in the royal bounty, being sustained with the lavish royal sustenance of the king's table, and being the privileged to have a place at the king's table.

9:8. Overwhelmed at the king's kindness, Mephibosheth prostrated himself again, using the derogatory metaphor **dead dog** in reference to himself.

2. Mephibosheth Eats Bread at the King's Table (9:9-13)

9:9-11. David instructed **Ziba**, Saul's servant, to **cultivate the land** and bring **the produce** to Mephibosheth. Mephibosheth's eating at David's **table** meant he was **as one of the king's sons.**

9:12-13. Mephibosheth had a young son named **Mica**. Mica himself later had five sons (cf. 1Ch 8:34-35). Even though the dynasty belonged to David's house, by the Lord's mercy Saul's line continued through Mica, his great-grandson. David's treatment of Mephibosheth was one of the great expressions of OT lovingkindness.

J. Hanun Spurns the Kindness of the King (10:1-19)

1. David's Servants Are Shamed (10:1-5)

10:1-2. When the **king of the Ammonites died**, his son **Hanun** became king in his place. Since Ammon was grieving, David desired to show lovingkindness to Hanun. David's gesture was surprising since Nahash was Hanun's father. Nahash was the king who threatened the men of Jabesh-gilead (cf. 1Sm 11:1-11). This Nahash showed lovingkindness to David. The narrator did not say when Nahash did so, but it probably took place when David was a fugitive. David and Nahash had peaceful relations. Even though Ammon at this time was subject to David (cf. 2Sm 8:12), David wanted to honor his commitments and diplomatic loyalty with them. The Ammonites lived on the east side of the Jordan River, occupying some of the same land of present-day Jordan.

10:3-4. Listening to the poisonous perceptions of his counselors, Hanun insulted David and his men, thinking they came as spies. The voluntary shaving of the beard was a sign of grief and mourning (cf. Jr 41:4-8), but to shave off half a man's beard by force was a biting insult. And to cut one's clothes in a way that exposed the buttocks, forcing him to go for miles in that condition, was a major affront (cf. Is 20:4). Hanun's mistreatment of David's servants shamed David and Israel as a whole; it was also a declaration of war.

10:5. David's envoys **were greatly humiliated**. David protected their dignity by allowing them to stay in **Jericho** until their beards grew back.

2. Ammon Becomes a Stench to David (10:6-8)

10:6. Ammon became **odious** (lit., "a stench"), like the smell of excrement in David's nostrils. Being a weaker nation, Ammon hired several thousand mercenary soldiers.

10:7-8. Instead of going to battle, David **sent Joab** and his **army**. The enemy armies split up. Some were in battle formation in front of the city of Rabbah, the Ammonite royal city (cf. 12:26-29), present-day Amman, the capital of Jordan.

3. Two Brothers Lead the Battle (10:9-14)

10:9-12. Joab selected some choice soldiers to face the Arameans, and he put other soldiers under Abishai, his brother, against the Ammonites (v. 10). Joab, being a strange mixture of treachery (cf. 2Sm 5) and faith (v. 12), somewhat unexpectedly committed the battle's outcome to the Lord. But perhaps David's life had a godly influence on Joab, who was his nephew.

10:13-14. The defeat of the fortified royal city required siege warfare. Joab returned from fighting against the defeated sons of Ammon. Then Joab completed this mission the following spring, when conditions were conducive to battle (cf. 11:1).

4. David Finds Victory over the Arameans (10:15-19)

10:15-16. Hadadezer brought Arameans from **beyond the River**, that is, from the east of the Euphrates River, drawing them from the lands of present-day eastern Iraq and western Iran.

10:17-18. The battle was so important that David himself went with his troops. They engaged Hadadezer's army in **Helam**, whose location is not clear. The text suggests that Helam was somewhere between the Jordan and the Euphrates Rivers. David defeated the Arameans, and **struck down** their commander **Shobach** as well. The death of an army's commander was a huge psychological blow.

10:19. Defeated by Israel, Hadadezer's vassals became vassals to David, fearing to come to Ammon's military aid again.

II. Great Sin, Great Grace, Terrible Consequences (11:1–12:31)

Chapters 11 and 12 record the dark incidents in David's life, the consequences of which he would bear the rest of his life. These sordid events may have been included for several reasons: (1) to show that even a godly person is not exempt from sin and to warn others to stand guard (Laney, *First and Second Samuel*, 106); (2) to show what happens when a ruler's power goes to his head (Chisholm, *1 & 2 Samuel*, 232); (3) to report a series of events necessary to understand the remainder of David's reign; and (4) perhaps to express shock that a man who had been presented to this point as the ideal servant of the Lord could become, for a brief time, a rebel against God's law (Bergen, *1, 2 Samuel*, 361).

A. War and Great Sin (11:1-27)

1. The King Is Intimate with Bathsheba (11:1-5)

11:1. The setting was **spring**, perhaps March or April. The warm weather facilitated siege warfare. **David sent Joab** and the army back out against the Ammonites, **but David stayed at Jerusalem**. This by itself signals a shortcoming on David's part, since spring was **the time when kings go out to battle**. It was his responsibility to lead his army (see also 1Sm 8:20 and the comments there). David's irresponsibility here put him in the wrong place at the wrong time, resulting in the greatest failure of his life.

11:2. At night David took a stroll on his **roof**. Since his royal residence was built on one of Jerusalem's highest elevations, and the hill that sloped away from the palace was steep, he had a terrific view of the city. From his vantage point he could look down upon many of the homes and buildings in the city. One night, he noticed **a woman** taking a bath. She **was very beautiful in appearance**, and David had a lustful attraction to her physical beauty.

11:3. So David **sent** someone to identify the woman. **Sent** is one of the keys words in chap. 11 (vv. 1, 3, 4, 5, 6 [twice], 14, 22, 27), and in 12:1. The narrator shows that while David gave all the orders and sent his servants and army wherever he wanted them to go, and everyone did his bidding, he was not the one in command of the situation. God was, later sending Nathan to rebuke David (cf. 12:1). The woman was a daughter of Eliam, one of David's mighty men, and she was the granddaughter of Ahithophel, one of David's most trusted advisors (cf. 23:34). And she was the **wife of Uriah**, one of David's chief warriors (cf. 23:8, 39). Though a **Hittite**, he had embraced faith in the Lord; in fact, his name "Uriah" means "Yahweh is light." Bathsheba was forbidden to David, and this information should have stopped David in his tracks.

11:4. But David **sent messengers and took her**. David abused his power, taking her as if she were spoils in a battle with a defeated foe. David committed more than adultery. Although there is no explicit statement in the text regarding Bathsheba's motives, it seems likely that David's actions could be construed as sexual abuse. In a world dominated by men, it was difficult for Bathsheba to refuse the most powerful man in the kingdom, or even the Middle East. In the context of sexual abuse and adultery, it is ironic to note that the text notes the law's ceremonial aspects. After the sexual relations in marriage, ritual bathing was required if there was a seminal emission (cf. Lv 15:18). Apparently that happened and that biological fact explains what follows.

11:5. Weeks passed. Bathsheba realized the unthinkable; she was pregnant. In the entire episode she voiced only two words in Hebrew (three in English): **I am pregnant**. Her few words overflow with scandal and disgrace.

2. David Tries to Deceive Uriah (11:6-13)

11:6-7. As a pretense, David called **Uriah** back to Jerusalem from the war zone and asked him for an update on the war.

11:8-9. David then sent Uriah home, telling him, **Go down to your house, and wash your feet**. These words were a polite way of saying, "Go have sexual relations with your wife." David was hoping that Uriah would have sex with his wife, and that Uriah would think the baby was his. But instead of sleeping at home with his wife, **Uriah slept at the door of the king's house**.

11:10-11. So David tried again. David's two questions (**Have you not come from a journey? Why did you no go down to your house?**) were designed to insult Uriah's manhood. Uriah's noble response (with the army in the field, how could he **lie with [his] wife?**) is filled with irony. What he refused to do out of principle is precisely what David had done.

11:12-13. David then sent for Uriah again, this time to have dinner with the king and become intoxicated. David hoped that in this condition, he would go home, have relations with his wife, and the problem of her pregnancy could be concealed. But the plan failed once again; Uriah **did not go down to his house**.

3. David Writes a Chilling Letter (11:14-21)

11:14-15. Realizing that his plan for Uriah was not going to work, David **wrote a letter to** general **Joab**, Uriah's commander. Later that morning, giving the letter to Uriah like a trusted advisor, David charged Uriah to take the letter to Joab. Uriah dutifully obeyed, not knowing that he was carrying his own death warrant.

11:16-17. Joab did what David commanded, but not exactly as he prescribed. Joab was a shrewd general. To make Uriah's death appear to be a result of battle, Joab placed some of his men with Uriah in a dangerous spot. The Ammonites killed Uriah and also some of David's other men.

11:18-21. In ancient warfare soldiers were not placed near the wall of a city being attacked because they would be vulnerable to the arrows of skilled archers. Joab knew that David would likely become angry at such a poor military move (v. 20). But Joab also knew that the news of Uriah's death would calm David's anger (v. 21).

4. Uriah the Hittite Dies in Battle (11:22-25)

11:22-25. The messenger sent by Joab reported on the battle and delivered the word that Joab knew David wanted to hear (vv. 22-24). If David was initially upset, he quickly and coldly expressed his concern that Joab not feel bad about what David ordered him to do. So David sent this word back to Joab: **Do not let this thing displease you** (v. 25). "Displease you" is literally, "be evil in your eyes." David tried to minimize in Joab's mind what happened by suggesting that **the sword devours one as well as another**.

5. The Lord Views David's Acts as Evil (11:26-27)

11:26-27. After Bathsheba's period of mourning the loss of **her husband** Uriah, David married her. Of course, to people unaware of David's adultery, his marital gesture looked like another expression of kindness. About nine months later, probably in December of that year, Bathsheba gave birth to **a son**. David's cover-up had worked—except for this ominous note: **But the thing that David had done was evil in the sight of the Lord** (v. 27). A cover-up on earth is an open scandal in heaven!

As Chisholm points out, David's actions created a "theological tension" in the story line. He violated the seventh and tenth commandments concerning adultery and coveting, and deserved death. Yet, "the Lord has made an irrevocable promise to [David], albeit with a stern warning regarding infractions (cf. 2 Sam. 7:11-16). So the reader wonders how the tension will be resolved" (Chisholm, *1 & 2 Samuel*, 236). The resolution will come in chap. 12. David's sins were heinous, hardly fitting his earlier description as a man after God's own heart. But his subsequent confession would reveal a heart that was still sensitive to God.

B. Great Grace, Terrible Consequences, and War (12:1-31)

1. The Lord Sends Nathan to David (12:1-15a)

12:1a. In chap. 11 David did virtually all the sending for people, but in chap. 12 **the LORD sent Nathan to David** with a divinely directed message (Bergen, *1, 2 Samuel*, 369), although the exact time or nature of the revelation was not recorded. Nathan wisely told David a story that penetrated his mind and heart before his defenses went up.

12:1b-3. Nathan told David a story about two men, one of whom was **rich** and one of whom was **poor**. The poor man had only **one little ewe lamb** (v. 3) that he had purchased. The lamb was like a member of the poor man's family. Nathan depicted the poor man's family life as the perfect image of countrified tranquility. The lamb **was like a daughter to him**. The image appealed to David's pastoral imagination.

12:4-5. Nathan introduced another character in the story, **a traveler** who was visiting **the rich man**. The traveler needed to eat, but the rich man refused **to take from his** flock or cattle. Instead he **took the poor man's ewe lamb and prepared it for the man**. Angered by this story, David said this man **deserves to die** (v. 5).

12:6. To **make restitution for the lamb fourfold**, as David demanded, meant that the rich man must pay four times the lamb's original cost. When someone stole a lamb, the thief had to pay four sheep for the one stolen lamb (cf. Ex 22:1).

12:7-8. Nathan then applied the story directly to David: **You are the man!** Nathan continued to speak to David, using the prophetic formula, **Thus says the LORD.** Nathan reminded David of the specific ways in which He had blessed him, and He **would have** done even **more** of the same for David (v. 8).

12:9-10. In light of what the Lord had done for David, Nathan asked David a searching question: **Why have you despised the word of the LORD by doing evil in His sight?** To "despise the LORD" suggests holding His Word in contempt and disrespect. David's contemptible actions with Bathsheba and Uriah were senseless. Although Joab carried out David's order to set Uriah up to be killed, the Lord said David struck him down because David gave the order. Although Ammonites killed Uriah in battle, the Lord said David killed him with an Ammonite sword (v. 9). David took Uriah's wife to be his wife (v. 10). David had taken; he had stolen; he had abused his power. Interestingly, the Lord referred twice to Bathsheba as Uriah's wife (vv. 9, 10; cf. Mt 1:6).

Since David killed Uriah with the sword, **the sword** would **never depart** from David's **house**. As a consequence of his sin, three of David's oldest sons would die violent deaths: Amnon (cf. 13:28-32), Absalom (cf. 18:6-15), and Adonijah (cf. 1Kg 2:19-25). It is possible that the death of David's unnamed son by his adulterous act with Bathsheba is the fourth part of the "fourfold" restitution (v. 6) David had unknowingly pronounced against himself (Youngblood, "1, 2 Samuel," 445; Bergen, *1, 2 Samuel*, 372).

12:11-12. The Lord would **raise up evil** (calamity) in David's own house. As David abused power and took Uriah's wife to be his own, the Lord would **take** David's **wives . . . and give them to** his **companion**, his rival for the throne. David's own son, Absalom, would claim the throne by having relations with David's concubines (cf. 16:20-22) **in broad daylight . . . before all Israel**, a fitting consequence of David's secret sexual sin and murder.

12:13-15a. The Lord does not diminish in the slightest way His sovereign hand in bringing about consequences for sin. In vv. 1-12, David had listened to his indictment and judgment, speaking only before he knew he was the guilty party. Now he responded to God's searching judgment with the words, **I have sinned against the LORD** (v. 13). After almost a year, David confessed his sin. Then Nathan uttered some of the most gracious words in the OT: **The LORD also has taken away your sin; you shall not die**. Under the OT theocracy, the penalty for adultery and murder was death (cf. Ex 21:12, 14; Lv 20:10). David may have expected to be put to death. But God had already put away David's sin and forgiven him. David acknowledged in Ps 51:16 that the law provided no sacrifice for murder and adultery, which were capital offenses. All David could offer were the sacrifices of a "broken spirit" and a "broken and a contrite heart" (Ps 51:17).

However, forgiveness does not eliminate consequences. David's sins caused the Lord's **enemies . . . to blaspheme** (v. 14). News of David's secret leaked out to pagans, causing them, the Lord's enemies, to speak ill of the Lord. So because of the Lord's honor and glory, David's recently born son would die. The text leaves no doubt about the severity and certainty of the consequence.

2. David's Baby Dies (12:15b-23)

12:15b-19. The Lord struck the child that Uriah's widow [lit., "wife"] **bore to David** (v. 15). The author emphasized that Bathsheba did not belong to David; she was Uriah's wife.

Although David had sinned grievously, he knew the Lord. And so he prayed and fasted for a week for his son's life. However, on the seventh day of David's fasting, the baby died (vv. 16-19).

12:20. When David learned of the child's death, he did not do anything desperate. David rose, **washed** his face, put on lotion, **changed his clothes**, and went **into the** Lord's **house**, that is, the tent area that David had set up for the ark, to worship.

12:21-23. David's behavior was an enigma to his servants. While the boy was alive, David fasted and prayed, thinking perhaps that God would be gracious and spare the child's life. Since the boy died, he no longer had reason to fast. David's words, **I will go to him** (v. 23), indicate that perhaps David had some understanding of life after death. The extent of David's understanding is much debated. Some have maintained that David was simply stating the inevitability and irreversibility of death (Merrill, "2 Samuel," 468). However, the personalization of David's expectation (saying **I will go to *him*** as opposed to stating that he would go to death, emphasis added) indicates that David had some expectation of a reunion after death. David would eventually die and join his son, but the son could not **return to** him this side of death.

3. David and Bathsheba Have Solomon (12:24-25)

12:24-25. David comforted his wife Bathsheba because of her pain and grief. In about one year Bathsheba's husband was killed and her baby died. For the first time in this chapter the writer referred to Bathsheba as David's wife. Then she conceived and **gave birth to a son**, whom David **named . . . Solomon**, whose name means "he has made peace," and is from the same Hebrew root as the word *shalom* (peace, wholeness). Peace and wholeness from the Lord is what David and Bathsheba needed. The author added that the Lord **loved** the baby boy, meaning that this child would have a special relationship with the Lord.

The birth of this child is part of the narrative strategy to trace the "Seed" of David (see comments about the Davidic covenant at 7:12-17). In fact, Solomon became David's successor and heir to David's throne. After learning about the special implications of God's love for Solomon, David (or perhaps the prophet Nathan) gave Solomon an additional name, **Jedidiah** ("beloved of the Lord").

4. David's Army Wins More Victories (12:26-31)

12:26-29. While David was involved in a scandal in Jerusalem, Joab was fighting against the Ammonites. Given David's awful sins, it might be expected that God would not grant victory to David in the Ammonite war. But Joab captured the royal city, the fortified city of **Rabbah**, and **the city of waters** (a fortified water source near the city; v. 27). Joab's control of the water source gave him a huge military advantage.

In the ancient world when a general conquered a city, he gave the city his name. Not willing to give the city his own name, Joab sent for David, asking him to bring the rest of the troops, capture the city, and take it so the city could be named in his honor (v. 28). So David brought the remaining troops from Jerusalem and conquered Rabbah (v. 29). Joab was loyal to David and sought glory not for himself, but for David.

12:30. David arrived and he **took the crown of their king**, a symbolic act indicating utter defeat and the transfer of power to the conquering king. Thus the domain of Ammon passed to David. The crown's weight indicated its great value. Its weight was a talent of gold, about 70 or 75 pounds.

12:31. David made the city's inhabitants become forced laborers. In their menial service they used **saws, sharp iron instruments, and iron axes, and [David] made them pass through the brickkiln**, meaning that they made bricks. David did this to **all the** Ammonite **cities**. Then David returned to **Jerusalem**. Including the stories of the birth of Solomon and the conquest of Ammon are narrative strategies to show that the Lord had indeed forgiven David and that He would continue to honor the covenant He had made with him.

III. More Fallout from David's Sin in His Own Family (13:1–20:26)

A. Rape, Vengeance, and Murder in the Family (13:1-39)

1. Amnon Desires His Sister (13:1-3)

13:1-2. Absalom and **Tamar** had the same mother. In polygamous families the children of the same mother were especially close, even though all the children had the same father. It is noteworthy that the narrator introduced Tamar as Absalom's sister instead of David's daughter, setting the stage for what was about to happen (Anderson, *2 Samuel*, 173). Chapters 13 and 14 record the beginning of the fulfillment of the disciplinary consequences foretold by Nathan ("the sword," 12:10) on David and his house for his sins of adultery and murder (Laney, *First and Second Samuel*, 110).

Amnon, David's firstborn son, the crown prince of Israel, loved Tamar, his half-sister, in a way a brother ought not to love his sister—although his emotions were actually lust, rather than true love. Amnon was frustrated (v. 2) because Tamar, a marriageable **virgin** daughter of the king, may have had a bodyguard so that Amnon had no access to her. Also he wanted to have relations with her, but the law of Moses strictly forbade sex between half-brothers and half-sisters (cf. Lv 18:11).

13:3. Jonadab was David's nephew and Amnon's first cousin and **friend**. Jonadab was a **shrewd** ("wise" in a negative sense), a cunning manipulator. When Amnon explained his problem to Jonadab, Jonadab gave him a plan that would enable him to fulfill his unlawful sexual desires with Tamar.

2. Amnon Rapes His Own Sister (13:4-19)

13:4-7. Jonadab suggested Amnon pretend to be sick and then ask David to have Tamar prepare him **some food** (v. 5). So when David went to see **Amnon**, Amnon made this request. So the king sent for **Tamar**, saying, **Go now to your brother Amnon's house, and prepare food for him** (v. 7). Being an adult, prince Amnon had his own house.

13:8-9. Amnon knew that he must be alone with Tamar to carry out his lustful design. So when he said, **Have everyone go out from me**, everyone left.

13:10-11. Continuing his ruse, Amnon asked his unsuspecting sister to come **into the bedroom** so he could **eat from** her **hand**. Tamar innocently complied with her big brother's wish. While she was standing next to the bed, he grabbed her and said basically the same words as Potiphar's wife said to Joseph (cf. Gn 39:7), **Come, lie with me**, but added **my sister** (v. 11).

13:12-14. Tamar refused for several reasons: (1) sexual relations between a brother and a sister were not to take place **in Israel** (v. 12a); (2) such action would be **disgraceful** (v. 12b); (3) she could not **get rid of** her **reproach** of being violated by her own brother (v. 13a); and (4) Amnon would be **like one of the fools in Israel** (v. 13b), like Nabal of 1Sm 25, who was also called a fool. She said she was willing to marry Amnon so they could legitimately engage in a sexual relationship. However, she seems to have forgotten that the law prohibited brothers and sisters from marrying each other. But Amnon refused to **listen**, and he overpowered and raped his own sister. Amnon was responsible for his own actions; yet his act was a consequence of David's own disobedience.

13:15-16. After raping Tamar, Amnon immediately experienced a dramatic emotional reversal. His violent act of rape left the taste of hate in his soul, drowning his love for Tamar. Still lying in the bed, no doubt traumatized by the violence, Amnon voiced four words to his sister: **Get up, go away!** (v. 15). Amazingly, Tamar refused to leave. Sending her away, she said, would be worse than the rape. Given the circumstances, Amnon should marry her (cf. Ex 22:16; Dt 22:28-29), but Amnon refused to listen.

13:17. So Amnon called one of his servants and told him to get rid of her **and lock the door behind her**. No longer did he refer to Tamar as his sister; he called her **this woman**.

13:18-19. Tamar **had on a long-sleeved garment** (lit., "a varicolored tunic"), similar to the one Joseph wore. The king's virgin daughters dressed themselves in this manner. Tamar's clothing symbolized her royal virginity. Then one of Amnon's servants put the king's daughter on the street, outside Amnon's home. Putting **ashes on her head** and tearing **her . . . garment** symbolized her grief and mourning over her personal tragedy.

3. Absalom Comforts His Sister and Hates His Brother (13:20-22)

13:20. Absalom suspected that Amnon had done something to hurt Tamar. He questioned her delicately. Then Absalom allowed **Tamar** to stay in his **house**.

13:21-22. When **King David heard** what Amnon had done, he was furious. He should have forced Amnon to marry Tamar. While the law forbade the union, it also insisted that if a man raped a woman, he must marry her (cf. Ex 22:16). Marriage was the better option. But inexplicably, David did nothing. He should have taken responsibility for Tamar, but she languished in the home of Absalom, the only person who seemed to care. Youngblood notes that the narrator's use of David's title in v. 21 is ironic, because he had the power to exercise justice for this crime ("1, 2 Samuel," 467). But David felt powerless, perhaps because of his own moral failure. Absalom refused even to talk with Amnon, but in his heart he **hated** him because he raped his **sister**.

4. Absalom Takes Revenge (13:23-36)

13:23-27. Absalom waited **two full years** (v. 23) to take his revenge on Amnon. But Absalom had to wait for the right time (Brueggemann, *First and Second Samuel*, 288-89). At sheep-shearing time (April and May), Absalom invited the king and his officials to his house for festivities (vv. 23-24). The king declined, feeling that providing a feast for the king and all his officials was a burden for Absalom (v. 25). Whether Absalom's invitation was part of his strategy to strike Amnon, or the opportunity simply presented itself when the king declined to attend, Absalom then asked for the next best request, the presence of **Amnon** (v. 26). David had misgivings about Absalom inviting Amnon. Against his better judgment, David permitted Amnon and all the king's sons to go with Absalom. But Absalom had an agenda, having waited two years to execute it, when guards were lowered, with little suspicion of malicious intent on his part.

13:28-29. As the king's son, **Absalom** had loyal **servants**. So when he told them to kill Amnon when he was **merry with wine**, they carried out Absalom's order and murdered Amnon. And then the **king's sons** all rode off on their mules.

13:30-31. The news about Amnon's murder reached Jerusalem before the king's sons did, but the initial report (that Absalom had killed all of David's sons) was inaccurate. Hearing that Absalom had struck down all his sons, David was grief-stricken.

13:32-33. However, the shrewd Jonadab, David's nephew, perceived immediately what happened. So he told David, **only Amnon is dead** (v. 33).

13:34-36. Jonadab's assessment was correct. A **watchman** saw David's surviving **sons** returning to Jerusalem in great anguish.

5. Absalom Flees to His Grandfather's House (13:37-39)

13:37-39. Absalom's mother was Maacah, the daughter of **Talmai . . . the king of Geshur**. Absalom was a fugitive in Geshur, where his maternal grandfather ruled, for three years (v. 38). David mourned for this son too.

B. David Restores Absalom to His Court (14:1-33)

1. Joab Enacts a Shrewd Plan on Absalom's Behalf (14:1-3)

14:1-3. Although Anderson says the narrator left his readers to draw their own conclusions regarding Joab's reason(s) for trying to reconcile David and Absalom (*2 Samuel*, 187), the text states that **Joab**, David's commander, perceived that David's heart was now lenient **toward Absalom**. Laney offers two other reasons for this event: Joab was concerned for the kingdom, since Absalom seemed to have the best chance to succeed David, and the friction between David and Absalom was having a demoralizing effect on the people of Israel (*First and Second Samuel*, 112). Joab therefore brought **a wise** (shrewd) **woman** from **Tekoa** (about 10 miles south of Jerusalem) to Jerusalem. Joab told the woman what to do and say. It was not uncommon for a person to go before the king to have a judicial matter settled. Under such circumstances the woman could have an audience with the king.

2. The Shrewd Woman Fabricates a Story (14:4-20)

14:4-7. When the woman entered the king's presence, she prostrated before David and said, **Help, O king** (v. 4). When David asked what was troubling her, she proceeded to tell him her fabricated story. The story's plot was simple, but full of pathos. She said she was a destitute widow. Modern-day economic safety nets were nonexistent for widows in the ancient world. Women depended on their husbands or their adult sons for financial security. Without those supports they became destitute. This woman from Tekoa said she **had two sons** (v. 6). They were fighting and one son murdered the other. The family members wanted to execute the guilty brother, but he was the woman's only heir. She said, **They will extinguish my coal which is left** (v. 7). "To extinguish her burning coal" was an idiom that meant her dead husband would have no name on the face of the earth, thereby dooming her to poverty.

14:8-11. David promised protection to the woman. **I will give orders concerning you** meant that he would protect her son from the avenger of blood (v. 8). But was this within David's authority if the son was truly guilty of murder? He also said, **Not one hair of your son shall fall to the ground** (v. 11).

14:12-14. The woman had thus emotionally manipulated David to be receptive to what she said next. In light of David's commitment to protect her son from the avengers, she told David that in not bringing back Absalom, he was acting like the avengers who wanted to kill her son. The woman's words about water being spilled on the ground suggested that David should restore Absalom before it was too late. Her observation that **God does not take away life** (v. 14) is not correct. She highlighted God's grace at the expense of His justice. Sometimes the Lord does take a life in His holy judgment.

14:15-17. The woman then returned to her fabricated story line. She flattered David, calling him **the angel of God** in being able to **discern** between **good and evil** (v. 17).

14:18-20. David discerned that Joab orchestrated his meeting with the woman. And when he asked her about Joab, she admitted that he had **put all these words in** her **mouth** (v. 19).

3. David Recalls Absalom to Jerusalem (14:21-33)

14:21-24. Joab's plan worked. Absalom returned **to Jerusalem**, but David did not restore him to his court. Perhaps still angry, David did not want to see him.

14:25-27. Like Saul, Absalom was the most **handsome** man in Israel. Absalom had no physical defects. He **cut** his thick head of **hair** once a year. The cut hair weighed **200 shekels**, that is, almost four pounds (v. 26). **By the king's weight** means that David had established his own measuring and weighing system. Absalom was married, for he had **three sons and one daughter** (v. 27). His beautiful daughter's name was **Tamar**, no doubt named in honor of his sister Tamar. His wife or wives are not named. All of Absalom's sons preceded him in death, judging by his own statement in 2Sm 18:18.

14:28-29. After **two full years** Absalom still had not seen his father. **Absalom sent for Joab**, thinking that he could facilitate his being restored to court, but Joab did not respond.

14:30-33. To get Joab's attention Absalom commanded his servants to set **Joab's** barley **field on fire**. There was a common field outside Jerusalem, in which landowners owned different portions of the field. Joab's portion was next to Absalom's. Then Joab went to Absalom's house, asking why his servants set his field on fire (v. 31). Absalom explained the action of his servants, saying that he wanted to see the king, adding, **if there is iniquity in me, let him put me to death** (v. 32). Absalom thought he had committed no sin in murdering his brother Amnon for raping his sister. Absalom had not seen his father for five years—the three years he was in Geshur (13:38) and the two years he was in Jerusalem.

Finally the king agreed to see his son. When they were reunited, **the king kissed Absalom** as an expression of reconciliation between father and son (v. 33). Since Amnon was dead, and assuming that David's second son, Chileab, died early in life (Chileab is mentioned only at his birth [2Sm 3:3] and never again), Absalom, David's third son, was the heir apparent to David's throne.

C. The Flight and Return of King David (15:1–20:26)

Two movements are highlighted in this section: the flight of David from Jerusalem during Absalom's revolt (15:13-37), and the return of David to Jerusalem (19:9-43). The episode's turning point was Absalom's decision to refuse Ahithophel's good counsel (17:14). If Absalom would have followed his counsel, he would have succeeded, humanly speaking, in dethroning his own father David. This section has two narrative purposes: First, to demonstrate that the consequences of David's sin in chap. 11 continued. And second, it shows David's continued faith in the Lord and trust in Him to accomplish His promises for him (cf. 7:12-17).

1. Absalom Dethrones David (15:1-37)

a. Absalom Steals the Hearts of the People of Israel (15:1-6)

15:1. Absalom began to present himself as king. He acquired **a chariot and horses** with **fifty men** running before it, riding through the streets of Jerusalem with the pomp and pageantry of royalty.

15:2-3. Absalom stood by the road not far from the gate to the king's house. One of David's role as king was similar to that of Moses, judging civil disputes. Evidently David had a chamber where he adjudicated such disputes. Solomon continued this practice with great distinction (cf. 1Kg 3:16-28). The narrator already stated that "David administered justice and righteousness for all his people" (2Sm 8:15). But Absalom misrepresented David and, when people came to David to adjudicate their cases, Absalom alleged that the king was corrupt and unjust: **No man listens to you on the part of the king.**

15:4-5. Absalom said in carefully chosen words, **Oh that one would appoint me judge in the land**. He did not say "king" because that would have been too inflammatory. Like a skillful politician, Absalom said just enough to get people on his side.

15:6. Absalom's public relations strategy at the city gate worked so well that he **stole away the hearts of the men of Israel**. Besides being a murderer, Absalom was also a thief. His stealing the hearts of the people is a classic example of political manipulation. Wanting his father's throne, he patiently waited to bring his evil plans to fruition.

b. Absalom Conspires against the King (15:7-12)

15:7-8. Four years elapsed between 15:6 and 15:7. Most scholars agree that the verse should read "four years," not **forty years**, the discrepancy likely a result of a copyist's error. Absalom fabricated a reason to leave Jerusalem and go to Hebron, about 20 miles south of Jerusalem. Hebron was the royal city of David when he reigned in Judah, and at the time was still the most distinguished city in Judah. Absalom said he had to pay a vow he had made while he was in Geshur, namely, **if the Lord shall indeed bring me back to Jerusalem, then I will serve the Lord** (v. 8). Absalom used pious language to hide his malicious intentions.

15:9-10. Absalom obviously had been quietly building his power base, and now he had **spies** in his service. He placed them strategically throughout all the tribes of Israel, with the following instructions: **As soon as you hear the sound of the trumpet, then you shall say, Absalom is king in Hebron** (v. 10). Although Absalom was the crown prince in birth order, the choice of David's successor was the Lord's decision, not Absalom's.

15:11-12. Two hundred invited **men** from Jerusalem joined **Absalom** in Hebron, but they **went innocently, and they did not know anything** (v. 11). **Absalom sent for Ahithophel**, David's wisest and most trusted advisor, and also the grandfather of Bathsheba. Perhaps Ahithophel revolted against David out of anger over what David had done to his granddaughter. Absalom's support was growing, indicated by the growing number of people joining him.

c. King David Flees Jerusalem (15:13-18)

15:13-15. In God's providence an unnamed person alerted David to the brewing conspiracy. David understood right away the significance of the messenger's words: **The hearts of the men of Israel are with Absalom** (v. 13). David did not underestimate Absalom—he knew his position in Jerusalem was vulnerable. Unless David and his servants fled right away, Absalom would overtake them. If David and his servants remained in Jerusalem, Absalom would **strike the city with the edge of the sword** (v. 14), resulting in the loss of many lives in Jerusalem.

15:16-18. David and his servants fled, but he left **ten** of his **concubines** to **keep the house** (v. 16). This may have included housekeeping duties, but Bergen suggests that David left these women in charge as a signal to his foes that he did not want any fighting to take place in Jerusalem (*1, 2 Samuel*, 403). Brueggemann sees this act as necessary to fulfill the judgment pronounced against David by Nathan in 2Sm 12:11 (*First and Second Samuel*, 302). Whatever the reason, the move had a negative result (cf. 16:21-22). David obviously expected to return sometime. As he **stopped at the last house** (v. 17), probably the house at the farthest eastern edge of Jerusalem (Youngblood, "1, 2 Samuel," 497), the king no doubt felt great emotion. The reality of what was transpiring sank in a new way: the king was fleeing from Jerusalem, under the threat of being killed by his own son. His servants and **six hundred men . . . from Gath** (David's old haunts; cf. 1Sm 27) fled with David.

d. David Receives Unexpected Loyalty: Ittai and Hushai (15:19-37)

15:19-23. David spoke to **Ittai**, the leader of the Gittites. The Gittites were Philistines, people from Gath who had recently arrived in Jerusalem. David tested their loyalty by encouraging them to **remain with the king**, that is, Absalom (v. 19). Ittai rejected David's suggestion, making an oath of loyalty to David in the Lord's name (v. 21). So they stayed with David. The 600 Gittites had their children with them and by implication, their wives as well (v. 22). Probably over a thousand people were in this Philistine contingent. The entourage **passed over the brook Kidron**, on the east side of Jerusalem at the base of the Mount of Olives. They went **toward the way of the wilderness** (v. 23), a barren area leading to the desert near Jericho.

15:24-26. Abiathar the priest stood with David until all of the people were out of the city. The dejected people must have been encouraged to see God's priest standing with David. David then told **Zadok**, **Return the ark of God to the city** (v. 25). David understood that God was sovereign, and if He wanted David back in Jerusalem, He would bring that about.

15:27-29. David balanced his sense of God's sovereignty with responsibility. He sent **Zadok** and his two sons back to the city to act as spies (v. 28). The **fords** were shallow parts of the Jordan River that could be crossed by wading.

15:30. For King David to walk outside with his head **covered** and without sandals were symbols of grief and pain. The whole group with David also went up the Mount of Olives in grief, **weeping** as they **covered** their heads.

15:31. In God's providence another unnamed person gave David the most important and troubling piece of information in the whole affair: **Ahithophel is among the conspirators with Absalom**. David then prayed about the most important concern in his troubling affair: **O Lord, I pray, make the counsel of Ahithophel foolishness**. If Ahithophel offered wise counsel, David knew it meant the undoing of his reign.

15:32-34. Hushai showed up, with the symbols of grief (**coat torn and dirt on his head**) about him as well (v. 32). **David** told Hushai, his friend, that he would serve David better if he returned and pretended to be loyal to Absalom. David even told Hushai what to say to Absalom. In Absalom's court, Hushai would be able to **thwart the counsel of Ahithophel** (v. 34). David had just asked the Lord in prayer to turn Ahithophel's counsel to foolishness. But David also had enough theological sense to know that God often works through people in exercising His sovereign will. Hushai was a part of the answer to David's prayer.

15:35-37. David told Hushai that if necessary, he could get any reports to David by relaying them to the priests, **Zadok and Abiathar** (v. 35). Going into the city at great risk to his own life in order to be a part of David's spy ring was evidence of Hushai's friendship with the king, an expression of covenant loyalty.

2. Ziba, Shimei, and More Sexual Abuse (16:1-23)

This chapter is a further fulfillment of God's judgment against David for his sin (cf. 2Sm 12:10-11), specifically, that the evil against David would come from his own household). David acknowledged his plight as God's work (cf. 16:10-11), and was willing to trust his future into God's hands (cf. 15:25-26; 16:12; Anderson, *2 Samuel*, 207).

a. The Opportunistic Ziba (16:1-4)

16:1-2. Ziba, Mephibosheth's **servant** arrived, but his presence was unexpected. Therefore, David questioned him about the many provisions he brought.

16:3-4. When David expected to see Mephibosheth, Ziba, who had been Saul's servant, explained that Mephibosheth was **staying in Jerusalem** hoping that his father Saul's kingdom would be restored to him (v. 3). When Ziba accused Mephibosheth of treason, David believed him and reversed the decision he made earlier concerning Mephibosheth (cf. 9:9). Thus, David gave Ziba all that belonged **to Mephibosheth**, causing Ziba to respond with the appropriate posture and words (v. 4).

However, Mephibosheth later would give David a completely different version of the story (cf. 19:24-30), accusing Ziba of slandering him to David (Peterson, *First and Second Samuel*, 211). David seemed to believe Mephibosheth's account, letting him live (cf. 21:7). The implication is that Ziba's story about Mephibosheth's disloyalty was false and slanderous, revealing Ziba as a greedy opportunist who was exploiting the political crisis for his own gain.

b. Shimei Curses David (16:5-14)

16:5-6. Bahurim was east of the Mount of Olives, on the road leading to the desert of Jericho. **Shimei**, a relative of Saul, attacked David verbally and physically. He did this despite David's mighty men being on his **right** and his **left**.

16:7-8. Shimei cursed David, saying, **Get out, get out**, that is, "Get out of Jerusalem, and go into exile." Shimei called David a murderer (**you man of bloodshed**, v. 7; cf. also v 8). And Shimei insulted David's character, calling him a **worthless fellow**! Shimei then explained that David's political crisis was because of the blood of Saul's family he had shed. Shimei's charges were wholly untrue. Nevertheless, some commentators affirm the truth of Shimei's charge. According to Brueggemann, there was "[a]n important body of opinion in Israel [which] maintained that David had complicity in the deaths of Saul, Ish-bosheth, and Abner" (Brueggemann, *First and Second Samuel*, 307). Brueggemann also argues that although the "pro-David" narrator was careful to exonerate David of any blame in these deaths, the mention of such charges may indicate the "vitality" of the accusation. He concludes, "We do not know" (Brueggemann, *First and Second Samuel*, 307).

However, the author of 2 Samuel was not a polemicist for David but an author of Scripture. His words are true. It is certain that David did not kill Saul when he had the opportunity (cf. 1Sm 24, 26) nor did he have any complicity in the deaths of Ish-bosheth and Abner (see also Merrill, "2 Samuel," 472, where he says David had been gracious to Saul when he had the chance to kill him). In the end, Shimei's charges are derived from his own bitterness and not the facts.

16:9-12. Abishai, one of David's mighty men, wanted to go and **cut off** (lit., "take off") Shimei's head for cursing the king. David, however, restrained Abishai with reasoned arguments (see in the introduction to this chapter). David had learned in his encounter with Nabal (cf. 1Sm 25) to allow the Lord to fight for him while he himself fought for the Lord.

16:13-14. On a hill parallel with them at a higher elevation, Shimei followed David and his people, cursing, and throwing stones and **dust**. Then David **arrived** at the ford of the wilderness, the desert of Jericho.

c. Absalom Takes David's Throne and Concubines (16:15-23)

16:15-19. The scene shifts from David at the fords to Absalom and the men of Israel entering Jerusalem. **Hushai**, David's counselor and friend, convinced Absalom that as he was loyal to his father, he would be loyal to him (vv. 16-19).

16:20-22. Ahithophel counseled Absalom, **Go in to your father's concubines**, that is, have sexual relations with them (v. 21). To have relations with the king's concubines was to claim the king's throne. The act had serious political implications, not just moral ones. By Absalom doing this, everyone would know that he and David were beyond reconciliation, thus strengthening the resolve of those with Absalom. It was bad enough to claim the throne by Absalom's sexual relations with the king's concubines, but that these women were his father's concubines made Absalom's actions all the more despicable.

A tent was set up **for Absalom on the roof**, that is, the roof of David's house. The roof setting was where the problem all started with David and Bathsheba (cf. 11:2). Without shame, Absalom had forced sexual relations with all ten of his father's concubines on the roof of the royal residence **in the sight of all Israel**. It is sobering to reflect that although Absalom was responsible for his sinful actions, this tragic experience for the concubines was the result of chastisement from God for David's sin (cf. 12:11).

16:23. Though **Ahithophel** had advised Absalom to have relations with David's ten concubines, many people viewed his counsel as guidance from the Lord Himself.

3. Hushai, Ahithophel, and Three Other Men (17:1-29)

a. Ahithophel Advises a Small Attack (17:1-4)

17:1-4. Ahithophel gave even more counsel to Absalom. He suggested 12,000 men—a massive force—pursue weak **and exhausted** David that very night. Wanting to exploit that weakness, Ahithophel felt that a show of military force would terrify David and that the people with David would flee in fear, making David an easy target (v. 2). By killing David, the kingdom and the people with him would belong to Absalom (v. 3).

b. Hushai Offers a Different Plan (17:5-14)

17:5-13. For some reason Absalom asked **Hushai the Archite**, David's friend and spy, for his advice (v. 5). In all likelihood Ahithophel was not present during Hushai's audience with Absalom. In the presence of his officials, Absalom related Ahithophel's counsel to Hushai (v. 6). Hushai's response was in two parts. First, he explained why he thought the counsel of Ahithophel was not good. David and his **mighty men** were **fierce** fighters who might well spring a surprise attack and achieve victory (vv. 7-10). Second, Hushai suggested his own plan, suggesting that Absalom himself lead the battle against David (v. 11), assuring Absalom of total victory (vv. 12-13).

17:14. Absalom and the men of Israel agreed that Hushai's counsel was better than Ahithophel's. The narrator explained why Absalom and his advisors embraced the counsel of Hushai: **For the Lord had ordained to thwart the good counsel of Ahithophel, in order that the Lord might bring calamity on Absalom.** The Lord answered David's prayer (cf. 15:31), thwarting Ahithophel's counsel through Hushai. The Lord would bring calamity on Absalom for his attempt to overthrow David.

c. Hushai Sends Word to David through the Spy Connection (17:15-22)

17:15-17. Hushai told the priests **Zadok** and **Abiathar**, who continued to be loyal to David, what **Ahithophel counseled Absalom** to do and what he, Hushai, counseled. Hushai told the priests to get a message to David not to **spend the night at the fords of the wilderness, but by all means cross over** [to the east side of the Jordan where David could be more secure], **or else the king and all the people who are with him will be destroyed** (lit., "swallowed up," v. 16). The priests got word to an unnamed and unsuspected **maidservant**, who was part of David's spy ring. She in turn took the information to **Jonathan and Ahimaaz**, the sons of Zadok and Abiathar (cf. 15:27), who **were staying at En-rogel** (on the southeastern corner of Jerusalem). Jonathan and Ahimaaz, like a relay team, stayed outside of Jerusalem to receive news passed to them from Hushai by means of the **maidservant**, and they carried the news out to David. The two men could not risk **entering** Jerusalem because by now it was known that they were on David's side (v. 17).

17:18-20. An unnamed boy saw Jonathan and Ahimaaz in En-rogel, and he informed **Absalom** that they were there. So they fled and arrived at a **house** in **Bahurim** (on the way to the wilderness outside of Jericho; v. 18). Providentially, there was a **well in** the **courtyard**. The well's mouth did not have a wall around it, so an unnamed **woman** spread a covering over the well and **scattered grain** on it to hide that the men were hiding in the well. Her plan worked (vv. 19-20).

17:21-22. After Absalom's servants left the area, Jonathan and Ahimaaz climbed **out of the well**, found David, and told him to **cross** the Jordan River **quickly**, for **Ahithophel has counseled against you**. Hushai was unaware that Absalom had chosen to follow his counsel.) Through the night David and the people **crossed** over to the east side of **the Jordan**.

d. Ahithophel Commits Suicide (17:23)

17:23. Ahithophel saw that his counsel was not followed and that Absalom and his men embraced the advice of Hushai. Therefore, Ahithophel must have known that letting David escape across the Jordan, instead of attacking the king as he had advised, meant Absalom had lost the advantage (Baldwin, *1 and 2 Samuel*, 267). If this were the case, Ahithophel would have sensed that Absalom's *coup d'état* was doomed to failure and that he himself would be executed for treason. Therefore he **set his house in order**, that is, he made arrangements about inheritance matters and other important issues. Then he took his own life by strangling.

e. The Lord Provides through Three Men (17:24-29)

17:24-26. Following Hushai's counsel, Absalom and his men **crossed the Jordan** (v. 24), preparing for a military confrontation with David and his men. Joab, the great military leader, was with David, and so Absalom placed **Amasa** over the army. Amasa was Absalom's cousin and one of David's nephews.

17:27-29. Three unexpected visitors arrived in Mahanaim (about 30 miles northeast of the Dead Sea and east of the Jordan River) and brought David and those with him supplies and food. The most unexpected person was **Shobi, son of Nahash**, from the capital city of **Ammon**. Given everything that Israel and Ammon had gone through in war (cf. 10:1; 11:1; 12:26-31), the appearance of one of King Nahash's sons was amazing. The reason for Shobi's kindness to David is not given, but there may be a hint in 2Sm 10:1-4. Shobi was the brother of Hanun, the Ammonite king who had replaced his father Nahash. David had attempted to show kindness to Hanun, but was rebuffed. Perhaps Shobi remembered that incident, and even disagreed with his brother's actions. Whatever the case, through these visitors' generosity, the Lord met David and his people's physical needs.

4. Defeat, Victory, and Guilty Grief (18:1-33)

The battle between the forces of David and Absalom was one of the most dramatic moments of David's life. God had promised David a perpetual kingship with an eventual heir who would fulfill Israel's messianic expectations. Yet now David was on the run, with his life at stake, just as he was years earlier while being pursued by Saul. The narrator had to answer the questions of how David's kingship would survive, and how God would deliver His anointed. Chapter 18 provides those answers.

a. David Assembles His Troops for Battle (18:1-5)

18:1-5. David placed **Joab** . . . **Abishai** . . . and **Ittai** over the soldiers, and assembled the men for battle. David's men convinced him not to go into battle because he was the main target. If he died in this battle, all would be lost (vv. 2-4).

David gave his three generals the following charge: **Deal gently for my sake with the young man Absalom**. The charge was loud enough for the people to hear (vv. 5, 12). David's fatherly sentiments were understandable. In these fives verses, David was referred to repeatedly as **the king**, leaving no doubt as to who was the legitimate ruler of Israel (Youngblood, "1, 2 Samuel," 522).

b. David's Servants Fight Israel; Absalom Murdered (18:6-18)

18:6. The battle between David's men and Absalom's men **took place in the forest of Ephraim**, a thickly wooded and treacherous forest on the east side of the Jordan River.

18:7-8. More of Absalom's soldiers lost their lives (**20,000** in all, v. 7) because of mishaps and accidents in the forest's dangerous terrain than from fatal wounds from David's soldiers' swords.

18:9. Absalom happened to meet David's **servants** in the forest. While riding, Absalom's thick head of hair (cf. 14:26) was caught in the **branches** of an **oak** tree. Consequently, **his mule**, the mount of royalty, trotted on without him, leaving him dangling in midair.

18:10-11. An unnamed person **saw Absalom hanging** in the tree. Joab was outraged because the man did not strike Absalom down and kill him. He would have rewarded him with **ten pieces of silver and a belt**, a substantial reward.

18:12-14. The unnamed man was a person of principle, unwilling to disobey the king by killing Absalom, but he was not naive. He sensed that if he had taken Absalom's life as Joab desired, Joab would have distanced himself from him. Wasting no time, **Joab . . . took three spears in his hand and thrust them** into Absalom's **heart** (v. 14).

18:15. Joab's thrusts did not kill Absalom. So, ten of Joab's armor bearers finished the job.

18:16-17. Absalom was not honored in burial. They took his corpse and threw it **into a deep pit in the forest**. It was dishonorable for a **heap of stones** to be placed over the spot where a person was buried (cf. Jos 7:25-26; 8:28-29).

18:18. Absalom . . . had . . . set up . . . a pillar . . . in the King's Valley (cf. Gn 14:17). Its location is uncertain, but it may have been near Jerusalem. Absalom had three sons, but all of them preceded him in death (see comments on 2Sm 14:25-27). Since he did not have an heir, he set up a monument for himself, calling it **Absalom's Monument** in order to keep his memory alive.

c. David Hears of Victory and Loss (18:19-33)

18:19-20. In the ancient world runners carried breaking news. **Ahimaaz the son of Zadok** the priest, wanted to **run** to David with the news that Absalom was dead. But Joab displayed unusual insight. Joab did not permit him, though the reason is not made clear. It may be that because of Ahimaaz's close relationship with David and the help that he had given him recently, Ahimaaz was in no position emotionally to bring to David all of the news about the day's events, including the news of Absalom's death.

18:21-23. Joab refused Ahimaaz's offer to deliver the bad news to David (vv. 19-20). Instead, Joab sent a **Cushite** (v. 21), a foreigner who may have been Joab's slave (Bergen, *1, 2 Samuel*, 423) to go tell David the news. The reason for Joab's decision was not given. Perhaps he feared that David would react violently, as he did with the runner who brought him news of Saul's death (cf. 1:15). If that proved to be the case, Joab did not want Ahimaaz, a loyal and valued servant of David, to be lost. However, Ahimaaz was determined to be the news bearer, so he took a shorter route, outrunning **the Cushite** (v. 23).

18:24-27. The scene switched back to Mahanaim (cf. 17:27). Gates in ancient Israel were complex structures, sometimes wide enough to have a roof. When **the watchman went up to the roof**, he saw **a man running by himself** (v. 24). This usually meant that he was bringing good news. Several runners together meant bad news. Since the runner was by himself, David believed he was bringing **good news** (cf. vv. 25-27, 31).

Then the watchman saw **another** runner. And since he was **by himself**, David interpreted this too as a sign of good news (v. 26). Observing the first runner's stride, the watchman concluded that it was like that of **Ahimaaz**, Zadok's son. Again David thought this was good news (v. 27). Perhaps this is why Joab did not want Ahimaaz to run in the first place, for he felt that when David saw Ahimaaz, David's hopes for Absalom's survival would be high.

18:28-30. Ahimaaz reached the king first, **prostrated himself before** David, and announced God's deliverance. But David wanted to know about Absalom's welfare. Ahimaaz knew that Absalom was dead, because Joab told him so (cf. v. 20). But sensing he could not tell the king the truth, he claimed ignorance about the details (v. 29).

18:31-33. When the Cushite arrived, he gave David the same basic message that Ahimaaz had given. David asked him the same question he asked Ahimaaz about Absalom. The Cushite responded in an indirect way. Instead of saying "Absalom, your son is dead," he said, **Let the enemies of my lord the king, and all who rise up against you for evil, be as that young man!** (v. 32). But this indirect approach did not ease David's pain. The chamber over the gate may have been David's temporary quarters. He went there and shed tears of grief. As he walked to the chamber he wailed, **O my son Absalom, my son, my son Absalom! Would I had died instead of you, O Absalom, my son, my son!** (v. 33). No doubt David realized that Absalom's tragic death was a consequence of his own sin. Once again, the sword of God's judgment (cf. 12:10-11) that pierced David's family had struck, this time piercing his heart. Peterson says, "David's words of mourning rank among the saddest, most heart-rending words ever spoken" (*First and Second Samuel*, 226).

5. Bringing the King Back (19:1-43)

In chaps. 19–20, in order to demonstrate God's faithfulness to His covenant despite David's sin, the narrator showed how the kingdom of David was reunited and he was reinstalled as king in Jerusalem. But there was one more threat to David's throne, albeit a short-lived one: revolt of a Benjamite named Sheba (Laney, *First and Second Samuel*, 118).

a. King David's Grief and Restoration (19:1-15)

19:1-2. David's grief was legitimate, but now was not the time to mourn. The victory's joy **was turned to mourning**.

19:3-4. Instead of celebrating joyously, the people sneaked back **into the city** like defeated soldiers. Brueggemann suggests that they wanted to give David plenty of space to grieve, and that his people's deep connection with the king made his loss their loss (*First and Second Samuel*, 323).

19:5-8. But Joab rebuked the king for placing his grief for his deceased rebellious son above his concern for those who had just contended successfully for his life. If David did not encourage his people now, his political situation would be worse than anything that had come on him since he was a youth (v. 7). So David took his place as king **in the gate**. Word got out, and **all the people came before the king** (v. 8).

19:9-10. The people were glad David had, early in his reign, defeated their enemies, but they were concerned that David had fled, in a show of dismal weakness, from his own son. But now that Absalom was dead, the fickle people wanted to bring King David back.

19:11-15. Israel wanted to bring the king back, but David received no word from Judah's **elders**. Since they were close relatives, they should not have been the last to bring David back to his throne (vv. 11-12). David took an oath, promising to make **Amasa** the commander of his army in the place of Joab (v. 13). This gesture strengthened David's alliance with Judah and penalized Joab for killing Absalom. David's decision won over Judah's elders (v. 15).

b. David and Shimei (19:16-23)

19:16-23. The same **Shimei** who cursed David and those with him now **hurried and came down with the men of Judah to meet King David** (v. 16). Shimei also had **a thousand men of Benjamin with him**, along with **Ziba the servant of** Saul's **house. They rushed to the Jordan before the king**, and Shimei **fell** at David's feet (vv. 17-18). Shimei begged for forgiveness. He pointed out to David that he was **the first of all the house of Joseph to go down to meet my lord the king** (v. 20). He did not, however, point out that he was the first of all the house of Saul to curse David (cf. 16:5-8). **Abishai**, not known for mercy, wanted to put **Shimei . . . to death**, but he was more diplomatic about it this time (v. 21).

But not wanting to put anyone to death in Israel that day, David swore to Shimei, **You shall not die** (v. 23)—at least not now (but see 1Kg 2:8-9, 36-46, and the comments there). Anderson believes that the "inherent danger" of Shimei's curse still hung over David's house, and later Solomon would remove both the effect of the curse and a potential enemy when he had Shimei killed at David's order (*2 Samuel*, 237–38). David never trusted Shimei (Baldwin, *1 and 2 Samuel*, 276), and when Shimei violated the terms of his "probation," knowing the penalty, Solomon had the reason he needed to execute Shimei.

c. A Conversation between David and Mephibosheth (19:24-30)

19:24-30. Mephibosheth met **the king** at the Jordan. A significant amount of time had elapsed in chaps. 15–19 since Absalom's conspiracy. David had one question for him: **Why did you not go with me, Mephibosheth?** (v. 25). Mephibosheth explained that his servant Ziba **deceived** him and slandered him (vv. 26-28, cf. 16:1-4). David seemed unsure about whom to believe, so he decided to split Saul's land and holdings between **Ziba** and **Mephibosheth** (v. 29).

d. Barzillai the Gileadite (19:31-39)

19:31-32. Among the people who met David at the Jordan to welcome him home was 80-year-old **Barzillai**. He had provided food for David while he was in **Mahanaim**. Barzillai's food provision was substantial, given the number of people with David at Mahanaim.

19:33-39. David wanted Barzillai to cross over with him to Jerusalem and live there, but Barzillai said he was too old and would be a burden to David (vv. 33-35). And he added that his thinking was no longer clear, he had lost his capacity to enjoy food, and his hearing was bad. The old man just wanted to return home and die in his **own city** near his father and mother's **grave** (v. 37). The noble old man returned home. David never forgot the kindness Barzillai showed him in his hour of great need and distress (cf. 1Kg 2:7).

e. Tensions between Judah and Israel over David's Reinstatement (19:40-43)

19:40-43. Contention erupted between the men of Judah and the men of Israel. The men of Judah escorted the king back, but the men of Israel felt they should have been involved in the process (vv. 41-43). Harsh words ensued over a triviality.

6. Sheba's Rebellion (20:1-26)

a. The Appearance of Sheba (20:1-2)

20:1-2. On the occasion of the tribal feuding between Judah and the ten tribes of Israel, Sheba, **a worthless fellow** (lit., "a man of Belial," meaning base, useless, wicked) was present (v. 1; cf. 19:41-43). The narrator related Sheba's rebellion not only to show that David's kingdom was in jeopardy again, but perhaps also to set the stage for the eventual breakup of the nation after Solomon's death. But here the time for the northern tribes to secede had not yet come (Youngblood, "1, 2 Samuel," 550), even though **all the men of Israel withdrew from following David and followed Sheba** (v. 2).

Significantly, the narrator mentioned Sheba eight times (vv. 1-2, 6-7, 10, 13, 21-22), signaling that, despite his worthless character, he must have been a person of influence (Unger, *The New Unger's Bible Dictionary,* 1171). Surprisingly, nothing else is known about him apart from this chapter. Sheba spoke divisive poetic words that caused a rift in the nation, with Israel following him but the men of Judah remaining faithful to David.

b. Providing for David's Violated Ten Concubines (20:3)

20:3. This parenthetical verse related how David took the **ten . . . concubines** whom Absalom had violated and **placed them under guard** to be sure they would never be taken advantage of again. The narrator added, but he **did not go in to them**, saying in a gentle way that David did not have sexual relations with these women. They lived **as widows**, as if David were dead. The treatment of these women may seem extreme for 21st-century sensibilities, but these women were in a legal relationship with David and he provided for them.

c. The Pursuit of Sheba (20:4-8)

20:4-8. The assembling of troops required three days. David ordered general **Amasa** to be present, but Amasa delayed for reasons unknown (v. 5). But David could not afford to wait on Amasa. So he sent Abishai in place of Amasa to pursue Sheba (v. 6). The **large stone** in **Gibeon** was a geographical landmark (v. 8).

d. Joab Murders Amasa (20:9-13)

20:9-13. Joab was ruthless, murdering Amasa probably out of envy for being replaced as the military leader by Amasa. Then Joab and Abishai pursued Sheba as if nothing happened.

One of Joab's young men sensed that Amasa's murder might cause division in David's ranks. So to prevent that he said, **whoever favors Joab and whoever is for David, let him follow Joab**. Joab's cruelty in leaving Amasa to wallow **in his blood** (v. 12) is stunning, even given what is known about Joab's character. Amasa's corpse, abandoned in the highway, was a distraction. So one of Joab's young men removed Amasa from the highway and covered him in the field with **a garment**.

e. Another Wise Woman (20:14-22)

20:14-15. The narrator did not identify the **he** in v. 14, but the context indicates that this was Joab since Joab and his actions were the focus of the narrative at this point. He and his men reached **Abel Beth-maacah** (about 25 miles north of the Sea of Galilee), the fortified city where Sheba was holed up. They besieged the city, and **all the people who were with Joab were wreaking destruction in order to topple the wall** (v. 15).

20:16-22. At Abel Beth-maacah we meet the second woman in 2 Samuel referred to as **a wise woman** (cf. 14:2). She cited a proverb to Joab, **they will surely ask advice at Abel** (v. 18). The proverb implied that the town of Abel had a long history of wise men and women. She personified her city as **a mother in Israel** (v. 19). Using the woman's imagery, Joab said he would not destroy her city. He only wanted the city to hand over guilty **Sheba.** So the woman convinced the people of the city to seize Sheba, cut off his head, and throw the head to Joab. This wise woman saved her city, and eliminated David's enemy.

f. A Summary of the Restored Kingdom (20:23-26)

20:23-26. The narrator named eight key administrators in David's restored kingdom. Mentioning David's bureaucracy was perhaps a way of signaling that the rebellion was over and the king was safe and his control once again firmly established (Brueggemann, *First and Second Samuel,* 332). Thus ends a major section of the book dealing with the consequences of David's sin.

IV. Epilogue: Final Thoughts about David (21:1–24:25)

Chapters 21–24 are not in historical sequence. They are drawn from different periods in David's reign, serving as an epilogue to the book. This section opens and closes with a narrative, with two poetic sections in between. Chapter 21 deals with how atonement resolved a sin problem that Saul caused. Chapter 24 deals with how atonement resolved a sin problem that David caused. The two poems in chaps. 22 and 23 are at the heart of this section, revealing that the Lord was the heart of David's life. Bergen describes these chapters as "a carefully arranged set of six accounts and lists that are chronologically detached from the previous narratives . . . [demonstrating that] David's career began with, was centered in, and ended with his relationship with the Lord" (Bergen, *1, 2 Samuel*, 441-42).

A. Atonement and Giant Killers (21:1-22)

1. Biblical Justice for the Gibeonites (21:1-9)

21:1-2. There was a famine in the days of David for three years. In agricultural societies a famine was a serious matter. And in Israel's theocratic society, famines also raised questions about causes. David prayed, asking the Lord about the cause of the three-year famine. The Lord answered, **It is for Saul and his bloody house, because he put the Gibeonites to death**. David therefore summoned **the Gibeonites**. These people were not Israelites, but a Canaanite people group who lived in the land at the time of Joshua's conquest. Centuries earlier, Joshua had made a covenant with the Gibeonites (cf. Jos 9:3-27). But Saul had put some of the Gibeonites to death **in his zeal for the sons of Israel and Judah** (v. 2), an event not recorded in Scripture, thus dishonoring the covenant Joshua had made.

21:3. David asked the Gibeonites, **How can I make atonement that you may bless the inheritance of the LORD?** Atonement was a central reality in the OT sacrificial system. The verb "make atonement" means to satisfy the Lord's holy demands for a sin that has been committed (cf. Lv 1:4; 4:20; 6:7; 16:6-3). Sin offends the Lord, and so in order to receive His forgiveness of sin, atonement must be made. The blood of a spotless sacrificial animal had to be shed so that the guilty person could then be forgiven. Ultimately, the sacrificial death of the Lord Jesus Christ on the cross ultimately, fully, eternally, and completely satisfied the Lord's holy justice against sin, making forgiveness and salvation possible for all who trust in Him (cf. Rm 3:25; Heb 10:1-14).

21:4-6. The Gibeonites did not want financial reparations, nor did they want to execute anyone **in Israel**. The man who committed the crime (in this case Saul) must pay for it. But Saul was dead. Therefore, the Gibeonites suggested that seven of Saul's sons (possibly including his grandsons) must take his place in death. The Gibeonites said they would **hang them** [lit., "expose them"] **before the LORD in Gibeah** (about four miles north of Jerusalem; v. 6). Exposing Saul's sons meant a public execution, maybe involving the dismembering of the corpses. Instead of being buried, they would be left out in the open for everyone to see.

21:7-9. The events recorded in this chapter probably transpired around the time when David spared Mephibosheth (cf. chap. 9).

Another concubine suffered in this grim event. This time it was **Rizpah**, Saul's concubine and mother of two of the executed men. Ironically, one of her executed sons was named Mephibosheth! Another daughter of Saul also suffered. **Merab**, Saul's oldest **daughter**, who should have been given to David in marriage, was given to **Adriel**, and she had **five sons** by this union (see comments on 1Sm 18:17-19). All five of her sons were put to death at once. The KJV translation substitutes Michal for **Merab** (v. 8) based on the reading of various Hebrew manuscripts. If this were the correct reading, it would contradict 2Sm 6:23 which states that Michal died childless. The NASB reading **Merab** follows various Hebrew manuscripts and the second-century BC Greek translation, the Septuagint, and is the correct reading.

On the surface it seems unfair to execute Saul's grandsons, when a spotless animal sacrifice was all that was required. But the only way to atone for murder and the consequent pollution of the land was for the person who committed the crime to be put to death (cf. Nm 35:30-34). Since Saul and his sons were dead, his grandsons had to replace them. To see God's displeasure turned away from Israel, justice could only be established through the shed blood of those who carried out the crime.

2. The Grief of Rizpah, Saul's Concubine (21:10-14)

21:10. Neither **birds** nor **beasts** could keep **Rizpah** from making sure the bones of her sons and relatives were protected. She stayed at the rock for months until the day it rained (v. 10).

Feeling the raindrops on her face, she knew that the Lord's wrath was turned away and that the famine was over.

21:11-14. Her actions moved David. So to honor the dead, he took Saul's and Jonathan's bones (he had to exhume them because the men of Jabesh-gilead had buried them; cf. 1Sm 31:11-13), and gathered the bones of those who had been **hanged**, and he buried them in **Benjamin** in **the grave of Kish**, Saul's **father**. The narrator added a significant statement: **after that God was moved by prayer for the land** (v. 14), indicating that God would now answer prayer in Israel. Similar words are recorded at the end of the book: "Thus the LORD was moved by prayer for the land" (24:25).

3. Renewed Conflict with the Philistines (21:15-22)

As great as David was, he still needed help. So the Lord surrounded him with men of faith and courage. Four of them are noted here. This section detailing David's deliverance from four giant foes prepared the reader for David's psalm of deliverance that followed in chap. 22 (Laney, *First and Second Samuel*, 125).

a. The Exploit of Abishai (21:15-17)

21:15-17. Fighting again against the Philistines, **David became weary**. A formidable Philistine named **Ishbi-benob**, who was a giant and one of Goliath's **descendants** was on the battlefield. Ishbi-benob had **a new sword**—normally his father Goliath would have passed his sword down to him, but David had taken Goliath's sword in battle (cf. 1Sm 17:54). Ishbi-benob **intended to kill David**, and in view of David's fatigue, he may have succeeded (v. 16).

But Abishai . . . helped him, and struck down the Philistine (v. 17). At this point David's men insisted that he no longer go out to battle with them. His death in battle would mean the extinguishing of **the lamp in Israel**. This metaphor indicates the moral and spiritual guidance that David, under God, provided for the nation.

b. The Exploit of Sibbecai the Hushathite (21:18)

21:18. The location of **Gob**, which means "pit," is uncertain. **Sibbecai the Hushathite**, one of David's men, **struck down** the Philistine **Saph**, **who was among the descendants of the giant**. He also killed Sippai (1Ch 20:4).

c. The Exploit of Elhanan (21:19)

21:19. War broke out again **at Gob**. This time **Elhanan the son of Jaare-oregim the Bethlehemite killed Goliath the Gittite, the shaft of whose spear was like a weaver's beam**. At first glance this account seems to contradict the account in 1Sm 17, which states that David killed Goliath. However, it was not uncommon for two different people to have the same name. And since the enemy soldiers in these verses were "descendants of the giant" (v. 16), it was also possible for David and Elhanan to have killed two different warriors each named **Goliath**, both having a spear like **a weaver's beam**.

d. The Exploit of Jonathan (21:20-22)

21:20-22. Another battle occurred in **Gath** in Philistia. This time there was a giant who had **six fingers on each hand and six toes on each foot** (v. 20). He **defied Israel** the way Goliath did, and **Jonathan the son of Shimei** [not the Shimei who cursed David in chap. 16], **David's brother, struck him down** (v. 21). David and his men thus defeated four of Goliath's descendants in battle (v. 22).

B. The Celebration in Song of the Lord's Deliverance (22:1-51)

1. The Lord's Central Place in David's Life (22:1-4)

22:1. It is well known that this chapter is virtually identical to Ps 18. The **day** that David composed this song **to the LORD** was not specified, but it was definitely much earlier in his life, perhaps after the battle of Gilboa when Saul was killed (cf. 1Sm 31:1-13, Baldwin, *1 and 2 Samuel*, 287). Thus the chapter is far out of chronological order; the narrator placed it here perhaps as a fitting counterpart to the song of Hannah (cf. 1Sm 2:1-10) with which his account began (Brueggemann, *First and Second Samuel*, 339). The song's placement also serves to show the reader that the history of both David and Israel were not just about power and conflict, but about God's sovereignty and deliverance (Brueggemann, *First and Second Samuel*, 339).

In this chapter, and in 23:1-7, the narrator moved from prose to poetry. This psalm, used in Israel's worship, is recorded here with some slight changes in Ps 18 (see comments above).

22:2-4. David used imagery to describe the Lord's central role in his life: **rock . . . fortress . . . refuge . . . shield . . . horn**, and **stronghold**. David drew these images from the physical setting where he spent his fugitive years. The song's theme is, **I call upon the LORD, who is worthy to be praised, and I am saved from my enemies** (v. 4).

2. Divine Rescue from Mortal Danger (22:5-20)

22:5-7. David described his fugitive years and near-death experiences as **waves of death** and

torrents of destruction. The word **destruction** (Hb. *belial*), means "worthless in character," thus underscoring the character of the people who tried to destroy David.

The word **Sheol** is usually, as here, a term for the grave. Sheol's coils wrapped themselves around David like a snake in the sense that he was about to die. David was in mortal danger, unable to deliver himself.

In **distress**, that is, in a cramped place because of his trials, David called on the Lord. His cry came to God's **ears**. Of course God is spirit, and does not have physical ears. The expression is an anthropomorphism, a description of God using terms of human anatomy to communicate a function like that of the human anatomy in question.

22:8-16. David framed the Lord's intervention on his behalf in language that was used to describe the exodus and other memorable events in Israel's history. This section is the psalm's central section. David is not mentioned here. The Lord's anger on David's behalf shook the entire universe.

Smoke from **His nostrils, fire from His mouth**, and kindled **coals** depict God's aroused righteous wrath (vv. 8-9). **He bowed the heavens**, that is, He split or parted the heavens (v. 10). **And He rode on a cherub and flew** (v. 11). Cherubim were ministers of God's throne, bearers of God's throne-chariot, which the Lord mounted and rode in rescue and in judgment (cf. Ps. 18:10; Ezk 1:4-28). The arrows (v. 15) were His bolts of lightning.

22:17-20. Much as Pharaoh's daughter lifted Moses out of the water (cf. Ex 2:10), so the Lord lifted David **out of** his **waters** of trials. David declared, **He also brought me forth into a broad place** (v. 20), a place no longer cramped by the constraints of distress.

3. The Moral Reasons for David's Deliverance (22:21-25)

22:21-25. The Lord rewarded David with deliverance because of his integrity and the consistency of his walk with God. David penned these words years before his moral failure recorded in chap. 11. The overall tenor of David's life at that time, and following the sin with Bathsheba, was devotion to the Lord.

4. God's Response to People Based on Their Character (22:26-30)

22:26-30. David wanted the readers of his songs to know that God's dealings with people were always just, in keeping with His righteous character (vv. 26-28). As one who had experienced God's righteous blessings, David could testify of the truths he had just stated. Using another metaphor for the Lord, David said God was his **lamp**, illuminating his **darkness** and helping him to walk in the light of life (v. 29). Also by Him, David could be agile in battle.

5. God's Blameless Way and Divine Enabling (22:31-37)

22:31-33. David put God's word to the test and found it be true. He is **a shield** (another metaphor) for all those who take refuge in Him, and **a rock** and a **fortress**, that is, the One in whom one can find protection. The questions in v. 32 underscored the Lord's uniqueness. Also, God's **way is blameless**, that is, whole, having integrity. Those who walk with Him reflect this character trait (v. 33; cf. vv. 24, 26). When David wrote that the **Lord** sets the **blameless in His way** (v. 33), he meant that God sets them free.

22:34-37. David praised God for strength, using a wonderful simile. **He makes my feet like hinds' feet, and sets me on my high places**. Like a hind (female deer) with strong legs and swift feet that go to high places on the mountains, so was David strengthened by God's enabling grace. God had trained him for battle so that his **arms can bend a bow of bronze** (v. 35). Bending a bronze bow is an overstatement, emphasizing that the Lord enabled David to achieve what he could not do in his own strength. God enlarged David's steps; because of the providential room for his feet, David had not slipped (v. 37).

6. The Victorious Pursuit (22:38-43)

22:38-43. David pursued and conquered his enemies because of God's work in him (girding him **with strength**, v. 40) and for him.

7. David's Exaltation from the Lord (22:44-46)

22:44-46. The Lord also made David a **head of the nations** (v. 44). The king recognized that all the supposed obedience from foreign leaders and peoples might not be sincere. Human **fortresses** (v. 46) were no match for the eternal God who is a fortress to those who trust Him.

8. Gratitude to the Lord among the Nations (22:47-50)

22:47-50. David continued to use **the rock** metaphor (cf. vv. 1-2, 32) to express the Lord's person and work. And David recognized that God gave him victory over his enemies (vv. 48-49). David did not want to limit God's praise to Israel; he wanted to celebrate the Lord among the nations.

9. Lovingkindness to David's Descendants Forever (22:51)

22:51. A **tower of deliverance**, that is, a tower of victories, is another metaphor for the Lord. David praised the Lord for the eternal scope and breadth of His **lovingkindness**. Eternity will not exhaust the display of the Lord's lovingkindness **to David and his descendants**, for the Messiah, the Lord Jesus Christ, *the* son of David, will reign over the house of Jacob **forever** (cf. Lk 1:31-33).

C. David's Last Words and His Mighty Men (23:1-39)

1. The Last Words (23:1-7)

Verses 1-7 are the last psalm spoken and written by David, apparently composed shortly before his death. The Lord preserved these words for posterity, in a sense to provide an author's guide for understanding the Psalms. Verse 1 does not mean these were the last words David ever spoke. The narrator framed them this way as a "fitting conclusion to the effective reign of David since 1Kg 1–2 depicts only a 'shadow' of the former king" (Anderson, *2 Samuel*, 268).

23:1. The ESV translates the Hebrew more accurately than the NASB here: "The oracle of David, the son of Jesse, the oracle of the man who was raised on high." The term "oracle" was usually used to describe a prophetic communication. David's last words were prophetic. He spoke as God's mouthpiece. It is commonly understood that David identified himself as the subject of his last words. (1) David was **the son of Jesse**. Saul had used these words in a pejorative way (see 1Sm 20:27-31; 22:7-29), but David may have used them here to indicate his humble beginnings and, by implication, God's work to exalt him from a mere shepherd boy. (2) He was **the man who was raised on high**, that is, the Lord had exalted David. (3) David was **the anointed of the God of Jacob**. God had anointed David, setting him apart and consecrating him to be king. (4) David was also **the sweet psalmist of Israel**. This is quite a free rendering of the Hebrew. A more literal approach would translate this as saying that David was "the delightful one of the songs of Israel," indicating that he himself was the favorite subject of the psalms he wrote. His psalms have influenced Israel's and the Church's worship for thousands of years, and have been a source of hope and strength for myriads of people. The Spirit of God spoke by him and put His Word on David's tongue. The Lord Himself was the source of David's psalms.

Despite the common interpretation of David's last words, as found above, there is a significant alternative interpretation that sees David's subject as not himself but the future Messiah. The difference centers on the Hebrew word *'al* (translated **on high**, v. 1). The Septuagint translates this with the Greek word *epi* ("concerning"), reading it with the same Hebrew consonants but with a slight vowel change in the Hebrew text (the vowels were not part of the original Hebrew manuscripts and were added in the early Middle Ages). This slight vowel difference results in a noteworthy difference in translation: "The oracle of David, son of Jesse and the oracle of the man raised up *concerning* the Messiah [Anointed One] of the God of Jacob, and the Delightful One of the songs of Israel." The significance is that while in the Masoretic Text, David appears to be talking about himself as the **anointed of the God of Jacob**, in the older Septuagint reading he is saying that his oracles are about "the Messiah (Anointed One) of the God of Jacob."

The internal evidence supports the Septuagint reading about the Messiah and is contrary to the view that David is writing about himself. In 2Sm 23:3-4, David proceeds to describe the righteous reign of the king. In 23:5, David makes a declarative statement (lit.): "For not so is my house with God." Most translations recognize the internal contradiction. In v. 1 David appears to be saying it is all about him, and then in v. 5, he plainly says it is not. Therefore, to harmonize this difficulty, most (but not all) English versions then translate v. 5 as a question: **Truly is not my house so with God?** The difficulty with doing so is that there is no Hebrew grammatical support for translating this verse as a question (it lacks the interrogative particle, the prefixed *h*).

Thus, it appears that the slightly different understanding of the vowel substantially changes the meaning of the text. It appears that David is saying that (1) the future Messiah was his favorite subject in his psalms (v. 1), (2) David could write of the Messiah because the Spirit of God spoke to him (v. 2), (3) the Messiah would be a righteous king with a righteous reign (vv. 3-4), (4) David was not that righteous ruler (v. 5), and (5) David was assured that the righteous King Messiah would indeed come because of the Davidic covenant (v. 5; For a thorough discussion of this, see Michael Rydelnik, *The Messianic Hope: Is the Hebrew Bible Really Messianic?* [Nashville: Broadman & Holman, 2010], 39-41, 168).

23:2-5. These verses are the words the Lord said to David; they are the heart of the poetic oracle. The Lord used a simile to describe the righteous and reverent rule of the king over people. The imagery of v. 4 speaks of the wonder of a refreshing and invigorating morning without clouds. A righteous rule is breathtaking, refreshing, and invigorating, and will be experienced under the reign and rule of the Messiah Jesus, the promised son of David.

Although the NASB translation has David asking a question in v. 5—**Truly is not my house so with God?**—this translation should not be understood as a question. It does not have the normal Hebrew grammatical indication of an interrogative, so it should be read as a statement: "For not so is my house with God" (lit., the NKJV has a similar declarative translation). David was not claiming that he was the righteous king described in v. 4. Rather, David was stating that although he had sinned, he was assured that God would fulfill His promise to him (**He has made an everlasting covenant with me, ordered in all things, and secure**, v. 5). The final phrase of v. 5 should not be translated as a question either (**Will He not indeed make it grow?**), but as a statement: "He has not yet made it sprout." In other words, despite his failure, David was assured, by the Davidic covenant, of the coming of the future Messiah **for all [his] salvation and all [his] desire** (v. 5), even though He had not yet "sprouted" (the verbal form of the messianic title "Branch," cf. Jr 23:5; 33:15; Zch 6:12). David's sins had not caused the Lord to abandon David or His promises to him. The Lord would indeed be faithful to his eternal covenant with David and one day, send the Son of David, the Messiah.

23:6-7. The wicked are like thorns being cast aside. The thorns are so sharp and jagged that those who remove them must be **armed with iron and the shaft of a spear** (v. 7). Thorns are to be burned with fire in a place designed for this purpose. This is the image of the fate of the wicked (cf. Mt 13:41).

2. David's Mighty Men (23:8-39)

23:8. After the last poetic oracle of David, the narrator discussed those who helped him. They were **mighty** (Hb. *gibbor*) **men**. The word *gibbor* means "mighty, valiant soldier." John N. Oswalt writes, "The Hebrew root is commonly associated with warfare and has to do with the strength and vitality of the successful warrior" (John N. Oswalt, "mighty," in *TWOT*, 148). These men were mighty warriors because of the Lord, who is also described as *gibbor* (cf. "mighty [*gibbor*] God," Is 10:21; the "strong [*gibbor*] arm" of God, Ps 89:13). The writer included these powerful warriors as one of the indications that God Himself was with David as a valiant, victorious soldier. Their names were given, along with some of their faith-based heroic exploits.

Heading the list is **Josheb-basshebeth a Tachcemonite, chief of the captains** (lit., "of the three"). Among David's 37 mighty men, three stand out. They had more authority and leadership among the mighty men. Josheb was the leader or head of the three. He was **called Adino the Eznite** because he slew **eight hundred** people in one battle. The odds were against him, but he fought in the Lord's name. The Lord granted him victory.

23:9-10. After Josheb was **Eleazar**. The men of Israel left him alone to fight **the Philistines**. Two of the other mighty men were also present, but the narrator did not identify them. The narrator focused on Eleazar, who **struck the Philistines until his hand was weary**. Exhausted, he **clung** to his **sword** until his hand froze to it. The Lord used him to bring about **a great victory** (v. 10).

23:11-12. The pride of third place went to **Shammah**. Lentils were a vegetable cultivated throughout the Middle East. **The people** were afraid to protect the lentil plot **where** a troop of **the Philistines were gathered**, and so they **fled**, leaving Shammah to face the Philistines alone. Shammah, however, defended it. Using Shammah, **the Lord brought about a great victory**. Though alone, Shammah held his ground.

23:13-17. As noted earlier, 37 mighty men are listed in this chapter, but among the 37 were 30 **chief men**, that is, those who had men under their leadership.

Three of the 30 went down to join David in a battle against the Philistines (v. 13). The time of the battle is unknown, but it may have occurred while David was at **the cave of Adullam** (cf. 1Sm 22). There was no water source near the cave, so David merely expressed a desire that someone would give him some water from Bethlehem's **well** (v. 15). He was not expecting anyone to do it; it was dangerous for anyone to attempt to do so, given the Philistine garrison at Bethlehem. But **the three mighty men broke through** the Philistine line, went to the well, **drew water** out of it, and took **it to David** (v. 16). Since these men risked their lives, David considered the water to be his men's lifeblood. The blood belongs to the Lord (cf. Lv 17:8-13). David therefore poured the water out as a sacrifice to God (v. 16-17).

23:18-19. Abishai, Joab's **brother . . . was chief of the thirty**. Joab is not listed as one of David's mighty men, but he is mentioned three times in connection with others (vv. 18, 24, 37). The narrator vividly described Abishai's exploit in battle, killing **three hundred** with his **spear**. He had justly merited a reputation like those of the first three named in this chapter. He was the leader of the 30, but he was not ranked among the first three in the list.

23:20-23. Another mighty man in the list was **Benaiah**. Benaiah's father carried out great exploits, mighty deeds. Like his father, Benaiah accomplished some mighty deeds. For example he **went down and killed a lion in the middle of a pit on a snowy day** (v. 20). Snowfall made the conditions slippery and dangerous to fight. But like David, who killed a lion (cf. 1Sm 17:34-35), Benaiah killed one in trying conditions. Also **he killed an Egyptian** who was **impressive** because of his physical stature and skill in warfare (v. 21). The Egyptian had the advantage. He had **a spear in his hand**, which he could use against Benaiah at a distance. All Benaiah had was a club, a clumsy weapon useful only in close battle. Using skill and speed, Benaiah snatched the Egyptian's own spear from him and killed him with it (v. 21), much like David who killed Goliath with the giant's own sword. Benaiah was honored among the 30, but did not attain to the stature of the first three on the list. Recognizing the faith and courage of Benaiah, David promoted him, placing him over his personal bodyguard.

23:24-39. Asahel, another brother of Joab, was among David's 30 mighty men (cf. 2Sm 2:18-23). Beginning in v. 24b and extending to the end of the chapter, the narrator named the men who were a part of David's mighty men. Several names are interesting. **Ittai** (v. 29) had some association with Saul, but was one of David's mighty men. **Eliam**, Ahithophel's son, was one of David's mighty men. Eliam was Bathsheba's father (v. 34; cf. 11:3). **Uriah the Hittite**, the last person on the list, was one of David's mighty men. His name was reminiscent of the dark period in David's life, but the Lord did not forget about Uriah's character and mighty deeds (v. 39).

D. David's Sinful Census and the Resulting Plague (24:1-25)

1. David Orders Joab to Number the People (24:1-10)

24:1. When this census was taken is not known. The Lord's **anger** again **burned** against Israel, though the reasons for His anger were not stated. The phrase **it** [apparently referring to the Lord's anger] **incited David** NASB; HCSB) is an incorrect translation of the Hebrew phrase, and should be rendered "He" (referring to the Lord) **incited David** (see the NIV; NET; ESV; KJV; and RSV). The Lord's anger cannot be properly understood as some impersonal force acting apart from the **Lord**. The writer understood God's governance and sovereignty even over David's sin in this instance. While God ordained the action, He was not blamed for the guilt of David's sin (cf. 24:10, where David blamed himself for the sin, not God). God is often presented as sovereignly governing people's sins, but, in possibly the most unfathomable mystery in all of Scripture, it is the people, not God, who are held morally responsible and thus guilty for the sins they commit. See the comments on Jb 1:21-22, where Job ascribed to God His providential role as the ultimate cause of what happened to him ("The Lord gave and the Lord has taken away. Blessed be the name of the Lord," Jb 1:21) without ascribing to God the moral guilt of those who attacked Job's holdings and family ("Job [did not] . . . blame God," Jb 1:22).

Some of this was complicated by Satan's role in this episode, according to 1Ch 21:1. Since the original readers of 2 Samuel would not have had a copy of 1 Chronicles on hand (1 Chronicles was written later), it is essential to interpret 2Sm 24 on its own, and in 2 Samuel Satan does not appear. For an explanation of the relationship of God in His sovereignty to Satan's actions and David's sinful choice in this episode, see the comments that introduce 1Ch 21:1–22:1.

David's numbering of Israel and Judah in these circumstances was an act of unbelieving pride, placing his faith in numbers.

24:2-9. The census counted every man 20 years old and upward who was able to go to war (cf. Nm 1:3; 2Ch 27:23). Women and children were not counted. Joab and the army commanders disagreed with the king's decision to count the people, but David's word prevailed. They **crossed** over to the other side of **the Jordan** River and **camped in Aroer** (v. 5). Aroer's location facilitated the counting of the people as groups of counters went from there to different parts of the country. It took Joab and his men almost 10 months to do the census because the counting covered such a wide area with vast differences in topography and terrain. They had a head count of 800,000 **valiant men** in Israel who drew the sword and 500,000 men in **Judah** (v. 9).

24:10. David's heart troubled him, that is, struck him with guilt before the Lord. Under a sense of guilt and conviction, David knew his act of counting was sin, so he confessed it to the Lord. But confession and forgiveness do not set aside consequences.

2. The Plague Strikes (24:11-17)

24:11-14. Gad was a **prophet** and a **seer** (v. 11). The word "seer" emphasized the way a prophet received his message from God; it was something he saw, a vision. Gad was David's prophetic advisor. The Lord told David through Gad to choose one of three consequences for his sin. David chose the option of falling into the Lord's hands because of **His** great **mercies**. David used the plural of "mercies" because of the infinite abundance of God's mercy. Given his depravity, man was the worse option. David's decision was wise and theologically informed.

24:15-17. The **pestilence** was not specified, but **seventy thousand men** died. Moving through the land with fierce wrath against the Lord's people, eventually **the angel stretched out his hand toward Jerusalem to destroy it**, but **the LORD relented from the calamity** (v. 16). The Lord stopped the angel from further destruction. The narrator then noted that **the angel of the LORD was by the threshing floor of Araunah the Jebusite**, indicating where the angel was when he ceased his destruction. Since this angel did not bring a revelation of God, it is likely that this was not a theophany or a pre-incarnate appearance of the Messiah.

3. David Offers a Sacrifice to the Lord (24:18-25)

24:18-25. Wrath was momentarily held back, but sin had to be dealt with through atonement. Gad therefore instructed David to **erect an altar to the LORD on the threshing floor of Araunah the Jebusite**, because this is where the angel had been when he withheld further judgment (cf. v. 16).

With royal officials David went to Araunah's **threshing floor**. This was a significant location. Later the purchased threshing floor of Araunah the Jebusite became the site of Solomon's temple (cf. 1Ch 21:18).

Araunah met David and his men and fell down before the king (v. 20). Still on the ground, Araunah asked the king why he had come. When David explained his presence, Araunah said he was willing to give the threshing floor free of charge and everything required to make the sacrifice (vv. 22-23).

But David refused to dishonor his Lord by offering Him a sacrifice that **cost** him **nothing** (cf. Is 61:6; Mal 1:13-14). David was emphatic in his insistence on buying the threshing floor. **I will surely buy it from you for a price** (v. 24). On Araunah's threshing floor **David built . . . an altar . . . and offered burnt offerings and peace offerings**. Atonement was made. So the Lord answered the **prayer** of His people for the land, and **the plague was** withdrawn.

Thus ends the two books of Samuel, with the story continuing immediately in the following books of Kings. Although named for Samuel, these books are essentially about David, the son of Jesse, the king of Israel. Samuel's role was to be the anointer of kings; Saul's role, as one who was not after God's heart, was a contrast to David; David, the central character, was depicted as the ideal king, the chosen one who was wholly devoted to the Lord.

Essential to the entire narrative of 1 and 2 Samuel was the covenant that God made with David, to give him a descendant who would have an eternal house, kingdom and throne (cf. 2Sm 7:12-17). In the following books of Kings, each Davidic king is compared to David but has a reign that ultimately fails. Therefore, up to that point, at the close of the books of the kings, no Davidic king fulfilled the promise to David. Even so, the covenant promise remained intact, looking to the day when the ultimate Son of David, the Messiah would come. It is only Jesus the Messiah, who was the Son of David (2Tm 2:8) and will one day return to sit on the Davidic throne (Is 9:7), who will totally fulfill God's eternal promise to David.

BIBLIOGRAPHY

See the Bibliography for 1 and 2 Samuel at the end of the commentary on 1 Samuel.

1 KINGS

HARRY E. SHIELDS

INTRODUCTION TO 1 AND 2 KINGS

Kings presents the history of Israel's monarchy, in the final days of the united kingdom and the later division into Israel and Judah. The book of 1 Kings opens at the end of the reign of David, Israel's greatest king. The deportation to Babylon of Jehoiachin, Judah's last king, closes the book of 2 Kings. The time span of the two books is a little more than 400 years (971–586 BC).

These historical narratives of Israel and Judah include interaction with the surrounding nations, the disasters of following false prophets, and the tragic Babylonian captivity. These books are a record of events in fulfilling God's promise of blessing for obedience (Dt 17:14-20) and judgment for disobedience (Dt 28–29). During the monarchy the prophets, particularly Elijah, Elisha, and Isaiah, proclaimed God's message. First and 2 Kings reveal God's faithfulness to His Word and His people. They are books of theological truth and great spiritual issues which ultimately remind Israel of the Davidic covenant (see 2Sm 7:12-16), the failure of all the kings in fulfilling it, and the resulting encouragement for Israel to keep looking for the coming Son of David, the messianic King.

Author. The books of Kings give no indication of the author's identity. However the style and word choice, recurring themes, and literary patterns in the book support the historic position of a single author. Rabbinic tradition ascribed authorship to Ezra or Ezekiel. The Babylonian Talmud says it was written by Jeremiah, since 2Kg 24:18–25:30 is exactly the same as the last chapter of Jeremiah (Jr 52). The actual writer is uncertain; however some facts about the author can be learned from the text.

It is clear that the author of Kings was familiar with the biblical text and other Jewish writings and referred to them in the composition of Kings. He referred to the "book of the acts of Solomon" (1Kg 11:41). He also referred to the "Book of the Chronicles of the Kings of Israel" (cf. 1Kg 14:19; 15:31; 16:5, 14, 20, 27; 22:39; 2Kg 1:18; 10:34; 13:8, 12; 14:15; 15:6, 11, 15, 21, 26, 31) and the "Book of the Chronicles of the Kings of Judah" (cf. 1Kg 14:29; 15:7, 23; 22:45; 2Kg 8:23; 12:19; 14:18, 28; 15:36; 16:19; 20:20; 21:17, 25; 23:28; 24:5). These Chronicles are not the OT books of 1 and 2 Chronicles but were official court records on the monarchy, no longer extant. Therefore the unidentified human author drew on a variety of secular records to record inspired history from God's perspective.

Some critical scholars have suggested Kings had multiple author/editors from various time periods in Israel's history who recorded events over this 400-year span from Solomon to Jehoiachin. Then a later editor added his own historical details and smoothed out rough transitions in the ultimate production of 1 and 2 Kings. The primary problem with multiple-author theories is that they do not provide sufficient evidence to explain the books' consistency in presenting a unified theological perspective or linguistic structure. Nor do they explain how these various editors were able to pass information along for a final composition, especially with so many supposed editors involved over several hundred years.

Therefore, the viewpoint of this commentary is that a single author wrote during the time of the exile, compiling what is known today as 1 and 2 Kings. This unidentified author drew on a variety of secular sources to record Israel's history. The people of Israel needed to understand theologically why they went into exile. Furthermore, all the failed kings of Israel and

Judah reminded them to keep looking for the Davidic King, the Messiah, who was yet to come.

Date. The date of composition, like the author, is difficult to ascertain. Nothing is stated in 1 or 2 Kings that pinpoints an exact date of writing.

Internal evidence, however, indicates the books were written during the exile. One piece of evidence is the last recorded event in 2 Kings, the release of Jehoiachin from prison to live out his life in Babylon. This occurred in the 37th year of his exile (cf. 2Kg 25:27-30; 560 BC). However, there is no mention of the return from Babylon, indicating the book was written while the Jewish people were still in captivity.

A second support for dating the books to the time of the exile is the phrase "to this day," which appears 13 times throughout the books (cf. 1Kg 8:8; 9:13, 21; 12:19; 2Kg 2:22; 8:22; 10:27; 14:7; 16:6; 17:34, 41; 20:17; 21:15). The phrase is significant because it describes a variety of situations and historical markers that were still in place or practice at the time of the writing. Again a specific date is not given, but internal evidence indicates that the writing had to be sometime after those events occurred, but not so far distant that they were no longer recalled. A date sometime during the exile, but prior to the return, best fits with the events described in 1 and 2 Kings. Therefore, a probable date for the writing of the books is between 560 and 550 BC.

Key dates in Israel's history are woven into the text: David died and Solomon became king in 971 BC; the kingdom was divided in 930 BC; the northern kingdom fell to Assyria in 721 BC; Judah fell to Babylon in 586 BC. However, an exact coordination of the kings of Israel and the kings of Judah can be confusing, despite chronology such as "in the third year that Jehoshaphat the king of Judah came down to the king of Israel . . ." (1Kg 22:2). This can be resolved in some cases by understanding coregency or vice-regency of kings. Also, Judah and Israel used two different systems of determining when the reign began, and even this system was sometimes altered over the years. Finally, Judah and Israel began their calendar years at different times, so the beginning of the new year does not coincide. (For a detailed discussion of this see, Edwin R. Thiele, *The Mysterious Numbers of the Hebrew Kings*, rev. ed., Chicago: University of Chicago Press, 1983.) The accounts of the reigns of the kings of Judah and Israel often alternate throughout the two books of Kings, with more details given about some of the monarchs and very little detail given about others. The dates and years of the reigns of the kings, along with the key parallel passages in 2 Chronicles, are included in the commentary.

Recipients. The recipients of 1 and 2 Kings are not specifically stated. However, the content and message of the book suggests it was written to the faithful remnant of Jewish people who had gone into captivity. The message of the book explains how and why the nation went into captivity, because of their failure to follow the Lord. It also presents God's faithfulness to His covenant to David to preserve a faithful remnant (cf. 2Sm 7:8-17). Although all of the kings of Judah had ultimately failed to fulfill the Davidic promise, the implication is that the people should keep looking forward for the messianic King, the greater Son of David.

Purpose and Theme. The historical narrative of Kings goes beyond a simple historical record of the 19 kings of Israel (all bad) and the 20 kings of Judah (only eight good—Asa, Jehoshaphat, Joash/Jehoash, Amaziah, Jotham, Azariah/Uzziah, Jotham, and Hezekiah). First, for the Jewish people in Babylon in 560 BC, and for the later Jewish community, reading Kings would provide insight into their circumstances, explaining the cause of the Babylonian conquest. The nation was taken into captivity for their wicked practice of idolatry: setting up a corrupted worship of the Lord with the golden calves in the northern kingdom, worshiping the gods of the pagan nations around them on the high places and in Jerusalem, and even sacrificing their children to Molech. After the return from exile, Israel would never again practice idolatry.

Second, these books are designed to reveal that each king failed, even the good kings of Judah, to be the ultimate heir to the Davidic throne promised by God in the Davidic covenant (cf. 2Sm 7:8-17). The messianic Son of David was yet to come. Furthermore, an understanding of Kings would give the Jewish people, and all readers up to today, renewed opportunity to fear God, live in devotion to Him, and look for the messianic King.

Background. The two books of Kings were originally viewed as one book in the Hebrew canon, called *melakim* (Hb. "kings"). The LXX (250 BC) divided both Samuel and Kings into two books most likely to make the length of the texts more manageable. The LXX referred to

1 and 2 Samuel as the "First and Second Reigns," while 1 and 2 Kings became the "Third and Fourth Reigns." The LXX division was quickly adopted by the Hebrew text and all subsequent translations.

The books of 1 and 2 Kings are similar in many ways to 1 and 2 Samuel. All four books were written primarily as historical narrative, but include the message of the prophets to the nation of Israel. In the Hebrew cannon, 1 and 2 Kings are placed with the last of the Former Prophets (Joshua, Kings, and Samuel), emphasizing the prophetic element of the books. The English canon places Kings between Samuel and Chronicles, thus emphasizing the historic element of these books.

The Latter Prophets (Isaiah, Jeremiah, and Ezekiel) also have a close connection with Kings in that 1 and 2 Kings provide the historical framework for all that the Latter Prophets proclaim. Both Kings and Chronicles cover Israel's history, yet they have different emphases. The books of Kings include details of all the kings from both the united and divided kingdoms. However, Chronicles focuses on the house of Judah during the Davidic monarchy. The northern kingdom of Israel is mentioned in Chronicles only in its relationship with Judah.

Note that equal length is not given to each of the kings identified in 1 and 2 Kings. The writer went beyond describing the various details of history to identify the spiritual condition of each king. Some of those spiritual conditions had great impact on the nation and were more important than others, earning more space in the text. After Solomon's reign the various kings were described by a fairly consistent six-fold formula: (1) the time of a king's ascension in relation to another king in Israel or Judah, (2) the length of the king's reign and the place of his capital, (3) the name of the king's mother in the case of the Judean kings, (4) a statement about whether the king was good or evil in the Lord's sight, often in comparison to David, (5) the source of further information about the particular king described, and (6) the name of the person who succeeded the king (Gordon D. Fee and Douglas Stuart, *How to Read the Bible Book by Book* [Grand Rapids, MI: Zondervan, 2002], 93).

The charts "Kings of Israel" and "Kings of Judah" provide an overview of the united monarchy, the kings of Judah and Israel. They include the years of reign and the text that records their history.

OUTLINE FOR 1 AND 2 KINGS

I. The United Kingdom under Solomon (1Kg 1:1–11:43)
   A. Solomon Anointed and Establishes Kingdom (1Kg 1:1–2:46)
   B. Solomon's Wisdom, Building, and Success (1Kg 3:1–10:29)
      1. Solomon Given Wisdom by the Lord (1Kg 3:1-28)
      2. Solomon Wisely Organizes His Kingdom (1Kg 4:1-34)
      3. Solomon's Building Programs: The Temple and Other Structures (1Kg 5:1–8:66)
         a. Solomon's Alliance with King Hiram and Organization of Workers (1Kg 5:1-18)
         b. Solomon Builds the Temple and His Palace (1Kg 6:1–7:51)
         c. Solomon Dedicates the Temple (1Kg 8:1-66)
      4. Solomon's Warning from the Lord (1Kg 9:1-9)
      5. Solomon's Splendid Kingdom (1Kg 9:10–10:29)
   C. Solomon's Divided Heart and Spiritual Decline (1Kg 11:1-43)

II. The Divided Kingdom: Northern Israel and Southern Judah (1Kg 12:1–2Kg 17:41)
   A. Rehoboam of Judah and Jeroboam of Israel (1Kg 12:1–14:31)
      1. Rehoboam's Reign: Foolish Choices and Their Consequences (1Kg 12:1-19)
      2. Jeroboam's Coronation as King of Israel (1Kg 12:20-24)
      3. Jeroboam's Self-Deception and Sinful Choices (1Kg 12:25-33)
      4. Jeroboam, God's Word, and Spiritual Rebellion (1Kg 13:1-34)
      5. The Consequences of Jeroboam's Disobedience (1Kg 14:1-20)
      6. Rehoboam's Reign in Judah (1Kg 14:21-31)
   B. The Kings of Judah and Israel until the Fall of Israel to Assyria (1Kg 15:1–2Kg 17:41)
      1. Abijam of Judah: A Bad King (1Kg 15:1-8)

2. Asa of Judah: A Good King (1Kg 15:9-24)
3. From Nadab through Omri: Increasing Spiritual Decline in Israel (1Kg 15:25–16:34)
4. Ahab and the Prophet Elijah: The Supremacy of God over Nature (1Kg 17:1–22:40)
   a. Elijah and the Prophets of Baal (1Kg 17:1–18:46)
   b. Elijah Fears for His Life and Is Comforted by the Lord (1Kg 19:1-21)
   c. Ahab and God's Supremacy over Military Power (1Kg 20:1-43)
   d. Ahab Covets Naboth's Vineyard and Learns of God's Justice (1Kg 21:1-29)
   e. Ahab Confronted by the Prophet Micaiah: God's Supremacy over Plans (1Kg 22:1-40)
5. Jehoshaphat of Judah: A Good King (1Kg 22:41-50)
6. Ahaziah of Israel: Elijah, and God's Supremacy over Health (1Kg 22:51–2Kg 1:1-18)
7. Elisha, Prophet to the Northern Kingdom (2Kg 2:1–6:23)
   a. Elisha Given the Prophetic Office of Elijah (2Kg 2:1-25)
   b. Elisha Confirms His Authority (2Kg 3:1-27)
   c. Elisha Performs Miracles to Substantiate His Message from God (2Kg 4:1–6:23)
      (1) The Miracle of the Widow's Oil (2Kg 4:1-7)
      (2) The Miraculous Healing of the Shunammite Woman's Son (2Kg 4:8-37)

Kings of Israel—Northern Kingdom

Name of King	Date of Reign (year) some coregent	Relation to Predecessor	Reign	1-2 Kings, 1-2 Chronicles Reference	Prophet
Jeroboam I	931-910 (22)	servant	bad	1Kg 11:26–14:20; 2Ch 9:29–13:22	
Nadab	910–909 (2)	son	bad	1Kg 15:25-28	
Baasha	909–886 (24)	none	bad	1Kg 15:27–16:7; 2Ch 16:1-6	
Elah	886–885 (2)	son	bad	1Kg 16:6-14	
Zimri	885 (7 days)	horse captain	bad	1Kg 16:9-20	
Omri	885–874 (12)	army captain	bad	1Kg 16:15-28	
Ahab	874–853 (22)	son	bad	1Kg 16:28–22:40; 2Ch 18:1-34	Elijah, Micaiah
Ahaziah	853–852 (2)	son	bad	1Kg 22:40–2Kg 1:18; 2Ch 20:35-37	Elijah
Jehoram/ Joram	852–841 (12)	brother	bad	2Kg 3:1–9:25; 2Ch 22:5-7	Elijah
Jehu	841–814 (28)	none	bad	2Kg 9:1–10:36; 2Ch 22:7-12	Elisha
Jehoahaz	814–798 (17)	son	bad	2Kg 13:1-9	Elisha
Jehoash/ Joash	798–782 (16)	son	bad	2Kg 13:10–14:16; 2Ch 25:17-24	Elisha
Jeroboam II	793–753 (41)	son	bad	2Kg 14:23-29	Hosea, Amos, Jonah
Zechariah	753–752 (6 months)	son	bad	2Kg 14:29–15:12	
Shallum	752 (1 month)	none	bad	2Kg 15:10-15	
Menahem	752–742 (10)	none	bad	2Kg 15:14-22	
Pekahiah	742–740 (2)	son	bad	2Kg 15:22-26	
Pekah	752–731 (20)	army captain	bad	2Kg 15:27-31; 2Ch 28:5-8	
Hoshea	731–722/21(9)	none	bad	2Kg 15:30–17:6	

(3) The Miracle of Healing the Poison Stew (2Kg 4:38-41)
(4) The Miracle of the Feeding of a Hundred Men (2Kg 4:42-44)
(5) The Miraculous Healing of Naaman the Leper (2Kg 5:1-27)
(6) The Miraculous Recovery of the Axe Head (2Kg 6:1-7)
(7) God's Miraculous Protection of Elisha (2Kg 6:8-23)

8. Elisha Predicts the Siege of Samaria Will End (2Kg 6:24–7:20)
9. Elisha Carries out the Prophecies Originally Spoken through Elijah (2Kg 8:1–9:13)
10. Jehu of Israel: A Bad King Who Takes Actions that Fulfill Prophecy (2Kg 9:14–10:36)
11. Athaliah and Joash of Judah: A Bad Queen and a Good King (2Kg 11:1–12:21)
12. Jehoahaz and Jehoash of Israel: Bad Kings in the Last Days of Elisha (2Kg 13:1-25)
13. Amaziah of Judah: A Good King; and Jehoash of Israel: A Bad King (2Kg 14:1-22)

Kings of Judah—Southern Kingdom

Name of King	Date of Reign (year) some coregent	Relation to Predecessor	Reign	1-2 Kings, 1-2 Chronicles Reference	Prophet
Rehoboam	931–913 (17)	Solomon's son	Bad	1Kg 11:42–41:31; 2Ch 9:31–12:16	
Abijam/Abijah	913–911 (3)	Son	Bad	1Kg 14:31–15:8; 2Ch 13:1-22	
Asa	911–870 (41)	Son	Good	1Kg 15:8-24; 2Ch 14:1–16:14	
Jehoshaphat	873–848 (25)	Son	Good	1Kg 22:41-50; 2Ch 17:1–20:37	
Jehoram/Joram	848–841 (8)	Son	Bad	2Kg 8:16-24; 2Ch 21:1-20	
Ahaziah	841 (1)	Son	Bad	2Kg 8:24–9:29; 2Ch 22:1-9	
Athaliah (Queen)	841–835 (6)	Mother	Bad	2Kg 11:1-20; 2Ch 22:1–23:21	
Joash/Jehoash	835–796 (40)	Grandson	Good	2Kg 11:1–12:21; 2Ch 22:10–24:27	
Amaziah	796–767 (29)	Son	Good	2Kg 14:1-20; 2Ch 25:1-28	
Azariah/Uzziah	792–740 (52)	Son	Good	2Kg 15:1-7; 2Ch 26:1-23	Isaiah, Hosea, Amos
Jotham	750–732 (16)	Son	Good	2Kg 15:32-38; 2Ch 27:1-9	Isaiah, Hosea, Micah
Ahaz	735–716 (16)	Son	Bad	2Kg 16:1-20; 2Ch 28:1-27	Isaiah, Hosea, Micah
Hezekiah	716/15–687 (29)	Son	Good	2Kg 18:1–20:21; 2Ch 29:1–32:33	Isaiah, Hosea, Micah
Manasseh	697–643 (55)	Son	Bad	2Kg 21:1-18; 2Ch 33:1-29	
Amon	643–641 (2)	Son	Bad	2Kg 21:19-26; 2Ch 33:21-25	
Josiah	641–609 (31)	Son	Good	2Kg 22:1–23:30; 2Ch 34:1–35:27	Jeremiah, Zephaniah
Jehoahaz	609 (3months)	Son	Bad	2Kg 23:31-33; 2Ch 36:1-4	Jeremiah
Jehoiakim	609–598 (11)	Brother	Bad	2Kg23:34–24:5; 2Ch 36:5-7	Jeremiah, Habakkuk
Jehoiachin	589–597 (3 months)	Son	Bad	2Kg 24:6-16; 2Ch 36:8-10	Jeremiah
Zedekiah	597–586 (11)	Son	Bad	2Kg 24:17–25:30; 2Ch 36:11-21	Jeremiah

14. Jeroboam II of Israel: A Bad King (2Kg 14:23-29)
15. Azariah (Uzziah) of Judah: A Good King (2Kg 15:1-7)
16. Zechariah, Shallum, Menahem, and Pekahiah of Israel: All Bad Kings (2Kg 15:8-26)
17. Pekah of Israel: A Bad King (2Kg 15:27-31)
18. Jotham of Judah: A Good King (2Kg 15:32-38)
19. Ahaz of Judah: A Bad King (16:1-20)
20. Hoshea of Israel: A Bad King and the Fall of the Northern Kingdom (2Kg 17:1-41)

III. The Kingdom of Judah after the Fall of Israel (2Kg 18:1–25:30)
- A. The Kings of Judah Prior to the Babylonian Invasion (2Kg 18:1–23:30)
  1. Hezekiah of Judah: A Good King (2Kg 18:1–20:21)
  2. Manasseh and Amon of Judah: Two Bad Kings (2Kg 21:1-26)
  3. Josiah of Judah: A Good King (2Kg 22:1–23:30)
- B. The Last Kings of Judah Prior to the Babylonian Captivity (2Kg 23:31–25:7)
  1. Jehoahaz and Jehoiakim of Judah: Two Bad Kings (2Kg 23:31–24:5)
  2. Jehoiachin of Judah: A Bad King (24:6-16)
  3. Zedekiah of Judah: A Bad King (24:17–25:7)
- C. The Fall of Judah and Jerusalem (2Kg 25:8-30)

COMMENTARY ON 1 KINGS

I. The United Kingdom under Solomon (1Kg 1:1–11:43)

The book begins with the transfer of the monarchy from David to Solomon and the latter's subsequent decisions in securing his reign over all Israel. Although he met with internal challenges from his brother Adonijah, Solomon soon learned that God alone had authority over who would lead His nation (cf. Ex 19:5-6). In addition, Solomon learned that the overwhelming task of leadership required more than human skill and expertise. He, like all leaders in Israel, would need the supernatural wisdom of God, if God's purposes were to be accomplished. And to carry out his father David's wishes, Solomon set out to build an earthly dwelling place for the Lord. But in the end Solomon's greatest accomplishments and his great wisdom would be overshadowed by his halfheartedness, led away by multiple pagan wives to worship other gods.

A. Solomon Anointed and Establishes His Kingdom (1Kg 1:1–2:46)

1:1-4. In typical narrative fashion a tension is established at the outset of 1 Kings, as **King David was old, advanced in age**, approaching seventy, and a new king would be required (cf. 2Sm 5:4; Ps 90:10). His strength and health in decline, the reign of Israel's greatest king was coming to an end. David's **servants** did everything in their power to care for the elderly monarch, but because of old age, and perhaps illness, **he could not keep warm**. So they sought out a **young virgin** to **attend the king and become his nurse** (v. 2). She may have been selected because she was old enough for care for an elderly person, but was not yet married with responsibilities to care for her own family. Her duties were not specified, other than to keep David **warm**, perhaps being sure he was kept covered with the duties of a constant attendant. The Hebrew term *'amad* for "attend" literally means "to stand before," or in this context, "to serve or nurse" the king. Even though **Abishag the Shunammite . . . was very beautiful** and **served** David, **the king did not cohabit with her** (v. 4).

1:5-7. David's imminent death quickly became known to many people in the royal household. As a result, **Adonijah the** fourth **son of** David with his fifth wife **Haggith** (cf. 2Sm 3:2-5; 1Ch 3:2) sought to make himself king (v. 5). David's older sons Amnon, Absalom, and Chileab (cf. 2Sm 3:3) were already dead (cf. 2Sm 13–18), so Adonijah **exalted himself, saying, "I will be king."** The Hebrew verbal form for "exalted" reveals that this was not a onetime event, but an ongoing activity on Adonijah's part ("he kept exalting himself"). His brazen behavior was fueled by his father's failure to **never** cross **him** (v. 6). This is yet another time in David's life, as with Absalom, when either from negligence or guilt over previous sins he allowed a son to go undisciplined. As a result, Adonijah behaved like a king in waiting (**he prepared for himself chariots**) and allied himself with an entourage of **fifty men** (v. 5). Also he conspired with **Joab**, David's military commander who had served faithfully for years (cf. 1Sm 26:6; 2Sm 2:13; 19:13; 20:10, 23), and **Abiathar the priest** (v. 7), who joined David after Saul commanded Doeg to slaughter the priests (cf. 2Sm 22:18-20). Adonijah wanted them to help make him Israel's next king.

1:8-10. However, **Zadok the priest** (cf. 2Sm 8:17), **Benaiah**, one of David's mighty men (cf. 2Sm 8:18; 23:20; 1Kg 2:25), **Nathan the prophet** (cf. 2Sm 12:1-25), David's trusted spiritual adviser, and **the mighty men who belonged to David were not with Adonijah** (v. 8). In a fashion similar to Absalom, another son of David who sought to usurp the throne (cf. 2Sm 15:11-12), Adonijah assumed he would be king and he called for a great celebration. He **sacrificed . . . and he invited** people who embraced the idea that he would be a worthy successor. **But he did not invite Nathan the prophet, Benaiah, the mighty men** (cf. 1Ch 11)**, and Solomon his brother** (v. 10). He excluded these people who he knew would not support his grab for the crown, since they supported David and knew God had revealed to David that Solomon would succeed him as king (cf. 1Ch 22:9-10).

1:11-14. When **Nathan**, the prophet and David's faithful adviser (cf. 2Sm 12:1-15; 1Ch 17:1-15), learned of Adonijah's conspiracy, he organized a plan to use both his own influence and that of David's wife, **Bathsheba** (cf. 2Sm 11; 12:24), to preserve what God had revealed years earlier regarding the successor to the Davidic line. Nathan said to Bathsheba, **Please let me give you counsel and save your life and the life of your son Solomon** (v. 12), for it was probable that Adonijah would kill any rivals to the throne if he became king. Nathan revealed the urgency of the situation by instructing her to **Go at once to King David and say to him, 'Have you not, my lord, O king, sworn to your maidservant . . . Solomon your son shall be king'** (v. 13). This oath is not recorded elsewhere; however, God told David who his successor would be, and possibly David had shared that news with Bathsheba (cf. 1Ch 22:9-10).

1:15-21. Bathsheba carried out Nathan's plan (introduced in vv. 11-14). She demonstrated her own respect for David as she **bowed and prostrated herself before the king** (v. 16). Referring to a previous statement by David, she said, **My lord, you swore to your maidservant by the LORD your God, saying, 'Surely your son Solomon shall be king after me and he shall sit on my throne'** (v. 17). David did not dispute her statement. Bathsheba knew that if Adonijah came to the throne she and Solomon would be **considered offenders** (v. 21), possibly killed as usurpers of the throne. The Hebrew *chatta'* (**offenders**) is frequently translated "sinner" and has a more secular connotation in v. 21, suggesting someone who is accused of breaking the laws of the state.

1:22-27. Part two of the plan (revealed in vv. 11-14) followed in quick succession. The only difference between Bathsheba's speech and Nathan's is that the prophet asked questions of David instead of making direct statements. He asked two diplomatic questions to alert David to the circumstances and motivate him to action: First, **My lord the king, have you said, 'Adonijah shall be king after me, and he shall sit on my throne'?** (v. 24). Second, he asked a question implying that David had kept something from two of his most intimate confidants: **Has this thing been done by my lord the king, and you have not shown to your servants who should sit on the throne of my lord the king after him?** (v. 27).

1:28-31. Following Nathan's inquiry David acted quickly. He called for **Bathsheba** and **vowed** in the strongest terms **As the LORD lives . . . Your son Solomon shall be king after me** (v. 30). Taking David at his word, Bathsheba **bowed with her face to the ground, and prostrated herself before the king**. Trusting David to do the right thing, she simply said, **May my lord King David live forever** (v. 31).

1:32-40. To demonstrate that Solomon had David's blessings as king, David's servants were to have **Solomon ride on** the king's **mule** to **Gihon**, just outside Jerusalem in the Kidron Valley (v. 33). Then Nathan would **anoint him there as king over Israel** (v. 34). This would make David's choice of Solomon known publicly.

A crowd gathered (v. 34). The people were **rejoicing with great joy, so that the earth shook at their noise** (v. 40). What David announced in the privacy of his bedroom was now known throughout Israel. The response of the people indicated that they approved of David's choice in making Solomon their new king [970–930 BC; cf. 2Ch 1–9].

1:41-48. The news of Solomon's coronation soon reached the ears of **Adonijah** and those who were prematurely celebrating **with him** (v.

41). The messenger, **Jonathan the son of Abiathar the priest**, reported what was happening (v. 42). He amplified the certainty and authority of Solomon's ascension to the throne with four facts: (1) Solomon was made to **ride on the king's mule**, which showed David's authorization of the decree (v. 44). (2) Solomon had been **anointed** king in Gihon, which signified a public declaration of intent (v. 45). (3) David's servants had extended a blessing, asking God to **make the name of Solomon better than** David's **name** (v. 47). (4) David **bowed himself on the bed**, indicating his recognition of Solomon as the new king (v. 47). The evidence was clear to Adonijah: his intentions were rejected and Solomon was to be the legitimate heir to the throne.

1:49-53. In fear for his life, **Adonijah** fled to the tabernacle. The law provided that anyone seeking asylum could be safe by taking **hold of the horns of the altar** (cf. Ex 21:12-14). Mercifully, Solomon agreed to let Adonijah live, although he made it clear that Adonijah was to prove that he was a **worthy man** (v. 52). That is, he was to renounce any claim to the throne and accept Solomon as the rightful king. Adonijah was then led into Solomon's presence, where he **prostrated** himself before the king (v. 53).

After Solomon's anointing as king, the aged King David gave some final advice to the new king. Throughout chap. 2, the narrator made it clear that Solomon "established" his kingdom (vv. 12, 24, 45-46), and this firm establishment was a direct result of God's plan and intervention.

2:1-4. Realizing the **time to die drew near**, David, as did Moses (cf. Dt 31:1-8), Joshua (cf. Jos 23:1-16), and Samuel (cf. 1Sm 12:1-2) near their time of death, **charged**, or gave important instructions to, his successor. The first challenge was for Solomon to **be strong** by depending on the Lord and His Word (Dt 31:7, 23; Jos 1:6-7, 9, 18) and to **show** himself **a man** (v. 2). The phrase "show yourself a man" literally means "to become a man." Solomon was to "become" all a king should be who would fulfill the conditions of Dt 17:14-20 by obeying the law. He was to **walk in** God's **ways**, and **keep His statutes . . . commandments . . . ordinances . . . and testimonies** (v. 3). These terms are frequently used together for obedience to covenant obligations (cf. 6:12; 8:58; 2Kg 17:37; Dt 8:11; 11:1; 26:17; 28:15, 45; 30:10, 16). When Solomon made himself a man obedient to the law, David informed him that **the LORD** would **carry out His promise** of the Davidic covenant (v. 4; cf. 2Sm 7:8-17). In addition, the kind of obedience enjoined by David reflected the conditions God established for fulfilling the Davidic covenant (cf. Ps 132:12), conditions which Solomon ultimately failed to meet.

2:5-6. David's second challenge for Solomon was to deal with the treacherous **Joab**. Although he had been a brave soldier in David's army, he had aligned himself with Adonijah (cf. 1:7). During his years of service to David, Joab often took matters into his own hands and usurped the will of King David. For instance, as David was seeking to unite his army with Saul's forces, Joab killed Saul's commander Abner in violation of a peace treaty David had enacted with Abner (cf. 2Sm 3). Also, Joab rashly executed Amasa, David's commander, for taking too long to return from a military assignment (cf. 2Sm 20). David told Solomon to exercise justice **according to** his **wisdom**, and not to let Joab's **gray hair go down to Sheol in peace** (cf. 2:28-35).

2:7. David then told Solomon to be kind **to the sons of Barzillai**. This family had assisted David when he fled from the attempted coup of Solomon's older brother, **Absalom** (cf. comments on 2Sm 19:31-39). David's counsel was to **let them be among those who eat at your table** because of the favor they had shown David in a time of great crisis.

2:8-9. Although **Shimei** seemed to be supporting Solomon, David knew Shimei's history and warned Solomon to protect himself from treachery. David remembered that Shimei was from Saul's family, a **Benjamite**, and had originally opposed David's kingship and then sided with Absalom against David. Shimei had **cursed** him **with a violent curse** (cf. 2Sm 16:5-13) in direct violation of the Mosaic command not to curse a ruler (cf. 2Sm 19:21; Ex 22:28). Later, after David defeated Absalom, Shimei hurried to meet David, pleading for mercy, and David spared his life (cf. 2Sm 19:18-23). Now with Solomon taking the throne, David again saw Shimei as a potential threat and cautioned for the good of Solomon's kingdom, **do not let him go unpunished**. Solomon did take action to protect himself from Shimei's treacheries (cf. 2:36-46).

2:10-12. Here are the first of several summary statements. David's death was announced—he **slept with his fathers** and the length of his reign (1010–970 BC). **Solomon sat on the throne of David his father, and his kingdom was firmly established**.

2:13-18. Even though the kingdom was secure under Solomon's control, when **Adonijah** approached **Bathsheba . . . peacefully**, he had a suspicious request. Adonijah's request was tinged with bitterness and remorse as he told her, **All Israel expected me to be king; however, the kingdom has turned about and become my brother's, for it was his from the LORD** (v. 15). He then asked her to ask **Solomon** to give him **Abishag the Shunammite**, who had been David's nurse (cf. 1:1-4), **as a wife** (v. 17). This request recalls a similar plot when Ahithophel advised Absalom to prove his right to the throne by sleeping with David's concubines (cf. 2Sm 16:21-23).

2:19-22. Apparently **Bathsheba** was unaware of **Adonijah**'s ulterior motive, for she presented his desire to marry Abishag to **Solomon** as **one small request** (v. 20). However, Solomon saw Adonijah's treachery immediately, knowing there might be "wickedness" (cf. 1:52). Solomon realized although David had not had sexual relations with Abishag, her intimate contact with the aged king (cf. 1:1-4) would cause her to be regarded by the people as part of David's harem. Marriage to her would strengthen Adonijah's claim to the throne (cf. 2Sm 3:7; 12:8; 16:21), so Solomon told his mother, **Ask for him also the kingdom—for he is my older brother** (v. 22), since many in the kingdom already had supported Adonijah's claim to the throne as the oldest heir (cf. 1:5-10). Solomon knew that if he granted Adonijah's request, then his brother's co-conspirators **Abiathar** and **Joab** (v. 22; cf. 1:7) would continue in the plot to seize the throne for Adonijah.

2:23-25. Solomon took swift and decisive action. He **swore by the LORD** (cf. comments on 1Sm 3:17) that Adonijah had declared his own death sentence (**spoken this word against his own life**) in making this grab for the kingdom. Solomon realized the Lord had **set** him **on the throne of David** his **father** (v. 24), so he sent **Benaiah**, David's military commander who continued this leadership role under Solomon (cf. 1:8-10; 2Sm 3:20), to execute Adonijah.

2:26-27. Solomon dealt with other conspirators who sided with and assisted Adonijah's plan to take the throne (cf. 1Kg 1:7). He ordered **Abiathar the priest** to be banished **to Anathoth**, his hometown three miles east of Jerusalem. Solomon reminded Abiathar that he **deserved to die**. But Solomon showed him mercy because of his loyalty to **David** over a number of years (e.g., 1Sm 22:20-23). He **dismissed Abiathar from being priest . . . in order to fulfill the word of the LORD**, a prophecy first mentioned regarding Eli's household (cf. 1Sm 2:27-36.)

2:28-35. It didn't take Solomon long to deal with a third individual of Adonijah's co-conspirators (cf. 1:5-10). When the news came to **Joab** about Adonijah's fate and Abiathar's banishment, he fled to **the tent of the LORD and took hold of the horns of the altar** (v. 28). This was the same tactic Adonijah employed for sanctuary (cf. 1:51). However, the right of asylum did not apply in conspiracy against the king, and Solomon did not extend mercy to him (cf. Ex 21:14). He quickly sent **Benaiah** to execute Joab (v. 29). The aging Joab was asked to come away from the altar and surrender (v. 30). But he refused, saying, **No, for I will die here** (v. 30). Not knowing what to do, Benaiah sent word to Solomon of the standoff and asked what to do. Solomon told Benaiah to do as Joab **has spoken and fall upon him** (vv. 31, 34). Solomon was obeying David's earlier warning about Joab, to "act according to your wisdom, and not let his gray hair go down to Sheol in peace" (2:5-6). Joab had **shed** blood **without cause** when he took the lives of both **Abner** and **Amasa** (v. 32; cf. 2Sm 3:27; 20:9-10). After wisely dealing with treachery in his administration, Solomon quickly **appointed Benaiah the son of Jehoiada over the army** in place of Joab, **and the king appointed Zadok the priest in place of Abiathar** (v. 35).

2:36-38. The final enemy about whom David warned Solomon was **Shimei** (cf. comments on 2:8-9), who cursed David when he was fleeing from Absalom and then became a reluctant ally when David returned to his palace. Solomon called for Shimei and offered him a plan of safety for life, as long as Shimei stayed within the boundary set by the king. He told Shimei to **build . . . a house in Jerusalem and live there, and do not go out from there to any place** (v. 36). However, on the day Shimei went beyond **the brook Kidron**, just east of Jerusalem before the Mount of Olives, he would be treated as an enemy **and know for certain that you shall surely die** (vv. 37-38). Keeping Shimei within the city of Jerusalem would allow Solomon to keep an eye on him and would prevent Shimei from gathering conspirators against Solomon.

2:39-46. Although Shimei agreed to the plan, after **three years**, when **two** of Shimei's servants **ran away** to **Gath**, the region of Israel's enemy, the Philistines (v. 39; cf. 1Sm 17), Shimei ignored his agreement with Solomon, went to Gath, and brought the escaped servants back to Jerusalem. He could have sent another servant to get the runaways, but foolishly took this opportunity to seemingly justify a trip to enemy territory beyond the limitation of his house arrest. When **Solomon** learned of the violation he summoned Shimei (v. 42) and reminded him of **the oath of the Lord** (vv. 41-43). Solomon also reminded Shimei of his past sins against David. So Solomon commanded **Benaiah** to execute Shimei (v. 46).

The section concerning the enemies of Solomon and of the house of David concludes with good news: **the throne of David shall be established before the Lord forever**. God was at work to fulfill His covenant and subsequently bless the reign of Solomon as promised (cf. 1Kg 1:47-48; 1Ch 22:9-10).

B. Solomon's Wisdom, Building, and Success (1Kg 3:1–10:29)

These chapters portray the reign of one of the greatest monarchs of all time. Chapters 1 and 2 show how Solomon became David's successor, but chaps. 3 and 4 reveal the reasons behind his legitimacy to the throne. His building programs are outlined in chaps. 4–9, with details about the building of the temple. Highlights of Solomon's magnificent reign include the visit from the Queen of Sheba and the descriptions of his splendors in chap. 10.

1. Solomon Given Wisdom by the Lord (1Kg 3:1-28)

3:1. Although Solomon's kingdom was established (cf. 2:46) and he would receive great wisdom from the Lord (cf. 3:6-15), he foolishly began his reign with the first of many marriages to foreign women who would eventually lead him astray into pagan worship (cf. 1Kg 11:1-8). Solomon **formed a marriage alliance with Pharaoh**. The clause literally reads "made himself a son-in-law of Pharaoh." Marriage alliances were common in the ancient world for a military and trade advantage; however they had been forbidden by the Lord (cf. Dt 17:17).

3:2-3. Although **Solomon loved the Lord**, he (along with the **people of Israel** who were **sacrificing**) sinned when he **sacrificed and burned incense on the high places**, pagan places of worship, instead of the one prescribed place, the tabernacle (cf. Dt 17:3-5).

3:4-5. At this time Solomon had a personal encounter with the Lord at **Gibeon** when he went to **sacrifice there**. Gibeon was a Levitical city about five miles from Jerusalem (Jos 18:25; 21:17). It was referred to as **the great high place** because the tabernacle of the Lord was there (v. 4; cf. 1Ch 16:39-40; 21:28-29; 2Ch 1:3, 5-6). Here **in a dream** God graciously appeared the first of two times in Solomon's life (cf. 9:2) and posed the most significant offer he would ever be given: **Ask what you wish me to give you**. Solomon's answer would change the course of his administration for good and for the good of the people.

3:6-7. Solomon responded to God by acknowledging that He had **shown great lovingkindness** to his father, **David**. He also hinted that the Davidic covenant was being fulfilled in him. But he quickly made his request, saying, **Yet I am but a little child; I do not know how to go out or come in**. This expression (Hb. *na'ar* means "immature person") reflected Solomon's youth and his virtual inexperience, not his chronological age. Since he reigned 40 years (970–930 BC) and did not die at a remarkable old age, he probably became king between the ages of 20 and 30 (cf. 1Kg 11:42-43). He felt overwhelmed by all that was placed on his shoulders in administering this kingdom.

3:8-9. Solomon proceeded to make his request, and God followed with an answer. First, Solomon identified himself as God's **servant**, and one of **Your people which You have chosen**, reflecting the Lord's unique relationship with the Jewish people (cf. Gn 12:1-3; Dt 7:7-8). He asked for **an understanding heart to judge Your people to discern between good and evil**. The word translated "understanding" comes from the Hebrew term *shome'* and can also be translated "hearing." Throughout the OT the words "hearing" and "obedient" were often intertwined. So what Solomon was asking for was the ability to "obey" what God had said in the law, and then to be able to distinguish **between good and evil** for the good of the Lord's people.

3:10-15. God responded that He had heard Solomon's prayer and that He would bless the new king. Solomon's request was **pleasing** to God because he had **not asked for [him]self** (v. 11), but was focused on the needs of the people to have **discernment to understand justice** (v. 11). God promised to give Solomon the **discerning heart** he requested, and He also promised that there would be **no one like you before you, nor shall one like you arise after you** (v. 12). God also promised Solomon he would have the very things he did not request—**both riches and honor** (v. 13).

Yet there was one conditional statement that Solomon would need to hear. It was the kind of condition his successors after him would also have to remember. These blessings would come **If you walk in My ways, keeping My statutes and commandments** (v. 14). God's desire was to bless Solomon, but the king was under obligation to obey the Lord in accordance with the stipulations of Dt 17:14-20. When Solomon awakened from his encounter with the Lord, he knew it was a dream, but he also realized God had spoken to him. So as a new act of obedience he went to the **ark of the covenant of the Lord** in Jerusalem and offered up sacrifices that were given in view of his sin, and also in view of God's great mercy (v. 15).

3:16-28. Immediately after the Lord gave Solomon great wisdom, the familiar story of the two **harlots** and the baby is recorded as evidence of King Solomon's wisdom (v. 16). This was a common procedure to inquire of a monarch in the ancient world and ask him to settle disputes. Both women gave birth to sons on the same day. There were no witnesses of the events that transpired. But in the middle of the night, one of the sons died because, according to one of the women, **she** [the second mother] **lay on it** (v. 19). While the other mother slept with the child that was still living, the mother of the dead child came and stole the living child away, replacing the child she took with the dead son (vv. 20-21).

After listening to both women, Solomon shocked the women by asking for a **sword** and suggesting that he cut the **living child in two** and **give half** to each (vv. 24-25). Maternal compassion became evident, along with ruthless evil. It was in the differing response of each woman that Solomon was able to "discern between good and evil" (cf. 3:9). Consequently, he gave the child to the mother who was willing to give up her son rather than see him die. Solomon's verdict not only impressed these women, but **all Israel . . . feared the king, for they saw that the wisdom of God was in him to administer justice** (v. 28). It was confirmation that Solomon was God's choice to be king and that God was clearly working in his life by giving him great wisdom.

2. Solomon Wisely Organizes His Kingdom (1Kg 4:1-34)

Solomon's divine wisdom was not only demonstrated in the execution of justice, but also in the way he brought order to the nation over which he was king. Prior to David's reign and under the leadership of Saul, Israel was little more than a loosely knit tribal confederacy. Under David's leadership the borders of Israel were expanded to come close to the land promises of the Abrahamic covenant. Captured nations were paying tribute, which brought great amounts of revenue into the nation. Under Solomon more administrative order was implemented.

4:1-6. Following David's successful reign, **Solomon was king over all Israel** (cf. 2Sm 8:15) and administered it with a well-organized government. Within Solomon's court, specific individuals were identified to provide the young king with spiritual, political, and military support. Perhaps Zadok (cf. 1:38) was too advanced in years to oversee the priesthood, so **Azariah the son of Zadok was the priest** (v. 2). The definite article "the" may indicate that Azariah was the high priest, while **Zadok** continued to serve in the priesthood. **Benaiah** replaced Joab as the commander over **the army** (v. 4). Although **Abiathar** had been dismissed as a priest by Solomon (cf. 1Kg 2:27), he apparently was given a somewhat emeritus role. It very well could be that some of the people mentioned served transitional roles in the new administration. Clearly, out of his God-given wisdom, Solomon saw a need to bring order to the daily activities of his court.

4:7-19. Solomon arranged for the financial support of his administration. **Solomon had twelve deputies over all Israel, who provided for the king and his household** (v. 7). These were not the twelve tribes of Israel, but administrative areas, perhaps based on agricultural productivity. Each of the twelve deputies **had to provide for a month in the year** (v. 7), as a means of providing equity in caring for the royal needs without overburdening any one area.

4:20-21. Solomon's reign was closely connected with the provision of the Abrahamic covenant (cf. Gn 12:1-9). The Israelites, **Judah and Israel**, had multiplied to the extent that they were **as numerous as the sand that is on the seashore in abundance** (v. 20), and Solomon **ruled over** the area God had promised.

4:22-28. The extent of Solomon's wealth is evident in the size of the **provision for one day** required for his court; one **kor** equals 10 bushels. So each day he needed 300 bushels of fine flour and 600 bushels of meal, plus hundreds of animals for meat to feed the royal house and administrative staff (v. 23). So **Judah and Israel lived in safety**, and they enjoyed individual prosperity as well from **Dan even to Beersheba**, meaning all across the land north to south (v. 25; cf. Jdg 20:1; 1Sm 3:20). Solomon had a military might of **40,000 stalls of horses for his chariots, and 12,000 horsemen** (v. 26). However, Solomon's multiplication of horses, a sign of military might, directly violated the Lord's command to depend on Him for security, and it would become a great problem in Solomon's later reign (cf. Dt 17:16; 1Kg 10:26-29).

4:29-34. Solomon was affirmed as having wisdom in the management of his kingdom greater than the men of the east, of Egypt, and the surrounding nations (vv. 30-31). His literary skills were also cited, since he wrote **3,000 proverbs, and his songs were 1,005** (v. 32). Solomon was also noted for his wisdom and expertise in plant and animal sciences (v. 33). As a result, **men came from all peoples to hear the wisdom of Solomon** (v. 34). Whether they knew it or not, Solomon's wisdom was really God's wisdom given to a young king to rule righteously.

3. Solomon's Building Programs: The Temple and Other Structures (1Kg 5:1–8:66)

a. Solomon's Alliance with King Hiram and Organization of Workers (1Kg 5:1-18)

Solomon's wisdom was displayed in the way he administered justice (cf. 3:16-28) and in the way he united the citizens into a highly functioning social unit. In chaps. 5–7 Solomon's wisdom and glory were put on display in his major building projects, the temple in particular.

5:1-12. News of Solomon's wise leadership reached Israel's northern neighbor. **Hiram king of Tyre** sent his servants to Solomon when he **heard that they had anointed him king in place of his father**. Hiram **had always been a friend of David** and had provided the wood for the construction of David's palace (cf. 2Sm 5:11). David had not been allowed by the Lord to build His house, the temple (v. 3), but now Solomon would **build a house for the name of the Lord my God** (v. 5). Solomon wanted only the best wood for the project, **cedars from Lebanon** (v. 6). The basis for this first building project was Solomon's obedience to the Davidic covenant (cf. 2Sm 7:12-13).

Hearing of Solomon's plans, Hiram affirmed that the Lord had given **David a wise son** and agreed to **do what you desire concerning the cedar and cypress timber** (vv. 7-8). Hiram would cut and transport the wood in the form of bundled rafts on the water, and then unload them at a designated site along the Mediterranean coastland. In turn, Solomon's workers would transport the wood after Hiram disassembled the logs at an appropriate place (v. 9). Payment for the wood and the work of transportation was to be carried out **by giving food to my [Hiram's] household** (v. 9). For this great building project **the Lord gave wisdom to Solomon** to start the construction of the temple. A covenant of **peace between Hiram and Solomon** sealed the transaction (v. 12).

5:13-18. Gathering resources for the temple was a major task. Solomon organized 30,000 **forced laborers** to work in **relays** of 10,000 men per team. The workforce came **from all Israel** (vv. 13-14). They would spend one month in **Lebanon** and two months in Israel. Also **70,000** individuals transported materials from their place of origin to a place of preparation, and **80,000** individuals served as stonecutters **in the mountains** (v. 15). Some of the workers were taken from the descendants of those whom the Israelites were not able to drive out of the land, while others were conscripted Israelites, but Solomon "did not make slaves of the sons of Israel" (1Kg 9:22; cf. 2Ch 8:9).

b. Solomon Builds the Temple and His Palace (1Kg 6:1–7:51)

6:1. The starting date for building the temple has three specific chronological markers associated with it. Scholars debate whether the **four hundred and eightieth year** was a rounded number or a symbolic expression of the number of generations from the exodus to the time of construction begun here. This brief time reference connects what Solomon was doing with the ongoing work of God's redemption for Israel, and the nation's promise from God to dwell in the land. The most important piece of information is that construction started in **the fourth year of Solomon's reign over Israel**. Most scholars believe that this would have been 967–966 BC. Therefore, a literal reading of the four hundred and eightieth year would make the date of the exodus to be 1447–1446 BC. Along with these two chronological markers is the fact that Solomon started this project in the **second month of Ziv** (April/May). It took Solomon seven years (seven years and six months) to build the temple (cf. 6:38).

6:2-10. By modern standards the temple was a fairly small worship facility: **its length was**

sixty cubits [90 feet] **and its width twenty cubits** [30 feet] **and its height thirty cubits** [45 feet] (v. 2). A **porch** was **in front of** the temple, and the temple had several **windows**, and **stories encompassing the walls . . . around both the nave and the inner sanctuary** (v. 5). The stones used in the basic structure were **prepared at the quarry**, so that no sound of tools was **heard in the house** (v. 7). The basic structure of the temple indicates from its outward appearance that it was a place of reverence (vv. 5, 8) and functionality (v. 7). The temple was enclosed completely with the construction of a roof or covering of **beams and planks of cedar** (v. 9).

6:11-13. As the temple was under construction **the word of the Lord came to Solomon** reminding him of the most important aspect of the **house which you are building**. Solomon was certainly building a great temple, but God was much more concerned with the condition of the heart—Solomon's heart, the hearts of his royal descendants, and the hearts of the people. God offered Solomon the following: **if you will walk in My statutes and execute My ordinances and keep all My commandments by walking in them, then I will carry out My word with you which I spoke to David your father** (v. 12). Obedience to the Mosaic and Davidic covenants was necessary for God to **carry out** His Word to the king and for Him to **dwell among the sons of Israel** (v. 13).

This passage plays a significant role in the development of the book's messianic message. In essence, God was offering Solomon that if he obeyed the Torah completely, God would fulfill the Davidic covenant through him (cf. 2Sm 7:12-16). At this point in the narrative, it appears that Solomon would be the son of David, the Promised One who would build the house for the Lord, who would have an eternal house, kingdom, and throne (cf. 2Sm 7:13). Further, he would go on to build the temple (but not the eschatological, messianic temple the prophets foresaw; cf. Zch 6:11-15; Ezk 40–48). The author's purpose was to raise the hope that the promise would be fulfilled in Solomon, but then reveal that Solomon would fail. He would multiply pagan wives who would turn his heart away from the Lord and cause him to follow foreign gods.

Clearly, Solomon was not to be the fulfillment of the promise to David. Afterwards, every Davidic king was compared to David, the ideal king, to see if he would be the promised Son of David. And in each case, even those who were deemed "good," the Davidic king would ultimately fail. Thus, at the end of the book of 2 Kings, the only conclusion to be drawn was that the promise to David had not yet been fulfilled. As a result, the message of the books of 1 and 2 Kings would be to keep looking for the fulfillment of the messianic promise to David in the future. In this way, 1 and 2 Kings point to the future with hope for a messianic Son of David who will yet fulfill the messianic promises, build the temple of the Lord (cf. Zch 6:11-15), and have an eternal house, kingdom, and throne.

6:14-18. Following God's reminder about the importance of obedience, details were given about the interior design and construction of its most revered sections. Solomon took the instructions given to him by his father David (cf. 1Ch 28:11-12) and prepared a structure that pointed to the glory and grandeur of God. The entire interior was covered with **cedar** and **cypress** wood, covering all the stone from **the floor of the house to the ceiling** (v. 15). These wooden paneled walls were also carved in the shape of **gourds and open flowers**, which pointed to God as the author of all creation. The whole stone building was covered by **cedar** and **there was no stone seen** (v. 18).

6:19-36. The most important part of the temple was the **inner sanctuary**, or the holy of holies, where the **ark of the covenant** (cf. Ex 25:10-22) would be kept (v. 19). The inner sanctuary was **twenty cubits** (30 feet) in length, width, and height (v. 20). In the center of the **inner sanctuary** were **two** wooden **cherubim** overlaid with gold. They were placed within the inner sanctuary in such a way that the wing of one cherub would touch one wall and the wing of the other would touch the other wall (vv. 23-28). The walls were also **carved** with **engravings of cherubim, palm trees, and open flowers** in both the outer and inner sanctuaries (v. 29). The grandeur of the gold-plated inner sanctuary along with the fact that Solomon **overlaid the floor of the house with gold** (v. 30), indicates that God was to be seen as exalted and majestic above all other gods. The inner sanctuary was His throne room where He would dwell with His people.

6:37-38. Solomon started temple construction in the **fourth year** of his reign, in the **month of Ziv** (cf. 6:1). The construction was completed in **the eleventh year, in the month of Bul, which is the eighth month** (Oct/Nov 959 BC). So it took the king seven years and six months to finish what he was commissioned by God to do.

7:1-12. Yet the construction of Solomon's **own house** took **thirteen years**, twice as long as it took to build the temple. The contrast in time devoted to the temple versus time spent on Solomon's private quarters and administrative buildings may indicate that he was already being tempted by his own self-importance (cf. Dt 17:19-20). Solomon's other building projects included five specific structures, three of which related to his administrative responsibilities as Israel's king (vv. 2-7). Two of the structures were designed for his own residential needs (vv. 8-12). The **house of the forest of Lebanon**, meaning it was built from the cedar trees of Lebanon (cf. 5:1-8), was 150 feet long, 75 feet wide, and 45 feet high, and served as an armory (cf. 10:17, 21; Is 22:8).

In addition there was **the hall of pillars**, which may have been part of a large palace complex (v. 6). This hall or colonnade served as a kind of portico that led into the **hall of the throne** or the **hall of judgment . . . paneled with cedar**, where Solomon rendered verdicts on issues of justice brought before him (v. 7).

The last two buildings are simply described as **his house** and **a house like this hall for Pharaoh's daughter** (v. 8). No detail is given, but Solomon may have gone to great expense and effort to build an individualized home for this wife above all the other women mentioned in 11:1. All five buildings were constructed out of **costly stones** and **cedar beams** (vv. 9-12). The complex would have been an impressive sight for the Israelites and foreign visitors to behold (cf. 10:11-13).

7:13-14. After describing the temple building, the inner sanctuary, and Solomon's palace, the author gave details of the temple furnishings. **Solomon** wanted the best craftsman, so he sent for **Hiram from Tyre**. Although they have the same name, this was not King Hiram (cf. chap. 5). This Jewish craftsman who lived in Tyre, also known as Huram-abi, was the son of a Danite woman (cf. 2Ch 2:13-14). He is identified as **a widow's son from the tribe of Naphtali, and his father was a man of Tyre** (v. 14). His genealogy is not a contradiction because by Solomon's time the tribe of Dan had moved north from their original allotment area in central Israel (cf. Jos 19:40-50; Jdg 18) and were incorporated into the general region of Naphtali (cf. Jos 19:32-39), making Hiram's mother's tribal identity both Dan and Naphtali. Hiram was **filled with wisdom and understanding and skill for doing any work in bronze**. This statement parallels the description of Bezalel (cf. Ex 31:1-5; 35:31), who built the tabernacle. The pairing of **wisdom and understanding** are often used to describe spiritual qualities, not just craftsmanship (e.g., Pr 4:7; 9:10; Is 11:2). A structure fit for the presence of God needed the influence of men who were also empowered by God.

7:15-22. Hiram designed **two pillars of bronze** about 30 feet high. Both pillars had carefully crafted capitals made for their tops and accompanying **lily design** (v. 22). But the striking feature of the pillars was that they were given names: **Jachin** (Hb. "he will establish") and **Boaz** (Hb. "in him is strength"). The names would serve as a reminder to the king and the citizen/worshiper that it was the Lord who would establish His people in accord with His strength as they lived lives of obedient worship.

7:23-26. Hiram also crafted a large **sea**, or basin, as a laver for the priests to wash as part of their ceremonial duties (cf. Ex 30:18-21; 40:30-32; 2Ch 4:6). It was **ten cubits** around and **five cubits** high (about 15 feet across and seven and one-half feet high, v. 23) and **stood on twelve oxen** (v. 25). This massive basin held **two thousand baths**, about 11,000 gallons of water (v. 26).

7:27-39. Hiram also crafted **ten stands of bronze** moveable on **four bronze wheels**, each one six feet square and about five and one-half feet high (**four cubits** square and **height** of **three cubits**). They were decorated with **lions, oxen**, and **cherubim** (vv. 27-30). On top of the stand was a **basin**, which held **forty baths** of water (v. 38), 230 gallons, used in the ceremony of the temple for purification.

7:40-47. Although no specific detail is given regarding their functions in the temple, **Hiram made the basins and the shovels and the bowls** used by the priests in temple service. The impressive nature of Hiram's work was seen in the statement: **Solomon left all the utensils unweighed, because they were too many; the weight of the bronze could not be ascertained** (v. 47).

7:48-51. The temple built by King Solomon, a permanent structure similar in design and parallel in purpose to the temporary tabernacle (cf. Ex 40), was now complete and ready to be used in worship of the true King, God Almighty.

c. Solomon Dedicates the Temple (1Kg 8:1-66)

With the temple construction completed, Solomon dedicated the temple to the worship of the Lord. The focus of the dedication was the greatness of God, and the fulfillment of His promises made to David and now completed under Solomon's reign (cf. 8:20-21). Solomon's desire was that "all the peoples of the earth may know that the LORD is God; there is no one else" (8:60).

8:1-2. For the sacred assembly **Solomon** called in the **elders . . . all the heads of the tribes** and **the leaders of the fathers' households**. Everyone in Israel, from the leadership to each family, was to be represented at the event. The focus of the assembly was **to bring up the ark of the covenant of the LORD** to the temple. It had been in the house of Obed-edom, the Gittite (2Sm 6:10), in **the city of David**, the part of Jerusalem built on the original Jebusite area, south of the Temple Mount. From now on the ark would reside in the holy of holies in the temple (cf. 2Sm 6:16-17). The dedication occurred at the time of sacred assembly **at the feast, in the month Ethanim** (Sept/Oct, also known as Tishri) **. . . the seventh** month, at the Feast of Booths (cf. Lv 23:33-36).

8:3-9. The **ark** and all the **holy utensils** from the **tent of meeting** (cf. Ex 40), the tabernacle, were brought into the temple by **the Levites** (vv. 3-4; cf. Nm 3, 4, 7; 2Sm 6:6-7). At the dedication of the temple there was so much sacrificing occurring simultaneously that the **sheep and oxen . . . could not be counted** (v. 5). As the priests carried the ark on **the poles**, it was eventually placed under **the wings of the cherubim** (vv. 6-8; cf. Ex 25:10-22). If Kings was written or ultimately completed during the time of the exile, then the phrase **they are there to this day** (v. 8) could not be referring to the existence of these poles at the time of the book's completion because the temple and its sacred contents were destroyed in 586 BC. However, as noted in Introduction: Date for this commentary, the author used several sources to compile 1 and 2 Kings. House suggests that when the author referred to these sources he used a phrase like "they are there to this day." In that sense the phrase is a kind of "footnote" referring to an original source (Paul R. House, *1, 2 Kings*, NAC [Nashville: Broadman and Holman, 1995], 30).

8:10-21. Once the ark was in place, **the cloud filled the house of the LORD** (v. 10), a phenomenon frequently associated with the Lord's presence (e.g., Ex 13:21-22; 16:10; 40:33-35; Ezk 10:3-5). Here the manifestation was so overpowering **that the priests could not stand to minister because of the cloud** (v. 11). God, Israel's Great King, had come to dwell with His people. Solomon explained the supernatural phenomenon as a sign of God's fulfilling His promises to David: **Now the LORD has fulfilled His word which He spoke . . . as the LORD promised** (v. 20; cf. 2Sm 7:8-16; 1Ch 22). Solomon also associated the presence of the glory of the Lord with the covenant made **with our fathers when He brought them from the land of Egypt** (v. 21; cf. Ex 15:1-18). Solomon's purpose was to remind the people that God had been true to His Word all along.

8:22-26. In view of God's faithfulness, Solomon offered a lengthy prayer of intercession for himself and his subjects standing **before the altar of the LORD** (vv. 22-53). He acknowledged the Lord's uniqueness: **God of Israel, there is no God like You**. He reiterated God's faithfulness: **keeping covenant . . . with Your servant, my father David** (vv. 23-24).

8:27-30. Solomon also emphasized God' great power: **The highest heaven cannot contain You** (v. 27). Yet intercession directed toward the temple was appropriate, since that was where God said, **My name shall be there** (v. 29; cf. 5:5). God's character was epitomized by the phrase "My name" (cf. Ex 33:19; Dt 12:5; 2Sm 6:2; 7:13; Ps 61:8). Here Solomon established the Jewish custom of turning toward Jerusalem, the location of the temple, **when they pray toward this place** and ask God to **hear in heaven Your dwelling place; hear and forgive** (v. 30; cf. 8:38, 44, 48; Dn 6:10; Ps 5:7).

8:31-40. Solomon interceded on behalf of citizens and underscored their relationship to the Lord as living in the **land** He gave them (vv. 34, 36, 40; cf. Gn 12:1-9). The people were to depend on Him in legal disputes with one another, coming **before Your altar in this house** (v. 31), asking that God would **hear in heaven and act and judge** (v. 32). He also asked for mercy when the nation sinned and were **defeated** in battle when **there is no rain** or **famine** (vv. 33-37). Solomon asked for forgiveness of sin, and for God to **teach them the good way in which they should walk** (v. 36). He asked that **they would fear You** (v. 40), recognizing God's great power and therefore obediently serve Him.

8:41-45. Solomon then prayed for Israel's relationship with non-Jewish people. First, he prayed for mercy for the **foreigner** who learns of **Your great name** (v. 42). This is a prime example of God's desire for the nations, the Gentiles, in the OT to know the Lord, **in order that all the peoples of the earth may know Your name, to fear You, as do Your people Israel** (v. 43). Next Solomon prayed for military victory when following the Lord's direction in **battle . . . whatever way You shall send them**, that He would hear their **supplication, and maintain their cause** (v. 45).

8:46-49. This part of Solomon's prayer was an instruction and warning that looked to the future regarding Israel's exile from the land. When they **sin** and they are taken **away captive**, an event that occurred almost 400 years later at the Babylonian captivity (586 BC), the people were to **pray to** God **toward their land** (v. 48) and repent.

8:50-53. Then Solomon asked God to have **compassion** on the people and **listen to them whenever they call to You** (v. 52; cf. v. 29; Dn 6:1; Ps 137). However, the prayer was not based on the merit of the king or the people, but on the reality that God had **separated** Israel **from all the peoples of the earth as Your inheritance** (v. 53).

8:54-61. With the prayer completed, Solomon turned and **blessed** the people, saying **Blessed be the Lord** (v. 56). This benediction had two elements. First Solomon wanted the prayer to be fulfilled **so that all the peoples of the earth may know that the Lord is God; there is no one else** (v. 60). In that sense his prayer had an outward, evangelistic focus to it. Second, He challenged the people **to be wholly devoted to the Lord our God**, having an inward spiritual focus (v. 61).

8:62-66. Solomon's prayer was followed by a series of sacrifices. The number of animals offered up to the Lord was so great that a minor change of venue had to occur. **The king consecrated the middle of the court . . . for the bronze altar that was before the Lord was too small** to care for the many offerings (v. 64). Great care and caution were undertaken to ensure that God was given the respect that His holy nature deserved. What started out as the observance of the annual seven-day **feast** of booths (8:2) ended up lasting for **fourteen days** (v. 65). However, the ongoing activities were not exhausting to either Solomon or his subjects, because he **sent the people away and they blessed the king**. They were **joyful and glad of heart** because they realized that God, their true King, had blessed them from the days their forefathers experienced Him at Sinai to the completion of the great temple (v. 66).

4. Solomon's Warning from the Lord (1Kg 9:1-9)

Solomon's reign as king had been magnificent in so many ways. God granted him wisdom beyond his years (cf. 1Kg 3:6-15). He had dedicated the temple, and his building projects were fast becoming world renowned (chaps. 6–8). Little did Solomon realize, even with all his wisdom, that he was in danger of making foolish, disastrous decisions. Yet, God would take the initiative to alert Solomon to dangers ahead.

9:1-5. After Solomon had **finished building** the temple, God appeared a **second time, as He had appeared to him at Gibeon** (vv. 1-2; cf. 3:4-15). God assured Solomon that He had heard his prayer at the temple dedication. God's statement, **My eyes and My heart will be there perpetually** (v. 3) refers to His constant presence with His people in the temple. Even though the highest heavens could not contain the living God, He would show His covenant love to His people by residing in a unique way in the temple. However, God's promise was tempered by two conditional warnings. The first warning was stated positively. God promised Solomon that if he would **walk . . . in integrity of heart and uprightness**, then God would establish his throne and he would **not lack a man on the throne of Israel** (vv. 4-5).

9:6-9. The second warning was stated negatively. If Solomon or his sons were to **turn away from following** God they would be **cut off** from the **land** and the **house** (i.e., the temple, v. 7). All would be lost if idolatry replaced the worship of God in the temple. After all, the behavior of the king was the example that the people were to follow (Dt 17:18-20), and that example was to be upright in every way. If the nation followed after other gods, **Israel** would **become a proverb and a byword among all peoples** (v. 7). That is, Israel would become the proverbial example of what life would be like when the Lord is abandoned. These exact predictions were fulfilled when Jerusalem fell to Babylon (cf. Jr 52).

5. Solomon's Splendid Kingdom (1Kg 9:10–10:29)

After the account of Solomon's second encounter with the Lord, there follows a rather lengthy description of what Solomon completed at the end of twenty years of his reign. This is the midpoint of Solomon's 40-year reign from 970–930 BC. Although his kingdom looked glorious, there were early indications of disaster ahead due to Solomon's attraction to foreign women and their idolatry.

9:10-14. After a long trade relationship with **Hiram**, **king of Tyre**, who had **supplied** the **cedar and cypress timber and gold** for Solomon's building projects (v. 11; cf. 5:1-12), instead of paying Hiram with cash and provisions Solomon **gave Hiram twenty cities in the land of Galilee**, the area of northwest Israel not far from Tyre (v. 12). However, these cities **did not please** Hiram, so he called them **Cabul**, a Hebrew word meaning "as good as nothing" (v. 13). Although the cities were worthless to Hiram, he supplied Solomon with **120 talents of gold** (v. 14). Solomon was the dominant monarch in the relationship, and his heart was revealed back in v. 11 in the statement that Hiram gave Solomon wood and gold **according to all his** [Solomon's] **desire**. Material desires were starting to influence Solomon's actions.

9:15-19. This section (vv. 15-24) provides clarification about the **forced labor** Solomon used in his building projects (cf. 5:13). These workers built **the house of the Lord,** as well as Solomon's **own house**. His other projects included **Millo**, probably Solomon's fortifications of Jerusalem, as well as his three chariot cities of **Hazor, Megiddo, and Gezer** (v. 15). These archaeological sites have been identified by their extensive stable areas and matching Solomonic gates. Some of the motivation for building may have come from Solomon's father-in-law, **Pharaoh king of Egypt** who captured **Gezer** (about 20 miles west of Jerusalem), and then gave it as a **dowry** to his daughter (v. 16). **So Solomon rebuilt Gezer** (v. 17) indicates that the gift led to Solomon's rebuilding of the city, perhaps a subtle pressure placed on Solomon by his wife or father-in-law. His other building projects include **cities for his chariots . . . and all that it pleased Solomon to build . . . in all the land under his rule**, indicating the self-focus of his projects.

9:20-24. The laborers who carried out these various building projects were **the people who were left of the Amorities, the Hittites, the Perizzites, the Hivites and the Jebusites** after the conquest under Joshua (cf. Dt 7:1-2). He used manpower not **of the sons of Israel** (v. 22) because Solomon did not turn his own people into **slaves**. His building projects, although impressive, did not endear him to his subjects (cf. 12:4).

9:25. In obedience to the law, **three times a** year, at the three annual pilgrim festivals (the Feast of Unleavened Bread, the Feast of Weeks, and the Feast of Booths; cf. Ex 23:14-17; Lv 23:34-43) **Solomon offered burnt offerings and peace offerings on the altar**. Because he was not a priest, he did not personally make these offerings, but the priests made them on his behalf, as they did for everyone who brought his or her offering to the temple.

9:26-28. Hiram not only supplied lumber for Solomon's buildings, he also supplied **gold** (9:14). Tyre was a sea merchant empire (cf. Is 23:1-8), so when Solomon needed sea power, he asked **Hiram** to send his **sailors** to man the ships. Solomon built a **fleet of** ships on Israel's **Red Sea** port of **Ezion-geber,** which is near Eloth (Israeli's modern port city of Eilat). In partnership with Hiram, ships were sent to **Ophir** (v. 28; the actual location is unknown, but the Arabian coast, the African coast, or India have all been suggested) to acquire **four hundred and twenty talents of gold**, about 16 tons. God had said He would give Solomon riches (cf. 3:13), but there was the serious danger of violating the precautions placed on Israel's king in Dt 17:17b.

10:1-5. Solomon's **fame** spread across the nations, and people wanted to have an audience with him. One such person was **the queen of Sheba**. Sheba was located in southwest Arabia in modern-day Yemen, about 1,200 miles from Jerusalem (not Ethiopia, as commonly suggested). Her arrival in Jerusalem was prompted by what she heard about Solomon's **fame** in connection with **the name of the Lord** (v. 1). She wanted **to test him with difficult questions**, meaning that she tested him with riddles. The Hebrew word translated **difficult questions** refers to a type of dialogue carried out by heads of state in the ancient world. In the course of her visit, the queen of Sheba asked questions and observed all that he had done. What she saw so moved her that **there was no more spirit in her** (v. 5), that is, she was overwhelmed with the splendor of Solomon's kingdom.

10:6-9. The queen of Sheba admitted that what she was told of **the king** was a **true report**, although she did not believe the reports until she heard of Solomon's wisdom firsthand. This led her not only to praise Solomon but also to proclaim the greatness of God. She said, **Blessed be the Lord your God who delighted in you . . .** and **made you king, to do justice and righteousness** (v. 9). Solomon was given a subtle reminder through this wise woman's words that what he had accomplished was the Lord's doing.

10:10-13. Sheba ended her visit by giving to Solomon gifts before returning home: **Never again did such abundance of spices come in as**

that which the queen of Sheba gave King Solomon. Solomon joined again in partnership with Hiram to bring **gold** from **Ophir**; Solomon was accumulating gold from a variety of sources (vv. 10, 11; 14; cf. 9:11). And yet God had warned all the kings of Israel to avoid what appeared to be the ever-increasing power of self-indulgence (cf. Dt 17:17)

10:14-25. Solomon's accumulation of **gold** is a key idea, mentioned 11 times in this section (vv. 14, 16-18, 21-22, 25). In **one year** alone Solomon received **666 talents of gold**, about 25 tons (v. 14). But in addition, Solomon was receiving tax revenues from **traders . . . merchants and all the kings of the Arabs and the governors of the country** (v. 15). Solomon put his accumulating wealth to impressive use in making **shields** (vv. 16-17), his **great throne** (vv. 18-20), and even **drinking vessels** (v. 21) out of gold. In comparison to the gold in his kingdom, silver **was not considered valuable in the days of Solomon** (v. 21). Those who were around Solomon in Jerusalem were impressed with his buildings, his **gold and silver, ivory and apes and peacocks** (v. 22). Not only had he been blessed with great wisdom, but also **King Solomon became greater than all the kings of the earth in riches and in wisdom** (v. 23). Yet no one except God, the true King, would see how all these material things were influencing Solomon's heart. Apparently, large amounts of wealth also came from those monarchs like the queen of Sheba when they had an audience with Israel's king (vv. 24-25).

10:26-29. The final section of chap. 10 summarized the high point of Solomon's reign. What God had promised Solomon (chaps. 3–5) had surely come to pass. However, Solomon appeared to be motivated perhaps more by material accumulation than by spiritual allegiance. Solomon imported **horses . . . from Egypt and Kue**, probably Cilicia in modern Turkey (v. 28). The king who was to meditate on God's law daily (cf. Dt 17:18-19) was living contrary to this same law by sending merchants back to Egypt, a place where the Lord told them to "never go back that way again" (Dt 17:16). Instead of growing closer to the Lord spiritually, Solomon's heart was headed in a different direction, propelled by luxury and fame.

C. Solomon's Divided Heart and Spiritual Decline (1Kg 11:1-43)

After an initial impressive reign, Solomon's monarchy came to a tragic end because he turned to the worship of idols. God had used him to build the temple and unite the people. People everywhere came to Israel's king to interact with his wisdom and to observe the great building projects he undertook. But in spite of great accomplishments, Israel's glory would never again be the same, for at the end of his reign Solomon's kingdom would be divided. Solomon's choices, both good and bad (but especially bad), would be repeated by his offspring. The people in exile, for whom 1 and 2 Kings were written, would read of Solomon's exploits and grieve over the consequences of his sin. But the ultimate aim of this record would be for the readers in exile to ponder the severe consequences of sin, to return to the Lord consistent with Solomon's prayer at the dedication of the temple (cf. 8:46-53), and to keep looking forward to the promised messianic King.

11:1-5. Solomon's downfall politically and spiritually was the result of his heart being turned away from the Lord because of his love for **many foreign women along with the daughter of Pharaoh**. He took these wives **from the nations concerning which the Lord** had clearly said, **You shall not associate with them . . . for they will surely turn your heart away after their gods** (v. 2; cf. Dt 7:3-4; 17:17). The magnitude of his spiritual betrayal was evident in the multitude of women whom Solomon married or had in his harem—**seven hundred wives, princesses, and three hundred concubines** (v. 3). A **concubine** was a female companion or slave with whom her master had rights to sexual relations, but who was not a legal wife; whereas a queen was a **wife** legally married to the king, and her children were legitimate heirs. Although the Lord created marriage to be between one man and one woman (cf. Gn 1:27; 5:2; Mk 10:5-9), by the patriarchal period it was not unusual for men to have more than one wife, often with disastrous consequences. However, in Solomon's case his multiple wives/concubines were unheard of in magnitude, and the disastrous results were likewise monumental. The severity of the problem was also amplified with the acknowledgement that Solomon **held fast to these** pagan women **in love**, and **his wives turned his heart away after other gods** (vv. 3-4).

11:6-13. The king's love for foreign women caused him to take even more heinous action. He built high places **for Chemosh the detestable idol of Moab** and **for Molech the detestable idol of the sons of Ammon** (v. 7; cf. Lv 18:21). These religions demanded vile worship practices including child sacrifice to these gods. Solomon made provision for **all his foreign wives, who burned incense and sacrificed to their gods** (v. 8). At the same time, God was true to His Word regarding punishment for idolatry (cf. 9:6-9). **The LORD was angry with Solomon because his heart was turned away from the LORD** (v. 9). The judgment for his sin was Solomon's loss of the kingdom, as the Lord said, **I will surely tear the kingdom from you, and will give it to your servant** (v. 11). The only comfort Solomon had was that God would not do it in his lifetime, but in the lifetime of his **son** (v. 12). The unexpected reprieve was **for the sake of My servant David** because of David's loyalty to God, and **for the sake of Jerusalem**, the city God had **chosen** as the place where His name would be exalted (v. 13; cf. 9:3; 2Sm 7:13; 2Kg 19:34; 21:4-8; Ps 132).

This entire section is the narrative proof that Solomon, despite building the first temple, did not fulfill the messianic promise of 2Sm 7:12-16. Hence, Israel was to keep looking for the Son of David who would obey the law perfectly and fulfill the promises made to David (cf. 2Sm 7:12-16, see discussion at 1Kg 6:11-13).

11:14-22. The LORD raised up three enemies as adversaries against **Solomon**. First, **Hadad the Edomite** was from the **royal line in Edom**. His bitterness toward the house of David originated when **Joab**, David's military commander, had gone to Edom **to bury the slain** (2Sm 8:13-18). Joab apparently went beyond his assignment and **struck down every male in Edom** (vv. 14-16). **Hadad fled to Egypt** with **certain Edomites** (v. 17) as well as men from **Paran**. While in Egypt, Hadad gained the favor of **Pharaoh**, who gave him **a house** . . . **land** . . . and a **wife** (vv. 18-19). He also had a son, **Genubath** (v. 20), whose name means "to steal," which may reflect Hadad's thinking that the household of David had stolen the lives and lands of people he loved. However, on learning of both David's and Joab's deaths, Hadad sought permission from the pharaoh to return to his own country (vv. 21-22). He was only one of three enemies of Solomon in the remaining years of his reign.

11:23-28. The second adversary God **raised up** was **Rezon**, who had **fled from his lord Hadadezer king of Zobah,** a city-state south of Damascus (v. 23; cf. 2Sm 8:3-6; 10:8) Apparently sometime after his escape from Hadadezer, Rezon organized a **marauding band** that became a thorn in Solomon's side **all the days of Solomon** (vv. 23-25). This was in the second half of Solomon's monarchy, since there was "safety" in the land during the earlier part of his reign, while he was building the temple (1Kg 4:25). Instead of being adored by visiting heads of state, now Solomon was confronted with the likes of Rezon, who **abhorred Israel** (v. 25) and her king from his kingdom in **Aram** (in modern-day Syria).

11:26-28. A third adversary was **Jeroboam the son of Nebat, an Ephraimite** and a **servant** of Solomon. This was the adversary who would eventually become king. The **reason** Jeroboam **rebelled against the king** is detailed (v. 27). Jeroboam was **a valiant warrior** and **industrious** (v. 28a). So Solomon **appointed him over all the forced labor of the house of Joseph** (v. 28b). As an Ephraimite, Jeroboam was a descendant of one of the sons of Joseph (cf. Gn 41:52; Joseph was not given his own tribal land allotment, but each of his two sons, Manasseh and Ephraim, was awarded territory, as detailed in Jos 16–17). Ephraim was one of the northern tribal areas in Israel. So it was expedient for Solomon to place Jeroboam over the **forced labor of the house of Joseph**; however, setting up Jeroboam in this area would lead to a division of Solomon's kingdom.

11:29-37. Jeroboam's life and the future of Israel are brought into focus by the God-ordained meeting with **the prophet Ahijah** (v. 29; cf. 12:15). Ahijah's presence was a subtle introduction to the influence that prophets would have in the two new kingdoms that were about to emerge. The prophet's message to Jeroboam took the form of an object lesson using the prophet's **new cloak, which** Ahijah **took hold of** in Jeroboam's presence and **tore it into twelve pieces** (v. 30). Jeroboam was then instructed to take **ten** of the **pieces**, because the prophecy informed Jeroboam that he would rule over **ten tribes** and Solomon's successor would rule over **one tribe** (vv. 31-32). But what about the twelfth tribe? The small tribe of Benjamin was viewed in such close association with Judah that it was counted together (cf. 12:21).

Ahijah said the reason for the upcoming division was **because they**, the people of Israel, had **forsaken** the Lord and worshiped the idols of the **Sidonians** . . . **Moab** . . . and **Ammon** (v. 33). However, the tribe of Judah would maintain a part of the kingdom, **one tribe, that My servant David** [his descendants] **may have a lamp** [a perpetual presence] **always** before the Lord **in Jerusalem, the city where I have chosen for Myself to put My name** (vv. 34-36; cf. 8:44, 48;

11:13, 32; 2Ch 6:34, 38; Zch 3:2). Even at the declaration of the division of the kingdom, God confirmed the Davidic covenant. The prophecy to Jeroboam was repeated to add emphasis to what was about to transpire: Solomon's kingdom would be divided and Jeroboam was to be **king over Israel** (v. 37).

11:38-40. Ahijah the prophet informed Jeroboam that if he was obedient to the Lord, He would give him **an enduring house**, that is, a lasting dynasty. However, the Lord's promise to David would not be broken, for although Judah would be afflicted, it would be temporary, **but not always** (v. 39). When Solomon learned of this prophecy of Jeroboam taking over the kingdom he **sought therefore to put Jeroboam to death**. The future king of the northern tribes fled to Egypt to live **until the death of Solomon** (v. 40). Because a new pharaoh, **Shishak**—not Solomon's father-in-law—was now ruler in Egypt, Solomon no longer had a matrimonial alliance with Egypt. This reference to another potential adversary heightened the political tensions for Solomon, who years earlier experienced peace all around his borders (1Kg 4:25).

11:41-43. The closing account of Solomon's reign introduced a formula that appears throughout the remaining accounts of the kings in 1 and 2 Kings. Four elements in the formula appear frequently. First, there is the identification of a resource for further inquiry. In this case the resource was **the book of the acts of Solomon** (v. 41). This first element subtly implied that the author was writing about historical events to provide *theological* insight as to why the nation would eventually end in exile. The original readers could check out historical facts through any one of three source documents—"the book of the acts of Solomon," "the Book of the Chronicles of the Kings of Israel" (cf. 14:19), and "the Book of the Chronicles of the Kings of Judah" (cf. 15:7). These chronicles were not the same as the biblical books of 1 and 2 Chronicles and are no longer extant. They were independent sources that monarchs in the ancient world kept for historical documentation (cf. 14:19).

The second element to define a given king's reign was the length of his reign and the place where he ruled. In Solomon's case it was **in Jerusalem** for **forty years** (v. 42). The third element identified the place of burial. When Solomon died, or **slept with his fathers** (v. 43), **he was buried in the city of his father David**, the original part of Jerusalem captured by David, where he had built his palace (cf. 2Sm 5:7-11). And the final element was the naming of the king's successor. In this case Solomon's son, **Rehoboam**, would rule in his place. But his reign would differ greatly from Solomon's. In fact, the days of Israel's glory were now gone, and a new age of spiritual, political, and economic decline was about to begin.

II. The Divided Kingdom: Northern Israel and Southern Judah (1Kg 12:1–2Kg 17:41)

The account of the divided kingdom of Israel begins in 1Kg 12:1, tracing the northern kingdom of 10 tribes under non-Davidic kings and the southern kingdom of Judah and Benjamin under kings from the line of David. However, there were two story lines in the record, one explicit and one implicit. The first had to do with the decisions that the human kings made in exercising what they assumed were their legitimate rights and responsibilities. At another level, the true King, God Almighty, was exercising His full authority over His people who were increasingly rebelling against His covenant reign over the nation and their lives. From this point onward, throughout 1 and 2 Kings, the kingdoms of Israel and Judah were in decline because of their disobedience to the Lord. The original audience of 1 and 2 Kings, the people in the Babylonian exile and beyond, could see why the nation ended up in exile, without a Davidic king on the throne, and needed to continue to wait for the promised messianic Son of David.

A. Rehoboam of Judah and Jeroboam of Israel (1Kg 12:1–14:31)

1. Rehoboam's Reign: Foolish Choices and Their Consequences (1Kg 12:1-19)

12:1-5. Rehoboam was 41 years old (cf. 14:21) when he **went to Shechem** to be made **king** (931–913 BC; 2Ch 9:31–12:16). Shechem was an important city in the northern tribal territory of Ephraim (cf. Gn 12:6; 33:18-20; Jos 8:30-35). It was here that Joshua renewed the covenant between the Lord and His people near the end of his ministry (Jos 24). Perhaps Rehoboam chose that location to identify himself with that former leader of Israel. Whatever the case, the majority of the nation's leaders, **all Israel**, gathered there to **make him king** (v. 1).

When **Jeroboam heard** of Rehoboam's coronation, he returned from **living in Egypt**, where he had **fled** from **King Solomon** (v. 2; cf. 1Kg 11:30-40). Jeroboam, along with **the assembly of Israel**, appealed to King Rehoboam to **lighten**

the hard service (the **yoke** was **hard**) Solomon had placed on them (v. 4). They told Rehoboam **we will serve you** if he would meet their request. This was not an unreasonable request in view of the massive building projects Solomon had undertaken that taxed the citizens in the form of labor and money. Rehoboam agreed to take their request under advisement for **three days**, then give them his answer (v. 5).

12:6-11. During the three-day interim, Rehoboam consulted with two groups. He first contacted **the elders who had served his father** (v. 6) and had observed the consequences of Solomon's extravagance. The elders counseled young Rehoboam to **speak good words** (v. 7) to his subjects, with the prospect of winning these citizens as his **servants forever**. But Rehoboam refused their counsel and sought the advice of the **young men who grew up with him** (v. 8). His peers suggested that even though Solomon had surely made their **yoke heavy**, Rehoboam was to **add to** their **yoke**. The words echoed the suffering that the Israelites had experienced at the hands of the Egyptians many years earlier when they were forced to make bricks without straw (vv. 10-11; cf. Ex 5:7-18). The Mosaic law instructed the king to fear the Lord and never put himself above his countrymen (cf. Dt 17:20), but Rehoboam's young advisers suggested that he was to say (v. 11), **My father disciplined you with whips, but I will discipline you with scorpions**. Rehoboam's young advisers were using hyperbole to make the point that life under his rulership would be even more demanding than what Solomon's reign had been.

12:12-15. On **the third day** Rehoboam **answered the people harshly**, just as his **young men** had advised (vv. 13-14). Although he refused to **listen to the people**, what was taking place **was a turn of events from the Lord** (cf. 11:11). This is one of the clear texts in Scripture that reveals God's sovereignty in bringing about His will, while also operating within what appears to be a personal sinful choice on the part of human beings. God had foretold what would happen to the kingdom (cf. 11:29-38). Yet, God also set before Rehoboam two choices—one that would endear him to the people, and another that would bring about serious harm to the kingdom that David and Solomon had united over the years.

12:16-19. Hearing of King Rehoboam's decision, **all Israel** gave their own verdict on what they had just heard. It is best to understand that **all Israel** referred to all the tribes of Israel, the majority of the people as a group. By responding, **What portion do we have in David?** (v. 16), they indicated they no longer felt allegiance to Rehoboam, the Davidic king. Then the people declared, **We have no inheritance in the son of Jesse** (cf. 1Sm 16:18; 1Ch 29:26). Solomon had placed the nation under oppressive economic conditions, and Rehoboam would make it worse. Therefore **Israel departed to their tents**, an idiom for their homes, rather than rallying in support of Rehoboam. Now, because of Rehoboam's foolish decision, the once-glorious kingdom of David was divided between 10 tribes who would sit under the reign of Jeroboam as Israel and two tribes of the **cities of Judah** that would follow **Rehoboam** as Judah (v. 17).

The prophet Ahijah stated that 10 tribes would come under the leadership of Jeroboam and one tribe would remain loyal to Rehoboam (cf. 11:31-32). Yet Rehoboam ruled over two tribes: Judah and Benjamin. At this time the tribe of Benjamin was counted as part of **Judah** (cf. 12:21, 23) because of its geographic proximity, its small size, and its loyalty to the house of David (see comments above on 11:29-37). Most important in the unfolding of God's revelation, and the record of the kings, is the significant role that Judah played in God's plan. Ten tribes would constitute the northern kingdom and one tribe, Judah, would be the primary player in the spiritual and political events of the southern kingdom, because the Davidic kings were from the line of Judah. The significance of the kings of Judah is apparent in the parallel texts of 1 and 2 Chronicles.

When **King Rehoboam** saw he had lost the majority of the nation, he apparently sent **Adoram** (cf. 2Sm 20:24; 1Kg 4:6; 5:14) as his representative to the rebels in a hopeful attempt to reunite the kingdom; however, **all Israel stoned him to death** (v. 18). Rehoboam **made haste . . . to flee to Jerusalem** for his safety.

So Israel has been in rebellion against the house of David to this day (v. 19). The term "rebellion" (*pasha'*) is often used in both a theological and a political sense. Certainly the ten northern tribes rebelled against the rule and reign of Rehoboam, the Davidic king. But the term implies spiritual rebellion as well. The temple was still in Jerusalem, and the people were to worship God in accord with His commandments in this one place (cf. 8:12-30; Dt 12:13-14). Failure to do so would be more than political treason; it would also be spiritual rebellion.

2. Jeroboam's Coronation as King of Israel (1Kg 12:20-24)

12:20-24. In response to Rehoboam's harshness, when **all Israel heard that Jeroboam had returned . . . they made him king over all Israel**, the 10 northern tribes (931–910 BC; cf. 2Ch 9:29–13:22). However, **the tribe of Judah followed the house of David**, ruled by Solomon's son, King Rehoboam (v. 20; cf. 12:17). After attempting to bring the tribes back into unity through his servant Adoram (v. 18), **Rehoboam** rallied **180,000 chosen men who were warriors** from **Judah** and **Benjamin . . . to fight against the house of Israel to restore the kingdom** (v. 21). Rehoboam tried to reunite his kingdom by force, but God had another plan. The **word of God came to Shemaiah the man of God** (v. 22; cf. 2Ch 12:15) to inform Rehoboam, **You must not . . . fight against your relatives the sons of Israel** (v. 24). Although Rehoboam had already refused wise counsel that led to division in the kingdom, he **listened to the word of the LORD** and civil war was temporarily prevented (cf. 14:30).

3. Jeroboam's Self-Deception and Sinful Choices (1Kg 12:25-33)

12:25. To defend his new kingdom, **Jeroboam built Shechem**, the key city in **the hill country of Ephraim** (v. 25; cf. 12:1) and made it his capital. This city was important not only for religious reasons, but also was on the main east-west trade route, making it a strategic city of the northern kingdom. The city of **Penuel** (also called Peniel, v. 25; cf. Gn 32:30-31) was also on a caravan route that went from Gilead to Damascus, a south to north route, and a key defensive city against attack from Damascus.

12:26-27. Jeroboam was concerned about defection as well as defense. He realized the **kingdom** (the people) **would return to the house of David** because they needed to **go up to offer sacrifices in the house of the LORD at Jerusalem.** To prevent the people from going back to **Rehoboam**, and worshiping in Judah, Jeroboam devised a plan in his **heart** for a whole new religious scheme (vv. 26-27, 33). Years later Jeremiah reminded the people that nothing good would come out of a corrupt, sin-infested heart (cf. Jr 17:9). And in Jeroboam's case, his unbridled fear of losing his kingdom (v. 27) led to a loss of faith in the Lord and the development of a new national religious system, a corrupted worship of the Lord, and increasing faith in his own devices.

12:28-33. Jeroboam's new religious system involved five elements: (1) new objects of worship in the form of the **golden calves** (v. 28); (2) new places of worship at **Bethel**, the center, and **Dan**, in the far north of his kingdom (v. 29); (3) new buildings of worship in the form of **houses on high places** (v. 31); (4) a new non-Levitical priesthood to lead in the newly established worship (v. 31); and (5) a new **feast** to compete with the Feast of Booths (v. 32). In affirming his new religion, King Jeroboam said: **Behold your gods, O Israel, that brought you up from the land of Egypt** (v. 28). Jeroboam combined the pagan calf symbol, familiar to the Arameans and Canaanites, with the worship of the Lord, and he used the same idea as Aaron had with the worship of the golden calf at the exodus (cf. Ex 32:4-5). The parallel account indicates that the Levitical priests sensed the corrupted religious practices in Jeroboam's plan, because they left the northern kingdom and joined with Rehoboam (cf. 2Ch 11:13-17). **This thing became a sin, for the people went to worship before the one as far as Dan** (v. 30), the farthest northern city. Jeroboam would soon have to face the consequences of his lack of faith and disobedience against Israel's true King.

4. Jeroboam, God's Word, and Spiritual Rebellion (1Kg 13:1-34)

God had promised Jeroboam that obedience to His Word would bring him an "enduring house," similar to the one He promised to David (cf. 1Kg 11:38). But the preceding chapter indicated that Jeroboam had greater fear of people than he did of God. This chapter now shows the serious consequences of refusing to take God at His Word.

13:1-10. The phrase **Now behold** is a rhetorical device to draw attention to the lesson given to **Jeroboam** as he stood by the pagan **altar** he had built at **Bethel** (cf. 12:32). Three primary characters appear in the narrative of chap. 13: **a man of God from Judah** (v. 1); Jeroboam, the king (v. 4); and an **old prophet . . . living in Bethel** (vv. 11-34). The **man of God** was a prophet who came with a special calling from God. Four times it is said he either came **by the word of the LORD** or delivered it (vv. 1-2, 5, 9), indicating both his calling from God and the authority behind his message. The prophet gave two signs to add powerful credibility to his words. A **sign** (Hb. *mopheth*, "wonder" or "portent") denotes a miracle that communicates a message from God. These were the same kind of miraculous interventions God worked through Moses and Aaron when they appeared before the pharaoh in Egypt (see the use of the same word in Ex 4:21; 7:3).

First, he gave a long-range sign, crying out **against the altar**, that a future **son** would be **born to the house of David** who would **sacrifice the priests of the high places** and **human bones** on this same altar (v. 2). He even went so far as to identify this future king as **Josiah**, who reigned about 300 years later and fulfilled the prophecy exactly (cf. 2Kg 23:15-20).

To prove the long-range prophecy would occur, he also gave a prophecy that had an immediate fulfillment. The prophet from Judah gave the **sign** that **the altar shall be split apart and the ashes which are on it shall be poured out** (v. 3). When Jeroboam ordered his guard to **seize** the prophet, the king's hand was paralyzed, **dried up** (v. 4). Immediately, the **altar split apart**, in front of King Jeroboam and those who came to worship with him, **according to the sign which the man of God had given by the word of the Lord** (v. 5). The destruction of the altar at Bethel demonstrated the Lord's rejection of this syncretistic worship (cf. Lv 6:10-11) This man who was attempting to exercise both political and religious power suddenly found himself under the power of Almighty God. Jeroboam sensed his helplessness, and in a panic he sought the aid of the prophet. **Please entreat the Lord your God, and pray for me, that my hand may be restored to me** (v. 6). God answered his request and **the king's hand was restored**. Significantly, Jeroboam referred to the Lord as **your God**, not as his God.

Apparently impressed by his hand being cured, King Jeroboam may have thought he could persuade the man of God to join forces with him. So he invited him to come to the king's home to refresh himself and to receive a **reward** (v. 7). But the prophet was under orders that **came by the word of the Lord** (v. 1). God had informed him that he was to **eat no bread, nor drink water, nor return by the way which** he **came** (v. 9). In other words, he was not to linger once his task was accomplished. The word "return" plays a key role in the rest of chap. 13 (it recurs in vv. 9, 10, 16, 17, 22, 33). However, he did "return" to another prophet's house and would face the consequences of disobeying God (vv. 18-19). And Jeroboam "did not return from his evil," and his high-handed disobedience would cost him his kingdom (v. 33).

13:11-19. The third major character in the narrative was introduced as **an old prophet . . . living in Bethel** (v. 11). He learned about the events at Jeroboam's altar through the eyewitness testimony of **his sons**. This prophet was not identified as a prophet of the Lord and his behavior indicated he was not a man of God. After learning the direction in which the **man of God** headed, the old prophet set out to meet him (v. 13). When the two men met, the old prophet asked the man of God, **Come home with me and eat bread** (v. 15). The man of God recited the same statement he had given to Jeroboam earlier, **I cannot return with you** (v. 16; cf. vv. 8-9 above). However, to add force to his invitation the old prophet stated that he had received information from **an angel** (v. 18) telling the man of God that he was to return. Surprisingly, the prophet from Judah did not inquire of the Lord or ask further questions, but accepted the invitation. But the text reveals that the old prophet **lied to him**, and the prophet of Judah believed the lie without question (vv. 18-19). God had spoken to a king and to a prophet from Judah. But both took the path of disobedience toward destruction.

13:20-25. After deceiving the man of God from Judah, **the word of the Lord came to the** [old] **prophet** (v. 20). The statement is strikingly familiar to what the man of God had originally received as **the word of the Lord** (cf. vv. 1-2, 5, 9). Just as the prophet from Judah had spoken God's very words to Jeroboam, now the old prophet **cried to the man of God who came from Judah** (v. 21). Two words capture the essence of this second prophecy. The man from Judah was told, **Because you have disobeyed the command of the Lord . . . your body shall not come to the grave of your fathers** (vv. 21-22).

The word translated "disobeyed" literally means "to rebel"; he had rebelled by failing to obey the word of the Lord spoken to him. His sin was as wicked as Jeroboam's, and it was ultimately against Israel's true King. The Hebrew word "grave" (*qeber*) refers to the family tomb. For a person to be buried away from the family tomb was a sign of dishonor, and in this case it was also an indication of the severe judgment of God. Although the prophet from Judah left the old prophet safely, **a lion met him on the way and killed him** (v. 24). However, contrary to usual lion behavior, it did not devour the prophet or kill the donkey, but **was standing beside the body**. As people passed by, they observed this strange scene and reported it **in the city where the old prophet lived** (v. 25).

13:26-32. Word eventually reached the old prophet, who said, **It is the man of God, who disobeyed the command of the Lord; therefore the Lord has given him** [the prophet from Judah] **to the lion . . . according to the word of the Lord** (v. 26). God was demonstrating to the residents of the northern kingdom that His Word is holy and that disobedience brings dire consequences. So the old prophet brought the body and placed it **in his own grave** (v. 30), bringing the younger prophet some respect despite his careless disobedience. But the old prophet recognized the gravity of all that had happened: **For the thing shall surely come to pass which he cried by the word of the Lord against the altar in Bethel and against all the houses of the high places which are in the cities of Samaria** (v. 32). The city of Samaria, seven miles northwest of Shechem (cf. 12:1), became the capital of the northern 10 tribes (cf. 16:24), but the name was more generally applied to the central area of Israel.

13:33-34. Although confronted by such dramatic examples of prophecy and judgment, Jeroboam did not repent of his sin of establishing an alternate religious system in Israel. Instead, he **did not return from his evil way** (v. 33). As a result, **This event became sin to the house of Jeroboam, even to blot it out and destroy it from off the face of the earth** (v. 34). The conditional promises in 1Kg 11:38 would not be fulfilled. God's word was to be heeded! Again disobedience resulted in serious consequences.

5. The Consequences of Jeroboam's Disobedience (1Kg 14:1-20)

14:1-5. Even though Jeroboam returned to his evil ways, God was not yet done with the first king of the northern kingdom. A third prophecy came to Jeroboam during the sickness of his son **Abijah**. So Jeroboam sent his wife to **Shiloh**, north of Bethel (cf. Jos 18; Jdg 21:19) to inquire of the now aged prophet **Ahijah** (cf. 11:29-39). The king apparently thought he could control his own destiny, or perhaps even manipulate the prophet of God, so he told her to **disguise** herself so that the prophet would **not know that** she was **the wife of Jeroboam** (v. 2). He also sent a personal gift to the prophet (v. 3). However, Jeroboam either forgot or simply did not know that God sees everything. Thus **the Lord** informed the aged, blind prophet (v. 5) that the king's wife was on her way to inquire of him. Ahijah was told, **say thus and thus to her**, a rhetorical device used for dramatic effect to condense the message that would be revealed in vv. 6-16. The Lord also told Ahijah, **she will pretend to be another woman** (v. 5).

14:6-11. Jeroboam's wife was met **with a harsh message** from Ahijah. The prophecy moved from the immediate situation in Jeroboam's life to the ultimate fate of the northern kingdom. Judgment was about to be delivered with: (1) the cause stated in vv. 7-9, (2) the impact of the judgment on Jeroboam's household, specifically in vv. 10-11, and (3) the impact for the northern kingdom of Israel in vv. 12-16. Ahijah announced that Jeroboam had **done more evil than all who were before** him by devising the religion of the golden calves (v. 9; cf. 12:25-33). Jeroboam had **made . . . other gods and molten images to provoke** the Lord **to anger**. The severity of his actions was captured in the words you **have cast Me behind your back** (v. 9). The series of metaphors highlights the gravity of what God was about to do in Israel. The Lord also announced through Ahijah that He would **cut off from Jeroboam every male person . . . and . . . make a clean sweep of the house of Jeroboam** (v. 10). The Lord would end Jeroboam's family line from any future leadership of Israel because of Jeroboam's wicked plan of leading Israel into idolatry.

The cause of the upcoming judgment was Jeroboam's establishment of the pagan alternative worship of the Lord with the golden calves—a direct violation of the Word of God (cf. Ex 34:17; Dt 27:15). Because of Jeroboam's sin, **the dogs** would **eat** his offspring who died in the city, a disgusting, tragic end (v. 11; cf. 16:4; 21:19, 24). In the ancient world, dogs were not domesticated pets. Left unfed, they became scavengers, roaming in feral packs, ready to eat anything. In Ahijah's prophecy the dogs amplify the defilement brought on by Jeroboam's religious apostasy, an apostasy that was deserving of the judgment of God.

14:12-14. Only Jeroboam's son, Abijah (v. 1), would be spared the horrid judgment because **the child** would **die** when his mother returned home from inquiring of the prophet, and **all Israel shall mourn for him and bury him** (v. 13). Despite Jeroboam's wickedness, his son was identified as a person in whom **something good was found toward the Lord God of Israel in the house of Jeroboam**. The treatment given the son indicated that there was grace from God even in the application of divine judgment. After the respectful burial of the child, **the Lord will raise up for Himself a king over Israel who will cut off the house of Jeroboam** (v. 14).

14:15-18. After God's condemnation of the house of Jeroboam, the prophecy expanded to include the future of the entire northern kingdom. The sinful acts propagated by Jeroboam would permeate the behavior of the entire citizenry. The nation would be unstable, the way **a reed is shaken in the water** (v. 15). They would be scattered **beyond the Euphrates River**. This scattering was fulfilled when the northern kingdom fell to Assyria in 721 BC (cf. 2Kg 17). Again the reason for God's condemnation was idolatry, specifically **their Asherim, provoking the LORD to anger** (v. 15; cf. v. 23; 15:13; 16:33). Asherim were wooden poles, phallic symbols, located near groves of trees and part of a pantheon of Canaanite gods. Asherah was one of the fertility goddesses worshiped by the northern tribes at their high places. When **Jeroboam's wife** returned **to Tirzah**, their home (cf. 1Kg 16:23), as she crossed **the threshold** of the royal household, the boy **died**. This was **according to the word of the LORD . . . through His servant Ahijah the prophet** (vv. 17-18; cf. v. 12 above).

14:19-20. The **acts of Jeroboam** were **written the Book of the Chronicles of the Kings of Israel**, not the biblical book of Chronicles, but a history of the kings of Israel, no longer extant, frequently referred to in 1 and 2 Kings (e.g., 15:31; 16:5, 14, 20, 27; 22:39; 2Kg 1:18; 10:34; 13:8, 11). The monarchy of the first king of Israel was summarized as **the time that Jeroboam reigned was twenty-two years** (v. 20). The mention of the succession of "Nadab his son "was a temporary reign that lasted two years (cf. 15:25), when Nadab was killed "according to the word of the LORD, which He spoke by His servant Ahijah" (15:29).

6. Rehoboam's Reign in Judah (1Kg 14:21-31)

The account of the reigns of the kings of Israel and Judah are often given in alternating sections in 1 and 2 Kings, and often their reigns were overlapping (cf. Introduction: Background). The following section continues the rule of Rehoboam in Judah (cf. 12:1-24).

14:21. King **Rehoboam**, after his foolish choices (cf. 12:1-19) at the time of his ascension (age **forty-one**), **reigned seventeen years in Jerusalem, the city which the LORD had chosen from all the tribes of Israel** (v. 21; cf. comments above at 8:29; 11:13).

14:22-24. A spiritual assessment of the kings is made throughout 1 and 2 Kings. From the outset of the divided kingdom, even **Judah did evil in the sight of the LORD** (v. 22). One would think that this would be said of Rehoboam, but the evaluation is of the whole southern kingdom—Judah— to show that what the king chose to do spiritually affected the entire nation. And the nation's choices **provoked** the Lord **to jealousy**. In terms of God's character, this emotion is related to His right to exclusive love and worship. His jealousy leads Him to warn His people about being spiritually unfaithful to Him. When they are unfaithful, He becomes "jealous"—a virtual synonym for "angry"—because His people have attached their affections to some false god, and He then judges them for their spiritual adultery.

The specific sins that motivated God to engage in His righteous jealousy were identified in as the **high places and sacred pillars and Asherim** (v. 23; cf. comments on 14:15 above). These were religious objects that probably had existed in the land for centuries, since Israel failed to dispossess the nations and their evil ways, according to 1Kg 9:20-21. The "sacred (stone) pillars" represented the presence of various gods, and the Asherah poles were symbols of various fertility gods, forbidden by the Lord (cf. Ex 23:24; Lv 26:1; Dt 16:21-22). There were also **male cult prostitutes**, as part of the pagan worship, **according to all** the pagan practices **of the nations** (v. 24). All of these practices prompted **the LORD** in righteous jealousy to act on behalf of His name (cf. 1Kg 5:5; 11:36; Is 48:11).

14:25-28. The Lord then raised up an adversary against Rehoboam, **Shishak the king of Egypt**. Prior to the reign of Shishak, peaceful relations existed between Egypt and Israel, especially after Solomon's marriage to Pharaoh's daughter (cf. 3:1). Paul House points out that the once-declining nation of Egypt experienced a short political and military revival when Egypt's 21st dynasty was overthrown by a popular Libyan noble named Shishak (House, *1, 2 Kings*, 195). No information was given as to why he attacked Judah, but for whatever reason, he came against Rehoboam and **took away the treasures of the house of the LORD and the treasures of the king's house** (vv. 25-26). The specific items that were surrendered to Shishak to avoid devastation of the city were the **shields of gold which Solomon had made** (cf. 10:17). To replace these, **Rehoboam made shields of bronze**. The change from gold to bronze, a much less expensive metal, indicated the decline in the wealth of the kingdom under Rehoboam after great glory under David and Solomon.

14:29-31. The details, **the rest of the acts of Rehoboam** during his reign of 17 years are recorded in **the Book of the Chronicles of the Kings of Judah** (cf. the comments on 11:41-43; 14:19). Two items of particular significance were mentioned. First, there was **war between Rehoboam** and **Jeroboam continually**. Despite the Lord's having forbidden civil war (cf. 12:14), there were battles between Israel and Judah until the alliance between Ahab and Jehoshaphat (cf. 2Ch 18:1–19:3). Second, Rehoboam's mother was **Naamah the Ammonitess** (v. 31; cf. v. 21; 2Ch 12:13), one of Solomon's wives from Ammon (cf. 1Kg 11:1). This pagan nation east of the Jordan was frequently in conflict with Israel (cf. Gn 19:30-38; Dt 23:3; 1Sm 11:1-15), and Ammonites were specifically forbidden to be part of the assembly of Israel (cf. Dt 23:3; Neh 13:1-2). Rehoboam's failure to follow the Lord was compounded by his mother's pagan influence. And what impacted the king would also have spiritual consequences for the people.

B. The Kings of Judah and Israel until the Fall of Israel to Assyria (1Kg 15:1–2Kg 17:41)

The reigns of Rehoboam and Jeroboam's successors demonstrated the consequences of spiritual compromises. Through the kings, God was calling His covenant people to rely on Him for all things. After all, He is the true King and protector of His people.

1. Abijam of Judah: A Bad King (1Kg 15:1-8)

15:1-2. The next king over **Judah** was **Abijam,** or Abijah as a variant spelling in some translations (913–911 BC; cf. 2Ch 13:1-22). The typical pattern for identifying the kings of Judah, including their mothers' names, follows: Abijam's mother was **Maacah the daughter of Abishalom** (v. 2). Since she is also identified as the daughter of Uriel (2Ch 13:2), it is likely she is the granddaughter of **Abishalom**, (that is David's son, Absalom), since biblical genealogical references often skip one or more generations.

15:3-8. Abijam **walked in all the sins of his father**, implying that the idolatrous practices Rehoboam modeled were now practiced by his son. And the reason for this was that **his heart was not wholly devoted to the Lord his God, like the heart of his father David** (v. 3), his great-grandfather. Although David fell into grievous sin (cf. 1Sm 11), he never swerved into paganism, but always worshiped only the Lord. Thus, David was the standard for devotion through Kings and Chronicles (cf. 1Kg 11:4, 6; 15:3, 11; 2Kg 14:3; 16:2; 18:3; 2 Ch 29:9).

Mention of David was important because on one hand the severity of sin was increasing, but on the other hand God was gracious to Judah **for David's sake** (v. 4). This was a subtle reference to the Davidic covenant (cf. 2Sm 7:12-14). God was gracious to Abijam in spite of his idolatrous ways because He had promised to give David **a lamp in Jerusalem** (v. 4; cf. 11:36)—an ongoing heir to the Davidic throne. The reason for God's kindness to David was **because David did what was right in the sight of the Lord** (v. 5). He had committed adultery and the horrible murder of **Uriah the Hittite** (2Sm 11:14-27), but David had never resorted to idolatry.

One consequence of the division of the kingdom was war between the tribes of Israel and Judah. The conflict was stated both as **war between Rehoboam and Jeroboam** (v. 6) and **war between Abijam and Jeroboam** (v. 7). That is, the northern and southern kingdoms, Israel and Judah, were engaged in a sin-induced conflict.

2. Asa of Judah: A Good King (1Kg 15:9-24)

15:9-10. Following Abijam's death after only a three-year reign (v. 2), **Asa** succeeded him as king in Judah (911–870 BC; cf. 2Ch 14:1–16:14). He **reigned forty-one years in Jerusalem**. A surprising introductory statement about Asa was that **his mother's name was Maacah the daughter of Abishalom** (v. 9). Possibly this is a statement of generational lapses as in Abijam's case (cf. 15:1-2). However, Provan makes the case that in view of all the idolatrous sins that Asa had to deal with in 1Kg 15, and in view of the removal of Maacah (v. 13), it is highly probable that Asa was the product of an incestuous relationship between Abijam and his mother, Maacah (Iain W. Provan, *1 and 2 Kings,* NIBC [Peabody, MA: Hendrickson, 1995], 126).

15:11-15. Asa was one of the eight good kings of Judah. He was commended because he **did what was right in the sight of the Lord, like David his father** (v 11; cf. comments above on 15:3-8). David was identified again as the great model of spiritual devotion. Whereas David fought against Israel's pagan enemies and ultimately united the tribes of Israel into one great nation, Asa was portrayed as the one who fought against idolatry. He **put away the male cult prostitutes . . . and removed all the idols which his fathers had made** (v. 12). Of particular note were his dealings with **Maacah his mother**, whom he **removed** as the **queen mother** because she had **made a horrid image as an Asherah** (v. 13; cf. 14:15, 23). Asa **burned** the horrid image (idol) she made **at the brook Kidron** outside of Jerusalem.

Asa attacked idolatry with a vengeance, and in turn, out of his devotion to the Lord, he even **brought into the house of the LORD the dedicated things** (v. 15). These were items presented as offerings and gifts in honor of God. The only apparent shortcoming in Asa's reign was that **the high places were not taken away** (v. 14), perhaps because they were so well established as part of the society (v. 14). This is another example of even the good kings of Judah failing to follow the Lord perfectly.

15:16-22. Asa also made important political decisions regarding his kingdom. **There was war between Asa and Baasha king of Israel all their days** (v. 16). The severity of Baasha's threat to Judah was that he started to fortify **Ramah in order to prevent anyone from going out or coming in** to renew an alliance with **Asa** (v. 17). **Ramah** was an important city in the tribal territory of Benjamin (cf. Jos 18:25), the other tribe allied with Judah against the 10 northern tribes (cf. 12:21). Ramah was also just four miles north of Jerusalem, making Baasha's activities a very serious threat to King Asa's reign. In an attempt to strengthen his kingdom, Asa **took all the silver and the gold which were left in the treasuries of the house of the LORD . . .** and **the king's house** and sent them by his servants to **Ben-hadad . . . the king of Aram** on Israel's northern border (v. 18). Asa sought to make a treaty with Ben-hadad, and also asked him to break an earlier treaty with Baasha (v. 19).

Ben-hadad agreed to the offer and **sent . . . his armies against the cities of Israel and conquered** the northern cities of **Ijon, Dan . . .** and **all the land of Naphtali** (v. 20). As a result, **Baasha . . . ceased fortifying Ramah** (v. 21). There is no mention here of a prophet who came and rebuked Asa for not seeking the Lord's help, and for relying instead on one who would become a growing threat against the tribes of Israel (cf. 2Ch 16:7-12). The broad purpose of Kings is history, while the purpose of Chronicles concerns the spiritual decision of the house of David (see Introduction). The omission of the record of a prophet's visit shows the political emphasis of Kings. However, the information in Chronicles reveals that even though most of his life was one of devotion to the Lord, Asa also suffered from bouts of spiritual amnesia, trusting in men rather than the promised strength of the Lord (cf. 2Ch 16:7-10; Dt 28:7).

15:23-24. Even though Asa was identified as a good and devoted king, his last years were not without difficulty. Because of his failure to call on the Lord for help, Asa faced war throughout his reign. Asa reigned 41 years (15:10), and in the 39th year of his reign, in **his old age he was diseased in his feet**, yet "he did not seek the LORD, but the physicians" to relieve his pain (2Ch 16:12). This health report, coupled with Asa's failure to seek the Lord's help from all his enemies, indicates his overall failure to depend upon the Lord in a variety of circumstances. This reminded the exilic audience that Asa was partially negligent in seeking the strong support of the Lord—physically, politically, and spiritually (cf. 2Ch 16:9), and that there were serious consequences as a result.

3. From Nadab through Omri: Increasing Spiritual Decline in Israel (1Kg 15:25–16:34)

This final section about the early days of the divided kingdom describes an obvious downward political and spiritual free fall. Seven kings over a period of 56 years are described in terms of their rise to power and horrid demise. But there is a phrase that holds the section together and explains why these historical events happened as they did. That phrase, "according to the word of the LORD," appears three times (15:29; 16:12, 34). What took place was not by chance. The Lord God of Israel ordained and predicted the ultimate outcome, and it happened in every case just as He said it would. The background to these events was Ahijah the prophet's rebuke of King Jeroboam for his idolatrous actions, telling the king's wife that God was about to "make a clean sweep of the house of Jeroboam" (14:10; cf. vv. 6, 20). Ahijah also prophesied events beyond Jeroboam's family. God consistently warned Jeroboam through the prophet that as evil increased, political stability would decrease, and that "the Lord will strike Israel, as a reed is shaken in the water" (14:15).

15:25-26. The end of the house of Jeroboam is recorded by reintroducing his son, **Nadab** (cf. 14:19-20). His reign lasted only **two years** (910–909 BC). As with all those who ruled in the northern kingdom, Nadab **did evil in the sight of the LORD, and walked in the way of his father**.

15:27-31. In fulfillment of Ahijah's earlier prophecy, **Baasha** (909–886 BC; cf. 2Ch 16:1-6) was also reintroduced after the brief explanation about his wars with Asa in 15:17-22 (cf. v. 32). Baasha **conspired against** his predecessor

Nadab and struck him down while the reigning king was attacking the Philistine-occupied town of **Gibbethon**, located between Jerusalem and Joppa (v. 27; cf. Jos 19:43-45). Baasha assassinated Nadab, and also **struck down all the household of Jeroboam**, not leaving a single heir alive (v. 29; cf. 14:10).

God in His providence ordained the demise of Jeroboam's kingdom and even the elimination of his heirs, but His providence never excludes the choices of people. Because God is sovereign, even the sinful acts of human beings coincide with His sovereign plans. Indeed, God uses people's sinful actions to accomplish His purposes. But this does not relieve the sinner of the guilt for his sin; God cannot be charged with the evil human beings commit (cf. Jms 1:13). This is one of the most profound mysteries in the Bible. Baasha's own determination was directly connected to his own spiritual decisions and the annihilation of Nadab's family (cf. 16:7). (For a brief discussion of the interaction between God's sovereignty and human responsibility, see the comments on Rm 9:18-23.) The details of the **acts of Nadab** are **written in the Book of Chronicles of the Kings of Israel** (v. 31; cf. comments above on 11:41-43; 14:19).

15:32-34. The account of Baasha's rise to power serves as a transition from the reign of Jeroboam to the lengthy reign of the dynasty of the house of Omri in 16:16. Even though Baasha was fulfilling the prophetic statements of Ahijah recorded in chap. 14, he **did evil in the sight of the LORD, and walked in the way of Jeroboam** (v. 34; cf. 16:2, 26; 22:52), worshiping idols. This phrase is in stark contrast to walking in the way of David (cf. 15:3).

16:1-5. Like his predecessor Nadab, Baasha pursued the idolatrous ways of Jeroboam. As a result, God sent a prophet in the person of **Jehu** to announce judgment on Baasha. Jehu informed him that as with Jeroboam God would **consume . . . his house** (v. 3). One reason for this divine judgment was Baasha's idolatrous lifestyle and because he "struck down all the household of Jeroboam" (15:29; 16:7). This was not simply a matter of removing Nadab from power. God was also condemning the intense brutality with which Baasha carried out his actions. This reveals the sovereignty and omniscience of God over human responsibility.

16:6-14. The transition to the dynasty of Omri continued with the rise of Baasha's son, **Elah** (886–885 BC) **who became king over Israel at Tirzah** (v. 8). He reigned only **two years**, until he was assassinated by **Zimri** his **commander** (vv. 8-10). When **Zimri** (885 BC) **became king in** Elah's **place,** he **destroyed all the household of Baasha, according to the word of the LORD, which He spoke against Baasha through Jehu the prophet** (16:12; cf. 16:7).

16:15-24. But Zimri's reign as king was one of the shortest of all of the kings of Israel. He ruled for only **seven days at Tirzah** (v. 15). When the people who were fighting against the Philistines heard of what happened, **all Israel made Omri** (885–874 BC) **the commander of the army, king over Israel** (v. 16). Ahijah's prophecy that Israel would be like a "reed shaken in the water" (14:15) came true. For a period of time there was political instability in the northern kingdom on several fronts.

First, Zimri realized that his power base was extremely weak. So **he went into the citadel of the king's house and burned the king's house over him with fire, and died** (i.e., he committed suicide, v. 18). But this was not simply an act of desperation, for this happened **because of his sins which he sinned** (v. 19). Zimri, like those before him, followed the idolatrous ways of **Jeroboam**.

Second, the **people of Israel were divided** (v. 21); half wanted to make **Tibni** king, while the other half **followed Omri**. Omri eventually prevailed and a second major dynasty to replace Jeroboam's rule came into existence. The record is simple: **Tibni died and Omri became king** (v. 22). Very little historical detail was given about Omri's rule, except that he **reigned twelve years; he reigned six years at Tirzah** (v. 23). Perhaps because a royal palace in Tirzah had been previously burned by Zimri, Omri may have felt compelled to establish a new royal palace. So he **bought the hill Samaria from Shemer . . . and built on the hill** the city of **Samaria** (v. 24). Samaria would become the key city that identified the place of residence for the northern kings, but also a symbol of intense religious apostasy against the Lord.

Although the biblical text is brief regarding Omri's reign, extrabiblical history indicates that he was a man of international importance. His name appears on the Moabite Stone, the black basalt memorial stone erected about 850 BC memorializing the deeds of King Mesha of Moab. There Omri is referred to as the one who captured a fertile and militarily strategic region known as the Moabite Plains (R. D. Patterson and Hermann J. Austel, "1 & 2 Kings," in vol. 4 of EBC [Grand Rapids, MI: Zondervan, 1988], 135). When Tiglath-pileser II of Assyria captured Israel, he referred to Israel in his annals as "the house of Omri."

16:25-28. Omri did evil in the sight of the Lord, and acted more wickedly than all those who were before him, thus showing the downward spiral of the kings of Israel (v. 25). After all, **he walked in all the way of Jeroboam** . . . (v. 26). After his death, **Ahab his son became king in his place** (v. 28).

16:29-33. Ahab (874–853 BC; cf. 2Ch 18:1-34), the son of Omri, Israel's most wicked king, reigned in Samaria for twenty-two years. As did his father before him, Ahab pursued a life of spiritual rebellion. He participated in evil more than all who were before him (v. 30). His sins are evident in four specific acts. (1) He married Jezebel the daughter of Ethbaal king of the Sidonians (v. 31). Like Solomon before him, Ahab's decision to marry Jezebel, who introduced Baal worship to Israel, was a clear violation of Scripture (cf. Dt 7:1-5). In Ahab's mind it was a trivial thing to commit sins such as marrying a pagan wife (v. 31). The word "trivial" is from the Hebrew word *qalal*, meaning "swift," "trifling," or "insignificant." Ahab did not care if his choice of a wife offended the Lord. (2) Ahab also went to serve Baal and worshiped him (v. 31). He did not just drift toward idolatry, he intentionally went **to serve** the fertility god of the Canaanites, and led the nation to follow in his idolatry (cf. 18:1-46; 22:53). (3) He also **erected an altar for Baal** in a temple he built in Samaria (v. 32). (4) He **also made the Asherah** (v. 33, cf. 14:15, 23). Thus Ahab is remembered as Israel's most wicked king because he **did more to provoke the Lord God of Israel than all the kings of Israel who were before him** (v. 33).

16:34. Jericho had been rebuilt as an unwalled city after Joshua's day (cf. Jos 18:21; Jdg 3:13; 2Sm 10:5). However, when **Hiel the Bethelite built Jericho** . . . **Abiram his firstborn** son died when **he laid** the **foundations** of the city and **his youngest son Segub** died when he **set up the gates**. His plan to rebuild a fortified city ended in tragedy, just as the Lord predicted. The rebuilding of Jericho was forbidden **according to the word of the Lord, which He spoke by Joshua** after God's supernatural destruction of that city, and the warning of the death of the firstborn was specific (cf. Jos 6:26). God had clearly spoken in Joshua's day, and He was still speaking in Ahab's lifetime. Rejecting God's ways was no "trivial thing" (cf. 1Kg 16:31). God was still the true King of Israel, and His word was to be heard and heeded. If the kings would not model God's will and ways, then the Lord would send His prophets, Elijah and Elisha, to call the people back to God's reign in their lives.

4. Ahab and the Prophet Elijah: The Supremacy of God over Nature (1Kg 17:1–22:40)

Following Solomon's spiritual demise, 1 and 2 Kings record few monarchs who were faithful representatives of God and His covenant. As a result, the Lord sent prophets to call the kings and the people to return to Him and His covenant promises. The two most notable prophets to the northern kingdom were Elijah and Elisha. Their mission was to bring various indictments against the northern kingdom. God used them to announce judgments and also to demonstrate His supremacy over absolutely everything.

a. Elijah and the Prophets of Baal (1Kg 17:1–18:46)

Although the divisions of chaps. 17 and 18 may imply different themes, the chapters together constitute one narrative unit. Chapter 17 introduces the tension of a famine brought on by God and introduced through the prophet Elijah. Chapter 18 brings resolution to the famine and demonstrates that God is supreme over nature and Baal, the god that Ahab and Jezebel so wickedly served. Baal worshipers believed that their god made rain and was responsible for fertility throughout the land. If a drought occurred, Baal worshipers believed that their god was residing in the place of the dead and needed to be brought back to life. However, Elijah would show that Baal was not dead or incapacitated for a season. He simply did not exist.

17:1-7. Elijah, whose name means "the Lord is my God," appeared on the pages of biblical history unannounced. He was **Elijah the Tishbite, who was of the settlers of Gilead**. Gilead was east of the Jordan River across from the Jezreel Valley (cf. Dt 34:1), but the exact location of Tishbi cannot be identified with any certainty. The prophet quickly announced to **Ahab** that there would be **no dew or rain**, except by the word of Elijah.

Almost as quickly as Elijah was introduced, he disappeared from King Ahab's presence because the Lord told him to **hide yourself by the brook Cherith**, east of the Jordan River (v. 3).

In the first of several demonstrations of His power over nature, the Lord **commanded the ravens to provide** for Elijah and they **brought bread and meat** to Elijah in the morning and evening (vv. 4-6). However, God was about to show His power to the prophet and a small Sidonian household in a still more dramatic way. So to move the prophet to his next task, **the brook dried up, because there was no rain in the land** (v. 7). God was using several aspects of nature to manifest His superiority over Baal.

17:8-16. A second miracle of provision occurred unexpectedly through a poor widow. Again God's influence was made known when He **commanded a widow . . . to provide** for Elijah (v. 9), and He enabled her to do so with a miraculous provision. The event occurred in **Zarephath**, a town in Sidon about 45 miles northwest of the Sea of Galilee on the Mediterranean coast. This was a Gentile region outside of Israel in the very center of Baal worship.

On his arrival Elijah met the woman appointed by God to provide for his physical needs (v. 10). When the woman proceeded to meet his request for water, Elijah asked the woman, **Please bring me a piece of bread in your hand** (v. 11). The request would reveal how severe the famine was both in Israel and in Sidon, as the woman acknowledged that she had **no bread**, and **only a handful of flour** (v. 12). In fact, the woman informed the prophet that she was about to prepare a final meal for herself and her **son**, so that they could **eat it and die**. However, Elijah encouraged her: **Do not fear** what might happen, but simply obey his request. She would then be able to **make** bread **for** herself **and for** her **son** (v. 13). Elijah informed her that if she did so the flour would not be **exhausted** . . . or the oil **empty** (v. 14). Miraculously, **the bowl of flour was not exhausted nor did the jar of oil become empty** (v. 16). There was an unending supply of four and oil to make plenty of bread. Her obedience quickly led to the revelation of God's power and faithfulness.

17:17-24. A third miracle-laden event soon followed: **Now it came about after these things** (v. 17). Good things had happened to Elijah, the widow, and her son. But now an even more severe crisis occurred when the widow's son **became sick** and eventually died. The widow interpreted her son's death as simply Elijah's way of bringing her **iniquity to remembrance** (v. 18). The widow felt that Elijah's presence in her home had caused God to recall her (unnamed) past sins, and the Lord was punishing her by putting her **son to death**.

Instead of answering her, Elijah confidently said, **Give me your son** and carried him to **the upper room** of the house **where he was living** (v. 19). He inquired of the Lord regarding the **calamity** (v. 20) and engaged in an unusual act in which life seemed to have been transferred from himself to the boy. He **stretched himself upon the child three times, and called to the Lord** . . . to **let this child's life return to him** (v. 20). In answer to his prayer, **the Lord heard the voice of Elijah, and the life of the child returned to him and he revived** (v. 21). As a result of the Lord's supernatural intervention, the woman made two important conclusions: (1) that Elijah was **a man of God**, and that (2) **the word of the Lord . . . is truth** (v. 24). The Lord was progressively building the case that He, not Baal, was the One who is supreme over nature and life.

18:1-2. A fourth miracle is introduced to convince the people of Israel that the covenant-keeping God is sovereign over everything. This miracle took place **in the third year**, which refers to the third year of the famine (cf. 17:1). In accord with the Lord's command, Elijah was told that he was to **show yourself to Ahab**, and in turn God would **send rain on the face of the earth** to end the drought and bring the famine, which was **severe in Samaria**, to a close. Obeying the Lord's command, Elijah proceeded to **show himself to** (meet) **Ahab**.

18:3-16. Although most of the northern kingdom had abandoned the Lord to follow paganism, a remnant remained faithful to the God of Israel. One of Ahab's servants, **Obadiah**, who was **over the household**, a high-ranking position, **feared the Lord greatly** (v. 3). Obadiah even risked his life by hiding **a hundred prophets** of the Lord **in a cave** to protect them from the annihilation policies of **Jezebel** (vv. 4, 13). Ahab had sent Obadiah to search for **springs of water . . . and keep the horses and mules alive** (v. 5). On the way, this godly servant met **Elijah** (v. 7), who had been in hiding from Ahab who was searching for him in every **nation** and **kingdom** (v. 10; cf. 17:3-24). The prophet told Obadiah to go announce to the king that **Elijah is here** (v. 8). Obadiah understood the command as an indictment of some sin in his life, because Elijah apparently had a reputation for appearing in one place and then disappearing to another (cf. 2Kg 2:16).

Obadiah was sure that if he announced Elijah was coming to Ahab, but then Elijah failed to appear, **he** [Ahab] **will kill me** (vv. 12, 14). Elijah reassured Obadiah that **as the LORD of hosts lives** (v. 15), he would surely appear before Ahab. Obadiah obeyed the prophet's order then, **and Ahab went to meet Elijah** (v. 16).

18:17-19. When the two men met, a debate ensued that centered on who was the true cause behind the devastating famine. Ahab called Elijah the **troubler of Israel**. Elijah in turn indicted Ahab as the real culprit, **because** he had **forsaken the commandments of the LORD and . . . followed the Baals** (v. 18). The word for "troubler" translates the Hebrew word *'oker*, used elsewhere in the OT to refer to individuals who brought spiritual pain and tragedy to the nation (cf. Jos 6:18; 7:25). To verify his claim that Ahab was the troublemaker, Elijah proposed a test to take place on **Mount Carmel**. Ahab was to bring from among the corrupt spiritual leaders of Israel **450 prophets of Baal and 400 prophets of the Asherah** (v. 19). Apparently only the prophets of Baal showed up (vv. 22, 25, 40).

18:20-24. In response, **Ahab . . . brought the prophets together at Mount Carmel** (v. 20), a hill close to modern-day Haifa that comprises the northwestern end of a range of hills known as the Carmel range. When the prophets of Baal arrived, Elijah spoke to **all the people**, for apparently there was a crowd assembled there to see the confrontation between the prophets and Elijah. The prophet challenged the populace immediately by asking them, **How long will you hesitate between two opinions?** (v. 21). The word translated as "hesitate" (Hb. *pasach*) literally means "to limp" or "to dance." It is used again to refer to the type of ritual dance the prophets of Baal engaged in to get their god's attention (v. 26). Overall, the word refers to the spiritual indecision that existed in the minds of the people.

For dramatic effect Elijah did two things. First, he stated that he alone was the only **prophet of the LORD** who was left with courage enough to come to meet the prophets of Baal (v. 22). The other prophets were in hiding (vv. 4, 13). Second, he proposed that the prophets of Baal would be given an **ox** for sacrifice, and he would also be given an **ox**. Then each would **prepare** the ox for sacrifice with **wood** but **not put a fire under it** (v. 23). He and the prophets of Baal would call on their respective deities to answer by fire to consume the respective offerings. Elijah stated, **the God who answers by fire, He is God** (v. 24). The people agreed that Elijah's proposal was good.

18:25-29. The subsequent events took place over an entire day. The prophets of Baal called on their god first, **from morning until noon saying, O Baal, answer us** (v. 26). By midday there was no answer, and Elijah **mocked** his opponents: **Call out with a loud voice . . . either he is occupied or gone aside, or is on a journey, or . . . asleep** (v. 27). The prophets of Baal **cried with a loud voice and cut themselves according to their custom**, as part of their religious ritual (v. 28). Although they **raved until . . . evening** there was **no voice** in answer from Baal (v. 29).

18:30-35. Then it was Elijah's opportunity to call on the Lord. **He repaired the altar of the LORD which had been torn down**, perhaps by Israelites who no longer worshiped the God of Israel but had torn down the Lord's altars to worship pagan gods (v. 30; cf. 19:14). Thus the construction of an altar was not a contradiction of earlier statements where the high places were condemned (cf. 12:31-32; 15:14). This was the **altar of the LORD**, not an altar for Baal worship. Elijah used **twelve stones** in its construction to symbolize the twelve tribes of Israel, **the tribes of the sons of Jacob**, and reminded the people that the Lord had said, **Israel shall be your name** (v. 31). Also when the **fire of the LORD fell**, it even consumed the stones that Elijah had used for his temporary altar (cf. v. 38).

Before actually calling on the Lord, Elijah heightened the tension even further by constructing what would appear like an impossible task. After arranging the wood and the sacrifice he poured **water . . . on the wood** and the sacrifice three different times so that **the water flowed around the altar and . . . also filled the trench** (vv. 33-35). It might seem that Elijah was sabotaging his own challenge for God to answer by fire. However, God was about to show His power and to force the people to identify with either Baal or the Lord.

18:36-40. After everything was in place, Elijah prayed (cf. Jms 5:18), addressing the Lord by his covenant name **O LORD, the God of Abraham, Isaac and Israel** (v. 36). He wanted four things to happen as a result of the upcoming miracle: (1) that the people would know that only the Lord was **God in Israel**, (2) that Elijah was His **servant**, (3) that all that was about to happen was according to the Lord's **word**, and (4) that the Lord would have **turned their heart back again** to follow Him (vv. 36-37).

Almost immediately and without Elijah having to cajole his God as the Baal prophets did with their god, the **fire of the LORD** fell and consumed everything on the altar—the **burnt offering**, the **wood**, the **stones**, and the **dust** and even **licked up the water in the trench** (v. 38). Without any prompting on Elijah's part, **when all the people saw it, they fell** down in worship and declared, **The LORD, He is God; the LORD, He is God** (v. 39). The verdict was in, and Baal had been defeated. **Elijah** immediately ordered, **Seize the prophets of Baal** and had them executed at **the brook Kishon** at the foot of the Carmel range (v. 40). The elimination of the prophets may have seemed like a brutal act, but these same individuals had been misleading God's covenant people for years, and drastic action had to be taken (cf. Dt 13:1-11). False prophets could not be allowed to exist in company with God's people.

18:41-46. The dramatic events at Mount Carmel led Elijah to take the first steps in announcing that the famine was about to end. In spite of Ahab's obvious humiliation, **Elijah** said to **Ahab**, to celebrate the end of the drought, **Go up, eat and drink; for there is the sound of the roar of a heavy shower** (v. 41). God's grace was being extended to the land. **Elijah went up to the top of Carmel**, where he **crouched down on the earth** (v. 42). The text does not give any further detail as to what Elijah was actually doing when he crouched down, but Jms 5:18 connects the events of 1Kg 18:43-44 with prayer (see the comments on Jms 5:15-18).

Finally a **small cloud** appeared on the seventh watch. With this small cloud in view, Elijah ordered **Ahab** to take his **chariot** to his palace in the **Jezreel** Valley (where he had his winter capital between Mount Carmel and Samaria; cf. 21:1), **so that the heavy shower does not stop you** (v. 44), making it impossible to travel by chariot. The prophet, apparently thinking that idolatry had been finally defeated, also headed in the same direction on foot. And because **the hand of the LORD** was on him, Elijah **outran Ahab to Jezreel** (v. 46). Baal worship had suffered a significant setback, but Elijah was soon to face a new challenge of his own when he finally arrived in Jezreel (cf. 19:1-2).

b. Elijah Fears for His Life and Is Comforted by the Lord (1Kg 19:1-21)

19:1-8. Elijah and the people of Israel had just witnessed the power of God over nature and the gods of Ahab and Jezebel. At Mount Carmel the people echoed the words, "the LORD, He is God; the LORD, He is God" (18:39). But things were about to change at Jezreel when **Jezebel** learned **all that Elijah had done**, particularly that **he had killed all the prophets** of Baal (v. 1). She sent **a messenger to Elijah** threatening to end his life by the next day (v. 2). Despite Elijah's recent victory over the false prophets, and the Lord's miraculous display of power, Jezebel now caused the prophet to be **afraid**, and he **ran for his life** (v. 3). He ran 120 miles south to **Beersheba**, one of the southernmost towns in **Judah** (cf. 1Sm 3:20). He concluded that he was no **better than** his deceased **fathers** (v. 4), a statement that simply means "Take my life; I am as good as dead already."

However, the Lord dealt with him the same way He did earlier (chap. 17), by providing him with food and protection. On this occasion an **angel** came to him twice to minister to his physical needs, saying, **Arise, eat** (vv. 5, 7). The Lord understood the emotional and physical exhaustion Elijah experienced after his confrontation with the prophets of Baal and the escape to Beersheba, **because the journey is too great for you** (v. 7). Under orders from the angel, Elijah **arose and ate and drank, and went in the strength of that food forty days and forty nights to Horeb, the mountain of God** (v. 8). **Horeb**, an alternate name for Mount Sinai, is in the wilderness about 250 miles south of Beersheba (cf. Ex 3:1; 19:1-3). **Elijah** was nourished the same length of time as Moses on Mount Sinai (cf. Ex 24:18; 34:28) and Jesus in the wilderness (cf. Mt 4:2, 11).

19:9-10. Elijah left Beersheba and **came to a cave** somewhere near Mount Horeb. This was the very same place where God had revealed His covenant stipulations to Moses, and here Elijah needed a renewed perspective on life. **The word of the LORD came to him**, asking a question to get his attention and to change his perspective. The Lord twice asked, **What are you doing here, Elijah?** (vv. 9, 13). In despair, Elijah concluded that his zeal for the Lord was futile. All he could think about was that, of all the prophets, he **alone** [was] **left**, and his life was in jeopardy (vv. 10, 14).

19:11-14. While still in a state of despair, Elijah was told to **stand on the mountain before the LORD**. The scene was similar to the one when God passed by Moses so that he could catch a glimpse of God's glory (cf. Ex 33:21-23). However, here Elijah was about to receive insight into how Israel's covenant-keeping God was able to reveal Himself. It was not in **a great and strong wind**, in **an earthquake**, or in a **fire** (vv. 11-12). The text does not even say that the Lord was in the **gentle blowing**. But by implication it seems that Elijah experienced a variety of natural forces on the mountain to show him that God can reveal Himself in a variety of ways. Elijah explained to the Lord the reason for his depression: **I have been very zealous for the Lord, the God of hosts; for the sons of Israel have forsaken Your covenant, torn down Your altars and killed Your prophets with the sword. And I alone am left; and they seek my life** (v. 14).

There are some remarkable parallels between Elijah's experience at Mount Horeb and Moses' experiences. First, while Moses spent 40 days on Mount Horeb (Ex 34:28), Elijah took 40 days to get there (1Kg 19:8); Elijah was in **a cave** (19:9), probably an allusion to the "cleft of the rock" in which Moses found himself in Ex 33:22. God was said to "pass by" both Moses (cf. Ex 33:22) and Elijah (1Kgs 19:11), the same word in both passages, and both received a vision of God (for Moses, see Ex 34; for Elijah, see 1Kg 19:11-13). Furthermore, like Moses, Elijah contended on behalf of God against apostates, called for a decision to follow God, and went to Horeb for reassurance. Elijah's theophany shared with the theophany given to Moses and Israel the elements of wind, earthquake, and fire (for these elements in Moses' experience, see Ex 19:9; 20:18-19; Dt 4:9-10; 5:24-25).

Despite these parallels, however, the writer of 1 Kings probably showed a fundamental disparity between the two individuals, not a correlation. In the exposure he had to God, Moses received encouragement for his work (cf. Ex 6; 19:1-25; 32:7-17; 33:23-23), but the interaction of Elijah and God was essentially a decommissioning of Elijah as a prophet. Elijah did not appear to have learned much, if anything, in the theophany he experienced, nor did he hear much in the **gentle blowing** (v. 12). Elijah was decidedly pessimistic about his brethren (1Kg 19:14 is a veiled condemnation of Israel by Elijah; see Rm 11:2, where Paul said Elijah "pleads with God *against Israel*"), rather than an intercessor on behalf of the people as Moses was. The question asked twice by God in 1Kg 19:9 and 13 suggests that God had not actually approved Elijah's trek to Mount Sinai. These differences indicate that Elijah was *not* a new Moses, and that God was not beginning a radically new movement through him.

All of this tends to emphasize the point made overtly in 1Kg 19:18, namely, that God Himself would preserve a faithful remnant that would not worship Baal, and that He would do this sovereignly and graciously apart from Elijah's work. Elijah was certainly a hero, but apparently toward the end of his ministry he had become worn out and needed to transfer the prophetic ministry to another (for more on this section, see Michael G. Vanlaningham, "Paul's Use of Elijah's Mount Horeb Experience in Rom 11:2-6: An Exegetical Note," *The Master's Seminary Journal* 6 [Fall, 1995]: 223-32).

19:15-18. The word of the Lord came again to Elijah, telling him to **return on** his **way to the wilderness of Damascus** (v. 15). He was God's messenger to the northern kingdom and needed to be about God's work. Specifically, he was to **anoint** three individuals: **Hazael king over Aram** (v. 15); **Jehu . . . king over Israel** (v. 16); **and Elisha . . . as prophet** in Elijah's **place** (v. 16). Only the last anointing was actually carried out by Elijah, while Elisha actually anointed the two kings, leading some commentators to ponder whether Elijah lived out his earthly ministry in disobedience (Provan, *1, 2 Kings,* 147), or that God chose to curtail Elijah's ministry in light of Elijah's determination to appoint himself as Israel's "new Moses" (see the comments on 19:11-14 above; Vanlaningham, "Elijah's Mount Horeb Experience," 229-30, n. 17).

However, the text does not actually condemn Elijah's behavior, and the nature of biblical prophecy does not demand that Elijah would actually anoint all three individuals identified in vv. 15-16. Both Elisha and John the Baptist would minister "in the spirit and power of Elijah" (Lk 1:17; and see the comments on Mt 11:13-15), that is, they would both serve with a special anointing from God and with a ministry akin to Elijah's. Elisha would complete the ministry of Elijah, but he would not be alone in following the Lord, for there would be **7,000 in Israel . . . that have not bowed to Baal** . . . or **kissed him** (v. 18), that is, they had not worshiped Baal. God was about to establish a new order in accord with His ways, and Elijah was the first to hear about it.

19:19-21. Elijah obeyed and **found Elisha, the son of Shaphat**, who would be the next major prophet to the northern kingdom. The fact that this farmer, who was about to become a prophet, had so many oxen—**Elisha . . . was plowing with twelve pairs of oxen before him**

(v. 19)—indicated that he and his family were people of substantial financial means. **Elijah . . . threw his mantle on** Elisha (v. 19), symbolically showing that the prophetic power was passing from one man to another. Also of significance is the fact that just as God passed by Elijah (v. 11) to reveal His ways to the prophet, now Elijah also **passed** by Elisha (v. 19) to communicate God's will.

Elisha **left the oxen and ran after Elijah**, indicating his desire to enter the prophetic office. His only request was that he might **kiss** his father and mother as a farewell gesture. He was abandoning his former life to become Elijah's servant and protégé (vv. 20-21). Elijah may have sensed that, despite his victory at Mount Carmel, Baal was not defeated. But God had now revealed that He was present and still about to do a mighty work in the northern kingdom.

c. Ahab and God's Supremacy over Military Power (1Kg 20:1-43)

Following the prophecies made to Elijah in 1Kg 19:15-16, one would expect that Hazael or Jehu would be anointed for their respective posts. But the narrative takes an unexpected turn as God continued His dealings with Ahab. The LXX reverses chaps. 20 and 21, apparently in an attempt to keep the relationship between Elijah and Ahab intact. However, the Hebrew text makes a strong connection between the king's attitude in 20:43 and what was revealed about him in 21:4. The reader must keep in mind the primary focus of the chapter, namely, that it was the Lord's intention to show His power to Ahab once again, so that the king would know that the Lord was God, the true King of Israel (20:13, 26).

20:1-6. One of the constant threats the northern kingdom faced was frequent invasions from **Aram** (Syria) in the north. **Ben-hadad** assembled an army of **thirty-two kings** and **went up and besieged Samaria and fought against it** (v. 1). Ancient extrabiblical records indicate that confederations of kings were common in the ancient Near East (Patterson and Austel, "1 & 2 Kings," 153). This **Ben-hadad** was not the same king of Aram identified earlier (cf. 15:17-20). More likely this is Ben-hadad II (c. 860–843 BC), because of the statement that he agreed to return to Ahab the cities his father had taken (cf. 20:34). Ben-hadad's military tactic was one of intimidation. He **sent messengers** to **Ahab**, telling him that he was about to take his **silver . . . gold** . . . and **your most beautiful wives and children** (vv. 2-3). Ahab agreed to the demands, saying, **I am yours, and all that I have** (v. 4). Then Ben-hadad sent messengers a second time to announce that he was coming **tomorrow** to take everything that was **desirable** in Ahab's eyes. The threat indicated that Ben-hadad wanted to reduce Ahab to his vassal (vv. 5-6).

20:7-12. Ahab, **the king of Israel**, suddenly realized the consequences of Ben-hadad's threat and sought the counsel of **the elders of the land** (v. 7). Their advice was to **not listen or consent** (v. 8). When Aram's king learned of Ahab's decision, he increased the verbal intimidation. Ben-hadad said, **May the gods do so to me and more also, if the dust of Samaria will suffice for handfuls for all the people who follow me** (v. 10). He was saying that total and complete destruction of Samaria would not satisfy his army. Ahab in turn cautioned Ben-hadad, **Let not him who girds on his armor boast like him who takes it off** (v. 11). The battle had not yet been fought, and Aram's king needed to remember not to boast too soon (v. 12).

20:13-21. Ahab had not sought the counsel of the Lord, but God in His grace sent **a prophet** to inform Israel's king that God would deliver him. Ahab in turn would **know that I am the LORD** (v. 13). When he inquired as to who would lead the battle, the prophet informed him that it would be **the young men** and Ahab himself (v. 14). The Hebrew term for "young men" (*na'are*) throughout 1 Kings always refers to those unschooled in military affairs; a youth in contrast to a trained warrior (cf. 1Sm 17:33). This lends itself to the drama of the passage where the enemy seemed to be overwhelmingly large and Israel appeared to be weak and inexperienced. The number **7,000** (v. 15) is the same as the number of the faithful remnant in 19:18. While these are not the same people, the writer of 1 Kings may be indicating that God has the power to preserve 7,000 faithful to Him, and He proved it by giving victory to Ahab's **7,000** soldiers.

Ahab clearly did not deserve this victory. God's spiritual preservation of the 7,000 faithful people and victory by the 7,000 soldiers of Ahab both exhibit God's profound grace. At the same time that Ahab talked with the prophet (vv. 13-14), Ben-hadad was **drinking himself drunk** along with his **thirty-two kings**, his army confederates (v. 16). When Aram's king heard that **Men have come out from Samaria**, he commanded, **If they have come out for peace, take them alive; or if they have come out for**

war, take them alive (vv. 17-18). His command played into the hands of Israel's army and the will of the Lord. **Ben-hadad** barely escaped with his life (v. 20). **The king of Israel went out and struck . . . and killed the Arameans with a great slaughter** (v. 21).

20:22-25. The same **prophet** who informed Ahab of the first battle plan came with a second, warning him that **at the turn of the year**, the spring time, Aram's king would return. Ben-hadad himself decided on a different strategy, having mistakenly been advised that Israel's gods were **gods of the mountains** (v. 23). His servants proposed that he fight against Israel on the plains and that he replace the kings he employed earlier and **put captains in their place** (v. 24). From a strictly military point of view the strategy seemed wise since Aram's military was larger and **stronger**, with many more horses and chariots than Israel would be able to assemble.

20:26-30. A second battle took place near **Aphek**, a few miles east of the Sea of Galilee. The contrast in armies was shocking: Israel's army was **like two little flocks of goats**, while Aram's army **filled the country** (v. 26). A **man of God** appeared to Ahab, **the king of Israel**, to again inform him that Aram's **multitude** would be given into his hand, so that he would know that **the Lord** had brought about the victory, not Ahab or Baal (v. 28). When the battle eventually took place Israel killed **100,000 foot soldiers in one day** (v. 29). Another group of Arameans **fled to Aphek**, where a **wall fell on 27,000 men** (v. 30). The scene hearkens back to other battles like Joshua's victory at Jericho. God's people went to battle, against great odds, but it was God who actually fought and gave the victory.

20:31-34. Ben-hadad also fled to Aphek to find protection (v. 30). Realizing that their lives were in jeopardy, some Arameans counseled Ben-hadad to consider terms of peace because they had **heard that the kings of the house of Israel are merciful** (v. 31). So to show their desire to surrender and not to fight, they girded **sackcloth on their loins and** put **ropes on** their **heads** (v. 32) in an attempt to find mercy (*chesed*), a Hebrew term consistently associated with covenant-keeping. However, God's covenant promises with Israel did not apply to their enemy neighbors. As in the case with Joshua (cf. Jos 6:15-20), Israel's pagan neighbors were to be destroyed, especially when God was the One who won the battle. Unfortunately Ahab forgot or simply did not know the ways of God and accepted Ben-hadad's pleas for mercy, saying of the king of Aram, **He is my brother** (v. 32). Ben-hadad made a deal with Ahab to **restore** territory and give him access to **Damascus**, so that Ahab **made a covenant with him and let him go** (v. 34).

20:35-43. Again Ahab was confronted by one of God's messengers—this time by **a certain man of the sons of the prophets** (v. 35). These men were students studying in the schools of the prophets, and this unnamed prophet was among them (cf. 2Kg 9:1). This prophet had a message for Ahab regarding his failure to punish Ben-hadad (vv. 32-34), and he delivered the message in the form of a drama. In a scene similar to 13:21-25, the one who received information **by the word of the Lord** asked a fellow prophet to **strike** him so as to give the impression that he had been one of the soldiers in battle against the Arameans (v. 35). When the second prophet refused to do so, he was told that a **lion** would **kill** him. And **as soon as he departed . . . a lion found him and killed him** (v. 36) as God had predicted. The prophet eventually found **another man** to assist him, and so the confrontation was put in place.

When the king met the prophet who had **disguised himself with a bandage over his eyes** (v. 38), the prophet told him a story about letting a prisoner escape. Ahab was told one of two things would happen to him: either he would have to pay with his **life**, or he would have to pay **a talent of silver**, about 75 pounds, an impossible sum for an ordinary soldier to pay (v. 39). **The king of Israel** was merciless, telling the prophet in disguise that the **judgment** would stand. At that point the prophet **hastily took the bandage away** and revealed his true identity to Ahab (v. 41). As the prophet Nathan had done when he told the parable to David regarding Bathsheba (cf. 2Sm 12), this prophet used his story of the escaped prisoner to accuse the king. Ahab was informed that because he had let his enemy **go out of** his **hand**, even though Ben-hadad was **devoted to destruction**, Ahab's life would be taken in place of Ben-hadad's (v. 42). The verdict was rendered, and Ahab was again aware that God alone is King! So he **went to his house sullen and vexed** as he came home to **Samaria** (v. 43). His emotional despair would follow Ahab as he now understood he was destined to live the remainder of his days under the judgment of God.

d. Ahab Covets Naboth's Vineyard and Learns of God's Justice (1Kg 21:1-29)

One would think that after seeing both God's judgment on Baal worship (cf. 18:30-40) and God's powerful deliverance over Aram (cf. 20:1-30), Ahab would have repented from his sinful ways. But Israel's king had consistently failed to acknowledge the Lord as King, and that Judah's and Israel's human monarchs were His servants. And so the spiritual education of the Babylonian exiles, the audience for whom 1 and 2 Kings was written, continued through yet another chapter related to Ahab's life.

21:1-4. The narrative history of Ahab's life continued with the transitional words **after these things** (v. 1). Ahab had been rebuked by one of the sons of the prophets and was sulking in Samaria over the thought that his end was at hand with little glory to accompany it. The king saw a garden belonging to **Naboth the Jezreelite** and wanted it for his own possession. Ahab offered Naboth what he thought was a reasonable deal—**a better vineyard** or **the price of it in money** (v. 2). Naboth refused all offers, claiming that the garden was **the inheritance of** his **fathers** (v. 3). Apparently Naboth understood that God said the land was His personal possession and He only entrusted it to His people (cf. Lv 25:23). The land was not to be traded as disposable real estate, but was to stay in the care of the families to which it was allotted (cf. Dt 25:5-10). When Ahab realized his wants would not be met, he again became **sullen and vexed** and went to **bed** and would not eat (cf. 20:43).

21:5-14. When **Jezebel** realized why Ahab was sulking (vv. 5-6), she came up with a plan. The queen resorted to a political power play, saying to him, **Do you now reign over Israel?** (v. 7). Perhaps she knew about the prophecies against him, but for **now** he was the king, and she was encouraging him to take advantage of his power base. Even more to her liking, Jezebel informed Ahab, **I will give you the vineyard of Naboth the Jezreelite** (v. 7). She then proceeded to send **letters** under the king's **seal** to the **elders** of Jezreel, encouraging them to proclaim a **fast** and invite Naboth (v. 9). The call for a citywide fast implied that some serious sin or legal infraction had occurred. In addition the elders were to invite **two worthless men** who would accuse Naboth of cursing **God and the king** (v. 10). Once the charges were made, Naboth was to be stoned to death. Jezebel's plan was executed perfectly, at least in her mind, and word came back to the queen that **Naboth** was **dead** (v. 14).

21:15-24. Jezebel then told **Ahab** that he could go **take possession of the vineyard of Naboth the Jezreelite** (v. 15). The property was still identified as belonging to Naboth, no matter what Ahab and Jezebel conspired. They assumed that all was going well with their scheme, but **the word of the LORD came to Elijah** (v. 17). He was told to go and confront **Ahab** who was on his way to take **possession** of the stolen vineyard. Elijah was told to inform Ahab that **where the dogs licked up the blood of Naboth** the **dogs shall** also **lick up** Ahab's blood (v. 19). Ahab realized he had been **found** by Elijah, and called him **O my enemy**, recognizing that the prophet spoke for the Lord, who had become the enemy of the wicked king. Elijah delivered his message: pronouncement of a horrible death that appears eight times in 1 and 2 Kings against those who would rebel against the precepts of the Lord (cf. 1Kg 14:11; 16:4; 21:19, 23-24; 22:38; 2Kg 9:10, 36).

Elijah made it clear that Ahab's demise was coming about **because** he had **sold himself to do evil in the sight of the LORD** (v. 20; cf. v. 22). Ahab had abandoned any righteous qualities he might have had to do evil for his own benefit and to the detriment of the kingdom. Therefore, the Lord would make Ahab's **house like the house of Jeroboam . . . because you have made Israel sin** with the worship of Baal (v. 22). Furthermore, **Jezebel** would also be judged for her wickedness in inciting Ahab to lead the nation into Baal worship and **the dogs shall eat Jezebel in the district of Jezreel**, a prophecy fulfilled exactly during the reign of Jehu (cf. 2Kg 9:30-37).

21:25-29. Here is an unexpected summary to Ahab's life. **Surely there was no one like Ahab who sold himself to do evil** (v. 25). Yet once Ahab heard Elijah's **words . . . he tore his clothes and put on sackcloth and fasted** (v. 27). The Lord acknowledged the king's repentant behavior to Elijah, and His willingness to extend mercy to Ahab. Specifically God would **not bring the evil** (*ra'ah*, "the disaster"), previously announced, to Ahab in his lifetime (v. 29). It would be Ahab's son, Joram/Jehoram, who would ultimately have to experience the fulfillment of the prophecies announced through Elijah against Ahab (cf. 2Kg 9:1-37). This event raises the question of the mercy and plan of God. Although God had pronounced judgment on Ahab, within His own plan He allowed for the modification of that judgment, all within His own omniscience.

e. Ahab Confronted by the Prophet Micaiah: God's Supremacy over Plans (1Kg 22:1-40)

Even though Ahab seemed to have a change of heart after Elijah confronted him (21:27-29), the events that followed indicate that a sinful worldview had control over much of the king's thinking. Ahab had been an eyewitness to God's supremacy over nature (chap. 17), over the prophets of Baal (chap. 18), and over his own secretive, unjust ways (chap. 21). In this section, Ahab would learn the hard way that God's prophetic word is superior to the manipulative words of his self-appointed prophets.

22:1-4. At this time there was a short-lived peace between Israel and Aram while they were in an alliance against the Assyrian king, Shalmaneser III, so **three years passed without war between Aram and Israel** (v. 1). A decisive victory against Shalmaneser took place at Qarqar in northern Syria in 853 BC. With the Assyrian campaign completed, Ahab wanted to complete the agreement made with Ben-hadad (cf. 20:34). He had specific concerns for **Ramoth-gilead**, one of the main cities belonging to Gad, about 30 miles east of the Jordan River and 15 miles south of the Sea of Galilee. Ahab asserted this area belonged to Israel but was still in **the hand of the king of Aram** (v. 3). At the same time Ahab was visited by **Jehoshaphat**, king of Judah (v. 4); because the daughter of Israel's king was married to the Judean king's son, there was a marriage alliance between Israel and Judah (cf. 2Ch 18:1). Military threats and a royal marriage brought the two men together.

22:5-12. Even though **Jehoshaphat** was willing to supply people and horses for the battle (v. 4), he insisted that the two kings **inquire first for the word of the Lord** (v. 5). The dialogue between the kings indicated that Jehoshaphat was much more spiritually sensitive to the Lord's wishes than was Ahab. So Ahab assembled about **four hundred** prophets (v. 6). This was about the same number as the prophets of Asherah who did not appear at Mount Carmel for the confrontation with Elijah; consequently they had escaped execution alongside the 450 prophets of Baal (cf. 18:19, 40). These pagan prophets clearly communicated to Ahab what he wanted to hear: **Go up, for the Lord will give** victory **into the hand of the king** (v. 6). But when Jehoshaphat challenged their report, the only prophet of the Lord Ahab could identify was **Micaiah son of Imlah** (v. 8). Ahab stated that his reluctance to bring Micaiah into his presence was that **he does not prophesy good concerning me, but evil** (*ra'*, i.e., "distress; calamity"). However, Jehoshaphat insisted that Micaiah be consulted, and plans were implemented to bring him to the royal assembly (v. 9). The tension of the meeting was heightened with the knowledge that another prophet, **Zedekiah**, and several other **prophets** encouraged Ahab and Jehoshaphat to fight for **Ramoth-gilead** by saying, **the Lord will give it into the hand of the king** (v. 12).

22:13-18. The messenger who went to summon Micaiah (v. 13) warned him that the other prophets were giving the kings a **favorable** report about going into battle. Their confidence resulted from the victories attained three years earlier, as well as the most recent victory against Shalmaneser III. But Micaiah did not have the same confidence. When the messenger warned him to speak favorably to Ahab, the prophet stated, **As the Lord lives, what the Lord says to me, that I shall speak** (v. 14). When Micaiah finally appeared before the two kings, he sarcastically agreed with the other prophets, saying: **Go up and succeed** (v. 15). But Ahab certainly detected something in Micaiah's voice or demeanor and demanded: **How many times must I adjure you to speak . . . the truth?** (v. 16). Micaiah then told of a vision that he had been given, revealing Israel's utter defeat at the hands of the Arameans. **I saw all Israel scattered on the mountains** (v. 17). Again Ahab whined that this prophet never said anything good, **but evil**.

22:19-28. Micaiah then explained how his prophecy came about. He referred to a heavenly vision with **the Lord sitting on His throne**, an image of the Lord in royal command (cf. Is 6:1; Jr 23:16-20; Ezk 1:26-28), a startling contrast to the two kings sitting on their thrones (v. 10). In this heavenly vision the prophet described a dialogue between the Lord and **the host of heaven** (v. 19). The Lord asked, **Who will entice Ahab to go up and fall at Ramoth-gilead?** (v. 20). Here **entice** means "to persuade or attempt to persuade." The Lord does not deceive people to accomplish His purpose. Micaiah's vision should be understood as the imagery of an ancient Near Eastern monarch seated upon his throne with his attendants and counselors around him. The Lord was not seated literally **on His throne** since He is an incorporeal spirit (cf. Jn 4:24), and as the One who is omniscient, He would not have required the input of other beings. The **deceiving spirit** is also unlikely to have been necessary for the sovereign God to accomplish something.

Instead, in this passage the **deceiving spirit** (v. 22) provides a theological "layer" between God and the false prophets. Because of the **deceiving spirit**, God is not depicted as directly causing the deceit Himself, though the writer of Kings clearly intended to indicate that He was superintending this situation (v. 23). In a mysterious way, God governed and ordained this event without Himself producing it as the direct, immediate cause (since "He Himself does not tempt anyone," Jms 1:13). Instead, He brought to fruition the episode as the "indirect," "ultimate cause," and the false prophets, who were responsible for their own moral deeds, are blamed for the guilt of their actions, not God.

The prophets and their words fed into the very thing that Ahab wanted to hear. But the vision was clearly made known to Ahab (vv. 17-23), and he had an opportunity to repent and do what was right before the battle. But Ahab refused to do so, choosing instead to put **Micaiah** in **prison**, and not be released **until I return safely** (v. 27). Micaiah had spoken the truth for the Lord; however, he suffered mistreatment at the hands of Ahab, and perhaps was left to die in prison because the prophet said, **If you indeed return safely, the LORD has not spoken by me** (v. 28). Ahab refused to listen and then marched to his death.

22:29-40. The prophecy must have had some sort of lingering impact on Ahab's thinking, because he proposed that he **disguise** himself before entering the battle, while Jehoshaphat would remain in his royal garments (v. 30). He wanted the king of Judah to be the target of the enemy, while he could move about the battlefield anonymously. The **king of Aram** gave specific orders for his **thirty-two captains** to **fight** only against Israel's king Ahab (v. 31). It was their mission to find and kill him. As the battle ensued, **a certain man drew his bow at random and stuck the king of Israel in a joint of the armor** (v. 34). This may have seemed like a **random** shot, but the arrow landed exactly where God wanted it to land. Despite being disguised in the battle, Ahab was mortally wounded and died **propped up in his chariot** (v. 35), as the **blood from the wound ran into the bottom of the chariot**. The prophecy of his death and that **the dogs licked up his blood** was fulfilled exactly (v. 38; cf. 21:19). Even his opulent **ivory house** and accomplishments as a monarch (v. 39) paled in contrast to the fact that Ahab tried to live his life independent of the God who is supreme over absolutely everything. After Ahab's death, **Ahaziah his son became king in his place** (v. 40). Ahaziah's reign is detailed in 2Kg 1.

5. Jehoshaphat of Judah: A Good King (1Kg 22:41-50)

22:41-50. The book closes with the account of **Jehoshaphat the son of Asa** becoming **king over Judah** (873–848 BC; cf. 2Ch 17:1–20:37). Unlike his counterpart in the northern kingdom, Jehoshaphat **walked in all the way of Asa his father; he did not turn aside from it, doing right in the sight of the LORD** (v. 43). Jehoshaphat was one of the good kings of Judah, although, like Asa, he failed to remove the **high places** (v. 43; cf. 15:14). By and large he was a king who sought to obey the Lord's will. His attempt to **go to Ophir for gold** failed because the ships were broken at **Ezion-geber** (v. 48; cf. comments on 10:20 and 2Ch 20), yet **Jehoshaphat was not willing** to enter into an alliance with Ahab's son, **Ahaziah** (v. 49).

6. Ahaziah of Israel: A Bad King (1Kg 22:51–2Kg 1:18)

22:51-53. In contrast to the righteousness revealed in Jehoshaphat's reign, the book of 1 Kings closes with a commentary on King **Ahaziah** (853–852 BC; cf. 2Ch 20:3-37), the son of **Ahab**, who **became king over Israel in Samaria in the seventeenth year of Jehoshaphat king of Judah** (v. 51). Like Ahab his father, **Ahaziah did evil in the sight of the LORD** (v. 52). He continued to serve Baal and **provoked the LORD God of Israel to anger** (v. 53). The details of his reign continue in 2Kg 1. His wicked behavior, along with that of the rest of the kings of Israel, led to the northern kingdom's demise (cf. 2Kg 17) and eventually led to the deportation of the southern kingdom of Judah to Babylon. In these closing verses the text gives sufficient evidence that the coming Babylonian captivity was deserved. God alone was their only righteous, sovereign King (cf. Ex 19:4-6; 1Sm 8:7). The **LORD God of Israel** alone deserves worship and allegiance, and the nation should continue to look for the messianic king, the Son of David.

The historic account and theological details of Israel's and Judah's kings continues uninterrupted in 2 Kings, beginning with details about Ahaziah's death.

BIBLIOGRAPHY FOR 1 AND 2 KINGS

Archer, Gleason L. *A Survey of Old Testament Introduction.* Chicago: Moody, 1964.

Arnold, Bill T., and Bryan E. Beyer. *Encountering the Old Testament.* Grand Rapids, MI: Baker, 1998.

Davis, John J. and Whitcomb, John C. *Israel: From Conquest to Exile.* Winona Lake, IN: BMH, 1989.

Devries, Simon J. *1 Kings.* Word Biblical Commentary, 2nd ed. Nashville: Thomas Nelson, 2004.

Fee, Gordon and Douglas Stuart. *How to Read the Bible Book by Book.* Grand Rapids, MI: Zondervan, 2002.

Harrison, R. K. *Introduction to the Old Testament.* Grand Rapids, MI: Eerdmans, 1969.

Hindson, Ed and Gary Yates, eds. *The Essence of the Old Testament: A Survey.* B & H Academic: Nashville, 2012.

Hobbs, T. R. *2 Kings.* Word Biblical Commentary. Vol. 13. Nashville: Thomas Nelson, 1986.

House, Paul R. *1, 2 Kings.* New American Commentary. Nashville: Broadman & Holman, 1995.

Howard, David M. *An Introduction to the Old Testament Historical Books.* Chicago: Moody, 1993.

Hubbard, Robert L. Jr. *First and Second Kings.* Everyman's Bible Commentary. Chicago: Moody, 1991.

Keil, C. F. and F. Delitzsch. *The Books of the Kings.* In Commentary on the Old Testament, reprint. Grand Rapids, MI: Eerdmans, 1975.

Patterson, R. D. and Hermann J. Austel. "1 & 2 Kings." In vol. 4 of The Expositor's Bible Commentary. Grand Rapids, MI: Zondervan, 1988.

Provan, Iain W. *1 and 2 Kings.* New International Bible Commentary. Peabody, MA: Hendrickson, 1995.

———. *1 and 2 Kings.* Understanding the Bible Series. Grand Rapids, MI: Baker, 2012.

Thiele Edwin R. *The Mysterious Numbers of the Hebrew Kings*, rev. ed. Chicago: University of Chicago Press, 1983.

Wiseman, Donald J. *1 and 2 Kings.* Tyndale Old Testament Commentaries. Downers Grove, IL: InterVarsity, 1993.

2 KINGS

HARRY E. SHIELDS

INTRODUCTION

See the Introduction to 1 and 2 Kings at the beginning of 1 Kings on p. 479. See the combined outline for 1 and 2 Kings on p. 481.

COMMENTARY ON 2 KINGS

1:1-8. Because 1 and 2 Kings were originally one book, the book of 2 Kings opens where 1 Kings left off, by giving more information about Ahab's son and successor to the throne of the northern kingdom of Israel, **Ahaziah** (853–852 BC). As was pointed out in the introduction, the Hebrew title *melakim* ("Kings"), indicates that the "book of Kings" was originally one book. That is why the statements about Ahaziah in 1Kg 22:51-53 serve as a natural transition into the events of 2Kg 1. Ahaziah's reign was short-lived—only two years (1Kg 22:51), and he provoked the Lord to anger because of his evil ways (v. 53).

In his brief reign, **Ahaziah** faced two major problems, one political and one physical (vv. 1-2). First, **Moab rebelled against Israel after the death of Ahab**. The actual details of this rebellion are described in 2Kg 3. Second, Ahaziah was seriously injured when he **fell through the lattice in his upper chamber** (1:2). A typical Middle Eastern **upper chamber** was a room on the roof, either with a window covered by latticework for privacy, or an open roof area surrounding latticework that served as a wall; this lattice could easily be broken. That may be one of the reasons the law provided practical legislation to minimize the kind of danger posed by these chambers (cf. Dt 22:8).

This injury became the central event in 2Kg 1. As a result of his illness, Ahaziah **sent messengers . . . to inquire of Baal-zebub, the god of Ekron** (v. 2). No reason is given as to why the king did not seek counsel from one of the prophets of Baal in his own country. Ekron was a major Philistine city, located between Jerusalem and Gath (cf. Jos 13:2; 1Sm 5:10). Some commentators suggest that he did so because he wanted to keep his illness private from the larger population, or wanted to go to the primary residence of the god from whom he was seeking counsel, or because **Ekron** was geographically close at hand (Patterson and Austel, "1 and 2 Kings," 172).

No matter what the cause, Ahaziah revealed his true character by inquiring of the pagan gods **whether I will recover from this sickness**. On their way the messengers were intercepted by **Elijah the Tishbite**, whom these individuals apparently did not know (cf. vv. 7-8). Elijah had a probing question, asked three times in the narrative to emphasize the king's spiritual condition: **Is it because there is no God in Israel that you are going to inquire of Baal-zebub, the god of Ekron?** (v. 3; see vv. 6 and 16, which have slight variations in wording). Ahaziah failed to learn from Israel's most recent events at Mount Carmel (the Lord's victory over the prophets of Baal, cf. 1Kg 18) and at Ramoth-gilead (Ahab's death as prophesied, cf. 1Kg 22) that the Lord alone was God and supreme over everything, including one's health.

Many commentators conclude that the name **Baal-zebub** means "Baal/lord of the flies," and was a deliberate corruption by Hebrew scribes to make light of the pagan deity. However, the original name was more likely Baal-zebul, meaning "Baal the exalted" (Provan, *1 and 2 Kings*, 170). This name, spelled "Beelzebul," appears several times in the NT as a synonym for "Satan" (cf. Mt 10:25; 12:24, 27; Mk 3:22; Lk 11:15, 18-19). The author's point was that Ahaziah was pursuing the wrong god. As a result, Elijah announced that the king would remain in his **bed** and he would **surely die** (v. 4).

Elijah was instructed by **the angel of the Lord** where to go (vv. 3, 15). The Hebrew word for **angel** (*malak*) simply means "messenger." This angel should not be assumed to be a preincarnate appearance of the Messiah who sometimes appeared to people in the OT to reprimand, encourage, or give instructions for specific tasks (cf. Gn 16:7-13; 18:1-33; Ex 3:2; Nm 22:22; Jdg 13:19-22; 16:3). When "the angel of the Lord" refers to the preincarnate appearance of the Messiah, His deity is acknowledged with acts of worship by those who see Him, or He is further identified with names of God. Since neither of these occurs here, this angelic messenger could have simply been a messenger from God telling Elijah where to go, in contrast to the messengers sent by Ahaziah to Ekron (vv. 5-8).

When the messengers returned, the king must have been surprised at such a quick turnaround, for he asked them, **Why have you returned?** (v. 5). They told how an unidentified **man came up to meet** them and told them to take a message to the king. The same inquiry about **no God in Israel**, (vv. 3, 6, 16), along with the prediction of the king's death, was repeated by the messengers. The king asked, **What kind of man was he . . . ?** (v. 7), and soon he realized from their description it was **Elijah the Tishbite** (v. 8).

1:9-16. One would assume that such a harsh indictment about the king's spiritual condition and his future would motivate Ahaziah to repent and call for mercy from the prophet (cf. 1:6, 8). Instead, **the king sent . . . a captain of fifty** with **fifty of his** soldiers **to** arrest Elijah (v. 9). Elijah's exact location was not identified, but the soldiers seemed to know **the hill** where he was stationed. The first captain identified Elijah as a **man of God**, and asked him to **Come down** per the king's command (v. 9). The phrase, **man of God** throughout 1 and 2 Kings refers to one who had a special message or prophetic office given by God (cf. 1Kg 12:22; 13:1; 17:18; 20:28; 2Kg 1:9; 4:7; 5:8). In scenes reminiscent of the events on Mount Carmel, **Elijah** said in response to the first two captains who came to arrest him, **If I am a man of God, let fire come down from heaven and consume you and your fifty** (vv. 10, 12).

Immediately **the fire of God** came down and consumed the first two captains and their soldiers. Just as the Lord had appeared on Mount Carmel (cf. 1Kg 17–18) as the God who controls nature and shows Himself in fire, so here He appeared again as the God who judges those who turn away from His grace and power to seek help from other gods. Even though Ahaziah and the first two captains did not comprehend the revelation of God in their midst, a third **captain** did understand the spiritual significance of all that was happening (v. 13). He **bowed down on his knees before Elijah, and begged him** for mercy on his life and the lives of his men. Many people in Israel were bowing their knees to Baal and the Asherah poles in their midst, but this soldier wanted to avoid the **fire . . . from heaven** (v. 14) and to experience mercy from the Lord.

Even though this officer bowed before Elijah, he was well aware that the prophet represented the true God. This captain's words and his posture reveal that he sought mercy from God (vv. 15-16). Elijah was then informed by **the angel of the Lord** (cf. 1:3) to go down with the third captain and appear before **the king**. Elijah was told not to **be afraid** (v. 15), and he responded to the angelic message with courage. Earlier the prophet was intimidated by Jezebel's threats on his life and ran as far away from Samaria as possible (cf. 1Kg 19:1-18). But life had changed for Elijah, and unlike Ahaziah, the prophet had come to know that God is supreme over kings and the force of nature. So it was the spiritually wise thing for him to obey the messenger.

1:17-18. The chapter closes with a summary of Ahaziah's life. The only additional information from what was recorded is that he **died according to the word of the Lord which Elijah had spoken** (v. 17; cf. 1Kg 22:51-53). Since Ahaziah had **no son, Jehoram became king in his place** (v. 17). This **Jehoram** was a brother to Ahaziah, and for that reason he is also referred to as a son of Ahab (cf. 2Kg 3:1). The time of ascension for this Jehoram of Israel was **in the second year** of a king by the same name in Judah. This other Jehoram was the **son of Jehoshaphat** (cf. 1Kg 22:41-50; 2Kg 3:1).

7. Elisha, Prophet to the Northern Kingdom (2Kg 2:1–6:23)

The various kings in Israel and Judah transitioned from one to another, and the same was true of the prophets: Elijah would eventually be replaced by Elisha (cf. 1Kg 19:16). Like Elijah, Elisha would perform miracles to authenticate the message the Lord gave him for the kings and people, primarily of the northern kingdom.

a. Elisha Given the Prophetic Office of Elijah (2Kg 2:1-25)

2:1-6. Though not stated directly, the actions of Elijah in vv. 1-14 indicate that he must have known that his departure was at hand. Here the miraculous conclusion to his life is presented without introduction: **And it came about when the Lord was about to take up Elijah by a whirlwind** (v. 1). On two different occasions (vv. 3, 5) the **sons of the prophets** knew that the time of Elijah's departure was at hand, so both **Elijah** and **Elisha** must have known as well.

Although Elijah was leaving, there was evidence that God would be present in Elisha's ministry. First, Elisha was persistently faithful to **stay** with Elijah, even when he was told to **stay here** and not continue on with Elijah, first to **Bethel**, then to **Jericho**, and on to the **Jordan** (vv. 2, 4, 6). But Elisha would have none of it. Each time Elijah asked him to remain while he himself moved on to another location, Elisha responded, **I will not leave you** (vv. 2, 4, 6).

2:7-14. As Elijah and Elisha traveled together, visiting **the sons of the prophets** along the way, they eventually reached **the Jordan** River where **fifty men of the sons of the prophets** also joined them (v. 7). In one last demonstration of God's hand on his life, **Elijah took his mantle** [his outer garment] **and folded it together and struck the waters** (v. 8). Immediately the waters were parted. Those looking on must have had thoughts of a similar time when God wanted to confirm the ministry of Joshua as he and the people crossed the Jordan and entered the promised land for the first time (cf. Jos 3:7-10). On this occasion, the **two** prophets **crossed over on dry ground** (v. 8).

When they were on the other side, Elijah asked Elisha what he could do for the man who was about to become his successor. Elisha responded, **Please, let a double portion of your spirit be upon me** (v. 9). The words "double portion" appear in Dt 21:17 as the amount that a firstborn son would inherit to assist in the care of the father's estate. In this context, where Elisha called Elijah his **father** (v. 12), the association with Dt 21:17 seems reasonable. Even though Elijah told his student that what he was asking for was a **hard thing** (v. 10), Elijah told Elisha that if he saw him when he was **taken from** him, the request would be granted.

Then as the two men kept walking, **a chariot of fire and horses of fire** appeared, and took Elijah **by a whirlwind to heaven** (v. 11). The chariot and horses were identified as the **chariots of Israel**, a manifestation of the presence of the Lord (v. 12; cf. Ezk 1:4-14, Hab 3:11). They are a demonstration of His strength, power, majesty, and protection. They **separated** Elijah and Elisha from each other, and then Elijah **went up** to heaven by the whirlwind. The power of the Lord is frequently associated with the power of fire, wind, and storms (e.g., Ex 13:21; Jb 38; 40:6-14; Pss 29:3-9; 77:18; 83:15; Is 19:1; Ezk 1:4). Like Enoch, Elijah went into the presence of the Lord without experiencing death (cf. Gn 5:24).

Elijah's ministry was suddenly concluded, but the question still remained as to whether God was still active in Israel. The first piece of evidence for God's continued presence in Israel and in Elisha's ministry came as an exclamation, when Elisha cried, **My father, my father, the chariots of Israel and its horsemen!** (v. 12). This expressed both Elisha's amazement at the manifestation of God's power and grief over the loss of his great mentor. But it was also confirmation that he had been an eyewitness to Elijah's being **taken up** (cf. v. 10), and therefore he would receive the **double portion** of Elijah's spirit that he had asked to receive.

As further evidence of God's presence in his life, Elisha **took hold of his own clothes and tore them in two pieces** as a sign of his grief (v. 12; cf. Gn 37:29, 34; 44:13; Jos 7:6). As Elijah was taken up, **the mantle of Elijah** fell to the ground. Elisha picked up the garment **and stood by the bank of the Jordan** (v. 13). Then Elisha **struck the waters . . . and crossed** back **over** the Jordan (v. 14). The Lord attested to Elisha's succession of Elijah's ministry by showing the two men had the same power to part the Jordan (vv. 8, 14). Another evidence of the transfer of power and spiritual leadership was the parallel of Elisha and Joshua parting the Jordan at the beginning of their ministries, probably in the same area near Jericho (vv. 4, 18; cf. Jos 3:13-17). There is even a link between their names: Elisha means "God saves," and Joshua means "the Lord saves."

2:15-18. The **sons of the prophets** who had observed this dramatic scene at the Jordan confirmed that a new prophetic leader was in their midst, saying, **The spirit of Elijah rests on Elisha** (v. 15). But they apparently still had doubts about whether Elijah had actually departed permanently. So they asked Elisha for permission to **go and search for** Elisha's **master** (v. 16) while he stayed at **Jericho**. After some resisting, Elisha let them go on a three-day search, in which they failed to find the departed Elijah (v. 17).

2:19-22. A second piece of evidence that proved that God was still at work in Israel and through Elisha occurred when **the men of the city** of Jericho approached him about a problem with their **water** supply. Apparently the curse enacted earlier (cf. Jos 6:26) was still posing problems for the people who lived in Jericho; in any case, the water of this **pleasant** oasis city was making the people sick. The city leaders stated that **the water was bad and the land . . . unfruitful** (v. 19). Elisha asked the men to bring him a **new jar** containing **salt** (v. 20). When they complied, he took the salt to the **spring** and **threw salt** on the water. He then stated on the Lord's behalf, **I have purified these waters; there shall not be from there death or unfruitfulness any longer** (v. 21). Elisha's action completely reversed the curse that had hung over the city for centuries. A similar act of water purification and spiritual renewal was recorded by Moses (cf. Ex 15:22-27). Again Elisha had demonstrated by his actions that God was present and working in great power.

2:23-25. The third piece of evidence confirming Elisha as the legitimate successor to Elijah is recorded in the prophet's response to the mockers. This event should not be misunderstood as the harsh actions of an irritable old man, because there is more to the story than first meets the eye. As Elisha returned to **Bethel . . . young lads came out from the city and mocked him** (v. 23). They yelled, **Go up, you baldhead; go up, you baldhead!** (v. 23). Elisha turned and **cursed them in the name of the Lord** (v. 24).

Two things need to be kept in mind when reading this account. First, Bethel was still one of the leading centers of idolatry in the northern kingdom (cf. 1Kg 12:29, 32-33; Am 7:30). The designation **young lads** (*qatan nahar)* is best understood from context to mean an "insignificant, untrained young adult," not a small child or little boy. This group of young adult lads represented the spiritual disregard that the citizens as a whole had for God and His prophets.

Second, the expression **go up** was an insult that may have meant, "Go away like Elijah" (House, *1 and 2 Kings,* 260). If that is the case, the insult was against not just Elisha, but against God, because they were saying Elisha should "go away and take his God with him!" When Elisha saw them, he pronounced a **curse** on them for their attitude toward the prophet of the God of Israel (cf. Lv 26:21-22). Almost immediately **two female bears came out of the woods and tore up forty-two lads**, so that they experienced the supernatural judgment of the Lord for their attitude (v. 24; cf. 36:16). At his parting from Elijah, Elisha had asked the question, **Where is the Lord, the God of Elijah?** (v. 14). Now, the answer was clear: the Lord was working in and through his servant, Elisha!

b. Elisha Confirms His Authority (2Kg 3:1-27)

In the previous chapter Elisha was clearly verified before the sons of the prophets as God's appointed successor to Elijah. In this chapter, the new prophet's sphere of influence extended to the political realm. Two important concepts must be kept in mind: (1) Elisha must be introduced to the kings of Israel and Judah to show that God is present and working through him. (2) The events were a further substantiation that God desires for His people to call on Him for divine assistance when they go into battle (cf. 1Kg 8:44-49). Jehoram/Joram, king of Israel, and Jehoshaphat king of Judah, joined forces to fight their common enemy, the king of Moab. Before they went to the battle, Jehoshaphat persuaded Jehoram to consult a prophet of the Lord.

3:1-3. Following the death of Ahaziah (cf. 1:17), his brother **Jehoram . . . became king over Israel. . . .** He **did evil in the sight of the Lord**, even though he removed a **sacred pillar** dedicated to **Baal** (v. 2). But God was opposed to him because he **clung to the sins of Jeroboam** (v. 3), who had established a corrupted system of worship in Israel with the golden calf altars at Dan and Bethel. Jeroboam had encouraged the northern kingdom to engage in various forms of self-made religion and a watering down of allegiance to God alone (cf. 1Kg 12:25-30).

3:4-8. King Jehoram soon faced a major test of his power by one of his vassals, **Mesha king of Moab** (v. 4). The Moabite Stone (cf. comments above on 1Kg 15:16-24) was constructed by this same King Mesha to report on his military achievements. The Stone refers to this battle, but with much more positive outcomes for Mesha and his army. Chapter 3 records the story from the vantage point of Israel's "theological history." And following the death of Ahab, **Moab**

rebelled against the king of Israel (v. 5). King Jehoram decided to take action by mustering his troops and heading south (v. 6).

Along the way he invited **Jehoshaphat the king of Judah** to join him in the ensuing battle. The request was a logical one, since Jehoshaphat's son—also named Jehoram—had married Ahab's daughter. Jehoshaphat enthusiastically agreed to go to battle. His only initial question had to do with the route they were to follow. There is no evidence of either king calling for prophetic insight, so Jehoram announced that they would travel **the way of the wilderness of Edom** (v. 8). This too seemed like a wise decision, since Judah controlled Edom (cf. 1Kg 22:47) and a vassal king had been appointed to give governance to the country.

3:9-12. The initial military strategy for the kings of **Israel . . . Judah** and **Edom** to join forces against Moab seemed like a good plan. But when **they made a circuit of seven days' journey, and there was no water** (v. 9), both soldiers and animals were now threatened. Jehoram concluded that the situation they were in was the Lord's doing **to give them into the hand of Moab** (v. 10). But Jehoshaphat, who still had spiritual insight, asked if there was a **prophet of the LORD** in their midst (cf. 1Kg 22:7). One of Jehoram's servants knew what the king himself did not know, namely, that **Elisha** was nearby. So at the urging of Jehoshaphat the three kings—**Jehoshaphat**, Jehoram, and **the king of Edom**—proceeded to gain an audience with Elijah's successor.

3:13-20. As soon as the kings came into Elisha's presence, the prophet was quick to express his disdain for Jehoram. **Elisha** sarcastically said to Israel's king, **What do I have to do with you? Go to the prophets of your father and to the prophets of your mother** (v. 13), meaning, "Why do you even bother consulting a prophet of the Lord God, when you worship the pagan gods of your father and mother; why don't you go seek advice from them?" Again, Jehoram gave his assessment that the Lord was going to hand them over to the people of **Moab**. His comment revealed how much Israel's king did not know about God and His ways.

So Elisha had to enlighten him, as well as to inform all three kings about what was going to happen next. Elisha expressed more disdain for Jehoram, by stating that if it were not for the presence of Jehoshaphat, he **would not look at** Jehoram (v. 14). As God's representative, Elisha was declaring God's utter contempt for the sinful practices carried out in the northern kingdom. However, Elisha did call for **a minstrel** and the **hand of the LORD came upon him** to deliver a prophecy (v. 15). Using musicians during times of prophetic disclosure was common in ancient Israel. However, Elisha's practice was not prescriptive for all generations of God's people. It was simply one resource he used until he heard from God (House, *1 and 2 Kings,* 263). And when the prophecy came to him, Elisha told the men to **make** the **valley full of trenches** (v. 16), because the valley was about to be filled with water. And exactly as Elisha had predicted, **water came by the way of Edom, and the country was filled with water** (v. 20). The miracle happened **about the time of offering the sacrifice** of the morning.

According to Ex 29:38-46, the priests were to provide daily sacrifices in the morning and near the end of each day. The offerings were to be a reminder that God is constantly present with His people and that He is the God of deliverance. Therefore, the presence of water coming in a miraculous way at the time of the morning sacrifice would have reminded the kings that God was still in their midst. Elisha not only predicted the provision of water in a miraculous way, but there were two other important details to his prophecy: (1) God's provision of water was a **slight thing in the sight of the LORD** (v. 18); and (2) once the Israelites engaged the Moabites in battle they were to **strike every fortified city . . . fell every good tree and stop all springs of water, and mar every good piece of land with stones** (v. 19). This second part of the prophecy would have some bearing on how the events of chap. 3 concluded.

3:21-27. When the Moabites learned of the military force coming against them, they prepared for battle. All the able bodied men **put on armor** and those too old for direct combat **stood** guard **on the border**. Early in the morning they looked in the valley, saw the water and mistook it **as blood** (v. 22). Their interpretation of what they saw was that the three kings had **fought together and . . . slain one another** (v. 23). As **Moab** proceeded to enter the scene and take the **spoil** that remained, they were surprised by the attack as the **Israelites arose and struck the Moabites, so that they fled before them** (v. 24).

In accord with Elisha's prophecy they **destroyed the cities; and each one threw a stone on every piece of good land and filled it** (v. 25) to totally disable the Moabite resources, **until** they got to **Kir-hareseth**, the capital of Moab (cf. Is 16:7, 11; Jr 48:31, 36) where **they left its stones**, but did not totally destroy the city. When the **king of Moab** realized that he was about to be defeated, he tried to attack the **king of Edom**, but was defeated (v. 26). In a final act of desperation the king of Moab offered **his oldest son . . . as a burnt offering on the wall** (v. 27). The abominable practice of child sacrifice was part of the Moabite worship of Chemosh (cf. 16:3; Nm 21:29; 1Kg 11:7; Jr 7:31; 48:46). At this detestable practice, **great wrath against Israel** occurred, **and they . . . returned to their own land**.

This is an obscure verse. Some commentators explain the **wrath** as divine wrath that resulted from Israel provoking the Moabites into engaging in human sacrifice, which was abhorrent to God (C. F. Keil and F. Delitzch, *The Books of the Kings* in COT reprint [Grand Rapids, MI: Eerdman's, 1975], p. 306). However, this seems unlikely in view of the fact that it was the King of Moab, not Israel, who engaged in this despicable act. Other commentators suggest that the wrath was superhuman strength extended toward Israel as the Moabites rallied around their king when they saw his willingness to sacrifice the heir to the throne (House, *1, 2 Kings*, 264). Still others see Israel turning away from the battle because they found the action of human sacrifice too despicable to watch. However, it seems preferable to view the wrath as divine wrath because Israel failed to fulfill everything Elisha had prophesied (cf. v. 19). At Kir-hareseth they went only to the fortress itself and stopped. They were to learn that when victory is snatched away by disobeying God's marvelous deliverance (cf. Ex 29:38-46), defeat will occur. The three kings were also learning that there was a new prophet in the land who would speak for God.

c. Elisha Performs Miracles to Substantiate His Message from God (2Kg 4:1–6:23)

Despite the division into chaps. 4–6, these passages have a common purpose of showing still further that Elisha was God's representative both to Israel and the surrounding nations. Through the use of seven selected miracle-laden events, the author laid out a case to verify to the first readers in the Babylonian exile that God is King, He is present, and His commandments are to be obeyed. These miracles might be referred to as "compassion-miracles," since they were administered to people facing very severe personal challenges, while at the same time verifying the ministry of the prophet.

(1) The Miracle of the Widow's Oil (2Kg 4:1-7)

4:1-7. The first of these miracles involved a widow, identified as **a certain woman of the wives of the sons of the prophets** (v. 1; cf. 1Kg 18:20; 20:25; 2Kg 2:3; 2:7; 9:1). She went **to Elisha** because her **husband** had died and **the creditor** had come to take her **two children** as **slaves** (v. 1). The scene indicates that a "school of prophets" came under the leadership and tutelage of men like Elijah and Elisha. Even so, these men carried out ordinary lives that included family life and work. But in the case of this woman, bills had mounted up and she was not able to meet her family obligations.

Hearing her request, Elisha inquired as to what she had **in** her **house**. This question implied that she may have had something that could be sold or traded to produce income. She said she had **nothing except a jar of oil** (v. 2). The prophet then told the woman to **borrow vessels** of different sizes and begin to fill them. Two things stand out in the orders he gave: first, he told her, **Do not get a few** (v. 3); and second, he told her, **Shut the door behind you and your sons** (vv. 4-5). The point of the second command was to help the woman see that the overflowing supply of oil was from the Lord and that the forthcoming miracle was not a public demonstration, but a private provision. The woman did as commanded and soon the borrowed **vessels were full** (v. 6). Only when the final vessel was full did **the oil** stop. Elisha then told the widow to **sell the oil and pay** her **debt** and **live on the rest** (v. 7). Through the Lord's (and the prophet's) compassion the woman and her sons were able to avoid a tragedy.

(2) The Miraculous Healing of the Shunammite Woman's Son (2Kg 4:8-37)

The second account in this series of miracles involved a Shunammite woman. **Shunem** was a town located in the Jezreel Valley (cf. Jos 19:18; 1Sm 28:4; 1Kg 1:3) in the heart of the Baal worshiping population of Israel. The story has similarities to Elijah's dealings with the widow of Zarephath (cf. 1 Kg 17). In both accounts women showed hospitality to the prophet, both had a need arising from the death of a son, and in both cases the Lord used the prophet to miraculously meet their need and raise the dead. Like the parallel accounts of the parting of the Jordan (cf. 2:8 and 14), the story of the two women confirmed Elisha's office following Elijah. The story is the longest one in 2 Kings 4, and it has two parts to it.

4:8-17. The first part introduced **Elisha** to a **prominent woman**, a woman of social and economic influence (v. 8) living in **Shunem**. Out of her apparently sizable economic resources she **persuaded** Elisha **to eat food** in her home (v. 8). In addition, after recognizing that he was a **holy man of God**, she persuaded her **husband** to **make a little walled upper chamber**, fully furnished, so when Elisha **comes to us, that he can turn in there** to have a place to stay (vv. 9-10). During one of Elisha's visits he instructed his servant, **Gehazi**, to inquire and see if there was anything he could do for her, either to speak **to the king** or to a **captain** on her behalf (v. 13). Gehazi reported his conversation with the woman to Elisha and pointed out that the woman had **no son and her husband** was **old** (vv. 11-14). Barrenness was a great tragedy in ancient Israel and the problem is often addressed in the OT (cf. Gn 11:30; 25:21; 29:31; Dt 7:14; Jdg 13:2; 1Sm 1:1-11). Acting out of compassion, Elisha announced to the woman that she would have a child in the **next year** (v. 16). The shock of the announcement prompted the woman to beg of the prophet that he **not lie** to her, for she would be too disappointed if his prediction failed. Miraculously, however, **the woman conceived and bore a son** the following **year** (v. 17). God and Elisha were true to their word.

4:18-21. The second part of the narrative introduces a tragedy that occurred many years later. **When the child was grown**, he was apparently working with **father** when he cried out, **My head, my head** (v. 19). Quickly a **servant** carried the young man to his **mother** and **he sat on her lap until noon, and then died** (v. 20). She laid him on the bed in Elisha's room and closed the door.

4:22-28. What followed revealed the commendable faith the woman had in God and Elisha—faith not readily seen in Israel. She called her husband and asked for a servant and a donkey to **run to the man of God and return** (v. 22). There was no mention of the child's death, but clearly she wanted help from Elisha because her son was so sick. Her husband, detecting that something was not right, asked why she would be seeking for Elisha when it was **neither new moon nor sabbath** (v. 23). These were biblical festival days when the faithful Jewish community would gather to worship (cf. Ex 16:23; 20:9-10; Nm 29:6; 1Sm 20:25; Neh 10:32-33; Ps 81:3; Ezk 46:1). Perhaps this woman often met with Elisha at those times, so her husband was surprised she would be seeking the prophet on an ordinary day, for he did not seem to know the gravity of his son's sickness. Her response to her husband's inquiry was simply, **It will be well**, indicating her faith in the power of God (v. 23).

The woman found Elisha on **Mount Carmel** (v. 25; cf. 1Kg 18). The prophet had already seen her coming from a **distance** and sent **Gehazi** to find out if everything was **well** with her and her family. Again she was evasive in her answer, saying, **It is well** (v. 26). However, Elisha discerned that something was wrong, even though the Lord had hidden the reason from him. She reminded Elisha that she did not **ask for a son** and she had also asked Elisha, **Do not deceive me**. The implication was that if God had given her this wonderful gift of a son, why was he now being taken from her?

4:29-37. Elisha's solution was to send Gehazi back to the woman's home and **lay** Elisha's **staff on the lad's face** (v. 29). Gehazi did so (v. 31), but the woman informed Elisha that she would **not leave**. She wanted the prophet at her son's side, and nothing else would suffice. So with Gehazi running ahead, while Elisha and the woman **followed** to the child's bedside. Sadly, Gehazi came back to report that **the lad** had **not awakened** (v. 31). Then Elisha arrived to find the **lad was dead** (v. 32). Elisha went into the boy's room, **shut the door . . . and prayed to the Lord**. The prophet also **lay** on the boy's body twice until the boy was finally raised from the dead (v. 35). Both **Gehazi** and the **Shunammite** mother were called to the room, so that the woman could **take up** her **son** (v. 36). Here in the ministry of Elisha, the Lord confirmed His power to raise the dead, just as He had done with Elijah and the widow of Zarephath (cf. 1Kg 17:8-34).

(3) The Miracle of Healing the Poison Stew (2Kg 4:38-41)

4:38-41. A third miracle of compassion occurred at the time **Elisha returned to Gilgal**. Once again, **there was a famine in the land** (v. 38); perhaps as in the days of Elijah, it was the direct result of God's judgment (cf. 1Kg 17–18).

Elisha met with some of the **sons of the prophets** and ordered **his servant** to prepare a pot of stew (v. 38). The command was carried out by one who **went out into the field to gather herbs** to add to the stew. Apparently the man retrieved **wild gourds** that were sliced . . . into the pot, but unknown to him they were poisonous (v. 39). Elisha was alerted to the poisonous food: **O man of God, there is death in the pot** (v. 40).

Elisha ordered that **meal**, that is flour, be added to the stew, and then the prophet ordered the people to **eat** because **there was no harm in the pot** (v. 41). Like purifying of the water of Jericho with salt (cf. 2:21), it was not the flour meal that made the food safe to eat; it was a miracle from the Lord. In God's compassionate mercy many people were rescued from harm.

(4) The Miracle of the Feeding of a Hundred Men (2Kg 4:42-44)

4:42-44. A fourth miracle was recorded when **a man came from Baal-shalishah** (a village in Ephraim, near Gilgal, v. 38)**, and brought the man of God bread of the first fruits** (v. 42). At the festival of **first fruits** people were to bring the first of their harvest to the tabernacle, and later to the temple (cf. Lv 23:17-21; Dt 18:3-5; Nm 28:26-31). They were to be brought to the priests for their regular provision, since the tribe of Levi had no land of their own as did the other tribes.

However, most of the priests in the northern kingdom under Jeroboam's reign had fled south to the kingdom of Judah (cf. 2Ch 11:14). So it was only logical that a man in the northern kingdom who loved the Lord would bring **first fruits** to Elisha, who was ministering like a priest in the northern kingdom. Immediately, Elisha ordered that the gift of food be used to feed **the people** (v. 42). However, **his attendant**, probably Gehazi, questioned whether there was enough food to feed the **hundred men** who were gathered (v. 43). Elisha responded, **Give them to the people that they may eat, for thus says the LORD, 'They shall eat and have some left over'** (cf. Mt 14:15-21). The attendant did as the prophet commanded, and food was available to eat and to collect afterward **according to the word of the LORD**.

(5) The Miraculous Healing of Naaman the Leper (2Kg 5:1-27)

One of the most memorable narratives in the Bible records Naaman the Aramean's healing from leprosy. The story contains a series of contrasts throughout: Naaman vs. the Jewish slave girl; the king of Israel vs. the king of Aram/Syria; Elisha vs. Naaman; and Naaman vs. Gehazi. But the climax and the purpose of the story is that Elisha refused to be rewarded for something God alone had done (vv. 15-16).

5:1-5. Naaman was introduced according to his position and reputation. He was **the captain of the army of the king of Aram** (Syria) on the northern border of Israel. He was **a great man . . . and highly respected** (v. 1). But anything Naaman accomplished was because **the LORD** was working through him. Even his victories came from the Lord's hand. But the one problem that stood out in Naaman's life was the fact that **he was a leper** (v. 1). The medical condition today called leprosy (or Hansen's disease) differs from the skin conditions described in Lv 13:1-46, which seemed to include a number of diseases of the skin. Hansen's disease would have been so debilitating that Naaman would not have been able to carry out his normal duties as a military officer. This was not the case with Naaman. So he may have had some other skin disease, possibly severe eczema or seborrhea.

The first major contrast in the passage placed Naaman alongside a **little girl from the land of Israel** who had been captured and placed in the care of Naaman's **wife** (v. 2). The girl had no power in contrast to Naaman, who had both social and military power. Yet she was the one God used to guide her master to discover the Sovereign of the universe (v. 3). When Naaman heard indirectly through the girl that there was a cure for his leprosy in Israel, he **went in and told his master**, the king of Aram, about what he had heard (v. 4). **The king of Aram** (Syria) sent Naaman with **a letter** for **the king of Israel**, along with **ten talents of silver and six thousand shekels of gold and ten changes of clothes** (v. 5). Both the king and the military commander believed that healing could be purchased.

5:6-7. When Naaman arrived in Israel, the **letter** he was carrying stated the intention of the trip, namely, that the **king of Israel** might **cure him of his leprosy** (v. 6). But King Jehoram interpreted the request as a provocation for war between Israel and Aram. Not knowing what to do, Jehoram **tore his clothes** in an expression of frustration and despair over being put in a position to be like **God** (v. 7), i.e., being responsible for momentous decisions.

5:8-14. The situation would be a platform for the living God to make Himself known. So when Elisha learned of Jehoram's response to the letter, he told the king to send Naaman to him. Elisha's purpose was to show **that there** was **a prophet in Israel** (v. 8). This expression is a way of saying, "So that he might know that there is a God in Israel."

Another contrast is seen in how Elisha handled the situation as opposed to Naaman's response to the prophet's orders given in v. 10. Elisha did not initially meet the Aramean commander face to face, but instead sent a **messenger**, telling him, **Go and wash in the Jordan seven times, and your flesh will be restored to you and you will be clean** (cf. Lv 13:6, 17, 23, 28, 37, 39), that is, "You will be healed." Elisha was responding on the basis of his faith in God, whereas Naaman primarily assumed he would be respected and healed on the spot. Naaman was insulted and **furious**; he interpreted the command as disrespectful to his station in life and as a mere religious ritual. From his perspective he could have carried out what he perceived as a ritual in one of the rivers in Aram, **Abanah and Pharpar** (v. 12).

But Elisha wanted the commander's thoughts to be directed elsewhere—to the God of Israel and His power. Naaman could have stormed away and provoked the very military conflict Jehoram feared (cf. v. 7). But **his servants** intervened to encourage him to do what the prophet directed (v. 13). Their reasoning was simply that if Elisha had asked Naaman to do **some great thing**, he would have done it; so why not **wash and be clean** as the prophet directed? Naaman listened to their advice, again being humbled by the words of people from lower stations in life and finding great benefit (cf. vv. 3-4, 13). What Naaman did was **according to the word of the man of God**, that is, according to God's direction. The result was that **his flesh was restored like the flesh of a little child and he was clean** (v. 14). The point was that from the perspective of the OT law, Naaman was restored both physically and spiritually. However, his spiritual condition would not be clearly revealed until later (vv. 15, 17).

5:15-19. Realizing that he had been healed, Naaman **returned to the man of God**, along with his entourage, and made a surprising confession. What was even more impressive was his change of attitude toward Elisha. He stated, **Behold now, I know that there is no God in all the earth, but in Israel** (v. 15). The story of Naaman illustrates God's faithfulness to Gentiles. Anyone who turns to the God of Israel, even in the period of the OT, would find grace, forgiveness, and a relationship with Him. Even citizens of Israel did not have the same conviction. And as a result of his healing, Naaman wanted to reward Elisha with the valuable gifts he had brought from Aram (v. 15). In another surprising move in the narrative, Elisha refused Naaman's offer (v. 16). In view of God's miraculous intervention and Naaman's profession of faith, this was not the time to receive money for something God had done.

Naaman apparently realized that God had healed him, but now he would be in a difficult situation when he returned to Damascus, where the God of Israel was not worshiped. So he asked Elisha for two things. The first was to provide him with **two mules' load of earth** (v. 17). It was a common idea in the ancient world that a deity could be worshiped only on its own home soil; so Naaman wanted to bring home with him the soil of Israel. His motives may have been good, but his understanding of the Lord was immature (Patterson and Austel, "1 and 2 Kings," 192). Naaman's second request was for forgiveness for future duties that would be imposed on him as a result of his position (v. 18). He knew that he would have to accompany the Aramean king to worship the Aramean false god of war, **Rimmon**. Naaman knew that God would see him going into the **house** (temple) of the pagan god, and so he asked for a special **pardon**. Elisha extended that pardon when he said, **Go in peace** (v. 19). The entire interaction with Naaman reflected back on the Abrahamic covenant and God's intentions to bless people from all nations (cf. Gn 12:3), as well as the fulfillment of Solomon's prayer that "all the peoples of the earth may know Your name" (1Kg 8:41-43).

5:20-27. A final contrast occurred in details between Gehazi, Naaman, and Elisha. **Gehazi** had been an eyewitness to a number of miraculous interventions from God through Elisha (cf. chap. 4). Unfortunately, Gehazi was troubled that his **master** had **spared this Naaman** (v. 20), and had not received from Naaman what he **had brought** to Israel as a gift. So Gehazi decided to take things into his own hands and get something for himself. He pursued **Naaman** on his way back to Aram, concocting a story of Elisha suddenly needing to feed guests who had come into his presence. Naaman accepted Gehazi's request and gave him **two talents** of **silver** and **two changes of clothes** which he had originally brought as a gift for Elisha (vv. 21-23).

The "rewards" were carried partway back to Gehazi's home, where he **deposited them in the house** (v. 24). Gehazi assumed that his plan was foolproof, but God sees everything! Nothing can be hidden from His sight. When Elisha asked Gehazi where he had been, Gehazi said, **Your servant went nowhere** (v. 25). Knowledge of Gehazi's deception was grievous to Elisha, for he said, **Did not my heart go with you, when the**

man turned from his chariot to meet you? (v. 26). The prophet implied that Gehazi's actions were inappropriate for all that God had done and revealed about Himself. It was not **a time to receive money... clothes... olive groves... vineyards and sheep and oxen and male and female servants** (v. 26). It was a time for worshiping and serving the God who miraculously intervened in a non-Israelite's life and made Himself known. As a result of Gehazi's brazen sin, **the leprosy of Naaman**, Elisha said, would **cling** to Gehazi and his descendants. Along with the grace showed Naaman for his faith, there was also chastisement of Gehazi for his greed.

(6) The Miraculous Recovery of the Axe Head (2Kg 6:1-7)

6:1-7. Earlier in his ministry, Elisha had been involved with great acts of personal compassion, as an expression of God's loving care. Here we see another aspect of the prophet's power and God's concern for the everyday issues of life. The miracle of the axe head reflects the value of tools to their workmen at this period. The setting for the account in these verses was in another meeting Elisha had with the **sons of the prophets** (v. 1). They expressed to their prophet-leader, **The place before you where we are living is too limited for us**. The Hebrew literally reads, "where we sit before you," and implies that some sort of place for instruction was being described. These students under Elisha's instruction said that where they were meeting was too small, and proposed that they **go to the Jordan** and build a larger facility (v. 2). Elisha agreed to the proposal, and after some urging, he agreed to accompany them on their journey.

However, in the process of cutting down some of the **trees**, a worker's **axe head fell into the water** (v. 5). He called out to Elisha, explaining that the axe head he was using **was borrowed** (v. 6). Loss of the tool would have put him in debt, and as with the widow in chap. 4, the indebtedness would have put him under a financial burden he would be unable to bear. Elisha asked where the axe head fell, then he threw **a stick** into the water, causing the axe head to **float**. The worker retrieved the axe head and presumably returned to his task. Skeptics can argue over the plausibility of such a miracle, but to do so is fruitless. The conclusion should be that God can do anything He chooses. And He is concerned about both "great" and "small" things in the lives of His people. Although the miracle involved the recovery of an axe head, the motivation for the miracle was compassion for the worker who had borrowed and lost it.

(7) God's Miraculous Protection of Elisha (2Kg 6:8-23)

6:8-12. The last of the "compassion-miracles" (for which, see the comments introducing chap. 4) tells of another time when **Aram was warring against Israel** (v. 8) and the Lord gave an amazing victory. One of the Arameans' strategies was to set up places to ambush the armies of Israel. The only problem was that Elisha, **the man of God** (v. 9), knew of the raids and would alert the king of Israel: **Beware... for the Arameans are coming down there** ahead of time so that his soldiers would avoid attack. This disclosure took place enough times that the king of Aram assumed that he had a traitor in his midst (v. 11). But one of the king's servants informed him that it was not a traitor but **Elisha, the prophet**, who even knew what the king would **speak in** his **bedroom** (v. 12). The point was that as the messenger of God, Elisha knew what God revealed to him, and God knew absolutely everything, including the most private things a king might say.

6:13-17. Learning that Elisha was the culprit who was frustrating the king of Aram's military strategies, he ordered his army to **Dothan**, a city northeast of Samaria near Mount Gilboa, where Elisha was staying. The Arameans **surrounded** the city at **night** so as to capture Elisha (v. 14). The next morning Elisha's attendant awakened to discover the Aramean forces ready to attack. He came to Elisha for insight as to what they should do. Elisha's response was, **Do not fear, for those who are with us are more than those who are with them** (v. 16). Then Elisha **prayed... and the LORD opened the servant's eyes and he saw the mountain... full of horses and chariots of fire** (v. 17), the very same phenomenon that Elisha himself saw when his mentor, Elijah, was taken up into heaven (cf. 2:11). The God who was with Elijah was confirming to both the prophet and his attendant that He was with them.

6:18-23. When the Aramean soldiers came down from the mountains to capture Elisha, the prophet prayed that God would strike them with blindness. And the Lord **struck them with blindness according to the word of Elisha** (v. 18). Elisha led the blinded troops into **Samaria**, the capital of the northern kingdom. It was Elisha's way of demonstrating to the **king of Israel** and his subjects God's power and compassion (vv. 19-21). When King Jehoram saw the Aramean soldiers, he asked Elisha, **Shall I kill them?** But

Elisha's orders were to treat them with compassion, like **those you have taken captive with your sword and with your bow**, and to set a **great feast for them** (vv. 22-23). Then with their sight restored, the once-captured men were allowed to return to their homeland. The result was that **the marauding bands of Arameans did not come again into the land of Israel** (v. 23). What a hostile king intended for evil, God worked through His prophet to bring about good. And He showed that nothing is obscure or hidden from the mind of God.

8. Elisha Predicts the Siege of Samaria Will End (2Kg 6:24–7:20)

Through a variety of miraculous events, it became clear that Elisha was the God-ordained successor to Elijah. Now the prophet's ministry was directed to King Jehoram and those living with him in the northern kingdom's capital city of Samaria, which was under attack.

6:24-25. Once again war had broken out and **Ben-hadad king of Aram** attacked **Samaria**. The narrative set the stage for what was about to follow, stating that the siege was so severe that the **famine in Samaria** made even food that would not usually be eaten, **a donkey's head**, an unclean animal (cf. Lv 11:2-7; Dt 14:4-8), be sold for an exorbitant price of **eighty shekels**, or two pounds, of silver; and a **forth of a kab**, or two quarts, of **dove's dung**, probably used for fuel, sold for **five shekels**, six months' wages of an average worker.

6:26-33. This section gives the bleakest report of the famine. While King Jehoram **was passing by on the wall** to survey all that was happening, **a woman** called to him for help. But the king himself was destitute, telling her, **If the Lord does not help you, from where shall I help you? From the threshing floor, or from the wine press?** (v. 27). He then inquired about her specific need. The scene portrayed a situation that was the opposite of what Solomon faced in the dispute between two women (cf. 1Kg 3:16-28).

However, Jehoram lacked the wisdom of Solomon. In fact, there was no hope in sight, outside of the merciful intervention of God, to help the people in their desperate circumstances. The **woman** informed the king that she had an agreement with another woman to cannibalize her **son** and then the next day they would eat the other woman's child. But the second woman reneged and had **hidden** her son so they would not **eat him** (vv. 28-29). This was the kind of sin God said would happen because of the rebellion of His people (cf. Lv 26:27-29). In his despair and anger over what he had just heard, Jehoram **tore his clothes**, a sign of grief (v. 30; cf. Gn 34:34) and announced a death sentence against **Elisha**, assuming that he was the cause of the siege, famine, and all that was happening (v. 31).

How quickly Jehoram had forgotten the prophet's earlier assistance in revealing the whereabouts of Aramean raiding parties (cf. 6:9). While **sitting in** his **house** with **the elders** of the city, Elisha revealed that a **messenger** from Jehoram was on his way to **take away my head** (v. 32). He told the elders to **shut . . . and hold the door shut against** the messenger, because the king was close behind him. The prophet made a subtle statement as to who was the real cause behind the famine when he referred to Jehoram as the **son of a murderer**, a reference to the murderous practices of the kings of Israel who had killed the prophets of God (v. 32; cf. 1Kg 18:4, 13-14; 21:10, 13). Jehoram blamed Elisha for the suffering, just as Ahab had blamed Elijah for the drought in his day (cf. 1Kg 18:10, 16; 21:20).

But when the messenger finally arrived, he appeared not to have Elisha's execution on his mind but cast blame on the Lord, stating that **this evil** was **from** Him (v. 33). As the ongoing narrative would reveal, the Lord was not to be morally guilty as if He had acted capriciously in ordaining the siege and its resultant famine. Instead, the idolatry of Jehoram and his subjects caused God to inflict such misery against Israel as a justifiable act of judgment (cf. 3:2).

7:1-2. After receiving the messenger, Elisha announced **the word of the Lord** for the elders and the king's messenger. By this time Jehoram himself may have appeared, because a **royal officer on whose hand the king was leaning**, meaning that he was Jehoram's "right-hand man," was within the hearing of Elisha's prophecy (v. 2). Elisha's prophecy had two elements. The first was that the previous high inflation caused by the Aramean siege would be totally reversed **tomorrow**, the next day. The statement implied that good things were about to happen. The second statement was a judgment against the doubting king's royal officer. When he heard what Elisha said, he responded by saying with great sarcasm: **Behold, if the Lord should make windows in heaven, could this thing be?** (v. 2). Because of the officer's skepticism Elisha announced that he would see the fulfillment of this prophecy, but he would **not eat of it** (v. 2).

No one could anticipate how quickly and accurately this prophecy would be fulfilled.

7:3-11. There were four leprous men at the entrance of the city **gate** (v. 3). They obviously were outcasts because of their physical condition, and they knew that their days were limited. They contemplated that if they tried to enter the city, the famine would overtake them with all the others held captive inside. So the other alternative was to **go over to the camp of the Arameans** and give themselves up. They reasoned that they had a 50/50 chance of living (v. 4). When they went to the Aramean camp as planned **at twilight** the next day, they were surprised to find that the camp had been deserted (v. 5). The Lord **had caused the army of the Arameans to hear a sound of chariots and a sound of horses, even the sound of a great army** (v. 6). The Arameans thought that Jehoram had hired the **Hittites** or the **Egyptians** to come to his aid, but clearly a direct, miraculous intervention of the Lord had caused the Arameans to think they were under attack and they **fled** for their lives (v. 7).

When the camp was deserted, livestock, food, **silver and gold and clothes** had been left behind, so the four lepers amassed the spoils with great excitement (v. 8). But as they were enjoying all that had been left behind, the lepers realized that they were not doing the right thing by keeping everything to themselves. They concluded, **This day is a day of good news, but we are keeping silent** (v. 9). So they left their discovery and went to the **gatekeepers** in Samaria and **told them** what they had found, announcing that the Aramean camp had been completely abandoned and abundant resources for the city's survival had been left behind (v. 10).

7:12-15. When the king got word about the lepers' discovery, he was skeptical of the report, thinking it was a military ambush to **get into the city** (v. 12). There was no indication that he recalled Elisha's earlier prophecy (v. 1). But starvation conditions in Samaria were so horrible, **one of his servants** suggested that they had nothing to lose in sending some men out to see if the lepers were telling the truth (v. 13). So he sent **two chariots with horses** to **go and see** if the report was accurate (v. 14). As they went, they learned that **all the way was full of clothes and equipment which the Arameans had thrown away in their haste** (v. 15).

7:16-20. When the news came back to the city, **the people went out and plundered the camp** (v. 16). And it **happened just as the man of God had spoken**; because of the abundance of good supplies in the camp, food would now be inexpensive (vv. 1, 18). In fact, the king even appointed his royal officer, who had **answered the man of God** with his mocking question (vv. 1, 18) **to have charge of the gate** as the people went out (v. 17). But stampede-like conditions occurred and the royal officer was **trampled** to death, **just as the man of God had said** (vv. 17, 20). He did see the abundance of food, but he did not eat it (v. 2). God's Word was fulfilled exactly, but in a most unexpected way.

9. Elisha Carries out the Prophecies Originally Spoken through Elijah (2Kg 8:1–9:13)

The pace of events in 2 Kings accelerated as Elisha's ministry continued. The argument made throughout this commentary has been that God is the true King over Israel and the world, and that human kings were to represent His will and ways as outlined in Dt 17:14-20. However, in the space of a lifetime, the average citizen in the kingdom might question whether God cared and would keep His Word. The chapters that follow make the case that God does care and is truthful in all that He says in most convincing ways.

8:1-6. The narration now returns to another event in the life of the Shunammite **woman whose son** Elisha **had restored to life** (cf. 4:8-37 and the comments there). The woman had been advised by Elisha, **Arise and go** elsewhere **for the Lord** has **called for a famine . . . on the land for seven years** (v. 1). The woman did as Elisha asked and **sojourned in the land of the Philistines seven years** (v. 2). When she finally returned, it appeared that her land had been confiscated, so she appealed **to the king for her house and for her field** (v. 3). Her actions would have been the right thing to do in view of the laws of restoration (cf. Ex 21:2-3; Dt 15:1-6). When she made her way into King Jehoram's presence, **the king was talking with Gehazi, the servant of the man of God** about how Elisha had raised this same woman's son from the dead (vv. 4-5). God's sovereignty and faithfulness would appear again and again in the remaining chapters of the book.

While Gehazi and the king were talking, the woman came to plead her case for the return of her land and Gehazi pointed her out, **This is the woman and this is her son, whom Elisha restored to life** (v. 5). When the king asked the woman to confirm Gehazi's story, she did so. Then the king ordered, **Restore all that was hers and all the produce of the field from the day that she left the land even until now** (v. 6). Nothing in the text indicates that Gehazi had been restored to health following the judgment of leprosy against him (cf. 5:27). However, this woman, because of her faithfulness in obeying the word of the Lord through Elisha, had seen both the restoration of life and property. God's sovereignty watches over those who care for His messengers.

8:7-10. Several years had passed since God's prophecy came to Elijah about anointing three men (cf. 1Kg 19:15-17). In God's encounter with Elijah, the prophet was told that he was to anoint three people to key roles in national and international events: Hazael was to be anointed king in Aram; Jehu was to be anointed king in Israel; and Elisha was to be anointed Elijah's successor. But Elijah carried out only one inauguration before he was taken up into heaven (cf. 2Kg 2). Had Elijah disobeyed God? Had the Almighty forgotten what He said He would do? This section (chaps. 7–15) shows that in spite of what Elijah was not able to do, God still carried out His will through Elisha in the spirit and office of Elijah.

At this point, without explanation, **Elisha came to Damascus**, where **Ben-hadad king of Aram was sick** (v. 7). King Ben-hadad learned of Elisha's presence and sent **Hazael** to inquire as to the prospects of his recovery. Ben-hadad also sent a very impressive **gift** for Elisha, apparently hoping to buy a good report (vv. 8-9). While addressing Elisha with the king's request, Hazael referred to the king as **your son Ben-hadad king of Aram** (v. 9). The title was a way of showing the respect the king had for both Elisha and the Lord.

In response to the question about the king's recovery, Elisha gave an unusual response: **Go, say to him, 'You will surely recover,' but the LORD has shown me that he will certainly die.** The prophet indicated that Ben-hadad would recover from the disease, but he would die from another cause (v. 10).

8:11-15. After giving Hazael the message for the king, Elisha looked **steadily** at him and **the man of God wept** (v. 11). Elisha explained he was weeping **because I know the evil that** Hazael would **do to the sons of Israel** (v. 12), and told him in details the horrible things he would do. In keeping with the prophecies, Hazael then **returned to his master**, gave him Elisha's message, and the **following day** assassinated Ben-hadad by smothering him. Just as the prophecy had said, **Hazael became king in his** place (v. 13; cf. 1Kg 19:15).

8:16-23. Now the focus shifts to political events in the southern kingdom of Judah. It is clear that spiritual apostasy was not simply an issue with the northern kingdom alone. The typical succession formula employed throughout the book was used here, noting that **in the fifth year of Joram the son of Ahab king of Israel . . . Jehoram the son of Jehoshaphat king of Judah became king** (v. 16). Two things were important in describing Jehoram's reign. First, **he walked in the way of the kings of Israel**, indicating he followed the pagan practices of the northern kingdom (v. 18). The reason for his orientation to evil was that **the daughter of Ahab became his wife**. The narrative that follows in chaps. 8–12 describes a steady spiritual decline in Judah that lasted for approximately 15 years.

However, the LORD was not willing to destroy Judah, for the sake of David His servant (v. 19). What God had promised to David in 2Sm 7:12-15 prompted years of mercy and patience for Judah. And yet Jehoram (called **Joram** in 2Kg 8:21) had his own troubles. **Edom** chose again to revolt against Judah (v. 20). Jehoram/Joram attempted to put a stop to the insurrection by taking his army into battle at **Zair**, near Edom, but his army was surrounded at night and they barely escaped (v. 21). Edom never came under Judah's control again (v. 22).

8:24-29. Following the reign of **Joram**/Jehoram, **Ahaziah his son became king** in Judah (841 BC; cf. 2Ch 22:1-9). His reign took place in the **twelfth year of Joram**/Jehoram **the son of Ahab** in Israel (v. 25). The succession description and the marriage alliances continued to explain why Judah faced spiritual decline. Ahaziah's mother, **Athaliah**, was the **granddaughter of Omri king of Israel** (v. 26) and the daughter of wicked Ahab (cf. 1Kg 16:1–22:40) who became a wicked queen of Judah (cf. 2Kg 11:1-16). Ahaziah's leadership was evil, **because he was a son-in-law of the house of Ahab** (v. 27). As he moved further away from a life shaped by the law of God, the more evil would have an influence on the land. Ahaziah of Judah was also drawn into further military campaigns with his northern counterpart (v. 28). In the battle with **Hazael king of Aram**, the Arameans wounded the king of Israel (Joram/Jehoram). Learning of his brother-in-law's injury, Ahaziah **went down to see** the king of Israel **because he was sick**. His presence providentially placed him in Jezreel and ultimately led to his own death as recorded in chap. 9.

9:1-3. So far in the historical narrative of 2 Kings, God fulfilled His word to Elijah concerning Elisha and Hazael (cf. 1Kg 19:15-17). These first two of three predictions were now fulfilled. The third prophecy, concerning Jehu, was about to unfold.

It may seem strange that Elisha did not have a more direct hand in what transpired in vv. 1-13. Instead, Elisha **called one of the sons of the prophets** and prepared him for an important task. The urgency of the mission was revealed in the words **Gird up your loins** (v. 1), meaning to gather up one's long outer garment and get ready for action. The mission must have had a high degree of danger associated with it, because this same messenger, after completing his assignment, was to **open the door and flee** (v. 3). His specific task was to **search out Jehu** and anoint him as king over Israel (cf. vv. 2-3). **Jehu** and his soldiers were in **Ramoth-gilead**, an important city east of the Jordan (cf. 1Kg 22), engaged in battle with Aram, a battle in which Israel's king Joram had been wounded (cf. 8:28).

9:4-10. When **the young man** who was sent by Elisha arrived he found Jehu sitting with **the captains of the army** (v. 5). The young man **poured the oil on his** [Jehu's] **head**, and told him, **Thus says the Lord, the God of Israel, 'I have anointed you king over the people of the Lord, even over Israel'** (v. 6). Jehu had a twofold task: (1) to **strike the house of Ahab**, and (2) **avenge the blood** of the Lord's servants, both the prophets and those who served Him in indirect ways (v. 7). Words originally spoken about the demise of Ahab's house (cf. 1Kg 21:21) were repeated for Jehu's benefit. The **house of Ahab** was to become like **the house of Jeroboam**, since both kings had led the people into spiritual rebellion for which the nations were now reaping the pain of their sin (v. 9). After giving Jehu this stark message the young man **opened the door and fled** just as Elisha had instructed (vv. 3, 10).

9:11-13. When Jehu **came out** from his meeting with the young man his **servants** asked, **Is all well?** In other words, "What happened?" Perhaps they saw the oil on his head and wanted to know more. They referred to the son of the prophet who had appeared to be a **mad fellow**, which shows the spiritual condition of Jehoram's/Joram's soldiers. At first Jehu dismissed their inquiries: **You know very well the man and his talk** (v. 11). But he finally admitted, **Thus and thus he said to me, 'Thus says the Lord, "I have anointed you king over Israel."'** Those who were with Jehu hurriedly took their garments, laid them at his feet, **blew the trumpet**, and declared, **Jehu is king!** (v. 13). God's word to Elijah had come to pass. What the Almighty says is to be taken as faithful and true—always!

10. Jehu of Israel: A Bad King Who Takes Actions that Fulfill Prophecy (2Kg 9:14–10:36)

The prophecy given to Elijah about Jehu's anointing as king of Israel, the northern kingdom, was now fulfilled. This section describes the purifying work of Jehu in five stages: (1) his assassination of Jehoram (9:15-26); (2) his assassination of Ahaziah (9:27-29); (3) the execution of Jezebel (9:30-37); (4) the execution of Ahab's 70 sons (10:1-17); and (5) the execution of Baal worshipers (10:18-28). The section closes with a summary of Jehu's own shortcomings and the beginning of the end of the northern kingdom (10:29-36).

9:14-20. Jehu had just been anointed as the new king of Israel by a representative of Elisha (841–814 BC; cf. 2Ch 22:7-12), and **conspired against Joram**/Jehoram, the reigning king of Israel. At this time, **King Joram**/Jehoram was on his way back to Jezreel to heal from his wounds (v. 15; cf. 8:29). At the same time **Ahaziah king of Judah**, had traveled to **Jezreel** to meet Joram because they were forming an alliance against the Aramean attack (v. 16). In his strategy to replace Joram, Jehu had secured **Ramoth-gilead** so that **no one** would **escape or leave the city** to run and inform Joram of Jehu's military threat to the throne (v. 15). Jehu himself set out in a chariot to apprehend Joram. As he approached Jezreel, a watchman standing on the city **tower** saw **a company** of people headed in the direction of the city.

Confused by the approaching military, King **Joram** sent a horseman to ask the purpose of this military approach: **Is it peace?** the rider asked Jehu (vv. 17-18). The first watchmen **did not return**, perhaps taken captive by Jehu's army. Finally, as the chariots got closer, the watchman reported that **the driving is like the driving of Jehu . . . for he drives furiously** (v. 20). The word translated **furiously** is the same word used to describe the son of the prophet as a "mad fellow" (v. 11). Jehu was a reckless charioteer and was easily recognizable by his distinct driving style. The watchmen did not understand why Jehu would be coming to Jezreel.

9:21-26. When **Joram**/Jehoram (king of Israel) realized that Jehu was on his way, both he and Ahaziah (king of Judah) **went out, each in his chariot . . . to meet Jehu** (v. 21). Interestingly, the meeting was at **the property of Naboth the Jezreelite** where Elijah prophesied the end of the line of Ahab (v. 21; cf. 1Kg 21:2-3, 13, 19). Joram again asked if Jehu's appearance was a peaceful one. Jehu responded, **What peace, so long as the harlotries of your mother Jezebel and her witchcrafts are so many?** (v. 22). Jehu identified the continuing occult ("witchcraft") sin and unfaithfulness to the God of Israel ("harlotries") of Ahab and Jezebel (cf. 1Kg 16:31), who were Joram's family (cf. 3:1).

Joram immediately realized the **treachery** of the situation (v. 23) and tried to escape, but Jehu **drew his bow . . . and shot** the king of Israel **through his heart** (v. 24). After Joram died in his chariot, Jehu, now Israel's new king, ordered **Bidkar his officer** to **cast** Joram's body on the property that Ahab had stolen from **Naboth** (v. 25; cf. 1Kg 21:2-3, 13-24). Jehu remembered Elijah's **oracle against him** (Ahab) and understood that everything that happened at Joram's death occurred **according to the word of the Lord** (v. 26). Although Elisha had spoken against Ahab, since Joram/Jehoram was the son of Ahab (3:1), his death was a fulfillment of Elijah's prophecy (cf. 1Kg 21:19).

9:27-29. When **Ahaziah the king of Judah** saw Jehu kill Joram, he tried to escape for his life. However, **Jehu pursued him** and Ahaziah was mortally wounded on his escape to **Megiddo** and **died there** (v. 27). He was eventually **carried . . . to Jerusalem** where he was buried **in the city of David** (v. 28). The summary of the reign of **Ahaziah** says he became king in Judah **in the eleventh year of Joram**, king of Israel (v. 29), but elsewhere it says that he became king in the "twelfth year of Joram" (cf. 8:25). The discrepancy is best resolved by understanding that ancient records handled partial years of a king's ascension in different ways (see Introduction: Background).

9:30-37. The next act of divine purification, and fulfillment of Elijah's prophecy, concerned **Jezebel**, King Ahab's wife and the mother of King Joram/Jehoram. The idolatrous queen **heard** of Jehu's arrival in Jezreel, and dressed for the occasion by painting **her eyes and** adorning **her head** to meet Israel's new king (v. 30). She referred to Jehu as **Zimri**, his **master's murderer** (v. 31). **Zimri** had taken the throne of Israel by assassination and had a brief seven-day reign in Israel (cf. 1Kg 16:8-20). Jezebel was mocking Jehu by associating him with the failed reign of Zimri, but that would not be the case with Jehu. Jehu asked Jezebel's officials, **Who is on my side?** (v. 32). They demonstrated their allegiance to him by obeying Jehu's command, **Throw her down** (v. 33). At once the **horses . . . trampled her** body **underfoot**. Later, when Jehu ordered Jezebel be given a decent burial, his attendants found that nothing was left except **her . . . skull and the feet and the palms of her hands** (v. 35). Jehu recognized what Elijah had prophesied about her had come to pass: **In the property of Jezreel the dogs shall eat the flesh of Jezebel** (v. 36; cf. 1Kg 21:23).

10:1-11. Jehu had not completed the task Elisha's messenger gave to him, for he had to finish dealing with the house of **Ahab** who **had seventy sons in Samaria** (v. 1). Up to this point, most of the events regarding Ahab's house took place in Jezreel. But since **Samaria** was the capital of Israel, Jehu needed to move to secure his authority there. One potential threat would have been anyone from Ahab's family who had a legitimate claim to the throne. To eliminate the threat, Jehu **wrote letters** to officials in both **Samaria** and **Jezreel**, specifically to those who were **guardians of the children of Ahab** (v. 1). He challenged them to identify **the best and the fittest of** Ahab's **sons,** and place him on the **throne** (v. 3). His tactic was to make the leaders of the former dynasty choose sides. Out of great fear (v. 4) they informed Jehu that they were his **servants** and would do whatever he asked of them (v. 5).

Apparently not accepting their word, Jehu **wrote a letter to them a second time**, telling them to combine their words with action. His specific challenge was to bring **the heads** of the **seventy** sons of Ahab to Jezreel where Jehu would meet them. The leaders **slaughtered them . . . and put their heads in baskets, and sent them to** Jehu **at Jezreel** (v. 7). Jehu then had his officials pile **the heads . . . in two heaps at the entrance of the** city **gate** (v. 8). A common practice in the ancient world was for conquering leaders to intimidate the citizens into obedience (House, *1, 2 Kings*, 292). When the citizens awakened the next **morning**, they observed a shocking display (v. 9). Jehu spoke to the people telling them, **Know then that there shall fall to the earth nothing of the word of the Lord**, that is, not one word spoken by the Lord will ever fail. He reminded them that what they saw before their very eyes was what **the Lord . . . spoke through His servant Elijah** (v. 10). Jehu wanted it to be clear that this change in regimes was not his doing, but the work of the Lord. Then **Jehu killed all who remained of the house of Ahab . . . until he left him without a survivor**, just as the Lord had said (v. 11; cf. 1Kg 21:20-24, 29).

10:12-17. Jehu then traveled from Jezreel to **Samaria**. On the way his entourage met **relatives of Ahaziah king of Judah**. They apparently were unaware of their own king's demise or the death of Joram of Israel. When they announced that they had come **to greet the sons of the king and the sons of the queen mother**, Jehu may have thought they too were potential rivals like the 70 sons of Ahab (v. 1). Therefore he seized all **forty-two** of them and killed them at the **pit of Beth-eked** ("the house of shearing"); apparently the shepherds were killed in a place, unidentified by archaeology, where their bodies would not quickly be found (v. 14).

While still on his journey to Samaria, Jehu **met Jehonadab the son of Rechab** (v. 15). Nothing is said about the man's background or political inclinations, other than the fact that he was **coming to meet** Jehu. The Rechabites were a Jewish sect who required that their followers not drink wine, and they were commended by Jeremiah for their spiritual devotion (cf. Jr 35:14-19). Both men had an interest in eliminating the ongoing threat of Baal worship , so Jehu invited Jehonadab to **ride in his chariot** and observe the zeal he had for the Lord (v. 16). When they arrived in **Samaria**, Jehu **killed all who remained to Ahab in Samaria, until he had destroyed him**, that is, the house of Ahab (v. 17). All that Jehu had done was in fulfillment of God's words through **Elijah** (cf. 1Kg 21:21).

10:18-28. Through the influence of his wife Jezebel, Ahab had introduced Baal worship to Israel (cf. 1Kg 16:31-32). With Jehonadab now part of his entourage, Jehu deceptively invited all the **prophets of Baal** and all his worshipers to come and join him in a **great sacrifice for Baal** (v. 19). His ruse was set up under the pretense that though **Ahab served Baal a little, Jehu** would **serve him much** (v. 18). In a general way, the scene has similarities to Elijah's confrontation of the Baal worshipers on Mount Carmel (cf. 1Kg 18), except that the prophet was open about his intentions and Jehu was deceptive.

When the worshipers arrived, Israel's new king made sure that **none of the servants of the Lord, but only the worshipers of Baal** were inside the **house of Baal** (v. 23). Prior to the gathering, Jehu **had stationed . . . eighty men outside** with orders to kill every single worshiper when he gave the command (v. 24). When the worshipers finished offering **the burnt offering**, Jehu gave the command and everyone inside the temple was executed. In addition, he made sure that other instruments of worship—**the sacred pillar of Baal** as well as the actual **house of Baal**—were destroyed completely and made into **a latrine** (vv. 26-27). What Elijah began, Jehu completed. **Thus Jehu eradicated Baal out of Israel** (v. 28).

10:29-31. Jehu was not like King David, however; although he ended Baal worship in Israel, **Jehu did not depart** from the worship of **golden calves that were at Bethel and that were at Dan** by which Jeroboam **had made Israel sin** (cf. 1Kg 12:26-32; 13:33-34; 14:16). Yet, for Jehu's zealous actions against the idolatry of Ahab and Jezebel, the Lord honored him for doing **what** was **right in** His **eyes** (v. 30). As a result, the Lord promised Jehu that he would have **sons of the fourth generation** who would sit on the throne of Israel (v. 30). However, this zealous king did not **walk in the law of the Lord . . . with all his heart**, and he continued in **the sins of Jeroboam** (v. 31).

10:32-36. Since Jehu and his successors did not follow the Lord completely, **the Lord began to cut off portions** of land **from Israel** (v. 32). **Hazael**, who had been appointed earlier by Elisha to rule in Aram, stepped up his attacks on the northern kingdom. Slowly the Israelites lost territory on their borders. Jehu's **twenty-eight years** began with great promise, but like so many kings before and after him, personal ambition kept him from leading the people in righteousness and blessing (v. 36).

11. Athaliah and Joash of Judah: A Bad Queen and a Good King (2Kg 11:1–12:21)

After detailing the major political and religious upheaval in the northern kingdom, the focus again moves to the southern kingdom of Judah. The text shows that political, national, and spiritual conditions always come back to "matters of the heart."

11:1-3. When news arrived in Jerusalem that Athaliah's son Ahaziah had been executed in Jezreel, she took immediate action to secure the throne for herself by destroying **all the royal offspring** (v. 1). **Athaliah** was the granddaughter of Omri and the daughter of Ahab (cf. 8:16-26) and had became the wife of the Judean king Jehoram. She reigned as the only queen of Judah (841–835 BC; cf. 2Ch 22:1–23:21). However, her wicked plan to be the sole heir to the throne was not foolproof, because another member of the royal family, **Jehosheba, the daughter of King Joram**, rescued a lone survivor, **Joash** (v. 2). Jehosheba was also the wife of the high priest, Jehoiada (cf. 2Ch 22:11). For **six years**, the child Joash was hidden by his aunt in the **house of the Lord**, unknown to the reigning queen (v. 3).

11:4-8. In the seventh year of Athaliah's reign, **Jehoiada sent and brought** a group of men who were assigned to serve as guards for the soon-to-be king, Joash. These men were identified as **the captains of hundreds of the Carites and of the guard** (v. 4). The Carites, also called Cherethites (cf. 1Sm 30:14; 2Sm 8:18; 15:18; 30:14) were possibly Phoenician mercenaries, who sometimes served as bodyguards to the king. Jehoida mustered his courage (cf. 2Ch 23:1) to protect the boy-king, and gave specific instructions to these Carites **to be with the king** at all times. Anyone who broke through their ranks to bring harm to Joash was to be **put to death** (v. 8).

11:9-12. Besides Jehoiada instructing the royal guard regarding their daily routines, he also supplied them with the necessary resources to carry out their orders. He gave them the **spears and shields that had been King David's** (v. 10). These were probably the gold shields that David brought with him after the defeat of the Aramean king Hadadezer (cf. 2Sm 8:7). At a specific point in time designated by Jehoiada the priest, **he brought the king's son out and put the crown on him and gave him the testimony** (v. 12). The **testimony** often referred to the tablets that Moses received from the Lord when he returned from meeting with God on Mount Sinai, and these were kept in the ark of the covenant. But in this context the term more likely refers to the copy of the law that the king was to read daily (cf. Dt 17:14-20). As the high priest placed the crown on Joash's head, and **anointed him** king of Judah, the people who had gathered **clapped their hands and said, "Long live the king!"** (v. 12).

11:13-16. The noise of cheering people got the attention of **Athaliah** as she **came to the . . . house of the Lord**, the temple (cf. 1Kg 3:1). Her immediate response to seeing the boy and the jubilant people was to **tear her clothes** in an act of grief. She shouted that what was happening was treason (v. 14). Earlier, the high priest had ordered that anybody who broke through the ranks of the guards was to be put to death (v. 8). And here was Athaliah defying the priest's orders. Therefore Jehoiada, the man now temporarily in charge of political and religious activities, ordered, **Bring her out between the ranks, and whoever follows her put to death with the sword** (v. 15). Athaliah was seized, taken away to the **horses' entrance of the king's house**, and **put to death** (v. 16).

11:17-21. With Athaliah no longer a contender for the throne, the high priest Jehoiada took a serious step in bringing about a spiritual renewal within the southern kingdom. He **made a covenant between the Lord and the king and the people** (v. 17). The details of the actual covenant were not included, but Jehoiada probably developed a covenant that was similar to the prayer Solomon prayed for the nation to be faithful to the Lord (cf. 1Sm 8). Also, this covenant probably reflected God's covenant with David in 2Sm 7:1-17 (House, *1, 2 Kings*, 299). Jehoiada's aim, however, was that all those gathered at Joash's coronation **would be the Lord's people** and not simply citizens focused on their self-interests (v. 17).

Two other events transpired on this important day in Judah's history. First, the people **went to the house of Baal, and tore it down** (v. 18). The purging activities that took place under Jehu in the north were not occurring in the southern kingdom. Second, those individuals who had been protecting Joash **brought** him **down from the house of the Lord . . . to the king's house . . . and he sat on the throne of the kings** (v. 19). At **seven years** of age, Joash became king to the delight of **all the people** (vv. 20-21). Following the coronation of Joash, **the city was quiet** (*shaqat* means "undisturbed" or "at peace"). Not only was there political peace, but after a long time of spiritual rebellion the people were at peace (quiet) with God, their true King, for the actions that they had taken against the encroachment of Baal worship.

12:1-3. Here Joash is identified by his other name, **Jehoash**. His rule is summarized, and the details of his activities given in vv. 4-21. He **did right in the sight of the Lord all his days in which Jehoiada the priest instructed him**. However, after the death of Jehoida, Joash/Jehoash "abandoned the house of the Lord . . . and served the Asherim and the idols" (2Ch 24:18; for details of Joash's rule and decline, cf. 2Ch 23–24). In spite of Jehoash's early noble efforts at keeping the Davidic covenant, he did not remove **the high places** (v. 3).

12:4-16. Under Jehoiada's influence, **Jehoash**/Joash was concerned about the care of the temple. At the time of Jehoash's reign the temple was well over a century old. The priests were responsible for collecting money for the regular maintenance of the building, but this duty had apparently been neglected. So Jehoash commanded them to take both the regular **assessment** of the worshipers as well as voluntary offerings that came from the people (**money which any man's heart prompts him to bring into the house of the Lord**, v. 4). But in the king's **twenty-third year** of his reign, the **priests had not repaired the damages of the house** (v. 6).

At that point Jehoash asked his mentor, Jehoiada the priest, to follow a different system. No longer were the priests to collect the money. Instead **Jehoiada . . . took a chest and bored a hole in its lid and put it beside the altar** (v. 9). The **king's scribe and the high priest** then took the money, **counted** it, and **gave** it to the workers to carry out necessary repairs (vv. 11-12). The priests **did not require an accounting from the men . . . for they dealt faithfully** with the money and the tasks assigned to them (v. 15). Other income collected **from the guilt offerings and . . . the sin offerings** continued to go to the priests for their regular care, since they had no land of their own to work as did other Israelites (v. 16). All these activities concerning the temple indicate Jehoash was following the Lord while he was under the influence of Jehoiada the priest.

12:17-18. Yet a person's spiritual orientation can change quickly, especially when threats and conflicts enter that person's life. And so it was with Jehoash. Near the end of his reign, after the death of Jehoiada, **Hazael king of Aram** was on a military campaign to capture new lands. Some commentators suggest that Hazael wanted to capture the southern trade routes that ran through Judah (e.g., House, *1, 2 Kings*, 303). Whatever the cause, **Jehoash . . . took all the sacred things** from the temple and from his own treasury **and sent them to Hazael king of Aram** as a bribe to keep him from attacking Jerusalem. **Then he** [Hazael] **went away from Jerusalem** (v. 18). The work that Judah's king put into repairing the temple was undone more quickly than it began. There is no indication that the king sought the Lord for strength or wisdom in dealing with the threat from Hazael; instead, Jehoash/Joash made a foolish decision. At the end of his reign he even had "Zechariah the son of Jehoiada the priest . . . stoned to death" when the priest confronted the king about his sinful behavior (2Ch 24:20-21).

12:19-21. In spite of a dramatic, and seemingly godly beginning, **Joash**/Jehoash's life came to a tragic end. In response to his murder of Zechariah (cf. 2Ch 24:25), **his servants arose and made a conspiracy and struck down Joash**/Jehoash (v. 20). He died at the **house of Millo**, the part of Jerusalem fortified by Solomon (cf. 2Sm 5:9; 1Kg 9:15) on his way to the nearby neighborhood of **Silla**. After Joash/Jehoash had been given a safe haven in the house of the Lord, it was the Lord who gave him over to judgment. The "quiet" that began with his reign (11:20) was replaced with the shouts of divine judgment, and he was **buried . . . with his fathers** [family] **in the city of David** (v. 21), but "not . . . in the tombs of the kings" (2Ch 24:25). Joash is a powerful illustration that there is no such thing as secondhand faith. He had never made his relationship with the Lord his own, and obeyed only as long as his mentor/spiritual leader Jehoiada was alive. However, once Jehoiada died, so did Joash's pretext of walking with the Lord.

12. Jehoahaz and Jehoash of Israel: Bad Kings in the Last Days of Elisha (2Kg 13:1-25)

13:1-9. Again the account moves back to events in the northern kingdom with the introduction to a new king, **Jehoahaz the son of Jehu**, who reigned for **seventeen years** (v. 1). Jehoahaz was the first of four descendants that the Lord told Jehu would sit on his throne. But as with the other kings of Israel, Jehoahaz also **did evil in the sight of the Lord**, following **the sins of Jeroboam** and leading the people to do the same (v. 2). As a result, the **anger of the Lord** came against the people. God is loving and forgiving, but His patience would not last forever (v. 3). The Lord responded to the sins of Jehoahaz and the people by giving them **continually into the hand of Hazael king of Aram** and his successor **Ben-hadad** II (v. 3). And the Lord's chastisement brought needed change, because in the depths of their suffering the king **entreated the favor of the Lord, who listened to him** as He watched the severe, horrible oppression that Hazael inflicted on His people (v. 4).

One of the consistent themes of 1 and 2 Kings is the Lord's compassion in response to the cries of His people. **The Lord gave Israel a deliverer, so that they escaped from under the hand of the Arameans** (v. 5), but no statement is made as to who this **deliverer** was. Keil argues that Jehoahaz's two successors, **Jehoash**/Joash (v. 10) and **Jeroboam** II (cf. 14:23), recaptured lands previously captured by the Assyrians (Keil, *The Books of the Kings*, 375). However, the one person who was consistently sought after by Israel's kings for help in times of political crisis was **Elisha** (cf. 13:14-21). One commentator writes, "It appears likely, then, that Elisha, the only figure in Israel's history who consistently makes Syria *fear him*, is indeed Israel's redeemer one last time" (House, *1, 2 Kings*, 306). The dark cloud that hung over Jehoahaz's noble attempt to seek the Lord is the fact that after a time of peace brought by Israel's **deliverer**, the people did **not turn away from the sins of the house of Jeroboam** (v. 6). As a result Jehoahaz's army was decimated, and he died as a king who apparently stopped pursuing the mercy and power of God in his activities (vv. 8-9).

13:10-13. King Jehoahaz was succeeded by his son, **Joash** (also referred to as **Jehoash**) as king of Israel. He too **did evil in the sight of the Lord** by pursuing the practices of Jeroboam (v. 11). After his death, **Jeroboam** [II] **sat on his throne**, succeeding him. After the summary statement regarding the death of Joash/Jehoash, the narrative looks back on Joash's reign to when he sought the aid of Elisha, just prior to the prophet's death.

13:14-19. King Joash approached **Elisha**, when the old prophet **became sick with the illness of which he was to die**, to talk with him about a military problem. Joash/Jehoash addressed the prophet, **My father, my father, the chariots of Israel and its horsemen!** (v. 14). The greeting showed the king's honor and deference toward Elisha, and his recognition of the power of the Lord to which Elisha had been an eyewitness (cf. 2:1-12; 6:17).

The king was looking for military help, but the prophet realized that help ultimately comes from God. Elisha proceeded to give Jehoash/Joash an opportunity to embrace the powerful work of God. He told him to take a **bow** and shoot an arrow out of a window **toward the east** (v. 17). After Jehoash did so, Elisha announced that the action was symbolic of the victory the Lord was about to give him over Aram at **Aphek**, about 40 miles northwest of Jerusalem (v. 17). Then the prophet asked the king to take the arrows nearby and to **strike the ground**. Elisha gave no indication as to how long Jehoash was to do this. But the king struck the ground only **three times and stopped** (v. 18). But Elisha announced **you should have struck five or six times**. Now, however, Israel would only experience three victories over their northern enemy when they could have seen Aram **destroyed** as an enemy (v. 19). God had given His servant, the king, an opportunity for greater blessing, but the blessing was limited by his lack of faith.

13:20-25. These verses address the ongoing power of Elisha, even after his death. Elisha ministered from the reign of Ahab (853 BC) to the reign of Jehoash (which began 798 BC), giving the prophet a ministry of about 56 years. After Elisha was **buried**, probably in a cave or tomb somewhere in the northern kingdom (the exact location is unknown), **bands of the Moabites** frequently invaded Israel **in the spring of the year** (v. 20). Following Israel's failed attempt to subdue the Moabites as a vassal state (cf. 3:1-27), the Moabites apparently attacked Israel at will. On one of these occasions some men were **burying a man** when the Moabites struck. In their haste to flee to safety they threw the dead man **into the grave of Elisha,** probably his cave-tomb. When the man's body **touched the bones of Elisha he revived and stood up on his feet** (v. 21). Just as Elisha had restored the Shunammite's son to life, even in death he was restoring life in a nation that was spiritually dying every day.

One of the themes in Elisha's ministry was that of the kindness and compassion of God. After Elisha's death, the **Lord was gracious** to Israel and **had compassion on them . . . because of His covenant with Abraham, Isaac, and Jacob** (v. 23; cf. Gn 12:1-3; 15:1-21; 17:1-27; 26:1-3). Also, God was not willing to **destroy them or cast them from His presence until now** (v. 23). The phrase **until now** is better translated "to this day," meaning "to this point in history," a declaration that God would always be faithful to His people (cf. Jr 31:31-37). Elisha had directed the people again and again to the covenants of the Lord. Therefore, even though Aram attacked Israel frequently, God bestowed His love on His covenant people. Even when **Ben-hadad** II came to power, God gave Joash/Jehoash king of Israel **three** opportunities to recover **the cities of Israel**, just as Elisha had predicted (v. 25; cf. 13:19).

God was consistently faithful to His people, even though Israel was not faithful to Him.

13. Amaziah of Judah: A Good King; and Jehoash of Israel: A Bad King (2Kg 14:1-22)

14:1-7. While **Joash**/Jehoash was ruling the northern kingdom, **Amaziah**, the son of Joash (not Joash, king of Israel) came to power in **Judah** (796–767 BC; cf. 2Ch 25:1-28). **He did right in the sight of the LORD, yet not like David.** But he **did according to all that Joash** [of Judah] **his father had done** (v. 3; cf. 12:4-12). Like his father, though, Amaziah did not remove the **high places**, and this encouraged the citizens to continue in their idolatry (v. 4). At the same time, Amaziah showed some preference for obeying the law, because even though he **killed** the **servants** who murdered **his father . . . he did not put to death** their sons (cf. Dt 24:16). In contrast to Jehu in Israel who went on a killing spree, Amaziah showed restraint and obedience to God's commandments. Likewise, he went to war against **Edom** and gained a measure of success (v. 7).

14:8-10. After **Amaziah** won battles against Edom, he challenged **Jehoash . . . king of Israel** to face him in battle. Jehoash responded with a parable. The strong **cedar** was Jehoash, and Amaziah was the **thorn bush** that could easily be **trampled**. The parable emphasized the foolishness of Amaziah's plan. Jehoahaz acknowledged that Amaziah had **indeed defeated Edom**, but he would not win a battle against the northern kingdom, but would **fall** in defeat **and Judah** with him (v. 10).

14:11-14. But Amaziah would not listen, and the two nations met near the Judean town of **Beth-shemesh**, about 15 miles west of Jerusalem (v. 11). **Judah was defeated by Israel** (v. 12), and Jehoash **tore down the wall of Jerusalem** where he **captured Amaziah** and **took all the gold and silver and all the utensils which were found in the house of the LORD** (vv. 13-14). Although Amaziah was remembered as one of the good kings of Judah, and this passage described his defeat in straightforward fashion, 2Ch 25:20 makes it clear that Amaziah's idolatrous ways led to his defeat.

14:15-22. Verses 15-16 summarized the reign of **Jehoash** king of Israel, then the text returned to a short description of **Amaziah**'s reign (vv. 17-20). Even though Amaziah had been captured by Jehoash, Amaziah still outlived his northern contemporary by **fifteen years** (v. 17). However, Amaziah was also subject to a conspiracy by his own people. After fleeing **to Lachish**, a fortress city 30 miles southwest of Jerusalem, he was captured and **killed there** (v. 19). His son, **Azariah**, also known as Uzziah (cf. 2Ch 26:1; Is 6:1) was made king in his place. He was instrumental in expanding Judah's southernmost borders when **he built Elath**, the port on the Red Sea (v. 22).

14. Jeroboam II of Israel: A Bad King (2Kg 14:23-29)

The events in this section (chaps. 14–17) recount the final reigns of the kings of Israel and their counterparts in Judah prior to the north's fall to Assyria (cf. 2Ch 25–28 as well as the books of Amos and Hosea). At this point in Israel's history her old arch-enemy to the north, Aram (Syria), was on the decline and the kingdom of Assyria was rising in power and influence, threatening the kingdom of Israel.

14:23-29. The continuing narrative of the northern kingdom provides a mixture of history and theological commentary. **Jeroboam** [II] **the son of Joash king of Israel became king in Samaria**, where Jehoram had also been made king (v. 23; cf. 3:1). Because Samaria was a major city of the northern kingdom, it was sometimes used as a synonym for Israel (cf. 1:3). Two things were said of Jeroboam II that revealed important theological markers. First, he was the second king to be called **Jeroboam**, and he was like his namesake in that **he did evil in the sight of the LORD** (v. 24). And yet, despite Jeroboam's evil during his **forty-one year** reign, he restored **the border of Israel** almost to the extent of the Solomonic kingdom (v. 25). In fact, the restoration was linked to **the word of the LORD** that the prophet **Jonah** had spoken (the same Jonah who traveled to Nineveh with God's message to the Assyrians, cf. Jnh 1). This is the only mention of Jonah's message or ministry in Israel before his mission to Nineveh. This event revealed the grace and kindness of God in the midst of spiritual rebellion.

A second important theological marker concerned the covenant-keeping character of the LORD. **The LORD saw the affliction of Israel**, and **did not say that He would blot out the name of Israel from under heaven, but He saved them by the hand of Jeroboam the son of Joash** (vv. 26-27). God graciously used an evil king to preserve His people. Israel had a short respite of prosperity and expansion, but like the kings before him, **Jeroboam slept with his fathers . . . and Zechariah his son became king in his place** (v. 29).

15. Azariah (Uzziah) of Judah: A Good King (2Kg 15:1-7)

15:1-7. It is important to read 2Kg 15 in conjunction with 2Ch 26. Two important details of Azariah's life are highlighted here and further explained in 2Ch 26. First, **Azariah** (also named Uzziah; vv. 13, 30, 32, 34; cf. Is 6:1) became king of Judah at the age of **sixteen** and served for **fifty-two years** (792–740 BC; cf. 2Ch 26:1-23). **He did right in the sight of the Lord** (v. 3). His shortcoming was that he did not remove the **high places** (v. 4), a common failure of the kings in Israel and Judah. The second item related to Azariah's reign was that **the Lord struck the king, so that he was a leper to the day of his death** (v. 5). The reason for the leprosy is detailed in 2Ch 26:16-21: Uzziah arrogantly entered the temple to burn incense, usurping the role of a priest. The books of 1 and 2 Kings are mainly a straightforward historical record, while 1 and 2 Chronicles provides more theological comments. At Azariah's death **Jotham his son became king in his place** (v. 7).

16. Zechariah, Shallum, Menahem, and Pekahiah of Israel: All Bad Kings (2Kg 15:8-26)

These four kings who reigned near the end of the northern kingdom were, like all the kings of Israel, evil rulers. Their reigns were not given in many details, but the highlights of their reigns showed their spiritual condition.

15:8-12. In brief, **Zechariah the son of Jeroboam became king over Israel in Samaria** (753–752 BC). His reign lasted only **six months.** Like the other kings in the north **he did evil in the sight of the Lord** and **did not depart from the sins of Jeroboam the son of Nebat** (v. 9). The significant factor in this turn of events is that at the end of Zechariah's six-month reign, **Shallum** conspired against him and **killed** him (v. 10). This was significant because it **was the word of the Lord which He spoke to Jehu** (v. 12; cf. 10:30). God proved again that what He said would certainly come to pass.

15:13-15. In a similar manner, **Shallum . . . reigned one month in Samaria** (752 BC). His reign was so short that his merits or shortcomings were not even mentioned. The quick change of administrations no doubt added to the increasing economic, political, and spiritual instability of the northern kingdom. Shallum was assassinated in **Samaria** by **Menahem,** who became king in his place (v. 14).

15:16-18. While Azariah was king of Judah, **Menahem** became **king over Israel** and reigned **ten years** (752–742 BC). Two of Menahem's actions revealed his extreme brutality. First, he attacked the region of **Tiphsah** ("Tappuah" in the LXX; cf. Jos 6:8; 17:7-8), on the border of Ephraim and Manasseh in the northern kingdom. When the people would not submit to his sovereignty, he attacked it with brutal violence (v. 16). Second, **he did evil in the sight of the Lord** (v. 18).

15:19-22. Menahem had to deal with the growing power of Assyria, whose leader at that time was **Pul**. This Assyrian king is identified in other historical records as Tiglath-pileser III (745–724 BC; Patterson and Austel, "1 and 2 Kings," 236). When Pul came against Israel, Menahem **gave** him **a thousand talents of silver** (v. 19). But the money was not simply to "buy off" an attack from Assyria. It was also **to strengthen the kingdom under his rule** (v. 19). That is, he wanted the backing of Assyria to strengthen his hold on the throne in Israel (Ibid.). The way he was able to pay for Assyrian assistance was to exact **the money from Israel** (v. 20). Assyrian military forces **did not remain** in the **land** of Israel, but Menahem did not win the favor of the people. This made things more difficult for his son **Pekahiah** who would rule after him (v. 22).

15:23-26. Menahem's son, **Pekahiah**, reigned just **two** years (v. 23). Like the kings before him in Israel, **he did evil in the sight of the Lord** (v. 24). The text does not state exactly, but perhaps the increasing economic pressure led to a conspiracy by **Pekah son of Remaliah** (v. 25). Joining with two other men and **fifty men of the Gileadites, Pekah** killed Pekahiah in his **castle**, and Pekah became king (vv. 25-26). The sins of the leaders were making life difficult for the northern kingdom. Eventually forces within and without the kingdom would destroy the nation altogether.

17. Pekah of Israel: A Bad King (2Kg 15:27-31)

15:27-31. The northern kingdom was in decline spiritually, following the sins of Jeroboam; socially, suffering from excessive taxation; and politically, under the constant threat of takeover by Assyria. Throughout **Pekah**'s reign of **twenty years**, his followed the common pattern: **he did evil in the sight of the Lord** and **he did not depart from the sins of Jeroboam** (v. 28). The Assyrian king **Tiglath-pileser** (cf. Pul in v. 19) was expanding his empire to control all of Mesopotamia. During Pekah's reign, **Tiglath-pileser . . . came and captured** several cities in the northern kingdom (v. 30). Even all the **land of Naphtali** was taken captive.

So Pekah made an alliance with **Rezin** king of Aram (Syria). Then they united **against Judah** under the rule of king **Ahaz** (cf. v. 37; 16:6). Their goal was to force Judah to join them in military action against Assyria, who was threatening both Aram and Israel (also known as Ephraim) at this time. This was the beginning of the so-called Syro-Ephraimite war, which figured prominently in the prophecies of Is 7–9. **Hoshea the son of Elah**, who became the last king of Israel (cf. 17:1-5), apparently thought if Pekah and his anti-Assyrian policies were to continue, it would just incite Assyria to take more territory from Israel. So he **made a conspiracy against** Pekah, **put him to death and became king in his place**.

18. Jotham of Judah: A Good King (2Kg 15:32-38)

15:32-38. After recording a series of kings in the northern kingdom, the text returned to events in Judah. During the **second year of Pekah**'s reign in Israel, **Jotham** replaced his father, **Uzziah,** as king of **Judah** (750–732 BC; cf. 2Ch 27:1-9). Again, two features characterized Jotham's life. First, his 16-year reign was associated in part with the fact that he **did what was right in the sight of the Lord** (v. 34). His only shortcoming, like the kings before him, was that **the high places** remained and the people resorted to idolatry and unsanctioned sacrifices (v. 35). The second important item related to Jotham's reign was that **the Lord began to send Rezin king of Aram and Pekah** of Israel **against Judah** (v. 37; cf. comments above on 15:27-31).

If Jotham did right in the Lord's eyes, why did the Lord send conflict into his life? Neither this chapter nor 2Ch 27 give specific reasons. However, Patterson and Austel speculate that the issue was designed by the Lord to become a test for Jotham's son and successor, **Ahaz** (Patterson and Austel, "1 and 2 Kings," 241). If that was the case, then Ahaz failed to display the spiritual qualities of his grandfather and father. The other possibility, and more in keeping with the ongoing theme of 1 and 2 Kings, was that many of the kings in Judah were only halfhearted in their devotion to the Lord, and this may have been the case with Jotham. Deuteronomy 17:14-20 makes it clear that the king was the representative of the true King. Halfhearted devotion would eventually lead to total corruption. God would allow whatever was necessary to call His people to rely on Him.

19. Ahaz of Judah: A Bad King (16:1-20)

16:1-4. The text first addressed the character and overall spiritual condition of **Ahaz** (735–716 BC; cf. 2Ch 28; Is 7). He reigned for **sixteen years in Jerusalem**, although the dates of his reign amount to 20 years, because some of those years were a coregency with his father (House, *1, 2 Kings*, 335–36). Although a king of Judah, **he walked in the way of the kings of Israel** (v. 3). What was slowly destroying the northern kingdom was now going to be a growing spiritual dynamic in the southern kingdom as well. More specifically, Ahaz **made his son pass through the fire**, that is, he offered him as a child sacrifice to a pagan god, an abominable act condemned by God (v. 3; cf. Lv 18:21; Dt 12:31; 2Kg 16:3). In addition, Ahaz participated in the idolatrous sacrifices that occurred on the **high places and on the hills and under every green tree** (v. 4).

16:5-9. The war described in these verses came about because **Ahaz** refused to join in an alliance with Aram and Israel against the growing threat of Assyria (cf. comments above on 15:27-31; Patterson and Austel, "1 and 2 Kings," 243). Other nations were also threatening the stability of Judah (cf. 2Ch 28:17-18). In the midst of these threats, Judah's apostasy was on the rise, and Ahaz elected to develop his own military strategy rather than call on the Lord for help, leading to unhealthy spiritual and regional alliances (cf. Is 7:3-17). Therefore, **Ahaz sent messengers to Tiglath-pileser king of Assyria**, requesting that he come and deliver him from Rezin and Pekah (v. 7).

The severity of the invasion from the north was so great that 120,000 soldiers from Judah were killed in one day (cf. 2Ch 28:5-6). After **Ahaz took the silver and gold** from **the house of the Lord and . . . the king's house**, and after sending **a present** to Tiglath-pileser, the Assyrians agreed to help Judah (vv. 8-9). A subsequent Assyrian invasion against Aram took place and **Damascus** was **captured**. But this alliance was not as good as it initially appeared. The Chronicler noted that although Ahaz gave silver and gold to Tiglath-pileser, "it did not help him" (2Ch 28:21). This short-term victory was soon to lead to great spiritual erosion.

16:10-18. Ahaz made a trip to meet with the victorious **king of Assyria** (v. 10). There the king **saw** an **altar**, made a **pattern** of it, and **sent** it **to Urijah the priest** to be constructed (vv. 10-11). On his return, Ahaz **approached the altar** and started to sacrifice on it (v. 12). He removed **the**

bronze altar Solomon had constructed for the purpose of daily sacrifices, and started to engage in temple worship in a way that differed from that set forth by the Lord (v. 14). Three specific sacrifices were mentioned: the **burnt offering** symbolizing forgiveness and communion; the **evening meal offering** symbolizing dedication; and the **drink offerings** symbolizing the joy of life poured out to God (v. 15; Patterson and Austel, "1 and 2 Kings," 244).

Ahaz engaged in the appearances of worship, but his heart was far from the Lord. This was an abomination to God (cf. Dt 18:10-13; Is 29:13). To make things even worse, Ahaz **cut off the borders of the stands . . . took down the sea from the bronze oxen . . . and put it on a pavement of stone** (v. 17). He even went so far as to remove **the covered way for the sabbath**, apparently a passageway for the king to walk from his palace to the temple on the Sabbath. All this was done **because . . . the king of Assyria** had made Israel a vassal state (v. 18).

16:19-20. The fourth and final excerpt from Ahaz's life described his death in the usual pattern of referring to another historical source for information: the **Book of the Chronicles of the Kings of Judah** (v. 19), and noting that **Ahaz slept with his fathers, and was buried**, followed by the name of his successor (v. 20). The one bright spot in the life of Ahaz was that he had a son, **Hezekiah**, who would reign in his place and bring spiritual light to bear on Judah's ongoing history.

20. Hoshea of Israel: A Bad King and the Fall of the Northern Kingdom (2Kg 17:1-41)

17:1-6. The last king in the northern kingdom was **Hoshea**, who reigned for **nine years** (c. 732–722 BC). Two things stand out about Hoshea. First, from a spiritual perspective **he did evil in the sight of the LORD, only not as the kings of Israel who were before him** (v. 2). God had been patient with His covenant people, but judgment had to be rendered in accord with His Word (cf. Dt 28:47-50). Second, there is a political/historical perspective regarding the events during the reign of Hoshea that culminated in the northern kingdom being taken captive by Assyria.

Initially, Hoshea was a vassal to **Shalmaneser king of Assyria** (v. 3), but he conspired against the Assyrian king by attempting to develop an alliance with **So king of Egypt** (v. 4). He is difficult to identify because by 722 BC Egyptian leadership had shifted several times, including Piankhy, Tefnakht, and Osorkon IV (House, *1, 2 Kings*, 339). What is clear is that **Shalmaneser** responded to Hoshea's attempted coup and **shut him up . . . in prison** (v. 4). **Then the king of Assyria invaded the whole land and went up to Samaria and besieged it three years** (v. 5). In 721 BC, the northern kingdom was captured and its citizens were **carried . . . into exile to Assyria**, a policy that had now become commonplace whenever the Assyrians took control (v. 6). Israel's deportation fulfilled God's Word that came through His prophets years earlier (cf. 1Kg 14:15-16). (For the Assyrian deportation policy, see the comments below on 17:24-41.)

17:7-17. This section is the low point of 1 and 2 Kings. Besides telling what happened, it also gives information on why it happened—the disaster that came on Israel and was yet to come on Judah (v. 19). The primary reason for defeat and exile was a failure to fear the Lord in accord with His covenant (cf. vv. 36-37). Following the description of Hoshea's demise, this chapter can be divided into three sections: (1) Israel's sinful choices (vv. 7-17); (2) the Lord's response to those choices (vv. 18-23); and (3) the ongoing sins that corrupted the land (vv. 24-41).

The cause of Israel's fall to Assyria was spiritual failure, not military or political failure. **The sons of Israel had sinned against the LORD their God . . . and they had feared other gods** (v. 7). They embraced the **customs of the nations whom the LORD had driven out . . . and the customs of the kings of Israel which they introduced** (v. 8). **The sons of Israel did things secretly** (v. 9) has the idea of "ascribing" things to the Lord that simply were not true—the kind of things Jeroboam did when he implied that it was acceptable to the Lord for Israel to worship the bulls he had constructed at Bethel and Dan (Patterson and Austel, "1 and 2 Kings," 249). This reveals that God's people feigned worship, but were actually rebelling against God by their forbidden religious practices: **They served idols concerning which the LORD had said to them, "You shall not do this thing"** (v. 12). The **LORD warned Israel and Judah** to turn from their evil ways or face the consequences described in Dt 28–29 (v. 13). But they refused and **stiffened their neck like their fathers** (vv. 14-17).

17:18-23. Initially the Lord responded to Israel's spiritual rebellion with grace and patience. He consistently **warned** them to turn away from their idols and back to His commandments (v.

13). When they refused to do so, **the LORD was very angry with Israel** (v. 18). In fact, this section is presented between two literary "bookends." The text states that the Lord in His anger **removed Israel from His sight** (v. 23; v. 18 says He **removed them**). This was true not only of the northern kingdom. **Judah** also **walked in the customs which Israel had introduced** (v. 19). The nation's ongoing sins resulted in terrible consequences in which Israel's descendants were **afflicted** and cast **out of His sight** (vv. 20, 23). The Lord gave them opportunities for repentance **through all His servants the prophets**, but they would not listen (v. 23). Therefore, the consequences of judgment were fair and certain: a life of **exile**.

17:24-41. However, even with Israel's deportation, the land was not completely void of spiritual rebellion. Assyria's policy was to take a captured nation's populace and relocate them in other places to reduce the possibility of insurrection, and to import people from other lands into the captured land. So **the king of Assyria** brought people from other nations and **settled them in the cities of Samaria in place of the sons of Israel** (v. 24). Early on in the resettlement process these nations **did not fear the LORD**. Like the Israelites they replaced, these new settlers did not worship the God of Israel. But this was the Lord's land, and He wanted that to be known, so He **sent lions among them which killed some of them** (v. 25). The new citizens somehow perceived that their affliction was from the Lord, even though they did not know His name or customs (v. 26). So they appealed to the **king of Assyria** for relief.

Under the providential hand of God, the Assyrian king sent back **one of the priests** of Israel **whom** he **carried away**, and this priest **taught them how they should fear the LORD** (vv. 27-28). The concept of fearing the Lord or fearing/worshiping other gods permeates the entire chapter (cf. vv. 7, 25, 33-34, 37-38). The Lord had called His people to fear Him from the very beginning of their covenant relationship (cf. Gn 17:1-5; Dt 1:17; 31:12). However, Israel, Judah, and the nations who resettled the land were always halfhearted in their worship. The author summarized the ongoing corruption of humanity by saying, **So while these nations feared the LORD, they also served their idols; their children likewise and their grandchildren, as their fathers did, so they do to this day** (v. 41). Centuries later Jesus dialogued with another citizen of the land about the quality of religion that occurred in Samaria and in Jerusalem (cf. Jn 4:7-45). Religious syncretism would continue for centuries. And only the true King who was to come would be able to transform the hearts of the citizens of the land. Only then would they be inclined to fear the Lord as He intended.

III. The Kingdom of Judah after the Fall of Israel (2Kg 18:1–25:30)

A. The Kings of Judah Prior to the Babylonian Invasion (2Kg 18:1–23:30)

The journey through 1 and 2 Kings takes its final turn at the beginning of chap. 18. The road laid out for Judah's monarchs looked much like the one laid out for their northern brothers. However, while all the rulers of the northern kingdom did evil in the sight of the Lord, there were a few good kings of Judah who followed Him. For example, Hezekiah and Josiah were intentional about serving the Lord by keeping His law (cf. 18:6 and 23:25); however, in the end even the good kings of Judah were disobedient. This led to the very disasters God had predicted (cf. Dt 28:15; 2Kg 17:19-20). In these remaining chapters, the case for God's judgment is clear; yet, at the same time, there are glimmers of grace and hope for the people of Judah who were bound together with a covenant-keeping God (cf. Gn 17:19; 2Sm 7:16).

1. Hezekiah of Judah: A Good King (2Kg 18:1–20:21)

Hezekiah's success was clearly the Lord's doing (v. 7). However, spiritual successes occur in the context of historical and political events. Hezekiah reigned from approximately 715 BC to 687 BC. During that time the Assyrians were the dominant force in the region. However, Israel also had its challenges with other powers in the region. The Assyrian king, Shalmaneser V (c. 727–722 BC), captured Samaria (vv. 9-10; cf. 17:5-6). He was followed by Sargon II (c. 722–705 BC), who was the Assyrian ruler during Hezekiah's early reign in Judah.

Sargon II faced growing opposition from Babylon as soon as he came to the throne. In fact, because of these problems with Babylon the Assyrians did not campaign in Judah's territory. When Sennacherib (c. 705–681 BC) ruled Assyria, insurrection in other parts of the Assyrian kingdom was suppressed and efforts were directed toward Judah. Perhaps while Assyria was preoccupied with Babylon, Hezekiah may have thought the timing was right to resist Assyrian power (House, *1, 2 Kings*, 352). Whether this was part of the Judahite king's reasoning or not, Hezekiah also had the Lord's empowerment on his side (v. 7).

18:1-3. Hezekiah's positive reign of **twenty-nine years** (716/15–687 BC; cf. 2Ch 29:1–32:33) was because **he did right in the sight of the LORD** (v. 3). Unlike his predecessors, he was favorably compared to **David.**

18:4-6. Hezekiah **removed the high places and broke down the sacred pillars and cut down the Asherah** (v. 4). But the item that is given the greatest attention was the destruction of the **Nehushtan,** meaning "a piece of bronze" (v. 4). This was **the bronze serpent that Moses had made** (cf. Nm 21:8-9) when the people of Israel spoke out against Moses and the Lord. In response the Lord sent poisonous snakes against the rebels. When they appealed to Moses for relief, the Lord told him to make a bronze serpent. When the afflicted people looked at the serpent in faith they would live. But apparently, this bronze serpent was kept among the temple furnishings and the **sons of Israel burned incense to it**. So Hezekiah **broke it in pieces** to allow for the proper worship of the Lord. So Hezekiah **clung to the LORD** and **kept His commandments** (v. 6).

18:7-12. Because of Hezekiah's faithfulness, **the LORD was with him; wherever he went he prospered**. The Lord gave Judah victory over their enemies. Hezekiah **rebelled against . . . Assyria**. He also **defeated the Philistines . . . from watchtower to fortified city**, a reference to the complete defeat of the nations directly west of Judah (vv. 7-8). At the time Judah was victorious over its enemies, there was a reminder of the subjugation of the northern kingdom by Assyria, when **Hoshea king of Israel . . . was captured** (vv. 9-12; cf.17:5-6). The repetition served as a literary device, contrasting the ways of Samaria with the dramatic, righteous ways of Hezekiah (cf. vv. 6, 12). Obedience brought blessing, whereas disobedience to the Lord brought disaster.

18:13-16. In his **fourteenth year** as king of Judah (701 BC), **Hezekiah** faced his greatest military threat, **Sennacherib** king of Assyria. After an extended campaign against Babylon, Sennacherib **came up against all the fortified cities of Judah and seized them** (v. 13). At that point, in an attempt to appease Sennacherib, Hezekiah confessed that he had done wrong in initially opposing Assyria, and asked for terms of peace to alleviate the impending threat. He was aware of what had happened to the northern kingdom and wanted to prevent the same disaster from befalling Judah. The Assyrian king **required of Hezekiah . . . three hundred talents of silver and thirty talents of gold** (v. 14). To pay this huge assessment, Hezekiah **gave him all the silver which was found in the house of the LORD, and in the treasuries of the king's house** (v. 15). He even stripped **the gold** he had previously placed over **the temple** doors and gave that to Sennacherib as well (v. 16).

18:17-25. Not satisfied with Hezekiah's payments, and seemingly wanting to dispose of the Judean king and his rebellious ways, Sennacherib sent a delegation of military leaders to challenge Judean sovereignty. One of the tactics of Assyrian warfare was to capture water sources and cut off access to the nation being invaded. Meeting at **the conduit of the upper pool** with Hezekiah's own delegation was a form of psychological warfare (v. 17). Hezekiah himself did not appear, but **Eliakim . . . and Shebnah . . . and Joah** served as the king's representatives (v. 18). The name **Rabshakeh** was a military term for the field commander of Assyria; he increased the pressure on Judah in three ways (v. 19).

First, he intimidated Hezekiah's delegation by wondering where they had mustered up the courage to challenge Assyria in the first place. He speculated out loud as to whether Judah would rely **on Egypt**, whom he described as a **crushed reed . . . on which . . . a man leans**, only to have it **go into his hand and pierce it** (v. 21). His point, one made by the prophets of Judah as well (cf. Is 36:6; Ezk 6–7), was that even if Judah did rely on Egypt, it would only be a matter of time until this weak ally would turn and afflict harm on God's people.

The Rabshakeh's second act of intimidation was to imply that Hezekiah had robbed Judah of spiritual strength. Even if God's people said, **We trust in the LORD our God,** the Rabshakeh pointed out that it was Hezekiah who had **taken away** the **high places . . . and altars**, and had told Judah that they had to worship in Jerusalem alone (v. 22). The Assyrians had assumed that such a tactic was against God's will and would weaken them further. The Assyrian commander even went so far as to state that it was the Lord's will for him to go **up against this land and destroy it** (v. 25).

His third act of intimidation was to emphasize Judah's lack of military strength and skill. Again the Rabshakeh asked for terms of surrender: **Come, make a bargain with my master the king of Assyria, and I will give you two thousand horses** (v. 23). Then he mockingly speculated as to whether Judah would be **able to . . . set riders on them**. He then pointed out that if Judah had no such **riders**, then how would they be able to **repulse one official of the least of** Sennacherib's **servants**? (v. 24). The Rabshakeh assumed this psychological warfare would certainly instill fear in the king's heart. But Hezekiah was not ready to surrender.

18:26-27. To combat the intimidating threats the Rabshakeh was hurling, Hezekiah's three diplomats asked him, **Speak now to your servants in Aramaic, for we understand it; and do not speak with us in Judean** [i.e., Hb.] **in the hearing of the people who are on the wall** (v. 26). They wanted to protect the people from falling further into a state of fear, but the request backfired. The Rabshakeh intensified his threats, this time going beyond diplomatic dialogue to appeal to the people.

18:28-35. First, he **cried with a loud voice** so that the common citizens within his hearing would consider surrender. He told them not to listen to Hezekiah and his promises that the Lord would deliver them. He asked them to **make your peace with** him and surrender (v. 31). If they did, he promised, they would be carried off to a land **like** their **own, a land of grain and new wine . . . bread and vineyards . . . olive trees and honey** (v. 32). This was a deceptive offer to entice the Judeans to surrender; in Assyrian warfare there is no evidence of such kind and prosperous treatment. Then to add more pressure, the Rabshakeh reminded the people that history was not on their side (v. 33). He pointed out Assyria's long record of victory, then hinted that the true and living God of Israel was just like the gods of the nations they had defeated: **Who among all the gods of the lands have delivered their land from my hand, that the LORD should deliver Jerusalem from my hand?** (v. 35).

18:36-37. Meanwhile, Hezekiah had ordered the people, **Do not answer him**. The delegation from Judah returned to the king obviously shaken and wondering what to do next. They appeared before Hezekiah in mourning attire, **with their cloths torn** (v. 37; cf. 6:30).

19:1. Hezekiah was obviously stressed by what had been reported to him. So he **tore his clothes, covered himself with sackcloth and entered the house of the LORD** (v. 1). This was the response of a king who knew that his nation was facing a terrible threat. Hezekiah was a godly king, so he turned his attention to the Lord and worshiped and sought His help.

19:2-7. Hezekiah also sent a message to **Isaiah the prophet** (v. 2; cf. Is 37–39), seeking his assistance in the matter. Just as the Lord had prophets ministering in the northern kingdom, most notably Elijah and Elisha (cf. 1Kg 16:29–2Kg 14:16), He had a series of prophets speaking to the kings of Judah as well. Isaiah ministered from the year King Uzziah/Azariah died (739 BC; cf. 2Kg 14:17) until after the death of Hezekiah (686 BC, cf. Introduction to Isaiah and comments at Is 6:1; 36–39). He began his ministry to Hezekiah when Judah was facing the Assyrian attack (cf. 2Ch 32).

The king's message to Isaiah had three parts. First, he described the severity of the siege that Sennacherib had placed on Jerusalem: **a day of distress, rebuke, and rejection**. It was so bad that when pregnant women were about to give birth, they had **no strength to deliver** (v. 3). It was as if they did not want their children to be born under such awful circumstances. Second, Hezekiah raised the possibility before Isaiah that perhaps the Lord would hear the blasphemies of the Assyrian king and **rebuke the words which the LORD your God has heard** (v. 4). Third, Hezekiah's appeal to the prophet was that he **offer a prayer for the remnant that is left**. Hezekiah's use of the term **remnant** referred to the inhabitants of Jerusalem in contrast to the people who had been seized in the other cities and towns of Judah (cf. 18:13).

19:8-13. These verses describe an interlude in the siege of Jerusalem. The **Rabshakeh** went to report how things were going with his war against Hezekiah, only to learn that King Sennacherib had moved to another battlefield in **Libnah** (cf. 8:22, near the Philistine border). Sennacherib had learned that the Egyptian army under **Tirhakah king of Cush** had come to fight against him (v. 9). But apparently out of concern that Hezekiah might come and attack him from behind while engaged with the Egyptians, he sent a letter to Jerusalem to try to intimidate Hezekiah. Sennacherib told Hezekiah not to let his **God . . . deceive** him into thinking that He would deliver Judah from the king of Assyria (v. 10). Little did Sennacherib realize that he was the one being deceived by his own arrogant heart. However, he returned to the Rabshakeh's previous taunt that the gods of the other nations he attacked were helpless in combating Sennacherib's power and might (vv. 12-13, cf. 18:33).

19:14-19. Sennacherib's messengers had communicated the Assyrian king's taunt in the form of a letter (v. 9). Hezekiah read the letter, then walked **to the house of the LORD and spread it out before the LORD** in a symbolic gesture of helplessness and intercession (v. 14). His words to the Lord consisted of an *affirmation* followed by an *appeal*. When Hezekiah stated that God was **enthroned above the cherubim**, he was saying that God was powerful and present with His covenant people. The king took comfort that God was not far away (v. 15). He went on to affirm that God was the exclusive God, the One who alone is the ruler: **You are the God, You alone, of all the kingdoms of the earth** (v. 15). In addition, Hezekiah acknowledged what he probably had prayed many times before, namely, that God is the One who **made heaven and earth** (v. 15). Therefore, if the Lord was present, Ruler, and Creator of all things, the only logical response for Judah's king was to call to Him for the help he needed.

From this simple affirmation, Hezekiah made his appeal to God (vv. 16-19). But he went beyond simply asking for deliverance and relief. He was more concerned with God's reputation. He acknowledged that Assyria had **devastated the nations and their lands** (v. 17). But those nations' gods were **not gods but the work of men's hands, wood and stone** (v. 18). Therefore Hezekiah's ultimate request was that through God's deliverance **all the kingdoms of the earth** would **know that You alone, O LORD, are God** (v. 19).

19:20-24. Hezekiah soon received an answer to his prayer through the prophet **Isaiah**, who announced in authoritative terms, **This is the word that the LORD has spoken against him** (v. 21). God knew Sennacherib's innermost thoughts and was about to reveal them. The song started with an indictment against the Assyrian king, who would be **despised . . . and mocked** by the **daughter of Jerusalem**, the city where the Lord had chosen to put His name (cf. 1Kg 8:44). The Assyrian king had continually **reproached and blasphemed** the Lord, identified as **the Holy One of Israel**, a title most commonly used by Isaiah of the Lord (v. 22; cf. Is 4:1).

19:25-28. Sennacherib had supposed his mighty strength and advanced weaponry had devastated nation after nation. But God revealed that **from ancient times** He **planned it**, and now He was bringing all these things **to pass** (v. 25). God is the omnipotent One, not Sennacherib! In addition, Isaiah revealed the omniscience of God in the words, **I know your sitting down, And your going out and your coming in, and your raging against Me** (v. 27). God knew all these things even if the Assyrian king only thought them secretly. And God was going to act in powerful ways.

In the past Assyria had treated their conquered subjects like animals, dragging and pulling them from one land to another. But God announced to Sennacherib, **I will put My hook in your nose, And My bridle in your lips, And I will turn you back by the way which you came** (v. 28). Assyria's butchery would come full circle, and they were about to experience what they had afflicted on others. And all at the hands of the true and living King of all the earth.

19:29-34. God's promise to Hezekiah would be demonstrated with a sign so that both the king and the citizens would know that what was about to happen was from the Lord. Hezekiah's father Ahaz had been given a sign by the same prophet (cf. Is 7:10-34), but he refused to accept it. Hezekiah was different and would believe. Apparently, under the Assyrian siege Jerusalem was unable to grow the usual crops, causing famine in the city (cf. 19:4). So the **sign** was agricultural: in the current year after the Assyrian withdrawal, the people of Judah would **eat what grows of itself**, and **in the second year** they would eat what came **from the same**. It was too late in the season to plant new crops, but at least they would be able to go out to the field to gather the produce. Then **in the third year** they would be able to **sow, reap, plant vineyards, and eat their fruit** (v. 29).

In other words, with every meal the people would have a reminder for three straight years that God was once again their mighty Deliverer. The point was that like these crops that were about to grow, so Israel would **again take root downward and bear fruit upward** (v. 30). Isaiah promised that the Assyrians would not come to **Jerusalem** or even **shoot an arrow** over its walls (vv. 31-32). Instead, the Assyrians would **return** to their own homeland, never to return to Jerusalem again (v. 33). Why? Isaiah announced that it was because of **the zeal of the LORD** on behalf of His **servant David** that He was doing these powerful acts of deliverance (vv. 31, 34). Human faithfulness and the promise of God were at work, and all the world would have a record of it.

19:35-37. Just as the prophet had predicted, the mighty Assyrians were defeated by the miraculous power of the Lord. In the middle of the night, **the angel of the Lord went out and struck 185,000 in the camp of the Assyrians** (v. 35). When Sennacherib and his officials awakened the next morning they saw dead bodies everywhere. Now that their army was destroyed, they had no choice but to return to Nineveh (v. 36). There Sennacherib was killed by his sons **Adrammelech and Sharezer** while worshiping **Nisroch**. This event is recorded in history as occurring some 20 years later (Patterson and Austel, "1 and 2 Kings," 268). Another son, **Esarhaddon . . . became king in his place** (v. 37). God's people were saved but not by the military skill of Judah's king or diplomatic efforts. God Himself was keeping His promises to David and honoring Hezekiah's passion for Him and His reputation. God was the true victor.

20:1-7. The account of Hezekiah's illness poses a chronological problem. The phrase **in those days** (v. 1) seems to connect the event with the preceding deliverance of Jerusalem from Sennacherib. But that seems unlikely because v. 6 suggests that Hezekiah's illness preceded Sennacherib's defeat, but also seems to hint that Sennacherib's invasion was imminent. The dates of Hezekiah's reign were 716–687 BC, assuming a 10-year coregency with Manasseh (697–643 BC). The fixed date for Sennacherib's invasion is 701 BC. The likely date for the visit of the Babylonian delegation was 703 BC.

Therefore, it is likely that Hezekiah received his 15-year extension of life (v. 6) shortly before the Babylonian delegation visited him. The illness, which occurred prior to the deliverance from Assyria, is recorded here after Sennacherib's siege as another demonstration of Hezekiah's righteous response to God, and served as a model of trust in God for the writer's original audience among those exiled to Babylon. The parallel account in 2Ch 32:25-26 indicates that Hezekiah's pride led to this illness (cf. Introduction to 1 and 2 Kings). In the Chronicler's account the king and the people humbled themselves, thus averting God's wrath that was probably coming in the form of Sennacherib's attack.

The narrative can be divided into three parts. First, there was the appeal that Hezekiah made on learning that he would die: **Remember now, O Lord, I beseech You, how I have walked before You in truth and with a whole heart and have done what is good in Your sight** (v. 3). There was no mention of Hezekiah's pride (cf. 2Ch 32:25-26), but the fact that he **wept bitterly** could indicate that he saw the error of his ways. Therefore, he called attention to his faithfulness in restoring Judah's worship of the Lord as it was intended it to be. The second part of the narrative was God's answer to the king's prayer. He sent Isaiah back to Hezekiah to inform him that He was about to heal him and **add fifteen years** to his life. But the rationale for doing so was God's own covenant-keeping character. The Lord stated, **I will defend this city for My own sake and for My servant David's sake** (v. 6).

20:8-11. In the third part of vv. 1–11, Hezekiah asked for a **sign** to affirm that the Lord's words through **Isaiah** were true. This was very different from Hezekiah's father, Ahaz, who refused to ask for a sign but was offered one anyway by Isaiah to confirm the Lord's promise to deliver Judah from the Assyrians (cf. Is 7:11). Hezekiah actually wanted a sign and the Lord accommodated his request. He asked him if he wanted the sun's **shadow** to **go forward ten steps or go back ten steps?** Hezekiah chose the option of the sun going **backward ten steps** (v. 10), assuming that this was the more significant, since the sun was already moving forward in its natural progression. The sun then moved backward, as seen on the **stairway of Ahaz** (v. 11). This was a special set of stairs that Ahaz had built as a kind of sundial (Patterson and Austel, "1 and 2 Kings," 274). The placement of Hezekiah's healing here in the text was intended to show that Hezekiah sought the Lord early in his reign, and this event strengthened his faith to call upon the Lord again when the Assyrians came against him later in his reign as recorded in chaps. 18 and 19.

20:12-15. Another chronological marker introduced an important meeting Hezekiah had with representatives from Babylon. The phrase **At that time** should be understood in general terms, meaning, at the time of Hezekiah's reign. **Berodach-baladan** (who ruled 721–710 BC) **a son of Baladan, king of Babylon, sent letters and a present to Hezekiah**. Sometime soon after the northern kingdom fell, while Assyria was still a regional power, but Babylon was on the rise, the king of Babylon wrote to Hezekiah **for he heard that Hezekiah had been sick** (v. 12). Hezekiah received the Babylonians, and **listened to them, and showed them all his treasure house**, perhaps to demonstrate the power and wealth of Judah (v. 13). This visit probably took place early in Hezekiah's reign when he "prospered" under the hand of the Lord (18:7; cf. 2Ch 32). Certainly it was prior to the siege of Jerusalem by Sennacherib (701 BC), when Hezekiah's treasuries would have been depleted. There would have been nothing to show (cf. 2 Kg 18:13-16).

20:16-19. This was the low point in Hezekiah's reign. He was foolish to show off his wealth to the Babylonian king's envoys. But why would the narrator want to record Hezekiah's healing followed by the king's apparent lack of discernment in showing off his riches? And why did Hezekiah not seem to be troubled by Isaiah's prophetic announcement of the time when **all that is in your house . . . shall be carried to Babylon; nothing shall be left** (vv. 16-18; cf. 24:10-16)? The narrator was not simply focusing on Hezekiah's actions, but on the plan of God as well. While the king was more righteous than his predecessors (cf. 18:5-6), he also had his weaknesses. And God had His purposes as well. Judah's spiritual rebellion would have its consequences, and God would be faithful to His word to judge them (cf. 2Kg 17:13, 19). Disobedience would lead to exile. Even if there were glimpses of righteousness in the kingly line of Judah, even the best of kings such as Hezekiah failed to be the promised Son of David, so this history served as a prompt to remind the readers of Kings to keep looking for the righteous Son of David who would be the messianic King. This was the way of Israel's true King.

20:20-21. Not only are the **acts of Hezekiah** recorded, but his construction work is still a testimony of his significance. The **conduit** which he built in Jerusalem to bring **water into the city** in time of siege was discovered in 1880. He carved a 1,700-foot tunnel from the Gihon spring (cf. 1Kg 1:33, 38) to a reservoir inside the city, the Pool of Siloam (cf. 2Ch 32:30). It includes the Siloam inscription noting the place where the workers met at the mid-point. This engineering marvel is open today for tourists to walk through in the City of David, Jerusalem.

2. Manasseh and Amon of Judah: Two Bad Kings (2Kg 21:1-26)

Despite his failure in showing the treasures to the Babylonians, Hezekiah's reign was impressive with respect to his personal devotion to the Lord and his desire to serve in righteousness. By contrast, his heirs, Manasseh and Amon, were the epitome of evil. Of both men it was said that they "did evil in the sight of the LORD" (vv. 2, 20). And for 57 years they led Judah away from the Lord, resulting in captivity to Babylon.

21:1-9. Manasseh came to the throne when he was **twelve years old** (v. 1). He ruled for 55 years (698/697–642 BC). This was the longest reign in Judah's history, part of which was a coregency with his father, Hezekiah (House, *1, 2 Kings*, 377). But it was his **evil** that is emphasized in the text. The specifics of that evil were recorded in four general areas. First, **he rebuilt the high places** that his father had torn down (v. 3). This in turn led the people to return to idolatrous practices. Second, he **built altars in the house of the LORD**; the seriousness of this is emphasized with, **of which the LORD had said, "In Jerusalem I will put My name"** (v. 4). Manasseh's act was contrary to what God had prescribed for worship (cf. 2Sm 7:13; 1Kg 8:29). Third, he resorted to all sorts of occult practices. **He made his son pass through the fire** (child sacrifice), and practiced **witchcraft . . . divination**, and the consulting of **mediums and spiritists** (v. 6). Fourth, **he set the carved image of Asherah that he had made, . . .** in the temple, the **house** in **Jerusalem** where God said **I will put My name forever** (v. 7).

This last act was contrary to the very conditions on which the Lord had promised blessing for Israel. He had told His people that He would bless them, only if they would **observe to do according to all that** He had **commanded them** (v. 8). But Manasseh led the people down a very different path. Tragically, **Manasseh seduced them to do evil more than the nations whom the LORD destroyed before the sons of Israel** (v. 9).

21:10-15. God was not absent while Manasseh promoted his evil ways. Rather, He made His will known **through His servants the prophets**, telling the people that He was about to bring a great **calamity on Jerusalem and Judah** (v. 12; cf. 21:1-3). The judgment to come would be so great that when a person heard about it, **both his ears shall tingle** (v. 12); the report of the disaster would figuratively hurt a person's ears to hear. This great calamity was described in the form of three **I will** statements used to paint a mental picture of the tragedy that would come in 586 BC.

First, God would evaluate the people: **I will stretch over Jerusalem the line of Samaria and the plummet of the house of Ahab** (v. 13). That is, He would use a plumb line, a standard measuring line, the same standards for judgment on Judah that He used in judging the house of Ahab. Second, He would use severe measures to purify all of Jerusalem, **as one wipes a dish, wiping it and turning it upside down** (v. 13). And third, God said **I will abandon** the Jewish people, **My inheritance** (cf. 1Kg 8:51; Dt 4:20) and **deliver** Jerusalem and Judah **into the hand of their enemies** (v. 14). This judgment was **because they have done evil . . . provoking Me to anger** (v. 15).

21:16-18. The true King was not turning a blind eye to Manasseh's sin. And in case the judgment to come might seem too harsh for religious malpractice, further evidence was given to prove that God's judgment would be just. Manasseh **shed very much innocent blood until he had filled Jerusalem from one end to another** and **made Judah sin, in doing evil in the sight of the LORD** (v. 16). This phrase is similar to the statement made about Ahab (cf. 1Kg 21:19; 22:35), who killed God's prophets. The announcement of impending judgment was just in every way. The case against Manasseh concluded by indicating that further information about his reign could be found in **the Book of the Chronicles of the Kings of Judah** (v. 17; cf. comments above at 1Kg 11:41-43; 14:19). Despite his long reign, Manasseh **was buried in the garden of his own house, in the garden of Uzza**, likely because his long history of evil deeds rendered him unworthy of burial with the other kings of Judah (cf. 1Kg 2:10; 2Kg 8:24; 8:28). The Uzza mentioned here is probably a shortened form of King Uzziah, in whose palace Manasseh lived, and not a reference to the Uzzah who touched the ark in transit and was struck dead (cf. 2Sm 6:1-8).

21:19-26. Very little information is given about the reign of **Amon**, Manasseh's son and successor. After becoming king at the age of **twenty-two,** he occupied the throne for only **two years** (v. 19). Certainly **he did evil in the sight of the LORD, as Manasseh his father had done** (v. 20). His servants then conspired against him and **killed the king in his own house** (v. 23). But the **people of the land killed all those who had conspired against King Amon,** and made **Josiah his son king in his place**. Like his evil father, Amon **was buried in the garden of Uzza** (v. 26; cf. v. 18). The repetition of Josiah's ascension to the throne (vv. 24, 26) served as a reminder that even though evil had prevailed for 57 years, there would be a respite of righteousness during the spiritual revival under Josiah. But Judah's destiny was certain. God would have to lead His people into exile to propagate a process of spiritual purification.

3. Josiah of Judah: A Good King (2Kg 22:1–23:30)

Israel's kings had continually provoked God to anger (cf. 2Kg 17:18-19; 23:26), and judgment was on the horizon. But there was also good news. A righteous king, zealous for the Lord's honor, was about to reign. Despite a short period of revival, however, God would not relent from the impending judgment He promised. Chapters 22 and 23 reveal exactly what God's intentions were. The account of King Josiah revealed both the heart of Israel's greatest reformer as well as the heart of God.

22:1-13. Josiah came to the throne at the age of eight and **reigned thirty-one years in Jerusalem** (v. 1). His reign was not as long as that of his evil grandfather, Manasseh, but he was to have a far superior influence. Clearly, he was not influenced by his immediate predecessors, but instead he **walked in all the way of his father David** (v. 2). At the age of 26, in his 18th year as king, he took steps to **repair the damages of the house** of the Lord (v. 5). But 2Ch 34:3 indicates that his zeal for God started even earlier, in his 12th year as king.

However, a major discovery in the temple was about to change everything that Josiah did. The high priest, **Hilkiah, found the book of the law in the house of the LORD** (v. 8). No explanation was given as to why this book (actually a scroll) was absent and where it might have been hidden or misplaced. Deuteronomy 31:24-26 stated specifically that the law was to be placed next to the ark of the covenant. In addition, the king was to have access to this law on a regular basis so that he would know God's will (cf. Dt 17:14-20).

Apparently, during the reigns of Manasseh and Amon, the law was deliberately set aside as pagan religious practices superseded the worship and law of the Lord. Not knowing how the young king might respond to this discovery, the high priest sent **Shaphan the scribe** to inform the king of what had just been found (vv. 9-10). He **read it** to Josiah, and when he did, the king **tore his clothes** in an act of repentance (v. 11). Almost immediately the king understood the implications of what he had heard. So he sent his officials to find out further what would happen. After all, the kings and the people had **not listened to the words of this book** (v. 13).

22:14-20. Four of Josiah's representatives went to **Huldah the prophetess** to hear how the Lord felt about Israel's sins and Josiah's repentance (v. 14). Other prophets, like Jeremiah and

Zephaniah, were contemporaries of the king, but a prophetess had Josiah's ear. Huldah would not give her own opinion, but she clearly gave the king an answer to his request. She began the response by saying, **Thus says the Lord** (v. 15). God's wrath was still burning against Judah, and it would not **be quenched** (v. 17). However, the heart of God was moved by Josiah's humility and zeal for God's honor. God said through the prophetess, **Because your heart was tender and you humbled yourself before the Lord . . . I will gather you to your fathers, and you will be gathered to your grave in peace, and your eyes will not see the all the evil which I will bring on this place** (vv. 19-20). Josiah would not live to see the destruction of Jerusalem and Judah taken captive to Babylon. Josiah would die in battle (cf. 23:29-30) but at peace with God.

23:1-3. On receiving Huldah's information, Josiah moved into action. The first thing he did was to implement the process of covenant renewal. He called for a national assembly with special invitations going to the **elders . . . all the men of Judah and all the inhabitants of Jerusalem**, along with **the priests and the prophets and all the people** (v. 2). No class distinctions were to keep people from coming to the assembly: **both small and great** were to attend (v. 2). Like Moses and Joshua in the past (cf. Dt 31:10-13; Jos 8:34-35), Josiah read **all the words of the book of the covenant** (v. 2). The ceremony must have lasted for quite some time. But in the end, the king himself pledged to keep the law, as did **all the people** (v. 3).

23:4-10. Following the covenant renewal ceremony, Josiah set out to purify the city and surrounding area, even going as far as to **Bethel** (v. 4), which had been resettled by the Assyrians (cf. 2Kg 17:24). Perhaps with a weakening Assyrian Empire, the Judean king thought he might be able to again unite the two nations of Israel and Judah (Patterson and Austel, "1 and 2 Kings," 287–88). But the reforms had both negative and positive aspects.

Josiah first destroyed all the **vessels that were made for Baal** worship (v. 4), burning them **outside Jerusalem**. Then he **did away with the idolatrous priests** who had assisted the kings in their idolatrous practices (v. 5). In an act similar to Moses' destruction of the golden calf, Josiah **ground** the burned **Asherah** pole **to dust** and then **threw its dust on the graves** (v. 6). Throughout these purification acts various elements were burned and thrown on graves, which in Israel was an extreme act of defilement and dishonor (cf. Nm 19:18). Josiah also destroyed **the houses of the male cult prostitutes** and the **high places**, along with those **priests** who encouraged the people in faulty worship (vv. 7-8). He purified Judea from **Geba** at its northern boundary to **Beersheba,** its southern boundary. Although later he killed the false priests in Bethel, he did not destroy those in Jerusalem. Instead, he refused to allow them **go up to the altar of the Lord** to serve at the temple, as part of their judgment (v. 9). He destroyed/**defiled Topheth**, the valley of Hinnom in Jerusalem dedicated to child sacrifice to **Molech** (v. 10).

23:11-14. Of particular interest were items not mentioned elsewhere in 1 and 2 Kings, namely, **the horses which the kings of Judah had given to the sun** (v. 11). Extrabiblical materials indicate that there was a strong association with horses, chariots, and the worship of the sun (Provan, *1 and 2 Kings*, 276). All these idolatrous objects, including **the altars . . . the high places** and **the sacred pillars** were destroyed (vv. 10-14).

23:15-20. In a grand fulfillment of the prophecy made about Josiah in 1Kg 13:26-32, he proceeded to destroy all of the idolatrous objects in **Bethel**, except for the **monument** that commemorated the coming of the man of God from Judah who had announced judgment on the altar at Bethel (cf. 1Kg 13:2).

23:21-23. Josiah's reforms led to a renewed celebration of the **Passover** (cf. Ex 12; 23:14-17). This feast celebrating God's redemption from Egypt had apparently been neglected, for **such a Passover had not been celebrated from the days of the judges who judged Israel** (v. 22). This does not mean Passover had not been celebrated at all since the times of the judges, but it indicates that the Passover under Josiah was more extensive than in the past (cf. 2Ch 25:1-19). The obvious point was that Josiah's celebration was grand in every way. He wanted to be sure the people reflected once again on the redemptive work of God among His people.

23:24-27. What Josiah wanted to do more than anything else was to **confirm the words of the law . . . that Hilkiah the priest** had discovered (v. 24). As the account of Josiah's life came to a close, two aspects of Josiah and the Lord are emphasized. First, Josiah was recognized for his commitment to the Lord: **before** Josiah **there was no king like him who turned to the Lord with all his heart and with all his soul and with all his might** (v. 25; cf. Dt 6:5). God honored

Josiah's zeal for His name. Second, in straightforward fashion the justice of the Lord was highlighted. Despite Josiah's faithfulness and his reforms, his influence on Judah was limited, for **the Lord did not turn from the fierceness of His great wrath . . . against Judah, because of all the provocations with which Manasseh had provoked Him** (v. 26). He did turn His heart toward a man who loved Him and His Word unequivocally, but He would **remove Judah . . . as I have removed Israel**. God's holy plans could not be thwarted.

23:28-30. The **acts of Josiah** are written in the **Book of the Chronicles** (cf. 14:19) and the events of his death are sketched out. In 609 BC Josiah moved his forces into the Valley of **Megiddo** to confront the Egyptian forces led by **Pharaoh Neco king of Egypt**. At the time Egypt had entered into an alliance with Assyria in an attempt to suppress various revolts within the western part of the Assyrian Empire. Josiah was able to stop Egypt from pursuing the alliance with Assyria, but he was **killed . . . at Megiddo**. But true to the prophetic word of God, Josiah was **brought . . . to Jerusalem and buried . . . in his own tomb** (v. 30; cf. 22:20).

B. The Last Kings of Judah Prior to the Babylonian Captivity (2 Kg 23:31–25:7)

After the death of Josiah there were no more good kings of Judah. The nation, which had began with so much promise under David, was now in a tragic spiritual decline which would culminate in its fall to Babylon. God's holy anger permeates every detail of these closing chapters; more details regarding the lives and spiritual condition of these final kings of Judah is recorded in 2Ch 36.

1. Jehoahaz and Jehoiakim of Judah: Two Bad Kings (2Kg 23:31–24:5)

23:31-33. After his father's death, **Jehoahaz**, the son of Josiah came to the throne in Jerusalem (609 BC). He reigned only **three months in** Jerusalem. Instead of following the righteous example of his father, **he did evil . . . according to all that his fathers**, the many wicked kings of Judah, **had done** (v. 32). He was captured by **Pharaoh Neco** as part of the Battle of Megiddo, and Judah temporarily came under the rule of Egypt (cf. 23:29-30). Once the people became vassals to Neco, the Egyptian king levied a tax **of one hundred talents of silver and a talent of gold** (v. 33). This imposed a heavy burden on the people that would weaken them even further. In addition, Neco deported Jehoahaz **to Egypt, and he died there** (v. 34). There would be another movement of God's people from the land to Egypt, ironically placing them in the very place where their history and covenant status started (cf. 25:26).

23:34-37. Jehoahaz's brother, **Eliakim**, was appointed by **Pharaoh Neco** to be his vassal king in Judah and **changed his name to Jehoiakim** (609–598 BC), a process of controlling another person's personality and reminding him who was in charge. The pressure to appease the Egyptian king must have been great as Jehoiakim **taxed the land in order to give the money** (v. 35). The prophet Jeremiah gave an even more harsh assessment of Jehoiakim by describing him as a king who oppressed, extorted, and shed innocent blood to accommodate his personal desires (cf. Jr 22:11-17; 26:20-24).

24:1-5. In the struggle for power, Egypt declined and Babylon gained dominance by defeating the Egyptian-Assyrian alliance at the battle of Carchemish on the Euphrates River (605 BC; cf. 24:7). Jehoiakim chose to switch his allegiance from Egypt to Babylon. **Nebuchadnezzar king of Babylon came up, and Jehoiakim became his servant for three years** (v. 1). It may have seemed like a reprieve from Egyptian oppression, but after three years Jehoiakim **rebelled against** Nebuchadnezzar. This led to the first Babylonian siege **against Judah to destroy it**. The attack not only included Babylonian/Chaldean forces, but an alliance of **Arameans . . . Moabites . . . and Ammonites**, some of Israel's historic enemies (v. 2). But it was **the Lord** (v. 3) who orchestrated the attack on Jehoiakim and Judah. Everything happened **according to the word of the Lord which He had spoken through His servants the prophets** (v. 2; cf. 21:12-15; 23:37).

2. Jehoiachin of Judah: A Bad King (24:6-16)

24:6-16. Following the death of Jehoiakim, his son, **Jehoiachin**, became king (v. 6). He **was eighteen years old when he became king, and he reigned three months in Jerusalem** (598–597 BC). During his reign, Nebuchadnezzar placed a second siege on the city of Jerusalem. Instead of trying to defend the city, **Jehoiachin the king of Judah went out to the king of Babylon . . .** that is, **the king of Babylon took him captive in the eighth year of his reign** (v. 12; cf. 2Ch 36:10; Jr 52:28). He surrendered himself, along with his family and several of his government officials (v. 12). But in spite of the surrender, Nebuchadnezzar used the occasion to take **all the treasures of the house of the LORD** and from **the king's house** (v. 13). All of this happened **just as the LORD had said** (v. 13; 22:14-16).

Besides taking the valuable items from the temple, Nebuchadnezzar also deported people, **all Jerusalem and all the captains and all the mighty men of valor**, totaling **ten thousand captives**, along with skilled workers of all kinds (v. 14). One of the people captured and taken away at the time of this second siege was the prophet Ezekiel (cf. Ezk 1:1-2). Babylon became the ruling power in Jerusalem. The glory that was established by Solomon was carried away to Babylon.

3. Zedekiah of Judah: A Bad King (24:17–25:7)

24:17-20. In Jehoiachin's place, Nebuchadnezzar **made his uncle Mattaniah king . . . and changed his name to Zedekiah**. He was just **twenty-one . . . when he became king** and **reigned eleven years in Jerusalem** (v. 18; 597–586 BC). He too **did evil in the sight of the LORD** (v. 19), being compared to Jehoiakim. Jeremiah's prophecy portrays Zedekiah as a spiritually confusing individual. In Jr 21:1-2, he asked God to save Jerusalem, while at the same time he was not worshiping Yahweh. In Jr 34:1-22, he heard and understood the prophet's message but did not obey it (cf. especially v. 17). Zedekiah appears to have lacked the consistency of mind and spirit to lead the people. Zedekiah foolishly **rebelled against the king of Babylon** (v. 20), and he would be the last king of Judah. (See the comments on the Jeremiah passages.)

25:1-7. Zedekiah's rebellion led to Nebuchadnezzar's third siege of Jerusalem (589–587 BC). During the **ninth year of** Zedekiah's **reign** the rebellion was underway, and Nebuchadnezzar himself came to put an end to the city and the kingdom once and for all (v. 1). A severe **famine** occurred because of the intensity of the Babylonian attack (v. 3). Then there was a break in one segment of the city and the Judahite warriors panicked. When the **Chaldeans** (Babylonians) **were all around the city**, Zedekiah's soldiers fled at night **by way of the gate between the two walls beside the king's garden** (v. 4). Nebuchadnezzar's army realized what had happened and set out in pursuit of the fleeing soldiers. They overtook Zedekiah in **the plains of Jericho and all his army was scattered from him** (v. 5). In the very place where Israel had its first victory in conquering the land, it suffered its final defeat before exile. And the king had to watch as the Babylonians **slaughtered** his sons before him and then they **put out** (blinded) his eyes. The killing of his sons was the last thing he saw before he was carried off to **Babylon** (v. 7).

C. The Fall of Judah and Jerusalem (2Kg 25:8-30)

25:8-21. With the army defeated and the capital city conquered, Nebuchadnezzar sent his representative, **Nebuzaradan the captain of the guard**, to finish what had been started two years earlier (v. 8). **He burned the house of the LORD, the king's house, and all the houses of Jerusalem** (v. 9; 586 BC). Even more people were deported to Babylon. Only **the poorest of the land** were left to serve as **vinedressers and plowman** (v. 12). And the things that Solomon had so carefully crafted were taken back to Babylon, including **bronze pillars . . . the stands** and **the bronze sea** (v. 13). The temple fixtures were described here in the same way they were portrayed at the building of the temple (cf. 1Kg 7:15-22).

In addition, Nebuzaradan rounded up the **chief priest**, the **king's advisers**, and several other city officials to take them to Nebuchadnezzar. The Babylonian king then **struck them down and put them to death at Riblah in the land of Hamath** (v. 21). The temple had been ransacked and the religious leaders were dead. The glory of the Lord's house was gone. A return to worship God, as required by the law of Moses with the required sacrifices, was now impossible. The tragic consequences of disobedience to the Lord had come to pass: **So Judah was led away into exile from its land** (v. 21).

25:22-26. The few people **who were left in the land of Judah** needed leadership, so Nebuchadnezzar **appointed Gedaliah** as governor. He was **the son of Ahikam**, who had served good king Josiah (cf. 22:11-20). The prophet Jeremiah described Gedaliah as an honorable man who wanted to serve Babylon (cf. Jr 40:7-16). As governor he appealed to the remnant left in Judea to **live in the land and serve the king of Babylon**. If they did, Gedaliah believed that it would **be well** for them (vv. 23-24). Not everyone agreed with this assessment, so a delegation led by **Ishmael the son of Nethaniah** came and killed Gedaliah, **along with the Jews and the Chaldeans who were with him at Mizpah** (v. 25; cf. Jr 40:13–41:15). Then the assassins were **afraid of the Chaldeans**/Babylonians and escaped to **Egypt** (v. 26).

25:27-30. With the destruction of Jerusalem, the destruction of the temple, and the people taken into captivity, everything seemed hopeless for God's people. But there was a glimmer of hope in the final treatment of imprisoned **Jehoiachin king of Judah** (v. 27; cf. 24:6-12). **Evil-merodach**, whose name means "man of (the Babylonian god) Marduk," was now the **king of Babylon**. In an unexpected act of mercy he **released Jehoiachin** from prison in the **thirty-seventh year** of his exile (561 BC). In addition, Evil-merodach **spoke kindly to him and set his throne above the throne of the kings who were with him in Babylon** and enabled Jehoiachin to have all **his meals in the king's presence regularly all the days of his life** (vv. 29-30).

It may seem strange to include Jehoiachin's experience of grace while living out his final days in exile. But it is important to keep in mind the theological perspective of the history of these kings. All of 1 and 2 Kings was written with Israel's law and covenants clearly in view. God had promised that rebellion would bring judgment, but repentance would bring God's blessings and the promise of return to the land (cf. Dt 30:1-10). At the same time, God's covenant with David held out the hope of an eternal kingdom for the heirs of David (cf. 2Sm 7:7-17). Therefore, Jehoiachin's exilic favors indicated in a small way that the "lamp of David" would not be extinguished (cf. 2Kg 8:19).

Israel's kings were leaders among the people, but the testimony of Scripture is that even these monarchs were simply God's servants and part of the larger kingdom of priests (cf. Ex 19:6). God would always be the true King! Therefore, it was important that these kings and their citizens alike obey the Lord in all they did. Israel's exile would not last forever, but it would be long enough to nurture repentance and eventually result in a return to the land of Israel. Although the Davidic line would not be placed on the throne after the return from Babylon, when Israel was back in the land, the people could focus their hearts on the coming of another king. One even greater than David, the promised King Messiah.

BIBLIOGRAPHY

See Bibliography for 1 and 2 Kings at the end of the commentary on 1 Kings.

● ● ● ●

1 CHRONICLES

KEVIN D. ZUBER

INTRODUCTION TO 1 AND 2 CHRONICLES

The books of 1 and 2 Chronicles, originally one book, were given the title *Chronicles* by Jerome in the fourth century AD, because it seemed to him to be a more descriptive title than the Greek (LXX) title *Paraleipomena*, "the things omitted." The Greek translators apparently considered these books to be something of an addendum or an appendix to the main historical accounts of Samuel and Kings. Unfortunately, that opinion about the books of Chronicles still prevails in many places today (and the fact that these books appear last in the Hebrew Bible has reinforced that idea.) It is something of a cliché to suggest that 1 and 2 Chronicles are among the most neglected, least read and studied (especially in key parts of the book such as the genealogies in chaps. 1–9), and least understood books in the Bible. Actually, the term *Chronicles* is a good idiomatic expression for the Hebrew title *dibre hayyamim* [lit., "the words of the days"]. The books of the Chronicles are "annals, records, histories" of the nation of Israel with a particular focus on the family and dynasty of David (cf. 1Ch 27:24). They are "theological histories." As such, they are an invaluable portion of the inspired Word of God, and it is a serious mistake to overlook them.

Author. Old Testament scholars generally speak of two major strands of historical narrative—the Deuteronomistic History (hereafter DH—Joshua, Judges, 1 and 2 Samuel and 1 and 2 Kings) and the Chronicler's History (hereafter CH—1 and 2 Chronicles, Ezra and Nehemiah). In broad terms the former is a history of Israel from a perspective that reflects preexilic and exilic views, and the latter from a generally postexilic perspective. For instance, the DH traces the history of Israel in the light of her faithfulness, or lack thereof, to the law, the Mosaic covenant. The failure of the nation as a whole to live by that covenant led to the exile as a judgment for serial idolatry. The CH understands the exile as a judgment on Israel for her failure to "seek the LORD," and for "forsaking the LORD" (see below under "Purpose and Themes"). These are not mutually exclusive concepts, but a matter of perspective. While this contrast is helpful in identifying different themes and emphases (especially where the two histories overlap) there are serious questions about the notion of a single "Deuteronomistic historian" and the identity of "the chronicler."

Jewish tradition, followed by a number of later scholars and commentators, attributes authorship of the books of Chronicles to Ezra the priest and scribe (Ezr 7:1-6), author of the book by the same name (and likely the author of Nehemiah). The strongest argument for this tradition is that the last verses of 2 Chronicles (2Ch 36:22-23) contain wording identical to that of the opening words of Ezra's book (Ezr 1:1-3). Furthermore, internal analysis of the books of the Chronicles makes it clear that there was a single author who used a variety of sources, a person who was intimately familiar with the temple and the services in the temple (cf. 1Ch 23, 24; 2Ch 2–5). There is a consistency of literary style and vocabulary, as the commentary will show, and a consistent theological perspective (cf. Payne, J. Barton, "1, 2 Chronicles," in vol. 4 EBC, ed. Frank E. Gaebelein. [Grand Rapids, MI: Zondervan, 1988], 305). This person was in a unique position to understand the need for such a book as Chronicles and also had the ability to write it.

While Ezra seems to fit all of these criteria, scholarship (evangelical and otherwise) is still divided on the question of his authorship of these books. The author of Chronicles appears to have had some ideas that were dissimilar to those of Ezra. The Chronicler (as it has become custom to refer to the author of these books) seems to have had a more open view with respect to mixed marriages (Jews and non-Jews) than does Ezra (see Neh 13:26; but not a word in protest appears about Solomon's wives from the Chronicler; 2Ch 8:11). Ezra, Nehemiah, and those who returned from the captivity often found themselves at odds with those who had remained in the land through the captivity (epitomized later in the conflict between the Samaritans and the Jews). Yet the Chronicler has given no evidence of such a conflict.

Indeed, the Chronicler seems to have intentionally included in his community any and all who could trace their heritage to the Israel of the United Monarchy. While his focus was on the Davidic dynasty and the southern kingdom of Judah, he regularly included, and had, in contrast to the author of Kings, a generally positive attitude toward the northern kingdom. The tribes of the northern kingdom are often included when he uses the expression "all Israel"; for instance, in the acknowledgment of the legitimacy of the Davidic king (1Ch 11:3) and the primacy of the temple in Jerusalem as the locus for true worship (1Ch 13:5; 28:1; cf. 2Ch 30:11, 18-19). These differences tend to militate against identifying Ezra as the Chronicler.

It seems best simply to affirm that the author of the Chronicles was likely a Levite, or at least one who served in the temple services, who sought by his extensive but selective history to bring encouragement and unity to the postexilic Jewish community.

Date. The internal evidence of the books of the Chronicles suggests that they were written sometime between 450 and 430 BC. The decree of Cyrus, King of Persia noted in 2Ch 36:22 was made in 538 BC, and the decree was carried out soon after that. In 1Ch 3, the genealogy of David's family is traced through Zerubbabel, the leader of those who first returned to Jerusalem (Ezr 2:2) around 520 BC. After Zerubbabel the Chronicler identified several more generations. If each generation is calculated to be 15 to 20 years, the dates for composition would be, as suggested, sometime in the second half of the fifth century BC. Furthermore, if we accept the view that 1Ch 9 is a genealogy of "the first who lived in their cities" after the exile (1Ch 9:2) and we compare this list to the lists in Nehemiah chaps. 11 and 12, we may legitimately presume that the books were written after the third generation of returnees, again in the range of 450–400 BC. While further precision in dating the book is probably unattainable, it seems that the Chronicles were written to the postexilic community of Jewish people living in the land promised by God to Abraham (see Gn 12:1-3; 15:18-21) near or in the city of Jerusalem.

The dating of the kings of Israel and Judah has been a source of frustration for the readers of the narrative and of scholarly debate for centuries. Many fine and detailed studies have attempted to unravel the complexities of the chronology of the Hebrew kings, and the reader is urged to consult them (cf. esp. Edwin R. Thiele, *The Mysterious Numbers of the Hebrew Kings,* new rev. ed. [Grand Rapids, MI: Zondervan, 1983]). No attempt will be made in this commentary to date the reigns of the kings or to correlate the narrative to other secular histories.

Purpose and Themes. As noted above, Chronicles was written using the Deuteronomistic history as a source and a guide for the "pure history" of the nation. That is, the Chronicler was not trying to rewrite the history but to give his generation a perspective on that history that would encourage and sustain them in difficult times. The genealogies were meant broadly to ensure the legitimacy of his generation's claim to the covenant promises (to Abraham and David) and specifically the legitimacy of the Levitical institutions that had been revived in his day. In both of these the legitimacy is proven by the continuity of the generational lines. In effect he was saying to his generation, "We are the legitimate heirs of those promises and institutions." His history was selective for the same reasons. He expected his readers to know the DH, and he selected those parts of the narrative that would support the claims of legitimacy and continuity with the nation's past—particularly the history of the Davidic dynasty based as it was on the Davidic covenant.

The Chronicler was not shy about his predilection for the Davidic dynasty. Throughout the entire work—from the genealogies to the accounts of the last kings of Judah—the Chronicler demonstrated his concern for the dynasty of David. He consistently sought to present a positive view of David and the descendants of David who sat on his throne after him, going so far as to omit accounts from Samuel and Kings that are unfavorable (e.g., David's sin with Bathsheba; the negative influences of Solomon's many foreign wives). Even where he had to acknowledge sin and apostasy, he was quick to interpret the matter in a providentially positive manner (i.e., David's census in 1Ch 21) or to offer a mitigating turn of events (i.e., Manasseh's repentance in 2Ch 33).

The Chronicler emphasized that God had chosen (elected) David and given him and his descendants the covenant (1Ch 17:1-15) that ensured a kingdom forever (17:14). That note would have had singular significance for the Chronicler's readers. This covenant was an extension of the Abrahamic covenant (Gn 17:6-8). In that covenant God had promised Abraham "kings will come forth from you" (17:6), and that "all the land of Canaan" would belong to his descendants "for an everlasting possession" (17:8). The Chronicler wanted his generation of Jews, those whose great-grandparents had come back into the land after the captivity, to know that the Lord was still faithful to those promises. His message was, "In accord with the promises He made to the Fathers, the Lord has chosen, made promises to, and preserved the Davidic dynasty through the tumultuous decades before the captivity. Therefore, we can be sure that He can be trusted to be faithful to those promises in our day." The Davidic dynasty was God's instrument for nurturing and preserving the promises and for maintaining the temple and its services as the place and means for the nation to experience the blessings of those promises.

The Chronicler was also devoted to the temple and took a keen interest in the worship and services of the temple. The temple was the locus of God's presence with His people. Proper worship was the outward evidence of a genuine inward faith in the Lord; proper worship was "seeking the LORD" and failure in proper worship was "forsaking the LORD." In this emphasis, the Chronicler was not advocating mere formalism, but he was concerned about true worship from the heart; the term "heart" appears some 30 times in Chronicles (Payne, "1 Chronicles," 318). For the Chronicler the temple was inextricably tied to the Davidic dynasty. The king was to establish and preserve the temple (as in the case of David and Solomon), and if need be restore it (as did Hezekiah and Josiah) and its proper services. For the Chronicler one of the main reasons for God's choice of David's line was to build, care for, and safeguard the temple. Part of this entailed the appointment of the proper functionaries in the temple—for example, the Levites, the priests, and the musicians (see 1Ch 23–26). For the Chronicler, when the kings took an interest in the temple it was a tangible expression of their faith and confidence in the promises the Lord made with David (1Ch 17).

The Chronicler was concerned to include "all Israel" in the restoration of the nation after the exile. All who will "seek the LORD" and who will acknowledge the temple as the only legitimate locus of worship are included in the blessings of the national relationship with the Lord. Accordingly, in his history the Chronicler downplayed the issues that divided the nation between northern and southern kingdoms and highlighted those institutions (David's regnancy 1Ch 11:1; Solomon's regnancy, 2Ch 1:2; the temple, 2Ch 6:3) and events (Hezekiah's restoration of Passover, 2Ch 30:1; Josiah's restoration of Passover, 2Ch 35:18) that brought "all Israel" together.

The Chronicler was concerned about the issues of faithfulness ("seeking the LORD") and apostasy ("forsaking the LORD"). These expressions appear regularly in his narrative—ideal Davidic kings "seek the LORD," and apostates "forsake the LORD." Failure to do the former while pursuing the latter brought the chastisement of the Lord. This was a key lesson from the nation's history that the Chronicler sought to teach his generation. It explained why the nation had gone into captivity and how those who returned could experience God's blessings. The Chronicler was very clear about retribution—the notion of "whatever man sows that shall he also reap." Yet he was equally interested in restoration—the notion that humble repentance and renewed obedience will restore a sinner (and the nation) to fellowship and blessing (see 2Ch 7:12-18). The experience of several later kings bore out this principle, and it was the message the Chronicler's generation needed to hear.

The Chronicler believed in prayer. Those who pray—from Jabez (1Ch 4:10) to David (17:1) and Solomon (2Ch 1:8; 6:12), to Rehoboam (12:6), Asa (14:11), Abijah (13:14), Jehoshaphat (18:31; 20:6-12), Hezekiah (32:20-21; 32:24), and even Manasseh (33:12-13, 18)—find that God hears and answers with blessing and forgiveness. The Chronicler was urging his generation to pray for God's blessing. This emphasis on prayer is a part of the general theme, noted several times already, of "seeking the LORD." The Chronicler was urging his generation to "seek the LORD" as David and his descendants had—through proper worship, through repentance, through prayer, and through obedience to the Word of God. The dangers of "forsaking the LORD" are also vividly (if minimally) noted by the Chronicler, not to warn of impending calamity (the perspective of the DH), but to encourage his generation to "seek the LORD" who is faithful to His promises (1Ch 16:11; 22:17; 28:9; 2Ch 15:2; 17:4; 30:9, 18b-19; 33:12, 19; 34:3).

The Chronicler was a man of hope and optimism, but this was not based on a superficial view of human nature or human history—a vague notion of "progress" and "prosperity." His hope was in the promise of God, in the covenants the Lord had made with Abraham and David. His hope was "Messianic" and will be vindicated when the Greater Son of David—the Lord Jesus Christ—fulfills those promises fully, literally, and forever.

Background. In composing his work the Chronicler used a number of sources, some of which he identified for the reader. It is likely that he used the canonical books of Samuel and Kings (1Ch 9:1; 2Ch 16:11; 20:34; 25:26; 27:7; 28:26; 32:32; 35:27; 36:8). He also used other canonical sources such as Genesis in the genealogies in chaps. 1 and 2 of 1 Chronicles and Psalms in 1Ch 16. He used a number of other sources identified as "chronicles" (1Ch 27:24, 29), "prophecy" (2Ch 9:29), "vision" (2Ch 9:29; 32:32), and "records" (2Ch 12:15; 33:19). The Chronicler has not simply "cut and pasted" his work from these sources, but has selected, crafted, and created from these sources his own skillfully composed literary product. First and Second Chronicles are not mere supplements to the histories of Samuel and Kings. The Chronicler had a unique message and provided his readers with a much-needed perspective on the history of his people. While he assumed that his readers were familiar with the histories in Samuel and Kings, he added a viewpoint intended to enrich their understanding and appreciation of that history.

A question related to the Chronicler's use of sources is the matter of historical accuracy and reliability. One area where the Chronicler has been questioned is his numerical citations. He has been accused of inflating the numbers (see 1Ch 18:4 compared to 2Sm 8:4; 1Ch 19:18 compared to 2Sm 10:18) and deflating the numbers (see 2Ch 8:10 compared to 1Kg 9:23; 2Ch 9:25 compared to 1Kg 4:26) and other anomalies. However, careful examination of these discrepancies shows that the apparent problem can be explained by scribal errors, or that the supposed discrepancy is a matter of alternative methods of counting (for an explanation of these details, see the comments on the relevant verses). The Chronicler has been shown to be highly reliable as a historian, even in somewhat incidental details (see J. B. Payne, "The Validity of the Numbers in Chronicles," *BibSac* 136 [1979], 109–28).

OUTLINE

I. The Genealogies of Israel (1:1–9:34)
   A. Adam to Esau (1:1-54)
      1. Opening Genealogies (1:1-27)
      2. Descendants of Abraham (1:28-54)
   B. David's Tribe and Family (2:1–3:24)
      1. Opening List (2:1)
      2. Genealogy of Judah (2:2-55)
      3. David's Family (3:1-24)
   C. Tribes of Israel (4:1–9:1)
      1. Judah (4:1-23)
      2. Simeon (4:24-43)
      3. Reuben, Gad, and Half the Tribe of Manasseh (5:1-26)
      4. Levites (6:1-81)
      5. Other Tribes (7:1-40)
      6. Benjamin (8:1-40)
      7. Summary (9:1)
   D. Postexilic Inhabitants of the Land (9:2-34)
II. History of David (9:35–29:30)

- A. David's Rise to Kingship (9:35–10:14)
  - 1. Genealogy of Saul (9:35-44)
  - 2. Defeat and Death of Saul and His Sons (10:1-14)
    - a. Saul's Last Battle (10:1-3)
    - b. Saul's Death and the End of His Dynasty (10:4-14)
- B. David Made King (11:1–12:40)
  - 1. David Is Made King (11:1-3)
  - 2. Jerusalem Is Made the New Capital (11:4-9)
  - 3. David's Mighty Men (11:10-47)
  - 4. Early Days (12:1-40)
- C. David and the Ark of the Covenant (13:1–16:43)
  - 1. David Moves the Ark: Part One (13:1-14)
    - a. David Sought Consensus to Retrieve the Neglected Ark (13:1-4)
    - b. Ark Began Trip in Celebration; but Not According to the Law (13:5-8)
    - c. Tragedy Ensued When Uzza Touched the Ark (13:9-10)
    - d. David Angered, Then Afraid; Halts Plan to Move Ark (13:11-14)
  - 2. David Consolidated His Regnancy (14:1-17)
    - a. David's Place among the Nations (14:1-2, 17)
    - b. David's Family Expands (14:3-7)
    - c. David's Victory over the Philistines (14:8-16)
  - 3. David Moves the Ark: Part Two (15:1–16:43)
    - a. Proper Preparation to Transport Ark (15:1-15)
    - b. Proper Reception of the Ark (15:16–16:6)
    - c. Proper Thanksgiving for the Ark (16:7-36)
      - (1) Call to Praise (16:7-13)
      - (2) Cause for Praise (16:14-22)
      - (3) Call to Praise (16:23-24)
      - (4) Cause for Praise (16:25-27)
      - (5) Call to Praise (16:28-33)
      - (6) Cause for Praise (16:34-36)
    - d. Proper Worship before the Ark (16:37-43)
- D. The Davidic Covenant (17:1-27)
  - 1. David Desired to Build a House (Temple) for the Ark (17:1-2)
  - 2. God Gave a Word to Nathan for David (17:3-15)
    - a. God Revealed His Mind to David His "Servant" (17:3-4a)
    - b. David Will Not Build the House (Temple) (17:4b-6)
    - c. God's Covenant with David (17:7-15)
      - (1) God's Choice and Protection of David Recalled (17:7-8a)
      - (2) God's Promise to David Revealed (17:8b-14)
      - (3) Nathan's Faithful Service (17:15)
  - 3. David's Prayer (17:16-27)
    - a. David's Humility (17:16-19)
    - b. David's Praise (17:20-22)
    - c. David's Prayer for God to Do as He Has Promised (17:23-27)
- E. David's Kingdom: Victories (18:1–20:8)
  - 1. David's Victories (18:1-13)
  - 2. David's Reign in Justice and Righteousness (18:14)
  - 3. David's Men (18:15-17)
  - 4. David Sought Peace with Ammonites but Had to Battle (19:1-19)
    - a. Delegation of Peace Is Abused (19:1-5)
    - b. Ammonites Prepared for War, Allied with Arameans (19:6-9)
    - c. Strategy and Faith of Joab Won the Day (19:10-15)
    - d. Arameans Called for Reserves but David Defeated Them (19:16-19)
  - 5. Victories Over Ammonites and Philistines (20:1-8)

F. David and the Temple (21:1–29:25)
  1. The Place for the Temple (21:1–22:1)
    a. Census (21:1-6)
    b. God's Displeasure; David's Sorrow (21:7-8)
    c. Consequences Fall (21:9-15)
    d. Consequences Mitigated (21:16-17)
    e. Consequences Turned to Good (21:18–22:1)
  2. David Made Preparations for the Temple (22:2–27:34)
    a. David's Initial Preparations (22:2-5)
    b. David Charged Solomon with Task (22:6-13)
    c. David's Closing Word to His Son (22:14-16)
    d. David Prepared Leaders to Assist Solomon (22:17-19)
    e. David Organized the Nation's Officials (23:1–27:34)
      (1) Solomon Made King; Officials Listed (23:1-6)
      (2) Levites in Non-Priestly Orders (23:7-32)
      (3) Levites Involved in Priestly Orders (24:1-19)
      (4) Remaining Levites Listed (24:20-31)
      (5) Musicians (25:1-31)
      (6) Gatekeepers (26:1-19)
      (7) Treasurers (26:20-28)
      (8) Other Officials (26:29-32)
      (9) Military and Civil Authorities (27:1-34)
  3. David's Final Addresses about the Temple (28:1–29:22a)
    a. First Address (28:1-10)
      (1) Assembly (28:1)
      (2) Davidic Covenant (28:2-8)
      (3) David's Charge to Solomon before the People (28:9-10)
    b. David Gave Solomon the Temple Plan and Encouragement (28:11-21)
      (1) The Plan (28:11-19)
      (2) Encouragement to Solomon (28:20-21)
    c. David's Second Address to Assembly and Their Response (29:1-9)
    d. David's Final Prayer (29:10-20)
    e. Closing of the Assembly (29:21-22a)
G. Death of David (29:26-30)

COMMENTARY ON 1 CHRONICLES

I. The Genealogies of Israel (1:1–9:34)

The genealogies of 1Ch 1–9 have several purposes: first, they are a prologue to the history to follow, providing a "background of heritage" for the narrative to follow. In a sense these genealogies are something like a "collapsed history" of Israel. (R. K. Duke, "Chronicles: Books of," *Dictionary of the Old Testament Historical Book*, ed. Bill T. Arnold and H. G. M. Williamson [Downers Grove, IL: InterVarsity, 2005], 172). In recording these genealogies the Chronicler expected his readers to have a working grasp of the narrative of Genesis and the rest of the Deuteronomistic History (see Introduction: Author). So, for instance, as he listed the names of Noah, Abraham, Israel, and the rest, he expected his readers to mentally review their stories.

Furthermore, the genealogies provide clues about the Chronicler's priorities; that is, they begin to point to some of his main concerns—the Davidic dynasty, worship, and prayer. But mostly they are intended to "define Israel's identity and promote the unity of all twelve tribes" of Israel. (Steven L. McKenzie, "Historiography, Old Testament," *Dictionary of the Old Testament Historical Book*, ed. Bill T. Arnold and H. G. M. Williamson [Downers Grove, IL: InterVarsity, 2005], 424).

A. Adam to Esau (1:1-54)

1. Opening Genealogies (1:1-27)

1:1-18. Beginning with Adam, the Chronicler moved quickly through the families of Noah, in order to come to Abraham and his descendants, and then shortly to David's main family line. By this device the Chronicler effectively tied world history to redemptive history. The Chronicler was mindful that God's purposes extend to all the nations (see Gn 12:3; Zch 8:22). "A summary of the 'generations' of Genesis, from Adam to Edom/ Esau, shows that all the nations were God's creation and therefore part of his special purposes for Israel" (Selman, Martin J., *1 Chronicles*. TOTC [Downers Grove, IL: InterVarsity, 1994], 86). In particular, the Chronicler is linking the house and line of David (and eventually the Greater Son of David, the Messiah) to Adam and the whole of mankind. Through the line of, and promise to, David, "God is reaching to all mankind" (Sailhamer, John, *First and Second Chronicles*, Everyman Bible Commentary [Chicago: Moody, 1983], 21). Luke was essentially making the same point in his genealogy of Jesus in Lk 3:23-38 (see the comments there).

The source of this first genealogy is apparently the "Table of Nations" in Gn 10. The sons of **Japheth** are the peoples of Europe along with northern and parts of western Asia. The sons of **Ham** are the peoples of Africa and parts of southwestern Asia. The sons of **Shem** are the peoples of west-central Asia and the Middle East.

1:19-27. The note about **Peleg** that **in his days the earth was divided** refers to the division that occurred at the tower of Babel (Gn 11:1-9). The name **Peleg** means "divided."

The climactic name on this list is, of course, **Abraham** (v. 27). Although the Chronicler does not specifically refer to the covenant promises made to Abraham (cf. Gn 12:1-3; 15:1-20; 17:1-14), the promises of many descendants and of the land are never far from his mind—those promises are the presuppositions of his narrative.

2. Descendants of Abraham (1:28-54)

1:28-54. The Chronicler next took up the descendants of Abraham, dealing first with the family of Ishmael (vv. 29-30) and the sons of his **concubine** (the term is not found in Gn 25; it means a sexual partner who is not on the same social level as a wife) **Keturah** (vv. 32-33). In Gn 25:1 Keturah was called "another wife." The title **concubine** was probably used here to make the point that the children she bore for Abraham were not children of the promise (see Gn 25:5-6 and the contrast with Isaac). The Chronicler then listed the sons of **Isaac**, dealing first with the family of **Esau**, from whom came the Edomites (vv. 34-54). Edom was an area southeast of the land of Israel/Judah on the other side of the Dead Sea, in the area of modern Jordan. The Edomites figured prominently in Israel's history all the way up to the time of Christ.

In the presentation of his genealogies the Chronicler employed a literary method (used in other Hebrew narratives such as Genesis) in which the author would carry the story, or describe the family, of a secondary character (here Esau, v. 34) to a suitable terminus and then backtrack to pick up the main story line at the point where the secondary character was introduced (compare 1:34 and 2:1). This gives a layered or segmented quality to the genealogy or narrative (see Braun, *1 Chronicles*, 1–2).

The Chronicler has used the lists from the book of Genesis (chaps. 5, 10, 25) to compile these opening genealogies. In doing this he not only gave evidence of his confidence in the historical reliability of Genesis, he was tying the narrative of David (1Ch 11–29) and the promises (covenant) the Lord would make with him (1Ch 17; cf. 2Sm 7) to the covenant promises God made with Abraham, Isaac and Jacob (Israel) (Gn 12:1-3; 15:1-21; 17:1-27; 28:13-15). He wanted his readers to see the continuity of God's purposes from the patriarchs to David's dynasty to their own place in that lineage.

B. David's Tribe and Family (2:1–3:24)

1. Opening List (2:1)

2:1. The Chronicler began a major section of his genealogical survey with a list of **the sons of Israel** (Jacob). The list in 2:1 is probably from the list in Gn 35:22b-26; cf. 46:8-25. However, the list given there is not followed exactly in the following genealogies. In the chapters that follow, the tribes of Dan and Zebulun are not included. While a number of explanations have been advanced to explain this, it seems best to see no negative implication in this omission since both tribes are included in this opening list and in the list in Ezk 48 (the distribution of the land in the millennium). Especially noteworthy is that Reuben is listed after Judah and Simeon. The Chronicler explained Reuben's demotion in 1Ch 5:1-2 (cf. Gn 35:22; 49:3-4). The most important variation is the promotion of Judah to the front of the list. This is because Judah was recognized as the line from which the kings of Israel will come (Gn 49:10) and thus Judah was the tribe of David (1Ch 2:15). The choice (election) of Judah and David and his descendants is a major theme of the Chronicler, exemplifying God's sovereign grace, as David later recognized about his own elevation to kingship and God's promise (see 1Ch 17:16-17).

2. Genealogy of Judah (2:2-55)

2:2-55. The genealogy of Judah reflects once again the Chronicler's use of Genesis (Gn 38). Here he also used the book of Ruth (compare 1Ch 2:11-15 with Ru 4:18-22) and possibly 1Sm 16. The Chronicler traces the line of Judah through his son **Perez**, grandson **Hezron** (vv. 5, 9), and great-grandsons **Ram** (vv. 10-17), **Jerahmeel** (vv. 9-42), and **Caleb** (**Chelubai** in v. 9) (vv. 18-20, 42-55).

3. David's Family (3:1-24)

3:1-24. Having traced out David's extended family line, the Chronicler turned to David's immediate family line and traced it through his sons **born to him in Hebron** (v. 1) and those **born to him in Jerusalem** (v. 5). The line is recorded through Solomon (v. 10), through Zerubbabel (v. 19), to the generations that were roughly the Chronicler's contemporaries. This family was of crucial importance: the line of David held the promise of God's continued blessing—the promise of the land, the kingdom, and the presence of God (see 1Ch 17:1-15; 2Sm 7:8-17). Ultimately, this line held the promise of the Messiah—Savior and King.

C. Tribes of Israel (4:1–9:1)

1. Judah (4:1-23)

4:1-23. Before turning to the genealogies of the other tribes, the Chronicler completed the family tree of Judah. The prayer of **Jabez** (v. 10) was noted as an example of the faith and reliance upon God that is blessed by God. His mother gave him the name **Jabez**—he causes **pain** (v. 9)—but his prayer "became an occasion of grace, so that God kept and blessed him" (Payne, "1 Chronicles," 341) so that his life did not live up to his name.

2. Simeon (4:24-43)

4:24-43. The tribe of **Simeon** lived close to Judah and was listed next in the genealogies of the tribes. The Chronicler here (vv. 28-31, 39-43) and in other places (2:22-23; 5:9-10, 16, 22, 23; 7:28-29) made a special note of the cities or the territory (the land) possessed by the tribes. He wanted his readers to know that their presence "in the land" was based on ancient tribal claims.

3. Reuben, Gad, and Half the Tribe of Manasseh (5:1-26)

5:1-26. Next the Chronicler listed the names of those tribes that settled in the territories east of the Jordan River—Reuben, Gad, and half of the tribe of Manasseh (see Nm 32). Reuben was the firstborn but lost the birthright because of his immorality (1Ch 5:1; see Gn 35:22; 49:4). This chapter contains notes about victory and blessing (1Ch 5:18-22) when the nation **cried out to God** in prayer and **trusted in Him** (v. 20) but also judgment and loss (vv. 25-26) when the nation **acted treacherously against the God of their fathers** by practicing idolatry (v. 25). This is a message and lesson that the Chronicler will deliver over and over—faithfulness and obedience bring God's blessing but disobedience, and especially idolatry, will bring God's discipline and captivity.

4. Levites (6:1-81)

6:1-53. The list of the Levites traces the family line from **Levi** (v. 1), through **Aaron** (v. 3), and through **Jehozadak** (v. 15) who was among those **carried . . . away into exile**. The emphasis is again on continuity, for it would be very important to the Chronicler's community to have qualified priests serving in the temple (see Neh 7:63-65). "Authentic genealogy, indeed, was essential for investiture (cf. 2:59-63)—hence [there was a] practical relevance of this chapter to the Chronicler's day" (Payne, "1 Chronicles," 350).

An important figure appears in this list of the Levites; he is **Zadok** (v. 8). While some critical scholars question Zadok's Hebrew/Levitical ancestry, this genealogy established him as a Levite, and he was a significant figure in David's administration (cf. 2Sm 18:17; 15:24). He appears later in 1Ch 12:28 and is described as "a young man mighty of valor," one of David's mighty men. At the time of Absalom's rebellion Zadok supported David (2Sm 9:11-14; 15:24-29, 36; 17:17-20; 18:19, 22, 27). David appointed Zadok to priestly service at the tabernacle in Gibeon (1Ch 16:39; cf. 29:22b), and he and his sons assumed the priestly administration of the temple until the time of the exile. Zadok was the priest who, along with Nathan the prophet, anointed Solomon as king (1Kg 1). Ezekiel prophesied that the priests who will serve in the millennial temple will be from "the sons of Zadok," who are "from the sons of Levi" (Ezk 40:46; cf. 43:19; 44:15; 48:11).

6:54-81. The list of the Levites is followed by a section detailing the allotment of the **cities** and **lands** of the Levites (vv. 54-81; see Jos 21). Once again the Chronicler showed that he was interested in the physical land and was very precise concerning its allotment. The promise of the land was always a central aspect of Israel's hope.

5. Other Tribes (7:1-40)

7:1-40. The genealogies of the tribes of Issachar (vv. 1-5), Benjamin (vv. 6-12), Naphtali (v. 13), Manasseh (vv. 14-18), Ephraim (vv. 20-27), and Asher (vv. 30-40) are recorded in a somewhat cursory fashion. As noted in the Introduction, the Chronicler's purpose is to bring "all Israel" into the narrative he is about to unfold.

6. Benjamin (8:1-40)

8:1-40. Here the Chronicler repeats and expands his genealogy of the tribe of Benjamin introduced in 7:6-12. This tribe is singled out for this extra coverage perhaps because of its close association with Judah or perhaps because it was the tribe of **Saul** (8:33), who will shortly, but briefly, become the focus of the narrative.

7. Summary (9:1)

9:1. This verse is a summary of the tribal lists the Chronicler has just completed and, somewhat enigmatically, notes **Judah was carried away into exile to Babylon for their unfaithfulness**. This note was probably meant to indicate that the list to follow concerns those who returned to the land after the captivity.

D. Postexilic Inhabitants of the Land (9:2-34)

9:2-34. This list of **the first who lived in their possessions in their cities** (v. 2) is a list of the Jewish people who had returned to repopulate the land of promise. The list of "common folk" (vv. 3-9), **priests** (vv. 10-13), **Levites** (vv. 14-16), **gatekeepers** (vv. 17-27), and other functionaries (vv. 28-34) was intended to show that among those who returned were those who could lead the people in government, establish true worship, and do the hard work of restoration. The Chronicler wanted his readers to be reassured that Israel had indeed survived the captivity. They, his readers, were not cut off from, but were vital participants in, God's ongoing purposes, and they were part of that nation with ongoing promises.

II. History of David (9:35–29:30)

A. David's Rise to Kingship (9:35–10:14)

Many commentators argue that the focus of this section is on the end of Saul, and there is much to be said for that view. In 9:35-44 the Chronicler recorded the genealogy of Saul, and in 10:1-10 he recorded Saul's defeat and death. However, given the overall emphasis on David in the Chronicles, it may be argued that the key verse is 10:14 and the main focus is not on Saul's end but David's rise to kingship.

1. Genealogy of Saul (9:35-44)

9:35-44. The mention of **Gibeon** was perhaps a subtle reminder that Saul's capital was *not* chosen by God—Gibeon is not Jerusalem. That the record of Saul's family line included several generations was a generous concession by the Chronicler. Since the Chronicler's history was in part meant to highlight the prominence of the Davidic line and given Saul's opposition to David, the Chronicler may have chosen to ignore the line of Saul altogether (thus diminishing that line's eminence). However, even though Saul was removed from the regnancy, his family remained a part of "all Israel" and his line is included among those who gave allegiance to David.

2. Defeat and Death of Saul and His Sons (10:1-14)

The Chronicler passed over the reign of Saul, although he apparently assumed his readers were familiar with the story. His main concern was the person and reign (and family) of David, and he moved quickly past Saul to begin David's story. Accordingly, the only significant part of Saul's reign as far as the Chronicler was concerned was its end.

a. Saul's Last Battle (10:1-3)

10:1-3. The accounts of Saul's last battle with the Philistines, the defeat of his army, and the deaths of his sons are starkly and sparely reported. The Chronicler does not revel in Saul's defeat. His readers were looking for encouragement and did not need to be reminded of the several "bad episodes" in the nation's history. (The Chronicler did his best to minimize the negative and accentuate the positive episodes of the nation's history.) There may be a "providential" element in that Saul was **wounded by the archers** (v. 3) (see 18:33). Thus it was the Lord and no other person who was responsible for Saul's defeat.

b. Saul's Death and the End of His Dynasty (10:4-14)

10:4-12. It is difficult, if not impossible, to discern with any certainty the Chronicler's view of Saul in his death. Was he a brave hero who preferred death at the hand of his servant, or even at his own hand, to humiliation and **abuse** by the **uncircumcised** (v. 4)? Or was he a coward who took the easy way out and left his defeated nation without a leader and at the mercy of its enemies (v. 7)? It seems that the Chronicler was deliberately ambivalent on these points (see 1Sm 31 for the more detailed account). Saul was the king, and for that he was to be honored, and his dismembered body was to be treated with respect (v. 12). Yet he was a flawed king, and for that he was defeated and mocked by his enemies (vv. 8-10).

10:13-14. The Chronicler's account concluded with his own distinctive summary, a theological explanation of why Saul was killed. He gave three reasons: (1) Saul was unfaithful to God (1Sm 15:11), (2) Saul did not obey God's Word (1Sm 13:8-14), and (3) Saul did not "seek the Lord" but sought **counsel of a medium** (1Ch 10:13; see 1Sm 28:6-7). Also, it was God's plan to turn **the kingdom to David** (1Ch 10:14). A man may give every outward indication, and posses all the natural capacities, that would point to success in service to God, but without faithfulness, obedience, and dependence on God he will fail (see 1Sm 15:22-23). Saul had not merely succumbed to the forces of the Philistines—the Lord **killed him** (v. 14). The Chronicler was well aware that God is in sovereign control of the events of history (cf. Eph 1:11; Dn 2:21).

B. David Made King (11:1–12:40)

The years of conflict and civil war (see 2Sm 1–4) are omitted from the Chronicler's account. This was not because the Chronicler thought he could remove that episode from the nation's memory of its history or because he thought it unimportant. Rather, he expected that his readers would know the actual history. Therefore, his purpose was as much, if not more, theological as it was historiographical—to "accentuate the positive," not rehash the negative in the nation's history. There is tacit recognition of David's reign over Judah from Hebron (11:1, 3) but that time of division did not interest the Chronicler, who was more concerned to highlight the unity of the nation.

The Chronicler introduced this key point in the very first verse of this two-chapter unit (chaps. 11 and 12) when he noted that David's ascension brought unity to "all Israel" (11:1). "This emphasis on Israel's unity under David must have had considerable implications for post-exilic Israel" (Selman, *1 Chronicles*, 137-38). After the captivity the divisions (north and south) and even the "tribal tensions" made less sense and were less consequential than they were before the captivity. The Chronicler knew that those returning to the land after exile needed a sense of "national identity" if the nation was to thrive as they faced the challenges of rebuilding. Part of his purpose was to unify these people. Thus the section begins and ends on this note of national unity.

1. David Is Made King (11:1-3)

11:1-3. The theme of the unity of "all Israel" was articulated in several ways. First, there was the unity expressed in the gathering of **all Israel** to David **at Hebron**, the headquarters of the first phase of his regency. Unity was expressed by the formula **Behold, we are your bone and your flesh** (v. 1). Unity was expressed too in the acknowledgment that even as Saul had remained king in name and title it was David who was the de facto leader of the armies. Unity also was expressed in the acknowledgment that David's reign was **according to the word of the Lord through Samuel** (1Sm 16). David's regnancy was described by two key terms: he was to **shepherd** and **be prince** (lit., "ruler") over the people (1Ch 11:2). The shepherd's task was to care for and protect the sheep. The "prince" (*nagid*) was a military designation and pointed to the task of "kingdom building" and national defense. Both terms may have been used to indicate that the Davidic king was to be a servant answerable to the Owner of the flock (cf. Selman, *1 Chronicles*, 139) and the True King of the nation, namely the Lord Himself. These are obviously rich biblical metaphors that point ultimately to the Messiah—the Great Shepherd, the Prince of Peace (cf. Is 9:6).

The Chronicler emphasized one other note, that is, the anointing of David was **according to the word of the Lord through Samuel** (1Ch 11:3). This makes the point that the events of this history are not random, nor are they the result of socioeconomic or political circumstances but are designed and directed according to God's sovereign will and purpose. David was the legitimate king of "all Israel" not by the nation's choice but by God's choice. The mention of Samuel was significant. Prophets play an important role in the narrative of Chronicles; "it is apparent that the Chronicler understood a major role of the prophets to be that of interpreting the hand of God in history" (Duke, "Chronicles," 178).

2. Jerusalem Is Made the New Capital (11:4-9)

11:4-9. Unity was further established through the new location for the capital city—Jerusalem. The choice of Jerusalem was wise. It was centrally located; it had to be conquered because it did not belong to either side—Saul's or David's—during the years of conflict between them (hence, it was a neutral site with no prior loyalties that could be questioned or championed over other cities); and its location had strong natural defenses.

3. David's Mighty Men (11:10-47)

11:10-47. Unity was further promoted by David's Mighty Men—**heads** (11:10), **chief**[s] (11:20; 12:3), **commander**[s] (11:21), **captains** (12:18), and fighting men who generally were loyal to David. An example of the fierce loyalty of these men to David, and of David's respect for them, appears in 11:15-19.

4. Early Days (12:1-40)

12:1-22. This chapter recorded something of a flashback to David's early days at **Ziklag** (vv. 1-22) and **Hebron** (vv. 23-40) (see 1Sm 27 to 2Sm 5) and is included here to complete the list of David's men. Several of these men are noted for their dexterity—a valuable asset for warriors (1Ch 12:2). That these were Benjaminites—**Saul's kinsmen**—is particularly significant, highlighting again the theme of unity around David (vv. 2b-7). Others are **from the Gadites** (vv. 8-14), and their bravery is noted in one remarkable incident when they **crossed the Jordan** during the flood season (v. 15) to win a victory. One man, Amasai, epitomized the affection and loyalty of David's men and was led by the Spirit (v. 18) to compose a verse expressing his loyalty to David: **We are yours, O David, And with you, O son of Jesse!** Still others, **from Manasseh** defected to David's side late in his conflict with Saul (v. 19). Although they were not needed in this battle against the Philistines (cf. 1Sm 29) they did serve David in a later skirmish (1Ch 12:21). In v. 22 the Chronicler explained that **day by day men came to David**—thereby increasing his stature and authority. David's army is "compared, poetically, with the heavenly hosts"—**like the army of God** (v. 22)—they were, so to speak, "on the side of the angels."

12:23-40. The list of the tribes in vv. 23-37 reinforced the main point—all Israel was with David, again, including even some of **Saul's kinsmen** from Benjamin (v. 29). This is the third time in this chapter the men of Benjamin have been mentioned (cf. vv. 2, 16-17). These men were warriors (vv. 28, 30), and the weapons they brandished are highlighted in these verses (vv. 24, 34, **shield and spear**; vv. 33, 37, **weapons of war**). Furthermore, they **understood the times** (v. 32)—that is, they knew these were David's times "thus they cast their lot with David rather than Saul" (Payne, "1 Chronicles," 378). They understood the tactics of warfare—**who could draw up in battle formation** (v. 38a). They all were of one mind, and when they **came to Hebron with a perfect heart** they made **David king over all Israel**. It was not only them but **all the rest also of Israel were of one mind to make David king** (v. 38b). The entire chapter celebrates—and ends with a celebration of (vv. 39-40)—David's kingship. With his reign **there was joy indeed in Israel** (v. 40c).

C. David and the Ark of the Covenant (13:1–16:43)

Unity as a theme is carried over into the next major section, centering on the ark of the covenant. David intended to promote the unity of the nation around the ark of God and the worship of God (13:2-3). Note again the emphasis on "all the assembly of Israel, all the people". However, David discovered that worship was not to be taken lightly and never as a means to an end. God's Word must be obeyed if worship is to be acceptable to Him. "The Ark was no mere symbol of God's presence. It was the place where God had chosen to center His presence among His people (Ex 25:22)" (Sailhamer, *First and Second Chronicles*, 38).

1. David Moves the Ark: Part One (13:1-14)

a. David Sought Consensus to Retrieve the Neglected Ark (13:1-4)

13:1-4. David desired to bring the nation together around the iconic symbol of the ark of the covenant. He consulted with the leaders (v. 1), rallied **all the assembly of Israel** (vv. 2-4), gathered "all Israel together" (v. 5), and proposed that the ark be brought from Kiriath-jearim (about 20 miles west of Jerusalem), where it had languished since its humiliating trip to the land of the Philistines and back. There the ark had remained through all the years of Saul's reign (see 1Sm 5–6 and 1Sm 7:1-2). David wanted to **bring back the ark of our God to us** (v. 3) and **the thing was right in the eyes of all the people** (v. 4).

b. Ark Began Trip in Celebration; but Not According to the Law (13:5-8)

13:5-8. Amid the celebration (v. 8) the Chronicler noted that the ark was the place where **God, the Lord . . . is enthroned above the cherubim, where His name is called** (v. 6). This solemn fact was stated just before the Chronicler incongruously noted that the ark was being moved on a **new cart** (v. 7) after the fashion of the Philistines (cf. 1Sm 6:7)! Even though the leaders and the people were quite happy with the event, God's Word was not being obeyed. Even though they had great respect for the ark (it was after all a *new* cart) they also displayed an unthinking, unacceptably cavalier attitude toward the ark and its significance. Genuine respect for the majesty and holiness of the ark required more than a consensus of what was pleasing to the people—it required obedience to God's Word on the matter (see the comments below on 13:9-10). It may have seemed a small matter, but God's Word is often very clear and specific on small matters. God does not make concessions even on small matters when matters of true worship and obedience are at stake.

c. Tragedy Ensued When Uzza Touched the Ark (13:9-10)

13:9-10. Nothing in the Chronicler's account to this point prepared the reader for the shocking turn of events that occurred next. Uzza (Uzzah in 2Sm 6) was one of the drivers of the cart (1Ch 13:7b). When the cart was nearly upset by the oxen he innocently reached out to steady the ark. While this might have seemed to be an act of concern for the ark, an innocent gesture—not meant to show disrespect, but in fact to protect the ark—it was a violation of the clear commands given in the law of Moses. The law stipulated the method and manner of transporting the ark (carried by means of acacia wood poles overlaid with gold inserted through rings on the base of the ark; Ex 25:12-15; Nm 4:5-14), as well as the persons authorized for moving it (the Levites; cf. Dt 10:8). God's Word, His utter holiness, and His awesome majesty must be acknowledged and respected. Good intentions are no substitute for obedience. David and the nation had focused on the ark itself and the celebration surrounding it and not on the God whose presence was being celebrated in the ark.

d. David Angered, Then Afraid; Halts Plan to Move Ark (13:11-14)

13:11-14. Uzza's death brought the celebration to an abrupt halt. David's response was shock, anger, and fear (vv. 11-12). The failure to be scrupulous in obeying the law resulted in a delay in bringing the ark to Jerusalem, and it was taken to the **house of Obed-edom the Gittite**—which means he was or had been "a resident of Gath" (Payne, "1 Chronicles," 381), a Philistine city. While David seemed to be afraid of the ark, Obed-edom found it to be a source of blessing (v. 14). The point seems to be that God's purpose for the ark was not judgment but blessing. Nevertheless, He will not allow His people to lose sight of His holiness and majesty. He is a God of power—for blessing upon obedience, for judgment upon negligence.

2. David Consolidated His Regnancy (14:1-17)

This chapter records events that took place prior to those in chap. 13. Once again the Chronicler, while not ignoring unpleasant historical events (like the debacle of the ark in chap. 13), arranged his material to highlight the favor and blessing God gave to David and his house. Thus, in keeping with this theme of the Lord's blessing of David, the Chronicler recorded three examples of that blessing.

a. David's Place among the Nations (14:1-2, 17)

14:1-2, 17. At both the beginning and conclusion of this chapter, the Chronicler gave a word about the respect (perhaps tribute) of other nations that David enjoyed at this time. This was a clear indication that **the LORD had established him as king** (v. 2).

b. David's Family Expands (14:3-7)

14:3-7. The note about the increase of his family is in the Chronicler's view a further indication of the Lord's blessing (cf. Ps 127:3-5), even though David's polygamy was not something the Lord endorsed and amounted to "a moral failure, directly contrary to the law (Dt 17:17)... This sin led to a whole series of disasters later on (2Sm 11:27)" (Payne, "1 Chronicles," 382). In spite of that, the Chronicler understood that in that time and culture, and in those circumstances, having a large family for a king was a sign of fertility and that was a sign of blessing (cf. 1Ch 3:5-9).

c. David's Victory over the Philistines (14:8-16)

14:8-12. David's victory over the Philistines takes up the bulk of this chapter and is another striking evidence of God's blessing. The Philistines had been a continual threat to the nation of Israel throughout Saul's reign, and they sought to continue that threat when David began his reign (v. 8). However, the Chronicler recorded that the forces that had defeated Saul and were used to end his reign were soundly defeated by Saul's divinely appointed successor. Two instances of Philistine incursions are noted. First they made a **raid in the valley of Rephaim**

(v. 9). The valley of Rephaim was "southwest of Jerusalem and formed part of the boundary between Judah and Benjamin (Josh 15:8)" (Payne, "1 Chronicles," 383).

14:13-16. Later they made yet another raid in that same valley (v. 13). In describing these two battles the Chronicler drew the contrast between Saul and David more clearly when he noted that when faced with the Philistine threat (vv. 8-9) David did what Saul had failed to do (cf. 10:14a), namely, **David inquired again of God** (14:14; cf. v. 10a). In the first instance David did not run ahead of God but looked for, and received, God's direction and promise—"Go up, for I will give them into your hand" (v. 10b). The Philistines were defeated, and the site was memorialized in the name Baal-perazim ("the Lord breaks through"). David acknowledged that the victory was the Lord's who "has broken through my enemies" (v. 11). In the second battle David was given the specific strategy of flanking the enemy and waiting for the sound of the wind (**sound of marching**) in **the balsam trees** (vv. 14-15a). Apparently, this resulted in some confusion in the Philistine camp since they were unable to perceive the direction of the attack from David, allowing David to achieve a complete victory. But the Chronicler was quick to emphasize that this victory was a result of God having **gone out before** David (v. 15b) and David having done **just as God had commanded him** (v. 16). David learned to "seek the Lord," and he found that "obedience brings blessing."

3. David Moves the Ark: Part Two (15:1–16:43)

David had learned the lesson—from his victories and from the tragedy of Uzza's death—that obedience, paying strict attention to the Word of the Lord, was the key to the blessing of the Lord. Thus when he resumed the project of moving the ark he instructed the proper authorities, the Levites (cf. Dt 10:8), "to carry the ark of God (1Ch 15:2) and to do so according to the ordinance (15:13) as Moses had commanded according to the word of the Lord" (15:15; cf. Ex 25:12-15). The account of moving the ark from the house of Obed-edom to the place David had prepared (1Ch 15:1) was recorded in three phases.

a. Proper Preparation to Transport Ark (15:1-15)

15:1-15. David simply and clearly laid out the instructions for moving the ark: **No one is to carry the ark of God but the Levites** (v. 2a). No similar preparation of any kind preceded the first attempt, the Chronicler noted (v. 13). The list of the names of the Levites here was designed to show the care with which this move was undertaken. Only those with proper credentials (that is, of the right tribe and ancestry) could perform the task of transporting the ark. Having the proper priestly credentials was very much an issue in the Chronicler's day; see Ezr 2:59-63. This time everything was done **according to the word of the Lord** (1Ch 15:15b).

In addition to making the obvious point that David and "all Israel" had learned the lesson of obedience to the Word, the Chronicler made another key point in this chapter: it was David who assumed the responsibility for ensuring a place for and proper respect for the ark. David also assumed the responsibility to organize the Levites and the musicians (in the next section). David assumed the role of a "second Moses" (Selman, *1 Chronicles*, 161), and the Davidic dynasty was henceforth understood as the patron and protector of the worship and services of the temple. This meant more than simply maintaining the proper forms and ceremonies. Temple worship was the heart of the relationship between the Lord and His people. Proper worship was the privilege and blessing of His people. Failure at, or forsaking of, that worship was the cause of calamity and chastisement. "For the Chronicler, the Levitical priesthood operated jointly with the Davidic monarchy in preserving the correct forms of seeking Yahweh, of maintaining the proper relationship with God" (Duke, "Books of Chronicles," 177).

b. Proper Reception of the Ark (15:16–16:6)

15:16-28. After scrupulous care had been taken to ensure everything was done according to the Word of the Lord to transport the ark, the Chronicler recorded that equal care was given to proper reception of the ark. This time, instead of "all Israel" celebrating "with all their might" (13:8a), everyone using whatever instrument they chose (13:8b), now the appointed musicians (15:16), those with skill (v. 22) were employed. Now proper and appropriate sacrifices were made (v. 26; 16:2). Now, **God was helping the Levites who were carrying the ark of the covenant** (15:26)—that is, since the ark was being transported in the manner prescribed by the law, God was with the Levites and "they were not struck down, as Uzzah had been (13:10)" (Payne, "1 Chronicles," 388). It was, in short, a time of enthusiastic and full-hearted worship; it was a joyful but mindful celebration "in spirit and in truth" (cf. Jn 4:24). David's **robe of fine linen** and **ephod of linen** (1Ch 15:27) were the garments of "priestly" dress, and they identified David as having a part in such service.

15:29. The brief reference to **Michal the daughter of Saul** (15:29) and her disgust over David's part in the activities (apparently his enthusiasm was too undignified for her taste) showed her insensitivity to the value and meaning of the ark (no doubt an attitude held by others) and was thus "a further demonstration of the unfitness of Saul's house to lead the people of God" (Selman, *1 Chronicles*, 166).

c. Proper Thanksgiving for the Ark (16:7-36)

This praise psalm is a compilation of Pss 105, 96 and 106. (For more detailed comment see the commentary on those Psalms.)

(1) Call to Praise (16:7-13)

16:7-13. The call to praise employs several imperatives: **give thanks**, **make known**, **sing**, **speak**, **glory**, **seek**, **remember** (16:8-13). For the Chronicler the keynote of this praise is found in 16:11 in the imperative to **seek the Lord and His strength; Seek His face continually**. (See Introduction: Purpose and Themes on the importance of the theme of "seeking the Lord.")

(2) Cause for Praise (16:14-22)

16:14-22. The covenant promise given to Abraham, Isaac, and Jacob was at the heart of the Chronicler's faith and hope (vv. 14-17). The experiences of the patriarchs were to be "remembered." The grace of God in calling and preserving the fathers was recalled and stood as a promise that by His grace believers during the Chronicler's day also shall be preserved. The note that this is **an everlasting covenant** (v. 17) would have been particularly important to the Chronicler and his generation. God's gifts—the **land of Canaan** (v. 18) and calling (His **anointed ones**, v. 22) are irrevocable (cf. the comments on Rm 11:28-29). The story of the sojourn of Abraham, Isaac, and Jacob (Israel) included encounters with kings, such as Abimelech (Gn 20; 26). But God protected His **anointed ones**, and **He reproved** those kings (vv. 21-22; cf. Gn 20:3, 7). Because His promises are everlasting His people can count on His continued protection.

(3) Call to Praise (16:23-24)

16:23-24. The call to praise employed more imperatives: **sing**, **proclaim**, **tell** (vv. 23-24). Here the breadth of the message was expanded to **all the earth** and **all the peoples**. This too was in keeping with the promise to Abraham, for in and through that covenant promise "all the families of the earth will be blessed" (Gn 12:3).

(4) Cause for Praise (16:25-27)

16:25-27. His superiority over idols and His transcendent majesty are noted as reasons that He is to be praised and feared (v. 25). The idols are impotent, but the Lord is the Creator God; He alone possesses **splendor and majesty** (v. 27; see Is 44:9-20 on the folly of idolatry and Is 6:1-6 on His majesty and glory).

(5) Call to Praise (16:28-33)

16:28-33. Again the Psalmist widened the picture and called for praise from the peoples of the earth as well as praise from the rest of God's creation. The threefold use of **ascribe** (lit., "give") (vv. 28-29) heightened the sense of worship; the focus is on the Lord. The nature of true worship was indicated by the call to **worship** (lit., "bow down") and **tremble** (vv. 29, 30), indicating the need for creaturely humility and submissiveness and at the same time the call to **be glad** and **rejoice** (v. 31) indicating the need for joy and celebration. The opposites **earth** and **heavens**, the **sea** and **field** (vv. 31, 32) indicate that worship is a primary responsibility of all creation, because His reign (v. 31b) is universal.

(6) Cause for Praise (16:34-36)

16:34-36. Thanksgiving appropriately concludes this hymn: He is **good** and loving, and He delivers (saves) and keeps His covenant. Once again, the emphasis is on the **everlasting** (vv. 34, 36) nature of His **lovingkindness** (*chesed*; meaning something like "loyal love," or "devotion in a covenant-based relationship"). The Chronicler's encouragement to his generation was very much in view: He is the **God of our salvation**, here specifically defined in terms of the people being gathered and delivered **from the nations** (v. 35).

d. Proper Worship before the Ark (16:37-43)

16:37-43. This brief note brings the reader back to the historical setting. Having established a place for the ark (v. 39; Gibeon is about five or six miles northwest of Jerusalem) David provided for a daily ministry centered on the ark and for proper care of the ark. The appropriate offerings are mentioned, and authorized priests are listed (vv. 37-42) to establish that a "primary sanctuary for sacrifice" (Payne, "1 Chronicles," 393) was now available. These verses simply reiterate the point that now (in contrast to the debacle with the ark recorded in chap. 13) all services done with respect to the ark were undertaken with the proper attention to detail and decorum. Everything was now in place—and in a better place since the ark was no longer in Philistine territory—in order for David and the nation to have a prosperous reign (v. 43).

D. The Davidic Covenant (17:1-27)

It would be difficult to overemphasize the significance of the contents of this chapter. Here the Chronicler recorded his version of the Davidic covenant (see 2Sm 7; Ps 89). This is "the heart of Chronicles" (Payne, "1 Chronicles," 395), the first of seven texts in Chronicles that state and restate this covenant (17:7-27; 22:6-16; 28:6-7; 2Ch 6:8-9, 16-17; 7:17-18; 13:4-5; 21:7). By his emphasis on this covenant the Chronicler gave it a greater significance than does the narrative of Samuel/Kings. In particular, and of special interest to his readers, the Chronicler emphasized two points: he was concerned to locate the fulfillment of the promise, Jerusalem; and he was concerned to emphasize that the promise was *forever* (a term used several times in this chapter; 17:12, 14). This promise has significance for David and his descendants, for the nation of Israel, and for all the nations of the earth. The reason is that this covenant promises that the Messiah will come (vv. 13-14; Lk 1:32-33) through David's line, to sit on David's throne, to rule in David's city, Jerusalem, over an everlasting kingdom, and that He will bring salvation that will "reach to the end of the earth" (Is 49:6; see the comments on Mt 3:1-4).

In form and even in expression, this unconditional promise to David and his descendants is noticeably and purposefully reminiscent of the Abrahamic covenant (Gn 12:1-3) on which it is built. The covenant with Abraham established the Lord's promise to make a great nation (Gn 12:2)—which He had done. The Lord had also promised Abraham that He would raise up kings (Gn 17:6)—which He was now doing with David. The unconditional nature of the promise is highlighted by the Lord's emphatic first-person pronouns describing His past but sovereign care of David ("I have gone" . . . "I have walked" . . . "I took") (17:5-7), combined with the personal promissory declarations for the future ("I will make" . . . "I will appoint" . . . "I will plant" and most vitally, "I will build") (vv. 8-10). While the author of 2 Samuel noted in his version of this promise that any particular individual descendant (king) of David (or one in the Davidic line) may fail to enjoy the promises of this divine blessing (cf. 2Sm 7:14), here in the Chronicler's version the Lord gave David unqualified assurance that One of David's descendants would enjoy a unique Sonship (cf. Heb 1:5; Is 9:6) and would experience the assured and permanent blessings of this covenant (17:11-14). Note the emphasis on the *throne* (vv. 12, 14). This speaks of the "place and right to rule." Emphatically (mentioned twice in this brief space), this part of the promise is *forever*. The term "covenant" (*berith*) does not appear in these verses, but the promises made here are referred to as a covenant in several later texts (see 2Sm 23:5; 2Ch 13:5; 21:7; 23:3; Ps 89:3, 28, 34, 39; Is 55:3; Jr 33:16-26).

1. David Desired to Build a House (Temple) for the Ark (17:1-2)

17:1-2. The account opened with David secure in his own **house** (v. 1; notice also the use of the term **house** in the previous transitional verse, 16:43). At first this seemed to be a somewhat mundane observation, but the various nuances of the word **house** (*bayit*) were meant to provide the reader with the focal points in this narrative and promise. The Chronicler used this term **house** (*bayit*) to refer to David's palace, to the temple (in prospect), and to David's dynasty. David drew the contrast between his **house of cedar** and the location of the ark **under curtains** (17:1b). He apparently considered his house of cedar to be a more appropriate dwelling for the ark than the tabernacle (of "curtains"); the Lord corrected David's perspective in the word from Nathan. David was exhibiting the quality of a good king and man of God by seeking the counsel of the prophet Nathan, but Nathan's encouragement (v. 2) was proven to be premature. Interestingly, Nathan was not rebuked for this presumption; nevertheless he received a timely correction.

2. God Gave a Word to Nathan for David (17:3-15)

a. God Revealed His Mind to David His "Servant" (17:3-4a)

17:3-4a. The opening expression, **It came about the same night** revealed the urgency of preventing David from proceeding with his plans. David was called **My servant** by the Lord, indicating that the Lord was not displeased with David's heart and intent.

b. David Will Not Build the House (Temple) (17:4b-6)

17:4b-6. Here in Chronicles the Lord's prohibition, **You shall not build a house for Me to**

dwell in (v. 4b), was much more directly, even bluntly, stated than in the parallel version in 2Sm 7. The Lord corrected David's estimate of the appropriateness of the ark's current abode by reminding him, **I have not dwelt in a house since the day that I brought up Israel to this day** (1Ch 17:5a). In other words, this was the Lord's plan from the beginning. The Lord chose this migratory arrangement by His own design. By this arrangement He **walked with all Israel** (v. 6). He had not asked for or commanded a **house of cedar** (a clear if mild reproof of David's estimate of the relative value of a house of cedar) to be built because His very presence is the glory of His people—not the container it comes in. (When Solomon later built the temple, he would make this same point: the presence of the Lord is more important than the earthly vessel in which He comes, no matter how grand or modest. When the Messiah came in humility essentially the same point was made once again; see Lk 2:11-12). The Lord was telling David, "I will choose the appropriate dwelling, for My reasons, according to My purpose, at the time of My choosing" (see Dt 12:5). The Lord deliberately chose the tabernacle that the people might be in awe of the presence of the Lord Himself, not the magnificence of the structure in which He manifested that presence. (See 1 Ch 22:8 for another reason for not allowing David to build the temple.)

c. God's Covenant with David (17:7-15)

The Lord then turned the tables and revealed His plans for David and David's "house."

(1) God's Choice and Protection of David Recalled (17:7-8a)

17:7-8a. The Lord recalled His election and elevation of David (and David would have no doubt recalled the events of 1 Samuel at this point). As with His choice of a dwelling, His choice of David was "contrary to expectation." God's man was not the people's choice—not Saul (1Sm 16:1), not one of David's elder brothers who would have been a more natural choice (1Sm 16:6, 8-10), but the young shepherd boy of the family (1Sm 16:11). "For God sees not as man sees, for man looks at the outward appearance," for God's house or God's leaders, "but the LORD looks at the heart" (1Sm 16:7). The Lord reminded David that his success in battle (a point to be reiterated in the next chapter) was because of His presence (**I have been with you**) and His power (**and have cut off all your enemies from before you**, 1Ch 17:8a), a point that reiterates God's sovereignty over all matters.

(2) God's Promise to David Revealed (17:8b-14)

17:8b-14. As noted, the Lord's covenant with David was reminiscent of the covenant promises the Lord gave to Abraham (Gn 12:1-3). The promises consisted of a word for David himself (1Ch 17:8), a word for the nation (v. 9), a word for both David and the nation (v. 10), a word to David's son Solomon (v. 11), and a word concerning David's Greater Son—the Messiah (vv. 12-14). Note again, the repeated phrase **I will**. As with the promise the Lord made to Abraham (see Gn 15) this promise was one-sided—the Lord obligated Himself. It was a promise based on sovereign grace, and it was unconditional—no obligation was laid on the recipient. David needed only to believe and trust God to keep this word (as with the Abrahamic covenant; see Gn 15:6). The Chronicler was well aware that neither Solomon nor any other Davidic descendant had ever met the requirement of full obedience ("If you will walk in My statutes, and execute My ordinances and keep *all* My commandments by walking in them, then I will carry out My word with you which I spoke to David your father," 1Kg 6:11-12 [italics added], cf. 1Ch 28:6-7). Therefore his narrative of the kings demonstrated that each one ultimately failed, even the good ones, and that the reader should continue to look for the messianic Son of David to fulfill the promise to David.

As a result, the prophets after David never saw the fulfillment of the Davidic covenant (found here and in 2Sm 7:12-16) in Solomon or any other Davidic king. Rather, they understood the Davidic covenant as the basis for an expectation that only the Messiah would fulfill this promise to David (cf. Is 9:6-7; 11:1, 10; 16:5; Jr 23:5; 30:9; 33:15-17; Ezk 34:23-24; 37:24-28; Hs 3:4-5; Am 9:11-15). Intertestamental Judaism also recognized the Davidic covenant as the basis for their expectation that the Messiah would be the Son of David (PsSol 17:21-25, 33-34, 44-45; 18:8; TLev 18:2-3; TJud 24:5-6; SibOr 3:652-53).

Thus the Chronicler was painfully aware that many of the kings, if not every king who followed David, had failed to enjoy the blessings of the Lord's promise. Therefore, in his rendering of the Davidic promise, the Chronicler chose to highlight the unqualified pledge of the Lord that assured his readers the Davidic dynasty had not been lost and the promise had not been voided. Men failed—but the promise remained, and a Greater Son of David would come (cf. Ps 89:24-29; Mt 1:1; Lk 1:32).

17:8b. David was promised a great **name** (again, very like the promise God had made to Abraham, Gn 12:2) **like the name of the great ones who are in the earth** (1Ch 17:8b). David's renown as a military leader (14:17), his singular stature as the model of the ideal, godly king (see 2Ch 28:1; 29:2; 34:2), and his reputation as a prophet (Ac 2:30) were all indications that this promise was literally fulfilled.

17:9-10a. The nation, **My people Israel**, was promised **a place** to dwell; the Lord affirmed, **I will plant them, so that they may dwell in their own place and not be moved again** (v. 9). No doubt this promise recalled the land promises of the Abrahamic covenant (see Gn 12:7; 15:18-21; 17:8). This promise would have had immediate significance for the generation of the Chronicler. That generation knew this was no guarantee that they, or any particular generation (or generations) would never be removed from the land. After all, their immediate forbearers had just returned from the captivity. But this promise meant they had a right to this land in their day and that future generations could look forward to a day when the promise would mean possession of the land forever. The nation was also promised rest from **all your enemies** (1Ch 17:10a). Both of these promises will be kept when the nation experiences the blessings of the millennial kingdom (Hs 2:18; Mc 4:3; Rv 20).

17:10b-11. To David and the nation the Lord promised to **build a house for you** (v. 10b). Here the term **house** refers to a dynasty; "God's promise to 'build a house' for David is a play on words: the king could not build God a house, i.e., a structure 'of cedar' (v. 6) but God would build him one, a dynasty of descendants" (17:11) (Payne, "1 Chronicles," 396). All in all, this would mean that the nation would continue to have a "servant," a shepherd for the people, a patron and protector of the temple (to come) and the Levitical institutions, a leader who would seek the Lord and bring the blessings of God's grace and lovingkindness.

17:12-14. Of course, this would be true only if the Davidic king continued to "seek the LORD" and did not "forsake the LORD." But that possibility (and the warning of 2Sm 7:14) is not in view here, as the Chronicler chooses to focus on the positive promise and the grace of God. The Lord promised **I will not take My lovingkindness** (*chesed*; "loyal love, covenant love") **away from him** (v. 13), not because of anything in the king himself, but solely because of God's word.

To David's son Solomon the promise was **He shall build for Me a house** (v. 12a). This promise would be reiterated and applied and fulfilled in later contexts in 1 and 2Ch.

Finally, there was a word about another, one who would be a Son to the Father (v. 13a; cf. Ps 89:27). That the Chronicler had in mind not Solomon (or any other of the kings named in the following history) may legitimately be understood because of the special nature of this promise: **I will settle him in My house and in My kingdom forever, and his throne shall be established forever** (v. 14). David's dynasty and Solomon's kingdom will be **established**, but this One will reign, His throne will last in perpetuity—**forever**. This is "a feature made possible by Jesus Christ, who, as God's Son (next verse), is the only one to possess a rule that is endless" (Payne, "1 Chronicles," 396). "No possibility is entertained that this covenant will be abrogated, or will need to be abrogated (v. 13); no less than five times the writer repeats that it will be forever" (Roddy Braun, *1 Chronicles*, WBC [Waco, TX: Word, 1986], 200).

The Chronicler was well aware that no king in his narrative fulfilled, or could fulfill, this promise. The promise was not, and could not be, fulfilled until the angel spoke to Mary and revealed that her Son "will be great and will be called the Son of the Most High; and the Lord God will give Him the throne of His father David; and He will reign over the house of Jacob forever, and His kingdom will have no end" (Lk 1:32-33). Only He, the One who lives forever and ever (Rv 10:6), can occupy a throne forever. "Ultimately it leads to Jesus, in whom this promise is finally and perfectly fulfilled. In the light of Jesus' resurrection and ascension, the early church constantly saw this as the supreme Old Testament promise concerning Jesus as the Son of God, frequently referring to this and similar passages (e.g. Acts 2:30; 13:22-23, 33-34; Rom 1:3-4; Heb 1:5, 8-9; 5:5)" (Selman, *1 Chronicles*, 179–80).

(3) Nathan's Faithful Service (17:15)

17:15. The note that Nathan carried out the task of communicating the word of the Lord to David completely (**all these words . . . according to all this vision**, v. 15) is another instance of the Chronicler's high regard for faithful prophets.

3. David's Prayer (17:16-27)

David responded in an extraordinary prayer of humility (17:16-19), of praise (17:20-22), and of faith in God's promise (17:23-27).

a. David's Humility (17:16-19)

17:16-19. David's humility here was remarkable: **Who am I . . . and what is my house** (v. 16). He knew that there was no inherent greatness in himself. David recognized that this great blessing was **a small thing in Your eyes** (v. 17a), that is, it took no effort or strain for God to accomplish something David could never have imagined by his own strength. David was given a "great name" only because the Lord **regarded** him as **a man of high degree** (v. 17b). David confessed that he was at a loss for words to express his humble appreciation for the Lord's utterly gracious promise (v. 18), a promise made solely **according to Your own heart** (v. 19), that is, utterly by grace. This promise was a demonstration of "the surpassing riches of His grace" (Eph 2:7), a promise "more abundantly beyond all that [David could] ask or think" (Eph 3:20).

b. David's Praise (17:20-22)

17:20-22. David's praise was in two parts. First he recognized the absolute uniqueness of God Himself, **O Lord, there is none like You** (v. 20), and second the uniqueness of God's choice of Israel (v. 21). David did not have a "sterile theology" but rather a rich appreciation of the sovereign, all-powerful gracious Lord. God had just given him a promise of incalculable value—and he was appropriately overwhelmed.

c. David's Prayer for God to Do as He Has Promised (17:23-27)

17:23-27. This part of the prayer betrayed no suggestion that David thought God's promise might not come to fruition. His prayer **let the word You have spoken . . . do as You have spoken** (v. 23) betokened his hearty approval and delight in the prospect. He desired that God fulfill His word in order that **Your name be established and magnified forever** (v. 24). In other words, "Do Your will, Lord, so that all the earth will acknowledge and exalt You." David concluded with another acknowledgment of the promise to **build . . . a house** (v. 25), and he specifically claimed one precious feature— the promise was **forever** (v. 27). This model prayer expresses humility, utter trust, rich theological confession, and simple trust. The Chronicler included it as a model prayer and attitude for his own people.

E. David's Kingdom: Victories (18:1–20:8)

These chapters record the expansion and consolidation of David's kingdom. The material here is not chronological and follows roughly "the sequence found in 2 Samuel" (Payne, "1 Chronicles," 398). In Chronicles the accounts of victory over enemies are intended to show David's military prowess (by the Lord's enablement), the loyalty and bravery of his men, and the unity of "all Israel" (cf. 19:17). The Chronicler was telling his generation that their victories would likewise require godly and divinely ordained national leadership, the loyalty and courage of each man (and woman), serving and working in unity—lessons for God's people of all ages. Thus, these accounts functioned as illustrations of the Chronicler's message and were not intended to be read as if they were in chronological order.

1. David's Victories (18:1-13)

18:1-13. David's victories over the Philistines (18:1), the Moabites (18:2), Hadadezer (18:3-11), and the Edomites (18:12-13) came about because **the Lord helped David wherever he went** (18:6b, 13b). This was in accord with the promise of 17:8. "The lesson of that collage of warfare is the same as that celebrated in Psalm 2: the kings of the earth can devise only an empty plan against the Lord and His Anointed (Ps. 2:1-2)" (Sailhamer, *First and Second Chronicles*, 51).

2. David's Reign in Justice and Righteousness (18:14)

18:14. This summary verse served to drive home once again the point that David reigned over **all Israel** and added that the success of his reign could be attributed to the qualities of **justice and righteousness** (v. 14). The Chronicler was not simply saying David's was a fair and equitable administration, that he was an even-handed ruler. He was all of that. But even more, these are the qualities of the perfect administration to come at the hand of the ultimate Son of David, the Messiah (Is 1:26-27; 11:1-5; 32:16; 33:5). David's reign was one that his descendants would either emulate, resulting in the nation's prosperity and blessing, or deviate from, to the nation's regret and judgment.

3. David's Men (18:15-17)

This brief listing of some of David's key men was placed here to prepare the reader for the role of Joab (18:15; 19:10) and the "choice men" in the next account. While there is much emphasis in Chronicles on the leadership of the king, the author also wanted his readers to be aware that leaders cannot win victories alone. God blessed David with loyal and courageous men from the beginning of David's reign (cf. 11:10-47).

4. David Sought Peace with Ammonites but Had to Battle (19:1-19)

This chapter shows not only that David was a fierce adversary militarily, but also that he could be diplomatic and cordial with his friends. However, when his overtures of friendship were rebuffed his power was to be feared.

a. Delegation of Peace Is Abused (19:1-5)

19:1-5. David sent what amounted to a "delegation of consolation" to **Hanun the son of Nahash** upon the death of Nahash (v. 2; cf. 1Sm 11:1, 2) the king of Ammon. The Ammonites had been enemies of Saul, and there had apparently been a treaty of some sort between Nahash and David during the period of their common enmity with Saul. This **kindness** is actually *chesed* or "loyalty," a term often used in covenants and treaties, and typically used for God's unending covenant love for Israel. David was not merely repaying an act of benevolence, but he also was living up to his treaty obligations. Hanun's advisers mischaracterized the purpose of the delegation and humiliated the messengers by having their beards shaved (specifically half-shaved in 2Sm 10:4) and their clothing cut (exposing them immodestly, 1Ch 19:4). These developments were reported to David (v. 5) setting the stage for the confrontation.

b. Ammonites Prepared for War, Allied with Arameans (19:6-9)

19:6-9. Each stage in the following account begins with the formula, "When [someone] saw that . . ." The Ammonites prepared for the battle by hiring mercenaries. David prepared for battle by sending out **Joab and all the army, the mighty men** (v. 8). David had neither desired nor invited this battle, but he was ready for it because he had previously cultivated the loyalty of a core of mighty men (fighters) and he had enlisted faithful generals (cf. 18:15-17). This was a battle between those who were paid to fight and those who fought on the basis of personal loyalty and for a cause greater than themselves.

c. Strategy and Faith of Joab Won the Day (19:10-15)

19:10-15. The battle array of the Ammonites was impressive (cf. 19:9), and when Joab saw it he embarked on a bold strategy. He himself led **all the choice men of Israel** (v. 10) against the mercenary Arameans (Syrians), and he set his brother **Abshai** against the main force of the Ammonites (v. 11). Each force was to act as the reserve for the other (v. 12). Joab's pre-battle speech is a motivational classic in three parts: First, he appealed for "personal courage"—**Be strong, and let us show ourselves courageous**. Second, he appealed on the basis of national pride—**for the sake of our people and for the cities of our God**. Third, his appeal was grounded in faith and trust in God—**and may the Lord do what is good in His sight** (v. 13). This was a message designed for the Chronicler's generation, and for all generations of God's people. Joab's faith was proven well-placed and his strategy well executed, and both the Arameans and Ammonites **fled before** him and his brother (vv. 14-15).

d. Arameans Called for Reserves but David Defeated Them (19:16-19)

19:16-19. The victory of Joab and Abshai was not the final battle. When the defeated Arameans called for reinforcements David himself **gathered all Israel** (v. 17), went across the Jordan river, **drew up in battle array**, and defeated them. This defeat was devastating (v. 18; on the numbers see Introduction), complete, and led to a time of peace with the leader of the Arameans, **Hadadezer** (v. 19).

5. Victories Over Ammonites and Philistines (20:1-8)

20:1-8. A final victory over the Ammonites and three vignettes from the wars with the Philistines conclude this record of David's victories. The Chronicler pointed out that while **Joab led out the army** and **David stayed at Jerusalem** (v. 1), yet the victory was David's **by the hand of his servants** (v. 8b). This presents a slightly different picture from that drawn in 2Sm 11:1. In that context there is an implication of negligence on David's part—he should have been out fighting with his men and instead he found himself at home tempted by Bathsheba (2Sm 11:2). The Chronicler, however, may be seeking to indicate that "plurality in leadership among God's people is essential, if only to make up for the deficiencies of others (cf. Eph. 4:11-13; Ac. 13:1-3; Phil. 1:1)" (Selman, *1 Chronicles*, 197).

The brutality indicated in 1Ch 20:3 may not be what it seems. The original is not altogether clear and the parallel in 2Sm 12:31 ("set them under" meaning "forced them to use") may indicate that this was an instance of forced labor (cf. Selman, *1 Chronicles*, 197); "David could be ruthless . . . but he was not cruel" (cf. Payne, "1 Chronicles," 402-403). The "giants" among the Philistines were apparently large men, with some physical oddities (v. 6) and some impressive weaponry (v. 5). However, these advantages were of no avail, and they were defeated **by the hand of David and by the hand of his servants** (v. 8b).

F. David and the Temple (21:1–29:25)

1. The Place for the Temple (21:1–22:1)

At this point the Chronicler chose to omit the account of David's sin with Bathsheba and the subsequent events: the murder of Uriah (2Sm 11), the rebuke of Nathan and loss of a child (2Sm 12), the turmoil in David's house (2Sm 13), including the revolt of Absalom (2Sm 14–19) and the lesser revolt of Sheba (2Sm 20). Between the end of 1Ch 20 and the account of the census to follow in 1Ch 21 (1Sm 24) there is a gap of about 20 years filled with these tumultuous events. The Chronicler is not attempting, by this intentional omission, to deny these events or rewrite history. He knew his readers were familiar with the accounts in 1 Samuel. "His reasons for a gap of this length are not difficult to surmise: little of what transpired during those two decades would encourage a postexilic Judah" (Payne, "1 Chronicles," 406). The Chronicler's purpose was to highlight the positive from Judah's past in order to give encouragement to her present.

Nevertheless, the Chronicler did include the narrative of David's sinful census (perhaps because to omit it would leave unexplainable gaps in the narrative). The Chronicler mitigated this surprising development somewhat by revealing that Satan (v. 1) instigated David's action. Satan is sometimes used by the Lord (in His sovereignty, yet with Satan doing just as he pleases) to accomplish His purposes (cf. Jb 1:8–2:10; Lk 22:31, 32). However, the parallel in 2Sm 24:1 indicates that it was the "anger of the LORD" (against David for relying on the number of his forces rather than on the Lord) that incited David to this action. In other words, it would appear that God, in His anger (for some unspecified sin, 2Sm 24:1), used the instrument of Satan, "the adversary of God's people" to incite David to sin. (Some suggest that this means simply "an adversary," indicating that Satan was used to provoke a rival nation to attack David.) This appears to be an instance of "compatibilist determinism" or the view that God can be the author of "nonconstraining causes" that nevertheless inexorably accomplish His will and yet do not make Him responsible for the free actions of men who act on those causes.

"Nonconstraining causes" are those that do not force a person to act against his will but are sufficient to assure a determined outcome—an outcome determined by God. Here the Lord sends a cause [the adversary] that does not force David to respond by this sinful act. Yet given David's propensity [self-seeking and sinful, as all men are] the Lord knows this cause is sufficient to move David to take this census—that is, David sins. In this case David sinned because of his own will [even though the provocation, the adversary sent by the Lord, ensured that that is exactly what he would do] and therefore he is responsible. "This view is often referred to as *soft-determinism* or *compatibilism*, for genuinely free [and responsible] action is seen as *compatible* with nonconstraining sufficient conditions which incline the will decisively in one way or the other" (John S. Feinberg, "God Ordains All Things," in *Predestination and the Will of God: Four Views on Divine Sovereignty and Human Freedom* [Downers Grove, IL: InterVarsity, 1986] 24-25). By ordering this census David brought the judgment of the Lord on the nation (1Ch 21:7, 14). Therefore, that David was "moved" (21:1) to order this census does not absolve him of personal responsibility, even if it explains his uncharacteristic disobedience. However, even this was not the final word, for upon David's confession and repentance the Lord not only mitigated the judgment but also turned the occasion to one of providential blessing—the place of the judgment became the location for the temple.

a. Census (21:1-6)

21:1. The appearance of **Satan** at this point is quite unexpected. Indeed, this is the first time *Satan* appears without the definite article in Scripture (see Jb 1–2; Zch 3:1-2, *hasatan* "the adversary"; but see comments above). In some fashion (perhaps through an intermediate means like a pagan nation in opposition) Satan **stood up against Israel** (1Ch 21:1). Whatever God's motives in using Satan for His purposes (see the discussion on God's use of non-constraining causes and free will) (or whatever *Satan* means) Satan remained malevolent and his intentions were always destructive of God's people (cf. 1Pt 5:8; for Satan as an instrument of chastisement under God's providential oversight, see 2Co 12:7; 1Tm 1:20).

21:2. David gave his orders for this census to **Joab and to the princes of the people** (21:2). The command was comprehensive—**from Beersheba** in the extreme south **even to Dan**, the northernmost point of the tribally occupied land. The phrase **that I may know their number**

may give a subtle clue as to David's motive: perhaps he was congratulating himself on the expansion of the kingdom, or perhaps this census was something of a poll of David's popularity, or perhaps designed to assess his military strength or economic power. Whatever the motive "he seems to have forgotten that the people were not his but God's" (Selman, *1 Chronicles*, 205). God had commanded that Moses number the people (Nm 1; 26) but He had not so commanded David. This census seems to be motivated by David's pride and self-importance.

21:3. Joab seems to have understood that this action was a mistake, and he said that such an act would **be a cause of guilt** (v. 3c). Because of this (and further showing he considered it a wrong thing to do) he attempted to dissuade David. His attempt was tactful (**But, my lord the king**...) but direct. He acknowledged that having a large population would be a blessing from the Lord, and he reminded David that they were all his servants no matter how many (or few). Perhaps Joab was thinking of the victories of the smaller Israelite forces over the larger armies of the Ammonites and Arameans. His subtle point would be, "We do not need to know the number. We need only to know they are your loyal servants." He then directly confronted David to inquire into his motives: **Why does my lord seek this thing?** In short, what purpose would this accomplish since the number of people was what it was by the Lord's will and blessing? Finally, he identified the real problem with this census: it amounted to **a cause of guilt to Israel**. The term **guilt** is a strong term usually used for acts that warrant God's wrath (2Ch 24:18; 28:10; 33:23).

21:4-6. Joab's boldness was commendable and his tact exemplary, but his objections did not change David's mind—**the king's word prevailed** (v. 4). The census went forward. However, Joab's heart was not in this task. In fact **the king's command was abhorrent** to him, and so the census was only partially done (v. 6) and not actually finished (cf. 27:24). No doubt the Levites were not numbered because they were never a part of the fighting forces (cf. Nm 1:47-55). Benjamin may have been left unnumbered simply because God's displeasure fell (1Ch 21:7) before the count could be completed and David stopped it. This was a sad and serious error on David's part that threatened the *esprit de corps* that existed between David and his men as the result of many years of fighting and serving together. The surest way for leaders to achieve excellence in God's work is to *enlist* likeminded and loyal coworkers (see the victories in 1Ch 18–20). But the surest way for leaders to undermine God's work is to *command* those under them to do as they are told while overruling their legitimate objections.

b. God's Displeasure; David's Sorrow (21:7-8)

21:7-8. The Divine's response to this census is startlingly and starkly recorded in v. 7: **God was displeased with this thing, so He struck Israel**. The principle that "the king stands for the nation" is behind this action. While it may seem unfair in this setting (and in every instance where the nation is punished for the king's disobedience), it is a principle that more often works in the nation's favor. Whatever this first "striking" was, it brought a swift and heartfelt confession from David. Here (v. 8) is a model of confession of sin. First, David called this act what it is in God's sight (a sin; David **sinned greatly**; cf. Ps 51:4). Second, he took personal responsibility—**I have done this thing . . . I have done very foolishly** (cf. Ps 51:1-3, noting the personal pronouns). Third, he asked for the removal of guilt, and for cleansing (cf. Ps 51:9-10).

c. Consequences Fall (21:9-15)

21:9-12. The confession and forgiveness of sin may bring God's mercy (cf. 21:13), but this does not eliminate all consequences for sin. Gad, the seer (prophet) made his first appearance in Chronicles here (vv. 9-10). The Lord called him to present David with three alternative punishments to be visited on the nation. One option was **three years of famine**; a second option was **three months to be swept away before your foes, while the sword of your enemies overtakes you** (v. 12; that is, three months of successive military losses); and the third was **three days of the sword of the LORD, even pestilence in the land**. (The parallel of "threes" makes it more likely that Chronicles is correct here as opposed to the "seven years" of 2Sm 24:13. The seven years in the latter text may simply be textual anomaly or a copyist error.) The alternatives ranged from relatively mild but extended hardship, to difficult but moderate losses, to intense but shortened catastrophe—in short, they were equally unpalatable. The last alternative was to be carried out by **the angel of the LORD** (v. 12b) also called "the destroying angel" (21:15). Since this angel did not come to bring a word of revelation from God (see Gn 16:7-12; 22:11-18;

Nm 22:22-35; Jdg 6:11-23; 13:2-5), it seems likely that this entity is not the same as the angel of the Lord in those other instances. Gad admonished David to weigh the answer carefully (v. 12c) indicating that no other alternatives were available.

21:13. David was unable to make a choice, being **in great distress**, and so he cast himself and the nation **into the hand of the LORD, for His mercies are very great**. This was a remarkable confession given the inevitability of the punishment to come. It was the confession of one who knew God well, for even if the judgment fell, David knew it would be just and it would come with mercy in its wake.

21:14-15. The Lord sent the third alternative, pestilence dispensed by the angel; **70,000 men of Israel fell** (v. 14), and then the angel approached Jerusalem itself (v. 15). The Chronicler built tension into his narrative at this point. The angel came to destroy, he was about to destroy, and then at the crucial moment the aforementioned mercy came into the narrative—**the LORD saw . . . and said . . . It is enough** (v. 15). The note that **the LORD saw and was sorry over the calamity** should not be taken to suggest that God "changed His mind"—this is not a contradiction to His immutability or omniscience.

Statements like these in Scripture are "anthropopathic," describing God using the terminology descriptive of human feeling. God does not alter His moral character to fit the circumstance, but He remains constant in *both* holy righteousness *and* compassionate mercy. However, the use of "anthropopathic language" is not meant to hide something (unfathomable) about God but to reveal something (true) about God. "When God is said to repent, it indicates his awareness that the human situation has altered and his desire to act in a way fitting to this changed situation." Furthermore, "when God is said to repent, it indicates his real experience, in historically unfolding relationships with people, of changed dispositions or emotions in relation to some changed human situation" (Bruce A. Ware, *God's Lesser Glory: The Diminished God of Open Theism* [Wheaton, IL: Crossway, 2000], 90-91). Thus, for example, in the circumstance of a truly repentant Nineveh (see Jnh 3–4), the unchanging purpose of a God who is always perfectly just *and* perfectly merciful may, from the human perspective, be described as "God relenting." When sin is confessed and repentance is genuine, just to be the "constant, faithful, good God" that He is, He will be merciful.

At the moment when the Lord called His angel to **relax your hand** (v. 15c) the angel was **standing by the threshing floor of Ornan the Jebusite** (v. 15d). Jebus was the ancient name of Jerusalem, and **the threshing floor of Ornan** appears to be the very place where the temple eventually would be built (see below on 21:18–22:1).

d. Consequences Mitigated (21:16-17)

21:16-17. Immediately David's heartfelt repentance was again in focus and appeared to be the reason for eliciting the Lord's mercy. At this climactic moment, as the angel of destruction stood poised to enact his calamitous mission with sword drawn, David offered himself as the substitute for further punishment, rightly arguing that the sin was his and the **sheep** should not suffer for his wickedness. David's sincerity was very much in evidence in the expression **O LORD my God, please let Your hand be against me** (v. 17).

e. Consequences Turned to Good (21:18–22:1)

21:18-27. In an amazing example of God's providence, the very place where the destruction of Israel was halted was to become the place of atonement for Israel's sin. The Lord commanded David **to build an altar to the LORD** on this very spot (v. 18). The significance of this act would not be lost on the Chronicler's readers. That David purchased the threshing floor of Ornan **for the full price** (v. 24) meant that as long as there was a Davidic line, this land belonged to the nation of Israel. Here is where David built the altar; here he offered sacrifices (v. 26a). The proof that the Lord approved of this was twofold: **He answered him with fire . . . on the altar**, and He commanded the angel to **put his sword back in its sheath** (vv. 26b, 27).

21:28–22:1. In what Selman calls "a brief theological supplement" (*1 Chronicles*, 210), the Chronicler first explained that the tabernacle was yet **in the high place at Gibeon at that time** (21:29). At the same time, the Chronicler noted that David had established an altar at the threshing floor of Ornan, and that he was afraid to abandon that location (v. 30). However, this arrangement could not last for David needed to **inquire of God** ("seek the LORD"). The solution was clear—the place of David's altar must become **the house of the LORD God** (22:1).

2. David Made Preparations for the Temple (22:2–27:34)

The remaining chapters of 1 Chronicles and the opening chapters of 2 Chronicles are focused on the temple. The Chronicler recorded first David's preparations for, and then Solomon's actual construction of the temple. Once again, the Chronicler expected his readers to have a grasp of the general flow of the nation's history with the narratives of 2 Samuel and Kings in mind. For his particular purposes he left out the details of 1Kg 1 and 2, which record the transition from the reign of David to Solomon.

The theme of chaps. 22 through 27 is "preparation" (cf. 22:3, 5, 14). The materials for the temple had to be gathered, the Levites and priests and temple personnel had to be organized, and preeminently the builder, Solomon, had to be prepared. Since David had purchased the place for the temple (21:24-26), it was time to prepare "to build the house of God" (22:2, 5, 6, 7, 8, 10, 11, 19). The Chronicler's emphasis on the temple had an application for his own generation. The people of his day were not as zealous for the temple as they ought to have been. The construction of the second temple after the exile, when the Chronicler wrote and his readers lived, was a difficult undertaking (cf. Ezr 3–6), and from time to time his people needed to be "shaken up" (cf. the comments on Hg 1:14; 2:7, 20) to keep working on it. They needed to be instructed on the seriousness of temple worship (cf. Mal 1:6-14) and the value of faithful adherence to the precepts of the law (cf. Zch 7–8; Mal 3:8-18).

The Chronicler's narrative was intended to reinforce those messages. He wanted his readers to understand that the fulfillment of the great promises of the Davidic covenant—promises on which they rested their hopes and included the guarantee of possessing their land—was intimately connected to the temple. The temple was the symbol, and more than a symbol, of the Lord's presence with His people. The temple ensured an ongoing relationship between the nation and the Lord. It was the place of God's mercy and of atonement, and the temple "was a permanent symbol that God had kept His promise about the land" (Selman, *1 Chronicles*, 215).

Taking the temple and its services and its worship seriously and devoutly meant taking the Lord seriously and serving Him devoutly. Ignoring it or "disdainfully sniffing" at its services (Mal 1:13, "taking lightly") meant ignoring *Him*, taking *Him* lightly. This would not only diminish their lives and corrode their hope, it also invited His chastisement. Second Chronicles records that those kings who honored the temple and sought the Lord were blessed, but those who defiled the temple and forsook the Lord were judged. The Chronicler wanted his generation to understand that for David, the temple was tied to the covenant promises—the assurance of the promise is the presence of the temple. For Christians the promise of salvation is tied to another temple—the resurrected Lord Jesus Christ (cf. Jn 2:21-22)—and the assurance of the believer's salvation is the resurrection!

The gathering of materials for the construction of the temple, and its actual building, as well as the transition from David to Solomon in 1Ch 22, may have been intended by the Chronicler to parallel Moses' preparation and building of the tabernacle as well as the transition from Moses to Joshua (the parallels will be noted in the comments below). The narrative here "does not have a parallel in the other historical books. The chronicler, drawing on his own sources of information . . . shows that David was responsible for gathering the building materials and workers (24:1-4, 14-19) and for ensuring that the temple plans corresponded to the promise of God (22:5-13)" (Sailhamer, *First and Second Chronicles*, 55).

a. David's Initial Preparations (22:2-5)

22:2-5. The preparations began with several mundane matters. First, David gathered skilled workers (cf. 2Ch 2:7; Ex 31:1-11) **to build the house of God** (1Ch 22:2). These **foreigners** may have been some who were taken as captives in battle or simply local artisans who, being familiar with the local materials were the best qualified for the technical and artistic aspects of the work. Second, David gathered the raw materials for building—**iron . . . bronze . . . timbers of cedar logs** (vv. 3-4). The note about **large quantities of iron** indicated that David had overcome the technology gap with the Philistines (cf. 1Sm 13:19-21). The **bronze** had been recovered as the spoils of war from the Arameans (1Ch 18:8). The timber came from Lebanon from David's ally Hiram (1Ch 14:1).

Third, David needed to prepare his son Solomon (v. 5). Solomon was probably in his mid-twenties at this time, but David's point does not pertain to his age so much as to his inexperience. From the comments that follow in this verse it seems David needed to impress his son with the magnitude of the undertaking and its significance. This temple was not to be built so as to please men but **for the Lord**. It was to be **exceedingly magnificent** (v. 5) so as to impress the nations with the magnificence and glory of the Lord. The emphasis was not on the greatness of the builder but the majesty of the Occupant—this temple was to be for "the name of the LORD" (cf. 22:7).

b. David Charged Solomon with Task (22:6-13)

22:6-10. David began his charge to Solomon with an explanation of his intent to build the temple and of God's restriction (vv. 6-10). In this statement he gave an interesting reason for the Lord's denying him the privilege of building the temple: David was a man of war and bloodshed (v. 8). There does not seem to be any ceremonial impurity attached to being a man of war (indeed, God had called David to the work of war and blessed him with victories). The restriction seemed to be simply a matter of what was more fitting for the temple—a man of war like David or a man of peace as Solomon was (whose very name is related to the word for "peace"; v. 9). The temple was to be a symbol of the **peace and quiet to Israel in his days** (v. 9).

Three items from the Davidic covenant (cf. 1 Ch 17:11-14) are noted in v. 10. First, it was the Lord's intent that David's son (here referring to Solomon) **shall build a house for My Name**. Second, this son would enjoy a unique filial relationship with the Lord. Third, the Lord reiterated the promise that the throne and kingdom established by God would be **forever**. "Alongside this direct focus on Solomon, the words *for ever* are an unmistakable hint that both covenant and temple have an eschatological dimension that will far outlast Solomon" (Selman, *1 Chronicles*, 215).

22:11-13. David's prayer (another example of "seeking the LORD") for his son (vv. 11-13) was a model of prayer for success in serving the Lord. It included a petition for the continued presence and guidance of the Lord through this project—**the LORD be with you**; a petition for **discretion and understanding**; a petition that Solomon would be **careful to observe the statutes and the ordinances** of the law; and a petition that he **be strong and courageous**, and that he should **not fear nor be dismayed**. Here are principles for success in the service of the Lord: communion with the Lord, wisdom from the Lord, obedience to the Lord, and courage from the Lord. The language here is reminiscent of the charge from Moses to Joshua (cf. Dt 31:1-7; cf. Jos 1:1-9). In addition, the charge in both circumstances follows an admission, whether by Moses or David, of failure to carry out his original intentions and the delegating of that task to a divinely appointed successor (Joshua and Solomon, respectively). If this parallel was intentional it would have served to remind Solomon of the importance of the task and to encourage him about the prospect for success.

c. David's Closing Word to His Son (22:14-16)

22:14-16. The theme of preparation continued and returned to mundane matters. Here David indicated to Solomon that the finances (v. 14) and the skilled workers (v. 15; cf. v. 2) had been assembled and it only remained for him to **arise and work** (v. 16). **The LORD be with you** (vv. 11, 16) "is not just conventional good wishes, but a vital piece of Old Testament theology; it guarantees Solomon's ultimate success" (Selman, *1 Chronicles*, 216).

d. David Prepared Leaders to Assist Solomon (22:17-19)

22:17-19. David knew that Solomon alone would not do the work, so he turned his attention to the leaders to enlist them in mutual service. He reminded them of the Lord's blessings of past victory and present rest (vv. 17-18). His admonition to them is a theme of Chronicles as a whole—**Now set your heart and your soul to seek the LORD your God** (v. 19a; see Introduction: Purpose and Themes). No enterprise undertaken for God will prosper if that dimension, the heart, is not right with God going in. He added, **arise, therefore, and build the sanctuary of the LORD God** (22:19b). Once the heart is set on God and His glory, the hands must work! Once again all are reminded that this **house** was to be **built for the name of the LORD** (22:19c). The Chronicler, through David's words in v. 19, drew several lines of the narrative together at this point. His objective was to bring the ark (chaps. 13–16) to the place (chap. 21) designated by the Lord as the location for His house (chap. 22).

e. David Organized the Nation's Officials (23:1–27:34)

These chapters highlight an often-overlooked quality of David. David's courage and military prowess are well known, as is his genius for worship and psalmody. But these chapters reveal that David was also a man of unusual administrative ability. The value of the details of organization revealed here may be lost on most readers today, but they would have been recognized and appreciated by the people of the Chronicler's generation as they sought to revive and restore the "practical workings" of the temple in their day. The basic organization that David established in these chapters served his successors in Judah for decades and even centuries. Here was the basic pattern and plan employed in the revivals of Hezekiah and Josiah (cf. 2Ch 35:3) and of the Levitical order in Nehemiah's day (cf. Neh 12). It "continued to meet the needs of God's worshiping people on into NT times (cf. 24:10 as reflected in Luke 1:5, 8)" (Payne, "1 Chronicles," 418).

David understood that "the people who serve God are just as important as the architectural splendor of the building in which they worship" (Selman, *1 Chronicles*, 222). Indeed, the worship leaders may have been *more* important than the building. The Chronicler had several purposes in relating all this information. First, he was highlighting David's wisdom (like that of Moses). Second, he sought to impress his readers with the importance of the temple services by indicating how much care David took for them. Third, and most practically, he was helping his own generation to "get organized" themselves. These chapters indicate that in Israel the worship of God is not something to be thrown together carelessly by any and all who desire simply to "participate." Although "nonprofessionals" may indeed lead worship in the church today, those who lead should understand its purpose, be spiritually prepared to do it, and strive to do it well.

(1) Solomon Made King; Officials Listed (23:1-6)

23:1-6. The note that David **made his son Solomon king over Israel** (v. 1) was probably placed here to make the point that the organization that David set in place began with his appointment of the king—the divinely established patron and protector of the temple and all who serve in it.

The Chronicler gave a brief inverted forecast of chaps. 23–26 in 23:2: **And he gathered together all the leaders of Israel** (see 27:1-34) **with the priests** (24:1-19) **and the Levites** (23:3-32; 24:20-31). In addition the Chronicler listed the musicians (25:1-31) and the gatekeepers (26:1-32). In the chapters to follow, the Chronicler moved from those closest (Levitical priests) to those who served furthest (military officers; 27:1-15) from the temple. All of this organizational activity took place in "the fortieth year of David's reign" (26:31), his last year of life (probably 971–970 BC).

The Chronicler noted that the total number of Levites was **38,000** (23:3). The age, **thirty years old and upward**, is based on Nm 4:3. The **38,000** were divided into four groups: **24,000 were to oversee the work of the house of the Lord** (23:4a), that is, they were the ones actually functioning as priests (24:1-19); **6,000 were officers and judges** (23:4b), that is, the ones assigned duties away from the temple (26:29-32); **4,000 were gatekeepers** (23:5a), that is guards along with "treasurers" (26:1-28); **4,000 were praising the Lord with the instruments** (23:5b), that is, the musicians (25:1-31).

(2) Levites in Non-Priestly Orders (23:7-32)

23:7-32. The Chronicler began this section with a census of the Levites (v. 24); three families are mentioned—that of Gershon (vv. 7-11), Kohath (vv. 12-20) and Merari (23:21-23). The Levites were originally assigned the task of carrying the tabernacle and its furnishings (v. 26) during the wandering in the wilderness. With the establishment of the permanent temple their duties were amended to the upkeep of the temple (v. 28), providing the appropriate elements for worship (v. 29), and offering daily prayers as well as regulating the festivals according to the prescribed calendar (cf. Nm 28–29). In sum, they were **to keep charge** of things (v. 32) in and around the temple.

(3) Levites Involved in Priestly Orders (24:1-19)

24:1-19. As noted, these lists show David's administrative ability, in turn serving as a model for the Chronicler's people. The work of the priests was limited to the **descendants of Aaron** (v. 1). "The duty of the priest was to attend to the altar and perform service 'inside the veil,' that is, within the temple itself (cf. Num. 18:1-7)" (Sailhamer, *First and Second Chronicles*, 57). The priesthood was divided into 24 divisions, 16 from the house of Eleazar and eight from the house of Ithamar (v. 4). They were chosen **by lot** (v. 5a) with witnesses, so as to avoid any suggestion of favoritism (vv. 5b-6). The **eighth** division, that of **Abijah**, was the division of Zacharias, the father of John the Baptist; cf. Lk 1:5. The summary statement in 1Ch 24:19 was meant to reinforce the point that these Levites, and *only* these Levites, were the legitimate priests. They alone had the right to serve in the temple. King Uzziah later discovered, to his great sorrow, that this restriction must be respected (see 2Ch 26:16-24).

(4) Remaining Levites Listed (24:20-31)

24:20-31. This list records the remainder of the Levites and once again is evidence of David's thoroughness in ordering the servants of the temple. No detail was too small to leave unaddressed. For the important character **Zadok**, see the comments on 6:8.

(5) Musicians (25:1-31)

25:1-7. The service of the musicians was a matter, no doubt, close to David's heart. The note that they were to **prophesy with lyres, harps and cymbals** (25:1) simply means they were "telling forth," that is, praising God with instruments. "Much of Hebrew poetry was religious and could be called 'prophecy'—not necessarily in the sense of special revelations from God's Spirit, but in the sense of general ascriptions of praise or of repetition in worship of prophecies or psalms that had already been revealed and recorded as Holy Scripture" (Payne, "1 Chronicles," 424). The musicians were said to be **all who were skillful** (25:7), perhaps a corrective to those who suggest one need only make a "joyful noise" (cf. Ps 66:1) to worship God. Apparently David required skilled musicians and singers.

25:8-31. The musicians were also divided by **lots** (v. 8) and divided into 24 divisions (vv. 9-31) on the pattern, no doubt, of the priests. "The singers 'cast lots' to determine without prejudice the arrangement of the twenty-four courses" (Payne, "1 Chronicles," 425).

(6) Gatekeepers (26:1-19)

26:1-19. The third branch of Levites included the gatekeepers, the guards. They are described only as **mighty men** (v. 6) and **valiant men** (v. 9) indicating something like "warriors" or "good fighters." Their other duties are listed in 1Ch 9:18-32. In keeping with the attention to detail, the very **gate** and hourly assignments are recorded in vv. 12-19, as were the other various locations (storehouses; gates; **Parbar** [precinct, court or colonnade]) where security was needed. The need for a "security detail" is not a modern phenomenon.

(7) Treasurers (26:20-28)

26:20-28. The treasurers were not "book-keepers" but, as they were associated with the guards, were the officials charged with protecting **the treasures of the house of God** (26:20). Much of this treasure was **spoil won in battles** (v. 27) by previous leaders of the Jewish people (v. 28).

(8) Other Officials (26:29-32)

26:29-32. The Chronicler listed the final branch of the Levites in a short paragraph that mentions **outside duties** (v. 29). It is not immediately clear what duties were in view, but they might have included Levitical duties that were required away from the temple, such as teaching the law (cf. Dt 33:10) or serving as magistrates (cf. Dt 17:9-10).

(9) Military and Civil Authorities (27:1-34)

27:1-34. The Chronicler finished the listing of temple servants and functionaries, and in characteristic thoroughness provided the reader with a listing of civil servants. Four groups are listed: first, the commanders of the army (vv. 1-15); second, the chief officers of **the tribes of Israel** (vv. 16-22); third, a list of officers in charge of the king's property (vv. 25-31); and finally, a list of David's counselors, in effect, his cabinet officers (vv. 32-34). While there was no direct purpose given for including this list, in the greater context of these chapters on "preparation for the temple," it seems likely that it indicated the nation's uniting to build the temple (see Selman, *1 Chronicles*, 244). Indeed, even as David's organizational genius is on display in these chapters, literally hundreds of people, in every conceivable occupation, were enlisted to facilitate the erecting of "the house . . . for the name of the LORD" (22:19d).

3. David's Final Addresses about the Temple (28:1–29:22a)

Up to this point David's preparations had been mostly physical and material. Now the account turned to what might be called the spiritual preparations. For the temple to be built one must have the necessary materials and sufficient skilled labor, but without a plan these provisions are of no value. Furthermore, the motivation for building the temple, one that would signify the presence of the Lord and symbolize God's promise to the nation, needed to be more than loyalty to David or an expression of civic pride. This temple had to be built for "the name of the LORD" (cf. 22:7, 19d). In chaps. 28 and 29, the Chronicler recorded David's final addresses and prayer. Here David was seeking to direct the hearts and minds of the people (the assembly, 28:1, 2; 29:1, 9, 14), the leaders ("all the officials," 28:1), and Solomon to the task of building the temple as an expression of obedience and devotion to the Lord, "for the temple is not for man, but for the LORD God" (29:1c).

a. First Address (28:1-10)

(1) Assembly (28:1)

28:1. The list in 28:1 was designed to indicate that the important leaders of the nation were firmly behind David and his intentions. The list does not indicate that only leaders were called to hear this address, since David addressed his audience by calling them "my brethren and my people" (28:2; cf. 29:1). The expression "the entire assembly" (29:1) included the "people" (29:9, 14).

(2) Davidic Covenant (28:2-8)

28:2-5. The address itself began with David rehearsing the history that led to this stage in building the temple. First, David reminded the assembly of his intention—providing a **permanent home** for the ark. In the Chronicler's history David's concern for the ark was the first priority after his reign was established (cf. 1Ch 13–16). The description of the ark as **the footstool of our God** (28:2; cf. Ps 132:7) introduces the theme of "rest." Instead of traveling in a tent, the ark will rest in the temple. For the Chronicler "rest" denotes "fulfilled promises" (cf. Is 14:1-3; 66:1; 30:10), for the nation then returned from captivity was "at rest". The final "rest" will not come through Solomon's or Herod's temple, but through the temple to be built by the Greater Son of David (Ezk 40–43; Zch 6:12-13), the One who is the ultimate fulfillment of the Davidic covenant (see comments above on 1 Ch 17:12-14). David's concern for the ark led him to make **preparations** for the temple. However, he was prevented, for David was a **man of war** (28:3; in contrast to Solomon, called a "man of rest" in 22:9).

Here, for a second time in his history, the Chronicler recorded the basic provisions of the Davidic covenant (1Ch 17:12-14; cf. 2Sm 7:12-16; Pss 89; 132). He emphasized two aspects, namely the Lord's sovereign election, and the everlastingness of His promise. The word "chose" or "chosen" occurs five times in this context (1Ch 28:4-10). In short order, David recalled a major theme of the Chronicler—God's sovereign choice of David. This theme began with the genealogies. The Lord chose Judah (v. 4; Judah was the first son of Jacob [Israel] in the genealogies, 1Ch 2:1). The Lord chose David (cf. 1Ch 2:9–3:24; 11:3), and the Lord chose Solomon (cf. 1Ch 17:11; 22:8-9). This promise was specifically stated to be **forever** (28:4, 7)—a provision that could be fulfilled only by the Greater Son of David (see comments above on 1Ch 17:12-14).

28:6-8. David's address turned to the one issue that was the catalyst for the enjoyment of the Davidic promises—obedience. The conditional element (**if he resolutely performs My commandments and My ordinances**, v. 7) and the admonition to obey (**observe and seek after all the commandments . . . so that you may possess the good land and bequeath it**, v. 8) are not suggesting that the ultimate fulfillment of the promise depends on Israel's obedience. If that were the case the late captivity would have indicated an end to the promises, rendering the Chronicler's history moot. The Chronicler understood the point: the promise to David's Greater Son is indeed unconditional based on the Word of the Lord —**I will be a father to him** (v. 6) and **I will establish his kingdom forever** (v. 7). However, any particular king or any particular generation of Israel may find they are not blessed to enjoy the benefits of the promise because they forsook the Lord, or disobeyed the **commandments of the Lord** (v. 8). The ultimate fulfillment of the promise was never in question. Yet for any specific generation to experience the blessings of the promise, to actually **possess the good land** (v. 8), required their obedience. In effect, this is a commentary on the history to follow in 2 Chronicles.

(3) David's Charge to Solomon before the People (28:9-10)

28:9-10. The final part of this address was directed toward Solomon, but the words were intended to be heard by the assembly. Five charges are laid on Solomon: He was to **know the God of your father**, to **serve Him with a whole heart and a willing mind**, to **seek Him** (v. 9), to **consider** (v. 10a; see below), and to **be courageous and act** (v. 10b).

Solomon was to **know** God, that is, to have both the theological depth of understanding (see David's prayer, 29:10-12) and a personal relationship with Him. Solomon was to **serve** the Lord as David had, with a **whole heart**, that is with the whole of his being—mind, body, emotions, will (cf. Ps 119:2, 10, 34, 58, 69, 145). He was to be "single minded" for the things of the Lord. He was to **seek Him**. This was a hallmark of the "good king," just as "forsaking the Lord" is the hallmark of the "bad king" (see Introduction: Purpose and Themes). He was to **consider**, that is, keep in mind his calling and election (cf. 2Pt 1:10) and to "stay on task." He was to keep his priorities for the Lord's work in mind at all times (cf. Hg 1:5, 7). Finally, Solomon was to **be courageous and act**. This again recalled the words of Moses to Joshua (cf. also 1Ch 22:13; Jos 1:6-9). David's admonition applies to all who undertake a service for the Lord. David reminded Solomon that his service was to be done with a **willing mind**, for the Lord **searches all hearts, and understands every intent of the thoughts** (1Ch 28:9).

The Chronicler, like his contemporary Malachi, knew that one of the failures of the nation before and after the exile was insincerity in worship (see Is 1:10-17; Mal 1:6-14). Such worship or service will be rejected by the Lord. He is not interested in "so-called worship" or service that is insincere. The service that pleases and honors the Lord is done in the "fear of the LORD," and He is to be served "in sincerity and truth" (Jos 24:14). This principle is illustrated in the next chapter, where the Chronicler emphasized the willingness of the people who gave sacrificially for the temple (1Ch 29:5c; 6, 9, 17).

b. David Gave Solomon the Temple Plan and Encouragement (28:11-21)

(1) The Plan (28:11-19)

28:11-19. This section is all about **the plan** (*tabnit*, vv. 11, 12; translated **model** in v. 18, and **pattern** in v. 19). This was not so much a set of blueprints as it was a verbal set of directives. These "plans" were given to David from the Lord. The description **the LORD made me understand in writing by His hand upon me** (v. 19) could mean that David received these directives in writing, that is, "they were given to him in written form from God" (Payne, "1 Chronicles," 437). Just as the plans for the tabernacle had been revealed to Moses directly by God (Ex 25:9, 40; 27:8), so David was indicating that the plans for the temple were revealed directly from God as well. They were **all that he had in mind** (1Ch 28:12). It seems that David was fulfilling a position in relation to the temple parallel to that of Moses in relation to the tabernacle. The main point is that this plan was the Lord's plan. Note, however, that "The plan itself is not included by the chronicler" (Sailhamer, *First and Second Chronicles*, 61). The description included some details concerning the architecture—the porch, the buildings and the rooms (vv. 11-12); concerning the personnel—the priests, Levites (v. 13); and concerning the utensils used **for every kind of service** (vv. 14, 13b-18). Of particular interest are the **cherubim** (v. 18) that **covered the ark of the covenant**. These were not the cherubim that formed the lid of the ark (Ex 37:7-9) but apparently were two larger cherubim to shelter the ark in the Holy of Holies in the temple. The picture was of the Lord riding the wings of the cherubim as one might ride a **chariot** (cf. Ps 18:10; Ezk 1:15).

(2) Encouragement to Solomon (28:20-21)

28:20-21. Once again David evoked the words given to encourage Joshua—**be strong and courageous, and act** (v. 20). David backed up this admonition with two supports on which Solomon could count. First, God promised to be with Solomon in an extraordinary way: **the LORD God . . . is with you**. The words **He will not fail you nor forsake you** were meaningful to Solomon and must have been a source of genuine optimism and hope for the Chronicler's generation. Second, David told Solomon that **every willing man of any skill will be with you** (v. 21), and **the officials also and all the people will be entirely at your command**. This note must have been particularly inspiring to the Chronicler's readers, and to ensuing generations of God's people—when the Lord commands them, no task, calling, or ministry need falter with the promise of an ever-present God and a group of like-minded, dedicated people (cf. Hg 2:4-5; 1Co 16:13).

c. David's Second Address to Assembly and Their Response (29:1-9)

29:1-5. David again addressed the assembly and again reminded the people of God's choice of Solomon and Solomon's need of their participation in the task of building the temple (v. 1). David next spoke of a matter that had not been emphasized to this point—namely, his contributions for the project out of his own personal resources. The amounts indicated here are staggering but well within the capacity of a victorious leader and king like David (vv. 2-5). His appeal was simple and direct: **who then is willing to consecrate himself this day to the LORD?** (29:5). This call to consecration used a word (**consecrate**) that was usually associated with an office such as the priesthood (e.g., Ex 28:41—of the priests "and consecrate them"; Ex 29:1—of the priests "to consecrate them"). Its use here indicated that David was not asking for an offering but for a heart commitment that would prove itself tangibly in a **willing** offering. In other words, this was not a "fund-raising" effort but a call to "spiritual commitment."

29:6-9. David's call was generously answered by leaders (and we may assume all the people, 29:6-9). The people rejoiced because this offering was generous, was made voluntarily (**willingly**, v. 6), and was an **offering to the LORD** (v. 9), that is, it was an evidence of devotion and a vital relationship with Him, made **with a whole heart** (cf. 28:9; 29:19). It brought joy to the King, and it encouraged others.

d. David's Final Prayer (29:10-20)

29:10-13. David's response to the generosity of the people was a prayer of thanksgiving (v.

13). "This magnificent prayer demonstrates beyond contradiction that Chronicles' priority is with the heart of worship rather than its form" (Selman, *1 Chronicles*, 259).

The prayer opened with a blessing on the Lord before the assembly (v. 10a). David's address—**O LORD God of Israel**—established the solemnity. The words **our father** refer to Israel (see v. 18).

David began the prayer with theologically rich declarations concerning God. The terms are not a list of divine attributes noted at random. They are the attributes of a Sovereign. The sovereignty of the Lord is the main idea: **Yours is the dominion, O LORD, and You exalt Yourself as head over all** (v. 11). In addition, David acknowledged the benevolence of the Lord. All the blessings of life he knows and his very kingdom come from God (v. 12). For all this God was to be thanked and praised (v. 13).

29:14-17. David next made humble acknowledgements about himself and the people. The phrase **who am I and who are my people** (v. 14a) was rhetorical and meant, "we are nothing in and of ourselves." He recognized that all of the wealth they had provided for the temple was actually **from Your hand** (v. 14b, 16). These were not vapid comments, but keenly felt sentiments of dependence and implicit, even plaintive, expressions of trust and hope.

"The truth that 'everything' we have 'comes from' God is the foundation for the doctrine of stewardship" (Payne, "1 Chronicles," 438). David added to this sense of utter dependence the recognition of the transience of humankind—**our days on the earth are like a shadow, and there is no hope** apart from the Lord (v. 15). The idea here is very much like Moses' in Ps 90—our transient and fleeting lives (Ps 90:2-10) will have meaning only if "the favor of the Lord our God be upon us" and He confirms (makes worthwhile) "the work of our hands" (Ps 90:17). The Chronicler's generation would be reminded that even living in the land they were still **sojourners . . . and tenants** (1Ch 29:15; cf. Ps 39:12). That is, they had rights to the land only through the promise given to the fathers (cf. 1Ch 29:18), and only on the basis of God's sovereign kindness and covenant faithfulness could they expect to continue to enjoy the blessings.

29:18-20. David knew that the people needed to keep their devotion and remain circumspect in their obedience, so he prayed that the Lord Himself would **preserve this forever in the intentions of the heart of Your people, and direct their heart to You** (v. 18). This emphasis on the heart continued with a petition for Solomon (v. 19)—**give to my son Solomon a perfect heart to keep Your commandments**. David knew better than anyone that "man looks at the outward appearance, but the LORD looks at the heart" (1Sm 16:7).

This prayer was not just evocative but motivational: how can God's people remain motivated for the task set before them? They must pray sincerely. Acknowledging God's sovereignty and their utter dependence, they must maintain a willing and obedient heart. The prayer closes with a blessing on the Lord by the people (1Ch 29:20).

e. Closing of the Assembly (29:21-22a)

29:21-22a. The assembly ended with sacrifices and offerings and with **great gladness** (29:21-22a). David had accomplished what he intended for this assembly—the people were unified and spiritually prepared for the great task of building the temple.

On the coronation of Solomon found in 1Ch 29:22b-25, see the commentary on 2Ch 1.

G. Death of David (29:26-30)

29:26-30. At the close of David's story, the Chronicler used a literary form that would serve him well in the narratives of the kings in 2 Chronicles. It was a "closing formula" that usually noted the sources of the narrative and other works with more information on the life of the king. It typically stated the length of the king's reign, noted the king's death, and often named his successor. The formula was not rigidly followed, and there were a number of variations to the basic outline.

The closing formula for David had many of the standard features. Of note is the mention of his seven-year reign in Hebron (v. 27), a part of the history that was barely mentioned in the Chronicler's narrative. Also, the note about **the chronicles** of the several prophets (v. 29; the terms **seer** and **prophet** refer to the same office) was intended to enhance the credibility and reliability of the Chronicler's accounts.

As noted, the Chronicler used the canonical books of Samuel and Kings as the sources for much of his narrative. The other noncanonical sources were not inspired, but they were apparently quite reliable. The death of David did not bring an end to his considerable influence on the nation. Instead, David became the model of Israel's ideal king, the picture against which every Davidic king would be compared until the coming of his Greater Son, the Messiah.

BIBLIOGRAPHY FOR 1 AND 2 CHRONICLES

Braun, Roddy. *1 Chronicles*. Word Biblical Commentary. Waco, TX: Word, 1986.

Dillard, Raymond B. *2 Chronicles*. Word Biblical Commentary. Waco, TX: Word, 1986.

Hill, Andrew E. *1 & 2 Chronicles*. NIV Application Commentary. Grand Rapids, MI: Zondervan, 2003.

Payne, J. Barton. "1, 2 Chronicles," in vol. 4 of The Expositor's Bible Commentary, ed. Frank E. Gaebelein. Grand Rapids, MI: Zondervan, 1988.

Pratt, Richard L. *1 & 2 Chronicles*. A Mentor Commentary. Fearn, Ross-shire, UK: Christian Focus, 1998.

Sailhamer, John. *First and Second Chronicles*. Everyman Bible Commentary. Chicago: Moody, 1983.

Selman, Martin J. *1 Chronicles*. Tyndale Old Testament Commentaries. Downers Grove, IL: InterVarsity, 1994.

Selman, Martin J. *2 Chronicles*. Tyndale Old Testament Commentaries. Downers Grove, IL: InterVarsity, 1994.

Tuell, Steven S. *First and Second Chronicles*. Interpretation: A Bible Commentary. Louisville: John Knox Press, 2001.

Wilcock, Michael. *The Message of Chronicles*. The Bible Speaks Today. Downers Grove, IL: InterVarsity, 1994.

● ● ● ●

2 CHRONICLES

KEVIN D. ZUBER

INTRODUCTION

For Introduction, see the Introduction to 1 and 2 Chronicles, pp. 553–556. Because 1 and 2 Chronicles were originally one book, the outline and commentary in this chapter of 2 Chronicles represent a continuation of the outline and commentary in 1 Chronicles. Therefore, the outline that follows begins with Roman numeral III and picks up with a portion of 1 Chronicles 29.

OUTLINE

III. History of Solomon (1Ch 29:22b-25; 2Ch 1:1–9:31)
- A. Solomon Made King (1Ch 29:22b-25)
- B. Solomon Consolidated His Regnancy (2Ch 1:1-17)
  1. Solomon Secured His Kingdom; the Lord Was with Him (1:1)
  2. Solomon Addressed All Israel (1:2-6)
  3. Solomon Asked for Wisdom (1:7-13)
  4. Solomon's Wealth (1:14-17)
- C. Solomon's Preparations for the Temple (2:1-18)
  1. Attention Turned to the Temple (2:1)
  2. The Workers (2:2, 17-18)
  3. Solomon Communicated with Huram King of Tyre (2:3-16)
- D. Solomon Built and Furnished the Temple (3:1–4:22)
  1. The Temple Plan (3:1-17)
  2. The Furnishings (4:1-22)
- E. Dedication of the Temple (5:1–7:22)
  1. The Ark and the Glory of God (5:1b-14)
     - a. The Ark Comes to the Temple (5:1b-10)
     - b. The Glory of God Comes to the Temple (5:11-14)
  2. Solomon's Dedicatory Speech (6:1-11)
     - a. Dedicatory Verse (6:1-2)
     - b. Dedicatory Address (6:3-11)
  3. Solomon's Dedicatory Prayer (6:12-42)
     - a. Prayer of Acknowledgment (6:14-15, 18)
     - b. Prayer of Petition (6:16-17, 19-21)
     - c. Prayer Regarding Various Situations (6:22-39)
     - d. Final Appeal (6:40-42)
  4. Fire and the Glory of the Lord (7:1-3)
  5. Sacrifices and Festival (7:4-11)
  6. Post-Dedication Appearance of the Lord to Solomon (7:12-22)
     - a. The Lord Confirms His Choice of the Temple (7:12, 16)
     - b. The Lord Extended His Promise to Include Restoration (7:13-15)

c. The Lord Reiterated His Promise to the House of David (7:17-18)
d. The Lord Warned of Exile for "Forsaking" His Law (7:19-22)

F. Solomon's Reign (8:1–9:31)
1. Solomon Secured His Kingdom (8:1-18)
a. Solomon's Building Projects (8:1-11)
b. Solomon's Temple Ceremonies and Personnel (8:12-15)
c. Summary Statement Regarding the Temple (8:16)
d. His Seaports and Trading (8:17-18; 9:10-11, 21)
2. Solomon Administered Kingdom in Wisdom, Amassed Great Wealth (9:1-28)
a. Solomon's Wisdom and Queen of Sheba (9:1-9, 12)
b. Solomon's Wealth and Power (9:13-20, 22-28)
3. Summary and Death of Solomon (9:29-31)

IV. The Kings of David's Line (10:1–36:23)
A. Rehoboam (10:1–12:16)
1. The Kingdom Divided (10:1-19)
a. Rehoboam Met with All Israel; Coronation Delayed (10:1-5)
b. Rehoboam Met with His Advisors (10:6-11)
c. Rehoboam Met with Jeroboam and All the People (10:12-15)
d. Kingdom Divided (10:16-19)
2. The Reign of Rehoboam (11:1-23)
a. Rehoboam Prevented from Attacking Israel (11:1-4)
b. Rehoboam Secured His Kingdom (11:5-13)
c. Jeroboam's Apostasy Led to Judah's Strength (11:14-17)
d. Rehoboam's Family (11:18-23)
3. Invasion of Shishak (12:1-12)
a. Invasion by Egypt (12:1-4)
b. Cause of Invasion Explained (12:5)
c. Repentance and Humility Avert Total Disaster (12:6-12)
4. Summary of Rehoboam's Reign (12:13-16)

B. Abijah (13:1–14:1)
1. Introductory Formula for Abijah (13:1-2a)
2. Abijah's War with Israel (13:2b-19)
a. Nations at War (13:2b-3)
b. Abijah's Speech to Israel (13:4-12)
(1) First Charge against Israel: Rebellion to Davidic Dynasty (13:4-7)
(2) Second Charge against Israel: Apostasy from True Worship (13:8-9)
(3) Justification of Southern Kingdom: Not Forsaking the Lord, True Worship Upheld (13:10-11)
(4) Appeal to Northern Kingdom: God Is with Us—Do Not Fight against Him (13:12)
c. The Battle Joined (13:13-19)
3. Concluding Formula for Abijah (13:20–14:1)

C. Asa (14:2–16:14)
1. The Lord Gives Godly King Asa Great Victory (14:2-15)
a. King Asa Did Right before the Lord (14:2)
b. Asa Instituted Religious Reforms (14:3-5)
c. Asa Instituted Nationwide Security Program (14:6-8)
d. Asa's War with Zerah the Ethiopian (14:9-15)
2. Asa's Response to Azariah's Prophecy (15:1-19)
a. Prophet Brings the Lord's Word to King and Nation (15:1-7)
b. Asa's Response to God's Word: Reformation, Revival (15:8-19)
3. Asa Sought Security in Treaty with Enemy (16:1-14)
a. Asa Made a Temporal Alliance (16:1-6)
b. Hanani the Seer (Prophet) Rebuked Asa (16:7-9)

    c. Asa's Reaction Inappropriate (16:10)
    d. Asa's Punishment (16:12)
    e. Concluding Formula for Asa (16:11, 13-14)
D. Jehoshaphat (17:1–20:37)
  1. Jehoshaphat Established His Kingdom (17:1-6)
    a. He Secured the Nation (17:1-2)
    b. He Devoted Himself to God (17:3-6)
  2. Jehoshaphat Administered His Kingdom (17:7-19)
    a. Jehoshaphat's "Spiritual" Administration (17:7-9)
    b. Jehoshaphat's "Temporal" ("Military") Administration (17:10-19)
  3. Jehoshaphat's Disastrous Alliance with Ahab (18:1–19:3)
    a. Alliance by Marriage (18:1)
    b. Alliance for War (18:2-27)
    c. Alliance in Defeat (18:28-34)
    d. Alliance and King Rebuked (19:1-3)
  4. Jehoshaphat's Reforms (19:4-11)
    a. Spiritual Renewal (19:4)
    b. Judges Appointed (19:5-7)
    c. Levites and Priests Appointed (19:8-11)
  5. Jehoshaphat Faced Invasion and War with Prayer, Faith (20:1-30)
    a. Surprise Invasion from the South (20:1-2)
    b. Spiritual Response by King (20:3-19)
    c. A Stunning Victory and Triumph (20:20-30)
  6. Jehoshaphat's Sad Ending (20:31-37)
E. Three Who Were "Bad" (Jehoram, Ahaziah, Athaliah) (21:1–23:15)
  1. Jehoram Succeeded Jehoshaphat (21:1-3)
  2. Jehoram's Evil and the Lord's Faithfulness (21:4-7)
  3. Jehoram's Punishment (21:8-19a)
    a. The Revolts of Edom and Libnah (21:8-11)
    b. Letter from Elijah (21:12-15)
    c. Punishments of the Letter (21:16-19a)
  4. Jehoram's End (21:19b-20)
  5. Reign of Ahaziah (22:1-9)
    a. Ahaziah Is Made King (22:1-4)
    b. Ahaziah's Alliance with Jehoram of Israel (22:5-6)
    c. Ahaziah's Destruction (22:7-9)
  6. The Reign of Athaliah (22:10–23:15)
    a. Athaliah's Bid for Power (22:10-12)
    b. Plan to Overthrow Athaliah and Establish Joash as King (23:1-11)
    c. Death of Athaliah (23:12-15)
F. Three Who Were "Mixed": Joash, Amaziah, Uzziah (23:16–26:23)
  1. Reign of Joash (23:16–24:27)
    a. Early Reforms of Joash by Jehoiada (23:16-21)
    b. Reign of Joash Under the Influence of Jehoiada (24:1-16)
    c. Reign of Joash after the Death of Jehoiada (24:17-22)
    d. The Lord's Judgment upon Joash: Defeat and Disease (24:23-27)
  2. The Reign of Amaziah (25:1-28)
    a. Amaziah's Reign Began with an Act of Reprisal (25:1-4)
    b. Amaziah's Battle with the Sons of Seir (Edom) (25:5-13)
    c. Amaziah's Idolatry (25:14-16)
    d. Amaziah Defeated by Joash of Israel (25:17-24)
    e. Amaziah's End (25:25-28)
  3. The Reign of Uzziah (26:1-23)
    a. Uzziah's Faithfulness (26:1-5)

b. Uzziah's Successes (26:6-15)
c. Uzziah's Pride and Fall (26:16-21)
d. Uzziah's End (26:22-23)

G. Six Kings Alternate between "Good" and "Bad" (27:1–35:27)
1. Good: Jotham (27:1-9)
2. Bad: Ahaz (28:1-27)
a. Ahaz's Evil Exposed (28:1-4)
b. Ahaz Defeated in Battle (28:5-7)
c. Captives Experienced Mercy (28:8-15)
d. Ahaz's Disastrous Alliance with Assyria (28:16-21)
e. Ahaz's Evil Expanded (28:22-25)
f. Ahaz's End (28:26-27)
3. Excellent: Hezekiah (29:1–32:33)
a. Hezekiah's Revival (29:1–31:21)
(1) Hezekiah Reopened, Consecrated the Temple (29:1-19)
(2) Hezekiah Restored the Temple Worship (29:20-36)
(3) Hezekiah Revived the Celebration of Passover (30:1-27)
(4) Hezekiah Reinstituted Tithes and Offerings (31:1-21)
b. Hezekiah's Victory over Assyria (32:1-23)
(1) Hezekiah Countered Sennacherib's Invasion (32:1-8)
(2) Hezekiah's Victory over Sennacherib (32:9-23)
c. Hezekiah's Last Days (32:24-33)
(1) Hezekiah's Illness and Pride (32:24-26)
(2) Hezekiah's Wealth and Pride (32:27-31)
(3) Hezekiah's End (32:32-33)
4. Bad, but Repentant: Manasseh (33:1-20)
a. Manasseh's Incredible Evil (33:1-9)
b. Manasseh's Humiliating Captivity (33:10-11)
c. Manasseh's Marvelous Repentance (33:12-13a, 18-19)
d. Manasseh's Attempted Revival (33:13b-17, 20)
5. Bad: Amon (33:21-25)
6. Very Good: Josiah (34:1–35:27)
a. Josiah's Reign—Seeking God, Purging Idolatry (34:1-7)
b. Revival Year: Repairing Temple, Rediscovering Law, Reviving Passover (34:8–35:19)
(1) Repairing the Temple (34:8-13)
(2) Rediscovering the Law (34:14-33)
(3) Revival of Passover (35:1-19)
c. Josiah's Tragic Death (35:20-27)
(1) Pharaoh Neco, on His Way to War, Warned Josiah to Not Interfere (35:20-21)
(2) Josiah Engaged Neco in Battle, Was Mortally Wounded (35:22-24c)
(3) Judah Mourned for Josiah (35:24d-25)
(4) Josiah's Reign Summarized (35:26-27)

H. Sons of Josiah (Jehoahaz, Jehoiakim, Jehoiachin, Zedekiah) (36:1-16)
1. Joahaz (36:1-4)
2. Jehoiakim and Jehoiachin (36:5-10)
3. Zedekiah (36:11-14)
4. Summary: Prophets Sent and Rejected (36:15-16)

I. The Captivity and the Decree of Cyrus (36:17-23)
1. The Captivity: Description and Rationale (36:17-21)
a. Description (36:17-20)
b. Rationale (36:21)
2. The Decree of Cyrus (36:22-23)

COMMENTARY ON 2 CHRONICLES

III. History of Solomon (1Ch 29:22b-25; 2Ch 1:1–9:31)

The books of 1 and 2 Chronicles were originally one work (see Introduction to 1 Chronicles), and 2 Chronicles picks up immediately where 1 Chronicles concluded. The last few chapters of 1 Chronicles centered on David's preparations for building the temple. The first chapters of 2 Chronicles deal with Solomon's work to finish the preparations, to actually build the temple, and to dedicate it. In a way "the reigns of the two kings are really a single unit" (Selman, *2 Chronicles*, 285). In the Chronicler's narrative, both David and Solomon are focused on building the temple, and this singular focus is the outworking of and response to the Davidic covenant (1Ch 17; 2Sm 7; Ps 89).

The Lord's promise to build a house (dynasty) for David foresaw that Solomon would build "a house to the name of the Lord" (see 1Ch 22:6-16; 28:6-7). By devoting themselves to the building of the temple, David in preparation and Solomon in construction, both kings affirmed their confidence and faith in the promise of God (the Davidic covenant) to build a house (dynasty) for David. For the Chronicler, the postexilic second temple had virtually the same significance—that if the new temple were to be raised up (after the exile) in the same place that David's/Solomon's temple was built, it would also affirm that the Lord had not forgotten His unconditional and everlasting promise to build a house for David. It would further assure that the Chronicler's generation would again enjoy the promise and the presence of the Lord.

David's house was not limited to the kings who followed Solomon, but would culminate in One who would "be a Son" to the Lord and occupy David's throne "forever." That One of course is Jesus Christ. In a way, the concern for the temple, as the concrete and visible embodiment of the Davidic covenant, both in the days of David and Solomon and in the days of the Chronicler, was the evidence of faith in the messianic aspect of the Davidic promise. In short, the temple was the focus of David and Solomon, and the Chronicler highlighted that focus in his history, because they had faith in all of God's promises. They were looking forward to the ultimate fulfillment of those promises by the Greater Son of David.

In the history of the kings after Solomon, the Chronicler differentiated the "good kings" by their concern for the temple and the purity of its services and the "bad kings" by their lack of concern for the temple and the introduction of false, idolatrous worship there. Here again, the kings' focus on the temple was the tangible expression of trust in the Lord and the promises of God.

With that focus in view, as with the life and kingship of David, the Chronicler did not include in his narrative several events from the reign of Solomon. In particular, he passed over the succession struggles (1Kg 1 and 2) and simplified the accounts about Solomon's power, wealth, and wisdom (compare 1Kg 3:16-28; 4:1-34 to 2Ch 1:14-17). He also left out the later accounts of Solomon's building of his own palace (1Kg 7:1-12) and the narrative about Solomon's many wives and how they led him away from complete devotion to the Lord (1Kg 11:1-40). As far as the Chronicler was concerned, "Whatever his weaknesses, Solomon had true greatness, and that greatness was seen in his devotion to the worship of God at the temple" (Sailhamer, *First and Second Chronicles*, 69). For the postexilic community, "it was Solomon's temple that captured their greatest concern" (Payne, "2 Chronicles," 443).

Of the nine chapters in 2 Chronicles that concern Solomon, only three (chaps. 1, 8, and 9) deal directly with him and his reign while the other six deal with his preparations for the temple (chap. 2), the building and furnishing of the temple (chaps. 3 and 4), and the dedication of the temple (chaps. 5, 6, and 7).

A. Solomon Made King (1Ch 29:22b-25)

1Ch 29:22b-25. The note that this was the **second time** Solomon had been made king was most likely meant to indicate that this was a public ceremony that took place after the private ceremony (cf. 1Kg 1:35-39). As with the accession of David (cf. 1Ch 11:1-3) the emphasis here is on the unity of **all Israel** (vv. 23, 25). Here too **all the officials** and **the mighty men** (v. 24; cf. 1Ch 11:1-3, 10) were solidly behind Solomon. This unity was the result of the Lord's gift to Solomon of honor and **royal majesty** (v. 25) **in the sight of all Israel**. The loss of David was mitigated by the Lord's continued involvement with and approval of Solomon and His faithfulness to His promise.

B. Solomon Consolidated His Regnancy (2Ch 1:1-17)

1. Solomon Secured His Kingdom; the Lord Was with Him (1:1)

1:1. The theme of the Lord's continued endorsement and approval of Solomon opens the narrative in 2 Chronicles. The notes that **the Lord his God was with him and exalted him greatly** (2Ch 1:1) are not pious fillers intended to give a sanctimonious patina to the realpolitik behind Solomon's accession to the throne of David. This was in reality the key to Solomon's success—his regency achieved security and stability *because* the Lord was with him.

2. Solomon Addressed All Israel (1:2-6)

1:2-3. The Chronicler's account of Solomon, centering on the temple, began with Solomon assembling **all Israel** in the form of the nation's officials (v. 2) at the tabernacle in Gibeon (v. 3; for the names of, and terms used to identify, the **tent of meeting** see commentary on Ex 25:1-5). This showed Solomon's sensitivity and care as he proceeded to move the locus of the nation's worship to Jerusalem. David had attempted to move the ark without such care, and the result was the tragic death of Uzzah (2Sm 6:1-11; 1Ch 13:5-14). Solomon will proceed with all due diligence.

1:4-6. The main point of the account is to show that Solomon sought the Lord. Even with all the indications of the approval and blessing of the Lord, Solomon was rightly careful to exhibit humility and deference to the institutions that have served the nation up to this point (v. 3). This was indicated by his care to seek out the **bronze altar** made by **Bezalel**, the Spirit-enabled artisan (Ex 31:1-11; 38:1-2), and to offer sacrifices upon it (2Ch 1:5-6). Those kings who did not seek the Lord and who ignored the divinely ordained institutions (temple, priesthood) found their reigns troubled and their legacies shamed. The Chronicler was concerned to teach his generation that God's blessings depended on respecting the ancient divine institutions. By coming to Gibeon to sacrifice and pray, "Solomon shows himself to be suitably qualified to build a temple which will be a 'temple for sacrifices' (2 Ch. 7:12; cf. 2:6) and a 'house of prayer' (Is. 56:7; cf. 2 Ch. 6:40; 7:14, etc.)" (Selman, *2 Chronicles*, 289).

3. Solomon Asked for Wisdom (1:7-13)

1:7. In one of the most famous conversations in Scripture, Solomon's careful and humble seeking was rewarded by an appearance and offer from God. In a dream (1Kg 3:5) God took the initiative and made an incredible offer, yet it was an offer that tested Solomon's heart: **Ask what I shall give you** (2Ch 1:7).

1:8-9. Solomon's reply began with the recognition that God had already been faithful to His promises: First, the Lord had shown **great lovingkindness** (1:8; *chesed*, a word that emphasizes God's characteristic of "loyal love" to those with whom He is in a covenant relationship [Dt 7:9, 12]). Moreover, God's "loyal love" is frequently linked with His forgiveness and mercy (Ex 34:6-7; Ps 103:4) to David. Second, He had kept His promise to Solomon and made him king (2Ch 1:8b-9a). Not only had the Lord been faithful to the Davidic covenant promises, Solomon acknowledged that He also had been faithful to the Abrahamic covenant promises as well in that He had been **made... king over a people as numerous as the dust of the earth** (v. 9b; cf. Gn 13:16; 28:14; cf. Nm 23:10). The reminder that God had fulfilled His promises, that He had been faithful to His ancient covenants, would have been a tremendous encouragement to the Chronicler's generation (and should be an encouragement to God's people in any dispensation).

1:10. Solomon's request for **wisdom and knowledge** (v. 10) was a humble acknowledgment of what David had affirmed about his youth and inexperience (1Ch 22:5; 29:1). "Wisdom and understanding" often appear in combination (cf. Pr 2:2; 3:13, 19; 4:5). The Hebrew notion of "wisdom" (*hokmah*) is something like "skill," even artistic ability (cf. Ex 31:1-3). The notion of "knowledge" is often simply "common, or practical sense" (derived from "obvious and observable facts") applied in a particular situation or occupation (e.g., the craftsmen who worked on the tabernacle, Ex 12:1-3; 35:1). Here Solomon was asking for "skill" and "practical competence" for leadership. He wanted to identify with the people—**that I may go out and come in before this people** (v. 10) that he might effectively **rule this great people**. Sailhamer suggests that the Chronicler and the author of the parallel passage in 1Kg 3:6-9 both had in view "the requirement of the king in Deuteronomy 17:18-20. The king was to know the law (*Torah*) of God and was to learn the fear of God and observe the will of God expressed in the law (*Torah*)" (Sailhamer, *First and Second Chronicles*, 70).

1:11-13. God responded to this humble and appropriate request by listing all the things for which Solomon could have asked, had he been selfishly motivated—**riches, wealth, honor**, revenge on enemies, **long life** (v. 11). The Lord was pleased with Solomon's request for **wisdom and**

knowledge (noted twice by the Lord). Therefore, He not only granted the request, He went beyond it to grant Solomon the riches and wealth that he had not requested. The Chronicler was not teaching the reader that the way to riches and wealth is to ask surreptitiously for more noble things like wisdom and spiritual understanding, hoping God will grant the lesser blessings as well. Rather, the point of these added blessings was to show that the Lord was pleased by Solomon's request for wisdom and understanding, because this indicated that Solomon's overarching desire was to be a good king. Solomon sought to honor God first and all the other things were added to him by God's goodness and grace (cf. Mt 6:33). Based upon the motive behind Solomon's request, God expected that the riches and wealth would not be selfishly used and abused but would also contribute to Solomon being a good king.

4. Solomon's Wealth (1:14-17)

1:14-17. Solomon's wealth was noted, and this demonstrated the fulfillment of God's answer to his request and gave tangible evidence that Solomon was "exalted greatly" (cf. 1Ch 29:25; 2Ch 1:1). The mention of **chariots** and **horsemen** (v. 14) is made without comment or explanation even though Dt 17:16 prohibited the kings of Israel from multiplying horses. The point of the prohibition was to keep the king from relying on his temporal power (cf. Zch 4:6). Apparently, at the outset of his regency Solomon was not relying on his chariots and horses, as they were more of a commodity to be bought and sold. He **imported** horses **from Egypt** and **Kue** (a region in Turkey) and **exported** them to the **Hittites** and the Arameans (v. 17).

C. Solomon's Preparations for the Temple (2:1-18)

David had made extensive preparations to build the temple (cf. 1Ch 22:1-5), centering on the enlistment of foreign leaders and workers (cf. 1Ch 22:2). The point is that Solomon had the good will and strong international relations that allowed him to concentrate on the temple as well as access to the skilled labor and engineering expertise necessary to accomplish the task. For the Chronicler the issue of maintaining good relations with other peoples and nations would be timely. The lesson was, to accomplish the Lord's work, "If possible, so far as it depends on you, be at peace with all men" (Rm 12:18).

1. Attention Turned to the Temple (2:1)

2:1. In the Chronicler's view the most important feature of Solomon's reign was his temple-building program, and he turned to that quickly in 2:1. He reiterated that the temple was to be **a house for the name of the LORD** (v. 1; cf. 1Ch 22:6, 19). A person's name stood for the whole person. The temple would be a place to "call on the name of the Lord" (cf. 1Kg 8:29; cf. Dt 12:11). Solomon's palace received a brief mention (cf. 1Kg 7), but the focus of the Chronicler remained on the temple.

2. The Workers (2:2, 17-18)

2:2, 17-18. The Chronicler noted the skilled foreign workers David had gathered (cf. 1Ch 22:2). Solomon also enlisted **the aliens who were in the land of Israel** (2Ch 2:17) for the unskilled labor necessary to do such work as **carry loads** and **quarry stones** (vv. 2, 18; this information began and ended the chapter). Such a massive undertaking as the temple would require large numbers of such workers, who were probably conscripted.

3. Solomon Communicated with Huram King of Tyre (2:3-16)

The inclusion of the correspondence between Solomon and Huram is an example of the care with which the Chronicler consulted and employed his sources.

2:3-10. Solomon's main "supplier" for the temple was Huram King of Tyre (called "Hiram" in the parallel account in 1Kg 5). Tyre was a major port city on the Mediterranean coast of Lebanon, about 20 miles south of Sidon and 23 miles north of Acre. It was an important mercantile location receiving and sending goods from all over the western Mediterranean basin as well as exporting the goods—mainly lumber and cedars—of Lebanon. Huram was Phoenician—a people mostly noted for their maritime prowess—and he had built his kingdom by trade mainly on the sea. Solomon's written communication with Huram was predicated on the friendship David established (2Ch 2:3). Solomon invoked previous treaty arrangements to encourage Huram to accede to the requests he was about to make. This letter was intended to accomplish three main goals: first, it was a request for materials, specifically timber (vv. 8-9), along with a negotiated price (v. 10; the cedars of Lebanon were world famous for their size and quality). Second, it was a request for skilled workers to work along with **the skilled men . . . in Judah and Jerusalem** (v. 7). Third, it was preeminently an apologetic, a theological justification for building the temple (vv. 4-6). The temple, again identified as a **house for the name of the LORD** (v. 4), was to be a place of worship, atonement and celebration of **the**

appointed feasts of the Lord our God (v. 4). Accordingly, in the light of these exalted purposes and owing to the superlative greatness of **our God than all the gods**, this house will **be great** (v. 5). Here, however, Solomon introduced a note he sounded again at the completion of the construction of the temple: as great as this temple will be, it will not be big enough to **contain Him**, indeed, **the heavens and the highest heavens cannot contain Him** (v. 6). This was not merely an affirmation of the immensity of God, or of His omnipresence. Solomon's focus was on the transcendence of God—the quality of God that puts Him beyond physical or temporal limitations, that puts Him beyond human comprehension. In effect, Solomon testified to Huram that the Lord was (and is) the only sovereign God.

2:11-12. Huram's reply to Solomon was more detailed in 2Ch 2 than the parallel in 1Kg 5:7-9. In this letter Huram responded to each point in Solomon's letter: first, he acknowledged in a blessing that **the Lord, the God of Israel** is the creator of **heaven and earth** (2Ch 2:12) and that it was this same **Lord** who **loves His people** and made Solomon king (v. 11). This need not be taken to indicate that Huram was a believer. Often the professions of truth about God from the mouths of unbelievers are recorded (2Ch 36:23; Ezr 1:2; 5:11-12; 6:10; Jr 10:11-12; Acts 4:24; 14:15; 17:24-26) to emphasize to the discerning believer that God has not left Himself without a witness to the whole world (cf. Rm 1:20).

2:13-16. Huram diplomatically praised Solomon (v. 13) and proceeded to answer his requests. The man to be sent by Huram was **Huram-abi**, a man especially qualified to assist in building the temple. He was not only uniquely skilled but he also was partly of Israelite ancestry. According to 1Kg 7:14, his mother was "from the tribe of Naphtali," whereas here in 2Ch 2:14a she was identified as **a Danite woman**. She was probably from the tribe of Naphtali by descent and from the area where the tribe of Dan settled (cf. Jdg 18). Finally, Huram promised delivery of the timbers (2Ch 2:16) upon receipt of the payment for them (v. 15). The mention of the port of **Joppa** (v. 16) indicated that this rather unpromising seaport had been sufficiently upgraded by Solomon to handle such large shipments.

D. Solomon Built and Furnished the Temple (3:1–4:22)

1. The Temple Plan (3:1-17)

Given the Chronicler's emphasis on the temple and the record of the many preparations for construction, it is "a little surprising" that the Chronicler's "account of the temple's construction is actually briefer than in Kings. Seventy-seven verses in 1Kg 6–7 (omitting the account of the royal palace, 7:1-12) have been condensed into 40 verses in 2Ch 3:1–5:1" (Selman, *2 Chronicles*, 303). By devoting more of his narrative to the dedication of the temple (see chaps. 5–7) than to its construction, the Chronicler indicated that its purpose was more important than its impressive size or spectacular furnishings. This would have been an encouragement to the generation of the Chronicler in their evaluation of the second temple (see Ezr 3:8-13; 6:16), a less impressive structure in appearance than Solomon's.

3:1. The note that **Solomon began to build** the temple (3:1) is climactic. The planning and preparation were over—the construction had begun. The Chronicler located the site of the temple with three increasingly specific designations—**Jerusalem** . . . **Mount Moriah** . . . **threshing floor of Ornan** (3:1). This served to remind the reader of the historically climactic events (cf. 1Ch 11:4-9; Gn 22:2—the sacrifice of Isaac; 1Ch 21:18) that took place at this specific spot and of God's providential choice of this location. This was a place of substitutionary sacrifice (cf. Gn 22:13-14; 1 Ch 21:26, 28) and where God had revealed Himself to two special servants who had received covenant promises from Him—Abraham and David. The construction began in 966 BC (Payne, "2 Chronicles," 450).

3:2-9. The project began **on the second day in the second month** (that is, sometime in the spring [April/May]; cf. 1Kg 6:1, 37) **of the fourth year** of Solomon's reign (2Ch 3:2). It was completed "in the eleventh year . . . the eighth month" (1Kg 6:38; cf. 2Ch 5:3; that is, sometime in the fall [Oct/Nov]). Thus the temple took seven and a half years to finish. (For exact dates see Thiele, *The Mysterious Numbers of the Hebrew Kings*, 51–52.) The account of the temple in 2Ch 3 is not a "blueprint" so much as a guided tour of the building. Beginning with the **foundations** (v. 3), the Chronicler recorded the description and dimensions of the building entrance, **the porch** (v. 4), **the main room** (vv. 5-7) corresponding to the holy place of the tabernacle, and **the room of the holy of holies** (vv. 8-9). The amount of gold used in this part of the temple is estimated at 23 tons (cf. Payne, "2 Chronicles," 451). The location of Parvaim

(v. 6) is uncertain. (This is the only reference to this geographical location in the Bible, and the term is not used in any other known literature, except for commentaries on this passage.) The "cubit" (*'ammah*) was by no means a standard length. It was generally the distance from a man's elbow to the fingertips (cf. Dt 3:11). There were Egyptian cubits, Babylonian cubits, and something called "Royal" cubit (Ezk 40:5)—these varied from about 17.5 or 17.6 inches to 20.6 or more inches. One talent was about 75 pounds, and one shekel was between two-fifths and one-half an ounce.

3:10-17. The Chronicler noted three unique features of the temple. First there were the **two sculptured cherubim** inside the holy of holies that covered the ark of the covenant, essentially filling the space above the ark (vv. 10-13; see comments on 1Ch 28:18). Cherubim were angel-like creatures whose presence symbolized the nearness of the transcendent. The second feature noted was the multicolored **veil** that separated the holy of holies from the holy place (cf. Ex 26:31-35). It was a reminder of the awesome presence of God, and its placement was a constant reminder that while God was indeed with them (see notes on 2Ch 6:11-14) yet none could approach Him without atonement. While the high priest entered the holy of holies every year on the Day of Atonement (see the commentary on Lv 16), only the sacrificial, substitutionary death of Christ would make a final way "through the veil" (cf. Heb 10:20).

The third unique feature of the temple, the **two pillars** (2Ch 3:15), were apparently highly ornamented, free standing (non-supporting), cast bronze pillars at the entrance of the temple. The note that they were 35 cubits high is certainly wrong and probably a result of a copyist's error (see 1Kg 7:15, specifying their height as 12 cubits). (This admission should not weaken the readers' confidence in the Bible's inerrancy since the claim of inerrancy is made only for the original writings, not for the many copies and manuscripts; cf. Paul D. Feinberg, "Bible, Inerrancy and Infallibility of," in *Evangelical Dictionary of the Bible*, ed. Walter A. Elwell [Grand Rapids, MI: Baker, 1984, 2001], 156-59.) The purpose was mainly to impress worshipers with the grandeur of the edifice. The significance of the names—**the one on the right Jachin** (he establishes) **and the one on the left Boaz** (in strength) (2Ch 3:17) is debated but may have to do with Hebrew terms of praise, and taken together they form a sentence: "He (God) establishes in strength."

The view that "Israel's small temple was to be understood to be a microcosm of the entire heaven and earth" (G. K Beale, *The Erosion of Inerrancy in Evangelicalism* [Wheaton, IL: Crossway, 2008], 164; cf. Beale, *The Temple and the Church's Mission* [Downers Grove, IL: InterVarsity, 2004] and John H. Walton, *The Lost World of Genesis One* [Downers Grove, IL: InterVarsity, 2009]) is based on certain premises about the nature and interpretation of the biblical text, especially Gn 1. Since the temple, and tabernacle before it, were intended to be suitable structures for the "cosmic presence" of the Lord, it may very well be that certain elements and aspects of those structures reflected the grand structure of the cosmos itself. However, this need not be taken to mean that the text of Gn 1 cannot be understood in a literal way (see commentary on Gn 1) or that this exhausts the tangible and practical use, the meaning and significance of the temple (and tabernacle) by the nation of Israel (historically)—or that there are no typico-prophetic elements of these structures (pointing to the substitutionary atonement of Jesus Christ on the cross) or that there will not be a literal rebuilding of the temple in the future (see Ezk 40–48).

2. The Furnishings (4:1-22)

4:1-22. The description of the temple furnishings was intended to indicate that Solomon was meticulous in following the plan for the temple delivered to him by David (see 1Ch 28:11-19). The pattern or floor plan of the temple followed that of the tabernacle, indicating the continuity of the ancient institutions with the new temple. The **bronze altar** (2Ch 4:1) of course, meant that approach to the Lord required atonement, as the **cast metal sea** (v. 2), a larger version of the laver (cf. Ex 30:17-21), indicated the need for cleansing. This feature of the temple will, in the millennial temple, be replaced with flowing waters (Ezk 47:1-12). The **ten basins** (2Ch 4:6) were not found in the tabernacle. The **ten golden lampstands** (v. 7) took the place of the single lampstand, and the **ten tables** (v. 8) for the showbread (**bread of the Presence**, v. 19) took the place of the single table of the tabernacle. These features were meant to indicate the larger size of the temple to accommodate the larger nation of Solomon's day. The lamps and the bread were symbols of the presence of God. The courts are mentioned (v. 9) as the place where the priests served, and the implements and utensils listed in vv. 11-22a were their tools. Bronze objects are listed in vv. 11-18, and golden objects are listed in vv. 19-22a. The priests' function was mainly intercessory by means of sacrifice and prayer. The sacred space and the preciousness of their tools indicated the supreme importance of their service for the nation. The golden doors of the temple completed the picture of a magnificent structure that was meant to focus the worshiper on the greatness and holiness of the Lord.

E. Dedication of the Temple (5:1–7:22)

5:1a. The dedication of the temple held much more interest for the Chronicler than did the details of construction. Therefore, he devoted three chapters to this most noteworthy event. The temple was begun in 966 BC and was completed in 959 BC, taking over seven years to complete (see 1Kg 6:1, 38). All of that was condensed to one verse—**Thus all the work that Solomon performed for the house of the Lord was finished** (2Ch 5:1a). By contrast the Chronicler devoted three chapters to the days (see 2Ch 7:8-9) of dedication. The actual celebration was delayed several months until "the feast that is in the seventh month" (5:3, September/ October 959 BC) so that the dedication might correspond to the Feast of Trumpets, the Day of Atonement (although Chronicles makes no mention of this), and the Feast of Booths (see Payne, "2 Chronicles," 4:459)

1. The Ark and the Glory of God (5:1b-14)

The final act of furnishing the temple was also the first act of dedication of the temple. The theme that ties these verses together is "the presence of the Lord." Both the ark and the glory indicate the presence of the Lord in the house that was built for the name of the Lord.

a. The Ark Comes to the Temple (5:1b-10)

5:1b. Solomon's first act of dedication of the temple was to bring **the things that David his father had dedicated** and the ark of the covenant to the temple.

5:2-3, 6. With the note that Solomon **assembled** the leaders of the nation **to Jerusalem** (v. 2a), the Chronicler focused on the theme of unity once again. This assembly effectively brought **all the men of Israel** (v. 3) together around *the* symbol of national pride and accord. In the rest of the narrative in Chronicles this type of national assembly was meant to indicate a time of revival of faith and fidelity to the Lord (cf. 2Ch 20:5-19; 30:13-27; 34:29-33). The many sacrifices offered by the king and **all the congregation of Israel** (v. 6) also served to bring a sense of unity to the entire proceeding.

5:4-5. The two accounts of David's attempt to move the ark (one ending in tragedy, 1Ch 13:1-14; and one ending in success, 1Ch 15:1-28) as well as the instructions in the law for transporting the ark (cf. Nm 4:15) are the historical and prescriptive backgrounds for the account recorded here. Solemn respect mixed with nearly breathless anticipation can be sensed in the description of the account of the transportation of the ark to the temple. That the priests involved were specially selected (not using the usual process)

Solomon's Temple

Adapted from *The New Moody Atlas of the Bible*. Copyright © 2009 The Moody Bible Institute of Chicago.

and consecrated for this task (see 5:11b) indicates the care taken in moving the ark.

Apparently the priests and Levites went to the tent where David had placed the ark (cf. 1Ch 16:1) and the **tent of meeting** (2Ch 5:5a; cf. 1:3) in Gibeon and brought **all the holy utensils** (v. 5b) to the temple, effectively uniting the ancient tabernacle with the new temple. It was important that the Chronicler demonstrate to his generation that the ancient institutions were not lost but preserved, and could be revived, in the rebuilt temple of their day.

5:7-10. The Chronicler related the placement of the ark with great precision, conveying the care that had been taken in the actual event. Four aspects of the ark are noted: its location, **the inner sanctuary . . . the holy of holies** (v. 7); its surroundings, **the cherubim** (vv. 7b-8; cf. 1Ch 28:18; 2Ch 3:10-13); its means of transport, the **poles** (5:9); and its contents, **the two tablets which Moses put there** (5:10). Payne notes, "the golden pot of manna (Ex 16:32-34) and Aaron's rod that budded (Nm 17:10-11; Heb 9:4) must have been lost" at some time over the years (Payne, "2 Chronicles," 460).

b. The Glory of God Comes to the Temple (5:11-14)

5:11-14. The Lord's presence symbolized by the ark now received an even more dramatic confirmation. As the priests (the ones specially selected and consecrated) who had transported the ark were exiting the holy place, as the singers were singing, the musicians playing—as the celebration was reaching a crescendo—**then the house, the house of the LORD, was filled with a cloud** (v. 13d), the *Shekinah* (divine presence). The dramatic event brought the ministry of the priests to a standstill for **the glory of the LORD filled the house of God** (v. 14). This was an unmistakable sign—as the Lord had come into the tabernacle in Moses' day (cf. Ex 40:34-38), so He had now graced Solomon's temple with His awesome presence. This "cloud" was a vivid and inimitable manifestation of God's presence (cf. Ex 13:31-32; Mt 17:5; Ac 1:9). Here it served as confirmation of the Lord's acceptance of and pleasure in this temple. (He will provide the same confirmation for the millennial temple according to Ezk 43:1-5.)

The praise of the priests—**His lovingkindness** (*chesed*) **is everlasting** (v. 13b)—recalls God's covenant loyalty (*chesed,* cf. 1:7-13 and comments there) to Solomon (see 1Ch 17:13) and so gives the credit for this completed temple to Him.

2. Solomon's Dedicatory Speech (6:1-11)

In recording the speech and prayer of Solomon, the Chronicler seemed particularly interested in relating to the reader the posture and orientation of the king and the assembly. His dedicatory verse (6:1-2) was apparently addressed toward the temple. His blessing and speech were delivered facing the standing assembly (6:3). For his prayer he began standing "before the altar" (v. 12) on a specially constructed bronze platform (v. 13; a detail not included in 1Kg 8:22-23) and then knelt and "spread out his hands" (vv. 12, 13c). These details were meant to convey the depth of dignity and solemnity of this moment. The presence of God was awe-inspiring, and the form of worship was vital to communicating the assembly's feelings of admiration, reverence, and respect. Solomon (and the Chronicler) knew that "posture in worship" could contribute to (or detract from) the depth, weight, and authenticity of worship.

a. Dedicatory Verse (6:1-2)

6:1-2. This "dedicatory verse" was uttered in response to the dramatic and climactic event of the glory of God filling the temple in the form of a cloud (cf. 5:13d). The image of a **thick cloud** (6:1) as the indication of God's presence is probably drawn from Moses' experience on Mount Sinai (Ex 20:21; cf. 2Sm 22:7-8; Ps 97:2). Now that the Lord, in the manifestation of this cloud, had come to the **lofty house** (2Ch 6:2a) Solomon had built, He demonstrated His approval of it and His intention to make it **a place for** His **dwelling forever** (v. 2).

b. Dedicatory Address (6:3-11)

6:3-4a. Solomon maintained the solemnity of the service by blessing the assembly and blessing **the LORD, the God of Israel** (v. 4). These blessings were not "pious words" but deeply felt petitions for joy and happiness (a beatitude) for the assembly and honor and thanksgiving toward the Lord.

6:4b-6. This address began with a series of remembrances of the Lord's promises and fulfillments. He spoke to David (v. 4b; cf. 1Ch 17:3-14), and He **fulfilled it with His hands** (2Ch 6:4c; that is, directly and literally). He spoke to Abraham and Moses (cf. Gn 15:13-14; Ex 3:7-10), and He fulfilled it when He **brought** His **people from the land of Egypt** (2Ch 6:5a). Again, He spoke to David and chose Jerusalem (vv. 5b-6a; cf. 1Ch 11:4ff.; 17:5; cf. 2Ch 12:13; Zch 1:17; 8:3), and he chose David (2Ch6:6b; 1Ch 28:4; cf. 1Ch 17:23, 27; cf. 1Sm 16:1-13). This list would have encouraged Solomon's audience and the Chronicler's readers to remember that the Lord's promises are certain (cf. Ps 105:1-8; Rm 11:29).

6:7-11. Solomon moved to the specific promise God made regarding the construction of the temple and its subsequent fulfillment. David had desired to build **a house for the name of the LORD**, and while this was commendable it was denied to him (vv. 7-9; cf. 1Ch 28:2-3). Rather, the honor for this task was granted to David's son (2Ch 6:9). This too **the LORD has fulfilled** (v. 10). Four aspects of Solomon's experience were specifically mentioned: first, he had **risen in the place of my father David**; second, he sat on **the throne of Israel**; third, he had **built the house for the name of the LORD**; and fourth, he had successfully **set the ark** of the covenant in the proper place. Each of these was the fulfillment of **His Word which He spoke** (v. 10). Besides the themes of promise and fulfillment, two other themes are touched upon: first, the Lord accomplished the fulfillment actively—by His "mouth" and His "hands" (6:4; cf. 6:15b) by His **word which He spoke** (v. 10). Second, those whom He uses to accomplish His work must be ready to serve in whatever manner He chooses—David not to build but to prepare—Solomon to build and to do all according to His Word. While Solomon considered himself to be the fulfillment of the promises regarding David's ultimate son (v. 10, **I have risen in the place of my father David and sit on the throne of Israel . . . and have built the house**), the Chronicler's readers would know from Israel's history that Solomon's failures disqualified him from being *the* Son of David, the Messiah (cf. 1Kg 11:1-13; see the comments on Mt 1:1).

3. Solomon's Dedicatory Prayer (6:12-42)

6:12-13. Solomon's prayer of dedication is one of the great prayers of the Bible. As noted, the solemnity and dignity of the moment were conveyed through Solomon's posture and attitude in prayer—he **knelt on his knees** (v. 13) indicating his humility before God and his reverence for God. The prayer itself is a model of praise and petition.

a. Prayer of Acknowledgment (6:14-15, 18)

6:14-15, 18. Solomon praised the **LORD, the God of Israel** (v. 14a) by acknowledging His transcendent uniqueness—**there is no god like You in heaven or on earth** (v. 14a)—His immensity—**Behold, heaven and the highest heaven cannot contain You** (v. 18), His covenant keeping "loyal love" ("lovingkindness," *chesed*, see comments on 1:7-13), and again, His promise fulfilled to David.

b. Prayer of Petition (6:16-17, 19-21)

6:16-17. Solomon made three petitions: first, he appealed to the Lord to **keep . . . that which You have promised** (v. 16), to **let Your word be confirmed which You have spoken** (v. 17). These were not expressions of doubt about whether the Lord would keep His Word. Solomon knew that God works through the prayers of His people to accomplish what He has decreed. Solomon was praying for God's promise to be kept, even as he prayed with God's promise as his assurance. He was in effect expressing his confidence in that promise.

6:19-21. Second, Solomon prayed for the Lord to **have regard** (v. 19a) to this prayer, to **listen to the cry**, to **the prayer**, to the **supplications** (vv. 19b, 21), to keep an open eye (v. 20a; cf. 6:40), to **hear** when prayers are made **toward this house** (i.e. the place of God's presence; v. 20). Again, these do not indicate that the Lord needed to be cajoled or prodded into hearing the prayers of His people. The key appears in the final expression in v. 21—**hear and forgive**. Solomon knew that he and the nation had access to God in prayer solely on the basis of God's grace. These are all pleas for God to be gracious—pleas from a sinner asking God to be forgiving and open to hearing the prayers of the penitent. Indeed, the prayers are made **toward this house**, this place of atonement for sin. They are the pleas of the unworthy to a gracious God to be forgiving in the light of the atonement to be accomplished in this temple. The theological idea behind these pleas is that the presence of the Lord in the temple was not merely "ceremonial" but that He would be taking an active role in the life of the nation and the experiences of the individual members of the community.

c. Prayer Regarding Various Situations (6:22-39)

Solomon next listed various circumstances for these pleas for a gracious hearing from God that might apply most. Selman notes, "Each paragraph follows the same pattern: (1) a situation of need, usually involving sin; (2) temple-based prayer and confession; (3) request for God to hear; (4) restoration and forgiveness" (Selman, *2 Chronicles*, 328).

6:22-39. Times when the Lord's active presence should be invoked include: (1) in the circumstance of those who take oaths, that the Lord may punish **the wicked** who break the oath and justify **the righteous** who keep the oath (vv. 22-23); (2) in the event of defeat by an enemy of the nation, that upon confession of the underlying sin He restore the nation **to the land** of promise (vv. 24-25); (3) in the event of drought (like a defeat it was a sign of God's chastisement for the nation's sin), that upon confession He **forgive the sin** and **teach them the good way** and **send rain on Your land** (vv. 26-27); (4) in the events of **famine . . . pestilence . . . sickness** when individuals or the nation—**any man or by all Your people Israel**—make supplication and pray, that He **render to each according to all his ways** and according to the sincerity of his heart (vv. 28-31); (5) in the case of foreigners, that when such a one who recognizes the truth of who the Lord is and His power, that He hear and answer them, so that **all the peoples of the earth may know Your name, and fear You** and thereby testify that the temple is indeed the **house** that **is called by Your name** (v. 33); (6) in the case of a war of conquest, **whatever way You shall send them**, that upon their prayers they be given success (vv. 34-35); (7) in the event of captivity, something only possible because of their sin, that when **they take thought** of **the land**, upon their repentance and confession, their **return to You with all their heart and with all their soul**, and their prayer **toward their land** and the city of the Lord's promise and choosing, He hear, and forgive, and restore them (vv. 36-39).

d. Final Appeal (6:40-42)

6:40-42. Solomon's confidence that the Lord would be **attentive to** this and all such prayers was predicated on the Lord's presence **in this place**—the temple. He concluded his prayer with a call for the Lord to take up **Your resting place**, and one final plea that He not **turn away** (vv. 41, 42).

4. Fire and the Glory of the Lord (7:1-3)

7:1-3. The Lord dramatically answered Solomon's prayer by sending down **fire . . . from heaven** to consume **the burnt offering and the sacrifices** and once again **the glory of the Lord filled the house** (v. 1). This was an unmistakable confirmation that the Lord had accepted the temple as His house and that He would deal with His people according to the ways Solomon had just petitioned Him. The reaction of the priests and people was fear—they **bowed down** in worship and praise (v. 3).

5. Sacrifices and Festival (7:4-11)

7:4-11. The assembly continued with sacrifices (vv. 4-5), music (v. 6), more offerings (v. 7), and celebration of the Feast of Booths (vv. 8-9). "Solomon had delayed the temple's dedication for a number of months (cf. 5:3) so that this might be celebrated along with the feast of Booths, when at the latter season all Israel would be coming in pilgrimage to Jerusalem (Ex 23:16-17" (Payne, "1 Chronicles," 464). Then Solomon dismissed the people **rejoicing and happy** (v. 10). The key to this rejoicing and celebration was the understanding of the people that the temple and all the blessings they were enjoying were grounded in the truth that **His lovingkindness** ("loyal love," *chesed*, see definition 1:7-13) **is everlasting** (7:3c, 6b). That is, they recognized with Solomon that as a people they deserved nothing, but that based on His covenant promises He would never forsake them. This was a message that the generation of the Chronicler (and all generations of God's people) needed to hear. The Lord will keep His promises. Of course, another note has been sounded in this paean of praise, namely, that the enjoyment of these blessings, for an individual or the nation, depends on obedience (cf. 6:16)—this point was soon to be driven home to Solomon.

6. Post-Dedication Appearance of the Lord to Solomon (7:12-22)

This nighttime appearance of the Lord to Solomon (v. 12) is the second recorded in 2 Chronicles (cf. 2Ch 1:7ff.) and was the occasion of another significant word from the Lord to Solomon in particular and to the Davidic dynasty in general. When the pertinent texts are considered (see 1Kg 6:38–7:1; 9:10), the note that the Lord spoke to Solomon after the completion of both the temple and the palace (2Ch 7:11-12) indicates that this appearance was some 13 years after the dedication ceremonies just recorded. It must have seemed more appropriate to the Chronicler that this divine confirmation be noted at the moment of the temple's dedication.

a. The Lord Confirms His Choice of the Temple (7:12, 16)

7:12, 16. The Lord made it clear that this appearance was in answer to Solomon's prayer of dedication—**I have heard your prayer**. He acknowledged that the temple was to be the place of mediation—of sacrifice and prayer. The nation could count on His promise—based on His choice of the temple—to hear their prayers because this was the place where His name, His **eyes**, and His **heart** (that is, His conscientious attention and affection) would be manifested **perpetually** (7:16b).

b. The Lord Extended His Promise to Include Restoration (7:13-15)

7:13-15. This awesome promise placed a compelling responsibility on the nation. The Lord anticipated a time of trial, one that would have been real to any nation in that time and place—a period of drought, **pestilence**, and famine (7:13). There is no indication that this eventuality was necessarily the result of sin—it might have been so, or it may simply have been an experience under God's providential direction. In any case, the promise meant that the nation had recourse to alleviate such disasters. In what is perhaps the best-known verse in all of Chronicles, the Lord outlined the proper attitudes and actions to regain and enjoy the blessing of the Lord. Although the promise was specifically directed to **My people**, the principles are applicable to all who call upon the name of the Lord (cf. Jl 2:32; Zph 3:9; Ac 2:21; Rm 10:13; 1Co 1:2) (cf. Selman, *2 Chronicles*, 338).

The four actions listed in 2Ch 7:14 were not intended to be understood as "steps in a process" but as contemporaneous "facets of an active attitude given tangible expression." These acts would be illustrated by several of the exemplary Davidic kings in the narrative to follow in 2 Chronicles, giving proof to the truth of this promise. A repentant people are, first, to **humble themselves**, that is they must refuse the stubbornness and pride so ever-present in the nation's history. Second, they are to **pray** and afford themselves of the great privilege represented by the temple itself. Third, they are to **seek My face**, again one of the key themes of the Chronicler—seeking God's face means the people are to reject self-seeking and self-reliance. Fourth, they are to **turn from their wicked ways**—this is repentance. These acts indicate that the Lord expects nothing less than a deeply felt rejection of self-reliance, self-trust, self-seeking, and a conscientious dependence upon Him, an active submission to Him, and a determined and active alteration of lives to be lived for Him.

The Lord's promise in response to this "active attitude" was threefold: first, He again promised to **hear from heaven**—an overwhelming reality if understood; to **forgive their sin**—the necessary step to restoration of the relationship with Him and the enjoyment of His covenant blessings; and third, to **heal their land**. This last element not only recalled the tangible aspect of the Abrahamic promise—the land—but also would have been especially encouraging to the Chronicler's generation as they were struggling in that very land—one badly in need of restoration. These promises were addressed to His covenant people Israel and reflect the Deuteronomic blessings and cursings promised in the law (cf. Dt 27, 28) and are therefore not appropriately enjoined for believers who do not live in a theocratic nation. Certainly God would long for the people of the United States (or any other country) to humble themselves and pray, and turn in faith to Jesus the Messiah. Although God would certainly forgive the sins of those people who turned to Him, there is no promise here that God would restore their respective nations or heal their lands.

c. The Lord Reiterated His Promise to the House of David (7:17-18)

7:17. The Lord next addressed Solomon personally, but in effect He was addressing the rest of David's dynasty. That is, while the Lord was speaking to Solomon, these words were equally relevant and urgent for each of the Davidic kings who would follow. While the promise to David was inviolable (v. 18b; cf. 1Ch 17), the enjoyment of it, in any individual king's reign, was contingent upon that king's obedience. The obedience expected was described in three terms: the king was to **walk**, to **do**, and to **keep** (2Ch 7:17). First, the obedience the Lord required was characterized as "walking"—behaving, serving, reigning—**as your father David walked** (v. 17a). David was the paradigm of covenant faithfulness. He was not perfect, but he was "a man after [God's] own heart" (cf. 1Sm 13:14; Ac 13:22). Second, the king was to **do according to all that I have commanded you**. The king was actually to serve as "vice-regent" under the sovereign Lord, the True King. Third, the king was responsible to **keep My statutes and My ordinances**. He was to obey the law as a guide to the will of God. "Keeping the law" did not mean keeping it as a legalistic code but rather adhering to it as the means for the Lord to bless the king and the nation (cf. Ps 1:1-3; 119:1-8). The exhortation here is remarkably similar to the description of Abraham in Gn 26:5: "Abraham obeyed Me and kept My charge, My commandments, My statutes and My laws." Surprisingly, Abraham is described this way even though the law was not given until hundreds of years later. Yet Abraham can be described in this way because he "believed in the Lord," and it was "reckoned ...

as righteousness" (Gn 15:6). The only reasonable explanation of Abraham is that because he lived a life of faith, he was able to carry out the law, even before it was given. Hence the message of the Pentateuch was to encourage faith leading to faithful obedience. Here Solomon is enjoined to obey as an expression of his faith.

7:18. The promise **You shall not lack a man to be ruler in Israel** (v. 18b) was (obviously) not a promise that there would always be a king over Israel. Indeed, the Chronicler was well aware that the nation had had no king since the captivity began (and still had no king in his day). The promise, however, was an expression of his messianic hope. While the covenant promises may not be enjoyed by a disobedient king, and the nation may fail to enjoy the blessings of having a descendant of David on the throne at any particular point in history, yet the Chronicler is sure this promise will find ultimate fulfillment in the Greater Son of David (cf. 1Ch 17:13-14), the Messiah who would come "to be ruler in Israel" (cf. Mc 5:2).

d. The Lord Warned of Exile for "Forsaking" His Law (7:19-22)

7:19-22. The Lord concluded the word to Solomon with a warning clearly articulating the themes "seeking the Lord" on the one hand and "forsaking the Lord" on the other hand (see Introduction: Purpose and Themes in 1 Chronicles). The history of the divided monarchy, beginning with the apostasy of Jeroboam I (cf. 1Kg 12:25-33) and running until the reign of Zedekiah (2Kg 24:17ff.) was checkered with disobedience to the law and the practice of idolatry. The warnings of exile and international ridicule were not potentialities to the Chronicler's generation—they were the tragic history the nation had actually suffered and from which they had returned relatively recently. The Chronicler's purpose "was not to rub salt in old wounds, [sic] rather his purpose was to show how to avoid the consequences of disobedience" and that when such consequences do fall, to show that "the proper recourse of the people is repentance" (Sailhamer, *First and Second Chronicles*, 78).

F. Solomon's Reign (8:1–9:31)

After 20 years on the throne (8:1), mostly consumed with building the temple and his own palace, Solomon was ready to enjoy the fruits of his labor. Being the king, however, meant that challenges and duties never stopped. The Chronicler concluded the narrative of Solomon by highlighting his activities in securing the kingdom and administering it in wisdom. His wealth and power are also noted.

1. Solomon Secured His Kingdom (8:1-18)

a. Solomon's Building Projects (8:1-11)

8:1-6. The Chronicler recorded the other, outlying building projects of Solomon, highlighting the cities he built for defense, **fortified cities** (v. 5), for **storage**—probably indicating places to secure his wealth (vv. 4, 6), and for bivouacking his **chariots** and **horsemen** (v. 6). The geographical notices indicate that Solomon extended his kingdom and secured it from attack.

8:7-10. The building of the cities indicates that Solomon secured his kingdom from external threats, and the note here about his labor forces indicates he secured his kingdom internally as well. All foreigners were conscripted as **forced laborers** (v. 8b; cf. 1Ch 22:2). This need not be understood in a way that envisions harsh conditions and severe taskmasters. It does indicate that Solomon kept close tabs on these people and did not allow them to advance to higher-level positions of authority. Those positions were reserved for **the sons of Israel** (2Ch 8:9). The purpose appears to be that only those who could be expected to have primary loyalty to the nation and the king would be in positions of responsibility and power.

8:11. Solomon also built a separate house for his Egyptian bride. The explanation seems to indicate that Solomon recognized the inappropriateness of having a foreign (possibly pagan) wife living in proximity to the holy places he had so recently consecrated for the ark. (On the matter of OT men having multiple wives see comments on 1Ch 14:3-7 and Gn 29, 30).

b. Solomon's Temple Ceremonies and Personnel (8:12-15)

8:12-15. The note here regarding the ceremonies and personnel of the temple must be understood in context as another feature of securing the kingdom. While the external and geopolitical steps taken for security were practical and important, the real security of the nation's people lay in their devotion to and trust in the Lord. These were given tangible expression in the sincere and faithful worship services in the temple. When all was done **according to the daily rule** (v. 13), and **according to the ordinance of . . . David** (v. 14a), and the priests served **according to the daily rule** (v. 14b), and when they **did not depart from the commandment of the king** (v. 15), the nation was assured of the Lord's continuing presence in the temple.

Solomon's Domestic Administration

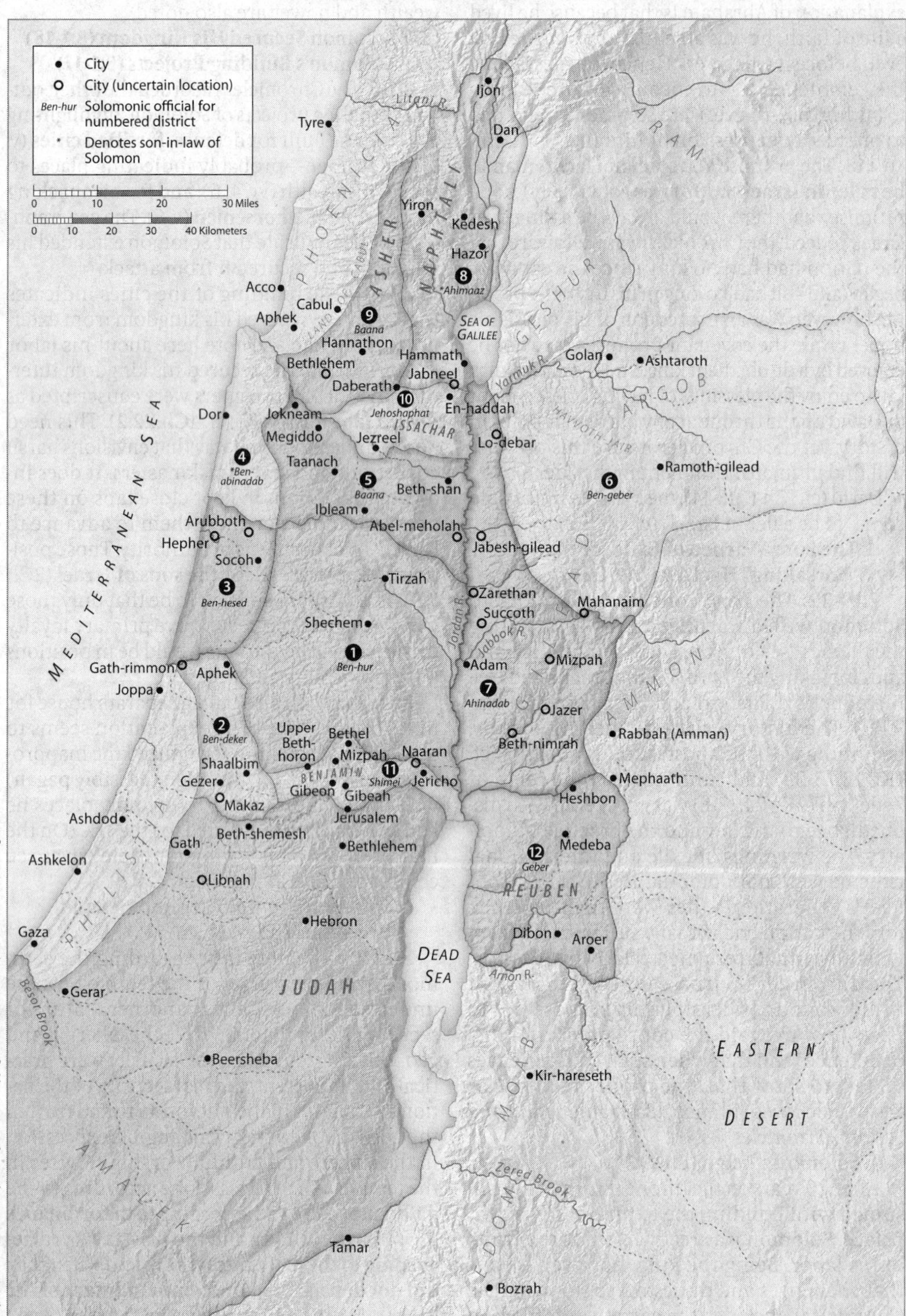

c. Summary Statement Regarding the Temple (8:16)

8:16. This final statement of the completion of the temple is not redundant. The Chronicler was driving home the point that Solomon's dedication to building the temple underlay the prosperity and security the king and the nation now enjoyed.

d. His Seaports and Trading (8:17-18; 9:10-11, 21)

8:17-18; 9:10-11, 21. The final note regarding Solomon's efforts to secure the nation concerns his establishment of seaports **Ezion-geber** and **Eloth** (modern Eilat) in the south, on the Gulf of Aqaba. These ports gave access to **Ophir** from which Solomon imported large amounts of gold and other riches (cf. 9:10-11). Since the Israelites were not seafaring people, Solomon employed the servants of Huram (King of Tyre) for this maritime enterprise. The location of **Ophir** and the mythical "King Solomon's mines" is unknown. Since the account of the seaports is linked to the visit of the Queen of Sheba it is probable that Ophir was located in or near Sheba—an empire that stretched from southern Arabia across the Red Sea to eastern Ethiopia (see Payne, "2 Chronicles," 4:470).

Another trade route was initiated to **Tarshish** (9:21a; cf. 2Ch 20:36). This was also manned by the **servants of Huram** and was also highly lucrative (9:21b).

2. Solomon Administered Kingdom in Wisdom, Amassed Great Wealth (9:1-28)

The narrative in this chapter demonstrated that the promise the Lord made to Solomon at the first night visit (1Ch 1:8-13) was completely fulfilled. The Lord promised Solomon wisdom and wealth—and Solomon indeed displayed unusual wisdom and amassed incredible wealth.

a. Solomon's Wisdom and Queen of Sheba (9:1-9, 12)

As Solomon's kingdom grew more secure and powerful it attracted the attention of other empires in the region. One such was the empire of Sheba. This empire of southern Arabia was built on intercontinental trade mainly between Africa and the Middle East (Asia). The attention devoted to the visit of the Queen of Sheba indicates the spread of Solomon's power and influence.

9:1-4, 9. Having **heard of the fame** of Solomon, the queen came to see for herself if the accounts of wisdom and wealth were true. In keeping with the social customs of visitors bearing gifts for their hosts, the queen brought **a large amount of gold and precious stones** (v. 1b). The queen's "gift, also recorded in 1 Kings 10:10" (**one hundred and twenty talents of gold**, 2Ch 9:9) "amounted to over four and a half tons of gold" (Payne, "2 Chronicles," 470).

The object of her visit was to **test Solomon with difficult questions** (v. 1a). This was not an attempt to "trip him up" but rather to discover for herself the depth of his wisdom and understanding. Solomon did not disappoint. He **answered all her questions** and gave her complete explanations (v. 2). This is more than a matter of historical interest to the Chronicler. Not only was this a specific instance of the fulfillment of the Lord's promise to Solomon (cf. 1:11-12) but also it is "reminiscent of the kind of messianic hope characteristic of the chronicler's day (Haggai 2:7)" (Sailhamer, *First and Second Chronicles*, 79). Indeed, the expectation of the Gentile nations coming to the Davidic King for instruction and enlightenment into the ways of the Lord was a significant feature of Jewish messianic expectation (see Is 60:3-6). The wisdom and splendor of Solomon left the queen **breathless** (2Ch 9:4c).

9:5-8, 12. The queen's personal visit proved to be a surprise to her, and she confessed that **the half of the greatness of** Solomon's wisdom **was not told** to her—his wisdom surpassed her expectations (v. 6). As earlier with Huram (cf. 2:11-12), the Chronicler recorded the remarkable theological insight of a non-Israelite—the Lord is the One responsible for this wisdom and splendor. Indeed, in this Davidic King and in this pagan queen there is the foreshadowing and portent of the promise that many nations will come to Jerusalem and "to the house of the God of Jacob" to receive "the word of the Lord" (Is 2:2-3).

The note in 9:12 indicates that in both physical and spiritual realms the queen returned home with more than **what she had brought to the king**.

b. Solomon's Wealth and Power (9:13-20, 22-28)

9:13-28. The record of the incredible wealth of Solomon was yet another indication of the fulfillment of the Lord's promise (1:11-13). The details of the golden **shields** (9:13-16), the **throne of ivory** and gold (vv. 17-19), and the golden **drinking vessels** (v. 20) gave evidence that Solomon was **greater than all the kings of the earth in riches and wisdom** (v. 22). Indicative of the same point, the Chronicler recorded that other kings followed after the example of the Queen of Sheba and came to witness Solomon's wisdom and bring him tribute (vv. 23-24, 28). Solomon's military might and the extent of his hegemony were also noted (vv. 25-26). The Chronicler recorded all of this as a message of hope for his generation. What God has done for Solomon in fulfillment of the Davidic promise, He will do fully, finally, and forever for the greater Son of David, the Messiah. While Solomon's power and authority reached the zenith in the extent of the kingdom in the OT (v. 26) his kingdom did not extend as far as the land promise to Abraham had indicated (here in 9:26—**border of Egypt**; cf. Gn 15:18-21—"river of Egypt"). Later prophets reiterated the promise (e.g. Am 9:11-15; Is 57:13; 61:7, indicating that they did not view the promise as fulfilled or abrogated), and the promise was ultimately meant to be "everlasting"—forever (Gn 12:1, 7; 13:15; 15:18; Is 60:21).

3. Summary and Death of Solomon (9:29-31)

9:29-31. The most striking aspect of this concluding formula is that it appears without the record of Solomon's failures toward the end of his reign (see 1Kg 11:1-43). Nothing is mentioned of his apostasy or that "the LORD was angry with Solomon because his heart was turned away from the LORD" (1Kg 11:9). As in the Chronicler's narrative of David, these more negative accounts in the narrative of Solomon were not included, though not in an attempt to deny them or rewrite history. Indeed, the Chronicler assumes the reader is aware of these parts of Solomon's story. His purpose, however, was to encourage his generation, and those negative details simply did not contribute to that end. For the Chronicler, the point of the narrative was not Solomon's success or failure but the Lord's promise and fulfillment of it. "Solomon was 'primarily exemplary.' Solomon was an example of *the* promised descendant of David, who in the chronicler's day had not yet come" (Sailhamer, *First and Second Chronicles*, 82). Nevertheless, Solomon's story did indicate that the Lord's promise would be fulfilled: the Greater Son of David would come, with wisdom and splendor even greater than Solomon's.

IV. The Kings of David's Line (10:1–36:23)

The fourth major division of the Chronicler's work essentially deals with the kings of the Davidic dynasty from the death of Solomon to the captivity. The focus is on the kingdom of Judah, and the references to the kings and kingdom of the northern tribes (Israel) are limited to those times when there was significant intercourse between the kingdoms. The Chronicler "was seeking not a comprehensive understanding of the past but a theological perspective on the present and the future" (Sailhamer, *First and Second Chronicles*, 83). The Chronicler was much less reticent in this section to recount the foibles and sins of the Davidic kings (when compared to his version of the lives of David and Solomon). However, while he did recount some serious problems with several of the kings in the Davidic line, he also presented a perspective that highlighted the benefits of "seeking the Lord" and presented that as a possibility even in the face of great failure (as in the case of Manasseh). While it was true that the Lord would chastise the king who failed to "seek the Lord," nevertheless the Lord responded favorably to sincere repentance and faith.

A. Rehoboam (10:1–12:16)

The reign of Rehoboam was set down by the Chronicler in three parts, each corresponding to the three chapters of 2Ch 10, 11, and 12. The first of these, delineated in 2Ch 10, corresponds closely to the parallel in 1Kg 12. This once again indicates that the Chronicler was not attempting to rewrite history—his retelling was meant to highlight certain aspects of the story to create an overall theological sense of the narrative. Much of the material in 2Ch 11 and 12 is unique to the Chronicler.

The division of the kingdom was a major event in the nation's history and an explanation was needed, especially in the light of the Davidic promise (1Ch 17). In Kings, it is clear that Solomon (cf. 1Kg 11:26-39, the account of the word of the Lord to Jeroboam through Ahijah the prophet), Rehoboam, and Jeroboam were each, in different ways, responsible for the division of the kingdom. However, the Chronicler highlighted one note from Kings to make it emphatically clear that the Lord predicted this division (2Ch 10:15; cf. 1Kg 12:15), so it "was a turn of events from God." As the Lord transferred kingship from Saul to David (cf. 1Ch 10:14), so He was also in control of even this unhappy phase of the nation's history. Thus, the Chronicler has indicated that the Lord is in charge of the great "turning points" in the nation's history.

1. The Kingdom Divided (10:1-19)

a. Rehoboam Met with All Israel; Coronation Delayed (10:1-5)

10:1-3. Rehoboam traveled to **Shechem** to meet with **all Israel** and be recognized as king.

Since the tribal divisions that would result in two kingdoms were already in place, the meeting's location at Shechem was significant. Shechem was about 30 miles north of Jerusalem in the territory of Ephraim and was already recognized as an important political center for the northern tribes. After the split, it became the first capital of the northern kingdom (cf. 1Kg 12:25).

It seemed that Rehoboam expected this coronation to proceed as his grandfather's had (cf. 1 Ch 11:1) since **all Israel** was in attendance. However, Jeroboam, who had been exiled to Egypt by Solomon (cf. 1Kg 11:26-40), had been recalled and had been appointed spokesman for the people. The atmosphere of this scene as recounted by the Chronicler was serious but not necessarily tense.

10:4-5. The statement **Your father made our yoke hard** and the reference to **hard service** (v. 4a) was a serious charge—essentially charging Solomon with "pharaoh-like" treatment (cf. the similar wording in Ex 6:6-7) of his countrymen in violation of the commandment directed at kings (Dt 17:20). However, the charge was immediately softened by a pledge that should this burden be lightened the people would be willing to serve the new king (2Ch 10:4b). Rehoboam acted prudently by delaying the response for time to consider the demand. At this point, humanly speaking, the division of the kingdom was not inevitable. The Chronicler may have been telling his readers that such disasters are avoidable and divisions are best healed while the breach is small.

b. Rehoboam Met with His Advisors (10:6-11)

If Rehoboam had been thinking of a previous assembly of "all Israel" (cf. 1Ch 1) he might have recognized the need to pray for wisdom as his father had done. The absence of prayer at this critical juncture in the nation's history and in Rehoboam's reign was glaring. Instead he met with his human advisors, and even then heeded the wrong ones.

10:6-7. The **elders** who advised Rehoboam were the men who **had served his father** (v. 6). Their advice was to do as the people had requested. "The parallel passage in 1Kg 12:7 quotes even stronger advice by the elders to the king: not simply that he 'be kind' and 'favorable' to the people, but that he 'be a servant' and 'serve' them" (Payne, "2 Chronicles," 4:474). What the people could endure for the great tasks of building the temple and palace could not be sustained indefinitely. Sacrifice for a grand project was one thing—constant subjugation for the king's personal aggrandizement was quite another.

10:8-11. The two times the text mentions that Rehoboam **forsook the counsel of the elders** (10:8a, 13) brackets the account and served to highlight his failure to "seek the Lord." He turned instead to **the young men who grew up with him**. Their self-serving loyalty was to him alone (**served him**) (v. 8b) and not the whole nation. Rehoboam's repetition of the people's charge (v. 9b) while leaving out the part about their promise to serve, distorted the issue and made the unreasonable advice of the young men seem more fitting. A challenge was met with a threat—always a bad policy! The bellicose advice of the young men, seen from the historical perspective after the division of the kingdom, was both immature and shortsighted.

c. Rehoboam Met with Jeroboam and All the People (10:12-15)

10:12-15. The parties reconvened and Rehoboam **answered them harshly** (v. 13). The repetition in these verses gave the sense that the scene had turned tense and adversarial. The Chronicler summarized with the words, **So the king did not listen to the people** (v. 15a). Rehoboam had clearly underestimated the seriousness of the challenge and overestimated his ability to carry out the threatened oppression. However, the Chronicler was quick to make clear that this **turn of events** (v. 15b) was of the Lord. "The reader is reminded that even a disastrous situation such as the division of the kingdom and the loss of the ten tribes of Israel was not without its place in God's plan" (Sailhamer, *First and Second Chronicles*, 84).

d. Kingdom Divided (10:16-19)

10:16-19. The reaction to Rehoboam's truculent and deprecating response was swift and unambiguous. The poetic question, **what portion do we have in David?** likely became a popular refrain among the people. The division between the **house** of **David** and **all Israel** reflects a rare time in Chronicles when the unity of the nation was shattered.

Rehoboam attempted to make good on his threat, but his man, **Hadoram** ("Adoram" in 1Kg 12:18) was stoned to death for his efforts. Rehoboam was forced to flee for safety to Jerusalem where he reigned over **the cities of Judah** (2Ch 10:17). The note about Israel being in rebellion **to this day** (10:19) most likely recounts the words of the Chronicler's source (cf. 1Kg 12:19). The Chronicler omitted the narrative of the coronation of Jeroboam (cf. 1Kg 12:20). From this point forward, he generally ignored the history of the northern kingdom (since his focus was on the Davidic dynasty), including the kings or events of the northern kingdom only when they related to the narrative of the Davidic kings of Judah. (The whole history of the rebellion, disobedience, and judgment of the northern kingdom did not serve the more optimistic view of the Chronicler. He was not interested in rehashing who was chastised, but he wanted his generation to "keep looking at the promise" and the Greater Son of David who would bring about the blessing on the nation.)

2. The Reign of Rehoboam (11:1-23)

At this point the Chronicler's account of Rehoboam's reign diverged considerably from that of Kings. The account in Chronicles is longer, with material not found in Kings. Furthermore, while the overall evaluation of Rehoboam is the same in both accounts (cf. 2Ch 12:14 and 1Kg 14:22) there is more place given to Rehoboam's albeit temporary repentance (2Ch 12:6) and to examples from Rehoboam's reign that indicate the Davidic promise endured despite the king's evil. Regardless of his folly and loss of the northern tribes, Rehoboam consolidated his kingdom (11:5ff.) just as David and Solomon had done. Furthermore, he gathered the priests and Levites (11:13) from all Israel and demonstrated a "Davidic" interest in the place of true worship—Jerusalem (cf. 11:16). Once again, the Chronicler was not attempting to rewrite history (he expects the reader to be familiar with the story as told in Kings), but he offered a perspective on Rehoboam that highlighted the Lord's faithfulness to His Davidic covenant promises.

a. Rehoboam Prevented from Attacking Israel (11:1-4)

11:1-3. Upon his return to Jerusalem, Rehoboam's initial response to the rebellion and to the outrage of the murder of his envoy was to assemble a force from **Judah and Benjamin** to **fight against Israel**. His objective was to restore ("to win back") the unity of the nation under himself (v. 1). The mention of **Judah and Benjamin** shows that it was these two tribes that made up the southern kingdom of Judah (cf. v. 3). Rehoboam had not yet learned from his folly and intended to force the northern tribes to submit.

The Lord put a swift halt to such intentions through **Shemaiah the man of God**, a prophet who ministered throughout the reign of Rehoboam and later wrote a noncanonical book about him (v. 2; cf. 12:5-7, 15). The message was addressed to the king and to **all Israel in Judah and Benjamin** (v. 3). The words **all Israel** (in contrast to "all the house of" in 1Kg 12:23) are significant. The Chronicler subtly shifts his use of this designation from its general application to the whole of the unified nation (2Ch 11:16) to those who are loyal to the Davidic dynasty and especially those who are devoted to the temple in Jerusalem. In other words, "all Israel" in a general sense means "all those who are descendants of the patriarchs," but a more "theologically centered" sense refers to those who "set their hearts on seeking the LORD God of Israel" (11:16) and proved their loyalty by going to Jerusalem to worship at the temple. The lesson for the Chronicler's generation was that those who returned from captivity, whose hope was in the Davidic promise, and whose worship centered on the temple, could legitimately be called "all Israel." (In 12:1 the shift is complete; there the terms are used to designate Judah alone.)

11:4. Shemaiah related the **words of the LORD** to Rehoboam and all Israel that it was not the Lord's will for them to go against their **relatives** ("brothers") (v. 4). The Lord's commands were sharp and clear: **You shall not go up or fight . . . return every man to his house** (v. 4a). His explanation was arresting: **for this thing is from Me** (v. 4b). This simple statement belies the complexity involved in the Lord's purposes for the division of the nation. The author of Kings made it clear that one reason for this division was chastisement for Solomon's apostasy (cf. 1Kg 11:29-33). Here, the Chronicler was indicating that the division was caused by the obstinacy and hubris of Rehoboam. But there is a subtler point: the division made a clear distinction between those "who set their hearts on seeking the LORD" (2Ch 11:16) and those who had forsaken the Lord. The positive effect of the division was the preservation of Judah from the apostasy of the northern tribes (cf. 11:14-15). Payne summarizes, "The overriding divine purpose was to separate the godly in Judah from the apostate in Israel (11:6-22) and to concentrate in the south those who remained faithful out of the northern tribes: 'thus they strengthened the kingdom of Judah' (v. 17)" (Payne, "2 Chronicles," 4:474).

The final word in this brief section recounted not an act of resignation by the king and the people but an act of obedience and submission: **So they listened to the words of the LORD** (v. 4c).

b. Rehoboam Secured His Kingdom (11:5-13)

11:5-13. Rehoboam's works of city building (11:5-10) and fortifying the nation (vv. 11-12) recall those of Solomon (cf. 8:2-6), and the underlying point is the same: the nation's security was a priority because only with security can the purpose of worship and service to the Lord proceed unhindered. Once the security of the nation was established then matters of true worship could be addressed (cf. 11:13, 16).

c. Jeroboam's Apostasy Led to Judah's Strength (11:14-17)

11:14-17. The Chronicler noted the apostasy of Jeroboam (v. 15), but his account highlights a providentially positive effect: since Jeroboam's idolatrous changes (cf. 1Kg 12:25-33) excluded the Levites, they were forced south to the Jerusalem temple, the center of true worship. This **strengthened the kingdom of Judah** (v. 17a) and helped Rehoboam. Sadly this effect lasted only three years (v. 17c), "an ominous reminder that Rehoboam was not to be the promised messianic Son of David" (Sailhamer, *First and Second Chronicles*, 85).

d. Rehoboam's Family (11:18-23)

11:18-23. The paragraph detailing Rehoboam's family was included not only to establish the line of succession through Abijah (a choice that did not follow the normal rules of succession). It also recorded how Solomon's disobedient (cf. Dt 17:19) and fatal error of multiplying wives, who turned the heart of the king from the fear of the Lord, was repeated by

Rehoboam's Fortified Cities

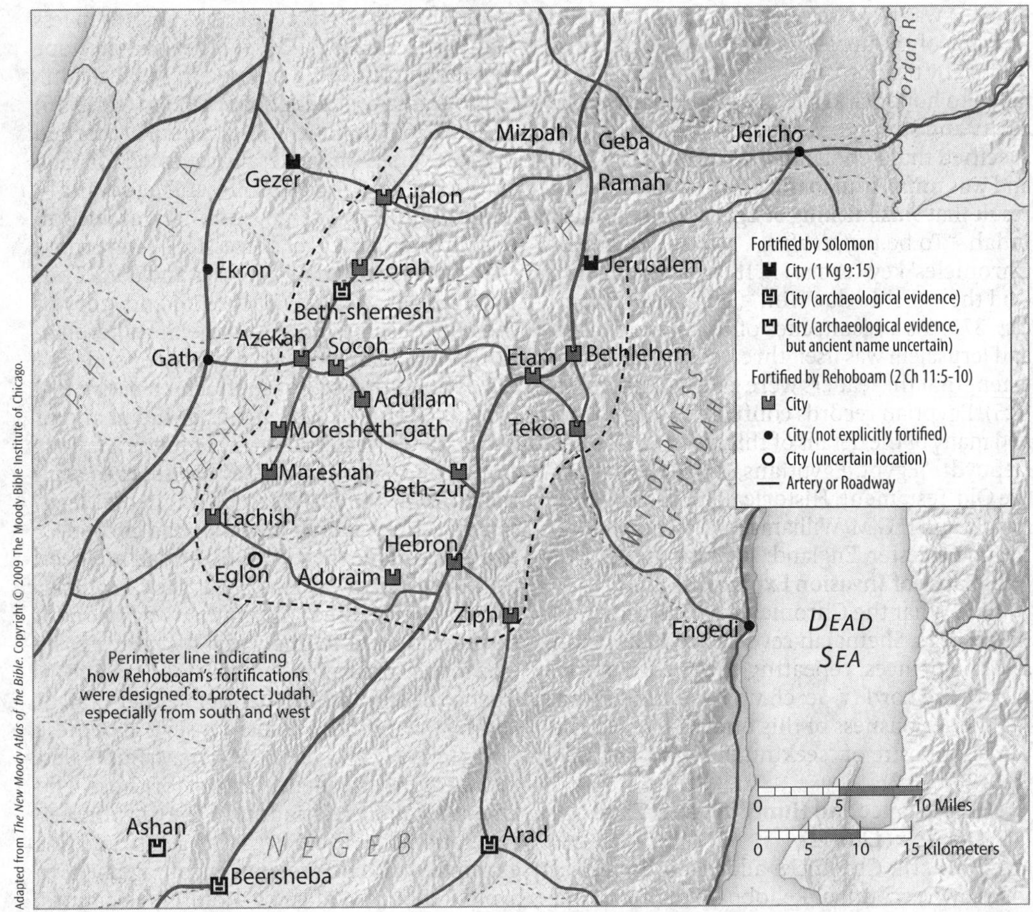

his son. Even though the Chronicler dutifully recorded that it happened, it is not to be inferred that it was acceptable to the Lord that Rehoboam married a half-sister.

3. Invasion of Shishak (12:1-12)

In some ways this chapter is the starting point for the rest of Chronicles (see Payne, "2 Chronicles," 4:477ff.). In this chapter the Chronicler regarded Rehoboam not so much as Solomon's successor but as the first in the line of historical kings of Judah that terminated with the captivity. This is not so much the (theocratic) Davidic line but the semi-cyclical (historical) line of Judah that toggled between "bad" and "good" rulers until the captivity by Nebuchadnezzar. Although the Davidic promise was carried by this historical line, these kings were at best mere representatives of the ideal, and actually often served as negative contrasts of the promised Greater Son of David, the Messiah.

a. Invasion by Egypt (12:1-4)

12:1-4. The opening statement of this chapter (v. 1) was to be recalled in a haunting echo in many of the accounts that followed: a king, blessed by the Lord with security and strength, failed to honor God and found the nation's security and strength weakened. The Chronicler specified that Rehoboam **forsook the law** (v. 1) and was **unfaithful to the Lord** (v. 2a) with the result that **Shishak king of Egypt** (v. 2b) invaded Judah. "To be *unfaithful* . . . to God is one of Chronicles' key terms. . . . It involves denying God the worship due Him" (Selman, *2 Chronicles*, 373). As a result, cites of Judah were taken and Jerusalem was itself threatened (11:4) to the extent that the leaders were gathered there (cf. 12:5). Egyptian records confirm the historicity and many of the details of this invasion (see Leo Depuydt, "Egypt, Egyptians," in Dictionary of the Old Testament, Historical Books, ed. Bill T. Arnold and H.G.M. Williamson [Downers Grove, IL and Leicester, England: InterVarsity], 243).

b. Cause of Invasion Explained (12:5)

12:5. What the Chronicler had already told his readers, Shemaiah revealed to Rehoboam and the princes, repeating the charge of forsaking the Lord (v. 5c; cf. v. 1) and underscoring the seriousness of this offense—it was the direct opposite of "seeking the Lord" (cf. 1Ch 28:9; 2Ch 15:2).

c. Repentance and Humility Avert Total Disaster (12:6-12)

12:6-12. The Chronicler added more material to his own account of Rehoboam than is found in 1Kg 14:25-28, and in doing so has offered a nuance to his story—there was repentance and humility on the part of the king and the princes (2Ch 12:6). This lesson is one the Chronicler's generation needed to hear. While "forsaking the Lord" brought chastisement, it was the loving purpose of a gracious God to bring about repentance through the "pain" and then, on the basis of the repentance and humility, to mitigate the penalty. Chastisement and even loss as the consequence of "forsaking the Lord" does not mean an end to His grace or His promises. While there was a heavy price to pay in treasure and gold (v. 9), nevertheless, because the king **humbled himself, the anger of the Lord** was averted and the destruction was minimized (v. 12). Indeed, even though the golden shields were lost, there were bronze shields to replace them, and in spite of the loss **conditions were good in Judah** (v. 12). The Chronicler's generation needed to know that the humbling experience of the captivity had not demonstrated the Lord's abandonment of His people. They had even less than the "bronze shields" but they had the hope that conditions could be good in Judah again.

4. Summary of Rehoboam's Reign (12:13-16)

12:13-16. The concluding formula recorded in these verses was generally repeated for each of the Judaic kings to follow. The details—length of life and reign, summary of accomplishments, matters of succession—were more than a mere record of statistics and data. They were a brief overview of the life and story of the king designed to set up the moral evaluation. In Rehoboam's case it was not good—**he did evil**. But it was not so much an active evil (as will be true of some kings of Judah and of Rehoboam's rival Jeroboam) as it was a failure to do good—**he did not set his heart to seek the Lord** (v. 14). Although he reigned in **Jerusalem, the city which the Lord had chosen . . . to put His name there** (v. 13b), he had not been wholehearted toward the Lord. The Chronicler may have noted that his mother was **Naamah the Ammonitess** to imply that his failure to be true to the Lord came from the non-Israelite influence of his mother. Then again, the detail of adding the mothers' names for several of these kings (cf. 13:2; 25:1; 27:1; 29:1) may simply be a means of precise identification for those who knew the family relationships. The Chronicler's generation once again lived in that city, and this example would be a solemn encouragement to avoid Rehoboam's fate by avoiding his failure.

The note concerning his sources (v. 15) would have increased the Chronicler's credibility and the power of his narrative.

B. Abijah (13:1–14:1)

1. Introductory Formula for Abijah (13:1-2a)

13:1-2a. Abijah was called "a great sinner" by the author of Kings (1Kg 15:3), but in accord with the general tenor of his work the Chronicler chose to highlight the positive in Abijah's brief reign—**three years** (2Ch 13:2a) from 913 to 911 BC. The name of his mother was **Micaiah** (Maacah, 1Kg 15:2) "and *Uriel* may be the son of Absalom ('Abishalom', 1Kg 15:2) making Micaiah/Maacah the granddaughter, though certainty is impossible" (Selman, *2 Chronicles*, 379). The Chronicler's account is longer than that of Kings, drawn from a source other than Kings, namely, "the treatise of the prophet Iddo" (2Ch 13:22b), and taken up mostly with the war between Abijah and Jeroboam (v. 2b). The account is less about Abijah himself than it is about the principle that humility and trust in God will bring victory and blessing since it is the Lord God of Israel (13:5) who brings victory. Because Abijah's reign was mostly concerned with rivalry and war with the northern kingdom, the Chronicler dated Abijah by the reign of his rival Jeroboam (v. 1). While this cross-dating of kings is a fairly constant feature in Kings, "It occurs only here in the books of Chronicles" (Sailhamer, *First and Second Chronicles*, 86).

2. Abijah's War with Israel (13:2b-19)

a. Nations at War (13:2b-3)

13:2b-3. The Chronicler simply and directly noted that **there was war** between the rival nations, indicating that Abijah and the southern kingdom were outnumbered by Jeroboam and the northern kingdom, two to one. Nevertheless, it was Abijah who **began** the battle (v. 3a).

b. Abijah's Speech to Israel (13:4-12)

The record of Abijah's speech is a typical literary device for the Chronicler. In fact, in narrative literature of the Bible, insight is regularly given through a speech by a primary character in the story.

(1) First Charge against Israel: Rebellion to Davidic Dynasty (13:4-7)

13:4-7. The exact occasion and location (**Mount Zemaraim**, v. 4a; cf. Jos 18:22) are uncertain, but apparently, while the two armies were lined up for battle, Abijah addressed his rival and **all Israel** (v. 4b). He delineated the charges against Israel and justification of this battle.

The first charge against Israel was her rebellion against the Lord's chosen Davidic dynasty. Abijah reminded the rebellious nation that the **Lord . . . gave the rule over Israel forever to David** (v. 5a). The reference to the **covenant of salt** (v. 5b) is probably to be understood as "a metaphor for permanence based on Nm 18:19" (cf. Lv 2:13) (Selman, *2 Chronicles*, 380). The primary use of salt in the ancient world was as a preservative—hence a covenant of salt would "last." Abijah scolded the northern kingdom for following Jeroboam, a traitor surrounded by **worthless men** and **scoundrels**, instead of siding with the legitimate heir of Solomon (vv. 6-7a). Abijah's characterization of his father Rehoboam was clearly biased but not inaccurate.

(2) Second Charge against Israel: Apostasy from True Worship (13:8-9)

13:8-9. The rebellion of the northern kingdom was not merely a political one but theological, thereby making it apostasy—a more serious matter for the Chronicler. It was not David's, nor Solomon's, nor Rehoboam's kingdom against which they have rebelled but **the kingdom of the Lord through the sons of David** (v. 8a). Their apostasy was expressed in the **golden calves** set up by Jeroboam. That these **gods** were **made for** them (v. 8b) made their naked idolatry more appalling. Additionally, the northern kingdom had employed illegitimate, self-proclaimed pagan **priests** (v. 9c; cf. 11:14-15), while the true **priests of the Lord, the sons of Aaron and the Levites** (13:9a; cf. 11:16-17) had been driven out of the northern territories. The idolatrous worship Jeroboam instituted was no better than the pagan idolatry of **the peoples of other lands** (13:9b). It was this defense of the Davidic dynasty and of the true worship of the temple that raised Abijah's reputation in the eyes of the Chronicler. It was of vital importance for the Chronicler and his generation to maintain the uniqueness of temple worship against the idolatry that had sent the nation into captivity and the paganism that continued to surround them. If they were to be blessed with success and security, they needed to be as bold as Abijah was in their regard for true worship.

(3) Justification of Southern Kingdom: Not Forsaking the Lord, True Worship Upheld (13:10-11)

13:10-11. Abijah mentioned a key theme of the Chronicler: **we have not forsaken Him** (v. 10). "This is extremely serious, for God would forsake those who forsook Him (1 Ch 28:9; 2 Ch

15:2; 24:20; cf. 2 Ch 12:1, 5)" (Selman, *2 Chronicles*, 381). Abijah could say **the LORD is our God** (13:10a) because he could point to the ongoing and faithful worship of the temple, just as that worship had been prescribed (vv. 10c-11).

(4) Appeal to Northern Kingdom: God Is with Us—Do Not Fight against Him (13:12)

13:12. In the same manner, Abijah could predict that the northern kingdom would not prevail (**you will not succeed**) because of their rebellion and apostasy. Those who worship and serve the Lord sincerely and in truth may expect His help. Those who forsake Him can expect to suffer loss. Not only the remainder of this account but the long history after the fall of the northern kingdom would drive home the truth of that assertion to the Chronicler's generation. Furthermore, it was a message to the opponents who may have been seeking to thwart the work of the Chronicler's generation in their efforts to rebuild Jerusalem and the temple.

c. The Battle Joined (13:13-19)

13:13-14. Even as Abijah was appealing to his wayward brethren, Jeroboam was busy flanking Judah's forces in preparation for a sneak attack behind them, so that Judah was surrounded. The Chronicler recorded that without a note of panic **they cried to the LORD, and the priests blew the trumpets** (v. 14). The presence of the priests in the line of battle indicated that Judah's trust was not in military might but instead well placed in the Lord.

13:15-17. Again, the events moved swiftly, but the men of Judah did not panic in this dire circumstance but rather **raised a war cry** (v. 15a; noted twice)—a confident and defiant gesture. Although the precise military details of the battle were not recorded, the underlying source of the victory was God Himself. Although no supernatural means is indicated, it was **God** who **routed Jeroboam and all Israel before Abijah and Judah** (v. 15b) and it was **God** who **gave them into their hand** (v. 16). At the end of the battle the forces of the northern kingdom were reduced to inferior numbers compared to Judah's.

13:18-19. The summary of Abijah's victory gave the Chronicler another chance to drive home the main point of this narrative: Abijah and Judah were victorious because **they trusted in the LORD, the God of their fathers** (v. 18). Israel had been **subdued** (lit., "humbled") and Abijah had captured her cities, most notably **Bethel** (v. 19, one of the places of the golden calves; cf. 1Kg 12:28-33) because the false gods could not defend themselves against the true God.

3. Concluding Formula for Abijah (13:20–14:1)

13:20. The summary of Jeroboam's loss and death was simply noted. The only detail was **the LORD struck him** (v. 20). Once again, the Chronicler provided his readers with a warning to those contemplating apostasy and an encouragement to not forsake the Lord.

13:21–14:1. The Chronicler noted Abijah's strength to explain why the northern kingdom did not counterattack and to preview the peace that prevailed in his son Asa's day (cf. 14:1b). It was the Lord who gave him prosperity and security (cf. 1Ch 26:5; 2 Ch 11:18-21).

C. Asa (14:2–16:14)

As with Abijah, the Chronicler gave more attention to Asa than did the author of Kings (compare 2 Chronicles' three chapters to 1Kg 15:9-24). Asa's example is a mixed one, however, and his reign exemplified both major themes of the Chronicler: at the outset of his reign Asa is one who is found "seeking the Lord" (e.g., 2Ch 14:2-3), but at the end of his reign he is one "forsaking the Lord" (16:7-10).

1. The Lord Gives Godly King Asa Great Victory (14:2-15)

a. King Asa Did Right before the Lord (14:2)

14:2. The Chronicler wasted no time in offering a hopeful beginning, by stating that **Asa did good and right in the sight of the LORD his God** (v. 2). This was a reminder that such beginnings must be followed by unflagging obedience.

b. Asa Instituted Religious Reforms (14:3-5)

14:3-5. Asa began his reign by a series of reforms designed to cleanse the nation from idolatry and to foster true worship. The centerpiece of his reforms (vv. 3-5, and literally at the center of these verses) was fostering the "seeking of the Lord." There was an encouragement to obedience to the law (v. 4) that was bracketed by the order to remove idolatrous forms of worship (see vv. 3 and 5). For the Chronicler, obedience to the law was anything but mere "legalism." "Since obedience is equated with seeking God, the law is viewed as a means of maintaining fellowship with God (cf. 6:16; 12:1, 5)" (Selman, *2 Chronicles*, 388).

c. Asa Instituted Nationwide Security Program (14:6-8)

14:6-8. Asa's security program involved

fortifications and a well-equipped standing army. However, his true security was based much more on **the LORD** who **had given him rest** (v. 6, cf. v. 7). The king wisely enlisted the people in his program and reiterated to them that the security they sought would come because they had **sought the LORD** their **God** (v. 7). The brief note that this needed to be done while **the land** was **still** theirs (v. 7b) would have pricked the ears of the Chronicler's first readers—a reminder of how the land had been lost and how it might be kept in the their own day.

d. Asa's War with Zerah the Ethiopian (14:9-15)

The preparations for security were soon tested by a threat from an unlikely source. The identity of Zerah is unknown outside of Chronicles. Most likely, this was a proxy war fought in behalf of the Egyptians who had ongoing conflicts with Judah and the other nations to its northeast.

14:9-10. The intimidating numbers of the enemy did not prevent Asa and Judah from proceeding out to the battlefield to face them. The battle plan, however, included a serious and determined effort at "seeking the Lord" before engaging the enemy. **Mareshah** was about 25 miles southwest of Jerusalem.

14:11. Asa's prayer began with acknowledgment of the singular power and strength of the Lord, thereby acknowledging his need and dependence on that power and strength. He expressed his and the nation's trust in the Lord, basing his petition not on anything in himself, nor in the nation, but only because the Lord had identified Himself with this nation. It was for the sake of God's **name** and because the Lord was their **God** that He should go before them in this battle. In effect, the enemy had not come against the king or nation so much as against the Lord. Therefore, Asa prayed **let not man prevail against You** (v. 11d).

14:12-15. The Chronicler left the reader with no uncertainty that the prayer was answered, and that the victory was itself achieved by the Lord: **So the LORD routed the Ethiopians** (v. 12a). The description of the extent of the victory and the plunder the nation **carried away** was an example of the Lord doing "exceedingly, abundantly above all" that the king had asked or expected.

2. Asa's Response to Azariah's Prophecy (15:1-19)

After the great victory the Lord sent His prophet Azariah to solidify the commitment and faithfulness of Asa and the nation. The description of Azariah's prophetic word and the covenant ceremony that followed are unique to the Chronicler's account.

a. Prophet Brings the Lord's Word to King and Nation (15:1-7)

15:1-2a. Azariah, who appears only here in Scripture, was empowered for his task by **the Spirit of God** (15:1a). This was a standard way to indicate the divine credentials of the man speaking for God. It recalled the way the Lord intervened in the days of the judges and kings—by Spirit-empowered leaders such as Othniel (Jdg 3:10) and Samson (Jdg 14:6) and Saul (1Sm 10:10; cf. 16:14).

15:2b. Seeking the Lord and not forsaking Him was a major theme of the Chronicler and the Asa narrative. As such this was the central verse in the whole of Asa's story (see Introduction: Purpose and Themes in 1 Chronicles).

15:3-6. Azariah recalled first the "bad old days" when the nation was without the direction and protection of the **true God** in the form of His priests mediating His law (v. 3). The description of the time indicated by Azariah seems best to fit the time of the Judges when the cycle of disobedience, distress, crying out to the Lord, and His deliverance was repeated several times over. This was a time of repeated **disturbances** (v. 5) and **every kind of distress** (v. 6).

15:7. Asa was admonished to avoid such a sorry cycle of "revival and relapse," and the phrase **be strong and do not lose courage** clearly recalled the words of the Lord to a leader who conquered and achieved victory, namely, Joshua (cf. Jos 1:6; cf. 1Ch 22:13b).

b. Asa's Response to God's Word: Reformation, Revival (15:8-19)

15:8-19. Asa **took courage** (v. 8a), and his response to the words of Azariah was immediate and dynamic. He embarked on an ambitious series of reforms that culminated in a gathering of the faithful, a rededication, and a covenant of commitment.

Asa removed idols (v. 8), restored altars (v. 9), and reinstituted sacrifices (vv. 10-11). He then strengthened the relationship with those who had defected from the northern kingdom of Israel (v. 9). He removed his own mother from power because she had encouraged idolatry (v. 16), and he added to the wealth and prestige of the temple (v. 18). But central to his reforms was the covenant he established between the Lord and **all Judah** (v. 9a) and all those from the northern kingdom who **saw that the LORD his God was with him** (v. 9b). This covenant of commitment **to seek the LORD God of their fathers with all their heart and soul** was the high point of Asa's reign. The Chronicler saw this as the reason Asa enjoyed many years of peace and success.

This then was the Chronicler's message to his own generation (and all subsequent generations)—security (cf. vv. 15c, 19) comes by committing oneself to the Lord with a **whole heart** and seeking Him **earnestly** (v. 15). Only by such sincere movements of heart, mind and soul can one expect that **He** will **let them find Him** (v. 15b). It goes without saying the Lord will be faithful to His promises—but the enjoyment of those promises by any generation requires the same level of sincerity and commitment exhibited by Asa and the nation at this point in the nation's history.

3. Asa Sought Security in Treaty with Enemy (16:1-14)

While the effects of Asa's revival lasted for many years (cf. 15:19–16:1) they did not last indefinitely, even for Asa himself. "Asa's last five years . . . completely reversed the pattern of the rest of his life" (Selman, *2 Chronicles*, 396).

a. Asa Made a Temporal Alliance (16:1-6)

16:1. The actions of Baasha, the king of Israel, in securing a border town of Ramah hardly seemed to offer much of a threat to Asa's or Judah's security. No doubt it was a provocative action, but it was designed to keep his own people from further defections to Judah more than to pose a threat to Judah.

16:2-3. In addition to the foible of depleting his and the nation's wealth, Asa's treaty with Ben-hadad displayed a lack of trust in the Lord and provoked a needless war for Israel.

16:4. It would appear that the idea to attack Israel came not from Ben-hadad but from Asa (16:4, **Ben-hadad listened to King Asa**). If so, it was ironic that having won a proxy war with Egypt (through Zerah), Asa himself initiated a proxy war with Israel (through Ben-hadad). The rather underhanded aspect of provoking this war was only the subtext for the main issue, however—namely, Asa was putting his security in alliances rather than in the Lord.

16:5-6. The final note regarding the battle again paints Asa in a poor light. He was opportunistic and disingenuous. He now threatened Israel more than he was endangered by Israel. All of Asa's actions at this point were based on "temporal calculations" with no evidence of seeking the Lord.

b. Hanani the Seer (Prophet) Rebuked Asa (16:7-9)

16:7-9. Hanani went to Asa and spoke directly: these actions were nothing less than a lack of faith in the Lord and a violation of Asa's previous covenant commitment to seek the Lord. Apparently the Lord had intended Judah to defeat Ben-hadad (Aram) (v. 7), but that was no longer possible since they were now in effect allies (and the threat from the Arameans would remain for subsequent kings, cf. 2Ch 18; 22:5). Asa's previous reliance on the Lord and victory over **the Ethiopians and the Lubim** (Lybians; 12:3; Nah 3:9) was held up by Hanani as the example of what Asa ought to have done in this case (2Ch 16:8). Hanani's description of the Lord's care over His own was not only memorably descriptive, it is also one of universal application: it shows a God who is intensely interested (**the eyes of the LORD move to and fro**, v. 9a) and deeply involved (**that He may strongly support**, v. 9b) in the lives of His people. The words **you have acted foolishly** (v. 9c) were a stinging rebuke to Asa, and would have made an unforgettable impression on the Chronicler's readers.

c. Asa's Reaction Inappropriate (16:10)

16:10. Where repentance to God's rebuke was in order Asa chose to retaliate against God's messenger. He had Hanani imprisoned and he oppressed the people, perhaps because they opposed this injustice toward the Lord's prophet.

d. Asa's Punishment (16:12)

16:12. The sad result of Asa's disobedience was a debilitating disease in his feet. Even with this, he failed to seek the Lord, relying rather on the physicians than seeking the Great Physician. This is not to suggest that seeking medical assistance was wrong in and of itself, but Asa was trusting only in the doctors, thus indicating his heart was no longer seeking the Lord. "Asa began his reign standing firmly in his trust in God. He ended his reign with diseased feet. Certainly part of the chronicler's intention in including this account of Asa's diseased feet was the picture it calls to mind of Asa's inability to stand firm" (Sailhamer, *First and Second Chronicles*, 91).

e. Concluding Formula for Asa (16:11, 13-14)

16:11, 13-14. Even though Asa's reign ended poorly he was honored in his death for the many years of his generally peaceful and prosperous reign. The notes concerning the funeral preparations indicate the nation's esteem for him despite his spiritual failures. "Asa, however, was still the most godly monarch to arise in Judah, from the division of Solomon's kingdom up to this point" (Payne, "2 Chronicles," 4:485). Unfortunately, this was not to be the last instance of a king who began well but ended poorly.

D. Jehoshaphat (17:1–20:37)

The reign of Jehoshaphat, whose name means "the Lord will judge," covers the next four chapters of 2 Chronicles. Unlike the record in Kings, where his story is ancillary to that of Ahab (of the northern kingdom of Israel), here in Chronicles Jehoshaphat takes center stage, being generally depicted as a good king. However, as with other generally godly kings, the Chronicler is forthright about his shortcomings and failures. He was a man of prayer (20:5ff.) who sought God (19:5b) and he "did not seek the Baals" (17:3b), but his unwise alliances with Ahab and Ahaziah brought serious rebukes from the Lord (cf. 19:1-2; 20:35-37). In several respects, the experiences and lessons (successes and failures) of his father Asa were repeated in the reign of Jehoshaphat.

1. Jehoshaphat Established His Kingdom (17:1-6)

a. He Secured the Nation (17:1-2)

17:1-2. When Jehoshaphat began his reign the tensions with the northern kingdom that had been evident during his father's reign were still present. He **made his position over Israel firm** by fortifying the border cities that his father Asa had conquered. This was not necessarily a provocative act and did not signal an aggressive stance toward the northern kingdom.

b. He Devoted Himself to God (17:3-6)

17:3-6. Jehoshaphat began his reign by demonstrating his devotion to God. He followed the example of **David's earlier days** (v. 3b; this seems an admission that David's later days were less than exemplary; cf. 2Sm 11 and 12). Jehoshaphat **did not seek the Baals** (2Ch 17:3b), that is, he did not lapse into idolatry, as did so many of his fellow kings. He **sought the God of his father** (v. 4a)—once again, a main theme of the Chronicler. He obeyed the commandments of the Lord. He **did not act as Israel did** (v. 4b)—that is, he did not follow the idolatry of Jeroboam I. He **took great pride in the ways of the LORD** (v. 6a), that is, he openly and sincerely served the Lord and sought to obey Him. Finally, he **removed the high places and the Asherim** (Canaanite female fertility goddesses, v. 6b), that is, he continued and expanded the reforms begun under his father Asa (cf. 15:16-17) by demolishing the places of pagan worship in Judah. Clearly, the Chronicler intended his readers to see in Jehoshaphat a list of acts of devotion that exemplify the best of the Davidic line.

For all this **the LORD was with Jehoshaphat** (17:3a), and **the LORD established the kingdom in his control** (v. 5a). This blessing was made tangible in that the nation **brought tribute** to Jehoshaphat (v. 5b)—not only **honor** but also **great riches.**

2. Jehoshaphat Administered His Kingdom (17:7-19)

Before beginning the actual narrative of Jehoshaphat's reign, the Chronicler noted his wise administration of the nation in two strategic areas.

a. Jehoshaphat's "Spiritual" Administration (17:7-9)

17:7-8. The placement of this note concerning the "spiritual" administration of Jehoshaphat before the note concerning the "military" administration of Jehoshaphat's kingdom indicates both the Chronicler's and Jehoshaphat's priorities. "Jehoshaphat was concerned that his kingdom be properly instructed in the law of God" (Sailhamer, *First and Second Chronicles*, 92). He understood that while military might had its place, there was no substitute for obedience to the Lord if the nation was to enjoy security and prosperity. With that mission in mind, he appointed **his officials**, Levites, and priests **to teach in the cities of Judah** (v. 7), a team consisting of five government officials, nine Levites and two priests (v. 8; the names were common, and precise identification with other persons with the same names is not possible).

17:9. This mission was intended to serve the people who could not make regular visits to the temple but still needed instruction in the Word of God. *What* they taught was **the book of the law of the LORD** (v. 9a)—not their own ideas or man's wisdom; *where* they taught was in **all the cities of Judah** (v. 9b)—that is, no community was excluded; and *who* they taught were **the people** (v. 9c)—indicating that even the common people were expected to know, understand, and obey the law. This formula would have greatly encouraged the leaders in the Chronicler's generation as they too were seeking stability and prosperity for those who had returned to the land—the way to true security is knowledge of and trust in the Word of God.

b. Jehoshaphat's "Temporal" ("Military") Administration (17:10-19)

17:10-19. Jehoshaphat also continued to secure the nation militarily. Because he prospered under the Lord's establishment of his kingdom (cf. v. 5a) the **dread of the Lord** (v. 10a) was upon the surrounding nations. Jehoshaphat's godly leadership prospered Judah, and the nations brought him tribute in an effort to forestall military conflict (v. 10b). The **Philistines** on the west brought the monetary wealth from their sea trading (v. 11a) and the **Arabians** on the east brought the wealth of livestock they had gained through the caravan trade on the eastern side of the Jordan River (v. 11b). This wealth served to make Jehoshaphat even stronger, and with it he **built fortresses and store cities** (v. 12) and a formidable, well-equipped army (vv. 13-19). The detailed notes of military strength anticipated the military conflicts to come in Jehoshaphat's reign.

3. Jehoshaphat's Disastrous Alliance with Ahab (18:1–19:3)

"The account of the alliance of Jehoshaphat and Ahab [18:1-34] is almost verbatim from 1 Kings 22:1-53 and is centered more on Ahab than on Jehoshaphat" (Sailhamer, *First and Second Chronicles*, 93).

a. Alliance by Marriage (18:1)

18:1. Jehoshaphat began his disastrous alliance with Ahab of the northern kingdom of Israel with the marriage of his son Jehoram to Ahab's daughter Athaliah (cf. 21:6; 2Kg 8:18). Such alliances were typical of the era, and Jehoshaphat may not have intended for this alliance to do more than secure peace between the two nations. However, the union was to be the source of a series of calamities for Jehoshaphat, his kingdom, and his family. It is a practical lesson on the reason a believer should "not be bound together with unbelievers" (2Co 6:14).

b. Alliance for War (18:2-27)

The remainder of the chapter concerns the ongoing war between the northern kingdom and the Arameans (Syria). This time the conflict concerned the disputed territory of **Ramoth-gilead**. This city, about 50 miles northeast of Jerusalem, was a significant city on the eastern side of the Jordan. It was on an important trade route and seems to have been a recurring source of tension between the two kingdoms.

18:2-3. The scene appeared at first to be no more than a "state visit" by one king to another (v. 2a). However, Ahab had ulterior motives. In the conversation and the ensuing conflict Jehoshaphat seemed somewhat naïve. After some "wining and dining" (v. 2b) Ahab **induced** (persuaded) Jehoshaphat to accompany him on an expedition to retake **Ramoth-gilead**. Impulsively, Jehoshaphat committed himself and his entire nation (v. 3b).

18:4-5. Even though to this point Jehoshaphat had acted naïvely and impulsively, he had enough spiritual sense to ask for some input from those who could give the kings some divine guidance before they embarked upon this military excursion (v. 4). Ahab may have expected such a request, for he produced no fewer than four hundred **prophets** who unanimously encouraged the kings to go into battle (v. 5).

18:6-7. Apparently it was clear to Jehoshaphat that this group, while large, was less than representative of the mind of the Lord. More than likely, they were employed by Ahab expressly to tell him what he wanted to hear. Jehoshaphat asked if **a prophet of the Lord** could be found (v. 6). Ahab was somewhat annoyed for he knew exactly what Jehoshaphat was seeking, namely, a prophet who would speak honestly and in accord with the mind of the Lord. Ahab knew that such a prophet could be found in **Micaiah, son of Imla** (v. 7b) and that this prophet would not endorse his plans. Ahab complained that this man **never prophesies good concerning me** (v. 7). Ahab even let his personal animosity toward Micaiah slip out (**I hate him**) drawing an instant (perhaps involuntary) rebuke from Jehoshaphat (**Let not the king say so**, that is, "You should not speak that way about a prophet of the Lord").

18:8-13. The prophet Micaiah is known to biblical history only through this incident. Nevertheless, his bold declaration, **As the Lord lives, what my God says, that I will speak** (v. 13) indicates that he was a true prophet.

While the kings were waiting for Micaiah to be brought before them (v. 8), Ahab had his false prophets continue to prophesy success for the campaign against the Arameans. One false prophet, **Zedekiah**, made an impressive visual aid, some iron horns (cf. Dt 33:17) and assured the kings that they would be victorious in the coming battle (2Ch 18:10), while all the prophets continued to add their assurances as well (v. 11).

Just before Micaiah was to speak to the kings he was advised that all the other prophets had spoken favorably and that he ought to do the same (v. 12). Many a prophet and preacher has had to face the same challenge—to agree with the "majority" or to speak the Word of God in truth and with courage. Micaiah assured his advisor that he intended to do the latter.

18:14-15. When he was called upon to give his prophetic answer to the question—to go to battle or to refrain (v. 14a)—he must have surprised everyone by his words **Go up and succeed** (v. 14b). His sarcasm, however, must have been clearly evident to everyone for Ahab admonished Micaiah to tell him the truth—that is, **to speak to me nothing but the truth in the name of the LORD** (v. 15). Ironically, it was Ahab who is adamant to have the prophet of the Lord speak the truth of the Lord. He probably insisted on this to prove his earlier claim that Micaiah never spoke good concerning him (v. 7, 17).

18:16-22. Micaiah forthrightly prophesied the defeat of this alliance. In a poetic verse, he **saw** that **all Israel** (a key term for the Chronicler that indicated both nations) would be **scattered . . . like sheep which have no shepherd** (v. 16a)—a clear prediction that these kings, as well as their nations, would be defeated. Then, in an intriguing description of the heavenly courts, Micaiah explained that God sent the false prophets to entice Ahab to undertake this war with the precise end of having Ahab **fall at Ramoth-gilead** (v. 19). The scene would have been particularly interesting to the Chronicler's readers as it was an insight into the "behind the scenes" work of the Lord to accomplish His purposes. Sometimes what seems like disaster from a human perspective is actually the Lord's work to accomplish His ends.

18:23-27. In a stunning breach of decorum, the false prophet Zedekiah struck Micaiah a blow to the face and boldly claimed that his prophecy was not of the Lord (v. 23). This act of violence itself indicated "that the Holy Spirit was not present with him (James 3:17)" (Payne, "2 Chronicles," 4:499). Micaiah's restrained and confident response showed that the Spirit was indeed with him (Gl 5:23; cf. Rm 12:17-19). Micaiah was promptly imprisoned by Ahab and treated harshly (2Ch 18:25-26). Micaiah's faith (like that of Daniel) was tested, but he expressed only assurance. He knew that his words were true and that Zedekiah would come to understand that (and be afraid, v. 24) and that Ahab would not return at all. His bold challenge, **Listen, all you people** (v. 27b) sounded like Elijah's challenge to exactly the same king and kingdom (cf. 1Kg 18:20-24).

c. Alliance in Defeat (18:28-34)

18:28-34. The account of the battle and defeat at Ramoth-gilead centered on the two kings—Ahab and Jehoshaphat. In a brazen display of duplicity mixed with cowardice, Ahab suggested he be disguised while Jehoshaphat was to go into battle with his full regalia (v. 29). The effect of this was predictable—the enemy would concentrate their forces on Jehoshaphat, identified as **the king** (v. 30), while Ahab could go undetected. However, the Lord thwarted this wicked plan. In a subtle change from his source (of 1Kg 22), the Chronicler noted that when Jehoshaphat was attacked and he cried out (1Kg 22:32b), **the LORD helped him, and God diverted them from him** (v. 31b). Furthermore, in one of the most poignant instances of divine providence over apparently insignificant events, there was **a certain man**, that is, no man in particular, **drew his bow at random**, that is, with no particular target, and shot his arrow in such a way that it not only hit the disguised Ahab but found **a joint of the armor** (v. 33a), inflicting what Ahab knew instantly to be a mortal wound (v. 33b). God delivered the king who cried out to Him, and God judged the king who defied Him.

d. Alliance and King Rebuked (19:1-3)

19:1-3. The events themselves were a rebuke of Jehoshaphat and exposed the folly of his unholy alliance with Ahab. Therefore, the Lord sent the prophet Jehu, the son of the prophet Hanani (who had rebuked his father Asa, for much the same folly of unholy alliances; cf. 16:7-10) to drive home the point. **Help**, **love**, and **hate** are terms related to covenant relationships. The principle behind Jehu's words is that one cannot **love** the Lord and ally with those who **hate** Him (19:2)—one cannot serve two masters (see the comments on Mt 6:24). This can only result in **wrath** from **the LORD** (v. 2b) in chastisement. This was strong language, but it was necessary to make the point to subsequent kings—faithfulness to the Lord is not optional. The rebuke by Jehu was mitigated by Jehoshaphat's previous reforms (v. 3), and it appeared to be the impetus for the reforms that followed.

4. Jehoshaphat's Reforms (19:4-11)

Jehoshaphat had the right attitude (a heart to seek God, v. 3b), and he responded to the rebuke of Jehu with reforms intended to strengthen his kingdom.

a. Spiritual Renewal (19:4)

19:4. The note in v. 4 is intended to indicate that Jehoshaphat not only carried out his reforms in the capital city, but he also extended them into the rural regions of his kingdom. His desire was to bring all the people **back to the LORD, the God of their fathers**. The constant need to return is a recurring theme for the Chronicler (and no doubt a need for God's people of any era.)

b. Judges Appointed (19:5-7)

19:5-7. To accomplish his goal of spiritual renewal Jehoshaphat **appointed judges** (v. 5; how this would assist in the renewal, see the comments on vv. 8-11). These judges were to work comprehensively (**in the land in all the fortified cites of Judah, city by city**; v. 5), conscientiously (**for the LORD**, in the presence of the Lord, with the **fear of the LORD** upon them, v. 6), and without **partiality** (v. 7).

c. Levites and Priests Appointed (19:8-11)

19:8-11. Apparently, the task of the judges out "in the land" (19:5) was like "small claims" or a "regional court," while the task of the Levites and priests and **heads of the fathers** in **Jerusalem** (v. 8) was like a "superior court" or "appeals court." The values imposed on the judges were reiterated and given more specific elaboration (vv. 9-10). Both spiritual (**all that pertains to the LORD**) and secular (**all that pertains to the king**) matters were to be taken up by these courts and resolved with integrity (v. 11b). Both the mere external organization of these courts and the signal values that were to guide them would have been of keen interest to the Chronicler's generation as they sought to forge a just and viable society in the postexilic period.

5. Jehoshaphat Faced Invasion and War with Prayer, Faith (20:1-30)

The narrative of the next major event in the reign of Jehoshaphat is introduced rather abruptly in 2Ch 20:1. The invasion by the forces of Moab, Ammon, and the Meunites (local tribes from the vicinity of Mount Seir, close to Petra in Edom, southeast of the Dead Sea; cf. 20:10) was itself unexpected and a shock to the nation. However, this account is exemplary of true faith under fire and depicts Jehoshaphat as the ideal Davidic king—a man who seeks God, a man of eloquent prayer and sincere faith.

a. Surprise Invasion from the South (20:1-2)

20:1-2. The route these forces took was from the eastern regions around the southern end of the Dead Sea. By the time news of their advance had reached Jehoshaphat, they were in Engedi, about halfway up the western side of the Dead Sea (20:2). They were a formidable force, a **great multitude**. This surprise attack found Jehoshaphat with little time for preparations and vulnerable, so the king **was afraid** (20:3a).

b. Spiritual Response by King (20:3-19)

Jehoshaphat's response was nearly as surprising as the invasion itself—but it showed him as an ideal Davidic King, a man of committed faith, and an exemplary leader of the nation whose God is the Lord.

20:3-4. Jehoshaphat may have been afraid, but he was not paralyzed with fear. He initially responded by calling for a fast in **all Judah** (v. 3). His previous programs to teach the Word in "all the cities of Judah" (17:9) and to appoint judges in all the cities (19:5) prepared the whole country. That the entire nation was well grounded in the Word and unified in its values is indicated by the repetition of the phrase **all Judah** (20:3, 13, 15, 18; cf. vv. 4, 17, 20, 27). They responded to the king's call and they gathered **to seek the LORD** (see Introduction: Purpose and Themes in 1 Chronicles) a signal feature of the ideal Davidic king (v. 4).

20:5-13. Besides the call to fast, Jehoshaphat offered a remarkable and exemplary public prayer (v. 5), heard by all but primarily directed to the Lord (v. 6). At the outset, Jehoshaphat acknowledged the Lord's sovereignty, noting His rule over the nations and His **power and might** over all (v. 6). Also, the king recognized the Lord's covenantal relationship to Israel, noting that He is the **God of our fathers** (v. 6a), the **friend** of **Abraham** (v. 7), and the One who promised the land, driving out the Canaanites to **give it to the descendants of Abraham . . . forever** (v. 7). Jehoshaphat then recalled the faithfulness of the nation to live to the Lord in this land—evidenced by the construction of **a sanctuary** (the temple) **for Your name** (v. 8). Next, Jehoshaphat recalled Solomon's prayer (at the dedication of the temple, cf. 2Ch 6:20, 28-31), asking for deliverance from **our distress** (v. 9). All of this was intended to say to the Lord, "You have the power, You made the promise, Your name is our concern"—**Your name is in this house** (v. 9)—the temple. In short, Jehoshaphat's main concern was the name—the reputation and honor—of the Lord. The invaders needed to be repelled for God to keep His promises and to uphold His **name** among the nations.

Accordingly, Jehoshaphat prayed specifically about this threat from **the sons of Ammon and Moab and Mount Seir** (v. 10a). These nations had been spared at the time of the conquest (v. 10b;

cf. Nm 20:14-21) but were now seeking to thwart God's intention to give Israel this land as **an inheritance** (v. 11). For this act of ingratitude and attempt to thwart God's purposes, Jehoshaphat implored the Lord, **will You not judge them?** (v. 12a). The king further acknowledged His nation's inability and cast himself and his whole kingdom at the mercy of the Lord—**our eyes are on You** (v. 12b). The poignant note in v. 13 that **all Judah**—men, women, and children—stood **before the Lord**, captured the sense of faith and hope of the nation as a whole in this time of distress. The point was clear: "We are powerless—so You, Lord, must fight for us." No doubt such a prayer echoed the faith and feelings of the Chronicler's generation as well.

20:14-17. The nation's faith and hope were rewarded with a word from the Lord through **Jahaziel** (v. 14b) who was a Levite (v. 14c). In true prophetic fashion, **the Spirit of the Lord came on Jahaziel** (v. 14a), and he spoke the actual words of the Lord (v. 15a). In one of the great clarion calls to faith, the Lord told His people, (1) **Listen** to Me (v. 15b); (2) **Do not fear** them (v. 15c), because (3) **the battle is not yours** (v. 15d) **but God's**. They could be sure that in spite of their weakness, they were strong (cf. 2Co 12:10) because the Lord intended to fight for them. The people were instructed to place themselves where they could observe the battle (2Ch 20:16, 17b), but it was reiterated that they were not to fight (v. 17a). They were given the supreme promise of security and victory—**for the Lord is with you** (v. 17c). The Chronicler no doubt wanted the reader to see this as another of the great instances of the Lord's promise to defend and preserve the nation (cf. Ex 14:13-14; Dt 20:4; 1Sm 17:37)—this was a promise the Chronicler's generation needed to hear and to trust.

20:18-19. The response to the Word of the Lord was, appropriately, humble worship (v. 18) and vociferous praise (v. 19).

c. A Stunning Victory and Triumph (20:20-30)

20:20-23. The king and the people prepared for the battle itself in several steps. First, they obeyed the Word of the Lord (they **went out to** the designated location, v. 20a). Second, Jehoshaphat again encouraged them to put their **trust in the Lord your God** and in His prophets (His Word to them) (v. 20b). Finally, they appointed "song and praise leaders" for the people and the army (v. 21). Apparently, these were the official singers (1Ch 25) and were to wear their **holy attire** (2Ch 20:21b; cf. 1Ch 16:29). This battle strategy was similar in intent, if not in form, to that of Gideon (Jdg 7), for the singers were to lead the army in a chorus of thanksgiving to the Lord (2Ch 20:21c)!

Once the singers had begun (v. 22a) confusion in the enemy forces was created, and they began to fight among themselves. Apparently, certain forces of the enemy had been positioned (intentionally by the enemy, providentially by the Lord; v. 22b) to ambush the army of Israel. However these forces were set upon by other enemy forces so that they **rose up against** each other (v. 23a) and they **helped to destroy one another** (v. 23b).

20:24-30. By the time Jehoshaphat and the army arrived on the scene, the destruction of the enemy was so complete (v. 24) that all he and the people had to do was pick up the spoils (v. 25). Days later they returned from the scene of destruction (now called **The Valley of Beracah**, v. 26, "blessing") to Jerusalem with joy and appropriately rejoiced in the temple (v. 28), for the Lord had given them victory. The news of this victory (as with others in the nation's history) spread to the surrounding nations and ushered in a time of peace (v. 30). The Chronicler was careful to emphasize that the nations knew that **the Lord had fought against the enemies of Israel** (v. 29b) and it was God who gave the king rest **on all sides** (v. 30). In contrast to the failed alliance with Ahab, Jehoshaphat had learned that absolute trust in the Lord was well placed and that only the Lord can bring the peace, prosperity, and security that the nation sought. This was a lesson the Chronicler's generation and all generations of God's people needed to know.

6. Jehoshaphat's Sad Ending (20:31-37)

20:31-37. The Chronicler finished his record of Jehoshaphat's reign with the typical concluding formula (vv. 31-33) and an atypical additional paragraph (vv. 35-37). In the latter the Chronicler recorded the sad fact that Jehoshaphat made yet another unwise alliance, this time with Ahaziah, the king of Israel. Jehoshaphat made an unwise economic alliance involving trade ships **to Tarshish** (v. 36), and the Lord sent the prophet **Eliezer** to tell him that the Lord had determined to thwart the enterprise. As a result, **the ships were broken** (v. 37) and the alliance came to nothing. The Chronicler was informing his readers that sometimes God thwarts the plans of men for His purposes—and that those purposes are ultimately gracious.

The record of Jehoshaphat's end was, therefore, mixed. He is credited with walking **in the way of his father Asa** (no doubt, thinking of the positive elements of Asa's reign) (v. 32). Yet, he did not undertake the reforms sufficiently to direct the hearts of the people completely back to **the God of their fathers** (v. 33b). His 25-year reign included some of the highest points of faith in the Lord and lowest points of failure to trust in the Lord.

E. Three Who Were "Bad" (Jehoram, Ahaziah, Athaliah) (21:1–23:15)

1. Jehoram Succeeded Jehoshaphat (21:1-3)

21:1-3. Upon the death of Jehoshaphat his son Jehoram became sole king in Judah (v. 1b, 3b). Before he died Jehoshaphat had made arrangements to secure his firstborn son's kingdom by the wise and judicial distribution of his wealth and power among his other sons. He gave Jehoram's brothers (v. 2) jurisdiction over the **fortified cites** (v. 3b) and the wealth necessary to administer them (v. 3a). The **fortified cities** were the border cities and settlements that provided the first line of defense of the kingdom. Having one's own brothers as the "border guards" should have been a source of security for Jehoram.

2. Jehoram's Evil and the Lord's Faithfulness (21:4-7)

21:4-6. Instead of building on the security left to him by his godly father, Jehoram committed several acts of evil. First, he slaughtered his brothers (v. 4) apparently in a foolish and wicked attempt to secure his throne from all potential rivals. Second, his eight-year reign (v. 5) was patterned, not after that of his godly father Jehoshaphat, but, generally **in the way of the kings of Israel** (v. 6) and specifically after his wicked father-in-law, Ahab. Here, the disaster of Jehoshaphat's alliance with Ahab (cf. 18:1) was brought home with terrible force. Years of wicked rule followed, and the nation suffered long after Jehoshaphat had passed from the scene. This lesson would not be lost on the Chronicler's generation, as it had suffered much for the sin and ungodliness of their national forbearers. Furthermore, Jehoram, in the pattern of the kings of the northern tribes, was the first king of Judah to actually establish places of idolatry (20:11). Finally, Jehoram's reign was characterized by the sweeping and devastating statement **he did evil in the sight of the LORD** (v. 6).

21:7. Nevertheless, the Chronicler was quick to add that in spite of this particular king's wickedness, the Lord remained faithful to His promise to David (v. 7). The Davidic covenant had its inviolability as a key provision. God would keep His promises to David and the nation even if a king sinned. However, a wicked king or a faithless generation might be denied the blessings and privileges of that covenant. There is blessing for obedience and humble godliness—there is chastisement for disobedience and prideful wickedness. Jehoram was a classic example of the latter.

3. Jehoram's Punishment (21:8-19a)

a. The Revolts of Edom and Libnah (21:8-11)

21:8-11. The revolts of Edom and Libnah (vv. 8, 10b; Libnah was a "semi-Philistine city . . . in the vicinity of Gath" [Payne, "1 Chronicles," 506]) were directly attributed to Jehoram's having **forsaken the LORD God of his fathers** (v. 10c). Instead of the security from such revolts that he might have enjoyed had he enlisted his brothers in the fortified cities, Jehoram had to endure this sort of rebellion for the duration of his reign (cf. v. 10a). Even though he was able to fend off such revolts (v. 9) he failed to enjoy the security and prosperity of the Lord's promise to a Davidic king.

b. Letter from Elijah (21:12-15)

21:12-15. Normally a letter from the Lord's prophet would be cause for joy—for Jehoram it was a prelude to more chastisement. Elijah is not mentioned elsewhere in Chronicles. But this is not surprising since his ministry was to the northern kingdom. Contrary to the conclusion of some critics, it was not impossible for Elijah to write such a letter since he was still alive during Jehoram's reign (cf. 2Kg 1:17; see Payne, "2 Chronicles," 506). Also, since Jehoram acted like one of the kings of Israel, it should be expected that he would attract the attention of the greatest prophetic opponent of those kings.

Elijah's rebuke went right to the heart of Jehoram's wickedness: he had failed to pattern his life and reign after godly kings of Judah (Asa, Jehoshaphat, v. 12b), while he *did* follow **the way of the kings of Israel** (v. 13a) and **the house of Ahab** (v. 13b). His idolatry and fratricide were specifically condemned (v. 13). For these iniquities he and his kingdom were to suffer: the nation was to experience **great calamity** (v. 14b), and he was to suffer a debilitating disease in his **bowels** (v. 15).

c. Punishments of the Letter (21:16-19a)

21:16-19a. The great calamity predicted by Elijah came in the form of yet another attack from foreign powers—**the Philistines and the** southern **Arabs** (v. 16). Once again, Jehoram's killing of his brothers was shown to be a short sighted and disastrous policy because it left the fortified border cities exposed. Those nations invaded and carried away all of his possessions and most of his family (v. 17). The disease predicted by Elijah (likely some form of dysentery) also came upon Jehoram and (described by the Chronicler in particularly graphic terms) eventually took his life (vv. 18-19a).

4. Jehoram's End (21:19b-20)

21:19b-20. The Chronicler recorded Jehoram's end with intentional brevity, in effect serving as a commentary on his repugnance toward this king. Jehoram received none of the customary honors accorded a deceased king. At his funeral there was **no fire** (no honorary funeral fire) and no **regret** (v. 20b). Moreover, as a final indignity, although he was buried in Jerusalem, he was not interred in the royal cemetery (v. 20c). In effect, the Chronicler's conclusion was that Jehoram was not a legitimate (even if he was a legal) member of the Davidic line.

5. Reign of Ahaziah (22:1-9)

The reigns of both Ahaziah, Jehoram's only surviving son (v. 1; cf. 21:17b; "Jehoahaz" was another name for Ahaziah; cf. 1Ch 23:25), and Athaliah, Jehoram's wife (granddaughter of Omri [2Ch 22:2b], daughter of Ahab [21:6b], mother to Ahaziah [22:10]) were recorded to show the consequences of Jehoram's terrible reign, and even further as consequences of the disastrous alliance Jehoshaphat had made with Ahab (cf. 18:1). The Chronicler viewed them as aberrations of the Davidic line, lacking full legitimacy. Both of these monarchs were essentially usurpers from the house of Ahab (cf. 22:3, 4, 7, 8), and their reigns were characterized by the same wickedness and evil as that of Ahab (vv. 3, 4).

a. Ahaziah Is Made King (22:1-4)

22:1-4. Ahaziah began his reign as a young man, only 22 years old (v. 2) and with no one from his father's side of the family to counsel him (v. 1). With only those from his mother's side of the family remaining, they, including his mother, counseled him **to do wickedly** (v. 3b), that is, to reign after the way of the wicked Ahab.

b. Ahaziah's Alliance with Jehoram of Israel (22:5-6)

22:5-6. Following the counsel of his family from the north, Ahaziah made yet another disastrous alliance with the northern kingdom, this time with Jehoram ("Joram," vv. 5c, 7) of Israel (v. 5), not to be confused with Jehoram of Judah, Ahaziah's deceased father. With this alliance, like that of his grandfather Jehoshaphat, the kings undertook to battle the Arameans once again at Ramoth-gilead (v. 5; cf. 18:8). As before, the king of Israel (Joram/Jehoram) was severely wounded and the battle was (presumably) lost. Apparently Ahaziah had not gone to the battle, but he did go to visit and support his wounded and ailing uncle Jehoram (22:6), whose sister Athaliah was Ahaziah's mother (cf. 21:6; 22:2-3). This indicates that Ahaziah was lending Jehoram the support and aid of Judah. **Jezreel** was located "at the head of the Esdraelon Valley, where . . . Ahab's palace was located" (1Kg 21:1) (Payne, "1 Chronicles," 508).

c. Ahaziah's Destruction (22:7-9)

22:7-9. The information supplied by the Chronicler is abbreviated (cf. 2Kg 9; for the whole account and exploits of Jehu, king of the northern kingdom, see 1Kg 19:16, 17) but sufficient to make the point that Ahaziah should not have made this alliance or offered his aid to Jehoram. This was so because the Lord had determined to destroy Jehoram and then turn the kingdom over to Jehu (2Ch 22:7b; 2Kg 9:6, 7). In effect, Ahaziah had made himself and his court a target of the vengeful Jehu (2Ch 22:8). Apparently, Ahaziah escaped the first wave of executions but was eventually caught and slain by Jehu (v. 9a). The Chronicler's association of Ahaziah with Jehoshaphat (v. 9b) is surprising but was included to demonstrate that no king of Judah had followed the way of Jehoshaphat **who sought the Lord with all his heart** (v. 9c). As a result of Ahaziah's death, there was no one to reign in Judah (v. 9d). The foolishness of Jehoshaphat's earlier alliance with Israel and the wickedness of Jehoram had brought the nation to a serious crisis.

6. The Reign of Athaliah (22:10–23:15)

The crisis of Ahaziah's death led to one of the most troublesome eras in the nation's history and brought the only regnant queen of Judah to the throne. Athaliah's reign was one of the lowest points in the history of the Davidic line.

a. Athaliah's Bid for Power (22:10-12)

22:10-12. The appalling indifference of Athaliah at the news of her son's death was exceeded only by her shocking cruelty and lust for power. Upon Ahaziah's death Athaliah began a systematic campaign to eliminate the Davidic line (v. 10). In terms of the main narrative of the Chronicler the matter could not have been more serious. The line of David had been reduced to one child—Joash, the son of Ahaziah (v. 11a). If he were to be killed with the rest of the **royal offspring of the house of Judah** (v. 10) then the promise to David (1Ch 17:10-14) could not be fulfilled.

Remarkably, the heroine of the moment turned out to be a sister of Ahaziah, Jehoshabeath, who rescued her nephew Joash (v. 11). Thus, it was one courageous godly woman who thwarted the evil of one wicked woman. At her own personal risk, Jehoshabeath **stole** the infant Joash and hid him **in the bedroom** (v. 11)—most likely a room used for storing the bedding. The Chronicler carefully identified Jehoshabeath (**daughter of King Jehoram**, **sister of Ahaziah** and **wife of Jehoiada the priest** v. 11b) as the heroine. This mini-genealogy was included to subtly but emphatically note that while wickedness and evil dominated in these years, there were still some who were faithful to the Lord and trusted in His promises. Apparently, after some time, the godly couple, Jehoshabeath and her husband Jehoiada the priest, took Joash and hid him in the temple (**the house of God**) for the duration of the six-year reign of Athaliah (v. 12).

Once again the Chronicler had tied the promise made to David and the fortunes of his line to the temple. In fact, "the temple was the vital link in the preservation of the Davidic dynasty" (Sailhamer, *First and Second Chronicles*, 99). This connection was important to the Chronicler and his generation. The nation would be restored only by the remnant of the Davidic line and the restoration of the temple. Thus, "the focus of the hope of the fulfillment of God's promise to David was centered on the temple" (Sailhamer, *First and Second Chronicles*, 99). In short, as long as the temple "existed" then God's promise to David "could be fulfilled"—if the one institution (Davidic dynasty or temple) thrived, the other would as well. This was the hope of the Chronicler's generation: by rebuilding the temple they were anticipating the revival of the Davidic promises and making the coming of Messiah possible.

b. Plan to Overthrow Athaliah and Establish Joash as King (23:1-11)

23:1-3. The plan by Jehoiada to place Joash on the throne was not without danger and required careful planning and preparation. Jehoiada first enlisted (made a **covenant with**) the armed forces of Judah (v. 1), and then he **gathered** the religious leaders (**the Levites**, v. 2) **from all the cities of Judah**. Finally he enlisted the **heads of the fathers** (v. 2), carefully planning and calculating the order of these enlistments. The five **captains of hundreds** (v. 1) were officers of "the Carites" (2Kg 11:4; or "Cherethites") who in turn were associated with the Pelethites (2Sm 20:23), all of whom were "elements of the royal guard" (Payne, "1 Chronicles," 510). That Jehoiada could make these key alliances demonstrated that Athaliah had little popular support in the nation. An assembly of all the parties was called and a **covenant** was made **with the king**—Joash—in the temple (v. 3a). In a dramatic moment in the history of the nation, Jehoiada proclaimed, **Behold, the king's son shall reign**, and he invoked the promise **the Lord has spoken concerning the sons of David** (v. 3b; cf. 1Ch 17:1-14).

23:4-11. Still, the dramatic proclamation needed to be backed up with action. Jehoiada divided his forces strategically so as to prevent access to the temple and to protect the young king (vv. 4-7). He gave the defenders of the true king the weapons of King David (v. 9b) that had been stored in the temple, and they formed an impenetrable human mass, making access to the king impossible (vv. 8-10). Finally, surrounded by the imposing forces of the armed Levites, Joash was brought into public view and crowned king. He was **anointed** and received the traditional adulation, **Long live the king** (v. 11b). The drama of the historic event and the significance of the preservation of the Davidic line made this a coronation of unusual importance for the Chronicler. That is the reason he provided more details for this coronation than any other in his books.

c. Death of Athaliah (23:12-15)

23:12-15. The adulation and celebration of the people (v. 13c) inevitably came to the attention of Athaliah (v. 12a). However, Jehoiada's preparations were impeccable, and by the time she understood what was happening it was too late for her to prevent the ascension of Joash. Her futile (and ironically illegitimate) cry of **Treason!** (v. 13c) only served to identify her for her executioners (v. 14). Her ignominious death, like that of her mother (cf. 2Kg 9:33-37), served as a fitting reminder of the end of the wicked, and all who attempt to thwart God's purposes.

F. Three Who Were "Mixed": Joash, Amaziah, Uzziah (23:16–26:23)

The sad and distressing era of Jehoram that ended with the death of Athaliah inaugurated an era that fluctuated between promise and failure. Each one of the next three kings began well but ended poorly. Of Amaziah it was said, "He did right in the sight of the LORD, yet not with a whole heart" (25:2), demonstrating the danger of partial spiritual devotion.

1. Reign of Joash (23:16–24:27)

The reign of Joash began with one of the most dramatic and significant events in the history of the nation—his coronation and anointing ended an era of wickedness and portended an era of faithfulness. However, the promise offered at the beginning of his reign departed by the end of it.

a. Early Reforms of Joash by Jehoiada (23:16-21)

23:16-21. The reforms Jehoiada undertook in Joash's name followed immediately upon the death of Athaliah. The **covenant** inaugurated by Jehoiada amounted to a rededication of the people **that they would be the LORD's people** (v. 16b)—worthy to be called "His people" (cf. 1Ch 22:18c; 23:35; 2Ch 22:11; 31:10; Ps 29:11 et al.). This would entail forsaking idolatry (2Ch 23:17), even to the extent that **Mattan**, a priest of Baal, was killed (cf. Dt 13:5-10) and restoring temple worship to the pattern and **order** established by **David** (2Ch 23:18; "David" is mentioned specifically twice). As was typical in the Chronicler's narrative, temple reforms and restoration of the Davidic regnancy went hand in hand. Thus, as the reforms of the temple were put into place (v. 19), so the rightful Davidic king was placed **upon the royal throne** (v. 20). The end of the upheaval of the recent past and the revival initiated by Jehoiada's covenant with the people brought about a time of rejoicing and hope for the future that the people had not known for many years (v. 21a).

b. Reign of Joash Under the Influence of Jehoiada (24:1-16)

24:1-3. The 40-year reign of Joash (v. 1) began as one of the most promising but ultimately ended as one of the most disappointing in the nation's history. The change in Joash from the days when Jehoiada advised him to the days when he was advised by the officials of Judah (cf. v. 17) was dramatic and disastrous.

Joash began well and **did what was right in the sight of the LORD** (v. 2a). However, the Chronicler was quick to add that this was during **all the days of Jehoiada the priest** (v. 2b). This godly advisor even arranged Joash's marriages (v. 3).

24:4-7. Once again, a favorite theme of the Chronicler is taken up as the Davidic king took a particular interest in the temple. Even as the temple had protected Joash, so now he oversaw its restoration (v. 4). Apparently, the temple had suffered not merely neglect but also vandalism and plunder during the reign of the wicked Athaliah (v. 7). At first Joash began a capital campaign (v. 5), and it seems this first effort lasted several years (as the use of the term **annually** in v. 5b implies; cf. 2Kg 12:6 "in the twenty-third year of King Jehoash [Joash]"). The note that **the Levites did not act quickly** (2Ch 24:5c) was a mild rebuke, but it made the point clearly—in some fashion the involvement of the Levites had slowed the collection of the revenues. Joash asked Jehoiada to explain the reason the revenues had not been collected according to the **levy** (tax) of **Moses** (cf. Ex 30:12-16). While the Chronicler recorded no detailed explanation, it seems apparent that the regular and prescribed revenues simply were not being collected efficiently.

24:8-14. Rather than accept this circumstance, Joash embarked upon a unique method of raising the necessary funds to restore the temple. Instead of depending on the priests and Levites to collect the revenues, Joash placed a large chest with an opening in the lid (cf. 2Kg 12:9) just outside the main gate of the temple (2 Ch 24:8). He instructed the officials and **all the people** (vv. 9-10) to place the Mosaic levies in this chest. When it was sufficiently full, this chest would be brought to the king, the monies collected, and the chest returned to its spot (v. 11). Apparently, this arrangement worked well, and soon the king hired the skilled workers and craftsmen needed to **repair the house of the LORD (God)** (vv. 12-14, the phrase "house of the LORD/God" appears six times in these three verses).

This scene would have appealed to the Chronicler as he sought to encourage his own generation to a similar respect and concern for the temple. The workers' efficient progress (v. 13a) contrasted with the Levites' inefficiency and resulted in the restoration of the temple (**house of God**) **according to its specifications** (v. 13b), meaning, according to its original design and purpose (cf. 1Ch 28:11ff.). Joash's fund-raising method was so successful that there were sufficient funds left over to restore the utensils for the temple service (2Ch 24:14a). The note concerning the **burnt offerings** (v. 14c) marked the high point of Joash's reign and was a warning to the Chronicler's generation—the revival of the temple service should not be taken for granted.

24:15-16. How soon Jehoiada died after the temple's restoration was not indicated but two facts related to his death were noted: first, Jehoiada lived a long life—**he was one hundred and thirty years old at his death** (v. 15). Such length of years at this point in history was unusual but not impossible (cf. Payne, "2 Chronicles," 4:514-15) and was recorded to emphasize the Lord's favor on such a significant figure. Second, he was buried in the royal cemetery—an unusual privilege for a priest but again, indicative of his importance and of the Lord's favor on him **because he had done well in Israel and to God and His house** (v. 16). This was in marked contrast to Joash's own fate (cf. v. 25c).

c. Reign of Joash after the Death of Jehoiada (24:17-22)

Few people in that day would have imagined that the death of Jehoiada could have precipitated the disastrous events that followed. It would have been predictable to assume that his years of influence on Joash would have carried the young king through many years of a godly and successful reign. Sadly, such was not the case. The Chronicler recorded the end of Joash's reign with a sharp brevity that conveyed a note of disappointment and a warning, reminding of the danger of secondhand faith.

24:17-18. Reminiscent of Rehoboam's foolishness (listening to foolish advice, cf. 10:6ff.), Joash **listened** (v. 17, in the sense of took their advice favorably) to those advising him to reinstitute idolatry. The Chronicler provided no details about this sad turn of events, only that they **abandoned the house of the LORD** and turned to **the Asherim** (Canaanite female fertility goddesses) **and the idols** (v. 18a). This brought swift and terrible consequences—the **wrath** of the Lord (v. 18b).

24:19-22. The pattern—apostasy followed by an appeal from the Lord's prophets—was well known to the Chronicler's readers, and the outcome was predictable. The prophets advised repentance, but **they** (the king and his advisors) **would not listen** (v. 19b). The lesson to the Chronicler's generation was "take care to whom you *listen*."

One of the prophets sent to the king and the nation was **Zechariah the son of Jehoiada the priest** (v. 20); "clothed" with the **Spirit of God** (v. 20a) Zechariah's message was in the form of a rhetorical question: **Why do you transgress the commandments** (v. 20b)? The simple incoherence of the act of idolatry was the point of this question—"What does idolatry do for you?" It actually caused the nation to **not prosper** (v. 20c) and their forsaking of the Lord led to His forsaking of them (20:20d; on "forsaking the Lord" see Introduction: Purpose and Themes in 1 Chronicles). However, like another generation of Israel, who heard the preaching of another Zechariah (son of Berechiah) they refused to *listen* (Zch 7:11, 13). In a shocking act of retaliation, the people **conspired against** (2 Ch 24:21a) the prophet of God. Then, with the complicity of Joash himself (against the prophet Zechariah, the son of his former, faithful mentor, Jehoiada) **they stoned him** (Zechariah) **to death** (v. 21b). To add to the repugnance of the act, it was accomplished **in the court of the house of the LORD** (v. 21c) adding desecration (of the same temple he had done so much to restore) to Joash's act of betrayal. To make sure that the reader did not miss the heinousness of Joash's duplicity toward Jehoiada, the Chronicler added the shocking conclusion—**but he murdered his son** (v. 22a).

Zechariah's final prayer—**May the LORD see and avenge** (v. 22b) was not one of forgiveness (cf. Stephen Ac 7:60; cf. Lk 23:34) but of vengeance. However, he was not seeking personal revenge—it was an imprecatory prayer asking for justice, not for himself, but from the Lord for His prophet (cf. Dt 32:35; Ps 94:1; Rm 12:19). Jesus' mention of "the blood of Abel to the blood of Zechariah" (Mt 23:35) has often been understood to refer to the murder of Zechariah, indicating guilt from the beginning of the Bible (Genesis, wherein Abel's murder is recorded) to the end (2 Chronicles, the last book of the Hebrew canon wherein Zechariah's murder was recorded). Yet there is a difficulty because Jesus called Zechariah "the son of Berechiah," and 2 Chronicles identifies him as "the son of Jehoida." Possible explanations for this discrepancy are: (1) perhaps Zechariah was the son of a Berechiah who was unmentioned and Jehoida was actually his grandfather; (2) perhaps a NT copyist confused Jesus' reference with the more famous prophet who was the son of Berechiah (see Zch 1:1) and mistakenly changed the text, so it was transmitted incorrectly; (3) perhaps Jesus was not referring to this incident in 2 Chronicles at all but referring to the prophet Zechariah, whose execution was not recorded in Scripture (Payne, "2 Chronicles," 515).

d. The Lord's Judgment upon Joash: Defeat and Disease (24:23-27)

24:23-24. Once again the Lord's judgment took the form of an invasion from Israel's enemies—here the Arameans (v. 23). **Now it happened** is a subtle way of saying "It did not just happen" but that the Lord was acting and was, in fact, exhibiting His wrath (cf. v. 18b). The Chronicler noted specifically that this calamity befell those who were the instigators of the idolatry—**all the officials of the people** (v. 23a) and that the calamity was devastating (v. 23b). The notice that the Arameans had the inferior force compared to Israel's **very great army** (v. 24a) indicates that this was not merely a defeat by a determined enemy but a judgment because **they had forsaken the Lord** (v. 24b). Once again the principle is illustrated—seeking the Lord brings blessing, while forsaking the Lord brings judgment (v. 24c).

24:25-27. The judgment was not limited to a national calamity. It also brought personal tragedy to Joash. Apparently, Joash was **very sick** (ESV "wounded;" the word can refer to the consequences of being injured in battle; cf. 2Kg 8:29) and confined to his bed after this defeat. This gave opportunity for those who resented his part in Zechariah's death to exact their revenge (2Ch 24:25). Since Joash had "conspired" against Zechariah, so **his own servants conspired against him** (v. 25a) and they **murdered him**. The naming of the servants indicates that they did not attempt to hide their involvement in the crime and they may have considered it a just act of retribution (v. 26). The final indignity for Joash was that he was not buried in the royal cemetery (v. 25b), an indication (in contrast to Asa, cf. 16:13-14) that the ungodliness of his latter reign overshadowed the good that he had done during the days of Jehoiada (v. 27).

2. The Reign of Amaziah (25:1-28)

The reign of Amaziah is well summarized: "He did right in the sight of the Lord, yet not with a whole heart" (25:2). The term "whole" (*salem*) means "complete, perfect, sound." To have a whole heart would mean (among other things) a "steadfast heart" (cf. Ps 57:7), an "upright heart" (cf. Ps 97:11), an "obedient heart" (cf. Ps 119:112), and a "devoted-to-God" heart (cf. Ps 9:1; 119:10, 69, 145). In effect, much of Amaziah's reign was a mixture of listening to, and submitting to the Word of God (the law, 2Ch 25:4a, or the word of a prophet, 25:7ff.) but also of rash decisions and self-serving pride.

"The date of Amaziah's reign is a seemingly intractable problem." (Selman, *2 Chronicles*, 459) In brief, the reference to his reign of twenty-nine years (v. 1; 2Kg 14:2) cannot be easily reconciled with the numbers from 2Kg 15:1, that is his 29-year reign added to the 52-year reign of his son Uzziah yields too many years when compared to the (northern kingdom) reigns of Jeroboam II (2Kg 14:23) and his son Zechariah (2Kg 15:8). "Jeroboam had a reign of forty-one years (2Kg 14:23), so his death occurred fourteen years after the death of Amaziah in Jeroboam's twenty-seventh year; however, when Zechariah succeeded Jeroboam II, Uzziah was already in his thirty-eighth year of reign" (Dillard, *2 Chronicles*, 198). The solution seems to be that Amaziah reigned only five years before Uzziah became his coregent (cf. Thiele, *The Mysterious Numbers of the Hebrew Kings*, 63–64). This long coregency may have been caused by the capture of Amaziah by Jehoash (2Ch 25:23). That would further indicate that the two wars of Amaziah occurred in the first five years of his reign.

a. Amaziah's Reign Began with an Act of Reprisal (25:1-4)

25:1-4. One of Amaziah's first acts was to exact vengeance (or justice depending on one's perspective) on those who had murdered his father Joash (v. 3). The Chronicler notes, however, that Amaziah did not kill the offender's families (as would have been customary in such cases at the time). This clemency was a result of Amaziah's observance of the **law in the book of Moses** (v. 4a) that the offender alone, not the father or the son of the offender, **shall be put to death for his own sin** (v. 4b; Dt 24:16). "God's mercy to thousands far exceeds his judgment to the third and fourth generations; cf. Ex. 20:5-6." (Selman, *2 Chronicles*, 459).

b. Amaziah's Battle with the Sons of Seir (Edom) (25:5-13)

25:5-8. Next, Amaziah began military preparations with intention to do battle with the sons of Seir (Edom) (cf. 25:11). A census of the able-bodied men in his kingdom revealed that Amaziah's forces were seriously depleted (**300,000**) from those in the days of Jehoshaphat (nearly 1.2 million, v. 5; cf. 17:14-19) and so, at great expense, he hired mercenaries from the northern kingdom of Israel (v. 6). This act was not acceptable to the Lord (**for the Lord is not with Israel**), so a **man of God** (v. 7), a prophet, brought a message to Amaziah to urge him to reconsider this action. Verse 8 appears confusing (probably because modern readers are not prepared for how the Lord's prophets use sarcasm). In effect the prophet was telling Amaziah that if he chose to go to battle with these mercenaries he should be prepared to **be strong for the battle** on his own because the Lord was not going to be helping him—in fact, he is told **God will bring you down before the enemy** (v. 8b)—he would loose the battle! The phrase **for God has power to help and to bring down** (v. 8c) means He, the Lord makes the winners win, and the losers lose. In short, if he wanted to win this battle Amaziah needed to send the mercenaries away.

25:9-10. Amaziah was apparently open to this, but he was concerned that the money already paid for the mercenaries would be lost (v. 9a). The man of God dismissed such concerns by reminding the king that the resources of the Lord were not limited to such pecuniary matters (v. 9b)—he was to cut his losses and dismiss these mercenaries. So Amaziah dismissed his hired troops, much to their displeasure (v. 10). Here again, the estimate of Amaziah is mixed as he readily turned away from his rash act of hiring mercenaries. However, the ill will this action created with the troops from the north had a devastating effect: even as Amaziah was engaged in fighting the Edomites in the south, these troops raided and despoiled the cities of Judah in the northern parts of Judah (v. 13). **Beth-horon** was a settlement about a dozen miles northwest of Jerusalem in the Valley of Aijalon and lay along one of the few good routes through the hill country between the north and south—it should have been protected. Amaziah may have avoided an outright defeat but his initial rash action of hiring the mercenaries still brought about calamitous results.

25:11-13. Thus reassured by the man of God, Amaziah went on the offensive and met the enemy in **the Valley of Salt** (v. 11), near the southern end of the Dead Sea. The defeat of the Edomites was complete with **10,000** of them killed in battle and another **10,000 captured** and executed (v. 12). The purpose of such a gruesome spectacle was to inflict a psychological wound on the minds of the Edomites to discourage any thought of retaliation.

c. Amaziah's Idolatry (25:14-16)

25:14. After defeating the Edomites, Amaziah, in a further rash act, retrieved their idols and **set them up as his gods** and **bowed down to them** (v. 14). "This is the only explicit reference to Edomite worship in the Bible." (Selman, *2 Chronicles*, 461) While it may seem to be a counterintuitive act (worship of the gods who could not bring victory to the devotees who had been worshipping them seems rather irrational), such practice was not unknown in the ancient Near East. When a nation suffered a defeat it was often taken as a sign of the displeasure of the gods with the devotion (or lack of it) by the nation. "Amaziah's action may" have been "intended to placate the presumed anger of the Edomite gods." (Selman, *2 Chronicles*, 461) Still such blatant idolatry was stunning. While it was not unheard of to take the idols of a defeated foe as plunder, it was rash and foolish to actually set them up as objects of worship (see Is 44:9-20 on the folly of idolatry).

25:15-16. The Lord's reaction was swift and severe: **Then the anger of the Lord burned against Amaziah** (v. 15a). At once a prophet was dispatched to confront the foolish king (v. 15b). The unnamed prophet's words were rightly ironic and their logic, perfect. In effect, he asked the king, "Why would you want to worship the gods of the people you just defeated? If those gods did not protect them from you, what promise do they have for protecting you?" (v. 15c). The prophet's sarcasm must have stung Amaziah, and in the middle of his rebuke to the king, Amaziah questioned the prophet's standing, shouted **Stop!** (v. 16b), and threatened the prophet (v. 16c). The disrespect shown to this prophet revealed Amaziah's heart (cf. v. 2b), and the prophet, in a terse and chilling statement, predicted the destruction of the king (v. 16d). Once again the Chronicler's theme is clear: those kings who heed the Word of God are blessed, those who do not are punished. The king may have stopped God's prophet, but he could not stop God's judgment—yet he did not listen (v. 16d; cf. v. 19).

d. Amaziah Defeated by Joash of Israel (25:17-24)

25:17-19. The exact nature of the message from Amaziah, king of Judah, to Joash, king of Israel, is unclear. It may have been a direct invitation to battle, or it may have been a (rather brash) method of diplomacy (v. 17). In either case, Joash took it as an affront and responded with a colorful but cutting "parable" (v. 18). Israel was compared to a mighty cedar tree, and Judah was compared to an insignificant thorn bush—the demands of the thorn bush were being ignored by the cedar when a **wild beast** came along and ignominiously trampled the bush. To make his meaning clear, Joash admonished Amaziah and said, in effect, "Just because you defeated Edom, you should not let your pride lead you to **boasting** and into trouble that will lead to your fall. You should **stay at home** and forget about conquests and battles" (v. 19).

25:20-24. The Chronicler made clear that Amaziah's decision to ignore Joash's sarcastic advice **was from God** (v. 20a) because the Lord had determined to use Joash to punish Amaziah for the latter's idolatry (v. 20b). The description of the battle indicates that it was brief but decisive (vv. 21-22)—Amaziah was captured (v. 23a) at Beth-shemesh "fifteen miles west of Bethlehem, on Amaziah's own picked ground" (Payne, "2 Chronicles," 519). Thus Jerusalem was deprived of her defenses (v. 23b), and much of the temple's treasure was looted (v. 24; **Obed-edom** was the name of the Levitical family [cf. 1 Ch 13:13-14; 26:4] of gatekeepers and musicians). "The raid on the temple must be seen as a punishment against idolaters in line with the principles of 2 Chronicles 7:19-22." (Selman, *2 Chronicles*, 464). Here again, the fortunes of the temple were tied to the fortunes of the king—and a bad king meant bad things happened to the temple.

e. Amaziah's End (25:25-28)

25:25-28. Joash's defeat of Amaziah left the southern kingdom defeated and depleted. Because of Amaziah's infidelity to the Lord, he was an unpopular king, and eventually conspirators turned against him and killed him (v. 27). While he was accorded burial **with his fathers in the city of Judah** (v. 28) his legacy was that of the rash and prideful (cf. Pr 16:18).

3. The Reign of Uzziah (26:1-23)

The Chronicler provided the bulk of the historical information on King Uzziah (cf. 2Kg 15:1-7, called there Azariah). Pride seems to have been a family trait for Uzziah, the son of Amaziah, who followed in his fathers' footsteps. At the outset, however, Uzziah showed great promise, and overall he fared better in the Chronicler's estimation (as compared to the account in Kings). Still, he followed the pattern of his two predecessors—he began well, but finished poorly.

a. Uzziah's Faithfulness (26:1-5)

26:1-5. Uzziah's long reign of 52 years (v. 3) began with great promise when he was **sixteen years old** (vv. 1, 3a). After noting a minor rebuilding project (v. 2; **Eloth**, or Elath, was a city on the eastern border of Judah), the Chronicler made an emphatic statement: **He did right in the sight of the LORD** (v. 4a), and he followed the good **that his father Amaziah had done** (v. 4b). As an exemplary Davidic king he **continued to seek God** (v. 5a; see Introduction: Purpose and Themes in 1 Chronicles) and followed (yet another prophet named) **Zechariah**, whose **understanding** of the Lord and His ways had come **through the vision of God** (v. 5b; the identity of this Zechariah is unknown). Much as Jehoiada had done for Joash, this prophet acted as mentor and guide. A theme of the Chronicler summarizes this part of Uzziah's reign: **as long as he sought the LORD, God prospered him** (v. 5c).

b. Uzziah's Successes (26:6-15)

26:6-15. The evidence of the Lord's prospering came early and often in Uzziah's reign. The lists of nations Uzziah defeated (vv. 6-7; the **Philistines**, the **Arabians**, the **Meunites**; for the Meunites, cf. the comments on 20:1; the location of **Gur-baal** is uncertain, possibly southern Edom), that brought him tribute (v. 8a; the **Ammonites**), and that knew his fame (v. 8b; **Egypt**), indicated the prosperity and power he achieved. His refortification of Jerusalem (vv. 9-10a) after the shame of Amaziah's defeat (cf. 25:23; he restored the **Corner Gate** that Joash had destroyed) and his refurbishing of the **army** (vv. 11-15b) testified to his strength and would have given the nation a solid sense of security. The note concerning the **engines of war** (v. 15a) indicates that Uzziah employed the most technologically advanced military of the day (cf. Payne, "2 Chronicles," 522)—perhaps a form of ancient trebuchets or catapults—the "heavy artillery" of the day. The Chronicler even included a brief note concerning his agricultural pursuits (v. 10) and gave a fleeting insight into the character of the king in the note that **he loved the soil** (v. 10b). This king was, literally, a down-to-earth man. In a unique and memorable summary of this period the Chronicler noted that because of all this success **his fame spread afar, for he was marvelously helped until he was strong** (v. 15b).

c. Uzziah's Pride and Fall (26:16-21)

The sweep of the summary of Uzziah's reign in the account so far, covering years and years of successes and repeated instances of the Lord's gracious gift of prosperity to the nation, is in stark contrast to the following account of a single event that brought the end of the reign of this otherwise good king. Many years of blessing and prosperity were overshadowed by one act of vanity and pride. It was a lesson to all of the Chronicler's readers that obedience and faithfulness must be constant and that one act of faithlessness can undermine a lifetime of service.

26:16-18. The opening words of this section indicate a disheartening turn of events: **But when he become strong, his heart was so proud** (v. 16a). The Chronicler first characterized the offense—**he acted corruptly, and he was unfaithful to the LORD his God** (v. 16b); and then described it—**for he entered the temple of the LORD to burn incense** (v. 16c). This was an act exclusively reserved for the priests (cf. Ex 30:1-10; Nm 18:1-7), and Uzziah would have been well aware of that restriction. The Lord considered breaches of the priestly function in matters related to tabernacle or temple worship as extremely serious (cf. Lv 10:1-3; Nm 16:1-40; 1Ch 13:9-10). In addition, for a Davidic king to violate the temple was to betray his greatest calling—to protect and uphold the temple and its institutions. Uzziah placed himself in great danger. **Azariah** the priest and the **eighty** brave **priests** (**valiant men**) with him were not only defending the integrity of the temple, but also were showing great concern for the king (2Ch 26:17-18a). The Chronicler recorded Azariah's rebuke to impress the reader with the specifics and seriousness of this violation (v. 18b). Azariah reinforced the character of the offense—Uzziah was being **unfaithful** to his calling as Davidic king and would **have no honor from the LORD God** (v. 18c).

26:19-21. The scene depicted was dynamic. The confrontation of the willful king with the concerned priests grew increasingly tense as the king began to add defensive anger to his willfulness and pride (v. 19a). To their horror the priests observed the judgment of the Lord befall Uzziah as **leprosy broke out on his forehead** (v. 19), right in front of them. "The disease [was] not leprosy as it is known today, but a general term for all kinds of skin diseases." (Selman, *2 Chronicles*, 471) The shock of this brought an immediate halt to the confrontation, and the king beat a hasty retreat out of the temple (v. 20). In a note of sad irony, this king who wanted to act the part of a priest was forever **cut off from the house of the LORD** (v. 21b), never allowed again even to worship there, because, as leper, he was confined to **a separate house** (v. 21a; Lv 13:46). The rest of his reign was accomplished through **his son**, while he remained in isolation (2Ch 26:21c).

d. Uzziah's End (26:22-23)

26:22-23. The Chronicler noted that the great **Isaiah, the son of Amoz** (v. 22) was one of his principle sources for the account of Uzziah. Uzziah's death was the occasion of the famous vision in Is 6. While accorded some dignity for his royal personage, Uzziah was nevertheless buried in a location near (**the field of the grave which belonged to the kings**, v. 23b), but not actually with the other kings, this on account of his leprosy (v. 23c). Sadly, in spite of his years of prosperous rule in Judah, the main feature of Uzziah's life, remembered for generations, was his one act of pride—an attitude contrasted with that of his biographer and mourner, Isaiah, who in the presence of the Lord cried, "Woe is me, I am ruined" (cf. Is 6:5).

G. Six Kings Alternate between "Good" and "Bad" (27:1–35:27)

As has been noted, a main theme of the Chronicler is that the when the Davidic king "seeks the Lord" there is blessing and prosperity—enjoyment of the blessings of the covenant promises. But when the king "forsakes the Lord" there is loss of blessing and chastisement for both the nation and the king. This theme is once again in focus in the accounts of the next six kings. The vacillation between "good kings" and "bad kings" was not merely a historical reality. It also provided the Chronicler the opportunity to drive the lesson home: faithfulness and obedience bring the blessing of the Lord, and disobedience brings His displeasure and loss of blessing.

The ultimate loss of blessing was the Babylonian captivity—the loss of enjoying the land itself. In these accounts the Chronicler began to foreshadow (what his generation knew all too well was) that inevitable reality. What if even the best Davidic king did not lead to the final and full promise of the Davidic covenant? What could the nation expect? The Chronicler's generation knew the answer to that question. However, the Chronicler wanted his readers to look *through* this history and their own experience—beyond the history of the past and the history they were living—to an ultimate fulfillment, to a Davidic son who would fully and finally bring to fruition those blessings of the Davidic covenant. As the kings of Judah came and went, some shone brightly (Hezekiah) while others were dreadful disappointments (Manasseh). Nevertheless, the historical process, the shifting and sifting of these kings is not without a point—each, in his own way, good or bad, helped to define the ultimate Davidic king so that when He arrives, the nation will know Him, and appreciate His achievement.

1. Good: Jotham (27:1-9)

27:1-2. Jotham's relatively brief reign was a relatively good reign. The Chronicler noted that **He did right in the sight of the LORD** (v. 2a) in that he followed the godly ways of his father Uzziah. In addition, he did not act unfaithfully—**he did not enter the temple of the LORD** (v. 2b) in disobedience as Uzziah had done (cf. 26:16b). However, the Chronicler also noted that **the people continued acting corruptly** (v. 2c). The corrosive influence of idolatry that had afflicted the nation during the reigns of Joash and Amaziah had not been overcome even during the long reign of Uzziah. Such are the pervasive and lasting effects of ungodliness and evil upon a nation. The Chronicler's generation was being warned, "Do not let the evil of idolatry take root again."

27:3-5. Jotham's reign was notable in two areas. First, he engaged in some important building projects. As a true Davidic king he took an interest in the temple—he worked on **the upper** (northern) **gate** (v. 3a) and he **built extensively**—that is, refurbished and extended—**the wall of Ophel** (v. 3b) on the southern side of the temple area, near the City of David. He also solidified the nation's security by building (fortress or outpost) **cities in the hill country of Judah** (v. 4a) as well as defensive structures—**fortresses and towers on the wooded hills** (v. 4b). Second, Jotham was engaged in a battle with the Ammonites, and **he prevailed over them** (v. 5a), yielding considerable tribute in silver and produce (v. 5b).

27:6-9. The short summary of Jotham's life—he **became mighty because he ordered his ways before the LORD his God** (v. 6) spoke well of the king personally. However, no revival happened in his reign. In keeping with his positive outlook and concern for the prosperity of the Davidic dynasty "The kings that interest the chronicler are those who bring revival" (Sailhamer, *First and Second Chronicles*, 104). Jotham was a good king but, because of his lack of positive spiritual influence, his reign fell short of the ideal for a Davidic king.

2. Bad: Ahaz (28:1-27)

The good king Jotham was followed by Ahaz, "one of the weakest and most corrupt of all the twenty rulers in Judah" (Payne, "2 Chronicles," 4:525).

a. Ahaz's Evil Exposed (28:1-4)

28:1-4. If Jotham fell short of the ideal for a Davidic king, Ahaz was David's complete opposite. For this reason the Chronicler reaches back to David himself when he gives the overall estimate of Ahaz—**he did not do right in the sight of the LORD as David his father** (v. 1b). Ahaz was the king for much of the time of the great prophet Isaiah (cf. Is 1:1; the same king to whom the prophecy of the virgin birth was delivered, cf. Is 7:14). Ahaz also reigned during the prophetic ministries of Hosea (Hs 1:1) and Micah (Mc 1:1). The Chronicler's treatment of this king was direct—he got right to the point of Ahaz' wickedness. "Chronicles has made Kings' (2 Kings 16) descriptions of Ahaz' failings much more explicit" (Selman, *2 Chronicles*, 476). Ahaz was, in fact, more like the kings of the northern kingdom of Israel than like the kings of Judah (2Ch 28:2a). He blatantly engaged in Baal worship (v. 2b; Baal was the name of the most prominent of the Canaanite gods), which often included "fertility rites," i.e. sexual acts, Jr 7:31; 19:4-6). Ahaz also participated in idolatrous worship **in the valley of Ben-hinnom** (2Ch 28:3a)—a place of noted pagan worship and later the site of Jerusalem's waste disposal site (cf. 2Kg 23:10. Thus it was a place of perpetual fires and ultimately a picture of hell itself, cf. the comments on Mk 9:43). Ahaz even joined in the utterly grotesque practice of child sacrifice—he **burned his sons in fire** (2Ch 28:3b; 2Kg 16:3). This unfathomably horrible practice was typical of the Canaanites who had been driven out of the land many years earlier (2Ch 28:3b) and was expressly forbidden in the law (cf. Lv 20:1-5). Finally, the extent of Ahaz' idolatry was noted in that he **sacrificed and burned incense . . . under every green tree** (2Ch 28:4).

b. Ahaz Defeated in Battle (28:5-7)

28:5-7. The Chronicler noted that Ahaz was defeated by the **king of Aram** (Syria; v. 5a) and by the **king of Israel** Pekah (v. 6a; cf. 2 Kg 16:5) without even giving any notice that there was conflict between Judah and these nations. This was clearly the Lord's retribution on Ahaz, delivering **him into the hand** (2Ch 28:5a, 6a) of the enemy. The nation suffered **heavy casualties** (vv. 5b-6a), and Ahaz lost a son and two close advisors in the battle (v. 7) **because they had forsaken the LORD God of their fathers** (v. 6b; see Introduction to 1 Chronicles on "forsaking the Lord").

c. Captives Experienced Mercy (28:8-15)

28:8-15. As the result of the overwhelming losses, Israel's army had taken many captives and much spoil (v. 8). An otherwise unknown **prophet of the LORD** named **Obed** intercepted the army of Israel with a message from the Lord. In effect, his message to Israel was: "Your victory was given to you because the Lord was **angry with Judah** (v. 9a). However, the Lord has taken notice of the **rage** displayed in the execution of this act and He is not pleased (v. 9b; cf. Is 10:15-16). And now you intend to enslave these captives from **Judah and Jerusalem** (2Ch 28:10a; cf. Lv 25:42-46). You should think better of that, for you yourselves are not innocent of transgression against the Lord (2Ch 28:10b). You should return the captives, because **the burning anger of the LORD is against you**" (v. 11).

This message was immediately taken to heart, and **some of the heads of the sons of Ephraim** (v. 12)—who realized their own guilt before the Lord (v. 13b)—stood up to the captors and convinced them to return the captives. So effective was this appeal that the **armed men** turned the captives over to the civil authorities (v. 14), who promptly cared for them and provided for their repatriation (v. 15). The message of "mercy is to be shown to the innocents" was not lost on the "innocents" of the Chronicler's generation—those repatriated captives of Judah and Jerusalem.

d. Ahaz's Disastrous Alliance with Assyria (28:16-21)

28:16-18. As other kings had done before, Ahaz foolishly sought an alliance with Assyria—a soon-to-be serious international threat—in the face of lesser threats from Edom and the Philistines (vv. 16-18. These are all towns on the eastern side of Judah in the foothills southwest of Jerusalem). Isaiah had strenuously advised against this action (cf. Is 7:3-9) not only because it was a foolish act in geopolitical terms but also because it was, more seriously, an act of unbelief and failure to trust the Lord. The truths that, beside the Lord "there is no one . . . to help in battle between the powerful and those who have no strength" (cf. 2Ch 14:11) and that "God has power to help and to bring down" (cf. 25:8), were lost on Ahaz.

28:19-21. The debilitating effects of Ahaz's evil and unfaithfulness (v. 19c) had demoralized and humbled Judah, effects brought by the Lord (v. 19a). As a result, the nation further declined morally as his policies **brought about a lack of restraint** (v. 19b), weakening the nation's ability to fend off aggression from the surrounding nations. Furthermore, Ahaz's attempt to bribe the Assyrian king (in a vain attempt to find security through compromise) accomplished nothing (v. 20-21). That Ahaz used a **portion out of the house of the LORD** (v. 21a) demonstrated his failure to be a true Davidic king. Soon after these events, just as Isaiah had foretold (cf. Is 7:17–8:22), Assyria destroyed the northern kingdom of Israel, took its people captive, and afflicted Judah in the days of Hezekiah.

e. Ahaz's Evil Expanded (28:22-25)

28:22-25. Judah's dramatic decline did not awaken repentance in Ahaz or cause him to reconsider his wicked idolatry. Instead, he persisted in and even increased his evil (v. 22). Perhaps in an attempt to appease his foes by the worship of their gods, Ahaz began to worship **the gods of Damascus** (v. 23a). That he attributed his defeats not to the Lord's judgment (cf. v. 5a) but to the supposed power of the pagan gods (v. 23b) proved how far he was from the faith of his fathers. "The reverence Ahaz paid 'to the gods of Damascus' (v. 23) took a particular form; he sacrificed on an altar patterned after the one he found there (2 Kings 16:10-13)" (Payne, *2 Chronicles*, 527). These may have been Assyrian deities. He discovered that idolatry is "futile," of "no profit" and brings all who engage in it "to shame" (cf. Is 44:9). Ahaz proved to be the quintessential anti-Davidic king when he destroyed the utensils of the temple and **closed the doors of the house of the LORD** (2Ch 28:24)—essentially shutting the temple down—while promoting false idolatrous worship as widely as he could (vv. 24b-25a).

f. Ahaz's End (28:26-27)

28:26-27. In his conclusion to the Ahaz narrative, the Chronicler associated Ahaz much more with "Israel" than with "Judah." It might be said that he was a true son of Jeroboam (cf. 2Kg 17:22) and not of David. He was not accorded a place of honor in burial (2Ch 28:27b), an indication not only of his unpopularity but also his unworthiness and a sign of the Lord's disapproval (cf. 21:20; 24:25; 26:33).

3. Excellent: Hezekiah (29:1–32:33)

The reign of Ahaz was the virtual lowest point of Davidic kingship (prior to the captivity itself). His reign gave little prospect of the revival to come under his son, the great Hezekiah. The reign of Hezekiah was a high point in the history of the nation, and the Chronicler devoted four extended chapters of his narrative to Hezekiah—more than to any other king except for David and Solomon. In stark contrast to Ahaz who "did not do right" and did not follow in the ways of David (cf. 28:1), Hezekiah proved himself an ideal Davidic king in that he "did right in the sight of the LORD, according to all that his father David had done" (29:2).

Much of the material in the Chronicler's record of Hezekiah is unique to him. The author of 2 Kings noted Hezekiah's reforms (cf. 2Kg 18:3-4), but he did not record the restoration of the temple (2Ch 29:3ff.) or the revival of the Passover (30:1ff.).

a. Hezekiah's Revival (29:1–31:21)

The key words and concepts describing Hezekiah's revival are "consecrate," "cleanse" and "celebrate." "Consecration"—the setting apart as "holy," being devoted to God—was understood to be the essence of genuine revival. Hezekiah's revival involved consecration of the priests, the temple, and the people themselves to the Lord and His service. The revival began with a restoration and cleansing of the temple from the desecration inflicted upon it by Ahaz and continued with a celebration of the sacrifices and of the long-neglected Passover.

(1) Hezekiah Reopened, Consecrated the Temple (29:1-19)

29:1-11. Hezekiah was an exemplary Davidic king, and nothing better demonstrated that than his immediate and active concern for the temple. The Chronicler emphasized that the restoration of the temple began **in the first year ... in the first month** (v. 3a) of Hezekiah's reign. Hezekiah wasted no time in reopening and repairing **the doors of the house of the LORD** that (v. 3b) that Ahaz had closed (cf. 28:24b). Rather than insist and demand by edict (from the position of an autocratic monarch), Hezekiah (in the model of a true "servant leader") enlisted those who could do the work of revival and restoration. He assembled the priests and Levites (v. 4) and gave a stirring address designed to motivate them for the work of consecration and renewal. His address began with (1) a call for consecration (v. 5; this was a call for "dedication"; *qadash* "to make a distinction between the common and the holy"), continued with (2) a confession of sin (vv. 6-7), was followed by (3) a description of sin's consequences (vv. 8-9), and concluded with (4) the initiating of a covenant (v. 10) to which he enlisted those in attendance (v. 11). In keeping with one of the major themes in Chronicles, the most serious sin of the fathers was a forsaking of the temple (v. 6b), bringing the **wrath of the LORD** (v. 8a) and defeat **by the sword** (v. 9a) by the nation's enemies. Only a renewed covenant (v. 10a) characterized by a return to devotion to the house of the Lord could turn away the **burning anger** of **the LORD God of Israel** (v. 10b). The Chronicler's generation would no doubt have understood how this prayer applied to their experience. The sin of forsaking the Lord had led to the captivity (cf. v. 9), and the present need was seeking the Lord. Hezekiah's words, **My sons, do not be negligent now** (v. 11), would have spoken as directly to the Chronicler's readers as they did to Hezekiah's listeners.

29:12-17. The list of names in vv. 12-14 indicates that Hezekiah's words were effective, since many of the priests and Levites responded enthusiastically. "Kohath, Merari, and Gershon were the three clans that made up the tribe of Levi (1 Chron 6:1" (Payne, "2 Chronicles," 534). Asaph, Heman, and Jeduthun were the three lines of Levitical musicians (1Ch 25:1). **Elizaphan** was "the leader of the Kohathites in the days of Moses" (Payne, "2 Chronicles," 534). They began the work of **consecration** and cleansing immediately (2Ch 29:17a—**the first day of the first month**; compare v. 3a). The cleansing amounted to hauling **every unclean thing** (v. 16b) out of the temple and disposing of it in the **Kidron valley** (east of the temple mount just below the Mount of Olives). The **Kidron** was a low point in the immediate geographical region, so the action may have been a symbolic demotion of the pagan symbols from the "high places" to the "low places" (cf. 15:16; 30:14; 2Kg 23:12). That the cleansing took 16 days (2Ch 29:17) shows the degree to which the temple had sunk into paganism under Ahaz.

29:18-19. In the end, the priests reported to Hezekiah that not only had they finished the cleansing but they also restored (vv. 18b-19) the utensils that Ahaz had previously destroyed (cf. 28:24). All of this work was accomplished **according to the commandment of the king by the words of the LORD** (v. 15b), that is, it was done under the direction of the Davidic king and according to the design of the temple and its services originally given to David (cf. 1Ch 28:12, 19). Once again the Chronicler emphasized the connection of the Davidic king to the temple: the prosperity of the nation depended on a Davidic king who took care to protect and preserve the temple, whereas failure in this matter would mean God's wrath and chastisement. Although the Chronicler's generation, as the remnant of the returning exiles, knew the truth of the latter point all too well, they would be renewed in their confidence by the narrative of Hezekiah's revival that if they would likewise care for the temple, they too could know prosperity from the Lord.

(2) Hezekiah Restored the Temple Worship (29:20-36)

29:20-34. As with those who had cleansed and refurbished the temple, Hezekiah lost no time reinstating the temple services. He **arose early** (v. 20a) and with the **princes of the city** (v. 20b, the civil leaders) **went up to the house of the LORD** (v. 20c). First there were sacrifices of atonement (vv. 20-24): the slaughter of the animals (vv. 22a, 22d, 24a), the sprinkling of the blood (vv. 22b, 22c, 24b), and the laying on of hands (in symbolic confession of sin) (v. 23b). These were all in accordance with the appropriate prescriptions of the Levitical sacrificial system (e.g., cf. Lv 1:1–7:38) **to atone for all Israel** (2Ch 29:24b). Then came the services of the musicians and the singers (vv. 25-28) to lead **the whole assembly** (v. 28a) in worship. They used the Psalms (that is, **the words of David and Asaph**, v. 30a; cf. David—Pss 3–9; 11–32; 34–41; 51–65; 68–70; 86; 101; 103; 108; 110; 122; 124; 131; 133; 138–145; Asaph—Pss 50, 73–83) and **sang praises with joy, and bowed down and worshiped** (2Ch 29:30). Finally, the services concluded with such a large number of burnt offerings of thanksgiving (vv. 31-35a) that the priests needed assistance from the Levites to accommodate all the worshipers (v. 34b).

29:35-36. The Chronicler's summary—**Thus the service of the house of the LORD was established again** (v. 35b)—was a triumphant note and would have been an encouragement to the Chronicler's generation, as those words could have described their own experience with the rebuilt temple of Ezra's day (cf. Ezr 6:16-18). Even more remarkable was the rapid accomplishment of restoration and renewal (2Ch 29:36b). This revival began and continued with heartfelt consecration to the Lord (cf. vv. 5, 15, 17, 19, 31, 33, 34), and yet it was what **God had prepared for the people** (v. 36a)—"for in the last analysis all spiritual achievements find their origin in God's grace" (Payne, "2 Chronicles," 536).

(3) Hezekiah Revived the Celebration of Passover (30:1-27)

For both the generation of Hezekiah's day and the generation of the Chronicler, the revival of the celebration of the Passover was an event wrought with deep significance.

30:1-5. The king began the revival of the Passover as He had the restoration of the temple by enlisting **his princes and all the assembly** (v. 2); "the assembly is especially important in Chronicles' version of Hezekiah (it occurs nine times in this chapter: vv. 2, 4, 13, 17, 23, 24, 24, 25, 25; cf. 29:4, 20, 23, 28, 31, 32; 32:18), and is one symbol of the people's unity" (Selman, *2 Chronicles*, 496). This group would have included common folk as well as certain officials (**his princes**, v. 2). Out of this meeting came a decision to send **letters to all Israel** (v. 1a), specifically including the tribes of **Ephraim and Manasseh** (v. 1b). This would have included those who had been left in the land or who had escaped (cf. v. 6d) from the captivity of the Assyrians after the invasion and captivity of 722 BC. These letters would carry a **proclamation throughout all Israel from Beersheba** (metaphorically the farthest point south in the southern kingdom) **even to Dan** (metaphorically the farthest point in the northern kingdom; v. 5b). The intent was to include and unify the whole nation around the temple and the proper observance of its services—especially the Passover (vv. 1c, 5c). Apparently, the Passover had not been regularly or widely celebrated (cf. v. 5d) according to the Torah (i.e., as **prescribed** (v. 5d). The decision **to celebrate the Passover in the second month** (v. 2b; April/May) (it was normally held in the first month, cf. Nm 9:2-5; March/April) was permitted by the provisions given in Nm 9:9-13 and was made necessary by the exigencies of the situation—a sufficient number of priests could not be consecrated in time nor could the people get to Jerusalem in time (2Ch 30:3).

30:6-9. The letters were delivered by **couriers** who went **throughout all Israel and Judah**. They carried a compelling message from the king and his princes (v. 6a). First, was the message of unity, as the letters were addressed to the **sons of Israel** and mention was made of the Patriarchs (reminding all of them of their common heritage, v. 6c). Next, the message came an invitation to repent, to **return to the LORD** (vv. 6b; 9a), and to **yield to the LORD** (v. 8b) and an appeal—**do not be like your fathers and brothers, who were unfaithful** (v. 7a)—**do not stiffen your neck like your fathers** (v. 8a). Here the message (and the Chronicler) identified the cause of the captivity—unfaithfulness to the Lord and rebellion against the Lord. This unfaithfulness had resulted in the **horror** (v. 7c) of the captivity as the result of the **burning anger** of the Lord (v. 8c). The message concluded with a promise of **compassion** (v. 9b) because **the LORD your God is gracious and compassionate** (v. 9c). The message most hopefully stated that upon repentance (indicated by a return to the temple and the Passover) the compassion of the Lord would mean an end to the captivity of **your brothers and your sons** (v. 9a, b).

30:10-12. Unfortunately, as the couriers carried this message to the northern tribes they found mostly that they were scorned and **mocked** (v. 10). However, some **humbled themselves and came to Jerusalem** (v. 11). In contrast, the appeal to celebrate Passover found ready acceptance in Judah (v. 12b), because **the hand of the LORD was also on Judah** (v. 12a)—thus proving that revival is a work of the Lord on the heart of those who repent from the heart.

30:13-15. When the celebration actually arrived it was evident that the effort to send the message to all Israel was a success—**a very large assembly** gathered in Jerusalem (v. 13). The **Feast of Unleavened Bread**, while technically a separate feast, was closely associated with Passover (cf. Ex 12; Mt 26:17; Lk 22:1). The zeal of the crowds (the average Israelites) apparently shamed the less enthusiastic priests and Levites (2Ch 30:15b), and so they again **consecrated themselves** (v. 15) to keep bringing sufficient offerings for the feast.

The celebration began and ended with the destruction of idols, first in the environs of Jerusalem itself (v. 14), then in Judah and Benjamin (31:1a) and, significantly, even in the areas of the northern kingdom (31:1b) where apostasy and idolatry had thrived since the days of Jeroboam I. By this the Chronicler emphasized that a sincere return *to* the Lord necessitated definitive turn *away from* idolatry and apostasy—"from idols to serve a living an true God" (1Th 1:9b). To do the one without the latter is not a true revival.

30:16-20. In spite of all the King's good intentions and the Levites' caring performance of their duties—**according to the law of Moses** (v. 16)—a problem arose concerning the worshipers from the northern tribes. Apparently, many of them **had not consecrated themselves** (v. 17a), meaning they were not permitted to slaughter the Passover lamb for themselves. Many who **had not purified themselves** (v. 18a) were actually violating the law by even eating the Passover (v. 18b). The solution to the first issue was having the Levites do the slaughtering (v. 17b). As for the second issue, Hezekiah himself offered a prayer, asking the Lord to pardon the infraction (v. 18c). Hezekiah's appeal amounted to asking the Lord to pardon and accept the worship of those who had come prepared in heart, if not strictly according to the law's prescriptions (v. 19). The Chronicler related God's response: **The LORD heard Hezekiah and healed the people** (v. 20). This shows that, while scrupulous adherence to the law was expected (as an indication of one's heart), the Lord was more interested in heartfelt worship than mere formalism, no matter how carefully performed (cf. Jn 7:22-23; 9:14-16).

30:21-22. The joyful celebration continued unabated **day after day** (v. 21). Hezekiah was careful to keep up the goodwill by commending the Levites who were working hard and showing **good insight** (v. 22)—that is, they did not let either the enthusiasm or the formalism of the celebration detract from its meaning and purpose. They kept the focus on the things **of the LORD**.

30:23-27. So successful was this celebration that it was extended for another seven days (v. 23). This recalled the seven-day celebration at the dedication of the temple in Solomon's day (v. 26; cf. 7:8-9). The great themes in these days were **joy** (vv. 23, 25, 26) and the unity of the nation—**all the assembly of Judah . . . that came from Israel** (v. 25) and the blessing that came from revival and renewal—the blessing of a restored relationship with the Lord (v. 27).

(4) Hezekiah Reinstituted Tithes and Offerings (31:1-21)

31:1-19. The reforms of Hezekiah included practical measures to ensure the continued performance of the temple services. Spiritual reforms could easily be lost if the practical concerns of caring for the priests were not also given serious attention. In accord with the orders and procedures established by David (v. 2; cf. 1Ch 24) and in obedience to what was **written in law of the LORD** (2Ch 31:3d, 4d) Hezekiah instituted reforms to ensure that the priests and Levites would receive **the king's portion of his goods** (v. 3a), that they would receive the tithes from the people (v. 4), and that these goods would be fairly distributed (vv. 11-19). Hezekiah himself followed up on his own orders (vv. 8-9) and found that the Levites were being more than adequately cared for (v. 10). Furthermore, it was reported that the provisions were distributed

faithfully (v. 15c) and **without regard to their genealogical enrollment**—without family preferences (v. 16a). This abundance and equity enabled the priests to dedicate **themselves faithfully in holiness** (v. 18c). The details of names and the order of authority specified in these verses indicated the stability and prosperity of Hezekiah's reign. Clearly Hezekiah was not only a godly king but he also had a range of administrative leadership skills as well.

31:20-21. This summary of Hezekiah's reign richly indicated the source of Hezekiah's success. He prospered because he **did what was good, right and true**. As a good Davidic king he took a keen interest **in the service of the house of God**, and most vitally he did all while **seeking his God** with **all his heart**. He followed David's advice (cf. 1Ch 22:19a; 28:9b) to obey the law and thereby found success (cf. 2Ch 22:11) and prosperity (cf. Dt 29:9). This was a message and an example the Chronicler's generation needed to hear.

b. Hezekiah's Victory over Assyria (32:1-23)

The Chronicler's transition from Hezekiah's revival ("these acts of faithfulness," v. 1a) to the story of the Assyrian invasion was abrupt. This however, was intended to highlight the connection between "faithfulness" and "victory," the point the Chronicler wanted to reinforce. Just as "forsaking the Lord" brought military defeat (e.g., Amaziah, 25:20ff.; Ahaz, 28:5ff.), so "seeking the Lord" brought military victory (e.g., Jehoshaphat, 20:20ff.). The account of the Chronicler is paralleled not only in Kings (cf. 2Kg 18, 19, and 20) but also by the "historical interlude" in Isaiah's prophecy (cf. Is 36-39). As usual, the Chronicler expected his readers to know something of the complexity of the historical events that took place between Hezekiah and the Assyrian empire. Yet for his own purposes he "simply envisage[d] a single Assyrian campaign, which is to be dated to 701 BC" (Selman, *2 Chronicles*, 508). The Chronicler has simplified the events to focus on the victory of the Lord over those who thought of Him as just another local deity.

(1) Hezekiah Countered Sennacherib's Invasion (32:1-8)

32:1. The Chronicler set up the situation facing Hezekiah quite simply: Sennacherib of Assyria had **invaded Judah and besieged the fortified cities** (v. 1b). Sennacherib ruled from 705 to 681 BC. He was a capable administrator, a superb military leader, and a ruthless overlord. Upon coming to the throne after his father, Sargon II, he faced a series of rebellions to Assyrian authority, and he spent several years reasserting his power and putting vassal states, including Judah, in their places. The danger to Judah was serious, as Sennacherib intended to **break into** these cites (v. 1c) **for himself**. This invasion was documented in Assyrian archives with the Assyrian king's boastfulness. Clearly he was not a conqueror with whom to be trifled. In fact, he mostly succeeded in accomplishing his boasts (cf. 2Kg 18:13; Is 36:1), except for Jerusalem.

32:2-8. Hezekiah well understood the danger this invasion posed for Jerusalem (v. 2), and he immediately began two kinds of preparations to counter it. First, he undertook the practical, tangible, and logistical matters to impede the Assyrian's progress. He had the water supplies cut so the enemy could not use them (vv. 3-4). Then he had the walls and fortifications rebuilt and reinforced (v. 5a, b). Next he restocked the arsenal and realigned the military chain of command **over the people** (vv. 5c-6a). Then he undertook to build morale and strengthen the courage of the people. He gathered the people to a rally (v. 6b). There his speech was encouraging and evoked the admonition of the Lord to Joshua (cf. Jos 1:6, 9) that David had invoked in his charge to Solomon (cf. 1Ch 22:13)—**Be strong and courageous** (2Ch 32:7a). He addressed directly the fear of the Assyrians' superior numbers (v. 7b) by reminding the people of the superiority of their God—**the one with us is greater than the one with him** (v. 7c). Thus, Hezekiah made the contest a spiritual one: the enemy had **an arm of flesh** (v. 8a; cf. Jr 17:5), but Jerusalem had **the Lord our God . . . to fight our battles** (2Ch 32:8b). In these actions Hezekiah demonstrated that he was an exceptionally spiritual, wise, and capable leader, and the people responded (v. 8c). The key theme of this battle for the Chronicler centered on the question, "Who is mightier, Sennacherib or the Lord?" In the story of the following contest, the Chronicler mostly narrated the events through Sennacherib to answer that question dramatically, showing the defeat of the Assyrian king.

(2) Hezekiah's Victory over Sennacherib (32:9-23)

32:9-19. Sennacherib's method of warfare included a "psychological attack" on the morale of his intended victims. While he was besieging the land of the Philistines, particularly the town of **Lachish**, 30 miles southwest of Jerusalem and midway between Jerusalem and Gaza (v. 9), he sent envoys (**his servants**, v.

9) to deliver discouraging messages to the inhabitants of Jerusalem. Several related themes appear in these messages. (1) Hezekiah could not be trusted to protect his people (vv. 10-11a, 15a)—he had prohibited the worship of all gods but One (v. 12)—an obvious limitation in the view of a polytheist like Sennacherib. (2) Devotion to the Lord would be insufficient to save them (vv. 11b; 15c)—perhaps Sennacherib was thinking that since the northern kingdom had (in part) trusted the Lord to no avail that Jerusalem should not think the Lord could protect them either. (3) Sennacherib had defeated all the gods of the other nations (vv. 13-14a) and would defeat their God as well (vv. 14b, 15b, 17). The relentlessness of this attack (v. 16) included **letters** (v. 17a) and public speeches (v. 18a), all intended **to frighten and terrify** the people (v. 18b) making it easier to conquer the city (v. 18c).

32:20-23. The response of Hezekiah and **Isaiah the prophet** (v. 20a) was precisely what was appropriate for this spiritual battle—they **cried out to heaven** (v. 20b), and the Lord heard "from heaven" (cf. 6:21, 23, 25, 27, 30, 33, 35, 39). By this time, the siege had actually begun and apparently the Assyrians had surrounded the city with a vast army (cf. 2Kg 19:35 notes 185,000). **The LORD sent an angel** (2Ch 32:21a) a messenger-warrior (otherwise unidentified) and destroyed the Assyrian forces—officers and men (v. 21b). While the exact means of the destruction was not identified, it was clearly a supernatural defeat and dramatic proof of the emptiness of Sennacherib's blasphemous boasts. Sennacherib returned home in shame and was ignominiously assassinated, ironically, in the act of worshiping his gods, who obviously could not save him (v. 21c). The Lord did save (deliver) the Davidic king and His city and proved that He, not the Assyrian king, is the true sovereign. The blessings that flowed to Hezekiah were the exceedingly abundant evidence that the Lord was keeping His promise to the Davidic king.

On the Sennacherib Prism, discovered in Nineveh in the 19th century, the Assyrian king boasted that he had trapped Hezekiah in Jerusalem "like bird in a cage." "As to Hezekiah the Jew, he did not submit to my yoke, I laid siege to 46 of his strong cities . . . Himself I made a prisoner in Jerusalem his royal residence, like a bird in a cage. I surrounded him . . ." (cited in A. Leo Oppenheim, trans., "Babylonian and Assyrian Historical Texts," in *Ancient Near Eastern Texts Relating to the Old Testament*, 3rd ed., ed. James B. Pritchard [Princeton: Princeton University Press, 1969], 288). In spite of the boastful tone, such language betrayed that Sennacherib had failed to conquer Hezekiah completely. Thus, even the pagan records gave reluctant testimony to the Lord, who could say "I am the first and last, and there is no God besides Me" (Is 44:6b).

c. Hezekiah's Last Days (32:24-33)

Following the order of the narrative from that of Kings (2Kg 20) and of Isaiah (Is 38 and 39), the Chronicler recorded the event of Hezekiah's illness and recovery after the defeat of the Assyrians, even though this event took place before the Assyrian siege. (This is clear from the promise given to Hezekiah by Isaiah: he will be healed *and* the Lord will "deliver you and this city from the hand of the king of Assyria," 2Kg 20:6; cf. Is 38:6). However, the Chronicler's account is much abbreviated. As throughout his narrative, the Chronicler expected his readers to be familiar with the narrative of Kings (see 2 Ch 30:32), while selecting and highlighting certain parts of that story to focus on his main interest—the person of the Davidic king. Hezekiah was an exemplary Davidic king—but he was not perfect. His imperfections were evident, and the Chronicler presented them in a light that could give exhortation and inspiration to his generation.

(1) Hezekiah's Illness and Pride (32:24-26)

32:24-26. The nature of Hezekiah's illness is not explained. It may have been some type of infection since a poultice of figs (cf. 1Kg 20:7) was applied to a "boil" (cf. Is 38:21) to attempt to bring healing. However, it was a mortal illness (2Ch 32:24). None of Hezekiah's depth of emotion—neither the dread prospect of death (cf. 1Kg 20:2-3; Is 38:2-3), nor the joy of healing (Is 38:9-20, Hezekiah's song of bitterness turned to joy)—is even hinted at in Chronicles. The **sign** given to him (the shadow on the steps of the temple went backwards; cf. 1Kg 20:8-11; Is 38:7-8) was also not explained. For the Chronicler's purpose, only that Hezekiah was healed as the result of his prayer and that he **gave no return for the benefit** (2Ch 32:25a) was important. This failure on Hezekiah's part was attributed to **his heart** being **proud** (v. 25b). The Chronicler's readers would have instantly understood the danger of this condition since the exact expression was used of Uzziah (cf. 26:16) and the Lord's wrath (cf. 2Kg 20:16-18; Is 39:6-7) had come upon the nation because of it. In contrast to Uzziah, however, Hezekiah repented. He **humbled the pride of his**

heart (2Ch 32:26a) and led the nation in this contrition (v. 26b). As a result, the Lord's wrath was averted, at least **in the days of Hezekiah** (v. 26c).

(2) Hezekiah's Wealth and Pride (32:27-31)

32:27-31. As expected for a faithful Davidic king, Hezekiah **prospered in all that he did** (v. 30b). He amassed wealth (vv. 27-29) and by it, wisely provided for the nation's security (v. 30). For instance, he commissioned the famous "Hezekiah's tunnel" so Judah would have a water supply that would be invulnerable to siege. This tunnel was cut through 1,700 feet of solid rock under Jerusalem to channel water from the Gihon spring on the east side to the pool of Siloam inside the city. In a remarkable confirmation of the accuracy of the biblical record, "Archeological confirmation of this engineering feat came in 1880 with the discovery at its lower portal of the Siloam Inscription, written in old Hebrew by the very workers who accomplished it" (Payne, "2 Chronicles," 542). The text reads in part "And when the tunnel was driven through, the quarrymen hewed (the rock) each man toward his fellow, axe against axe . . ." (William F. Albright, trans., "Palestinian Inscriptions," in *Ancient Near Eastern Texts Relating to the Old Testament*, 3rd ed., ed. James B. Pritchard [Princeton: Princeton University Press, 1969], 321). All this was to be expected from an exemplary Davidic king. Once again, however, Hezekiah succumbed to pride. In this case, his pride was not mentioned explicitly but it was illustrated by the foolish act of parading his treasures and the nation's defenses before **the envoys of the rulers of Babylon** (v. 31a; cf. 2Kg 20:12-13; Is 39:1-4). Those rulers had come to **inquire of the wonder** (2Ch 32:31b) of Hezekiah's illness and recovery (and possibly the sign) (cf. 2Kg 20:12b; Is 39:1b). While the two parallel accounts in Kings and Isaiah record the rebuke of Isaiah for this foolishness (cf. 2Kg 20:16-19; Is 39:5-7), the Chronicler reveals that the Lord ordained this to test Hezekiah (2Ch 32:31c). The Lord wanted to know if Hezekiah's trust was in the Lord or in a potential alliance with Babylon—the rising power in the east. Apparently, Hezekiah's heart was divided on this matter (cf. Is 39:8-9).

(3) Hezekiah's End (32:32-33)

32:32-33. The Chronicler completed his account of Hezekiah by noting his **deeds of devotion** (v. 32a). That his narrative is told not only in the **Book of the Kings** but also in the prophecy of Isaiah (v. 32b), and the honor bestowed on him in his burial (v. 33), indicated that Hezekiah was an outstanding example of the Davidic ideal. Although Hezekiah was not a perfect king, the Chronicler would have concurred with the lofty evaluation by the author of Kings, that "after him there was none like him among all the kings of Judah, nor among those who were before him" (2Kg 18:5).

4. Bad, but Repentant: Manasseh (33:1-20)

The Chronicler's record of Manasseh is decidedly brief—despite that Manasseh "had the longest reign of all the Hebrew monarchs" (Payne, "2 Chronicles," 4:544). In stark contrast to his father Hezekiah, arguably the best of the kings of Judah, Manasseh was the worst. He did more to promote the idolatry that led to the Babylonian captivity than any other single individual (cf. 2Kg 23:26; Jr 15:4) and was rightly condemned by the Lord and vilified in the memory of the author of Kings. The Chronicler, however, presented material not found in Kings that highlights Manasseh's repentance.

a. Manasseh's Incredible Evil (33:1-9)

33:1-9. The term **evil** (vv. 2a, 6b, 9) began, centered, and concluded the Chronicler's description of Manasseh's reign. Manasseh's idolatry was characterized as a revival of the paganism of the nations that had once occupied the land (vv. 2b, 9c). It included blatant Baal worship on newly restored altars on **the high places** (v. 3), the building of pagan altars even in the temple (vv. 4a, 5a), and the setting up of idols there (v. 7a; for Baal worship see comment on 28:2; **Asherim** were Canaanite female fertility goddesses). Manasseh even engaged in the despicable act of child sacrifice (v. 6a) in combination with vile occult practices (v. 6b). The Chronicler noted that (1) the temple was to be the place where the Lord put His **name . . . in Jerusalem, forever** (vv. 4b, 7c), that (2) the temple was the focus of His promise to preserve the nation and the Davidic king (vv. 7b-8a), and that (3) obedience to **the law, the statutes and the ordinances given through Moses** (v. 8c) was expected. These observations made the profanations of Manasseh all the more abhorrent and foreshadowed the reason for the captivity. It was shocking that the Davidic king, of all people, had so forsaken the Lord and so profaned the temple. This was especially heinous in light of the Lord's desire not to **remove the foot of Israel from the land** again (v. 8a). With this degree of wickedness and disobedience it was evident that the promise of security was not going to be kept for this king or this generation. The Chronicler's generation was painfully aware that this sort of evil idolatry, temple sacrilege, and disobedience to the law of Moses had caused their struggle to recover from grinding captivity.

b. Manasseh's Humiliating Captivity (33:10-11)

33:10-11. In spite of this horrendous apostasy the Lord was still gracious to speak to the king and the nation, calling them, to no avail, to repentance (v. 10). The resulting captivity of Manasseh was brutal and humiliating (v. 11).

c. Manasseh's Marvelous Repentance (33:12-13a, 18-19)

33:12-13a, 18-19. The Chronicler's generation did not need to dwell on the causes that sent their fathers into captivity—they needed to know how they could recover from it. Therefore, the account of Manasseh's repentance would have been a genuine encouragement to them. Apparently, even in captivity in Babylon (v. 11d) Manasseh was given the opportunity to hear from **the seers who spoke to him in the name of the LORD God of Israel** (v. 18b), just as the nation had its prophets (Daniel and Ezekiel) in captivity. As a result of the preaching of these seers, Manasseh became a remarkable example of true repentance. First, as just noted (1) he was receptive to the word of God in his distress (v. 12a), (2) he turned to God in prayer (vv. 13a, 19a), (3) in this prayer he confessed his sin (implied in the content of v. 19), and finally (4) he **humbled himself greatly before the God of his fathers** (v. 12b), indicating a complete change of heart and mind and will. The Lord **was moved by his entreaty and heard his supplication** (v. 13a)—a note of utter grace and mercy. Clearly, the lesson for the Chronicler's generation was that forgiveness and grace are available to the worst of sinners! As disobedience and evil bring the Lord's judgment, so repentance and trust in the Lord bring His blessing.

d. Manasseh's Attempted Revival (33:13b-17, 20)

33:13b-17, 20. The blessing of the Lord upon repentance indicated by the return of Manasseh to Jerusalem (v. 13b) would have been a historical note of keen interest to the Chronicler's generation. What had secured their return was the Lord's faithfulness, but they too needed to follow in the footsteps of repentant Manasseh. The genuineness of Manasseh's repentance is seen in (1) the statement he **knew that the LORD was God** (v. 13c), (2) his attempts at revival of the true worship of the Lord (vv. 15-16), and (3) his efforts to fortify the city (v. 14)—all acts of a true Davidic king. The effects of this effort were sadly minimal, as the people continued the practices of idolatry that Manasseh had previously introduced, even if they intended to direct them toward the Lord (v. 17). Manasseh's experience was a hard lesson that keeping worship pure, while difficult, is preferable to attempting to reintroduce pure worship.

Manasseh ended his reign with the stigma of his previous life affecting his legacy, and he was not accorded the honor of burial in the royal cemetery (v. 20). Nevertheless, his was a story of the possibility for repentance for even the most unlikely of persons and a story of the incredible grace of God.

5. Bad: Amon (33:21-25)

33:21-25. Amon's brief reign of two years (v. 21) was told only briefly by the Chronicler. This was probably because the lessons to learn from this evil king were not unique. Amon followed in the wickedness and idolatry of his father Manasseh (v. 22) but did not follow his father in the path of humble repentance (v. 23a). This serves as a warning to all parents—not just those of royalty. Whatever is impressed upon them in youth will in all likelihood set their path in adulthood, and children can be trained for righteousness (cf. Pr 22:6). Amon actually did worse than Manasseh (2Ch 33:23b), so much so that his own servants assassinated him (v. 24). This act of treason was avenged (v. 25). While the birth of Josiah was a harbinger of better days, the kingdom itself had taken a precipitous decline from the days of Hezekiah.

6. Very Good: Josiah (34:1–35:27)

The darkest days, from a human perspective, are often the days most propitious for a fresh work of the Lord to begin. After the dreadful days of Manasseh and even more despicable days of Amon, the Lord was gracious to send good king Josiah and the bright days of revival.

a. Josiah's Reign—Seeking God, Purging Idolatry (34:1-7)

34:1-2. Josiah began his reign as a young boy of only eight years (v. 1). In the pattern of Jehoshaphat (cf. 17:3) and Hezekiah (cf. 29:2) **he did right in the sight of the LORD** (v. 2a) and conducted himself after the example **his father David** (v. 2b). The expression that he **did not turn aside to the right or to the left** (v. 2c) indicated that he did not deviate from David's godly example. He showed unusual spiritual maturity at a young age.

34:3-7. When he was 16, **while he was still a youth**, he sought the Lord (v. 3a; see Introduction to 1 Chronicles), and at the age of 20 (v. 3b) he began to purge the nation of the idolatry that had plagued it for many years. His manner of dealing with the idols was not gentle: they **tore down** the idols' altars (vv. 4a, 7a), **chopped down** the **incense altars** (vv. 4b, 7c), ground the pieces to powder (vv. 4c, 7b), and spread the dust on the graves of the idol worshipers (v. 4d). This act demonstrated his utter contempt for the idols and their worshipers. He even took the bones of the pagan priests (buried near the pagan shrines) and burned them (v. 5) in fulfillment of the word of the Lord to Jeroboam that human bones would be "burned" on the false altars he set up at the time of the division of the kingdom (cf. 1Kg 13:2). Josiah's purge did not stop at the borders of Judah but extended to the territories of the former (at this time exiled) northern kingdom as well (2Ch 34:6). These were bold actions for the day and would have been a great encouragement to people like Jeremiah and Habakkuk. Josiah knew what many of God's men have not known over the years: idolatry and ungodliness are never defeated by half measures but require bold, stern, and definitive purging.

b. Revival Year: Repairing Temple, Rediscovering Law, Reviving Passover (34:8–35:19)

The eighteenth year (34:8a; 35:19) of Josiah's reign was a "banner year," one of the most memorable in the entire the history of the nation. It is all the more remarkable that Josiah made it so great when he was only 26 years old (cf. 34:1a plus 34:8a).

(1) Repairing the Temple (34:8-13)

As was typical for a true Davidic king, Josiah took an immediate interest in the temple. The man of God must not stop merely with "purging" evil—he must be about "promoting" godliness. This is best done through the promotion of true worship. The monies collected for the repair and restoration of the temple came from the former northern kingdom as well as from Judah (34:9b). This detail picks up again a major theme of the Chronicler, namely, that "all Israel" was involved in this enterprise. The unity of the nation after the captivity was vital to its success and wellbeing, and the Chronicler knew that the locus of that unity needed to be the temple and the true worship of God. The Chronicler was telling his generation that true unity could be achieved if the whole nation was devoted to the true worship of the true God in the temple He Himself had chosen for His name.

34:8-13. The details of the restoration project (cf. vv. 9a, 10-13) indicate that the temple had been allowed to decline significantly (cf. v. 11c, **had let go to ruin**)—the result of the paganism and idolatry of the several ungodly kings. Several principles contributed to the success of the project to repair and restore the temple. The project was undertaken with sufficient resources (vv. 9a; 11a), by a team with various skills (cf. v. 10 **workmen**; v. 11 **carpenters** and **builders**; v. 13a **burden bearers**), and assisted by some with no evident skills for building (cf. vv. 12b, 13c **Levites** and musicians, scribes, etc.), but who had an incentive and a desire to do the work. The Levites were determined to beautify their place of service. The work was led **faithfully with foremen . . . to supervise** (v. 12a) and proceeded in an orderly fashion—**from job to job** (v. 13b). These details would not be lost on the Chronicler's generation—people facing a daunting "restoration" project of their own.

(2) Rediscovering the Law (34:14-33)

34:14-18a. The account of the discovery of the book of the law is astounding but reads "true to life." It is astounding that the law could be lost at all! However, it must be remembered that without printing presses copies of the law were rare—and made even more so by the waves of apostasy that the nation had suffered. The loss of the law as a way of worship and life would have inevitably led to the loss of the physical book. The book Hilkiah discovered was identified as **the law of the LORD given by Moses** (34:14b) and **the book of the covenant** (34:30c). Various attempts have been made to identify which portion or portions of the Pentateuch are in view here, but few are convincing and it may be that the whole Pentateuch is in view. It should also be noted that Mosaic authorship is indicated without question or argument. (See Payne, "2 Chronicles," 551).

As noted, the short account of the "physical" discovery of the book reads "true to life." That is, it seems that at first the discoverers did not realize what they had found. Apparently, in the process of restoration (cleaning out an unused cluttered, storeroom perhaps) the priest Hilkiah, as he was going about his duties, discovered the book and almost as an afterthought passed it on to Shaphan, the scribe. The conversation between Shaphan and the king, (v. 16a) as he reported on the progress of the restoration (v. 16b) and the dispersion of the finds (v. 17) seemed to indicate that there was no urgency attached to the discovery of **a book** (v. 18a). The skill of the Chronicler's narrative should be noted: the reader knows the significance of this book, but as yet no one handling it seemed to realize it and the narrative builds suspense. Will anyone recognize this book for what it is, or will it be laid aside as some curiosity to be investigated later?

34:18b-21. In climactic fashion, the scribe Shaphan **read from** the book **in the presence of the king** (v. 18b), and the king's reaction was dramatic. When he heard **the words of the law** he immediately **tore his clothes** (v. 19; cf. Gn 37:34; Jb 1:20) as an act of deep repentance and serious remorse. Significantly, it was the Davidic king who recognized the book's meaning and significance. "Acknowledging the word of God for what it is, is always an essential step towards seeing God at work" (Selman, *2 Chronicles*, 532). Instantly, Josiah understood a project more vital than the restoration of the temple needed to be undertaken, namely, the restoration of the nation to obedience. Hilkiah, Shaphan and others were reassigned to **inquire of the LORD** (2Ch 34:21a), to study the law to see what was required of the nation to avert God's **wrath** (v. 21b). Josiah knew that ignorance of the law was no excuse and that the years of disobedience left the nation in serious danger. The law was clear: blessings could be expected only if the nation did **according to all that is written in this book** (v. 21c).

The idea that this book was actually (what is now known as) Deuteronomy and that it was created much later in Israel's history by temple priests seeking reform was originally proposed by Wilhelm Martin Leberecht de Wette (1780–1849), a German critical-biblical scholar. However, later studies have shown that the philological arguments of de Wette were deficient. The notion that the reforms of Josiah were purely "Deuteronomic" has been shown by Kitchen to be false since Josiah's reform "could have been sparked off as easily by one version of the Sinai-covenant (Exodus-Leviticus) as the other (by forty years only: Deuteronomy)." Thus, "this ancient canard of 1805 should be quietly given a decent burial." Kitchen adds, "And the *modern* data on treaty, law, and covenant put both versions [of the Sinai-covenant—Exodus/Leviticus and Deuteronomy] squarely in the late second millennium, *not* in the late seventh century, and not as a pious fraud either" (Kenneth A. Kitchen, *On the Reliability of the Old Testament* [Grand Rapids, MI: Eerdmans, 2003], 40001; see also his summary dismissal of the JEDP theory: *Reliability of the Old Testament*, 492–96).

34:22-28. In the process of seeking the mind of the Lord, an inquiry was made to the prophetess **Huldah** (v. 22a). With no note of explanation for the presence, much less the importance, of a female "prophetess" and that she was clearly a well-known person (note the details of her identity, v. 22b), it must be assumed that the "idea of discrimination based on sex" was "foreign" to the "spirit of the OT," at least for a prophetess (Payne, "2 Chronicles," 4:551). Huldah gave her prophecy in two parts. First she revealed what the king had feared: because of the nation's continued apostasy, the exile was inevitable. In a way, in order to be faithful to His word, he would bring on **all the curses written in the book** that had been read to the king (v. 24; Lv 26:14-45; Dt 28:15-68). God's **wrath [would] be poured out on this place** because of the apostasy and idolatry (2Ch 34:25). But second, she revealed that because Josiah had shown humility, true remorse, and heartfelt repentance (v. 27) the necessary judgment would not come during his lifetime—he would **not see all the evil** that God would **bring on this place and on its inhabitants** (v. 28). The Chronicler's generation knew the truth of the first part of Huldah's prophecy, and they needed to know the point of the second part—namely, God's curses and wrath are not unavoidable. His chastisement becomes inevitable by persistent disobedience to the Word, but His blessings are just as sure if the nation will consistently practice obedience. It was still true that if the nation and people would humble themselves, seek the Lord, pray and "turn from their wicked ways," then He would forgive and heal them (cf. 7:14). The Chronicler's generation knew they had a choice: follow the ways of Josiah's ungodly predecessors or follow Josiah in humility, repentance, and faithful obedience.

34:29-30. Even in the face of the first part of Huldah's prophecy, Josiah led the people in a public reading of the law. This was not an afterthought for a nation in inevitable decline but the only proper faithful act of God's people, regardless of time or circumstance.

34:31-33. The reading of the law led to a nationwide "covenant renewal." The king's self-dedication was genuine and exemplary: it was public (he **stood in his place**, v. 31a), focused on the Lord (**before the LORD . . . after the LORD**, v. 31b), specific (**commandments . . . testimonies . . . statutes,** v. 31c), heartfelt (**with all his heart . . . soul**, v. 31d), and followed by action (**to perform the words of the covenant**, v. 31e). As a good leader he brought others with him in his dedication (v. 32a) and influenced others to follow as well (v. 32b). This rededication led to further reforms (v. 33a) and a lifetime of service and obedience (v. 33b). Although the obedience among many may have been only external (cf. Jr 11:1-13), nevertheless Josiah's example proved the power of one leader's complete dedication over the direction of the entire nation.

(3) Revival of Passover (35:1-19)

Following in the steps of his great-grandfather Hezekiah (cf. 30:1ff.), Josiah capped his restoration and reformation project off with a revival of the Passover. The celebration took place on the fourteenth day of the first month (35:1b), indicating that Josiah made sure the ceremony took place according to the law (cf. Ex 12:6), not allowing the adjustment made by Hezekiah (cf. 2Ch 30:2) to set a precedent.

35:1-10. Preparations for the Passover were made in several steps. First, Josiah **set the priests in their offices and encouraged them** (v. 2), amounting to a royal reconsecration for their ministry. He wanted them to undertake this solemn service knowing they had the full support of the Davidic king. Second, Josiah ordered that the ark of the covenant be replaced in the temple (v. 3a, b). Apparently, it had been removed from the temple, either by faithful priests to protect it during the reigns of Manasseh (cf. 33:7) and Amon, or by those who worshiped other gods by means of other tokens, or perhaps it had simply been removed for safekeeping during Josiah's reconstruction project. The note that the ark would **be a burden on your shoulders no longer** (v. 3c) may suggest that, for some undisclosed reason, the ark was being carried in and out of the temple (according to the law, cf. Ex 25:14, 15) but would once again find a permanent home in the restored temple. Another possibility is that this was a symbolic act of removing the ark and returning it as a symbol of the temple's reconsecration. Third, Josiah reordered the priests according to the **divisions** established by David and Solomon (2Ch 35:4-5, 10b) and commanded them to perform their duties **according to the word of the LORD by Moses** (v. 6). "Josiah's goal was to prevent the sort of confusion that had arisen during the more precipitous reform and Passover of his godly great-grandfather, some 103 years earlier (cf. 30:16-18)" (Payne, "2 Chronicles," 4:553). Fourth, Josiah and his officers supplied the animals for the offerings and sacrifices to be made for the Passover (v. 7-9). **So the service was prepared** (vv. 10a; 16a).

35:11-19. The Chronicler recorded this Passover celebration in two parts: First, there was the record of the sacrifices made and distributed (vv. 11-15). The details indicate that every person knew his part and performed it accordingly (**as it is written in the book of Moses**, v. 12c; **according to the ordinance**, v. 13a; **according to the command of David** and others, v. 15a). Second, there was the note of the significance of this particular Passover (vv. 16-19). The celebrants of that particular Passover were aware that such a full national celebration (**all Judah and Israel who were present**, v. 18c) had not been celebrated **since the days of Samuel the prophet** (v. 18b). As such it was a high point in the nation's history. But to the generation of the Chronicler this meant they could recapture this moment in their own day as those who had returned to Jerusalem as representatives of "all Israel." Everything rested on how they regarded the temple. The restoration of the temple in their day would mean that they too could participate in a singularly significant, nationally historic, Passover.

c. Josiah's Tragic Death (35:20-27)

Josiah's death was faithfully recorded by the Chronicler as a historical fact. But the transition to this tragic ending may indicate that the Chronicler did not want this death to be Josiah's legacy. He first noted "when Josiah had set the temple in order" (v. 20a) and then began the narrative of Josiah's last days.

(1) Pharaoh Neco, on His Way to War, Warned Josiah to Not Interfere (35:20-21)

The Battle at Carchemish (on the Euphrates 250 miles northeast of Damascus) between Neco of Egypt (allied with Ashuruballit of Assyria) and Nebuchadnezzar of Babylon in 605 BC was one of the great turning points in world history. Neco eventually lost that battle and Babylon became the ascendant world power, affecting both world and biblical history in profound ways. Josiah was a minor player in this saga—one who did not actually need to be involved at all.

35:20-21. When Josiah was apprised of Neco's plans he determined to engage him in battle. Perhaps he feared an Egyptian-Assyrian alliance or maybe he wanted to assist Babylon, hoping to secure favorable terms from the rising power in the east. Neco attempted to dissuade Josiah by assuring him that he, Neco, had no animus toward Josiah (**I am not coming against you**) and by appealing to divine providence (**God has ordered me . . . God who is with me**, v. 21b). The sincerity of this last appeal has been questioned, but as recorded by the Chronicler, it seems that Josiah should have seen the working of God's providence (v. 22b). There is a tragic and ironic parallel to the fate of the ungodly Ahab (cf. 18:29-34) in this account.

(2) Josiah Engaged Neco in Battle, Was Mortally Wounded (35:22-24c)

35:22-24c. Josiah proceeded to engage Neco (**would not turn away** . . . did not **listen to the words of Neco from the mouth of God**) on the **plain of Meggido** (v. 22), the enormous plain through the hill country in Israel from northwest to southeast (and future site of the battle of Armageddon; Rv 16:16). Josiah took the futile precaution of disguising himself (2Ch 35:22b); nevertheless **the archers** mortally **wounded** him (v. 23a; cf. the fate of Ahab, 18:33). Josiah was able to be transported to Jerusalem before he died (v. 24b)—evidence of the Lord's favor on this godly Davidic king—and he was **buried in the tombs of his fathers** (v. 24c) in honor of his godly faithfulness.

(3) Judah Mourned for Josiah (35:24d-25)

35:24d-25. The unusual details about the mourning for Josiah, the listing of mourners (**all Judah and Jerusalem**, v. 24d . . . **Jeremiah** . . . **male and female singers**, v. 25a) the terms used to express the mourning (**chanted a lament**, v. 25a . . . **lamentations**, v. 25b), and the note about the **ordinance** of mourning (v. 25c) indicate the high level of honor and respect the nation had for Josiah. The book **Lamentations** (v. 25d), noted here is not the biblical book of "Lamentations."

(4) Josiah's Reign Summarized (35:26-27)

35:26-27. The sad events that led to his death were not the last word about Josiah for the Chronicler. A word about his revival of temple worship (v. 20a) and a note about his **deeds of devotion** to **the law of the Lord** (v. 26) bracketed the account of his tragic death. However, Josiah's godliness, his devotion to the law, and his revival were soon overshadowed by the precipitous decline of the nation following his death.

H. Sons of Josiah (Jehoahaz, Jehoiakim, Jehoiachin, Zedekiah) (36:1-16)

Josiah's revival was the nation's last opportunity to avoid the inevitable chastisement (cf. 34:23-25) of the captivity. The Chronicler's readers were already well aware that the nation did not build on that revival but instead quickly declined and did not listen to the prophets (Jeremiah in particular; cf. Jr 1:1-3) sent to them (cf. 2Ch 36:15-16). The readers knew well that the captivity was not a happenstance of history but the righteous chastisement of the Lord. Therefore the Chronicler did not record the history of the last kings of the nation in great detail, and the final chapter of his work moved swiftly to the foregone conclusion. However, a note of hope arose. The decree of Cyrus was given to round out his message to his generation: the God who promised to build the house of David was not about to prove Himself faithless to that promise. He would bring (as the generation of the Chronicler knew He had brought) the nation back to the land. The promise remained (and remains) in effect for His chosen people.

1. Joahaz (36:1-4)

36:1-4. Joahaz was elevated to the throne by popular acclaim (v. 1), but he reigned only three months (v. 2). Probably to prevent him from doing the same ill-fated act of his father, Pharaoh Neco **deposed** Joahaz (v. 3a) and took him captive to Egypt (v. 4b). To recoup some of his expenses for the late war (cf. 35:20) Neco also imposed a levy on the nation (v. 3b). He set up Joahaz's brother **Eliakim** on the throne and, in an act that would remind him of his servile position, the Pharaoh changed Eliakim's name to Jehoiakim (v. 4a).

2. Jehoiakim and Jehoiachin (36:5-10)

36:5-10. Jehoiakim proved to be an evil (v. 5b; 8a) and weak king. During his reign Nebuchadnezzar of Babylon invaded Judah and took Daniel and his friends into captivity (vv. 6-7; cf. Dn 1:1-2). The loss of the wealth and articles of the temple would have been particularly devastating and an indication of the Lord's displeasure with the house of David. Throughout the Chronicler's record the fortunes of the temple were tied to the fortunes of the Davidic king. For God to allow the glories of the temple to be sacked indicated He was chastising the Davidic king for unfaithfulness. Jehoiakim, a puppet of Neco, was deported and Jehoiachin, his son, was made king (2Ch 36:9a). Jehoiachin reigned only **three months and ten days** (v. 9b), and for his evil (v. 9c) he suffered exactly the same fate as his father (v. 10a).

3. Zedekiah (36:11-14)

36:11-14. The last king of the nation was another son of Josiah (uncle to Jehoiachin), Zedekiah (also called Mattaniah, cf. 2Kg 24:17), who also became a puppet king of Nebuchadnezzar (2Ch 36:10b). He too did evil (v. 12a). The Chronicler specifically noted he did not listen (**did not humble himself** v. 12b) to the preaching of **Jeremiah the prophet who spoke for the Lord** (v. 12c). He compounded his errant ways by rebelling against Nebuchadnezzar (v. 13a) and by hardening his heart against the Lord (v. 13b).

He led the nation in pagan practices (**abominations of the nations** v. 14a) and committed the epitome of faithlessness for a Davidic king—he **defiled the house of the Lord** (v. 14b).

4. Summary: Prophets Sent and Rejected (36:15-16)

36:15-16. In a summary statement (vv. 15-16) that not only described the last days before the captivity, but in effect the whole history of the nation, the Chronicler recorded that the Lord—in His deep compassion—had sent messengers again and again to call the people—**His people**—to repentance, only to have them **mocked** and **scoffed at** and His words **despised** (vv. 15-16a). This pattern in the nation's history would be recalled on more than one occasion by Jesus Himself (cf. Mt 23:29-35). The failure of the nation to heed God's Word resulted in His **wrath** and **no remedy** (2Ch 36:16b).

I. The Captivity and the Decree of Cyrus (36:17-23)

The Chronicler's conclusion of his history conveyed a stark realism and note of hope for his generation.

1. The Captivity: Description and Rationale (36:17-21)

a. Description (36:17-20)

36:17-20. The account of the captivity related the brutality of the Chaldeans (Babylonians) (v. 17, **no compassion on young man or virgin, old man or infirm**) and the completeness of the destruction of the temple and the city (v. 19, **burned . . . broke down . . . burned**). The looting of the temple (v. 18) and captivity of the remnant not slain (v. 20) are details that corroborate the accounts in other books, such as Daniel (cf. Dn 1, 5).

b. Rationale (36:21)

36:21. The rationale for the captivity (in addition to the implicit rationale articulated throughout the Chronicler's work—namely the failure of the nation and the evil kings to seek the Lord while seeking other gods and neglecting the temple) was drawn from the prophet Jeremiah (v. 21a). Since the nation had not obeyed the law of giving the land its **sabbath** rests (cf. Lv 26:34-35, 43) the nation would be held in captivity until all the missed **sabbath** years had been made, a period calculated to be **seventy years** (2Ch 36:21b).

2. The Decree of Cyrus (36:22-23)

36:22-23. While the prophecy of Jeremiah's 70-year captivity was heavy for those going into captivity, that same prophecy brought hope to those at the end of the captivity (v. 22). The Chronicler's generation knew well the significance and the challenges of Cyrus's decree. Once again, it was not the purview of an earthly king but that of a heavenly sovereign who ordered the events of captivity and return (cf. v. 23a). The final call, **Whoever there is among you of all His people, may the Lord his God be with him, and let him go up!** (v. 23b) was still being made by the Chronicler to his generation.

In the order of books in the Hebrew Bible, 2 Chronicles is the final book and the Persian King Cyrus's decree, the final words. The phrase **let him go up** finds its subject in the previous phrase, "he whose God is with him." This wording is based on the Hebrew Bible, which literally reads, "He whose God is with Him, let Him go up!" (The NASB renders it more as a prayer, "may the Lord his God be with him.") Cyrus's decree concerns God's people in captivity and exile in Babylon, which later came under the rule of Persia. The decree ended their 70-year captivity, fulfilling the prophecy of Jeremiah (Jr 29:1-10), and letting the people return to rebuild the temple in Jerusalem. Yet it also seems that the Chronicler is using Cyrus's decree to end here with a messianic image (cf. 1Ch 17:12), saying that of all the people who were to go up, one prominent figure, He whose God is with Him (the Messiah), should go up to Jerusalem to build the messianic temple (Ps 110; Zch 6:9-15). In this way, readers at the close of the OT, are being pointed forward immediately to the NT, which opens with a genealogy in the Gospel of Matthew (linking it to the genealogy at the beginning of the books of Chronicles), identifying Jesus as the one whose God is with Him and therefore "God with us" (Immanuel). He is the fulfillment of the messianic promise to David. Thus, the Hebrew Bible concludes with hope, not just in the faithfulness of God in restoring Israel in the past, but even more, with hope for the future. It is a reminder to keep looking for the messianic son of David, the redeemer of Israel and the world.

BIBLIOGRAPHY

See Bibliography for 1 and 2 Chronicles on p. 582

EZRA

J. BRIAN TUCKER

INTRODUCTION

Author and Date. The work does not identify an author; however, Ezra was likely responsible for the so-called Ezra memoir, Ezr 7:28–9:15, written in the first person. A significant portion of canonical Ezra includes official documents and letters, which would indicate the work of a compiler; Ezra may well have been the editor of these documents (cf. Ezr 1:2-4; 4:11-16, 17-22; 5:7-17; 6:2b-5, 6-12; 7:12-16). All are written in Aramaic with the exception of Ezr 1:2-4. Some argue that the similarity of 2Ch 36:22-23 with Ezr 1:1-3 and the priestly perspective in both works point toward one person involved in the creation of both (cf. Joseph Blenkinsopp, *Judaism, the First Phase: The Place of Ezra and Nehemiah in the Origins of Judaism* [Grand Rapids, MI: Eerdmans, 2009], 166; H. G. M. Williamson, *Ezra, Nehemiah*, WBC, vol. 16 [Waco, TX: Word Books, 1985], xxi-xxiii). The opening of Neh 1:1 indicates the separate literary creation of that work; however, the books of Ezra and Nehemiah were combined into one quite early on (cf. Josephus, *Contra Apion* 1.40; *Baba Bathra* 15a; Eusebius, *Hist. Eccl.* 4.26.14). Second Maccabees 2:13 provides a plausible scenario in which Ezra would have had access to the type of documents evident in Ezra-Nehemiah (e.g., the Nehemiah memoir in Neh 1:1–7:5). If one accepts this framework, then one may date the composition of Ezra, and by extension Nehemiah, to some time between 440 BC and 430 BC (cf. Neh 1:1; 8:2; 12:2; 13:6; Ezr 7:8).

Ezra offers the canonical retelling of the return of the Judeans from the Babylonian captivity. It comes after 2 Chronicles in the English Bible, but the Hebrew Bible places it before Chronicles. This raises the question, why is Ezra-Nehemiah canonically before Chronicles in the Hebrew Bible? Chronicles was probably written after the events narrated in Ezra and Nehemiah. The conditions were such that they continued to reflect exile rather than restoration (Ezr 9:6-15; Neh 9:32-36). So the question of Israel's place in God's plan and the continuing relevance of the promises made to David were significant communal concerns. Thus Chronicles provides an interpretation of Israel's history that addresses the specific concerns of postexilic Israel. In this way, Ezra-Nehemiah serve as excellent canonical introductions to 1 and 2 Chronicles. As just alluded to, in the Hebrew Bible, Ezra forms one book with Nehemiah (Ezra-Nehemiah), as it does in the Septuagint, where it is called "Esdras B." This is distinct from 1 Esdras, which is an apocryphal book that served as a source for Josephus in the writing of his *Jewish Antiquities*. Esdras is the Greek equivalent of the Hebrew name "Ezra."

Theme and Purpose. The theme of the book of Ezra is the restoration of the covenant identity of Israel through God's providence. The purposes of the book flow from this theme. (1) Ezra wrote because he wished to narrate the way God fulfilled His promises to restore His covenant people to the land of Judah after the Babylonian captivity. (2) He wrote to reveal God's providential care of His children and illustrate the way imperial powers can be used to further God's redemptive purposes. (3) He wrote so that the process of restoration involved in the rebuilding of political and religious structures necessary to secure the continuity of Judean covenantal identity during the Persian period would be remembered. (4) He wrote in order to detail the rebuilding of the temple and the reconstitution of the people of God living in accordance with the law of Moses. (5) Ezra wrote because he (and

Ezra-Nehemiah combined) understands the return from captivity as a promise of an even greater return. That is to say, Ezra presents the return from the exile as a fulfillment of prophecy (Ezr 1:1-4), but the conclusion to Nehemiah shows how Israel had still not kept the Mosaic covenant. So, although the return from exile was part of God's graciousness to Israel, it did not tell the entire story. Rather, it pointed to an eschatological day of fulfillment, when Messiah would fulfill all the promises God made to His people.

Contribution. Ezra contributes to the biblical narrative in four ways. (1) It provides the narrative description of the return of the Judeans from the Babylonian captivity and thus continues the story that began in 1 and 2 Chronicles. (2) It explains the presence of the Judeans in Israel, and the religious and political events that took place for their resettlement in the promised land and the rebuilding of the temple. (3) It provides the historical context for the prophetic ministries of Haggai and Zechariah; without Ezra their prophetic oracles would lack significant context. (4) It reveals the origins of early Judaism and the contours of Jewish identity that are central to the later biblical-theological context.

Ezra is a historical narrative or chronicle that presents a theological interpretation of the events it narrates. This does not mean that the book is unhistorical; its events parallel quite nicely the inscriptional and archaeological records (e.g., Elephantine papyri, *ANET*[3], 491-92; Cyrus Cylinder, *ANET*[3], 315-16). It does mean that it provides its audience with a theological interpretation of salvation history. It includes sources from administrative documents, letters, lists, and genealogies; however, it lacks the prophetic discourse evident in Haggai and Zechariah, two works that describe similar postexilic circumstances.

Background. The events narrated in Ezra occurred during the Persian imperial period, and opened with Cyrus II, who reigned from 550 to 530 BC. He had overthrown the Neo-Babylonian king Nabonidus in 539 BC and then consolidated his power throughout Mesopotamia, reinforcing the political domination of the Achaemenid dynasty (named after Achaemenes, who ruled Persia from 705 to 675 BC, and founded the royal family of whom Cyrus was a member). Cyrus reversed the forced migration policies of the Babylonians and initiated a program of repatriation. The Judeans living in Babylon, as new citizens of the Persian Empire, benefited from this change in imperial policy. In 538 BC, Cyrus issued a proclamation that allowed the Judeans to return to the province of Judah for the purpose of rebuilding the temple and reinhabiting Jerusalem (Ezr 1:1-4; 6:3-5).

Cambyses, who ruled from 530 to 522 BC, is not mentioned in the narrative, but Darius I, who reigned from 522 to 486 BC, plays a significant role. He received a letter from a provincial official concerning the rebuilding of the temple (5:6-17), and after investigating Cyrus' original proclamation, he decreed that the construction project should continue (6:1-12). The narrative also mentions complaints made to Xerxes, who reigned from 496 to 465 BC, concerning the Judeans (4:6). Artaxerxes I, who was emperor from 465 to 424 BC, ruled during the mission of Ezra. The nature of the opposition during this period related to the building of the walls rather than the temple, which had been completed during the reign of Darius I. The arguments of Rehum and Shimshai convinced Artaxerxes I, and he ordered the rebuilding of the walls to stop (4:8-23). He eventually reversed his decision and allowed Ezra to lead another group of exiles to Jerusalem in 458 BC. Though outside the narrative of Ezra, Nehemiah arrived in Jerusalem 13 years later, in 445 BC, to inspect the walls (Neh 2:1) and returned again in 433 BC (Neh 5:14; 13:6). The combined narrative time of Ezra-Nehemiah is around 105 years and covers the reign of five Persian kings (Edwin M. Yamauchi, *Persia and the Bible* [Grand Rapids, MI: Baker, 1996], 395–6).

OUTLINE

I. Returns of the Exiles and Restoration of the Temple (1:1–6:22)
   A. Initial Return of the Exiles (1:1-11)
      1. Proclamation of Cyrus (1:1-4)
      2. Leadership of Sheshbazzar (1:5-11)

B. Initial List of the Exiles Who Returned (2:1-70)
C. Renewal of Ritual and Worship (3:1-13)
  1. Restoration of the Altar and Sacrifices (3:1-7)
  2. Reconstruction of the Foundations of the Temple (3:8-13)
D. Opposition to God's Renewing Work (4:1-24)
  1. Opposition During the Time of Cyrus (4:1-5)
  2. Imperial Oppositions (4:6-24)
E. Prophetic and Political Events and the Temple (5:1-17)
F. Imperial Protection and the Completion of the Temple (6:1-22)
  1. Record of the Decree of Cyrus Found in Ecbatana (6:1-7)
  2. Decree of Darius (6:8-12)
  3. Temple Finished and Dedicated (6:13-18)
  4. First Observance of the Passover (6:19-22)

II. Return of Ezra and Reformation of the People (7:1–10:44)
A. Ezra's Journey to Jerusalem Under the Authorization of Persia (7:1-28)
  1. Journey from Babylon to Jerusalem (7:1-10)
  2. Imperial Authorization for Ezra's Mission (7:11-28)
B. Ezra's Return to Jerusalem (8:1-36)
C. Threat of Mixed Marriages to Covenant Identity (9:1-15)
  1. Mixed Marriages Among the Community (9:1-5)
  2. Ezra's Confession of the Community's Sins (9:6-15)
D. Communal Reformation and Renewal (10:1-44)
  1. Consent of the Community to End Mixed Marriages (10:1-17)
  2. Listing of Those Implicated in Mixed Marriages (10:18-44)

COMMENTARY ON EZRA

I. Returns of the Exiles and Restoration of the Temple (1:1–6:22)

Ezra 1:1–6:22 describes the initial and subsequent returns of the exiles from Babylon, as well as the reconstruction of the temple. The events narrated here occurred about 80 years before Ezra arrived in Judah; the temple had been restored for almost 60 years. These chapters provide a theological interpretation of history and emphasize God's providence and sovereignty.

A. Initial Return of the Exiles (1:1-11)

Chapter 1 shows the way a small postexilic community of Jews could understand themselves as the covenant people of God. God's fulfillment of the promises proclaimed by Isaiah and Jeremiah restored significant continuity in the ritual life of the preexilic community. The worship articles were from the previous temple, and some of the diaspora group members were Levites. God's providence and sovereignty were evident, as He used an imperial power and an obscure Babylonian Jew to accomplish His salvation goals in history and lead the exiles out of captivity into the promised land.

1. Proclamation of Cyrus (1:1-4)

1:1. In 538 BC, God moved on the heart of **Cyrus king of Persia** to allow the Jews in exile to return to the land of Judah, a course of action that Isaiah had prophesied (Is 44:28; 45:1, 13). This **proclamation** also provided an initial and partial fulfillment of the prophecy of **Jeremiah** concerning the length of Babylonian captivity (cf. Jr 25:11-12; 29:10; 51:11; 2Ch 36:20). The timing of these events is often a matter of scholarly dispute; however, if the first captives were taken to Babylon in 605 BC (cf. Dn 1:1; Jr 25:1), then 536 BC would have been the seventieth year (Ezr 3:8). Thus, God remembered His covenant people and fulfilled His promise to them, even by the agency of an imperial power (Mervin Breneman, *Ezra, Nehemiah, Esther* [Nashville, TN: Broadman & Holman, 1993], 67).

1:2-4. The proclamation of Cyrus provided freedom for the Jews and allowed them to return to **Jerusalem, which is in Judah** to rebuild the temple. An Aramaic version of this proclamation occurs in 6:2-5. This latter declaration is more of an administrative "memorandum" and parallels quite closely the Elephantine papyrus, dated to 407 BC, requesting permission from the governor to rebuild a temple in that Egyptian city (Edwin M. Yamauchi, "Ezra and Nehemiah," in John H. Walton, ed., *1 & 2 Kings, 1 & 2 Chronicles, Ezra, Nehemiah, Esther*, ZIBBC, vol. 3 [Grand Rapids, MI: Zondervan, 2009], 399).

The original proclamation of Cyrus was part of his broader political strategy that allowed conquered peoples to return to their homeland and rebuild their cities. This is evident in the Cyrus Cylinder, an inscription struck in 539 BC on the occasion of Cyrus's capture of Babylon. On the cylinder, written in Akkadian, Cyrus declared himself the great and benevolent king over all, the one who restored peoples to their land and returned the religious objects that had been stolen from their temples (*ANET*[3], 316). In this way, God used the political inclinations of Cyrus to further His purposes with regard to His covenant people. The Jews in Babylon were now free to return and **rebuild the house of the LORD, the God of Israel**, while the Jews who chose to remain in Mesopotamia were encouraged to support those returning **with a freewill offering for the house of God which is in Jerusalem**.

2. Leadership of Sheshbazzar (1:5-11)

1:5-8. God now moved the hearts of some of the Jews to return to Jerusalem to **rebuild** the temple. This explanation provides a theological reason that some Jews chose not to return to Judah—God had not **stirred** their hearts to do so. The return was organized through existing kinship structures, which relied on **the heads of fathers' households** for social control and cohesion. Continuity with previous expressions of Jewish identity is evident with the further description of these people as being from the tribes of **Judah and Benjamin**, as well as those who were **priests** and **Levites**. Jewish identity had proven to be remarkably stable throughout the Persian period, and the ritual life of this covenant community embodied that identity.

Echoing an exodus motif, **all those about them**, i.e., the exiles' Babylonian neighbors, gave them gifts, supplies, and food for their journey back into the land of promise (cf. Ex 3:21-22; 12:35-36; Ps 105:37). Furthermore, **King Cyrus brought out the articles** from the temple, which had been removed by **Nebuchadnezzar** (Ezr 6:5; 2Ch 36:7, 10, 18). Removing religious items from a defeated foe's sanctuaries communicated domination by putatively showing that the group's deity was no longer able to protect them (1Sm 5:2; Jr 27:16, 21-22; Dn 5:23). Returning the items that were part of the ritual life of the community provided continuity of worship. **Cyrus** had **Mithredath the treasurer** give an accounting of the items to **Sheshbazzar, the prince of Judah**. He was a Babylonian Jew who led the returnees on the four-month journey to the land of Judah in 537 BC (Ezr 1:11; 7:8-9). **Sheshbazzar** served as the deputy governor of Judah under the satrap, a name given to governors in the Persian Empire, in Samaria (5:14, 16). Josephus wrongly conflated him with Zerubbabel (*Ant.* 11.13-14 or 11.1.3), and others have tried to identify him with Shenazzar in 1Ch 3:18, though there is little basis for this identification (Williamson, *Ezra, Nehemiah*, 17-19).

1:9-11. Mithredath provided a count of the utensils from the temple; the listing totaled 2,499, but the complete inventory resulted in 5,400 objects. Most English translations describe these as **dishes** and **bowls**; however, the Hebrew terms are either obscure, or loan-words that could also refer to basins, censers, and possibly even knives (David John Alfred Clines, *Ezra, Nehemiah, Esther*, NCBC [Grand Rapids, MI: Eerdmans, 1984], 41-3). The text is clear that worship items included **gold** and **silver** vessels (5:14; 6:5) but not the less valuable bronze items, which may have been melted down for reuse (2Kg 24:13; 25:13-17). The list points out significant links between preexilic and postexilic ritual practice. The ark of the covenant (1 Ch 28:13-18; 2Ch 5:1), however, is conspicuously absent (Edwin M. Yamauchi, *Africa and the Bible* [Grand Rapids, MI: Baker, 2004], 102). After enumerating the temple articles, **Sheshbazzar brought them all up with the exiles**, and this small group, those "whose spirit God had stirred" (Ezr 1:5), departed for **Jerusalem**. God used **Sheshbazzar**, an otherwise unknown and obscure historical figure, as He worked in history to restore His covenant people and lay the foundation for the origins of what became, during the Second Temple period, Judaism (Blenkinsopp, *Judaism: The First Phase*, 9-11).

B. Initial List of the Exiles Who Returned (2:1-70)

In Ezra, the genealogy prepared for the rebuilding of the temple and the reestablishment of worship in accordance with the law of Moses. A genealogy may not seem the most effective way to address this issue; however, it clarified questions of ethnic identity and provided a framework by which to interpret God's expectation for purity and His restorative work among the covenant people now situated within the land He had promised them. How does a genealogy accomplish this? First, it assures members of the community that they are valued and numbered among God's people. Second, as members of the covenant people, their ethnic identity is central to God's continuing plan for ethnic Israel, and a genealogy provides a reminder of this for the returnees. Third, this list provides legitimization for those in Israel who find themselves in a culture not oriented toward God's standards of purity (Breneman, *Ezra, Nehemiah, Esther*, 73-5).

2:1-2a. Scholars often note that the genealogical listing in 2:1-70 is quite similar to the listing in Neh 7:6-73 (1 Esdras 5:4-46), but each has a different rhetorical purpose. Many scholars think the Neh 7 version came first, though there is no consensus on this issue (F. Charles Fensham, *The Books of Ezra and Nehemiah*, NICOT [Grand Rapids, MI: Eerdmans, 1982], 49). The composite list in Ezr 2 probably included prominent individuals who returned at various times between 537 and 515 BC. It indicated the reconstitution of the tribes of Israel in the Promised Land (cf. Neh 7:7). The list in 2:2a provided further information only for **Zerubbabel** and **Jeshua**. Ezra 3:2, 8 describes **Zerubbabel** as the son of Shealtiel; but 1Ch 3:19 lists him as the son of Pedaiah, Shealtiel's younger brother. Two ways to resolve this exist. (1) Shealtiel died early, and Pedaiah became the head of the household. (2) This is an instance of a levirate marriage (Dt 25:5-6). It is hard to determine which of the two is more likely when 1Ch 3:19 is taken into consideration, following Thompson, "The explanation may be that Shealtiel died childless and Zerubbabel was born to Pedaiah by a levirate marriage with Shealtiel's widow" (J. A. Thompson, *1, 2 Chronicles*, NAC [Nashville: Broadman & Holman, 2001], 70). **Zerubbabel**, a descendant of King David, became the governor of Judah (Hg 1:1) subsequent to Sheshbazzar holding the position (Ezr 5:14), though it is not clear when that change occurred. Sheshbazzar started the work on the temple (5:16), then **Zerubbabel** became the governor (3:2) and finished the temple in 516 BC (6:15). **Jeshua**, who is called "Joshua" in Hg 1:1, was the high priest and grandson of Seraiah, the final high priest prior to the exile (2Kg 25:18). The person described as **Nehemiah** is most likely not the leader who arrived in Jerusalem around 80 years later in 445 BC.

2:2b-35. This group of well-known family and place names is organized under the covenant name **Israel**. This was a reminder that God is faithful to His covenant promises. Israel's ethnic identity also had a geographical component to it, and specific locations were identified with the groups in vv. 21-35. The towns described were within the region given to the tribe of Benjamin and located, with the exception of **Netophah** and **Bethlehem**, north of Jerusalem (Breneman, *Ezra, Nehemiah, Esther*, 78). These probably were the villages that the returnees and/or their ancestors had originally left, which leaves open the question as to whether they returned to these specific locales. While the alternate means of identification may represent different ways of registering people during the various returns between 537 and 515 BC, the importance of the land in the formation of Jewish social identity provides another possible explanation. These newly arriving **people of Israel** needed a sense of roots; this could come by identification with their tribal linage (vv. 3-20), and these preexilic locations provided them with a constant reminder of God's covenant faithfulness (vv. 21-35).

2:36-58. The social function of the genealogy is quite evident in the next list, those ministering within the temple. The priestly families of **Jedaiah**, **Immer**, **Pashhur**, and **Harim** also appear in 10:18-22. **The Levites** were descendants of Levi, subordinate to the descendents of Aaron, who made up the priestly families (8:15-20; 1Ch 24:26-28). **The Levites**, **singers**, and **gatekeepers** all engaged in tasks associated with temple worship (Ezk 44:10-44; 1Ch 9:17; 15:16). **The temple servants** and **sons of Solomon's servants** assisted the Levites with the more routine temple duties (1Ch 9:2; Ezr 7:24).

2:59-63. The need for communal holiness required the reconstitution of a group set apart for ritual-communal purposes. This action drew a boundary around those who **were not able to give evidence of their fathers' households**. These lay and priestly families were separated from the community of **Israel** and **considered unclean**. **The governor** directed them not to partake of the sacred food **until a priest stood up with Urim and Thummim**. The high priest kept these small objects, possibly different colored pebbles, with inscriptions indicating "yes" or "no," in his garments; they helped him determine God's will (Ex 28:30;

Nm 27:21). It appears they had fallen into disuse after the time of the early monarchy and were revived during the time of Ezra (1Sm 14:41; Neh 7:65). Some suggest this disuse occurred because of the presence of prophetic revelation; however, they were introduced during the time of Moses, and prophetic revelation was active during that period. More likely, argues Fyall, the reinstatement of the Urim and Thummim at this time was done to emphasize continuity with Israel's past and "provided a way of access to God" (Robert S. Fyall, *The Message of Ezra and Haggai: Building for God* [Downers Grove, IL: InterVarsity, 2010], 51). The resolution with regard to these six families is unclear from the text. The point, however, is clear: purity concerns would predominate in the formation of identity within the postexilic community, just as within the preexilic one, except now genealogical records would determine whether or not one was part of **Israel** (Ezr 2:59).

2:64-70. The whole assembly numbered 42,360. The combined total of the preceding list is 29,818; however, the aggregate nature of the lists and the likelihood of inadvertently omitting some names may plausibly explain the discrepancy (Breneman, *Ezra, Nehemiah, Esther*, 85). The number **42,360** is nonetheless correct and detailed those considered part of the **assembly**, with the numbers of **servants**, singers, and animals listed separately. The presence of **servants** and various animals indicates economic diversity among the people of Israel, although later, in 520 BC, Haggai would point out that their neglect of the house of God had brought economic distress on the community (Hg 1:7-11). Some heads of various kinship groups **offered** significant financial resources to restore the **foundation** of the temple. The majority of the exiles settled in the villages around Jerusalem, while those associated with the temple settled within the city proper. The initial group of exiles was now ready to rebuild the temple and reestablish proper worship of God as Moses had laid it out in the law, which is the concern of chap. 3.

C. Renewal of Ritual and Worship (3:1-13)

Sheshbazzar led the exiles into a time of renewal in their ritual and worship life. He delegated Zerubbabel and Jeshua to oversee the initial stages of this project. After living in Judah for about six months, they restored the sacrifices on the rebuilt altar. After seven months, they laid the foundation for the restoration of the temple. This engendered different expressions of worship, and it served as a catalyst for those who opposed God's activity among His people.

1. Restoration of the Altar and Sacrifices (3:1-7)

3:1-7. The events described in this section, **when the seventh month came**, occurred during the sacred month of Tishri (Sept–Oct), probably in 537 BC. Specifically, 3:6 says sacrifices were restored on the first of the seventh month—this is the date of the first fall feast, Trumpets. These fall feasts culminated in the Feast of Booths (v. 4). Two terms indicate the salience of their social identity: **the sons of Israel** and **as one man**. The emerging sense of community had its source in their common identity expressed in their worship of the God who chose Israel (Ex 19:5; Lv 11:44; Dt 14:2, 21).

Two of the key leaders in the restoration of the ritual life of the community were **Jeshua** and **Zerubbabel** (see discussion at 2:1-2a). Their initial worship focus, following the earlier example of David (2Sm 24:25), was to build **the altar of the God of Israel**. They built this in accordance with **the law of Moses** (Ex 20:25). This implicitly criticized those who had continued to offer sacrifices at the defiled altar in Jerusalem during the Babylonian captivity (cf. Jr 41:5; Ezr 4:2). The exiles committed themselves to ritual purity and to line up their worship practices with **the law of Moses**. The desire to show continuity with the identity of the preexilic community led the Israelites to build **the altar on its foundation**, i.e., in the exact location of the preexilic altar. They offered **burnt offerings morning and evening**; this was also in accord with **the law of Moses** (Nm 28:2-4). The return of the exiles did not please everyone; **the peoples of the lands**, i.e., the Samaritans and those foreigners who had lived in this region prior to the Israelites' return, became increasingly hostile to the restored community (Breneman, *Ezra, Nehemiah, Esther*, 92).

The Israelites **celebrated the Feast of Booths** from the 15th to the 21st days of Tishri (Lv 23:34). This was the last of the three pilgrimage festivals (Ex 23:14-16), and **the law of Moses** contained detailed prescriptions for its observance, which the returnees followed **as it is written** (Nm 29:12-38). The feast reminded the worshipers of God's providential care in the past and their ongoing need to trust Him for protection, security, and deliverance. Living for seven days in huts covered with branches draped with fruits and vegetables physically reminded them of their dependence on God and also served as a communal embodiment and memorial of the exodus (Lv 23:40). In a later observance of this feast, Ezra read the law of Moses to the people (Neh 8:13-18).

The restoration of a comprehensive program of sacrifices preceded the first attempt to rebuild the temple. It involved the entire community, as they **offered a freewill offering to the Lord**. As the formation of this community continued, worship would serve as the primary way to express the ongoing transformation of their identity. This process was just beginning, however. **The foundation of the temple of the LORD had not been laid**; significant work still remained, but God was with them. They would have to accomplish this work in the midst of hostile neighbors; however, they had **the permission** of **Cyrus king of Persia** (Ezr 6:3-5), and more important, they had experienced the presence of God even before the rebuilding of the temple.

2. Reconstruction of the Foundations of the Temple (3:8-13)

3:8-13. The returnees began to rebuild the temple **in the second year**, i.e., 536 BC, **in the second month** (April–May); this is the same month in which Solomon began to build the first temple (1Kg 6:1). Due to opposition (Ezr 4:1-5), they did not complete this project during this time, though they laid the foundations. A second period of temple rebuilding started in 520 BC, and the completion of the temple itself came in 516 BC (5:2; 6:15; Hg 1:14,15). **Zerubbabel**, **Jeshua** and others from the **captivity . . . began the work**. The leaders delegated some of it to others, e.g., **the Levites**, and reduced their qualifying age to **twenty**, probably because of the paucity of their numbers (cf. Ezr 2:40; Nm 4:1-3; 1Ch 23:3, 24). They, then, managed **the workmen in the temple of God**.

Once the workers had **laid the foundation**, the community gathered to praise God for what He had allowed them to accomplish. This postexilic community showed significant continuity with the ritual and worship life of the preexilic one, so much so that they not only ordered their worship according to the law of Moses, but more specifically **according to the directions of King David of Israel** (1Ch 25:1). The psalm they sang came from Ps 100:5, and had previously signaled anticipation of God's glory and presence (1Ch 16:34; 2Ch 5:13). They had not yet rebuilt the temple, but they had laid **the foundation of the house of the LORD**, and that resulted in great shouts of praise and celebration. Some, on the other hand, **wept with a loud voice** when they saw the extent of the foundations in comparison to the earlier temple, an experience repeated in 520 BC when temple construction restarted a second time (cf. Hg 2:3; Zch 4:8-10). The foundation of the temple served as a concrete reminder that the Israelite's community belonged to God, and His call formed the foundation of their identity as God's chosen people (Dt 7:6-8). Two points of application emerge from Ezr 3:1-13. (1) A way to deal with personal hurts from the past is to unite with others who want to make a spiritual impact. (2) Spend money for kingdom purposes, and then celebrate what God can do through generous giving. The returnees quickly learned that God's renewing work did not please everyone; this becomes evident in chap. 4.

D. Opposition to God's Renewing Work (4:1-24)

Chapter 4 is a thematically-ordered listing of the opposition that the various communities in Judah experienced from their arrival in Judah led by Sheshbazzar until the time of Nehemiah and the building of the walls around Jerusalem almost 100 years later. This chapter examines the unrelenting hostility of those opposed to God's renewing work and the challenges faced by those called to fulfill God's purpose in the world.

1. Opposition During the Time of Cyrus (4:1-5)

4:1-5. The opposition in vv. 1-5 occurred during the reign of Cyrus and covered the period from 536–530 BC. **The enemies** were the people from Samaria who asked **Zerubbabel** to allow them to **build** the temple with the returning exiles (Yamauchi, "Ezra and Nehemiah," 405). The Samaritans descended from those deported by Sargon II to repopulate Israel after the fall of the northern kingdom in 722 BC, along with a later forced migration of Egyptians by **Esarhaddon** in 671 BC. They were syncretistic in their worship, combining the worship of Yahweh with other gods in the ancient Near East (cf. 2Kg 17:24-33; Jr 41:5). Concerns for ritual purity led **Zerubbabel** and the other leaders to conclude that these outsiders should **have nothing in common** with those working on the temple. Furthermore, they reminded these so-called willing volunteers that **Cyrus, the king of Persia** had allowed this building project, implying that their interference would go against Persian imperial policy.

The opposition, however, did not cease. **The people of the land**, those already introduced in Ezr 3:3, **discouraged** and **frightened** the builders. They **hired counselors** to delay the rebuilding process. **The enemies** continued these tactics through the reigns of **Cyrus**, Cambyses, and Darius I (Matthew Levering, *Ezra & Nehemiah*, BTCB [Grand Rapids, MI: Brazos Press, 2007], 64–6). The actual work on the temple ceased in 530 BC (Ezr 4:24) and did not start again until 520 BC (Ezr 5:2). It was then completed during the reign of Darius I in 516 BC (Ezr 6:15).

2. Imperial Oppositions (4:6-24)

4:6-24. Though the exiles had permission to return to Judah, they still lived under an imperial power, and the Israelites' enemies relied on that as a way to thwart their progress. The following section is a rhetorical digression, diverting from the primarily chronological narrative in order to reinforce the theme of persistent opposition experienced by the returning exiles, whether in rebuilding the temple or in the later building of the walls. The Jewish leaders had rejected offers of assistance from the people of the land, and vv. 6-23 provides a case study that reveals that these people were disingenuous in their offer; their motivation was to hinder rather than support progress. This revelation justified the leaders' rejection of their overtures of help.

During his **reign**, **Ahasuerus**, i.e., Xerxes (486–465 BC) received complaints concerning those living in **Judah and Jerusalem**. The nature of the **accusation** is unclear, but some relation to the rebellion in Egypt remains a conjecture. The next accusation occurred during the **days of Artaxerxes** I (465–424 BC) and consisted of a letter written in **Aramaic**, which had become the *lingua franca* in the Persian Empire (Yamauchi, *Persia and the Bible*, 244). The **Aramaic** text extends from 4:8 to 6:18. The letter, which begins in v. 12, came from the officials in Samaria and accused the Jews who sought to rebuild Jerusalem's walls of subversive behavior. The writers contended **that if the city is rebuilt and the walls are finished**, those in Jerusalem would cease paying their required **tribute, custom or toll** to the Persians—an effective economic argument. Next, they employed the notion of honor and shame, which played a dominant role in public life, to assert that these exiles were seeking to dishonor the king. This public challenge to his honor required a response—an effective cultural argument. There was only one solution: since a Persian king had issued the initial proclamation to allow these subversive exiles to rebuild, likewise the Persian king should use his authority to put an end to the project. Otherwise, when they completed the walls, then the Persian Empire would lose Judah, and in light of the trouble in Egypt and Greece it could not allow this to happen. The letter convinced him, and consequently **Artaxerxes** I issued a decree to cease the rebuilding of the walls immediately. **Rehum**, **Shimshai**, and the others entered Jerusalem and **stopped them by force of arms**.

What were the rhetorical purposes of this digression and these letters? (1) They indicated that if the rebuilding of Jerusalem were going to happen, it would come from God's power and not by political might (Ps 127:1). (2) They explained the reason the rebuilding stopped for a period of time. (3) They provided a reminder that the rulers of this age did not understand the ways of God (see 1Co 2:6-9).

The digression ends in v. 24, and the narrative comes back to the original opposition from vv. 1-5 in the time of Sheshbazzar, during the reign of Cyrus in 530 BC. The effectiveness of the initial opposition by the enemies of Jerusalem and Benjamin was evident: the **work on the house of God in Jerusalem ceased**. It would not begin again until 520 BC, a time of relative peace and stability after Darius I had consolidated his power through two years of military conquests, recounted on the Behistun Inscription, a massive trilingual monument, which shows a life-size Darius dominating diminutive figures, representing his enemies (Yamauchi, "Ezra and Nehemiah," 408-9). Those involved in God's renewing work will experience opposition from those who do not understand His ways. So it should not be a surprise when opposition comes; however, God's plans ultimately will not be thwarted (Ex 14:13-14). Ezra 5 makes this truth clear.

E. Prophetic and Political Events and the Temple (5:1-17)

This section begins with the introduction of the prophetic ministries of Haggai and Zechariah. These served as the revelatory impetus for the completion of the temple. God continued to work through the imperial powers and their local collaborators to accomplish His desire for the rebuilding of the temple. For this to take place the returned exiles had to recount the way Cyrus had originally allowed them to return and build.

5:1-2. Work on the temple had ceased for ten

years when the prophets **Haggai** and **Zechariah** emerged to call the **Jews** to begin again to rebuild the temple (Hg 1:1; Zch 1:1). Led by **Zerubbabel** and **Jeshua**, the two **prophets of God were with them supporting them** by offering motivation, encouragement, and perspective concerning the importance of completing this task (Ezr 6:14). Haggai's message provided encouragement in three ways. (1) It pointed out that the rebuilding of the temple would ameliorate the Judeans' current dire economic situation (cf. the comments on Hg 1:10; 2:18-19). (2) It reminded them that even though this temple was small in comparison to Solomon's, God's glory and the wealth of the nations (or perhaps the Desired One of the nations, the Messiah) would fill it (see comments on Hg 2:3, 7-9). (3) It encouraged the people about their future security and protection. Zerubbabel, son of Shealtiel, was from the Davidic line (1Ch 3:17), and God had chosen him as a vessel through whom He would provide victory over Israel's enemies. Zechariah's message resonated with these same three themes (cf. Zch 1:16; 4:9; 8:3, 12-13), but also addressed three further topics. (1) God would fulfill His promises to Abraham (Zch 2:11). (2) God would no longer remember their sins (Zch 3:9). (3) The ultimate transformation of history would come through God's Messiah (cf. Zch 3:8; Is 11:1-10; Mk 8:29). Both of these **prophets** were able to see the way God's specific plans for the returned exiles fit into His broader plans for salvation history (Levering, *Ezra & Nehemiah*, 69–73).

5:3-5. The Jews began to rebuild the temple; however, immediately the provincial rulers and their local collaborators challenged their actions. **Tattenai** and **Shethar-bozenai** had no awareness of Cyrus's decree, and thus Zerubbabel and Jeshua's reimplementation of it rightly troubled them. **Tattenai** probably functioned in the broad sense as a **governor** under the satrap Ushtannu, who ruled the province of Babylon and Beyond the River, while **Shethar-bozenai** may have been Tattenai's scribe (cf. Shimshai, 4:8) or more likely one of the Persian imperial officials responsible for inspecting the provinces for the king (4:9; 6:6). This broad interpretation of **governor** still allows for the description of Zerubbabel as governor of Judah (Hg 1:1, 14; 2:2, 21), though perhaps with limited authority. The Persian officials enquired about the **structure**, and about those involved in its reconstruction. The officials allowed them to continue to work until they received a response from **Darius** I, which thus showed that **God**, in His providence, was watching over them—**the eye of their God was on the elders of the Jews**.

5:6-17. The Persian officials composed **a report** to Darius I, and this section recounts the contents of the letter. The Elamite texts in Persepolis, dating to the time of Darius I, include administrative reports such as this (Williamson, *Ezra, Nehemiah*, 78). They addressed the mundane aspects of provincial life as it intersected with imperial concerns. The report included the following: (1) a review of the physical structure, with its **huge stones** and **beams** (cf. Ezr 6:4; 1Kg 6:36); (2) a recounting of the enquiries put to the Jewish leaders, i.e., **elders**; (3) an extensive detailing of the responses given by the men, which mirrors the narrative in Ezr 1:1-11; (4) a request for verification of the **decree** issued by **King Cyrus**. The religious identity of the leaders is brought to the fore in 5:11-12 as they assert key aspects of their worldview: (1) they are servants of the God of heaven and earth; (2) they are rebuilding the house of the God who is involved in history; and (3) they understand the way the failures of the previous generation led to the captivity of their people.

F. Imperial Protection and the Completion of the Temple (6:1-22)

Darius I had his officials search for the original proclamation allowing the Jews to return and rebuild the temple in Jerusalem; they found it in Ecbatana. After reading the decree, Darius I issued a further proclamation to allow the Jews to complete their work and to prevent the local officials from interfering with their progress. With renewed imperial support and vigorous prophetic encouragement, the people finished and dedicated the temple. The community then celebrated the Passover and the Feast of Unleavened Bread as initial expressions of their renewed identity as the covenant people of God.

1. Record of the Decree of Cyrus Found in Ecbatana (6:1-7)

6:1-7. The search for Cyrus' proclamation began in **Babylon** since the Jews left from there to go to Judah. It ended in **Ecbatana** (located 200 miles southwest of the Caspian Sea), the capital of **Media**, the summer residence for the Persian kings, with the discovery of **a scroll** containing a relevant **memorandum**. This was probably not the original decree, which a scribe would have written on a clay tablet, but rather a record of the decree with further administrative details (cf. 1:2-4; Xanthos Charter, c. 358 BC; Yamauchi,

"Ezra and Nehemiah," 411–2). It stipulated the size of the rebuilt temple, though if followed would have resulted in one larger than the original (1Kg 6:2). The financing would come **from the royal treasury**, and the **gold and silver utensils** previously taken would regain their proper location within the **temple** (Dn 5:2-4). Darius I then ordered his provincial officials to **keep away from there**, i.e., not to interfere any further with the rebuilding of the temple, and to let Zerubbabel and **the elders of the Jews rebuild this house of God on its site**. They were to rebuild the temple in its original location; an inscription of Nabonidus indicates that he rebuilt the temple of Sippar, a city of Babylonia on the Euphrates, over the foundations of the earlier temple of Sargon II, king of Assyria and Babylonia from 721 to 705 BC (*COS*, 2.123A).

2. Decree of Darius (6:8-12)

6:8-12. The Persian kings were interested in the restoration of indigenous religious sanctuaries throughout their empire, and Darius's proclamation fit within that context (cf. *ANET*[3], 491-92). This was an adroit political maneuver, because it secured the loyalty of their subjects, while offering putative support for foreign cults—notice also that he required the Jews to **pray for the life of the king and his sons**. The end of the Cyrus Cylinder included this strategic request for all those repatriated to their sacred cities. Herodotus attested to this imperialistic intrusion into accepted ritual life. As the sacrifice was being offered, the one involved, "prays that it may be well with the king and all the Persians" (1.132). The financial and ritual resources necessary for the completion of the temple were to come from Tattenai's provincial coffers. This would result in the offering of **acceptable sacrifices to the God of heaven**. The decree included a sentence of death on anyone **who violates this edict**. Darius I impaled some of his enemies (cf. Herodotus 3.159; the Behistun Inscription), so this was no idle threat. Coupled with Darius' curse on anyone who tried to **destroy this house of God in Jerusalem**, this dire warning served as an effective means of social control throughout the Persian Empire.

3. Temple Finished and Dedicated (6:13-18)

6:13-18. The provincial officials and the local collaborators **carried out the decree with all diligence**, providing much needed political and economic support. The prophetic and spiritual support continued from **Haggai** and **Zechariah** (Hg 1:12-15). As a result, **they finished building** the temple, a project completed through God's **command** and the political proclamations of the Persian emperors on March 12, 516 BC, **the sixth year of the reign of King Darius**.

Next, the community gathered to dedicate **this house of God with joy** (cf. 1Kg 8 for the first temple's dedication). The hundreds of animal sacrifices offered were small in comparison to previous dedications (1Kg 8:5, 63; 2Ch 30:24; 35:7). Also, the **sin offering for all Israel** indicated social identification with **the tribes of Israel**. The leaders organized ritual life in a manner consonant with the preexilic community and in accordance with **the book of Moses**. The returned exiles thus embodied the identity of the covenant people of God.

4. First Observance of the Passover (6:19-22)

6:19-22. A month later, with the temple dedication complete, the community **observed the Passover**. This was the first time in 70 years that the reconstituted **sons of Israel** were able to observe, in Jerusalem, the feast that commemorated their liberation from Egyptian oppression (Ex 12:1-14) and redemption as a nation. The joyous, worship-focused seven-day **Feast of Unleavened Bread** followed (Lv 23:5-6; Ps 105:42-43; Neh 8:10). **The priests and the Levites had purified themselves** with the washings outlined in the law of Moses (Ex 29:4; Nm 8:7).

The returned exiles, though committed to purity within their community, included among their group others **who had separated themselves from the impurity of the nations of the land**. These inhabitants of Judah had to make two decisions. (1) They had to reprioritize any aspects of their social identity inconsistent with their identification with the people of God. (2) They had to reorient their religious and political focus and **seek the Lord God of Israel**, because it was God who **had turned the heart of the king of Assyria** (Pr 21:1; Herodotus 1.178). This unexpected title for Darius, king of Persia, rhetorically connected him with the history of Israel, where in 2Kg 17, with the fall of Samaria, the northern tribes were deported to Assyria. Also, Kidner points out Assyria is functioning here as the quintessential oppressor (see Neh 9:32) (F. D. Kidner, *Ezra and Nehemiah*, TOTC [Downers Grove, IL: InterVarsity, 1979], 60). The reference to Assyria also provided a subtle reminder that God's providence oversees the course of history (Breneman, *Ezra, Nehemiah, Esther*, 122). The renaissance of Jerusalem during the Persian period occurred because of God's faithfulness to His promises (Jr 23:3).

II. Return of Ezra and Reformation of the People (7:1–10:44)

Ezra 7:1–10:44 recounts another migration of Judeans from Babylon, during the time of Artaxerxes I under the leadership of Ezra. The events narrated here occurred about 80 years after the first migration under Sheshbazzar. Much of this section reflects the personal memoirs of Ezra and is intensely personal. These chapters emphasize the importance of purity to the identity of God's people and how living according to God's law results in reformation and renewal.

A. Ezra's Journey to Jerusalem Under the Authorization of Persia (7:1-28)

The narrative moves forward several decades to describe another group of immigrants led by Ezra, under the patronage of the Persian King Artaxerxes I. Ezra was a different type of leader from Sheshbazzar, the prince of Judah. A priest, a scribe, and one who knew the law of God, he was also politically clever and navigated the Persian imperial context in a manner that allowed God's people to return with the financial, judicial, and spiritual resources necessary to address the challenges awaiting them.

1. Journey from Babylon to Jerusalem (7:1-10)

7:1-10. The narrative first orients itself to what preceded it. The completion of the temple had occurred in 516 BC (6:15); however, Ezra arrived in Jerusalem in 458 BC (vv. 7-9). Thus, a span of 58 years had passed since the completion and dedication of the temple. Darius I reigned from 522–486 BC and was followed by Xerxes (486–465 BC), referred to as Ahasuerus in 4:6, which recorded opposition to the rebuilding of the foundations of the temple (Est 1:1-2; Herodotus 3.89; 7.138-239). Xerxes had married Esther, who secured the safety of the Jews by thwarting the plans of Haman (Est 7:1-10). The events associated with Esther occurred during the time between chaps. 6 and 7 of Ezra. Artaxerxes I ascended to the throne in 465 BC and reigned until 424 BC. Thus, if the events narrated in Ezr 7 occurred in the **seventh year of King Artaxerxes** I, this would place Ezra's arrival in Jerusalem in 458 BC (v. 7). The text provides a genealogy for **Ezra son of Seraiah** that traced his linage back to Aaron the chief priest (1Ch 6:7-10). This provided spiritual legitimation for his mission and established continuity with the preexilic people of Israel. Ezra's home was in **Babylon, and he was a scribe skilled in the law of Moses**. Thus, he was well-trained and capable of teaching the Israelites concerning the social implications of the Torah. In spite of the decree against the returned exiles (4:19-22), Ezra found favor with Artaxerxes I, and **the king granted** his request that he and others could return to Judah and Jerusalem—possibly to verify whether or not there was a subversive intent by the Judeans (4:21). A brief travelogue narrates the 118-day journey with its 11-day delay and concludes with Ezra and a new group of returned exiles arriving safely in **Jerusalem** (cf. 8:31). Once in Jerusalem, Ezra committed himself **to study the law**, **to practice it**, and **to teach** it to those living in Jerusalem. This provides an apt description of those who are likewise committed to God's mission (Breneman, *Ezra, Nehemiah, Esther*, 130-1).

2. Imperial Authorization for Ezra's Mission (7:11-28)

7:11-20. Artaxerxes' decree authorized Ezra's journey to Jerusalem, and the Aramaic text follows. The proclamation declared that **the people of Israel**, **priests**, and **Levites** could go to **Jerusalem**. Notice the designation "Israel" rather than "Judah" (cf. 1:2), which might have indicated Persian awareness of an emerging national identity. Ezra's purpose was to **inquire** and determine the extent to which the returned exiles lived in accordance with **the law of [their] God**. This followed Persian imperial policy, which sought to exert hegemonic control over the local expressions of religious devotion (Herodotus 1.132). Artaxerxes reinforced his imperial legitimation by providing the economic means to maintain ritual life in Jerusalem (Williamson, *Ezra, Nehemiah*, 100). He positioned himself as the patron of the Jewish people. He provided **the silver and gold** necessary to purchase the sacrifices in the temple to maintain a robust worship life among these Persian citizens in the province of Judea. The resources provided would more than cover the costs of the sacrifices, so Artaxerxes allowed the leaders to use the finances for purchasing **utensils** for the house of God. Finally, in one last expression of his beneficence, the king declared that **the royal treasury** would cover any other **needs** for the temple.

7:21-26. Artaxerxes I further legitimized Ezra's mission by allowing him to request resources from the **provinces beyond the River**.

Ezra, who functioned as the royal patron's broker, did have set limits, a subtle reminder that it was Artaxerxes I who had allowed all of this to occur (cf. Josephus, *Ant.* 12.3.3). The Persian king had now positioned himself as the patron of the Judeans in hope that their God would favor him and extend his reign in peace and prosperity even unto **his sons**. Furthermore, to ensure that **the God of heaven** would favor the king, he released the **servants of this house of God** from **tax, tribute or toll**. Thus the workers in the temple could offer their service without hindrance, distraction, or delay. His task as the king's broker included a commission for Ezra to **appoint magistrates and judges** throughout the province. This would ensure that those who opposed the law of God or the law of the Persians would face appropriate consequences. Moreover, Ezra was to **teach** those who did not know the law. Artaxerxes rhetorically exerted imperial power in declaring that those who did not obey the conjoined laws of God and the Persians would face death, expulsion, imprisonment, or seizure of property (Fensham, *The Books of Ezra and Nehemiah*, 108). Obedience to the emperor, religious devotion, and ethical behavior combined to provide legitimation for Ezra's mission as Artaxerxes' broker. The narrative, however, also provides an alternative explanation: legitimization for Ezra's mission came, he said, "because the good hand of his God was upon him" (7:9).

7:27-28. The text returns to Hebrew at this point. The text from here to Ezr 9:15 may have reflected Ezra's personal journal; this conclusion follows primarily from the presence of first-person pronouns beginning in Ezr 7:28 (Breneman, *Ezra, Nehemiah, Esther*, 136). Ezra first worshiped God for the favor he had found with the **king** in that he would allow the beautification of the temple—a fulfillment of Is 60:7,13. This probably accounts for Artaxerxes' intrusion into the narrative in Ezr 6:14, and brings to the fore Ezra's understanding of God's providential care for His people. The personal application of this truth **strengthened** Ezra as he **gathered leading men** to lead a new group of immigrants to the Persian province of Judea.

B. Ezra's Return to Jerusalem (8:1-36)

This section provides a further description of Ezra's return to Jerusalem, including the interplay between God's providence and human action. Its purpose is to address the issues of identity continuity, the lack of incentive to return to Jerusalem, and why those in exile should return. Its function within the book is to connect two important theological themes: (1) the hand of our God (7:6, 9, 28; 8:18, 22, 31) and (2) God's demand for holiness (2:58-63; 4:1-3; 6:20-22; 8:24-30; 9:1–10:44). This chapter outlines the individuals who participated in the immigration and the way Ezra recruited more Levites for temple service. It records the prayers offered for the journey and ends with a recounting of the delivery of the articles for the temple and the reaffirmation of Israel's covenant identity.

8:1-14. Ezra began by describing those who returned with him. He listed the descendants of 15 individuals, totaling around 1,500. However, if that number included the Levites (8:15-20), women, and children, it would rise to around 5,000, a significantly smaller number than the 42,360 who composed the initial return (2:64). **Gershom** and **Daniel** descended from Aaron through **Phinehas** and **Ithamar**, respectively (Ex 6:23-25; 28:1), while **Hattush** descended from David (1Ch 3:22). By placing the priestly family before the royal family, Ezra, also of the family of Phinehas (Ezr 7:5), showed that he viewed them as more important. The primary concern of this restored community was purity (Nm 25:7-8), though a desire for a Davidic ruler in Judah could occupy them as well. Ezra next included 12 other families; this may represent a full complement of the house of Israel, i.e., rhetorically the 12 tribes of Israel had returned to the land (Williamson, *Ezra, Nehemiah*, 111). Ezra 2, a listing from 80 years earlier, contained all the names on this genealogy with the exception of Joab (8:9). Thus, the initial group of returnees included those who left family members in Babylon, and the descendants of many of those families had now returned with Ezra.

8:15-20. Ezra **assembled** those who returned by the **river that runs to Ahava**. The exact location is unknown, but it was most likely near the city of Babylon. Then he noticed the absence of **Levites** among them (cf. 2:36-42). So he sent for the **leading men** and **teachers** and instructed them to journey to **Casiphia** (exact location unknown but probably close to Ahava) with a message for **Iddo and his brothers**. They obeyed and found **a man of insight . . . Sherebiah**, and 37 other Levites, including **Hashabiah**, and **220 temple servants** willing to leave Babylon and return to Israel (8:24). These Levites would serve in the temple (Nm 3:5-8), but, of equal importance, they would interpret God's law for the people (e.g., Sherebiah, Neh 8:7-8; 9:4-5; 12:8, 24). Furthermore, they would guard the integrity of the worship of the people of Israel even as their Levite ancestors did (Ex 32:26-29).

8:21-23. Ezra prepared the people both spiritually and physically for the journey back to the promised land. To accomplish this, the narrative, as in Ezr 1–3, draws on motifs from the exodus (Blenkinsopp, *Judaism: The First Phase*, 165). Ezra **proclaimed a fast** that would result in a spirit of humility as well as God's protection on their journey (cf. 10:6). There would be no pillar of cloud by day, or a pillar of fire by night (Ex 13:21-22), but **the hand of God** would rest upon them (cf. Is 40:3). Ezra then recognized that his previous statements to the king concerning God's protection would not allow him now to request an imperial escort (cf. Neh 2:9). The returnees continued to fast and pray, and God heard them (cf. Ezr 9:31; Jos 1:7-9). Leaders should follow Ezra's example here: humble trust in God's guidance and protection actually signal a leader's strength, not weakness (Ac 14:23; 2Co 12:9-10).

8:24-30. The physical preparation for the journey began by weighing the **silver**, **gold**, and the **utensils** donated to the temple by Artaxerxes I. This provided a baseline amount and would reveal any losses or thefts during the journey. These articles were **holy** and reflected **a freewill offering to the Lord**. How did these articles become holy? First, notice the people and the objects both are considered holy (v. 28). Second, the idea here is "consecrated" or "set apart" (*qodes*), not just in a generic way, but **to the Lord** (vv. 24, 28). Third, in this situation, holiness is imputed to both groups by God's Word, emphasizing that they are separated from profaneness and uncleanness (cf. Lev 20:26; 22:2-3; Hab 1:13a). Therefore, only **the priests and the Levites**, also described as **holy**, would handle and protect these "consecrated" articles. Ezra delegated to them the responsibility that these offerings, from the emperor and those staying in Babylon, came safely **to Jerusalem to the house of our God**. Ezra's leadership had both spiritual and administrative challenges, but he proved himself a capable leader, and now this group of exiles was ready to return to Judah and Jerusalem (Breneman, *Ezra, Nehemiah, Esther*, 144).

8:31-34. With the preparations complete, Ezra and the returning exiles left their encampment **on the twelfth** day of Nisan, i.e., April 19, 458 BC. They made the four-month, 900-mile journey without incident because **the hand of our God was over us**. The focus on the hand of God is evident in 8:18, 22, 31, and brings to the fore the idea of God's providence, defined by Culver as, "the continuous going forth of God's power whereby He causes all features of the created universe to fulfill the design for which He created them" (Robert Duncan Culver, *Systematic Theology: Biblical and Historical* [Fearn, Ross-shire, UK: Mentor, 2005], 194). God's providence was evident in the beginning and ending details of their return (8:18, 31; cf. Neh 9:6), but also served as a warning to those "who forsake Him," while also serving as a comfort to those "who seek Him" (Ezr 8:22). They arrived in **Jerusalem** on August 4 (7:8) and rested for **three days** (cf. Neh 2:11). They **weighed** the **silver**, **gold**, and the **utensils** before the temple leadership and accounted for and **recorded** everything—now their journey was complete. Ezra followed expected Persian accounting practices by recording everything in detail. His commitment to integrity is an important model for those reading this narrative today.

8:35-36. The returned **exiles**, following the instructions of the king, engaged in worship (7:17). They offered **bulls**, **rams**, **lambs**, and **goats**, all of which the people had offered when they dedicated the temple 57 years earlier (6:17). After they completed their worship, they **delivered** Artaxerxes' decree to the surrounding **satraps** and **governors**. The provincial officials and their local collaborators followed the king's directive and **supported the people and the house of God**.

C. Threat of Mixed Marriages to Covenant Identity (9:1-15)

With the covenant identity of the people of God now reaffirmed (chap. 8), these new inhabitants in Jerusalem would have to negotiate existing identity structures in order to maintain their identity as a holy community. That is the concern of chap. 9.

Ezra identified a threat to Israel's covenant identity. He discovered that the Judeans had intermarried with idolatrous non-Judeans. Ezra continued his previously established pattern of prayer and then action. He interceded for the Judeans and confessed their sin before God, and then acted.

1. Mixed Marriages Among the Community (9:1-5)

9:1-2. Within four months of his arrival in Jerusalem (10:9), **the princes approached** Ezra with a major threat to the identity of the covenant community—Judeans had taken **wives** from among **the peoples of the lands** (Gn 15:19-21; Ex 3:8,17). The group that informed Ezra of this situation would not have consisted of **the princes and the rulers**, themselves implicated in this repudiation of covenantal identity. Malachi had prophesied prior to the arrival of Ezra, but he also indicated that the Judeans had divorced their wives in order to take foreign ones in their place (Mal 2:10-16). Notice the two associated actions: (1) They had **not separated themselves**. (2) They participated in the **abominations** of the foreign nations. The issue not only concerned intermarriage, but also communal purity and idolatry (Ex 34:11-16; Dt 7:3-4). **The holy race** refers to the Jewish people. "Race" is an incorrect translation. Literally, the word means "holy seed," and it refers to the distinctive lineage of the Jewish people as used in the Abrahamic covenant (Gn 17:7, where the NASB translates it "descendants"), and described Israel's unique covenant identity. This type of ethnic reasoning points to the very real possibility that cultural and social integration at this level would result in a lack of purity within the community—a loss of covenant identity (cf. Ps 106:35; Ex 19:6). The **princes** who approached Ezra characterized the offenders as people who embodied **unfaithfulness**, those who had violated their covenantal identity (Jos 7:11; 22:16, 20-22).

9:3-5. When Ezra heard of this situation, he expressed mourning and outrage by ritually tearing his **robe** (Gn 37:34; 2Kg 19:1) and pulling out his **hair** (cf. Neh 13:25; Is 22:12); he **sat down appalled** (cf. Josephus, *Ant.* 11.142). One group existed, however, whose covenantal identity remained salient; they **trembled at the words of the God of Israel**, i.e., they continued to obey the law of Moses (Ezr 10:3; Is 66:2, 5). The group **sat appalled until the evening offering**, i.e., 3:00 p.m., when Ezra decided to speak (cf. Ac 3:1). Ezra then **fell on** his **knees** and **stretched out** his **hands** in a prayer of confession.

2. Ezra's Confession of the Community's Sins (9:6-15)

9:6-9. Ezra's prayer was intensely personal; he was **ashamed and embarrassed** because of the community's **iniquities** and **guilt** (Jr 31:19). He recounted the history of the disobedience of the covenant people and concluded that their sin had resulted in exile at the **hand of the kings of the lands**, i.e., the imperialistic powers that had subjugated Israel (cf. Dt 28:15-68; 2Kg 17:20; Jr 24:9-10). Here Ezra's confession brings to the fore both the individual and corporate guilt. While it is clear that individual sin must be addressed, all too often, collective sin is ignored. Sin, however, is also corporate, and our individual sinful acts contribute to the broader communal ethos of sinfulness. Ezra recognizes the interconnected nature of individual and corporate guilt. Fyall further applies this idea by stating, "We cannot escape the effect of the sins of earlier generations nor the consequences of our sins for future generations" (Fyall, *Ezra and Haggai*, 125). However, Ezra interpreted the events associated with Cyrus's edict as **a brief moment** of **grace** given by **God**. His beneficence resulted in a **remnant** who embodied their covenantal identity (cf. Is 10:20-22; Jr 24:4-7). This grace allowed the Judeans to find favor with **the kings of Persia**, and even though Israel was still in **bondage** to the Persians, they had restored the temple in **Jerusalem**. God had **not forsaken** His people (Is 44:26).

9:10-15. Ezra confessed that the community had **forsaken** God's **commandments**, especially with regard to intermarriage with foreigners. He employed scriptural reasoning, and gathered a catena of commands drawn from Israel's Scriptures to describe the nature and extent of Israel's disobedience (e.g., Lv 18:25; Dt 4:5; 7:1-5; 11:8; 18:9; 23:6; 2Kg 16:3; 21:16; Is 1:19; cf. Mal 2:10-16). Ezra's mediatory role is reminiscent of Moses' with regard to the sin of worshiping the golden calf (Ex 32:10-13). Ezra recognized that God would be just if He were to destroy them and bring renewed judgment on the Judeans (Williamson, *Ezra, Nehemiah*, 137). He also saw the existence of the **remnant** as an indication of God's mercy (Dt 32:4). The conclusion of Ezra's prayer not only functioned as a petition for divine clemency, but also exerted social influence within the community and motivated them to reconcile with God.

D. Communal Reformation and Renewal (10:1-44)

Shecaniah suggested to Ezra that they make a covenant with God to divorce their foreign wives. The community gathered together and delegated a group to investigate the matter. Two months later, priests and Levites put away 27 wives, while the rest of the community divorced 83 wives. The result of these actions included reformation and renewal within the covenant community and a reaffirmation of their particular identity as the people of God.

1. Consent of the Community to End Mixed Marriages (10:1-17)

10:1-4. Ezra continued to pray and intercede for the people who had **gathered to him from Israel** and they **wept bitterly**. This iniquity had apparently gone on for a considerable time since it involved **children** (10:3, 44). However, the people began to realize that they had not followed God's law and had neglected their identity as a people set apart for God, choosing to live like the foreign nations. **Shecaniah** spoke for the group and declared that they **have been unfaithful to our God**. His solution was **a covenant with our God**. This renewed covenant would require the Judeans to **put away all the** foreign **wives and their children**. Shecaniah was confident that this act would renew **hope for Israel**. With the use of the group descriptor **Israel**, their covenant identity began to emerge. The community agreed to order their social life **according to the law**. The communal reformation occurred as they renewed the covenant; a similar situation had occurred during the revival at Shechem in Jos 24:2-27. Shecaniah provided support to Ezra and exhorted him to **be courageous and act** (Jos 1:7).

Often the question of whether this episode provides interpretive texture for Paul's instructions in 1Co 7:12-14 arises (Breneman, *Ezra, Nehemiah, Esther*, 165). (1) The narrative here is descriptive and not prescriptive, and one should thus be hesitant to invoke this over Paul's teaching in 1Co 7 (see the comments on 1Co 7:10-16). (2) The situations in view are too dissimilar; one considers those who had disobeyed God's law by taking foreign wives, while the Corinthian correspondence addresses individuals who began to follow Christ after they had already married. Nevertheless, for followers of Christ who intentionally marry those who are not believers, it would still be inappropriate to follow Ezra's pattern rather than the clear directions of the apostle Paul.

10:5-8. Ezra had the people **take** an **oath** to follow through with the covenant they had made. **Ezra rose** and withdrew from the people to fast and mourn by himself because of the **unfaithfulness of the exiles**. While Ezra continued to fast and pray, the **leaders** and **elders** of Israel called **all the exiles** to an assembly in **Jerusalem**. Any who did not come to the gathering would forfeit their property rights and be **excluded from the assembly of the exiles**, i.e., they would lose their identity as a member of the covenant community (Lv 7:21).

10:9-12. The Judeans gathered in the temple **square**, **trembling** on account of the situation and the **rain**. Ezra began by pointing out that the people **have been unfaithful** to God because they had **married foreign wives**. This section simply restates previously introduced material (9:1-2, 4, 6-7; 10:2). The return from exile had indicated that God had forgiven Israel's sin (Is 40:1-3), but their actions added to the **guilt of Israel**. Ezra called the assembly of the exiles to **make confession** for their sin and then: (1) to withdraw from **the peoples of the land**, and (2) to divorce their **foreign wives**. Upon hearing Ezra's instructions, the returned exiles agreed to the suggested course of action.

10:13-17. The complete implementation of the renewed covenant took three months (vv. 16-17). The **assembly** of the exiles suggested that their **leaders** should determine who had actually married a foreign woman and discern the possible presence of proselytes. The community was unified in their decision to put away the foreign wives, but a small group did oppose it, though their reasons are not clear. Ezra organized the **heads of fathers' households** to **investigate the matter**. This group determined that a little over 100 couples were involved in marriage to pagans. Collectivist societies ascribe social identity based on group membership and social categorization. The social-spiritual dilemma associated with mixed marriages exemplifies the way individual sins can affect communal life (cf. Jos 7:1, 11). Ezra was concerned with the formation of Jewish identity during the Persian period. This explains why Ezra and the assembly of the exiles had to go to such so-called extreme measures: the very identity of the covenant people of God was at stake—there was no other solution.

2. Listing of Those Implicated in Mixed Marriages (10:18-44)

10:18-43. The list included **priests**, **Levites**, and elite Judean families; these would have experienced the temptation to intermarry with non-Jews the most strongly. For example, the **sons** of the high priest Jeshua (2:1; Hg 1:1), once found guilty, divorced their wives and sacrificed a **ram** as a guilt offering (Lv 5:17-19). Only the priestly offense required the pledge and the sacrifice; however, the Leviticus passage addresses unintentional sins. This could indicate that they did not understand fully the social implications of following the law of Moses. If this was the case, it points to the importance of Ezra's teaching ministry (7:10) and calls for contemporary teachers of God's Word to commit themselves to the accurate exposition and application of the Scriptures.

10:44. The list of the men implicated in the mixed marriages, which covers around 110, concludes **that some of them had wives by whom they had children**. This statement has greatly contributed to negative characterizations of early Judaism and the reforms enacted by Ezra. The issue that this solution sought to address, however—mixed marriages—would have obliterated Jewish covenantal identity. Building on the identity framework mentioned earlier from Herodotus 8.144, mixed marriage could have broken Jewish kinship ties, diluted speech patterns, led to syncretism with foreign gods, and changed the common way of life that had its basis in the law of Moses. The problem Ezra faced did not go away, and the characteristics of social identity mentioned by Herodotus are still at issue in Neh 13:23-29. While these painful reforms created emotional havoc for the families involved, the text is silent concerning these foreign family members. Many would have returned to their original household. Others would begin the process of proselyte conversion and assimilate into the assembly. Finally, people could choose to live by the standards of the Israelite community and dwell among them as resident aliens; in that case they would have access to the financial and material support evident in the law (Dt 10:18; 14:29; 24:19-21).

In dealing with mixed marriages, Ezra has addressed the need for covenant faithfulness among the returned exiles. This fits with the overall theme of Ezra—restoration of the covenant identity of Israel through God's providence. The book of Ezra has demonstrated not only how the Lord returned His people to their land, but also, now that they had returned, how the Lord sought to keep them faithful to Him and His Word.

BIBLIOGRAPHY

Blenkinsopp, Joseph. *Judaism, the First Phase: The Place of Ezra and Nehemiah in the Origins of Judaism*. Grand Rapids, MI: Eerdmans, 2009.

Breneman, Mervin. *Ezra, Nehemiah, Esther*. Nashville, TN: Broadman & Holman, 1993.

Clines, David John Alfred. *Ezra, Nehemiah, Esther*. New Century Bible Commentary. Grand Rapids, MI: Eerdmans, 1984.

Culver, Robert Duncan. *Systematic Theology: Biblical and Historical*. Fearn, Ross-shire, UK: Mentor, 2005.

Fensham, F. Charles. *The Books of Ezra and Nehemiah*. New International Commentary on the Old Testament. Grand Rapids, MI: Eerdmans, 1982.

Fyall, Robert S. *The Message of Ezra and Haggai: Building for God*. Downers Grove, IL: InterVarsity, 2010.

Hallo, William W., and K. Lawson Younger. *The Context of Scripture, vol. 2*. Monumental Inscriptions from the Biblical World. Leiden: Brill, 2000.

Kidner, F. Derek. *Ezra and Nehemiah*. Tyndale Old Testament Commentaries. Downers Grove, IL: InterVarsity, 1979.

Levering, Matthew. *Ezra & Nehemiah*. Brazos Theological Commentary on the Bible. Grand Rapids, MI: Brazos Press, 2007.

Pritchard, James Bennett. *Ancient Near Eastern Texts Relating to the Old Testament*. Princeton, NJ: Princeton University Press, 1992.

Williamson, H. G. M. *Ezra, Nehemiah*. Word Biblical Commentary, vol. 16. Waco, TX: Word Books, 1985.

Yamauchi, Edwin M. "Ezra and Nehemiah," in John H. Walton, ed., *1 & 2 Kings, 1 & 2 Chronicles, Ezra, Nehemiah, Esther*. Zondervan Illustrated Bible Backgrounds Commentary, vol. 3. Grand Rapids, MI: Zondervan, 2009.

———. *Africa and the Bible*. Grand Rapids, MI: Baker, 2004.

———. *Persia and the Bible*. Grand Rapids, MI: Baker, 1996.

NEHEMIAH

BRYAN O'NEAL

INTRODUCTION

The book of Nehemiah contains narratives that deal with the last events of the Hebrew Scriptures, recounting the circumstances of the third wave of Jewish people returning from the Babylonian exile in 444 BC, the rebuilding of the walls of Jerusalem, and the rededication of the temple and people to godliness. The book begins in the Persian city of Susa, with Nehemiah hearing of the ongoing disrepair of the walls and gates of Jerusalem, which leads to his request to King Artaxerxes that he be allowed to lead a return to Jerusalem to see to the reconstruction of the city. That request being granted, the book then details Nehemiah's successful work as governor in rebuilding the walls, the opposition that the people faced, and the spiritual renewal that followed that successful labor. The book concludes with an account of Nehemiah's final efforts to sustain that commitment to spiritual faithfulness. The close of the book includes information that marks the conclusion of the biblical history of the OT, though 2 Chronicles serves as the last book in the Hebrew canon. Nehemiah has the records of the last actions of the OT, marking the beginning of the silence of divine revelation lasting until the first events opening the NT, namely Luke's record of the angel Gabriel appearing to Zacharias in Lk 1.

Author. In the Hebrew Bible the books of Ezra and Nehemiah are treated as a single book ("Ezra-Nehemiah"), spanning nearly a century of history. The latter part, separated as a distinct book in the English Bible ("Nehemiah"), contains the "Nehemiah memoirs" which purport to be the first-person writings of Nehemiah, the two-term governor of Judea in the fifth century BC. Some of the material contained in the book (particularly most of chap. 7, which is a near-exact repetition of the earlier writing of Ezr 2) is obviously drawn from other sources, which the author/editor chose to include in the text. This commentary adopts the traditional view that Nehemiah is the author/editor of the book bearing his name.

Date. The events recounted in Nehemiah range from the report of the disrepair of Jerusalem coming to Nehemiah in 445 BC, through his first term as governor of Judea (a period of approximately twelve years), followed by a period of undetermined length during which Nehemiah was presumably back in Persia, and a brief account (chap. 13) of several corrective actions Nehemiah takes in an apparent second term as governor. All told, the events of the book span approximately 15-20 years, bringing its events to a close about 425 BC and the book in its final form before the end of the fifth century BC.

Recipients. Nehemiah wrote his book to the faithful remnant of post-exilic Israel to show them God's gracious restoration of the Jewish people from captivity. By revealing God's blessing in recapitulating the conquest as in the days of Joshua, he also looks forward to the ultimate blessing of restoration at the end of days (see comments at the end of chap. 13).

Purpose and Theme. One obvious purpose of the book of Nehemiah is to chronicle the history of the Jewish people during the period of the return from exile to see them reestablished in the land of promise and awaiting the coming of Messiah. Too often the book is seen as mere history, or as a leadership manual using Nehemiah for a character study. Additionally, prayer is a common theme in Nehemiah as the narrator prays several times (1:5-11; 2:4; 4:9) and regularly brackets a section of the text with "Remember me, O my God" or "Remember them" (5:19; 6:14; 13:14, 22, 29, 31).

Yet, the book is primarily a recapitulation of the initial conquest of the land of Canaan under Joshua, as will be detailed throughout the commentary. This understanding of Nehemiah as a "second Joshua" parallels the common portrait of Ezra as a "second Moses," one who restores the law to the people. Just as Moses brought the law to the people but it was left to Joshua to bring the people into the land, so Nehemiah completes that which Ezra initiates. Much textual evidence supports this interpretation, including: (1) Nehemiah's opening appeal to Dt 20:2-4 (Neh 1:8-9); (2) Nehemiah's secret scouting of Jerusalem's walls in 2:13-15 (compare the spies' visit to Jericho in Jos 13:16); (3) the division of the labor of the walls in Neh 3 paralleling the division of the conquest of the land in Jos 13–19 (note Nehemiah's explicit but rare usage of "portion" in Neh 2:20, and "inheritance," in 11:20; for the use of "portion" in Joshua, see Jos 14:4; 15:13; 17:14; 19:9; 22:25; for some of the uses of "inheritance," see Jos 11:23; 13:6-8, 14-15, 23-24, 28-29, 32-33); (4) the restoration of the Feast of Booths, explicitly reminiscent of similar celebrations in the time of Joshua (Neh 8:17), and culminating in the dedication of the walls as the Jewish people marched around the city led by trumpet-blowing priests (Neh 12). This march clearly echoes a similar procession initiating the prior conquest under Joshua with the defeat of Jericho (Jos 6). For these reasons, the central theme of the book of Nehemiah is "the reconquest of Canaan."

Contribution. Nehemiah completes the historical record of God's great narrative of His work with the Jewish people in the OT—from the call of Abraham and the exodus from Egypt, through the initial conquest and the reigns of the kings, to the Babylonian exile and the return of the Jewish people to the promised land. As the book concludes, Israel is a purified people, restored to the land of promise, worshiping in a rebuilt temple—all things necessary and in preparation for the coming of Messiah.

Background. Nehemiah is about events during the end of the Babylonian exile, during the period when, under the Persians who conquered the Babylonians, the Jewish people were allowed to return to the land of Israel. The northern kingdom of Israel, comprised primarily of ten Jewish tribes, had been defeated and scattered by the Assyrian conquest in 721 BC. The southern kingdom of Judah, made up primarily of the tribes of Judah and Benjamin with substantial numbers of Levites, endured until the Babylonian conquest under Nebuchadnezzar in 586 BC. Nebuchadnezzar took captive much of the population of Jerusalem, including the noble and royal families, deporting them to Babylon. With the later fall of the Babylonian empire to that of the Medes and Persians (beginning in 539 BC), the Jewish people were eventually allowed to begin returning to their homeland after the 70 years of exile prophesied by Jeremiah (Jr 29:10). The first return under Zerubbabel (a descendant of David) occurred in 538 BC, followed by a later return led by Ezra the priestly scribe in 458 BC. Thus, some of these Jewish people had been back in the land for over 90 years as the book of Nehemiah opens (445 BC), explaining his surprise and lament that the walls and gates of Jerusalem remained in shambles, and prompting Nehemiah's request of Artaxerxes that he might lead an expedition to restore Jerusalem. In the absence of a strong political presence in Judea, local power devolved to several petty nobles, among them Sanballat the Horonite, Tobiah the Ammonite, and Geshem the Arab (the descendants of many of Israel's ancient enemies); these figures became Nehemiah's nemeses in his work of reconstruction and restoration.

OUTLINE

I. The Plight of Jerusalem and the Jewish People (1:1–2:20)
  A. Nehemiah Is in Babylon and Hears of Jerusalem's Plight (1:1–2:8)
    1. Jerusalem's Plight (1:1-3)
    2. Nehemiah's Prayer (1:4-11)
    3. Artaxerxes' Permission (2:1-8)
  B. Nehemiah Travels to Jerusalem and Surveys the Situation (2:9-20)

1. Travel to Jerusalem (2:9-10)
2. Surveying the Walls of Jerusalem (2:11-16)
3. Beginning the Work of Rebuilding (2:17-20)

II. The Rebuilding of the Walls (3:1–6:19)
- A. Nehemiah Leads the Rebuilding of the Walls (3:1-32)
- B. Opposition: the Military Challenge (4:1-23)
  1. The Mockery of the Opposition (4:1-6)
  2. The Threat of Violence (4:7-15)
  3. The Renewed Work (4:16-23)
- C. Opposition: The Moral Challenge (5:1-19)
  1. The Problem of Usury (5:1-13)
     - a. The People's Complaint (5:1-5)
     - b. Nehemiah's Response (5:6-13)
  2. The Example of Nehemiah (5:14-19)
- D. Finishing the Wall (6:1-19)
  1. The Physical Threat (6:1-9)
  2. The Political Threat (6:10-14)
  3. The Wall Complete (6:15-19)

III. The Rebuilding of the People (7:1–10:39)
- A. Genealogies (7:1-73)
  1. The Instructions for Security (7:1-4)
  2. The Genealogical Record (7:5-65)
     - a. The Returned Exiles with Genealogical Records (7:5-60)
     - b. The Returned Exiles without Genealogical Records (7:61-65)
  3. Summary (7:66-73)
- B. The Public Reading of the Law (8:1-18)
  1. The Reading of the Law (8:1-8)
  2. The Sacred Feast (8:9-12)
  3. The Feast of Booths (8:13-18)
- C. The Confession and History of Israel (9:1-37)
  1. The Assembly of the Levites and People (9:1-5)
  2. Creation and the Call of Abraham (9:6-8)
  3. The Exodus and Wandering (9:9-22)
  4. The Conquest under Joshua and Subsequent Unfaithfulness (9:23-31)
  5. Confession and Repentance (9:32-37)
- D. The Establishing of a New Sacred Covenant (9:38–10:39)
  1. The Signers of the Covenant (9:38–10:27)
  2. The Content of the Covenant (10:28-39)

IV. The Dedication of the People, Walls, and Temple (11:1–13:31)
- A. Populating Jerusalem and Its Region (11:1-36)
- B. Dedicating the Walls of Jerusalem (12:1-47)
  1. The Priests and Levites Who Returned from Exile (12:1-21)
  2. The Leading Levites (12:22-26)
  3. Purification of Levites, People, and Wall (12:27-30)
  4. Two Choirs (12:31-43)
     - a. First Choir under Ezra (12:31-37)
     - b. Second Choir under Nehemiah (12:38-43)
  5. Worship and Celebration (12:44-47)
- C. Purifying the Promised Land (13:1-31)
  1. Purifying the Temple (13:1-14)
  2. Purifying the Sabbath (13:15-22)
  3. Purifying the People (13:23-29)
  4. Purifying the Priests (13:30-31)

COMMENTARY ON NEHEMIAH

I. The Plight of Jerusalem and the Jewish People (1:1–2:20)

A. Nehemiah Is in Babylon and Hears of Jerusalem's Plight (1:1–2:8)

1. Jerusalem's Plight (1:1-3)

1:1-3. The book claims to be written by **Nehemiah the son of Hacaliah**. Three Nehemiahs are mentioned in the text: a Jewish exile who returned to Jerusalem in the first return led by Zerubbabel and Joshua, in 538 BC (7:7); the son of Azbuk who was a local official (3:16), and Nehemiah son of Hacaliah, narrator of the book bearing his name. For more on authorship, see Introduction. The **month** of **Chislev** of the Jewish calendar corresponds to the period from about December 5 to January 3. The **twentieth year** refers to the twentieth year of the reign of Artaxerxes, which would place the events of the opening verses of Nehemiah in December of 445 BC. There is some controversy regarding the accuracy of the dates in the first two chapters of Nehemiah; for more information, see the comments on 2:1. **Susa the capitol** has caused some confusion among interpreters. It is well known that the capitol of the Persian Empire was the city of Babylon, taken over by the Persians when they conquered the Babylonian empire in 538 BC. Susa, however, served as a winter palace and fortress for Persian kings, and was located east of the city of Babylon and about 150 miles north of the Persian Gulf. Fellow exile Daniel experienced a vision of himself in Susa (Dn 8:2). Susa is likewise the setting for the story of Esther.

Hanani, one of my brothers was likely an actual blood brother or relative of Nehemiah, and there is record of a Jewish administrator of that name in Jerusalem during this period. It is unknown whether that person is the figure mentioned here. As for the **Jews who had escaped and had survived the captivity**, Nehemiah inquires about those who had earlier returned from exile, and is surprised that they remain in a distressing situation in Jerusalem. On the fall of Jerusalem and the subsequent exile, see Jr 39. and 2Kg 24. During the reign of the Persian kings, the Holy Land was subdivided into four administrative districts, with **Jerusalem** serving as the local capitol of Judah. It was in this period after the exile that the descendants of Abraham, Isaac, and Jacob began to be known as "Jews." The distress of Jerusalem extends to the **remnant** (the people God had preserved through the exile and brought back to Jerusalem), the **gates**, and the **wall**. It is significant that the bulk of the book of Nehemiah focuses more on the rebuilding of the remnant than on the walls, indicating that God's greater desire was the faithfulness and obedience of His people.

2. Nehemiah's Prayer (1:4-11)

1:4-5. Nehemiah seems surprised by the report, coming as it does nearly a century after the first return of exiles in 538 BC. When Nehemiah identifies with **those who love [God] and keep His commandments** (v. 5), he is bringing to mind the promise of God's faithfulness to his people expressed in the Mosaic covenant (see specifically the Ten Commandments, the first commandment in Ex 20:6 being reflected here in Nehemiah's prayer about "loving God" in v. 5).

1:6. In the beginning of Nehemiah's prayer he confesses **the sins of the sons of Israel**, including his own. One of the main sins that had led to Israel's exile was idolatry (e.g., 2 Kg 17:7-20). It has been said that the Babylonian captivity "cured" Israel of her centuries-long struggle with idolatry. Though the post-exilic Jewish religion had its problems (such as the legalism of Jesus' day), idolatry does not seem to have been among them (the end of idolatry was foretold in Hs 3:3-4).

1:7-10. The **commandments**, **statutes**, and **ordinances** (v. 7) of Moses refer not only to the Ten Commandments but to the whole of the Pentateuch, delivered explicitly to Israel before the initial conquest of the promised land. Along with idolatry, Israel's failure to honor the law led to God's judgment in the exile (cf. Lv 26). Nehemiah knows that restoration to and security in the land will require renewed adherence to the Mosaic covenant. This renewal, and the related "reconquest" of Canaan under Nehemiah, is the major theme of the book. In vv. 8-9 Nehemiah explicitly quotes Dt 30:1-4 (also Lv 26:33), effectively Moses' last words to Israel before Joshua's conquest, and in so doing identifies with the promises of restoration to the land, which would partly take place under Nehemiah's own leadership. The regular mention of the people **You** [God] **redeemed by Your great power and by Your strong hand** (v. 10) is the language of Passover and the exodus (Ex 12–14).

1:11. A **cupbearer** (v. 11) was not a waiter, but a highly trusted servant. Just as modern Secret Service agents constantly guard the US president, so the cupbearer was ever present. Given the history of assassinations in the Persian court, Nehemiah's job was to be sure the wine was not poisoned. Additionally, he did more than protect—he also served as companion and confidant to the king, much like a modern "counsel to the president."

3. Artaxerxes' Permission (2:1-8)

2:1-4. The month of **Nisan** (v. 1, March/April) is the first month of the Jewish calendar; this presents some difficulty reconciling Nehemiah's audience with the king still **in the twentieth year** with the earlier report from Jerusalem in the ninth month, Chislev (1:1). Apparently, Nehemiah is using a Persian dating system that likely calculated the king's reign from the precise month that it began, so that a single year in his reign would span two normal calendar years. Thus the events of v. 1 still take place in **the twentieth year of King Artaxerxes**, though they occur in the following Jewish calendar year. The text says that Nehemiah's request to Artaxerxes is made three months after the report from Jerusalem, in March/April 444 BC.

Nehemiah was **afraid** (v. 2) for two reasons. First, it is assumed that to live in the presence of the king is an unqualified privilege and pleasure, so to exhibit any negative expression is to dishonor the king (cf. Est 4:11; 5:2-3). Second, Nehemiah is about to ask the king to permit the rebuilding of Jerusalem in direct contravention of his earlier decree to cease such labor (Ezr 4:21). Nehemiah does not really want Artaxerxes to **live forever** (v. 3)—this is just the proper way to address Persian royalty. He credits his sad face to a politically safe cause: the poor condition of his native land. When the king invites Nehemiah's request, he prays **to the God of heaven** (v. 4)—but this is not a sudden and surprised prayer, but instead a recapitulation of the sustained prayer of 1:4-11 (that is, his "quick" prayer in 2:4 is basically a "Now, please, Lord" based on the earlier prayer).

2:5-8. Nehemiah had the extended three months of prayer before making his request of the king, so he was prepared with exactly the correct petition and precisely the appropriate answers to Artaxerxes' expected questions. He knew he would need the king's support for security (**allow me to pass through**, v. 7) and building supplies (**beams for the gates of the fortress**, **the wall of the city**, **the house**, v. 8). With striking understatement the text says that **the king granted** the requests. In so doing he committed financial, political, and military support to the rebuilding of Jerusalem. Perhaps more significantly, this decree initiates one of the most important prophetic timelines for the coming of Messiah. Daniel had previously prophesied that "from the issuing of a decree to restore and rebuild Jerusalem until Messiah the Prince there will be seven weeks and sixty-two weeks" (see Dn 9:25 and the comments on Dn 9:24-27).

This passage offers several points of theological and practical significance. Extended times of prayer, and delayed answers from God may be a manifestation of grace to make us ready for when the time is right. If Nehemiah had rushed impetuously and impatiently to Artaxerxes upon receiving the report from Jerusalem, he would have been ill prepared to answer thoughtfully when the king invited his request. Similarly, Nehemiah's years spent becoming and serving as a cupbearer were not wasted. He was being prepared for a distinct ministry, much like Esther being readied "for such a time as this" (Est 4:14). It is less important what title one bears, or how one intends to serve God, than what one does when the opportunity for service is presented. Nehemiah's years at court not only gave him access to the king at a time of need, but also equipped him for the political and administrative challenges he was about to encounter.

B. Nehemiah Travels to Jerusalem and Surveys the Situation (2:9-20)

1. Travel to Jerusalem (2:9-10)

2:9-10. Nehemiah's pathway from Susa to Jerusalem mirrors that of Abram's journey: across the Fertile Crescent from Babylon, northwest to Haran, and then west and south into Judah and Jerusalem. Beyond **the River** (v. 9) refers to the lands west of the Euphrates, the horizon of Babylonia's traditional realm. The **letters** from the king were validated by **officers** and **horsemen** from the king. **Sanballat** (v. 10) was governor, subject to Artaxerxes, over Samaria, the region or province north of Jerusalem. **Tobiah** was governor (one of many of this powerful family) of Ammon, east of the Jordan River. Judah in these days was underserved and underrepresented; the appointment of a governor and champion (seeking the **welfare**) of Judah, Jerusalem, and the Jewish people represented a corresponding diminishing of the power of the other governors in the area. Hence, their adverse reaction to

The Persian Empire

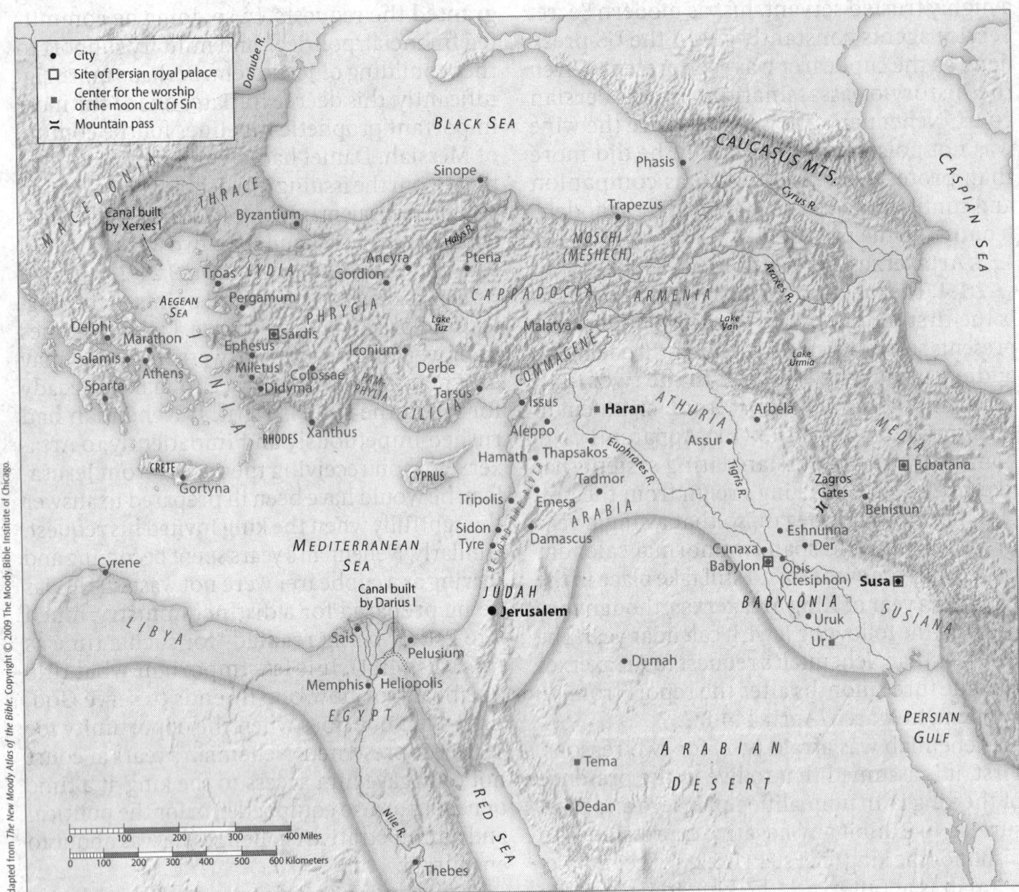

these new developments under Nehemiah is understandable although certainly inappropriate.

2. Surveying the Walls of Jerusalem (2:11-16)

2:11-12. Waiting **three days** (v. 11) may have given Nehemiah time to settle into his home and identify the local leaders and power structures. Waiting a few days may also have begun to lull the opposition into thinking that he was not any immediate threat. Verse 12 and v. 16 serve to bracket the intervening verses, and emphasize that Nehemiah had **not** told **anyone** his intentions (v. 12), that is, what God had put into his heart. After being in the land and city for nearly 100 years, the disrepair of the walls and corresponding spiritual poverty of the people had sadly become normative. Nehemiah's audacious intent to reverse both of those conditions would require a clear understanding of the situation and a specific plan to address it. Scouting the walls alone in secret gave him the time to come up with a plan to follow. That there is **no animal with** him (i.e., he walked inconspicuously) is in contrast to v. 9 where Nehemiah travels with the king's horsemen.

2:13-16. Nehemiah does not circumnavigate the whole of Jerusalem, but only surveys the southern portion. The **Valley Gate** (v. 13) faced southwest towards the Hinnom Valley; the **Dragon's Well** likely refers to a spring at the junction of the Hinnom and Kidron Valleys on the southeast edge of Jerusalem. The Dung Gate or **Refuse Gate** would have been at the southernmost tip of the city, as deep into the valley and far from the temple area to the north as possible, accessing the garbage dump to the south. The **Fountain Gate** (v. 14) faced southeast, toward the Kidron Valley, and the **King's Pool** may be a reference to the Pool of Siloam (cf. Jn 9) at the southern edge of Jerusalem.

The state of the walls, gates, and approaches to the city were so poor that even a single horse was unable to navigate the area. Not only is this a dangerous situation (enemies can approach unobserved, criminals can slink in and out of the city), but also it is a reflection of a people without self-respect or hope. Compare this to the earlier and later comments (in Neh 1:3 and 2:17) that the people suffer reproach. In keeping with the book's theme of the reconquest of Canaan (see the Introduction), the author may have included the record of Nehemiah's puzzling nighttime inspection of the walls as a parallel to the spies' secret visit to Jericho before Joshua's conquest (cf. Nm 13 and Jos 2).

3. Beginning the Work of Rebuilding (2:17-20)

2:17-18. The reproach of the people (v. 17; cf. 1:3) is personal shame, corporate disgrace, and a reflection on the nation and its God. Here Nehemiah announces his bold plan to rebuild the wall of Jerusalem. It may be that although the local governors knew of Nehemiah's royal support, the people and priests did not yet know of his intent to rebuild the city. Even upon hearing of it, they may have felt the task was impossible, or would be merely more of the same in accordance with previous failed attempts. However, upon hearing of the king's direct sponsorship of the project, and understanding that this must indeed be an instance of divine provision (**the hand of my God had been favorable**, v. 18) they were strengthened to do the good work.

2:19-20. Sanballat and Tobiah begin a public mockery of the work (v. 19). They are joined by **Geshem the Arab**, whose province comprised the regions south of Judah, thereby completing the circle of political opposition around Nehemiah and Jerusalem. This collection of opponents recalls the nemeses of Israel from their time of wandering and conquest: Ammon (Dt 23) and Jericho with Samaria (Joshua). The meaning of **portion** includes the idea of inheritance as well as ownership. **Portion** occurs more often in the book of Joshua than any other OT book (Jos 14:4; 15:13; 17:14; 19:9; 22:25), and is used here to signal the reclaiming of Israel's inheritance under Nehemiah. Further, talk here of an inheritance immediately precedes the assigning of sections of the walls to various families, paralleling the division of the land to various tribes and clans under Joshua. Nehemiah looked beyond what **Jerusalem** was in his day (a wrecked town) to what it would become—a great city in which these opponents would have no part.

Though this section is historical, it has practical application for today. There is such a thing as a proper use of secular power, and practical wisdom. Certainly Nehemiah was convinced that the success of his endeavors would come by the abiding hand and favor of God; however, he did not presume upon the favor of God by acting foolishly and assuming that God would work everything out. Instead, he marshaled his resources, acted circumspectly, and then was prepared to act boldly when the proper time came. Also, those who expect to enjoy a portion in God's blessing (in contrast to those opponents who have no such expectation) should also anticipate taking a portion of the labor, as the following chapter illustrates with the rebuilding of the wall.

II. The Rebuilding of the Walls (3:1–6:19)

A. Nehemiah Leads the Rebuilding of the Walls (3:1-32)

Having previously stated that "the God of heaven will give us success" (2:20), the purpose of this chapter is to demonstrate the evidence of that claim. It recounts the builders and their tasks in reconstructing the walls and gates of Jerusalem. The description proceeds geographically in a counterclockwise direction around the city, starting and ending at its northeastern corner near the temple area. Though the whole of the rebuilding requires 52 days to complete (6:15), this chapter anticipates the completion of the work, as described in chaps. 4 through 6. The workers came from many cities and towns, spanning the whole of Judea, indicating the broad popular support and political success Nehemiah enjoyed.

3:1-2. This is the first mention of **Eliashib the high priest**, the grandson of Jeshua, the high priest during the initial return under Zerubbabel (cf. Ezr 3; see also Neh 12:10-12). Fittingly, he and his priests are mentioned first, and the account begins with the rebuilding of the **Sheep Gate**, at the eastern edge of the north wall of the city. It was through this important gate that sacrificial sheep would enter the temple courts. The **Tower of the Hundred** and the **Tower of Hananel** (perhaps the "fortress . . . by the temple" of 2:8) were fortifications on the north side of the city, as this area did not enjoy the natural protection of a steep ascent. Also prominent by their early mention are the **men**

Jerusalem during Nehemiah's Rebuilding of the Walls

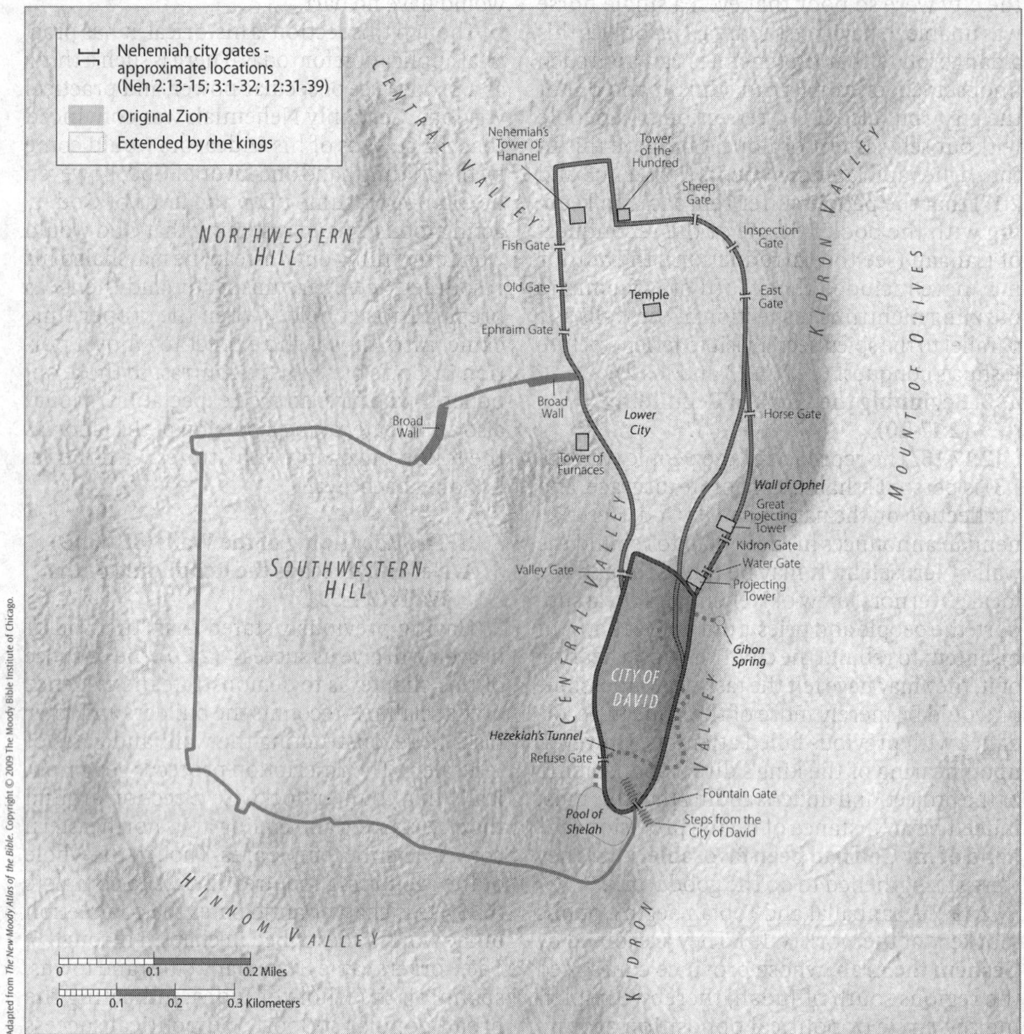

of Jericho—recalling, perhaps, that Joshua's conquest began with the defeat of Jericho and now her men are numbered with Israel.

3:3-5. The **Fish Gate** was on the northwest side of the city, in the direction of the "Great Sea" (the Mediterranean), and allowed easy passage to the city's fish market. This gate also led out into the territory of Ephraim, and so may be another name for the Gate of Ephraim (8:16; 12:39). Many builders are listed here, and in the remainder of the chapter, who are otherwise unmentioned in Scripture and little known to us. It would be a mistake to try to draw theological significance from the etymology of their names. The **Tekoites** (citizens of Tekoa, about five miles southeast of Jerusalem, Amos' hometown) participate, but their **nobles** do not. Perhaps these nobles feared the wrath of Geshem the Arab (2:19).

3:6-12. Towards the northern end of the west wall is the **Old Gate** (v. 6). That its **beams**, **doors**, **bolts** and **bars** are mentioned indicates that the gate was wholly restored. Explicitly mentioned are the **men of Gibeon** (v. 7), for their work on the western wall. Known from the Joshua narrative as those who deceived Joshua and were thus forced into subjugation (Jos 9:22-27), they remained conquered, as did the men of Jericho in Neh. 3:2. The **governor of the province beyond the River** (possibly Nehemiah) has a residence or "seat" along the wall, which these men repaired. Also singled out are the **goldsmiths** and **perfumers** (v. 8) for their work toward the **Broad Wall**. At this point and in the following verses, it becomes evident that, by the participation of the priests, the conquered people, the common Israelites, and the wealthier professionals (the goldsmiths and perfumers), this labor is genuinely a community effort and requires everyone's active contribution. Along with many others, the officials **of Jerusalem** (vv. 9, 12), including some **daughters** (v. 12), worked to rebuild. Evidently, everyone was capable of making some important contribution to the work. The **Tower of Furnaces** (v. 11) is the section of the city wherein baking ovens and/or pottery kilns would be located, indicating the participation of these guilds as well (with the goldsmiths and perfumers mentioned earlier, v. 8).

3:13-14. The **Valley Gate** through which Nehemiah began his nighttime inspection (2:13) is so named because it leads to the Tyropoeon Valley to the west of Jerusalem. This southwesterly section of the wall and its gates seemed to be in the best repair, as indicated by Nehemiah's ability to traverse this section on horseback in the preceding chapter, and by the relatively few workers mentioned for a large section of the wall (**a thousand cubits**, or 500 yards) to the **Refuse Gate**. This is the section least threatened geographically by Sanballat, Tobiah, and Geshem, which may explain its relatively good condition (or its relatively low priority) for allocating workers and resources for repair. The Refuse Gate, sometimes called the Dung Gate, is at the southernmost point of the city, farthest from the temple precinct and allowing the most immediate access downhill and downstream from the city. It is a bad idea to discard rubbish and dung upstream from one's water source.

3:15-27. The **Fountain Gate** (v. 15) is also at the far southern point of the city, probably oriented toward the Kidron Valley along the eastern wall as the wall begins its northerly course. The **Pool of Shelah** may be identified with the NT Pool of Siloam (Jn 9:7) into which the water from Hezekiah's tunnel flowed, apparently part of a park or garden area (**the king's garden**) in Jerusalem; this area would be part of the original **city of David**. The **Nehemiah** mentioned in Neh 3:16 is not the narrator of the book (see 1:1). This area, including **the tombs of David**, **the artificial pool** (v. 16; possibly the "King's Pool" of 2:14), **and the house of the mighty men** mark the limits of Nehemiah's prior nighttime inspection. Apparently this section of the city recalls Israel's golden age under David and Solomon. The work on this eastern wall is delineated now primarily from house to house rather than gate to gate, reflecting some large distances between gates to the east. This is understandable as the eastern slope of Mount Moriah (upon which Jerusalem was built) is quite steep and does not permit many roads allowing entrance into the city. The **Levites** build as well (v. 17), paralleling their brothers the priests (3:1, 22), showing again that all tribes share in this labor.

3:28-32. The last segment of the wall completes the circuit of the city, along the temple courts and back to the Sheep Gate in the northeast corner. The **Horse Gate** (v. 28; cf. 2Ch 22:15) allowed access to the former royal courts (horses were a mark and measure of wealth). The **East Gate** (v. 29; cf. Ezk 10:19) may be the predecessor to the current Golden Gate of Jerusalem. One of the builders, **Meshullam** (v. 30), is later identified (6:18) as a relative by marriage to Tobiah, one of Nehemiah's constant nemeses. Ultimately, the end of the book finds Tobiah actually living in the temple storerooms whose construction is described here (13:4-9).

The various workers here—priests, goldsmiths, prominent political families— underscore once more the complete participation of the community in the labor. Finally, the **Inspection Gate** (v. 31) is listed, so named possibly due to its proximity to the temple. The faithful would bring their sacrifices through this gate, and the animals had to "pass inspection" according to the dictates of the law (see for example Dt 17:1); alternatively, this area may have been the place of "muster" or "inspection" for the guard or army (as the word is used in 2Sm 24:9).

As noted previously, the book of Nehemiah serves to recapitulate much of the history of Israel. This section is reminiscent of the conquest of Canaan led by Joshua, and serves a similar function for the people of Judah. Just as the conquest would not be complete, and Israel would not fully possess the land in peace, unless each tribe secured its own assignment in the land, so also the walls would not be complete and none of the citizens of Jerusalem would be safe unless each family or group successfully completed the rebuilding of their section of the wall.

Additionally, this project brings to mind the saying that "a chain is only as strong as its weakest link." The same can be said for Jerusalem's walls: they are only as secure as their weakest section. Obviously, no builder in the city can take undue pride in the significance of his task, but must recognize how critical every section is. This anticipates the NT attitude toward the interdependence of the varying members of the Church. Sometimes the Church is described with a building metaphor, where every believer is a living stone being built together into a temple in which God takes delight to dwell (Eph 2:21-22). The Church is also described as a "body," and Paul instructs his readers that every part of the body is significant, even critical, to the proper function of the whole (1Co 12:14-26).

B. Opposition: the Military Challenge (4:1-23)

The following report about opposition was designed to highlight the success God was granting. At the end of chap. 2, Nehemiah claimed that God "will give us success" (2:20). Chapter 3 demonstrated the success God had granted. Here in chap. 4, the point is to emphasize that, even with opposition, success did indeed come from the Lord. At the heart of Nehemiah and the people's victory lay this crucial fact: "we prayed to our God" (4:9).

1. The Mockery of the Opposition (4:1-6)

4:1-3. On Sanballat and Tobiah (v. 3) see comments on 2:9-10 and 2:19-20. Sanballat's fury (v. 1) literally made him "hot" and he was once more very angry—as he was in 2:19 when he heard of Nehemiah's plans. Disproportionate anger remains a common response to the work of God and to His people. Mockery is often enough to dissuade people who are only weakly committed to a task. Sanballat's mockery takes the form of five questions, and reflects a keen understanding of the weaknesses of the human psyche. The forms his ridicule takes remain effective discouragers today. He first asked, **What are these feeble Jews doing?** Calling the Jewish people feeble (v. 2) is objectively accurate of those who had returned, surrounded by enemies as they were and in economically tenuous circumstances.

His second question, "Can they restore it by themselves (HCSB)?" gives voice to the enormity of the task. Sometimes verbalizing an objective reveals its audacity. The third question, **Can they offer sacrifices?** has a twofold effect: it points out the disconnection between the walls and the spiritual work of the temple, and mocks the devotion of the Jewish people. There are those today who agree that the Church ought be concerned only about spiritual work and ignore tasks of a secular nature. Fourth, with the question **Can they finish in a day?** Sanballat misrepresented the time frame, again attempting to demoralize the people. Many worthwhile projects cannot be completed in a day; God's people must be on guard against an impatience that makes them unwilling to sustain a difficult task. Finally, Sanballat wonders whether the Jewish people can build a wall using **burned** stones weakened by the fires of Nebuchadnezzar's assaults. Here he again misrepresents their challenge. It was not as bad as that, with many available stones perfectly suitable for (re)use in the walls.

These questions bring to mind the spies' initial report of Canaan, that its people were "giants," or of the daily discouragement of the army of Israel when subjected to Goliath's taunts. Sanballat began by saying the returned number of Jewish people was too small (v. 2). He now concludes by saying their task was too great.

Tobiah's mockery in v. 3 undermines itself. If the walls were so weak that even a small animal would topple them, then Jerusalem's enemies should have no worries. The concern of Sanballat, Tobiah, and others should have encouraged the Jewish builders that their labor was significant.

4:4-6. Once more, Nehemiah prays and *then* he works. His is an "imprecatory" prayer, asking God to judge and punish the enemies of God's people. Compare Pss 5, 28, 31, 35, 58, 59, 69, 79, 83, 109, 137, 139, 140, as well as Jeremiah's prayers (in this same city!), particularly in Jr 11, 15, 17, 18. Note particularly the close parallel between Neh 4:5 and Jr 18:23. When Nehemiah notes that the people **are despised** (v. 4), he implies that if God's people are despised, it is really God who is being mocked. As such, his prayer is that God act on His own behalf. A believer's attitude and prayer regarding "enemies" ought to be motivated by a concern for God's name, and not individual reputation.

The theme of **reproach** returns here (4:4). It is a subtle form of prayer that genuinely looks to the defeat of God's enemies without seeking to take its own revenge, but instead trusts in God to use many mysterious means to produce His judgment. Compare Habakkuk's confusion that God would use the Chaldeans to discipline Israel (Hab 1–2). The God who turns the heart of the king and can hurl Babylon in judgment against His own people can certainly intervene on behalf of His people in any age. Despite the mockery of their enemies, and according to the strength that came by prayer, the Jewish people were able to reach the halfway point of the walls' reconstruction. This seems to have provoked an intensified concern on the part of their enemies, as they began to plot violence. Godly success often begets increased opposition. The **people had a mind to work** (v. 6). "Mind" here is literally "heart."

2. The Threat of Violence (4:7-15)

4:7-9. In the face of the ridicule of Sanballat, Tobiah, and the others, the Jewish builders sustained their work, prompting their opponents to intensify their opposition with threats of violence. As **the breaches began to be closed** (v. 7), the window of successful opposition shrank as well. In the face of the opposition, Nehemiah reacts with a spiritual as well as a military response: **we prayed to our God** and **we set up a guard** (v. 9). This was an appropriate balance—trusting God for success but taking appropriate action as well. Sanballat hoped to disrupt the work enough (fight and cause a disturbance) to perhaps influence Artaxerxes to withdraw his support for the project (as in Ezr 4:19-22).

4:10-15. The situation was so bleak that the Jewish workers began to sing a song of discouragement (v. 10) even as they labored, ironically echoing the lament of Psalm 137 recently sung in Babylon, longing to return to this very city. The **Jews who lived near them** (v. 12) refers to the Jewish people who dwelt outside Jerusalem, in geographic proximity to the ring of Israel's enemies. They brought word of the plotters' devices: **told us ten times** might be a literal ten times, or perhaps something repeated several times (cf. Gn 31:7, 41; Nm 14:22). These plots were not in secret—even the reports become a sort of propaganda campaign of discouragement to the people.

Nehemiah reallocated some of his workforce to defense and **stationed men . . . behind the wall** and in **the exposed places** (v. 13) while others continued the work. Ultimately, Nehemiah encouraged the people by first calling them to **remember the Lord who is great and awesome** (v. 14)—Israel's best hope has always been in the Lord rather than physical strength—and to be prepared to fight for their families and land. Nehemiah's **do not be afraid of them** is reminiscent of Moses' charge to Israel and Joshua before the conquest in Dt 31:6ff. In the end, it is Israel's enemies who become discouraged, although Nehemiah is careful to acknowledge that **God had frustrated their plan** (v. 15).

3. The Renewed Work (4:16-23)

4:16-18. Encouraged by their ongoing success, the Jewish builders applied themselves to the labor with renewed vigor. "Each one to his work" (v. 15) recalls the significance of the labor of each participant. For the remainder of the task, half of Nehemiah's forces were on constant military alert (with **spears**, **shields**, **bows**, and **breastplates**), while even the half that continued building did so with the other hand **holding a weapon** (v. 17). This militarization of all of Israel turns even the mundane task of stonemasonry into a military campaign. Israel is certainly at war, with her **captains** who were **behind the whole house of Judah** (v. 16) directing the forces.

4:19-23. Even with this, the forces were spread thinly, so Nehemiah retained a trumpeter to remain near him to summon defenders if enemies arose at a point of weakness. Divine providence and human responsibility are closely juxtaposed: **At whatever place you hear the sound of the trumpet, rally to us there. Our God will fight for us** (v. 20). This vigilance is epitomized by the scope of readiness throughout the day (**from dawn until the stars appeared**, v. 21), the complete social strata of Israel (**each man with his servant**, v. 22), and through every detail of the day (**even to** [get] **water**, v. 23). This latter phrase may bring to mind Gideon's likewise outnumbered army, selected randomly by God even as they drank (see the comments on Jdg 7:1-8). Ultimately, during these critical weeks of construction, the worker-warriors become an armed camp, staying in Jerusalem around the clock—**a guard for us by night and a laborer by day**.

This passage reminds us that not all opposition is physical—Sanballat's initial "attacks" were psychological—and that struggles are not always against flesh and blood, but against spiritual forces (cf. Eph 6:12). And often, those who threaten with great bluster are rebuffed by simple confidence in the Lord's sufficiency. Moreover, perseverance through trials leads to greater successes (as 1Pt 1:7 instructs, perseverance through trials purifies and strengthens faith). Confidence in the Lord does not negate the role of practical and applied wisdom: Nehemiah models what it is to trust God, take wise action, and credit God with any successes that follow. Finally, the demands of faithfulness may include total dedication to the Lord's cause, all of one's resources and time, at least for a season.

C. Opposition: the Moral Challenge (5:1-19)

There is a practical piety in the book of Nehemiah. While Nehemiah and the people had confidence in God granting them success, particularly through prayer, they also took up weapons for defense even as they trusted God. In the continuing description of God's work of rebuilding the walls, though the people take up their own defense (previous chapter), they also need strong leadership. The following two brief narratives about Nehemiah's godly leadership illustrate this point, reinforcing the importance of practical piety.

1. The Problem of Usury (5:1-13)

a. The People's Complaint (5:1-5)

5:1-4. In the midst of external opposition from Sanballat and his cohorts, an even more insidious challenge comes from within the Jewish community: the economically oppressed—including their wives—cry out against their Jewish brothers (v. 1). Economic distress comes in many forms. One is a basic lack of food: **let us get grain that we may eat and live** (v. 2). Another symptom of distress is the mortgaging of property—**fields**, **vineyards**, and **houses** (v. 3). Some of the Jewish people had been back in the land long enough to establish themselves economically, but the present distress was forcing them to forfeit even those meager gains. A combination of growing population, concerns over physical safety, attention to the labor of the walls, and the disrepair of the fields had led to famine. High taxes, such as **the king's tax** (v. 4), were a third source of economic distress. Multiple sources recount the oppressive taxes of kings in the ancient Near East. For example, one common estimate is that the Persian king collected twenty million darics per year in taxes (high-quality gold coins introduced by Darius the Great around 500 BC that continued in use until Alexander the Great's conquests in 330 BC).

5:5. So extreme were the economic challenges that family members, **sons** and **daughters**, were sold into bondage to satisfy creditors. Jewish law required that such "hired servants" be released in the seventh year (Dt 15:12-18). A vicious downward spiral prevailed as the people lost possession of their fields and vineyards, and ultimately their own freedom, and lacked the means to repay debts or provide for their families. To some minds, the conditions of restored Israel were worse than those of exiled Israel. At least in Babylon families were together and could live with relative provision. This recalls the complaints of the Jewish people even in the aftermath of the exodus from Egypt, facing the hardships of the wilderness (cf. Nm 14).

b. Nehemiah's Response (5:6-13)

5:6-8. Nehemiah became **very angry** (v. 6) because he was focused on the walls and the needs of the city and was shocked that any would capitalize on the hard economic circumstances for personal profit. It is one thing when the threat is external, as with that of Sanballat and Tobiah—that is to be expected. It is much worse when the "threat" to a community is internal. Here Nehemiah contends with the **nobles and the rulers** (v. 7). He first **consulted with** himself to be sure that his actions and words would be just and fitting. He held the nobles and rulers up to public censure by calling a great assembly against them. Already Nehemiah has reduced the size of his workforce by separating the people into guards and laborers (4:15-23); now he had to spend precious time by calling everyone away from the work to assemble together. However, both actions increase the effectiveness of the labor, as the people are ultimately freed to labor first in physical, and then in economic, security. Nehemiah accuses the rulers of the most egregious of offenses: **usury**, the charging of exploitive interest. This is different from a secured loan. (cf. Dt 24:10; Pr 22:26). It is one thing, even an act of mercy perhaps, for one Jewish person to take on another as a bondservant. It is a great tragedy however, as in this case, when Jewish brothers are **sold to the nations** (v. 8) in order to cover their debts. Nehemiah accuses the nobles and rulers of being indifferent to this tragedy, against which they **could not find a word to say**.

5:9-13. The testimony of Scripture (Ex 21:8; Dt 23:20) and the courage of "speaking truth to power" was enough to prevent any attempt at self-justification by the nobles and rulers. Believers are reminded that they live on a greater stage than their own interests suggest. They must live righteously before **the nations**, even **our enemies** (v. 9). More fundamentally, believers must live in the proper **fear of our God**. These leaders were valuing their own economic interests ahead of their testimony among the Gentiles and the favor of God.

Nehemiah sets the example (v. 10) by lending **money and grain** (note that it is lending with interest, not lending without interest, that is condemned). He calls his fellow leaders to join with him in so doing, but without usury. Nehemiah was not giving away his material goods—he expected to be repaid (and those who borrow should expect to repay) in equal value. What he desired was to end the practice of ruinous usury, demanding back more than the value of the thing loaned.

In inflationary times, the collecting of interest may be just if it reflects the current real value of the object lent. In non-inflationary contexts, to charge interest is to demand back more than the value of the amount lent (usury). In inflationary economic contexts, the future "cash value" of an item is higher than the present "cash value," so an equal repayment may in fact require a higher cash repayment. For example, if someone borrows two dollars to buy bread today, and that bread costs three dollars a year later, the "fair" repayment is three dollars a year later. This principle allows the distinguishing today between appropriate interest charges (like savings accounts, CDs, and most home mortgages) and exploitive usury. Of course, best of all is for believers, when they have the resources, to give freely and demand no return (cf. Lk 6:35).

Nehemiah urges the restoration of the possessions lost through the period of economic distress (v. 11). Notably, Nehemiah's request is couched as an appeal (**Please**, v. 11), not a demand or command; this is an "in-house" matter among the Jewish people. This reflects the twofold principle that judgment and righteousness begins with the household of God, and that believers must be cautious about expecting, much less demanding, spiritually righteous behavior from those outside the people of God.

The **hundredth part** (v. 11) is probably a one-percent (perhaps monthly) interest charge, and Nehemiah tells the lenders to return that interest as well as the principal. The settling of these economic matters is ultimately a spiritual issue, as indicated by the involvement of the **priests** (v. 12). Oaths are ultimately before the all-seeing and all-hearing God. Again, God is the ultimate guarantor of these sacred vows. Nehemiah's warning (v. 13) is dramatized by shaking out his robes, as one does when removing crumbs or brushing dust off of trousers. The symbolism is clear: may God "shake off" these people if they fail to adhere to that which they agreed to. This sort of "judgment by shaking" is later repeated in Jesus' instructions to his disciples (Mt 10:14).

The people's response is threefold: they accepted the terms (**Amen**), they **praised** God (v. 13, moral reconciliation freed them for genuine worship), and they **did according to this promise** (it was not mere "talk").

2. The Example of Nehemiah (5:14-19)

5:14-18. This second narrative demonstrates that God gave the people success through Nehemiah's sacrificial leadership. Though he had the legal right, Nehemiah did not take from the people during the twelve years of his governorship. (Compare Paul's words that he worked "night and day so as not to be a burden to any of you," 1Th 2:6, 9.) Some have understood **former governors** (v. 15) as a reference to the Samaritans and other local rulers. More recent evidence, however, demonstrates that there were governors in Judah before Nehemiah who did take advantage of their position for economic gain. If some of those governors were themselves Jewish, this further highlights Nehemiah's exasperation with his countrymen. Nehemiah was ultimately concerned about God's judgment (cf. 5:9, 19) and was guided by the vision for what he was called to accomplish without being distracted or captivated by the opportunities for personal gain afforded by his position (v. 16). The size and scope of Nehemiah's household and responsibilities is evident (v. 17) by his having **one hundred and fifty Jews and officials** at his table. Not only did Nehemiah offer "internal" service in leading Judah, he also had an "external" testimony of diplomacy to **those who came to us from the nations**. Even here, in a narrative closely focused on God's preservation of the Jewish people, there is a reminder of God's concern—and the concern of godly people—for all the nations. Despite Jewish economic hardship, the Jewish people, through Nehemiah, were a source of blessing to the nations. Offerings to the governor (**the governor's food allowance**, v. 18) are referred to in God's rebuke of these same Israelites through the prophet Malachi (Mal 1:8).

5:19. Throughout this chapter, Nehemiah's greatest concern was his consciousness of living before God's eyes, and for His approval: **Remember me, O my God**. This theme will be repeated at the close of the book (13:14, 22, 31).

Often the greatest and most discouraging challenges for believers today come from within the community. This is the reason that "judgment [begins] with the household of God" (1Pt 4:17) and that Paul is more concerned about the impurity within the Corinthian church than the corruption outside it (1Co 5:11-13). Furthermore, those who pursue God's purposes cannot do so for their own material gain (1Tm 3:3; Ti 1:7). Finally, we see in Nehemiah a willing model of righteousness, forfeiting his "rights" to impel others to holiness. True leadership is found more in such actions than in lofty speeches or daring deeds.

D. Finishing the Wall (6:1-19)

Having shown that God used Nehemiah's servant leadership skills to aid in the success that God was granting in the building project, what follows is designed to show God's fulfillment of Nehemiah's claim (2:20) that God would grant them success. Thus, the chapter shows the completion of the wall, even in the midst of threats. The first verse (6:1) serves as an outline of the chapter: the opposition of Sanballat and Geshem (vv. 2-9), Tobiah's treachery (vv. 10-14), and the dismay of **our enemies** (vv. 16-19).

1. The Physical Threat (6:1-9)

6:1-4. As the walls neared completion (**no breach remained**, though Nehemiah had not yet **set up the doors in the gates**, v. 1), time grew short for effective opposition. The town and plain of **Ono** (v. 2) was most likely some distance northwest of Jerusalem (seven miles southeast of Lod, near modern Joppa). Sanballat and Geshem were undoubtedly trying to lure Nehemiah far from the security of Jerusalem (though still technically within his territory of Judah) in order to harm or assassinate him. Nehemiah used the great distance, and the time lost to travel, as his reason for not complying. Sanballat's persistence (five invitations) probably confirmed Nehemiah's suspicions. Letters in these days were typically sealed to guard their privacy and the authenticity of their source.

6:5-9. The **open letter** (v. 5) made public the charges against Nehemiah, that he was aspiring to kingship and rebellion against Artaxerxes (v. 6), and was a form of political blackmail. Obviously, the Persian king would tolerate no aspirations of rebellion. It is likely that the true audience for this letter was the Jewish people, in hopes that their fear of Artaxerxes might impel them to take matters into their own hands by restraining Nehemiah. Previous Israelite kings had hired false prophets to testify in their favor (1Kg 11:29-31; 2Kg 9:1-3), which is part of what Amos condemned in his ministry (Am 7:10-17). Nehemiah's response in v. 8 was direct: the charges are not true; these things **have not been done**. The intent of the psychological attack (v. 9) was to weaken the morale and resolve of the builders. Although the closing words of v. 9 (**O God, strengthen my hands**) seem to record a prayer, this is not likely. The "O God" that appears in many English versions (usually in italics) does not appear in the original text. Contrast this with Nehemiah's known prayers, which typically include "Remember me" or "Remember them." A better translation would be, "I carried on with even greater determination." Indeed, in the face of accelerating opposition, Nehemiah had greater reason than ever to finish the task before his enemies took concrete action.

2. The Political Threat (6:10-14)

6:10-12. The second line of subterfuge against Nehemiah came through Shemaiah, who was **confined at home** (lit., "shut up," v. 10). Multiple explanations of this difficult phrase have been proposed; the most compelling is that Shemaiah was feigning personal danger to develop a supposed identification with Nehemiah in order to convince him that they needed to flee together to the temple. Shemaiah seems to have had access to the temple, perhaps as a priest; he may also have been recognized as a prophet, which could have been the reason that Nehemiah was willing to visit him. However, like the false prophets of Israel (1Kg 22:5-6), Shemaiah was willing to tailor his messages to serve political and personal ends. It is his counsel here—that Nehemiah believe the false political threat and illegally hide in the temple (Num 18:7)—that convinced Nehemiah that this was no word from God (**God had not sent him**, v. 12). Nehemiah's reasons for rejecting the counsel are twofold: a leader (**a man like me**, v. 11) should not flee from danger, and only priests (i.e., not **one such as** Nehemiah, who was not a priest) were allowed this intimate access to the temple. Indeed, had Nehemiah taken this counsel and unlawfully barricaded himself in the temple there was a chance his own life would have been forfeit for profaning the sacred space, causing the plots of his enemies to succeed.

6:13-14. Tobiah and Sanballat had initiated this plot. Tobiah had much influence in Jerusalem (see comments on 2:10 and 3:28-32), a point reemphasized in 6:17-19. Here, he was exploiting his resources to trap or discredit the governor. Nehemiah was concerned that he not bear the appearance of guilt or fear by fleeing to the temple, away from weak or nonexistent enemies. Furthermore, Nehemiah recognized that the suggested course of action was not just politically inexpedient, but actually **sin** (v. 13). This is yet another example of Nehemiah's knowledge of the Scriptures. The closing of this section includes the familiar formula **Remember** . . . (v. 14), here in an imprecatory application against the various individuals opposing the work. Perhaps Nehemiah is applying Dt 32:35 in which the Lord says, "Vengeance is Mine." In summary of the various enemies arranged against him, it is surprising to discover that even **Noadiah the prophetess and the rest of the prophets** were also arrayed against Nehemiah (v. 14).

3. The Wall Complete (6:15-19)

6:15-16. Finally, though with some understatement, the walls were completed. **Elul** is the sixth month of the Jewish calendar; the twenty-fifth of Elul is October 27, 445 BC. **Fifty-two days** (v. 15) is a remarkably low figure for such a large task; its accomplishment reflects well on both the industry of the people and the favor of God, as noted in 6:16. **Enemies** (v. 16) probably refers to Sanballat and the other named adversaries; **nations** probably refers to their peoples. The work of Nehemiah and the builders was so rapid that the various plots not withstanding, the **nations** were astonished and demoralized by the quick completion. Part of what makes this accomplishment astonishing is that any great work requires unselfish cooperation, and such cooperation is often rare (as anyone who serves on a committee can testify!).

The point of these two verses is to show the fulfillment of Nehemiah's earlier claim that God would grant success (2:20). Now even Nehemiah's enemies, seeing the wall complete, **recognized that this work had been accomplished with the help of our God** (v. 16).

6:17-19. The discussion about Tobiah's letters (vv. 17-19) applies to the whole of the rebuilding period (**in those days**, v. 17). Nehemiah had accomplished his task in a context marked by constant intrigue and treachery. His experience ranged from those who actively opposed him to those who actively supported him. There were also several positions in between, such as **Meshullam** (v. 18), who was an active builder of the walls (3:4, 30), even while retaining political ties to Tobiah. Tobiah had secured many political and personal allies through marriage contracts and other personal relationships. These mediators spoke in favor of Tobiah, whereas ironically Tobiah's own words (via **letters to frighten me**, v. 19) reinforced Nehemiah's distrust of him.

No matter how charismatic a speaker is, or how compelling his message, the words must be measured against the word of God. Nehemiah is an early "Berean" (Ac 17:10-13) who rejected Shemaiah's counsel because it contradicted the revealed Scriptures. The book of Nehemiah is often read as a study in leadership; it could just as well be seen as a catalog of the sorts of opposition common to humanity—personal, physical, psychological, and political. Nehemiah demonstrates the truth of 1Co 10:13: that these temptations are common, and there is always a way for the man of God to act righteously in response.

III. The Rebuilding of the People (7:1–10:39)

A. Genealogies (7:1-73)

Much of Neh 7 matches almost exactly the list of the original returnees in Ezr 2 (see the notes on Ezr 2). With the walls complete, Nehemiah now turns his attention in the second half of his book to the rebuilding of the people who will occupy Jerusalem. To connect his present work with the original returnees from exile, he opens this section with the same list of them that opened Ezra's account of the first return under Zerubbabel and Jeshua. His purpose in doing so was to demonstrate that the repopulation of Jerusalem would be with genuine Jewish people, truly descended from Abraham, Isaac, and Jacob. Hence, Nehemiah carefully included this genealogy.

1. The Instructions for Security (7:1-4)

7:1-3. The establishment of civil function was not complete until the **gatekeepers**, **singers**, and **Levites** (v. 1) were appointed to their proper offices. There is some ambiguity in v. 2: how many men did Nehemiah put **in charge of Jerusalem**? Most English versions suggest two—Nehemiah's brother **Hanani** (cf. 1:2) and the citadel commander **Hananiah**. In favor of this understanding is the slight difference in names as well as the additional description of Hananiah as one who was **a faithful man and feared God more than many**. Hanani is already known, having been introduced in the first chapter. Hananiah's suitability for this office is further explained. He had administrative experience as the leader of the **fortress**, moral excellence (**faithful** as it related to integrity, literally in Hb., "truthful"), and genuine spirituality (**feared God**).

Another reading of this verse suggests only one man as "mayor" of Jerusalem. On this interpretation, the verse reads "my brother Hanani, that is, Hananiah, the commander of the citadel." In favor of this reading is the only slight variation in the name (perhaps Hanani was known popularly or familiarly as "Hananiah"), and the unwieldiness of sharing this office. Recall from chap. 3 that Jerusalem was already divided into sub-districts administered by Rephaiah and Shallum (3:9, 12). All things considered, the former interpretation seems preferable—for example, Nehemiah speaks to **them** (v. 3), indicating a plural audience.

There are multiple readings possible for v. 3 as well. On the one hand, perhaps it reads that the gates are not to be opened **until the sun is hot**, meaning later in the day than first light. As a measure of heightened security, the gates were not to be opened until the city was completely awake. Alternatively, some suggest the gates were not to be opened "when" **the sun is hot**—that is, during the heat of the day. The midday period is another time of vulnerability, as guards and others might seek shade as relief from the scorching sun. On either understanding, Nehemiah is instituting unusual security measures owing to the ongoing precariousness of the people in Jerusalem, as well as the very underpopulated condition of the city (to be addressed shortly).

7:4. The **city was large** only relative to its small population. The area enclosed by the walls was substantially smaller than the former city under Solomon and Hezekiah. The **people in it were few**, a situation Nehemiah begins to rectify (see 11:1 where residents of the surrounding towns are "drafted" via lottery to move into Jerusalem). Though the **houses were not built** (v. 4), obviously some houses remained as habitable—just not enough for an appropriately repopulated city. By rediscovering (**I found the book of the genealogy**, v. 5) and republishing the list of original returnees, Nehemiah is connecting his current project of city-building and populating to the task of the original return. Here Nehemiah is showing that his work is not distinct from God's plan of restoration but the actual completion of it.

2. The Genealogical Record (7:5-65)

For the most part, 7:5-73 is a nearly identical summary of the same material found in Ezr 2. See also the commentary on Ezra in this volume.

a. The Returned Exiles with Genealogical Records (7:5-60)

7:5-60. Why was so much material, and of such pedantic nature, repeated in the Nehemiah text? Essentially, as noted, the inclusion of this genealogy closely links the earlier returns (under Zerubbabel and Ezra) with this third return and project under Nehemiah's leadership. Sometimes Nehemiah (the man and the book) is erroneously relegated to merely material and pragmatic concerns such as building walls and administering a city, while Ezra is seen as focused on "spiritual" matters such as the temple and the law. A careful reading of the history of Israel will reveal a consistent association of the people (the nation), its worship (the tabernacle and the temple), the law, and the land. God's work with the Jewish people demonstrates the regular interrelationship of these concerns. Indeed, the people's recent exile from the land was occasioned by their idolatry and disobedience to various elements of the law. In the book of Nehemiah, only the initial focus is on the rebuilding of the walls of Jerusalem (securing "the land" once again), a focus that is substantially complete by the end of chap. 6, less than halfway through the book. This indicates that the book as a whole is as much concerned with the issues of the law, the temple, and the purity of the people as it is with the walls and other critical matters addressed in the first six chapters of the text. Transitioning to concerns such as law, temple, and purity by here recalling the original returnees provides a context and justification for the deeply theological agenda of the remaining balance of the book.

b. The Returned Exiles without Genealogical Records (7:61-65)

7:61-65. Though it seems harsh, those practicing priests who could not establish a family tie to historic and ethnic Israel were **excluded from the priesthood** in Judah (v. 64). This is consistent with God's intention to establish a "holy priesthood," sanctified and set apart for particular service (Lv 8–9). This provides the backdrop for the renewed prohibition of mixed marriages to follow later (Neh 13:23-29) in which the Jewish people are required to refrain from marrying foreigners.

3. Summary (7:66-73)

7:66-73. These verses summarize the offerings recorded in Ezr 2:68-69. The discrepancies are probably caused by the "conversion," for example, of the value of things like bowls and garments into cash values. This section ends by noting that many of the people, including **priests, Levites, gatekeepers, singers, temple servants, and all Israel** (v. 73) remained in the cities surrounding Jerusalem. The need to repopulate the rebuilt city of Jerusalem becomes the focus of chap. 11, but first Nehemiah turns his attention to the spiritual restoration of the people in chaps. 8–10.

Despite the strength of its walls or other fortifications, the real strength of a city or a community is its people. Nehemiah's work had only begun with the completion of the walls; it would be completed in the construction of a people to occupy the city. Revisiting the list of returnees served to remind the people who they were, and why they were in Judah: to rebuild the temple and the city, and to testify to the power and grace of God.

B. The Public Reading of the Law (8:1-18)

Having highlighted the people's genealogical descent, showing their genuine Jewish identity, Nehemiah wanted to focus on the spiritual lives of the people. Physical descent from the people of Israel was insufficient without a spiritual relationship with the God of Israel. Thus chaps. 8–10 focus on the spiritual lives of those who had returned, beginning with the input of the Word of God as foundational to their spiritual revitalization.

1. The Reading of the Law (8:1-8)

8:1-4. The whole people **gathered . . . at the square which was in front of the Water Gate** (v. 1) rather than the temple court, where only men were allowed. It was **on the first day of the seventh month** (v. 2), the date of the Feast of Trumpets (Lv 23:23-25; Nm 29:1-6), a festival that began the penitential season for Israel. The blowing of trumpets functioned to call the nation to repentance in preparation for the Day of Atonement nine days later. Ezra was instructed to **bring** out (and read) **the book of the law of Moses** (v. 1). The reading of the law may have been part of the origins of the reading cycles that developed in the synagogue shortly thereafter. As Ezra read on this occasion for only six hours or so (see v. 3), he only read portions, not the whole Pentateuch. Assuming the literary and theological agenda of the book of Nehemiah includes an attempt to recapitulate the conquest of Joshua (see also v. 17), a reading of Deuteronomy—Moses' reproclamation of the law to the people prior to the conquest—would be appropriate.

The makeup of the assembly is noteworthy, consisting of **men and women, those who could understand** (v. 3). This was not a male-only event, or even an adult event. Children who could understand were present and participating as well (this might count as a challenge to the contemporary practice of excusing children from church services prior to the sermon). **From early morning until midday** spans about six hours, implying that the people had traveled to Jerusalem from their houses "in their cities" (7:73) early in order to be assembled and ready to hear by daybreak. The **wooden podium** (v. 4, better "platform") upon which Ezra stood is also translated "tower" (JPS); it is thought to have had a broad, flat surface at the top in order to have space for the men standing with him. The text lists six men on Ezra's right, and seven on his left, totaling thirteen. This has been a cause of some concern to interpreters because of the lack of symmetry and because the expected number would be twelve. As a result, there has been some disagreement about the significance of the thirteen leaders with Ezra. The most likely explanation is that this is an attempt to associate this event with the conquest. The most prominent gathering of "thirteen" tribes in Israel's history occurred at the mustering prior to the conquest, recorded in Jos 2–4, where twelve tribes plus the Levites (totaling 13) were assembled (Jos 4:1-10). In the present text, the assembly of thirteen behind Ezra represents the whole of the reconstituted people of Israel in Nehemiah's day. There is almost certainly a deliberate parallel between the episode at the conquest and this one, thereby associating the present restoration of the land to the past gift of the land.

8:5-8. There appears to have been a specific liturgy of Judah's worship for this special feast day. As **Ezra opened the book . . . all the people stood up** (v. 5), presumably in respect for the Word of God (a practice adopted in many contemporary churches when the Scriptures are read aloud). Ezra led the people in prayer and praise, and they responded with the double **Amen** (v. 6). Some find in these verses (including vv. 7-8 to follow) the beginnings of the synagogue system that would figure prominently in the NT because here is a service of worship and biblical instruction happening outside of (but close to) the temple courts. (For some reason, many contemporary churches that adopt the practice of standing for the reading of the Word do not also adopt the practice of bowing low and worshiping the Lord **with their faces to the ground**, v. 6.) In vv. 7-8, a different group of men who were **Levites** (again numbering thirteen) dispersed among the people and **explained the law to the people** . . . giving them **the sense**. It seems that after Ezra would read, these men would explain, answer questions, and address issues of application. Also, because the people now spoke Aramaic, the Levites would have needed to translate or paraphrase the meaning of the Hebrew text. This pattern of assembly in smaller groups for the reading and discussion of the law became the basis of Israel's later synagogue system, as well as for Bible study and Sunday school classes for contemporary believers.

2. The Sacred Feast (8:9-12)

8:9-12. The initial response to the law was one of grief, likely because of the penitential day and also the realization of how much of the law had been disobeyed. It was so much that Ezra and Nehemiah had to intervene and encourage the people to celebrate instead: **This day is holy to the LORD your God; do not mourn or weep** (v. 9). It was a reminder that this holy day, the Feast of Trumpets, was a festival of joy as well. This suggests that "holy" need not equal "somber." Indeed, the people were commanded to go and **eat**, **drink**, and **send portions** (to those without the means to do so—**him who has nothing prepared**, v. 10). These words are counter to the situation Paul later discovers in Corinth, where the celebration of the Christian love feast had become an occasion of excess for the wealthy and exclusion for the poor (see the comments on 1Co 11:17-22). Celebration of God's grace should be inclusive of those without the same means to celebrate. Further, there is an appropriate consumption of **fat** (foods) and sweet drinks, against those who think that godliness requires abstaining from all physical and sensory pleasures. The people responded with great joy (v. 17) when they actually understood the words of the law. A right understanding of God's law, and the grace it contains, should lead to joy.

3. The Feast of Booths (8:13-18)

8:13-18. On the **second day** of the (seventh) month, the people found in the law instructions concerning the Feast of Booths (Tabernacles) (Lv 23: 33-44; Dt 16:13-16), and immediately reinstituted the celebration. There is some thought here that they began this celebration a few days too early; the feast was supposed to begin on the fifteenth day of the month and last for eight days. More likely, the text here records the timely discovery of the instructions for the feast, which the people were able to appropriately celebrate beginning two weeks later. When the text notes that the people kept the Feast of Booths, it does not say that this was the first time they had done so in centuries (v. 17); indeed, there are biblical accounts of various Booths celebrations throughout Israel's history (Jdg 21:19; 1Sm 1:3; 1Kg 8:2; Ezr 3:4; Zch 14:16). However, Booths had not been celebrated "like this" (NIV) since **the days of Joshua the son of Nun** (v. 17). Perhaps the distinctive relates to the "correctness" of the celebration, or the extent of the joy on this occasion. In any event, the author once more draws the reader's attention to the correspondence between the conquest of Joshua and the reconquest of Nehemiah. Each day included a reading from the law (perhaps in this context Ezra was able to read through the whole of it), as well as ongoing celebrations.

This eighth chapter of Nehemiah contains a surprising amount of historic precedent, laying the groundwork for the teaching and worship of a more geographically diverse Israel in the NT period (the synagogue system), and ultimately much of the shape of early and contemporary Christian worship. From Israel's earliest days the people had been instructed that the "book of the law shall not depart from your mouth, but you shall meditate on it day and night" (Jos 1:8). By the time of the return from exile Israel had fallen far from this lofty standard, even to the point of needing to rediscover and reinstitute the law itself. In the intervening years before the coming of Jesus the Messiah, the Jewish people sustained this attention to the Scriptures so that Jesus and the apostles were able to initiate their own ministries by entering into synagogues and reasoning from the Scriptures to proclaim the fulfillment of them in Jesus. Admittedly, however, this attention to the Hebrew Scriptures had become tragically obscured by the religious leaders' obsession with oral tradition (see the comments on Mt 15:1-20). This "Scripture-centered" faith has remained a hallmark of the true people of God for the last 2,400 years.

C. The Confession and History of Israel (9:1-37)

The message of chap. 9 continues the focus on the spiritual lives of those who had returned (chaps. 8–10). The author moves from the nation needing the input of the Word of God as a foundation for their spiritual revitalization to their need for genuine repentance to renew their walk with their God (chap. 9). Based on the reproclamation of the law and the reinstitution of Jewish ceremonial and celebratory practices like the Feast of Booths (Neh 8), the Jewish people realize they have broken covenant with God and then seek to reestablish this sacred covenant (chap. 10). Preparatory to the covenant renewal is the assembling of the people and a recitation of Jewish history here in chap. 9, which is an account of God's repeated grace and their repeated rebellion, culminating with a confession of their corporate national sin.

1. The Assembly of the Levites and People (9:1-5)

9:1-3. Despite the temporary celebration of Booths at the close of the prior chapter, the returned nation's need for confession and repentance remained, as well as a rededication to covenant faithfulness. The **twenty-fourth day of** [that same] **month** was two days after the end of Booths. **Sackcloth** was a rough material made of goat's hair; **dirt** was also a sign of shame and mourning, in this case for the sins of the people. The confession was exclusive to the community, so Israel **separated themselves from all foreigners** (v. 2) since God's covenant had been with Abraham and his descendants (see vv. 7-8 to follow). There is a close connection between the Word of God (**they read from the book of the law** for three hours), and the application that follows (they **confessed and worshiped** for three hours). An understanding of Scripture leads to a realization and acknowledgement of estrangement from God (confession), as well as the access available to Him by grace (worship).

9:4-5. Surprisingly, the spiritual leaders of the nation were not singled out (cf. chaps. 4–5) until after this description of corporate confession and worship. This reminds us that a relationship with God is ultimately personal, and not one that can be maintained by the vicarious actions of spiritual leaders. Here, it is the **Levites** (priestly descendants of the tribe of Levi) who assume a leadership role; in the chapter to follow, as the renewed covenant includes political and administrative commitments, Nehemiah and other governing officials are recognized as well. These Levites led the worship in two groups, with some members (five) participating in both.

2. Creation and the Call of Abraham (9:6-8)

9:6-8. Israel's covenant is with the only God of the Universe: **you alone are the LORD. LORD** here is God's covenant name with Israel, appropriately used as the people reinvoke their particular and unique relationship with Him. God's work with His people is set in the context of His sovereignty. God is the maker of the **heavens**, the **earth**, and the **heavenly host**—a reference to the stars or the angels (or both), as well as everything that lives on the earth or in the sea. Amid the scope of such a vast creation, God singled out **Abram** (later **Abraham**) as the father of the Jewish people (Gn 11:31ff.) and brought him out of the Chaldean land, from where the Jewish people in this narrative had just come. The returned Jewish exiles recalled the promise that God made to Abraham to give them the very land in which they were standing (Gn 12, 15, 17).

3. The Exodus and Wandering (9:9-22)

9:9-13. Without mentioning the other patriarchs, Joseph, or the movement of the twelve tribes to Egypt at the end of Genesis, the prayer next turns to the events of the exodus and journey toward the promised land. Indeed, in the whole of the prayer, the focus is continually on the placement of the people in the land, with all other events secondary to this central concern. The exodus from Egypt (Ex 12) was the singular event forming the national identity of ancient Israel, commemorated annually in the Passover feast. God **saw the affliction of** their **fathers** and **heard their** cries (v. 9), just as these fifth-century Jewish descendants continued in affliction and crying out. God demonstrated His presence and faithfulness to His people, leading them through **the sea** and with a **pillar of cloud** by day and a **pillar of fire** (vv. 11-12) by night (Ex 13–14). God's visible presence was localized in the tabernacle and later the temple; the people were calling on God to once more dwell among them and return to the temple of Jerusalem. God also gave them His **ordinances**, **laws**, **statutes**, and **commandments** (v. 13) at Mount Sinai (for example, Ex 20), as they had recently been reminded through the reading of the law (Neh 8).

9:14-22. Furthermore, God demonstrated weekly and even daily provision in the **sabbath** and with manna (vv. 14-15), good news indeed to a weary, oppressed, and hungry people who longed to be restored to such provision. These things were supposed to culminate in the provision of a homeland: **You told them to enter in order to possess the land which You swore to give them** (v. 15). Here ancient Israel balked, overwhelmed by the threat of the Canaanites and preferring to return to Egypt (v. 17) rather than conquer the land as instructed. However, even in the face of the people's rebellion and idolatry (Ex 32), God remained **a God of forgiveness, gracious and compassionate, slow to anger and abounding in lovingkindness** (v. 17). People cannot unilaterally restore a broken relationship with God—nothing they can offer can earn His favor. The only hope is that God will forgive because He cannot forget or ignore sin. This hope is well-founded because He is gracious, blessing beyond what is deserved, and compassionate and merciful, withholding punishment that is deserved. God demonstrated this to Israel by remaining faithful to the nation during the forty years of desert wandering (vv. 18-21, as seen especially throughout the book of Numbers).

4. The Conquest under Joshua and Subsequent Unfaithfulness (9:23-31)

9:23-31. God's intention in preserving Israel through the wanderings was that they would eventually enter the land of promise, as indeed occurred under Joshua. **Numerous as the stars of heaven** (v. 23) recalls God's promise to Abraham (Gn 15). Joshua's conquest (Jos 11) is described here (**subdued** . . . **inhabitants of the land, the Canaanites** . . . **captured fortified cities and a fertile land** . . . **took possession of houses**) in matter-of-fact terms (vv. 24-25), as if it were a simple thing for God to accomplish, as indeed it was. These latter-day Jewish people recognized that Joshua's conquest was the work of God, that their challenges were similar, and that God could again give them the land. The Jewish people in the past **became disobedient and rebelled** . . . **and they committed great blasphemies** (v. 26): these words summarize the repeated cycles of falling away through the times of the judges and the kings. Significantly, the great victories of the judges, the reigns of Saul, David, and Solomon, the prophetic ministries of Elijah and Isaiah—in fact all the high points of Israel's history—are omitted. Instead, Israel's core history is not measured by these political victories or the accomplishments of the prominent heroes of the people, but by either periods of faithfulness or unfaithfulness among the people as a whole. Faithfulness is rewarded by peace (**rest**, v. 28) in the land, unfaithfulness is judged by oppression and ultimately exile from the land. Such is the consistent history of Israel, paralleled by God's consistent history of **great compassion** (v. 31). Every instance of rebellion is matched by a further outpouring of God's mercy.

5. Confession and Repentance (9:32-37)

9:32-34. Now comes the central petition of the prayer (**Now therefore**, v. 32), though it has been implicit throughout: that God would once more show mercy to His people. The appeal is both to the Word of God, that He keep His covenant (v. 32), and to the character of God, that he be merciful once more (**lovingkindness**). The whole of Israel is at fault (**us, our kings, our princes, our priests, our prophets, our fathers and** . . . **all Your people**), culminating in the great judgments of the Assyrian (v. 32) and Babylonian conquests. There is no fault in God, however (**You are just**, v. 33). The appeal is not for a just treatment but a merciful one. Believers should be careful when crying out to God for what they believe they deserve, as opposed to casting themselves on His mercy.

9:35-37. Land (v. 35) is mentioned nineteen times in Nehemiah, thirteen of which are in this prayer. Indeed, possession, provision, and peace in the land are the key markers of God's favor to these people and the central petition, after forgiveness, of this prayer. The passage concludes with the request that they be allowed to dwell in freedom and in plenty in the land (just as Joshua was to have established the nation). The agreement (v. 38) to follow is the expression of their commitment to return to the terms of the prior covenant.

This passage is a reminder that sin has consequences that often endure for generations. The Jewish people of the Bible, acting as all people do, had presumed upon the goodness of God (they had "grown fat" in the land) and taken for granted His mercy toward their sin. Perhaps they had even settled into a sort of "cheap grace" attitude that when things got bad enough, they could easily repent and God would quickly restore them. They failed to recognize that one effect of sin is to "stiffen necks" and make people even less inclined towards God and repentance. In this case, it required the radical "tough love" of God's chastening through exile to finally cure Israel of idolatry and spiritual adultery. While this passage models what it is to cry out to God in true repentance, it also warns us of the destructive effects of sin on individuals and communities.

D. The Establishing of a New Sacred Covenant (9:38–10:39)

The revitalization of the people continues in this next section. Their renewal began by hearing the Word of God (chap. 8), continued with their repentance (chap. 9), and now culminates with a covenant renewal with God (chap. 10).

1. The Signers of the Covenant (9:38–10:27)

9:38. Following the recitation of history and confession of sins in the previous section, here the people respond by committing themselves to God and one another. Literally, **making** a binding **agreement** means "cutting an amen," with "cutting" serving as a reminder of ancient covenant practices (cf. Gn 15 where God makes a covenant with Abram and passes between divided or cut animals), and the "amen" referring to a "sure, trustworthy statement" signifying permanence or constancy. The seals (v. 38; 10:1) refer not to a closed, **sealed** document, as some translations imply, but instead to the affixing of personal seals as signatures. These served as guarantees of leadership participation in the agreement. The seals contained the names of the **leaders**, **Levites**, and **priests**.

10:1-13. Nehemiah the governor's name appears first on the sacred covenant at the beginning of chap. 10. **Zedekiah** (10:1) is not mentioned elsewhere; commentators suggest that he is the scribe who is recording the agreement. The list of priests begins with v. 2 (**These were the priests**, v. 8). In distinction from the other lists of this section, this designation occurs at the end of the list of priests, most of whom are known from other sections of the book (see, for example, 12:1-7). Twenty-one priests are listed. First Chronicles 24:7-18 describes a structure by which the priests are divided into 24 groups serving the temple in rotation. This rotation leads directly 400 years later to Zacharias taking his turn in temple service in Lk 1:8. Next (vv. 9-13) are listed **the Levites**, seventeen of whom are named here.

10:14-27. Finally, in vv. 14-27, there are the **leaders of the people** (v. 14). This list includes substantial overlap with those of Ezr 2 and Neh 7. It is misguided to try to ascertain spiritual significance from the etymology of the names listed here. What is important is the actual flesh-and-blood men who committed themselves and the community to the terms of the covenant (see further comments below).

2. The Content of the Covenant (10:28-39)

10:28-29. The comprehensive list that begins this section includes **the rest of the people** (v. 28), meaning that this was not solely a "representative" covenant, but that the whole of the community—**all those who had knowledge and understanding**—joined itself in this covenant. Similarly, we find comprehensive commitments **to walk in God's law . . . to keep and to observe all the commandments of God our Lord, and His ordinances and His statutes** (v. 29). The extended readings of the law had brought to mind the details of God's law for His people (the components of immediate significance are identified in the section to follow). Compare Dt 27–29, wherein Israel recommits to the covenant of God in light of a series of curses and blessings. Once more, the text recapitulates the language of the conquest in the reformation of Israel in Canaan.

10:30-39. Several specific points are emphasized. First, the threat of the loss of national identity through mixed marriage requires Israel to commit to ethnic purity in marriage in v. 30 (see also Ezr 10 and Neh 13:23-28). Second, one of the Jewish nation's most public expressions of collective identity was the keeping of the **sabbath** (affirmed here in v. 31); this had become a point of extreme legalism by the time of Jesus (cf. Jn 5:1-9 and Jn 9:14-16). Similarly, a renewed commitment to the Sabbath rest of the land— "let [land] rest and lie fallow" (Ex 23:10-11; Lv 25:2-7)—served to distinguish Israel radically from her contemporaries and highlighted her faith in God's provision. Third, the law commanded a half a shekel (Ex 30:13-14) to provide for needs associated with the tabernacle and later the temple. Here (vv. 32-33) the people promised to support the temple through a "tax" of **one third of a shekel**. The discrepancy has been explained by appeal to either the harsh economic circumstances, or a variation in how shekels were weighed and valued. The constant sacrifices required a regular **supply of wood** for burning, hence the explicit commitment in v. 34. Furthermore, the law required the offering of **first fruits** (Ex 23:16; 34:19-20; Dt 26:1-11), which applied to cattle and people (v. 36) as well as to plants (v. 37). The many commodities required for the service of the temple and the maintenance of the priests were to be supplied through the people's tithes. This priority of the first fruits, and of the tenth or tithe, reflect for Israel the central prominence of the temple and its service in the renewed community. As a concluding comment, the people declare, **we will not neglect the house of our God** (v. 39).

This section of the book seems anti-climactic, being concerned with seemingly insignificant housekeeping issues like maintaining a supply of wood for the temple. Yet, this section of the text underscores the critical role chap. 13 will play, as Nehemiah becomes distraught over Israel's failure to keep the terms of the covenant listed here: marriages mixed, the Sabbath profaned, tithes uncollected, and even wood unsupplied for the temple offerings. The point in chap. 13 is to show that although Israel had returned from captivity, the nation's final restoration was not to be seen in the return from Babylon but to be expected at the end of days (this will be discussed in greater depth in the comments on chap. 13).

Contemporary readers may question the devotional value of long lists of difficult names as included in 10:2-27 (as well as in 11:4-36 and 12:1-26 to follow). Indeed, does not 2Tm 3:16 assure that "All Scripture is . . . profitable for teaching, for reproof, for correction, for training in righteousness"? Where is the profit in a record such as this? Rather than seeing this as a wearisome and tedious section of Scripture (or worse, mere fodder for Bible trivia games!), believers should reflect on (1) the nature of a God who knows His people by name, (2) on the power and responsibility of an individual to represent his family and community through spiritual headship, and (3) ultimately on the Judeo-Christian affirmation of each person as an intrinsically valuable divine image-bearer. Furthermore, faith in Christ and belief in the Bible is historically grounded, not based on legendary figures. It has been passed from generation to generation by genuine people with real names and specific circumstances. Though today these people are unknown and their names unrecognized, they would have been extremely significant to the first readers and hearers of Nehemiah's book. They would have reminded them that they were the inheritors of a particular covenant history with God. Believers today stand many generations later in that exact same spiritual lineage, through the faithfulness of many other committed followers of the Lord, not immortalized by a single mention in Scripture.

IV. The Dedication of the People, Walls, and Temple (11:1–13:31)

The initial problem that prompted Nehemiah's return to Jerusalem was that those who returned from captivity were "in great distress and reproach" because of the broken walls and burned gates of Jerusalem (1:3). Therefore, Nehemiah returned to rebuild the walls physically (chaps. 3–6) and revitalize the people spiritually (chaps. 7–10). At this point the author wants to show the outcome of these efforts. A few specific challenges were that the people needed to act on the previous corrections by populating Jerusalem, dedicate the rebuilt walls of the city, and purify the promised land, all subjects that will be addressed in the last three chapters of the book (chaps. 11–13).

A. Populating Jerusalem and Its Region (11:1-36)

The consecration of the people is now followed by the record of their consolidation, applying their consecration in a practical way. This was to show that it was insufficient to build walls and commit to spiritual faithfulness without also helping repopulate and fortify Jerusalem, the center of worship of the covenant people.

11:1-2. At the end of chap. 7, the various religious leaders (priests, Levites, temple servants) were living outside Jerusalem in their own towns (7:73). Now, chap. 11 declares that the leaders **lived in Jerusalem** (11:1), but the people remained scattered, with the result that Jerusalem was severely underpopulated, preventing the city from serving as the administrative and spiritual center of the Jewish people. In fact, a "tithe" of the people, determined through casting **lots** (11:1), served to require ten percent of the population of the land to take up residence in the city. This involved moving from established houses and agricultural fields. As a result, the majority of Jewish people who did not move commended (**blessed**, v. 2) those who volunteered to move to Jerusalem (presumably because their actions allowed the others to remain in their cities). Estimates of Jerusalem's population in this day range from 4,800 to 8,000, a far cry from the estimated population of 20,000 before the Babylonian conquest.

11:3-24. What follows is an accounting of the most prominent residents of Jerusalem and its precincts. As expected, the tribes of Judah (vv. 4-6) and Benjamin (vv. 7-9), as well as the priests (vv. 10-14), Levites (vv. 15-18), gatekeepers and temple workers (vv. 19, 21) are explicitly mentioned. As discussed earlier regarding chap. 10, contemporary eyes glaze over at the extended recitation of unfamiliar names. It bears reflection, however, that these names represent real people and families who made sacrificial life changes for the good of the broader community. They may merit only these single mentions in Scripture, but they were genuine heroes to their countrymen for their willingness to take up the mantle of difficult service in Jerusalem. Sometimes the most heroic task to perform is not the one that others are incapable of doing, but rather the task others are unwilling to do.

11:25-36. Next, there is a record of the broader circle of Judah's residents who populate the cities found in the territory of the tribes of Judah and Benjamin (vv. 25-35), including cities **from Beersheba as far as the valley of Hinnom** (v. 30); that is, from Israel's traditional southern boundary, north to the Hinnom Valley, adjacent to Jerusalem on its southern side. Benjamin's expanse ranges north and west of Jerusalem (vv. 31-35). An accounting of the population of Benjamin's cities reveals that this tribe's populace was underserved by resident Levites, necessitating a move into the region by some of the divisions of the Levites of Judah (v. 36).

Apart from the census-type accounting of Israel, and some redistribution of the population as necessary, chap. 11 reports life in Judah settling into a normal routine. The affirmation that the **rest of Israel, of the priests and of the Levites, were in all the cities of Judah, each on his own inheritance** (v. 20) can only be understood as an allusion to the conquest of Canaan under Joshua. Of the 192 OT uses of the Hebrew word for inheritance (*nachalah*), 97 are in Numbers, Deuteronomy, and Joshua, and only five are postexilic: three in Chronicles (1Ch 16:18; 2Ch 6:27; 2Ch 10:16), one in Malachi (Mal 1:3), and here in Nehemiah. This reapportioning of the people in keeping with their ancient tribal lands gives a sense that all is once again as it should be in Israel, and serves as the antecedent to the climactic celebration of God's faithfulness in chap. 12.

B. Dedicating the Walls of Jerusalem (12:1-47)

1. The Priests and Levites Who Returned from Exile (12:1-21)

12:1-9. These verses list the spiritual leaders (priests and Levites) who returned from the exile as a part of Zerubbabel's return in 538 BC, as well as the sequence of high priests from Zerubbabel's time to Nehemiah's, and the heads of priestly families during the intervening years. The Ezra listed here (v. 1) is not the same scribe who led the second return eighty years after Zerubbabel's in 458 BC. There are 22 leaders of priestly courses (vv. 1-7); the division of priests into 24 groups for service dates perhaps to the time of David (cf. 1Ch 24). Similarly, vv. 8-9 record how the Levites were also divided into their service divisions. This section provides some insight into the historical background regarding the formal division of worship leadership responsibilities, as **Mattaniah** is named (v. 8), with his brothers, as having charge over the **songs of thanksgiving**. Attention to thanksgiving is particularly appropriate at this stage of Israel's history, after years of longing and lament (cf. Ps 137).

12:10-21. Also listed is the line of high priests from **Jeshua** to **Jaddua** (vv. 10-11). **Jeshua** was high priest at the construction of Zerubbabel's temple (518 BC, cf. Hg 1:1, 12; 2:2; Zch 3:1-10; 6:11-15). **Eliashib** (v. 10) was Nehemiah's contemporary. As particular attention is given to the priestly families during the service of the high priest **Joiakim**, perhaps he was high priest during the return and early ministry of Ezra. A number of the 22 priestly families (cf. vv. 1-7) are repeated (vv. 12-21). The general intent of vv. 1-21 is to connect the returnees under Zerubbabel with the Levitical leadership in the time of Nehemiah, to indicate that the events soon to be recounted are in continuity with and in completion of the original return. It is a way of showing that the "distress and reproach" of Jerusalem had been relieved.

2. The Leading Levites (12:22-26)

12:22-26. The **Darius** mentioned (v. 22) might be either of a pair of similarly named Persian rulers whose reigns fall within the period bounded by the returns of Zerubbabel and Nehemiah, depending on variant spellings of different high priests' names appearing in some of the extra-biblical records. **With their brothers opposite them** (v. 24) probably indicates antiphonal singing. **As prescribed by David** is probably drawn from David's organization of priestly liturgy (1Ch 16:4; 23:27-31; 2Ch 8:14). The **gatekeepers** of the temple (v. 25), attending to the basic coming-in and going-out of the worshipers, occupy an unprestigious role in the Levitical hierarchy. However, the psalm writer had said that he would rather serve as a gatekeeper in the house of the Lord than to dwell in the more luxurious dwellings of the wicked (Ps 84:10). This list of temple workers is summarized as those who **served in the days of Joiakim** and **Nehemiah the governor** and **Ezra the priest and scribe** (v. 26).

3. Purification of Levites, People, and Wall (12:27-30)

12:27-30. The dedication of the wall of Jerusalem by the restored priesthood and people of Israel, culminating with the reconsecrated temple, stands as the spiritual climax of the book of Nehemiah. The word **dedication** (v. 27) in Aramaic is *Chanukah*. The Jewish holiday of Chanukah is a celebration of the Jewish people's later recovery and dedication of the temple from the Seleucids (165 BC). That celebration stands in the tradition of the dedication of Solomon's temple (1Kg 8), the initial dedication of the Second Temple under Zerubbabel (Ezr 6:13-18), and this parallel dedication of the whole of the city and the people. Though some of the Levitical tribe had volunteered to live in Jerusalem, and others had been relocated to places of service throughout the land of Judea (recall for example 11:1-2, 36), the Levitical singers were summoned from throughout the land to participate in the celebration. **Cymbals** and stringed instruments (v. 27; **harps** had strings of differing lengths; **lyres** had strings of the same length with differing diameters and tensions) were common in religious services. Purification (v. 30) restored a person or object to ritual holiness after it had become unclean or unholy. The order of purification is important—only when first having been made clean themselves are the Levites able to extend the sanctification to the **people, the gates and the wall** (v. 30). This principle remains instructive for those in ministry today. This purification and dedication reflects an expanding idea of the "holy place" beyond the temple and the people to the whole of Jerusalem—a holy city.

4. Two Choirs (12:31-43)

a. First Choir under Ezra (12:31-37)

12:31-37. The **two great choirs** gathered in the southwest portion of the city, perhaps near the Valley Gate. Nehemiah had begun his nighttime inspection of the city's walls by leaving from the Valley Gate (2:13). This walk serves as an *inclusio*, a literary bracketing to show the completion of Nehemiah's work. First he examined the shame and reproach of Jerusalem, and now he shows that it is over.

The first choir, with Ezra (v. 36), moved along the wall in a counterclockwise direction, past the **Refuse Gate** and on to the **Fountain Gate** (vv. 31, 37), and then directly up the steps to the **Water Gate** leading to temple precincts. The second choir, with Nehemiah (v. 38), moved clockwise along the wall above the **Tower of Furnaces**, along the **Broad Wall**, above the **Gate of Ephraim**, by the **Old Gate**, the **Fish Gate**, the **Tower of Hananel** and the **Tower of the Hundred**, as far as the **Sheep Gate**; and they stopped at the **Gate of the Guard** (vv. 38-39). The listing of these gates and landmarks conveys a sense of remembering a series of hard-won battlefields—the people are celebrating their prior victory in the rebuilding of these very walls described in chaps. 3–6. Nothing like this movement of choirs is recorded in the two other dedications mentioned before (1Kg 8:22-66; Ezr 6:16-18). This movement around the perimeter of the city is reminiscent of the capture of Jericho under Joshua. Perhaps this important event from Israel's history was on the people's minds as the army marched around the city accompanied by the **priests with trumpets** (v. 34; see Jos 6:4, 6, 8, 13, 16, 20).

Two deviations from the descriptions in chap. 3 bear mention: in Neh 12:39 the Inspection Gate is called the **Gate of the Guard**, lending credence to the military function of that northwest gate; second, the **Gate of Ephraim** is not mentioned in chap. 3. Either it was not in need of repair then, or it is another name for one of the other gates, probably the Old Gate (3:6). A gate thus positioned would be oriented toward the traditional inheritance of the tribe of Ephraim, hence its name. If a major theme of the book of Nehemiah is to describe a reconquest of Canaan along the lines of the original conquest, it is worth recalling that Joshua was an Ephraimite (1Ch 7:20-27). The substitution here of this name is a subtle reminder of that connection. This theological thesis would be confirmed beyond reasonable doubt if it could be demonstrated that Nehemiah also was a member of the tribe of Ephraim.

b. Second Choir under Nehemiah (12:38-43)

12:38-43. The two choirs were reunited in the **house of God** (v. 40). There the ceremony climaxed as the officials, priests, and people **offered great sacrifices and rejoiced** with **great joy** (v. 43). Indeed, the repeated theme of these concluding verses is emphatic rejoicing. This rejoicing is for "all the people," including the **women and children**, even those far away from Jerusalem.

5. Worship and Celebration (12:44-47)

12:44-47. In these concluding verses of the chapter, Israel begins well in following through on the obligations of supporting the restored and repurified temple. In keeping with the rejoicing of the previous paragraph, the people of Judah **rejoiced over the priests and Levites who**

served in the temple (v. 44), and manifested that joy in stocking the storerooms with the **first fruits** and **tithes** (this recalls the stipulations of the sacred covenant of 10:28-39). Sadly, the following chapter will record that after some intervening years, these tithes had become sporadic, and these same storerooms had become the dwelling place of Tobiah, the erstwhile enemy of Judah (13:8-9). For a time, however, this chapter presents Israel as having come into her proper glory—worshiping according to the law and dwelling in the land in the spirit of Israel's golden age under **David** and **Asaph** (v. 46; David appointed Asaph as a temple musician who became the father of the clan of musicians that served throughout the history of the temple; for the songs of Asaph, see Pss 50, 73–83).

Most readers of this book think Nehemiah's major work was the rebuilding of the walls of Jerusalem and the attendant relative security the people then enjoyed. However, it is the clear emphasis of the text that while that work was urgent and immediate, Nehemiah believed that the task of rebuilding the people of Israel spiritually was in fact the more important and enduring work. Had the walls been merely rebuilt, but not placed in the service (dedicated) to the spiritual health of Israel, they would have instead been a stumbling block and obstacle to Israel's greater need for right relationship with God. Believers need to retain such spiritual priorities, affirming the value of material success but never allowing such to substitute for spiritual aspirations. Also, this text affirms the community value of those who minister in the house of God, with the whole of Israel materially supporting the Levites in their full-time service in the temple. The application for believers today is twofold, and a matter of degree. Those who work hard at teaching and shepherding the household of God are worthy of material as well as verbal reward (1Co 9:4-14; Gl 6:6; 1Tm 5:17-18). However, as the apostle Peter explains, all Christian believers have collectively become a royal priesthood and temple of God (1Pt 2:9) and thus have ongoing responsibilities akin to those of Israel's Levitical tribe: worship of God and service to the community.

C. Purifying the Promised Land (13:1-31)

The outline of this final chapter is clear—each of its sections concludes with Nehemiah's refrain, "Remember me/remember them . . . O my God" (vv. 14, 22, 29, 31). Nehemiah is not concerned that God will forget the facts of his service; instead, his requests are that God will act in blessing or judgment on the basis of His knowledge of the facts. Despite the emotional and spiritual high of the dedication of the walls in chap. 12, the ongoing, daily work of faithful holiness requires daily vigilance; the triumphs of a great day of celebration and accomplishment are eroded by small acts of compromise. Furthermore, in the intervening years between the affirming of the details of the sacred covenant in 10:28-39 and Nehemiah's return to the land in his second term as governor (recorded here in chap. 13), Israel had managed to violate every explicit provision of the covenant: tithing had been neglected, Sabbath rest was regularly ignored, mixed marriages were being permitted, and even the wood for the temple offerings was not being supplied as promised. Nehemiah acted immediately to correct these violations, lest Israel fall quickly again under God's curse.

1. Purifying the Temple (13:1-14)

13:1-3. From **the book of Moses** (v. 1; see Dt 23:3-6) the people recall God's declaration that the children of mixed marriages with Ammonites or Moabites cannot enter the assembly, "even to the tenth generation" (in contrast to the children of Edomites and Egyptians, who gain access in the third generation). Even though it had been well over ten generations since Ammon and Moab had failed to assist Israel (Nm 22–24), the recent opposition of Tobiah the Ammonite had rekindled the ancient prohibition. This rediscovery of the law led to a general, but not complete, exclusion of residents of foreign descent.

13:4-9. It seems unlikely that **Eliashib the priest** (v. 4) was the high priest, as it is unlikely that the high priest would be administering storerooms. In contrast to the intent to exclude enemies of Israel (particularly of Ammonite descent), here **Tobiah** is found actually dwelling in the temple precincts (v. 5)! Furthermore, it is telling that there was available a large (and empty) storeroom **formerly** used for the storage of tithes and offerings; the eager generosity of the last chapter (12:47) had substantially waned by this time. This backsliding occurred in Nehemiah's absence, as he had returned to Babylon (as intended, cf. 2:6) **in the thirty-second year of Artaxerxes** (v. 6), completing his first term of twelve years (cf. 1:1; 2:1). How long the intervening absence was is unknown, nor is the length of Nehemiah's second term known. Extrabiblical data indicates that Bagohi was governor of Judah by 407 BC. As Nehemiah **threw** out all of Tobiah's property (v. 8), he prefigured Jesus' cleansing of that same temple 400 years later (Mt 21:12-13).

13:10-14. The Levites and singers were forced to return to their fields to provide their own sustenance because the tithes had been neglected (v. 10). As a consequence, **the house of God** had been **forsaken** (v. 11; i.e., neglected). Nehemiah recalled the temple servants, restored the tithe, and restructured its administration (vv. 11-13). This section illustrates two important matters: first, the collective responsibility for the maintenance of godly worship, and second the need for trustworthy oversight of the community's resources (cf. Ac 6:1-5 where the same principle is applied to the selection of the Church's first deacons). Nehemiah was bold, and confident that he was acting before God's eyes and for God's favor; the fourteenth verse is the first of four brief benedictory prayers in this final chapter (vv. 14, 22, 29, 31).

2. Purifying the Sabbath (13:15-22)

13:15-18. Both labor (**treading wine presses**, v. 15) and commerce (selling food, vv. 15-16) had encroached upon the Sabbath rest. Nehemiah held responsible not just those who violated the Sabbath directly in these ways, but also those who permitted it— **the nobles of Judah** (v. 17). Nehemiah connected Israel's former Sabbath violations to her recent exile and punishment, and wanted to act to avoid a repeat of God's chastisement. Again, the many—all **Israel** (v. 18)—would suffer if the actions of a few were allowed to continue unchecked.

13:19-22. The Jewish people count days from sundown to sundown (cf. Gn 1, evening and morning). The Sabbath begins at nightfall on Friday and continues until dark Saturday. On it there was to be no buying or selling or ordinary work. To enforce this code against commerce, Nehemiah shut the city gates and threatened violence against those who would violate it (v. 21). After a short time the merchants realized Nehemiah was serious about this injunction. Once more, Nehemiah invited God's evaluation and approval of his actions, this time the purifying of the Sabbath (v. 22).

3. Purifying the People (13:23-29)

13:23-27. The compromise and intermarriage with foreigners was not limited to Tobiah; there were many mixed marriages with women from **Ashdod, Ammon and Moab** (v. 23). Ezra had had to confront the problem of the ethnic and spiritual dilution of Israel through intermarriage some thirty years earlier (Ezr 10). So once more Nehemiah vigilantly needed to guard the purity of Israel in this next generation. That the concern is not merely ethnic is reflected in the concern for the children that **none of them was able to speak the language of Judah** (v. 24); they were being cut off from the law and heritage of Israel. Whereas Ezra had decreed the forced divorcing of foreign wives (Ezr 10:10-12), Nehemiah intervenes only to the extent of prohibiting further mixed marriages.

13:28-29. One of the grandsons of **Eliashib** the high priest's participation in the mixed marriages (v. 28), having married the daughter of Sanballat the Horonite, one of Nehemiah's primary adversaries (2:10), was especially grievous, and Nehemiah **drove him away**. Given his privileged position and heritage, it was reasonable to hold him to a higher standard. As Nehemiah prayed this third time, it is in light of his efforts to purify the priesthood (v. 29). In contrast to his other prayers inviting God's blessing for his faithfulness, here his prayer is imprecatory, inviting judgment on those who would defile the priesthood.

4. Purifying the Priests (13:30-31)

13:30-31. These final verses summarize Nehemiah's desire and attempt to purify and restore godly practice in Israel, and recall the concluding verses of chap. 12. Even the apparently trivial matter of the collection of **wood** for the offering (v. 31) is not too unimportant to merit Nehemiah's attention, as it was a component of the sacred covenant of chap. 10. Beyond that, wood is actually critical for the burnt offerings that would play so central a role in Israel's history until the destruction of the temple in AD 70. In his closing words, Nehemiah asks that God would **remember** him, even as he has constantly acted in conscious awareness of God's presence and will.

The dedication of the walls of Jerusalem, as recorded in chap. 12 of Nehemiah, is really the literary and theological climax of the book. From a literary perspective, the falling action of the final chapter is somewhat anticlimactic. Chapter 13:1-31 seems to deal only with various administrative actions, including the eviction of a foreign temple squatter, the restoration of tithes, the Sabbath, and the prohibition of mixed marriages. After these matters, the texts ends abruptly, with almost nothing save a short prayer by way of formal conclusion. To one who reads Nehemiah as a recapitulation of Joshua's conquest, however, this conclusion is not so odd. The emotional high of the initial conquest was at the beginning, with the fall of Jericho. As one reads the rest of Joshua, there is the impression that the remainder of the campaign was basically a mopping-up operation as each portion of the conquest was completed. There is a notable exception, however. Immediately after the fall of Jericho, Israel was surprisingly defeated at Ai because of what turned out to be impurity and unfaithfulness in the ranks. It was not until Achan's sin was discovered and punished that Israel was restored to victory. Nehemiah is a good student of history, and he refuses to wait to suffer for any impurity in the camp. Immediately after recording the great triumph of Jerusalem's walls, Nehemiah actively scours the camp for any deviation from the law of God, quickly acting to remove and prevent the violations of temple holiness, tithes, Sabbaths, and marriage, lest the defeat at Ai be repeated. This conquest will not be like the former, if Nehemiah can prevent it.

As governor, Nehemiah had the best motives for trying to deal with Israel's breaking of their covenant. But his purpose as author for including chap. 13 in this text has a distinct literary purpose for the readers, namely, to show that the promised restoration of Israel had not been fulfilled with the return from Babylon. In the law of Moses, Israel's dispersion for disobedience had been predicted (Dt 4:27) along with their future repentance and restoration "in the latter days" (Dt 4:30). Upon their restoration, God promised that He would circumcise their hearts so they could love God with all their heart and with all their soul that they might live (Dt 30:6).

Had Nehemiah ended with chap. 12, it may have been thought that the end of days had come and the final restoration of Israel had been accomplished. By including chap. 13, with its specific breaking of the renewed covenant of chap. 10, Nehemiah was proving that the return from Babylon was not the restoration anticipated in Deuteronomy—that one was yet future, at the end of days. Although God was indeed blessing His people by bringing them back to their land, this was not the final, full restoration for which they had hoped. Thus, Nehemiah includes a significant eschatological (end of days) perspective. God would indeed fulfill His promises to Israel and the Jewish people would indeed respond in faith and obedience, but it did not occur in Nehemiah's day. Rather, it would take place in the distant future, when Messiah would come. Hence, the ultimate literary message of the book of Nehemiah is not focused on the past but on the future messianic age.

Finally, this book contains the record of events that come at the chronological close of God's special revelation to Israel in the Hebrew Scriptures. It is fitting that there is a sense of incompletion or non-resolution, as the whole of the Hebrew Bible awaits the fulfillment of the Davidic covenant and the Messiah promised in it. In this sense even the book of Nehemiah is preparatory to the coming of the Messiah. The particular work of Nehemiah serves explicitly that end, containing therein the reconstitution of the people of Israel, the reconquering of the land of promise, living under the law, and worshiping at the rebuilt temple. And it is indeed at the location of that very temple, where the OT narrative ends, that God breaks back into the affairs of men by sending the angel Gabriel to speak to the priest Zacharias (Lk 1:5-20), to announce to him the birth of John the Baptist, heralding the immediate coming of the promised Messiah.

BIBLIOGRAPHY

Boice, James Montgomery. *Nehemiah: Learning to Lead.* Grand Rapids, MI: Baker, 1990.

Breneman, Mervin. *Ezra, Nehemiah, Esther.* The New American Commentary. Nashville: Broadman & Holman, 1993.

Clines, D. J. *Ezra, Nehemiah, Esther.* The New Century Bible Commentary. Grand Rapids, MI: Eerdmans, 1984.

Fensham, F. Charles. *The Books of Ezra and Nehemiah.* New International Commentary on the Old Testament. Grand Rapids, MI: Eerdmans, 1982.

Kidner, Derek. *Ezra & Nehemiah.* Tyndale Old Testament Commentaries. Downers Grove, IL: InterVarsity, 1979.

Levering, Matthew. *Ezra & Nehemiah.* Brazos Theological Commentary on the Bible. Grand Rapids, MI: Brazos, 2007.

McConville, J. G. *Ezra, Nehemiah, and Esther*. The Daily Study Bible Series, Old Testament. Philadelphia: Westminster, 1985.

Myers, Jacob M. *Ezra, Nehemiah: Introduction, Translation, and Notes*. The Anchor Bible. New York: Doubleday, 1965.

Williamson, H. G. M. *Ezra, Nehemiah*. Word Biblical Commentaries. Waco, TX: Word, 1985.

Yamauchi, Edwin. "Ezra, Nehemiah." In The Expositor's Bible Commentary, edited by Frank E. Gaebelein, vol. 4, 563–771. Grand Rapids, MI: Zondervan, 1988.

● ● ● ●

ESTHER

Multiple Faculty Contributors

INTRODUCTION

Author and Date. The book of Esther was apparently compiled from several different sources. This is *not* to say that the book is exclusively the product of *human* activity, but rather that the writer-compiler(s) was superintended by the Holy Spirit to express the *precise meaning* that God intended. Evidence of this compilatory aspect of Esther (even if the compiling and writing were undertaken by one person) is suggested by: (1) the relating of the specific content and procedural enactment of royal decrees (3:12-15; 8:9-13); (2) the references to various events in the book being recorded in the royal "chronicles" (2:23; 6:1-2; 10:2); and (3) the references to Purim (the holiday commemorating the redemptive events in Esther) as a well-established, yearly "custom" (9:19, 27-28), implying the passing of some time since the initial recording of the events.

Nevertheless, several facts show that the book was compiled or written during the Persian period (559–330 BC). Although many scholars say that the book is primarily a fictional narrative written during the period of Greek rule over Judaea (330–63 BC), the following reasons argue for a date in the Persian period. (1) The writer-compiler(s) clearly had intimate knowledge of administrative practice and life in the Persian court. (2) The Hebrew of Esther is similar to that of the other Persian-period narratives in Ezra-Nehemiah (originally one book) and Chronicles. (3) More Persian loanwords are in Esther than in any other Bible book (i.e., about 60 Persian words for the book's 165 verses. (4) The book has a few syntactical Persianisms, instances in which a Hebrew phrase is constructed in a manner reflective of either Old Persian or Persian Aramaic syntax, as in the expression "invited by her" (*qaru' lah*) in 5:12, the omission of the definite article from "Pur" in 3:7, and the double entendre of Haman's request in 6:8 (for the details, see comments there). According to early Jewish tradition, Esther (along with Ezekiel, the Minor Prophets, and Daniel) was "written down" by "the men of the Great Synagogue" (Babylonian Talmud, *Bava' Batra'* 15a), a Persian-period institution traditionally ascribed to (i.e., founded by) Ezra.

Purpose. Most conservative scholars conclude that the purpose of Esther is to highlight the providence of God, that is, God's sovereign ability to provide for His people. If, however, one takes the rest of Scripture into account, it becomes apparent that the goal, of the book is to express His *faithfulness*—all the more so, since the benefactors of His faithfulness, Israel, are in the land of their exile on account of their sins. God is faithful in upholding His unconditional covenant with Abraham, in blessing His people Israel (Gn 12:1-3; Jr 31:36; Zch 3:9; 12:10) and to "all families of the earth" (Gn 12:3; Gl 3:8). The latter is seen in the mass conversion by Gentiles from multiple ethnicities in Est 8:17: "And many among the peoples of the land became Jews" (without question describing a *religious* conversion). Of course, God's providence is present in the book, but His providence is both founded on and directed toward the expression of His covenant faithfulness.

Background. The book of Esther is among the most—if not in fact *the* most—disparaged book in the Bible with respect to its canonicity and inspiration. That is due in no small part to Esther being the only book of the Bible that has no explicit reference to God. In the writings of the early church fathers Esther is often simply ignored. Yet among later writers appears the statement by Martin Luther (AD 1483–1546) in his

De servo arbitrio (ed. Jena, 3:182) that, "though they [i.e., the Jews] have this (book) in the canon, in my judgment it deserves more than all to be excluded from the canon." And Franz Delitzsch stated that "in the book of Esther we perceive nothing of the impulses which the exile was to give to the people in the direction of the New Testament, nothing of prophetic afflation" (*Old Testament History of Redemption* [Edinburgh: Clark, 1881], 158-59).

The first piece of evidence that Esther was not yet considered canonical in the first century is derived from the Babylonian Talmud, a collection of ancient rabbinic legal discussions (codified around AD 500). The evidence consists of two statements in which a dissenting opinion is given either about Esther's canonicity (in B. Tal. *Megilla* 7a, by Rav Samuel—who nonetheless affirms Esther's inspiration) or its sanctity (in B. Tal. *Sanhedrin* 100a—though this may also simply be a question of canonicity, *not* inspiration—by Rav Levi bar Samuel and Rav Huna bar Hiyya). In both instances, however, these dissenting opinions by ancient rabbis are clearly presented as *unacceptable*—in the first instance because it contradicts the established view of the older rabbinic majority, and in the second instance because it is immediately dismissed as *heretical* by the principal rabbi (i.e., Rav Judah bar Ezekiel). Moreover, both of these dissenting opinions, which stem from the *third* century AD, run contrary to the older (i.e., no later than the *second* century) talmudic statement explicitly listing Esther among the accepted canonical books in B. Tal. *Bava' Batra'* 14b (and by implication in the *first*-century sources represented by Josephus in his *Against Apion* i.37-43, and the apocryphal work 2 Esdras 14:45-46).

The second main piece of evidence suggesting Esther's unestablished canonicity at the time of Christ is its *absence* from the biblical fragments of the Dead Sea Scrolls, among which every other one of the 39 books of the Old Testament (enumerated as 24 books in Jewish tradition) is represented. However, in addition to the obvious weakness of such "evidence," a careful study of the *parabiblical* Scrolls (i.e., apocryphal and apocrypha-like works based on the figures and events contained in the canonical books) reveals that Esther was in all likelihood viewed as canonical by the Dead Sea Scrolls community. Among such parabiblical scrolls is a work that is apparently based on the book of Esther and intended to be read as a (fictional) "prequel" to it. Since such apocrypha-type works are based, as a rule, on recognized canonical books, the implication of such a "prequel" is that Esther was indeed viewed as canonical. These factors indicate that the book of Esther is inspired by God and deserves to be included in the Hebrew canon.

Finding God in the Book of Esther

A. Finding God in Hiding

The Mosaic foundation. As is well known, Esther is the only book of the Bible in which there is no explicit mention of God—either by name or title/common noun. Rather than a "drawback," however, this may well be an intentional reflection of one of the book's central points. This omission should be understood as a device meant to underscore God's faithfulness in fulfilling His promise (i.e., threat) to hide His presence ("face," *panim*) in the place of Israel's exile (cf. Dt 31:17; Is 59:2). Moreover, excluding God's name is a literary strategy used to demonstrate that, even when Israel forgot their God (hence the exclusion of His name), God did not forget Israel, and acted covertly through His providence to show His covenant faithfulness.

The terminological allusion. This theme of God hiding His "presence" is borne out on a terminological level by the unmistakable similarity between the name of the book's central protagonist—*'ester* ("Esther")—and the phrase by which God expressed His threat—*'astir* ("I will hide"; Dt 31:18; cf. Ezk 39:23-24). Moreover, the Hebrew *consonants* of these two terms makes them almost identical, as the name "Esther" was *'str* and the phrase "I will hide," *'styr*. This similarity, as a reminder that God (both in name and in deed) is *meant* to be hidden in the book, was recognized and affirmed early in Jewish interpretive history, as attested in the Babylonian Talmud *Chullin* 139b.

B. Finding God in Israel's Deliverance

The Abrahamic foundation. The book's central narrative event of the deliverance of the Jewish people from complete annihilation by Haman's decree (3:13) is itself a testimony to God's active involvement in the events described. The divine orchestration of Israel's deliverance in Esther is also borne out by the clear, compelling, and unquestionably intentional parallels between the various elements, both textual and historical, surrounding that deliverance and those surrounding God's first covenant-motivated deliverance of the nation as recorded in the book of Exodus.

The Exodus connection. The book of Esther has clear signs that it is meant to be viewed as a parallel to the deliverance narrative in Exodus.

The close parallels between Esther and the Exodus narrative show that the two were meant to be juxtaposed. Parallels are seen in content (including phraseology), and in the festal commemoration of the narrative events. Content parallels include the following:

- Both narratives concern the comprehensive deliverance of the entire Jewish people, set outside the promised land.
- In both narratives the deliverance comes through a specific Jewish individual strategically placed in the Gentile king's own family (Moses and Esther) with the assistance of an immediate family member (Aaron and Mordecai).
- In both narratives the key protagonist is initially hesitant to mediate the deliverance (Ex 3:11; 4:13; Est 4:11-14).
- Both narratives are peppered throughout with references to either the key protagonist or Israel as a whole enjoying "favor" (*hen*) or "grace" (*chesed*) with the king, key officials, or the Gentiles at large—with the consistent difference that in Exodus God is explicitly identified as the one "granting" (*natan*) that favor (Ex 3:21; 11:3; 12:36), whereas in Esther it is always "found" (*naśa'* or *masa'*) by the benefactor (Est 2:9, 15, 17; 5:2; 8:5).
- In both narratives the "turning point" from affliction to deliverance is initiated in the same month, apparently on the *same day* of that month (i.e., Nisan 14, underscoring as well the uniquely shared typology of these two events.
- In both narratives the deliverance of the Jewish people results in the large-scale evangelism and/or proselytism of Gentiles to faith in the true God (Ex 12:38; Est 8:17).

Festal parallels include the following:

- The feasts elaborated by the two narratives—i.e., Passover (Unleavened Bread) and Purim—are the *only* yearly feasts (of eight in the Hebrew Bible) commemorating past events of deliverance of the Jewish people.
- Passover (Unleavened Bread) and Purim are the *only* yearly feasts celebrated in the months of Nisan and Adar, which are juxtaposed by virtue of their being the first and last (12th) months, respectively.
- Passover and Purim are the *only* yearly feasts that are celebrated on the 14th day of any month (see Ex 12:18; Est 9:19).

Thus linked, the two feasts may be seen as "mirrored bookends," occurring as they do on the same day in the first and last month of the Jewish calendar, at opposite ends of Israelite biblical history (and of the traditional Jewish canon). In this way they call attention to the year-round—and hence "circular" or unending—faithfulness of God toward the people He has sworn eternally to preserve.

C. Finding God in Queen Esther

The typological starting point. There is no direct messianic prophecy in Esther, which is consistent with God's promise/threat to "hide" His presence through a prophet or supernatural phenomena. This does not mean, however, that Esther has no contribution to the presentation of the Messiah in the Hebrew Bible. In fact it *must* have something to say about the Messiah, as is clear in Lk 24:27, that "He explained to them the things concerning Himself in *all* the Scriptures" (italics added). Since the Scriptures of Jesus' day included Esther, it logically follows from this statement that there is something "concerning Himself" in the book of Esther. If it is not in the form of direct, or verbatim, prophecy, then it must be in the form of indirect or non-verbatim prophecy—what is designated by the expressions "shadows" (Heb 10:1) or "types" (Heb 11:19). The specific presence of such "shadows" or "types" in Esther is further indicated by Paul's statement in Col 2:16–17 regarding *all* of Israel's holy days: "Therefore let no one act as your judge in regard to . . . a festival [*heortes*] or a new moon or a Sabbath day—things which are a mere shadow [*skia*] of what is to come, but the substance [*soma*; lit., "body"] belongs to Christ." Since Purim is one of Israel's eight yearly "festivals" (to which the Gk. term *heorte* is clearly applied in the LXX, cf. Lv 23) so must the events underlying that feast as described in Esther contain prophetic "shadows" that outline the "substance" belonging to Messiah.

The typology. The "shadows" or "types" in the book of Esther that center on the protagonist herself may be summarily presented in the following seven pairs of "shadow" and "substance" (all of which, except the first pair, are discussed in detail by the present writer in *Bibliotheca Sacra* 154 [1997], 275–84).

Shadow	Substance
Esther was prepared as the mediator of deliverance before the need for it (i.e., before Haman's promotion and ensuing decree) had arisen (Est 2:17-18).	Jesus was prepared as the mediator of salvation before the need for it (i.e., before man's creation and ensuing sin) had arisen (Rv 13:8).
Esther's three-day period of fasting began during the daylight hours of Nisan 14, the first day of Passover (Est 3:12).	Jesus' three-day period of physical death, initiated on the cross, is identified in Scripture as the period of His "humiliation" or "affliction" (Php 2:8).
Fasting in general—and thus Esther's fast—is identified in Scripture with "humiliation" or "affliction," and since mourning was involved, the fast may also be viewed as representing a temporary "state of death" (Lv 23:27-29).	Jesus' three-day period of physical death, initiated on the cross, is identified in Scripture as the period of His "humiliation" or "affliction" (Php 2:8).
Esther's period of "affliction" ended on the third day, Nisan 16 (Est 5:1).	Jesus' period of "affliction" ended on the third day, Nisan 16 (Ac 10:40; 1Co 15:4).
At the end of her fast (i.e., after "arising" from her symbolic state of death), but before presenting herself before the king, Esther was clothed in royalty (Est 5:1; LXX: "glory").	At the end of His three-day period of death, but before presenting Himself before God the Father in heaven, Jesus was resurrected in royal "glory" (1Co 15:20, 43).
On the basis of her fast, Esther entered the king's presence in "the inner court of the king's palace" and was accepted into his presence with favor (Est 4:16; 5:2).	On the basis of His atoning self-sacrifice, Jesus entered the Father's presence in the true holy of holies in heaven and was accepted into His presence to sit "at the right hand of the throne of God" (Heb 2:9-10, 14; 9:12, 24; 10:12; 12:2).
The result of Esther's acceptance by the king was the salvation of her people Israel, with the further result that many among the Gentiles turned in faith to the true God and became one with the people of God (Est 8:17).	The result of Jesus' acceptance by the Father was the salvation of His people Israel ("the lost sheep of the house of Israel"; Mt 15:24), with the further result that many among the Gentiles turned (and are turning) in faith to the true God to become one with the people of God (Rm 2:28-29; Eph 2:14-15; Col 2:11; Ac 2:10-11; 11:18; Gl 3:8).

OUTLINE

I. The Preparation of the Jewish People (1:1–2:23)
  A. Vashti's Removal (1:1-22)
  B. Esther's Elevation (2:1-20)
  C. The King's Debt to Mordecai (2:21-23)

II. The Crisis of the Jewish People (3:1–5:14)
  A. Haman's Elevation (3:1)
  B. Haman's Plot against the Jews (3:2–4:17)
  C. Haman's Plot against Mordecai (5:1-14)

III. The Deliverance of the Jewish People (6:1–10:3)
  A. Neutralizing the Threat (6:1–8:14)
  B. Strengthening the People (8:15–9:18)
  C. Establishing the Commemoration (9:19–10:3)

COMMENTARY ON ESTHER

I. The Preparation of the Jewish People (1:1–2:23)

This first section lays the groundwork for the narrative. In accordance with His covenant faithfulness, God providentially prepares the circumstances so that the Jewish people will be protected and preserved when the attack comes against them. To set matters in motion to protect the Jewish people, God's hand arranges for Vashti to be removed as queen, Esther to replace her, and the king to become indebted to Mordecai.

A. Vashti's Removal (1:1-22)

1:1-8. The events in Esther are dated to **the days of Ahasuerus** (probably the same as in Ezr 4:6). This name is an English form of a Hebrew transcription of the Old Persian *Khshayarsha*, otherwise known by Greek transcription as Xerxes (the Great), who ruled the Persian empire from 485 to 465 BC. This was **the Ahasuerus who reigned . . . over 127 provinces** (v. 1). This distinguishes him from the Median (not Persian) ruler of the same name who was the father of Darius the Mede (Dn 9:1), ruler of Babylon from 605 to 562 BC, and whose empire was somewhat lesser in extent than that of the Ahasuerus in Esther, encompassing only 120 provinces (Dn 6:1). The reason for the **banquet** (lit., "drinking party," *mishteh*) that Ahasuerus gave **in the third year of his reign** (Est 1:3) is not stated. It may have been: (1) a celebration of the consolidation of his rule, or (2) a morale-boosting prelude to his military campaign against Greece in his fourth year (Herodotus, vii.20). Whatever the reason, it was managed by God to prepare the way for Esther (and Israel's deliverance) by the ensuing dethronement of Vashti. As Solomon wrote, "The king's heart is like channels of water in the hand of the LORD; He turns it wherever He wishes" (Pr 21:1).

1:9-22. Consistent with ancient and Middle Eastern custom, **Queen Vashti** and the rest of **the women** had their own **banquet** in a separate location (v. 9). This customary separation of the sexes was maintained across the ranks of society. That custom is further indicated in that the king's command **to display** Vashti's **beauty** to the men was given only on the seventh day of the banquet **when** his **heart . . . was merry with** (i.e., under the influence of) **wine** (vv. 10-11). To a certain degree, therefore, it must have been in adherence to this custom that **Vashti refused to come at the king's command** (v. 12). In deciding on an appropriate response to this refusal, the king turned in his anger to his **seven** closest advisors (on which number see Ezr 7:14; Jr 52:25) **who understood the times** (i.e., what happened in past times, namely case law, based on precedent, and/or common law) as well as **law and justice** (i.e., statutory/legislative law; Est 1:13-15). However justified Vashti may have been in refusing the king's unseemly command, concern over the precedent it might set for more general (and less justified) disobedience of their husbands by wives throughout the kingdom prompted the advisors to recommend that Vashti be permanently banned from **the** king's **presence** and **her royal position** given **to another** (v. 19). The effect of this decree, when made known to the public, was **that every man** continued to **be the master in his own house** (v. 22).

B. Esther's Elevation (2:1-20)

2:1-4. When some time had passed and **the** king's **anger . . . had subsided**, his thoughts of Vashti took a more positive, loving turn, and his thoughts of **what had been decreed against her** took a more grievous turn. To console him and divert his attention from these thoughts **the king's attendants** prompted him to implement the suggestion of his advisors recorded in 1:19, namely, that he have **every beautiful young virgin** in the kingdom brought **to . . . Susa** the capital and make the one **who pleases** him **queen in place of Vashti**.

2:5-7. Mordecai is described as a **Jew** (*yehudi*, which literally means "Judaean"). This term is used only in the later books of the Hebrew Bible (for the first time in Jr 32:12), when the northern kingdom and its Israelite ethnic majority had dissolved and those that remained of God's people in the Abrahamic line of promise were represented in the southern kingdom of Judah alone. This is not to say, of course, that every "Jew" so-called in Scripture is descended from the tribe of Judah. Thus though described as a **Jew** (i.e., Judaean), Mordecai was ethnically **a Benjamite** (from the tribe of Benjamin), and was in fact born in exile, someplace in Babylon or Persia. This is indicated by three facts. First, he was described as Esther's first cousin, and Esther herself was described as a "young woman" (*na'ara*; Est 2:7), which typically denotes a woman between adolescence and her early 20s at the latest, and hence Mordecai could not have been much older. Second, the pronoun **who** at the beginning of v. 6, probably refers to **Kish**, not Mordecai, as the one who was **taken into exile** by Nebuchadnezzar **with Jeconiah king of Judah**. This conforms with the timing of Jeconiah's exile in 605 BC, whereas the events of Esther took place between 485 and 465 BC. Third, Mordecai (a Babylonian name probably related to the Babylonian god Marduk) apparently had no given Hebrew name, since none is ever mentioned, as is Esther's in v. 7. Had he not been born in exile he would certainly have had one. In Esther's case, her Hebrew name was **Hadassah**. The writer added, **that is Esther** and referred to her afterward exclusively by this Persian name (which means "star"), since it was by this name that she would have been best known to the book's readers.

2:8-18. The gathering of the virgins began sometime just after the middle of the king's third year (see 1:3-4 and 2:1-4). Esther—who lived in the same city as the king himself—is **taken to the king's palace** only toward the end of his sixth year (i.e., more than *three years* later). This is implied by her audience with the king having been **in the tenth month** of his **seventh year**, after twelve months of cosmetic preparation (v. 12) This timetable suggests either that Esther had just attained adolescence when she was taken (though this is unlikely in view of her description as a "young woman" in v. 7, see comment there), or, as deduced by many medieval commentators, that Mordecai, not wanting her to be taken into a pagan's harem, did his best to "hide" her for as long as he could. In the end, however, Esther **was taken** (lit., "seized") along with the other **young ladies**. Nonetheless, consistent with His plan in preparing Israel's deliverance, God ensured that Esther **found favor with** her custodian Hegai (vv. 8-9) and **all who saw her** (v. 15), including ultimately **the king** himself (v. 17). Then **he set the royal crown on her head and made her queen instead of Vashti**.

2:19-20. These two verses constitute one complex sentence; v. 19 contains two dependent clauses (lit., "During the period when the virgins were being gathered," [and] while **Mordecai was sitting at the king's gate**). Verse 20 contains the main clause (properly: "Esther would not make known her kindred or her people . . ."). This functions as a narrative "flashback" that serves three purposes: (1) It smoothly transitions from the previous section that focuses on Esther to the following section that focuses on Mordecai (vv. 21-23, in which the wording of the first verse is precisely parallel to v. 19b: while **Mordecai was sitting at the king's gate**. (2) It clarifies how Mordecai would have found out the plot of the king's personal chamberlains. He was an established court official himself (he was **sitting at the king's gate**). (3) It clarifies the extent of Esther's concealment of her family information, which led in turn to the natural inference that she continued to conceal this information. The later revelation of this information (in chap. 7) ultimately played such a crucial, climactic role in the downfall of Haman and consequent deliverance of the Jews. Mordecai may have enjoined this concealment because he anticipated some future benefit to his people (consistent with his characterization in 10:3). Yet it is more likely, as often advanced by traditional Jewish commentators, that by such concealment Mordecai intended that Esther be able to follow the ritual-legal precepts of her faith without harassment or interference from the Gentiles among whom she lived.

C. The King's Debt to Mordecai (2:21-23)

2:21-22. The reference to Mordecai **sitting at the king's gate** constitutes a quasi-technical statement indicating that he filled an official role in the king's court—just like Daniel, to whom the corresponding expression is applied in Aramaic (Dn 2:49; see also Xenophon's use of "gate" [Gk., *thyras*] in the technical sense of "court" in the context of Old Persian royal history in his *Cyropaedia* viii.1.6, 16, 33, 34; viii.3.2; viii.6.10; viii.8.13, and *Anabasis* i.9.3). Probably because of his privileged position at the royal court, compounded by his relative "inconspicuousness" as a regular presence there for several years (at least four, as implied in Est 2:19), Mordecai was able to uncover the plot of **Bigthan and Teresh, two of the king's officials** [i.e., his chamberlains or personal attendants] . . . **who guarded the door**.

2:23. Mordecai then warned the king through the mediation of Esther, rather than bringing the news to him directly (which he may not have been permitted to do) or through another court official. This course of action attested to Mordecai's wisdom, righteousness, and paternal solicitude, since it would have ensured that: (1) the plot was accurately relayed to the king, as others in the court may also have been involved (similar intrigues were not uncommon among the Persians, and in fact later conspirators did succeed in murdering Ahasuerus/Xerxes, on which see Herodotus, iii.118); and (2) the king's faith in—and favor for—Esther would be strengthened, thus ensuring his readiness to believe any future unfavorable report she might bring to him, such as that of Haman's own plot. Indeed, the divine hand at work in the management of this event, preparing His people's deliverance from upcoming danger, is further borne out by its similarity to the circumstances of the OT Joseph who, like Mordecai, was also "forgotten" until the opportune time, so that he could affirm in retrospect what was hidden from him in the past: "God sent me before you to preserve life" (Gn 45:5; see also 50:20).

II. The Crisis of the Jewish People (3:1–5:14)

A. Haman's Elevation (3:1)

3:1. Israel's danger is here introduced with the promotion of **Haman, the son of Hammedatha** approximately five years **after** the **events** of the previous two chapters. This chronology is implied in that those previous events took place no later than the king's seventh year (2:16). At the beginning of the king's 12th year Haman issued his decree to annihilate the Jews because of Mordecai's refusal to bow down to him according to "the king's command." The issuing of this decree coordinated with Haman's promotion **over all the** other **princes** (i.e., to a rank second only to the king—the same role that Mordecai later filled after Haman's downfall; 10:3). The additional reference to Haman as an **Agagite** has been explained by many scholars in connection with Agag, king of the Amalekites at the time of Saul (1Sm 15:8). This connection implies that Haman was a descendant of Agag. Thus the conflict between him and Mordecai represents the final "playing out" of the ancient conflict between Agag and Saul. Alternatively, Haman has been identified not as a descendant of Agag, but rather as one of the same kind of notorious biblical archfoes of Israel. In this case, the term **Agagite** is applied to Haman by association (i.e., as an alternate name). Most likely, however, the term **Agagite** refers to Haman's origin in a certain region of Persia or Media, that is the district of Agag, the existence of which is affirmed by an archeological inscription from the time of the Assyrian king Sargon (725 BC). This in turn enhances all the more the *theological* magnitude of Mordecai's/Israel's victory over Haman/Israel's enemies. The victory indicates that Israel's God is not only sovereign over the gods of the Amalekites, a minor Canaanite tribe, but over the gods of the most powerful empire on earth at that time, the Persians and the Medes. The theological significance of the victory helps explain the *unprompted* conversion to Israelite faith by "many among the peoples of the land" (Est 8:17).

B. Haman's Plot against the Jews (3:2–4:17)

3:2-4. The reason Mordecai **neither bowed down nor paid homage** to Haman, even though **the king had commanded** all his **servants who were at the king's gate** (thus including Mordecai) to do so, was not because of some alleged personal or Jewish pride, but rather because these actions were intended expressions of *worship* and not just respect. Five facts support this point: (1) Mordecai himself explained that he refused to bow down and pay homage to Haman because **he** [Mordecai] **was a Jew**. Of course, Jews were permitted to bow down to other people out of simple respect (Gn 23:7; 33:3; 1Sm 24:8), but they were forbidden to worship more than one God (Dt 6:13-14). (2) The Hebrew verbs here translated **bowed down** and **paid homage**, when used together, are attested *only* in the sense of *worship* (2Ch 7:3; 29:29; Ps 95:6); (3) That Mordecai would be sinning is implied by the almost exact literal phraseological parallel between Est 3:4b (**Now it was when they had spoken daily to him** [that] **he would not listen to them**) and Gn 39:10 ("As she spoke to Joseph day after day, he did not listen to her"). Just as Joseph resisted the temptation to listen to Potiphar's wife, so Mordecai resisted the temptation to bow down. (4) Herodotus stated that a custom among the ancient Persians was that "if one is of much less noble rank than the other, he falls down before him and does worship [*proskyneei*] to him" (Herodotus, i.134). (5) Such worship is entirely consistent with the Zoroastrian (Mazdean) religion. This dualistic religion was founded by the Persian prophet Zoroaster in the late seventh or early sixth centuries BC, based on the concept of a continuous struggle between Ormazd [or Ahura Mazda], the god of creation, light, and goodness, and his archenemy, Ahriman, the spirit of evil and darkness, and it was well established by the time of Ahasuerus/Xerxes. In the words of a 10th-century Jewish commentator and native of Persia, it was believed of an accomplished individual, like Haman, "that something of the Divine Light existed within him, and so they would deem fit to worship him in a special fashion."

3:5-15. In response to Mordecai's continued refusal to bow **down** and pay **Haman homage**, Haman determined not only **to lay** his **hands on** (i.e., "kill," the same idiom used in 2:21) **Mordecai**, but in fact **to destroy all the Jews**. The most reasonable explanation for this seemingly unbalanced response (the extermination of an entire nation for one man's disobedience) is that Haman, who clearly had some knowledge of the Jewish faith (v. 8), correctly recognized that Mordecai's refusal, was symptomatic of the Jewish mindset at large. So since Mordecai refused to worship Haman because of his faith, so too would every Jew, thereby constituting a potentially grave threat to Haman's authority and status in a culture where appearances and outward protocol were so highly regarded (cf. 1:11-12; 5:1-2; 6:7-12).

This theological-religious substratum of the ensuing conflict, and of Haman's response in particular, is still further borne out by his immediate appeal to the **Pur**, an Old Persian term that means **the lot**. The reason for using the Persian term must lie in some feature of the **Pur** other than its mere physical nature as "something that is cast." In surveying the use of the lot (Hb., *goral*) and lot-casting (*happalat goralot*) in Scripture, it becomes evident that this distinction must have been theological, for in Israelite culture "the lot is cast into the lap, and [not "but," as in some translations] its every decision is from the LORD" (Pr 16:33; cf. Lv 16:8; Jos 18:6; Neh 11:1). Haman, however, was certainly not appealing to "the LORD" ("Yahweh"), Israel's God, by casting lots, but rather, by the implied juxtaposition of the Persian "Pur" with its Hebrew counterpart, the *goral*, to his own god(s). This is perfectly consistent with the Zoroastrianism of ancient Persia, in which all the days of the year were regarded as either favorable and propitious, or unfavorable and unpropitious. Hence **the lot was cast before Haman** (probably by a magus, one of the Zoroastrian sacerdotal caste) as a *religious* act intended to divine the will of Ahura Mazda, the one creator-god of Zoroastrianism, in selecting the most auspicious day for destroying the Jews. On Zoroastrianism, see comments on Est 3:2-4.

Once that day was determined (Adar 13, cf. v. 12), Haman wasted no time in moving his plot forward. He immediately secured the king's approval by painting the Jewish people as a potentially serious source of sedition, especially since they were spread throughout **all the provinces of** his **kingdom**. At the same time he sought to portray himself as deeply committed to the welfare of the king and his kingdom. He was even willing to **pay ten thousand talents of silver** from his own pocket. This enormous sum was perhaps intended to offset the loss of tax revenue for the government resulting from the genocide. Once the king's permission was given, Haman summoned **the king's scribes** to produce copies of the official edict, which was then immediately published throughout the kingdom by government **couriers** (v. 13). The first location to hear of this decree was **the city of Susa**, which surrounded the royal compound or "fortress of Susa" (see 1:2; 2:8). The city reacted with **confusion** (or "agitation," "aimless wandering," the reference probably being both to the Jews of Susa as well as the Gentiles with whom they had regular social and economic interaction). Later on, by contrast, the city of Susa was also the first location to hear of Mordecai's decree, to which the Jews reacted with glad shouting and rejoicing (8:15).

4:1-17. The opening syntax of v. 1 is circumstantial rather than sequential, and is thus properly translated not, **when Mordecai learned all that had been done, he tore**, (NASB; ESV; HCSB), but rather, "Now Mordecai was aware of all that had been done, and so he tore" (NET). In other words, as an established official in the king's own court, Mordecai would have learned of the plot to destroy the Jews almost as soon as it went beyond the private counsel of Haman and the king. Hence this chapter shows Mordecai's immediate reaction on the same day the decree was issued. That, in turn, further clarifies the messianic typology surrounding Esther's fast and its chronology (see section C. in Introduction). Interestingly, the first thing Mordecai did—and in which he was joined by **many** of the other Jews in Susa (as eventually those in **every province** when they learned of the decree)—was to **put on sackcloth and ashes, and** wail **loudly and bitterly**. These actions are characteristic of an appeal to God in response to potential danger and impending calamity (cf. Jdg 20:26; Ezr 8:21).

In seeking Esther's intervention, Mordecai needed first to **inform her** (Est 3:8), of Haman's decree. She was unaware of it because of her seclusion in the women's quarters of the palace. He communicated through the eunuch **Hathach**, who was **appointed to attend her**. At the same time Mordecai exhorted her to **implore** the king's **favor and to plead with him for her people** (v. 8). Esther was initially recalcitrant—recalling the similar response of Moses in Ex 3:11 and 4:13, and she sought to excuse herself by pointing out that the king had not summoned her for the past **thirty days** (Est 3:11). Though the point of her citing this number was to imply that the king's interest in her was apparently waning, it also served as yet another subtle testimony to the historical veracity of the book, for 30 days prior to this conversation (which took place on Nisan 13) she would indeed have been in the king's presence for the royal observance of the important Zoroastrian *Farvardigan* (welcoming the spirits of the dead) festival, celebrated at that time from Adar (Old Persian *Viyahna*) 11–15 (mid-April in our calendar).

Mordecai, however, was not dissuaded, and he again exhorted Esther to intercede with words intended both to reprove and to encourage her. The reproof was that she, though the queen, should **not imagine that** she **can escape any more than all the Jews** (v. 13) and, moreover, should she **remain silent**, the Jews would still be delivered whereas she and her **father's house will perish** (v. 14). The encouragement was that the Lord is sovereign in all circumstances to preserve His people from destruction—as is unquestionably implied by Mordecai's confident expectation, not mere hope or wish, that **relief and deliverance will arise for the Jews from another place**. His confidence can be explained by his faith in God's promise to bless Israel and preserve them forever as a people before Him (Gn 12:1-3; Jr 31:35-37). Also he was certain that God had already been at work by ensuring that she **attained royalty for such a time as this**. Esther thus acquiesced and enjoined a preparatory fast (again as a specific appeal to God) on her behalf that was to be undertaken by **all the Jews . . . in Susa . . . for three days, night or day**. Allowing Mordecai the minimum amount of time necessary to assemble the Jews of Susa for this fast, as well the urgency of the situation, it is reasonable that this fast began on Adar 14 (cf. Est 3:12). This was either later that night per biblical-Jewish reckoning in which days began at sunset, or, at the latest on the following morning (dawn was in fact the usual time when public fasts began, according to the Babylonian Talmud, *Pesahim* 2b)—both possibilities would still have been Adar 14. Esther's fast was thus observed *during the first three days of Passover*, an observation that is central to an appreciation of the book's typology.

C. Haman's Plot against Mordecai (5:1-14)

5:1-8. Implicit in the statement that Esther **put on her royal robes** is that, until then, she had been dressed in the vesture that often accompanies fasting, similar to that of Mordecai and the other Jews (cf. 4:1-3), which in turn brings Esther's fast more clearly into focus as a type. Fasting, in other words, and its outward accompaniment by disgraceful attire (such as sackcloth and ashes), is intended throughout the Bible as an expression of *self-denial* and *self-affliction*. This is reflected, for example, in God's command that on the Day of Atonement "you shall humble [lit., "afflict"] your souls" (Lv 16:29, 31; 23:27, 32; Nm 29:7). In this respect Esther's fast both anticipated and paralleled the self-denial and affliction of Christ Himself, the One who, "although He existed in the form of God humbled Himself by becoming obedient to the point of death, even death on a cross" (Php 2:6, 8). This typological aspect of Esther's fast may also have been recognized by the first-century church father Clement of Rome, who wrote of Esther that "by fasting and self-affliction she besought the Master [and] seeing the affliction of her soul, delivered the people for whose sake she put herself in jeopardy" (*1 Clement.* 55:6). Like that of Christ, moreover, so too Esther's affliction ended **on**, not *after*, **the third day** (Ac 10:40).

As to the reason Esther deferred her request until the following day (Est 5:8), see comments on 7:1-10.

5:9-14. On his way **out** from Esther's banquet, Haman saw **Mordecai in the king's gate**, from which it may be deduced that Mordecai, like Esther, had ceased wearing sackcloth and ashes, since no one thus clothed was permitted in the king's gate (i.e., court, cf. 4:2). This further underscores the strength of Mordecai's faith and spiritual maturity. Having made his appeal to God he left the matter in His hands and moved on, confidently trusting in God's absolute sovereignty and covenant faithfulness. Indeed, Mordecai's confidence is further borne out by his refusal to even **tremble before** Haman, despite Haman's *apparent* power and "sealed" plan to destroy the Jews. The verb **tremble** (*za*) is employed elsewhere in Scripture to denote the trembling produced by *fear* (see Ec 12:3; Dn 5:19; 6:26 [Hb., v. 27]).

The role and actions of Haman in these verses attest a clear symmetry with those of the king in chap. 1, serving as testimony to (1) the narrative's high degree of literary sophistication, (2) the underlying facts of Haman's status and circumstances as a preeminent courtier, and (3) Haman's implicit thirst for emulation, perhaps even eventually to replace the king himself. The individual components of this parallel with the king are as follows: (1) The great wealth of both Ahasuerus and Haman is explicitly emphasized (1:4; 5:11). (2) Both men were characterized at the outset by feeling "merry of heart" from wine (1:10; 5:9). (3) Both were described as having (or intending to have) their wives "brought" to them (1:11; 5:10). (4) Both were refused the obedience of another member of the royal court (1:12; 5:9). (5) The immediate reaction of both was that they were filled with "anger" (1:12; 5:9). (6) Both immediately sought the counsel of those closest to them (1:13-14; 5:10). (7) In both instances the advice was to permanently remove the offender (1:19; 5:14). (8) In both instances "the advice was pleasing" to the men and they "did" accordingly (1:21; 5:14).

III. The Deliverance of the Jewish People (6:1–10:3)

A. Neutralizing the Threat (6:1–8:14)

6:1-14. The deliverance that God had prepared for the threat of Haman's decree now began to unfold in the first of a series of reversals ("return on his own head," 9:25) hearkening back to God's promise/threat in Gn 12:3 to curse the one "who curses" [lit., belittles] Israel. The impetus for this first reversal is the king's insomnia—implicitly effected by God, the giver of sleep (see Ps 127:2). So **the** Persian **book of records** was brought out and **read before** him (to both dispel boredom and induce sleep). When the reader comes to the record of Mordecai's good deed in reporting the plot of **Bigthana and Teresh** (see Est 2:21-23) and made no mention of his being rewarded (as implied by the king's question in v. 3a), the king naturally became preoccupied with correcting his oversight at once. At that precise moment, by divine appointment, Haman entered **the outer court** to request permission to execute Mordecai. Haman's conceited drive for advancement was emphatically demonstrated both by his assumption that the king's question in v. 6a (**What is to be done for the man?**) concerns himself, as well as his response to that question, which entailed the public bestowal of royal accoutrements—things that had so far been outside Haman's grasp. Then the king commanded that these things be given to Mordecai *by* Haman, who was to lead Mordecai about on horseback while walking before him and proclaiming his honor (vv. 10-11).

Mordecai's ascendancy over Haman became clearly manifest, leading his wife and his friends to say to Haman afterward that he had **begun to fall** before Mordecai (v. 13). Haman's *actual* fall or derogation of status is referred to in their ensuing declaration that he (i.e., Haman) **will surely fall before him** (Mordecai). This declaration, based on Mordecai's **Jewish origin**, may at first seem completely out of place as coming from pagans—especially those who just advised that he be put to death (5:14). Yet their reasoning may be explained by the Zoroastrian preoccupation with signs and omens, and their attendant belief that the beginning of an event is often a reliable portent of its end (for more on Zoroastrianism, see comments at 3:2-4). Thus, Mordecai's temporary exaltation over Haman signified a final (permanent) exaltation, in which position Mordecai would certainly do all he could to remove "the enemy of the Jews" (3:10) from power.

7:1-10. Haman's fall, as anticipated by his wife and "wise men" in the previous chapter, took place in quick and complete fashion. At the same time it provided a vivid biblical example of the "reversal" principle that so often characterizes God's retribution of the wicked in general and Israel's enemies in particular. **At the** second **banquet**, when the king reiterated his intention to grant Esther anything she might request, **even to half of the kingdom**, she implored the king to **let** her **life be given** her (i.e., preserved) along with the lives of her **people**. She immediately proceeded to give the reason for her request—**for we have been sold . . . to be destroyed**. By this she paved the way for the king's response in v. 5 (**Who is he?**). She also cleverly and bravely implied a certain measure of culpability on the part of the king himself, since the selling is an obvious reference to the transaction of 3:9: Haman filling the role of purchaser (by his offer to "pay ten thousand talents of silver" for the genocide) and the king filling the role of seller. Afterward the king would have realized a degree of his own culpability, motivating him to make restitution). When the king then asked **who** and **where** the culprit is, Esther pointed to **Haman** as the **foe** and the **enemy**. In reaction, just as the Jews in every province were "in mourning" at Haman's decree in 4:3, so now in clear reversal Haman was **terrified before** the Jewish **queen** and her **king**. This reversal was brought to a dramatic conclusion when, after misconstruing Haman's attempted appeal as an attempt to **assault the queen**, the king had Haman hanged (i.e., "impaled," as was the Persian practice; Ezr 6:11) on the very **gallows** (actually, "stake") **which he had prepared for Mordecai**.

Why did Esther defer her petition until the second banquet? This was not due to trepidation, indecisiveness, or fear on her part, because she had committed for her people to intercede regardless of the cost to herself, as expressed in Est 4:16: "and if I perish, I perish." Her deferment, rather, was perhaps because she was possibly waiting for a sign of God's involvement in the denouement. This sign was in the event which took place between the two banquets, that is, Mordecai's public elevation over Haman. This clear reversal—and hence its eventual culmination in Haman's execution and Mordecai's taking his position (8:2)—would be viewed by the Jews as a sign of encouragement that God was still as faithfully concerned for them as ever. Gentiles (especially in Persia) would view the reversal as a sign that the God of Israel is indeed the true God, since He is sovereign over even the gods of the dominant Persian Empire. And Mordecai's public elevation over Haman in chap. 6 was logically affirmed by the ensuing confidence of the Jews in gaining "mastery over those who hated them" (9:1) as well as by the ensuing conversion to faith in Israel's God by "many among the peoples of the land" (8:17).

8:1-14. The theme of reversal appears in five places in this chapter: (1) **The king took off his signet ring which he had taken away from Haman, and gave it to Mordecai** (v. 2a). This represents yet another parallel to the Joseph narrative (see Gn 41:42 and Est 8:15). (2) Mordecai was placed **over the house** (i.e., property) **of Haman** (v. 2b). (3) Esther further petitioned the king **to revoke** (*le-hashib*) **the letters devised by Haman** (v. 5). (4) Mordecai issued a second decree giving the Jews the right **to defend their lives** and **to destroy, to kill and to annihilate** any who **might attack them** (v. 11). This effectively reversed the first decree of Haman, which gave the Jews' enemies the right "to destroy, to kill and to annihilate all the Jews" (3:13). Though Persian laws were irrevocable (v. 8; 1:19; Dn 6:8), the king's favor clearly lay with Mordecai's decree. (5) As with Haman's decree (Est 3:15), so too with Mordecai's did the couriers go out **impelled** (v. 14). On the famously fast and efficient Persian postal system see Herodotus, viii.98.

B. Strengthening the People (8:15–9:18)

8:15-17a. Once the thorn at the center of Israel's affliction (i.e., Haman) was removed, God's salutary plan for His people continued to unfold with their consequent strengthening in three vital areas: psychological well-being, numeric growth, and physical security. The first of these, Israel's psychological well-being, was emphatically represented (vv. 15-17a) not only by Israel's jubilant response to Mordecai's decree, but also by its clear juxtaposition with their opposite psychological response to Haman's decree. Thus whereas the *immediate* response to Haman's decree was that "the city of Susa was in confusion" (3:15), the immediate response to Mordecai's promotion was that **the city of Susa shouted and rejoiced** (v. 15). When Haman's decree was issued, "there was great mourning among the Jews, with fasting, and weeping and wailing" (4:3). But the response to Mordecai's decree was that **in each and every province . . . wherever the king's commandment and his decree arrived, there was gladness and joy for the Jews, a feast and a holiday** (v. 17a).

8:17b. This half-verse offers a profound picture of Israel's numeric growth, for it is the only time that Scripture refers to a historical event in which **many among the peoples of the land became Jews**. This was accomplished by the substantial increase, not simply of the populace of Israel, but specifically the populace of *believing* Israel. For a Gentile to "become a Jew" is not simply to join oneself to an ethnic community, but also to a *spiritual* one. In practical terms this entailed circumcision on the part of males (Gn 17:10; Ex 12:48). This understanding is reflected in the Septuagint translation of the expression **became Jews** in this verse as "were circumcised." On the typological significance of this event see section C. in Introduction.

9:1-18. The strengthening of Israel's *physical security* is represented in these verses by the removal of hostile people and hence further potential threats in the places where the Jewish people lived. Some may be inclined to criticize the Jews for their supposed "vengefulness" killing upwards of 75,000 individuals (v. 16). But they killed only the worst of the worst throughout the entire Persian Empire—defending themselves not only against **those who hated them** (v. 1), but also against those who still decided to take advantage of the permission granted by Haman's decree and actively **sought** the Jews' **harm** (v. 2). The wisdom of Esther's petition (v. 13) that **the Jews who are in Susa** be permitted to take up arms against their enemies on Adar 14 as well is evident in that Susa was the source of both influence and policy on matters pertaining to the Jews. She also asked that **Haman's ten sons** (slain already on Adar 13; vv. 6-10) be hanged on the gallows (i.e., by the very stake on which Haman had been impaled). When viewed canonically, this action no more reflects excessive retribution than God's decision to destroy Sodom and Gomorrah in such a way that they too might serve as a visible "example to those who would live ungodly lives thereafter" (2Pt. 2:6). Also, whereas Mordecai's decree (Est 8:11) granted the Jews permission to kill *everyone* among those "who might attack them, including children and women" as well as to "plunder their spoil" (parallel to Haman's decree in 3:13), the text refers explicitly only to the Jews killing **men** (Hb. *'ish*; vv. 6, 12, 15) and also states repeatedly that the Jews **did not lay their hands on the plunder** (vv. 10, 15-16). Undoubtedly Mordecai highlighted this contrast to what Haman intended and what the Jews' enemies *would* have done (3:13). About 800 men "who hated" the Jews were killed in Susa (500 on Adar 13 + 300 on Adar 14; see vv. 6, 15), and about **75,000** were killed in the rest of **the king's provinces** (v. 16).

C. Establishing the Commemoration (9:19–10:3)

9:19-32. Just as the festival of Passover was instituted as "a memorial" (Ex 12:14) to Israel's deliverance recorded in Exodus, so too was a festival instituted to memorialize Israel's deliverance recorded in Esther. These two deliverance events are connected by their being the *only* biblical events of comprehensive Jewish deliverance set outside the promised land (on the theological significance of this connection/canonical juxtaposition see further our discussion in section B. in Introduction). In the absence of a direct word from God (on which see ibid., and section A.), this feast is enjoined by Mordecai, with the further backing of Esther (Est 9:29), by means of **letters** that he sent **to all the Jews who were in all the provinces of King Ahasuerus**. The divine "backing" of this festival is, of course, implied by the inclusion of this record in the biblical canon (an admittedly circular view, since it is based on the unempirical [i.e., faith-based acceptance of the canon as inspired]). Early Jewish tradition also supports the tradition recorded in the Jerusalem Talmud (*Megilla* i.5) that the proto-Sanhedrin at the time of Esther, comprised of 85 elders, were enlightened by God Himself to accept the institutionalizing letters of Mordecai and Esther.

The name given to the festival is **Purim**, so-called **after the name of** the **Pur** (v. 26)—that is, the Persian lot that was cast before Haman (see 3:7 and comments there). Rabbi Elijah ben Shlomo Zalman Kramer, an early-modern Jewish commentator (known as the "Vilna Gaon"; 18th century), commenting on the choice of name, says, "The *Pur* was the pivotal axis of the miracle by which God overturned [Haman's] calendrical divination." Moreover, in addition to its observance on **the fourteenth day of the month Adar** (v. 19), this festival was also observed on Adar 15 by the Jews of Susa to commemorate their additional day of "enemy-ridding" (see 9:15, 18). In early postbiblical tradition (and continuing up to the present) this additional day was enjoined more broadly upon Jews living in any city "encircled by a wall since the days of Joshua" (Mishna, *Megilla* i.1)—in practical terms today, only in Jerusalem.

To this day, Jewish people continue to celebrate their deliverance by God from the genocidal plans of Haman. The celebrations include reading the scroll of Esther in the synagogue, complete with noisemakers to drown out the name of Haman every time his name is read. It is also customary to deliver baskets of foods and sweets to neighbors (v. 22), to eat tri-cornered pastries reminiscent of Haman's hats (or some say his ears), and to perform plays reenacting the defeat of Haman. In light of Hitler's Holocaust, these celebrations have broadened their meaning to remember God's care to preserve His people at other times, for as the Jewish Passover liturgy states, "In every generation, they rise up to destroy us, but the Holy One, blessed be He, always delivers us from their hands."

10:1-3. These final three verses—which effectively constitute the book's epilogue—contain a final commemorative reference *not* to the festival of Purim or the specific events leading up to it, but rather to **the greatness of Mordecai** in general, as fully **written in the Book of Chronicles of the Kings of Media and Persia** (one of the possible sources utilized—under inspiration—by the writer, on which see Author and Date in the Introduction). In his position as **second only to King Ahasuerus**, Mordecai used his authority in the manner first exemplified by Joseph in the *same* position under Pharaoh. The same term "second" here [*mishneh*] is also used with reference to Joseph in Gn 41:43), namely, to seek **the good** (or "benefit") **of his people** and to speak **for** their **welfare** (lit., "peace"). Both of these activities, moreover, canonically describe a person who is motivated by *the fear* (i.e., slavish love) *of the Lord* (cf. Pss 34:11-14 [Hb. 12-15]; 85:8-9 [Hb. 9-10]; 122:8-9). Thus, the book ends with a sense of God's *enduring* concern for His people Israel, and the expectation that He will sovereignly continue to manage both events and individuals, whether great or small, in ongoing demonstration of His faithful love—with the result that one day His people will see it and say, in the words of Malachi (Mal 1:5), "The LORD be magnified beyond the border of Israel!"

BIBLIOGRAPHY

Anderson, Bernhard W. "The Place of the Book of Esther in the Christian Canon." *Journal of Religion* 30 (1950): 32-43. Reprinted in Carey A. Moore, ed. *Studies in the Book of Esther.* New York: KTAV, 1982.

Beckwith, R. *The Old Testament Canon of the New Testament Church and Its Background in Early Judaism.* Grand Rapids, MI: Eerdmans, 1985. Esp. chap. 7, "The Identity of the Canonical Books."

Conti, M. *et al*, eds. *1–2 Kings, 1–2 Chronicles, Ezra, Nehemiah, Esther.* Vol. 5 in *Ancient Christian Commentary on Scripture: Old Testament.* Downers Grove, IL: InterVarsity, 2008.

Huey, F. B., Jr., "[Commentary on] Esther." Vol. 4 in *The Expositor's Bible Commentary*. Ed. F. E. Gaebelein *et al.* Grand Rapids, MI: Zondervan, 1988.

Keil, F. C. "The Book of Esther." In Biblical Commentary on the Old Testament. Trans. S. Taylor. Grand Rapids, MI: Eerdmans, 1966.

McClure, W. J. *The Book of Esther: Prophetic Foreshadowings from the Book with No Divine Name in It.* Kilmarnock: John Ritchie, 1990.

Walfish, B. D. *Esther in Medieval Garb: Jewish Interpretation of the Book of Esther in the Middle Ages.* Albany, NY: SUNY Press, 1993.

Wechsler, M. G. "Shadow and Fulfillment in the Book of Esther." *Bibliotheca Sacra* 154, no. 615 (1997): 275–84.

JOB

EUGENE J. MAYHEW

INTRODUCTION

Author. The authorship of Job has been debated for centuries among both Jewish and Christian scholars. Traditional views within Judaism hold that the book of Job is of Mosaic origin, an ancient tradition that appears in the Babylonian Talmud, *Tractate Baba Bathra* 15 a-b. The problem with this view is that there is no such claim to authorship found in the book of Job. The book does not identify its author. Yet from the book's manner and viewpoint, it would seem that the author was not Job.

From the earliest discussions and OT canonical lists, the book of Job has been included and its canonicity upheld. Over time, in printed Hebrew Bibles, Job was placed between Psalms and Proverbs in order of decreasing [scroll] length (*Babylonian Talmud,* Ber. 57b). A quotation of Jb 5:13 by the apostle Paul in 1Co 3:19 is "introduced by a formula that indicates that Job was canonical Scripture in the first century AD" (Robert L. Alden, *Job,* NAC [Nashville: Broadman & Holman, 1993], 25). No evidence exists that the canonicity of the book of Job was questioned or disputed in Judaism or Christianity.

Date. The historical setting for the events of the book of Job was the development of the nations (Gn 10–11). This time period was post-flood and post-Babel, as well as patriarchal (Gn 11:32–12:1-3). The prophet Ezekiel confirmed that Job was a real man and not a fictitious character (Ezk 14:14-20). A plethora of historical indicators within the book of Job (see chart) also confirms the historicity of the man and the events (Alden, *Job,* 31).

Based on this internal evidence and other biblical evidence, a pre-patriarchal or patriarchal date for the lifetime of Job is not unreasonable. However, one must distinguish between when Job lived and when the account was written. Just as Moses lived from approximately 1527 to 1407 BC and (by inspiration of God) was able to write accurately about Adam or Abraham who lived centuries or millennia before his time, so is the situation with the book of Job. Several items in the account show that both the text and events are very old. (1) Job's lifespan places him solidly in the time of the early relatives of Abraham (Gn 22:20-24). (2) Neither the nation of Israel nor anything Israelite is mentioned in the book of Job because Job lived before or at the time of Abraham (Gn 11:32). (3) Many of the customs found in the book of Job are the same as those practiced by the patriarchs of ancient Israel. (4) New discoveries have shown that the Aramaic used in the book is ancient in date (Alden, *Job,* 26). It would appear from the evidence that Job lived in the land of Uz c. 2400–2100 BC. However, the book could have been written much later (as with the book of Genesis and Mosaic authorship).

The book of Job existed prior to these elements. (1) In AD 100 a copy of the *Targum of Job,* written in Aramaic, was shown to Rabbi Gamaliel. (2) At least four Job manuscripts were discovered among the Dead Sea Scrolls of the Qumran community (177 BC–AD 100). (3) Jesus ben-Sirach (c. 132 BC), referred to Job in his writings in Ezk 14:14-20. (4) The Greek translation of the OT, the Septuagint (LXX), written c. 200 BC, included the book of Job. (5) Ezekiel referred to Job as a past example of righteousness (Ezk 14:14). (6) Jeremiah wrote about a specific nation ruled by kings in the land of Uz which was still well known in 600 BC, likely Syria (Jr 25:20).

Purpose. The aims of the author are quite clear as the book of Job sets forth a polemic against a wholesale approach to retribution—cause and effect for all sin in a person's life. It

Historical Indicators in the Book of Job

Places	People	Proper Names/ Family	Customs	Sociological Infrastructure
Uz (Jb 1:1)	Men of the east (1:3)	Job (1:1)	Taking turns hosting feasts in homes (1:4)	Respect of older members (15:10)
Tema (6:19)	Sabeans (1:15)	7 sons 3 daughters (1:2)	Purification for sin after feasts (1:5)	Princes (29:9)
Sheba (6:19)	Chaldeans (1:17)	Age hierarchy (1:13, 18)	Traveling in caravans (6:19)	Nobles (29:10)
The east (1:3)	Temanites (2:11)	Wife (2:9)	Casting lots (6:27)	Tribes (30:12)
Jordan [River] (40:23)	Shuhites (2:11)	Eliphaz (2:11)	Loin cloth (12:18)	Bartering (41:6)
	Naamathites (2:11)	Bildad (2:11)	Cult Prostitutes (36:14)	Merchants (41:6)
	Men of the west and east (18:20)	Zophar (2:11)	Mourning Customs: tearing robe, shaving head (1:20), sitting in ashes (2:8), sprinkling dust on head (2:12-13)	Slave/master (3:19)
	Buzite (32:1)	Elihu, son of Barachel, family of Ram (32:2)	Cult and Shrine (36:14)	Kings of the earth (3:14)
	Mockers (17:2)	Siblings (42:11)		Cities (15:28)
	Servants (1:3)	Jemimah, Keziah, Keren-happuch (42:14)		
	Past Generations (8:8)			

also shows how a believer can triumph over tragedy even when much is unknown about the true God. The reader is given several visual snapshots into the unseen world of the throne of God and His workings (Alden, *Job*, 38–39).

Theme. The book of Job deals with a major problem area of fallen human existence, namely suffering. Why do people suffer (especially righteous people) if God is righteous and good? This book gives a larger perspective on the issue of theodicy (God's justice in light of evil in the world) and demonstrates that sometimes suffering comes because of the supernatural conflict between God and Satan. In this ongoing conflict humanity often serves as the playing field for these supernatural matches of the strength, power, and stamina of the kingdom of God versus the kingdom of darkness. Ultimately, the book teaches God's sovereignty over all.

God is in wise control (Jb 28) of the universe and of all issues in a believer's life, both normal and abnormal, including triumphs and tragedies, affluence and poverty, adversity and prosperity. Even when those closest to the sufferer give wrong counsel and challenge the reasons for the misfortune, a righteous believer can stand confident that he is in God's hands by understanding God's work in creation. Therefore questioning or arguing with Him is unreasonable, but praising and repenting before Him is in order.

Chapters 1–2 and 42 are written in prose (narrative), and chaps. 3–41 are written in poetry, "except for brief introductions of the friends of Job just ahead of their addresses" (Alden, *Job*, 35). With the high density of poetry, Job has an impressive number of *hapax legomena* (terms used only one time in the book of Job or in the OT), and sometimes it is a challenge to grasp their meaning.

Critical scholars have tried to set forth the case that the book of Job was a mosaic that took shape over time as new portions of it were added. They view chaps. 1–2 and 42 as the original account, with all the poetic sections added later. But C. Hassell Bullock states, "The book of Job defies all efforts to establish its literary genre. While it has been viewed as an epic, a tragedy, and a parable, upon close analysis it is none of these even though it exhibits properties belonging to each of them" (C. Hassell Bullock, *An Introduction to the Old Testament Poetic Books* [Chicago: Moody, 1979], 69).

Contribution. The book of Job draws back the curtain on a dynamic glimpse of the throne of God and interaction between God and Satan. God appears not only in control of Job's suffering, but also omniscient and wise in the matter—wisdom belongs to God even in the most difficult aspects of life. As Job said, "With Him are wisdom and might" (Jb 12:13). The account demolishes the false ideas that the true God is aloof and unconcerned about human dilemmas. Rather, He is highly involved in a person's life beyond our wildest imagination.

The facets of sin and suffering are greatly expanded in this early, inspired book. Many layers of suffering were unknown to the debaters as they tried in vain to sort out Job's dilemma. Job 2 demonstrates the extent to which the adversary can assault the believer, even to the point of death (Rv 1:18-19; 20:11-14). And Job 2 shows the extent to which the believer is to trust God in the tragedies and uncertainties of life. This chapter informs the reader of the realm of supernatural conflict between God and the adversary. The awesome fact in the prologue of Job is that God set forth Job for the contest, and He is the One who initiated the challenge and contest. Yet God did this without removing His hand or His love from Job's life. God appears as wisely sovereign and good in both the positive and negative aspects and events of individuals' lives.

The account of Job shows us that God was active among humanity from the time of the flood until Abraham appeared on the stage of history, by the following facts: (1) The true God was well known to many people, and their knowledge of theology was extremely intricate and discussed among themselves. (2) Job appeared as a Gentile believer like Melchizedek and Jethro, who had knowledge of the true God apart from Abraham and Israel. (3) The interaction between God and Satan was clearly described, and the facets of suffering came into a clearer perspective. (4) Even a righteous believer could misunderstand God's work and hurl false accusations against Him.

Where did the author of Job receive his either pre-Israelite or non-Israelite information? Very simply, there had to have been a body of truth orally transmitted from generation to generation from the time of Adam and Eve to the time of Moses.

The book of Job can be viewed as a beautiful and balanced seven-part chiasm. Beyond God's sovereignty and His control over suffering is the assurance that suffering has meaning and purpose for the believer. Job 28, the psalm on wisdom, is at the heart of the book of Job (Elmer B. Smick, "Job," in EBC [Grand Rapids, MI: Zondervan, 1988], 4:848).

Many scholars see the chiastic structure as the key to understanding the book's strategy. It shows God's wisdom (Jb 28) and the need for total dependence and trust in Him. See the chiastic structure of Job below:

The Book of Job Chiastic Structure Outline

A. Prologue: Righteous Job Sees His Life Go from Tremendous Triumphs to Phenomenal Tragedies (1:1–2:13)
   B. The Lament of Job before His Friends concerning His Serious Sufferings (3:1-26)
      C. The Rounds of Counseling with His Friends: Eliphaz, Bildad, and Zophar (4:1–27:23)
         D. The Heart of the Message of the Book of Job: The Bastion of Wisdom Is Known Only by the True God (28:1-28)
      C'. The Rounds of Counseling with His Younger Friend, Elihu (29:1–37:24)
   B'. God's Rhetorical Questioning of Job concerning His Intricate Care of Creation (38:1–42:6)
A'. Epilogue: Righteous Job Saw His Life Go from Phenomenal Tragedies to Tremendous Triumphs (42:7-17)

OUTLINE

I. Job's Circumstances and Calamities (1:1–2:13)
  A. Job's Status before His Calamities (1:1-5)
  B. Satan's Challenge to God about Job (1:6-11)
  C. God's Permission to Satan to Afflict Job's Possessions (1:12-22)
  D. God's Permission to Satan to Afflict Job's Body (2:1-6)
  E. Job's Reaction to His Losses (2:7-10)
  F. Job's Three Friends Arrive to Comfort Him (2:11-13)

II. First Round of Speeches between Job and His Three Friends (3:1–14:22)
  A. Job Laments His Condition (3:1-26)
  B. Eliphaz Delivers His First Speech (4:1–5:27)
  C. Job Responds to Eliphaz's Charges (6:1–7:21)
  D. Bildad Delivers His First Speech (8:1-22)
  E. Job Responds to Bildad's Charges (9:1–10:22)
  F. Zophar Delivers His First Speech (11:1-20)
  G. Job Responds to Zophar's Charges (12:1–14:22)

III. Second Round of Speeches between Job and His Friends (15:1–21:34)
  A. Eliphaz Delivers His Second Speech (15:1-35)
  B. Job Responds to Eliphaz's Charges (16:1–17:16)
  C. Bildad Delivers His Second Speech (18:1-21)
  D. Job Responds to Bildad's Charges (19:1-29)
  E. Zophar Delivers His Second Speech (20:1-29)
  F. Job Responds to Zophar's Charges (21:1-34)

IV. Third Round of Speeches between Job and His Three Friends (22:1–26:14)
  A. Eliphaz Delivers His Third Speech (22:1-30)
  B. Job Responds to Eliphaz's Charges (23:1–24:25)
  C. Bildad Delivers His Third Speech (25:1-6)
  D. Job Responds to Bildad's Charges (26:1-14)

V. Job Continues His Speeches (27:1–31:40)
  A. Job's Final Speech to His Friends (27:1-23)
  B. Job's Message concerning God's Wisdom (28:1-28)
  C. Job Reviews His Life (29:1–31:40)

VI. The Speeches of Elihu (32:1–37:24)
  A. His First Speech about Job, His Friends, and God's Work (32:1–33:33)
  B. His Second Speech (34:1-37)
  C. His Third Speech (35:1-16)
  D. His Fourth Speech (36:1–37:24)

VII. God Speaks to Job (38:1–42:17)
  A. God's First Speech about His Knowledge (38:1–40:2)
  B. Job's Response to God's First Speech (40:3-5)
  C. God's Second Speech about His Power (40:6–41:34)
  D. Job's Repentance before God (42:1-6)
  E. Job's Restoration by God (42:7-17)

COMMENTARY ON JOB

I. Job's Circumstances and Calamities (1:1–2:13)

Chapters 1 and 2 are part of the prose section of Job, setting forth the issues and characters in quick succession. Job's sterling spiritual character, his family and possessions, Satan's accusations and attacks on Job, Job's reactions, and the arrival of his friends—all are set before the reader in rapid fashion, like an edited film speeding through the preliminaries. Everything happens quickly, yet the dialogue that follows unfolds at a very studied pace. The pace slows, and the plot is simple. The prologue is necessary background told in rapid narrative style to get the reader quickly to Job's agonizing confrontations with his friends and with God.

A. Job's Status before His Calamities (1:1-5)

1:1. Job lived in the land of Uz. The location of Uz is disputed, as there are three people with that name in the book of Genesis (10:23; 22:21; 36:28). However, the only one who could have lived, become famous, and had a land named after him by the time Job existed would have been Uz son of Aram (Gn 10:23). Aram had settled the area now known as Syria, and it appears from the evidence that his son Uz had a large portion of ancient Syria named after him.

As noted in the introduction, writing after Syria had been conquered by the Assyrians, Jeremiah referred to Syria as "the land of Uz" (Jr 25:20). Therefore at the time of Jeremiah, Uz was an ancient name that referred to the area formally known as Syria before it fell to the Assyrians. There is a second biblical reference to Uz as a possession or neighbor of Edom (Lm 4:21).

Other theories on the location of Uz are northwest Arabia and Edom. However, Jeremiah referred to it as a nation with many kings (Jr 25:20). Thus Uz was not an alternative name for Edom, or for Philistia, Moab, or Ammon because they are listed apart from the land of Uz (v. 21). Gleason L. Archer notes: "in *Berlin Execration Texts* . . . **Job** *('Iyyob)* appears as the name of a Syrian prince living near Damascus" (*Encyclopedia of Bible Difficulties* [Grand Rapids, MI: Zondervan, 1982], 236). There is not enough evidence to establish that this refers to the biblical Job, but from this discovery the exact personal name is used in the region of ancient Aram (Syria) where Aram had a son named Uz (Gn 10:23). Unger adds, "The most likely location of Uz is Syria (Aram), rather than Edom, Idumea, or another area. The Uz of Gn 10:23 is apparently the only biblical person who could have established an area bearing his name by the time Job lived, apparently in the Abrahamic or pre-Abrahamic age" (*Unger's Commentary on the Old Testament* [Chicago: Moody, 1981], 1:679).

The time frame of Job was patriarchal (see discussion in introduction). The book yields at least seven facts about Job's age:

1. Job had ten grown children with sons who owned their own houses.
2. He had the reputation as being the greatest man of the east before his suffering took place (1:2-4).
3. He sat with the elders at the gate of his city (29:1-12).
4. Job was an elder, and younger Elihu was hesitant to speak up about his suffering.
5. He had ten additional children after his suffering (42:13).
6. His name *'iyyob* was a common name during the time of the patriarchs and even before as it appears in texts discovered at Ugarit, Mari, and among the *Amarna Letters* and the *Egyptian Execration Texts*.
7. Job lived 140 years beyond his sufferings and saw his next generations born (42:16-17).

A conservative estimate of the lifespan of Job based on this internal evidence would be that he lived to be much older than Abraham, since Jb 42:16-17 informs the reader that Job's lifespan was 140 years, after his sufferings, almost equal the length of Abraham's total life of 175 years (Gn 25:7). This would place Job as living after the Noahic flood and before the time of the patriarch Abraham.

Roy B. Zuck (*Job* [Chicago: Moody, 1978], 10) adds these reasons for Job having lived in the time of the patriarchs:

1. Job's wealth was reckoned in livestock (1:3; 42:12), which was also true of Abraham (Gn 12:16; 13:2) and Jacob (Gn 30:43; 32:5).
2. The Sabeans and Chaldeans (Jb 1:15, 17) were nomads in Abraham's time, but not in later years.
3. The Hebrew word *qesitah*, translated "piece of money" (42:11), is used elsewhere only twice (Gn 33:19; Jos 24:32), both times in reference to Jacob.
4. Job's daughters were heirs of his estate along with their brothers (Jb 42:15). This, however, was not possible later under the Mosaic law if a daughter's brother(s) were still living (Nm 27:8).
5. The name *Shaddai* is used of God 31 times in Job (compared with only 17 times elsewhere in the OT) and was a name familiar to the patriarchs (Gn 17:1; also cf. Ex 6:3). Edersheim wrote this about the years

before Abraham: "It will be readily understood that the number of those 'born out of season,' as it were, from among the Gentiles, must have been larger the higher we ascend the stream of time. The fullest example of this is set before us in the book of Job, which also gives a most interesting picture of those early times" (Alfred Edersheim, *The Bible History* [Grand Rapids, MI: Eerdmans, 1969], 1:5–6).

1:2-3. The true God blessed Job's life and work. In addition to his 10 children, Job also had many possessions, including 7,000 sheep, 3,000 camels, 500 yoke of oxen, 500 female donkeys, and many servants. He was both wealthy and godly—two characteristics not often found together. He was a remarkable man indeed.

Perhaps Job was like many patriarchs who were ancient teamsters, moving goods in the lucrative caravan business, as large caravans used hundreds of animals. The camels, oxen, and donkeys were the standard beasts of burden in the ancient Near East at that time. One would become well known over a vast region by being in that business. His wealth, like that of Abraham and others, was stated in animals owned (Gn 13:2, 6; 24:28-35; cf. 1Sm 25:2; 2Kg 3:4).

It is written that Job **was the greatest of all the men of the east** (v. 3). According to other biblical authors the east (*qedem*) refers to a definite area or region during the time of the OT. In later times the east had ominous overtones for the people of Israel because it was from the east that God summoned the great Babylonian king, Nebuchadnezzar, to come and destroy Jerusalem and carry the people away into captivity. But this would be many centuries after the time of Job.

Other references to "the east" include (1) Gn 10:30, referring to where Shem, Noah's son, settled after the flood; (2) Jdg 6:3, 33; 7:12-8:10, referring to the area of the Midianites; (3) Jr 49:28, referring to a region near Kedar; and (4) Ezk 25:2, 4, referring to an area of the Ammonites. Therefore **the east** encompassed the district from Damascus to Arabia and over to what later became Assyria. Job's great stature in that ancient society resulted not only because of his accumulation of goods and animals, but also because he obeyed the true God and was a man of integrity (Jb 1:1).

1:4-5. The strong evidence that Job lived during or even before the classic patriarchal period of the OT appears in his spiritual activities on behalf of his children. He served as Abraham did as the family priest (1:4-5; 42:8) (Alden, *Job,* 26, 31, 52). Unger notes, "He offered burnt offerings, as symbolic of the messianic expiation of sin, to make atonement for sins his children might have committed" (*Unger's Commentary on the Old Testament,* 1:680, cf. *Deuteronomy Rabba,* II). Regarding making offerings, the text states, **thus Job did continually**. This shows, as Albright concludes, "that Job may have been a contemporary of the patriarchs in the pre-Mosaic age" (William Albright, "The Old Testament and Archaeology," in *Old Testament: A General Introduction to Commentary of the Books of the Old Testament,* ed. Herbert C. Alleman and Elmer E. Flack [Philadelphia: Muhlenberg Press, 1948], 155; see also William F. Albright, *Yahweh and the Gods of Canaan,* [London: Athlone Press, 1968], 67–71).

Archer concludes, "There are no tenable grounds for the theory of a fictional Job. The Apostle James was therefore quite justified in appealing to the example of the patriarch Job (James 5:11), in his exhortation to Christian believers to remain patient under tribulation. It is needless to point out that the Lord could hardly have been merciful and compassionate to a fictional character who never existed" (Archer, *Encyclopedia of Bible Difficulties,* 236–37).

B. Satan's Challenge to God about Job (1:6-11)

1:6-8. Satan came into the court of heaven as one of **the sons of God** permitted to stand before God. From other Scriptures we know that angels, both unfallen and fallen (Satan in Jb 2), were allowed to appear before Yahweh in heaven. In Zch 6:5, the prophet is told that his vision of the four chariots represents "the four spirits of heaven, going forth after standing before the Lord of all the earth." While this reference does not identify angels by name, this is a legitimate interpretation. There is no question, however, about Lk 1:19, when Gabriel declared to Zacharias, "I am Gabriel, who stands in the presence of God."

The expression "sons of God" is used of both godly people and godly angels who follow the true God. Here the expression is used of angels, based on Jb 38:7. In this particular heavenly audience **Satan** was also allowed to attend (Eph 2:2; 2Pt 2:4; Jd 9; Rv 12:7-9). The root verb for the Hebrew word *satan* has the potential meanings of "to oppose, to come in the way," "to treat with enmity." In the book of Job, this opposer or adversary always occurs with the definite article, hence, *hassatan*—"*the* opposer" or "*the* adversary." In Rv 12:7-9; 20:2, it is another name for the fallen cherub that relates back to Gn 3; it is not a late postexilic concept or doctrine. Other occurrences of the title in the OT are in 1Ch 21:1 and Zch 3:1-2. Delitzsch notes, "But, the conception of Satan is indeed much older in its existence than the time of Solomon; the serpent of paradise must surely have appeared to the inquiring mind of Israel as the disguise of an evil spirit" (Franz Delitzsch, *Biblical Commentary on the Book of Job,* 3 vols., trans. F. Bolton [Grand Rapids, MI: Eerdmans, 1949], 1:28). When God asked Satan where he had been, Satan replied that he had been **roaming about on the earth** (Jb 1:7). Satan may have been doing this while "prowl[ing] around like a roaring lion, seeking someone to devour" (1Pt 5:8), which is his constant goal.

It is clear that God was the One who introduced Job into the scene of His audience with Satan (v. 8). The Lord referred to Job as **My servant**, which Zuck calls an "honorable title" (*Job*, 15). God praised Job's devotion, and was confident that Satan would also discover that Job's piety was far more than a superficial devotion.

1:9-11. Satan could not deny Job's devotion to God, but he asked the question, **Does Job fear God for nothing?** This is an issue human beings have wrestled with for generations. From Job's day to the message of the so-called health and wealth preachers of today, there has been no lack of people to suggest that those who serve God can expect to reap material benefits in this life as well as eternal life in heaven.

After Jesus' disciples watched a rich man come and ask Jesus about inheriting eternal life, and then go away sadly (Mk 10:17-22), they wondered what they would receive for giving up all to follow Jesus. The Savior responded, "Truly I say to you, there is no one who has left house or brothers or sisters or mother or father or children or farms, for My sake and for the gospel's sake, but that he will receive a hundred times as much now in the present age, houses and brothers and sisters and mothers and children and farms, along with persecutions" (vv. 29-30). Jesus' promise of persecutions for His faithful followers does not fit with the theology of the "name it and claim it" teachers who say that material prosperity is guaranteed by God.

Satan knew he could not impugn Job's demonstrated piety, so he impugned Job's motives instead. The adversary complained to God about three aspects of Job's faithfulness. (1) God had **made a hedge** of protection around Job and all he possessed. (2) Job worshiped God because of what he was receiving from Him. (3) If God allowed Job's blessings to be taken from him, he would **curse You to Your face** (v. 11).

From ancient times Satan has been the grand accuser of the servants of God (Rv 12:10). However, God, not Satan, made the initial challenge and set the boundaries for the testing of Job of Uz. Many Bible teachers miss this foundational truth and end up with false conclusions about Job's ordeal. It was God who challenged Satan concerning Job.

In the first assault that was negotiated and authorized in heaven, God allowed Satan to test Job, but limited Satan's testing to Job's possessions and family. Delitzsch states, "There is in nature an entanglement of contrary forces which Satan knows how to unloose, because it is the sphere of his special dominion; for the whole course of nature, in the change of its phenomena, is subject not only to abstract laws, but, also to concrete supernatural powers, both good and bad" (*Biblical Commentary on the Book of Job,* 1:28).

Several key questions are raised by these early verses of Job. Zuck summarizes them well: "Will Job be seen as one who will serve God even if he gets nothing in return? Will *anyone* serve God for no personal gain? Is worship a coin that buys us a heavenly reward? Does man serve God to get blessings, fearing that failure to worship will bring punishment? Is piety part of a contract by which to gain wealth and ward off trouble?" (*Job*, 15, italics original).

C. God's Permission to Satan to Afflict Job's Possessions (1:12-22)

1:12-19. In rapid succession Job saw many of his earthly possessions taken from him—and finally all 10 of his children were killed in one moment. The **Sabeans** may have come from the region of Sheba, in southwest Arabia, or from a town named Sheba, near Dedan, in Upper Arabia (Gn 10:7; 25:3). The **Chaldeans** were fierce marauding inhabitants of Mesopotamia.

Four servants came to Job to report the losses he had incurred. Delitzsch summarizes, "Satan has summoned the elements (nature) and men for the destruction of Job's possessions by repeated strokes. That men and nations can be excited by Satan to hostile enterprises is nothing surprising (cf. Apoc. xx.8); but here, even the fire of God and the hurricanes are attributed to him" (*Biblical Commentary on the Book of Job,* 1:63).

1:20-22. A solid faith perspective is extremely important when suffering comes into a believer's life. Job **worshiped** God when these tragedies struck him and his wife. He acknowledged that the true God can give or take and that a believer should not blame God for any misfortune. William Dyrness adds, "Job deals with the ancient problem of the innocent sufferer. It faces squarely the reality of evil and human suffering but shows the futility of calling God to account (Jb 40:6-14) . . . the attitude of sufferers is more important than the answer to their questions" (*Themes in Old Testament Theology* [Downers Grove, IL: InterVarsity, 1979], 192–93). Job expressed both his grief and his submission to God when he **tore his robe and shaved his head** and **fell to the ground and worshiped** (v. 20).

The LORD gave and the LORD has taken away (v. 21) was Job's declaration of trust. This statement indicates that Job saw God as the ultimate cause of his misfortunes, though not the immediate, direct cause, which came from the other participants. This is an important consideration for the entire book—God is presented as the One who ordained and sovereignly stood behind Job's situation.

Equally important is the statement in v. 22: Job . . . did not **blame God**. The Hebrew word translated **blame** connotes "unsavoriness, foolishness." It is probably used metaphorically here with the sense of "moral repugnance" or "reprehensibility." In addition, it sometimes carries the sense of "repulsiveness," i.e., a state or condition which causes feelings of abhorrence and loathing (Jr 23:13).

While Job ascribed to God the ultimate causation of his losses (**The LORD has taken away**), he did not hang upon God the moral culpability (the guilt) of them. God is rightly seen in Scripture as the ultimate, not *direct*, cause of the sin, evil, and suffering in the world (that is, He is sovereign over them, ordains them, and brings them about indirectly through the free actions of people or demons as part of His providence; see Gn 50:20; Ac 2:22-23; 4:27-28). But God is never blamed for the moral guilt of evil—even by Job—and is never the One who tempts people to sin (Jms 1:13). Moral guilt is always ascribed to people and demonic beings. This is part of the mystery of God's sovereignty, and its interaction with the moral responsibility of moral agents, whether human or demonic.

In the first assault by the adversary, Job felt the tremendous loss of his children, herds and flocks, and many servants (1:16-22). In chap. 2 the angelic adversary requested authorization and received permission to launch a second assault against Job since his first assault did not cause him to **curse** God (Jb 1:11, 22; 2:5). As Zuck points out, "Job was subjected to two tests—one on his possessions and offspring (1:6-22) and one on his health and his reputation (2:1-10). In each test were two scenes, one in heaven and one on earth. Each scene in heaven included an accusation by Satan against Job, and each scene on earth included an assault by Satan against Job" (*Job,* 15).

Satan failed in his first attempt to discredit Job's faith and expose him as a person who worshiped God only for the protection and possessions He provided. Job's response proved Satan to be completely wrong in his confident prediction that Job would curse God if calamity befell him. Job's humble submission and his worship of God at a moment of supreme grief and despair verified God's words that Job was, indeed, unlike any other person on earth. However, Satan was not ready to quit the attack.

D. God's Permission to Satan to Afflict Job's Body (2:1-6)

Once again, Satan called God's word into question and impugned Job's motive for worshiping Him—even though Job had nothing left at this point but his life. This was enough for Satan to accuse Job a second time of serving God only for personal benefit.

The text of Job provides no time frame between Jb 1 and 2; therefore, the elapsed time between the first assault in chap. 1 and the second major assault in chap. 2 is uncertain. However, it would seem that the two assaults were somewhat close together (v. 11), as reflected in: (1) the statement of Job to his wife about accepting adversity (v. 10); (2) the reference that seems to include the bad events recorded in 1:6-22 and 2:7; and (3) the reference in 2:11 to "all this adversity." However, as Robert Gordis notes, "For the news to reach the friends in their several countries and for them to arrange for a meeting suggests that Job's suffering had extended over a considerable period of time" (*The Book of God and Man: A Study of Job* [Chicago: University of Chicago Press, 1965], 22). The context necessitates a period of time consisting of

The Attack of the Adversary: Before and After

Pre-supernatural Testing and Job's Prosperity		Post-supernatural Testing and Job's Prosperity		
Blessings	**Description**	**Losses**	**Description**	**Increased Blessing**
Jb 1:2	7 sons 3 daughters	1:13, 18-19	7 sons 3 daughters	42:13
1:3	7,000 sheep	1:16	14,000 sheep	42:12
1:3	3,000 camels	1:17	6,000 camels	42:12
1:3	500 yoke of oxen	1:14-15	1,000 yoke of oxen	42:12
1:3	500 donkeys	1:14-15	1,000 donkeys	42:12

at least several months to over a year. As chap. 2 opens, Job is in the midst of dealing with his heavy losses and grief when the physical affliction (the second assault) comes on him (vv. 7-8).

2:1-6. The context of chap. 2 is in the aftermath of Job's horrible losses described in chap. 1. Meanwhile, back in heaven Satan appeared a second time, and God again set forth a challenge to him. To set the stage for this challenge, Satan snarled, **Skin for skin!** (v. 4). If Job's body can be touched with adversity, **he will curse You to Your face** (v. 5). To this, God issued another limitation: the adversary could touch Job's body, but not kill him: **only spare his life** (v. 6).

E. Job's Reaction to His Losses (2:7-10)

2:7-10. Then the adversary went from heaven to earth and inflicted Job with a boil-type disease. Job initially tried to alleviate the pain and mourn, in ancient Near Eastern style, for the calamities he had encountered. The author noted, **And he took a potsherd** [a broken piece of pottery] **to scrape himself while he was sitting among the ashes** (v. 8). Even Job's **wife** became part of the problem by telling him to give up, to **curse God and die** (v. 9). Responding to his wife, Job stated that believers in their misfortunes can expect both **good** and **adversity** from God (v. 10). This fits with the strong statement of the psalmist who wrote, "Let the sound of his praise be heard; he has preserved our lives and kept our feet from slipping. For you, God, tested us; you refined us like silver. You brought us into prison and laid burdens on our backs. You let people ride over our heads; we went through fire and water, but you brought us to a place of abundance" (Ps 66:8b-12 NIV).

A Jewish legend states that "Job was stricken by Satan with fifty plagues" *(Targum Yerushalmi; Exodus R., xxiii, 10),* and another that says his suffering endured for a year (*Testament of Job, v. 9*; Isadore Singer, "Job," in *The Jewish Encyclopedia* [1904], 7:194). Others make Job the all-time sufferer of humanity. However, from Job's symptoms, one of several known diseases could have been the culprit Satan used to cause terrible pain and suffering. The chart on the following page lists the symptoms that the text of Job indicated he had.

The angelic adversary actively struck Job with a physical disease identified as *shechin* (v. 7). This term means a boil or eruption (Francis Brown, S. R. Driver, and Charles A Briggs, *Hebrew and English Lexicon of the Old Testament* [Oxford: Clarendon Press, 1906], 1006, hereafter *BDB*), and occurs in other Semitic languages, such as Akkadian, Assyrian, Ugaritic, and Aramaic, denoting "heat, fever, inflammation and the like." It stems from the verb "to be inflamed." The writer states that Satan **smote Job with sore boils from the sole of his foot to the crown of his head** (v. 7). The Hebrew word for "sore" is *ra'* meaning "bad, noxious, hideous" (Dt 28:7; 2Ch 21:6; Ec 6:1). The Septuagint translator chose the term *elkos,* which is used in the NT of an ulcer (Lk 16:20; Rv 16:2). In the OT the term is applied to skin diseases (Marvin H. Pope, *Job* [Garden City, NY: Doubleday, 1973], 2). The differences of opinion among various biblical scholars and medical doctors concerning the range and precise designations of *shechin* arise from its use in relation to different skin diseases in the OT and in other ancient Near Eastern literature.

Numerous theories have been advanced concerning Job's disease: leprosy, elephantiasis, acute dermatitis, oriental sore, Egyptian boil, smallpox, pemphigus foliaceus, ecthyma, erythema, multiple disease, psychosomatic, unique adversary theory, and no disease theory.

Summation of the Symptoms - Exegetical Evidence

Passage	Particular	Pathology
2:1-6	Deals with losses and grief	Depression
2:7	Struck with *shechin*	Boil-type disease
2:8	Scraping	Skin
7:4-6	Insomnia, worms in sores, scabs, hopelessness	Insomnia, skin, depression
7:14-16	Nightmares, choking, death wish, weakness	Nightmares, weight loss, growing depression
16:8	Continued weight loss	Weight loss
18:13	Skin eaten by disease	Disease progresses
19:17	Bad breath	Halitosis
19:20	Continued weight loss	Disease progresses
19:26	Skin is location of problem	Epidermis
30:17	Insomnia, constant pain	Inorganic/organic
30:18	Pus-saturated garment	Coagulating white blood cells
30:27	Diarrhea	Irritable bowel
30:30	Skin turns black	Skin discoloration

Zuck for one favors pemphigus foliaceus, an auto-immune blistering disease of the skin and mucous membranes with characteristic lesions that are scaly, and crusted erosions (*Job*, 19). The "Egyptian boil" is taken from a reference to "the boils of Egypt" in Dt 28:27. Later, the same words as in Jb 2:7 are used in Dt 28:35 to describe the suffering that would come to Israel because of disobedience: "The LORD will strike you on the knees and legs with sore boils, from which you cannot be healed, from the sole of your foot to the crown of your head."

It is best to understand that *shechin* is a general word that describes a number of boil-type skin diseases (the context of the book indicates that it was a serious skin disease). In Jb 18:13 Bildad said of Job, "His skin is devoured by disease. The firstborn of death devours his limbs." No one can state the exact nature of the disease. A number of diseases can cause boils all over the body and reveal the symptoms listed in the book.

The phrase **from the sole of his foot to the crown of his head** has been taken to mean that the boils occurred all over Job's body. This merism—similar to "And in His law he meditates day and night" (Ps 1:2) and "from Dan even to Beersheba" (2Sm 3:10)—is employed to describe the extent of the boil outbreak on the skin of Job without listing every body part where a boil erupted. The boils were multiple and every region of Job's skin was affected by them. Thus the adversary inflicted Job with a horrible physical disease in this second assault.

Realizing that he had contracted a serious boil-type disease, Job responded by scraping himself with a **potsherd** as he sat in **the ashes**. Job's reaction reveals the seriousness of the disease and of his emotional state. Job's skin problem produced itching to the point of morbid aggravation. This word **scrape** or "scratch" occurs in Aramaic and Phoenician to refer to "flesh-scrapers." In this gruesome scene Job selected a ragged-edged potsherd with which to scrape himself to alleviate the pain and itching. Broken pieces of pottery were used for makeshift tools such as scrapers and scratchers.

To v. 8 LXX translators added the last three words "without the city." Since lepers were required to live outside a camp or town, these three words have added support to the view that Job's disease was leprosy. Acknowledging such an interpretation, Gordis adds, "Job sits on the ash-heap outside the city, not as a sign of mourning, but rather because of the contagious character of his disease and his loathsome appearance" (*The Book of Job* [New York: Jewish Theological Seminary of America of 1978], 21).

However, Edward J. Kissane is right to argue against the LXX addition: "The Greek text adds 'without the city' and this has given rise to the common view that Job retired outside the city. But the text itself does not say this, and the presence of his wife would indicate rather that he was still at his own house" (*The Book of Job* [Dublin: Browne and Nolan, 1939], 10). Job's sitting "among" the ashes was a custom in the ancient Near East that indicated mourning. In a time of mourning, an easterner could simply take ashes from a campfire or fireplace and put them in a convenient location and begin the mourning process. Therefore Job could have been mourning at his home.

If Job had been on the dunghill or the city dump, then the following would seem to be true: (1) Job's friends spent an entire week either on the dunghill or in or near the dump; (2) the entire conversation between Job and his friends took place there as well, since 2:12 shows them joining him in this custom; and (3) ashes presuppose the dunghill. But a more plausible interpretation is that Job went outside his home and participated in a well-established custom that pictured the inner turmoil of the mourner or sufferer. When his friends came close to his home, they joined him in his mourning near his dwelling. Then Job's suffering was intensified from yet another angle.

In addition to the anguish of suffering with an acute boil-type disease, the adversary also used Job's wife in the assault, and in the near future would also use his relatives and friends. She asked, **Do you still hold fast your integrity?** Then she uttered her famous command that aligns with the contest in heaven between the adversary and God. She should have been Job's greatest strength apart from God, but she told him to **curse God and die!** The Hebrew text uses the word *barakh,* bless, as a euphemism for "curse" since the idea of cursing God was unthinkable.

Concerning the use and understanding of the words **curse God**, E. Dhorme comments:

> The sharp reply which Job's wife gets in v. 10 excludes the translation of *curse* as "bless Elohim" (Targ. and Vulg.). As has been understood by Syriac and some Greek interpreters, the word ["**curse**"] is a theological euphemism which we have found in the whole of the narrative (v. 5 and 1:5, 11). Hence we shall continue to read *curse* as before: "Curse Elohim and die!" It is not necessary to see death as a consequence of the suggested cursing. It is simply a matter of succession in time (*Commentary on the Book of Job* [Nashville: Thomas Nelson, 1967], 20).

Smick writes that the word "die"

> is a universally used Semitic root for dying and death . . . the literal demise of the body in death is usually in view. . . . The Canaanites employed it as the name of the god of death and the netherworld, Mot (cf. *ANET*, 138–142). . . . In Ugaritic, the god Mot was a well-defined figure who ruled the netherworld, a land of slime and filth. ("Job")

In addition to this command by Job's wife, the LXX places a lengthy speech in her mouth. About the origin of her speech H. H. Rowley states: "Ball suggests that it may go back to a Hebrew original, but there is no reason to suppose it belonged to the authentic text" (*Job,* The Century Bible [New York: Thomas Nelson, 1970], 39).

Some commentators have understood the advice of Job's wife as compassionate rather than contemptible, a wish for a quick death instead of prolonged suffering. But this idea does not do justice to the context, since her statement would require Job to abandon his integrity and his trust in God—the very outcome Satan also tried to bring about. It is preferable to view Job's wife as expressing bitterness toward God.

Job responded that his wife spoke **as one of the foolish women**, as a person with no spiritual discernment. Delitzsch states: "The answer of Job is strong but not harsh, for the [spiritual insensitivity] is somewhat soothing. The translation 'as one of the foolish women' does not correspond to the Hebrew; [*nabal*] is one who thinks madly and acts impiously" (*Biblical Commentary on the Book of Job*, 1:72). The word *nebalaah,* meaning "foolish or senseless," is used of a person who lacks moral and spiritual perception.

Job then said to his wife, **Shall we indeed accept good from God and not accept adversity?** Besides accepting "good" benefits from God, Job also realized that believers must **accept adversity**. The term *ra'* means "distress, evil, wrong, injury, calamity," and this verse once again indicates God's providence over evil and suffering in the world (see the comments on 1:21-22). Job's stance points up the need for perseverance in the midst of trials and problems. As the second assault progressed in intensity, Job continued to trust in his relationship with his God. But the calamities, the first and second assaults that Job had experienced, stretched him to the breaking point.

Nevertheless, **in all this Job did not sin with his lips**. The word "sin" is *chata'*, which means "miss, go wrong, sin, commit a mistake, miss the mark" (*BDB*, 306).

In Akkadian the verb *hatu* means "to sin, to neglect," and in Ugaritic the verb refers to "sin" three times (Cyrus H. Gordon, *Ugaritic Textbook* [Rome: Pontifical Biblical Institute, 1967], no. 19/952). Regarding the phrase **with his lips**, Gordis states, concerning Job, "Purity of speech reflects the integrity of one's spirit" (*The Book of Job*, 22).

F. Job's Three Friends Arrive to Comfort Him (2:11-13)

2:11-13. This section concerning the entrance of his friends closes one episode and begins a new one with Job's friends entering the scene. The men who came to visit are referred to as **friends**, that is, companions. Job's friends Eliphaz, Bildad, Zophar, and Elihu demonstrated that they believed that problems and turmoil were always a result of serious kinds of sin. However, the account shows that this approach to suffering is both theologically shallow and often wrong.

Gordis states, "For the news to reach the Friends in their several countries and for them to arrange for a meeting suggest that Job's suffering has extended over a considerable period of time" (*The Book of Job*, 22). **They made an appointment** together, that is, the three friends worked as a team in planning to come as a group to help Job. The reason for their visit was to **sympathize with** and **comfort** Job. Obviously they came with good motives. When they saw Job's condition, they were moved to identify with his situation, and they entered the well-established custom of mourning.

Seeing his horrible condition, his friends **raised their voices** (v. 12). At the same time they **wept**, and tore their garments. Leonard Coppes comments that this "has to do with rending cloth or a similar substance.... Most frequently, it refers to an act of heartfelt and grievous affliction (tearing one's upper and under garment, "*qara'*," in *Theological Wordbook of the Old Testament*, ed. R. Laird Harris, Gleason L. Archer, Jr., and Bruce K. Waltke [Chicago: Moody, 1980]: 2:816).

When they saw his condition, they were overwhelmed and joined him in a week of silent mourning before they began to speak (v. 13). They were moved to tears because of the condition of their friend Job.

No doubt the week of silent mourning allowed time for the friends to contemplate possible causes of Job's catastrophes as they witnessed his physical agony and inner despair. Previously in 1:20-21, Job had responded by participating in some outward expressions of mourning by tearing his robe, shaving his head and sitting on the ground. But unlike these three friends, Job did not throw **dust** or ashes on his head. Instead he worshiped God and did not blame Him.

II. First Round of Speeches between Job and His Three Friends (3:1–14:22)

A. Job Laments His Condition (3:1-26)

3:1-4. Totally distraught with his condition, Job started to lash out at his existence. Cracks started to develop at this point in his physical, emotional, and spiritual stamina. He began as a sterling example of dealing with personal disasters, but as the intensity of the tests increased, Job began to doubt, and he started to target God. In lament fashion he bemoaned (1) his conception and the night he was conceived in the womb (vv. 2-10); (2) his birthday and wondered why he did not die the moment he was born (vv. 11-15); and (3) that he was not miscarried at some point during his mother's pregnancy (vv. 16-19).

Job began his lament by **curs[ing] the day of his birth**, literally "the day" (v. 1). He did not curse God, as Satan had hoped and his wife had advised him to do. His wish was that the day on which he was born could have been blotted off the calendar. He even went back farther in time to bemoan the night of his conception, personifying the night as announcing the gender of the child who was conceived (v. 3). By wishing that **God above** would **not**... **care for it** (v. 4), Job was saying that perhaps if God did not take notice of the day of Job's birth, perhaps He would not take notice of Job now in his suffering.

3:5-10. These verses draw heavily on the image of darkness, to which Job referred five times. The word "blackness" is a *hapax legomenon* meaning the darkness that results from an event in nature that darkens the sky, such an eclipse or a tornado. In v. 7, Job continued his strong lament by wishing that his mother had gone barren on the night he was conceived. The **Leviathan** (v. 8) was a seven-headed sea monster in ancient Near Eastern mythology (although some commentators believe it referred to a crocodile of the Nile River). The mythological understanding fits the context better, since the Leviathan was believed to swallow the sun or moon, thus causing the darkness that would occur in an eclipse, for example. Job was not expressing his belief in mythology, but simply using a common idea of his day to illustrate his desire for the day of his birth to be swallowed up and disappear. Because the womb of Job's mother did open at his conception, he was forced to see trouble rather than having it hidden from his eyes (v. 10).

3:11-19. Job continued to pour out his complaint, wondering why he was not stillborn. Short of this, he also lamented that he had been welcomed as a newborn. The question, **why did the knees receive me?** (v. 12) could refer to his mother taking him in her lap, or the patriarchal custom of placing a newborn on his father's knees as a symbol of the child's acceptance (cf. Gn 48:12; Zuck, *Job*, 25). Job continued by saying that he could have achieved the same goal of death if only his mother had not nursed him (v. 12). Job was so distraught that he felt it would have been even better had he been a **miscarriage** at some point during his mother's pregnancy (vv. 16-19). Either way, Job could have enjoyed **rest** in the grave.

3:20-26. Job's lament differed significantly from the wise counsel for which he was known in the east. As he questioned, **Why is light given to him who suffers, and life to the bitter of soul?** (v. 20) he obviously longed to die. This was the third "Why?" question in Job's lament (the first two were in vv. 11-12). Job's remorse was, **For what I fear comes upon me** (v. 25). The translation "For the thing which I greatly feared" (KJV) looks backward, possibly to the beginning of Job's trials, as the news of one loss spurred his fear of the next one. The NASB translation used points to Job's present suffering, which seems to better fit the context.

B. Eliphaz Delivers His First Speech (4:1–5:27)

4:1-2. Eliphaz is identified as a **Temanite** (4:1). Teman was an important city in Edom, known as a center of wisdom studies (Jr 49:7; cf. Jb 6:18-20; Is 21:14; Jr 25:23; and Ob 8-10). He addressed Job's turmoil and immediately confronted Job's conclusions. He attempted to clear the air and to counter Job's thinking. In fact, he said, **But who can refrain from speaking?** (Jb 4:2b). After a week of silently observing, Eliphaz said he could not refrain from speaking even if he so desired. He had come to some conclusions of his own to present to Job. Bullock says, "[Eliphaz's] basic contribution to the dialogue was probably the universal principle that he propounded: the universe operates according to the law of cause-effect (4:7-11). . . . A second principle put forth by Eliphaz was that suffering may be viewed as the chastisement of God with the purpose of correction and healing (5:17-18)" (*An Introduction to the Old Testament Poetic Books*, 90–91).

4:3-11. Eliphaz was most likely the oldest of Job's three visitors, since he spoke first; protocol of the day would demand it, in fact. He reminded Job of the wisdom and excellent counsel for which Job was known, while helping so many people in the past (vv. 3-4). However, now that tremendous misery had come on him, Job failed to take the counsel he had given to others. He was **impatient** and **dismayed** (v. 5). Often it is easier to give good advice than to apply the same advice to personal issues and problems. Eliphaz reminded Job that his **fear of God** should be his **confidence** (v. 6; see Pr 9:10).

Again, where had Eliphaz acquired his theological information? The book of Job gives evidence of passed-down theological truths or theology in general. One needs to remember that Job, Job's wife, Eliphaz, Bildad, Zophar, Elihu, and Job's extended family and society, as far as is known, were not trained theologians as one would understand today. However, Job was a patriarchal priest for his household, sacrificing animals to cover and deal with human sin. This too is seen in the lives of Abraham, Isaac, Jacob, and later in the Israelite nation (Alden, *Job*, 89).

Then Eliphaz affirmed that the **innocent** do not perish and **the upright** are not **destroyed** (v. 7). The implications were that because Job was suffering intensely, surely he was not innocent of sin, and that God was angry with him (v. 9). Since people reap what they sow, Job was suffering the consequences of some wrongdoing (vv. 7-11). Gordis states, "Undoubtedly, Eliphaz, the most dignified and urbane of the friends, is the profoundest spirit among them; his intense religious convictions have not robbed him of sympathy for the distraught and suffering Job" (*The Book of God and Man*, 77). Eliphaz had a mechanical view of sin and punishment. So, since severity of sin is balanced with severity of punishment, there is no answer for Job's situation other than some truth known only by God or based on what was the view of retribution in the ancient Near East (Alden, *Job,* 85–86). Eliphaz posed the problem in a rhetorical question, "If you are blameless, should you not have **confidence** and **hope**?" (v. 6). Eliphaz said Job was like a lion dying for lack of food (vv. 10-11).

4:12-21. Claiming some kind of an unusual encounter, Eliphaz lapsed into an eerie report that his answer came as a faint **whisper** in a night vision when a **spirit** approached him and said, **Can mankind be just before God? Can a man be pure before his Maker?** (v. 17). Alden notes, "The dreamer from Teman continued to detail the picture of his eerie vision. Lacking the words 'goose pimples,' Eliphaz described the same phenomenon with the rare word 'stood on end' [v. 16], a term that occurs elsewhere only in Ps 119:20" (*Job, 87)*. Also, humans are less reliable than God's **angels** (v. 18). When Eliphaz referred to dust in v. 19, it is likely he acquired the information to connect dust with the Maker of man and the habitation of man, not to mention the material the Maker used to create man, from Genesis (Gn 2:7). Even angels, God's servants (possibly fallen angels and Satan), are not perfect, so certainly humans are perishable and **die, yet without wisdom** (v. 21).

Zuck comments on Eliphaz's dream: "Are the words from Eliphaz's dream true? Yes, in one sense. Man by himself cannot be righteous and pure before God; God charges man with sin more so than the angels; and man is mortal, easily perishing. However, Eliphaz seems to be wrong in applying those words to Job as if he were a willful sinner. To say 'The reason you are perishing, Job, is that you are mortal and unclean; there is no hope for you' runs counter to God's evaluation of Job's character (1:1, 8–2:3)" (*Job*, 33–34).

5:1-16. Eliphaz continued his diatribe against Job by hinting that he was a fool (vv. 2-3) who could not count on intervention by the angels. He then "mercilessly reminded Job of his calamities by speaking of the loss of his children and the marauding of his wealth" in vv. 4-5 (Zuck, *Job*, 34). Job was born for **affliction** (v. 6); therefore, he needed to **seek God** (v. 8) about his tragedies because He assists and answers the helpless (the **lowly**, those who **mourn**, v. 11, and **the poor**, v. 15). However, God deals with **the shrewd** and **the wise** (vv. 12-13) by confounding their schemes and cleverness.

Verse 7, **For man is born for trouble, as sparks fly upward**, has occasioned discussion among commentators. If it is simply a statement of the human condition as imperfect beings born in an imperfect world, then it is incongruous with Eliphaz's view that people bring trouble on themselves by their own actions, not as a consequence of their environment (Bullock, *An Introduction to the Old Testament Poetic Books*, 91). Bullock favors the view that Eliphaz was quoting a popular, pessimistic view of life that he himself did not believe; thus the idea of the verse is, "Some people say, 'Man is born ...'" (Bullock, *An Introduction to the Old Testament Poetic Books*, 91). Zuck agrees that the verse teaches that man brings trouble on himself by his sin, but adds that it is only "a partial truth," citing Jesus' statement in Lk 13:4 that people killed by the falling tower "were no more sinful that the survivors" (*Job*, 34).

Concerning Jb 5:13, Alden points out, "This is the only quotation from Jb in the New Testament (with the possible exception of Job 41:11 in Romans 11:35), quoted in 1Co 3:19" (*Job,* 94). The apostle Paul referred to Jb 5:13 when he concluded that the wisdom of the world will not open the door for salvation. In fact the wisdom of the world will turn a person not to God but to arrogant pride.

5:17-27. Eliphaz warned Job not to **despise the discipline of the Almighty** (v. 17). The Hebrew word for the "Almighty" is *Shaddai*. As Walter C. Kaiser Jr. writes, "In the book of Job, *El Shaddai* is used some thirty times beginning in (5:17), and was used frequently in Genesis as a description of the God of the patriarchs [Gn 28:3; 41:14; 48:3; 49:25]. This is not unexpected, for the prologue and epilogue ... have such clear credentials for placing the events of Job in the patriarchal era" (*Toward an Old Testament Theology* [Grand Rapids, MI: Zondervan, 1978], 97).

Eliphaz's advice to Job to endure God's chastening instead of despising it (v. 17) was based on the mistaken assumption that Job's troubles resulted from God's discipline for Job's sin. Therefore, Eliphaz's counsel in v. 18, that Job should admit his guilt so that God could give him **relief** and **heal** him, was also incorrect.

According to Eliphaz, Job needed to remember that if he would acknowledge his sin, he would have security and need have no fear that God would heal Job's **wounds**, deliver him from **famine**, **war**, **violence**, and abuse by wild **beasts of the field** (vv. 18-23). Job would also enjoy security, many **descendants**, and the **full vigor** of life (vv. 24-27). Eliphaz used the picture of a plentiful harvest to explain to Job how he would come to **the grave** in **vigor** (v. 26), "old . . . and full of days" (42:17), if he would only admit to his sin.

Eliphaz summarized his first discourse in v. 27. He was saying, "Friend Job, we have examined the situation, and what we are saying is true" (Alden, *Job,* 97). All of this blessing and healing assumed, of course, that Job would seek God (v. 8).

C. Job Responds to Eliphaz's Charges (6:1–7:21)

6:1-13. Job's reply to Eliphaz's charges included a prayer to God (7:7-21) that He would forgive Job before he died from his troubles. Job actually began his reply by restating his complaint and defending the rightness of his position. He disagreed with Eliphaz, and saw his life miserably coming to an end.

Job's **grief** was so heavy it was like **sand** (vv. 2-3). He defended his **rash** words (the complaint of chap. 3) by saying that they were nothing compared to the heavy weight of his grief. He perceived that the Almighty's terrors were like poison **arrows** in him (v. 4). Job said he would not be complaining if he had no problem. When a donkey or ox has food, it does not bray (v. 5), so unlike them, Job is complaining with reason. His afflictions have caused him to lose his taste for life (vv. 6-7), which was now as unsatisfying as unseasoned or bland food, such as **the white of an egg**. "Figuratively speaking, Job found the meal that God served so unpalatable that he refused it altogether. The motif of food that began in v. 4 concludes here with Job's total rejection of the menu. It made him sick (Jb 6:7; Ps 41:1-4)" (Alden, *Job,* 99).

In vv. 8-9, Job expressed the desire that God answer his prayer by killing him (**crush me . . . and cut me off**). Even though Job believed he had **not denied the words of the Holy One** (v. 10), he felt no strength. Zuck notes, "If God would let [Job] die, freeing him from life, Job would have one point of consolation, namely, that he did not deny God's words" (*Job,* 37). Job also felt that no **help** or **deliverance** from his problems was forthcoming (v. 13). Eliphaz might have thought that Job was made out of **stones** and **bronze** so as not to feel suffering, but it was not true. To the contrary, as Alden adds concerning v. 9, "Like Moses (Nm 11:15) and Elijah (1Kg 19:4), Job wished to die" (*Job,*100). The Hebrew expressions "crush" and "cut off" (Jb 6:9) often served as metaphors for death.

6:14-30. Job used the important Hebrew word translated **kindness**, or loyal love—the kind of loyal love and faithfulness God shows to His people—to describe the kind of response he expected **from his friend**. Bullock observes, "Outside of our Lord's own bitter loneliness during His passion, there must be no keener sense of having been forsaken by one's friends expressed in Scripture than here" (*An Introduction to the Old Testament Poetic Books,* 91).

Job compared his friends to a desert **wadi** (a dry river bed in the summer when water was needed most) instead of a freshwater river. They **acted deceitfully** by pretending to help him while offering no real help, or even loyalty to him in his suffering (v. 15). Just as travelers look forward to getting water for themselves and their animals but are sadly **disappointed** when they find the wadis dry (vv. 17-20), so now his friends were disappointing him. He challenged them to show him where he had **erred** (v. 24), and even said he could stand the pain of **honest words** if only his friends would speak them to him (v. 25). Instead, they sought to reprove his words because they considered them worth only to blow away in **the wind** (v. 26).

Despite Eliphaz's assertion that trouble comes about only as a result of sin, Job urged his friends, **Now please look at me, and see if I lie to your face** (v. 28). It would take a particular type of bald-faced liar to do that to his friends, and Job invited his friends to search his face for any trace of falsehood.

Assuming that they would find no such evidence, Job called on them to **desist** (v. 29) in their accusations—that is, to change their minds and the approach they were taking of accusing him of wrongdoing. **Is there injustice on my tongue? Cannot my palate discern calamities?** (v. 30) was Job's way of saying that he would know before anyone else if his sufferings were justified. Of course, as far as he was concerned they were not, and so he did not expect a reply from his friends.

7:1-19. Starting to lose hope, Job returned to his bitter complaint as he dealt with the agony of his boil-type disease. He had devalued his existence to a state of futility and worthlessness, referring to himself as a **hired man** and a **slave** (vv. 1-2) who had been given **months of vanity** (v. 3). He was suffering terribly (v. 5), and he viewed his short life as **swifter than a weaver's shuttle** (v. 6). Consumed in misery, he believed he would not experience any benefits again (v. 7). Since his time on earth appeared short at hand, like a mere **breath** (v. 7) and a **cloud** (v. 9), Job asked why God was constantly guarding him as if he were **the sea monster** (v. 12), a reference to the common ancient Near Eastern mythological beliefs held by the Canaanites and their northern counterparts in Lebanon. As Alden notes,

> As in 3:8 Job again alluded to characters in popular mythology. "The sea," *yam*, was personalized and deified by second millennium BC Canaanites at Ugarit. The terms "monster of the deep" (Heb. *tannin*), Leviathan (Ugaritic *Lotan*; cf. 3:8; Ps 74:13-14; Is 27:1), and Rahab [not the harlot of Jericho] (9:13; 26:12; Is 51:9) were also mythological sea deities. According to the Ugaritic myth, *Yam* was the boisterous opponent whom Baal captured. Job protested that he was not such an unruly foe that he needed constant guarding. (*Job*, 111)

Job would not be silent even though he was having terrible nightmares, saying to God, **You frighten me with dreams and terrify me by visions** (v. 14). In his view, his death was impending. As a cloud can seem to disappear in the sky because of the intensity of the wind or sun, Job connected that observation with his apparent near demise (cf. 7:9 with 10:21 and 16:22). He would rather die than continue in his pains (7:15). God would not leave him alone long enough to **swallow** his saliva (v. 19), that is, for a mere second. When he is dead, he said, God will look for him but he **will not be** (v. 21).

7:20-21. Observing that he was physically wearing away, Job pondered whether he had sinned and why God had made him His **target**. Job mentioned the three classic categories of wrongdoing: sin, **transgression**, and **iniquity**. As noted in the comments on Jb 2:10, the word "sin" is *chata'*, which means "miss, go wrong, sin, commit a mistake, miss the mark" (*BDB*, 306). "In Judges 20:16 the left-handed slingers of Benjamin are said to have the skill to throw stones at targets and 'not miss.' In a different context, Proverbs 19:2 speaks of a man in a hurry who 'misses his way.' A similar idea of not finding the goal appears in Proverbs 8:36; the concept of failure is implied" (Herbert G. Livingston, "*chata',*" in R. Laird Harris, Gleason L. Archer, and Bruce K. Waltke, TWOT, 277). By using this word, Job was asking God where he had missed the mark of what God wanted for him. "How have I failed to miss the way you wanted me to go?" might be one way to state Job's perplexity.

The word **transgression** is *pesha'*, or "rebellion." The root idea is a breach of relationships between two parties. The noun denotes a person who rejects God's authority by rebelling against it. This word suggests the need for reconciliation to remedy the rebellion. "[A]s far as God is concerned, there are two ways the rebellion may be ended; it may end with punishment or the renewal of the relationship (Livingston, "*chata',*" 743)." Job did not use **transgression** in a question (7:21). Instead, he was saying, "God, if I have rebelled against You, why have You not forgiven me?" As Zuck states the issue, "Why all the big the fuss about a little sin—if I have even sinned at all?" (*Job*, 42).

Job's third word for sin (v. 21) is *'awon*, or "iniquity." The noun form used here refers to "infraction, crooked behavior, perversion, iniquity, etc. . . . *'awon* is definitely not a trait of God's character nor of his dealing with man . . . but it is an overwhelming trait of man's character and actions, including consequences of those actions" (Carl Schultz, "*'awon,*" TWOT, 650). Although Job was not aware of committing iniquity, any more than he was aware of missing the mark or rebelling against God, he asked why God had not forgiven and removed his **iniquity** and its guilt.

Job wondered if he had violated all three categories of sin at once. Or had he crossed an invisible line into an unknown category of sin? He was disillusioned by the growing influence of evil on his life, his family, his reputation, his work, and his theology. In asking, **Have I sinned?** (v. 20), Job was grappling with the massive issue of sin. What is sin? Is it negative actions, negative thinking, the absence of good, the lack of education, the lack of understanding? Is it simply a human issue? Is sin an issue people can deal with strictly on a human level? Very simply, sin is any thinking or activity that is contrary to the character of God and the boundaries He has established.

D. Bildad Delivers His First Speech (8:1-22)

8:1-14. Job ended his lament in chap. 7 with the statement, "For now I will lie down in the dust; and You will seek me, but I will not be" (v. 21). His complaint and questioning of God brought a stinging rebuke from one of his visiting friends, **Bildad**, who is identified as **a Shuhite** (v. 1). In cuneiform tablets, an area near the Euphrates River is called Suhu. Some see Bildad as a member of the tribe named for Shuah, the son of Abraham and Keturah (Gn

25:2). Bildad addressed Job's turmoil and responded in a much harsher tone and attitude than did Eliphaz.

As did Eliphaz, Bildad believed that a person's calamities result from his or her sins. Bildad also echoed Eliphaz in saying that Job might be able to recover from his woes if only he would acknowledge his sin. But in contrast to Eliphaz's appeal to personal experience ("I have seen," 4:8) and his dream (4:12-21), Bildad appealed to the experience of previous generations in this speech. And while Eliphaz began his first speech with a question that was "soft and courteous . . . Bildad's opening query was blunt and discourteous" (Zuck, *Job*, 43).

Bildad directly stated that Job harbored perverted ideas about God's justice, for apparently his children got what they deserved (vv. 1-4). Bildad was angry at Job's insistence on his innocence, his expressed frustration with his three friends, and his statements that God was hounding him despite his lack of wrongdoing. Bildad was also apparently upset that Job had rejected Eliphaz's gentle rebuke. He characterized Job's defense to Eliphaz in chaps. 6–7, as just a **mighty wind** (v. 2) producing nothing of value. In v. 3, Bildad strongly argued that if Job's accusations about God were true, then that would make God unjust since He would be afflicting one who did not deserve it (cf. 40:8). The only explanation for the death of Job's children was that God **delivered them into the power of their transgression** (v. 4)—a charge that must have wounded Job deeply. But as far as Bildad was concerned, if God is God as presented by Job and his friends in this theological debate, then the only conclusion anyone could come to was that Job must be the one who is wrong.

Bildad then confronted Job, maintaining that *his* sin had to be the cause of the death of his children. Alden notes, "The most cruel and least tactful part of Bildad's confrontation is just a restatement of the basic theology of retribution that the three friends held to so tenaciously" (*Job*, 116). Bildad told Job to **seek God** and if he did, God would restore his **estate** (vv. 5-7). Bildad also encouraged Job to seek the sound wisdom of **past generations** (v. 8) and not to forget it because one's life is like a mere **shadow** (v. 9). Bildad directed Job to consider a body of truth handed down from former generations. Apparently Bildad believed that truth and wisdom were not limited to their generation. His statement that Job would learn from past generations by studying the **words from their minds** may have been Bildad's way of "sarcastically hinting that Job's words were from his mouth only [v. 2] and not from his mind" (Zuck, *Job*, 44).

These statements by Bildad also help to place these events in history. They reflect what Alden calls "well-established, long-held wisdom," and adds, "While former generations have passed away, their accumulated wisdom remains, and to that old wisdom Bildad made his appeal" (*Job*, 118–19). Bildad seems to have had Job in mind when he referred to all who **forget God** and are **godless**. They are like a **papyrus** plant withering **without water** (vv. 11-13). The confidence of such people is as **fragile** as a **spider's web** (v. 14).

8:15-22. Job had no respite from Bildad's accusations. The latter said the wicked person **trusts in his house, but it does not stand**—perhaps suggesting that Job was trusting in his estate as his confidence. Bildad also suggested that Job was like a thriving plant that was then uprooted (vv. 16-18), to be replaced by other plants (v. 19). But God honors people of **integrity** (v. 20). If Job were to repent, God would enable him to laugh and the wicked would be abolished (vv. 21-22).

E. Job Responds to Bildad's Charges (9:1–10:22)

9:1-12. Now it was Job's turn to respond to Bildad's withering attack. Despite the searing nature of the latter's charges against him, Job replied, **I know that this is so**, that is, that evil people are cut off from before God (v. 2). "All bad things that happened to the world or to people were viewed as expressions of God's anger" (Alden, *Job*, 127). Job and his friends initially assumed that God always punishes evil. But knowing this, the question for Job was, **But how can a man be in the right before God?** Eliphaz had asked virtually the same question in his first speech: "Can mankind be just before God? Can a man be pure before his Maker?" (Jb 4:17). Job's dilemma was that even if he had his "day in court" before God, there was no answer he could give to the One who could remove **mountains**, shake the **earth**, and command **the sun not to shine** (vv. 3-7).

Furthermore, Job argued that since God created the constellations, how would he even know if God passed by him, or how could he know if it was God's voice since He is so powerful that He created **the Bear, Orion and the Pleiades** (v. 9; cf. 38:31-33). Later in biblical history the prophet

Amos affirmed that it was God who made the Pleiades and Orion (Am 5:8). S. C. Hunter noted, "The writer of the book of Job seemed to have a surprising familiarity with celestial matters" ("Bible Astronomy," *Popular Astronomy* 2 [1912]: 288). As Alden points out, "All these references to the world around—sun, stars, sea, heaven, and earth—attest to Job's monotheism. Unlike the neighbors of ancient Israel, who attributed each of these domains to separate deities, Job and all the Bible's authors believed that God alone was responsible for their creation and regulation" (*Job*, 125). In chaps. 9 and 10 Job defended his conclusions to Bildad by noting God's magnitude in creation (W. D. Reyburn, *A Handbook on the Book of Job* [New York: United Bible Society, 1992], 781–83).

In v. 10, Job again recalled the words of Eliphaz, quoting almost verbatim the latter's statement concerning God, Who **does great and unsearchable things, wonders without number** (Jb 5:9 HCSB). Job asked, "In the face of a God like this, whose power is unfathomable, and who does whatever He pleases, how could I possibly expect to win my case against Him?"

9:13-24. Job described God's power as being so great that He conquered **the helpers of Rahab** (v. 13; cf. Ps 89:10; Is 51:9). This reference is to a sea monster in Babylonian myth who was defeated by Marduk, who then captured her helpers (Zuck, *Job*, 48). **Rahab** is another name for Leviathan, the sea monster of Jb 7:12. God's power is so great that He can defeat all the forces of evil, real or mythical.

How, then, could Job expect to present a case before such an Almighty (and seemingly aloof) God and expect to even be heard, much less vindicated? Job realized his only hope was to throw himself on the mercy of his **judge**, regardless of the merits of his plea that he was, after all, **right** in his claim of innocence (vv. 14-16). Job was not confident that God would listen to him, even if He called on Job to speak. As Zuck notes, "God is so overwhelming, Job argued, that he was afraid he would become confused and witness against himself (9:20)!" (Zuck, *Job*, 49). Job's **righteous** position would count for nothing in the court of heaven.

There was only one understandable conclusion from Job's standpoint: God destroys the **guiltless** with the **wicked**, even though that seems to be a great theological contradiction (v. 22). Alden notes, "'Innocent/blameless' and 'wicked' are words laced throughout this portion of Job's complaint (vv. 20-24). The two are opposites, but not to God, fretted Job (cf. Matt 5:45). They are one and the same. . . . That God destroys the wicked would be affirmed by Job's friends, but that he treats the godless and the godly alike is what separated Job's position from theirs (cf. Mal 3:18)" (*Job*, 130).

9:25-35. Sensing his life was slipping away (vv. 25-26), Job resolved to try to forget his troubled circumstances. But he knew this would be useless because his pain would make him sad again, and he knew that God would not **acquit** him (vv. 27-28). Job longed for an **umpire** to arbitrate between God and himself in a **court** (v. 33). Walter C. Kaiser Jr. maintains that this is the first hint of messianic expectation in Job. A mediator between God and a human being could not be a mere mortal but had to be divine. "One can see the logic building for some person who will be no less than the Son of God if he is to bridge the gulf created by this situation" (Walter C. Kaiser, *The Messiah in the Old Testament* [Grand Rapids, MI: Zondervan, 1995], 62). And as Alden adds,

> Job also used other terms to describe his need for someone to come to his aid: "arbitrator" (9:33); "witness, advocate," (6:19); "intercessor, friend," (16:20); and, "redeemer" (19:25). The Christian reader of these passages cannot help but think that the one Job sought for has come to us in Jesus Christ (Compare Lk 1:74; Rm 7:24; Gl 1:4; 2Tm 4:18; 2Pt 2:9). (Alden, *Job*, 136–37)

This section emphasizes Job's struggle with understanding the reason for his suffering. As Smick notes, "the text hints at some unknown reason for Job's suffering above and beyond the dispute over Job's motives described in the prologue. . . . Neither Job's friends nor his readers are truly able to access fully the reason for his suffering" ("Job," 263). Ancient and modern-day believers in the Lord must remember that suffering serves a spiritual purpose. At times, God chooses to bring believers to spiritual maturity through suffering, to help strengthen their integrity toward Him. Paul testified to this when he declared, after asking God three times to remove his "thorn in the flesh" . . . "Most gladly, therefore, I will rather boast about my weaknesses, so that the power of Christ may dwell in me" (2Co 12:7, 9).

Yet, at other times God permits suffering to bring glory to Himself. The blind man of Jn 9 illustrates this truth. To the disciples' Job-like question, "Who sinned, this man or his parents, that he would be born blind?" (v. 2), Jesus replied, "It was neither that this man sinned, nor his parents; but it was so that the works of God might be displayed in him" (v. 3). The ultimate explanations for suffering are in God's hands.

10:1-7. Job pleaded with God to tell him why He was contending with him in this severe manner, because based on Job's knowledge of the true God, he had not changed his lifestyle or relationship since the time when he abundantly prospered—and God knew that (v. 7).

Therefore, Job challenged God with a series of questions in an attempt to discover why God was afflicting him. Job's first question implied that God was acting unjustly by punishing Job, whom He had created, while looking favorably on the schemes of evil men (v. 3). Perhaps God was even acting like a finite human being, like someone who was limited in his lifespan and knowledge and so had nothing to go on but the **eyes of flesh** and **the days of a mortal** (vv. 4-6). Job accused God of knowing that he was **not guilty** of any behavior worthy of such calamity, and yet Job experienced **no deliverance from [God's] hand** (v. 7).

10:8-17. Job reflected on the marvels of how God fashioned him in the womb and **made** him from **clay** and **dust** (cf. Gn 2–3). Yet, God also seemed intent on destroying this marvelous work of His hands. Why would God create Job so intricately only to destroy him (v. 8)? Job reminded God that He made Job out of the dust into a **clay** pot. Was it God's plan to smash Job **into dust again?** (v. 9). The questions continued in vv. 10-11 as Job described his creation by God's hand. Job also remembered how God showed him **lovingkindness** (lit., "loyal love," v. 12).

But it seemed that all the while, even from the moment of Job's creation, God had planned the calamities that befell Job—and therefore, Job felt that he was justified in holding God accountable for his suffering. He proposed that perhaps it made no difference with God whether he was **wicked** or **righteous** (v. 15). He felt that God opposed him **like a lion**, showing Job His **power** and **anger**. Not only that, but even if Job were given his day in court, God would gather more **witnesses** against him and only become angrier with him. No wonder Job felt as if he was experiencing one **hardship after** another (vv. 16-17).

10:18-22. Job's despair was such that he digressed to the complaint in his original lament, "Why did I not die at birth?" (Jb 3:11). It would have been better for him if he had been carried **from womb to tomb** (v. 19b). Since his days were so few and so miserable, Job wondered why God would not leave him alone so that he might have a few moments of **cheer** before he returned to **the land of darkness and deep shadow** (death, vv. 21-22). Frustrated by his frailty, Job slowly drifted into being a poor example of dealing with catastrophe. He used a series of words "to depict the horrible prospect of death, which is envisioned by Job as better than life with its miseries. . . . Thus far, each of Job's speeches has ended on a gloomy note, with reference to death (3:21-22; 7:21; 10:21-22)" (Zuck, *Job*, 52).

F. Zophar Delivers His First Speech (11:1-20)

Zophar, the third friend who had sat with Job for a week, was the next to speak. He was even more blunt than Bildad, brushing off Job's claims to innocence as against what Zophar considered to be common sense, and implying that Job was an idiot for trying to understand God's ways (11:12). Alden uses a series of adjectives to describe Zophar's invective: "He was impetuous, tactless, direct, [and] unsympathetic," although he also notes that Zophar's first speech "is "not altogether without some contribution to make to the friends' case" (*Job*, 141).

11:1-12. Zophar is identified as a **Naamathite** from a tribe whose identity is unknown, but was probably in the east. He addressed Job's turmoil and responded, as noted above, very caustically. He also had some added warnings for Job.

Even though Zophar's speech would be blunt and pointed, he maintained that he had not planned to speak until Job's foolish outpouring of words compelled him to speak up. Zophar was angry because Job had scoffed at the rebukes of Eliphaz and Bildad, and because Job insisted that he was blameless and deserved to be **acquitted** before God (v. 3). Someone had to answer Job and defend his friends—and presumably, defend God.

Zophar confronted Job as being guilty and not **innocent** as he claimed (v. 4). The problem, in his opinion, was that Job was trying to justify himself by evaluating his situation only with human wisdom. Zophar wished that God would, in fact, speak to Job, for His words would condemn rather than vindicate Job (v. 5), so proving the rightness of his friends' claim that he was guilty of some sin. Zophar was certain that if God revealed to Job **the secrets of wisdom**, Job would see how foolish and wrong he was.

Zophar pointed out that **sound wisdom has two sides** (v. 6), and Job knew only the human side of wisdom, what can be seen and known by finite beings. But there is another side of wisdom that only God knows, that which is hidden to the eyes of men. God's wisdom is so inscrutable that for mankind to try and fathom it is utterly fruitless. God's wisdom reaches to and goes far beyond every known limit (vv. 7-9). God is so immense that Job would be frustrated in trying to discern the Infinite. In fact in God's omniscience, **He knows false men** and sees their **iniquity**, and Zophar implied that Job was among them (vv. 10-11). Then Zophar added insult to injury with his sarcastic proverb that implied that Job was an **idiot**.

11:13-19. Leaving his harsh language aside, Zophar counseled Job along much the same lines as his other friends (vv. 13-19): Repent if you have sinned and you will enjoy God's favor once again. His troubles would end, and his life would be bright (cheerful) without **darkness** (troubles). People would even **entreat [Job's] favor**, as they had no doubt done before Job's troubles came. Bullock says, "As hopeless as Job appeared to Zophar . . . he had an appropriate admonition couched in conditional language . . . holding forth hope to Job as had the other two members of the friendly trilogy" (*An Introduction to the Old Testament Poetic Books*, 95).

11:20. But like Bildad, who ended his first speech by warning, "The tent of the wicked will be no longer" (8:22), Zophar also ended his speech with a stern warning to Job. If he continued in sin, he would die soon.

In the postflood and postBabel era, a strict cause-and-effect relationship between sin and judgment probably became the normal way of explaining havoc in a person's life. Job's friends were convinced that this explained that Job's suffering was God's punishment for his sin. Elmer Smick succinctly points out, "A superficial acquaintance with the dialogues of the book of Job will convince anyone that Job and his friends were theologically somewhat confused especially in the matter of theodicy" ("Mythology in the Book of Job," JETS 13 [1970]: 101). A major issue for Job, based on his prior walk before God, was that he could not identify any sin(s) that would warrant such devastation in his life—if God was truly punishing him in a cause-and-effect manner, as his friends were suggesting.

Job's three friends have had their initial say, and all three came to the same conclusions. Job had obviously committed some grievous sin to bring such chastisement from God, who punishes only wrongdoers. If Job would simply admit his sin instead of futilely protesting his innocence and charging God with injustice, his suffering would end and he would be restored to his former estate. Eliphaz appealed to a dream he had; Bildad pointed to the wisdom of their forefathers in ages past; and Zophar argued from the basis of God's infinite wisdom. These were hard to refute; as Zuck says, "Who could refute someone else's dream? Who could argue with forefathers who are no longer alive? Who could debate with the infinite wisdom of God Himself?" (*Job*, 55).

G. Job Responds to Zophar's Charges (12:1–14:22)

But as chaps. 12–14 reveal, Job was not ready to be silenced. Instead, he began his reply with a severe criticism of their ideas. This section divides into two parts: 12:1–13:19 is addressed to the three friends; 13:20–14:22 is addressed to God. This response is longer, but as Alden points out, "[T]he issues Job raised are essentially the same. Large sections deal with exceptions to the generalized rules of retributive theology, with God's sovereignty over the world, and with complaints addressed to God because Job received no hearing and would rather die than live" (*Job*, 148).

12:1-6. Several times Job asked God to show him his sin (6:24; 10:2; 13:23). Now, in 12:2, Job demonstrated that he was capable of some sarcasm of his own. He mocked his friends' counsel by saying, in effect, "It is obvious that all of the world's wisdom resides in you three. What a shame that wisdom will perish from the earth when you die!" Verse 3 shows the reason for Job's biting comment. He was not about to let his friends get away with implying that he was **inferior** to them in **intelligence** (even stupid, cf. 11:12). He already knew **such things as these** (v. 3), so they were not enlightening him on anything about the universe or God's dealings with humanity. Yet Job was like a joke to them, even though he was **just and blameless** (v. 4). Job chided his counselors further by saying how easy it is for those who are **at ease** to look with **contempt** on the person who is suffering **calamity** (v. 5)—an allusion to their charge that evil comes only to those who have sinned. But Job said that assumption does not square with the facts because there were **destroyers**, or "robbers," who prospered despite their evildoing.

12:7-12. Verses 7-8 may be addressed to Zophar. Zuck suggests that Job's reference to learning from animals, the earth, and fish was in reply to Zophar's insulting comment that Job was "being more stupid than a wild donkey (11:12)" (*Job*, 56). Job even suggested that these "witnesses" were smarter than Zophar, because even the animals and the earth itself knew that God had brought about his turmoil (v. 9) and that wisdom was resident in God, though His actions sometimes seem paradoxical. Verse 12 appears to contradict what Job had been arguing, since he accused his three **aged** friends with lacking **wisdom**. Job may have been expressing sarcasm or quoting his friends' own words back to them.

12:13-25. God's control over the earth and everyone on it refutes the claim of Job's friends that He always acts in predictable ways. God's **wisdom . . . might . . . counsel . . . and understanding** are beyond dispute (v. 13). Both the deceived and the deceiver are under His control (v. 16). Yet God often acts in surprising ways. If Job's friends are correct, then wise leaders would always be rewarded. Yet "God, it seems, delights in undoing human doings" (Alden, *Job*, 153). For example, He often reverses the roles of earthly leaders (including **counselors . . . judges . . . kings . . . priests . . . nobles** . . . and **chiefs**; vv. 17-25). God raised up nations and destroyed them, seemingly without a reason other than His sovereign choice. When He plunges nations and their leaders into **darkness**, they have no escape.

13:1-12. Job told his friends that they had yielded no new insights into his dilemma as he languished in terrible suffering. He repeated the claim he had made in 12:3, saying in v. 2, **What you know I also know; I am not inferior to you**. Not only was Job equal to them in knowledge, he wanted to bypass their advice altogether and take his case directly to God and **argue** with Him (v. 3). Job's friends had done nothing but **smear [him] with lies**; they were **worthless physicians** (in 16:2 he would call them "sorry comforters"), who only added to his suffering with their outright lies (v. 4). He urged them to be **silent** (v. 5), which would be the best demonstration of their **wisdom**. Job's admonition calls to mind the words of Pr 17:28, "Even a fool, when he keeps silent, is considered wise; when he closes his lips, he is considered prudent."

Job wanted his friends to keep silent so he could present his **argument**. He also urged them not to **show partiality for** God over against him. It was distressing enough for Job that his friends presumed to speak for God. But to do so using **unjust** and **deceitful** words, putting them on God's lips, as it were, was unconscionable (vv. 6-8). To Job, the proof of their deceit was that God would reprove and terrify them because their words of counsel were nothing but **proverbs of ashes** (v. 12). This was an ironic statement since Job was seated among the ashes. "Job correctly believed that it was wrong to use lies and false reasoning even in the service of truth" (Alden, *Job*, 157).

13:13-19. For a second time in this chapter Job asked his friends to **be silent** and let him present his argument (v. 13). He was willing to take his life in his hands by presenting his case before God and accepting whatever verdict God would decree, even if it meant his death (vv. 14-15). The first half of v. 15 is arguably the most famous statement in the entire book of Job: **Though he slay me, I will hope in Him**. It is a ringing affirmation, at least in most English translations—of Job's trust in God even if He puts Job to death.

But the Masoretic Hebrew text is uncertain, and there are two main possibilities for understanding this verse. The first option is just to translate the words of the Hebrew text literally: "Behold, He will slay me, I will *not* wait." The second and alternative translation is derived from an ancient marginal note in the Hebrew text, indicating that the word "not" should be read as "for Him." Moreover, the word "behold" could be alternatively translated as "although." These two factors yield the second option "Although He slay me, I will wait for Him."

In defense of the first option, Zuck argues that "Behold, He will slay me; I do not have hope" makes better sense in light of the preceding verse (*Job*, 61). Also, it can be argued that the alternate reading was merely the work of a pious scribe hoping to neutralize a problematic text (as noted by John E. Hartley, *The Book of Job*, NICOT [Grand Rapids, MI: Eerdmans, 1988], 221). As a result, Zuck explains the verse to mean that "Job fully anticipated that his self-defense would result in his being killed by God. But he was more concerned for maintaining justice than for maintaining his life" (*Job*, 61).

Nevertheless, the second possibility seems more likely for the following reasons: First, it can be argued that "though He slay me, yet I will wait for Him" can make perfect sense in the context. Second, the verb "wait" in the verse requires an object, i.e., for what is Job waiting or not waiting? This is resolved by accepting the Masoretic alternative reading, "I will wait *for Him.*" Further, this same Masoretic alternative reading is accepted with virtually no dispute in Is 63:9. Additionally, this reading was accepted by the ancient Targums, the Syriac, and the Vulgate. Hence, in this verse, despite Job's suffering, he is expressing confidence in both his own righteousness and God's justice (Francis I. Andersen, *Job: An Introduction and Commentary*, TOTC [Downers Grove, IL: InterVarsity, 1980], 166–67). Therefore, Alden maintains this statement is one of the "glimmers of hope and flashes of faith that punctuate these otherwise depressing chapters" [chaps. 12–14] (*Job*, 160).

Regardless, Job is determined to argue the innocence of his case before God regardless of the risk (13:15b). He expected to be vindicated rather than killed, because he knew that a **godless man** could not stand in God's **presence**. Therefore, Job pled a second time (v. 6) for his friends to **listen** to his argument (v. 17). He had carefully prepared his case to bring before God in court; he was confident of acquittal because no one could present a valid charge of wrongdoing against him. If God brought charges against Job, then and only then was he willing to accept a verdict of death (vv. 18-19).

13:20-28. Job's response changes the direction in v. 20, from his friends, Zophar in particular as the last speaker, to God Himself. Job was ready to appear before God to argue his case, but he requested first that God would remove His **hand** of punishment from Job, and not **terrify** him by His awesome presence (vv. 21-22). If Job was a sinner then, he reasoned, God should reveal his **iniquities** and **rebellion** and **sin** (v. 23; see discussion above of these terms at 7:20-21). He continued to be puzzled as to why it appeared that God considered him His enemy (v. 24). God's silence, especially in light of the way He was tormenting Job, was especially perplexing to Job since he was nothing more than a **driven leaf** and **dry chaff** (v. 25). Job was so frustrated that he even accused God of unjustly keeping a **bitter** record of his wrongs and punishing him for sins committed decades earlier. Job made no protest of innocence here, since he knew that he had not been sinless throughout his entire life. He felt like a prisoner in God's custody, locked up and watched carefully. The thought of it all caused Job to sink into despair (v. 28).

14:1-6. Job lamented that **man . . . is short-lived and full of turmoil**, living a very short time like a **flower** or **shadow** (vv. 1-2). More than that, Job felt himself under God's condemning gaze. In this situation, Job said he had no hope of being acquitted (v. 4). Man's existence is not only fleeting, but **his days are determined** beforehand by God so that when they are completed, he cannot live another day (v. 5). Given the brevity and frailty of man's existence, the best Job could hope for was that God would avert His **gaze**, or lift His hand of judgment, so that Job could find some rest before he was cut off the from the land of the living (v. 6).

14:7-17. The finality of death is the theme of these verses, although v. 14 seems to offer hope of life beyond the grave. Job mused that **a tree** that dies can **sprout again** and grow with access to some **water**, but if a **man dies . . . where is he?** (vv. 7-10). These verses suggest the permanence of death, as do vv. 11-12. Job's reference to **the heavens** being **no longer** may mean that he believed man would never **be aroused** from the grave, since the heavens were considered to be permanent (Zuck, *Job*, 65).

But with v. 13, it seems that Job was encouraged by a sudden thought: what if there were life after death? If that were possible, then Job would consider his time **in Sheol** (the grave) not as a permanent condition, but as a resting place until God's **wrath returns to** Him, or is lifted from him, and the limit of his days in death is reached, just as God had set a limit to his days on earth (v. 5).

This is the context in which Job asked the well-known question, **If a man dies, will he live again?** (v. 14). This is one of the ongoing philosophical and theological questions of humanity. Is the grave the end of human existence spiritually and/or physically? In modern society people often say, "When I die, they will put me in a hole in the ground, cover up the hole, and walk away and forget me." Is there life after death? In the midst of his catastrophe Job wrestled with the same question. Commentators are divided on whether 14:14 affirms a belief in resurrection (Alden, *Job*, 168), or whether Job was asking a question for which the book of Job provides no firm answer, or even a negative answer. An argument for the latter view is that after wondering about the possibility of resurrection, in vv. 18-22 Job proceeded to describe how God destroys human life (Bullock, *An Introduction to the Old Testament Poetic Books*, 96) and, in the process, also destroys **man's hope** (v. 19).

However, it is more likely that Job did indeed believe he was going to live beyond his earthly life. This is seen in his hope-filled statement that even though he struggled through life (the Hb. for **struggle** is "warfare"), he could go to the grave with hope because he would **wait until** his **change** came from God (v. 14), that is, he would wait to be resurrected. This hope led Job into what Zuck calls a "brief rhapsody of anticipated fellowship with God" (*Job*, 66) in vv. 15-17, anticipating the time when God would **long for** fellowship with Job, watching over him for good and not for calamity, and sealing up his **transgression** and **iniquity** to cover them from His sight.

14:18-22. However, for the present time it appeared to Job that God wanted to wear him down and **destroy** his **hope**. His body was still experiencing **pains**, and he mourned (like a crumbling **mountain** or **stones** worn away by **water) only for himself** with no one to comfort him.

III. Second Round of Speeches between Job and His Friends (15:1–21:34)

A. Eliphaz Delivers His Second Speech (15:1-35)

The second round of speeches by Job's three friends, and Job's response to each, occupy chaps. 15–21. For the most part, the three men repeated their earlier contention that sin was the reason for Job's suffering. Eliphaz's tone changed noticeably in his second speech (chap. 15). He abandoned any effort to be gracious toward Job and assaulted him immediately with a flurry of accusations. All three speeches are more abrasive, showing more intolerance toward Job for insisting he was innocent and refusing to repent. His friends were also disturbed by Job's bold challenge to God to prove His case against him. They used more insulting language and, interestingly, in this cycle they did not call for Job to repent and thus end God's heavy hand of seeming chastisement on his life.

15:1-6. Eliphaz began his second address to Job with a withering frontal attack, accusing Job of being nothing more than a windbag, filled with hot air like the **east wind** that blows in from the desert. Instead of speaking as a wise man, Job relied on **useless talk** and **words which are not profitable** (vv. 2-3). Even worse, Job's words were impious, without a proper respect (**reverence**) for God. Job spoke out of the **guilt** of his heart, relying on clever words instead of sincere speech (vv. 4-5). Eliphaz felt justified in this charge, since in his view Job had condemned himself with his own words. Like a triumphant prosecutor, Eliphaz felt all he had to do to prove his accusation was to point at Job the defendant and say, "There, you heard it for yourself from his own lips."

15:7-16. Eliphaz was disturbed that Job thought he alone had special access to the counsel and wisdom of God (vv. 7-9). Eliphaz attacked Job's presupposition that God knew he was innocent, and that Job was wasting his time talking to his friends when he ought to be addressing God himself (cf. 13:3). Eliphaz also assailed one of the foundations of Job's argument, by asking **What do you know that we do not know? What do you understand that we do not?** (v. 9). Twice Job had used the argument that he knew everything his friends knew, making him their equal in terms of wisdom (cf. 12:3; 13:2). But Eliphaz threw Job's assertion back in his face, accusing him of disdaining the counsel of his elders. Eliphaz even described his words as **the consolations of God** (v. 11) that he had spoken **gently** to Job—at least in his first speech.

However, instead of welcoming his rebuke as the message of God, Eliphaz said that Job had let his emotions get the best of him—causing his **eyes** to **flash** in anger, his **spirit** to turn **against God**, and mouth to pour out evil **words** (vv. 12-13). Then Eliphaz posed a rhetorical question with which Job would have agreed: **What is man, that he should be pure, or . . . righteous?** (v. 14) before God. In fact, Job had expressed the same view in 7:17 and in 14:4. Eliphaz answered his own question in vv. 15-16; no person can be pure in the sight of a God who does not **trust** His angels, and before whom **the heavens are not pure**. How much less would God hold guiltless human beings who are **detestable** and **corrupt**—like Job, whom Eliphaz no doubt had in mind as the primary example of his argument. He was direct and blunt in his accusations against Job.

15:17-35. Lest Job miss his point, Eliphaz concluded his second speech with a lengthy reminder that the **wicked man** (v. 20) will suffer a terrible fate. Job had argued that the wicked actually prosper (12:6), to counter his three friends' dogged insistence that God uniformly rewards the righteous and punishes the unrighteous. But Eliphaz threw his verbal weight against this foundation of Job's defense by affirming that **wicked** people do not prosper, but are constantly in **pain** (v. 20), suffer anxiety that robs them of **peace** (v. 21), go hungry (v. 23), and experience terrifying **distress** and **anguish** (v. 24). Verses 25-26 explain the reason the wicked suffer all of these ills. It is because they have **stretched out** their **hand** in pride and arrogance **against God** and rushed **headlong at Him** in a fierce, determined attack. Clearly, Eliphaz saw Job as the attacker in this war with God, the exact opposite of Job's contention that God was at war with him (cf. 7:20; 13:24).

Even though the wicked are fat with self-indulgence and are not hesitant to live in **desolate cities** that God has cursed (cf. Jos 6:26; 1Kg 16:34 [Zuck, *Job*, 74]), they will experience the failure of their crops (v. 29), **darkness** (v. 30), **emptiness** (v. 31), and barrenness (v. 34)—all because they are godless (v. 34), mischievous, and deceptive (v. 35). Once again, it becomes obvious that the theology of Eliphaz and his friends was slanted toward a strictly retributive theology. If a person is a sinner, God will punish him, and if he is not, God will not.

B. Job Responds to Eliphaz's Charges (16:1–17:16)

Job's reply to Eliphaz heightened the tension in his deteriorating relationship with his three friends/enemies. It is not surprising that he rejected Eliphaz's speech, dismissing it as the same rhetoric he had previously heard. The opening verses of chap. 16 contain Job's response to Eliphaz, after which Job plunged headlong into another lament in which he sharply, and wrongly, accused God of hounding him to the grave despite his clean record. Job also called on God again to give him a hearing so that he might present his case and end God's unfounded persecution of him.

16:1-17. Job wasted no time dismissing Eliphaz and his friends, accusing them of monotonously repeating their attitudes and arguments. Their words were of no help; in fact Eliphaz and his friends were **sorry comforters** (v. 2). Job turned Eliphaz's accusation that he was a windbag (cf. 15:2) around on his three unhelpful friends, lamenting that there seemed to be no end to *their* hot air. In v. 3, he asked them, **what plagues you that you answer?** Job wanted to know the reason his visitors were so irritated with him and his desire for a hearing before God. To him, this seemed the only right way to get to the bottom of his troubles and prove once and for all that he was innocent, despite their accusations that he had sinned. He chided them with the reminder that if the situation were reversed, it would be easy for him to sit in the judge's seat and make accusations. Instead, Job said he would speak words of **solace** that would **lessen** their **pain** (vv. 4-5), just as Eliphaz said Job had done in the past (cf. 4:4). Now Job could not even lessen his own pain, whether he spoke or remained silent (v. 6).

But as painful as were the accusations and insults of Job's three counselors, vv. 7-9 (also vv. 11-14, see below), they reveal that Job's greatest agony was a result of the way God had **exhausted** him, **laid waste** his life, and **shriveled [him] up** through His relentless attacks. Job viewed his troubles as a **witness** against him, evidence that his friends considered to be proof of God's judgment against Job for the sin that he refused to admit. Job felt there was not much he could do to counter this seemingly ironclad evidence, since his **leanness**, his shriveled sore-encrusted body, was evident to all and spoke against him. He was like a helpless prey whom God, depicted here as a savage predator, tore apart with His teeth.

Far from being helpful, Job's counselors had become condemners whom God had used against him (vv. 9b-11). Their rebukes were like a slap in the face to Job, the ultimate act of **contempt** in many cultures. Were Eliphaz, Bildad, and Zophar the **ruffians** and **wicked** men into whose hands God had given Job? Alden believes so, although he also suggests that they may have been the Sabeans and Chaldeans (cf. 1:14-17) who ravaged Job's property (*Job*, 184). But again, more painful than the insults or attacks of other men were what Job called the attacks that God launched against him, seemingly from nowhere and without cause while Job was **at ease** (v. 12). Job used vivid word pictures to describe what he had experienced, from God shaking him **by the neck** to direct assaults that created **breach after breach** in Job's life into which God rushed **like a warrior** to conquer his enemy (vv. 12-14). Job's response was to don sackcloth, lower his horn (a figure for his strength) in the dust, a sign of defeat, and weep until his face was **flushed** and his **eyelids** were a **deep** dark color, signs of mourning (vv. 15-16). Job's lack of **violence**, or wrong actions, and his **pure** prayer made his ordeal even harder to endure (v. 17).

Job was mistaken in his assumption that God was his enemy, assaulting him for no reason. These verses are a reminder that one must be extremely careful when trying to comfort a person whose world has suddenly come apart "at the seams." The comforter may or may not have a clear understanding of the ordeal their acquaintance is undergoing. Often when a person is in the middle of an ordeal, that is not the time to try to explain why the suffering has occurred. Sufferers do not want answers. They want their suffering to vanish, and as important as good answers are, those answers will often not alleviate the anguish.

16:18-22. God, Job said, was his **witness** (v. 19), but his **friends** were his antagonists (v. 20). Sensing that he would soon die, he longed for someone to **plead** his case with God—a heavenly **witness** who would testify to Job's integrity, even after he was dead and gone (vv. 21-22). In asking for an **advocate on high**, Job is looking for a divine intercessor. As such, "Job wants nothing less than an advocate with the Father, a longing that will find expression much later in 1 John 2:1" (Kaiser, *Messiah in the Old Testament*, 63).

17:1-5. The thought of death reminded Job that he already felt as if he had "one foot in the grave." Even though his eyes were dark from crying, he had to gaze upon the charges and insults of his three tormenters—they were right under his nose. Job accused his so-called friends of being **mockers** (v. 2), and then longed for God to **pledge** his safety as a **guarantor** (v. 3). That Job did not expect his friends to fulfill this role is clear from his statement in v. 4 that God had **kept their heart from understanding** his situation (v. 4). Even worse, Job charged them with turning against him from the selfish motive of wanting to secure some of his property for themselves, a despicable act that would bring harm down on the heads of their **children** (v. 5).

17:6-9. Job said he had become **a byword of the people** (v. 6), that is, they mocked him and spat on him, another despicable action in the ancient Near East. He was grieving, and losing weight (his body was like a **shadow**, v. 7), so that **upright** people were astonished (v. 8). This thought seemed to give Job a temporary spark of hope that when godly people saw the way he was being abused without cause, they would rally to his side. It is also possible that Job was being ironic in v. 8. Whereas his friends should have been **appalled** at a righteous man's mistreatment, they had acted like the **godless** by pulling away and denouncing him (Alden, *Job*, 190). **Nevertheless**, Job seemed to gain a sense of strength just when he felt he was at his weakest.

17:10-16. Job's rally in spirit may be behind his invitation to his critics to accuse him once again (v. 10). Job seemed ready for their next assaults because he was confident that there was no truth in their accusations. There was not **a wise man among** them. But lest anyone think Job had overcome his agony, he immediately returned to the hopelessness of his situation (vv. 11-16) in a "dirge about death" (Zuck, *Job*, 80). **Plans** and **wishes** he had for his life were now gone. Making **night into day** may refer back to 11:17, where Zophar had said that Job's "darkness would be like the morning." Once again, Job wondered if death (the meaning of **Sheol** here) would be his answer (vv. 13-14). He felt himself so close to death that he considered the **pit**, or grave, and the **worm** as his family. ("Pit" could be from another Hb. root meaning "corruption" [cf. Ps 16:10], and based on the parallel with "the worm" this is more likely.) In death his body would be consumed by worms, and any **hope** he had would go to the grave with him.

How can Job's statement of the finality and hopelessness of death here be reconciled with his belief in resurrection (see comment on 14:14)? Job's emotions ebbed and flowed throughout his ordeal, sometimes giving him hope and at other times dragging him down to the pit of despair. Thus it should not be surprising that one can find a wide range of Job's beliefs and observations on a number of subjects—including resurrection—throughout the book, depending on his state of mind at the moment. With regard to the resurrection of the body, a few chapters later comes Job's strong affirmation of his belief that he would live again after he died (cf. 19:26-27).

C. Bildad Delivers His Second Speech (18:1-21)

Bildad was the next to answer Job, betraying great impatience at the latter's words by his question, How long will you continue to babble (v. 2)? But Bildad offered little in the way of fresh ideas in his second speech, largely repeating Eliphaz's theme in his second speech of the fate of the wicked. One difference was that while Eliphaz said evil people are brought down by God, Bildad said they bring about their own downfall (cf. 18:7b-8 [Zuck, *Job*, 81]). Another difference in Bildad's second speech is that he was even more sharp-tongued toward Job than he was in his first response.

18:1-4. Bildad the Shuhite was clearly disturbed by Job's defense. He had waited impatiently for Job to finish so he could speak. (**How long . . . ?** was also the question with which Bildad opened his first speech, v. 2; cf. 8:2.) Bildad was also offended by Job's comparison of his three friends to carnivorous **beasts** (cf. 12:7-9), implying that they were more **stupid** than animals who unthinkingly hunt and tear at their prey (v. 3). Job had said that God tore at him and hunted him down (16:9), likening God to a predator. But Bildad contended that Job was tearing himself by his **anger** toward God and his friends. Bildad also scornfully asked Job if he thought the earth should stand still just for him (v. 4).

18:5-21. Bildad then cited the many ways the wicked are judged, a thinly veiled reference to Job (note the change from second person [vv. 2-4] to third person in the remainder of the chapter). God is not mentioned until the end of this speech (v. 21), but these judgments can be viewed as His activity. They include the **light** of the wicked being snuffed **out** (vv. 5-6), a picture of a person suddenly being plunged into darkness. This extinguishing of the light, or prosperity, in a wicked person's life is well deserved, given that person's evil scheming against others. The wicked are caught in the **net** . . . **snare** . . . **trap** . . . and **noose** that they lay for others (vv. 8-10).

As a result, they experience **terrors** (v. 11), their **strength** is gone and their **skin** is diseased (vv. 12-13), certainly a reference to Job on the ash heap. Job had been **torn from the security of his tent** as everything he had was reduced to nothing (vv. 14-15). Job was, in Bildad's view, one of the wicked of whom he spoke, so Job could expect to be forgotten (v. 17) and have no **offspring** (a biting reminder of Job's loss of his ten children, v. 19). The end of a wicked person would be so terrible that people far and wide who heard of it would be **appalled at his fate** (v. 20).

D. Job Responds to Bildad's Charges (19:1-29)

Job's reply to Bildad began in a familiar way, with his rejection of the latter's relentless accusations. He even used Bildad's favorite question, "How long . . . ?" (19:2), to indicate his own impatience. Bildad accused Job of creating his own grief, but Job strongly repudiated that charge, saying, in effect, "This is all God's doing." Job then turned to lament his condition again in a powerfully emotional word picture of a man utterly rejected. But the chapter also includes a high note of hope (19:25-27).

19:1-12. Job began his reply to Bildad with a hyperbole, saying that they had crushed and insulted him **ten times** with their useless words, without any remorse (vv. 2-3). Job raised the hypothetical question, **Even if I have truly erred**, his sin did not harm the three men sitting with him (v. 4). But he quickly denied any wrongdoing on his part, saying (foolishly) that it was God who had committed the wrong (v. 6). Though he called for **justice** and the restoration of his **honor**, (vv. 7-9) he did not get it. God had broken Job, considering him an enemy to be surrounded and defeated (vv. 10-12).

19:13-22. Seeing himself as abandoned and even attacked by God, Job recounted the hostility he had suffered at the hands of his family, including his wife (v. 17), his friends, and even his household servants. Job's sad plea, **Pity me, Pity me, O you my friends** (v. 21) came from the mouth and heart of a sufferer who believed that **the hand of God** was against him and who longed for human affection (vv. 21-22).

19:23-26. Feeling utterly alone, Job wished that the **words** of his defense would be permanently inscribed in a way that "would allow future generations to judge the justice of his case" (Zuck, *Job*, 89). Yet even in his horrific circumstances, Job was confident that his **Redeemer** lived and that when he died, he would see Him **from my flesh** (vv. 25-26). Admittedly, this is a highly controversial passage, particularly the two statements of v. 26. Commentators differ widely on the identity of Job's Redeemer and the question of whether Job states a clear belief in bodily resurrection. On one point all seem to agree: these verses are "the crescendo of faith to which Job attains" (Gordis, *The Book of Job*, 204).

The first difference of opinion concerns the identity of the **Redeemer** (v. 25). Several views have been suggested through the centuries: (1) a heavenly witness (Reyburn, *Handbook on the Book of Job*, 363; Hartley, *Book of Job*, 293); (2) God as kinsman and friend (Harris, et al., "ga'al," in TWOT 1:144–45); (3) Job's innocence personified (David J. A. Clines, Job 21–37. WBC [Dallas, TX: Word, 2006] 1:445); (4) an arbiter or blood avenger; (5) God (Andersen, 194; Dhorme, *Commentary on the Book of Job*, 283; Pope, *Job*, 146; Elmer Smick, "Job," 4:786-87); or (6) the Messiah (Alden, *Job*, 207; Kaiser, *Job*, 63). Several reasons support the idea that it refers to the Messiah. First, the meaning of the word **Redeemer** points to a messianic idea. It refers to a close relative upon whom fell the responsibilities of levirate marriage, restoring property that was in danger of being lost to a family, or avenging the murder of a relative. Hence, Job is looking for a human Redeemer. Further, this Redeemer is described as a living person (**I know that my Redeemer *lives***). Second, the Redeemer will **stand on the *earth***, which points to a human vindicator. Third, the Redeemer is an eschatological figure, who will appear **at the *last*** (all emphases added). Finally, the Redeemer appears to be divine, in that Job said, when he sees the Redeemer, he will **see *God***. As Kaiser states, "This 'Redeemer' will be a living person whom God will raise up 'in the end,' i.e., who will appear on the earth at the end of all things. At that time, he will stand on the earth as the final vindicator of the beaten-down Job and vindicate him" (Kaiser, *The Messiah in the Old Testament*, 63). This is likely the advocate for whom Job previously longed (cf. Jb 9:33; 16:19-21).

As for the second area of contention, Job's anticipation of resurrection, it seems that Job was also confident that "in" his flesh, even if he died, he would see his Redeemer (v. 26). This suggests a solid belief and "awareness of the bodily resurrection that awaits all redeemed believers in the Resurrection" (Archer, *Encyclopedia of Bible Difficulties*, 240–41). Archer's statement points to a key issue in v. 26, the meaning of **from** in the phrase, **from my flesh**. The word translated "from" may mean from the perspective of Job's **flesh**, that is, from the vantage point of his present life on earth. Or it could suggest "apart from" his flesh, signifying that Job expected to have conscious communion with the eternal God after his death without reference to a bodily resurrection (Bullock, *An Introduction to the Old Testament Poetic Books*, 99). However, "from" could also be rendered "in," suggesting that Job would see God in a resurrected body. Translated in this way, the word virtually demands that Job have a resurrected body when he sees God, since he had already stated in v. 26a that his expectation of seeing God was after his physical death. This early belief in the future resurrection is exhibited in Job's belief system that existed at the time of or before the patriarchs (Gn 12–35), when this book was written.

Job's hope was that despite the direction his life had taken, in the end, the Messiah would vindicate his claim of innocence (cf. 9:21, "I am guiltless"). He knew that God is pure and righteous, even if Job's vindication did not occur in his lifetime, though he hoped that would be the case. In 13:18 he declared, "I have prepared my case; I know that I will be vindicated." Job believed that the vindication he longed for (19:23-24) would come from his **Redeemer** (v. 25), even though his life (**skin** and **flesh**) was being destroyed. If Job's anticipated vindication did not come in his earthly lifetime, it would basically require his resurrection because God's holy governance of the universe would not leave an innocent man unjustly condemned.

19:27-29. Job was overwhelmed at the thought of seeing God for himself (v. 27). He then turned to his friends and warned them that their unjust accusations against him would turn on them and they would experience the severe judgment they believed Job had so richly deserved.

E. Zophar Delivers His Second Speech (20:1-29)

Zophar then spoke up for the second time (20:1-29), seething with anger against Job. His second speech was another diatribe against wicked people, except that this time he developed the thought that the wicked would lose their wealth and see their lives shortened as God judged them severely for stealing from and defrauding others to get rich. He pictured the wealth of evil people as food that turns in the stomach of the eater, making him sick enough to vomit it up. Other than taking a slightly different tack, Zophar's message came to the same conclusion as those of his first speech and the speeches of Eliphaz and Bildad: God always rewards the righteous and punishes the wicked. It was obvious to Zophar that Job's sudden loss of wealth made him the wicked person of Zophar's description.

20:1-3. Zophar felt disquieted, agitated, and reproved by Job's insult (v. 3), apparently his warning to the three friends in 19:28-29 to think twice before condemning him lest the sword of God's judgment fall on them.

20:4-11. Zophar's description of the wicked person's brief enjoyment of life is captured in words like **short . . . momentary** (v. 5), a life that vanishes quickly **like a dream** (v. 8). Job was sitting on the refuse heap, which apparently served for Zophar as an apt picture of Job's demise as one who was so clearly wicked, or so his friends thought. The wicked man's sons would repudiate his greed by acting charitably toward **the poor**, while the man himself would have to return the **wealth** he earned by oppressing **the poor** (v. 10; cf. v. 19). The **vigor** of the wicked person's life also evaporates while he is still in his youth (v. 11).

20:12-19. To the wicked, Zophar said, **evil is sweet**, something to be savored (v. 12). However, while this one may enjoy his ill-gotten **riches** for a while, in the end he loses them (he will **vomit them up**, v. 15). The reason is clear: God brings judgment on the wicked because they have **oppressed and forsaken the poor** (v. 19), gaining their wealth by evil means that God will surely punish.

20:20-29. Then Zophar repeated his point that the prosperity of the wicked does not last. Everything he **desires** will be taken away from him (v. 20). God in His anger **will pierce him** with His **bronze bow** of judgment (v. 24). Verse 25b, **the glittering point from his gall**, is a difficult expression in Hebrew. It seems to picture the gleaming point of the arrow fired from the **bronze bow** piercing the wicked man's stomach and having to be pulled out—"a ghastly picture of the end of a man who is the object of God's wrath" (Zuck, *Job*, 96). And if this were not enough, Zophar said God would also bring **terrors** and **darkness** on those who do evil (vv. 25-26), and their iniquity would be attested both by **the heavens . . . and the earth** (v. 27), a sad **heritage** of God's judgment on evildoers (v. 29).

In this second round of debates these three friends all aligned Job's future with that of the destiny of evildoers (Eliphaz, 15:17-35; Bildad, 18:5-21; Zophar, 20:12-21). In fact, in his first speech Eliphaz had emphasized that suffering is never the experience of the innocent or the upright (4:7).

F. Job Responds to Zophar's Charges (21:1-34)

In chap. 21, Job answered the continued insistence of Zophar, and of all three men, that judgment and suffering are always and ever the lot of wicked people, because God always rewards good and punishes evil in life. Therefore, in their view Job had to be a great sinner to have suffered the way he was suffering. Zophar had responded angrily in his second speech (chap. 20), but Job's reply is more measured and thoughtful. He built a solid case that, in fact, evil people often seem to thrive in life and suffer little in the way of retribution for their sins. Job's previous two defenses had been concerned with his charge that God had made Job His enemy with no justification. In this chapter, however, Job took a more probing look at the issue of evil.

His complaint that the wicked often prosper calls to mind a similar complaint made centuries later in Ps 73:1-14, where the psalmist lamented the prosperity of the wicked and said he had kept himself pure for nothing—a charge that he reverses when he saw the truth from God's perspective (Ps 73:15-28). The experiences of Job and the psalmist reveal that the seeming triumph of evil is a problem people have wrestled with since the earliest times.

21:1-6. Job addressed his counselors and inferred that "with friends like these, who needs enemies?" He begged for their attention because he had something worthwhile to say, not just a further defense of his innocence or charge that God was attacking him without cause. "Listen to me," Job said, "and then if you still think what I have to say is worthless, go ahead and mock me again" (vv. 1-3). He said his **complaint** was to God anyway, and not to them, so they had no reason to become so angry at his words. His ghastly appearance should have shocked them into silence. Job himself was horrified at the way he looked (vv. 4-6).

21:7-16. Job unfolded a long list of the ease, comfort, financial success, and other aspects of the good life that wicked people enjoyed (vv. 7-13). Job disagreed strongly with Zophar, who had said the wicked lose their wealth and die or live short lives. In Job's view **the wicked . . . continue on** (v. 7). Their livestock increase, they enjoy life, and they prosper, while all the time refusing to have anything to do with God. Even more puzzling, they do all this while openly rejecting God and challenging Him to His face (vv. 14-15). Yet Job did not want his friends to think that he envied the wicked or followed their example (v. 16).

21:17-26. Job's contention that the wicked often live full lives and seem to suffer no judgment for their sin (vv. 17-18) was another refutation of his friends' theology of retribution, which says that sin always brings swift and sure judgment (cf. 20:5, 8, 11). And lest they should protest that the judgment for an evil person often falls on his children, Job asked, **What does he care for his household after him**? (v. 21). A wicked person who dies does not know or care about what his descendants may have to endure. The mysteries of God's dealings mean that Job's friends cannot presume to tell God what to do (v. 22). Sometimes a person **dies in his full strength** (v. 23), and **another dies with a bitter soul**, but both die (v. 26). Job's perspective, of course, does not take into account God's final judgment of the wicked.

Today believers must be careful not to covet the lifestyle and material wealth of those who do not follow God, and who have gained it by evil means.

21:27-34. Job said he knew what his friends were thinking, how they were planning to continue attacking his integrity (v. 27). Rather than viewing the wicked as prosperous, Job's friends needed to see that **the wicked** will face days **of calamity** (v. 30). Yet he said that despite this, evil men are often honored in death and beyond. In view of these facts, Job concluded that all the advice of his friends had been useless and **full of falsehood** (v. 34).

IV. Third Round of Speeches between Job and His Three Friends (22:1–26:14)

A. Eliphaz Delivers His Third Speech (22:1-30)

Commentators seem to agree that the third round of speeches by Eliphaz and Bildad, beginning in chap. 22, do little to advance the case. Alden says flatly, "There is not much new in Eliphaz's third speech" (*Job*, 229). Bullock notes, "In his original speech Eliphaz had acknowledged Job's benevolent conduct (4:3-4), but now the intervening arguments and emotions had come to so dominate his objectivity that he was fully convinced that Job had required illegal pledges [cf. Ex 22:26; Dt. 24:10-13] and had taken undue advantage of the poor generally" (*An Introduction to the Old Testament Poetic Books*, 100). These allegations are among the specific sins with which Eliphaz charged Job, charges Job vigorously denied.

22:1-11. As far as **Eliphaz** was concerned, Job's righteousness and **reverence** had little impact on God, who was above being affected by human actions (vv. 1-4). Eliphaz believed that God was afflicting Job not because he was pious, but because he was a great sinner (v. 5) who had gained his wealth by abusing the helpless and downtrodden (vv. 6-7, 9). In fact, there was no end to Job's **wickedness** and **iniquities**, which Eliphaz then enumerated in withering detail. There does not seem to be a category of people whom Job did not mistreat: **his brothers . . . the weary . . . the hungry . . . widows . . . orphans.** Charging Job with mistreating these last two groups was especially cruel of Eliphaz, for as Zuck says, "To reject widows and orphans was an atrocious felony, because widows and their children (orphans were usually fatherless children living with their mothers) were subject to social and economic losses, being without male protection" (*Job*, 104). For these crimes, Eliphaz contended, Job was suffering the catastrophic judgments that had come upon him (vv. 10-11). Job later refuted this specific charge (cf. 31:16-22).

22:12-20. Eliphaz was indignant that Job was not only guilty of terrible sins, but that he committed them in defiance of the God who is in heaven (vv. 12-14). The unrighteous view God as being detached and uninterested in human affairs (vv. 13-14), so that they can conduct their underhanded business without fear of divine retribution. Given what Eliphaz saw as Job's wanton contempt for God's power and justice, he warned Job that the One who **walks on the vault of heaven**, that is, God (v. 14), was mocked by the wicked, meaning by Job, who will be **cut off** (v. 20) in the end. Eliphaz's point is that Job will be among them.

22:21-30. Eliphaz's call for Job to return to God (vv. 21-24) could, as Alden notes, "easily be turned into a sermon for today. Results from these imperatives ('submit, accept, return, assign') are all desirable outcomes ('peace, prosperity, restoration, [spiritual] gold and silver'). Eliphaz's error, which could be ours, was preaching this fine sermon to one who already knew the Lord. The message that Job needed God himself would deliver in chaps. 38–41" (*Job*, 235–36). Job certainly was not enjoying **peace with [God]** at the moment (v. 21), but not for the reason Eliphaz assumed, that is, Job's sinfulness. The path to Job's restoration was to **receive instruction from** God and allow Him to **establish His words** in Job's **heart** (v. 22). Eliphaz named Job's problem as **unrighteousness**, which if true would need to be removed from Job's **tent**, his life. Job also needed to renounce his trust in material wealth (v. 24), another erroneous accusation from Eliphaz—which Job answered later (cf. 31:24-28). The benefits of this repentance are spelled out in vv. 25-30 (also **good** in v. 21), and they are impressive. Job would enjoy restored fellowship with **the Almighty**, who would hear his prayers (vv. 26-27), which, his three friends assumed, God was not doing for Job as he sat on the ash heap. He would also experience success (v. 28), and **the humble person** would be blessed by Job's righteousness (v. 29). Even those who are **not innocent** would be delivered through Job's uprightness (v. 30).

B. Job Responds to Eliphaz's Charges (23:1–24:25)

In his third reply to Eliphaz, "Job does not dignify Eliphaz's accusations with a direct denial. Instead, he tells of his efforts to find God, hoping to be vindicated through this confrontation. Even in his extremity Job still believes that if he could meet his divine Adversary, God would recognize his essential uprightness" (Gordis, *The Book of Job*, 253). The problem, Job said, was that although he longed to find God and present his case, God was nowhere to be found. Evidently Job had abandoned the approach of trying to persuade his friends of his innocence. He wanted to try his case in the court of God. Eliphaz had told Job to "return to the Almighty" (22:23), "but for Job that counsel was pointless" (Zuck, *Job*, 107). In chap. 24, Job presented his point once more that his friends' rigid view of retribution was unsupported by the realities of life. More than that, Job "lambast[ed] God for being so apathetic about injustice . . . [and] God's apparent neglect to use [His] majesty to correct the world's wrongs" (Zuck, *Job*, 109).

23:1-7. Job wanted to present his case to God, to make his **complaint** about the way God was treating him, even though he believed that doing so would be counted as **rebellion** against God. Job lamented that God's **hand** was **heavy** on him in judgment, despite the intensity of Job's **groaning** in pain of body and anguish of soul (v. 2). Job's desire for a hearing before God was so strong that he had already filled his **mouth** with arguments to present, though he would also be careful to listen to what God had to say to him (vv. 4-5). Job's confidence in his innocence and God's acquittal had grown to the point that instead of worrying about God overwhelming him with **the greatness of His power**, Job was certain that God would listen to him and he **would be delivered** from God, his **Judge** (vv. 6-7).

23:8-17. But Job's hope for a hearing was futile, because he could not find God no matter which way he turned (vv. 8-9). But he knew God could find him (**He knows the way I take**, v. 10). Job's declaration in the second half of v. 10, **When He has tried me, I shall come forth as gold**, has, as Alden notes, "lent strength to believers through the ages as they passed through fires of tribulation and trial" (*Job*, 241). However, other commentators see in this Job's confidence of his innocence rather than a declaration of steadfastness in trial. Zuck represents this viewpoint: "When God would appear in court and try Job's case, it would be evident, Job asserted, that he was gold and would shine like it. . . . Although trials may help to purify the believer's faith . . . that does not seem to be what Job was saying here" (*Job*, 108). This view seems to be confirmed by vv. 11-12, in which Job reasserts his faithfulness to God's requirements.

But Job's confidence faded (v. 13) when he lamented that God is a Sovereign who acts according to His own **desires**, despite whatever evidence Job might present of his innocence. Therefore, Job was **terrified** and **dismayed** (v. 15) at the thought of appearing before God, for it was God who had made his **heart faint** and had **dismayed** Job by what he saw as God's unjust punishment of him. Still, Job asserted that he was not going to be **silenced** by the **darkness** and **gloom** that had enveloped his life (v. 17).

24:1-12. This chapter presents Job's complaint that God seems to tolerate the terrible evil in the world. He asked why God did not have specific times for judging the ungodly so that those who know Him could see Him at work, dispensing divine justice (v. 1). Job was concerned that God did not seem to do anything about people who, for example, **remove the landmarks** of their neighbors in an attempt to expand their own property illegally, a sin that was forbidden in the law of Moses (v. 2; cf. Dt 19:14; in 27:17, the person who does this is cursed). An equally heinous crime in an agricultural society was to steal another's **flocks**, and to mistreat **the poor** (vv. 3-4). As a result of this mistreatment, the poor had to scratch and beg for food, being reduced to gleaning **in the vineyard of the wicked**, those who were oppressing them (vv. 5-6). At night, the poor had **no covering against the cold**, leaving them to get soaked by the rain and **hug the rock** in a desperate attempt to gain shelter (vv. 5-8).

Job continued his litany of oppression by describing how a fatherless baby was snatched from its mother, and how **the poor** were made to work and yet were not allowed to eat or drink from the fruits of their labor (vv. 9-11). Yet even in the face of these terrible injustices, Job charged God with **not pay[ing] attention to folly** (v. 12).

24:13-17. In contrast to these visible evils are those who sin in secret: **the murderer** . . . **thief** . . . **adulterer** (vv. 14-15). They may wait for the cover of darkness to do their evil, but even though their sins are hidden from the eyes of others, surely God must see what is being done. "Therefore, how can God withhold retribution?" (Zuck, *Job*, 111).

24:18-25. These verses express such a seemingly opposite view from vv. 1-17 that some commentators assign this section to one of Job's friends, either Zophar or Bildad, or view this as

Job quoting his friends, with the introductory words "You say" and vv. 18-20 in quotation marks, with vv. 21-25 being Job's rebuttal (Zuck, *Job*, 111). But a sudden change of perspective need not signal a different source for these verses that the text includes in Job's response. A similar change is seen later in Ps 73:16-20, where the psalmist turned from lamenting the success and ease of the wicked to their sudden destruction at God's hands. Job did not say the wicked would never be judged, only that **they are exalted a little while** before being forgotten and **cut off** like heads of grain (v. 24). Job's point is that God appears to treat the wicked and the poor in much the same way. He appears detached and uninvolved, and everyone fades away in the end. Job's friends had argued that evildoers are judged immediately, but Job countered that the realities of life proved their theology of retribution to be in error. If that were not the truth, Job challenged any one of his friends to **prove** him to be a **liar** (v. 25).

C. Bildad Delivers His Third Speech (25:1-6)

Bildad's final speech (25:1-6) is something of a last gasp from Job's accusers, an attempt by Bildad to say something by way of defense of the three men's "one-tracked" theology (Zuck, *Job*, 113) of retribution rather than being silenced. That Zophar did not make a third speech is also evidence that the three had run out of ideas and had no answer to Job's realistic portrayal of the inequities of life. One difference in this speech is that instead of speaking about the fate of the wicked, Bildad extolled the greatness of God.

25:1-6. God is a great Sovereign, Bildad said, to whom **dominion and awe belong** (v. 2). **His troops**, whether referring to angels or stars, are innumerable, befitting the Ruler of the universe, and His **light** shines upon every creature He rules (v. 3). Given the awesome majesty of God, the question becomes, **How then can a man be just with God?** (v. 4). Bildad's rhetorical question suggests no positive answer. The second halves of vv. 4 and 6 strengthen his claim that all the human race is sinful and unclean before God—including Job. And lest Job miss the point, Bildad indirectly called him a **maggot** and a **worm**, which would have been extremely painful references for Job in his pitiful physical condition (v. 6).

D. Job Responds to Bildad's Charges (26:1-14)

Job's third reply to Bildad is in chap. 26. The latter's extremely brief speech brought the words of the three friends to a close, since Zophar did not venture to speak for a third time (see below). Their argument never advanced beyond their basic syllogism: Only the wicked suffer at God's hand; Job is suffering at God's hand; therefore, Job must be wicked. Job resisted their conclusion to the very end of the argument. He dismissed Bildad's final words with biting sarcasm, which Alden terms "Insult with Irony" (*Job*, 257). Bildad offered no new insights on Job's case, and the brevity of his speech signaled that Job's accusers had no meaningful response to him.

26:1-4. Job sarcastically chided Bildad for his unhelpful words. Verses 1-3 drip with irony: "Where in the world would this poor soul be without your amazing counsel and wisdom!" Job cried out in mock awe. Verse 4 delivers the punch line. Job told Bildad his words were not even his own. He was simply parroting what others said. He continued by informing Bildad that his comfort had been worthless.

26:5-14. Job continued by claiming that he understood more about the greatness of God than did Bildad, or any of the three friends, for that matter. Verses 5-14 are a declaration of God's majesty that rightly describes His power and omniscience. "Bildad had stated that God was majestic [25:1-6]; Job responded with statements about God's majesty that were far more majestic than Bildad's" (Zuck, *Job*, 115). Job asserted that nothing is hidden from Him: **Naked is Sheol before Him, and Abaddon has no covering** (v. 6).

He knew that God had: (1) **stretch[ed] out the north over empty space** and suspended **the earth on nothing** (v. 7). The first statement could be a reference to Mount Zaphon (the word for "north"), where in the Canaanite mythology of Job's day the gods dwelled (Gordis, *The Book of Job*, 278–79; Zuck, *Job*, 117). Job's statement would then be a polemic against the mythology of pagan religion, showing that the mountain of the gods in myth was "the majestic heavens in divine cosmology" (Zuck, *Job*, 117). And v. 7b is an amazingly accurate statement of the earth's suspension in space, a fact that was not known scientifically until several millennia after Job lived; (2) **inscribed a circle on the surface of the waters**, that is, marked out the boundaries of the oceans (v. 10a); (3) **shattered Rahab,** a sea god in Babylonian mythology that stood for the raging sea (v. 12; cf. 9:13). In Isaiah 51:9, God is the One who "cut Rahab in pieces," signifying

God's power over pagan deities; and, (4) **pierced the fleeing serpent**, which may parallel Job's reference to the shattering of Rahab. Yet, for all of this, what people know of God is limited (v. 14). Job's point is that all of creation, and all earthly creatures, derive from God and are subject to His sovereign dictates.

From the exchange of addresses between suffering Job and non-comforting Eliphaz, Bildad, and Zophar, they concluded it was evident that he had sinned in a terrible way to have so much havoc in his life. Also, because they logically jumped to unsupported conclusions based on partial evidence and generalizations, they did not accomplish their purpose in coming to comfort their friend Job. As Bullock observes,

> Their defense of God turned into a defense of their own theology at the expense of their friend Job . . . Job taught that although he could not see through the mystery of his suffering, he must still hold fast to the fear of the Lord, and that those who feared Him must be judged by a different principle than the cause-effect principle that the friends had used. (*An Introduction to the Old Testament Poetic Books*, 73, 75)

V. Job Continues His Speeches (27:1–31:40)

A. Job's Final Speech to His Friends (27:1-23)

27:1-6. Job took a strong oath, **As God lives** (v. 2), to reassert his innocence. He was convinced enough of his purity to invoke God's name and existence, yet he also said that it was **the Almighty** who had made his life bitter. Nevertheless, Job was determined to cling to his innocence as long as he had breath (v. 3), and he declared that he would not utter any lies (v. 4). That is why he would not say his accusers were **right** in what they had spoken against him, charging him with sin (v. 5). On the contrary, Job asserted that his conscience was clear (v. 6).

27:7-10. Some commentators regard vv. 8-23 as Zophar's third speech, although there is no evidence for this in the text. Instead, vv. 7-10 are Job's curse on his enemies, whom he likens to **the wicked** in that he desires for them to have the same fate. Bildad had accused Job of being **wicked** (18:5, 21), but now Job turned the charge around and prayed "that Bildad (or all three friends) might be punished as the wicked deserve" (Alden, *Job*, 263). **The godless** have no hope when they cry to God (vv. 8-9), nor will they find any delight in the **Almighty**. As Alden notes further on this section, "Verses 8-10 are somewhat out of character for [Job] since they describe bad things happening to bad people. This is what the friends usually said, not Job" (Alden, *Job*, 263).

27:11-23. Eliphaz had urged Job to receive instruction from God (22:22). But now Job reversed that suggestion, telling his three accusers that he would instruct them about God's power and teach them about **the Almighty** (v. 11). Since they already knew what Job was going to tell them, it was foolish for them to accuse him falsely (v. 12).

Job then recounted the fate of **a wicked man** (v. 13). Both his family (vv. 14-15) and his wealth (vv. 16-23) will be lost, despite that **his sons are many** (v. 14) and **he lies down rich** (v. 19). The wicked man himself will suddenly be swept away as if by a strong **east wind** from which he is unable to escape. Those who see the wicked man swept away in judgment will clap their hands in derisive joy that he is gone.

B. Job's Message Concerning God's Wisdom (28:1-28)

Job 28 is regarded rightly by many scholars as the theological and literary heart of the entire book (see, for example, Elmer Smick, "Job," 4:848; Dorsey, *The Literary Structure of the Old Testament* [Grand Rapids, MI: Baker 1999], 72; Alan Cooper, "Narrative Theory and the Book of Job," *Studies in Religion* 11 [1982]: 42). It is sometimes seen as an intrusion into the book. It presents a loftier view of God's providence and skill than is found elsewhere in the book, and it forecasts some of what is found in chaps. 38–42 when God confronts Job with how little Job actually knows. But Kaiser points out, "Rather than viewing Job 28 as an inserted interruption in the flow of the argument between Job and his friends, it was rather the writer's attempt to give his readers a revelatory perspective in the midst of so much talk which was devoid of divine wisdom" (*Toward an Old Testament Theology*, 169).

The chapter extols God's wisdom, an attribute of God that concerns His sovereign skill and knowledge with which He creates and administers the universe, including human affairs. In Wisdom literature and Hebrew poetry, wisdom is often personified as an associate or agent of God. Job indicates that while human technology can be astonishing (e.g., mining, vv. 1-11), no one can discern how or why God does what He does in the world. Part of the motivation for Job noting these truths about God's wisdom relates to the presumption of Job's friends, who thought they "had it all figured out" when in fact they did not. Their belief in retributive justice—that people suffered because of their sin—was too reductionistic and put God in a box.

Sin can and does bring God's retribution in the form of human suffering. Yet at other times, God designs suffering to be disciplinary and remedial (see Heb 12:1-11), and sometimes suffering is intended strictly for God's glory (see Jn 9:3). It is not always and only a divine reaction to human sin. In contrast to his friends, Job demonstrated that God is not nearly so one-dimensional, and that his own circumstances did not fit their erroneous theology. It was only the true God and His wise control of the universe who knew why the turmoil had entered Job's life and what purpose it had for Job. But His purposes remained inscrutable for Job and, though they denied it, for his friends as well.

28:1-14. Men have penetrated the earth in search of precious metals and stones, often facing danger in the process. They dig precarious mines and shafts into the earth, and they descend with the aid of ropes and **hang** from them (v. 4) while they are excavating. They labor in the cracks and crevices of the mountains, searching for metals and stones that have human value. They will go where no **bird of prey** or **fierce lion** has ever gone in search of riches (vv. 7-8). But while humanity has been successful in searching for precious metals and stones (**what is hidden he brings out to the light**, v. 11), man has not been successful in finding godly wisdom.

Where is the source of **wisdom** (v. 12)? It seems to be hidden, not found in the **deep** or in the **sea** (v. 14). Wisdom has ultimate value and is not found under a mountain, or a rock. Meredith Kline asserts, "Man's reverent acknowledgement that he and his world are subject to the Creator is so much the lifeblood of human wisdom that it can be identified with wisdom. A man begins to be wise when he ceases to strive for wisdom independently of God and in his own power" ("Job," in *The Wycliffe Bible Commentary*, ed. Charles F. Pfeiffer and Everett F. Harrison [Chicago: Moody, 1990], 480). Parsons adds,

> Job said that the wondrous acts of God in nature are inexplicable to him. He could not perceive God's nature in these sovereign works (see: 9:10-12; 26:14; and perhaps Job 28). Rather, God's sovereign control of nature (creation) appears to indicate an arbitrary abusive power and wisdom (9:12, 14-24; 12:13-25; also, 30:18-23). At the same time, Job appeals to nature to be a witness for him of [what Job considered to be] the obvious injustices of God against him (12:7-10; 16:18-19) and his own ethical purity (see: 31:8, 12, 38-40). (Gregory W. Parsons, "The Structure and Purpose of the Book of Job," *BibSac* 138 (1981): 146)

28:15-22. The value of wisdom is vastly beyond that of **precious** stones (v. 16) that have human value, and cannot be purchased with **gold** . . . **silver** . . . **onyx** . . . **sapphire** . . . **coral** . . . **crystal** . . . **pearls** . . . **topaz** . . . or even **pure gold**. From where wisdom comes, only God knows.

28:23-27. God was not just sovereign and in control of Job's turmoil and catastrophes; He was *wisely* in control. Only God knows what God plans: **God understands its** [wisdom's] **way, and He knows its place** (v. 23). Job began to fathom that there might be a reasonable design for what had befallen him, and vv. 23-27 reflect in a superficial, initial sense what God makes explicit in chaps. 38–41 about His skill and knowledge in running the universe. However, the details as yet escaped him.

28:28. True wisdom teaches a person how to live skillfully before God both in the triumphs and the tragedies of life and all points in between (28:28; Ps 111:10; Pr 1:7; 9:10). God established wisdom and said that **the fear of the Lord** is wisdom. God's wisdom is His divine skill and knowledge in how to manage the affairs of all creation. Human wisdom is skill for living and managing one's life—skill that is ultimately derived from **the fear of the Lord**, the need to respect Him so profoundly that one will **depart from evil**.

C. Job Reviews His Life (29:1–31:40)

The recurring theme in these three chapters is Job's adamant claim that he was upright enough that the suffering he endured was undeserved. He recalled the happy days of the past when God had blessed him (29:1-25), recounted the pain of his present suffering (30:1-31), and disavowed once again any wrongdoing on his part (31:1-40).

29:1-7. Job yearned for the return of his prosperous and happy times before calamity befell him. Those were **the days when God watched over** him (v. 2) and Job walked in the **light** of God's favor (v. 3). God was his friend; **the Almighty** was with him (vv. 4-5a). Job was also surrounded by his ten **children**, a picture of a father (and perhaps, grandfather) delighting in his sons and daughters. Job also recalled his great prosperity; even **the rock poured out for**

me streams of oil! (v. 6). He also had great status and influence as a respected elder at the **gate** of his city (v. 7).

29:8-16. In former days, when he was a leader among his peers, Job was well known for his wisdom. When he came to the gate of the city, both young and old stood, and talking ceased as even **the nobles** fell silent to hear what Job had to say (vv. 8-11). He was also known for the justice and mercy he gave those in need (**the poor**, **the orphan**, **the widow**, **the blind**, **the lame**, **the needy**, vv. 12-16). No one who had a need of any kind was turned away from Job's door, and he made sure that justice was done even for those whose situation **he did not know**, perhaps strangers (v. 16b).

29:17-25. Job opposed **the wicked** (v. 17) who oppressed the poor and needy, picturing himself as rescuing the **prey** from the **jaws** and **teeth** of the wrongdoer. Job felt he would live on (that his days would **multiply**, v. 18) in strength and blessing because he had been a defender of the weak. His **root** would always reach **the waters** and **dew** perpetually rest on his **branch** (v. 19). His **bow**, "representing strength and resilience" (Alden, *Job*, 285), would stay fresh with him. "Job said that he expected to continue with God's blessing on him right up to his death" (Zuck, *Job*, 128). He was highly esteemed by the masses as he encouraged them with his **words** (vv. 21-25).

30:1-10. Chapter 29 described what God had given Job; chap. 30 describes what God had taken away (cf. 1:21). **But now those younger than I mock me**, Job complained (v. 1). And even worse than being dishonored by his juniors, Job's mockers were the sons of contemptible men Job would have **disdained** in his days of prosperity and blessing. Verses 2-8 describe this rabble crowd in vivid terms, picturing them as acting like animals and so being **driven from the community** as troublemakers (v. 5). How painful for Job that those who were of no account, and whom he may have even helped at one time, now taunted him, considering him even lower than themselves (vv. 8-9). Once *he* judged *them*, but now they passed by, even spitting at his **face**, the worst of insults (v. 10).

30:11-15. Job felt that God had left him defenseless against his opponents by loosening his **bowstring** (v. 11), leaving him without any way to defend himself. Seeing Job's vulnerability, his **brood** of enemies came at him in full fury, knocking him off his feet and building a siege ramp against him (v. 12). They managed to destroy him without any outside help ("restrains" here means "helps" [Zuck, *Job*, 130–31]). They broke through **a wide breach** in the walls of Job's life, and rushed in upon him like a marauding army (v. 14). Little wonder that Job was seized with **terrors** (v. 15) in the face of this relentless assault.

30:16-23. Job then turned to bemoan the physical and emotional suffering he was experiencing at the hands of God (vv. 16-18). Job's bodily agony was constant, causing him to writhe at night in pain until his **garment** was twisted around him. Job felt that God had cast him **into the mire** (v. 19). Job cried out to God for help, but instead of receiving help, Job charged God with being **cruel** to him, persecuting even to death (vv. 20-23).

30:24-31. Having been abandoned and even ill-treated by God, Job lamented that he had also been abandoned by people. This was especially painful to him because he had been deeply concerned about the needs of others (v. 25). Yet when he needed help, all he got in response was **evil** . . . **darkness** . . . and **affliction** (vv. 26-27). He had no **comfort** though he cried **for help** (vv. 28-29). His physical suffering was accompanied by **mourning** that left Job in grief (vv. 30-31).

31:1-8. Job ended **his words** (v. 40) with a lengthy defense of his innocence in various areas of his life. He couched his defense in the strongest of terms, a self-malediction, invoking curses on himself if he were guilty of any of the sins he named in this chapter. "So convinced was Job of his integrity and freedom from sin that he listed here about seven categories of crimes, whose consequences he would be glad to suffer" (Alden, *Job*, 297). Job's first claim was freedom from sexual sin. He claimed that he had made and kept a **covenant** with his eyes concerning sexual lust, and therefore had not sinned even with a lustful glance (v. 1). Job was restrained from sin by the thought that the God who meted out **calamity** to evildoers had His eye on Job, seeing everything he did (vv. 2-4). Verse 5 begins Job's series of self-maledictions (the word **If** occurs at least 14 times in chap. 31). **If** he had been guilty of **falsehood** or **deceit** in his actions or dealing with others, then let God **weigh** Job, judge his actions, and carry out whatever consequences Job had coming (vv. 5-6). But Job maintained that he was upright, confident that not even a **spot** of wrongdoing was on his hands (v. 7). But if he was found guilty, he was willing to let his **crops be uprooted** (v. 8), the ruining of his income as a farmer.

31:9-15. Job added that he had not been **enticed** into an illicit relationship with another **woman**, as that would be **a lustful crime** and **an iniquity** deserving the kind of treatment he was receiving from God (vv. 9-11). But this was Job's point; contrary to the charges of his friends, who accused him of the crimes he outlined in chap. 31, Job was free of guilt—which in his mind proved that the treatment he was receiving from God was unjust. Job also asserted that he had been fair in the treatment of his servants, recognizing that they were also the creation of God's hands even as he was (vv. 13-15).

31:16-23. The poor and needy also were blessed by Job's care. In 29:12-17, Job had claimed that his concern for orphans, widows, the hungry and others suffering need was the reason God had blessed him with material abundance. He reasserted that claim here, saying **the poor** . . . **the widow** . . . **and the orphan** had been cared for at his table and from his flock (vv. 16-20). He also said that he had never used his clout at the city gate for self gain or to take advantage of the downtrodden (v. 21). Again, in the matter of the needy, Job said if he had failed to help them, he was willing to suffer physical agony (v. 22). But his fear of the Lord kept him from doing evil (v. 23).

31:24-28. Job further claimed that he had not placed his trust **in gold**, nor had he **gloated** despite God having blessed him with wealth (vv. 24-25). He also disavowed any involvement in idolatry or astrology (vv. 26-27), sins that would also merit God's judgment.

31:29-40. Job added revenge against his enemies to the catalog of sins of which he was innocent (vv. 29-30), a disavowal for which his three friends might later give thanks to God! Neither was Job miserly with his wealth, he claimed (vv. 31-32), nor had he tried to cover up his sins the way **Adam** had done by hiding from God (Gn 3:9-10). Job said he had no reason to hide from the gaze of others, because he had done nothing wrong (vv. 33-34). Therefore, he longed for God to answer him so he could approach God in confidence **like a prince** (vv. 35-37). He closed his testimony by claiming that he was innocent of any gross wrongdoing worthy of the suffering he had undergone (vv. 38-40).

Development of Aggression toward Job

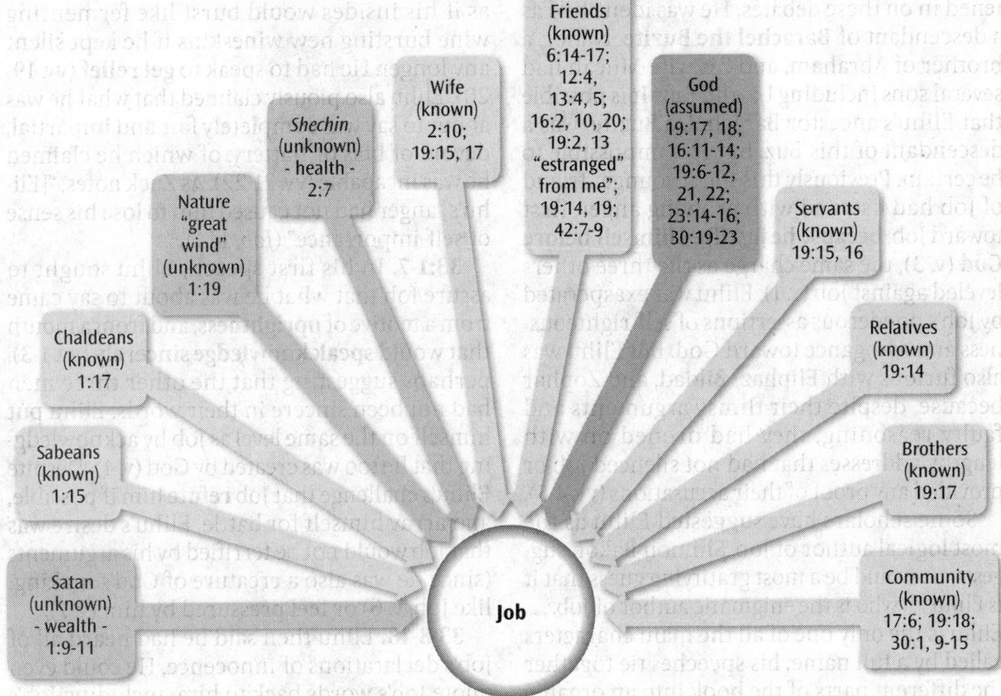

Following the rigid cause-and-effect mindset of Job's friends regarding sin, judgment, and suffering, God was quickly reduced in their eyes to being merely a rewarder or a punisher. But this does not explain human existence in a fallen world. How would one explain the life of Joseph (Gn 37–38), Jesus (the Gospels), Lazarus (Lk 16:20-25), or the righteous poor widow (Mk 12:41-44)? The pressure was building in Job's life by way of known and unknown aggression. The chart "Development of Aggression toward Job" portrays the many individuals and groups with whom Job had contact, and illustrates the many-sided attacks and accusations he faced. In light of these "enemies" massed against him, it becomes easier to see why Job retreated into a fortress of self-defense and self-justification.

VI. The Speeches of Elihu (32:1–37:24)

A. His First Speech about Job, His Friends, and God's Work (32:1–33:33)

32:1-5. Job's three so-called friends had heard enough from Job, and they agreed the main problem was that Job was proud and **righteous in his own eyes**. This was a serious flaw in Job's character, as far as they were concerned, especially given their certainty that he was guilty of sinning and then trying to deny it. At least one more friend by the name of **Elihu** had listened in on these debates. He was identified as a descendant of **Barachel the Buzite**. Nahor, a brother of Abraham, and his wife Milcah had several sons including Uz and Buz. It is possible that Elihu's ancestor Barachel, a Buzite, was a descendant of this Buz, but it is impossible to be certain. Previously this silent younger friend of Job had listened with growing anger, first toward Job, **because he justified himself before God** (v. 3), the same charge as the three others leveled against Job (v. 1). Elihu was exasperated by Job's ponderous assertions of self-righteousness and arrogance toward God. But Elihu was also furious with Eliphaz, Bildad, and Zophar because, despite their flimsy arguments and faulty reasoning, they had droned on with lengthy addresses that had not silenced Job or provided any proof of their accusations (vv. 4-5).

Some scholars have suggested Elihu as the most logical author of Job. Shimon Bakon suggests, "It would be a most gratifying guess that it is Elihu . . . who is the enigmatic author of Job. . . . Elihu is the only one of all the main characters called by a full name; his speeches tie together the different parts of the book into an organic entity that gives it a distinct expression to one of the main themes in the book of Job—to suffer for the sake of purification" ("The Enigma of Elihu," *Dor le Dor* 12 [1984]: 228).

32:6-14. Despite his burning anger, Elihu began by acknowledging his "junior" status in the presence of his elders. He even described himself as **shy and afraid** to speak up because he thought that wisdom would come from the three older men (vv. 6-7). But he confronted Job and the three friends with the reminder that being older did not guarantee that wisdom would be understood or used, because it came from **the breath of the Almighty** (vv. 8-9). So Elihu said, **Listen to me** (v. 10). "In view of his daring assertion that his elders were ignorant, he found it necessary to plead for a hearing" (Zuck, *Job*, 143). Elihu said again that the three friends had failed to refute Job (cf. v. 3), concluding that they lacked wisdom from God. But since Elihu had such wisdom, he claimed, he would argue against Job using that wisdom (vv. 11-14).

32:15-22. Elihu felt compelled to speak up because the other three men had run out of **words** in their attempt to prove Job was a sinner who deserved his fate (vv. 15-16). But Elihu had some ideas and opinions of his own to share, and he was ready, **full of words**, and eager to speak (vv. 17-18). He was so pent up, in fact, that he felt as if his insides would burst like fermenting wine bursting new wineskins if he kept silent any longer. He had to speak to **get relief** (vv. 19-20). Elihu also piously claimed that what he was about to say was completely fair and impartial, devoid of bias or flattery, of which he claimed he was incapable (vv. 21-22). As Zuck notes, "[Elihu's] anger had not caused him to lose his sense of self-importance" (*Job*, 144).

33:1-7. In his first speech, Elihu sought to assure Job that what he was about to say came from a motive of **uprightness**, and from a mouth that would **speak knowledge sincerely** (vv. 1-3), perhaps suggesting that the other three men had not been sincere in their words. Elihu put himself on the same level as Job by acknowledging that he too was created by God (v. 4). Despite Elihu's challenge that Job **refute** him if possible, and **array** himself for battle, Elihu's desire was that Job would not be terrified by his arguments (since he was also a creature of God's making, like Job, v. 6) or feel pressured by him (v. 7).

33:8-18. Elihu then said he had heard all of Job's declarations of innocence. He could even quote Job's words back to him, including Job's charge that God had made up charges against Job and treated him like an **enemy** and a prisoner, watching him closely to seize the opportunity to charge him with wrongdoing (vv. 8-11). But Elihu declared Job was wrong in saying that God was against him (v. 12). Then he launched a strong rebuttal of Job. God does speak, Elihu asserted, even using dreams, all in an effort to **keep man from pride**, which would lead to his destruction (vv. 14-18). Eliphaz claimed that a dream provided the authoritative content with which to confront Job. Job claimed he had been terrified with nightmares from God. Elihu's point is that God used dreams to speak to people but, by implication, Job had failed to hear His message. The primary contents of the dreams from God included the need to avoid sin (vv. 17-18).

33:19-22. Besides communicating through dreams, God also communicates through sickness. Here Elihu used an illustration that "struck nearer to home for Job" (Alden, *Job*, 328). He had experienced continued **pain on his bed** and **unceasing complaint in his bones** (v. 19), to the point that he not only had lost interest in eating, but his body revolted at the sight of even his **favorite food** (v. 20; cf. 3:24; 6:7). Verse 21 also describes the wasting disease afflicting Job, which he felt more than once was bringing him close to death (v. 22).

33:23-28. Here Elihu offered a word of hope in the form of **an angel** who may intercede for the afflicted person and **deliver him** from death through the payment of a ransom (vv. 23-24), whether "the repentance of the sick person or a gracious atonement" (Zuck, *Job*, 147). The sufferer who is ransomed in this way will regain his **youthful vigor**, his physical health, and undergo a spiritual renewal so that he can **pray** again and **sing** (vv. 25-27) because God has **redeemed** his life from going down into the pit of death (v. 28).

33:29-33. God's purpose in this restoration is to reestablish the sufferer's fellowship with Him. Elihu concluded his first speech by pleading with Job to **listen to** him, because he wanted to **justify** Job and because he had **wisdom** to offer.

Elihu's theology differed slightly from those of Job's three friends. They saw suffering as a result of God's retribution for one's sin. But Elihu asserted that suffering can be instructive, calling attention to one's sins, and can serve as a preventive measure whereby one is warned and can escape death. Illness, said Elihu, is designed by God to woo people back to Him (**Then he will pray to God, and He will accept him**, v. 26). This wooing could be mediated through angelic beings in Elihu's thinking (v. 23). As did Job's three friends, Elihu connected suffering with sin. But unlike them, he saw a more tender, restorative purpose in it than they did. And as Job's friends did, Elihu misunderstood the situation as it related to Job, who was not guilty of sin that warranted such suffering.

B. His Second Speech (34:1-37)

34:1-9. In his second speech, Elihu answered Job's accusations that God was unjust. Verses 1-15 are addressed to Job's three friends, and vv. 16-37 are spoken to Job (the "you" is singular). Elihu asked again for a hearing from the group and called on them to decide, based on what he had to say, whether Job was right or wrong in charging God with being unjust toward him (vv. 1-4). Elihu then quoted Job's basic defense (vv. 5-6), and took the side of the friends by saying that he **drinks up derision like water** (v. 7), similar to the charge Eliphaz had made in 15:16. Elihu criticized Job for being irreverent, and later for being spiritually ignorant (vv. 34-37). He also accused Job of keeping company with **the workers of iniquity** and walking with **wicked men** (v. 8). Elihu offered no proof of that charge, but he was right in repeating Job's contention that it had done him no good to maintain his integrity before God (v. 9). Elihu reproved Job for his claim that no tangible good comes from one's relationship with God (see Job's earlier comments in 21:15), and in chap. 35 gave a lengthy response to the allegation (see the comments there).

34:10-15. Sounding like Bildad, Elihu defended God's justice. It was unthinkable that **God . . . the Almighty** would **do wickedness** or **do wrong** (v. 10). He does not pervert justice. Elihu maintained that God is just in His dealings with humankind (v. 11), is answerable to no one because of His sovereign authority over the earth (vv. 12-13), and has the right to sustain life or to take it away as He determines (vv. 14-15).

34:16-30. God is **righteous** and impartial, showing no favoritism to **a king**, **to nobles**, or to **the rich**, because they are all the creations **of His hands** whom He can remove **in a moment**. God does not need the aid of a human **hand** to carry out His judgments (vv. 16-20). In His omniscience He sees everything everyone does (v. 21); there is no **darkness** dark enough or **shadow deep** enough for **the workers of**

iniquity to hide themselves from God's all-seeing eyes. He can judge righteously in an instant without having to investigate a matter further or bring the person into His court (vv. 23-24). Evildoers should take warning, because God can overthrow them either **in the night**, when others do not see them, or **in a public place** where their punishment can be seen (vv. 25-26). God judges the wicked because they turned away from **following Him** and **had no regard for any of His ways** (v. 27). As a result of their arrogance in thinking God would not see or punish them, the wicked proceeded to oppress **the poor** and **the afflicted**, who cried out to God for justice (v. 28). But even if God keeps silent when people are downtrodden without cause (as Job accused Him of doing to him), that does not give Job the right to condemn Him (vv. 29-30).

34:31-37. In these verses, Elihu applied the attributes of God he presented in vv. 10-30 to Job and his situation. Elihu presented Job with a hypothetical prayer he could pray as a way of admitting to God that he had committed **iniquity** (vv. 31-32). Elihu then gave Job an indirect ultimatum: it was up to Job, and no one else, to let go of his insistence on his innocence and submit to God's evaluation of him (v. 33). Elihu contended that Job was speaking **without knowledge** and **without wisdom** (v. 35) and was being rebellious against God who is all-powerful and sovereign. Far from being wise, Job needed to be judged **to the limit**—"a cruel statement [that] sounds like Zophar's cutting words that God was not giving [Job] all the punishment he deserved" (Zuck, *Job*, 151). Job had taken a wrong turn in his theological thinking and, in Elihu's opinion, needed to confess it. Like his three older friends, Elihu felt Job had lied about his innocence. He strived to defend God based on an inaccurate knowledge of Job's situation—which started with the dispute in heaven and not with his own gross sin.

C. His Third Speech (35:1-16)

35:1-8. In this paragraph Elihu continued (cf. 34:9) his response to Job's insistence that a relationship with God brings no benefits (cf. 21:15). Elihu's response was that: "(1) God is supreme, and thus He is not affected by or dependent on man's innocence or sin, and (2) God's lack of response to Job's cries was because of his pride" (Zuck, *Job*, 152–53). Elihu charged Job with being inconsistent. Job claimed to be righteous (v. 2). But a person who was truly righteous would not say there is no **profit** in seeking to live righteously before God. Elihu used the same approach he had used earlier, quoting Job (vv. 2-3) and then refuting his logic (vv. 4-8). It did not make sense for Job to claim that he was righteous before God, and then turn around and argue that being righteous in God's sight brought him no advantage. But as noted above, God remains essentially unscathed by human actions, whether good or evil. He judges all impartially. An evil person cannot scare God into treating him well (v. 6), nor can anyone bribe God to be kind to him (v. 7). God has impartially and objectively determined that people "get what they deserve," whether wickedness for wicked people (by implication, Job) or righteous treatment for righteous people (v. 8). Human attempts to intimidate or bribe God have no influence whatsoever with Him.

35:9-13. According to Elihu, people tend to **cry for help** to God when they suffer. But He does not always answer these cries, he continued, because they were just pleas for deliverance from trouble instead of a true prayer of humility to God. Then Elihu enumerated three benefits God gives to those who trust in Him (vv. 10b-11). First, He **gives songs in the night**, suggesting how a believer can find true comfort even in the midst of trouble. Second, He **teaches** people **more than** He teaches the animals. Third, He makes humans **wiser than the birds**. As Alden points out, "These two sentences [in v. 11] are not very profound, but they are one more hint of the upcoming revelation of God, who will interrogate Job about the 'beasts of the earth' and the 'birds of the air' (38:39–39:27)" (*Job*, 345).

Elihu continued his subject of unanswered prayer by saying that God did not respond to the prayers of the oppressed because they were offered in **the pride of evil men** (v. 12), possibly demanding that God provide relief for them. This was no doubt an indirect reference to Job, whom his friends saw as a proud protestor crying out to God not in humility and repentance, but in arrogant pride demanding a hearing and an acquittal from the Almighty.

35:14-16. Such prayers from someone who said God had been unfair to him would **much less** be answered. Elihu advised Job to wait for God to rule on his case. Elihu believed that Job babbled on without knowledge of what he was talking about (cf. 34:35 and therefore, it was time for him to be silent and see what God would say. In v. 15, Elihu responded to Job's assertion in 21:14-21 that God does not punish the wicked as evidenced by their easy lives. As he said in 35:1-8, God does judge the unrighteous, for His impartiality requires it. In v. 16, Elihu may have turned to Job's friends in a sort of aside to give his opinion of Job's words (they are empty and ignorant). This charge "was Elihu's chance to turn this phrase against Job, and he did, although Job had not said anything since Elihu began speaking one hundred verses ago. Thus Elihu showed himself to be of the same mold as the other three" (Alden, *Job*, 347).

D. His Fourth Speech (36:1–37:24)

36:1-4. In his final speech, Elihu claimed to speak with the authority of God (v. 2), asserting that there is an advantage to living a righteous life. Alden calls this "a new tack," and says,

> [Elihu's] tone smacks of arrogance, a sin he indirectly accused Job of in 35:12. Insofar as he went on to speak of God's greatness, his veracity cannot be questioned, but scattered throughout the speech are innuendoes that indicate his assessment of Job's problems has not changed. (*Job*, 347)

Elihu's arrogance is on display in his declaration, **One who is perfect in knowledge is with you** (v. 4).

36:5-11. Elihu emphasized God's strength, mercy, and justice, the latter seen in judging the wicked (v. 6), something which Job had questioned. God not only keeps **His eyes** on **the righteous**, but exalts them like kings (v. 7). If they encounter hardship, it is because of their sin, but those hardships are God's means for providing spiritual instruction for them so that they will repent and find full restoration (vv. 8-11). Once again, Elihu's view of suffering is much more positive than that of the three older friends. It can be remedial and redemptive, not just retributive, and those who return to God and serve Him will benefit from such action (see also vv. 15-16). His statement that the righteous can respond to God's chastening by repenting of their **transgressions** (v. 9) and **evil** (v. 10), and enjoying His renewed blessing, was clearly meant for Job's ears. The other three friends must have been nodding in agreement, since their relentless message to Job was to confess his sins and regain God's favor.

36:12-16. Elihu also presented the alternative to repentance and restoration of God's blessing for those who have sinned: death **by the sword**, dying young, and **without knowledge** (v. 12), that is, without ever learning the lessons God had for them in their suffering. This was another warning aimed at Job, and a not-so-subtle call for him to repent while there was still time. Elihu cautioned Job not to react to his trials as the **godless** do, becoming angry at God but not crying out to Him for **help** in their distress, dying **in youth** in shameful circumstances (vv. 13-14). Yet He relieves **the afflicted**, enabling the oppressed to obey (**opens their ear**). And Elihu said God gave Job **a broad place** (that is, a life with blessings) and food in abundance (vv. 15-16).

36:17-25. At this point, Elihu began to apply vv. 1-16 to Job. Verse 17 is notoriously difficult. The NET translates it, "But now you are preoccupied with the judgment due the wicked, judgment and justice take hold of you" (see also the HCSB). It is possible that the Hebrew means, "You are full of the wicked person's judgment"—that is, often you have judged others as an unrighteous person would judge them when you executed your magisterial tasks. As a result, God's judgment has justly come together and landed upon Job. The **ransom** of v. 18 is often translated "bribe" (see 1Sm 12:3; Am 5:12; Pr 6:35), and Elihu was probably warning Job not to allow even a large bribe to deter him from full repentance and restoration with God. The reason is that **riches** are not a buffer to **distress** (v. 19). Elihu's final warning to Job is **do not turn to evil**, which he believed Job had **preferred** by complaining about his suffering rather than repenting and finding God's restoration. Instead of stubbornly clinging to his claims of innocence, Job should turn to God and learn from Him rather than accusing Him of wrongdoing in the way He was dealing with Job (v. 23). Elihu also said that Job needed to exalt God's works, about which godly people sing praises, and which **all men** have seen, even if from **afar** (vv. 24-25).

36:26-33. Beginning with 36:26 and continuing to the end of his speech in 37:24, Elihu turned from considering Job's plight to the majesty of God. **God is exalted** and infinite. He controls all aspects of nature, including evaporation of **rain** water, **clouds**, thunder, and **lightning**, and He provides food for mankind. Some commentators see in these closing verses a prelude to the storm that speaks of God's power, and out of which He will soon speak to Job (cf. 38:1). Alden says, "[T]he storm is evidence of divine power. Awesome in its power, it speaks to the difference between God's control over the elements and human inability to cope with them when they are stirred up" (*Job*, 357). God's greatness should lead people, including Job, to revere Him and not reject Him. In this section Elihu foreshadows much of what God will say about Himself and His governance of the world in chaps. 38–41.

37:1-13. Elihu continued his vivid word picture of a storm, which speaks so eloquently of God's sovereignty in nature: **thunder**, **lightning**, **snow**, **rain**, storms, cold, and **ice**. The thought of God's overwhelming majesty and power caused Elihu's heart to palpitate and leap **from its place** in fear and awe (v. 1). When God unleashes His thunder and lightning, people must stop their work (v. 7) and seek shelter, knowing that the storm is the work of God, and the animals retreat to their dens (v. 8). God sends these phenomena of nature both for **correction** and for **lovingkindness** (v. 13), as He sees fit. As people focus on God's power apparent in creation, they will adopt the correct attitude of reverence and submission to him, according to Elihu's theology.

37:14-20. In vv. 1-13 Elihu spoke of God's work in nature in the winter. Now he spoke of God's sovereignty in the summer: **lightning**, **clouds**, **south wind**, **skies** bright like a **mirror**. Once again, Elihu paused to call for Job's attention so he could apply his words to the sufferer. As long-winded as Elihu had been, his advice in v. 14b, **Stand and consider the wonders of God**, was ultimately what Job would have to do. It is also good advice for God's people in any age under any circumstances. All believers need to be reminded that they are the work of the great God who, in His grace, has chosen to bestow His love and favor on them. The **darkness** here (v. 19) probably refers to the moral and intellectual dimness that besets humanity, rendering a legal argument against God futile. Verse 20 could be paraphrased, "Should someone say to God, 'Listen up'? If someone does that, any audience he would have with God would result in him being devoured."

37:21-24. These are Elihu's final words, and with them the arguments of Job's four visitors are ended. God's **awesome majesty** is seen in the **skies** and **the north**. God stretches out the clouds in the sky (v. 18), but also brings the wind to clear the skies so the sun, moon, and stars can be seen (v. 21). But God cannot be seen, and therefore no one can **find Him**. He is both powerful and just. Therefore people should **fear Him** and put away pride, a final call to Job to abandon his stubborn refusal to admit his sin and bow humbly before the Lord in confession and repentance.

Did Elihu's speeches advance the case against Job or deepen his understanding of God and His ways? Neither the other three men, nor Elihu persuaded Job to relinquish his position, although most commentators acknowledge that Elihu went deeper into the character and ways of God than did the older men—by pointing out that suffering can be a teaching tool leading to healing and restoration instead of simply being retributive. Zuck says,

> Elihu thus prepared the way for God to speak. Although he stressed aspects of suffering and of the character of God beyond those mentioned by [the other men], he did not have total insight into Job's situation. In fact . . . no man could. It was therefore necessary that God speak. (*Job*, 162)

VII. God Speaks to Job (38:1–42:17)

Perhaps the most fascinating portion of Scripture on general revelation is Job 38–41, because God was using it to address Job's arguments, accusations, and questions.

Gordon R. Lewis and Bruce A. Demarest write:

> General revelation refers to the disclosure of God in nature, in providential history and in the moral law in the heart, whereby all people at all times and places gain a rudimentary understanding of the Creator and His moral demand. (*Integrative Theology* [Grand Rapids, MI: Zondervan, 1987], 1:61)

In Jb 38–41, Job found himself in God's "interrogation room" of the universe. After asking Job more than 60 rhetorical questions on many aspects of general revelation, God finally brought Job to silence. What exactly can be said about how God used general revelation in this particular passage of Scripture? Can the reason for this extensive barrage of interrogative statements be discerned? Do we learn anything substantial about the proper use and understanding of the place of general revelation? What is God doing with general revelation in His response to Job? What did Job comprehend, and what answers did God provide? Roland E. Murphy notes, "It has been well-said that when the Lord 'replies' to Job, He lets nature do the talking (Job 38–41)" (*Tree of Life* [New York: Doubleday, 1990], 3–4).

A survey of the positions on this section of Job immediately places the reader in a torrential rainstorm of material. One is reminded of the conclusion of the Czechoslovakian scholar,

Milos Bic, when he stated almost 45 years ago, "There is an unmanageable mass of literature on the book of Job" (*Review of Alfred Jepsen: Das Buch Hiob und seine Deutung* [Berlin: Evangelische Verlogsanstalt, 1963], 46–47). As one examines the views concerning the 'Speeches of Yahweh,' Bič's conclusion has been seen as valid. Leo G. Perdue cogently states, "While the 'Speeches from the Whirlwind' (38–42:6) provide the climax of the poetic book, no consensus of their interpretation has emerged" (*Wisdom in Revolt* [Sheffield: Almond Press, 1991], 196). James G. Williams helpfully notes, "There has been an explosion of interpretations of Job in the modern Western world. Most interpreters will agree on one thing: the theophany or addresses of God in Job 38–41 provide the key to the book" ("The Theophany of Job," in *Sitting with Job: Selected Studies on the Book of Job*, ed. Roy B. Zuck [Grand Rapids, MI: Baker Book House, 1992], 359). Based on the structure of the book of Job and that Jb 28 is the apex of the book with its wisdom theme, Williams is not fully correct, but Jb 38–41 is an important factor in understanding the account as it supports the central apex in Jb 28.

Yahweh's questions are designed to expose the impotence of all rival deities and individuals. The addresses were a defense against Job's accusations. As Job pressed God for an answer in the preceding chapters, his attitude became sinful as he began to view his affliction as a travesty by God. Therefore Yahweh asked questions to bring Job to realize his ignorance and God's wise omniscience and omnipotence in all the affairs of nature and humanity. Job needed to repent before God, based on what had been revealed.

Parsons points out that

> a main function of the Lord's speeches is to show the absurdity of Job's attempt to manipulate God by a "lawsuit," which assumed that his relationship to God is a juridical one. . . . In 40:8-14, God demonstrated the fallacy of Job's impugning His justice in order to vindicate himself. (Parsons, "Structure and Purpose," 149)

Initially, Job was a great spiritual example as he responded to his losses. However, as the months wore on (7:2; 29:3), the afflictions and disasters started to take their toll. He became worn down physically, mentally, emotionally, and even spiritually. Job started out as a strong spiritual example, but over time cracks began to appear in his theological mindset as he questioned, challenged, and wrongfully accused God of being unjust, uncaring, and malicious.

The Yahweh Speeches (hereafter referred to as *YS* for brevity) are filled with rhetorical questions. Michael Fox explains: God is not quizzing Job. . . . Rather, God is saying to Job, "You know very well that I and I alone created order and maintain it in the world, and I know that you know and you know that I know you know" ("Job 38 and God's Rhetoric," *Semeia* 19 [1981]: 58–59).

How have the *YS* fared in the interpreter's fire over the past 2,000 years? There are two millennia of Jewish and Christian interpretations of this interesting but perplexing section of the book of Job, and their significance is debated. The following are several of the major views commentators have taken on the *YS* of Jb 38–41. No one position captures every feature, and some positions are stronger than others. But each of the five views listed below has something to commend it, along with its limitations.

1. The Grand Paradox Viewpoint. *Yahweh's actions are paradoxical and indiscernible by humans; therefore the only way out of this dilemma is to align with Yahweh and hope for the best. The YS demonstrate a host of paradoxes, from simple to complex, that bring Job to a dead end in seeking to understand God.* Perdue notes,

> God's actions in the world are paradoxical: He nurtures but limits the Yam [the sea], checks the power of death by the recurring of birth, and feeds the offspring of eagles with the dead flesh of other creatures. In a world of paradoxes, Job's speeches rooted in the idea of retribution make no sense and thus are dismissed. (*Wisdom in Revolt*, 197)

It is impossible and ridiculous to judge Yahweh's actions or to try to figure Him out. The numerous references throughout Job to the inscrutable ways of God testify to the thesis that His ways are past finding out. Job's experience, and the rigid view of God's retribution proposed by his three friends—which Job demonstrated to be untenable—prove that God's sovereign will cannot be reduced to a humanly created formula.

2. The Maintenance-Mode Viewpoint. *Yahweh maintains justice in creation and history despite the presence of chaos and imperfection. The YS portray Yahweh as in the maintenance-mode concerning moral order in the universe, thus giving Job an indirect response to his questions.*

Robert Gordis states, "The vivid and joyous description of nature is not an end in itself: it underscores the insight that nature is not merely a mystery, but is also a miracle, a cosmos, a thing of beauty. From this flows the basic conclusion at which the poet has arrived: just as there is order and harmony in the natural world, though imperfectly grasped by man, so there is order and meaning in the moral sphere, though often incomprehensible to man. . . ." (*The Book of Job*, 133).

There is no question that God maintains moral order in His universe, although this view does not seem to speak to the issue of how mankind should respond to the revelation of God's purpose in creation and in history.

3. The Lawsuit Viewpoint. *Yahweh responded to Job in the context of a courtroom atmosphere since Job had leveled charges against God's management of his life and the universe. The* YS *stand as the testimony of Yahweh, the defendant, in the lawsuit brought by Job.* Sylvia H. Scholnick states:

> As many scholars have recognized, the poet chooses the court of justice as the setting for the dialogue between Job and his friends. He dramatizes the hero's search for an acceptable definition of the meaning of divine justice by structuring the work around a lawsuit which the man from Uz initiates against God. The case is comprised of several interwoven complaints. But when God speaks from the whirlwind, the setting of the drama appears to shift to what Alter calls the "arena of creation." ("Poetry in the Courtroom: Job 38–41," in *Directions in Hebrew Poetry*, ed. Elaine Follis [Sheffield: JSOT Press, 1987], 185–86)

This is a very common view of the *YS*, and one for which strong evidence appears in the text. That Yahweh twice used the "gird up your loins" metaphor of a challenge in 38:3 and 40:7 supports the lawsuit viewpoint. Job had repeatedly pled for a hearing before God, and said he had marshaled his arguments so as to win a "not guilty" verdict from the Almighty. So this viewpoint has the strength of offering a fitting conclusion to Job's case, although God did not respond in the way Job or his friends thought He would. Job was not called to testify!

4. The Legal Challenge Viewpoint. *The book of Job is similar to a challenge motif concerning who is "god," whether Yahweh or the gods of the nations.* The questions in the *YS* are designed to expose the impotence of all rival deities. In Job the opposing parties are Yahweh and Job; therefore the *YS* are a defense against Job's accusations. Henry L. Rowold noted that "the questions in Job 38–41, as in Is 40–66, do not seek information. Instead they are challenges to the opponent" ("Leviathan and Job in Job 41:2-3," *Journal of Biblical Literature* 105 [March 1986]: 104–9). This lawsuit format is not a covenant court trial *(rib)* in which Yahweh prosecutes His people for breach of covenant. Instead it is a challenge to an opponent. This view takes a different approach to the legal argument of Jb 38–41 in that Job's situation is not the issue.

5. The Lawsuit/Lament Viewpoint. *The book of Job is in the form of an expanded lament and lawsuit. The YS are the "salvation oracle" to the individual in need of help or deliverance.* Claus Westermann states:

> The full significance of God's answering Job becomes apparent only when viewed against the background of the book's structure. We have seen how the element of a summons to a lawsuit is contained in the wish that God might answer Job. Here converge two lines that have run through the whole book so far: the legal proceedings and the lament. In line with the legal proceedings, Job, who was accused by the friends of being a transgressor, appeals to that higher court which is at the same time, however, the very opponent he summons to a lawsuit. In line with the lament, that point is now reached at which, in the genre of the lament psalm, the answer of God is expected. . . . (*The Structure of the Book of Job,* trans. Charles A. Muenchow [Minneapolis: Fortress, 1981], 105–6)

J. E. Hartley adds, "The Yahweh Speeches thus relate to the two dominant elements in Job's speeches, lament and lawsuit. . . . As a result Yahweh wins the lawsuit by reducing Job to silence. As for lament, Yahweh delivers to Job a word of hope, similar to an oracle of salvation" (*The Book of Job*, 489). Proponents of this view note that Job cried for litigation, not deliverance. The lament and lawsuit elements of Job's speeches have been noted throughout this work, and they are clearly two key motifs. Whether the *YS* constitute a "salvation oracle" is open to debate.

6. The Traditional Viewpoint. *Yahweh is the sovereign Creator and Master of the universe; therefore questioning or arguing with Him is* *ridiculous, but repenting and praising Him are in order. The YS illustrate these two essential ideas: Yahweh is Creator and Master of the universe.* If these two ideas are true, then Job needs to adjust his attitude if he truly wishes to be correct about his notion of what is going on in his situation as it concerns the Almighty. Included in this adjustment is the need he had, not only to correct his attitudes about God, but also to *embrace and accept what God had ordained for his life.* Lewis and Demarest summarize, "The vast expanse . . . clearly reflects the infinite Mind that created and orders all these phenomena. . . . Through the medium of a magnificent cosmos the observer plainly perceives the reality of the God who made and who upholds all that is" (*Integrative Theology*, 1:67). This view may have the most to commend it in terms of bringing together the various elements of the *YS*.

Bullock notes concerning the *YS*,

> Significantly, the answer to the question "Why do the innocent suffer?" is nowhere spelled out in the God Speeches. The Lord did not accommodate Himself to so simplistic a formulation of so profound a mystery. Job had begun with the challenge that God explain his own personal dilemma. . . . [But] the Lord's answer was phrased almost altogether in universal terms. (*An Introduction to the Old Testament Poetic Books*, 107)

A. God's First Speech about His Knowledge (38:1–40:2)

38:1-3. When God finally responded to Job, He **answered . . . out of the whirlwind.** This may have been frightening to Job. The word **darkens** means "to distort something, to place something in a false or bad light." **Counsel** means "a plan, design, purposeful scheme." **Without knowledge** suggests that there is no way Job could have known all the facts about God's confrontation with Satan. Job's comments about God were thus based upon ignorance of God's plans and actions, and yet Job's comments had put God and His providential rule of the universe in a bad light. God challenged Job, **gird up your loins** like a soldier and get ready for an intellectual and spiritual battle! God was ready to do battle (9:34; 10:2-9; 23:3-9; 31:35), and He was up to the challenges of his human contender, Job. God said He would ask Job, and ironically, He challenged him to **instruct** Him. "Job the plaintiff had suddenly become the defendant!" (Zuck, *Job*, 165).

38:4–39:30. Although God had told Job to be prepared to answer Him, He began immediately with a tremendous series of questions for which Job had no answer at all. God questioned Job about his relationship to the physical universe, here inanimate creation. God asked him about the creation of **the earth** (vv. 4-7); the origin and limits of **the sea** (vv. 8-11); Job's ability to cause the sun to rise each **morning** (vv. 12-15); the hidden aspects of creation not visible to humankind (vv. 16-18); the location and properties of the sun (vv. 19-20); the spasmodic tendencies of the weather (vv. 22-30); how the stars operate (vv. 31-33); and details related to droughts (vv. 34-38).

God also questioned Job about his *comprehension* of the mechanical function of these aspects of the creation (vv. 4, 18, 20-21, and 33). If Job could not answer these questions, he had no right to question God's design of the universe. In addition, vv. 10-11, 12-15, 26-27, and 37-38 emphasize God's goodness as advertised in creation. Job had questioned and doubted God's wisdom and knowledge in how He ran the world, especially in light of Job's undeserved suffering. Job also questioned God's goodness. Here, in chap. 38, using numerous features of inanimate creation, God refuted Job's allegations by asking him to account for where he was when God created or determined the various elements of the natural world where Job resided. So God put Job to the test. "Job, can you pass this rhetorical quiz? Answer if you are able." The 18 questions in this quiz, which continues all the way to the end of chap. 39 are not only impressive, but unanswerable by any human being.

1. Where were you when I designed and built the earth? (38:4-6)
2. Where were you when the sons of God sang about it? (38:7)
3. Where were you when I set the oceans and their boundaries? (38:8-11)
4. Have you ever commanded . . . the dawn to appear? (38:12-15)
5. Have you ever explored the depths of the oceans? (38:16-18)
6. Have you understood the expanse of the earth? (38:18)
7. Do you know where light and darkness dwell? (38:19-21)
8. Do you know where snow and hail are stored? (38:22-24)
9. Do you know about thunderbolts, rain . . . ice . . . frost? (38:25-30)

10. Do you control each constellation and its orbit? (38:31-33)
11. Do you cause rain and lightnings and give people wisdom? (38:34-38)
12. Do you feed lions and their cubs or the ravens and their young? (38:39-41)
13. Do you know when mountain goats and deer are born?(39:1-4)
14. Did you loose the wild donkey and care for each one? (39:5-8)
15. Do you control the wild ox or does he obey you? (39:9-12)
16. Did you give the female ostrich low intelligence? (39:13-18)
17. Did you give the war horse abilities for battle? (39:19-25)
18. Did you give the hawk and the eagle incredible eyesight? (39:26-30)

In the second part of God's quizzing of Job, He interrogated him about his relationship to and knowledge of *animate creation* (questions 12-18). As noted above, God asked Job about lions (38:39-40); ravens (38:41); mountain goats (39:1-4); wild donkeys (39:5-8); wild oxen (39:9-12); the ostrich (39:13-18); the horse (39:19-25) and predatory birds (39:26-30). It would be impossible for Job to know much about "what makes these animals tick," their skills, behavior, instincts. But God knows about these creatures. Furthermore, the description of each animal also includes a description God's goodness to the animal—either by providing what these animals need to stay alive (for example, lions and ravens in 38:39-41; the hawk and eagle in 39:26-30), or by giving these animals the physical dexterity necessary to live (the mountain goat's inherent toughness in 39:1-4; the horse's strength and speed in 39:19-25).

40:1-2. These verses are Job's first response to God. God asked Job, **Will the faultfinder contend with the Almighty?** (vv. 1-2), that is, "Will you continue to indict me for injustice?" (Zuck, *Job*, 175). **Faultfinder** means "one who reproaches or scorns, who censors" another. It is a noun related to a verb that means "to admonish" or "correct."

B. Job's Response to God's First Speech (40:3-5)

40:3-5. In 10:2 and 23:6, Job accused God of contending with him unjustly, and thus reproached Him. But in the first encounter with God, Job saw God's skill, knowledge, power, and *goodness* in nature. How could he then continue to find fault with God? Job was deficient in his knowledge of God's ways and incompetent to control the universe, so how could Job presume to expect God to give an account of His actions to him? **Reproves** is a legal term that means "to incriminate, criticize, make a charge against" another. Job had no right to do this against God since he was God's inferior.

Faced with God's question for which he had no answer, Job wisely chose silence (vv. 3-5). He was ashamed because he realized he had already said too much in charging God with treating him unjustly. Admitting that he could not instruct God (cf. 38:3), Job confessed, **I am insignificant**, meaning "light" or "slight." In essence Job stated, "In comparison to you, God, I am a nobody!" Job's former self-confidence and pride (see 13:22) are now shriveled into humility, for he said, **What can I reply to You?** In 31:37, Job said that he would act like a prince and approach God with no thought of bowing to Him (Jb 31:37). But here he is put in his proper place. **I lay my hand on my mouth** indicates that Job realized he needed to remain silent before God. He had spoken critically of God on more than one occasion (**Once I have spoken . . . Even twice**), but now realized he must say nothing more. Nevertheless, however much Job was humbled at this point, he was not as yet repentant. To bring him to that point, God would interrogate him.

C. God's Second Speech about His Power (40:6–41:34)

God made His second speech to Job, again out of the storm (40:6). In a pattern similar to the first speech, God challenged and questioned Job, and Job responded.

40:6-9. God shouted to Job from the storm, **Now gird up your loins like a man** (40:6-7) to face His interrogation, a repetition of God's challenge in 38:3. God's justice, which Job had questioned previously (see, e.g., 9:24), is touched on briefly by God. **Annul** means "to break, dissolve, destroy." Job had blamed God for being unjust in his misfortune. But any mortal's alleged superiority that would enable him to criticize God for His apparent lack of justice must be accompanied by a similar superiority of power (v. 9). God challenged Job to assume the role of Deity. But it is apparent that God has no equals in power, especially not in Job. Job is not only inferior to God, he is not even remotely God's equal (v. 9). He does not have the strength (**arm**) or voice (**thunder**) needed to contend with Him. Job had no choice but to stand silently while the **thunder** of God's **voice** broke over him.

40:10-14. Continuing the idea of Job's

inferiority stated in v. 9, God challenged him to run the universe better than God did. God's assignment to Job was to bring **down the wicked** and **proud** by unleashing his anger, humiliating them just by looking at them, demolishing them, burying them. If Job could do this, which Job had accused God of neglecting (see 21:7-26), God would praise Job as one superior to Him, and Job could justify himself. But humankind cannot do this. Therefore, one must simply depend on God, even though people cannot comprehend God's ways. As Zuck states,

> Because Job was unable to assume God's managerial responsibilities over the wicked, it became clear that he could not save himself. Hence it follows that man, dependent on God, must not question Him, even though he cannot fully comprehend His ways. (*Job*, 177)

40:15-24. Job had impugned God's justice (9:24, as noted above; cf. also 10:3; 12:6, 16:11), and challenged His sovereignty by saying he would happily go to court with God and present a case against Him—and win (cf. 13:3; 23:1-7, 10). Here God addressed those very aspects of His nature, challenging Job to find any fault with His justice and, by implication, present his challenge if he thought there was any way he could contend successfully with God.

The ancients were well aware of the Canaanite and Chaldean creation myths— epics and symbols of the enemies of the stability in the cosmos and the chaos they could inflict. As Dyrness explains, "Old Testament writers borrowed Canaanite and Babylonian mythical elements to use them in their picture of the world" (*Themes in the Old Testament Theology*, 69). God could cut or dismember Rahab, the personification of the raging sea (Jb 26:12; 38:8-11), and could pierce through the mythic dragon (Is 51:9; cf. Rv 12:7-9). Nevertheless, for the following reasons, Zuck suggests that it is more likely that the **Behemoth** and the **Leviathan**, described in this section, were actual beasts and not merely mythological (*Job*, 177–78). (1) In His speech, God declared that He had made Behemoth (40:15) and Leviathan (41:1). (2) The descriptions of these animals' anatomies are so precise that they appear to be real. (3) Mythical animals were based on actual animals, albeit with exaggerated or added features. (4) All the animals God listed in His first speech were real. (5) The Bible speaks of both Behemoth and Leviathan in other parts of the Bible without any mythological connotations (Ps 104:26; Jl 1:20).

As to the significance of God's citing these animals, Zuck states, "The purpose in this zoom-lens photography of Behemoth (40:15-24) and Leviathan (chap. 41) was the same as in the first speech: to impress Job with his feeble puniness in contrast to God's majestic power" (Zuck, *Job*, 177).

Attempts to identify **Behemoth** have run the gamut. This creature has been identified as the elephant (Aquinas), the buffalo (Couroye), or the hippopotamus (Archer; Zuck), but none of these fits all the description of this creature. Some believe it was a creature that is now extinct, or as mentioned above, mythic (Alden, *Job*, 395–96). Whatever the identity of this animal, its impressiveness is beyond doubt. God called it **first** in His **ways**, probably in reference to its size and strength. Verse 19b could refer to the Behemoth being so large and powerful that only his **maker** could approach him with the idea of engaging him in combat or trying to subdue him.

41:1-34. Some believe the **Leviathan** to be a mythical monster identical to Lotan mentioned in texts at Ugarit among the Canaanites. Baal, the Canaanite storm god, is reported to have killed the crooked serpent with seven heads (cf. Ps. 74:13-14; Is 27:1-3). More likely, the Canaanites created their mythic Leviathan from some sort of real animal. Like Behemoth, the identity of **Leviathan** baffles interpreters. It has been called a whale (Aquinas), dinosaur (Whitcomb), or crocodile (Archer; Zuck). But in the list of the characteristics of both creatures below, none of these identifications fully satisfies the descriptions. It is popular to argue that both animals are dinosaurs, but this is unlikely.

In vv. 10b-11, God inserted a question to Job in the middle of His description of Leviathan. He challenged Job to **stand before** Him in light of His greatness, which of course Job could not do. Job had come to realize the truth of God's declaration, **Whatever is under the whole heaven is Mine**, including Job and his circumstances. Job had declared more than once that he would be ready to present his defense if God would give him the opportunity. But now that Job had that opportunity, he had nothing to say!

The description of **Leviathan** continues in v. 12. Those who favor the dinosaur view are somewhat inconsistent in how they view the characteristics with which they are described. They view some of the features as literal (the Leviathan's mouth is ringed with fierce **teeth**, 41:14), but view others as being figurative (his

breath can ignite **coals**, 41:21). It is preferable to view these as creatures that would prove vastly inferior to God. However, Leviathan was so terrifying that all other creatures, including man, cowered in terror before him (v. 22).

The animals that God described to Job in chaps. 38–41 were "a grand zoological exhibition to help Job sense that because he had nothing to do with making, sustaining, or even subduing them, it was unthinkable that he could question their Creator" (Zuck, *Job*, 183). Job met God's final challenge with contrition and regret that he had said as much as he did (Alden, *Job*, 392). In 40:15–41:34 Job was confronted with two ferocious beasts that only God could create and control. Just as Job would tremble in fear in the presence of these creatures, he was wise to tremble in fear and submission to God.

D. Job's Repentance before God (42:1-6)

42:1-6. In Job's second response to God, he acknowledged that God is sovereign, and he confessed that he had contended with God in ignorance (vv. 1-3). He recognized his need to be instructed by God (not for him to teach God anything). Then he admitted that what he now knew about God compared with what he knew before was like a contrast between hearing someone and then seeing that individual in person (v. 5). So he repented **in dust and ashes** (v. 6).

It would be natural to ask, "Why does God speak to Job without answering his questions directly?" Nowhere does God offer an explanation about the cosmic challenge made by the devil. Why is this? In response, David McKenna writes,

> The answer is that Job is casting a dark shadow between his mind and God's mind with the *why* of ethical questions about his suffering, which the human mind cannot comprehend or understand. We lack the perspective of God's view in *creating* the universe, *controlling* its forces, and *caring* about its creatures. Job needs to learn that the issue is not ethical, the question is not *why*, and the need is not understanding. The issue is spiritual, the question is *who*, and the need is trust. (*Job*, CCSOT, vol. 12 [Waco, TX: Word, 1986], 293)

When believers face the kinds of suffering that Job faced, it is not answers to intellectual questions that are really necessary. The tendency is to ask, "Why did this tragedy happen?" Yet the *answer* is not what is truly sought. Believers want their sons or daughters or spouses back, their marriages restored, their financial losses reversed, or their bodies healed. The answer to the question would not satisfy. But a deepened sense of God's love, sustaining tenderness, sovereign goodness, and gladsome presence will steady us. John Piper writes,

> Pain and loss are bitter providences. Who has lived long in this world of woe without weeping, sometimes until the head throbs and there are no more tears to lubricate the convulsing of our amputated love? But Oh, the folly of trying to lighten the ship of suffering by throwing God's governance overboard. The very thing the tilting ship needs in the storm is the ballast of God's good sovereignty, not the ... [casting off] of [this] deep and precious truth. What makes the crush of calamity sufferable is not that God shares our shock, but that his bitter providences are laden with the bounty of love. (*Misery of Job and the Mercy of God* [Wheaton: Crossway, 2002], 8–9)

E. Job's Restoration by God (42:7-17)

42:7-17. Walther Eichrodt faults Job's friends for believing in what he refers to as "a mechanical doctrine of retribution" (*Theology of the Old Testament* [Philadelphia: Westminster Press, 1967], 2:88). Yes, some suffering is a result of personal sin, but there are other reasons for its occurrence in the life of a believer or unbeliever. One purpose for suffering is that the glory of God might be displayed both in the life of the sufferer and to others, as Jesus said concerning the man born blind (Jn 9:3, cf. commentary above for Jb 9:25-35). It is instructive that in this case, the man's blindness also became the vehicle for leading him to faith in Christ. Elihu's speeches also pointed out that God sometimes uses suffering in the life of a believer to bring about repentance and restoration.

God told **Eliphaz the Temanite** that He was angry with him and his two friends because they misrepresented Him to Job. Eliphaz was singled out probably because he was the eldest and spoke first. Although the three men had related many truths about God, they also mistakenly insisted that God always sent suffering in retribution for sin, limiting His sovereignty and reducing Him to a Deity who always acts in predictable ways. In this way they had **not spoken ... what is right** of God (v. 7), as Job had done. Twice in these verses, God affirmed that Job had **spoken ... right** about Him. How did Job earn this commendation, since he had accused God of being unjust to him? The answer seems to be that God saw "the thoughts and intents of Job's heart" (Alden, *Job*, 412), knowing that Job was innocent of sin. Also note that Job repented of anything he had said that impugned God's goodness. The three friends apparently repented only after God commanded them to sacrifice **seven bulls and seven rams** as **a burnt offering** in the presence of Job for their sins and to ask Job to **pray** for them.

God **accepted Job** and did not judge his friends for their **folly**. They did as the Lord told them, and Job was restored to fellowship with God and to even more prosperity than he had known before his trials.

Job's siblings came and **comforted him** and **gave him . . . money** and each a **ring of gold**. Though they apparently had done nothing before to comfort Job, at least his extended family responded then with acts of mercy.

The Lord blessed Job's **latter** years more than the earlier years of his life with **14,000 sheep . . . 6,000 camels . . . 1,000 yoke of oxen, and 1,000 female donkeys**, exactly twice what he had before (1:3). Job and his wife also had **seven** more **sons** and **three** more **daughters**, and Job lived to see his offspring to the fourth generation.

Since he lived **140 years** after his calamities, and since he was probably 40 or 50 years of age when the calamities struck, he lived close to 200 years; he **died . . . full of days**. It is also possible that Job was closer to 70 years of age when he lost everything, which would make his remaining 140 years twice what he had lived before, in accordance with God's **twofold** blessing (cf. v. 10). Interestingly, Eliphaz had prophesied Job's longevity and it came true—but not for the reason Eliphaz suggested. He had said to Job, "You will come to the grave in full vigor, like the stacking of grain in its season" (5:26), providing that Job would acknowledge and repent of his sin. Job's long life put him the company of the great patriarch Abraham, who also died "in a ripe old age, an old man and satisfied with life" (Gn 25:8).

Some readers of Job might conclude that God's goodness to Job was a reward for his upright behavior. But it is important to understand that "God was freely bestowing His goodness, not obligingly rewarding Job's piety" (Zuck, *Job*, 188). Job's latter blessings were not in payment of a debt that God owed to him. That idea brings one closer to the mechanical view of God's actions that Job's three friends propounded, that God always rewards piety with blessings just as He always punishes sin with calamity, because He cannot do otherwise.

But that idea was shown to fall far short of God's infinite, incomparable, and often (to humans) incomprehensible wisdom, which is on display throughout the book of Job. Delitzsch states,

> This is the twofold point of view from which the suffering of Job was to be regarded. It was designed, first of all, that Job should prove himself in opposition to Satan, in order to overcome him; and since Job does not pass through the trial entirely without sinning, it has the effect at the same time of purifying and perfecting him. In both respects, the history of Job is a passage from the history of God's own conflict with the evil one, which is the substance of the history of redemption, and ends in the triumph of the divine love (*Biblical Commentary on the Book of* Job, 1:32).

Here are several truths based on Job that apply to believers today.

1. Believers' *service for God should never depend on what they receive from Him*. Many believers in the affluent Western world believe that God guarantees our enjoyment of life. However, the book of Job is a large banner *against* the health-and-wealth theology of the 21st century.

2. In times of *severe suffering* sometimes a believer cannot trust the counsel of closest friends and even his spouse, for they may not be thinking properly. Job's wife had suffered most of the same losses Job experienced, but her advice was inappropriate.

3. *Believers often go to the wrong sources for counsel and help*. Advice from television talk shows, movies, novels, wayward friends, and a secular society often usurp the wisdom of God and His Word. When believers experience suffering, they should be sure Jb 28 is in proper focus.

4. *Suffering believers need not be afraid to counter their friends, relatives, or spouses when receiving foolish advice from them*. Several of Job's claims have become solid advice for the ages (1:21; 2:9; 14:14: 19:23-27; 31:6; 42:1-6). Margaret Clarkson makes an excellent point when she states,

> A new error is deceiving many evangelicals and leaving a trail of destruction. Though promoted as truth, it distorts biblical teaching. The myth is that salvation is accompanied by instant health. Christians experiencing

anything less either lack faith, are out of God's will, or maybe are not really Christians. (Clarkson, "It's No Sin to Be Sick," *Moody Monthly*, November 1978, 52)

She notes that promoters of this view tell their audiences that Jesus wants everyone well, and that their pain can be eliminated by an instant miracle if they have enough faith.

5. *The Bible mentions over 30 reasons that believers suffer in this life.* A major problem with the counsel of Job's friends is that they focused on too few categories.

6. *Though Satan is not omniscient, he knows everyone's name and where each person lives.* He is skilled in tripping up people, but God sets boundaries on what he can do to believers. His works are bound under God's sovereignty, and he is a spiritual loser, as seen in his failed strategy against Job.

7. *Because each person has a nervous system, physical suffering and pain will be part of human existence in this fallen world.* Even Jesus participated in pain, suffering, and physical death.

8. *Being righteous and having integrity does not mean that anyone is perfect or without any fault.* The book of Job is clear that Job did sin, but he did not curse God to His face as Satan had predicted. In fact at the end of the account he confessed to God that he had sinned in several different ways (42:2-3). Believers today are not perfect, and yet they should be careful not to accuse God of wrongdoing.

9. *The spiritual health of believers is not determined by their wealth or poverty.* The book of Job makes clear that wealth and poverty are products of God's divine sovereignty.

10. *Believers may ask God for answers without sinning.* Job was entirely justified to ask God why He was allowing all this evil to befall him. He only sinned when he began to demand answers from God, as if God were answerable to him.

11. *Suffering can help lead believers to deeper levels of spiritual maturity and can strengthen their integrity before God.* Job, although righteous at the outset of the book, grew spiritually because of the suffering he endured. He became even more godly.

12. *Suffering can strengthen the believer's resolve to remain faithful to the Lord, regardless of the circumstances.* Job was stretched and came to the brink. Yet he refused to curse God and die. Therefore, his resolve was strengthened for his spiritual good.

The message of the book of Job is frequently understood to be an explanation of suffering in this life. Yet the book never does explain suffering. Instead it emphasizes the sovereignty of God and the need for all sufferers to submit to that sovereignty. Furthermore, God's sovereignty is not depicted as ruthless or capricious. He is loving and caring and knows what He is doing—He just does not reveal His purposes to suffering believers. A truly righteous sufferer will ultimately come to trust the Eternal Just One to know what He is doing, and with Job, to declare, "Though He slay me, I will hope in Him."

BIBLIOGRAPHY

Alden, Robert L. *Job.* New American Commentary. Nashville: Broadman & Holman, 1993.

Andersen, Francis. *Job: An Introduction and Commentary.* Tyndale Old Testament Commentary. Downers Grove, IL: InterVarsity, 1976.

Bullock, C. Hassell. *An Introduction to the Old Testament Poetic Books.* Chicago: Moody, 1979.

Clines, David J. A. *Job 21–37.* Word Biblical Commentary. Dallas: Word, 2006.

———. *Job 38–42.* Word Biblical Commentary. Dallas: Word, 2006.

Delitzsch, Franz. *Biblical Commentary on the Book of Job,* 3 vols. Translated by F. Bolton. Grand Rapids, MI: Eerdmans, 1949.

Gordis, Robert. *The Book of Job: Commentary, New Translation, and Special Studies.* New York: Jewish Theological Seminary of America, 1978.

Hartley, J. E. *The Book of Job.* New International Commentary on the Old Testament. Grand Rapids, MI: Eerdmans, 1988.

McKenna, David. *Job.* The Communicator's Commentary Series: Old Testament, vol. 12. Waco, TX: Word, 1986.

Rowley, H. H. *Job.* The Century Bible. New York: Thomas Nelson, 1970.

Smick, Elmer B. "Job," In *The Expositor's Bible Commentary,* vol. 4, rev. ed. Edited by Tremper Longman III and David. E. Garland. Grand Rapids, MI: Zondervan, 2010.

Zuck, Roy B. *Job.* Chicago: Moody, 1978.

———, ed. *Sitting with Job: Selected Studies on the Book of Job.* Grand Rapids, MI: Baker, 1992.

PSALMS

Multiple Faculty Contributors

INTRODUCTION

The Hebrew title of the book of Psalms is *Tehillim*, literally "praises." However, the English title Psalms is adopted from the Septuagint (LXX) Greek Bible in the intertestamental period, which titled the book *Psalmoi*, meaning "songs to the accompaniment of a stringed instrument," or simply "songs of praise." The LXX Greek word translates the Hebrew word *mizmor* ("song") that occurs in the titles of 57 of the psalms as the title. The English translators transliterated the Greek *Psalmoi*, resulting in the title "Psalms" in English Bibles.

Author. There is a distinction between God as the author and originator of the ideas and intentions of the text (2Tm 3:16-17), and the individual human psalmists as the writers (2Pt 1:21). This is illustrated in the NT with respect to Psalms in Ac 1:16, where Peter cited Pss 69:25 and 109:8 as "Scripture . . . which the Holy Spirit foretold by the mouth of David" (see also Ac 4:24-25, cf. Pss 1–2; Heb 4:7, cf. Ps 95:8).

Certain psalms begin with a superscription/heading, which is part of the text indicating the author. King David is explicitly named in the headings of 73 psalms, as well as having his authorship identified in the NT for three other psalms (Pss 1–2 in Ac 4:25; Ps 95 in Heb 4:7). Asaph is the author of 12 psalms, predominantly with postexilic content (50, 73–83). He was one of three heads of the three families of Levitical singers in the time of David (see 1Ch 25) and was also a seer/prophet (2Ch 29:30).

The sons of Korah, a branch of the Levitical singers who led temple worship (2Ch 20:19), are identified in Pss 42, 44–49, 84–85, and 87–88. King Solomon wrote two psalms (72, 127). Ethan, a wise man, Levitical singer, and probably the same as Jeduthun (1Kg 4:31; 1Ch 2:6; 15:19; 2Ch 25:1) wrote one psalm (89). Heman who has co-attribution to the sons of Korah in one psalm (88), was a singer and wise man in Solomon's court (1Kg 4:31; 1Ch 15:19). Moses wrote one psalm (90).

Of the 46 remaining psalms for which no headings are supplied perhaps three more (Pss 96, 105, and 106) were written by David on the testimony of 1Ch 16:7-36, which ascribes to David ("David first assigned") a psalm of thanksgiving selectively derived from those three (i.e., Pss 96; 105:1-15; and 106:1, 47-48). The remaining 43 psalms are anonymous, without headings, although tradition has attributed several of them to David.

Date. Historically the individual psalms were written over a period of about 1,000 years, from the time of Moses (c. 1400 BC) to the Israelites' return from exile (c. 450 BC).

There is no definitive indication of the person or persons responsible for compiling and ordering the psalms in the form of the book, though it seems likely that the bulk of this work was undertaken by an editor after the return from Babylon.

The central implication of this distinction is that Psalms, particularly the royal psalms, must be read from this postexilic perspective when there was no Davidic king on the throne. As a result, the psalms are to be read not looking back at past kings of Israel but forward to the coming of the anticipated son of David, the messianic King.

Structure. In the Hebrew manuscripts, and as reflected in most translations, Psalms is subdivided into five distinct "books." Though the individual psalms were written by different people at different times (see "Date" above), they were, through divine guidance, eventually compiled and organized around this five-book framework in the postexilic period. Each of the books ends with a doxology (cf. Book One, 41:13; Book Two, 72:18-19; Book Three, 89:52; Book Four, 106:48; and Book Five, Ps 150, which is a doxology to the whole Psalter).

The most likely structure is an intentional paralleling of the five-book subdivision of the Torah. This is affirmed not only by early Jewish tradition but also by the thematic parallels in the content of the corresponding books of the Torah and Psalms, as illustrated in the chart below.

In addition to each of the five books of Psalms being explicitly indicated in the Hebrew text by the headings "Book One," "Book Two," etc., the ending of each book is indicated by a clear doxology, the first four of which are variations of the formula "Blessed be . . . the LORD/His name . . . forever/to everlasting" (Pss 41:13; 72:18-19; 89:52; 106:48). The last of these is appropriately expressed by a grand doxology, the all-encompassing exhortation, "Let everything that has breath praise the LORD" (Ps 150:6). The individual unity of each of the five books is also underscored (often in quite subtle and sophisticated ways) by the use of similar literary forms and language.

A further structural parallel between Psalms and the Torah is evident in the way both compilations begin and end. Just as the first two chapters of Genesis focus on God's intended ideal for man, both individually and collectively (i.e., "to worship and to obey"; see the commentary on Gn 2:15), so too do the first two chapters of Psalms focus on God's intended ideal for man, both individually and collectively; i.e., to cultivate "delight . . . in the law" (Ps 1:2) suggests obedience, and to worship ("do homage," Ps 2:12). Also just as the last two chapters of Deuteronomy express praise for God's overall concern for Israel (Dt 33:3: "Indeed, he loves the people"), His judgment of her enemies (Dt 33:29: the Lord is "the sword of your majesty! So your enemies shall cringe before you"), and His anticipated future, messianic redemption (Dt 34:10: "Since that time no prophet has risen in Israel like Moses"), so too do the last two psalms express praise for God's overall concern for Israel (Ps 149:4: "For the LORD takes pleasure in His people"), His judgment of her enemies (149:6: "Let the high praises of God be . . . a two-edged sword in their hand, to execute vengeance on the nations"), and His anticipated future—and final—redemption (149:4: "He will beautify the afflicted ones with salvation").

Place in the Canon. In modern Christian Bibles, Psalms is the second book in the books of Poetry section (following Job). This organization of Law (Genesis–Deuteronomy); History (Joshua–Esther); Poetry (Job–Song of Songs); and Prophets (Isaiah–Malachi) is derived from the tradition of categorizing the biblical books adopted by Hellenistic Jewry and reflected (with some differences) in the Septuagint (the earliest Greek translation of the OT).

In manuscripts of the Hebrew Bible, Psalms is located in the section known as the Writings (or Hagiographa), the third and last division of the Hebrew Bible. The Hebrew Scriptures are divided into three sections: Torah (Genesis–Deuteronomy), the Prophets (Isaiah–Malachi) and Writings (Psalms, Proverbs, Job, Song of Songs, Ruth, Lamentations, Ecclesiastes, Esther, Daniel, Ezra–Nehemiah, Chronicles). Though the traditional place of Psalms in this third division

The Torah (Pentateuch)	Psalms
Genesis: God's sovereign creation of man and election of Israel.	Book One (1–41): expressions of worship focusing on God's sovereign election.
Exodus: God's protection of His nascent national son, Israel, and His provision of the fundamental/general laws intended for their material and spiritual nurture.	Book Two (42–72): expressions of worship focusing on God's protective nurture.
Leviticus: God's granting of specific laws intended to instruct the people in the importance and obligations of holiness.	Book Three (73–89): expressions of worship (of which all but Ps 86 are attributed to Levites) focusing on God's instruction in holiness.
Numbers: God's fatherly chastisement of His national son Israel over the course of their 40-year sojourn in the desert.	Book Four (90–106): expressions of worship focusing on God's fatherly chastisement.
Deuteronomy: God's prologue to the fulfillment of His promise concerning the land of Israel and His final preparation of the people to enter in faith.	Book Five (107–150): expressions of worship looking ahead to the ultimate fulfillment of God's promises.

varies between first (the modern Jewish consensus) and second (after Ruth or Chronicles), it is universally treated (as also in Christian tradition) as a distinct subgroup together with the two successive books of Proverbs and Job.

The prominent place of Psalms in the organization of the Hebrew canon is also evident in Luke 24:44, where, most likely because of its size, "the Psalms" is probably intended as a reference to the entire third division of the Writings (a figure of speech known as synecdoche, substituting a part for the whole). A similar reference—which is also highly significant as a testimony to the early canonization of the OT (earlier, at least, than many modern scholars have been prone to believe)—is also now known from a period more than 100 years before the previously cited reference by Luke, in one of the Dead Sea Scrolls, where the Scriptures are referred to as "the book of Moses and the books of the Prophets and (the Psalms of) David" (4QMMT, C 10).

Purpose and Themes. Almost every biblical theme and theologically significant idea is to be found in Psalms. However, the overarching purpose of the book is indicated by Pss 1 and 2, which were intended to be read together as an introduction to the entire book of Psalms. These two psalms are joined by the literary device in the Hebrew Bible known as an *inclusio* (or "book ending"), whereby the identical term or expression is intended to highlight the main theme of the "framed" unit—in this case, "blessed" (lit., "O, the blessedness of"), denoting primarily a state of spiritual—and only secondarily material—well-being (not necessarily emotional happiness), equivalent to the blessedness indicated by Jesus in the Beatitudes (Mt 5:3-11).

As an introduction to the book, Ps 1 focuses on worship at the individual level and is grounded in God's Word, whereas Ps 2 focuses on worship expressed at the corporate level and is grounded in submission to God's Son, the Messiah King.

As a general introduction, therefore, these two psalms note that the book's overarching purpose is to instruct believers in the ways of expressing both personal as well as collective worship, grounded in the study of God's Word and directed toward the Anointed One, the Messiah. It is the Messiah who is the central theme of the book of Psalms, as the last words of David indicate (2Sm 23:1). The future Messiah was "the Delightful One of the songs of Israel," or David's favorite subject in the psalms (cf. comments on 2Sm 23:1).

Genre. The book of Psalms is Hebrew poetry. However, Hebrew poetry is not recognized by rhyming patterns as in English language poetry. Instead, several other characteristics typify this poetry:

1. *Poetic language.* The beauty and power of the psalms are evident in their rich concise word choice, poetic language, and powerful word pictures—as seen in these examples: "the wicked are . . . like chaff" (1:4); "you have shattered the teeth of the wicked" (3:7); "the LORD is my shepherd" (23:1); "as the deer pants for the water brooks, so my soul pants for You, O God" (42:1); "as the mountains surround Jerusalem, so the LORD surrounds His people" (125:2); and "He gives snow like wool; He scatters the frost like ashes" (147:16).

2. *Inclusio.* This literary device serves as "book ending" or "bracketing" of ideas with identical or parallel phrases to create a poetic unit of thought. For example, "how blessed is the man . . ." (Ps 1:1) / "how blessed are all . . ." (Ps 2:12) and "hope in God, for I shall again praise Him for the help of His presence" / "Hope in God, for I shall yet praise Him, the help of my countenance and my God" (42:5, 11).

3. *Parallelism.* Another important feature of Psalms (and of all biblical Hebrew poetry) is parallelism, one idea presented in relation to another through parallel thoughts. Generally, parallelism is of three types:

(a) synonymous parallelism, in which consecutive lines (each of which is usually a half-verse) present the same or similar idea in different words—

He raises the poor from the dust,
And he lifts the needy from the ash heap.
(Ps 113:7)

(b) antithetical parallelism, in which consecutive lines present contrasting or opposite ideas, usually revolving around a shared point of contact—

The LORD keeps all who love Him,
But all the wicked He will destroy.
(Ps 145:20)

(c) synthetic parallelism, in which consecutive lines present different, yet complementary ideas, which together provide a fuller and more specific idea than either line alone—

He trains my hands for battle,
So that my arms can bend a bow of bronze.
(Ps 18:34)

4. *Acrostic Structure.* In an acrostic, each verse in the psalm begins with a consecutive letter of the Hebrew alphabet (e.g., Pss 9–10 together are an acrostic poem; so are Pss 25; 34; 37; 111–112; and 145). Psalm 119, the longest psalm, is an acrostic praise to the Lord and His Word. It has 22 stanzas of eight verses; each stanza begins with the same letter. Acrostic structure is a helpful memory device, and reflects God's truth from A to Z.

5. *Musical Instruction.* The psalms were written to be sung, and 30 psalms are identified as "songs" (e.g., Pss 45, 48, 92). The musical connotation *mizmor*, often translated "psalm" in the heading, occurs 57 times and only in the headings of psalms. It probably indicates a psalm that was sung by the Levites in the temple to the accompaniment of musical instruments (e.g., Pss 3, 48). Fifty-five of the psalms include musical instructions in their heading; e.g., "For the choir director" (Ps 5); "with stringed instruments" (Ps 67); "A Song of Ascents" (Pss 120–134). These songs of ascents are arranged in poetic units to be sung as the worshipers approach the temple in Jerusalem.

Types of Psalms. Because the subject matter and content are so varied in the Psalter, a number of types or categories of psalms have been suggested. For an overview of the approaches to studying Psalms see Allen Ross, *A Commentary on the Psalms, Volume 1: Psalms 1–41*, Kregel Exegetical Library (Grand Rapids, MI: Kregel Academic, 2012), 65–80. Because of the complex content of the psalms, some may be categorized as more than one type. A helpful classification of the psalms is:

1. *Psalms of Praise and Thanksgiving.* This is often thought of as the typical psalm, because these are frequently the most familiar; examples are Pss 21, 30, 32, 34, 40, 146, and 148.

These psalms often are related to specific incidences of personal deliverance. They include a proclamation of praise to God, a report of deliverance, a renewed determination to praise, and often instruction for corporate praise.

2. *Hymnic Psalms.* Some praise psalms are more specifically hymnic in structure, rather than related to personal deliverance. These have the common elements of: (1) call to praise; (2) cause for praise; and (3) concluding exhortation to praise. They often include a superscription regarding the choir or a musical notation. Examples are Pss 33, 36, 105, 111, 113, 117, 135.

3. *Songs.* The headings/superscriptions of 15 psalms specifically identify them as *songs* (18, 45–46, 48, 65–68, 75–76, 83, 87–88, 92, 108). These psalms were to be sung, and some include additional musical direction. These are all psalms of praise, except Pss 83 and 88. A specific group of songs are the songs of ascents (Pss 120–134).

4. *Laments.* The most numerous and common psalms are laments, making up about a third of the psalms. These psalms are cries or prayers of help in times of distress. The lament psalms include (1) an introductory plea to the Lord; (2) the specific lament describing the issue; (3) confession of trust in the Lord despite the circumstances; (4) petition for help; and (5) conclusion of a vow to praise the Lord despite circumstances and regardless of deliverance. Examples of personal laments are Pss 3, 4, 12, and 22.

There are a number of national lament psalms as well. These are focused more specifically on the circumstances faced by the nation of Israel as a whole and follow the same pattern. Examples are Pss 44, 60, and 83.

5. *Imprecatory Psalms.* Some of the lament psalms have an imprecatory element, calling for specific judgments to fall on the enemy. The verb "imprecate" means "to pray evil against" or "to invoke disaster upon." These prayers are the plea of God's people for justice for atrocities committed against them personally or against the nation of Israel by the Lord's enemies; examples include Pss 5, 10, 17, 35, 58, 59, 69, 70, 79, 83, 109, 129, 137, and 140. These psalms may seem unloving and contrary to a biblical perspective. However, they are truthful and transparent expressions by the righteous, asking God to act on behalf of His people and for His name's sake. This is particularly true in times of warfare when destruction of the enemy was essential to the survival of the king and his people. Moreover, in these psalms, the psalmists do not take vengeance into their own hands but pray for God to execute just judgment. Imprecatory psalms were prayers for God to act according to the righteous requirements of His Word in its laws and covenants.

Some have thought that these prayers are contrary to a NT ethic. However, martyred believers in heaven offer an imprecation, asking how long before God will bring just retribution on their murderers (cf. Rv 6:10-11). Both OT and NT believers did not rejoice in the death of evil people. However, they did look forward to God's justice, when God would bring judgment on the wicked in accordance with His word, and make the world right (2Th 1:6-10).

Background. As originally written, and in the oldest manuscripts, the psalms were not numbered, nor were there verse divisions (as is true for the whole Bible). The helpful divisions were added much later. When reading or comparing different versions of the Bible, there may be a slight discrepancy in the numbering (though not the content) of the psalms. The Septuagint—an early Greek translation of the Bible produced in the intertestamental period by and for Hellenistic Jewry—has a verse division slightly different from the Hebrew. The early church adopted the Septuagint divisions in the OT and this has been followed by Roman Catholic tradition. Later, during the Reformation, there was a return to the Hebrew enumeration of the Psalms (Geneva Bible, Luther's German Bible, KJV), and this is the common division in Protestant Bibles.

In addition, the Christian English versions do not number the heading/superscriptions as the first verse, whereas the English translations of the Hebrew/Jewish Bible do, thus resulting in a one-verse difference in the psalms (e.g., in Ps 3 the Hebrew Bible has nine verses, whereas Christian Bibles have eight).

By recognizing Psalms as a coherent collection of writing, organized in the postexilic period, the message of the entire book becomes clearer. Certainly the later organization did not alter the original meaning of the individual psalms, but it deepened and clarified the focus to be on the coming messianic King of Israel. At the time of the final redaction, there was no Davidic king on the throne of Israel, so the psalms, especially those which speak of a King (with a capital K), are all looking forward to the future messianic King. Based on the postexilic compilation of Psalms, David C. Mitchell concludes, "the messianic theme is central to the purpose of the collection" (David C. Mitchell, *The Message of the Psalter: An Eschatological Programme in the Book of Psalms* [Sheffield, England: Sheffield Academic Press, 1997], 87). This would explain the way the NT writers frequently see Jesus the Messiah as the fulfillment of the psalms. They understood that He was the eschatological Davidic King anticipated in the book of Psalms.

OUTLINE

I. Book One: Responding in Worship to God's Sovereign Election (Pss 1–41)
   Psalms 1–2: The Introduction to Psalms: Properly Expressed Worship and Its Resultant Blessing
   Psalm 1: A Model of Personally Expressed Worship
      A. Developing the Habit of Walking with the Lord through His Word (1:1-2)
      B. Producing the Fruit of Walking with the Lord through His Word (1:3)
      C. Attaining the Reward of Walking with the Lord through His Word (1:4-6)
   Psalm 2: A Model of Collectively Expressed Worship
      A. Expressing Our Shared Persecution by the Nations (2:1-3)
      B. Expressing Our Shared Confidence in the Victory of the Son (2:4-9)
      C. Expressing Our Shared Commission to Worship the Son (2:10-12)
   Psalm 3: A Paradigm of Personal Lament
      A. Express Your Trouble to the Lord (3:1-2)
      B. Declare Your Confidence in the Lord (3:3-6)
      C. Present Your Petition to the Lord (3:7-8)
   Psalm 4: A Paradigm of Expressing Trust in the Lord
      A. The Basis of Trust in the Lord (4:1)
      B. The Challenge of Trust in the Lord (4:2-5)
      C. The Result of Trust in the Lord (4:6-8)
   Psalm 5: A Paradigm of Morning Devotion
      A. Affirming Submission to God (5:1-3)
      B. Declaring Praise of God (5:4-7)
      C. Presenting Petition before God (5:8-12)
   Psalm 6: A Paradigm of Petitioning God for Mercy
      A. Fully Admitting One's Spiritual Position (6:1-5)

- B. Fully Expressing One's Circumstantial Anxieties (6:6-7)
- C. Fully Affirming One's Covenantal Expectation (6:8-10)

Psalm 7: A Paradigm of Imprecation
- A. Know What to Expect (7:1-5)
- B. Appeal to the Lord for Vindication (7:6-16)
- C. Thank the Lord Regardless of His Answer (7:17)

Psalm 8: A Paradigm of Praise
- A. Reflect on How God Uses Men (8:1-2)
- B. Reflect on Why God Cares for People (8:3-5)
- C. Reflect on What God Has Given People (8:6-9)

Psalm 9: A Meditation on God's Justice: God as the Vindicator of the Righteous
- A. Declaring One's Confidence in the Vindicator (9:1-2)
- B. Affirming the Established Record of the Vindicator (9:3-12)
- C. Making One's Appeal to the Vindicator (9:13-20)

Psalm 10: A Meditation on God's Justice: God as the Judge of the Wicked
- A. Affirming the Need for the Judge (10:1-11)
- B. Making One's Appeal to the Judge (10:12-15)
- C. Declaring One's Confidence in the Judge (10:16-18)

Psalm 11: An Anatomy of Trust
- A. The Temptation against Trusting God: The Strength of the Wicked (11:1-3)
- B. The Basis for Trusting God: Who God Is and What He Does (11:4-7a)
- C. The Ultimate Hope of Trusting God: Beholding His Face (11:7b)

Psalm 12: Reflecting on Divine Deliverance
- A. Reflecting on the Need for Deliverance (12:1-2)
- B. Reflecting on the Process of Deliverance (12:3-5)
- C. Reflecting on the Provider of Deliverance (12:6-8)

Psalm 13: A Prayer for Personal Deliverance
- A. Express Need for God's Deliverance (13:1-2)
- B. Express Appeal for God's Deliverance (13:3-4)
- C. Express Confidence in God's Deliverance (13:5-6)

Psalm 14: An Anatomy of Human Folly
- A. The Essence of Human Folly (14:1)
- B. The Pervasiveness of Human Folly (14:2-6)
- C. The Antithesis of Human Folly (14:7)

Psalm 15: An Anatomy of the Truly Faithful
- A. The Desire of the Truly Faithful (15:1)
- B. The Qualities of the Truly Faithful (15:2-5a)
- C. The Final State of the Truly Faithful (15:5b)

Psalm 16: Confidence in Life and Death
- A. The Confidence of the Psalmist (16:1)
- B. The Prayer of the Messiah (16:2-11)
  1. The Lord Is His Delight in Life (16:2-8)
  2. The Lord Is His Deliverer in Death (16:9-11)

Psalm 17: Praying for Protection
- A. Asking God for an Audience (17:1-6)
- B. Appealing to God for Protection (17:7-14)
- C. Affirming God's Promise (17:15)

Psalm 18: A Psalm of Praise for God's Personal Deliverance
- A. David Affirms His Relationship with the Lord (18:1-29)
  1. Affirming One's Devotion to God as the Deliverer (18:1-3)
  2. David Affirms the Personal Nature of God's Deliverance (18:4-19)
  3. David Affirms the Depth of God's Interest in the Delivered (18:20-29)
- B. David Affirms the Deliverance by the Lord (18:30-50)
  1. Affirming the Depth of God's Interest in the Delivered (18:30-36)

2. Affirming the Personal Nature of God's Deliverance (18:37-45)
3. Affirming One's Devotion to God as the Deliverer (18:46-50)

Psalm 19: A Meditation on Divine Revelation
- A. The Revelation of God in Creation (19:1-6)
- B. The Revelation of God in His Word (19:7-11)
- C. The Revelation of God in Man (19:12-14)

Psalm 20: Expressing the Assurance of Victory in God
- A. The People's Assurance of Victory (20:1-5)
- B. The King's Assurance of Victory (20:6-8)
- C. The Collective Assurance of Victory (20:9)

Psalm 21: A Meditation on the King Who Trusts in the Lord
- A. The Blessing of the King Who Trusts in the Lord (21:1-6)
- B. The Strength of the King Who Trusts in the Lord (21:7-12)
- C. The Praise of the King Who Trusts in the Lord (21:13)

Psalm 22: A Prophetic Perspective on the Crucifixion of the Messiah
- A. The Suffering Messiah's Prayer (22:1-21)
  1. Questioning God (22:1-10)
  2. Petitioning God (22:11-21)
     - a. Seeking God's Presence because There Is No One Else to Help (22:11-18)
     - b. Seeking God's Presence because Only God Can Help (22:19-21)
- B. The Exalted Messiah's Praise (22:22-31)
  1. Praise before Israel: God Is Not Deaf, He Hears! (22:22-26)
  2. Praise before the Nations: God Is Not Dead, He Lives! (22:27-31)

Psalm 23: The Lord as Shepherd of His People
- A. The Shepherd's Provision of Rest (23:1-3)
- B. The Shepherd's Provision of Comfort (23:4-5)
- C. The Shepherd's Provision of Confidence and Care (23:6)

Psalm 24: The Return of the King of Glory
- A. The Extent of His Dominion (24:1-2)
- B. The Characteristics of His People (24:3-6)
- C. The Glory of His Reign (24:7-10)

Psalm 25: A Prayer for God's Protective Care
- A. Affirm the Relational Basis of the Petition (25:1)
- B. Express the Specific Content of the Petition (25:2-21)
- C. Consider the Broader Application of the Petition (25:22)

Psalm 26: A Meditation on Personal Integrity
- A. Affirming God as the Determiner of One's Integrity (26:1-2)
- B. Affirming God as the Goal of One's Integrity (26:3-10)
- C. Affirming God as the Enabler of One's Integrity (26:11-12)

Psalm 27: A Meditation on Personal Confidence
- A. Affirming God as the Basis of One's Confidence (27:1-3)
- B. Affirming God as the Goal of One's Confidence (27:4-6)
- C. Affirming God as the Developer of One's Confidence (27:7-14)

Psalm 28: A Paradigm of Appeal for the Demonstration of God's Love
- A. As Demonstrated in His Unmerited Attention to the Beloved's Cry (28:1-3)
- B. As Demonstrated in His Ongoing Judgment of the Beloved's Enemies (28:4-5)
- C. As Demonstrated in His Final Salvation of the Beloved's People (28:6-9)

Psalm 29: A Meditation on God's Awe-Inspiring Power
- A. The Unequivocal Ascription of God's Power (29:1-2)
- B. The Universal Attestation of God's Power (29:3-9)
- C. The Eternal Application of God's Power (29:10-11)

Psalm 30: Thanksgiving and Dedication after Discipline
- A. The Transience of God's Discipline (30:1-5)
- B. The Pain of God's Discipline (30:6-9)

- C. The Goal of God's Discipline (30:10-12)

Psalm 31: Appealing to God for Deliverance from Oppression
- A. Affirming the Insurmountable Strength of God's Deliverance (31:1-5)
- B. Expressing the Present Need for God's Deliverance (31:6-22)
- C. Sharing the Praiseworthy Hope of God's Deliverance (31:23-24)

Psalm 32: A Paradigm of Forgiveness
- A. The Nature of Divine Forgiveness (32:1-5)
- B. The Availability of Divine Forgiveness (32:6-7)
- C. The Attraction of Divine Forgiveness (32:8-11)

Psalm 33: A Paradigm of Collectively Proclaiming God's Praise
- A. The Obligation of Collective Praise (33:1-3)
- B. The Reasons for Collective Praise (33:4-19)
- C. The Application of Collective Praise (33:20-22)

Psalm 34: A Paradigm of God's Providence
- A. Praise for God's Providence (34:1-7)
- B. An Invitation to God's Providence (34:8-14)
- C. The Object of God's Providence (34:15-22)

Psalm 35: A Petition for Personal Vindication
- A. Expressing the Desire for Personal Vindication (35:1-8)
- B. Considering One's Merit for Personal Vindication (35:9-26)
- C. Affirming the Goal of Personal Vindication (35:27-28)

Psalm 36: A Meditation on God's Covenant Love (*Chesed*)
- A. The Absence of Lovingkindness (36:1-4)
- B. The Embodiment of Lovingkindness (36:5-9)
- C. The Ongoing Need for Lovingkindness (36:10-12)

Psalm 37: A Celebration of Satisfaction with God's Reward
- A. God's Reward Is Sure (37:1-15)
- B. God's Reward Is Best (37:16-26)
- C. God's Reward Is Everlasting (37:27-40)

Psalm 38: Responding to God's Chastisement
- A. Implore God's Mercy (38:1-8)
- B. Admit Personal Weakness (38:9-12)
- C. Affirm Continual Dependence on God (38:13-22)

Psalm 39: The Brevity of Life and the Sin of Silence
- A. Understanding the Sin of Silence (39:1-3)
- B. Realizing the Brevity of Opportunity and Life (39:4-6)
- C. Repenting of the Sin of Silence (39:7-13)

Psalm 40: Deliverance and Distress
- A. Praise for Deliverance (40:1-10)
- B. Prayer for Deliverance (40:11-17)

Psalm 41: A Meditation on God's Grace
- A. Individual Blessing of God's Grace (41:1-3)
- B. Individual Need for God's Grace (41:4-9)
- C. Individual Encouragement from God's Grace (41:10-13)

II. Book Two: Responding in Worship to God's Protective Nurture (Pss 42–72)

Psalm 42: Longing for God's Care
- A. Depth of Yearning for the Lord (42:1-5)
- B. Deep Need for the Lord (42:6-11)

Psalm 43: The Goal of God's Nurture

Psalm 44: A Prayer for Divine Deliverance by Reviewing Israel's History
- A. Affirming God's Proven Record (44:1-8)
- B. Expressing One's Present Need (44:9-22)
- C. Appealing to God's Lovingkindness (44:23-26)

Psalm 45: Affirming the Precedence of God the Son

- A. His Precedence Affirmed by His Role as the Bridegroom (45:1-9)
- B. His Precedence Affirmed by the Response of the Bride (45:10-15)
- C. His Precedence Affirmed by the Position of His Children (45:16-17)

Psalm 46: A Meditation on Divine Refuge
- A. Permanence of Divine Refuge (46:1-3)
- B. Accessibility of Divine Refuge (46:4-7)
- C. Comfort of Divine Refuge (46:8-11)

Psalm 47: A Public Praise of the Divine King
- A. Challenge of the Divine King (47:1-4)
- B. Praise of the Divine King (47:5-7)
- C. Preeminence of the Divine King (47:8-9)

Psalm 48: A Praise for Zion, the City of the Divine King
- A. Preeminence of Zion (48:1-8)
- B. Praise of Zion (48:9-11)
- C. Challenge of Zion (48:12-14)

Psalm 49: Affirming God's Grace as the Redeemer
- A. Man's Inability to Redeem Himself Spiritually (49:1-9)
- B. Man's Inability to Redeem Himself Physically (49:10-14)
- C. God's Ability to Redeem Man Completely (49:15-20)

Psalm 50: God as the Judge of Humanity
- A. Introduction of the Divine Judge (50:1-6)
- B. Ruling of the Divine Judge (50:7-21)
- C. Final Warning of the Divine Judge (50:22-23)

Psalm 51: David Affirms God's Forgiveness
- A. Recognition of Personal Sin (51:1-6)
- B. Request for God's Mercy (51:7-13)
- C. Response of Thanksgiving (51:14-19)

Psalm 52: The Problem of Evil in Perspective: Man's Place in Eternity
- A. Identity of the Wicked (52:1-4)
- B. Final Place of the Wicked (52:5-7)
- C. Final Place of the Righteous (52:8-9)

Psalm 53: The Unchanging Anatomy of Human Folly
- A. Essence of Human Folly (53:1a)
- B. Pervasiveness of Human Folly (53:1b-5)
- C. Antithesis of Human Folly (53:6)

Psalm 54: Appealing to God for Help
- A. Consider Motivation (54:1-3)
- B. Affirm Confidence (54:4-5)
- C. Express Thanksgiving (54:6-7)

Psalm 55: Finding Solace from the Persecution of "Friends"
- A. Express Emotion to God (55:1-8)
- B. Implore Vindication from God (55:9-15)
- C. Affirm Your Confidence in God (55:16-23)

Psalm 56: Affirming God's Intimate Concern over You
- A. Affirming God's Intimate Concern over Circumstances (56:1-7)
- B. Affirming God's Intimate Concern over Your Sorrow (56:8-12)
- C. Affirming God's Intimate Concern over Your Future (56:13)

Psalm 57: Finding Refuge in the Transcendent God
- A. Finding Refuge in God's Transcendent Power (57:1-3)
- B. Finding Refuge in God's Transcendent Glory (57:4-6)
- C. Finding Refuge in God's Transcendent Praise (57:7-11)

Psalm 58: A Meditation on Divine Justice
- A. Need for Divine Justice (58:1-5)
- B. Demonstration of Divine Justice (58:6-9)

C. Reaction to Divine Justice (58:10-11)

Psalm 59: A Personal Petition for Divine Deliverance
A. Honestly Expressing the Need for Divine Deliverance (59:1-8)
B. Humbly Considering the Purpose of Divine Deliverance (59:9-15)
C. Unconditionally Praising the Giver of Divine Deliverance (59:16-17)

Psalm 60: Affirming Our Utter Dependence on God
A. Affirming God's Chastisement (60:1-5)
B. Affirming God's Promises (60:6-8)
C. Affirming God's Actions (60:9-12)

Psalm 61: A Cry to God from the Faint of Heart
A. For Unbreakable Protection (61:1-4)
B. For Life-Giving Love (61:5-7)
C. For Enduring Purpose (61:8)

Psalm 62: A Meditation on True Salvation
A. True Salvation Is Found in God Alone (62:1-4)
B. True Salvation Is Available from God at All Times (62:5-8)
C. True Salvation Is Dispensed by God Sovereignly (62:9-12)

Psalm 63: Expressing Yearning for God
A. For His Presence (63:1-5)
B. For His Protection (63:6-8)
C. For His Praise (63:9-11)

Psalm 64: Finding Solace from Tormentors
A. Unburdening the Torment of Heart to God (64:1-6)
B. Affirming the Judgment of Tormentors by God (64:7-8)
C. Anticipating the Glory of the Future with God (64:9-10)

Psalm 65: God's Grace toward Man
A. As Expressed in His Sovereign Forgiveness (65:1-4)
B. As Expressed in His Miraculous Works (65:5-8)
C. As Expressed in His Continuous Provision (65:9-13)

Psalm 66: An Exhortation to Praise God for His Concern
A. In Delivering His People (66:1-7)
B. In Refining His People (66:8-15)
C. In Hearing His People (66:16-20)

Psalm 67: Praise from All Peoples
A. Based on His Spiritual Concern for Israel (67:1-2)
B. Based on His Administrative Concern for All Peoples (67:3-5)
C. Based on His Material Concern for Israel (67:6-7)

Psalm 68: A Procession of Praise for the Triumphant God
A. As the Head of Israel's Triumph over Physical Distress (68:1-14)
B. As the Head of Israel's Triumph over Spiritual Distress (68:15-23)
C. As the Head of All Nations' Triumph over All Distress (68:24-35)

Psalm 69: The Distress of God's Servant
A. Appealing for Deliverance from the Distress (69:1-21)
B. Imprecating the Cause of the Distress (69:22-28)
C. Thanking the One Who Relieves the Distress (69:29-36)

Psalm 70: A Paradigm of Dependence on God's Deliverance
A. Imploring Deliverance from God (70:1–3)
B. Encouraging Rejoicing in God (70:4-5)

Psalm 71: A Paradigm of Dependence on God in Old Age
A. Affirming Confidence in God (71:6-16)
B. Declaring Gratitude to God (71:17-24)

Psalm 72: A Paradigm of Prayer for the King
A. The Messiah's Righteous Reign (72:1-7)
B. The Messiah's Universal Reign (72:8-14)

- C. The Messiah's Abundant Reign (72:15-17)
- D. Conclusion to Book Two (72:18-20)

III. Book Three: Responding in Worship to God's Instruction in Holiness (Pss 73–89)

Psalm 73: On the Worth of Holiness
- A. The Apparent Futility of Holiness (73:1-14)
- B. The True Futility of Unrighteousness (73:15-20)
- C. The True Worth of Holiness (73:21-28)

Psalm 74: Appealing to God for Relief from Affliction
- A. Recognizing God's Correction (74:1-11)
- B. Affirming God's Sovereignty (74:12-17)
- C. Requesting God's Deliverance (74:18-23)

Psalm 75: Praise for God's Sure Justice
- A. Thankfully Affirm God's Sure Justice (75:1-3)
- B. Boldly Share God's Sure Justice (75:4-8)
- C. Continually Declare God's Sure Justice (75:9-10)

Psalm 76: God's Defense of Israel
- A. Among His People in the Land (76:1-3)
- B. Among His People outside the Land (76:4-10)
- C. Beyond His People throughout All Lands (76:11-12)

Psalm 77: Finding Comfort in God
- A. Express Need (77:1-10)
- B. Affirm the Principle (77:11-15)
- C. Select an Example (77:16-20)

Psalm 78: A Celebration of the Lord of History
- A. The Purpose: To Teach Later Generations of God's Faithfulness (78:1-8)
- B. The Record: The History of God's Faithfulness to Israel (78:9-64)
  1. Divided Kingdom History/Exodus History (78:9-16)
  2. Wilderness Wandering History (78:17-33)
  3. Period of Judges History (78:34-39)
  4. Exodus History (78:40-53)
  5. Conquest History (78:54-64)
- C. The Triumphant Culmination of God's Choice in the Messianic Line (78:65-72)

Psalm 79: A Collective Appeal for Deliverance
- A. Acknowledging God's Judgment (79:1-7)
- B. Imploring God's Mercy (79:8)
- C. Focusing on God's Glory (79:9-13)

Psalm 80: God's Shepherding of His People Israel
- A. The Reality of the Correction (80:1-7)
- B. The Basis of the Correction (80:8-13)
- C. The Goal of the Correction (80:14-19)

Psalm 81: The Characteristics of God's Collective Call to Renewal
- A. A Customary Event (81:1-4)
- B. A Commemorative Event (81:5-7)
- C. A Confessional Event (81:8-16)

Psalm 82: God's Sovereignty over the Nations
- A. God's Position (82:1)
- B. God's Challenge (82:2-4)
- C. God's Judgment (82:5-8)

Psalm 83: Imprecation as Affirmation of God's Gracious Promises
- A. To Make Israel an Eternal Nation (83:1-8)
- B. To Give Israel an Eternal Land (83:9-15)
- C. To Bless All Peoples with Eternal Life (83:16-18)

Psalm 84: The Threefold Aspects of True Blessedness
- A. Dwelling in God's Presence (84:1-4)

B. Living in God's Strength (84:5-7)
C. Trusting in God's Grace (84:9-12)

Psalm 85: The Three Tenses of Divine Love
A. Divine Love in the Past (85:1-3)
B. Divine Love in the Present (85:4-7)
C. Divine Love in the Future (85:8-13)

Psalm 86: Prayer to the Sovereign Lord from His Servant
A. Affirming the Lord as His Sovereign (86:1-5)
B. Affirming the Lord as the Only Sovereign (86:6-13)
C. Affirming the Lord as the Perfect Sovereign (86:14-17)

Psalm 87: On the Preeminence of Zion
A. Zion the Place of God's Choice (87:1-3)
B. Zion the Place of God's People (87:4-6)
C. Zion the Place of God's Salvation (87:7)

Psalm 88: The Reasons for Seeking Relief from God's Correction
A. Plea for Restoration of Vitality (88:1-9)
B. Plea for Restoration of Worship (88:10-12)
C. Plea for Restoration of Relationship (88:13-18)

Psalm 89: God's Faithfulness to the Davidic King
A. God's Faithful Character (89:1-18)
B. God's Choice of David as King (89:19-29)
C. God's Unconditional Covenant with David (89:30-37)
D. God's Discipline on the Davidic Throne (89:38-52)

IV. Book Four: Responding in Worship to God's Fatherly Discipline (Pss 90–106)

Psalm 90: A Prayer to God Eternal in Response to the Brevity of Life
A. Affirming the Eternality of God (90:1-2)
B. Acknowledging Man's Mortality and Need for Wisdom (90:3-12)
C. Asking for God's Favor and Blessing (90:13-17)

Psalm 91: Concerning Personal Security
A. The Believer's Source of Security (91:1-4)
B. The Extent of Security in the Lord (91:5-13)
C. The Intimacy of Security in the Lord (91:14-16)

Psalm 92: A Song of Weekly Praise
A. A Song for the Privilege of Praise (92:1-4)
B. A Song for the Lord's Justice (92:5-9)
C. A Song for the Lord's Great Love (92:10-15)

Psalm 93: Affirming God's Rule as the King of Creation
A. By His Work of Creation (93:1-2)
B. By His Transcendence over Creation (93:3-4)
C. By His Special Revelation within Creation (93:5)

Psalm 94: Praying for God to Judge
A. For the Sake of God's Glory (94:1-7)
B. With Recognition of God's Mercy (94:8-16)
C. In the Light of God's Plan (94:17-23)

Psalm 95: Rejoicing in the Lord's Beneficial Works for Humanity
A. The Lord as the Creator (95:1-5)
B. The Lord as Good Shepherd (95:6-7a)
C. The Lord as the Rest-Giver (95:7b-11)

Psalm 96: An Exhortation to Praise the World's Once and Future King
A. Let Israel Praise the Lord, the King (96:1-6)
B. Let the Nations Praise the Lord, the King (96:7-10)
C. Let all Creation Praise the Lord, the King (96:11-13)

Psalm 97: God, The Ruler of the Universe
A. His Reign over Creation (97:1-6)

B. His Reign over the Supernatural World (97:7-9)
C. His Reign over His People (97:10-12)

Psalm 98: A Challenge to Praise the Messianic King
A. The Basis of the Challenge (98:1-3)
B. The Extent of the Challenge (98:4-8)
C. The Consummation of the Challenge (98:9)

Psalm 99: The Exaltation of God's Royal Holiness
A. The Lord Reigns in Zion (99:1-5)
B. The Lord Gave His Priests and Prophets (99:6-9)

Psalm 100: A Song of Thanksgiving to God
A. Thanking God for His Sublime Uniqueness (100:1-3a)
B. Thanking God for His Gracious Election (100:3b-c)
C. Thanking God for His Faithful Love (100:4-5)

Psalm 101: King David's Resolve to Reign Righteously
A. The King Is Committed to Personal Righteousness (101:1-4)
B. The King Is Committed to Establish Righteousness in the Land (101:5-8)

Psalm 102: Prayer from the Corrected Believer
A. Affirming God's Correction (102:1-11)
B. Affirming God's Compassion and Grace (102:12-17)
C. Affirming God's Purposes (102:18-28)

Psalm 103: Blessing God for His Benefits in Dealing with Humanity
A. The Scope of His Benefits in Dealing with Humankind (103:1-14)
B. The Duration of His Benefits in Dealing with Humankind (103:15-18)
C. The Purpose of His Benefits in Dealing with Humankind (103:19-22)

Psalm 104: Blessing God for His Work as Creator and Sustainer of Life
A. Bless the Lord for His Work as Creator (104:1-23)
B. Bless the Lord for Sustaining the Life of All Creation (104:24-35)

Psalm 105: Praise to the God of the Abrahamic Covenant
A. Praise for Choosing the People of Israel and Giving Them the Land of Israel (105:1-15)
B. Praise for Preserving His People outside Their Land (105:16-41)
C. Praise for Establishing His People within Their Land (105:42-45)

Psalm 106: Praise for God's Faithfulness to His Unfaithful People
A. The Basis of God's Faithfulness (106:1-5)
B. The Expression of God's Faithfulness (106:6-46)
C. The Goal of God's Faithfulness (106:47-48)

V. Book Five: Responding in Worship to God's Ultimate Faithfulness (Pss 107–150)

Psalm 107: A Call for the Redeemed to Praise the Lord
A. Praise the Lord for Restoring His People to Their Land (107:1-3)
B. Praise the Lord for Correcting His People for Their Sins (107:4-22)
C. Praise the Lord for Preserving His People through Their Distress (107:23-43)

Psalm 108: Reaffirming Our Total Dependence on God
A. Reaffirming God's Praise (108:1-6)
B. Reaffirming God's Promises (108:7-9)
C. Reaffirming God's Actions (108:10-13)

Psalm 109: A Prayer for Justice against a False Accusation
A. As an Occasion for Appealing to God's Justice (109:1-20)
B. As an Occasion for Appealing to God's Lovingkindness (109:21-29)
C. As an Occasion for Expressing God's Praise (109:30-31)

Psalm 110: Deliverance through the King Messiah
A. Messiah, the Divine King (110:1-3)
B. Messiah, The Priest-King (110:4)
C. Messiah, the Victorious Warrior (110:5-7)

Psalm 111: A Call to Worship God for His Unfailing Righteousness

A. The Response of Worship (111:1)
B. The Motivation for Worship (111:2-9)
C. The Attitude in Worship (111:10)

Psalm 112: The Benefits of Fearing the Lord
A. The Call to Fear the Lord (112:1)
B. The Blessings of Fearing the Lord (112:2-9)
C. The Contrast with Fearing the Lord (112:10)

Psalms 113–118: The Hallel Psalms
A. Psalm 113: Praise the Lord for His Sovereign Concern for Mankind
B. Psalm 114: Praise the Lord for His Deliverance of His People at the Exodus
C. Psalm 115: Praise the Lord for His Sovereignty over Israel and the Nations
D. Psalm 116: Praise the Lord the Sustainer of Life
E. Psalm 117: Praise the Lord All Nations
F. Psalm 118: Praise the Lord for His Lovingkindness is Everlasting
1. A Call to Thanksgiving (118:1-4)
2. An Explanation of Deliverance (118:5-21)
3. The Identity of the Deliverer (118:22-29)

Psalm 119: A Psalm of Praise to the Word of God
A. *Aleph:* The Blessing of Walking in God's Word (119:1-8)
B. *Beth*: God's Word Provides Protection Against Sin (119:9-16)
C. *Gimel*: God's Word as a Source of Comfort (119:17-24)
D. Daleth: God's Word as a Source of Strength (119:25-32)
E. *He*: God's Word Deserves Respect (119:33-40)
F. *Vav*: God's Word is the Source of Reply to the Wicked (119:41-48)
G. *Zayin*: God's Word is the Source of Hope (119:49-56)
H. *Heth*: God's Word is Sufficient (119:57-64)
I. *Teth*: God's Word is Good (119:65-72)
J. *Yodh*: God's Word Gives a Clear Testimony (119:73-80)
K. *Kaph*: God's Word is Faithful (119:81-88)
L. *Lamedh*: God's Word is Settled in Heaven (119:89-96)
M. *Mem*: God's Word is Sweet (119:97-104)
N. *Nun*: God's Word Gives Guidance (119:105-112)
O. *Samekh*: God's Word is a Refuge (119:113-120)
P. *Ayin*: A Prayer for Vindication (119:121-128)
Q. *Pe*: God's Word is Wonderful (119:129-136)
R. *Tsadhe*: God's Word is Righteous (119:137-144)
S. *Qoph*: God's Word is Truth (119:145-152)
T. *Resh*: A Call for Deliverance (153-160)
U. *Shin*: God's Word is a Source of Peace (119:161-168)
V. *Tav*: God's Word Provides Help (119:169-176)

Psalm 120–134: The Psalms of Ascent
A. Psalm 120: A Prayer for Deliverance and Peace
1. Trusting the Lord for Deliverance (120:1-4)
2. Desiring Peace in Conflict (120:5-7)
B. Psalm 121: Affirming the Lord is the Keeper of Israel
1. The Lord Is the Source of Israel's Security (121:1-2)
2. The Lord Guarantees Israel's Security (121:3-4)
3. The Extent of Israel's Security (121:5-8)
C. Psalm 122: A Hymn of Peace for Jerusalem
1. Peace for the Purpose of Worship (122:1-4)
2. Peace by the Rule of His Son (122:5)
3. Peace through the Prayers of His People (122:6-9)
D. Psalm 123: Looking to the Lord for Help
1. The Object of the Hope (123:1)

2. The Manner of the Hope (123:2)
3. The Motivation for Hope (123:3-4)

E. Psalm 124: A Song of Thanksgiving for God's Help
1. Recalling God's Deliverance in the Past (124:1-5)
2. Thanking God for His Deliverance Today (124:6-8)

F. Psalm 125: The Lord's Protection of His People
1. The Lord's Protection is as Permanent as Mount Zion (125:1-2)
2. The Lord Will Protect His Land from the Wicked (125:3)
3. The Lord will Protect His People (125:4-5)

G. Psalm 126: Rejoicing at God's Restoration of Zion
1. Looking Back with Thanksgiving at Past Restoration to Zion (126:1-3)
2. Looking Forward with Hope to Future (and Final) Restoration (126:5-6)

H. Psalm 127: A Song of Praise for the Lord for Daily Care
1. The Lord is the Source of Protection and Purpose (127:1-4)
2. The Lord is the Source of Blessing in the Family (127:3-5)

I. Psalm 128: The Blessing of Walking with the Lord
1. The Personal Blessings of Walking with the Lord (128:1-4)
2. National Blessing of Walking with the Lord (128:5-6)

J. Psalm 129: An Imprecatory Psalm Against the Enemies of Israel
1. Praise God for Preventing the Destruction of Israel (129:1-4)
2. Pray to the Lord to Punish the Persecutors of Israel (129:5-8)

K. Psalm 130: A Cry to the Lord for Mercy
1. The Human Need for Mercy (130:1-3)
2. The Divine Gift of Mercy (130:4-6)
3. Response to the Mercy and Forgiveness of God (130:7-8)

L. Psalm 131: David's Personal Faith in the Lord
1. David's Humility before the Lord (131:1)
2. David's Dependence on the Lord (131:2)
3. David's Admonition to Israel (131:3)

M. Psalm 132: Affirming the Davidic Covenant
1. The Request to Remember David's Zeal (132:1-10)
2. The Request to Remember the Davidic Covenant (132:10-18)

N. Psalm 133: The Beauty of Unity among the People of Perfected Jerusalem
1. The Beauty of Unity (133:1)
2. The Illustrations of the Blessings of Unity (133:2-3a)
3. The Blessing of Immortality (133:3b)

O. Psalm 134: The Final Ascent: Praise the Lord for Complete Blessing
1. The Affirmation of Blessing (134:1)
2. The Source of Blessing (134:2)
3. The Dissemination of Blessing (134:3)

Psalm 135: Praise for God's Manifest Kindness toward Israel
A. Praise God for Choosing Israel (135:1-7)
B. Praise God for Preserving Israel (135:8-14)
C. Praise God for His Relationship to Israel (135:15-21)

Psalm 136: Superlative Praise for God's Lovingkindness
A. Praising God as the Source of All Lovingkindness (136:1-3)
B. Praising God for His Lovingkindness Expressed in Creation (136:4-9)
C. Praising God for His Lovingkindness for Israel (136:10-22)
D. A Finale of Praise to God, the Source of Lovingkindness (136:25-26)

Psalm 137: Lamenting the Victory of God's Enemies over Zion
A. Grieving over the Conquest of Jerusalem (137:1-3)
B. Affirming the Ongoing Centrality of Jerusalem (137:4-6)
C. Envisioning the Just Judgment of the Enemies of Zion (137:7-9)

Psalm 138: A Hymn of Thanksgiving for the Faithfulness of God

- A. Praise God for His Faithfulness and Strength (138:1-3)
- B. Praise God, All the Nations of the Earth (138:4-6)
- C. Praise God for His Future Faithfulness (138:7-8)

Psalm 139: David's Praise for the Presence of the Lord
- A. God Is Present in Everyday Experiences (139:1-12)
- B. God Is Sovereign in Planning Personal Existence (139:13-16)
- C. God Is Active Guiding into the Everlasting Way (139:17-24)

Psalm 140: A Prayer when Oppressed by the Wicked
- A. David's Request for the Lord's Help (140:1-8)
- B. David's Request for Vengeance on the Wicked (140:9-11)
- C. David's Confidence in the Lord's Justice (140:12-13)

Psalm 141: Imploring God's Protective Guidance
- A. In Diverting from Iniquity (141:1-4)
- B. In Chastising for Iniquity (141:5-7)
- C. In Preserving from the Doers of Iniquity (141:8-10)

Psalm 142: A Prayer for Deliverance
- A. Boldly Pour Out Complaint to the Lord (142:1-6)
- B. Affirm God's Glory as Motivation for Rescue (142:7)

Psalm 143: A Prayer for Guidance and Deliverance
- A. The Appeal for Help in the Present (143:1-4)
- B. The Memory of Help in the Past (143:5-6)
- C. The Plea for Help Immediately (143:7-12)

Psalm 144: Affirming God's All-Encompassing Provision
- A. God's Provision of Personal Care (144:1-4)
- B. God's Provision of Protection (144:5-11)
- C. God's Provision of Ongoing Life (144:12-15)

Psalm 145: The Threefold Basis of Blessing God's Name
- A. The Blessing of God's Power (145:1-7)
- B. The Blessing of God's Kindness (145:8-14)
- C. The Blessing of God's Faithfulness (145:15-21)

Psalms 146–150: The Conclusion to Psalms
- A. Psalm 146: Praise the Lord Forever
  1. The Praise of God (146:1-2)
  2. The Power of God (146:3-6)
  3. The Provision of God (146:7-10)
- B. Psalm 147: Praise the Lord for His Care of Jerusalem
  1. Praise the Lord for Building up Jerusalem (147:1-6)
  2. Praise the Lord for His Daily Care (147:7-11)
  3. Praise the Lord, O Jerusalem (147:12-20)
- C. Psalm 148: Praise the Lord, All the Earth
  1. Let the Heavens Praise the Lord (148:1-6)
  2. Let the Earth Praise the Lord (148:7-12)
  3. Let the People of Israel Praise the Lord (148:13-14)
- D. Psalm 149: Praise the Lord All Israel
  1. Israel Should Rejoice in Their King (149:1-5)
  2. The Lord Will Execute Judgment on the Enemies of Israel (149:6-9)
- E. Psalm 150: The Great Hallelujah
  1. Praise the Lord in the Sanctuary (150:1-2)
  2. Praise the Lord with Music and Dancing (150:3-5)
  3. Let Everything Praise the Lord (150:6)

COMMENTARY ON PSALMS

I. Book One: Responding in Worship to God's Sovereign Election (Pss 1–41)

Psalms 1–2: The Introduction to Psalms: Properly Expressed Worship and Its Resultant Blessing

These two psalms are united by the use of the same phrase, "How blessed," at the beginning of the first (1:1) and at the end of the second (2:12). They serve as an introduction to the book of Psalms, introducing the theme of the importance of meditation on Scripture. As an introduction to the book, these two psalms orient the reader to the purpose of the Psalms generally, which is to model the various ways to express individual and collective worship of the Lord, and the resulting blessing the righteous will find from studying God's Word.

Psalm 1: A Model of Personally Expressed Worship

Though not supplied with a heading, this psalm may be definitively identified as an utterance of David since it is thematically united with Ps 2, which is explicitly attributed to David in Ac 4:25-26.

A. Developing the Habit of Walking with the Lord through His Word (1:1-2)

1:1-2. The psalm (and the book of Psalms) begins by linking the blessings of God to those who **walk** by (i.e., live, indicating a daily practice of life) and meditate (think about in all circumstances) on His Word, the Scriptures, **the law of the LORD . . . day and night**. The phrase **How blessed** (lit., "O, the blessedness of"; Hb. *ashre*) is parallel to the expression used in the Beatitudes (Mt 5:3-11), both signifying not material or circumstantial blessing (i.e., wealth, position, happiness, etc.), but the deeper and enduring blessing of a dynamic relationship with God on a daily basis. The psalmist presents a contrast of the righteous **man** who does not associate with the **wicked**. This sequence of the verbs **walk**, **stand**, and **sit** moves from denoting activity to denoting a state of being and indicate a whole lifestyle. The word **sinners** is the same word found in Gn 13:13 for the sinners in Sodom, suggesting a hardened commitment to wicked behavior.

In bright contrast to the wicked, the godly individual has an overall course of life or habit: he **delight[s]** in and **meditates** on the **law of the LORD**. The word **law** (*torah*) is an elastic term, generally translated "law" or "instruction." It can refer to an individual law, the laws of Sinai, the Pentateuch, the Hebrew Bible, or spiritual instruction. Here it means all of God's Word, not just the Pentateuch. His greatest joy in life is to think about, fill his mind with, and obey the Word of God. The verb **meditates** means "to mutter something under one's breath," referring to the quiet recitation of Scripture to one's self. It signifies the filling of the mind with the biblical text and careful consideration of both what the text means and how it applies. In the Bible, "meditation" is often equivalent to the term "study." This command was given to Joshua when he assumed leadership of Israel (Jos 1:6-9).

B. Producing the Fruit of Walking with the Lord through His Word (1:3)

1:3. Meditation on the Word of God is thus presented, by virtue of its inclusion in this first introductory psalm, as a basic act of worship, or, more precisely, as the foundation on which all expressions of worship must be based. The blessing of obedience is metaphorically presented as a **tree** producing **fruit**. For the one who habitually meditates and delights in God's Word, **in whatever he does, he prospers**. The word **prospers** primarily refers here, not to immediate material prosperity, but to success—that is, spiritual success in one's life through applying and adhering to "the law of the LORD" (v. 2). The same word is used in Is 53:10 ("and the good pleasure of the LORD will prosper in His hand") of the success of the Messiah in reconciling people to God, accomplished in the "crushing" and "putting to grief" of Messiah as the "guilt offering" (hardly a picture of immediate material prosperity or ease).

C. Attaining the Reward of Walking with the Lord through His Word (1:4-6)

1:4-6. The fruitful life of the righteous is contrasted with the worthless life of the **wicked**, which is like **chaff**, the husk of grain blown away by the **wind**. The perspective (and motivation) for studying and living by God's Word is ultimately eternal, not any immediate material prosperity. This is underscored by David's reference to **the wicked** (lit., "wicked ones," parallel to **sinners** in the next line) not standing **in the judgment**, referring to God's judgment of all the assembled unrepentant at the Day of Judgment (cf. Mt 12:41-42; Lk 10:14; 11:31-32; Rv 20:11-15).

The reward and blessing of the righteous, by contrast, consists not only in their being able to stand in the Day of Judgment—because of their faith they are not condemned (Rm 8:1)—but also that **the LORD knows the way of the righteous**. This is the reality of an intimate and loving relationship with the heavenly Father. The connotation of the Hebrew verb **knows** generally signifies the most thorough and/or intimate knowledge (often described as a thorough experiential knowledge) of what is known. This is the typical verb used to describe conjugal relations between a husband and wife (e.g., Gn 4:1). For God to **know** the way of the righteous indicates His loving concern for them.

Psalm 2: A Model of Collectively Expressed Worship

This is identified as a psalm of David (cf. Ac 4:25). It is one of the several directly "messianic" utterances (as likewise applied in Ac 13:33; Heb 1:5; 5:5; cf. 2Sm 23:1 comments) that readers, either out of carelessness in interpretation or specific apologetic concerns, have often taken as referring directly and only to David—and only indirectly (typologically) if at all to Jesus. While there are, to be sure, several parallels to David's experiences as king in this psalm, what is stated far transcends what is ever said of David. This was already recognized long ago by the early rabbinic interpreters, who also understood this psalm as applying to the King Messiah, though for polemical purposes this view was later rejected in favor of the application to David—as exemplified in the following comment on this psalm by Rashi (Rabbi Solomon ben Isaac), who flourished in the second half of the 11th century and greatly influenced the course of subsequent Jewish interpretation of the Bible: "Our ancient sages expounded the theme of this psalm with reference to the King Messiah, yet . . . as a rebuttal to the Christians, it is proper to explain it as referring to David."

A significant interpretive presupposition for understanding Ps 110 as messianic is that David himself, in his last words (2Sm 23:1-5), identified the Messiah as his favorite subject in the Psalms. There David reveals, by his own authorial intent, that his psalms refer to the Messiah. This interpretation of David's last words is not as evident in the Masoretic Text of 2Sm 23:1 as it is in the Septuagint (LXX). The LXX reading is a result of a variant vowel (cf. comments on 2Sm 23:1-7) and yields the following translation:

These are the last words of David:
The oracle of David the son of Jesse,
The oracle of the man raised up,
Concerning the Messiah [Anointed One] of the God of Jacob,
And the Delightful One of the songs of Israel (2Sm 23:1).

In his last words, David said that the Messiah was his favorite subject in the Psalms. This gives a crucial clue to reading Davidic psalms in general and Ps 2 in particular. David claimed that he had a messianic focus in writing the Psalms. This should guide the understanding of Ps 2. Moreover, the postexilic compilation of the book of Psalms, when there was no Davidic king, should emphasize that the Psalm is not looking back at David but forward to the messianic King (see Introduction: Background).

One of the thematic connections between Pss 1 and 2 is found in the recurrence of the word "blessed" in 1:1 and 2:12. Meditation on the law of the Lord (1:1-2) leads to blessing and leads one to apprehend the source of the greatest blessings—namely, the Messiah (see especially 2:12).

A. Expressing Our Shared Persecution by the Nations (2:1-3)

2:1-3. In the Hebrew Bible, opposition to God and His people typically proceeds from the **nations** (lit., "Gentiles"), designating the pagan nations, directed by their **kings** and **rulers** who consistently **take their stand . . . against the LORD and against His Anointed**. The citation of this passage by the nascent church in Ac 4:25-26 is significant, for it not only clarifies that the **Anointed** (Hb. *mashiach*, from which is derived the English word "messiah") in this passage is intended as a specific, predictive reference to Jesus Himself (the Hebrew term is also applied in the OT in a more general, nonpredictive sense to kings and priests; cf. Lv 4:3; 1Sm 24:10), but it also implies that opposition to God and Messiah Jesus are inseparable. The "chief priests and the elders" of the Jewish people to whom the early Jewish-Christian community applied this passage (Ac 4:23) would certainly not have claimed to reject the God of Israel whom they worshiped as their heavenly Father. Yet from God's perspective one's acceptance and worship of Him is bound up with one's acceptance and worship of His Son, the Messiah, Jesus of Nazareth (see comments on Ps 2:11-12a). "Whoever denies the Son does not have the Father; the one who confesses the Son has the Father also" (1 Jn 2:23; see also Lk 10:16; Jn 5:23).

The verb **take their stand** (v. 2) was used for Goliath's haughty posture against the Jewish warriors in 1Sm 17:16. As the giant Philistine opposed David's people, so also the godless nations will oppose David's prominent Son, the Messiah.

B. Expressing Our Shared Confidence in the Victory of the Son (2:4-9)

2:4-5. The Lord is in complete control despite the rebellion of the nations. The Lord **sits in the heavens** ("is enthroned") and **scoffs at them** for their foolish behavior (cf. Ps 59:8). He will answer their uproar with **His anger** and **fury** in judgment for their wickedness and rebellion, an expression of God's righteousness (cf. 7:11).

2:6. The Lord's victory is certain because His Son, the King Messiah, will rule the earth from Jerusalem: **I have installed My King upon Zion, My holy mountain**. The location of **My holy mountain** is the Temple Mount in Jerusalem (cf. 2Ch 33:15; Pss 15:1; 43:3; 99:9; Is 52:1; 56:7). It is strongly suggestive of the king's priestly character, linking it to the Temple Mount (further affirming the application to Jesus, the only one in whom both offices unite). The verb **installed** (Hb. *nasakhti*, lit., "poured out," a synonym of "anointed" with a specifically Levitical connotation as in Ex 30:9; Hs 9:4) indicates the Lord's setting up the messianic King.

2:7. The statement **I have begotten You**, which is directed from God the Father to God the Son, signifies not the production of Sonship (since all three persons of the Godhead are uncreated and eternal), but rather the Father's declaration of the Messiah's Sonship as announced later by Gabriel (Lk 1:32), reiterated at Jesus' baptism (Lk 3:22), and confirmed by His resurrection (Ac 13:33; Rm 1:4). In the ancient near east, a king was considered "begotten" when he entered into kingship. This unique Person of the divine Son is the basis of the confidence of God's people in the Lord's victory.

2:8-9. Victory by the King (v. 6) is certain because ultimately the **nations . . . and the very ends of the earth** are His **inheritance**—something that is never ascribed to any Davidic king but only to the divine Messiah Himself (cf. Ps 110:6; Zch 14:9; Rv 21:22-24). He will judge the wicked and **break them with a rod of iron . . . shatter them** (cf. Gn 3:15; Nm 24:17; Ps 110:2, 5-6; Rv 2:27; 19:15).

C. Expressing Our Shared Commission to Worship the Son (2:10-12)

The collective expressions of shared persecution (vv. 1-3) and shared confidence (vv. 4-9) are here counterbalanced and completed by the expression of what has always stood at the heart of God's self-revelation to man: God's empathetic and loving desire that everyone—both Jew and Gentile—come to know and worship Him as the one, true God (cf. Gn 12:3; Dt 4:6-8; Ps 22:27; Is 45:22-23; 49:6; 56:7; Zch 14:16). As in the previous two expressions, so too here David focuses this collective expression on the person of God in His Son.

2:10. The section opens with a challenge to the Gentile **kings** to recognize God's truth and **show discernment** to obey Him. This is a **warning** to all the **judges** ("leaders") **of the earth**. The message is to those who had counseled together against the Lord (cf. 2:1-3) and for everyone who decides to rebel against His rulership (2:3).

2:11. The point of the inseparability of "the LORD" (God the Father) and "His Anointed" (God the Son) is here reiterated by David as an evangelistic challenge: to truly **worship the LORD** in a way acceptable to Him.

2:12. The commanded requirement is **Do homage to the Son** (lit., "kiss the Son"). Some suggest "kiss" be understood as a more affectionate synonym for the verb "worship" in the previous verse to which it clearly stands in parallel (another reason that the Son in this psalm can refer only to the divine messianic King). However, the use of the verb "to kiss" as a euphemism for "to worship" is also attested and would affirm the understanding of **Do homage to the Son** (cf. 1Kg 19:18; Jb 31:27; Hs 13:2). Some scholars contest this understanding, pointing out that the word translated "(the) son" (*bar*) is Aramaic, whereas the proper Hebrew word for "son" is *ben*. Since this psalm (like all the rest) is in Hebrew, it is sometimes argued that *bar* here should be understood as the Hebrew adverb "purely," giving the sense "kiss purely." However, two flaws oppose this view: (1) The Hebrew of David's day had many Aramaic loan words (Abraham himself was an Aramean; Dt 26:5), one of which was indeed *bar*, "son," as employed thrice by Solomon in Pr 31:2, (2) every one of the remaining 31 OT occurrences of the Hebrew verb "to kiss" has an explicit direct or indirect object, which would be unaccountably missing from the present verse if *bar* is taken as the Hebrew adverbial expression "purely." It is better to see the phrase not as "kiss purely" but as "kiss the Son," that is, **Do homage to** the Son.

Psalm 3: A Paradigm of Personal Lament

Psalm 2 deals with the promises God made to David in what is called the Davidic covenant regarding his future supreme Son, the Messiah (see comments on 2Sm 7:12-17). In Ps 3, David struggled with how that covenant could be fulfilled in light of the sinful rebellion of David's son Absalom (for this connection, see John H. Sailhamer, *NIV Compact Bible Commentary* [Grand Rapids, MI: Zondervan, 1994], 315).

The heading/superscription identifies this as a **Psalm of David**. Of the 41 psalms in Book One (Pss 1–41), 37 are identified as a **Psalm of David**; Pss 1–2, 10, and 33 are the only exceptions. In total 73 are directly attributed to him in the superscriptions. Additionally, the NT identifies David as the author of Pss 2 and 95. The word for "psalm" in the heading is *mizmor*; the term occurs 57 times and only in the headings of psalms. It probably indicates a psalm that was sung by the Levites in the temple to the accompaniment of musical instruments. Furthermore, Ps 3 is one of 14 psalms linked in the superscription to a specific event in David's life (3, 7, 18, 30, 34, 51, 52, 54, 56, 57, 59, 60, 63, 142). This psalm was written by David **when he fled from Absalom his son** (cf. 2Sm 15–19).

A. Express Your Trouble to the Lord (3:1-2)

3:1-2. The **adversaries** to whom David referred were not Canaanites or other hostile Gentiles (e.g., the Arameans; see 2Sm 10), but his fellow Israelites, **many** of whom were **rising up against** him in rebellion under the leadership of his son, Absalom. These **many** were vividly described by Absalom's advisor Hushai as "all Israel . . . from Dan even to Beersheba, as the sand that is by the sea in abundance" (2Sm 17:11). By their statement, **There is no deliverance for him in God**, these adversaries of David were not denying God's power to save, but rather His will to deliver David from his circumstances (see 2Sm 16:8).

B. Declare Your Confidence in the Lord (3:3-6)

3:3-4. David affirmed, nonetheless, that God is his **shield**, the one who will protect him, **and the One who lifts** his **head**—that is, the one who will give him victory (on this sense of "lifting the head" see also Pss 27:6 and 110:7). For God's answer to his cry of distress, David looked to **His holy mountain**, referring to Zion, and the Temple Mount in particular (see the comment on 2:6), which the Lord had chosen as His dwelling place. The source of David's comfort was the Lord Himself (Ex 40:34; 2Sm 24:24-25; 1Kg 8:11).

3:5-6. By affirming that it was **the Lord** who **sustains** him—as opposed to David's own ingenuity and ability—his mind was set at ease and he was able to sleep soundly, even though his adversaries numbered in the **ten thousands** (cf. 1Sm 18:7).

C. Present Your Petition to the Lord (3:7-8)

3:7. David's petition, **Arise, O Lord**, could be translated "Rise up, O Lord," and is a word play on his opening cry, "Many are rising up." It sets in perspective the threat posed by David's adversaries. The opposition that "rises up" against one, as long as that one is conducting himself according to the will of God, will be met and defeated by the "rising up" of God Himself. The concept of defeat is underscored by David's reference to God having **smitten all my enemies on the cheek**—an act that is closely associated in Scripture with abasement and subjugation (cf. 1Kg 22:24).

3:8. David concluded his psalm in characteristic fashion on a theocentric (God-focused) rather than an egocentric (self-focused) note, declaring that **salvation** (lit., "deliverance," as in v. 2) ultimately **belongs to the Lord**. That is, God determines whether, when, and how to bestow deliverance (David does not presume this will always immediately and completely resolve his affliction). David's concern is for his people (the very ones who are his adversaries!), that God's **blessing** be upon them and that God be glorified as a result. In spite of Absalom's rebellion, David continued to hold on to God's faithfulness and His promises in the Davidic covenant to provide salvation and deliver His people even though it looked as if the covenant could not be fulfilled through Absalom (Sailhamer, *NIV Compact Bible Commentary*, 315).

Psalm 4: A Paradigm of Expressing Trust in the Lord

Psalm 4 continues the theme of Ps 3, focusing on the David's trust in the Lord. David continues his longing for the fulfillment of the Davidic covenant when David himself will be vindicated from his opponents, including Absalom (Ps 3) (Sailhamer, *NIV Compact Bible Commentary*, 315).

The heading states that this is a **Psalm of David** (Hb. *mizmor*; see introduction to Ps 3) and intended for the **choir director**—a designation that occurs 55 times in the headings of the Psalms and once at the end of Habakkuk. It probably signifies the conductor of the entire company of priestly musicians and singers whose job it was to enhance worship for the Jewish people.

A. The Basis of Trust in the Lord (4:1)

4:1. David began by emphasizing his spiritual dependency on God, employing the designation **God of my righteousness** (not, as in the NIV, "my righteous God"), which is meant to indicate that (1) God (as opposed to man) is the only true source of righteousness (cf. Ps 71:16; Ec 7:20; Jr 23:6; Rm 3:10), and (2) as true righteousness is found only in God, He "reckons" (i.e., "legally extends") it to whomsoever He chooses (whether David or anyone else) as a gift (cf. Gn 15:6; Rm 3:22; 4:3-6, 24). David trusted not only in who God is (His attributes of righteousness and grace), but also in what He does—specifically, what He already did for David when He relieved him **in** his past **distress**. The specific wording here is significant, for it indicates that based on his past experience David did not expect that God would fully remove the **distress**, but rather that He would extend relief to David **in** the midst of it (cf. 1Co 10:13; 1Th 1:6; 2Tm 1:8; 1Pt 4:19; 5:10). David's request that God **hear** him refers not to the act of listening (for God knows what people need even before they ask; Mt 6:8), but rather the act of providing what is most needed by the petitioner.

B. The Challenge of Trust in the Lord (4:2-5)

4:2-5. David next addressed the **sons of men** (lit., "sons of man"), which may refer to men of status and wealth who were failing to trust God, but instead were loving **what is worthless**, and aiming **at deception** (counterfeit gods). Whatever their precise identity, these men are unquestionably Israelites, since David exhorted them to offer **sacrifices of righteousness** (v. 5)—that is, sacrifices consisting not only of the proper material elements but also offered with the proper heart attitude, without which the sacrifice is meaningless (cf. Ps 51:16-19; Is 29:13). David warned them to **tremble** [lit., "be angry"] and **do not sin** (v. 4). Anger, which can be an overpowering emotion, has the potential of strengthening the temptation to sin. God had cautioned Cain in his anger to be careful, for "sin is crouching at the door; and its desire is [to master] you, but you must master it" (Gn 4:7). The wise course for anyone who becomes angry is to **meditate in** one's **heart upon** one's **bed** (v. 4), but, as Paul wrote, "Do not let the sun go down on your anger" (Eph 4:26).

C. The Result of Trust in the Lord (4:6-8)

4:6-7. David here directed his address back to the Lord, expressing the desire on behalf of himself and the **many**, the "godly" of v. 3. Verse 6 is literally, "Oh that someone would provide us what is good." This understands the Hebrew clause as a hope (see the same expression in 1Sm 23:15), and is preferable to the more pessimistic interrogative translation of the NASB (**Who will show us any good?**). The godly, like David, know full well that God alone is the source of all good (Jms 1:17), though by phrasing their petition in this hopeful manner, they are expressing both respect and leaving room for God to respond how and when He deems best. This psalm emphasizes both the source and the blessing of trust in the Lord by adopting phraseology from the Aaronic and Mosaic benedictions (v. 1: "be gracious to me" [cf. Nm 6:25b]; v. 5: "offer the sacrifices of righteousness" [cf. Dt 33:19]; v. 6: **Lift up the light of Your countenance upon us** [cf. Nm 6:25a]; v. 7: **when their grain and new wine abound . . . sleep** [cf. Nm 6:26; Dt 33:28]).

4:8. David's confidence that God, and God **alone**, will fully provide all that is necessary for his good enabled him to **lie down and sleep** even in the midst of his distress. This may well allude to David's experience when God intervened to save his life by putting Saul and his army into a sound sleep (1Sm 26:12). In two other OT passages, God brought a deep sleep onto someone in connection with sovereignly meeting a great need (cf. Gn 2:21; 15:12).

Psalm 5: A Paradigm of Morning Devotion

Psalm 5 continues the theme of Ps 3, which is revisited in Ps 7 as well. In part, it is written against the rebellious (5:10), which may have included Absalom. But as in Ps 2:12, the righteous, like David, will be blessed as they continue their trust in God to fulfill the Davidic covenant when they will find refuge in the Anointed (5:11; see 2:2, 12) (Sailhamer, *NIV Compact Bible Commentary*, 315). In its heading this psalm (Hb. *mizmor*) is directed to the **choir director** (see introduction to Ps 4) and is attributed to **David**. That it was sung in connection with the regular morning offering in the temple is suggested by the repeated reference in v. 3 to this prayer being uttered "in the morning." And, indeed, the phraseology of this psalm is employed in traditional Jewish morning prayers. The order of the thematic parts of this psalm is also significant in that it clearly establishes the precedence of praise to petition (focusing on God first, then one's need). This principle is reflected not only in the Lord's Prayer (Mt 6:9-13), but also in the early Jewish approach to prayer: "A man should always first express his praise of the Holy One, blessed be He, and only afterward express his petition" (Babylonian Talmud *Berakhot 39a*).

A. Affirming Submission to God (5:1-3)

5:1-3. David began by imploring God to **give ear** (i.e., "to attend carefully to someone or something" with the intent of responding for the petitioner's benefit) to his **words**, and to **consider** his meditation (not **groaning**, as in the NASB). He followed this with reference to God as his **King**, underscoring that God is the true king of Israel, whereas David, like his son Solomon and all the human kings after him who "sat on the throne of the LORD" (1Ch 29:23; see also 28:5) were only custodians of God's kingship. This opening sentiment is paralleled by the opening affirmation of God's kingship in Jesus' own model of prayer (Mt 6:9-10).

B. Declaring Praise of God (5:4-7)

5:4-6. In his praise David here focused on two attributes of God: His holiness and His fatherly (i.e., relational) compassion. God's holiness is indicated by David underscoring that God is the opposite of all that is unholy. He is **not a God who takes pleasure in wickedness; no evil dwells** (resides, sojourns) **with You**. The Lord hates **iniquity**, **falsehood**, and **deceit**.

5:7. David emphasized that the only reason he can **enter** the Lord's **house** and worship **at** His **holy temple** (lit., "temple of holiness," see the comment on Ps 2:6) is because of God's **abundant lovingkindness** to him. The term **lovingkindness** is *chesed*, which specifically indicates God's covenant love, His faithful and continual expression of what is best for those who are His own under the promise of the Abrahamic covenant (see Gn 12:1-3 and discussion of this term in the Introduction to the book of Ruth). The word may also reflect David's understanding of God's loving choice of him as the vehicle for the Davidic covenant that includes the future coming of David's supreme son, the Messiah (see 2Sm 7:16), which will come about through God's faithfulness in spite of Absalom's rebellion (see the comments on the superscription of Ps 3).

C. Presenting Petition before God (5:8-12)

5:8-10. In his petition David noted that **righteousness** is not found in himself or attainable on his own, but rather finds its source only in God and is attainable only by His leading (see also comment on Ps 4:1). This is a stark contrast to his wicked foes who are not **reliable** and whose **throat is an open grave**. This refers to the deceitfulness of David's foes (see the parallelism with **There is nothing reliable in what they say**) who, according to several ancient Jewish sources, are sinners from among the Jewish people (in *Midrash on Psalms*, Ps 49:5, where Ps 5:9 is cited, referring to the "wicked" among the Jewish people, distinct from the "saints" and "the nations"; see William G. Braude, *The Midrash on Psalms*, [New Haven: Yale University Press, 1959], 383–384). David's petition therefore is not only that God would protect him from physical harm (as in his military campaigns against the Philistines), but also that God would **lead** him in **righteousness**, including the Lord's restraining him from taking merciless retribution on Israelites outwardly opposed to him (like Nabal; 1Sm 25:26) as well as granting him discernment so as to avoid the counsel (see the same word in Jb 29:21; Pr 1:31, "devices") of ungodly allies and advisors (like Joab; see 2Sm 3:24-30, 39). David also prays that God's judgment would fall on his foes because **of their transgressions** and **rebellious** behavior toward God (v. 10). God's justice would be especially evident if they would fall **by their own devices**, being destroyed by the plots they laid for others (later in the Bible, Haman experienced this kind of justice, being hanged on the gallows he built for Mordecai, cf. Est 7:9-10). See Introduction: Types of Psalms for discussion of imprecatory psalms.

5:11-12. David is confident of the good outcome of following the Lord. Those who **take refuge** in Him will **be glad . . . sing for joy**. The Lord will bless **the righteous** and **surround him with favor**.

Psalm 6: A Paradigm of Petitioning God for Mercy

In its heading this psalm is directed to the **choir director** (see introduction to Ps 4) and attributed to **David**. This psalm continues the theme of David's patience with which he awaited God's deliverance from his enemies (see 6:3), which may have included Absalom (Ps 3). David is confident of God's unfailing covenant love (6:4), expressed to him in the Davidic covenant (see 2Sm 7:8-17) (Sailhamer, *NIV Compact Bible Commentary*, 316).

A. Fully Admitting One's Spiritual Position (6:1-5)

6:1-3. David begins his petition for God's mercy by fully and sincerely admitting his guilt. He asks for the **LORD** to be merciful and **not**

rebuke and **chasten** him in the Lord's **anger** or **wrath** (cf. Pr 3:11). David made this admission with the heartfelt conviction that he was confessing his sin not to a distant, wrathful God, but rather to the God who looks on him as a father looks on his son. This is the implication of the terms **rebuke** and **chasten**, which in the Bible are primarily the responsibility of the father to administer to his children (see, for example, Pr 3:12). David's spiritual condition caused physical consequences so that his **bones** were **dismayed**. His **soul**, or his mental condition, is **greatly dismayed** because of his distress. Asking **how long** (or "when" or "why") is an expression of anguish asking for relief; it shows the psalmist's intimate relationship with the Lord and the confidence the righteous can have in inquiring of the Lord for mercy, help, and understanding. (Asking **how long** is a common question, cf. 13:1-2; 35:17; 74:10; 79:5; 80:4; 89:46; asking "why" is common as well, cf. 10:1; 22:1; 42:9; 43:5.)

6:4-5. Indicative of his relationship is David's appeal to **Return, O LORD, rescue my soul** based on God's **lovingkindness** (see the comment on this word in 5:7). David makes fivefold use in this opening section of God's covenant name **LORD** (Yahweh). He pleads for mercy in life, for there is no opportunity to **mention** the Lord **in death**. Regarding **Sheol**, see the comment on Ps 49:10-14, 15.

B. Fully Expressing One's Circumstantial Anxieties (6:6-7)

6:6-7. Though David's distressing circumstances may have been a just expression of God's loving chastisement for his sin(s), they were nonetheless a source of anxiety and—to a certain extent—even depression. These are natural human responses to ongoing and unfavorable circumstances, which can take a toll on both body and mind: **I am weary . . . I dissolve my couch** (bed) **with my tears** . . . he **has become old because of all [his] adversaries**. Such responses are not sinful, and, as modeled here by David, are an acceptable—even incumbent—part of worship to bare one's turmoil and distress to God, who as a loving and sympathetic Father (cf. Heb 4:15) earnestly desires to hear His children (see the comments on Ps 142). This act of baring his heart to God serves as a balm to soothe David's distress. Although God had not yet resolved the negative circumstances and removed David's **adversaries**, David was beginning to experience the Lord's comfort.

C. Fully Affirming One's Covenantal Expectation (6:8-10)

6:8-9. David separated himself from **all . . . who do iniquity** and was confident that God, because of His covenantal relationship with David, had **heard** his **weeping** and **supplication** (i.e., this specific supplication) and, in general (as indicated by the present/imperfect tense), **receives** his **prayer**.

6:10. Typical of David's psalms of lament, complaint, and petition, he ended on a positive note, characterized not by a look back at what God had done to resolve his situation, but rather by a look forward to what God would do—if not in this life, then unquestionably in the next, when **all my enemies will be ashamed**. They will finally be judged and David, in the company of those who love God, will stand in the full light of His presence (cf. Pss 16:11; 142:7).

Psalm 7: A Paradigm of Imprecation

The heading identifies this psalm as **A Shiggaion of David**. The term **Shiggaion** occurs only here in the Bible and the meaning is unclear. It perhaps means "to be exhilarated," as a similar Hebrew word is used in Pr 5:19-20 and Hab 3:1. Thus it would designate a highly emotionally charged type of psalm. This psalm presents David's emotional response to the news of Absalom's death. The content of this psalm concerns a certain **Benjamite** named **Cush**, who is mentioned nowhere else in the Bible. Yet he is almost certainly to be identified as one of Saul's soldiers who was seeking, with his king, to kill David, since (1) the psalm deals with David's enemies, individually (vv. 2-5, 12-16) as well as collectively (vv. 1, 6-9), and (2) there are several clear verbal parallels to the two situations in which David was cornered by Saul and his men in 1Sm 24 and 26. For example, for Ps 7:1, "Save me from all those who pursue me," see 1Sm 24:14; 26:24. For 7:3, "If there is injustice in my hands," see 2Sm 24:11; 26:18. For 7:8, "The LORD judges the peoples," see 1Sm 26:12, 15; and "Vindicate me, O LORD, according to my righteousness" (cf. 1Sm 26:23).

Another possibility is identifying **Cush, a Benjamite** with the Cushite who notified David of the death of Absalom in 2Sm 18:21-33. This forges a link with Ps 3 and here expresses David's reaction to his son's death (Sailhamer, *NIV Compact Bible Commentary*, 316).

A. Know What to Expect (7:1-5)

7:1-4. David declares his trust in the Lord in dangerous times: **O LORD my God, in You I have taken refuge**. After an initial appeal to

God's sovereign protection (**Save me**), David affirmed the possibility that his distressing circumstances were in fact a merited expression of God's chastisement (**if I have done this**) for some **injustice** or **evil** that he had committed, and of which he was either unaware or unrepentant.

7:5. If such were the case, David was not only willing to submit to God's chastisement, but he also earnestly encouraged it: **Let the enemy pursue my soul and overtake it** . . . and **trample my life**. For David, what was most important was that his situation bear out the righteousness of God (on which note he ended this psalm in v. 17), not David's own comfort and political-military success. This sentiment is likewise evident in David's words in 1Sm 26:19, where he suggested that Saul was "stirred" up against him by the Lord, in which case he asked that the Lord "accept an offering," David's sin offering.

B. Appeal to the Lord for Vindication (7:6-16)

7:6-8. Recognizing that his **adversaries**, who may have included Absalom, were motivated by evil, David implored God to **arise** in His **anger** and **lift** Himself **up** against them. This phrase is used in the Pentateuch to describe Israel's divinely championed military victory (cf. Nm 23:24; 24:9). David asked God to **vindicate** him completely, but only **according to** his **righteousness and** the **integrity that is in** him.

7:9-11. David also affirmed that God judges not only men's actions, but also their **hearts and minds**, that is, the thoughts and motives that underlie actions, whether good or bad. He appeals to the Lord as the **righteous judge**. The Lord's judgments are not reserved only for a future time, but He has **indignation every day**.

7:12-16. God is ready to act against a **man** who **does not repent**. He will prepare, **sharpen His sword**, and bend **His bow** to judge the wicked. His evil (**wickedness, falsehood**, v. 14) and **mischief will return upon his own head** when the Lord judges him.

C. Thank the Lord Regardless of His Answer (7:17)

7:17. Again David ended his petition by giving **thanks to the Lord**. He is expressing gratitude and **praise** for whatever God chooses to do; no matter what it is, it will be consistent with God's perfect **righteousness.** God chose not to resolve David's persecution by Saul for several years. Nevertheless, God kept His promises to David and vindicated him before his opponents and made him the king of Israel.

Psalm 8: A Paradigm of Praise

David concluded Ps 7 with praise for God's righteousness exhibited in his vindication of David and the bringing down of David's adversaries, whether Saul or Absalom. Psalm 8 continues praising God, including "the son of man" (v. 4), a concept linked to the Son in whom the righteous find refuge in 2:12. Psalm 8 is appropriately understood as a messianic psalm (Sailhamer, *NIV Compact Bible Commentary*, 316).

Psalm 8 is cited four times in the NT, where it is recognized as a prophecy of Messiah, three of which are in direct application to Messiah (1Co 15:27; Eph 1:22; Heb 2:6-10; additionally Mt 21:16 cites this psalm). The psalmist understood that this song would be fulfilled directly by the Messiah. "The son of man" is a direct link to the "Son" of Ps 2:7, 12, and appears to be associated with the "Son of Man" in Dn 7:10-14. As a royal figure, He is crowned with "glory and majesty," and rules over all creation (vv. 5-6). As a human being, He is "a little lower than God" (v. 5), not in His essence but in His human attributes (here the word "God" likely has its less common meaning, "angels" [LXX] or "the angels" [NIV], as it does in Ps 82:6 and 1Sm 28:13—hence the Son of Man in His incarnation is less powerful than angels although greater in His essence as God). As the Son of Man, the Lord Jesus fulfills humanity's ideal (all that humanity was meant to be and do) and directly fulfills this Psalm. Only by being "united with Him" (Rm 6:5) through faith—and hence "in Christ" (one of Paul's favorite expressions; cf. 1Co 1:30; 3:1; 4:10, 15, 17; 15:18-19, etc.)—are believers able to experience the application of this ideal as "fellow heirs with Christ" (Rm 8:17).

For the heading of this psalm, see the comments introducing Ps 3. A Gittith was a stringed musical instrument, mentioned here and in the heading of Pss 81 and 84.

A. Reflect on How God Uses Men (8:1-2)

8:1-2. The opening phrase, **O Lord, our Lord, How majestic is Your name in all the earth** is repeated at the end of the psalm (8:9) as a literary device (an *inclusio*; see Introduction: Genre) highlighting the main theme of the psalm, which is to praise God for His majesty as expressed in His creation of and interaction with humanity. In this opening clause, David affirmed God's **majestic** name, which is indicative of His power and glory evident **in all the earth**. David also affirmed Israel's submission to the one true God. This is indicated by the first

LORD (Hb. *Yahweh*) that represents the unique covenant name of the true God, which is conjoined to the second **Lord** (Hb. *adonenu*), which represents the Hebrew term for "master" (one to whom the speaker is subject). Verse 2a is cited by Jesus in Mt 21:16 (see the comments there).

B. Reflect on Why God Cares for People (8:3-5)

8:3-5. The **heavens** and all that is in them, including **the moon and the stars**, are described by David as **the work of** God's **fingers**. God is declared and acknowledged as Creator. On the application of vv. 4-6 to Messiah in Heb 2, see above and the comments on Heb 2:6-10.

C. Reflect on What God Has Given People (8:6-9)

8:6-9. God gave the son of man to rule over what is described as **the works of** His **hands**, denoting products intended for use and enjoyment (cf. Gn 1:28). The second half of v. 6 is cited twice in the NT (1Co 15:27 and Eph 1:22), in both instances with direct reference to Christ and (redeemed) humanity's fulfillment in Him of their ideal to rule over "all things" (see esp. Eph 1:22-23, "and [God] gave Him as head over all things to the church, which is His body, the fullness of Him who fills all in all"). The emphasis on man's **rule over the works of** God's **hands** also naturally indicates man's precedence over all other parts of creation, that mankind was created as the pinnacle and crown of God's creative work and the object for which all that work was intended (see the comments on Gn 1:26-27).

Psalm 9: A Meditation on God's Justice: God as the Vindicator of the Righteous

Regarding the heading of this psalm, see introduction to Ps 4. The word **Muth-labben** occurs only here. If taken as a literal Hebrew phrase, it means "on the death of a son" (perhaps Absalom, 2Sm 18:33). Or it could be a word for a musical instrument. The meaning is unclear. It is helpful to take the meaning of "death of the Son" when read in context with the exaltation of the Son of Man in Ps 8:5, and in fact the writer of Hebrews indicates that the death of the Son resulted in Him being crowned with glory and honor and providing salvation for His people (Heb 2:8-9). The theme of Ps 9 is God's reign in Zion, the location of the kingdom of the messianic Son; thus, reading and understanding Pss 8 and 9 together is most helpful (Sailhamer, *NIV Compact Bible Commentary*, 316–317).

Pss 9 and 10 together are written as a modified acrostic, with the stanzas beginning with a consecutive letter of the Hebrew alphabet. Moreover the two psalms share certain parallels in structure, phrasing, and themes that suggest both were composed as a unit. Structurally, the beginning of Ps 9 mirrors the ending of Ps 10 (an *inclusio*), with a declaration of confidence in God. Also, both psalms employ several of the same or closely parallel expressions.

A. Declaring One's Confidence in the Vindicator (9:1-2)

9:1-2. David begins by expressing his determination (**I will**) to **give thanks to the LORD . . . tell of** His **wonders . . . be glad and exult in** Him and **sing praise to** His **name**. God's **wonders** is a term in its various forms that denotes God's powerful actions (i.e., miracles; see also, e.g., Ex 34:10). Because of His **wonders** (and wonderfulness) David affirmed that God is the **Most High** (preeminent over any other existing authority), which in turn established the basis of David's ensuing appeal to God as the preeminent judicial authority and ultimate vindicator of the oppressed.

B. Affirming the Established Record of the Vindicator (9:3-12)

9:3-4. David proclaims his confidence in God as he sees his **enemies turn back**. The Lord is the preeminent vindicator who **maintained my just cause**. He affirms the Lord's past and present record as a judge of righteousness (literally, as opposed to the NASB's **judging righteously**; elsewhere this expression occurs only in Jr 11:20, again referring to God), as consistently and comprehensively borne out from the following three perspectives: first, God's vindication of David personally (vv. 3-4), in which David's words **you have maintained my just cause** "as a judge of righteousness," hearkens specifically to his words in 1Sm 24:15 ("The LORD therefore be judge and decide between you and me; and may He see and plead my cause and deliver me").

9:5-10. Second, God vindicates the oppressed generally. He has **rebuked the nations** (cf. 2:1-6) and His blotting **out** the **name** of **the wicked** recalls God's judgment and annihilation of all the wicked among humanity during the flood (cf. Gn 6:7; 7:4, 23). God's vindication is based on His eternality: **the LORD abides forever**, and **He will judge the world in righteousness** and **equity**.

Third, the Lord is **a stronghold in times of trouble** and He will never forsake **those who know [His] name . . . trust [Him]** and **seek** Him. Trusting in His **name** means to trust in His whole character and identity. God's vindication of His people is implied by the expression **those who know Your name**, which is elsewhere applied to the nation of Israel, the ones to whom God's name was "made known" (cf. Ex 3:13-15; 6:2-6; 1Ch 28:9; Ezk 20:5). The expression **those who seek You** is applied in the OT to Israelites and proselytes (cf. Ex 18:15; Ezr 4:2).

9:11-12. The response to God's righteous judgment is the exhortation to **sing praises to the Lord, who dwells in Zion**. God's heavenly throne (v. 7) has a counterpart in the place He has chosen as His earthly residence, Jerusalem (2:6; 3:4; 20:2; 132:13-14). The message is to declare **among the peoples His deeds**, which recalls the specific OT mission of Israel (cf. 1Ch 16:8; Ps 105:1 [with v. 6]; Is 12:4).

C. Making One's Appeal to the Vindicator (9:13-20)

9:13-16. On the basis of his confidence in God and His proven record as the preeminent and perfectly righteous judge, David now made his appeal, imploring that God **be gracious to** him and **see** (in the sense of assessing and responding to David's need; see the comments on Ps 4:6 and Gn 1:4-5) his **affliction**. David's motivation, as always, is not his own ease or comfort, but rather that the glory of God might be manifest—that he might have yet one thing more to speak of when he tells **of all** God's **praises**, both for His granting **salvation** to David as well as for executing **judgment** on **the wicked**.

9:17-20. The fate of the **wicked** and those who **forget God** is to **return** (more literally "turn") **to Sheol**. On David's reference to **Sheol** (v. 17), which is not to be confused with the "hell" or "Hades" of the NT, see the comment on Ps 49:14-15. In contrast, the **needy** and **afflicted** have hope in the Lord, who will judge the wicked.

Psalm 10: A Meditation on God's Justice: God as the Judge of the Wicked

The omission of a heading from Ps 10 is probably because of its composition link to the previous psalm, with which it shares clear structural, verbal, and thematic parallels (see introduction to Ps 9). This psalm would also have been written by David.

A. Affirming the Need for the Judge (10:1-11)

10:1-4. The psalmist opens with a heartfelt expression of anguish and dismay, **Why do You stand afar off, O Lord?** It seems as if God is hidden in the face of the ongoing activity of **the wicked**. Yet the psalmist's complaint is ultimately motivated not by the desire that the wicked be punished or **the afflicted** be relieved of their distress, but by the glory and honor of the Lord. God's holding back punishment, even though the wicked man **curses and spurns** Him (v. 3), seems to encourage the **thoughts** of the wicked that **there is no God** (v. 4).

10:5-11. The wicked person sees that he **prospers at all times** and God's **judgments** are **out of his sight** (v. 5). He does many wicked things such as killing **the innocent** and catching **the afflicted**, causing the **unfortunate** to fall into his clutches (vv. 8-10); yet he believes God will not judge him, for he believes either He **has forgotten** or **He** is unable to **see it** (v. 11; see the comments on Ps 142). The wicked in view here includes both Jew and Gentile (sin being a human, not an ethnic problem), as v. 7 is cited and applied in Rm 3:14.

B. Making One's Appeal to the Judge (10:12-15)

10:12-15. The psalmist implores God to take action using the same phrase as the previous psalm (**Arise, O Lord**, cf. 9:19), pleading for God's judgment, for "they are but men" (9:20). The psalmist followed up his appeal with an affirmation that God has **seen** the mischief of the wicked (contra their assertion in v. 11, "He will never see it") and has **been the helper** (from the same Hebrew root as "helper" in Gn 2:18, 20) to the **unfortunate** (lit., "dejected") and **the orphan** (v. 14). The question is not if, but when, God will **break the arm** (an idiom signifying the crushing of both power and glory; cf. Jb 22:8-9) **of the wicked** and **seek out** (lit., "requite") **his wickedness** (contra the assertion in v. 13: **You will not require it**).

C. Declaring One's Confidence in the Judge (10:16-18)

10:16-18. The psalm concludes with a declaration of praise: **The Lord is King forever and ever**. He has a confident look at the final, future state, when everyone will recognize **the Lord** for who He is and always has been—the true King of all the earth (cf. 47:7)—and **nations** (lit., "Gentiles," i.e., those opposed to the true God and His people) will **have perished from His land** (i.e., all of the redeemed/recreated "new earth"; cf. Zch 14:9; Rv 21:1). The use of the past (i.e., perfect) tense verbal expression—in this case, **have perished**—is a common feature of prophetic-predictive statements in the OT and is intended to underscore the absolute certainty of a future event. Such events are described, as it were, from God's timeless perspective, as if they had already happened. The LORD had **heard** the request of the **humble** and would **vindicate the orphan and the oppressed**. The **man who is of the earth**, the person who is not following God, will no longer **cause terror** because they will no longer be in power over the righteous and innocent (cf. 49:12, 29; 56:4, 11; 62:9; 118:6-9).

Psalm 11: An Anatomy of Trust

For the heading of this psalm, see introduction to Ps 4. Though no historical event is mentioned in the heading, the imagery of David's words in v. 1 ("Flee as a bird to your mountain") bear a close similarity to his words in 1Sm 26:20 ("the king of Israel has come out . . . just as one hunts a partridge in the mountains"), suggesting the latter as a likely venue. As in Ps 10, the theme of trust in God when the wicked are powerful continues here. In 2:12 blessedness belongs to the one who seeks refuge in the Anointed. In Ps 11 the future deliverance from the Lord (vv. 4-7) also involves refuge (11:1), with such refuge coming from the Lord through the Anointed One here as well (Sailhamer, *NIV Compact Bible Commentary*, 317).

A. The Temptation against Trusting God: The Strength of the Wicked (11:1-3)

11:1-3. The psalm begins with a declaration of intent: **In the LORD I take refuge**. But the temptation not to trust God is represented by the apparent overpowering strength of **the wicked**. Their power is here underscored by the contrast between David as **a bird** (lit., "sparrow," the smallest of birds) set on by a multitude of **wicked** (the Hb. is plural). They have locked him in their sights, suggested by the figure of bowstrings pulled back and ready **to shoot**. In such a situation it seems that even **the foundations**—a figure of speech for societal order and authorities (cf. Pss 75:3; 82:5; Ezk 30:4; Gl 2:9)—**are destroyed** and there is nowhere **the righteous** can turn for true justice.

B. The Basis for Trusting God: Who God Is and What He Does (11:4-7a)

11:4-7a. However bleak the situation might seem, David found assurance and relief for his anxiety in the sure knowledge that **the LORD is in His holy temple**, that is, heaven, of which the earthly temple was only "a copy and shadow" (Heb 8:5). This point is further driven home by the parallel statement, **the LORD's throne is in heaven**. This indicates God's dual role, embodied and eternally fulfilled in the Anointed One, the Son of God as both king (His **throne**) and priest (His being in the **holy temple**), a combination of offices otherwise forbidden among the Israelites (see the comment on 2:6). David found relief from his distress, in other words, from the knowledge that just as God's holy throne is beyond the realm of man, permanently established and untouchable, so too is His will (and hence His promises to David) beyond the ability of man to rescind. They are untouchable by those who oppose it.

While God **tests** (a verb used for refining metals to determine their quality) **the righteous and the wicked**, in the end He will bring just punishment in this life or the next on **the wicked** and **the one who loves violence** (a word always denoting wicked violence, as in Gn 6:11 and Is 53:9). He will **rain snares** (bird traps) upon them. The variant reading in Symmachus (author of an ancient Greek translation of the OT), "coals of fire," makes more sense in context. Yet this seems to be an attempt to harmonize this word with the phrases that follow. Therefore, it is best to stick with the Masoretic reading, which pictures the Lord hurling **snares** to trap the wicked—they will be caught like birds (in contrast to their telling David to flee like a bird, v. 1). God will also bring them judgment—**Fire and brimstone and burning wind** (v. 6).

C. The Ultimate Hope of Trusting God: Beholding His Face (11:7b)

11:7b. By contrast, the ultimate hope of **the upright** is to **behold His face**. This is a unique (and perhaps the greatest) hope for believers, looking forward not simply to worshiping an eternally transcendent God, but enjoying intimate fellowship with Him (see the comments on Gn 1:26; 2:7; 3:8). In seeing God's **face**, His person and presence are revealed. Jesus Himself referred to this same idea in the sixth beatitude: "Blessed are the pure in heart (synonymous with the Hb. term here translated **upright**), for they shall see God" (Mt 5:8).

Psalm 12: Reflecting on Divine Deliverance

For the heading of this psalm, see introduction to Ps 4. This psalm expands on the theme of times of trouble and oppression for God's people (vv. 1-4), and here God's help is both a present one and will also come in the future when the kingdom is established on earth as it is in 11:4-7 (Sailhamer, *NIV Compact Bible Commentary*, 317).

A. Reflecting on the Need for Deliverance (12:1-2)

12:1-2. David's call for deliverance is prompted by the increasing scarcity of **the godly man** and

faithful . . . **from among the sons of men**—which leaves a void inevitably filled by a corresponding increase of ungodliness. By virtue of the implied contrast between these two verses, the godly/faithful are not simply those who do what God requires, but those who strive to do so with their whole heart (i.e., devoted and sincerely "faith-filled"). As depicted in the OT, both one's thoughts and one's words proceed from the heart (i.e., the "heart" and the "mind" are synonymous in the OT), and hence one who thinks one thing and says or does another is described as having "two hearts," or **a double heart**. Those to whom David here refers may well have been saying and even doing what God required, yet their hearts were not motivated by commensurate faith and devotion, and therefore God wanted none of it (cf. Ps 51:16-17; Is 29:13; 64:6; and comment on Gn 4:3-5). The concept of deceit and double-mindedness is further underscored by the statement in v. 2, **They speak falsehood to one another** (lit., "a man toward his neighbor"), which recalls the ninth commandment in Dt 5:20: "You shall not bear false witness [lit., "a witness of falsehood"] against your neighbor."

B. Reflecting on the Process of Deliverance (12:3-5)

12:3-5. By his appeal **May the Lord**, David was not addressing whether God would bring deliverance, but when. David wanted this deliverance to be nothing less than the final deliverance that will attend the establishing of God's kingdom, as indicated by (1) the expression **all flattering lips** and (2) the verbatim repetition of the words **"Now I will arise," says the Lord** in Is 33:10, in a clearly eschatological context. This is also seen in God's declaration, **I will set him in the safety** [lit., "I will establish him in the deliverance"] **for which he longs**, and in the description of His coming kingdom in Is 26:1: "In that day . . . He sets up walls and ramparts for security."

C. Reflecting on the Provider of Deliverance (12:6-8)

12:6-8. David's eschatological perspective continues into this last section, but these verses also contain the promise of present comfort for the afflicted righteous (see v. 7). Here David focuses on (1) the purity of **the words of the Lord** (i.e., revelation) that are compared to **silver** . . . **refined seven times**, emphasizing their superlative quality (i.e., to the highest degree possible: the purest) and (2) the Lord's faithfulness to His promises grounded in those **pure words** (cf., e.g., the promises of the Davidic covenant in 2Sm 7:12-17) that He **will keep** and **preserve** the one who loves Him, like David, **from this** wicked **generation forever**. This promise does not guarantee the preservation of the godly from affliction and oppression by the wicked in this life, but rather from the fate of the wicked (cf. Pss 37:28 and 97:10).

Psalm 13: A Prayer for Personal Deliverance

For an explanation of the heading of this psalm, see introductions to both Pss 3 and 4. The psalm is divided structurally into three parts, each part containing three components: first, David felt God had forgotten him (v. 1). David then realized God had not, and was considering David's situation (v. 3a), resulting in David, once again, trusting in God (v. 5a). Second, David's heart was grieved about his situation and that of the righteous (v. 2a), until God enlightened David (v. 3b) so that David's heart rejoiced (v. 5b). Third, David's enemies appeared to be exalted over him (v. 2b). David appealed to God lest his adversaries "overcome" him (v. 4). Finally, David sang to the Lord when he realized God would deliver him (v. 6).

A. Express Need for God's Deliverance (13:1-2)

13:1-2. David once again expressed a heartfelt lament to God, **How long, O Lord? Will You forget me forever?** It is spoken as a son to his father with whom he shared a deep emotional and psychological bond. David's anguish, **having sorrow in my heart all the day**, comes from feeling forgotten by God—a figure of speech known as "anthropomorphism" (attributing a human quality or characteristic to God). Rather than being the victim of disinterest or fickleness on God's part, this disruption is further characterized by David as an act of divine chastisement for (his) sin, as implied by his reference to God hiding (not removing) His **face** (i.e., "presence"). Just as this hiding of God's presence is presented in Dt 31:17-18 as the culminating chastisement for the sins of God's national son, Israel, so too does it apply to the individual son (or daughter) of God (cf. 1Co 10:11). And just as one of the ways by which God hid His presence was to abstain from communication with His sinning people—whether directly or indirectly through dreams, lots, and prophets (see the introduction to the book of Esther)—so too does He abstain from such communication with David, explaining why David referred to taking **counsel in** his **soul** (i.e., with himself).

B. Express Appeal for God's Deliverance (13:3-4)

13:3-4. David implored God to **consider** his situation and **answer** him. The verb **consider** is typically employed in the OT to indicate not just careful attention to something, but also a sense of affinity with, acceptance of, and pleasure in the object of that attention (as in Gn 19:26; Ps 119:6; Am 5:22—all of which are generally rendered by the verb "look"). Without God's help, David knew there was no hope.

C. Express Confidence in God's Deliverance (13:5-6)

13:5-6. In this final section, as characteristically in his psalms, David concluded on a note of trust, gratitude, and praise of God: **But I have trusted in Your lovingkindness**. Despite God's not yet having answered David's appeal, indeed He is more than deserving of David's praise and gratitude for (1) who He is (i.e., a God characterized by **lovingkindness**; cf. 5:7 comments), (2) what He has promised ultimately to do (i.e., bring full and final **salvation**, as in Ps 12:5), and (3) what He has already done (**dealt bountifully** with David [lit., brought David redemption]; for this word, see the comment on Ps 116:7).

Psalm 14: An Anatomy of Human Folly

This psalm is repeated, with minor variations, in Ps 53, the repetition being intended to emphasize the unchanging nature of human folly. For the heading of this psalm, see introduction to Ps 4. Though the focus of the psalm is on the lack of faith of the Gentile nations in and around Canaan and their opposition to the God of Israel and His people (see especially vv. 4-7), verbal parallels between vv. 1-3 and other OT passages, as well as the citation of these verses in Rm 3:10-12, indicate that the indictment for lack of faith (i.e., folly, biblically defined) applies in principle to all people, "both Jews and Greeks" (Rm 3:9).

A. The Essence of Human Folly (14:1)

14:1. This psalm begins with a key idea for life: **The fool has said in his heart, "There is no God."** The word **fool** (Hb. *nabal*), biblically defined, refers to one who is morally deficient. He lives his life believing that **there is no God**—which may refer either to the denial of His existence (i.e., atheism), for which there is no excuse (cf. Ps 19:1; Rm 1:19-20), or to the denial of divine justice (cf. 10:4). A vivid biblical illustration of just such a **fool** is the man whom David solicited for help, Nabal, whose very name is the same word employed here, meaning "fool" (cf. 1Sm 25). Nabal's rejection of the sovereignty of the Lord and His anointed—just like that of the fool depicted in this psalm—is ultimately, inevitably requited by God: "the LORD struck Nabal and he died" (1Sm 25:38). People with this attitude **are corrupt** and there is **no one who does good**.

B. The Pervasiveness of Human Folly (14:2-6)

14:2-3. Despite the foolish denial of God's existence, He does indeed exist. David's poetic description of God having **looked down from heaven... to see** refers not to the physical act of seeing from an upward location, but rather to His ongoing assessment of the heart of humanity. The unchanging conclusion of this assessment is that there are none **who seek after God** (cf. Jr 17:9-10). This is a universal reality of the sinfulness of the human condition: **They have all turned aside... become corrupt** (cf. Rm 3:23). The full truth of God's Word, and the gospel in particular, will never be understood and accepted "unless the Father... draws him" (Jn 6:44).

14:4-6. The contrast here is between the **workers of wickedness** who **do not call upon the Lord** and **the righteous** who make **the LORD** their **refuge**.

C. The Antithesis of Human Folly (14:7)

14:7. Here is a hope and call for **the salvation of Israel** that will come **out of Zion** (cf. comments on 2:6; 9:11). Bearing out the statement that "faith is the assurance of things hoped for" (Heb 11:1), David focused on the object of faith for the righteous among his people (vv. 4-5), namely, the future and final **salvation of Israel** when God **restores His captive people** (lit., "restores the fortunes of His people"; cf. 126:1-3). To "restore His captive people" is often interpreted wrongly as a restoration from the Babylonian captivity several hundred years after this was written. To restore Israel's fortunes refers to that time when the Lord Himself smelts away Israel's remaining dross (cf. Is 1:25) and makes them what they were always intended to be: "a kingdom of priests and a holy nation" (Ex 19:6), redeemed, righteous, and at rest (see the comment on Ps 95:11). At that time **Jacob will rejoice, Israel will be glad** (cf. Ps 53:6). These are two names for the nation of Israel, taken from the patriarch, and indicate all the people of Israel (Gn 32:28; e.g., Pss 20:1; 46:7, 11; 146:5; Is 46:13).

Psalm 15: An Anatomy of the Truly Faithful

For the heading of this psalm, see the comments on Ps 3. Thematically it serves as a link between the previous and the following psalms, presenting the counterpart of the fool (i.e., the unrighteous) described in Ps 14 while at the same time anticipating the specific content of faith described in Ps 16. The righteous whom God will rescue is mentioned in 14:5. In Ps 15, the characteristics of the righteous are presented (Sailhamer, *NIV Compact Bible Commentary*, 318).

A. The Desire of the Truly Faithful (15:1)

15:1. David began this psalm with a question related to the note he introduced in Ps 14 regarding God's relationship to the wicked and the righteous: **Who may abide in Your tent. . . . dwell on Your holy hill?** This asks who would be permitted in the tabernacle (**tent**) of God or have access to the temple mount (**holy hill**; see the comment on Ps 2:6). In sum, David is asking who can worship the Lord in His dwelling place.

B. The Qualities of the Truly Faithful (15:2-5a)

15:2-3. A person who has access to God **walks with integrity** (cf. Ps 1) and practices **righteousness**, as well as **speaks truth in his heart** (cf. Ps 1:2)—that is, his thoughts and motivations are characterized by righteousness and love. This point of making God the priority of life and loving Him with a whole heart is a central theme throughout the Bible, and is emphasized just as much in the OT as in the NT (e.g., Gn 6:5; Dt 6:4-9; 30:6, 10; Ps 51:17; Pr 23:7; Is 29:13), and epitomized in both testaments by the two great commandments: to love God and one's neighbor (Lv 19:18; Dt 6:5; Mt 22:36-40). The second of these is here intimated by the statement that the righteous **does** no **evil to his neighbor**.

15:4-5a. This section is somewhat of an illustration of Ps 1. The righteous man will despise **a reprobate**, but **honors those who fear the Lord** (cf. 111:10). Furthermore, he always keeps his word, even when difficult (**swears to his own hurt**) and is always ethical in **money** matters, consistently showing concern for the **innocent**.

C. The Final State of the Truly Faithful (15:5b)

15:5b. The hope of the truly faithful, whatever he may experience in this life, is that he **will never be shaken**, that is, he will never lose or be separated from his promised inheritance of life in the new creation in the presence of God (cf. Rm 8:38-39). Implicit in this affirmation, as highlighted in the following psalm where the same phraseology is employed, is that the faithful **will never be shaken** because the Lord Himself is at their right hand (Ps 16:8), referring to the believer's reliance on God (including His Word and His character), the only unshakable foundation in this corrupt and crumbling world (the same phraseology is used in Pss 21:8; 112:6; 125:1; Pr 10:30; 12:3).

Psalm 16: Confidence in Life and Death

One of the characteristics of the righteous is confidence in God's ability to resurrect, exhibited in David's confidence that God would not abandon him, or his supreme Son, the Messiah, to the grave (Sailhamer, *NIV Compact Bible Commentary*, 318). Because David was a prophet he "looked ahead and spoke of . . . the Christ [the Messiah]" (Ac 2:31). In this messianic psalm, the emphasis is on the resurrection of Messiah (see Introduction: Background).

In its heading, this psalm, attributed to **David**, is identified as a **Mikhtam**, a designation that is also applied to Pss 56–60 (all also by David). Though the meaning of this term is not entirely clear, several of the ancient translations (LXX, the Targum, and the Vulgate) construe it as the designation for an engraving or inscription in stone, suggesting that this psalm played an especially prominent role in the liturgy and ritual culture of ancient Israel—as indeed it does play in later rabbinic Judaism, being appointed for recitation on various occasions and cited in connection with ritual and theological fundamentals in the writings of prominent rabbinic authorities (e.g., Maimonides, Moses Isserles).

A. The Confidence of the Psalmist (16:1)

16:1. At the outset, David gives a summary statement of his prayer to the Lord, that God would keep him safe. He is affirming not just the identity but also the exclusive sovereignty of the **God** (Hb. *el*) in whom He takes **refuge**. David's confidence in the Lord rests on understanding of the promise of Messiah, as demonstrated in the following verses.

B. The Prayer of the Messiah (16:2-11)

Although the English versions generally read "I said to the Lord" (v. 2), the Hebrew reads "You said to the Lord." The "You" of whom David spoke is the Messiah (see the comments on 2Sm 23:1, explaining how the Messiah was David's favorite subject in the Psalms, as well as comments on Ps 2), indicating that the rest of the psalm contains the words of Messiah to the Lord. The Messiah's prayer deals with two aspects of His life. First, He expresses His delight in the Lord in this life (16:2-8). Then He reveals His confidence in the Lord when facing death (16:9-11).

1. The Lord Is His Delight in Life (16:2-8)

16:2. David is the author of this psalm but he is writing the prayer of the Messiah (see previous comments). Hence the Messiah gives several reasons He delights in the Lord in this life. First, He delights in the Lord's goodness (**I have no good besides You**), indicating that God alone is the source of anything truly **good** (or "beneficial," as the term may also be translated) for Him, and hence for anyone.

16:3-4. Second, the Messiah expresses His delight in the Lord's people. He speaks of the faithful who were His **delight**. They are identified as those who share his faith in the sovereignty of God and who demonstrated such through their obedience to His Word (cf. Nm 15:40; Pss 34:9; 89:5, 7). They are also called **saints who are in the earth**, that is, people who live their daily life focused on the Lord, set apart in their attitudes and actions to serve the Lord (cf. Lv 20:7-7; Ps 1); it does not mean individuals who have been canonized. These godly associates are further called **majestic ones**, or noble ones. In contrast to following the Lord, there are **sorrows** for **those who have bartered** (more correctly translated "hastened") to follow after **another god**. The messianic King rejected their evil idolatry, refusing their pagan worship.

16:5-6. Third, the Messiah explains His delight in the Lord's **portion**. This is an allusion to the tribe of Levi, which did not receive a portion in the land for an **inheritance**. Instead, the Lord was their portion (Dt 10:9). Therefore, He rejoices that **the** (boundary) **lines have fallen to me in pleasant places**, meaning He, like the Levites, has received a spiritual inheritance and **heritage**.

16:7-8. Fourth, the Messiah finds His delight in the Lord's presence. His Father is present with Him as a guide. As such, the Lord **counseled** Him and **instructs** Him. The Father is also present with Him as a guard—the Lord is at His **right hand**, guarding and protecting.

2. The Lord Is His Deliverer in Death (16:9-11)

16:9-10. Besides the Messiah's delight in the Lord in this life, He also affirms His confidence when facing death. First, He declares that God will protect Him, making His **flesh . . . dwell securely**, granting Him safety until death (v. 9). But, second, when He does die, the Messiah affirms that the Lord will deliver Him from death. He has confidence in God's sovereign power that God **will** not **allow** His **Holy One to undergo decay**. Some interpreters say this statement refers only to David (i.e., the expectation of his own resurrection) and later symbolically or typologically is applied in the NT to Jesus. Yet, in light of this entire prayer reflecting the perspective of the Messiah, it is more likely directly messianic. Additionally, Walter C. Kaiser points out that the self-description **Your Holy One** (lit., "favored one") is "a messianic term . . . only surpassed by 'Servant of the Lord' and 'Messiah' in the OT" (Walter C. Kaiser, Jr., *The Old Testament in the New* [Chicago: Moody, 1985], 330). Moreover, the expectation here was that the **Holy One** would not **undergo decay**, an expectation not true of or possible for David. Therefore, this statement was knowingly intended by David to refer directly and exclusively to the resurrection of the Messiah. The NT confirms this, for this is precisely what Peter said regarding this passage in Ac 2:30-31: "he [i.e., David] was a prophet and . . . he looked ahead and spoke of the resurrection of the Christ" (see also Ac 13:35-37). Also, Peter pointed out that the terminology employed by David in the psalm indicates that it could not apply to him, for David died and was buried, and his body would naturally have undergone substantial decay. Yet David declared that God's **Holy One** would not **undergo decay**. David understood that it was essential for the Messiah to be raised from the dead first, as the "first fruits of those who are asleep" (1Co 15:20), and that in doing so he would serve as the model and guarantee for those who believe. For what the NT adds to the understanding of Ps 16:10, see the comments on Ac 2:24-32. On **Sheol** see the comments on Ps 49:14-15.

16:11. Not only would God preserve the Messiah until death and resurrect Him from death, the Lord assured Him of eternal life afterwards. Messiah looked forward confidently to what he knew God would do (not to what He hoped God might do). He stated in no uncertain terms, **You will make known to me the path of life**. Also, He was certain to experience full joy (lit., "the satisfaction of [all] joys") in God's presence. This bliss would be at God's **right hand** and would last **forever**.

Psalm 17: Praying for Protection

This psalm **of David** (cf. introduction to Ps 3) is described as a **Prayer**. Four other psalms are designated as prayers: Pss 86 (also attributed to David), 90 (attributed to Moses), 102 (anonymous, though framed by Davidic psalms), and

142 (attributed to David). A comparison of these five psalms bears out certain similarities that serve to reinforce and clarify the content of each psalm individually. Especially prominent in each of these psalms is the combination of three themes: (1) an appeal that God "hear" or "give heed" (v. 1)—or, in the case of Ps 90, to "return" with a compassionate answer to the psalmist's cry/supplication (17:1; 86:6; 90:13 [where "be sorry for" should be "show compassion on"]; 102:1; 142:6); (2) a description of the affliction, trouble, or distress of the psalmist or the people of Israel collectively (17:9; 86:1; 90:15; 102:2; 142:2); and (3) an appeal to God's lovingkindess, compassion, and/or grace (17:7; 86:5; 90:14; 102:13; 142:1 [where "make supplication" means lit., "seek grace for myself"]). David knew his own resurrection was dependent upon that of the "Holy One" (16:10), and he expressed confidence that in his own resurrection he would awake to see God (17:15b) (Sailhamer, *NIV Compact Bible Commentary*, 318).

A. Asking God for an Audience (17:1-6)

17:1-2. David began by humbly asking God to **Hear a just cause, O Lord, give heed to my cry**, that is, "Favorably answer my prayer" (not presuming that God will do so, for the presence of unconfessed or unrecognized sin on the part of the petitioner will ensure that God does not "hear" his petition; see Is 59:2; Jr 14:12). By saying that his prayer **is not from deceitful lips** David was not claiming that he was not a sinner (or had not sinned), but rather that he had confessed his sin(s) sincerely, without "a double heart" (see the comment on 12:2), and had humbly received and responded to his heavenly Father's chastisement for those sins.

17:3-6. His point is emphatically indicated by the three-clause parallelism: **You have tried** . . . **You have visited** . . . **You have tested**, each expression employed elsewhere to denote divine chastisement (cf. Ex 32:34; Zch 13:9). As a result of this chastisement, David affirmed that God would find **nothing** in him that remained of unconfessed sin. There is therefore no apparent reason God should not favorably **answer** him and protect him from further chastisement.

B. Appealing to God for Protection (17:7-14)

17:7-12. David acknowledges the Lord's character and power when he asks him to **Wondrously show Your lovingkindness** (v. 7; cf. 9:1; 5:7 comments). He identifies the Lord as **Savior of those who take refuge** in Him (v. 7). His request for God to **keep me as the apple of the eye** (as one protects the pupil of the eye) and **hide me in the shadow of Your wings** (as a mother bird protects her chicks, v. 8) are familiar biblical metaphors for protection (cf. Dt 32:10; Ru 2:12; 3:9; Pss 36:7; 57:1; 61:4; 63:7; 91:1; Pr 7:2). Although in danger of **enemies who surround** him (v. 9), David was seeking the Lord's protection.

17:13-14. David referred to them as "the wicked, Your sword" (not, as in the NASB, **with Your sword**; there is no preposition in the Hb. text). That is, these enemies were the **sword** of God's chastisement. He even saw this difficult circumstance within the hand of the Lord.

C. Affirming God's Promise (17:15)

17:15. Despite any circumstances, David was confident in the Lord: **As for me, I shall behold Your face**. David concluded this psalm in characteristic fashion by looking beyond the present life to his guaranteed future state in eternity, a state characterized by perfect **righteousness** (*sedeq*). This bookends the psalm with the same term in v. 1, though there the NASB translates *sedeq* by **just cause**. He will then **behold** the **face** (or "presence") of God (see Pss 16:11; 142:7). Implicit in this conclusion is the recognition that God may choose not to protect him from further affliction by the wicked, but rather—as in the case of Job—to permit it for David's further refinement (not necessarily chastisement), and in the end therefore for God's greater glory.

Psalm 18: A Psalm of Praise for God's Personal Deliverance

This psalm repeats, with minor variations, David's psalm in 2Sm 22. For the heading of this **Psalm of David**, see the comments on the heading of Ps 3. David here is described as the **servant of the Lord**, a description elsewhere applied to him only in the heading of Ps 36. This description serves to identify David with a select group of others in the Bible who are similarly described. Those individuals include Moses and Joshua, to whom the identical phrase is applied (see Dt 34:5; Jos 24:29), Caleb, Zerubbabel, and Jonah (2Kg 14:25). The Messiah is also called "My servant" (see Nm 14:24; Hg 2:23; Zch 3:8). The heading also indicates that this psalm was spoken by David on **the day that the Lord delivered him from the hand of all his enemies and from the hand of Saul**. This refers not to the day when Saul died (1Sm 31:6), nor even the day when David was finally enthroned king of all Israel (2Sm 5:3), but at that point much later in his reign after Saul's death, as well as his many victorious wars with the Philistines and others and after the revolts of Absalom (2Sm 18) and Sheba (2Sm 20).

A. David Affirms His Relationship with the Lord (18:1-29)

1. Affirming One's Devotion to God as the Deliverer (18:1-3)

18:1-3. David began this psalm by affirming his devotion to God, **I love You, O Lord, my strength** (v. 1). Then he acknowledges **God** as his **rock**, **fortress**, and **deliverer** (v. 2).

Identifying God as **my rock** (cf. comments on 18:46) is a frequent poetic figure for God, indicating His unfailing strength as a refuge and defense (cf. 2Sm 23:3; Pss 19:14; 28:1; 31:2-3; Is 26:4; 30:29). David's devotion is characterized not by a formal reverence, such as one might show toward a respected yet distant superior, but rather by love—as indicated by his opening words **I love You** (*erhamekha*), which is derived from the same root as the Hebrew word for "womb" (*rehem*), and denotes a deep and emotionally charged sense of personal attachment and commitment (hence the translation elsewhere of *rahamim*, the plural of *rehem*, as "mercies" [cf. Ps 145:9]). This expression recalls Dt 6:5: "You shall love the Lord your God with all your heart and with all your soul and with all your might" (cf. Mt 22:36-38). The term **horn** in the expression **horn of my salvation** (v. 2) symbolizes strength and victorious power (see Dt 33:17; 1Kg 22:11).

2. David Affirms the Personal Nature of God's Deliverance (18:4-19)

18:4-6. In this section first-person forms predominate (**me** and **my**), with David emphasizing God's deliverance and love for him personally. By stating that **I called . . . to my God for help; He heard my voice**, David was describing God's favorable response to his petition (cf. comment on 17:1-6).

18:7-15. The phrases and figures of speech in this section highlight the awe-inspiring power of God's deliverance: e.g., **the earth . . . quaked** (v. 7); **The Lord also thundered** (v. 13; cf. the same phraseology in Am 1:2); **lightning flashes in abundance** (v. 14). Other phrases highlight God's speed: **He rode upon a cherub** (v. 10), hearkening to the imagery of the divine cloud of glory dwelling over the ark, which was crowned with cherubim (see Ps 99:1), **and He sped upon the wings of the wind** (v. 10). Still others focus on God's thoroughness: **the foundations of the mountains were trembling** (v. 7, paralleled in v. 15), **and the foundations of the world were laid bare** (v. 15; cf. Ex 15:8; Jb 4:9; Ps 106:9; Nah 1:4).

18:16-19. The Lord's powerful rescue is further described as **He delivered me from my strong enemy** (v. 17). The basic explanation of God's actions in David's defense is **He rescued me, because He delighted in me** (v. 19).

3. David Affirms the Depth of God's Interest in the Delivered (18:20-29)

18:20-24. David presents a link between the Lord's actions and his behavior. **The Lord has rewarded me according to my righteousness.** David is not claiming sinlessness or perfect righteousness, but presents his devotion to the Lord and his desire to live with integrity as other OT figures have done (e.g., 1Sm 12:3; 2Kg 20:3; Jb 13:23; Pss 17:3-5; 19:14). He affirmed that God is interested not only in the improvement of his outward (i.e., physical-material) life (achieved by His deliverance of David from political-military distress), but also in the improvement of his inner (i.e., spiritual) life. This is emphatically indicated by David's repeated assertion that the Lord has rewarded (v. 20) and recompensed (v. 24) him according to his **righteousness** and **the cleanness of** his **hands . . . in His eyes**. By this he meant that God delivered him according to his need for growth in righteousness, which only God could fully perceive and meet. The deliverance may not have come at the time or in the manner David would have preferred, yet in the end, as David affirmed, it was exactly what it should have been to supply David's needs as aligned with the furtherance of God's glory.

18:25-29. David presents the Lord's reciprocal response to man. **With the kind You show Yourself kind.** Although God's mercy is not limited to rewarding man's righteousness, David points out a correlation between obedience and blessing: **For You save an afflicted** (humble) **people, but haughty eyes You abase.**

B. David Affirms the Deliverance by the Lord (18:30-50)

1. Affirming the Depth of God's Interest in the Delivered (18:30-36)

18:30-36. In this section, which mirrors the previous one, David affirmed God's character, **His way is blameless**, and the depth of God's concern for him, **He is a shield to all who take refuge in Him**. The Lord not only **girds** him **with strength**, that is, grants him political-military deliverance (cf. Jb 38:3; 40:7), but He also **makes** his **way blameless**, that is, He intervenes to keep him from acting rashly or vindictively (and hence in less than **blameless** fashion) toward his enemies (see 1Sm 25:26, 32-34). David further affirmed God's interest in his spiritual well-being by declaring that He has **given** him **the shield of** His **salvation**, which parallels the military-spiritual phraseology in Is 59:17 (cf. Eph 6:16-17). The Hebrew term for **salvation** (*yeshah*) is one that often signifies comprehensive deliverance (i.e., both internal-spiritual and ultimately external-physical; cf. David's use of the term in 2Sm 23:5; 1Ch 16:35; Pss 24:5; 25:5). Not surprisingly, therefore, this term is employed (in verbal form) in the name of David's seed, the Savior Himself, Jesus (His Hebrew name is *Yeshuah*, "he saves/will save"; cf. Mt 1:21).

2. Affirming the Personal Nature of God's Deliverance (18:37-45)

18:37-42. Here David recounts his victory over his **enemies**. In this section, which mirrors the second section of the "first movement" above (vv. 4-19), David affirmed God's role in granting him deliverance as manifested in the victories God gave him. He emphasized the power of these victories, **You have girded me with strength . . . You have subdued under me**, as well as their speed, **I pursued my enemies and overtook them**, and their thoroughness, **until they were consumed. . . . I shattered them, so that they were not able to rise. . . . I beat them fine as the dust before the wind.**

18:43-45. David acknowledges God as the source of his victory: **You have delivered me . . . You have placed me as head of the nations.**

3. Affirming One's Devotion to God as the Deliverer (18:46-50)

18:46-50. As in the opening section of this psalm (vv. 1-3), David closed with an affirmation of his love and devotion to God: **The Lord lives, and blessed be my rock; and exalted be the God of my salvation**. God is the One who **delivers** him (v. 48; cf. v. 2), both physically and spiritually. The permanence of this deliverance is underscored by David's characterization of the Deliverer as his **rock** (v. 46; Hb. *sur*, as in v. 2, cf. 18:2). This common biblical designation of God signifies a massive rock formation that is humanly impossible to move, such as a cliff, quarry, or the side of a mountain (cf. Ex 33:22; 1Ch 11:15; Jb 18:4; Pss 31:3; 71:3; Is 2:10; 51:1). In loving response to God's acts of deliverance—and affirming the central motivation for His election of Israel (cf. Gn 12:3; 1Kg 8:43)—David declared (v. 49) that he **will give thanks . . . among the nations** (lit., "Gentiles"). By this statement, in view of its citation in Rm 15:9, David meant specifically that he would proclaim among the Gentiles (1) God's faithfulness in upholding "the promises given to the fathers," Abraham, Isaac, and Jacob (see Gn 12:1-3; 15:8; 17:7-8), which includes God's promise to David (see 2Sm 7:8-17), and (2) God's "mercy"—both of which find their greatest expression in the person and work of Messiah, the Promised One.

Psalm 19: A Meditation on Divine Revelation

For the heading of this **Psalm of David** see introduction to Ps 3. As in Ps 1, God's Word is powerful (see 19:7-14) and points the way to salvation. God's Word also leads one to seek refuge in the Son who brings that salvation (2:12; see the comments introducing Ps 2). In Pss 19 and 20 one finds a similar connection. God's Word is powerful to save (19:7-14) and leads one to the Anointed (20:6) (Sailhamer, *NIV Compact Bible Commentary*, 319).

A. The Revelation of God in Creation (19:1-6)

19:1-6. This psalm focuses on the works and word of God. The terms **heavens** and **expanse** are synonyms, the joint use of which alludes back to their initial occurrence in Gn 1:7-8, where God created the **expanse** and called it "heaven." The point of this and the ensuing verses is that the heavens and all that with which God has filled them, like the entirety of creation, constitute ongoing testimony to **the glory of God** (v. 2: **day to day** and **night to night**) and to the existence of the Creator (cf. Ps 8:3). The created order testifies to the existence of God and His eternal power (i.e., omnipotence), and there is no place where the evidence of creation is not seen. The glory of all that is seen makes known His invisible attributes (see the comments on Rm 1:18-23).

B. The Revelation of God in His Word (19:7-11)

19:7-11. Following the testimony of creation, God's character, works, and will for humanity are further specified by His Word, which **is perfect**. The first and foundational part of God's Word is **the law** (see the comment on 1:3-4), here described by the various other biblical synonyms including **testimony**, **precepts**, **commandment**, and **judgments** ("ordinances," as in Ex 21:1). Through this verbal/written revelation man is instructed in **the fear** (i.e., worship) **of the Lord** (cf. 111:10; 2Kg 17:28). Two key biblical concepts of worship and obedience (i.e., "keeping/obeying"), presented at the outset of the Torah, are reiterated here (see the comment on Gn 2:15; cf. also Ec 12:13). God's words are a guide and a warning for how to live, and **in keeping them there is great reward** (cf. Ps 1).

C. The Revelation of God in Man (19:12-14)

19:12-14. Whether one's **errors** are **hidden** or committed in open arrogance (**presumptuous sins**), God brings conviction because nothing is hidden from Him (Dt 29:28; Ec 12:14). David concludes with a request to be kept away from sin and that God not allow it to **rule over me**. Then he asks the Lord to **Let the words of my mouth and the meditation of my heart be acceptable in Your sight**. On the meaning of **meditation** (19:14) see the comment on Ps 1:2; on **rock** as a divine title see the comment on Ps 18:46.

Psalm 20: Expressing the Assurance of Victory in God

On the heading of this **Psalm of David**, see the heading of Ps 3. Just as one can find deliverance in God's Word (19:7-14), one can find deliverance in the Anointed One, the Messiah, whom God will bless and preserve (20:6; Sailhamer, *NIV Compact Bible Commentary*, 319).

A. The People's Assurance of Victory (20:1-5)

20:1-5. The thematic focus in this psalm is on victory in God, calling on the **LORD**/King to **answer you**/us (on this "framing" technique, known as *inclusio*, see Introduction: Purpose and Themes). The expression **the name of the God of Jacob** (v. 1) relates specifically to the association between God's self-disclosed name (i.e., the Hebrew four-letter name for God, commonly written in English as *Yahweh*, usually translated "the LORD") and His provision of deliverance and victory (both physically and spiritually; cf. Ex 3:13-17). It also relates to the various names (i.e., titles, which in the OT are the same as names) applied to God by the beneficiaries of His gracious intervention (cf. Gn 16:13; 22:14; Ps 18:2; Is 9:6; etc.).

B. The King's Assurance of Victory (20:6-8)

20:6-8. David expresses his confidence, **I know that the LORD saves His anointed**, referring to God's **anointed** king (cf. 1Sm 16:13). David underscored his personal experience—and hence confident assurance—of God's deliverance, since the verb in the expression **I know** denotes experiential knowledge (see the comment on Ps 1:6; for parallel phraseology and meaning see Gn 22:12; Ex 18:11; Jdg 17:13). Through God's deliverance of David, David anticipates the Lord's deliverance of the future Davidic Messiah. Though His cloud of glory may dwell in the tabernacle, David affirmed that God's true habitation is **His holy heaven** (lit., "the heaven of His holiness," which is distinct from the created "heaven" of Gn 1:6-8; cf. Dt 26:15; 1Kg 8:39; Heb 8:5; 9:24). David contrasted his and his people's complete reliance on God in military matters to the reliance of **some** (the Gentiles nations, especially those surrounding Israel, such as the Philistines, Amalekites, Moabites, and Ammonites) on their **chariots** and **horses** (i.e., the size and strength of their military). This wording hearkens specifically to God's command that the king of Israel "not multiply horses" (cf. Dt 17:16).

C. The Collective Assurance of Victory (20:9)

20:9. David concluded by affirming the absolute dependence of God's people not on their human king, David, but on their true King, God, crying out, **Save, O LORD; may the King answer us in the day we call**. That **the King** here refers to God is indicated by (1) the clear parallelism between this statement and the opening statement in v. 1, where the subject is "the LORD"; (2) God's desire that He Himself be affirmed as Israel's king (see 1Sm 8:7), a desire shared by David (cf. 1Sm 21:2, in which the "king" is implicitly God, not Saul, since only God "commissioned" David, in 1Sm 13:14); (3) David's use of **us**, indicating that he was speaking for himself as well as his people; and (4) the expression **we call** (lit., "of our calling out") in the OT is typically directed to God, not man.

Psalm 21: A Meditation on the King Who Trusts in the Lord

On the heading of this **Psalm of David**, see the comments on the headings to Pss 3 and 4. This psalm (v. 1) picks up where Ps 20:7 left off, describing the king's trust in the Lord. Another link between Ps 21 and Ps 20 are the ideas of the prayer for God to "grant you your heart's desire" (20:4) and the praise that God has "given him his heart's desire" (21:2). David presents a picture of an elevated king, who enjoys God's presence and eternal blessings (21:6). Moreover, the direct address to the king (v. 9ff.) depicts His coming in fiery judgment. Hence, this is not a presentation of a generic king but the Messiah, promised to David (cf. 2Sm 7:12-17; Sailhamer, *NIV Compact Bible Commentary*, 319). This depiction of the messianic King introduces the presentation of the suffering Messiah in the psalm that follows (Ps 22).

A. The Blessing of the King Who Trusts in the Lord (21:1-6)

21:1-6. David began by affirming that it is only **in** God's **strength** that a **king will** (i.e., can) **be glad**, that is, find true satisfaction in his royal office. And only **in** His **salvation** can **he** truly **rejoice**, both in this life and the next. This eternal-spiritual aspect of God's **salvation** is emphatically affirmed by (1) the reference to **blessings** (vv. 3, 6), the biblical concept of blessing ultimately entailing the greatest possible qualitative enhancement of life in all its senses (see the comment on Gn 1:22); (2) the reference to God having given (the past tense indicates that the gift is irrevocably given) the king **life . . . forever and ever** (v. 4); and (3) the reference to being **blessed forever . . . in** God's **presence** (v. 6), epitomizing the expectation of the eternal King and the hope that His followers will also experience it in the hereafter (see the comments on Pss 11:7b and 15:5b). His work of **splendor and majesty** are terms that are elsewhere associated with God's saving work and priestly ministry (cf. Pss 21:5; 45:3; 96:6; 104:1; 145:5).

B. The Strength of the King Who Trusts in the Lord (21:7-12)

21:7. Because **the king trusts in the Lord**, therefore **the lovingkindness** (cf. comment on 5:7) **of the Most High** will be applied to him, and **he will not be shaken**, referring to the eternal state in God's presence (Ps 15:5b).

21:8-12. Now addressing the king directly (**Your hand . . . Your right hand**, v. 8), the psalmist anticipates the messianic King coming in judgment. The concept of God's sovereignty in maintaining His promised concern (*chesed*) toward His faithful is seen in the king's judgment of his **enemies** who the **Lord will swallow . . . up in His wrath**. Although the wicked **devised a plot, they will not succeed** (cf. Is 54:17).

C. The Praise of the King Who Trusts in the Lord (21:13)

21:13. The psalm concludes with praise to God, **Be exalted, O Lord**. The expression **in Your strength** (applied to God in Is 12:2) here serves as a bookend (*inclusio*; see Introduction: Genre) with the same phrase at the beginning of this psalm, and underscores the true and only enduring source of strength of the godly messianic King (cf. 1Sm 2:10).

Psalm 22: A Prophetic Perspective on the Crucifixion of the Messiah

On the heading of this **Psalm of David**, see the comments on the headings to Pss 3 and 4. The elliptical instruction **upon Aijeleth Hashshahar** (lit., "Hind/Doe of the Dawn"), though not entirely clear, probably refers to the psalm's melody. It has also been suggested that it is the name of a musical instrument or an allegorical allusion to the subject of the psalm.

Since David is the author of this psalm, some commentators suggest that he was writing about his own experience of suffering, or about the suffering of the righteous generally. However, this psalm transcends the experiences of David or his contemporaries. David was never brought to the "dust of death" (v. 15), nor were his "hands" and "feet" ever pierced (v. 16). There is no record of his ever having had his "garments" divided or "lots" cast for them (v. 18). Moreover, his suffering did not bring universal righteousness (vv. 27-31). Therefore, Ps 22 is better understood as a messianic psalm, presenting the future suffering of the Messiah, fulfilled in the experience of Jesus—to whom portions of this psalm are directly applied in the NT (in Heb 2:11-12, v. 22 of this psalm is introduced as a direct utterance of Messiah). This application to the Messiah is even evident in the medieval rabbinic compilation of commentaries known as the *Yalkut*, which identifies the mockery of v. 7 ("all who see me sneer at me; they separate with the lip, they wag the head") as the sufferings and derision experienced by the Messiah (*Yalkut Shimoni* on Is 60, paragraph 499).

David, in his last words (2Sm 23:1-5), affirmed that he was a prophet and that his favorite subject in the Psalms was the Messiah (see comments at 2Sm 23:1-5 and the introduction to Ps 2). Likely David wrote from the perspective of his own significant experience of suffering, but he also referred beyond that to the far greater suffering of the Messiah. As such, the psalm is written in the first person, but expresses the words of Messiah in His greatest suffering. The overall structure of Ps 22 is twofold. It begins with the suffering Messiah's prayer (vv. 1-21) and follows with the exalted Messiah's praise (vv. 22-31)

A. The Suffering Messiah's Prayer (22:1-21)

The first section of the psalm is a lament or prayer. It begins with the suffering Messiah's questioning of God (vv. 1-10) and is followed by His petition to God (vv. 11-21).

1. Questioning God (22:1-10)

There are two stanzas in this section (vv. 1-5 and 6-10), each using the same pattern of a complaint followed by a statement of confidence.

22:1-5. This psalm begins with a complaint (vv. 1-2). David writes from the perspective of Messiah—or, more precisely, with the Spirit of Messiah (i.e., the Holy Spirit; see Rm 8:9) foretelling "by the mouth of David" (Ac 1:16; 4:25)—precisely the last words He would utter on the cross: **My God, My God, why have You forsaken me?** (Mt 27:46; Mk 15:34). In the two instances that the NT cites these words, they are given in their original Aramaic as well as in Greek translation (rather than only in Greek translation, like almost all Jesus' other words recorded in the NT). The reason may be to highlight the special significance of this statement as the culminating expression of His first advent in which He became a sin offering (2Co 5:21).

The question asked regarding God's forsaking of the Messiah (v. 1) is not literal but rhetorical, for certainly the Messiah would have understood the reason for His own suffering. Moreover, it is only an emotional expression, since God did not in reality abandon the Messiah. Some have suggested that God is "too pure to look upon evil" (Hab 1:13) and therefore He literally abandoned the Messiah when the sin of all the world fell upon Him at His crucifixion and the eternal fellowship of the Father and the Son was broken. This explanation is problematic in that the words in Habakkuk mean that God will not "look with approval" upon sin, not that God cannot look upon evil, else He could not look upon the world or people. Additionally, Messiah did not literally become sinful at the cross, but rather the elliptical phrase in 2Co 5:21 means that God made the sinless one to be "a sin offering," not literally sinful. The eternal fellowship of the Father and the Son was never broken.

Having expressed a complaint, the suffering Messiah next states His confidence (vv. 3-5). He looked back at the **fathers** (or ancestors) and affirmed that they trusted in the **holy** God, who is **enthroned upon the praises of Israel** (v. 3), and were **delivered** (vv. 4-5). The reference to the **fathers** should not be limited only to the patriarchs, but to the ancestors (a valid translation of the Hebrew) of Israel, whose walk of faith is recorded in Scripture (for a similar viewpoint of the "men of old" [Heb 11:2], see Heb 11:3-40).

22:6-10. The suffering Messiah continues His complaint, stating that He had been forsaken by men (vv. 6-8, in contrast to His complaint in vv. 1-2 that He was forsaken by God). He has experienced human **reproach . . . sneer[ing]** and derision (cf. Mt 27:38-44).

Having stated a complaint, the suffering Messiah once again gives His confidence. Previously He remembered the past experience of Israel's fathers (vv. 3-5); now He bases His confidence on His own experience with the Lord (vv. 9-10). He can confidently expect God's care because God has always cared for Him since His birth.

2. Petitioning God (22:11-21)

There are two stanzas in this petition, both pertaining to seeking God's presence. The first is in vv. 11-18 and the second in vv. 19-21.

a. Seeking God's Presence because There Is No One Else to Help (22:11-18)

22:11. The first verse in this section functions as a summary, indicating that while **trouble is near**, help is far away. Therefore, the suffering Messiah petitions God to **be not far from me**. What follows is a description of the trouble that is surrounding Him.

22:12-13. In describing His troubles, the suffering Messiah first describes His enemies (vv. 12-13) and then depicts His suffering (vv. 14-18). In describing His enemies, He uses a figure of speech called zoomorphism, ascribing animal qualities to human beings. Hence, those who oppress Him are called **bulls** (v. 12), who gore or pierce those they attack. Their threats and verbal attacks are compared to **a ravening and a roaring lion**, circling for the kill.

22:14-18. Having described His enemies, the Messiah next depicts His suffering. His physical pain is great (**all my bones are out of joint**) as is His fear (**my heart is like wax . . . melted within me**, v. 14). His **strength** is as absent as moisture in a **potsherd**. In fact, He realizes that He is about to die (**You lay me in the dust of death**, v. 15).

The culminating statement of this suffering is **they pierced my hands and my feet** (v. 16), representing one of the most specific predictive references to Messiah's crucifixion (paralleled only by Zch 12:10). Yet this is one of the most debated passages in the Bible. The debate centers on the key Hebrew word *ka'aru*, rendered **they pierced**, though in most (but not all) medieval Hebrew manuscripts this word is written *ka'ariy*, meaning "like a lion." The first reading, however, is to be preferred for five reasons. First, it is supported by three of the four ancient translations (LXX, the Peshitta, and the Vulgate; the fourth translation, the Targum to Psalms, was translated in the second century AD by non-Christian Jews). Second, even for Hebrew poetry, the phrase "like a lion" is far too elliptical and makes no sense without a verb—which supporters of this reading are forced to supply (e.g., "like a lion *they bite* my hands and my feet"). Third, were the symbol of a lion intended, it would have been employed in the plural, not the singular, in order to agree with the plural subject ("evildoers") in the verse (as in Jr 50:17 and Zph 3:3). Fourth, one of the leading medieval Jewish scribal authorities (Jacob ben Chayyim) himself affirms that the older and better manuscripts read *ka'aru* ("they pierced") rather than *ka'ariy* ("like a lion"). Fifth, the reading *ka'aru* ("they pierced") is attested in the earliest manuscript of this psalm (5/6 HevPs) from the Dead Sea Scrolls, which predates the medieval manuscripts by approximately one thousand years. Therefore, the suffering Messiah's words predict His own death by crucifixion at a time when crucifixion was unknown.

There are other specific predictions here. Notable is the specific use of the verb **stare** (*yir'u*, meaning "to look at thoughtfully," v. 17)—here describing the people's willful rejection of Messiah. This is the same verb used in Zch 12:10 (the only other specific OT crucifixion prophecy) to indicate the people's willful acceptance of the pierced Messiah. Additionally, the suffering Messiah predicted that His tormentors would **divide [His] garments** and **cast lots** for His **clothing** (v. 18). This specific prediction was fulfilled by the Roman soldiers who cast lots for Jesus' robe (cf. Jn 19:23-24).

b. Seeking God's Presence because Only God Can Help (22:19-21)

The second stanza of the suffering Messiah's petition is different from the first in that He previously stated there were no others to help, but here He notes that so dire are His circumstances that God alone can help Him.

22:19-21. As above (cf. v. 11), the suffering Messiah petitions God to be near (**be not far off**, v. 19). The petition then follows a similar pattern as above, but begins with a depiction of His suffering (v. 20) followed by a description of His enemies (v. 21). Only God can **deliver** Him from death (**the sword . . . the power of the dog**). His enemies are again described with zoomorphism (cf. vv. 12-13 above) as a **lion**, whose teeth would pierce, and as **wild oxen** (v. 21), whose horns would gore. The certainty of Messiah's deliverance is underscored in v. 21 by the use of the past (perfect) tense verb, literally, "You have answered me" (as in the NET Bible, also see the comment on Ps 10:16 regarding the prophetic perfect).

B. The Exalted Messiah's Praise (22:22-31)

There is a dramatic change in tone here from the plaintive cries of the previous verses to the exultant praise that follows. Although there is no specific reference to resurrection, in light of the references to death in the previous verses ("dust of death," v. 15; "they pierced my hands and my feet," v. 16), this seems to hint at a miraculous resurrection.

1. Praise before Israel: God Is Not Deaf, He Hears! (22:22-26)

22:22-24. The exalted Messiah promises that He will praise God **to my brethren**, a reference to the people of Israel. God delivered the Messiah from death and as a response He praises God **in . . . the assembly** (v. 22). Besides His own praise, the exalted Messiah calls upon Israel to **glorify** God with Him (v. 23). The reason is that God has **not despised nor abhorred** nor **hidden His face**, but rather He has answered the Messiah's petition. Thus, when **he cried to Him for help, He heard** (v. 24).

22:25-26. Recognizing that His exaltation comes from God (v. 25), the exalted Messiah calls all sufferers (**the afflicted**) to trust God even as He did. Thus, they too will experience deliverance and **praise the Lord** (v. 26).

2. Praise before the Nations: God Is Not Dead, He Lives! (22:27-31)

22:27-31. There is an expectation of the messianic age here, when **the ends of the earth will . . . turn to the Lord** (v. 27), that is, when the Lord will rule **over the nations** (v. 28). At that time, all will worship the Lord, even the wealthy (v. 29a), the dead (who will be raised, v. 29b), and all **posterity** (vv. 30-31), who will recognize and serve the living God. These words fulfill the promise made to Abraham that "in your seed all the nations of the earth shall be blessed" (Gn 22:18).

Psalm 23: The Lord as Shepherd of His People

On the heading of this **Psalm of David**, see the comments on the heading to Ps 3. Here David metaphorically described God as a shepherd—a profession with which David was intimately familiar (see 1Sm 16:11, 19; 17:20). This metaphor of shepherd is frequently applied to God throughout the OT and to the Messiah Jesus in the NT (e.g., Gn 48:15; 49:24; Pss 28:9; 80:1; Ec 12:11; Is 40:11; Ezk 34:12,23; 37:24; Mt 2:6; 26:31; Jn 10:1-16; Heb 13:20; 1Pt 2:25; 5:4; Rv 7:17).

Identifying both the God in the OT and Jesus in the NT by this same title is another intimation of Messiah's deity.

The Afflicted One of Ps 22 nevertheless has God's ongoing attention and love, and is ultimately vindicated in that affliction as suggested by Ps 23. The one who is vindicated is the Anointed One (v. 5) who will someday return (not "dwell in," v. 6) to the house of the Lord forever. In context with Ps 22, Ps 23 is messianic as well (Sailhamer, *NIV Compact Bible Commentary*, 319).

A. The Shepherd's Provision of Rest (23:1-3)

23:1-3. This psalm begins with its subject, **The Lord . . . my shepherd**, then throughout the psalm describes His qualities and relationship with those under His care. Although speaking in terms of sheep, the actual subject of this psalm is the people of Israel (and by application all who love the Lord). This literary image is used in Ps 95:7 and Ps 100 as well.

David began by describing how God fully provides for the needs of His sheep: (1) **I shall not want**, because He will supply the needs of those under His care (cf. Ps 34:9; Mt 6:25-34); (2) **makes me lie down in green pastures**, providing a safe place to rest and eat (cf. Is 14:30; Jr 33:12-13; Zph 3:12-13); (3) **leads me beside quiet** (or "still") **waters**, which literally means "waters of rest," in which the Hebrew word for "rest" is what is used elsewhere to denote spiritual rest (i.e., salvation, one's relationship with God, as in Ps 95:11; Heb 4:1-10); (4) **He restores my soul; He guides me in the paths of righteousness**; that is, under His care my spiritual condition is constantly refreshed by following His instructions (cf. Ps 1; Mt 6:33) for His glory and consistent with His plan (cf. 1Kg 8:41-42; Ezr 20:9, 14, 22; Is 48:8; Jr 14:21). David was not asserting here that God always provides (in this lifetime, at least) for believers' physical needs, but rather that He will always supply what is necessary for the believer's spiritual well-being.

David is confident that the Lord will take action **for His name's sake**. The **name** of the Lord is not distinct from Him, nor is it just a title or description; rather, His name is a manifestation of Himself and His character (cf. Ex 3:14-15; 34:6-7); His name is synonymous with Him. Thus, the Scriptures speak of "praising His name" (e.g., Pss 7:17; 18:49), "loving His name" (e.g., 69:36), "trusting in His name" (e.g., 20:7), and so on. Often the Lord is described as taking action "for Your name's sake" or "for His name's sake" (e.g., Pss 25:11; 31:3; cf. 1Kg 8:41-42; Jr 14:21; Ezk 20:9, 14, 22) in order to manifest His glory, power, and reputation in relation to Israel or among the nations.

B. The Shepherd's Provision of Comfort (23:4-5)

23:4-5. That God will not necessarily deliver His sheep from all affliction and distress is underscored by the affirmation that **I walk through the valley of the shadow of death** (cf. 107:14). The **shadow of death** was described in the previous psalm, as the suffering Messiah stated that He had been placed in "the dust of death" (22:15). In those difficult circumstances of life, those under His care should not **fear** any **evil** because **You are with me** (cf. 27:1; 118:6). God's care is described using the image of the shepherd's tools: the **rod** (an instrument of authority, the thick wooden pole used to count and protect the sheep, cf. 2:9; 45:6) and the **staff** (the longer, often curved walking stick used for reaching and support, cf. Ex 21:19; Zch 8:4). God will always be available in such situations to **comfort me** by His care (cf. Pss 71:21; 86:17; Is 12:1; 40:1; 4:13). There is safety in the presence of the Lord because He is the one who will **prepare a table** (provide a meal) even **in the presence of my enemies**. To anoint **my head with oil** was a symbol of consecration, refreshment, and rejoicing (cf. Pss 45:7; 104:15; 133:2; cf. Ex 28:14; 30:30; 2Sm 16:3). This identifies the individual spoken of here as the Anointed One who had experienced suffering and death in the previous psalm.

C. The Shepherd's Provision of Confidence and Care (23:6)

23:6. David's confidence in this future inheritance, guaranteed by God's unshakable **goodness and lovingkindness** (cf. 5:7 comments), brings him comfort in this life, regardless of the situation. The fatherly aspect of the relationship between the divine Shepherd and His sheep is underscored by the verb **follow** (sometimes translated "pursue," elsewhere used to describe the active pursuit of one army by another; e.g., 1Sm 17:52). Under God's care, His followers will be constantly pursued or faithfully followed after by His **goodness and lovingkindness**.

The closing verse has two interesting words in translation. Commentators frequently suggest the meaning here has to do with spending eternity in heaven. However, this idea does not originate in this text. Rather than to **dwell** (Hb. *yashav*), the Hebrew should be translated "return" (*shuv*), so this is likely an expectation of return to the **house of the LORD**, the usual name for the sanctuary (tabernacle or temple; e.g., Pss 15:1; 26:8; 27:4; 134:1; 135:2), for a lifetime (**forever**, lit., "for length of days") of worship and fellowship with God. This anticipates the time when the Anointed One will return to the temple in Jerusalem, a common messianic theme (cf. Zch 9:9). Not surprisingly, the next psalm will take up this theme, celebrating the return of the "King of glory" (cf. Ps 24:9-10) to the temple in Jerusalem.

Psalm 24: The Return of the King of Glory

On the heading of this **Psalm of David**, see the comments on the heading to Ps 3. This psalm connects with the previous in that Ps 24 describes the return of the King to the house of the Lord and His reception by His people at that time (Sailhamer, *NIV Compact Bible Commentary*, 320).

A. The Extent of His Dominion (24:1-2)

24:1-2. In the opening statement of praise David affirmed that **The earth is the LORD's, and all it contains** (its "fullness"), recalling God's statement to Moses in Nm 14:21, "all the earth will be filled with the glory of the LORD" (see also Ps 72:19; Is 6:3; 1Co 10:26). The implication of this parallel phraseology is that, in addition to denoting the extent of the Lord's dominion, the present statement also implies that the fullness (everything within) of that dominion attests to the glory of God (cf. Ps 19). Furthermore, it highlights God as the Creator, **for He has founded it upon the seas**.

B. The Characteristics of His People (24:3-6)

24:3-5. This section closely parallels the entirety of Ps 15 and provides an excellent example of intertextual interpretation (i.e., juxtaposing parallel passages so as to derive a fuller understanding from both together that may not be evident from either alone). The question, **Who may ascend into the hill of the LORD?**, the temple mount, corresponds to 15:1. Likewise the response, **He who has clean hands**, to 15:2-5. This depicts those who will welcome the Messiah, the King of glory, into Jerusalem. For more interpretive specifics see the comments on Ps 15.

24:6. The reference to **Jacob** specifies **those who seek . . . Your face**—i.e., the faithful remnant of Israel (the people), for which **Jacob** is a poetic description (see Ps 14:7). This is especially appropriate since the patriarch Jacob struggled with God and saw Him "face to face," and only afterwards was his name changed to "Israel" (see Gn 32:28-30 and the comments there).

C. The Glory of His Reign (24:7-10)

24:7-9. The **gates** and **ancient doors** are parallel images of the king entering into Jerusalem, heading to the temple mount. David concluded by emphasizing the Anointed One of the previous psalm (23:5) as **the King of glory** (a title repeated in vv. 7, 8, 9). The focus is specifically on His military glory, as indicated by his repeated use of the word **mighty** (the Hb. term *gibbor*) which, though usually translated **mighty**, is in fact a noun specifically used to designate warriors characterized by highly distinguished military prowess (e.g., David himself [1Sm 16:18], Goliath [1Sm 17:51], Saul and Jonathan [2Sm 1:19, 25, 27], and David's inner circle of 30 mighty men [1Ch 11:10]). This is no ordinary warrior—rather He is the divine messianic King, taking His seat in the temple after His military victories at the end of days.

24:10. The point is that God, **the LORD of hosts** (that is, Lord of the armies of heaven), is presented as the mighty warrior King returning victorious in battle (e.g., 1Sm 17:14). He is the mightiest warrior of all—as indicated both by the miraculous military victories He had already won for Israel (from the exodus [see Ex 15:3] up to David's day [see 2Sm 5:24]) as well as by what He will one day do in the person of Jesus who will "strike down the nations, and . . . [tread] the wine press of the fierce wrath of God" (Rv 19:15).

Psalm 25: A Prayer for God's Protective Care

This **Psalm of David** (cf. comments on the heading of Ps 3) is parallel to Ps 34 (also attributed to David) in theme (both focus on God's providence), phraseology (both refer, e.g., to "fearing the Lord" [25:12, 14; 34:7, 9, 11], "taking refuge" in Him [25:20; 34:8], the Lord being "good" [25:7-8; 34:8], God "delivering" His own [25:20; 34:4, 17, 19], "the humble" [25:9; 34:2], "eyes" being "toward" [25:15; 34:15], and a concluding reference to God "redeeming" His people, employing the same specific Hebrew verb), and structure (both are acrostics, following the order of the Hebrew alphabet).

Plainly David is identified as the author of this psalm. However, its placement here reflects the postexilic perspective of the final compiler of the book of Psalms. At that time, a significant theme was that Israel and the nations would come to Jerusalem and be instructed by God (Zch 8:20-23; Is 2:2-4). Hence, this psalm follows the description of the King of glory and includes a prayer that God would "lead me in Your truth and teach me" (25:5). The final verse of the psalm anticipates the great hope of the psalmist, that God would redeem Israel through the coming of the Messiah (v. 22) (Sailhamer, *NIV Compact Bible Commentary*, 320). Nevertheless, the psalm is a model prayer for believers, teaching how to ask God for one's needs.

A. Affirm the Relational Basis of the Petition (25:1)

25:1. David's opening simple statement, **To You, O LORD, I lift up my soul**, is an idiom used elsewhere to express deep longing, desire, and need (cf. Dt 24:15; Jr 22:27). David did not begin by immediately presenting his need or focusing exclusively (and selfishly) on God's interest in him, but instead he appealed to God on the basis of His merciful character.

B. Express the Specific Content of the Petition (25:2-21)

25:2-3. David stated his **trust** in God as the basis for his request for deliverance from his **enemies** (vv. 2, 19). David is confident that all who **wait for You will** never **be ashamed** or disgraced (repeated here and again in v. 20).

25:4-7. Here David prays for guidance to **know Your ways . . . teach me Your paths. . . lead me in Your truth**. The basis of his request is his relationship with the Lord because **You are the God of my salvation**. David was depending on the Lord's **compassion** and **lovingkindness** (*chesed*, in vv. 6, 7, 10; cf. 5:7 comments). At the same time, he asked for forgiveness of **sins** and **transgressions**. The basis of his request to **remember me** is God's character. David's motivation in making a request of the Lord was **For Your goodness' sake**, on the basis of God's character and for God's honor.

25:8-9. Beginning with the key idea **Good and upright is the LORD**, these verses express confidence in God's faithfulness to instruct **sinners in the way** (of following the teachings of the Lord).

25:10-11. The Lord leads those who trust in Him (v. 9). Specifically, **All the paths of the LORD are lovingkindness and truth**; even experiences that might seem like the "valley of the shadow of death" (23:4) are part of His good plan for **those who keep His covenant and His testimonies** by obeying Him and living according to His word.

25:12-15. Here is a profile of the rewards for **the man who fears the LORD** (cf. 111:10). The Lord **will instruct him in the way he should choose**. Instruction comes through the Scriptures (32:8; Pr 9:10). The focus is not material **prosperity**, but what is fundamentally good (i.e., the best) for man, namely, God Himself and/or the knowledge of Him (see Gn 2:9 and Ps 16:2). In this same way, a righteous man's descendants **will inherit the land**, that is, retain their tribal/family inheritance (cf. Pss 37:9, 11, 18, 22, 29, 34; 69:36; Is 60:21); this further anticipates the promise of receiving a place in the future millennial kingdom on earth following the second coming, as directly cited by Messiah (Mt 5:5; see the comments there) from Ps 37:11 (see the comments there).

25:16-21. Here is a request for emotional relief: **be gracious** for I am **lonely** and **afflicted** and **the troubles of** his **heart** are **enlarged**. He requested God to **forgive all my sins** (cf. vv. 7, 11, 18) and to protect him from his **enemies**. But he primarily wants the Lord to **guard** his **soul** on the basis of his having taken **refuge in [Him]** (cf. 86:2) and having behaved righteously before God (with **integrity and uprightness**).

C. Consider the Broader Application of the Petition (25:22)

25:22. David began the psalm with a declaration of trust in God. He concludes with a prayer for the nation of **Israel**, that God would make His glory known by redeeming (rescuing and protecting) them **out of all** their **troubles**. Hence David implored God to **redeem Israel**, employing a verb that specifically denotes the paying of an outstanding debt, and which elsewhere denotes the work of complete spiritual and physical redemption that only God in His grace can supply (see Ps 49:7-8; Is 1:27; Jr 31:11). This anticipates the ultimate redemption of Israel by the Messiah.

Psalm 26: A Meditation on Personal Integrity

This **Psalm of David** has a threefold approach and contains parallels to Ps 27 (see the outline for that psalm). Both psalms begin by focusing on God as the foundation (both the establisher and determiner) of the central concept of the respective psalms—one's integrity in Ps 26, and one's confidence in Ps 27, and then present God as its goal, and conclude by affirming God as its ongoing enabler and developer. This parallel approach serves to emphasize the relationship between the central theme of this psalm and that of the next. Additionally, the psalmist had confidence that God would redeem him (26:11).

A. Affirming God as the Determiner of One's Integrity (26:1-2)

26:1-2. David began by entrusting himself entirely to God's perfect justice. He implores God to **vindicate** him, to take account of David's moral integrity and judge him on that basis. David recognized his integrity was less than perfect by his use of the phrase **my integrity**, in which the possessive pronoun indicates his adherence to integrity as he understood it, yet which was still not unadulterated by sin; David is not claiming perfection but his best intentions to follow the Lord **without wavering**. God would **examine** (as in a court of law) and **try** (as precious metals are tried for the quality of the ore) not only his actions, but his **mind** (seat of knowledge/understanding) and **heart** (seat of emotions/affections and the active inner person).

B. Affirming God as the Goal of One's Integrity (26:3-10)

26:3-7. David sought to order his life by the **lovingkindness** (God's loyal love) of the Lord and referred to his having **walked** (i.e., "lived," cf. v. 11) in God's **truth**. Moreover, he does **not sit with deceitful** (lit., "without spiritual worth"; see also v. 5b) **men**. He never descended to the point of "sitting" (i.e., identifying wholeheartedly) with them (on these concepts/verbs see the comment on Ps 1:1). The goal of his lifelong endeavor to walk in integrity and truth was not to promote his own merit or worth, but to express **thanksgiving** for what God had done (v. 7), namely, His **wonders** of deliverance both personally for David and for His people throughout history (cf. 9:1).

26:8-10. David proclaims **I love the habitation of Your house**, the temple of God, **the place where Your glory dwells** (Ex 24:16; 33:22; 40:35; 1Kg 8:11). He requests deliverance from **men of bloodshed** and **wicked** schemers so that he can continually "stand . . . in the congregations" and "bless the LORD" (v. 12).

C. Affirming God as the Enabler of One's Integrity (26:11-12)

26:11-12. While recognizing his imperfection and failings, David, rather than succumbing to despair, determined to continue to **walk in my integrity** and appealed to God's mercy to **redeem me**, implying forgiveness, not requiting the full penalty that his sins merited (cf. Ezr 9:13), and asks God to **be gracious to me** (grant him the help he does not merit). Thus, he will be able to continue his attempt to **walk in [his] integrity**. In this respect it is important that he spend time **in the congregations** of the faithful (as opposed to "the assembly of evildoers" in v. 5) praising God with those who were of the same mind as he, who affirmed their need for God's mercy and grace and would therefore encourage him along in his walk—no doubt often meeting at the tabernacle to do so (cf. v. 8).

Psalm 27: A Meditation on Personal Confidence

This **Psalm of David** mirrors the expository structure of Ps 26 (see the introductory comments there). David once again alludes to the theme broached in 23:6 in which he anticipated being able to live in the house of the Lord with the Anointed One (see 27:4) (Sailhamer, *NIV Compact Bible Commentary*, 320–21).

A. Affirming God as the Basis of One's Confidence (27:1-3)

27:1-3. David's confidence was based on **the LORD** (rather than man or a group of men) who was his **light and . . . salvation**. The word **light** here, as elsewhere in the OT, is a metaphor for comprehensive salvation, spiritual and physical, both present and eternal. This metaphor of God as light also includes the concept of God illumining David's darkness (cf. 2Sm 22:29) and directing his life toward obedience to the Lord (e.g., Pss 18:28; 119:105). Furthermore **salvation** encompasses not just deliverance from enemies, but more significantly spiritual redemption as well (e.g., Pss 3:8; 9:14; 13:5; 18:2, 46; 27:9). David's dependence on God as **the defense of [his] life** is further emphasized by his specific use of the two verbs **fear** and **dread** (v. 1). This recalls the uses of both verbs when God urged the Israelites to take confidence that they would succeed in possessing the land not because of any ability on their part, but because God Himself will "put the dread and fear" of them "upon the peoples everywhere" (cf. Dt 2:25; Est 8:17). No matter what happens (**enemies**, **a host**, or **war**), he **shall be confident**.

B. Affirming God as the Goal of One's Confidence (27:4-6)

27:4-6. David has one request: **that I may dwell in the house of the LORD all the days of my life**. His request is for never-ending fellowship with the Lord by worship in the **temple**. This is an allusion within the Psalms to 23:6. Just as the Anointed One anticipated returning to God's house, so the psalmist looks forward to that time as well. David wanted greater intimacy with the Lord **to behold the beauty of the**

Lord and **offer . . . sacrifices** and **sing praises to the Lord**. The verb **to meditate** (v. 4) refers to giving careful, close, and absorbed attention and consideration to something, in this case the Lord and His Word (cf. 77:12; 119:15, 48; Lv 13:36; 27:33; Pr 20:25; Ezk 34:11; 39:14).

C. Affirming God as the Developer of One's Confidence (27:7-14)

27:7-10. David seeks God's answer (**Hear, O Lord**) by pointing out his obedience to God's command to **seek My face**. The face of God is a key word in this section, appearing three times (vv. 8-9); to seek His face indicates a determination for intimate fellowship with the Lord. On the basis of that behavior David again points to the **God of my salvation** (cf. 27:1). He uses the extreme example of rescue from abandonment, **For** (better translated "if") **my father and my mother have forsaken me, but** (better translated "then") **the Lord will take me up**.

27:11-14. To be taught the **way** of the Lord will **lead me in a level path**, a phrase associated with walking righteously (cf. 26:12; 143:10; Is 26:7). Just as God taught him, so too might he instruct and encourage others to **be strong** and **take courage** (v. 14; cf. Dt 31:7; Jos 1:7). To **wait for the Lord** means to depend on Him; it does not indicate passivity or inaction, but rather trust and confident anticipation that He will take action (e.g., Pss 25:3, 5, 21; 37:7, 9, 34; 59:9; 62:5; cf. Gn 48:18).

Psalm 28: A Paradigm of Appeal for the Demonstration of God's Love

On the heading of this **Psalm of David**, see the comments on the heading to Ps 3. Though a cursory reading might seem to suggest that his appeal for help is based on his own merit, a closer reading of how key phrases are used elsewhere in the OT reveals instead that his help is based on God's mercy, grace, and covenant faithfulness—in short, on His love as it is expressed in His covenant promises (see 2Sm 7). In its overall structure this psalm parallels God's own description in Mal 1:2-5 of the three ways in which His love for Israel is demonstrated (1) in His accomplished gift of unmerited intimacy (Ps 28:1-2; Mal 1:2), (2) in His ongoing judgment of their enemies (Ps 28:3-5; Mal 1:3-4), and (3) in His future restoration and blessing of the nation (Ps 28:6-9; Mal 1:5).

A. As Demonstrated in His Unmerited Attention to the Beloved's Cry (28:1-3)

28:1-3. Rather than hold back his distress and anguish, David poured it out fully: **To You, O Lord I call**, not to anyone else (see the comments on Ps 142:1-6). He identified God as his **rock** (cf. 18:2 comments). David did not demand that God **hear** (meet his need) his **cry . . . for help** as if he merited such a hearing because of his righteousness. Instead he requested that God hear him on the basis of His mercy and grace—even though David did not merit God's positive response. This is indicated by David's admission of the real possibility that God might choose to **be deaf** and **silent to** his appeal (v. 1) as well as that He might **drag** David **away with the wicked** (signifying judgment, not chastisement).

The logical implication of this is that David is also wicked, for the Lord would never "sweep away the righteous with the wicked" (Gn 18:23; see the comments on David's admission of wickedness in Pss 7:1-5 and 13:1-2). Also the Hebrew word usually translated **supplications** (*tahanunim*) in v. 2 (and again in v. 6) signifies "pleas for grace" (from the Hb. *hen*, "grace"), implying the granting to David of what he did not deserve. Yet, that David could appeal to God with the hope of being shown grace indicates a preexisting relationship (see the comments on Pss 6:1-5; 23:6; 51).

B. As Demonstrated in His Ongoing Judgment of the Beloved's Enemies (28:4-5)

28:4-5. David further asks for judgment of his enemies, **Requite them according to their work**. Just as the love of a parent will prompt him to fight against those who seek to injure his child, so too David implored God to demonstrate His love by "requiting" (judging, both militarily and spiritually) his enemies. Those enemies were the Gentile nations around Israel, as indicated by (1) David's description of them as those who **do not regard** [lit., "discern"] **the works of the Lord nor the deeds of His hands** (v. 5a), employing the same phraseology used to describe these nations in Dt 32:27, and (2) his expectation that the Lord **will tear them down and not build them up** (v. 5b), which parallels the phraseology of God's declaration concerning Edom in (Mal 1:4). David's reason for imploring God to **requite** his and Israel's enemies is not that they are his and Israel's enemies as such (or even that they are more depraved than the Israelites), but that, as reflected by their opposition to Israel, they are opposed to the person, standards, and work of God Himself (cf. Ps 83).

C. As Demonstrated in His Final Salvation of the Beloved's People (28:6-9)

28:6-9. As a final demonstration of God's love, David implored God to **save Your people**, the people of Israel, who are identified as His **inheritance**. Of all the nations and people groups on the earth, the people of Israel alone are identified as the inheritance of the Lord, indicating His unique relationship with them. The people of Israel are frequently identified as God's inheritance (Dt 9:29; 32:9; Pss 33:12; 74:2; Is 63:17; Jr 10:16; 51:19). That this (v. 9) is intended as a reference to complete (material and spiritual) blessing is seen in the parallel reference to God as **their shepherd** who will **carry them forever** (cf. comments on Ps 23; Mal 1:5).

Psalm 29: A Meditation on God's Awe-Inspiring Power

On the heading of this **Psalm of David**, see the comments on the heading to Ps 3. According to early Jewish tradition, this psalm, which concerns God's transcendent power and its ultimate application to the full restoration of His people, was recited by the Levites on the Feast of Booths (cf. Lv 23:33-44; Babylonian Talmud, *Sukka* 55a). This festival likewise commemorates God's power and ability to supply His people's needs in the desert wandering as well as His ultimate application of that power to fully restore Israel and establish His tabernacle over all creation (see Zch 14:16-18; Col 2:16-17; Rv 21:3; and see the comment on Ps 15:1). The theme of God's strength in both 28:7 and 29:1, 11 suggests that Ps 29 may be the very song David wrote and sang in response to that strength (Sailhamer, *NIV Compact Bible Commentary*, 321).

A. The Unequivocal Ascription of God's Power (29:1-2)

29:1-2. This psalm is a call to praise God: **Ascribe to the LORD** (repeated 3 times for emphasis) . . . **glory and strength** . . . **glory due to His name**. David affirmed the absolute sovereignty and preeminence of God, in both **glory and strength**, not just over all men but also over all other gods. This is indicated by the phrase **sons of the mighty** (v. 1a), better translated "sons of gods." The term **mighty** (*elim*), which occurs only three times elsewhere (Ex 15:11; Ps 89:6; Dn 11:36), refers to pagan gods (see Ex 15:11). Scripture denies the existence of such divine beings (that is, there is no such supernatural being as "Dagon" or "Baal"), but sometimes posits them for the sake of the discussion and in dialogue with pagan practices (e.g., Gn 31:19; 35:2; Ex 23:32; Nm 33:4; Dt 6:14; Jos 24:16; Ru 1:15). The word "sons" in this expression does not denote descendancy but rather association or characterization (cf., e.g., 1Sm 25:17; Pr 31:5; Mk 3:17), the reference being here to anything (e.g., idols or concepts) associated with or characterized by pagan deities. The call is for even those who have followed paganism to acknowledge the Lord, and **worship the LORD in holy array**, in a proper manner.

B. The Universal Attestation of God's Power (29:3-9)

29:3-9. These verses extol the manifestation of God's **glory** and power in creation, (similar to Ps 19:1-6)—though in this case these verses allude to the deliverance, provision, and guidance of His fledgling people Israel at the exodus. Hence God's **voice** (or "sound," as the word is often translated) "thundering" **upon the waters** (v. 3) alludes to His deliverance of Israel from Pharaoh's army. In the exodus, He "rebuked the Red Sea and it dried up" (Ps 106:9; cf. Ex 15:8-10; Ps 114:3-5; Nah 1:4). His voice also is described as making **Lebanon** (i.e., the mountains of Lebanon) **skip like a calf** and **Sirion** (the Sidonian name of Mount Hermon; Dt 3:9) skip **like a young wild ox** (v. 6). This parallels the poetic depiction of creation's reaction to God's power revealed at the exodus in Ps 114:4-6. The reference to His voice hewing **out flames of fire** parallels the description of the seventh plague (fiery brimstone) in Ps 105:32: "He gave them . . . flaming fire in their land" (cf. Ex 9:23). And the reference to God "shaking" **the wilderness of Kadesh** (v. 8) alludes to God's chastising of the exodus generation at Kadesh (Nm 14:1-45; 20:1-13). On everything **in His temple** saying **Glory!** (v. 9), see Is 6:1-4 (where even "the foundations of the thresholds" are said to respond to God's glorious presence).

C. The Eternal Application of God's Power (29:10-11)

29:10-11. David concluded by affirming God's glory and sovereign power: **The LORD sits as King**. He reigned even before **the flood**, the first historical event of divine deliverance and judgment. That **the LORD** sat (i.e., exercised full authority and control as judges in biblical times might; Ex 18:13; Ru 4:1; 1Kg 2:12; Jr 26:10) at that worldwide event (see the comments on Gn 6:13-20) assures that He has sat as King over all human affairs ever since then, and that God will continue to sit over all Creation **as King forever**. As such, He is certainly able to control all matters relating to the welfare of **His people**, ultimately fulfilling all He promised them by blessing **His people**—both the remnant of ethnic Israel and those joined to them by faith (cf.

28:6-9)—**with peace** (*shalom*, signifying "completeness" and the presence of restful well-being in every sense, both physically, circumstantially, and spiritually; cf. 2Sm 7:11; Pss 28:9; 95:11).

Psalm 30: Thanksgiving and Dedication after Discipline

On the heading of this **Psalm of David**, see the comments on the heading to Ps 3.

Psalm 30 is described as a **Song** (see Introduction: Genre) for **the Dedication of the House**. Several of the psalms mention rejoicing in God's presence in the temple (cf. 23:8; 27:4). In addition, the rescue David experienced that he described in this psalm (vv. 1-5) was apparently selected by the postexilic editor of Psalms to serve as a reassurance to the exiled community that God would be faithful to them and someday restore them and the temple in Jerusalem (for this, see Sailhamer, *NIV Compact Bible Commentary*, 321). At issue is whether this psalm refers to the dedication of David's palace (2Sm 7:1) or the Lord's temple. The latter seems more likely since the vast majority (hundreds) of references to a specific "house" in the OT are to the temple, whether in the phrase "the house of God" (Ezr 2:68), "the house of the LORD" (2Kg 25:16), or, as here, "the House" (cf. 1Kg 8:13; Jr 26:18). That the intended reference is to the dedication of the temple is also supported by early Jewish tradition, according to which this psalm was recited in the temple on the eight days of Hanukkah (as it still is in many synagogues to this day), commemorating the (re) dedication of the temple in the intertestamental period after the victory of the Maccabees over the Greeks who sought to eradicate Jewish practices in Israel at that time.

Although David may have written this psalm in anticipation of the future dedication of the temple, it is more likely that this superscription was included by the postexilic editor of the Psalms, since there is no specific reference to the temple in it. His intention would have been to link David's restoration after being disciplined to Israel's return and rebuilding of the temple after the discipline of the exile.

A. The Transience of God's Discipline (30:1-5)

30:1-3. David begins with praise for personal deliverance: **I will extol You, O LORD, for You have lifted me up**. David affirms God as the source of deliverance from his **enemies** and from **Sheol** (the general OT description of the place of the dead; see comments on 49:10-14, 15). He praised God because He **kept me alive** and did not let him **go down to the pit** (grave). At some point David was on the brink of death at the hands of his enemies, but the Lord rescued him.

30:4-5. David's response to rescue is to encourage all **His godly ones** (corporately, the faithful of Israel) to join him and **sing praise to the LORD**. Specifically, they are to **give thanks to His holy name** (cf. 4:3). There is a sharp contrast between God's **anger** (for correction and discipline) that **is but for a moment**, and **His favor** (of blessing after restoration) that **is for a lifetime**.

B. The Pain of God's Discipline (30:6-9)

30:6-7. As a result of his **prosperity** David almost forgot God, considering himself invincible (**I will never be moved**, v. 6). As is so often the case, God's blessings often divert a believer's attention from Him and reduce reliance on Him, ultimately leading to the sin of self-dependence rather than relying on the Lord.

In fact this very self-reliance led David to take the census of fighting men in Israel, so that God chastised him (see 2Sm 24). David described that discipline by the expression **You hid your face** (v. 7; on this expression as the description of God's discipline, not judgment, see the Introduction to Esther), so that he **was dismayed** or brought to a full realization of his sin.

30:8-9. Adverse circumstances prompted David to reset his focus from assessing his material circumstances to praising God (**To You, O LORD, I called**). David realized his own mortality, that he could not praise the Lord from **the pit**.

C. The Goal of God's Discipline (30:10-12)

30:10-12. Having come to the full realization of his sin, David implored, **Hear, O LORD, and be gracious to me** and begged God to **be** his **helper** (lit., "be a helper to me"). This phrase alludes to God's promise and self-disclosure of His name to Moses in Ex 3:12 ("I will be with you"), which in turn implies that David, like Moses, was here affirming his own fundamental inability to undertake God's charge to him of ruling Israel (cf. Ex 3:11, "Who am I . . . that I should bring the sons of Israel out of Egypt?") as well as his consequent dependence on God to help him do so. The goal of God's chastisement of David was thus realized in that David recognized and affirmed his utter dependence on God, and in the process he would **sing** his **praise** to Him (v. 12 is lit., "Glory will sing to You," i.e., David's song of glory would be lifted up to God. This reflects the same concept and wording in 29:9b: "And in His temple everything says, 'Glory!'").

Psalm 31: Appealing to God for Deliverance from Oppression

On the heading of this **Psalm of David** see the comments on the headings to both Pss 3 and 4.

A. Affirming the Insurmountable Strength of God's Deliverance (31:1-5)

31:1-5. The declaration **In You, O Lord, I have taken refuge** (v. 1) is David's affirmation that his trust is completely and solely in the God of Israel (1Sm 26:19). God is the only impenetrable **refuge**, as highlighted by the expressions **rock** (v. 2; see comment on Ps 18:46) **of strength, a stronghold** (a place of protection), and **fortress** (v. 3; a fortress on a cliff or mountain; cf. Ps 71:1-3 for similar terms). Another reason for David's confidence is that God, **in** His **righteousness**, will do what is best to **deliver** (v. 1) David. David understood the faithful and just character of the Lord and remembered the covenant God had established with him (2Sm 7:16). David wanted the Lord to take action on his behalf **for Your name's sake** (cf. Ps 23:3 comments). David employed the same phraseology, **You will lead me and guide me**, as in Ps 23:3. God's best does not necessarily include immediate deliverance from physical distress or persecution as is evident in Jesus' words on the cross, "INTO YOUR HANDS I COMMIT MY SPIRIT" (Lk 23:46).

B. Expressing the Present Need for God's Deliverance (31:6-22)

31:6-8. Hating **those who regard vain** (empty, powerless) **idols** is a rejection of paganism. In contrast, David is determined to **trust in the Lord**, a life characterized by the attitude of **I will rejoice** in God's lovingkindness (cf. 5:7) because the Lord had **known** his **troubles** (cf. comment on 1:6) and delivered him from **the enemy**.

31:9-13. The expression **be gracious** implies that David's distress may have been intended as chastisement for his sins (cf. comment on 28:2), or just a cry for relief. David expressed his natural desire for immediate relief from his **distress** that is described as: **grief, sorrow, sighing** . . . **like a broken vessel**. The source of his trouble was his **adversaries** who **schemed to take away** his **life**.

31:14-22. Despite his dire circumstances, David declares his faith and trust in God: **But as for me, I trust in You, O Lord** . . . **You are my God**. He recognizes **My times are in Your hand**, the Lord is in control of every aspect of his life. His request, **Make Your face to shine upon Your servant** recalls the Aaronic benediction (cf. Nm 6:25). He anticipates deliverance by saying **He has made marvelous His lovingkindness to me in a besieged city**. . . . **You heard the voice of my supplications when I cried to You**.

C. Sharing the Praiseworthy Hope of God's Deliverance (31:23-24)

31:23-24. David characteristically concluded with devotion, praise, and exhortation to worship: **O love the Lord, all you His godly ones!** The concept with which David began this psalm—God's covenant faithfulness serving as the source of constant strength and deliverance for His people—is reiterated by David in the closing verse, **Be strong and** . . . **take courage** (cf. 27:14; Jos 1:9).

Psalm 32: A Paradigm of Forgiveness

This **Psalm of David** (see the comments on Davidic authorship in the heading to Ps 3) is a ***Maskil*** (lit., "enlightenment" or "to impart wisdom"), a type of psalm focusing specifically on instruction in practical wisdom or contemplation. This term occurs as a specific designation in the headings of 12 other psalms (Pss 42, 44, 45, 52–55, 74, 78, 88, 89, 142), and in Ps 47:7 as a general designation of this type of psalm ("Sing praises with a [*maskil*]"). On parallels between Pss 32 and 33 to Pss 1 and 2, see introductory comments on Ps 33.

A. The Nature of Divine Forgiveness (32:1-5)

32:1-2. David affirmed **how blessed** (see the comment on Ps 1:1) the man is **whose transgression is forgiven**. This verb, when used with any of the words denoting sin (e.g., **transgression** [rebellion against God], **sin** [missing the mark of God's standard], **iniquity** [behavior that is bent or twisted]), represents the standard biblical idiom used to express the concept of forgiveness in the following. The parallel statement, **whose sin is covered**, likewise expresses confidence in forgiveness of sin. It is a figurative expression characteristic of Hebrew poetry, and should not be taken to mean that sin in the OT period was in reality only covered up but not forgiven. In the OT, forgiveness is expressed in terms of complete atonement and removal for those who offered their sacrifices in faith (e.g., 2Sm 12:13; Is 6:7). Romans 4:4-8 cites this passage regarding forgiveness of sin (see the comments there).

32:3-5. David not only learned of the happiness of forgiveness, but also the effects of unconfessed sin. It caused physical difficulties for him (**my body wasted away**, v. 3) and emotional strain (**my vitality was drained away**, v. 4). These difficulties persisted until he **acknowledged** his **sin** and confessed his **transgressions** (v. 5), so that God **forgave the guilt of [his] sin**.

B. The Availability of Divine Forgiveness (32:6-7)

32:6-7. On the basis of his experience, **therefore**, David called **everyone who is godly** to **pray**. The image of **great waters** depicts extreme distress (Ps 18:16; Is 8:7-8). More particular allusions to the flood are indicated by the surrounding statements: **let everyone . . . pray to You in a time when You may be found**, paralleling the clearly defined period of "evangelism" and potential repentance by the people alive during Noah's building of the ark (cf. Heb 11:7 and comments on Gn 7:1-10), and **You are my hiding place; You preserve me from trouble**, paralleling the preservation of Noah and his family from—that is, through—the flood (cf. 1Pt 3:20 and the comments there).

C. The Attraction of Divine Forgiveness (32:8-11)

32:8-11. The expression **I will instruct you and teach you in the way which you should go** indicates that God's forgiveness fosters spiritual perception and moral clarity revealed by God in His Word. The phrase **I will instruct** signifies the imparting of wisdom as expressed by Joshua (Jos 1:8) in connection with the law of God. There must be a response to God's instruction, however, so that the person is not **as the horse or as the mule which have no understanding**. In other words, do not resist repentance and hold back confession. The challenge is to be wise and learn from the Lord, because **many are the sorrows of the wicked,** but God's fatherly **lovingkindness** (*chesed*; cf. comments on Ps 5:7) surrounds the believer. The result for the person **who trusts in the Lord** will be experiencing God's grace (**lovingkindness**). That person will be **glad in the Lord . . . rejoice . . . and shout for joy**.

Psalm 33: A Paradigm of Collectively Proclaiming God's Praise

The absence of a heading for this psalm is possibly because it was intended "as a piece" with the previous psalm—just as Ps 2 is intended to be read "as a piece" with Ps 1 (see comments there). Strengthening this possibility is the observation that this and the previous psalm attest clear parallels to Pss 1 and 2, both *thematically* (Ps 32, like Ps 1, focuses on personally expressed worship, whereas Ps 33, like Ps 2, focuses on collectively expressed worship) and in *phraseology* (e.g., "How blessed" [1:1; 32:1]; "day and night" [1:2; 32:4]; "streams of water" / "great waters" [1:3; 32:6]; closing comparison between the circumstances of "the wicked" and "the righteous" [1:5-6; 32:10-11]; "the nations . . . the peoples . . . take counsel together against the Lord" / "the Lord nullifies the counsel of the nations . . . the plans of the peoples" [2:1-2; 33:10]; "He who sits in the heavens laughs" / "the Lord looks from heaven . . . from His dwelling place" [2:4; 33:13-14]; "the very ends of the earth" / "all the earth" [2:8; 33:5, 8, 14]; and "blessed are all" / ". . . is the nation" [2:12; 33:12]).

A. The Obligation of Collective Praise (33:1-3)

33:1-3. The opening **Sing for joy in the Lord, O you righteous ones** is a closely linked idea to the close of the previous psalm (32:11). There is a reiteration of the call to collective **praise** and **thanks** (the theme of Ps 33) in the form of a **new song** (a song of worship that gives a fresh expression to the believer's continued experiences with God). These songs celebrate God's character and salvation (cf. 40:3; 96:1; 98:1; 144:9; 149:1, Is 42:10; Rv 5:9; 14:3) and are offered by **righteous ones** to God for His gracious gift of personal forgiveness (the theme of Ps 32).

B. The Reasons for Collective Praise (33:4-19)

33:4-5. This is a song of praise to **the Lord**, the Creator, with seven distinct reasons for collectively praising God: (1) His attributes (vv. 4-5)—specifically His imitable attributes of being **upright**, His **faithfulness**, His **righteousness**, His **justice**, and His **lovingkindness** (cf. 5:7 comments); the terms **righteousness and justice** are often linked in Scripture regarding God's character and obedience to His Word (e.g., Gn 18:19; 2Sm 8:15; 1Kg 10:9; 1Ch 18:14; Pss 89:14; 97:2; 99:4; Pr 1:3; 2:9: 21:3; Is 1:27).

33:6-19. Furthermore, (2) His power is exhibited in His creation of the world: **He spoke, and it was done**, by His **word** (vv. 6-9); (3) the sovereign permanence of His **counsel** (i.e., His will, vv. 10-11); (4) His election of Israel **for His own inheritance** (v. 12; see Ps 28:9); (5) His intimate understanding of **the hearts of** all people (vv. 13-15); (6) His superiority to any other basis of **hope** or deliverance (vv. 16-17); and (7) His special concern for **those who fear** (i.e., worship; cf. 111:10) **Him** (vv. 18-19; see Ps 40).

C. The Application of Collective Praise (33:20-22)

33:20-22. There is a resulting collective reliance on God, highlighted by plural pronouns: **Our soul waits for the LORD** knowing **He is our help and our shield** (cf. Jdg 5:8; 2Kg 19:32; Ps 35:2). There is a strengthening of collective **trust** in God's **holy name** (cf. comments Ps 23:3) and the fostering of collective joy (**our heart rejoices**) among God's people—whatever the circumstances might be.

Psalm 34: A Paradigm of God's Providence

This **Psalm of David** (see the comments on Davidic authorship in the heading to Ps 3) is parallel to Ps 25 in its theme, phraseology, and structure (for specifics see introduction on Ps 25). The heading also indicates that this psalm was written when David **feigned madness before Abimelech**—referring to the episode recorded in 1Sm 21:10-15 (see comments there). This psalm should thus be understood not only as an expression of David's thanksgiving and praise for God's providence and faithful concern, but also as an implicit confession of guilt for fearing Achish (see 1Sm 21:12) more than he feared the Lord ("fear" of the Lord is a prominent motif in this psalm; see vv. 7, 9, 11; 111:10). With the exception of v. 22, this psalm is an acrostic (each line begins with the succeeding letter of the Hebrew alphabet). Verse 22 explicitly links the hope of the faithful to the messianic expectations fostered in Ps 2:12 ("Do homage to the Son . . . How blessed are all who take refuge in Him"; see the verbal parallels in 34:22: "and none of those who take refuge in Him will be condemned") (Sailhamer, *NIV Compact Bible Commentary*, 322).

A. Praise for God's Providence (34:1-7)

34:1-3. David's declaration **I will bless the LORD at all times** is especially significant when seen in response to his failure to trust God in the Abimelech situation. The depth of David's praise is underscored by the fact that it will **continually be in** his **mouth** (v. 1); that is, in his everyday speech he will make a conscious effort to affirm God's character and activity. He will make his **boast in the LORD**, not in anything he has accomplished (cf. Ps 44:8; Jr 9:23-24; 1Cor 1:31). As a result, when others **hear it**, they will **rejoice**. Then they will **magnify the LORD** and **exalt His name** with David.

34:4-7. David praises God because He **delivered me from all my fears**. The description **poor man** (v. 6; better translated "afflicted" or "oppressed" because it does not indicate financial circumstances but affliction) indicates David's spiritual condition of neediness and distress. When he **cried** (called out), the **LORD heard** (responded to his prayer) and **saved him out of all his troubles**. David vividly underscored God's personal role in rescuing him by the reference to **the angel of the LORD**, which often refers in the OT to the temporary manifestation in human form of God (known as a *theophany*)—often of the preincarnate Son of God and always for the purpose of meeting a personal or collective need (see the comments on Gn 16:7-12). This is not about guardian angels in the popular Hollywood sense. **Encamps around** speaks of the security the Lord provides His people collectively.

B. An Invitation to God's Providence (34:8-14)

34:8-14. The invitation here, in poetic terms, is to experience the goodness of the Lord: **O taste and see that the LORD is good**. The expression typically translated **taste** may be more precisely understood to mean "acquire/derive discernment" (as also in Ps 119:66 and 1Sm 25:33). The sense of the verse is that one should derive discernment from the Lord's work and word and consequently **see** (perceive or assess) **that** He **is good**, that is, the only true good, the best that man can ever have (see the comment on Ps 16:2). The best life, the most **blessed** life (cf. Ps 1), is available to the **man who takes refuge in Him**. Those who **seek the LORD shall not be in want of any good thing**. This is not a promise of prosperity, but the principle of God's more enduring provision for **the man who desires life and loves length of days** in which "life" and "length of days" signify the quality and quantity of life with God. These principles of wise living, similar to those found in Proverbs, conclude with the general statement **Depart from evil and do good; seek peace and pursue it**.

C. The Object of God's Providence (34:15-22)

34:15-18. Although both the righteous and the wicked have **troubles**, the outcome of their circumstances is different because of their different relationship with the Lord. God knows and sees everything, and is concerned for the good of those who love Him: **The eyes of the LORD are toward the righteous . . . His ears are open to their cry . . .** He **delivers them out of all their troubles**. In contrast, **the face of the LORD is against evildoers**. Describing believers as **the**

brokenhearted and the **crushed** [or "contrite"] **in spirit** does not indicate depression/despair in this context, but rather it is intended to describe their ongoing attitude of repentance and humility before God (cf. Ps 51:17).

34:19-22. Here **bones** represents the whole person (cf. Ps 6:2). At the crucifixion the phrase **not one of them is broken** was applied to Jesus (Jn 19:36) to emphasize Jesus was not only the Passover Lamb (cf. Ex 12:46; Jn 1:35) but also the righteous sufferer whom **the LORD redeems**.

Psalm 35: A Petition for Personal Vindication

This **Psalm of David** (see the comments on Davidic authorship in the heading to Ps 3) contains many verbal and conceptual parallels to Ps 34 (34:1 = 35:28; 34:2 = 35:9; 34:7 = 35:5-6; 34:20 = 35:10).

A. Expressing the Desire for Personal Vindication (35:1-8)

35:1-3. David's appeal **Contend, O LORD, with those who contend with me** has a specific legal connotation (as in Pss 43:1; 74:22; Pr 22:23; Is 3:13). David's request is to God alone, since it is (1) according to God's standards, not man's, that everyone will be judged, and (2) God alone will ultimately sit as judge over everyone (cf. v. 24, as well as Pss 7:8; 9:8; 75:7; 96:10, 13; 110:6; Ec. 3:17; 12:14; Ac 17:31; Rv 20:13). The Lord, identified as **your salvation**, is portrayed as a warrior who will **fight** for the righteous with specific military images: **buckler and shield**, **spear**, and **battle-axe**.

35:4-8. The defeat of those **who devise evil against me** is that they should be **ashamed, dishonored, and humiliated**. They should be like **chaff** (cf. Ps 1:5-6). The **angel of the LORD** (cf. comments on 34:4-7) is the instrument of judgment **pursuing them**.

B. Considering One's Merit for Personal Vindication (35:9-26)

35:9-12. David is confident of justice: **my soul shall rejoice in the LORD. . . . who delivers the afflicted . . . and the needy**. Certainly David did not consider himself sinless (1Sm 25:32-33; 2Sm 12:1ff.), yet he affirmed his innocence in the face of **malicious witnesses** (a legal term) and those who **repay** him **evil for good**. Then David gives the example of his kind behavior toward his enemies when they were in trouble (vv. 13-14) in contrast to their evil behavior toward him in similar circumstances (vv. 15-16).

35:13-14. When his enemies were **sick**, he had concern for them, offering repeated prayers (as indicated by the phrase **returning to my bosom**) in **sackcloth** and **fasting**, a sign of deep concern for their condition. He cared for them as he would for those whom he loves, as if they were a **friend or brother**, as concerned as if in deep **sorrows for a mother**.

35:15-16. The psalmist's enemies, in contrast, **rejoiced** at his **stumbling**. This is not moral failure, since this would not be an issue for the wicked, but being brought down by circumstances (e.g., 9:3; 27:2; 37:34).

35:17-18. Under these circumstances, David asks **Lord, how long** (see comments on 6:3). He asked for the Lord to **rescue** him, not for his own glory, but so that he could give **thanks in the great congregation . . . among a mighty throng**, that is, in communal worship with the people of Israel in the tabernacle/temple.

35:19-26. To underscore the wickedness of his foes, David further referred to them as **those who hate me without cause** (cf. 69:4). This is another appeal for judgment: **You have seen it, O LORD, do not keep silent** (v. 22). The Lord is always near us (He is everywhere, omnipresent), but in difficulties God's people may feel as if He is **far** away.

C. Affirming the Goal of Personal Vindication (35:27-28)

35:27-28. The motivation of David's personal vindication was that **the LORD** would **be magnified**, not that he might be proven right.

Psalm 36: A Meditation on God's Covenant Love (*Chesed*)

On this **Psalm of David** see the comments on the headings to Pss 3 and 4. **David** is described here as **the servant of the LORD** (a description also applied to him only in the heading of Ps 18). The central theme of this psalm is God's *chesed*, traditionally translated "lovingkindness"—God's unshakable covenant love (cf. 5:7 comments).

A. The Absence of Lovingkindness (36:1-4)

36:1-4. The core/**heart** of the **ungodly** is rejection of the Lord. **There is no fear of God before his eyes**. To the ungodly, **transgression** serves as the authoritative guide in all aspects of life. Instead of fearing the Lord, he **flatters** himself to soothe his conscience, and thereby approves of all his own **wickedness and deceit**. Having no fear of God, **he does not despise evil** (cf. Pr 8:13).

B. The Embodiment of Lovingkindness (36:5-9)

36:5-9. In God, **lovingkindness** (*chesed*, loyal love) receives its fullest expression and stands as the enduring model for us to follow. David underscored (1) the endless supply of God's **lovingkindness** that **extends to the heavens . . . skies**—it is inexhaustible (cf. Lm 3:22-23); (2) the unfathomable extent of God's **lovingkindness** so that it even affects His **judgments**, rendering them as inscrutable as the **great deep** (oceans; Gn 1:2; 7:11). Further, God's **righteousness is like the mountains of God**, like the mountains surrounding and protecting Jerusalem (cf. 125:2); (3) the consistent application of God's **lovingkindness**—both generally, to **preserve** the physical lives of both **man and beast** (per the Noahic covenant of Gn 9:9-11; Mt 5:45), and specifically, in holding out the ongoing gift of spiritual life (per the greatest provision of the Abrahamic covenant; Gn 12:3 and its crystallization in the new covenant). This is implied by the reference to taking **refuge in the shadow of Your wings** (see the comment on Ps 17:8). For humanity, God is the only source of **light**, which in the Bible is employed as a symbol of life and/or salvation, whether physical or spiritual (cf. Ps 49:19; Is 9:2; Jn 1:4-9; Eph 5:8; Rv 21:22-23).

C. The Ongoing Need for Lovingkindness (36:10-12)

36:10-12. There is continuing need for the Lord's **lovingkindness to those who know You** because believers are always longing to experience the Lord's kindness. To **know** signifies an intimate relationship (see the comment on Ps 1:6). Further, David implored God not to let his oppressors hurt him with their arrogant feet (**the foot of pride**; this metaphor may derive from ancient military commanders placing their feet on the necks of those they had conquered; cf. Jos 10:24) nor with their wicked hands (**the hand of the wicked**). David anticipates God's answer to his prayer, pointing to the place of victory where these **doers of iniquity have fallen . . . been thrust down and cannot rise.**

Psalm 37: A Celebration of Satisfaction with God's Reward

This **Psalm of David** (see the comments on Davidic authorship in the heading to Ps 3) is an acrostic. Its central theme is divine reward, with specific focus on (1) the nature of that reward as epitomized by the eternal inheritance of the land of Israel and (2) the character of those so rewarded, who represent only a portion (a remnant) of the people of Israel.

Both of these aspects of the reward motif punctuate the psalm at various points by synonymous descriptions of those who receive the reward—i.e., "those who wait for the LORD" (v. 9), "the humble" (v. 11), "those blessed by Him" (v. 22), "the righteous" (v. 25), those who "keep His way" (v. 34), followed by the repeated declaration that they will "inherit the land" (vv. 9, 11, 22, 29, 34); these themes reiterate those of Pss 1 and 2. Not surprisingly, Jesus quoted from this promise of future reward in His own exposition of the topic in the Beatitudes (Mt 5:5; see the comment on Mt 5:1-6). To facilitate memorization of this psalm, it is arranged as an acrostic.

A. God's Reward Is Sure (37:1-15)

37:1-15. David's admonitions, **do not fret** (repeated vv. 1, 7, 8) and **be not envious toward wrongdoers**, addressed the problem of God's justice—how can a good God allow good things to happen to bad people, and bad things to good people? The reasons for this admonition not to be distressed because of the prosperity of the wicked are presented in the following three parts of this psalm.

First, there is the certainty that as any good (e.g., wealth, position, power) enjoyed by evildoers in this world is only temporary—**for they will wither quickly like the grass** (v. 2; see also vv. 9, 10, 20). On the other hand, so too it is certain that those who **delight . . . in the LORD** (v. 4) . . . **commit** their **way to the LORD**, **trust also in Him** (v. 5) . . . **rest in the LORD** (v. 7) . . . **will inherit the land** (v. 9; cf. v. 3, 22; see comments on 25:15) and **will delight themselves in an abundant prosperity** (v. 4-5, 7, 9, 11). **Prosperity** (Heb., *shalom*) is better translated "peace," for it refers to spiritual (inner) as well as material-physical (outer) completeness (see the comment on Ps 29:11). Jesus included this text in His Sermon on the Mount message (see comment on Mt 5:5).

B. God's Reward Is Best (37:16-26)

37:16-26. Having affirmed the abundant bestowal of peace upon the righteous and final depriving of the wicked, David next presented the second aspect of divine reward: that by comparison to the temporary prosperity of the wicked, God's reward is **better** (**Better is the little of the righteous than the abundance of many wicked**; v. 16; biblical Hebrew syntax denoting the comparative, i.e., "better," may semantically extend to the superlative, i.e., "best"). There can be nothing better than the relationship of the righteous with the Lord: He **sustains** them (v. 17) and . . . **knows** their **days** (v. 18) and knows that . . . **their inheritance will be forever** (v. 18). Specifically this future inheritance is best because it entails the complete fulfillment of all one's physical needs (vv. 19, 25) and the complete fulfillment of all one's spiritual needs (epitomized by the terms **blessed** and **blessing** (vv. 22, 26). God's blessing also entails the complete fulfillment of one's relational-emotional needs, as vividly indicated by the imagery in v. 24, where God is depicted as the believer's Father who **holds his hand** with a gentle and unslackened grip even **when he falls** (v. 24).

C. God's Reward Is Everlasting (37:27-40)

37:27-40. The third and final aspect of divine reward regarding God's justice is that of eternality: **Depart from evil and do good, so you will abide forever** (v. 27). Whatever one may experience in this life is minor in comparison to one's experiences in the hereafter, which will endure eternally. The **wicked will be cut off** (vv. 28, 38)—a biblical idiom denoting death (perhaps here referring to "the second death"; Rv 20:14)—whereas the righteous (i.e., the remnant of Israel and Gentiles: those who put their faith in the God of Abraham, Isaac, Jacob, and ultimately the Messiah Jesus) **will abide** [live] **forever** (v. 27). No matter what circumstances arise the admonition and encouragement is to **wait for the Lord and keep His way** (v. 34) because **the salvation of the righteous is from the Lord; He is their strength in time of trouble** (v. 39).

Psalm 38: Responding to God's Chastisement

On the heading of this **Psalm of David**, see the comments on the heading to Ps 3. This psalm is also identified **for a memorial** (lit., "for bringing to remembrance"), which suggests that it may have been recited in connection with the Feast of Trumpets (known today as Rosh Hashanah, the Jewish New Year festival), which is specifically described as "a memorial" (Lv 23:24 KJV, ESV). This psalm may describe the kind of anxiety over evil people that David warned about in Ps 37:40, emphasizing how God "helps" them and His action "saves" the righteous, and Ps 38:22—it contains an earnest request for God's "help" and "salvation" (37:40; Sailhamer, *NIV Compact Bible Commentary*, 322–23).

A. Implore God's Mercy (38:1-8)

38:1-8. The opening plea to the Lord not to **rebuke me . . . in Your wrath, and chasten me not in Your burning anger** is almost identical to that of Ps 6, with a petition for God's mercy combined with a sincere admission of guilt, implied by the verbs **rebuke** and **chasten** (see comments on Ps 6:1). David affirmed that he had sinned: **my iniquities . . . are as a heavy burden** and **they** are **too much for me** (vv. 3-4). . . . **I groan because of the agitation of my heart** (v. 8) and hence deserved God's discipline. The effects of his guilt for sin are described physically and emotionally as **no health in my bones** (v. 3; cf. Jb 33:19) and **no soundness in my flesh** (v. 7) along with emotional pain, **I go mourning all day long** (v. 6; cf. Ps 32:3-4).

B. Admit Personal Weakness (38:9-12)

38:9-12. David was transparent about his sin (**Lord, all my desire is before You**; v. 9), admitting his inability to resolve, on his own, the broad aftermath of his sin. He mentioned (1) his personal sense of distress and guilt (**My heart throbs, my strength fails me**; v. 10), (2) the distance his sin created between him and his friends (**my loved ones and my friends stand aloof**; v. 11), and (3) the opportunity that his sin had given to his opponents to attack him (**Those who seek my life . . . devise treachery all day long**; v. 12).

C. Affirm Continual Dependence on God (38:13-22)

38:13-22. David, by saying he was **like a deaf man . . . like a mute man**, indicated that he will not listen to the attacks of his enemies nor reply to them (v. 13). Instead he will wait for the Lord. This affirmation of dependence on God is epitomized by David's frequent statement **for I hope in You, O Lord** (v. 15; cf. 31:24; 33:18, 22; 69:3; 131:3; see also 42:5, 11; 43:5; 71:14; 130:5, 7; 147:11). On David's concluding reference to the **Lord** as **my salvation** (33:22), see comments on Ps 3:8.

Psalm 39: The Brevity of Life and the Sin of Silence

On the heading of this **Psalm of David**, see comments on the headings to Pss 3 and 4.

The choir director is **Jeduthun**, the father of one of the three families of Levitical singers (see 1Ch 16:41; 24:1). This psalm, especially v. 11, looks at David's afflictions from the vista of eternity (Sailhamer, *NIV Compact Bible Commentary*, 323). This psalm also has thematic and verbal parallels both to the previous psalm (e.g., 38:13 = 39:2, 9; 38:11 = 39:10; 38:1= 39:11), as well as to the words of Job (e.g., 39:4 = Jb 6:11; 39:13 = Jb 10:20-21)

A. Understanding the Sin of Silence (39:1-3)

39:1-3. David reviewed his past when he said, **I will guard my ways that I may not sin with my tongue**, and he was determined to **guard** his **mouth . . . while the wicked** were **in** his **presence** (v. 1). Knowing his own tendency to meet injustice with quick-tempered outbursts rather than more thoughtful and discerning responses, David determined to refrain from rash pronouncements that he might later regret as excessive and hence sinful (as in 1Sm 25:21-22, 33). While this determination was a good thing and consistent with biblical wisdom (see Pr 14:29; 17:27), David took it too far by remaining **silent** when he should have spoken and in so doing **refrained even from good** (therefore, his **sorrow grew worse**; v. 2; cf. Lv 19:17).

B. Realizing the Brevity of Opportunity and Life (39:4-6)

39:4-6. He prayed, **LORD, make me to know my end . . . the extent of my days** (v. 4). He desired to know how to use his time and his opportunities to speak or be silent. He realized that **every man at his best is a mere breath** (cf. Pss 49:10-12; 62:9; 89:47; 90:3-6; Ec 1:2-4; 6:12; Is 40:6-8). This does not, however, justify or exonerate David from the sin of remaining silent when he should have spoken.

C. Repenting of the Sin of Silence (39:7-13)

39:7-13. David threw himself on God's mercy for forgiveness of sin: **And now, Lord, for what do I wait? My hope is in you** (v. 7). David acknowledged his **transgressions** (v. 8)—his "manner" of having kept silent when he should have spoken—and he affirmed the justness and necessity of God's correction (v. 11, **with reproofs You chasten**; see comments on Ps 6:1). Significantly as part of his repentance, David affirmed both his relationship with and his desire for God, as indicated by his statement **I am a stranger with You** (v. 12). This psalm ends on a note of despair (**turn Your gaze away from me**; v. 13) because he felt so ashamed to be in God's presence. However, Ps 40 contains the record of God's answer to David's prayer, which included His promise to send a Deliverer for him (Sailhamer, *NIV Compact Bible Commentary*, 323).

Psalm 40: Deliverance and Distress

On the heading of this **Psalm of David**, see the comments on the headings to Pss 3 and 4.

This psalm divides in two sections. The first contains the psalmist's thanksgiving for deliverance (vv. 1-10), and the second includes his prayer for deliverance (vv. 11-17). The prayer for deliverance is, for the most part (vv. 13-17), repeated in Ps 70. The structure of the psalm may seem inverted. Some have maintained that David should have first prayed for deliverance and then praised God for providing it. However, this psalm more likely begins with David remembering a past deliverance (vv. 1-10) as the basis for praying for the same in a present difficulty that still requires God's help (vv. 11-17).

A. Praise for Deliverance (40:1-10)

40:1-5. This psalm is a joyful description of David's deliverance from the circumstances of Ps 39. The expression **the LORD . . . heard my cry** (v. 1) here signifies, as does every biblical reference to God "hearing" (or "seeing"), God's compassionate attention to human need (see the comments on Ps 34:15-18). The description of the **pit of destruction** (v. 2) is likely figurative for the problems David faced, in much the same way that contemporary believers would use this expression in a song. God's deliverance gave David a **new song . . . of praise** (v. 3; see comments on a **new song** at 33:1-3), which should motivate many to **trust in the LORD** (cf. 33:3; 96:1; 98:1; 144:9; 149:1).

The song of praise then expresses a general principle: **How blessed is the man who has made the LORD his trust** (v. 4). Then David identified his own deliverance with those **wonders** God has done for His people in the past and will do in the future (v. 5).

40:6-8. Having mentioned the wonder of God's deliverance, David remembered what was written **in the scroll of the book** about the future Deliverer (vv. 6-8). Quoting what that Deliverer would say, David used the first person, in the voice of the Deliverer, referring to the book of the **Law** (Torah). The message of the Torah was not to emphasize its many sacrifices but that God actually desired Israel's service, as seen in the slave who had his own ear pierced to demonstrate his willing service to his master (Ex 21:6). Thus, the Hebrew text says, "ears you have *dug out* for me" (not **opened** as in the NASB, though the translator's notes for Ps 40:6 indicate lit., "dug," or possibly "pierced").

The LXX of vv. 6-8, is cited in Heb 10:5-10 as the direct utterance of the Messiah ("when He comes into the world, He says . . ."; v. 5) with exclusive application to the culminating work of His first advent in the offering of Himself as "one sacrifice for sins for all time" (Heb 10:12). By saying that God has **not desired** a **sacrifice** or **required** a **burnt offering and sin offering** (v. 6), the Messiah was not repudiating the unchanging divine requirement of substitutionary (life-for-life) atonement. Instead He was affirming that (1) when sacrifice is offered, it must be accompanied by the right heart attitude (faith-filled contrition, delight, and gratitude) or else it means nothing (see Ps 51:16-19), and (2) the animal sacrifices never in fact satisfied God's requirement for sin, "for it is impossible for the blood of bulls and goats to take away sins" (Heb 10:4). Only the one sacrifice that was qualified by the spiritual purity (i.e., a soul untainted by sin and depravity) to do so—that of Messiah Jesus Himself—was an acceptable sacrifice. Once this sacrifice was made—and vindicated through Jesus' resurrection (Rm 1:4)—God required no other sacrifice from humans but their faith in His Son and spiritual service (Rm 12:1). Further, Heb 10:5 also quotes the LXX translation "a body You have prepared for Me." This is a paraphrastic translation of the Hebrew "my ears you have dug" (v. 6). The LXX's wording is an acceptable translation in that both LXX and the Hebrew are speaking of the Messiah's complete devotion to serving God.

40:9-10. Having anticipated the coming of the future Deliverer, the psalm returns to celebrating the **glad tidings** of God's deliverance (v. 9; cf. 35:17-18). His message was about God's **lovingkindness** and **truth**.

B. Prayer for Deliverance (40:11-17)

40:11-12. Here a shift occurs from praise to urgent supplication: **You, O Lord, will not withhold Your compassion from me** (v. 11). David's need was great because of his own **iniquities** (v. 12; cf. 25:17-18; 38:2-14).

40:13-17. David implored God to intervene: **Be pleased, O Lord, to deliver me; make haste . . . to help me** (v. 13; cf. Ps 38:22). He then specified what he would like the Lord to do to his enemies, that they would **be ashamed and humiliated . . . be turned back and dishonored** . . . and **be appalled** in **shame** (vv. 14-15). On the other hand, for the righteous he asked God, **Let all who seek You rejoice**. Finally he expressed his overall goal in every circumstance: **the Lord be magnified!** (v. 16; cf. 35:27; 70:4).

Psalm 41: A Meditation on God's Grace

On the heading of this **Psalm of David**, see the comments on the headings to Pss 3 and 4. Ps 40 contains David's plea for deliverance and help. In Ps 41 the ancient editor of the book of Psalms concludes the first "book" (the first major division of Psalms, Pss 1–41) with a psalm emphasizing David's unfailing trust in God for deliverance. Because God is faithful to His Word, David could rely on Him (Sailhamer, *NIV Compact Bible Commentary*, 323).

A. Individual Blessing of God's Grace (41:1-3)

41:1-3. With the opening words of v. 1, **How blessed is he** . . . , Book One of Psalms concludes in the same way it began—with explicit reference to individual blessing (see comments on Ps 1:1). The blessings of Ps 1 are also tied to Ps 2:12 and the theme of finding refuge in the Son. The intentional "bookending" of this key phrase both there and here serves not only to emphasize the motif of individual blessing, but also to clarify that the concept of worship that leads to individual blessing, as introduced in Ps 1, includes, among other things, the specific demonstration of compassion and grace (per 41:1, **he who considers the helpless**). In other words, the worship resulting in personal blessing (Ps 1) should include acts of compassion and grace (Ps 41). Worship should be expressed in obedience to the second greatest commandment ("You shall love your neighbor as yourself," Mt 22:39; cf. Lv 19:18), which follows the first commandment, to "love the Lord your God with all your heart, and with all your soul, and with all your mind" (Mt 22:37; cf. Dt 6:4-5).

B. Individual Need for God's Grace (41:4-9)

41:4-9. David asked that God would show him grace: **As for me, I said, "O Lord, be gracious to me . . . for I have sinned against You."** To persist in expressing worship (and experiencing blessing) in showing compassion and grace toward others, believers must persist in affirming the expression of God's compassion and grace toward them. The focus here is on the individual believer's continuing need for God's compassion and grace. Specifically this includes God's grace in healing his **soul** when he has **sinned** (v. 4), that is, God's responding to sin with fatherly correction intended to lead the believer to repentance and restoration to a healthy, growing walk (life) in godliness (see Pr 3:11-12; Heb 4:4-17, and comments there). God's compassion and grace is also seen in relieving the believer of emotional distress when he is persecuted for living a godly life, whether by those **who hate** him (v. 7) or a **close friend** whom he **trusted** (v. 9). The Lord Jesus applied this passage to His own experience at His final Passover (the Last Supper) when he spoke of Judas Iscariot's betrayal (Jn 13:18).

C. Individual Encouragement from God's Grace (41:10-13)

41:10-13. David asked for grace again: **O Lord, be gracious to me and raise me up** (e.g., 4:1; 6:2;

25:16; 57:1). The experience of God's grace brings with it an inseparable encouragement. In this case, being delivered from his **enemy** was evidence that God had upheld him **in** his **integrity** (vv. 11-12a). God **set** him (better translated, "have set," per the Hebrew verb in past tense) **in** His **presence forever** (v. 12b). The righteous will someday see God face to face and enjoy Him forever, but until that time fellowship with the Lord is possible on a daily basis through knowing the Scriptures and walking with Him in obedience. David began with a focus on the Lord's gracious blessing on him, and concluded with a doxology by emphasizing the importance of a believer's never-ending lifestyle of blessing God: **Blessed be the LORD, the God of Israel, from everlasting to everlasting** (v. 13; cf. 106:48). The final words **Amen and Amen** ("so be it," "truly") conclude four of the books of the Psalms (cf. 72:18-19; 89:52; 106:48).

II. Book Two: Responding in Worship to God's Protective Nurture (Pss 42–72)

Psalm 42: Longing for God's Care

Psalms 42 and 43 constitute one cohesive thought, as indicated by (1) their use of the same refrain (42:5, 11; 43:5); (2) their focus on the same theme (longing for God's fatherly protection and nurturing); (3) their clear structural division, when taken together, into three parts (42:1-5; 42:6-11; 43:1-5) consistent with the typically attested psalmic structure; (4) their being treated together as a single unit in early rabbinic sources and presented as such in most Hebrew manuscripts and printed Hebrew editions of the psalms; and (5) their being recited as a single unit in long-standing eastern (Sephardic) Jewish tradition on the Feast of Booths (which likewise commemorates God's nurturing of the Israelites). Consistent with its placement at the beginning of the second of the five "books" of Psalms, this psalm focuses on and hence introduces the main theme of Book Two: God's fatherly care, both material and spiritual. This is parallel to the second book of the Pentateuch (Exodus) with the same theme.

This psalm is described as a **Maskil** (see introduction to Ps 32 and Introduction: Genre) and attributed to **the sons of Korah** (see Introduction: Author). They were the Levites who were faithful to the Lord and were not "swallowed up" by the earth for rebelling against Moses as their father was along with some 250 other men (Nm 26:10-11; see also Nm 16:1-40). From the days of David onward, they were among the Leitical singers in the temple (see 1Ch 6:22-28, 31; 2Ch 20:19).

A. Depth of Yearning for the Lord (42:1-5)

42:1-5. The focus of this psalm is yearning for the Lord: **As the deer pants** (lit., "longs for") **water . . . so my soul** longs **for You, O God**. This image of a thirsty deer illustrates the urgency of the psalmist's craving for God, which is essential to life, just as water is to the deer. The psalmist's specific comparison of **the deer** to **my soul** (rather than the more general "to me") also indicates God's nurture extends not merely to physical needs but more significantly to spiritual needs (cf. **my soul** vv. 2a, 4a, 5a, 6a, 11a). The phrase **the living God** links to Israel's encounter with the Lord at the fiery mountain when God made Himself known in a powerful, personal way (Ex 19:16, 18; 20:18-21; cf. Dt. 5:5, 25-26). In his time of need, the psalmist recalled his struggle and said, **My tears have been my food day and night**, as he constantly prayed. The wording in v. 4 (**procession**, **thanksgiving**, **keeping festival**) is suggestive of the Feast of Booths, which was one of Israel's three pilgrimage festivals (the other two being Passover and Pentecost) and was specifically intended as a time of thanksgiving for God's protective care of the Israelites during their 40-year sojourn in the desert (Lv 23:34-43).

B. Deep Need for the Lord (42:6-11)

42:6-7. The psalmist portrayed the depth of his need for and trust in God's nurture by asking "Why are you in despair?" (v. 5) rather than trusting in the Lord. He reminded himself, "Hope in God, for I shall again praise Him" (v. 5). No matter where he was in Israel—whether at its eastern border in **the land of the Jordan** or in its northern reaches among **the peaks of Hermon** (a mountain containing three peaks, one of which is **Mount Mizar**)—he would **remember** (i.e., "call to mind," or "invoke") the Lord (v. 6). The psalmist noted that **deep calls to deep at the sound of** God's **waterfalls . . . and** His **waves ha[d] rolled over** him, expressions that carry through the theme of the Lord quenching the psalmist's spiritual thirst through His abundant water supply (v. 7). This image captures the **waterfalls** from the Hermon mountain range, as well as the **waves** of the Jordan River.

42:8. The psalmist was confident of God's fatherly protection and care. His statement that **the LORD will command** (send forth His love, like a military messenger to do His will) **His lovingkindness** to care for him indicates the psalmist's confidence (see comments on Ps 5:7). Furthermore, the Lord's care is continual, **in the daytime . . . in the night.**

42:9-11. Despite his expression of confidence in God, David openly admitted his struggles and asked: **Why have You forgotten me? Why do I go mourning because of the oppression of the enemy?** David realized his circumstances were causing his enemies (those who do not know the Lord) to mock: **Where is your God?** (see comments on Ps 6). Ultimately the psalm ends with David's admonition/encouragement to himself: **Hope in God**, despite any circumstances, **for I shall yet praise Him**. He identified the Lord as **the help of** his **countenance and** his **God.**

Psalm 43: The Goal of God's Nurture

For evidence that Ps 43 should be read as part of a single unit with Ps 42, see the introductory comments to Ps 42. There is an implicit allusion to personal guilt in David that caused God to seemingly but not actually reject him (43:2).

43:1-2. After expressing his hope in the Lord (42:11), the psalmist opened this psalm with an appeal to God's protective care in order to **vindicate** him and **plead** his **case** (as in Ps 35:1; see the comment there). The request was that he be delivered from an **ungodly nation . . . the deceitful and unjust man** (v. 1). David's **enem[ies]** here are the Gentile nations and their people who are **oppress[ing]** him (v. 2).

43:3-5. The further appeal to God to **send out** His **light and** His **truth** underscores the comprehensive vitality of God's care (v. 3). **Light** is what God created first for humanity's specific benefit and is a symbol of God's overall redemptive provision (see Pss 27:1; 36:9; Gn 1:3-4; also see comments there), whereas **truth** refers specifically to God's moral provision and absolute holiness (the necessary revelation for godly living). These provisions, of following the Lord's **light** and **truth**, will **bring** the psalmist and those of like mind to God's **holy hill** (i.e., the Temple Mount, see comment on Ps 2:6), which is the **dwelling** place of God's glory (v. 3; cf. 1Kg 8:27-30; Ezk 43:7). The goal of God's provision is to lead believers permanently into His presence and to the **joy[ful] praise** of their **God** (v. 4). The concluding verse is a refrain of Ps 42:11 (see comments there).

Psalm 44: A Prayer for Divine Deliverance by Reviewing Israel's History

On the heading of this **Maskil of the sons of Korah**, see comments on the headings to Pss 3, 32, and 42.

In the previous psalm, there is an implicit allusion to personal guilt in David that caused God to seemingly but not actually reject him (43:2). Psalm 44 deals with guilt and its consequences, even when it is not clearly visible (see especially vv. 9-19; Sailhamer, *NIV Compact Bible Commentary*, 324).

A. Affirming God's Proven Record (44:1-8)

44:1-3. The psalmist's words are directed to the Lord, but they remind his readers of Israel's history: **O God, we have heard with our ears, our fathers have told us the work that You did in their days, in the days of old** (v. 1). The psalmist affirmed that the **fathers** of his generation **have told** them (their children) about **the work that** God did throughout the history of the nation of Israel (e.g., Ex 10:2; 12:14-27; 42; Dt 32:7; Est 9:23-32). The subsequent verses review God's past victories and miracles by which God delivered Israel, provided for them, and established them in the land of Canaan. God **drove out the nations** and then **planted** his people there instead. He **spread them** throughout the promised land (v. 2). This was not accomplished by the might of the people of Israel, not **by their own sword**, but by God's **right hand and** His **arm and the light of** His **presence**—phrases closely linked to Israel's exodus from Egypt (v. 3; cf. Ex 6:6; 3:20; 7:5; Jos 24:13). God did deliver Israel by (1) His **right hand and** His **arm** (synonyms denoting His majestic and redemptive power; cf. Ps 77:15; Ex 15:6, 16; Is 53:1), (2) **the light of** His **presence** (signifying privileged position, i.e., relationship, as the recipient of God's salvation and love; cf. Jn 1:4-13; 3:19-21; 1Jn 2:8; and comments on Pss 11:7b; 13:1; 41:12), and (3) God's favor (i.e., His unconditional, love-motivated, and merciful blessing, as in, e.g., Ps 85:1; cf. Dt 7:8; 33:11a, 23-24).

44:4-8. The declaration of God as **King** is followed by a request for **victories for Jacob** (the people of Israel; v. 4; cf. 14:7 and comments there). The psalmist declared that Israel will succeed (**push back our adversaries**) only through God's work in and through them (v. 5). Therefore, he said, **I will not trust in my bow, nor will my sword save me** (v. 6; cf. 20:7), as God alone will grant victory. He affirmed that God had **saved** them; the Lord had answered his request, so **in God** they had **boasted all day long** (vv. 7-8; cf. 5:11).

B. Expressing One's Present Need (44:9-22)

44:9-10. The statement **You have rejected us** (v. 9; 60:1), expresses the psalmist's feelings at that time, in the midst of Israel's distressing situation, and is not a statement of actual fact (which would contradict a host of other biblical passages; cf. Lv 26:44; Is 49:15; Jr 31:35-37).

44:11-16. God had **scattered** his people **among the nations** (v. 11). This is the same wording in the Pentateuch (see Lv 26:33), where God warned the Israelites of the correction He would bring on them for their disobedience (cf. Lv 26:22; Dt 28:36-37). This statement suggests a situation in which Israel had begun to be taken into exile—though not completely, since they were still struggling to push back their adversaries (Ps 44:5). The conquest and deportation of the people in the northern kingdom of Israel took place under the Assyrian king Sargon II, and this threatened the southern kingdom of Judah under Sargon's successor Sennacherib. That this is the situation of which the psalmist here lamented is further suggested by the parallel wording in v. 16a (**because of the voice of him who reproaches and reviles**) and God's description of Sennacherib (cf. Is 37:23).

44:17-19. The psalmist affirmed **but we have not forgotten**; the people were faithful to God's **covenant** (the Mosaic covenant; v. 17). Therefore he considered the alternate possibility that the distressing situation facing His people was not intended as correction, but rather as an occasion for testing, or refinement, as in the case of Job. Saying **our steps have not deviated from Your way** (v. 18) is closely parallel to that of Job in defending his own integrity (cf. Jb 31:5-7)

44:20-22. This perspective of refinement rather than correction is underscored: **But for Your sake we are killed all day long** (v. 22). They were suffering, although they **had** not **forgotten the name of** their **God** (v. 20; cf. 23:3 and comments there). This is applied elsewhere in Scripture to the believer's temporal (i.e., this-worldly) experience of "tribulation, or distress, or persecution, or famine, or nakedness, or peril, or sword" (Rm 8:35-36) and counterbalanced by the eternally grounded belief that "in all these things we overwhelmingly conquer through Him who loved us" (Rm 8:37).

C. Appealing to God's Lovingkindness (44:23-26)

44:23-26. Just as the idea of God "rejecting" His people (v. 9) is an emotional question, here is a clearly figurative expression: **why do You sleep, O Lord?** (v. 23)—for the Lord who keeps Israel "will neither slumber nor sleep" (Ps 121:4; cf. Is 27:3). Whether the distress experienced by the psalmist and his people is intended as correction or refinement—or a mixture of both—their relationship with God is a reality, grounded not in Israel's obedience but in the Lord's faithful love, or **lovingkindness** (cf. comments on Ps 5:7). Hence the psalmist appealed **for the sake of** (i.e., to maintain the integrity of) the Lord's **lovingkindness**, and not his or his people's own comfort or reputation (v. 26; cf. 3:7; 6:4; 25:22). This call for deliverance is answered in Ps 45 with the promise of a coming divine King who will bring about this salvation (Sailhamer, *NIV Compact Bible Commentary*, 324).

Psalm 45: Affirming the Precedence of God the Son

On the heading of this **Maskil of the sons of Korah**, see the comments on the headings to Pss 3, 4, 32, and 42. The concise instruction **according to the Shoshannim** ("Lilies") likely designates the melody of this psalm (see introductory comments to Ps 60; cf. headings of Pss 69 and 80). It is **A Song of Love** in celebration of the king's marriage. This and other psalms indicated as *songs* were to be sung, and some included additional musical direction (see the comments on songs under Introduction: Types of Psalms). Some have proposed that the psalm describes David's marriage, perhaps to Michal, or Maacah of Geshur, or even to Bathsheba. But David was not king when he married Michal nor was he over all Israel when he married Maacah; and Bathsheba was not of a royal family (as v. 9 requires). Others have proposed Solomon as the kingly groom at his marriage to an Egyptian princess. But this is unlikely for three reasons: (1) this king was a warrior (vv. 3, 5) and Solomon was not; (2) none of Solomon's sons were made princes over the whole earth (v. 16); and (3) Solomon's marriages to pagan princesses would not have found the approval that this wedding does (cf. 1Kg 11:1-13).

It is far better to take the wedding described in the psalm as symbolic. The wedding is not that of the Davidic king but rather that of the Son of God (the "bridegroom") and His people (the "bride"). According to Walter C. Kaiser, Jr., there are four reasons that this psalm refers to the Messiah: (1) this is a *divine ruler*, addressed directly as "O God" (v. 6); (2) the king has an *eternal kingdom* (v. 6); (3) the king is a divinely *anointed ruler* (v. 7); and (4) the king is a *righteous ruler* (v. 6) (Walter C. Kaiser Jr., *The Messiah in the Old Testament* [Grand Rapids, MI: Zondervan, 1995], 128–29).

A. His Precedence Affirmed by His Role as the Bridegroom (45:1-9)

45:1-2. This psalm indicates its subject: **I address my verses to the King** (v. 1). Although some suggest this is addressed to David or Solomon, the identity of the king as shown above can only refer to the divine King, the Son of God, as seen in the content of the psalm.

45:3-5. The description of the king as **Mighty One**, riding in **splendor** and **majesty** (v. 3; cf. 21:5 comments) for the **cause of truth and meekness and righteousness** and doing **awesome things** (v. 4) are all terms often used to describe the Lord. The psalmist affirmed that the divine King is "fairer" than anyone else (v. 2; cf. Ps 27:4 and see comment there). He will one day be affirmed by all (Is 33:17), in marked contrast to the initial assessment of His people (Is 53:2). "Grace is poured upon [lit., "by"] Your lips" (v. 2), that is, His speech is imbued with grace and purity throughout (see the similar wording in Pr 22:11, as well as the clear application of this concept in Lk 4:22 to Jesus and His speech).

Calling the king the **Mighty One** (lit., "hero," "valiant warrior") ascribes to Him an important divine messianic title, also employed in Ps 24:8 (see comment there) and Is 9:6. And He is clothed in **splendor** and **majesty** (see Ps 110:3 and comment there). He is further qualified by the messianic combination of **truth** (cf. Jn 1:14), **meekness** (i.e., nonarrogance; cf. Zch 9:9), and **righteousness** (v. 4; cf. Is 9:7). Also attributed to Him are the exclusively messianic attributes of receiving the obedience of **the peoples** (v. 5; i.e., all human ethnic groups, as in Gn 49:10, an allusion strengthened by the reference to the royal scepter in v. 6b) and reigning forever (v. 6a; see 2Sm 7:13; Lk 1:33; cf. Rev. 5:9-10).

45:6-7. This previous section accordingly focused on the preeminence of the divine King to all others—whether men or angels—which is precisely the intended point in Heb 1:8-9, where the culminating thought of this section, in Ps 45:6-7, is cited. The phrase **Your throne, O God** is the key and indicates that the King who is being addressed is God. While it might be possible to understand v. 6 in the sense "Your throne is divine" or "God is your throne," the traditional understanding (**Your throne, O God**) is best for several reasons. Both in the verses before and after v. 6, the second person "you" predominates, and those uses refer to the King (see v. 1). When the King is referred to in v. 6 as being upon His throne, He is then called "God," suggesting that this King is divine. Then, in v. 7b, when God is clearly referred to, the psalmist uses the third person (**Your God** [He]**, has anointed You**), thus distinguishing God from the (divine) King. In v. 7, the phrase **God, Your God** is instructive after the use of **God** in v. 6. While the King may be divine, He must not forget that God is still His God. Implicit here is a distinction between the divine King Messiah and the divine Father.

One might object that no monotheistic Jewish poet would ever use "God" in the full sense of the word for a king of Israel. But the psalmist could speak of this King's "splendor" and "majesty" (45:3) as well as God's magnificence and grandeur (96:6; the same words are used in both passages). Likewise, the psalmist could speak of the King's proclivity to support "truth" and "righteousness" (45:4, 6) as well as God's same activity (33:5; 99:4; Is 61:8); the King's ability to judge uprightly (Ps 45:6b) as well as God's ability to do the same (67:4; 99:4); and this King has a throne that is eternal (45:6), just as God does (10:16; 93:2; 145:13). It seems reasonable that the king who is extolled in Ps 45 might be *the* Davidic King, presented in Ps 45 as divine.

45:8-9. The king is symbolically depicted as experiencing a glorious wedding day, attended by **noble ladies** and a **queen in gold** at His right hand. This is not the wedding of Solomon but a symbolic picture of the greater Son of David, the Messiah, when He unites with His faithful people, as a groom with a bride, at the future messianic banquet (cf. Is 25:6-8; 54:4-5).

B. His Precedence Affirmed by the Response of the Bride (45:10-15)

45:10-15. If the king in this psalm is the Son of God, the Messiah, then the bride described in this section can only be His people, redeemed Israel. It finds a parallel with the depiction elsewhere in the OT of national Israel as the wife of the Lord (see Hs 2:19-20; Is 54:5). This is a royal bride, dressed in gold, as a royal priesthood (Ex 19:5-6). She must cut ties with her past (v. 10) and **bow down to** her King, the **Lord**. She will then be privileged to **enter into the King's palace** (v. 15, the word typically designating the sanctuary—the place of God's eternal throne; see Ezk 43:7 and comments on Ps 11:4-7a).

C. His Precedence Affirmed by the Position of His Children (45:16-17)

45:16-17. Continuing (and slightly mixing) the metaphor, the psalmist concluded by focusing on the eternal testimony to God's redemptive glory, namely, the **sons**, or "children" of the messianic King (i.e., His people, believers). As a result of the King's sacrificial-atoning work, they will be brought into relationship with Him (cf. Is 53:10; Rm 8:16) and partake of His royal status as **princes** (as well as priests; see 1Pt 2:9 and comment on Ps 110:4). The psalmist then affirmed that **the peoples will give You thanks** [lit., "praise You"] **forever** (v. 17). This employs the same phraseology Jacob gave in his messianic blessing on Judah and his seed (Gn 49:8-12): "Your brothers shall praise You . . . and to him shall be the obedience of the peoples" (vv. 8, 10). When Israel comes to know the divine King, so also will the nations share in the messianic blessing (Gn 12:3b; 22:18).

Psalm 46: A Meditation on Divine Refuge

On the heading of this **Psalm of the sons of Korah . . . A Song**, see comments on the headings to Pss 3, 4, and 42. This and other psalms indicated as *songs* were to be sung and some included additional musical direction (see comments on songs under Introduction: Types of Psalms). The musical instruction, **set to Alamoth** (lit., "maidens"), likely refers to the melody of the psalm (cf. 1Ch 15:20). The description of the divine King who will rescue Israel (Ps 45) is followed by this psalm that describes the King's city, Jerusalem, when He comes (Sailhamer, *NIV Compact Bible Commentary*, 325).

A. Permanence of Divine Refuge (46:1-3)

46:1-3. The depth of God's concern as the **refuge** and **strength** of Israel is stressed by the description of Him as being **a very present** [i.e., always available] **help in trouble**. The permanence and inviolability of God as Israel's **help** is certain (v. 1). Nothing can happen, **though the earth should change**—due to earthquakes, avalanches, raging **waters, quak[ing] mountains**, or any other natural disaster, with all the chaos and emotional turmoil brought about by such disasters, that will ever keep the Lord from being the refuge of Israel (vv. 2-3).

B. Accessibility of Divine Refuge (46:4-7)

46:4-7. The imagery in this section turns to the hope of intimate accessibility to God's presence in the future, when the Messiah reigns from Jerusalem, **the city of God**, when He establishes His throne in Zion (Ezk 43:7) and ultimately remakes all creation in purity and at rest in Him (Rv 21:1-5) The **river whose streams** [or "divisions"] **make glad . . . the holy dwelling places** (i.e., the temple compound and all its compartments, as in Ps 43:3) **of the Most High** (Ps 46:4) parallels both the phraseology and specific concepts surrounding, first, the garden of Eden. Eden is described as having "a river" that "flowed out" of it and was "divided" where there was communion with God's "presence" (Gn 2:10; 3:8). Second, also similar to Eden is the reestablishment of God's presence through the divine King in the most holy place (v. 5), where He will dwell among the sons of Israel and at which time a river will open up just below the altar and bring the gladness of life and healing to all along its course making alive even the Dead Sea (Ezk 43:1-12; cf. Is 35:1). And third, when creation is renewed it will be God's holy tabernacle where people will commune with **the God of Jacob**. (v. 7; cf. Rv 21:3, 22; 22:1-2).

C. Comfort of Divine Refuge (46:8-11)

46:8-11. The psalmist closed this psalm with words of encouragement to **behold the works of the LORD** (v. 8), referring specifically to His works of redemption on behalf of Israel (66:5-6). In these closing words of comfort God also included a challenge: to **cease striving** [lit., "cease," "relax"] **and know that I am God** (v. 10). Here the verb **know** signifies experiential knowledge (see the comment on Ps 1:6). The believer is commanded to cease worrying when faced with problems, persecution, and circumstances; instead the command is to remember that **the LORD of hosts is with us; the God of Jacob is our stronghold** (v. 11; also v. 7).

Psalm 47: A Public Praise of the Divine King

On the heading of this **Psalm of the sons of Korah**, see comments on the headings to Pss 3, 4, and 42. Thematically and structurally Pss 47 and 48 are closely linked. Both psalms concern divine kingship, already introduced in Pss 45 and 46, with Ps 47 focusing on the person of the divine King, and Ps 48 focusing on the city of the divine King. In both psalms the same three aspects of the person (Ps. 47) and the city (Ps. 48) are considered, reinforcing each other by their chiastic organization: challenge—praise—preeminence; preeminence—praise—challenge.

A. Challenge of the Divine King (47:1-4)

47:1-4. The psalmist began by addressing **all** the **peoples**, so that the nations of the earth are called to **joy[ful]** worship (the plural **peoples** signifying distinct religio-ethnic groups; v. 1; see comments on Ps 45:17) with the challenge of affirming the sovereign reign of the true "God of Abraham" (cf. v. 9). Clapping the **hands** and the verb translated **shout** in v. 1 are elsewhere employed in Scripture in connection with the crowning and recognition of a king (1Sm 10:24; 2Kg 11:12). The expression **Most High** is one of the many biblical titles of God and underscores His supreme greatness and transcendence over all creation (v. 2; cf. Dt 28:1; Ps 83:18). Hence this affirms His prerogative to (1) choose Israel's **inheritance**—i.e., the promised land of Canaan (see Gn 13:15; 17:8; Pss 105:11; 135:12), despite the claims of anyone else there, and (2) bestow His irrevocable love by sovereign grace on **Jacob** (Israel, the Jewish people; v. 4; cf. Ps 105:8-10; Rm 9:11-13; 11:29).

B. Praise of the Divine King (47:5-7)

47:5-7. In his exuberance of praise, the psalmist described God as having **ascended with a shout** (the same root as in v. 1, specifically affirming God's kingship; v. 5; cf. 1Kg 10:19; 1Ch 28:5). On the expression **skillful psalm** (*maskil*), see introduction to Ps 32.

C. Preeminence of the Divine King (47:8-9)

47:8-9. In this concluding section the psalmist looked forward to that future time when the whole world will recognize **God reigns over the nations** (v. 8; cf. comments 10:16). The willing submission of all humanity to God's preeminent kingship is underscored by **the princes of the people**; the Hebrew term translated **princes** literally signifies "willing ones" or "volunteers" and derives from the same root as the term "freewill offerings" used to describe Messiah's people (i.e., the same group as here) in Ps 110:3. All will worship **the God of Abraham** (v. 9; cf. Gn 12:2-3; Ex 3:6; Mt 22:32).

Psalm 48: A Praise for Zion, the City of the Divine King

On the heading of this **Song . . . a Psalm of the sons of Korah**, see comments on the headings to Pss 3 and 42, and 46. Thematically and structurally it is closely linked to Ps 47 (see introduction there). During the period of the second temple (c. 530 BC–AD 70) this psalm was recited by the Levites in the temple during the daylight hours of the Sabbath (*m. Tamid* 7.4).

A. Preeminence of Zion (48:1-8)

48:1-8. The preeminence of **Zion** (another name for Jerusalem) among all places in creation is tied to its being **the city of our God**, who is the preeminent King. More precisely, the preeminence of Zion derives from **His** [God's] **holy mountain** (vv. 1-2). This mountain is Mount Moriah, the temple mount (see 2Ch 3:1), where God's tangible presence dwelt historically and where the throne of His physical presence will once again be established for all eternity (see comments on Pss 2:6; 46:4-7). Here on Mount Moriah, the earthly focal point of His gracious provision, God **has made Himself known** (v. 3; see comments on 1:6 and 46:10). As in the last section of the previous psalm, the psalmist concluded this parallel section with a look forward to that time when **God will establish** Zion **forever** (v. 8) as the universally recognized seat of His rule over creation.

B. Praise of Zion (48:9-11)

48:9-11. Those who worship God **have thought on** (or "pondered," "contemplated") **[His] lovingkindness** (Hb. *chesed*; see comment on Ps 5:7), on Mount Zion, **in the midst of [His] temple** (v. 9). The reference to the **name** of **God** concerns His reputation. As His reputation is known throughout the whole earth, so His **praise** will be **to the ends of the earth** (v. 10). The idea of **Zion be glad**, described here, is the praise of the residents of Zion directed to their divine King. Specifically, as described by the psalmist, this is the praise expressed by all (v. 11).

C. Challenge of Zion (48:12-14)

48:12-14. The psalm concludes with a command to **walk about Zion . . . count her towers** and **consider her ramparts.** This would involve a worship procession, reflecting on the actual structures of Jerusalem as God's chosen beloved city (v. 2; Pss 14; 87:2-3; 102; 1Kg 11:13, 32-36; Is 24:23). They are to consider how this city was established by a fledgling people as the capital of their fledgling nation (under Joshua and later David); how it was maintained intact against much larger and more powerful forces (such as the Arameans and Assyrians ; cf. Is 7:1-2; 37:36); and how, after the dramatic exile of its inhabitants as an expression of divine chastisement, it was again reestablished as Israel's capital city against overwhelming odds (Neh 6:15-16). This observation of Jerusalem should not be limited to personal worship and reflection, but it should be told **to the next generation** (v. 13). Each generation is to do this and pass their knowledge of the Lord on to the next generation, **for such is God, our God forever and ever**. Because of His faithful love **He will guide us until death** (lit., "over death"; v. 14).

Psalm 49: Affirming God's Grace as the Redeemer

On the heading of this **Psalm of the sons of Korah**, see comments on the headings to Pss 3, 4, and 42. Psalm 48 concluded with God's care for His own even to the point of death. This psalm extends that care beyond death (Sailhamer, *NIV Compact Bible Commentary*, 325).

A. Man's Inability to Redeem Himself Spiritually (49:1-9)

49:1-4. This beginning exhortation of the opening words **hear this** emphasized the importance of paying attention to what was to follow (vv. 1-2), described by the overlapping terms **wisdom**, **meditation**, **proverb**, and **riddle** (vv. 3-4; cf. Pr 1:6).

49:5-9. This section is one of the most concise biblical declarations of the human dilemma: **Why should I fear in days of adversity?** God alone is eternal and sovereign, whereas even those with **abundance of their riches** cannot **live on eternally** (vv. 5-6, 9). Everyone needs to be redeemed from eternal and spiritual death (cf. Ec 7:20; Ezk 18:4; Dn 12:2; Rm 3:23; 6:23), but also no one is able to pay his own soul's **redemption** (v. 8; or "redemption price," elsewhere used only in Ex 21:30 and in parallel to "ransom") much less that of someone else (v. 7). Since this dilemma is universal, then the solution must be divine.

B. Man's Inability to Redeem Himself Physically (49:10-14)

49:10-14. Not only are riches useless, even **wise men die**, along with the **stupid and the senseless** (v. 10). The bleakness of the human dilemma is here highlighted by focusing on **the way of those who are foolish** (v. 13), that is, those who believe that all the real property they amass in this life (i.e., **houses . . . dwelling places . . .** and **lands**) will enable **their own names** (signifying "reputation") to endure **forever** (v. 11; cf. Gn 11:1-9, esp. v. 4). In the end, **their form** (i.e., their souls / spiritual essence), and any reputation they may have, are **appointed for Sheol** (OT designation for the place to which all people, righteous or wicked, go after death; v. 14; cf. Gn 37:35; 44:29; Nm 16:30-31; Pss 9:17; 16:10; 55:15; Pr 23:14; Ezk 31:16).

C. God's Ability to Redeem Man Completely (49:15-20)

49:15. On the other hand, the psalmist commenced this last section of the psalm with the affirmation that **God will redeem my soul from the power of Sheol** (v. 15). The concept conveyed by the term *she'ol* in the OT is a complicated one, partly because both the righteous (see Jacob, Gn 37:35) and unrighteous (such as Korah and Dathan, Nm 16:30-31) go there as mentioned above. This led some early Church fathers to invent an improbable "two compartment" view of Sheol in which the wicked suffer, but the righteous reside in Abraham's bosom until Christ's resurrection when the righteous are led by Him into heaven. This unlikely view is also fueled by a misunderstanding of Lk 16:19-31; Eph 4:9-10; and 1Pt 3:19 (see comments there). The evidence is that the biblical term *she'ol* refers to the grave, where the bodies (not the souls) of all people, righteous and wicked alike, go at death. *She'ol* appears to be a synonym for another Hebrew word, *qeber*, used 71 times for "grave" (see the parallels between *she'ol* and *qeber* in Ezk 32:21-27). In Jb 17:13-16, the word *she'ol* denotes a downward place that is dusty, infested with worms, typified by decay—what one expects from a description of the grave (although disembodied souls notably are not eaten by worms nor do they rot). See also Jb 21:13. For this understanding of the term *she'ol*, see the helpful article by R. Laird Harris, "*she'ol*," in vol. 2, TWOT, ed. R. Laird Harris, Gleason L. Archer Jr., and Bruce K. Waltke (Chicago: Moody, 1980), 2:892–93.

Complicating this understanding of *she'ol* is the psalmist's confidence that God would **redeem** his **soul from the power of Sheol** (v. 15). Often when *nephesh* (the word wrongly translated in this verse as **soul**) is used as the object of a verb (here it is the object of the verb **redeem**), it refers not to one's immaterial nature (soul) but to a person's life or to the entire individual himself, soul and body (see Jos 2:13; 1Sm 19:11; 2Sm 19:6; Pss 6:4; 72:13). On this Bruce K. Waltke wrote, "Here too belongs Lev 17:11, one of the most decidedly theological and distinctively meaningful passages where the word *nephesh* is of major significance, and one which certainly defines the term as meaning life [sic] 'for the life (*nephesh*) of the flesh (*basar*) is in the blood'" ("*nephesh*," in TWOT, 2:589–90). In addition, in the advancing parallelism between v. 15a and 15b, **me** corresponds to **my soul** (*nephesh*), suggesting that **soul** refers to the psalmist's entire personhood and life, who he was both in body and soul. It is better to translate v. 15: "But God will rescue my life [or *me* (*nephesh*)] from the power of the grave [*she'ol*]." In contrast to the righteous person, who will finally be delivered from the grave at the resurrection of the righteous (see comments on 1Co 15:50-57), the wicked "will never see the light" (v. 19).

49:16-20. This section is a reminder never to worry about anyone else's better situation: **Do not be afraid when a man becomes rich**, this should not threaten or concern you, but instead trust in the Lord (cf. Pss 37 and 73; see comments there).

Psalm 50: God as the Judge of Humanity

On the heading of this **Psalm of Asaph**, see comments on the heading to Ps 3. This psalm is attributed to **Asaph** (see Introduction: Author), who was a prophet (2Ch 29:30), as demonstrated in the many first person utterances of the Lord in this psalm (e.g., vv. 5-23).

A. Introduction of the Divine Judge (50:1-6)

50:1-6. This psalm begins like an oracle, a prophetic utterance: **The Mighty One, God, the LORD, has spoken** (cf. Jos 22:22). His credentials are presented in several ways. He is the Creator: He **summoned the earth from the rising of the sun to its setting** and **summons the heavens above** (vv. 1, 4). Also, He rules **out of Zion** in magnificent power (v. 2; cf. 48:2). He is so powerful that **fire devours before Him** (v. 3), a frequent description of God's manifest power and judgment (e.g., 18:12-13; 97:3; Is 6:6-7, 13; 66:24; Zch 3:2).

B. Ruling of the Divine Judge (50:7-21)

50:7-15. This is another prophetic call: **Hear, O My people, and I will speak** (v. 7; cf. Dt 6:5). The pronouns in the phrases **My people . . . your God** (v. 7) reflect the relationship between God and His people (cf., e.g., Ex 19:3-6; Lv 19:2-4, 10, 25, 31, 34; 23:22). However, God does **testify against** (better translated "warns"; v. 7) His people Israel to be alert not only to their outward obedience, as epitomized by their **sacrifices** and **burnt offerings** (vv. 8-13), but also to their motives: **offer to God a sacrifice of thanksgiving** (v. 14a) that express gratitude and display righteousness in various areas of life (e.g., in fulfilling their vows, v. 14b). Especially prominent here is the need for His people to rely on Him (**call upon Me in the day of trouble**) and, with that attitude of utter reliance, to worship Him (**you will honor Me**; v. 15). These points are taken up again in Ps 51:13-19.

50:16-17. These words of judgment, **but to the wicked God says, "What right have you . . . ?"** (v. 16), are directed to Israelites not Gentile nations, because pagan Gentiles would not be worshipping the God of Israel. These **wicked** presumed to **tell of** God's **statutes** (a term applied elsewhere in Scripture to the law of Moses; cf. Lv 10:11; Dt 4:6) or **to take** His **covenant in** their **mouth** (i.e., to appeal to the Abrahamic covenant as granting them a special relationship with the Lord; Gn 12:1-3; cf. Mt 8:10-12; Lk 3:8), but they had no right.

Rather than loving God's instruction, they **hate discipline** and **cast** God's **words behind** them; they might give verbal assent and rote obedience to worshipping the Lord, but in actuality they reject His Word and rule (v. 17; see Ps 1:2; cf. Pr 5:12).

50:18-21. The wicked interpersonal behavior of God's wayward people demonstrates their inner moral corruption. They (1) approve of the behavior of **a thief**; (2) **associate with adulterers**; (3) speak **evil** and **deceit**; and (4) **slander** their own brother. At the same time, the wicked wrongly thought the Lord **was just like** them, making God into their image—a common error (cf. 10:3-6, 11). Instead the Lord will **reprove** them and will begin by stating **the case in order** right **before** their **eyes**, in the form of a legal indictment.

C. Final Warning of the Divine Judge (50:22-23)

50:22-23. In concluding His "ruling," God addressed both groups, asking them to **consider** His message, which combines warning, exhortation, and promise. First, there is a warning to those **who forget God** (i.e., who ignore His statutes and offer Him no true worship), **or** He **will tear** them **in pieces**, an image of judgment (cf. Ps 7:1-2, this may indicate eternal condemnation; cf. Dn 12:2). The conjunction **or** (lit., "lest") signals God's grace by giving them the possibility of escaping this fate through repentance and worship. Second, an exhortation that **He who offers a sacrifice of thanksgiving honors** God; to go through the actions of worship and sacrifice with the right motives is to offer sacrifices truly expressive of **thanksgiving** to the Lord and sparked by trust in God and the recognition of His deliverance (as in Ps 50:15). Worshiping the Lord with a pure heart will result in one **who orders his way aright**, lives a godly life. Finally, God promises to the one who does sincerely worship the Lord and lives according to His Word that He **shall show** him **the salvation of God** (cf. 1:1-3). The verb **show** (lit., "cause to see") here has the sense of "provide." It is often translated this way elsewhere, and when applied to God it always refers to His active interaction with people (or a person) to give them what is best (see comments on Ps 4:6, where the same verb is used).

Psalm 51: David Affirms God's Forgiveness

On the heading of this **Psalm of David**, see comments on the headings to Pss 3 and 4. The occasion for this psalm was **when Nathan the prophet came to** David to reprove him and prompt him to repent **after [David] had gone in to Bathsheba**, which is related in 2Sm 12.

A. Recognition of Personal Sin (51:1-6)

51:1. David's plea for God to **be gracious to** him is based on the Lord's character: **according to Your lovingkindness** and **the greatness of Your compassion** (cf. 6:4). One thing that undoubtedly qualified David as "a man after [God's] own heart" (1Sm 13:14) was not that he was sinless, but that when confronted with his sin, he sincerely confessed and repented of it, rather than excusing, diminishing, or ignoring it. Such was exactly his response when called out by Nathan on his sins of murder and adultery. His request to **blot out my transgressions** pictures forgiveness with the image of writing being removed from a papyrus scroll (cf. v. 9; 9:5; Is 43:25; Jr 18:23).

51:2-3. David's request for forgiveness is further illustrated with the images of **wash me** in terms of the removal of filth and **cleanse me** in terms of ritual purification for participation in temple worship (v. 2). Once David was confronted by Nathan, he recognized reality: **my transgressions, and my sin is ever before me** (v. 3).

51:4. The depth of David's spiritual sensitivity is clear: **Against You, You only** [Hb. "You alone"]**, I have sinned**. That is to say, "Against You, who alone (i.e., set apart, unparalleled) is the eternal and holy God, I have sinned." He was not denying that he sinned against Uriah and Bathsheba; he knew he had committed the sin of adultery and murder. Instead he is affirming the grievous nature of his sin against the Lord, as did Joseph when he refused the offer made by Potiphar's wife to sin sexually with her. Joseph asked, "How then could I do this great evil and sin against God?" (Gn 39:9). David recognized that in addition to the people against whom he had sinned, his primary sin was against the Lord, who alone is the source and standard of righteousness (cf. Ps 71:16; Ec 7:20; Jr 23:6; Rm 3:10) and who alone is the judge of all human sin (see Ps 50 and comments there).

51:5-6. By saying **I was brought forth in iniquity, and in sin my mother conceived me** (v. 5; see also Gn 8:21; Ps 58:3; Is 48:8), David did not indicate that he was conceived during some sinful act by his mother. Rather, the better understanding is that David bemoaned the possession of a sin nature, which came to him through natural generation at the moment of his conception. David contrasted his sinful nature with the Lord, who desires **truth in the innermost being**. Therefore David desired **in the hidden part** for God to **make** him **know wisdom** (v. 6; cf. 37:30-31; 139:13-16).

B. Request for God's Mercy (51:7-13)

51:7-9. Following his confession of sin, David returned to his plea for forgiveness. David implored God's mercy, which meant not giving him the death penalty he deserved for both murder and adultery (cf. Gn 9:6; Ex 21:12; Lv 20:10). David recognized that God in His justice cannot simply ignore sin, and that the penalty it requires (i.e., life) must still somehow be paid (Lv 17:11; Ps 49:7-8). So he implored God to forgive him and to **purify** him **with hyssop** (v. 7). Hyssop is an important shrub mentioned in the Bible. Jewish slaves dipped a bunch of hyssop in the blood of a slain lamb and applied some on both the lintel and doorposts of their houses prior to the Passover (Ex 12:22). Hyssop was also used in ceremonial cleansing from skin disease (Lv 14:4-7) and in making the red heifer offering (Nm 19:6). Thus, the symbolism of hyssop portrayed spiritual cleansing. The request to **wash me, and I shall be whiter than snow** is for complete purity (v. 7; cf. Is 1:18). To **hide Your face from my sins** is parallel to **blot out all my iniquities** (v. 9; cf. v. 1), or in other words, remove my sins from before You.

51:10-11. Along with his request for the forgiveness and removal of sin, David asked that God **renew a steadfast** [lit., a "right-thinking"] **spirit within** him (v. 10; cf. v. 6). His request that God **not take** His **Holy Spirit from** him (v. 11) has often been explained as a petition by David that God not revoke his salvation. This is a misunderstanding of the work of the Holy Spirit in the OT. Under the old covenant, the Spirit would come upon individuals to enable them to do remarkable work (see, e.g., Ex 31:3; 35:31; 1Sm 11:6), but He could also depart from them (as in the case of Saul in 1Sm 16:14, after which Saul's decisions as king were consistently unwise, even though he himself was still "saved"; cf. 1Sm 28:19). Nowhere is the Spirit promised such that He might take up permanent residence in the rank-and-file OT believer. In David's case, the Spirit came upon him so he could function skillfully as Israel's king (1Sm 16:13-14). There is every reason to believe that David was saved in an OT sense before the coming of the Spirit upon him. What David was therefore requesting was that God not take away His special empowerment through the Spirit to function wisely in the role of Israel's king. Under the new covenant after the day of Pentecost, the Holy Spirit permanently comes upon and resides in believers, never to be taken away (see Jesus' promise of this to the disciples in Jn 14:16-17; Rm 8:9, 37-39).

51:12-13. After being forgiven and restored to fellowship with the Lord, David asked to have the **joy of [God's] salvation** returned (v. 12). People identified as **transgressors** and **sinners** were Israelites who had stopped following the Lord. David wanted to **teach [them God's] ways** (cf. 25:4). For the sinner to be **converted** (lit., "turned back" or "turned around," the most frequently used OT term for turning to the Lord) **to You** does not mean a change in ethnic identity, but to turn away from sin and toward the Lord; to have a change of heart/mind about one's behavior and henceforth to follow the Lord.

C. Response of Thanksgiving (51:14-19)

51:14-17. In response, David promised that if God would **deliver [Him] from bloodguiltiness**, then he would **joyfully sing** of God's **righteousness** (v. 14) and **declare** God's **praise** (v. 15). He would also bring Him "righteous sacrifices" (v. 19). David's assertion **You do not delight in sacrifice** (v. 16) does not negate the sacrificial system, but rather indicates the Lord's rejection of sacrifice offered without a proper heartfelt attitude and foundation of sincere faith (cf. 40:6). Once that foundation of right attitude is laid, the **sacrifice** becomes acceptable to God. But God finds the offering of **sacrifices** without **a broken spirit** and **a broken and a contrite heart** (v. 17) repugnant to Him (see Is 1:13-15).

51:18-19. This prayer for **Zion**, requesting to **build the walls of Jerusalem** . . . so **then young bulls will be offered on Your altar** is probably a postexilic addition to this psalm from the time of Nehemiah.

Psalm 52: The Problem of Evil in Perspective: Man's Place in Eternity

On the heading of this **Maskil of David**, see comments on the headings to Pss 3, 4, and 32. The occasion of the psalm is **when Doeg the Edomite came and told Saul . . . "David has come to the house of Ahimelech"** (see 1Sm 22:9, 22; see also 1Sm 21:7).

On the concept of theodicy, which concerns the vindication of God's justice in the face of what would seem to be His allowance and on occasion even enacting of injustice, see comments on Ps 37 (as well as Rm 9:14-29, which addresses this topic in an especially pointed fashion). In this case the seeming injustice in view is what occurred when (1) God ordained that Doeg communicate David's whereabouts, thereby placing David in greater danger and distress, followed by (2) Doeg's massacre of the priests at Nob, underscoring the seeming folly of God's withdrawing from Saul the ability to lead effectively.

On this psalm, John Sailhamer commented, "The note about Doeg is probably intended to bring David's words into the larger messianic picture of the fall of the house of Edom at the hands of the house of David (cf. Nm 24:18). It had long been an important part of the messianic hope of Israel that the Messiah's coming would be marked by the destruction of Israel's enemies, principally, the Edomites (e.g., Am 9:12; Ob 18). Edom was particularly singled out, not because its people were excessively evil, but for what was in fact a literary reason: 'Edom,' similar to the Hebrew word for humankind ('Adam'), was used in order to form a wordplay. Hence, in speaking of the defeat of Edom (v. 5), the psalmist naturally calls to mind God's judgment of all humanity" (Sailhamer, *NIV Compact Bible Commentary*, 326). While the reference is to Doeg the Edomite, he serves as an example of what will happen in the future to all humanity under the hand of David's supreme Son.

A. Identity of the Wicked (52:1-4)

52:1-4. The **mighty man** in view here is Doeg the Edomite, whose character and actions David immediately contrasted with God's own. Whereas Doeg boasted **in evil . . . the lovingkindness of God endures all day long** (i.e., even when man is sleeping, since God never does; v. 1; cf. Ps 121:4; Is 27:3; on **lovingkindness**, see comments on 5:7). David focused his description of Doeg on imagery connected with speech (v. 2, **your tongue**; v. 3, **speaking**; v. 4, **words that devour . . . deceitful tongue**) since the injustice Doeg committed was instigated by his report about David (1Sm 22:9-10). David therefore condemned what Doeg said as being **evil** (v. 3), whereas doing **good** sometimes requires saying nothing at all.

B. Final Place of the Wicked (52:5-7)

52:5-7. God's justice is ultimately vindicated in that He will one day, inevitably, **break . . . down** the wicked **and uproot** them **from the land of the living**, plus this will be their state **forever** (v. 5), that is, eternal condemnation and separation from the presence of God (see Dn 12:2; Mt 25:46). The latter (eternal separation from God)—which is unquestionably the essence of the final torment of the wicked—is signaled by David's assertion that God **will snatch**

you up and tear you away from your tent (v. 5). Though some translations, including the NASB, insert the pronoun **your** (which is not in the Hb. text) before **tent** here, more likely David was referring here to God's **tent**. God does not always "tear away" the wicked from their "tent," though He will ultimately tear down their "house," that is, their dynasty (as in Pr 15:25). Also the use of "tent" in this context parallels David's use of the same word in Ps 27:5, where it clearly refers to God's "tent" (the tabernacle), and, as in the present psalm, is paralleled by reference to God's "house" (the temple; see v. 8 and Ps 27:4).

C. Final Place of the Righteous (52:8-9)

52:8-9. Just as God's justice is ultimately vindicated by the eternal separation of the wicked from His presence, so too is it vindicated by the establishment of the righteous in His presence. Here the righteous are pictured **like a green olive tree in the house of God** (referring to the "tabernacle" of the new creation; see comments on Ps 15:1), where David will rest **in the lovingkindness of God forever** (v. 8), and **give** Him **thanks forever** in the company of His **godly ones** (i.e., the righteous, like him; cf. Ps 142:7 and see comment there).

Psalm 53: The Unchanging Anatomy of Human Folly

This **Maskil of David** repeats, with minor variations, Ps 14, apparently to emphasize the unchanging anatomy of human folly (its essence and pervasiveness). On the heading of this **Maskil of David**, see comments on the headings to Pss 3, 4, and 32. The concise instruction **according to Mahalath** probably designates the melody to which the psalm was to be sung, though the meaning of the term **Mahalath** is uncertain (suggestions include "sickness," "entreaty," or "pardon"). If Doeg the Edomite in Ps 52 stands for all humanity apart from and contrary to God and facing His judgment, this psalm continues the theme of God's universal judgment of humanity (Sailhamer, *NIV Compact Bible Commentary*, 326).

A. Essence of Human Folly (53:1a)

53:1a. See the comments on Ps 14:1a.

B. Pervasiveness of Human Folly (53:1b-5)

53:1b-4. See the comments on Ps 14:1b-6a.

53:5. The main variation from Ps 14 complements the emphasis on God's sympathy and proximity to the righteous in the structurally parallel passage in Ps 14:5-6. Both in 14:5-6 and 53:4-6, the psalmist emphasizes God's judgment and rejection of those (i.e., the Gentile nations, who in the OT are generally identified with the enemies of the true God; see the comment on Ps 2:1) **who encamped against** David's people (v. 5).

C. Antithesis of Human Folly (53:6)

53:6. See the comments on Ps 14:7.

Psalm 54: Appealing to God for Help

On the heading of this Maskil of David, see the comments on the headings to Pss 3, 4, and 32. This psalm was to be sung with the accompaniment of **stringed instruments**. The occasion for this psalm was **when the Ziphites came and said to Saul, "Is not David hiding himself among us?"** This refers to the situation introduced in 1Sm 23:19, in which the wording is identical to that in the heading of this psalm (hence not the situation introduced in 1Sm 26:1). The Ziphites were Israelite residents of Ziph (identified with the modern site of Tel Zif), a city situated in the tribal region of Judah about 25 miles south of Jerusalem (see Jos 15:55). The Ziphites are thus to be numbered among the fools mentioned in Ps 53 (Sailhamer, *NIV Compact Bible Commentary*, 326).

A. Consider Motivation (54:1-3)

54:1-3. David implored God, **Save me . . . by You name**, in which the term **name** signifies not merely the collection of labels by which God is known, but His reputation as revealed in who He is and what He does (see Gn 11:4; 12:2; Ex 3:13-16; see also comments on Pss 20:5; 23:3). David was asking God to act on His covenant love (Hb. *chesed*; see Ps 5:7) as previously affirmed and demonstrated toward him. David's motivation was driven by God's reputation ("by Your name," i.e., for His name's sake; cf. Pss 23:3; 25:11; 143:11) and not his own. David's enemies (v. 3, **violent men . . . have not set God before them**) had not sought to live their lives in the fear of God (cf. 111:10), in contrast to the righteous who "set the LORD continually before" them (Ps 16:8). By vindicating David (v. 1) God would ultimately be vindicating Himself.

B. Affirm Confidence (54:4-5)

54:4-5. David's confidence—as he affirmed so frequently throughout his psalms—was his relationship with God. Based on God's own words and promises to him David was convinced that whatever may transpire in his role as Israel's king, **God** was his **helper**. The personal intimacy of this relationship is indicated by the use here of a variant form of the same word used for Eve as Adam's wife (i.e., "a helper suitable to him"; Gn 2:18, 20) and by the additional descriptive phrase **sustainer of my soul** (v. 4; cf.

Pss 37:17, 24; 145:14). Against his **foes** David also had confidence in God's **faithfulness** to bring **recompense** on them for their **evil** deeds and ultimately to **destroy them** (v. 5).

C. Express Thanksgiving (54:6-7)

54:6-7. In closing, David reiterated his God-centered perspective. He ended this psalm (as he did so many others; e.g., Pss 7:17; 13:6; 26:11-12; 41:13) by affirming what he will do: **I will sacrifice . . . I will give thanks** to the Lord (v. 6), regardless of how and when God might resolve his present **trouble**. Despite any circumstances, ultimately God will deliver David, and he will look back **upon** his **enemies** with the knowledge that God's name has been eternally vindicated (v. 7).

Psalm 55: Finding Solace from the Persecution of "Friends"

On the heading of this **Maskil of David**, see comments on the headings to Pss 3, 4, and 32. This psalm was to be sung with the accompaniment of **stringed instruments**. Whereas Ps 54 expresses David's confidence that God would vindicate him, Ps 55 embodies a prayer for sustenance against the pressures that his opponents brought while David waited for God to act (see esp. 55:1-3).

A. Express Emotion to God (55:1-8)

55:1-5. The severity of David's situation and the depth of his desire that God resolve it is immediately evident in his four-phrase parallelism (i.e., repetition of the same thought) in vv. 1-2: (1) **give ear**, (2) **do not hide**, (3) **give heed**, and (4) **answer me**. In the ensuing verses David then described in detail the emotional and psychological torment that he was experiencing (knowing that God, his heavenly Father, the Almighty, could help him—and, indeed, that He wanted to hear his child express his need for Him), so much so that even his **heart** was **in anguish** (v. 4, lit., "trembling," as in Ps 114:7, here denoting the tremors brought on by anxiety).

55:6-8. Though the situation underlying this psalm is unspecified, a clue as to what it may have been is indicated by David's wish that he **had wings like a dove** that he might **fly away and be at rest** (v. 6; doves are prone to fly about and dwell in places inaccessible to hunters). This idea of escape recalls David's words in 1Sm 26:20, when he was cornered by Saul in the wilderness of Ziph (see the comments immediately below).

B. Implore Vindication from God (55:9-15)

55:9-11. Further suggesting that this psalm reflects the situation narrated in 1Sm 26, when Saul with his 3,000 men closed in on David with his 600 (1Sm 23:13), is the phrase **Confuse, O Lord, divide their tongues** (i.e., their ability to communicate and act efficiently against David; v. 9). Saul and his army could be stopped only by God's direct intervention (cf. 1Sm 26:12).

55:12-15. David's adversary was **not an enemy who reproaches me** (v. 12), but instead the attacks came from his **companion and** his **familiar friend** (v. 13), terms that sometimes described Saul's attitude toward David (cf. 1Sm 16:21; 18:27). On **Sheol** (v. 15), see comment on Ps 49:14-15.

C. Affirm Your Confidence in God (55:16-23)

55:16-23. Ultimately, typical of his psalms of lament and complaint, David affirmed his confidence in the Lord: **As for me, I shall call upon God, and the LORD will save me**. His confidence in speaking of his situation to the Lord, even if he had to **complain and murmur**, was continual—**evening**, **morning**, and **at noon** as well. He found solace despite his situation by affirming what he knew God would do. David did not presume on God with what he wanted Him to do, but rather relied upon what God Himself had said He will do: **He will hear my voice**. Because God is faithful to His Word, His children have every right to expect Him to do what He said He will do. And what He has promised is to deliver His children from all the distress and persecution of this world (Is 25:8; Rv 21:4), in the hereafter if not before. And until He chooses to do so, his children, like David, can **cast** their burdens **upon the LORD**, knowing that **He will sustain** them throughout and **never allow** them **to be shaken** (see comment on 15:5b, cf. 1Pt 5:7).

Psalm 56: Affirming God's Intimate Concern over You

On the heading of this **Mikhtam of David**, see the comments on the headings to Pss 3, 4, and 16. It is accompanied by the instruction, **according to Jonath elem rehokim** (lit., "The Dove of the throng [or "silent one"; cf. Ps 38:11] of the distant ones"). This most likely refers to the melody by which it was to be sung. Also the occasion for this psalm was **when the Philistines seized** David **in Gath**, (cf. 1Sm 21:11-15). David concluded Ps 55 by urging others to follow his example in relying on the Lord. Here he recounts an experience when he had to do this very thing (Sailhamer, *NIV Compact Bible Commentary*, 326).

A. Affirming God's Intimate Concern over Circumstances (56:1-7)

56:1-2. David implored God to **be gracious to** him, an expression found frequently in psalms of entreaty (e.g., Pss 4:1; 6:2; 9:13; 26:11; 30:10; 31:9; 41:4; 51:1). This request embodies those foundational convictions on which all his entreaties to God are based, including (1) the conviction of an existing relationship between him and God, (2) the conviction that he did not merit God's favor, and (3) the conviction that because of their existing relationship (and despite the lack of merit), God desired to be gracious to David, his child. The psalm uses poetic repetition to emphasize David's serious circumstances: **man** had **trampled upon** him, and he was under attack **all day long** (v. 1); his enemies **trampled upon** him **all day long** (v. 2).

56:3-7. Despite his circumstances, David said, **When I am afraid, I will put my trust in You** (v. 3; **afraid** is repeated for emphasis in vv. 4, 11). David's trust in God is based on His **word** (v. 4a). With the Lord on his side, no matter what his enemies do (**distort** his **words**, plan **evil**, **attack**, **lurk**, wait for his **life**; vv. 5-6) David is still able to ask, **what can mere man do to me?** (v. 4b).

B. Affirming God's Intimate Concern over Your Sorrow (56:8-12)

56:8-12. God was concerned not only with what was happening around David but also, and more important, with what was happening within David. Hence he affirmed that God had **taken account of** [lit., "counted"] his **wanderings**, that is, David's wanderings about Israel as he "fled ... from Saul, and went to ... Gath" (1Sm 21:10). And in one of the most poignant and picturesque examples of such in the Bible, he appealed to God's intimate concern and empathy: **Put my tears in Your bottle. Are they not in Your book?** (v. 8). This is an image of God collecting David's tears in a wineskin, indicating that God remembered his suffering. Not one tear of His child is ever shed without evoking the most heartfelt empathy and compassion of God. Jesus likewise endured sufferings and tears (Lk 19:41; Jn 11:35) so that He might sympathize with humanity in every respect and pioneer our way "to the throne of grace, so that we may receive mercy and find grace to help in time of need" (Heb 4:1-16).

C. Affirming God's Intimate Concern over Your Future (56:13)

56:13. Characteristic of David at the end of his psalms of entreaty and complaint, he looked ahead not to the hoped-for resolution of his immediate situation, but beyond it to that for which his heart truly longed: that time when he and all God's children will do what man was meant to do in Eden—to **walk** [lit., "walk about," "stroll;" the same verb as in Gn 3:8; see comments there] **before God in the light of the living** (or "life"; cf. Ps 116:9). This signifies qualitative ideal life, for which the tree of life was meant to seal man forever (see comments on Gn 3:22) and one day will (Rv 22:2). On the symbolism of **light** here, see comments on Ps 27:1.

Psalm 57: Finding Refuge in the Transcendent God

On the heading of this **Mikhtam of David**, see the comments on the headings to Pss 3, 4, and 16. This psalm is to be set to **Al-tashheth** (lit., "Do not destroy"; likewise Pss 58; 59; 75) and probably refers to the now unknown melody to which it was to be sung. The occasion for this psalm's composition was **when [David] fled from Saul in the cave**, referring to either or both of the events recorded in 1Sm 22:1 and 24:3 (cf. Ps 142). As in the previous psalm, David found deliverance from the hand of Saul on this occasion as well and celebrated that deliverance with this song (Sailhamer, *NIV Compact Bible Commentary*, 327).

A. Finding Refuge in God's Transcendent Power (57:1-3)

57:1-3. David's opening entreaty, **be gracious to me**, is repeated for emphasis here as in a number of other psalms (cf. comment Ps 56:1). This entreaty is balanced by his subsequent assertion that, despite his present situation (and whether or not it was soon resolved), his **soul takes refuge in** God. This underscored the point David employed in a favorite familial expression: **in the shadow of Your wings I will take refuge** (v. 1; cf. Pss 17:8; 36:7; 61:4; 63:7; 91:4). This poignant poetic imagery was first employed by Moses (Dt 32:11) and then by David's own great-grandparents Ruth and Boaz (Ru 2:12; 3:9), and it suggests unreserved submission, reliance, and selfless devotion, grounded in a warm relationship. David also affirmed that **God will send forth His lovingkindness** (cf. comment on Ps 5:7) **and His truth** (v. 3; cf. comment on Ps 43:3), as if they were angels sent ahead of David to prepare his way.

B. Finding Refuge in God's Transcendent Glory (57:4-6)

57:4-6. Again despite his distressing circumstances as a fugitive from Saul's wrath, the focus of David's heart was the **glory** of **God**, whom he declared to **be exalted above the heavens** (v. 5). Implicit in this declaration—and also a source of encouragement to David—is the idea that God, being in the heavens and hence above all nations, will do as He pleases despite the will and opposition of man (cf. Pss 113:4; 115:3). So too, all that happens—regardless of when and how God resolves David's situation—will ultimately contribute to the manifestation of God's **glory . . . above all the earth**.

C. Finding Refuge in God's Transcendent Praise (57:7-11)

57:7-11. See comments on Ps 108:1-5, which repeats, with minor variations, these five verses.

Psalm 58: A Meditation on Divine Justice

On the heading of this **Mikhtam of David**, see comments on the headings of Pss 3, 4 and 16. The psalm is to be set to **Al-tashheth** (see comment on heading to Ps 57).

A. Need for Divine Justice (58:1-5)

58:1-5. This does not begin by addressing God "the LORD" (Yahweh). Rather, the words **O gods** are occasionally applied to human authorities (judges and leaders) serving as intermediaries for God (see Ex 22:8-9; Ps 82:6). But the term used here is "aggregate/throng" (Hb. *'elem*, as in Gn 37:7, where it is usually translated "sheaf," i.e., a collection of stalks). Therefore, the sense of David's opening words is, **Do you indeed speak righteousness**, O throng? (a throng of people, parallel to **sons of men** in the next line; v. 1). Hence the need for divine justice is immediately introduced—and further emphasized by David's subsequent reference to **violence** (v. 2, signifying "wicked violence"; see the comment on Gn 6:11) and **the wicked** being **estranged from the womb** and going **astray from birth** (v. 3; i.e., depraved from birth, as in Ps 51:5; see comment there). This is a poetic passage and does not mean that week-old infants sin. The idea is that because of human depravity, from early on people do that which is wicked.

B. Demonstration of Divine Justice (58:6-9)

58:6-8. David thus urged **God** to manifest his justice (for His glory, as is made clear in the next section), using a number of figures of speech for destroying the enemy. David prayed that God will (1) **shatter their teeth** and **break out the fangs of the young lions**, actions that would render both the serpent (mentioned in v. 4) and attacking **lions** powerless (v. 6); (2) let them **flow away like water that runs off** and is absorbed in the ground; (3) make their attacks miss their aim like **headless** arrow **shafts** (v. 7); (4) let them be as powerless as **a snail**; and (5) let them be as fruitless as **miscarriages** (v. 8). See comments on imprecatory psalms under Introduction: Types of Psalms.

58:9. God's judgment will be fast: **before your pots can feel the fire of thorns** (the kindling to start the fire), God will quickly and ultimately manifest His justice and **sweep them away** as a **whirlwind** that carries everything away in its path.

C. Reaction to Divine Justice (58:10-11)

58:10-11. The response to God's justice that **the righteous will rejoice** (v. 10), not because the wicked have been destroyed as such (for in the death of the wicked God takes no delight, and so neither should His people; Ezk 18:23, 32; 33:11), but rather because God Himself has been vindicated (see comments on Pss 52:8; 54:7). Even more the sovereignty of **God who judges** all the **earth** (v. 11; cf. Gn 12:3; 18:15; 1Sm 17:46; see comments on Pss 2:10-12; 18:46-50; 22:27; 36:5-9; 45:16-17; 48:9-11).

Psalm 59: A Personal Petition for Divine Deliverance

On the heading of this **Mikhtam of David**, see comments on the headings of Pss 3, 4 and 16. The psalm is to be set to **Al-tashheth** (see the comment on heading to Ps 57). The occasion for this psalm was **when Saul sent men** to watch **the house** in which David lived with his first wife, Michal, **in order to kill him**, recounted in 1Sm 19:11-17.

A. Honestly Expressing the Need for Divine Deliverance (59:1-8)

59:1-8. David earnestly implored God to **deliver** him **from** his **enemies** (v. 1), referring not to Saul's soldiers in general but to those among Saul's followers whose desire for social and political favor by supporting the king was greater than their desire for righteousness. Hence David described them as **those who do iniquity** (v. 2) and **who are treacherous in iniquity** (v. 5). The futility of their schemes is underscored by his use of the same words as in Ps 2:4 (v. 8, namely, **laugh** and **scoff**), implying that in their opposition to David, God's newly anointed king (1Sm 16:13), they are ultimately opposed to God Himself.

B. Humbly Considering the Purpose of Divine Deliverance (59:9-15)

59:9-15. David was unjustly hunted by Saul and vastly outnumbered, yet he trusted in the

Lord: **because of his strength I will watch** [anticipate/expect] **for You** (v. 9). David was motivated not by his own glory (that he might be recognized and respected for who he is, God's newly anointed king), but rather by the advancement of God's glory, that He might be recognized and respected for who the Lord is: (1) a God who is characterized by **lovingkindness** (Hb. *chesed*, loyal covenant love), by which He **will meet** him (lit., "go before Him," as vividly illustrated in 2Sm 5:24) as one who is under His covenant (v. 10); (2) the **Lord** who is **our shield** (v. 11); and (3) a God who is characterized by justice, for He will never let the wicked (unrepentant) go unpunished (Ex 34:7; Pr 11:21), but will **destroy them in wrath** (v. 13, again hearkening to the wording of Ps 2, in this case 2:12). The result will be that believers will worship and unbelievers will fear. And it is hoped unbelievers will submit and turn to Him as the only true God (as in Est 8:17), **know[ing] that** He **rules in Jacob**, the people of Israel, **to the ends of the earth** (v. 13).

C. Unconditionally Praising the Giver of Divine Deliverance (59:16-17)

59:16-17. David concluded in typical fashion with unconditional praise. **As for** him, regardless of how and when God answers him, he **shall joyfully sing of** God's **lovingkindness** [*chesed*, cf. v. 10 above] **in the morning** (v. 16, for every morning they "are renewed"; see Lm 3:22-23 and comments on Ps 36:5-9) and **sing praises to God**, his **strength** (v. 17).

Psalm 60: Affirming Our Utter Dependence on God

On the heading of this **Mikhtam of David**, see comments on the headings of Pss 3, 4 and 16. The **choir director** is instructed that the psalm is **according to Shushan Eduth** (lit., "Lily of Testimony"), an expression also occurring (though in the plural) in the heading of Ps 80 (cf. headings of Pss 45 and 69). In both cases it probably designates the melody according to which the psalm was to be sung. In this unusually lengthy heading, the psalm's purpose is to teach, used only here in the headings of the psalms, but true of all of Scripture (2Tm 3:16-17). In light of how the same expression is used in the preface to David's funeral song for Saul and Jonathan (2Sm 1:18), this psalm was probably meant to be taught to the sons of Judah in commemoration of the many Israelites who fell in the difficult battle (**when he struggled**) with **Aram-naharaim** and with **Aram-zobah** (referring to the events of 2Sm 8 and 1Ch 18). David had a decisive victory over Edom during that time (see 2Sm 8:12-13), and the defeat of Edom has important messianic implications (see introductory comments to Ps 52).

A. Affirming God's Chastisement (60:1-5)

60:1-4. Since this psalm, according to a natural reading of the heading, was composed in the course of Israel's ongoing battle with the Arameans at a point when the former was struggling against the latter, David uttered a gut-wrenching cry of despair, **O God, You have rejected us** (v. 1). This is an expression of the depth of David's despair in response to the horrific circumstances. It is not a contradicting theological truth, however, for the Lord will never reject His people or break His covenant with them (cf. comments 44:23). Because of God's unique relationship with Israel, as His people, He will correct them, not abandon them. The difference is a crucial one: the concept of rejection (or abandonment), which in the Bible is synonymous with condemnation (cf. Ps 37:33; Rm 8:1, 38-39), takes place only in the absence of a relationship with God, whereas correction takes place only within the existence of a relationship (even if the existence of the a relationship is not felt by the one being corrected; cf. Heb 12:5-11 and comments on Ps 23:6 and Ps 30).

60:5. That a relationship indeed exists between Israel and God is indicated by the relational expressions "Your people" (v. 3) and **Your beloved** (v. 5, the name David means "beloved"; this is the plural from the same root as David's name). For comments on this verse, see 108:6.

B. Affirming God's Promises (60:6-8)

60:6-8. These verses are parallel to Ps 108:7-9; see comments there.

C. Affirming God's Actions (60:9-12)

60:9-12. The question **Who will bring me . . . ?** (v. 9) is rhetorical, and the implied answer is the Lord, who will **go forth with our armies** (v. 10). The Lord will give the **deliverance** (v. 11) and by His might **He . . . will tread down our adversaries** and deliver His people (v. 12; cf. Ps 20:7; Nm 24:18; Is 14:19, 25: Jr 12:10; Zch 10:5).

Psalm 61: A Cry to God from the Faint of Heart

On the heading of this **Psalm of David**, see comments on the headings to Pss 3 and 4. This psalm was to be sung with the accompaniment of **a stringed instrument**. In Ps 60, David expressed confidence in God's final victory over his enemies (60:12). Here he prayed that God would prosper the divine King who will bring about this final victory (61:5-8) and who will provide the refuge David and the righteous seek (Sailhamer, *NIV Compact Bible Commentary*, 327; cf. 61:4 with 2:12).

A. For Unbreakable Protection (61:1-4)

61:1-3. This is an earnest prayer: **Hear my cry, O God; give heed to my prayer** (v. 1). The images underscore David's vulnerability; he is calling out to God as if from a distant land, **from the end of the earth . . . when** his **heart is faint** (v. 2a). He therefore looks to God for the most intimate familiarity (his internal emotional needs) and the most impenetrable security (his external physical needs). For security he implored God and said, **Lead me to the rock that is higher than I**, that is, to God Himself (v. 2b). A **rock** is a common biblical image of the Lord and a place of safety (cf. 18:2; 31:2; 62:2, 6-7; 71:3; 94:22). The Lord is specifically called "the Rock of Israel" (2Sm 23:3; Is 30:29). David knew that God was **a refuge** (cf. 2:12) and **a tower of strength** (v. 3; cf. 18:1-3).

61:4. He implored God to **let** him **dwell in** His **tent forever** (v. 4a), that is, to have intimate fellowship with Him in the tabernacle (cf. 15:1; 23:6; 27:4). David then asked God to **let** him **take refuge in the shelter of** His **wings** (v. 4b; see comments 57:1). Both of David's petitions envision worship and joyful intimacy in the presence of God.

B. For Life-Giving Love (61:5-7)

61:5-7. Notwithstanding his opening appeal that God "hear" him, David affirmed that God had already **heard**, that is, He had already provided what was best for David (see comments on Ps 34:15; cf. Gn 16:11). This "best," as David affirmed, entailed **the inheritance of those who fear** God's **name** (v. 5; cf. 111:10). **Inheritance** usually refers to land but is used here metaphorically to refer to the spiritual rewards given to **those who fear** (have appropriate awe) for God's reputation. He also prayed for God's eternal King to come forth and be established, based on the promises God had made to David of an eternal King and kingdom described in 2Sm 7:11-17. David expected a descendant whose reign God **will prolong**, a reign in which the King's years will be as **many generations** (v. 6), a poetic idiom for "forever" paralleled in v. 7a: the King will **abide before God forever** (cf. Dt 32:7). The prospect of this eternal King made it possible for David to anticipate eternal life with God (to "dwell in Your tent forever"; v. 4a) and to "take refuge" under God's "wings" (v. 4b).

C. For Enduring Purpose (61:8)

61:8. David affirmed the essential motivation for his petition as well as the goal for which he earnestly yearned: to **sing praise to [God's] name forever** (on the significance of God's **name**, see comments on Ps 20:5; see also Gn 11:4; 12:2).

Psalm 62: A Meditation on True Salvation

On the heading of this **Psalm of David**, see comments on the headings to Pss 3 and 4. This psalm's heading also includes the phrase **according to Jeduthun**, referring to a certain melody or a musical instrument, or that the psalm was somehow under the direction of one of the three families of Levitical singers (see the introductory comments to Ps 39). Though there is no explicit mention of the Messiah in this psalm, there is hope for a future salvation and of finding refuge in God, which according to Ps 2:12 is a refuge found in "the Son." This taken in connection with the context of Pss 60 and 61, which are messianic, indicates the messianic hope of this psalm as well (Sailhamer, *NIV Compact Bible Commentary*, 328).

A. True Salvation Is Found in God Alone (62:1-4)

62:1-4. David asserted confidently that his **soul** "finds its tranquility" (a preferable translation to the NASB's **waits in silence**) when he directed his thoughts toward God. Not only was his **salvation** (a word that, as in Ps 13:5, denotes full and final salvation) from God (v. 1), but in fact it **is** God—and **He only** (v. 2). Because God was David's **rock** (see the comment on 61:2), he could declare with confidence that he **shall not be greatly shaken**. Whatever might befall him in this life would never be severe enough to dislodge the promises of future glory that God had given him, especially about his supreme Son (see comments on the parallel phraseology in Ps 15:5b). This initial assertion set David's situation—oppression by those who **delight in falsehood** (v. 4)—in proper perspective and diminished the emotional sway it might otherwise have held over him.

B. True Salvation Is Available from God at All Times (62:5-8)

62:5-8. David began this second section by reiterating (in vv. 5-6) the comforting confidence with which he began the psalm, the only difference being that here he substituted **hope** for "salvation." He thus affirmed that the "salvation" of which he spoke in v. 2 was still unrealized (and hence a reference to future and final salvation), just as **hope**, by definition, pertains to what is yet unaccomplished and unseen (cf. Heb 11:1, where "things hoped for" is parallel to "things not seen"; cf. also Rm 8:24-25). Nonetheless, on the basis of his confidence in God who is the unshakable source of his hope, David exhorted his **people** to **trust in Him at all times** (v. 8a)—not just as an unshatterable **rock of... strength** (v. 7), but also with a compassionate and ever-attentive ear, eager for His children to **pour out** their **heart before Him**, who is their **refuge** (v. 8b). This word **refuge** (Hb. *machseh*) is from the same root as the verb "to take refuge" (Hb. *chasah*), as in Pss 17:7-8; 36:7; 52:1; 61:4; 91:4, and employs the imagery of a fledgling bird finding refuge in the shadow and security of its parent's wings (cf. 63:7).

C. True Salvation Is Dispensed by God Sovereignly (62:9-12)

62:9-12. David exhorted his people (those he addressed in v. 8) to look beyond the apparent prosperity of the wicked (v. 9, **men of low degree**), because **power** (v. 11) and **lovingkindness** (Hb. *chesed*; v. 12) **belongs to God** (i.e., they are His to the utmost degree), and by them He will eventually **recompense** every **man according to his work** (culminating at that time when Jesus returns in glory and wrath; see Mt 16:27 and Rm 2:6).

Psalm 63: Expressing Yearning for God

On the heading of this **Psalm of David**, see the comments on the heading to Ps 3. The background of this psalm is the time **when** David **was in the wilderness of Judah**, which refers to either or both of the periods when he was a fugitive from Saul (1Sm 23:14, 24; 24:1; 25:1) or his son Absalom (see 2Sm 15:28). David's being in the wilderness sets the stage both for his thirst for God (v. 1) and for drawing a parallel to Israel's wilderness wandering with the hope of entering and subduing Canaan. The mention of the king at the conclusion of the psalm (v. 11) puts this psalm in the context of the Torah's (Pentateuch's) anticipation of the deliverance brought by the great King who will arise from Judah and rescue God's people (see Gn 49:8-12; Nm 24:7, 17) (Sailhamer, *NIV Compact Bible Commentary*, 328).

A. For His Presence (63:1-5)

63:1. In the expression **You are my God** in Hebrew is arranged grammatically as "My God You are," by which he underscored not simply the deity of the Lord but also the comforting and joy-giving truth that the Lord, who is the only real deity, was his God, personally and intimately. His longing for God is deep: **my soul thirsts for You, my flesh yearns** [lit., "faints"] **for You**. The description is heightened by the image of desperate thirst **in a dry and weary land where there is no water** (cf. 42:1).

63:2-5. Although when David was in the wilderness removed from God's presence (i.e., His cloud of glory; cf. Ex 40:34), he had **seen** Him **in the sanctuary** and knew of God's **power and** His **glory** (v. 2). By the statement **Your lovingkindness is better than life** (v. 3), David meant that God's *chesed* (cf. comment on 5:7), which will bring him into the glory and complete joy of the next life, is better than anything that the present life has to offer (cf. 84:10). In this hope his **soul is satisfied as with marrow and fatness** (v. 5), that is, highly valued and nourishing food sources (see Gn 4:4; Ps 36:8).

B. For His Protection (63:6-8)

63:6-8. David said he will **remember** God **on** his **bed** and **meditate on** God **in the night watches** (v. 6), emphasizing the importance (and benefit) of meditating in all wakeful hours of the night, i.e., filling one's mind with the Word of God (see comments on Ps 1:2; Dt. 6:5-9; Jos 1:8). **In the shadow of Your wings** (v. 7, cf. comments on 17:8) is one of David's favorite phrases, since it so beautifully and concisely expresses his sense of relationship with, security in, and submission to the Lord. This sense of personal intimacy is poignantly emphasized by the statement **my soul clings to You** (v. 8)—in which the verb **clings** is the same one used to express the bond between husband and wife (see Gn 2:24 and comments there).

C. For His Praise (63:9-11)

63:9-11. Ultimately, David is confident that **those who seek** his life will be defeated by the Lord (v. 9). His hope is evident in the sudden reference to the King, reminding of the Torah's mention of this king, who would come from Judah and rule the nations (Gn 49:8-12; Nm 24:7, 17). **Everyone who swears by** (i.e., places their confidence in) this future King **will glory** (lit., "boast," as in Ps 105:3; cf. 1Kg 20:11), for He will fulfill all that He has promised, and so **the mouths of those who speak lies** [i.e., who contradict what God has said] **will be stopped** (v. 11).

Psalm 64: Finding Solace from Tormentors

On the heading of this **Psalm of David**, see comments on the headings to Pss 3 and 4. As with the preceding psalms, in Ps 64 David anticipated a future salvation, yet here it is a salvation that incorporates people from every ethnic group (v. 9), but still involves finding refuge in Him, that is, in the divine messianic King (see "take refuge" in 2:12; cf. comments on 62:8) (Sailhamer, *NIV Compact Bible Commentary*, 328).

A. Unburdening the Torment of Heart to God (64:1-6)

64:1-6. To express a **complaint** (v. 1) to God, provided one does so in the manner modeled by Scripture, is not only an acceptable part of worship (see comments on Pss 10:1-11; 28:1-2; 142) but is also an essential part. In doing so the child of God finds healthy release for the concerns that inevitably attend living in an ungodly world (cf. Mk 4:19; Jn 16:33; Ac 14:22; 2Tm 3:12), and in the process it strengthens the bonds of intimacy and dependence on one's heavenly Father. David affirmed that **the inward thought and the heart of a man are deep** (v. 6), too deep for David to discover (and so take up his guard against), but never too deep for God who knows the innermost secrets of all men's hearts (see Pss 17:3; 44:21; 139:1-4; Ac 15:8).

B. Affirming the Judgment of Tormentors by God (64:7-8)

64:7-8. Because God knows the heart and because He is just and all-powerful, David will say with confidence that **God will shoot at** his enemies and **suddenly they will be wounded** (lit., "smitten down"; v. 7). The words of this verse recall what David had said to Goliath: "This day the LORD will deliver you up into my hands, and I will strike [lit., "smite"] you down and remove your head from you" (1Sm 17:46). The battle indeed was the Lord's, and He quickly gave the giant into Israel's hands (vv. 47-51).

C. Anticipating the Glory of the Future with God (64:9-10)

64:9-10. David had also said to Goliath that he will be defeated so "that all the earth may know . . . and that all this assembly may know" that God alone is supreme (1Sm 17:46-47). Here too in Ps 64 David affirmed the consequent manifestation of God's glory, which was cause for fear among unbelievers (v. 9, **then all men will fear**) and cause for gladness and a sense of solace among believers (v. 10, **the righteous man will be glad . . . and will take refuge in Him**). That solace, of course, is found ultimately for those who "do homage to the Son" and "take refuge in Him" (Ps 2:12) (Sailhamer, *NIV Compact Bible Commentary*, 328–29).

Psalm 65: God's Grace toward Man

On the heading of this **Psalm of David . . . A Song**, see comments on the headings to Pss 3, 4, and 46. This psalm reiterates the theme of God's universal rule expressed in Ps 64 (especially 64:9) (Sailhamer, *NIV Compact Bible Commentary*, 329). One of the reasons "all men will fear," declare God's works, and glory in Him (64:9-10) is because God will make available the forgiveness of sins to the ends of the earth (65:3-5).

A. As Expressed in His Sovereign Forgiveness (65:1-4)

65:1-4. This song of praise is set **in Zion**, the temple (v. 1). It is arranged into three sections, each expressing God's grace toward humanity. First, the greatest of all, His forgiveness of sin: God will **hear prayer**, and as for **our transgressions**, He **forgive[s]** the sin of all men (lit., "all flesh," meaning any human being, whether Jew or Gentile; cf. Gn 6:19; Is 49:26; Jr 32:27; Jl 2:28) who **come** to Him (v. 2). This wording parallels Solomon's prayer (following in his father's footsteps!) at the dedication of the temple (see 1Kg 8:41-43). **How blessed** (see comment on Ps 1:1) **is the one whom** God thus **choose[s]** (v. 4) to **forgive** (v. 3). And if such forgiveness comes about by God's choice, then it cannot come about through the striving or merit of man; it is simply and magnificently a gift of God (Eph 2:8-9).

B. As Expressed in His Miraculous Works (65:5-8)

65:5-8. Second, God's grace is expressed in His **awesome deeds** (v. 5), that is, the awe-inspiring miracles He performed to deliver His people Israel (v. 8), as recalled in Ps 106:22, where the same term is applied to all He did "by the Red Sea" (i.e., halting Pharaoh's army with a pillar of fire, splitting the sea in half, bringing Israel across on dry land [Ex 14:10, 19-20, 22; 15:19; Ps 66:6], and then drowning Pharaoh's army). Just as Israel affirmed in their song of response that God "has become my salvation" (Ex 15:2), so too did David affirm in this song (as the psalm is called in its heading) that the Lord is the **God of our salvation** (Ps 65:5; cf. 27:1; 85:4; Is 12:2).

C. As Expressed in His Continuous Provision (65:9-13)

65:9-13. Finally, God's grace is seen in His providential care. David said that God **visit[ed] the earth** (v. 9), recalling the wording in Ru 1:6 that "the LORD had visited His people in giving them food." He gives them **grain**, ensuring that seed is available and that it grows, and He brings **water** (i.e., rain) on the earth's **furrows** (v. 10). And He does so in His grace, for both the righteous as well as the unrighteous (Mt 5:45), and in response the land and everything on it **shout**

for joy (v. 13). Here David focused on God's grace as expressed in His ongoing provisions for His people—and for humankind in general—by upholding the natural order (cf. Col 1:17).

Psalm 66: An Exhortation to Praise God for His Concern

On the heading of this **Song** . . . **A Psalm**, see comments on the headings to Pss 3, 4, and 46. The vast salvation God makes available for all flesh (65:4-6) calls for every human being who receives it to sing praises to Him (66:1-4) (Sailhamer, *NIV Compact Bible Commentary*, 329).

A. In Delivering His People (66:1-7)

66:1-7. The psalmist exhorted **all the earth** to **shout joyfully** (that is, in praise) **to God** (v. 1) for His **awesome** . . . **works** (v. 3), referring to His works of redemption (see comment on the same expression in Ps 65:5). In particular the psalmist specified God's awe-inspiring miracle of **turn[ing] the sea into dry land** (v. 6; see Ex 14:21-22)—a miracle performed on such a grand scale that it set fear and trembling into the hearts of the peoples all around (Ex 15:14; cf. Jos 5:1) and serves through all Scripture as a symbol of the salvation God provides (see, e.g., 1Co 10:1-10). Yet though these people, the **enemies** of God and Israel, then **feigned obedience to** God out of fear of His great **power** (v. 3), the psalmist affirmed that one day **all the earth will** truly **worship** God (v. 4), a goal no force of history can preempt (cf. Is 11:10; Zch 14:9, 16; Rv 22:3-4).

B. In Refining His People (66:8-15)

66:8-15. The psalmist next praised God for having **tried** and **refined** His people (v. 10)—a process that is like **an oppressive burden upon our loins** (v. 11), yet those who have been trained by it come **into a place of abundance** (v. 12). **Abundance** more precisely signifies "satisfaction" and "rest" (of waiting on the Lord and finding one's strength in Him). All these points are developed in Heb 12:4-13, which explicitly adds, citing Pr 3:11-12, that divine correction in the end is a cause for rejoicing, for it is evidence of God's fatherly love.

C. In Hearing His People (66:16-20)

66:16-20. The psalmist praised God for hearing him when He had every reason not to listen. Regarding the **wickedness in** his **heart**, he correctly determined that **the Lord will not hear** (v. 18, cf. Is 59:2). Yet for those who have repented and submitted in faith to God's Word, God will give **heed to the voice of** their **prayer** (v. 19) and **not** turn **away** His **lovingkindness** (Hb. *chesed*) **from** them (v. 20).

Psalm 67: Praise from All Peoples

On the heading of this **Psalm** . . . **A Song**, see comments on the headings to Pss 3, 4. This psalm was to be sung **with** the accompaniment of **stringed instruments**. Structurally and thematically this psalm is organized in a beautifully chiastic fashion:

A God's care for Israel brings worldwide praise (vv. 1-2)
  B Praise is the correct response by the peoples (v. 3)
    C God's sovereignty over the nations (v. 4)
  B' Praise is the correct response by the peoples (v. 5)
A' God's care for Israel brings worldwide praise (vv. 6-7)

In chiastic structures, the central element(s) is emphatic, here the sovereignty of God over the world expressed as His right to judge them. This structure underscores that this is not only a picture of what the nations should ideally do (taking up this theme from the contrasting description of what the nations say and do in Ps 2:1-6, 10-12), but also what they will one day really do when God establishes His kingdom on earth.

A. Based on His Spiritual Concern for Israel (67:1-2)

67:1-2. The psalmist adopted the wording of the priestly (or "Aaronic") benediction (Nm 6:24-26) in which the key expressions **be gracious**, **bless**, and **cause His face to shine upon** (v. 1) all specifically signify both physical and spiritual provision regardless of outer circumstances, "rest" in the salvific sense (see Gn 2:15 and comments there), and intimacy with God (see comments on Pss 1:1; 2:12; 36:9; 44:3; 56:1, 13). God's covenant faithfulness in spiritually redeeming Israel is intended **that** His **way may be known on the earth**, that is, His **salvation among all nations** (v. 2), in fulfillment of God's greatest promise to Abraham (in Gn 22) to bless the world through his Seed, the promised Messiah (see comments on Gn 22:18). And indeed God's ongoing salvation of individual Jewish people—as His future salvation of the entire nation—stands as one of the greatest testimonies in this world that "the word of God has [not] failed" (Rm 9:6; see 11:1-32 and comments there).

B. Based on His Administrative Concern for All Peoples (67:3-5)

67:3-5. The result of the Lord's "salvation" being "known on the earth" (v. 2) will inevitably culminate in all **the peoples** of the earth offering their **praise** to God (vv. 3, 5; on the universal and spiritual significance of the term **peoples** in the plural; see comment on Ps 45:17). This will happen when, in the person of His Son, God will establish His kingdom permanently and physically on earth, **judg[ing] the peoples with uprightness** (reminding of the messianic imagery of Is 11:3-4; cf. Jn 7:24), and He will **guide** with compassion and concern as a shepherd guides his sheep and a father his children (on this specific sense of **guide** see, e.g., Ex 15:13; Pss 27:11; 43:3; 77:20; 107:30; 139:24) **the nations on the earth**, indicating God's love for all mankind (Ps 67:4; cf. Is 9:6; 56:7; Lk 2:32).

C. Based on His Material Concern for Israel (67:6-7)

67:6-7. The psalmist affirmed God's material concern for Israel, including both (1) His provision of food, since it is by His will that **the earth has yielded its produce** (v. 6a; cf. Ps 85:12), and (2) His protection, since an inseparable part of the blessing by which God **blesses** the psalmist and his people Israel (v. 6b) is not only by giving them food (see Ps 132:15) but also by ensuring that they never cease from being a people before Him (see Jr 31:37, reiterating His eternal promise to Abram in Gn 12:2-3; see also Gn 17:7-8; Ps 105:8-10). God's protection and preservation of Israel will in turn serve as a worldwide testimony to His sovereign power, causing people in **all the ends of the earth** to **fear Him** (v. 7)—as the Egyptians did at Israel's redemption from Pharaoh (Ex 12:33), as many of the people did at Israel's redemption from Haman (Est 8:17), and as we should do in the face of Israel's miraculous existence (as both a nation and a people) to this day. These are promises made to the nation and people of Israel. They require a fulfillment that includes the Jewish people's presence in the land as a national entity. Promises such as this cannot be fulfilled by a "new Israel" or a "spiritual Israel," i.e., the Church consisting of many nations, as it is sometimes argued. Only when Israel as a restored nation among other nations exhibits God's sovereignty and grace can such promises as those here in Ps 67 be fulfilled. At that time, Israel as a nation will mediate God's blessings to other nations of the world, and thus the families of earth's nations will be able to receive the same salvation (cf. Gn 12:3; 22:18; 26:4; Is 42:6; 49:6; Gl 3:8; Ac 26:23).

Psalm 68: A Procession of Praise for the Triumphant God

On the heading of this **Psalm of David. A Song**, see the comments on the headings to Pss 3, 4, and 46. This psalm is linked to the previous one (with which it also shares several similar wordings) by continuing the same theme of God's worldwide praise (both from Israel His people [vv. 7-8] as well as from the all the kingdoms of the earth [v. 32]). This psalm focuses on the processional expression of that praise while also introducing the focus of the following psalm, with which it shares a specific and direct messianic application (see the citation of v. 18 in Eph 4:8).

A. As the Head of Israel's Triumph over Physical Distress (68:1-14)

68:1-6. This psalm opening, **Let God arise, let His enemies be scattered** (v. 1), is an indirect quotation/adaptation of Moses' exhortation to Israel to move on from Mount Sinai, following "the cloud of the LORD" (Nm 10:35; cf. 9:16). This is similar to how Ps 67 begins by employing the wording of Aaron when he blessed Israel (Nm 6:24-26). These are excellent examples of intertextuality, how later writers of Scripture employed earlier texts of Scripture.

68:7-14. So this psalm continues the theme of the previous one, that God will lead His **people** triumphantly through their present distress just as He led their ancestors **through the wilderness** (v. 7). And not just those distant ancestors were blessed. The successive generations were blessed, to whom He **confirmed** (i.e., gave) His **inheritance**, that is, the land of Canaan that He gave to the Jewish people as an eternal inheritance (Gn 17:8; Ps 105:10-11), in which He brought them **plentiful rain** (v. 9) and caused the **armies** of their enemies to **flee** (v. 12). Resting under the **wings of a dove covered with silver . . . pinions with glistening gold** (v. 13) is a poetic image of Israel under God's bountiful and beautiful protection (cf. 17:8; 57:1; 91:4).

B. As the Head of Israel's Triumph over Spiritual Distress (68:15-23)

68:15-18. From imploring (vv. 1-3) and then affirming (vv. 4-14) God's provision of temporal blessings, David moved on to affirming God's provision of spiritual triumph to Israel. This is introduced in v. 18 with the observation that God crushed the enemies of Israel during the conquest of the land of Canaan. In turn, this supports the concept that He also has the power to save his people (vv. 19-20). In vv. 15-18, the psalmist describes the victory God provided over the opponents of the Jewish people in Canaan during the conquest. God gained the victory for them then, and likewise had been victorious over Zion on behalf of David in his time (see 2Sm 5:6-10). God, who had been present at Sinai (v. 17), subdued Zion (the **mountain** of God's **abode**) and will reside there **forever** (v. 16). But doing so required taking many **captives** (v. 18) from those who were the enemies of Israel defeated in the conquest. **You have received gifts among men** should be understood as God, and His people, receiving the spoils of war or tributes from the vanquished kings of Canaan in the land that came to be called Israel (similarly, see v. 29). In Eph 4:8, the apostle Paul adjusts **You have received gifts among men** to "HE GAVE GIFTS TO MEN." On this adjustment, Harold W. Hoehner wrote, "Although the two renderings seem to be opposites, they are not incompatible. If God receives the spoils of war from the enemies in Ps 68, it is not beyond understanding that he would give gifts to those who are on his side as a provision from him as is portrayed in Eph 4:8. Furthermore, if this is considered only an indirect quotation summarizing the whole psalm, then there is no need to harmonize completely the specific verse but rather to show that it is consistent with the content of the whole psalm. Thus, the essence is that God is the one who gives gifts to his children" (Harold W. Hoehner, *Ephesians: An Exegetical Commentary* [Grand Rapids, MI: Baker, 2002], 529).

68:19-23. All of this serves to substantiate the promise of God's spiritual and physical deliverance that He will bring to His people as forecast in vv. 19-23: **Blessed be the Lord, who daily bears our burden** (cf. 55:22; 1Pt 5:7)**, the God who is our salvation** (v. 19; cf. Ps 27:1) . . . He is **to us a God of deliverances** (v. 20; cf. 18:50; 32:7).

C. As the Head of All Nations' Triumph over All Distress (68:24-35)

68:24-35. As a result of God's triumph over all distress, both material and spiritual, as seen in His victory **procession** . . . **into** His **sanctuary** (v. 24). God's victory will be recognized by all, both people from all Israel, indicated by the sample of the tribes **Benjamin**, **Judah**, **Zebulun**, and **Naphtali** (vv. 24-28), as well as the Gentile **kings** (vv. 29-35). Regarding the Gentiles, David looked forward to that culminating procession of praise when, in fulfillment of his exhortation in Ps 2:10, the nations are led in example by their **kings** (v. 29) to **sing praises to the Lord** (v. 32) and to **ascribe strength to God** (v. 34), who rules **from** His **sanctuary** (v. 35) in Jerusalem (see Rv 21:24-26; cf. Ezk 43:7; Zch 14:9-21).

Psalm 69: The Distress of God's Servant

On the heading of this **Psalm of David**, see comments on the headings to Pss 3 and 4. The psalm is accompanied by the instruction **according to Shoshannim** ("Lilies") (see introductory comments to Ps 45; cf. headings of Pss 60 and 80).

Psalm 69 is among those psalms more frequently referenced in the NT (directly in five instances and indirectly in at least seven more; for specific citations, see comments below) with application to the Messiah and His circumstances—concerning which David, being a prophet, could "look ahead" with clarity and speak of in detail (see Ac 2:30-31; see also Introduction: Background). Although David likely was writing about the Messiah, he was using some circumstance in his own life to describe or make allusions to Him. This may be called "symbolic realism" in which the real David becomes a symbol of the Messiah. Hence, David used his own flawed experience as the symbol of the Messiah and therefore included his own confession of guilt (Ps 69:5). Nevertheless, after David wrote this psalm, it was likely applied to every Davidic descendant as a possible fulfillment of the Davidic covenant (cf. comments on 2Sm 7:11-17). However, they all failed in the end, and Israel went into captivity without the messianic Seed of David ever taking His throne.

As a result, at the return from exile, when there was no Davidic king, a great hope and expectation for His coming emerged and began to grow. So when the psalms were redacted into a book (after the exile), these Davidic psalms (like Ps 69) were viewed as referring to the future Son of David, the Messiah. The NT goes even further, making explicit reference to Ps 69 in a variety of ways, each time showing that Jesus the Messiah was the referent who literally fulfilled these words (see Bruce K. Waltke, "A Canonical Process Approach to the Psalms" in *Tradition and Testament: Essays in Honor of Charles Lee Feinberg*, ed. John S. and Paul D. Feinberg [Chicago: Moody, 1981], 3–18). This explains the specific citations of this psalm in the NT as referring to Jesus.

As in Ps 68, the psalmist looks forward in Ps 69 to God's deliverance of Zion and the establishment of God's kingdom (vv. 34-36), both of which are contingent upon the fulfillment of the Davidic covenant (cf. 2Sm 7). This psalm, however, concentrates on the lamentable spiritual conditions among the people while awaiting the kingdom of God (Sailhamer, *NIV Compact Bible Commentary*, 330).

A. Appealing for Deliverance from the Distress (69:1-21)

69:1-3. This psalm begins with a cry: **Save me, O God** (v. 1a). Poetically it then describes David's situation: **waters, mire** and **deep waters** (vv. 1b-2), all of which indicated great distress. He was **weary with** his **crying**. Despite his sadness and distress he was still waiting for **God** to act (v. 3).

69:4. David was innocent, and yet he was **hate[d]... without a cause** (cf. 35:19) by a multitude of enemies, **more than the hairs of** his **head**. The Lord Jesus applied the first part of v. 4 to Himself when he taught the disciples on the night he was betrayed (cf. Jn 15:25).

69:5-7. Although he had not done the things his enemies were persecuting him for (vv. 4), David recognized his sin: **my wrongs are not hidden from You** (v. 5). His prayer was that his circumstances and the mockery of his enemies would not cause the Lord to **be dishonored through** him (vv. 6-7; cf. 22:6-8; 42:3; 79:10; 115:2).

69:8-12. Because of his innocent behavior, although attacked by his enemies, David had **become estranged from my brothers**—even his family avoided him (v. 8; cf. Mk 3:21; cf. vv. 31-35). A primary catalyst for this rejection was that his **zeal for** God's **house consumed** him (Ps 69:9). This is not limited to the literal temple but encompasses obedience to the Lord as epitomized by the temple, where the presence of God dwelt. For example, David's commitment to honor Saul as the Lord's king, prevented him from rebellion against Saul, to the consternation of David's family and followers (see, e.g., 1Sm 24; 26; 2Sm 1). This **zeal** for the Lord was even truer of Jesus, and this text was applied to Him (cf. Jn 2:17). Jesus' zeal led Him to do and say things that, unless perceived in light of zeal for God, were highly divisive and offensive to His contemporaries: for example, cleansing the temple (Jn 2:13-22) and calling religious leaders a brood of vipers (Mt 3:7).

Furthermore, the statement **the reproaches of those who reproach You have fallen on me** (Ps 69:9) was also applied to Jesus (cf. Rm 15:3 and see comments there) and refers to those who implicitly reject God the Father (despite their outward obedience) by offering Him only rote worship while inwardly rejecting the claims on their heart of His Word and now of His Son (Is 29:13; Mt 5:20; Jn 8:18-19; Heb 1:1-2).

69:13-19. This **prayer** repeats many of the images of distress from the opening prayer (vv. 1-3). David depended on **the greatness of** God's **lovingkindness** (vv. 13, 16) to deliver him (cf. 5:7; 6:4; see comments on 5:7).

69:20-21. The **reproach** of those who hate him without cause (v. 1-4) had **broken** his **heart**, and there was no **sympathy** from anyone, nor any **comforters** (v. 20). When he was hungry and thirsty, it would have been better to have been given nothing than given **gall** ("bitter" or "poisonous") **for** his **food and... vinegar** ("sour wine") **to drink** (v. 21). These are metaphors of the scorn and opposition he faced. This experience of suffering and mistreatment is used in all four Gospels to illustrate the culmination of the Messiah's rejection on the cross (Mt 27:34, 48; Mk 15:23, 36; Lk 23:36; Jn 19:28).

B. Imprecating the Cause of the Distress (69:22-28)

See comments on imprecatory psalms under Introduction: Types of Psalms.

69:22-23. The **table before them** may be a reference to meals. In any case, the wicked behavior of David's enemies was a mockery of worship. So David prayed that even their **peace** may **become a snare** and **a trap** to them in their sin (v. 22). The passage **may their eyes grow dim so that they cannot see** is cited in the NT (from the LXX) by the apostle Paul to explain the reason the majority of his fellow Jewish people had rejected Jesus as the Messiah (v. 23; cf. comments on Rm 11:9-10). Yet Paul had further explained that the blindness was partial and that there was and always would be a remnant of Jewish people who believed in Jesus as the Messiah (cf. Rm 11:5, 23-25).

69:24-28. The references here to God's **indignation** and His **burning anger** are phrases often associated with judgment (v. 24; cf. 79:6; Jr 10:25; Ezk 20:8). David's imprecation calls for the homes/communities, **camp[s]**, and **tents** to become **desolate** as the result of God removing the wicked (v. 25). This image of divine judgment is applied to Judas Iscariot (cf. Ac 1:16-20). It is important to understand, however, that the reference to being **blotted out of the book of life** (v. 28a; cf. Rv 3:5) does not mean that one can lose his salvation. Rather, as indicated by the parallelism in the second line of the verse, the petition **may they not be recorded with the righteous** is intended to emphasize that such individuals were never **recorded** in the book of life **with the righteous** in the first place (v. 28b).

C. Thanking the One Who Relieves the Distress (69:29-36)

69:29-33. God's deliverance of His servant (see vv. 17, 36) would serve not only as another occasion for the servant Himself to offer the Father **praise** and **thanksgiving** (v. 30), but it would also cause **the humble** who **have seen it** (i.e., accepted it) to be **glad** (v. 32). On the basis of the servant's deliverance, the **heart** of these **humble** ones (i.e., those **who seek God) will revive** (lit., "be made alive"; v. 32), language that anticipates the promise and blessings of the new covenant (Jr 31:33; Ezk 11:19; 36:26-27).

69:34-36. The exhortation to **let heaven and earth praise Him . . . for God will save Zion and build the cities of Judah** looks forward to the time when God's kingdom will finally be established and the divine King, Messiah Jesus, will reign forever (see Pss 9:11; 20:5; Is 56:6; Rv 21:1-8; 22:1-5; see also comments there).

Psalm 70: A Paradigm of Dependence on God's Deliverance

On the heading of this **Psalm of David** see the comments on the heading to Ps 3. This psalm is **for a memorial** (see introduction to Ps 38, the only other psalm for which this instructional note is given). Psalm 70 appears to be an introduction, and Pss 71 and 72 (like Pss 42 and 43) seem to constitute a single cohesive unit of thought. Psalm 70 repeats with minor variations Ps 40:13-17.

Psalm 70 is a fitting follow-up to the prayer of David for God to deliver Israel and establish His kingdom. In this psalm, David asks that God would answer the prayer of Ps 69 quickly. In its context between Pss 69 and 71–72, Ps 70 reiterates the plea for God's swift return to establish His worldwide reign and establish the divine King upon His throne (Sailhamer, *NIV Compact Bible Commentary,* 330).

A. Imploring Deliverance from God (70:1-3)

70:1-3. See the comments on Ps 40:13-15, the parallel passage.

B. Encouraging Rejoicing in God (70:4-5)

70:4-5. See the comments on Ps 40:16-17.

Psalm 71: A Paradigm of Dependence on God in Old Age

Psalm 71 has no superscription, but may have been viewed by the redactors of the Psalms as ascribed to David, since the contents of the psalm are clearly Davidic. It is David's final prayer in this section of the book. Here he is an old man (cf. vv. 9, 18), still trusting in God's promises, many of which David had seen fulfilled, and still looking forward to the salvation God would bring in fulfillment of the promises He made to him decades before (cf. 2Sm 7) (Sailhamer, *NIV Compact Bible Commentary,* 330).

A. Affirming Confidence in God (71:6-16)

71:1-5. David began by asserting unconditionally his confidence in God. **In You, O LORD, I have taken refuge**. For this section see the comments on Ps 31:1-5.

71:6-16. Just as God had **sustained** him with life and strength from his **birth**, even **from [his] mother's womb** (v. 6, indicating life begins in the womb, so David asked for God to continue sustaining him even now that he had arrived at **old age** (v. 9, and was "old and gray," v. 18). David's **enemies** (v. 10) were seeking to take advantage of his physical weakness. Old age, like "youth" (vv. 5, 17), is a blessed time of life in which one is inclined to greater dependence on God (cf. 92:14; Pr 16:31). No matter what happened, David kept the Lord uppermost in his thoughts and speech: **But as for me, I will hope continually, and will praise You yet more and more . . . I will make mention of Your righteousness, Yours alone** (vv. 14, 16; cf. vv. 2, 5, 8).

B. Declaring Gratitude to God (71:17-24)

71:17-24. David's goal in life was to **declare Your strength to this generation** and **to all who are to come** (v. 18). In typically Davidic fashion, this psalm of entreaty concludes with an unconditional declaration of thanksgiving and **praise** (vv. 14, 22; **praises**, v. 22, 23), both for who God is (i.e., characterized by perfect **righteousness**; vv. 15-16, 19, 24) and for how He delivered David in the past and would **revive [him] again** (v. 20, cf. 9:1 comments). David was determined to **praise You . . . Your truth . . . O Holy One of Israel** (v. 22; this is a powerful name of God used 25 times by Isaiah [e.g., Is 1:4; 5:19; 41:14, 16, 20; 60:9, 14] and elsewhere only by Jeremiah [Jr 50:29; 51:5] and in 2Kg 19:22 as well as in Pss 78:41; 89:18). David would **shout for joy** and **sing praises to** God from his **soul**, **which** God had **redeemed** (v. 23; see comments on Pss 25:22 and 26:11).

Psalm 72: A Paradigm of Prayer for the King

This is the first **Psalm of Solomon** (the other being Ps 127). It was probably composed at his ascension to the throne, perhaps in connection with the prayer he offered when God appeared to him in a dream (cf. comments on 1Kg 3:6-9). Psalm 72 has several parallels to 1Kg 3 (Ps 72:1a//1Kg 3:9a; Ps 72:1b//1Kg 3:6; Ps 72:2a//1Kg 3:9). Just as Ps 2 looked forward to the fulfillment of the messianic promises, Ps 72 reiterates many of the same themes. And this psalm was written by Solomon, a son of David. His authorship would have evoked messianic hopes in those who read it (Sailhamer, *NIV Compact Bible Commentary,* 330–31). This final psalm in Book Two is a royal psalm. It is not primarily about David or Solomon, but is a description of the Messiah, with extravagant descriptions that go far beyond either of those kings. It was understood as messianic by early Jewish tradition, but is not cited in the NT.

A. The Messiah's Righteous Reign (72:1-7)

72:1-4. Solomon requested that God would **Give the king Your judgments** (better "justice") and **righteousness**, evoking memories of Solomon's request for himself (v. 1; cf. 1Kg 3:9). The prayer is that the righteous king would **judge** the people with **righteousness** and **justice**, **bring peace** to the people, **vindicate** and **save the** people, **and crush the oppressor** (vv. 2-4). These are all descriptions of a messianic reign and bring to mind the depiction of the King in Is 11:1-16.

72:5-7. The prayer for the messianic King continues, but the NASB reading of v. 5 based on the Masoretic Text (**Let them fear You while the sun endures**) is likely incorrect. It is preferred to follow the LXX (LXX), as does the HCSB: "May he continue while the sun endures and as long as the moon throughout all generations." There are several reasons to follow the LXX reading. (1) There is no clear reason for the MT to change the pronoun from the surrounding verses, where there is a consistent reference to the king ("let him"); only in this verse is there an unexpected change to the second person ("let them fear you"). (2) There is no clear antecedent to the pronoun "them" in the MT. (3) The LXX verb "continue" makes more sense than the MT "fear," because of all the temporal allusions in vv. 5-7. Some might argue that the MT is the harder reading and therefore to be preferred. However, it would be necessary to show a literary basis in the context for the MT reading, but there is none. Thus, v. 5 is calling for the establishment of an eternal King, whose reign would last as long as the sun and moon. And with His reign, He would bring **abundance of peace till the moon is no more** (v. 7).

B. The Messiah's Universal Reign (72:8-14)

72:8-11. The petition for this King is not that He would reign over all Israel alone, but that He would **rule from sea to sea and from the River to the ends of the earth** (v. 8). This King's enemies will **lick the dust** (v. 9), alluding to the promise of the victorious Messiah in Gn 3:15 (see comments there). **Kings** and **nations** will worship Him (vv. 10-11).

72:12-14. The Messiah's worldwide reign will be characterized by justice for the **needy** and the **afflicted** (v. 12). Those who oppressed the weak and defenseless will have to face a righteous King who will rescue the downtrodden from **oppression and violence** (v. 14).

C. The Messiah's Abundant Reign (72:15-17)

72:15-17. This section begins with another prayer for the messianic King to have abundance (**the gold of Sheba** and **abundance of grain**). The Messiah's kingdom will not only be righteous but exceptionally prosperous, with a population that will **flourish like vegetation of the earth** (v. 16). This King will be so glorious that His **name** will **endure forever . . . as long as the sun shines**. All humanity will **bless themselves** by Him, a clear allusion to the messianic promises in Gn 12:3; 22:18; and 26:4. This King is the one through whom all nations of the earth will be blessed.

D. Conclusion to Book Two (72:18-20)

72:18-20. Though enumerated as the last verses of 72, these are an epilogue to Book Two (42–72). **Blessed be the Lord God, the God of Israel** is a similar doxology to the end of Book One (cf. 41:13). It includes a forward look to the end of days when **the whole earth [will] be filled with His glory** (cf. 85:9; Is 11:9; Hab 2:14). Even though several of the psalms in Books One and Two were written by others, they are all collectively identified here as **the prayers of David** since he wrote the majority of them.

III. Book Three: Responding in Worship to God's Instruction in Holiness (Pss 73–89)

Psalm 73: On the Worth of Holiness

On the heading of this **Psalm of Asaph,** see Pss 3 and 50. Consistent with its placement at the beginning of the third of the five "books" of Psalms, this psalm focuses on and introduces the main theme of Book Three, which parallels the third book of the Pentateuch (Leviticus): the importance and obligations of holiness (see Introduction: Structure).

A. The Apparent Futility of Holiness (73:1-14)

73:1-2. The psalmist began by affirming what he knew to be true: **God is good to Israel**, and especially **to those who are pure in heart!** Yet at the same time he confessed a theological dilemma (vv. 2-14) that brought his **feet . . . close to stumbling** (failing to follow the Lord).

73:3-12. The dilemma was that **the arrogant** and **the wicked** appeared to prosper (v. 3). They enjoyed good health into old age (**no pains in their death**, v. 4); were **not in trouble** (v. 5), and **increased in wealth** (v. 12; cf. v. 7), even while ignoring the Lord and asking, **How does God know?** (v. 11).

73:13-14. Seeing the easy life of the wicked caused the psalmist to think that keeping his **heart pure** (i.e., holy, unstained by sin; cf. Pr 20:9) was a **vain** exercise (v. 13; the classic problem of the justice of God and the existence of evil; see the comments on Pss 37 and 52). The wicked were enjoying a prosperous easy life while the psalmist had **been stricken all day long**.

B. The True Futility of Unrighteousness (73:15-20)

73:15-20. The psalmist's perspective changed when he **came into the sanctuary of God** (v. 17, lit., "holy places," referring to the temple, cf. 68:35) and was confronted with the holy presence of God. Then he **perceived** the **end** of the wicked, that ultimately the Lord would judge their wickedness, **despise their form** (v. 20), and they would be cut off from Him. What was obscuring the psalmist's spiritual perspective was quickly burned away by the blinding holiness of God. As Franz Delitzsch aptly summarizes, "[H]is eyes [were] opened to the holy plans and ways of God [and] the sad end of the evil-doers was presented to him" (Franz Delitzsch, *Commentary on Psalms*, in *Commentary on the Old Testament in Ten Volumes* by C. F. Keil and F. Delitzsch, Trans. James Martin [Grand Rapids, MI: Eerdmans, 1980], 318).

C. The True Worth of Holiness (73:21-28)

73:21-28. God's holiness was impressed on the psalmist even in the midst of his affliction. He realized he was **continually with** God (v. 23; cf. v. 28) and **afterward** (i.e., after he died) God would **receive** him **to glory** (v. 24). This is a great contrast to the **sudden terrors** (v. 19) of the fate of the wicked. The psalmist was able to reconcile his adversity—his loss of station, possessions, and perhaps even his health (as suggested by vv. 14, 26)—because, when compared to what he already had in God (i.e., a present relationship and the hope of glory), all their value evaporated. Thus, with redoubled yearning he affirmed that, **besides** God, he **desire[d] nothing on earth** (v. 25; cf. 16:2). No matter what might happen to him, or what he might observe around him, **as for me, the nearness of God is my good; I have made the Lord God my refuge** (v. 28; cf. 14:6; 46:1; 61:3; 62:7-8; 71:7; 91:2, 9).

Psalm 74: Appealing to God for Relief from Affliction

On the heading of this **Maskil of Asaph** see the comments on Pss 32, 50. The content of this psalm concerning the perpetual ruins of Jerusalem and the damage to the sanctuary (vv. 3-11) indicates that it was written sometime after the Babylonian destruction of Jerusalem (586 BC).

A. Recognizing God's Correction (74:1-11)

74:1-2. By the opening expression, **why have You rejected us**? (cf. v. 11), the psalmist did not mean that God had forsaken His people. Rather, he was describing his feelings in the midst of Israel's affliction at the hands of their enemies (cf. comments on 44:9, 60:1). Despite his emotions, the psalmist had an unshakable conviction that Israel, **the sheep of Your pasture** (cf. 23:1; 100:3), were always God's people. Asaph prayed, **Remember Your congregation, which You have purchased of old, Which You have redeemed** (v. 2). This is the same terminology used by Moses at the time of the exodus (cf. Ex 15:13-18) to describe God's relationship with Israel, His **inheritance** (cf. comment on Ps 28:9). He also asked the Lord to remember **Mount Zion, where You have dwelt** in the temple (cf. 2:6; 9:11).

74:3-11. The Lord's **footsteps** is poetic personification calling for God to **Turn** and help Jerusalem. The city was in **ruins**, because **the enemy ha[d] damaged everything . . . burned Your sanctuary** and **defiled the dwelling place of Your name** (vv. 3, 7). The destruction of Jerusalem by Babylon is detailed in 2Kg 25:1-21; Jr 52. The enemies said, **Let us completely subdue them**, oppressing the people of Israel (v. 8). Plus, there was no **prophet . . . among us who** knew how long these terrible events would last (vv. 9-10).

B. Affirming God's Sovereignty (74:12-17)

74:12-17. Despite this worst of all events, the destruction of Jerusalem and the temple, **God is my king from of old, Who works deeds of deliverance** (v. 12). This section focuses on God's absolute sovereignty on Israel's behalf at the exodus from Egypt (**You divided the sea by Your strength**, vv. 12-15; cf., Ex 14–15), and on behalf of humanity in general at creation (**You have prepared the light and the sun . . . established all the boundaries of the earth**, and **made summer and winter** (vv. 16-17; cf. Gn 1:1-31). The reference to **the heads of Leviathan** in v. 14 is a figurative description of the manifold forces (Pharaoh and his military units) that came against Israel at the exodus, just as Leviathan is also used as a figurative label for all the world's forces that will one day array themselves against Israel before God's final judgment (cf. Is 27:1).

C. Requesting God's Deliverance (74:18-23)

74:18-23. It is not ultimately Israel whom **the enemy has reviled**, but the God of Israel, whose **name** they had **spurned** (v. 18; cf. 83:2-3; 1Sm 17:45).The psalmist affirmed that his motivation for imploring God's deliverance of His people was God's glory and honor (cf. comments on Ps 23:30). God's enemies are called **foolish** because they refuse to believe God (vv. 18, 22; cf. comment on 14:1). The psalmist prayed, **Arise, O God, and plead Your own cause** (v. 22), that is, defend Your reputation against **those who rise against You** (v. 23; cf. 2:1-3) by acting on Your covenant with Abraham, which entailed the survival and blessing of Israel. The answer to this prayer request is in the next psalm.

Psalm 75: Praise for God's Sure Justice

On the heading of this **Psalm of Asaph**, see the comments on the headings of Pss 3–4, 50. On the phrase **a Song**, cf. Ps 46. This psalm is also accompanied by the instruction that it be set to **Al-tashheth** (cf. Ps 57). In Ps 74, Asaph asked how long God would delay in vindicating His people. As a response, in Ps 75 (cf. esp. vv. 2-5), God makes it clear that He chooses to act on His own timetable (Sailhamer, *NIV Compact Bible Commentary,* 332).

A. Thankfully Affirm God's Sure Justice (75:1-3)

75:1-3. God's nearness and justice are acknowledged in the opening: **We give thanks to You, O God, we give thanks, For Your name is near** (cf. 5:11; 23:3; 25:11; 31:3). God's **wondrous works** (lit., "wonders") designates His acts of deliverance as a judicial response to the affliction of His people by those who transgress His revealed standards and authority (cf. comments on 9:1-2; 40:5). And just as His justice has already been executed in history, so too does God Himself promise that in the future, at **an appointed time** (v. 2) known only to Him, He will deliver His people and execute inevitable, final judgment on the **earth and all who dwell in it** (v. 3; cf. comments on 46:4-7).

B. Boldly Share God's Sure Justice (75:4-8)

75:4-5. Addressing **the boastful** and **the wicked**—both among the Gentiles as well as among God's people Israel—and in light of His already proven and inevitable final justice, Asaph exhorted evil people **not** to **lift up** their own **horn on high**, that is, not to assert their own strength and ability (as symbolized by a **horn**, cf. Dt 33:17; 1Kg 22:11; Ps 18:2).

75:6-8. The wicked should not **speak with insolent pride** (v. 5) because there is no **Judge** greater than God—not **from the east, nor from the west** (comprising all geographical distance), **Nor from the desert comes exaltation** (lit., "from the wilderness of mountains"). These inclusive geographic phrases introduce that **God is the Judge** over all; He alone ultimately **puts down... and exalts** (v. 7). The **cup** is a metaphor here referring to **the LORD['s]** judgment (cf. 60:3; Is 51:17; Jr 25:15; Hab 2:16) which **all the wicked of the earth must drain and drink down its dregs** (v. 8), meaning to experience God's judgment fully.

C. Continually Declare God's Sure Justice (75:9-10)

75:9-10. Asaph affirmed the goal of God's justice in wondrous works of the deliverance of Israel by judging their enemies at the exodus (vv. 1-3) as well as by His final judgment of all the wicked of the earth (vv. 4-8). The psalm begins with giving thanks (v. 1) and concludes with the declaration to **forever... sing praises to the God of Jacob** (v. 9; cf. 14:7; 20:1).

Psalm 76: God's Defense of Israel

On the heading of this **Psalm of Asaph**, see the comments on the headings to Pss 3–4. This is also a **Song** (cf. introduction to Ps 46) to be accompanied by **stringed instruments**. On the thematic connections of this psalm with those that surround it, Sailhamer writes, "With Ps 73, he [God] is the God whose dwelling place is Zion, the site of the temple. With Ps 74, he is the God who comes in judgment upon those who have oppressed the godly. With Ps 75, he is the God who acts at his appointed time and thus is the one who is to be feared [76:11]..." (Sailhamer, *NIV Compact Bible Commentary,* 332).

A. Among His People in the Land (76:1-3)

76:1-3. The psalmist affirmed the special sense in which **God is known in Judah**. He is not merely among them in the omnipresent sense whereby He is everywhere and "in Him all things hold together" (Col 1:17), but He **is** also **known**, indicating the intimate familial relationship of God to Israel corporately and to the righteous within her individually (cf. comment on Ps 1:5). This special relationship is visibly highlighted by **His tabernacle** (the temple) **in Salem** (Jerusalem; cf. Gn 14:18)and **His dwelling place . . . in Zion**. This speaks of God's manifest presence within creation both historically, as the site where His cloud of glory dwelt (cf. Ex 40:34-38), as well as for all eternity, when He will establish His kingdom on earth (cf. Ezk 43:7; Rv 21:22-27).

B. Among His People outside the Land (76:4-10)

76:4-8. God is presented as **resplendent, More majestic than the mountains** (cf. Ex 15:6, 14; Pss 8:1, 9; 29:4; Is 63:1). His triumphant defense of His people is illustrated by the destruction of the Egyptian army at the exodus: **Both rider and horse were cast into** the deep (v. 6; cf. Ex 15:1; Ps 74:12-15). The Lord **caused judgment to be heard from heaven; The earth feared and was still** (v. 8; cf. the Introduction to Esther and comments on Est 8:17).

76:9-10. Even the most difficult circumstances, **the wrath of man**, as exemplified by the wicked Egyptians, **shall praise You**. The outcome of God's judgment on the wicked will ultimately bring Him praise (cf. 2:6-8).

C. Beyond His People throughout All Lands (76:11-12)

76:11-12. The psalm culminates by affirming that not only is God known in Judah (v. 1), but ultimately He is (and will be) **feared** (recognized as "awesome") **by the kings of the earth** (Gentile nations) when they acknowledge the sovereign rule of the God of Jacob (v. 12; cf. v. 7; 2:4-12; Is 45:23; Rm 14:11; Php 2:10).

Psalm 77: Finding Comfort in God

On the heading of this **Psalm of Asaph**, see the headings of Pss 3– 4. For the instruction **according to Jeduthun**, see introduction to Ps 62. Although there was scant evidence of God's miraculous intervention in his own day (cf. 74:9), Asaph chose to meditate on God's mighty deeds from the past (cf.; 77:5-12; (Sailhamer, *NIV Compact Bible Commentary,* 332).

A. Express Need (77:1-10)

77:1-2. The psalmist expressed his heartfelt need for comfort: **My voice rises to God, and I will cry aloud . . . and He will hear me**. He turned to the Lord, the only One who could truly bring his **soul** comfort. Both **in the day of . . . trouble** and **in the night**, he **stretched out** his hand **without** growing weary of pleading with the Lord for help.

77:3-8. Asaph held nothing back in his prayers, but in **remember[ing]** (turning to) **God**, he was **disturbed** (v.3, better translated "distressed"). **I sigh** would be better translated "I pour out my complaint," as in the headings of 102 and 142:2 (see comments there). Instead of being comforted when he recalled **the days of old . . . the years of long ago** when he had a **song in the night** (vv. 5-6), now (in the midst of unanswered prayer and problems) he wondered if God's **lovingkindness [had] ceased forever**, if **His promise [had] come to an end** (v. 8).

77:9-10. Asaph also wondered, **Has God forgotten . . .** has **the right hand of the Most High . . . changed**? The **right hand** is the image of God's power, which He uses on behalf of His people (cf. Ex 15:6, 12). These are emotional questions arising from circumstances (cf. comments on Ps 44:9; 60:1; 74:1).

B. Affirm the Principle (77:11-15)

77:11-15. With a determined attitude Asaph applies the essential principle of finding the Lord's comfort in difficult times by refocusing on the Him. Asaph will **remember** His **deeds** and His **wonders** (the word here has a collective sense, as again in v. 14) **of old**. Instead of allowing the present difficult circumstances or unanswered prayer to: (1) cause distress when remembering the Lord (vv. 3-6), or (2) cause doubt about the very character of God (vv. 7-10), instead remember the truth: **Your way, O God, is holy . . . You have by Your power redeemed Your people** (vv. 13, 15; cf. comments on 9:1; 40:5; 75:1), The "remembering" here entails meditation (v. 12, **I will mediate**; cf. comment on 1:2). God's lovingkindness is grounded in His unconditional covenant with Abraham, Isaac, and Jacob, here identified as **the sons of Jacob and Joseph** (cf. comment on 74:1-11).

C. Select an Example (77:16-20)

77:16-20. Two specific example of God's concern and deliverance are given. The first is God's power at the parting of the Red Sea: **the waters saw You, O God . . . the earth trembled and shook** (vv. 16-18) as God took action on behalf of His people Israel at the exodus (referred to by Asaph also in 74:13-15; 76:5-7; 78:13; 80:8a; and 81:6, 10a). The second is His character as the Shepherd of Israel, leading His **people like a flock** (cf. 100:3) under the leadership of **Moses and Aaron** (v. 20; cf. Ex 4–6).

Psalm 78: A Celebration of the Lord of History

This psalm, a **Maskil** (cf. introduction to Ps 32) of **Asaph** (cf. introductory comments on Ps 50), is especially appropriate following Ps

77 where Asaph determined to meditate on God's mighty deeds from the past. Here he did that explicitly with the intent of educating a younger generation about the works of the Lord on behalf of His people Israel throughout their history (vv. 2, 4; (Sailhamer, *NIV Compact Bible Commentary,* 332). This is an acrostic psalm, composed of 77 lines in Hebrew in seven symmetrical stanzas following an 11-line introduction: 8 lines/16 lines/9 lines/16 lines/9 lines/8 lines.

A. The Purpose: To Teach Later Generations of God's Faithfulness (78:1-8)

78:1-2. The psalmist described his **instruction** as **a parable** ("teaching stories/illustrations") and **dark** (lit., "riddles/enigmatic") **sayings.** The phrase **dark sayings** does not mean something sinister or negative, but rather an enigmatic saying used for instruction. This does not imply that the meaning of his words was unclear, but that the meaning would be clear only to those who had the spiritual capacity to understand it, namely, those whose heart was right before the Lord. To those whose heart was not right, (i.e., the unfaithful whose heart had not been circumcised; cf. Dt 10:16; 30:6; Jr 4:4), the truth of this psalm—which concerns a fundamental aspect of the expressed relationship between God and those whom He has chosen—would remain obscure and seem like "foolishness" (1Co 1:18). Precisely for this reason v. 2 is cited (in typical paraphrase) in Mt 13:35 to describe Jesus' periodic teaching in parables (cf. the citation of Is 6:9-10 in Mt 13:10-17 with a similar point).

78:3-4. The purpose of this psalm is to recount God's faithfulness throughout Israel's history, to **tell . . . the generation to come the praises of the LORD, And His strength and His wondrous works that He has done.** The history is presented somewhat chronologically, yet with significant overlapping of historical periods and events.

78:5-8. Foundational to this history is that God **established a testimony in Jacob and appointed a law in Israel** (v. 5). Surprisingly, the psalmist did not start with the creation of the world or the covenant with Abraham, Isaac, and Jacob. Rather, he began with God's gift of the law to Moses. The purpose of the law was to teach the next generation to know the Lord, and in turn teach the same to the next generation (v. 6). Thus, each generation, would learn to **put their confidence in God** (v. 7). The point of this psalm was to teach this later generation to learn from Israel's history and **not be like their fathers** who were **stubborn and rebellious . . .** and were **not faithful to God** (v. 8). Through the history of God's faithfulness and Israel's rebellion, this generation would learn to follow the Lord.

B. The Record: The History of God's Faithfulness to Israel (78:9-64)

This large section is parallel to, and quite likely the exemplar for, Stephen's defense in Ac 7:2-53. The point in both cases was to review the record of God's faithfulness for the consistently rebellious people whom He had chosen. Like Asaph in the present psalm, Stephen also focused his review on the early generations of Israel (especially in the wilderness), highlighting their culminating expressions of sin and God's consequent correction (cf. vv. 17, 40-43, 58 with Ac 7:39-43), and concluding with God's gracious establishment of the Davidic monarchy and the building of the temple in Jerusalem (vv. 69-70; cf. Ac 7:46-50).

1. Divided Kingdom History/Exodus History (78:9-16)

78:9-16. The **sons of Ephraim** were the northern ten tribes of Israel. Saying **they turned back in the day of battle** (v. 9) is a metaphor for Israel's betrayal of her **covenant** to worship God as He commanded at the temple in Jerusalem. Instead, they **refused to walk in His law** (v. 10) by worshiping false gods in Samaria and Bethel under the leadership of Jeroboam when the kingdom divided (cf. 1Kg 12; 2Ch 10). Many of the miraculous events of the exodus, which they should have remembered, are recounted here (cf. Ex 7–17; Nm 20:8-11).

2. Wilderness Wandering History (78:17-33)

78:17-33. Despite God's faithful deliverance and care (vv. 11-16), the Israelites **still continued to sin against Him** (v. 17). This is an overview of their rebellion **against the Most High in the desert** during the 40 years of wilderness wandering (cf. Nm 11). Because the generation that came out of Egypt sinned and **did not believe in God** or **trust in His salvation** (v. 22), they all died in the wilderness, **their days** came to an end in **futility** (v. 33; cf. Nm 14:22-23, 28-35).

3. Period of Judges History (78:34-39)

78:34-39. When Israel entered the promised land of Canaan, they were under the leadership of the judges. This period was characterized by a cycle of sin and judgment: **He killed them** for their sin (v. 34), so they **returned** to Him for a short time before they were again **[un]faithful** to **His covenant** (v. 37; cf. Jdg 3:7-8; 17:6; 21:25).

4. Exodus History (78:40-53)

78:40-53. This is a summary review of rebellion **in the wilderness** (v. 40), looking back again with a general overview of the plagues in **Egypt** (v. 43). The Passover was the central miraculous event in Israel's history (cf. Ex 12:1-23). The Lord commanded Israel to celebrate the Passover each year and to teach its significance to each generation (cf. Ex 12:24-27). God **smote all the firstborn in Egypt** and **led forth His own people like sheep** (vv. 51-52).

5. Conquest History (78:54-64)

78:54-64. After the exodus and 40 years of wilderness wandering, **He brought them to His holy land** (v. 54). The land of Israel, or Canaan, is specifically identified as God's **holy land** (cf. Lv 25:23; Zch 9:16), which He gave to the Jewish people by His covenant forever (cf. Gn 12:1-3; Jr 7:7; 25:5). The Lord **drove out the nations before them** (v. 55; cf. Jos 11:16-23), **Yet they tempted and rebelled against the Most High God** (v. 56). This section gives a similar sad account as vv. 34-39.

C. The Triumphant Culmination of God's Choice in the Messianic Line (78:65-72)

78:65-66. The Lord's defense of Israel begins with a poetic description that says **the Lord awoke as if from a sleep**. Of course, the Lord does not sleep (cf. 121:4). The phrase **as if from** indicates the feeling that the Lord had been inactive/asleep; finally, at last, the Lord was defending His people after a period of seeming inactivity. He began by driving **His adversaries backward**; these enemies of Israel were the enemies of the Lord (cf. 83:2-5) and **He put on them an everlasting reproach** (v. 66). God's decisive victory will come when the messianic King rules the earth (cf. 2; 146:10; Lk 1:32-33).

78:67-69. This section presents God's choice of Judah, the tribal line of Messiah; the location of Zion, the ultimate messianic royal city; and the line of David, the dynasty of the future Messiah. God **rejected the tent [household] of Joseph**, although the Lord was with him (v. 67; cf. Gn 39:2-3, 19, 23). Likewise God did **not choose the tribe of Ephraim** for the messianic line (cf. Gn 48:5; 20; Is 7:17).

Instead, God **chose the tribe of Judah** (v. 68), not by virtue of the birth order of Judah, (he was the fourth-born son, not the first-born, cf. Gn 29:35), nor by reason of his righteousness, but by God's sovereign choice. Within the tribal territory of Judah, God **chose . . . Mount Zion**, beginning with Abraham's offer of Isaac there (cf. Gn 22:2; 2Ch 3:1; Ps 132:13-14). God then directed David to buy the land for the temple (cf. 2Sm 24:18-25) and directed Solomon to build the temple there (cf. 2Ch 3:1-2). He chose **Mount Zion** as the place **which He loved** (v. 68; cf. 87:2); there the Lord **built His sanctuary** both historically (cf. 1Kg 6; Ezr 3) and for all eternity (cf. Ezk 43:7; Rv 21:22-27).

78:70-72. God also **chose David** (cf. 1Sm 13:14; 16:1, 3, 7; Ac 7:46; 13:22) as the head of the messianic line (cf. Ru 4:18-22; 2Sm 7:8-16; Mt 1:1, 6; 9:27). David, who had been a **shepherd**, was called by the Lord **to shepherd Jacob His people** (v. 71). David was the prototype of the Good Shepherd, the Messiah Jesus (cf. Jn 10:11; Rv 7:17).

Psalm 79: A Collective Appeal for Deliverance

On the heading of this psalm of **Asaph**, see the comments on the headings to Pss 3 and 50. This psalm continues the history from Ps 78. it is a national lament for a catastrophe that struck Jerusalem, probably the Babylonian destruction of the city and the Solomon's temple and the captivity in 586 BC. Psalm 79 describes the subsequent apostasy and judgment of Judah (esp. vv. 1-7) to indicate the spiritual unworthiness of the entire nation, both northern and southern tribes. The psalmist thereby emphasized the need for, and his confidence in, God's unfailing grace and covenant faithfulness in the midst of the current disaster (Sailhamer, *NIV Compact Bible Commentary,* 333).

A. Acknowledging God's Judgment (79:1-7)

79:1-4. The description of Jerusalem is dire: **O God, the nations have invaded Your inheritance** (v. 1; cf. comments on 47:4; 68:9). The Gentile nations around Israel had **defiled Your holy temple** and **laid Jerusalem in ruins** (the destruction by Babylon; cf. 2Kg 25). People were lying dead in the streets as **food to the birds**; **their blood** was poured out **like water round about Jerusalem** (vv. 2-3). The disaster had made the survivors **a reproach to** their Gentile **neighbors**.

79:5-7. The question **How long, O Lord? Will You be angry forever?** indicates these tragic events were the result of God's judgment. Acknowledging the LORD was **angry** at His people implies the recognition of God's judgment on their sin. Moreover, the word **jealousy** in v. 5 is not the petty emotions of an insecure heart, but rather God's zeal for the full devotion and worship of His people (cf. Dt 4:24-31). The situation was so terrible the psalmist pled for God, **Pour out Your wrath upon the nations which do not know You**, and have **devoured Jacob** (v. 6), the people of Israel. See comments on imprecatory psalms in Introduction: Types of Psalms.

B. Imploring God's Mercy (79:8)

79:8. Having affirmed God's chastisement and therefore their sins which caused the judgment, the psalmist now led his people in petitioning God: **Let Your compassion** (mercy out of love, cf. 25:6) **come quickly**.

C. Focusing on God's Glory (79:9-13)

79:9-12. The motivation for this petition—and, of course, the ultimate goal of Israel's (as any believer's) chastisement—is **the glory of** God's **name** (i.e., God's "name" is often used by metonymy for God Himself; see comment on 20:5). By reproaching Israel, these enemies were ultimately reproaching God Himself. Jerusalem had become a **reproach** to her **neighbors** (v. 4), yet **the reproach with which they have reproached** was against **You, O Lord** (v. 12). Therefore, by delivering His people, God was vindicating (i.e., proving the infallibility of) His covenant promises to preserve His people (cf. comments on 76, 83).

79:13. The psalm centers on the Lord's relationship with His people. It begins by identifying Israel as God's inheritance (v. 1) and ends by identifying them as **Your people and the sheep of Your pasture** (cf. 74:1; 100:3). God's deliverance would serve as another occasion for **all generations** (cf. 78:4) to **tell of** His **praise**.

Psalm 80: God's Shepherding of His People Israel

On this **Psalm of Asaph**, see introductory comments to Pss 4 and 50. This psalm is **set to El Shosahannim** ("Lilies," cf. introductory comments on Ps 60; cf. headings on Pss 45 and 69). **Eduth** is a legal term meaning "testimony," probably because it serves to provide a legal testimony regarding the just historical basis for God's correction of His people. Psalms 78 and 79 describe God's judgment of the apostate northern and southern tribes, casting some doubt on the possibility of the fulfillment of the Davidic covenant and the future restoration of the nation. But Asaph reassured his readers that there would be such a restoration under the supreme Son of David (called "son of man" in v. 17).

Psalm 80 indicates that the hope of this future restoration did not hang on any of the previous sons of David. Since the book of Psalms was edited into its final form in post-exilic times, Israel had no king to fulfill its hopes at this point in its history, giving this psalm a decidedly prophetic and messianic flavor (Sailhamer, *NIV Compact Bible Commentary*, 333; also see Introduction: Background and introductory comments to Ps 69).

A. The Reality of the Correction (80:1-7)

80:1-3. Israel's relationship with the Lord is immediately indicated by the description of God as the **Shepherd of Israel, You who lead Joseph like a flock** (v. 1; cf. 23:6; 77:20; 78:52). God is portrayed in great majesty **enthroned above the cherubim** (cf. 1Sm 4:4; Ezk 1:22-28). The request **God, restore us** indicates that God was correcting His people (cf. Pss 28:1-2; 50:7, 21). To **cause Your face to shine upon us** (v. 3; cf. vv. 7, 19) is requesting God to bless them and is drawn from the Aaronic benediction (cf. Nm 6:22-27; Pss 4:6; 31:16; 67:1).

80:4-7. Addressing God as **Lord God of Hosts** further indicates His majesty (cf. v. 1; 1Sm 17:34; 1Ch 17:24; Pss 46:7; 69:6). Israel's suffering is described with words like **bread of tears . . . drink[ing] tears**, and being made an **object of contention** (vv. 5-6; cf. 79:4). Asking **How long will You be angry**? (v. 4) forms one of the links connecting this psalm to the previous psalm (see comments on 79:5). The intended goal of chastisement was that God would **restore** them to spiritual health (v. 7 is parallel to v. 3).

B. The Basis of the Correction (80:8-13)

80:8-13. This section of the psalm is in the form of a parable. The **vine** metaphor was frequently used of Israel (cf. Is 3:14; 5:1-7; 27:2; Jr 2:21; 12:10; Ezk 15:1-8; 19:10-14; Hs 10:1; 14:7). Here the vine describes Israel in terms of the exodus from **Egypt** and settling in Israel. The basis of God's correction was His unconditional, sovereign election of Israel, grounded in His covenant with and promises to Abraham, Isaac, and Jacob (cf. Gn 12:2-3; 17:7-8; Ps 105:8-10; Rm 9:7-8; Gal 3:18-19). This point is vividly portrayed by the image of Israel as **a vine**, being **removed**/transplanted by God from Egypt to Canaan, His holy land (v. 8, cf. 78:54-55). In Canaan, God also **cleared the ground** (v. 9) of the Gentile nations to provide space for the vine of Israel, so it **took deep root and filled the land** (cf. comments on 74:1-11). At one time the Israel the vine flourished so that **the mountains were covered with its shadow** (v. 10), but now God had **broken down its hedges** that protected the vineyard and **whatever moves in the field feeds on it** (v. 13), indicating that Israel was being oppressed by the nations.

C. The Goal of the Correction (80:14-19)

80:14-15. Again the prayer, directed to the **God of hosts**, was for Him to **take care of this vine . . . which Your right hand has planted** (vv. 14-15; cf. v. 8). Israel was called **the son** [lit., "branch"] **whom You have strengthened for Yourself**.

80:16-18. Although the vine had been **burned with fire** and **cut down**, this was because of **the rebuke of Your countenance**. The goal of God's correction was to restore Israel to Himself. **Then** afterwards, **we shall not turn back from You; Revive us** (lit., "give life") so we will **call upon Your name**.

80:19. The psalm concludes with the image of restoration by God using the phrase that unites the psalm: **Cause Your face to shine upon us** (v. 3, 7, 19; see comments at v. 3; 11:7b; 15:5b; 44:3; 56:13) **and we will be saved** (v. 3, 7, 19). The Lord is the only hope of salvation.

Psalm 81: The Characteristics of God's Collective Call to Renewal

On the heading of this **Psalm of Asaph**, see the comments on the heading to Ps 50. It is for the **choir director; on the Gittith**, see the comments on Ps 8. Written from exile, Ps 80 contained a plea for God to restore the people of Israel and their nation (see esp. vv.1-7, 14-19). Now Pss 81 and 82 are the Lord's reply. Israel's national restoration (not personal salvation) was conditioned upon their need to become obedient to Him (81:12-14). If they would do this, God would bless them (v. 16; Sailhamer, *NIV Compact Bible Commentary*, 333).

According to ancient Jewish tradition, based on the blowing of trumpets (v. 3), this psalm is recited on The Feast of the Trumpet Blowing (also called *Rosh Hashanah*, the Jewish New Year; cf. Lv 23:24-25; Nm 29:1). In a sense, this is a hymn to challenge the people of Israel to covenant faithfulness. It gives an overview of the history of the covenant, using the Torah/Pentateuch.

A. A Customary Event (81:1-4)

81:1-2. The psalm begins with a call to worship: **Sing for joy to God our strength; Shout joyfully to the God of Jacob**, and encourages worship with a variety of instruments.

81:3-4. The **trumpet** (Hb. *shofar*), the ram's horn trumpet (cf. Ex 19:13), was to be blown at appointed feasts, at the **new moon** (cf. Nm 10:10; 28:11-15), at the **full moon** (cf. Lv 23:34), and at God's appointed times (cf. Lv 23:34). As a supplement to—and reinforcement of—the individual obligation to continually "renew" (maintain the vibrancy of) one's walk in righteousness, God also commanded the regular collective observance of a **feast day**. **For it is a statute for Israel, An ordinance of the God of Jacob** (v. 4). This **feast day** is *Rosh Hashanah*, as noted above, which falls on the **new moon** (i.e., the first day) of the seventh month. The focus of this festival is national spiritual renewal—as in this psalm—through repentance (cf. vv. 8-9, 11-13) and praise (cf. vv. 1-2).

B. A Commemorative Event (81:5-7)

81:5-7. As an impetus to spiritual renewal, God reminded His people of His past concern for them in their early days as a people—how He **went throughout the land of Egypt** (v. 5, an allusion to His judgment of the Egyptians by the 10th plague, cf. Ex 11:4) and **relieved** their **shoulder of the burden** of slavery, freeing their **hands . . . from the basket** of straw they would gather for making bricks (v. 6; cf. Ex 5:7). He did all this, moreover, even though the people did not deserve it—as seen in that God **proved** them (i.e., refined them [through correction]; see the verb also in Zch 13:9 where the NASB translates it "test" and "tested"). When the people of Israel **called in trouble** the Lord **rescued** them (v. 7).

C. A Confessional Event (81:8-16)

81:8-10. The Lord called His people to Himself: **O Israel, if you would listen to Me!** This is reminiscent of the *Sh'ma*, the watchword of Israel (cf. Dt. 6:4), where He reminded them to be faithful to Him. **Let there be no strange god[s] among you** because **I, the Lord, am your God** (vv. 9-10)). Just as He fed the people with manna in the wilderness of **Egypt** (cf. Ex 16:14-21), so God commanded them, **Open your mouth wide and I will fill it** (v. 10), not with manna this time, but with His own goodness.

81:11-16. Despite the record of God's care, **Israel did not obey** the Lord**.** The key idea here is that God wanted Israel to **listen** (vv. 11, 13) to Him. If they would **walk in [His] ways**, He would **subdue their enemies** and richly bless them, using the poetic imagery of satisfying them with **honey from the rock** (v. 16; cf. Dt 32:13), meaning divine providence.

Psalm 82: God's Sovereignty over the Nations

On the heading of this **Psalm of Asaph**, see the comments on the headings to Pss 3 and 50.

In Ps 82, God continued to respond to the pleas of His people in Pss 80 and 81 by continuing to call them to obey Him (Sailhamer, *NIV Compact Bible Commentary*, 333).

A. God's Position (82:1)

82:1. The **congregation** in which **God takes His stand** (i.e., to execute judgment, as God's "standing" is elsewhere intended; cf. Is 3:13) was the congregation (i.e., people) of Israel, to whom this same expression "congregation (of the LORD)" is elsewhere applied (cf. Nm 27:17; Jos 22:16-17). So too the **rulers** (Hb. *elohim*, lit., "gods") **in the midst of** whom **He judges** were the leaders of Israel to whom the ministry of teaching, modeling, and enforcing God's Word was entrusted, such as the judges and priests in the OT and the scribes and Pharisees in the NT. The gods (v. 6a) here were the same contextually as those Jesus cited cf. Jn 10:34). He further defined "gods" as those "to whom the word of God came" (Jn 10:35; see comments there). Both on the lips of Jesus and here, the word referred to men such as Moses (designated *elohim* in Ex 4:16), the judges who assisted him (designated *elohim* in Ex 21:6; 22:7-8, 27), and the subsequent judges and leaders of Israel (cf. Jdg 5:8; Ps 138:1). In all these instances where the epithet "gods" (*elohim*) is applied to men, it should be understood in the sense of "proxies or representatives of God." The point of this verse is thus to underscore God's preeminent position as the final Judge who will pass judgment on all other judges.

B. God's Challenge (82:2-4)

82:2-4. God's challenge here essentially repeated the injunction of Lv 19:15-16 in which God instructed His people at the outset of their nationhood and spoke to them continually thereafter through His prophets (cf. Is 1:17; Mc 6:8). His message was that they not **judge unjustly** or **show partiality to the wicked** (v. 2), but rather that they **vindicate** (i.e., plead the cause of) **the weak and fatherless** (or "orphan"; this word elsewhere is translated "orphan," referring to a pre-adolescent who has no father), **the afflicted and destitute** (v. 3), those who have no one else to help them or plead their cause (see Jb 29:12, where "orphan" is also used).

C. God's Judgment (82:5-8)

82:5-8. The psalmist affirmed the Lord's inevitable judgment of those judges and leaders (v. 6), designated **gods** in v. 1, who continue to judge unjustly (v. 2), at which time **all the foundations of the earth** will be **shaken** (v. 5), for He is the One who laid them (cf. 75:3; 104:5). This imagery points to the final judgment of Rv 20:11-15 that immediately precedes God's remaking of the heavens and the earth. Asaph's closing affirmation that **it is You who possesses all the nations** (cf. Ps 2:8) further emphasizes God's right to enact this final judgment, as well as that this judgment will be enacted by the Son of God.

Psalm 83: Imprecation as Affirmation of God's Gracious Promises

On the heading of this **Psalm of Asaph** see the comments on the headings to Pss 3 and 50. It is described as **A Song** (see introduction to Ps 46). Thematically, the three parts of this psalm parallel the three essential provisions or, more precisely, promises (cf. Gal 3:17-18) of the Abrahamic covenant: an eternal land, an eternal people, and eternal blessing (for Israel and all nations). The fulfillment of these promises, and not the destruction of the psalmist's enemies as such, drove his imprecation in this psalm.

One of the central themes of Asaph's psalms (73–83), of which this is the last, is imploring God to deliver His people, city, and temple. These all lay in ruins and provided the Gentile nations grounds for mocking Him. Asaph therefore called upon God to judge those nations so they would recognize His supremacy (Sailhamer, *NIV Compact Bible Commentary*, 333-34).

A. To Make Israel an Eternal Nation (83:1-8)

83:1-5. The opening of this psalm is a plea: **O God, do not remain quiet . . . silent . . . still**, but instead take action against **Your enemies**. The expression **exalted themselves** (v. 2) is lit., "lifted up (their) head," referring to the mustering and counting of soldiers in preparation for battle against God's people. They **make an** uproar against the Lord (cf. Ps 2). The threat was against Israel by her many enemies, who collectively **conspire together** against the people of Israel to **wipe them out . . . That the name of Israel be remembered no more** (vv. 3-4).

However, because the plans were made by the enemies of the Lord, these words were ultimately directed against God Himself, since He established Israel as a distinct people (cf. Gn 12:2) and promised that they would remain so forever (cf. Jr 31:35-37). It was He who gave them their name (cf. Gn 12:2; 32:28), the name itself bearing witness to the character of God. "Israel" literally means "God strives," that is, "strives for Israel"; (see comment on Ps 32:28). These people who **hate You** (v. 2) conspire together (v. 2, **conspired together**, v. 5) and **Against You they make a covenant** (v. 5). These words indicate that hatred against the people of Israel was in actuality hatred of the God of Israel.

83:6-8. The enemies were Gentile nations which had a history of aggression against Israel: **Edom** (cf. Am 1:11), **the Ishmaelites** (cf. Gn 25:12-18), **Moab** (cf. Is 16), **the Hagrites** (cf. 1Ch 5:10), **Gebal** (cf. Ezk 27:9), **Ammon** (cf. Am 1:13-15), **Amalek** (cf. Dt 25:17-18), **Philistia** (cf. 1Sm 17), **Tyre** (cf. Ezk 26:1–28:19), and **Assyria** (cf. 2Kg 17:1-6). The statement that these nations had **become a help to the children of Lot**, the Moabites and Ammonites (cf. Gn 19:36-38), is a summary of the coalition of enemies against Israel. Although they had all opposed Israel in the past, this assault appears to refer to the end of days, when the nations will gather against Israel (cf. Ps 2:1-2; Zch 14:2).

B. To Give Israel an Eternal Land (83:9-15)

83:9-15. This is a plea for the Lord to **Deal with them** (those nations listed vv. 6-8) as He did with **Midian . . . Sisera and Jabin** during the time of the Judges (cf. Jdg 4, 7). The mention of those **destroyed at En-dor** (cf. Jos 17:11) . . . **Oreb . . . Zeeb . . . Zebah and Zalmunna** (cf. Jdg 7–8) is another list of enemies defeated by the Lord.

Consistent with their collective intention to wipe out the people of Israel, the enemies of God's people also sought to **possess** the **pastures of God**, the land of Israel, for themselves (v. 12)—an intention that was likewise ultimately directed against God since He gave Israel that land as an everlasting possession (cf. Gn 13:15; 17:8; Ps 105:10-11). This same intention continues unabated to the present day among Israel's many enemies

C. To Bless All Peoples with Eternal Life (83:16-18)

83:16-18. Counterbalancing the imprecation in this psalm (as also, even if implicitly, in any other imprecatory psalm or statement in Scripture) is God's final and greatest promise to Abraham, Isaac, and Jacob, that through them all nations of the earth will be blessed (cf. Gn 12:3; 22:18; 26:4; 28:14). This promise was here explicitly affirmed by Asaph, who implored God to **fill** the **faces** of Israel's enemies **with dishonor**, with the goal **that they may seek** God's **name** (v. 16) and **know that** it is He **alone, whose name is the LORD,** is **the Most High** (cf. 14:19) **over all the earth** (v. 18; cf. Gn 11:4; 12:2; Pss 20:5; 23:3; Mal 1:11).

Psalm 84: The Threefold Aspects of True Blessedness

On the heading of this **Psalm of the sons of Korah**, see the comments on the headings of Pss 3–4; 42–43, and Introduction: Author. The three parts of this psalm comprise those three concurrent aspects (not progressive "steps") of the believer's walk with the Lord, as presented in terms of worship in Zion. Whereas Asaph's psalms mourned the destruction of the nation and the temple, this psalm anticipated the temple's restoration and the prospect of glorious worship there (Sailhamer, *NIV Compact Bible Commentary*, 334).

A. Dwelling in God's Presence (84:1-4)

84:1-4. The first aspect of true blessedness is proximity to the **LORD of hosts** whose presence on earth was centered in His **dwelling places**—the plural form referring to the temple compound and all its distinct sections (as in 43:3; 46:4). The psalmist's **soul longed and even yearned for the courts of the LORD** (v. 2; cf. 42:1), a poignant indication of the psalmist's focus on being in God's presence All those who love God should yearn to **dwell in** God's **house**, not simply as the priest who served there, but as the Lord's guest enjoying His presence (v. 4; cf. comments on 15:1; 23:6).

B. Living in God's Strength (84:5-7)

84:5-7. True blessing accrues to the person (Hb. *adam*, which, though usually translated **man**, is properly a designation for any human individual) who finds his **strength . . . in** God alone (v. 5; cf. 1Sm 30:6). No matter what happens, even **Passing through the valley of Baca** ("weeping," v. 6), the saddest of times, those who trust in the Lord can transform those tears and **make** the valley of weeping into **a spring** of water. People such as this **go from strength to strength** (v. 7a). No matter where they go or what their circumstances may be, God's strength is always available to them; and to "recharge" this strength they appear regularly **before God in Zion** (v. 7b). This refers to the three pilgrimage festivals (Unleavened Bread, Weeks [Pentecost], and Tabernacles), when God commanded that every man in Israel "appear before the LORD your God in the place which He chooses" (Dt 16:16). Likewise, today we should seek God's presence through study of His Word as our resource of fellowship, refreshment, and strength.

C. Trusting in God's Grace (84:9-12)

84:9-10. After praising God (vv. 1-7), the psalm transitioned with a prayer that was likewise focused on the joy of fellowship with God in His presence. **For a day in Your courts is better than thousands outside** away from Him (v. 10).

84:11-12. The Hebrew in the phrase **the LORD gives** denotes an ongoing/unending action; **grace** indicates it is God's consistent, never-ending supply to His people throughout the OT, both by protecting and providing for them, as well as by granting them **grace** (or "favor") in the eyes of others (cf. Gn 39:21; Ex 3:21; 11:3; 12:36; Dn 1:9). The description of God as **a sun** reinforces the concept of God's grace as the giver of life; being a **shield** indicates that He is the One who protects life (v. 11).

Psalm 85: The Three Tenses of Divine Love

On the heading of this **Psalm of the sons of Korah**, see the comments on the headings of Pss 3–4; 42–43. This psalm reiterates the hope of God restoring Israel in the future, but the righteous must prepare for this coming deliverance by continued obedience and faithfulness (cf. 85:8; Sailhamer, *NIV Compact Bible Commentary*, 334).

A. Divine Love in the Past (85:1-3)

85:1-3. In the past the **Lord . . . showed favor to** the . . . **land** of Israel. God's showing of **favor** is specifically associated in Scripture with His "compassion" or "tender love" (cf. Is 60:10). This tender love was expressed toward Israel in the past by His having **restored the captivity** (better translated "fortunes") **of Jacob**—referring to God's restoration of the people to an outward state of prosperity following a period of correction or testing during the Babylonian exile (cf. the same expression in Jb 42:10; Ezk 16:53). But more importantly, He **forgave the iniquity of [His] people [and] turned away from [His] burning anger** (v. 3). The Babylonian exile was a judgment for failing to obey the Lord (cf. Jr 25:1-11), and return to the land of Israel was an evidence of the Lord's forgiveness.

B. Divine Love in the Present (85:4-7)

85:4-7. Based on the example of God's past expression of love toward His covenant people, the psalmist expectantly implored God's present expression of the same. During the current difficulties, he asked God to **revive us again, that your people may rejoice in You**. That God did **show** them **lovingkindness** (*chesed*, a synonym of the word translated favor in v. 1) is evident from God's declaration through Malachi "I have loved [denoting action begun in the past and continuing unabated into the present] you" (Mal 1:2).

C. Divine Love in the Future (85:8-13)

85:8-13. There is a confidence in the future under the Lord's loving command: **He will speak peace to His people**; those who are obedient to the Lord are called **His godly ones** (v. 8). That God will continue to express His compassion and love toward Israel in the future is emphasized by the phrase, **Lovingkindness and truth have met together; righteousness and peace have kissed each other**. These are especially poignant and memorable because all these ideal qualities and attributes are ultimately fulfilled and eternally exemplified in the Messiah (cf. Is 11:1-5; Zch 6:13).

Psalm 86: Prayer to the Sovereign Lord from His Servant

In its heading this psalm is **of David** (the only Davidic psalm in Book Three of the Psalms) and described as **A Prayer** (see introduction to Ps 17). The psalm's theme of God's sovereignty (i.e., lordship) and the psalmist's corresponding servanthood, is emphasized by the sevenfold repetition (signifying perfection and completion) of the word Lord (Hb. *adonai* lit., "my Lord/Master/Sovereign," as opposed to LORD = Yahweh; vv. 3a, 4b, 5a, 8a, 9a, 12a, 15a), and by the threefold repetition (signifying the "utmost" of something, equivalent to the English superlative) of the expression Your servant (vv. 2b, 4a, 16a; on these repetition methods see introduction to 110. This psalm of David may have been inserted here into the "Korah psalms" to illustrate that God does hear the prayers of the righteous in which they cry out for deliverance and forgiveness (Sailhamer, *NIV Compact Bible Commentary*, 334).

A. Affirming the Lord as His Sovereign (86:1-5)

86:1-5. The psalm begins with a direct request, **Incline Your ear . . . and answer me** (cf. 17:6; 31:2). The request for an answer to prayer is predicated on the character of the Lord. Prefacing the concept of God's perfect sovereignty, as signified by the sevenfold repetition of **Lord** (*adonai*) throughout the psalm (as in Ps 85, see introduction to Ps 86), is the concept of God's unique sovereignty (that He is the sovereign of all creation with no one of superior authority or ability over Him). This is signified by the threefold repetition of **Lord** in this opening section. David also employed two other common biblical designations of the Lord in this section: **LORD** (*Yahweh*, in v. 1a) and **God** (*elohim* in v. 2b), whereas in v. 5 he employed descriptions of

God that are more relational: a Sovereign who is **ready to forgive** (v. 5; cf. Ex 34:7) as well as one who is **abundant in lovingkindness** (v. 5; cf. Ex 34:6). On the expression, **Be gracious to me** (v. 3), see comment on 56:1.

B. Affirming the Lord as the Only Sovereign (86:6-13)

86:6-10. Again there is a request: **Give ear, O Lord, to my prayer** and **supplications!** In this section David emphasized the uniqueness of his Sovereign—not only that there is no one above Him, but also that **there is no one like** Him (v. 8; cf. Ex 15:11). No other sovereign can be credited with having **made** all the **nations** (v. 9, referring both to His material creation of humanity as well as to His division of humanity into distinct linguistic and political entities at Babel; cf. Gn 11:9). And there is no other sovereign whom **all nations** . . . **shall** one day **come and worship before** (v. 9; for only God is to be worshiped; cf. Ex 34:14; Lk 4:8). This statement refers specifically to the nations' worship of Messiah, to whom this passage is applied in Rv 15:4.

86:11-13. In order to begin to understand the sovereignty of the Lord, it is essential to know Him better daily by obeying the instruction: **Teach me Your way, O Lord; I will walk in Your truth; Unite my heart to fear Your name** (v. 11; cf. Ps 1; 111:10). David's affirmation that God had **delivered** his **soul from** . . . **Sheol** (v. 13) expressed his confidence in his relationship with the Lord even unto death. It was also a foreshadowing of David's confidence in the resurrection of the coming Messiah, as he "looked ahead" and understood that truth (cf. Ac 2:31 and comments on Pss 16:10; 49:14-15).

C. Affirming the Lord as the Perfect Sovereign (86:14-17)

86:14-17. At this point, the psalm turns to address David's enemies, characterized as **arrogant men** who **have risen up against** him and **have not set [God] before them.** David affirmed the perfection of his Sovereign—perfect in His divine attributes (such as omniscience and omnipresence) not possessed by people, and in His attributes that people may also have (such as His righteousness, holiness, or faithfulness). David also affirmed God's attributes most important to the Jewish people, such as His loyal love (**You, O Lord, are** . . . **abundant in lovingkindness**, v. 15), **truth** (v. 15), mercy (**You, O Lord, are** . . . **merciful**; v. 15), grace (**be gracious to me**, v. 16; **gracious**, v. 15), and His imparting of help and comfort (**You, O Lord, have helped me and comforted me**, v. 17).

Psalm 87: On the Preeminence of Zion

On the heading of this **Psalm of the sons of Korah. A Song**, see the comments on Ps 3, 42–43; 46. This psalm is a celebration of Zion (Jerusalem) as the city of God and affirms that God will restore Israel someday. When He does, the Gentile nations also will receive great blessings along with Israel. Israel will be a people of supreme blessing, and will exhibit God's majesty most powerfully because of His faithfulness to His covenant with David and Abraham (Sailhamer, *NIV Compact Bible Commentary*, 335).

A. Zion the Place of God's Choice (87:1-3)

87:1. The opening phrase **His foundation is in the holy mountains** (cf. 2:6; Is 56:7) reflects that the Lord founded Zion (cf. Is 14:32). He chose the location for the temple and when it was built there on Mount Moriah (cf. 2Ch 3:1), the glory of the Lord filled the temple (cf. 2Ch 7:1-3). The plural of **mountains** may be a plural of majesty, or it may indicate the location being surrounded by mountains like Mount of Olives and Mount Scopus. Furthermore, the mountain is **holy** because the Lord will return in glory and holiness to the temple (cf. Ezk 43). That glory had been visible in the past in the tabernacle (cf. Ex 40:34 and comment on Ps 2:6) and will come again to the temple in the future.

87:2-3. The Lord loves the gates of Zion more than any other place in **Jacob** (the land of Israel). He chose **Zion** (cf. comments on 2:6; 3:3-4; 9:11-12; 48:2) to be the focal point of His visible presence on earth, not just in history during the days of the two temples, but also when He returns to establish His kingdom on earth and for all time thereafter (cf. Jr 3:17; Ezk 43:7; Rv 21:22-27). For the meaning of **loves**, see the comment on Ps 78:65-72. Biblically, Mount **Zion** is synonymous with Mount Moriah. It was the site of the binding of Isaac (cf. Gn 22), and the location purchased by David for the temple at the Lord's direction. Today, the area identified as Mount Zion in Jerusalem, outside the walls of the Old City, is not on the same location as the biblical site.

B. Zion the Place of God's People (87:4-6)

87:4-6. In the future, when the Messiah returns to rule on earth in Jerusalem, Zion will be the focal point of God's rule when people of the Gentile nations will worship the Lord at His holy mountain (cf. Is 56:7). Although this list is brief—and hence necessarily selective—the expansiveness and force of God's mercy and grace (in fulfillment of His promise in Gn 12:3b) are poignantly emphasized by calling attention to the promise that some of Israel's archenemies will be numbered **among those who know Me** (i.e., who have a relationship with God; see comment on Ps 1:6). Those nations include **Rahab** (a poetic designation for Egypt; see Ps 89:9-10; Is 51:9-10), **Babylon** (destroyer of Jerusalem, cf. Ps 137:1-9), and **Philistia** (cf. Is 19:19-25).

C. Zion the Place of God's Salvation (87:7)

87:7. The psalm concludes with a brief glimpse of the praise and rejoicing that will characterize that future time when God rules from Zion, when **those who sing as well as those who play the flutes** (or "who dance")—both of which activities are associated in Scripture with rejoicing and praise (cf. 1Sm 18:16; 1Kg 1:10)—will say, **All my springs of joy are in you**. This may look forward to the life-giving waters which will flow from the temple in the Messianic Age, making the Dead Sea fresh (cf. Ezk 47:1-12; Ps 46:6; Rv 22:1-3), or to springs of salvation (as in Is 12:3). Either way, the **springs** are a source of life flowing from God Himself and Messiah the Lamb on His throne in Zion (cf. Rv 22:3).

Psalm 88: The Reasons for Seeking Relief from God's Correction

On the lengthy heading of psalm, **A Song. A Psalm of the sons of Korah**, see the comments on the headings to Pss 3–4, 42–43, 46. For **according to Mahalath** see Ps 53; **Leannoth** ("for singing loudly," as in Ex 15:21; 1Sm 21:11; Ps 147:7; cf. "I have cried out" in 88:1, 13). In his **Maskil** (see introduction to Ps 32) **of Heman the Ezrahite** (see Introduction: Author), Heman lamented his suffering which he saw as coming from God's sovereign hand. Since God was sovereign over his sufferings, Heman also viewed God as equally sovereign over their removal—hence he cried out to Him for relief. The righteous must learn to remain close to God even during difficult times, and Heman's pleas to God mirror the feelings and prayers of all those who are still awaiting the fulfillment of God's promises (Sailhamer, *NIV Compact Bible Commentary*, 335).

A. Plea for Restoration of Vitality (88:1-9)

88:1-5. This prayer to the **Lord, the God of my salvation** was so urgent that the psalmist **cried out by day and in the night**. The psalmist described his **troubles** (v. 3) as feeling like he was **forsaken among the dead** (v. 5). Thus, this psalm is a response to God's discipline. On **Sheol** (v. 3) see the comment on 49:14-15.

88:6-9. The drowning image of **You have put me . . . in the depths . . . You have afflicted me with all Your waves** (vv. 6-7) is similar to Jonah's experience (cf. Jnh 2:3). Yet even worse, the psalmist understood the Lord had done this: **You have** (vv. 6-8). He recognized that he was under **[God's] wrath** (v. 7); nonetheless, the psalmist **called upon [Him] every day** (v. 9; cf. 22:2; 86:3).

B. Plea for Restoration of Worship (88:10-12)

88:10-12. Using four rhetorical questions, typical of disputation arguments, this section is an appeal to God to help the psalmist before he died. The questions imply a "no" answer, but are not denying the resurrection or hope of the afterlife as revealed in the OT (cf. 16:11; 23:6; Is 26:19; Dn 12:1-3). Rather, this was an appeal to the Lord to allow the psalmist to continue living, so God could bless him and allow him to worship God on earth. **Abbadon** (v. 11; lit., "place of destruction") is a synonym for hell.

C. Plea for Restoration of Relationship (88:13-18)

88:13-18. This section reviews the early part of the psalmist's prayer, but from the perspective of crying out **in the morning**. The themes in vv. 13-18 are similar to vv. 1-9: e.g., **You reject my soul** (v. 14/v. 6); **I suffer Your terrors** (v. 15-16/v. 6); I am overwhelmed by waves of **water** (v. 17/v. 7); I am **removed** from **lover . . . friend . . . acquaintances** (v.18/v. 8).

The psalmist lamented what was to him the most distressing of all the consequences of God's discipline, namely, his sense of broken relationship with God (vv. 7, 14) This is not to say the psalmist believed that because of the sin(s) for which he was being corrected, his relationship with God had been severed or annulled. Rather the proper (i.e., healthy, unhindered) experience of that relationship had been diminished or hindered. The psalmist's reference to God rejecting him (v. 14) is thus not an actual statement of a theological fact, but was an expression representing the tortured depth of how he felt at the time (see comments in 44:9; 60:1). His reference to God's hiding His face draws directly from the wording of God's threat of chastisement (not rejection or abandonment) to the fledgling nation (cf. Dt 31:17-18 and "Finding God in the Book of Esther," in the Introduction to Esther).

Psalm 89: God's Faithfulness to the Davidic King

For background on **a Maskil of Ethan the Ezrahite** see Ps 32 and Introduction: Author.

Ethan the Ezrahite appears to have been a poet or wise man from the court of King Solomon (cf. 1Kg 4:31). He appears to have written an ode to the glorious nature of the Davidic covenant. Perhaps he longed for the covenant to be fulfilled through Solomon. However, the failures of Solomon (cf. 1Kg 11) and the rest of the Davidic kings caused the fulfillment of the promise to be found much later, by the messianic Son of David.

The key idea in this psalm is the unconditional and inevitable fulfillment of the Davidic covenant, grounded in God's lovingkindness (*chesed*) and faithfulness. This is underscored by the sevenfold repetition of each of these words (lovingkindness in vv. 1, 2, 14, 24, 28, 33, 49; faithfulness in vv. 1-2, 5, 8, 24, 33, 49).

Not all of God's people wait for His deliverance with great hope, as Ps 88 made clear. Psalm 89 emphasizes that this deliverance will come someday, and the righteous can console themselves with its certainty and its glory when it arrives. Its arrival will take place in connection with the fulfillment of the Davidic covenant in the seed, or descendants, of David (89:3-4, 29, 36), the Messiah (Sailhamer, *NIV Compact Bible Commentary,* 335).

A. God's Faithful Character (89:1-18)

89:1-4. The themes of God's **lovingkindness** . . . and **faithfulness** are introduced, then linked to the **covenant** the Lord had **sworn to David** (see comments on 2Sm 7:11-17). The three aspects of the Davidic covenant are an eternal house (i.e., dynasty), an eternal kingdom, and an eternal throne—all fulfilled in Messiah Jesus the Son of David (cf. Lk 1:32-33). The unconditional nature (and hence inevitable fulfillment) of this covenant is indicated by: (1) the repeated references to God's **lovingkindness** (cf. comment on 5:7) and **faithfulness** (on its unconditional nature see the comment on 88:11); and (2) the singular form of the verb translated **I have made** in v. 3, indicating that the fulfillment of all aspects of the Davidic covenant depended on God alone, and thus its unconventional nature. The **seed** introduced in Gn 3:15 can be traced throughout the whole OT and refers ultimately to the supreme Son of David, the Messiah (cf. Ac 2:20). The phrase **build up your throne** (v. 4) is a promise of the Davidic covenant.

89:5-10. This stanza of the psalm is **praise** to the Lord for His **wonders** and **faithfulness**, the fact that He is **awesome above all** and **rule[s] . . . the sea** (creation) and **crushed** and **scattered [His] enemies**. In summary, it depicts the incomparable **LORD God of hosts** (v. 8; **who is like you, O mighty LORD?**; cf. Pss 35:10; 71:19; 77:13; 89:6; 113:4; Ex 15:11; Mc 7:18).

89:11-14. The stanza begins with an overview of God's greatness. The Lord **created** everything (vv. 11-12). He rules the world with **a strong arm . . . righteousness . . . justice . . . lovingkindness** and **truth**.

89:15-18. The focus narrows to the Lord's relationship with His people Israel. **How blessed are the people who . . . walk** (cf. Ps 86:11) **in the light of Your countenance** (cf. 1; 44:3) and know **the Holy One of Israel** (v. 18; cf. 71:22).

B. God's Choice of David as King (89:19-29)

89:19-29. The Lord chose **David** to be king of Israel (vv. 20-21; cf. 1Sm 13:14) and be **anointed**—according to God's direction—by Samuel (cf. 1Sm 16:1-3). Because God's covenant with David is unconditional, there is no doubt that He **will keep** (or "preserve," "uphold") it **for him forever . . . establish his descendants** [lit., "seed," referring to an individual, the messianic King] **forever**, and establish **his throne as the days of heaven** (a poetic phrase meaning "forever"). These are all aspects of the Davidic covenant (vv. 28-29; cf. 2Sm 7:12-13).

C. God's Unconditional Covenant with David (89:30-37)

89:30-32. The future Davidic kings (Solomon and the 20 kings of Judah, cf. 1Kg 11:42–25:30; 2Ch 9:31–36:21) often failed to follow the Lord, and He **punish[ed] their transgression with the rod**, culminating in the Babylonian captivity.

89:33-37. But the Lord will always be faithful not to **violate** the covenant He had made with David and swore **by** His **holiness** (vv. 34-35). There can be no stronger guarantee, because the Lord would **not lie to David**. The covenant is fulfilled in **His descendants** (lit., "seed", cf. comments on v. 29), that is, the Messiah (cf. Mt 1:1, 17; Lk 1:32; 20:42-44). The Davidic covenant **shall be established forever like the moon** (cf. Jr 31:35-37).

D. God's Discipline on the Davidic Throne (89:38-52)

Psalm 89 begins with praise to the Lord and joyful celebration of David and the Davidic covenant. The conclusion of the psalm (vv. 38-52) is a radical shift into questions and sorrow. This final section seems to have been added in the postexilic period, when the psalms were made into a book and when Jerusalem was in ruins, the nation was in exile in Babylon and there was no king on the throne of David (vv. 38-45 describe a situation much later than the time of Ethan the Ezrahite, the Davidic crown was in the dust [v. 39], his throne had been cast to the ground [v. 44], and the walls and strongholds of Jerusalem were destroyed [v. 40], all indicating that this was a post-exilic addition to the psalm). Yet it ends in anticipation of the coming of the Messiah, listening for the footsteps of Your anointed (v. 51), a rabbinic phrase for the coming of the Messiah.

89:38-45. At this point it seemed God had **cast off** the nation of Israel and **rejected** His people, and was **full of wrath against [His] anointed** kings (v. 38). Each verse in this section except v. 41 contains the refrain **You have**…, indicating all the dire circumstances that had befallen Jerusalem were the result of God's judgment. The prophets as well as Kings and Chronicles provide the details of Israel's behavior which led to this judgment. It seemed (although impossible, cf. vv. 36-37) that God had **spurned the covenant of [His] servant** David (cf. vv. 3, 20), for God had cast **his crown in the dust**… **broken down** the **walls** of Jerusalem, **made all his enemies rejoice** and **cast his throne to the ground**.

89:46-50. This section asks **How long, O Lord?** (cf. 6:3) will these awful condition prevail; **Will You hide Yourself forever?** (cf. 10:1; 13:1; 27:9). The psalmist then recalled God's **former lovingkindnesses** and **faithfulness** to **David** (v. 49). Since he could not live forever, the author appears to be asking God to fulfill the Davidic covenant by sending the Messiah, the Son of David.

89:51-52. Because of God's judgment on His people, God's **enemies** had reproached the Lord's reputation, particularly concerning the promised coming of the Messiah. They disbelieved that they would soon hear **the footsteps of Your anointed** (Hb., *Messiah)*. Thus, after the exile, it appears that this addition to the psalm is calling for the Lord to fulfill the Davidic covenant, not by restoring the Davidic line, but by sending the messianic King.

This psalm, which concludes Book Three, ends with the short doxology: **Blessed be the Lord forever! Amen and Amen** (cf. 41:13; 72:18-19; 106:48; 50:6).

IV. Book Four: Responding in Worship to God's Fatherly Discipline (Pss 90–106)

Psalm 90: A Prayer to God Eternal in Response to the Brevity of Life

Consistent with its placement at the beginning of the fourth of the five Books of Psalms, this psalm focuses on and hence introduces the main theme of Book Four, which, parallel to the fourth book of the Pentateuch (Numbers), concerns God's fatherly correction of His national son Israel. This is **a Prayer of Moses, the man of God**, (see Ps 17 introduction). That this psalm is attributed to **Moses** reinforces the parallel between Book Four of the Psalms and God's discipline of Israel in the wilderness wanderings. In addition to this psalm's prayer, Moses wrote at least three other psalmic compositions: two "songs" (Ex 15:1-18; Dt 31:30–32:43) and one blessing (Dt 33:1-29).

A. Affirming the Eternality of God (90:1-2)

90:1-2. The prayer begins by affirming Israel's relationship with God: **Lord, You have been our dwelling place in all generations**. God's right to bring correction (detailed vv. 3-12) is based on His character and relationship with Israel. That God has been Israel's **dwelling place** (their impregnable source of refuge and protection; cf. Pss 71:3a; 91:9b) **in all generations** was proven in the past and promised in the future. Moses employed the same expression in Dt 32:7 (where it is parallel to "eternity"). Moses referred figuratively to God as Creator, having given **birth to the earth and the world**. The **world** refers here not just to the inanimate world, but to all of creation, particularly to humanity (cf. Pss 96:13; 98:9). He emphasized God's eternality: **Even from everlasting to everlasting, You are God**.

B. Acknowledging Man's Mortality and Need for Wisdom (90:3-12)

90:3-6. In this section Moses acknowledged the justice of God's disciplinary correction of Israel, beginning with an allusion to His first act of corrective discipline: **You turn man back into dust** (v. 3; cf. Gn 3:19). He also illustrated God's eternality: **For a thousand years in Your sight are like yesterday**… **Or as a watch in the night** (v. 4; cf. Jdg 7:19).

90:7-12. Sin was explicitly acknowledged and confessed with the words, **You have placed our iniquities before You, our secret sins in the light of Your presence** (v. 8). The eternality of the Lord (vv. 1-2) is a dynamic contrast to the descriptions of the brevity of human life: (1) as brief as a **sigh** (v. 9; lit., "whisper"); (2) the average length of **life** being only **seventy years, or if due to strength, eighty years** (v. 10); and (3) **soon**… **we fly away** (or die; v. 10). In light of the shortness of life the plea to the Lord is: **teach us to number our days, That we may present to You a heart of wisdom** (v. 12). In order to make the most of their short lives (even the longest life is short in contrast to eternity), those who love the Lord need to be aware of how they spend time. This text urges believers to make the most of each day by obeying the Lord and living according to the wisdom in His Word (cf. Pss 1:1-3; 86:11; Pr 9:10; 19:23).

C. Asking for God's Favor and Blessing (90:13-17)

90:13. Having confessed Israel's sin on their behalf, Moses implored God to **return** and comfort His people (cf. 6:3-4); to **be sorry for** (lit., "appeased" or "propitiated") [His] **servants**, in that their confession of sin was genuine and the judgment had lasted long enough.

90:14-16. When fellowship with the Lord is restored, then it is possible to be satisfied with the Lord's love (**O satisfy us in the morning with Your lovingkindness**, v. 14). The Lord had never ceased to love His people, but their sin had prevented their experiencing His goodness. The motivation for this petition, ultimately, was not simply that Israel's circumstances might be improved, but **that** they **may sing for joy and be glad** (v. 14), that is, that they might proclaim God's glory through their worship (cf. 32:11; Jr 31:7; Zch 2:14).

90:17. In the closing request, **Let the favor** (lit., "beauty," cf. 27:4) **of the Lord our God be upon us**, Moses was reflecting his brother Aaron's famous blessing on Israel (cf. Nm 6:22-26). In asking the Lord to **confirm** . . . **the work of our hands** Moses was requesting approval of and blessing for all their efforts to serve Him (cf. Dt 14:29; 16:15; 24:19).

Psalm 91: Concerning Personal Security

Though this psalm has no heading in the Hebrew text, early Jewish tradition has given it several attributions: to David (LXX), to Solomon (the Midrash on Psalms), to Moses (Midrash on Psalms), or as a joint composition by David (vv. 3-8, 10-16) and Solomon (vv. 1-2, 9; (the Targum). A theme in Ps 90 is God as the refuge of Israel (90:1) and the brevity of life (90:7-12). Psalm 91 encourages the readers to find their refuge in God when they have not yet experienced the fulfillment of all God's promises (Sailhamer, *NIV Compact Bible Commentary*, 336).

A. The Believer's Source of Security (91:1-4)

91:1-2. The source of one's security is found in the Lord: **He who dwells in the shelter of the Most High Will abide in the shadow of the Almighty**. Security is not in one's circumstances or personal ability, but in God. Believers are to turn to Him not only in times of distress or need, but continually, as indicated by the opening reference to **He who dwells** (i.e., a person who sees himself, whether awake or asleep, as being in the Lord, and hence protected by Him from any lasting harm, whether physical or spiritual).

Abiding **in** His **shadow** (cf. v. 4), suggesting both His proximity to His people and the relief He provides from scorching heat, indicates protection and security (cf. 121:5; Is 30:2-3; 49:2; 51:16). The Lord will be his **refuge** (cf. Ps 46:1) and **fortress** (cf. 31:3).

91:3-4. Yet this protection is as gentle and warm as a mother bird sheltering her young. **He will cover you with His pinions . . . under His wings you may seek refuge** (v. 4; cf. Pss 17:8; 36:7; 57:1; 68:13). The protection provided by the Lord is **His faithfulness** (cf. Dt 7:9; 36:5, 89:2; 98:3). This is an image of protection used by Messiah Jesus regarding the Jewish people (cf. Mt 23:37).

B. The Extent of Security in the Lord (91:5-13)

91:5-6. The psalmist here gave examples of threatening situations (both day and night) from which the Lord will keep the believer safe, so he should **not be afraid of** the **terror by night . . . arrow that flies by day . . . pestilence that stalks in darkness**, or **destruction that lays waste at noon** (v. 6).

91:7-8. The parallel numeric poetic construction of **a thousand** and **ten thousand** expressed security against outrageous odds: **it shall not approach you**.

91:9-10. The extent of the security afforded to the individual is rooted in making **the Most High** his **dwelling place**. The image of **No evil will befall you, Nor will any plague come near your tent** (lit., "dwelling"), is a link back to the Lord's protection of Israel during the plagues on the Egyptians at Passover (cf. Ex 11:6-12). This verse is not a universal promise of safety for all believers. It might be paraphrased, "No disaster or trouble will come upon a believer except if it is part of God's loving plan."

91:11-13. This illustration is of the Lord's care as quoted by Satan to Jesus during His temptation in the wilderness (cf. Mt 4:6; Lk 4:10-11, see comments there). If this principle was true of any believer, how much more would it be true of the Messiah, the Son of God? Additionally, the words **He will give His angels charge concerning you** is a strong OT support for the concept of guardian angels (cf. Heb 1:14 for NT support).

C. The Intimacy of Security in the Lord (91:14-16)

91:14-16. This last section highlights the importance of relationship with the Lord: **Because he has loved Me, therefore I will deliver him.** To know **My name** (v. 14) means to know the Lord (cf. 5:11; 23:3; 25:11; 31:3). The intimacy of being in a relationship with God is emphasized by His reference to being **with him** (with individual believers) **in** his **trouble** (v. 15; cf. vv. 5-8). God affirms the full and final **salvation** (v. 16; cf. 62:1) of the one who trusts in Him and whom therefore He **will set** . . . **on high** (v. 14), in an unassailable place—that is, in Him, the Most High, who is the believer's dwelling place (vv. 1, 9).

Psalm 92: A Song of Weekly Praise

On the heading of this **Psalm, a Song**, see the comments on the headings to Pss 3 and 46. It is to be sung on **the Sabbath day**. According to ancient Jewish tradition, this psalm was sung by the Levites in the Second Temple period at the time of the daily Sabbath offering (Mishnah, *Tamid* vii.4). This unique psalmic association with the Sabbath (seventh day) is underscored by the observation that this is also the only psalm in which the four-letter name for God (called the Tetragrammaton and typically translated Lord or Yahweh) is repeated seven times (vv. 1, 4-5, 8-9, 13, 15), a number that signifies perfection or completion. In Ps 90, the psalmist drew attention to God's attributes of power and authority as they relate to humanity's, especially Israel's, accountability to Him. Psalm 91 emphasizes God's power and authority, but as they relate to His tender care of Israel. In Ps 92 emphasis is placed upon God's love and steadfastness, as well as His blessings upon the righteous and judgment upon the wicked. Its exalted description of God paves the way for the hymns portraying God's sovereign power and authority in Pss 93–99 (Sailhamer, *NIV Compact Bible Commentary*, 336).

A. A Song for the Privilege of Praise (92:1-4)

92:1-4. The psalmist praised God because **it is good to give thanks to the Lord and to sing praises to Your name, O Most High.** He praised God for being able to **give thanks** to Him (v. 1). He recognized that doing so (like worship in general) was not a right but a privilege, granted not on the basis of the psalmist's personal merit, but of God's **lovingkindness** (v. 2; *chesed*, see Ps 5:7) and **faithfulness** (see Ps 88:11). These terms are elsewhere paired or employed in parallel to underscore God's unconditional mercy and grace (cf. 89:1-2, 24, 33, 49; 98:3) which the psalmist is eager **To declare**. The **LORD** had **made [the psalmist] glad by what** He had **done**, specifically, **the works of [His] hands** (v. 4).

B. A Song for the Lord's Justice (92:5-9)

92:5-9. Since persecution by the ungodly is an inevitable component in the lives of "all who desire to live godly" (2Tm 3:12), this model of weekly prayer—which is intended to contribute to the spiritual and emotional recharging of the believer—here reminds the worshiper that this life is but a drop in the ocean of eternity, and that the **sprout[ing] up** (i.e., flourishing) of **the wicked** is **like** the **grass** (v. 7). In contrast, God is eternal (**You, O LORD, are on high forever** (v. 8; cf. 92:2). Though God in His forbearance may allow some among those **who do iniquity** (v. 9; cf. v. 7, lit., "those doing iniquity," i.e., an ongoing unrepentant lifestyle) a brief time to flourish so that they might repent, He will inevitably requite them should they not repent with destruction **forevermore**, that is, with eternal condemnation (v. 7; cf. 83:17; Dn 12:2).

C. A Song for the Lord's Great Love (92:10-15)

92:10-15. The reminder of God's inevitable condemnation of the wicked in the previous section is here counterbalanced by focusing on what God had already done for the psalmist in exalting his **horn** (symbolizing the giving of strength based in God's salvation; see 17:3; 74:5) and having **anointed** him **with fresh oil** (symbolizing the giving of joy; see 23:5). The condemnation of the wicked is also counterbalanced by what God will yet do for the righteous, that is, that he will be **planted** (lit., "transplanted," as in Ezk 17:8, 23) **in the house of the LORD** and **flourish in** His **courts** (v. 13; on the eschatological sense of this thought, see the comments on 23:6 and 84:1–4).

Psalm 93: Affirming God's Rule as the King of Creation

Though this psalm has no heading in the Hebrew text, early Jewish tradition (the LXX) attributes it to David and also identifies it (in both the LXX and the Babylonian Talmud, *Rosh Hashanah* 31a) as the psalm that was recited by the Levites in the Second Temple period on the sixth day of the week (i.e., Friday) because on it "He completed His work (of creation) and commenced reigning over (all) of them (i.e., His 'creations')." God's universal rule is also a primary theme of this psalm. Psalm 93 emphasizes

God's powerful creation and governance of the world, themes forecast in Pss 91–92 (Sailhamer, *NIV Compact Bible Commentary*, 336-37).

A. By His Work of Creation (93:1-2)

93:1-2. The opening declaration, **The LORD reigns**, affirms God's ongoing reign, not just at the present time, as the present tense translation **reigns** equals "on-going/unending." Furthermore, His eternal reign is associated with God as Creator, by the explicit reference to **the world** being **firmly established** (cf. 24:2; 104:5). Implicit in the concept of God having **established** the world, moreover, is the concept of His preexistence (**You are from everlasting**, v. 2; lit., "from eternity"). The word **everlasting** signifies no ending, whereas "eternity" signifies both no ending and no beginning, spanning eternity past to eternity future.

B. By His Transcendence over Creation (93:3-4)

93:3-4. God's great power as Creator is vividly depicted by the reference to **the floods** (repeated three times for emphasis in v. 3; cf. 86:1-5), **pounding waves . . . many waters** and **mighty breakers**, symbolizing the unstoppable and overwhelming power of creation as perceived by humanity (cf. 2Sm 22:5; Jnh 2:3-5). Yet these roaring waters are not as **mighty** as **the LORD on high** whose power is **more than the sounds of many waters, than the mighty breakers of the sea** (v. 4; cf. 18:15-16; 29:3-4; 77:19; 88:7; Is 8:7-8).

C. By His Special Revelation within Creation (93:5)

93:5. God's rule is affirmed by His **testimonies**, that is, the specific revelation of His Word, and the law in particular (cf. Dt 4:45; 6:20; Neh 9:34; Pss 78:56; 119:22, 24, 59, 79). The law clearly testifies both to God's universal rule as the Creator of heaven and earth (cf. Ex 20:11; 31:17) and to the **holiness** that resides exclusively in Him (cf. Lv 10:3), and distinguishes Him perhaps more than anything else from His creation. Hence the three-fold repetition of "holy" in Is 6:3 and Rv 4:8. No other attribute of God has such a three-fold attribution.

Psalm 94: Praying for God to Judge

This psalm, as the previous one, has no heading in the Hebrew text. Early Jewish tradition (the LXX), as with Ps 93, attributes it to David. Psalm 94 is identified in both the LXX and the Babylonian Talmud (*Rosh Hashanah* 31a) as being recited by the Levites in the Second Temple period on the fourth day of the week (i.e., Wednesday). This is so because on the fourth day God created the sun and the moon, and He will one day take vengeance on those who worship them (consistent with how the psalm begins: O Lord, God of vengeance). Since God is the sovereign King (Ps 93), it is appropriate to draw attention to His role as sovereign Judge (Ps 94) (Sailhamer, *NIV Compact Bible Commentary*, 337).

A. For the Sake of God's Glory (94:1-7)

94:1-3. The Lord is presented as a **God of vengeance** (twice for emphasis in v. 1). The English term **vengeance** is often associated with cruelty, insensitivity, and unreasonable or excessive retribution for some perceived injustice. This is not the meaning of the Hebrew term, which indicates strictly and justifiably upholding or carrying out justice or righteousness against wrongdoing. So a more appropriate translation would be "vindication." God, the **Judge of the earth** (v. 2; cf. Gn 18:25), is being called upon to take action against those **who do wickedness** (v. 4). By asking **How long[?] . . . How long[?]** in vv. 3-4, the psalmist leaves the act of vindication, along with its timing and means, up to God (cf. Dt 32:35; Rm 12:19; Heb 10:30).

94:4-7. The offense to God Himself is further emphasized in that the wicked **crush Your people . . . and afflict Your heritage** (v. 5; cf. 28:9; 33:12; 72:4; 79:1). The wicked are acting in defiance, knowingly or not, of God's covenant promises to Abraham, Isaac, and Jacob, with regard to both His choice of Israel and His faithfulness to His people (see the comments on 74:1-11; 77:11-15; 88:10-12). **They have said, "The LORD does not see, nor does the God of Jacob pay heed"** to their wicked behavior, especially in relation to their persecution of the people of Israel (v. 7; cf. 3:2; 10:11).

B. With Recognition of God's Mercy (94:8-16)

94:8-11. This warning was to those among the people of Israel who thought God had abandoned them to the wicked. The **senseless among the people**, are those among His own people, Israel (as indicated by the singular noun for **people**, typically used to designate the nation of Israel, as opposed to the plural used for the Gentiles, often designated by the plural term **nations**). These **stupid** ones, like the fool in Ps 14, doubted the reality of divine justice because they believed God was incapable of perceiving and responding to human injustice, or else He was simply not there (atheism). To these people who did not **understand** (v. 8; cf. 14:2), the psalmist pointed out that God not only does **hear** and **see** (v. 9) all that is said and done, He also **knows** (understands at the deepest level) even **the thoughts of man**, **that they are** a **mere breath** (v. 11; i.e., transient; see the citation of this verse in 1Co 3:20 and the comments there).

94:12-13. The psalmist contrasted the foolishness of those Israelites who denied God's justice or power to act with the godly man who understood the necessity of the Lord dealing with sin in Israel: **Blessed is the man whom You chasten, O LORD . . . whom You teach out of Your law.** The nation's present affliction was an expression of God's discipline rather than His inability to protect them against the wickedness of their enemies.

94:14-16. Ultimately, God would deal with the wicked oppressors of Israel, and thereby turn His people back to Him. No matter what happened, **the LORD will not abandon His people, nor . . . forsake His inheritance** (v. 14). The **judgment** of the Lord would cause the **upright** to follow Him and they are called to **take** a **stand** against **those who do wickedness** (v. 16).

C. In the Light of God's Plan (94:17-23)

94:17-23. When affliction by the wicked and the apparent delay of divine justice caused **anxious thoughts** to **multiply within** him (v. 19), the psalmist found **consolations** for his **soul** in at least two sources: (1) God's **lovingkindness** (*chesed*, v. 18; cf. comment on 5:7) toward him; and (2) his confidence that God **will destroy** those who do wickedness (cf. vv. 4, 16) **in their evil** (v. 23). The psalm begins by calling on the Lord to avenge the wrong done to His people (v. 1) and concludes with the assertion **The LORD our God will destroy them.**

Psalm 95: Rejoicing in the Lord's Beneficial Works for Humanity

Though this psalm has no heading in the Hebrew text, early Jewish tradition (the LXX) attributes it to David (cf. 93–94, 96, 99). Davidic authorship is confirmed by the explicit reference to him in Heb 4:7 as the one through whom this psalm was revealed. Several themes from previous psalms (namely God as Creator, Judge, Deliverer, Object of worship) are woven into this one. But Ps 95 also includes a more explicit warning (starting at v. 7b) to God's people in light of these attributes He possesses. As mighty as He is, and as faithful as He is to Israel, He is not to be trifled with (Sailhamer, *NIV Compact Bible Commentary*, 337).

A. The Lord as the Creator (95:1-5)

95:1-5. David began by exhorting his people Israel, **O come, let us sing for joy to the LORD** (cf. v. 6; 66:1). God is worthy to be praised because He is: (1) **the rock of our salvation** (the Secure and Stable One who brings our deliverance; v. 1; cf. 18:2); (2) **a great God** (the only true One; v. 3; cf. 48:1); (3) **a great King above all gods** (v. 3; cf. 10:16); and (4) the One whose **hand** created the **earth . . . mountains . . . sea** and **dry land** (vv. 4-5; cf. Gn 1; Pss 124:8; 134:3). To **sing for joy** typically signifies the joyful singing attending worship (cf. 20:5; 63:7; 92:4; 132:16; Is 35:2; 52:8).

B. The Lord as Good Shepherd (95:6-7a)

95:6-7a. Here David called the people of Israel to express submission to the Lord by their posture and attitude in worship: **Come, let us worship and bow down . . . kneel** before Him. To **bow down** and **kneel** is to do homage to and acknowledge God's sovereignty. Again the Lord is presented as Creator, **our Maker** (cf. vv. 4-5), and the Great Shepherd, for **we are the people of His pasture and the sheep of His hand** (cf. 23; 28:9; 80:1). This highlights not so much god's sovereign power over creation as His specific, intimate, and consistent role in caring for His covenant **people**, Israel. To emphasize this concept of relationship, the psalmist referred to Israel as **the people** of God's **pasture**.

This term is employed elsewhere in two ways: (1) by metonymy it substitutes **pasture** for "sheep" since the two are closely related, and designates the focus of the shepherd's action (i.e., the flock that is in the pasture, as in Jr 10:21); and (2) as the shepherd's action itself (pasturing the sheep), it entails the provision of all that is necessary for the well-being of the flock (i.e., land, ample food, protection from enemies). This OT imagery of God as the Shepherd of Israel was applied by Jesus to Himself (Jn 10:11-17, 26-30) in one of the few NT passages where He explicitly affirmed His co-equality with God the Father. See the comments on Jn 10.

C. The Lord as the Rest-Giver (95:7b-11)

95:7b-11. The psalms often entreat the Lord to hear the request of His people (cf. 4:1; 27:7). However, this last section is an urgent admonition to listen **today** and obey the Lord, to **hear His voice** (cf. Dt 6:4; Ps 50:7). The word **hear** indicates obedience, not just processing information. The warning is **Do not harden your hearts**

as at Meribah . . . in the day of Massah in the wilderness (v. 8; cf. Ex 17:2-7; Nm 20:13). This refers to the event after the exodus from Egypt when the people of Israel refused to listen and obey the Lord to enter the promised land (cf. Nm 13:1-33; regarding the land promise cf. Gn 12:1-3; 50:24). Therefore, the Lord disciplined them with **forty years** of wandering the wilderness, until all those in that doubting generation died and did **not enter** into the promised land (vv. 10-11; cf. Nm 14:20-35). The promised land is the place where God will give His people rest (cf. Ex 33:14; Dt 3:20; 12:10; 25:19; Jos 1:13). This passage is quoted in the NT as a warning to followers of Messiah against unbelief and disobedience (cf. comments on Heb 3:7-11; 4:1-7). The **rest** in view here is not merely a physical rest (peace and tranquility), but rather the rest of a right relationship with the Lord, and in the ultimate sense signifies the rest of the messianic kingdom when King Messiah rules on earth (cf. Is 11:1-16).

Psalm 96: An Exhortation to Praise the World's Once and Future King

Though the Hebrew text of this psalm has no heading (like Pss 93–94, 95, 99), it is almost certainly to be attributed to David because: (1) the entirety of the psalm is given with minor variations in 1Ch 16:23-33 as part of a psalm of thanksgiving ascribed to David cf. 1Ch 16:8-36); and (2) early Jewish tradition (the LXX) attributes it to David. As in Ps 95, God's sovereign governance of the world is made clear (cf. 95:1-7a; 96:1-9), as is His authority to judge the world (vv. 10-13; cf. 95:7b-11; Sailhamer, *NIV Compact Bible Commentary,* 337). Each of the three stanzas of Ps 96 begins with a call to give praise to the Lord.

A. Let Israel Praise the Lord, the King (96:1-6)

96:1-6. This is a hymn (**Sing** is used three times in the first two verses) celebrating God's kingship over all creation, similar to Ps 93, and begins with a call to worship: **Sing to the Lord a new song** (cf. comments on 33:3); **Sing to the Lord, all the earth**. The word **earth** (Hb. *eretz,* "land") is often used specifically for the land of Israel, thus indicating that this psalm is directed specifically to the people of Israel. They are to **Tell of His glory among the nations . . . among all the peoples** (v. 3) who had been worshipping **idols** instead of **the Lord [who] made the heavens** (v. 5; cf. Gn 1–2; Ps 89:11-12). (For **splendor and majesty** see comments on 21:5).

B. Let the Nations Praise the Lord, the King (96:7-10)

96:7-10. Here the Gentile nations, the **families of the people**, are invited to worship the Lord, to **Ascribe to the Lord the glory of His name** (v. 8; cf. comments on 5:11). Once the nations acknowledge God, they are invited to **Worship [Him] in holy attire** (v. 9; lit., "splendor of holiness" elsewhere applied to God's people; cf. 1Ch 16:29; Pss 29:2; 110:3). This point is further emphasized by the universal challenge to **say** (i.e., affirm) that **the Lord reigns** (as in Ps 93:1, the tense of the verb is translated better as "has been reigning," i.e., ever since the beginning of creation until now).

C. Let all Creation Praise the Lord, the King (96:11-13)

96:11-13. Because God is King over Israel and the nations, all creation is called to praise Him. The inanimate creation is pictured with anthropomorphic qualities: **Let the heavens be glad . . . the earth rejoice . . . the sea roar . . . the field exult** and **the trees . . . sing for joy** (vv. 11-12; cf. Is 55:12). They are the retinue **Before the Lord, for He is coming . . . to judge the earth**, and at that time every knee will bow before the righteous Judge (cf. Pss 7:11; 9:8; 50:4; 67:4; 75:7; Is 11:4-5; 45:23; Rm 14:11; Php 2:10; Rv 19:11). In the future the Lord will establish His righteous reign on earth, when Messiah Jesus will reign from Zion and the knowledge of the Lord will cover the earth as the waters cover the sea (cf. Ps 2; Is 11:9).

Psalm 97: God, The Ruler of the Universe

Though the Hebrew text of this psalm has no heading, early Jewish tradition (the LXX) attributes it to David (also Pss 93–94, 95–96, 99). As in Pss 95 and 96, the theme of God's good governance of the universe (97:1) is followed by His authority to judge it and the people in it (97:2-12; Sailhamer, *NIV Compact Bible Commentary,* 337).

A. His Reign over Creation (97:1-6)

97:1. The first verse of this psalm, linked in theme to 96, sets its tone: **The Lord reigns, let the earth** [Hb., *eretz,* land] **rejoice**, **let the many islands be glad**. The **earth** refers to the land/people of Israel (cf. 96:1 and comments there), while the **islands** (lit., "coastal regions") is a common synonym for the nations around the Mediterranean Sea, which serve as representatives of all the Gentile nations (cf. Is 42:4).

97:2-6. The description of the features attending God's manifest presence parallels other passages regarding the display of His power: **Clouds and thick darkness**: (v. 2; cf. Dt 4:11; 5:22; Ezk 1:4-28); **Fire** (v. 3; cf. Ex 13:21; Lv 9:24); a **burn[ing]** (v. 3; cf. Mal 4:1); **lightnings** (v. 4; cf. Ex 19:16; Ezk 1:13-14);and a **melt[ing]** (v. 5; cf. Am 9:5). Regarding **Righteousness and justice** (v. 2; cf. 33:5 and comments there), He is **the Lord of the whole earth** (v. 5; cf. Is 6:3).

B. His Reign over the Supernatural World (97:7-9)

97:7-9. The psalmist affirmed God's dominion over the **gods** of the Gentiles, represented by their **graven images** and **idols** (v. 7). The reality of these **gods** was granted here for the sake of argument, because they were perceived as gods by the pagans (cf. Ex 12:12; 18:11).

C. His Reign over His People (97:10-12)

97:10-12. God's dominion over His **godly ones** (lit., recipients of Hb. *chesed*, "lovingkindness") is underscored by the fact that He **preserves** their **souls** and **delivers them from the hand of the wicked** (v. 10), and that His people are **glad** to **give thanks** (a component of worship) and obey God (v. 12). They **hate evil**, a concept that is associated with doing and keeping God's Word (cf. Pr 8:13; Am 5:15).

Psalm 98: A Challenge to Praise the Messianic King

On the heading of this psalm, see the comments on the heading to Ps 3. Early Jewish tradition (the LXX) attributes this psalm to David (as is true of Pss 93–94, 95–96, 97, 99). Psalm 97 ended on a note of the righteous rejoicing at the prospect of God's coming in judgment (cf. vv. 10-12). Psalm 98 continues this theme. Sailhamer writes, "God's judgment of the wicked means salvation for the righteous (vv. 1-3)" (Sailhamer, *NIV Compact Bible Commentary*, 337).

A. The Basis of the Challenge (98:1-3)

98:1-3. The exhortation is to **sing to the LORD a new song** (cf. comments on 33:3; Is 42:10). As at the beginning of Ps 96, moreover, this exhortation is directed not only to the assembly of Israel, but to all the earth. The basis for this exhortation and challenge is twofold: (1) because God has done **wonderful things** (v. 1; see comments on 9:1; 40:5; 96:3) entailing the display of His universally preeminent power over humanity (symbolized and emphasized by God's **right hand** and **holy arm** in v. 1b (cf. 44:3; 77:15; Ex 15:6, 16; Is 53:1); and (2) because He has displayed His gracious and faithful pursuit of intimacy with humanity, represented by **His lovingkindness and His faithfulness to the house of Israel** (v. 3a), on whose behalf He **has made known His salvation** to **the nations** (vv. 2-3; cf. Ps 96).

B. The Extent of the Challenge (98:4-8)

98:4-8. The extent of the psalmist's exhortation is vividly underscored by the sources of God's praise, which extend from **all the earth** (Hb., *eretz*, v. 4) including its animals (v. 7a, **all** the sea **contains**), its people (v. 7b, **those who dwell in it**), and even its inanimate parts (v. 7a, **the sea**; v. 8a, **the rivers**; v. 8b, **the mountains**), and the diversity of God's praise, represented by the multifaceted ways in which that praise is produced: by shouting **joyfully** (vv. 4a, 6b), by singing (vv. 4b, 8b), **with the lyre** (v. 5), **with trumpets** and **the horn** (v. 6a), by roaring (v. 7a), and by clapping (v. 8a).

C. The Consummation of the Challenge (98:9)

98:9. The universal challenge to praise God will not remain open forever, but will come to an end (though, of course, the praise will continue among the righteous) when He comes **to . . . judge the world with righteousness**. This refers (as in 96: 10, where similar wording is used) to the advent of the messianic King, who will judge all those who have rejected Him (cf. 2:9, 12; Heb 9:27; Rv 20:12).

Psalm 99: The Exaltation of God's Royal Holiness

Though the Hebrew text of this psalm has no heading, early Jewish tradition (the LXX) attributes it to David (as is true of Pss 93–98). The primary theme in Pss 93–98 was God's governance of the world. Here the primary focus is upon God's unique love for and forgiveness of Israel, demonstrated especially in His selection and use of Moses and Aaron to provide expert leadership for Israel (cf. vv. 6-9; Sailhamer, *NIV Compact Bible Commentary*, 337).

A. The Lord Reigns in Zion (99:1-5)

99:1-3. The psalmist continues one of the central, unifying themes of the preceding psalms in Book Four: **The LORD reigns** (v. 1; cf. 93:1; 96:10; 97:1). In Ps 99, the theme of God's rule is considered, specifically how the various expressions of God's holiness reflect His universal rule (as emphasized by the repeated refrain **Holy is He** in vv. 3b, 5b and holy is the LORD in v. 9b). In this opening section the universal aspect of God's rule is correlated with the manifestation of God's holiness in creation—signaled first and foremost by the reference to Him being **enthroned above the cherubim** (v. 1, cf. 97:1-6 and comments there).

This description of the Lord refers not only to His presence in the cloud of glory over the **cherubim** that crowned the ark of the covenant (cf. Ex 25:22; 1Sm 4:4; Ezk 1), but also to His preeminent position on the throne of heaven (over all creation) over the surrounding cherubim who stand in readiness to do His will within creation (cf. Ezk 10:1-15; Is 6:1-13). This thought of God's holiness on the worldwide level is also indicated by the exhortations to **let the peoples tremble** and **let the earth shake**! The shaking of the earth is like the response of the heavenly temple itself to the holiness of God in Is 6:4 (where "trembled" can also be rendered "shook"). The **Lord is great in Zion** (v. 2; cf. 2:6; 9:11 and comments there) . . . **Holy is He** (vv. 3, 5).

99:4-5. The **strength of the King**, the Lord, is characterized by His love of **justice**, His **equity** (or "uprightness") and **righteousness**, all here in relation to His people, **Jacob** (cf. 14:7 and comments there). Following naturally on the concept of God's holy rule over creation as represented by His enthronement over the cherubim, the psalmist next reflected upon God's holy rule as represented by His code contained within the ark, that is, the law as epitomized by the two tablets of testimony (cf. Ex 25:16; Dt 10:5; 1Kg 8:9). The terms **justice**, **equity**, and **righteousness** are often linked to the law and are characteristics of the Lord and His Word (cf. Ps 33:5 and comments there). To **worship at His footstool** (cf. 132:7) is a metaphor for worshiping at His feet, because **Holy is He** (vv. 3, 5).

B. The Lord Gave His Priests and Prophets (99:6-9)

99:6-7. The reference to **Moses and Aaron** (both Levites; cf. Ex 2:1) concerns the Lord's provision of the **priests** and tabernacle with the sacrificial system for sin (cf. Lv 17:11). Then **Samuel** was included **among those who called on His name** as a priest who was the last of the judges and the first in the office of prophet of Israel (cf. 1Sm 7:15-17; 12:19-25). The brief history of God's care for Israel is from the **pillar of cloud** during the exodus (cf. Ex 33:3; Nm 12:5) to those faithful unnamed individuals who **kept His testimonies**.

99:8-9. God's relationship with faithful individuals in Israel is clear, for **O Lord, our God, You answered them**. The reference to God as **a forgiving God** highlights the result of that priestly work in which God's holiness is most often encountered and affirmed by the common Israelite in atonement. The reference to **His holy hill**, where the temple was located on Mount Zion (cf. 2:6, 9:11 and comments there), highlights the exclusive location where sacrifices were offered and atonement accomplished.

Psalm 100: A Song of Thanksgiving to God

On the heading of this **Psalm for Thanksgiving** (or more literally "a thank offering"), see the comments on the heading to Ps 3. Given both the Levitical and temple context of the Psalms' original compilation (see Introduction: Date) and the frequent use of the Hebrew term translated here as **Thanksgiving** to designate a "thanksgiving sacrifice" (cf. Lv 7:12; 22:29; Jr 17:26; Am 4:5), this psalm was probably sung in connection with temple sacrifices. God was celebrated as the sovereign Governor of all creation in Pss 93–99. It is fitting that here He be praised as the One who, in His sovereign power, chose Israel as the recipient of His covenantal blessings (vv. 3-5; Sailhamer, *NIV Compact Bible Commentary*, 338).

A. Thanking God for His Sublime Uniqueness (100:1-3a)

100:1-3a. The psalm beings with the call to praise: **Shout joyfully to the Lord** (cf. 32:11; 33:3). The psalm is addressed to the people of Israel; **all the earth** *(*Hb. *eretz,* land*)* is the particular name for the land of Israel, which is a metonymy for the people of Israel. They are to **serve** (in the service of worship) the **Lord** for who He is, focusing on the fact of His deity in general as opposed to any specific attribute(s), that is, because He is **the Lord** [Hb. *Yahweh*, His uniquely revealed name] **Himself is God**. The pronoun **Himself**, which is usually not supplied except for emphasis, underscores that **the Lord** alone is God. Both in concept and wording, this fundamental basis of worship recalls the central confession of biblical faith: "Hear, O Israel! The Lord is our God, the Lord is One!" [unequaled or unique; Dt 6:4].

B. Thanking God for His Gracious Election (100:3b-c)

100:3b-c. The psalmist continued his exhortation to praise and thanksgiving by declaring, on behalf of Israel, that **It is He** (the one and only God as affirmed in the previous clause) who **has made us**. This refers not to God's creation of humankind in general, but rather to His choice of Israel as His unique people (cf. Dt 32:6, 15; 1Kg 8:51; Pss 28:9; 74:2). Furthermore, the psalmist affirmed that because God had **made** them, they are **His people and the sheep of His pasture** (cf. comments on 23 and 95:6-7).

C. Thanking God for His Faithful Love (100:4-5)

100:4-5. Drawing out the implication of Israel as being the "sheep" of God's "pasture," the psalmist exhorted his people to offer God **thanksgiving** and **praise** because of His **lovingkindness** and **faithfulness** toward them (see comments on 5:7; 88:11). The conclusion is God's faithfulness to Israel forever: **The LORD is good; His lovingkindness is everlasting and His faithfulness to all generations** (v. 5; cf. 36:5-7; Jr. 31:34-37).

Psalm 101: King David's Resolve to Reign Righteously

On the heading of this **Psalm of David**, see the comments on the heading of Ps 3. This psalm is an expression of King David's commitment to reign righteously, and to establish this pattern for future kings of Israel. The psalm is built around seven "I will" statements. The first stanza (vv. 1-4), is the king's commitment to reign righteously by giving heed to the blameless way; the second stanza (vv. 5-8) is the king's commitment to punish the wicked but reward the blameless under his rule. Ultimately only Messiah Jesus, the great Son of David, can and will fulfill the commitments and ideals of Ps 101.

In Pss 93–99, God's universal rulership and authority to judge in righteousness were emphasized. Here, in this devotional psalm by David, the reader encounters not just the king of Israel, but the child of God earnest to walk in righteousness as befitting one who loves the righteous God, and who was loved by Him (Sailhamer, *NIV Compact Bible Commentary,* 238).

A. The King Is Committed to Personal Righteousness (101:1-4)

101:1-2. In light of God's everlasting **lovingkindness** (Hb., *chesed,* loyal love) and **justice** extolled in the previous psalms (cf. 98:9; 99:1-4; 100:5), Ps 101 develops a new and complementary theme of King David's commitment to live and reign with personal righteousness: **I will give heed to the blameless way** (or "behave purely"; cf. 18:32; 119:1; Pr 11:20; 13:6); **I will walk within my house in the integrity of my heart** (v. 2). David's pursuit of the Lord began with the determination to live his life daily (**walk**; cf. 1:1; 86:11; 89:15) by developing **integrity** (or "purity," signifying moral wholeness based on emulation of God's character as revealed in His Word) in his **heart**, his conscious inner self.

101:3-4. David's determination to **set no worthless thing** (Hb. *Belial,* often translated "wicked"; cf. 1Sm 10:27; 30:22; 1Kg 21:10, 13) before his **eyes** indicates a determination not to be drawn away to wickedness. In obedience to the Lord, the righteous will **hate the work of those who fall away** into apostasy from the Lord (cf. Ps 26:5; 97:10). A **perverse heart** is the opposite of a blameless/godly heart. By departing from these sinful practices, David **will know** [participate in/be intimately involved with] **no evil** (cf. Pr 11:20).

B. The King Is Committed to Establish Righteousness in the Land (101:5-8)

101:5. David vowed he would be careful about the character of his people (vv. 5, 7), as well as who he engaged as personal friends or allowed to have influence in his administration. Pure speech is an evidence of a pure heart, but anyone who **secretly slanders his neighbor** is committing serious sin (cf. Ex 20:16; Ps 15:3; Is 32:7) which can irreparably damage the innocent, so the righteous king will **destroy** (lit., "silence") that wicked person. Likewise, the person who has a **haughty look** and **an arrogant heart** (the second phrase expands on the first) were under condemnation because they were unwilling to submit to the leadership of God's anointed king. These are attitudes David would not **endure**, but he would **destroy** the wicked. These were serious issues because they violate the Lord's command to "love your neighbors as yourself; I am the LORD" (Lv 19:18; cf. Mt 22:34-40).

101:6-8. Just as the king would take action against slander and pride, so too he would keep his **eyes . . . upon the faithful . . . that they may dwell with me.** A person who is faithful **walks**, or lives, a life characterized by obedience to the Lord (see comment on Ps 1:1; cf. Gn 5:22; 6:9; Ps 26:11; 81:13; 86:11). To walk **in a blameless way** (v. 6) does not mean living a sinless life, but a determination to consistently obey the Lord. Such a person **is the one who will minster to me**, that is, serve as an attendant or personal advisor to the king of Israel. On the contrary, anyone who **practices deceit** or spreads **falsehood** would not have a **position** in David's court or in his friendship. He had a serious plan **Every morning** to **destroy** ("silence") **all the wicked** and **those who do iniquity** (v. 8). David would not allow them to have a place in **the land** (of Israel), so he would remove them **from the city of the LORD**, Jerusalem (cf. 46; 48; 87).

Psalm 102: Prayer from the Corrected Believer

Regarding the heading of **A Prayer of the Afflicted** (better, "an afflicted one," not **the Afflicted** as in the NASB), see the Ps 17 introduction. This prayer is intended as a model for any afflicted (i.e., chastised; see v. 10) believer when he or she is faint (signifying not only physical, but also emotional ebbing, despair, and depression, as in 61:2; 77:3) and pours out (signifying a full and sincere confession) his complaint (see 142:2) before the LORD. The content of the psalm calling for compassion on Zion, which was in ruins (vv. 13-14), suggests the psalm was written or edited following the Babylonian destruction of Jerusalem. This psalm, in which the psalmist yearned for the restoration of Zion (Jerusalem), is placed between two psalms of David, a fitting location since it is ultimately the Son of David who will provide final deliverance of the city and the nation (Sailhamer, *NIV Compact Bible Commentary,* 338).

A. Affirming God's Correction (102:1-11)

102:1-7. Consistent with the verb in the heading, the psalmist presents the reader in this opening section with a model of a sincere and deeply personal complaint: **Hear my prayer, O LORD! . . . Do not hide Your face from me in the day of my distress** (vv. 1-2). This models any believer's lament or complaint as a valid component of prayer. This complaint is expressed to God and God alone. Because God, ultimately, directs the steps of everyone (cf. Pr 20:24), any resolution of one's situation is in His hands to effect in accord with His will. The psalmist presented his situation with poetic descriptions of suffering: **days . . . consumed in smoke . . . bones . . . scorched like a hearth . . . heart . . . smitten like grass and withered . . . bones . . . cling to my flesh** (vv. 3-6). The closing images of **a pelican of the wilderness** and **an owl of the waste places** present the idea of a **lonely** situation.

102:8-11. The psalmist affirmed that the reason his **enemies** had **reproached** him to such an extent that he had **eaten ashes** (ashes were put on one's head as a sign of mourning, cf. Is 44:20) **like bread** (so these ashes of mourning had become mixed with his food) **and mingled my drink with weeping** (cf. Pss 42:3; 80:5) was just. It was **Because of Your indignation and Your wrath** (v. 10; see comment on Ps 30:5; cf. Is 60:10). The psalmist's agony was his sorrow at feeling **cast . . . away** from the Lord.

B. Affirming God's Compassion and Grace (102:12-17)

102:12-17. The psalmist had hope even in the midst of his difficult circumstances and the disaster which had befallen Jerusalem: **But You, O LORD, abide** [lit., "sit enthroned"] **forever. . . . You will arise and have compassion on Zion** (vv. 12-13). The **LORD** is not only just and righteous, but is also compassionate (see comment on 26:11) and gracious. Because of the unconditional nature of the Lord's covenant with Israel (cf. Gn 12:1-3; Ps 100:3), the psalmist declared with absolute confidence, no matter what the timing or events, that the Lord would **arise and have compassion on Zion** (see comments on 2:6; 9:11), for **it is time to be gracious to her** (v. 13); cf. 18:1; 30:5).

The remarks about **Zion** indicate that this psalm expressed national as well as personal distress, arising from the Babylonian exile. Although Jerusalem was in ruins after the destruction, **Surely Your servants find pleasure in her stones and feel pity for her dust** (v. 14; cf. 48:2; 12; 87:2; 137:5). When the Lord **has built up Zion . . .** and **appeared in His glory** (v. 16, an event so certain it is written in the Hb. prophetic perfect tense as if it had already occurred), then **the nations will fear the name of the LORD and all the kings of the earth Your glory** (v. 15; cf. 2). The psalmist found encouragement for his own situation by looking to God's relationship with Israel collectively as a paradigm of His relationship with the psalmist individually, both relationships being based on the same divine expressions of mercy, grace, and unconditional choice.

C. Affirming God's Purposes (102:18-28)

102:18-22. Verse 18 is unique in the Psalms in calling for a record to be **written for the generation[s] to come.** No matter what happened, the Lord would be faithful to all future generations, so that **a people yet to be created may praise the LORD . . . and tell of the name of the LORD in Zion** (vv. 18, 21). Although at the time of the writing of the psalm Jerusalem was in ruins and the Jewish people in exile, these future celebrations of **praise** will take place in **Jerusalem**, and at that time the Gentile **kingdoms** will **serve the Lord** (v. 22), which seems to be an eschatological perspective of the millennial kingdom when all the nations will worship the Lord in Zion (cf. 2:4-8; Is 56:7; Zch 8:23)

102:23-28. The psalm shifts back at this point to the psalmist's personal circumstances, when

God had **weakened [his] strength** and **shortened [his] days**. Simultaneously, there is praise to the Lord as Creator, **You founded the earth** (v. 25), and as the Eternal God, **You are the same . . . Your years will not come to an end** (v. 27, descriptions applied to the Lord Jesus, cf. Heb 1:10-12; see comments there). The psalm concludes with confidence in the survival of the Jewish people: **The children of Your servants will continue, And their descendants** [lit., "seed"] **will be established before You** (v. 28; cf. Gn 12:1-3; 2Sm 7:24; Is 49:15-16; Jr 31:35-37).

Psalm 103: Blessing God for His Benefits in Dealing with Humanity

On the heading of this **Psalm of David**, see Ps 3. This hymn of praise celebrating the great goodness of the Lord is connected to the restoration of Zion (cf. 102) and the spiritual restoration of the people of Israel. This spiritual restoration comes only through the forgiveness, grace, and mercy of God, the primary themes of this psalm (Sailhamer, *NIV Compact Bible Commentary,* 338).

A. The Scope of His Benefits in Dealing with Humankind (103:1-14)

103:1-5. The opening clause, **Bless the LORD, O my soul**, is repeated again at the end of the psalm, serving to emphasize its central idea (cf. "inclusio" in Introduction: Genre; cf. 104:1). Humanity is obligated and privileged to bless (i.e., to express praise and thanksgiving to) **the LORD** for the manifold **benefits**, and should be careful not to **forget** any of these blessings. In their scope, God's benefits are both spiritual and physical; David began by pointing to the central benefit of the Lord being the One (i.e., the only One; cf. Ps 49:7-9; Is 43:25) **who pardons all** man's **iniquities** and **redeems [his] life from the pit** (v. 4, death and separation from God; cf. 30:1). The psalm also praises God as the One who (ultimately; cf. Is 33:24; 35:5-10; Rv 21:4) **heals all your diseases** (v. 3). The blessings are personal and relational: the Lord **crowns you with lovingkindness and compassion** and **satisfies your years** [lit., "desires"] **with good things** (v. 5). Describing **youth** being **renewed like the eagle** is appropriate because the eagle is a symbol of strength, vitality, and endurance (cf. Is 40:31).

103:6-10. God's **righteous deeds** are illustrated by the Passover, alluding to God's revelation to **Moses** (cf. Ex 34:6) and His **acts to the sons of Israel** during the exodus. His character is summarized: **The LORD is compassionate and gracious, Slow to anger and abounding in lovingkindness** (v. 8; cf. 86:5, 15; Ex 34:6-7). The warning that God **will not always strive with us** provides another view of the Lord, who is just and will not overlook sin, yet in His mercy will not deal with us **according to our iniquities** if we trust Him to forgive our sins (vv. 9-10).

103:11-14. God's **lovingkindness [is] toward those who fear Him** (cf. 111:10) and **as far as the east is from the west** so far will He remove our **transgressions from us** (v. 12). This was accomplished in the OT by the offering of sacrifices with a faithful heart, and in the NT by faith in Messiah Jesus the final sacrifice (cf. Heb 10:1-18). Then God's kindness is illustrated **as a father** who has **compassion on his children** (v. 13).

B. The Duration of His Benefits in Dealing with Humankind (103:15-18)

103:15-18. To underscore the unending duration of God's benefits to **those who keep His covenant**, David pointed to man's temporary physical nature; **his days are like grass** (v. 15; cf. 102:11; Is 40:6-8). He then contrasted mortal humanity with God's eternal **lovingkindness** (Hb. *chesed*; cf. 5:7) which is **from everlasting to everlasting** (v. 17; cf. 90:2). The expression **those who keep His covenant** (v. 18) refers to those who, like Abraham, believe in the truth of God's Word and strive, however imperfectly, to uphold it (see comment on Gn 15:6; 26:5).

C. The Purpose of His Benefits in Dealing with Humankind (103:19-22)

103:19-22. David referred to the Lord as the Creator who **established His throne in the heavens** (cf. Ps 9:7; 11:4; Ezk 1) and as the King who in **His sovereignty rules over all** ("everything" more accurately signifies every created thing, whether animate or inanimate, material or immaterial). To affirm His benefits, compassion, forgiveness, eternality, and lovingkindness, the only response must be the threefold **Bless the LORD** (vv. 20-22), punctuated by the climactic declaration, **Bless the LORD, O my soul!** (v. 22).

Psalm 104: Blessing God for His Work as Creator and Sustainer of Life

Though the Hebrew text of this psalm has no heading, likely its attribution to David is suggested by: (1) its close thematic and verbal parallels to Ps 103, which is explicitly a Davidic psalm; and (2) the ascription of this psalm to David in early Jewish tradition (i.e., the LXX and the Midrash on Psalms, v. 1 [§2]). This hymn of praise is offered to God as Creator and Sustainer. The last line of the psalm is a reminder that the earth is not yet perfect and awaits the rule of the messianic King to eliminate the wicked and provide final redemption (cf. Rm 8:22-24).

A. Bless the Lord for His Work as Creator (104:1-23)

104:1-2a. As in the previous psalm, so in this one the psalmist began and concluded (v. 35) with the exhortation, **Bless the Lord, O my soul!** (see comment on 103:1). He was thus signaling at the outset that the theme of the present psalm was intended to complement that of the previous one. Whereas Ps 103 affirmed the praise due to God for His benefits to humankind, Ps 104 affirms the praise due to God for His creation of the world. The Lord is described as glorious **very great . . . clothed with splendor and majesty** (cf. comments on 21:5). These poetic descriptions of His glory (cf. 8:1, 3; 104:1, 131; Is 2:10, 19, 21; Jb 38–41) are linked to His eternality in the phrase, **Covering Yourself with light as with a cloak.** God alone is creator of the world.

104:2b-3. These verses continue the overview of creation in poetic terms: **stretching out heaven . . . lay[ing]s the beams** of the **waters**, making the **clouds His chariot**, and **walk[ing] upon the wings of the wind**.

104:4. God creates **winds** (better translated "angels") and **flaming fire** (or "ministers of flame") to obey Him (cf. 102:21). Hebrews 1:7 uses the LXX translation of v. 4a in a passage showing that Jesus receives higher honor than the angels.

104:5-9. The creation overview concludes with general statements of God's great power: **He established the earth** and **set a boundary** for the oceans (**the deep**, v. 6).

104:10-13. The Lord's provision for and the beauty of His creation is the emphasis of this stanza. He provides **springs** of water for **every beast of the field** so that **the earth is satisfied with the fruit of His works**.

104:14-23. God provides everything humanity needs in the process of caring for the earth. He gives food for the **cattle** (referring to a category of animal created specifically for man's use; cf. Gn 1:24); **vegetation for the labor of man** (cf. Gn 3:23), plus **wine which makes man's heart glad** (cf. Pr 3:20; although wine is a gift from the Lord, drunkenness is forbidden, cf. Pr 20:1) and **the moon for the seasons** (v. 19, referring to the regular observance of Israel's festivals of redemption at God's "appointed times"; cf. Lv 23:2, 4, 37, 44; Neh 10:33; the idea of seasons of the year is too ambiguous; see comment on Gn 1:14); and the cycle of life, **work**, and rest for humanity and animals (vv. 20-23).

B. Bless the Lord for Sustaining the Life of All Creation (104:24-35)

104:24-30. A summary statement **O Lord, how many are Your works! In wisdom You have made them all** speaks of God's creation of **the earth . . . the sea** and the **animals** (vv. 24-15). The Lord supplies all **their food** and either gives them life or **take[s] away their spirit** (which should properly be translated "breath," since "spirit" may be taken to signify a soul, which animals were never given; cf. comment on Gn 2:7;), and they **return to their dust** (v. 29; cf. Gn 3:19).

104:31-35. The response to glorify God as Creator is **Let the glory of the Lord endure forever . . . I will sing to the Lord as long as I live** (vv. 31, 33). This glorification is achieved both through the **praise** and worship of those who love God and truly know Him (cf. 1:6; this is, of course, the psalmist's personal perspective as expressed in vv. 33-34 and 35b), as well as through His just judgment of **sinners** and removal of **the wicked** from His presence forever (v. 35a; see comments on 69:22-28). The psalm closes with the well-known exhortation to praise, *Hallelujah* (**Praise the Lord**), which occurs only in Psalms, and here for the first time.

Psalm 105: Praise to the God of the Abrahamic Covenant

Though the Hebrew text of this psalm has no heading, evidence for its partial, if not complete, attribution to David is attested by: (1) the presentation of vv. 1-15 in 1Ch 16:8-22 as part of a psalm of thanksgiving ascribed to David ; and (2) the attribution to David of v. 38 (and by implication the rest of the psalm) in Jewish tradition (i.e., the Midrash on Psalms, v. 38 [§11]).

A. Praise for Choosing the People of Israel and Giving Them the Land of Israel (105:1-15)

105:1-11. The opening verses are a call to **give thanks to the Lord, call upon His name . . . Let the heart of those who seek the Lord be glad . . . Remember His wonders** (vv. 1, 3, 5). The psalm is addressed to the **seed of Abraham . . . sons of Jacob, His chosen ones!** (v. 6). The Jewish people are God's chosen people through the covenant the Lord made with Abraham (cf. Gn 12:1-3) and confirmed with Isaac (cf. Gn 26:23-25) and Jacob (cf. Gn 35:9-12; Dt 7:6-7). This psalm focuses on God's faithfulness in upholding the three promises/provisions of the Abrahamic covenant: possession of the Holy Land, a numerous people, and multi-faceted blessings (cf. comments on Gn 12:1-3).

The psalmist began by exhorting his audience (Israel) to **make known [the Lord's] deeds** (i.e., His sovereignty and character as borne out by His deeds of salvation and judgment) among all the **peoples** of the earth. This reflects God's primary motivation in making His covenant with Abraham, namely, to bless all peoples through him, and ultimately through his seed, the Son of God. To provide a defined venue through which to bring this seed of blessing, God: (1) sovereignly chose the line of **Abraham . . . Isaac**, and **Jacob** (vv. 9-10). From the patriarchs God created "a people for His own possession" (Dt 7:6; a choice based on God's grace alone; see the comments on Rm 9:6-8); and (2) sovereignly gave them **the land of Canaan** as their everlasting **inheritance** (v. 11). That the land is an everlasting inheritance of the nation of Israel follows logically from the Abrahamic covenant under which it was promised, being **an everlasting covenant** (v. 10; cf. Gn 17:7-8).

105:12-15. In addition to Israel's creation as a distinct people, God's covenant with Abraham also involved their preservation as a people regardless of whether they conducted themselves in a manner worthy of their being called **His people** (vv. 24, 43). This section includes a quick review of God's care for His people when **they were only a few . . . in number**, and protected them (**He permitted no man to oppress them**, v. 15) even when Abraham made bad decisions (cf. Gn 12:11-20; 20:2-7).

B. Praise for Preserving His People outside Their Land (105:16-41)

105:16-24. This is an overview the time there was **a famine upon the land** of Israel. This was followed by the experience of **Joseph** from his time as a **slave** until he became **ruler over all his [Pharaoh's] possessions**, until **Israel [Jacob] also came into Egypt** (also called **Ham**; cf. v. 27; 78:51; 106:21-22; Gn 10:6). The psalmist explored specifically how God provided for and protected the people of Israel so that they became **very fruitful** (v. 24) The narrative account of this is found in Gn 39–41.

105:25-36. This is the retelling of the call of **Moses** after the people of Israel had been slaves in Egypt for 400 years, culminating with the plagues on the Egyptians and the deliverance of the Jewish people at Passover when the Lord **struck down all the firstborn** of Egypt (v. 36). The narrative account of this is found in Ex 1–13.

105:37-41. What follows is a sketch of the deliverance from Egypt. **He brought them out**, followed by the Lord's guidance with the **cloud** and provision of **quail . . . the bread of heaven** (manna), and **water** from the **rock** on their way to the promised land (cf. Ex 14–17). God cared for His people even when they were outside of their homeland for a period of about 400 years (cf. Gn 15:13).

C. Praise for Establishing His People within Their Land (105:42-45)

105:42-45. The psalmist reflected on God's faithfulness in restoring His people to their land as **He remembered His holy word with Abraham His servant** so that **He brought forth His people with joy, His chosen ones** (cf. v. 6) to **the lands of the** Canaanite **nations** that **He gave them** (v. 44) as an everlasting inheritance according to His promise to Abraham, Isaac, and Jacob (cf. vv. 8-11). God's blessing was expressed not only by His giving Israel land, but also by His giving them a land already prepared to live in by the **labor** of the Canaanite **peoples** (v. 44; cf. Dt 6:10-11). This continues the pattern already presented in God's original creation of mankind's home in which everything was fully prepared for humanity before their creation, and also anticipates the same scenario for the final home of God's people in the hereafter (cf. Jn 14:2-3). On the concluding exhortation **Praise the LORD!** see the comment at the end of Ps 104.

Psalm 106: Praise for God's Faithfulness to His Unfaithful People

The Hebrew text of this psalm has no heading. Verses 40-47 bear the hallmarks of an exilic perspective, and quite likely represent the words added at or after the Babylonian exile to continue and hence emphasize the picture of God's unbroken correction of and lovingkindness toward His people. Similar to Ps 105, this psalm is a historical psalm that reflects the psalmists understanding of God's faithfulness as demonstrated in the Abrahamic covenant in the Pentateuch, and appeals to God to provide salvation to His people based upon His faithfulness to that covenant (v. 4; Sailhamer, *NIV Compact Bible Commentary*, 339).

A. The Basis of God's Faithfulness (106:1-5)

106:1-5. The psalmist began with a call to **Praise the LORD!** for those aspects of His character that undergird His faithfulness to Israel. His goodness (**He is good**) is a term that first occurs in the creation account and describes what is of utmost good for mankind; see comment on Gn

1:4; also **His lovingkindness** (cf. comments on (Ps 5:7). On the basis of these two divine attributes, God chose Israel as "a people for His own possession" (Dt 7:6). This is emphasized by four descriptive titles applied to Israel in vv. 4-5: **Your people . . . Your chosen ones . . . Your nation**, and **Your inheritance** (cf. 105:6 and comments there; Dt 9:27-29; 1Kg 8:53).

B. The Expression of God's Faithfulness (106:6-46)

106:6-12. Certainly the Lord is faithful (cf. comments on 23:6; 85; 88) but His people often fail to be obedient to Him. The majority of this psalm focuses on the ongoing cycle of God's correction of sinful Israel beginning with the exodus generation: **We have sinned like our fathers . . . in Egypt [who] did not understand Your wonders . . . but rebelled by the sea** (vv. 6-7). Despite their sin **He saved them for the sake of His name . . . He saved them from the hand of the one who hated them** (vv. 8, 10; cf. 23:3 and comments there).

106:13-27. The history continues to review the journey to the promised land when **They quickly forgot His works, tempted God in the desert** (vv. 13-14), **made a [golden] calf in Horeb** (v. 19, cf. Ex 32:4), and **forgot God their Savior** (v. 21). When the 12 spies were sent to evaluate the promised land, **they despised the pleasant land** (v. 24); only Joshua and Caleb trusted the Lord while the other 10 spies **did not listen to the voice of the Lord** (v. 25; cf. Nm 13:32-33).

106:28-31. During the wilderness wanderings, instead of faithfully following the Lord their God, many people worshiped the pagan god **Baal-peor** (cf. Nm 25). Yet, the priest **Phinehas** led a faithful remnant in following the Lord, and **it was reckoned to him for righteousness** (vv. 30-31), using the same phrase that described Abraham's faith (cf. Gn 15:6). Righteousness comes by faith in the Lord, and this is true for **all generations forever** (v. 31).

106:32-33. Israel also **provoked** God's **wrath** at the **waters of Meribah** (cf. Ex 17:1-7; Nm 20:2-13). Twice the people complained about the lack of water in the wilderness, this one likely referring to the event at the end of the wilderness wanderings (cf. Nm 20). Although Moses demonstrated a lack of faith by striking the rock (cf. Nm 20:12), there are no allusions here as to responsibility. It was the people who rebelled against God's **Spirit**.

106:34-43. When they finally entered the land of promise, the Israelites **did not destroy the** pagan **peoples** who lived in there **as the Lord commanded them** (v. 34; cf. Jos 16:10; 17:13; Jdg 1:21 and the following chapters). As a result, the people of Israel **learned** the **practices** of the pagan nations and **served their idols**, even falling to the abominable sin of sacrificing **their sons and their daughters to the demons**, the god Moloch (v. 37; cf. 2Ch 28:3; 33:6; Jr 7:31, 19:2-6). Unfaithfulness to the Lord is described as playing **the harlot in their deeds** (v. 39; cf. Jdg 2:17; Ezk 23:3-8; Hos 5:3; 6:10).

106:40-46. The righteous **anger** of God's judgment led to the period of the exile when God **gave them into the hand of the nations** (v. 41), a reference to the Babylonian exile (cf. Lv 26:25-26, 33-38, 42-44; Neh 9:30). Even in exile, the Lord **looked upon their distress . . . heard their cry . . . remembered His covenant** (with Abraham) and **also made them objects of compassion in the presence of all their captors** (vv. 44-46; cf. the words of Solomon, anticipating the future exile, in 1Kg 8:50).

C. The Goal of God's Faithfulness (106:47-48)

106:47-48. The psalm concludes with a plea to deliver Israel from Babylonian captivity: **Save us, O Lord our God, and gather us from among the nations.** The present psalm, like Ps 90, focuses on the ultimate goal of God's correction and deliverance. The Israelites were to **give thanks to** His **holy name and glory in** His **praise** (v. 47). Verse 48 is employed as a compound doxology by which both this psalm and the Fourth Book of Psalms (90–106) are brought to a close with the exhortation **Praise the Lord!** (cf. 104:35.)

V. Book Five: Responding in Worship to God's Ultimate Faithfulness (Pss 107–150)

Psalm 107: A Call for the Redeemed to Praise the Lord

This psalm has no heading. Consistent with its placement at the beginning of Book Five of Psalms, this psalm focuses on, and hence introduces the main theme of the fifth book, about the ingathering of the people of Israel to the land of Israel. The design of the book of Psalms parallels the Pentateuch (see Introduction: Title, Structure, and Place in the Canon). Thus this fifth book of Psalms parallels Deuteronomy, the fifth book of the Pentateuch, and concerns the arrival of God's people to the promised land (see v. 3) and their living under the perfect and intimate rule of their divine King. God revealed these truths to those who came out from Egypt.

They are repeated in Deuteronomy for the subsequent generation born in the wilderness who did not witness them first hand. "Deuteronomy," the name for the book in the LXX, means "repeated or reiterated Law."

Book Five of Psalms often focuses on the ingathering of God's people after the exile, with some references to the advent of God's kingdom on earth. This theme is emphasized by the repetition of the key expression "Hallelujah," (of which 20 of its 24 biblical occurrences are in Book Five, the other four being in Pss 104:35; 105:45; and 106:1, 48).

Ps 106 closed with a prayer for God to regather His people from the nations (see 106:47). Ps 107 contains an expression of thanks for God regathering the people after exile (107:1-3).

A. Praise the Lord for Restoring His People to Their Land (107:1-3)

107:1-3. This psalm opens with the call **O give thanks to the LORD, for He is good**. This call to give thanks is repeated throughout the psalm (cf. vv. 8, 15, 21, 31). The psalm emphasizes that God's **lovingkindness is everlasting** (also repeated in vv. 1, 8, 15, 21, 31). This statement is the most repeated qualification of praise in the book of Psalms, occurring most often in this fifth book (see 118:1-4, 29; 136). God's **lovingkindness** (*chesed*; cf. comments on 5:7) more than anything else is represented by His regathering of Israel to their land of Israel and the consequent fulfillment of all that He promised to do for them ultimately under the reign of King Messiah.

That this has in view the final fulfillment of all God's promises (per the Abrahamic covenant) both to and through Israel is evident from: (1) the past tense (perfect) verbal forms **has redeemed** and **[has] gathered** (vv. 2-3), which indicates that these actions are viewed as completed (whereas from the time of the Babylonian exile to the present they are still ongoing); (2) the specific phraseology describing Israel's regathering from all points of the compass, **east/ west/ north/south**, using prophetic phraseology to describe Israel's final regathering and redemption, not just the return from Babylon (cf. Is 43:5-6; 56:12; Ezk 11:17; 20:33ff.); and (3) the specific use (in v. 2) of the term **redeemed**, signifying (Is 35:9; 62:12), both spiritual and physical redemption

B. Praise the Lord for Correcting His People for Their Sins (107:4-22)

107:4-9. This is an overview of Israel's history of the exodus as they **wandered in the wilderness** yet when **they cried out to the LORD . . . He delivered them out of their distresses** (vv. 4, 6, cf. vv. 13, 28). Therefore **Let them give thanks to the LORD for His lovingkindness** (v. 8).

107:10-16. The reference to **those who dwelt in darkness and in the shadow of death** (cf. v. 14; 23:4) begins a graphic image of distress (cf. 18:28; Jb36:8; Is 5:30; 8:22; 59:9; Jr 13:16; Lm 3:7). The reference to **prisoners in misery and chains** relates to Israel being taken away to captivity in Babylon (cf. 2Ch 36:6; Jr 52:12-30). They were judged because they **rebelled against the words of God** yet when **they cried out to the LORD in their trouble** (vv. 11, 13; cf. vv. 6, 28) He **brought them out of darkness and the shadow of death** (v. 14; cf. v. 10). Therefore the psalmist exhorted his people to **give thanks to the LORD for His lovingkindness** (v. 15; cf. vv. 9, 21) not only for redeeming them from the afflictions of those disciplines but also for bringing those corrections on them in the first place (cf. Pr 3:11-12; Heb 12:4-11).

107:17-22. These **fools**, people who had refused to believe in and follow the Lord (cf. 14:1; 53:1), were suffering physically for their **iniquities**. They had lost their appetites, **abhorred all kinds of food**, coming almost to the point of **death** (v. 18). When **they cried out to the LORD in their trouble** (v. 19; cf. vv. 6, 28) He **healed them** (v. 20). Therefore they were exhorted to **give thanks to the LORD for His lovingkindness** indicating the people will be back in the Land of Israel with a rebuilt temple, the place to **offer sacrifices of thanksgiving** with a heart of worship (vv. 21-22; cf. Lv 7:12-15; 22:29-30; Pss 50:7-15; 116:17).

C. Praise the Lord for Preserving His People through Their Distress (107:23-43)

107:23-38. In keeping with the overall theme of Book Five, the psalmist moved on from focusing on God's lovingkindness as expressed in the process of correction throughout Israel's history to focusing on God's lovingkindness as expressed in God's absolute dominion over nature. He is in control of the **wonders in the** oceans, the **stormy wind** and **waves of the sea** (vv. 24-25) as well as the **rivers . . . springs . . . fruitful land** . . . so people can **establish an inhabited city** . . . **sow the fields** because **He blesses them** (vv. 33-34; 36-38). Therefore, they should **give thanks to the LORD for His lovingkindness** (vv. 31-32; cf. 8, 15, 21).

107:39-43. Because of God's dominion, He cannot be impeded either by events in nature nor from human agency (from political or social sources) in the process of restoring His people to their land. **He set the needy securely on high . . . and makes his families like a flock** (v. 41; cf. Ps 23 and comments there). The conclusion of this psalm is in the style of a proverb: The **wise** person will **give heed** (carefully watch/meditate upon) the instruction of this psalm and **consider the lovingkindness of the Lord** (v. 43).

Psalm 108: Reaffirming Our Total Dependence on God

On this **Psalm of David**, or **Song**, see the comments on the headings to Pss 3 and 46. The psalm represents a combination of the parts of two previous psalms. Verses 1-5 correspond to Ps 57:7-11, and vv. 6-13 correspond to Ps 60:5-12. This repetition and recombination, with slight variation further reinforces the parallel between Book Five of Psalms and Deuteronomy (see introduction to Ps 107). Psalms 108–110 are psalms of David that develop the dual themes of the oppression of God's people at the hands of their enemies and God's promise to rescue them. Ultimate deliverance from oppression will come through the inauguration of the messianic kingdom. In Ps 108, David requests God's help in the midst of defeat (v. 6), and God responds by promising to deliver Israel (vv. 7-9) (Sailhamer, *NIV Compact Bible Commentary*, 340).

A. Reaffirming God's Praise (108:1-6)

108:1-6. Regardless of circumstances, David is determined to thank and praise the Lord: **My heart is steadfast, O God . . . I will give thanks to You, O Lord**. The final line of this stanza, **That Your beloved may be delivered** indicates some unspecified trouble. God's **lovingkindness** (v. 4) ensures not only what is materially best, but also what is spiritually best, including correction, as affirmed in the previous psalm. Because all believers, like David, are viewed by God as His **beloved** (the word is used to describe those in the position of the most intimate relationship with God; cf. Dt 33:12; Ps 127:2; Is 5:1).

B. Reaffirming God's Promises (108:7-9)

108:7-9. David here affirmed that the God of Israel, who **has spoken in His holiness**, has given the Land of Israel to the people of Israel forever. His promises regarding the land are underscored by the Lord's possession of all the region, indicated by the possessive pronouns (**Mine**, **My**). The areas of **Shechem** (cf. Gn 33:18-19; 1Kg 12:1, 25) **Succoth** (cf. Gn 33:17; and **Gilead** (cf. Ps 34:1; Jos 17:6) belong to Israel. During the divided monarchy **Ephraim** was the Northern Kingdom, being the **helmet of My head**. The Davidic kings ruled (held **My scepter**; cf. Gn 49:10) in **Judah,** the southern kingdom. Israel's most prominent enemies in the land are mentioned: **Moab**, **Edom**, and **Philistia** (cf. 60:6-9 and comments there) as areas over which the Lord will have dominion: Over Edom I will **throw My shoe** (likely a symbolic action, indicating ownership, cf. Dt 11:24), **Over Philistia I will shout aloud**, with dominance (v. 9).

C. Reaffirming God's Actions (108:10-13)

108:10-13. These verses repeat the refrain of the final stanza of Ps 60. See comments in the parallel text, 60:9-12. The question **Who will bring me . . .** is rhetorical. Clearly it is the Lord **God who will . . . go forth with our armies** (v. 10).

Psalm 109: A Prayer for Justice against a False Accusation

On the heading of this **Psalm of David**, see the comments on Pss 3 and 4. David's hope of deliverance for himself and his people (see 108:10-13) will occur only when God acts to bring this about (Ps 109).

A. As an Occasion for Appealing to God's Justice (109:1-20)

109:1-5. Although in difficult circumstances, David begins his focus on the Lord: **O God of my praise, Do not be silent!** (cf. Dt. 10:21; 28:1-2). Wickedness is an inseparable component of this life, even for those who follow the Lord (2Tm 3:12). Here is a model for transforming, as it were, the black coals of unjust persecution into the brilliant diamonds of worship. One way in which this can be done is by petitioning God **in prayer** (v. 4), to manifest His justice in bringing retribution on the **wicked and deceitful** who oppress the righteous by repaying **evil for good and hatred for . . . love** (vv. 2, 5).

Though this may initially seem to contradict Jesus' emphasis on loving one's enemies (Mt 5:44), several considerations bear out its consistency with NT teaching. First, throughout this psalm, as typically in the other "imprecation" psalms, the psalmist appeals to God to bring just retribution on his oppressors, rather than expressing the intention to take the matter of vengeance into his own hands ("Vengeance is Mine;" Rm 12:19). Second, nowhere in this psalm or any other imprecation psalm did the psalmist require a timetable for God's retribution against his oppressors, but instead he leaves the "when" and "how" to God. Third, the same standard of divine justice applies equally to both believers like himself as well as to the wicked who oppress them, and under this perfect standard all people stand justly condemned to God's severest retribution. In the present section this point is vividly made in v. 6, the imagery and even phraseology of which parallels that in Zch 3:1. See comments on imprecatory psalms in the introduction to Psalms.

109:6-13. This imprecatory psalm requests specific harsh judgments on his wicked enemies, that each one would suffer the punishments he deserves. These requests include that the wicked: be found **guilty**; have his **prayer** unanswered because of his sinful actions; have someone else **take his office**; be executed for his crime and thus leave **his children . . . fatherless** and **his wife a widow**. David asks that his enemy be deprived of all his property so his **children** have to beg from **their ruined home**; that **creditors** and **strangers** take **all that he has**; and even that no one be **gracious to his fatherless children** (vv. 11-12), so that by the next **generation** the family **name will be blotted out** (v. 13; cf. 9:5). The phrase about letting **another take his office** (v. 8) is applied to Judas Iscariot in Ac 1:20. This is not a direct prediction and fulfillment. Rather, the principle of this psalm, that wicked men should be replaced by someone else, is applied to Judas. Therefore, to prove that Judas was a wicked man, another had to be appointed to replace him as an apostle.

109:14-20. This section continues the imprecation by asking the Lord to **cut off their memory from the earth**, because the wicked man **did not remember to show lovingkindness but persecuted the afflicted and needy man** (vv. 15-16).

B. As an Occasion for Appealing to God's Lovingkindness (109:21-29)

109:21-29. Another way in which believers can turn oppression by the wicked into worship is by appealing to God to **Help me . . . save me according to Your lovingkindness** and manifest His kindness in such a way that the wicked will **know that this is Your hand** (vv. 26-27). The psalmist requests that his accusers be put to shame as that is their only hope of turning to the Lord in repentance.

C. As an Occasion for Expressing God's Praise (109:30-31)

109:30-31. A third way in which believers can turn their oppression into worship is by taking it as an occasion not only to implore God to do something (such as bringing just retribution on oppressors and showing lovingkindness toward believers by relieving their affliction), but also to **give thanks** to God and to **praise Him** for what He has already done. The psalm ends with confident expectation of the Lord's answer, **For He stands at the right hand of the needy, To save him from those who judge his soul.**

Psalm 110: Deliverance through the King Messiah

On the heading of this **Psalm of David** see the comments on Ps 3. Like Pss 2 and 22, this psalm refers directly and exclusively to the Messiah (see Introduction to the Psalms). That this is so is more than evident, not only from a careful reading of the psalm itself, but also from its treatment in the NT, where it is cited directly with exclusive reference to Messiah nine times (cf. Mt 22:43-45; Mk 12:36-37; Lk 20:42-44; Ac 2:34-36: Heb 1:13; 5:6-10; 7:11-28). This number is surpassed only by Ps 118, which is directly cited 11 times. Considering other allusions to it, Ps 110 unquestionably emerges as the most prominent of all. Also the theological centrality of this psalm is evident from its role in Heb 7 (see comments there) in which the writer emphasizes the soteriological point that the atonement afforded by the priestly work of the Messiah is not only perfectly efficacious but is also eternal.

Even the structure of this psalm points to its centrality. The psalm has three units of thought, each describing the messianic King. The first three verses describe Him as the divine King (vv. 1-3), the central verse shows Him as the eternal priest (v. 4), and the final three verses identify Him as the victorious warrior (vv. 5-7). The central verse (v. 4), about the eternal priest, in its brevity provides the literary focal point of the Psalm. The main idea of Psalm 110 is that "the Lord has granted universal dominion to the messianic Priest-King" (Michael Rydelnik, *The Messianic Hope: Is the Hebrew Bible Really Messianic?* [Nashville: B&H Publishers, 2010], 171).

Book Five of the Psalter (107–150) opens with seven psalms, 107–113, that have a clear unit of thought. The seven are linked, and Ps 110 is the thematic and central unifier. Psalms 107–109 plead for God to deliver Israel while Psalms 111–113 praise God for having delivered Israel. Between these psalms sits Ps 110, revealing the Messiah as the answer to the pleas for deliverance (107–109) and the reason for the praise for deliverance (111–113).

A. Messiah, the Divine King (110:1-3)

The first stanza of Ps 110 emphasizes the kingship of Messiah, depicting Him in a variety of His royal roles.

110:1. As consistently explained in the NT (Mt 22:44; Mk 12:36; Lk 20:42-43; Ac 2:34-35; Heb 1:13), this opening verse describes the determination of God the Father (**the LORD**) regarding the ultimate victory and dominion of God the Son (**my** [David's] **Lord**), hence establishing the parameters by which to understand the rest of the psalm. Though some critics claim that the NT writers (and Jesus Himself) construed this verse—and the psalm generally—in a manner inconsistent with the semantics of the Hebrew text and how it has always been naturally understood in pre- and post-NT Jewish tradition, those claims are untrue.

That the first **LORD** refers to God is beyond all question, since the Hebrew term used is "Yahweh." But the following expression **my Lord** (Hb. *adoni*) is less clear. In purely lexical terms it designates one's sociocultural superior (i.e., "my master"). The only other place David employed this expression was of Saul (1Sm 30:13). The support for seeing the word as referring to deity is threefold. (1) Although generally used of a human authority, this word can be used of deity, being used of the Lord God appearing as the angel of the Lord in two places (Jos 5:14; Jdg 6:13). (2) The word intended may have been the normal word for Lord (God). As Robert Alden observed, the psalm was originally written only with consonants (the vowels being added between the eighth and tenth centuries AD). But it is possible that the original consonantal text understood the vowels to refer to *Adonay*, the normal word for God (Robert L. Alden, *Psalms: Songs of Discipleship*, vol. 3 of Everyman's Bible Commentary [Chicago: Moody, 1976], 331–32). (3) In v. 5, the one at the right hand is called *adonay* (the word for Lord that indicates deity) just as the Lord in v. 1 is said to be at the right hand of God. Verse 5 therefore identifies the one at the right hand of the Lord as also being deity.

Some interpreters object that this psalm in its "natural" Hebrew sense has never been understood as referring to the Messiah. The rabbinic consensus was that the expression **my LORD** refers to Abraham or perhaps David. However, these are neither the only nor the earliest views. Among the Dead Sea Scrolls (most of which were written in Hebrew by Jews) is one (11Q13) in which Melchizedek, the central personage of this psalm, is clearly depicted (in a manner closely parallel to that in Heb 7) as filling the role of the Messiah (see comments on Gn 14:17-24). Some medieval Jewish interpreters have also recognized that what is said in this psalm far transcends whatever did or can apply to either Abraham or David, and therefore they conclude that David "composed this psalm about the Messiah" (Obadiah ben Jacob Sforno [d. 1550]). That the Messiah was divine, however, no rabbinic interpreter can admit, since such would contradict one of the foundational tenets of rabbinic Judaism).

As to the Father's declaration that David's Lord **sit at** His **right hand**, the place of greatest favor, power, and preeminence, this is a point of central importance in the NT, as indicated by the many direct citations and allusions to it (see Mt 26:64; Mk 14:62; 16:19; Lk 22:69; Rm 8:34; Eph 1:20; Col 3:1; Heb 1:3; 8:1; 10:12). It serves as explicit affirmation of the inevitable and ultimate victory of Messiah over all earthly opposition. The divine messianic King will one day rule over His **enemies** (vv. 1, 2). The word for **enemies** is used regularly in the Psalter of God's enemies (8:2; 21:8; 66:3; 74:23; 89:10, 51; 92:9), giving support that the King here is viewed as deity. These enemies will one day become his **footstool**, a word that depicts the King's victory (cf. 47:3; Jos 10:24; Is 49:23). The word **footstool** is also frequently used as belonging to God (1Ch 28:2; Pss 99:5; 132:7; Is 66:1; Lm 2:1), indicating that these enemies will one day be a *divine* footstool. It seems that this depiction could not describe anyone other than an exalted, eschatological, divine, messianic King.

110:2-3. Initially the King was depicted in the throne room of God in heaven (v. 1), now it shows him descending to earth (**Zion**, v. 2). There He receives dominion over His **enemies** and leads His servants into battle. His scepter extends (**stretches forth**) **from Zion**, indicating a reign from earthly Jerusalem. Moreover, the King leads His **people** who **volunteer freely** to fight on the day of battle. This is an eschatological army, in **holy array** (lit., "splendors of holiness" *hadre qodesh*), referring, like the similar expression (*hadrat qodesh*) in 1Ch 16:29 and 2Ch 20:21, to the "holy attire" worn by the Levitical priests in praising the Lord. The specific scenario in view here is indicated by the expression **in the day of Your power** (v. 3), in which the term **power** (*hayil*) literally signifies "military might," thus relating this depiction to the Messiah's coming in power ("the day of His wrath" in v. 5) as portrayed in Zch 14:3-5 and Rv 19:11-16. Thus, the psalm is depicting the Messiah Jesus at His return, not His first coming.

The last phrase of v. 3 **from the womb of the dawn, Your youth are to you as the dew**, is virtually unintelligible in the Masoretic Text. Much to be preferred is the LXX reading, "from the womb of the dawn, I have begotten you." Although some would argue for the MT, following the text critical axiom of taking the harder reading, this is to be rejected. There is a difference between a harder reading and an unintelligible reading. The variant reading is also supported by the Syriac and a number of Masoretic manuscripts. The phrase "I have begotten you" would then be a clear allusion to Ps 2:7, another significant messianic psalm. The King is said to be begotten **from the womb of the dawn**, indicating that this divine King comes from the heavenly realms from eternity past, before the creation of morning light.

B. Messiah, The Priest-King (110:4)

110:4. The center of this psalm (v . 4) is also—and most importantly—the focal point, for this verse establishes the Father's ordination of the Son **according to the** priestly **order of Melchizedek**, rather than Levi (cf. Heb 5:6, 10; 6:20; 7:11, 17, 21). For a detailed discussion of the significance of this unique priestly order (and the meaning of Melchizedek's name) see the comments on Gn 14:17-24 and Heb 7. Beginning with the promise of the Lord, the psalmist focuses on the certainty of God's oath to the King. Since **the LORD has sworn**, He will assure that it will happen and He will not be sorry. This refers to God's irrevocable establishment of the King as priest.

The reason an oath was necessary was because the promise is unusual—God will unite the offices of king and priest in this divine King. This is unusual in that these offices were always separate in Israel. Another surprising feature is that the King will not be a Levitical priest but a priest **according to the order of Melchizedek.** This mysterious individual from Gn 14, served as a priest-king of God Most High. Just as Melchizedek was a priest-king, so this messianic figure will likewise be a priest-king, in the same manner.

The most significant aspect of this priesthood is that, unlike the transitory Levitical priests, this Priest-King would be **a priest forever.** This refers to His eternal nature and the permanent effects of His work. As the focal point of the psalm, this verse emphasizes the eternal priesthood of the messianic King. The verses both before and after v. 4 depict the King at war. Hence, the Priest-King is one who offers up the enemies of God in a great sacrificial feast (Ezk 39:17-20) to the Lord at the end of days.

C. Messiah, the Victorious Warrior (110:5-7)

The last stanza depicts Messiah's victory over the nations in the great end-of-days war. Verses 5-6 begin the stanza by identifying those whom the Messiah will defeat, while v. 7 depicts His refreshment after battle.

110:5-6. At the outset, v. 5 states, **The Lord is at your right hand**. Unlike v. 1, the Hebrew word for "Lord" uses the vowels indicating that a divine Lord is being described. But this is not Yahweh at the King's right hand but the King at the right hand of Yahweh. This is evident in that all the third person singular pronouns that follow refer back to the word "Lord." But, plainly it is the King who will **shatter kings, judge . . . the nations** and **shatter the chief men**. If the King is the subject of all these verbs, He must be the one called **Lord**. This clearly fits with v. 1. There He was said to be at the right hand of Yahweh even as He is once again depicted at God's **right hand** here in v. 5. The logical conclusion is the warrior King is being called **the Lord** *(Adonay)*, a title reserved for God alone.

In these two verses the victorious divine King is described as defeating all those who have rebelled against God. He crushes kings and rulers, judges people, and heaps up **corpses**. The violence of the imagery recalls Is 63:1-6, where the messianic King tramples the wine press of the nations, staining His garments with blood and crushing nations in His wrath. The psalmist says all this will occur on **the day of His wrath** (v. 5). This phrase ("day of wrath") occurs in only six verses in Scripture (Jb 20:28; Lm 2:1, 21-22; Zph 2:2-3) and in each case refers to God's wrath. Thus, it implies that the victorious King of Ps 110 is indeed a divine King.

110:7. The last verse uses a refreshment metaphor, depicting the King as **drink[ing] from the brook** after the last battle. In contrast to v. 1, where the King sits, awaiting the day when His enemies are defeated and made a footstool, in v. 7, having defeated the enemies, He is refreshed by drinking from the brook—thus **He will lift up His head**, surveying His great victory on the battlefield.

Psalm 110 as a whole depicts the divine, eternal Priest-King of Israel who will rule all the nations from Zion, crush all rebellion against Himself, and bring peace to the world. This elevated depiction eliminates Abraham, David himself, Solomon, or any other suggested human king as the subject of this psalm. It points to the return of the divine Messiah, the Lord Jesus, when He returns in power and glory.

Psalm 111: A Call to Worship God for His Unfailing Righteousness

Psalms 111 and 112 are closely connected by parallel themes, both expressing praise to God for having provided deliverance (see introductory comments to Ps 110). Psalm 111 focuses on the object of worship, and Ps 112 focuses on those offering worship. Both are alphabetic acrostics. The purpose of an acrostic is to repeat a single theme for each letter of the alphabet, totaling twenty-two times. Although David is mentioned as the author of only Ps 110, these following psalms (Pss 111 and 112) are so closely linked in content, tradition suggests David as the author of these three psalms.

A. The Response of Worship (111:1)

111:1. The purpose of the psalm is direct: **Praise the Lord!** The psalmist affirmed that God's creation is obligated to give Him worship, specifically the praise and thanksgiving to which He is entitled. The psalmist emphasized the quality of his worship by referring not to his use of a certain formula or special wording, but rather that it is to be given **with all** his **heart**. The worship of God should not be just personal and private; it should also be public, expressed collectively with other believers: **In the company of the upright**.

B. The Motivation for Worship (111:2-9)

111:2-6. The essential motivation or basis for all worship is **Great are the works of the Lord**. He is to be worshiped for His **righteousness** that **endures forever**. Moreover, He is **gracious and compassionate**, a phrase used to describe the Lord ten times in the Scriptures, highlighting His mercy and kindness (cf. Ex 34:6; 2Ch 30:9; Neh 9:17, 31; Pss 112:4; 116:5: Jl 2:13; Jnh 4:2). His faithfulness to Israel in **giving** to them **the heritage** [*lan*] **of the nations** refers to the land of Israel provided by the Lord from the seven Gentile nations in the promised land of Canaan (cf. Dt 7:1).

111:7-9. All **the works of His hands are truth and justice**, and **His precepts** (cf. 19:8) are **sure** (certain and unfailing; 19:7). He is to be praised because **He has sent redemption to His people** by the giving of His **covenant forever** (v. 9) beginning with the promise of the Redeemer in the Abrahamic covenant (cf. Gn 13:1-2; Ex 2:24). **Holy and awesome is His name** (cf. comments on Pss 5:11; 23:3).

C. The Attitude in Worship (111:10)

111:10. The psalm concludes the attitude that should guide worship: **The fear of the Lord** as **the beginning of wisdom**. This is a concept more familiar from Proverbs but central to worship in the Psalms (cf. Pr 1:7; 9:10). To fear the Lord is be in awe of Him based on understanding His righteousness (v. 3), wonders (v. 4), justice (v. 7), holiness (v. 9), and awesomeness (v. 9). When one worships God in this manner He is glorified. Those who fear and worship Him will grow in **wisdom** and **understanding**, and the wiser people become, the more able they will be to **do**/obey **His commandments** (v. 10).

Psalm 112: The Benefits of Fearing the Lord

This psalm is closely related in both content and structure to Ps 111 (see introduction to Ps 111). It also is an acrostic, extolling God's faithfulness to the righteous.

A. The Call to Fear the Lord (112:1)

112:1. Opening with a call to **praise the Lord** and to be one **who fears the Lord**, this psalm continues the thought with which the previous one ended (cf. Pss 1 and 111:10 and comments there). The proper perspective in fearing the Lord is that such a person **greatly delights in His commandments**; learning more of the Lord each day and daily becoming more obedient is the greatest joy in life (cf. 1:2; 19; 119). The terms **fears** and **commandments** are closely related to the terms "worship" and "obey" in Gn 2:15, epitomizing man's original purpose and relationship to the Lord (see comments there).

B. The Blessings of Fearing the Lord (112:2-9)

112:2-3. The **descendants** of the righteous man will be **mighty on earth**, having influence for good as they continue as the **generation of the upright**, following the Lord, then passing the godly heritage to their own children so that **his righteousness endures forever** (cf. 37:36; 127:3-5; 128:3-4; Pr 13:22; 14:26; 31:28).

112:4. Stating that **Light arises in the darkness for the upright**, the psalmist employs the image of light as God's guidance (cf. 4:6; 18:28: 27:1; 43:3; 44:3; 89:15; 97:11; 119:105, 130; Pr 4:18) revealing the clear pathway in the midst of **darkness**, a metaphor for confusion, uncertainty, trouble or even evil (cf. 107:10 and comments there). Because the Lord is **gracious and compassionate and righteous** (cf. 111:4 and comments there), there is no need to fear anything.

112:5-6. A characteristic of the **man** (person) who fears the Lord (cf. 111:10) is his generosity and sympathy. He is **gracious and lends** to the poor and needy (cf. v. 9) and is concerned for justice in **judgment** (cf. 33:5; Pr 1:3; 8:20; 21:3, 15). This person **will never be shaken** by the circumstances of life (cf. v. 7; 15:5; 16:8; 21:7; 46:1-2; 55:26). Therefore, **the righteous** will have a good reputation into future generations and be **remembered forever** (cf. v. 2).

112:7-9. Those who fear the Lord will be blessed by the Lord. They are **trusting in the Lord** (cf. v. 1; 9:10; 31:14) and **will not fear evil tidings** (cf. v. 5; 56:3-4) because they have confidence in the Lord's good protection and plan. Therefore they **will not fear** bad news or uncertainty concerning the present or the future (cf. v. 4 and comments there; 25:10; Pr 3:5-6). The Lord will take care of all circumstances and bring justice on their **adversaries.** The righteous person will have an excellent reputation—**his horn will be exalted in honor** (Ps 112:9; cf. 89:17).

C. The Contrast with Fearing the Lord (112:10)

112:10. The psalm concludes with a contrast between the man who fears the Lord (vv. 1-9) and the **wicked**, a contrast introduced in Ps 1. When the **wicked . . . see it**, God's blessing on the righteous, they will be **vexed** (lit., "become angry") and **gnash** their **teeth** (cf. 35:16; 37:12). Yet their anger will **melt away**, have no effect, and the **desire of the wicked will perish** (cf. 1:4-6; 9:3; 37:20; 68:2).

Psalms 113–118: The Hallel Psalms

In very early Jewish tradition these six psalms are known collectively as *Hallel* psalms ("The Praise"), because of the Hallelujah! ("Praise the Lord") endings (113:9; 115: 18; 116:19; 117:2). This *Hallel* reading tradition was already established by the NT period as a fixed part of the Passover, Pentecost and Tabernacles celebrations (Lv 23; Nm 10:10). These were probably the hymns Messiah Jesus and His disciples sang after their Passover seder (cf. Mt 26:30; Mk 14:26). (Psalms 113–114 were sung before the Passover meal and Pss 115–118 after it.)

The author of these psalms is unknown, but thematically they form a unit of thought in Book Five of Psalms. They share common themes of the exodus/Passover events; the Lord's covenants with Israel; and they emphasize the obligation and desire to offer God praise and thanksgiving for His lovingkindness and sovereignty. Those twin attributes of God are demonstrated by His protection and restoration of Israel to their Land (Pss 113–15), His provision of all their most intimate needs (Ps 116), and in recalling the provision of the Abrahamic covenant of blessing through Israel to all other nations of the world (Pss 117–118; Gn 12:1-3).

A. Psalm 113: Praise the Lord for His Sovereign Concern for Mankind

113:1-4. The words **Praise the Lord** in the opening of this psalm serves as an introduction both to the *Hallel* Psalms generally (see Pss 113–118: The Hallel Psalms above), as well as to this first section emphasizing praising the Lord for His sovereign concern. The obligation to praise God is emphasized in the opening verse by the threefold repetition (signifying the superlative) of the exhortation **Praise**/*hallelu* (**Praise** you!). The extent of this exhortation is **from this time . . . and forever**, then specified as **from the rising of the sun to its setting** (vv. 2-3). To **praise the name of the Lord** is synonymous to praising everything about the Lord (cf. comments on 7:17; 18:49; 5:11; 20:5; 23:3; 31:3). The focus is on God's absolute sovereignty over all things: **above all nations . . . above the heavens** (v. 4).

113:5-9. The Lord is **enthroned on high** (cf. Ex 15:11; Pss 11:4; 103:13), yet He **humbles Himself to behold**, to take note of and show concern for people's need (cf. comment on Gn 16:13-14). Raising the **poor from the dust . . . needy from the ash heap** means from the most destitute circumstances (cf. 1Sm 2:8; 1Kg 16:2; Jb 30:19; Is 47:1; Jr 25:34). God chooses to **make them sit with princes of His people** (vv. 7-8). Even more remarkable and wonderful is God's kindness that makes **the barren woman . . . a joyful mother of children** (v. 9). Barrenness in biblical culture was regarded as a great tragedy a woman could suffer (cf. Gn 21:2; 25:21; 30:1, 23; 1Sm 1:6-7, 10), surpassed only by the destitute condition of a childless widow who would have no one to care for her in her old age (cf. Ru 1:11-13; 2Kg 4:14). With these examples of God's character and care, the psalm ends: **Praise the Lord!** (Hallelujah!).

B. Psalm 114: Praise the Lord for His Deliverance of His People at the Exodus

For introduction to this psalm see Pss 113–118: The Hallel Psalms.

114:1-2. This psalm focuses on the specific expression of God's concern for **the house of Jacob,**

a frequent synonym for Israel and the Jewish people in the Psalms (e.g., 14:7; 22:23; 46:11; 114:1). It highlights Israel's history, beginning with when God redeemed them from **Egypt** to lead them to the land of Canaan. The Psalm continues with a reference to the divided kingdom (1Kg 12) consisting of **Judah**, which comprises the two southern tribes of the southern kingdom, where **His**/God's **sanctuary**/temple in Jerusalem was located and the Davidic kings ruled; and **Israel**, the ten northern tribes, **His dominion**, under God's rule during the divided kingdom.

114:3-8. The remainder of the psalm returns to the exodus events. It presents poetic imagery of how God exercised His sovereign power in Israel's redemption from Egypt: **the sea looked and fled**, referring to the dividing of the Red Sea (v. 3; Ex 14:21; cf. Ps 77:16); **the Jordan turned back**, referring to crossing through the Jordan on dry land to enter the promised land under Joshua (vv. 3, 5; Jos 3:13, 16); the **mountains... skip** refers to the quaking of Mount Sinai when the Lord gave Moses the Commandments (v. 6; Ex 19:18; Jdg 5:5; Ps 29:8; Is 64:1); God providing **water** in the desert to nourish and sustain the people (v. 8; Ex 17:6; Nm 20:11; cf. Dt 8:15).

C. Psalm 115: Praise the Lord for His Sovereignty over Israel and the Nations

For introduction to this psalm see above: Psalms 113–118: The Hallel Psalms.

115:1. Because of all the Lord has done (as presented in Ps 113 to needy individuals and in Ps 114 in delivering Israel from Egypt), the **glory** (the thanksgiving, praise, and adulation) for these benefits belongs **not to us**, but to God's **name** (cf. 113:1-2; see comment on 20:5). All these benefits are ultimately an expression of God's **lovingkindness** (cf. 5:7 and comments there) and **truth** (cf. 92:2).

115:2-3. The pagan **nations** may mock Israel for having a God who cannot be seen by saying **Where now, is their God?** (cf. 2; 79:10), but they fail to realize **our God is in the heavens** the position of complete sovereignty (cf. 113:3-4). The Lord is all powerful, **He does whatever He pleases.**

115:4-8. The Lord should not be mistaken as having the qualities of **idols**, which are made of **silver and gold** by **man's hands.** Idols are powerless, and they **cannot speak... hear... smell... feel... walk... make a sound** (vv. 5-7). Anyone who **trusts in them... will become like them** (v. 8), useless and dead.

115:9-14. Instead of trusting in lifeless idols and becoming like them, the people must **trust in the LORD** as **their help and their shield** (vv. 9, 10, 11; cf. comments on 33:20). The psalmist then moves from addressing the nation as a whole (**Israel** vv. 9, 12) to his exhortations and reminders that God **will bless** (vv. 12, 13, 15) **the house of Aaron** (vv. 10, 12) since the priests were responsible for teaching the rest of the nation (cf. Dt 33:10). People **who fear the LORD** (v. 11; parallel to the **small** and **great**, v. 13) are called upon to **trust in the LORD** (cf. comments 111:10).

115:15. Rather than being the work of man's hands (v. 4), the **LORD** is the **Maker of heaven and earth** and He is the source of all blessings.

115:16-18. The psalm concludes with a doxology to the Lord as creator and sustainer of life. The **dead do not praise the LORD** (v. 17) is not a denial of the afterlife, which is clearly taught in Scripture. Rather in the framework of the psalm it means the dead are no longer active on the **earth**, and so cannot praise Him here, but **go down into silence**. In contrast, **But as for us,** as long as we are alive, **we will bless the LORD from this time forth and forever. Praise the LORD!** (Hallelujah!).

D. Psalm 116: Praise the Lord the Sustainer of Life

For introduction to this psalm see above: Psalms 113–118: The Hallel Psalms.

116:1-4. The declaration **I love the LORD, because He hears my voice** sounds somewhat self-serving but it actually is appropriate. People can only love the Lord in response to His initiating a relationship ("Not that we loved God, but that He loved us," 1Jn 4:10). His love towards people is not based on anything within humanity, but is derived from His own sovereign will and choice. That love causes Him to listen to His children, prompting their responsive love. God **inclined His ear**, and the psalmist is determined to **call upon Him as long as** he would **live** (v. 2). Facing some deadly circumstance (v. 3), the psalmist **beseech[ed]** God to **save** his **life** (v. 4).

116:5-11. The Lord answered the call for help in v. 4, and the psalmist praised God as **gracious ... righteous... and compassionate**. Identifying Him as **our God** suggests the psalm is to be read in the congregation (cf. vv. 14, 18). Because of his situation the psalmist had been **brought low**, but God **saved** him (v. 6; cf. v. 4) from a list of problems (vv. 7-11).

116:12-14. In acknowledging all the Lord had done for him, the psalmist realizes, **What shall I render to the Lord for all His benefits toward me?** In response he will worship the Lord by (1) **lift[ing] up the cup of salvation**, related to the thank offering and/or the Passover meal (cf. vv. 17-18; 22:26, 29; Ex 29:40-41; Nm 15:5, 7; Lv 7:11-21; Mt 26:26-29; 1Co 10:16); (2) **call[ing] upon the name of the Lord**, in praise and thanksgiving (cf. 9:2; 18:49; 44:8; 56:12-13); (3) **pay[ing]** ("fulfill") **my vows to the Lord**, that is, keeping all commitments to obedience and offer all the proper sacrifices (cf. 7:17; 50:14; 66:13-15; 116:18); and (4) worshiping **in the presence of all His people**, where others would be encouraged (cf. 22:25).

116:15. The word **precious** implies "value" and therefore "worth protection." This comforting verse **Precious in the sight of the Lord is the death of His godly ones** indicates the Lord's love and care for those who have put their trust in Him, to preserve their life on earth for His service and to welcome them into His presence after death. The term **godly ones** is often misunderstood to be those who have been recognized for having an exceptional degree of holiness, sanctity, and virtue; the biblical designation means people who have been sanctified (set apart, declared righteous) by the grace of God through their faith in Him.

116:16-19. The psalm concludes with a commitment to service, **surely I am Your servant**, a person devoted to you (cf. 19:11, 13; 86:4), with vv. 17-18 being a summary restatement of vv. 2-14. Praise will be offered **in the courts of the Lord's house, In the midst of you, O Jerusalem** (v. 19), thus indicating this psalm was intended to be read in the temple at the festivals (cf. Pss 113–118: The Hallel Psalms). **Praise the Lord!**

E. Psalm 117: Praise the Lord All Nations

For introduction to this psalm see above, Psalms 113-118: The Hallel Psalms.

117:1-2. This shortest of all the psalms calls for **all nations** (Gentiles) to **praise the Lord**. The Gentiles' praise of God is the result of God's **lovingkindness**, which **is great toward us**, the people of Israel. The psalm is cited in the NT as evidence of Jewish and Gentile followers of Messiah Jesus worshiping together (cf. Rm 15:11, see comments there). One aspect of the Abrahamic covenant (Gn 12:1-3) was God's promise that in Abraham "all the families of the earth will be blessed" (Gn 12:3). This blessing to the Gentiles was fulfilled in the coming of the Redeemer, Jesus the Messiah, the "son of David, the son of Abraham" (Mt 1:1). The phrase **is great toward us** is literally "has prevailed over us" (cf. 5:7; 103:11). All nations are called on to worship the God of Jacob, and bend the knee to Messiah Jesus, the Son of David (cf. Is 45:23; Rm 14:11; Php 2:10; Is 56:7) to acknowledge the extent of the Lord's lovingkindness.

117:2. These short verses encapsulate the great truth that the destiny of all nations is linked to God's faithfulness and work among His people Israel, culminating in the reign of King Messiah Jesus on earth (cf. 2:8-12; 47:9; 67:2; 72:17; 102:15; 110; Dt 32:43; 1Kg 8:41-43; Is 2:2-4; 11:10; 14:2; 25:6-7; 52:15; 56:7; 60:3; 66:18-24; Jr 3:17; 33:9: Am 9:11-12; Zph 3:8-9; Zch 2:10-11; 8:20-23; 9:9-10; 14:2-3, 9; Mal 3:12; Rv 5:9; 7:9).

F. Psalm 118: Praise the Lord for His Lovingkindness is Everlasting

For general introduction to this psalm see above: Psalms 113–118: The Hallel Psalms. Psalm 118 closes the Hallel psalms and was possibly written to celebrate the Feast of Booths or the dedication of the rebuilding of the temple when the Jewish people returned to Israel from the Babylonian exile (cf. Ezr 3:3, 6:16-21).

Psalm 118 is cited 11 times in the NT (v. 6 in Rm 8:31 and Heb 13:6; v. 15 in Lk 1:51; v. 17 in 2Co 6:9; v. 19 in Ac 22:14; v. 20 in Jn 10:9; v. 22 in Mt 21:42; Mk 8:31; 12:10; Lk 20:17; Ac 4:11; 1Pt 2:4, 7; v. 24 in Ac 19:7; v. 25 in Mt 21:9; Mk 11:9; Jn 12:13, and v. 26 in Mt 23:39; Lk 13:35; 19:38). It is cited more than any other single psalm (though see introduction to Ps 110), with reference both to general theological principles as well as to the Messiah in particular.

1. A Call to Thanksgiving (118:1-4)

118:1-4. This psalm begins and ends (vv. 1, 29) with a call to **Give thanks** to God for two reasons: His goodness and **His** eternal **lovingkindness** (*chesed*, loyal love, cf. 5:7). The call is directed to **Israel** (v. 2), to the priesthood (v. 3), and finally to all **who fear the Lord** (v. 4), including Israel and even those who know Him among the nations.

2. An Explanation of Deliverance (118:5-21)

118:5-9. In explaining his call to praise, the psalmist declares that God has delivered him from **distress**. The Lord's **help** (v. 7) has taught him the lesson that trusting in God's help is better than trusting in man's help; God's help is even better than the aid of powerful people, even that of **princes** (v. 9).

118:10-14. Next the psalmist specifies from what distress the Lord saved him. Although surrounded, he was able to defeat his enemies. Three times he declares that he **cut them off**. This verb is typically translated "circumcised" in all places but here and 58:7 and 90:6. It is not a literal circumcision in view here but a poetic image of his enemies being cut off and cast aside. He could only accomplish this victory because he acted **in the name of the LORD**. Then, with a direct address to his enemies, he tells them, **You pushed me violently** but the **LORD helped** him (v. 13). This made God his **strength** (his source of strength in battle), his **song** (his reason for singing and the one of whom he sings), and his **salvation** (his deliverer in battle).

118:15-21. The psalmist offers a threefold tribute to God's **right hand** (the right hand represents God's power; cf. 20:6). Thus, his life was saved by God's power. Whatever difficult circumstances he was in, he recognizes that it was a result of God's discipline (v. 18). Nevertheless, the Lord led him through **the gates of righteousness** (v. 19), likely a reference to God's deliverance and his expectation to return to worship in the temple. God is indeed his **salvation** (v. 21).

3. The Identity of the Deliverer (118:22-29)

118:22-27. Next the psalmist will identify through whom the Lord grants deliverance. It is **the stone which the builders rejected** who also will **become the . . . corner stone** (v. 22). This indicates that the Lord has a Deliverer who will be rejected by the leaders of Israel (a likely reason not to trust in princes, cf. v. 9) but will be the one individual through whom the whole house of Israel will one day be established. He is the **blessed . . . one who comes in the name of the LORD** (v. 26). When Israel beseeches this One to **save** them and recognizes that He comes in the name of the Lord, the nation will be delivered (vv. 25-26).

Sailhamer states, "Though the psalm itself does not identify who this One is, the larger context within the Psalms makes it clear that he is the Promised Seed of the house of David, the Messiah. It is for this reason, this psalm is frequently alluded to in the NT" (Sailhamer, *NIV Compact Commentary*, 342). Moreover, the Lord Jesus also reminded Israel that He would not return to deliver them until the nation's leadership reversed their rejection of Him and instead recognized Him, saying "Blessed is He who comes in the name of the Lord" (Mt 23:37-39, cf. comments there).

118:28-29. The psalm concludes where it began, with thanksgiving. The psalmist will express his own thanksgiving, saying **you are my God, and I give thanks to you** (v. 28). Then he calls all others to **give thanks to the Lord, for He is good** (v. 29), the very words with which he began this song of thanksgiving.

Psalm 119: A Psalm of Praise to the Word of God

This longest of the psalms is an acrostic organized in the order of the Hebrew alphabet. It has twenty-two sections of eight verses, each verse of each section beginning with a letter of the Hebrew alphabet in sequence (hence 22 letters x 8 verses = 176 total verses). That is, each line of vv. 1-8 begins with a word that starts with the first letter of the Hebrew alphabet (see **Aleph** in the NASB), each line of vv. 9-16 begins with a word that starts with the second letter of the Hebrew alphabet (see **Beth** in the NASB), and so on throughout the alphabet.

While the Psalter overall praises the Lord for His powerful acts as Creator and Redeemer and Sustainer, Ps 119 extols the Lord in relation to His Word and the Word as a guide to life. It is a celebration of God's gift of the Scriptures and uses ten synonyms for God's Word: "law" (*torah*/25 times), "testimonies" (*'edot*/22 times), "ways" (*derakhim*/5 times), "precepts" (*piqqudim*/21times), "statutes" (*chuqqim*/ 21 times), "commandments" (*misvot*/21 times), "judgment[s] (which are judicial edicts, not acts of judgment); *mishpat* /19 times), "word(s)" (*debar* / 25 times), "sayings" (*imrah*"/19 times), and "path" (*'orah*/5 times). The frequently used word "law" (*torah*) should be understood to mean all of the Hebrew Scriptures, not just the Five Books of Moses/Pentateuch (cf. Jn 10:34).

The psalmist refers to himself as God's servant (Ps 119:17, 23, 38, 49, 65, 76, 84, 124-25, 135, 140, 176). He gives several responses to the Scriptures: obey/keep/observe His Word (vv. 4, 5, 8, 17, 34, 44, 56-57, 60, 67, 88, 100-101, 129, 134, 145, 158, 167-68); meditate on His Word (vv. 15, 23, 27, 48, 78, 97, 99, 148); rejoice in the Scriptures (vv. 14, 162); delight in God's Word (vv. 16, 24, 35, 47, 70, 77, 92, 143, 174); love God's Word (vv. 47-48, 97, 113, 119, 127, 159, 163, 165, 167). He frequently asked the Lord to revive him as he obeyed the Word or by the Word (vv. 25, 40, 88, 107, 149, 154, 156, 159).

There are, as Sailhamer observes, three psalms that focus directly on the Scriptures as the means of living a righteous life before God: Pss 1, 19, and 119. Each of these is followed by a unit of psalms that focuses on the coming Messiah: Ps 1 by the messianic concepts in Ps 2; Ps 19 with the messianic ideas of 20–24; Ps 119 by the messianic emphasis of the Psalms of Ascents (120–134). The compiler of the book of Psalms was intentionally ordering the psalms to show that if readers search the Scriptures, they will find the Messiah. This strategy is further employed by the "lost sheep" in the final verse (119:176), which lead into the opening of the Psalms of Ascents with their focus on the Lord's faithfulness to David and the fulfillment of the messianic promise (Sailhamer, *NIV Compact Commentary*, 342–343).

A. *Aleph:* The Blessing of Walking in God's Word (119:1-8)

119:1-8. This introductory section begins by summarizing and emphasizing the blessings of those **who walk** (cf. 1:1) **in the law of the LORD.** There are deliberate similarities to the positive aspects of Ps 1 for those who **seek** the Lord with **their** whole **heart** and **walk in His ways.**

B. *Beth*: God's Word Provides Protection Against Sin (119:9-16)

119:9-16. These verses focus on what may be called the preparatory benefits of God's Word. It is essential for **a young man** to **keep his way pure** and resist temptation before theological doubt is encountered rather than during it or after it. For this reason the psalmist opened this section with an explicit reference to **a young man**, beginning in youth and establishing a pattern throughout life to walk with God. This way entails both treasuring (zealously guarding; cf. Jos 2:4; Ps 27:5; Pr 10:14) God's **word . . . in** one's **heart** (v. 11) as well as meditating **on** it (v. 15, internalizing, memorizing it, pondering it over time, and considering how it applies to one's situation). This should form a lifelong habit of hiding God's word in his **heart** so as to **not sin against** the Lord (v. 11).

C. *Gimel*: God's Word as a Source of Comfort (119:17-24)

119:17-24. The psalmist requested God's blessing (**deal bountifully with Your servant**). He knew that the source of that comfort was for God to **Open** his **eyes that** he might **behold wonderful things from** God's **law** (v. 18). No matter how difficult his circumstances, he was determined to **observe** God's **testimonies** and make them his **delight** and have them function as his **counselors** (vv. 22, 24).

D. *Daleth*: God's Word as a Source of Strength (119:25-32)

119:25-32. The psalmist poured out his sad heart, telling his **ways** to the Lord. He asked God: **Make me understand the way of your precepts** to enable him to **meditate on Your wonders** (v. 27). Although he was in deep **grief**, he asked for the Lord to **strengthen** him **according to** (by the power of) His **word** (v. 28). Confronted by temptation, he implored God to **remove** that **false way** (the way of sin by which he was tempted) **from** before him (v. 29).

E. *He*: God's Word Deserves Respect (119:33-40)

119:33-40. The requests of this stanza are essential to a meaningful life: **Teach me, O Lord, the way . . . Make me walk in the path of Your commandments** (vv. 33, 35). In order to respect God's word, the dangers of **dishonest gain** and **vanity** (anything that is worthless, either materially or morally) must be avoided or eliminated. **Establish Your word to Your servant . . . which produces reverence for You** (v. 38). Much in life is worthless, but God's **ordinances are good** (v. 39).

F. *Vav*: God's Word is the Source of Reply to the Wicked (119:41-48)

119:41-48. Experiencing God's **lovingkindness** (cf. vv. 64, 76, 88, 124, 149, 159; see comments at 5:7; 6:4) will allow the righteous person to **have an answer for** one **who reproaches** him. Instead of being overcome or confused by the skeptic or the wicked person, the righteous will **trust in** God's **word . . .** and **not be ashamed** (vv. 42, 46) because they **love** and **meditate on** God's **statutes** (see introduction to Ps 119).

G. *Zayin*: God's Word is the Source of Hope (119:49-56)

119:49-56. This stanza continues the issue of need for **comfort in . . . affliction** (cf. vv. 19-23, 42). The source of comfort is God's word through which God gives **hope.** The psalmist **remembered** God's **ordinances from of old . . .** and recalled God's **name** (referring to His character and reputation; cf. comments on 23:3) **in the night** (cf. 42:8; 92:2).

H. *Heth*: God's Word is Sufficient (119:57-64)

119:57-64. Here **the LORD** is acknowledged as the psalmist's **portion** (cf. 16:5; 73:26). **Portion** refers to the allotment of land given to each tribe of Israel (Nm 18:20), meaning He is all that one needs in life. The righteous do not simply obey the Lord by habit or out of duty, but **hasten . . . to keep Your commandments** (v. 60). Although surrounded by the **wicked**, the godly person will be **a companion of all those who fear You** . . . and **keep Your precepts** (v. 63; cf. 111:10; 52:9; Pr 13:20; Heb 10:25). The stanza reaffirms God's sufficiency: **The earth is full of Your lovingkindness, O LORD; Teach me Your statutes.**

I. *Teth*: God's Word is Good (119:65-72)

119:65-72. The Lord's character and His Word are inseparably linked. The psalmist realized that God had **dealt well with Your servant** even though he had been **afflicted** by the judgments of God because he had gone **astray** (vv. 65, 67). Through that experience he came to understand as never before that God is **good and** He does **good** (v. 68; cf. 16:2; 25:8; 73:28; 86:5; 100:5; 106:1; 118:1, 29; 135:3; 145:9). As a result, he learned that **the law of Your mouth is better to me than thousands of gold and silver pieces** (v. 72; cf. 37:16; Pr 15:16).

J. *Yodh*: God's Word Gives a Clear Testimony (119:73-80)

119:73-80. This section begins by acknowledging God as the source of life, **Your hands made me and fashioned me** (cf. 100:3; 138:8: 139:15-16) and He wants people to **learn** His **commandments**. The result of a godly life is a clear testimony: so that **those who . . . see** the life of the righteous will **be glad** if they also know the Lord; or **ashamed** for trying to **subvert** the righteous **with a lie** if they do not know God (vv. 74, 78). No matter what the response of others, he is determined to **be blameless** (have integrity) **in Your statutes**, so he will never be **ashamed** of his behavior (v. 80).

K. *Kaph*: God's Word is Faithful (119:81-88)

119:81-88. The psalmist confessed that his **soul languishe[d]** as he waited for God to **comfort** him. After describing himself feeling like **wineskin in the smoke**, dried up and useless and calling for **judgment on those who persecute** him, he concludes with faith: **All Your commandments are faithful**, they are true and unchanging.

L. *Lamedh*: God's Word is Settled in Heaven (119:89-96)

119:89-96. Although external circumstances may change and affliction may come, **Forever, O LORD, Your word is settled** (lit., "stands firm/unchanging") **in heaven** (the poetic description of everything in God's realm). There is no end of His **faithfulness.**

M. *Mem*: God's Word is Sweet (119:97-104)

119:97-104. The open declaration: **O how I love Your law!** (see introductory comments to Ps 119) is the outcome of meditating on the **testimonies**/Scriptures **all the day**. Knowing the Word of God has several results: it gives **more insight than all my teachers**; more understanding **than the aged**; **restrained my feet from . . . evil** (vv. 99-101). Loving God's Word should be the attitude of the righteous because the Lord Himself instructs His followers (**You Yourself have taught me**) through His Word and His **words** are **sweet . . . sweeter than honey** (vv. 102-103; cf. 19).

N. *Nun*: God's Word Gives Guidance (119:105-112)

119:105-112. God's **word is a lamp to my feet and a light to my path** means the Scriptures give us direction and guidance in all circumstances of life. The section continues with a brief account of the psalmist being **exceedingly afflicted**; nonetheless, God's Word is **the joy of [his] heart** and the psalmist is determined to **perform [His] statues forever** (vv. 111-112).

O. *Samekh*: God's Word Is a Refuge (119:113-120)

119:113-120. The psalmist has made the Lord his **hiding place and . . . shield** (v. 114; cf. 33:3; 7:10; 31:20). Instead of being like the **double-minded** or **evildoers**, the righteous will **observe the commandments**. The statement **You have removed all the wicked of the earth like dross** (v. 119) refers to God's future final judgment of the wicked; this event is so certain it is presented as accomplished fact (cf. Is 1:24-25; Jr 9:7; Zch 13:9; Mal 3:2-3). One of the reasons the righteous will **wait** (confidently hope for the fulfillment) of God's Word is because of an understanding of the fear (awesome nature) of God who is a refuge against the wicked and a judge of the wicked: **My flesh trembles for fear of You, and I am afraid of Your judgments** (v. 120).

P. *Ayin*: A Prayer for Vindication (119:121-128)

119:121-128. The psalmist declares he has **done justice and righteousness** yet was **oppress[ed]** by the **arrogant** (a term often used of those who mock God and behave as a law unto themselves, cf. 10:2-11). Therefore he says: **It is time for the LORD to act, For they have broken Your law** (v. 126). This is a prayer that God would intervene with judgment to vindicate His word.

Q. *Pe*: God's Word is Wonderful (119:129-136)

119:129-36. The Hebrew word for *wonderful* usually used of God's character or His redeeming acts (cf. Ex 15:11; Is 9:6; 25:1; Pss 9:1; 77:11, 14; 78:12; 89:5). Here God's **testimonies are wonderful** demonstrating the link between God's character and His Word (vv. 18, 27). The **unfolding** (the revelation and interpretation of the Scriptures) **of Your words gives light**, direction for life (cf. v. 10). The request to **Make your face shine upon Your servant** (v. 135) is allusion to the Aaronic benediction (cf. Nm 6:22-26; cf. 13:1).

R. *Tsadhe*: God's Word is Righteous (119:137-144)

119:137-144. This stanza describes the **Lord** as **righteous** and His **righteousness is an everlasting righteousness.** At the same time, His **testimonies** are **righteous forever**. God's character, His very essence, is linked to His word. In order to know the Lord, those who love the Lord are those who love the Scriptures.

S. *Qoph*: God's Word is Truth (119:145-152)

119:145-152. The **commandments** of the Lord are **truth** (v. 151, cf. v. 160). The psalmist had a custom of crying to the Lord, praying and meditating **before dawn** . . . and during the **night** (vv. 147-148). As the psalmist felt the wicked **draw near**, he could be confident of the Lord's care because he had knowledge of God's **testimonies**, which were **forever**, established in the unchanging moral righteousness of the Lord (v. 152; cf. 119:89, 144, 152, 160).

T. *Resh*: A Call for Deliverance (153-160)

119:153-160. Here is another request for **rescue** from **persecutors and . . . adversaries**, a theme that increases as the psalm concludes. The content of this stanza is similar to vv. 145-152, with an emphasis on **Great are Your mercies, O Lord.**

U. *Shin*: God's Word is a Source of Peace (119:161-168)

119:161-168. This stanza is similar to vv. 145-152 and vv. 153-160; see comments there. Although persecuted, the psalmist **stands in awe of** God's **words** (cf. 22:23; 65:8). No matter what the circumstances, the righteous should **rejoice at Your word** (v. 162). Furthermore, **Those who love Your law have great peace** (v. 165; cf. 23; 29:11; 46:1-7).

V. *Tav*: God's Word Provides Help (119:169-176)

119:169-176. The final stanza is a conclusion to the whole psalm. It affirms the need for **understanding** of God's **word** and asks the Lord to **teach me Your statutes**, so that the psalmist can **sing of Your word**. The psalm ends with a request for God to **deliver** according to Your word . . . and **help** from Your ordinances because **I have gone astray like a lost sheep** (cf. Ps 23; Is 53:6). This is an acknowledgement that despite the psalmist determination to live according to God's righteous word, he failed and needed the Good Shepherd to **seek** for him.

Psalm 120–134: The Psalms of Ascents

Psalms 120–134 form a collection of 15 psalms identified in their headings as the Songs of Ascents. Regarding songs, see comments at Ps 46. Four are attributed to David (122, 124, 131, 133) and one to Solomon (127); the others are anonymous. They are a carefully selected group of psalms arranged here in the text around the theme of the Lord's messianic promise to David (cf. 2Sm 7:11-17). The central psalm of the unit is Ps 132, which recounts the Davidic Covenant.

The meaning of the "Ascents" has several possible implications. It could refer to: (1) ascending the steps leading up to the altar in the temple, so these psalms would have been sung by the Levitical priests offering sacrifices; (2) worshipers going up (ascending) to Jerusalem during one of the annual pilgrimage festivals (cf. Passover, the Feast of Weeks, and the Feast Tabernacles; see Dt 16:5-17; Lv 23; Ps 122:1), when these psalms would have been sung as part of these appointed feasts; or (3) the Jewish people coming up out of the Babylonian exile and back to the land of Israel, sung en route in hope of return and again in celebration after return (126:1).

Within the context of the Psalms these options are not contradictory, as this collection of psalms was organized as a unit in the final postexilic arrangement of the Psalter. Throughout the OT, the return from the Babylonian exile is seen as a precursor of the time of Messiah (cf. Is 40), so reading the Psalms of Ascents in this matter is an expression of the hope of God's faithfulness to fulfill the Davidic Covenant with the reign of King Messiah, Son of David.

A. Psalm 120: A Prayer for Deliverance and Peace

1. Trusting the Lord for Deliverance (120:1-4)

120:1-4. The opening cry (**In my trouble**) to the Lord is a link to the statement of wandering away from the Lord at conclusion of Ps 119. This first psalm of ascents opens with the assurance that the Lord **answered me** and had already delivered him from his adversaries. His enemies were **lying** using their **deceitful tongue** (i.e., slander and false accusation) against him. Since this is likely a postexilic psalm, the reference to verbal opposition may be a reference to the actions of Sanballat and Tobiah against Nehemiah's rebuilding of the walls of Jerusalem at the return from exile (cf. Neh 4; 6). The phrase **What more shall be done to you** is common oath formula (e.g., 1Sm 3:17; 14:44; 2Sm 3:9; Ru 1:17), here indicating the certainty of God's judgment on the enemy. The tongue is described as dangerous as arrows (cf. 64:7; Pr 25:18; Jr 9:8), so the judgment of God will likewise be **sharp** as **arrows of the warrior** and as consuming as **burning coals of the broom tree**, a large desert shrub that would quickly burn.

2. Desiring Peace in Conflict (120:5-7)

120:5-7. The psalmist expression of lament, **Woe is me** is because **I sojourn** (live temporarily as an alien) **in Meshech**, an area in Asia Minor (cf. Gn 10:2) and **Kedar**, in Arabia (cf. Gn 25:13; Is 21:16). These areas are emblematic of the barbaric foes of Israel, so the psalmist uses their names to express his sorrow at dwelling . . . **too long . . . with those who hate peace**. This may be a reference to being back in the land of Israel under constant attack while trying to rebuild Jerusalem (cf. vv. 1-4), or if written in exile, a statement of condition living in Babylon. The psalmist concludes **I am for peace** (cf. 29:11) . . . but **they are for war**. The pagans among whom the psalmist was dwelling did not know the God of **peace**, and did not understand the Lord's plan for His people, so they were **for war** (cf. Jr 27:9, 11).

B. Psalm 121: Affirming the Lord is the Keeper of Israel

See introductory remarks to the Psalms of Ascents. Psalm 121 continues the theme of Ps 120 related to the psalmist's hope and trust in God. Despite his difficult circumstances, the psalmist remains confident in God's salvation (Sailhamer, *NIV Compact Bible Commentary*, 343).

1. The Lord Is the Source of Israel's Security (121:1-2)

121:1-2. As the psalmist said **I will lift up my eyes to the mountains** and asked **From where shall my help come from**, he knew his help was **from the Lord**. By looking to the mountains surrounding Jerusalem (as in 125:2), and in particular Mount Moriah, the site of the temple (2Ch 3:1) and the focal point of God's abiding and manifest presence on earth (i.e., the cloud of glory, cf. Ex 40:34-38), he made God the focus of his help. The returning exiles will see this mountain and know their **help comes from the Lord, Who made heaven and earth**.

The Lord's power to help is often illustrated by His power as Creator; if He could create the earth, He also has the power to defend His people (cf. 33:6; 89:11-13; 96:4-5; 104:2-9; 124:8; 134:3; 136:1-9). Hence, David, like Daniel (Dn 6:10), directed his gaze, whether literally or emotionally, toward Jerusalem (1Kg 8:27-30), though at the same time recognizing that God is not restricted to one place, for He is the One **who made heaven and earth** and as such He transcends it (cf. 57:4-5; 83:18; 93:3-4; 115:3). In addition, if God possesses the power to create the **mountains**, **heaven** (the sky and the cosmos) and **earth**, then He has the power to establish Israel in the Holy Land in spite of her enemies.

2. The Lord Guarantees Israel's Security (121:3-4)

121:3-4. Just as God **will not allow** the **foot** of the individual who trusts in Him **to slip** (or "be moved, shaken"; see the same word in Pss 17:5; 30:6; 62:6; 112:6; 125:1; see comment on 15:5b), neither will He allow Israel to ever be out of his sight. The Lord does **not slumber**, so He is always awake to **keep** watch over **Israel**. This is a military image of a guard vigilant and every watchful, never sleeping, on duty. **Keeps** (v. 3, the verb being repeated in vv. 4, 5, and 7) means "to exercise diligent, watchful, protective care over" or "to guard" someone or something. The repetition of the verb emphasizes God's awareness of His people and the threats they face, as well as His commitment to protect them in the end.

3. The Extent of Israel's Security (121:5-8)

121:5-8. The extent of God's guarding and protecting Israel is twofold. On the one hand, it is physical, as indicated by the poetic imagery of God being the individual Israelite's **shade on** his **right hand** (cf. 16:8; 73:23; 109:31) so that **the sun will not smite** him **by day** (cf. Is 49:10; Jnh 4:6-8) **nor the moon by night**, indicating God's care day and night. The affirmation that **the Lord will protect you from all evil** (v. 7) shows the Lord's total care. God's spiritual care is explicitly indicated by the statement **He will keep your soul** (v. 7; soul includes both one's material [body] and immaterial [soul] elements; cf. comments on 49:15).

Both aspects of God's "keeping" (i.e., His overall concern) are summed up in the concluding verse. **Going out and . . . coming in** speaks of daily life (cf. Dt 28:6; 1Sm 29:6), and the living of life from **this time forth and forever** (in God's "keeping"), indicates God care throughout life and even into eternity for the redeemed.

C. Psalm 122: A Hymn of Peace for Jerusalem

See introductory remarks to the Psalms of Ascents (in the section prior to Ps 120). The psalmist longed for God to deliver his people in Ps 121. That salvation includes the restoration of Jerusalem and reconstituting the dynasty of David, ultimately fulfilled through His promised Son (122:5). To pray for the peace of Jerusalem is to pray for the coming of the Son of David, the Messiah Prince of Peace who will bring peace. He will secure Israel and enable the nation to experience perpetual peace and prosperity (see the promises of the Davidic covenant in 2Sm 7:10-16; 1Ch 17:9-14) (Sailhamer, *NIV Compact Bible Commentary*, 343).

1. Peace for the Purpose of Worship (122:1-4)

122:1-3. The opening **I was glad when they said to me, Let us go to the house** [i.e., temple] **of the Lord** expresses David's joy at worshiping the Lord in His temple (cf. 84:10; 95), whether starting in Jerusalem or outside it. The reference to **the house of the Lord** provides the structural frame of the psalm (vv. 1, 9). This hymn of peace for Jerusalem expresses David's joy over the city and his longing for her welfare, a frequent theme in the Psalms (cf. 42–43; 46; 48; 84; 87; 137).

122:4-5. The . . . **tribes of the Lord** are the twelve tribes of Israel (cf. Gn 49:1-28); to keep the **ordinance for Israel** refers to obeying God's command to Jerusalem to celebrate His appointed feasts (Dt 16:1-17; Lv 23; (see introductory remarks to the Psalms of Ascents in the section prior to Ps 120).

2. Peace by the Rule of His Son (122:5)

122:5. The **thrones set** up **for judgment . . . the thrones of the house of David** refers to Jerusalem, the city of the Lord and the royal capital of Israel, from which the Davidic kings governed the land and from which the messianic King will rule in the future (2:2, 6-7; 89:3-4, 18-37; 110; 2Sm 7:8-16; Ezk 43:7). Ultimately that perfect, righteous judgment will be discharged during the eternal rule of the messianic King, the Lord Jesus during the messianic, millennial kingdom (see Jr 23:6; Is 9:7; 11:4; 16:5; Ac 10:42; 2Tm 4:1).

3. Peace through the Prayers of His People (122:6-9)

122:6-9. The exhortation to **pray for the peace of Jerusalem** (v. 6a) includes not simply the city itself, but the Jewish people, the tribes of Israel that regularly go up to it (v. 4) as the political and religious capital of the land given to them as an eternal inheritance by God (cf. Gn 13:15; 17:8; Ps 105:10-11; Rm 11:29). The link between Jerusalem and the Jewish people is so close that the former is often employed as a personified substitute (metonymy) for her Jewish residents or the Jewish people in general (cf. 48:11; 97:8; 126:1; Is 40:2; 51:16; 52:9; Jr 4:14). He calls for those **who love you** to pray, that is those who love Jerusalem because they are devoted to the Lord who also loves Jerusalem (cf. 87:2 and comments there) and its people. The prayer for peace is all inclusive **within your walls . . . within your palaces . . . for the sake of my brothers and my friends**. His emphasis on this central concept of **peace**, one that is permanent, complete, and inclusive, is indicated by its being mentioned three times in the psalm (vv. 6, 7, 8). The statement, **May they** [the Gentile nations and individuals] **prosper who love you** (v. 6) is linked to God's promise to Abraham: "I will bless those who bless you" (Gn 12:3).

122:9. David's prayer is ultimately motivated **for the sake of the house of the Lord**. This is similar to the idea of "for His name's sake (cf. 5:11; 23:3; 25:11; 31:3), that is, for the sake of the Lord Himself. It is the determination of the psalmist and of the admonition of the psalm to **seek your good**, the welfare and God's blessing on Jerusalem (cf. Neh 2:10; Ex 10:3).

D. Psalm 123: Looking to the Lord for Help

See introductory remarks to the Psalms of Ascents (in the section prior to Ps 120). In Ps 123, the writer expresses his intense attentiveness to God in anticipation of God's signal that He will act to save His people (v. 2). The salvation that is craved in Pss 121 and 122 here in Ps 123 is acknowledged as provided by God alone (Sailhamer, *NIV Compact Bible Commentary*, 343).

1. The Object of the Hope (123:1)

123:1. To You I lift up my eyes is similar to the opening of Ps 121, however here the Lord is described as **enthroned in the heavens** as Almighty King (cf. 2:4; 11:4 and comments there). Our hope is in the Lord.

2. The Manner of the Hope (123:2)

123:2. The psalmist compared the manner in which he and those like him looked to their divine King to the manner in which servants look **to the hand of their master**, and **a maid to the hand of her mistress**. In each statement **the hand** signifies the supply of all that is needed (cf. Php 4:19). Here it is the **Lord our God** who is a merciful sovereign to whom the needy should look to/depend upon **until He is gracious to us** (gracious is threefold for emphasis, vv. 2, 3). The word **gracious** ("mercy" ESV) means a heartfelt, merciful response to a need by someone who has the power or materials to meet that need; it is technically an undeserved positive treatment by a superior to one who is unworthy. Some thirty times in the Psalms the Lord is requested to be **gracious** (e.g., 6:2; 9:13; 27:3; 30:10).

3. The Motivation for Hope (123:3-4)

123:3-4. The psalmist realizes his hope is in the Lord, so he begs the **Lord, be gracious to us** (cf. comments on v. 2). He is suffering, by being **greatly filled with** (suffering under the) **contempt** of mockers (cf. 119:22) and the **scoffing of those who are at ease** (cf. 73:6-9; 94:2). Ultimately the vindication of God's justice, as manifest in His condemnation of the wicked and in rewarding His servants, will bring glory to him.

E. Psalm 124: A Song of Thanksgiving for God's Help

See introductory remarks to the Psalms of Ascents (in the section prior to Ps 120). The theme of God's deliverance of Israel is a focal point of this psalm as it was Ps 123. Just as God saved His people before the Egyptians could destroy them at the Red Sea (vv. 4-5), so God will save Israel in the future before she is destroyed (Sailhamer, *NIV Compact Bible Commentary*, 343).

1. Recalling God's Deliverance in the Past (124:1-5)

124:1-2. This psalm is to the community of Israel to encourage them to always trust God's faithfulness in preserving the Jewish people. They are to consider what might have happened if **the Lord** had **not been on** their **side** (v. 1, 2 repeated for emphasis). This is not unhealthy but a positive reminder: **Let Israel now say**, that is, recall what might have happened if it were not for the Lord's loving care **when** men (their enemies) **rose up against** them.

124:3-5. The illustration of the Lord's protection is the escape from the Egyptians at the Red Sea (cf. Ex 14). The phrase "when men rose up against us" (v. 2) is similar to the phrases in the Song of Moses after the escape from Pharaoh's army (cf. Ex 15:1-18). If the Lord had not been on Israel's side their enemy (the Egyptians at the exodus and other enemies throughout the ages, such as Assyria, cf. Is 8:6-8, or Babylon or modern enemies up to the present time) would have **swallowed us alive . . . the waters would have engulfed us . . . the stream would have swept over our soul . . . raging waters** (repeated for emphasis) **would have swept over our soul** (cf. Pss 18:16-18; 32:6; 69:1-2). In fact these more powerful enemies served as proof of God's past faithfulness to His unconditional promise to Israel through Abraham (Gn 12:2-3; Jr 31:35-37). This in turn was a historical precedent enabling Israel to expect the same continued faithfulness, especially preservation from destruction, both then and in the future.

2. Thanking God for His Deliverance Today (124:6-8)

124:6-7. David commenced his review of what God had done by declaring praise and thanksgiving. He said, **Blessed be the Lord** (cf. comment on 103:1), **who has not given** Israel **to be torn by** the enemy's **teeth**. Rather He enabled them to escape intact **as a bird out of the snare of the trapper**. David applied this bird imagery to himself in 1Sm 26:20, suggesting that he was here extrapolating his personal experience of God's faithfulness to that of the nation as a whole.

124:8. Reviewing what God had done reinforced David's confidence in what God will do. The psalm ends with a declaration of God's faithfulness: **Our help is in . . . the Lord** (cf. 22:19; 29:9; 40:17; 46:1; 121:2), **Who made heaven and earth** (cf. 121:2 and comments there; Gn 1:1).

F. Psalm 125: The Lord's Protection of His People

See introductory remarks to the Psalms of Ascents (in the section prior to Ps 120). The salvation of Israel and restoration of Jerusalem, a primary theme of the Songs of Ascents, (cf. Ps 122) is, once again, tied to the fulfillment of the Davidic covenant and the presence of David's divine Son in Ps 125 (Sailhamer, *NIV Compact Bible Commentary*, 343).

1. The Lord's Protection is as Permanent as Mount Zion (125:1-2)

125:1-2. The psalmist uses a landmark familiar to his readers to illustrate an important spiritual truth: **Those who trust in the Lord are as Mount Zion, which cannot be moved but abides forever**. The most appropriate symbol to illustrate the permanence of God's people (that they cannot be moved; see the comment on 15:5) is Mount Zion (cf. 2:6 and comments there). Despite any geographic changes God may make when He renews heaven and earth (cf. Is 65:17; 66:22; Rv 21:1), Zion will abide **forever** as the same distinct Zion of previous redemption history. This permanence of Zion is ultimately grounded in the permanence of Zion's King, the divine Messiah, who will establish His throne in Zion (on the Temple Mount) before renewing Creation, and will maintain His throne there forever (cf. Ezk 43:7; Rv 22:3-5).

2. The Lord Will Protect His Land from the Wicked (125:3)

125:3. The Lord will protect **the land** from the **scepter of wickedness**. The scepter is a symbol of authority (cf. Gn 49:10; Est 5:2). A wicked scepter is rule by ungodly authority. The statement **the righteous will not put forth their hands to do wrong** looks forward to a time when the Lord will rule with His righteous scepter (cf. Ps 2:6; 45:6; 60:7; 110:2).

3. The Lord will Protect His People (125:4-5)

125:4-5. The psalmist prayed that God would **do good . . . to** (or "for") **those who are good** (parallel to "the righteous" of v. 3, as in Pr 2:20). Because they have been reckoned as righteous they are therefore able to do good. On the other hand the Lord will judge those who **turn aside to their crooked ways** along with **the doers of iniquity**.

G. Psalm 126: Rejoicing at God's Restoration of Zion

See introductory remarks to the Psalms of Ascents (in the section prior to Ps 120). This psalm, as with the previous ones, looks forward to when God will deliver Israel. Psalm 126 parallels that future, eschatological rescue with the joy the Jewish people experienced at the end of the Babylonian exile that replaced the tears at the start of the exile. "This psalm, with its direct allusion to the return from Babylon, shows that Israel's troubles remain. God has still to fulfill his promise to David. The Messiah has not yet come. Nevertheless, the righteous remain faithful in their trust in God's promises" (Sailhamer, *NIV Compact Bible Commentary*, 344).

1. Looking Back with Thanksgiving at Past Restoration to Zion (126:1-3)

126:1-3. The psalmist reflected on the past event of God's restoring (lit., "returning") **the captive ones** (lit., "the returning ones") **of Zion**. This refers to those who returned to **Zion**/Jerusalem (cf. 2:6; 9:11 and comments there) after 70 years of exile/captivity in Babylon (2Ch 36:22-23; Jr 25:11; 29:10; Dn 9:2 see comments in these texts). The return to Israel was like a **dream** come true; the people were filled with gladness, **laughter** and **joyful shouting**. When the surrounding Gentile **nations** saw the Jewish people back in their land they recognized **The LORD has done great things for them**. This same statement of praise was echoed by the Jewish community, **The LORD has done great things for us; We are glad**.

2. Looking Forward with Hope to Future (and Final) Restoration (126:5-6)

126:4. The restoration prayed for here, **Restore our captivity, O LORD** seems to look forward to a time in the future when the Lord will bring all of the Jewish people back to the land. This request may seem puzzling since he referred to those who had already returned from the 70-year exile (vv. 1-3). The reason for this entreaty becomes evident, however, when realizing that many of the Jewish exiles did not return to the promised land from Babylon, and continued to live outside of Israel, in the Diaspora. Furthermore, since the Roman expulsion of the Jewish people from Israel (AD 70), the majority of the Jewish community has lived outside the land of Israel. Only in the modern period and since the rebirth of the modern state of Israel has there started to be a more widespread return to the land, although the majority of the Jewish people are still living in the Diaspora yet to return (cf. Ezk 37 and comments there). That this is looking to a final eschatological restoration is suggested by the image of **streams in the South**, a reference to the fruitful transformation of that land from the waters that will emerge from the temple with the Messiah's advent as the worldwide King (see Ezk 47:1-12).

126:5-6. The psalm concludes with a poetic agricultural description of the joy of this final return to the land. There will be a period of **weeping** (cf. Zch 12:10) prior to the final **joy** of the messianic restoration (e.g., Is 25:8-9; 35:10; 51:11; Rv 21:4); but that joy is certain, it **Shall indeed come** when God restores "the fallen booth of David" through David's supreme Son the Messiah (cf. Am 9:11-15; Zch 9:16-17; 14).

H. Psalm 127: A Song of Praise for the Lord for Daily Care

See introductory remarks to the Psalms of Ascents (in the section prior to Ps 120). This psalm, written by Solomon, continues the theme of God taking care of His people (cf. Ps 121). Further, the restoration of Israel and its capital, Jerusalem (the theme of Ps 126), will take place only when God determines and acts to make it happen. "The house" in v. 1 may have application to one's home and "children" to one's family (vv. 3-4), but within the context of the Psalms of Ascents, the main reference is to "the house of David," that is, to David's dynasty as fully realized through his Seed, his matchless Son, the Messiah (Sailhamer, *NIV Compact Bible Commentary*, 344).

1. The Lord is the Source of Protection and Purpose (127:1-3)

127:1-3. This psalm emphasizes the importance on relying on the Lord for purpose and meaning in every aspect of life. Hard work and personal goals in life are important; however, depending on anything or anyone other than the Lord for purpose and success is **vain** (v. 2). Any labor undertaken to meet one's needs, no matter how industrious, if undertaken in a manner and for a purpose inconsistent with God's Word will in the end be unsatisfying and even unsuccessful.

Solomon supports his conclusion with three illustrations (v. 2): (1) it is **vain** to labor and **build the house** apart from **the Lord**; (2) it is **vain** if the **watchman keeps awake** unless he recognizes **the Lord guards the city** (cf. 121); and (3) it is **vain** to work day and night at **painful labors**, for without the Lord, who **gives to His beloved even in his sleep**, there is no success. The concept of the utter vanity of living life apart from God is emphasized by the threefold repetition of the key terms "vain" and "in vain" in vv. 1-2a (on the use of threefold repetition in the Bible, see comments on Pss 86 and 110). In the book of Ecclesiastes Solomon wrote in detail concerning the vanity of living apart from dependence on the Lord.

This opening verse clearly affirms, on the one hand, the general principle of including God (through prayer, the counsel of His written Word, and the advice of godly believers) in one's decision of when, where, and how to build one's **house** (referring not just to the act of building the structure, but to the family that fills it). But it could also be taken as referring specifically to God's involvement in the building of the temple and Jerusalem in the future, as suggested by three facts. First, the psalm is attributed to Solomon, who built the temple and established Jerusalem (uniquely in his time) as the greatest capital city of any kingdom on earth (to which "all the earth" came to seek his presence, 1Kg 10:23). Second, the exilic and pilgrimage setting of this psalm (see introduction to Ps 120) implies a natural focus on Jerusalem and the temple. Third, the only **house** and the only **city** God was directly involved in establishing and building was the temple and Jerusalem.

2. The Lord is the Source of Blessing in the Family (127:3-5)

127:3-5. In the agrarian culture of Israel, children were the key to a successful family, and the absence of offspring was a family disaster. The point is that, if God does give children, they are to be viewed as **a gift** (lit., "the inheritance or property") **of the Lord**. This inheritance He has in turn entrusted to human parents for proper care and nurture, both physically and spiritually. Children, **the fruit of the womb**, are a **reward**, because only the Lord can create life. Godly people throughout the Scriptures valued, protected, and taught their children as the Lord commanded (cf. Dt 6:4-9).This does not suggest that children are the only or even the best gift God can give, or that if one does not or cannot have children one is lacking an important gift of God and is somehow less favored by Him. Yet children were a blessing (v. 5) in ancient times and compared to **arrows in the hand of a warrior** (v. 4), for like arrows, adult children could provide protection for the family in times of danger, and would provide honor to the family at **the gate** of the city (cf. Dt 17:5; 21:19; Ru 4:1; Is 29:21; Am 5:12). Depending on how these arrows (children) are shaped, drawn, and aimed, they may either miss the intended target or hit it on the bull's-eye (cf. the principle in Pr 22:6).

Given the messianic context of this psalm (see introduction to Ps 127), Solomon may be indicating that the final realization of the Davidic covenant is "given to His beloved" (v. 2; i.e., Israel) as **a gift of the Lord** (v. 3), that is, at a time to be decided by Him alone and apart from the work of His people.

I. Psalm 128: The Blessing of Walking with the Lord

See introductory remarks to the Psalms of Ascents (in the section prior to Ps 120). This psalm is a wish for fruitfulness and prosperity, but "How blessed is everyone" parallels Ps 2:12 and a promise of blessing for those who "kiss the Son" (of David, the Messiah). Thus Ps 128 will find its ultimate fulfillment of blessing "from

Zion" only when the promises to David are realized (2Sm 7:10-16; 2Ch 17:10-14).

1. The Personal Blessings of Walking with the Lord (128:1-4)

128:1 The godly will experience God's best, His blessing, first of all in their home (cf. 127:3). **How blessed** parallels the basis for success in life found in Ps 1:1 and 6, where **blessed** (1:1) and **way** (1:6) are used as they are here in v. 1. A person **walks** in the way of the Lord because he has a proper attitude and understanding of the Lord, so that he **fears the LORD** (cf. comments on 36:1; 111:10. The psalmist connects being blessed with fearing the Lord (vv. 1, 4), just as it is found in 112:1.

128:2. The blessings of the Lord are illustrated by His blessing upon his work, **you shall eat the fruit** (lit., "labor") **of your hands** (cf. Dt 28:1-6). This is emphasized by the description **You will be happy and it will be well with you.**

128:3-4. The blessings of the Lord are further illustrated in terms of wife and children. If a man truly fears the Lord then he will find satisfaction and joy in (1) his **wife**, who will certainly be affected by the godliness of her husband and **shall be** to him **like a fruitful vine**. This refers to her "fruitfulness" in all those venues that are open to her, whether or not childbearing is one of them (see the comments on Ps 127:3-5 and the application of "fruitfulness" beyond childbearing in such passages as Pr 31:31; Is 11:1; Dt 29:18). Also a man who fears the Lord will find satisfaction and joy in (2) his **children**, who, being reared in the fear of the Lord, will be to their parents **like olive plants**, often a symbol of blessing (cf. 52:8; 144:12; Dt 8:8; Jr 11:15-16). The metaphor suggests the great promise that such young ones possess, just as sapling olive trees have the promise of great bounty when they mature.

2. National Blessing of Walking with the Lord (128:5-6)

128:5-6. This benediction is a summary of the blessings: **The LORD bless you from Zion** (cf. 2:6; 9:11; 20:2; 34:3; 50:2; Is 2:3). In this final section the psalmist was not only expressing the wish that those who fear the Lord experience continued blessing in this life but primarily the extension of God's blessing to the outward circumstances of Israel. In short, the psalmist desires that they would live to see the advent of the Messiah and God's kingdom established on earth. Only then would they **see** Jerusalem's full and secure **prosperity** (a collective noun signifying all things that are good, and inevitably hearkening back to the ideal of God's filling the world at creation with what was perfectly good; esp. Gn 1:31) and **peace** (*shalom*; see the comments on Pss 29:11; 35:27). **Peace be upon Israel** (cf. 125:5; Nm 6:22-26).

J. Psalm 129: An Imprecatory Psalm against the Enemies of Israel

See introductory remarks to the Psalms of Ascents (in the section prior to Ps 120). Psalm 129 is a song of confidence in God's protection of Israel, similar to Ps 124, against her enemies. In Ps 124 Israel is admonished to realize it was only the Lord who prevented them from being destroyed by her enemies. Psalm 129 not only praises God for His protection, but includes an imprecatory prayer against the enemies of Zion.

1. Praise God for Preventing the Destruction of Israel (129:1-4)

129:1-3. Historically **many times** the enemies of Israel **have persecuted me**. This psalm begins by underscoring the tragic historical fact (both biblical and postbiblical, up to the present day) that **many times** various groups and individuals **have persecuted me**—Israel, the people, here personified as God's "national" son—beginning in his **youth** (referring to Israel's affliction in Egypt; see Ex 1:11-14; Hs 2:15). Nonetheless Israel's adversaries **have not prevailed against** him (to wipe him out as a people), nor will they ever do so, for Israel's continued existence is guaranteed by God's eternal and unconditional promise to Abraham, Isaac, and Jacob (Gn 12:1-3; Jr 31:35-37; Rm 11:29). Persecution is presented by the poetic images of **plowers plowed upon my back**.

129:4. Despite the attempts of the wicked to destroy Israel, **The LORD is righteous** (74:1-11; 77:11-15; 88:11-12; 96:13) and thwarted their plan. Therefore because God is righteous and faithful, **He has**, and will continue to **cut in two the cords of the wicked**. This is similar to the phrase used to depict God's response to general worldwide opposition and enmity toward the LORD and His Anointed (cf. 2:3).

2. Pray to the Lord to Punish the Persecutors of Israel (129:5-8)

129:5-8. The psalmist can utter **May all who hate Zion** (Jerusalem and its people, cf. 2:6; 9:11) **be put to shame** because the enemies of Israel are held responsible as the enemies of the God of Israel (cf. 5:10; 83 and comments there). Concerning the requests for judgment, **be like grass . . . which withers before it grows up** (cf. Introduction: Types of Psalms). The concluding language emphasizes the withholding of **the blessing of the Lord** from Israel's persecutors, reflecting specifically on the Abrahamic covenant (Gn 12:3; 27:29; Nm 24:9), in which God promises to bless those who bless Israel and to curse those who curse Israel (cf. Gn 12:3, and comments there). The concept of curses means to withhold good, or think less of, and is not indicating an eternal separation from God; it is not blasphemous language nor occult cursing (which is forbidden in Scripture, Lv 19:26, 31; 20:6, 27; Dt 18:9-14).

K. Psalm 130: A Cry to the Lord for Mercy

See introductory remarks to the Psalms of Ascents (in the section prior to Ps 120).

1. The Human Need for Mercy (130:1-3)

130:1-3. This penitential psalm is a cry for mercy from **out of the depths** (cf. other penitential Psalms 6:25; 32; 38; 51; 69). The **depths** out of which the psalmist cried to the Lord were not physical depths, but rather, expresses the low point of his emotional condition (cf. 69:2, 14). He acknowledged the contrast between his **iniquities** and God's righteousness, so that if it were not for God's mercy, no one **could stand** before the Holy One; this is the universal problem of sin for all humankind (cf. 49:7-8; Ec 7:20; Ac 3:23). **If You, Lord, should mark iniquities**, that is count all sins against the sinner, **who could stand**, under Your righteous judgment? The answer to this rhetorical question is "Absolutely no one could stand in God's presence."

2. The Divine Gift of Mercy (130:4-6)

130:4-6. The Lord is holy **but there is forgiveness with** God (cf. Neh 9:17; Dn 9:9), **that** He **may be feared** (cf. comments on 19:9; 34:9, 11; 111:10; 128:1; Ex 34:6-7). The purpose of His attribute of mercy with its resulting forgiveness, along with His many other attributes, is that He might be **feared**, that is, worshiped with reverence and awe. The personal experience of this divine forgiveness underlies the psalmist's affirmation, **I wait for the Lord... and in His word I do hope**. He is eagerly expecting the Lord's continued goodness. He compares his attitude to that of **watchmen** who are awake on the job all night, eagerly waiting for the **morning**.

3. Response to the Mercy and Forgiveness of God (130:7-8)

130:7-8. In response to the forgiveness of God, Israel is reminded to **hope in the Lord** (cf. v. 5). This **hope** is linked to the **lovingkindness** (cf. comments on 5:7). While this exhortation certainly includes the general desire to see his people blessed spiritually (i.e., "saved" in the sense typically intended in the NT, as in Rm 10:9) in every age and generation, the psalmist's primary reference in this last section is to that day when God **will redeem Israel from all his iniquities**, that same day of which Zechariah and Paul wrote (Zch 12:10-13:1; Rm 11:25-27; see comments there).

L. Psalm 131: David's Personal Faith in the Lord

See introductory remarks to the Psalms of Ascents (in the section prior to Ps 120). This short psalm concisely highlights the qualification of David as "a man after God's own heart" (1Sm 13:14; see comments there). Despite his sins, David understood clearly and accurately who he was in relation to (and in contrast with) God, and how he was therefore to relate to God.

1. David's Humility before the Lord (131:1)

131:1. David humbly confesses his status before the Lord saying **O Lord, my heart is not proud**. Although chosen by the Lord to be the King of Israel (cf. 1Sm 16), and renowned among the people of Israel (cf. 1Sm 18:7), David was humble before God knowing that pride was opposed to the Lord (cf. Dt 8:14; 2Ch 26:16; Is 9:9-10; 10:12-14; Hs 13:6). David presents evidence of his humility by saying **I** do not **involve myself in great matters** (i.e., incomprehensible, not more important)... **or... things too difficult** (lit., "too wonderful," i.e., unattainable, as in Gn 18:14); that is, he did not make any claim to godlike power or understanding.

2. David's Dependence on the Lord (131:2)

131:2. David pictures his determination to obey and trust the lord as **I have composed and quieted my soul**. Just as a **weaned child**, a toddler of three or four, is content to be by **his mother**, so David is content, satisfied to be in the presence of the Lord (cf. 23; 84:10).

3. David's Admonition to Israel (131:3)

131:3. In conclusion, David shifts from recounting his dependence on the Lord, to admonishing the nation **O Israel, hope in the Lord** (cf. comments on 130:5, 7-8).

M. Psalm 132: Affirming the Davidic Covenant

See introductory remarks to the Psalms of Ascents (in the section prior to Ps 120). This psalm is the climax of the Psalms of Ascents. In it the psalmist emphasizes that all of Israel's future hopes are dependent upon the fulfillment of the Davidic covenant (vv. 1, 11-12, 17-18; see 2Sm 7:8-17; 1Ch 17:7-15 and comments there).

David's sons did not qualify spiritually to fulfill those promises (v. 12), so the promises remained intact and awaited the supreme, future Son of David, the Messiah, who will successfully keep God's covenant (Sailhamer, *NIV Compact Bible Commentary*, 344–45).

The content of the psalm is structured around the Davidic covenant aspects of house/throne/kingdom (2Sm 7:2-16). The Psalm begins with a plea "O Lord remember David" followed by: (1) David's desire to make a house for God to dwell (vv. 2-10), but instead the Lord said he would make a house for David; (2) the promise of a king to reign on David's throne (vv. 11-12); and (3) the promise of an eternal kingdom in Zion (vv. 13-18).

There are some parallels in this psalm to Solomon's prayer at the dedication of the temple (cf. 2Ch 6), so perhaps this psalm was originally composed and sung during the "bringing up" (from the same root as the word "ascents" in the heading of the psalm) of the ark from the tabernacle in the city of David to its place in the inner sanctuary of Solomon's temple (1Kg 8:4-6).

1. The Request to Remember David's Zeal (132:1-10)

132:1-2. The opening verses are a plea for the Lord to **remember . . . on David's behalf** (cf. v. 10) . . . **how he swore to the LORD and vowed to the Mighty One of Jacob**. This is a poetic call to remember the covenant the Lord made with David (cf. comments on 2Sm 7:12-17). There are three aspects of the Lord's unconditional covenant with David: (1) an eternal house/dynasty; (2) an eternal throne/sovereignty; and (3) an eternal kingdom/nation.

132:3-5. This section recalls David's desire to **find a place for the LORD**. David's desire was to build the temple, a permanent **dwelling place** for the worship of the Lord and no longer maintain the transportable tabernacle.

132:6-9. The ark was lodged for twenty years in area of **Ephrathah** at the village of Kiriath-Jearim, here identified as **Jaar** (cf. 1Sm 7:2). The location for the temple had been chosen by the Lord (cf. vv. 13-14; Gn 22; Dt 12:14; 2Sm 24:18-25), although the building of the temple there was delayed until the reign of David's son, Solomon (cf. 2Sm 7:1-7; 1Ch 22:7-9). Nevertheless, it was David's desire for the Lord to **arise . . . to your resting place** (cf. 2Ch 6:41), **You and the ark of Your strength** (v. 8). Then **priests** will be **clothed with righteousness**, reflecting not just their garments, but their spiritual condition, and the **godly one** will **sing for joy** (cf. v 16). In the Lord's covenant with David, He promised to build a house for David.

2. The Request to Remember the Davidic Covenant (132:10-18)

132:10-12. Having asked the Lord to remember David's zeal for Him, the psalmist next asks the Lord to remember His response to David, which was the Davidic covenant. He pleads with the Lord not to **turn away** from His **anointed**. The reason is that the Lord had **sworn to David** that his descendants would rule from the Davidic line, so David makes another request, based on the Davidic covenant: **For the sake of David Your servant** (cf. v. 1) remember his **sons . . . shall sit upon your throne forever**. There was a continual line of Davidic kings from David to the Babylonian captivity. However, after the return there was not a son of David on the throne until the coming of Messiah Jesus, and ultimately He will reign from Jerusalem (cf. Lk 1:68-79; Ezk 37:24).

132:13-16. Coinciding with the choice of David's house, was the Lord's election of Zion as the center of worship and rule (**For the LORD has chosen Zion** [cf. 2:6; 9:11] . . . **This is My resting place forever** . . . **Here I will dwell** [vv. 13-14; cf. Dt 12:4-14]). Here the psalmist longs for the restoration of Zion and the priesthood (v. 16; cf. v. 9).

132:17. The eschatological aspect of the psalm comes into focus regarding the Lord's promise of the eternal kingdom through the messianic Son of David. He promised **I will cause the horn of David to spring**. The **horn** is commonly a symbol of strength and dignity (18:2; 89:17, 24; 92:10). But in Dn 7:7, 8, 24, the horn represents a king. Hence the horn of David likely represents a powerful and dignified king from the house of David, or the messianic King. This is further supported by the use of the verb **spring** (lit., "branch forth"), which alludes to the messianic prophecies concerning the "Branch" of David (cf. comments at Is 4:2; Jr 23:5; 33:15; Zch 3:8; 6:12). The Lord also **prepared a lamp for Mine anointed**. The **lamp** is a metaphor for an heir (cf. 1Kg 11:36, when a man did not have an heir, and it was said that his lamp went out). This verse is a promise that the Lord will send a future messianic Son of David, who will be the ultimate heir for David, who was the anointed king.

132:18. Those who oppose the messianic King, the **enemies** of the Lord, God **will clothe with shame**, indicating judgment (cf. 2:4-12; 35:26; 109:29). In contrast **upon himself**, the horn of

David, the messianic King, **his crown shall shine**. The singing of this psalm after the return from the Babylonian exile, when there was no longer any Davidic king, was a proclamation of faith that God would keep His covenant with David and send King Messiah, Son of David, to reign on David's throne. Certainly this was the expectation and understanding of Zecharias, father of John the Baptist, who prophesied that "the Lord God of Israel . . . has raised up a horn of salvation for us, in the house of David His servant" (cf. Lk 1:68-70).

N. Psalm 133: The Beauty of Unity among the People of Perfected Jerusalem

See introductory remarks to the Psalms of Ascents (in the section prior to Ps 120). In connection with Ps 132, Ps 133 describes the consequences of the fulfillment of the Davidic covenant when the Messiah is present (unity [vv. 1-3a, b]—perhaps even including the reunification of the northern and southern tribes as well as the blessing of salvation [v. 3c] which will flow from Zion (Jerusalem) and the joy of eternal life (Sailhamer, *NIV Compact Bible Commentary,* 345).

1. The Beauty of Unity (133:1)

133:1. The opening, **Behold**, calls attention to something important to follow; it then uses double adjectives in describing the event. Coupling **good** and **pleasant** is used elsewhere to describe who God is, what He gives, or the worship that He receives from His people (cf. 135:3; 147:1; Gn 13:6; 36:7; 49:15; Jb 36:11). Considering the Messianic focus of the Songs of Ascents (see introductory remarks to the Psalms of Ascents, in the section prior to Ps 120), the **unity** of **brothers** has several implications. In the future, the land will be fruitful enough to support all the people in every tribal division so there will be no disputes over territory (cf. Ezk 48:1-8). This unity refers to the reuniting of the northern and southern kingdoms in the Messianic Age (cf. Ezk 37:15-22). More immediately, it may refer here to the spiritual unity of the various Israelite worshipers traveling to celebrate the feasts, who have come together to worship their one Lord and Father at the temple in Jerusalem. Finally, the personal application of the unity here is not just to intra-Jewish unity, but to the spiritual unity of Jew and Gentile united by faith in Messiah Jesus (cf. Is 19:23-25; Zch 14:16; Eph 3:11-16).

2. The Illustrations of the Blessings of Unity (133:2-3a)

133:2. The goodness and pleasantness of unity is illustrated in two ways. First, unity has a consecrating effect. It is compared to **the precious oil . . . coming down upon . . . Aaron's beard**. This highlights the holiness of that unity or, more precisely, the priestly holiness of the people who dwell in that unity. The **precious oil** indicates a specific kind of oil. It is not the ordinary oil used for other anointing purposes (cf. Ec 9:8). This is the precious anointing described in Lv 8:10-13 which, after being applied to the tabernacle and all that was in it, was poured on Aaron's head to consecrate him, setting him apart as high priest. This unity is like the **oil upon . . . Aaron's beard**. Hence this blessing of unity is referring to the consecrating effect of unity on the nation.

133:3a. The second way that unity is good and pleasant is that it is refreshing to the people of God. The next illustration compares the unity of the brothers to the dew **coming down** from Mount **Hermon**, the tallest mountain in Israel. It is always snowcapped and is consistently characterized in its lower parts by an abundance of **dew**—which symbolizes fresh and vigorous life (cf. 110:3; Hs 14:5). These waters do ultimately descend to **the mountains of Zion** (cf. Ps 2:6). The snow runoff from Hermon seeps through the limestone substrata and provides the headwaters for the Jordan River, the life-giving artery of Israel. In the dry and hot seasons, this dew provides cool water and refreshment for the nation. Likewise the unity of the people will be refreshing to the people of God. The reference to **Zion** as the source of this eternal blessing alludes specifically to the presence of God therein as the eternal King and source of all that is best for His people (cf. Ezk 43:7; Rv 21:6, 23-24; 22:1-5, 17).

3. The Blessing of Immortality (133:3b)

133:3b. This psalm closes with the essence of biblical blessing which entails the full experience of blessing as originally intended by God when He blessed mankind to walk with Him in the Garden of Eden (cf. Gn 1:28): **life forever** (i.e., eternal life qualified by all that is good).

O. Psalm 134: The Final Ascents: Praise the Lord for Complete Blessing

See introductory remarks to the Psalms of Ascents (in the section prior to Ps 120). This psalm concludes the unit of Psalms of Ascents, and reinforces the blessing of the Lord upon His people by the threefold repetition (once in each verse) of the verb "bless" (on the use of such threefold repetition see introductory comments on Pss 86 and 110). It calls on all who worship the Lord, the Creator of Heaven and earth in Zion and to look for His blessing to come from Zion. This call for praise at the conclusion of the Songs of Ascents is answered in the following two psalms, 135–136 (Sailhamer, *NIV Compact Bible Commentary,* 245).

1. The Affirmation of Blessing (134:1)

134:1. This Psalm of Ascents ends with a clear call to worship: **Behold** (cf. 133:1) **bless the LORD, all servants of the LORD.** Those who have been blessed by the Lord with the guarantee of "life forever" (133:3b) should respond in worship. The expression those **who serve** [lit., "stand"] . . . **in the house of the LORD** certainly includes the Levites who ministered in the temple, since stand is the typical verb used to describe their temple service (cf. Dt 10:8; 18:5; 2Ch 29:11). Considering the context and culminating place of this psalm, it also unquestionably includes reference to all Israelite worshipers and pilgrims to the temple who sought to worship God in gratitude and praise. The reference to this worship taking place **by night** underscores the unbroken continuity of this worship, not only as expressed by the Levites in their temple ministry (see 1Ch 9:33), but also as expressed by all Israelites (e.g., Anna in Lk 2:36-37). Everyone was to be drawn in their devotion to God's presence on earth. This would have been especially true during the pilgrimage festivals (Passover, Pentecost, and Booths), for in the time of the second temple, built after the return from exile, according to early Jewish tradition, "on the pilgrimage festivals, before (the time of) the cockcrow drew near, the Temple Court [i.e., "the Court of Israel" for Jewish men who were not priests] would already be filled up with Israelites" (Mishnah, *Yomah* i.8).

2. The Source of Blessing (134:2)

134:2. Part of serving in the temple was worship, to **Lift up your hands to the sanctuary** (lit., "holiness," an abbreviated reference to "the holy of holies"; Ex 26:34) **And bless the Lord**, or give Him honor and praise. The worshiper's focus on the temple, whether in orientation only (cf. 1Kg 8:30) or in actual attendance, as most notably on the pilgrimage festivals, was to be motivated not by the structure itself, but by the presence of God Himself in it. In history His presence was in the cloud of glory (Ex 40:34-35), but in the future His presence would be seen in the Son of God (cf. Ezk 43:7; Rv 21:22-27). To **lift up** one's **hands** to Him, moreover, highlights that important relational facet of worship characterized by the worshiper's utter submission to and dependence on God as the one who is both able and willing to meet His child's deepest needs (cf. the parallelism between "I lift up my hands" and "my supplications" when "I cry . . . for help" in Ps 28:2; this is also the likely significance in 1Tm 2:8).

3. The Dissemination of Blessing (134:3)

134:3. This opens with a call for those who love the Lord to bless the Lord; it closes with a parallel request: **May the LORD bless** (cf. Nm 6:24) **you from Zion.** The psalm, and hence the Song of Ascents, concludes most fittingly on the note of blessing going forth from **the LORD** Himself, the Source of all blessing. The blessing will be imparted from His place in **Zion**, the reference being not just to what was in the days of the First and Second Temples but also inevitably to what will always be from the days of Messiah's advent to the Third Temple and beyond. On the two parts of this verse represented verbatim in previous Songs of Ascents, see the comments on Ps 128:5a (134:3a) and Pss 121:2b and 124:8b (134:3b). The Lord is identified as **He who made heaven and earth** indicating His sovereignty as Creator and sustainer of the world (cf. 121:1; 124:8; 146:6).

Psalm 135: Praise for God's Manifest Kindness toward Israel

Psalms 135–136 are praise psalms, and are placed here in the Psalter in response to the call to worship in Psalm 134. In Ps 135 God should be praised specifically because of His power demonstrated in the creation and governance of all that there is (vv. 5-7) and in His work to redeem Israel from Egypt and establish them in the land of Israel (vv. 8-21; Sailhamer, *NIV Compact Bible Commentary,* 345).

A. Praise God for Choosing Israel (135:1-7)

135:1-3. The declaration **Praise the Lord!** is the focus of this psalm and the apt response to 134. Though this psalm is not part of the "Songs of Ascents" (Pss 120–34), it is closely connected to the previous psalm by its opening exhortation, addressed to the **servants of the LORD** (cf. Ps 134:1) . . . **who stand in the house of the LORD.** So too the application to God of the adjectives **good** and **lovely** (or "pleasant") recalls the use of the same two adjectives applied to God's people in 133:1, suggesting that the "good and lovely" unity between His people comes ultimately from His own "good and lovely" nature.

135:4. The central reason for praising God begins with the essential fact that God chose

His people Israel: **the LORD has chosen Jacob for Himself, Israel for His own possession** (cf. Dt 7:6; 10:1; Ps 105:6; Rm 9:4-5; 11:29). The rest of this first section focuses on that expression of God's concern for Israel, which stands at the foundation of their identity as His people, because of His sovereign and unmerited choice.

135:5-7. The psalmist offers other reasons for praising the Lord: (1) His supremacy (**the Lord is great . . . above all gods**); (2) His omnipotence (**Whatever the LORD pleases, He does**); and (3) His sovereignty as the Creator and sustainer of life, (**He causes the vapors to ascend . . . makes lightnings . . . wind**; cf. Jr 10:131; Jb 28:25, 26; 38:35, 36; Zch 10:1).

B. Praise God for Preserving Israel (135:8-14)

135:8-14. The description of God's protection of Israel begins with highlights of the exodus and continues in His care for His people throughout their conquest of the promised land. God expressed His concern for Israel by (1) defeating their enemies from **Egypt** (vv. 8-9; cf. Ex 1–14) and the **Amorites** and the people of **Bashan** (v. 11a; cf. Nm 21:21-35) to **all the kingdoms of Canaan** (v. 11b); (2) giving them the **land** of Canaan (and all it contained for their sustenance) **as a heritage** (or "inheritance") forever (v. 12; cf. Gn 17:8; Ps 105:8-11; cf. also Dt 9:6); and (3) promising to **judge His people** (a better translation is "vindicating" as in such translations as ESV, NIV, TNIV, HCSB, and RSV) and showing **compassion** on His people, that is, manifesting His deeply felt concern and care (see "vindicate" and "compassion" in Dt 32:34, cf. Pss 102:13; 106:46; Ex 33:19; 34:6).

C. Praise God for His Relationship to Israel (135:15-21)

135:15-18. The Lord is truly God, not like **the idols of the nations** . . . which are **the work of man's hands**. This section is parallel to 115:4-8; see comments there.

135:19-20. The psalm concludes with a call for **Israel**, the people in general . . . **Aaron** and **Levi**, the priesthood . . . and all **You who revere the LORD**, to **bless the** Lord (cf. 115:9-11 and comments there).

135:21. The psalm concludes with a call of **Blessed be the LORD from Zion, who dwells in Jerusalem** (cf. 128:5; 132:13-14 and comments there).

Psalm 136: Superlative Praise for God's Lovingkindness

This psalm is a continued response to the call for praise in Ps 134:1. The focus of praise in Ps 135 is on the Lord's lovingkindness, mentioned in each of the 26 verses, a repetition that occurs more so than in any other biblical passage. That divine attribute epitomizes any and all the good that God has ever done for humanity (cf. 5:7 and comments there). The structure is: God's greatness as Creator (vv. 4-9); God's Redemption of Israel from Egypt (vv. 10-16); God's provision of the land of Israel to the people of Israel (vv. 17-22) (similar to the structure of Ps 135). This is a liturgical psalm composed around the phrase repeated throughout: "For His lovingkindness is everlasting."

A. Praising God as the Source of All Lovingkindness (136:1-3)

136:1-3. The opening call to **Give thanks to the LORD, for He is good** and the rest of the psalm form a liturgy of praise to the Lord as Creator (vv. 4-9) and Israel's Redeemer (vv. 10-25). The focus of praise is on **His lovingkindness**, which is **everlasting** (cf. 5:7 and comments there; 1Ch 16:41; Pss 100:5; 107:1). He is the only god, **God of gods** . . . and **the Lord of lords** (cf. Dt 10:17).

B. Praising God for His Lovingkindness Expressed in Creation (136:4-9)

136:4-9. God doing (or "making") **great wonders** is a phrase that signifies God's manifest acts of deliverance (see comments on 9:1; 40:5). He is the Creator, and His awe-inspiring works on the second through the fourth days of the creation week (cf. comments on Gn 1:9-16) are highlighted: **the heavens**, the **earth** and **the great lights**—that is, **the sun** and **the moon**—and the **stars**. In addition to the obvious benefit of these to humanity, the "goodness" component of God's lovingkindness, manifest in His creation of these, is intimated by the psalmist's initial reference, in v. 4, to God doing (or "making") **great wonders** (*nifla'ot*), a term specifically signifying God's manifest acts of deliverance (see comments on 9:1; 40:5)—often in connection with these celestial parts of creation (cf. comment on Gn 1:14).

C. Praising God for His Lovingkindness for Israel (136:10-22)

136:10-15. God demonstrated His **lovingkindness** to the people of Israel by delivering them from their enemies. The arrangement of this historical survey of deliverance begins with the deliverance from **the Egyptians**, specifically the slaying of **their firstborn** on the night of Passover and the escape from **Pharaoh** at the **Red Sea** (vv. 10, 13-15; cf. Ex 1–14).

136:16-22. The history continues with recalling that the Lord **led His people through the wilderness** (cf. Ex 3:18; 15:22). He gave them victory over various **mighty kings** (vv. 17-18), from **Sihon, king of the Amorites** and **Og, king of Bashan** (vv. 19-20; cf. Nm 21:21-35), and from the Canaanites, whose land He **gave** to Israel **as a heritage** (or "inheritance") forever (vv. 21-22; cf. Gn 13:14-15; 17:8; Dt 6:22-23; Ps 105:8-11).

136:23-24. These two verses reiterate in abbreviated fashion the entire spectrum of God's **lovingkindness** expressed in Israel's deliverance, from Egypt, as indicated by the expression **Who remembered us** (cf. Ex 2:24). It continues to the postexilic period, with the expression He **has rescued us**. This phrase is not speaking of the exodus, since this verb form for **rescued** is used in the sense of "rescue/deliver" elsewhere only in Lm 5:8, with reference to the nation not yet having been delivered from exile. Hence, here it is saying, God **rescued us** from exile.

D. A Finale of Praise to God, the Source of Lovingkindness (136:25-26)

136:25. The psalmist concludes by once more praising God as the Creator and sustainer (parallel to vv. 4-9) **Who gives food to all flesh**. His giving (the verb here indicating an ongoing action) food to all flesh signifies both mankind and animal life (cf. Gn 6:17; 7:21; Ps 147:9, to animals; and Ps 145:15, to people).

136:26. The final **give thanks** concludes the psalm as it began, but here it describes the Lord as **the God of heaven**. This fairly rare divine title recalls the expression of God's transcendent **lovingkindness** throughout the OT history of Israel, whether in overcoming spiritual and geographical obstacles to provide a godly bride for Isaac (Gn 24:3, 7), natural and ethnic obstacles to provide salvation to a despised Gentile people (Jnh 1:9), or political and spiritual obstacles to provide the restoration of His people to their land (Ezr 1:2; 5:11, 12; 6:9, 10; 7:12, 21; Neh 1:4, 5; 2:4, 20; 2Ch 36:23). Its use in this psalm suggests a postexilic time of writing, as the majority of the uses of the **God of heaven** title are from that time period.

Psalm 137: Lamenting the Victory of God's Enemies over Zion

This sad song of the exiles looks back on the circumstances of the Jewish people living in Babylonian captivity remembering Zion (vv. 1-6) and concludes with an imprecatory stanza (vv. 7-9). Psalm 137 forms a "bookend" with Ps 120 regarding the Babylonian exile. This bookending suggests that while Ps 137 is not one of the Songs of Ascents, the psalms in the Songs of Ascents that present the themes of Israel's ultimate restoration and salvation (virtually all of Pss 121–134) must be understood against the backdrop of the exile (Pss 120, 137). While the return from the Babylonian exile was not the final fulfillment of all the promises of Israel's ultimate deliverance, it nevertheless provided a rejuvenated hope that God would, in the future, fulfill all of His promises to Abraham and David (Sailhamer, *NIV Compact Bible Commentary*, 345).

A. Grieving over the Conquest of Jerusalem (137:1-3)

137:1-3. This somber psalm begins recalling the sorrow of life in captivity, **By the rivers of Babylon . . . we sat down and wept**. This sorrow arose as they (1) remembered **Zion**, i.e., what Jerusalem and Israel were before the Babylonian conquest, not only in their material splendor, but even more so as the site of God's presence on earth in the temple, now destroyed (cf. comments on 2:6; 9:11); and (2) their being under the dominion of pagan **captors**, **tormentors** who mocked and **demanded** that the Jewish captives express **mirth** and **sing . . . songs of Zion** (v. 3) against their will (such as Pss 48 and 87, each of which is designated a "song" in its heading).

B. Affirming the Ongoing Centrality of Jerusalem (137:4-6)

137:4. How did the exiles respond to their captors' demand to sing "one of the songs of Zion" (v. 3)? By asking rhetorically: **How can we sing the LORD's song in a foreign land?** Of course it would be impossible to sing the sacred songs of worship to the Lord as entertainment for pagans.

137:5-6. This is the heart of this psalm: **If I forget you, O Jerusalem . . . If I do not remember you, If I do not exalt Jerusalem above my chief joy** then let judgment fall upon me, may I become lame in **my right hand** and may I become unable to speak. Their determination to remember Jerusalem is founded in their worship of God who chose Zion as the seat of His earthly rule as Israel's true King (cf. 2:6, 9:11). The affirmation in turns bears out the reason for the exile which, though accomplished by means of an ungodly people, was intended by God as correction for Israel's failure to recognize Him as their ultimate authority—a failure epitomized by their idolatry (Ezk 20:27-32) and failure to observe God's command concerning the land's sabbatical rest (2Ch 36:21).

C. Envisioning the Just Judgment of the Enemies of Zion (137:7-9)

137:7-8. This final imprecatory stanza opposes the enemies of Israel. **Edom** had a long history of enmity against Israel, and the prophets portray Edom as the epitome of Israel's enemies, slated for judgment by the Lord (cf. Is 63:1-4; Jr 49:7-22; Ezk 25:8, 12-14; 35; Ob). When the Babylonians attacked **Jerusalem** they were supported by Israel's neighbor Edom, **who said, "Raze it, raze it to its very foundation."** Edom's cruelty to Jerusalem was unprecedented (cf. Ob 11-14). Likewise the psalm calls for the destruction of the **daughter of Babylon**, a personification of the empire that destroyed Jerusalem and would be judged for its cruelty (cf. Jr 51–52 and comments there).

137:9. By these actions and attitudes, these enemies of Israel had placed themselves under the inevitable and just wrath of God (cf. Jr 30:11; 50). The psalmist appealed for the execution of divine justice in vv. 7-8, which he concluded with the admittedly shocking statement, **How blessed will be the one who seizes and dashes your little ones against the rock**. This statement, however, is meant to be shocking, just as shocking as the destruction of Sodom and Gomorrah and all their inhabitants (Gn 19:25). This was intended as an example not of God's supposedly barbaric and warlike nature, but rather of His perfect holiness and justice (cf. Rv 18:1–19:4; see comments on imprecatory psalms in the Introduction to Psalms). Even so, the longing for the brutal destruction of Babylonian children seems especially harsh. It is likely that the psalmist was not actually speaking of **little ones** in a literal sense, but rather, the descendants of Babylon as a whole, that is, all the citizens of "the wicked mother Babylon" (Alden, *Psalms: Songs of Discipleship*, 3:85).

Psalm 138: A Hymn of Thanksgiving for the Faithfulness of God

Psalm 138 is the first of eight consecutive Davidic psalms (cf. Pss 2–3 heading) near the close of the Psalter. The themes of these psalms reaffirm David's confidence in God's promise to uphold His covenants. They seem to have been written during a time when the Jewish people were suffering under the wicked. The psalms emphasize David's own need, and that of the Jewish people corporately. And they encourage them to continue to trust in God to accomplish all that He promised, especially with regard to the Davidic covenant Thus this unit of psalms affirms the messianic hope (Sailhamer, *NIV Compact Bible Commentary*, 346).

Psalm 138 has many parallels to the oracles of blessing in Isaiah (cf. Is 40–60). Some of the LXX manuscripts link this psalm to the period of Haggai and Zechariah.

A. Praise God for His Faithfulness and Strength (138:1-3)

138:1-3. David's asserts that he **will give . . . thanks with all** his **heart . . . before the gods**, in the presence of **the gods**. There are three possible meanings to this expression: (1) "gods" may refer to angels, i.e., supernatural beings in the presence of God (cf. 8:5), which is how the LXX translates this; (2) it could refer to human rulers (cf. 82:1); or (3) it could be false gods. In light of the setting being worship in the temple, the first option seems most likely. On bowing **down toward** God's **holy temple** see comment on 134:2. God's **name** represents a summary reference to His character and all the past deeds for which He is known cf. 5:11; 20:5; 23:3; 31:3). Praise is expressed for His **lovingkindness** (cf. comment on 5:7) and **truth** (v. 2; cf. comment on 43:3), as when He redeemed David from Saul (cf. 57:3; 1Sm 22:1; 24:3). There is a link between the **word** of God, which is truth (cf. Ps 119:160) and his **name**, which epitomizes His character.

B. Praise God, All the Nations of the Earth (138:4-6)

138:4-6. This section looks forward to the time when **all the kings of the** earth, the Gentile nations they represent, **will give thanks to You**. The motivation for their praise is their having **heard the words of Your mouth** so the Gentiles might also come to know and worship the Lord with Israel (cf. Is 19:24-25; 56:7; Eph 2:13-18). Together the redeemed of the Gentile nations and the people of Israel **will sing of the ways of the Lord** (cf. Rv 5:9-10; Pss 2:10-12; 22:27-31; 68:32). The concept of God's spiritual provision is also affirmed by David's statement that **He regards the lowly** (v. 6). The verb translated "regards," when used with God as the subject, typically signifies His assessment and provision of what is most needed (see comments on 4:6).

C. Praise God for His Future Faithfulness (138:7-8)

138:7-8. As in Ps 23, David expresses his confidence in the Lord, **Though I walk in the midst of trouble** (cf. Ps 23 and comments there). God will **stretch forth** His **hand** is a frequent expression of

God's judgment (cf. Ex 7:5; 15:12; Is 5:25; Jr 51:25) against the **wrath of my** (David's, and by extension, Israel's) **enemies.** But in contrast, David concluded with the confident assertion, **Your right hand will save me** (cf. Pss 20:6; 60:5; 118:25) and that God would **accomplish what concerns me** (cf. 57:2). His affirmation that God **not forsake** him and His people, **the works of Your hand** (cf. 100:3), alludes to the promise of Dt 31:6.

Psalm 139: David's Praise for the Presence of the Lord

On the heading of this **Psalm of David**, see the introduction to Ps 138 above. The faith exhibited so clearly by David in Ps 138 is explored more fully here, as Ps 139 gives the specific characteristics of God that engendered faith in David (Sailhamer, *NIV Compact Bible Commentary*, 346).

A. God Is Present in Everyday Experiences (139:1-12)

139:1-6. David begins this intensely personal psalm by praising God's omniscience (that He knows everything) and omnipresence (that He is always present, at all times and in all places), **O Lord, You have searched me and known me** (an expression of personal involvement and knowledge). Therefore, David affirmed that God's involvement in his active life, **when I sit down and when I rise up** (cf. Dt 6:7, meaning every minute of his life) was personal not abstract. He said the Lord had **enclosed me behind and before and laid Your hand upon me** (v. 5), a gentle touch of blessing (cf. 48:14).

139:7-12. David is comforted by the assurance of God's presence even in times of chastisement, **Where can I go from Your Spirit ? Or. . . flee from your presence?** The phrase **Sheol** and the **sea**, are similar to Jonah's experience (cf. Jnh 2:2-3; Ps 49:14-15).

B. God Is Sovereign in Planning Personal Existence (139:13-16)

139:13-16. One aspect of David's confidence in the Lord is related to his knowledge that he was created by the Lord from conception to birth: **You formed my inward parts . . . wove me in my mother's womb**. David notes that he is **wonderfully** (or "divinely") **made**. *Wonderfully* is applied in the Bible to what God is and does (cf. comments on 119:121-128).The phrase **in the depths of the earth** (v. 15) is a poetic reference to the womb, not to geography. David confirms that not only did the Lord plan his life from the womb, but he knows the precise number of **days** that he would live, **when as yet there was not one of them** (v. 16). This verse strongly supports that there is actual human life in the womb, which should be protected.

C. God Is Active Guiding into the Everlasting Way (139:17-24)

139:17-18. When reviewing all the Lord knows about him, David exclaims **How precious also are Your thoughts to me, O God!** (cf. 36:7; 40:5). David finds comfort and encouragement in God's care for him: **If I should count them** [your thoughts toward me], **they would outnumber the sand**; they are innumerable. Asleep or **awake, I am still with You**.

139:19-22. David's deep love for the Lord motivates him to hate everything that is contrary to God. So he called an imprecation on all who stand opposed to the Lord: **O that You would slay the wicked, O God . . . For Your enemies take Your name in vain** (cf. Ex 20:7). David in this psalm, as he did when he fought Goliath, hates and **loathe[s] those who rise up against You** (v. 21; cf. 1Sm 17:26, 45-47). See comments on imprecatory psalms in the Introduction to Psalms.

139:23-24. The psalm ends as it began with an acknowledgement of God searching and knowing him. Although David was determined to hold to God's holy standard, at the same time, he knew his motives and obedience were imperfect. So, David concluded by asking that God **see if there be any hurtful way in** him (cf. 17:3-5) and, if so, **lead** him **in the everlasting way**—i.e., the "upright" way of God (cf. 27:11).

Psalm 140: A Prayer when Oppressed by the Wicked

On the inscription of this Psalm of David, see Ps 138 introduction above. This psalm continues David's character as a righteous man being persecuted by evil (cf. 139:19-22), violent men. The structure of the psalm is threefold: David's request for help from the Lord (v. 8); David's request for vengeance on the wicked (vv. 9-11); and David's confidence in the Lord's justice (vv. 12-13).

A. David's Request for the Lord's Help (140:1-8)

140:1-3. Almost as a follow-up to David's commitment to defend God's honor by slaying the wicked (cf. 139:19-22), here David implores the Lord to **Rescue me . . . from evil men; preserve me from violent men**. The term here translated **violent** (lit., "violence," i.e., the plural form of the word *hamas*) signifies violence characterized by wickedness (cf. comment on 11:5). These evil men **devise evil . . . in their hearts . . . stir up war**. They have tongues sharp **as a serpent** (speak violent lies, cf. 57:4; 64:3). The phrase describing wicked speech as the **poison of a viper** [or asp] **is under their lips** (v. 3) is cited in in Rm 3:13 to underscore the concept that both Jews and Greeks are all under sin. Possibly David had in view here include both Israelites as well as Gentiles.

140:4-5. The prayer, **Keep me, O Lord, from the hands of the wicked** is David's request not to fall into the **trap** . . . **net** and **snares** the wicked had set for him.

140:6-8. David made his statement of faith: **You are my God** . . . **God the Lord, the strength of my salvation** (cf. 3:2; 18:1-3). He recalled past times of protection when God had **covered** [his] **head in the day of battle**. Then, upon the basis of his faith in God, he pleaded for God's protection: **Give ear, O Lord** . . . **Do not grant** . . . **the desires of the wicked** (vv. 6, 8).

B. David's Request for Vengeance on the Wicked (140:9-11)

140:9-11. David appealed to God to have the plans of the wicked **cover them**, that is, fall on their own wicked **head** (v. 9). This is what happened with Haman's evil plan to hang Mordecai—it was reversed so that Haman himself was hung on the gallows he built for Mordecai (cf. Est 6–7). The word **mischief** is better translated "evil plots." He requested the Lord not to grant "the desires of the wicked" lest they "be exalted" (or "become lofty or high," as, e.g., Is 52:13), not only so that the individuals are not exalted, but also so that wickedness in general is not promoted and further corrupt society. The judgment of the wicked includes **burning coals fall[ing] upon them** . . . being **cast into fire** . . . and caught in **deep pits**. These are images sometimes used of the judgment of the Lord (cf. 21:9; 97:3; Is 12:31; 26:11; 36:12). See comments on imprecatory psalms in the Introduction to Psalms.

C. David's Confidence in the Lord's Justice (140:12-13)

140:12-13. As typical of David's psalms of lament, complaint, imprecation, and petition, he ends on a positive, confident note, **I know that the Lord will maintain the cause of the afflicted**. This looks forward to what God will do—if not in this life, then unquestionably in the next, when **the upright will dwell in** God's **presence** (cf. comments on Pss 1:5-6 and 11:7b).

Psalm 141: Imploring God's Protective Guidance

On the heading of this **Psalm of David**, see Ps 138 introduction above. Psalm 141 contains a similar theme as that found in Ps 140, requesting protection from the wicked. This lament psalm, however, deals with more internal struggles than external foes. David once again (as in Ps 140) presents himself as a model of sincere trust in God when suffering at the hands of the wicked or wrestling to achieve personal righteousness.

A. In Diverting from Iniquity (141:1-4)

141:1-2. David began with the urgent request: **hasten to me** . . . **give ear to my voice when I call to you** (i.e., meet his need in the best way possible as signified by the synonymous expression "hear my voice" in v. 2). His prayer is presented in terms of worship **as incense** (cf. Ex 30:8; Lk 1:10; Rv 5:8) and **the lifting up of my hands** (cf. Ps 28:2; 63:4: 119:48: 134:2) . . . **as the evening offering** (cf. Ex 29:41).

141:3-4. Here are a series of prayer requests: (1) **Set a guard, O Lord, over my mouth (the door of my lips** is a prayer for pure speech, cf. 19:14); (2) keep my **heart** from desiring **any evil thing** (cf. 119:36) is prayer for protection from temptation; and (3) protect me from the **practice** of **deeds of wickedness with men who do iniquity**; this is a prayer for protection against evil influences (cf. 1; Pr 1:8-19; 13:20)

B. In Chastising for Iniquity (141:5-7)

141:5-7. The relationship of God's guidance is here extended by David by the instruction and chastisement of his godly friends: the **righteous** who **smite** him **in kindness** (Hb. *chesed*; see the comment on 5:7). His righteous companions would **reprove** him for his own good as a sign of genuine friendship (cf. Pr 3:11-12; 27:6). The result will be refreshing as **oil upon the head** (cf. 23:5; 133:-2). While enjoying the fellowship and correction of the righteous, his **prayer** is **still** against the **wicked** (cf. 140:9-11). His imprecation on the wicked is for their unrighteous **judges** to be **thrown down** to their deaths on **the rock** (cf. 2Ch 25:12). See comments on imprecatory psalms in the Introduction to Psalms.

C. In Preserving from the Doers of Iniquity (141:8-10)

141:8-10. David's absolute trust in God is emphasized by his declaring **my eyes are toward You, O God, the Lord** (cf. 25:15; 123:2). The conclusion of the psalm concerning taking **refuge** in God and praying for escape from the **trap** and **snares** of the enemy is parallel to 140:4-5 (see comments there).

Psalm 142: A Prayer for Deliverance

On the heading of this **Maskil of David**, see Psalm 138 introduction above as well as the headings of Pss 17 and 32. The occasion for the psalm was David's situation **when he was in the cave**, referring either to the cave of Adullam (1Sm 22:1-5) or the cave at Engedi, among the Rocks of the Wild Goats (1Sm 24:1-7). Both incidents occurred during the early period of David's flight from the murderous jealousy of Saul. This psalm, like the others around it (esp. 140 and 141) contains the similar theme of unshakeable trust in God when one suffers at the hands of the wicked (Sailhamer, *NIV Compact Bible Commentary*, 347).

A. Boldly Pour Out Complaint to the Lord (142:1-6)

142:1-2. It is an act of worship for David to **cry aloud** . . . **to the LORD** . . . to **make supplication with my voice** . . . **pour out** his **complaint before** God (cf. 77:3; 102), for in doing so he was affirming both God's willingness to listen and His power to take action. The **complaint** (i.e., lamenting his situation) was to God alone (cf. Hab 1:1-17).

142:3-4. The specifics of his complaint are: his **spirit was overwhelmed** . . . his enemies **have hidden a trap for [him]** . . . **there is no escape** . . . **no one cares for [his] soul**. Under his circumstances, David felt alone, in danger and despair (cf. 38:11; 140:4-5).

142:5-6. David continues his petition, declaring **You are my refuge** (cf. comments on 17:7; 27:13; 73:26; 91:2, 9) . . . **my portion in the land of the living** (cf. 16:5; 73:26 and comments there).

B. Affirm God's Glory as Motivation for Rescue (142:7)

142:7. The request is for the Lord to **bring my soul out of prison**. This is not a literal jail but a poetic description of his circumstances, being held captive in the cave. The goal in deliverance from all his troubles was not simply for the sake of his personal comfort and ease but **so that** he might **give thanks to** God's **name**. By resolving this situation, God would enable David to: (1) express his worship in the way that God legislated by offering Him sacrifice at the tabernacle (which he was prevented from doing as a fugitive from Saul); and (2) enhance the basis of God's praise by yet another distinct act of His redemption. Furthermore, then he could experience the benefits of being with the **righteous** who would **surround** him (cf. 140:13).

Psalm 143: A Prayer for Guidance and Deliverance

On the heading of this **Psalm of David**, see the introductory paragraph to Ps 138. Although not specified in the heading, the LXX identifies the occasion for this psalm as the time when David was forced to flee Jerusalem by his son Absalom (2Sm 15–18). This psalm of confession is one of the Penitential Psalms (cf. 6, 32, 38, 51 102, 130). If the righteous suffer at the hands of the wicked (Pss 140–142), it is important nevertheless to seek to do God's will, as is modeled in his psalm by meditating on God's word (v. 5) and seeking guidance from God Spirit (v. 10) (Sailhamer, *NIV Compact Bible Commentary*, 347).

A. The Appeal for Help in the Present (143:1-4)

143:1-4. David began his **prayer** by imploring God to **hear** him not because he merited a hearing but on the basis of God's own **faithfulness** and **righteousness**. This spiritually honest and accurate attitude of self-introspection, which is one of the main qualifiers of David as "a man after (God's) own heart" (see the comments on 1Sm 13:14), continued in his affirmation in v. 2 that his current persecution by **the enemy** (v. 3) may well be an expression of **judgment** (a general term signifying justice as in Is 9:7) or discipline. **In** God's **sight** (lit., "before You," i.e., by comparison with God) **no man living** (i.e., neither David's enemy nor David himself) **is righteous** (v. 2). God is the only measure of true righteousness, before whom even a prophet like Isaiah could do nothing but immediately confess that he was unclean (Is 6:3-5; cf. Ec 7:20; Rm 3:23).

B. The Memory of Help in the Past (143:5-6)

143:5-6. The psalms recalled God's past faithfulness. The statement **I remember** is more than a general awareness of past faithfulness, but linked to a specific event, as in God's intention that the exodus be remembered or memorialized (cf. Ex 12:14). There are close parallels between **the days of old** . . . **Your doings** . . . **the work of Your hands** and the exodus, one of the most vivid examples of God's covenant faithfulness (cf. 44:1-2 and comments there). His recollection of these is because **I meditate** on Your doing, even on the word of God that was written in the Torah (cf. 77:12; 118:27). Knowing the Lord made his **soul** long for **You, as in a parched land** (cf. 42:1-4), David was thus affirming his confidence in God's faithfulness. Just as He upheld His promise to the Israelites through the patriarchs, so too would He uphold His promise to David (2Sm 7:8-16). On the significance of stretching **out** his **hands to** God, see the comment on Ps 134:2.

C. The Plea for Help Immediately (143:7-12)

143:7-9. David needed deliverance **quickly**. In a quick succession of requests, he cried out with his need for help: **do not hide your face** . . . **let me hear Your lovingkindness** . . . **teach me the way** . . . **deliver me**.

143:10-12. Throughout it all David expressed his trust (v. 8) in God and simply wanted for God to **teach me to do Your will, for You are my God**. Most important to David was not that his persecution be resolved or his enemies annihilated, but that God's glory be manifest in his life **for the sake of Your name, O Lord**. For this reason he affirmed (as in v. 2) the need for God's correction, yet asked God to bring that discipline to an end—"Do not hide Your face [or "presence"] from me" (v. 7), while at the same he confidently affirmed **I am Your servant** (v. 12; cf. 116:16).

Psalm 144: Affirming God's All-Encompassing Provision

On the heading of this psalm, see the introductory paragraph to Ps 138. David continues with similar themes found in Pss 140–143 (see the introductions there). The distinction here, however, relates both to the imminence and the nearly apocalyptic sense of God's coming to rescue His people (vv. 5-8). It thus reflects a similar sense of the hope of the Lord's victory over His enemies and the coming of the Messiah to rule the earth (cf. Dn 7:14 and Hab 3:3-6; see the comments there; Sailhamer, *NIV Compact Bible Commentary,* 347).

A. God's Provision of Personal Care (144:1-4)

144:1-4. After opening with the expression **Blessed be the Lord** (see the comment on 103:1), David underscored both the depth and all-encompassing nature of his personal connection to God by describing Him with expressions in which the possessive pronoun "my" predominates: **my rock** (see the comment on 18:46), **my lovingkindness** (see the comment on 5:7), and **my fortress** (see the comment on 31:3). In vv. 3-4 David expanded and enhanced his devotional focus by pondering God's intimate love and concern not just for him personally but for humans as such. He wondered why God would condescend to enter into an intimate relationship (this being the sense of **take knowledge of**; see the comment on Ps 1:6) with any human being. The implicit answer is, of course, that God is not only holy, righteous, and just, but also merciful, gracious, and loving.

B. God's Provision of Protection (144:5-11)

144:5-11. The Lord has ultimate control, thus the psalmist says **Bow Your heavens** (an idiom meaning "make the sky bend down even as You descend") **O Lord, and come down** . . . **stretch forth Your hand** . . . and **rescue me and deliver me** (vv. 5, 7). In this section David affirmed God's role as the one who both protects Israel and determines her military success. God's absolute sovereignty in this respect was repeatedly impressed on David throughout the course of his career, both in his pre-reign years as a fugitive from Saul (see 1Sm 23:2, 10-12; 30:8) as well as in his throne years when leading Israel against their enemies (see esp. 2Sm 5:19, 23-24). As in Is 8:7, the enemies of Israel are described by the imagery of **great waters** (v. 7), emphasizing their greater number and military prowess, and hence David's ultimate reliance on God to **rescue** him and his people (see the comments on 124:4-5). Also, as attested in early Jewish tradition (i.e., the Targum to Psalms), the reference to **the evil sword** (v. 10) may allude to the sword of Goliath (cf. 1Sm 17:45, 51), who is a biblical symbol of Gentile opposition to God and His people.

C. God's Provision of Ongoing Life (144:12-15)

144:12-15. In this section David implored God's continued concern in providing for his people's physical and material needs, using a variety of poetic images: (1) **Let our** young **sons** be as strong as **grown-up plants**; (2) **our daughters** be **as** strong and beautiful **corner pillars** in a **palace**; (3) **our garners** (storehouses) **be full**; (4) **our flock** be so fruitful they will **bring forth thousands and ten thousands**; (5) **our cattle bear** healthy calves **without mishap**; and (6) **no outcry in our streets**, i.e., peace in the land. The psalm closes with a twofold declaration: **How blessed are the people** (cf. 2:12; 33:12 and comments there).

Psalm 145: The Threefold Basis of Blessing God's Name

On the heading of this **Psalm of Praise, of David**, see Psalm 138 introduction above. This psalm forms an alphabetic acrostic, each verse beginning with a successive letter of the Hebrew alphabet—although excluding the 14th letter *(nun),* which enables the psalm to be organized into three stanzas of seven verses each.

This is the last of David's psalms in the entire book. In his final psalm, David expresses praise to God and calls his people to praise the Lord as well. His praise of God focuses on His power (vv. 1-7), kindness (vv. 8-13), and faithfulness (vv. 14-21). An important element in Ps 145 is the scope of the kingdom David envisioned (vv. 11-13). It cannot be equated simply with the kingdom David or his sons would rule. This kingdom is the messianic kingdom that the Lord will establish and over which He will rule. It is a literal, physical, geopolitical kingdom that will last forever as David's Great Son rules over Israel and the nations (Sailhamer, *NIV Compact Bible Commentary*, 348). This indeed is a worthy subject for which to praise God!

A. The Blessing of God's Power (145:1-7)

145:1-7. The words **I will extol You, My God, O King** sets the tone for this psalm. The repetition at the end of the psalm of David's opening declaration, **And I [all flesh] will bless Your name forever and ever**, underscores the theme of the psalm itself. The specific reference in v. 1 to **God's name** (rather than just "God") indicates a specific focus on God's reputation based on His acts of deliverance and victory (both spiritual and physical; see the comments on 20:5; Gn 11:4; 12:2). On David's affirmation of God as the true King (v. 1), both of Israel as well as of creation in general, see the comments on 137:4-6.

Especially prominent in this section is the concept of God's greatness as borne out by the threefold use of "great" words (v. 3, **Great is the LORD . . . His greatness is unsearchable**; and v. 6, **I will tell of Your greatness**). On **splendor of Your majesty** (cf. 21:5 and comments there) and the sense of David's reference to God's **wonderful works** (v. 5); see comments on 9:1 and 40:5.

B. The Blessing of God's Kindness (145:8-14)

145:8-14. This section emphasizes the **gracious and merciful** character of the Lord and His majestic reign. The glory of God's name (reputation) is manifest in His kingdom, specifically as characterized by (1) the **glory** (vv. 11, 12) and **everlasting** extent (v. 13) of that over which He rules; (2) the rule itself, signified by **power** (lit., "sovereign power"; vv. 11b, 12a) and **dominion** ("sovereign might"; v. 13b), which, like the Ruler, is **gracious and merciful** (v. 8; cf. **mercies** in v. 9), **slow to anger and great in lovingkindness** (v. 8; for **lovingkindness**, see comment on 5:7); and (3) the "citizens" of His kingdom, the **godly ones** (lit., "recipients of *chesed*"). This kingdom focus of the psalm goes beyond David himself, so when he says **the LORD is faithful to all His promises** (v. 13) the psalmist is looking forward to the establishment of God's everlasting kingdom which **endures thoughout all generations** under the rule of the Messiah, the Son of David (cf. Is 9:6-7; Lk 1:33; Rv 11:15).

C. The Blessing of God's Faithfulness (145:15-21)

145:15-21. David concluded by focusing on the specific ways in which God's lovingkindness is expressed toward the citizens of His kingdom, both now as well as in the future. At that time, **the eyes of all** will **look to [God]**. He supplies their need for physical sustenance **in due time** (v. 15; i.e., consistent with His glory); He satisfies their **desire** (vv. 16, 19; esp. when such is in alignment with His own); He **is near to** them (v. 18); and He **save[s]** them (v. 19).

Finally, He **keeps** (or "preserves," "guards") them (v. 20), meaning that, from the moment that their status as citizens in God's kingdom is granted, as appropriated and expressed through their faith, He maintains that status forever (cf. Jn 10:28-29; Rm 8:38-39).

Psalms 146–150: The Conclusion to Psalms

These final five psalms are a panoply of praise for the God of glory. They are intended to be a distinct unit, as indicated by all five psalms beginning and ending with "Praise the LORD" (Hallelujah!). This identical exhortation, "Praise the LORD!", reflects the shared focus of each psalm on the praise of God. An established practice in early Jewish tradition continued to this day is to recite these five psalms, together with Ps 145 as part of the daily morning liturgy (see the Babylonian Talmud, *Shabbat* 118b; *Massekhet Soferim* xviii.1). Though none of these five psalms has a heading, thus reinforcing their cohesion, the LXX attributes the first three to the postexilic prophets Haggai and Zechariah, leaving the last two anonymous.

All the psalms in this last section of the Psalter are connected thematically. In fact, many of the themes of the entire book of Psalms are found in Ps 146: God's power as seen in creation (v. 6), His lovingkindness toward His people (vv. 7-9), and the kingdom He promised David that will be established in Zion (v. 10). Psalm 147 especially notes God's continual care for Israel as observed in His work to restore them to their land following the Babylonian exile (vv. 2-6) and to provide them with His Word (vv. 19-20). The psalmist poetically calls upon creation to praise

God in Psalm 148, because "He has lifted up a horn for His people," (v. 14; see comments on Ps 132:17) which, in the context of the entire Psalter, is a reference to the seed of David who will rescue and secure Israel (see Ps 110:7). Psalm 149 emphasizes the need to praise God for the future restoration of Israel under His sovereign and gracious hand (vv. 1-4) when He vanquishes Israel's enemies (vv. 5-9).

Psalm 150 appropriately concludes the Psalter. In that psalm, God is in His sanctuary (v. 1) receiving praise from His people (vv. 3-6) in what is best understood as an eschatological setting, providing a parallel with Dn 7:27 and Rv 4 (Sailhamer, *NIV Compact Bible Commentary*, 348). How fitting to conclude the book with a glimpse of the praise that will attend God for all eternity.

A. Psalm 146: Praise the Lord Forever

1. The Praise of God (146:1-2)

146:1-2. The culminating focus of this psalm is on God's praise, immediately signaled in the opening two verses by the threefold repetition: **Praise the Lord** (expressing utmost emphasis; see the comment on 17:3). The act of praising the Lord is lifelong: **while I live . . . while I have my being**.

2. The Power of God (146:3-6)

146:3-6. The psalmist followed this call to praise by exhorting Israel, **Do not trust in princes** who are mere **mortal** men, and **in whom there is** therefore **no salvation** (cf. comments on 118:8). In contrast, **How blessed is he whose help is** in the **God of Jacob** reflect the main themes of Pss 1:3 and 2:12 of blessedness found in **hope . . . in the Lord his God** (v. 5), revealed in God's Word and in David's future Son. The words **how blessed** in v. 5 are literally "O, the blessedness of," and refer to distinct spiritual happiness or joy. Such a person adheres to the principle of trusting and hoping in God rather than in human leaders. The Lord can be trusted, as opposed to human beings, because of His infinite power (He **made heaven and earth**) and His faithful character (He **keeps faith forever**; cf. 115:15; Rv 14:7).

3. The Provision of God (146:7-10)

146:7-9. The psalmist then considered the various ways in which God's concern is expressed as provision for His people: He provides justice (**executes justice for the oppressed**), food (**gives food to the hungry**), liberty (**sets the prisoners free**), healing (**opens the eyes of the blind**) restoration (**raises up those who are bowed down**) protection (**protects the strangers**), care (**supports the fatherless and the widow**), and moral justice (**thwarts the way of the wicked**).

146:10. The Psalm culminates with the words, **The Lord will reign forever, your God, O Zion, to all generations**, an allusion to that coming messianic kingdom. It will be manifest when He establishes His **reign** over Zion **forever** (cf. Ezk 43:7-8; Zch 14:9-11; Rv 21:2-4).

B. Psalm 147: Praise the Lord for His Care of Jerusalem

For an introduction, see Psalms 146–150: The Conclusion to Psalms above. The focus of Ps 147 is God's faithfulness to Israel in terms of His care for Jerusalem and the future of His chosen city. This is a hymn of praise without a line of lament.

1. Praise the Lord for Building up Jerusalem (147:1-6)

147:1-2. It is **good** and **pleasant** to praise the Lord (on the use of these two terms as poetic parallels, see comments on 133:1). Psalm 147 continues the focus of 146:6-10, reviewing the various expressions of God's concern for Israel—for which Israel's responsive praise is obligated, as the psalmist in his ensuing review, affirms that **the Lord builds up Jerusalem**. This is not referring to His construction of the actual city but rather to establishing the city in peace at the end of days (cf. 89:4; Is 62:10-12). This is indicated by the parallel line **He gathers the outcasts of Israel**, a statement linked to the end times promises of the messianic kingdom (cf. Is 11:12; 56:8; Ezk 39:27-28). The return from Babylon was only a preview of Israel's ultimate regathering to the land of Israel from all nations (cf. Is 11:2; Ezk 36:22-28)

147:3. The Lord is to be praised for His merciful care of Jerusalem. He **heals the brokenhearted** refers to His acts of delivering His people from oppression and distress (e.g., 34:18) and comforting them as the Lord will do in the Messianic Age (cf. Is 61:1). The Lord **binds up their wounds** (lit., "sorrows") is further image from the Messianic Age (cf. Is 30:26; 53:4; Jr 30:17).

147:4-6. The Lord is to be praised for His sovereign authority: **He counts the number of the stars** and **gives names to all of them** (cf. Gn 15:5; Is 40:26); **Great is our Lord and abundant in strength** (cf. 47:2; 48:1; 95:3; 96:4); **His understanding is infinite**. On the basis of His power and might, He is worthy to be praised; He can be depended upon to keep His promises, care for the **afflicted**, and destroy the **wicked**.

2. Praise the Lord for His Daily Care (147:7-11)

147:7-9. It is good to **sing to the LORD with thanksgiving**. He controls the **earth** as indicated by the mention of **clouds** . . . **rain** . . . **mountains** (v. 8). He supplies every need: **gives to** every **beast** (referring to land animals generally) **its food** . . . as well as to the **ravens** (as an example of the birds).

147:10-11. The Lord **does not delight in the strength of the horse** (cf. 20:7; 33:16) nor **take pleasure in the legs of man** (cf. 18:33; Am 2:14-15). This is a statement regarding war horses and military men, as indicated by the next statement **The LORD favors those who fear Him** (cf. Ps 34:8-14) and **wait for His lovingkindness** (cf. comment on 5:7). God's delight is in those who worship and trust in Him, not in those who depend upon themselves.

3. Praise the Lord, O Jerusalem (147:12-20)

147:12. Jerusalem . . . **Zion** is commanded to **Praise the LORD** . . . **your God**. Jerusalem, symbol of the Jewish people, has a unique and privileged relationship with the Lord (cf. v. 20; see 9:11 and comments there).

147:13-14. This section highlights God's care for Jerusalem. He **strengthened** . . . **your gates** (cf. 87:2), provided security, **blessed your sons, makes peace** (cf. 29:11), and gives prosperity by causing the land to produce the **finest wheat**.

147:15-18. He provides care for Jerusalem as He oversees the whole weather spectrum (cf. 33:4; 104:4-5) when **He sends forth His command to the earth** (*eretz*, "land," often used specifically of Israel) and **gives snow**. . . **frost** . . . **ice** . . . **cold** . . . warmth to **melt** . . . **wind**. . . **and the waters**.

147:19-20. Among these gifts the Lord gave His people, the most significant gift was His Word (cf. 119; 138:2): **He declares His words to Jacob** (cf. comments on 14:7), **His statutes and His ordinances to Israel** (cf. Dt 6:4-9; 31:9-14; 33:3-4; Rm 3:1-2; 9:4-5). The Jewish people are unique in their relationship with the Lord as His chosen nation, and His faithfulness to them is unending (cf. Jr 31:35-37). **He has not dealt thus with any nation** . . . **Praise the Lord!**

C. Psalm 148: Praise the Lord, All the Earth

For an introduction, see Psalms 146–150: The Conclusion to Psalms above. In Ps 148, the psalmist underscored the praise due to God from all His creation. The psalm is organized into three distinct venues: in the heavens (vv. 1-6), on earth (vv. 7-12), and concluding among His people, Israel (vv. 13-14).

1. Let the Heavens Praise the Lord (148:1-6)

148:1-6. The key word is **Praise**, used nine times in this section. This section concerns **Prais[ing] the LORD from the heavens**. Concerning God's work in **the heavens** (v. 1a, introducing the entire venue) the psalmist moved from highest to lowest, starting with **the heights** (v. 1), the "third heaven" where God dwells (2Co 12:2) and which is also inhabited by **His angels** (explained as **His hosts** in v. 2). Then the psalmist mentioned the **highest heavens** (v. 4), that is, the universe beyond the earth's atmosphere (v. 4a) including the **sun and moon** and **all the stars** (v. 3), and the sky (as depicted by the **waters** . . . **above**, i.e., the clouds). All that fills these three heavens are obligated to praise God because He created and **established them**.

2. Let the Earth Praise the Lord (148:7-12)

148:7-10. Praise the LORD from the earth is the key idea of this section. Commanding these nonhuman elements of the **earth** to praise the Lord is personification, giving them human emotional characteristic in order to make the point that the Lord deserves praise for everything He has created (cf. 150:6). The psalmist started with the waters around the edges of the land (inhabited by the **sea monsters**, lit., "creatures"; see the comment on Gn 1:21) **and all deeps**, including the depths not just of oceans but also of lakes and rivers (cf. Ex 15:5). Then the psalmist catalogued the inanimate things that both affect the land, **fire**. . . **hail** . . . **snow** . . . **clouds** . . . **wind**; and the geography and vegetation that cover it, **mountains** . . . **hills** . . . **trees** (cf. Is 55:6); as well as animal life, **beasts** . . . **cattle** . . . **creeping things** . . . **fowl** (cf. 89:11; 90:1-2; 96:11-12; 113:6; 136:5-6).

148:11-12. This is a general call for all people and human authorities, **Kings** . . . **Princes** . . . **judges**, and all people of every age, **both young** . . . **and old**, to praise the Lord.

3. Let the People of Israel Praise the Lord (148:13-14)

148:13-14. The psalm culminates with the truth that **His name**, the name of the Lord (cf. 23:3; 31:3 and comments there) **alone is exalted** (cf. Ex 15:1, 21; 2Sm 22:47; Ps 18:46; 108:5; Zch 14:9, 16). Then it focuses on the Lord's relationship with **His people** (cf. Ps 147:19-20). Concerning God's work among **His people** Israel, the psalmist emphasized God's perpetual concern for His people and Israel's consequent obligation of praise by (1) affirming that God has **lifted up a**

horn for them (v. 14; i.e., granted them strength; [see the comments on 17:3; 74:5]) especially strength as found in the "horn of David" (132:17; Lk 1:69), the Messiah; (2) referring to them as **His godly ones** (lit., "recipients of *chesed*," see Ps 97:10); and (3) describing them as **a people near to Him**, an allusion to Dt 4:7, signifying access to God on the basis of their relationship to Him. As the fulfillment of His promises to Israel, God would send the Messiah Jesus, through whom individual Jewish people and Gentiles would have access to forgiveness of sin and eternal life.

D. Psalm 149: Praise the Lord All Israel

For an introduction, see Psalms 146–150: The Conclusion to Psalms above. The focus of this hymn of praise is Israel's celebration at the establishment of the messianic kingdom. At that time Zion will be restored and the enemies of Israel vanquished. Psalm 149 mirrors the content of Ps 2.

1. Israel Should Rejoice in Their King (149:1-5)

149:1-3. The opening praise of the Lord in this psalm narrowed the focus from the universal of Ps 148, to **Israel** and **Zion**. The call is to **be glad in** their **Maker** (cf. 95:6), to **rejoice in their King** (cf. 2:6; 145:1). To **praise His name** (v. 3) is to praise the Lord for His excellent reputation (cf. 23:3; 31:3 and comments there), and they are to do so with **dancing . . . let them sing praises . . . with timbrel and lyre** (cf. 150:1-5). **Godly ones** occurs three times (vv. 1, 5, 9) in this psalm. There has always been a remnant of godly people in Israel (e.g., 1Kg 19:18), but the focus of this psalm together with the following one is ultimately on the future. Then **the sons of Zion** (all Israel) will **rejoice in their King** (Jesus the Messiah; see comments at Zch 12:10 and Rm 11:26). Then, the kingdom of Messiah Jesus will be established.

149:4-5. The Lord created humanity (cf. Gn 1:27) and chose Israel to be His inheritance because He loves her (cf. Dt. 7:7-8; Ps 100:3). So it is fitting that **the LORD takes pleasure in His people** (cf. 22:3; 147:11). In His loving care, He will **beautify** ("adorn"' cf. Is 61:3) **the afflicted** ("humble"; cf. Ps 147:6), those who are totally dependent upon Him, with **salvation** (cf. 3:8; 18:46; 24:5). Certainly in light of the Lord's attitudes and actions (v. 4), **the godly ones** (cf. v. 1) should **exult in glory** and **sing for joy on their beds**.

2. The Lord Will Execute Judgment on the Enemies of Israel (149:6-9)

146:6-9. While **the high praises of God** are **in their mouth**, at the same time the people are to act in divine retribution and take up the **two-edged sword . . . to execute vengeance on the** pagan **nations** who are the enemies of the Lord and His people Israel. This will occur at the end of days (cf. Is 34; Jr 46:10-12; Mc 5:7-15) and **the judgment written**, that is, their final judgment will take place, as recorded in Scripture (Is 45:14-17; Zch 12:6-9; Ps 110:3, 5-7). Just as when David slew Goliath to honor the reputation of the Lord (1Sm 17:1-47), so this judgment will be **an honor for all His godly ones.**

E. Psalm 150: The Great Hallelujah

For an introduction, see Psalms 146–150: The Conclusion to Psalms above. This final psalm is the great hallelujah, not only as the conclusion of Book Five (cf. 41:13; 72:18-19; 89:52; 106:48), but as the culmination of the whole Psalter.

1. Praise the Lord in the Sanctuary (150:1-2)

150:1-2. The psalmist here concluded the Psalter with a final, emphatic exhortation to offer praise to God. The venue for His praise is **His sanctuary** (lit., "holiness," which may also refer to the holy of holies, or, perhaps His "holy height" [Ps 102:19; i.e., the "third heaven"] as indicated by the parallelism with **His mighty expanse** (the sky, as in Gn 1:7-8). Thus, the location of praise may be God's heavenly sanctuary as well as the earthly temple.

2. Praise the Lord with Music and Dancing (150:3-5)

150:3-5. The enumeration of instruments in vv. 3-5 with which to accompany this praise—the **timbrel** and **lyre**—alludes to the span of praise offered to God throughout the OT, from "the lyre and the pipe" first mentioned in Gn 4:21 and the "dancing . . . timbrel and lyre" of Ps 149:3 (cf. Miriam and women of Israel, Ex 15:20); to the "cymbals, harps and lyres" that accompanied the praise of the restored exiles (cf. Ezr 3:10; Neh 12:27). These instructions for joyful praise will be fully carried out during the rejoicing in the messianic kingdom (cf. Is 35:10; 51:11).

3. Let Everything Praise the Lord (150:6)

150:6. Consistent with his focus on the citizens of God's future kingdom, the psalmist concludes with a final exhortation, not to the godly ones of Israel alone, but to **everything that has breath** (i.e., humanity at large, comprised of redeemed Jewish people and redeemed Gentiles; cf. Is 56:7; Eph 2:15; Rv 5:6-10, 12-13). Together they will one day lift up their voices in unison before the throne of God and cry out, **Praise the LORD!** (*Hallelu-Yah!*).

BIBLIOGRAPHY

Alden, Robert L. *Psalms.* 3 vols. Everyman's Bible Commentary. Chicago: Moody, 1976.

Anderson, A. A. *Psalms.* 2 vols. The New Century Bible Commentary. Grand Rapids, MI: Eerdmans, 1981.

Goldingay, John. *Psalms.* 3 vols. Baker Commentary on the Old Testament. Grand Rapids, MI : Baker, 2008.

Kidner, Derek. *Psalms 1–72* and *Psalms 73–150*. Tyndale Old Testament Commentaries. Downers Grove, IL: InterVarsity, 2009.

Ross, Allen. *A Commentary on the Psalms, Volume 1: Psalms 1–41* and *Psalms 42–89*. Kregel Exegetical Library. Grand Rapids, MI: Kregel, 2012, 2013 respectively.

Sailhamer, John H. *NIV Compact Bible Commentary*. Grand Rapids, MI: Zondervan, 1994.

VanGemeren, Willem. *Psalms*. The Expositor's Bible Commentary, revised edition, Grand Rapids, MI: Zondervan, 2008.

Waltke, Bruce K., and James M. Houston. *The Psalms as Christian Worship: An Historical Commentary*. Grand Rapids, MI: Eerdmans, 2010.

Wilson, Gerald H. *Psalms Volume 1*. New International Version Application Commentary. Grand Rapids, MI: Zondervan, 2002.

PROVERBS

DAVID FINKBEINER

INTRODUCTION

When people think of the OT Wisdom literature (which includes Job, Ecclesiastes, and some Psalms) they usually first think of Proverbs, and for good reason. This book does indeed live up to its reputation as a treasure trove of biblical wisdom.

Author. Proverbs is an anthology of wisdom that explicitly includes the voices of Solomon (1:1; 10:1; 25:1), the "wise" (22:17; 24:23), Agur (30:1), and Lemuel (31:1). There was also the editorial work of the "men of Hezekiah" (25:1) along with, presumably, a final editor or editors who put the whole collection together in its finished form. And when one considers the international borrowing of proverbs among different peoples, one can readily recognize that Proverbs does not relay the thought of only a single human author.

Nevertheless, it is also true that the most significant authorial voice in the book is that of Solomon. Several factors support this claim. First, when comparing its structure with the structure of other works of wisdom in the ANE, Pr 1:1–22:16 displays a unity as the work of Solomon. "The corpus conforms precisely in its structure with many of the ancient Near Eastern 'instruction' documents: main title with preamble (1:1-7), a prologue (collection 1: 1:8–9:18), a subtitle to collection 2 (10:1), and the main text (10:2–22:16)" (Bruce Waltke, with Charles Yu, *An Old Testament Theology: An Exegetical, Canonical, and Thematic Approach* [Grand Rapids, MI: Zondervan, 2007], 905). Second, the words of the wise (22:17–24:34) most likely are Solomon's own compilation and adaptation of wisdom from other sources, appended to 1:1–22:16. After all, since its author is not named (which is not typical of works of wisdom instruction in the ANE), the "I" (22:19) who introduces this section most naturally accords with the Solomonic "I" of chaps. 1–9 (Waltke, *OT Theology*, 905). Third, chaps. 25–29 are another section of Solomonic proverbs, this time collected by scholars in the time of King Hezekiah (25:1). Fourth, Solomon's work in collecting and disseminating the wisdom in Proverbs fits well the biblical picture of him as a famous sage and composer of wisdom writings (1Kg 4:29-34; cf. 1Kg 3).

Hence, with the exception of chaps. 30–31, all the previous sections of the book have a direct connection with Solomon. This makes the superscription in 1:1, "the proverbs of Solomon," an appropriate description of the book as a whole.

Date. The authorship of the book gives parameters to its date. Given the conclusion above regarding chaps. 1–24, this section would be dated to the time of Solomon (around 950 BC). The compilation of chaps. 25–29, as indicated in the text itself, would be dated at the time of Hezekiah (716–687 BC). What about chaps. 30–31? There is no external or internal evidence to date this material. Consequently, no firm date can be affixed to the final editing of Proverbs, though it is possible that it was as early as the time of Hezekiah.

Recipients. The authorship question also gives direction to the setting and audience of the book. The prominence of Solomon, as well as the influence of Hezekiah's men and King Lemuel make a royal court setting for the compilation of much of Proverbs evident. But the proverbs do not deal solely with court life. Indeed, in regard to the transmission of the wisdom in Proverbs, the setting of the book seems more attuned to the family—a father addressing his son (or a mother her son in chap. 31). "Solomon intended to transmit his wisdom to Israel's youths by putting his proverbs in the mouths of godly parents

(1:8-9), even as Moses disseminated the law in the home (cf. Dt 6:7-9)" (Bruce K. Waltke, *The Book of Proverbs, Chapters 1–15*, NICOT [Grand Rapids, MI: Eerdmans, 2004], 63).

Structure and Genre. The text of Proverbs clearly indicates that it is a collection of different works of wisdom, each of which is usually headed by a title of sorts. This sets up the basic organization of the book.

After a short preface to the book as a whole (1:1-7), the first nine chapters (1:8–9:18) are a collection of lengthy discourses on wisdom. These discourses differ markedly from the two line aphorisms people usually associate with Proverbs. They are a collection of lengthy poems primarily in the form either of a father addressing his son or of a personified wisdom herself calling for people to follow her ways. These discourses usually have three parts: (1) a call to the addressee exhorting him to listen to the lesson and providing him motivation to do so (e.g., 2:1-11), (2) a lesson commending the way of wisdom and/or warning against the way of folly (e.g., 2:12-19), and (3) a conclusion that summarizes the teaching (e.g., 2:20-22) (Tremper Longman III, *Proverbs*, BCOT [Grand Rapids, MI: Baker, 2006], 30). This section primarily functions to exhort the reader to embrace the way of wisdom rather than the way of folly, making it a fitting beginning to Proverbs as a whole.

The next section (10:1–22:16) is called "the proverbs of Solomon." The majority of this section is made up of the two-line proverb so familiar to many. There are four major questions to consider in connection with this literary form.

First, what exactly is a proverb? A proverb (Hb. *mashal*, "comparison," "parable," "proverb") is a short wisdom saying—"wisdom in a nutshell" (M. Salisbury, quoted in Michael V. Fox, *Proverbs 1–9: A New Translation with Introduction and Commentary*, AB [New Haven: Yale University Press, 2000], 15). The Hebrew term itself likely picks up on the idea of a comparison, perhaps referring to metaphors and similes in the proverb or to how the lines of the proverb relate to one another, but more likely referring to how the wise reader connects his situation to the message of the proverb (Waltke, *Book of Proverbs 1–15*, 56).

Second, what are some characteristics of a proverb? Proverbs share the characteristics of all Hebrew poetry. They are quite concise, but their brevity is dense with meaning and motivation. Moreover, like much good poetry, they are filled with figures of speech and laden with imagery, creating pictures with words. This helps the reader not only to remember but also to reflect further on what is said.

Proverbs are also characterized by another key feature of Hebrew poetry, parallelism, not rhyme schemes familiar in English poems. Hebrew poetry is arranged in groups of two or more lines that are parallel in structure, though they do not merely say the same thing. They are "juxtaposed in such a way that the words and images play off against each other and suggest a web of meanings" (Fox, *Proverbs 1–9*, 15). So in a two-line parallelism (as are most proverbs in this section), the second line might, for example, intensify, specify, reinforce, expand on, or contrast with the first line (William W. Klein, Craig L. Blomberg, and Robert L. Hubbard, *Introduction to Biblical Interpretation* [Dallas: Word, 1993], 225). The majority of the proverbs in this particular section of the book have *antithetical* parallelism (a contrast between the two lines). In any case, the key task for the interpreter is to seek to understand how the lines interact with one another.

Beyond these characteristics that proverbs share with Hebrew poetry in general, a proverb has a distinctive feature. A proverb, by its very nature, presents a general principle, a rule of thumb. This feature leads to a third question: how should one construe a proverb? Christians often misconstrue a proverb by understanding it as a rigid command or a fixed promise. On this view, a proverb could not have any exceptions. But this fundamentally misunderstands the genre. For "the proverb form, no matter the cultural background, presupposes the right circumstances for its proper application" (Tremper Longman III, *How to Read Proverbs* [Downers Grove, IL: InterVarsity, 2002], 48). That is, proverbs have a range of application. Some may virtually always apply; many others do not apply to every situation. But it takes a wise person to know when each applies. For example, in light of 26:4-5, should one answer a fool according to his folly (v. 5) or not (v. 4)? It depends on the situation. "A wise person knows the right time and the right situation for the right proverb" (Longman, *How to Read Proverbs*, 49). This was one of the problems with Job's friends. Many of the principles they articulated were proverbially true, but they inappropriately applied those principles to Job's situation.

Finally, how are the proverbs in this section (10:1–22:16) related to one another? Many have argued that the proverbs in this section are put together randomly, with no particular arrangement. On a cursory reading, this certainly seems to be the case. Recently, however, several scholars have argued that there are literary units within this section, although there is no widespread consensus on how those units might be delineated precisely because no unit is obvious on a cursory reading. Advocates appeal to various features like literary devices (e.g., chiasm or *inclusio*), repeated sounds (e.g., alliteration, assonance), or repeated words or ideas as the basis for a literary unit.

It is quite possible that, as they were collected, some of these proverbs were put together in small literary units. However, as a general rule, it seems more prudent to approach this section as a random collection of proverbs. After all, when used originally in their oral context, they did stand alone (this section is a *collection* of proverbs, after all). Furthermore, they do not usually appear to be grouped together in terms of their actual content. Moreover, their largely random arrangement reflects real life, which is muddled and resistant to neat categorization (Longman, *How to Read Proverbs*, 40). In this sense, these "proverbs are presented in the seemingly haphazard way we encounter the issues with which they deal" in real life (Duane Garrett, *Proverbs, Ecclesiastes, Song of Songs*, NAC [Nashville: Broadman & Holman, 1993], 46).

This is a significant question because it directly influences how one interprets these proverbs. In short, what precisely is the context? As suggested above, this commentary will usually approach each proverb on its own without reference to a larger context. However, comments will also sometimes take account of two types of contexts to nuance the interpretation of certain proverbs. When a proverb does seem to be grouped in a unit with other proverbs, we will consider the *literary* context. And when a proverb deals with a certain topic, we will sometimes take into consideration the *topical* context (i.e., other proverbs that deal with the same topic).

The next section in Proverbs is the "sayings of the wise" (22:17–24:34). Four features are notable in this section. First, this section is different in style from the previous one. Most of the sayings are more extended than the two-line proverbs that dominate the previous section, and they reflect the style of a father's address to his son (so prominent earlier in chaps. 1–9). Second, this section has two parts, the "thirty sayings of the wise" (22:17–24:22) and "more sayings of the wise" (24:23-34). Third, there is some disagreement over the exact delineation of the "thirty sayings" in part one (an issue that will be addressed within the commentary itself). Fourth, parts of this section are strikingly parallel with the words of the Egyptian wise man Amenemope. Whichever work was written earlier, this feature is a reminder of the international character of wisdom in the ancient world, as previously noted.

The "sayings of the wise" are followed by another collection of Solomon's proverbs (25:1–29:27). These sayings were collected during the reign of Hezekiah (25:1). They are similar in style to the first collection of Solomon's proverbs (10:1–22:16).

The last two chapters of Proverbs consist of three separate sections. The first of these is the sayings of Agur (30:1-33). The identity of Agur is obscure; he may have been an unknown Israelite or even a Gentile wise man. One interesting feature of this section is the repeated use of numerical proverbs (e.g., 30:18-19). The second section in these chapters is the sayings of King Lemuel (31:1-9). Like Agur, Lemuel's identity is obscure, as is his kingdom. But he too may have been a Gentile. The words in this section actually reflect the teaching of Lemuel's mother, and they focus on the characteristics of an ideal king. The third section deals with another ideal, that of the ideal wife. This is an acrostic poem (each line of the poem beginning with a subsequent letter of the Hebrew alphabet) describing the virtuous woman. As argued in the commentary, this poem is likely a continuation of the words of King Lemuel.

Themes. When considering the theology of Proverbs, one could profitably explore numerous specific topics addressed in the book (e.g., wealth, laziness, speech, etc.). Unfortunately, space precludes this commentary from such investigations (see Longman, *Proverbs*, 549–578 and Derek Kidner, *Proverbs: An Introduction and Commentary*, TOTC [Downers Grove, IL: Tyndale, 1964], 31–56, for good examples). However, certain theological themes are so important in understanding the book as a whole that they need to be addressed here at the outset.

The Nature of Wisdom. Though contemporary Americans value wisdom (just check out the self-help section of a local bookstore), America is not a proverbial society. For Americans, proverbs are trite and infrequently used. But this is not the case in many other cultures. It certainly was not the case in ancient Israel where proverbs were a part of everyday life for all levels of society.

Israel was not alone in valuing proverbial wisdom. The larger culture of the ancient Near East, of which Israel was a part, also greatly valued proverbs, and there was a good deal of interchange between ANE cultures. So even though Israel's wisdom was distinct in important ways, it also intentionally included international dialogue partners. For example, one can see direct parallels between several proverbs (particularly in 22:17–24:22) and the instructions of the Egyptian wise man Amenemope (an Egyptian government official probably sometime before 1000 BC). This should be no surprise in light of Solomon's great wisdom, which was known across the ancient world (1Kg 4:29-31). "While the Old Testament scorns the magic and superstition which debased much of this thought (Is. 47:12,13), and the pride which inflated it (Jb. 5:13), it can speak of the gentile sages with a respect it never showed towards their priests. Solomon outstripped them, but we are expected to be impressed by the fact" (Kidner, *Proverbs*, 17).

What does Israel's interchange with its neighbors imply about the nature of wisdom? Wisdom focuses on living in this world and in that sense has a foundation in general revelation. This is why non-Israelite wise men could look at the world and make wise observations. In looking long and hard at this world, the sage might make general conclusions, seeking to interpret what is happening in life broadly (as in Job or Ecclesiastes), or he might make more concrete conclusions, seeking to provide guidelines for living life skillfully (as in much of Proverbs). Nevertheless, this world is *God's* world, and so biblical wisdom is superior to other wisdom, for it acknowledges that God is central. While pagan wisdom sought to control and manipulate the world order in favor of one's own interests, biblical wisdom is rooted in the fear and worship of the living God (Pr 1:7; 9:10).

Wisdom as Theology. It was pointed out above, in connection with the international flavor of ANE wisdom, that wisdom has a particular interest in truth gleaned from observing life in this world. Yet this point should not be overstated. The book of Proverbs is no more just another piece of ancient wisdom than a priceless masterpiece is just another painting. Nor is Proverbs just a collection of practical, secular advice with a few references to the Lord tacked on here and there to give it a pious veneer. Biblical wisdom is fundamentally theological precisely because it is rooted in the Lord Himself. Consider the following two crucial points.

First, biblical wisdom is revealed from God Himself. It is not merely the product of man's insights into the world. Solomon received his wisdom from God (1Kg 4:29), as Solomon himself acknowledges (Pr 2:6). It is this divine wisdom that has been God's ever-present companion from the beginning of time (8:22-31). Indeed, Agur makes clear that God's wisdom, revealed in His Word, far exceeds the limitations of human capacities (30:2-6). Little wonder that Agur and Lemuel both consider their sayings to be an "oracle" (i.e., a prophetic revelation) from God (30:1; 31:1; see commentary below) (Waltke, *OT Theology*, 915–921).

Second, biblical wisdom reflects the worship of God Himself. This is why the fear of the Lord is the key to wisdom (cf. 1:7). Longman has pointed out that Pr 1–9 is really a hermeneutical guide for understanding the rest of Proverbs. Its major focus is to contrast wisdom with folly and extol the advantages of wisdom. This contrast is most pronounced in the comparison between Lady Wisdom and Woman Folly (chap. 9). Both invite the passerby (the reader) to join her for a fellowship meal. Both of their houses are situated on the highest point of the city, the place where temples were situated in the ancient world. Ultimately, both are calling the reader to worship either the Lord (in the case of wisdom) or idols (in the case of folly) (Longman, *Proverbs*, 58–61). This makes the decision between wisdom and folly a matter of life and death. Those who choose wisdom will inevitably fear (or worship) the Lord (1:7; 9:10) and put their trust in Him (3:5-6; 14:26; 16:3, 20; 18:10; 19:23; 22:19; 28:25). In the end, the wisdom sayings are effective because of the Lord who has revealed them to His sages and because He sustains them (Waltke, *OT Theology*, 921).

The Wise. Although it is not possible here to survey thoroughly the teaching of Proverbs on wisdom and the wise, consider three broad points. First, Proverbs uses a vast array of terms to describe wisdom and the wise. The full array of terms will be seen in the commentary below (e.g., 1:2-6), but Kidner's survey provides a helpful sample. The wise are *disciplined*, having received wise "instruction" (*musar*; e.g., 1:2-3) and accepted "reproof" (*tokachat*; e.g., 1:23; 3:11). The wise are also *discerning* because they have "understanding" (*binah*; *tebunah*; e.g., 1:2; 2:2). Moreover, they demonstrate practical *common sense* ("wise behavior"; *sekel*; e.g., 1:3; 12:8). This term was used of Bezalel, the craftsman whom the Lord gave *skill* for the building of the tabernacle (Ex 31). Hence, its usage in Proverbs should be understood as "skill for living." The proverbs speak of "sound wisdom" (*tushiyyah*; e.g., Pr 2:7; 8:14) in times when resourcefulness is needed. Similarly, the wise have *shrewdness* ("prudence";*'ormah*; e.g., 1:4) and "discretion" (*mezimmah*; e.g., 1:4); they understand the situation and plan accordingly. Finally, they have "knowledge" (*da'at*; e.g., 2:5; 3:6) and "learning" (*leqach*; e.g., 1:5) of God and His truth (Kidner, *Proverbs*, 36–37).

Second, because the wise by definition fear and trust the Lord, Proverbs inextricably links being wise with godliness. Wisdom is fundamentally spiritual and ethical. The wise are thus righteous (*tsedeq*; e.g., 1:3), just (*mishpat*; e.g., 1:3), and fair ("equity"; *mesharim*; e.g., 1:3). Similarly, they are also characterized as blameless ("integrity"; *tom*; e.g., 2:7), "good" (*tob*; e.g., 2:20), "upright" (*yashar*; e.g., 2:7). They also exemplify kindness ("steadfast love"; *chesed*; e.g., 3:3) and faithfulness ("truth";*'emet* ; e.g., 3:3) (Waltke, *Book of Proverbs 1–15*, 97–100).

Third, wisdom is both compelling and accessible. Wisdom is shown not only as having innumerable benefits and rewards (and folly its dangers), but it is often pictured as a regal lady who is utterly incomparable and yet also available to all who seek her. For those willing to turn from folly and seek wisdom and the Lord who gives it, wisdom may be found.

The Fool. As with the wise, there is also a wide variety of terms for the fool. The mildest is the "naive" (*peti*; e.g., 14:15), who is gullible, aimless, and easily led astray. But he is not incorrigible and can be taught wisdom if he will listen. More intransigent is the typical "fool" in proverbs, called the *kesil* (e.g., 17:16) or the *'ewil* (e.g., 24:7). This type includes "people with morally deficient characters that prompt their irrational behavior. They are blockheads because, deaf to wisdom, from their distorted moral vision, of which they are cocksure, they delight in twisting values that benefit the community" (Waltke, *Book of Proverbs 1–15*, 112). Even worse is the "scoffer" (*lets*; e.g., 9:7-8), who is utterly arrogant and hardened against wisdom and correction. His sneering attitude is repulsive, and his influence in society is noxious. Another type of fool deserving special mention is the "sluggard" (*'atsel*; e.g., 26:13-16), whose laziness makes him a menace to himself and others. These terms make clear that, as with wisdom, so too folly is fundamentally spiritual and ethical. So, for example, the "wicked" (*resha'im*; e.g., 10:3), the *perverse* (*tahppukot*; e.g., 6:14), the "devious" (*luz*; e.g., 3:32), and the "treacherous" (*bogedim*; e.g., 11:3, 6) are all fools as well.

Life and Death. A major theme in Proverbs is the two paths, those of wisdom and folly. Wisdom's path is straight and smooth and leads to life; folly's path is crooked and hard and leads to death. But what exactly does Proverbs mean by "life" and "death," and do these concepts include *eternal* life and death?

In Proverbs, "life" sometimes refers merely to physical life (e.g., 31:12). But typically it goes beyond that to include a quality of life that involves material, social, psychological, moral, and spiritual well-being (3:21-22; 8:35; 10:16; 15:27; 16:15; 19:23; 21:21; 22:4). At its heart, life is tied inextricably to fellowship with the Lord (e.g., 2:5-8; 8:35). While Proverbs does not explore life after physical death in detail, it does indicate that abundant life in fellowship with the Lord continues after physical death (12:28; 14:32; 15:24; 23:17-18). This eternal, qualitative nature of life is why Proverbs consistently describes the wicked who are still physically alive as partaking not in life, but in death (Waltke, *Book of Proverbs 1–15*, 104–107; Kidner, *Proverbs*, 53–55).

What, then, is "death" in Proverbs? When taken in light of the entire OT, Proverbs included, "death is a whole realm in conflict with life, rather than a single and merely physical event" (Kidner, *Proverbs*, 55). To be sure, the death that folly and wickedness bring may well be physical (e.g., the result of capital justice for adultery, Lv 20:10; Dt 22:22). But death continues to endure in the grave (Sheol and Abaddon), and it can also come to those physically alive "in the forms of sickness (e.g., Ps. 116:3), calamity (Dt. 30:15) and above all, sin (Gn. 2:17)" (Kidner, *Proverbs,* 56). Most significantly, death has no part in the kind of abundant life that pertains to never-ending fellowship with God (Waltke, *Book of Proverbs 1–15*, 105), with all its attendant blessings. For a similar understanding of death in the NT, see the comments on Rm 6:15-20; 7:14-25; 8:12-13.

Retribution. Besides life and death, various rewards and punishments are said to follow from wisdom/righteousness and folly/wickedness respectively (e.g., Pr 3:2, 9-10; 10:3; 21:7). This theology of retribution, so common in Proverbs, must be qualified by four important considerations. First, these retributive statements are proverbial. As discussed above, proverbs are not mechanistic promises but statements with a range of application. And that application may need to be qualified by other proverbs and biblical teaching that present mitigating factors. "A single proverb does not intend to address all the nuances of a situation; it just gives a snapshot of life to motivate proper behavior" (Longman, *Proverbs*, 85). So, for example, though God blesses the righteous and judges the wicked, Proverbs (as well as Job, Ecclesiastes, and Psalms) also indicates that there are times when the wicked do seem to prosper (cf. 10:2; 11:4) and the righteous suffer (24:16).

This leads to a second consideration. Retributive statements must be understood with a long-range perspective. Any gains for wicked fools and any setbacks for the righteous wise are short-lived (cf. 24:15-16). Put differently, viewed in light of eternity, it is certainly the case that wisdom/righteousness is blessed and wickedness/folly is cursed. While that blessing/cursing may not always be seen immediately, it will be seen inevitably. This long-term perspective fosters complete trust in the Lord (Waltke, *Book of Proverbs 1–15*, 109; cf. 3:5-6).

However, third, one usually does not need to wait until eternity to see the principles of retribution at work. For example, generally speaking, experience even in this fallen world demonstrates that those who are self-controlled, diligent, wise in their speech, and gracious to others will prosper far more than those who are not. While mitigating factors may exist (see above), they are exceptions to a rule that generally pertains.

Finally, God Himself stands behind retributive justice. The general principles pertain because the Lord built the world that way (Longman, *Proverbs*, 84). And, in any case, in the end God will bring all things into judgment (cf. Ec 12:14). This is why the wise will fear and trust in the Lord.

OUTLINE

- I. Solomon's Collection (1:1–24:34)
  - A. Introduction (1:1-7)
    - 1. Title (1:1)
    - 2. Purpose (1:2-6)
    - 3. Theme (1:7)
  - B. Extended Discourses on Wisdom (1:8–9:18)
    - 1. Lesson 1: Beware of Violent Companions (1:8-19)
    - 2. Wisdom's First Call (1:20-33)
    - 3. Lesson 2: Wisdom's Protection (2:1-22)
      - a. Wisdom's Conditions: Receive and Seek It (2:1-4)
      - b. Wisdom's Benefits: Protection (2:5-11)
      - c. What Wisdom Protects From (2:12-19)
      - d. Summary (2:20-22)
    - 4. Lesson 3: Wisdom as Worship (3:1-12)
    - 5. Poem: the Value of Lady Wisdom (3:13-20)
    - 6. Lesson 4: The Benefits of Wise Dealings (3:21-35)
      - a. Wisdom's Safety (3:21-26)
      - b. Wise Dealings with Others (3:27-31)
      - c. Motivations for Wise Dealings (3:32-35)
    - 7. Lesson 5: A Grandfather's Lesson on the Value of Lady Wisdom (4:1-9)
    - 8. Lesson 6: Keeping on the Right Path (4:10-19)
    - 9. Lesson 7: Guarding Your Heart (4:20-27)

a. Guarding the Receptive Organs (4:20-22)
b. Guarding the Heart (4:23)
c. Guarding the Active Organs (4:24-27)

10. Lesson 8: Passion's Proper Place (5:1-23)
 a. Introductory Exhortation (5:1-2)
 b. The Seductress: Passion's Improper Place (5:3-14)
  (1) The Danger of the Seductress (5:3-6)
  (2) The Central Exhortation (5:7-8)
  (3) The Results of Not Heeding the Exhortation (5:9-14)
 c. One's Wife and Passion's Proper Place (5:15-20)
 d. Conclusion (5:21-23)
11. Warnings against Foolish People (6:1-19)
 a. Warning Concerning Becoming a Guarantor (6:1-5)
 b. Warning Concerning the Lazy Man (6:6-11)
 c. Warning Concerning Troublemakers (6:12-19)
  (1) Describing Troublemakers (6:12-15)
  (2) The Lord's View of Troublemakers (6:16-19)
12. Lesson 9: Warnings against the Adulteress (6:20-35)
 a. Introduction (6:20-24)
 b. Central Exhortation (6:25)
 c. Supporting Reasons for the Exhortation (6:26-35)
13. Lesson 10: More Warnings against the Adulteress (7:1-27)
 a. Introductory Exhortation (7:1-5)
 b. The Story of the Seductress and the Simpleton (7:6-23)
  (1) The Setting (7:6-9)
  (2) The Seductress (7:10-12)
  (3) The Seduction (7:13-21)
  (4) The Surrender (7:21-23)
 c. Epilogue: Concluding Exhortation (7:24-27)
14. Wisdom's Second Call (8:1-36)
 a. Preface to Wisdom's Address (8:1-3)
 b. Wisdom's Opening Exhortation (8:4-11)
 c. Wisdom's Autobiography (8:12-31)
  (1) Wisdom's Autobiography in History (8:12-21)
  (2) Wisdom's Autobiography before History (8:22-31)
   (a) Wisdom's Existence before Creation (8:22-26)
   (b) Wisdom's Participation in Creation (8:27-31)
  (3) Lady Wisdom and Christ
 d. Final Exhortation (8:32-36)
15. Conclusion: Two Invitations (9:1-18)
 a. Lady Wisdom's Banquet Invitation (9:1-6)
 b. Interlude (9:7-12)
 c. Woman Folly's Banquet Invitation (9:13-18)

C. The Proverbs of Solomon (10:1–22:16)
D. Thirty Sayings of the Wise (22:17–24:22)
E. More Sayings of the Wise (24:23-34)

II. The Collection of Solomon's Proverbs by King Hezekiah's Scribes (25:1–29:27)

III. Agur's Collection (30:1-33)
 A. Prologue (30:1-9)
 B. The Proverbs of Agur (30:10-33)

IV. King Lemuel's Collection (31:1-31)
 A. Title (31:1)
 B. Admonitions to a King (31:2-9)
 C. The Excellent Wife (31:10-31)

COMMENTARY ON PROVERBS

I. Solomon's Collection (1:1–24:34)

A. Introduction (1:1-7)

1. Title (1:1)

1:1. Although this verse serves structurally as the superscription of Solomon's collection, it is a fit title for the book as a whole given that **Solomon the son of David, king of Israel** had the dominant influence in Proverbs. For further discussion of the nature of proverbs and of the book's authorship, see Introduction.

2. Purpose (1:2-6)

These verses lay out the purpose of the book, demonstrating the benefits that heeding its teachings will bring. It is probably best to see these benefits addressed to three audiences: readers in general (vv. 2-3), the simple (v. 4), and the wise (vv. 5-6) (Longman, *Proverbs*, 95). Generally, this section shows that Proverbs was written to impart wisdom in its various aspects both to those devoid of it and to those who can continue to grow in it. Furthermore, it was written to spur its readers to carefully ponder and grow in understanding and applying the profound words of the wise, for by doing so comes wisdom.

1:2-3. Proverbs is written with three purposes for the general reader. First, it helps the reader **know wisdom and instruction** (v. 2a). *Knowing* here is more than acquiring information; it is a personal, internalized knowledge in which a person possesses wisdom and heeds instruction and makes them one's own. Here the term **wisdom** (*hokmah)* is used in its broadest sense, the umbrella term for the various facets of wisdom discussed below (Kidner, *Proverbs*, 36). But **instruction** (*musar*) is more specific, "a chastening lesson" that invokes the character and discipline necessary to take correction to heart (Waltke, *Book of Proverbs 1–15*, 175).

Second, Proverbs is written to help its readers **discern the sayings of understanding** (v. 2b). The verb **discern** (*habin*) involves the capacity to truly understand something beyond the superficial level, and in that sense to gain genuine perceptiveness. The language here is repetitive for emphasis (lit., "to understand sayings of understanding"). Proverbs thus encourages its readers to gain *insight* into its *insightful* sayings about life, to truly *perceive* the *perceptive* sayings of the wise. They will, in turn, become insightful about life themselves.

Third, Proverbs is written to general readers so that they would **receive instruction**, accepting in their hearts the kind of correction that produces **wise behavior** (v. 3a). Wisdom produces a change in action, not just an accumulation of knowledge. But truly wise behavior is neither self-centered nor unscrupulous. Proverbs thus also instructs its readers in **righteousness, justice and equity** (v. 3b). These terms remind us that true wisdom entails both personal moral integrity and social consciousness.

Taken together, these three purposes show that Proverbs will shape the thinking, attitude, moral character, and behavior of the general reader.

1:4. Beyond the general reader, Proverbs is written more specifically to the **naive**. Their naiveté, associated especially with **youth**, is "inexperienced, easily seduced, but needing instruction and capable of learning" (Ludwig Koehler, Walter Baumgartner, Johann Stamm, *The Hebrew & Aramaic Lexicon of the Old Testament*, CD-ROM-Edition, trans. M. Richardson [Leiden: Brill, 2000], 989). Such people at least are teachable, unlike fools and mockers. To these, Proverbs is able **to give prudence** (that is, good judgment), **knowledge and discretion**. Proverbs imparts truth and skill for living that they did not previously know, so that they can act with wise deliberation and foresight when facing life's challenges and temptations.

1:5-6. Proverbs is also written more specifically to the **wise**. Unlike the naïve person, the wise person is able to build on the wise foundation he already has. So Proverbs exhorts the wise person not only to **hear** its wisdom, but to **increase in learning** and **acquire** even more wisdom (v. 5). The wise man realizes he never arrives but continually needs to grow in wisdom. As he grows more wise he will also grow in his understanding of all kinds of wisdom sayings, whether a **proverb**, a **figure**, or the **riddles** and **words of the wise** (v. 6). After all, many proverbs are broad, ambiguous, or enigmatic, and all of them need to be applied to the specific circumstances of life. Consequently, those who are wise in the first place are best suited to truly understand what proverbs are saying and how they best apply.

Verses 4-6 therefore indicate that there is a kind of chicken-and-egg relationship to wisdom sayings and being wise. On the one hand, we need to understand wisdom sayings in order to act wisely (v. 4), but as we act wisely we grow in our capacity to understand wisdom sayings (v. 5-6). No human being ever graduates from the school of Proverbs!

3. Theme (1:7)

1:7. Even more importantly, no truly wise human being can abandon God in his pursuit of wisdom because **the fear of the Lord is the beginning of knowledge** (v. 7a). **Knowledge** here is closely associated with "wisdom" (cf. 1:4). The **fear of the Lord** is a reverential awe toward Him. It involves taking Him seriously, both fearing His just judgment and holding Him in the highest respect and love. The term likely has both rational and relational aspects. Rationally, it refers to knowledge of the Lord's special revelation (cf. Pss 34:11ff.; 19:7-9). Relationally, it involves the wise man's worship of the Lord, a worship that entails reverent fear, love, and trust (cf. Dt 5:29 and Dt 6:2; Dt 6:5 and Jos 24:14) (Waltke, *Book of Proverbs 1–15*, 100–101). **Beginning** (*re'shit*) indicates that the fear of the Lord is the foundation, the first principle, the presupposition of all wisdom. Here, then, Solomon indicates that a person can only be truly wise when he acknowledges that wisdom ultimately comes from the Lord Himself, and when he roots his pursuit of wisdom in worship of the Lord. "What the alphabet is to reading, notes to reading music, and numerals to mathematics, the fear of the Lord is to attaining the revealed knowledge of this book" (Waltke, *Book of Proverbs 1–15*, 181). It is little wonder, then, that only great **fools** would **despise wisdom and instruction** (v. 7b). For in showing contempt for biblical wisdom, the fool is rejecting the Lord Himself. And in denying the Lord, the fool is arrogantly denying reality itself—a fool's errand indeed.

This verse thus makes a sweeping statement about the very nature of true wisdom. As such, it functions as the motto for the whole book of Proverbs, and for good reason. "It stands in front of the rest of the collection as the quintessential expression of the basic spiritual grammar for understanding the book" (Waltke, *Book of Proverbs 1–15*, 180).

B. Extended Discourses on Wisdom (1:8–9:18)

This section is made up of a series of fifteen poems. Most of them are in the form of a father's instruction to his son. Typical elements in these instructions include the presentation of a lesson, an admonition to listen to the lesson, and motivations for heeding the lesson. Other poems in this section acclaim wisdom's value by presenting it as a lady who calls naïve young men to follow her ways. This section as a whole serves as an interpretive key for the rest of the book.

1. Lesson 1: Beware of Violent Companions (1:8-19)

1:8-9. This lesson begins with the urgent appeal to listen: **Hear, my son, your father's instruction**. It follows the typical pattern in Proverbs with an admonition to the one lacking wisdom to obey the instruction in the lesson. Also typical is the parental imagery: the father addressing his young and naïve **son**. He is exhorted to heed rather than reject what *both* his parents have taught him (v. 8). The motivation for doing so is that their teachings bring to the obedient son honor like an appealing garland (**a graceful wreath to your head**) and prosperity like an expensive necklace (**ornaments about your neck**) (v. 9).

1:10. The lesson is summarized: **Do not consent** when **sinners entice you**. A "sinner" is one who offends against God and, by extension, the community (Waltke, *Book of Proverbs 1–15*, 189). Here the term refers specifically to violent criminals as is evident by the enticements they offer in the following verses. Not in our day only has the young man been tempted by the lures of the gang. He therefore faces a choice: either listen to the wise advice of his parents or the destructive enticements of the gang.

1:11-14. Taking on the persona of the gang recruiter, the father summarizes the temptations offered by the gang. First, the recruiter offers easy gain. They will **ambush** the **innocent** who are unsuspecting and therefore defenseless against robbery (v. 11). This will bring them **all kinds of precious wealth** and abundant **spoil** (v. 13). Second, the gang offers a sense of power. The language of v. 12 is bombastic. They claim to have the power of death itself (**Sheol** is the grave), able to **swallow** their victims **alive** and **whole** (v. 12). The gang describes their victims as **those who go down to the pit** (i.e., the grave). Yet it is quite possible that this statement is ironic. Rather than merely describing their victims, they are really inadvertently describing themselves; in destroying others, they ultimately destroy themselves (Garrett, *Proverbs*, 70; cf. v. 18). Third, the recruiter offers a feeling of belonging. If the young man will **throw in** his **lot with** them—join them—they will **all have one**

purse (v. 14). That is, he offers an equal share to everyone who is part of the group. What he does not say, once again ironically, is that everyone also gets an equal share of the group's guilt (Longman, *Proverbs*, 107; cf. v. 18).

1:15. Having described the gang's appeal, the father now warns his son not to **walk in the way with them** but to **keep** his **feet from their path**. The imagery of the **way** and the **path**, so common throughout Proverbs, points both to one's lifestyle and the destiny of that lifestyle (cf. 4:10-19). This includes that lifestyle's nature, context, choices, behavior, and consequences (Waltke, *Book of Proverbs 1–15*, 193–194). As the next few verses show, the destiny of the lifestyle offered by the gang provides the motivation for going on a different, better path.

1:16-18. The word **for** gives the reason or motivation for the exhortation of the previous verse. The fundamental motivation the father presents in these verses is that the lifestyle of the gang leads to the gang member's own destruction. This is implied in the ambiguous wording of v. 16. The gang is eager to pursue **evil**, but the term can refer either to moral wickedness perpetrated against others or the calamity they bring on themselves. In addition, these violent men **hasten to shed blood**, but it is not entirely clear whose blood they are actually shedding—others', or their own. Quite possibly, then, in their eagerness for evil and murder against others, they are really pursuing their own calamitous end. This becomes clearer in the next two verses. Even a **bird** has the good sense to avoid an obvious trap (v. 17). But not the foolish gang member. The trap he sets for others entraps him; the **ambush** he sets for others is really his own (v. 18). His passion to pursue violent wickedness leads to his own violent end.

1:19. In this summation, the father lays out a general principle. The self-destructiveness of v. 18 is the destination of **everyone who gains by violence**. The idiom translated in the NASB as **gains by violence** is better translated "greedy for unjust gain" (ESV). Thus the principle is even broader than vicious robbery by violent men, though such greed certainly exemplifies it. All who seek to profit unjustly at the expense of others find that their unjust gain ultimately destroys them (**takes away the life of its possessors**).

2. Wisdom's First Call (1:20-33)

This section has three parts: the setting of wisdom's address (vv. 20-21), her second-person address to the foolish (vv. 22-27), and her first-person reflection on that address (vv. 28-33) (Waltke, *Book of Proverbs 1–15*, 201–13).

1:20-21. These verses introduce a central character in the first part of Proverbs, the personification of wisdom, who is addressed as **she**, and often identified by commentators as Lady Wisdom. Sharing the same worldview as the wise father, she is "the personification of the Lord's wisdom," reminding us that one cannot be wise apart from a real relationship with wisdom, and ultimately, with God Himself (Longman, *Proverbs*, 111; cf. 1:7). Like a street preacher, she **shouts**, **lifts her voice**, and **cries out** her message in public so it can be heard above the din of city life. And she does so in the most prominent places of the city where all can hear—**the street**, **the square**, and **the entrance of the gates in the city**. Her message, therefore, is accessible to all, even if there is much in the **noisy streets** to distract people from it. All need the Lord's readily available wisdom, whether they recognize it or not.

1:22-25. Addressed directly to fools, the message of Wisdom contains three elements. First, she begins with a rebuke of three kinds of people most in need of her message (v. 22). All of them share the complacency of ignorance, though they differ in the degree of their complacency. The worst of these are **scoffers** (*letsim*) who **delight themselves in scoffing** because they are so arrogant and jaded that they mock wisdom. The broadest category, **fools** (*kesilim*) who **hate knowledge**, are not much better, though their rejection of wisdom is due less to cynicism than to their being smug, thick-headed dolts (Fox, *Proverbs 1–9*, 98). The **naive ones** (*petayim*) who **love being simple-minded**, like the young, are gullible in their ignorance, but unlike the scoffer and fool, are teachable. They are probably a special object of Wisdom's address because they are less committed to folly than the other two, though their danger is no less if they persist in their ignorance.

Second, Wisdom issues the heart of her message to them, a call to repentance (v. 23). If they **turn** or change direction at her **reproof**, she **will pour out** her **spirit** (*ruach*) **on** them and **make** her **words known to** them. That is, she will help them understand and take to heart her wise message. Real change is possible for them. It is noteworthy that, in the wider context of Scripture, such wisdom is associated with the Spirit of God (Ex 31:3; Is 11:2-3) who will be poured out on God's people in the "last days" (Is 32:15; Jl 2:28; cf. Ac 2:16-21). When Christians (in whom the Spirit of God dwells) walk by the Spirit, they walk in wisdom's path.

Third, Wisdom issues a warning: the opportunity for repentance is limited (Pr 1:24-27). This warning consists of a description of fools' rejection of her (vv. 24-25) and the results of their rejection (vv. 26-27). Even though Lady Wisdom has repeatedly **called** and **stretched out** her **hand** to them inviting them to repent (v. 24), the foolish have rejected her. They have persistently **refused** her (v. 24a), not **paid attention** to her warnings (v. 24b), **neglected all** her **counsel** (v. 25a), and rejected her **reproof** (v. 25b). These four descriptions of rejection probably reflect an escalating hardness of heart against her message (Waltke, *Book of Proverbs 1–15*, 205).

1:26-27. Lady Wisdom then describes the resulting judgment they face because of their stubborn rejection. The consequences of their foolish lifestyle are **calamity**, **dread**, **distress**, and **anguish**, and these will be as devastating to them as a terrible **storm** and a **whirlwind**, images frequently associated with God's judgment (e.g., Ps 83:15; Jr 23:19; Zch 9:14). These terms highlight not only the disasters that fools face, but also the emotional horror these consequences elicit in them. And as they face these horrific results, Lady Wisdom, whom they have scorned, will **laugh** and **mock** (cf. Pss 2:4; 59:8). There is good reason for this. Her response reflects "the inward joy and disdain a mighty conqueror feels" in his victory over his enemies, a "victory so lopsided that there is a comic aspect to the reversal of fortunes, provoking mockery over the enemy. Truth has a harsh edge, and Wisdom does not dull it. Her shock tactics aim to persuade the young to turn to her" (Waltke, *Book of Proverbs 1–15*, 207).

1:28. Lady Wisdom continues to speak in this section, only now she no longer addresses the fool directly. Instead, she reflects on her address and the fools' failure to respond. The upshot of her reflection is that, having suffered the consequences of their folly, Wisdom can no longer help them (v. 28). Though they **will call on** her and **seek** her **diligently** in their distress, she **will not answer** them. Once they face calamity and are desperate to escape from it, they will be "at last ready to listen to advice, but it is too late" (Garrett, *Proverbs*, 73).

1:29-31. It is too late to call to the Lord to answer because **they hated knowledge**. They rejected wisdom when it could have made a difference. But worse even than rejecting Wisdom's **knowledge**, **counsel**, and **reproof** (vv. 29a, 30), they have rejected Him who is the source of wisdom. That is, they **did not choose the fear of the Lord** (v. 29b). Their foolish lifestyle choices had inevitable consequences. They **shall eat of the fruit of** the path they have chosen and of their godless schemes (**devices**), and they will be filled (**satiated**) with that fruit (v. 31)—no doubt until it makes them sick.

1:32-33. Lady Wisdom brings her reflection to a close with a general principle that compares the wise and the fools. There are two kinds of turning and two kinds of ease. Fools of all stripes turn away from God's wisdom in their **waywardness** and are comfortable in their **complacency**, little realizing that their path will **kill** and **destroy** them (v. 32). In contrast, the godly wise turn away from folly and listen to wisdom. As a result, they **live securely** and are **at ease from the dread of evil**, for they never have to face the inevitable consequences of folly. In the end, Lady Wisdom confronts the reader with a choice between wisdom/life and folly/death, a choice far too urgent to postpone

3. Lesson 2: Wisdom's Protection (2:1-22)

This chapter develops the protective benefits of wisdom. After exhorting his son to pursue wisdom (vv. 1-4), the father declares that wisdom provides protection (vv. 5-11), and then discusses what it protects from (vv. 12-19). His conclusion exhibits the superiority of wisdom's path (vv. 20-22).

a. Wisdom's Conditions: Receive and Seek It (2:1-4)

2:1-4. This section, introduced by **if** (vv. 1, 3, 4), and followed by "then" in the next section (vv. 5, 9), sets up the conditions for receiving the benefits of wisdom. To receive wisdom's benefits one must first know well and fully accept wisdom's teachings (vv. 1-2). The father's **words** and **commandments**, which refer to his lessons throughout chaps. 1–9, are equivalent to **wisdom** and **understanding**. Second, one must also actively seek wisdom, pursuing it fervently like a supplicant in need of help (v. 3) or a treasure-seeker bent on his trove (v. 4). **If** one does so, the result then will be life-changing reward from the Lord.

b. Wisdom's Benefits: Protection (2:5-11)

The two sections in this part of the lesson (vv. 5-8 and 9-11), both introduced by "then," present the benefits of seeking wisdom. Together they promise protection to the one who is wise, although the first seems to have a more vertical focus, in relation to the Lord, and the second a more horizontal one, in relation to people (Garrett, *Proverbs*, 75).

2:5-8. Wisdom is the priority of life because the pursuit of wisdom leads to the **knowledge of God** Himself and a genuine understanding of the **fear of the LORD** (v. 5). Wisdom is inextricably bound to a relationship with the Lord, the pursuit of either one leading to the other (cf. 1:7; Longman, *Proverbs*, 120). This is because **wisdom** (and its counterparts, **knowledge and understanding**) comes from the Lord, who bestows it to seekers (v. 6). Indeed, the father here equates his lessons in Proverbs with the inspired words of the Lord Himself, which come **from His mouth**.

Those who are in right relationship with God consequently experience protection from folly (vv. 7-8). They are described as the **upright**, as **those who walk in integrity** and in **the paths of justice**, and as **His godly** (or faithful) **ones**, reminding us that biblical wisdom clearly has both moral and covenantal dimensions. The Lord provides for them an abundance of **sound wisdom**, resourcefulness "to help one escape a fix" (Fox, *Proverbs 1–9*, 114). This is why He is a protective **shield** for them, **guarding** and preserving them on life's path.

2:9-11. If the previous section focused on the vertical dimension of wisdom's benefits in relation to the Lord, this section focuses on its horizontal aspects in relation to others. Acquiring wisdom and knowing God will result in one's being able to **discern** how to act in **righteousness and justice and equity** (or fairness) (v. 9; cf. 1:3). These terms describe the ethical aspects of wisdom, particularly in one's dealings with others. Together they constitute **every good course**, summarizing a desirable way of life that "encompasses the full gamut of ethical behavior that leads to life, peace, and prosperity (see 3:1-12)" (Waltke, *Book of Proverbs 1–15*, 227).

The wise man develops this God-given moral sense so that his **heart** and affections are transformed (v. 10). **Wisdom** and **knowledge** become part of who he is and are therefore **pleasant** to him. Along with a changed heart he also develops **discretion** and **understanding** that serve to protect him from evil (v. 11). **Discretion**, used in parallel with **understanding**, refers to a shrewdness that involves "thinking through the consequences of an action and choosing the way of integrity" (Longman, *Proverbs*, 122; cf. Fox, *Proverbs 1–9*, 117). Together these terms describe a perceptiveness that is vital when facing temptations.

c. What Wisdom Protects From (2:12-19)

This section expands on the protection afforded by wisdom. Wisdom protects from succumbing to the temptations of the evil man and the immoral woman, the young man's two main sources of temptation. In both cases, wisdom is able "to deliver" (vv. 12, 16) or save the wise son from these two types of people. This deliverance is not a removal of the temptation but the insight and capacity to reject what they offer.

2:12-15. Wisdom rescues the wise one **from the way of evil** (v. 12a). The term **evil**, used in parallel with **the man who speaks perverse things** (v. 12b), likely refers not to evil abstractly, but specifically to wicked persons. The wicked man is described in several ways. First, he **speaks perverse things** (v. 12b). What he says, particularly in tempting others to follow his way of life, is twisted and distorted, rooted in values that turn wisdom on its head. In addition, the wicked prefer an evil lifestyle, abandoning **uprightness** in pursuit of moral **darkness** (v. 13). Furthermore, the wicked actually **delight** and **rejoice in** their acts of **evil** and **perversity** (v. 14). They "not only do evil for the sake of its supposed rewards, they positively enjoy it" (Fox, *Proverbs 1–9*, 117). Finally, the wicked's way of life is **crooked** and **devious** (v. 15). In contrast to the smooth, straight way of wisdom, their **paths** are twisted. They contort the truth (cf. v. 12b). Ironically, they not only deceive others in promoting their wicked **ways**, but they also deceive themselves about the roughness of their self-chosen path.

2:16-19. Wisdom also delivers the wise one from the immoral woman. This section describes her in several ways as well. First, she is **strange** and foreign (v. 16). The term translated in the NASB as **adulteress** literally means "a foreign woman" (Koehler et al., *HALOT*, 700). What makes her strange and foreign is "her willingness to operate outside the bounds of moral, legal, and customary restraints" of the laws given by the Lord to Israel (Longman, *Proverbs*, 124). Second, she **flatters with her words** (v. 16b). By appealing to her victim's ego she seduces and deceives him for her own ends and to his own destruction. Third, her lack of restraint manifests itself in her unfaithfulness to her husband and the Lord (v. 17). So she abandons **the companion of her youth**, her husband, and she **forgets the covenant of her God**, ultimately displaying infidelity to God Himself by her adultery (cf. Mal 2:13-16). Fourth, she is deadly to all who heed her seductions (Pr 2:18-19). Although her promises are enticing, those fools who **go to her** and **her house** will go **down to death**, with no hope of escape. It is as if she dwells on the threshold of the grave itself, the pathway to her leading **to death** and away from **the paths of life** (for more on life and death, see Introduction: Themes).

d. Summary (2:20-22)

2:20-22. This concluding section brings this lesson to an end. Wisdom not only protects from the destructive ways of folly and wickedness, but it also sets one in a very different direction. In contrast to the foolish wicked, those who **walk in** wisdom's **way** and **keep to** its **paths** are described as **good** and **righteous** (v. 20). Such people are commendable (**good**) because they remain faithful to God's covenant (and in this sense they are **righteous**), living in such a way that "their character and conduct comport to doing what is right toward others in a covenant relationship with God" (Waltke, *Book of Proverbs 1–15*, 234).

As a result, these **upright** and **blameless** people **will live in the land** and **remain in it** (v. 21), in contrast to the **wicked** and **treacherous**, who will be **cut off** and **uprooted from it** (v. 22). The **land** (*erets*) here may refer to the world, namely, the land of the living, with its attendant blessings (Fox, *Proverbs 1–9*, 123; Waltke, *Book of Proverbs 1–15*, 234–235). But since wisdom is closely connected to a relationship with the Lord Himself, it is more likely that the reference to the land alludes more specifically to the covenant promises and curses in the Mosaic law (see Dt 27–28). These resulted from Israel's continued covenant faithfulness or unfaithfulness to the Lord, respectively. For the Israelite, the promised land, the land of Israel, was the place to experience God's blessing in relationship with the Lord; to be cut off from it was to be cursed. If Israel would obey the law of Moses, the nation would be blessed both materially and spiritually in the land. Disobedience would bring discipline in the land and, as the ultimate discipline, would bring dispersion from the land of Israel. As is evident throughout Proverbs, there are really only two kinds of paths in life. So the son is presented a choice: the ways of folly, wickedness, cursing, and death (even while he is alive), or the ways of wisdom, righteousness, blessing, and the abundant life. The right choice is obvious.

4. Lesson 3: Wisdom as Worship (3:1-12)

The twelve verses of this lesson can be divided into six groups of two verses. Each of these verse groups has an exhortation followed by the results of heeding that exhortation. At their heart, these exhortations encourage the son to be wise by worshipping the Lord.

3:1-2. The opening exhortation, so typical of the lessons in the first part of Proverbs, encourages **my son** to heed his father's **teaching**. Rather than ignoring or rejecting (**do not forget**) what the father instructs, the son should obey (**keep**) his father's **commandments**, not perfunctorily, but with all his **heart**. The result of doing so **will add** to the **length** of one's life (cf. Ex 20:12) and improve the quality of that life through increased **peace** (*shalom*) or well-being. This is the kind of full, rich life associated with the blessings of fellowship with God, in contrast to the way of death associated with folly (cf. comments on Pr 2:16-19 above).

3:3-4. The son here is encouraged never to **let kindness and truth leave** him. Indeed, he is told to **bind** these virtues **around** his **neck** like a necklace and to **write them on the tablet of** his **heart**, a reflection of the teaching of the Shema (Hb. word meaning "to hear," from Dt. 6:4), given by the Lord to Moses with the command to keep God's Word "on your heart" and "bind them . . . on your hand" (cf. Dt. 6:4-9). By doing so he is making these virtues a permanent part of his inward character. But what exactly are these virtues? **Kindness** (*chesed*) refers to loyalty and covenant love, and **truth** (*'emet*) involves faithfulness. Together they speak of loving faithfulness.

And whose loving faithfulness is this? Some have argued that this pair of virtues refers to *God's* loving loyalty (so Fox, *Proverbs 1–9*, 144-145). But since the exhortation is directed to the son, it is more likely that these virtues belong to him. So the son should be loyal and faithful in his relationships with other people and, more fundamentally, with God. Still, because this pair of virtues is often used of God (cf. Gn 24:7; Ex 34:6; Pss 86:15; 115:1; 138:2), it may be that the text is purposely ambiguous (so Longman, *Proverbs*, 132). That is, by living a life characterized by loving faithfulness to God and others, the son will also be keeping himself close to God Himself, who truly epitomizes loving faithfulness. This kind of lifestyle will **find favor and**

good repute in the sight of God and man (Pr 3:4). Those who are lovingly loyal to God and man are well-regarded by both.

3:5-6. These verses represent the heart of the exhortations. The son is admonished to **trust in the LORD with all** his **heart** (v. 5a). Such trust completely believes what God says, including accepting His words of wisdom while rejecting the way of folly, obeying His commands, and embracing His promises. Trust also involves resting secure in God's loving, protective care and relying completely on His resources. Thus the trusting one will **not lean on** his **own understanding** (v. 5b). "In acknowledging one's own lack of resources, one becomes open to God's power and wisdom, which is a better guide to life" (Longman, *Proverbs*, 133).

The one who trusts God and not his own wisdom will also **acknowledge** God **in all** his **ways** (v. 6a). To **acknowledge** God is to know Him personally and to be in fellowship with Him (Kidner, *Proverbs*, 63-64). The trusting one thus pursues his relationship with the Lord in everything he does (cf. 1Co 10:31).

The result of trusting and pursuing the Lord is that **He will make your paths straight** (Pr 3:6b). As the lifestyle of the wicked is crooked in both a moral sense (they live corruptly) and a pragmatic sense (they face difficulties of their own making) (see 2:15), so the lifestyle of the righteous is straight in both senses. His way of life is straight morally (i.e., he lives in a God-honoring way) and smooth pragmatically (i.e., he faces fewer obstacles to a successful, joyful life).

3:7-8. This group of verses complements the preceding one. In a similar vein, the wise one will **not be wise in** his **own eyes** (v. 7a). He will not be impressed by his own capacity for shrewdness (cf. Is 5:21), thereby relying on his own resources. Instead, he will **fear the LORD** (Pr 3:7b; see the comments on 1:7). He will worship Him, trusting in His resources and reverently obeying Him. He therefore also will **turn away from evil**, a sure sign of a worshipping heart.

Interestingly, such spiritual health can result in physical well-being (v. 8). What's more, the imagery of **healing** and **refreshment** involving one's **body** (lit., "navel") and **bones** probably suggests that such well-being is both external ("navel") and internal ("bones"), extending from a person's physical state to his mental and emotional state (Waltke, *Book of Proverbs 1–15*, 26–27; cf. Garrett, *Proverbs*, 81, n. 51). Generally speaking, those intimately close to the Lord experience a spiritual refreshment that has enormous benefit to their whole being.

3:9-10. Worship is reflected in one's finances. So the son is admonished to worship God in giving (v. 9). To **honor the LORD** in general is to value Him as He deserves and pay Him homage, but here it more specifically implies doing so by giving Him gifts (cf. Nm 22:37; 24:11; Jdg 9:9) (Fox, *Proverbs 1–9*, 151). These gifts not only come out of what one owns (**your wealth**), but they also reflect the **first** and best (Koehler et al., *HALOT*, 1170) of **all** one's possessions. A person's financial generosity displays who or what he truly values. Such generosity in honor of the Lord results in generosity from the Lord, expressed here in agricultural terms—and abundant ones at that (Pr 3:10). Giving to the Lord does not foster financial ruin; it promotes fiscal prosperity. In Kidner's words, "a dedicated income" (v. 9) becomes "a multiplied one" (v. 10) (Kidner, *Proverbs*, 64). This reflects the blessings of the Mosaic covenant (Dt 28:8). Note that such giving is done precisely in honor of the Lord, not as a means of manipulating Him to get rich.

3:11-12. Surprisingly, following the Lord also brings another expectation: **discipline** and **reproof** from **the LORD**. The Lord is active in training His people, sometimes with verbal correction (through the wise) and sometimes through hardship. And so the son is commanded not to **reject** nor **loathe** this painful training (v. 11). This is because such discipline is an evidence of God's love toward His people, as in the case of a loving **father** who disciplines **the son in whom he delights** (v. 12). These verses are a powerful reminder that difficulties are part of life and sometimes one of the blessings God gives us is life-shaping affliction (cf. Heb 12:4-11 that quotes these verses). God promises His worshippers unfailing love, not unmitigated prosperity or comfort (cf. Jb 5:7; Jn 16:33). Therefore, one who worships the Lord will trust in Him and "accept suffering as an act of divine love, not repudiate it and rebel against one's condition" (Fox, *Proverbs 1–9*, 153).

5. Poem: the Value of Lady Wisdom (3:13-20)

In this section Lady Wisdom emerges once again. This poem interrupts the series of instructions in order to promote the value of wisdom, not only to man (vv. 13-18), but even to God (vv. 19-20).

3:13. The poem begins with a beatitude, **How blessed is the man**, to motivate the young to pursue wisdom. Those who attain **wisdom** and **understanding** are truly **blessed**. If a young person wishes to be similarly happy, he should emulate the example of the wise (cf. Ec 12:1). The rest of the poem explains why: wisdom is incredibly valuable.

3:14-15. Lady Wisdom's value is evident when comparing her to items typically associated with great wealth: **silver**, **fine gold**, and **jewels**. She is incomparably **more precious** than these or anything else of value in the world that one might typically **desire**. Job 28:12-22 explains why wisdom is more valuable than wealth. Unlike wealth, which mankind can attain on their own through great effort, wisdom is unattainable through human effort alone. God alone possesses it, and He alone can grant it to those who fear Him (Longman, *Proverbs*, 137; Waltke, *Book of Proverbs 1–15*, 258).

3:16-18. Lady Wisdom's value is also evident when considering the gifts she brings in each **hand** (cf. 3:2). First, she gives an extended life (**long life**, v. 16; **a tree of life**, v. 18), keeping the wise from the destructive ways of the fool. Second, she gives a better quality of life (**riches and honor**, v. 16; **pleasant ways** and **peace**, v. 17), fostering a lifestyle that promotes prosperity, a good reputation, and enjoyable well-being. Little wonder, then, that **all who hold her fast** are **happy**.

3:19-20. Lady Wisdom is valuable not only to man, but even to the Lord Himself. Anticipating 8:22-31, v. 19 indicates that **by wisdom** God created **the earth** and **the heavens**. In addition to His work of creation, God makes use of His wise **knowledge** in His work of providence (v. 20). He controls His cosmos, as when He breaks **the deeps** so that waters can gush forth, either in judgment (Gn 7:11) or blessing (Jdg 15:19; Ex 17:5-7; cf. Is 35:6). He also sustains the earth with life-giving **dew**. In short, if the Lord could accomplish the wonders of creation and providence with wisdom, think of what He could also do with wisdom in His people's lives (David A. Hubbard, *The Preacher's Commentary: Proverbs* [Nelson: Nashville, 1989], 75). For more on wisdom, God, and their relationship in creation, see the comments on Pr 8:22-31.

6. Lesson 4: The Benefits of Wise Dealings (3:21-35)

In encouraging the son to deal wisely with others, this section promotes the safety that wisdom provides (vv. 21-26), describes what wise dealings with others involves (vv. 27-31), and presents motivations for doing so (vv. 32-35).

a. Wisdom's Safety (3:21-26)

3:21-22. The opening exhortation of this lesson encourages the **son** to be diligent in pursuing wisdom (v. 21). Like a guard who is ever vigilant with his charge, the son must constantly **keep** (or guard) wisdom's words and never allow **them** to **vanish from** his **sight**. The kind of wisdom highlighted here is **sound wisdom**, a resourcefulness for dealing with difficulties, and **discretion**, a shrewd circumspection that helps keep one out of trouble in the first place. Little wonder that such practical capacities result in the best of **life** from the Lord (v. 22).

3:23-26. If the son heeds the previous exhortation, then he can expect security by day or by night. He does not have to fear getting tripped up in his daytime **walk** (v. 23), and he can **sleep** securely and comfortably at night (v. 24). Hence, he should **not be afraid**. He will not face the shock (**sudden fear**) that **the wicked** experience when calamitous ruin (**onslaught**) inevitably comes their way (v. 25). For his **confidence** is found in **the Lord**, who is present to protect him (v. 26). "If the son will 'guard' the Lord's wisdom (v. 21), the Lord will 'guard' him" (v. 26) (Waltke, *Book of Proverbs 1–15*, 263).

b. Wise Dealings with Others (3:27-31)

There are five commands in this section, each involving wise relationships with others, highlighting wise behaviors that promote a healthy and safe community.

3:27-28. The first two involve sins of omission towards others. First, **do not withhold good** from others (v. 27). The good here is generic, involving anything that benefits another who needs it. But there are two conditions: (1) the person is someone **to whom** that good **is due** (i.e., you have a moral obligation to help them), and (2) it is something that you have the **power to do** (i.e., you are not required to do what you cannot do). The second command (v. 28) intensifies the first. That is, do not delay doing the good due to those around you (**your neighbor**) when there is no good reason for the delay.

3:29-30. The next two commands involve sins of commission toward others. Third, do not plot against an unsuspecting neighbor who has no reason to expect **harm** from you (v. 29). Fourth, **do not contend** (or quarrel) with others for no good reason (v. 30). Strife of this sort does not necessarily involve a legal setting (Koehler et al., *HALOT*, 1224), although it could include frivolous lawsuits (Garrett, *Proverbs*, 84). Selfishly taking advantage of others and being contentious only serve to undermine peace, harmony, and safety in a community.

3:31. The last command involves an attitudinal sin, namely, choosing the wrong role model. While it may appear that **a man of violence** benefits from his wicked behavior at others' expense (cf. Ps 73), this is only a "surface impression" masking a path that really leads to death (Longman, *Proverbs*, 143; cf. Pr 2:18-19). Only a fool would **envy** such a person and **choose any of his ways**.

c. Motivations for Wise Dealings (3:32-35)

3:32-35. These verses explain why one should deal wisely with others by promoting harmony in one's community. In short, doing so puts one on the Lord's side rather than in opposition to Him. **The Lord** finds the **devious**, who perversely seek to take advantage of others in the ways described above, to be **an abomination**. On the other hand, He is on **intimate** terms with the **upright** who deal honestly with others (v. 32). "The Lord abhors intrigue, but people who are candid and upright, who know the virtue of openness and simplicity, have his ear. A council of this sort will triumph over its Machiavellian rival" (Waltke, *Book of Proverbs 1–15*, 271). Consequently, such **wicked** people should only expect the Lord's **curse** on them and all that they hold dear, rather than the blessing He gives to those who are **righteous** in their dealings with others (v. 33). Similarly, the Lord will get the last laugh on **scoffers** who consider themselves so strong that they can revel in the misfortune of others (cf. Ps 2:4). In contrast, the **afflicted**—those who humbly see themselves as needy before the Lord (Koehler et al., *HALOT*, 856)—can expect His gracious favor when turning to Him (Pr 3:34). In sum, those who are **wise** in their dealings with others will **inherit honor** from the Lord and the community, while those who are foolish in their dealings with others can expect **dishonor** (v. 35). The verb translated **display** in the NASB is probably better translated as "acquire" (Waltke, *Book of Proverbs 1–15*, 254, n. 43; Fox, *Proverbs 1–9*, 169). Thus, such fools earn the disgrace they receive from the community and the Lord.

7. Lesson 5: A Grandfather's Lesson on the Value of Lady Wisdom (4:1-9)

Like other lectures in this part of Proverbs, in Lesson 5 the father continues to exhort his son to pursue wisdom. But unlike the other lessons this one spans three generations: the father speaks to the son of what his grandfather had taught, thus presenting a heritage of wisdom.

4:1-2. The opening in which **sons** are exhorted to listen to **the instruction of a father** is more generic, lacking the use of personal pronouns (v. 4a). This likely suggests what becomes clearer below, that the advice is intergenerational. If the sons persistently heed their father's **sound teaching** and **instruction**, they would **gain understanding** (vv. 1b-2).

4:3-4a. Here the father transitions to autobiography, introducing an exhortation that his father gave to him **when I was a son to my father**—when he was learning from his loving parents. The wisdom his father **taught** him and that has served him so well he still considers appropriate for his own son. Therefore, in the rest of this lesson he simply communicates the words of the grandfather so that the grandson also might benefit from them.

4:4b. The grandfather introduces his exhortation with an exhortation similar to the father's in vv. 1-2. He exhorts his son to **keep** and **hold fast** his life-giving **words** of wisdom. The lesson itself is made up of two sections (vv. 5-6; vv. 7-9), each comprising a command to acquire wisdom with accompanying motivations. Lady Wisdom appears prominently in the lecture, pictured as a worthy bride and a generous patroness (Waltke, *Book of Proverbs 1–15*, 278–279).

4:5-6. The command to **acquire wisdom** (v. 5a) is linked to the idea of Lady Wisdom as a valued bride for whom a dowry must be paid. Wisdom—closely associated with the grandfather's wise **words**—is not something attained once-for-all (Longman, *Proverbs*, 150). The son can **forget** or **turn away** from wisdom. And so, treating her like his treasured bride, the young man is to **love her** and **not forsake her**. If he does so, she will reward her lover with protection (v. 6).

4:7-9. The admonition to **acquire wisdom** is repeated, emphasizing the foundational importance of gaining wisdom and **understanding**. The first step in seeking wisdom is to understand its great value, above anything else that one might seek to **acquire**. Yet does it not say elsewhere in Proverbs (e.g., 1:7; 9:10) that the fear of the Lord is wisdom's beginning (1:7)? Clearly the pursuit of the Lord and the pursuit of wisdom are closely intertwined, in no small measure because only the Lord can grant wisdom. "One must seek wisdom, but when one finds it, one realizes that it was not because of the effort, but because it was a gift of God" (Longman, *Proverbs*, 150).

A man who wins his desired beloved as his wife will naturally cherish (**prize**) her and intimately **embrace** her. This the son must do with Lady Wisdom (v. 8). In response, she will grant him great **honor**. His wisdom, and the benefits it brings, will be as evident to the community as an attractive **garland** or beautiful **crown** on one's **head** (v. 9; cf. Is 61:3, 10).

8. Lesson 6: Keeping on the Right Path (4:10-19)

This section addresses the two paths so prominent throughout Proverbs (See "Life and Death" in Introduction: Themes). After an opening exhortation, this lesson discusses the benefits of the right path (vv. 10b-13) and the horror of the evil path (vv. 14-17) before closing with a final comparison (vv. 18-19).

4:10. Once again the father exhorts his **son** to **hear** and **accept** his wise **sayings**. By doing so, the son will "adopt a lifestyle that promotes life and avoids situations that might lead to premature death" (Longman, *Proverbs*, 151).

4:11-13. The **way of wisdom** is nothing new for the **son**, for the father has already been directing his son along its upright path (v. 11b). This track is firm and straight—both morally and practically (Kidner, *Proverbs*, 67). Its traveler can confidently **walk** or even **run** along it without fear of twists, turns, and obstacles that would impede him or cause him to stumble (v. 12). It is the safe path. Hence, the son would be wise to continue on that path, since it leads him to **life** (v. 13). He must continually **hold** on to discipline (**instruction**) without letting go; he must **guard** wisdom. Otherwise, he might stray from this path.

4:14-17. In the strongest possible terms, the father then warns his son **not** to **enter the path of the wicked** (vv. 14-15). Indeed, he should actively **avoid** the evil path because sometimes its twisted way may for a time veer very closely to the path of life, or even cross it (Fox, *Proverbs 1–9*, 180–181). Opportunities for evil abound, even for the wise, and they must be aggressively shunned. The results of following the evil way are not pretty, for the wicked who go that way become consumed by evil (vv. 16-17). They are restless at night, unable to **sleep** because they cannot **do evil** or lead someone else to **stumble** in evil (cf. 1:10-11); the best they can do is plot (cf. Ps 36:4; Mc 2:1). During the day, they are sustained by their own **wickedness** and **violence** towards others; evil is their food and drink. In presenting this picture of these "evilaholics," no doubt "the father assumes that his son's moral appetite will draw back in horror from this gruesome picture of their craving for wrongdoing" (Waltke, *Book of Proverbs 1–15*, 286).

4:18-19. This lesson concludes with a final comparison between the two paths. Their contrast is as great as the difference between **light** and **darkness**. The **path of the righteous** is **like** the increasing light of a cloudless **dawn** emerging into the **brighter** light of the full day (v. 18). Light is probably picturing morality, safety, and clarity (Waltke, *Book of Proverbs 1–15*, 292; cf. Jb 29:2-3; Ps 43:3; Is 42:16). As the righteous walk life's path, they can see ever more clearly the way God would have them walk, a clarity that only increases their security and well-being. The **way of the wicked**, in contrast, **is like darkness** (Pr 4:19). The wicked **stumble** blindly in murky gloom, unable to negotiate dangers on the path nor even know why they fall. They are lost in immorality, ignorance, and disaster.

9. Lesson 7: Guarding Your Heart (4:20-27)

In connection with the previous lesson, this one underscores the importance of staying on the straight path of life. But it also primarily stresses a central element of discipleship, the heart. This is "the anatomy of discipleship" (Hubbard, *Proverbs*, 87), a "medical inspection" of sorts that examines various parts of the person (Kidner, *Proverbs*, 68). This examination first considers the passive or receptive elements of the body (vv. 20-22) before moving to the active ones (vv. 24-27). Serving as the transition between the two sections is v. 23, which functions as the center of the lesson (Waltke, *Book of Proverbs 1–15*, 296–301). Appropriately, it focuses on the heart, which is the center of the person.

a. Guarding the Receptive Organs (4:20-22)

4:20-21. The father's standard opening invitation to his **son** to pay **attention to** his **words** is here presented in terms of the human faculties of reception. He must **incline** his **ear** to his father's wise **sayings**, **not let them** out of the **sight** of his eyes, and **keep them** locked within his **heart** by keeping them on his mind.

4:22. There are advantages to heeding the father's wisdom, advantages stressed in several lessons already—namely, **life** and overall **health**. Wisdom really is the best medicine, as it safeguards us from life-threatening evils.

b. Guarding the Heart (4:23)

4:23. The core of the examination is a stress test of the **heart**. "Sometimes the 'heart' may emphasize one aspect of the core personality, especially the mind but also the emotions or will, but typically it refers to the whole inner self" (Longman, *Proverbs*, 131, n. 4). It is therefore not only receptive (see v. 21b) but also active, since **from it flow the springs of life**. This expression reminds us that all of life's activities originate from, and are produced by, the heart (Waltke, *Book of Proverbs 1–15*, 298). This is why the son must **watch over** his **heart** as his highest priority (the phrase **with all diligence** is better translated as "above all else," as in the HCSB; cf. Koehler et al., *HALOT*, 649). In particular, he must guard it diligently from devising evil (cf. 6:14, 18; Mk 7:20-23).

c. Guarding the Active Organs (4:24-27)

4:24. By taking his father's wisdom into his heart and protecting it from evil intentions, the son is better equipped to monitor his active faculties. The father starts with the **mouth**, probably because its speech is the clearest indicator of what is in the heart (Lk 6:45; Rm 10:10; cf. Fox, *Proverbs 1–9*, 186). The son must shun **deceitful**, **devious** speech. Such talk not only reflects the heart, but it can also bounce back to influence the heart. "Superficial habits of talk react on the mind; so that, *e.g.*, cynical chatter, fashionable grumbles, flippancy, half-truths, barely meant in the first place, harden into well-established habits of thought" (Kidner, *Proverbs*, 68).

4:25-27. The son must also keep his **eyes** (his attention) fixed on the right path. He must maintain a tunnel vision, not allowing his focus to be distracted by evil from what is **straight in front of** him (v. 25). He must keep his **feet** on the path of life (v. 26) rather than **turn** off that path onto the way of **evil** (v. 27). Taken together, these admonitions are a reminder once again that walking in wisdom "entails a lifetime of work and not a single decision" (Longman, *Proverbs*, 155).

10. Lesson 8: Passion's Proper Place (5:1-23)

Warnings against promiscuity are prominent in Proverbs, especially in chaps. 1–9. This theme appears indirectly in sections comparing wisdom to a chaste wife and folly to a crude seductress (e.g., 1:20-33; 3:13-20; 9:1-18). It has appeared directly as well (e.g., 2:16-19), although this is the first of three extended discourses devoted to that topic (cf. 6:20-35; 7:1-27). While the discourse throughout is male-centered (a father speaking to a son about women), these same lessons apply to young women as well.

a. Introductory Exhortation (5:1-2)

5:1-2. The father once again begins with a typical exhortation that the **son** pay attention to the **wisdom** he seeks to impart to him. Though in one sense this wisdom belongs to the father (**my wisdom**, **my understanding**; cf. 1:8; 2:1), it certainly derives ultimately from God Himself (cf. 1:7). The result of heeding it will lead to the son's internalizing that wisdom in what he does (**observe discretion**) and says (**lips may reserve knowledge**), giving him the resources for dealing with the seductress. Like Joseph with Potiphar's wife, the son must be able to confront her with words of truth in order to resist her allure (Gn 39:8-9).

b. The Seductress: Passion's Improper Place (5:3-14)

(1) The Danger of the Seductress (5:3-6)

5:3. For indeed, the seductress is alluring. Her appeal here comes particularly through her **speech**, as is indicated by the reference to her **lips** and mouth. Her flattering words are as sweet as **honey** and as smooth as olive **oil**, making her company pleasant and inviting. Beyond that, the language in the verse suggests a double-entendre of a sensual nature. Thus the **lips** here (cf. v. 2) also probably suggest kissing, as in Sg 4:11 (Longman, *Proverbs*, 159). Some scholars argue that there may be other erotic images here as well (see Waltke, *Book of Proverbs 1–15*, 308–309).

5:4-6. Appearances can be deceiving, and Proverbs reminds us consistently that "nothing can be judged by its first stages" (Kidner, *Proverbs*, 69). This is particularly so in the case of the adulteress. The sweetness she promises leads in the **end** to a **bitter** aftertaste, like the very bitter oil from the **wormwood** shrub, which is poisonous in large doses (v. 4a). So too, despite her smooth allure, she is really as **sharp** and dangerous **as a two-edged sword** (v. 4b). To pursue her is to follow her on the descending pathway to **death** (v. 5). After all, her lifestyle demonstrates that she has turned away from the **path of life** (v.6a). She finds herself wandering aimlessly in her sin toward devastation without even realizing it (v. 6b; cf. 4:17). "She is a self-destructive fool, as is whoever follows her" (Fox, *Proverbs 1–9*, 194).

(2) The Central Exhortation (5:7-8)

5:7-8. As if to stress the importance of what he is about to say, the father once more (cf. v. 1) calls his **sons** to **listen** to his **words** without ever abandoning them (v. 7). Most likely, in referring to his **sons** the father is thinking of successive generations of his descendants. This advice needs to be passed on from generation to generation (cf. 4:1-9). His advice is direct: Keep **far** away from the adulteress (v. 8). This is the best way to avoid her temptations. Only the fool loiters **near the door of her house**, a place of grave danger (cf. 2:18-19; 7:6-23).

(3) The Results of Not Heeding the Exhortation (5:9-14)

5:9-10. The foolish son who fails to heed this advice faces three consequences (Kidner, *Proverbs*, 70). First, he finds himself exploited, but it is a voluntary exploitation, something he will freely **give** away to **others**. To them he yields his youthful **vigor** and his **hard-earned goods** produced by the **strength** of his labor. These others are **strangers** and aliens, and they are **cruel**. They thus care little about the son because they have no genuine connection with him. But they are connected to the adulteress in some way—whether her outraged husband and family seeking redress from the man, or her friends or handlers seeking to benefit financially from her promiscuity at the man's expense. Several scenarios are possible, but the general point is clear: sexual debauchery "leads to personal degeneration and financial depletion" (Garrett, *Proverbs*, 92).

5:11-13. Second, the foolish son will end up with a regretful, guilty conscience. Toward the **end** of his life, when his **body** is **consumed** either by sexual disease or hard living resulting from his sinful choices, he will **groan** in despair. Only too late does he come to regret his foolish decision not to heed the wise advice of his **teachers** who warned against such adulterous entanglements.

5:14. Third, the foolish son will end up publicly humiliated. The word translated **almost** here more likely means "quickly" (Fox, *Proverbs 1–9*, 199). His secret dalliance quickly becomes public humiliation before his community, a devastating fate in the ancient world as well as our own. "Made public, adultery brings personal shame, humiliation to loved ones, and loss of respect in the larger community" (Hubbard, *Proverbs*, 93).

c. One's Wife and Passion's Proper Place (5:15-20)

For the wise son, there is a far better way. He need not deny the reality of his sexual passions, but fulfill them in the right place—with his wife. The imagery of these verses is erotic, referring to the sexual relationship between a husband and wife in ways reminiscent of the Song of Solomon. "In the love language of the poem, the wife is portrayed as unique, like no one else, to be treasured for herself alone, to be shared with no other. . . . If the husband can appreciate the companionship of his wife, the attractions of the outside woman will disappear" (Richard J. Clifford, *Proverbs: A Commentary*, OTL [Louisville, KY: Westminster John Knox, 1999], 71–72).

5:15-17. Throughout these verses, lovemaking is compared with drinking water (cf. 9:17). A man's wife is like his **own** private **cistern** and **well** (v. 15). The best place to satisfy his heated sexual thirst is to **drink** the cool, satisfying **water** his wife alone provides for him (cf. Sg 4:10-15). Verse 16 is ambiguous, eliciting multiple interpretations (for a sample, see Garrett, *Proverbs*, 93), but if the metaphor remains consistent throughout these verses, then the son's **springs** and **streams of water** most likely refer to his sources of sexual pleasure (Waltke, *Book of Proverbs 1–15*, 319). That is, why should he seek to satiate his sexual thirst with public water sources that he inevitably shares with others? He would be a fool to take up with wayward women who surely have multiple paramours when he can enjoy far more satisfying and exclusive intimacy with his wife (**let them be yours alone**).

5:18-20. In light of the importance of the son's relationship with his wife, the father prays the son's sexual relationship with her—his **fountain**—would **be blessed** (v. 18a). Some think that this is a prayer for many children (e.g., Fox, *Proverbs 1–9*, 202), but the immediate context indicates that it primarily is a call for a satisfying sexual relationship. So the son is exhorted to **rejoice**, or take pleasure in the **wife of** his **youth** (v. 18b). She is to be the sole object of his passionate affection (v. 19). He is to think of her **as a loving hind and a graceful doe**, images which in that culture suggest that to him she is "graceful, lovely, and *sexy*" (Fox, *Proverbs 1–9*, 202, emphasis retained; cf. Sg 2:9, 17; 4:5). His lovemaking with her should completely satisfy his passionate thirst **at all times**; indeed being with her should **always** leave him **exhilarated.** The verb translated **exhilarated** (*shagah*) means "to stagger" as if intoxicated (Koehler et al., *HALOT*, 1413). "Love and lovemaking make one lightheaded, similar to the effects of drinking wine" (Longman, *Proverbs*, 162). In comparison to such joys in the marriage bed, **why should** the son ever seek to **embrace** the **adulteress** (Pr 5:20)? It is a foolish, and far less satisfying, alternative. In our own day, the pursuit of adultery and immorality in the form of pornography only reinforces the emptiness of the world's alternatives to the blessings of God-ordained marriage.

d. Conclusion (5:21-23)

5:21-23. If the son needs any more motivation to avoid the adulteress, his father gives him the strongest motivation in the conclusion. The **Lord** is omniscient; He sees all **the ways of a man** (v. 21), even when those **paths** include sexual sins done behind closed doors. This means that judgment for such sins is inevitable, though it is a judgment of the sinner's own making. **His own iniquities will capture** him (v. 22). His great folly will lead him **astray** ultimately to his own death (v. 23). The verb *shagah* (translated by the NASB here as **go astray**) is probably picking up on the same sense that was used in vv. 19-20 where it is translated "exhilarated" with the sense of intoxication (see the comments there). That is, if would-be adulterers "are not inebriated by the love of their wife, then they will be inebriated by their own stupidity, and that will result in their death" (Longman, *Proverbs*, 163).

11. Warnings against Foolish People (6:1-19)

Like the poems in 1:20-33 and 3:13-20, this section differs from the standard lesson format so typical in the first nine chapters of Proverbs. Rather, it describes three types of foolish people who, like the sexually promiscuous in lessons 8 (chap. 5) and 9 (6:20-35), either destroy themselves, others, or both.

a. Warning Concerning Becoming a Guarantor (6:1-5)

Though these verses do not share all the elements of the standard lesson, where the father is addressing his son directly, they continue to follow the typical "if-then" pattern. *If* the son gets into a foolish situation (vv. 1-2), *then* he should do the following (vv. 3-5).

6:1-2. The first foolish situation involves loans. The **son** allows himself to **become surety** for someone else (v. 1). This involves cosigning, or guaranteeing, the loan of another. Because of the distinction between a **neighbor** and a **stranger**, commentators dispute over the precise scenario described here (e.g., who is loaning the money, and who is borrowing it?). It is probably best to see the two lines in v. 1 as parallel, with **neighbor** and **stranger** functioning as two extremes that include everything in between (Longman, *Proverbs*, 170). That is, do not become a guarantor for anyone else, whether friend, stranger, or anyone in between. To do so is to become **snared** by one's own **words** or verbal pledge (v. 2).

The Scripture certainly does not discourage generosity to the needy, nor does it forbid offering collateral for a loan (cf. Dt 24:10-13) or even paying someone else's past debts (cf. Phm 18-19). But what it does discourage here is something akin to gambling (Kidner, *Proverbs*, 71–72). For when a man becomes surety for another's debt obligation, he exposes himself and his own assets to future situations completely outside of his own direct control—a foolish legal entanglement indeed (Garrett, *Proverbs*, 96; cf. Pr 27:1).

6:3-5. When caught in such a trap of one's own making, the wise son should do everything he can to **deliver** himself from the situation (v. 3a). He has foolishly "handed himself over to the debtor, who may unmercifully throw him into the hands of the creditor" (Waltke, *Book of Proverbs 1–15*, 333) (v. 3b). So the son must **humble** himself and **importune** his **neighbor** to get out of this obligation; he must grovel before him and badger him (v. 3c). The matter is so urgent that he should act immediately and be willing to lose sleep in his effort to extricate himself from the situation (v. 4). He should be as eager to escape this arrangement as a **gazelle** or **bird** escaping from the traps of those who hunt them (v. 5).

b. Warning Concerning the Lazy Man (6:6-11)

This section addresses laziness for the first time in Proverbs (cf. 24:30-34; 26:13-16), which is another kind of behavior that is self-destructive.

6:6-8. Proverbs often makes use of features in the natural world to teach wisdom principles. Here the writer urges the **sluggard** (i.e., the lazy man) to **observe** the **ant** to learn wisdom from it (v. 6). In particular, even though the ant has no obvious overseer who continually drives it in its labors (v. 7), it nevertheless diligently stores up **food** in the **summer harvest** in order to prepare for the winter dearth (v. 8).

6:9-11. The industrious foresight of the little ant sharply contrasts with the lazy man (cf. 10:5). The rhetorical questions (v. 9) are aimed at stirring the **sluggard** to get to work in the harvest and to ridicule his preference to stay in bed and **sleep**. But rather than getting to work, he prefers just **a little** bit more **slumber** (v. 10).

He does not exactly refuse to work; he just does not want to get started yet. "All he knows is his delicious drowsiness; all he asks is a little respite" (Kidner, *Proverbs*, 42). But he is deceiving himself, and setting himself up for disaster. Utter destitution is his inevitable fate (cf. 19:15; 20:13), but he neither expects it nor prepares for it. Because of his refusal to take responsibility to work, **poverty will come** and is presented with two illustrations. It will come upon the person silently **like a vagabond** who creeps in to steal, or like **an armed man** who forcibly imposes **need** (v. 11). Laziness will inevitably result in poverty and need.

c. Warning Concerning Troublemakers (6:12-19)

Unlike the previous two foolish types of people, this one is more nefarious. He draws others into his dangerous schemes, leading them to disaster as well.

(1) Describing Troublemakers (6:12-15)

6:12a. The foolish person dealt with in this section is identified as a **worthless person** (*'adam beliyya'al*), a term "used of troublemakers of all sorts" who agitate "against all that is good" (Waltke, *Book of Proverbs 1–15*, 342). "*Belial* [a component of the second word in the phrase] always implies wickedness as well as worthlessness (1Sm 2:12; 1Kg 21:10); sometimes sheer destructiveness (Nah 1:11, 15; Ps 18:4); eventually it becomes a name for the devil (2Co 6:15), who is the father of all such qualities" (Kidner, *Proverbs*, 72–73). Little wonder that he is also called **a wicked man**.

6:12b-14. Here the troublemaker is described in more detail. First, his way of life displays his **perverse mouth**, spreading lies and gossip that destroy relationships and undermine society (Longman, *Proverbs*, 174) (v. 12b). Second, his gestures indicate his sinister intentions (v. 13). These gestures—winking, foot signals, pointing—might refer to his involvement in black magic and casting curses, or in part reflect his inner shiftiness and turbulent spirit (so Fox, *Proverbs 1–9*, 220–21). But most likely they refer to non-verbal, surreptitious signals to his co-conspirators, whether to ridicule someone else behind his back or to instigate and direct a sinister plot. Third, his outward actions are rooted in the **perversity in his heart** (v. 14). With this destructive bent in his character he continually plots **evil** and **spreads strife** (cf. Gn 6:5).

6:15. Troublemakers usually end up bringing troubles on themselves. The tumult he unleashes inevitably results (**therefore**) in **his** own **calamity**, which will be sudden (**suddenly**), abrupt (**instantly**), and irreversible (**there will be no healing**). He sows the wind and reaps a whirlwind (Hs 8:7) in which **he** ends up **broken**.

(2) The Lord's View of Troublemakers (6:16-19)

This section is the first of the numerical lists in Proverbs, so prominent particularly in Pr 30. Numerical proverbs follow an "x, x + 1" formula. That is, they begin with a two- line proverb that mentions a certain number of similar items in the first line (e.g., six things the Lord hates), followed in the next line by a restatement of those same items with their number increased by one (e.g., seven things the Lord finds abominable). Although the number in the second line is the true number of items, the formula may serve sometimes to place the emphasis on the last item in the list (cf. 30:18-19) (Longman, *Proverbs*, 173). Some commentators treat this list as a distinct section. But while it likely did originate independently, its placement right after 6:12-15 is no accident. This list of seven things that the Lord hates also applies to the troublemaker because "no other type of person satisfies the description" (Waltke, *Book of Proverbs 1–15*, 345).

6:16. This verse introduces the list. What all the items share in common is that **the LORD hates** them. Anything that is an **abomination to** the Lord is extremely offensive to Him, violating His ritual, legal, or moral order and eliciting His most severe judgment. The language here is exceptionally strong; these items truly disgust God. Garrett calls these "Israel's Seven Deadly Sins" (Garrett, *Proverbs*, 97).

6:17-18. The first five items involve body parts, going from top to bottom. **Haughty eyes** betray an arrogant pride that exalts self over others (v. 17a). A **lying tongue** spreads falsehood that manipulates and hurts others (v. 17b). **Hands that shed innocent blood** exemplify violence against those who do not deserve it (v. 17c). At the center of this evil person is a **heart that devises wicked plans** at others' expense (v. 18a). His **feet that run rapidly to evil** indicate that he is eager to implement his evil schemes (v. 18b).

6:19. The last two items involve two types of people. A **false witness** perjures himself to corrupt justice (v. 19a). And **one who spreads strife among brothers** (v. 19b) "attempts to break apart the bonds that hold a society [or family] together" (Garrett, *Proverbs*, 98). People with characteristics like these seven (vv. 16-19) are the worst sorts of troublemakers. Although they make trouble for others, their own condition is far worse since they have made themselves objects of God's wrath, because they "are an abomination to Him" (v. 16).

12. Lesson 9: Warnings against the Adulteress (6:20-35)

This lesson is the second extended discourse devoted to warning the son against the adulteress (cf. chap. 5). It includes a typical introduction (vv. 20-24), a central admonition (v. 25), and arguments in support of that admonition (vv. 26-35).

a. Introduction (6:20-24)

6:20-21. The lesson begins with a typical exhortation to **observe** and **not forsake** what the son's parents are teaching him (v. 20). He is to carry this teaching along with him **continually**, like a pendant hung around his **neck** and over his **heart** (Fox, *Proverbs 1–9*, 228–229; cf. Dt 6:4-8). This teaching should become a part of who he is.

6:22-23. The wisdom imparted by his parents is personified as his constant female companion who guides, protects, and counsels him (v. 22). Though the NASB uses the third person plural here (**they**, usually thought to have parental "commandments" and "teachings" as the antecedent), the Hebrew text uses the third person feminine singular ("she"). As will be evident shortly, wisdom is a far better consort than the adulteress. The commandment of the Lord is a **lamp** and a **light**, and heeding the **discipline** of the Lord and His word should become habitual (cf. Pss 19:8; 119:105). Thus, wisdom is a fine companion because it illuminates **the way of life** (see the comments on 4:10-19) and corrects him so that he does not wander into danger (v. 23).

6:24. The particular danger the father has in mind in this lesson is **the adulteress**. Despite her **smooth** talk, she is **evil**, a deadly pitfall from which wisdom will protect him.

b. Central Exhortation (6:25)

6:25. Given the pressing danger the adulteress represents, the father then explicitly states his warning: Do not let **her capture you with her eyelids** so that you are tempted to lust after her beauty. At that time the eyes were considered one of the most beautiful and captivating parts of a woman (e.g., Sg 1:15; 6:5). She can seduce with words or by nonverbal means. To covet or **desire her beauty in your heart** directly violates the tenth commandment not to covet one's neighbor's wife (Ex 20:17; cf. Mt 5:28). Sin and death begin with the inordinate desires of the heart (cf. Jms 1:13-15).

c. Supporting Reasons for the Exhortation (6:26-35)

6:26. Here the father distinguishes two types of immoral women: the prostitute and the adulterous wife. In terms of the dangerous effect on the son, the latter is even worse than the former. Against the NASB, NET, KJV, and other translations, the verse is not saying that the son **is reduced to a loaf of bread** by the **harlot**, but that the prostitute's services can be purchased in exchange for a loaf of bread or what it costs to purchase one (see Koehler et al., *HALOT*, 141; so also ESV; RSV; HCSB). In contrast, the adulterous wife **hunts** for something far more **precious**, her paramour's very **life**. This verse is certainly not minimizing prostitution, which is forbidden and destructive (cf. 23:27; 29:3). But unlike the quick business transaction with the harlot, an affair with a married woman enters a man into "an entangling alliance" that is even more costly and harmful (Hubbard, *Proverbs*, 107).

6:27-29. Adultery with a married woman inevitably brings punishment. A man who sleeps with another's wife is playing with **fire**, and he will surely get **burned** (vv. 27-28). Verse 29 makes the point of these images crystal clear: a sexual relationship (euphemistically pictured as **goes in to** and **touches**) with another man's **wife** inevitably leads to punishment, as the verses to follow illustrate.

6:30-32. Adultery with a married woman is also inexcusable. People **do not despise a thief** who **steals to satisfy** his hunger (v. 30). Of course, despite people's pity, if he is caught he must **repay**. Although Mosaic law demanded no more than fivefold payment for theft, this **sevenfold** indicates an even fuller restitution of damages (cf. Ex 22:1-9; Waltke, *Book of Proverbs 1–15*, 358). A thief must repay though it cost him all that he owns, **all the substance** (lit., "wealth") **of his house** (Pr 6:31). Still, one can at least comprehend the starving thief's decision. Not so the adulterer. Unlike the thief who makes a rational calculation to steal in order to survive, the adulterer makes stupid decisions (i.e., he **is lacking sense**) by which he will **destroy himself** (v. 32).

6:33-35. These verses explain how he destroys himself. First, he can expect public disdain (v. 33). This may be demonstrated in physical pain. **Wounds** refer to a painful, "violent assault" whether by other human beings, God, or disease (Waltke, *Book of Proverbs 1–15*, 359). It may well be the result of a judicial verdict or even a jealous husband (see vv. 34-35). Beyond the physical pain, he will also find **disgrace** and **reproach**. Unlike the thief, the adulterer's community has nothing but contempt for him, and they "denigrate his significance, worth, and potential influence" because he has undermined the family and social cohesion (Waltke, *Book of Proverbs 1–15*, 359). Worse still, this stigma will never **be blotted out**.

Second, he can expect to create an implacable enemy. In his **jealousy**, the enraged husband of the adulteress **will not spare in the day of vengeance** (v. 34). The term for **man** here (*geber*) implies strength; the wronged man is a considerable foe. He will be in no mood for pity when it comes time to exact revenge. Perhaps he will take matters into his own hands. Or at the very least, he will use the legal system (v. 35). According to the Mosaic law, the penalty for adultery is death (Dt 22:22), although the law seems to imply that in such cases a substitute fine might be paid to avoid capital punishment (cf. Ex 21:30; Nm 35:31-32; Longman, *Proverbs*, 181). But the wronged husband will not be placated by **any ransom**, no matter how great. He will want the harshest penalty: death. In either case, the adulterer should expect a shortened life.

13. Lesson 10: More Warnings against the Adulteress (7:1-27)

This final lesson of the father to his son, while similar to the previous one (6:20-35; cf. 2:16-19; 5:1-23), comes in the form of a story, and once again solemnly warns the son against the adulterous wife. It focuses particularly on her seductive stratagems, presented in dramatic form. This drama of the Seductress and her Simpleton is preceded by a prologue and followed by an epilogue (Kidner, *Proverbs*, 75).

a. Introductory Exhortation (7:1-5)

7:1-2. Once more, the father exhorts the son to **keep** his **commandments** and **treasure** them (v. 1). He is to guard (**keep**) them with the greatest of care, as he would protect the very sensitive pupil (**apple**) **of** his **eye**, since his very life is at stake (v. 2).

7:3-4. The son needs to pay diligent attention to his father's teachings. So he should **bind them on** his **fingers** and **write them on the tablet of** his **heart** (v. 3; see comments on 3:3-4). That is, he should allow them to transform his external actions (**fingers**) and internal character (**heart**) (Longman, *Proverbs*, 186). Moreover, he needs to treat **wisdom**—personified once again as a woman—like his **sister** and **intimate friend** (v. 4). The latter image refers to a relative (Koehler et al., *HALOT*, 550), and the former may actually be an intimate "term of endearment for a girlfriend or wife" (Garrett, *Proverbs*, 102; cf. Sg 4:9). In any case, wisdom is to be treated as an intimate companion.

7:5. This verse tells us why. He should keep his father's wise words so **that they may keep** him **from an adulteress**. Her primary allure, as the drama below makes evident, is her flattering **words**.

b. The Story of the Seductress and the Simpleton (7:6-23)

The father's realistic drama about the seductress has the effect of "making his son feel her seduction, yet in such a way that she becomes utterly repugnant to him" (Waltke, *Book of Proverbs 1–15*, 367). It should be noted that this lesson (as well as the other ones warning about the wayward woman) presuppose that the son, while inexperienced, is on the right path and must be exhorted to remain there. It does not intend a sexist portrait of all women as seductive vixens and all men their hapless victims. More often than not, the roles are reversed—and wise "daughters" should heed a similar warning. If the address assumed that the son was already on the wrong path (as many men are), he would need to be rebuked for his own predatory behavior (Longman, *Proverbs*, 181).

(1) The Setting (7:6-9)

7:6-9. The father's story begins with a scene he observed while looking out onto the street **through** the **lattice** in **the window of** his **house** (v. 6). Among the **naive** young men (see the description of this type of fool in Introduction) he **saw**, he noted one in particular who lacked **sense** (v. 7) because he did not maintain suitable caution in his surroundings. He happens to wander **near** the street **corner** where she lives (v. 8). Worse still, it is **twilight** as the **darkness** of the **night** is quickly setting in (v. 9), a darkness that conceals evildoers and their deeds (cf. Jb 24:15). While he is not intentionally seeking out the adulteress—she does go to great lengths to seduce him, after all—he certainly does put himself in the wrong place at the wrong time.

(2) The Seductress (7:10-12)

7:10-12. But "if *he* is aimless, his temptress is not" (Kidner, *Proverbs*, 75). At this point, the narrative becomes quite vivid. **A woman** rather suddenly appears **to meet him** (v. 10a), and her intentions are quickly evident. She is described in several ways. First, though presumably not a prostitute by trade (cf. vv. 19-20), she is **dressed as a harlot** to let all comers know that she is sexually available (v. 10b). Yet, second, her provocative attire hides a cunning **heart** (v. 10c). Her ultimate motives are closely guarded, although love for the young fool is certainly not one of them, her flattering words to him notwithstanding. Third, she is unrestrained (v. 11a). Lacking "all grace and refinement" (Hubbard, *Proverbs*, 113), she is **boisterous and rebellious**, willing to defy authority and social norms. Fourth, she is predatory (vv. 11b-12). Not content to **remain at home**, she wanders about town and **lurks by every corner** looking for conquest; her goal is to capture a young fool. This is only reinforced if the reference to **her feet**, which want to wander about town rather than staying home, has sexual connotations (cf. 6:28).

(3) The Seduction (7:13-20)

7:13. Her seduction begins with bold action, a kind of "shock treatment" (Kidner, *Proverbs*, 75). The woman **seizes him and kisses him**. She is utterly shameless, and so **with a brazen face** she bluntly begins to proposition him. Verses 14-20 are her words of seduction.

7:14. Strangely, she begins her seduction on religious grounds, informing him that she has offered **peace offerings** and **paid** her religious **vows**. Some suggest that she is a pagan inviting him to participate in pagan fertility rites (which included sex), or even that she falsely claimed that she needed to prostitute herself for the money to pay her vows (so Garrett, *Proverbs*, 103-104). More likely, however, she is perverting the Levitical system. In Lv 7:16-18, a worshipper who had fulfilled a vow would present a peace offering to the Lord and then be able to eat some of what had been offered that day or the next. In short, the immoral woman is inviting him to a celebratory feast. Her attitude reveals the "bland secularization of her religion," much like today's secularization of Christmas (Kidner, *Proverbs*, 75), and her adulterous intentions indicate that "she is also blaspheming the holy things of God" (Longman, *Proverbs*, 190).

7:15. She proposes that the celebratory meal be a romantic dinner for two. Her flattery here is astonishingly absurd. She suggests that she only has eyes for him—**I have come out to meet you**; he is the one she has been looking for. In reality, she is repeatedly on the prowl for fresh lovers, and just about anyone will do.

7:16-18. But clearly she has more than food on her mind, and so she moves in for the kill. She stimulates his senses of sight, smell, and touch by describing her **bed** as soft and lovely (v. 16) and fragranced with expensive, alluring perfumes, **myrrh, aloes and cinnamon** (v. 17; cf. Sg 4:14). Then she directly invites him to "a night of luxurious lovemaking" (Garrett, *Proverbs*, 104) (Pr 7:18). But the **love** and **delight** she promises are a trap and poor substitutes for biblical love (cf. 5:15-19): "The temptress promises sexual love without erotic restraint, but she refuses to make the fundamental commitment of self to him that is required of true love" (Waltke, *Book of Proverbs 1–15*, 380).

7:19-20. She then tells him how easy this all will be. There are no worries because they can get away with it. Her husband **is not at home** but away **on a long journey** (v. 19). His business dealings will keep him away until the **full moon** (v. 20), probably about two weeks away (Fox, *Proverbs 1–9*, 248). He will never know. Of course, conveniently, she mentions neither the possibility of witnesses nor her option, like Potiphar's wife (Gn 39), to allege rape if they are caught (Waltke, *Book of Proverbs 1–15*, 382).

(4) The Surrender (7:21-23)

7:21-23. But he is too stupid to see through her arguments and flatteries (v. 21). Fool that he is, her invitation proves too much. Impulsively (**suddenly**) **he follows her** to disaster (v. 22a). He is compared to an unsuspecting dumb **ox** on his way **to the slaughter** (v. 22b). He is also comparable to an unwitting stag stepping into a noose/**fetters** (v. 22c; this reading of the line in the LXX and ESV is preferable to that of the NASB of "the discipline of a fool"; cf. Fox, *Proverbs 1–9*, 249–250; Waltke, *Book of Proverbs 1–15*, 365, 383). Once caught, the stag will be killed when **an arrow pierces through his liver** (v. 23a). Or he is like a senseless **bird** that **hastens to the snare** and its death (v. 23b). Like all three ignorant animals that are oblivious to the dire end that awaits them, so also the naive is oblivious to the consequences of adultery (**does not know** that his adultery **will cost him his life**; v. 23c).

c. Epilogue: Concluding Exhortation (7:24-27)

7:24-25. The father closes his lesson with an admonition to his son (and presumably, his son's **sons** as well) not to follow the path of the simpleton described in the story. He should heed his father's wise **words** (v. 24) instead of being snared and slaughtered by the seductress's siren call. He must guard his **heart** lest he **turn aside** and **stray into her paths** (v. 25). "You are in danger as soon as your thoughts wander in this fatal direction" (Kidner, *Proverbs*, 76).

7:26-27. The motivation for this exhortation is straightforward: the adulteress, and the act of adultery, is deadly. The adulteress' captivating veneer masks a monster who is both seductive and bloodthirsty (Garrett, *Proverbs*, 104). Her many **victims**, though mighty in number, lay **slain** before her (v. 26). **Her house** is no palace of delights but a vestibule leading down to the grave (**Sheol**) and **the chambers of death** (v. 27). This graphic discussion of the consequences of the simpleton's encounter with the adulteress assumes the more detailed expositions of the practical effects of sexual sin (cf. 5:9-14; 6:32-35; Waltke, *Book of Proverbs 1–15*, 366). Contemporary Western culture, which glamorizes sex without restraints, rejects this wisdom from Proverbs by ignoring immorality's devastating effects on people's lives.

14. Wisdom's Second Call (8:1-36)

In this lengthy poem, Lady Wisdom directly addresses the reader, and it is a stunning contrast to the adulteress's words to the simpleton in chap. 7. It is also her second address to the reader. Though the two addresses share similarities, the first address (1:20-33) primarily is negative, demonstrating the folly of rejecting her, while this is primarily positive, exemplifying the wonderful benefits Lady Wisdom brings.

a. Preface to Wisdom's Address (8:1-3)

8:1-3. Wisdom and **understanding** is again presented in this section (cf. 1:20-33) as a lady addressing the public. She speaks loudly and clearly so she can be heard. She stands **on top of the heights beside the way** so she can be easily seen (v. 2a). She **takes her stand** at the crossroad **where the paths meet** so that many will hear her before making a decision about which path to take (v. 2b). And **she cries out** beside the city **gates**, the hub of an ancient city's legal, political, social, and commercial business, much like a city's center or town hall today (v. 3). Wisdom is thus seen as eager for adherents, widely accessible for all who would receive her, relevant for all facets of life, and crucial for one's way of life.

b. Wisdom's Opening Exhortation (8:4-11)

8:4-5. Like the father in his lessons, Lady Wisdom also begins her address by encouraging listeners to heed her words. Wisdom's words are directed to all **men** (v. 4). But they are particularly appropriate for the **naive**, who are young, gullible, and inexperienced, and the **fool**, who is just plain thickheaded (Fox, *Proverbs 1–9*, 268). All men need the **prudence** that Wisdom teaches (cf. 1:4).

8:6-9. Here, Lady Wisdom describes the characteristics of her words, to which all would be well advised to **listen**. Her words are **noble** and **right** (v. 6) because she speaks the **truth** and considers **wickedness** an **abomination** (v. 7). Rather than being **crooked or perverted**, **all** her **utterances** are spoken **in righteousness** (v. 8). And they resonate with the discerning and knowledgeable (Fox, *Proverbs 1–9*, 270) who find them **straightforward** and **right** (v. 9). After all, one's attitude toward wisdom reflects whether or not one is wise.

8:10-11. Lady Wisdom tells her listeners how valuable her **instruction** is. She may be widely accessible, but she is by no means cheap (Garrett, *Proverbs*, 107). She is more valuable than **silver**, the **choicest gold**, or **jewels** (vv. 10-11a). Indeed, her worth is incomparable, worth more than **all** material **things** one might consider **desirable** (v. 11b).

c. Wisdom's Autobiography (8:12-31)

This section is the heart of Lady Wisdom's address. In essence, it is her autobiography. It serves as a tribute to wisdom, intended to motivate the reader to pursue her. It has two sections that describe Wisdom in history and before history (Waltke, *Book of Proverbs 1–15*, 393).

(1) Wisdom's Autobiography in History (8:12-21)

8:12-16. Lady Wisdom describes her characteristics. She first mentions herself, then three of her companions: **prudence**, **knowledge**, and **discretion** (v. 12). Wherever you find her, you find them (Longman, *Proverbs*, 201). Yet in her these qualities are never separated from **the fear of the Lord**, which will always **hate evil** in its various forms—**pride**, **arrogance**, **evil** behavior, and **perverted** speech (v. 13; cf. 1:7; 3:7; 16:6). True wisdom should never be confused with mere cleverness; Lady Wisdom despises the arrogant pride "to which shrewd and clever persons are especially prone" (Hubbard, *Proverbs*, 122). Wisdom is also where one can find good **counsel**, **sound wisdom**, **understanding**, and **power** (v. 14). These attributes suggest a competence that not only can discern the best course of action but has the strength of purpose to carry it out. Wisdom's qualities are particularly appropriate for statecraft. **All** those with power—**kings**, **rulers**, **princes**, **nobles**—need

Lady Wisdom if they are to rule effectively and justly (vv. 15-16).

8:17-21. Lady Wisdom promises great reward to those who pursue her. She promises to **love those who love** her and to be found by **those who diligently seek** her (v. 17). She does not play hard to get with those who steadfastly pursue her (cf. Jms 1:5-8). And her love is rewarding. To her "lovers" she bestows **enduring** material prosperity (**riches** and **wealth**), **honor** (rather than shame), and **righteousness** (Pr 8:18). While **righteousness** could be understood simply as "prosperity," the context suggests more—a prosperity that is only "part of a far bigger whole, which will be specified in [verse] 35 as life and divine favour" (Kidner, *Proverbs*, 78). Hence, what she produces (her **fruit** and **yield**) is more valuable than **pure gold** and the **choicest silver** (v. 19). While they do prosper materially, her lovers are not crass materialists seeking ill-gotten gain. After all, if they accompany her, they too will **walk in the way of righteousness** and **justice** (v. 20). In return, she grants them **wealth** and abundant treasure that probably includes much more than material prosperity, which alone never quite satisfies (Hubbard, *Proverbs*, 124). Thus, Lady Wisdom is presented here as a "majestic patron and benefactor" who "moves in the most esteemed circles, among the rich and the powerful" and the righteous. She is, in fact, "an intimate of God himself," comparable to a "darling" daughter (Fox, *Proverbs 1–9*, 278–279).

(2) Wisdom's Autobiography before History (8:22-31)

(a) Wisdom's Existence before Creation (8:22-26)

This passage may well be the most controversial in all Proverbs. Debate on it has gone back at least as far as the ancient Christian church. Clearly Wisdom is being personified in this chapter as a whole, but some have argued that this section takes Wisdom beyond mere personification. They maintain that Wisdom in this section is an actual person who, as it turns out in later biblical revelation, is Jesus Christ. This theological question directly affects the interpretation of the text itself, and so we will return to it after going through the text.

However, the basic message of the text should not be missed. First, Lady Wisdom is older than creation itself (vv. 22-26), enjoying a greater dignity. Second, Lady Wisdom observed and even participated in God's work of creation (v. 27-31). All this means that if one is going to understand, successfully navigate, and enjoy life in God's world, wisdom is indispensable. The main point of these verses is clear enough: Wisdom existed prior to the universe, and she is distinct from creation, closely associated with the Lord Himself.

8:22. This controversial verse has two key interpretive questions. First, what is the meaning of **possessed** (*qanah*)? While its basic sense is "to get or acquire" (e.g., 1:5), here commentators typically debate whether it means "to possess" (i.e., "to have already acquired something") or "to create" ("to have acquired by making"). Neither quite captures the more likely sense. On contextual grounds (esp. vv. 24-25), it is best understood in terms of "begetting" (as in having children).

The second interpretive question actually pertains to the whole stanza (vv. 22-26). Is Wisdom pictured as eternal, like the Lord Himself, or does she have a beginning, like the rest of creation? Here we must tread carefully. On the one hand, since Wisdom is begotten, the text likely does indicate that the Lord's begetting her is "the first of his works" (v. 22a, NIV) and "the first of his acts of old" (v. 22b, ESV). On the other hand, the implications of the temporal language in these verses must not be misunderstood. The language does not imply that God at first "lacked it and had to create it or learn it," a notion "both alien to the passage and absurd" (Kidner, *Proverbs*, 80). Nor should it be construed to undermine wisdom's distinctiveness from the rest of creation. The temporal language lays stress on Wisdom's preexistence, not on the timing of her origin (cf. Daniel J. Treier, *Proverbs and Ecclesiastes*, BTCB [Grand Rapids, MI: Baker, 2011], 48–49). Wisdom is unique in God's world, having existed before its creation.

Lady Wisdom is thus pictured in these verses as God's "daughter" begotten before creation but unique within it. It therefore makes the best sense to see her as a personification of God's revealed wisdom. For "wisdom comes from God's essential being; it is a revelation that has an organic connection with God's very nature and being, unlike the rest of creation that came into existence outside of him and independent from his being. Moreover, since this wisdom existed before creation and its origins are distinct from it, wisdom is neither accessible to humanity nor can it subdued by human beings, but it must be revealed to people and accepted by them" (Waltke, *Book of Proverbs 1–15*, 409; cf. 86-87, 127–130).

8:23. This verse essentially restates the previous verse. The verb in this verse (**I was established**) is also debated. The two major options (depending on the identity of the verb's root) are "to appoint" (similar to the NASB) or "to weave." While the former would appropriately suggest Wisdom's royalty and parallel Ps 2:6-7 (where regal appointment and being begotten are placed together), the context more strongly favors the latter. The image of weaving, which is used in Ps 139:13 for David's formation in his mother's womb, directly parallels the picture of wisdom's being begotten in Pr 8:22, 24, and 25. Wisdom was woven together primordially, **from everlasting.**

8:24-26. These verses stress Wisdom's preexistence, predating all creation. Wisdom declares twice in these verses that she **was brought forth**, a verb that evokes the imagery of childbirth. God brought her forth **before** He created the world. The references to the waters (v. 24), **mountains** (v. 25), and **fields** (v. 26) recall the creation account in Gn 1–2 (see Longman, *Proverbs*, 205–206).

(b) Wisdom's Participation in Creation (8:27-31)

8:27-29. Wisdom not only predated creation, she was present with God before creation. The main point in these verses is that she **was there** to see **when** God created the cosmos. Once again, God's work of creation is described in several actions reminiscent of the creation of the heavens and the earth in Gn 1. She was there when God **established the heavens** (Pr 8:27a), created the horizon separating sky from sea (v. 27b), strengthened the clouds of the sky and the fountains **of the deep** (v. 28), and created the land by setting the sea's **boundary** (v. 29). Wisdom observed the whole thing and "was privy to the how's and what's and who of those mysterious beginnings—prime credentials for any teacher" (Hubbard, *Proverbs*, 126).

8:30-31. These verses take Wisdom's role further. She was not only an observer in creation, but she was also **beside Him** as a companion in his work (v. 30a). But what kind of companion? Once again we encounter debate, this time over the term *'amon* (translated **master workman** in the NASB). Some believe that it means "child" who joyfully plays in God's creation. Others suggest it should be understood as "constantly,"—that is, Wisdom is God's constant companion. Most commonly the term is understood to mean "artisan" (NASB). It is difficult to decide between alternatives, though the last is probably to be preferred since Wisdom participates in God's work of creation (cf. 3:19) so that "the principles of wisdom are woven into the fabric of the created order" (Garrett, *Proverbs*, 110). Little wonder, then, that she celebrated with God His very good creation (vv. 30b-31). She did so each day of creation, possibly bringing Him delight as well (v. 30b), depending on whether or not it is *His* **delight** or *hers* (each is possible). Her celebration was playful, constant, and worshipful (v. 30c). To rejoice has the idea of dancing and playing (Koehler et al., *HALOT*, 1315), and doing so **before** the Lord probably suggests worship (Waltke, *Book of Proverbs 1–15*, 421; cf. 2Sm 6:5, 21). Her celebration also focused on the world God made, particularly **the sons of men** who inhabit it (Pr 8:31). Wisdom thus "laughs before him (God) and laughs and plays with the human race," suggesting that she is "a mediating figure between the human and the divine" (Longman, *Proverbs*, 207).

(3) Lady Wisdom and Christ

The comments above make clear that this commentary does not support the view that Wisdom in this section is Jesus Christ. Lady Wisdom here is no more than a personification of the wisdom that the sage has received, a wisdom revealed by God and rooted in His very own character. The context simply does not justify interpretations that go beyond the personification of wisdom here. Furthermore, while the text does indicate that Lady Wisdom is unique and preexistent, its language cannot sustain the idea that she is eternal in the sense that Jesus Christ is as God. Indeed, the ancient Arian heresy identified Wisdom as Jesus and used this section to argue that Jesus was not eternal and therefore not God. In order to avoid Arian implications, orthodox Christians who actually agree that Wisdom is Christ have sought to interpret this section in a way consistent with the eternality of Wisdom/Christ (see Treier, *Proverbs*, 44–57). But as seen above, this is difficult to do successfully.

Still, it is true that the Christian tradition has commonly identified Christ with Wisdom here, and that is not without some justification. After all, Wisdom is pictured in the text as preexistent, exalted, and distinct from the rest of creation. Moreover, the NT does appear to make a connection between Christ and Wisdom in Pr 8 (cf. Mt 11:18-19; Col 1:15-17; 2:3; 1Co 1:24, 30; perhaps Jn 1 and Rv 3:14; see Longman, *Proverbs*, 210–212; Treier, *Proverbs*, 49–57 for further discussion). It is therefore best to say that Lady Wisdom shares similarities with Christ, but Christ is even greater than she. In short, the sage's wisdom is a type of Christ. "In typology the antitype [Christ] shows both similarities and superiority to the type [the sage's wisdom]" (Waltke, *Book of Proverbs 1–15*, 131; see his extensive list of similarities and superiorities between the two on pp. 130–32). The exalted picture of personified wisdom, "far from overshooting the literal truth, was a preparation for its full statement" in the person of Jesus Christ (Kidner, *Proverbs*, 79).

d. Final Exhortation (8:32-36)

Having narrated her autobiography, Lady Wisdom concludes her address with final advice.

8:32. As a consequence of her autobiography (**therefore**) she exhorts her audience to **listen to** her, that is, to **keep** her **ways**. The motivation for this is a beatitude: those who do so will be **blessed** or happy. In living like her, they will enjoy God's world as much as she does (cf. vv. 30-31).

8:33-34. The pattern of exhortation and motivating beatitude is repeated here. Her audience should **heed** rather than **neglect** her **instruction**, and thereby grow **wise** (v. 33). If they **listen to** her with eagerness, they will be **blessed**/happy (v. 34). The idea of eagerness is portrayed by a man keeping vigil by the door of her house, probably in the sense of a lover waiting to see his beloved (Fox, *Proverbs 1–9*, 290).

8:35-36. Why is the one who heeds Wisdom blessed? Positively, to **find** her is to find abundant life and God's **favor** (v. 35), much like finding a good wife (see 18:22). Negatively, a person only **injures himself** when he does not find her (v. 36a). The verb translated **sins against** here means "to miss." And ultimately, by missing her, they **hate** her and, perversely, **love death** (v. 36b). One either loves Wisdom or hates her. There is no middle ground, and life and death are at stake (Garrett, *Proverbs*, 110). The reader faces a dramatic choice, and chap. 9 will lay it out starkly.

15. Conclusion: Two Invitations (9:1-18)

This chapter is an appropriate epilogue to the first part of Proverbs, and Lady Wisdom's call. It proffers a concluding choice between wisdom and folly in the form of an invitation. It has three sections of six verses each. Lady Wisdom (vv. 1-6) and Woman Folly (vv. 13-18) both issue parallel invitations to their banquets, each reiterating themes previously addressed. An intervening section (vv. 7-12) contrasts the two ways through direct instruction, picking up on themes in the prologue (1:1-7).

a. Lady Wisdom's Banquet Invitation (9:1-6)

9:1-3. These verses describe Wisdom's preparation for her banquet. She **has built her house**, which has **seven pillars** (v. 1). Her house may suggest the imagery of a temple, a place to come worship the Lord (so Hubbard, *Proverbs*, 133), but also indicates a large, solid house, the grand mansion of a wealthy, noble lady, with plenty of room for lots of guests. In addition, she personally and meticulously arranges the feast itself, which is extravagant and delightful (v. 2). So she **prepared her food**—or more precisely, "arranged a slaughter" (Koehler et al., *HALOT*, 368)—that involved butchering and cooking meat, a luxury in the ancient world appropriate for feasts; she **mixed her wine** with honey and spices to taste good; and she **set her table** for her guests' enjoyment (Longman, *Proverbs*, 216-17). Furthermore, she aggressively and publicly issues an invitation to her feast (v. 3). She sends **out her maidens** to issue the invitation, but she also does so herself, probably calling out from the **tops** of the city walls (Waltke, *Book of Proverbs 1–15*, 436)—a vivid reminder that wisdom is widely available.

9:4-6. She issues her invitation directly to **whoever is naive**, those who lack **understanding** (v. 4). Though they have not yet chosen wisdom, neither have they yet been hardened in folly, so she wants to win them over, urging them to **turn** aside from their way. She then invites them to **eat** and **drink** of her banquet feast (v. 5). In doing so, she may also be inviting them to an intimate relationship with her (Longman, *Proverbs*, 217; cf. 3:18; 7:4). In any case, her cuisine is far different from that of the wicked (4:17) and foolish (9:17-18). For her food is life-giving (v. 6). But it is also costly, for its participant must **forsake** folly and commit himself to continuing **in the way of understanding**. God's banquets are always so (Is 55:1; Lk 14:15-24; Jn 6:41-59).

b. Interlude (9:7-12)

This collection of wisdom sayings between the two parallel invitations of Wisdom and Folly may at first seem out place both in style and even in substance. However, this interlude actually fits the context as it displays the stark contrast between those who have chosen wisdom and those who have chosen folly. The choice between Wisdom and Folly is not "an isolated, impulsive decision"; it "is seen ripening into character and so into destiny" (Kidner, *Proverbs*, 82).

9:7-9. Ostensibly, these verses seem directed to wise teachers regarding whom they should instruct, but they are really less about teachers and more about the students. The **scoffer** is really the worse kind of fool, "so full of himself and contemptuous of others that he will not humble himself under any authority, not even under that of the Lord" (Waltke, *Book of Proverbs 1–15*, 140). The last thing he wants is constructive criticism. So anyone who **corrects** the mocker should expect **insults** and abuse from him (v. 7). A wise teacher should therefore choose his students carefully (v. 8; Hubbard, *Proverbs*, 135). On the one hand, it is a waste of time to **reprove a scoffer** because **he** will only **hate you** all the more for trying to correct him; he is not teachable. On the other hand, **a wise man** actually **will love you** for doing so. He will appreciate you because you are helping him to **increase his learning** and become **still wiser** (v. 9). This is a reminder that a truly wise person is humble and teachable because he knows that he is always in process. He is also **righteous**, as the next verse makes clear.

9:10. Reiterating the theme verse of Proverbs, this verse shows the inextricable connection between wisdom and worship (see 1:7). **The fear of the LORD** is here equated with **the knowledge of the Holy One**. Those who worship and know the Lord submit to His authority and consequently grow in wisdom and righteousness.

9:11-12. There are consequences to heeding Wisdom—or not. "The righteous course is in fact the prudent course" (Kidner, *Proverbs*, 83). Essentially, Wisdom brings **life** (v. 11; cf. 3:2; 4:10; for more on life and death, see Introduction: Themes). The words **by me** make this clear, and they may also suggest that personified Wisdom has been speaking the whole time (from vv. 5-12). The single greatest beneficiary of a person's choosing wisdom is the person himself (v. 12a). But all this also implies what becomes more explicit below, that folly brings death. And so the scoffer, who blatantly rejects wisdom, has no one to blame but himself, for he **alone will bear** folly's fruit (v. 12b). While one's choices might affect others (e.g., 10:1), "the ultimate gainer or loser is the man himself" (Kidner, *Proverbs*, 83).

c. Woman Folly's Banquet Invitation (9:13-18)

9:13-15. Lady Wisdom's rival is here introduced, and **the woman of folly** does not fare well in the comparison. Folly is, however, just like the adulteress in chap. 7. She is a **boisterous**, gullible ignoramus (v. 13). She may have much to say to the naïve, but what she says demonstrates that she is just as clueless as they are. Unlike Lady Wisdom's diligent preparations for her feast, Woman Folly does not even bother to get up; she just **sits at the doorway of her house** (v. 14a). But her laziness does not mitigate her bombast. Her **seat by the high places of the city** is probably a kind of public throne (v. 14b). "The pretentious imposter presents herself as an empress who rules a city, and the gullible bow to her authority" (Waltke, *Book of Proverbs 1–15*, 444). Alternately, she may be pictured as a kind of pagan priestess lounging outside her temple (so Hubbard, *Proverbs*, 173). In any case, she is in reality little more than a prostitute selling herself in public. **Calling to** passersby who are minding their business with no intention of going astray, she hopes to waylay the gullible among them (v. 15).

9:16-17. She directs her invitation to the **naive**, the one **who lacks understanding** and does not know better (v. 16). She is vying for the attention of the same audience as Lady Wisdom. But her appeal is base and tawdry. True, **water** and **bread** can hardly compare to the sumptuous feast offered by Lady Wisdom, but Woman Folly still claims her meal is **sweet** and **pleasant** (v. 17). Her offer of **stolen water** likely refers to an adulterous sexual liaison (cf. 5:15-18; 7:18). Her offer of **secret** bread may also have adulterous overtones (cf. 30:20), or it may refer to illicit schemes for profiting at other's expense (Garrett, *Proverbs*, 116; cf. 1:11-14; 4:14-17). But Folly's seductiveness "applies to illicit gratifications of all sorts" (Fox, *Proverbs 1–9*, 303)—alluring precisely because they are forbidden.

9:18. Adam and Eve discovered death as the consequence of illicit gratification; so too the simpleton who succumbs to Woman Folly. Hers is the dinner of the **dead**, held in the hall of the grave (**Sheol**). But the simpleton's ignorance is not bliss, because he will join **her** dead **guests** at the banquet.

This section of Proverbs therefore closes with a sharp choice, particularly proposed to the young and naïve. They can either choose the Lord, Wisdom and her blessings, and ultimately, life. Or they can choose Folly, evil, and finally death. It is either one or the other. The remainder of the book is for those who have chosen well.

C. The Proverbs of Solomon (10:1–22:16)

10:1a. This major section of the book (10:1–22:16) is introduced here as **the proverbs of Solomon**. Some have noted that the letters of the Hebrew alphabet have numerical value, and the name "Solomon" has the value of 375, the same number of proverbs in this section (10:1–22:16), suggesting an intentional organization. It is a collection of various proverbs, with little explicit organization (see Introduction: Structure and Genre).

10:1b-c. The first proverb in this section is an appropriate transition from the previous section of the book. It reiterates the contrast between wisdom and folly (as in chap. 9), and it replays the parent-son relationship so prominent in the previous section. The opening statement seeks to motivate the **son** to choose wisdom out of love for his **father** and **mother**. If a son has even a modicum of consideration for his parents—for their affection for him, their reputation, and their support when old—then he will choose wisdom. His choice will thus either bring joy or **grief** to his parents. "Your choice may be lonely [9:12]; it cannot be private" (Kidner, *Proverbs*, 84).

10:2-3. Money has its limitations. Ultimately there is no **profit** in **ill-gotten gains** (v. 2a). **Righteousness** here probably refers specifically to one's generosity toward others, in contrast to ill-gotten gain (Waltke, *Book of Proverbs 1–15*, 453, 99). Such generosity is a far better investment because it **delivers from death**, either now, or more importantly, in the hereafter (v. 2b). Money will be of no use to the wicked in the face of death. The next proverb clarifies (v. 3). The **righteous** have wisely put themselves on the Lord's side; the wicked oppose Him. All things being equal, God will take care of the former, but the appetites of the latter will go unfilled. Behind these proverbs is the realization of God's wrath (cf. 11:4). When it comes time for God to pour His wrath on such wickedness, either now or in the hereafter, the wise know which side to choose.

10:4-5. The issue of laziness is again addressed (cf. 6:6-11) and makes its first appearance here in this section (cf. v. 26; 12:24, 27; 13:4; 15:19; 18:9; 19:15, 24; 20:4, 13; 21:25; 22:13). While it pays to be **diligent**, the only dividend a **negligent** shirker should expect is dire poverty (v. 4). Diligence manifests itself in the foresight to gather and store up food in the **summer** and season of **harvest** rather than sleeping soundly through it all, as does the slacker (v. 5). By his folly, the latter not only affects himself but also disappoints and brings shame to his parents. The former is accredited a wise **son**, pleasing not only his parents (cf. 10:1) but also the Lord, with all that entails—such as not going hungry (cf. v. 3).

10:6-7. The **righteous** act justly and graciously toward others. By doing so, they enrich their community, and the community responds in kind (Waltke, *Book of Proverbs 1–15*, 457). So the righteous are crowned with **blessings** (v. 6a). Although these could come directly from God Himself (cf. v. 22), here they more likely are realized through the relationships with and prayers of grateful neighbors (Waltke, *Book of Proverbs 1–15*, 457; Kidner, *Proverbs*, 85; cf. 11:26; Ru 2:4; 3:10). In contrast, the **wicked** mistreat others for their own gain, even to the point of **violence**. Yet before the public they seek to conceal their actions with their words (Pr 10:6b). But the effect of such public relations is at best temporary; legacy tells a fuller story. Although **the righteous** will be remembered as a **bless[ing]**, . . . **the name of the wicked will rot** (v. 7). Their memory **will rot** because it will decay away entirely and be forgotten, or like a putrid carcass, its repugnant odor may linger. It may be that people will continue to use the name of the righteous and wicked in pronouncing blessings or cursings, respectively (Michael V. Fox, *Proverbs 10–31: A New Translation with Introduction and Commentary*, AYB [New Haven: Yale University Press, 2009], 515).

10:8. Those who are truly **the wise of heart** continue to grow wiser still because they are eager to **receive** wisdom's **commands**. They are humble, receptive, teachable, and obedient. The **babbling fool** is too busy spouting his own opinions to even hear wisdom, let alone obey. He will end up ruined.

10:9-10. One's **walk** is tied to one's chosen path (cf. 4:10-19) and therefore involves one's way of life (cf. Gl 5:16-26). So to walk **in integrity** is to live innocently and purely (Koehler et al., *HALOT*, 1744). Because such people have "nothing to hide" they have "nothing to fear" (Kidner, *Proverbs*, 86). The wicked person **who perverts his ways** has no such confidence. Try as he might to hide who he really is, his true character **will** eventually **be found out**. There are two illustrations of wicked people whose character eventually becomes evident. The evil conspirator who **winks** with **the eye** (cf. Pr 6:13) will be recognized by the **trouble** he **causes**, and the **babbling fool** by the **ruin** he brings on himself (cf. 10:8).

10:11-12. In their desire to help others, **the righteous** speak words that, like **a fountain** of fresh water in a dry land, are **life**-giving (v. 11a). Their words, whether of rebuke or encouragement, promote wisdom and godliness in others, and hence their very life. In contrast, rather than helping others, what **the wicked** say only **conceals** their violence against others (v. 11b; see comments on the identical line v. 6b). However, there is an appropriate kind of "cover up," rooted in love rather than self-promotion and wickedness (v. 12). In contexts where one person wrongs another, **hatred** toward the wrongdoer only makes matters worse because it **stirs up strife**. But **love covers** over **all** kinds of **transgressions** for the sake of peacemaking (cf. 1Co 13:4-7). Because it "cherishes the wrongdoer as a friend to be won, not as an enemy with whom to get even," love does not exact revenge by exposing his faults for all to see. It rather "endures his wrongs to reconcile him and save him from death (cf. Pr 25:21-22; 1Co 13:4-7; Jms 5:20) and to preserve the peace" (Waltke, *Book of Proverbs 1–15*, 461; cf. Pr 19:11).

10:13-14. Discerning people display their **wisdom** in what they say (v. 13a). Unfortunately, to get through to him, the thickheaded dolt needs something more dramatic than wise words, such as **a rod** on his **back** (v. 13b). The next proverb expands on these ideas. **Wise men** can communicate wisdom because they are a storehouse of **knowledge**, which they no doubt learned from other sages (v. 14a). In contrast, the fool's **mouth** displays the folly that he has stored up, and his subsequent **ruin** will dramatically demonstrate just how foolish he is (v. 14b).

10:15. Wealth certainly has its advantages. Like a **fortress**, it can provide protection and resources to get one through tough times. Anyone trying to save up a nest egg knows this. In that sense, **the rich man** is better off than **the poor**, whose **poverty** leaves them exposed with no fortress, but only a **ruin**. But if this proverb rightly warns us not to "embrace poverty out of laziness or romanticism" (Kidner, *Proverbs*, 87), it also may subtly warn the rich man not to trust too much in ***his* fortress** of resources (emphasis added; cf. 11:28) rather than in the Lord (cf. 18:10-11). That is the continual temptation of the rich man (cf. 30:7-9; see also 1Tm 6:17-19).

10:16. There is another kind of wealth and poverty, and the wise know where to make their investment. "The righteous and the wicked are the wise and the fool, described by their ethics" (Longman, *Proverbs*, 236). The **righteous** are truly rich, their **wages** being **life** itself, in all its fullness. The wicked's **income** is meager indeed. It is sin (a better translation of *chatta't* than the NASB's **punishment**), which itself leads to death (cf. Rm 6:23; 5:12; Jms 1:15).

10:17. Life-giving wisdom is also manifested in heeding corrective **instruction** rather than rejecting **reproof**. To follow the Lord's wisdom, is to walk on the **path of** life (cf. 6:23). Those who fail to learn from their mistakes will wander about in their own folly. The verb **goes astray** is perhaps better understood here as "leads others astray" (e.g., ESV). If so, the fool's wandering is even worse, because he leads others astray as well as himself.

10:18-21. The next several proverbs revolve around one's speech. The KJV probably captures the grammatical structure here better than the NASB. It describes a **fool** as someone who lies to **conceal** his **hatred** of someone else when they are together, but **spreads slander** about that person behind his back. Fools are also verbose, speaking **many words**, whereas the **wise** use words with careful restraint, knowing that the more one speaks, the greater the chance to sin with one's words (v. 19; cf. 13:3; 17:28). More broadly, a person's core character (**heart**) will reflect itself in one's words (v. 20; cf. Mt 12:33-37). Your words "are worth what *you* are worth" (Kidner, *Proverbs*, 88). So the words/heart of **the righteous** are precious as **choice silver** in comparison to those of **the wicked**, which are a pittance. One reason they are so precious is their effect on others (Pr 10:21a). The nourishing, life-giving words of **the righteous feed many**, teaching, rebuking, encouraging, and edifying them. In contrast **fools** starve to death **for lack of understanding**. Lacking wisdom, they cannot feed themselves, let alone others, and they do not have the good sense to go to the righteous for nourishment.

10:22. This verse reminds the wise who ultimately **makes** one **rich**. Wealth comes from **the blessing of the Lord** (v. 22a; cf. Dt 8:18). In the second half of the verse, **sorrow** is better translated "strenuous work" (Koehler et al., *HALOT*, 865), and it should be seen as the subject of the verb (i.e., "strenuous work does not add to the blessing that come from the Lord"). That is, one's own strenuous efforts "can give a man no more than God's blessing provides" (Fox, *Proverbs 10–31*, 523; cf. Dt 8:17). This hardly encourages laziness, since Proverbs does make clear that God uses a person's "righteous diligence" as a "means of God's blessing" (Waltke, *Book of Proverbs 1–15*, 473). But wise people know who really provides such blessings and who deserves the praise for them.

10:23-25. The foolish and the wise have different tastes (v. 23). The **fool** takes pleasure in **doing wickedness** (it is **like** a **sport to** him). He enjoys "any crass offense against people and community" (Waltke, *Book of Proverbs 1–15*, 474; cf. 2:14; 15:21; 26:19). On the other hand, the wise delight in **wisdom** (v. 23). One's pleasures reveal one's heart (Mt 6:21). Their destinies differ as well (Pr 10:24). The **wicked** fool's laughter only masks his deeper fear, a guilty conscience that dreads his getting his just deserts. Certainly he will, whether here or in the hereafter, for God is just (cf. Ec 12:14). In contrast, what the **righteous** wisely desire **will be granted** to them—wisdom, blessing, life, and ultimately, the Lord Himself. The **wicked** have good reason to be afraid because they are vulnerable, unlike the **righteous** (Pr 10:25). When life's devastating disasters come like a **whirlwind**, the wicked will be blown away whereas the righteous have enduring foundations to survive life's worst difficulties (cf. Ps 1; Mt 7:24-27).

10:26. A **lazy** person is infuriating. **Like** acidic sour wine (**vinegar**) which irritates **teeth** (particularly bad teeth; Waltke, *Book of Proverbs 1–15*, 476) or **smoke** which stings the **eyes**, a sluggard sent on a mission is entirely unreliable and therefore exasperating.

10:27-30. These proverbs all pertain to the futures of the righteous and the wicked. First, the righteous, those who wisely **fear . . . the LORD**, can expect prolonged **life**, but the life of the wicked **will be shortened** (v. 27). As a general principle, living in rebellion to God and the way He has ordered His world leaves one vulnerable in this present age to the debilitating effects of sin and folly. Second, they have different expectations (v. 28). The **righteous** can expect the kind of **gladness** that only God Himself can provide, both in His blessings but more particularly in His very presence (Ps 16:11). The wicked can expect disappointment, their hopes dashed. Third, they experience God's just rule differently (Pr 10:29). The **way of the LORD** generally involves His standards of morality and wisdom for human beings, but here it likely focuses on His commitment to uphold those standards in the world, i.e., "his moral government of the world" (Waltke, *Book of Proverbs 1–15*, 479). This explains why the **upright** or blameless find comforting security (**a stronghold**) in the **way of the LORD** whereas it means horrifying **ruin** to the **workers of iniquity**. No matter what outward circumstances may come, **the righteous will never be shaken** (cf. Pss 46; 125). In contrast **the wicked will not** live securely (**dwell in the land**), for the Lord has stipulated that one of the consequences of disobedience is removal from the land of Israel (cf. Dt. 28:63; Ps 37:9, 28; Longman, *Proverbs*, 244).

10:31-32. These proverbs focus on the words of the righteous and wicked. Like a fruitful plant, **the righteous** man "brings forth" (a better translation for the NASB's **flows with**) **wisdom** in what they speak (v. 31a). In contrast, the **perverted tongue** of the wicked distorts God's truth and can anticipate being stilled (**cut out**) in judgment (v. 31b). In a similar vein, v. 32 compares the character of each of their speech. To **bring forth** is best translated "to know" (*yada'*), in the sense of knowing something by experience because one is well practiced in it (Longman, *Proverbs*, 245). So the **lips of the righteous** are well practiced in **what is acceptable** whereas the **mouth of the wicked** is well practiced in perversities. Unlike the distorted speech of the wicked, the righteous speak in ways appropriate to the situation, thereby gaining "the approval of God and other wise persons" (Longman, *Proverbs*, 245).

11:1. Proverbs is an unendingly practical book to guiding daily life. Here it demonstrates that God is profoundly concerned about ethics in business. **A false balance**, when measuring or weighing items for purchases is cheating. Such unjust business practices are **an abomination to the LORD**. Dishonesty is serious because it is in the same category as other abominations, including sexual immorality, idolatry, occult practices, child sacrifice, and lying (cf. Lv 18:22; Dt 7:25; 18:9-14; Pr 3:32; 12:22; Jr 32:35). Although it might be easy to cheat in business, and it might not seem like a major sin, God utterly abhors such crooked practices but He **delight[s]** in honest business practices, a **just weight**. The wise know that the Lord's favor is more important than a quick buck.

11:2. Proverbs repeatedly asserts that the wise person is teachable (cf. 13:1, 10; 15:5). The **pride** of fools will bring them **dishonor** because they are too arrogant (and self-deceived) to be taught by those wiser than they are. The wise are **humble**. Being self-aware, they are teachable and therefore grow in **wisdom**.

11:3. This is the first of several proverbs (vv. 3-9) that address the fate of the righteous and the wicked. Those who are **upright**/blameless have **integrity** that will **guide** their decisions in life on the path of wisdom; they are honest and without guile. However, the **crookedness** of the **treacherous** twists and perverts the truth, making life choices that will **destroy them**.

11:4. The contrast between **riches** and **righteousness** is striking. Righteousness is more valuable than money (cf. 16:8; Ezk 7:19). This proverb probably applies the principle especially to ill-gotten gain (cf. Pr 10:2). Those who gain wealth at others' expense cannot bribe their way out of **the day of wrath**, which includes God's judgment in both the here and the hereafter. The righteous avoid that fate altogether (see comments on 2:20-23). **Righteousness** puts them on the path of life and so **delivers from death**.

11:5. The two paths, so prominent in chaps. 1–9 (see esp. 4:10-19), are reviewed here. The paths are altogether different. For the righteous and **blameless**, it is smooth. For **the wicked**, it is treacherous and strewn with stumbling blocks to make him stumble and **fall**. Granting that this is a fallen world and often the righteous are persecuted, Solomon and others who love Lady Wisdom have observed generally that the righteous have a more peaceful and contented life—and certainly a better destiny—than do the wicked (see Introduction: Retribution).

11:6. From what will the **upright** be delivered by their **righteousness**? Probably from the very thing that ensnares the treacherous, their own "evil desires" (NIV). This translation of *behawwat* is stronger than the NASB's **greed**, which is too narrow (although greed is certainly one kind of evil desire). Such cravings are ultimately deadly (cf. Jms 1:14-15).

11:7. The aspirations of the **wicked man**—no doubt shaped by his cravings—cannot survive death. That which he expects and hopes for (namely, his own pleasure and security) will remain unfulfilled **when** he **dies**. The second line explains why, though its translation is admittedly difficult. The NIV probably best captures the idea: "all he expected from his power comes to nothing." Whatever resources he trusted to get his way will prove to be wanting.

11:8. The **righteous** man has a far better resource: the Lord Himself. **Trouble** in this life is only temporary because he will be **delivered** from it by the Lord either in this life or the next. **His** short-lived **place** of trouble will be taken more permanently by **the wicked**, whose destiny is trouble because of God's judicial action against the wicked perhaps in this life and certainly in eternity.

11:9. The **godless man** does not just ruin himself. He also **destroys his neighbor** by what he says. Most likely the wicked man does so by communicating to his unwary associates the destructive folly he himself lives by, which spreads like a disease. But because they are wise and know better, the **righteous** are not taken in by his noxious counsel and so **will be delivered** from it.

11:10-11. Two things can make a **city**/community rejoice: the prosperity of **the righteous** or the perishing of **the wicked** (v. 10). Verse 11 explains why. The **blessing of the upright** may refer either to God's blessing on the righteous (which has positive effects on his neighbors) or the righteous man's effectual prayer for blessing to come upon his neighbors (Waltke, *Book of Proverbs 1–15*, 492). Either way, his **city** will benefit through its righteous citizens. In contrast, the wicked's words are a destructive instrument in his community. "The wicked slander, deceive, and abuse others, and this engenders conflict, uncertainty, and oppression all around them" (Fox, *Proverbs 10–31*, 535).

11:12. This proverb deals a devastating blow to judgmentalism. Only a fool **despises his neighbor** and so insults him. In contrast, **a man of understanding keeps silent**. Wise people do so because they are not proud. "The most misleading way to feel wise is to feel superior . . ., for one is denying that God is the only competent judge of human worth" (Kidner, *Proverbs*, 91). In addition, the wise respect and love their neighbors because every person bears the image of the Lord, the Creator of all (Waltke, *Book of Proverbs 1–15*, 493). And even if one's neighbor is a fool who deserves rebuke, the wise man will still be slow to speak his mind.

11:13. Choose your confidants carefully. A **talebearer** is a slanderer, one who is "malicious rather than indiscreet; he is an informer, out to hurt" (Kidner, *Proverbs*, 91; cf. Lv 19:16; Ezk 22:9). So for his own selfish ends he **reveals secrets** given to him in confidence, even if another is harmed by it. A true friend, one

who is trustworthy and faithful, **conceals** those confidences.

11:14. This proverb pertains particularly to a political and military context because it is talking about a people rather than individuals and so refers to a nation (hence involves political or military matters). That sense picks up on the impact of the righteous in the city (vv. 10-11). If a **people** do not want to **fall** but to have **victory** ("deliverance"), they need wise **guidance** best provided by an **abundance of counselors**. It is best to "get all the advice you can" because it is "fatally easy to shut out disquieting voices" (Kidner, *Proverbs*, 91–92). What goes for a people also goes for a person.

11:15. Here is wise counsel about cosigning a loan for a casual acquaintance. The implication is that when the debt is not paid by the **stranger**, the **guarantor** will be responsible for the debt and so **suffer** financial loss. Better to **hate** those kinds of financial agreements and be financially **secure** (see 6:1-5).

11:16-17. A **gracious woman** is reminiscent of the excellent wife (cf. 31:10-31) and of wisdom herself (chap. 8). Surprisingly, she is compared to a gang of **ruthless men** because both she and they can take hold of (**attain**) something apparently desirable. The gang can seize **riches** by their brutality, but such wealth is limited (11:4, 28), probably short lived (13:11), and ultimately self-destructive (2:8-19). What she gains is **honor**, which is not only more valuable and permanent than wealth (22:1), but often includes it (3:16; 8:18; 22:4). Hers is the better way. This becomes more apparent in v. 17. Like her, a **man** who is **merciful** and kind to others will actually benefit himself, whereas the **man** who is **cruel** to others ultimately ends up hurting **himself**.

11:18-19. It really does not pay to be **wicked**. Such a man **earns deceptive wages** that are both "unsatisfying and transitory" (Fox, *Proverbs 10–31*, 538). In contrast, **he who sows righteousness** will reap a far more reliable, **true reward**. The beginning of v. 19 is best translated "Yes indeed!" (Hb. *ken*) (Waltke, *Book of Proverbs 1–15*, 502) and suggests that this proverb unpacks v. 18. The righteous reap **life** itself. The wicked reap **death**—deceptive wages indeed!

11:20-21. God detests the **perverse in heart** but finds **delight** in those whose **walk** is **blameless**. One who is perverse "is set against God and community to serve self" (Waltke, *Book of Proverbs 1–15*, 502). One's character (**heart**) will inevitably manifest itself in one's behavior (**walk**). It is sometimes said that God hates the sin but loves the sinner, but this proverb (v. 21) does not make such neat distinctions. God's disposition toward sinners has sobering implications. For the **evil man**, there is the certainty that he **will not go unpunished**. God's wrath is finally inescapable (cf. Rm 1:18–2:16). But **the righteous will be delivered** from that fate. The **descendants** do not refer to progeny of the righteous but to individuals who live according to this wisdom principle.

11:22. Physical beauty is overrated. Dress a sow up with **a ring of gold**, and you still have a **swine**—a most detestable creature in ancient Israel because pork was the epitome of nonkosher food (Lv 11:1-8). So too is **a beautiful woman who lacks discretion**, "the God-given gift of discrimination enabling good judgment (1Sm 25:22; Jb 12:20; Ps 119:66)" (Waltke, *Book of Proverbs 1–15*, 504). Her tasteless behavior defaces her beauty. No matter how beautiful a woman might be, she becomes abhorrent to those around her if her character and behavior is loathsome. Those concerned with outward appearance should take note and prioritize wisely.

11:23. This proverb is ambiguous in comparing the **righteous** and **wicked**. The issue of the comparison is either the *nature* or the *result* of their aspirations. Although both are possible (perhaps even at the same time; cf. Waltke, *Book of Proverbs 1–15*, 505–6), the second line makes the latter, the result, more likely. The NIV captures well the idea: "The desire of the righteous ends only in good, but the hope of the wicked only in wrath." The proverb is thus a reminder of God's righteous judgment.

11:24-27. The wise are generous. A person **who scatters** is someone who gives freely, particularly to those in need (cf. Ps 112:9; Pr 19:17), and he contrasts directly with the miser **who withholds what is justly due** (cf. Dt 15:7-11; 1Tm 6:17-19). Paradoxically, the resources of the generous **increase** whereas the resources of the hoarder will only dwindle, **result[ing] . . . in want**, (Pr 11:24). So the altruist's generous giving will rebound back to him all the more (v. 25). Verse 26 specifies the principle. In a time of want, a grain dealer **who withholds grain** to drive up the price is compared to the one **who sells it** to those who need it. **The people will curse** the former and bless the latter in prayers to the Lord, who presumably repays in kind. Verse 27 captures a similar idea: "what you seek for others you will get yourself" (Kidner, *Proverbs*, 94). The one who **diligently seeks** to do **good** to others will receive **favor** from the Lord Himself, resulting in His blessing. The one **who seeks** after **evil** to inflict on others will suffer similar harm. Seek and you will find, so be careful what you seek.

11:28. It is folly for a man to **trust in his riches** because in doing so he **will fall**. Money is notoriously unreliable for those who rely on it (23:5; 10:2; 1Tm 6:17). In contrast **the righteous will flourish** like healthy foliage, because they trust in the Lord who is altogether reliable (Pr 3:5; 16:3, 20; 22:19; 28:25; 29:25).

11:29. This proverb probably profiles a foolish son. He **troubles** his family, **his own house**, whether by bad decisions, wasting resources, alienating relationships, turning away from the Lord, or something else. As a result, he will **inherit** the **wind**, that is, nothing. Left in poverty, without an inheritance, he **will** become a **servant to the wisehearted**, those too wise to get themselves into such straights.

11:30. He who is **righteous** and **wise** is a great blessing to others. His **fruit**—the beneficial effects of his words and deeds—are a veritable **tree of life** (cf. 3:18), conferring "healing and abundant, eternal life" to the community (Waltke, *Book of Proverbs 1–15*, 513). Furthermore, he **wins souls**. This disputed phrase more literally means to "take souls," that is, through his words and deeds he wins others over to the way of wisdom, righteousness, obedience to the Lord, and life.

11:31. This proverb deals with God's retribution here **in the earth**. The two lines present a "stronger-to-weaker" argument: if the first line is true, **how much more** the second. The **righteous will be rewarded**, is better translated "repaid" (ESV) or "receive their due" (NIV) for their behavior. It carries a negative sense of warning here. This is the way Peter (following the LXX) understood this proverb (1Pt 4:15-19; see comments there). That is, even the righteous cannot escape judgment for sin on this earth. If so, **how much more** should **the wicked and the sinner** expect punishment. "In other words, nobody sins with impunity; not even a Moses or a David, much less the confirmed rebel" (cf. Jr 25:29; Ezk. 18:24; Kidner, *Proverbs*, 95).

12:1. This proverb assumes we all make mistakes; the only question is what we do with them. Those who are humble enough to eagerly receive **discipline** and correction demonstrate their wisdom. Those who in pride **hate** such **reproof** are brutishly **stupid**.

12:2-3. Wisdom has a moral dimension, and so the wise know to choose what is right. They know that **the Lord** as judge will **favor** the **good man** and **condemn** the **evil** schemer. Moreover, they know that righteousness is far more stable and secure than **wickedness**.

12:4. Here is good advice for the bachelor. Find **an excellent wife**, or more literally, "a woman of strength" (*chayil*) and godly character. She is described in more detail in 31:10-31 and illustrated by Ruth who is also called a woman of excellence (Ru 3:11). To her **husband**, such a noble woman is like a valuable **crown**, bringing him honor. In contrast is a wife **who shames** her **husband** in public and private. She is like a cancerous growth that is **rottenness in his bones**. "She undermines him by being unfaithful (Pr 2:17), contentious (19:13; 21:9, 19) and/or impious and incompetent (cf. 31:10-31)" (Waltke, *Book of Proverbs 1–15*, 522). And rather than her being a source of pride for him before others, he suffers with her in private (Fox, *Proverbs 10–31*, 548).

12:5-6. The righteous have **just** intentions (**thoughts**). The selfish intentions of **the wicked** lie hidden in their **deceitful** advice. Verse 6 may be talking about the effect of their respective advice on others when the goals of the wicked (personal advancement through harming others) in contrast to those of the upright (serving and strengthening the community) become clear. Like a bloody ambush, the deceptive **words** of the **wicked** will destroy those who heed them, in contrast to the words of the **upright**, which will **deliver** those who listen. But the wording of this proverb is ambiguous, and so it may be talking about the effect of their words on themselves, either as self-destructive or self-preserving. The former of the two seems more likely, though the ambiguity may be intentional to include both.

12:7. This proverb again compares the instability of the **wicked** with the stability of the **righteous** (cf. 10:25; 12:3). The former are **overthrown** and destroyed, presumably by God, whether directly or indirectly. The stability of the latter extends even to their **house** (one's dwelling or line of descendants or both; see comments on 14:11).

12:8-9. Wisdom is noteworthy. **A man** with **insight**—"the ability to recognize the true nature of a situation or circumstance" and act appropriately (Longman, *Proverbs*, 273)—**will be praised** by others who take note, and for good reason. In contrast, the person with a **perverse**

mind is incapable of thinking clearly and also acts accordingly, only to earn contempt from others. But social esteem has its limits (v. 9). Verse 9 is a "better this than that" proverb that establishes priorities. Here there is a priority higher than reputation. In short, it is better to have food without an impressive reputation among one's peers than to engage arrogantly in self-promotion when one does not have food. A person with a **servant** in ancient Israel may not necessarily have been rich, but he would probably have enough to feed himself (cf. Waltke, *Book of Proverbs 1–15*, 525–26). Even if he is **lightly esteemed** in society, he is still better off than a starving pauper who **honors himself**, that is, who tries to "play the great man" (ESV).

12:10. This proverb compares the sensitivities of the **righteous** and the **wicked**. In his disposition to look out for the needs of others, the righteous even considers the needs of his **animal** and cares for it. In stark contrast, the self-absorbed wicked man is just plain mean, **cruel** even in his most compassionate moments. Thus the righteous is compassionate even to the most insignificant, whereas the wicked is cruel even at his best.

12:11. Dreamers beware! "Frivolity fills no cupboard" (Kidner, *Proverbs*, 96). The person who works hard in productive pursuits, such as working **his land**, will have **plenty** to eat. **But** it is foolish nonsense to chase **worthless things** instead, vain pursuits or fantasies that cannot put **bread** on the table.

12:12. There are several textual and interpretive difficulties in this proverb, and so there are also several possible interpretations. But broadly speaking, the proverb may be comparing the wicked and righteous either in regard to what they *produce* or in regard to their *stability* (Waltke, *Book of Proverbs 1–15*, 529). The noun **booty** is better translated "net" (so KJV) or "snare," although both translations are connected (booty being what one snares). If the proverb focuses upon what they produce, then the wicked will accumulate things by means of his violence against others. In contrast, the Lord produces a thriving life for **the righteous**. If stability is the point, then it maintains that the wicked are pursuing their own deadly trap whereas the healthy **root of the righteous** continually yields fruit for the righteous. Interestingly, both ideas are picked up in the next two proverbs in regard to words.

12:13-14. An **evil man['s]** offending words (**the transgression of his lips**) bring **trouble**, but to whom? The Hebrew text is more ambiguous than the NASB. So it may be that they ensnare the gullible, a trap that the righteous **escape**. Or, as the NASB indicates, the wicked's offending words (whether slander, gossip, or lying) bring trouble on his own head, whereas the words of the righteous keep him out of such **trouble**. The latter is more likely, particularly in connection with principle of retribution laid out in v. 14. What you sow you reap, whether in word or deed. The principle is applied particularly to the righteous, who finds satisfaction in the **good fruit** produced by his words and deeds.

12:15. The **fool** is cocksure. He is convinced that what he is doing (his **way**) is **right**. Why would he need anyone's corrective counsel when he already has everything figured out? The **wise man** knows that he does not have it all figured out, so he is teachable, seeking and heeding the wise counsel of others.

12:16. The fool displays his **anger** at **once** because he is proud and lacks self-control. In contrast, the **prudent man** demonstrates a humble self-control that **conceals dishonor** in the sense that he overlooks insults (cf. 10:12; 17:9; 19:11).

12:17. The statement that a truthful witness **tells what is right** whereas a **false witness** deceives may seem like mere truism. But the point is more profound: one's words reflect one's character—and affect others. Wise people of honest character are particularly important in a legal setting, since justice requires reliable witnesses and is subverted by false ones.

12:18. Rash outbursts (like that of Moses referred to in Ps 106:33) can be as harmful to others as **thrusts of a sword**, whereas **wise** words, spoken with soothing care, bring **healing**. The **wise** are peacemakers, effecting reconciliation and not inciting conflict.

12:19. Truth endures, providing a sure foundation, **established forever**. Lies eventually are discovered, and any of their gains are only temporary, **for a moment**. The proverb may also be talking about the fate of those who engage in either behavior, thereby reiterating the theme of the stability of the wise/righteous and the insecurity of the foolish/wicked.

12:20. The two lines of this proverb contrast those who **devise evil** and **counselors of peace**. On the one hand, those who plot **evil** are deceptive at heart. They promote strife in the community, ultimately to their own misery (perhaps because the evil they plot boomerangs back on them; Waltke, *Book of Proverbs 1–15*, 538). On the other hand, those who counsel **peace** are honest at heart. They promote harmony in their community, and experience a fulfilling sense of **joy** as a result.

12:21. This proverb may be a broad statement of retribution: God keeps **the righteous** from all **harm** (the kind of harm that afflicts the wicked when He judges them), but the **wicked** get their fill of trouble (punishment in judgment). If so, then it is a general principle, not an ironclad contract—a mistaken interpretation Job's friends made. But the proverb may be more specific than that, bearing a close connection with the previous proverb. The term **harm** (*'awen*) "always refers to wickedness (e.g., 6:12; 10:29; 17:4) or (less frequently) to its consequences (e.g., 22:8; Jb 21:19; Ps 41:7)" (Fox, *Proverbs 10–31*, 557). Here it may involve harm that is a result of evil scheming. If so, by not lingering in evil, the righteous never experience the kind of harm that backfires on the wicked.

12:22. This proverb provides all the motivation one should need to be honest. **The Lord** deplores liars and their **lying**, but He **delight[s]** in those whose dealings are honest (cf. v. 17).

12:23. A **prudent man** is not a self-promoter. A man of careful words, he does not show off his **knowledge**, but keeps it in store for the right time. The **fool**, in contrast, has no such caution. Careless with words, he **proclaims** his **folly** and thereby reveals his true self (his **heart**).

12:24. Diligence pays off. Those who are **diligent will rule**, attaining authority and independence by their hard work. **But** the slacker **will be put to forced labor**. In ancient Israel, forced labor was a kind of tax (e.g., 1Kg 5:13), and it may be that local leaders would have chosen their least productive members to meet their quota of laborers (Fox, *Proverbs 10–31*, 558). In any case, though the slacker seeks to avoid work, he is forced to do the most menial, onerous chores. So "the diligent rise to the top and the lazy sink to the bottom" (Allen Ross, *Proverbs*, EBC 5 [Grand Rapids, MI: Zondervan, 1991), 973).

12:25. An encouraging word is powerful, a **glad** antidote to an **anxiety** that **weighs down** the **heart** (very core of a person). The **good word** that encourages may take many forms depending on the circumstances, from giving the person a wider perspective (so Longman, *Proverbs*, 279) to strengthening him to face the cause of his anxiety (Kidner, *Proverbs*, 99).

12:26. The translation and interpretation of this proverb, particularly the first line, is disputed. The NIV paraphrases one option: "A righteous man is cautious in friendship." The NASB gives another one: **The righteous is a guide to his neighbor**. Although both are possible, the NASB is preferable since it fits better with the second line. If so, the **righteous** and **wicked** differ markedly in their sense of direction. The former knows the right way so well he is able to guide others; the latter do not know the right way and so wander astray to their destruction.

12:27. This proverb contrasts the slacker with the diligent (cf. v. 24) and presents another interpretive conundrum (cf. v. 26). The image in the first line may be that the **lazy man** is too slothful either to cook what he has caught or even to bother hunting it in the first place. The word **roast** could also be translated "catch." So the proverb is either about cooking the food or catching the food, but in either case, he has nothing to eat. The Hebrew text of the second line is difficult grammatically, but the ESV may best capture its sense, particularly in contrast to the first line: "the diligent man will get his precious wealth." The proverb would thus contrast the starvation of the slacker with the prosperity of the diligent.

12:28. The first line is clear enough, and it reiterates a major theme in the first section of Proverbs. The **way of righteousness** is the path of **life** (cf. 3:1-20; 4:10-19). The Hebrew of the second line is difficult to interpret, depending in part on whether one understands the text to say **no death** or "to death." In the latter sense, the line would present another contrast and read: "But another path leads to death" (HCSB). Yet the NASB probably represents the stronger interpretation: **And in its pathway there is no death**. If so, this proverb indicates that the way of righteousness includes immortality—a powerful motivation indeed!

13:1-3. It is crucial both to listen and speak wisely. The **wise son** is contrasted with the most intransigent of fools, the **scoffer**. The wise son is teachable, accepting correction from his father. The incorrigible mocker is so set in his folly that he scoffs at such correction. Verse 2 may be intentionally ambiguous. If the subject of the first line is indefinite (*one* rather than ***he* enjoys good** things [emphasis added]), then the proverb addresses both listening and speaking, forming a transition from listening in v. 1 to speaking in v. 3 (Waltke, *Book of Proverbs 1–15*, 552–53). A wise man speaks wise words; this produces (the sense of **fruit**) **good** things both for himself and for those who heed him (like the wise son in v. 1). Conversely, because a **treacherous** person (like the mocker in v. 1) craves **violence**, his words aim to hurt others while ultimately coming back to harm himself. For these reasons, a wise man guards his words carefully whereas the fool has a big mouth (v. 3). It really is a matter of **life** and death because rash words—be they hasty "promises, assertions, disclosures"—produce **ruin**, whether "financial, social, physical, spiritual" (Kidner, *Proverbs*, 101).

13:4. This is another contrast between sloth and diligence (cf. 12:24, 27). The **sluggard** is left only with whatever things he **craves**, which remain unfulfilled because he is too lazy to fulfill them. But **the diligent** will have his "desires" (better than the NASB's **soul**) fully satisfied (**made fat**). Hard work pays off (cf. 13:25).

13:5. The **righteous man hates falsehood**, which implies at least that he will not be ashamed and may even be honored for his honesty. In contrast, since the **wicked man** presumably is loose with the truth, he will be disgraced. He **acts disgustingly** (brings a stench) and so becomes shameful. Think, for example, of a man who never gets around to keeping his promises.

13:6. Here **righteousness** and **wickedness** are given human qualities. Personified Righteousness protects **the one whose way is blameless**, whereas personified Wickedness leads **the sinner** astray to his own ruin. The better companion on life's path is obvious for anyone with sense.

13:7-8. Real wealth is not always obvious. Sometimes a person who is really poor **pretends to be rich** and someone who is quite wealthy **pretends to be poor**. The verbs here are ambiguous: both persons may be pretenders, or paradoxically they may actually be rich (or poor) monetarily and yet poor (or rich) in more important ways (cf. Lk 12:21; 2Co 6:10). At the very least, this proverb demonstrates that appearances can be deceiving. Proverbs 13:8 reiterates the point. One would think that the wealthy would enjoy greater security, but this is not necessarily so. The word **rebuke** probably carries the connotation of "threat." Thus, whereas the rich may have the resources to pay off a kidnapper or blackmailer, the poor man is not vulnerable to such threats in the first place. Lacking resources, he "offers too small a target" (Kidner, *Proverbs*, 102).

13:9. Light and **lamp** are metaphors for life, including quality of life (cf. Jb 18:5-6; 21:17; Pr 24:20). In the case of the **righteous**, their **light rejoices**. Though the verb *yismach* regularly does mean "to rejoice," here it probably carries the meaning "to shine brightly" (Koehler et al., *HALOT*, 1335). Nevertheless the two are interconnected. The righteous receive life and enjoy it. The prospects of the wicked are grimmer: an extinguished **lamp**. They thus face catastrophe and death.

13:10. Insolence is always present when there is **strife**; pride drives quarrels. Those who are wise have a humble spirit that listens first and is willing to accept good **counsel**, thus avoiding quarrels. Kidner notes that strife is not a difference of opinion but a "clash of competing and unyielding personalities" (*Proverbs*, 102).

13:11-12. Patience is a virtue. Its advantage is seen in the accumulation of wealth (v. 11). Occasionally, some lazy people actually produce wealth, short lived though it might be. The NASB's **wealth obtained by fraud** is probably too specific. Better to think of it as wealth acquired "by unsound means," or "easy money" (Waltke, *Book of Proverbs 1–15*, 561). This could include anything from legal get-rich-quick schemes (such as gambling) to fraudulent ventures to blatant robbery. Such wealth **dwindles**. **One who gathers by labor** (lit., "by hand") is one who works diligently and patiently. Unlike the fool's "easy come, easy go" wealth, this wise man's wealth will **increase**, even if gradually. Patience is also advantageous in a broader sense (v. 12). When one's hopes and expectations are delayed, one becomes **heartsick**—discouraged, frustrated, even depressed. When one's hopes and expectations are **fulfilled**, it brings to one's soul joyful vitality, like **a tree of life**. This general observation counsels patience to the righteous and wise (who will not finally be disappointed) and warns the wicked and foolish, whose hopes will remain elusive.

13:13-15. The wise are not just teachable; they are also obedient to that teaching (v. 13). The teaching is described as **the word** and the **commandment**, referring to God's Word in general and to wisdom teaching in particular (Longman, *Proverbs*, 287–88). To **fear** those teachings is to respect them so that one obeys, in contrast to one who **despises** and disregards those teachings. The latter "will pay for it" (the NIV's helpful paraphrase of the NASB's more literal **will be in debt to it**) in judgment; the former will be rewarded. Verse 14 clarifies why. **The teaching[s] of the wise**, like a bubbling fountain, give life and vitality. They also help those who listen to avoid **death** traps laid by the wicked and foolish.

Verse 15 continues in the same vein. A person with **good** sense wins **favor** from both God and man. In contrast, the **way of the treacherous** or unfaithful ends in their destruction. In the second line, the NASB's **hard** is difficult to justify, and so it is best to go with "destruction," following the LXX.

13:16. Jesus said that a good and bad tree are recognized by their fruit (cf. Mt 7:20); the same could be said for the wise and foolish. Even if the **prudent man** is not a self-promoter (cf. Pr 12:23), his **knowledge** is still evident in how he **acts**. Similarly, the **fool** inevitably puts his **folly** on display, both in word and deed. One's character is thus "written all over one's conduct" (Kidner, *Proverbs*, 104).

13:17. In the ancient world, messengers played crucial roles in government, commerce, and personal relationships. Much therefore depended on reliable, **faithful** messengers. **A wicked messenger** gets into **adversity**/trouble, either while trying to accomplish his mission or after he botches it. Because he is unreliable, he arrives late or distorts the message or just does not bother delivering it at all, bringing harm both to himself and to those who employ him. In contrast, the **faithful envoy brings healing**. His task well done, he fosters well-being in the community and for himself.

13:18. There are huge advantages to those who are disciplined enough to accept correction (reproof) (cf. 12:1; 13:1). Wealth and honor (note the connection in 3:16) come to them, as opposed to the **poverty and shame** awaiting proud fools who disregard corrective advice.

13:19. This proverb may be contrasting the desires of the righteous, which when inevitably **realized** will be **sweet** to them, with the **evil** desires of **fools**, which prevent them from experiencing the joy of the righteous. But the first line seems like a general principle: it is a joy to have one's legitimate **desire realized** (whatever the nature of that desire). That being the case, **fools** find delight in **evil** realized. The point is that one's desires reveal one's character.

13:20. A man is shaped by his friends. If he hangs around with **wise men** then he will become **wise**. If he associates with **fools**, the results are equally predictable. Becoming a fool himself, he will **suffer** the **harm** that fools should expect. The proverb may also suggest that one's character is demonstrated by one's choice of friends.

13:21-22. The next two proverbs address recompense for the sinner and the righteous. The first personifies evil (**adversity**) and good (**prosperity**). "In this personification the evil that sinners inflict on others turns around to destroy them, and the good that the righteous bestowed on others justly rewards them" (Waltke, *Book of Proverbs 1–15*, 572). So like a relentless stalker, **adversity pursues sinners**, and it will inevitably find them. In the second line, against the NASB, **prosperity** is likely the subject, and the verb (**will be rewarded**) is active rather than passive. That is, **prosperity** will reward the **righteous**. The next proverb addresses the staying power of that prosperity (v. 22). The blessing of the **good man** endures, left as **an inheritance** for subsequent generations of his family. In contrast, any **wealth** that the sinner might **store up** is short lived for him, only to be passed on ultimately to **the righteous**.

13:23. People are not always poor because of laziness or foolishness; sometimes they are just plain victims of **injustice**. Diligently working one's field, which can produce plenty of **food**, may not be enough to keep one out of poverty if there is **injustice** in the land. For the rich and powerful may sweep **away** the land's yield, leaving one destitute.

13:24. Parents who love their children discipline them. If folly is bound up in the heart of a child (22:15), and that folly is deadly, then a parent who **withholds** (spares) **his rod** not only spoils **his son**, but he may even push him toward his death (23:14; 19:18). This is hate indeed. But loving one's child calls for diligent discipline to root out the folly in his heart, and sometimes "it will take more than words to dislodge it" (Kidner, *Proverbs*, 51). The **rod** may be a metonymy for discipline of various sorts, but it clearly includes, and probably emphasizes, physical discipline. This text supports neither the physical abuse of children nor the abandonment of physical discipline. Neither extreme is loving because neither looks out for the child's best interests (see 19:18-19; 20:30; 22:15; 23:13-14 and comments there).

13:25. This proverb connects righteousness with plenty, and wickedness with want. As in 10:3, here too God's retributive justice stands behind the saying. God gives **the righteous . . . enough to satisfy his appetite**, but the wicked starve, their appetite unfulfilled. Although this may apply literally, it surely carries emotional and spiritual applications as well. Jesus made a similar point (Mt 6:25-34, esp. v. 33).

14:1. It is crucial that a man choose his wife carefully, not only because she directly affects his life (cf. 12:4) but because she directly shapes his whole household. The **wise woman** promotes the well-being of her family in a variety of ways (cf. 31:10-31) and thereby **builds her house**. The foolish woman destroys her household in the various ways that folly manifests itself—such as arrogance, foolish speech, impatience, incompetence, lack of self-control, or unfaithfulness (Waltke, *Book of Proverbs 1–15*, 584). Each kind of potential wife recalls either Lady Wisdom or Woman Folly (cf. chap. 9).

14:2. One's walk is a matter of worship. Fearing the Lord, wisdom, and ethics are all interconnected (cf. 1:7; 9:10). So a man whose lifestyle is upright (keeping within ethical boundaries) demonstrates that he **fears the Lord**, and one whose lifestyle is **devious** reveals that he **despises Him**.

14:3. The first line is ambiguous. The NASB and other translations emend the Hebrew text to read **rod for his back**. But without emendation the text reads "rod of pride," and there seems no good reason to justify the emendation. The image may suggest that the fool's words are like a shoot (cf. Is 11:1) which sprouts from pride, and in light of the parallel, the **rod** likely has a punitive connotation. Thus the fool's words not only display his pride, but also bring their own punishment, a fate the wise avoid. In contrast, the words **of the wise will protect them** from trouble.

14:4. Productivity requires investment. This proverb uses an agricultural illustration. **Oxen** are needed to produce an increase in crops, but oxen require feeding and clean up. Having **no oxen** requires no investment because the feeding trough remains empty and therefore **clean**. But if one wants the **revenue** that **comes by the strength of the ox**, then one needs to invest the labor and resources to own oxen.

14:5-6. One's character makes a difference on what *comes out of* a person (v. 5). An honest person does not utter lies; a dishonest person **utters lies**—or better, "breathes out lies" (so ESV; cf. 12:17). Furthermore, one's character makes a difference on what *goes into* a person. A **scoffer** is too arrogant and intractable to ever really take **wisdom** to heart, even though he **seeks** it on his own terms. But **one who has understanding** has an **easy** time taking in more wise **knowledge**.

14:7. This proverb exhorts those who would be wise to **leave the presence of a fool**. The fool's companion will never find any **words of knowledge** with him, and his foolishness may rub off on his companion (cf. 13:20; 1Co 15:33).

14:8. Self-awareness is crucial. **The wisdom of the sensible** gives him insight into **his** own **way** of life. He knows what he is about, where he should go, and the blessings that result. In contrast, the **foolishness of fools** deceives the fool himself so that he is not aware of how foolish he is, or the disaster that awaits him on his path.

14:9. The word **sin** here is better translated "guilt," or even "guilt offering." Although some argue that "guilt" is the subject (i.e., guilt mocks fools), it is more likely the object (as in the NASB). In mocking guilt, **fools** care not a whit about incurring guilt before God and man, much less about making amends. Clearly, the upright do, and so they enjoy acceptance (or **good will**) from God and **among** themselves.

14:10-13. These four proverbs each relate to the idea that appearances can be deceiving.

14:10. No one really knows the internal experiences of another. The gamut of a person's feelings, from **bitterness** to **joy**, cannot be fully shared with another human. Our dealings with each other must reflect our awareness that in some sense we are each something of a **stranger** to the other, no matter how close we are. Only the Lord fully knows the human heart (15:11)—in all its individuality and complexity.

14:11. This proverb compares the destinies of the **wicked** and righteous in a rather paradoxical sense. The wicked's **house** may seem more permanent and prosperous than the **tent of the upright**. Nevertheless, the former **will be destroyed** whereas the latter **will** not only endure but also **flourish**. One's house or tent here are synonymous terms for all that belongs to a person—his life, family, and possessions.

14:12. A man may judge a particular path to be **right** *(yashar)*. Since this term can also mean "straight" or "smooth," it is probably intentionally ambiguous, referring to a **way** that seems ethical and/or prudent. That is, the path one chooses may seem to be the easiest path or the best way to success or morally acceptable. But in the **end** it leads to **death**. Since a foolish, immoral path can appear to be neither foolish nor immoral, the wise man will not lean on his own understanding but trust in the Lord, seeking His insight and wisdom (cf. 3:5-6).

14:13. "Outward merriment may mask heartache, but in the end grief will manifest itself" (Waltke, *Book of Proverbs 1–15*, 592). This side of glory, happiness has its limitations (v. 13a) and is not permanent in any case (v. 13b). This sobering proverb reminds the wise not to accept people's **laughter** at face value and to look for a more enduring **joy** (cf. Jn 16:20-24; 17:13; Rv 21:3-4).

14:14. This verse compares **a good man** with a **backslider**, one who rebelliously turns away from the Lord and His way. Each face the same outcome: they will both get their **fill of** their **own ways** (the main verb in the second line is implied from the first line). This may simply refer to retributive judgment; each type will fully reap what he sows (cf. Gl 6:7). Or it may mean that each finds satisfaction in what he does, which in the case of the rebel is shortsighted, foolish, and ultimately deadly (so Peter A. Steveson, *A Commentary on Proverbs* [Greenville, SC: BJU Press, 2001], 189–90; Longman, *Proverbs*, 301).

14:15-17. In various ways, the next three proverbs reinforce the idea that the wise are cautious before the Lord.

14:15. The **naive** are gullible. They take things at face value and do not bother to ponder matters more carefully before acting, inevitably getting into trouble. The **sensible man**, in contrast, avoids such trouble because he **considers** matters more carefully before he acts. Look before you leap!

14:16. The NKJV better captures the Hebrew text of this proverb: "A wise man fears and departs from evil, but a fool rages and is self-confident." The **wise man** fears the consequences of foolish and evil decisions and so **is cautious** to avoid evil. This would contrast with the **fool** who is so arrogantly overconfident that he exercises little self-control over his temper. More likely, in this proverb the **wise man** fears the Lord (cf. 1:7) and so **turns away from evil** (cf. 3:7). The **fool**, then, rages against the Lord—arrogant overconfidence indeed!

14:17. A quick-tempered man acts foolishly because he is rash and careless. But being more intentional is not enough, because there is someone even worse: the **man** who intentionally plots **evil**. To be sure, he is far more deliberate than the hothead, but his discipline is bent toward evil purposes. Such a person **is hated**, certainly by others who catch him in his schemes, but more importantly by the Lord, who will judge him.

14:18-19. Wisdom is prestigious. It brings honor (i.e., the wise are **crowned with knowledge**). Those who are **naive**, and remain so, **inherit foolishness**. They can expect the shame that is the fool's lot—some inheritance! In contrast, the **knowledge** of the **sensible** is like a crown, which is not only plainly evident in their lives but also honors them. Wisdom (manifested in righteousness) also brings triumph. The **righteous** will rule over wicked (v. 19). The **gates of the righteous** probably allude to the city gates, where the righteous dispense justice to the wicked (Fox, *Proverbs 10–31*, 580). This is a general principle (e.g., Joseph and Mordecai) that has exceptions in our fallen world but is inevitably true in the long run (Longman, *Proverbs*, 303; cf. Lk 16:19-31; Rv 5:10; 20:4; 22:5).

14:20-21. Verse 20 makes a general observation about human life. "It is a principle of human nature that most people would rather be in the company of wealthy persons than of poor persons. The latter typically have needs that require attention, whereas the former have resources that may prove a benefit to others" (Longman, *Proverbs*, 303). Obviously, then, being **poor** is not advantageous. But being rich has its disadvantages as well, since **the rich** person is besieged by **many** "fair-weather friends" (Kidner, *Proverbs*, 109) who hang around for what they can get out him (cf. Ec 5:11). The righteous go against the grain of this reality (Pr 14:21). Realizing that it is a **sin** to **despise** one's **neighbor**, particularly the needy **poor** around him, he is **gracious** to them. That is, he "esteems his neighbor as worthy of favor, and so actively accepts him and does acts of kindness for him" (Waltke, *Book of Proverbs 1–15*, 599). Such a person is indeed blessed (**happy**), enjoying the Lord's favor.

14:22. Those who plan **good** or **evil** will be "paid in their own coin" (Kidner, *Proverbs*, 110). Plotters of evil will **go astray** from the path of life to their destruction. But **those who devise good** will encounter loving **kindness** (*chesed*) and faithfulness (**truth**; *emet*) from others and from the Lord.

14:23-24. Being foolish is not worth it. All hard work is profitable, but a fool's **mere talk** is worthless and **leads only to poverty** (v. 23). Sluggards take note. Moreover, with wisdom comes honor (a **crown**; cf. v. 18) and wealth (cf. 3:16), but **folly** is its own, and only, reward (v. 23).

14:25. The proverb in 14:5 described the character of honest and dishonest witnesses; this proverb speaks to what is at stake. In a legal context, people's lives are at stake. Truth-telling **saves lives**, but perjurers threaten lives by their selfish deceit.

14:26-27. The wise man fears **the LORD**. Doing so brings him protection from folly and evil, and through his influence, protects his family as well (v. 26). **The fear of the LORD** is thus like a **fountain of life** that saves him (and those whom he influences) from **death** (v. 27).

14:28. A wise **king** promotes the good of his **people**. A prosperous, vital people who grow numerous only increase his splendor. But a king whose policies cause his people to waste away or abandon him is ruined. "A king without much of a nation is not much of a king" (Longman, *Proverbs*, 306). Wise leaders know that policies that are good for their followers are good for them.

14:29-30. Self-control is enormously beneficial. In the form of patience, it promotes **great understanding**, while impatience only promotes **folly** (v. 29). Patience exhibits a self-control that leaves room for deliberate action, depends on trust in the Lord, and reflects His own patience (Waltke, *Book of Proverbs 1–15*, 605–6). In the form of a **tranquil heart**—an emotional stability—self-control promotes physical health (v. 30). Those whose **passion** runs hot (such as those with fervid jealousy) literally undermine their physical well-being.

14:31. Though poverty may sometimes result from folly and wickedness, that is not always so (cf. 13:23), and in any case does not justify mistreating the **poor**. All human beings, rich and poor alike, are created as ones who bear the image of God. So to **oppress** the **needy** ultimately shows Him contempt, and to be **gracious** to them **honors Him**. Abusing the poor is thus not only wicked, it is foolish, putting one under divine censure. The righteous wise treat the poor with dignity and generous love as to the Lord Himself (cf. Mt 25:31-46).

14:32. This proverb looks toward the ultimate end of the **wicked** and **righteous**. The former will finally be **thrust down** to ruin. **The righteous**, in contrast, has different expectations **when he dies**. He **has a refuge** in the Lord. That is, the righteous trust in the Lord when they die, knowing that they will not be cast down to destruction.

14:33. This difficult proverb has occasioned several interpretations, including adding "not" to the second line (following LXX). But it is probably best to see this as two very different responses to **wisdom** (so Waltke, *Book of Proverbs 1–15*, 610). The NIV captures the sense: "Wisdom reposes in the heart of the discerning, and even among fools she lets herself be known." Personified Wisdom reveals herself to all (9:1-6), even to **fools**, but only the discerning take her to **heart**. She is at rest there because she belongs with those who are like her.

14:34-35. A nation needs both righteousness and wisdom. A truly great **nation** is characterized by **righteousness**, exercising a concern for and justly dealing with others (v. 34). In contrast, a sinful nation **is a disgrace**. "Ultimately a nation's exaltation depends on its piety and ethics, not on its political, military, and/or economic greatness" (Waltke, *Book of Proverbs 1–15*, 612). A nation also needs wise officials, and kings who want their nation to prosper know this. So an insightful **servant** of the king enjoys his **favor**, but a foolish official who inevitably **acts shamefully** will face the king's **anger** (v. 35).

15:1-2. Wise speech is both restrained and edifying. In confrontational situations, it takes self-control to respond (**answer**) gently (v. 1), but doing so is constructive. It **turns away wrath**, which can sabotage fruitful dialogue, sour relationships, and damage others. Far worse is to escalate **anger** with a **harsh** response that seeks to hurt others. Wise, thoughtful speech is also edifying because it promotes **knowledge** and does so in a winsome way (v. 2). In contrast, unrestrained "fools just vomit up their nonsense" (Fox, *Proverbs 10–31*, 589), damaging others as well as themselves.

15:3. The LORD sees everything everywhere. His omnipresence and omniscience should be a warning to **the evil** and an encouragement to **the good**.

15:4. Words can be **soothing** and healing, like **a tree of life** (cf. Ezk 47:7, 12; Rv 22:2). But life-fostering words never distort or deceive. Such **perversion** of speech **crushes the spirit**, devastating one's emotional and spiritual well-being. The wise speak sensitively, but they speak the truth nonetheless.

15:5. A young man who **rejects his father's** correction may consider himself too clever to need it, but really he is a **fool**. It is the one who takes **reproof** to heart who becomes truly shrewd (**sensible**), having the capacity to "maneuver his way through life to his best advantage" (Fox, *Proverbs 10–31*, 590).

15:6. The **righteous** accrue **great wealth**, their **house** like a great vault containing many kinds of valuable resources. The **wicked** simply accrue **trouble** or ruin. The resources of the former bless both themselves and others, since the righteous are concerned for others. Similarly, the wicked brings trouble to others, but then ultimately that trouble rebounds back on himself (Waltke, *Book of Proverbs 1–15*, 619).

15:7. The parallel between **lips** and **hearts** suggests that one's words flow from who one is. Since the **wise** have taken **knowledge** to heart, their words **spread** it. **Fools** simply have no knowledge to spread, but only foolishness.

15:8-9. The Lord delights in the righteous but deplores the wicked. Merely being religious is not enough (v. 8). The **wicked** may offer a **sacrifice**, but **the Lord** considers it an **abomination** (cf. 1Sm 15:22). Yet even a **prayer** offered by the **upright is His delight**. "It is the sacrificer, not the sacrifice, that is the issue" (Roland Murphy, *Proverbs*, WBC [Nashville: Nelson, 1998], 112). What goes for their religious practice also applies to their way of life, which reveals the character of each (Pr 15:9). Note how the one enjoying the Lord's loving favor actually **pursues righteousness**—a truly devoted heart indeed!

15:10. The Lord may despise the wicked's way (v. 9), but the wicked apostate—he **who forsakes the way** of the Lord—returns the favor. He finds discipline (**punishment**) rooted in God's wisdom to be distasteful. Though the NASB and other translations indicate that the wicked should expect stern discipline (**grievous punishment**) in the first line, Longman's translation (*Proverbs*, 315) is probably better: "Discipline is evil to those who abandon the way" (cf. KJV). That is, he considers such **reproof** to be evil (cf. vv. 5, 12) and so he **hates** it (cf. Clifford, *Proverbs*, 152). His end is made clear: **he . . . will die**.

15:11. Sheol is the grave and **Abaddon** the place of destruction. Together they refer to the realm of death. This dark, distant, impenetrable place (cf. Ps 88:11-12) **lie[s] open before the Lord**; His omniscience—and by extension, His sovereignty—reaches even here. If so, then **how much more** does He know and rule over human **hearts** (cf. Pr 15:3). "The Moral Governor's probing, penetrating, all-seeing gaze tests the motives governing their actions (16:2; 17:3; 21:2; 24:12), and no one can escape his demand for an answer" (Waltke, *Book of Proverbs 1–15*, 623).

15:12. A scoffer dislikes anyone **who reproves him** so he stays away from **the wise**. Being the most arrogant kind of fool, he has no interest in wisdom's correction, nor the courage to change.

15:13-15. These three proverbs all deal with the human heart. First, the heart affects one's exterior and interior life (v. 13). Joy in one's **heart** typically shows in one's **cheerful** countenance (though not always; cf. Ec 7:3), whereas a **sad heart** is dispiriting, leading to "a crushed, downtrodden, attitude" (Murphy, *Proverbs*, 112–13) and sapping one of vitality. Second, the character of one's heart is reflected in what one finds satisfying (Pr 15:14). The NIV better captures the first line: "the discerning heart seeks knowledge." In contrast, the **fool** at heart simply feeds his face with **folly**. Third, the heart shapes one's outlook on circumstances (v. 15). A person who is **afflicted** with poverty or in some other way may have a very difficult daily life, and yet with **a cheerful heart** he can still enjoy life as if it were a **continual feast** of celebration (cf. Php 4:4-13; 2Co 12:7-10; Heb 10:34). This proverb thus reverses the typical assumption that circumstances determine the heart's outlook.

15:16-17. There are certain things more valuable than wealth. **The fear of the Lord** certainly is (v. 16). It more than compensates for a lack of wealth (Fox, *Proverbs 10–31*, 595). Indeed, even **great** wealth without it brings **turmoil**. After all, one who rests in the Lord does not face the anxiety of those who trust in their riches (cf. Ec 5:10-19). Love is also more valuable than wealth (Pr 15:17; cf. 17:1). A simple meal **of vegetables**, served with **love**, is far more pleasant than a sumptuous feast garnished with **hatred**. Just ask anyone whose home is torn by strife.

15:18. "Quarrels depend on *people* far more than on subject-matter," and so the "storm-centre" of strife is the **hot-tempered man** (Kidner, *Proverbs*, 115). The patient, self-controlled man has the opposite effect; he **calms a dispute** and defuses contentious situations.

15:19. The lazy is contrasted with the **upright**. This is a reminder that laziness is not only a wisdom issue but also a moral one. The slacker's **way** is like **a hedge of thorns** blocking his path. It may be that this is his silly excuse for not going anywhere (so Clifford, *Proverbs*, 153; cf. 22:13; 26:13). But more likely it indicates that although a sluggard craves an easy life, he can expect a difficult and painful one. This contrasts with the **path of the upright**, which is clear and smooth like a **highway**.

15:20. This proverb reiterates the idea in 10:1 that the **wise son makes** his **father glad** and certainly his mother as well. But this proverb extends the idea further: **a foolish man** actually **despises his mother** (and father) by actions that not only grieve his parents, but also demonstrate a callous disrespect for them. He rejects their wise teaching (cf. v. 5) and cares not a whit for how his folly affects them.

15:21. The fool is so senseless that **folly is** a **joy to him** and that is his doom (cf. 10:23). It is the only joy he will get. "The wise, who realize the danger, **walks** the **straight** and narrow" (Clifford, *Proverbs*, 153, emphasis added), and by implication, enjoys the far greater blessings of that path.

15:22. Good, successful planning requires **many counselors** (cf. 11:14). This, of course, assumes they are wise—no small matter, as Rehoboam found out (1Kg 12; Longman, *Proverbs*, 320). More counselors are better in order "to offset the weaknesses, ignorance, and limitations of each individual" (Waltke, *Book of Proverbs 1–15*, 633).

15:23. It is a great **joy** for someone to give an **answer** that is appropriate to the situation and to do so in a **timely** manner. Obviously, an **apt**, timely **answer** requires wisdom. But it also reflects the right approach to wisdom's sayings, which must be applied to the right situation at the right time (see "Structure and Genre" in Introduction; cf. Longman, *Proverbs*, 320).

15:24. The two ways of Proverbs are in view here, with the **path of life** going **upward** and the way of death descending to **Sheol below**. The **wise** person knows to take the former and **keep away** from the latter. The upward direction of the path of life means more than just success; its ultimate destination is heaven, where God dwells and eternal life is found, as Scripture teaches elsewhere (e.g., Php 3:20; Col 3:1-2; 1Jn 5:11-12, 20; cf. Longman, *Proverbs*, 321).

15:25-27. In biblical times, widows were among society's most vulnerable. Here a **proud**, wealthy man is portrayed greedily adding to his holdings by annexing the property (removing the **boundary** marker) of a poor **widow** who has no one to defend her (cf. 23:10-11; Dt 19:14; 1Kg 21; Is 5:8-9). His triumph, however, is short lived, because **the Lord will tear down** his **house** and preserve the **boundary** of her land. "The reliable Lord himself, not fickle chance or uncertain social safety nets, assumes responsibility to take away from the proud their family, fame, and fortune and to restore life to the widow" (Waltke, *Book of Proverbs 1–15*, 636). The broader principle in Pr 15:26 explains why. The wicked's **evil plans** reflect his desire to harm others, and **the Lord** deplores this. In contrast, the **pleasant** or friendly (Koehler et al., *HALOT*, 706) **words** and actions of those who are kind to others are **pure** and therefore well pleasing to Him. Verse 27 presents a similar idea. The one who is greedy for illicit **profits**, such as taking **bribes**, usually does so at others' expense. Putting himself under God's wrath, he can expect to bring ruin on himself and **his own house**, in contrast to the one **who hates** such behavior (cf. 1:10-19).

15:28. Prudent speech is a moral issue, reflecting one's character. Before he speaks, the **righteous** first reflects on what he will say, and how and when he will say it. He exercises self-control and a concern about the effect of his words on others. The **wicked** cares about neither, and his glib, **evil** words show it.

15:29. The **wicked** are on their own. **The Lord is far from** them. "Distance and closeness are here not a matter of space but of the ability to communicate, to speak and be heard" (Clifford, *Proverbs*, 154; cf. Ps 145:18). Thus the Lord **hears** and responds to **the prayer of the righteous**. The wicked miss out on the blessing of His presence and His help in time of need.

15:30. Joy is contagious. A person with **good news** and the happy demeanor to show it (**bright eyes**) brings joy to another. The messenger's happy communication, both verbal and nonverbal, cheers (**gladden[s] the heart**) the other person and refreshes his whole person (**puts fat on the bones**).

15:31-33. To be wise one must be teachable. He who accepts wise **reproof** fosters his own **life** and shows that he belongs in good company, the community of **the wise** (v. 31). This is why someone who refuses to listen (**neglects discipline**) simply **despises himself** (v. 32a). His self-destructiveness demonstrates that he lacks the good sense (**understanding**) of the one who will accept **reproof** (v. 32b). In the end, it takes humility to be wise (v. 33). **The fear of the Lord**—reverentially worshipping Him in submission—makes **instruction** leading to **wisdom** possible. This disposition is tied closely to **humility** (cf. 22:4). So if someone wants the **honor** that comes with being wise, he must humbly receive instruction from the Lord and His sages.

16:1-9. These proverbs all address the theme of God's sovereignty over human affairs. Verses 1 and 9 are similar, forming a literary envelope for the section.

16:1. A **man** may plan in his **heart** what he is going to say, but what he actually ends up saying **is from the Lord**. The same could be said for his actions (cf. v. 9). Nothing that a person plans to do can come to pass apart from God's sovereign will.

16:2. Human beings have an almost unlimited capacity to justify and rationalize anything they do, but such evaluations are superficial. "Deeper within lies the spirit and the heart, and God sees into them (15:11), even when a man can not or will not do so himself (1Sm 16:7b)" (Fox, *Proverbs 10–31*, 608). So **the LORD weighs** people's **motives**, or more literally, their "spirits," which includes but is not limited to motives. The weighing imagery likely reflects "an ancient Egyptian belief that a person's heart is weighed against truth after death" (Bruce K. Waltke, *The Book of Proverbs, Chapters 15–31*, NICOT [Grand Rapids, MI: Eerdmans, 2005], 10). God alone is true evaluator of human action, a reality that the wise recognize (cf. 1Co 4:4).

16:3. Given God's sovereignty (v. 1) and human limitation (v. 2), the wise entrust (**commit**) all that they do **to the LORD**. Such trust includes submitting one's **plans** to the Lord. When those plans accord with His will, they will be realized. It is a principle Christians articulate every time they pray, "if it be your will" (cf. Mt 6:10; Lk 22:42; Ac 18:21; Jms 4:15).

16:4. In God's sovereign plan, **everything** has **its own purpose**. This **even** includes **the wicked**, who were made **for the day of evil**. Some maintain that this proverb attests to God's retributive justice (i.e., the wicked and righteous will each get their due), whereas others hold that God uses all things (including evil) to accomplish His good purposes (Ec 3:1-8; Gn 50:18-20; Rm 8:28). More likely, the proverb is broad enough to include both: everything, including evil, "will be put to some use and matched with its proper fate" (Kidner, *Proverbs*, 118).

16:5. The "proper fate" of one kind of wicked person, the **proud in heart**, is laid out here. Because the Lord considers this disposition such **an abomination**, He guarantees that all such people **will not** go **unpunished**. Since He is sovereign, their judgment is assured.

16:6-7. A right relationship with the sovereign Lord has profound significance. First, it addresses the sin problem (v. 6). Some argue that the covenant love (**lovingkindness**) and faithfulness (**truth**) here belong to the Lord (Fox, *Proverbs 10–31*, 612), or that they belong to humans but are directed toward other humans, effecting reconciliation (so Murphy, *Proverbs*, 121). More likely, they are the human response to God, particularly in light of their parallel with **the fear of the LORD**. Mere ritual sacrifice is not enough (cf. 1Sm 15:22; Hs 6:6; Mc 6:6-8); **iniquity is atoned for** in the lives of those whose trust in God is expressed by their love and faithfulness to Him. Similarly, the believer's ongoing **fear of the LORD** will help to keep him **away from evil** in the future. Second, a right relationship with God brings favor with God and man (Pr 16:7). The God-fearer's **ways** being well **pleasing to the LORD**, God also brings him into good favor with other human beings, including **even his enemies** who come to be **at peace with him**. Some argue that this peace may actually be more like forced surrender (Waltke, *Book of Proverbs 15–31*, 14–15) or that at least his enemies are no longer a factor for him to worry about (Kidner, *Proverbs*, 119; cf. 29:25; Rm 8:31).

16:8. Righteousness—being just in dealing with others—is more valuable than wealth. Unjust gain is worthless; it is **better** not to have it at all. Surely the Lord Himself, though unmentioned, stands behind this principle. In His economy, unjust gain is short lived and perilous (cf. 10:2; 11:4).

16:9. What is true of a man's answers (cf. v. 1) is true of his actions as well. The Lord sovereignly **directs** a man's **steps**. "Human beings can plan, but plans do not get put into operation and do not find success unless Yahweh so decrees it" (Longman, *Proverbs*, 331).

16:10-15. These proverbs cluster around life under the rule of a king.

16:10. The king's judicial verdict has the practical force of a **divine** oracle. When he is just, he bears God's authority and speaks, as it were, for God Himself (cf. 1Kg 3:28). Citizens should take note (Rm 13:1-7). But so should the king. He "should not betray justice" (Pr 16:10b NIV) because he too "is a man under authority" (Kidner, *Proverbs*, 119; Dt 17:18-19).

16:11. Fair commerce depends on accurate **weights** and measurements, and the **LORD** Himself takes great **concern** for this matter (cf. 11:1). "God is the ultimate source of standards, and any distortion in their accuracy offends him directly (Prv 20:10, 23)" (Fox, *Proverbs 10–31*, 615). A wise king who fears the Lord will share the same concerns in his realm.

16:12. Although it is **an abomination *for* kings to commit wicked acts** (emphasis added), just as it is for any person, the emphasis of this verse is perhaps better translated it is "an abomination *to* kings." Kings should hate evil deeds in their kingdom (cf. 20:26). This is because a righteous, just kingdom is in their own best interests, establishing their **throne**. Any king who tolerates injustice in his domain—or worse, promotes it himself—may foster rebellion—or worse, bring God's righteous justice down on his own unjust administration.

16:13. Wise **kings** also **delight** in certain things, like the **righteous lips** of one **who speaks right**. To speak in such a way is to speak with integrity. A prudent king loves such wise, honest advisors because they do not misrepresent reality but help him craft a successful policy (Longman, *Proverbs*, 332).

16:14. A **king** is powerful, and so his **fury** is dangerous, a harbinger of **death** as if delivered by **messengers**. Here is another benefit of a **wise** counselor. He can **appease** that wrath, whether against others or even himself. This has obvious advantages to the wise man or any other possible object of the king's wrath, but it may even benefit the king himself in the long run (cf. 1Sm 25; Dn 2).

16:15. The king's **favor** is as **life**-promoting as his wrath is deadly. **The light of a king's face** marks his goodwill and favor. This presages abundant prosperity for the object of his favor, much like **a cloud with the spring rain** anticipated an abundant harvest, which in Israel's climate was so dependent on those late rains.

16:16. Wisdom is simply more valuable than **gold** or **silver**. Without wisdom, wealth may well be morally tainted and is certainly ephemeral. In contrast, wisdom regularly delivers God's favor, life, and honor as well as wealth. This verse marks the midpoint of Proverbs and so may serve to reiterate one of the book's major purposes: the admonition to **get wisdom** (Longman, *Proverbs*, 334).

16:17. The path of the **upright** is a clear, smooth **highway** leading inexorably to life. The wise man will be careful to remain on it (**watches his way**). In doing so, he avoids **evil** and its consequences and ultimately **preserves his life.**

16:18-19. Arrogant **pride** is self-destructive (v. 18). The **haughty** will "stumble to their perdition" (Waltke, *Book of Proverbs 15–31*, 26). They are foolishly self-sufficient and unwilling to humbly receive the instruction and correction so necessary for wisdom's blessings. This is why humility is so valuable (v. 19). Those who **divide the spoil** have been triumphant and share the booty among themselves; they are contrasted with those who are **lowly** and needy—perhaps even as a result of being defeated in battle (Clifford, *Proverbs*, 160). Yet humility even in demeaning poverty is **better** than profitable victory when accompanied with pride. Pride makes victorious gain short lived. This is true particularly if it is an ill-gotten gain that the arrogant wrest from the poor (Waltke, *Book of Proverbs 15–31*, 27).

16:20. The statement that **he who gives attention to the word will find good** is ambiguous and could be understood in at least two ways. The first of these is captured in this rendering: "The one who understands a matter finds success" (HCSB). This suggests that the wise bring their insight into a situation and have success. A second interpretation could be: "Whoever gives heed to instruction prospers" (NIV). That instruction, translated more literally, is **the word** of God as revealed through the sages. Although the first view is certainly taught in Proverbs, the second view is preferable because it is more directly parallel with the second line. So the person who fears and **trusts in the Lord** will also heed His instruction and, becoming wise, will prosper greatly.

16:21-24. Wise people influence others positively. They certainly are noticed (v. 21). Being **wise in heart**, they develop a reputation for being discerning (**understanding**), and their wisdom rubs off on their community through their pleasing, winsome (**sweetness of**) **speech**. Their influence is like a **fountain of life**, promoting full, abundant living for **one who has it** (v. 22). On the other hand, fools do not possess the good sense (**understanding**) of the wise but instead the only training (**discipline**) fools offer others is in **folly** (cf. 13:13-16). The influence of the wise derives from their very character (v. 23). Their wise **heart instructs** them to speak prudently and persuasively. And what they have to say is compelling (v. 24). Like a **honeycomb**, their wise **words** are both **pleasant** and **healing** to **the soul** and body (**the bones**).

16:25. See 14:12 (and comments there), which is identical. Its repetition here may implicitly compare the beneficial sweetness of wisdom in v. 24 with the deadly sweetness of folly here (Fox, *Proverbs 10–31*, 621).

16:26. A worker's **appetite** and **hunger** (lit., "mouth") is advantageous to him because it **urges him on** in his efforts. Such appetites have their limits to be sure. They are insufficient to stir the sluggard (13:4), and when viewed more broadly are not finally satiated (Ec 6:7). Thus Scripture presents us with other motivations for hard work as well (see Eph 4:28; 6:5-9).

16:27-30. There are several kinds of troublemakers. First, there is the **worthless man** (v. 27). He works hard to **dig up evil**. This metaphor may suggest mining and thus looking for evil to use against others (Fox, *Proverbs 10–31*, 622); or it may suggest digging a pit for others to fall into and thus plotting against them (Clifford, *Proverbs*, 161–62; cf. NIV; ESV). In either case, his harmful words are as devastating to others as a **scorching fire**. Second, there is the **perverse man** (v. 28). Because he "turns the moral order on its head" (Waltke, *Book of Proverbs 15–31*, 33), he actually sets out to foment **strife** and undermine community. The **slanderer** illustrates such perversity by separating even **intimate friends** through his calumnies. Third, there is the **man of violence** (v. 29). In this case, the evil he perpetrates is not so much against the victim of his violence as it is against **his neighbor** whom he seduces to join him in his crime (cf. 1:10-19). But his **way** is **not good** because it is both evil and self-destructive. Verse 30 could be understood in two ways. It may be saying that troublemakers can be recognized through subtleties of body language, like winking one's **eyes** or pursing one's **lips** (at least in the culture of that day). Or, it may be that these actions are nonverbal signals passed between conspirators to plot and carry out evil. If so, then it may refer to the signals shared by violent gang members in v. 29 (so Waltke, *Book of Proverbs 15–31*, 34), or it may just describe another kind of troublemaker: the conspirator.

16:31. Gray hair, an indication of old age, is a glorious **crown**. It marks the blessing of a long life that results from following **the way of righteousness** (cf. 3:1-2, 16). In that sense, the elderly who have lived long in righteousness and wisdom should be honored and respected.

16:32. A patient man, one **who is slow to anger**, is truly self-controlled (**rules his** own **spirit**). He is **better than** a **mighty** man **who captures a city**. He is better primarily because the self-controlled man demonstrates a *power* even greater than a conqueror might have. For a mighty man may still lack self-control, which is a sign of true weakness (25:28). Furthermore, the self-controlled man displays what only *wisdom* can bring. But a mighty man may unwisely trust his own strength (Ps 33:16), oppose God (Ps 52), or demonstrate his folly in other ways (e.g., Abimelech, Jdg 9).

16:33. Though the exact nature of the **lot** is unclear, it was probably something like dice used to determine God's will in decision-making (e.g., Lv 16:8; Nm 26:55; Est 3:7; 1Ch 25:8; 1Sm 14:40-42; Pr 18:18; Ac 1:26). This proverb explains why: **its every decision is from the Lord**. "The underlying belief is that the Lord, who determines all things, also determines the way the lots turn out" (Murphy, *Proverbs*, 124). The wise recognize and trust in God's sovereign providence.

17:1. A peaceful home is of great value. It even makes an unsavory **morsel** of **dry** bread palatable in comparison to **feasting with strife**. This phrase literally reads "sacrifices of strife," and it probably alludes ironically to peace offerings. These offerings left the worshipper with meat for a celebratory feast. But if the peace offering meal becomes a "strife offering" meal, one is **better** off with a quiet snack of dry bread.

17:2. It was rare for a **servant** to be adopted into a family, much less to experience a role reversal with a **son**. Yet wisdom is so powerful that it "can transcend natural boundaries and expectations" (Clifford, *Proverbs*, 164). Folly can have an equally potent effect as well, and any **son who acts shamefully** should take note lest he become subject even to his own slave.

17:3. The **Lord tests** human **hearts**. Workers in precious metals heat **silver** or **gold** to purify them or to demonstrate their purity. Similarly, the sovereign Lord uses trials of life to the same ends. Since He already knows the human heart (cf. 15:11), the Lord uses those trials "not for finding a person out but for sorting him out" (Kidner, *Proverbs*, 123). Furthermore, they may prove revelatory to the person himself, who needs God's refining work on his own deceptive heart (Jr 17:9) in order to reveal the sin that needs to be addressed (Ps 139:23-24).

17:4. An **evildoer** and **liar** not only dispenses **wicked, destructive** words (lies, gossip, slander, etc.), he also **pays attention** to them, revealing his evil character. "Evil words die without a welcome; and the welcome gives us away" (Kidner, *Proverbs*, 123).

17:5. One might show contempt for others overtly (**mocks**) or covertly (**rejoices at calamity**). But in either case, showing contempt for other human beings who experience misfortune, whether poverty or some other **calamity**, is both wicked and foolish. It is wicked because, in ridiculing an image-bearer, it actually **taunts** the **Maker** Himself. It is foolish because it makes the one showing contempt liable to God's just punishment.

17:6. When wisdom permeates a family, blessings flow between generations. Righteous, wise **old men** (cf. 16:31) will rightly take pride in their wise **grandchildren** as a glorious **crown** (cf. 10:1). Similarly, later generations return the favor by glorying in the wise heritage of their ancestors (**fathers**). It truly is a mutual-admiration society, and for good reason.

17:7. The **fool** here (*nabal*) is an "overbearing, crudely godless man as in Psalm 14:1 or 1 Samuel 25:25" (Kidner, *Proverbs*, 123). The notion that such a person would communicate with eloquence "is as grotesque as a ring of gold in a swine's snout (11:22)" (Waltke, *Book of Proverbs 15–31*, 47). But even more outrageous is a nobleman (**prince**) who lies. Both types speak in a way out of keeping with their nature, or at least what they purport to be (in the case of the prince). Worse still, both are dangerous to others, though the lying prince probably more so (given his greater power).

17:8. Here is the viewpoint of one who offers bribes. To him, **a bribe is** like **a charm** or, literally, a magic stone that brings favor (Koehler et al., *HALOT*, 332). He expects it to bring prosperity **wherever** he uses it. For him, "money talks" (Kidner, *Proverbs*, 123). Proverbs gives a negative verdict on this viewpoint. Bribes pervert justice (v. 23) and so put one under God's judgment (v. 15). Thus any "success" is short lived.

17:9. Since love "bears all things" (1Co 13:7), loving others requires overlooking (**conceals**) their offenses. And if one wishes to maintain an **intimate** friendship, he never **repeats** such offenses. This could involve either gossiping about that person's faults to others or harping on that person's faults in front of him. Both actions alienate.

17:10. A wise man gets it, but fools don't. A person with **understanding** allows a wise **rebuke** to penetrate deep into his soul and effect change. **A fool** is so dense that even **a hundred blows** (more than twice the legal limit, Dt 25:1-3) are not enough to get through to him and effect change. David repented with a word (2Sm 12:1-7; 24:13-14) and Peter by a mere look (Lk 22:61-62), but far more dramatic steps were still not enough for Pharaoh (Ex 9:34-35), Ahaz (2Ch 28:22), or Israel (Is 1:5; 9:13; Jr 5:3) (Charles Bridges, *An Exposition of Proverbs* [1846; repr., Marshallton, DE: National Foundation for Christian Education, n.d.], 261–62).

17:11. At heart, an evil man is a rebel against God. As such, he can expect that **a cruel messenger will be sent against him**, whether angelic (cf. Ps 78:49) or human (cf. Pr 16:14). Rebels will not go unpunished.

17:12. A she **bear robbed of her cubs** is surely dangerous (2Sm 17:8). But more dangerous still is a **fool in his folly**. This humorous proverb encourages people to avoid fools as they would an enraged beast.

17:13. Proverbs warns against paying back evil for evil (cf. 20:22). But some people are so wicked that they actually go much further, practicing a perverse "gratitude" that **returns evil for good.** This proverb maintains that such a person will sow far worse than he reaps. **Evil** will visit him like an unwanted house guest who refuses to leave (Waltke, *Book of Proverbs 15–31*, 53–54). "He will suffer harm unremittingly, and his family with him" (Fox, *Proverbs 10–31*, 631). How much better the way of Christ (Mt 5:43-45; cf. Rm 12:14, 17, 21).

17:14. Starting a **quarrel** is like the **letting out** of **water**, that is, opening a sluice gate or breaching a dam. "Opening such a sluice lets loose more than one can predict, control or retrieve" (Kidner, *Proverbs*, 125). **So** it is wise to **abandon the quarrel before it breaks out** in the first place. Wisdom defuses potentially explosive **strife** rather than stirring it up (cf. 15:1; 20:3).

17:15. The Lord detests injustice; all those who judge others unjustly are **an abomination** to Him. Injustice turns the law on its head (cf. Lv 19:15; Dt 16:18-20; 25:1; Is 5:20; Hab 1:4). In a legal setting, it involves declaring the guilty to be innocent (**justifies the wicked**) or the innocent to be guilty (**condemns the righteous**). Such injustice is possible outside the courtroom as well. It can happen whenever people pronounce an unjust verdict on someone else's character (cf. Pr 28:5; Ps 11:3).

17:16. You cannot **buy wisdom** with money. **A fool** might think he can. But lacking **sense**, he lacks the capacity and character to receive wisdom, so he is just wasting his money. It is a mistaken notion too often repeated in modern education.

17:17. Some see the two lines of this proverb as antithetical; that is, it is better to have a **brother** than a **friend** in times of real **adversity**. But the two hardly need compete. Anyone who truly **loves** us—friend or family—does so **at all times**, including the hard times. "The saying does not identify true love with family relationships as such but, more generally, with constancy in difficult times" (Clifford, *Proverbs*, 166).

17:18. Whereas a true friend helps the one he loves, he does not do so foolishly. To become a **guarantor**, providing surety for another's loan is **lacking sense** (cf. 6:1-5). "Risking one's present security on the fidelity of the neighbor to pay back his loan and on an uncertain future is the mark of a senseless person" (Waltke, *Book of Proverbs 15–31*, 58). There are better ways to help those in need, like simply giving generously.

17:19. A person who **loves transgression** either enjoys offending people or relishes harping on other people's past offenses. In either case—and it may well be purposely ambiguous—such a person presumably also **loves strife** because he must enjoy being in the midst of the turmoil and conflict his behavior creates. To raise one's **door** in the second line likely refers to an ostentatious doorway and home, and by extension, to pride. Taken together, both lines may suggest that it takes arrogance to be itching for a fight; and in seeking to destroy others, such people are ultimately aiming for their own **destruction**.

17:20. A **crooked mind** manifests itself in a **perverted** tongue. The wicked person twists the truth in his character and speech. As a result, he **falls into** calamity (**evil**) rather than finding prosperity (**good**).

17:21. A **fool** is sure to disappoint his **father** (or mother) (cf. 10:1; 13:1; 15:20). Indeed, his parents will suffer anguish over him (see similar comments on v. 25; 10:1b-c).

17:22. There is a close connection between body and soul. **Good medicine** and **drie[d] up bones** depict good and bad health respectively. The difference between a **joyful heart** and **broken spirit** "depends more on a person's spiritual resources than on his circumstances" (Waltke, *Book of Proverbs 15–31*, 61; cf. 15:15; Ac 16:25).

17:23. The phrase **receives a bribe** is ambiguous in Hebrew. The phrase "takes a bribe from the bosom" captures the ambiguity of the Hebrew. That is, one might take a bribe secretly from one's own pocket to *offer* a bribe or from another's pocket to *receive* it. The ambiguity is probably purposeful. One who *offers* or *receives* bribes **to pervert the ways of justice** is **wicked** indeed, and his surreptitious behavior shows that he knows it.

17:24. This proverb may be saying that the wise man focuses on attaining wisdom whereas the fool's attention wanders, distracting him from such worthwhile pursuits (cf. NIV). But it is likely that the proverb deals more with proximity than concentration. So for a perceptive man (**one who has understanding**) **wisdom** is already close at hand (**in** his **presence**); being receptive, he is attentive to and takes advantage of wisdom's lessons in daily life. In contrast, wisdom is far away to the **fool**. He "may search the world for wisdom, but he will not find it, because he does not realize its proximity" (Fox, *Proverbs 10–31*, 636), nor is he prepared to receive it even if he did (cf. v. 16).

17:25. A **foolish son** brings **grief** and **bitterness** to his parents (see similar comments on v. 21; 10:1b-c.)

17:26. This proverb clearly deals with injustice, but it presents three key interpretive issues. First, **also** (Hb. *gam*) is better translated "even," applying directly to the infinitive: i.e., "even to fine" (cf. Waltke, *Book of Proverbs 15–31*, 46n66). Second, **for** in the second line is better translated "against." That is, it is "against what is upright" to **strike the noble** (Longman, *Proverbs*, 351). Third, **the noble** in Hebrew parallels **the righteous** and so speaks of one noble in character rather than a member of the nobility. Therefore, this proverb indicates that it is not right even **to fine** those who are righteous, much less to **strike** or flog them. Government officials who act in such ways are an abomination to the Lord (cf. v. 15).

17:27-28. One who is wise is self-controlled (v. 27). He **restrains his words** and his temper (i.e., he is not hotheaded but **has a cool spirit**). Such restraint can even help a **fool** (v. 28). Keeping his mouth shut can actually make him appear to be **wise**, at least for a time before his words finally erupt and betray him (cf. 10:8; 18:2). In any case, the point is clear enough: if restrained words benefit the fool, how much more the wise (Waltke, *Book of Proverbs 15–31*, 65).

18:1-2. A person needs others to be wise. Radical individuality—doing your own thing—is foolish (v. 1). When one **separates himself** from others to pursue his own agenda (**desire**), he **quarrels against** or "defies" (NIV) **all sound** judgment. Absent the wisdom of many counselors (cf. 15:22), his only counselor is a fool—himself. This is a warning to the wise "against headstrong, self-centered decisions" (Steveson, *Commentary on Proverbs*, 241). Similarly, the **fool** has a "closed mind, open mouth" (Kidner, *Proverbs*, 127) (v. 2). He has no taste for learning **understanding** from the wise (cf. 2:2; 5:1). He is far more interested in spouting his own opinions, thereby **revealing** the fool that he is.

18:3. In this proverb, **a wicked man** is parallel with **dishonor** (or shame), and **contempt** is parallel with **scorn**. The proverb thus indicates that a wicked person acts shamefully, and in so doing rightly receives the contempt and reproach of the community.

18:4. The interpretation of this proverb hinges on whether **deep waters** is a negative or positive image. If negative, it indicates that a **man's words** conceal what is **deep** within him (cf. 20:5), in contrast to the accessibility of life-giving wisdom. More likely, however, the image is positive, and the two lines are synthetic rather than antithetical. If so, the entire proverb describes the **words** of a *wise* man. The image of **deep waters** would therefore suggest that his words are refreshing (Fox, *Proverbs 10–31*, 639), or they are "profound and sometimes mysterious, requiring reflection and interpretation" (Longman, *Proverbs*, 354; cf. 1:6). Moreover, they are a source of wisdom to others (a **fountain of wisdom**) and are a life-giving **bubbling brook**.

18:5. This proverb again addresses injustice (cf. 17:15, 26). **To show partiality to the wicked** is to pardon them; **to thrust aside the righteous in judgment** is to condemn them (Clifford, *Proverbs*, 170). Both judicial acts are **not good**. Clearly this is a moral judgment (as 17:15 makes clear), but it may also have a pragmatic nuance. Injustice is "not useful" and "downright deleterious" (Fox, *Proverbs 10–31*, 639).

18:6-7. A fool talks himself into trouble (Kidner, *Proverbs*, 128). His words **bring strife** that hurts himself and possibly others (v. 6). It is as if he is asking for a beating; **his mouth calls for blows**. Worse still, his words destroy him (v. 7). They bring on **his ruin** and trigger a deadly **snare** for **his** life/**soul**.

18:8. A whisperer is a gossip. The gossip he spreads is as irresistible to others as **dainty morsels** of fine food. That is why gossip spreads; people enjoy it. Indeed, they greedily devour it so that it goes **down into** their **innermost parts**. Such penetration inevitably shapes the hearer's thought and character for the worse. Gossip is thus "dangerous because of the flaw in human character which ensures that it is avidly listened to and remembered" (R. N. Whybray, *The Book of Proverbs*, CBC [Cambridge: Cambridge University Press, 1972], 104–5). The wise will neither spread gossip (17:9) nor keep company with gossips (20:19) but will follow Jeremiah's better example of devouring the words of the Lord, not the morsels of a whisperer (Jr 15:16).

18:9. The Lord values hard, diligent work (cf. 10:4; 13:4). A person **slack in his work** bears a family resemblance to a person who **destroys** the work of others. The one who in his laziness fails to complete a work or do it well is little better than the villain who **destroys** it. They both end up with much the same result. It is not a family tree to be envied.

18:10-11. The wise trust in the Lord, and for good reason (v. 10; cf. 3:5-6). He is a **strong tower** who keeps His people **safe**. God's **name** describes who He is and therefore refers to **the Lord** Himself (cf. Ex 3:14-15; 6:3; Ps 135:13). The **righteous** wisely **run** to Him in difficult times for His protection. In contrast, the wealthy man trusts in his own **wealth** (v. 11; cf. 10:15). To him, his riches are a **strong**, fortified **city** to get him out of trouble in difficult times. But wealth is unreliable in difficult times (see 11:28 and comments there), and its efficacy is limited in any case (cf. Ps 52:5-7). So his security is a "castle in the air," more imagined than real. "The world thinks that the unseen is the unreal. But it is not the man of God (10) but the man of property, who must draw on *his imagination* . . . to feel secure" (Kidner, *Proverbs*, 128–9).

18:12. Haughty pride precedes **destruction** (cf. 16:18), **but humility** precedes **honor** (cf. 15:33). There is a causal connection between the elements in each pair. This proverb may relate to the previous two, comparing those who humbly rely on the Lord with those who arrogantly trust their own resources (so Waltke, *Book of Proverbs 15–31*, 77–78); or it may be comparing those too proud to hear wisdom with those humble enough to receive wise correction (so Longman, *Proverbs*, 357); or its application may be more general.

18:13. This is another reminder that the wise are slow to speak, unlike the fool. In this case, the wise man listens to others and **hears** them out. The fool is so interested in airing his own views (cf. v. 2), and so uninterested in listening to others, that he speaks prematurely or even rudely interrupts. His words therefore display his **folly** and thus bring **shame** on himself.

18:14. The unity of a person's inner and outer man appears once again (cf. 17:22); this proverb emphasizes the inner. There is something worse than physical **sickness**: **a broken spirit**. The **spirit of a man** is his inner emotional, psychological, spiritual life. It can sustain him even when he is physically ill. But an anxious, depressed, disturbed spirit is unendurable. Too often, the Christian's prayer requests have the priorities exactly backwards (cf. Kidner, *Proverbs*, 129).

18:15. The wise are ever eager to learn of the Lord (cf. 1:5; 9:9-10; 16:20). They make it a priority to acquire **knowledge** and **seek** it (cf. 15:14). "Those who know most know best how little they know" (Kidner, *Proverbs*, 129).

18:16. This proverb is unabashedly realistic. **Gift**-giving secures opportunities and access to **great men**. It has always been that way. Commentators dispute whether these gifts are distinguishable from bribes and so whether this proverb encourages or discourages this practice. But since such gifts are given by those with means to gain an advantage over those who do not have those means, and since this promotes favoritism, such a system amounts to bribery and violates the principles of justice in Proverbs (Waltke, *Book of Proverbs 15–31*, 81–82). This proverb thus presents the way things *are*, not the way they *should be* (as in 14:21). Of course, realities may force wise people at times to work within an unjust system to get things done, but they must be wary of any such accommodation lest it make the injustice worse.

18:17-19. These three proverbs all relate to disputes.

18:17. Here is a good reason not to make snap judgments. Listening to only one side of the argument (**the first to plead his case**) can be misleading. It may **seem right**, but it is better to hear all the facts and arguments before deciding. This is true whether in a law court or in life.

18:18. According to 16:33, **the . . . lot** expresses the Lord's decision in a matter. In difficult disputes involving **strife** that are hard to settle, particularly when the disputants are **mighty**, it is best to let the Lord decide **between** them, in this case through use of the lot. "It would be particularly important to resolve conflicts between powerful people because their disagreements could lead to the most widespread damage, not only to themselves as individuals but also to society at large" (Longman, *Proverbs*, 358). The principle here is that all (including the mighty) should submit to the Lord's will, however that will is revealed. Today, the Holy Spirit guides us particularly through His Word.

18:19. Contentions with an intimate such as **a brother** are especially difficult. This **offended** person is "a party in the closest human relation with another, whether by blood or choice, who feels wronged and has cut himself off from the other with a deep sense of personal injury" (Waltke, *Book of Proverbs 15–31*, 84). Reconciliation is so difficult because his hard feelings make him as impenetrable as a **strong city** or **the bars of a citadel**. Better to prevent such conflict in the first place (cf. 17:14). After all, "family feuds are the bitterest conflicts and civil wars are the bloodiest wars" (Clifford, *Proverbs*, 172).

18:20-21. A man's words have repercussions for himself. He will feed on the produce of his **mouth** and **lips**: his words and their consequences (v. 20). In fact, he will have his fill of them. This proverb may be positive: wise words are satisfying to the speaker as well as the hearer. But the verb translated **will be satisfied** is ambiguous, much like the English verb "to be filled." So the proverb may also suggest that the fool will get his fill of his foolish words and their consequences. Verse 21 makes the consequences of both types explicit. In short, the **tongue** has the **power** to bring **death and life** to the speaker. **Those who love** making use of **it** (i.e., the tongue), whether for good or ill, will **eat its fruit**. That is, they will live, or die (i.e., forfeit the "abundant life"), with the consequences of their words.

18:22. A man **who finds a wife** has also found a blessing (**a good thing**). Of course, the proverb assumes that she is a good wife (cf. 19:13-14; 21:9; 31:10-31). The language of this proverb parallels 8:35, which suggests that finding a good wife is much like the blessing of finding Lady Wisdom herself. A man is wise to search for such a wife, but when he finds her, he should not forget that ultimately this **favor** ("goodwill," "delight") is from **the Lord**.

18:23. Because of his need, the **poor man** is forced to **utter supplications**, pleading for help, from **the rich man**. The rich, however, **answers** the poor man **roughly** or harshly. Perhaps because he is a callous man, unmoved by the need of the poor and to discourage appeals in the future (from this beggar or others) or perhaps because he is arrogant and stingy . . . in any case he does not help. The lesson is: Those who might fall into poverty because of foolishness should pursue wisdom and avoid such dire straits because they are unlikely to find help from the rich. At the same time, those who are wealthy should righteously emulate the Lord, who is merciful to those in need and obey His commands to care for the poor (Ps 28:2, 6; Pr 14:21, 31: 19:17).

18:24. The choice of one's friends shapes one's life (cf. 12:26; 13:20). If a **man** only makes casual friendships, this will bring him to **ruin** because his gaggle of fair-weather **friends** will let him down in difficult times. A true **friend** is one who **sticks closer than a brother** through thick and thin (cf. 17:17). The wise cultivate the latter kind of friendship.

19:1. This "better this than that" proverb asserts that "ethical qualities are more important than material possessions" (Longman, *Proverbs*, 364). Though being **poor** is a disadvantage, if the poor man is honest (**walks in his integrity**) he is still far better off than the lying **fool** whose words distort the truth—even if such a fool is wealthy (cf. 28:6). Long term, and certainly in light of eternity, honesty is the best policy (cf. 17:20; 22:5).

19:2. In the context, **person** (*nephesh*) here is better translated "desire" (so ESV), and **also** (Hb. *gam*, "even") may indicate a lesser to greater argument (Waltke, *Book of Proverbs 15–31*, 88, 98). So **it is** bad (**not good**) when one's desires are foolish (i.e., **without** wise **knowledge**). It is even worse when one is hasty to carry those desires out. A person who acts without planning guarantees that he will miss out on what he wants (i.e., he **errs** or misses his goal). Thus a fool not only pursues foolish desires, but he is also too hasty even to get them.

19:3. When a fool **ruins his way** due to his own **foolishness**, he then turns around and gets angry with (**rages against**) **the Lord**. He blames God for his problems. This blame-shifting only compounds his folly because it prevents repentance and wise change.

19:4. This proverb describes the kind of fair-weather "friends" presented in 18:24a. When a person has **wealth**, he can expect to have lots of **friends** who hang around for what they can get. But poverty has the opposite effect; any such **friend** will no longer associate with **a poor man**. The wise therefore will seek the kind of friends who stick closer than a brother (18:24b), even in times of adversity (17:17).

19:5. Proverbs indicates that liars are fools (v. 1); this proverb explains one reason why. Liars, particularly those who perjure themselves in court, **will not escape** judgment. Even if they get away with their lies in this world, they **will not go unpunished** before God's bar of justice (cf. v. 9).

19:6-7. These proverbs once again compare the "friends" of the rich and the poor (cf. v. 4). On the one hand, the rich are popular (v. 6). **A generous man** (*nadiyb*) could also be translated "ruler" or "nobleman." Here it suggests a powerful, wealthy man who is generous. He has many **friend[s]** who seek his **favor** because he **gives** them **gifts**. But these "friends" are sycophants who are in it for themselves. The wealthy should take note. On the other hand, the **poor man** is not very popular because he is so needy (v. 7). People cannot get anything out of him, and they do not want to be bothered with his needs. Even his **brothers** (relatives) **hate him** and wish to be rid of him. **How much more do his friends**, who do not even share an obligation of family, keep their distance from **him**. Although the poor man **pursues** his friends and family **with words**, no one sticks around to hear his pleas for help. Both rich and poor alike need truer friends than these.

19:8. It is in one's own best interest to acquire **wisdom** by heeding **understanding**. Such a person **loves** himself because he **will find** what is good, i.e., the blessings that come from the Lord's wisdom.

19:9. This proverb is identical to 19:5, except for the last verb in the proverb, which specifies the judgment the liar faces: he **will perish** in the end.

19:10. It is inappropriate, indeed absurd, for a **fool** to enjoy the **luxury** of wealth. This only encourages him in his folly. It is even more absurd for **a slave to rule over princes** because this has a more widespread effect. The statement assumes that the slave is incompetent to rule (like 12:24 rather than 14:35 and 17:2). Such a one becomes an insufferable despot who brings "incompetence, mismanagement, abuse of power, corruption, and injustice; in brief, social chaos (cf. Eccl. 10:5-7)" (Waltke, *Book of Proverbs 15–31*, 105). Both states of affairs turn the world upside down, at least until God eventually restores order (Waltke, *Book of Proverbs 15–31*, 104; cf. 1Sm 25:2, 25, 27).

19:11. It does a man credit to be **slow to anger** (self-controlled), which gives him the ability to **overlook a transgression** (offense) against him. This behavior not only demonstrates his **discretion** (insight) but also makes him praiseworthy (**his glory**), since he is reflecting God's own patience (Ex 34:6; Mc 7:18). Paradoxically, then, "one gains glory by giving up a common means of protecting it—argument" (Clifford, *Proverbs*, 177), and in this way actually displays "the glowing colours of a virtue which in practice may look drably unassertive" (Kidner, *Proverbs*, 133).

19:12. Better to gain the king's **favor** rather than provoke his **wrath**. **The king's wrath** signals danger to life and limb, **like the roaring of a lion**. In contrast, his favor indicates blessing, **like dew on the grass**, which is so crucial to life in Israel's arid climate (cf. Gn 27:28; Ps 133:3). Although this proverb certainly encourages royal officials to act prudently before the king, it may also encourage kings to be patient, if read in light of v. 11 (Fox, *Proverbs 10–31*, 654).

19:13-14. One's home life is critical. A dysfunctional home life can deliver two possible sources of domestic misery to a man (v. 13). First, his **foolish son** brings him **destruction**, whether that involves his emotional life (e.g., 10:1), his family legacy (cf. v. 14a), or some other sort of catastrophe. Second, the relentless **contentions of** his nagging **wife**, like **a constant dripping** of a leaky roof, wear him down and drive him to despair. On the other hand, a healthy home life is a source of tremendous blessing (v. 14). Absent a foolish son, **fathers** can pass on the family **inheritance** and thereby preserve the family's **house and wealth**. Even better, at its heart is the **prudent wife** (cf. 14:1; 31:10-31). "A man's fortune depends on her moral competence to grasp the problems involved in running a household and their solutions and to throw all her energies into their successful management (see 1:2; 12:4; 14:1; 18:22)" (Waltke, *Book of Proverbs 15–31*, 108). Wise fathers and sons may be able to ensure the preservation of family property, **but** only **the Lord** can bequeath to a husband the treasure of a wise wife (cf. 18:22). Of course, though stated from the man's perspective, both proverbs could apply equally well to a woman's experience as well.

19:15. His **laziness casts** the **idle** slacker into a **deep sleep**. He is in such a stupor that he is useless (Fox, *Proverbs 10–31*, 655), unable to meet his most basic needs such as satisfying his **hunger**. Indeed, he would rather sleep than eat (cf. v. 24).

19:16. Obedience to the word of God given through His sage is life giving. The word **keeps** (*shomer*) is used in two senses. The one who **keeps** (i.e., heeds) God's wise **commandment keeps** (i.e., preserves) his life. He contrasts with the one **who is careless of**—or more literally, who *despises*—his **conduct**. Disrespectful and unconcerned about his lifestyle and its consequences, he engages in foolish, wicked behavior that leads to his demise (i.e., he **will die**).

19:17. The Lord cares for the poor, even if others do not. So to be **gracious to a poor man** by giving to him is like **lend[ing] to the Lord**. God will honor this debt by repaying the benefactor **for his good deed**. This proverb anticipates a "faithful recompense, not necessarily one's money back" (Kidner, *Proverbs*, 134), whether here or in the hereafter.

19:18-19. Sometimes "compassion" can be foolishly misplaced. Parents can exercise a "deadly leniency" (Kidner, *Proverbs*, 134) by failing to **discipline** their **son** (v. 18). In so doing, they allow the child to follow his own natural inclinations toward folly (cf. 22:15 and comments there), which ultimately lead to his **death**. Yet there is a window of opportunity, ***while* there is hope** (emphasis added), to affect one's child for good before he is set in his foolish ways. Failure to enact timely discipline is not loving (see 13:24; 20:30; 23:13-14 and comments there); it is more like attempted murder (**do not desire his death**). Similarly, you do the hothead no great favor **if you rescue him** from the consequences of his **great anger** (v. 19). His anger habitually gets him into trouble, so delivering him **again** and again only enables him. Better to let him **bear the penalty** of his own behavior. Maybe then he will learn and change.

19:20. Becoming **wise** does not happen overnight. It requires the humble, ongoing commitment to **listen to counsel and accept discipline** from the wise. Then sometime in the future you will become **wise**. **The rest of your days** is better translated "your future days," and the line probably suggests that as young and experienced alike continue to hear wisdom, they grow wiser still (cf. 1:5; Longman, *Proverbs*, 370).

19:21. People may make **many plans**. They can change, and they may or may not come to fruition. In contrast, the **Lord['s]** plan **will stand** firm and surely come to pass (cf. Ps 33:10-11). The wise will make their plans in submission to the will of God (see 16:1-9 for similar proverbs and comments there).

19:22. Kindness (*chesed*) here probably carries the connotation of *loving loyalty*, so characteristic of the Lord Himself (e.g., Ex 15:13; 34:6-7; Ps 103:17; Is 54:10) rather than simple human kindness. People rightly desire or value loyalty. Indeed, it is more **desirable** and valuable than wealth. That is why it is **better** to be **poor than** to be **a liar** who is unfaithful and does not keep his promises.

19:23. The fear of the Lord brings great blessing (cf. 9:10). It **leads to life**. This includes a sense of contentment (**sleep satisfied**) because the

Lord meets one's needs and security (**untouched by evil**) because the Lord delivers from calamity.

19:24. This humorous proverb pictures **the sluggard** as too lazy even to feed himself. Put a **dish** of food before him and he may summon the strength to **bur[y] his hand in** it, but he will never get around to lifting the food into **his mouth**. Perhaps he thinks himself too exhausted to do so or he does not want to be bothered or maybe he just falls asleep (Steveson, *Commentary on Proverbs*, 263). In any case, his sloth will lead to his starvation. The proverb may also suggest that the sluggard is too lazy to take advantage of good opportunities (Fox, *Proverbs 10–31*, 660).

19:25. The **scoffer** is so closed minded that a beating will make no impression on him. Still, even if the punishment does the scoffer no good, seeing it can teach **the naive** to be **shrewd**, or at least shrewd enough to avoid such a beating (Fox, *Proverbs 10–31*, 660). But a wise man of **understanding** is so sensitive that he needs no shock treatment like being beaten; a word of rebuke (**reprove**) is enough for him to **gain** even more **knowledge**. The wise are humbly teachable.

19:26-27. One kind of fool who brings grief to his parents (cf. 10:1) is the one **who assaults his father and drives his mother away** (v. 26). He might do so "by passive sloth (10:5), actively squandering the family fortune in riotous living (29:3), and/or by the overt crime of plundering the father and evicting the mother to seize the inheritance (20:20; 28:24; 30:11; 17)" (Waltke, *Book of Proverbs 15–31*, 123). Such a **son** shames and disgraces not only his parents but himself. Verse 27 explains how a **son** might sink so low. He stops **listening to** his parents' **discipline** and so **stray[s]** away **from the words of knowledge**. But what goes for a son goes for anyone. The wise man never arrives, and he knows it. So he is always prepared to be corrected lest he wander further from wisdom.

19:28-29. A **rascally** (worthless) **witness** mocks **justice** by his false testimony (v. 28; cf. 1Kg 21:10, 13). He does so because he is **wicked** to the core. The verb **spreads** is better translated "swallows." He ingests **iniquity**; his **mouth** spouts what it swallows. But such wicked **scoffers** should not be too smug (Pr 19:29). Though they mock it, justice will be served. God will not be mocked. They can expect divine **judgments** or even human justice (**blows for the back of fools**), which they deserve.

20:1. The Bible does not condemn all uses of alcohol (cf. 3:10; 9:5; Ps 104:15; 1Tm 5:23), however, drunkenness is always condemned (cf. 21:17; 23:19-21, 29-35). Here **wine** and **strong drink** are personified as **a mocker** and **a brawler**. The one who **is intoxicated** (lit., "staggers") **by it is not wise** because drunkenness makes one lose control and act in an impudent, rowdy, or some other foolish way.

20:2-3. Like **the growling of a lion** poised to strike its prey, **a king** in his fury strikes **terror** in the heart of the subject **who provokes him to anger**—and for good reason, since the subordinate's **own life** is endangered (v. 2; cf. 19:12). It is therefore wise not to upset him in the first place. Yet even if one does not rub shoulders with the king, it is still wise to avoid **strife** (v. 3). **Any fool** is quick to **quarrel**, but a wise **man** gains **honor** from being a peacemaker. Paradoxically, the fool is quick to defend his honor and loses it, but the wise who humbly refrains from that fight gains honor (Clifford, *Proverbs*, 182).

20:4. The sluggard has no foresight. He does not bother to do the hard work of plowing in the appropriate season. The phrase translated **after the autumn** indicates the proper time in Israel to **plow**. Having planted nothing, he will also reap **nothing during the harvest** and is forced to **beg** for food. His hunger will likely continue indefinitely, since, lacking any crop, he also lacks the seed for next year's planting (Waltke, *Book of Proverbs 15–31*, 130–31).

20:5. The interpretation of this difficult proverb hinges on three factors. First, **deep water** (as in 18:4) may signal something that is hidden (Clifford, *Proverbs*, 182) or mysterious and profound (Longman, *Proverbs*, 377) or refreshing (Fox, *Proverbs 10–31*, 664). Second, the noun, **plan** (*'etzah)* may refer either to a person's plan or his advice. Third, the character of the **man** with the plan is not specified, so he could be an evil schemer, a befuddled counselee, a wise man, or the sage himself. What, then, is the **man of understanding** doing when he **draws a plan out**? He may be discerning (1) his own hidden insight (Murphy, *Proverbs*, 150), (2) the intentions of another person who lacks such insight (Kidner, *Proverbs*, 137), (3) the machinations of an evil schemer (Waltke, *Book of Proverbs 15–31*, 131), or (4) the wise advice of a fellow sage, which is refreshing (Fox, *Proverbs 10–31*, 664–65) or profound and challenging (Longman, *Proverbs*, 377). The fourth option is most likely (cf. comments on 18:4), although this "riddle of the wise" (1:6) may be purposefully ambiguous.

20:6. Talk is cheap. **Many** claim to be loyal and faithful, but a truly **trustworthy man** is rare. It is the difference between claims of friendship untested and those tested by adversity (Clifford, *Proverbs*, 182), between the fair-weather friend and the true intimate (cf. 17:17; 18:24).

20:7. A righteous man lives **in his integrity** (blamelessly) in that he fears and loves the Lord and strives to please Him. As such, he is a good role model for his **sons** and daughters, who follow his example and are **blessed** as a result

20:8. This verse depicts a righteous and wise **king** who rules with **justice**. Thus, **disperses** here carries the connotation of winnowing or sifting with his discerning **eyes**. Because he both has the power to execute justice (**sits on the throne of justice**) and the insight to recognize evil, he roots out all evil and expels it (cf. 25:5). This ideal will be fully realized in the messianic kingdom under the rule of King Messiah (Is 11:1-5).

20:9. This proverb clearly attests to human depravity and moral incapacity before the Lord. The rhetorical question in this verse demands the answer: no one. Before the Lord, no one has **cleansed** his **heart** so that he is **pure from . . . sin** (cf. 1Kg 8:46; Ec 7:20; Jr 17:9; Is 53:6; Rm 3:9-20). True, Proverbs repeatedly maintains a difference between the wicked and the righteous, who pursue moral purity, blamelessness, and justice (e.g., Pr 20:7-8 above). But this proverb reminds the righteous that perfection is impossible, that their purity is relative, that they cannot cleanse themselves. In short, they recognize that they are still sinners in need of God's merciful forgiveness (cf. 28:13).

20:10. This passages again emphasizes the importance of honesty in business (cf. 11:1; 16:11). **The Lord** abhors **differing weights and differing measures**. These reflect corruption, using an unfairly large weight and measure for buying (and therefore getting more from the seller than one is due) and an unfairly small one for selling (and therefore giving less to the buyer than he is due). Such corruption, whether on the individual or governmental level, draws the Lord's ire.

20:11. The phrase **distinguish himself** (*yitnakker*) can mean either "to be recognized" or "to dissemble." Thus even the **conduct** of a **lad**, a young person, reveals one's character, whether it is **pure and right**. The ESV captures both nuances of the word: "Even a child makes himself known by his acts, by whether his conduct is pure and upright." If the verb means "to be recognized," the proverb would be saying that young person (**a lad**) can be recognized **by his deeds**, whether they are **pure and right** or not. That is, one's **conduct** reveals one's character. The ESV reading in the margin says, "Even a child can dissemble in his actions, though his conduct seems pure and upright." If the verb means "to dissemble," the proverb would be saying that a young person can dissemble by his actions, even if those actions seem pure and right. That is, one can be a hypocrite. Both interpretations are possible, and they would carry the same force: if this is true even of children, it is certainly true of adults as well.

20:12. The hearing ear and the seeing eye indicate true perceptiveness, "the ear that *really* hears and the eye that *really* sees" (Fox, *Proverbs 10–31*, 668). This perceptiveness is necessary for wisdom: "It is through the ready hearing of the right teaching, and through the observant eye, that one becomes wise" (Murphy, *Proverbs*, 151). It may also come in handy in situations like those in v. 11. The proverb stresses, however, that such insight is not self-generated but only comes from **the Lord** who **made both of them** (cf. Is 6:9-10; Mt 13:14-15).

20:13. Because he loves to **sleep** rather than work, the sluggard become **poor** (cf. 6:10; 24:33). In contrast, the diligent stay awake (**open** their **eyes**) when it is time to work and have plenty of **food**. This proverb commands the wise to follow the example of the latter rather than the former.

20:14. This proverb warns against the shady **buyer** rather than the shady salesman (Longman, *Proverbs*, 381). This kind of **buyer** is not interested in offering a fair price. He claims the product is poor quality (**Bad, bad**) in order to drive its price down below market value, and then **boasts** about his shrewdness once he has closed the deal, when he **goes his way**. He "is both a deceitful liar and an impious boaster" (Waltke, *Book of Proverbs 15–31*, 143). In bargaining, a wise businessman will take such a buyer's complaints about his wares with a grain of salt.

20:15. Wisdom is **more precious** than **gold** and many **jewels** (cf. 3:14-15; 8:10-11). The comparison suggests more than wisdom's greater value; it also suggests wisdom's greater attractiveness. The word **thing** is better translated "ornament" paralleling the imagery of jewels (Fox, *Proverbs 10–31*, 669). It is more appealing to be adorned with **lips of knowledge** (i.e., to speak with wisdom) than merely to be bedecked with jewelry.

20:16. It is foolish to guarantee the loan of **a stranger** (cf. 6:1-5; 11:15; 17:18; 22:26; 27:13). The one who does so can lose everything, even the **garment** off his back, his primary article of clothing. These may be the words of a judge or the creditor regarding the loan guarantor (Fox, *Proverbs 10–31*, 669).

20:17. Bread obtained by falsehood literally reads "bread of deceit." This food is deceptive in two senses. First, it is obtained by fraudulent means. Second, it deceives the deceiver. It seems **sweet** and satisfying at first, **but afterward** it is as unpleasant and destructive as eating **gravel** (cf. the "sweet water" of Folly that actually kills, 9:17-18). "Food obtained through deceptive behavior provides deceptive nourishment" (Clifford, *Proverbs*, 184). What goes for food could also be extended to one's possessions (Longman, *Proverbs*, 381) or that which fulfills any human drive (Waltke, *Book of Proverbs 15–31*, 146).

20:18. The **plans** of the wise succeed because they seek wise **consultation** (cf. 11:14). This general principle is applied to battle preparation. A wise king or military leader will **make war** only after he seeks the **wise guidance** of counselors. Failure to seek counsel can have disastrous results for a nation and individual alike.

20:19-20. Fools harm others with their speech. One kind, the **slanderer**, **goes about reveal[ing] secrets** (v. 19). This is one reason people are tempted to **associate with** him, but it is foolish to do so. The **gossip** has a big mouth (more lit., he is one who "opens his lips"; Koehler et al., *HALOT*, 985). So it is far better to stay away from him altogether. Otherwise, he will end up spreading your secrets! Another kind of fool **curses** his parents (v. 20). Cursing them involves disparaging and insulting them publicly (Fox, *Proverbs 10–31*, 672). Consequently, "his lamp will be snuffed out in pitch darkness" (NIV; cf. Ex 20:12). This probably suggests that he will die prematurely (Clifford, *Proverbs*, 185), or it might indicate that he will have no descendants (Fox, *Proverbs 10–31*, 672). In any case, he will be judged. "As he cursed his parents, the Lord curses him" (Waltke, *Book of Proverbs 15–31*, 151; cf. Dt 27:16).

20:21. An inheritance gained hurriedly at the beginning indicates that it is bequeathed prematurely. The text is not clear why it is premature. If connected with cursing the parents (v. 20), it suggests ill-gotten gain, a wicked son fraudulently acquiring his inheritance early (see comments on 19:26-27). Or it could indicate that the son receives his inheritance when he is too young to handle it, possibly like the situation of the prodigal son (cf. Lk 15:11-32) or because his parents died early (Longman, *Proverbs*, 383). In any case, the inheritance **will not be blessed in the end**.

20:22. The short warning here is against personal revenge. **Do not say, "I will repay evil."** "The disciple looks to God to right wrongs no matter how long he must wait for divine intervention" (Waltke, *Book of Proverbs 15–31*, 153; cf. Ps 37:34; Rm 12:19-21). Far wiser than personal revenge is trusting the Lord (**wait for the Lord**). When He does intervene, **He will save** His disciple. This deliverance probably entails both caring for the victim and judging the offender. It should be noted that this proverb addresses only personal vengeance, as indicated by the first-person **I** (Longman, *Proverbs*, 383). It does not reject a government's legitimate role in taking action for justice as God's minister (cf. Rm 13:1-7).

20:23. This proverb reiterates the idea that God despises unfair **weights** (cf. v. 10), but it adds the thought that such **a false scale is not good**. **Good** probably has a pragmatic nuance here (Fox, *Proverbs 10–31*, 674), that is, cheating is not ultimately profitable because God will take vengeance on cheaters (cf. v. 22).

20:24. Proverbs frequently encourages the wise to plan (cf. 11:14; 14:22; 15:22; 20:18; 21:5; 24:6, 27), but this cannot mitigate God's sovereignty over all of one's life. A **man's steps** are from **the Lord**. Consequently no man **can understand his way**. "Man cannot fully plan or control the course of his life, for God is ultimately in control, and God's plans are not transparent" (Fox, *Proverbs 10–31*, 674). Human action (cf. 16:1, 9) and wisdom are limited (cf. Ec 3:11; 8:17; 11:5), so the wise plan and act in humble submission to God's will (cf. Pr 16:3).

20:25. This proverb pertains to rashness in making vows to the Lord, or in any area of his spiritual life (cf. Dt 23:21; Ec 5:1-7). The wise will first carefully consider, **make inquiry**, before making **vows** to consecrate some gift to the Lord (saying, **It is holy!**). Those who foolishly get it backwards by vowing **rashly** before counting the cost **trap** themselves, because God expects them to fulfill the vow (Dt 23:21-23). One thinks of Jephthah (Jdg 11:29-40) and of Saul, for example (1Sm 14). Such behavior is presumptuous as well as foolish.

20:26. Ancient farmers drove a **threshing wheel** over grain stalks to separate or winnow the grain itself from the lighter chaff, which is then scattered to the wind. The **wise king winnows the wicked**, scattering and expelling them from his kingdom (cf. v. 8). The imagery may also imply punishment/destruction (so Fox, *Proverbs 10–31*, 676). In any case, the wise king will not tolerate evil in his kingdom.

20:27. The basic point of this proverb is that God knows man inside out (cf. 15:11). **The lamp of the Lord** sheds light on **the innermost parts of his being**. This **lamp** is identified as a man's breath (*nishemat*), which may refer to a man's life (e.g., Gn 2:7), his **spirit** (cf. Jb 32:8), or even his words (which he breathes out). The second option makes best sense in the context, particularly if a man's spirit refers to his conscience. Thus, the human conscience is used by the Lord to penetrate into our inmost being so that we can begin to see it as He does. As such it is a gift of God to expose the sin in our lives so that we do not remain ignorant of it (Steveson, *Commentary on Proverbs*, 279).

20:28. A king is preserved on **his throne** by *chesed* (translated **loyalty** in line 1 and **righteousness** in line 2) and *'emet* (translated **truth** in line 1). These refer to steadfast love and faithfulness. But is this *God's* steadfast love and faithfulness to the king, or the *king's* steadfast love and faithfulness to God and/or to the people? The ambiguity may be purposeful, involving all parties in a God-honoring kingdom. "It is through the kind of constant faithfulness between all the parties that productive governance can take place and the king himself can avoid usurpation or assassination" (Longman, *Proverbs*, 385).

20:29. This proverb compares what brings **glory** to **young men** and **honor** to **old men**. The young can take pride in **their strength** (cf. Lm 3:27); the old can take pride in **their gray hair**, an evidence of their wisdom, righteousness, and successful life (cf. Pr 16:31; Lv 19:32). The young should seek the old to grow wise, and the old should not begrudge the young their vigor (cf. 2Tm 2:2; 1Tm 4:12). After all, although both are good, wisdom is even better than strength (cf. Pr 24:5-6). So viewed in the context of Proverbs, the old probably have the better deal (Longman, *Proverbs*, 386).

20:30. Corporal punishment (**stripes that wound**; **strokes**) can do more than force external compliance; it can **scour away evil** even in **the innermost parts** of a person. Although it may refer to criminal punishment in the context (so Garrett, *Proverbs*, 179), it surely applies to parental discipline as well (cf. 13:24; 22:15). This certainly does not advocate child abuse! Appropriate corporal discipline is viewed as a good teaching tool with other forms of instruction. For a parent, it is an act of love, its effect edifying rather than deleterious (see 13:24; 19:18-19; 22:15; 23:13-14; and comments there).

21:1. This is a testimony to the "King of kings" (Kidner, *Proverbs*, 141). God's sovereignty extends even to the king and the nation he leads. Just like a farmer can direct irrigation **channels of water** to areas in his land of his choosing, so **the Lord** directs **the king's heart wherever He wishes**. **Water** is often pictured as a mighty, chaotic force in the OT, something requiring great power and skill to control (Waltke, *Book of Proverbs 15–31*, 168). But it is also a life-giving blessing. So too the Lord masters the king, powerful though he may be, and directs him in ways that bless—or redirect blessing away from—his nation.

21:2-4. The wise are concerned foremost with the sovereign Lord's evaluation. Verse 2 is almost identical to 16:2 (see comments there). Humans misjudge whether their **way is right**, either through self-deception or rebelliously turning God's moral order on its head (cf. Gn 3:1-7). It is the Lord's just verdict on one's **heart** that counts. Proverbs 21:3 gives an important instance of God's standards of evaluation. **The Lord** values **righteousness and justice** even **more than sacrifice**. He favors ethics over religious ritual. Indeed, ritual shorn of ethics is unacceptable to him (cf. 15:8-9; Is 1:11-17; Hs 6:6; Mc 6:6-8; 1Sm 15:22; Longman, *Proverbs*, 390). The NT may have set aside ceremonial laws of the OT (cf. Mt 12:7; Ac 10:34-35), but not its moral laws (Mt 22:27-29) (Waltke, *Book of Proverbs 15–31*, 170). Proverbs 21:4 is another example of God's evaluative standards. He considers **haughty eyes, a proud heart**, and **the lamp of the wicked** all to be **sin**. The key interpretive question here relates to the last image. The word *nir* might be translated "lamp" or "tillage/plowing". Commentators are divided, but either image seems to arrive at the same point. Lamp may be an image for one's life (so Kidner, *Proverbs*, 141; cf. 20:20), and tillage may be used as one example of a common activity standing for all of one's undertakings. The point is that all of the activities of the **wicked**—indeed, their very life—is considered sinful to the Lord. Read in light of v. 2, they are also **proud** through and through (externally: eyes; internally: heart) because they judge their actions right against God's standards.

21:5-7. If the previous proverbs dealt with God's standards of judgment, these deal with the results of His judgment on various types of wicked people.

21:5. Rather surprisingly, diligence here is contrasted with hastiness, not laziness. Perhaps rashness should be understood as a form of laziness: someone who acts with haste is too lazy to plan. In any case, **the diligent**, who do take time to plan, will prosper whereas the **hasty** will come **to poverty**. Haste does make waste.

21:6. Liars can sometimes amass **treasures**, but it is fool's gold. Fraudulent gain is as **fleeting** as a windblown **vapor**. Worse still, those who pursue it are really pursuing **death**, the deceptive reward of their deceit.

21:7. Wicked men will act with **violence** against others in an unjust cause, but that violence will rebound back on them. It **will drag them away** like a fish caught in a dragnet (cf. Hab 1:15). They become "their own executioners" (Kidner, *Proverbs*, 142; cf. Jdg 9). Jesus Himself made a similar, if more general, point (cf. Mt 26:52).

21:8. The difference between **a guilty man** and a **pure** one is evident in their **way** of life or conduct. The former's **way** is **crooked**, the latter's **upright** or straight. The different paths they follow may suggest God's judgment or blessing as well (i.e., a crooked path is much harder than a straight one), particularly in light vv. 5-7. Some commentators understand the admittedly difficult first line very differently and interpret the whole proverb accordingly. Clifford's translation (*Proverbs*, 187) captures this alternate, though less likely, interpretation: "A person's path may zigzag and be strange, but his actions are blameless and right."

21:9. Having a good wife is a blessing (18:22); having a **contentious** wife is not. A contentious person is always quick to quarrel. So it is **better to live in a corner of a roof** alone. Since roofs were flat, a man might live on one, but it would be a lonely, cramped, uncomfortable, exposed existence. Still, living in **a house shared with a contentious** wife is comparatively worse. The same could be said of a wife and her contentious husband. Singles who wish to get married and are wise should pray for the Lord's blessing in finding a good mate and wait patiently for such a person. After all, being lonely is better than being in a strife-torn marriage. Just ask someone with a contentious mate.

21:10. The **wicked** person makes a terrible neighbor. He has a craving for **evil**. He is so absorbed by his own evil passions that, at best, he neglects his neighbor; at worst, he abuses him. But in neither case does he love his neighbor. The wicked person's **neighbor** can expect no **favor** from him.

21:11. The hard-hearted **scoffer** gains little from his well-deserved punishment, but at least the **naive** onlooker can learn something and become **wise** (cf. 19:25). The second line is more ambiguous. Who **receives knowledge when the wise is instructed**? It may refer to the **wise**, who continue to grow in wisdom without needing to be shocked into attention (similar to 19:25). Or it may refer to the **naive**, who can grow in wisdom both through negative and positive examples. The latter seems preferable, since one of wisdom's purposes is to win the naive over to wisdom (Murphy, *Proverbs*, 159; cf. 1:4).

21:12. Who is the **righteous one** in this proverb? Some maintain he is a righteous *man*. But it is difficult to see how he could bring **the wicked to ruin**, since it is the Lord who justly brings about their downfall (cf. 13:6; 20:22). The **righteous one** therefore is a reference to God Himself (Is 24:16). Nothing in the wicked man's household escapes His notice, and He will judge them justly.

21:13-15. The following proverbs present various attitudes towards justice and injustice.

21:13. What goes around comes around, at least for the one who hardens his heart (**shuts his ear**) and fails to respond **to the cry of the poor**. When his time of need comes—and it will—his cries for help will receive no response. No human will pity the man with no pity; why should they? Worse still, God Himself will not respond. God cares for the poor (19:17; 22:22-23), and He expects people to do so as well (14:31). Failure to do so is wicked, and calls for His judgment, not help.

21:14. Despite the reality of v. 13, the man without pity may think he has a good reason not to respond to the cry of the poor for justice. With a **gift** given **in secret**—a **bribe**—he may be able to circumvent justice for a time. Some commentators argue that this proverb merely makes an observation that bribes assuage **anger**; since appeasing wrath is a good thing (15:1, 18), sometimes bribes may be appropriate. But Proverbs discourages bribes (15:27;

17:8, 23; 19:6; see comments on 18:16), and in this context the anger placated is probably righteous indignation (Waltke, *Book of Proverbs 15–31*, 179). That is, the one who is righteously angry should allow his anger over injustice to lead him to right those social wrongs that incense him rather than take a bribe from a perpetrator to look the other way. So this proverb is reiterating the observation that bribes pervert justice (17:23) and the righteous hate them (15:27).

21:15. One reason the **righteous** hate bribes is because they love **justice**. The **exercise of justice** brings **joy for the righteous, but** it brings **terror** to **workers of iniquity**. After all, justice served means the wicked man's own ruin (the word **terror** could be translated "ruin"). Even merely observing justice served to other wicked people reminds him of what he faces.

21:16. This proverb reiterates the two-path theology of the first nine chapters. The one **who wanders** away **from the way of understanding** will die. The rebel's "moral wanderlust" (Kidner, *Proverbs*, 144) will end with his rest—**in the assembly of the dead** (cf. 9:18)!

21:17. Pleasure is the same word as joy in v. 15, but the parallel **wine** and **oil** clarify the kind of joy this proverb addresses. Drinking **wine** and anointing the body with fragrant **oil** are associated with festive celebration, with what we could call "partying" today (Longman, *Proverbs*, 395). **He who loves** and pursues such pleasures as an end in themselves is foolish. Pleasures cost lots of money, and being preoccupied with them discourages thrift and industry. Poverty is the result. Pleasure seekers beware.

21:18. A **ransom** is a penalty paid **in the place of** the person ransomed in order to free him. Here **the wicked** and **the treacherous** become such a substitute for the **righteous** and **upright**. This may be referring to God's punishment of a people corporately: the **wicked** will bear the brunt of that punishment on behalf of the righteous, who are preserved through it (Fox, *Proverbs 10–31*, 687). Or it may be referring to punishment unjustly plotted or meted out against the righteous: in the end, the tables will be turned on the wicked (Waltke, *Book of Proverbs 15–31*, 181–82; cf. the story of the Jews' deliverance told in the book of Esther). In both cases, this proverb is similar to 11:8.

21:19. This proverb is similar to v. 9 (see comments there), but with a different metaphor. In this case, living in a **desert** is a more preferable than living with a **contentious and vexing woman**.

21:20. Precious treasure may suggest a collection of fine wine (Clifford, *Proverbs*, 192; cf. 1Ch 27:27), particularly in connection with olive **oil**. Together these elements suggest that this proverb lends further commentary to Pr 21:17. The **wise** man deals prudently with his resources so that they can accumulate. The **foolish** pleasure seeker **swallows** them **up** right away. He consumes rather than conserves. No wonder he comes to poverty.

21:21. He who pursues righteousness and loving **loyalty** (*chesed*) will find them, and more (cf. 1Kg 3:10-13; Mt 6:33). The repetition of **righteousness** suggests that he will find what he seeks; in treating others justly, kindly, and loyally he will find others treating him the same. The addition of **life** and **honor** indicates he receives great blessings beyond what he sought.

21:22. In picturesque language this proverb indicates that wisdom is powerful (cf. 24:5-6; Ec 9:13-16). It pictures the **stronghold** of a **city** defended by **mighty** warriors. Its citizens confidently **trust** in its seemingly impenetrable defenses. Yet through wise strategy, the **wise man** somehow **scales** the city's defensive walls, overcomes its **mighty** defenders, and **brings** it **down** to defeat. "Wisdom may succeed where brute force fails" (Kidner, *Proverbs*, 144).

21:23. There is a play on words with **guards** (*shomer*) in this proverb. **He who guards** (*shomer*) **his** speech *watches* what he says very carefully. In doing so he **guards** (*shomer*) **his soul** by *protecting* himself **from trouble.**

21:24. Proverbs says much about the **scoffer**/mocker, but this proverb actually defines him. The HCSB best captures the meaning: "The proud and arrogant person, named 'Mocker,' acts with excessive pride." He has an incredible overabundance of **pride**, so he makes fun of others and never accepts any correction.

21:25-26. The desire of the sluggard kills him because he **refuse[s] to work**. It may be that his desire for the necessities of life is somehow insufficient to motivate him to work (and eat). Or it may be that any motivation to work (and eat) is overwhelmed by his desire for something else—such as chasing some empty fantasy or just trying to avoid any work! The first line of v. 26 also addresses someone's desire (**craving**), but it is not clear whose. It may belong to the wicked in general, whose selfish, greedy cravings are never ending. More likely it continues to describe the desire of the sluggard, who is left with nothing but his incessant (**all day long**) craving. In any case, neither has any capacity to give to others. Therefore, neither is a **righteous** person, who **gives** to the needy and does so generously (he **does not hold back**).

21:27. The Lord is not impressed by mere religious practice without a heart devoted to Him (cf. Is 1:11; Jl 2:13; Am 5:21; Mt 15:8). He considers **the sacrifice of the wicked** to be **an abomination** (cf. 15:8). Perhaps they are simply going through the motions or offering carelessly or trying to maintain a hypocritical veneer. That is loathsome enough. But God considers a sacrifice offered **with evil intent** to be even **more** loathsome. This probably involves the wicked's actually trying to solicit God's help in some evil scheme (Fox, *Proverbs 10–31*, 691). Attempting such a bargain only "adds insult to injury" (Kidner, *Proverbs*, 145).

21:28-29. Both proverbs discuss the liar. The **false witness will perish** and will be defeated (v. 28). The first line is clear enough, but the second line is more difficult, spurring several interpretations. It mentions **the man who listens**, but to what does he listen? By adding the phrase **to the truth**, the NASB indicates that he listens to what is true. However, it is more likely that he listens carefully to what the false witness claims. Then the discerning listener **will speak** *lanetzach*. Here this term more likely means "victoriously" rather than **forever** (Waltke, *Book of Proverbs 15–31*, 163–64n44). The second line is therefore probably saying that the careful listener will be able to discern the perjurer's lies and then expose those lies when he finally speaks, thereby winning his case (cf. Fox, *Proverbs 10–31*, 691). Verse 29 is similar. Here the liar is described as **a wicked man** who **displays a bold face**. That is, he is an evil, bald-faced liar (Garrett, *Proverbs*, 185). The ESV translation nicely captures the second line: "but the upright gives thought to his ways." He understands the ways of the liar and sees right through his charade (Garrett, *Proverbs*, 185). An alternate, though less likely interpretation (following the NASB) applies the proverb to the wicked more generally: they boldly follow their evil path to destruction, in contrast to the **sure** path of the righteous (see Longman, *Proverbs*, 399–400).

21:30-31. Since **the Lord** makes them possible, there can be **no wisdom**, **understanding**, or **counsel** without Him (cf. 1:7), nor can feeble human attempts at wisdom prevail **against the Lord** (v. 30). Verse 31 applies the principle to war. The war **horse** (as well as chariots) represented the best in military technology of the time (Clifford, *Proverbs*, 194). Yet human resources are not conclusive in determining the outcome of warfare. No success is possible apart from God's will; **victory belongs to the Lord** (cf. Ps 33:16-17). "Neither wisdom (v. 30) nor might (v. 31) can attain its aims if these are contrary to God's designs" (Fox, *Proverbs 10–31*, 693).

22:1-2. Wealth should not be valued above reputation (v. 1). A good reputation (**a good name**, **favor**) is worth more. Wealth alone cannot secure it. Only wisdom can (cf. 3:1-4), and wisdom can bring wealth to boot (cf. 3:14; Waltke, *Book of Proverbs 15–31*, 199). Wealth also should not give one superior airs (v. 2). The **rich and the poor have a common bond**: both are created by **the Lord** and so both are image-bearers. This reality should be a "school of virtue" for both: "the poor shall not envy the rich (Prov. 3:31), and the rich shall not despise the poor" (C. F. Keil and F. Delitzsch, *Proverbs, Ecclesiastes, Song of Songs*, trans. M. G. Easton, COT 6 [1874–75; Peabody, MA: Hendrickson, 1996], 322).

22:3. The word **evil** might refer to moral evil or to harm/danger. Either option is probably too narrow; the word is intentionally broad here (something like the word "trouble"). The **prudent** have the foresight to avoid trouble (evil and/or unnecessary difficulties). The naive, lacking such insight, head right towards trouble, and end up finding it. They are **punished for it**, either because they fall into moral evil and its consequences, or they get enmeshed in unnecessary problems that could have been avoided.

22:4. The end result (**reward**) of wisdom is **riches**, **honor**, **and life** (cf. 8:18, 35). And wisdom depends on a **humility** associated with **the fear of the Lord**. The humble who revere the Lord renounce self-sufficiency (Waltke, *Book of Proverbs 15–31*, 202) and humbly receive wise instruction and correction from His sages.

22:5. The way of the perverse, crooked person is difficult. It is filled with **thorns** and deadly **snares**, making their life miserable—and short (Fox, *Proverbs 10–31*, 697). The way to protect (**guard**) oneself—and one's very life—is to keep **far from** those **thorns and snares** by avoiding the lifestyle of the crooked in the first place.

22:6. This well-known proverb raises several important considerations. First, to **train**

up (or "to dedicate") a child, "means to start the youth off with a strong and perhaps even religious commitment to a certain course of action" (Waltke, *Book of Proverbs 15–31*, 204). Second, the meaning of a child's **way** (lit., "his way") has been disputed. Some suggest it refers to training in accord with the child's abilities and capacities. Others suggest it ironically refers to the child's own desired way; let them do what they want and you will never change them (so Clifford, *Proverbs*, 197). But it surely refers to the way of wisdom, (**the way he should go**). After all, there is only one right way in Proverbs, and the second line suggests that the child does get old, which is a reward for that right way (cf. 20:29; Waltke, *Book of Proverbs 15–31*, 205). Third, as is true of proverbs in general, this one also is a general rule of thumb, not an unmitigated promise. This is a proverb, and proverbs describe the common experiences of God's people over long periods of time. Typically, a child whose parents dedicate him to the right path through careful training will continue in that way to old age. This proverb does not treat children mechanistically as if a child cannot choose to walk away from the faith (e.g., 2:13), nor does it assume that humans can force God's hand (16:1-9). Other factors outside parental control may affect outcomes as well. But this proverb stresses "parental opportunity and duty" (Kidner, *Proverbs*, 147), encouraging parents to do their part by raising their children well. Even parents of children who may become prodigal (Lk 15:11-32) can have real hope that **when he is old he will not depart** from what he has been taught as a child.

22:7. This proverb urges extreme caution about indebtedness in order to avoid becoming **the lender's slave**. The first line is a frank observation: "Those with material means usually call the shots in a society" (Longman, *Proverbs*, 405). The same dynamic happens to **the borrower**: the lender has the power in the relationship. After all, the borrower owes the lender money, and should he fail to pay, in that society he could quite literally become enslaved as a debtor. The Bible does not forbid making or taking out loans (see Lv 25:35-36; Mt 5:42; Lk 6:35); however, financial and social bondage can be the result. Extreme caution is wise when incurring debt.

22:8-9. Oppression is a poor investment (v. 8). **Iniquity** has the connotation of injustice here (Koehler et al., *HALOT*, 798), particularly when seen in parallel with a **rod of fury** used for oppression. **Will perish** is better translated "will fail." Thus **he who sows** injustice **will reap** nothing (**vanity**) except failure. Generosity is a much better investment (v. 9). A **generous** (lit., "good of eye") man who **gives some of his** own **food to the poor will be blessed**. That blessing comes from the Lord Himself, who cares for the poor (cf. 19:17), and perhaps also from the poor, who thank him and speak well of him to God and man.

22:10. The scoffer has a terrible effect on the community. He is a troublemaker because he thinks he is never wrong, is defensive, and likes to **dishonor** others and stir things up. So when a community expels him, they also expel the **contention**, **strife**, and **dishonor** that accompany him. "It is often not the situation but rather the people involved in a situation who cause problems" (Longman, *Proverbs*, 407). A similar principle should operate in church life (cf. Mt 18:17; Ti 3:10 and comments there).

22:11. Here is some advice on how to win friends and influence people—particularly important people like **the king**. Become a person **who loves purity of heart** and who can speak graciously at the same time. Effective speech without integrity makes one a manipulative hypocrite; integrity without effective speech makes one's influence ineffective. "It is the equal partnership of integrity and charm, the one not diminishing the other, that is the rarity" (Kidner, *Proverbs*, 148). It is a powerful combination that attracted the king's favor in the past and is just as winsome today.

22:12. The **LORD['s] eyes** keep watch over **knowledge**. To keep watch is to guard, and by extension, to **preserve**. **Knowledge**, in contrast to **the words of the treacherous**, probably refers to the words spoken by the wise. God therefore makes sure that wisdom succeeds whereas He brings the teachings of those who treacherously subvert wisdom to failure (Fox, *Proverbs 10–31*, 701).

22:13. The **sluggard** shamelessly uses excuses to avoid work, no matter how absurd (cf. 6:6-11). Here he claims that **a lion** is stalking the city **streets**. Ancient Israel had its lions, but they hardly ever wandered city streets!

22:14. Another kind of man-eater really does stalk city streets: the adulteress (Waltke, *Book of Proverbs 15–31*, 215; cf. 7:12). Her **mouth** refers to her seductive kisses and words (cf. 7:13-21). Those who succumb to her temptations **fall into** the **deep** deadly **pit** she places before them.

Worse still, they place themselves under the **LORD['s] curse**. The wording of the second line probably does not mean that the Lord curses them *so that* they succumb to her. More likely, it stresses that she is the means of God's judgment on those who disregard Him and heed her seductions.

22:15. The depravity of humanity is evident in the natural inclination of children (cf. Ps 51:5). **Foolishness** is inherently **bound up** in the very character (**heart**) **of a child**. This "doctrine of 'original folly'" (Whybray, *Book of Proverbs*, 125) is no small matter; foolishness is hard to remove, and it is ultimately deadly. But there is hope for the parents who love their child: **the rod of discipline will remove it far from him**. It takes early, dramatic preemptive action to deal with folly, and physical discipline is a significant part of that (cf. Pr 13:24; 19:18-19; 20:30; 23:13-14 and comments there).

22:16. This proverb gives two examples of ill-gotten gain that lead ultimately ***to* poverty** (emphasis added). The first is oppressing **the poor** in order to enrich oneself (cf. 14:31; 17:5; 19:17). The second is offering bribes **to the rich** and powerful in order to get ahead. In the end, both of these are "expensive tactics" (Kidner, *Proverbs*, 149).

D. Thirty Sayings of the Wise (22:17–24:22)

This section differs in style from the previous section, almost like a brief version of the first nine chapters. It consists of 30 sayings of the wise, presumably collected from various wisdom teachers (22:17–24:22). Notably influential in 23:22-34 (sayings 17-19) is the Egyptian wise man Amenemope, but there are also Aramaic and Akkadian similarities as well (Waltke, *Book of Proverbs 15–31*, 217; cf. also Fox, *Proverbs 10–31*, 705). Of course, Solomon adapted international wisdom sayings in a way consistent with the fear of the Lord. Scholars differ to some degree about how this section should be organized, but the structure below is fairly typical. (Each of the 30 sayings will be designated after their respective passage with a number enclosed in brackets.)

In addition, 24:23-34 comprise a brief addendum, identified as the "also sayings" of the wise so-called because of the "also" of 24:23a and discussed in the next section.

22:17-21. [1] This first saying functions as a prologue to the whole section. Like the lessons in the first section of Proverbs, this section begins with an exhortation to **incline your ear and hear** (diligently heed) these teachings (v. 17). They are called the sayings or **words of the wise**, but they are also described as **my knowledge**, suggesting that Solomon used and adapted the wisdom of other sages (Waltke, *Book of Proverbs 15–31*, 222). The learner has ample motivation for heeding these teachings: they will have **pleasant** consequences for his life (v. 18). But this will only happen if he so internalizes them—**keep them within**—that he can readily articulate them—**ready on your lips** (cf. 2:10).

There are two purposes for these teachings (vv. 19-21). The first and most important is that the learner might **trust . . . in the LORD** (v. 19). This involves a personal, ongoing commitment to and reliance on Him (Waltke, *Book of Proverbs 15–31*, 223; cf. 3:5-6), and nothing is more pleasant than that! The centrality of fearing the Lord is a crucial difference between biblical wisdom from its ANE counterparts. The sage's other purpose for writing his **counsels and knowledge** (v. 20) is that the learner would know **truth** and speak honestly and reliably (v. 21). Honest, wise, reliable people are valuable to anyone who commissions them and are beneficial to society. The **excellent things** of v. 20 is better translated "thirty sayings" (cf. Waltke, *Book of Proverbs 15–31*, 219-20, n. 113; Fox, *Proverbs 10–31*, 710–12)—hence the title of this section.

22:22-23. [2] This saying forbids ill-gotten gain (v. 22) and then gives a motivation: God is on the side of the poor and oppressed (v. 23). These verses form a chiastic structure. So wicked, powerful people may **rob** the **poor because**, being **poor, he** lacks the money and power to defend himself (v. 22a). But then in turn **the LORD** will literally rob **the life of those who rob** the poor (23b). Similarly, the powerful may **crush the afflicted** in legal proceedings **at the gate** of the city, where such proceedings were held (v. 23b). But then in turn **the LORD will plead their case** against their oppressors (v. 23a), and He always wins His case (v. 23b)! Taking advantage of the poor and oppressed is not wise.

22:24-25. [3] A wise person will **not associate or go** about with an angry, short-**tempered man** (v. 24). And there is good reason not to. **Anger** is contagious, and so are its dire results (v. 25). The hothead's associate **will learn his ways**, and becoming like him, will fall into the same deadly **snare**.

22:26-27. [4] As elsewhere in Proverbs (e.g., 6:1-5), here again making **pledges** (more literally, "shaking hands" in a contractual agreement) to **become guarantors for** other people's **debts** is discouraged (v. 26). After all, the time may come that **you have nothing with which to pay** when the loan is called, and the creditor may **take** the very **bed from under you**. At that point, you are left with nothing.

22:28. [5] To **move** stones marking the **boundary** of family property represents seizing that property by fraud (when, for example, it is done little by little over time) or by brute confiscation (when oppressors take from the powerless, e.g., 15:25). In Israel, these boundaries were **ancient**, arranged by lot for Israel's **fathers** (see comments on Jos 14–19) when Israel received the land in fulfillment of the Abrahamic covenant and assigned by tribal allotment by Joshua (Gn 12:1-3; 15:18; Jos 11:23ff.). The Lord considered the preservation of this allotted property important (Dt 19:14; 27:17; Lv 25:24-34), as would the wise (cf. 23:10-12).

22:29. [6] A **man skilled in his work** is noticed. And he is going places. **He will stand before kings** and **not . . . before obscure men**. That is, his skillful services come to be in such demand that he can serve only the upper echelons of society—and only they can afford him! It is a good motivation to work hard, continue to grow in one's skills, and push for excellence.

23:1-3. [7] The context of this saying is a banquet with a **ruler**, a king, or some other important government official (Fox, *Proverbs 10–31*, 720) (v. 1a). The wise will **consider carefully what** or who (the Hb. is ambiguous) **is before** him (v. 1b). That is, he will pay cautious attention to that context, and act accordingly. In particular, he will not overindulge (v. 2-3a). To **put a knife to** one's **throat** does not suggest mere threat, but is akin to slicing one's throat. In that situation, any **man** inclined to gluttony (**great appetite**) had better put a stop to it and not crave the **delicacies** the ruler places before him. And for good reason, **for it is deceptive food** (v. 3b). Why is it deceptive? It may be that overeating has disagreeable side effects after the fact, or that the food comes with strings attached (so Garrett, *Proverbs*, 195). More likely, however, the food is more than it seems: "it points to the wily character of the host, who is testing the character of the guest" (Murphy, *Proverbs*, 174). Demonstrating his lack of self-control, the glutton will make a poor impression on the ruler and undermine the hope of career advancement. The wise make good impressions at opportune times.

23:4-5. [8] "When wealth is acquired through wise effort such as diligence (10:4) and modesty (21:17) and given by the Lord," Waltke wrote, "it is a positive blessing" (Waltke, *Book of Proverbs 15–31*, 240; cf. 3:16; 10:22; 12:27). After all, in those cases it is a consequence of fearing the Lord. But wealth pursued as an end in itself is a fool's errand. So v. 4 advises against exhausting oneself **to gain wealth**. To **cease from your consideration** literally says: "cease from your understanding." This is an encouragement to stop relying on your own understanding or schemes to acquire wealth (so rightly Waltke, *Book of Proverbs 15–31*, 240; cf. 3:5-6). That is, people often pursue riches to be self-sufficient and secure (cf. 18:11). But wealth is unreliable (v. 5). **Set your** sight **on it**, and it may well sprout **wings** and disappear, **like an eagle that flies** into the sky.

23:6-8. [9] Dining in the home of a stingy, **selfish man** (cf. 28:22), even though the menu contains **delicacies**, is unpleasant. It is best to avoid his banquet altogether (**do not eat** his bread) much less to **desire** the opportunity, because the hypocritical skinflint is really "the kind of person who is always thinking about the cost" v. 7 (NIV) and really does not want you there. Although he urges his guest to **eat and drink**, in **his heart** (which reveals his true identity) he resents his dinner guest. The result is a very unpleasant meal, where the guest feels like he wants to **vomit up** the dinner. Duty may demand that the guest converse pleasantly (**compliments** is literally "pleasing words") with the host, but that conversation is a **waste**. Every invitation is not worth accepting.

23:9. [10] Wise **words** are wasted on **a fool**. Good intentions notwithstanding, the sage's only thanks for instructing him will be the fool's contempt for his **wisdom** (cf. Jesus' similar point in Mt 7:6). Still, Pr 26:5 indicates that there may be times to do so anyway.

23:10-11. [11] In words reminiscent of 22:28, this saying prohibits land grabs, particularly against vulnerable people like **the fatherless** (also widows, 15:25; cf. 22:28). But they are not powerless, because they have a strong **Redeemer** and advocate, the Lord Himself (cf. 22:22-23). A needy person's redeemer (*go'el*) was a relative who advocated for him, protected his property, kept him out of slavery, and avenged his murder (Lv 25:25-25, 47-54; Nm 35:19-27; Ru 3-4; Waltke, *Book of Proverbs 15–31*, 245). In a surprising turn, therefore, the oppressor foolishly places himself in a precarious and vulnerable position.

23:12. [12] This saying exhorts the hearer to receive **discipline** and **knowledge**. He must bring the wisdom he receives through his **ears** to bear on his **heart**, rather than listen and forget.

23:13-14. [13] Parental **discipline** is difficult, but vital. Parents may be tempted to **hold back discipline from** their **child**, particularly if it includes spanking **him with the rod**. But if they do discipline him, **he will not die** (v. 13). This is probably has a double meaning: "the child will not only survive it, he will survive *because* of it" (Kidner, *Proverbs*, 152). So he will not die because wise parents love their children and exercise moderation; they are not abusive. He also will not die (i.e., **you shall . . . rescue his soul from Sheol**) because it will drive the foolishness from his heart (22:15), which, if left unchanged, will be his death (v. 14; cf. 13:24; 19:18-19; 20:30; 22:15; and comments there).

23:15-16. [14] A **son** or daughter who is **wise** and speaks wisely will make their parents **glad**. If the previous saying dealt with negative reinforcement, this is positive reinforcement. "The joy of giving one's parents or teachers a sense of pride and satisfaction should serve as a motivation to pursue the right path" (Garrett, *Proverbs*, 196).

23:17-18. [15] The wise man should **not . . . envy sinners** in his **heart** (v. 17a), even if they seem to prosper for a time (cf. Ps 73, esp. v. 3, and Ps 37). Instead, he will "look up (17b) and look ahead (18)" (Kidner, *Proverbs*, 152). Looking up, the wise will **always** be zealous for **the fear of the Lord** (v. 17b). The NASB suggests that live is the implied verb in this line. But more likely the verb **envy** in the first line carries over into the second as well, only here it has the sense of being "zealous for" **the fear of the Lord always** (Nm 25:11, 13; Ezk 39:25). Looking ahead, the wise realize that they have good reason for their passion. Unlike the wicked, who face destruction, those who worship the Lord have **a future** and a **hope** that **will not be cut off** (v. 18). In the end, it is nothing short of eternal life.

23:19-21. [16] The father encourages his son to heed wisdom and **direct** his **heart in** its **way** (v. 19). This could be a separate saying in its own right, but its invitation for the **son** to **listen**, reminiscent of chaps. 1–9, anticipates the message the father wants his son to hear in the verses to follow (Waltke, *Book of Proverbs 15–31*, 256). In this case, wisdom's way is to not join in with **heavy drinkers** or **gluttonous** men (v. 20). And for good reason: dissipation leads to **poverty** (v. 21). Overindulging wastes resources rather than using them wisely (cf. 21:17, 20). Moreover, it fosters a slothful lethargy (**drowsiness**) that discourages work (cf. 6:10; 23:33-34). For Christians today, it is truly sobering that the saying considers gluttony no better than drunkenness.

23:22-25. [17] This saying encourages the son to embrace wisdom (vv. 22-23) so that he makes his parents glad (vv. 24-25). He should **listen to** his wise parents' teachings (v. 22). Their being **old** implies that his parents are righteous and wise, and failure to listen to them is tantamount to showing contempt both for parents and wisdom—and for the commands of the Lord (cf. Ex 20:12; Eph 6:2). In commercial terms, he should **buy truth**, which includes **wisdom and instruction and understanding** (cf. Pr 1:2); they are too valuable to **sell** (v. 23). "Selling out" involves rejecting wisdom in favor of some foolish worldview (Waltke, *Book of Proverbs 15–31*, 259). When a son embraces his parents' teachings, becoming **righteous** and **wise**, he will cause his **father** and **mother** to **rejoice** and **be glad** (v. 24). Therefore, the wise son will seek to bring them joy in this manner (v. 25). The saying assumes that making his parents proud will motivate the son (Longman, *Proverbs*, 429)—a safe assumption, all things being equal.

23:26-28. [18] Here a father tenderly requests his son to **give me your heart** and **let your eyes delight in my** wise **ways** (v. 26). He wants his son to take delight in wisdom rather than be attracted to **a harlot** or someone's **adulterous** wife—because these women are like **a deep pit** and **narrow well** (v. 27). Falling into either was certain death (cf. 5:5; 7:27; 9:18). These images probably also have sexual connotations. But she is more than a passive danger; she is an active one as well, like a **robber** who **lurks** in ambush (v. 28a). "She is at once the lure and the trap" (Fox, *Proverbs 10–31*, 739). She **increases the faithless among men** (v. 28b) because there are plenty of fools willing to heed her siren song. She only serves to undermine the moral character of society (Garrett, *Proverbs*, 197). Of course, the playboy is no better than she is.

23:29-35. [19] This saying on drunkenness, and ultimately alcoholism, begins with six interrogatory riddles (v. 29). **Who** cries out **woe** and alas (**sorrow**), because of all the suffering he brings on himself? **Who** gets into quarrels and **has** complaints, needless **wounds**, and bloodshot **eyes**? The answer is obvious: drunks (v. 30)! They are described as **those who linger**

long over wine and **who . . . taste** or examine it. The tone is sarcastic. "The sots come to 'inspect' or 'investigate' **wine**, as it were. We can picture them hunched over their cup, staring duly at the object of their 'study'" (Fox, *Proverbs 10–31*, 741). The problem is not in drinking wine per se but in becoming enamored with its charms and overindulging, something the wise **do not** do (v. 31). Like the seductress above, wine captivates the foolish drunk. He looks longingly at the **wine**, sparkling **red** in the **cup**, and dreams of **it** going **down** his throat **smoothly**. There is a word play here; the word for wine's "sparkle" usually means "eye." So the alluring gaze of wine's red "eye" will be returned by the fixed stare of the drunk's bloodshot eyes (Fox, *Proverbs 10–31*, 741).

In the end, wine for the drunk is as poisonous as a striking **serpent,** or **viper** (v. 32). The harmful effects of intoxication include distorted perception (v. 33a) and the breakdown of appropriate inhibitions (v. 33b). In addition, it gives the drunk a nauseating lack of balance, like a person grasping the deck or rigging of a ship tossed to and fro on the high seas (v. 34; Waltke *Proverbs 15–31*, 266). Moreover, it anesthetizes him to all the damaging beatings he has taken, at least temporarily (v. 35a). But the worst part of the alcoholic's addiction is his incorrigibility (v. 35a). He longs to **seek another drink** as soon as he awakens from his drunken stupor, only to repeat the process in a downward spiral. The whole dark comedy thus turns tragic—a sobering picture indeed.

24:1-2. [20] The admonition **not** to **be envious of evil men nor desire** their company appears elsewhere in Proverbs (cf. 3:31; 13:20; 23:17-18; vv. 19-20). But here the motivation for not doing so focuses on the character of the evil men themselves. The violent schemes of **their** hearts (**minds**) are reflected in their malicious words. Such characters are repulsive. Anyone with sense would neither want to become like them nor share their ultimate fate. Yet the proverb implies that close companions will become alike and share the same fate (cf. 3:31; 23:17-18; 24:19-20; Pss 37; 73). The next two sayings show that wisdom's way is better.

24:3-4. [21] **By wisdom** one builds, establishes, and fills **a house** with **precious and pleasant riches**. This is true literally, of course, since it takes wisdom to produce the wealth needed for such costly endeavors (cf. 3:13-20; 8:18). However, even more significantly, it applies to the incalculable blessing of a loving, harmonious, stable family life that can only come by wisdom (cf. 14:1; 31:10-31).

24:5-6. [22] A **wise man is strong** in ways that go beyond brute strength. Therefore, wisdom and strength are a powerful team; working together (8:14), wise **knowledge increases power**. Verse 6 illustrates the point. A king may have the power to **wage war**, but only when he does so with **wise guidance** and an **abundance of counselors** can he be confidant of **victory** (cf. 11:14; 15:22; 20:18). Prudence and power make a potent combination.

24:7. [23] Wisdom is **too exalted,** out of reach, **for a fool** (*ewil*). He "lacks the wings of piety and humility" needed to soar to such heights (Waltke, *Book of Proverbs 15–31*, 273). So **in the** city **gate**, the forum where public policy, justice, and business was conducted, **he does not open his mouth**. It is not that he is unwilling to speak; the fool is always ready to spout his folly (cf. 15:2). It is rather that in such weighty matters he simply has nothing to contribute, and the leaders of the community do not give him a platform to be heard. Lacking wisdom, he is unable "to speak well, authoritatively, and constructively" (Waltke, *Book of Proverbs 15–31*, 273), and everyone knows it. In such settings, he is way out of his league.

24:8-9. [24] While the community may readily dismiss some fools, they will come utterly to despise others. The one who, for his own benefit, **plans to do evil** at others' expense will develop a reputation as **a schemer** (v. 8). This is no small matter. His community recognizes his foolish scheming as **sin** (v. 9a). And though he may mock at violating the norms of God and society, the **scoffer** will suffer as a despised outcast of his community, being an **abomination to men** (v. 9b).

24:10-12. [25] Times of **distress** will test a person's character (v. 10). If he is **slack** in difficult times, due to cowardice, laziness, or indifference he proves his **limited strength** of character (Waltke, *Book of Proverbs 15–31*, 275). One such time of crisis would involve intervening on behalf of **those who are being taken away to death** (v. 11). The particulars of this scenario are not clear. It may involve intervening with fools whose behavior is leading them inexorably to death (e.g., 7:22-23; Longman, *Proverbs*, 438). More likely, it involves delivering people from life-threatening injustice, such as victims of violent criminals, evil people, and corrupt governments (so Fox, *Proverbs 10–31*, 747). In any case, flimsy excuses to avoid any involvement will be judged by the Lord (v. 12). The slacker may feign ignorance (saying **we did not know this**), but God, **who weighs the hearts**, perceives the truth. More ominously, God, who **keeps** watch over one's life (**soul**), **will** also **render to man according to his work**. If a man "turns a blind eye to helping victims and does nothing to help them, the Protector of Life will turn a blind eye to him in his crisis" (Waltke, *Book of Proverbs 15–31*, 278).

24:13-14. [26] This saying draws a parallel between eating **honey** and knowing **wisdom**. To **eat honey** is **good**, like tasty medicine, because it not only was considered to have medicinal value for one's body, but it also has a **sweet**, pleasant **taste** (v. 13). In a similar sense, wisdom is also both pleasant and beneficial to one's **soul** (v. 14; cf. 16:24). To **know** and appropriate **wisdom** secures a person's **future** rather than disappointed **hope**. This is because it fosters life itself, and an enjoyable life to boot. When seen in connection with the fear of the Lord and the larger biblical witness, it is also nothing less than the bliss of eternal life with the Lord Himself (cf. 23:18).

24:15-16. [27] Attacking the righteous is a fool's errand. This warning is probably directed to the **wicked** man: criminals should not target the home and possessions of **the righteous** (v. 15). Verse 16 explains why: the **righteous man** is resilient. This does not mean he is untouchable, for even **a righteous man falls** into difficulty. But that difficulty is never permanent. "No matter how many times (the proverbial **seven**) the just one falls, he will rise again, in contrast to the stumbling of the wicked" (Murphy, *Proverbs*, 181–82). Their **stumble** into **calamity** is permanent. The difference between them is clear. The righteous have wisdom and, more important, the Lord to carry them through; the wicked are bereft of all such resources.

24:17-18. [28] If the previous saying predicted the downfall of the wicked, this saying discourages gloating when it happens. The wise person will **not rejoice when** his **enemy falls** (v. 17). But sometimes the righteous wise person rightly does that very thing (cf. 1:26; 11:10; Ex 15; Jdg 5; Ps 52:5-7), so what is different here? The clue may be found in the motivation clause in Pr 24:18. When **the Lord** sees it, He will **be displeased** by it—or more literally, it is "evil in His eyes." The son may rejoice at deliverance from oppression or the display at God's justice, but he should never revel in human suffering itself, even of his enemies. True, his wicked enemy may be on the receiving end of God's just **anger**, but his own vindictive glee over his enemy's suffering is no better than his enemy's sin (Kidner, *Proverbs*, 155). He becomes like his enemy.

Hence, in such cases, God may, at least for the time being, **turn away His anger from** the son's enemy, lest He perpetuate the situation that feeds the son's own malevolent attitude (Waltke, *Book of Proverbs 15–31*, 285). Worse still, the saying may also imply that God will turn His anger back on the son himself. It is much better, then, to "place justice in the hands of God and stand back in silent dread of God's power" (Garrett, *Proverbs*, 199; cf. 20:22; 25:21-22; Jb 31:29-30).

24:19-20. [29] If the previous saying encourages proper attitudes when God delivers justice, this saying encourages proper attitudes when such justice seems delayed. In times when **evildoers** seem to prosper, the righteous wise should **not fret**, that is, become agitated, infuriated, enraged. Nor should they become **envious of the wicked** (v. 19; cf. 3:31-33; 23:17-18; 24:1-2; Ps 73). This is because any prosperity for the wicked is short-lived, a striking contrast with that of the righteous (v. 20; cf. 23:18). Having **no future** because his **lamp** (i.e., his life) **will be** snuffed **out**, the wicked man's long-term prospects are premature death—and worse in eternity. In times when the wicked prosper, then, righteous people will trust in the Lord rather than give way to fretting and envy, which is only "to play the fool by confusing their temporary lot with their permanent reward" (Hubbard, *Proverbs*, 386).

24:21-22. [30] Rebellion against **the Lord** and **the king** is dangerous. The wise person will thus **fear** them both rather than **associate with** rebels (v. 21; cf. 16:14; 19:12; 20:2; 1Pt 2:17). The phrase **those who are given to change** (*shoniym*, "change", "altered") is difficult, but the context indicates they are rebels. Verse 22 explains why subjection to God and king is the wiser course. Both of them will bring certain and sudden disaster (**calamity**) on rebels, with the resulting **ruin** too great to fully understand. This proverb assumes, of course, that the king himself is not a rebel to His King, the Lord, but is exercising legitimate authority derived from the Lord (cf. Rm 13:1-7).

E. More Sayings of the Wise (24:23-34)

24:23a. This clause introduces another section, similar in style to the previous one.

The section is **also** called **sayings of the wise**, an addendum affixed to the previous section (22:17–24:22).

24:23b-25. The first of these "also sayings" pertains to the law court, and the basic principle is stated initially in v. 23b: for a person sitting **in judgment**, it **is not good to show partiality** (cf. 17:15, 23, 26; 18:5; 28:21). Two reasons for impartial judgment are given, one negative, one positive. Negatively, a judge who shows favoritism to someone who is guilty (**wicked**) by declaring him innocent (**righteous**) will be universally reviled; **peoples** and **nations** will **curse** and **abhor him** (v. 24). It is not just that blatant injustice is offensive; it is also detrimental to society. Positively, judges **who rebuke** and convict the **wicked** will receive **a good blessing** (v. 25). The people will honor rather than curse them. But beyond the praise of people, the text implies the blessing and cursing is from the Lord Himself.

24:26. This saying compares giving **a right answer** with kissing **the lips**. A right answer is a straightforward, honest response to an inquiry (Koehler et al., *HALOT*, 699). Such words reflect love, respect, and intimacy toward the inquirer, much like a kiss on the lips. "The greatest sign of affection and respect for another is to tell the person the truth" (Clifford, *Proverbs*, 217).

24:27. This saying is akin to the modern proverb, "first things first" (Fox, *Proverbs 10–31*, 772). More particularly, the wise son will first attend to his labors **outside** before trying to **build** his house. In an agrarian context, this means preparing his **field** so that its yield can support his household (cf. 27:23-27). More broadly, the wise will not undertake a project without appropriate preparation.

24:28-29. If taken separately, these two verses would be warning against giving false testimony (v. 28) and taking revenge (v. 29). More likely, however, they should be taken together as a unit. It pictures a person who witnesses falsely **against** his **neighbor** for revenge. Because he has no valid legal **cause** for testifying against his neighbor, (as in Lv 5:1), he testifies deceptively (v. 28). Yet he justifies his false testimony as payback (what **he has done to me**) for a previous wrong (v. 29). Unfortunately, such behavior destroys one's personal integrity and undermines the justice system, which depends on honest testimony. Worse still, it displays a lack of trust in the Lord who judges justly in His timing (cf. 20:22; 24:12).

24:30-34. This last saying follows a story (cf. 7:6-23), and its teaching echoes 6:6-11. The wise father recalls a **field**, or more precisely a **vineyard**, owned by a **sluggard** who lacks **sense** (v. 30). His lazy neglect of his property is evident by the weeds that have overtaken it (**overgrown with thistles** and **covered with nettles**) and by the dilapidated state of (**broken down**) the **stone wall** meant to protect it (v. 31). This implies that the prosperity is no longer productive and that the lazy owner is left in poverty. On observing this example, the wise person takes the lesson to heart: **I reflected . . . looked, and received instruction** (v. 32). The lesson itself is stated clearly: because of the sluggard's lazy neglectfulness (i.e., his preference for **sleep** and **slumber** instead of working), **poverty** will inevitably overtake him like a **robber** or **armed man** (vv. 33-34; cf. 6:9-11; these verses are almost identical; see comments there).

II. The Collection of Solomon's Proverbs by King Hezekiah's Scribes (25:1–29:27)

25:1. This title introduces a second collection of Solomonic proverbs that the **men of Hezekiah, king of Judah, transcribed**. Hezekiah ruled Judah from about 715–687 BC. In the wake of Assyria's destruction of the northern kingdom (721 BC) and apostasy in Judah, he devoted himself to the Lord and led a revival (2Kg 18:1-12). Likely as part of this Hezekiah commissioned wise scholars to copy, collect, and arrange this group of proverbs from among Solomon's 3,000 proverbs (1Kg 4:32). The proverbs of Pr 25:2-7 cluster around interacting with the king.

25:2-3. When it comes to power and wisdom, there is a hierarchy from God to king to human subjects (Waltke, *Book of Proverbs, 15–31*, 310). It is true that **God** and the **king** have **glory**, though God's clearly outstrips the king's (v. 2). God's glory is displayed in the mysteries of His creation, which stress His incomprehensibility and transcendence (cf. Dt 29:29) and bring all human beings to an appropriate humility before Him (Fox, *Proverbs 10–31*, 778). Still, wise governing means that the king must try **to search out** some of these mysteries (**a matter**). So his glory is seen in his capacity to use God-given wisdom to understand some of those mysterious matters of God's creation, particularly those pertaining to affairs of state and to administering justice (Waltke, *Book of Proverbs 15–31*, 311–12; cf. Solomon in 1Kg 3:9, 16-28). Similarly, **the heart of**

kings is as inscrutable to their subjects **as** the mysteries of the heights of **the heavens** and the depths of **the earth** (Pr 25:3). The motivations, thought processes, and emotions behind what he does are hard to fathom, and the subject should give him due deference. Since "those who do not have either the responsibility or information for massive decisions will always be puzzled by those who do," it is best to "be humbly appreciative of the magnitude of the tasks that wise leaders perform" (Hubbard, *Proverbs*, 400).

25:4-5. To get silver pure enough to make a lovely silver **vessel**, the silversmith must remove the **dross from the silver**. Similarly, if the king wants his rule to be securely **established in righteousness**, he must remove **the wicked** from his royal court (cf. 20:8, 26; Ps 101:6-8). If the proverb is also addressed to his advisors, they should seek to promote righteousness in the king's administration so that both king and nation prosper.

25:6-7b. This is direct advice to the king's courtiers against self-promotion. In the context of the king's court, unbridled ambition may spur a courtier to **claim honor** for himself or consider himself the equal **of great men** of high dignity and rank, but this is foolish (2Sm 1:1-16). Far **better** to let others promote you to higher rank than be demoted and humiliated (Pr 25:7; cf. 22:29). Jesus makes the same point (Lk 14:7-11).

25: 7c-10. When addressing conflicts with a **neighbor**, the wise will not be quick to escalate the conflict. For one thing, the wise person will be sure he has his facts straight (vv. 7c-8). The last line of v. 7, **whom your eyes have seen**, is better connected to the idea of presenting your case. If so, the ESV captures the idea: "What your eyes have seen do not hastily bring to court." A rash case based on mere cursory observation rather than careful investigation is foolish. In court, such rashness will be exposed, bringing "shame" (v. 8 ESV) to the one who brought suit. What is true in a court setting is also true in life generally. Don't be quick to argue with another based on hastily drawn conclusions, or you will make a fool of yourself.

Moreover, the wise will deal confidentially and directly with his neighbor with whom he has a dispute (vv. 9-10). In times of conflict with a **neighbor**, it is foolish to gossip to others about your complaint against him, (to **reveal the secret of another**) rather than going directly to him (v. 9). Verse 10 explains why. Those others who hear your accusations will brand you a complainer or a gossip, and that reputation will stick. If the background to these verses is the courtroom, they may be encouraging settling out of court rather than airing one's dirty laundry publicly in the courtroom, to the shame of all involved.

25:11-12. The wise person speaks the right words at the right time (cf. 15:23). **Settings of silver** only enhance the inherent value of golden **apples** (probably in reference to jewelry or some work of art). Similarly, the inherent value of a wise **word** is enhanced when it is **spoken in right circumstances** (v. 11; Longman, *Proverbs*, 453). This principle is evident when it comes to giving **wise** reproof to someone (v. 12). Reproof given to someone unwilling to receive it is wasted. But it is altogether different when rebuke is given to someone with **a listening ear**, willing to receive correction. He will find the **wise reprover** a valued treasure, like jewelry made of **fine gold**.

25:13-14. Reliability is a great blessing (v. 13). Working the wheat **harvest** in May-June was hot labor. If it were possible, no doubt the sweating laborer would welcome the refreshing **cold of snow** in the midst of his hot work. **A faithful messenger** is similarly refreshing **to those who send him** (cf. 13:17). "Business transactions, political decisions, not to speak of personal communication—all depended on the reliability" of messengers (Longman, *Proverbs*, 454). With so much at stake, it is little wonder that senders would find refreshing comfort in a messenger who could be counted on. In contrast, unreliability is a great curse (v. 14). Some people are big talkers, but they cannot back up their promises. **Clouds and wind** promise rain, a huge blessing to an agrarian people living in Israel's arid areas. So if they bring no **rain**, they are a huge disappointment. Similarly a man who **boasts** about the **gifts** he promises to give but does not follow through is a terrible disappointment. The wise will follow through with what they promise, and look warily on big talkers.

25:15. This proverb is counterintuitive because one would expect that the best way to deal with tough people—like a **ruler**, who is as hard and rigid as **bone**—is to be similarly tough. Yet the best approach is **forbearance**, patience. Wise, persistent, **soft** words can break through to tough people and **persuade** them (cf. 15:1, 4, 18; 16:14). The wise man "can bring another to his way of thinking through a patient, open, and warm disposition and through sensitive, tactful speech" (Waltke, *Book of Proverbs 15–31*, 325).

25:16-17. Too much of a good thing is no good. **Honey** is pleasant and beneficial to eat, but **eat** too much, **have it in excess** (*saba*, "to be overfilled"), and you will **vomit** (get sick, v. 16). Similarly, visiting a **neighbor** is enjoyable for both parties, but make a nuisance of yourself by pestering your friend or overstaying your welcome and you will destroy your friendship because **he will become weary** (*saba* "to be overfilled"). Even good friends need private space. Moderation preserves the pleasure of pleasant things; overindulgence destroys it (cf. v. 27; 27:7).

25:18. A **club**, **a sword**, and **a sharp arrow** were weapons of war meant to wound and kill others. **A man who bears false witness against his neighbor** is just **like** such weapons. Perjury is no small matter. "The perjurer is a dangerous weapon" (Garrett, *Proverbs*, 208) who is destructive or even deadly to others (cf. 14:25; 19:28; 1Kg 21).

25:19. A man relies on his teeth to chew and his feet to walk. So a **bad** or broken (Koehler, *HALOT*, 1271) **tooth** and **an unsteady foot** will fail him when he needs them, disappointing him and causing him pain (Longman, *Proverbs*, 456). Similarly, when one puts **confidence in a faithless man in time of trouble**, he will be disappointed and hurt by his friend's treacherous failure in times of need. The wise will choose their friends more carefully (cf. 17:17; 18:24; 20:6).

25:20. This proverb contains two metaphors. The first is taking **off a garment on a cold day**. This action is inappropriate and only makes the person colder. The second is pouring **vinegar on soda**. There are two issues for interpreting this image. First, *nater* is usually translated as **soda**, but it could also be translated as "wound" (e.g., NLT). Second, if **soda** is the proper translation, what effect of mixing vinegar (acid) with soda (base) is highlighted? Is the point that the two do not mix well and react against each other, or is it that the two neutralize each other's effects? It is more likely that the former is intended, particularly in light of the first image. Pouring vinegar on soda—or on a wound—is inappropriate and only stirs things up. In a similar vein, it is insensitive and inappropriate to sing joyful **songs to a troubled heart**. Doing so displays a callous impropriety that only makes the suffering of the depressed person worse. "Seasonable songs can be therapeutic (cf. 1Sm 16:15-23; 19:9; Jb 30:31; Pr 12:25), but when sung unseasonably they are painful and damaging to the spirit (cf. Ps 137:1-4; Sir 22:6a). The sensitive know how and when to sorrow and to rejoice (Ec. 3:4; Rm 12:15; 1Co 12:26: Heb 13:3)" (Waltke, *Book of Proverbs 15–31*, 329).

25:21-22. It is human nature to take vengeance on one's **enemy**, particularly if that enemy is vulnerable. But the admonition here calls for a radically different way: showing kindness to one's vulnerable enemy (v. 21). **If your enemy is hungry**, feed him, and **if he is thirsty, give him water**. There are two reasons given for doing this (v. 22). First, doing so **will heap burning coals on his head**. This image is obscure, and commentators differ widely on its meaning. It is unlikely that it represents an inverted form of vengeance, an act of purported kindness motivated by a vindictive desire actually to gall them. After all, Proverbs discourages taking vengeance (cf. 17:13; 19:11; 20:22; 24:17-18, 29), and the second line here indicates that this is something the Lord considers good (Waltke, *Book of Proverbs 15–31*, 331). Whether or not the image picks up on an Egyptian ritual of penitence, as some suggest, it probably does involve bringing shame to one's enemy—painful though that may be for him (cf. 6:27-28)—with the goal that he would repent. What is clear is that such behavior pleases the Lord and so brings **reward**. Paul quotes these verses in Rm 12:20 as a support for not taking vengeance but overcoming evil with good.

25:23. The difficulty with this proverb rests with the very idea that the **north wind brings forth rain**. In ancient Israel, rain was associated with the west wind (e.g., 1Kg 13:41-46) rather than the north wind. Some suggest that it is simply a reference to a northwest wind. But a better solution is implied by the possible word play in Hebrew between *tsaphon* (**north**) and *sater* (**backbiting**), both of which suggest hiding (Waltke, *Book of Proverbs 15–31*, 332–3). The image implies that the rain brought by the north wind is unexpected and unwelcome (Pr 26:1; 28:3). In a similar vein, the gossip produced by a secretive (**backbiting**) **tongue** is also unexpected and unwelcome, producing **angry** people.

25:24. See the comments on the virtually identical proverb in 21:9. Waltke suggests that its repetition in this context may highlight the idea that such conflict is also "unexpected and unwelcome." (Waltke, *Book of Proverbs 15–31*, 334).

25:25. A drink of **cold water** satisfies the craving of a thirsty person **weary** from hard labor (**weary soul** could be translated as "thirsty throat"). Similarly, in a time when any **news from a distant land** was painfully slow in arriving for those anxiously awaiting it, word of **good news** was particularly satisfying to the hearer. One effect of this proverb may have been to encourage those traveling in a distant land to send good news back to their loved ones (Longman, *Proverbs*, 459).

25:26. In ancient Israel **a trampled spring** or a **polluted well** was a disaster (cf. Gn 26:15; Ezk 34:17-18). The righteous man is compared to a "fountain of life" because his words promote the wisdom and righteousness that brings the life to others (cf. Pr 10:11). But what happens when **a righteous man . . . gives way before the wicked**? It is as if the life-giving **spring** is **trampled** and muddied and the **well** of pure water **polluted**. This may refer to the wicked man's triumph over the righteous man, which, though ultimately temporary (cf. 24:16), still removes his life-giving influence. More likely, however, it refers to the moral corruption of the righteous man himself, who gives in to the pressures of the wicked. "His despicable compromise disappoints, deprives, and imperils the many who have learned to rely on him for their spiritual life" (Waltke, *Book of Proverbs 15–31*, 336). Spiritual leaders take note!

25:27. Too much of a good thing, like overeating **honey**, is **not good** (cf. v. 14). The same principle is applied to self-promotion in the second line, which is best captured by the ESV's translation: "nor is it glorious to seek one's own glory." That is, while it is good to be honored, it is neither good nor honorable to be foolishly consumed with **search[ing] out** praise/**glory** for yourself.

25:28. This proverb compares a man who has **no** self-**control** with **a city that is broken into and without walls**. In biblical times, the key to a city's security was its strong walls. A city with **broken . . . walls** has clearly been defeated, disgraced, and left vulnerable to further attack. The fool without self-control is in similar straits, although his conqueror is the passions of **his** own **spirit**. They overwhelm him, disgrace him, and leave him vulnerable to further shameful outbursts. A man controlled by the Holy Spirit has far better prospects (Gl 5:22-23).

26:1-12. This section describes the fool (see Introduction: The Fool).

26:1-3. Though v. 2 is the only proverb in this section that does not specifically mention the fool, it is grouped with vv. 1 and 3 because each deal with the topic of what is appropriate and deserved. Verse 1 pertains to the fool. In Israel, the primary **harvest** time took place in the **summer**, which was hot and dry. Therefore **snow** in **summer and . . . rain** in **harvest** would be out of place, or worse, do significant damage to crops (1Sm 12:17-25). Similarly, giving **honor** to a **fool** is **not fitting**, and could do serious damage, indicating as it does that values are seriously skewed among people that would honor such a person. It is a fitting warning to pop culture today. Though Pr 26:2 is the only proverb in this section that does not specifically mention the fool, it is grouped with these verse (vv. 1, 3) because each deal with the topic of what is appropriate and deserved.

Verse 2 pertains to what is not fitting for the innocent. A **flitting sparrow** and a **flying swallow** do not land. Neither does a **curse without cause**. People may issue curses, calling down judgment on others, but unless the righteous Lord Himself backs them up, they are mere superstition—and He will not curse the innocent. Cursing the innocent is thus inappropriate and a fool's game. "Balaam is the reluctant witness against all superstition" (Kidner, *Proverbs*, 162; Nm 23:8; Ps 109:28).

Proverbs 26:3 pertains once again to what is fitting for the fool. The way to control and subdue beasts like **the horse** and **donkey** is through harsh force, such as the **whip** and **bridle**. Similarly, **fools** are little better than beasts in their response to instruction; words are not enough to get them to restrain their folly. The only language they understand is harsh force, such as **a rod for** their **back** (cf. 10:13; 18:6; 19:25, 29)—and sometimes even that may not be enough (17:10; 27:22)! The wise know a better way to learn (cf. Ps 32:8-9).

26:4-5. Apart from the negative **not** (v. 4), the first lines of vv. 4 and 5 are virtually identical in Hebrew. To **answer a fool according to his folly** is to present wisdom in response to the fool's nonsense in word or deed. The competing advice in these proverbs about whether to do so seems contradictory, but the juxtaposition of the two is a reminder that being wise involves not only knowing the proverbs themselves but also how and when they best apply. Taking the two proverbs separately, whether or **not** the wise should **answer a fool according to his folly** depends on the circumstances. Sometimes it is wise not to respond, lest the wise get caught up in the argument and be dragged down to the fool's level of boorish bickering (v. 4). In such cases, the wise becomes just **like** the fool, and observers may consider his wisdom as no better than the fool's nonsense. Sometimes it is better simply to avoid or ignore the fool.

At other times the wise must respond to the fool (v. 5). "If you leave the fool unchallenged, he will assume that he has impressed, intimidated, or confounded you, and he will be even more obnoxious than usual" (Fox, *Proverbs 10–31*, 793). A fool made more cocksure of himself is an even greater danger to anyone he might influence, much less to himself. In such circumstances, the wise cannot keep silent. If taken together, the two proverbs may be urging the wise "to show the fool's folly for what it is" without ever "lowering himself to the fool's level in a debate" (Waltke, *Book of Proverbs 15–31*, 349).

26:6. This proverb uses hyperbole to make the point that a fool makes a terrible messenger. Given the important role that messengers had, anyone who makes use of a fool for such a purpose is himself foolish. When carried by a fool, the sender's **message** will surely not get through, which is like cutting **off his own feet**. And with his message lost, he is harming himself, much like drinking poison (drinking **violence**).

26:7. A **lame** man's **legs** are useless to him for walking. So **a proverb** is useless for **fools**. Even if the fool can utter a proverb, it does him no good. After all, he is unable to understand and apply it to himself in the right way at the right time, and he is unwilling to do so even if he could. Nor does his regurgitating it to others do them good either, because he cannot communicate it skillfully to them at the right time (cf. 15:23; 25:11-12).

26:8. Honoring a fool is clearly unfitting (cf. v. 1). In the ancient world, slings, leather straps used for the hurling of rocks, were useful for hunting as well as war (Jdg 20:16; 1Sm 17:37-49; 1Ch 12:2). The phrase **one who binds a stone in a sling** is not entirely clear. The word **bind** might refer simply to putting a stone in a sling. The idea would be that an honored fool becomes as dangerous to others as a stone thrown from a sling, due to the influence he will wield (Fox, *Proverbs 10–31*, 795). Or, more likely, binding may refer to tying the stone to the sling's pouch so that it *cannot* be thrown, making the sling useless. It is a ridiculous thing to do, counterproductive to the purpose of the weapon. Similarly, giving **honor to a fool** is absurd, promoting that which is counterproductive to the good of society. Better to cast him out of society rather than honoring him within it (Kidner, *Proverbs*, 162).

26:9. This verse revisits the idea of **a proverb in the mouth of fools**, where a proverb proves ineffective for both the fool and those who hear him (cf. v 7). In this verse, a proverb in the mouth of a fool proves dangerous for himself and others (cf. 12:18; 13:16; 14:3; 25:20; Jb 16:1-4). A **thorn which falls into the hand of a drunkard** is likely not referring to a **drunkard** who gets his **hand** pierced by a **thorn**, but to a drunkard who puts his hand on a "stick with thorns" (cf. HCSB). He will cut himself and others when he brandishes it about. So too the fool will hurt himself and others when he communicates and applies it inappropriately (Longman, *Proverbs*, 466).

26:10. Here the person who **hires** a **fool** or one **who pass[es] by**, a stranger, is compared to **an archer who wounds everyone**. This archer lacks any sense of discrimination, so he fires upon friend and foe alike, causing chaos. Similarly, **he who hires a fool** or any passerby lacks any sense of discernment. Neither will serve him well, thus causing havoc for him and his business interests. Wise employers will know whom they hire and avoid hiring fools or untested strangers.

26:11. This proverb intentionally uses repulsive imagery to show how incorrigible the fool is. A **dog** was often considered detestable in the ancient world (cf. 1Sm 17:43), but its predilection to return to eat **its vomit** only made it more disgusting. Even though what the dog ate made it sick, the dog wants to go back to consume it once more. The fool's proclivity never to learn but to repeat **his folly** is equally as disgusting, and makes just as little sense. Peter uses this analog of false teachers (2Pt 2:22).

26:12. In one sense, there is someone worse than the **fool**. It is **a man wise in his own eyes**. This person proudly thinks he has arrived at wisdom and needs no more instruction. He leans to his own understanding (3:5). There is **more hope** for a **fool**, because at least the fool might respond to some form of correction (e.g., 26:3). "Worse than a fool is a deluded fool" (Waltke, *Book of Proverbs 15–31*, 355). There may be an implicit warning to those considered wise: "As soon as the wise person can say that he is wise, he turns out to be *worse* than a fool" (Murphy, *Proverbs*, 201).

26:13-16. This cluster of verses is a "mirror of sluggards" as the previous section was a "mirror of fools." The reflection is not flattering, even if it is humorous (Waltke, *Book of Proverbs 15–31*, 355).

26:13. Any flimsy excuse is enough to keep the **sluggard** from working. See comments on 22:13.

26:14. The **sluggard** is as attached to **his bed** as a **door** that **turns on its hinges**. His only activity is to turn in his bed. He is no more likely to get up from his bed and go to work than is a door to leave its hinges.

26:15. As the similar 19:24 (see comments there), here too the **sluggard** is too lazy to feed himself and faces starvation. Even eating makes him **weary**.

26:16. If the previous proverbs in this section show **the sluggard** to be a buffoon, this proverb shows that some are smug, self-deceived, and incorrigible. He is wise **in his own** eyes (cf. v. 12). In fact, he actually believes his "clever" excuses to get out of work make him **wiser . . . than seven men who . . . give a discreet answer**. The number seven here probably suggests a council of many wise men coming to unanimous agreement on just the right answer. The sluggard is so deluded he considers himself wiser than their corporate wisdom, so there is little hope for him (cf. v. 12).

26:17-28. These proverbs broadly address people who cause trouble, primarily through their words.

26:17. A person who grabs a passing dog (and in that cultural context, probably a wild one at that) by its sensitive ears may well get bitten. So too the busybody who **meddles with** a conflict not his own will regret it. Better to mind one's own business than get caught up in someone else's fight for no good reason.

26:18-19. A madman who shoots flaming and deadly **arrows** recklessly toward others causes them havoc and terrible, senseless harm (v. 18). The **man who deceives his neighbor** is no different, even if he claims it was just a joke (v. 19). "Deception is no laughing matter" (Fox, *Proverbs 10–31*, 799). It too causes havoc and harm to others for no good reason. The callous deceiver may claim that he was just having fun, but his idea of a good time only displays the foolish perversity of his heart (cf. 10:23). More broadly, harming others by word or deed should never be passed off as a joke.

26:20-21. Strife is like fire, and it needs certain kinds of people to stir it up. First, it requires slanderers (v. 20). Where there is no **wood the fire goes out**. Similarly, because the slandering **whisperer** only fuels **contention**, his absence **quiets** it **down**. "His tools of trade are innuendoes, half-truths, and facts distorted and exaggerated beyond recognition (cf. 10:18; 11:13, 28; 16:28; 18:8; 20:19)" (Waltke, *Book of Proverbs 15–31*, 360). Second, **strife** needs **contentious** people (v. 21). They **kindle strife** the way that charcoal fuels **hot embers** and wood a dying **fire**. Such people are itching for a fight, and they usually find one and always make a tense situation worse. Both types of troublemaker are best avoided.

26:22. This proverb is a repetition of 18:8 (see comments there). Here it probably serves to highlight the point that gossips are best avoided, not only because they stir strife, but also because they negatively shape the hearer.

26:23-28. These proverbs warn against evasive or deceptive speech. Such speech is like a glaze of **silver dross** covering **an earthen vessel** (v. 23). The vessel may look impressive, even expensive, but it is not what it seems. In truth, it is nothing but a cheap clay jar covered by a worthless sheen. Dissembling speech is here described as **burning lips**. In light of the parallelism, it is possible that it refers to speech that presumably burns with fervent affection (cf. ESV). Some, however, follow the LXX here and translate this as "smooth lips" (e.g., HCSB), i.e., deceptive speech. Either way, the point is much the same: speech that feigns friendship may look good, but it hides a malicious, **wicked heart**. The wise will take such smooth talk with a grain of salt because an enemy will use just such tactics (v. 24). He **disguises** his hatred by what he says, even though **in his heart** he plans deceptive stratagems to harm his intended victim. This is why the wise will **not** be quick to **believe** gracious, charming speech; it may hide **seven abominations in** an enemy's **heart** (v. 25). "His heart is crammed full ('seven' speaks of utmost completeness) of 'abominations' (3:32), acts and attitudes of the most hateful horror" (Hubbard, *Proverbs*, 420).

Such **hatred**, though concealed **with guile**, cannot remain hidden forever (v. 26). Eventually, **his wickedness will be revealed** in public. While this proverb does not clarify whether this public disclosure will harm the deceiver or the deceived (Longman, *Proverbs*, 471), the next two proverbs suggests the ambiguity is purposeful, with the emphasis on the former. On the one hand, the trouble the liar plans for others will **come back on him** (v. 27). He **will fall into** the pit he dug to entrap another. And the large **stone** he tries to roll up a hill to drop on another **will** fall **back on him** and crush him. Of course, this retributive or "'poetic justice' is in the hands of the Sovereign (e.g., 10:3, 29; 16:4; cf. Job 5:13)" (Waltke, *Book of Proverbs 15–31*, 366). On the other hand, it is true the liar **hates** and **crushes** his victims (v. 28a). In this sense, it appears that the **flattering** liar **works ruin** for his victim (v. 28b). But the ambiguity of this second line actually suggests retributive justice as well. Seen in light of v. 27, the liar who works for the ruin of his victim is ultimately bringing about his own ruin (Waltke, *Book of Proverbs 15–31*, 366).

27:1-2. The wise man is no braggart. He certainly does not brag about what he has not even yet accomplished. Only a fool will **boast about tomorrow** (cf. 1Kg 20:11; Jr 9:23), since no one can **know** for certain even **what** today **may bring forth**. Humans lack the knowledge and power to control what is most immediate to them, let alone what will come later. Since both the present and future are in God's hands, the wise make plans in the fear of the Lord, humbly trusting His disposition of events (cf. Pr 16:1, 3, 9, 33; Ps 37; Lk 12:16-21; Jms 4:13-16). Furthermore, the wise man does not brag about himself at all (Pr 27:2). Self-praise not only reflects pride but also self-deceit. **Praise** from **another**, particularly a disinterested **stranger** who has no cause for flattery, is more credible (Waltke, *Book of Proverbs 15–31*, 374). Better still is the Lord's "well done" (Jn 12:42-43). Self-praise is also misdirected. Anything praiseworthy in a man is a result of the grace of the Lord, who alone is truly worthy of praise (Jr 9:23-24; 1Co 1:26-31). Taken together, these two proverbs "espouse an attitude of humility before the sovereignty of God and the judgment of the community" (Garrett, *Proverbs*, 216).

27:3-4. These proverbs describe two "unbearable personalities" (Garrett, *Proverbs*, 216). The first is the **fool** who is easily provoked or angered (v. 3). Although **the provocation of a fool** might refer to the anger he incites in others, it more likely refers to his own bent toward feeling provoked (cf. 12:16; 29:9, 11). He is more unbearable than the physical burden of carrying a **heavy stone** or bag of **sand**. Who wants to be around the thin-skinned fool who is easily offended and knows nothing of the gracious spirit of the wise? The second unbearable type is the jealous person (v. 4). **Fierce** cruelty **and** a **flood** of **anger** are very difficult to withstand, but wrath driven by **jealousy** is overwhelming to both its possessor and target (Fox, *Proverbs 10–31*, 804). "Dealing with ordinary ire is hard enough, but a fury that stems from jealousy is not open to reason or moderation" (Garrett, *Proverbs*, 216). The wise will avoid those who are easily aroused to jealousy and will certainly not stir it up in others (cf. 6:32-35).

27:5-6. A true friend is willing to rebuke his companion. Thus **open rebuke** is **better than love that is concealed** (v. 5). After all, correction is the way to wisdom and life; this is why both the Lord and parents will discipline their beloved children (3:11-12; 13:24). Hidden love is unwilling to reprove but remains silent in the face of needed correction. Whatever the reason for this silence—whether fear, selfishness, or negligence—it really is not very loving at all, because it does one's friend no good. Surprisingly, this timid silence is little better than an enemy's deceptive displays of affection (v. 6). This proverb contrasts "friendly wounds" with "wounding kisses" (Waltke, *Book of Proverbs 15–31*, 376). The former demonstrates true, **faithful** friendship aimed at correction, painful though it may be. The latter is diametrically opposed to friendship. Whether the **kisses** here are **deceitful** (NASB) or "excessive" (HCSB)—the Hebrew term is unclear—the point is much the same. The one who lavishes outward displays of affection on his "friend" when he should rebuke him shows that he is nothing more than a treacherous **enemy**.

27:7. This proverb makes the observation that what one considers appealing depends on one's appetites. The proverb contrasts two people: one who is satisfied, or **sated**, and the other who is **famished**. But what kinds of appetites are being compared? The proverb may be contrasting sated with deprived appetites. If a man's appetite is completely satisfied, he does not even find something good and beneficial like **honey** appealing. But if he is starving, he will even consider **any bitter thing . . . sweet**. "Hunger is the best sauce" (Clifford, *Proverbs*, 238). In this case, moderation is the way of wisdom, neither overindulging in what is pleasant (cf. 25:16-17) nor always avoiding what may be unpleasant but needful (e.g., vv. 5-6) (Fox, *Proverbs 10–31*, 806). Or the proverb may be describing two kinds of sick appetites. "Both a person so sated in wrong things that he despises good things and a person so hungry that he perceives *every* bitter thing and harmful thing as sweet are sick" (Waltke, *Book of Proverbs 15–31*, 377). In this case, a healthy appetite will crave the good and reject the bad. Either nuance has a wide range of possible applications.

27:8. A **bird** away from **her nest** is unsettled, isolated, and vulnerable; so too **a man** away **from his home**. After all, his home is where he belongs. It is not clear whether the verb *nadad* (**wanders**) carries the connotation of fleeing from a troubled place or merely straying from where one belongs. Either way, the message remains: A man should value and protect his home life so that he can remain there, safe and secure.

27:9. The first line clearly states that people find costly amenities like **oil** and **perfume** pleasant. The second line mentions something equally as pleasant, but the Hebrew text is unclear about what that something is. The HCSB captures one possible way to translate it: "the sweetness of a friend is better than self-counsel," suggesting that having a friend to counsel you is more pleasing than being left alone with your own counsel. Probably more likely is the alternative, captured in the ESV (and reflected less clearly in the NASB): "and the sweetness of a friend comes from his earnest counsel." A friend who cares enough to give you fervent, heartfelt counsel is truly a blessing.

27:10. This proverb continues with lessons about friends. It has three lines (rather unusual in Proverbs), with the third line clarifying the first two. It states that a friend who is a **near neighbor** is **better than a brother** who lives **far away** (v. 10c), presumably because the friend is more available in times of **calamity**. Most likely the closeness of the friend and distance of the relative could be either spatial or emotional (Garrett, *Proverbs*, 218). In such cases, the wise will cultivate rather than **forsake** close relationships with personal and family friends (v. 10a) rather than rely on distant relatives for help in difficult times (v. 10b). Thus while it is true that "a brother is born for adversity" (17:17), there are friends who stick "closer than a brother" (18:24), and sometimes it is more prudent to rely on friends than depend exclusively on relatives.

27:11. A father is affected by the character of his **son** (cf. 10:1). If the son is **wise**, he will make his father **glad** because he thwarts an enemy's attempt to denigrate his father. The son is the best proof of the wisdom of his father (cf. 2Co 3:1-3; 1Th 2:19-20; 3:8).

27:12. A prudent man has foresight that the **naive** lack. This proverb repeats 22:3 almost verbatim (see comments there), although here it may be used in support of v. 11 (Waltke, *Book of Proverbs 15–31*, 381)—either encouraging the wise to train their children well or the son to think ahead about how his chosen way of life affects his parents.

27:13. This proverb is very similar to 20:16 (see comments there). The only notable difference is that the "foreigner" in 20:16 is the **adulterous woman** here. The wise will not become entangled with people like her, alluring though her words may be (cf. chap. 7).

27:14. A true friend is not obnoxious. It is irritating for a person still groggy with sleep to be met with a loud greeting, well-intended though it might be. The second line is ironic: not only does the sleepy man find his loud friend's **bless[ing]** to be a **curse** to himself, he will also be tempted to return his insensitive friend's blessing with a curse.

27:15-16. Also annoying is a **contentious woman**. As in 19:13b (see comments there), she is compared to the **constant dripping** of a leaky roof on very rainy **day** (v. 15; cf. 21:9, 19; 25:24). Like the leak, she is irksome, unpleasant, and discouraging to her husband. Verse 16 intensifies her baleful effect on her husband, though its translation is difficult. In the first line, the verb translated **restrain[s]** in the NASB is probably better translated "shelters" (Koehler et al., *HALOT*, 1049). Apparently, then, a man with such a wife has, in effect, brought the windstorm under his own roof rather than keeping the storm out. In short, she wreaks destructive havoc within his home (Waltke, *Book of Proverbs 15–31*, 383). Like trying to grasp **oil** with **his right hand**, the husband cannot restrain or control the contentious woman. Any hope for a more harmonious household is a fantasy.

27:17. The wise are not lone rangers. **Iron** was used to sharpen the edge of other **iron** instruments, making them more effective. In the same way, **one man** can sharpen **another**. Productive interaction with others can make people more effective and wise, particularly when it includes constructive criticism and mutual encouragement toward righteousness (cf. 13:20; 27:6). "The wisdom enterprise is a community effort" (Longman, *Proverbs*, 481).

27:18. This proverb compares the farmer who faithfully **tends** his **fig tree** with the faithful servant who **cares for his master**. As the farmer enjoys the **fruit** of the tree, so the servant will enjoy the honor bestowed on him by his master. Both are rewarded for their labor.

27:19. When a person looks into a still pool of **water**, he can see a reflection of his own face. Likewise, a man's **heart reflects** the **man**.

Although multiple interpretations of this proverb have been proffered (Fox, *Proverbs 10–31*, 812), two seem more likely than the rest. It may mean that a person sees himself reflected in other people so that he interprets them in light of his own **heart**. For example, a cynical person projects his cynicism on others. Even more likely, however, the proverb likely indicates that the human heart reflects the whole person. A person's heart defines his true identity.

27:20. Death (**Sheol and Abaddon**; cf. the comments on 15:11) is **never satisfied**. Everyone dies, and yet death still wants more (cf. 30:15-16). A man's **eyes** are equally insatiable. One's **eyes** here refer to one's desires and appetites (cf. Ec 2:10; 4:8; 1Jn 2:16). Comparing such desires to death is not coincidental (Clifford, *Proverbs*, 240; cf. Gn 3:6; 1Jn 2:16-17). Ecclesiastes reminds the reader that desires for things under the sun can neither be satisfied nor are they satisfying. They simply distract us from a better way: the fear of the Lord and the life He brings.

27:21. The Lord uses trials to refine a person's character like **the crucible . . . for silver** and **the furnace for gold** (cf. 17:3). This proverb suggests that one such refining test is **the praise accorded** to a man, a phrase that is somewhat ambiguous in Hebrew (literally, "a man is tested by his praise"). Some suggest from this ambiguity that a man's character is revealed by what he praises or by the kind of people who praise him. But the kind of testing here is actually a trial used to refine people (Kidner, *Proverbs*, 168), and so the proverb actually indicates that people are tested by how they respond to praise they receive. Those who remain humble and thankful to the Lord, and who do not continually crave for more, are strengthened in the process (cf. 1Sm 18:7; Jn 12:42, 43).

27:22. Using a **mortar** and **pestle** was not a typical way to separate grain from its husks but suggests extreme methods (Clifford, *Proverbs*, 240). Yet even severe means, such as physical punishment, are still not enough to separate the incorrigible **fool** (*ewil*) from **his foolishness** (cf. 9:7-10; 12:15; 17:10; 26:11).

27:23-27. This section about diligence uses an agricultural illustration, though its principles have wider application. It begins by admonishing the farmer/shepherd to **pay** careful **attention** to the **condition of** his **flocks** and **herds** (v. 23) rather than neglecting them. Doing so requires the kind of discipline, hard work, compassion, and savvy that only wisdom can give (Waltke, *Proverbs 15–31*, 391). The next four verses give two reasons to support the admonition. First, **riches** do not last (v. 24)—not even if they derive from some kind of high position (as exemplified by **a crown**). A nest egg is **not forever** and can easily disappear (cf. 23:5). Second, unlike a nest egg, flocks and herds are renewable resources when cared for (vv. 25-27). "The ecosystem of animals and grassland provides sustenance for human beings. Year after year beast and field provide clothing, money to purchase more pastureland, and food for an entire household" (Clifford, *Proverbs*, 241). The point of the whole poem is to encourage the wise to "take care of your own business, and it will take care of you" (Garrett, *Proverbs*, 221) rather than foolishly depending on resources that are fleeting.

28:1. This proverb recalls the covenant curses of Lv 26:17, 36. **The wicked** have no rest. Their past activities have only created enemies—both divine and human—and a guilty conscience, so they **flee** even **when no one is pursuing**. They can expect a reckoning, and this leaves them paranoid and fearful. But not **the righteous**: they are **bold**—or better, confident—like **a lion**, who has no predators to fear. Because they fear the Lord (Pr 1:7), the righteous have nothing else to fear because they are in His good hands. They are not chased by enemies but are followed by a rearguard of goodness and mercy (Kidner, *Proverbs*, 168; cf. Ps 23:6).

28:2. The situation described here is social and political chaos, with competing **princes** jockeying for power. This is the result of a land's transgression, which likely describes a rebellious spirit in general and against the Lord ultimately. Rebellion fosters rebellion and chaos. Stability comes through stable leadership, through a leader who is **a man of understanding and knowledge**. A wise and godly king truly is a blessing to a land.

28:3. People expect rain eventually to produce food, so there is something perverse about **a driving rain that leaves no food** because it damages the crops. A **poor man who oppresses** other poor people is equally perverse. It is so bizarre to think of poor people oppressing other poor people that some opt for an alternate understanding of the oppressor (e.g., NIV: "a ruler who oppresses the poor," a translation which misses the lesson). But a poor person who acts to oppress other poor people is precisely the point. He is an "unnatural tyrant" (Kidner, *Proverbs*, 169) who ought to commiserate with fellow sufferers rather than try to make their situation worse by wringing whatever little he can from them.

28:4. One's attitude toward **the wicked** is a reflection of one's values, and one's values are measured by one's assessment of **the law**. The law at least includes the instruction of the wise, though it may refer more specifically to the Mosaic Law (e.g., Ex 13:9; Ps 1:2; 19:7; 119:1; Longman, *Proverbs*, 488). Either way, one's treatment of wisdom instruction/law reflects one's appraisal of God. People therefore who **forsake the law** will **praise the wicked**, who display similar disdain toward God. But the righteous who fear the Lord and observe His instructions/law will oppose the wicked. A person's friends and enemies say much about him and his view of God (cf. Rm 1:18-32).

28:5. Justice here probably refers to that which is right (Waltke, *Book of Proverbs 15–31*, 410), likely in relation to the treatment of other people in particular. **Evil men** simply **do not understand** it. They do not recognize the need to deal fairly with others, nor do they realize that they themselves will be subject to God's justice as a result. In contrast, **those who seek the Lord** also fear Him and find wisdom (cf. 1:7). They thus **understand all things**, that is, in the context, all things related to justice. "The pious find their abilities to distinguish good from evil and right from wrong and to proceed with equity by seeking the Lord through his revelation" (Waltke, *Book of Proverbs 15–31*, 410).

28:6. This proverb is similar to 19:1 (see comments there). A **poor** honest man is **better than** a **rich** man whose ways are **crooked. Crooked** ways suggest both a dishonest and difficult lifestyle (Fox, *Proverbs 10–31*, 822)—despite one's wealth. Thus **integrity** is more valuable than wealth, for the latter has definite limitations while the former aligns one with the Lord.

28:7. The background to this proverb is Dt 21:18-21. There a rebellious son, one who "will not obey his father or his mother," is identified as a "glutton and a drunkard" and is sentenced to stoning. In context, **the law** here refers to the father's wise instruction. A son who heeds his father's instruction is **discerning** and by extension, brings joy to his parents (Pr 10:1; 27:11). In contrast, a son **who is a companion to gluttons** by implication has rejected his father's wisdom for his compatriots' folly (cf. 13:20; 23:20-21). And folly it is, because such profligates "squander all that is precious—life, food, and instruction" (Waltke, *Book of Proverbs 15–31*, 412). Little wonder he **humiliates his father**. (Similar themes are developed in 23:19-25.)

28:8. The Mosaic Law forbids Israelites from charging interest to fellow Israelites (Ex 22:25; Dt 23:19-20), particularly the poor among them (Dt 15:1-8). This proverb likely pictures a person enriching himself at the expense of the poor by charging them usury for life's necessities (cf. Pr 22:16). But this is a bad long-term investment, for the rich oppressor only **gathers it for him who is gracious to the poor**. Behind this retributive justice stands the Lord, who blesses those who are generous and provides for the needy through them (cf. 13:22; 14:31; 19:17).

28:9. God refuses to heed the requests of those who refuse to listen to Him. As in v. 4, **the law** refers to instruction from the Lord, whether the teachings of the wise or the Mosaic Law more specifically. Failure to heed God's instruction is rebellious, and God finds the **prayer** of the rebellious fool to be repulsive (cf. 15:8, 29).

28:10. Evil people are not satisfied in being evil themselves; they want to bring others along with them (e.g., 1:10-19). They often delight in leading **the upright astray** into an **evil way** through deception. But they only end up falling prey to their own machinations. "We are to picture a sneaky man laying a trap in a path and leading another onto it, but as they walk along, the deceiver himself also falls in" (Fox, *Proverbs 10–31*, 824). Such people are their own worst enemies because, in making themselves God's enemy, they subject themselves to His retributive justice (cf. 26:27; Mt 5:19; 18:6; Lk 17:1-2). The **blameless**, who **will inherit good**, have chosen a much better way. But they must be vigilant, lest they fall prey to the deceptive machinations of the wicked and go astray.

28:11. His success in accumulating wealth tempts the **rich man** to think himself **wise**. Perhaps sycophants reinforce his self-perception. But wealth is not a sure sign of wisdom, and a man wise **in his own eyes** surely lacks wisdom (26:12; cf. 3:7; 12:15; 26:5). A **poor** man **who has understanding** is able to see right **through** the rich fool's wise pretense. In that sense, his clear-sighted wisdom is more valuable than the fool's deceptive wealth.

28:12. The **triumph** of **the righteous** in a community is a blessing to that community (cf. 11:10-11; 28:28; 29:2, 16). Because they are godly and wise, when the righteous come to power they implement policies that are good for the community and bring the blessing of God. The community therefore prospers with **great glory**. The opposite is true as well, **when the wicked rise** to power, people **hide themselves** in their attempt "to avoid danger, oppression, and corruption" (Fox, *Proverbs 10–31*, 825) inevitable under such evil leaders.

28:13. This is a powerful proverb about addressing one's own sins. Cover-ups are foolish. A man may be inclined to conceal **his transgressions**, but he **will not prosper** on this path. There is a better way, which is a quintessential summary of a truly repentant person (cf. Ps 32). First, he **confesses** his sin, acknowledging what he did and his need for forgiveness. Such confession also entails glorifying God by acknowledging "his greatness (i.e., one cannot hide sin from him), his justice (i.e., he has the right to punish the transgressor), and his grace (i.e., he forgives and delivers; cf. Josh. 1:9)" (Waltke, *Book of Proverbs 15–31*, 417). Second, he **forsakes** his sins, strong evidence that he truly finds his sin evil. The resultant blessing of true repentance cannot be overstated: he will receive **compassion**, mercy, and forgiveness. While God Himself is the primary one who grants such mercy, this proverb may also include other people who respond compassionately to repentance.

28:14. This proverb is a beatitude for **the man who fears always**. But what does he continually fear? This could refer to the fear of the Lord. However, that is not clear, since "fear" here is a different Hebrew word than that usually used in the phrase "the fear of the Lord," and the Lord is not specifically mentioned here. The antithetical second line helps to clarify. A person who **hardens his heart** to his foolish sin **will fall into calamity**. He is boldly arrogant in his sinful way, unwilling to repent (cf. v. 13) and to hear wise reproof. Lacking sensitivity and insight, he has no fear of the dreadful consequences of his sinful ways. The wise, in contrast, will fear the consequences of such a sinful lifestyle. In the end, of course, that kind of fear is really inextricably bound to the fear of the Lord as well. Proverbs 14:16 is similar, although it seems to lay greater emphasis on the fear of the Lord (since "fear" there is the same Hb. term as the "fear of the Lord").

28:15-16. These two proverbs describe the tyrant. First, such a **wicked ruler** is dangerous like **a roaring lion and a rushing bear** (v. 15). He preys on his own **people**, impoverishing them by his ravenous appetites rather than working for their good. Second, the tyrant is a fool (v. 16). Lacking good sense (**understanding**), he oppresses his people for his own gain. But he only undermines himself. In contrast, the honest ruler who wisely **hates unjust gain** will also **prolong his** own days. His rule draws neither the ire of his people nor the judgment of the Lord.

28:17. This proverb is a sobering picture of justice. **A man who is laden with the guilt of human blood** likely describes a murderer with a guilty conscience. His guilt drives him to **be a fugitive until death**, or more literally to "flee to the pit" (that is the grave/death). Whether in guilty despair he is hastening toward death, or whether he is forced for the rest of his life to flee as a fugitive from avengers real or imagined, the advice here is the same. Do not **support** or help **him**, because he is facing his just deserts. This advice contrasts with the compassion that is to be shown to the innocent (24:11-12).

28:18. Here once again the two paths so prominent in Proverbs appear (cf. 4:10-19). One can walk **blamelessly** or follow the **crooked** path. The former **will be delivered** from the pitfalls into which the crooked suddenly **fall** (cf. v. 14).

28:19. This proverb is similar to 12:11 (see comments there), but this proverb further explains why the one **who follows empty pursuits** "lacks sense." Unlike hard work, which produces **plenty of food**, frivolity only produces **plenty** of **poverty**.

28:20-25. These proverbs all address those with an inordinate love for money.

28:20. A **faithful man** here refers to the one who is trustworthy, diligent, and reliable in his responsibilities, because of his ultimate trust in the Lord to bring him abundant **blessings** (Fox, *Proverbs 10–31*, 829; cf. v. 25). He is sharply contrasted with **he who makes haste to be rich**. A penchant for get rich quick schemes displays a haste that inevitably fosters foolish actions (cf. 19:2; 20:21; 29:20). Worse still, it displays a passion for and trust in money that overwhelms any love for God and neighbor. Such a man thereby places himself in opposition to the Lord and consequently **will not go unpunished**.

28:21. One way to get rich quickly is to receive a bribe. But **to show partiality is not good** (cf. 24:23b-25), particularly when the person doing so is **a man** in a position of strength over others, such as a judge. He may be willing to **transgress** against others for personal gain, but he only demeans himself. Once he is willing to sell his integrity, he will often sell his services cheaply, even **for a piece of bread**.

28:22. A man with an evil eye likely refers to a greedy skinflint (cf. 23:6; 22:9, where the generous person is described as "good of eye"). He is not looking toward the Lord or seeking His wisdom, but only focusing on money. His avarice makes him hasten **after wealth**, always foolishly and often at the expense of others. Consequently, he falls under the judgment, for he will unexpectedly meet **want** (cf. v. 20). He has bad eyes indeed, since he cannot see the poverty coming toward him (Clifford, *Proverbs*, 247).

28:23. In the context of the other proverbs around it, this proverb likely refers to those who think they can gain power and wealth through flattery (Garrett, *Proverbs*, 227). But that is a fool's errand. Granted, honest correction may be painful and meet resistance at first. But in the long run (**afterward[s]**) the wise man **who rebukes** another **will find more favor than** the flatterer (cf. 17:10; 19:25; 25:12; 27:5-6). This favor certainly comes from God and probably also from the one rebuked as well (cf. 3:4)—unless he is a fool (13:1; 15:12; cf. Waltke, *Book of Proverbs: 15–31*, 425–6). In any case, any benefit from flattery is short-lived.

28:24. Some love money so much that they are willing to rob their **father** and **mother**, and do so without remorse (saying **it is not a transgression**). This stealing might be active (taking their property) or passive (withholding support from them when they need it) (Waltke, *Book of Proverbs 15–31*, 426). "Such children may think that they are simply taking what belongs to them by virtue of being members of the family, but in reality they are no better than a criminal from outside the family" (Longman, *Proverbs*, 496).

28:25. Arrogant here is better translated "greedy" (literally, "wide of throat"). Such a **man** has a voracious appetite for more. He is not reluctant to stir **up strife** to get what he wants, though the conflict will likely frustrate the prosperity he craves. He contrasts directly with the one **who trusts in the Lord**. "Greed is a repudiation of trust in God, for he who trusts in God accepts what God gives and does not crave more" (Fox, *Proverbs 10–31*, 831). Indeed, this man finds satisfaction in God Himself, and so finds prosperity as well (cf. Mt 6:19-34).

28:26. Contemporary thought often advocates, "Just trust your heart." Nothing could be farther from the truth of Scripture. This proverb describes a person **who trusts in his own heart**, relying on his own understanding and resources, as a **fool**, since the human heart left to its own devices is depraved, foolish, and limited (cf. Jr 17:9). In contrast, one **who walks wisely** is implicitly trusting in the Lord (cf. Pr 3:5-6), who is the source of all wisdom. Such a wise man **will be delivered** from the inevitable, disastrous fate of the fool.

28:27. The idea of greed in v. 25 is now picked up again here. God will supply the needs of the generous one **who gives to the poor**. But the stingy one **who shuts his eyes** to the needy around him **will have many curses**, if not from the poor whom he neglects, certainly from the Lord who judges justly. Trust stands behind either behavior. The miser trusts in his own resources, but the generous man trusts in the Lord to provide for his needs and so is free to give away resources.

28:28. This proverb is very similar to v. 12 (cf. 29:2). People lay low (**hide themselves**) **when the wicked rise** to power because their rule is disastrous to the community. But their downfall brings about the flourishing of **the righteous**, and that is a great boon to the community.

29:1. Proverbs repeatedly teaches that the wise heed rebuke and fools do not (e.g., 12:1; 13:1, 18; 19:25, 27). This proverb continues this theme by describing a stubborn fool who, though repeatedly reproved, refuses to listen (**hardens his neck**). At some point, **suddenly** and unexpectedly for him, his opportunity for change ends and he reaps catastrophic results, with no hope of **remedy** at that point.

29:2. Essentially restating the idea in 28:12, 28, this proverb highlights the emotional state of people in two different societies. A society in which the **righteous** flourish (**increase**) brings the community great joy (**the people rejoice**) because it is blessed. In contrast, a **people** led by a **wicked** ruler **groan** under his oppressive and foolish policies. Voters today should take note.

29:3. A man who loves wisdom will certainly not love cavorting with prostitutes. A man who **keeps company with** them only **wastes his wealth** and that of his family, thereby displaying a foolishness that grieves his parents. Lady Wisdom has much more to offer, wealth included (cf. 3:16). No wonder a man who cherishes wisdom **makes his father glad**.

29:4. A just **king** whose administration upholds the law equitably and fairly brings long-term **stability** to his **land**/nation. He contrasts with "a man of contributions." Whether this is a government official who taxes unfairly (so Longman, *Proverbs*, 502) or one who simply **takes bribes** (NASB) both reflect corrupt government officials concerned only with their own profit. Such a corrupt system only tears down (**overthrows**) the realm it is supposed to serve.

29:5. Unlike encouragement, which is rooted in truth, a person who **flatters** is deceptive and destructive (cf. 5:3-4; 6:24; 7:5, 21; 26:28; 28:23). Like a hunter trying to ensnare his prey, the flatterer is **spreading a net** to entangle the **steps** of his **neighbor**. Rather than disseminating wise, honest instruction or even rebuke (cf. v. 1), he tells people what they want to hear for his own gain. Ironically, the antecedent of **his steps** is ambiguous. Clearly, the victim is ensnared in the flatterer's deceptions, but as the next proverb suggests, his web of deceit likely also endangers the flatterer himself.

29:6. This proverb can be understood in close connection with the previous one, though it also has broader application. More specifically, an **evil man** (such as the flatterer) **is ensnared** by his own deceptions while **the righteous** man who rejects foolish flattery **sings and rejoices** because he escapes the deceptions of the flatter. More broadly, "sin complicates life, setting traps for the sinner" (Longman, *Proverbs*, 503). The righteous one avoids such traps and benefits from the long-term blessings of righteousness.

29:7. The **righteous** man is truly **concerned** for **the rights of the poor** and powerless. Such concern "involves an investment of time, patient research, and willingness to risk himself in confronting injustice (cf. Job 29:12-17)" (Waltke, *Book of Proverbs 15–31*, 435). The **wicked** man is too callous and self-absorbed to concern himself with the plight of the poor nor even to **understand such concern**. But his ignorance is not bliss, for his heartlessness makes him culpable before the ultimate Judge of all.

29:8. Most likely this proverb pertains particularly to the political realm. So the **scorners** here likely refer to arrogant cynics with some political influence whose rhetoric inflames social unrest in **a city** (Murphy, *Proverbs*, 221; cf. Is 28:14). Their effect is disastrous to the community. Much better for society are **wise men** who are able to assuage **anger** in tense political situations, allowing space for cooler heads, and peace, to prevail. "The fanning of party strife which brings a quick sense of power" cannot compare to the "'peaceable wisdom' [which] must work and wait (see Jas. 3:13-18)" (Kidner, *Proverbs*, 174).

29:9. This proverb concerns the outcome of **controversy** between the **wise man** and the **foolish man**. Some translations (e.g., NIV, HCSB) suggest that the controversy occurs in a courtroom setting, but the verb here is likely more generic, referring to any kind of controversy. Sometimes it is best for a **wise man** *not* to engage a fool in debate (cf. 26:4) because the fool will not learn. Instead, he sometimes **rages**, a Hebrew term also used to describe an angry bear (cf. 17:12) or the stormy seas (cf. Is 57:20-21). Or at other times he **laughs**, mocking the wisdom of the wise. In both cases he is restive in the face of wise reasoning, incapable of settling down to actually receive it.

29:10. The first line of this proverb is fairly straightforward. **Men of bloodshed hate the blameless** because their innocence represents everything that murderers are not (Fox, *Proverbs 10–31*, 837). The second line is more difficult because neither the subject of the clause nor the meaning of the verb (lit., "seek his life") is clear. One view, reflected in the NASB, sees **the upright** as the subject and interprets "seeks his life" positively as being **concerned for** the life of the blameless. But the expression "seeks his life" is typically idiomatic for seeking to kill someone, not preserve someone's life (unless it is an ironic reversal of an idiom). A second view also sees the upright as the subject of the clause but maintains that they seek to kill, not the blameless, but the murderer (i.e., they want to see justice done) (Longman, *Proverbs*, 504). A third view sees the bloodthirsty as the subject of the sentence, who then seek to kill the upright as well as the blameless. The ESV reflects this interpretation: "Bloodthirsty men hate one who is blameless and seek the life of the upright." Though all three views are possible, the last view is most likely, making the proverb a powerful sketch of the depraved character of violent people.

29:11. The **fool** lacks self-control, so he **always loses his temper**. He differs dramatically from the **wise man**, described as one who **holds it back**, although the precise meaning of the line is disputed. If the word *be'achor* (translated "back" in the NASB's translation of the phrase **holds it back**) means "in the end," or "afterwards" (so Koehler et al., *HALOT*, 31; Waltke, *Book of*

Proverbs 15–31, 439), it would suggest that the wise man is able eventually to quiet the turmoil generated by the raging fool (cf. v. 8). More likely, however, *be'achor* means simply means "back", suggesting that **a wise man holds** . . . **back** or controls his own temper.

29:12. A ruler sets the atmosphere for his whole administration. **If** he lets himself be influenced by **falsehood**, his government will become corrupt. Ultimately **all his ministers** will **become wicked**, due to the ruler's lack of concern for integrity and justice in his government. David's attitude is a vivid contrast (Ps 101:6-8).

29:13. Although at opposite ends of the social spectrum, **the poor man** and his wealthy **oppressor** share something **in common** (cf. 22:2). **Both** of them receive their very life (**light to the eyes**) from the **Lord**. This proverb likely functions both to encourage the poor and to warn the oppressor that both their lives are in God's just and wise hands.

29:14. This proverb picks up on ideas in the previous two proverbs. A wise **king** who wishes to have a stable reign and enduring dynasty **judges the poor** faithfully (**with truth**). Therefore, he will not tolerate corrupt advisors (v. 12), nor will he be a respecter of persons (v. 13) when it comes to justice. He realizes that his strength comes not from currying favor with the rich and powerful but from dealing fairly with all, including "those who can put least pressure on him" (Kidner, *Proverbs*, 175). Such a king not only generates respect but also reflects the ultimate King who judges fairly (e.g., Gn 18:25).

29:15. Parents are neither wise nor loving if they let their **child** get **his own way**. For he will become a fool who **brings** them **shame** (cf. 13:24). The proverb assumes inherent human sinfulness and foolishness; children do not need to be taught sinful folly. This is why they need correction (**rod and reproof**), whether verbal or physical (Waltke, *Book of Proverbs 15–31*, 442). Of course, in the hands of loving parents who wish to inculcate wisdom, neither of these are weapons of abuse but tools of love.

29:16. When **the wicked increase** in number and influence, their dominance is pervasive but short-lived. For with their rise also comes rising **transgression** against God and man, which undermines public order and stirs divine wrath (cf. v. 2 and comments there). This state of affairs is inherently unstable. In contrast, the **righteous** endure to **see** the wicked **fall**. This proverb is both a warning to the wicked and an encouragement to the righteous in times when the wicked seem dominant (Longman, *Proverbs*, 506).

29:17. Like v. 15, this proverb also stresses the importance of correcting one's child, although here the motivation is entirely positive. Parents who do so will raise a wise **son** who brings them **comfort** and **delight**. These terms "suggest the image of a parent taking a deep breath and letting out a sigh of relief and pleasure at a child who has turned out well" (Fox, *Proverbs 10–31*, 840).

29:18. The term **vision** (*chazon*) is typically used of prophetic visions. In the context of Proverbs this term, like its parallel *torah* (**law** or teaching), "refers here to the sage's inspired revelation of wisdom" (Waltke, *Book of Proverbs 15–31*, 446). Without a message from the Lord, the **people** will be **unrestrained** or running wild with disastrous consequences for the nation as a whole (Ex 32:25; Jdg 17:6). Conversely, any individual who obeys wise instruction (**keeps the law**) will be **happy** as a result of the blessings that wisdom brings.

29:19-20. Words have limitations, but their effect should never be underestimated. On the one hand, **words alone** are not enough to **instruct a slave** in wisdom (v. 19). The problem is not intellectual; **he understands** the instruction. The problem is volitional; there is **no response** to it. Thus disciplining a slave in wisdom requires a multifaceted approach going beyond words in order to motivate change. Similarly, whether it is a child facing punishment, a student facing grade reductions, or employees facing reduced pay or loss of job, words often are not enough; there may need to be other incentives (Steveson, *Commentary on Proverbs*, 411).

On the other hand, the power of words should not be underestimated (v. 20). A foolish **man who is hasty in his words** displays a reckless arrogance that fails to appreciate both the power of words and his own propensity to misuse them (cf. 10:19; 17:27-28; 26:12; Jms 1:19). A wiser man is much more cautious about himself and his words. Being hasty in word is one manifestation of being wise in one's own eyes, which makes one worse than **a fool**, who might at least respond to some form of correction.

29:21. This proverb returns to the theme of disciplining slaves (cf. v. 19). A master does **his slave** no favors if he pampers the slave **from childhood**. If he does so, there will be problems **in the end**. The pampered slave will become *manon* (NASB: **a son**). This word is used only once in the OT, and its precise meaning is uncertain—an uncertainty reflected in the English translations (see Fox, *Proverbs 10–31*, 844 for a summary of options). Translating it as "arrogant, insolent, rebellious" (Koehler, *HALOT*, 600) is probably best, judging from the context. Failure to discipline a household slave early on will only end up frustrating both the slave and the master in the long run. It is a form of fostering unrealistic expectations.

29:22. An **angry**, **hot-tempered man** is looking for a fight (cf. 15:18; 28:25). So he readily **stirs up** conflict and quickly offends other people, making **transgression abound**. He is offensive to society and is best avoided (cf. 6:14; 15:18; 22:24-25).

29:23. Ironically, the proud **man**, who craves to be exalted, will be brought **low** while a man of lowly or **humble spirit** will be exalted with **honor** (cf. Jb 5:11; Jms 4:10). There may be many reasons for this: the proud depend on themselves and go their own way while the humble depend on God and submit to His moral order (Waltke, *Book of Proverbs 15–31*, 450); the humble are teachable while the proud refuse to learn from their mistakes (Longman, *Proverbs*, 509); society finds the proud obnoxious and the humble winsome (Clifford, *Proverbs*, 255); or the Lord judges the proud and blesses the humble. But whatever the reason, the general principle stands.

29:24. The **partner** of a **thief** actually **hates his own life**. Since the partner was involved in the crime, he is unable to testify against the **thief** because if he testifies he will show himself guilty as well. On the other hand, his failure to testify even when **he hears the oath** puts him under the sanction of Lv 5:1: "If you are called to testify about something you have seen or that you know about, it is sinful to refuse to testify, and you will be punished for your sin" (NLT). His failure to testify puts him under divine judgment for protecting the wicked, thus endangering his very own life. It is a "suicidal complicity" (Kidner, *Proverbs*, 177).

29:25-26. The wise should trust God and not **fear . . . man**. To fear man is to be anxious about what other people think and what they can do, it is the opposite of trust in God (Fox, *Proverbs 10–31*, 846–47; cf. Jr 15:5-8; Ps 56:5; Is 51:12-13). Therein lies the **snare**, for the fear of man easily overwhelms fear of the Lord and so promotes sin and folly (Clifford, *Proverbs*, 255). The solution is to trust **in the LORD**, recognizing that human power and opinion are inconsequential in comparison to the LORD. **He who** puts his trust in the Lord **will be exalted**, not in the sense of being honored but in the sense of being protected, elevated "beyond man's reach" (Kidner, *Proverbs*, 177). Therefore, trusting in God protects a person from human power and from the sin and foolishness that results from fearing human opinion (cf. Ps 37:3-5; Pr 3:5-6; 18:10).

Verse 26 illustrates the point. **Many** people scramble to get into a **ruler's** presence and **seek** his **favor** to find **justice** for their cause. To be sure, seeking help from other humans is not inappropriate in proper measure. But the wise never forget that **justice for man comes from the LORD**, who controls even the heart of the king (cf. 21:1). Since only the Lord Himself can ensure justice, "people should be clamoring to get into the presence of Yahweh" to seek His help (Longman, *Proverbs*, 510).

29:27. The **righteous** and **wicked** find each other's way of life **abominable**. The former, **who is upright in the way**, serves God and others; the latter, who is **unjust** in his dealings with others, serves only himself (Waltke, *Book of Proverbs 15–31*, 453–54). Their lifestyles have nothing in common. It is a fitting way to end this section of Proverbs. There are only two paths, and they are radically different. The wise will choose the path of righteousness and expect opposition from the wicked (Fox, *Proverbs 10–31*, 848).

III. Agur's Collection (30:1-33)

Scholars debate the contours of this section. Some end it at v. 9, others at v. 14, others still at the end of the chapter. But apart from the first verse, in this chapter there is no other explicit indicator (such as a title) that delineates the start or end of a new section. This commentary therefore treats the whole chapter as part of one collection by Agur.

A. Prologue (30:1-9)

30:1. This verse functions as the title of the section. It is described as **the words of Agur the son of Jakeh**. His identity is unknown. Traditionally both Jewish and non-Jewish commentators speculated that this name is a pseudonym for Solomon; however, most modern commentators reject this idea, and suggest that he was a now unknown Israelite wise man or even a Gentile proselyte. This latter option would be confirmed if one were to slightly amend *massa'* (**oracle**) in the Hebrew text to mean "the Massaite" (i.e., a tribe descendent from Ishmael), suggesting that he was a follower of the Lord outside of the nation of Israel. However, whether or not he is a Gentile proselyte, there is no good reason to amend the text. The combination of *massa'* (**oracle**) and *ne'um* (rightly translated by HCSB as "the man's oration" rather than the NASB's **the man declares**) indicate that these words are prophetic divine revelation (cf. Waltke, *Book of Proverbs 15–31*, 454-55, 464-67; Fox, *Proverbs 10–31*, 852-53; cf. Zch 12:1; 2Sm 23:1; Nm 24).

There is widespread disagreement over how to translate the second line. Are the Hebrew words proper names, as in the NASB's **to Ithiel, to Ithiel and Ucal**? If so, Agur is directly addressing certain people, possibly his sons or disciples. Or are these words statements, such as the ESV's "I am weary, O God; I am weary, O God, and worn out"? Such statements do fit nicely with the words to come. No definitive answer is possible, but Waltke's solution (which sees the first Ithiel as a proper name but then the remaining two terms as statements) is intriguing (Waltke, *Book of Proverbs 15–31*, 454–55; 467–68, esp. notes 100–101; see Murphy, *Proverbs*, 225, for another option).

30:2-3. Agur's words in vv. 2-3 are humble and self-abasing. He claims to be **more stupid than any man**, lacking human **understanding** and **wisdom**, bereft of **knowledge** of God. If this follows the statements of his weariness (v. 1), it may suggest that Agur has come to the end of an exhausting search for human wisdom in a spirit reminiscent of Qohelet in Ecclesiastes (see Introduction in Ecclesiastes). The hyperbolic tone of these verses highlights two points. First, true wisdom is not a mere human endeavor; it can only come from God to those humble enough to receive it from Him. Second, divine wisdom so received is far greater than man's "wisdom" gained through pretentious human effort (Fox, *Proverbs 10–31*, 854).

30:4. There are four rhetorical questions (similar to Jb 38–39) meant to highlight the gap between God and man (v. 4). They each call for the answer: no one but God. No one but God can bring divine knowledge and wisdom down to man from **heaven**. No one but God controls the **wind** and rain. No one but God **has established the ends of the earth**. Agur challenges the reader to name this one who reveals knowledge and controls the cosmos. (**Surely you know!**) This is a reminder of God's covenant name—Yahweh—and the relationship that entails with His people. Only in relationship with Him can wisdom be found (Waltke, *Book of Proverbs 15–31*, 474–75). "To know the name, especially the covenant name 'Yahweh' is to know the person of God as Creator and Redeemer (Ex. 3:13-14)" (Hubbard, *Proverbs*, 471)—and Revealer of wisdom.

This may help explain the puzzling reference to **His son's name**. In Proverbs, the son is the one who learns wisdom from his father. This probably suggests that those who want to receive divine wisdom must be in relationship to God as father. Beyond Proverbs, in the OT the imagery of son is applied to Israel, those in covenant relationship with the Lord (e.g., Ex 4:22; Dt 14:1; Jr 3:19; Hs 11:1).

Some have taken this reference to the Son as a reference to the Messiah. As support, it is maintained that the earlier questions allude to Pr 8:27-30, describing wisdom as the architect of creation. Agur appears to be raising the idea of a Son (Ps 2:7, 12) who is with God and mediates His word (cf. Pr 30:5) to humanity. This approach sees an intentional attempt to direct attention to Israel's messianic hope. The wisdom of the entire book and the wisdom found in the words of Solomon become representative of the Wisdom of the divine Son of God. Thus the practical wisdom of Proverbs serves an even more significant purpose than providing skill for everyday living. Rather, they point to the Son, the Messiah Himself, in whom are hidden all the treasures of wisdom and knowledge (Col 2:2-3).

It is tempting to interpret Agur's question about the **son** as a reference to the Messiah, and therefore, Jesus Christ. After all, He is God's Son *par excellence*, who creates and sustains the world, reveals the Father, and personifies true wisdom. Moreover, the biblical theme of sonship in the OT also has Messianic overtones in places (e.g., Ps 2). Still, such rich connections should most likely not be read into Agur's words here. Instead, Agur's words contribute to an incipient theology of sonship that finds its richest, fullest expression in later NT revelation concerning Jesus Christ.

30:5-6. Picking up on the two key ideas in vv. 2-4, Agur encourages his readers to place their trust in God and His word. God's infinite greatness means that **every word of God is tested** (v. 5a; cf. Ps 18:30). The word **tested** refers to the end of a metallurgical refining process which removes all impurities from metal; the **word** is thus completely pure and true. True protection (**shield**) can only come to those who trust completely (**take refuge in**) the Lord, heeding

His word rather than their own understanding (v. 5b; cf. 3:5-6; 18:10). Given the purity and reliability of God and His Word, it would be foolish to **add to His words** (v. 6a; cf. Dt 4:2; 12:32; Rv 22:18-19). Such alteration only sullies the pure word with impure, false human wisdom and therefore betrays a lack of trust in God. Consequently, anyone who does so will be judged (**reprove**) and **proved a liar**.

30:7-9. Agur then turns to God in prayer with **two** requests (v. 7). These requests reflect the themes of God's true wisdom and trust in God from the previous verses. The phrase **before I die** probably carries the sense "as long as I live" and indicates a desire for ongoing help (Hubbard, *Proverbs*, 473). First, he asks God to **keep deception and lies far from me** (v. 8a). Agur wants nothing to do with falsehood in the way he believes, speaks, and lives; he wants rather to be a man of God's word in these ways. Second, he wants **neither poverty nor riches** but enough **food** to meet his daily needs as apportioned by God (v. 8b-c; cf. Mt 6:11; 1Tm 6:8). Proverbs 30:9 provides the explanation for his second request. Both extremes present spiritual dangers, particularly a failure to trust in the Lord in either times of need or plenty. To be filled beyond what is needed promotes a self-sufficiency that tempts a person to foolishly think he has no need to depend on the Lord. To be **in want** of God's daily allotment tempts a person to take matters into his own hands and **steal**. Thievery dishonors God's **name** because it violates His command and demonstrates lack of trust in Him (cf. Ex 20:15; Mt 6:9-11).

B. The Proverbs of Agur (30:10-33)

Agur presents several different kinds of proverbs in this section, the most notable and common of which are the so-called "numerical proverbs" (see comments on 6:16-19).

30:10. This proverb has less to do with unwarranted meddling than with oppressing the powerless. To **slander** involves speaking against someone furtively, whether true or not, for malicious rather than constructive purposes. It is bad enough to slander anyone, but slandering **a slave** before **his master** is a form of oppression against the powerless. The slave's only option is to **curse** his slanderer. But this should not be taken lightly, since the slanderer will **be found guilty** by the Lord and punished accordingly.

30:11-14. These verses describe four types of fools of the worst order. The first is the **kind of man who curses his** parents rather than blessing them (v. 11; cf. 20:20). Such behavior—demonstrating rebellion against God and man—violates the Ten Commandments and actually calls for the death penalty in the Law (Ex 20:12; 21:17). The second type is the deluded self-righteous person who is **pure in his own eyes** even though his moral **filthiness** remains (v. 12). "Having adopted their own evil nature as their standard (cf. 4:16-17), they consider wrong as right" (Waltke, *Book of Proverbs 15–31*, 485). The third type is the arrogant person whose proud **eyes** are the telltale sign of his haughtiness (v. 13; cf. 6:17; 21:4). He looks down on others and certainly does not humbly fear the Lord. The fourth type is the cruel oppressor. Violent men like him are pictured as ravenous beasts which greedily **devour** their prey, with **teeth like swords** and **knives** for devouring **the afflicted** and **needy**, whom they brutally oppress for personal gain.

30:15a. This one sentence proverb is a fitting transition between the previous proverb and the next one. **The leech** has a sucker on either end of its body, its **two daughters**, both of whom are named **Give** and who perpetually cry **give** (Fox, *Proverbs 10–31*, 867). The leech gorges itself insatiably on the blood of its host. Similarly, wicked oppressors (such as those in v. 14) are as rapacious as this despicable bloodsucker, as are the following three things that will not be satisfied (15b-17).

30:15b-16. These verses, the first of the numerical proverbs in this chapter (see comments on 6:16-19), describe four other items similarly insatiable. **Sheol** (the grave) continually craves more dead (cf. 27:20); the barren womb hungers unceasingly for a child (e.g., Gn 30:1); land (esp. for farming) always needs more **water**; and **fire** cannot ever get **enough** fuel. This proverb is probably making the observation that the world is full of all kinds of insatiable desires. Perhaps it is an implicit warning against uncontrolled coveting and cravings (Hubbard, *Proverbs*, 477; cf. Ex 20:17; Php 4:11).

30:17. Behaving respectfully toward one's parents is a serious responsibility in Scripture (cf. Ex 20:12; Pr 15:20; 20:20; 30:11). The arrogant person who **mocks** and **scorns** his parents faces a gruesome judgment. He dies dishonored and unburied, left as carrion for **ravens** and **eagles** (a fate associated with judgment of the wicked; e.g., .Is 18:6; Jr 16:4; Ezk 32:4)—his haughty **eye** a particularly tasty morsel for the scavengers. His parental disrespect is "so unnatural that nature itself carries out the punishment" (Clifford, *Proverbs*, 266).

30:18-20. Agur finds **four things** in the world to be wondrous and mysterious (v. 18). The first three climax in the fourth (v. 19). The **way of an eagle in the sky**, **a serpent on a rock**, or **a ship in the middle of the sea** all share something in common, although it is not entirely clear what that is. Most likely, all three operate in an easy, appropriate—even lovely—way in their environment (Kidner, *Proverbs*, 180), even though it may not be readily evident how they do so. **The way of a man with a maid** (i.e., a virgin), likely referring to courtship and marital love, is similar. There is something wonderfully appropriate and lovely about a husband's joining with his new bride, even though there is something mysterious about marriage as well.

The conclusion is a jarring contrast (v. 20). The **adulterous woman** is equally at home in her environment of adultery. Gratifying her lusts is no more remarkable than enjoying a meal; after her sinful behavior **she . . . wipes her mouth**. Perhaps the notion of eating has sexual overtones (cf. 9:17). Unlike the previous beautiful examples, there is no joy, wonder, or beauty here. The mystery, however, is how the adulteress can be so blind, callous, and smug in thinking she has **done no wrong**.

30:21-23. This numerical proverb lists **four things** that turn the social order upside down (like when **the earth quakes**), thereby creating an unbearable situation (v. 21). First, a **slave**, who is not equipped to be king and can only come to power through upheaval of the kingdom, creates havoc in the realm **when he becomes king**. Second, a boorish **fool** becomes only more unbearably obnoxious and overbearing **when he is satisfied with food**, that is prospers. Third, a **woman** who is **unloved**—or more literally, "hated"—will also be more intolerable once **she gets a husband**. Perhaps because of the pressures of marriage itself she is both cruel to her husband and haughty to her community (cf. 15:17; 17:1; 19:13; 21:9; 25:24;). Fourth, a **maidservant** who **supplants her mistress** becomes unbearable to the household in general and to the woman she dispossessed in particular (cf. Gn 16:4).

30:24-28. Here Agur names **four small** creatures, common in Israel, that are **exceedingly wise** despite their small size (v. 24). Together they show that wisdom is better than power. Though they lack strength, **ants** embody disciplined planning and hard work: **they prepare their food in the summer** to give them provision for the future (v. 25; cf. 6:6-8). "Rock badgers" (ESV), or coneys (*hyrax syriacus*, rabbit size rodents native to Israel), though they **are not mighty** and are basically defenseless, wisely choose to **make their houses** high **in the rocks**, where they are safe from predators (v. 26). Though **locusts have no king**, they prudently remain unified and organized, making them formidable despite their size, as is evident in the destruction of swarms of locust (v. 27; cf. Jl 2:1-11). The **lizard** (probably a gecko) can easily climb walls and ceilings; it is small and vulnerable enough to be captured in one's **hands** (v. 28). Yet their physical skills and tenacity pay off because they gain access even to **kings' palaces** (v. 28).

30:29-31. This numerical proverb lists **four things** that **walk** with a **stately** bearing (v. 29). Each displays power and fearless confidence within their realm and the list climaxes in the fourth example. First, the **lion**, being so **mighty among beasts**, has no need to **retreat before any** enemy (v. 30). Second and third, the **strutting rooster** (although the exact meaning of this Hb. word is uncertain) and **the male goat** are similarly confident as they move about the barnyard. All three of these animals aptly illustrate a mighty **king** accompanied by **his army**. His confidence is evident because none can stand against him, and only a fool would try. The lesson here is not entirely clear and is probably ambiguous on purpose (to call the wise reader to make multiple applications). Thus it may be a call for leaders to display confidence (Hubbard, *Proverbs*, 481), or for the wise to be confident in the Lord (Waltke, *Book of Proverbs 15–31*, 499), or for rebels against the king to think twice!

30:32-33. Confidence is a good quality; **foolish** arrogance (**exalting yourself**) is stupid. Someone who wishes to exalt himself, and plots to do so at other people's expense, ought to shut up instead, **put** his **hand** over his **mouth**, and stop self-promoting (v. 32). If he does not, he will only stir up anger in others, with inevitable results (v. 33). Just like **the churning** [*miytz*] **of milk produces butter** and **pressing** [*miytz*] **the nose brings forth blood**, so **churning . . . anger produces strife**. Plotting self-exaltation inevitably will have a bad effect, leaving one with a bloody nose—or worse!

IV. King Lemuel's Collection (31:1-31)

Although there is some dispute over the division of the verses in this concluding section of

Proverbs, some suggest vv. 1-9 is one section by King Lemuel, about whom little is known; and the poem on the excellent wife is likely a separate section, possibly by an anonymous author (vv. 10-31). However, the collection more likely includes the entire chapter since the concluding excellent wife poem is not introduced with a new title and its topic is "appropriate to the concern and experience of a queen-mother" (Hubbard, *Proverbs*, 485).

A. Title (31:1)

31:1. This section is described as **the words of King Lemuel**. His name means "for/belonging to God," but nothing is known of his identity. There is no record of any Hebrew king with this name, but some traditional interpreters have argued Lemuel is an alternate name for Solomon. It is also possible that Lemuel is a Gentile proselyte who ruled elsewhere (see comments on Agur's identity in 30:1). If *massa'* here refers to a location, he would have been King of Massa. But here the word is better translated as **oracle**. Like Agur's words, Lemuel's words are revelatory as well. They are also described as that **which his mother taught him**. While in Proverbs mothers instruct their sons, it is unusual to find such instruction independent of the father. "The topic of her conversation is something that a wise mother, especially the wise mother of a leader, would want to drive home to her child: women and drink are two large temptations to a man with power and money" (Longman, *Proverbs*, 538).

B. Admonitions to a King (31:2-9)

31:2. The opening exclamations display all the passion that only a mother could have for her son. Three times she asks King Lemuel, **What**? Whether she is implicitly rebuking him (e.g., ESV's "What are you doing?") or just introducing her words (e.g., HCSB's "What should I say?"), she is certainly getting his attention. Her description of him as **son**, **son of my womb**, and **son of my vows** reflects their closeness and her right to address him forthrightly, king though he may be (Longman, *Proverbs*, 538–9). Indeed, she was the one who bore him. Moreover, perhaps because she had difficulty conceiving (as Hannah did; cf. 1Sm 1:11), she presumably vowed repeatedly to dedicate him to God. After all, the name Lemuel means "belonging to God" (Koehler, *HALOT*, 532).

31:3. She first addresses the topic of his relationship to **women**. Clearly she is not warning Lemuel about all women; the final poem demonstrates that some women are great gifts to their husbands. She is rather warning him about a certain kind of woman, a kind **which destroys kings**. She is probably thinking here of his engaging in illicit sexual liaisons (e.g., 7:24-27) or maintaining a large harem (e.g., David, 2Sm 12:9-10; Solomon, 1Kg 11:1-11). Indulging his sexual desire in such ways would waste his energies and resources (**strength** and **ways**) and distract him from the business of state.

31:4-5. For similar reasons, then, it is **not** appropriate **for kings** to crave **wine** and **strong drink** (v. 4). Drunken kings can hardly maintain the sound judgment they need to uphold the law (i.e., not to **forget what is decreed**) and render just verdicts, particularly on behalf **of all the afflicted** (v. 5). Drunken kings make poor rulers, allowing injustice to flourish, and making them liable to divine judgment (cf. 20:1; 23:29-35).

31:6-9. A king certainly does not need strong drink (vv. 6-7). Although the advice here may suggest a principle that in some cases alcoholic **drink** (or by extension, an opiate) may be appropriate to alleviate people's desperate sufferings (particularly those who are dying, or **perishing**), more likely it is sarcastic (Waltke, *The Book of Proverbs 15–31*, 508). Certainly a king would not face such dire circumstances. So if a king wants to **give strong drink** to anyone, it should be to the destitute embittered in misery and facing starvation (i.e., they are **perishing**) rather than himself. Then at least they can **forget** something worth forgetting, their **poverty** and **trouble**. Of course, getting drunk will not solve the poor man's crushing poverty (cf. 20:1; 23:29-35). There is a more constructive course of action commanded of the king (v. 8-9). The king can **open** his **mouth**, not to imbibe liquor, but to speak up on behalf of those too **unfortunate**, **afflicted and needy** (cf. 24:11-12) to speak up for themselves (i.e., they are **mute**). Only the king can **judge righteously**, **defend** them, and alleviate their suffering from oppression.

C. The Excellent Wife (31:10-31)

This famous poem is an acrostic in Hebrew. Each verse begins with a consecutive letter of the Hebrew alphabet, giving the reader the impression of a complete "A to Z" picture of this godly woman (Waltke, *Book of Proverbs 15–31*, 514). It is probably a heroic poem, a genre which typically sings the praises of a military hero (Longman, *Proverbs*, 539–40). She is no less valiant, being a reflection of Lady Wisdom herself. Young men need to be reminded of the kind of women they should seek for a spouse. Plus, she serves as an example for women of all ages to emulate as well.

31:10. The **excellent wife** is literally called a "woman/wife of strength or valor" (*'eshet chayil*). She is strong in competence and character (Fox, *Proverbs 10–31*, 891; cf. Ru 3:11; Pr 19:14). The rhetorical question (**who can find** such a woman?) does not deny her existence. It rather highlights how rare and precious she is, even **far** beyond **jewels** (cf. 8:11). A man with such a wife has a rare treasure indeed (cf. 12:4).

31:11-12. Her husband can readily see her worth. He **trusts in her** completely, with full confidence (v. 11a). And he has good reason, for through her **he will have no lack of gain** (v. 11b). **Gain** is a military term meaning "spoil" or "booty." This suggests that she is like "a warrior in the battle of life" who wins plunder for her family, to their benefit (Longman, *Proverbs*, 543). Indeed, **all** throughout **her life** she is a great asset to him, committed to consistently do **him good and not evil** (v. 12).

31:13. Wool and flax were needed to make clothes for her family. She not only seeks to secure those materials, quite possibly by overseeing their production herself (Clifford, *Proverbs*, 275), but she also makes those clothes willingly and with **delight**, having joy in her family and her work.

31:14. She is industrious and resourceful. **Like merchant ships**, she trades goods she has produced domestically for **food** she cannot produce at home. She is thus able to secure "tasty foreign delicacies" **from afar**, provisioning a bountiful table that "replicates in miniature that of fabled King Solomon" (Waltke, *Book of Proverbs 15–31*, 524; cf. 1Kg 4:21-23).

31:15. Unlike the sluggard, who cannot get out of bed to feed himself (26:14-15), the excellent wife **rises** early before dawn (**while it is still night**) to make sure the entire **household**, including **her** maidservants, has the **food** they need. This shows that she is compassionate, sacrificial, and hard working. The word translated **food** (*terep*) often means "prey." This may suggest she is like a lioness—strong, cunning, skillful—in providing for her own.

31:16. She is entrepreneurial. She makes sound judgments (**she considers** thoughtfully) in choosing the right **field** for development. Then, using **her** own **earnings** from her domestic labors, she **buys** the property and **plants a vineyard** on it. Presumably, the vineyard then produces grapes, wine, and raisins for her family as well as creates a profitable agribusiness.

31:17. This verse uses language that reiterates her strength and vigor. Halfhearted effort is not for her. The Hebrew text literally says that **she girds** her loins **with strength**. Girding the loins involved tucking one's floor length tunic into one's belt in order to allow for free movement of one's legs for fighting or hard work. Similarly to make **her arms strong** may mean "that she tucks in her sleeves so that they will not encumber her in her work" (Fox, *Proverbs 10–31*, 895). She thus prepares herself to energetically engage any task that she undertakes (cf. 10:4).

31:18-20. Her efforts pay off as she senses the **gain is good** from her business ventures. The image of **her lamp . . . not** going **out at night** could suggest that she works well into the night (i.e., her business success spurs her on to work harder). Or, that she is prosperous enough to keep the lamp burning (i.e., her successful efforts ensure the prosperity of her household and the oil does not run out). Either way, her success does not go to her head (vv. 19-20). Working the **distaff** and **spindle** (tools for spinning fabric) with **her hands** indicates that she personally continues to spin fabric. That is, she does not neglect her domestic responsibilities (cf. v. 13) despite her profitable business ventures (Garrett, *Proverbs*, 250; cf. Fox, *Proverbs 10–31*, 895). She wisely cares for the **poor** and is compassionate, **stretches out her hands to the needy** (cf. 14:21; 19:17; 28:27; 29:7).

31:21-22. She has foresight to provide clothes for **all her household**. She therefore does not have to be **afraid of the** cold weather (**snow**), because their clothes are warm. That they are also dyed **scarlet** suggests that their clothing is expensive and of the highest quality, since **scarlet** die was very expensive, and often used on wool (2Sm 1:24). Although she has been scrupulous in caring for others, as a dignified woman she takes appropriate care of herself as well (Fox, *Proverbs 10–31*, 896). Her bed **coverings** and **clothing**, made of **fine linen and purple**, are also expensive and of highest quality—even luxurious—as befits a woman of her status. While not all women could aspire to her financial status, all can emulate her industriousness and commitment to providing the best care for her family within whatever monetary means she has. She is the example of a wise woman who builds her house, and any woman who likewise wants to honor the Lord with her life in relation to her family can follow her example (cf. Pr 14:1).

31:23. The excellent wife is a credit to **her husband**. She only makes him better, brings him greater respect in the community (cf. 12:4), and frees him up for worthwhile pursuits. He therefore is a highly respected leader in society, one of **the elders of the land** who sit **in the** city **gates**, the government and business center of the city where the **elders**, as city leaders, made decisions for the community. Behind this great man is a great woman, and any young man with high aspirations should take note to pray for and pursue a wife like this (cf. 12:4; 18:22).

31:24. Part of her business efforts includes producing **linen garments** and **belts** and selling them to **tradesmen**—a truly enterprising woman indeed.

31:25. Even better than the fine clothes she produces is the fine character that adorns her like fine **clothing**. She is a woman of **strength** and **dignity** (honor), which are "the advantages of both youth and old age" according to 20:29 (Waltke, *Book of Proverbs 15–31*, 531). With these qualities **she smiles at the future**, facing all her tomorrows with confidence. This is no cocky self-confidence or dreamy hopefulness; it reflects her wise confidence in the Lord whom she reveres (cf. v. 30).

31:26. Not only does she live wisely, but she also teaches **wisdom** to others. Her wise instruction is described as **the teaching of kindness** (*chesed*). This phrase probably indicates that all her instructions "to her staff, family, and friends are motivated by covenant love that treats others with the loyal consideration that characterizes God's dealings with His people" (Hubbard, *Proverbs*, 496).

31:27. She diligently watches over (**looks well** on) everything that goes on (**the ways**) in **her household** without ever letting **idleness** distract her from her supervisory responsibilities. This highlights her organizational skill, attentiveness, persistence, and hard work.

31:28-29. Her family rightly recognizes what a treasure she is. **Her children** and **husband rise up**, perhaps in respect (Waltke, *Book of Proverbs 15–31*, 543) or to make a public proclamation (Hubbard, *Proverbs*, 497), and praise her (v. 28). Her husband's words of praise are: that of all the **many** women (**daughters**) who **have done nobly**, she excels **them all** (v. 29). The word **nobly** is the same word (*chayil*) translated "excellent" in v. 10. He says that she is the most excellent of all excellent wives, the rarest of all rare jewels. In many observant Jewish homes today, it is customary on Friday evening (the beginning of Sabbath) for the husband to stand and recite (or sing) this blessing over his wife—a lovely custom indeed acknowledging her worth to him, the family, and the community.

31:30. This wife is praiseworthy from the inside, not just because of external **charm** and **beauty**. An attractive outward appearance can be **deceitful** because it reveals nothing about a person's true quality and may in fact mask character deficiencies. Moreover, it is **vain** in any case because it is fleeting. Of course, beauty is not a negative quality, and a husband should find his wife attractive (cf. 5:19-20). But attractiveness is relatively insignificant when compared to the decisive factor making the excellent wife so praiseworthy. What matters most is that she **fears the Lord** (cf. 1:7; 9:10). Her relationship with the Lord makes her such an exemplar of wisdom and righteousness.

31:31. This kind of woman deserves to be rewarded (**give her the product of her hands**) and publicly praised (**let her works praise her in the gates**). A society would be wise to promote such women and the values they represent.

In sum, the excellent wife fears and trusts the Lord. More specifically, she is trustworthy, industrious, resourceful, enterprising, ebullient, sound in judgment, successful, responsible, generous, dignified, strong, kind, and supportive to her husband and family. A wise son would be wise to pursue such a wife. For in doing so he embraces Lady Wisdom. After all, the excellent wife exemplifies Lady Wisdom herself. In this sense, this description of the excellent wife is a good way to end the book of Proverbs. Only a fool would not want a companion like her.

BIBLIOGRAPHY

Bridges, Charles. *An Exposition of Proverbs*. Marshallton, DE: National Foundation for Christian Education, n.d. First published in 1846.

Clifford, Richard J. *Proverbs: A Commentary*. Old Testament Library. Louisville, KY: Westminster John Knox, 1999.

Fox, Michael V. *Proverbs 1–9: A New Translation with Introduction and Commentary.* Anchor Yale Bible. New Haven: Yale University Press, 2000.

———. *Proverbs 10–31: A New Translation with Introduction and Commentary*. Anchor Yale Bible. New Haven: Yale University Press, 2009.

Garrett, Duane. *Proverbs, Ecclesiastes, Song of Songs*. New American Commentary. Nashville: Broadman & Holman, 1993.

Hubbard, David A. *The Preacher's Commentary: Proverbs.* Thomas Nelson: Nashville, 1989.

Keil, C. F. and F. Delitzsch. *Proverbs, Ecclesiastes, Song of Songs*. Commentary on the Old Testament, vol. 6. Translated by M. G. Easton. Peabody, MA: Hendrickson, 1996. English translation originally published in 2 vols. in 1874–75.

Kidner, Derek. *Proverbs: An Introduction and Commentary*. Tyndale Old Testament Commentaries. Downers Grove, IL: Tyndale, 1964.

Klein, William W., Craig L. Blomberg, and Robert L. Hubbard. *Introduction to Biblical Interpretation.* Dallas: Word, 1993.

Koehler, Ludwig, Walter Baumgartner, Johann Stamm. *The Hebrew and Aramaic Lexicon of the Old Testament.* CD-ROM-Edition. Trans. M. Richardson. Leiden: Brill, 2000.

Longman, Tremper, III. *How to Read Proverbs*. Downers Grove, IL: InterVarsity, 2002.

———. *Proverbs.* Baker Commentary on the Old Testament. Grand Rapids, MI: Baker, 2006.

Murphy, Roland. *Proverbs.* Word Biblical Commentary. Nashville: Thomas Nelson, 1998.

Ross, Allen. *Proverbs.* The Expositor's Bible Commentary, vol. 5. Frank E. Gabelein, ed. Grand Rapids, MI: Zondervan, 1991.

Steveson, Peter A. *A Commentary on Proverbs*. Greenville, SC: BJU Press, 2001.

Treier, Daniel J. *Brazos Theological Commentary on the Bible: Proverbs and Ecclesiastes*. Grand Rapids, MI: Baker, 2011.

Waltke, Bruce K. *The Book of Proverbs, Chapters 1–15*. New International Commentary on the Old Testament. Grand Rapids, MI: Eerdmans, 2004.

———. *The Book of Proverbs, Chapters 15–31*. New International Commentary on the Old Testament. Grand Rapids, MI: Eerdmans, 2005.

———, with Charles Yu. *An Old Testament Theology: An Exegetical, Canonical, and Thematic Approach.* Grand Rapids, MI: Zondervan, 2007.

Whybray, R. N. *The Book of Proverbs*. The Cambridge Bible Commentary on the New English Bible. Cambridge: Cambridge University Press, 1972.

• • • •

ECCLESIASTES

DAVID FINKBEINER

INTRODUCTION

Bible readers have often been surprised by what they find in the book of Ecclesiastes. Yet while it is controversial for scholar and layman alike, it more than repays careful study of its beneficial teachings.

Author. The authorship of Ecclesiastes is probably the single most important consideration for understanding the date, message, and interpretation of the book as a whole. Unfortunately identifying the human author is no easy task because of several factors.

First, the bulk of Ecclesiastes represents the thinking of "Qohelet," the "Preacher." Traditionally it has been argued that Qohelet is Solomon. This seems reasonable for several reasons. (1) Qohelet is called the son of David, king in Jerusalem, and king over Israel (1:1, 12). These designations most naturally apply to Solomon. (2) The great wisdom, wealth, and power by which Qohelet explored life's meaning in 1:12–2:26 best match Solomon's, whose resources were unsurpassed in Israel's history (cf. 1:16; 2:7-8). (3) The apparently cynical, world-weary words of Qohelet seem best explained as the words of Solomon later in life when he turned away from the Lord (1Kg 11). (4) Early Jewish and Christian interpreters believed Qohelet to be Solomon.

In spite of these arguments many interpreters today do not believe that Qohelet is Solomon. Why? (1) Some scholars have argued that the unusual grammar and vocabulary of Ecclesiastes reflect a Hebrew much later than Solomon's time, although more recent research has seriously undermined this argument. (2) Qohelet is never called Solomon, nor is Solomon even mentioned—something one would expect if he were the author (cf. Pr 1:1; 10:1; Sg 1:1). (3) In places Qohelet's self-description does not easily match that of Solomon. For instance, though David was the only king of Israel prior to Solomon who reigned in Jerusalem, Qohelet implied that a string of kings preceded him (e.g., Ec 2:9—assuming that he was not referring to the line of Canaanite kings who reigned in Jerusalem before David). In addition, although Solomon died in office as king, Qohelet may imply that his kingship was in the past (depending on how one translates 1:12), and he does distance himself from his kingly persona after chap. 2. (4) As described by Qohelet, his day seems to be characterized by injustice and abuse of power by those in authority (3:16-17; 4:1-3; 8:2-11; 10:5-6, 20), characterizations that seem inconsistent with Solomon's golden age.

A solution here is not easy, since there are solid arguments on both sides, and Ecclesiastes is anonymous. So it is possible that Qohelet was a wise man well after Solomon's time who took on a persona reminiscent of Solomon in chaps. 1–2. Still, on balance, it seems more likely that Qohelet's words reflect the words of Solomon himself. Beyond the arguments that support identifying Qohelet with Solomon, the arguments against doing so are not decisive. Most of them can be explained by recognizing that Qohelet might be employing a literary device to distance himself from his role as king in order to highlight his role as wise teacher. In this role he can reflect critically even on his own reign and its weaknesses (Duane Garrett, *Proverbs, Ecclesiastes, Song of Songs*, NAC [Nashville: Broadman & Holman, 1993], 264).

A second complication in identifying the author of Ecclesiastes is that Qohelet is not the book's only voice. His words run from 1:2–12:8. But there is also a narrator whose words insert themselves occasionally (1:2; 7:27; 12:8) and, more important, frame Qohelet's thoughts (1:1;

12:9-14). The book's epilogue, where the narrator assessed Qohelet's words and concluded the book, makes it clear that the narrator's voice is significant for the theological message of the book as a whole. The reader is expected to adopt the viewpoint of the narrator.

This leads to a third complication. Does the narrator agree with Qohelet, or is he a critic? How interpreters answer this question will have enormous impact on how they interpret Qohelet's words, which make up the bulk of the book. Those who see the narrator as critical of Qohelet will often characterize the latter as cynical and even unorthodox. In the epilogue then the narrator emerges to set the record straight, stating that in contrast to Qohelet's perspective, it is wise to fear God and keep His commandments.

The other basic interpretation finds Qohelet and the narrator in fundamental agreement. Those who take this approach believe that Ecclesiastes presents a unified message and that Qohelet's statements are consistent with the orthodox viewpoint of the narrator. In fact some believe that Qohelet and the narrator are the same person in different personas, though the text itself does not explicitly indicate this.

In the end the answer to this question hinges on how one interprets the epilogue. As will be seen below, the narrator seems to commend the words of Qohelet as wise, beneficial, and rooted in God Himself. This commentary therefore argues that Ecclesiastes presents a unified message and that readers need to heed all Qohelet's teachings rather than to be wary of his skeptical, cynical words.

Date and Recipients. The date and audience of Ecclesiastes are closely bound to the question of its authorship. Obviously those who identify Qohelet with Solomon date the book to the 10th century BC, whereas those who reject Solomonic authorship date the book to the postexilic period. Strictly speaking, even if Qohelet is identified as Solomon, the book itself may be later than his reign, since the author of the book (the narrator) is differentiated from Qohelet himself. Therefore one cannot be definitive here.

Still, identifying Qohelet as Solomon does at least suggest an earlier date, tying Ecclesiastes to the wisdom milieu of the ancient Near East associated with the court of Solomon. Indeed scholars have identified parallels between sections of Ecclesiastes and ANE literature like the *Epic of Gilgamesh*. Given this earlier date, then, Garrett may well be right in arguing that the primary audience of Ecclesiastes was the Solomonic court, "the intellectual elite of Ancient Jerusalem" (Garrett, *Proverbs, Ecclesiastes, Song of Songs*, 266).

Purpose. Although Ecclesiastes has a unified message, that message is complex because of two features in Qohelet's approach. First, Qohelet presupposed both that God is the creator and ruler of this world and that it is still fallen. The world's fallenness explains the frustrations, uncertainties, mysteries, and paradoxes that Qohelet saw in life. He acknowledged that this is still God's world—a world He created and controls. So God cannot be ignored. If anything, His lordship over the world only compounds its mysteries.

Second, Qohelet approached the world *primarily* from the perspective of life "under the sun;" his interest is life here on earth. He explains this approach in 1:13: by wisdom he set out to explore what is done "under heaven." Qohelet raised deeply disturbing questions about this life without quickly reverting to theological truisms. His approach might therefore best be categorized as "essentially empirical" (Michael V. Fox, *Qohelet and His Contradictions* [Sheffield: Almond, 1989], 85). This does not mean that Qohelet was *exclusively* empirical; at times he gave a God's-eye perspective. But he honestly looked at life in this fallen world without flinching, and he wanted his readers to do the same. Only then would they be able to appreciate the relevance and propriety of his advice.

And only then will readers be able to appreciate the concluding message of the book, as summarized by the narrator. In the end Ecclesiastes rests in the knowledge that God will finally set the world aright. In the meantime people face the difficulties of life in this fallen world under the sun, and as they anticipate the final judgment, wisdom calls on everyone to fear God and keep His commandments (12:13-14).

The structure of Ecclesiastes, like so many other matters in this book, is also difficult. Proposed outlines are legion, none gaining widespread consensus. This is partly because the structure of Ecclesiastes is not linear but episodic, repetitive, and developmental. That is, the discussion often moves abruptly from one topic to another, sometimes with little transition or even connection (episodic). In addition, a topic is presented in one section of the book, only to be revisited in later sections of the book (repetitive). Furthermore different occurrences of the same topic are often approached from different perspectives (developmental). These characteristics are reflected in the commentary's outline below.

OUTLINE

I. Prologue (1:1-2)
II. The Profitless Cycle of Life (1:3-11)
III. The Search for Meaning (1:12–2:26)
  A. The Investigator and His Investigation (1:12-13a)
  B. Summary Reflections (1:13b-18)
  C. The Search Itself (2:1-11)
  D. Death's Impact on the Search (2:12-23)
  E. A Breath of Fresh Air (2:24-26)
IV. Examples of Futility under the Sun (3:1–6:12)
  A. Futility in Light of Time and Eternity (3:1-15)
    1. The Rhythms of Life (3:1-8)
    2. Assessing the Rhythms of Life (3:9-15)
  B. Futility in Injustice/Oppression (3:16–4:3)
  C. Futility in Labor under the Sun (4:4-12)
  D. Futility in Advancement (4:13-16)
  E. Futility in Improper Worship (5:1-7)
  F. Futility in Governmental Dealings (5:8-9)
  G. Futility in Amassing Wealth (5:10–6:9)
  H. Concluding Reflections on Futility under the Sun (6:10-12)
V. Wisdom: A Taste of Proverbs (7:1–8:1)
  A. Things to Value in Life—But Not Too Much (7:1-14)
  B. An Extended Reflection on Wisdom and Righteousness (7:15–8:1)
VI. Life's Frustrations (8:2-17)
  A. Frustrations Dealing with the King (8:2-9)
  B. Frustrations Dealing with Injustice (8:10-15)
  C. Frustrations in Not Knowing God's Plan (8:16-17)
VII. Life's Common Destiny (9:1-12)
VIII. More Wisdom: Its Limits, Benefits, Observations, and Advice (9:13–11:6)
IX. Advice to the Young: On Youth, Old Age, and Impending Death (11:7–12:7)
  A. On Youth (11:7-10)
  B. On Old Age and Impending Death (12:1-7)
X. Epilogue (12:8-14)

COMMENTARY ON ECCLESIASTES

I. Prologue (1:1-2)

1:1. The narrator began Ecclesiastes by introducing the reader to the predominant voice in the book, Qohelet (**the Preacher** or Teacher), one who convenes an assembly to address them. The English title for the book comes from the Greek translation of Qohelet (*ekklesiastes*). This designation is likely a functional title. So although Qohelet, as both **the son of David** and **king in Jerusalem**, is probably Solomon (see Introduction), in this book he is taking on the role of a teacher addressing his hearers with wisdom (cf. Garrett, *Proverbs, Ecclesiastes, Song of Songs*, 264).

1:2. This verse presents the theme of Qohelet's entire discourse. Its importance is evident not only because it is repeated throughout the book but also because it comes at the beginning (here) and end (in 12:8) of Qohelet's discourse, forming an inclusio (a literary envelope) around Qohelet's words.

The Hebrew term for **vanity** is *hebel*, the most important term in the book. It literally means "breath" or "vapor," but it clearly has a metaphorical sense in Ecclesiastes. In various contexts it can be translated as transitory, worthless, empty, incomprehensible, absurd (Michael Fox, *A Time to Tear Down and a Time to Build Up: A Rereading of Ecclesiastes* [Grand Rapids, MI: Eerdmans, 1999], 28). No one English term—such as **vanity**, meaningless (NIV), or futile—can capture the different nuances of *hebel* in every occurrence throughout Ecclesiastes. Qohelet intensified the term by twice using its superlative, **vanity of vanities**, which means "completely or utterly vain or meaningless." Qohelet declared this verdict on **all** within his frame of reference. Repeatedly throughout Ecclesiastes Qohelet uses phrases like "under the sun" (e.g., 1:3, 14) to indicate that his observations pertain to human life in this fallen world (see Introduction).

So Qohelet's thesis is that everything in human life in this fallen world, taken as a whole, is utter **vanity**. It is a jarring way to begin his discourse, and yet it is crucial for the message of the book. Elsewhere in the OT the term *hebel* is applied to idols (e.g., Jr 14:22), which are vain, worthless, absurd. But because people in this fallen world naturally seek to find meaning in things under the sun, it is equally true that those vain things become idols. Qohelet will show that pursuing these worthless idols is a fool's errand. The conclusion will then be obvious: worship the true God (Ec 12:13).

II. The Profitless Cycle of Life (1:3-11)

1:3. The rhetorical question in this verse introduces a prominent theme in Ecclesiastes closely connected with the thesis that life **under the sun** is vanity (*hebel*). Qohelet claims that there is no net profit (**advantage**) in **all** one's hard **work** in life. The rest of this section unpacks this claim.

1:4. Since labors under the sun are profitless, it is no surprise that human effort would make no lasting difference here. Much happens, but nothing really changes. As developed in this section, **generation** refers both to human generations and the processes of the natural world. So neither changing events nor changing generations of people in the world leave a lasting change under the sun.

1:5-7. Qohelet gives three illustrations of the natural world's "ceaseless round" (Derek Kidner, *The Wisdom of Proverbs, Job, and Ecclesiastes: An Introduction to Wisdom Literature* [Downers Grove, IL: InterVarsity, 1985], 97). Day after day, **the sun rises and the sun sets**, only to repeat the process again. The **wind**, which seems so changing and unpredictable, really just goes in circles. **Rivers** keep flowing **into the sea**, but it never fills.

1:8. To the honest observer, this ceaseless round is **wearisome** beyond description (**man is not able to tell it**), much like a difficult but pointless task. Worse still, it is frustrating because it reminds people that nothing under the sun can fully satisfy. One can never see or hear enough. This frustration only adds to the weariness.

1:9-11. What is true of the earth's wearying cycles is also true of human history. Despite all that happens in human life, **there is nothing new under the sun** (v. 9). Someone might object that human life includes much that is new (v. 10a). Qohelet denies this. Allegedly new occurrences actually have a long pedigree (v. 10b). They only seem novel because humans tend to forget the people of the past and their actions. Nor should people expect anything different in the future; people of this generation will not be remembered by future ones (v. 11). "Like ants on a rock, we leave no trace of having been here" (Garrett, *Proverbs, Ecclesiastes, Song of Songs*, 285).

Qohelet's words here drive the reader to look beyond life under the sun. Qohelet is not denying the possibility of human invention but is analyzing the fundamental human condition, much like the well-known proverb, "The more things change, the more they stay the same" (Derek Kidner, *A Time to Mourn, and a Time to Dance* [Downers Grove, IL: InterVarsity], 1976, 26). So one who hopes to find something new and satisfying under the sun—that fundamentally alters the human condition—is on a fool's errand. This is merely trying to gain the world while losing the soul (Mk 8:36).

III. The Search for Meaning (1:12–2:26)

A. The Investigator and His Investigation (1:12-13a)

1:12-13a. Qohelet here switched to the first person, as if giving his personal journal about his search for meaning under the sun. His investigation was extensive, involving **all that has been done under heaven**. And it is competent. If Qohelet is Solomon, one can scarcely imagine a more qualified investigator for this task. As **king over Israel in Jerusalem**, he had all the resources necessary to conduct the search (v. 16). And with his **wisdom** he could conduct his investigation carefully, thoroughly, and accurately.

B. Summary Reflections (1:13b-18)

Before narrating his search for meaning, Qohelet gave two summary reflections based on his investigation.

1:13b-15. His first reflection was that **God** has **afflicted** man with a **grievous task** (v. 13b). All man's **works**... **under the sun** are not only vanity (*hebel*) but are also a **striving after wind** (v. 14). The imagery of chasing after the wind connotes both frustration (one can never capture it) and futility (and even if one did catch it, he would have nothing). The supporting proverb (v. 15) highlights two points: (1) there is something fundamentally wrong with the world (it is **crooked** and **lacking**), and (2) man can do nothing to change it (because God is behind this; cf. 7:13).

1:16-18. After recounting his Solomonic credentials for investigating life's meaning (v. 16) and his full participation in the search (v. 17a), Qohelet gave his second summary reflection. He maintained that even the pursuit of **wisdom and knowledge** is frustrating and futile because it only brings greater **grief** and **pain** (vv. 17b-18). After all, Qohelet's search for meaning always led to meaninglessness and an inability to truly understand life under the sun, except for its troubles and sorrows (see below).

C. The Search Itself (2:1-11)

2:1-3. Qohelet's search for meaning began with basic **pleasure** (**laughter** is roughly synonymous). That is, he wanted to **enjoy** himself, particularly as he sought **to stimulate** his **body with wine** (v. 3). The use of wine for pleasure may well connote both the refined pleasure of the wine connoisseur and the drunken debauchery of the carouser. Even so, since he was conducting an experiment, his **mind** was engaged in the process and **guiding** him with wisdom (v. 3). He found here already what he would find at the end of his investigation: these things lead to **futility** (v. 1).

2:4-8. Qohelet then described other elements of his search. He engaged in grand building projects typical of great kings (vv. 4-6). He amassed a fortune, as seen in the unsurpassed **slaves**... **flocks**... **herds**... **silver, and gold** he **collected** (vv. 7-8a). He also demonstrated his power as a great king in his ability to collect **the treasure of kings and provinces** (v. 8a). He enjoyed hearing **male and female singers** (v. 8b) as a connoisseur of fine arts. And he partook of the sexual **pleasures** of his harem (v. 8c).

2:9-10. Qohelet then summarized his search for meaning. Because he was the greatest king of his era (v. 9a), he had all the resources necessary to engage in this search. And it is clear that his investigation was extensive, because he **did not refuse** any **pleasure** he **desired** (v. 10a). Indeed he greatly enjoyed his search (v. 10b), even though he never stopped using his wisdom to evaluate everything he was doing (v. 9b).

2:11. Qohelet's verdict on his search is that none of the pleasures he pursued provided meaning in life. They are **all**... **vanity**, a **striving after wind**, and without ultimate **profit**. Since most people today spend their lives living for one or more of these pleasures, Qohelet's conclusion is still relevant.

D. Death's Impact on the Search (2:12-23)

2:12. Throughout his search Qohelet has made use of wisdom. Now he made wisdom itself the subject of his investigation. The rhetorical question of v. 12b is notoriously difficult to translate, though the NASB's translation is fairly literal here. The verse likely conveys the idea that if even the king cannot find meaning in life, who can? Since Qohelet was uniquely equipped as king to undertake the investigation in vv. 1-11, his conclusion was the last word. It was therefore time to press on to investigate other matters, like wisdom itself.

2:13-17. Wisdom does have its advantages over **folly**. If nothing else, the wise do not stumble blindly into difficulties, as do fools (vv. 12-13a). And yet there is a certain futility even in gaining wisdom. In the end, both the wise man and the fool share the same physical fate: death (vv. 14b-15). And once gone, the wise and the fool alike will be forgotten (v. 16; cf. 1:11). This also shows the futility of life.

2:18-23. Just as the reality of death had tempered Qohelet's enthusiasm for wisdom, so too it tempered his enthusiasm for life's pursuits (vv. 17-18a). Qohelet gave three warnings to ambitious people who live to achieve greatness. First, at death the achiever gives control over the **fruit** of his **labor** to someone who may well squander it in his folly (vv. 18-19). Second, the achiever never really benefits from the fruit of his labor; his heirs do (vv. 20-21). Third, the achiever has little chance to enjoy his achievements in this life; mostly he just has hard work and worries (vv. 22-23). Workaholics, be warned!

E. A Breath of Fresh Air (2:24-26)

2:24a. This statement is a brief respite from Qohelet's brutally honest observations of life under the sun. Qohelet encouraged people to enjoy life's simple pleasures (e.g., to **eat and drink**), including the fruit of one's **labor**. This is not a cynical call for people to wring as much pleasure as they can from this futile world before they die. There really is a legitimate place for life's simple pleasures. So this is a call to faith, to a perspective that looks beyond life under the sun. How else could one enjoy life's small pleasures in the face of a futile world?

2:24b-25. These verses spell out that perspective. Life's small pleasures and the capacity to enjoy them are a gift from **God**, and **without Him** such **enjoyment** is impossible. Qohelet's words reflect a strong sense of God's sovereignty and even of His grace.

2:26. Qohelet took the perspective further, reflecting on Deuteronomy (blessings for the obedient in Dt 28:1-15, curses for the disobedient in 28:16-68) and Proverbs (success and happiness to the one who fears God and is wise in Pr 3:1-12, for example). The one who pleases God (i.e., **who is good in His sight**) will be blessed with **wisdom and knowledge**, and the capacity to enjoy life. This person is one who is rightly related to God, described later in Ec 12:13 as one who fears God and keeps His commandments. In contrast, **the sinner** fully experiences life's futility. This is because in the end he finds his meaning for living in something under the sun.

IV. Examples of Futility under the Sun (3:1–6:12)

In this sobering section Qohelet presented an unflinching tour of life under the sun to force his readers to face life's futility.

A. Futility in Light of Time and Eternity (3:1-15)

1. The Rhythms of Life (3:1-8)

3:1. The wise man not only knows the principles of wisdom, but he also knows when they apply (cf. Pr 26:4-5). Wisdom is thus about proper timing. Qohelet recognizes that the same is true of life under the sun. **Every event** under the sun has its proper **time**, as is seen in the poem that follows.

3:2-8. Each verse in this poem has two pairs of opposite events in life. Each opposite pair is a merism, a literary device highlighting the totality of something by indicating its two extremes and everything in between. The two pairs of opposites in each verse are probably related thematically and focus on a significant feature of life under the sun.

What features did Qohelet address? He started with the most basic one, the beginning and end of life, whether of humans (birth and death) or plants (planting or uprooting) (v. 2). Similarly, he dealt with destruction and construction, whether of living creatures (killing and healing) or inanimate objects (tearing down and building up) (v. 3). As regards **a time to kill** *human beings*, Qohelet was probably thinking in the context of capital punishment or warfare. Verse 4 addresses the emotional life, moving from grief (weeping and mourning) to joy (laughing and dancing). What follows (v. 5) is more difficult. While obscure in their meaning, throwing and gathering stones most likely refer to sabotaging a field in war (cf. 2Kg 3:19, 25) or clearing a field in peace (Is 5:2) (Tremper Longman, III, *The Book of Ecclesiastes*, NICOT [Grand Rapids, MI: Eerdmans, 1998], 116). In connection with the second pair of opposites (embracing and refraining from embracing), this seems to refer to the gamut of relationships running from intimacy to belligerence. The next verse (v. 6) pertains to possessions. Sometimes possessions are worth keeping or searching for when lost; sometimes they are not. The two pairs in v. 7 might be unrelated, but more likely they pertain to mourning in a funeral context. "Mourners tore their clothes, and their comforters kept silent during times of grief, but people were free to repair clothes and freely converse at other times" (Garrett, *Proverbs, Ecclesiastes, and Song of Songs*, 298). Finally, the two pairs of v. 8 address attraction and repulsion, whether in personal relations (love and hate) or corporate relations (war and peace).

This poem affirms that no state of affairs under the sun is permanent. Life's activities are changing and fleeting, not static and enduring. Moreover, no one can ultimately control these seasons of life. They are in God's hands.

2. Assessing the Rhythms of Life (3:9-15)

3:9-10. Life's fleeting activities reminded Qohelet once again that the results of one's labors are also fleeting (v. 9). And yet **God** Himself **has given** people life's labors **to occupy** them, so they cannot escape the rhythms of life.

3:11. In this complex verse Qohelet first affirmed that God has a sovereign plan that extends to everything under the sun (cf. Eph 1:11). So there is something **appropriate**—even beautiful (*yapeh* could be translated this way)—in the way **everything** is ordered. God **has also set eternity in** the human **heart**. One's **heart** is the core of a person, but to what does the much-debated term **eternity** (*olam*) refer? Some have suggested alternate meanings such as "world" or "ignorance/darkness" (Longman, *The Book of Ecclesiastes*, 120). But given the immediate context, "eternity" is the best translation, and it probably refers to an eternal, God's-eye perspective on life's changing rhythms. Humans thus inherently long to understand God's plan and its meaning. However, God's eternal plan and purposes are inscrutable. Simply no one can **find out** what **God has done** from **beginning** to **end**. In short, humans know God has a plan, they want to know what it is, and yet they cannot. Frustration indeed!

3:12-15. Though no one can have a God's-eye perspective on all of life, people can at least gain some perspective from God on some aspects of life under the sun. To this end Qohelet made two basic points in these verses. First, he claimed that although God gave this unfulfilled eternal longing, He also gave a consolation, a **gift** to counterbalance that longing (vv. 12-13). He gives the capacity to find enjoyment and a measure of satisfaction in life's changing rhythms, a way of "making the most of life as it is" (Kidner, *A Time to Mourn*, 39). Second, Qohelet maintained that there is a vast difference between God and man (vv. 14-15). God's work and plan are eternal and shape all reality (v. 14a); they need no tinkering or change (v. 14b). In contrast, man's efforts are fleeting and incapable of changing what God has determined to do (vv. 14b-15). In fact, God Himself has ordered the world this way (v. 15c)! Why? **God has so worked that men should fear Him**. The *fear* of the Lord is a central theme in the wisdom literature, referring to a proper reverence or better, the worship of the living God (cf. 12:13-14). The radical distinction between God and man, between His infinite understanding of and power over the changing rhythms of life in contrast to finite man's, should issue forth in reverence for God.

B. Futility in Injustice/Oppression (3:16–4:3)

3:16. Here Qohelet introduced the injustice theme that he developed later in 4:1-3. **The place of justice** and **righteousness** refers to law courts. Is there anything more outrageous than the miscarriage of justice in the court of law? God certainly is outraged (cf. Pr 17:15).

3:17. Here is some encouraging news. While human beings may be unjust, believers can have confidence that God will bring everything into judgment. Why? Since there is a proper **time for every matter**, presumably there is a proper time for divine judgment in the future. For Qohelet, this future divine justice is almost certainly eschatological, but it may well also include the expectation of more immediate judgment under the sun (i.e., "what goes around comes around" even in this life).

3:18-22. Qohelet now considers the reality of death, which complicates the expectation of future divine judgment. Some have found Qohelet's observations in these verses troubling because it sounds as if he was questioning the reality of an afterlife for human beings. But readers must keep in mind once again that Qohelet's comments reflect his observations from the limited vantage point of life under the sun (see Introduction). Qohelet maintained that **God has surely tested** humanity by exposing it to the hard reality that, in at least one important way, people are like animals (v. 18). In terms of mortality they have no advantage over the animals (vv. 19-20). Like them, humans receive life's **breath** from God, and when He withdraws it they die, and their bodies return to **dust** (cf. Ps 49:12-13; 104:27-30). Humans and animals both **go to the same place**, the grave. In the creation narrative in Gn 1–2, the author distinguishes between people and animals. The earth brought forth animals (Gn 1:24-25), but in Gn 2:7 God breathed the breath of life into man. Yet, Qohelet seems to link people and animals into the same category, contrary to Genesis. Some even cite this passage as a support for the idea that animals will be in heaven, because they have the same destiny as people. However, the background of this text is not the biblical strand of teaching highlighting man's distinctiveness from animals as image bearer, but a biblical strand of teaching that highlights commonality of humans and animals. Moreover, Qohelet was precisely not addressing the question of an afterlife for animals but the similarity between humans and animals. Furthermore, from the perspective of life under the sun, no one knows directly what happens after death nor has any living person yet experienced the afterlife. From humanity's vantage point under the sun, people can only observe that men and animals both die (Ec 3:19-21). The powerful reality of death should encourage people to enjoy in the here and now what they have been given by God as their **lot** in life (v. 22a; cf. Ps 90:10-12).

Seen in the larger context, death complicates the hope for future divine judgment against those who are evil. People might die before they can witness any temporal fulfillment of divine judgment against the wicked. Worse still, death conceals the reality of final divine judgment. These facts thus lead inexorably to the conclusion of the book (Ec 12:13-14), which calls people to a faith that rests on the One who is beyond life under the sun (Ps 49:12-15). Only then can people fear Him, enjoy what they have been given, and leave future judgment in His hands. Finally, the paragraph ends with the rhetorical question, **who will bring him to see what will occur after him?** The expected answer is that human beings cannot see beyond this life, but God alone does indeed see.

4:1-3. Only confidence in God can help people cope with the injustice and brutal realities of oppression under the sun. **The oppressed** find no joy in their lot in life, but only **tears**. Furthermore they have **no one to comfort** them or alleviate their suffering. And they cannot stop their **oppressors**, who have all the **power** over them (v. 1). In fact the horror of oppression is so great that from one perspective, it is **better** to die or even to have **never existed** than to experience such **evil activity** (vv. 2-3). If this is so, then why does God bring people into the world? Although the Scriptures teach that life is a gift from God (Gn 2:2-8; Jb 10:12; Ps 139:12-14), the point of these verses is to highlight the horror of oppression and the discouraging nature of living under it. This certainly is not the final biblical word on the subject, nor does Qohelet intend it to be. But he does intend the reader to feel the bite of this observation. Why God brings people into an oppressive world is one of those matters Qohelet considers inscrutable. This is Qohelet's graphic way of saying that living under intense oppression is simply no way to live.

C. Futility in Labor under the Sun (4:4-12)

4:4-6. In the normal style of Qohelet, an abrupt shift of topic follows. These three verses work closely together to give a helpful perspective on **labor** in this futile world. On the one hand, working hard to succeed is prompted by **rivalry**, the desire to have greater success than one's peers (v. 4). This desire is **a striving after wind**, if for no other reason than that success is fleeting and unsatisfying. On the other hand only a **fool folds his hands** (stops working hard) and starves as a result (v. 5). Verse 6 brings the two competing thoughts together. Qohelet contended that a person is better off settling with less (one handful) than seeking for more (two handfuls). The one who diligently labors but settles for something less than the workaholic still has something to enjoy (unlike the lazy fool) without the cares and time constraints of the one driven by rivalry to succeed at all costs (cf. 2:22-24; Pr 15:16-17). In the next several verses, (Ec 4:7-12) Qohelet gave a negative (vv. 7-8) and a positive (vv. 9-12) example of this principle.

4:7-8. The negative example is Qohelet's sketch of the lonely miser, whose insatiable lust for more leaves him all alone, bereft of the pleasures associated with one's family and companions. His only friend is money (Garrett, *Proverbs, Ecclesiastes, and Song of Songs*, 307).

4:9-12. Qohelet's positive example is a stark contrast to the lonely miser. The one who is not an ambitious workaholic has room for life's blessings, such as companionship. Companions make labors easier while increasing reward (v. 9). They also help in times of need (v. 10), give comfort in the face of life's harshness (v. 11), and add to one's strength in dangerous times (v. 12).

D. Futility in Advancement (4:13-16)

4:13-16. Making another abrupt shift of topic, Qohelet used the story in these verses to illustrate that political advancement under the sun is also futile. Though not entirely clear, the plot line of this story seems to go as follows. There is an old king who is a fool because he does not listen to advice or warning (v. 13). He is replaced by a youth who is far wiser, even though he once was poor and even imprisoned (v. 14). But even this young king's wisdom is not enough, because he is replaced by another youth who is very popular (vv. 15-16a). The popularity of this third king, however, is only temporary (v. 16b). This loose narrative indicates that people can attain power through seniority, wisdom, or popularity (Longman, *The Book of Ecclesiastes*, 147). But in each case the result is the same. Political power is vanity (*hebel)* because it is fleeting.

E. Futility in Improper Worship (5:1-7)

Qohelet argued in this section that improper worship is both foolish and futile. So, he gave four pieces of advice regarding worship.

5:1. First, Qohelet warned people to approach God with reverence. To **guard your steps** is reminiscent of Moses' reverence in approaching the burning bush (Ex 3:5). Such reverence will lead one to **listen** submissively to God and not to **offer the sacrifice of fools**, the presumption that external sacrifice without heartfelt contrition will avail with God (cf. Ps 51:16-17). Such flippant externalism only exacerbates the fool's guilt.

5:2-3. Second, Qohelet urged his readers to pray with reverence (v. 2a). Irreverent prayer is **hasty** and **impulsive**. Its many words reflect the fool's desire to manipulate God (cf. Mt 6:7-8) or his flippancy toward God (cf. Pr 10:19). Such attitudes fail to appreciate God's exalted greatness (Ec 5:2b). The proverb in v. 3 illustrates this point. While its exact meaning is obscure, its basic point is clear. The many words of the fool only display his folly; they gain him nothing with God.

5:4-6. Third, picking up on Dt 23:21-23, Qohelet urged people not to vow rashly. Tied to temple worship, a vow was "a promise to consecrate something, normally either a sacrifice or a money payment (as in Lv 27:1-25) to God in return for the granting of a favor" (R. N. Whybray, *Ecclesiastes*, NCBC [Grand Rapids, MI: Eerdmans, 1989], 94). Vowing was voluntary, but failure to fulfill a vow once taken offended God. Therefore hasty, unfulfilled vows are another example of foolish worship, because like the previous two examples, they demonstrate a lack of respect for God and bring judgment down on the worshiper.

5:7. Finally, echoing the conclusion of the book, Qohelet urged his readers to **fear God**. This is true worship, which stands in stark contrast to the improper worship summarized in v. 7a. The flippant multiplying of **words** in improper worship is as empty as the **dreams** of a fool. Such improper worship in our day is summarized nicely by Kidner (*A Time to Mourn*, 52): "This writer's target is the well-meaning person who likes a good sing and turns up cheerfully enough to church; but who listens with half an ear, and never quite gets round to what he has volunteered to do for God."

F. Futility in Governmental Dealings (5:8-9)

5:8-9. Qohelet considered government to be frustrating because it was a necessary evil, something deeply flawed but indispensable. On the one hand people should **not be shocked** when they see **oppression** and injustice in a governmental **province** (v. 8a). After all, bloated governmental bureaucracy tends to frustrate justice (v. 8b). On the other hand, government has its advantages (v. 9). Some believe this verse continues the negative assessment of government (cf. the NIV's translation), but it is probably better to understand it more positively (as reflected in the NASB) since it fits with Qohelet's normal pattern of "on the one hand, on the other . . ."

Since Qohelet seemed to say that on balance (**after all** is literally, "in all"), the king (i.e., the whole government) is an advantage for the land. Even a corrupt government is better than anarchy, which devastates an agrarian economy and leads to starvation (Garrett, *Proverbs, Ecclesiastes, Song of Songs*, 312).

G. Futility in Amassing Wealth (5:10–6:9)

Qohelet's various reflections on wealth in this section are tied together by a common purpose, to show that the pursuit of wealth for meaning in life is futile.

5:10-16. Qohelet gives several reasons that pursuing wealth is futile. First, pursuing wealth creates an insatiable appetite for more (v. 10). In addition, greater wealth simply encourages greater expenditures (v. 11). Furthermore wealth increases anxiety and decreases rest (v. 12). Wealth can also encourage self-destructive hoarding (v. 13) while still providing no real security (v. 14). Moreover, wealth is not permanent; no one can take it with him beyond the grave (vv. 15-16).

5:17. Beginning with this verse and running through 6:6, Qohelet presented another reason that wealth is futile: it simply cannot bring happiness or enjoyment. In this verse he sketched a picture of a rich man, whose miserable, embittered existence demonstrated that he was unable to enjoy the wealth he loved.

5:18-20. The contrast in these verses with v. 17 could not be starker. Those who do not focus on life's many cares but enjoy what they have—whether their **labor**, life's simple pleasures, or even **wealth**—do so by God's grace and power, as a **gift** from Him. Qohelet said that living this way is **good and fitting**.

6:1-2. Qohelet gave a **prevalent** example of wealth's inability to bring enjoyment. He presented someone to whom God has granted everything he wants: **wealth**, possessions, **honor**—except He has withheld the ability to enjoy them. Instead someone else, a stranger, actually gets to enjoy his wealth. This truly is a horrible state of affairs.

6:3-6. Qohelet then showed just how horrible it is. Take a man who is rich, lives a long time, and has many children. Yet even though he meets "the three traditional conditions for happiness" in Hebrew thought (Garrett, *Proverbs, Ecclesiastes, Song of Songs*, 315), he is not happy. In fact, he makes those around him so miserable they do not even give him a **proper burial**. A miscarried child is better off than he is (v. 3). This is a staggering assessment in light of Ps 58:8, where "the Psalmist could not think of a more horrid fate to wish upon his enemies" than a fate like the stillborn child (Longman, *The Book of Ecclesiastes*, 171; cf. Ps 58:8). Why is the stillborn better off than this rich man? While both die in the end, at least the stillborn has the advantage of never experiencing the miserable frustration of the rich man who cannot enjoy his wealth (Ec 6:4-6).

6:7-9. While some commentators consider them unrelated to the previous section, these verses likely present another reason that pursuing wealth is futile (reminiscent of 5:10): wealth does not satisfy. Like one's hunger for food, which keeps returning even after he eats, the **appetite** for money is never **satisfied** (v. 7). Verse 8 seems to presuppose the idea (common in wisdom literature) that the wise often accrue wealth. But if wealth cannot satisfy, then there is no **advantage** in being wise for money's sake. So in the end, it is best then simply to be content with what one has than to strive constantly for more (v. 9).

H. Concluding Reflections on Futility under the Sun (6:10-12)

6:10-12. At first glance, these verses may seem unrelated, but they are tied together by an ongoing comparison between God and man (a comparison which clearly favors God). Qohelet first asserted that man is no match for God. The ability to name involves both knowledge and control of a person or thing. Though God gave Adam the authority to name the animals (Gn 2), man's ability to name pales in comparison to God's. Given **what man is**, God is much **stronger than he is** (Ec 6:10). So it is simply pointless to **dispute** with God about what happens under the sun, even if one persists with **many words** (vv. 10b-11). Verse 12 tells why ongoing contention with God is a waste of time. In comparison to God, who perfectly knows His plan (cf. 3:1-11), humans are ignorant of the present (**what is good for a man** under the sun) and the future (**what will be after him under the sun**). God's cursing the world in humanity's fall (Gn 3) is likely the background of these verses. By showing how pointless it is to resist or dispute with God about His cursing the world under the sun to futility, these verses are a fitting conclusion to this whole section.

V. Wisdom: A Taste of Proverbs (7:1–8:1)

This section is a collection of wise statements about life and about wisdom itself.

A. Things to Value in Life—But Not Too Much (7:1-14)

7:1. Like **ointment** or perfume, which was desirable and expensive, a secured reputation is quite valuable (see Pr 22:1), but only relatively so. It will not be finally secured until after one's **death**, so people should not become obsessed by it.

7:2-4. Pondering death is valuable too. Since it is the **end** all people face, the **wise** person does not avoid the **sorrow** and sober reflection prompted by a funeral (**the house of mourning**), as does the fool. Such reflection is good for the **heart**. In that sense, even a **face** that **is sad** at a funeral can reflect a **heart** that **may be happy**.

7:5-7. The rebuke of a wise man is also far more valuable than the unwarranted **song** of praise and frivolity (**laughter**) of the fool (vv. 5-6). In contrast to the benefit of a wise man's correction, the fool's contribution is as annoying and worthless as **thorn bushes** in a fire (v. 6), which "provide quick flames, little heat, and a lot of unpleasant noise" (James Crenshaw, *Ecclesiastes*, OTL [Philadelphia: Westminster, 1987], 135). Unfortunately the value of a wise rebuke can be mitigated, for example, in a political context by extortion or bribery (v. 7).

7:8-9. Patience should be valued as well. It takes **patience** rather than proud presumption to bring a **matter** to its completion (v. 8). And it takes patient self-control to avoid the destructive quick temper of **fools** (v. 9).

7:10. One common aspect of life that is neither valuable nor wise is pining for the "good ole' days."

7:11-14. Wisdom too is an **advantage** in life just like **money**, because both are a **protection** (vv. 11-12a). In fact wisdom is even more advantageous because it stays with you through the hardest times, when money runs out (v. 12b). Still, God's sovereign plan exposes wisdom's limits (vv. 13-14). No one—not even the wisest person—can change God's plan or predict what will happen in it. So people should **be happy**

in good times as a gift from God. And **in the day of adversity** one should **consider** that God's plan encompasses that as well (cf. 3:1-8); this is a cursed world after all.

B. An Extended Reflection on Wisdom and Righteousness (7:15–8:1)

7:15-18. Qohelet began this section by arguing that there are exceptions under the sun to the retribution principle, which maintains that the righteous prosper and the wicked suffer (e.g., Pr 3:1-2) (Ec 7:15). So one should avoid a zealous, excessive legalistic religiosity (disguised as zeal for righteousness) and a fanatical pursuit of wisdom driven by the retribution principle (Garrett, *Proverbs, Ecclesiastes, Song of Songs*, 323). Otherwise a person will **ruin** himself trying to achieve an impossible standard (supreme righteousness and wisdom) for an end that is not even guaranteed (prosperity) (v. 16). The limits of the retribution principle do not mean, however, that one is justified in being **wicked** and foolish. Retribution is still generally true, and foolish villains often do get their just deserts (v. 17). So a person **who fears God** will reject both extremes (v. 18). One should be godly and wise without becoming a cheerless, frustrated legalist. This way life can be enjoyed without falling into sinful, destructive license.

7:19-22. Similarly Qohelet encouraged his readers to seek wisdom but not to overestimate one's ability to be wise and righteous. **Wisdom** (skillful living in the fear of the Lord) is powerful, more so than even political power (v. 19; cf. Pr 24:5-6). But it is not powerful enough to defeat human sinfulness, to create even one **righteous man on earth who continually does good and who never sins** (Ec 7:20). So it is important to act wisely in light of human sinfulness. For example one should not be eager to hear what others say about him (v. 21a). Since it is characteristic of sinful humans to speak against other people, one may likely hear someone speak against him as well (vv. 21b-22).

7:23-24. Given **all** he has observed, Qohelet still believed wisdom is worth pursuing. And yet, even for someone as wise as he, wisdom is elusive in some sense. Qohelet thus recognized that he lacked the wisdom to understand God's **mysterious** plan (cf. 3:11).

7:25-29. While Qohelet's wisdom had its limitations, pursuing it did teach him about **evil** and **folly** (v. 25). In particular he discovered that a relationship with an immoral woman leads to a **bitter** end (cf. Pr 2:16-19), so the wise God-fearer **will escape from her** (Ec 7:26). In addition, Qohelet discovered the gender conflict resulting from the curse (cf. Gn 3:16). Told from the male perspective, Qohelet finds harmonious community rare with other men, but rarer still with women (Ec 7:27-28). No doubt, a female Qohelet would hold a similar opinion of men (Garrett, *Proverbs, Ecclesiastes, Song of Songs,* 325). Most significantly Qohelet discovered human depravity. Though God created them **upright**, fallen humanity has pursued sinful **devices** (v. 29).

8:1. Qohelet concluded this section with a qualified endorsement of wisdom. True, no one has ultimate wisdom. Still, the limited wisdom people possess is advantageous, and thus better than folly.

VI. Life's Frustrations (8:2-17)

Qohelet presented various examples of frustration under the sun.

A. Frustrations Dealing with the King (8:2-9)

The dangerous world of ancient monarchical politics (in which the king has the power of life and death) is foreign to people in Western democracies today. Nevertheless, anyone who has experienced an arbitrary and abusive superior can identify in part with Qohelet. This section involves advice for people in such a system, advice that illustrates how frustrating it can be to try to negotiate one's way wisely while dealing with a difficult superior.

8:2-4. Qohelet's basic point in these verses is clear enough: treat the king carefully because he is so powerful. His specific advice, however, is more difficult to interpret. Most likely, Qohelet's advice is as follows. Show proper reverence for authority by obeying the king, as promised (v. 2). And do not be quick to abandon the king in pursuit of a rebellious plot (**an evil matter**). Because he is so powerful, it will probably fail (vv. 3-4).

8:5. Two guiding principles underlie Qohelet's advice. First, a person is better off being obedient to the king, because it is the best way to avoid harm. Second, since subordinates are dealing with such a powerful person, they also need wisdom to know how best to obey him.

8:6-8. The second principle is rooted in the way God has ordered reality, in which everything has a **proper time and procedure** (v. 6a; cf. 3:1-8). But this raises a problem. In the court, as in all of life, wisdom has its limits. Wisdom is needed if one is to safely obey the king, but since human wisdom is limited, a person still might lose his head! No wonder **man's trouble is heavy upon him** (v. 6b). Not even the wise can anticipate with certainty the future ramifications of their actions (v. 7). This is all part of the larger truth that human beings are weak and limited. Their weakness is illustrated in their inability to control the **wind**, **the day of death**, events that overtake them (like **war**), or the consequences of the **evil** that they **practice** (v. 8).

8:9. In sum, Qohelet maintained that life under tyranny is not a happy condition. Any wise man who does his best to please a tyrannical king (or workplace superior) without any guarantees knows this.

B. Frustrations Dealing with Injustice (8:10-15)

8:10-15. Qohelet here considered the problem of delayed justice. Granted, the **wicked** die and are **forgotten**, so there is some justice under the sun. But during their lifetime, they may well be regarded as religiously respectable citizens of the city who even receive the honor of a proper burial. Justice delayed like this is frustrating (v. 10). Worse still, it only encourages increased wickedness among human beings (v. 11). In spite of such cases in which justice is delayed (v. 12a), Qohelet still maintained that **those who fear God** will be better off than the wicked, whose life will be cut short (vv. 12b-13). Qohelet thus affirmed the principle of retribution while also acknowledging that there are frustrating exceptions under the sun, the most vexing of which are those cases in which the **righteous** get what the **wicked** deserve, and the wicked get what the righteous deserve (v. 14). Since no one can understand these exceptions, Qohelet encouraged everyone to enjoy life's good gifts **given** by **God**, leaving the question of ultimate justice to Him (v. 15).

C. Frustrations in Not Knowing God's Plan (8:16-17)

8:16-17. Having carefully and comprehensively observed life under the sun, Qohelet concluded that no one simply can understand what God is doing; God's plan is beyond human comprehension (vv. 16-17a). Indeed no matter how **wise** a **man** may be or how hard he searches, in the end no one can comprehend what God is doing (v. 17b).

VII. Life's Common Destiny (9:1-12)

Qohelet returned to the topic of death in this section.

9:1. Summarizing the previous section, Qohelet contended that the **righteous** and **wise** are ultimately under God's control (in **the hand of God**), and His plan is not predictable. But that led Qohelet to another thought. No one knows what future **awaits** him in this life, whether **love or hatred** (i.e., favorable or unfavorable circumstances). In short righteousness and wisdom cannot guarantee good times in life. God will not be manipulated.

9:2-3. But one future is guaranteed under the sun: death. This is the great leveler, regardless of how a person lives (v. 2). **It is the same for all . . . there is one fate for all men** (vv. 2-3) in this life. Yet this horrid fate does not stifle human sinfulness. **Throughout their lives** depraved human **hearts** are **full of evil and** the **insanity** of sin. Humanity is in a sorry state indeed.

9:4-6. Since death is inevitable, is there any advantage in living? Qohelet agreed that there is, even though in statements about death elsewhere (e.g., 6:3-5) he indicated there may be times when life's difficulties sap life of those advantages. Qohelet thus asserted that even a creature as wretched as a **live dog**—ancient Israelites despised dogs—**is better than** a noble creature (such as a **lion**) that is **dead** (v. 4b). Why? Although living people **know they will die**, that death is yet future, and in the meantime they have the **hope** of being able to enjoy that which is good under the sun (vv. 4a, 5a). In contrast the dead are gone and **forgotten**, and they have no thoughts (**do not know anything**) or temporal benefits (**a reward**) in this life. In short, they no longer partake **in all that is done under the sun** (vv. 5b-6). Once again, it is important to keep in mind that Qohelet was considering death from the perspective of life under the sun; questions about the nature of the afterlife are outside his purview here.

9:7-10. Since life has its advantages, Qohelet exhorted his readers to enjoy its blessings (in **happiness** and **with a cheerful heart**), something God has **approved** (v. 7). And people should do so whenever possible (v. 8). This is why he urged people to wear **white** and put on **oil**, which were marks of festivity (Whybray, *Ecclesiastes*, 144). One of life's blessings is the joy of marital love (v. 9). People should participate in life and its joys (like marriage), not with half measure but **with all** their **might** (v. 10), because life is **fleeting**. **Sheol** refers to the grave, not to a gathering place of disembodied souls in the afterlife. Here as elsewhere, he focused only on life under the sun, not on the afterlife. His point is simply that people are all headed to the grave when all opportunities under the sun cease (v. 10).

9:11-12. Life is unpredictable, which is why ability is no guarantee of success under the sun (v. 11). Similarly death is also unpredictable. **Man does not know** his time of death. Death and disaster can overtake a **man** as **suddenly** as **fish** or **birds** are captured (v. 12).

VIII. More Wisdom: Its Limits, Benefits, Observations, and Advice (9:13–11:6)

This section covers a variety of material, all related once again to the theme of wisdom.

9:13-18. In discussing wisdom's relative benefits and limits, Qohelet started with an example of a story that **impressed** him (v. 13). A powerful **king** attacked **a small city** (v. 14). Against all odds, a **poor wise man** somehow delivered the city, whose people then promptly forgot him once they were delivered (v. 15). This episode highlights both the power and limits of wisdom (v. 16). Wisdom is so powerful that even the quiet words of a wise man are more effective than the ranting of a foolish king, who tries to ram through his foolish will by sheer force (v. 17). Therefore **wisdom is better than weapons of war** (v. 18a). And yet wisdom is not invulnerable; **one sinner** can ruin **much good** wrought by wisdom.

10:1-3. Wisdom is powerful, but so is folly. Little **dead flies** can make a **perfumer's** batch of ointment ferment and **stink**. Similarly it takes only a **little foolishness** to undermine the good, like wisdom or honor (v. 1). Wisdom and folly simply do not go together (v. 2). And if a little folly can be destructive, a lot can be humiliating (v. 3). So folly should be avoided at all costs.

10:4-7. Here Qohelet gave wise advice for dealing with difficult superiors, who themselves can limit wisdom's benefits. When encountering an *angry* superior, the best a wise man can do is to allay his anger with **composure**, not panicked retreat (v. 4). And when encountering a *foolish* superior, the wise man should not be surprised by his actions or their results. Instead of promoting the deserving (the **rich** is probably a metonymy for the wise), a foolish ruler will promote undeserving fools to **exalted places** (vv. 5-6). Such foolish management has dire consequences, leading to social upheaval (v. 7).

10:8-11. Qohelet also commended wise perspectives on life's accidents. Wisdom cannot prevent *every* accident; some accidents (Qohelet gives four examples) happen no matter how wise we are (vv. 8-9). In such cases it is not wise to seek blame but recognize that even work done wisely can have a snake bite in it. Yet wisdom can prevent *some* difficulties in life. So sharpening one's **axe** will save a lot of work (v. 10). And snake charmers who are wise (i.e., who know what they are doing) will lose neither their job nor their life (v. 11).

10:12-14. Though wisdom does have its limitations, Qohelet here showed the even greater problem of foolishness, considering the way of the fool as a foil to wise living. The first example of foolishness is the fool's words. Wise talk is **gracious**, in contrast to the self-destructive words of the **fool** (v. 12). In fact while the fool's words might seem silly at first, in the **end** they are devastating in their **wicked madness** (v. 13). Worse still, **the fool** speaks too much and does not know when to shut up (v. 14a). Furthermore, his excessive verbosity addresses matters he knows nothing about, like the future (v. 14b).

10:15. The second example of folly is the fool's work, which is no better than his words. He does his work the hard way (cf. 10:10), even in his commute home from work. "The reason why fools are so tired after a long day's work is that they are so stupid that they get lost and walk a longer distance than necessary to return to their homes in the evening" (Longman, *The Book of Ecclesiastes*, 248).

10:16-20. The third example of folly is the fool's leadership. A land with a wise, noble **king** will make sure that his subordinates work hard for the good of the land and use their resources to strengthen them in their task. Such a **land** is **blessed** (v. 17). In contrast a **land, whose king is a lad**—someone immature and foolish—is under **woe** (v. 16a). He allows his nobles to use their resources inappropriately to **feast in the morning**, a sure sign of dissipation (v. 16b). The foolish laziness of leaders like this brings disaster on both **house** and land (v. 18), but they are too enamored with money and parties to care (v. 19). They only squander the resources of the land. And there is no relief in sight because one has little recourse with such a foolish king. To whom can one complain? Even to criticize him in the most private settings may get back to him—and bring great grief to the complainer (v. 20).

11:1-2. Life in all its unpredictability has risks. While wisdom cannot remove life's uncertainties, it can help people cope with them. Qohelet addressed two areas of uncertainty. First, in the area of finances, Qohelet encouraged investing wisely. To **cast your bread on the surface of the waters** is an image from maritime trading, which was risky business but could be extremely profitable. So the wise investor will not always be averse to taking risk, especially when there is a genuine possibility of real gain (v. 1). But as a safeguard, he will also diversify his investments rather than putting all his proverbial eggs in one basket (v. 2) (Garrett, *Proverbs, Ecclesiastes, Song of Songs,* 338).

11:3-6. Second, in the area of farming, Qohelet maintained that the farmer must act wisely despite the uncertainties of nature. Farming is fraught with risk. Some aspects of nature are relatively predictable (rain **clouds** bringing **rain**). But others are unpredictable (for example, wherever a **tree falls**), and most are out of human control (v. 3) (Whybray, *Ecclesiastes,* 159). Farmers cannot allow their inability to predict or control nature to paralyze them into inaction (v. 4). Since God's ways are as inscrutable as the formation of the baby in the womb or the direction of the wind (v. 5), the wise farmer will work hard and wisely plan for many possible contingencies (v. 6).

IX. Advice to the Young: On Youth, Old Age, and Impending Death (11:7–12:7)

A. On Youth (11:7-10)

11:7-8. Light (along with its parallel, seeing **the sun**) and **darkness** are metaphors for life and death respectively. So Qohelet once again maintained that life is good (v. 7); so people should enjoy it as long as possible because it is so short (v. 8). There will be **many** more **days** of death than of life for a person under the sun, and what remains of life is fleeting (*hebel,* translated **futility,** carries this connotation here).

11:9-10. Qohelet focused his exhortation to enjoy life on those best positioned to do so: the young. He first counseled them to enjoy life to its fullest, to participate with gusto in what brings them joy (v. 9a). However, the advice to **follow the impulses of your heart and the desires of your eyes** is not a license to sin. Qohelet thus also advised them to recognize God's **judgment** over **all these** activities. A person who is aware that God is assessing what he does will not allow his celebration of life to become sinful (v. 9b). God is no celestial killjoy; rejecting a "sow your wild oats" philosophy "robs joy of nothing but its hollowness" (Kidner, *A Time to Mourn,* 99). Those who fear the Lord are best suited to enjoy life. Qohelet also encouraged the young to remove impediments to enjoying life, like fixating on its **grief** and **pain** (cf. 5:20). The joy of youth is simply too **fleeting** to squander (v. 10).

B. On Old Age and Impending Death (12:1-7)

12:1a. Given life's brevity and God's approaching judgment, Qohelet exhorted the young to **remember** their **Creator**, to commit to Him in "passionate fidelity" (Kidner, *A Time to Mourn,* 100-01) before old age (vv. 1b-5a) and death (vv. 5b-7) arrive.

12:1b-5a. Qohelet characterized approaching old age in a series of descriptions and images. It is a time of **evil** (or better misery) when physical incapacity hinders enjoyment (v. 1b). Like the gloom of a dark, rainy day, it clouds life's pleasures (v. 2). The loss of physical capacities in old age is described in metaphors related to a large household (vv. 3-4a): trembling hands (**watchmen of the house**), weakening of major muscles in the legs and back (**mighty men**), loss of teeth (**grinding ones**), loss of eyesight (**those who look through windows**), and loss of hearing (**doors on the street**). Qohelet then continued to describe old age using other metaphors (vv. 4b-5a): the loss of sleep (to **arise at the sound of the bird**), the decreased capacity to sing (**daughters of song will sing softly**), loss of confidence (**men are afraid**), graying hair (the **blossoms** of an **almond tree** are white), the difficulty of physical movement (**the grasshopper drags himself along**), and the loss of appetite, sexual and otherwise (**the caperberry is ineffective**; the caperberry was believed to stimulate appetite, particularly sexual desire).

12:5b-7. Once again Qohelet used several images to describe death's relentless approach. The **mourners** of a funeral indicate that **man** goes to the grave (**his eternal home** from the perspective of "life under the sun") (v. 5b). A **broken silver cord** and a **crushed golden bowl** refer to the loss of something valuable at death, namely, life (v. 6a). The broken **pitcher** or **wheel** at the **well** or **cistern** means that it is impossible to draw more water for life (v. 6b). In language reminiscent of creation and the curse, when man dies God withdraws the breath (**spirit**) of life, and man returns to the **dust** from which he was taken (v. 7).

X. Epilogue (12:8-14)

12:8. One final time Qohelet reiterates his theme, forming with 1:2 a literary envelope (*inclusio*) around his words. Everything in this life under the sun is *hebel*, vain, meaningless, absurd, frustrating, futile, fleeting.

12:9-10. Now the narrator's voice speaks. He started with an evaluation of Qohelet (**the Preacher**), considering him a **wise man** who imparted **knowledge** and who understood and collected **proverbs**. And not only was Qohelet a **delightful** writer, but also his words also communicated **truth correctly**. Far from considering him an unorthodox cynic, the narrator commended Qohelet.

12:11-12. What effects do **the words of wise men** like Qohelet have? They are **like goads**, perhaps with **nails** imbedded in them (cf. Fox, *Qohelet and His Contradictions*, 324-25). Goads are long sticks that sting cattle, prodding them to move. Similarly even if wise words sting, they still spur the disciple into wise, moral behavior. Ultimately all these wise words **are given by one Shepherd** (v. 11). This may simply refer to God as the source of and authority for all wisdom (cf. Pr 1:7), although some argue that its referent is more specific. Michael Rydelnik, for example, maintains that the phrase **one Shepherd** is used elsewhere in Scripture only as a messianic appellation (Ezk 34:23-24; 37:24-25), and so the narrator was claiming here that the divine Messiah specifically is the source of all wisdom (Michael Rydelnik, *The Messianic Hope*, NACBT [Nashville: Broadman & Holman, 2010], 78-79).

As helpful as **books** of wisdom might be, one could study them endlessly to great **wearying** effect (Ec 12:12). So there is a time to ponder wise sayings, and there is a time to move on to conclusions.

12:13-14. What, then, is the narrator's **conclusion** to **all** Qohelet's wise words? **Fear God and keep His commandments**. To fear God is to "respect, honor, and worship" Him (Longman, *The Book of Ecclesiastes*, 282). Keeping God's commandments is the fruit of fearing Him. The narrator gives two reasons to do this. The first is that **this applies to every person** (v. 13b). A more literal translation reads, "this is the whole of humanity." As image bearers, to fear and obey God is at the core of what it means to be human (Garret, *Proverbs, Ecclesiastes, Song of Songs*, 344). This is what humans were made for. But if that is not enough, the narrator then gave a second, more negative reason: God's final **judgment** (v. 14). This judgment is comprehensive (including **everything**, public or private, **good or evil**) and assured (it **will** occur). Only the fool would not fear and obey Him.

Ultimately then the only place to find meaning in this meaningless life under the sun is in the One who is beyond life under the sun: God Himself.

BIBLIOGRAPHY

Crenshaw, James. *Ecclesiastes*. Old Testament Library. Philadelphia: Westminster, 1987.

Eaton, Michael A. *Ecclesiastes*. Tyndale Old Testament Commentaries. Downers Grove, IL: InterVarsity, 1983.

Fox, Michael V. *Qohelet and His Contradictions*. Sheffield: Almond, 1989.

Garrett, Duane A. *Proverbs, Ecclesiastes, Song of Songs*. New American Commentary. Nashville: Broadman & Holman, 1993.

Goldberg, Louis. *Ecclesiastes*. Bible Study Commentary. Grand Rapids, MI: Zondervan, 1983.

Kaiser, Walter C., Jr. *Ecclesiastes: Total Life*. Everyman's Bible Commentary. Chicago: Moody, 1979.

Kidner, Derek. *A Time to Mourn, and a Time to Dance*. Downers Grove, IL: InterVarsity, 1976.

_____. *The Wisdom of Proverbs, Job, and Ecclesiastes: An Introduction to Wisdom Literature*. Downers Grove, IL: InterVarsity, 1985.

Longman, Tremper, III. *The Book of Ecclesiastes*. New International Commentary on the Old Testament. Grand Rapids, MI: Eerdmans, 1998.

Whybray, R. N. *Ecclesiastes*. New Century Bible Commentary. Grand Rapids, MI: Eerdmans, 1989.

Wright, Addison, G. "The Riddle of the Sphinx: The Structure of the Book of Qoheleth." *Catholic Biblical Quarterly* 30 (October–December 1950): 313–34.

SONG OF SOLOMON

MICHAEL RYDELNIK AND TIM M. SIGLER

INTRODUCTION

Title. The title "Song of Solomon" is from the opening words in the Hebrew text, *Shir hashirim asher l'sholomo* (lit., "Song of Songs which belongs to/concerns Solomon"). Many English versions identify the book as Song of Solomon (NASB, AV, RSV, NKJV, KJV), while other versions title the book Song of Songs (NIV, TNIV). The Latin Vulgate translates the Hebrew as *Canticum Canticorum*, or in English, Canticles (Catholic Bibles).

Author. Solomon is identified as the author in the opening verse, "The Song of Songs, which is Solomon's" (*l'sholomo* = "of/concerning Solomon"). Solomon, King David's son (1Kg 2:2-4), ruled Israel during the high point of the united kingdom (970–930 BC) and is a central figure in the book (Sg 1:1, 5; 3:7, 9, 11; 8:11-12). God gave Solomon great wisdom and he spoke 3,000 proverbs, many recorded in the book of Proverbs, plus 1,005 songs (1Kg 4:29-34). This superlative form (Song of Songs) is common in biblical Hebrew, as seen in the phrases "King of kings," "Lord of lords," and "holy of holies." It indicates that of all of Solomon's many songs, these are his best.

Although a great king, Solomon is infamous for his 700 wives and 300 concubines (1Kg 11:3), so it is puzzling that he would write a book extolling faithfulness in marriage. Sadly, many people do not practice the wisdom they know, and this may account for the contradiction between Solomon's wise words and his foolish behavior.

However, though Solomon is a central figure, he may not have written the Song in its final form. As Pr 25:1 describes Hezekiah's men recording Solomon's proverbs well after his time, so too the Song may be a later recollection of Solomon's love poems. That Solomon wrote numerous such songs is clear from 1Kg 4:29-34. Regardless, Solomon's songs of love were not based on his own experience but rather intended to depict an "ideal" marriage.

Date. The book was probably composed while Solomon was king (970–930 BC) or some time shortly thereafter. Although it lacks the historical reference points found in the Pentateuch, Prophetic Books, and many of the Psalms, the interpretation of the Song does not depend upon chronology.

Theme and Purpose. Like Ps 45, which is titled "A Song of Love" and celebrates a royal wedding, the Song is a celebration of marital love. Its association with Solomon allows it to be read in light of other wisdom books as both a song of celebration and caution—celebrating divinely created and encouraged marital love as well as cautioning against its misuse or exploitation. Just as Solomon repeatedly pleaded with future Davidic rulers, employing the phrase "my son" throughout Pr 1–7, the Song cautions the "daughters of Jerusalem" to be wise about sexuality (Sg 2:7; 3:5; 8:4). Thus the Song may be read as a female counterpart to Proverbs. Sadly, though Solomon did not always follow the wisdom of Proverbs or the Song, God did use him to write of both wisdom and love despite his failures.

The Song borrows imagery from plant and animal life, food and beverage, geography, colors, fragrances, and many other aspects of the natural order that idealize a paradise-like landscape, reminiscent of the garden of Eden. Marital love, though tainted and troubled by the fall, is still a part of God's creation and a good gift intended for husband and wife to fully enjoy.

Despite the Song's obviously sensual content, it should not be reduced to a manual on romantic love. The Song warns those who would approach sexuality carelessly that "love is as strong as death, jealousy is as severe as Sheol" (8:6). These very cautions found throughout the Song demonstrate that it is overwhelmingly a celebration of marital love.

Therefore, the major purpose of the Song is to exalt the love and marriage between a husband and wife. Like Hosea and Proverbs, this book teaches the importance of faithful, pure love in marriage, which is also reflected in the NT: "Marriage is to be held in honor among all, and the marriage bed is to be undefiled" (Heb 13:4).

In addition to the depiction of the celebration of ideal marital love, as Hamilton maintains, its secondary purpose could also be to symbolize the messianic hope of recovery of spiritual intimacy after the alienation of sin (J. M. Hamilton, Jr., "The Messianic Music of the Song of Songs: A Non-Allegorical Interpretation," *WTJ* 68 [2006]: 331).

Genre. The Song is written in Hebrew poetry. Although called "Song," the Hebrew word refers to a poem, much more like a sonnet than a musical composition. This literary style, found throughout the OT, is rich in repeated words, linguistic patterns, and parallelism. As poetry, the Song is built on imagery and symbolism, intended to portray themes and ideas outside the scope of the literal descriptive words (e.g., "Your teeth are like a flock of newly shorn ewes . . .", 4:2). Robert Gordis notes the significance of the use of poetry: "The essence of poetry employs symbolism, not allegory, to express nuances beyond the power of exact definition. . . . The language of symbolism, on the other hand, is superior to literal speech as well, because its elements possess both existential reality and a representational character" (*The Song of Songs and Lamentations*, revised edition [New York: Ktav, 1974], 36–38).

Interpretation. Scholars and theologians have offered numerous suggestions to understand the challenging poetic message of the Song. Their presuppositions determine how the book is understood.

First, allegory has historically been the most common approach to the Song. Jewish tradition sees it as a story of God's love for Israel. Christian tradition has seen it as Christ's love for the Church. Although love is a key element in the Song, forcing an allegory strains the message of the text and imposes arbitrary meanings. Therefore, allegory has generally been rejected by modern scholarship as a valid approach to the Song.

Second, it is common to interpret the Song as a drama. As a drama, Solomon and the Shulammite (see comments at 6:13 for this name) have the main roles with a chorus as minor speakers. The lack of plotline in the Song and the subjective imposition of scenes make a dramatic reading forced. Most importantly, full-fledged dramatic literature of this type was not known among the ancient Israelites.

Third, some critical scholars see the Song as a sacred marriage story drawn from ancient pagan Near Eastern fertility cults. However, annual fertility rituals are absent from the Song. Furthermore, it is doubtful that the sacred monotheistic Scriptures would borrow from pagan fertility rituals.

Fourth, a common current interpretation of the genre of the Song is that it is an anthology of love poems. The Hebrew title of the book provides readers with a literary clue to the book's genre—and therefore its interpretation. *Shir Hashirim* (the Song of Songs) is a collection of love poems or a song composed of many songs—thus a "song of songs." Those who differ with this interpretation argue it fails to see the intrinsic unity in the Song as well as the intertextual links within it.

Fifth, recently it has been again suggested that the Song should be read as a messianic document. John Sailhamer and James Hamilton have both argued that the Song was written from a messianic perspective in order to nourish a messianic hope.

Sailhamer views the Song as an allegory not of Messiah's love for the Church, but for His love for divine wisdom. He cites "Beneath the apple tree I awakened you . . ."(8:5b) as an intertextual reference to the prologue of the book of Proverbs and the fall in Gn 3 (J. H. Sailhamer, *NIV Compact Bible Commentary* [Grand Rapids, MI: Zondervan, 1994], 359–60). In his view the beloved is understood as "wisdom" and Solomon represents the promised seed of Gn 3:15.

Hamilton proposes a more likely messianic view. He posits a nonallegorical but symbolic interpretation, with King Solomon, as the son of David, representing "the ultimate expression of David's royal seed . . . the Davidic king, with all the messianic connotations that status carries" (Hamilton Jr., "The Messianic Music of the Song of Songs," 331). Hamilton sees the theme of the Song as the "recovery of intimacy after alienation, which appears to match the hope engendered by Gn 3:15 for a seed for the woman who would come as the royal Messiah to restore the gladness of Eden" (339-40).

After demonstrating the development of this theme of recovered intimacy through the Song, Hamilton points out that "I am my beloved's, And his desire is for me" (Sg 7:10) functions as the climax to the Song, using the same word for "desire" as in Gn 3:16. This word (Hb. *tesuqah*) is used only three times in the Hebrew Bible (Gn 3:16; 4:7; Sg 7:10). The first two uses refer to the alienation of the fall. Thus the Song appears to be making a direct allusion to the alienation found in the curse of Gn 3:16, suggesting that the messianic king will ultimately reverse the curse on the woman.

These views notwithstanding, it remains best to understand the Song as primarily a poetic presentation of a biblical view of ideal love and marriage. This is not to treat the book as a sex manual, but rather as divine guidance for the most sacred earthly relationship created by God. It treats marital love as a spiritual creation. Roland Murphy correctly concludes that "the eventual canonization of the work . . . can best be explained if the poetry originated as religious rather than secular literature" (Roland E. Murphy, *A Commentary on the Book of Canticles or the Song of Songs*, Hermenia—A Critical and Historical Commentary on the Bible [Minneapolis: Augsburg Fortress Press, 1990], 94–95). Love and marriage are divinely ordained and not mere cultural mores.

Unity and Structure. Scholars approach the structure of the Song in two ways. The first holds that the Song is a loose collection of songs/poems without a chronological or narrative flow. The second maintains that there is a logical flow of thought, based on a chiastic structure, suggesting a subtle, almost dramatic, progression.

Regarding the first approach, while the Song is often seen as a loose collection of songs/poems, the scholars who hold this view do not see it as completely devoid of order. The repeated refrains (2:7; 3:5; 8:4) and parallel structures (2:10-13 with 7:12-13; 2:14 and 17 with 8:13-14; 3:1-5 with 5:2-8; 3:6-11 with 5:9-16; and 4:1-7 with 6:4-10) indicate an internal coherence and structural unity in relation to its themes. Those who interpret the Song as an anthology of love poems identify the various poems as follows:

1. Title / Superscription (1:1)
2. Rejoicing in You (1:2-4)
3. The Black Beauty and Her Brothers (1:5-7)
4. A Lovely Mare (1:8-11)
5. Sensual Scents (1:12-14)
6. Beautiful Darling, Handsome Beloved (1:15-17)
7. Flowers, Fruit, and Trees (2:1-7)
8. A Gazelle in Springtime (2:8-17)
9. Searching for Her Love (3:1-5)
10. Solomon's Wedding (3:6-11)
11. His Descriptive Song of Beauty (4:1-7)
12. The Garden of Love (4:8–5:1)
13. Searching for Her Love Once More (5:2–6:3)
14. Comparable but Ultimately Unique (6:4-10)
15. In the Orchard (6:11-12)
16. The Dancing Shulammite (6:13–7:10)
17. Her Invitation to the Countryside (7:11-13)
18. A Song of Yearning (8:1-4)
19. More Powerful than Death (8:5-7)
20. Brothers (8:8-10)
21. My Vineyard Is Mine Alone (8:11-12)
22. Be Like a Gazelle! (8:13-14)

Nevertheless, the book's multiple intertextual links argue against this anthological interpretation (a loose collection of poems) but rather reflect an internal unity. First, the same characters appear and speak throughout the book: the maiden, the lover, and the daughters of Jerusalem. Second, similar figures of speech are used throughout: e.g., love is better than wine (1:2; 4:10); fragrant perfume (1:3, 12; 3:6; 4:10); lovely cheeks (1:10; 5:13); eyes like doves (1:15; 4:1); teeth like sheep (4:2; 6:6); admonitions for purity (2:7; 3:5; 8:4); gazelles (2:9, 17; 8:14); Lebanon (3:9; 4:8, 11, 15; 7:4). Third, the book is united by the rich, consistent poetic imagery of flora, fauna, fragrance, and color, suggesting the beauty of Eden.

David A. Dorsey correctly maintains, "The sophistication and homogeneity of the Song's surface-structure design strongly suggests a unified poem that was composed by a single author" (*The Literary Structure of the Old Testament* [Grand Rapids, MI: Baker, 1999], 213). Dorsey's chiastic outline demonstrates the symmetry that many interpreters have observed in the Song.

A Opening words of mutual love and desire (1:2–2:7)
  B Young man's invitation to the young woman to join him in the countryside (2:8-17)
    C Young woman's nighttime search for the young man (3:1-5)

D The crest: their wedding day (3:6–5:1)
C' Young woman's nighttime search for the young man, and their speeches of admiration and longing (5:2–7:10)
B' Young woman's invitation to the young man to join her in the countryside (7:11–8:4 [7:12–8:4])
A' Closing words of mutual love and desire (8:5-14)

The A, B, and C sections reflect the courtship phase of this ideal marriage; D is the focal point of the poetic book and focuses on the actual wedding, while C', B', and A' describe the maturation of marital love in an ideal marriage. The interpretation that will undergird this commentary is that the book is a collection of love poems arranged or structured to depict these three phases of marriage: courtship (1:1–3:5), wedding (3:6–5:1), and maturation of marital love (5:2–8:4).

Background. As part of the Hebrew Bible, the Song is one of the *megillot* (scrolls) in the Writings section. The book had early acceptance and was included in the LXX translation. The Mishnah indicates certain portions of the Song were used during the Passover festival celebrated in the temple before AD 70 (*Ta'anit* 4:8).

In AD 90, the rabbinic scholars of Yavneh debated the Song, not regarding its inclusion, because it was already included, but rather re-examining it to verify its canonical status. There, Rabbi Akiba upheld the Song's divine inspiration using allegorical interpretation as a means to justify its spiritual value (cf. Gleason L. Archer, Jr., *A Survey of Old Testament Introduction* [Chicago: Moody, 2007], 541).

Although not quoted in the NT, the early Church recognized the Song as Scripture. The Church fathers attested to its canonicity and interpreted it primarily as an allegory. Throughout Church history, the Song has stimulated debate.

A longstanding objection to the Song's canonicity is that the name of God is used only once (8:6). Yet the name of God does indeed appear in the book. Moreover, having the name of God in the text is not a criterion for inclusion in the canon—the canonical book of Esther lacks the name of God in its text.

Critical scholars also object that the language of the Song is too descriptive of physical characteristics and sexual intimacy. In response, the Song does indeed include references to sexual intimacy and romantic love in poetic form; but these images have been given exaggerated sexual meaning by some recent interpreters. Despite the Song's obviously romantic content, it should not be reduced to a sex manual. The Song warns against approaching sexuality irresponsibly (cf. 2:7; 8:4, 6). Instead, the book is overwhelmingly a celebration of marital love.

Despite these objections to the Song's place in the canon, it can confidently be recognized as a canonical book. The Song should be read as God's Word on wisdom applied to marriage.

OUTLINE

The chiastic structure (see above on Unity and Structure) of the Song reflects a subtle "beginning-middle-end" arrangement, progressing from courtship (A, B, C), to wedding (D), to the maturing of the marriage (C' B' A'). The outline below reflects that view of the structure, and is the one on which this commentary is based.

I. Courtship: the Beginning of the Relationship (1:1–3:5)
  A. Introduction of Solomon and the Shulammite (1:1-11)
    1. Superscription: Song of Solomon (1:1)
    2. The Shulammite (cf. 6:13) Longs for Solomon (1:2-4)
    3. The Shulammite Is Insecure about Her Beauty (1:5-7)
    4. The Shulammite Is Praised by Solomon (1:8-11)
  B. Growth of Love between Solomon and the Shulammite (1:12–3:5)
    1. The Shulammite and Solomon Describe and Praise One Another (1:12–2:6)
    2. The Refrain of Warning to the Daughters of Jerusalem (2:7)
    3. The Shulammite and Solomon in the Country (2:8-17)
    4. The Shulammite's Fear of Losing Solomon (3:1-4)
    5. The Refrain of Warning to the Daughters of Jerusalem (3:5)

II. Wedding: the Consummation of the Relationship (3:6–5:1)
   A. The Wedding Procession (3:6-11)
   B. The Wedding Night (4:1–5:1)
      1. The Beauty of the Shulammite, the Bride (4:1-7)
      2. The Request of Solomon, the Groom (4:8)
      3. The Praise of the Bride's Beauty by the Groom (4:9-11)
      4. The Praise of the Bride's Purity by the Groom (4:12-15)
      5. The Consummation of the Marriage by the Bride and Groom (4:16–5:1)
III. Marriage: the Maturation of the Relationship (5:2–8:4)
   A. The Problem and Resolution of Indifference (5:2–6:13)
      1. Apathy and Absence (5:2-8)
      2. Renewed Affection and Attractiveness (5:9-16)
      3. Affirmation of Affection in the Garden (6:1-3)
      4. Restoration of Intimacy (6:4-13)
   B. The Expression of Maturing Love (7:1-10)
      1. The Wife Is Praised for Her Beauty (7:1-6)
      2. The Husband Expresses His Desire for His Wife (7:7-9a)
      3. The Mutual Expression of Desire and Commitment (7:9b-10)
   C. The Wife's Longing for Intimacy (7:11–8:4)
      1. Her Initiation of Intimacy (7:11-13)
      2. Her Desire for Greater Intimacy (8:1-4)
IV. Conclusion (8:5-14)
   A. The Strength of Love between a Husband and Wife (8:5-7)
   B. The Continuing Love between Solomon and the Shulammite (8:8-14)

COMMENTARY ON SONG OF SOLOMON

The book opens by introducing Solomon, the author, followed by a series of songs describing the courtship (1:1–3:5) between the king (1:1, 4, 16) and a young woman. She is later identified with the title "the Shulammite" (see the explanation at 6:13) and, for the sake of clarity, will be called this throughout this commentary. From the beginning of the book there is a chorus of "we" (1:4b), the "daughters of Jerusalem" (1:5), who reiterate key ideas. Most notably, this section describes the growth of love between Solomon and the Shulammite prior to marriage and before their marital consummation.

I. Courtship: the Beginning of the Relationship (1:1–3:5)

A. Introduction of Solomon and the Shulammite (1:1-11)

1. Superscription: Song of Solomon (1:1)

1:1. The first words in the Hebrew text, *shir hashirim*, introduce the work as "**Solomon's** best song" or "**Song of** all **Songs.**" This superlative form (singular noun + article + plural version of the same noun) is also seen in the phrases "King of kings," "Lord of lords," and "holy of holies." Of all of Solomon's many songs (cf. 1Kg 4:32), these lyrics make up his very best.

2. The Shulammite (cf. 6:13) Longs for Solomon (1:2-4)

1:2-4. The woman expresses her romantic desires for Solomon (**The king**) in a poem of invitation that focuses on his many attractive qualities (his **kisses**, **his mouth**, his **love**, his **fragrance**, and even his **name**). The verb in the clause **the king has brought me into his chambers** should be translated as a precative perfect indicating longing or request, not an accomplished event. Therefore, the phrase should be translated "O that the King would bring me into his chambers" (cf. HCSB). This is a better understanding because their wedding would not be consummated until a future time.

The **daughters of Jerusalem** (cf. 1:5; 3:10; 5:8, 6) approve: **We will rejoice in you and be glad** (1:4b), and **extol** the appropriateness of her love for him. **Better than wine** (v. 2) and **more than wine** (v. 4), a frequent image in the Song (1:2, 4; 4:10; 5:1; 7:2, 9; 8:2), suggests their relationship is more enjoyable than the joy of wine (Pr 5:18-19). In Scripture, wine is associated with gladness (Ps 104:15; Zch 10:7) and worship (Ex 29:40; Nm

15:1-10). In the Song, wine is always mentioned positively (Sg 1:2, 4; 4:10; 5:1; 7:2, 9; 8:2). This opening indicates a physical longing of unfulfilled romantic love; such desire is a good gift from God when expressed within the bounds of His moral values.

3. The Shulammite Is Insecure about Her Beauty (1:5-7)

1:5-7. The woman addresses the **daughters of Jerusalem** to whom she defends her appearance as well as introduces her brothers, who have contributed to her self-neglect by sending her to perform a task normally assigned to men within this ancient culture (vv. 5-6). **My own vineyard** is a metaphor for "my body, femininity, or womanly charm." The brothers do not reappear in any other poem until the close of the Song in 8:8 where they again are not mentioned positively. Even here she distances herself from them by calling them **my mother's sons**. Thus, the brothers are mentioned here as part of the city motif that is often an obstacle to the lovers within the Song. They, like other onlookers, are not helpful or approving of the young woman's romantic interest. The woman compares her sun-darkened skin to two exotic and luxurious dark images: the Bedouin **tents of Kedar** (constructed of black goat hair) and **the curtains of Solomon**. Solomon's curtains are described in 2Ch 3:14, "He made the veil of violet, purple, crimson and fine linen, and he worked cherubim on it." Like these exotic furnishings, the woman is at once dark yet beautiful. Her self-description as **black** says nothing of her ethnicity or origin from any place outside of Israel. Here the thought is clearly of skin that has become blackened by the sun and not of a possible African origin. Though she has not enjoyed the pampering of the more sophisticated daughters of Jerusalem, the rustic maiden is aware of her own charm. In v. 7, she wants to know **where** her beloved is pasturing his **flock** and where he will rest **at noon**. It was a common practice for shepherds to rest during the heat of the day. Her description of **one who veils herself** means she does not want to be without Solomon, looking sad and dressing as a person in mourning (Ezk 24:17, 22).

4. The Shulammite Is Praised by Solomon (1:8-11)

1:8-11. Like lovers in other generations or cultures, this couple speaks in imaginary terms in which they at times give themselves make-believe identities (e.g., shepherds, peasants, animals, brother and sister—and at other times as royalty). The images of shepherd and shepherdess have caused confusion for interpreters, but ancient kings often identified with this trade and idealized it. As if a shepherd, the man responds playfully and invites her to come looking for him. While comparing a woman to a horse is no compliment in the modern age, the point is that the woman is like one female horse (**My mare**) entering the company of many male chariot horses—completely distracting! The mention of **Pharaoh** continues the Song's royal imagery and is followed by lavish descriptions of her appearance. In v. 11, the daughters of Jerusalem (**We**, cf. 1:5) say they will make beautiful jewelry, **ornaments of gold** and **silver** for her—a distinct change of opinion from their prior mocking (cf. 1:6).

B. Growth of Love between Solomon and the Shulammite (1:12–3:5)

This section shows the progression of the courtship in a series of shorter poems. Their attraction to and longing for each other intensifies throughout the section.

1. The Shulammite and Solomon Describe and Praise One Another (1:12–2:6)

1:12-14. Appealing fragrances provide the theme for this three-verse poem. First, the woman's **perfume** (nard) gives off its scent. Her lover is then likened to a sachet of fragrant **myrrh** lodged between her breasts, and further to **a cluster of henna blossoms in the vineyards of Engedi**—a tropical oasis in the rough Judean desert close to the Dead Sea that was known for producing aromatic plants. Likewise, she was surrounded by the pleasant thoughts of her beloved. In addition to the sensation of smell, Engedi's topographical appearance also contributes visually to the poem: it is a refreshing oasis that might serve as an ideal location for lovers.

1:15-17. A key to romance in the Song and in life is the giving and receiving of kind words of appreciation. While many translations insert headings to suggest who is speaking throughout the Song, at times it is impossible to be certain who it is. The NASB consistently translates the female lover as **darling** (Hb. *ra'ayah*, or *ra'ayati*, "my darling") and the male as **beloved** (Hb. *dod*, or *dodi*, "my beloved"). The couple's dialogue of mutual admiration takes place on a **luxuriant** (lit., "green") **couch** (or bed) in a house **of cedars** (idealizing a nature scene with fragrant flora). **Eyes** like **doves** are mentioned in 1:15; 4:1; and 5:12. In each instance the eyes are appreciated for some quality also shared by doves—perhaps their softness or the way they flutter.

2:1-4. The woman compares herself to a flower and her lover to an apple tree. The exact identification of the flowers in vv. 1-2 is debatable. She implies that she is fruitful—a wild flower of the fertile **Sharon** plain (a lush, fertile area on Israel's Mediterranean coast; cf. Is 33:9; 35:2), a **lily of the valleys** (the definite article is absent from the Hb. text). The man answers in Sg 2:2 by insisting that she is more than a lily among other lilies. She is **like a lily among the thorns** in comparison to other girls. She responds appreciatively in praise of his uniqueness, stating that he is **like an apple tree** (perhaps better translated "apricot" because there is no evidence apples were grown in Israel in antiquity) among the more simple non-fruit-bearing **trees of the forest** (v. 3).

This poem reveals several especially important requirements for a developing relationship. First, women value a sense of protection. Sitting in **shade** is an image of protection throughout the Scriptures (cf. Ps 36:7; 91:1; Is 16:3). Second, couples need to cultivate the joy of being together. The Shulammite enjoyed his company, taking **great delight** and sitting with him. Third, couples should cultivate a growing knowledge of each other. The importance of intimate personal experience is captured in the image of **his fruit** of the **apple tree** being **sweet** to her **taste** (cf. Ps 34:8). This depicts an in-depth interpersonal involvement, short of sexual intimacy. Fourth, couples need public commitment. Solomon publicly proclaimed his love for her by bringing her into his **banquet hall**. Here he declared his love with a **banner** (Hb. *degel*, a flag or ensign used to identify or direct troops). Flying the **banner** indicated possession and leadership. The intimacy and commitment of courtship are developed by these expressions of protection, communication, knowledge, and dedication, building a strong sense of security and self-worth for a future stable marriage. (These four principles were developed from the observations of Jack Deere, "Song of Songs," BKCOT edited by John F. Walvoord and Roy B. Zuck [Wheaton, IL: Victor Books, 1985], 1014–15).

2:5-6. She described her emotional reaction as **lovesick**, being consumed by love. She communicated her condition by requesting **raisin cakes** and **apples** (or apricots, cf. 2:3), ancient symbols of love, to give her strength. As they approached marriage, the Shulammite longed for her beloved, desiring **his left hand** under her **head** and his **embrace** (lit., "caressing") with the **right hand**, signaling her readiness and anticipation of physical affection in their future marriage (cf. 8:3).

2. The Refrain of Warning to the Daughters of Jerusalem (2:7)

This unit concludes with the first of three refrains of admonition (2:7; 3:5; 8:4). These adjurations function as structural markers in the book, indicating the end and beginning of units of thought.

2:7. I adjure you (placing the **daughters of Jerusalem** under oath and requesting their promise) suggests that love is a serious matter and should not be entered into foolishly or casually. If the virgin girls of Jerusalem are to enjoy the type of relationship described in the Song, they should be careful not to **arouse or awaken** sexual passions prematurely. **Until she** (better, "it") **pleases** suggests the appropriate time for such enjoyment. Forcing or hurrying sexual experience can bring disastrous results and should be reserved for the time it can develop naturally within the security and faithfulness of the marriage covenant. Wild animals associated with fertility, **the gazelles** and **hinds** (does) **of the field**, were called on as witnesses to this oath—perhaps as a circumlocution to continue the Song's avoidance of the divine name.

3. The Shulammite and Solomon in the Country (2:8-17)

2:8. The Song often portrays the couple as either together in joyful companionship or apart in longing anticipation—emotionally expressed in terms of desire and fulfillment. They look forward to their reunion and the exciting intimacy of marriage. In v. 8 the two have been apart but are now within sight, and their reunion is cause for elation. The woman compares her lover to a gazelle or a young stag leaping **on the hills**—a motif repeated at the beginning and end of 2:8-17, providing an enclosing structure (*inclusio*) that sets off the poem as a distinct unit. The poem portrays a couple excited with the anticipation of marrying and consummating their marriage, but facing certain fears, awkwardness, and obstacles that they eventually overcome.

2:9-13. She imagines her lover's journey like the actions of a quick and agile **gazelle or a young stag** (v. 9; see also v. 17; 8:14). She cannot wait for his arrival, and he is making no detours in his undistracted determination to reach her quickly. While the mountains and hills are correctly understood as obstacles, her lover dances rapidly over them in order to enjoy her company.

On his arrival, he waits outside her family home, **standing** . . . **looking** . . . **peering through the lattice**, anxious for their reunion (v. 9). From here, he offers the invitation (vv. 10-14), beckoning his lover to join him in the countryside. He assures her that nature's seasonal indicators make it evident that their **time has arrived** (v. 12). The idyllic nature descriptions are reminiscent of the garden of Eden.

Our land (v. 12) hints at the theological dimension of Israel's connection to the land as promised to the patriarchs and their descendants. Their land, then, is the ideal place for them to be, the spring is the ideal time for them to be there, and the couple view each other as the ideal people to be enjoying all that the land has to offer as it becomes their lovers' paradise.

2:14. Verse 14 climaxes the springtime poem as the lover pleads with his beloved to accept his invitation to their countryside rendezvous. His pet name for her is **my dove**, a bird that loyally bonds with its mate for life (cf. 1:15; 2:14; 4:1; 5:2, 12; 6:9). Doves often sought refuge **in the clefts of the rock, in the secret place of the steep pathway**, and he wanted to be with his beloved in such a secluded place. Her beloved's encouraging words reassure her, and she is overcome with a sense of security and desire for him (2:16-17). In time she is able to confidently assert, "My beloved is mine, and I am his" (v. 16; cf. 6:3).

2:15-17. Walled and tree-lined **vineyards** provided seclusion and natural protection from view along with the fragrance of blossoming vines (cf. 2:13)—ideal for romantic encounters. But the image of **little foxes** living in a vineyard and damaging the tender blossoms is a warning to **catch** relationship problems before they damage the growing bonds of deeper intimacy. Lovers must protect themselves from such harmful elements. The poem concludes with the woman's restatement of mutual belonging (**My beloved is mine, and I am his**, v. 16) and her inviting call (reminiscent of v. 9) encouraging him to be like **a young stag** and speed his way to her.

4. The Shulammite's Fear of Losing Solomon (3:1-4)

3:1-4. After their time of courtship in the country, perhaps Solomon left the Shulammite and returned to Jerusalem. The woman recounts a repeated experience in which **night after night** she **sought him** in what is probably a dream scene or a nightmare. During their betrothal, she was longing to have and to hold her groom and felt she could no longer endure their separation. In the dream, her unmet desire was so great that it drove her out into the dangerous nighttime city streets and squares. Since criminals and prostitutes are normally found in such areas at night (cf. Pr 7:8, 12), **the watchmen who make the rounds in the city** were unhelpful in her quest as seen even more clearly in the parallel scene at 5:2-8. When they **found** her, in her urgency she took the initiative to question them: **Have you seen him whom my soul loves?** These bold actions illustrate how the powerful force of romantic love can drive people to risk their safety, security, and status in society. The Song alludes to several obstacles to committed lovers (e.g., family members in 1:6 and 8:8-9; relational conflicts in 2:15; or a disapproving public in 8:1-2), but she is allowing nothing to diminish her love for him.

Her actions on finding him seem odd to modern readers: **I held on to him and would not let him go until I had brought him to my mother's house, and into the room of her who conceived me**. These strange actions should not be mistaken for the brazenness of prostitutes (cf. Pr 7:13; Hs 2:7). Rather, in the retelling of her dream she is indicating that the marriage covenant is the appropriate response to romantic desire. She does not want anything to separate them until they can wed and consummate their marriage. The **mother's house** is mentioned twice in the Song and two other times in the OT (Sg 3:4; 8:2; Gn 24:28; and Ru 1:8)—all in the context of marriage. In the ancient Near East, it was often the mother who arranged the wedding.

5. The Refrain of Warning to the Daughters of Jerusalem (3:5)

3:5. This refrain concludes the courtship section (1:1–3:5) and transitions to the wedding portion of the Song (3:6–5:1). Her adjuration to the **daughters of Jerusalem** has the effect of charging them not to **arouse or awaken** sexual passions before they can be consummated in marriage (cf. 2:7; 8:4). This exhortation is a reminder for contemporary singles that sexual purity can be maintained more readily if sexual experimentation is avoided until sexual expression can be legitimately fulfilled in marriage.

II. Wedding: the Consummation of the Relationship (3:6–5:1)

In ancient Israel, marriages were arranged by parents (e.g., Gn 24:1-67). On the day of the wedding there would be procession of the groom to the bride's home (cf. Mt 25:1-13), followed by the wedding ceremony and party. This section depicts the wedding procession (Sg 3:6-11) and the consummation (4:1–5:1).

A. The Wedding Procession (3:6-11)

3:6-11. The focus turns from adjuration (v. 5) to description (vv. 6-11). This poem celebrates the luxurious views of King Solomon's wedding procession using the common poetic device of question and answer: **What is this . . .? Behold, it is . . . .** The descriptions suggest an elaborate convoy of sight and scent featuring the procession of the groom, **King Solomon**, on his **sedan chair** (v. 9; a decorated seat carried on poles).

A number of biblical connections related to temples and royal gardens begin to emerge from this description. The furniture of the tabernacle, like Solomon's chair, was overlaid in **silver** and **gold** (Ex 26:32; 36:36). Similarly, Solomon's palace and temple were constructed from **timber** imported from **Lebanon** (1Kg 5:6; 10:17; 2Ch 2:8, 10), as was his **chair**. The Hebrew term *olah* (**coming up**, Sg 3:6), describing the ascent **from the wilderness**, most likely to Jerusalem, also evokes temple imagery since it is the term for the whole burnt offering that *goes up* as a sweet-smelling aroma to the Lord (e.g., Lv 3:5). That the **columns of smoke** were perfumed **with myrrh and frankincense** (Sg 3:6) and every other spice that was sold recalls the Song's "mountain of myrrh" and "hill of frankincense" (4:6), where these conceptual images integrate temple and garden imagery. Both are places of renewal and fellowship. The poem provides a scene that is at once majestic, luxurious, and holy.

The daughters of Jerusalem (synonymous with Zion) who were cautioned in 3:5 are now encouraged in v. 11: **Go forth, O daughters of Zion, and gaze on King Solomon with the crown with which his mother has crowned him**. These majestic scenes demonstrate the importance of **the day of his wedding**, described here as **the day of his gladness of heart** (cf. Ps 45:1). The heart that yearns with passion for oneness, commitment, and an honorable union is gladdened by marriage.

One must wonder how this wedding Song of gladness and commitment relates to other biblical portraits of King Solomon who was not known for his marital faithfulness. Two explanations may help piece together this puzzle: (1) These love poems, among other things, may be an expression of an idealized marriage extolled by Solomon without necessarily suggesting this was his actual experience. (2) Solomon may have once been a more wise and loyal king in his younger years. But he eventually succumbed to the pressures about which God warned Moses, such as taking wives as guarantees of political treaties (Dt 17:17; 1Kg 11:4). Like many today, Solomon knew far better than he acted. Nevertheless, the biblical ideal of one wife and one husband united for a lifetime in the covenant of marriage is praised and upheld in the Song despite Solomon's tragic legacy concerning the sanctity of marriage.

B. The Wedding Night (4:1–5:1)

1. The Beauty of the Shulammite, the Bride (4:1-7)

Three times in this unit Solomon tells the Shulammite she is beautiful (vv. 1 [twice], 7). Although these comparisons of beauty are unfamiliar to the modern mind, they were lovely poetic images in Solomonic Israel. In this section Solomon praises seven areas of her beauty: eyes, hair, teeth, lips/mouth, temples, neck, and breasts.

4:1-7. Descriptive poems such as this were commonly employed in ancient Near Eastern wedding songs and are still in use in the Middle East today. Such poems praise the wonders of the bride's attractive form, poetically describing her beautiful body part by part and making figurative comparisons in which *x* (one of her physical attributes) is like *y* (a lovely element found in nature). Three poems in the Song describe the woman (4:1-7; 6:4-10; and 7:1-9), and one describes the man (5:10-16). The interpreter must answer the question, How is *x* like *y*? And with poetry, the answers can be many. In light of the cultural and historical distance between the reader and Solomon, modern readers may find these points of comparison strange, yet they were appealing images of beauty in ancient times. Modern lovers can learn much in the Song about the importance of kind words of praise from one another.

The man's praise begins with admiration of his beloved's **eyes** and **hair** (v. 1), and moves to her **teeth** (v. 2), **lips**, **mouth**, and **temples** (v. 3). For further details on the repeated images of hair, teeth, and temples, see the commentary on 6:5-6. Her **hair** is seen as **a flock of goats** moving down **Mount Gilead**, a mountain range east of the Jordan River known for its pastureland (cf. Mc 7:14). From a distance, it would be beautiful to see a herd of black goats cascading down those mountains. Her **eyes** are compared to doves, perhaps because of their softness or the way they flutter. Her **lips**, like a scarlet thread, are red and narrow. Unlike the other items in this list, no simile is employed to describe the woman's **mouth**. He simply states that her mouth is **lovely**—a term of affectionate appreciation.

His positive description descends next to her **neck** (apparently prominent, like David's tower, about which Scripture says nothing else, Sg 4:4) and climaxes with a vivid appreciation of her **two breasts**, which are likened to **twins of a gazelle which feed among the lilies** (v. 5)—probably a reference to the agile animal's soft, supple form, or a view of the pair's rounded hind quarters which became conspicuous when feeding with their heads down. A majority of interpreters understand the description of the two aromatic mountains (**I will go my way to the mountain of myrrh and to the hill of frankincense**) in v. 6 as an elaboration of the man's admiration of his lover's breasts. Verse 7 affectionately summarizes the poem. It reiterates its main idea: **You are altogether beautiful**, and the man sees **no blemish** in her (cf. 5:2). Every husband should view his wife in this way. The standard of beauty should be his love for her, not the shifting cultural norm of appearance or the passing of years. A husband's appreciation of his wife's physical beauty and intrinsic value should be a lifelong hallmark of their relationship (cf. Pr 5:18; Mal 2:14).

2. The Request of Solomon, the Groom (4:8)

4:8. This poem of invitation, description, and acceptance/consummation is often seen as the centerpiece of the entire book. The request to **come** is an invitation to the wedding night. In this section Solomon calls her **my bride** six times (4:8–5:1), indicating a change in relationship from courtship to marriage. The groom requests that his bride join him in consummating their marriage as though she were coming from the distant mountainous wonderland of **Lebanon** near the peaks of **Amana**, **Senir**, and **Hermon**. Unlike the famous Mount Hermon that straddles the borders of modern Israel, Syria, and Lebanon, the exact locations of the peaks of Amana and Senir are debated and were even confused by different groups in Bible times (cf. Dt 3:9). They are likely distinct peaks in the ridge known as Mount Hermon.

3. The Praise of the Bride's Beauty by the Groom (4:9-11)

At this point the bride granted the groom's request to join him and now Solomon praises her physical expression of love for him. The metaphors depict the purity and virginity of the bride prior to the wedding night.

4:9. He is taken captive by her love. She **made my heart beat faster**. Calling his **bride** his **sister** throughout this section (cf. vv. 10, 12; 5:1-2) is an affectionate term for her. It seems to have been a common phrase of endearment between couples in the ancient Near East, and does not indicate a true sibling relationship.

4:10-11. The Hebrew word for **love** (*dod*) is used here for physical expressions of intimate romantic love (cf. 1:2, 4; 5:1; 7:12; Pr 7:18; Ezk 16:8). Intimacy between the husband and wife is **better** than **wine** (cf. Sg 1:2, 4) and the **fragrance** of all kinds of perfume. Her kisses are like **honey** and **milk**, an allusion to the sweetness of the promised land (cf. Ex 3:8; Lv 20:24; Dt 6:3). Her clothing had the **fragrance of Lebanon**, rich with aromatic cedar (1Kg 5:6; Pss 29:5; 92:12; 104:16; Is 2:13; 14:8; Hs 14:5). Their love involves all the senses from sight, to taste, to touch, to smell.

4. The Praise of the Bride's Purity by the Groom (4:12-15)

4:12. The images of a **garden** (cf. 4:12, 15; 5:1; 6:2) **locked** and **spring** (4:12, 15) **sealed up** depict privacy, refreshment, and virginity. It has been observed that "The most obvious feature of the Song of Songs is the sexually explicit nature of the material, sensitively guised in figurative language" (J. Paul Tanner, "The Message of the Song of Songs," *BibSac* 154 [April-June, 1997], 145).

4:13-14. Solomon amplifies the garden metaphor by picturing the beauty of an **orchard**, meaning a park-like, enclosed garden (cf. Neh 2:8; Ec 2:5), not the typical garden where fruit is grown. The bride is compared to a pomegranate (cf. Sg 4:3), **henna** (cf. 1:14), and **nard** (cf. comments on 1:12). **Saffron** is a costly spice made from the pistils of the crocus; **calamus** is possibly sweet cane (cf. Is 43:24; Jr 6:20; Ezk 27:19); **cinnamon** (Ex 30:23; Pr 7:17) was imported from Egypt; **myrrh** (cf. Sg 1:12) and **aloes** were fragrant plants from the Red Sea area. These aromatic, costly spices call to mind the beauty, desirability, and value of the bride.

4:15. She is further described as **a garden spring** (cf. 4:12) and a precious **well of fresh water**, the most valuable resources in Israel's arid climate. This wholesome, fresh, and pure bride is now accessible to Solomon.

5. The Consummation of the Marriage by the Bride and Groom (4:16–5:1)

4:16. This section gives a delicate poetic invitation by the bride to her groom. She wants her **garden** (cf. 4:12) to send out (**breathe out**) an alluring **fragrance** to attract Solomon. She invites her **beloved** to **come into his garden**. The garden that was once hers is now his to enter and enjoy its **choice fruits**, a poetic invitation to sexual union of husband and wife.

5:1. The string of four past-tense verbs in 5:1 (**I have come . . . I have gathered . . . I have eaten . . . I have drunk**) indicates completion and the satisfaction of sexual desire. The garden of sexual delights that was closed to all others in 4:12 is now completely open exclusively for him to enjoy. The repetitive phrases **my garden, my sister, my bride** poetically communicate his feelings of contentment, closeness, and commitment as well as the appropriateness of these emotions since she is *his* bride (repeating the claim of 4:8). While the bride is not his biological sister, the groom employs a common Semitic term of family closeness in calling his beloved his "sister" to express his deep feelings for her. Approval of their union is declared in the closing words of the poem—**Eat, friends; drink and imbibe deeply, O lovers**—which have been attributed by commentators to the daughters of Jerusalem, wedding guests, or even to God Himself as the author of marital love (Gn 2:18-25). Similar approval of sex in marriage is expressed in Pr 5:18-20.

III. Marriage: the Maturation of the Relationship (5:2–8:4)

This section of the Song concerns the couple's maturing marital relationship. After the anticipation of courtship (1:1–3:5) and the delight of the wedding (3:6–5:1), this section provides a template for a maturing marriage. It includes an interpersonal problem and its resolution, showing how couples can learn to resolve difficulties (5:2–6:13). Furthermore, the poems that follow express the deepening of love as the marriage matures (7:1-10) and the deepening of romantic intimacy as the years of marriage progress (contrary to contemporary ideas that romance must decline with familiarity).

A. The Problem and Resolution of Indifference (5:2–6:13)

1. Apathy and Absence (5:2-8)

5:2-8. The Song indicates there are seasons of greater and lesser passion in marriage. Like the parallel poem of 3:1-5, **I was asleep but my heart was awake** describes a dream or a nightmare. The husband affectionately requests her sexual availability: **Open to me, my sister, my darling, my dove, my perfect one!** But she describes how her excuses and hesitation caused his passions to subside and the opportunity to be lost by the time she warmed up to his advances: **I opened to my beloved, but my beloved had turned away and had gone!** (v. 6). Now more appreciative of his desires (**My heart went out to him as he spoke**), she misses him and ventures into the dangerous nighttime **city** to search for him (v. 7). Sadly, watchmen mistake her for a prostitute and, in this nightmare, beat her as a means of crime deterrence. As in the parallel scene of 3:1-5, she charges the **daughters of Jerusalem**, but this time she requests their assistance: **If you find my beloved, as to what you will tell him: For I am lovesick** (v. 8).

2. Renewed Affection and Attractiveness (5:9-16)

After the dream, the Shulammite realizes how much she loves and desires her husband, and gives a loving description of him.

5:9-16. Her adjuration elicits questions from the daughters of Jerusalem (v. 9; cf. v. 16): **What kind of beloved is your beloved . . . that thus you adjure us?** In other words, they ask, what is so special about your lover that you so desperately seek our help? Their question in turn prompts her to offer the descriptive poem of vv. 10-16 within the larger poem of 5:2–6:3. This is the second of four poems of description in the Song and the only one in which the man is described (see comments on 4:1-7; 6:4-10; 7:1-9). She states that he stands out uniquely in a group of even **ten thousand** other men and describes **his head, locks** of hair, **eyes, cheeks, lips, hands, abdomen, legs**, overall **appearance**, and **mouth**—concluding that **he is wholly desirable**. The description of the man as **dazzling** may be because of his clear complexion. He is described as **ruddy** (Hb. *adom*), a word that often means "red" or "a burnished dark color" like the stony land of Edom, whose mountains and crags are a reddish color. His **head** (v. 11a), like pure gold, is impressive and without defect. Ruddy cannot be a reference to red hair, as v. 11 compares his **locks** to clusters of ripe dates that are **black as a raven**. Just as the groom compares the bride's eyes to doves in 1:15 and 4:1, so the bride likens his **eyes** (v. 12) to this soft and fluttering creature. Birds, both the raven and the dove, are often impressive and enjoyable to observe. His eyes seem to be calming with a healthy white sclera (thus sitting **beside streams of water** and **bathed in milk**). His **cheeks** (v. 13a), like most Israelite males (Lv 19:27; 21:5), were probably bearded, thus resembling a sprouting bed of herbs. It is uncertain how his **lips** (Sg 5:13b) are to be likened to lilies, but the garden imagery is consistently idealized in the Song. His **hands** (v. 14a), **abdomen** (v. 14b), and **legs** (v. 15a) are likened to strong, firm materials, suggesting his muscular strength and virility. Yet his strong and impressive appearance is tempered by the tender description of his **mouth—full of sweetness** (v. 16a). All this would profit her little if not for his mutual appreciation for and commitment to her. **This is my beloved and this is my friend** (v. 16b). The term **friend** (Hb. *reyah)* is used here in the sense of "intimate companion," "compatriot," "partner in task," and "close friend" (cf. Pr 27:9-10, 14, 17). It is unlikely that a marriage could survive on sexual attraction alone. But even if it could, friendship helps a couple grow in their love for one another and greatly enhances romance.

3. Affirmation of Affection in the Garden (6:1-3)

6:1-2. The couple was originally separated because of the indifference of the beloved (5:2-8). Waking from her dream, the Shulammite realized her love for and need of her husband, and this is expressed in her song of praise (5:10-16). After waking from her dream, the daughters of Jerusalem now offer to assist (6:1) in the poem's original search of 5:6-8. They ask, **Where has your beloved gone, O most beautiful among women?** Her reply employs the garden imagery of 5:1—a metaphor for their sexual delights. This is reminiscent of the garden of Eden where the first human couple was naked and unashamed in their one-flesh union. **My beloved has gone down to his garden, to the beds of balsam, to pasture his flock in the gardens and gather lilies** (6:2). In this context, pasturing (lit., "feeding") refers to the satisfaction of the sexual appetite. Apparently she has found him, and their lovemaking has resumed.

6:3. The words of exclusivity, mutuality, and commitment in 6:3 supply the famous lover's aphorism cited often in Jewish marriage contracts and inscribed on wedding rings: **I am my beloved's, and my beloved is mine**. Above friends and other family (even children, which are not mentioned in the Song), marriage is the only bond that causes two people to become one flesh (Gn 2:24).

4. Restoration of Intimacy (6:4-13)

6:4. The third of the Song's four poems of description is found in 6:4-10 (see comments on 4:1-7; 5:10-16; 7:1-9). Like its counterparts this poem contains many comparisons describing the Shulammite. She is **as beautiful as Tirzah** (a city once chosen as a capital for the northern tribes whose name means "pleasantness" because of its location on a beautiful hill bounded on three sides by a river, the Wadi Farrah), and **as lovely as Jerusalem** (with all of its regal and spiritual nostalgia). The phrase **awesome** (Hb. *ayom*, lit., "terrible or terrifying"; thus "dreaded" in Hab 1:7) **as an army with banners** occurs both in Sg 6:4 and 6:10, each time illustrating how overwhelmed the man is with his **beautiful** bride.

6:5-7. Her **hair is like a flock of goats** [which are often black] **that have descended from Gilead** (perhaps suggesting it cascaded onto her shoulders and was wavy and black). Though the ancients did not possess cosmetic dentistry, and missing **teeth** was a common phenomenon (cf. Ex 21:24, 27; Pr 25:19; Lm 3:16), she had all of hers (her upper and lower teeth matched like **twins, and not one among them** was missing). Her **temples are like a slice of a pomegranate**—perhaps a reference to the rosy color of her cheeks, or as an example of blossoming springtime fruit often associated with sexuality and fertility (see also Sg 4:3, 13; 6:7, 11; 7:12; 8:2), or because of its use in the ancient world as an aphrodisiac, or all of the above.

6:8-10. The Shulammite is uniquely beautiful among every category of women **without number**. There might be **sixty queens** (women married to the king), **and eighty concubines** (women having sexual relations with the king, but not married to him), **and maidens** (young women of marital age, but still virgins; Hb. *almah*, cf. Is 7:14). Yet she alone is called **my perfect one** (Hb. *tam*, "one who is morally innocent and ethically pure, lacking nothing in beauty or strength") and **unique**. She is the most beautiful in the land—none can compare to her.

Harems (**sixty queens and eighty concubines, and maidens without number**) were a fact of life among ancient royalty and their inclusion here is not a biblical sanction of polygamy. Rather, the poem extols her exclusive place in comparison to other women: **But my dove, my perfect one, is unique**. Even in an ancient culture that tolerated polygamy, the biblical ideal of one man and one woman united exclusively in marriage is elevated. God strictly forbade kings, as the example to the nation, from polygamy (Dt 17:17). Although the Scriptures recount that the patriarchs and kings had multiple wives, this should be understood as a true record of events, not a model of family life. Solomon is evaluated negatively for his foreign wives (1Kg 11:1-6), and Scripture reveals numerous details of the domestic strife that entered into the lives of others who were known for their polygamous relationships (cf. the vindictive baby-naming contest between Rachel and Leah in Gn 30; the rivalry between the mothers of Ishmael and Isaac; the emotional trauma brought on by Hannah's co-wife, Peninnah). Some forms of immorality are so obviously against the grain of Scripture that a clear biblical command against such activity is unnecessary. The poem concludes (Sg 6:10) with these other women (v. 9), perhaps the daughters of Jerusalem, echoing the man's praise of his unique lover.

6:11. Like 7:12, this brief poem looks to nature to signal the timing when marital joys should no longer be delayed: **I went down to the orchard of nut trees to see the blossoms of the valley, to see whether the vine had budded or the pomegranates had bloomed**. The blossoming orchards and vineyards indicate to the woman that springtime has arrived (cf. 2:11-13 where "winter is past"), and flora and fauna alike know that it is the season for love. Nature's readiness is symbolic of her own readiness.

6:12. This verse uses common Hebrew words, but the syntax is unusual. (For a deeper look at the issues, see Jill Munro, *Spikenard and Saffron: A Study in the Song of Songs* [Edinburgh: T & T Clark, 1995], 30.) At the end of their reconciliation, the Shulammite (**I, my, my**) picturesquely expresses her joy. Her husband had gone down to her garden (v. 2), and she experienced an affirmation of his love (vv. 4-10). She was enraptured, beside herself with joy: **before I was aware, my soul set me**. In modern language she might have said, "Before I knew what happened, I felt on top of the world." She compares her exaltation to being chief over all of Solomon's great army (1Kg 10:26) of 1,400 **chariots**, overseeing **my noble people** in full view of a crowd. Their reconciliation was complete and public.

6:13. As they left the garden, the onlookers begged them to **come back** (four times) . . . **that we may gaze at you!** They wanted to enjoy her beautiful presence, just as contemporary crowds want celebrities to stay on stage for an encore. And the request for her return appears to come from the daughters of Jerusalem. Earlier, in 6:9, the maidens saw her and called her blessed. Similarly, these local girls do not want their heroine to flee away from view but to return to them so they can continue to delight in her beauty.

Throughout the Song, the female lover is referred to as "my sister," "my bride," "my darling," "my dove," "my perfect one," but only at v. 13 is she identified as (the) **Shulammite**. Opinions abound about how to understand this word: (1) it is the girl's proper name; (2) it is a geographically-based name for the girl (since the letters *l* and *n* can be exchanged in Semitic languages at times, the girl could be from Shunem in the Jezreel Valley—home to the beautiful maiden Abishag in 1Kg 1:3 and the Shunammite woman who fed Elisha in 2Kg 4:8); (3) it is a pet name derived from the root letters of Solomon's name, since she is his counterpart in the love poems (i.e., "the Solomoness"); or (4) it should be translated as "perfect one," since the root word for Solomon and Shulammite, like the word "shalom," means "perfect" or "complete." Views 3 and 4 are the most compelling. They are not mutually exclusive (i.e., they could both be correct) in that the meaning of the words Solomon (Hb. *Shlomo*) and Shulammite (Hb. *Shulamit*) both derive from the root "shalom," meaning "perfect" or "complete." Such a complimentary term for the lovers seems appropriate in the context of the praises they offer one another. View 1 is suspect because this verse would provide the only attestation of the proper name "Shulammite" in biblical or extra-biblical ancient Hebrew (despite the name's popularity in modern Jewish communities). Against view 2, the only other Shunammite women in the Bible are mentioned by that designation. There are no other references to "Shulammite" women, as if from Shulam/Shunem. But the more likely view is that the name is a title using the feminine version of "Solomon." Support for this view is twofold: (1) the presence of the article "the" (Hb. *ha*) indicating that it is a title meaning "Solomon's wife," and (2) the similarity to the Ugaritic designation of Daniel's wife, understood as "Lady Daniel" (for a full discussion of the options, see Marvin H. Pope, *Song of Songs*, AB [Garden City, NY: Doubleday, 1977], 596-598).

While the first lines of Sg 6:13 appear to be the words of the daughters of Jerusalem pleading with the Shulammite to return to them, the final lines of the verse seem to be the woman's reply. No specific **dance** is associated with **two companies** (6:13), but perhaps the imposing sight of two armies about to engage in battle continues the military imagery of 6:4, 10. The modest Shulammite asks why the daughters of Jerusalem would want to gaze at her the way they might at two armies engaged in battle.

The daughters of Jerusalem ask many questions in the preceding context: "what kind?" (5:9), "where?" (6:1), and "who?" (6:10). Now, as if in response, the man poetically defends his choice of the Shulammite.

B. The Expression of Maturing Love (7:1-10)

As a marriage matures, difficulties will arise and should be resolved. Likewise, the expression of love should grow. In this section, Solomon praises his wife's beauty (7:1-6) and then expresses his longing for her (7:7-9a), followed by a mutual expression of love and commitment (7:9b-10).

1. The Wife Is Praised for Her Beauty (7:1-6)

7:1-6. The Song's fourth poem of description is embedded within the larger poem of 6:13–7:10. In the other descriptive poems (4:1-7; 5:10-16; 6:4-10), the descriptions begin at the head with the eyes or hair and descend downward. However, here the man's description begins at his bride's **feet** and ascends to her **hips**, **navel**, **belly**, **breasts**, **neck**, **eyes**, **nose**, **head**, **locks** of hair, stature, breasts again, breath, and mouth. It has been suggested that his attention was drawn to her feet as she danced for him. Her **hips** are likened to artistically designed jewels, likely a reference to their perfect shape. While not specified, the **artist** or master-craftsman hints at God as the creator of all (cf. Pr 8:30 where the same term is used in the context of God's wisdom in creation). He compares her **navel** to **a round goblet which never lacks mixed wine** as a symbol for abundance and that which continuously brings satisfaction (Sg 7:2). Her **belly** is likened to a **heap of wheat** bordered by **lilies**—all images associated with health and fertility. But overwhelmingly he desired to enjoy her **breasts.** He mentions her breasts briefly in v. 3, continues his descriptive poem working his way up her form to her neck, nose, head, hair, and overall stature (vv. 4-7a)—but returns to focus again on her breasts in vv. 7b-8 before concluding with her mouth and lips in v. 9. It is not as though these other body parts are not of interest. Her **neck** is both strong or prominent and beautiful like a tower of ivory (v. 4a); her **nose** is also compared to a tower—this time with geographical locations that protrude just outside of Israel's borders into Lebanon in the north and Damascus to the northeast; her **eyes** are desirable and appropriately moist like the pools of the fertile Transjordanian Medeba Plateau at Heshbon (v. 4b); her **head** crowns her body like the Carmel mountain range that sits prominently on Israel's northern coast (v. 5a); and her **flowing locks** of hair are like **purple threads**—a royal color which captivates the king—even though this does not state that her hair was purple!

2. The Husband Expresses His Desire for His Wife (7:7-9a)

7:7-9a. The husband longs for his wife and refers to her **stature** being **like a palm tree** (Hb. *tamar*), fitting well with his vertically ascending description of the woman's form. This tree was idealized as a symbol of beauty and fertility throughout the ancient Near East because it can grow even in a harsh desert if a water source is available. The palm tree is therefore a fitting image of marriage as a refreshing oasis in a harsh world. He desires to scale the palm tree of her body and enjoy her breasts as if they were fruit to be eaten (v. 8). His description concludes with this statement of determination and a final word about her **mouth**. It is **like the best wine** (v. 9a).

3. The Mutual Expression of Desire and Commitment (7:9b-10)

7:9b-10. The bride responds positively to her groom and picks up on the wine imagery: **It goes down smoothly for my beloved, flowing gently through the lips of those who fall asleep** (v. 9b). While wine is often the precursor to wrongdoing in Scripture (Gn 9:20-27; 19:30-38; Is 28:7), and its excesses cautioned against (Pr 20:1; 23:29-30; 31:4-5), it is also associated with gladness (Ps 104:15; Zch 10:7) and worship (Ex 29:40; Nm 15:1-10). In the Song, wine is always mentioned positively (Sg 1:2, 4; 4:10; 5:1; 7:2, 9; 8:2). Apparently the word **it** at 7:9b in the NASB refers to their kisses and caresses, which were **flowing gently** and **smoothly** between them. The poem concludes (v. 10) with a statement of rightful belonging: **I am my beloved's, and his desire is for me** (similar to 2:16; 6:3).

C. The Wife's Longing for Intimacy (7:11–8:4)

In response to Solomon's praise for the Shulammite and his expression of desire for his beloved, she responds with her longing for intimacy with her husband.

1. Her Initiation of Intimacy (7:11-13)

7:11. Throughout the Song, the husband instigates sexual intimacy and invites his wife to enjoy his advances, but here the wife is the instigator: **Come** . . . **let us** . . . . Such freedom is an indicator of a healthy marriage in which both partners give and receive, instigate and cooperate, invite and accept invitations. And the mutuality shared by the Song's lovers illustrates both the joy of having one's sexual desires met in marriage as well as the joy of being desired sexually in marriage. Thus the Song subtly offers instruction about love for both husbands and wives.

7:12-13. She looked to the signals of the created order to determine the season of love in 6:11. And in 7:12 she invites him to **see whether the vine has budded**. She promises that when he accepts her invitation to the countryside, **There I will give you my love**—the love she has **saved up** for her **beloved**. The **mandrakes** (from the common root word meaning "beloved," Hb. *dod*) are mentioned in this romantic vineyard scene as a love-enhancing aphrodisiac and serve a similar function to the other sweet fruits mentioned throughout the Song (cf. 2:3; 4:13, 16; 8:2). This plant has a sweet bloom and parsnip-like root, often branched in the shape of a man, thus the English name. The Hebrew name, *dudaim*, literally means "love plant," and was considered to possess aphrodisiac qualities (Gn 30:14-16). By pointing out the **fragrance** of **mandrakes**, the Shulammite is saying the atmosphere is right for love. They would share **fruits**, both **new** spring produce, and **old**, dried fruits of the previous spring (e.g., dates, raisins, and apricots, typical delicacies in the Middle East), indicating that their love is creative and fresh, yet familiar and comfortable. It was a love she had **saved up** for her **beloved**.

2. Her Desire for Greater Intimacy (8:1-4)

In this section the Shulammite builds on the initiative described in the previous section and expresses her desire for even greater intimacy with her husband-lover.

8:1. Jewish standards of modesty in the Old Testament era limited public displays of affection to certain family members, but excluded husbands and wives. Therefore the Shulammite wished her husband **were like a brother** so that she could **kiss** him **outdoors**, in public. Here **outdoors** refers not to the remote scenes of the countryside that have often provided privacy for the couple. This location suggests a public place where she was not free to demonstrate her affections without being shamed by others and where disapproving onlookers would **despise** them. However, according to her proposed solution in the poem, if he were merely like a brother, rather than a lover, no shame would be attached to tame displays of affection.

8:2-3. She continues this thought by casting herself in the role of an older sister who would **lead you**—the verb (Hb. *nahag*) is always used of a superior leading an inferior. She would take the initiative and bring him to her **house** and **give** him **spiced wine** (cf. 1:2), made from the juice of **pomegranates** (cf. 4:3), a specifically romantic drink. She openly invites him to totally embrace her, with his **left hand** and **right hand**.

8:4. These hindrances and difficulties prompt the final exhortation refrain: To experience the intimacy that she and her beloved share, the **daughters of Jerusalem** should not stir up sexual passion before the appropriate time but instead reserve such intimacy for their husbands (cf. 2:7; 3:5).

IV. Conclusion (8:5-14)

This final section summarizes the message of the Song, first with a statement on the strength of marital love (8:5-7), and then a summary of the specific love relationship between Solomon and the Shulammite (8:8-14).

A. The Strength of Love between a Husband and Wife (8:5-7)

8:5-7. Various images describe the nature and power of love. First, love is like a **seal**, or signet ring. In the ancient world, this was an engraved stone or metal stamp used to prove ownership and indicate the value of a possession. The Shulammite wanted to be her husband's most valuable treasure. Having the seal over his **heart**, the place of his affections (e.g., Ps 9:1), and over his **arm**, the source of his strength (e.g., Dt 7:19), demonstrated her priority in his life.

Second, love is **as strong as death**. If love is true, nothing can stop love or change love. Third, love, described as **jealousy**, is as **severe as Sheol** (the place of the dead). In English, **jealousy** usually has negative connotations, but in Hebrew (*qinah*) also indicates "ardor, zeal, passion." For example, the Lord is jealous for His people (e.g., Ex 20:4-5; Nah 1:2). Here love is depicted as powerful and inescapable because the **flame of the Lord** Himself is the source of love. This is the only use of God's name in the Song, and is significantly associated with the strength of love. This pictures love's serious intensity and resolute devotion. Fourth, love is pictured as unconquerable (Sg 8:7). It cannot be swept away or drowned by **many waters**. Fifth, love is priceless and cannot be bought by great **riches**.

B. The Continuing Love between Solomon and the Shulammite (8:8-14)

The conclusion of the book looks back on their relationship. First it explains the protection of the girl by her brothers when she was a child (8:8-9). Next it reviews her first encounter with Solomon (8:10-12). The Song ends with statements showing the couple's ongoing intense love (8:13-14).

8:8-10. While families play an important role in protecting girls from sexual harm, the absence of a father in the Song may be the reason the brothers are overzealous in their desire to protect their **sister**—even though she is ready for marriage. A **wall** suggests that she has fortified herself against promiscuity. A **door** suggests easy access, in which case she will need assistance in protecting her purity. But she assures her brothers, **I was a wall**, and then asserts her readiness to give herself only to her marriage partner.

8:11-12. Just as **Solomon** had the prerogative to entrust his literal **vineyard** in **Baal-hamon** (an unknown location), the Shulammite had her **very own vineyard**, a metaphor for her own person, which she would now give to Solomon. The vineyard's name (meaning "lord possessor of abundance") implies that it was fruitful. Solomon **entrusted**, or leased, this to her brothers as **caretakers** (cf. 1:6). **Each one** was required to produce fruit valued at a **thousand shekels of silver**, for which they would be paid wages of **two hundred** shekels each. This vineyard was where the Shulammite first met Solomon.

8:13-14. He asks to hear her **voice—Let me hear it!** And she requests that he make no delay in joining her: **Hurry, my beloved, and be like a gazelle or a young stag on the mountains of spices.** The cautious warnings and acknowledgments of harsh realities are set aside in preference of risking to choose love's joys. The Song concludes on the high note of the lovers' great expectations.

The Song is significant for contemporary readers as a marriage metaphor for the love between God and His people. As such, it can be instructive about the virtues and joys of fidelity to the marriage covenant (see Is 54:6-7; Jr 2:1; Ezk 16; 23; Eph 5:22-33; Rv 19:6-8). The book's poems suggest that marriage—like the gardens of which they speak—can be viewed as a microcosm of the garden of Eden and by extension God's temple. Such harmony and communion between husband and wife is not only reminiscent of the blessings and gifts of God to mankind in Eden (Gn 1–2), but also the fellowship with God that was to be known through the tabernacle and temple (Ps 16:11).

Yet, above all, the Song of Solomon remains significant for understanding human marital love. Frequently, contemporary perspectives toward marriage diminish its value and disrespect the need for permanent commitment. In dramatic contrast, in the Song, Solomon presents an outstanding picture of emotional commitment and physical love between a husband and wife. God's beautiful design for men and women is purity prior to marriage, then a monogamous, sacrificial, passionate loving relationship between one man and one woman for life (Gn 2:24). Solomon described the marriage relationship as God intended it, proclaiming, "This is my beloved and this is my friend" (Sg 5:16).

BIBLIOGRAPHY

Bloch, Ariel, and Chana Bloch. *The Song of Songs: A New Translation with an Introduction and Commentary*. Berkeley: University of California Press, 1998.

Carr, G. Lloyd. *The Song of Solomon: An Introduction and Commentary*. Tyndale Old Testament Commentaries. Downers Grove, IL: InterVarsity, 1984.

Deere, Jack. "Song of Songs." Bible Knowledge Commentary. Old Testament. Edited by John F. Walvoord and Roy B. Zuck. Wheaton, IL: Victor, 1985.

Garrett, Duane. *Song of Songs*. Word Biblical Commentary. Edited by Bruce M. Metzger. Nashville: Thomas Nelson, 2004.

Gledhill, Thomas. *The Message of the Song of Songs*. The Bible Speaks Today. Downers Grove, IL: InterVarsity, 1994.

Glickman, Craig. *Solomon's Song of Love*. West Monroe, LA: Howard, 2004.

Hess, Richard S. *Song of Songs*. Baker Commentary on the Old Testament: Wisdom and Psalms. Grand Rapids, MI: Baker, 2005.

Longman, Tremper, III. *Song of Songs*. The New International Commentary on the Old Testament. Grand Rapids, MI: Eerdmans, 2001.

Munro, Jill. *Spikenard and Saffron: A Study in the Song of Songs*. Edinburgh: T & T Clark, 1995.

Murphy, Roland E. *A Commentary on the Book of Canticles or the Song of Songs*. Hermenia—A Critical and Historical Commentary on the Bible. Minneapolis: Augsburg Fortress Press, 1990.

Pope, Marvin H. *Song of Songs*. Anchor Bible Commentaries. Garden City, NY: Doubleday, 1977.

Roberts, D. Phillip. *Let Me See Your Form: Seeking Poetic Structure in the Song of Songs*. Studies in Judaism. Lanham, MD: University Press of America, 2007.

Tanner, J. Paul. "The Message of the Song of Songs." *Bibliotheca Sacra* 154 (April–June, 1997): 145.

Trible, Phyllis. *God and the Rhetoric of Sexuality*. Overtures to Biblical Theology Series. Philadelphia: Fortress, 1978.

● ● ● ●

ISAIAH

MICHAEL RYDELNIK AND JAMES SPENCER

INTRODUCTION

Author. Some have suggested that the book of Isaiah is the product of multiple authors working independently. They have posited two or three "Isaiahs" normally identified as first, second (or "deutero"), and third (or "trito") Isaiah, whose works were ultimately united into the book as it is now. Generally, first Isaiah corresponds to chaps. 1–39, a section thought to have an Assyrian background. Second Isaiah comprises chaps. 40–55, which are assumed to have a Babylonian background. Third Isaiah is identified as chaps. 56–66, considered to be a postexilic section. The division of Isaiah into three separate parts is based on notoriously difficult to demonstrate stylistic criteria as well as a presumption that predictive prophecy is not possible (John N. Oswalt, *The Book of Isaiah, Chapters 1–39* [Grand Rapids, MI: Eerdmans, 1987], 23–29).

Though the prophecies recorded in the book of Isaiah originated with the prophet himself, the author of the book of Isaiah is more difficult to identify. Early interpreters often identified Isaiah himself as the author of the book. Josephus, an early Jewish historian, suggests, "Now as to this prophet [Isaiah], he was by the confession of all, a divine and wonderful man in speaking truth; and out of the assurance that he had never written what was false, he wrote down all his prophecies, and left them behind him in books" (Josephus, *Antiquities* X, ii). While it is possible that Isaiah recorded his own visions and recorded them in this book, it is also possible that an editor compiled Isaiah's visions into a single work.

In either case, the prophecies of Isaiah would have been transmitted in oral or written form from the preexilic period regardless of when the book was finally compiled. One support for the unity of the book is that every extant version of the book of Isaiah, including the scroll dating to the first century BC found among the Dead Sea Scrolls at Qumran, presents all 66 chapters of Isaiah as a unified whole. That the prophecies originated prior to the exile preserves the predictive nature of Isaiah's oracles and underlines their divine source. Despite those hypotheses positing multiple Isaiahs, the traditional view maintains that the book of Isaiah, whether written by the prophet himself or by an editor who compiled his prophecies, forms an organic whole which stands as a witness to God's exhaustive knowledge and faithfulness.

There are several reasons for maintaining the traditional view of Isaiah's authorship. First, those suggesting chaps. 40–55 have a Babylonian background fail to recognize that oracles against Babylon also occur in chaps. 1–39 (cf. 21:1-10). In fact, the word "Babylon" occurs more frequently in chaps. 1–39 than in 40–55, with nine occurrences in the former and only four in the latter (cf. 13:1, 19; 14:4, 22; 21:9; 39:1, 3, 6-7; 43:14; 47:1; 48:14, 20). The use of "Babylon" in chaps. 1–39 and 40–55 suggests that the identification of 40–55 as Babylonian based on the appearance of this term is wrongheaded.

Second, the recurrence of the name "the Holy One of Israel" throughout the book of Isaiah supports the unity of the book. This title for the God of Israel is only used six times outside of the book of Isaiah (cf. 2Kg 19:22; Pss 71:22; 78:41; 89:19; Jr 50:29; 51:5). But Isaiah utilizes the term 25 times. The phrase is used in chaps. 1–39 (1:4; 5:19), 40–55 (41:14, 16, 20), and 56–66 (60:9, 14). The frequency with which the book of Isaiah uses the term suggests that the holiness of God is central to Isaiah's theology. The title is in accordance with Isaiah's call in which the God who is "Holy, Holy, Holy" (6:3) purifies Isaiah's lips before sending him out as His prophet.

Third, as mentioned above, the Isaiah scroll found at Qumran preserved the book as a unified whole. Fourth, the NT attributes both sections of the book to Isaiah. Note the NT passages and the corresponding portion of Isaiah to which they refer in the chart "Quotation of Isaiah."

Quotation of Isaiah

New Testament Reference	Isaiah Passage Quoted
Matthew 13:14-15	Isaiah 6:9-10
John 12:37-38	Isaiah 53:1
John 12:39-40	Isaiah 6:10

Date. Isaiah's ministry began around 740 BC and ended after the death of Hezekiah around 680 BC. The book was likely written shortly afterward, in the early to middle seventh century. There is no record of Isaiah having a public ministry during the reign of Manasseh, who ascended to the throne of Judah in 697 BC. Various strands of Jewish tradition suggest that Isaiah was killed by King Manasseh. Though the accounts vary in certain details, there are common elements. According to tradition, Manasseh discovered Isaiah hidden in a cedar tree and cut the tree and Isaiah in half, likely referenced in Heb 11:37 (for the accounts of Isaiah's death see *Yebamoth* 49b, *Sanhedrin* X, and the Targum of Isaiah).

If the traditions are correct, Isaiah would have died between 687 and 642 BC. As noted above, the book of Isaiah was likely compiled sometime after the death of Hezekiah in 686 BC, likely in the early to middle seventh century. This dating assumes that the audience of the book was not the same as the audience to whom the prophet Isaiah originally delivered his message. Instead, the message of the prophet was preserved and passed on as a continual reminder, exhortation, and witness to future generations.

Recipients. The book of Isaiah is different from the personal ministry of Isaiah. The book was written for the faithful remnant of Israel in order to engender comfort, hope, and faith in them by reminding them that the Holy One of Israel would judge sin and ultimately comfort and restore Israel according to His promise.

Theme and Purpose. The book of Isaiah covers a great deal of ground in its 66 chapters. Theological themes, including messianic expectation and trusting in God, are discussed and developed throughout this book. While it is difficult to identify a single, unifying theme in the book, it seems appropriate to recognize Isaiah's depiction of God as "the Holy One of Israel" and faithful deliverer of His people as a common element uniting the book. The God of Isaiah is the holy God who faithfully restores His people and fulfills His promises. This understanding of God underlines the book's desire to remind the people of God that living in the presence of a holy, faithful God empowers them to live obedient, joyful, peace-filled lives. It inspires them not to accept that which appears to be prudent, rational, or expedient, but to think with a theological rationale that calls them to trust in God to intervene, to protect, and to rule.

The enduring message of Isaiah is that God's people would continue to live in the knowledge that He is the holy God who delivers those faithful to Him. This message is interwoven in the various discussions about the remnant, the coming Messiah, and the eventual restoration of all creation. Recognizing that God is the holy God who delivers those faithful to Him empowers believers of all generations to live lives of obedience and love regardless of the circumstances in which they find themselves. It continues to remind the faithful to trust in God and to follow Him even when it appears to be irrational, inconvenient, or dangerous.

Structure. In addition to those proposals associated with the historical-critical division discussed above, several proposals for the book of Isaiah's structure have been suggested, based on more thematic analyses. Dorsey, for instance, identifies a chiastic structure, in which themes from one section of the book are mirrored by the same themes in another section. (See chart in David A. Dorsey, *The Literary Structure of the Old Testament: A Commentary on Genesis–Malachi* [Grand Rapids, MI: Baker, 1999], 234.)

Another approach to structure sees the book opening with a prologue (chaps. 1–6) followed by two main sections, the first emphasizing the judgment of Israel and the nations (chaps. 7–35) and the second emphasizing the blessing of Israel and the nations (chaps. 36–66). Both of the main sections contain a narrative about a Davidic king, who is facing a military threat and then receives

Structure of Isaiah

an offer of a sign from God. In the first narrative (chaps. 7–12), the king rejects the sign, so what follows are oracles emphasizing judgment (chaps. 13–35). In the second narrative (chaps. 36–39), the king believes the sign and what follows are narratives emphasizing blessing (chaps. 40–66). See the chart "Structure of Isaiah."

Genre. The book of Isaiah is comprised of several different literary forms. These include the prophetic oracle (chaps. 13–23), autobiographical narrative (chap. 6) and biographical narratives (chaps. 37–39), and visions (chap. 6), as well as various other forms such as prayers and doxologies. Isaiah's oracles generally include either words of judgment or comfort spoken to Israel, Judah, or other groups of people or individuals within Israel and Judah. Phrases such as "thus says the LORD" or "The word of the LORD came to Isaiah" are characteristic introductions to prophetic oracles. Isaiah's oracles also contain predictive prophecy.

Visions are less common within the prophetic literature and often overlap with the autobiographical form. Isaiah's vision in chap. 6 is a good example of the merging of vision and autobiography. Isaiah's call to prophetic ministry was relayed to his audience through the narrative description of his vision of Israel's holy God on His heavenly throne.

Biographical and autobiographical narratives within Isaiah point to the importance of Isaiah's activities and interactions throughout his prophetic ministry. As noted above, Isaiah's call was narrated in an autobiographical style. This narrative authorized Isaiah's prophetic ministry, but it also provides a vivid, compelling picture of God and highlights the significance of Isaiah interaction with the Lord at the beginning of his ministry. The autobiographical and biographical narratives provide a context for the surrounding oracles, offering a framework in which the prophetic pronouncements may be understood.

Background. Isaiah 1:1 places the beginning of Isaiah's ministry during the reigns of Uzziah and Jotham around 750 BC. Uzziah's military campaigns against the Philistines and building projects in Jerusalem (cf. 2Ch 26:6-15) established Judah as an economic and military power. He fortified Jerusalem through the construction of towers "at the Corner Gate and at the Valley Gate and at the corner buttress" (2Ch 26:9). Uzziah also trained and equipped an army of more than 300,000 soldiers to solidify Judah's position as having influence in ancient Near Eastern politics.

Uzziah's success in the early part of his reign may be attributed to his willingness to do "right in the sight of the LORD" (2Ch 26:4). Uzziah's early faithfulness was paired with turmoil in Assyria, a growing power within the ancient Near East. Internal struggles and famines kept the Assyrians from expanding their territory and encroaching on Judah (A. Kuhrt, *The Ancient Near East: c. 3000–300 BC,* II [New York: Routledge, 1995], 490–93). With the Lord's blessing and the absence of competing national entities, Uzziah was able to overcome the Philistines, Meunites, and Ammonites (cf. 2Ch 26:6-8). Despite the Lord's blessing, Uzziah became prideful, overstepped his bounds, and burned incense at the temple. As a result God struck him with leprosy and he was prohibited from entering the temple for the rest of his reign. After Uzziah contracted leprosy, Jotham, Uzziah's son, reigned as king over Judah. Jotham "did right in the sight of the LORD" (2Ch 27:2). Though Jotham's reign was marked by economic and political success, he was not able to institute widespread spiritual reform in Judah, leaving the southern kingdom prosperous financially but spiritually fragile.

Ahaz became king after the death of Jotham (c. 735 BC). Ahaz did not follow the example of Jotham his father. Instead, "He walked in the ways of the kings of Israel; he also made molten images for the Baals. Moreover, he burned incense in the Valley of Ben-hinnom and burned his sons in fire, according to the abominations of the nations whom the LORD had driven out before the sons of Israel. He sacrificed and burned incense on the high places, on the hills and under every green tree" (2Ch 28:2-4). Ahaz's disregard for the Lord did not go unpunished. His reign was characterized by pressure and political scheming as he attempted (and failed!) to maintain the security and independence of Judah.

While Ahaz mistakenly cast his lot with the Baals (false gods of Canaan) and the other enemies of the Lord, the Assyrians were beginning to grow in power under the leadership of Tiglath-pileser III, who reigned in Assyria from 745–727 BC. Under his guidance, Assyria acquired several vassal states from which Assyria received tribute. King Rezin of Damascus and King Pekah of Israel formed an alliance against Assyria in an attempt to resist Assyrian conquest. After Ahaz refused to join the alliance of Rezin and Pekah, the two kings set out to dethrone Ahaz in order to place a king on the throne of Judah who would join with them against Assyria. The campaign against Ahaz was devastating to Judah (cf. 2Ch 28:6-8). The attacks of Rezin and Pekah combined with Edomite invasions eventually prompted Ahaz to enlist the help of Tiglath-pileser III and the Assyrians to defeat Rezin and Pekah. But while Ahaz was no longer in danger from Syria and Israel, Tiglath-pileser III turned Judah into an Assyrian vassal state (cf. 2Kg 16:7-18).

Judah continued its downward spiral under the leadership of Ahaz, who continually refused to depend upon the Lord. Instead, he sacrificed to the gods of Damascus, defiled and closed the temple of the Lord, and promoted idolatry in Jerusalem and Judah (cf. 2Kg 16:10-20; 2Ch 28:1-4). Ahaz died in 715 BC, leaving his kingdom to his son Hezekiah.

The continual growth and influence of the Assyrian empire cast its shadow over Hezekiah's reign. Although Assyria did not directly affect Judah until 701 BC when King Sennacherib (704–681) confronted the alliance between Egypt, Philistia, and Judah (cf. 2Kg 18:7), Assyrian activity under Sargon II (721–705 BC) produced turmoil in the region and created uncertainty in Judah. Judah's leaders watched as the Assyrians conquered other states. One example was Azuri, king of Ashdod, who attempted to break away from Assyria. Thinking that Egypt would protect him from Assyrian retaliation, Azuri refused to pay tribute to the Assyrians. Unfortunately for Azuri, Egypt did not come to his aid and Assyria conquered Ashdod around 711 BC. Isaiah's three years of nakedness (20:2-3) were prompted by Sargon II's invasion of Ashdod, and served as a sign to Hezekiah that he should not put his faith in the Egyptians. Hezekiah listened to Isaiah and did not depend on Egypt, which was eventually defeated by Assyria.

Second Kings 18:7-8 record the anti-Assyrian acts of Hezekiah. He refused to pay tribute to Sargon II and took control of a portion of Assyria's territory in Philistia. Hezekiah's actions were not addressed until the reign of Sennacherib, which began in 705 BC following the death of Sargon II. Sennacherib's campaigns in Philistia put pressure on Hezekiah, who eventually paid tribute to Assyria (cf. 2Kg 18:14-16). Having received this payment, Sennacherib turned his attention to Egypt. The payment provided only temporary relief and Sennacherib ultimately returned to Judah. He sacked Lachish and Libnah (about 25 and 20 miles southwest of Jerusalem, respectively; cf. 2Kg 19:8; 37:8) and laid siege to Jerusalem. Hezekiah's attempts to fortify Jerusalem against Sennacherib were successful, and he maintained control of Jerusalem until 686 BC (cf. 2Ch 22:8-11; 32:3-5, 30).

In addition to his decision to trust God against Assyria, Hezekiah succeeded in instituting several spiritual reforms (cf. 2Ch 29:3-11, 15-36; 30:1-11, 18-21; 31:1; 32:6-8, 20-21; 2Kg 18:4). Despite these reforms, other books of Scripture record Hezekiah's missteps (cf. 2Kg 18:14-16;

20:12-18; 2Ch 32:25-26). Though Isaiah applauded Hezekiah for choosing to trust God to defeat the Assyrians, he painted a less-than-positive picture of the spiritual state of Judah and its leaders. Judah's actions would bring judgment on Jerusalem (cf. Is 29:1-4), yet Jerusalem was not blameless. Jerusalem also needed to turn back to God in obedience and trust in the Lord to defeat the Assyrians (cf. 30:31-33; 31:8-9).

Isaiah confronted a nation whose identity as God's chosen people had become confused. The erosion of Judah's faith in the face of heavy political pressures provided the impetus for Isaiah's prophecies. As Judah's leaders struggled to imagine a world in which political alliances were not necessary, Isaiah called them to recognize a theological reality. That reality was rooted in the sovereignty of God and His desire to glorify His name through Israel.

Contribution to the Bible. Isaiah is the most cited prophetic book in both the NT and in rabbinic literature. The book of Isaiah's impact on the theology of the OT and NT is difficult to overstate. Often referred to as the "fifth gospel," Isaiah's messianic prophecies, as well as the book's development of remnant theology, anticipate the coming of Messiah and the restoration of Israel.

OUTLINE

I. Prologue: The Indictment of Israel and Call of Isaiah (1:1–6:13)
  A. Israel's Rebellion and the Hope of Restoration (1:1-31)
  B. Israel's Present Judgment and Coming Glory (2:1–4:6)
  C. Israel's Judgment and Exile (5:1-30)
  D. Isaiah's Call to Prophesy (6:1-13)
II. The Judgment of Israel and the Nations (7:1–35:10)
  A. A Narrative of a Sign Rejected: Ahaz Chooses to Trust the Nations (7:1–12:6)
    1. The Messianic Sign of Immanuel: His Birth (7:1-16)
    2. An Oracle of Judgment on Judah, Damascus, and Samaria (7:17–8:22)
    3. The Messianic Son of God: His Nature (9:1-7)
    4. An Oracle of Judgment on Samaria and Assyria (9:8–10:34)
      a. The Judgment of Samaria (9:8–10:4)
      b. The Judgment of Assyria (10:5-34)
    5. The Messianic Branch of the Lord: His Reign (11:1-16)
    6. A Hymn of Praise (12:1-6)
  B. The Oracles of Judgment (13:1–35:10)
    1. The Oracles against the Nations (13:1–23:18)
      a. The Oracle against Babylon (13:1–14:27)
      b. The Oracle against Philistia (14:28-32)
      c. The Oracle against Moab (15:1–16:14)
      d. The Oracle against Syria and Ephraim (17:1-11)
      e. The Oracle against Cush (17:12–18:7)
      f. The Oracle against Egypt (19:1–20:6)
      g. The Oracle against Babylon (21:1-10)
      h. The Oracle against Edom (21:11-12)
      i. The Oracle against Arabia (21:13-17)
      j. The Oracle against Jerusalem (22:1-25)
      k. The Oracle against Tyre (23:1-18)
    2. The Little Apocalypse (24:1–27:13)
      a. The Judgment of the Earth (24:1–25:12)
        (1) The Description of the Judgment (24:1-23)
        (2) The Responses to the Judgment (25:1-12)
      b. The Establishment of God's Kingdom (26:1–27:13)
    3. The Book of Woes (28:1–33:24)
      a. The First Woe: For Drunken Mocking (28:1-29)
      b. The Second Woe: For Religious Hypocrisy (29:1-14)

c. The Third Woe: For Attempting to Deceive God (29:15-24)
d. The Fourth Woe: For Stubborn Rebellion (30:1-33)
e. The Fifth Woe: For Failure to Trust (31:1–32:20)
(1) God (Not Egypt) Will Deliver Israel (31:1-9)
(2) God Will Establish His Righteous Messianic King (32:1-20)
f. The Sixth Woe: For Destructive Opposition (33:1-24)
4. The Summary of Judgment and Blessing (34:1–35:10)
a. The Power of the Gentiles Will Be Broken (34:1-17)
b. The Redeemed Will See the Kingdom of God (35:1-10)
III. The Blessing of Israel and the Nations (36:1–66:24)
A. A Narrative of a Sign Accepted: Hezekiah Chooses to Trust the Lord (36:1–39:8)
1. Hezekiah and the Assyrians (36:1–37:38)
a. The Attack of Assyria (36:1-22)
b. The Defeat of Assyria (37:1-38)
2. Hezekiah and the Babylonians (38:1–39:8)
a. Hezekiah Healed by the Lord (38:1-22)
b. Hezekiah Reveals His Treasures to the Babylonians (39:1-8)
B. The Oracles of Blessing (40:1–66:24)
1. Deliverance from Babylon (40:1–48:22)
a. God's Comforting Message (40:1-31)
b. God's Powerful Deliverance (41:1-29)
c. God's Chosen Servant (42:1-25)
d. God's Comforting Assurance (43:1–44:5)
e. God's Sovereign Authority (44:6-23)
(1) God's Declaration of His Unique Sovereignty (44:6-8)
(2) Satire on Trusting in Useless Idols (44:9-20)
(3) Admonition to Remember and Return to God (44:21-22)
(4) Concluding Hymnic Praise of God. (44:23)
f. God's Human Agent (44:24–45:25)
(1) The Description of Cyrus (44:24–45:13)
(2) The Effect of Cyrus (45:14-25)
g. God's Righteous Judgment (46:1–47:15)
h. God's Predicted Restoration (48:1-22)
2. Deliverance from Sin (49:1–57:21)
a. The Encouragement of Israel (49:1–52:11)
(1) The Servant's Roles (49:1-13)
(2) The Lord's Reassurance of Faithfulness (49:14-26)
(3) The Servant's Example (50:1-11)
(4) God's Promised Deliverance (51:1–52:12)
b. The Sacrifice for Israel (52:13–53:12)
(1) God Speaks: The Servant Will Be Exalted Despite His Humiliation (52:13-15)
(2) Israel Speaks: The Servant Was Not Recognized because of His Humiliation (53:1-9)
(3) God Speaks: The Servant Will Be Exalted because of His Humiliation (53:10-12)
c. The Salvation of Israel and the Nations (54:1–57:21)
(1) The Salvation of Israel (54:1–55:13)
(a) The Promise of Salvation (54:1-17)
(b) The Offer of Salvation (55:1-13)
(2) The Salvation of the Nations (56:1–57:21)
(a) The Inclusion of the Gentiles (56:1-8)
(b) The Condemnation of the Wicked (56:9–57:21)
3. Deliverance in the End (58:1–66:24)

COMMENTARY ON ISAIAH

I. Prologue: The Indictment of Israel and Call of Isaiah (1:1–6:13)

The first six chapters of the book of Isaiah function as a prologue to the entire book, introducing the relationship between God and Judah. Its main emphasis is an indictment of Judah for sin. God offered a message of impending doom and future hope for Israel by describing the nation's identity in the present and the future. Their ignorance of God and His desires would result in disaster, but that disaster was not complete. God would sustain a remnant and restore Israel, but only through judgment and discipline. As a culmination of the indictment, the story of the call of Isaiah was recounted. Having indicted Judah, demonstrating a need for a prophet, God called Isaiah to bring His message to His wayward people.

A. Israel's Rebellion and the Hope for Restoration (1:1-31)

1:1. The superscription introduces the book of Isaiah as the vision given to the prophet Isaiah concerning Judah and Jerusalem. This verse locates the vision within the reigns of **Uzziah, Jotham, Ahaz, and Hezekiah, kings of Judah**, thereby offering a life setting for Isaiah's visions. Isaiah's relatively easy access to the kings of Judah has prompted some commentators to speculate that Isaiah was of royal lineage. More significantly, the visionary quality of the message sets it apart from other critiques of Israel's situation and from the visions of false prophets.

1:2-9. Isaiah began delivering his message in v. 2 when he called the heavens and the earth as witnesses to God's indictment. The language is similar to that found in the announcement of a formal "legal case" (cf. Dt 30:19; 31:28; 32:1; Ps 50:4). Isaiah described the charges that God was bringing against the people and called into question the wisdom of continuing to suffer when repentance would bring relief.

God's first charge was that the Israelites were rebellious. The comparison of Israel to the ox and the donkey (v. 3) highlighted the nation's ignorance of God's ways and their refusal to adhere to them. The refusal to turn back to God results in suffering described as a beating (**stricken**, v. 5). The prophet questioned where the next blow would land since Judah was covered with wounds and bruises from head to toe (v. 6). The land of Judah was destroyed and was being overthrown by strangers (v. 7). Judah has become like an abandoned hut in a harvested field (v. 8). These images spoke to the relationship between God and Israel, yet the suffering of Israel was not without a glimmer of hope. Despite their rebellion, God would not make them like **Sodom** and **Gomorrah** (v. 9). He would not destroy them completely, but would leave a remnant to rebuild the nation.

1:10-20. In v. 10, the **rulers of Sodom** and the **people of Gomorrah** were called to hear (Hb. *shama*) just as previously the heavens and the earth were called to "listen" (Hb. *shama,* 1:2). The identification of Israel with Sodom and Gomorrah in v. 10 was designed to underline the depravity of Judah's people and leadership. The characterization of Israel as a prototypical pagan and wicked city was followed by God's rejection of Judah's empty worship (vv. 11-14), resulting in God's temporary abandonment of Judah (v. 15). The hands of Judah, covered in the blood of unwanted sacrifices and oppressed peoples, caused God to turn away and to ignore their prayers. God would not grant the requests of those who engaged in hollow worship and harsh oppression.

Verse 16 shifts from a demonstration of the people's iniquity to a call for them to **wash** themselves **clean** of sin and turn back to God. Repentance involved turning from sin to the practice of justice and righteousness, particularly in relation to the oppressed, the orphan, and the widow, who were the weakest members of that society (v. 17). God's people did not need to seek to gain advantage through subjugation. God would remove the crimson stain of sin and provide all they needed and more if they would trust and obey Him (vv. 18-19). They would eat the **best** of the land if they turned and obeyed (v. 19). But if they did not repent, they would be **devoured by the sword** (v. 20).

1:21-31. Having described the alternatives associated with obedience and rebellion in vv. 19-20, the focus shifted to the unfortunate state of Jerusalem. Verses 21-23 present a stark contrast between the Jerusalem of the past and the Jerusalem of the present. God lamented the fall of the once faithful city into unfaithful practices. While harlotry or prostitution is often used to refer to idolatry in the OT (cf. Jr 2:20; 3:1; Ezk 6:9; 16:15-16; Hs 4:12; Nah 3:4), in this case it was linked to the oppressive, immoral social practices being carried out in Jerusalem. The deprivation of Jerusalem's leadership was highlighted by their willingness to trade justice for bribery and to ignore the cause of the widow and orphan. Such practices were unimaginative and reflected a lack of trust in God that was characteristic of many of those to whom Isaiah prophesied. The drive for more power, more security, and more wealth in the present limited the leaders' ability to envision a future in which all the people would experience God's blessing.

The depraved activities of Judah's leaders caused God to come against them to re-establish order within Jerusalem and to reassert His rightful claim as ruler in Jerusalem. **The Lord GOD of Hosts, The Mighty One of Israel** (v. 24), would fight against those who oppressed the vulnerable within society. He would console Himself (v. 24) by coming against His enemies within Jerusalem. Once order was restored, God would **smelt away** Jerusalem's impurity (v. 25) and transform the city of harlotry into the city of righteousness (v. 26). The wicked leaders of the city would be replaced by leaders whose trust in God would be reflected in their honest dealings and wise counsel. The presumption is that this transformation of Jerusalem would take place at the return from captivity. However, even a cursory examination of the postexilic prophets demonstrates that the people of Jerusalem continued to struggle with righteous living (cf. Hg 1:1-11; 2:10-14; Zch 1:4-5; 7:4-14; Mal 1:6-14; 2:1-9; 2:10-17). Therefore, it is more likely that the promise to make Jerusalem a city of righteousness will be fulfilled in the distant future, in the messianic kingdom.

In Is 1:27, the prophet reveals that in this distant future, justice and righteousness will redeem Zion and those within her who repent. Zion, a poetic term for Jerusalem and the surrounding region, denotes "the chosenness, hope, and beauty which belong to those who are in God," will be freed by the just and righteous actions of God (Oswalt, *The Book of Isaiah, Chapters 1–39*, 109). As God judges fairly and restores order to Zion, those who seek their own selfish agendas will be crushed (v. 28), and those who commit to God's way will live in peace and prosperity. When God brings judgment, those who rebelled against Him will be ashamed or disappointed by **the oaks which [they] have desired** and **the gardens which [they] have chosen** (v. 29).

These oaks and gardens are likely associated with the worship of foreign gods. The Septuagint (LXX), an ancient Greek translation of the OT, translates "idols" rather than **oaks**, suggesting that the translators understood this reference to be aimed at the worship of false gods. The shame and disappointment the people will feel is related to the inability of their gods to sustain them through the onslaught of the true God. The gods on whom they depended to sustain their way of life will fail them. This embarrassment is underlined by the comparison of v. 30 in which the fragility of the oak and garden are used to describe the people who wither under the judgment of God. The vitality of living plants is replaced by dry, dead tinder that will burn easily and will not be put out (v. 31).

B. Israel's Present Judgment and Coming Glory (2:1–4:6)

The message in these chapters exhibits a

chiastic structure, a literary device used to relate multiple clauses, in which the establishment of the kingdom in 2:1-4 and 4:2-6 surround the condemnation of the proud in 2:6-22 and 3:1–4:1. Note the chart of the chiasm taken from Gary V. Smith (*Isaiah 1–39,* NAC [Nashville: Broadman & Holman, 2007], 122).

Chiastic Structure 2:1–4:6

2:1-5 God's kingdom will be established
 2:6-22 Condemnation of pride
 '3:1–4:1 Condemnation of pride
 '4:2-6 God's kingdom will be established

The chiastic structure underscores the inevitability of God's kingdom. Regardless of the supposed strength and glory of humanity, God's kingdom will come. Attempts to gain wisdom and security through human alliance (2:6), to amass wealth (2:7), and to create gods that will not oppose their efforts (2:8) only result in humiliation as God comes to establish His majesty. The day of the Lord will bring low the esteem of man and exalt God's majesty.

2:1-5. Verse 1 is not described as a "vision," but as a **word** ("message") depicting the glorious eschatological future for Israel and Jerusalem. The prophet announced what he had seen concerning Jerusalem and Judah. The picture of Israel in chap. 2 inspires hope that God will bring about His promised blessing by making the temple mount, or **the mountain of the house of the Lord** (v. 2, cf. v. 3), the highest of the mountains. The height of the mountain was a significant factor because of the ancient Near Eastern perspective suggesting that the peaks of the mountains were associated with the presence of the gods. Mountains, in particular the temple mount, were viewed as the junction between heaven and earth. That the mountain of the house of the Lord will be higher than any other mountain speaks to its prominence and, in this context, the glory of the temple and the truthfulness of the worship that occurs there.

As the law is proclaimed from Zion (v. 3), the mountain of the Lord, the nations will call one another to worship at the temple so that they may learn God's ways and live obediently (v. 3). Although God's law is eternal, it has various expressions. This likely does not indicate that the law of Moses will be reinstated in the messianic kingdom. More likely, the word **law** should be translated "instruction" (HCSB) and refer to the laws God establishes for the future eschatological kingdom. The nations will finally recognize God as the true God who will judge the world with righteousness and bring peace to the nations, signified by turning their implements of war into agricultural tools. While the first four verses of the chapter present the glorious future of Zion without reference to the sin and rebellion of Israel, v. 5 appears to be a call for the house of Jacob to return to Zion. The depiction of the nations streaming to Zion in vv. 2-4 is utilized to motivate Judah to walk obediently **in the light of the Lord** (v. 5).

2:6-11. This section, through v. 22, begins the first condemnation of pride, to be followed by a second one (3:1–4:1), as part of the chiastic structure (see above). Some commentators suggest that the depiction of the nations in vv. 2-4 is designed to make the Jewish people jealous so that they will return to follow God (Oswalt, *The Book of Isaiah, Chapters 1–39,* 118). It seems more likely, however, to function as a critique of Judah, given the contrast between the foreign practices associated with Judah in 2:6-9. The phrase beginning with **for** (v. 6) provides the reason that Judah must turn and walk in the light of the Lord. God has abandoned them temporarily and Judah needs to repent in order to be restored.

The NASB translates v. 9 **so the *common* man has been humbled and the man *of importance* has been abased, but do not forgive them**. Although the italicized words have been supplied in the translation for clarity, this translation may actually be misleading. The grammar of v. 9 suggests that it is continuing the description of the action in vv. 6-8. If this is the case, the emphasis would be on the activities of those who worship idols. They bow down and are humbled before their idols. In the final phrase of v. 9, the prophet exhorts God not to "lift them up" (Hb.). The NASB correctly translates this phrase with its intended meaning of **forgive**, imploring God not to forgive idolaters.

Verse 9 offers a play on words, as do vv. 11 and 17, utilizing the same Hebrew terms for **humbled** and **abased** as v. 9. In these latter verses the terms are used with reference to pride, suggesting that God will humble those whose arrogance has produced rebellion. In v. 9, it seems that these terms foreshadow those in vv. 11 and 17, perhaps suggesting that the sort of humility that humanity currently exhibits before idols is a false humility that will be corrected in the coming day of the Lord.

Verse 11 also marks the first instance of the phrase **in that day**, one of the most frequently used phrases in the book of Isaiah. It appears 45 times throughout the book and generally refers to the events associated with a coming day of reckoning. The worship of and dependence on the Lord (cf. 2:11; 10:20; 12:1, 4; 17:7; 19:18-19, 21, 23-24; 25:9; 26:1; 27:13), the removal of idols, the loss of wealth and security and the destruction of cities (cf. 2:20; 3:18; 17:9; 19:16; 20:6; 22:25; 31:7), the arrival of enemies (cf. 7:18, 20, 23; 17:4), the deliverance of God's people (cf. 10:27; 11:11), and the establishment of Israel's leadership (cf. 4:2; 11:10; 22:20) all will occur in that day.

This day is a day of punishment and victory in which God will overcome His enemies (cf. 2:11, 17; 24:21; 27:1, 12). It will be a time of difficulty that gives way to justice, prosperity, and wholeness (cf. 28:5-6; 29:18; 30:23). Isaiah also uses similar phraseology, for example, referring to a day or the day (cf. 2:12; 14:3; 30:8), the day of punishment (cf. 10:3), the day of the Lord (cf. 13:6, 9), the day of His burning anger (cf. 13:13), and the day of a great slaughter (cf. 30:25). Each appears to be pointing to the same time frame as that denoted by the phrase "in that day." Isaiah 22:5 also refers to a day of tumult, trampling, terror, a day of battering down walls, and of crying out to the mountains.

The "day of the LORD" is frequently a reference to God's eschatological judgment of the earth, when the nations will be judged and Israel fully restored (cf. Is 13:6-16, 9; 34:8; Jl 1:15; 2:1,11; 3:14; Am 5:18, 20; Ob 15; Zph 1:7, 14; Zch 14:1; Mal 4:1-6; 1Th 5:2; 2Th 2:2; 2Pt 3:10). However, it can also refer to God's temporal judgments (cf. Lm 2:21-22), even as Judah and Israel had experienced God's temporal judgment when punished for their sins (cf. Ezk 7:1-14).

2:12-22. There will be a day of reckoning to humble the proud (v. 12). Isaiah went on to associate the proud with prominent symbols of power and security, including the well-known **cedars of Lebanon** and **oaks of Bashan** (v. 13), **lofty mountains** and high **hills** (v. 14), **fortified wall[s]** and **tower[s]** (v. 15), and impressive **ships** (v. 16). These associations underline the misplaced security of the proud. If the majesty and implied permanence of the trees, mountains, walls, and ships will fall to the power of the Lord, human power cannot hope to stand. In the end, only God will be lifted up (2:17).

In addition, the idols that the people serve will finally be found worthless in the coming day of the Lord (v. 18). The people will abandon them and hide from the judgment of the Lord (v. 19). Their human sources of security will fade and their trust in human potential will be revealed as misplaced. The rhetorical question in v. 22 underscores the futility of elevating human prowess. There should be no particular esteem given to the capacity of humankind whose power is ultimately fleeting. The day of the Lord as described here is not addressing temporal judgment but rather, the eschatological day of the Lord. This is evident from its universal scope (note the uses of "and" in vv. 13-16), the absolute end to all idolatry (vv. 20-21), and the ultimate exaltation of the Lord over all (vv. 11, 17).

3:1-7. A second section (3:1–4:1) condemning pride begins here. This is part of the chiastic structure discussed above. Verse 1 offers support for God's claim that humanity's power is fleeting and conditioned upon His provision, and provides God's response to human exaltation and pride. God will strip away everything upon which Jerusalem and Judah depend. Food, water, prophets, and leaders will all be taken from Judah (vv. 2-3). The country will fall into disarray under the leadership of inexperienced **lads**, **capricious children**, and **women** (vv. 4, 12) as an indication of God's judgment against them. The prosperity of Judah will be diminished to the point that a man with a coat will be made leader of the people (v. 6). God will remove everything that inspires the pride of Judah and replace it with desperation, uninspired leadership, and poverty.

3:8-15. The people's widespread rebellion and arrogance against God will bring divine judgment (v. 9), but just as the wicked will eat the fruit of their actions, so will the **righteous ... eat the fruit of their actions** (vv. 10-11). Though the nation will experience judgment, it will go well for the righteous. As Judah's rulers oppress and lead astray, the Lord will come to convict His people and to punish those who have sought security through oppression and theft (vv. 14-15).

3:16-23. This section announces God's judgment of the women of Jerusalem. The extravagance and haughty attitude of the women are the focus of the condemnation and would result in the reversal of their fortunes. God would bring shame upon them and, as Childs notes, "the horrors of war—rape, disease, and famine—will replace the luxurious life of opulence and self indulgence" (Brevard S. Childs, *Isaiah: A Commentary* [Louisville: Westminster John Knox, 2001], 34). The reference to the women's hair in v. 17 reflects ancient Near Eastern practices in relation to the treatment of prisoners. Shaving off a woman's hair, or portions of it, was considered an act of public humiliation. Verses 18-23 continue the theme of humiliation as the woman's decadent trinkets are removed from them.

3:24–4:1. After describing the garments worn by the daughters of Zion, these verses portray Zion as women who will lose their men and be deserted (vv. 25-26). The shortage of men would result in desperation on behalf of Zion's women. Attempting to escape the shame and insecurity of being without a husband, the women of Jerusalem would suspend normal social convention in order to find a husband (4:1). Left in a socially compromising position, these women were seeking a mate even if they had to pay their own way. Husbands were to provide their wives with food and clothing. These women are pictured as offering to provide for themselves, suggesting that their desire for a husband had less to do with economic concerns and more to do with a desire to legitimize their position in society through marriage.

The irony of the section should not be overlooked. The beautiful, well-adorned women described in previous verses would no longer be alluring and self-sufficient. Their physical appearance would no longer be enough to sustain them. Instead, they must resort to paying their own way to find companionship and social standing. These decadent women who once had every luxury must now share one man. This section paints a vivid picture of the end awaiting those who rely on their own wealth rather than on the Holy One of Israel.

4:2-6. As part of the previously mentioned chiastic structure of this section, this paragraph again speaks of the messianic kingdom (as did 2:1-5). Despite the degradation of Israel, God will not abandon the nation. The phrase **in that day** links 4:2-6 to the previous portions of Isaiah's prophecies in which Isaiah described the coming day (cf. 2:2; 11-12, 17; 3:7, 18; 4:1). Here, however, the day is characterized by restoration rather than discipline. Though **the Branch of the LORD** is often used as a reference to Messiah (cf. Jr 23:5; 33:15; Zch 3:8; 6:12), several modern commentators suggest that the reference in 4:2 is a more general reference to the land's vegetation because of the parallel phrase **the fruit of the earth**.

There are three possible interpretations for these phrases. (1) They may be entirely literal, and both phrases would refer to the glorious gardens Israel will have in the future. In light of the other prophets using the word **Branch** as a messianic title, and the seeming incongruent nature of depicting the glorious future of Israel with mere agriculture, this seems unlikely. (2) Both phrases may be figurative and depict the future Messiah. But this is problematic in that the Messiah is nowhere else called **the fruit of the earth**. (3) They may be partially figurative and partially literal, with the first phrase about the **Branch** referring to the Messiah and the second about **the fruit of the earth** referring to agriculture in the messianic kingdom. Some argue that this is inconsistent, but it is not unusual for the prophets to depict the coming of the future Messiah with agricultural blessings (cf. Is 30:20-23). Therefore, this seems to be the most likely option. Nevertheless, whether or not the Messiah is in mind, the passage highlights the coming glorification and abundance given to the remnant of Israel by God (4:3). The remnant of Israel will experience a reversal of fortune as God's punishment turns to blessing. Through judgment, God will wash away the disgraceful filth and bloodshed that previously stained Zion, the city of Jerusalem. He will then bring protection to Zion through the provision of cloud and **flaming fire** (v. 5) as He had done previously in the wilderness (cf. Nm 9:15-23).

C. Israel's Judgment and Exile (5:1-30)

5:1-7. While God will restore Israel, specifically the faithful remnant, the time of their restoration is still future. Chapter 5 highlights the condition of Israel at the time of Isaiah's prophecy. These verses use an extended metaphor or parable to underscore the strained relationship between Israel and God, with Israel depicted as a vineyard and God as the vinedresser. God had cared for His vineyard and provided it with everything necessary to prosper (vv. 2, 4), but the vineyard did not produce **good grapes** (v. 4). Because the vineyard had not produced, all the provisions would be taken from it (v. 5). The vinedresser would **lay it waste** so that it no longer had the opportunity to bring forth produce (v. 6). Verse 7 offers a summary interpretation of the metaphor in which the house of Israel and the men of Judah are identified as the vineyard and the vines. The fruit they were to produce, justice and righteousness, never sprouted. Instead of this good fruit, Israel produced bloodshed and a cry of distress.

5:8-23. The parable of vv. 1-7 is followed by a series of six woes against the people of Judah, specifically those who greedily accumulated wealth and power (vv. 8-17) and those who mocked God and recognized evil as good (vv. 18-30). A similar parable of a vineyard is found in 27:2-6 and is also followed by six woes, but these are on the leaders of Judah (chaps. 28–33). The other distinction is that the first parable describes the judgment of the vineyard and the second depicts its preservation.

The word **woe** is more of a lament than a judgment—it could be paraphrased "How sad for you." The Lord lamented for six specific sins in Judah. The first sin was greed (vv. 8-10). Amassing houses and land would become vanity when the Lord came to destroy many houses and leave great and fine houses empty. The Lord also lamented their second sin: debauchery (vv. 11-17). The people of Judah's love of beer (the meaning of **strong drink** in the NASB; distilled liquor had not yet been developed) and **wine** and banquets (vv. 11-12) caused a lack of regard for God. This would be the downfall of the people as their fundamental misunderstanding of the world's order and of God's role as Sovereign within that order would be their undoing (vv. 12-13). Their security in earthly power and wealth was a false security that would eventually result in the humbling of humankind (vv. 14-15). Humanity would be humbled, but God would be exalted in justice and righteousness (v. 16). The return of the sheep and the lambs is a bold image in which the meekest of animals would overtake the stronghold of the rich and powerful. The land that was overtaken by the powerful would be given back to the weak.

Verses 18-19 continues the lament of those who stood against God by identifying their third sin, blasphemy. In contrast to the previous sins, the following sins were less related to greed and more to the perversion of reality. The people blasphemed because they were tied to their sin, dragging it with **cords of falsehood**. The cords, along with the ropes mentioned in the next line, describe the inextricable attachment the people had to their sins (v. 18). In light of their sin, they challenged God to come quickly and to show His plan. Their blasphemy was that they sinned boldly and then challenged God to do something about it. The people's arrogance in their own ability and their lack of respect for God's power led them to disregard the supposed plans of God. Such disdain would be their undoing.

Judah's fourth sin was perversion, in that they called **evil good, and good evil** (v. 20). The people's inverted value system caused them to reject God's standards of righteousness. With a fifth woe, God lamented their sin of arrogance (v. 21), being **wise in their own eyes**. Their sixth sin was corruption (vv. 22-23). They were **heroes in drinking wine** but failures at justice, taking bribes and invalidating justice for **the ones who are in the right**.

5:24-30. As a result of Judah's sins, God promised to judge those who were incapable of viewing the world in proper order. The reference to the rejection of God's law in v. 24 suggests more than simple disobedience to God's commands. It was a rejection of God's wisdom, of His way of ordering the nation of Israel. Obeying the law is an act of trust in the Lord. The woes came upon those who refused God's view of the world (v. 20), who saw themselves and their own capacities as a source of wisdom (v. 21), who excelled at excess (v. 22), and who corrupted justice for money (v. 23). God would punish Israel for their rejection of His law (v. 25). His instrument of punishment would be the nations that would come swiftly and powerfully with no yielding (vv. 26-30).

D. Isaiah's Call to Prophesy (6:1-13)

The prologue of the book culminates in Isaiah's call to ministry. Some have understood this account chronologically, assuming that Isaiah was called to ministry after his initial messages in chaps. 1–5. This is unlikely. Rather, after giving the particulars of God's indictment of Judah, Isaiah included this statement of the prophet's call. It was because of Israel's sin that the Lord was sending His prophet to His people.

6:1-7. The account of Isaiah's call refers to Uzziah's death, providing a marker for dating the call of Isaiah at approximately 740 BC. Isaiah saw God in a vision, seated on His high throne with **seraphim** standing above Him. The seraphim have often been identified as a category of angelic beings along with the cherubim. Despite this identification, the term "seraphim" is a transliteration of a Hebrew word and not a translation. While it is certainly possible to identify the seraphim as angelic beings, it may also be translated as "burning ones" or, as is the case in other biblical passages, used to refer to poisonous (fiery) snakes (cf. Nm 21:6; Dt 8:15; Is

14:29; 30:6). Isaiah 14:29 and 30:6 describe the snakes as flying, which may lend weight to the identification of the seraphs mentioned in 6:2 as serpentine in appearance. However, to depict these angelic beings as flying serpents with feet, wings, and a face is unlikely. The association of the word "seraph" with the word "fiery" would make the translation "burning ones" more likely. The text provides specific descriptions of the seraphim and their activities. They had six wings, with two covering their faces and two covering their feet. Even the fiery seraphim cannot be fully exposed in the presence of the God who is **Holy, Holy, Holy**.

The threefold repetition of **Holy** ("that which is utterly separated from all evil and possessing moral perfection") in v. 3 is not a reference to God's Trinitarian nature, but a device meant to underscore the degree of God's holiness. A similar device is used in Ezk 21:27 ("A ruin, a ruin, a ruin I will make it", meaning a complete and total ruin). The essence of this proclamation is that God is completely and totally holy, in every way distinct and wholly apart from all that He rules. The threefold repetition in combination with the description of God on His throne highlights the separation of God from His creation, yet **the whole earth is full of His glory** (v. 3).

It is the Lord's drastic separation from sinful humanity that prompted Isaiah's reaction before Him. Gazing upon the holiness of God, Isaiah became aware of his own uncleanness (v. 5). He quickly identified his lips as unclean. This reference might be associated with his coming call to prophesy, but his reference to the unclean lips of the people suggests otherwise. It is more likely that Isaiah was referring to the praise of the seraphim, or burning ones. Isaiah was unable to worship, as were the people of Israel, because of their unclean lips. In response to his pronouncement, a burning one flew to Isaiah to touch his mouth with a burning coal. The coal purified Isaiah and made him fit to worship and to serve (v. 7). Of course, the law prescribed a sacrifice for atonement (cf. Lv 17:11). This, however, is a vision and not literal; therefore the burning coal depicted God's removal of sin.

6:8-13. God's mobilization of the nations described in 5:26-30 was not His final act against the people of Israel. Having cleansed Isaiah and accepted him as His messenger (vv. 7-8), God gave him a message. The content of the message has troubled commentators because of its apparent command to offer a message that would harden the hearts of the people to whom it was given. Even ancient translations and commentaries change the text of chap. 6, suggesting discomfort with the text. For instance, the Dead Sea Scrolls change the command in v. 9 so that Isaiah is called to assist the people to understand.

The Septuagint, the ancient Greek translation of the OT, changes the imperatives or commands in v. 9 into descriptive, future verbs translating, "you will hear but you will not understand; you will see, but you will not perceive." In each case, the change away from the Hebrew text reflects an attempt to make v. 9 more palatable by shifting the blame of Israel's sin from God and Isaiah to Israel itself. While it is possible that the message should be read as ironic, the overall context, particularly that of chap. 5, suggests the inevitability of God's coming judgment on His people. The proclamation of Isaiah would only serve to harden the people's hearts further, and the evidence of the text, as presented above, indicates that God governed this process.

In v. 11, Isaiah asked how long the message would harden the people of Israel. Though some have suggested that the question is more objection than inquiry, it seems best to understand the question as part inquiry and part lament (Ivan Engnell, *The Call of Isaiah: An Exegetical and Comparative Study* [Uppsala, Sweden: A.B. Lundequistska Bokhandeln, 1949], 69). God's response revealed that the people's hardening would continue through the destruction of cities, the desolation of the land, and the deportation of the people. Near the end of the book, the prophet once again asked God to explain His decision to harden Israel (65:17). Here God reminded Isaiah that despite these punishments, there would remain a tenth of the population in the land (v. 13). After a second desolation, only a **stump** would remain, the holy seed, or remnant, of Israel. This group is crucial to understanding the audience of Isaiah. In every generation, God retained a faithful remnant of Israel (10:21; 65:8-10; cf. 1Kg 19:18; Rm 11:1-6). This faithful remnant was proof that God would be loyal to His promises to Israel.

II. The Judgment of Israel and the Nations (7:1–35:10)

The prologue (chaps. 1–6) was designed to demonstrate the specific sins of Judah (chaps. 1–5) and the Lord's call of the prophet Isaiah (chap. 6) to bring the nation to account. That being completed, what follows is the body of the book. The two main sections of Isaiah begin with narratives containing similar content. In each one, a king from Judah is facing a military threat and Isaiah brings them each a sign of hope. The primary difference between these two narratives is that in the first (chaps. 7–12), wicked King Ahaz rejects the Lord's sign, while in the second (chaps. 36–39), good King Hezekiah trusts the Lord's sign. Both narratives are followed by sections of oracles; after the rejected sign the oracles emphasize judgment (chaps. 13–35), whereas after the accepted sign, they emphasize blessing (chaps. 40–66).

A. A Narrative of a Sign Rejected: Ahaz Chooses to Trust the Nations (7:1–12:6)

The first main section of the book (chaps. 7–35) begins with a narrative about a sign rejected (chaps. 7–12) and is followed by a series of oracles emphasizing judgment (chaps. 13–35). In chaps. 7–12, there is a cycle of messianic blessing followed by oracles of judgments, moving repeatedly from mountain peaks to valleys (see accompanying chart, "Messianic Blessings and Judgments Chapters 7–12").

1. The Messianic Sign of Immanuel: His Birth (7:1-16)

This chapter contains one of the most controversial messianic predictions in the Hebrew Bible. Interpreters differ over a number of issues, such as the meaning of the Hebrew word *'almah* (translated "virgin" [v. 14] in the NASB), the way Isaiah's sign (v. 14) relates to the context, how the original audience would have understood Isaiah's words, and Matthew's intention in citing this passage as a prediction of the virgin birth of Jesus (cf. Mt 1:18-25).

As a result of these disputed meanings, there are three primary interpretations of this passage, and even among these three, expositors have their own distinct perspectives. The first approach, held by many traditional Christian interpreters, sees the prophecy as a direct prediction of the virgin birth. Although there are a variety of ways that these interpreters come to this conclusion, they all agree that the word *'almah* means "virgin" and refers to the virgin mother of the Messiah. A second view, frequently held by traditional Jewish scholars and biblical critics, sees the passage as purely historical. In this view, a young woman in the eighth century BC would give birth to a child in a completely natural way. A third explanation of the passage, held by many other Christian interpreters, understands the passage as having dual or multiple fulfillments. These interpreters understand the passage to refer to the natural birth of a child in the eighth century BC. Nevertheless, they contend that this does not exhaust its meaning. Rather, by double fulfillment, typology, and progressive fulfillment, the prophecy also refers to the virgin birth. This commentary will argue for the traditional interpretation, that the passage contains a direct prediction of the virgin birth of the Messiah.

7:1-9. After Isaiah's call, the first narrative of the book depicts his prophetic ministry. Moreover, Ahaz's refusal to heed the sign given by Isaiah appears as an outworking of the ministry to which Isaiah has been called. Ahaz was hardened and would not receive the prophet's message. As predicted (6:9-10), he listened, but did not understand; he looked, but did not perceive. His denial of the sign served as an example of those who cannot see past their current circumstances to imagine the reality that God

Messianic Blessings and Judgments Chapters 7–12

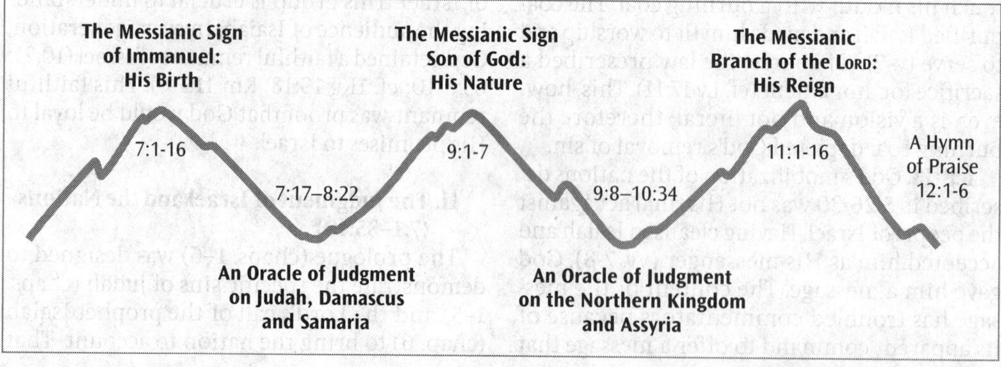

would bring about if humankind would only trust Him.

The situation in which Ahaz found himself was not trivial. His refusal to form an alliance with Syria, the northern kingdom of Israel, and Egypt caused King Rezin of Syria and King Pekah of Israel to march against Judah (v. 1). Their goal was to dethrone Ahaz in order to set another king on the throne, **the son of Tabeel**, who would be more sympathetic to their cause (v. 6). Ahaz was faced with a difficult situation in which his throne and his kingdom were in jeopardy. Judah could not stand before the combined forces of Syria and Israel. Ahaz's fear was well described—the house of David is pictured as trembling like **the trees of the forest shake with the wind** (v. 2), since replacing Ahaz would also entail the murder of the entire house of David. Michael Rydelnik explains:

> This threat provides a significant detail in understanding the passage. While some have contended that there would be no reason to foretell the coming of the Messiah, the danger to the house of David explains the messianic concerns of the passage. It was the Davidic Covenant (2 Sam 7:12-16; 1 Chron 17:11-14) that led to the expectation of a future Messiah who would be a descendant of David. Therefore, if Ahaz and the entire royal house were to be destroyed, it would bring an end to the Messianic hope. A long-term prophecy of the birth of Messiah would assure the Davidic house and the readers of the scroll of Isaiah that the Messianic hope was indeed secure (Michael Rydelnik, "An Example from the Prophets: Interpreting Isaiah 7:14 as Messianic Prophecy", In *The Messianic Hope: Is the Hebrew Bible Realy Messianic?* [Nashville: Broadman & Holman, 2010], 148).

While Ahaz formulated a plan to survive the impending threat of Rezin and Pekah, God sends Isaiah to present a divine possibility to Ahaz. God commanded Isaiah to take his son **Shear-jashub** with him to meet Ahaz at the end of the upper pool's aqueduct (v. 3). Introducing Shear-jashub was no trivial detail—he would play a significant role in the prediction later in the passage. The aqueduct was outside the city, but it was a strategic point from a military perspective as it was Jerusalem's water source. Military strategies in the ancient Near East often entailed sieges in which an attacking army trapped their opponents inside a walled city (Israel Eph'al, *The City Besieged: Siege and Its Manifestations in the Ancient Near East* [Leiden: Brill, 2009], 35–113). Those inside the city could hold off an attack if they were adequately stocked with food and water.

While it is not stated in the text, the implication is that Ahaz was actively planning to resist Rezin and Pekah by preparing for a siege. When Isaiah arrived with Shear-Jashub, which means "a remnant will return," he told Ahaz not to worry about Rezin and Pekah. These two kings are described as two stubs of smoldering firebrands, suggesting that they were about to die out (v. 4). While his enemies plotted against Ahaz and sought to take over his kingdom, God proclaimed another plan (vv. 5-9). The disjunction between the two plans is important. Ahaz was presented with two potential outcomes. The first involved defeat at the hands of Rezin and Pekah, who would dethrone him, take over Judah, and ally Judah and Israel with Egypt against Assyria. The second involved trusting God, who would protect Ahaz and Judah from Rezin and Pekah so that their threat would **not stand nor . . . come to pass** (v. 7).

While Judah's enemies appeared to be powerful, God declared that in **65** years, Ephraim (the independent northern kingdom of Israel) would be shattered, so that it was no longer a people (v. 8). This prediction came to fruition in three phases. (1) Tiglath-pileser, the king of Assyria, sent many captives from Israel to Assyria when he conquered Israel in 732 BC (cf. 2Kg 15:29). (2) Assyria destroyed the kingdom of Israel in 721 BC, sending a large portion of the population to Assyria and replacing them in Israel with other peoples (cf. 2Kg 17:24). (3) The fulfillment was completed when Ashurbanipal made the final population transfers between Israel and Assyria (cf. Ezr 4:2, 10). Thus, in exactly 65 years, the kingdom of Israel was **shattered, so that it [was] no longer a people** (v. 8).

The power of Rezin and Pekah, those **stubs of smoldering firebrands** (v. 4), was to be fleeting. If Ahaz would only trust in the Lord, his kingdom would stand (v. 9).

7:10-15. Ahaz was given the opportunity to confirm God's words by asking for a divine sign, or proof that what the Lord had declared would actually come about. But Ahaz refused to ask for a sign, with false spirituality (v. 12). The use of the word **test** suggests some connection with Dt 6:16, although the latter text refers to the testing at Massah when the Israelites complained against the Lord. They were challenging the Lord's claims concerning His ability to care for them in the wilderness.

In contrast, Ahaz was given the opportunity to ask for a sign, with no restrictions. Ahaz could ask for anything—a sign as **deep as Sheol or high as heaven** (v. 11). Although the word **sign** in Hebrew can refer either to a miraculous or a natural sign, this offer indicates that it was to be viewed as a miraculous sign. Ahaz was not constrained from asking for a sign because of a limited amount of options, but by his lack of faith. By refusing, Ahaz revealed that he was not interested in entertaining the possibility that God could protect him from Rezin and Pekah. It represented his implicit choice to deny the Lord.

Ahaz's rejection of Isaiah's offer caused Isaiah to address the house of David. This is evident not just by the use of the vocative **Listen now, O house of David** (v. 13), but also in the use of the second person plural pronoun **you**, evident in Hebrew but not in English since English does not have a distinct word for the second person singular and plural pronouns ("you" serves as both). The rhetorical questions in v. 13 highlight the ironic result of Ahaz's refusal to ask for a sign. While he did not want to test God, the king exhausted God's patience by not asking for a sign. What appeared to be a pious decision was revealed as false piety.

Since Ahaz refused to ask for a sign, now the entire house of David, under a threat of destruction because of Ahaz's lack of faith, would receive a sign: **a virgin will be with child and bear a son, and she will call His name Immanuel** (v. 14). This was the first of two signs. The first sign was addressed to the entire house of David and gave a long-term prophecy of the coming Messiah (vv. 13-15) to reassure them of God's preservation of the nation. The second sign was a short-term prophecy addressed to Ahaz about the immediate situation he was facing.

The term **sign** occurs elsewhere in Isaiah with reference to various objects, people, or non-miraculous events that are identified as having particular significance (8:18; 19:20; 20:3; 37:30; 55:13; 66:19). While non-miraculous events can be used as signs, Isaiah also used the word **sign** to refer to miraculous events. For example, later in the book Hezekiah would be given a sign that his life would be extended, namely, that the shadow on the stairway would retreat ten steps, clearly a miraculous event (38:7-8, 22). Hence, the way to determine if the word refers to a miracle is by the context. Since Isaiah had previously offered a sign as **deep as Sheol or high as heaven** (v. 11), it appears that this sign now would also be miraculous.

The Lord called special attention to the ensuing sign with the word **behold** (v. 14). When used in similar constructions in the Hebrew Bible (cf. Gn 16:11; 17:19; Jdg 13:5-7), this word serves to bring attention to a birth of special importance. The sign the Lord promised the house of David was that "the" virgin would conceive. The use of the definitive article (frequently untranslated in modern English versions) with the word *'almah* indicates that the Lord had a particular woman in mind. She was not some nameless woman in the court of Ahaz, but one whom the prophet specifically saw.

Controversy has long surrounded the translation of *'almah*. Does it mean "young woman" or "virgin?" Etymologically, *'almah* is derived from a word which means "to be sexually strong, sexually mature, sexually ripe or ready," emphasizing the age of the woman (pubescent) rather than indicating whether she was sexually active. However, the best way to determine the meaning of *'almah* is by examining its usage throughout the Hebrew Bible. If there were but one place in Scripture where *'almah* were to refer to a non-virgin (that is, as some maintain, "a young woman of marriageable age who is engaging in intercourse and on the verge of conception"), then it would dismiss the translation of the word as "virgin." However, in every usage, the word is used either of a virgin (a woman who has not had sexual relations) or in a sense that is indeterminate, meaning it does not address the sexual experience of the young woman (cf. Gn 24:43; Ex 2:8; 1Ch 15:20; Pss 46:1; 68:25; Pr 30:19; Sg 1:3; 6:8).

The passages that speak to the sexuality of the *'almah* always indicate that she was not sexually active. For example, in Gn 24, Rebekah is called an *'almah* (v. 43) and a *betulah* (general word for virgin, v. 16). In Ex 2:8, Miriam, Moses' sister, is described as an *'almah*, and she is young and plainly a virgin. In Sg 6:8, the king's harem is described as having sixty queens and eighty concubines, and maidens [*alamot*, plural of *'almah*] without number. The queens were those married to the king, the concubines those with whom he has had sexual relations, and the *alamot* were virgins who would either become concubines or queens. In Pr 30:19, the word *'almah* is used to describe the pure, romantic attraction between a maiden and a young man. Since the following verse (v. 20) contrasts that attraction with an immoral woman, it would be unlikely that the attraction in 30:19 was anything other than wholesome, and the word *'almah* would refer to a virgin.

Beyond usage in the Hebrew Bible, in the intertestamental period the Septuagint (second-century BC Greek translation of the Hebrew Bible) translated *'almah* as *parthenos* in Mt 1:23, an undisputed Greek word for virgin. (See the extended word study in Rydelnik's *The Messianic Hope,* 151-55; see also the comments on Mt 1:22-23.) Based on the use of *'almah* in the Hebrew Bible, the meaning of the word is precise and specific, referring to a maiden who has just arrived at puberty but has not been sexually active. She is a virtuous maiden in the truest and purest sense.

The virgin of Is 7:14 would be **with child**. However, the Hebrew is even more emphatic, using the feminine singular adjective *harah* ("pregnant"). This should more accurately be translated "the virgin is pregnant" or "the pregnant virgin." Were it not for the context calling for a miraculous sign, such a translation would seem impossible. However, the prophet, by a vision, saw a specific pregnant virgin before him who would be the sign of hope for the house of David. Indeed, this would meet the miraculous requirement of being **deep as Sheol or high as heaven** (v. 11).

The virgin mother would recognize the special nature of the child and **call His name Immanuel**, meaning "God is with us" (cf. Mt 1:22). The message to Judah was that God would be with them in a special way through this child. Since the next great vision of the future Davidic king describes Him as "Mighty God" (9:6), Immanuel should also be read as a divine title.

By describing the virgin-born Davidic Messiah as eating **curds and honey** as He matured (v. 15), the oracle gives a clue to the situation into which He would be born. Later in the chapter it speaks of the coming Assyrian oppression when Assyria would shave the land (v. 20). At that time, fields would not be cultivated and instead would become pastures for oxen and sheep (vv. 23-25). The effect of this would be an overabundance of dairy (indicated by the word "curds") because of the pasturing of livestock, and an excess of honey because bees would be able to pollinate the wild flowers. Therefore, **because of the abundance of the milk produced . . . everyone that is left within the land will eat curds and honey** (v. 22). So in this passage, curds and honey do not represent the food of royalty, but rather the food of oppression. The point then of v. 15 describing the future virgin-born Davidic king eating curds and honey is not to emphasize His royalty, but to accentuate that He would be born during a time of political and economic oppression.

Thus, Matthew's quotation of Is 7:14 (cf. Mt 1:23) in his narrative of the virgin birth was derived from a careful reading of Isaiah. He recognized that the prediction given to the house of David had found its fulfillment in the virgin birth of Jesus of Nazareth. Immanuel had come just as prophesied eight centuries earlier. God was with Israel.

7:16. What follows is the second of the two signs in this passage, this one focused on the short-term crisis facing Judah. Verse 16 should not to be understood as a direct continuation of the prophecy in 7:13-15, but rather as a contrast. The opening word **for** can have an adversative nuance in Hebrew, showing an obvious distinction between the child described in vv. 13-15 and the one described in v. 16. The NIV and NLT (first edition) are two recent English versions that have caught this, beginning 7:16 with the words "But before" reflecting the contrast. There is a different child in view in v. 16.

So who is the child in 7:16? In light of Isaiah being directed to bring his own son to the confrontation with the king at the conduit of the upper pool (cf. v. 3), it makes most sense to identify the lad as Shear-jashub. Otherwise, there would be no purpose for God directing Isaiah to bring his boy. Thus, having promised the virgin birth of the Messiah (vv. 13-15), the prophet next pointed to the small boy that he had brought along and said, **[But] before the boy** [this lad, using the article with a demonstrative force] **will know enough to refuse evil and choose good, the land whose two kings you dread will be forsaken**. In this way, Shear-jashub functioned as a sign to King Ahaz about matters in his own day.

This prediction was directed to King Ahaz. This is evident in the Hebrew text, but not necessarily in the English translations. In v. 16, the prophet returned to using the second person singular pronoun (**the land whose two kings you [sg] dread**). In vv. 10-11 Isaiah used the singular to address King Ahaz. Then, when addressing the House of David with the prophecy of Messiah, he shifted to the plural. But in

v. 16, he used the singular pronoun once again, addressing Ahaz and giving him a near prophecy: before Shear-jashub would be able to discern good from evil, the northern confederacy attacking Judah would fail. Within two years, Tiglath-pileser defeated both Israel and Syria, just as the prophet had predicted.

This short-term prophecy had a distinct purpose for the reader. Just as God faithfully fulfilled the prediction of Shear-jashub, so He could be trusted to fulfill the prediction about Immanuel. He recorded these so the prophet's readership could have confidence in the distant prediction by observing the fulfillment of the near one.

2. An Oracle of Judgment on Judah, Damascus, and Samaria (7:17–8:22)

What follows is an oracle of judgment on all three nations involved in this regional dispute. Nevertheless, the judgment focuses primarily on God's people, Judah.

7:17-25. Though the destruction of Rezin and Pekah was good news for Judah, Isaiah's message indicated that Judah was not left unscathed. Verse 17 offers an ominous prediction concerning Judah's future and the coming terror accompanying the king of Assyria. Verses 18-19 describes Judah's future metaphorically as a destination for the flies of Egypt and the bees of Assyria. The swarms of flies and bees would overtake the land (7:19). The imagery then shifts to that of a razor in v. 20. Since shaving off portions of hair was used to humiliate offenders or enemies (cf. 2Sm 10:4), the reference in this context likely denoted Judah's coming disgrace.

Judah would be left with little when the Lord came (v. 21). They would survive on the milk of a young cow and two goats. The recurrence of **curds and honey** in v. 22 reinforces the understanding of vv. 13-15 offered previously. The coming judgment would not lead to annihilation, but to oppression. Israel would be crippled as the land refused to bring forth produce (v. 23). The land would become wild and the farmland trampled by cattle and sheep.

8:1-4. Given the prophecy of the child in chap. 7, it is often suggested that the child of chap. 8 is one of the boys predicted in chap. 7. However, there are some potentially critical differences between the descriptions of the children in chaps. 7–8. First, the names Immanuel or Shear-jashub never appear in chap. 8. Instead, the child here is to be named Maher-shalal-hash-baz, or **swift is the booty, speedy is the prey** (v. 1; cf. v. 3). Second, it is clear that the prophetess, unidentified in the context, was not the *'almah* from chap. 7, since she had already given birth to Shear-jashub and so was not a virgin. Third, both Immanuel (7:14-15) and Shear-jashub were described as refusing evil and choosing good, but the child in chap. 8 would witness the destruction of Syria before he **knows how to cry out 'My father' or 'My mother'** (v. 4). Finally, the discipline of Judah in chap. 7 was that the Lord would bring on Judah **the king of Assyria** (v. 4).

But the judgment in chap. 8 would be that **the wealth of Damascus and the spoil of Samaria will be carried away** (v. 4). Clearly, these are distinct prophecies and different children. This prophecy entailed writing on **a large tablet** the words **swift is the booty, speedy is the prey** (v. 1) before witnesses to confirm the truth of the prophecy (v. 2). Not only were these words the name of the child that Isaiah's wife would bear (**Maher-shalal-hash-baz**), but they would also be the words that soldiers would cry as they defeated Aram and Israel.

The significance of Maher-shalal-hash-baz was as a sign of the impending defeat of the alliance of Aram and Israel against Judah. These two nations would be defeated by Assyria before the child was old enough to have full speech. The prophecy was fulfilled less than two years later, when Assyria plundered both Damascus and Samaria in 732 BC.

8:5-10. God addressed Isaiah with another message in v. 5. It was addressed to the nation of Judah, which, under the leadership of Ahaz, had rejected God's protection and continued to fear Rezin and Pekah. This rejection would cause Judah to be overcome by **the strong and abundant waters of the Euphrates**, the king of Assyria (v. 7). The water imagery in v. 7 is juxtaposed to that in v. 6. The **gently flowing waters of Shiloah** had been rejected, so the Lord would give them the floodwaters of the Euphrates. If Judah would not trust in God's protection, He would demonstrate His power through Assyria. The appearance of the name **Immanuel** in v. 8 denotes that God would have His people in the land, which actually belonged to the messianic King promised in 7:13-15. **Immanuel** also reminded the nation that although judgment was coming, God would not forget His covenant or break faith with His people. He would still be with them.

Israel's enemies would not go unchecked. The cry to Immanuel in v. 8 turned the prophet's attention toward God's faithfulness to Israel and His ultimate plans for Zion. The nations may plan to come against God's people. They may be allowed to wage war against Israel, but they would not do so without suffering the retribution of the Lord who is with Israel. God's presence is denoted by an echo of Immanuel. God's faithfulness and continued presence with Israel will ultimately bring redemption to Israel, **For God is with us** (v. 10).

8:11-18. The next paragraph reveals God's encouragement to Isaiah to remain separate from the rest of Judah. He must not fear what the people fear, or get caught up in conspiracy theories. Instead, the Lord exhorted Isaiah to fear Him and to regard Him as holy. Isaiah must remember God as Isaiah saw Him in his initial vision, sitting on His great throne among the seraphim praising Him with the refrain of "Holy, Holy, Holy" (6:3) ringing out. By fearing God and regarding Him as holy, Isaiah recognized God as his **sanctuary** (v. 14). The term translated **sanctuary** is used 75 times in the OT, including three other uses in the book of Isaiah (cf. 16:12; 60:13; 63:18). It generally denotes the place of God's dwelling, with connotations of strength and refuge (cf. Ps 27:5; Ezk 11:16). Isaiah's experience of God as sanctuary is contrasted to the way those who do not fear God experience Him. For them, He will be a stone over which Judah and Israel will stumble (v. 15). For those who fear Him, God will be a refuge, but for those who refuse to trust Him, God will be their undoing.

In v. 16 God commanded Isaiah, **Bind up the testimony, seal the law** (or "instruction"), meaning "to care for the prophetic messages" that God had given him. Preserving these prophecies provided a way to authenticate the divine proclamation against the people of Israel and Judah. Some suggest that vv. 16-18 narrate a break in Isaiah's ministry in which he no longer prophesied publicly for a few years (George Buchanan Gray, *A Critical and Exegetical Commentary on the Book of Isaiah 1–27* (Edinburgh, Scotland: T&T Clark, 2001). Though such an understanding is possible, particularly given the reference to Isaiah's patience in v. 17, it may be best to understand Isaiah's patience in relation to the people's hardening against his message (cf. 6:9-10). The people's rejection of Isaiah's message required him to persevere and to wait for God's action while ensuring that he and his followers maintained their faith in the Lord.

8:19-22. It is difficult to determine whether it is Isaiah or the Lord who is speaking in this section. If it is the Lord speaking, this section resumes the discourse begun in vv. 12-15 in which the prophet and his followers were exhorted to fear the Lord and revere Him as holy. Given that Isaiah is speaking to his followers in vv. 16-18, it seems best to read vv. 19-22 as a continuation of Isaiah's encouragement to his followers.

Though the people sought **mediums** and underworld spirits to determine the future (v. 19), true knowledge and security concerning the future could only come from the Lord. Seeking the dead to determine the fate of the living was far inferior to the law and to the testimony (v. 20). Whether seeking refuge from human powers, or seeking guidance and insight concerning one's fate, God has provided the answers in His Word to humankind. Without His law and testimony there is no knowledge, no insight, and no dawn. Instead, those who do not speak according to the Word of God will find no answers and no comfort (v. 21). Ultimately, their dire situation will lead them to curse their God and their king. Having put their trust in something other than God, they will find no solace in the world, no mechanism through which the **distress and darkness, the gloom of anguish** may be lifted, and no hope for anything but continued suffering (v. 22).

3. The Messianic Son of God: His Nature (9:1-7)

After the prediction of Messiah's birth (7:1-16) and the judgment of Judah and the surrounding nations (7:17–8:22), the prophet next returned to the promise of the messianic King.

9:1-5. Though those who refuse to live in accordance with the Word of the Lord will live in continual distress (8:22), those who were once distressed will experience comfort (v. 1). The tribes of **Zebulun** and **Naphtali** refer to the northern region of Galilee in which invading nations would have first come against Israel. These territories were seized by Tiglath-pileser in his campaign against Israel in 733 BC (cf. 2Kg 15:29). Zebulun and Naphtali may be roughly equated to **the way of the sea, on the other side of the Jordan**, and **Galilee of the Gentiles** (Yohanan Aharoni, *Land of the Bible: A Historical Geography* [Philadelphia: Westminster, 1967], 374). The humbled lands will be glorified and their fortunes will be reversed.

Verse 2 utilizes the images of **light** and **darkness** common in Isaiah. In several instances light and darkness are used in association with judgment and deliverance or justice. Isaiah 45:7

places light and darkness in parallel with prosperity and disaster. The association of light and salvation is also available in several other passages (cf. 5:20; 13:10-11; 49:6; 51:4; 58:8). Verse 2 makes a similar association between light and darkness. Those walking in **darkness**, or judgment, **will see a great light**, or deliverance. The reference to the nation's growth and increased joy in v. 3 further suggests the connection between darkness and judgment and light and salvation. The joy of the people is compared to that experienced at the time of a great harvest, or when soldiers bring back plunder from war. God's victory over Midian served as a paradigmatic instance of God's deliverance in the past. He will crush the oppressive yoke of Israel's new enemy just as he defeated Midian (v. 4; cf. Jdg 7:19-25 and the comments on it). The blood-covered clothes will be burned in an act of dedication to God (v. 5).

9:6-7. The joys described in vv. 1-5 are grounded in the birth of a child within the Davidic line. The child's birth will bring deliverance, and the titles bestowed upon him are impressive. The first given is that of **Wonderful Counselor**. The word **Wonderful** (extraordinary to the point of being miraculous) is not meant in the colloquial usage of contemporary society. Rather it refers to the supernatural work of God. A good example is its usage in Jdg 13:15-21, wherein the angel of the Lord does a "wonderful" thing (v. 18) and ascends to heaven in the flame of Manoah's sacrifice (v. 20).

The title of **Counselor** does not carry the same sense as the modern English word, which is often associated with a therapist or social worker. Instead, the word means "one who advises, who serves as a consultant to help and lead others." The title here must be construed as denoting this child's capacity to guide the people of the nation, particularly with reference to military endeavors. Though the child's guidance of the nation would not be limited to warfare, it does suggest that his skill in making decisions for the nation exhibits a divine or miraculous character that would not be possible through simply human devices (Smith, *Isaiah 1–39*, 240). The word "wonderful" stands in epexegetical construct to "counselor," and could be translated "a wonder of a counselor" or "a wonder-counselor."

The second title, **Mighty God**, is repeated in Is 10:21 and applied to God Himself. Although the Hebrew word for **Mighty** can refer to a valiant warrior, this close usage to 10:21 seems to indicate a reference to deity. The word means "valiant military hero" or "champion." Similar phrases are also used in Dt 10:17 and Jr 32:18 with reference to God. Oswalt notes, "This king will have God's true might about him," being so powerful so as to be able to absorb all evil and defeat it (Oswalt, *The Book of Isaiah, Chapters 1–39*, 247).

The child is also called **Eternal Father**. Filial relationships, such as father and son, were emphasized in the ancient Near East. The king was generally the son in such relationships and the deity the father (John H. Walton, et al., *IVP Bible Background Commentary: Old Testament* [Downers Grove, IL: InterVarsity, 2000], 518). Kings, however, also claimed to be the "father" of those they ruled (Oswalt, *Isaiah 1–39*, 247). The notion of a human king as father of his people is not foreign to the OT. Note, for instance, 1Sm 24:12 in which David calls Saul his father. But this one is not merely the royal father of His people. The adjective **Eternal** speaks to the idea of one who is forever or eternal. He is the "Father of eternity," indicating that He is the author or creator of time. The child born here is not to be confused with the Father in the triune Godhead. Rather, the Son of God is the creator of time, the author of eternity.

The final title given to the child is **Prince of Peace**. This child will have a reign characterized by peace. There will be no more war under this king. Instead, the child will usher in an era of rest from conflict that is noted in 2Sm 7:10-11.

Some have suggested that these titles are merely a theophoric name, a name that embeds God's name in a human name. Hence, "Isaiah" ("The Lord saves") is theophoric, but does not indicate that Isaiah is deity. If this is so here, then the child is not necessarily deity, but rather a royal human figure with a long name, similar to Maher-shalal-hash-baz ("Swift is the booty, fast is the prey," Is 8:1), containing names of deity. They translate this as "A wonderful counselor is the Mighty God, the eternal Father is the Prince of Peace."

This explanation is unlikely for three reasons. (1) The name in 8:3 is dependent on 8:1 and is not parallel syntactically to 9:6. All the words in 9:6 are substantives that do not have subjects and predicates. (2) Titles such as this one frequently reflect the nature of the person (cf. 2Sm 12:24-25; Is 1:26; Hs 1:10). (3) Frequently, the verb "call" with a name indicates the nature of the one named, either by a play on words (cf.

Gn 5:29) or direct meaning (cf. Is 1:26). Hence, this usage in v. 6 indicates that the names are related to the nature of the child born. Robert Reymond is correct in stating that there is no reason, "except dogmatic prejudice," to prohibit the conclusion that Isaiah meant nothing other than unabridged deity here (Robert L. Reymond, *Jesus, Divine Messiah: The OT Witness* [Fearn, Ross-shire, Scotland: Christian Focus Publications. 1990], 51).

The child will fulfill the promise of the Davidic covenant (cf. 2Sm 7:12-16), and establish the messianic kingdom through justice and righteousness. This kingdom will not be the outworking of a king with human wisdom and power. The child will rule with the wisdom, power, and peace of God. The final statement in v. 7 notes that the Lord will accomplish all that has been described. Isaiah again underscores that trust in the Lord is the key to receiving the promised blessing.

4. An Oracle of Judgment on Samaria and Assyria (9:8–10:34)

Isaiah continues the cycle of hope followed by judgment. Having promised the birth of the messianic King (7:1-16), foretold judgment on Judah and the surrounding nations (7:17–8:22), and predicted the nature of the future messianic King (9:1-7), he now returned to an oracle of judgment. The two nations facing judgment are Samaria (9:8–10:4) and Assyria (10:5-34).

a. The Judgment of Samaria (9:8–10:4)

This section promises judgment on the northern kingdom of Israel for four specific sins. Each of the four sections ends with the refrain, "In spite of all this, His anger does not turn away and His hand is still stretched out" (9:12, 17, 21; 10:4).

9:8-12. The first sin to be judged is human pride and self-sufficiency. Having described the coming glory of the child's kingdom, Isaiah turned to those whose pride and sin would not stand beneath God's regime. Jacob, otherwise known as Israel, received a message from God that condemned those whose arrogance and pride refused to allow them to admit defeat, even when God's judgment had taken away their prosperity (vv. 8-9). They looked at the devastation of God's judgment, yet they continued in their self-sufficiency.

The plans of the arrogant, however, would be met with opposition. God would stand against Israel and bring foreign enemies against the nation (v. 11). The Arameans and the Philistines would turn and devour Israel (v. 12). Despite this punishment, the Lord's anger would not be assuaged and would continue to burn against His people (v. 12).

9:13-17. The second sin to be judged was misleading leadership. Even after they experienced the consequences of not trusting the Lord, the people refused to return to the Lord (v. 13). The leaders of the nation, the elders and the prophets, would all be eliminated for leading the nation astray (v. 14). Because the people followed leaders who led them away from the Lord, the Lord would not spare them either. Even the groups on whom the Lord normally has compassion, such as **orphans** and **widows**, would not be spared (v. 17).

9:18-21. The northern kingdom of Israel would be judged for a third sin: social anarchy. The severity and completeness of this punishment did not calm God's anger and the situation in Israel continued to worsen as God destroyed the nation (vv. 18-21). The nation was divided, with each person taking advantage of the other (v. 20). The nation was so divided that the only area of unity was in their opposition to Judah (v. 21).

10:1-4. The fourth sin to be judged was unjust oppression. Although many in Israel had accumulated wealth and power, they had done so through unjust practices and oppression of the weak. Therefore, their position and wealth would not help them in the day of judgment. They would ultimately be enslaved **among the captives** or slaughtered **among the slain** (v. 4), underscoring the uselessness of their ill-gotten gains. This, as with Isaiah's other prophecies, highlighted the value of trusting in the Lord rather than trusting in one's own wealth and power. Efforts to gain human advantage through injustice will be shown futile in order to display the sovereign power of God and His capacity to bless and punish.

b. The Judgment of Assyria (10:5-34)

God would not only judge His own people but, as predicted in what follows, He would bring devastation upon Assyria, His instrument of judgment upon Israel.

10:5-12. While God's anger against His people would be made manifest through Assyria, that nation would be punished for its role in the devastation of God's people (v. 5). God's use of Assyria was for a specific purpose. He called them to punish those among His people who had angered Him. Assyria, however, took advantage of God's authorization to implement a larger plan of destruction (v. 7). But God will not allow Assyria to implement its own agenda without retribution. Though the Assyrians had powerful commanders (v. 8) and a track record of victory over the idols of other nations (v. 9), the Assyrian assumption that the defeat of Jerusalem and Samaria constituted a defeat of the God of Jerusalem and Samaria reflected their ignorance of their true task. They were not empowered by their own inherent strength or by their national gods, but by the Lord. He would not allow their arrogance to continue, but would punish them for not recognizing and following Him (v. 12).

10:13-19. The punishment of Assyria's pride may be compared to the pride of God's people. Assyria claimed to defeat the nations by their own **power** and **wisdom** (v. 13). But the celebration of Assyrian power was misguided, because it is God who orchestrates the activities of the nations. The rhetorical questions of v. 15 express this well. **Is the axe to boast itself over the one who chops with it? Is the saw to exalt itself over the one who wields it?** Of course not—they are only tools. Assyria's boasting would result in humiliation as the Lord debilitated the nation's mighty warriors with **a wasting disease** (v. 16). **The light of Israel**, the Lord who guides Israel, would **become a fire** to burn Assyria in judgment. God is **his** [collective Israel's] **Holy One**, who will be **a flame** burning Assyria as **thorns and . . . briars** (vv. 17-19). God's control over the Assyrians provided an odd sense of comfort as the fate of Israel was not based on the mercy of Assyria, but upon the steadfast faithfulness of God. God would punish, but not annihilate, His people. His desire was to discipline, not destroy.

10:20-27. This sense of comfort was confirmed in the following paragraph. A remnant of Judah would be preserved through the Assyrian strike, and they would no longer depend upon their oppressors, but upon the Lord (v. 20). Those who remain would no longer look to foreign political powers, or, by extension, any power aside from the Lord. The remnant would not make the fundamental mistake made by Israel and its leaders of trusting human power rather than God. Despite this glimmer of hope, the consequences of Israel's sin were regrettably evident. The once numerous nation with a population as numerous as the sand by the sea would be reduced to a vestige of Israelites who had been allowed to survive the Lord's destruction, **overflowing with righteousness** (vv. 22-23).

Verses 24-27 offer words of encouragement to Israel. Though the Assyrians were coming to destroy, God reminded His people that He wielded Assyria and that there was no need to **fear** them. Israel's fate did not rest upon the mercy of Assyria, but upon the mercy of the Lord. God was in complete control of Assyria and would deliver Israel as He had in the past (vv. 25-26). The final phrase in v. 27, **the yoke will be broken because of fatness**, is difficult to interpret though it appears to be related to the coming blessing of the Lord. Assyrian oppression would end as the Lord blessed His people and made it impossible for Assyria's yoke to remain upon Israel.

10:28-34. This last paragraph describes the path that the invading army would take as it moved toward Judah and Jerusalem. The northernmost cities were mentioned first as the army moved south. As the invaders reached Zion, the Lord intervened. His actions were described using the imagery of a forest being cut down. The reference to Lebanon recalled the coveted cedars that grew in Lebanon, which were prized for their size and quality (Walton, et al., *IVP Bible Background Commentary*, 36).

5. The Messianic Branch of the Lord: His Reign (11:1-16)

The prophet continues the cycle of messianic hope—followed by judgment—followed by messianic hope. This chapter returns to the theme of messianic hope found in chaps. 7 and 9.

11:1-5. The passage begins with a description of a **shoot** that **will spring from the stem of Jesse**. This description stands in contrast to the imagery of a mighty forest that would be cut off in 10:33-34. The cedars of Lebanon, which elicit images of strength, size, and power, have been destroyed, so that the seemingly fragile bud sprouting from the root of Jesse may rule. Likely it describes the King as coming from **Jesse** rather than David to emphasize His humble ancestry. This new ruler will be empowered by **the Spirit of the LORD** (v. 2). The presence of the Lord's Spirit denotes the human ruler's access to supernatural resources that will give Him a more-than-human capacity to rule. It also legitimizes His rule as divinely ordained.

The Spirit of the Lord is characterized by three sets of paired attributes: (1) **wisdom and understanding**, (2) **counsel and strength**, and (3) **knowledge and the fear of the LORD** (v. 2). The first pairing (**wisdom and understanding**) speaks to the Spirit's empowering of the King to make godly decisions as the ruler of Israel. The second pairing (**counsel and strength**) is likely related to the capacity given to the King to devise and implement plans for the nation. **Counsel** here brings to mind Is 9:6 in which the title "Wonderful Counselor" was also applied to the coming King (see the comments there). The final pairing of **knowledge and the fear of the LORD** suggests an intimate relationship of loyalty to God that is rooted in reverence for the Lord. That the King's delight will be in the fear of the Lord highlights the intensity of the King's loyalty to and dependence on God (v. 3). The King's judgments are not driven by appearance or rumor, but by a deep commitment to God's righteousness. In relying upon God, the King will look beyond appearances to see the heart of the matter. The King will not favor the rich and the powerful in His judgments, but will offer right judgments regardless of station. The poor and the weak will receive justice (v. 4).

The phrase **fear of the LORD** and those similar to it are used often in Scripture (cf. 2Ch 19:9; Pss 19:10; 34:12; 111:10; Pr 1:7, 29; 2:5; 8:13; 9:10; 10:27; 14:26-27; 15:16, 33; 16:6; 19:23; 22:4; 23:17), though more rarely in Isaiah (vv. 2-3). While the use of **fear** could suggest the sort of terror elicited when one is faced with sudden death or loss of some kind, in Scripture this fear denotes a healthy, overwhelming reverence for God. It is an orientation toward God that overshadows any desire for earthly position or possession. As Sheriffs notes, "'The fear of the Lord is hatred of evil', and the evil concerned is not demonic or cosmic, but the down-to-earth evil of human 'pride,' 'arrogance' and 'perverted speech.' It is in this sense of moral choice that 'the fear of the Lord is a fountain of life, so that one may avoid the snares of death'" (Deryck Sheriffs, *The Friendship of the Lord* [Eugene, OR: Wipf and Stock, 2004], 163).

11:6-10. The descriptions of the kingdom found in vv. 6-9 paint an idyllic picture of the King's reign. These descriptions speak to the uniqueness of this King's reign and the restorative regime that He will bring with Him. The King's capacity to bring forth peace moves beyond the kings of the past. Isaiah is not simply looking forward to the installation of the next Davidic monarch, but to the installation of *the* Davidic monarch, the *supreme* Son of David, who will live in full obedience to God and rule with God's wisdom, strength, and justice (v. 5). Not only will the root of Jesse bring the peace and harmony described in 10:6-9, but His reign will also initiate God's gathering of the remnant from the four corners of the earth (v. 11). This new King's wise rule will attract even the nations and serve as a banner around which the nations will rally to hear His counsel (v. 10).

11:11-16. Under this King's rule, the divided kingdoms (Israel in the north; Judah in the south) will set aside past animosity and unify to defeat their common enemies (vv. 13-14). The previously mentioned peace will come through the unification of Israel and Judah and the removal of all wickedness from the land (cf. v. 4). The conquest of Philistia, Edom, Moab, and the Ammonites refers to the accomplishment of security in the nation of Israel. The nations mentioned lie on the east, west, and south of Israel. Their continued presence would represent a remaining threat to the nation. The defeat of these nations secures peace under the hand of a single sovereign.

Verses 15-16 portray the acts of God that will make the return of the remnant possible. Nothing will stand in the way of God's people and their return. God will create a highway that will lead His people out of Assyria, just as there was for Israel **in the day that they came up out of the land of Egypt** (v. 16). Chapter 11 offers a powerful picture of Israel's future that is ultimately rooted in God's acts on behalf of the nation in the past. The reference to the exodus from Egypt, one of the most foundational events in the history of Israel, anchors the predicted events in Israel's past experience of God. The identity of the nation will be preserved not because Israel is a powerful nation, but because Israel's God desires it to be so. His acts on behalf of Israel will come to fruition. This prophecy, the future that it reveals, and the past in which it is rooted, solidifies Israel's identity and offers assurance of the nation's continued existence and prosperity as God's covenant people.

6. A Hymn of Praise (12:1-6)

At the end of this cyclical section, the prophet concludes with a hymn of praise. This paragraph functions as a fitting conclusion or epilogue to the section frequently called "The Book of Immanuel." Having cycled back and forth between God's gracious promise of Messiah and His just judgment of Israel and the nations, the author concludes with an exultant song of thanksgiving to God.

12:1-2. This passage represents a song of victory celebrating the Lord's defeat of Israel's enemies and His deliverance of Israel. The song begins with an acknowledgement of God's **anger**, which has **turned away** resulting in comfort and salvation (v. 1). It continues with the affirmation that the people's salvation is found only in God. Verse 2 does not point to the activities of God that have led to salvation, but to God Himself as salvation (Smith, *Isaiah 1–39*, 282). As such, the people will no longer look to more powerful nations, political alliances, or their own wealth and strength for salvation, but to God alone. The people will finally trust and fear the Lord, acknowledging Him as the source of all refuge and strength (v. 2).

12:3-6. The revelation that God is salvation prompts the call to proclaim the Lord's prowess throughout the nations. Having seen God move powerfully to restore the remnant and to establish a king and kingdom of wisdom, justice, and peace, Israel finally recognizes God as the only one on whom Israel needs to depend. Nations like Assyria are tools of God that cannot offer any true deliverance. Instead, Israel must learn to trust in the Lord despite the appearance of the economic and political landscape.

B. The Oracles of Judgment (13:1–35:10)

The first main section of Isaiah (chaps. 7–35) is about the judgment of the nations. This is developed with a narrative (chaps. 7–12) in which King Ahaz rejected God's offer of a sign. Although the Lord gave the sign as well as other signs, the outcome of faithless Ahaz's decision was a series of oracles that emphasize God's judgment of the nations (chaps. 13–35).

1. The Oracles against the Nations (13:1–23:18)

The first part of the judgment section of Isaiah emphasizes God's oracles against all of the nations surrounding and including Judah. However, the judgment focuses on Babylon more than the other nations mentioned (there are 55 verses dealing with the judgment of Babylon, but not more than 38 for any other nation). Though other views are possible, it appears that Is 13:1–23:18 forms a unit devoted to prophecies against specific nations.

J. A. Motyer's observations concerning this section are helpful in that they offer a sense of cohesion to the oracles against the nations (J. A. Motyer, *The Prophecy of Isaiah* [Downers Grove, IL,: InterVarsity, 1993], 131–32). He suggests that the oracles be organized into two groups of five oracles each, with each group beginning with an oracle against Babylon. The chart below depicts Motyer's organization of the ten oracles.

While many of these oracles prophesy against nations other than Israel, their record here suggests that the condemnation of the nations and their practices contain a message for Israel. Given that Israel's leadership exhibited a tendency to cast their lot with the nations, it may be that these oracles were designed to remind Israel's leaders that partnering with foreign powers was futile. The oracles would also have encouraged the remnant, those within Israel who trusted the Lord. No nation, regardless of its perceived power, will stand before God.

a. The Oracle against Babylon (13:1–14:27)

13:1-10. First and foremost among these nations was Babylon. This is the first of two oracles against Babylon (it ends in 14:27; the second appears in 21:1-10). Babylon's prominence in this section is probably tied to the nation's prominence on the geopolitical stage after the domination of the Neo-Assyrian empire in 627 BC when Nebuchadnezzar rose to power in the newly established Neo-Babylonian empire (Walton, et al., *IVP Bible Background Commentary*, 601). Babylon also gained significance in Isaiah through Hezekiah's interactions with Babylon in 39:1-8.

After the introduction to the oracle in 13:1, it shifts between the voice of God (13:2-3, 11-18)

Motyer's Organization of the Oracles in Isaiah 13:1–23:18

Group 1			
13:1–14:27	Oracle against Babylon	21:1-10	Oracle Against Babylon
14:28-32	Oracle against Philistia	21:11-12	Oracle Against Edom
15:1–16:14	Oracle against Moab	21:13-17	Oracle against Arabia
17:1–18:7	Oracle against Damascus/Israel	22:1-25	Oracle against Jerusalem
19:1–20:6	Oracle against Egypt	23:1-18	Oracle against Tyre

and the voice of the prophet (13:4-10, 19-22). God recounted the call of His **consecrated ones** and **mighty warriors** to stand against Babylon (vv. 2-3). The prophet then proclaimed the coming of the Lord's massive army which would destroy Babylon (vv. 4-5). There would be no mistake that the destruction was divine in its origins as it would bring the sort of terror, fury, and natural disruption that only the judgment of God could bring (vv. 6-10).

13:11-18. God's speech in this section highlights His intention to **punish** the people of the world for their **evil** and display Himself as the sole Ruler of the earth. The tyrants and the proud who have rebelled against God will be humbled. Pride is again pictured as the object of the Lord's wrath. The vanity of human pride will be revealed as God shakes the very foundations upon which human dynasties have been built. God will make people scarce (v. 12). He will shake **the heavens** and **the earth** (v. 13). Those who try to escape will be caught and killed (vv. 14-15). Horrendous acts will be performed against women and children (v. 16). God appointed the Medes as His attackers. Their lack of concern for silver and gold neutralized the rich and eliminated any attempts at bribery. The Medes' desire for blood pushed out all pity and compassion, so that even children were not spared (vv. 17-18).

13:19-22. The third-person reference to God in v. 19 (**God overthrew**) suggests that the prophet was once again speaking about God, rather than God speaking about Himself. Babylon is described as **the beauty of kingdoms** (v. 19), the glory of the Babylonians' pride, but its fate would be the same as that of **Sodom and Gomorrah**. It would be made desolate so that not even nomads and shepherds would use the location. Only wild animals would live in Babylon after God was done with it. This sort of description was typical of the manner in which demolished cities were described in the ancient Near East (Seth Erlandsson, *The Burden of Babylon: A Study of Isaiah 13:2–14:23* [Lund: CWK, 1954], 118). The once proud city would soon be disgraced (v. 22) as the Medes under the leadership of Cyrus overcame Babylon in 538 BC. This invasion, however, was relatively peaceful and did not produce the sort of destruction described in chap. 13. Babylon was destroyed by Sennacherib during an earlier Assyrian invasion and was rebuilt under Esarhaddon between 681 and 669 BC. The city's ultimate eschatological destruction is also mentioned in Rv 18.

So when did or will this destruction of Babylon take place? For several reasons, it seems best to view Isaiah's depiction of Babylon's destruction as eschatological. First, Babylon's defeat will be in "the day of the LORD" (vv. 6, 9), which is generally an eschatological expression. Moreover, the signs in the heavens (v. 10) and the whole earth (vv. 9, 11) align with the eschatological signs of the end of days. Second, Babylon's fall will be violent destruction (vv. 15-18), but as noted above, no historical defeat of Babylon matches that description. It is likely to happen at the end of days. Third, Babylon's defeat will coincide with Israel's end-time restoration (14:1-2), an event related to the end of days.

The difficulty with understanding Babylon's defeat as eschatological is the reference to the Medes participating in its destruction (v. 17). This would automatically lead to the conclusion that Babylon's fall, described here, took place at the hands of Cyrus the Great and his Medo-Persian kingdom in 539 BC. However, in light of the evidence pointing to an eschatological defeat in this passage and the rest of the Bible (see the comments on Jr 50–51 and Rv 17–18), it is preferable to view the mention of the Medes as a reference to one of the nations at the end that will come against Babylon.

14:1-4. The oracle against Babylon continues with a statement of God's loyalty to Israel and the reconstitution of the nations (vv. 1-21). When God brings eschatological relief to Israel, they will look upon those who once oppressed them, particularly Babylon, and mock them (vv. 1-4). The rest of the passage is dedicated to recounting Israel's taunting. The taunt reinforces several of the prominent themes that have been previously introduced in Isaiah's prophecy. The arrogance of Babylon is epitomized in its leader's attempts to elevate himself to the level of the Most High (v. 14). Despite its lofty aspirations, the nation does not achieve the heavens, but is brought down to Sheol.

14:5-23. This passage uses language reflecting ancient Near Eastern cosmic geography. **Sheol**, which is mentioned several times throughout the passage (vv. 9, 11, 15), was the place lying beneath the earth where those under divine judgment would spend eternity (Philip S. Johnson, *Shades of Sheol: Death and Afterlife in the Old Testament* [Downers Grove, IL: InterVarsity, 2002], 83.). While the Babylonian leaders wished to ascend to the heights of the gods (vv. 13-14), they would descend into Sheol (i.e., the grave; see the comments on Ps 49:15 for a discussion of the word *sheol*). They would be humbled and people would be amazed that these men were ever capable of mastering the earth (vv. 15-17). This drastic reversal of fortune in death and defeat highlights the degree of pride and arrogance exhibited by Babylon. Unlike other kings, the leader of Babylon would not rest **in his own tomb** (vv. 18-20), his offspring would be executed cutting off the king's lineage (vv. 21-22), and all memory of Babylon would be erased (v. 22).

Some have understood the words of 14:12-15 as an address to Satan, describing his fall. The support for this is found in Dn 10, where demons and angels are associated with nations, influencing the affairs of humanity. Hence, as the power behind Babylon, Satan's fall is described as desiring to make himself **like the Most High** (v. 14). The difficulty with this interpretation, and what makes it unlikely, is that there is no change of address syntactically—it all appears to be addressed to the king of Babylon.

14:24-27. Although seemingly a separate oracle against **Assyria**, this is not so because the word "oracle" is not here as it is in the other oracles to the nations. This is likely because Assyria is linked to Babylon, with Babylon being the successor empire to Assyria. The Lord's judgment of Assyria is certain (**just as I have planned so it will stand**, v. 24). Although Babylon's defeat of Assyria certainly judged that nation, this is more eschatological in nature. It will take place in Israel, **in My land . . . on My mountains** (v. 25) when the Lord gathers the nations there to execute eschatological judgment (cf. Ezk 39:4; Zch 14:2). This is part of God's plan for **the whole earth** (v. 26). In the end, the Lord's plans will come to fruition. No power may stand against God and no nation can frustrate His plans (v. 27).

b. The Oracle against Philistia (14:28-32)

14:28. The oracle about the Philistines was given for Judah's benefit. The time marker in v. 28 marks the shift from the oracle against Babylon to that against Philistia. Israel had a long history with the Philistines. Uzziah had brought Philistia under Judean control during the first part of the eighth century BC (cf. 2Ch 26:6). During the reign of Ahaz, the Philistines gained their independence (cf. 2Ch 28:18). While Philistia was one of Israel's opponents during the reign of Ahaz, it was also plagued by the Assyrians.

14:29-32. Philistia was not to celebrate because **the rod that struck you is broken** (v. 29). This is not a reference to Ahaz, but to Uzziah. However, with the death of Ahaz, the house of David was further weakened as was Judah, and the Philistines had hope of greater conquest. However, a **viper** (a metaphor for a deadly foe) and a **flying serpent** (indicating a deadly and speedy conquering nation) would strike Philistia, referring to Assyria (v. 29). In but a few short years after this oracle (711 BC) the Assyrian king Sargon II conquered Philistia and made it an Assyrian province. Judah's response to this news would be that **the LORD has founded Zion** (v. 32). Assyria would not be able to conquer Jerusalem (cf. chaps. 36–37) and the Babylonians would not conquer Judah until many years afterwards (586 BC).

c. The Oracle against Moab (15:1–16:14)

15:1-9. Moab, like Philistia, was no stranger to Assyrian domination. Moab was noted in the prophecies of other Israelite prophets (cf. Jr 48; Am 2:1-5). Several of the cities noted in vv. 1-4 were in northern Moab including **Kir**, **Nebo**, **Medeba**, **Heshbon**, and **Elealeh** (vv. 1-4). The southern cities of **Dibon** (v. 2) and **Jahaz** (v. 4) were distant participants in the destruction occurring in Moab. The people of Dibon performed the classic activities associated with morning: lamenting at the high places and the removal of the hair on one's head and face (v. 2) (Walton, et al., *IVP Bible Background Commentary*, 605). The distance between the northern and southern cities served to highlight the extent of the devastation and anguish felt in the northern cities (v. 4).

In vv. 5-9 the people of Moab are pictured as fleeing from the coming destruction. They ran away with whatever they could carry in search of a place where they could find safety. The reason for their flight is given in v. 6. The waters of **Nimrim** likely refer to an oasis of sorts north of Zoar southeast of the Dead Sea. The location was known for its abundant resources (David Noel Freedman, et al., *Eerdman's Dictionary of the Bible* [Grand Rapids, MI: Eerdmans, 2000], 965). The announcement in 15:6 that the waters of Nimrim have dried up offers a powerful image of destruction. The drying up of Nimrim prompted the people's departure with their wealth over the **brook of Arabim** (v. 7), which should likely be identified as the Wadi el-Hesa between Moab and Edom at the southern border of Moab (Walter A. Elwell and Philip W. Comfort, *Tyndale Bible Dictionary* [Carol Stream, IL: Tyndale, 2008],

1302). The entire country would be engulfed with the cries of the people from **Eglaim** and **Beer-elim** in the north to Wadi el-Hesa in the south. Those fleeing the north would find no refuge in the south. As the refugees flee southward to escape the invaders from the north, they would feel as if **a lion** was pursuing them (v. 9).

16:1-5. The oracle against Moab continues with a call to send a tribute to Jerusalem (v. 1). Moab now sought Judah's protection from their enemies. The Moabites compared themselves to birds without nests who were trying to find a new home. The once proud Moabites had been reduced to begging Judah for support and protection (v. 3), so Moab pled for a decision from Zion. This request speaks to the theological perspective presented in this oracle. As Young notes, "If there is to be deliverance Moab must be covered with Zion's shadow. Indeed, all who will find deliverance must be covered with Zion's shadow" (Edward J. Young, *The Book of Isaiah* (3 Volumes). Grand Rapids, MI: Eerdmans, 1965–1972, 463). If the Moabites were allowed to take shelter in Judah, they could escape the coming destruction as they waited for the establishment of that Davidic King, the Messiah, whose reign will usher in an age of justice (v. 5, cf. 11:1-16).

16:6-12. Next, the sin of **pride** once again becomes the focus of Isaiah's prophecy. The Moabites were a proud people. Their excess and abundance were a source of boasting, which would be proven empty (v. 6). Moabite pride and the devastation of their land came together to produce the lamentation of the nation (vv. 7-8). The destruction was so great that even the prophet had sympathy for Moab (vv. 10-11). Not only had the Moabites lost the security that came from abundance and excess, but they had also lost the security, however false, that was once drawn from their gods. Their pleading and praying would be forever ineffective (v. 12).

The oracle against Moab reflects again the futility of trusting and reveling in human accomplishments. The pride of Moab, embodied and emboldened by their lavish lifestyle, their vineyards, and their gods, did not save them from the coming destruction. The attempt to befriend Judah and the condemnation of Moab's pride stand in juxtaposition. The oracle calls those who read it to join themselves to Zion and the Lord who reigns there rather than trusting in human accomplishments.

16:13-14. This previous message is underscored by the Lord's pronouncement of Moab's demise. The glory of Moab would disappear and the nation's population would be devastated. This short-term prophecy was fulfilled as predicted. Within three years, Sennacherib destroyed Moab (701 BC). This example of short-term fulfillment was offered to give greater confidence with regard to the fulfillment of the previous long-term prophecies.

d. The Oracle against Syria and Ephraim (17:1-11)

17:1-11. The oracle against **Damascus** included judgment against **Ephraim**, the northern kingdom, Israel (v. 3). This is likely because of the alliance between Syria and Israel (cf. 7:1). This oracle differs from the ones previously delivered against Babylon and Moab in that it does not refer to the pride of the nation (aside from the reference to **the glory of Jacob**; v. 4). Instead, the nation's trust in the Lord rather than idols appears to be at issue (vv. 7-8). The altars and Asherah poles of the Israelites had produced a situation in which God had been forgotten. Asherah poles were pagan fertility symbols that were used in idolatrous worship. The production and prosperity of Israel would come to nothing because they had ignored God (vv. 10-11). Therefore, God ordained discipline for Israel, to motivate them to **look to the Holy One of Israel** (v. 7). Under God's hand, Tiglath-pileser III was swift in responding to Ahaz's gift. He conquered Damascus, killed King Rezin, and made the city a ruin (cf. 2Kg 16:7-9). Even so, Isaiah's repetition of the phrase **in that day** (vv. 4, 7, 9, 11) seems to point to an "end of days" fulfillment of this prophecy. In that case, Tiglath-pileser III's conquest would be a mere foreshadowing of a far more serious conquest at the end of days.

e. The Oracle against Cush (17:12–18:7)

17:12-14. While it is possible to view vv. 12-14 as the conclusion of the oracle begun in v. 1, the similarity in imagery and perspective between 17:12-14 and 18:1-7 make it reasonable to view these verses as a single unit. There is also a noticeable shift between 17:1-11 and 17:12-14. Whereas vv. 1-11 concern the sins of Damascus and Ephraim, which are primarily concerned with idolatry and the abandonment of God, vv. 12-14 focus on the raging nations and their inevitable failure. There is also a repetition of the term **Alas** in both 17:12 and 18:1, linking these sections together (the word is literally "woe" as in the NIV, an expression of lament that could be paraphrased "how sad for you"). These factors suggest that 17:12-14 be viewed as presenting an oracle distinct from 17:1-11 and joined to 18:1-7.

The apparent power of the nations is introduced in v. 12. Their **roaring** and raging are powerful, but they are no match for the Lord (v. 13). The juxtaposition of imagery in v. 13 contrasts the perceived roar of the nations that will crash down like powerful waves with the harmless chaff on the hills or tumbleweed that is driven along by the wind. Rather than dominating, the nations find themselves dominated by the Lord's "sudden terror" (17:14, NIV). Such is the fate of the enemies of the Lord and His people (v. 14).

18:1. This verse identifies the oracle as directed against Cush, modern Sudan and Ethiopia. The phrase **whirring wings** has been variously interpreted. The most likely understanding seems to be that offered by the Septuagint and the Targumim (Aramaic paraphrases of the OT by ancient rabbis) which interpret the phrase in relation to boats. Such an understanding plays on the prominence of insects in the land of Cush and on the reference to boats in v. 2. The imagery of **whirring wings**, then, suggests that the speedy "ships of the Ethiopians whiz up and down the rivers like winged insects" (Oswalt, *The Book of Isaiah, Chapters 1–39*, 359).

18:2-7. While it has been suggested that Cush is the one that sent envoys to Judah, it seems best to see an unknown group sending messengers to Cush in order to request their aid against other enemies. Perhaps this is a reference to Damascus and Ephraim and their alliance with Egypt, though the lack of a specific referent makes this identification difficult to confirm. In any case, the description of the nation and its people (v. 2), in combination with the command to **Go**, seems to picture Cush as a likely savior whose strength would provide safety. Such a description is only perceived since the *woe* saying of 18:1 is against Cush. Verse 3 critiques the unnecessary preparations for war. If the Lord were preparing an army, it would not be a secret. The whole world would see His banner and hear His **trumpet**. The verse appears to be a condemnation of the human efforts to prepare for battle rather than wait on the Lord.

Instead of making furious preparations for war, the Lord waits in silence until the time of pruning before the harvest (vv. 4-5). He will **cut off** portions of the vine and leave them for the birds and other wild animals to eat. The growth of God's enemies will only result in pruning. In the end, God will have His tribute as the nations, including the mighty Cush, will come to Zion. It seems that this is addressing Cush as experiencing eschatological judgment with the rest of the nations of the world (vv. 1-6). Nevertheless, a remnant of Cush will believe in the God of Israel and worship at **Mount Zion** in the millennial kingdom (v. 7).

f. The Oracle against Egypt (19:1–20:6)

The oracle against Egypt has two main sections. The first contains a long-term prophecy of events that will occur at the end of days (19:1-25) and the second has a near-term prophecy of events in eighth century BC (20:1-6). In the first section, there is a prediction of eschatological judgment (19:1-15) followed by eschatological blessing (vv. 16-25).

19:1-10. The events predicted in this chapter refer to the end of days. This is likely because the judgments described have yet to occur, such as the drying of the Nile River (vv. 5-8). Also, the future blessing described, when Egypt will come to know the God of Israel, has never happened. Further, the repetition of the eschatological phrase, **in that day** (vv. 16, 18, 21, 23-24) indicates that the oracle points to both judgment and blessing at the end of days. At the end of days, Egypt will also become subject to the Lord's actions. The weakness and worthlessness of their idols will be revealed and the whole nation will be in turmoil, with neighbor turning against neighbor (vv. 1-3). Despite their attempts to find answers by consulting their **idols . . . mediums and spiritists** (v. 3), Egypt is still at the mercy of the Lord (v. 4). Although some have identified the king of Assyria as the **cruel master** and **mighty king** who will oppress Egypt (v. 4), the eschatological nature of the chapter seems to point instead to the future world ruler called the little horn in Daniel (see the comments on Dn 7:8, 11-12, 19-27; 11:36-39). The Nile River is the primary resource on which Egypt depends, but at the end it will no longer be available to sustain the nation and its people (vv. 5-10).

19:11-15. The foolishness of Egypt's leaders is displayed in their inability to rightly direct the nation (vv. 11-13). Their inability to lead is ultimately attributed to the action of the Lord, who has mixed within her a spirit of distortion (v. 14). Egypt will appear as a drunk who **staggers in his vomit** (v. 14). This picture offers a vivid depiction of Egypt's confused, pitiable, and helpless state (v. 15).

19:16-22. The phrase **in that day** (v. 16), as well as the introduction of Judah (v. 17), marks a shift in the message to Egypt from end of days judgment to end of days blessing. The comparison between Egypt and women reflects the general understanding of women's social status in the ancient Near East. Women were not generally involved in military endeavors. The Egyptians have become delicate. They no longer have the illusion that they are capable of protecting themselves. Instead, they **tremble** as they watch the Lord come against them (v. 16). Judah will become the instrument of God's terror not just for Egypt, but also for **everyone to whom [Judah] is mentioned** (v. 17). This reversal of fortune in which the previous world powers tremble before the small, insignificant nation of Judah is achieved through the revelation of the Lord God of Israel.

The trembling of the Egyptians **in that day** will give way to a newly found allegiance to the Lord. **Five cities in the land of Egypt will be speaking the language of Canaan and swearing allegiance to the LORD of hosts** (v. 18). The reference to the five cities has been a source of confusion as the number of cities is relatively small in comparison to the number of cities actually in Egypt. The relative number of cities, however, may be of less significance. Note, for instance, the use of the number "five" in Lv 26:8: "Five of you will chase a hundred, and a hundred of you will chase ten thousand, and your enemies will fall before you by the sword." The use of five and one hundred to chase one hundred and ten thousand, respectively, suggests that though the number is small, the Lord will bring victory. Oswalt suggests that the number is meant to highlight the "radical nature of the turn" from idols to the Lord (Oswalt, *Isaiah 1–39*, 377). The adoption of Hebrew, **the language of Canaan**, does not indicate that Egyptians will stop speaking their own language, but that the Egyptians' turn to the Lord will cause them to worship in Israel and learn that language.

Of additional significance in this instance is the phrase **City of Destruction** or "city of the sun" in v. 18. The Hebrew phrase more traditionally translated as "city of destruction" is difficult to understand given the repentant response of the five cities with which it is included. Other ancient sources, including Isaiah scrolls found among the Dead Sea Scrolls, certain medieval Hebrew manuscripts, Aramaic translations (Targumim), Latin translations (Vulgate), and certain Greek translations of the text, suggest that the phrase be translated as "City of the Sun." If this latter translation is accepted, the reference would likely be to the city of Heliopolis. Heliopolis was the center for the Egyptian priesthood when Onias's temple was built in the nearby city of Leontopolis in the second century BC. Because the words "sun" and "destruction" look similar in Hebrew, it may be that there is a play on words here suggesting that the City of the Sun is, in fact, also the City of Destruction and refers to the destruction of Egypt's idols.

An altar to the Lord and a sacred pillar will replace the Egyptian cultic structures in the middle and border of Egypt. Because it is often assumed that the OT requires a central location for worship, this prediction may seem strange. However, the OT appears to make concession for worship at sites apart from the central sanctuary even when the central sanctuary was functioning. Vogt notes, "[T]the validity of a place of worship is determined not by the inherent sanctity of a place . . . but by the endorsement of the site by Yahweh. . . . 'The place' had to be one that Yahweh chose" (Peter T. Vogt, *Deuteronomic Theology and the Significance of Torah* [Winona Lake, IN: Eisenbrauns, 2006], 177). Once the altar and sacred pillar are established, they will serve as **a sign and a witness to the LORD of hosts in the land of Egypt** (v. 20). The altar and pillar could be construed as a sign for God or as a sign to the people. In either case, God will become Egypt's protector and Egypt will acknowledge God and His sovereignty in worship (v. 21).

19:23-25. The next section describes the millennial peace between Assyria, Egypt, and Israel. When the Messiah Jesus returns and establishes His earthly kingdom, these three nations will be united in worship of the Lord. The turning of Egypt and Assyria to the Lord represents another affirmation of God's coming triumph. Israel need not fear these other national powers. Instead, Israel must wait for the nations to recognize God's authority. They must focus on remaining faithful to God rather than making political alliances. God will bring unprecedented peace through the unification of the nations in worship of Him.

20:1-6. The prophet shifts from the idyllic picture of peace amongst the nations at the end of days to one of soon-coming judgment against Egypt. Isaiah went about **naked and barefoot** for **three years** as a symbol of the devastation of Egypt when Assyria would come against her. Likely the word **naked** only refers to the prophet going without an outer garment and not without any clothing whatsoever. This judgment fell in 711 BC when Egypt handed over the king of Ashdod, who had been granted asylum in Egypt, to the Assyrians. The message is that those who trust in Egypt trust in a nation that has already fallen. Again, the emphasis is placed on turning back to the Lord.

g. The Oracle against Babylon (21:1-10)

21:1. This oracle speaks against the nation of Babylon, or the **wilderness of the sea**. Why Babylon is referred to as such is difficult to ascertain. Ancient translations vary, with the Dead Sea Scrolls reading "words of the sea." The replacement of **wilderness** with "words" is based on the similarity of the two words in Hebrew, with only one letter differentiating the two. The Aramaic Targum expands the phrase to read "armies that come from the desert like water from the sea." Other more modern commentators have suggested that the reference is related to southern Mesopotamia's identification as "the Sealand" with **wilderness** having a predictive function and referring to Babylon's inability to help other nations (Oswalt, *Isaiah 1–39*, 340).

21:2-10. Isaiah identified the vision he had received as **harsh** (v. 2). Babylon would be defeated by the **treacherous one** and the **destroyer**. While the enemy is not specifically identified, the word "treacherous" is used of Assyria in Is 33:1. Isaiah's reaction to the vision reflected his dismay over the coming destruction of Babylon. Smith suggests that the prophet was frustrated because "the defeat of Babylon meant that Judah would probably have to face Assyria by itself, with little hope to defend itself against Assyria" (Smith, *Isaiah 1–39*, 372). Such an interpretation seems to stand in tension with the message of God's sovereignty that the rest of Isaiah provides.

It is, however, difficult to understand why this message of judgment had such an impact on Isaiah. Perhaps it is best to understand the description of the prophet's attitude in juxtaposition to the relatively carefree attitude of Babylon (v. 5). The Babylonians appeared to be too busy feasting and drinking to prepare for war. Isaiah called for guards to be posted to watch for the coming onslaught, only to report the complete destruction of Babylon along with the nation's idols. Babylon and its idols were not invincible. Judah could not rely on Babylonian power, but must rely on God.

Identifying the time when Babylon would fall is more challenging. Some have taken it to refer to the fall of Babylon to the Assyrians in 689 BC (because of Israel's lack of joy; vv. 3-4). Others view it occurring when Babylon fell to the Persians in 539 BC (because of the reference to the Medes in v. 2). A third more likely view is to understand this judgment as a combination of the first two views and events (Oswalt, *The Book of Isaiah, Chapters 1–39*, 390). But since the previous description of the fall of Babylon (cf. Is 13–14) referred to an end-of-days judgment, this oracle likely does as well. Additionally, the repetition of the phrase **fallen, fallen is Babylon** (v. 9) in the book of Revelation, both times referring to the eschatological end of Babylon (cf. Rv 14:8; 18:2), likely identifies this as an end of days destruction as well.

h. The Oracle against Edom (21:11-12)

21:11-12. The thrust of the oracle against **Edom** appears to be that while the morning is coming, night will overtake it again. The language of **morning** and **night** is probably symbolic, representing distress and deliverance respectively. The watchman's response to the concern may reflect the ambiguity of the situation and the necessity of diligent watchfulness.

i. The Oracle against Arabia (21:13-17)

21:13-15. This next oracle is about Arabian tribes. Speaking to the **Dedanites** (a tribe from southern Arabia) and the **inhabitants of the land of Tema** (an oasis in northwestern Arabia), the prophet directed them to bring water and food to the fugitives fleeing from battle whom they would soon encounter.

21:16-17. The prophet then made a specific prediction about Arabia. **In a year**, the people of Arabia, specifically, the men of **Kedar** (in northern Arabia) as representing all the tribes, would become fugitives. Some have suggested that this was fulfilled with the invasions of Tiglath-pileser (738 BC), Sargon II (715 BC), or Sennacherib (703 BC). Although it is not clear which invasion caused the prophecy to be fulfilled, the ancient original readers would know. As such, this prophecy, with its near-term fulfillment, functions as a reminder to trust God to fulfill the many long-term prophecies found throughout the book.

j. The Oracle against Jerusalem (22:1-25)

22:1-14. Isaiah now turned his attention to Jerusalem. Because the rest of the oracles included in Is 13–23 were aimed at non-Israelite nations, the inclusion of the oracle against Jerusalem, as well as its position within chaps. 13–23, raises questions concerning its overall function and purpose. Adding to the difficulties associated with this passage is the use of the term **valley of vision** (v. 1) to identify Jerusalem. While Jerusalem is often referred to as a mountain, or Mount Zion in particular, it is seldom identified as a valley. Furthermore, the exact phrase **valley of vision** is only used here in the OT. Young connects the use of the term vision with revelation, noting that Jerusalem was the place in which revelation was given (Young, *The Book of Isaiah*, 2:86). Others have suggested that the phrase refers to the Hinnom Valley. This valley is normally understood to run along the west and south side of the Old City south of the Jaffa gate. Another possibility is that it refers to the Kidron Valley that runs between the city proper and the Mount of Olives to the east. The identification of this valley as the **valley of vision** is justified geographically, but may not have any particular bearing on the interpretation of chap. 22.

The oracle begins with a rhetorical question that highlights the contradictory nature of Jerusalem's rejoicing. The people had not been destroyed. The dead were not killed by the sword (v. 2), but they were dead just the same. The rejoicing of the people over their successful siege and the brilliance of their defense lacked imagination (vv. 6-11). The defenses of Jerusalem were flawed because the city **did not depend on Him who made it nor . . . take into consideration Him who planned it long ago** (v. 11). The mention of making **a reservoir** (v. 11) is a reference to the well-known Hezekiah's tunnel, carved by King Hezekiah from solid rock in order to connect the Gihon Spring to the Pool of Siloam (cf. 2Ch 32:30) and provide water for Jerusalem in time of siege. Nevertheless, rather than rejoicing in their success, God expected Judah to repent (vv. 12-13). The inappropriate reaction of the people reflected their disrespect for God, which was unpardonable (v. 14).

22:15-25. That vv. 15-25 continue the oracle of vv. 1-14 is suggested by the repetition of the title **the Lord GOD of hosts** (v. 15) from vv. 5 and 12 (note also the shortened title **the LORD of hosts** in v. 14). The people were called to address the steward **Shebna**. The Hebrew term translated **steward** is only used here in the OT, making its meaning difficult to determine. It is clear, however, that Shebna was a high-ranking official in Jerusalem. Despite his self-interested behavior, which was exemplified through the building of the hillside tomb (v. 16), Shebna would be tossed aside and would not retain his position (v. 19). In 1953, a tomb, dating from the eighth century BC, in the Silwan (Siloam) section of Jerusalem was discovered that many identify as the one described in this passage as belonging to Shebna.

When Shebna was removed, the Lord would place His servant on the throne. The significance of the "servant" terminology in the book of Isaiah will be further addressed in relation to its application to Israel and to the suffering servant in Is 40–55, and again to Israel in chaps. 65–66. By identifying **Eliakim** as **My servant** (v. 20), God authorized his leadership. Eliakim, a godly palace administrator, would benefit from God's blessing as he governed Judah, yet he too would fall (v. 25). Despite the honor bestowed upon him, Eliakim would not be able to bear the weight of Judah in that day. Eliakim was not to be trusted because he also was human. Instead, Judah must place their trust in God.

k. The Oracle against Tyre (23:1-18)

The final oracle in this section was levied against Tyre. This city, just north of Israel on the shore of the Mediterranean, was the bookend to ancient Babylon to the east. Both cities epitomized the arrogance and pride that pits itself against the one true God. Hence, Tyre would come under judgment.

23:1-14. This first part of the oracle focuses on the fall of Tyre. The people of the Mediterranean were called to mourn at the fall of this city, since its demise would hinder the economies of the entire Mediterranean world. Tyre's defeat would affect trade and therefore bring sorrow to **Tarshish** (vv. 1, 6) in Spain and to **Cyprus** (vv. 1, 12), as well as to the **Nile** in the land of **Egypt** (vv. 3, 5). The once great civilization would suffer at the hands of the Lord (vv. 8-9). The punishment of Tyre is again linked to God's plan to bring low those honored by humanity (v. 9).

23:15-18. Just as Babylon was conquered by Assyria in 689 BC, so Tyre would also be destroyed **for seventy years** (vv. 13-15). Some have proposed that the 70 years refers to the time of Judah's captivity, but that period of time did not affect Tyre. It has also been speculated that this period of time was not a specific amount of time, but rather an idiom for fullness or completeness. Yet it seems most likely, because of the specificity of the date, that the prophet was speaking of the period from about 700 to 630 BC when the Assyrians greatly restricted Tyre's trade. However, with the decline of Assyria, Tyre would return to her **harlot's wages**, a reference to Tyre's return to her economic power (v. 17). Yet, when Tyre's strength returned, it would be used in service to God's people (v. 18), aiding Israel in the rebuilding of the temple.

This series of oracles underscored the prophet's message concerning the nations. They were not to be trusted. Nothing the nations had was of any permanent value. Their belongings, wisdom, strategies, and military might were fleeting and deceptive. The critique of the nations was designed to point the people of Judah back to the Lord. Alliances may be politically expedient, foreign idols may bring momentary comfort, and foreign wealth may offer the allure of a decadent lifestyle, but they cannot last, nor can they compare to the security, assurance, and abundance of the Lord's blessing.

2. The Little Apocalypse (24:1–27:13)

Here the prophet changed his focus from the nations surrounding Israel to that of the whole earth. In so doing, his perspective changed from the near term to the long term and from his days to the end of days.

These chapters are also often identified as Isaiah's "Little Apocalypse." Despite this more traditional ascription, many modern interpreters do not consider the material in this section of Isaiah as genuine apocalyptic literature. However, apocalyptic literature is difficult to define, and generally there are several characteristics present in the apocalyptic genre. John J. Collins identifies apocalyptic as "[A] genre of revelatory literature with a narrative framework, in which a revelation is mediated by an otherworldly being to a human recipient, disclosing a transcendent reality which is both temporal, insofar as it envisages eschatological salvation, and spatial insofar as it involves another, supernatural world" (John J. Collins, *Apocalyptic Imagination* [Grand Rapids, MI: Eerdmans, 1998], 4).

Several elements within Is 24–27, including, but not limited to, the defeat of Leviathan and the reactions of the sun and moon, and the presence of eschatological salvation, have been identified as apocalyptic. However, there is no angelic messenger. Sweeny suggests that "these chapters can hardly be characterized as apocalyptic in the fullest sense, although they may represent an early stage in the development of apocalyptic" (Marvin A. Sweeney, *Isaiah 1–39* [Grand Rapids, MI: Eerdmans, 1996], 313–14). Therefore, some have identified this section as "proto-apocalyptic" suggesting that it is a precursor to full-blown apocalyptic literature (Paul Hanson, *The Dawn of Apocalyptic* [Minneapolis, MN: Augsburg Fortress, 1989], 27). It seems best to refer to this section of Isaiah as eschatological prophecy, since it utilizes images similar to those found in apocalyptic literature. The similarities indicate that it is still appropriate to title this section "The Little Apocalypse."

Despite the disputes concerning the genre of Is 24–27, the message of this section is relatively clear. God will triumph, bringing destruction to His enemies and peace and restoration for God's people. These chapters continue the call for Israel to trust in the Lord rather than in the nations.

a. The Judgment of the Earth (24:1–25:12)

In chaps. 24 and 25 Isaiah discussed God's judgment of the earth. First, the prophet described the judgment of the earth (24:1-23), after which he took up the responses to that judgment (25:1-12).

(1) The Description of Judgment (24:1-23)

The earth as inhabited by humanity is depicted as a city. As such, the city of man, guided and directed by human perspectives rather than God's counsel, becomes a city of chaos (v. 10). Though the city is not identified, the 17 uses of earth suggest that the city is representative of the nations as a whole. The nations' adherence, or lack thereof, to the law of the Lord determines their fate (vv. 1, 3, 5, 14, 21).

24:1-3. The first part of the description of judgment is the future, eschatological devastation of the earth. As such, the earth is **laid waste and completely despoiled** (v. 3). The emphasis of v. 2 is that this devastation will affect all classes of society—none will be spared.

24:4-13. The second aspect of the judgment is that the earth mourns (v. 4). The world will come under this judgment for breaking **the everlasting covenant** (v. 5). Some have considered this phrase to refer to the Mosaic covenant, but since it is the inhabitants of the earth breaking it and not Israel, this is unlikely. More likely it refers to the Noahic covenant (cf. Gn 9) with its requirements for righteousness for the whole world. Another possibility is this refers to the law of conscience, broken even by those who do not have the law of Moses (cf. Rm 2:14-16). Regardless, the judgment of God will turn all the revelry of sin into sorrow and mourning (vv. 6-13).

24:14-16a. A third aspect of God's judgment is worship. The believing remnant will respond by glorifying Him for His judgment. These worshipers are not limited to the remnant of Israel, but include all the faithful **from the west . . . in the east** and **the coastlands of the sea**. In fact, **from the ends of the earth** they will sing **Glory to the Righteous One**. God will be glorified because He is righteous and just in His judgment.

24:16b-20. The fourth way that the judgment of God is described is with sorrow. The prophet himself laments when he foresees God's judgment, crying out, **Woe to me! Woe to me! Alas for me!** (v. 16b). Isaiah saw all the treacherous people upon whom judgment must fall. Seeing that **terror and pit and snare** was their destiny (v. 17), the prophet grieved at their destruction and the violent devastation of the earth that was yet to come (vv. 18-20).

24:21-23. The last aspect of God's judgment of the earth is its finality. **The Lord will punish the host of heaven** (likely a reference to fallen angels or spiritual powers that oppose God) and **the kings of the earth** (referring to the political opposition to God in the last days; v. 21; cf. Ps 2). At that time, the Lord will take His throne on **Mount Zion**, and His glory will supersede the glory of the **moon** and **sun** (v. 23).

(2) The Responses to Judgment (25:1-12)

25:1-5. This chapter represents the response of God's people to the judgment of the earth in chap. 24. Their first response to God's judgment is thankfulness for His activities among the nations. Their grateful praise derives from the execution of God's plans that were decreed **long ago** (v. 1). It is clear that the destruction of the nations was not done on a whim, but was planned beforehand. The promised redemption is sure. Just as the earth was previously described as a chaotic city (cf. 24:10), in response God will take that city and make it **into a heap** and **a ruin** (v. 2). God's destruction of the nations will bring about the nations' worship and fear. The nations' reverence is not only rooted in their respect for God's power, but for His treatment of the poor and needy. In contrast to a tyrant, the Lord cares for those whom He rules. His reign is not characterized by oppression and difficulty, but by protection and care (vv. 4-5).

25:6-8. The second response to God's judgment will be triumph. This is depicted as **a lavish banquet for all peoples**, a reference to the great messianic banquet (not the marriage supper of the Lamb in Rv 19, but the millennial kingdom on earth) with abundance and community (v. 6) and the removal of death and disgrace (vv. 7-8). With the onset of the messianic kingdom, God will bring comfort, wiping **tears away from all faces** and restore Israel, removing **the reproach of His people from all the earth** (v. 8).

25:9-12. The third response to God's judgment will be joy. The song of God's people shifts the focus from the universal perspective offered in vv. 6-8 to the reaction of Israel. They recognize the fulfillment of God's long-awaited promise of deliverance (v. 9). The **hand of the Lord will rest on this mountain** and provide security, but **Moab** will be destroyed beneath it **as straw is trodden down in the water of a manure pile** (v. 10). Swimming in manure is strong imagery that highlights the depth of Moab's humiliation. Moab serves as an archetype of the enemies of Israel. In the end of days, regardless of all the nations' **trickery**, they will be brought low (vv. 11-12).

b. The Establishment of God's Kingdom (26:1–27:13)

Having demonstrated that God would establish His righteousness through judgment in the previous two chapters, the author points beyond that judgment to the blessing of God's kingdom that will follow.

26:1-6. To begin the focus on God's kingdom, the author presents Judah's song of joy and thanksgiving to the Lord. Judah sings praises for God's acts on its behalf. In contrast to the chaotic city described in 24:10, this city, built by God, is strong because the Lord has provided genuine **security** (v. 1). Its walls offer security for the righteous nation and those who are **steadfast of mind** (vv. 2-3). Trust in the Lord is of paramount importance for Judah. Their continued security depends on the nation's ongoing faithfulness to the God who will bring low **those who dwell on high** (v. 5). The proud have no standing before the Lord. Instead, the lowly and the poor will trample the proud and mighty. The poor and the needy who trust God will overcome their apparently powerful opponents.

26:7-11. In the discussion of God's kingdom, the author shifts from thanksgiving to an expression of dependence during the time while God's people wait for His kingdom to be established. The Lord makes paths straight for the righteous. Those who trust in God wait patiently for the Lord's judgment to teach those on earth righteousness (vv. 8-9). The wicked learn righteousness only through judgment. Despite the favor of the Lord, they are blind to God's majesty (v. 10). Even as the Lord prepares to judge the people, they are unaware. The prophet calls God to show them **Your zeal for the people** (v.

11). Two other potential senses of this phrase are possible. First, the phrase may refer to the nations' jealousy against Israel. Second, it may refer to Israel's zeal against the enemies of the Lord. Yet the NASB rendering appears most likely given the context of judgment on the nations and the mention of the fire that will devour God's enemies.

26:12-19. Not only do those who trust wait for God to act, they also have confidence in the Lord to renew His people. He will bring **peace** to His people and, unlike their previous rulers, God will show them graciousness and be good to them (vv. 12-13). The other nations have not stood the test of time. They challenged the Lord and He **destroyed** them (v. 14). By contrast, the Lord has expanded His territory (v. 15). God is the just ruler whose reign is everlasting and whose past activities instill confidence in His people that He will deliver them.

The prophet's message shifts back to the present in vv. 16-19. Whereas vv. 12-15 highlighted the certainty of God's deliverance and a hopeful future, vv. 16-19 compares the distress of the people to a woman in childbirth. The Lord brought an agony upon His people similar to that of a woman bearing a child (v. 17). Unlike a woman in child **birth**, however, the anguish of God's people produced nothing. It brought neither **deliverance** nor conquest (v. 18). The agony resulted only in death. Yet God will restore the dead to life. Those in the dust will experience life-giving power like that of the dew (18:4; Hs 14:5-6). The resurrection of OT saints will take place at the return of Jesus the Messiah (cf. Dn 12:2 and the comments there) and they will enter and enjoy His millennial kingdom.

26:20–27:1. Besides the song of joy (26:1-6) and the expression of trust (26:7-19), the author offers an exhortation to the faithful to wait for God's judgment and future blessing. It is written as an oracle of salvation. Though salvation will come, God's people must wait patiently. God calls them to seek shelter and to hide **until** His **indignation runs its course**, or His wrath is complete (26:20). At various times in their history, God's people have been preserved from judgment. Noah and his family were shut up in the ark (Gn 7:16) and the Israelites were spared at the Passover (Ex 12:13). Even Rahab was spared because of her willingness to aid the Israelite spies (Jos 2:12-20). God's preservation of His people reflects His commitment to accomplish His purposes and bring His people faithfully through to the end. The Lord will come in judgment against the sin of the people of the earth. The bloodshed produced by the swords of men will no longer be hidden in the earth. The sins committed by those who challenged God's rule will be brought to light. Isaiah 27:1 makes reference to Leviathan. Leviathan is consistently associated with chaos and the sea (Jb 26:13; 41:1; Ps 74:13-15; 104:26). Other civilizations in the ancient Near East such as Ugarit and Babylonia have stories of similar creatures that were also associated with chaos and death.

In slaying Leviathan, the Lord vanquishes the great symbol of chaos and antagonism toward God. Though the powers of this world appear to be prevailing, they will not be victorious in the end. God will triumph in the end. Those who have trusted in Him will be preserved. Those who continue in their sin will be destroyed. Those who rebel against God, who oppose God in the manner of Leviathan, will be defeated.

27:2-6. This section speaks of a day when the Lord will deliver Judah. The passage portrays Israel as a **vineyard** protected and cared for by the Lord (vv. 2-3). It speaks of a day in which the Lord's anger has subsided and He longs for enemies, represented by **thorns** and **briars**, to come against Judah so that He can defend the nation (v. 4). Better still, He desires that the nations would come to Him and make **peace** as Jacob becomes secure and expands upon the earth (vv. 5-6).

The previous use of vineyard imagery came in 5:1-7 and depicted Israel as a wild and untamed vineyard that would only produce worthless fruit. Here, the vineyard depicts Israel as redeemed. The Lord will care for the vineyard and bring forth produce. God's judgment will be supplanted by His deliverance as the new vineyard prospers under His care. The return of the vineyard imagery highlights the dramatic turn that will come about for God's people. The assurances given in 27:2-6 underscore the coming restoration of Israel and sets Israel's situation into relief with that of the nations.

27:7-13. The rhetorical question of v. 7 highlights the difference between God's treatment of the nations and God's treatment of Israel. As Brueggemann notes, "Yahweh's punishment of Yahweh's own has indeed been harsh, but not as harsh as punishment given to others" (Walter Brueggemann, *Isaiah 1–39*, Westminster Bible Companion (Louisville: Westminster John Knox Press, 1998), 214). Despite this encouragement, however, v. 8 affirms that God will bring discipline on Israel. The Lord is said to have **contended** with Israel by **banishing** them. An alternative translation takes the word "banishing" as "measure," with which the ancient Jewish Targum concurs. Oswalt also translates "measure," arguing that the punishment fits the crime. Lexically, the Hebrew form can be translated either way. In light of the phrase that follows (**driving them away**) and the Hebrew penchant for parallelism, it seems that the appropriate translation is "banishing." Therefore, this speaks of God's discipline of Israel by exile.

The reference to the **east wind** in v. 8 gives weight to the coming discipline upon God's people. This punishment will not be a slap on the wrist, but will come with the severity of the east wind, which provides an ominous presence at various points in Scripture (Gn 41:6; Jb 27:21; Ps 48:8; Jr 18:17; Ezk 27:26; Hs 13:15). Winds from the east of Israel originated in the scorching temperatures of the desert, and could be destructive for crops and animals. The east wind here likely appears as a symbol for violent, unstoppable, divine judgment.

Regardless of the precise meaning it is clear that God will judge His people, yet it is through this judgment that **Jacob's iniquity will be forgiven** (v. 9; see the comments on Rm 11:27, where this verse is cited by the apostle Paul). The people's sins will be forgiven and they will turn back to God. The passage illustrates not only the necessity for forgiveness, but the need for accompanying acts that reflect a renewed commitment to follow God. The people, perhaps in response to God's judgment and the forgiveness that it brings will respond by removing the idolatrous altars and Asherah poles. This action represents a renewed commitment to the Lord and a sole devotion to the God of Israel.

The identification of the **city** in v. 10 is unclear but it seems likely that the city is symbolic for God's enemies. The description of the city as **fortified** may suggest an element of self-sufficiency, particularly when combined with the familiar punishment of abandonment and forsakenness that has been utilized in previous passages in Isaiah (cf. 1:7; 24:10). The imagery of animals grazing on the land of a once-great city is also found in other passages within Isaiah (cf. 5:17; 7:25; 17:1-2). Eventually, the animals will strip the city's vegetation bare and women will use the dry wood to make fires. This picture of a deliberate, ongoing march toward final destruction is caused by the people's lack of understanding (27:11). This lack of understanding results in a lack of **compassion** from their **Maker**.

The people's inability to live under the rule of God, to recognize their Creator, and to obey Him brings unhindered punishment. By contrast, the Israelites will find deliverance. Isaiah 27:12-13 speaks of the great gathering of Israel. As the nations are punished, the people of Israel will be assembled from the nations in order to worship the Lord in **Jerusalem**. The **great trumpet** will sound as all of God's people are called there. The trumpet blast appears in relation to several events in Scripture. It is perhaps most known for its associations with war (Jos 6:16, 20; Jdg 6:34), particularly with the final battle against all evil (Zch 9:14). In this context, however, this association is less likely as it would appear that the battle has ended before the trumpet is blown. In other instances, the trumpet blast is associated with the installment of a new king (1Kg 1:34, 39; 9:13) and with more general calls to attention (Lv 25:9; Jl 2:1, 15). In this context, the trumpet marks a call to come out from exile to **worship** the Lord (Is 27:13).

3. The Book of "Woes" (28:1–33:24)

In Is 5:1-6, Israel was depicted as a vineyard that would only produce worthless grapes. Afterwards, in 5:7-30, six woes were declared on the people for their sins. In chap. 27, Israel was again depicted as a vineyard, but this time as a protected one, indicating God's permanent preservation of His people. Now in Isaiah 28–33, six woes are again declared but now upon the leaders of Israel for their sins.

a. The First Woe: For Drunken Mocking (28:1-29)

28:1-6. The first of six woes is for the drunkenness and mockery found in Israel's leaders. The word **woe** is an interjection or exclamation of lament. It generally (but not always, cf. Is 55:1) precedes a warning of God's coming judgment and contains within it an expression of sympathy or pity. It could be paraphrased, "How sad for you!" The **proud crown** (v. 1) is a symbol of power and sovereignty. It is the crown, or the glory, that sits on the head of those whose drunken behavior blinds them to the coming destruction. The city of Samaria is likely in mind here. Samaria served as the capital of the northern kingdom in the eighth and ninth centuries BC. The city was located on a hillside overlooking a fertile valley. Its elevated location made Samaria difficult to overtake, although it was besieged on several occasions (1Kg 20:1-21, 28-34; 2Kg 7:1-20). The city was eventually overtaken by the Assyrians in 722/721 BC. The future onslaught will come at the hands of the Lord's **strong and mighty agent** (28:2). The storm imagery used in v. 2 suggests the force with which Samaria will be brought down. The images of windblown hail being driven into the ground and rain pounding into the dirt depict vividly the power with which Samaria will be destroyed.

The once-beautiful wreaths worn by the drunkards will soon wither and fade. That which was worn on the top of one's head as a sign of carefree self-indulgence will fall to the ground and be **trodden under foot** (v. 3). This trampling will come quickly as the comparison of Samaria to the ripe fig makes clear. Figs and fig trees are used in other prophetic passages to denote divine punishment (cf. Jr 8:13; Jl 1:7, 12; Am 4:9; Hab 3:17). It is also used as a figure of restoration (Jl 2:22). Figs could have ripened twice a year, with the winter crop ripening in June and the summer crop in August and September (David C. Hopkins, *The Highlands of Canaan: Agricultural Life in the Early Iron Age* [Sheffield: Sheffield Academic, 1985], 228). As Wildberger notes, "The pride of the lords of Samaria would be gone quickly and it would be demonstrated, with uncanny speed, that all the hopes by which the people tried to comfort themselves would be comparable to the euphoric expectations of drunks" (Hans Wildberger, *Isaiah 28–39: A Continental Commentary* [Minneapolis: Fortress, 2002], 11).

In Is 28:5 the Lord will become a **crown** for the remnant of His people. God will provide the needed resources for those ruling His people. He will be a **spirit of justice** (v. 6) for those who judge in Israel and a source of **strength** to those who defend God's people. The Lord will replace the pride and drunkenness of the people with justice and power that will protect the remnant of his people. God will empower His people to overcome their enemies.

28:7-13. The priests and prophets who were supposed to guide Israel spiritually, offer the nation discernment, and serve as a conduit for the Word of the Lord instead are drunken fools. Their drunkenness was influencing their official duties as they would **reel** and **stagger** during their decisions and visions (v. 7). The tables at which the officials sat were covered with **vomit** due to their excessive drinking. The pleasure-seeking behavior of the rulers had come to a degrading end as they sat reveling in their own filth (v. 8). Despite their unfortunate state, the drunken prophets and priests rejected the Lord's teaching. The **He** of v. 9 most likely refers to God and to the message delivered by His prophet. The sarcastic response of the priests and prophets in v. 9 reflects both their arrogance and ignorance. They are proud of the way they are living and reject the way of righteousness. They view themselves as men who have no need of the Lord's rebuke rather than what they actually are—"babies" who require the guidance given by God's prophet.

The disdain of the priests and prophets is given an ironic twist in v. 10. The teaching that they assumed was given to children and babes just **weaned from milk** (v. 9) will become unintelligible to them. It will be like the babbling of a child in their ears. The paired phrases in v. 10 exhibit a literary characteristic of assonance and alliteration in which there is a repetition of vowel and consonantal sounds respectively to create a patterned whole. The Hebrew text reads as follows with the "ts" at the beginning of some of the words being pronounced as the "ts" combination in English words like "nuts" or "hits": "tsav latsav, tsav latsav, qav laqav, qav laqav." Though several English translations, including the NASB, provide a translation of each of these terms, it is likely that they were meant to represent the speech of a young child just learning to talk.

Not only will God speak in the unintelligible gibberish of children, He will speak in a foreign language (v. 11). While the babbling of children would be impossible to understand, the **foreign tongue** will be far more discernible. The reference to the stammering lips and strange tongue in v. 11 refers to the language of the Assyrian empire. The failure of the leaders to listen to God's message through the prophet will force God to make them hear Him through the sword of Assyria. When they hear the foreign language of Assyria, they will know judgment is upon them. Paul also cited this example of a foreign language in the context of a sign pointing to the truth of God's message (see comments on 1Co 14:20-25). The babbling comes to bring judgment and punitive consequences (28:13).

28:14-16. The **therefore** at the beginning of v. 14 suggests a causal relationship between the events described in 28:5-13 and the message delivered in 28:14-29. Given the coming destruction, the prophet calls the rulers to listen to God's Word. Rather than trust in the Lord for protection, the rulers of Jerusalem have made a foolish pact with Sheol or "the grave" (v. 15; for an explanation of Sheol, see the comments on Ps 49:15). The pact is rooted in lies and will never be able to protect the people from their enemies or from the judgment of God. Their agreement with death has made **falsehood** their refuge. While such a pact is obviously a misguided act of disobedience, God graciously offers an alternative. He will place in **Zion** a stone or a **cornerstone**. The stone is described as being **tested** and **costly** (28:16). It will offer a foundation firmly placed and the one who believes in it will not be **disturbed**. Unlike the false covenant made with death, which could offer nothing except false assurances, the cornerstone offers everlasting security to those who lean upon it.

The imagery of the cornerstone was used previously in 19:13 where the unreliable cornerstones of Egypt deceive the nation and lead it in the wrong direction. The term is also used in Jr 51:26 in an oracle of judgment against Babylon and in Zch 10:4 as a reference to the messianic ruler who will come from Judah. One of the most well-known uses of the cornerstone imagery is the messianic reference found in Ps 118:22, which is applied to Christ in Mt 21:42; Mk 12:10; Lk 20:17; Ac 4:11; Eph 2:20; and 1Pt 2:7. It seems Isaiah is also using the term as a figure for the ultimate son of David, the messianic King.

28:17-20. The cornerstone will provide safety from the implementation of God's just rule, which will **sweep away the refuge of lies** (v. 17). The reference to the **lies** in conjunction with **refuge** alludes to the false covenant with death. The people's hiding place will be submerged with no hope of protection. As God establishes His new order, the covenant with death will be terminated. Its uselessness will be revealed as the Lord brings the **overwhelming scourge** upon the people and it will not stop (vv. 18-19). Nothing will stop the onslaught except trust in the cornerstone. The people's securities and comforts are no more. Even their beds do not provide comfort (v. 20).

28:21-23. This section likely refers to God's activities against the Philistines at Baal-perazim (2Sm 5:20) and against the Canaanites (Jos 10:10-11). As God came against the Philistines and the Canaanites, so He will come against Israel in judgment. Such activities against Israel seem strange and unfamiliar in comparison with the punishment of the nations. Regardless of its oddity, God will accomplish His unusual task of disciplining Israel. The Lord will not continue to bear the people's foolish mocking. Instead, the discipline of Israel will only increase until the whole land is destroyed if they refuse to turn back to the Lord (v. 22). The prophet calls Israel to obey his word, to listen, and to follow the Lord (v. 23).

28:24-29. The rhetorical questions (vv. 24-25) bring focus to the foolishness of the leaders' rebellion against God. The picture painted is one of a farmer who has been taught by God to care for his fields and to sow and harvest its produce. The farmer does not plow the field forever. After plowing and breaking up the ground, the farmer begins to sow. The ground can only be cultivated for so long before the farmer must take the next step and sow seeds. The seeds in question each require specific planting techniques. The farmer understands the needs of each of the seeds and cares for them to secure his harvest.

Cummin (v. 25) was generally scattered by hand over cultivated ground, but the **wheat**, **barley**, and **rye** may have been planted with a seed drill as they would have needed to be separated from one another (Walton, et al., *IVP Bible Background Commentary*, 620). The farmer would plant the seeds appropriately based on the instruction of the Lord (v. 26). The **dill** and **cummin** mentioned take on a greater significance in v. 27 where the process for threshing is described. **Dill** and **cummin** are too delicate to use large threshing tools. For more resilient seeds, such as **wheat**, the Israelites would have employed a process in which wood sleds were used to crush the wheat. Threshing forks were then utilized to toss the wheat into the air. The chaff was blown away by the wind and the heavier grain fell to the ground and was collected and stored (William G. Dever, *The Lives of Ordinary People in Ancient Israel: Where Archaeology and the Bible Intersect* [Grand Rapids, MI: Eerdmans, 2012], 199).

The simple farmer has been taught by God to care for his field and to do what is necessary to care for his produce. The knowledge of planting, harvesting, and threshing does not come from an agrarian god, but from the **Lord of hosts**. There is a contrast being made between the pastoral imagery used in 28:23-28 and the terms used to describe the Lord in v. 29. The phrase **Lord of hosts** translates a Hebrew phrase that associates God with war, or as the commander of armies (John Goldingay, *Songs from a Strange*

Land: Psalms 42–51 [Toronto: Clements, 1972], 60). God is not simply a God who provides the techniques necessary to inform a farmer's planting and harvesting. Instead, He is a powerful God of armies who provides counsel and wisdom.

The Hebrew term translated **counsel** (v. 29) is related to that translated "counselor" in the phrase "Wonderful Counselor" in 9:6, though it is not clear that a specific connection is intended. The point of the contrast just noted is twofold. First, the agrarian cycle exhibits the sort of wisdom and order that God brings to those who listen to Him and learn from His word. Second, the use of **LORD of hosts** (lit., "Lord of armies") highlights God's capacity to function in realms other than that of agriculture. The same God who teaches the farmer to care for his wheat and cummin is also the God who does battle. The leaders whose covenant with death will be overturned must realize that their security does not lie in a misguided agreement, but in the God who commands armies. The passage calls the leaders and all those who read it to see the truth and to abandon false allegiances that offer only the appearance of safety.

b. The Second Woe: For Religious Hypocrisy (29:1-14)

29:1-4. The second **woe** of the six woes is for religious hypocrisy in Israel, particularly among the spiritual leaders. Isaiah continues his prophecy against Israel by turning his attention to **Ariel**. Though it is clear that the prophecy is addressing Jerusalem (29:8), the term **Ariel** can be understood as either a reference to the altar hearth where sacrifices were offered (Ezk 43:15-16), or as a compound noun combining the Hebrew words for lion (*ari*) and God (*el*). The first interpretation is supported by the reference to the feasts in 29:1, which could suggest a cultic context for the passage as a whole. The latter more likely understanding of Ariel is supported by the numerous uses of "lion" in conjunction with Judah or the Judean king (Gn 49:9; 1Kg 10:19-20; Is 31:4).

Ariel is also identified as the city where David once camped. There is some dispute over this translation as the Hebrew word translated **camped** (29:1) is used again in v. 3 with the sense of "besiege." While it is possible that the two terms should be translated similarly, it is not required. In this case, translating the two instances of the same term differently offers a contrast. In 29:1, the reference to David may be read as a source of pride or distinction. Ariel is the place of David and where he camped, but it will also be the place that is besieged by God (vv. 2-3). The city that continually celebrates feasts "year to year" will be overtaken by God. It will no longer celebrate, but it will be **lamenting and mourning** (v. 2). The city's fortunes will be reversed and God will humble it so that it speaks from the dust (v. 4).

29:5-8. Despite the severity of God's acts against the city, its enemies' punishment will be even harsher (v. 5). They will be ground to **dust**. They will be blown away as easily as **chaff**. This description of the enemies not only points to their coming punishment, but to their ultimate inability to destroy Jerusalem. Their apparent power will be devastated when the Lord comes. The description of God's appearance in v. 6 is characteristic of ancient Near Eastern descriptions of theophany, or divine appearances, particularly the description of "natural upheaval" (Jeffrey J. Niehaus, *God at Sinai: Covenant and Theophany in the Bible and Ancient Near East* [Grand Rapids, MI: Zondervan, 1995], 27-28). The elements of nature respond to the Lord's presence as a sign of His power and control over all creation (Ex 19:16-19; 1Kg 19:11-13; Ezk 20:47-48). Though God's visitation on Israel will certainly have the dual impact of discipline and deliverance, God's discipline appears to be most prominent here. Israel will suffer the punishment of God. This passage has been thought to foretell the defeat of the Assyrians (Is 37), yet the emphasis on the **multitude** (29:5) of Judah's enemies and the **multitude of all the nations** (vv. 7, 8) indicates that this clearly has eschatological elements.

After the Lord's coming, the **multitude of all the nations** (vv. 7, 8) will wake as from a dream. Just as one who dreams of eating or drinking but awakes to have done neither (v. 8), the enemies besieging Jerusalem at the last battle will **dream** that they have destroyed the city and people, only to awake and see that the destruction has not occurred.

29:9-14. What follows is a description of the serious spiritual impairments of Israel's leadership. They are deaf and blind. Those who should be guiding the nation toward God wander about with no senses to guide them. God's capacity to deliver His people, to work within the seeming impossibilities of history, and to defeat the political powers that threaten Israel regardless of the size or capacity of Israel's armies is ignored by Israel's leadership. Those who should be most aware of God's ability to work outside the boundaries of the world are incapable of imagining a way of life with God that could overcome political realities. All that God has spoken and given through the prophetic message will fall on those without the sensitivity to understand it (vv. 9-10). The message of the prophet is like a **sealed** scroll that the leaders of Israel cannot open or **read.** The sealed words have no effect for those who cannot open the scroll and comprehend its message (vv. 11-12).

Without divine words, the people are left with only human rules. God's message to the people is of no use because only the spiritually deaf and the blind lead the nation. They hear the words but do not believe them. They see the events around them, but do not look to God to deliver them. Without the ability to hear God, there is no chance for the people to honor God. Their superficial reverence of God had become a vain activity comprised only of ritual.

If, as Proverbs asserts, the "fear of the Lord is the beginning of wisdom" (Pr 9:10), wisdom cannot be founded on human rules. The people appear to have been fooled into thinking that their reality is the only reality. God will once again shake up their perceptions. He will astound them "with wonder upon wonder" (NIV, Is 29:14). The human **wisdom** (v. 14) that has driven the lives of Israel will be removed. God will so explode the people's understanding of reality that what once counted as wisdom and intelligence will be overshadowed by God's wisdom, knowledge, and power. God's people must be reminded that life with God is never without possibility. There is always hope, always potential. God's astonishing acts are designed to call God's people to believe once again that God does not operate within the limits of human possibility or vision.

c. The Third Woe: For Attempting to Deceive God (29:15-24)

29:15-16. The third **woe** of six is for Israel's leaders' attempted deception of God. Israel's leaders have some sort of hidden plan that they are attempting to keep from the Lord (v. 15). The language of hiddenness and darkness suggests that the plans were not simply hidden from the Lord, but from everyone. Though it is not explicit within the text what plan has been made, it may be that a secret political alliance is in mind (cf. 30:1-2; 31:1). In any case, the nature of the plan is secondary to the manner in which it was conceived.

The hiddenness of the plan and the exclusion of God from the planning process is a sign of disrespect (v. 16). It represents yet another instance of the leaders' rejection of God, as well as highlighting the leaders' hubris in relation to their own knowledge. The **clay** has said of the potter **He has no understanding**. Here again, the leaders reveal their lack of imagination and trust in God's sovereignty. Paul addresses the principle of God's sovereignty over humanity when he explains election using this passage (see comments on Rm 9:19-21). Nevertheless, Israel's leaders lack recognition of God's sovereignty over them and therefore solve their current difficulties based on their rejection of God and their skewed understanding of the relation between Creator and creation.

29:17-24. Having attempted to deceive God, what follows is a depiction of the coming reversal of their human assumption. That which humanity took as an absolute will become unreliable. The divine surprise will overturn established knowledge and wisdom. It will showcase the possibilities available through the power of God. A series of reversals illustrates the futility of plans that exclude God and, instead, limit potential options to those that seem to be within the realm of human control. With God involved, the great forests of **Lebanon** will become **fertile** fields and the fertile fields will grow into a great **forest** (v. 17).

The reference to the **book** in v. 18 echoes the previous referent to the sealed book in vv. 11-12. While the leaders could not read the scroll, God will allow others to receive His message. He will empower the eyes of the blind to see despite the darkness. These lines may refer to the transformation of a spiritually insensitive nation. There will be yet another reversal as God who previously "shut your eyes" and "covered your heads" (v. 10) will now open the eyes of the blind and make the **deaf** hear (v. 18). Though the generation to whom the prophet's message was delivered was blind and deaf to God's word, there will come a day when the blind and deaf will see and hear.

Even those who have no cause for rejoicing under the current regime will find cause for worship. The blind and the deaf, the humble and the needy represent the downtrodden of Israelite society. They have no opportunity to abuse their power or to lead the nation astray because they have no position, no influence, and no hope within human government. God will change the situation of those who have no standing in the nation and give them reason to rejoice (v. 19). By contrast, those who have done evil and benefited through injustice will be destroyed.

The first two categories of people noted in v. 20 are mentioned at other points in the book of Isaiah. The Hebrew word translated **ruthless** in v. 20 is also used in 13:11; 25:3-5; 29:5; and 49:25. The term refers to those who practice wickedness. In 25:3, "cities of ruthless nations" are used in parallel with "a strong people," suggesting that they occupy a privileged place in society. The **scorner** is only mentioned in 28:14 ("scoffers"), but the description is used numerous times in Proverbs to refer to those who mock godliness and degrade the wisdom of God (e.g., Pr 1:22; 14:9). The deeds of those who watch and do evil are made explicit in 29:21. They use empty arguments (the word **meaningless** is the same word as used in the creation narrative [Gn 1:2], indicating that the new creation was "formless and void") to pervert justice while actively oppressing and mistreating their countrymen. Each of these groups, then, stands against God and opposes His moral order.

These reversals will result in the removal of shame from Jacob (29:22). The reference to God's redemption of Abraham is likely designed to remind Israel of God's steadfast faithfulness to them. God has been working on Israel's behalf since He called their first forefather out of the desert. Just as He redeemed Abraham, so He will redeem Jacob, a reference not to the patriarch but to the nation by way of metonymy. The allusion to Abraham may also have a second purpose related to vv. 22-23. Jacob's shame and embarrassment will be lifted because of the children God will produce among them. Much like God's provision of children to Abraham, He will now bring prosperity to a new generation of Abraham's descendants with offspring. The people of Israel will turn and honor God when they see the children He has provided (vv. 23-24).

d. The Fourth Woe: For Stubborn Rebellion (30:1-33)

The fourth woe is for the stubborn rebellion of God's people. First, there is a description of Israel's rebellion (30:1-5), followed by God's judgment of their rebellion (30:6-17), and concluded by a prediction of Israel's future restoration (30:18-33).

30:1-5. After a brief message of hope related to God's provision of children, the prophet returns to a message of **woe** against **the rebellious children** (v. 1). The reference to making plans becomes more specific than that in 29:15. These plans, like those mentioned in 29:15, have been made without consulting God. The **alliance** with **Egypt** is misguided. Not only were alliances with Egypt forbidden (Ex 13:17; Dt 17:16), the planners have not planned with the Lord. Seeking out Egypt's assistance is problematic for a number of reasons. Theologically, the alliance with Egypt suggests that God is less than capable of caring for the people He has chosen. Politically, the alliance is doomed because Egypt cannot hope to defeat the Assyrians.

The Israelites' rejection of God reflects an ignorance of God's power and an unwillingness to wait on the Lord's deliverance. The alliance will not bring victory but shame to Israel (v. 3). The certainty of this result is driven home through the use of a merism, "a literary device that uses an abbreviated list to suggest the whole" (Tremper Longman III, "Merism," in *Dictionary of the Old Testament: Wisdom, Poetry and Writings*, ed. Temper Longman III and Peter Enns [Downers Grove, IL: InterVarsity, 2008], 464). **Zoan** was located in northern Egypt and **Hanes** in the south. Referring to a city in the north and the south suggests that the whole country of Egypt is in mind. No location in Egypt will be immune to the coming defeat. Rather, the whole of Egypt will be **ashamed** along with anyone who puts his trust in Egypt (v. 5). Despite the perceptions of the Israelites, Israel's fate will be unfavorable because of their alliance with Egypt. Israel will suffer because of this misguided partnership.

30:6-7. Judgment would come upon Israel for three reasons. The first reason was the alliance with Egypt. The **oracle concerning the beasts of the Negev** highlights the lengths to which Israel had to go to court their worthless ally. Hezekiah sent ambassadors from Judah to Egypt carrying **riches on the backs** of donkeys and camels (v. 6). Because Assyrian forces would have been blocking the coastal routes, the envoys would have been required to go to Egypt by travelling "south to Aqaba and across the Sinai to Egypt" (Walton, et al., *IVP Bible Background Commentary*, 621). The envoys were carrying the riches of Israel to a people who could not profit them. The investment of time and resources would not result in positive dividends. Israel's leaders were funneling their wealth into a bottomless pit that would eventually collapse and bury Israel inside.

Egypt's inability earned it the nickname **Rahab who has been exterminated** (v. 7). **Rahab** is used throughout Scripture to denote a mythical chaos monster (Jb 9:13; 26:12; Ps 89:11; Is 51:9). It is also used as a poetic name for Egypt (Ps 87:4). Though this latter use is certainly in mind in 30:7, the former use may also be in mind, particularly given the later reference to Rahab in 51:9. The description of Rahab as she **who has been exterminated**, or "the Do-Nothing" as translated by the NIV, reflects not only the uselessness of Egypt, but the nation's lack of any power, mythic or otherwise. There is no alliance that Israel can make that will bring salvation. Uniting with the Lord and Him alone is the only path to deliverance.

30:8-14. The second reason given for Israel's judgment is for rejecting God's truth. Verses 8-11 call for the creation of a permanent record to remind the **rebellious people** and **false sons** of their folly (vv. 8-9). The everlasting witness against the people is designed to record the people's unwillingness to follow the Lord. It will also allow the prophet to illustrate that God warned His people of the coming judgment. The people's deceitfulness goes beyond individual fraud to a concerted effort to silence those who might offer words of truth to challenge their falsehoods. They call the prophets to ignore their **visions** and to deliver only **pleasant** messages. They want to hear lies over the truth (vv. 9-10). The statement in v. 11 is a bold affirmation of Israel's desire to avoid the word of God: **Let us hear no more about the Holy One of Israel**. The people's active rejection of the Word of the Lord will not go unpunished.

The consequence for rejecting God's message of truth will be the shattering of the nation. The people's unwillingness to accept the truth and their embrace of deceit will create an illusory defense. The instability of deceit is compared to a **high**, cracked **wall** that will not provide protection. Instead, it will **collapse**. Its apparent strength is a fantasy. The wall constructed by their sin is fragile like pottery. The fragility of the strategy will lead to complete and total brokenness (v. 13) to the point that there will not be a piece large enough **to take fire from a hearth or to scoop water from a cistern** (v. 14).

30:15-17. The third reason for judgment is for the nation's self-reliance. All the lying and plotting, the silencing of the prophets, and the delusional behaviors have been useless. The attempts to form alliances, to gain profit through oppressive acts, and to position the nation among the rest of the world powers are wrongheaded. Instead of scheming and hiding and trusting in their own plans, God's people should have been trusting in Him for deliverance. The people's refusal to repent and to wait for the Lord was their downfall (v. 15). Their adoption of customary, worldly means of deliverance effectively eliminated God from the equation. Their deliverance was not in activity and power, but **quietness and trust** (v. 15). It was not in hard-hearted rebellion, but in repentance and trust in their Lord.

This wisdom, while available to the people, was buried and marginalized to the point that it became unavailable. Rather than trusting God to act, the people chose **horses**. The horses appear to be a strategy for escape that God assures the people they will need to use. But no matter how fast they run, it would not be fast enough (v. 16). Their efforts are futile, but they can see no other way. The people will flee from forces of **one** or **five**, so that only a small force is left atop a **mountain**. God's people will be like a flagpole and a banner there (v. 17). While the imagery could be a positive reference to a remnant of the people, the negative connotations of the preceding verses suggest that the comparison is meant to be taken negatively.

30:18-22. Having described Israel's rebellion and promised judgment, the prophet turns to a message of hope. Although 30:1-17 condemns the Israelites for their rebellious, foolish, and deceitful activities, 30:18-26 holds out a hopeful offer of deliverance. The transition in v. 18 also suggests that God longs to overturn the preceding message of judgment with His restoration. God wants to pour out His grace on His people if they will only wait on Him. Regardless of their mistakes and betrayals, God will be merciful and just if Israel will turn to Him. Jerusalem can yet find hope in three ways. First, hope is to be found through the great messianic teacher who is to come (30:18-22); second, mercy will be experienced through the abundance God will provide at that time (30:23-26); and third, justice will be found through the judgment of Assyria (30:27-33).

The note of comfort offered to **Zion** begins with God's gracious offer that if Israel turns to Him for help, God will respond to the cries of His people (v. 19). His discipline is given for a reason. Israel is not being forced to eat the **bread of privation** and drink the **water of oppression** without purpose. It is through their burden that they will turn to the message of truth revealed by their great messianic **Teacher**.

Some versions understand the word "teacher" (v. 20) as plural, referring to many teachers (NIV, NET), while others translate it as singular, "Teacher," and interpret it as the Messiah. The difficulty of v. 20 is that the Hebrew verb **hide Himself** (*yikkanep*) is a third-person masculine singular form, but the noun corresponding to it, **your Teacher**, appears to be a plural. Hence some versions translate this as "your teachers will no longer be hidden," indicating that the verse promises true teachers (but not the Messiah) who will be revealed to Israel. However, this does not resolve the problem of the singular verb, which ought to agree in number with the noun. One possibility is that the noun is a plural of majesty, hence only plural in form but not in meaning, and therefore should be translated as "Teacher." Another possible resolution of the difficulty is to recognize that the Hebrew suffix **your** on the noun **Teacher** begins with a consonant. According to Gesenius, Kautzsch, Cowley, in biblical Hebrew, when a suffix begins with a consonant, it can yield a form change so that a true singular is formed as a plural but remains singular (W. Gesenius, *Gesenius' Hebrew Grammar*, ed. E. Kautzsch and A. E. Cowley, 2nd English ed. [Oxford: Clarendon Press, 1982], 273–274). This would therefore yield the translation, **your Teacher will no longer hide Himself, but your eyes will behold your Teacher**. This seems to be the appropriate resolution of the grammatical difficulty. Thus, when Israel turns to the Lord, the Messiah will no longer hide Himself from His people. Instead, as a Teacher, He will guide His people, whispering in their ears, **This is the way, walk in it** (30:21; see also the discussion of the parallel messianic passage in Jl 2:23).

30:23-26. God will not only reveal the messianic Teacher to the people, at the time the nation finds Messiah, God will also bring prosperity. **Rain** will water the ground and bring forth produce that will feed even the people's livestock lavishly (v. 23). The provision of rain at this time is also a support for the messianic interpretation of this passage. In similar fashion, according to Jl 2:23, when the great messianic Teacher comes to Israel, God will provide both the former and the latter rains, and will bring them great agricultural abundance (see comments on Jl 2:23). The **salted fodder** (30:24) is particularly extravagant feed for the animals, suggesting that God has blessed the Israelites with such abundance that they are even willing to share with their livestock. Verse 25 connects two events: the destruction of the **towers** and the provision of **streams** of **water**. Ordinarily, these two events would seem contradictory as the felling of the towers and the destruction they imply do not fit with the abundance suggested by the resulting streams of water. The connection between the two events here may hinge on understanding the towers as a remnant of the people's human security. They are relics from a time when God was not trusted in Israel. The toppling of the towers allows the people to experience God's blessing as their trust in Him is now no longer prohibited by illusions of human power.

God's healing activities will be accompanied by unprecedented illumination. God will usher in a time of **light** that will drive away darkness. The sevenfold increase in the sun's light highlights its intensity. The combination of healing and light is opposite to that of disease and darkness. The coming light and the healing of God's people is a symbol of the coming restoration. God is now pictured as a physician who will heal the wounds of **His people** (v. 26). While physical healing is certainly in mind, the holistic nature of God's restorative work in the messianic age, encompassing all aspects of creation, should not be missed.

30:27-33. God's blessing is not only available to Israel through the coming of the messianic teacher (vv. 18-22), and the provision of abundance (vv. 23-26), but also through the expectation of judgment on Assyria. Shifting away from the focus on God's restoration of His people, Isaiah now directs attention toward the devastation of Assyria. The Lord, who was just portrayed as the gentle physician who brings healing and light, is now depicted as a fierce warrior. He is described as burning in **His anger** and **dense** with **smoke** (v. 27). Although the NASB, along with many other English translations, use the word **smoke**, the underlying Hebrew is somewhat ambiguous. A more formal translation of the Hebrew would be "heaviness of elevation," but such a translation makes little sense in English. It may be that the phrase should be understood as a reference to God's coming wrath, particularly given its connection with God's burning anger. A description of the Lord's foreboding presence follows. It is said that God's breath is like **an overflowing torrent**, meaning it will overcome His enemies like a flood (v. 28). In Israel, the imagery of an overflowing torrent is likely drawn from the sudden floods associated with wadis, which are dry stream and river beds that flood with devastating force and surprising suddenness. To this day flash floods still overcome people in Israel. This vision of the rushing torrent would have been a familiar and powerful image to those in Israel.

God will also **shake the nations back and forth in a sieve** (v. 28), with the word **sieve** drawing on agricultural imagery. As the wheat is separated from the tares, so will the nations be sifted. There were two types of sieves used in ancient Israel during the time in which Isaiah prophesied. Concerning the first type of sieve, Borowski notes, "the first sieve has large holes and is used by moving it sideways and in a circular manner, which distributes the heavy particles, such as small stones, to the sides while the grain falls through the middle (Oded Borowski, *Agriculture in Iron Age Israel* [Winona Lake, IN: Eisenbrauns, 2009], 66). The second sieve, which is likely in mind in v. 28, has "small holes and is used by moving it up and down. This motion lets the small particles fall through the holes while the grain is left inside the sieve (Borowski, *Iron Age*, 66-67).

This image is combined with that of the horse and **bridle** (v. 28). The nations will be led along by the Lord to a place of destruction. The destruction of Israel's enemies will result in rejoicing. Joy over an enemy's destruction is not uncommon in Scripture (cf. Ps 96). The people's happiness is compared to the time **when one marches to the sound of the flute** (30:29), to go up to the **mountain of the LORD**, to the **Rock of Israel**. God will not come in secret, but will make His voice heard. It is God's **voice** that will destroy Assyria, which here represents all the nations that have oppressed Israel (vv. 30-31). He will come with visible signs that cannot be missed (v. 30). The coordination of **the rod** of punishment (v. 31) and the music of **tambourines and lyres** (v. 32) illustrates the joy that the defeat of the Assyrians will bring.

Topheth (v. 33) refers to a location near Jerusalem that was used as a burial ground (cf. Jr 7:32; 19:11). As such, the Hebrew might also be translated "burial place." The reference to the **pyre of fire with plenty of wood** would then be associated with some form of a funeral rite. In this sense, the passage ends on a note of despair for those who oppose Israel. In the end, even **the king** will fall (v. 33).

e. The Fifth Woe: For Failure to Trust (31:1–32:20)

This **woe** contains two elements—a condemnation for relying on Egypt and failing to trust God (31:1-9), followed by a promise that God would still fulfill all His promises to Israel and send the messianic King (32:1-20)

(1) God (Not Egypt) Will Deliver Israel (31:1-9)

31:1-3. Once again, the alliance with **Egypt** is the subject of the prophetic message. Reliance on Egypt and **horses** is again seen as a misguided strategy. Large forces, strong armies, and political partnerships are of no use if there is no loyalty to the **Holy One of Israel** (v. 1). The exclusion of God from Israel's strategy is a fatal flaw. Verse 2 begins with an affirmation of God's wisdom that is likely aimed at the supposed wisdom of those who seek to form an alliance with Egypt. Regardless of the leaders' attempts to protect Israel, God will not allow it (v. 2). The fallacy of depending on people for aid is highlighted in v. 3. The problem with people is that ultimately their military prowess, wealth, and apparent position among the world powers still pale in comparison to the power of God. The mutually dependent relationship between Egypt and Israel will not allow either to stand. Instead, both nations will fall.

31:4-5. These verses offer a far different fate for Jerusalem. The NASB translation correctly identifies that **the LORD of hosts** will **wage war** on behalf of, and upon, Mount Zion rather than against it. While some commentators suggest that v. 4 describes God's acts *against* Zion, this position is difficult to maintain given the description of the Lord as Jerusalem's shield in v. 5. God is depicted as a growling **lion** that will not back down regardless of the odds against him. He is the fearless defender of Zion who will deliver Jerusalem. God's salvation is fundamentally different than that of Egypt. The inability of Egypt to save stands in stark contrast to God's guarantee to save. In fact, as a further reminder of God's greatness compared to Egypt, the prophet promises that God **will pass over and rescue** Jerusalem (v. 5). The Hebrew word translated **pass over** is the same word used in the Exodus narrative of God's promise "to pass over" those homes with the blood of the lamb on the doorpost (Ex 12:23). It is a deliberate allusion to God's redemption of Israel from Egypt, and this future rescue is painted with the same brush as that historic one to encourage the Jewish people that there will be a future deliverance just as there was a past one.

31:6-9. With these two alternatives in mind, vv. 6-9 call Israel to **return** to the Lord. When the Israelites stop revolting against the Lord, they will get rid of all their idols (v. 7). Verses 8-9 reveal Assyria's fate. They will be destroyed by the hand of God as will anyone who touches **Jerusalem**. Jerusalem is depicted as a hearth that will hold God's fire. The heat from that fire is being prepared against any who seek to harm God's people and will be unleashed from Jerusalem (v. 9). This promise of God's protection of Jerusalem establishes the foundation for the promise of the coming messianic King, found in the next chapter.

(2) God Will Establish His Righteous Messianic King (32:1-20)

32:1-8. This chapter presents Israel with an alternative future. The results associated with the formation of an alliance with Egypt have been described as disastrous. Trusting the Lord, however, creates new possibilities for Israel's future. At the outset, the prophet describes the characteristics of the righteous King (vv. 1-8). First, God will provide a refuge for His people through the King and His princes (vv. 1-2). In the messianic kingdom, the messianic **king** (see 33:17) **will reign righteously** (32:1; see also 11:1-16; Jr 23:5) along with other **princes** (or rulers) under Him. The word **each** (32:2) should be understood as a reference to the rulers who will truly protect the nation as opposed to the previous regime that oppressed the people and cared only for the needs of the ruling class. The new leadership will keep people from harm. Secondly, the righteous King's reign transforms the nation (vv. 3-8). He will usher in a healing influence in which the blind will see and those who were previously deaf will now be able to hear. With the messianic King on the throne, His restorative influence will be released within Israel. The healing of the deaf and blind will be accompanied by the granting of discernment to those who act without restraint. Not only will the King transform the nation physically, but He will cause the value system of the people to change. Those who were once honored for their foolish rebellion will be seen for what they are (vv. 3-5). Verses 6-7 provide the rationale for the reversal. Fools will no longer have a privileged position because they only speak foolishness and seek evil. Under the righteous King, there will be no room for people who **speak error against the Lord** (v. 6). The **fool** and the **rogue** are both opposed to God. Their continued activities pose a threat to the new order, so they can no longer be viewed as wise members of society. Fools and rogues refuse to live according to God's order. They care only for their own needs and are willing to sacrifice the safety and security of those in need in order to get what they want (v. 7).

By contrast, v. 8 upholds **the noble man.** Nobility can denote a particular standing within society, but, in this context, it is more likely that a particular sort of character is in mind. The dual reference to noble plans suggests more than societal conventions associated with a privileged class. Instead, the noble man lives with integrity. His behavior is distinct from the fools and scoundrels, honoring God and benefitting society.

32:9-14. Having first described the messianic King (32:1-8), the prophet then describes the cry of the Israelite **women** (see also 3:16-26). The justice and righteousness that will come with the institution of a new ruler will not come without loss. Those who have been living complacently and with false security will see that all their human dependencies will fail them. The devastation is promised to arrive **within a year and a few days** (v. 10). One possibility is that this refers to one of the 46 cities Sennacherib destroyed in 701 BC. Or if it refers to the destruction of Jerusalem (**the jubilant city**, v. 13), then perhaps it marks the siege of Jerusalem by Sennacherib in 701 BC as the beginning of Jerusalem's destruction that was completed by Nebuchadnezzar 115 years later in 586 BC.

The comfortable residents will grieve. The reference to **sackcloth** (v. 11) likely refers to ancient mourning practices in which clothing made of goat or camel hair was worn as a symbol of grief and repentance. Those who are **complacent** will long for the produce that once sustained them. The land will be overtaken by thorns and thistles. While the land of God and the people of God are connected, the abundance of the land cannot be simply assumed. Rather, the land's prosperity is conditioned upon the people's continued loyalty to the Lord. He is the key to the richness of His people and the land on which they dwell. Given the covenantal relationship between God and Israel, it may be that the people's complacency derives from false assumptions about the Lord and what He actually desires.

In Deuteronomy, the people of Israel were warned not to "forget the LORD" when they crossed into the land and received His abundant blessing (Dt 6:10-15). The concern was that the people would be lulled into a false sense of security and lose sight of their dependence on the Lord. This situation came about in Isaiah's time as the complacent people neglected their God. They had not given Him gratitude or praise. Instead, they had transferred their trust from the God who gives to the gifts that He had given. This transference would not produce continued abundance, but mourning, grief, and destruction (Is 32:14). An abandoned fortress, a deserted city, and a newly formed wasteland will replace the once impressive city and its confines. It will become **a delight for wild donkeys** and **a pasture for flocks** (v. 14). Although the land's devastation is described as lasting **forever**, the Hebrew words *'ad 'olam* do not always refer to eternity. In fact, since immediately afterwards the author saw a time when the devastation would end, these words likely mean "for a very long time."

32:15-20. The tone shifts in v. 15 from destruction to restoration. In describing the messianic kingdom, the author moves beyond the description of the future messianic King (32:1-8) and the cry of the Israelite women (32:9-14) to the certain coming of the messianic kingdom (3:15-20). The devastation just described will only last until **the Spirit is poured out upon us from on high** (v. 15). The prophets frequently link the establishment of the millennial kingdom with the coming of the Spirit upon God's people (Ezk 36:27; Jl 2:28-32). God's Spirit will perform a reversal of fortune, transforming the city and the people and all that has been destroyed. The progression from desert to fertile field to forest is similar to that in 29:17 and appears to denote extraordinary growth.

Not only will the region be restored physically, **justice** and **righteousness** will be restored within it. Divine blessing and restoration will come with an infusion of virtue and loyalty to the divine order. Justice and righteousness will **dwell** in this restored civilization (32:16) and be fixtures in the land. The return of justice and righteousness represents the true transformation of the land. Righteousness will usher in **peace** and security (v. 17). When injustice is banished from the land, the people will experience God's continued abundance, peace, and security. This security will bring lasting rest.

For Israel, such rest represents the fulfillment of God's promise to establish His people in the millennial kingdom. This righteousness will only come when Israel will turn in faith to the Lord at the end of days (see comments on Dt 4:30 and Hs 3:4-5). The hail must destroy the forest and the city must be ruined (32:19), indicating the pain and difficulty that must come before deliverance, yet deliverance will come. Isaiah 32:20 offers a picture of limitless blessing. Farmers would not normally plant near streams for fear of flooding, but in this new world, there is no fear of destruction. They can even allow their flocks to "range free" (NIV) without fear of them eating too many crops. There will be plenty of produce to go around, so allowing the flocks to roam and eat need not be curtailed. In the end, the people will be blessed without measure.

f. The Sixth Woe: For Destructive Opposition (33:1-24)

The litany of woes continues, but this final lament is not upon Israel but against her enemies. The structure of this chapter is as follows: A woe upon Israel's enemies (33:1), a prayer for God to judge Israel's enemies (33:2-9), followed by a description of God's response to the prayer for judgment (33:10-24).

33:1. After the promise of restoration at the end of Is 32, a woe statement begins chap. 33. In this case, however, the **woe** is not against Israel, but against the **destroyer** (v. 1). It is the destroyer who will now be destroyed and the betrayer who will finally be betrayed. The identity of the destroyer is not made explicit in the passage. One option is to identify the destroyer as Assyria, which has been noted as particularly vicious throughout Isaiah. A more likely possibility is that the term refers to the collective of the nations or **peoples** mentioned in v. 3. This identification is likely for at least two reasons. First, the proximity of the mention of the **nations** in v. 3 suggests that the characteristics of verse one refer to the nations. Second, the message of Isaiah has frequently referred to the surrounding nations as a danger to Israel, as well as predicting that one day the instrument of God's destruction would be punished. The difficulty with this identification is that the plural **nations** is also called the **destroyer**, a singular noun. The stronger option is to see the nations as viewed collectively, as a single entity in v. 1, thus the use of a singular to describe a single source of opposition to God.

33:2-4. These words likely represent the prayer of the righteous remnant, awaiting God's deliverance of Israel. The interjection in v. 2 is identifiable as a prayer with the use of the imperatives **be gracious** and **be their strength**. A third imperative is implied through the use of ellipsis, which is a literary technique in which a clause or word is omitted that would ordinarily be required by the other parts of the literary context. In this case, the Hebrew includes a conjunction translated as **also** or "even" and appears before the final clause in the verse. A more helpful translation might be "*also be* our salvation in time of distress." In any case, the imperative is implied in this final line calling God to be Israel's **salvation**, as well as its strength. Although the NASB states that Israel has **waited** (v. 2) for the Lord, the NIV captures the eager desire that characterizes their waiting by translating the phrase "we long for you." The righteous remnant of Israel are not sitting by idly or complacently. Instead, they recognize that God's appearance is the only thing that will deliver them. Their waiting, then, is charged with a desire for restoration and a disdain for the current state of things. They long to see God overturn the status quo and to bring a new, revived world into existence, a world in which the destroyer is destroyed and the nations are subdued.

Verse 3 describes how the **peoples** will run from God when He acts to deliver Israel because such action is terrifying, even to those who are rescued. But they resolve to trust in God's ability to do what no army or political strategy can ever achieve. God will defeat the nations. Having prayed, the remnant addresses the **nations** and declares that their plunder will be taken from them as when the crops are taken by **locusts** (v. 4). Locusts normally appeared after the cereal crops had grown, sometime between late winter and early spring. Borowski notes, "Damage to vegetation by locusts occurs when they band into swarms" (Borowski, *Iron Age*, 154). Locust imagery would have been powerful to the ancient world, as locusts posed a significant threat to the agricultural stability of Israel. The locust imagery is more fully developed in Jl 1:4-12 and in Am 7:1-2.

33:5-6. The prayer of the righteous remnant continues with their exaltation of the Lord, offering assurance that God will protect and restore Zion. The first statement concerning the Lord's exalted nature likely highlights God's capacity to rule because of His position in heaven. The progression from God's exaltation to the assertion that **He has filled Zion with justice and righteousness** suggests that governance is in mind (v. 5). Further, God is a source of stability for Israel that will not ebb and flow as their human allies do (v. 6). The Lord is constant and He provides **salvation** and wisdom and knowledge abundantly. Though the NASB translates **wisdom and knowledge**, these terms may form a hendiadys, or the use of two words linked by a conjunction to express a more unified idea. Here, **wisdom and knowledge** should be understood as great or superior wisdom. All of this is available to those who **fear** the Lord, who allow the fear of the Lord to be the foundational orientation to life that "gives balance to the individual as he relates both to his world and God" (C. Hassell Bullock, *An Introduction to the Old Testament Poetic Books* [Chicago: Moody, 1988], 25).

33:7-9. The end of the prayer is that God is implored to listen because the enemy, described as the destroyer (v. 1), has arrived and is upon the city. It appears that all hope is lost. The people, physical resources, and bastions of safety and prosperity that had once made Israel forget their dependence upon the Lord will fail. In v. 7a, the NASB adopts the translation **brave men**. The underlying Hebrew term here, however, is unknown. Other English versions adopt similar translations. The KJV and ASV versions translate "valiant ones" and the NIV, like the NASB, translates "brave men." The Septuagint translation takes a number of liberties with the underlying Hebrew. Translated to English the Septuagint reads something like the following: "See now! They themselves will fear you, those you feared will fear you, for messengers will be sent requesting peace, weeping bitterly calling out for peace." This translation appears to fit better as a conclusion to 33:5-6 than as an introduction to this section as it suggests that Israel's enemies will come to Israel calling for peace. Though possible, the expansive nature of the Septuagint's translation is difficult to accept in this instance.

In any case, it may be best to translate v. 7a as something similar to "envoys of peace" given that the lines are in parallel with v. 7b (**ambassadors of peace**). This translation focuses the entire verse on diplomatic efforts and may refer to Assyria's double-crossing of Israel during

Sennacherib's campaign against Lachish (see Introduction: Background). Oswalt suggests this setting as a likely historical context for Isaiah 33 (Oswalt, *Isaiah 1–39*, 595). Essentially, Sennacherib agreed to leave Jerusalem untouched if tribute was paid, but continued on with his campaign against Jerusalem despite the payment of tribute. With the diplomatic efforts exhausted and military action being untenable, it would have become clear to Israel that they were without human options. Such an understanding of the historic scenario fits with the mention of both the "destroyer" and "he who is treacherous" in v. 1 and, potentially, with the reference to the broken treaty in v. 8.

Highways (v. 8) is used frequently in Isaiah. Of the term's 27 uses in the OT, nine appear in Isaiah (7:3; 11:16; 19:23; 40:3; 49:11; 59:7; 62:10). The use of a similar term also translated as "highway" appears in 35:8. Although it usually indicates a conduit for the deliverance of God's people (11:16; 19:23; 40:3; 49:11; 62:10), now **the highways are desolate** and in need of the Lord to act. As in 59:7, the word **highway** in 33:8 takes on a negative nuance in which the highway is empty and, presumably, incapable of being traversed. In contrast to the highways that bustle with the returning remnant (11:16) and the coming and going of Assyrians and Egyptians (19:23), the highway on which the Lord will come (40:3) now stands desolate. It is clear that the highway appears as a symbol of coming deliverance but is depicted here, before that time, as an abandoned path on which the people are afraid to travel.

With the affirmation of the broken treaty it is not surprising that no one is willing to travel on the highway. The looming threat of military invasion combined with the inability of Israel's leaders to fend off the attack would likely have created a sense of dread. Because the human means for peace have failed, the people's false sense of security is exposed and they are unable to recognize that the highway could be a path to deliverance if only they would trust the Lord.

Not only are the people in disarray, the land is also in turmoil. The connectedness between the land and the people is here brought to the forefront. All creation will suffer and the proud cities will wither and be ashamed. Verse 9 names four locations: **Lebanon**, **Sharon**, **Bashan**, and **Carmel**. **Sharon** was a fertile plain on the Mediterranean coast that would no longer be fertile, but turn to desert. **Bashan** was also known as a fertile area in the far north due to its volcanic soil and high precipitation. **Lebanon** is mentioned in connection with **Bashan** in 2:13. The "oaks of Bashan" are mentioned in parallel with the "cedars of Lebanon," suggesting that Bashan's vegetation was also impressive. The final location of **Carmel** had a reputation similar to that of Bashan. The two locales are mentioned together in other places in the OT (Jr 50:19; Nah 1:4). Verse 9 highlights the reversal of the normal order of things. The lands that could normally be depended upon to produce vegetation and that had come to be known as symbols of power and stature will fail. Any sense of security that may have existed for Israel will be eliminated.

33:10-13. After all is hopeless, the Lord speaks, in answer to the prayer of the remnant. First, God states that He will judge the nations. He will come and establish Himself as **exalted** ruler of all things. With the people's security removed, the way is clear for the Lord to show Himself worthy of praise. Verse 10 asserts God's exalted status in contrast to the **chaff** conceived by the nations in v. 11. That the nations are in view is suggested by use of the second person plural verbs in v. 11 (**you** [plural] **have conceived . . . you will give birth**). All the plans that the nations have made against God's people will backfire and bring about their destruction (v. 12). The work of the Lord will be recognized by everyone. The universality of this recognition is suggested by the reference to those who are **near** and those who are **far** (v. 13). Mentioning these two groups in parallel denotes those who are far and near, as well as implies all those who are in between.

33:14-16. The second part of God's answer to the remnant is that He will purify Judah. Those who continue to disobey the Lord in **Zion** now feel the pressure of living with a Holy God. **Sinners** will tremble once they acknowledge their inability to survive in the presence of the Lord. They cannot survive unquenchable **fire**. Their sinful disobedience will result in their destruction (v. 14), whereas those who practice righteousness will experience the safety and provision of the Lord (vv. 15-16). The list of actions provided in v. 15 is instructive. Those who will receive God's blessings speak truthfully and with integrity; they disdain ill-gotten gains, and they refuse to participate in planning evil. These men and women refuse to engage in the sort of activities that characterize Israel's current leadership. Their avoidance of these activities will yield the security of a mountain fortress and the provision of daily needs as denoted by the supply of **bread** and **water** (v. 16).

33:17-22. God's third response to the remnant's prayer is that He will send the messianic King to reign over Israel. The nation **will see the King** (v. 17), the Messiah. His reign will be characterized by peace and stability in which those who once oppressed the nation no longer have a place. The messianic reading of the passage is suggested by the declaration that the Lord is indeed the **king** (v. 22). Given that the Messiah has been previously described as divine (cf. 7:14; 9:6), it makes the most sense to recognize that the Messiah is in view in 33:17. The kingdom will be empowered by the divine Messiah on His throne. The human rulers will no longer be found and their **unintelligible speech** will no longer be heard and the arrogant no longer seen (v. 18-19). The other uses of "unintelligible speech" in the OT refer to non-Israelites (Is 28:11; 36:11; Jr 5:15; Ezk 3:5-6). Here, the usage may be taken as a reference to foreign invaders who have dominated Jerusalem. Given that foreigners are in view here, it is likely that those referred to in 33:19 are non-Israelites who collected tribute from Israel.

When the Messiah comes as King, the foreign oppressors will be removed and Jerusalem will be a place of stability and peace (v. 20). The people will not wander and their **tent** will **not be folded**. The image of the **tent** could refer to the tabernacle. However, the word translated **tent** does not necessarily denote the tabernacle, but is used of any tent. It may be that the image of a tent is meant to stand in contrast with the more stable structures of the day. Many times God utilizes weaker structures, such as a smaller armed force (cf. Jdg 7:6-8), to demonstrate His glory. Here the reference to a mobile dwelling's permanence could evoke a similar understanding. God does not need fortresses with high walls and strong towers. Instead, He is the strong tower, the permanent structure and dwelling place for Israel.

A similar point appears to be in mind in 33:21 in which Zion is said to be **a place of rivers and wide canals**. Regardless, no ships will be capable of sailing against Zion. Verse 22 reinforces the reason that **no boat with oars will go** and **no mighty ship will pass**. It is because the Lord, the divine Messiah, is **judge**, **lawgiver**, and **king**. He will save His people. While waterways could certainly serve as a strategic geographic defense against attack, they could also serve as an opportunity for enemies to strike via boat. In this instance, however, the messianic King's presence precludes any such offensive.

33:23-24. The Lord's final response to the prayer of the remnant is that He will provide abundantly for His people. Those ships that attempt to attack God's people will have their apparatus fail and will become **abundant spoil** for Israel. There will be so much bounty that even **the lame** will be there in time to receive **the plunder** (v. 23). The Lord will not only provide materially, but He will also provide physically—**no resident will say, "I am sick"** (v. 24). More importantly, however, is the expansion of this final line to include forgiveness of sins. Beyond physical deliverance, Israel needs to be delivered from their sin. This deliverance is coming. When the divine Messiah asserts His position as ruler of His people, He will bring forgiveness and restore the people materially, physically, and most importantly, spiritually.

4. The Summary of Judgment and Blessing (34:1–35:10)

After beginning the book of Isaiah with an introduction itemizing the particulars of Israel's disobedience (chaps. 1–6), the first half of the book (chaps. 7–35) emphasized judgment (although it does include promises of blessing as well). The first half began with the narrative found in the book of Immanuel (chaps. 7–12), showing Ahaz's rejection of the offer of a sign from God. As an outgrowth of that rejection of the sign, the sections that followed all emphasized that God would judge Israel and the nations (chaps. 13–35). There are four sections emphasizing judgment: The oracles against the nations (chaps. 13–23), the promise of end-time judgment and blessing (often called "The Little Apocalypse," chaps. 24–27), the book of Woes (chaps. 28–33), and what follows now, the summary of end-time judgment and blessing (chaps. 34–35). This section marks the end of the first half of the book, summarizing its overall message of judgment and blessing. The first part of this summary pertains to God's judgment of the nations (chap. 34) and the second part highlights God future blessing of Israel (chap. 35).

a. The Power of the Gentiles Will Be Broken (34:1-17)

34:1-4. In describing God's judgment of the nations, the prophet moves from the general (God's punishment of the nations, vv. 1-4) to the specific (God's punishment of Edom, vv. 5-17). The overall message of this section is concerned with the results of trusting in the nations. The chapter begins with an oracle against the nations that proclaims their coming judgment and ultimate downfall. The call to **listen** is a common feature in the context of judgment (Is 1:10; 28:14; 32:9). In this case it is addressed to the foreign nations who have denied Israel's God. These nations have sought Israel's destruction, thereby standing against God. This message is not simply delivered to the nations. It is heard throughout creation by the **world** and **all that springs from it** (34:1).

It is possible to understand the call for the earth to hear as a call for creation to stand as witness to the oracle against the nations (cf. Dt 4:26; 30:19). In this case, however, it may be best to understand the text as a reference to all humanity. The key phrase is **all it contains** (v. 1), which translates a Hebrew term used four other times throughout Isaiah (Is 6:3; 8:8; 31:4; 42:10). Each of the other uses in the book appears to have a meaning different from that in 34:1. The term can refer to everything on the earth (Ps 89:12) or in the sea (Ps 96:11) or to more limited subsets within creation (cf. Ps 24:1; 50:12; 98:7). Though it is not explicit in Is 34:1, on the basis of this unique use in Isaiah, it seems most likely that the text refers to humanity as part of creation in a manner similar to Ps 24:1 or Ps 98:7.

Such a reading also maintains the linkage between the first and second portions of Is 34:1. The first section addresses the **nations** and **peoples** whereas the second refers to the **earth** and **world**. In both instances the call is to listen to the warning that will be delivered in the following verses. The two portions of v. 1 are parallel statements that reinforce each other, maintaining the overall tone of judgment. This involves not simply a set of nations, but all those who oppose the Lord, His people, and His plans.

The next verse (v. 2) begins with the conjunction **for**, giving the reason for the previous call to listen. In this case, the nations are called to listen because of the Lord's anger and the coming destruction that will ultimately arrive as a result. The term translated **utterly destroyed** is used in several places throughout the OT to refer to the "ban," or the setting aside of something or someone for total destruction (Nm 21:2-3; Dt 2:34; 3:6; Jos 6:18, 21; 11:11-12, 20). The use in v. 2 underscores the severity of God's punishment of the nations.

Isaiah 34:3 depicts the humiliation and indignity that the once-proud nations will suffer. They will not even be able to bury their dead. Instead, the decaying bodies will simply be thrown out where both the sight and the stench will reveal the undoing of the nations' power.

The translation **the mountains will be drenched with their blood** (v. 3) is somewhat misleading. The term translated **drenched** is used in other contexts to denote melting or dissolution. There are several figurative references to "hearts melting" (Dt 20:8; Jos 2:11; 5:1; 7:5; 2Sm 17:10; Ps 22:14; Is 13:7; 19:1; Ezk 21:12), as well as several uses in which the melting of material is in view (Ex 16:21; Jdg 15:14; Ps 68:3). The term is also used to describe the melting away of the mountains in Ps 97:5 and Mc 1:4. While there is no reference to blood in either Ps 97:5 or Mc 1:4, it is clear in both passages that the mountains are "melting away." As such, the translation of Is 34:3 should likely be understood as "the mountains will melt with the blood." Oswalt suggests that the image is drawing on the erosion that takes place as water dissolves soil (Oswalt, *Isaiah 1–39*, 609). This understanding also fits well with the dissolution of the stars, or hosts, of heaven in 34:4. In each case, it is clear that God is giving the nations an idea of His sovereign, cosmic reach.

34:5-17. The discussion of judgment continues through the lens of **Edom**, which becomes the representative of all the nations. The choice of Edom as the representative nation is to be expected. Edom stands as Israel's opponent throughout the OT (Ob 11-14; Ezk 35:1-15; Mal 1:2-3). Even in Rebekah's womb Israel (Jacob) and Edom (Esau) battled for position (Gn 25:23). The use of Edom in Isaiah depicts the choice that must be made. All humanity must choose the way of Edom or the way of the Lord. Either choice brings with it a specific set of consequences that are made clear through the prophetic word.

The certainty of Edom's punishment is established through the prowess of the Lord's sword, which **is satiated** in the heavens (v. 5). This sword will come from the heavens to destroy Edom. Its heavenly origin suggests that Edom does not stand a chance against God. The sword is further described in v. 6 in terms drawn from the sacrificial system. The location of **Bozrah**, included here as the place in which the sacrifice will occur, is disputed. Some believe it is modern Buseirah, some 35 miles southeast of the

Dead Sea. In support of this view is that Buseirah sounds as if it retains the ancient Hebrew name for the city and that it was the ancient capital of Edom. Others maintain that Bozrah should be located in the ancient Nabatean stronghold of Petra. This is an isolated area, accessible via a narrow canyon that opens into a wide space. This seems the more likely location because: (1) The name "Bozrah" means "sheepfold" and the city of Petra is located in a basin within Mt. Seir with surrounding mountains and cliffs, creating a natural "sheepfold." (2) Right next to Petra is the Arab site of Butzeira, a name that more accurately retains the Hebrew form of Bozrah. Some have conjectured that Bozrah is the place to which Jewish people in the future tribulation will flee for safety from the pursuit of the antichrist (see Rv 12:6). Therefore it would make sense for end-time judgment to begin with the Lord's deliverance of the Jewish people there. So great will be God's warfare that even the **strong** among Edom will fall and the land will be **soaked with blood** (34:7). The next verse provides the reason for the Lord's attack—He has planned a **day of vengeance** in which He will take up Zion's cause (34:8; see 63:1-6 and comments there for the chronology of the events in Bozrah). As a result, destruction and confusion will follow as described in vv. 9-17. The natural resources of the land and even the land itself will turn against the people of Edom throughout their generations (vv. 9-10). Verse 11 draws on the imagery of the measuring or plumb line. In other instances, these images are normally employed in relation to God's judgment (2Kg 21:13; Is 28:17; Jr 31:39; Lm 2:8). Those who rule Edom will have nothing left to oversee when the fortified towers and cities are besieged by nettles and thistles (34:12-13). Desert creatures and wild animals will settle there since Edom will be abandoned with no other life present (vv. 13-15). These events will certainly come about because the Lord has decreed it. Edom's destruction is coming just as the word of the Lord has declared (vv. 16-17).

b. The Redeemed Will See the Kingdom of God (35:1-10)

This section shifts the focus from judgment in the land of Edom to blessing in the land of Israel, called "Zion" in v. 10. The picture of the renewed land in the messianic era is one of peace, security, and abundance.

35:1-4. The image of the happy and rejoicing desert in v. 1 could refer figuratively to the happiness and spiritual fertility of the people when they are restored, but more likely refers to the spectacular and unexpected change in the desert's landscape. No longer will the desert be a place without vegetation, but a lush, blossoming space. Its seeming limitations will be overcome by the Lord and become like the fertile sites of **Lebanon**, **Carmel**, and **Sharon** (v. 2). The reversal of the situation in the desert should result in comfort. Those who fear may find strength in God's coming vengeance and deliverance (vv. 3-4).

35:5-10. In the messianic era, God's work will open the **eyes of the blind** and **the ears of the deaf**. Those who were once physically disabled will celebrate and use their faculties as never before (vv. 5-6). God's deliverance will not only transform the people of the land, but it will affect the land itself (vv. 6-7). Even **the Arabah**, the desert area by the Dead Sea, will be transformed from barrenness to a lush area, where **waters will break forth in the wilderness and streams in the** desert (v. 6). The desert, habitable only for **jackals** (v. 7), will become fertile and refreshed with water. This seems to indicate a contrast with Edom in the previous chapter. There, Bozrah, or Petra, in the messianic age will become the haunt of jackals (34:13), but the wilderness of Israel will no longer be that. All these changes seem to culminate in the creation of the **Highway of Holiness** that will lead those in need of help safely to Zion (vv. 8-10). All the Lord's activities will result not only in the safety and prosperity of Zion, but in the establishment of a sanctuary for those the Lord has rescued, likely referring to His deliverance of the Jewish people from Bozrah (34:6). Under the reign of Messiah, the Lord will provide much for Israel, specifically, holiness (35:8), safety (v. 9), and **everlasting joy** (v. 10). The **ransomed** of the nation will be welcomed with singing and experience the ongoing joy of living in the presence of the Lord.

III. The Blessing of Israel and the Nations (36:1–66:24)

The simple structure of Isaiah is a prologue (chaps. 1–6) followed by two main sections (chaps. 7–35 and 36–66). The second of the two main sections of Isaiah starts here (36:1). Each of the two sections begins with narratives containing similar content. In each one, a king from Judah is facing a military threat and Isaiah the prophet brings them each a sign of hope. The primary difference between these two narratives is that in the first narrative (chaps. 7–12), wicked King Ahaz rejects the Lord's sign, while in the second (chaps. 36–39), good King Hezekiah trusts the Lord's sign. Both narratives are followed by sections of oracles: after the rejected sign the oracles emphasize judgment (chaps. 13–35), whereas after the accepted sign they emphasize blessing (chaps. 40–66). The next section contains the second narrative of a sign accepted (chaps. 36–39), to be followed by the oracles of blessing (chaps. 40–66).

A. A Narrative of a Sign Accepted: Hezekiah Chooses to Trust the Lord (36:1–39:8)

The stories about the reign of King Hezekiah, including the Assyrian threat, the king's recovery from deadly illness, and his foolish exhibition of Israel's wealth to the Babylonians are designed as a parallel to the events in the reign of King Ahaz (see chaps. 7–12), the chief difference being that Hezekiah, unlike Ahaz, is a godly king. Both were offered signs from God but Ahaz refused (7:12), while Hezekiah willingly received signs from the Lord (37:30; 38:7-8).

The content of this part of the book is virtually identical to 2Kg 18:13–20:19, with the exception being that the Isaiah account includes Hezekiah's prayer of thanksgiving (38:9-20). This whole narrative section is integral to Isaiah's book. Since the book of Isaiah predated the books of 1 and 2 Kings, this makes it likely that this section of Isaiah was the source of the 2 Kings account.

The events in chaps. 36–37 chronologically follow those in chaps. 38–39. This is plain from 38:6, which anticipates the threat and defeat of the Assyrians (described in chaps. 36–37) as yet future. Moreover, extrabiblical historical records agree, placing Sennacherib's siege of Judah (recounted in chaps. 36–37) in 701 BC but the visit of Merodach-baladan's delegation (39:1) in 703 BC.

There were several literary purposes for the non-chronological arrangement of this section of the book. First, the narrative portion functions as a bridge from the previous oracles to the following oracles. Isaiah 36–37, with its emphasis on the Assyrian threat, provides closure to the first part of the book (chaps. 7–35), in which Assyria was prominent. Isaiah 38–39, with its emphasis on the Babylonian visit, anticipates the second part of the book (chaps. 40–66), in which Babylon is prominent.

A second structural purpose for the non-chronological arrangement is so that the historical narrative would end with Hezekiah's great failure (showing the treasures of the temple to the Babylonian ruler) rather than his greatest act of faith. After reading the first part of the book, a reader might conclude that Hezekiah was the great king anticipated in 7:13-15; 9:6-7; and 11:1-16. Therefore, at the end of the narrative about Hezekiah, the author wanted to clarify that despite being a godly king with great faith, Hezekiah was not the messianic King anticipated earlier in the book.

A third purpose was to focus on the future rather than the past. Although linking the fulfillment of some of Isaiah's prophecies to historical events (such as the Assyrian defeat), the narrative's true focus is to look forward to Babylon, anticipating the coming Babylonian captivity. This focuses the book on the future rather than the past or the present. John Sailhamer states: "[A]s is suggested at numerous points in the prophecies themselves, their scope is messianic and eschatological. They look forward to a time after the exile in Babylon, when God would judge the nations and bring peace to Jerusalem by means of his promised King" (John H. Sailhamer, *NIV Compact Bible Commentary* [Grand Rapids, MI: Zondervan, 1994], 367).

1. Hezekiah and the Assyrians (36:1–37:38)

The first story about Hezekiah looks at the attack and defeat of the Assyrians. This brings closure to the first half of the book that emphasized Assyria.

a. The Attack of Assyria (36:1-22)

36:1-3. The first narrative of Hezekiah is dated as taking place **in the fourteenth year of King Hezekiah**. The dates of Hezekiah's reign were 715–687 BC, assuming a ten-year co-regency with Manasseh (697–643 BC). The fixed date for Sennacherib's invasion is 701 BC. The likely date for the visit of the Babylonian delegation (39:1) was 703 BC. Therefore, Hezekiah received his 15-year extension of life (38:1-8) shortly before the Babylonian delegation visited him. In 701 BC, the Assyrian king Sennacherib had captured several of Judah's fortified cities (36:1) and placed **Lachish** under siege. The city, located approximately 30 miles southwest of Jerusalem, was used by Judah as a stronghold and a strategic military site. Anticipating success there, the Assyrian king sent **Rabshakeh**, literally "chief cupbearer" but a term that came to refer to the vizier or chief officer of the empire, **with a large army** (v. 2) to threaten and dishearten Jerusalem so that it would surrender without a fight. He gave his message by the conduit of the upper pool on the highway of the fuller's field, the exact location that Isaiah gave his prophecy of Immanuel to Ahaz (7:3). Citing this location is designed to associate this narrative with the previous one. Hezekiah sent a high-level delegation of **Eliakim** and **Shebna** (who are mentioned in 22:15-25 as the present and future stewards of the royal household) and **Joah . . . the recorder** to negotiate with him.

36:4-10. The message delivered to Hezekiah via Sennacherib's chief advisor is designed to highlight the weaknesses of Hezekiah's resistance. He questions Hezekiah's source of confidence, pointing to the weakness of Judah's military potential and the total lack of allegiances that could actually save the kingdom from Assyria (vv. 5-6). His explicit reference to Egypt reminds the reader of Ahaz's attempt at an alliance and confirms the weakness of the Egyptians.

The comments made by Sennacherib's advisor in v. 7 get to the heart of the issue. The Assyrians do not fear or understand the Lord. Hezekiah's reforms are viewed as a rejection of God. If Hezekiah had not honored Judah's God, how can he trust in the Lord for salvation? Without the strength of a strong military, the support of other nations, and the backing of their God, the Israelites have no choice but to negotiate with the Assyrians. Continuing his argument, the advisor claims to have been sent against Israel by the Lord (v. 10).

36:11-22. The request of Eliakim, Shebna, and Joah for the messenger to speak to them in Aramaic rather than in Judean (i.e., Hebrew) in the hearing of the people **who are on the wall** (v. 11) is seemingly motivated by a desire to prevent panic among the people by excluding them from the discussion. The Assyrian response suggests that the message is intentionally designed to inspire unrest among the people of Judah. All of Judah, even those who are not making political decisions, will reap the consequences of what the Assyrians are portraying as the futile resistance of Judah to Assyria's assault.

Instead, the Assyrian commander calls the people to make peace with Assyria and to experience the blessings of Sennacherib (v. 16). Under Sennacherib the people will be able to eat their own produce and drink from their own cisterns until they are whisked away to the wonderful land of grain and new wine, **a land of bread and vineyards** (v. 17). While Sennacherib and his messenger are to be commended for their ability to put a positive spin on national deportation and exile, his promise to the people is an empty one.

In a final attempt to convince the people to turn on Hezekiah, the Assyrian messenger calls upon a historical analogy (v. 18). The Assyrians had conquered numerous nations with little or no resistance. Pointing to these conquered nations, the Assyrians suggest that Judah and its God will not stand against them. If the gods of the other nations cannot oppose Assyria, then there is no reason to believe that the Lord can protect Judah. This reasoning does not result in the surrender of the people whose loyalty to Hezekiah held despite the apparent threat (vv. 21-22). Nevertheless, the threats had a fearful effect on the delegation, who returned to Hezekiah with **their clothes torn** in mourning to relay the message of Rabshekah.

b. The Defeat of Assyria (37:1-38)

37:1-7. In the face of a looming Assyrian threat, Hezekiah tore his clothes and **covered himself with sackcloth** in symbolic acts of mourning and sent **Eliakim** and **Shebna** to Isaiah (vv. 1-2). Hezekiah hopes that God has been listening to the Assyrian's blasphemy and is ready to take action against them (v. 4). Already this response is far superior to that of Ahaz. Hezekiah sought the consultation of the prophet whereas Ahaz rejected the sign offered by the prophet.

The message sent from Hezekiah to Isaiah was an entreaty for the prophet to pray for Judah. Hezekiah's words recognized the foolishness that the Assyrians had spoken against God. He saw the coming slaughter and hoped that the Lord would hear the words of the Assyrians and punish them for taunting the Lord (vv. 3-4). Isaiah's response to Hezekiah is encouraging. The king of Assyria will be diverted by a report to return to Assyria and **fall by the sword**, while Judah will be spared (vv. 5-7).

37:8-13. The scene quickly shifts back to the chief advisor of the Assyrians who has received reports of Assyria's departure from **Lachish** (v. 8). Despite learning that Ethiopian troops (from **Cush**, v. 9) were coming against him, the king of Assyria sends a second message, via letter, to Hezekiah calling him to remember the Assyrian victories over the gods of **Gozan**, **Haran**, **Rezeph**, and **Eden**. Surely if Assyria could defeat these nations and their gods, Judah and its God would not stand a chance (vv. 11-13).

37:14-20. After reading the letter, Hezekiah **spread it out** before the Lord and prayed. His prayer recognized God as the **LORD of hosts** and as the only God of all the earth. The reference to God as creator of heaven and earth underscores not only God's uniqueness, but His control over all kingdoms (v. 16). He calls God to hear the insults of Sennacherib and to act so that the world may know **that You alone, LORD, are God** (v. 20). The emphasis of the prayer is upon God's universal sovereignty. Hezekiah recognizes that the Assyrians have defeated other nations and their gods, but the Lord is stronger than all gods and nations combined. He cannot be defeated. Hezekiah calls God to prove His power against the Assyrians by delivering Judah from the seemingly invincible Assyrian army. The boldness and public nature of the Assyrian claims would make a Judean victory serve as a moment of humiliation for Assyria in which their claims to power would be shown to be false.

37:21-29. Isaiah's message to Hezekiah provided confirmation that the Lord would respond to the Assyrians' taunting. Hezekiah's prayer, faithful response, and dependence upon God are cited as the impetus for God's action against Sennacherib. Rather than an act of divine frustration against Assyria, the Lord's response is to a faithful prayer (v. 21). **Zion** will mock the mighty Assyrians because Sennacherib has spoken falsely about **the Holy One of Israel** (vv. 22-23). The Assyrian faith in their military prowess and the memories of their past conquests and achievements skew their vision so that Judah's God has become just another weak force that is easily overcome (vv. 24-25). Assyria's success, however, was not of its own doing. Instead, their success is part of God's sovereign plan. The rise and fall of all nations, not just Israel, is governed by the Lord (vv. 26-27). The Assyrians' insults do not escape God either (v. 28). It is the raging of the Assyrians against the Lord that brings them to His attention and will ultimately be the Assyrians' downfall (v. 29).

37:30-35. In v. 30, the Lord shifts from addressing Sennacherib and the Assyrians to addressing Hezekiah. He offers signs to Judah to serve as a reminder of what was previously spoken. The people will eat wild crops for two years and then they will plant and harvest their own crops and **vineyards**. This sign recalls the previous sign the Lord offered Ahaz through Isaiah (see the comments on chap. 7). The difference is that Ahaz rejected the offer but Hezekiah readily receives it. The sign promises that a remnant of Judah will be restored through the Lord's **zeal** (vv. 37:31-32). The Hebrew word translated "zeal" is also often translated "jealousy." In this context, however, it appears that the Lord's unending devotion to His people is in mind.

Hezekiah need not fear Sennacherib because the Lord has declared that he will not attack Jerusalem or enter the city. Instead, he will go back to Assyria (vv. 33-34). The Lord will protect the city because of His promise to David (v. 35). This promise is surely a reference to the covenant that the Lord made with David when God installed him and assured him that he would have a descendant on the throne forever (see the comments on 2Sm 7:12-16).

37:36-38. Isaiah 36-38 concludes the narrated episode, describing the actions of the **angel of the LORD** who went out and fought against Assyria. He is mentioned numerous times throughout the OT (Gn 16:7, 9, 10-11; 22:11, 15; Ex 3:2; Nm 22:22-27; Jdg 2:1, 4; 1Kg 19:7; 2Kg 1:15; 1Ch 21:12, 15-16; Ps 34:8; 35:5-6; Hg 1:13; Zch 1:11-12; Mal 2:7) and the term generally refers to a theophany or christophany, a preincarnate appearance of the Messiah. Furthermore, the term translated **angel** could also be translated "messenger," as it is rendered in Is 37:9. As indicated by the common usage of this phrase, this likely is a pre-incarnate appearance of Messiah, but it also may serve as something of a play on the use of "messenger" in 37:9. Assyria's messenger brings an empty threat, whereas the Lord's "messenger" kills **185,000** Assyrians.

These actions prompted Sennacherib's retreat from Judah to **Nineveh**, thus fulfilling God's word concerning the fate of Judah and Assyria. The story also relates the ultimate end of **Sennacherib** whose worship of **Nisroch** does not protect him from the assassination plot of his sons twenty years later (v. 38) in fulfillment of Isaiah's prophecy in 37:7. The inclusion of this verse at the end of this episode has a ring of irony. Sennacherib's god, whose power was going to destroy Judah, could not even protect one man who stood worshiping in his presence. This final description of Sennacherib's death highlights the supremacy of the Lord and, ultimately, the futility of quests for power.

The Taylor Prism (a clay prism inscribed with the annals of Sennacherib, c. 691 BC) gives extrabiblical confirmation to this narrative. It states,

As to Hezekiah, the Jew, he did not submit to my yoke, I laid siege to 46 of his strong cities, walled forts and to the countless villages in their vicinity, and conquered (them) by means of well-stamped (earth-)ramps, and battering-rams brought (thus) near (to the walls) (combined with) the attack by foot soldiers, (using) mines, breeches as well as sapper work. I drove out (of them) 200,150 people, young and old, male and female, horses, mules, donkeys, camels, big and small cattle beyond counting, and considered (them) booty. Himself [i.e., Hezekiah] I made a prisoner in Jerusalem, his royal residence, like a bird in a cage. I surrounded him with earthwork in order to molest those who were leaving his city's gate (J. B. Pritchard, ed., *Ancient Near Eastern Texts*, 2nd ed. [Princeton: Princeton University Press, 1968], 287-288).

Ancient Near Eastern despots would never admit or include their defeats in a victory monument such as this prism. Therefore, the text portrays this as a victory and makes no mention of the 185,000 dead. But there is a subtle admission that Hezekiah was not defeated but only besieged, a confirmation of the biblical history recorded in Is 37 and 2Kg 20.

2. Hezekiah and the Babylonians (38:1–39:8)

These stories describe events that preceded the ones described in the previous chapter. They are placed here out of chronological order for thematic purposes, namely, to point forward to the focus on Babylon in the second half of Isaiah.

a. Hezekiah Healed by the Lord (38:1-22)

38:1-8. After the deliverance of Jerusalem from the imminent threat of the Assyrians, the prophetic text shifts to a narrative of Hezekiah's illness. **Hezekiah** contracts a terminal disease and receives a visit from **Isaiah** who tells Hezekiah to prepare for his impending death (v. 1). Rather than passively accepting the word of Isaiah, Hezekiah prays **to the Lord** (v. 2). The content of Hezekiah's prayer calls God to remember Hezekiah's faithfulness and devotion. Calls to remember in the OT are seldom simply requests to revisit information cognitively, but to act upon the memories that are summoned. In this case, Hezekiah is calling on God to act because of Hezekiah's past faithfulness. Following on the heels of the narrative describing Hezekiah's acts in relation to Assyria, such a request seems imminently justified, particularly in contrast to Ahaz. His example of faith in regard to Assyria is reflective of his character, even though those events actually took place after his illness and healing.

God is moved by Hezekiah's prayer and sends a message through Isaiah granting Hezekiah an additional 15 years of life, as well as promising to defend the city from Assyria (vv. 4-6). The sign that the Lord will do as He has said is given in v. 8. The shadow on the steps of Ahaz will move back ten steps. The precise nature of these steps is not altogether clear. The stairway is also mentioned in the parallel narrative of Hezekiah's illness in 2Kg 20:9-11, but no additional details are provided. Tadmor suggests that the steps functioned as a type of sundial, citing medieval translations that spoke of the "stairs of the sundial" (Hayim Tadmor and Mordechai Cogan, *II Kings* [New Haven: Yale University Press, 1988], 108). A similar interpretation is available in the Qumran scrolls translation of Is 38:8, which renders it "on the dial of the Ahaz roof chamber." This function would make more sense of the sign offered by the Lord, as well as bringing an element of time into the prophecy, thereby resonating with the 15 years that Hezekiah is about to be granted. This miracle involved either reversing the earth's rotation or refraction of the sun's rays. In either case, this was a supernatural sign that Hezekiah received and believed, in contrast to Ahaz, who rejected Isaiah's offer of a supernatural sign (7:11-12).

38:9-20. The prayer of King Hezekiah contained in vv. 9-20 depicts Hezekiah's joy after his recovery from illness. Verses 10-15 describe the illness of Hezekiah and his grief over his impending death, while vv. 16-20 discuss God's deliverance of Hezekiah. Whereas Hezekiah fears that his years will be cut short and that he will never again see **the Lord in the land of the living** (vv. 10-11), God's deliverance brings with it new worship and celebration (v. 20). Hezekiah sees his bitterness transformed into joy. His suffering was for his benefit as he may now thank the Lord as a living human rather than an inhabitant of Sheol (vv. 18-19).

The focus on worship and thanksgiving is telling. Hezekiah is certainly concerned with his own loss of life, but this loss is not simply material. Instead, Hezekiah regrets that he will no longer be able to participate in the very human activity of worship and thanksgiving. As he is given over to Sheol, he sees that there is no longer a capacity to celebrate God. In the OT, Sheol is depicted as the abode of the dead, a place in which the blessing of God is not experienced and so there is no praise of Him. It is not equivalent to hell as developed in the NT (for an explanation of Sheol in the OT, see the comments on Ps 49:15). In any case, Hezekiah's deliverance from death will allow him to continue to worship the Lord. His salvation will result in singing and celebration in the house of the Lord **all the days of his life** (38:20).

38:21-22. Isaiah 38:21-22 would appear to fit better at another point in the narrative. In the parallel passage in 2Kg 20, these phrases occur prior to the provision of a sign confirming the Lord's promise (2Kg 20:7-8). This arrangement, if transferred to Is 38, would mean that Is 38:21-22 would be placed between 38:6 and 38:7. Such a view, while making sense of the verses in question and harmonizing the accounts found in 2 Kings and Isaiah, is difficult to sustain due to a lack of textual evidence. As the text stands, it is perhaps best to take these verses as a reference to the healing of Hezekiah's boil, which would have precluded him from entering the temple. Hezekiah's request for a sign is thus motivated by his newfound desire to worship in the Lord's temple as was expressed in his prayer. Though the placement of Is 38:21-22 seems odd, it must also be read in relation to the events that follow in which Hezekiah gives the Babylonian delegation a tour of the temple. Hezekiah's zeal to enter the temple once again is manifested in his willingness to showcase his wealth and the contents of the temple to the Babylonians.

b. Hezekiah Reveals His Treasures to the Babylonians (39:1-8)

39:1-2. Hezekiah's interactions with his Babylonian visitors are narrated in this section. While this narrative is often understood as an act of pride on the part of Hezekiah, it is not clear from the narratives included in Isaiah, 2 Kings, or 2 Chronicles that Hezekiah was motivated by pride. The reference to the events related to the Babylonians in 2Ch 32:31 suggests that Hezekiah failed a test designed by God to know "all that was in his heart," but, even here, pride is not mentioned explicitly. Given Hezekiah's reaction to the prophetic proclamation recorded in Isaiah and 2 Kings, it may be better to identify Hezekiah's failure as one of self-centeredness. He had only a concern for the prosperity of his reign rather than the ongoing prosperity of the people. In any case, it is not clear why Hezekiah decided to show his whole house to the Babylonians. Given the flow of Isaiah, it may be that such a gesture is motivated by Hezekiah's joy at his recent deliverance.

39:3-8. Regardless of his reasons, Hezekiah's act becomes the impetus for a prophetic proclamation. As Hezekiah showed all that was in his house to the Babylonians, so the Babylonians will eventually come and carry it all away. Even some of Hezekiah's sons would be taken and **become officials** in the Babylonian king's court (v. 7). The word **officials** is literally "eunuchs," a word that may have meant only "royal official" or may have been intended literally as men who were castrated. If literal, then Isaiah's pronouncement indicated a danger to the continuation of the Davidic line by a physical threat to the ability of the descendants of David to reproduce. Hezekiah's reaction to this pronouncement is somewhat surprising given that it focuses solely on his own reign. The **peace** and security that will characterize Hezekiah's lifetime seems to be Hezekiah's primary concern (v. 8). His vision for God's ongoing activity amongst the people and the continuation of the Davidic dynasty is overshadowed by present concerns.

Such a reading adds nuance to the interpretation of Hezekiah's prayer in which he mourns his own loss of life and the capacity to worship God only to rejoice in his ability to worship again at the temple. Perhaps even in his praise of God after being healed from his illness, Hezekiah does not recognize the importance of the enduring worship of God throughout the generations of Israel. Instead, his own ability to worship God and to enjoy the blessings of God in his lifetime was enough.

Also, the Babylonian visit may not have been a simple social call. Interpreters as early as Josephus suggested that the Babylonians came to form an alliance between Babylon and Judah (*Antiquities* X.II.2). This suggestion is strengthened by similar episodes in 1Kg 15:16-20 and 2Kg 16:5-9 in which Asa and Ahaz respectively form alliances with foreign nations. If Hezekiah is portrayed as making an alliance with Babylon, the episode resonates with the dynamics between God and king that have been highlighted throughout Isaiah. When the human king trusts in God completely, God will bring peace and security. When the human king seeks to place his faith in the power of the nations, God will discipline the nation. In this case, the deportation of Israel and the stripping away of all the riches of the temple offer a vivid contrast between the fruits of God's rule and that of Babylon. Babylon's rule results in displacement and deprivation. God's rule is one of prosperity and peace in which the Messiah will reign. Aligning the nation with any power except the Lord's is a near-fatal misstep with far-reaching implications. Here, Hezekiah's shortsightedness foreshadows Judah's fall to the increasingly powerful Babylonian Empire.

B. The Oracles of Blessing (40:1–66:24)

Having completed the narrative of Hezekiah's faith in the signs of deliverance granted him by God (chaps. 36–39), the prophet turns to oracles emphasizing God's blessing for Israel and the world (chaps. 40–66). This is in contrast to the first major section of the book, consisting of a narrative wherein Ahaz refuses to have faith in the signs granted him by God (chaps. 7–12), followed by a series of oracles emphasizing judgment (chaps. 13–35).

The oracles of blessing have three major sections, each ending with a phrase emphasizing God's judgment of the wicked (as opposed to the blessing of the righteous) (48:22; 57:21; 66:24). These function as markers, indicating the end of each section.

1. Deliverance from Babylon (40:1–48:22)

The first section in the oracles of blessing promises restoration to Israel. For the most part, this restoration pertains to God's promise to restore Israel from captivity in Babylon, but occasionally looks beyond that to the messianic restoration.

a. God's Comforting Message (40:1-31)

This section represents the first part of a broader prophetic message spanning chaps. 40–48 and offering comfort to God's exiled people. Despite their current situation under Babylon, there is hope because Babylon will not determine the fate of God's people. Instead, God lies behind Babylon, maintaining oversight of His people and their time in exile. Whereas Babylon cares nothing for the continuation of the Jews, God wants His people to survive and to thrive as a nation under His rule. This section provides comforting assurance to Israel (40:1-11) because God is incomparable (40:12-31).

40:1-2. Isaiah begins by bringing a word of comfort to Israel. The imperative **comfort** is likely directed by God to the prophet (v. 1). Targumim, ancient Aramaic rabbinic paraphrases of the OT, follow this interpretation by including "O, prophets" at the beginning of the verse. God calls Isaiah to deliver a message that will remind Israel and Judah of God's commitment to His covenant and to the reestablishment of the Israelite nation. God will bring relief that is threefold (40:2): the nation's **warfare has ended** (God will provide peace), **her iniquity has been removed** (God will forgive), and **she has received . . . double for all her sins** (God will end the national discipline and restore her). The repetition of **comfort** serves to highlight the coming consolation and reminds Israel and Judah that their God desires to soothe them and restore them. Isaiah is to speak **kindly** to Jerusalem and reveal that the entire nation's suffering will come to an end and that the nation's sin has been paid for (40:2). The reference to the **double** payment **for all her sins** at the end of the verse emphasizes the severity of Israel's exile. Though the exile has been hard on the people, it will not last forever. The God who brought forth punishment will come to reveal His glory (40:5).

40:3-5. After a message of comfort, the prophet next brings words of hope, beginning with the proclamation of the coming of the Lord. Though it is tempting to identify the one whose voice **is calling** out (v. 3) as Isaiah, the prophet is not specifically identified. Isaiah 40:3 is utilized in the NT in a reference to John the Baptist (cf. Mt 3:3; Mk 1:3; Lk 3:4; Jn 1:23), but in a slightly different form. The Hebrew text suggests that the phrase **in the wilderness** modifies the verb **clear**. In this case, the **way** in question is to be prepared in the desert. The NT translation takes **in the wilderness** as modifying the verb **calling**, thus suggesting that the source of the voice is in the desert. In the NT, John the Baptist is identified as the fulfillment of Is 40:3. This identification need not control the understanding of the passage in its original context of Is 43 where it functions less as a piece of predictive prophecy and more as a description and guarantee of the coming glory of God. The predictive element is, however, implied insofar as the **voice** is never identified. The NT adoption of the passage then is designed to summon the picture first developed in the context of Isaiah. A smooth way should be prepared for the coming of the Lord and the revelation of His glory. All will see this glory because the Lord Himself has said it will be so (40:5).

Some hold that Isaiah 40:3-5 only refers to God coming to Israel and not to the return of the exiles. Such a view, however, appears to be at odds with Is 35:8-10 in which the ransomed of the Lord will return on the highway of the Lord. Therefore, the way in the wilderness will serve both as the way the Lord will come to Jerusalem and as the way the people will return from exile. This way will be characterized by the reunion of God and His people.

40:6-8. A second aspect of hope for Israel is that the word of God is eternal. Regarding the two voices (vv. 3 and 6), they are likely the same voice because of their similarity in position at the beginning of the verses. Regardless, the command to call out prompts Isaiah's question concerning the topic of the cry. The answer given reinforces the certainty of the events in vv. 3-5 by underlining the permanence of the Lord's word. While **grass withers** and flowers fade, **the word of** the Lord **stands forever** (v. 8). The imagery of grass drying up and falling flowers suggests the fragility of humanity. Grass and flowers have no permanence, but the Word of the Lord will never fail.

40:9-11. A third source of hope for Israel is that God will powerfully protect the nation. This is so important that Zion (Jerusalem) is called to proclaim the **good news** from a **high mountain** and tell **the cities of Judah** not to fear because God is about to deliver them. The herald is to announce the arrival of the Lord and present Him as the great protector to the people of Judah. The translation **Lord God** captures the strength and majesty of Israel's God (v. 10). **His arm** is an image of His military power. Similar imagery is used elsewhere in Isaiah (51:9-10; 63:5), though the references are specifically to God's right hand. God's military might is also evident as He brings His reward with Him to Jerusalem (40:10), but such spoils are not the Lord's true treasure. Instead, the Lord's gain comes in His renewed embrace of His people (v. 11).

The use of shepherding imagery was commonly used to describe kings and deities in the ancient Near East and in the OT. There are a number of instances in which the image of a shepherd was employed as a royal title for Mesopotamian kings. The gods are also described in these terms. For instance, in the ancient lament over the destruction of Ur, the gods are described as shepherds who have abandoned their flocks. This more negative image is also present in the OT, but only with reference to earthly kings (cf. Jr 10:21; Ezk 34:2-3; Zch 11:3-17). The Lord is always pictured in positive terms (cf. Gn 49:24; Ps 8:2; 23:1; 78:52-55, 70-72). The image of Is 40:11 displays God's care for His people as being like a **shepherd** who cares for His sheep.

40:12-17. The second half of the chapter presents the reason that Israel can trust God for the nation's comfort and hope, depicting the Lord as incomparably superior to all creation. God is first described as incomparable as Creator (vv. 12-17). Through a series of questions, God is shown to be the meticulous and powerful Creator (v. 12), to have a mind that no human can understand or advise (v. 13), and to determine the course of the world through the manifestation of His own wisdom (v. 14). In vv. 15-17, God is compared to the nations that pale in comparison to His majesty. They are dust that does not even register on the Lord's scale (v. 15). Even Lebanon, regarded for its massive cedars, offers nothing to God. The riches of the nations are insignificant to God (vv. 16-17).

40:18-20. Second, God is incomparable as the Eternal One. After comparing **God** to the nations, the conversation turns toward handmade idols (vv. 18-20). Idols were common in the ancient Near East. Though they varied depending on the culture in which they were produced as well as the god they were intended to represent, they were generally carved from wood (v. 20), overlaid with **gold** and **silver** (v. 19), and then, in some cases, dressed in fine clothes. Because idols represented the physical site in which a particular god manifested his or her presence in a special way, they were constructed with great care. They were a means of communicating with the gods and were, in many ways, revered. The comparison between God and idols, then, should not be taken lightly. While it seems difficult to believe that physical idols, which were made with human hands, would be viewed as having power and authority, the comparison between God and idols was not simply one between a trinket and a supernatural being in the eyes of the ancient world. Instead, from the perspective of the ancient Near East, it was a comparison between two providers.

40:21-24. God is incomparable in a third way—in His transcendence. Verse 21 challenges the people's decision to create idols, suggesting that the knowledge of God has already been communicated to them. God is transcendent, standing far **above** the **earth** and **its inhabitants**. It is His creation (v. 22). His control over the world extends to its seemingly powerful rulers who, despite appearances, are **sown**, take **root**,

wither away, and are swept off like chaff (v. 24), not unlike grass and flowers (see v. 8). No creature or man-made idol can truly be compared to the Lord. He has no equal (40:25).

40:25-26. Fourth, God is incomparable as ruler of the heavens. As proof of His incomparable superiority, He calls the people to examine the heavens and think of the **One** who created them. God here is pictured as being a powerful military leader (note **the greatness of His might and the strength of His power**), the one to whom even the **stars** show their obedience, who has the capacity to preserve Israel. No idol can make the same claim, and certainly no leader who is a mere mortal.

40:27-31. Having comforted Israel (vv. 1-11) by describing God's incomparable superiority (vv. 12-26), the prophet seeks to apply this message of hope to the despondent state of Israel in captivity. They should know that God's strength offers comfort to His people. Their difficulty does not correspond to some weakness in God or to His neglect of their cause (v. 27). Instead, God is inexhaustible. The depth of His understanding is beyond comprehension (v. 28). God will provide for Israel. He is a limitless source of strength that transcends even the energy of young men (vv. 29-30). Verse 31 concludes the chapter with a declaration that it is not those who have wasted their energy on idols, on plotting, or on developing their own strength that will win the day. Instead, those who wait for the Lord to take action will find additional strength. The imagery of being carried on the wings of eagles also appears in Ex 19:4 within a context of deliverance. Deuteronomy 32:11 also uses the imagery of the eagle to denote protection. In Is 40:31, the reference to the eagle's wings appears to capture the effortless power of the eagle in flight in contrast to futile human efforts. The final two lines of v. 31 reinforce this understanding of the eagle's wings. Those who trust in the Lord will be sustained by Him.

This section underscores the power and wisdom of God, offering these characteristics as a source of comfort for Israel. God's unlimited control over His creation stands in contrast to the supposed sovereignty of earthly rulers or false idols. It is in this God that all of Israel's hope rests. Israel's plight cannot be solved through dependence on political or military power. Instead, Israel will be delivered by waiting for the Lord to act. They must trust that the all-powerful Lord of all things will ultimately bring salvation and vigor. God is the source of all things. He is the one in whom all men must trust. He is the Lord who brings rest and vitality to all those who faithfully endure as they wait for Him to save them.

b. God's Powerful Deliverance (41:1-29)

The words of comfort to Israel conveyed in Is 40 shift to a challenge to the nations in Is 41:1-7 as God calls the nations to recognize His power, authority, and control over world events. Despite this turn, Is 41 supports the words of comfort spoken previously. God's control over world events implicitly emphasizes His ability to bring about the good of His people Israel. By dismissing the seemingly evident power of the nations, it becomes clear that the people of Israel's lives are not left to cruel human regimes, but are sustained and guided by the Lord.

Watts suggests that Is 41 is structured based on a chiastic arrangement with vv. 8-9 serving as the central pivot around which the rest of the chapter is arranged. (See chart in John D. W. Watts, *Isaiah 34–66*, WBC [Waco, TX: Word, 1987], 101.) This arrangement highlights Israel's servanthood as a central concept within Isaiah's message. Though the servanthood of Israel and the Messiah rises to greater prominence in later chapters, its appearance here offers a sense of consolation and comfort. Despite the scattering of God's corporate servant Israel, they will be brought back. The nation has not been rejected (41:9).

41:1-7. This first unit of thought describes Cyrus, who in a sense functions as a political servant for God. To begin, the islands are to be silent and to listen to the argument that the Lord is mounting against the nations (v. 1). The **judgment** mentioned at the end of v. 1 could refer to the Lord's pronouncement against the nations, but in this context could denote the conversation as a whole. Note also the contrast between the call to **silence** and the call to **speak** (v. 1). The nations are not excluded from the conversation, but will be engaged through a series of questions in vv. 2-4. The first set of questions calls the nations to consider who rouses the **one from the east** (v. 2). The **one from the east** is almost certainly a reference to Cyrus the Great, the Persian king who is the rising star on the ancient Near Eastern stage. This Persian nation led by Cyrus is certainly in mind in later texts within Isaiah (44:28–45:6; 46:11; 48:14-16). Persia and her emperor, regardless of military strength, has not become a superpower of its own accord. Instead, God has called Cyrus and the Persians and it is He who has made them successful (41:2-3). For more on Cyrus, see the comments on 44:24-28.

A new question is asked (41:4), which appears to broaden the scope of God's activity from the contemporary conquests of the Persians to the entirety of world history. It is not simply that God has orchestrated Persia's success in this generation, but that He has done so throughout the generations. God was with the first generation guiding and moving them toward His intended purposes (v. 4). He asserts Himself as the one who has controlled world events from the beginning. God is not simply the ruler of Israel, but the sovereign ruler over all nations.

After God makes Himself known as the one who rules over history, the prophet describes the reaction of the coastlands, a reference to the distant lands beyond the sea and the nations that live there (v. 5). The reaction of the nations could be construed as positive. Fear and trembling are not inappropriate responses to seeing the coming of the Lord. Yet their reaction to the Lord's instrument, Cyrus, could more likely be construed as negative, driven by fearful panic. In vv. 6-7 the people of the coastlands do not depend on God but on one another for support and they turn to false idols. This shows that they are not repentant but fearful. Nailing down the idols so that they do not fall over suggests that the people are still loyal to their idols. Their efforts to keep the idols upright betray their continued trust in them (v. 7).

41:8-13. Next, the prophet describes Israel, God's national servant (41:8-24), a nation with a different story than the coastlands. Verse 8 offers a rich description of Israel's identity, specifically calling **Israel** God's **servant**. The phrase **My servant** is also used of Isaiah (20:3), of Eliakim (22:20), of David (37:35), and of a distinctive redemptive Servant (42:1; 52:13). Israel is not identified as God's servant until the second half of Isaiah. Using the patriarchal name **Jacob** for the nation, the prophet identifies the nation as God's servant (cf. 44:1-12; 45:4; 48:20). Yet, Israel is only infrequently described as God's servant in the rest of the OT (cf. Ps 136:22; Jr 30:10). The servant language here denotes Israel's special position in relation to the Lord and in relation to the rest of the nations. It also suggests that Israel is God's representative that will showcase His strength by obeying the Lord and trusting in Him.

Israel is special among all the people of the world because God has chosen them. Israel's chosen status should be understood in relation to Abraham, who is called God's friend—literally, "beloved one." This friendship is seen at various other occasions in Scripture (cf. 2Ch 20:7; Jms 2:23). Friendship in this context suggests at least that there is a bond of mutual affection between God and Abraham. The close covenantal connection between God and Israel, as well as the reference to Israel's chosen status in the near context, makes it likely that Abraham's friendship signifies him as God's covenantal partner. Abraham is God's friend or "beloved" because of God's choice of Abraham. In Scripture, the language of love and hate indicates choice and rejection (see Mal 1:2-5 and Rm 9:13 and the comments there). God's unconditional election of Abraham and his descendants explains the promise that God will reconstitute the nation from the places where they have been scattered (Is 41:9). Israel's identity is rooted in the Lord, His activity, His choosing, and His designation of the nation as His servant. It is this identity that has the potential to truly comfort Israel. God's actions on behalf of Israel are intended to draw attention away from the military prowess of Israel's enemies and Israel's current subjugation to them. The promised regathering of Israel proves God's capacity to care for the nation and showcases the benefits of servanthood to the Lord.

Israel has no reason to fear because the Lord is with the nation. The very presence of Israel's God should drive out fear. Israel's confidence is not rooted in its own ability, but in the Lord's strength. This call not to be afraid is repeated several times in Isaiah (40:9; 41:13-14; 43:1, 5; 44:2, 8; 51:7; 54:4), but in this context the fear is not simply concerned with defeat by an enemy nation, but also with divine abandonment (41:9). God will remove all of Israel's enemies and provide His chosen nation with safety and security. The Lord's help will deliver and sustain Israel (vv. 11-13).

41:14-16. The prophet reiterates the call for Israel not to fear (v. 14). Israel, despite being despised and insignificant, as the designation **worm** implies, may take comfort in the Lord's assistance. The term **worm** can refer to an actual creature (cf. Dt 28:39; Jnh 4:7), but often metaphorically refers to a person's or humanity's state of destitution or despised status (cf. Ps 22:6). It seems unlikely that God is calling Jacob a worm from His perspective, but rather that Jacob is a worm in the eyes of the world. Israel is not a privileged nation on the world stage, but God will still care for the nation even if, or perhaps *because*, it is not powerful enough to care for itself.

The Lord is called Israel's **Redeemer** and **the Holy One of Israel** (v. 14). This is the first time in Isaiah that **Redeemer** has been applied to the Lord. **Redeemer** had a secular as well as a theological meaning. God's redemption of Israel began in Ex 6:6 when God acted on behalf of Israel to protect the nation from the Egyptians. The term means "one who buys back" and is primarily associated with the concept of the kinsman-redeemer that is displayed in the interactions between Ruth and Boaz in the book of Ruth. The role of the kinsman-redeemer was to preserve and recover a particular Israelite tribe member's losses. For more on the kinsman-redeemer, see the introduction to the commentary on Ruth.

God's provision and distribution of tribal lands, as well as His concern for the continuation of the various tribal seed lines, provided the rationale for the practices related to the kinsman-redeemer. A family member was enlisted to protect the broader tribal interests. When used in reference to God, the term denotes His ongoing protection of Israel's interests. The covenant that God established will be sustained and its provisions will come to pass. Israel's exile and its inability to stand against its enemies do not constitute a rejection of the covenant. Israel's situation does, however, require a redemptive act of God.

God will reverse Jacob's status as a worm (41:15). Israel, which was once weak and helpless, will be made into a powerhouse, metaphorically described as a **sharp threshing sledge with double edges**. There were two types of sledges used for threshing in the ancient Near East. Oswalt states: "One was simply a frame of heavy timbers with sharp stones or pieces of metal driven into the underside. The other was a frame holding one or two heavy rollers into which the stones or metal was driven" (John N. Oswalt, *The Book of Isaiah, Chapters 40–66* [Grand Rapids, MI: Eerdmans, 1998], 94). Whether the first or second threshing instrument is in view is largely inconsequential. The significance of the image is located in the implement's function and quality. This new threshing implement will chew through the nations that then will be blown away by the wind (41:16).

41:17-20. Israel's newfound strength will result in rejoicing as the nation will give God the glory for its success. Beyond military victory, the Lord will provide nourishment for the oppressed and the poor (v. 17). Though success in war and care for the downtrodden are not always mentioned together in this manner, their association in this case suggests that the reign of Israel will not be characterized by socioeconomic inequality or oppressive societal practices. God will answer the prayers of the people. He will not abandon those who need Him, but will supply them with great abundance (vv. 18-19). God's acts, despite their humanitarian impact, are not done explicitly for humanitarian reasons. Instead, God's work on Israel's behalf is designed to proclaim His sovereignty and power to the world (v. 20). Taking Israel from insignificant worm to world power in the future millennium will showcase God's power and let the nations know that it is Israel's God who controls the course of history.

41:21-23. Following on the heels of God's acts on Israel's behalf, the Lord calls the pagan gods to defend themselves and their legitimacy (v. 21). These gods have no evidence of their power, no proof of their sovereignty or their ability to deliver and sustain (v. 22). They do not control world history. They do not even have the capacity to act (v. 23). The inability of the gods stands in stark contrast to the power of the Lord that will be made manifest in the exaltation of Israel whose strength is only to be found in the faithfulness of their God.

41:24. The critique of the gods leads to the condemnation of the worshiper. The gods do nothing. They have no proof of their power or authority. This lack of evidence will cause those who worship these gods to be **an abomination**. These detestable gods are mere idols. The pagan gods cannot sustain those who worship them from the onslaught that God Himself will bring upon them. Israel will be preserved and will prosper, but those who trust in false idols will fall.

41:25-29. The prophet returns to the servant described at the outset of the chapter, Cyrus the Great, the Lord's political servant. The **one from the north**, referring to Cyrus, will bring devastation as he treads on rulers (v. 25). The coming of Cyrus should not have come as a surprise. The Lord had previously spoken of it (vv. 1-7). Foretelling Cyrus's impending encroachment will ultimately prove that God is right (v. 26). The pagan gods failed to warn those who worship them. Instead, God was the first to speak it and to proclaim it in Zion (v. 27). Jerusalem was given a messenger and warned of the coming destruction by their God, unlike the other nations whose gods failed to give them the news. The absence of counsel and warning offers additional proof of their falsehood (v. 28). These gods are not present with their people. Worshiping these idols amounts to vanity. It has no value. Trusting in those gods results in vanity and confusion (v. 29). In contrast to the Lord, the shortcomings of other gods become painfully obvious. They do not stand up to scrutiny.

c. God's Chosen Servant (42:1-25)

Though God has designated Israel as His servant in chap. 41, 42:1-9 represents the first of Isaiah's so-called "Servant Songs." The other songs appear later in the book (cf. 49:1-13; 50:4-11; 52:13–53:12). These songs describe the ministry of God's servant whose unique functions set Him apart to accomplish God's work. The Servant Songs have received a great deal of attention in the history of scholarship related to the book of Isaiah, with the identification of the servant being a central concern. Earlier commentators such as Gerhard von Rad suggested that the Servant Songs recalled the ministry of Moses (Gerhard von Rad, *Old Testament Theology: The Theology of Israel's Historical Traditions* [Louisville, KY: Westminster John Knox, 2001], 238–262). Others have questioned whether the servant is a single individual or a group of people. Those who see the servant as an individual have identified men as diverse as Hezekiah, Isaiah, Cyrus, or the coming Messiah. Israel, or a segment thereof, is most commonly identified with the servant (Shalom M. Paul, *Isaiah 40–66*, Eerdmans Critical Commentary [Grand Rapids, MI: Eerdmans, 2012], 18).

Despite these potential options, it appears best to identify the servant in the Servant Songs of the book of Isaiah as a prediction of the Messiah. As such, the NT identifies Jesus of Nazareth as the referent to these passages. The NT's acknowledgement of Jesus as Messiah and, thus, as the Servant of the Lord, makes clear that He is the true referent of the Servant Songs (cf. Mt 8:14-17; Lk 22:37; Ac 8:30-35; 1Pt 2:21-25). The chart below shows the development of the message of the Servant Songs.

42:1-4. For this passage, see also the comments on Mt 3:15-16 and Mt 12:15-21. The message of the first Servant Song (42:1-9) is that the **Servant** is God's chosen agent to establish justice in all the earth and deliver both Jew and Gentile from darkness and bondage. Just as in the fourth Servant Song (52:13–53:12), this Song is written in the third person. The first part of the Song (42:1-4) declares that the Lord has chosen the Servant to provide **justice** for Israel and **the nations** (v. 1). The Song's first four verses move from designation to mission. Verse 1 designates the Servant as God's chosen, describes God's equipping Him for service, and declares His mission. Verse 1 begins by presenting the Servant as the special agent of the Lord, His **chosen one**. The Servant is sustained by God. He is not delivered by His own strength, but by the power of the Lord. He, like Israel, has been chosen. The mention of the **Spirit** suggests anointing, though the specific language of anointing is not used in this context (cf. Is 11:1; 61:1). The Servant is given the Spirit in order to bring forth justice for the nations.

Isaiah 42:2-3 addresses the activity and behavior of the Servant. Despite the power He has been given, the Servant will not flaunt His strength (v. 2). His reign will not be characterized by oppression. Instead, He will be gentle enough to care for the **bruised reed** and the **dimly burning wick** among the people. These groups symbolize the downtrodden in Israel who suffer under unjust rule. The Servant's reign will be characterized by His gentle care for the oppressed (v. 3). This clearly distinguishes the Servant from Cyrus the Great, whom Isaiah describes as crushing others with weapons (41:2-3).

Verse 4 speaks to the **justice** resulting from

The Message of the Servant Songs

The Responsibilities of the Servant: He will establish justice and enlighten the darkened.	The Roles of the Servant: He will restore Israel and reach the Gentiles.	The Rejection of the Servant: He will trust God for vindication in the face of humiliation.	The Redemption by the Servant: He will be exalted by God because of providing atonement through death.
Biography	Autobiography	Autobiography	Biography
42:1-9	49:1-13	50:4-11	52:13–53:12

the Servant's rule. Justice is a characteristic task of royal figures throughout the OT (cf. 1Sm 8:5, 20; Ps 72:1-2, 4; Is 9:6; Jr 21:11; 22:3, 15; 23:5). Bringing justice will also bring peace as even the nations (**the coastlands**) will wait to hear the Servant's instruction. The Servant will persevere until He completes His mission. He will establish justice on **the earth** and the nations will no longer set their own rules. Instead, they will align themselves with the **law** of the Servant.

42:5-7. The second part of the Song declares that the Lord calls the Servant to enlighten and liberate Israel and the nations (42:5-9). These verses underscore the Lord's commissioning of the Servant and amplify the expectations of the Servant. The description of God in v. 5 focuses on God's position in relation to creation. This focus is designed to support the word of God proclaimed concerning the Servant. God has created all things. He gives and sustains all life. Therefore, His word is to be trusted. In v. 6, the Lord commissions the Servant. His appointment is twofold—**as a covenant to the people** and as **a light to the nations**. The phrase **covenant to the people** has three possible interpretations. First, those who take the Servant as referring to the people of Israel give it the sense of "a covenant people." This is unlikely because the Hebrew word order is wrong for this translation. It would have to read "a people of the covenant" (*'am berith*), not as it does, lit., "a covenant of the people" (*berith 'am*). A second view is that this phrase describes the Servant as a covenant representative for the nations. This is doubtful because the word **people** is singular, and as such it is generally a reference to the people of Israel. This is clearly the case when the same phrase is used in the next Servant song (49:8). The third and most likely interpretation is to see the Servant as a covenant mediator for Israel. The phrase **a covenant to the people** is a figure of speech, a metonymy of effect (covenant) for cause (mediator), and means a "covenant mediator for the people." Like Moses, the Servant will mediate a covenant for Israel's benefit, specifically the "new covenant" for the messianic age (cf. Jr 31:31-34). Since the Servant is the mediator of the covenant for Israel, the Servant clearly cannot be Israel.

The second aspect of the Servant's commission is as **a light to the nations** (v. 6). Messianic expectation always anticipated the nations coming to know the true God of Israel. The Servant Messiah will be the one to bring this light to the Gentiles. This concept is developed further in the second Servant Song (49:1-13).

Verse 7 continues to list the results of the Servant's commissioning. Not only will He serve as covenant mediator for Israel and be a light to the Gentiles, He will also open **blind eyes**, liberate captives, and free those who are imprisoned **in darkness**. Though each of these may be understood to refer to physical conditions, the metaphorical value of these actions should not be dismissed. Blindness is often utilized to denote spiritual blindness (cf. Is 29:18; 35:5; 42:16). The darkness mentioned in the final line of v. 7 refers to the darkness of spiritual bondage.

42:8-9. As a conclusion to the first Servant Song, there is a declaration of God's power. God will disrupt the human praise of idols who steal His praise. The references to fulfilled prophecy echo the declarations of chaps. 40–41, connecting the Servant Song to its context. God can do what the idols cannot, so He will not share His **glory** with them. God calls again on His predictive oracles as a proof of His ability to see what will come to pass and to support what He has just foretold (42:9). The readers of Isaiah can trust this prophecy because the God of glory has predicted Messiah's coming.

42:10-13. Having described the Servant-Messiah (vv. 1-9), the next section offers a song of praise (vv. 10-13) followed by a depiction of the Servant's ministry to Israel. The call to praise (vv. 10-12) directs all the inhabitants of the earth and sea to sing praises to the Lord. The **new song** (v. 10) is prompted by the new oracles that will be fulfilled by God's continued work. The call expands beyond the nation of Israel and encompasses all **who go down to the sea** (v. 10). This likely refers to people at the end of the earth (John Goldingay, *The Message of Isaiah 40–55: A Literary-Theological Commentary* [New York: T & T Clark, 2005], 169). The islands that were previously called upon to listen to the Lord (41:1) are now called to respond to what they have heard (42:10). All the world is called to give glory to the Lord (vv. 11-12). God is then depicted as a **warrior**, indicating His great power (42:13).

42:14-17. This section shifts from the previous call to praise to a description of the Lord and His activity. This image of the Lord depicts God as an unstoppable soldier prepared for battle. God contrasts His seeming silence in the past (v. 14) to the powerful actions He will take in the future (vv. 15-16). The imagery of the **woman in**

labor suggests that the Lord's silence will not continue. His eagerness to fight will not be held back for long. His inactivity should not lull the world into a false sense of security because the Lord will come and overturn nature's strength (v. 15).

The reference to the **blind** (v. 16) harkens back to v. 7 in which the blind will see and those in darkness will be released. God proclaims that He will lead the blind down new **paths**. The blind will not be left helpless as God comes in fury, but will be led to safety. The blind here could refer to Israel, or to the nations who will now be led by God's light. Though the previous context focused on all the earth's inhabitants, it is significant that the perspective of 42:18-25 shifts to Israel, referring to God's people as deaf and blind. Verse 17 reveals the reaction of idol worshipers who will see the actions of the Lord and be ashamed that they ever bowed down to a lifeless piece of wood.

42:18-25. Next, God reasons with His people Israel. The blind and deaf are identified as God's **servant**. Whereas the previous mention of a servant in 42:1-4 seemed to refer to an individual figure, the servant in this case is the nation of Israel. Far from being triumphant and like the coming servant of the Lord described in 42:1-4, the servant described here is the epitome of deafness and blindness. The rhetorical questions in this case assume that no one is more deaf or blind than this servant of the Lord. The word translated **at peace** (v. 19) is problematic as the specific verbal form only occurs here in the OT. Oswalt suggests rightly that the term should be translated "one in covenant peace" (Oswalt, *Isaiah 40–66*, 128). The servant's senses are not gone, but they are of no real use. Though the servant's eyes can see and their ears can hear, there is no understanding, no faithfulness, and no obedience (v. 20).

Israel's sluggish response to the Lord's revelation stands in conflict with the great and glorious **law** that God has provided **for His righteousness' sake** (v. 21). The law was given to display God's justice to the world through the obedience of God's people. The servant was meant to prosper by obeying God's law. Instead, Israel has been imprisoned, pillaged, and **plundered** (v. 22). Their unwillingness to act on what they have seen and heard has resulted in their degradation. They appear to have been abandoned with no one calling out to rescue them (v. 22).

Having spoken the truth, the Lord steps back to question who among the Israelites will actually **heed** His warnings and listen to His instruction (v. 23). The question is legitimate as those to whom God is speaking have already heard the message. They have already refused to follow the ways of the Lord, prompting God to turn them over to their enemies (v. 24). Even as He **poured out** His anger on His people, they remained ignorant, confused, and blind so that they did not recognize or respond to the work of God (v. 25).

d. God's Comforting Assurance (43:1–44:23)

The stark picture painted at the end of chap. 42 leaves Israel's future in a moment of ambiguity. Isaiah 43 and 44 addresses this ambiguity by assuring Israel that God will protect His people.

43:1-4. At the outset, the prophet grants Israel assurance of God's continued loving presence. God is Jacob's **Creator** and Redeemer. His actions against Israel are not permanent. The nation will not be imprisoned in exile forever because no one may steal God's possession (v. 1). The reference to Israel's redemption in v. 1 may be intended to recall the exodus from Egypt. Moreover, the imagery of passing through waters is reminiscent of the exodus (v. 2). The Targumim make specific reference to the Exodus: "When you first passed through the Red Sea my word sustained you, Pharaoh and the Egyptians, who were like the waters of the river, did not stand against you." Though the Targum's paraphrase is not definitive, it does suggest that certain segments of the broader interpretive community understood v. 2 as referring to the exodus.

While it is tempting to agree with the Targum, other factors must be taken into account. For instance, the second half of the verse does not refer to water, but to walking through fire, which does not appear to have any particular connection to the exodus from Egypt. The reference to Egypt in v. 3 is not related specifically to the exodus, either. Instead, Egypt is given as **ransom** for Israel. In addition neither **Cush** (Ethiopia) nor **Seba** (modern Yemen) appear in the Exodus narrative. It may be best to recognize that the exodus from Egypt, which would be ingrained in Israel's memory, is difficult to avoid in this context. Activating this memory, however, does not require that the entire verse be connected to the exodus. Instead, the passage brings to mind the ongoing protection of the

Lord with an echo from the exodus reinforcing the point. God promises to redeem Israel because the nation is **precious** to God (v. 4). The word "precious" describes that which has great value either because of rarity or intrinsic worth. Since there are many nations, likely here, Israel is precious to God because of the nation's value to Him. Nevertheless, it was God's choice of Israel that gave the nation its intrinsic value (Dt 7:7-8). God considers Israel so precious, honored, and loved that He will sacrifice other nations, namely Egypt, in its stead.

43:5-7. God's comforting assurance includes the promise of Israel's regathering. The call not to fear appears once again (v. 5) and is associated with the Lord's promise to regather Israel from across the world. The mention of **east** and **west** (v. 5) and of **north** and **south** (v. 6) underscores the completeness of the return. God's scattered people will be reconstituted from the four corners of the earth. They will be rescued because they are God's special possession, His creation formed for the **glory** of God (v. 7). Surely they will not remain hidden as prisoners of the nations but will be reconstituted as an independent nation.

43:8-13. God's comforting assurance also promises that He will not change Israel's calling. This section begins with the familiar imagery of those who have eyes and ears, but cannot see or hear. Though this description has previously been used of Israel (42:19), it appears that all the nations are in view in this case (43:9). The nations are again pictured as incapable of predicting what has happened to them. They could not have foreseen their fate. The nations cannot produce **witnesses** to prove they were right about the way things would turn out. Their means did not produce the expected ends, so they cannot claim that they were right.

Though the nations have no witness to defend them, God calls His **servant** Israel as His witness. Service as God's witness was part of Israel's mission. As Kaiser notes, "... Israel herself was a standing witness to the power and reality of who Yahweh was and what he had done in their history" (Walter C. Kaiser, Jr., *Mission in the Old Testament: Israel as a Light to the Nations* [Grand Rapids, MI: Baker, 2012], 54). The obedience and ultimate success of Israel stands as the testimony to God's uniqueness. God is not only the God of Israel, but the only God in existence, period. This testimony becomes clear in the assertion that no god was **formed** before the Lord and none will be formed **after** (v. 10). Verse 11 sharpens God's uniqueness. He is not simply the only God, but also the only **savior**. Israel's calling stands as witness that the Lord alone has **declared** and **saved** and **proclaimed** (v. 12), in contrast to the so-called gods of the foreign nations. God is the ruler of all and there is nothing that can stand against Him. His will is irresistible (v. 13).

43:14-15. Israel is further assured of God's promise of redemption. Having proven and proclaimed His sovereignty, the Lord now proclaims the next events He will orchestrate on the world stage. For the **sake** of Israel, God will bring the Babylonians low. Babylon's rejoicing will turn to mourning as the powerful nation is subjected to the hand of the Lord (v. 14). Furthermore, God declares both His position as Lord, as well as His special relationship to **Israel** (v. 15). Though it is not explicitly stated, God's position as Lord gives power to His position in Israel. **The Lord** in this context is God's covenant name, but it is also a proclamation of His universal sovereignty. This God, who has committed Himself to Israel through the covenant and stands above all supposed gods, is also Israel's **Holy One**, **Creator**, and **King**. He will protect His people as proven by His actions against Babylon.

43:16-21. The references to making a pathway **through the sea**, the chariots and horses, and the **army** (vv. 16-17), allude to the exodus from Egypt. This powerful event holds a special place in the narrative of Israel's history as the nation's defining moment. At the exodus, Israel was delivered from slavery in order to fulfill its destiny and dwell with God in the land forever. The exodus was crucial for Israel, yet God calls Israel not to dwell on the **former things** (v. 18). Rather than looking to the past at what the Lord has done, Israel is called to see what God is doing now and will do in the future (v. 19).

The implication is that the exodus, a defining event in the life of Israel, will be overshadowed by **something new** (v. 19) that God is planning for the present. This new thing effectively reverses the exodus. Whereas God caused the sea to turn to dry land to save His people from the Egyptians, now He will make paths and streams in the desert to deliver His people (vv. 19-20). God does not wish Israel to miss the present while they are looking to the past. Instead, He wants Israel to praise Him in the present for His coming provision of streams in the desert (v. 20-21). God's sovereign control of nature stands in stark contrast to the inability of the idols.

43:22-24. God additionally grants Israel the comforting assurance of His total forgiveness. The tone of this section shifts from a proclamation of God's sovereignty to an indictment of Israel's sin. Beginning with a contrastive **yet** (v. 22), the prophet signals the turn from the blessings that God will bring to Israel to Israel's failure to respond to God despite His actions on their behalf. The nation did not seek God. While it may appear that Israel did not provide the appropriate **sacrifices** to the Lord, such a view is difficult to maintain given Israel's exile. The exile would have precluded religious ritual, making it difficult to expect that Israel could perform appropriate sacrifices. Since other passages suggest that Israel offered excessive sacrifice prior to the exile (Is 1:11-14; Jr 6:20; Am 4:4-5; 5:21-23), it seems best to understand this verse as a comment on the worthlessness of Israel's religious expressions (Christopher R. North, *The Second Isaiah: Introduction, Translation and Commentary to Chapters XL–LV* [Eugene, OR: Wipf and Stock, 2005], 127). God's people did not honor the Lord with sacrifices and gifts. Instead, they **burdened** Him with transgression (43:24).

43:25-28. God describes Himself as the God **who wipes out your transgressions for My own sake** (v. 25). Israel is not forgiven based on its own merit or for its own sake, but for the sake of the Lord. God has been good to Israel, forgetting their sins and bearing the nation's iniquity (v. 25). Israel is called to bring evidence of its faithfulness. The nation is asked to review the past and to prove its innocence (v. 26). Before the nation can answer and bring evidence, God declares that Israel has been sinful from the beginning (v. 27). The NASB translation of **first forefather** (v. 27) suggests that the text is referring to one of the patriarchs. It is unlikely, however, that the text intends to indicate Abraham as the **first forefather** since he is presented positively at other points in Isaiah (29:22; 41:8; 63:16). Given that Jacob is referred to as the father of the nation (58:14) and is, at times, portrayed in a negative light, it is likely that Jacob should be identified as the **first forefather**. But it was not only the patriarch who sinned against the Lord. The nation's **spokesmen** have also rebelled. Israel's leadership has failed to remain faithful to God, resulting in the downfall of these leaders and the destruction of the nation (v. 28).

44:1-5. God further grant[illegible] ance to Israel with the promise [illegible] Spirit. This section announces [illegible] Israel. **Jacob** is used in parallel with [illegible] 1, identifying the nation with its patr[illegible] well as playing off the two names given to [illegible] (cf. Gn 32:28). Again we see the use of serv[illegible] language in reference to the nation of Israel, as well as the identification of Israel as God's chosen people. Each description underscores the special relationship between God and Israel. **Servant**, as has been mentioned in previous sections, designates Israel as God's representative whose purpose is to display God's glory and to adhere to His wisdom as an example to the nations. As God's chosen one, Israel has been uniquely selected for this task and will experience the protective hand of God even as they are subjected to God's discipline.

God's choice of Israel is emphasized using the poetic term **Jeshurun** in parallel with Jacob (v. 2). **Jeshurun** is only used here in Isaiah. The other three occurrences of the term are found in poetic portions of Deuteronomy (32:15; 33:5; 33:26). The Septuagint translates **Jeshurun** as "beloved" or "one who is loved," whereas most of the Targumim and the Peshitta (a fourth- or fifth-century Syriac translation of the Bible) translate it "Israel." Only the Targum Yerushalmi translates **Jeshurun** in Dt 32:15. Regardless of the translation, most commentators agree that **Jeshurun** should be identified with Israel. This identification is clear from the term's parallelism with **Jacob** (44:2).

Aside from the reference to Israel's chosen status, the prophet identifies the Lord as Israel's creator: **the Lord who made you and formed you from the womb, who will help you** (v. 2). Israel has no need to fear because God has created and helps Israel. He will provide for the people of Israel and ensure the nation's continuance across its generations. One way God will provide is by pouring **water on the thirsty land** (v. 3). Though it is certainly possible to understand this as a metaphor, introducing the coming offspring promised to Israel in the second half of the verse (v. 3) and in v. 4, it may be best to view the reference as a literal restoration of the land. The metaphoric interpretation is difficult to sustain given the similarity with the other depictions of God's transformation of the land of Israel (41:17-20; 43:19-21).

Regardless, a connection is made between the water and God's **Spirit** through the repetition of

. Just as God will bring barren, dry ground, so He ile throughout the nation's 's descendants are compared ut up in the **grass** and to **pop-** mns, suggesting both posterity and NASB translation does not refer to ring the verse as **they will spring up e grass** (v. 4). This rendering is based on soretic Text of the OT that reads **among.** e text of 1QIsa[a], which was found along n the other Dead Sea Scrolls at Qumran, has a different Hebrew word suggesting the translation "like a binu-tree." The two phrases, while strikingly different in English, are similar in Hebrew and could have easily been confused by one or the other textual tradition. Though it is possible to argue for either rendering of the verse, retaining the translation of "like a binu-tree" forms a parallel with the **poplars** in the following line, suggesting that it may be the correct reading since poplars were a type of willow tree, which grew next to flowing bodies of water.

Next the prophet describes the words of **this one** (v. 5). The identity of **this one** has been the focus of considerable scholarly attention with some suggesting that the individual referred to is not an Israelite, but a foreign proselyte who has believed in the God of Israel (Roger N. Whybray, *Isaiah 40–66* [Grand Rapids, MI: Zondervan, 1981], 95). Others suggest that **this one** is a reference to the nation of Israel as God's servant. Given the contextual mention of the offspring of Israel in the near context, however, it seems best to identify **this one** as referring to future Israelites collectively who will affirm their allegiance to the Lord. This collective group ultimately chooses to identify as the Lord's people and as part of the remnant of Israel. The practice of writing on one's **hand** has precedence among slaves in the ancient Near East, denoting a sense of permanence and loyalty to a particular master.

This paragraph has underscored the coming refreshment of the land and restoration of Israel by God's Spirit (v. 3). God, who has chosen and formed Israel to be His servant will not abandon His people, but will pour out His Spirit on them. Future generations will experience God's blessing and proudly identify themselves as belonging to the Lord and as members of Israel.

e. God's Sovereign Authority (44:6-23)

On the heels of God's promise to restore Israel in Is 44:1-5 comes a statement of God's sovereignty, and with it, a condemnation of idolatry. According to Smith (Gary V. Smith, *Isaiah 40–66*, NAC [Nashville, Broadman & Holman, 2007], 224), this section of the prophecy may be divided into four major sections: (1) God declares His uniqueness (44:6-8); (2) satire on trusting in useless idols (44:9-20); (3) admonition to remember and return to God (44:21-22); and (4) concluding hymnic praise of God (44:23).

(1) God's Declaration of His Unique Sovereignty (44:6-8)

44:6-8. Verse 6 depicts God as Israel's **King** and **Redeemer**, as well as the **Lord of hosts**, or Lord of armies. Each of these titles recognizes God's sovereign position over Israel. God's authoritative statement at the end of the verse underscores God's position as the only sovereign. God is the first and the last of divine beings. There are no other gods.

If the statements in 44:6 reflect God's sovereignty and separation from any other so-called "gods," the question **Who is like Me?** (44:7) emphasizes God's incomparability. Though false idols may claim to be like God, they cannot predict the future nor determine the events that will take place. God, in comparison, governs the events of history and sets life in order. Once again, the idols are shown to be powerless to aid those who serve them. The idols cannot offer sure advice or security to their followers because the idols do not know or control the future.

In contrast, God may give comfort to His people. Isaiah 44:8 encourages Israel not to fear. They have God's declarations from times past. The verb translated **do not tremble** (v. 8) is generally used to describe the fear that results from divine action (cf. Ex 15:6; Is 19:16; 33:14). The verb translated **do not be afraid** is used only in v. 8, though its meaning can be deduced through its connection to the other verb translated **do not tremble**. There is no need to fear because God has foretold what will happen to Israel. God's declaration cannot be threatened because God is the only **Rock**. Not only is God capable of proclaiming what will come about in the course of history, He is also incapable of being thwarted as He conforms world events to His will. God is, like a rock, a source of stability and strength. He is Israel's immovable foundation (cf. Dt 32:3, 15, 18, 30, 37; 1Sm 2:2; Ps 18:31). God is not one foundation among many, but the only foundation period. There is no other rock.

(2) Satire on Trusting in Useless Idols (44:9-20)

Despite God's incomparability, humanity

insists on trusting in the gods that are formed with human hands. Isaiah 44:9-20 represents a condemnation of those who trust in handmade idols.

44:9-11. At the outset, the prophet declares in no uncertain terms the worthlessness of idols and the folly of trusting in them. The question in v. 10 should be taken as a moment of satire since no one who forms idols profits. The idol makers and their associates cannot benefit from building their own god because the makers themselves are only human (v. 11). As Brueggemann notes, "These gods have no inherent power or force but are manufactured. As a consequence, they can have no more power or force than their 'makers' can bestow upon them, which is nil" (Walter Brueggemann, *Isaiah 40–66* [Louisville: Westminster John Knox, 1998], 68). In the end, anything that these human idol makers create will be beset with human limitations that cannot provide comfort. Unlike the Lord, who forms and sustains Israel throughout its generations (cf. v. 2), the humans who form idols cannot hope to see their work last. They will be brought together to display their humiliation.

44:12. The satire about idols continues by describing the construction of idols and highlighting their manufactured nature. The detail provided concerning the production of the idols emphasizes the inherent weakness and worthlessness of the gods. While the powerful **iron** tools, the heat of the **coals**, and the strength of the maker's arm are undeniable, the text also notes the frailty of the builder whose strength fails because of hunger and thirst. Rather than bringing **strength**, the idol weakens the one who builds it so that even in its construction the idol reveals its inability to sustain those who trust in it.

44:13-17. The description of the construction of a wooden idol is steeped with irony. Whereas the man who makes the idol of metal is weakened by his efforts, the man who makes an idol of wood is sustained by the same material that he uses to create his god. The **wood** worker measures and designs the idol to look like **a man**. Concerning the woodworker's process, Smith notes: "Although the author makes no comparison with God, any Hebrew person in the audience would see the dramatic contrasts. In 40:12 and 22 God stretches out a line to mark off the breadth of the heavens, but in this text the idols are made by a man who stretches out a short line to make the outline of the idol (Smith, *Isaiah 40–66*, 232).

The idol is made in the likeness of a human **so that it may sit in a house** (v. 13). The NASB translation of **house** as opposed to the NIV translation of "shrine" suggests a more profane understanding of the underlying Hebrew term. This profane understanding, however, may obscure the sacred nature of the idol. As such, it seems better to translate "shrine" in this instance. That the idol is made in the likeness of a human (when in fact humanity is made in the image of God) in order to sit in a shrine speaks to the underlying self-worship that characterizes idolatry. God, unlike the idol, is holy. He is unique and incomparable. His presence in a mundane environment would be readily noticed and, as was evident in Isaiah's vision of God in 6:1-13, awe-inspiring. Humans could not bear to stand in His presence without terror. The wooden idol, however, is crafted in a manner that is familiar to humankind. It brings no dread or terror, but a sense of complacency that does not challenge its maker. Instead, the idol reaffirms its maker and whatever lifestyle he chooses to live.

The process for creating a manmade idol demonstrates the impotence of the idol and the self-sufficiency of humankind. **Rain** caused the trees to grow (v. 14). After the trees have grown the woodworker cuts them down. He uses some of the wood to build a fire for warmth and baking and the rest to form an idol (v. 15). The man cares for his own needs and then fashions his god and cries out to it for salvation (v. 17).

This depiction of the idol's construction highlights a paradox in the life of the idol's creator. He is capable of supplying his own needs from the trees that grow because of **the rain** that falls upon them. This reference to the rain in v. 14 suggests that God, who is identified as the source of rain throughout Scripture (cf. Gn 2:5; 7:4; Lv 26:4; Dt 11:14; 28:12; 1Sm 12:17-18; Jb 5:10; Is 30:23; Zch 10:1), lies behind the growth of the tree that is used to sustain the woodworker and to form his idol. The idol does not provide sustenance, but is drawn from the very material that gives warmth and heat for baking bread.

44:18-20. Those who form idols, however, are blind and do not see or understand the foolishness that comes with the making of idols (v. 18). The irony of the idol's formation goes unnoticed. Smith suggests that this blindness is a condition of the people's participation within a particular culture. He notes, "The prophet does not attribute this blindness to any specific factor, but if these people were raised to believe these things by their parents and religious leaders, they would naturally be somewhat bound by that culture's false interpretation of reality" (Smith, *Isaiah 40–66*, 235).

Regardless of the reason, the people are incapable of recognizing that the idol is made of the same material as that used to keep warm and to cook food (v. 19). Idol worshipers are unable to form the sort of questions that would free them from the deceptive trap of idolatry. The practice of idolatry ensnares those who participate in it by deceiving them so well that they are no longer able to ask, **is there not a lie in my right hand?** (v. 20).

(3) Admonition to Remember and Return to God (44:21-22)

44:21-22. Jacob (i.e., the nation of **Israel**) is called to remember both God's formation of Israel and humanity's formation of idols. The juxtaposition between God's relationship to Israel and that of the idol to its maker is one that Israel cannot afford to forget. The Lord is the only God. He is incomparable. The call to remembrance is reinforced by God's assurance that He will not forget His special servant, His chosen nation. The Lord summons Israel to **return to Me, for I have redeemed you** and **wiped out your transgressions like a thick cloud** (v. 22).

(4) Concluding Hymnic Praise of God (44:23)

44:23. As a response to the satirical portrayal of idolatry, Israel is not simply called to remember, but to rejoice along with the whole of God's creation. The reason is that the one, true God, has **redeemed Jacob and in Israel He shows forth His glory**.

f. God's Human Agent (44:24–45:25)

In the oracles that continue to describe Israel's deliverance from Babylon, this section identifies the human agent God will use for that deliverance. He is Cyrus the Great, the emperor of Medo-Persia. The point in this section is that although Israel will suffer loss at the hands of the Babylonians, God's people must remember that the power of Babylon will only last as long as the Lord allows. The coming of Persia is far from a coincidence. It is the will of God made manifest in the ongoing events of human history. Isaiah 44:24–45:25 may be divided into several smaller units. The first major section begins at 44:25 and ends at 45:13, emphasizing God's use of the foreign king Cyrus. The second major section describes the effect of Cyrus on Israel—he is a harbinger of happier times in the future. The description of those times foreshadows the messianic kingdom, a time in which both Israel and the nations will worship the Lord (45:14-25).

(1) The Description of Cyrus (44:24–45:13)

44:24-28. The description of Cyrus begins with a paragraph that is structured through a series of descriptive statements that clarify God's identity as Israel's Redeemer. The redemption of Israel from Egypt was a foundational event in Israel's past, but it also reminded Israel that God could act as the nation's Redeemer again. In these five verses God's identity is expressed in a series of relative clauses. The first relative clause, **the one who formed you from the womb** (v. 24), occurs outside of the Lord's speech which constitutes the bulk of the content in 44:24-28. The emphasis on formation reminds Israel once again that God has been with His people from the beginning.

God's proclamation begins with the assertion **I, the Lord, am the maker of all things** and continues with the declaration identifying God's activities as including **stretching out the heavens by Myself and spreading out the earth all alone**. God's position as Creator implies His capacity to maintain order within creation. God's acts of creation were comprehensive, meaning that no other god created anything. God created alone. He needed no help in stretching out the heavens or spreading out the earth. He brought it about by His power alone. No god stood before God, against God, or with God in the formation of the world.

Moving from creation to the fulfillment of prophecy, the Lord demonstrates His sovereignty through His control of history. The false words spoken by false prophets are revealed as deceptions. God reveals the foolishness of those who are considered wise. He disrupts human logic (v. 25). Not only does He undermine the musings and predictions of humanity, but also He confirms **the word of His servant** (the prophet Isaiah) and performs **the purpose of His messengers** (v. 26), i.e., the prophets. God will protect and prove true those who speak for God and live in accordance with God's wisdom.

God is also the one who confirms the fate of Jerusalem. The Creator of the world and the One who controls history proclaims that Jerusalem will one day be inhabited and that the ruins of Judah will be restored (v. 26). The declaration that Jerusalem will be restored carries with it an undeniable sense of certainty because it is connected to God's identity. God has committed Himself to the renewal of Israel.

God is presented as the one **who says to the depth of the sea, Be dried up! And I will make your rivers dry** (v. 27). There are several possible ways to understand the reference to the **depth of the sea**. The most obvious possibility is to identify it as the waters of creation, which were drawn together to form the dry land. It is also possible to view this as an allusion to Noah's flood or to the Red Sea that swallowed up the Egyptians. The watery deep might also be a veiled reference to Cyrus' diversion of the Euphrates to capture the Babylonians (Goldingay, *Message of Isaiah 40–55*, 259). Symbolic references should not be discounted, as Assyria, too, is referred to as a flood that comes against God's people (Is 8:7-8; 17:12-13; 28:2; 30:28). It may be that the depth of the sea represents a coming military attack that will be dried up by the Lord.

The more likely view is that it refers to Cyrus' defeat of Babylon, because he is the central figure in this entire section and is mentioned by name in the very next verse. Moreover, these verses describe what specifically happened in Cyrus' defeat of Babylon. So v. 27 is saying that the God who gathered the waters to make the dry land will also dry the river and make Cyrus's conquest possible. In v. 28, God is described as the one who says of Cyrus, **He is My shepherd! And he will perform all My desire**. Part of God's pleasure includes Cyrus's declaration that both Jerusalem and the temple will be rebuilt. The identification of Cyrus as God's shepherd identifies Cyrus as a royal figure who will serve God and care for God's people. Cyrus's rule, in this sense, will not be his own, but will belong to and be guided by the Lord and His purposes.

45:1-7. The description of Cyrus continues with a surprising title for the pagan emperor. It may indeed seem strange to apply the title of "My shepherd" (44:28) to Cyrus, but it is even more unexpected to identify him as the Lord's **anointed** (45:1), or the Lord's messiah. The English term "messiah" is a transliteration of the underlying Hebrew word. It is used of priests (Lv 4:3, 5, 16; 6:15), kings (1Sm 2:10, 35; 12:3, 5; 16:6; 2Sm 1:14, 16; 19:22; Ps 2:2; 18:51; 132:10) and prophets (Ps 105:15). The title of **anointed** is used only here (45:1) in Isaiah, although the verbal form is used later to speak of the Lord's anointing of the herald who preaches good news to the poor (61:1). In general, the title is given to someone of Israelite origin, but in Is 45:1 a Persian is identified as God's **anointed**. Though this strategy might be employed as an affront against Israel (cf. comments on Is 2:6-22 above), it seems best to view the identification of Cyrus as **His anointed** as a sign of God's universal sovereignty over the nations. Even the foreign rulers of the world are conscripted for service to God (cf. Is 10:5).

Westermann suggests that this passage represents the commissioning of Cyrus as ruler over Israel (Claus Westermann, *Isaiah 40–66* [London: SCM, 1969], 157). Commissioning, however, does not appear to be in mind, since God is simply conveying what He plans to do with Cyrus. Instead, the passage presents Israel with a picture of a hopeful future that will come through the rule of the Persian Empire. It points beyond the earthly rule to the sovereign God who truly controls the course of history. As Smith notes, "The name or identity of this ruler is not the focus of these verses (it is mentioned only once); instead, the main emphasis of this paragraph is on God's sovereign work of accomplishing his will through this king" (Smith, *Isaiah 40–66*, 254-255).

The oracle concerning Cyrus (vv. 1-7) reveals that Cyrus will be God's tool for restoring Jerusalem (44:28). The Lord addresses Cyrus directly, while the Israelite readers see God speaking to His anointed Gentile king by whom He will deliver kings and nations and Israel. Cyrus will experience the protection of the Lord who will clear the way for Cyrus, providing him with open doors, moving mountains, and breaking gates of bronze and bars of iron (45:1-2). The **treasures of darkness** (v. 3) likely refer to the spoils of war that God will give to Cyrus **so that you may know that it is I, the Lord, the God of Israel, who call you by your name**.

Concerning this purpose, Brueggemann notes, "The daring expectation of this poetry is that Cyrus may come to acknowledge that the move west by the Persian Empire is not just imperial policy but belongs to the larger purpose of the real Governor of international politics" (Brueggemann, *Isaiah 40–66*, 76). Though the Lord expresses His intention to Cyrus, the oracle in which it is included is meant for Israel. Acknowledging God as Lord, then, is not simply God's intention for Cyrus, but also His intention for Israel as the nation watches the events of world history unfold.

Cyrus has been summoned for the sake of Israel even though Cyrus does not know God v. 4). God declares **I am the Lord, and there is no other; besides Me there is no God** (v. 5). This statement of exclusivity highlights that it is God alone who will strengthen Cyrus even if Cyrus does not acknowledge God. That God alone is the Lord and there are no other gods must cause Israel to recognize that Cyrus's activities are superintended by God for the sake of Israel, Even if Cyrus claims to have been given victory by one of the gods in the Persian pantheon, the Israelites will see that it is the Lord who enabled Cyrus to conquer. Isaiah's message expands the original intention of God's activity on Cyrus's behalf to include the men from all corners of the earth (v. 6). The Lord is the creator of light and darkness, **well-being** and **calamity** (v. 7). The Hebrew word for **calamity** is literally "evil." As a result, some translations state that God creates evil, and as a result, some identify the Lord as the author of evil. But the NASB correctly translates the word as **calamity**, since the Hebrew can mean both "moral evil" as well as "disaster," "calamity." God is not the author of moral evil, nor is He held morally culpable for it (cf. Jms 1:13-14).

This is a declaration of God's sovereignty—He conforms all things, good and bad, to His will. This section ends by emphasizing God's control over all aspects of creation (v. 8). In language reminiscent of the fertility described in Dt 28:11-12, God calls for rain showers of deliverance and the growth of salvation. Oswalt summarizes the force of Is 45:8 well, stating, "[J]ust as the sky that God has created cannot help but pour forth rain, and the earth that God has created cannot help but bring forth plants, so God the Creator can only pour out on his people right dealing and mighty deliverance in all his relations with them" (Oswalt, *Isaiah 40–66*, 206).

45:8-13. After the extended description of Cyrus, a warning is given to those who would attempt to oppose the Lord. Using the imagery of the pot and the potter, the prophet describes the foolishness and futility of arguing with the Lord. The NASB translation of **earthenware vessel** (v. 9) might be better rendered as "shard" to make clear that what is in mind is a fragment of pottery. These shards are not unique, and no one shard is more significant than another. Those who quarrel with their maker will only find anguish and grief. After all, the clay does not have a right to question the potter's intentions or question his skills (**He has no hands**, v. 9; see the comments on Rm 9:19-21).

Shifting from the image of the potter and the clay to that of the parents and the child (v. 10), the prophet reiterates his point. Children have no right to question their parents for giving birth to them. God's speech applies the principle to Himself, expressing His own disapproval of those who question what He is doing with His creation (vv. 11-13). As Creator, He may choose what to do with His creation. As if He is answering an unspoken objection against His use of Cyrus, God defends His decision to appoint Cyrus to deliver Israel (v. 13). God will use whomever or whatever He desires to accomplish His purposes. In this case, He has chosen Cyrus whom He will empower to rebuild Jerusalem (**My city**) and to free the Israelites from Babylon. Cyrus will not be paid nor rewarded—he will simply serve as God wills.

(2) The Effect of Cyrus (45:14-25)

Having described Cyrus as the Lord's shepherd and anointed, chosen to deliver Israel from Babylon, the prophet next turns to the effect of Cyrus's work. The Persian ruler is a harbinger of better times. In the description of those better times, clearly the impact of his work is far greater than what actually happened for Israel. Here the return from captivity is depicted as a foreshadowing of the future messianic kingdom.

45:14-19. As a result of God's redemption, the Gentile nations will acknowledge (**bow down to**, v. 14) Israel. This prophecy begins with the depiction of three nations, the Egyptians, Cushites (modern Ethiopia), and Sabeans (modern Yemen), that will bring their tributes to the people of Israel. They follow behind the Israelites in chains and will bow down before the people of Israel. The image of people in chains suggests that Israel, like other ancient Near Eastern powers, will receive both the tribute and the loyalty of subservient nations. Israel is viewed as a mediator between the nations and God receiving the prayer of the nations which recognize that **God is with you** (v. 14) and that God is incomparable.

God is next presented as Israel's deliverer **who hides Himself** (v. 15). Though God's hiddenness has often been construed as a complaint against God for His inaction (cf. Ps 10:1, 11; 13:1; 27:9; 30:7; 55:1; 69:17; 88:14; 89:46; 102:2; 143:7), it does not appear that the nations' statement here is designed as a critique against God.

Instead, it seems to be an insight concerning the unexpected nature of ways of God, **who hides Himself** (v. 15). The Egyptians, Cushites, and Sabeans have come to humble themselves before Israel, while others, specifically those who fashion idols, **will go away together in humiliation** (v. 16). Taken with the statement in v. 17 that the Israelites will be delivered and never again be ashamed, the mention of the idol makers in v. 16 suggests again that the idols of the nations will ultimately fail those who worship them.

God, the Creator of the heavens and the earth, declares that His creative work was not done on a whim or without purpose (vv. 18-19). Using one of the terms employed to describe the "formless" world of Genesis 1:1-2 (here translated **a waste place**), the text asserts that God did not create the world to exist without order, but to be inhabited. God's statement in v. 19 returns to the previous mention of His hiddenness in v. 15. God has not kept His will from Israel. He did not create the world and then stand in the shadows as if He were a clockmaker who, having completed a new timepiece, leaves it to run on its own. Instead, God has maintained a hand in the history of His creation to bring about order. He has spoken to Israel with **righteousness** and reliability (v. 19).

45:20-25. Not only will the nations acknowledge Israel (v. 14), but a second, more important consequence of God's redemption is that the nations will acknowledge (bow, v. 23) and revere the God of Israel. God calls to those who worship idols and have no guidance, telling them that they have no god to call upon for deliverance (v. 20). The true God, the God of Israel, is unique (v. 21). The foreign idols cannot predict the future or deliver people from destruction. God is the only righteous **Savior**. As such, He calls the **ends of the earth** to come to Him for salvation. He is the only God and the only shelter for all people (v. 22). God's irresistible, irrevocable word proclaims that **every knee will bow** before the Lord (cf. v. 14) and that **every tongue will swear allegiance** (v. 23).

This is the basis of Paul's eschatological expectation that every knee will bow before the Lord Jesus, either in worship or submission (see comments on Rm 14:10-12 and Php 2:10-11). Bowing the knee and swearing allegiance are both acts of fidelity to the Lord, as is suggested by the words that the people will speak when God has asserted His authority: **Only in the Lord are righteousness and strength** (v. 24). The content of the people's confession is not simply related to power, but to the correctness of God's judgments. When those who were angry with Him stand in His presence, they will be humiliated. But all of Israel living in the messianic kingdom will be declared righteous and will worship **and will glory** in the Lord for His great deliverance (v. 25).

Isaiah 45:13-25 ultimately provides a source of comfort for those who choose to follow the Lord. Recognizing that God is the Creator, and that He has not left His creation to determine its own path, emphasizes and explains God's continued activity within creation. Though the events, powers, and strategies of the world may hide God's work, God has made promises to His chosen people Israel to remind them that God has not abandoned them. Turning to idols in an attempt to order the world is a futile exercise. Deaf and dumb gods have no control of history, nor did they have any hand in creation. Even when it appears that the powers of the world are in flux, this passage recognizes that God uses the world's superpowers to bring about deliverance for those who remain faithful to Him.

g. God's Righteous Judgment (46:1–47:15)

This section of Isaiah stresses once again the sovereignty of the Lord, His ability to deliver Israel and judge the nations. The references to Bel and Nebo in 46:1, as well as the explicit mention of Babylon in 47:1, 48:14, and 48:20, suggest that at this point God is dealing with the Babylonian Empire, which had taken Israel into exile. Chapters 46 and 47 resemble the oracles against the nations that appeared in Isaiah 13–23 (Chris A. Franke, "Reversals of Fortune in the Ancient Near East," In *New Visions of Isaiah*, ed. R. F. Melugin and M. A. Sweeney [Sheffield: Sheffield Academic, 1996], 104-23). As with the oracles against the nations, the critique of Babylon in chaps. 46 and 47 is provided for the benefit of Israel. Babylon is not the indestructible power that it appears to be. Instead, its idolatrous, unjust practices are an affront to the Lord, practices that will ultimately bring about the nation's downfall. The first part demonstrates God's righteous judgment by defending His authority over idols (46:1-13).

46:1-7. Bel was a Babylonian title ascribed to various Babylonian gods including Enlil, the father of the gods, and Marduk, the head god of the city of Babylon. Marduk was depicted as defeating Tiamat, the Babylonian goddess representing primordial chaos, and was subsequently named king of the gods. Though Marduk is never mentioned explicitly, it seems likely that Bel is a reference to this Babylonian god. That Marduk is in mind is suggested by the reference to Nebo, Marduk's son, in the parallel line. Nebo, or Nabu, was "god of the scribe and of intellectual pursuits" and was head over the city of Borsippa south of Babylon (Oswalt, *Isaiah 40–66*, 228).

These prominent gods of Babylon are now bent low. Their images are carried off by animals and, rather than empowering the people, they burden those who carry them (v. 1). Their inability to remove the burden results in captivity. Those who once took captives are now brought **into captivity** (v. 2). In contrast to these idols, God is capable of upholding His people. Israel (**Jacob**) is also called to remember that it is the Lord who has sustained Israel from their youth and into their old age (vv. 3-4). The so-called gods of Babylon do not compare to the Lord (v. 5). Whereas God carries His people from age to age, those who commission the construction of idols with gold and silver must carry their gods (v. 7). The precious god that was skillfully formed by the blacksmith is inanimate and cannot move or speak. The idol cannot respond to the prayers of those who cry out to it. The idol's inability to act should serve as a warning to those who seek to rebel against the active God of Israel.

46:8-13. God, on the other hand, is supremely powerful. God's past actions demonstrate that He is God Almighty. He has exercised His will without opposition. His will and His purposes will come to pass (vv. 8-10). His capacity to predict future events showcases His ability to bring about whatever He chooses (vv. 10-11). As Hanson notes, "The principle underlying this interpretation of history and enabling the prophet to discern a creative, redemptive pattern is theological. It revolves around faith in the divine promise, 'I have planned, and I will do it'" (Paul D. Hanson, *Isaiah 40-66* [Louisville: John Knox, 1995], 115). God will summon a **bird of prey**, or **the man of My purpose from a far country** (v. 11). The identity of this bird is not stated in the text. Though Cyrus is the likely explanation, ancient sources, specifically the Targum (ancient rabbinic paraphrase), suggest that the call of the **bird of prey** refers to the call of Abram and to the ingathering of the exiles. In light of the frequent mentions of Cyrus being raised up to accomplish God's purposes in restoring Israel (41:2, 44:28, 45:1) this makes the most sense in context. Regardless, the point of the text is clear. God does not issue empty threats but instead will execute His plans (v. 11).

The **stubborn-minded** people of v. 12 should be identified with the Babylonians, the idolatrous rebels in 46:6-8. Their paganism led them to believe that God's perceived inactivity had resulted in disbelief in God's ability to deliver Israel. This rebuke, although addressed to Babylon in the text, was included to give hope to the readers of this book, the remnant of Israel. Despite Babylon's skepticism, God's deliverance was near and would come to pass. Zion will be saved and God's glory will be displayed in Israel (v. 13).

47:1-7. Having defended that God is righteous in judgment because of His authority over Babylonian idols (46:1-13), the next section announces God's righteous judgment of Babylon, indicating that the empire's fall was imminent (47:1-15). At the outset, the reasons for Babylon's judgment are described (47:1-17). Babylon is presented as an arrogant woman of great beauty whose status in the upper echelon of society is revoked. This beautiful, pretentious woman must now take the place of a slave. In v. 1, the **virgin daughter** (Babylon) is commanded to abandon her throne and to get down in the dust. Sitting in the dust is a sign of Babylon's humiliation and, potentially, mourning (3:26; 25:12; 26:5). In any case, the image of Babylon sitting in the dust communicates the nation's imminent lowly status.

Identifying Babylon as a **virgin** does not speak to the nation's innocence, but to the nation's delicate beauty. Smith suggests, "The title 'Virgin Daughter of Babylon' and 'Daughter of the Babylon [Chaldeans]' are honorific titles which do not refer to the young age of Babylon but draw on the image of a virgin as someone who is beautiful, desirable, and unconquered" (Smith, *Isaiah 40–66*, 301). No longer will Babylon be beautiful and unconquered. Instead, Babylon's beauty will fade as the nation is forced to work as slave. The circumstances that allowed Babylon to remain **tender and delicate** will be removed (v. 1).

The prophet foretells that this "delicate daughter" will participate in the hard labor of grinding flour with the millstone (v. 2). This labor is not conducive to the prominence to which Babylon has become accustomed. As such, she is commanded to remove her veil and to lift her skirts. She has become profane to the point that her nakedness will be uncovered, indicating that once proud Babylon will be shamed (v. 3). In the ancient world, appearing naked was a sign of shame and could refer to an act of sexual violation (cf. Lv 18:6-19). The point is that Babylon's nakedness refers to her ultimate humiliation.

God's vengeance on Babylon will be complete (v. 3). The NASB's translation of **I will . . . not spare a man** interprets the literal Hebrew "I will not meet a man." The Hebrew verb for "meet" carries the nuance of "meet with mercy" or "meet with kindness" (cf. Is 64:5). God will show no pity when He encounters Babylon. Verse 4 does not appear to have any specific connection to v. 3. The Septuagint adds the verb "says" before **our Redeemer** in v. 4, clarifying that it is God speaking in v. 3. Though the verb for "say" is not included in the Hebrew text, there is evidence to suggest that the verb could have been omitted through the process of transmission because the presence of a similar looking word at the end of v. 3. Inserting "says" at the beginning of v. 4 identifies the Lord as speaker. This verse could also be an outburst of joy by the prophet, celebrating that God will redeem Israel and punish the nation's oppressor, Babylon.

God is characterized as Israel's Redeemer, as **the LORD of hosts** (Lord of armies), and as the **Holy One of Israel** (v. 4). The God who redeemed Israel from Egypt is the same God who will redeem Israel from Babylon. The designation of **LORD of hosts** depicts God as the unstoppable general who leads heaven's army. God's titles reinforce His ability to save His people.

Returning to the message of judgment on Babylon, next God condemns the arrogant, unreflective activities of Babylon. The Lord commands Babylon to sit (as in v. 1), but also to be silent and to **go into darkness** (v. 5). Though some commentators (see Christopher R. North, *Isaiah 40–55* [London: SCM, 1964], 99) have suggested that imprisonment is implied by these phrases, the lack of specificity in the text does not demand such an interpretation. In any case, Babylon will lose its prominent place among the nations and the moniker of **queen of kingdoms** will be taken away (v. 5). What follows are the events that led to Babylon's rise to power and fall from grace (v. 6). God's anger prompted Him to hand His people over to Babylon.

Presumably, Babylon was to serve as an agent of divine justice, but Babylon refused to temper its level of punishment inflicted on the nations it subdued. Babylon did not show mercy even to the aged, but laid a **very heavy** yoke on them (v. 6). Babylon's hubris grew to the point that the nation boasted about its permanence (v. 7). The nation, however, neglected to evaluate the consequences of their actions against God's people. They did not recognize that Israel was God's special possession and that even in punishment Israel was to be treated with respect.

47:8-15. Having given the reasons for Babylon's downfall, the prophet describes the specifics of God's judgment against her. Babylon did not weigh the consequences of their actions, so they will now experience the results of treating Israel harshly. God tells Babylon, the **sensual one**, to listen. He mocks Babylon's delusion of security, treating them like any other nation. Despite Babylon's boasting to the contrary, the nation will gain widows and lose children in a single day (vv. 8-9). The magical resources so crucial to the Babylonian religion will prove useless. Smith describes the various magical practices as occurring in conjunction with divination, or the attempt to determine the future (Smith, *Isaiah 40–66*, 306). Young notes, "The certainty of the coming calamities cannot be denied. Though there is an abundance (possibly referring to inherent strength) of magic and a vast array of spells, these cannot help, for the coming will be strong" (Young, *The Book of Isaiah*, 3:238-239).

Rather than trusting God, Babylon has trusted in its own wicked practices (v. 10). These practices likely include the **sorceries** mentioned in v. 9, as well as the oppression of God's people and the harsh practices associated with Babylon's rule. Koole suggests that the wickedness is related to Babylon's arrogance described in vv. 6-8, noting the quotation of v. 8—**I am, and there is no one besides me**—in v. 10 (Jan L. Koole, *Isaiah III* [Leuven: Peeters, 1998], 540). The assumption that **no one sees me** (v. 10) does not necessarily suggest that the Babylonians believed that their activities would never be noticed, but that no one existed who could judge those activities. Yet again, Babylon wrongly asserts its sovereignty. Babylon's folly is rooted in its inability to recognize that its wisdom and knowledge are actually foolishness. The nation believed itself to be unique, incomparable, and eternal, but such thoughts are deceptive. They cultivated arrogance and blinded Babylon to the coming destruction (v. 11).

Babylon is challenged, with a fair bit of irony, to continue its worthless pagan and occult practices so that, perhaps, one day those practices will become effective (v. 12). Oswalt notes, "The city that has made itself the equal of God has no alternative—it must trust its vaunted intelligence, there is nothing else. It has invested too much hard, exhausting labor for too many years . . . to abandon the effort now" (Oswalt, *Isaiah 40–66*, 253). The challenge to maintain its current course "seems to mock or taunt the Babylonian effort to try to avert God's judgment" (Smith, *Isaiah 40–66*, 308).

The **many counsels** referred to in v. 13 likely come from inside Babylon. It may refer to the continued activities related to the Babylonian cult as suggested by Young (Young, *The Book of Isaiah*, 3:242). This counsel has resulted in nothing but expended energy. Mistaking foolishness for wisdom is not unique to Babylon, but is a deception to which others have also fallen prey (cf. Is 5:18-19; 8:10; 16:3; 19:3, 11; 23:8-9; 29:15; 30:1; 32:7-8; 36:5; 40:13-14; 41:28; 44:26; 45:21). The Babylonians are called to trust in **the astrologers . . . who predict by the new moons** for salvation (v. 13).

This message to the Babylonians was given for the benefit of the nation of Israel. It also appears to reinforce the previous discourses related to idolatry. Israel should not believe that the Babylonians' cultic efforts will deliver this vicious nation. Instead, Israel must again recognize that their God will come in vengeance. This vengeance is described in v. 14 as an all-consuming **fire** from which Babylon's religious officials will not even be able to deliver themselves. Instead, the magicians of Babylon will fuel the fire (cf. 30:30; 31:9; 33:14; 66:16, 24).

The mention of the **coal** at the end of v. 14 likely refers back to the discourse concerning idol makers in 44:15-19. In that passage the idol maker uses part of his wood to construct his idol and the other part to build a fire. In Is 47:14, however, there are no coals to warm food because the material that is burning is so worthless that it cannot even be used to bake bread. **Stubble**, which represents the Babylonian astrologers and magicians, has less use than the wood used to build false idols. In the end, the only gift that the religious men of Babylon will provide is a fire that gives no heat and has no usefulness—they cannot **save** (v. 15). The fate of Babylon is tragic. The entire existence of the Babylonian people and everything that they had done to safeguard their nation and to ensure its security has been an exercise in futility. When God's judgment comes, the wise advisors of Babylon will fall into terror and be unable to save the people of Babylon.

Despite its rich history and its fervent religious activities, Babylon will fall. Its traditions, prayers, counselors, and rituals only appeared to be connected to the nation's success. Babylon, however, failed to recognize that it was God who had given them power over Israel. It is God who will punish Babylon for its harsh treatment of His people. For Israel, this message clarifies God's control over Babylon. The success of the nation could have easily validated the nation's beliefs and practices as effective. God's declaration against the nation, however, reveals that the nation survives only by the grace of God. It was God who handed Israel over to the Babylonians and it is God who will deliver His people from their hand.

h. God's Predicted Restoration (48:1-22)

After addressing the Babylonians in Is 47, the prophet turns to address the people of Israel in exile. Despite God's anger toward Babylon and the imminent judgment that will be unleashed on that nation, Israel also must answer to God. Yet despite's Israel's spiritual obstinacy, God predicts deliverance and restoration.

48:1-11. This first paragraph reminds Israel of the certainty of God's Word. At the outset, with a blunt description of the exilic audience's spiritual hypocrisy (v. 1), the prophet commands for Israel to hear, calling the people to attention. The verb translated **hear** is repeated ten times in the next sixteen verses, suggesting that the people should be paying close attention to God's message. The people are portrayed in ways that emphasize their genealogical descent (**who came forth from the loins of Judah**), as well as their present devotion (**who swear by the name of the Lord**, v. 1) and identity (**for they call themselves after the holy city**, v. 2). The people have every reason to believe that they are part of God's family and that they may rely on the God of Israel. This belief, however, is undermined by their own lack of truth and righteousness. There is no authenticity in their claims.

Though it should not be assumed that all the exiles were insincere in their faith, the charge levied against them is a solemn reminder that one's ethnicity and claims to religious devotion do not guarantee deliverance. Instead, there must be a correspondence between word, heart, and action. The claims and practices of the exilic community must be sincere. The Israelites must recognize that God is the Almighty. Oswalt suggests that the final statement of 48:2 represents an "implicit charge" noting, "although the people profess to depend on the God of Israel, they have not truly recognized the he is *the Lord of Hosts*, the Almighty God . . . They are not living out the implications of their monotheism" (Oswalt, *Isaiah 40-66*, 261).

Verse 3 returns to the recurring claim that God foretells and controls the course of history. This control is evident in His announcement of **former things** that have come to pass. In this context, God's ability to predict future events is not designed as a comment on God's omniscience, but a statement of His sovereign mastery over His creation. God reveals the way that things will come to pass despite the stiff **neck** and bronze **forehead** of the Israelites (v. 4). The image of the stiff **neck** is used several times in the OT in relation to Israel (cf. Ex 32:9; Dt 9:6, 13; Ps 75:5). The stubbornness of the nation has been a perennial problem for Israel despite God's actions on the nation's behalf and His prediction of the events that have come to pass.

God gives two reasons for His predictions of the return from Babylon. The first reason God announces these events beforehand is so that Israel will not credit their idols for deliverance from Babylon (v. 5). Only the God in control of history could foretell an event like the return from captivity. Had God not predicted this, Israel might be tempted to give their idols credit. The word of the Lord continues to be confirmed in the fall of Babylon and, ultimately, in the ingathering of Israel. The evidence is clear. All Israel needs to do is affirm its truthfulness (v. 6). God, however, is not finished declaring what is to come. He will prophesy new things and hidden things to Israel (v. 6).

The second reason God gives prophecies of the return from captivity (**new things**, v. 6) is so Israel could not boast that they knew of this all along (v. 8). Oswalt suggests, "Just as prophecy was given so as to refute the claims of idols, so not all prophecy was given at once in order to refute the claims of human omniscience" (Oswalt, *Isaiah 40–66*, 268).

Now God declares not only why He predicted the restoration from captivity, but also why He would even bring Israel back at all. Despite the nation's rebellion against God (v. 8b), Israel has been spared because of God's concern for His own reputation (v. 9). Instead of destroying Israel, God has chosen to refine and test the nation through affliction. Refinement through affliction is a common occurrence throughout the OT (cf. Ps 66:10; Jr 9:7; Zch 13:9; Mal 3:3). This refinement process is designed to purify the people of Israel and to strengthen their faith in the Lord. God does not do this for Israel but rather for His own sake and for His own reputation (v. 11). God does not want His name to be defiled by Israel in rebellion or by the nations in their disdain. He will not share His glory with another (v. 11; cf. 42:8).

48:12-16. Having been reminded of the certainty of God's Word (48:1-11), Israel is next challenged to recall the nature of their Redeemer (vv. 12-16). Israel's Redeemer is the Eternal One, **the first** and **the last** (v. 12). The mention that God has called Israel reminds the reader that Israel does not enjoy its relationship with the Lord of its own volition, but by the hand of God. The God who was there in the beginning (the first) and will continue till the end (the last) has summoned Israel to be His special possession.

Building on the assertions of His own nature and identity, God points again to His role as Creator (v. 13). As such, the God of all creation calls everyone to listen to His word and to recognize that He has declared these things (v. 14). The rhetorical question includes a reference to **them**, referring to false gods who are unable to declare the future. But the Lord controls the course of history. It is because of God's nature that He can predict Israel's deliverance and will accomplish it through the one He **loves**, or, the more preferable translation in the NIV, through His "chosen ally." It is likely that the "ally" in question refers to the Persian Cyrus (cf. 41:2, 44:28, 45:1) who will fulfill God's desire to judge Babylon (v. 14). God empowers the one who carries out His will against Babylon so any success that the individual has should be attributed to God (v. 15).

As a result of God's prediction of Israel's deliverance through His instrument Cyrus, He now calls Israel to draw near and listen to Him (v. 16a). God again asserts the clarity of His message. He has not hidden His plans from His people. Having stated this, the second half of the v. 16 describes one **sent** by **God** and **His Spirit**. Commentators differ in identifying the speaker. Possibilities include Isaiah, Israel, Cyrus, and the Messiah. The first two possibilities have nothing in the context to support them. Cyrus, just mentioned as God's chosen ally, is possible. But the mention of the Spirit of God makes it more likely that the Servant-Messiah is the speaker here. God and His Spirit will send Him, reminding of the Messiah's sevenfold anointing by the Spirit (11:1) and the Spirit's anointing of the Servant to ministry (61:1-3). This anointing assures that the Servant-Messiah will succeed in the task that God gives Him (52:13). It also functions as preparation for the second Servant Song in the next chapter (49:1-7).

48:17-19. This Servant-Messenger reminds Israel of the need to obey God's counsel. The message offered emphasizes that God offers Israel wisdom (v. 17). If Israel had taken God's counsel to heart, they would have experienced peace and righteousness (v. 18). The descendants of Israel would have multiplied and experienced God's continual blessing (v. 19). The comparison of Israel's children to the **sand** recalls God's promise to Abraham (Gn 22:17), highlighting the connection between the covenant and the blessing. Instead, Israel rejected God's counsel and went their own way. Unfortunately, Israel's "wisdom" led them to Babylon.

48:20-22. The final part of the chapter represents a moment of hope for Israel. While their unwillingness to trust the Lord has resulted in the nation's exile in Babylon, they will not stay there forever. Instead, God calls them to flee from the Babylonians and to leave Babylon (v. 20). The Lord's redemption of Israel from Babylon is to be proclaimed with joy over the whole earth. Israel may not remain silent about God's acts on their behalf, but must rejoice before all the nations to witness to God's preservation and deliverance of His people. Such actions are more necessary when it is remembered that God will use the Persian Empire and its ruler Cyrus to free Israel. Israel must not stay silent, but must proclaim to the world that the God of Israel is the master of history. He is the one who has rescued Israel and redeemed the people once again from the hands of foreign powers. The linking of the return from Babylon to God's previous redemption of Israel from Egypt and the subsequent wilderness wanderings is deliberate. The reference to the provision of water from the rock is an inner-biblical link to that earlier redemption (Ex 17:6) when God commanded Moses to strike a rock so that the people may drink.

The NASB translation of the verbs in v. 21 in the past tense suggests that the verse is referring to the events that occurred when the Israelites were brought out of Egypt. In the context of this passage, however, it seems best to translate v. 21 in the present tense so that it refers to the coming redemption from Babylon noted in v. 20. The present tense should be read not as what was happening at the moment, but as what will come to pass, what is as good as done. Though past events are certainly in mind, the passage should be read as describing God's provision of water for those returning from Babylon and redeeming Israel (40:20). In other passages the English versions translate the same Hebrew construction with the English future tense (cf. Jdg 1:2; 1Sm 2:16; Is 6:5). Though none of the major English versions translate these verbs in the present tense, the Septuagint translation begins with a condition ("If they thirst . . .") that is followed by a series of verbs in the future tense. Goldingay follows this interpretation suggesting that the verb in cf. 21 is an "instantaneous or prophetic perfect" and translates the verse: "Yahweh is restoring his servant Jacob; they are not thirsty as he leads them through the wastes. He is making water flow from a rock for them; he is splitting rock and water is gushing" (Goldingay, *The Message of Isaiah 40–55*, 360).

The words of the final verse of the chapter (**there is no peace for the wicked**) function as a literary marker, bringing to a close this section on deliverance from Babylon (chaps. 40–48). A virtually identical phrase concludes the next major section (deliverance from sin, chaps. 49–57; see 57:21) and a similar but stronger theme closes out the last unit of the book (deliverance in the end, chaps. 58–66; see 66:24). The message of this verse brings a dose of reality into the context of hope created by vv. 20-21. Regardless of God's coming deliverance, Israel is reminded that **there is no peace for the wicked** (v. 22). The nation must still turn to their God and follow Him.

2. Deliverance from Sin (49:1–57:21)

This section of Isaiah is the second major section (of three) in the oracles of the second half of the book (see chart of Isaiah's structure in "Structure" in the introduction to this commentary). Each part of this oracular section emphasizes Israel's deliverance—from Babylon (chaps. 40–48), from sin (chaps. 49–57), and in the end of days (chaps. 58–66). The significant element of this section is that it contains three of the four Servant Songs in Isaiah (49:1-13; 50:4-11; 52:13–53:12, the first being in the previous section, 42:1-9).

a. The Encouragement of Israel (49:1–52:11)

When the book of Isaiah was written, Israel was facing the gloom of anticipated captivity.

In this section the prophet seeks to give encouragement to Israel, emphasizing the coming deliverance and restoration of Israel. The first part of that encouragement pertains to the Servant-Messiah's roles in God's plan for Israel and the nations.

(1) The Servant's Roles (49:1-13)

Three sections comprise Is 49:1-13. The first depicts the Servant's call to go to Israel (49:1-4); the second reveals the expansion of the Servant's ministry to the Gentile nations (49:5-7); and the third indicates the Servant's ultimate deliverance of Israel (49:8-13).

49:1-4. There has been some debate concerning the identity of the speaker in 49:1-13. The first view is that there are multiple entities called in chap. 49. Beginning with servant (vv. 1-4), the speaker shifts to servant Darius in vv. 5-6 and then to a herald (vv. 7, 13), the Lord (vv. 8-12, 15-21), and Zion (v. 14) in the rest of the chapter (Watts, *Isaiah 34–66*, 182–84). The identification of the various speakers is based on a reconstruction of the passage's alleged historical background rather than specific elements in the text. A second view is that it was written by an individual prophet (Oswalt, *Isaiah 40–66*, 289). Yet the depiction of the speaker is too exalted to be a human prophet. A third possibility identifies the Lord as the speaker based on the similarities between the exhortation to **listen to Me** (v. 1) and the similar exhortations in other parts of Isaiah (46:3, 48:1, 12, 14, 16; Goldingay, *The Message of Isaiah 40–55*, 365).

It appears that the first half of v. 1 (**Listen to Me, O islands, and pay attention, you peoples from afar**) represents a direct exhortation from the Lord to pay attention to the message that will be spoken. The exhortation is universal in scope, thus emphasizing the scope of the Servant's vocation. Beginning with the second half of v. 1 (**The Lord called Me from the womb; from the body of My mother He named Me**), a new speaker, identified as **My Servant, Israel** (v. 3), describes His calling. That the speaker is identified as **Israel** has caused some to suggest that the nation of Israel collectively is the servant of the Lord in view here. More likely the servant in this context is not the nation as a collective, but that the servant is the representative of Israel, the epitome of all that Israel was to be (see below for a defense of this view).

The **Servant** begins by describing His own calling to Israel. Using the first person, the Servant initially describes His preparation by God. First, God predestined His ministry, calling Him from the womb (v. 1). Second, God also equipped the Servant for ministry to Israel (v. 2) in two ways: (a) God enabled Him to speak effectively, making His mouth **like a sharp sword**. (b) God made the Servant like **a select arrow**, with the ability to penetrate the spiritual heart of the nation with His message. Third, God preserved the Servant for His ministry to Israel, with the Servant saying of God **in the shadow of His hand He has concealed Me** and **He has hidden Me in His quiver**. Both of these expressions are used of the care and protection of the Lord (cf. Ps 17:8; 27:5; 31:20; 64:2; Jr 36:26). Fourth, God proclaimed that the Servant would be the epitome of Israel that would glorify the Lord (v. 3). What Israel corporately was designed to do, the Servant will do for her, without, however, eliminating a future role for corporate Israel.

Calling the Servant by the name **Israel** has caused some to maintain that the Servant should be identified as the nation of Israel. This is unlikely because then the nation of Israel would have a mission to itself (see vv. 5-6). Moreover, the Servant is described as one who is "abhorred by the nation" (v. 7), indicating that He cannot be the nation. Therefore, the Servant-Messiah is called "Israel" because He is the true King of Israel and the epitome of what Israel ought to have been. He will succeed in all the ways that Israel the nation failed.

Besides His preparation, the Servant also describes His own frustration (v. 4). He felt He **toiled in vain**, reflecting His disappointment at Israel's failure to receive His ministry. All His labor appeared to be wasted (**for nothing and vanity**).

49:5-7. In light of Israel's rejection of the Servant, the Servant next declares the expansion of His calling to the Gentiles. In so doing, the Lord began by reaffirming the Servant's ministry to Israel. Despite Israel's rejection, the Servant is still called **to bring Jacob back to** the Lord (v. 5). But this was **too small** a task for one as glorious as this Servant. Not only will He **raise up the tribes of Jacob and . . . restore the preserved ones of Israel**, but He will also be **a light to the nations** (v. 6). This is so the **salvation** provided by God would not be limited to Israel but **reach to the end of the earth**. As a response to the previous frustration of the Servant (v. 4), the Lord reassured the Servant of His ultimate success. Although **despised** and **abhorred by the nation** of Israel, the Servant will be worshiped by the Gentile nations—**kings will see and arise, princes will also bow down** (v. 7). The word **despised** is the same root as used in the fourth Servant Song (53:3). He would be **abhorred** (which means "to be rejected as unclean or an abomination") by the nation (i.e., Israel; Hb. *goy*, when used in the singular as here, usually refers to Israel; see Gn 12:2; Ex 19:6; Dt 4:6; Mc 4:7; Zph 2:9). God's faithfulness will cause the Gentile nations (**kings, princes**) to worship Him.

49:8-13. Despite Israel's prophesied rejection of the Servant in vv. 4-6, this final part of the Servant's call looks to the more remote future when Israel will ultimately believe in Him and experience redemption. At the appointed time, God will make the Servant **a covenant of the people** . This is the same expression used in the first Servant Song, meaning that the Servant would be a covenant-mediator for the people of Israel. The phrase is a figure of speech (metonymy of effect [covenant] for cause [mediator]) for "covenant-mediator" (see a more full discussion at 42:5-7). This refers to the "new covenant" which includes both spiritual and material elements (Jr 31:31-34).

Associated with the new covenant are the restoration of the land of Israel and the granting of tribal allotments (v. 8). The servant will also free prisoners (v. 9). The reference to **those who are in darkness** is also likely a reference to the dispersed of Israel being kept in dungeons as it is in parallel with **those who are bound** referred to in the first line of v. 9. Those who are set free will experience the fruit of God's blessing of the Servant's work (vv. 9-11). God, through the Servant, will provide food and water for the people as they travel from exile back to the land of promise, as well as a safe, easy passageway on which the people may travel. God's provision of sustenance is elsewhere associated with flocks of animals (Is 17:2; 40:10-11; 63:11), but, in this case, there are no flocks in mind, suggesting that God will provide for their needs and those of their animals, as they return to the Holy Land. Verse 10 describes God's gracious provision of water and the protection of God's people from the heat and sun. This restoration is linked to the Servant's work and therefore does not refer to the return from Babylon (539 BC) but looks forward to the end-of-days restoration of Israel in the messianic kingdom.

The intended result of the Servant's work now comes to fruition as those who have been freed **come from afar** and **from the north and from the west**, indicating that this is a worldwide restoration (v. 12). The location of **Sinim** is debated, and the ancient versions give a variant reading here using the word "Syene." The Masoretic, or Hebrew Text, reads **Sinim**, but the location of the **land of Sinim** is unknown. The name "Syene" is found in the copy of Isaiah among the Dead Sea Scrolls at Qumran. Several modern versions have adopted "Syene" in the translation of v. 12 (e.g., ESV; NIV has "Aswan"), whereas the NASB, the NET, and the HCSB retain **Sinim**. Syene is a town in Egypt near modern Aswan in southeastern Egypt. Those who come from afar should be identified as God's people, given the reference to them in v. 13. God's comfort of Israel is to be met with the praises of all creation represented in the sky, earth, and mountains (v. 13).

This Servant Song presents in prophetic form what Paul described in Rm 11. Israel (in part) rejected the promised Servant-Messiah, then God gave the message of Messiah to the Gentiles, of whom many received Him; but in the end, God will open the hearts of Israel so as a nation they will believe in Messiah Jesus and experience all the covenant promises. "Now if their transgression is riches for the world and their failure is riches for the Gentiles, how much more will their fulfillment be! . . . For if their rejection is the reconciliation of the world, what will their acceptance be but life from the dead?" (Rm 11:12, 15; see the comments there).

(2) The Lord's Reassurance of Faithfulness (49:14-26)

God continues to encourage Israel. The first part of that encouragement pertained to the Servant-Messiah's roles in God's plan for Israel and the nations (vv. 1-13). Now, the Lord encourages the nation by reassuring them of His loyalty to the covenant promises made to the nation.

49:14-16. In reply to Zion's accusation of the Lord's abandonment of the nation, **The LORD has forsaken me, and the Lord has forgotten me** (v. 14), the Lord states that He will always remember Israel. God uses a rhetorical question, **Can a woman forget her nursing child and have no compassion on the son of her womb?** (v. 15), to respond. Though it seems clear that the implied answer to the rhetorical question is no, the remainder of the verse offers an additional rhetorical flourish. Surely a mother could not forget her child, yet the text states that even these may forget, for the love of a woman for her child is not as sure or consistent as the love that the Lord exhibits toward His people. God will never forget Zion.

Aside from the hypothetical comparison between a woman and her child and the Lord and Zion, God states that He has inscribed the name of Zion **on the palms of My hands** (v. 16). Engraving Zion on His palms suggests a sense of immediacy, which is confirmed by the second poetic line of v. 16, stating that **your walls are continually before Me**.

49:17-21. God will not only remember, but He will also fully restore Israel. Zion will experience an influx of people as the sons of Jerusalem return and those who destroyed the city will leave it (v. 17). The sons will be like ornate jewels on a bride for the city of Zion, marking a reversal of fortune for the city (v. 19). The city that was once abandoned will now be bursting at the seams to the point that Zion will be confused about where all the people have come from (vv. 19-21). This is referring to the restoration of Zion in the millennial kingdom, not to the return from Babylon.

49:22-26. The Lord reassured Israel not only with the promise that He would remember and restore Israel, but also that He would ultimately exalt Israel. The repopulation of the city will be assisted by the Gentiles (v. 22). The nations will serve the sons and daughters of Zion. They will care for Israel and **bow down** in humility before the people of Israel (v. 23). When these things take place, the people of Israel will recognize that their hope in the Lord has not disappointed. The ferocity of Israel's enemies makes no difference to the Lord (vv. 24-25). He will rescue Israel from those who **contend** with them. The defeat of Zion's enemies will be brutal. The reference to Zion's enemies eating **their own flesh** and being **drunk with their own blood** (v. 26) may be a reference to radical siege warfare in which the enemy is starved out to the point that they resort to cannibalism. It could also suggest, as Oswalt argues, that without anyone for them to attack "the bloodthirstiness of the oppressors becomes so strong that . . . [the oppressed] must turn on themselves" (Oswalt, *Isaiah 40–66*, 314). Whatever the reference, this behavior marks the moment in which all humanity recognizes that God is Lord, the **Redeemer** of Israel.

(3) The Servant's Example (50:1-11)

The encouragement of Israel continues. Having reassured the nation of the Servant's ministry to Israel and the world and the Lord's faithfulness to Israel, the Lord now encourages Israel to follow the example of the Servant in facing dark times.

50:1-3. This paragraph functions as an introduction to the third Servant Song (vv. 4-11). The Lord declares Israel's disobedience and unbelief is the cause of the people's imminent exile to Babylon. Once again addressing the assertion that God had forgotten Zion (49:14), the Lord reminds the nation that He never broke His covenant with Israel or gave Israel **away**. The rhetorical questions included in v. 1 negate any suggestion that God was guilty of the evil of breaking His covenant which led to Israel's exile. God did not **divorce** Israel or sell them to the nations because of some debt. Instead, it was the rebellion of Israel that resulted in their captivity, and God's action in governing the exile was a judgmental reaction to Israel's sin.

Verse 2 consists of four rhetorical questions followed by a set of assertions that continue into v. 3. The rhetorical questions highlight Israel's culpability in the exile. God came, but no one welcomed Him. He called for the nation to repent and to trust Him for deliverance, but no one responded. God did not lack the capacity to rescue Israel. Instead, Israel refused to obey and trust in the Lord whose power has no equal. Now, facing the darkness of discipline, the Lord gives the example of the Servant-Messiah in His darkest hour to teach Israel how to respond to the trauma of exile (v. 4-9). The poem has two parts, the first giving the example of the Servant (vv. 4-9) followed by the exhortation to Israel based on the Servant's example (vv. 10-11).

50:4-9. This brief section of the two-part poem presents the Servant as an example of trust in the Lord, persevering despite opposition. Written in the first person, the section has four parts, each introduced by the divine name **the Lord God** (vv. 4, 5, 7, 9). First, the Servant affirms that He is a disciple of the Lord (v. 4). He states that the Lord has given Him **the tongue of disciples**, instructing Him as a spokesman, in order to help those who need comfort. God has also given Him special attentiveness, allowing Him to **listen as a disciple**. The Lord, the Servant's Father, awakened Him **morning by morning** to instruct Him personally as a disciple.

Second, the Servant affirms that He is submissive to the will of God (vv. 5-6). This emphasis on submissive obedience is evident in the life of the Servant. The Lord **opened** His **ear**, indicating that He listened to God and **was not disobedient** (lit., "rebellious," v. 5). In saying that He had not rebelled, the Servant cannot be identified as the nation of Israel. There is only one place where the expression is used of Israel as not being rebellious (Ps 105:28) and that describes Israel before the exodus. Every time afterward the Scripture describes Israel as rebellious (cf. Is 3:8; 63:10).

Remarkably, the Servant's submissive obedience is not enacted in a comfortable world free of confrontation and anguish. Instead, the Servant is persecuted, but refuses to fight back, offering Himself to His oppressors (v. 6). The NT depiction of the trial and crucifixion of Jesus demonstrates His submission to His Father's will and to the beating and mockery of the Roman soldiers and even the religious leaders (Mt 26:67; 27:27-31, 39-44; see the comments there).

Third, the Servant affirms His confidence in His vindication by God. He recognizes that God's aid will keep Him from experiencing shame and disgrace, giving the Servant an unwavering sense of purpose. The Lord will **vindicate** the Servant and defend Him from those who seek to accuse Him (vv. 7-8). Using legal terms (**vindicates**, **contend**, **case**), the Servant anticipates a "not guilty" verdict. Of course, Jesus was condemned in trial before Pilate. His vindication would come not from Pilate but from the Lord (v. 9), when He would raise from the dead and the stone would be rolled away from His empty tomb.

Fourth, the Servant expresses confidence that He would be avenged. Those guilty of condemning Him would wear out like a garment and be eaten up by moths (v. 9). His false accusers would all face judgment from the Lord.

50:10-11. Having given the example of the Servant's faithfulness during a time of deep trouble, the song next turns to exhort Israel, calling the nation to follow the example of the Servant in its time of trial. The exhortation has a positive (trust God in the darkness) and negative (do not trust oneself in the darkness) aspect. The positive exhortation begins with a question, asking Israel to identify who among them fears the Lord and obeys His Servant, but still **walks in darkness and has no light** (v. 10). Though the language of darkness is often used with reference to evil or blindness, in this case, it is likely that the darkness here refers to the difficulties the nation is facing. If the term is taken in this fashion, the force of the verse is exhortative. It calls those experiencing difficulty (i.e., darkness) to trust in the Lord. In this sense, it offers an answer to the question at the beginning of v. 10: those who fear the Lord and trust His Servant are those who trust in the Lord even in the absence of light. In darkness (suffering) they are to trust God even as the Servant did so they can experience the same glorious outcome. As Motyer writes, "Those who commit to the servant way will have a servant experience, normative for them because true of Him" (Motyer, *The Prophecy of Isaiah,* 401).

The negative exhortation is to those who attempt to light their own way, using human manipulations rather than trusting God in the darkness. In their attempt to make their own **light**, they will be burned by that light and ultimately will lie down in torment (v. 11).

(4) God's Promised Deliverance (51:1–52:12)

Having encouraged Israel by revealing the Servant's roles (49:1-13), reminding of the Lord's faithfulness (49:14-26), and reviewing the Servant's trust (50:1-11), the prophet next provides encouragement to Israel with a reminder of the Lord's promise of deliverance and restoration.

51:1-3. The Servant's calling, activity, and example provide the launching point for an articulation of Israel's hopeful future. The now-familiar exhortation to listen is addressed to those who **pursue righteousness** and **who seek the Lord** (v. 1). They are called to contemplate their origins, which are pictured metaphorically with mining imagery (**the rock from which you were hewn . . . the quarry from which you were dug**). Abraham and Sarah are cited as an example of God's past action on behalf of His people. The certainty of the Lord's comfort to Zion is confirmed by the past blessing of Abraham and Sarah and God's covenant with them. The restoration of Zion will go beyond mere rebuilding. Instead, the city's surroundings will become **like Eden** and **her desert like the garden of the Lord** (v. 3). Certainly this would not be fulfilled at the return from Babylon but awaits the appearance of the messianic kingdom. At that time, God's care for the city will exceed any human expectations and will restore it to the glorious state of creation.

51:4-8. God gives another call to listen (v. 4), but in this case the Israelites are to hear the Lord's "instruction" (Hb. *torah* may be translated "instruction"—its use here is not a reference to the Mosaic law but God's instruction at the end of days; see comments on 2:3.) It is

God who will be the source of justice and order that will become a light to the peoples (v. 4). God's righteousness and justice will not be unwelcome. Instead, **the coastlands** (see Is 41:1) **will wait** in anticipation of His coming (v. 5). God's justice is not transitory like the things of the world, or even like creation itself. God will usher in an everlasting salvation that will not **wear out**, but will continue to offer security and prosperity (v. 6). Israel is encouraged not to be afraid of the insults of humanity (v. 7). The description of the people of Israel as knowing what is right and having God's law (instruction) in their hearts suggests that such knowledge can eliminate fear. Those who are obedient have no need to fear because those who mock and taunt will not last. They will be like moth-eaten clothes that are devoured over time (v. 8). The vindication of the Lord will last through **all generations** (v. 8; cf. v.6). The contrast between the permanent and the transient in these verses is designed to highlight the value of the Lord's righteousness over the so-called treasures of temporal society.

51:9-10. Next, God is addressed and called to awake and put on strength. The reference to the **arm of the LORD** is to God's military prowess. Here, God is called to prepare for action to defend His people as He did in times past when He defeated the proud and brought order to chaos. **Rahab** refers to the primordial sea monster representing chaos and disorder. Beyond its most familiar reference to the prostitute and woman of faith (Jos 2; 6: 22, 25; cf. Hb 11:31), **Rahab** appears six times in the OT. Two of these occurrences refer to Egypt (Ps 87:4; Is 30:7) while the other occurrences refer to the mythic sea monsters (Jb 9:13; 26:12-13 [see the comments there]; Ps 89:8-10; Is 51:9). In this context, the reference to Rahab emphasizes God's command over all created forces, regardless of how powerful. The point of the rhetorical question is to highlight God's capacity to act and to anticipate His doing so.

A similar implication may be drawn from v. 10 in which the events associated with the Exodus are cited as additional evidences of God's ability to control creation. The sea, in a manner similar to **Rahab**, is associated with the powers of chaos: "The image of a raging personified cosmic deep is perhaps the most pervasive symbol of chaos in ancient mythological texts" (F. J. Mabie, "Chaos and Death," *Dictionary of the Old Testament: Wisdom, Poetry and Writings*, ed. Tremper Longman III and Peter Enns [Downers Grove, IL: InterVarsity, 2008], 44). God also demonstrated His power over the Red Sea in the deliverance of Israel from Egypt. The call for God to awake is rooted in the powerful memories of His past acts of deliverance for Israel.

51:11-16. God's response to the plea for Him to rouse Himself on Israel's behalf follows. It is, in many ways, a call by Him for Israel to maintain faithfulness and to wait on the Lord. Those whom the Lord has promised to rescue will be rescued, restored, granted posterity, and given **everlasting joy** (v. 11). God declares Himself to be the One who **comforts** Israel (v. 12a). The two questions that follow reflect God's frustration over the peoples' continued anxiety about the nations. Though these questions should not be understood as diminishing the difficulties of the people of Israel, they do challenge the doubts previously expressed concerning God's apparent inactivity (vv. 9-10). If God is the One who brings comfort, then there is no need to fear humanity. Those die and are as fragile as grass. Israel must remember the Lord who created and continues to control all of creation (v. 13). There is no danger or oppression that can overwhelm the comfort of God. God's people need only to exercise faithful patience, trusting in the Lord for comfort.

Verse 14 underscores God's willingness to act as He declares that the exile will soon be set free and will be given provision. This release is grounded in the Lord's identity as the One **who stirs up the sea** (v. 15). The imagery of the sea points to the Lord's power over the chaotic aspects of life. The turmoil that Israel has experienced, in other words, is not solely the result of powers that stand in opposition to God, powers that He must defeat. Instead, it is also God who makes the **waves roar**, that is, He ordains these difficulties encountered by Israel because of their sin. But despite their difficulties, the people of Israel have been commissioned to speak for the Lord and to be called God's people. Jerusalem is called to awake and to rise.

51:17-23. In this section, Zion is challenged to rouse itself, like a drunkard awakening from a binge. In this case, however, the cup of His anger, not alcohol, has caused Jerusalem's senselessness. Israel's experience of God's discipline has left the nation's senses dull, its reactions slow. Not only is Jerusalem drunk, but she is also alone—there is no one to help guide Jerusalem home. None of Jerusalem's children are available to help their drunken parent.

There is no consolation for Jerusalem whose children lie in the street **full of the wrath of the Lord** (v. 20). Just as Israel has come to her lowest point, God, her defender, declares that the cup of His wrath which has left Israel reeling will be taken away and that the nation will never drink it again (v. 22). Instead, the cup will be passed to those who have tormented Israel. Israel's oppressors truly walked on the backs of the bruised calling Israel to lie on the ground so that they could walk across them. They will feel the disorientation and hopelessness that comes from drinking too much of God's wrath (v. 23). Plainly none of these promises were fulfilled at the return from exile in Babylon. Although some argue that the prophet is using hyperbole here, because the author gives no hint of using a figure of speech, it is better to still anticipate the fulfillment of God's permanent restoration of Israel in the future messianic kingdom.

52:1-2. Now Zion is called to wake up, to put on strength and **beautiful garments**, because that which defiled the city (the uncircumcised Gentiles and the unclean pagans) will no longer enter it to bring it harm. Zion will now experience freedom from oppression and the influence of those who do not fear the Lord. They can now **shake** themselves **from the dust** and **rise up** (v. 2). The description of the conditions that resulted in Israel's newfound freedom follow (52:3-6).

52:3-6. First, Israel will be redeemed. She who was **sold for nothing and . . . will be redeemed without money**. As Oswalt notes, "Since God had not been forced to hand over Judah to satisfy some creditor, nor had he sold her in order [to] get cash to pay his debts, but purely on his own volition, then on his own volition he could redeem her . . . There is no third party involved; it is strictly a matter between him and his people" (Oswalt, *Isaiah 40–66*, 361–362).

Second, God will punish Israel's oppressors (vv. 4-5). These verses discuss the history of Israel's time in Egypt and Assyria, as well as their imminent exile under rulers who mock God's people. Such a situation is untenable because the Lord's name is blasphemed. The Septuagint, which is quoted in Rm 2:22-24 (see the comments there), adds the phrase "because of you among the nations" suggesting that God's people are at fault for the blasphemy of the nations. Nevertheless, the actions of the nations will prompt God's action, so that Israel, who has questioned God's delay in deliverance, will know that it is God who is rescuing them (52:6). God declares, "Here I am showing that I am with you in your distress."

52:7-10. The prophet next proclaims God's kingship over Israel. The beautiful feet of the messenger and the **good news** He proclaims to the people of Israel result in praise. The Septuagint and the NT translate the Hebrew phrase rendered **good news** as "gospel." Therefore, the term "gospel" carries with it a royal nuance that is frequently overlooked. In the context of Isaiah, the royal nuance of the good news is certainly in mind as God is identified as the One who reigns.

The watchmen of the city are the first to see the Lord's restoration of Jerusalem (v. 8). The joy of the watchmen will be matched by the **waste places of Jerusalem** because of the comfort and redemption that the Lord will finally bring to Jerusalem. Jerusalem's rejoicing will be preceded by the baring of God's **holy arm** (v. 10), which is a metaphor of His military power. Jerusalem did not rescue itself—her newfound salvation is the work of the Lord.

52:11-12. God's call for Israel to depart is likely a call for Israel to leave Babylon. The concern with purity is a statement against carrying foreign practices back to Jerusalem. When the Israelites leave Babylon, they must also leave behind the Babylonian practices. The Israelites need not leave Babylon in a rush or in secret since the Lord will guard them in the front and the rear, so there is no need to be fearful, since their return to Canaan would not be characterized as **haste** or flight (not **as fugitives**) (v. 12). Despite the call to leave Babylon, this should be viewed as a precursor to the events described throughout chaps. 51–52 which describe Israel's ultimate restoration at the end of days.

b. The Sacrifice for Israel (52:13–53:12)

This section of Isaiah is focused on the exaltation and humiliation of the Servant. The second group of deliverance oracles, focusing on deliverance from sin (chaps. 49–57), began with oracles that were designed to encourage Israel (49:1–52:12). This poem at the center of the deliverance oracles presents the fourth Servant Song, depicting the Servant-Messiah as a sacrifice offered for Israel's redemption. Whereas Is 42 described the responsibilities of the Servant, Is 49 His roles, and Is 50 His rejection, Is 52:13–53:12 describes the culmination of the Servant's mission. He would be a sacrifice for Israel and thereby provide redemption for the nation and the whole world (see the chart on the Servant Songs with the comments regarding Is 42).

The structure of the poem is as follows: There are five stanzas, each consisting of three verses. The first (52:13-15) and last stanza (53:10-12) function as a prologue and epilogue to the poem; each has God speaking about the Servant's exaltation. The main body of the poem contains three stanzas at the center (53:1-9), as the repentant nation of Israel speaks about the Servant's humiliation.

The Jewish interpretation of this Song is significant. In the ancient Rabbinic literature, the Servant was frequently identified as the Messiah (e.g., Targum Jonathan ben Uzziel [written c. AD 100–200] on Isaiah 52:13 states, "Behold, my Servant the Messiah will prosper"; also, Bab. Sanhedrin 98a identifies the Messiah as the subject of Isaiah 53). However, the influential medieval Jewish interpreter Rabbi Shlomo Yitzchaki (Rashi, AD 1040–1105) identified the Servant as Israel. Today, most Jewish interpreters follow Rashi, as do most critical scholars. The following are six reasons the Servant in the fourth Song cannot be identified as Israel.

First, the pronouns of the Song would be inconsistent. In the body (53:1-9), the people of Israel are speaking and uniformly identify themselves in the first person (we, our, us). They also describe the Servant in the third person (He, Him). Thus, Israel cannot be the Servant.

Second, the Servant is said to die for "my people" (53:8). Isaiah's people were the people of Israel. Therefore, the Servant cannot be Israel and also die for Israel.

Third, the Servant is described as completely innocent ("He had done no violence, nor was there any deceit in His mouth," 53:9). Yet, throughout Isaiah, Israel is called guilty (e.g., 1:16-20; 5:7). The nation cannot be the innocent Servant.

Fourth, the Servant suffered for the sins of others (53:6). But the nation of Israel suffered for her own sins (40:2).

Fifth, the Servant was a willing sufferer, rendering "Himself as a guilt offering" (53:10). But Israel did indeed suffer, in fact, twice as much as she deserved (40:2), but never did so willingly.

Sixth, the Servant actually died ("cut off out of the land of the living," 53:8). Certainly many in Israel did die but the nation collectively did not perish. In fact, God promised that the nations could never totally destroy His people (Jr 31:35-37). On the whole, it seems best to maintain the earliest Jewish view that the Servant should be identified as the Messiah.

(1) God Speaks: The Servant Will Be Exalted Despite His Humiliation (52:13-15)

The first stanza functions as a prologue or introduction to the Song. God is the speaker and He declares that the Servant will be exalted despite His suffering and humiliation.

52:13-15. The passage begins with the affirmation that the Servant's actions will be in accordance with divine wisdom. Although translated that the Servant **will prosper** (v. 13a), the Hebrew is literally stating that He will "act wisely." This is a metonymy of cause for effect, indicating that He will be successful or prosper. His exaltation is described with the glorious language of Is 6:1. There it states that God is "lofty and exalted." Although translated as **high and lifted up** (52:13b), the same Hebrew words are used of the Servant as are used of God. It even goes further, adding the expression **and greatly exalted**, a phrase not used in Is 6:1.

In addition to the Servant's exaltation, He is also said to have an appalling and disfiguring death: **His appearance was marred more than any man** (v. 14). The question arises as to who is being addressed. The NASB adds the italicized *My people*, indicating that the words were added and are not in the original text. There are several possibilities for dealing with the address to **you**. First, it is possible that this is a comparison—just as people would be appalled at the suffering of Israel, so they would be when seeing the disfiguring of the Messiah. Second, many ancient Hebrew manuscripts have the word "Him," as in **just as many were astonished at** Him. This would make more sense in the context. A third possibility is that at times to heighten the drama in Hebrew poetry, the speaker can begin to address directly the individual being described throughout in the third person. In essence, it is as if for a moment the Lord stopped describing the Servant and instead spoke directly to Him. To capture the sense in English, it should be translated in the third person. It seems best therefore to translate this as the NIV and NLT do, that many would be appalled or amazed at "Him."

It is through the Servant's disfiguring death that He will accomplish His work and destiny, that **He will sprinkle many nations** (v. 15). There is a dispute about the meaning of the word translated here as **sprinkle** (*yazzeh*), with some translations indicating that the word should be "startle."

The basis for the alternate translation "startle" is that this fits the parallelism with appalled or amazed in the previous verse as well as the parallelism with the line that follows: **Kings will shut their mouths** [in astonishment]. Furthermore, while it is agreed that the Hebrew word used here consistently means "sprinkle" throughout the Hebrew Bible (e.g., Ex 29:16; Lv 17:6; Nm 18:17; Ezk 36:25), it always has a preposition following it ("to sprinkle something *on*"), indicating what object is being sprinkled. However, there is no preposition in this passage. Perhaps this is why the Septuagint translated this word "astonish." Some have conjectured an Arabic cognate word to support this.

The argument for the traditional translation "sprinkle" is (1) that it is the plain definition of the word; (2) taking it as "startle" requires identifying it with a root completely unattested in the Hebrew language; (3) the word need not be parallel to "appalled" but could rather mean that the Servant's disfiguring death would be the way He would "sprinkle" the nations; and (4) as a causative verb, it could be an exception to the general rule of needing a preposition, with the idea "He besprinkles many nations." This verb is unattested in Hebrew for the concept of being "astonished" or "startled." It seems best, therefore, to translate *yazzeh* as **sprinkle**. This is the same word used in Leviticus for sprinkling sacrificial blood (Lv 4:6; 16:14, 19), indicating that the Servant's disfiguring death would function as a sacrifice for many nations. As a result, when Gentile kings understand the sacrificial reason for the Servant's death, they will **shut their mouths** in reverence and submission.

(2) Israel Speaks: The Servant Was Not Recognized because of His Humiliation (53:1-9)

The speaker changes from God to Israel in 53:1, and the nation continues speaking through the three stanzas of the body of the poem (53:1-9). Israel speaks from the perspective of finally understanding the identity of the Servant after many years of rejection. This is penitential Israel, finally recognizing the long-rejected Messiah. In a parallel passage, Zechariah predicts that when Israel finally recognizes the Messiah, the nation will repent with great mourning (Zch 12:10). The words in this section aptly express that mourning and repentance. In the body of the song, penitent Israel gives three reasons for failing to recognize the Messiah in the past.

53:1-3. *Israel states that the Servant was too plain to be the Messiah.* It was difficult for Israel to believe in the Servant (**Who has believed our message?**, v. 1) because He was not what was anticipated. **The arm of the LORD**, previously mentioned in Isaiah (44:12; 48:14; 50:2; 51:5; 51:9; 52:10), was unrecognizable even to those who know it is coming. The **tender shoot**, or **root** (v. 2), did not meet the people's expectations of a Deliverer. Oswalt describes the **shoot** as "the normally unwanted shoot that springs up from an exposed root of a tree" (Oswalt, *The Book of Isaiah, Chapters 40–66*, 382). Such an understanding is suggested by the following parallel lines in which the Servant is described as having **no stately form or majesty**. The entire verse emphasizes the Servant's seeming insignificance. While Israel was looking for a royal deliverer, the Servant appeared ordinary. His appearance was unimpressive. No one would have any reason to **be attracted to Him**. Rather the Servant **was despised and forsaken of men**; sorrow and suffering characterized His life (v. 3). He knew **grief**. The term **grief** is often rendered "sickness" (HCSB; Dt 7:15; 28:59, 61; 1Kg 17:17; 2Kg 1:2,4; 8:8-9; 13:14; 2Ch 16:12; 21:15, 18-19; Ps 41:3; Ec 5:16; 6:2; Is 1:5; Jr 6:7; Hs 5:13). Since the Servant was not physically ill, it may be best to translate the term as "suffering" and understand it to refer to the physical pain of a tortured and disfiguring death that He endured (52:14).

Describing the Servant as **one from whom men hide their face** (v. 3) suggests that those who rejected the Servant considered Him contemptible. Therefore He was **despised** and did not receive proper esteem. The term **despised** is the same Hebrew word used of the singularly contemptible Antiochus Epiphanes (Dn 11:21, translated "despicable").

53:4-6. *Israel states that He was punished for His own sin.* The despised Servant bore **our griefs** (better translated "suffering"; see comments on 53:1-3) and carried **our sorrows**. The words may contain the idea of sickness, leading some to believe that faith in the Servant guarantees immediate healing of all diseases. However, this does not mean that all sicknesses will immediately be cured because of the Servant's vicarious suffering. Rather it is promising that the Servant's death would ultimately provide deliverance and healing for all who believe in Him. The Servant did indeed take the punishment for sin and therefore would provide immediate forgiveness to someone who trusts in Him. However, removing the penalty for sin will not remove the presence of sin in a believer's life until after the resurrection. In the same way, the forgiveness of the sins that cause sickness does not guarantee healing from diseases until the presence of sin is removed at the resurrection at the end of days.

Israel now confesses that upon viewing the Servant's suffering, the nation had concluded that the Servant was undergoing divine punishment. He was **stricken, smitten of God, and afflicted** (v. 4), all terms that indicate punishment for sin. The word **stricken,** meaning "to smite with disease for sin," was used when both Miriam (Nm 12:9-10) and Uzziah (2Kg 15:5) were stricken with leprosy for sin.

Penitent Israel now recognizes that while the Servant was indeed being punished for sin, it was not for His sins but theirs. The Servant's suffering included being **pierced through for our transgressions** (v. 5). The Hebrew word translated **pierced** (*mekholal*) means "wounded to death" and conveys a violent and painful death (Dt 21:1; Is 51:9). The Servant was **crushed for our iniquities**. Although the word **crushed** means "broken" or "shattered to pieces," it is not generally used in a literal way but with a metaphorical sense, as in a "contrite [lit., "crushed"] spirit" (Is 57:15) or "contrite heart" (Ps 51:17). Israel now understood that the Servant took the punishment (**chastening**) they deserved, that He was flogged (**by His scourging**) in order to bring their spiritual healing. The substitution of the Servant for the people certainly foretells the sacrifice of the Messiah Jesus as a sacrifice for the sickness of sin (1Pt 2:24).

Penitent Israel now summarizes what they have learned: They are the ones who have strayed from God **like sheep** and followed their own desires. Consequently, the Lord has caused the punishment for the **iniquity** (guilt) **of us all to fall on Him** (v. 6).

53:7-9. *Israel states that the Servant was too passive to be innocent.* The Servant's silence at His trial and His submission to death demonstrates His acceptance of suffering and His willing participation. The Servant did not proclaim His own innocence, making those who observed Him mistake His behavior for passivity and acquiescence brought about by His own guilt. But the real reason for the Servant's acceptance of His suffering was that He understood that His suffering was coming upon Him to fulfill God's purpose. As Goldingay notes, "He 'bore' and 'carried' not because he had to but because he agreed to. So there was no basis for or logic in protest . . . he was at every point a victim, but he maintained a form of control of his destiny, not letting anyone else determine his reaction to it" (Goldingay, *The Message of Isaiah 40–55*, 506).

Additionally, the Servant submitted to a crooked trial (v. 8). The phrase **by oppression and judgment** is a hendiadys, two separate words describing just one subject; they are better translated "oppressive judgment," indicating a corrupt legal procedure. As a result, His contemporaries (**His generation**) considered that He brought His death upon Himself by His own sin rather than understanding the real reason for His death: to bear the punishment **for the transgression of** the **people** of Israel.

After His death, the Servant's grave was assigned with wicked men (v. 9). The implication is that even after the Servant died, His innocence was not recognized and He would be buried as a common criminal. Instead, however, **He was with a rich man in His death**. This was because the Servant was genuinely innocent (**He had done no violence, nor was there any deceit in His mouth**; It was as if God had said, "This far and no farther," and spared His Servant the final humiliation of a dishonorable burial. The Servant's innocence caused the Lord to place Him in the tomb of a rich man (cf. Mt 27:57-60).

(3) God Speaks: The Servant Will Be Exalted because of His Humiliation (53:10-12)

The final stanza of the Song serves as an epilogue. The Lord is once again the speaker, just as He was in the opening stanza. Just as the first stanza depicted the Servant's exaltation, this one does as well. The difference is that in the first stanza the Servant is promised exaltation despite His humiliation but now He is promised exaltation precisely because of His humiliation.

53:10. *The Servant will be restored because of His humiliation in serving as a substitutionary sacrifice for sinners.* Just before the oracle proper where the Lord begins to speak, the prophet Isaiah states that the will of the Lord will be accomplished through the Servant's sacrifice and ultimate exaltation. Although the NASB states that **the LORD was pleased to crush Him**, the Hebrew word translated "pleased" may also be used to indicate will or purpose (cf. Jdg 13:23) and therefore translated "willing." That this is so here is indicated by the active voice (lit., "The Lord willed") and the grammatical construction (to be precise, an active voice verb ["willed"] followed by an infinitive ["to crush"] with a pronominal suffix in the accusative ["Him"], these elements typically expressing purpose). God took no pleasure in the death of His Servant but He "willed" to crush (cf. 53:5) Him for the ultimate purpose of providing salvation.

The Servant's exaltation would come as a result of His making Himself **a guilt offering** (v. 10). This is a reference to the restitution offering (cf. Lv 5:14-6:7) when one wronged God or other people. A sacrifice was offered to God providing atonement for the wrong done (Lv 5:15, 18; 6:6; 19:20) along with a restitution or fine to the offended human party. Regardless, this sacrifice did provide expiation for sin. The use of this term in relation to the Servant identifies His death as an atonement for the damage and injury done by sin.

As a result of His atoning death, the Servant will experience restoration as the first aspect of His exaltation. The Servant's restoration has three components. First, He will have followers, not rejecters. Although He was despised and forsaken of men (53:3), the Servant is promised that **He will see His offspring** (lit., "His seed"). Normally this term refers to physical progeny, but the context about rejection and the timing of this after His death indicates that the word "seed" should be taken figuratively for "followers" (as it is used in Is 57:4).

The second aspect of the Servant's restoration is that He will have life, not death. Despite the gruesome death described previously (52:14, 53:8-9), here He is promised prolonged days (v. 10), indicating an indirect reference to the resurrection. Third, the Servant's restoration will include God's pleasure and prosperity in His life rather than suffering and sorrow.

53:11. *The Servant will be satisfied because of His justification of sinners.* The Servant's exaltation will also include His own satisfaction with what He accomplished. He will not consider His death as a sign of failure, but rather **be satisfied** with the forgiveness He provided. From His anguish, **He will see *it*,** but the object *it* is not in the Hebrew text. In fact, there is no object to the verb **see**. Both the Septuagint and the Qumran scroll of Isaiah do have the word "light" as the object. This reading, which is more likely, indicates that after **anguish** the Servant will see light. The NIV translation correctly translates this as a reference to resurrection: "he will see the light of life."

It is **by His knowledge** that the Servant will **justify the many**. This should more likely be read in the objective case ("knowledge of Him"), indicating that many people will come to know (believe in) the Servant. As a result, God's righteous Servant will provide justification. This is a play on the words, as both **righteous** and **justify** have the same Hebrew root word. The **Righteous One** will "declare righteous" (**justify**) those who know Him. As a result, **He will bear their iniquities**. This is what brings the Servant satisfaction—knowing that His suffering and death will bring forgiveness to those who turn to Him. It is almost universally recognized by Pauline scholars that Is 53:11 is what provides the theological basis for much of what Paul says about the atoning, justifying death of Jesus Christ (see Rm 3:21-29).

53:12. *The Servant will be rewarded because of His intercession on behalf of sinners.* The Servant's ultimate exaltation will not only include His restoration (53:10) and satisfaction (53:11) but also His reward. This verse uses the imagery of victory after battle. First, the Servant will receive **a portion**, not meaning "a part" but "spoil, inheritance." The content of that portion is not **with the great**, but as the HCSB translates it, "the many." The word "many," used five times in this Song (52:14, 15; 53:11, 12), here indicates the many people He has redeemed. The Servant will receive the redeemed as His reward after His deadly battle with sin. His spoil will also include the nations ("He will receive the mighty as spoil," HCSB).

All this will be His because of His willing **death** and identification with **transgressors** (rebels against God). As such, the Servant bore the sin of those He redeemed (the **many**) and **interceded** for them. This intercession likely refers to the Servant's perpetual priestly mediation for those who know Him (cf. Heb 7:25). The ultimate message of this Song is that God will bring glory and reward to His Servant, who endured a humiliating and horrific death to redeem sinners.

F. B. Meyer correctly states, "There is only one brow upon which this crown of thorns will fit" (F. B. Meyer, *Christ in Isaiah: Expositions of Isaiah XL-LV* [New York: Revell, 1895], 158). Only Jesus of Nazareth fulfilled the specific prophecies of this remarkable Song. What follows are ten specific fulfillments of prophecy:

1. Jesus suffered an appalling, disfiguring death (52:14).
2. Jesus' blood sprinkled nations and brought kings to submission (52:15).
3. Jesus was rejected by Israel for being too plain (53:1-3).
4. Jesus' suffering was considered to be punishment for His sin by Israel (53:4-6).
5. Jesus suffered and died without resistance, accepting God's will to provide atonement for Israel and the world (53:7-8).
6. Jesus was buried in a rich man's tomb (53:9).
7. Jesus was resurrected from the dead (53:10-11).
8. Jesus was given innumerable followers (spiritual seed) (53:10).
9. Jesus is satisfied today with the forgiveness His death provided (53:11).
10. Jesus has been rewarded by God the Father as the victor over sin (53:12).

c. The Salvation of Israel and the Nations (54:1–57:21)

The second group of deliverance oracles, focusing on deliverance from sin (chaps. 49–57), began with a section designed to encourage Israel (49:1–52:12) and were followed by the fourth Servant Song (52:13–53:12), depicting the sacrifice of the Servant for the sins of Israel. Now the prophet turns to the third section, emphasizing the salvation of Israel and the nations. First he speaks of the salvation of Israel (54:1–55:13) and then addresses the salvation of the Gentiles.

(1) The Salvation of Israel (54:1–55:13)

The prophet begins by describing the promise of salvation (54:1-17) and then will invite Israel to receive it (55:1-13).

(a) The Promise of Salvation (54:1-17)

54:1-3. The first aspect of the promise is that God will enlarge and repopulate the land of Israel. Zion is told to rejoice, **Shout for joy**! (v. 1). The imagery of the barren woman whose offspring will be more numerous than that of a woman who has a husband implies that there is a reversal of fortune coming. Those who had no hope will now experience abundant blessing. After the call to rejoice, Israel is told the reason: **Enlarge the place of your tent** . . . **lengthen your cords and strengthen your pegs** (v. 2). All three phrases depict the expansion of a **tent** and direct them to the Lord's promise that Israel will one day widen their borders and take control of the nations (54:3).

54:4-10. The second aspect of the promise of salvation is that, in the day when the entire nation will turn to the Servant for deliverance, Israel will be fully restored. The nation will no longer feel shame or humiliation because of the nation's relationship with the Lord (vv. 4-5). **The shame of your youth** (lit., "maidenhood," from the same root as the word for "virgin" in 7:14) and **the reproach of your widowhood** both indicate times when a woman was ashamed in that culture because she had no husband (v. 4). This humiliation will be removed because the Lord will become Israel's husband. Alongside the descriptions of God as **the Holy One of Israel** and as **your Redeemer** (v. 5), the relationship between God and Israel is depicted in terms of a marital relationship, with God, Israel's creator, as Israel's husband. This imagery is also used here (cf. 54:6) and elsewhere in the Hebrew Bible (cf. Is 50:1; Jr 3:8, 14, 20; 31:32; Hs 2:2, 16). The relation is often stated negatively in the context of divorce and unfaithfulness, but ultimately suggests the permanence of Israel's relationship to God and implies the protection and security that was available to God's spouse. The restoration of the relationship will occur when God's call for Israel to come from dispersion will resemble a husband calling his wife back to him after she was **rejected** (v. 6). Although it might be thought that this was fulfilled at the return from Babylon, the full restoration of Israel did not occur then. Therefore, this certainly points to the restoration of Israel in the messianic kingdom.

Israel's restoration reflects the permanence of God's reunion with His estranged wife. Her time of abandonment had been relatively short and will ultimately result in a compassionate regathering (v. 7). A similar sentiment is further expressed, but God's anger at their sin is identified as the reason for Israel's temporary abandonment (v. 8). The comparison to the time of Noah (v. 9) offers Israel assurance that God's anger has subsided and that He will never again rebuke Israel. Just as God promised never again to discipline the earth with a flood and gave the rainbow as a sign of this covenant (Gn 9:8-17), so God promises never to rebuke again. Since Israel did indeed endure discipline after the return from Babylon, this promise must be understood as referring to the end of days when Israel turns to the Messiah in faith (cf. Hs 3:4-5).

It is a reference to the promise not to abandon or discipline Israel once they have been restored in the millennium. The elaboration of the promise in v. 10 clarifies this understanding by depicting the stability of God's **lovingkindness**, which stands firm when the mountains are shaken and the hills removed. The Hebrew term translated **lovingkindness**, used 245 times in the OT, would best be translated "loyal love." It is linked to God's "covenant faithfulness" or God's steadfast loyalty to His people.

Just as God made the rainbow covenant with Noah, so He indicates that He will establish a covenant of peace with Israel. The phrase **covenant of peace** (v. 10) occurs elsewhere in the OT (cf. Nm 25:12; Ezk 34:25; 37:26). In Nm 25:12, the phrase appears to denote the agreed upon peace between God and Israel. The "covenant of peace" in Ezekiel is associated with security and blessing (see the comments on Ezk 34:25). Given the other uses of the phrase in Numbers and Ezekiel, the **covenant of peace** as used here refers to the new covenant (cf. Jr 31:31-34), when Israel will be at peace with God and experience the security having been re-established in the land.

54:11-17. The third aspect of the promise of salvation is that Israel will be renewed. The description of the future rebuilding of Jerusalem, here called the **afflicted one** (v. 11), underscores the peace and security that God will bring to the people. Jerusalem will be rebuilt with precious stones and jewels, suggesting luxuriousness and highlighting the unique love that God has for the city (vv. 11-12). God will not simply rebuild Jerusalem, but will construct it from extravagant materials that will set it apart from any other city. In the coming idyllic state of Jerusalem (vv. 13-17), Israel's children will experience peace, having been **taught of the Lord** (54:13). In this context, being **taught** likely assumes that the students have also learned what the teacher seeks to convey. The children of Israel will not simply hear the Lord's teachings, but will obey them (see Is 30:20-21 and the comments there).

Not only will the next generation of Israelites obey the Lord, but also God will usher in an unprecedented era of peace and safety. Israel will not be ruled by tyrants. They will have no need to be afraid any longer because God will protect them **from oppression** . . . **and from terror** (v. 14). In the millennial kingdom (the one-thousand-year reign of Messiah Jesus literally and physically on the earth; cf. Rv 20:1-6, and see the comments there) God will not allow any nation to defeat Israel. In the past God allowed the destroyer (Babylon) to ruin. But in the end of days, **no weapon that is formed against you will prosper** (v. 17). There is no blacksmith in the world who can forge a weapon that will defeat Israel in those days. God's people have been vindicated and stand before God as part of an everlasting covenant. God's role in the formation of Israel's enemies has been emphasized throughout the book. His involvement offers comfort to Israel since God's wrath will be checked by His mercy and compassion for His covenant people.

(b) The Offer of Salvation (55:1-13)

Having promised salvation to Israel, the Lord next offers Israel an opportunity to receive the gift. However, the offer is also extended beyond Israel to the nations as well (cf. Is 49:6).

55:1-5. At the outset, the Lord invites Israel to come and enjoy the nourishing presence of God and His blessing, and thereby experience spiritual satisfaction. This section highlights not only the amazing provisions of God, but also that these provisions are free. In contrast to those who charge the thirsty for drink, God offers water and wine at no charge (v. 1). The rhetorical questions (v. 2) continue the previous thought, emphasizing the futility of spending hard-earned money on food that will not nourish. God calls His people to eat what is good and rich without charge. The figurative nature of the previous verses is evident in what follows (v. 3). Though physical sustenance will surely be provided, Israel will be sustained through their obedience to the Lord and His provision of the everlasting covenant, a reference to the new covenant (see Jr 31:31-34), guaranteeing God's ongoing nourishment. Next, the Lord explains how to respond to the invitation, namely by turning to the Servant, the Davidic Messiah (v. 4). In this verse, the Lord shifts from addressing Israel (you, your, v. 3) to speaking of the Servant-Messiah (**him**). He is described as **a witness**, **a leader**, and a **commander**. That these are to be understood as messianic is evident in that: (1) this language is too exalted for any other ruler and (2) the word **leader** (*nagid*) is specifically used of the Messiah (Dn 9:25). That the antecedent to these titles is **David** (v. 3) does not negate the messianic interpretation in that the prophets frequently call the Messiah "David" (cf. Jr 30:9; Ezk 36:23-24, 37:24-25; Hs 3:4-5) by metonymy because He and David are so closely connected and He is the fulfillment of the Davidic covenant (called here **the**

faithful mercies shown to David, 55:3; cf. 2Sm 7:12-16). The word **witness** refers to one who speaks truthfully. **Leader** means "ruler" and is used as a synonym for "king" (see 1Sm 9:16; 10:1; 1Kg 1:35). **Commander** refers to a leader with authority to issue commands, a royal lawgiver. The Lord's Servant-Messiah is addressed directly (55:5) where God tells Him that He will have command over a nation that He does not know because the Lord **has glorified** Him. When the Servant-Messiah takes His throne, He will not only rule Israel but the Gentile nations as well.

55:6-7. Having invited Israel to find spiritual nourishment from the Lord (55:1-3) and identifying the Servant-Messiah as the source of that nourishment (55:4-5), God now calls on all to repent and turn to Him. The promise here is plain: if people will **seek the Lord** in a timely manner, turn from wickedness and **return to the Lord**, then **He will abundantly pardon**. These phrases are not calls for works righteousness but are calling for genuine faith leading to divine forgiveness and transformed behavior. This is evident from the opening words of this Song (vv. 1-2), calling Israel to obtain salvation freely (not by works) since it is only available by God's gracious gift.

55:8-11. What follows is an answer to an implicit question concerning the repentance of the wicked. The question is, "How will repentance produce God's pardon?" The answer comes in a series of explanatory clauses beginning with the word **for**. The first two clauses assert that God's way of thinking cannot be constrained by humanity's understanding of it (vv. 8-9). As Oswalt puts it, "Our understanding is not the measure of what God can do" (Oswalt, *Isaiah 40–66*, 434). Another reason is related to the certainty of God's Word, which is highlighted through a comparison with rain and snow. Beyond certainty, however, God's word produces repentance and pardon, just as the rain and snow water the earth so that it yields vegetation (vv. 10-11).

55:12-13. In the final two verses of the chapter God's assurance of pardon brings **joy**. A transformed creation, including **the mountains and the hills** praise God, even as **the trees . . . clap their hands**. The replacement of plant life associated with the curse (i.e., thorn bush and nettle) with cypress and myrtle trees (v. 13) suggests the removal of toil and trouble. All this is done as a memorial to the Lord and will be an everlasting sign. This indicates that this restoration is accompanied by the repentance and restoration of God's people whose ongoing faithfulness will yield God's blessing.

(2) The Salvation of the Nations (56:1–57:21)

That Gentiles would be included in Messiah's kingdom was broached in the previous chapter (55:5). Now, however, this promise becomes the focus of the prophet's message.

(a) The Inclusion of the Gentiles (56:1-8)

56:1-2. God's attention turns from Israel to the foreigner and the eunuch. The initial call to promote justice and to obey the Lord is rooted in God's readiness to deliver (v. 1). The inclusive nature of the Lord's blessing (v. 2) suggests that, regardless of one's ethnicity, the obedience of faith is God's means of blessing to every individual. Obedience that day would include keeping **the sabbath** (v. 2). Sabbatarians have used this verse to maintain that Gentile believers today are required to keep Israel's Sabbath while some, having moved the Sabbath requirements to Sunday, still use it to argue for a renewed Christian Sabbath. However, the Sabbath was a sign of the Mosaic covenant (Ex 31:12-17) and is not commanded of believers in the Church. Nevertheless, this verse indicates that Sabbath requirements will be renewed in the messianic kingdom.

56:3-8. The natural question an Israelite would ask is how could foreigners or eunuchs be included in God's kingdom. Addressing this question, the prophet indicates that when those excluded from the promises bind themselves to the Lord, they will receive **a memorial, and a name better than that of sons and daughters . . . an everlasting name which will not be cut off** (vv. 4-5). All who obey the Lord and respect His ways will experience life with the Lord forever (vv. 6-7). That this brief discussion of the nations was addressed to Israel is evident in that the Lord tells Israel that she will not be the only nation regathered to God, but He will also gather Gentiles (v. 8). This is a fulfillment of the promise to Abraham to bless all nations through him and his seed (cf. Gn 12:3; 22:18; see also Is 60:3-11; 66:18-21; Jn 10:16).

(b) The Condemnation of the Wicked (56:9–57:21)

The preceding section's affirmation that foreigners will be saved alongside Israel heightens the denunciation of Israel's paganism that follows. Together the passages highlight the need for unconditional faithfulness to the Lord.

56:9-12. It was not enough for Israel to have a covenant with God; the nation also needed to follow Him. Yet Israel's leaders, the spiritually blind **watchmen** (v. 10), had led the nation astray. They were selfish **shepherds** (v. 11) who drank their days away, thinking that life would continue unchanged (v. 12) and that God would not intervene to hold them accountable.

57:1-6. These foolish leaders of Israel were insensitive to the death of the godly and would not experience the blessing of the Lord. Though the upright would experience blessing (vv. 1-2), those who practice the shameful sexual sins of paganism described in vv. 3-5 would ultimately experience God's punishment (v. 6a). He will not relent in judgment.

57:7-13. The prophet continues his condemnation of paganism. The Israelite's sacrifice **upon a high and lofty mountain** refers to hilltop shrines with idolatrous altars, as well as the placement of the pagan symbols within their homes and their tireless efforts to deliver sacrifices to the king. Some suggest that **king** (v. 9) should be amended to "Molek" (NIV), the Ammonite god to whom children were sacrificed. There is no textual support for this but **the king** in question was likely a pagan god—this idolatrous worship was but one of many of paganism and betrayal of the Lord (cf. vv. 7-10). The Israelite journey to sacrifice to the king prompts rhetorical questions in v. 11. The Israelites, who have not heard from the Lord, forget God and do not fear Him. As such, God will surrender Israel to their idols, but save those who trust in Him (vv. 12-13), thereby underscoring that faithfulness to God will yield God's blessing.

57:14-21. The tone of Is 57:14-19 shifts to one of hope in which God promises to heal humanity and to bring rest despite human rejection of Him. The **high and exalted** God promises that He also dwells with the penitent. They are called **contrite and lowly of spirit** (v. 15). The word **contrite** literally means "crushed" and refers to those who have been brought low by discipline from God. He will revive the heart of the contrite. Here the verb is the same as that found in David's psalm of confession, "a broken and a contrite heart, O God, You will not despise" (Ps 51:17). The grace and mercy of God is evident in that He who is exalted above all will descend and dwell with the lowly when they turn to Him. He promises to discipline those who keep **on turning away** (v. 17) but will also **restore comfort** (v. 18) upon repentance. There will be prosperity and peace when God's anger relents and He puts praise on the lips of the mourners in Israel (v. 19). The contrast between the penitent and the wicked is evident—God's peace will not be upon those who oppose His ways (vv. 19-21).

The words of the final verse of the chapter (**there is no peace . . . for the wicked**) function as a literary marker, bringing to a close this section on deliverance from sin (chaps. 49–57). A virtually identical phrase concludes the previous major section (deliverance from Babylon, chaps. 40–48) and a similar but stronger theme closes out the last unit of the book (deliverance in the end, chaps. 58–66, 66:24).

3. Deliverance in the End (58:1–66:24)

This section of Isaiah is the third major section (of three) in the oracles of the second half of the book (see chart of Isaiah by Rydelnik in the introduction). Each part of this oracular section emphasizes Israel's deliverance—from Babylon (chaps. 40–48), from sin (49–57), and in the end of days (58–66). The significant element of this section is that it takes a theme that has been raised throughout the book, eschatology, and makes it the central message. Above all, this final unit of Isaiah demonstrates that God will be faithful to His promises to Israel despite the nation's failures and that He will be King over all the earth.

a. God's Initiative Delivers Israel (58:1–60:22)

The final unit of Isaiah (chaps. 58–66) begins by demonstrating that God's initiative will produce His end-of-days deliverance (58:1–60:22). It is not Israel's righteousness but God's faithfulness and grace that accomplishes His purposes.

(1) God Describes Israel's Sinfulness (58:1–59:8)

The prophet presents God's words, depicting God as speaker in this section. The Lord presents Israel's primary sin as hypocrisy.

58:1-12. The first way Israel behaved hypocritically was in fasting. God describes Israel as manipulative worshipers who attempt to fool God into thinking they are truly seeking Him (vv. 1-2). They appear to have been impressed by their own activities to the extent that they are offended that God has not noticed their fasting (v. 3a). The peoples' fasting, which they count as an act of humility, is tainted by their ongoing quest to obtain their own selfish desires (v. 3b). This manipulation was compounded by their oppression of workers (v. 3c). Moreover, the point of fasting was not contrition but merely a means of covering their contentious behavior (v. 4). The command which follows demands that the fasts not be used **to make your voice heard on high**. The fast has become an attempt to manipulate Yahweh in order to gain or sustain advantage over others. Their fasts were not acts of humility, but were political tools employed in an effort to obtain blessing.

God did require fasting that would be accompanied by penitence and changed behavior. Those fasting would allow **the oppressed** to **go free** (v. 6) and care for the downtrodden (v. 7). These acts of repentance will result in messianic blessing. The **light** (a metaphor for the Messiah, cf. Is 9:2) will come as will their **recovery** (literally, "healing" referring to spiritual and physical restoration) (v. 8). The nation will experience **righteousness** and **the glory of the Lord**. Most importantly, **the Lord will answer** their prayers and **guide** them (vv. 9, 11). At that time, the nation will **rebuild the ancient ruins** of Israel (v. 12). Although it is certain that genuine repentance will always bring God's blessing, this passage is speaking of God's blessings in the end, in the messianic age.

58:13-14. The second way Israel practiced hypocrisy was in Sabbath observance. The Sabbath was not acceptable as long as the people observed it in a self-serving way and maintained oppressive labor practices. God called Israel to turn from hypocritical Sabbath practices to those that honor the Sabbath as a holy day resulting in enjoyment of God. Rather than legalistic Sabbath observance, true faith would bring God's messianic blessing—then Israel would truly honor the Sabbath. At that time God would provide for the nation. The phrase **ride on the heights of the earth** (v. 14) is an allusion to Dt 32:13 and refers to the provision of food. God will also **feed** them **with the heritage of Jacob** indicates that the land promised to Jacob will provide all the food the nation will need.

59:1-8. Besides hypocritical fasting and Sabbath observance, Israel is indicted for general hypocrisy. This section identifies Israel's true problem: disobedience. God is strong enough to deliver them, but the disobedience of the nation has alienated the people from God (vv. 1-2). Isaiah 59:3-7 describes the unjust practices of this "religious" people, encompassing both word and deed, as represented by the mention of the people's **hands** and **tongue[s]** (v. 3). The people's lack of concern for justice results in false witness as is commensurate for those who refuse to trust God. Self-interested logic permeates society as the people in power do whatever they must in order to ensure their own comfort and security. Their actions are rarely benevolent, nor do they have the capacity to be (vv. 5-6). Their activities result in injustice and a lack of peace. They desire only to preserve themselves through oppressive, selfish acts that disregard the justice of God (vv. 7-8).

The point of this section (58:1–59:8) has been to show the hypocritical sinfulness of Israel. It proves that they are too sinful to initiate their own redemption.

(2) Israel Confesses Its Own Sinfulness (59:9-15a)

59:9-11. The shift from the third person ("they"; 59:1-8) to the second person ("us"; 59:9-15) indicates that Israel is now speaking. The nation recognizes their sinful behavior (described in vv. 1-8) that has kept them from experiencing God's **light** of salvation (v. 9). Instead, the people fumble about aimlessly in the dark (v. 10) and make the inarticulate sounds of bears and doves (v. 11). The bear imagery is not used elsewhere in Scripture, but the image of the cooing, or mourning, dove is found in biblical laments (cf. Is 38:14; Ezk 7:16; Nah 2:7).

59:12-15a. Israel's people confess their sin and rebellion against God. Since this confession initiates eschatological redemption, these words will be offered by Israel at the end of days. The nation will confess that they have committed **transgressions** (meaning "rebellion" or "violation of rights"; cf. Gn 31:36; 50:17; 1Sm 24:11; 25:28), indicating they have rebelled against God and violated His right to their submissive behavior. They also recognized their **sins**, a word that means "to miss the mark" (Jdg 20:16) of God's righteous standard. They also know their **iniquities**, a word that refers to being twisted or bent and indicates that they had behaved perversely or crookedly. Israel's sins caused societal virtues such as **justice**, **righteousness**, **truth**, and **uprightness** to be absent (v. 14). As a result, if even one person repents and turns aside from evil, that person places himself in danger from the rest of corrupt society (v. 15a).

(3) God Initiates Israel's Redemption (59:15b-21)

59:15b-19. The corrupt situation will not stand because the Lord's displeasure will ultimately reverse it (vv. 15b-16). God was displeased that Israel's sin required a mediator but there was no one capable. Therefore God determined to bring Israel's salvation by His own strength (**His own arm**) (v. 16). God alone can initiate redemption for His people. The description of the body armor, helmet, and garments represents the girding up of God for battle against all that plagues Israel (v. 17). God **will repay . . . His adversaries** and punish **His enemies** (v. 18). This punishment extends beyond the sin of Israel as the mention of **coastlands** suggests. As a result of the Lord's coming, even the Gentile nations, from the west and east, will fear the name of the Lord (v. 19). God will come with an unstoppable ferocity that cannot be stopped.

59:20-21. God declares that He will be the **Redeemer** who **will come to Zion**. Therefore, those who **turn from transgression in Jacob** will experience God's salvation (v. 20). Paul the apostle quotes this verse in Rm 11:26, depicting the day when Israel turns to the Lord Jesus for deliverance prior to the second coming of Christ. When the entire nation repents, then all Israel will be saved (see comments on Zch 12:10; Mt 23:37-39; and Rm 11:26-27). At that time, God will enact the new covenant (cf. Jr 31:31-34) with Israel that will guarantee God's presence with the nation throughout her generations (Is 59:21). The permanence of the Spirit and the Word among the people speaks to the promise of ongoing faithfulness and of the removal of sin.

(4) God Will Redeem Israel for His Glory (60:1-22)

When Israel recognizes her own sinfulness, the nation will turn to the Lord in repentance (59:9-15a). At that time, the Lord will initiate Israel's final redemption (59:15b-21). What follows is the glory that God will share with Israel when He brings about Israel's redemption.

60:1-3. When God redeems Israel, He will bring His **light** (a metaphor for Messiah, cf. 9:2) to the nation in darkness. Zion will be so illumined that the **nations will come to your light** (v. 3). Not only will Israel know the Lord in the messianic kingdom, but so will the Gentile nations.

60:4-14. When God redeems Israel, He will bring the Gentile nations to His people. Zion will find itself in a privileged position as the powers of the world will bring Israel's children back to Zion along with the wealth of the nations (60:4-7). The Lord will use the wealth that the nations bring to establish God's millennial temple (vv. 6-7, 13; see comments under "A New Temple" introducing the comments on Ezk 40–43). Surrounding nations will bring precious gifts to Zion, including **gold and frankincense** (v. 6; this is not likely a prediction of the visit of the magi in Mt 2:1-12) because God **has glorified** His people (v. 9). Jerusalem will be a restored city as the nations will work to restore it and bring their wealth to it (vv. 10-11). This is not Israel's doing but a result of the Lord having had **compassion** on His people. Those nations that opposed Zion will have been judged and destroyed—they **will perish** and **be utterly ruined** (vv. 11-12; see comments on the judgment of the nations, Mt 25:31-46). God promises Israel the ultimate reversal. The sons of those who afflicted you will come bowing to you and recognize that it was the Lord who accomplished this. They will call Jerusalem **the city of the LORD** (v. 14).

60:15-22. When God redeems Israel, He will bring millennial blessings to the nation. The once **forsaken and hated** people and land of Israel will be a perpetual **joy from generation to generation** (v. 15). The hope of Zion does not come through the prerogative of the nations, but through the restoring presence of the **Redeemer, the Mighty One of Jacob** (v. 16). God will grant peace and prosperity to His people instead of warfare and suffering (vv. 17-20). He will give His people wealth (60:17), peace (60:18), God's light (vv. 19-20), and righteousness, even as He enlarges the nation (v. 21). The permanence of this peace and prosperity is secured through the continued righteousness of the people who are depicted as the special branch of God's hands planted to reveal God's splendor (vv. 20-21).

b. God's Messiah Delivers Israel (61:1–63:6)

The final unit of Isaiah, which is about God's deliverance in the end (chaps. 58–66), began by demonstrating that God's initiative will produce the end-of-days deliverance He will provide (58:1–60:22). Not only will He initiate but He will accomplish His purposes for Israel through His messianic King (61:1–63:6).

(1) The Messiah's Ministry to Israel (61:1-11)

61:1-3. As a whole, Is 61 describes the coming deliverance of God's people and the subsequent worship of God amongst the nations. This passage is the address of God's messianic Servant (42:1-9; 49:1-13; 50:4-11; 52:13–53:12) who proclaims His own role in God's redemption of Israel. Jesus began His ministry by quoting this passage to identify Himself as the Servant Messiah (cf. Lk 4:18-21, identifying Jesus of Nazareth as the passage's referent). This passage will be fulfilled by Jesus in His two advents. This is evident in that Jesus' quotations of these verses do not mention **the day of vengeance** (v. 2; Lk 4:18-21). Jesus inaugurated this messianic ministry but it will not be fulfilled in its entirety until His return. The passage addresses the release of Israel from captivity, not just from Babylon but from around the world (vv. 1-2). This will be possible because the Spirit of the **Lord** will anoint the Servant to make it happen. The word **anointed** is the same as the Hebrew word for "Messiah" and refers to the consecration of someone or something to a specialized task. Note that the triune God is hinted at in this verse (the **Spirit**, **The Lord God**, and the Servant [Me]). The Messianic Servant will comfort all the mourners of Zion (v. 3) by His restoration of Israel.

61:4-11. The Servant Messiah's ministry will also include the rebuilding of **the ancient ruins** of Israel, the elevation of Israel above the nations, and the renewal of Israel to her proper place as a nation of **priests** (cf. Ex 19:5) mediating the knowledge of God to the nations (Is 61:6; see Zch 8:23 and the comments there). Israel will receive a **double portion** of inheritance (v. 7) as the first born of the Lord (cf. Ex 4:22; Dt 21:17). This is fair and just since Israel has also received "double for all her sins" (Is 40:2). God will make **an everlasting covenant** (v. 8) with Israel, a reference to the new covenant (Jr 31:31-34). The reason for this turn of events rests in God's faithfulness to His covenant, which will bring blessing to God's people across their generations (vv. 8-9). The Lord's Servant will give praise to God for His luxurious **garments of salvation** and His **robe of righteousness** (v. 10). Endowed with these, the Servant will accomplish God's purposes for Israel and the world. Therefore, God **will cause righteousness and praise to spring up before all the nations** (v. 11).

(2) The Messiah's Restoration of Israel (62:1-12)

62:1-9. The deliverance of Israel by the Messiah sent by God continues. Not only will the Messiah minister to Israel (61:1-11) but He will also provide full restoration of Israel (62:1-12), emphasizing God's commitment to the vindication of Jerusalem. When Messiah Jesus returns to Israel, He will transform Jerusalem. He will change her from darkness to light so that **her salvation** will be **like a torch that is burning** (v. 1). From sin and humiliation, the Messiah will change Jerusalem to embody **righteousness** and **glory** (vv. 2-3). Other alterations will include changed names, from **Forsaken** and **Desolate** to **My delight is in her** and **Married** (v. 4). The Lord's delight in Jerusalem will be comparable to the love of a bridegroom for his bride (v. 5). Israel's depiction as the wife of the Lord does not imply that Israel and the Church (the Bride of Christ) are one and the same. This is merely a metaphor that depicts the covenantal relationship between God and Israel just as the metaphor applies to Christ and the Church. That is not to say that God is a bigamist, married to both Israel and the Church, just that the metaphor is used distinctively of both Israel and the Church. Ultimately, God will make all people, with all their distinct ethnicities, part of His family (note that God promises that one day even Egypt will be called His people, Is 19:25). At that time, God will not dissolve His special relationship with Israel, but will always keep Israel as a distinct and beloved people, in whom He delights (62:4-5). Though God's commitment to Jerusalem is sure, God's people must continue to pray for Him to fulfill these promises for Israel and make Jerusalem the **praise in the earth** (vv. 6-7). God's people today would do well to become the watchmen on the walls of Jerusalem, praying for the Lord to bring Israel to know their Messiah and fulfill all these good promises. God's promise to care for Jerusalem will be accomplished by God's might (**His right hand** and by **His strong arm**). He will provide for Israel and not give their produce to foreigners again (vv. 8-9).

62:10-12. The last section of this Song of Messiah's transformation of Israel is a call to respond. The faithful of the nations should first remove the obstacles to Israel's restoration (v. 10). This is a figurative depiction of the nations making it possible for Israel to return to their God. Some of these obstacles include the sad history of Christian anti-Semitism or the common Christian denial of Israel's distinctive place in the plan of God. Second, the faithful should proclaim the message of the Lord's salvation to Israel (v. 11). The reward noted could refer to a reward for Jerusalem's faithfulness, but more likely refers to the dispersed of Israel who will accompany the Lord back to Jerusalem—they are the Lord's reward. Third, the faithful are to remind Israel of their future destiny as **The holy people, the redeemed of the Lord**, and **a city not forsaken** (v. 12).

(3) The Messiah's Judgment of Edom (63:1-6)

63:1-6. The Messiah will deliver Israel, not only by restoration of the nation but by judgment of the enemies of Israel. The backdrop is the future tribulation, when Israel will flee to the wilderness to escape the attack of the future world ruler, also known as the Antichrist (see Ezk 20:34-36; Rv 12:6). Likely, the place in the wilderness is in **Edom** (modern Jordan) in the city of **Bozrah** (Petra; see Is 34:5-17 for evidence to support this). The nations will pursue Israel there leading to a bloody war (previously depicted in 34:1-7). God is once again depicted as a conquering hero covered in the blood of those He has trampled in the winepress of His wrath (63:1-3). Not only did Isaiah previously draw this picture in Is 34, but the book of Revelation draws it as well (cf. Rv 14:19-20; 19:13-15). These passages identify Jesus the Messiah as the One coming in judgment of the enemies of Israel. From the above passages, it appears that Jesus returns to Bozrah at the end of the tribulation to deliver Israel. Having defeated the nations that attacked Israel in the wilderness, the Messiah will then lead them to Jerusalem (Mc 2:12-13), where His feet will stand on the Mount of Olives, and deliver besieged Jerusalem (Zch 14:3-4). God has acted alone because no one else was willing to take up the cause of beleaguered Israel (Is 63:4-5). The destruction of the nations will come through the singular activity of the Son of God (vv. 5-6; cf. Ps 110:5-7).

c. God's Covenant Faithfulness Delivers Israel (63:7–66:24)

The final unit of Isaiah that describes God's deliverance in the end (58-66) begins by demonstrating that Israel's deliverance at the end of days would come as a result of God's initiative, not Israel's (58:1–60:22). The emphasis on the next part was on the way God would bring Israel deliverance in the end, specifically through His messianic King (61:1-63:6). Now in the third and last section, the prophetic message emphasizes the basis of God's final deliverance: God's covenant faithfulness.

(1) God's Faithfulness Remembered (63:7-14)

63:7-14. This section remembers the Lord's deeds on behalf of Israel in the past, in Egypt and the wilderness wanderings (vv. 7-8). It recalls God's participation with them in their suffering while they were slaves in Egypt. At that time, **the angel of His presence saved them** (v. 9; also see Ex 23:20-26 and comments there), likely a preincarnate appearance of the Messiah. In response, Israel rebelled in the wilderness (cf. Nm 20:10), grieving God's Spirit deeply (Ps 106:32-33) and causing Him to turn them over to their foes (v. 10; cf. Ps 106:40-41). The rebellion of Israel placed the nation in opposition to God. Yet the nation remembered the care and deliverance of God in the past, from the parting of the Red Sea (vv. 11-12) to the provision in the wilderness (v. 13) and ultimately to giving them rest in the promised land (v. 14). The recital of God's acts on behalf of the nation ends with the declaration that God has made a **glorious name** (v. 14).

(2) God's Forgiveness Requested (63:15–64:12)

63:15-19. In light of God's past faithfulness, the prophet pleads for God to take note of His people and act on their behalf again (v. 15) because the Lord was their **Father** and **Redeemer**. He questions God's purpose for making His people stubborn and disobedient (v. 17; cf. 6:9-10). God is indeed sovereign over hearts, and just as Pharaoh was both hardhearted toward God and also hardened by God, so Israel was as well (see comments on Ex 7:3). Yet God is never held culpable for Israel's rebellion, even though He ordained and governed it—one of the most profound mysteries in all of Scripture. Israel's sin would make their control over God's sanctuary only short-lived (v. 18). While Israel has been God's possession, God occasionally treated Israel as if it were simply another Gentile nation because of its sin (v. 19). This final statement appears to continue the tone of the questioning in v. 17 as it seems that God has abandoned His people to ruin while the nations prosper.

64:1-12. The prophet calls God to come down as He did in the past (vv. 1-4). Just as God revealed Himself on Mount Sinai (v. 3; Ex 19:16-18) and delivered Israel and made His name known in the days of Deborah (Jdg 4:15) and Gideon (Jdg 7:20-21), Isaiah pleads for God to act again. God always has acted on behalf of those who wait for the Lord and obey Him with a joyful heart, whereas those who sin against the Lord have no reason to believe that God will save them (vv. 4-5). Yet the prophet acknowledges that God hides His face from those who refuse to walk in His way or call on His name (v. 7). The fundamental dynamic expressed here reflects the need for God's people to trust in Him rather than attempt to secure their own future when doing so leads them to ignore God's laws.

Despite their shortcomings and rebellion, God is called upon to show mercy upon those whom He has created by forgetting (i.e., forgiving) their sins (vv. 8-9). The plea is based on God's covenant faithfulness, because Israel is His **people**. When the Babylonians conquer, they will bring desolation and destruction on Israel, Jerusalem, and the temple (the **holy and beautiful house**; vv. 10-11). This is written in a "prophetic perfect," describing a future event that is so certain it is described by the prophet as a completed action. The chapter ends on a note of confusion as God is asked whether or not He will act. Have the sins of the people alienated them from God to the point of destruction? Will God not act on behalf of that which He has formed (vv. 8, 12)?

(3) God's Deliverance Described (65:1-25)

65:1-7. God responds to the prophet's plea by explaining that He would judge Israel's idolaters. The passage begins with a declaration that God always was available to the nation of Israel (v. 1). He has made Himself known to them even though the nation has rejected Him through their idolatry, which included their obstinacy, false worship, unclean practices, and hubris (vv. 2-5). Their unfaithful deeds cannot go unpunished, but must be repaid (vv. 6-7).

65:8-10. Despite the coming judgment of the Lord, God will not destroy His people completely—a remnant will be saved. God always works this way, preserving Israel for the remnant in the past (1Kg 19:18) and in the present Church (Rm 11:1-6; see the comments there). Instead, God, who preserved the faithful remnant in Isaiah's day (**My servants**) also promises **not to destroy all of them** (the as-yet unbelieving majority; vv. 8-9). Similarly, the apostle Paul wrote that God had preserved a remnant in his day, similar to Isaiah's, but that eventually "all Israel will be saved" (see the comments on Rm 11:1-6, 25-28). God's promise of preservation extends to the land of Israel. **Sharon** (v. 10) refers to a plain along the Mediterranean coast between Joppa in the north and Carmel in the south, while the **valley of Achor**, which may be translated "Valley of Trouble," was the site of Achan's execution (Jos 7) near Jericho in the east. The locations of **Sharon** and the **valley of Achor** in the west and the east of the nation respectively suggest that the whole nation is in view. The contrast between **Sharon**, which was a fertile area, and the **valley of Achor**, which was barren, may also suggest that regardless of the state of the land previously, God will transform it so that life can thrive there.

65:11-16. God assures that He will both judge and deliver Israel. Those who have rejected the Lord (vv. 11-12) form a sharp contrast to "My people who seek Me" and dwell in Sharon and the valley of Achor in v. 10. Those who neglect the Lord and worship other gods will be destroyed. The reason for their destruction is directly related to their disobedience to the Lord. They have not responded to God's call or obeyed His word but have chosen to live according to their own wisdom and to displease God. This judgment will take place at the end of days. Jeremiah calls this "the time of Jacob's distress" (Jr 30:7), and Ezekiel describes it as the time when God will enter into judgment with Israel and make the nation pass "under the rod" (Ezk 20:33-38). Zechariah depicts this time as the time of purging for Israel, when the remnant of Israel is refined and will call on the name of the Lord (Zch 13:8-9).

In contrast to those who will be judged, the Lord proclaims that His servants, or those loyal to Him, will have all that they need to sustain themselves (v. 13). They will worship the Lord and He will give them a special name (vv. 14-15). In contrast, those who disobey the Lord will go without sustenance. Instead of worship, those who reject God will be in anguish. Their situation will be so desperate that they will be the perfect picture of what it means to be cursed (v. 15). In the messianic kingdom, the remnant will be redeemed. At that time, every good thing in the land will be recognized as God's work. No other god will be addressed or invoked, and God will forgive the violations of the past (v. 16).

(4) God's Glory Descends (65:17–66:24)

The final section of the book depicts the end of days when God recreates the world as "new heavens and a new earth" (65:17). These descriptions frequently fuse together the earthly millennium, the literal thousand-year reign of Christ on the earth following His second coming (see the comments on Rv 20:1-6), and the eternal state ("a new heaven and a new earth"; see the comments on Rv 21:1–22:9). Also, the depictions of the descent of God's glory combine the descent of renewal for the redeemed versus the descent of judgment for the wicked.

65:17-25. At the outset, *God's glory descends with a new creation for His people,* a reference to what He does at the conclusion of the millennial kingdom and the start of the eternal state. God announces that there will be a final judgment that will destroy all that was and remake the heavens and the earth into a place of peace, harmony, and order. Jerusalem will be remade so that it becomes God's delight (vv. 19-20). Although it is possible for people to **die** in the messianic age (the millennial kingdom), people will live much longer and premature death will be banished (v. 20). This is possible because at the return of Jesus the Messiah, when He judges the nations, compared to separating sheep and goats, the redeemed nations will enter the kingdom without yet having been glorified (Mt 25:34). In the same way, when Israel calls for the Lord Jesus to save them at the end of the future tribulation, they will be redeemed and enter the kingdom without glorified or resurrected bodies (cf. Zch 12:10; Rm 11:25-27). Thus, these peoples will all be able to reproduce and, as Is 65:20 indicates, even **die**. Even so, they will live much longer in kingdom conditions.

At that time, the land will be secure from enemies, free from fears of having **another inhabit** or bearing **children for calamity** (vv. 21-23). The people will experience the closeness of God who **will answer** and **will hear** (v. 24), and all creation will exhibit an unprecedented peace, free from **evil or harm** (v. 25). Even the animal kingdom will change, removing the curse on it, so that predators will become herbivores. One aspect of the animal world will remain—serpents will still eat **dust**. This will be a perpetual reminder of the curse on the serpent (Gn 3:14), fulfilling the promise that the serpent would be "more cursed" than the rest of the animal kingdom. The picture of the new creation is a powerful statement of the restoration of God's order. In the first creation, God made an idyllic environment in which the entire world worked together to achieve harmony in accordance with God's wisdom and will. The second creation represents a return to this state that will allow all God's people to glorify Him forever.

66:1-6. *God's glory will also descend with judgment for the wicked.* This section begins with two rhetorical questions designed to emphasize God's position above humanity. The seeming critique of temple-building (i.e., **a house you could build for Me**) should not be taken as a prohibition against building a holy temple. Instead, God is calling humanity to remember that His favor cannot be obtained through the construction of a house for the Lord. God is the maker of the heavens and the earth, so a temple made with human hands will not impress Him. Rather, God will show His favor to the one who recognizes God's sovereignty over the heavens and the earth and **is humble and contrite of spirit, and who trembles at** God's **word** (v. 2). Using slightly different Hebrew words, Isaiah has previously made this point (57:15). Religious ritual that is not matched by respect for life and for the law of God will bring about God's punishment (vv. 3-4). In fact, the offerings of those who rebel against God will make Him view them as if they were unacceptable and unclean (v. 3). Even a lamb sacrifice will be **like the one who breaks a dog's neck**. Thus, a clean sacrifice (lamb) will be viewed as unclean (dog). Even the ritual acts that were in alignment with God's requirements were tainted and viewed as an affront by God because of the people's disobedience.

It is not clear when the judgment described here will take place. It likely is describing the final judgment before the "great white throne" (Rv 20:11). We conclude this because Scripture indicates that redeemed but unglorified people will enter the millennium. They will be able to reproduce and, therefore, their offspring will also need to trust in Jesus the Messiah. Those who do not become genuine followers of Messiah Jesus will be those who will not offer acceptable sacrifices. They will face the white throne judgment after the millennial kingdom, as described in Rv 20:11-15.

The critique against dichotomous practice is reaffirmed (Is 66:5) with the condemnation of exclusionary practices performed while proclaiming allegiance to the Lord. The declaration of those who exclude the faithful (v. 5b) refers to some in the community who were neglecting the needs of others. Instead of helping, they simply continued to worship the Lord, telling those in need to wait for God's glorious return in order to find their joy. God will not stand by, however, and allow displeasing practices to infect His temple. His glory will descend and He will judge those who oppose Him even though they hide in His temple (v. 6).

66:7-13. *God's glory will descend with a rebirth for Zion.* The metaphor used in v. 7 in which a birth occurs with no pain symbolizes the coming restoration of Jerusalem that will require no effort by the people (v. 8). Interestingly, the Targum (ancient rabbinic paraphrase) renders the final line of this verse as "her king will be revealed," which suggests a messianic reading referring to what happens immediately following the second coming of Christ. The series of rhetorical questions in vv. 8-9 underscore the uniqueness of the events that will occur, so that it is clear that only God could bring them (v. 8) and that God is certain to restore Zion (v. 9). Moreover, those who love Jerusalem are called to rejoice with the city (v. 10a). Jerusalem's restoration and prosperity will benefit those who have loved the city and mourned her destruction (vv. 10b-12). God's consolation of Jerusalem will be like that of a mother providing comfort for a child (vv. 12b-13). This metaphor emphasizes God's great compassion and connection to His people.

66:14-18. *God's glory descends with wrath for the wicked,* at the second coming of Jesus the Messiah (see Rv 19:11-21 and the comments there). In contrast to God's joy giving acts of consolation, **His anger** and **rebuke** will descend **with flames of fire** . . . to **execute judgment** (vv. 15-16). The reasons for God's wrath were the idolatry of the wicked, special purification rituals, eating forbidden meat and **detestable things** (v. 17). The disobedient will see God's glory descend in judgment as God gathers all nations to Jerusalem (v. 18).

66:19-23. *God's glory will also descend with compassion for the nations.* God proclaims that He will send a sign or act mightily against the nations (cf. Ps 78:43; Jr 32:20) but will also show compassion to them. The sign will evidently devastate but not destroy the nations as the reference to **survivors** (v. 19) suggests. Some of the survivors will be sent to the nations to proclaim the glory of God and to bring back Israelites from among the nations to serve the Lord as priests and Levites in the millennial temple (vv. 20-21; see the discussion under "A New Temple" that introduces the comments on Ezk 40–43). It is sometimes argued that believing Gentiles, along with believing Jews, comprise the eschatological "new Israel" based on vv. 19-21. It is maintained that Gentiles (vv. 19-20) are drafted by God to be **priests** and **Levites** (v. 21), indicating that no ethnic distinctions persist in the kingdom.

Some theologians view this as the Church Age. Such a view cancels out the prominent place of Israel in the future kingdom. Notice that when God says, **I will also take some of them for priests and for Levites** (v. 21), the closest antecedent for **them** is not the Gentiles of vv. 19-20a, but **the sons of Israel** in v. 20b. It is an unwarranted leap to say that Gentiles become Jews or part of the "new Israel" (**priests** and **Levites**), and that this eliminates ethnic distinctions in some sort of an amalgamated "new Israel."

In the end, the nations will be instruments used to accomplish the restoration God will oversee for Israel and the world. This restoration will be permanent (vv. 22-23). As the **new heavens and the new earth** will last forever, so the people and name of Israel will endure. More importantly, the whole world will worship God forever—**all mankind will come to bow down before Me** (v. 23).

66:24. *Finally, God's glory will descend with eternal judgment for the rebellious.* The oracles of the second half of Isaiah each conclude with a warning of judgment (48:22; 57:21; 66:24). In the previous two major sections of Isaiah (chaps. 40–48, deliverance from Babylon; chaps. 49–57, deliverance from sin), a virtually identical phrase ("there is no peace . . . for the wicked") concluded each (48:22; 57:21).

Here an even stronger statement, warning about eternal judgment for the rebellious, functions as a literary marker closing both this section (on deliverance in the end, chaps. 58–66) and the entire book. The repulsive sight of those whom the Lord has defeated will be an ever-present reminder to all humanity that the Lord is not to be mocked or opposed. This reference to the lake of fire, where the **fire will not be quenched** and the unredeemed wicked will suffer eternally, is not merely an OT concept. In fact, Jesus the Messiah repeated this phrase from Isaiah (**their worm will not die and their fire will not be quenched**) as a warning of eternal judgment (cf. Mk 9:43-48; Jesus also taught elsewhere about eternal suffering separated from God; cf. Mt 13:41-43; 25:31-46; Lk 16:24; Rv 20:15).

The book of Isaiah records the message of the Holy One of Israel to Israel and Judah. It calls the people to be faithful to the Lord whose arm controls the course of world events. It reveals that the exile of Israel and Judah is not a permanent removal from the promised land, but a temporary situation from which God will deliver those who trust in the Lord. The contrast between those who trust the Lord and those who do not underscores the prophet's basic message: trusting the Lord frees humanity from oppressive, selfish, destructive behavior and offers resources to patiently wait for the coming righteousness and justice of God. It also frees humanity from the judgment of God. The Lord will showcase His glory through Israel, the Messiah-King He will send, and the final judgment. As Israel fulfills its destiny as the witness to God's way, the nations will turn and glorify God.

Finally, all creation will be cleansed, sin will be taken away, and God's order will be restored as all that God has created finally recognizes that He is the Holy One of Israel.

BIBLIOGRAPHY

Bultema, Harry. *Commentary on Isaiah.* Translated by Cornelius Lambregtse. Grand Rapids, MI: Kregel, 1981.

Childs, Brevard S. *Isaiah: A Commentary.* Louisville: Westminster John Knox, 2001.

Deilitzsch, Franz. *Isaiah* in *Keil and Deilitzsch Commentary on the Old Testament,* vol. 7. Translated by James Martin. Grand Rapids, MI: Eerdmans, 1980 Reprint.

Goldingay, John. *Isaiah.* New International Bible Commentary. Peabody, MA: Hendrickson, 2001.

———. *The Message of Isaiah 40–55: A Literary-Theological Commentary.* New York: T&T Clark, 2005.

Grogan, G. W. "Isaiah." *Isaiah–Ezekiel.* Vol. 6 of *The Expositor's Bible Commentary.* Edited by Frank E. Gaebelein. Grand Rapids, MI: Zondervan, 1986.

Hindson, Edward E. *Isaiah's Immanuel: A Sign of His Times or the Sign of the Ages.* Grand Rapids, MI: Baker, 1979.

Lindsey, F. Duane. *The Servant Songs.* Chicago: Moody, 1985.

Martin, Alfred, and John Martin. *Isaiah: The Glory of the Messiah.* Chicago: Moody, 1983.

Motyer, J. A. *The Prophecy of Isaiah.* Downers Grove, IL: InterVarsity, 1993.

Oswalt, John N. *The Book of Isaiah, Chapters 1–39.* Grand Rapids, MI: Eerdmans, 1986.

———. *The Book of Isaiah, Chapters 40–66.* Grand Rapids, MI: Eerdmans, 1998.

Rydelnik, Michael. *The Messianic Hope: Is the Hebrew Bible Really Messianic?* Nashville: Broadman & Holman, 2010.

Smith, Gary V. *Isaiah 1–39.* Vol. 15a of *The New American Commentary.* Nashville: Broadman & Holman, 2007.

———. *The New American Commentary: Isaiah 40–66,* Vol. 15b. Nashville: Broadman & Holman, 2009.

Wolf, Herbert M. *Interpreting Isaiah: The Suffering and Glory of the Messiah.* Grand Rapids, MI: Zondervan, 1985.

Young, Edward J. *The Book of Isaiah,* 3 Vols, Grand Rapids, MI: Eerdmans, 1965–1972.

● ● ● ●

JEREMIAH

CHARLES DYER WITH EVA RYDELNIK

INTRODUCTION

Author. Jeremiah the prophet was, as early tradition maintains, the author of this book. It is an extensive collection of the prophet's oracles opening with "The words of Jeremiah" (1:1) and stating, just before the historical epilogue of the book, "Thus far are the words of Jeremiah" (51:64). Thus, the book contains the words Jeremiah received from the Lord and includes the writings of Baruch ben Neriah, Jeremiah's companion and scribe (36:4), to whom the prophet dictated some of his messages (36:32).

Perhaps Jeremiah, at different stages of his ministry, collected his prophecies and rearranged them in a definite pattern (cf. 25:13; 30:2; 36:2, 32). Maybe he completed the final form after he was taken hostage to Egypt (cf. 51:64), or possibly Baruch could have collected and organized Jeremiah's writings, adding chap. 52 (from 2Kg 24:18–25:30) after Jeremiah's death.

The text clearly states the book is "The words of Jeremiah," and it is by and about "Jeremiah the son of Hilkiah" (Jr 1:1). He was the foremost prophet of Judah during the dark days just prior to the Babylonian destruction and captivity. His heart was broken over Jerusalem's sin and the judgment they had brought upon themselves, and his great sorrow earned him the title "the weeping prophet" (9:1). His book is the most autobiographical and spiritually transparent of the prophetic writings. Despite his circumstances and sorrow, Jeremiah had unwavering confidence in God's faithfulness to His people (3:23).

Jeremiah is a common name, found nine times in the OT (eg., 2Kg 23:31; 24:18; 1Ch 5:23; 12:4, 10, 13; Neh 10:2; 12:1; Jr 35:3); but this prophet is the most significant person of that name. The meaning of the name is possibly uncertain, perhaps: "the Lord throws" in the sense of laying a foundation; or "The Lord establishes."

Jeremiah was from a priestly family, as were Moses (Ex 6:16-20), Ezekiel (Ezk 1:3), and Zechariah (Zch 1:1). Anathoth, a small village about three miles northeast of Jerusalem, was his hometown, and his father was Hilkiah, a Levite (Jr 1:1; Jos 21:15-19; 1Kg 2:26). Hilkiah was likely a descendant of Abiathar, the sole survivor of the priests of Nob (1Sm 22:20), who later was exiled by Solomon to Anathoth (1Kg 2:26). His father was probably not the same Hilkiah who discovered the law in the temple during the reign of Josiah (cf. 2Kg 22:3-14), since he was not living in Jerusalem, and because this key event is not mentioned in relation to him.

Although from a priestly family, Jeremiah does not seem to have served as a priest. But he was called to be a prophet when he was "a youth" or a young man, probably under 25, calculated from the time he began his ministry (Jr 1:6-2). The Lord commanded him not to marry, as an object lesson to the nation of the impending disaster (16:1-2). His ministry extended from the 13th year of the reign of Josiah (1:2) to the reign of Zedekiah, "until the exile" (1:3). Thus he prophesied from about 627 BC till at least 582 BC, after the fall of Jerusalem. He continued to minister to the survivors in Jerusalem and in Egypt, where he was taken against his wishes, after Gedaliah's murder (41:2). He wrote his final prophecies in Egypt (chaps. 43–44), and according to tradition he died there by stoning.

Throughout his ministry, Jeremiah was hated, persecuted, and imprisoned for his message. He declared Jerusalem would fall to the Babylonians, as a judgment from the Lord and advised surrender to Nebuchadnezzar (18:18; 37:15; 38; 40:1). After the fall of Jerusalem, he delivered God's message for the remnant to stay in Judah and not go to Egypt, but he was ridiculed and ignored. Jeremiah was a man of outstanding courage, who boldly and unwaveringly proclaimed the Lord's message despite almost total national opposition.

Date. Jeremiah began to prophecy during the 13th year of Josiah in 627 BC (1:2) and continued past the fall of Jerusalem in 582 BC. Thus, like Moses, he prophesied 40 years. He was a contemporary of Zephaniah, Habakkuk, Daniel, and Ezekiel. There were three phases of his prophetic ministry: (1) while Judah was under the threat of Assyria and Egypt, 627–605 BC; (2) while Babylon was threatening and laying siege to Judah, including the fall of Jerusalem, 605–586 BC; (3) while staying with the survivors in Jerusalem until the assassination of Gedaliah, and then forced to go with the exiles to Egypt, where he died 585–580(?) BC.

Recipients. During Jeremiah's ministry his primary audience was Judah and Jerusalem. He spoke to the population in general (2:2; 3:17; 7:2; 18:11); and also directly addressed Judah's kings (13:18; 21:3, 11; 22:1-2, 11, 18, 24); her priests (20:3-6); and her prophets (23:9; 28:15). In addition, Jeremiah served as God's messenger to those nations surrounding Judah responsible for persecuting her (chaps. 46–51). The book in its final form, as gathered by Baruch, addressed the faithful remnant of Israel in captivity. However, the writer of Scripture knew the message was profitable for all who read it (2Tm 3:16).

Purpose and Themes. The purpose of Jeremiah is to encourage repentance and faith by revealing the Lord's faithfulness to His promises both to discipline and restore Israel. Judgment, based on the holiness of the Lord, is one of the pervading themes of the book, but a parallel theme is the call to repentance and restoration (Jr 7:1-11, 23; 9:12-16, 23-24; 19:1-4) .

The promise of restoration goes beyond the immediate return from Babylon after the 70-year captivity (29:10). The phrase "days are coming" (see comments on 16:14-15 and 31:27-40) looks forward to the reign of Messiah, the Righteous Branch, on the earth in the millennial kingdom (23:3-6; 30:1-9; 33:14-15).

An outstanding emphasis in Jeremiah's ministry is the priority of a right relationship with the Lord, in contrast to external religious practices (4:4; 7:21-26; 11:1-13). The people of Jerusalem were outwardly religious, but they were following false prophets, not the Word of the Lord (7:28; 14:13-16). It was essential to have a circumcised heart that promoted genuine worship and obedience, in addition to physical circumcision, and other outward practices of obedience (9:23-26).

In addition to the holiness and righteousness of God as seen in His judgments, Jeremiah presented the Lord as: Creator (5:22; 10:12-16; 27:5; 31:35-37; 32:17; 51:15-19); the all powerful LORD of hosts (9:7; 10:6; 27:5; 31:35; 32:17, 27); everywhere present (23:23-24); Savior and Redeemer (3:23; 14:8; 31:11; 50:34), and loving and compassionate (12:15; 30:18; 31:3, 13). The Lord will always be faithful to His covenant with Israel, His chosen people, who are His inheritance (10:16; 12:14-15; 31:35-37; 33:14-21; 51:5). God is the LORD the God of Israel (11:3; 19:3; 24:5) and of the nations (5:15; 10:6-7; 18:7-10; 25:17-28; chaps. 46–51).

Jeremiah introduced the new covenant in his "Book of Consolation" (chaps. 30–33), using the formulaic expression "days are coming" and showing his readers the future. These chapters portray the Messianic restoration of Israel and Judah (chap. 30). They present the future change in God's relationship with His people: It will not be on the basis of the Sinai/Mosaic covenant but instead a new covenant inaugurated by the Messiah (31:31-34; Lk 22:20).

Although Messianic prophecy is not as prominent in Jeremiah as it is in Isaiah, Daniel, or Zechariah, the Messianic hope is essential in Jeremiah. He described events that will occur "in those days": (1) Jerusalem will be called "The Throne of the Lord" (Jr 3:14-17) and the Lord's presence there will replace that of the ark of the covenant; (2) the righteous Branch of David (23:1-5; 33:15) "shall reign as king . . . and do justice and righteousness in the land"; (3) the deity of the Messiah is seen in 23:6 because "He will be called 'The LORD our righteousness'"; (4) He will bring in the new covenant (31:31-34), which will fulfill God's covenant with Abraham (Gn 12:1-3; 17:1-8), Moses and Israel (Dt 28-30), and David (2Sm 7:1-17).

Jeremiah has been an accepted book of the canon, first in the Jewish Scriptures before the advent of the Messiah Jesus, then in the complete Scriptures of the OT and NT.

The Hebrew canon is divided into three main sections: Law (***Torah***), Prophets (***Nevi'im***), and Writings (***Ketuvim***). An acronym formed from the first Hebrew letter of each section results in the Hebrew word for the OT: the *Tanakh, (TaNaK)*. The Prophets are divided into the Former Prophets (Joshua, Judges, Samuel, Kings) and the Latter Prophets (Major and Minor Prophets).

In many ancient Hebrew manuscripts, as noted in the Talmud (*Baba Bathra* 14b), Jeremiah is the first book of the Major Prophets, so the Hebrew order is Jeremiah, Ezekiel and Isaiah. The location of Jeremiah in the Hebrew canon explains Matthew's phrase, "that which was spoken through Jeremiah the prophet was fulfilled" (Mt 27:9), when the verse quoted is from Zechariah, not Jeremiah. As the first book of the Major Prophets, Jeremiah could be used to represent all of the prophets. Using the first book of a section to represent all the books of that section was a common Jewish practice. Matthew was using this method of taking the first book of a section, Jeremiah in the Prophets, to identify the whole group of prophets and quoting Zechariah. A paraphrase of Mt 27:9 would be, "as it was spoken by the prophets." In addition, this is what Jesus did when He used the word "Psalms" to represent the entire section of the Writings (Lk 24:44), because Psalms is the first book of the Writings. There Jesus was saying that the whole *Tanakh*, Law, Prophets, and Psalms (Writings), spoke of Him (Lk 24:44-46). English and Greek versions of the OT, as well as contemporary Jewish Bibles, Tanakh (JPS), place Jeremiah after Isaiah and before Lamentations and Ezekiel.

Unlike Ezekiel or Isaiah, whose prophecies are chronological, Jeremiah's messages are not chronological, but are arranged more by emphasis, developing the theme of God's judgment. The judgment on Judah is the theme of chaps. 2–45; the judgment on the Gentile nations is the theme of chaps. 46–51. The book ends with a supplement, not written by Jeremiah, almost identical to 2Kg 24:18–25:30, recording events at the end of the exile. Jehoiachin's release foreshadowed God's promises of restoration and blessing for Israel. The promised Redeemer had not yet come, but His coming was certain.

The book includes narrative, poetry, sermons, addresses, and parables. Object lessons are a major teaching tool of Jeremiah: the linen belt (chap. 13); the potter's clay (chap. 18); the baskets of figs (chap. 24); the yoke (chap. 27); and the large stones in the Egyptian delta city of Tahpanhes (chap. 43). Jeremiah's life itself was used by the Lord as a daily illustration to Judah (13:1-14; 14:1-9; 16:1-9; 18:1-8; 19:1-13; 24:1-10; 27:1-11; 32:6-15; 43:8-13).

Background. During the years of Jeremiah's ministry, Judah was caught in a three-cornered international crisis as Assyria, Egypt, and Babylon struggled for world dominion. These historical events formed the backdrop to Judah's situation and Jeremiah's messages.

Internally, Judah experienced her final spiritual renewal in Josiah's reign (622 BC; 2Kg 22:3–23:25). Prompted by the discovery of a copy of the Mosaic law in the temple in his 18th year as king, Josiah worked to rid the nation of the idolatry that had taken root during the 55-year reign of wicked King Manasseh (2Kg 21:1-9). Josiah succeeded in removing the outward forms of idolatry, but his efforts did not reach the hearts of his people. After Josiah's untimely death, Judah returned to idolatry.

Internationally, the Assyrian Empire had taken the northern kingdom of Israel captive in 721 BC (2Kg 17) and had dominated the ancient Near East for centuries. At the outset of Jeremiah's ministry, it was on the brink of collapse. Babylon, a new force in the region, had destroyed the Assyrian capital city, Nineveh, in 612 BC. A realignment of power was on the horizon.

Egypt, which had long been in decline, now saw an opportunity for expansion in Assyria's weakness. If Assyria could be kept as a buffer state to halt Babylon's advances, Egypt hoped to reclaim her former kingdom, including Judah. So Egypt allied with Assyria against Babylon, expecting to dominate a weakened Assyria and block Babylon's advances.

King Josiah wanted to stop the alignment of Egypt and Assyria, seeing that allegiance as a threat to Judah. A decisive battle took place on the plain of Megiddo between Egypt and Judah, where Josiah was killed and Judah was defeated (2Ch 35:20-24). Meanwhile, Babylon was growing stronger and Assyria ceased to be a major empire.

Egypt assumed control of the area after Judah's defeat. Pharaoh Neco deposed King Jehoahaz, (Josiah's son) then plundered the treasuries of Judah and appointed Jehoiakim, another son of Josiah, as Egypt's vassal king (2Kg 23:34-35).

Babylon and Egypt wrestled for power, but Babylon's defeat of Egypt at Carchemish (605 BC; Jr 46:2) signaled the end of Egyptian military supremacy in the region. Jehoiakim became a vassal king under Babylon as Nebuchadnezzar solidified his rule in the area by appointing kings and taking hostages to assure continued loyalty. At this time, Nebuchadnezzar took Daniel and the other select young men captive (Dn 1:1-6). Judah remained a vassal state of Babylon until 605 BC, when Nebuchadnezzar made another advance through Judah, engaged Egypt in battle, but was defeated by Egypt.

The World of Jeremiah and Ezekiel

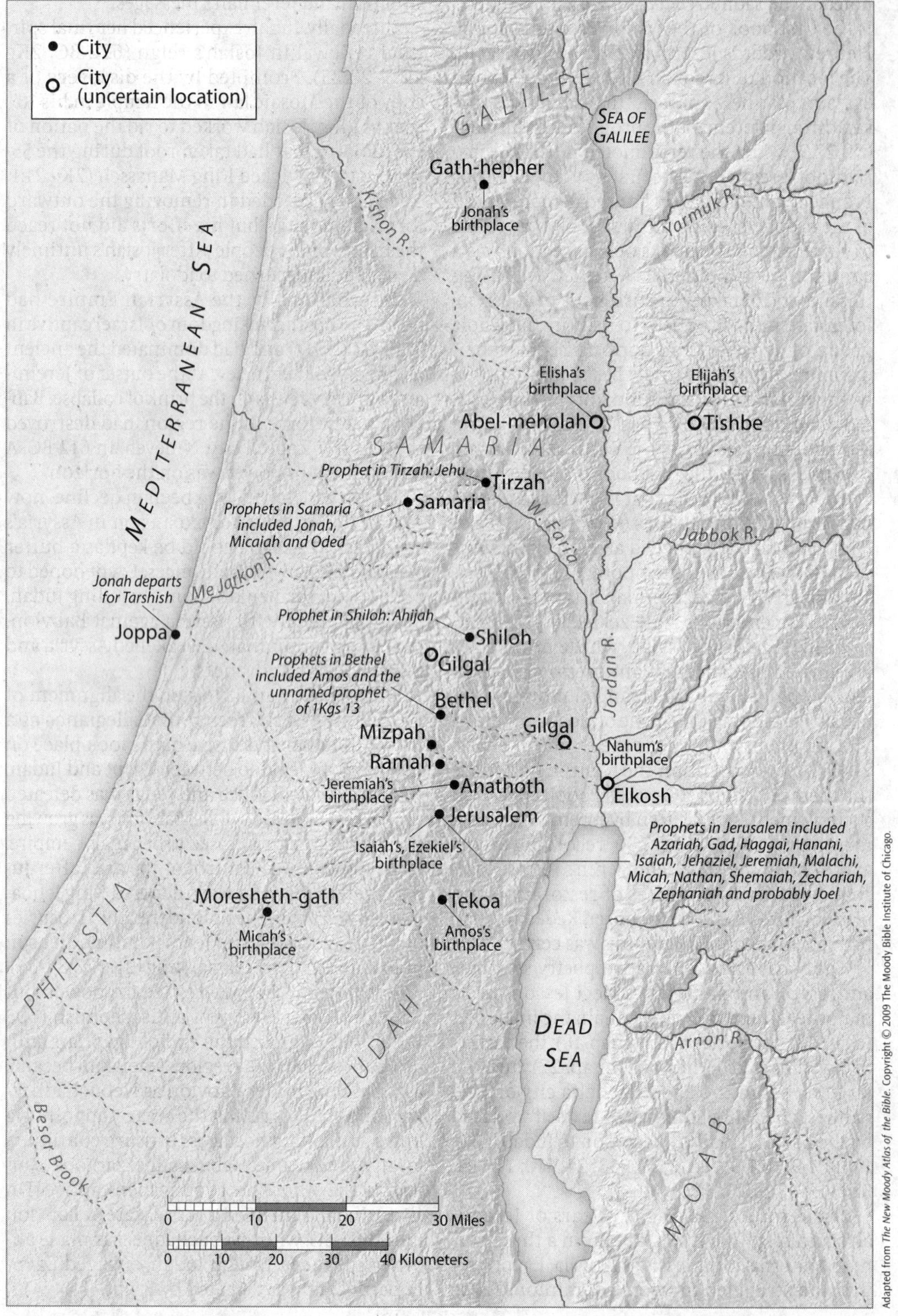

Thinking the Egyptian-Babylonian balance of power was shifting, Jehoiakim switched allegiance back to support Egypt (cf. 2Kg 24:1). This was a disastrous decision. By 597 BC Jerusalem was under Babylonian attack for her rebellion. Jehoiakim died during the Babylonian assault, and Jehoiachin, his son, became king.

Nebuchadnezzar looted the city and took the chief individuals captive. After a three-month reign, Jehoiachin was deported to Babylon along with 10,000 leaders, skilled laborers, and soldiers (cf. 2Kg 24:12-16). This was probably when the prophet Ezekiel was taken to Babylon, where five years later he began his prophetic ministry.

Zedekiah was placed on the throne by Nebuchadnezzar as Judah's vassal king. His 11-year reign was marred by spiritual decline and political instability (2Kg 23:26). With the enthronement of Pharaoh Hophra in Egypt (588 BC) Judah was once again enticed to revolt against Babylon (2Kg 24:1-4). This was a fatal mistake.

Nebuchadnezzar determined to make an example of Jerusalem to show the awful consequences of rebelling against Babylon. Nebuchadnezzar's response was swift and brutal. The army of Babylon surrounded Jerusalem and began a long siege (2Kg 24:20–25:1; Jr 52:3-4). From 588 to 586 BC Babylon's army ground away at Jerusalem's defenses (2Kg 25). Quickly Egypt, Judah's ally, was defeated and Judah was alone in her defense. One by one, the cities of Judah were crushed (Jr 34:6-7) until only Jerusalem remained before the mighty Babylonian war machine.

As the army of Jerusalem fought to defend her walls and gates against the sword, inside the city was swept with disease and famine (14:12) so severe that mothers ate their own children (19:9; Lm 2:20; 4:10). Idolatry flourished as people cried out to any and every god for deliverance (7:30; 10:1-16), but they refused to turn to listen to Jeremiah and his message from the Lord God. Paranoia gripped the people until they were willing to kill God's prophet as a traitor and spy just because he spoke the truth (37–38).

The 30-month siege ended in August 586 BC when the walls were breached (2Kg 25:2-4) and on August 14, 586 BC the destruction of the city began (2Kg 25:8-10). The temple, the king's palace, and all other major buildings in Jerusalem were burned and the walls of the city torn down (Jr 52:13). The majority of the survivors of the siege were carried into Babylon for the 70-year exile (2Ch 36:21; Jr 25:11; 29:10; 39:9). Jeremiah was an eyewitness to all of these tragic events (39:1-14; 52:12-14).

The main link between Jeremiah and the NT is the new covenant (31:31-34; Lk 22:20; 1Co 11:25; 2Co 3:6; Heb 8:8-12; 10:16-17). However, the NT alludes to Jeremiah dozens of times with explicit and implicit references to his prophecy, e.g., Mt 2:17-18 (Jr 31:15); Mt 21:13, Mk 11:17, Lk 19:4 (Jr 7:11); Rm 11:27 (Jr 31:33); Heb 8:8-13 (Jr 31:31-34).

The Septuagint (LXX) is the ancient Greek translation of the Jewish Scriptures, made in Alexandria, Egypt by a team (according to tradition) of 70 rabbis in the intertestamental period (third and second centuries BC). It was translated for the large Hellenistic Jewish community that spoke Greek, not Hebrew.

Jeremiah, of all the OT canon, shows the most striking divergences between the Greek LXX and the Hebrew Masoretic Text (MT). The LXX of Jeremiah is about one-eighth shorter than the MT of Jeremiah (about 2,700 words), and the chapters in the LXX are in a different sequence. Discoveries at Qumran among the Dead Sea Scrolls (DSS) have revealed manuscript fragments from both the proto-masoretic text and the Hebrew text that lay behind the LXX.

According to Gleason Archer, the divergent traditions stem from the development of the book of Jeremiah. He proposes (and the book of Jeremiah itself seems to indicate) that scrolls of Jeremiah's writings were circulated during the time of the prophet's ministry (36:32). Furthermore, Jeremiah dictated to Baruch, his scribe (36:4), all the words of the scroll Jekoiakim had burned and added "many similar words" (36:32). It is reasonable to assume that, to this earlier composition, Jeremiah continued to add the messages given him by the Lord during the reign of Zedekiah and after the fall of Jerusalem. Thus, it is likely that the prophet himself composed an earlier, shorter, edition of his own book. This version was available in the prophet's own lifetime and likely circulated in Egypt where he was living after the fall of Jerusalem. This could be the basis of the LXX translation.

After Jeremiah's death, it appears Baruch gathered and edited Jeremiah's work and made a more comprehensive collection of the prophet's writings. He rearranged the material in the current order and added the text of 2Kg 24–25 as a conclusion to the book. This became the final composition of the book of Jeremiah. As Archer concludes: "The MT doubtless preserves this posthumous edition of Baruch" (Gleason Archer, Jr., *A Survey of Old Testament Introduction* [Chicago: Moody Publishers, 2007], 342).

In the final analysis, the Masoretic text contains the canonical version of the book of Jeremiah. C. Hassell Bullock notes that although "the LXX readings may occasionally be preferred over the Hebrew, the opposite is more often the case." If the LXX translator used an earlier edition of Jeremiah, "it was not superior to the Hebrew" Masoretic version (C. Hassell Bullock, *An Introduction to the Old Testament Prophetic Books* [Chicago: Moody, 1986], 206).

OUTLINE

I. Introduction to the Book of Jeremiah (1:1-19)
- A. The Prophet's Background (1:1-3)
- B. The Prophet's Call (1:4-10)
- C. The Prophet's Confirming Visions (1:11-16)
  - 1. The Blossoming Almond Branch (1:11-12)
  - 2. The Boiling Pot (1:13-16)
- D. The Prophet's Challenge (1:17-19)

II. Prophecies Concerning Judah (2:1–45:5)
- A. Divine Judgment on Judah (2:1–25:38)
  - 1. Jeremiah's Nine General Prophecies of Judgment (2:1–20:18)
    - a. First Prophecy of Judgment—Jerusalem's Faithlessness (2:1–3:5)
    - b. Second Prophecy of Judgment—Judah's Call to Repentance in Light of Coming Judgment (3:6–6:30)
      - (1) The Summons to Repent (3:6–4:4)
      - (2) The Warning of Coming Judgment (4:5-31)
      - (3) The Reasons for Coming Judgment (5:1-31)
      - (4) The Certainty of Coming Judgment (6:1-30)
    - c. Third Prophecy of Judgment—Judgment on False Religion and Its Punishment (7:1–10:25)
      - (1) The Temple Address: Judah's False Worship (7:1–8:3)
      - (2) The Temple Address: God's Retribution on the People (8:4–10:25)
    - d. Fourth Prophecy of Judgment—The Broken Covenant (11:1–12:17)
      - (1) The Violation of the Covenant (11:1-17)
      - (2) The Consequences of Violating the Covenant (11:18–12:17)
    - e. Fifth Prophecy of Judgment—The Object Lessons of the Linen Belt and the Wineskins (13:1-27)
      - (1) The Illustration of the Linen Waistband (13:1-11)
      - (2) The Parable of the Wineskins (13:12-14)
      - (3) The Message on Sin and Its Results (13:15-27)
    - f. Sixth Prophecy of Judgment—The Drought and Prayer (14:1–15:21)
      - (1) The Fate of Jerusalem (15:5-9)
      - (2) Jeremiah's Complaint (15:10-21)
    - g. Seventh Prophecy of Judgment—Jeremiah's Restrictions and Judah's Sin (16:1–17:18)
      - (1) Jeremiah's Restrictions (16:1-9)
      - (2) Judah's Sin (16:10–17:18)
    - h. Eighth Prophecy of Judgment—For Failure to Keep the Sabbath (17:19-27)
    - i. Ninth Prophecy of Judgment—Object Lesson of the Potter and the Broken Jar (18:1–20:18)
      - (1) The Message at the Potter's House (18:1-23)
      - (2) The Message of the Broken Jar (19:1-15)
      - (3) Pashhur's Response (20:1-6)
      - (4) Jeremiah's Complaint (20:7-18)

2. Jeremiah's Four Specific Prophecies of Judgment (21:1–25:38)
    a. The Rebuke of the Kings of Judah (21:1–23:8)
        (1) The Rebuke to Zedekiah (21:1–22:9)
        (2) The Rebuke to Shallum (22:11-12)
        (3) The Rebuke to Jehoiakim (22:13-23)
        (4) The Rebuke to Coniah (Jehoiachin) (22:24-30)
        (5) The Hope of Messiah, the Righteous Branch (23:1-8)
    b. The Rebuke of the False Prophets (23:9-40)
        (1) The Character of the False Prophets (23:9-15)
        (2) The message of the false prophets (23:16-40)
    c. The Two Baskets of Figs (24:1-10)
        (1) The Vision of the Two Baskets of Figs (24:1-3)
        (2) The Explanation of the Good Figs (24:4-7)
        (3) The Explanation of the Poor Figs (24:8-10)
    d. The Seventy-Year Captivity in Babylon (25:1-38)
        (1) Warnings Ignored (25:1-7)
        (2) Judgment Described (25:8-14)
        (3) Wrath Promised (25:15-29)
        (4) Universal Judgment Affirmed (25:30-38)

B. Jeremiah's Personal Conflict with Judah (26:1–29:32)
    1. Jeremiah's Conflict with the People (26:1-24)
        a. Jeremiah's Message (26:1-6)
        b. Jeremiah's Arrest and Trial (26:7-15)
        c. Jeremiah's Deliverance (26:16-24)
    2. Jeremiah's Conflict with the False Prophets in Jerusalem (27:1–28:17)
        a. Jeremiah's Prophecy (27:1-22)
            (1) The Message to the Ambassadors (27:1-11)
            (2) The Message to Zedekiah (27:12-15)
            (3) The Message to the Priests and People (27:16-22)
        b. Hananiah's Opposition (28:1-17)
            (1) Jeremiah's Conflict with Hananiah (28:1-11)
            (2) Jeremiah's Message to Hananiah (28:12-17)
    3. Jeremiah's Conflict with the False Prophets in Exile (29:1-32)
        a. Jeremiah's First Letter to the Exiles (29:1-23)
            (1) The Introduction (29:1-3)
            (2) The Announcement of a Long Exile (29:4-14)
            (3) The Warning against False Prophets (29:15-23)
        b. Jeremiah's Second Letter to the Exiles (29:24-32)
            (1) The Report of Shemaiah's Letter to Jerusalem (29:24-29)
            (2) The Condemnation of Shemaiah (29:30-32)

C. Future Comfort for Israel and Judah (30:1–33:26)
    1. The Restoration of Israel and Judah Declared (30:1-24)
        a. Physical Deliverance of Israel and Judah (30:1-11)
            (1) The Nation's Restoration to the Land (30:1-3)
            (2) The Time of Jacob's Distress Prior to Restoration (30:4-7)
            (3) Restoration and Deliverance by the Lord (30:8-11)
        b. The Spiritual Healing of Zion (30:12-17)
            (1) Israel's Sin Caused Her Wounds (30:12-15)
            (2) God Would Heal Israel's Wounds (30:16-17)
        c. The Nation's Material and Spiritual Blessing (30:18-22)
        d. The Judgment on the Wicked (30:23-24)
    2. The New Covenant: Israel's Future Hope (31:1-40)
        a. The National Restoration of Israel (31:2-22)
        b. The National Restoration of Judah (31:23-26)

c. The New Covenant (31:27-40)
3. The Restoration of Israel and Judah Illustrated (32:1-44)
a. The Illustration: Buy a Field in Anathoth (32:1-12)
(1) Jeremiah's Circumstances (32:1-5)
(2) The Purchase of the Field at Anathoth (32:6-12)
b. The Explanation of the Purchase (32:13-15)
c. The Prayer of Jeremiah (32:16-25)
(1) His Praise for God's Greatness (32:16-23)
(2) His Puzzlement over God's Promise (32:24-25)
d. The Answer of the Lord (32:26-44)
(1) The City Will Be Destroyed (32:26-35)
(2) The City Will Be Restored (32:36-44)
4. The Restoration of Israel and Judah Reaffirmed (33:1-26)
a. The Coming Judgment and Future Restoration (33:1-13)
(1) The Judgment (33:1-5)
(2) The Restoration (33:6-13)
b. The Covenants with David and the Levitical Priests (33:14-26)
(1) The Covenants (33:14-18)
(2) The Confirmation of God's Covenant Promises (33:19-26)
D. Present Catastrophe of Judah (34:1–45:5)
1. Before the Fall of Jerusalem (34:1–36:32)
a. The Inconsistency of the People (34:1-22)
(1) The Warning to Zedekiah of His Exile (34:1-7)
(2) The Warning to the People for Enslaving Their Countrymen (34:8-22)
b. The Consistency of the Rechabites: An Object Lesson to Judah (35:1-19)
(1) The Fidelity of the Rechabites (35:1-11)
(2) The Example of the Rechabites (35:12-17)
(3) The Reward of the Rechabites (35:18-19)
c. Jehoiakim's Scroll-Burning (36:1-32)
(1) The Writing of the Scroll (36:1-7)
(2) The Reading of the Scroll (36:8-19)
(3) The Burning of the Scroll (36:20-26)
(4) The Rewriting of the Scroll (36:27-32)
2. During the Fall of Jerusalem (37:1–39:18)
a. Jeremiah's Message to Zedekiah about Egypt (37:1-10)
b. Jeremiah's Imprisonment (37:11–38:28)
(1) Jeremiah's Arrest and Confinement in a Dungeon (37:11-16)
(2) Jeremiah's First Meeting with Zedekiah and Transfer to the Courtyard of the Guard (37:17-21)
(3) Jeremiah's Confinement in a Cistern (38:1-6)
(4) Jeremiah's Rescue from the Cistern (38:7-13)
(5) Jeremiah's Second Meeting with Zedekiah (38:14-28)
c. Jerusalem's Destruction (39:1-18)
(1) The Fate of the Jews (39:1-10)
(2) The Fate of Jeremiah (39:11-18)
3. After the Fall of Jerusalem (40:1–45:5)
a. Jeremiah's Ministry to the Remnant in Judah (40:1–42:22)
(1) The Governorship of Gedaliah (40:1-12)
(2) The Assassination of Gedaliah (40:13–41:15)
(3) The Leadership of Johanan (41:16–42:22)
b. Jeremiah's Ministry to the Remnant in Egypt (43:1–44:30)
(1) The Remnant's Flight to Egypt (43:1-7)
(2) The Prophecy of Nebuchadnezzar's Invasion of Egypt (43:8-13)
(3) The Warning of God's Judgment (44:1-30)

c. Jeremiah's Ministry to Baruch (45:1-5)

III. Prophecies Concerning Nations (46:1–51:64)
  A. Prophecy against Egypt (46:1-28)
    1. Egypt to Be Defeated at Carchemish (46:1-12)
    2. Egypt to Be Invaded and Exiled (46:13-26)
    3. Israel to Be Regathered (46:27-28)
  B. Prophecy against Philistia (47:1-7)
  C. Prophecy against Moab (48:1-47)
    1. Moab's Land to Be Destroyed (48:1-10)
    2. Moab's Complacency to Be Shattered (48:11-17)
    3. Moab's Cities to Experience Catastrophe (48:18-27)
    4. Moab's Pride to Cease (48:28-39)
    5. Moab's Destruction to Be Complete (48:40-47)
  D. Prophecy against Ammon (49:1-6)
  E. Prophecy against Edom (49:7-22)
  F. Prophecy against Damascus (49:23-27)
  G. Prophecy against Kedar and Hazor (49:28-33)
  H. Prophecy against Elam (49:34-39)
  I. Prophecy against Babylon (50:1–51:64)
    1. The Announcement of Judgment (50:1-10)
    2. The Fall of Babylon (50:11-16)
    3. The Restoration of Israel (50:17-20)
    4. The Attack on Babylon (50:21-40)
    5. The Anguish of Babylon (50:41-46)
    6. God's Vengeance against Babylon (51:1-14)
    7. God's Sovereignty over Babylon (51:15-26)
    8. The Summons to the Nations against Babylon (51:27-33)
    9. God's Revenge on Babylon (51:34-44)
    10. The Warning to the Remnant in Babylon (51:45-48)
    11. The Certainty of Babylon's Fall (51:49-53)
    12. God's Repayment of Babylon (51:54-58)
    13. Seraiah's Symbolic Mission (51:59-64)

IV. Conclusion: Historical Supplement (52:1-34)
  A. The Fate of Jerusalem (52:1-23)
    1. The Fall of Zedekiah (52:1-11)
    2. The Destruction of the City (52:12-16)
    3. The Destruction of the Temple (52:17-23)
  B. The Fate of Certain Individuals (52:24-34)
    1. The Fate of Those in Jerusalem During Its Fall (52:24-27)
    2. The Fate of the Exiles (52:28-30)
    3. The Fate of Jehoiachin (52:31-34)

COMMENTARY ON JEREMIAH

I. Introduction to the Book of Jeremiah (1:1-19)

Jeremiah is introduced as the prophet at the opening of the book. His background and call into the prophetic ministry set the stage for his prophecies and eyewitness account of the fall of Jerusalem recorded in the book.

A. The Prophet's Background (1:1-3)

1:1-3. Jeremiah was the **son of Hilkiah**, a Levitical **priest**. The name Hilkiah ("portion of the Lord") was a common OT name for priests or Levites (2Kg 22:2-14; 1Ch 6:45-46; 26:10-11; 2Ch 34:9-22; Neh 12:7). Jeremiah's hometown was **Anathoth**, a Levitical city in the **land of**

Benjamin, about three miles northeast of Jerusalem. Solomon exiled Abiathar the priest to Anathoth for supporting Adonijah as David's successor (Jos 21:15-19; 1Kg 1:7; 2:26-27).

There is no mention of Jeremiah serving as a priest; he was called as a prophet when **the word of the LORD came** to him. This phrase is a typical introduction of divine calling (cf. Ezk 1:3; Jnh 1:1; Hg 1:1; Zch 1:1) of a prophet, someone through whom God spoke directly to His people.

The Lord called Jeremiah in the **thirteenth year** of the reign of **Josiah, . . . king of Judah**, the last righteous king of Judah (2Kg 22). Josiah became king in 640 BC, so Jeremiah received his call as prophet in 627 BC.

Jeremiah continued as God's spokesman in the **days of Jehoiakim, the son of Josiah**, who did evil in the sight of the Lord (2Kg 22:32), down to the fifth month of the **eleventh year** of King **Zedekiah**, Judah's last king, who reigned 597–586 BC, **until the exile of Jerusalem in the fifth month** (July–August 586 BC). Thus Jeremiah's ministry lasted at least 41 years during the reign of five kings of Judah: Josiah, Jehoahaz, Jehoiakim, Jehoiachin, and Zedekiah. The phrase **until the exile** refers only to Jeremiah's ministry to the nation of **Judah, until the exile of Jerusalem**, but does not mean his ministry ended with the fall of the city in **the fifth month**, ninth of Av in the Jewish calendar, August 14, 586 BC (2Kgs 25:3-10). Jeremiah continued to minister to the remnant who remained in Jerusalem (Jr 39:11–44:30) after the fall. Following the assassination of Gedaliah (41:1-3), he went with the exiles to Egypt (43:7) and continued to speak for the Lord there (44:1-30).

B. The Prophet's Call (1:4-10)

1:4-5. God revealed His choice of Jeremiah: **Before I formed you in the womb** (Ps 139: 13-16). Before Jeremiah was **born** God **knew** (*yada'*) him. This is not just general knowledge, but indicates the sense of close relationship, and includes the idea of being "chosen" (Am 3:2) and having God's protection or God "watching over" him (Ps 1:6). God had set him apart, **consecrated** him to be His spokesman to Israel. Consecration describes being set apart for holy service and is used to describe the Sabbath and the tabernacle and its furnishing (Ex 16:23; 20:8; 30:30; 40:9). This message would give Jeremiah courage and motivation for God's task.

Jeremiah was **appointed**, commissioned, as **a prophet to the nations**. Though Jeremiah proclaimed God's word to Judah (chaps. 2–45), his ministry as God's spokesman extended to the Gentile nations (chaps. 46–51).

1:6. Jeremiah's response of **alas**, an exclamation of pain or sorrow, indicates his self-doubt when God called him, articulated by two protests. First, Jeremiah objected: **I do not know how to speak**, similar to Moses' response to the Lord at the burning bush (Ex 4:10). Jeremiah was not claiming that he was mute, but that he lacked the ability to be God's spokesman. Second, he objected that he was **a youth**, a word used of infants as well as young men (Ex 2:6; 1Sm 4:21; Gn 14:24). Jeremiah's exact age is not given, but his objections, and the length of his ministry, indicate that he was in his late teens or early twenties at the time of his calling. By using the term **youth** he emphasized his lack of experience and his feeling unprepared to be God's spokesman.

1:7-10. God answered Jeremiah's objections in three ways. First, the Lord stressed Jeremiah's call to be a faithful messenger, to go **everywhere I send you**, obey **all that I command**, and **speak** the Lord's message. Second, God told Jeremiah **do not be afraid of them** (the people) to whom he was sent because He promised to be with him and **deliver** Jeremiah even when people tried to kill him (cf. 11:18-23; 12:6; 20:1-2; 26:11; 36:15-56; 37:4-6). Third, God showed Jeremiah that He was the source of the message. **The LORD stretched out His hand and touched my mouth** (perhaps in a vision; cf. Ezk 1:1). This visible manifestation of God was His object lesson to tell Jeremiah that the Lord Himself would **put** His **words in** Jeremiah's **mouth**. God would provide the very words he would speak and the exact protection he would need.

God graciously taught Jeremiah, and all believers, that He specializes in using ordinary people to accomplish His extraordinary work. The Lord will use people who: (1) trust Him in spite of fears; (2) obey Him in spite of inexperience; and (3) proclaim His Word in spite of feelings of inadequacy.

God then repeated Jeremiah's calling, **I have appointed you this day**, and summarized the content of His message. It would be a message of judgment and blessing to **nations** and **kingdoms**, using two metaphors to describe his mission (cf. Jr 31:28). First, he compared Jeremiah to a farmer who would **pluck up** (announce judgment), then **plant**, (announce blessing). Next, He compared Jeremiah to a carpenter who would **break down**, **destroy**, and **overthrow**, announcing judgment—then **build**, announcing blessing.

C. The Prophet's Confirming Visions (1:11-16)

God gave Jeremiah two visions to confirm his calling. The first (vv. 11-12) focused on the nature of the message, and the second (vv. 13-16) on the content of the message.

1. The Blossoming Almond Branch (1:11-12)

1:11-12. The Lord's first confirming vision was **a rod** (branch) **of an almond tree**. The Hebrew word for "almond tree" (*saqed*) is from the word meaning to "watch" or "to wake" (*saqad*) because in Israel the almond is the first tree to bud and awaken in January as the first sign of spring. The almond branch represented God, who was **watching over** His **word to perform it**. The vision of the "awake tree" reminded Jeremiah that God was awake (Ps 121:4) and watching over His message to bring it to pass.

2. The Boiling Pot (1:13-16)

1:13. The Lord's second confirming vision was of a **boiling pot**, literally a "blown upon" kettle, indicating a wind blowing on the fire to keep the caldron's contents boiling. The pot was **facing away from the north**, so that its contents were about to be spilled out toward the south.

1:14-15. This tilting represented **evil** about to **break forth** on **all the inhabitants of the land**. God was summoning **kingdoms of the north** to punish **Jerusalem** and **Judah**. This refers to the coming invasion of Babylon and her allies (cf. 25:8-9). Although Babylon was located in the east geographically, the invading armies followed the routes along the Euphrates River in their march to Judah. So the enemy did approach from **the north** (cf. 4:6; 6:1, 22; 10:22; 13:20; 15:12).

When they conquered the city, Babylon would set **his throne at the entrance of the gates of Jerusalem**, thus replacing Judah's royal authority (43:10; 49:38). Babylon took **all the cities of Judah**, not just Jerusalem.

1:16. The Lord's **judgments** fell on Judah for idolatry; they **offered sacrifices to other gods**, **worshiped the works of their own hands**, and had **forsaken** God (Dt 28). The judgment of Judah was a fulfillment of the blessings and cursings laid out when they entered the land of Israel (Dt 28).

D. The Prophet's Challenge (1:17-19)

1:17-19. Once his call was clear, God challenged Jeremiah to **gird up** his **loins**, a picture of tying up the long garments to be able to move quickly and to get ready for the task (cf. Ex 21:11; 2Kg 4:29; 9:1; Lk 12:25; Eph 6:14; 1Pt 1:13). God pictures His strength in three ways. First, He gave Jeremiah the needed strength to **arise**, to stand up against the people of Judah and **not be dismayed** (afraid). Next, through God's enablement Jeremiah would be as strong as **a fortified city and as a pillar of iron and as walls of bronze**. Jeremiah could be confident that his enemies would not **overcome** him. By God's power he could withstand those who attacked him and his message from the Lord. Finally, God assured him that He was **with** Jeremiah **to deliver** him. There is no greater assurance of victory than to know the Lord is standing with us.

II. Prophecies Concerning Judah (2:1–45:5)

This section begins with Jeremiah's 13 oracles of divine judgment against Judah (chaps. 2–25), usually introduced with the phrase "the word of the LORD came" or "the LORD said" (e.g., 2:1; 3:6; 7:1). Following the messages of judgment, Jeremiah recorded the rejection of his message and the ensuing conflict (chaps. 26–29). The judgment of Judah was sealed, but before Jeremiah chronicled the execution of that judgment, he inserted God's message of future comfort for Israel and Judah in what is often called the Book of Consolation (chaps. 30–33). Though Judah would go into captivity, God would never abandon His chosen people. He gave the hope of the new covenant and the certainty that He would fulfill the good word He had spoken concerning the house of Israel and Judah. After the message of hope, Jeremiah then recorded the fall of Judah to Babylon (chaps. 34–45), and God's judgment pronounced by Jeremiah was fulfilled.

A. Divine Judgment on Judah (2:1–25:38)

1. Jeremiah's Nine General Prophecies of Judgment (2:1–20:18)

Jeremiah's nine general prophecies of judgment begin this opening section of prophecies concerning Judah.

a. First Prophecy of Judgment—Jerusalem's Faithlessness (2:1–3:5)

2:1-3. Jerusalem, as a representative of the whole nation, was confronted with her waywardness. For emphasis, Jerusalem's sinful condition was contrasted with her former **devotion** to the Lord. The Hebrew word for **devotion** (*chesed)* refers to the most intimate degree of loyalty, love, and faithfulness that can exist between two people or between an individual and the Lord. In Israel's early history, in her **youth**, she was **following after** the Lord **in the wilderness** (the exodus), and **holy to the LORD**, set apart for His service. Despite Israel's grumbling, she was the chosen nation, the **first of His harvest**, dedicated to the Lord (Lv 23:9-14). Anyone who **ate of it** was as guilty as those who ate of the first fruits dedicated to the Lord, and **evil came upon them**. They were judged for their mistreatment of Israel (Gn 12:3; Ex 17:8-16).

2:4-6a. The faithfulness of **Jacob** (a synonym for **Israel**) did not last. They **went far from [God] and walked after emptiness** (*hebel*, "worthlessness, uselessness, vanity"; the word is often used for idols and is used in Ecclesiastes 30 times for the vanity of life without God). These people became **empty**, like the objects of their worship, for whatever we worship shapes our lives. They followed **empty** idols (2:5, 8, 11; 8:19; 10:8, 14-15; 14:22; 16:19; 18:15; 51:17-18) forgetting the **LORD who brought** them **out of . . . Egypt**.

2:6b-8. The Lord had brought them from Egypt and the wilderness **deserts**, **pits**, **drought**, **and darkness** to **the fruitful land**, a synonym for the land of Israel (cf. 4:26; 48:33). The Lord identified the country of Israel as **My land**, and He holds the deed to it as the God of Israel. It is His **inheritance** According to Walter Elwell, in the theological sense, to inherit means to "receive an irrevocable gift" with an emphasis on the special relationship between the benefactor and the recipients (Walter Elwell, "Inheritance," in *The Evangelical Dictionary of Biblical Theology* [Grand Rapids, MI: Baker, 1996], 374). God has made Israel His inheritance, and He has a unique, permanent relationship with the land of Israel and the people of Israel as indicated throughout Scripture (3:18; 10:16; 16:18; Lv 25:23; Dt. 32:9; 1Sm 10:1; 2Sm 21:3; Pss 78:54, 71; 94:14; Is 19:25; Zch 2:12; 9:16). But the land was defiled, **made an abomination**, ceremonially unclean with idolatry (Jr 3:1; 16:18; Lv 4:12).

Jeremiah singled out the three groups who failed in their leadership duties, and he exposed their lack of obedience (2:8). First, the **priests did not say,** Where is the LORD? They should have instructed the people, but they **did not know** God themselves; "know" indicated intimate, personal knowledge, not just intellectual information.

Second, the **rulers**, (literally "the shepherds," meaning the political and civil leadership, including the king), **also transgressed**. Ironically the ones who were to lead Judah were in rebellion against the One who had appointed them to the task of leadership.

Third, the **prophets**, who should have been giving the word of the Lord, now **prophesied by Baal**, the chief deity of the Phoenicians and Canaanites. Jeremiah constantly warned against Baal worship (7:9; 11:13; 12:16; 19:5; 23:13, 27; 32:29, 34). Baal was the male deity (Asherah, the female deity in the Baal cult) and was worshiped for fertility, crops, and rain. Worship of Baal was on high places or in temples with ritual, incense, animal, and even human sacrifices (1Kg 16:31-33; Jr 19:5; 32:35). Israel was constantly lured into this pagan worship rather than staying true to the Lord and therefore suffered dire consequences (1Kg 18:18-40; 2Kg 10:18-28; 21:1-3). Their false teaching led Israel astray as they **walked after things that did not profit** (Jdg 2:11-13).

2:9-12. Jeremiah used the image of a court case to focus on the seriousness of Israel's sin. God would **yet contend** (used twice, or "bring charges" or "I will bring a case against you," HCSB) with Israel. This is a legal term for presenting a lawsuit (Hs 4:1-4; Mc 6:1-2).

Jeremiah asked for an investigation from as far away as **the coastlands of Kittim** (the ancient name for Cyprus, but it came to be used for the lands around the Mediterranean Sea in general, and in Dn 11:30 it refers to the Romans) in the west to **Kedar** (Arabia) in the east. The rhetorical question: **Has a nation changed gods when they were not gods?** clearly expects a negative answer and points out the foolishness of Judah's actions. Idolatrous nations surrounding Israel were more faithful to their false gods than Israel had been to the true God. Israel had **changed their glory**, the True and Living God, for dead idols, **that which does not profit**, that which is worthless, without the slightest benefit (see comments on Rm 1:18-24 for an allusion to this, where Paul targets both Gentiles and even the Jewish people).

2:13. God's people had **committed two evils**. The first was a sin of omission: She had **forsaken** God, **the fountain of living waters**. Her second sin was one of commission: She replaced her true God with idols, described as **broken cisterns,** they had hewn (cut, carved) for **themselves.** Cisterns were large pits dug into the rock with walls sealed with plaster. They were used to collect and store rainwater. The stored water could become brackish, and during droughts, cisterns often dried up. Cisterns could develop cracks in their walls, and the water would leak out. Jeremiah compared Israel's actions to a man abandoning a **fountain of living waters**, a fresh, plentiful, reliable stream, to go to **broken cisterns** that would **hold no water**. To turn from a dependable, pure stream of fresh running water to a broken, brackish cistern was idiotic. Yet that is what Judah did when she turned from the living God to worship idols.

2:14-16. Another rhetorical question highlighted Judah's apostasy and its consequences: **Is Israel a slave?** She could no longer live as a free person, but as a **slave**, purchased in the market or a **homeborn servant**. She became **prey** to other nations, and her land was **a waste** because of foreign invaders who here were compared to **lions**. Her **cities** were **destroyed** and **without inhabitant**.

The Egyptian cities of **Memphis and Tahpanhes** (Ezk 30:13, 16, 18) could refer to Pharaoh Shishak's invasion of Judah in 925 BC (1Kg 14:25-26) or more likely to the more recent event of Pharaoh Neco's killing of King Josiah in the battle at Megiddo (609 BC; 2Kg 23:29-30). Either way, Egypt had triumphed over Judah or had **shaved the crown** of Judah's head, a figure of mourning, disgrace, and devastation (cf. Jr 47:5; 48:37).

2:17-19. Judah had not only been **forsaking the LORD** for false gods, she had also forsaken the protection of the Lord. He had **led** her **in the way**, but now Judah made false alliances with **Egypt** and **Assyria** to guarantee her safety (cf. v. 36; Ezk 23; Hs 7:11). Like the broken cisterns (Jr 2:13), the waters of the **Nile** or **Euphrates**, referring to those alliances, could not protect Judah from her enemy or her sin. Only after she received her judgment would Judah realize how **evil and bitter** it was to **forsake the LORD**.

2:20. Judah's spiritual apostasy was pictured as spiritual adultery, acting like **a harlot**. Jeremiah painted four verbal pictures of Judah's wayward state and insatiable lust for false gods (vv. 20-28). First, Judah was rebellious, breaking her bonds with the Lord. It would be better to translate the opening of the verse according to the LXX: **For long ago [you]** (not "I") **broke your yoke** (NIV; NET Bible), implying that Israel had thrown off all restraint. This translation is clarified by Judah's statement: **I will not serve!** Israel broke away, **tore off**, the **yoke** that bound her to the Lord. "The yoke of the law" is a common rabbinic phrase to indicate obedience to the Lord (cf. Mt 11:29). Instead of worshiping the Lord, she followed heathen practices of worship (cf. 3:2; Ezk 6:1-7, 13) **on every high hill**, frequently called "high places," where she had **lain down as a harlot**. Spiritually, Judah was acting like a prostitute giving herself to foreign gods, and committing spiritual adultery against the Lord.

2:21. Second, Judah is pictured as a **choice vine** from **faithful seed** that God had **planted**. Often described as God's vine (Is 5:1-7; Ezk 15). Judah had transformed herself by choosing to forsake God, follow idols, and turn herself into a **degenerate**, **foreign vine** incapable of producing any good fruit.

2:22. Third, Judah had a **stain** of **iniquity** that could not be washed away, even with **lye**, a strong mineral cleaner, or **much soap**, a strong vegetable alkali. Her iniquity was ingrained.

2:23-25. Fourth, Judah is likened to animals in heat: a **swift young camel** running fast, **entangling** and tripping up, running after a mate, and a **wild donkey** in **heat** ready to breed, who **sniffs the wind in her passion**, seeking mates. Judah likewise vigorously pursued her false gods and could not be restrained in her **passion** for the idols of **strangers**.

2:26-28. Israel was **shamed** by her pursuit of false gods who could not help her, just as a **thief is shamed when he is discovered**. She declared **a tree** and **a stone** to be her creator: **You are my father . . . You gave me birth**. Yet when **trouble** came, Israel cried to God, **Arise and save us!** Her idols were powerless to help, although Judah had as many idols as **the number** of her **cities** (cf. 11:13).

2:29-31. Judah eventually became so spiritually irresponsible that she dared to **contend with** God. Earlier God had brought charges against Judah. Now she brought charges against Him (cf. 2:9). God's judgment was necessary to curb their transgression, but His **chastening** (discipline, correction) was **in vain**. The people still refused to respond. They even killed (**your sword has devoured**) the prophets. When Jesus wept over Jerusalem (Mt 23:37), He said "Jerusalem, who kills the prophets," referring to Israel's sad history of rejecting and even killing the messengers the Lord sent to bring the nation back to Him. Likewise, Jeremiah pled, **O generation, heed the word of the LORD**, but they would not **come** to the Lord and instead proclaimed their freedom **to roam** away from Him.

2:32-33. Judah's unreliability was evident when she forgot God's past goodness. This sin is introduced by another rhetorical question:

Can a virgin forget her ornaments, or a bride her attire? Certainly a woman going to be married would never forget her wedding **ornaments** (jewelry), or wedding **attire** (her dress); but Judah had **forgotten** the Lord for a long time, **days without number**. She did not remember who had adorned her and set her apart from the other nations. Judah had become so skilled at illicit **love** that even **wicked women** have been **taught** secrets of seduction from her.

2:34-37. Judah also displayed her irresponsibility in acts of injustice and murder by spilling **the lifeblood of the innocent poor**. Perhaps this is a reference to the murder of the prophets (cf. 26:20-23) or taking advantage of the poor in the land (Is 3:14; Am 4:1-5). Though her clothes (**skirts**) were covered in blood of the guiltless, she claimed, **I am innocent**. Had the poor been found **breaking in** to another's house to find provisions and had then been killed, the one responsible for the death would be guiltless (Ex 22:2). But the ones Judah killed were **the innocent poor**. These murderers were destined for judgment because they said, **I have not sinned**.

Another indication of Judah's inconsistency was her fickle foreign policy, constantly **changing [her] way** in making alliances with **Egypt** (Ezk 23) and **Assyria** (2Kg 16:7-9; Is 7:13-25). But because the Lord had **rejected** these nations, Judah would **not prosper with them**. She could not be helped by them.

3:1-5. The spiritual harlotry of Judah is exposed by Jeremiah and linked to the Mosaic law. If a couple divorced and the wife married another man, and then was divorced or widowed from her second husband, she was prohibited from ever remarrying her first husband (Dt 24:1-4). This law seemed to have been given to protect the sanctity of marriage by discouraging hasty divorce. Judah had separated from her husband, the Lord, and had been **a harlot with many lovers**. Judah had been unfaithful in marriage to the Lord and had no right to **turn to** Him or expect Him to **still return to her**. Her unfaithfulness was evident in that the **land** was **completely polluted** with idols, and she had sat as a harlot by the roads (cf. Gn 38:13-14, 20-21)—an image of a cult prostitute. However, God's faithfulness to His word is greater than Judah's unfaithfulness to Him, as Jeremiah later recorded God's promise of Israel's national restoration under the new covenant (cf. Jr 3:18; 31:33-33).

God judged Judah by withholding **showers** and **spring rain** (Dt 28:23-34; Jr 14), yet Judah **refused to be ashamed**. Although Judah **called** God **My Father**, and **the friend of my youth**, her words were hypocritical and manipulative, not repentant, because she continued to do **evil things**.

b. Second Prophecy of Judgment—Judah's Call to Repentance in Light of Coming Judgment (3:6–6:30)

Jeremiah was given this prophecy to call Judah to repentance during the days of Josiah, probably before the discovery of the law in 621 BC (cf. 11:1-8).

(1) The Summons to Repent (3:6–4:4)

3:6-11. The prophecy is built around the story of two sisters—**Israel** and **Judah** (cf. Ezk 23). The northern kingdom, **Israel**, was **faithless** and a **harlot** on **every high hill**, under **every green tree**. God waited for her to **return to** Him, but she did not and Judah, **her treacherous sister**, observed her behavior.

God **sent her** (Israel) **away** into captivity to Assyria (2Kg 17:5-20; 722 BC). Judah did not learn from Israel, **but she went and was a harlot also**. Judah became even worse than Israel by committing the same sins, but **in deception** (hypocrisy) pretending to follow the Lord.

The northern kingdom practiced a form of false worship of the Lord, instituted by their first king, Jeroboam (1Kg 12:25-33). They worshipped golden calves and did not go to Jerusalem to offer sacrifices. Yet Judah pretended to be faithful to the Lord, and followed the sacrificial system in Jerusalem, but practiced idolatry at the same time. God called **faithless Israel . . . more righteous than treacherous Judah** (Ezk 16:51-52; 23:11).

3:12-15. At this point in his message about condemnation because of sin, Jeremiah paused to offer a proclamation of hope and repentance to the **north** (the northern kingdom). If **Israel** would **return** (repent) to her God (7:3; 26:13), He would **not look upon** her **in anger** but would extend mercy. The term "return" literally means "to turn back" "to turn around" (*shuv),* and is a technical term that means "to repent." First used in Dt 4:30 and throughout the Pentateuch as a call to come back to the Lord, it is a common phrase in Jeremiah (Jr 3:12, 14, 22; 4:1; 8:5; 15:19; 24:7).

If they repented, God promised to gather a remnant from the north (**one from a city and two from a family**) and bring them to **Zion**, Jerusalem. This remnant would have **shepherds** (cf. 10:21; 22:22; 23:1-2, 4) who would provide leadership **after** God's **own heart**.

3:16-18. Using the phrase **in those days**, an eschatological term that often introduces prophecies about more remote future events (cf. 16:14-16; 23:5-6; 30:3, 24; 31:17, 31), Jeremiah described Israel's end-time restoration. Then Judah and Israel will be reunited (after having been divided since 931 BC) as a nation serving the Lord (31:31-33).

Further describing end-time circumstances, Jeremiah predicted that in the messianic kingdom the **ark of the covenant**, lost at the destruction of the temple (586 BC), would **not come to mind** or be missed. Rather, the very **Throne of the Lord** (Ezk 43:7) will be present with Messiah also ruling in Jerusalem as King (Zch 14:16-19), extending His dominion over all nations. In the kingdom there will be complete obedience to King Messiah, and no one of an **evil heart** will be found there. **Judah will walk with . . . Israel** and **all the nations will be gathered** to worship there in the land of Israel, which God gave Israel's **fathers** (Abraham, Isaac, and Jacob; Gn 15:18) **as an inheritance.**

3:19-20. Although the Lord wanted to bless the **house of Israel** like **sons** and give them a **beautiful inheritance**, they were unwilling to return to Him. Instead, they acted like a treacherous **woman** unfaithful to her **lover** (*rayah*, "faithful companion, imitate friend" not sexual partner) indicating the breach of a committed matrimonial relationship.

3:21-25. The voice of **weeping and the supplications** of repentance will be prompted because they **perverted their way** and because **they** had **forgotten the Lord their God**. In Jeremiah's ideal picture of repentance the nation would finally realize the depth of the pit into which they had fallen. God would respond to the cry by offering to **heal** their **faithlessness** if she would return.

Verses 22c-25 are an indication of the sort of repentance God wanted to see from Israel. Israel was to **come** to **the Lord . . . God**, admitting that the **shameful thing** (idolatry) **has consumed** them. She must confess that she **sinned against the Lord**. This heartfelt confession of sin did not seem to occur in Jeremiah's day. Instead it still awaits the future repentance of the nation when the Messiah returns as King (Zch 12:10–13:1).

4:1-4. While God promised to respond if Israel and Judah would return to Him, their repentance had to be genuine. They had to remove their idols and stop pursuing false gods. He pictured this in two ways. First, Jeremiah used the metaphor of farming to show the need to prepare their hearts, **break up your fallow ground**, a field that has been unplanted, but do not **sow among thorns**. The second metaphor, **remove the foreskins of your** heart, is a reference to circumcision, the sign of the Abrahamic covenant, the symbol of the Jewish people's relationship with God (Gn 17:9-14). Though circumcised physically, the men of Judah needed to circumcise their hearts so that their inward condition matched their outward profession (Dt 10:16; 30:6; Jr 9:35-56; Rm 2:28-29). If Judah did not repent, God vowed that His **wrath** would burn against them because of their evil deeds.

(2) The Warning of Coming Judgment (4:5-31)

4:5-9. Judgment was certain, so it was time to **blow the trumpet** of warning and go into the **fortified cities** for defense because the judgment was coming **from the north . . . great destruction**. The approaching army of Babylon was like **a lion** that would destroy the land because of **the fierce anger of the Lord**. Certainty of the coming destruction would cause the people to mourn: **put on sackcloth, lament and wail**. Fear would paralyze the leadership of the people, **the king**, **princes**, **priests**, and **prophets** (cf. 2:26; 4:9; 8:11) as they watched the annihilation of their country. Yet the destruction would come in part because of their own leadership failure (cf. 2:8).

4:10. This verse is one of the most challenging in the book to interpret. Jeremiah claimed that God had **deceived this people** by promising they would have **peace** when in fact a **sword** was at their throats. It is better to understand that Jeremiah was complaining that God had ordained the false prophets to proclaim their message of peace (cf. 6:14; 14:13-14; 23:16-17). Scripture is clear that it is not in God's nature to lie (cf. Nm 23:19). But God is sovereign over all that happens in creation, even the false prophecies given by the deceptive teachers and leaders, though He is never blamed for the moral guilt of their sin, while *people are* (see comments on Rm 9:13-23). God ordained the deception of the false teachers as one of the rungs in the ladder leading up to the judgment they deserved for abandoning the Lord. In fact God's true prophets had been predicting judgment, not peace (cf. Jr 1:14-16; Mc 3:9-12; Hab 1:5-11; Zph 1:4-13). Only the false prophets had been proclaiming peace. Thus, it is better to understand Jeremiah's complaint that God, in His providence, ordained these false prophets to proclaim their false message.

4:11-14. Jeremiah gives two pictures of the coming invasion of Judah. First, the invading armies are pictured as a **scorching wind** that blows in from the **wilderness**, the desert (Ezk 17:10; 19:12). This wind does not cool, and it cannot be used to winnow because it is too strong and would blow the grain away with the chaff. Instead, this **scorching** wind withers vegetation (Gn 41:6) and causes extreme discomfort (Jnh 4:8). Second, the advance of Babylon's army is pictured as an approaching storm of **clouds** sweeping into Judah, and their **chariots** as a **whirlwind** pulled by **horses** as fast as **eagles**. Both images are of rapid, powerful invasion (Jr 4:13-14).

In light of Judah's certain destruction God again graciously called the people to repentance. If they were to **wash** the **evil from** their **heart** they would be **saved** (delivered) from judgment.

4:15-18. A **voice**, a messenger from **Dan**, the northernmost tribe of Israel and from **Mount Ephraim**, 35 miles north of Jerusalem, would signal the approach of Babylon's army These areas would be the first to see the **besiegers** approach, and their **watchmen** would sound the alarm. God sent Babylon to punish **the cities of Judah** because she had **rebelled** against Him.

4:19-22. Jeremiah cried out in **anguish** at the news of the coming invasion. His **heart** pounded, and he could not **be silent** because he heard the coming **alarm of war**. The repetition **disaster on disaster** indicated the seriousness of the coming events, pictured as **tents devastated** in **an instant**. God said, **My people are foolish**, because they did not know Him. In an ironic reversal of wisdom living, the people were **shrewd**, skilled **to do evil**, but ignorant in knowing good (cf. Pr 1:2-3).

4:23-28. Jeremiah compared the coming judgment to a cosmic disaster. The description of the land as **formless and void** evokes images from the creation account, the chaos that preceded God's work in creation (Gn 1:1-2). Jeremiah indicated that no aspect of life would remain untouched: **heavens**, **mountains**, **man**, **birds**, **land**, and **cities**. Jeremiah pictured the land as barren as it had been before the formation of the earth (Gn 1:11-13, 20-26).

The imagery was so stark that some might think He would totally destroy Israel. To guard against this misunderstanding, God qualified His statement: **Yet I will not execute a complete destruction** (Jr 4:27; cf. 5:18). Though the whole **earth shall mourn** as He judged the people, and the Lord would **not change [His] mind** (4:28), yet Israel as a people and a nation would not be eradicated (31:35-37).

4:29-31. Jeremiah warned that when the armies of **horseman and bowman** marched to attack, people in **every city** would flee for safety, hiding in **thickets** and **among the rocks**. Then addressing Jerusalem's leaders collectively as the **desolate one**, Jeremiah challenged their plan for dealing with Babylon. These Jewish leaders thought if they would figuratively dress as a harlot (in **scarlet** with jewels of **gold,** and cosmetic **paint** on their **eyes**) they might seduce, or politically persuade, Babylon to prevent their attack (cf. Ezk 16:26-29; 23:40-41). But it was **in vain**; her former **lovers** (allies) now **despise[d]** her.

As the Babylonians pressed their attack, the **daughter of Zion** (the people of Jerusalem) cried out in **anguish** like a **woman in labor** (cf. Is 13:8; 21:3; 26:17; Jr 6:24; 13:21; 22:23; 30:6; 48:41; 49:22, 24; 50:43; Mc 4:9-10). She stretched out **her hands** for help that never came as she died at the hands of **murderers**.

(3) The Reasons for Coming Judgment (5:1-31)

In chap. 4, Jeremiah described the inevitability and reasons for the coming judgment. Here he has presented the extensiveness of the sin in Judah for which God would judge them.

5:1-3. Judah faced judgment because every person was guilty. Jeremiah was challenged to look **through the streets of Jerusalem** for just **one man** who did **justice.** But unlike Abraham looking for a righteous person in Sodom, Jeremiah could not find even one (Gn 18:26-32). They all **refused correction**, had hearts **harder than rock** toward God, and **refused to repent**.

5:4-6. Jeremiah thought perhaps **only the poor**—the **foolish** or uneducated masses did not **know the way of the Lord**. He decided if he went to the **great**, the leaders, they would **know the way of the Lord**. Sadly, the leaders had joined the people (cf. 2:8) and had broken off the yoke of service to God (cf. 2:20). So God would judge leaders and followers alike for their sin, using the image of three wild animals (the **lion**, the **wolf**, and the **leopard**) to symbolize the coming ravages of the Babylonian attack on Judah.

5:7-9. God asked Judah two rhetorical questions. First, **Why should I pardon you** (Judah)? (v. 7). Second, **Shall I not punish these people**?

(v. 9). Between the two questions, Judah's character is described in a way that made the answers obvious. God could not forgive Judah because she had **forsaken** Him and **sworn by** false gods, committing spiritual **adultery**. Though God had provided for them, the people were acting like **lusty horses**, each of whom went after **his neighbor's** wife. God would not pardon, but would punish Judah for her idolatry and adultery.

5:10-19. God's choice vine, Judah, had become a wild vine (2:21), so God called His invaders to **go up through** Judah's **vine rows** and **strip away** the **branches**.

The people refused to believe that God would ever destroy Jerusalem, saying **misfortune will not come on us** (v. 12). The people said that the prophets—Jeremiah, Ezekiel, and others who were predicting doom—were just full of **wind** (v. 13). They did not believe judgment would ever fall on them or their city, Jerusalem. Yet Jeremiah's words became **fire**, and the **people** were as **wood** to be consumed in judgment (v. 14).

God would bring a **nation** (Babylon) **from afar** against Judah—a nation whose **language** the Judahites did **not know** (v. 15). Similarly, Isaiah had earlier predicted that Judah would know they were under judgment when the Assyrians arrived, speaking a language they did not know (Is 28:11; cf. 1Co 14:21). These warriors would **devour** the **harvest**, children, livestock, **vines**, and **fig trees** and would **demolish** the mighty **fortified cities** that Judah trusted for protection (Jr 5:16-17).

Yet again God emphasized that He would not destroy Judah completely (cf. 4:27) but would preserve a remnant. When these captives would ask, **Why** has **God done all** this to us? Jeremiah was told to say, "Because you had **forsaken** God to serve **foreign gods** in your own land." Therefore God would have them **serve strangers** (the Babylonians) in a foreign land (v. 19). His punishment fit their sin.

5:20-31. The **house of Jacob**, namely **Judah**, was willfully ignorant, **foolish, and senseless**. Though she had **eyes** and **ears**, she did not **see** or **hear** (i.e., comprehend) the true character of God (cf. Ezk 12:2). She refused to **fear** God (cf. Pr 1:7). Even the **sea** remains within its **boundary** (cf. Jb 38:10; Ps 104:9), yet the **people** of Judah refused to stay within God's covenant limits. Instead they **turned aside**. They did not acknowledge God's gracious hand at work—He who **gives rain in its season** and appoints the **weeks of . . . harvest** (Jr 5:23-25).

Specifically, the people were **fat** and **sleek** (rich and powerful), excelling in **wickedness**, waiting to take advantage (**set a trap**) of the poor. They refused to help the **orphan . . . or defend the rights of the poor** (vv. 26-27). The **prophets**, who were to proclaim God's word of truth, were prophesying **falsely**, and the **priests** who were to instruct the people in the ways of God, were instead ruling **on their own authority** (cf. 2:8). Rather than resisting this poor leadership, the people **love[d] it**. All the elements of society preferred wickedness to righteousness (vv. 26-31).

(4) The Certainty of Coming Judgment (6:1-30)

6:1-3. Warning of coming danger was given in two ways. First, a **trumpet** of alarm would announce an impending attack (cf. 4:5-6). The people of **Benjamin**, Jeremiah's home area (cf. 1:1) just north of Jerusalem, were to **flee . . . from the midst Jerusalem** for safety instead of going into the walled city. It would be safer to be outside the city than inside it. The warning **trumpet** would be sounded at **Tekoa**, about 11 miles southeast of Jerusalem (cf. Am 1:1). The second type of warning was **signal** fires at **Beth-haccerem**, a vantage point midway between Jerusalem and Bethlehem, lit to warn people to flee. Jerusalem would be destroyed so completely that **shepherds** would **pitch their tents** and **pasture** their herds on its site. This extensive destruction was confirmed by Nehemiah (cf. Neh 1:3; 2:3, 11-17).

6:4-9. As the enemy gathered against Jerusalem, they were prepared (eager) to **attack at noon** or even **by night**. Most armies would wait until daybreak to begin, but the Babylonians decided to begin their attack that night. **The LORD of hosts** directed the soldiers of Babylon as they built **siege** ramps to breach the city's defenses (cf. Ezk 4:1-2).

Jerusalem had to be punished because of her sin. Her wickedness poured forth like **fresh waters** from a well. Unless she would heed the warnings and repent, she would become a **desolation**. God would have Babylon **thoroughly glean** (Lv 19:10; Ru 2:2, 7) the **remnant of Israel**; when grapes were picked some were left either inadvertently or purposefully on the vine for use by the poor, but Babylon would **pass** over the land **again** to be sure none were left, as one would pick all the grapes from a vine. The attack would be merciless.

6:10-15. Behold their **ears are closed**, literally *uncircumcised* (cf. 4:4), not open to hearing the word of the Lord, **and they cannot listen**. Jeremiah responded in amazement to Judah's unbelief—that no one would **listen** to him as he tried to warn them of the coming calamity.

This is the first of more than three dozen times Jeremiah recorded that the people did not listen to (i.e., disobeyed) God's word. It was **a reproach to them** and they had **no delight in it**. Jeremiah was **weary** of holding in God's message **of . . . wrath**, and had to **pour it out** for everyone to hear (cf. 20:9). God vowed that His wrath would be felt by all—from **the children** to **the very old**.

Both the **prophet** and the **priest . . .** dealt **falsely**, and the nation was injured by their bad leadership. The **brokenness**, or wound (v. 14) refers to the people's spiritual condition and its physical effects (cf. 8:11, 22; 10:19; 14:17; 15:18; 30:12, 14, 17). The false prophets were proclaiming, **peace, peace, but there [was] no peace** (cf. 8:11; 23:17). God's message was not of peace, but of judgment. These charlatans were **not even ashamed** and **did not even know how to blush** when their sin was exposed. God would **punish them** because they led Judah astray.

6:16. Judah had strayed from **the ancient paths** of God's righteousness (cf. 31:21; Is 30:18-21). The Lord urged her to follow the **good way** and **walk in it** (Jr 7:23) to **find rest for** their **souls**. This important idea is by quoted by Jesus in Mt 11:29 (see comments there).

6:17-21. Because they would **not listen** (v. 17) to God's instruction and **rejected** God's **law**, they brought **disaster** upon themselves. They were reaping the **fruit of their plans** (v. 19). Judah had rejected God's law, thinking she could substitute rituals for sincere obedience. God rejected faithless sacrifices made with **frankincense** imported from **Sheba**, in southwest Arabia (1Kg 10:1-13; Ezk 27:22) and of **sweet cane** (Ex 30:23; Sg 4:14), an ingredient in anointing oil imported from **a distant land**, perhaps India. The elaborate burnt offerings, divorced from genuine love for God, were **sacrifices . . . not pleasing to** Him (Jr 6:20).

6:22-26. Jeremiah warned against the foe **coming from the north** who would be **cruel** and show **no mercy** (Hab 1:6-11), as he concluded his second message. Their target was **you, O daughter of Zion**! (people of Jerusalem). This report would bring **anguish**, like the pain of **childbirth**, and grief (cf. Jr 4:31). The people would be afraid to go **into the field**, or on the **road**, because **the enemy has a sword**. They should stay home and mourn for their sin and for the coming disaster—mourning **as for an only son**, with **bitter lamentation** (v. 26).

6:27-30. Jeremiah was appointed as **an assayer and a tester**, not of metal ore, but to test the moral quality of God's **people**. They were found to be **corrupt**, and the **refining** efforts were useless. The **wicked** were not **separated** out. The smelting process separated silver from **lead**, so like impure, **rejected silver, . . . the LORD . . . rejected them**. The nation refused God's call to return to Him, so judgment was inevitable.

c. Third Prophecy of Judgment—Judgment on False Religion and Its Punishment (7:1–10:25)

Jeremiah's "Temple Address" focuses on God's judgment on the people for their false religion. They believed that God's punishment would never extend to Jerusalem or to them (cf. 5:12-13) because the temple was in Jerusalem and, they believed, God would never allow it to be destroyed (notice the repetition "the temple of the LORD" in 7:4). The Temple Address shattered this false hope and exposed the festering sore of idolatry that was producing spiritual gangrene in the people. The events in chap. 26 indicate the people's response to this message.

(1) The Temple Address: Judah's False Worship (7:1–8:3)

7:1-7. God summoned Jeremiah to go to the **gate of** the temple, **the LORD's house**, and **proclaim** His message to all who **enter by these gates to worship the LORD**. The message was designed to help the people **amend** ("to make pleasing," "to do right") their **ways**, and Jeremiah gave three specific actions to assist them (vv. 1-7). The first two concern interpersonal relationships, and the third related to the Lord. First, the people should **not oppress** the helpless in society, **the alien, the orphan, or the widow** (cf. Dt 14:19; 16:11; 24:19; Ps 94:6). Second, they were **not** to **shed innocent blood** (cf. Dt 19:19-13; 21:1-9). Third, they were to stop idolatry and not to **walk after other gods**. The blessing of obedience would be permission to **dwell . . . in the land** peacefully. Here the land of Israel is described as God's gift to Israel, having given it **to your fathers forever and ever**. The phrase **forever and ever** (*min olam v'ad olam*) is the strongest expression in Hebrew to describe perpetuity and eternality. It is generally used of God's nature and character (e.g., 1Ch 16:36; Pss 90:2; 103:17). The only exceptions to this general usage are found in this verse and Jr 25:5, describing God's gift of the land of Israel to the people of Israel as being "from everlasting to everlasting."

7:8-15. Jeremiah warned that Judah's trust in **deceptive words** would not help. Her hypocrisy was being spotlighted. She felt so secure because of the presence of the temple that she believed she was safe, saying, **We are delivered!** Yet they practiced **all these abominations**. This catalog of disobedience includes fully half of the Ten Commandments (cf. Hs 4:2). They **steal, murder, . . . commit adultery and swear falsely, . . . offer sacrifices to Baal and walk after other gods** (Jr 7:9). Her vileness had actually turned **this house, which is called by My name,** into a **den of robbers**. This problem arose in NT times, and Jesus quoted this passage when He observed inappropriate activity in the temple (cf. comments on Mt 21:12-13).

What Judah failed to realize was that God had **seen it** and was aware of all her deeds. The people presumptuously trusted in the temple building for protection (repeated three times in v. 4 to emphasize their belief) rather than trusting in the God of the temple and obeying Him. The temple (v. 14) was **called by My name**, (cf. vv. 10, 12, 30) in the sense that it was a symbol of God's presence (His **name** refers to His revealed attributes).

Judah was told to remember what God did to **Shiloh**, where the tabernacle had dwelt (Jos 18:1; Jdg 18:31; 1Sm 4:3-4). Because of Israel's **wickedness**, that city was destroyed (cf. 2Kgs 17:5-20). If Judah did not repent, the Babylonians would destroy her just as the Assyrians had taken Israel, the northern kingdom, in 722 BC.

7:16-20. Judah's sin was so serious that God told Jeremiah **do not pray, do not lift up cry or prayer, do not intercede** for her because He would not **hear** (cf. 11:14; 14:11-12). This does not mean that the Lord literally was incapable of hearing Jeremiah's prayer. The Lord hears everything. The point was that Jeremiah's pleas were futile because God had determined not to answer Jeremiah's prayer on behalf of sinful Judah.

Throughout Judah, whole families (**children, fathers, women**) were uniting in pagan worship. They prepared **cakes** of bread (flat cakes possibly formed into the image of the goddess, cf. 44:17-19, 25) for the **queen of heaven** (cf. 44:17-19, 25). This pagan goddess is possibly Ishtar, the Babylonian goddess of love, sexuality, and fertility, who is also identified with Astarte, the Canaanite high goddess of sexual love and fertility. Israelites adopted her worship at the time of the conquest, and it continued through the monarchy (Jdg 2:13; 1Kg 11:5). The worship of Ishtar/Astarte included temple prostitution, lewd sexual promiscuity, sacrificial libations, and offerings of food. The Lord admonished the Jewish people because they would **pour out drink offerings** (wine) **to other gods** (cf. Jr 19:13). Yet such idolatrous rituals were only harming those who participated in them. Their false worship did not damage God. The people would bear the consequences of their actions when God's anger and **wrath** would be **poured out** on all Judah, on both **man** and **beast**.

7:21-26. Although the people of Judah offered all the technically correct **burnt offerings** in the temple, they failed to understand God's most important **command** given at Sinai **in the day** He **brought them out of . . . Egypt**. God **commanded them** to **obey** His **voice** and **walk in all the way** He commanded (cf. 6:16). Tragically, Israel **did not obey** or pay attention (**incline their ear**) to this command, and instead **walked in their own counsels**. Since the time of the exodus, when their ancestors **came out of the land of Egypt until** Jeremiah's **day**, God continually **sent [His] servants**, the prophets like Jeremiah, to warn the people, but they **did not listen** (cf. 25:4-7).

7:27-31. God told Jeremiah the people **will not listen** to him. So Jeremiah was to go into mourning: **cut off** his **hair** (cf. Jb 1:20; Jr 48:37; Ezk 7:18), and **take up a lamentation** (*qindh*, "a funeral dirge") for the nation. He was to begin mourning because the destruction of Judah was certain, **for the Lord has rejected and forsaken the generation** because of **His wrath** against their **evil** actions. Specifically, they had **set their detestable things**, idols, in the temple itself, **the house which is called by My name, to defile it** (cf. Jr 7:14; Ezk 8:3-18).

Outside the city they **built the high places of Topheth** (cf. Jr 14) in the **valley of the son[s] of Hinnom** (cf. 19:2, 6; 32:35; the Valley of Ben-hinnom) in worship of Molech the Phoenician god. Molech had the most evil of worship rituals of any god in history, demanding parents **to burn their sons and their daughters** alive **in the fire** in a brass statue of the god as child sacrifice. This cruel practice was specifically forbidden by God (cf. Lv 18:21; 20:2-5) but practiced by some of the evil kings of Israel and Judah (cf. 2Kg 16:2-3; 21:6; 23:10; Jr 19:5). Worship of Molech was often combined with Baal worship (19:5; 32:35).

The word **Topheth** is possibly a word for a "cookstove" or "oven." The place of sacrifice was a fire pit, or a metal idol with outstretched arms, into which the living children were sacrificed. The Valley of Hinnom (Hb., ge'-*hi'nom)* is immediately south and west of Jerusalem, and in this valley the refuse of the city was burned. In Greek times the valley was called "Gehenna" (*gehennah*), and the name became synonymous with the picture of the fiery corruption of hell because of the children burned alive in sacrifice there to Molech (cf. comments on Mt 18:7-10; 2Pt 2:4).

The horror of child sacrifice was so abhorrent to the Lord, He explicitly said concerning it, **I did not command, and it did not come into My mind** (cf. 32:35). This expression does not mean that the Lord is not all knowing but rather that He totally disapproved of this wickedness. Compounding the phrases **not command** and **did not come into My mind** emphasizes God's loathing of the abhorrent practice of child sacrifice.

7:32-34. God declared that the name of this place would be changed to **valley of the Slaughter** because of the number of **dead bodies** that would be burned after the destruction of Jerusalem. The prediction about **birds** and **beasts** eating the carcasses affirms the judgment of the Mosaic covenant for disobedience (cf. Dt 28:26). To remain unburied was an abomination in the Jewish community (cf. 2Kg 9:10, 30-37). **Joy** and **gladness** would **cease**, and the **land will become a ruin** (cf. Jr 16:9; 25:10).

8:1-3. The bones of **the kings of Judah and the bones of its princes** who worshiped **the host of heaven**, pagan gods, would be removed from their graves and exposed to the **sun** and **moon**, **which they [had] loved**, and they would not be **buried** again, but **will be like dung on the face of the ground** (cf. 25:33). The **remnant** who survived the fall of Jerusalem would be **driven** away and would have **chosen** death over life in exile.

(2) The Temple Address: God's Retribution on the People (8:4–10:25)

This poetic section of the Lord's message highlights Judah's spiritual condition and her attitude toward her sin.

8:4-7. God posed a series of questions to expose Judah's refusal to turn back to Him. When people **fall** do they not try to **get up again**? When a person turns away from the right path, will he not turn around (**repent**)? People should learn from instruction, but **Jerusalem turned away in continual apostasy** . . . and **refuse[d] to return**. They refused to acknowledge any wrongdoing. **No man repented** . . . **everyone turned to his** own way. She pursued her own ways with determination like a **horse charging into** . . . **battle**. Even birds, **stork**, **turtledove**, **swift**, **and thrush**, know **the time of their migration**, but Judah did **not know** that it was time to return to her God. She had less wisdom than a bird!

8:8-12. God asked Judah another question to point out her foolishness: **How can you say, We are wise?** Judah felt superior in her wisdom to other nations because she had the **law of the Lord**. Unfortunately false **scribes** had twisted that law and **made** it **into a lie**. Their rejection of the **word of the Lord** would bring judgment (cf. Dt 28:30-45) on **everyone**, from the least to the greatest.

The leaders treated the **brokenness** of God's people **superficially**. They would dress (or bandage) the wound (cf. Jr 8:22 and comments on 6:14) as if it were not serious when in fact it was terminal. They proclaimed **peace, peace, but there [was] no peace** (vv. 10b-12 repeats the message the prophet had given in 6:12-15; cf. comments there). The truth was repeated for emphasis.

8:13-17. God would punish the nation by taking from them the blessings of the harvest, **grapes** and **figs** that He had earlier **given them**. When God's judgment began, the people would flee in panic **into the fortified cities**. They would realize they were **doomed** by the Lord because they had **sinned against** Him. Their hopes for **peace** and **healing** were replaced by **terror**.

The **snorting of** (the enemy) **horses** was heard from Dan in the north (cf. 4:15), moving across the **whole land** to come to **devour** . . . **the city and its inhabitants**. God sent the Babylonians, compared to **serpents**, to **bite** the Judahites without a remedy (**no charm**).

8:18–9:2. Jeremiah cried out to the Lord with **sorrow** . . . **beyond healing**, and his **heart** was **faint** at the suffering of his people. He implored God to **listen** to the cry of his people who had been deported to a **distant land**. In anguish they questioned if their King, the **Lord**, was **not in Zion**. God responded that Jerusalem's destruction was brought about by their sin, not by His absence. God brought the army of Babylon because Judah had **provoked** Him to anger with **their graven images** and **foreign idols**.

Judah continued to rebel, although God gave her every opportunity to repent. The people realized the seasons were passing (the Babylonian siege lasted 30 months), and they were **not saved**. They failed to repent and take God's provision for deliverance from judgment when it had been available, now they were without hope.

Jeremiah's reaction to Judah's fate was sadness and despair. He so identified with his people that he was crushed by their certain destruction. In vain he sought for **balm** from **Gilead** to heal the wound of his people (cf. v. 11 and comments on 6:14). "Balm" was the resin of the storax tree that was used medicinally. Gilead, east of the Jordan River, was famous for its healing balm (cf. Gn 37:25; Jr 46:11; 51:8; Ezk 27:17). He longed for the **health of the daughter of my people** to be **restored.**

Jeremiah is known as the "weeping prophet" because of the tears he cried over the sin and fate of his people (cf. Jr 13:17; 14:17). The grief caused Jeremiah to wish his **eyes** would become a **fountain of tears** so he could weep continually (**day and night**) for those who had been **slain**. He spoke of the Jewish people with tender sympathy, while recognizing their sin. An isolated lodging place in the desert was preferable to living with the unfaithful people of Judah.

9:3-6. God commanded truth (Ex 20:16), but in Judah lying was a way of life. They would **bend** their **tongue like their bow**, using deception like a weapon, so that **lies and not truth** prevailed **in the land**. No one could be trusted, and all refused to **know** the Lord.

9:7-9. Because of Judah's deceit, God sought to **refine** and **assay** (test) her because of her sin (cf. 6:28-30; Is 48:10; Ezk 22:18-22). Metal was heated in a crucible to melt it and test its purity. Likewise, God would place Judah in the crucible of judgment to test her integrity and deal with her deceit. God rhetorically asked Jeremiah if He should not **punish** their sin and **avenge** Himself on the nation.

9:10-16. Jeremiah was **weeping** and **wailing**, crying silently and aloud, over the condition of the land **laid waste** and untraveled, and **Jerusalem a heap of ruins** (cf. 10:22; 49:33; 51:37) because of the Babylonian attack. God asked **the wise** men of Judah to explain why was the **land ruined, laid waste**. The Lord replied with the obvious, **because they have forsaken My Law** and had followed **the Baals** (see comments on 2:23). This was why God would **scatter them among the nations** (cf. 13:24; 18:17; 30:11; 46:38; Dt 28:64) and why many in Judah would be killed by the **sword** (cf. Ezk 5:2, 12). But the Lord is faithful, and would not **annihilate** them completely because of His faithfulness to His people (cf. Jr 5:10; 31:35-37).

Although the Lord is faithful to preserve a remnant of His people, yet Jerusalem will certainly be judged and suffer the dire consequences of the city's sin. Not only did Jeremiah weep; in the next section, the Lord calls for the people, **mourning women**, to join in the lamentation for the nation's sin and the coming ruin.

9:17-24. This section contains three separate pronouncements from the Lord, each beginning with the phrase, **Thus says the LORD**. In the first section (vv. 17-21), God called for the **mourning women**, professional mourners (cf. 2Ch 35:25; Ec 12:5; Am 5:16), to lament for Jerusalem. The content of their lament was **the word of the LORD . . . the word of His mouth**, which they should then **teach** their **daughters**. This funeral dirge happened because death had **cut off** (killed) **children** and the **young men**.

In the second pronouncement (v. 22) God pictured the severity of the massacre by Babylon. The **corpses of men will fall like dung** in a field, or like sheaves of grain behind a **reaper**, so that unburied bodies would be everywhere (cf. 7:32-34). The Lord revealed this picture of certain future destruction of Judah by the armies of Babylon.

The third declaration (vv. 23-24) showed the response God expected from the people. The people were not to **boast of** their own **wisdom** or personal **might** or **riches**. Instead a person should boast only in the fact that he **understands and knows** the Lord (cf. 1Co 1:29-31). Again the word "know" (*yada'*) pictured an intimate knowledge of God (cf. Jr 1:5). God wanted the people to be intimately acquainted with His **lovingkindness, justice and righteousness. Lovingindness** (*chesed*) refers to God's loyal love (cf. 31:3; 33:11; Lm 3:22). God would stand by His commitment to His people, even in the midst of their sin. **Justice** (*mispoṭ*) is a broad term that pointed to governing justly, with fairness and equity. God would vindicate the innocent and punish the guilty. **Righteousness** (*akqah*) conveys the idea of conforming to a standard or norm. God's standards of conduct were supposed to be Israel's norm.

9:25-26. A theme of Jeremiah is the contrast between external religious practice and internal righteousness. If personal achievement or ability would not please God (v. 23), neither would outward conformity to religious rituals (being **circumcised** only in the flesh) without a right heart of true obedience (being **uncircumcised** in the heart, i.e., without sincere trust in and obedience to the Lord; cf. 4:4). The uncircumcised Gentile nations of **Egypt**, **Edom**, **Ammon**, **and Moab** were compared to faithless **Judah** and **all the house of Israel** who were similarly **uncircumcised of heart**. Judah's idolatrous, evil actions exposed the fact that although their foreskin was circumcised in obedience to the Abrahamic covenant (Gn 17:1-14), they indicated by their behavior that they were **uncircumcised** . . . in **heart** (cf. Jr 4:4). The apostle Paul also wrote that circumcision of the heart made Jewish people into true Jews (Rm 2:25-29, see comments there).

10:1-16. The series of Temple Messages concludes with a poetic section contrasting the vast difference between idols and the living God. It is a parenthetical address on the greatness of God before the judgment of God continues.

10:1-5. The poetic section begins as **the Lord speaks** to the whole **house of Israel**, both the northern kingdom already in exile and Judah, soon to be in exile, and explains the foolishness of idolatry. Israel was not supposed to **learn the way of the nations**, nor was she to be **terrified by the signs in the heavens**, as were the **nations**. "Signs" such as eclipses or comets were thought to be omens from the gods.

Such idolatrous practices were a **delusion** (*hebel*, "breath," "vanity," cf. Ec 1:2) because these gods were created by their worshipers (cf. Is 40:18-20). A person would **cut from the forest** a tree, then a **craftsman** would carve and **decorate it with silver and with gold** and **fasten** it with **nails** . . . **so it will not totter**. The Lord compared idols to a lifeless scarecrow in a cucumber field. It **cannot speak** to give knowledge and cannot **walk**, but has to be **carried** around and can do neither **harm** nor **good**. So Israel is exhorted to **not fear them**.

10:6-7. In contrast to idols, there is a burst of praise for God: **there is none like You, O Lord**. The uniqueness of God is an important theme in Scripture (cf. v. 7; Ex 15:11; Dt 33:26; Ps 86:8, 10; Is 40:18, 25). God alone is **great** and should be feared, for the Lord is **King of the nations**, that is, He is the King of kings (cf. Pss 47:8-9; 96:10).

10:8-9. The **stupid and foolish** wooden idols (10:15) were decorated with **silver** . . . **from Tarshish and gold from Uphaz**. **Tarshish** was a city probably in southern Spain, and the name was a technical term for a "mineral-bearing land" (Jnh 1:3; Ezk 27:12). **Uphaz** is mentioned only here and is either unknown or possibly a textual variant for *Ophir*, possibly a region in Arabia known for its gold (cf. 1Kg 9:28; Jb 22:24; Ps 45:9), though certain identification is impossible.

10:10-11. Unlike gold-plated wooden idols, the **Lord is the true God**, genuine in contrast with the false idols. He is **the living God and the everlasting King**, but they were lifeless, not speaking, not walking (cf. v. 5), and temporary, carved into existence by craftsmen and destined to decay. Idols were powerless and harmless (cf. v. 5), but by **His wrath the earth quakes, and the nations cannot endure His indignation**.

Aramaic, a language similar to Hebrew was the trade language of the day. Verse 11 is the only Aramaic verse in Jeremiah. Probably it is in Aramaic because it was directed to the pagan idolaters surrounding Israel. The message to these idolaters, in a language they could understand, was that their false gods **did not make the heavens and the earth** and were temporary, sure to **perish from the earth**.

10:12-15. In distinction from the powerless idols, the Lord is Creator who **made the earth by His power** (vv. 12-13). He **established the world by His wisdom** . . . **and** . . . **stretched out the heavens** (10:12-16 is virtually the same as 51:15-19). This focus on the awesome nature of a thunderstorm with its **clouds**, **lightening**, and **wind** illustrates the continuing power of God (cf. Jb 38:22; Pss 33:7; 5:7).

In comparison with the Creator, **every goldsmith** who made idols would be **put to shame by his idols**, which are **worthless, a work of mockery** ("errors and delusion"). These idols and their makers will be judged and **will perish**.

10:16. In contrast, the Lord **is not like these** lifeless idols; they can make nothing! The Creator is **the portion of Jacob** (cf. Jr 51:19). A "portion" (*heleq* "share") usually referred to something allotted to an individual (cf. Gn 14:24; Lv 6:17; 1Sm 1:5). God, in a sense, belonged to Israel. But at the same time Israel belonged to God. She was, and remains, His inheritance, and He was her inheritance. God is also the **Maker of all** (cf. Gn 1:1; Jb 4:17; 32:22; 35:10; Ps 121:2; Ec 11:5) including **Israel**, His chosen people, **the tribe of His inheritance** (Dt 4:20).

This parenthetical portion (vv. 1-16) contrasting the living God and the everlasting King (v. 10) with the worthless (v. 15) idols concludes by a proclamation of who God is: **The Lord of**

hosts is His name, a title of God often connected with His power as Creator and Redeemer (cf. Jr 31:35; 32:18; 50:34; Is 54:5; Am 4:13).

10:17-22. The Temple Address goes on to describe Jerusalem's coming destruction and exile. The people **under siege** were to **pick up** their **bundle**, indicating their meager belongings, because God was **slinging out the inhabitants of the land** (cf. Ezk 12:3-16) so they would **be found** by the Babylonians.

The people responded in anguish: **Woe is me**. The **wound** she had suffered was **incurable** (cf. Jr 6:14). Jerusalem, the mighty, fortified city was pictured as a **tent** that had collapsed. Her **sons** were deported, and there was no one to **stretch out** the tent again.

The shepherds (*ro'im*, "leaders"; cf. 2:8) who were to guide the flock had failed because they had **not sought the Lord** and the flock was scattered (cf. 23:1-2; Ezk 34:1-10). The attack from **the north** (cf. Jr 4:5) would make the **cities of Judah a desolation, a haunt of jackals** (cf. 9:11).

10:23-25. The Temple Address concludes with Jeremiah's prayer acknowledging God's control: **I know, O Lord** that a **man's way**, a person's life, cannot be considered his own, **not in himself**, nor is he free to **direct his steps**. God is in command, and only those who let God direct their ways will be truly blessed (cf. Pr 3:5-6; 16:9; 20:24; Ps 37:23).

Judah's judgment was unavoidable, therefore compassionate Jeremiah pleaded that it might come only with God's **justice** and **not with** His **anger**. He asked for God's patience and leniency in dispersing judgment lest the nation be reduced **to nothing**. By saying **me** (v. 24), Jeremiah was identifying with and representing Judah. Then Jeremiah asked that God's judgment of Judah be accompanied by His **wrath on the nations**, who refused to call on God's **name**, and had **devoured** and **consumed** God's covenant people, **Jacob**.

d. Fourth Prophecy of Judgment—The Broken Covenant (11:1–12:17)

Jeremiah's fourth general prophecy of judgment focused on Judah's sin of breaking covenant with her God. Though the message does not contain a chronological marker, several points help date the events described in the passage at around 621 BC, six years after Jeremiah's ministry began. The temple was being repaired by King Josiah that year, as part of his reforms, and a copy of the law was discovered in the renovation (cf. 2Ch 34:14-33). Several of Jeremiah's references allude to this discovery of God's law and the realization of the broken covenant (cf. Jr 11:3-5). Jeremiah called on the people to obey the words of the covenant that Josiah read to them (11:6; 2Ch 34:19-32).

(1) The Violation of the Covenant (11:1-17)

11:1-5. The word came **to Jeremiah from the Lord** to **hear the words of this covenant** and **speak to . . . Judah and . . . Jerusalem.** The covenant was the Sinai (Mosaic) covenant, which God gave when He **brought them out of the land of Egypt**. God commanded obedience, saying, **Listen to My voice** (cf. Dt 28). God reminded them of His promise to **give them a land flowing with milk and honey**, a common description of Israel, picturing agricultural prosperity (cf. Jr 32:22; Ex 3:8, 17; 33:3: Lv 20:24; Nm 13:27; Dt 6:3; Jos 5:6; Ezk 20:6, 15). Jeremiah replied **Amen, O Lord**, reflecting the "amens" given at the conclusion of each of the curses recorded in Dt 27:15-26.

11:6-11. Jeremiah called the people to **hear the words of this covenant and do them**. He also reminded them of their past failure: **Yet they did not obey**. Though God had **persistently** warned them to **listen to** His **voice** they **refused to hear** His **words** and both Israel and Judah had **broken** the Sinai **covenant**. Therefore, He would be **bringing disaster on them**, all the curses of the covenant (cf. Dt 27:15-26) to which they had said, "Amen." Israel's history was one of rebellion and correction. The book of Jeremiah is an outworking of the judgments for disobedience to this covenant.

11:12-13. With disaster on the way, the people would **go and cry to the gods to whom they burn incense**. They would seek help from the idols, but idols **will not save them** (cf. 10:1-16). Now it was too late to plead with God, for He would not listen to them (cf. 7:16). Though Josiah tried to rid the land of idolatry (2Ch 34:33), the **incense** altars devoted to **Baal** (cf. Jr 11:17) were still as numerous as the **streets of Jerusalem.**

11:14-17. Again Jeremiah was told **do not pray for this people** because their sin was so pervasive (cf. 7:16; 11:11; 14:11). Although God called Judah, **My beloved** (v. 15), the nation's wickedness took away their **right** to be in God's **house**, the temple. With **many vile deeds** of spiritual hypocrisy Judah continued to offer **sacrificial flesh**, while refusing to genuinely love and obey the Lord. She thought this feigned obedience would prevent **disaster**, so she could continue to **rejoice**. The Lord called Judah **a green olive**

tree (v. 16) described as **beautiful in fruit and form**. But His judgment would be like a **tumult**, the noise made by an attacking army (cf. Is 13:4; Ezk 1:24). God **kindled fire**, to set Judah aflame and make her **branches . . . worthless** (cf. Ezk 31:12). Judgment would fall because of the **evil** of **Israel** and **Judah** when they offered **sacrifices to Baal** (v. 17).

(2) The Consequences of Violating the Covenant (11:18–12:17)

11:18-23. Instead of heeding Jeremiah's warning, the people of **Anathoth** (his hometown, cf. 1:1) tried once again to kill him (cf. 1:8, 17-19). He was like a **gentle lamb led to the slaughter**, unaware of their plot against him. They did not want to hear him **prophesy in the name of the Lord**.

However, God **made it known** to Jeremiah and he escaped, all the while praying for vengeance on his enemies. God promised to **punish** the wicked of Anathoth with the **sword, famine**, and **disaster** because they opposed God's messenger.

12:1-6. After being delivered from the plot against his life, Jeremiah proclaimed, **Righteous are You, O Lord**, in thanksgiving for answered prayer.

Jeremiah then brought a **case** (*rib*, cf. 2:9, 29), a legal proposition before God, because he had an important question for the Lord. Jeremiah wanted to know **Why has . . . the wicked prospered**, and why are the treacherous **at ease** if God is truly angry about their sin (cf. Jb 21:7; Pss 73:3-5, 12; 94:3)? Why had God **planted them** and allowed them to produce **fruit**? They were hypocrites in their devotion to God, praying with their **lips**, but obedience was **far from their mind** (cf. Mt 15:8). Jeremiah asked God to drag them off **like sheep for the slaughter** because they treated Jeremiah like "a gentle lamb led to slaughter" (Jr 11:19).

God had judged the nation for sin with drought. Lack of rain was causing **the land to mourn** because of the **wickedness** of the people (cf. 14:1-6; Lv 26:19-20; Dt 28:22-24). The people believed that God was indifferent to their sin as they claimed that **He [would] not see** what happened (cf. Pss 73:11; 94:7).

Instead of giving real comfort or a direct answer to Jeremiah, God indicated that if Jeremiah found his present circumstances difficult, his future situation would be even worse (v. 5). God used two metaphors to make this point—a race, and a cross-country walk. If Jeremiah had **run with footmen** and become **tired**, how could he compete later with **horses**? Or if Jeremiah would **fall down**, stumble, in a **land of peace**, how could he manage if he were in the **thicket** by the **Jordan**? The idea of this second question could possibly be paraphrased: If Jeremiah could trust in God only in a time of peace, how would he manage in the midst of difficulties?

God told Jeremiah the bad news that even his own family, his **brothers** and **household**, had **dealt treacherously** with him and warned Jeremiah not to **believe them** even if they said **nice things**. Evidently they had joined the plot against Jeremiah at Anathoth (cf. 11:18-23).

12:7-9. After presenting the plot against Jeremiah (11:18–12:6), God continued His pronouncement of judgment. God tenderly described Judah as **My house**, and **My inheritance** and **beloved of My soul**. By depicting the nation in this way God was indicating that their judgment would not come from a hardened heart of a capricious king but from a loving Sovereign (cf. v. 16; Dt 4:20). Though He had wanted to bless, the people's sin would force the Lord to judge Judah (**forsaken, abandoned, given . . . into the hand of her enemies**). The nation had become **like a lion** that had **roared against** Him in opposition to His loving commands (cf. Jr 11:10). He had come to **hate her**, i.e., He had chosen to withdraw His love from her because of her sin.

God's **inheritance** had become **like a speckled bird of prey** to Him. A speckled bird's markings were different from the other birds of prey. Consequently those other birds would surround and attack this strange bird. Judah had become so estranged from God that He would call **the birds of prey against her**, and the **beasts of the field** would **devour** her.

12:10-11. The coming devastation of Jerusalem was compared to **shepherds** (cf. 2:8) and their flocks ruining a **vineyard** (cf. 2:21) as they **trampled down** God's **pleasant field**. The **desolation** of the land resulted from the false shepherds leading the people into idolatry and disaster. God's once productive nation would become a **desolate wilderness. Desolate** (*shamem)*is used three times in this verse. It is used elsewhere of the utter destruction of the temple in Jerusalem (Dn 9:17) and the devastation of Judah by the Babylonians (Jr 44:6). The repetition emphasizes the certainty and totality of the coming devastation.

12:12-13. The **destroyers** were the Babylonians, but the action was ultimately caused by the judgment of the sovereign God, hence the invaders are called the **sword of the Lord** (i.e., the Babylonians' swords were wielded as God's instruments). **There is no peace for anyone** throughout the land. All would be forced to bear the shame of their harvest of judgment **because of the fierce anger of the Lord**.

12:14-17. The fourth message closes with hope and compassion. God identified the countries around Israel as **My wicked neighbors**, indicating the Lord's unique relationship with the land of Israel (cf. Lv 25:23; Dt 32:43; Ps 78:54; Zch 2:12; 9:16). Those **wicked neighbors** of the Lord had seized Israel's God-given **inheritance** (cf. Jr 10:16). Therefore, the nations would also be uprooted **from their land** (cf. 25:12-14, 27-29; chaps. 46–51). In contrast, God would later **uproot the house of Judah** from **among them**, the Gentile nations where they had been scattered, and would **bring . . . back** Judah to **his land** (cf. 31:7-11; Ezk 37:1-14).

Though God would judge these Gentile nations, He will later have **compassion**, if they **learn the ways** of **My people** and **swear by My name** (cf. Is 56:7). Then God will restore them to their own lands. This will happen when Messiah returns to establish His millennial kingdom on earth. Those nations that follow the Messiah of Israel will be **built up in the midst of My people**. However, God would **destroy** any nation that **will not listen** (cf. Zch 14:9, 16-19).

e. Fifth Prophecy of Judgment—The Object Lessons of the Linen Belt and the Wineskins (13:1-27)

To clarify the message of judgment, the Lord directed Jeremiah to instruct the people with a series of object lessons and parables. These unusual means of communication were designed to provoke interest from unresponsive Judah (cf. 7:24, 28; 11:8; 32:33). Likewise Ezekiel was commanded to use similar techniques in Babylon to communicate truth from the Lord (cf. Ezk 4:1-5:4).

(1) The Illustration of the Linen Waistband (13:1-11)

13:1-7. God commanded Jeremiah to buy **a linen waistband**, and wear it, but not **put it in water**. A **waistband** was a sash or cloth tied around one's waist as the innermost garment (cf. 2Kg 1:8; Is 5:27). Those observing Jeremiah's actions would notice its significance—**linen** was the fabric used for the priestly garments (cf. Lv 16:4; Ezk 44:17-18).

After wearing the belt for a time, God told him to take it to **the Euphrates** (*parah)* and **hide it there in a crevice of the rock**. There are two possible meanings of *parah*. First, it may refer to the Euphrates River in Babylon, as reflected in the NASB translation. In this case, Jeremiah would have walked to the Euphrates River, a round-trip journey of about 700 miles, to bury this sash. However, a second possibility is that Jeremiah traveled to the village of Parah (*pardh*) about three miles northeast of Anathoth in the tribe of Benjamin (cf. Jos 18:21, 23). A deep wadi in this area, known today as 'Ain Farah, fits the description of a place with crevices and rocks. This seems the more likely explanation for the following reasons. First, in Hebrew the spellings for "to Parah" and "to Euphrates" are identical (cf. Jr 13:4-7). Second, by using a location so close to home the people would be able to observe Jeremiah's symbolic actions. Third, the similarity of name would remind the nation of the army of Babylon from the **Euphrates** that was coming to destroy them.

After many days, an unspecified but significant amount of time, God told Jeremiah to retrieve the belt from where he had **hidden it**. (Another round-trip walk of 700 miles would have been necessary if Parah is the Euphrates. This adds further support to the view that the place where Jeremiah was sent was the nearby village of Parah.) As he dug up the **waistband** he found that its exposure to the elements had made it **totally worthless**. The waistband was ruined.

13:8-11. The Lord explained the lesson of the waistband. Just as the linen was ruined, so would God **destroy the pride of Judah and . . . Jerusalem**. The belt represented **the whole household of Israel and . . . Judah**. It was a symbol of their formerly intimate relationship with God, as they were to **cling** to Him and be His people for **renown**, **praise**, and **glory**. However, when they became **wicked people who** refused **to listen** to God's words, they were **just like this waistband which** was **totally worthless**.

(2) The Parable of the Wineskins (13:12-14)

13:12-14. The next object lesson is more direct. Jeremiah declared, **Every jug is to be filled with wine**. The people scoffed at Jeremiah's self-evident proverb. Of course every wine jar should be filled with wine. Then Jeremiah drove home the point of the parable. The empty jars represented **all the inhabitants of this land** including Davidic **kings**, **priests**, and **prophets**. God would **fill** them **with drunkenness**, a symbol of judgment (cf. Is 49:26; 63:6; Jr 25:15-25; 51:7, 39), **dash them against each other**, and they would be broken without **pity** or **compassion**.

(3) The Message on Sin and Its Results (13:15-27)

13:15-17. The **haughty** people were admonished to **give glory to the LORD your God** before He brought the **darkness**, **deep darkness**, and **gloom** of certain judgment (cf. Ezk 30:3,18; 32:7-8; 34:12; Jl 2:12; Am 5:18-20; Zph 1:15). If they refused to **listen** and repent, Jeremiah would **sob** (Jr 14:17) because their foolish **pride** would cause the **flock of the LORD** to be **taken captive**.

13:18-19. Jeremiah's earlier message had been to the people, now he addressed the **king and the queen mother**. The reference is probably to King Jehoiachin (also known as Jeconiah) and the Queen Mother Nehushta, the widow of King Jehoiakim (cf. 29:2; 2Kg 24:8, 12, 15). They were exhorted to humble themselves (**take a lowly seat**). Because **your . . . crown has come down from your head**, and **Judah has been carried into exile, wholly carried into exile** (repeated for emphasis). Since they went into captivity in 597 BC after his reign of just three months (2Kgs 24:8), the events in this prophecy must have taken place during that three-month period.

13:20-21. The king was urged to **lift up** his **eyes** and see the armies **coming from the north** (1:14; 4:6; 6:1, 22; 10:22) who would remove the **flock**, the people of Judah (cf. 10:21; 13:17). Those with whom Judah had once tried to be aligned, her **companions**, would become her cruel task-masters (cf. Is 39:1-7; Ezk. 23:14-27). As a result, Judah would be in pain **like a woman in child-birth** (cf. Jr 4:31).

13:22-27. The reason for **these things**, the coming disasters, was because of **the magnitude of your iniquity**. The people would be put to open humiliation, disgraced publicly like a common prostitute, **skirts . . . removed and . . . heels . . . exposed** (vv. 26-27; Is 47:3; Hs 2:3, 10). Judah was incapable of doing **good**. Just as an **Ethiopian** could not **change his skin** color nor a **leopard his spots** (Jr 13:23), neither could Judah change herself. Because they had **forgotten** God and **trusted in falsehood** (v. 25), they would certainly go into exile, scattered **like drifting straw to the desert wind** (v. 24; cf. 4:11-12). Using language to match Judah's lewd conduct, God declared that He would pull her **skirts . . . over** her **face** (cf. v. 22). Her **adulteries** and **lustful neighings** (like wild animals in heat, cf. 2:23-24) characterized the **lewdness of** their **prostitution**. Her **abominations** of idolatry had been seen by God, and would lead to judgment (**Woe to you, O Jerusalem!**).

f. Sixth Prophecy of Judgment—The Drought and Prayer (14:1–15:21)

14:1-6. At the time of the exodus, God warned the Jewish people of judgment for disobedience. **Drought** was one of the covenant curses God said He would send on them for sin (cf. Lv 26:18-19; Dt 28:22-24; Jr 3:3; 12:4). The poetic section pictures the land of Israel suffering severe **drought**. **Judah mourns** because there was no water in the **cisterns**, where rain was collected for time of emergency.

There was **no water** because there was **no rain**. The **ground is cracked**, dried out, the animals suffered, the crops failed (**the farmers have been put to shame**). Both the people in the city and the farmers in the country **covered their heads**, a sign of grief or shame (cf. 2Sm 15:30). Those who had rejected the "living waters" of life for false cisterns (Jr 2:13) now found their physical water supply matching the useless spiritual water supply to which they had turned.

14:7-9. The severity of the drought forced the people to cry to God for deliverance. They implored Him to **act for** His **name's sake**, calling on the Lord to honor His Name (cf. v. 21; Jos 7:9; Pss 25:11; 79:9; 106:8; 109:21; 143:11; Is 48:9-11) despite their **iniquities**. They admitted their many **apostasies** and asked God to intervene and supply rain. By calling God the **Hope of Israel** (cf. Jr 17:13; 50:7) and the **Savior** (cf. Is 19:20; 43:3, 11; 45:15, 21; 49:26; 60:16; 63:8) the people acknowledged the Lord as the only One who could deliver them.

Though God had the power to help, He did not answer the people's pleas for rain. The people accused God of acting like a **stranger in the land**, or **traveler** who had no real concern for the country through which He was traveling. God's failure to act reminded them of a man who had been **dismayed**, ambushed, and overcome before he could defend himself, or a **mighty man** who was powerless. Despite God's silence, they acknowledged He was **in** their **midst**, and the nation was **called by Your name** (cf. Jr 7:10). So the people pleaded with Him not to **forsake** them. Times of adversity were driving the people back to seek God.

14:10-12. Instead of responding to their confession and plea, the Lord reminded them that they **have loved to wander**. He upbraided them for their waywardness. God knew that their confession was only superficial. They claimed God as their Lord, but they refused to keep **their feet in check**. Because of their continued bent toward sin, God said He did not **accept them** or their superficial confession. Instead, He would **remember their iniquity** and punish them for their sins.

God again told Jeremiah **not to pray for . . . this people** (cf. 7:16; 11:14). Their feeble efforts to manipulate God to answer them took several forms. They would fast and **offer burnt offering**, hoping to appease the Lord and avert His wrath. But God cannot be bought or tricked. He vowed to destroy, **make an end**, to the wicked with the **sword**, **famine**, and **pestilence**, the three hammer blows of divine judgment (cf. Lv 26:23-26; Jr 21:6-7, 9; 24:10; 27:8, 13; 29:17-18; 32:24, 36; 34:17; 38:2; 42:17, 22; 44:13; Ezk 5:12; 6:11; 7:15; 12:16; Rv 6:8).

14:13-16. Jeremiah interrupted the Lord: **But, Ah, Lord God!** The false **prophets** were contradicting His message. Instead of the **sword** or **famine**, they were announcing that God would give **lasting peace** to Jerusalem (cf. 5:12-13; 6:13-14; 7:4, 9-10; 27:16; 28:2-4). God explained that the messages of these false prophets were **falsehood[s]** because they had not been **sent** by Him (14:14,15). Their messages were **false visions** and **the deceptions of their own minds**. God would judge them for their lies by destroying both the false prophets and those who listened to them. They would **be thrown out into the streets of Jerusalem**, and all would perish by **famine** and **sword** (cf. vv. 13, 18). No one would even survive to bury them (cf. 7:33; 9:22) because God **will pour out their own wickedness on them**.

14:17-18. At the thought of this suffering, Jeremiah began to weep once more, and his eyes were filled **with tears night and day** over Jerusalem's fall (cf. 9:1, 18; 13:17; Lm 3:48-51). He pictured the city as a **virgin daughter** (cf. Is 37:22; Jr 8:21; Lm 1:15) who was **crushed with a mighty blow**, a mortal wound (cf. Jr 6:14), and Jeremiah's heart was broken for her. Conditions were terrible in and around the city. The **country** surrounding Jerusalem was covered with the corpses of those **slain with the sword**. People who escaped to the **city** were slowly falling to the ravages of **diseases** and **famine**. **Both prophet and priest**, who should have set the people aright, were **roving**, wandering **about in the land**, and had nothing to teach because they did **not know**.

14:19-22. In light of their circumstances, the people asked God two related questions: **Have You completely rejected Judah?** and **Have You loathed Zion?** They were puzzled as to why God would despise them and why He afflicted them (cf. "why" in vv. 8-9). Though they hoped for **peace**, they had experienced only **terror**. Their circumstances prompted them again to acknowledge their **wickedness** (cf. v. 7) and **iniquity** and to ask God to help them.

Again, they appealed for God's help based on His personal character (**for Your own name's sake**; cf. v. 7), His temple (**throne of Your glory**; cf. 3:17; 17:12), and His **covenant** (cf. 11:2-5). The people were quick to remind God of His obligations to the nation, but failed in their own obligations to Him. They finally admitted that the **idols of the nations**, the pagan gods (cf. 2:5) they had worshiped, could not **give rain** to quench the drought. They acknowledged the only source of rain was the **Lord our God**, **therefore we hope in You** (cf. 1Kg 17:1; 18:18-46).

15:1-4. Here **the Lord** responded to an earlier plea, "Have you completely rejected Judah?" and the related question, why "terror" instead of "healing"? (14:19-22). The nation's sin was so habitual that judgment was inevitable. Even the intercessory prayer of **Moses and Samuel** could not stop God's judgment. These two men were remembered in Israel for their leadership and intercession for the people. **Moses** pled for God to turn away His wrath from Israel when they sinned in the wilderness (Ex 32:9-14; Nm 14:11-20; Dt 9:18-20, 25-29). **Samuel** interceded to defeat their Philistine enemies and turn away God's wrath when the nation sinned (1Sm 7:3-11; 12:19-25). The condition of the nation was so dire at this point, that even the prayers of **Moses** or **Samuel** would be useless.

The fate of Jerusalem was certain. The future held **four kinds of doom** (Jr 15:3). Some were **destined** to **death**, probably death by plague. Others would be cut down by the **sword**, killed by the Babylonian army, while others would die from **famine** when the city was under siege. However, those not appointed to death (cf. 14:12) would be taken into **captivity**. The future of **four kinds of doom** included the dead being devoured and destroyed by **dogs**, **birds**, and wild **beasts** (cf. 16:3).

The consequences of Judah's sin were irreversible, because she followed the ways of **Manasseh, the son of Hezekiah** (cf. 2Kg 21:1-18; 2Ch 33:1-20). **Manasseh**, whose name means "causing to forget" ruled Judah for more than 50 years (697–643 BC). He was Judah's most wicked king, and he led the nation "to do evil more than the nations whom the LORD destroyed before the sons of Israel" (2Kg 21:9-17). Even Josiah's reforms could only postpone her certain destruction (2Kg 22:16-20).

(1) The Fate of Jerusalem (15:5-9)

15:5-7. The people of **Jerusalem** are questioned by God: **Who will have pity** when you are judged? The only One who had ever cared for her was God, but she had **forsaken** Him. Therefore God vowed to **destroy** her without **relenting**. He would **winnow** her as a farmer winnowed grain to remove the unbelievers who were like chaff because **they did not repent**.

15:8-9. In judgment, all the people would be struck by the **destroyer**. **Widows** would become more numerous than the **sand of the seas**, as the Babylonians slaughtered the men. To be a mother of **seven sons** symbolized a zenith of happiness and security. But she would **pine away** at the loss of her children. Though this "mother" could mean a physical mother, it is possible that Jeremiah was picturing Jerusalem as a mother who felt secure, but suffered tragic loss. Even the initial **survivors** would die by the **sword**. In either case, Babylon would shatter her security by destroying the city and those who lived in it.

(2) Jeremiah's Complaint (15:10-21)

15:10-11. As Jeremiah considered the seriousness of Judah's sin and the message he had to give, the prophet wished he had never been born: **Woe to me**, he lamented. He pictured the whole land against him, though he had not **lent** or borrowed, actions that could arouse tensions and conflicts (cf. Neh 5:1-13; Pr 22:7). The prophet was innocent of any wrongdoing, but the people despised him because of his unpopular message.

God assured him of vindication. In the future his **enemy** would **make supplication** to him when the times of **distress** arrived. This promise was fulfilled specifically by the requests of King Zedekiah to Jeremiah (cf. Jr 21:1-7; 37:1-10, 17-20; 38:14-26).

15:12-14. This rhetorical question emphasized the inevitability of judgment. Just as a man cannot **smash iron** or **bronze** with his bare hands, so the people of Judah would be unable to break the power of the Babylonian attack.

Indeed all their **wealth** would be plundered as **booty**, spoils of war (cf. 17:3; 20:5), by the invaders. The Babylonians would enslave the Judahites and deport them to a **land you do not know** (cf. 14:18; 15:2; 16:13; 17:4) because God's **anger . . . will burn upon** them.

15:15-18. Jeremiah asked God to **Remember** and **take notice** of him. God had promised to deliver and vindicate Jeremiah (v. 11), but in light of the coming calamity (vv. 12-14) Jeremiah asked for speedy help and **vengeance**. He wanted to be vindicated before God would **take [him] away** in death.

Jeremiah's request was based on his relationship with God. In contrast with the people of Judah who despised God's word (cf. 8:9), Jeremiah accepted and internalized (**ate**) God's **words**, his **joy** and **delight** (cf. Ps 1:2). He loved and identified with God, **for I have been called by Your name, O LORD God of hosts**. Jeremiah refused to associate with the company of **merrymakers** (cf. Ps 1:1), choosing instead to sit **alone** and be guided by God's **hand**. He shared God's indignation over the people's sin.

Jeremiah ended this address by sadly recounting his pitiful condition. He wanted to know why his **pain** was **perpetual** and his **wound incurable**. He felt that God was protracting his suffering. Worse yet, he wondered if the God who claimed to be a spring of living waters (cf. Jr 2:13), had become like a **deceptive stream** with **unreliable** water. These tragic and harsh circumstances caused Jeremiah to waver in his hope in God. The difficult circumstances of both Elijah (1Kg 19) and John the Baptist (Mt 11:1-19) had a demoralizing effect upon them, just as Jeremiah's deflated him. But like these men, Jeremiah was ultimately comforted and strengthened by the Lord.

15:19-21. God responded to Jeremiah's discouragement. He instructed him to **return**, to refocus on the Lord, and God would **restore** him. His focus would have to be on the Lord to **extract the precious from the worthless**. Understanding God's Word and His promises would enable Jeremiah to understand what was eternal and what was temporary (cf. 2Co 4:18). He was to remain steadfast before God so the people would turn to Jeremiah; in no case was he to **turn to them**.

God ended by restating the promises He made when He commissioned Jeremiah as a prophet (cf. Jr 1:18-19). He would strengthen Jeremiah as a **wall of bronze** so that those opposing him could **not prevail** over him. Though opposition would come, God reminded him, **I am with you to save you**, and promised to **deliver** Jeremiah from **the grasp of the violent**.

Like Jeremiah, we must remember that living for the Lord is not always easy. We must be prepared for trials, obstacles, and opposition, sometimes even from our own family (see 12:5-6). However, we have God's Word and know that He is always faithful to us. Sometimes God needs to take us back to the basics to remind us of what He has promised (v. 16).

g. Seventh Prophecy of Judgment—Jeremiah's Restrictions and Judah's Sin (16:1–17:18)

(1) Jeremiah's Restrictions (16:1-9)

16:1-4. To make God's message graphically clear, Jeremiah was instructed to proclaim the warning not only with words, but also with his own life as an object lesson. God placed several restrictions on Jeremiah's personal life that were object lessons for Judah. The first restriction on Jeremiah (vv. 1-4) concerned his personal life. He was commanded **not to take a wife** or to **have sons or daughters**. God's purpose was to show that the coming catastrophe would disrupt all normal relationships because children born in Jerusalem **will die** by **sword and famine** (cf. 14:15-16; 15:2). The carnage would be so extensive that those killed would not even be mourned or buried, but their **carcasses will become food for the birds . . . and for the beasts** (cf. 15:3; 16:6; 25:33).

16:5-7. The second restriction on Jeremiah concerned his activities. He was not to enter a **house of mourning** or **lament** (mourn) or **console** the bereaved (cf. Ezk 24:15-24). He was not to display the normal emotion of grief or to offer comfort when someone died. There were three purposes in this restriction. First, it was to show that God had **withdrawn [His] peace . . . lovingkindness and compassion**. Second, it served as a reminder to Judah that those who would die during the fall of Jerusalem would **not be buried** or **lamented** (cf. Jr 16:4). The survivors would find no one to **comfort** them in their grief, for the devastation would be too widespread. To **gash** oneself and to **shave** one's **head** were signs of grief (cf. 41:5; 47:5; 48:37) though the law forbade these practices (Dt 14:1) because of their pagan associations (cf. 1Kg 18:28).

16:8-9. The third restraint on Jeremiah was not to enter a house where there was **feasting**. This prohibition indicated that times of **rejoicing** and **gladness**, even celebrations at a wedding, would soon cease (cf. 25:10).

(2) Judah's Sin (16:10–17:18)

16:10-13. God forewarned Jeremiah of the peoples' response to his message. Naively they asked **for what reason** they deserved such judgment. God's answer underscored the root problem throughout Israel's history. It was **because** the previous generations (**forefathers**) had **forsaken** the Living God and **followed other gods** and Jeremiah's generation **too** had **done evil**. Instead of learning from their ancestors' errors, the current generation was going further astray. Each person was following the **stubbornness** within his **evil heart** rather than **listening to** God.

Because of their continued rebellion, God vowed to **hurl** the people of Judah **out of this land**, (cf. 1Sm 18:11; 20:33; Jr 22:26-28). The people would be violently thrust into a **land which you have not known** (cf. 14:18; 15:2, 14; 17:4) where they would **serve other gods** (cf. 5:19). Because they rejected God He would show them **no favor** (cf. v. 5).

16:14-15. Again God interrupted His pronouncement judgment to present a word of hope. In case the people interpreted His previous words to mean that Israel would no longer have any place in His covenant program, God stated clearly that the judgment by Babylon was not permanent (cf. 4:27; 5:18). Jeremiah introduced God's promise of future blessing for Israel with the phrase the **days are coming**. This is an eschatological formula the prophet frequently used (cf. vv. 14-16; 23:5, 7; 30:3; see comments on 31:27-40; 38; 33:14; 51:47, 52; Am 9:13) to speak of events occurring in the distant future during the end times. Here the prophet is telling of a time, after Judah's return from captivity in Babylon, when there would be a new "exodus." No longer would the people look back to the first exodus when God brought Israel out of Egypt. Ultimately, at the end of days, Israel as a nation would be restored to her land and would then enjoy God's blessing.

Although the Jewish people would return from the 70-year Babylonian exile (516 BC; cf. 29:10) and live in the land until the Roman expulsion in AD 70, they would then suffer an even more extensive expulsion from their homeland. So the return from Babylon did not fulfill the specifics of this prophecy. Rather, this passage predicts the ultimate return of the Jewish people to their land at the end of days. This return and blessing is yet to take place. In the millennial reign of Christ the nation will experience the full benefits of the Davidic covenant (cf. 1Ch 17:9) as well as the new covenant (Jr 31:31-34). In the messianic kingdom, the Jewish people will not just celebrate the return from **Egypt**, but will also point back to the time when God brought them back from the **land of the north** and **from all the countries where He had banished them**. Following the Babylonian exile the Jewish people returned from Babylon—though not from a worldwide dispersion that Jeremiah is here describing. This is a future return at the end of days, beyond the return from the Babylonian exile. Thus God affirmed His promise ultimately to **restore** Israel **to their own land which I gave to their fathers** (cf. Gn 15:18; 17:8; 26:3-5; 35:9-12).

Because the texts of vv. 14-15 and 23:7-8 are nearly identical, some scholars suggest this may be a scribal error. It is better to understand that Jeremiah used the same or similar wording in several places throughout his book, for emphasis (cf. 1:18-19 with 15:20; 6:13-15 with 8:10-12; 7:31-32 with 19:5-6; 15:13-14 with 17:3-4).

16:16-18. After assuring Israel of her future blessing, Jeremiah foretold the means the Lord would use—persecution—to draw His people back to their ancient homeland. When the Jewish people returned to Israel from Babylon, it was by the decree of Cyrus (Ezk 1:1-8; Jr 25:12, 29:10). The return was peaceful and even aided by the Persian king. This passage is describing a different, post-Babylonian, return to the land and uses metaphors for persecution to describe it. First, there is the image of (v. 16), **fishermen** who would **fish for them**, catching them against their will. Also **many hunters** would **hunt them from every mountain** . . . **hill** . . . **clefts**, a terrifying image, but none could escape. God's **eyes** saw all of their **iniquity** (32:10) and He would **doubly repay** . . . **their sin**.

It is likely that these verses found their fulfillment in the restoration of the Jewish people to the land of Israel beginning in the 19th century and continuing to today. In the modern era, Jewish people have fled from pogroms in Russia, Nazi persecution in Germany, and Soviet oppression. As a result of these **hunters** and **fishermen**, the Jewish people made their way back to their ancient homeland Israel, even before the rebirth of the modern state of Israel. This remarkable return to the land of Israel through persecution from around the world has caused greater marvel than the much earlier exodus from Egypt or the peaceful return from Babylon.

The people will return to the land of Israel, God identifying it as **My land** and **My inheritance** (cf. 2:7; 3:18). This compounds the significance that they had **polluted** ("defiling," "desecrating" "make ceremonial unclean"; cf. 3:2, 9; 23:11) His holy land (Ps 78:54) with **their detestable idols** and **abominations**.

16:19-21. The prophet Jeremiah interjected words of hope and praise, and he affirmed his trust, identifying God as **my strength** . . . **stronghold** . . . **refuge** (cf. Ps 18:2). He emphasized the protection God provided for him.

After affirming his trust in God, Jeremiah looked forward to the day when all the **nations** of the world **will come** to know the God of Israel (Jr 12:14-17; Is 56:7). They will admit their former objects of worship were **futility**, nothing but false gods (cf. Jr 2:5). At that time God will **make them know** (used three times for emphasis) of His **power** and **might** so they will understand His character and will **know that My name is the Lord** (cf. Ezk 36:22-23).

17:1-4. God would not overlook the sin of the Jewish people and their defilement of His land. He would enter into judgment with them, so they would know Him. He described the seriousness of the **sin of Judah** as being **written** with an **iron stylus** with a **diamond point**. This pictures the method used to engrave the most permanent writing into stone (cf. Jb 19:24). Judah was so entrenched in her ways that it was as if **sin** was **engraved** on the **tablet of their heart** and expressed itself on the **horns of their altars**. The **horns** were projections at the top of each altar on the four corners where sacrificial blood was sprinkled for forgiveness of sin (Lv 16:18).

Idolatry was so pervasive that even their **children** participated in worship to the **Asherim**. Asherah was the Hebrew name for the Canaanite fertility goddess who was worshiped in various parts of the ancient Near East. The biblical writers sometimes did not make a clear distinction between references to Asherah as a goddess and **Asherim** as objects of worship. The worship of Asherah was associated with sacred groves of trees and the erecting of wooden fertility poles of male or female sexual imagery (Dt 7:5; 16:21-22; 1Kg 15:13). Although the Lord strictly forbade the worship of Asherah, throughout the preexilic period Israel often sinned by worshiping this pagan deity (1Kg 14:23). Wicked King Manasseh had placed an Asherah pole in the temple (2Kg 21:7; cf. Dt 16:21). Though he ultimately removed it (2Ch 33:13, 15), it was evidently reinstalled, because Josiah took it out during his reforms and burned it (2Kg 23:6). However, after Josiah's death the people resumed their idolatry, and again worshiped the Asherah (cf. Ezk 8:5). They worshiped their idols under **green trees** on the **high hills**, traditional places of pagan worship (cf. Ezk 6:13).

Because of Judah's sin, God would **give over** the city of Zion, His **mountain**, and the **wealth** of its inhabitants, as **booty** to the invaders. The image of **mountain of Mine** expands the geographic location of the temple mount to refer to the whole city of Jerusalem (cf. Jr 15:13; 20:5). The people of Judah would be forced to **let go** of their **inheritance**, the land God **gave** them. He would make them **serve** their **enemies** in **the land** they did **not know** (cf. 14:18; 15:2, 14; 16:13).

17:5-8. Judah's sin centered on her trust in false gods and foreign alliances, rather than in the Lord. This short poem contrasts the way of the wicked, who fail to trust in God (vv. 5-6), with the way of the righteous, who trust only in Him (vv. 7-8). It is similar to the message of Ps 1, but in reverse order.

Judah had been trusting false gods and foreign alliances for **strength**, but God said anyone who **trusts** in man (**flesh**) for protection is **cursed** because his **heart turns away** from God. Instead of prospering, he will be like a **bush in the desert**, living in a harsh **wilderness**. By contrast, a righteous person is **blessed** because he **trusts in the Lord**. He will flourish **like a tree planted by the water**, which puts down deep **roots by a stream**, and not be troubled by **drought**. When difficulties (represented figuratively by **heat** and **drought**) come, he will not fear, but will bear **fruit**. Jeremiah used the warning concerning disobedience and the consequences of drought as judgment to communicate the seriousness of Judah's sin (Jr 2:13; 14:1-9)

17:9-11. The source of Judah's problem was her **heart**. It was so **deceitful** and **desperately sick** that Jeremiah wondered **who can** even **understand it**. God informed Jeremiah that He alone understands it, that He alone has the ability to **search the heart** and **test the mind**. God knows those innermost thoughts and motives that an individual might hide from all others. Therefore God could justly render to each person what his deeds deserve **according to his ways**.

Jeremiah used a proverb to illustrate the point of cause and effect. If a **partridge**, perhaps a type of sand grouse, hatched the eggs of another bird, the offspring would soon desert the mother and fly away. Similarly, A man **who makes a fortune, but unjustly**, will also lose his wealth. **It will forsake him**, and the one who had been hoarding it would be exposed as **a fool**. This will happen when God brings the Babylonian destruction to discipline Judah.

17:12-13. The prophet contrasted the foolishness of trusting in wealth or human wisdom with the wisdom of trusting in the Lord. Here the focus shifts to the majesty of God. **A glorious throne** pictures His grandeur (cf. 14:21; Is 6:1). The location is **on high . . . the place of our sanctuary** (Ex 15:17), the temple on Mount Zion, the "high mountain of Israel" and the "joy of the whole earth" (Ezk 20:40; Ps 48:2). God's eternality is accentuated with the phrase **from the beginning** (Ex 3:14; Dn 7:9). The Lord reigns and is **the hope of Israel** (cf. Jr 14:8; 17:13).

All who **turn away** from trust in the Lord would be **written down**, but not in the Book of Life (Ex 32:32-33; Ps 69:28). They deserved this fate at the hands of the Babylonians because they had **forsaken** the **fountain of living water** (cf. Jr 2:13; Is 12:1-6), **even the Lord**.

17:14-18. After the warning not to forsake the Lord, Jeremiah concluded with a personal lament, calling on God for help in two ways: **Heal me, O Lord, and I will be healed** and **Save me and I will be saved**. He confirmed his confidence in the Lord regardless of the people's response to his message. Jeremiah reminded the Lord, **I have not hurried away from being a shepherd after You.** He was confident in God, **For You are my praise** (cf. Dt 10:21; Ps 109:1).

Jeremiah contrasted his faithful devotion to God with the unbelief of those persecuting him. They scoffed at his predictions (**Where is the word of the Lord?**) and demanded that those prophecies now be fulfilled at once (**Let it come now!**) if they were true. Yet, in spite of this opposition, Jeremiah had **not hurried away**; he faithfully served as God's **shepherd** and looked to Him for **refuge** when judgment fell in **the day of disaster**.

Therefore Jeremiah asked God to put his persecutors **to shame** by bringing on them the **day of disaster** he had been predicting. Because they refused to accept his message, he asked God to bring the full measure of judgment against them (**twofold destruction**; cf. Jr 16:18).

h. Eighth Prophecy of Judgment—For Failure to Keep the Sabbath (17:19-27)

Jeremiah's previous message was against the general sin and rebellion of the people; it highlighted idolatry, sin against the temple, and the hypocritical sacrifices. This message of judgment focuses on one specific command in the Mosaic law, the Sabbath (cf. Ex 20:8-11; Dt 5:12, 14). Because the Sabbath was more than a component of the covenant (it was one of the primary "signs" of the Mosaic covenant; cf. Dt 5:15; 31:16-17), breaking of the Sabbath was exemplary of breaking the whole covenant, and showed how far the nation had departed from God. Again there is an explicit offer of repentance. Blessing will follow obedience, but judgment will follow disobedience.

17:19-20. The Lord commanded Jeremiah to **stand** in the **public gate**. The specific gate is unknown, though it is the gate through which the **kings of Judah . . . and all inhabitants of Jerusalem** go in and out. Because it was so busy, many people would hear his message. After delivering his message there, he went to **all the** other **gates of Jerusalem** as well.

17:21-23. Jeremiah stood at the **gates** of Jerusalem and could observe people perpetually violating the Sabbath by carrying loads **on the sabbath day**. He cautioned them to not **bring anything in through the gates**, meaning that they should not conduct business, nor **bring a load out of your houses** (do work at home), on the Sabbath. The Sabbath was given to Israel as a sign of the Mosaic covenant, with the seventh day designated as a time of complete rest, holy to the Lord (Ex 31:15-17). Their **forefathers** had violated this command, and Jerusalem now followed their example. Keeping the Sabbath was an essential visible test of Israel's faithfulness to God's covenant since it marked God as Creator (Jr 10:11-16), served as a witness against idolatry, and marked the covenant relationship between God and Israel.

17:24-27. Blessing would come from faithfulness to the law: **If** Israel would **listen** and obey God's commandments, **then** God would bless Jerusalem with three distinct, conspicuous blessings: First would be the continuation of the Davidic dynasty, **kings . . . sitting on the throne of David**. Second, people would **come** to the city from all around the country, the **land of Benjamin**, the **lowland**, the **hill country** (the hills of the Shephelah in southwest central Israel), and **Negev** (the far south wilderness of the Dead Sea and desert), and Jerusalem would be **inhabited forever**. All of this suggests the spiritual and financial health of the land and the city of Jerusalem. Third, the temple will be the center of worship as the people **bring . . . offerings . . . incense . . . sacrifices of thanksgiving to the house of the Lord**. King David's dynasty will last forever when Messiah, Son of David sits on the throne of David (cf. 23:5-6; 30:9; 33:15; 2Sm 7:12-17), Jerusalem will be inhabited for all time (Zch 2:2-12; 8:3; 14:11), and the nation will live under the new covenant, worshiping the King (Jr 31:33-34). However, if they would **not listen** to **keep the sabbath day holy**, judgment would fall, and God would **kindle a fire** to **devour . . . Jerusalem** (cf. 49:27).

i. Ninth Prophecy of Judgment—Object Lesson of the Potter and the Broken Jar (18:1–20:18)

Jeremiah's ninth general message of judgment was a series of parables and events that climaxed the first section of the prophecies of judgment. Rather than giving a direct message of judgment, Jeremiah delivered this section of judgment oracles in the form of parables and object lessons.

The lesson of the potter (18:1–19:15) demonstrated God's sovereign rule over Judah (18:1-23) and its impending judgment (19:1-15). A pivot in the book, chap. 20 prepares the reader for the open opposition to Jeremiah's messages and specific prophecies of judgment that follow.

(1) The Message at the Potter's House (18:1-23)

18:1-12. God told Jeremiah to **go down to the potter's house** (v. 1-3) and watch him molding clay into his wheel reshaping unsatisfactory pots (for a similar use of this imagery, see Rm 9:20-21 and comments there). The potter pressed the clay **into another vessel, as it pleased the potter** (Jr 18:3-4). The potter and the clay illustrated the Lord's relationship with Israel: **like the clay in the potter's hand, so are you in My hand** (v. 6). God has the right to **uproot** (v. 7) or **plant** (v. 9) a nation as He pleases. He had promised the nation blessing; but since she continued to do **evil**, He would reconsider, **think better of the good**, and bring about **calamity** (18:10-11). However, if Judah would **turn back** her **evil way** God would also revoke the disaster He threatened to send. But the people of Judah would say, **It's hopeless!** (v. 12; cf. 13:23) and would stubbornly continue to **follow** their **own plans** of their **evil heart[s]**.

18:13-17. Even the **nations** around **Judah** would testify of her **appalling** acts as she refused to follow her God (cf. 2:10-11). Even the **snow of Lebanon** and the **cold flowing water** were more dependable than fickle Judah. She had **forgotten** God to worship **worthless gods** (cf. 2:5), which only caused her to stumble away and abandon the **ancient paths** of obedience to God's Word (cf. 6:16; Is 2:3-5; 30:21). God's judgment would **make their land a desolation**. She would become the **object of perpetual hissing**—mockery (Jr 19:8) by people **astonished** at her condition (cf. 9:8; Lm 2:15). The Lord vowed to **scatter** the nation like the **east wind** (cf. Jr 4:11-12; 13:24). They should expect God's judgment (His **back**), not His favor (His **face**).

18:18-23. Instead of heeding Jeremiah's warning, they devised **plans against** him. His message conflicted with their false teachers of **the law** . . . **the priest** . . . **the sage** and **the prophet**. Their solution was to attack him with their **tongue**, to mock, slander, and malign his message, and not **heed** his **words**. Evidently their plans were more sinister because Jeremiah prayed to the **Lord** for help, **for they have dug a pit for me** (they were plotting to take his life; vv. 20-21; cf. 11:18-21).

Judah had rejected both God and His messenger; Jeremiah could do no more for them. They would experience **famine** and **the sword** (v. 21). Jeremiah had earlier asked God to **turn** His **wrath away** (v. 20; cf. 7:16; 8:20-22), but now he called on God to deal with them in His **time of** . . . **anger** (v. 23).

(2) The Message of the Broken Jar (19:1-15)

19:1-6. Again Jeremiah used an object lesson to teach the leaders of Judah. God instructed him to buy an **earthenware jar**, then **take some of the elders and** . . . **senior priests** to the **valley of Ben-hinnom** (cf. 7:31) just outside the **potsherd gate**. The Hinnom Valley ran along the south and west of the city and served as Jerusalem's community dump. The gate at the south of the city that opened into the valley was called the Potsherd Gate because people carried their potsherds (broken pieces of pottery) and other refuse through this gate to throw it in the Hinnom Valley. The Targum (ancient Jewish paraphrases of Scripture) identifies the Potsherd Gate with the Dung Gate (cf. Neh 2:13; 3:13-14). The modern Dung Gate in Jerusalem is also located on the southern wall, but the present walls are several hundred yards north of the walls in Jeremiah's day.

With the Hinnom Valley as his backdrop, Jeremiah delivered his message. God vowed to **bring a calamity** so shocking that **the ears of everyone that hears of it will tingle**. They had **forsaken** the Lord and **burned sacrifices in it** [the Hinnom Valley] **to other gods**. The Valley itself was a witness against the people because it contained the **high places of Baal** where people would **burn their sons in the fire** as sacrifices. Because of these wicked deeds, God again (cf. Jr 7:32-33) vowed to rename the place the **valley of Slaughter**, as He would destroy the people there.

19:7-9. God declared Judah's future. He would **cause them to fall by the sword**, and their **carcasses** would serve **as food** for the **birds** and **beasts** (cf. 7:33; 16:4; 34:20; Dt 28:26). The city's **disasters** would cause those who **pass by** to **hiss** in scorn (Jr 18:16). As Babylon's siege choked off the supply of food, famine would decimate the city to the point that people would resort to cannibalism (**eat the flesh of their sons** and **daughters**; cf. Lv 26:27-29; Dt 28:53-57; Lm 2:20; 4:10). All the curses God promised would overtake the people because of their sin (cf. Lv 26:14-39; Dt 28:15-68; Jr 11:1-8).

19:10-13. To illustrate the message, God commanded Jeremiah to **break the jar** in the valley **in the sight of the men**. God said He would smash **this people and this city**, both the nation of Judah and the city of Jerusalem, just as Jeremiah smashed the potter's jar. Jerusalem would become like **Topheth** (cf. comments on 7:31). Its once-beautiful dwellings would be reduced to rubble, and the entire area would be defiled with decaying bodies of the slain. The cause for the destruction was their sin of offering **sacrifices to all the heavenly host and** . . . **other gods**.

19:14-15. Jeremiah went directly to the temple court from **Topheth**. He reiterated the message he gave the leaders (cf. v. 1) **to all the people**. God's judgment would come against Jerusalem and the **towns** around it because the people refused to **heed** the Lord's **words**.

(3) Pashhur's Response (20:1-6)

20:1-2. Pashhur, **son of Immer** who is otherwise unknown in Scripture was one of the priests who served in the temple in the years immediately prior to the fall of Jerusalem to Babylon. He was the **chief officer** in the temple and was probably assigned to maintain order within the temple area (cf. 29:26). Pashur heard and rejected Jeremiah's message of judgment from the Lord to take place in the Valley of Hinnom (19:1-6). As an official of the temple, Pashur seized Jeremiah and had him **beaten** and **put him in the stocks** for public ridicule near the busy **Benjamin Gate**. This was the first of several instances of open opposition against Jeremiah's ministry.

20:3-6. On the next day Jeremiah was **released**, and he confronted Pashhur. Although

Pashhur's name means "freedom," Jeremiah told him **the LORD has called you . . . Magor-missabib** "terror on every side." Because Pashhur refused to heed God's message, he would not see freedom but instead God's judgment. He would watch in **terror** as his own **friends** fell by the sword, and he would see Babylon carry away all the wealth of Jerusalem as plunder (cf. 25:13; 17:3). Pashhur and his family would **go into captivity** in **Babylon** and would **die there**.

This judgment was not just because he had Jeremiah beaten, but also because Pashhur prophesied lies (v. 6), denying the truth of Jeremiah's message. The exact fulfillment of Jeremiah's prophecy about Pashhur was not given, but it is possible Pashhur was taken to Babylon during the second deportation (597 BC) along with Ezekiel (cf. 2Kg 24:15-16; Ezk 1:1-3).

(4) Jeremiah's Complaint (20:7-18)

20:7-10. After his arrest by Pashhur, Jeremiah was feeling low. The NASB says he felt that God had **deceived** (*pathah*) him. However, the word can mean to be "enticed," "coerced," or "persuaded" (Hs 2:13). A more helpful translation would be "you coerced me into being a prophet, and I allowed you to do it. You overcame my resistance and prevailed over me" (NET Bible). At his call by God, Jeremiah pointed out he was not qualified to be a prophet, but God persuaded Jeremiah to obey His call (Jr 1:1-7). God did not deceive Jeremiah but persuaded him to become a prophet. God even told Jeremiah that his message would be rejected (1:8, 17-19). Here Jeremiah complained that the Lord **prevailed** in His plan for Jeremiah, a plan that the prophet did not like. Since he was beaten and made a **laughingstock** for his message, Jeremiah was discouraged (cf. 15:15-18). He had faithfully warned Judah of the coming violent destruction; but he was rewarded with **reproach and derision all day long.**

Disheartened, Jeremiah considered withholding God's word to avoid persecution (**I will not remember Him or speak anymore in His name**). But he loved the Lord and His word too much to disobey, and the word became **like a burning fire shut up in my bones** (23:29; cf. Jb 30:17; 33:19). The intensity of God's word in his soul made it impossible for him to hold **it in**—he had to keep proclaiming the word of the Lord.

The people were **whispering** (Jr 18:18) against him, and Jeremiah wanted to quit. His message of **terror on every side** (6:25; 17:18; 20:3-44; 46:5; 49:29; Lm 2:22) was now being hurled back at him (Ps 31:13). Even his **trusted friends** betrayed him, **watching** for him to **fall** and give a wrong prediction so they could take their **revenge** on Jeremiah by accusing him of being a false prophet (cf. Dt 18:20).

20:11-13. Jeremiah expressed his confidence in God, despite these attacks. He realized **the LORD is with me like a dread champion**. God is described with the word **dread** (*'ariyts*, "awe-inspiring, terror-striking, awesome, terrifying, ruthless, mighty"). Jeremiah had a powerful **champion** (defender), and he could have confidence his **persecutors** would **stumble and not prevail**.

God does **test** (*baw-khan'*, "examine" or "prove") **the righteous**, not in the sense that He is looking for failure. The purpose of His testing is to show the worth of **the righteous**, like a builder testing the strength of a bridge. He sees the **mind** and **heart** and was looking after Jeremiah's **cause**. This assurance of God's care and vindication allowed Jeremiah to **sing to the LORD** and **praise the LORD**, for He had encouraged Jeremiah, (**delivered the soul**), and would rescue Jeremiah **from the hand of evildoers.**

20:14-18. Jeremiah again plunged from a height of confidence (vv. 11-13) to the depths of despair. Perhaps he realized that the vindication he sought could come only through the destruction of the city and nation that he dearly loved. His agony made him again **curse . . . the day** he **was born** (cf. 15:10; Jb 3:1-19). He was brokenhearted at the **trouble and sorrow** he was experiencing and also because of the calamity that would occur in Jerusalem's near future. Jeremiah's self-pity could not erase the fact that he had been consecrated "in the womb" for service to the Lord (cf. Jr 1:5).

2. Jeremiah's Four Specific Prophecies of Judgment (21:1–25:38)

Pashhur's hostility (20:1-6) is a pivotal episode or bridge in the book of Jeremiah. Through a series of nine general, undated prophecies (spanning chaps. 2–20; see Outline in Introduction), Jeremiah had denounced Judah's sin, foretold judgment, and offered hope if the people would repent. Though he had been opposed (11:18-23; 12:6; 15:10; 17:18; 18:19-23), he had not suffered serious physical persecution. After Pashhur's opposition, however, Jeremiah's messages become more specific, directed against particular individuals and groups. At the same time, Jeremiah's hope that Judah would repent was replaced by the certainty of God's judgment.

a. The Rebuke of the Kings of Judah (21:1–23:8)

Jeremiah first addressed the kings, those appointed by God to be shepherds of the flock of Judah (cf. 2:8; 10:21; 23:1-8; Ezk 34:1-10). After rebuking the wicked kings who had ruled Judah (Jr 21–22), he offered hope in the future righteous King, the Messiah, who would come to restore Judah (23:1-8).

Jeremiah's messages to the wicked kings were arranged in an atypical order. Zedekiah, the first king addressed, was Judah's last king (597–586 BC; cf. 21:1–22:9; 2Kg 24:17–25:7). The other kings were arranged chronologically beginning with Shallum (his more commonly known name being Jehoahaz; 609 BC; Jr 22:10-12), continuing with Jehoiakim (609–598 BC; 22:13-23), and ending with Coniah (598–597 BC; also known as Jehoiachin or Jeconiah, 22:24-30).

There are two reasons for the order of these rebukes. First, by discussing Zedekiah at the beginning, he linked it to the story of Pashhur the son of Malchijah (21:1), who was the grandson of Zedekiah (38:6). He was part of a group that later had Jeremiah imprisoned for treason (38:1-6). This Pashhur is not the same as Pashhur, son of Immer mentioned earlier (20:1-2).

Second, the accounts were arranged so that the prophecy against Coniah would climax God's judgments against the kings. The line of the wicked kings would be cut off (22:30) until God would raise a Righteous Branch to rule the nation, King Messiah (23:1-8), who would not come from the line of Coniah (22:28-30). The Messiah would be born from the line of Nathan the third of four sons born to King David and Bathsheba in Jerusalem (2Sm 5:14; Lk 3:31). So the arrangement of these prophecies provided both continuity and climax.

(1) The Rebuke to Zedekiah (21:1–22:9)

21:1-2. King Zedekiah sent two priests, **Pashhur**, **son of Malchijah** (see above) and **Zephaniah**, **son of Maaseiah**, to inquire of Jeremiah (some time between 588 BC and 586 BC). Zephaniah's duties included determining the veracity of a prophet's message (29:25, 26). Shemaiah the Nehelamite later asked this priest to rebuke Jeremiah for the prophet's message concerning Jerusalem's fate (29:27). Here these officials asked Jeremiah to **inquire of the Lord** regarding **Nebuchadnezzar** and his planned attack on Jerusalem. Though Jeremiah was to ask God what the outcome would be, they hoped that God would perform **wonderful acts** as He had done in the past and make Nebuchadnezzar withdraw. Probably Zedekiah and his advisers were thinking of God's rescue in the reign of King Hezekiah, when the Assyrians had threatened Jerusalem (2Kg 18:17–19:37; Is 36-37) but withdrew after King Hezekiah asked Isaiah for the Lord's intervention (Is 37:2-7).

21:3-7. Jeremiah did not have the same good news for Zedekiah that Isaiah had for Hezekiah. Instead of rescuing Jerusalem, God would **war against** it with His own **outstretched hand and a mighty arm**. This phrase echoes God's powerful redemption of Israel at the exodus (32:21; Ex 32:11; Dt 4:34; 5:15; 7:19; 26:8), but here God's might is turned *against* Israel. Those who were huddled for protection in the city would die of a terrible **pestilence** (plague), **sword**, or **famine** (cf. Jr 14:12).

Those who did **survive** the siege would fall into the hands of Nebuchadnezzar. They could expect no **pity** or **compassion**, for he would kill them. This was fulfilled in 586 BC after the city fell. King Zedekiah's sons were slain before his eyes; he was then immediately blinded and taken in chains to Babylon (39:5-7; 2Kg 25:7). The other city leaders were captured and sent to Riblah, where they were executed (Jr 52:24-27).

21:8-10. The people had two clear choices: **the way of life** and **the way of death**. The **way of death** was selected by those who chose to remain in the city. They would die by **sword**, **famine**, and **pestilence**. The **way of life** was selected by those who surrendered (the one who **goes out** to the **Chaldeans**, another name for Babylonians). This was the only hope for those still alive because God had **set [His] face against this city for harm and not for good**.

21:11-14. Jeremiah next focused on the sin of the remaining **king of Judah**, Zedekiah. The **house of David** was supposed to **administer justice every morning** and to **deliver** the rights of those who were oppressed. Since the king refused to heed God's warning, God would **punish** him for his evil deeds, and **kindle a fire** to **devour** Jerusalem and its **forest[s]** and **environs** (cf. 4:4; 17:4; 21:12).

Evidently the king felt secure in Jerusalem, which had been impenetrable, and asked, **who will enter into our habitations**? He saw no need to obey God's injunction. Because of this proud self-reliance coupled with arrogant disobedience, God would punish the king and his people.

22:1-5. God instructed Jeremiah to go down from the temple to the **house of the king of Judah**. His message was to the **king . . . who sits on David's throne**, his **servants**, and all the **people who enter these gates**. The message was simple: **Do justice and righteousness, and deliver the** oppressed (cf. 21:12; Mc 6:8). The Lord demanded that the ruler on the Davidic throne make justice his primary goal.

If the king would **indeed perform** this justice, the Davidic dynasty would be uninterrupted in Jerusalem (cf. Jr 17:25-27). **But if** he did **not obey**, his **house** (i.e., his dynasty, not just his place of residence) would become a **desolation**. To emphasize the truth and solemnity of this command, the Lord swore by Himself, and there could be no stronger ratification of a decree (49:13; 51:14; Gn 22:16; Is 45:23; Am 6:8; Heb 6:13-18).

22:6-10. Here, with the phrase **house of the king of Judah**, Jeremiah was referring to the royal palace, not the dynasty. Both **Gilead** and **Lebanon** were famous for their cedar forests (Jdg 9:15; 1Kg 4:33; 2Ch 2:8). The royal palace in Jerusalem was known as the "House of the Lebanon" (1Kg 7:2-5; Is 22:8) because it was constructed of this luxurious wood. But after God's judgment the palace would be as desolate as a **wilderness**. The Babylonian **destroyers** would **cut down** the palace's **choicest cedar** beams and **throw them on the fire** (cf. Jr 52:13).

Jerusalem was such a **great city**, and so beautiful, that people from **many nations** would see her destruction and ask, **Why has the Lord done thus?** The answer was simple: **Because they forsook the covenant of the Lord** and practiced idolatry. The covenant they violated was the Mosaic covenant (confirmed in Dt 27–30), referred to throughout the book of Jeremiah, which was conditional.

In contrast to the Mosaic covenant, the Abrahamic and Davidic covenants were unconditional. The sign of God's unconditional covenant with Abraham was circumcision. It had no conditions but was solely based on God's work and faithfulness (Gn 12:1-3; 15:18-21). Failure to circumcise their sons did not abrogate God's guarantee of the Abrahamic covenant. The Davidic covenant likewise was based on God's faithfulness (2Sm 7:8-17; 1Ch 17:7-15). The obedience of David and his descendants affected the level to which they enjoyed the blessing of God's covenant; however, the Lord guaranteed the fulfillment of the "house, kingdom, and throne" promise, which would ultimately find its fulfillment in the King Messiah Jesus and His yet future reign on the earth.

The extensive devastation of Jerusalem would be a lesson to the nations of the power and holiness of the God of Israel. The people were told not to **weep for the dead**, those killed in battle or siege, for they would be free from pain. Instead **weep continually for the one who goes away** into captivity. The 70-year captivity would mean the exiles deserved pity, for they would **never return** or **see** their **native land**, again.

(2) The Rebuke to Shallum (22:11-12)

22:11-12. King **Shallum**, also called "Jehoahaz," was a **son of Josiah** and came to the throne after Josiah was killed by Pharaoh Neco II (2Kg 23:29-33). After a reign of only three months, Shallum was deposed by Pharaoh Neco.

Jeremiah penned this prophecy after Shallum had been taken into Egyptian captivity (609 BC; 2Kg 23:34). Shallum would **never return** to Jerusalem but instead would **die** in captivity (the first ruler of Judah to die in exile) and **not see this land again**.

(3) The Rebuke to Jehoiakim (22:13-23)

22:13-14. Jehoiakim was appointed king by Pharaoh Neco (2Kg 23:34–24:5) to replace his exiled brother Shallum. He ruled as a corrupt, petty king who cared only for personal gain and nothing for the will of the Lord. His legacy was to build **his house without righteousness**.

He built an actual palace for himself at the expense of his subjects through taxation and **services without pay**. Jehoiakim paneled his palace with **cedar** and painted it **bright red**, a costly color. Judah was already under economic stress because she was paying heavy tribute to Egypt during the early part of his reign.

22:15-17. Jeremiah rebuked Jehoiakim for his **cedar** dwelling and contrasted him with his **father**, King Josiah, who ruled with **justice and righteousness** and **pled the cause of the afflicted and needy**. In contrast, Jehoiakim cared only for **dishonest gain**, **shedding innocent blood**, **oppression, and extortion**.

22:18-19. Because of Jehoiakim's oppression of his people, they would not **lament** for him at his death. Instead of the lavish funeral normally given a king, Jehoiakim would have a **donkey's** burial. He would be dragged away and thrown outside **beyond the gates of Jerusalem** to rot. Jehoiakim died in late 598 BC as Nebuchadnezzar was advancing on Jerusalem to punish the city for rebellion, and there is no record of his burial. The new king, Jehoiachin (also known as Coniah), surrendered and was taken to Babylon, and the city was spared temporarily (2Kg 24:1-17).

22:20-23. Because of Jehoiakim's foolish leadership, Jeremiah called on Jerusalem to **cry out** and lament her fate. This passage should probably be dated in late 598 to early 597 BC, since it focused on the imminent invasion of Babylon in retaliation for Jehoiakim's rebellion. Jerusalem's cry would be heard throughout the mountains of the land. From **Lebanon** in the north, to **Bashan** in the northeast, to **Abarim** in the southeast, Judah's lament would sound when her **lovers** (allies) would be **crushed** by Babylon.

God had warned Jerusalem of the consequences of disobedience when she felt secure **in** her **prosperity**, but, as usual, she would **not listen** (6:17; 7:26-27; 13:11; 17:23). Now she could only watch in sorrow as her **shepherds** (kings) were taken away along with her **lovers**, pagan political allies, possibly Egypt (cf. 2Kg 24:7).

Jeremiah referred to the people of Jerusalem as those **who dwell in Lebanon**. So much cedar had been imported to build palaces and mansions in Jerusalem from Lebanon (cf. Jr 22:6-7, 13-15) that living in Jerusalem was like dwelling among Lebanon's cedars. Yet those **nested in** these **cedar** homes would **groan** when the **pangs** of God's judgment came on them **like a woman in childbirth** (4:31).

(4) The Rebuke to Coniah (Jehoiachin) (22:24-30)

22:24-27. Coniah (also called both "Jehoiachin" and "Jeconiah") succeeded Jehoiakim as king (598–597 BC), and surrendered to Nebuchadnezzar after a three-month reign. He was deported to Babylon where he lived the rest of his life (cf. 52:31-34). God said that if Coniah was as valuable as a **signet ring** to Him, He would nevertheless **pull [him] off**. A signet ring was valuable because it was used to stamp the owner's seal on official documents. Even if Coniah were this important to God (and the clear implication is that he was not), God would **give** him to **Nebuchadnezzar** as judgment for his sins. He and his **mother** (Nehushta, the widow of King Jehoiakim, 2Kg 24:8) would be exiled **into another country** (Babylon) where they both would **die**. This is Jeremiah's second prophecy of their deportation (cf. Jr 13:18-19).

22:28-30. God had another message for **Coniah** (also known as Jeconiah and Jehoiachin) and **his descendants** that went beyond being **cast into a land that they had not known** (14:18; 15:2, 14; 16:13; 17:4). The Lord foretold severe judgment in the distant future and demonstrated **Coniah[’s]** rejection by the Lord in the near future. Jeremiah's focus is on the Davidic line rather than Coniah personally. There are several components to this judgment.

First, some of the false prophets saw Coniah as deserving of his kingship (he was not, in their opinion, a **shattered** [worthless] **jar**, v. 28; cf. 28:1-4). But this was not God's plan because in His eyes he was worthless as a ruler, and the kingly line of Coniah was at an end.

Second, some asked, **Is he an undesirable vessel? Why have he and his descendants been hurled out?** He was taken into captivity with the royal house (24:1) and did have a son, Shealtiel (1Ch 3:17-18; Mt 1:12). Since Coniah had sons who could serve as heirs to the Davidic throne, some thought one of them should become king (Jr 29:1-32), but this was not God's plan. Coniah's wickedness would keep his descendants from ruling on Judah's throne.

Before posing the third component of the judgment, Jeremiah called on the **land** three times to bear witness and **hear the word of the Lord.** The repetition indicates the strongest intensity and seriousness of the statement (cf. 7:4). The whole nation was to notice carefully and remember this judgment of the Lord.

The third component begins, **Thus says the Lord**, focusing on the importance of the proclamation. The phrase **write this man down childless** relates to a register of citizens (Is 4:3), or a census list. Coniah did, in fact, have seven sons recorded by name (cf. Jr 22:28; 1Ch 3:17-18; Mt 1:12), but none succeeded him to the throne. He was to be *considered* childless because **no man of his descendants will** . . . sit **on the throne of David**. He was dynastically **childless** because he was the last of the Davidic kings in his family. This prophecy had both immediate and long-range significance. No offspring of Jehoiachin (also known as Coniah) followed him to the throne. Zedekiah, who replaced Coniah, was Judah's last king, but Zedekiah was Coniah's uncle, not his son.

The long-range significance is seen in the line of the Messiah, the exalted Son of David, because Jesus was not *physically* related to Coniah/Jechoniah. This prophecy helps explain the genealogies of the Messiah in Mt 1 and Lk 3. Specifically, Matthew recorded the legal line of

Messiah through Joseph, his stepfather. Joseph was a descendant of David through Shealtiel, who was a son of Jeconiah/Coniah (Mt 1:11-12; cf. 1Ch 3:17). Had Jesus been a physical descendant of Joseph and not virgin-born, He would have been disqualified as Israel's King based on the prophecy that **no man of** Coniah's **descendants** would . . . **sit on the throne of David**. Luke recorded the physical line of Jesus the Messiah through His mother, Mary. She was descended from David through the line of Nathan, son of David (Lk 3:31; 1Ch 14:3-4). Being virgin-born of Mary, Jesus was not under the curse of Coniah, and was qualified to rule on the throne of David. However, since Jesus was a physical descendant of David through Nathan, He was the rightful Son of David.

(5) The Hope of Messiah, the Righteous Branch (23:1-8)

23:1-4. The prospects for the house of David were ominous in light of the sinfulness of the last Davidic kings. But the outlook was not completely hopeless, and vv. 1-8 contains a message of hope for the Jewish people.

Jeremiah pictured the false leadership of Israel and the unrighteous kings as **shepherds who** were **destroying and scattering the sheep of** God's **pasture**. The shepherds deserved punishment because of the **evil** they had done (cf. Ezk 34:1-10).

Jeremiah presented a two-part picture of God's plan for caring for His flock once the evil shepherds were removed. First, God Himself would **gather the remnant** of the people who were dispersed and would bring **them back**. The term **remnant** originally meant simply "the few survivors," but it came to have a more specific meaning of "the ones who are faithful to the Lord" (Is 4:2-6; 10:20-22; 28:5; Rm 9:27–10:4; 11:1-6). The Lord would assume responsibility for Israel's regathering (cf. Jr 31:10; Mc 2:12; 5:4; 7:14). Just as the scattering of the people was literal, so their regathering would be. The promise of restoration goes beyond the return from Babylon, to bringing them back from **all the countries** (cf. Jr 16:14-15), indicating an eschatological return.

Second, God would raise up new **shepherds** over them who would **tend them** and care for the people the way God intended. When the Messiah reigns in His millennial kingdom, Israel will be assured of peace. The phrase **nor will any be missing** means there will be righteous shepherds in Judah, future leaders who will care for the Jewish people and keep them safe and obedient to the Lord, so that none of them will be lost. Jesus expressed this comforting idea during His earthly ministry (Jn 6:39; 10:27-28).

23:5-8. God promised **the days are coming** (often an eschatological term, here referring to the Messianic Age; cf. comments 16:14-15; 23:7; 30:3; 31:27-40) when He would **raise up for David a righteous Branch**. This is a key messianic passage in Jeremiah, and the promise centers on the Davidic covenant (2Sm 7:8-16). The image of the **Branch** is a frequent and important image of the promised Messiah (cf. Jr 33:15-15; Is 4:2; 11:1; 53:2; Zch 3:8; 6:12). For more on this messianic title, see comments on Zch 6:12-13. Jesus of Nazareth is the fulfillment of this prediction.

King Messiah will reign **wisely** and with **justice** and **righteousness** (cf. Ps 72:2). The name of this coming King is **the Lord our Righteousness** (*Yahweh tsideqenu*). This is a powerful messianic title, as it presents Him as the righteous King, as God, and as Redeemer (cf. Is 45:24; Jr 33:16; 1Co 5:21). Though Jesus offered Himself as Israel's Messiah at His first advent and provided the way of salvation, this prophecy's fulfillment awaits His rule and reign in the millennial kingdom following His second advent. At that time, He will rule over **the sons of Israel** regathered **back . . . from all the countries where** they had been scattered, to **live on their own soil** (*adama*, land). Israel will again be delivered (cf. Is 59:20; Zch 12:6-9; Rm 11:26) from oppression and reunited as a single nation and will live in safety (cf. Ezk 37:15-28).

The future restoration of Israel (Jr 23:6) is directly and inseparably related to the messianic hope (**the days are coming**; cf. comments on 16:14-15; 23:5; and see comments on 30:3; 31:27-40). It will be so dramatic that the people will **no longer** look back to the time when God brought them **from the land of Egypt**. The first exodus, a biblical watershed in Jewish history, will pale in comparison with this new exodus when God will bring the Jewish people out of **all the countries** where they have been and will restore them to their own land (cf. 16:14-15).

b. The Rebuke of the False Prophets (23:9-40)

Jeremiah refocused his message from Judah's kings to deliver God's judgment message against the false prophets. These pseudo-seers opposed Jeremiah's declaration of doom (cf.

6:13-14; 8:10-11; 14:14-16; 28:1-4, 10-11; 29:8-9, 20-23, 31-32) and offered instead a false promise of peace.

(1) The Character of the False Prophets (23:9-15)

23:9-12. Jeremiah's **heart** was **broken**, his body became weak, his **bones tremble[d]**, and he staggered **like a drunken man** when he thought of God's **holy words** abused by the false prophets. They claimed authority to speak (cf. 28:2, 15-16), but the **land mourns** under God's judgment of drought (Dt 28:23-24), by which the land **dried up** (cf. Jr 14:1-6, 22). This was due in part to the teachings of the false prophets whose influence contributed to Judah's waywardness, resulting in God's curse upon them.

Judah's spiritual leaders (both **prophet and priest**) were **polluted**, defiled (cf. 3:1-2, 9). They had such a low view of God's holiness that they even profaned His temple with their **wickedness**. God vowed to bring **calamity** on them because of their sin.

23:13-15. Jeremiah compared the **prophets of Samaria** to the **prophets of Jerusalem**. The prophets of the northern kingdom of Israel (**Samaria**) had **prophesied by Baal**, leading the nation **astray** (cf. 1Kg 18:16-40; 2Kg 10:18-29; 17:16). Because of their wickedness, God destroyed the northern kingdom by the hand of the Assyrians (721 BC).

The prophets of Judah continued in similar paths of sin, committing spiritual and moral **adultery**, telling lies, and strengthening **evildoers**. Their repulsive conduct made them like **Sodom** and **Gomorrah** to God. He had to judge them for their sin and would **feed** them **wormwood** and **poisonous water** because of the lying messages they were teaching, by which **pollution** (spiritual corruption) came to **all the land** (cf. Jr 9:15; Lm 3:15, 19).

(2) The message of the false prophets (23:16-40)

23:16-22. The false prophets fabricated their own message, and Jeremiah warned the people not **to listen** to them. Their **vision[s]** came from their **imagination** (cf. v. 26) **not from the mouth of the LORD**. They proclaimed **peace** (cf. 6:14; 8:11) and said **calamity will not come**. This was not from God. **The storm of the LORD** would judge the wicked—it was coming and would destroy those in its path. **The anger of the LORD** would **not turn back** until He finished His judgment. Only then would the people understand God did **not send** these false prophets. If they had **stood in** God's **council** they would have **announced** His words to turn Judah from her **evil . . . deeds**.

23:23-32. The false prophets misrepresented God's character. They saw Him as some localized deity from whom they could **hide** and He would **not see** (v. 24). Indeed, God in His omniscience fills **the heavens** and **earth** so that no place is outside His realm. He had heard what the false prophets had said when they spoke lies in His **name** (v. 25). The prophets also claimed that God had given them revelation in a **dream**, but their visions were imaginary (cf. v. 16). Their **dreams**, false prophetic visions, were designed to make Judah **forget** God's **name** (v. 27), just as earlier prophets did through **Baal** worship (cf. v. 13). Their prophetic messages were as worthless for meeting spiritual needs as was **straw**, instead of **grain**, for meeting physical hunger (v. 28). Their words had no force, while God's **word** is penetrating **like fire** (v. 29; cf. 20:9) and as effective as a **hammer** that **shatters a rock**.

God set Himself **against the prophets**, which is repeated three times (vv. 30, 31, 32) for intensity. They **led My people astray**, they were not sent by Him, and they did not **furnish . . . the slightest benefit**.

23:33-40. An **oracle of the LORD** was a revelatory message from God. The Hebrew word for **oracle** in daily use referred to the "load" or "burden that someone had to lift or carry" (Ex 23:5; Neh 13:19). The burden the prophet had to carry was the message or oracle given by God (Is 13:1; 14:28; Nah 1:1; Hab 1:1) often of judgment (cf. Is 15:1; 17:1; 19:1; 21:1, 11, 13; 22:1; 23:1). When the **people**, **prophet**, or **priest** asked Jeremiah, **What is the oracle of the LORD?** (Jr 23:33), he was to say, God **will abandon you** because the false prophets **perverted the words of the living God** (v. 36). The prophets who continued to claim divine oracles would be judged (vv. 38-40). God vowed to **cast** them **away** from His **presence** along with all Jerusalem (v. 39). Furthermore, these false prophets faced **everlasting reproach . . . and humiliation** for their wicked words (v. 40).

Much of what Jeremiah recorded is relevant in the contemporary world. The people of Judah were led astray because they believed the false teachers and prophets who presented an appealing—but wrong—message supposedly from the Lord. They rejected Jeremiah because they did not like his message. Similarly, people today must guard against the tendency to become attached to a religious leader based solely on outward appearances or the presentation of endlessly inspiring and engaging messages that ignore sin and its consequences. God's people then and now must always evaluate every teacher, message, and book by the contents of Scripture, which means they must spend time digesting God's Word in order to know what it says, and thinking with discernment about what they are taught to determine if it concurs with Scripture. If it does not, then followers of Christ must align themselves with those who teach and live the truth as found in God's Word, an adjustment Jeremiah's audience failed to make, with appalling consequences.

c. The Two Baskets of Figs (24:1-10)

(1) The Vision of the Two Baskets of Figs (24:1-3)

24:1-3. Although written at a later time, the vision of the **two baskets of figs** was given to Jeremiah after **Jeconiah** and the **officials**, **craftsmen**, and **smiths** were carried into **Babylon** (cf. 2Kg 24:8-16) sometime in the beginning of the reign of Zedekiah (597 BC).

In the vision Jeremiah saw two **baskets of figs**, each representing a group whose conditions would be different under the Babylonians. The vision is like the offering of the first fruits set **before the temple of the Lord** (cf. Dt 26:11). In one basket the figs were **very good**, like the **first-ripe figs**, the best of the crop (cf. Is 28:4; Hs 9:10; Mc 7:1), the first fruits that were to be offered to the Lord (Dt 14:22). The second basket contained bad figs, which could not **be eaten** because they were rotten. Such fruit was unacceptable to the Lord for sacrifice (cf. Mal 1:6-9).

(2) The Explanation of the Good Figs (24:4-7)

24:4-7. The Lord explained that the basket of **good figs** represented the **captives** from Judah who had been carried away to the **land of the Chaldeans**. This explanation was contrary to the belief of the people of Jerusalem who thought the people taken into in captivity were taken away from the nurturing of the Lord (cf. Ezk 11:14-15). But Jeremiah explained they were **sent out** of Jerusalem, exiled by God, and He regarded this plan as **good**. God promised to **set My eyes on them for good**, and **bring them again** to the land (cf. Ezk 11:16-17). The Lord also promised to give the Jewish people a new **heart** so they would **know** Him (cf. Jr 4:22). At that time they would be His **people** spiritually as well as nationally (cf. comments on 30:22) and would **return** to Him **with their whole heart**. Although God did restore a minority of the people to the land after the Babylonian captivity, following the exile they never experienced the full blessings of fellowship God had promised (cf. 31:31-34; Ezk 36:24-32). This awaits a still-future fulfillment when God again will regather Israel at the beginning of the Messiah's millennial reign on earth (Mt 24:29-31).

(3) The Explanation of the Poor Figs (24:8-10)

24:8-10. The basket of **bad figs** represented **Zedekiah** and the other survivors (cf. 29:17-19), including those in Israel and those who fled to **Egypt** (cf. 43:4-7). God vowed to make them **a terror**, **evil for all the kingdoms of the earth**. They would be despised **as a reproach and a proverb**, ridiculed and cursed wherever they went, as Jeremiah often predicted (cf. 25:9, 18; 26:6; 29:18; 42:18; 44:8, 12, 22; 48:39; 49:13, 17; 51:37). God would send His three instruments of judgment, **sword**, **famine**, and **pestilence** (cf. 14:12; 15:2-4), until they were all **destroyed**.

d. The Seventy-Year Captivity in Babylon (25:1-38)

Jeremiah's 13 messages of judgment spanning chaps. 2–25 were arranged topically, not chronologically. The prophecy about the 70-year captivity (25:1-38) was placed last because it was the climax of all Jeremiah's judgment messages.

(1) Warnings Ignored (25:1-7)

25:1-3. Jeremiah's final message concerned **all the people of Judah**. The time when it was given was recorded because of the significance of the message. It was delivered in the **fourth year of Jehoiakim . . . king of Judah (that was the first year of Nebuchadnezzar king of Babylon)**. Calculating the Jewish and Babylonian calendars with ascension designations along with the modern calendar, that would have been between September 7, 605 BC and September 25, 604 BC. Jeremiah had been prophesying for **twenty-three years** (cf. 1:2), and though he had spoken to the people **again and again**, they had **not listened** to God's warnings to repent.

25:4-7. God had also sent other **servants** and **prophets** who warned the people to turn from their **evil . . . deeds**. If they had heeded the prophets' warnings, God would have allowed them to stay in the land in peace and would have done them **no harm**. Yet the people did **not listen** to God. They continued in their sin to **provoke** God to **anger** with the **work of [their] hands**, making and worshiping idols (10:8-9).

(2) Judgment Described (25:8-14)

25:8-11. Because Judah had repeatedly **not obeyed** God's **words** of warning, God would **send** for the Babylonians, under **Nebuchadnezzar**, called God's **servant** (v. 9), to bring judgment on Judah. This pagan king was God's **servant** (cf. 27:6; 43:10) in the sense that, even without acknowledging the Lord, he would carry out God's sovereign plans by destroying Jerusalem and **all** the **nations** who had been her allies.

The sounds of **joy** and **gladness** would cease (cf. 7:34; 16:9) in Jerusalem because the **whole land** would become a **desolation**. Famine would replace wedding celebrations, and there would be no grain to grind in the **millstones** or olive oil to light the **lamp**. The **whole land** and surrounding **nations** would serve the Babylonians **seventy years** (25:11; 29:10; 2Ch 36:21; Dn 9:2; Zch 7:5).

The judgment was for idolatry, but the length of **seventy years** was a consequence of specific disobedience about the land. The captivity was destined to last seventy years (605–536 BC) because the Jewish people had failed to observe God's law of a Sabbath rest for the land for the previous 490 years, the number of years of between Saul and the fall of Jerusalem at the hand of the Babylonians. God had decreed that every seventh year the land was to lie fallow (Lv 25:3-5). The people were not to sow their fields or prune their vineyards each seventh year to allow the land to rest. Failure to obey would result in expulsion from the land, and an enforced Sabbath rest for the land (Lv 26:33-35). The seventy-year Babylonian captivity did "fulfill the word of the LORD by the mouth of Jeremiah, until the land had enjoyed its sabbaths. All the days of its desolation [the land] kept sabbath until seventy years were complete" (2Ch 36:20-21).

25:12-14. When the 70 years were **completed** God would also **punish the king of Babylon and that nation** because of their **iniquity**. He would fulfill all the judgments **written in this book** against Babylon by Jeremiah (cf. chaps. 50–51). **This book** may refer to the scroll mentioned in chap. 36:1-4. The LXX places chaps. 46–51, the judgment on the nations, at this point, a slightly different order of the chapters (see "Background" in Introduction of Jeremiah for the Septuagint /LXX issues). Babylon fell to the Medo-Persian empire in 539 BC, and the Babylonians were made their **slaves**; God would repay Babylon **according to their deeds**.

(3) Wrath Promised (25:15-29)

25:15-25. The coming wrath of God is presented in a vision to Jeremiah: He saw **the LORD** holding in His hand a **cup of the wine of wrath** (v. 15). God would **send** Jeremiah to specific **nations** to make them **drink it** (cf. Lm 4:21; Ezk 23:31-33; Rv 16:19; 18:6) and experience judgment **because of the sword** that God would send **among them** (v. 16). The first to drink God's wine of wrath were **Jerusalem** and the **cities of Judah** (v. 18). Other nations (vv. 19-26) would follow Judah in judgment by the hand of the Babylonians. These included **Egypt** (v. 19), whose feeble assistance prompted Judah to rebel against Babylon (cf. Ezk 29:6-9). **Uz** (v. 20) was probably east of Edom in northern Arabia (cf. Jb 1:1). The Philistines' key cities of **Ashkelon**, **Gaza**, **Ekron**, and **Ashdod** (v. 20) were on the lower coastal shore of the Mediterranean, west of Judah. **Edom**, **Moab**, and **Ammon** (from south to north, v. 21) were the nations east of Judah to the Jordan River and the Dead Sea. The Phoenician cities of **Tyre** and **Sidon** (v. 22) were north of Israel on the Mediterranean coast. **Dedan**, **Tema**, and **Buz** (v. 23) were cities in the northern Arabian Peninsula associated with the **kings of Arabia** and **all . . . the foreign people** (mixed multitude) in the desert (v. 24). The location of **Zimri** (v. 25) is uncertain, but it is associated with Elam (Gn 14:1-9; Is 11:11; Dn 8:2) and **Media** (2Kg 16:6; 18:11; Dn 6:8,15), two countries east of the Tigris River, north of the Persian Gulf, an area now included in parts of Iran and Iraq. All these nations fell to Babylon.

25:26. Despite Babylon's extensive conquest of **all the kings of the north, near and far**, ultimately she too would fall to God's judgment (cf. 51:48-49). God would make the **king of Sheshach . . . drink after them**. The name **Sheshach** is a cryptogram, an *atbash* cipher, for the word "Babylon" in Hebrew. An *atbash* cipher substitutes the first letter of the alphabet for the last, the second letter for the next to last and so. For example, in English *z* would be an *a*, *y* would be a *b*, and so on; thus, the name *Abby* as an *atbash* would become *zyyb*. Using this cipher, **Sheshach** is a Hebrew *atbash* for "Babylon." Perhaps it was unsafe to speak directly against Babylon during the exile, so an *atbash* was used for safety. God would judge Babylon after judging the other nations (cf. vv. 12-14). Another *atbash* cipher is used in 51:1 for the word "Chaldea" ("Leb-kamai").

25:27-29. The nations told to **drink** from the cup of God's wrath would be like a man who has become **drunk**. They would **vomit** and **fall**, because of the wine of God's wrath and die by the **sword** He would **send among [them]**. His judgment could not be avoided (they **shall surely drink!**). If God would bring **calamity** on Jerusalem (which is **called by My name**) because of its sin, then these pagan **inhabitants of the earth** could not escape the **sword** of His judgment.

(4) Universal Judgment Affirmed (25:30-38)

25:30-33. Here in poetic form, **the LORD** is portrayed as a lion who **will roar mightily** (cf. Am 1:2; 3:4, 8) in judgment and would **shout** from **His holy habitation** in heaven **against all the inhabitants of the earth**.

God had a **controversy** with these **nations** and would enter **into judgment** against them. He would bring charges (cf. 2:9) that would extend beyond Judah to all humankind (**all flesh**). This judgment was pictured as a **great storm** that would envelop all nations. In its wake the **slain** would be scattered everywhere. Their corpses would be like **dung** lying on the ground, just as the citizenry of Jerusalem would be after the Babylonian siege (cf. 8:2; 14:16; 16:4-6).

25:34-38. The **shepherds**, the leaders of these many nations, would **cry** and **wallow in ashes** (a sign of deep grief, cf. 6:26; Mc 1:10), mourning because the **days of [their] slaughter** and **dispersions** had **come**. The judgment of God's **fierce anger** (25:37-38) would make each **land . . . become a horror**.

B. Jeremiah's Personal Conflict with Judah (26:1–29:32)

Although there was some opposition to Jeremiah's message earlier in his ministry (cf. 11:18-23; 15:10; 20:1-6), the focus of chaps. 1–25 was on God's coming judgment if the people refused to repent. In this section (chaps. 26–29) Jeremiah refocused on Jerusalem's response to his message. Both he and his message were rejected by the leadership and the people of Jerusalem.

1. Jeremiah's Conflict with the People (26:1-24)

a. Jeremiah's Message (26:1-6)

26:1-3. This message was delivered early in the reign of **Jehoiakim, . . . king of Judah**, who ascended to the throne in 609 BC. The message is probably part of the Temple Address (cf. chaps. 7–10), and the focus here is on the response to the message. The Temple Address is summarized here as God's warning of judgment so the people would **listen**, then **turn from** their **evil way**, so that God would not carry out His threatened judgment if the people obeyed His commands. The word **repent** is an anthropomorphic term—ascribing to God human emotions and thoughts—and should not be understood literally, for God does not repent (Nm 23:19). He would not bring **calamity** on them if they changed (cf. 7:3-7). Certainly the all-knowing Lord God knew what they would do.

26:4-6. The message was of judgment for disobedience. **If** the people refused to follow God's law and **to listen** to God's **servants the prophets** (cf. 7:21-26), God would make the temple (**this house**) as desolate as **Shiloh** (cf. 7:14), and the Gentile **nations of the earth** would use the **this city**, Jerusalem, as a **curse** (cf. 24:9).

b. Jeremiah's Arrest and Trial (26:7-15)

26:7-11. When the **priests**, the **prophets**, and **all the people heard** the Temple Address (see chaps. 7–10) they **seized** Jeremiah just as he **finished** his message and demanded that he **must die** for his words. They accused Jeremiah of being a false prophet because he had spoken in the **name of the LORD**. They believed that such a negative and condemnatory prophecy could never have come from God.

The charges against Jeremiah had to be brought to the **officials of Judah** who heard the case at **the entrance of the New Gate**. The city gate was where the leaders sat to administer justice and to conduct official business (cf. Dt 21:18-19; Ru 4:1-11; Jr 39:3). The mob demanded a **death sentence** because he had **prophesied against this city** of Jerusalem.

26:12-15. Jeremiah gave a three-part self-defense to the charges. First he announced, **The LORD sent me to prophesy** the message they had heard, so he was not a false prophet. Second, he announced that his message was conditional. If the people would **amend** their ways (cf. 3:12; 7:3) God would **change His mind** about the disaster (26:3). It was within God's plan to be merciful if the people repented. Thus Jeremiah's message did offer some hope for the city. Third, he warned that if they **put** him **to death** they would bring the guilt of **innocent blood** on themselves. He made a strong closing statement of self-defense: **truly the LORD has sent me to you**.

c. Jeremiah's Deliverance (26:16-24)

26:16-19. After hearing Jeremiah's defense, the **officials** along with **all the people** sided with Jeremiah against the religious leadership of **priests** and false **prophets**. They declared that Jeremiah did not deserve the **death sentence**. This verdict was supported by some **elders** who reminded the people that **Micah of Moresheth** (the prophet Micah) had given a similar message nearly seventy years earlier in **the days of Hezekiah** (Mc 3:12). This is the only place in the OT where one prophet quotes another and identifies his source. Instead of seeking to put Micah to **death**, King Hezekiah listened to Micah's words and sought **the favor of the LORD**. In response to Hezekiah's request God did not bring the disaster predicted by Micah. Failure to follow Hezekiah's example was to bring a terrible disaster, **great evil**, on Judah.

26:20-23. Although Jeremiah's life was spared, other prophets were not so fortunate. The prophet **Uriah the son of Shemaiah** (mentioned only here in the Bible) spoke **words similar to all those of Jeremiah**, but **King Jehoiakim ... slew him with a sword** and **cast his dead body** into a grave for **common people**.

26:24. Ahikam the son of Shaphan protected Jeremiah so the people did not **put him to death**. The family of Shaphan played an important part in the final years of Judah (2Kg 22:3-13) and Ahikam's son, Gedaliah (Jr 40:5, 9), was appointed governor of Judah by Nebuchadnezzar after the fall of Jerusalem.

Sometimes God delivers us from our trials, while at other times He sustains us through them (Heb 11:32-40). In both instances our response must be the same: trust and obey!

2. Jeremiah's Conflict with the False Prophets in Jerusalem (27:1–28:17)

The nation was reluctant to believe Jeremiah's message that God's judgment would result in the fall of Jerusalem to wicked Babylon. They opposed Jeremiah to the point of physical violence. In this section, the opposition to Jeremiah's message is a counterattack by false prophets who contradicted Jeremiah's message and gave the people false hope of deliverance.

a. Jeremiah's Prophecy (27:1-22)

Jeremiah refuted the false prophets with three messages of truth and used an object lesson of yokes to make God's point clear.

(1) The Message to the Ambassadors (27:1-11)

27:1-7. Early in **the reign of Zedekiah** (probably 593 BC; cf. below) God commanded Jeremiah to make **yokes** like those used to hitch together teams of oxen and to **put them on [his] neck**. This was an object lesson to envoys from **Edom, Moab, Ammon, Tyre**, and **Sidon** who had **come to Jerusalem** to meet with **Zedekiah**. They were probably meeting to discuss the possibility of uniting together in a revolt against Babylon.

This meeting occurred sometime between May and August 593 BC (cf. 28:1). The *Babylonian Chronicles* (a series of stone or clay tablets in cuneiform text written during the biblical period in Babylon, recording major events in Babylonian history, now in the British Museum) recorded that just over a year earlier a rebellion had occurred in Babylon. Evidently Nebuchadnezzar had to defend himself against an attempted coup. Certainly such unrest within Babylon might cause the various vassal states, like those mentioned here, to consider throwing off Babylon's yoke of domination.

While Jeremiah wore the **yoke**, he gave the message that God had **made the earth** so He could **give it** to anyone He pleased (v. 5). For now, these nations should wear the yoke of Babylon. God selected **Nebuchadnezzar king of Babylon** (v. 6) as His instrument of judgment and **all ... nations shall serve him** (v. 7). Later Babylon's **time** of judgment would come. Only then would other **great kings** be able to **make him their servant** (v. 7). For a set time Babylon would rule the world, but later even mighty Babylon would be conquered and serve an even greater nation, the Medo-Persian empire (539 BC).

27:8-11. With Nebuchadnezzar's divine appointment clearly established, Jeremiah warned against rebellion. Any nation that refused to **put its neck under the yoke** of Babylon would be punished by God with **sword**, **famine**, and **pestilence** (cf. v. 13; 14:12). For the first of three times in this chapter, Jeremiah warned his audience not to listen to the false **prophets** (vv. 9, 14, 17), who might present themselves as **diviners**, **dreamers**, **soothsayers**, or **sorcerers**. The false teachers presented a **lie** when they promised a successful rebellion against Babylon. God had vowed to remove any nation who rebelled. Only those that would submit to the authority of Babylon (**bring its neck under the yoke**) would be allowed to remain **on** their **land**.

(2) The Message to Zedekiah (27:12-15)

27:12-15. Jeremiah gave the same message to **Zedekiah king of Judah** in two parts. First, God commanded Zedekiah to **bring** his **necks** under **the yoke of the king of Babylon** and to continue to serve as a vassal king. If he refused to serve Babylon, the judgment of God would come on Judah by **sword, famine and pestilence**. Second, God warned him not to trust the false **prophets** who predicted victory and prophesied a **lie** because God had **not sent them**.

(3) The Message to the Priests and People (27:16-22)

27:16-22. Jeremiah's message to the **priests** and **all this people** was slightly different. He cautioned them **not** to **listen** to the false prophets who were predicting that the **vessels of the LORD's house** that had been taken to Babylon (cf. 2Kg 24:13; Dn 1:1-2) would soon be brought back (v. 16). In fact, just the opposite would happen. The furnishings still remaining in the house of the LORD (along with those of the king's palace) that had not been removed during the deportation of **Jeconiah** would be **carried to Babylon** and remain there until God's judgment was complete (vv. 19-22). Only then would He **bring them back** (cf. 2 Kg 25:13-17; Ezr 1:7-11).

b. Hananiah's Opposition (28:1-17)

(1) Jeremiah's Conflict with Hananiah (28:1-11)

28:1-4. There are no chapter breaks in the original Hebrew manuscripts, and this is clearly a continuation of the previous message. It was given **in the same year** as chap. 27, and specifically in **the fifth month** of **the fourth year of King Zedekiah** (August–September 593 BC). Jeremiah was careful in noting the date because of the events that happened later (v. 17).

Hananiah son of Azzur challenged Jeremiah. Perhaps Hananiah was a brother of "Jaazaniah son of Azzur" who was denounced by Ezekiel (Ezk 11:1-3); he was **from Gibeon**, about six miles northwest of Jerusalem, another town assigned by Joshua to the priests (cf. Jos 21:17-18), so possibly Hananiah, like Jeremiah, was from a priestly family.

Hananiah directly contradicted Jeremiah's prophecy. He stated that God had **broken the yoke** of Babylonian oppression and urged Judah to rebel against Babylon, not to submit to her (cf. Jr 27:2, 8, 11-12, 17). Hananiah promised that the rebellion would be followed by restoration. **Within two years**, he said, God promised to bring back to Judah **all the vessels of the LORD's house** (cf. 27:16-22). These would be accompanied by King **Jeconiah** and **all the exiles**.

28:5-11. Jeremiah wished he could say **amen** to Hananiah's words (v. 6), **yet** he knew Hananiah's prophecy was false. The ultimate test for prophets was whether their prophecies were fulfilled. A prophet was known to be sent by God only **when the word of the prophet comes to pass** (vv. 8-9; cf. Dt 18:20-22).

To demonstrate that he was right, Hananiah **took the yoke from the neck of Jeremiah** (cf. Jr 27:2) and **broke it** (v. 10). This dramatically visualized his prophecy of God breaking the **yoke of Nebuchadnezzar . . . within two full years**. **Jeremiah** did not respond publicly to this insult, but **went his way** (v. 11).

(2) Jeremiah's Message to Hananiah (28:12-17)

28:12-14. Jeremiah spoke privately to Hananiah with a three-part message from **the LORD**. First, Hananiah's actions increased the harshness of the coming judgment. The false prophet had **broken the yokes of wood**, but God would replace them with **yokes of iron** that could not be broken (v. 13). These iron yokes, figuratively speaking, would be fastened to the necks of **all these nations** who gathered in Jerusalem **that they may serve Nebuchadnezzar** (27:3), as would **the beasts of the field**.

28:15-17. Second, Jeremiah revealed Hananiah's lack of credentials as a prophet. God had **not sent** Hananiah as His spokesman, but through his eloquent speech the false prophet had **made** the nation of Judah **trust in a lie**.

Third, as a judgment on Hananiah, because he **counseled rebellion against the LORD**, he would be removed **from the face of the earth (die)**. It was already the "fifth month" (v. 1), and Hananiah died **in the same year in the seventh month** two months later (v. 17). With this death, God vindicated His true prophet Jeremiah, and judged the false prophet Hananiah, and demonstrated to the priests and all the people Jeremiah's accuracy.

3. Jeremiah's Conflict with the False Prophets in Exile (29:1-32)

a. Jeremiah's First Letter to the Exiles (29:1-23)

(1) The Introduction (29:1-3)

29:1-3. The words and influence of false prophets like Hananiah had spread even to the Jewish exiles in Babylon. Jeremiah therefore wrote a letter to neutralize this influence if possible. Jeremiah inserted into his book the **words of the letter** that he **sent from Jerusalem** to the **elders of the exile, the priests, the prophets**, and those deported with **King Jeconiah and the queen mother** (cf. 2Kg 24:8-17; Jr 13:18; 22:24-27; Dn 1:1-2). This deportation occurred in 597 BC, so Jeremiah's letter was written after that date.

(2) The Announcement of a Long Exile (29:4-14)

29:4-9. God told the exiles to prepare for a long stay in Babylon, completely opposite of the teaching of the false prophets. In exile they were to **build houses**, **plant gardens**, **take wives**, and have **sons and daughters . . . multiply there and do not decrease** (v. 6). They were to settle down and make a life for themselves in exile. Instead of hoping for Babylon's quick collapse they were commanded to seek the **welfare of the city** (v. 7). Jeremiah even told them to **pray to the Lord on . . . behalf** of Babylon! Those **prophets** and **diviners** (cf. 27:9) who were predicting a soon return to Judah were prophesying **falsely in** God's **name** (vv. 8-9). God made it clear: **I have not sent them**.

29:10-14. The exiles would return to Judah only **when** God's **seventy years** of judgment had **been completed** (cf. 25:11-12). Then God would **fulfill** His **good word** to **bring** the exiles **back** to their land. The seventy-year exile was a part of God's **plans** to give Judah **a future and a hope** (v. 11). The people were to be encouraged when they realized that, at the end of the exile—at the end of the time of judgment—God would provide for their **welfare and not** bring them **calamity**.

The judgment prompted the exiles to **seek** God wholeheartedly (cf. Dn 9:2-3, 15-19), and He promised that when they **call upon** Him, he would **listen**; and when they **seek** Him with all their heart, they would **find** Him. These verses are sometimes used to support the idea that even a person who never hears about Christ can be saved apart from conscious faith in Christ if he or she responds correctly to the light of God in creation and seeks Him sincerely. But such an understanding wrests this promise from its theological and literary context. These Jewish exiles had *special revelation* from God which had forecast such an exile, and which had forecast a restoration to the land after exile *when they repented*, when the *Jewish people* returned to the Lord and "searched for Him with all their heart." See, e.g., Lv 26:33-45; Dt 4:25-29; 30:1-3. This is a guarantee God made to a people already in a covenantal relationship with Him and cannot be applied to those who are not. This text is not helpful when it comes to considerations of those who never hear about Jesus. For more relevant passages, see comments on Rm 1:18-23; 3:9-19, where it is apparent that no one, apart from the intervening work of God, would begin a search for God based on the dictates of his or her own unregenerate heart.

Once they had turned back to the Lord, He would **gather** them **from all the nations** where they had been banished and **restore** them to their land (Jr 29:14).The Jewish people did not return from Babylon because of spiritual revival, but because of Cyrus's decree. However, in the **future** the whole people of Israel will call upon the Lord and recognize Jesus as their Savior (Zch 12:10). This restoration is **from all the nations**, so it seems to look beyond the return from Babylonian exile to the future regathering of Israel at the end of days when Messiah will establish His kingdom.

The purpose of casting Israel out of their land, whether to Babylon or after the Roman expulsion, was more than judgment for sin. The larger purpose was to force Israel back to her God (cf. Dt 30:1-10). Whenever we face difficulties in our lives, we must remember God has a good plan for us, a plan that includes even the difficulties themselves. We should call on Him, pray to Him, and know that He is listening. Instead of being angry and shutting God out when we encounter trials, we should seek Him with our whole heart, keep reading the Bible, stay in fellowship in our local church, and anticipate a good outcome from the Lord (Jr 29:11-14; Rm 8:28; Jms 1:2-4; Heb 10:19-25).

(3) The Warning against False Prophets (29:15-23)

29:15-20. The people rejected Jeremiah' s message because it contradicted the message of the Jewish false **prophets . . . in Babylon**. Evidently these prophets were proclaiming the safety of Jerusalem and the swift return of those in captivity (cf. 28:2-4). Jeremiah shattered their optimistic forecasts by announcing that those who had not been exiled were destined for the **sword**, **famine**, and **pestilence** (cf. comments on 14:12). He reminded them of his earlier vision of the **figs** (cf. 24:1-2). Those remaining in Jerusalem were like **split-open**, rotten **figs**, destined to be thrown away because they were not good for anything. Still they would **not listen** (cf. 24:8-9).

29:21-23. Jeremiah singled out two of the false prophets in Babylon, **Ahab the son of Koliah** and **Zedekiah the son of Maaseiah** who were **prophesying . . . falsely** and committing **adultery with their neighbors' wives**. The Lord would judge them by delivering **them into the hand of Nebuchadnezzar**. For rebellion against Babylon, they would be publicly executed, **roasted in the fire**, a form of execution often used in Babylon (cf. Dn 3:6, 11, 15, 17, 19-23). Their death by fire would give rise to a **curse** the captives would use. These false prophets had said Nebuchadnezzar would not capture the city; when Babylon captured Jerusalem they were among the first to die for their insolence against mighty Babylon.

b. Jeremiah's Second Letter to the Exiles (29:24-32)

(1) The Report of Shemaiah's Letter to Jerusalem (29:24-29)

29:24-29. Evidently after Jeremiah's first letter to the exiles (vv. 1-23) another prophet in Babylon, **Shemaiah**, wrote to **Zephaniah, the priest**, and to **all the priests** in Jerusalem urging them to **rebuke Jeremiah** (vv. 25-28). However, the **letter** was **read** to Jeremiah (v. 29) who then wrote a second letter to the exiles, quoting the text of Shemaiah's letter.

(2) The Condemnation of Shemaiah (29:30-32)

29:30-32. Jeremiah quoted the text of Shemaiah's letter (vv. 24-28), delivering God's word of judgment against the false prophet. God would punish both **Shemiah . . . and his descendants**. They would **not** live to **see the good** the Lord was **about to do** for His **people** (explained in chaps. 30–33). Because Shemaiah had **preached rebellion** and caused the people to **trust in a lie**, he had forfeited his right to the blessings of the Lord.

C. Future Comfort for Israel and Judah (30:1–33:26)

This section of Jeremiah's prophecy is called "The Book of Consolation." It is a poetic description of the ultimate restoration and blessing of Israel and Judah. Certainly there would be a time of judgment for God's people, but after the "time of Jacob's distress" (30:7) Israel and Judah would be returned to their land, reunited as a nation, and restored to their God. Here is the promise of the new covenant and redemption. These prophecies look beyond Judah's imminent situation and point to the Messianic Age.

1. The Restoration of Israel and Judah Declared (30:1-24)

a. Physical Deliverance of Israel and Judah (30:1-11)

(1) The Nation's Restoration to the Land (30:1-3)

30:1-3. The Lord, the God of Israel told Jeremiah to **write** His promises of comfort in a **book** so they would be available to the exiles after Jerusalem fell. This book would declare a note of hope that the **days are coming** when God **will restore the fortunes** [i.e., deliver them from captivity] **of** His people **Israel and Judah**. The phrase **the days are coming** is an eschatological marker, looking forward to the end times and goes beyond the immediate future of the return from Babylon (3:16; cf. comments on 16:14-16; 23:5-6; 31:3, 31; 31:27; 50:1).

However, as in all prophetic material one must keep in mind the principle of "foreshortening" or "telescoping." That is, though Jeremiah saw all these predictions as one continuous series of events, they were fulfilled over a long period with intervening gaps of time. Thus, for example, prophecies about the suffering Messiah and the ruling Messiah appear together, though they describe two different advents of Christ (e.g., Is 9:6-7; 61:1-2) separated by at least 2,000 years. In the same way Jeremiah described the restoration of Judah after the Babylonian captivity and the still-future restoration of Judah in the Messianic Age within some of the same passage (Jr 31:15-20, cf. comments on 50:1). Therefore one should be cautious in interpreting the various parts of Jeremiah's predictions about "the coming days" as having already been fulfilled at the return from the Babylonian captivity (see comments on 50:1).

God's first promise, related to the first day, was to **restore** the nations of **Israel** and **Judah** back from captivity. God promised to **bring them back to the land** He had given them (cf. Dt 30:3-5). This promised return of both the northern and southern kingdoms served as an introduction to these chapters and provided hope to those who would soon be dispossessed from their land.

(2) The Time of Jacob's Distress Prior to Restoration (30:4-7)

30:4-7. The final return of **Israel** and **Judah** to the land will be preceded by a time of national distress, "Cries of **terror** will be heard among the residents of Israel in the latter days, during the time of Jacob's distress, and there will be **no peace**. Jeremiah compared the anguish of men clutching themselves in fear to a woman in **childbirth** (cf. 4:31; 6:24; 13:21; 22:23; 49:24; 50:43). The coming calamity will be so awful that there is **none like it** (cf. Mt 24:21; Dn 12:1).

This is **the time of Jacob's distress**, also known as the day of the Lord, or the great tribulation. It is a time of judgment that will culminate in Israel's physical and spiritual deliverance when the nation will recognize Jesus as the Messiah of Israel (see comments on Zch 12:10–13:1). The period includes a unique time of judgment on the nation for their sin (cf. Mt

24:21; Dn 12:1; Ezk 30:3; Jl 1:15; 2:1-2, 11; Am 5:18-20; Mc 1:2-5; Zph 1:2–3:8), including events more extreme than the fall of Jerusalem to Babylon (586 BC) or Rome (AD 70) (see comments on Mt 24:21-22).

The use of **Jacob** represents the whole nation, and this eschatological song looks to the Lord's faithfulness. Despite the distress, all will not be lost because God guaranteed that the nation **will be saved from it** (Zch 14:1-8, 12-15), for He has guaranteed the survival and ultimate blessing of His chosen people (Gn 12:1-3; 17:1-14; Is 41:8-11; 31:35-37).

Some interpreters consider the **time of Jacob's distress** to be the coming fall of Judah to Babylon. However, this is unlikely because these events are linked to **that day**, an eschatological term. A better solution is to see Jeremiah referring to the still-future tribulation period, when the remnant of Israel and Judah will experience a time of unparalleled persecution (**there is none like it**; Dn 9:27; 12:1; Mt 24:15-22). The result of this tribulation will be that Israel will call on Jesus the Messiah in faith (Zch 12:10–13:1). Then He will appear, rescue Israel (Rm 11:26), and establish His kingdom (Mt 24:30-31; 25:31-46; Rv 19:11-21; 20:4-6), providing Israel with their ultimate physical and spiritual deliverance.

(3) Restoration and Deliverance by the Lord (30:8-11)

30:8-9. God will come to rescue the nation **on that day**, and **strangers will no longer make them their slaves**. In addition, **they shall serve the Lord** and submit to the authority of **David their king** whom God will **raise up** for them. Many scholars view this, and the passages below, as a reference to Christ who is from the line of David. Others see this literally as David resurrected because he is referred to by name. However, it seems best to understand this and other passages like it (cf. Ezk 34:23-24; 37:24-25; Hs 3:5) as referring to the future restoration of a united Israel (see comments on Jr 50:1). The name David is not about resurrected King David but the scion of the house of David, the Messiah Jesus (see comments on Ezk 34:23-24). In the messianic kingdom, King Messiah, the Son of David will rule on the throne of David. Jesus is frequently identified as the Son of David in the NT (Lk 1:31; Mt 1:22; Mk 10:47; Ac 4:12; 2Tm 2:8; Rv 5:5).

This is a reference to the future millennial kingdom (**on that day**) when King Messiah, the Son of David, will rule from Jerusalem. From the Babylonian captivity until the coming of Messiah there was no king in Israel, just as the prophets foretold. Today we await the return of the King, the second coming of Jesus the Messiah to rule in His kingdom on earth (Hs 3:4-5). Here Jeremiah is speaking of restoration (Jr 30:3) in the remote future during the Messianic Age, when God will bring Judah and Israel into a new relationship with Him, and when He will judge the Gentile nations (cf. 3:16, 18; 16:14; 23:5, 7, 20; 30:3, 24; 31:27, 29, 31, 33, 38; 33:14-16; 48:12, 47; 49:2, 39; 50:4, 20; 51:47, 52). Both of these days, **the time of Jacob's distress** and **that day** when **they shall serve the Lord... and David their king** are yet future. In that day God will purify Israel, judge the nations, and fulfill the blessings of restoration promised in Dt 30:1-10 and Jr 31.

30:10-11. Jacob is told **not** to **fear**, and God's promise of restoration was designed to give **Israel** hope. She had no need to **be dismayed** because God promised to **save** her **from afar**. No country would be too distant for God to reach and rescue His people. When He brings them back to their land they will live in **quiet and at ease**, with the peace and security that was absent in Jeremiah's day (cf. 8:11), and for which Israel is still waiting.

God will **destroy completely all the nations** where Israel and Judah had been **scattered**. Though He would **chasten** Israel and Judah, He assured them that He would never **destroy** them **completely**. Any judgment would be done **justly** (cf. 10:24; 46:28) so that the punishment for His chosen people would be tempered with His faithfulness.

b. The Spiritual Healing of Zion (30:12-17)

This period of spiritual healing looks not to the return from Babylon but to the future end times. It is only then that God will destroy Israel's enemies and remove the iniquity of Israel.

(1) Israel's Sin Caused Her Wounds (30:12-15)

30:12-15. Israel's condition was critical. Her **wound** appeared **incurable** (6:14), and **no one** was available to provide a **healing for [her] sore**. There appeared to be **no recovery** possible. The **lovers**, her allies, in whom the nation had placed such great hope, had **forgotten** her. Even God had **wounded** her as **an enemy** would and punished her **because** of her **iniquity**.

(2) God Would Heal Israel's Wounds (30:16-17)

30:16-17. Israel's condition appeared hopeless, but God promised to reverse her misfortunes. Those who were devouring the nation would themselves **be devoured** by God. He would send her **adversaries . . . into captivity** and **plunder** those who sought to make spoil of her. At the same time God promised to **restore** Israel to spiritual **health**. He would intervene for His outcast people. Although the nations said **no one cares for her**, the Lord cared for **Zion**.

c. The Nation's Material and Spiritual Blessing (30:18-22)

Events described in this section go beyond the return from Babylon and detail a set of events that will take place at the end of days (cf. comments on 50:1).

30:18-20. God Himself will be involved in rebuilding **the tents of Jacob** (32:44; 33:11, 26; cf. Dt 30:3). The city of Jerusalem will be **rebuilt on its ruin**, including the king's **palace**. The festive sound of **thanksgiving** and the **voice of those who celebrate**, which had been silenced by Babylon (cf. Jr 7:34; 16:19; 25:10), will once again be heard in the city, and God will increase Judah numerically (cf. Dt 30:5). The nation will be secured and established before God, and He will **punish all their oppressors.**

30:21. Their leader will be **one of them . . . from their midst** instead of some foreign despot (cf. v. 9). This ruler will come close to God as the Lord brings **him near** into His service and will **approach** the Lord. Since unauthorized approaches to God's presence were punishable by death (Ex 19:21; Nm 8:19) this leader's proximity to God indicated spiritual qualifications for leadership.

Walter Kaiser identifies this passage as a picture of the Messiah. The Hebrew word translated **leader** (*'addir*) can be translated "glorious one" and indicates divine origin; it is used four times of either the Lord or God. Nevertheless, this coming glorious ruler will **come forth from their midst**, be from the Jewish people, as predicted of the Messiah (Gn 49:10; Dt 18:15). The phrase **I will bring him near and he shall approach Me** indicates a priestly office of this ruler. To come **near** or **to approach** (Ex 24:2; Nm 16:5) means "to engage in the work of a priest." The privilege of drawing near to God in this technical sense belongs only to those persons whom God had set apart for the task. The closing challenge, **who would dare to risk his life to approach Me?** implies that only the Messiah would be qualified for the task of Glorious Ruler-Priest (W. C. Kaiser Jr., *The Messiah in the Old Testament* [Grand Rapids, MI: Zondervan, 1994], 189–90).

30:22. Immediately Jeremiah pictured the result of the Messiah's ministry: **You shall be My people and I will be your God**. This ideal relationship between Israel and her God was expressed several times in the OT (cf. Lv 26:12; Dt 7:6; 26:16-19; Jr 7:23; 11:4; 24:7; 31:1, 33; Ezk 11:20; 14:11; 34:30; 36:28; 37:23, 27; Hs 2:23; Zch 8:8; 13:9). Israel will finally experience the relationship with God that He had always intended under the leadership of King Messiah.

d. The Judgment on the Wicked (30:23-24)

30:23-24. Jeremiah repeated a similar message to that written in 23:19-20. Before God's blessing can be experienced, He must judge sin. His **wrath** will burst out against the **wicked**. Though these words applied to false prophets in 23:19-20, here they may refer to God's judgment on the wicked nations who opposed Israel (cf. vv. 16-20). God's **fierce anger** has accomplished the **intent of His heart**. The full meaning of this message will be understood only **in the latter days** (an eschatological expression pointing to the day of the Lord; 23:20; Gn 49:1), and points to a time after the judgment has passed.

2. The New Covenant: Israel's Future Hope (31:1-40)

31:1. This verse should be connected with the text about the "latter days" in 30:23-24, as there are no chapter breaks in the original manuscript. It explains the results of God's judgment on the earth and also serves to introduce the section on national restoration that follows. God promised that when He would judge the world for its sins He would also restore all Israel to Himself in the Messianic Age. All the **families of Israel**, not just the tribe of Judah, will be known as God's people (cf. 30:22). An integral component of that restoration involves His establishment of the new covenant, the main topic of chap. 31.

a. The National Restoration of Israel (31:2-22)

31:2-6. God assured restoration even to the northern kingdom, which had fallen to Assyria in 721 BC. Those who had **survived the sword** would yet experience God's **grace** as He led them into the desert for their new exodus (cf. 16:14-15; 23:7-8; Hs 2:14-15). The turmoil of their long years of exile would cease when God intervened to give **rest** to the nation Israel.

God would restore the nation because of His **everlasting love** (*ahabah*; Jr 31:3), which He will freely bestow on His people (cf. Hs 11:4; 14:4;

Zph 3:17) and His **lovingkindness** *(chesed*; cf. Jr 9:24; 32:18; Lm 3:32; Dn 9:4). God had made unconditional covenants with Abraham (Gn 15:7-21) and with David (2Sm 7:12-16), as well as another covenant with Israel at Sinai (Ex 19:3-8; Lv 26; Dt 28:1–30:10). He vowed to stay faithful to His commitments. Therefore, Israel could look forward to experiencing God's blessing. The people were called the **virgin of Israel** (Jr 31:4)—God will one day see them as pure and innocent, because in the future, by His grace, she will be forgiven and **rebuilt**.

Jeremiah drew three word-pictures of God's restoration of Israel. First, it will be *a time of renewed joy*. Israel will once again take up her **tambourines** with **dances** and **merrymakers** (v. 4). The times of sadness will cease when the captivity ends and Messiah sets up His kingdom (cf. Ps 137:1-4; Jr 16:8-9; 25:10-11). Second, it will be *a time of peace and prosperity* as the people **plant vineyards** on the **hills of Samaria** (v. 5). Free from external threats, they will be able to enjoy their fruit (cf. Lv 26:16; Dt 28:33; Mc 4:4; Zch 3:9-10). Third, even more splendid, it will be *a time of renewed commitment* to the Lord. The **watchmen** stationed on the **hills of Ephraim** (Jr 31:6) will direct those from the northern kingdom to go **up to Zion** to worship the **Lord our God**. Not since the split of the northern kingdom from Judah (930 BC) had there been united worship in Zion by Israel and Judah. In the messianic age, the people will once again be united in their worship in Jerusalem.

31:7-9. The great salvation provided by the Lord is described with five joyful verbs: **sing**, **shout**, **proclaim**, **praise**, and **say**. The people will call out, **O Lord, save** (Pss 20:9; 28:9; 86:2). The same Hebrew word for **save** is the basis of the word "Hosanna," the cry of the people of Jerusalem to Jesus on Palm Sunday (Mt 21:9). God's restoration will be accompanied by songs of joy and the praises of the people for His deliverance. God will **gather** His people from the **remote parts of the earth**. No one will be too insignificant or weak for the Lord to deliver. God will restore the **blind** and the **lame** as well as the mother with **child** and women **in labor** (i.e., those who are most vulnerable). A **great company** will **return** to the land, **weeping** tears of repentance (Jr 31:9) for their sin will be overcome with tears of joy at God's salvation.

As God leads His people home to Israel, He will provide for their every need. He will guide the people beside **streams of waters** (cf. Ex 15:22-25; Nm 20:2-13; Ps 23:2; Is 41:18; 49:10) and they will travel on a **straight path** so they will **not stumble**—images of spiritual supply and guidance. God will do all this because of His special relationship to Israel. He is **a father to Israel** (Jr 31:9; cf. Dt 32:6; Is 63:16; 64:8; Jr 3:4, 19; Mt 6:9), and **Ephraim** (emphasizing the northern tribes of Israel) is His **firstborn** son (cf. Ex 4:22). Jeremiah used the image of a father/son relationship to show God's deep love for His people (cf. Hs 11:1, 8).

31:10-14. The Lord will **gather** Israel, as a **shepherd keeps his flock** (cf. 23:3; Mc 2:12; 5:4; 7:14) with tenderness and compassion. **Jacob** will be blessed spiritually, **ransomed** *(padah)* suggesting financial payment to buy out of slavery (Hs 13:14), and **redeemed** (*gaal*, used of a family member acting on behalf of a relative to remove trouble, avenge wrong, or pay a debt; Ru 4:1; Hs 13:14) by the Lord. **They will come and shout for joy on the height of Zion** (Jr 31:12). They will be **radiant** over the **bounty** (*tov*, "goodness") of **the Lord**. There will be material blessings of crops (cf. v. 5) and flocks. Israel will enjoy such a **life** of material blessing that she will be compared to a **watered garden** that would never **languish again**. This outpouring of blessing will produce gladness from **young** to **old**, as **mourning** and **sorrow** are replaced by **joy** (cf. vv. 4, 7; 33:10-11). The prosperity will be so great that the **priests** will have **abundance** from the many sacrifices brought by the worshipers (Lv 7:34).

31:15-17. The nation's future hope is certain. It is in stark contrast to her misery in Jeremiah's day. The cry from **Ramah** was one of **lamentation and bitter weeping—Rachel . . . weeping for her children**. It presents a heartbreaking picture of a mother's grief. **Rachel**, Jacob's favorite wife, was the mother of Joseph and Benjamin. Joseph was the father of Ephraim and Manasseh, who became two major tribes in the northern kingdom of Israel. Benjamin was the father of one of the two tribes that made up the southern kingdom. Thus Jeremiah was picturing Rachel as a symbol of mothers of the northern kingdom watching their children being carried into Assyrian exile (722 BC) and mothers of Judah who would see their children slaughtered or exiled to Babylon (586 BC) and be **no more**.

Significantly, near **Ramah**, a town in Benjamin five miles north of Jerusalem, Nebuchadnezzar established his headquarters on the plain of Hamath (39:5) and used it as the deportation point where the captives were assembled before removal to Babylon (cf. 40:1). Those considered too weak for the journey were immediately slaughtered there.

But as the women of Israel and Judah wept for their exiled children, God offered a word of **hope** and comfort: **Restrain your voice from weeping . . . they will return . . . There is hope for your future** (cf. comments on 29:11). Their children would return to their own land of Israel because God would bring about the restoration. This is a promise to be fulfilled in the Messianic Age, more than with a return from Babylon (see comments on 50:1).

This passage is most familiar because it is quoted in the NT regarding Herod's slaughter of the all the baby boys "in Bethlehem and its vicinity . . . two years old and under" when Jesus was born (Mt 2:16). When Herod learned of the birth of Jesus from the Wise Men, he killed all the innocent male children age two and younger in Bethlehem in an attempt to kill the baby Messiah. Matthew identified this tragedy as fulfilling that which "had been spoken through Jeremiah the prophet" (Mt 2:17-18).

Understanding Matthew's use of the word "fulfilled" (*pleroo*) in Mt 2:17 is important. Although Matthew did use the verb to record direct fulfillment of OT predictions (cf. Mt 21:4-5 with Zch 9:9), he also used the word to indicate a variety of other categories of fulfillment of prophecy. (For the different ways that Matthew uses the verb "to fulfill," and other ways he indicates fulfillment in his Gospel, see Michael Rydelnik, *The Messianic Hope: Is the Hebrew Bible Really Messianic?* [Nashville: B&H, 2010], 95). Specifically, in this quotation, Matthew used the word "fulfilled" in the sense of applicational fulfillment. This sort of usage highlights the contemporary relevance of an ancient prophetic text. Therefore, Matthew cited Jr 31:15 to show that Scripture had a continuing relevance, simply applying the language of this prophecy to the tragic situation of the slaughter of the innocents. Even as Jeremiah had described Rachel, representing Jewish motherhood, weeping at the death and exile of her sons, so Jewish motherhood once again mourned when wicked Herod murdered her children. And Rachel has continued to lament and has refused to be consoled for her children as they have been murdered by Crusaders, Nazis, and modern terrorists. Sadly, this Scripture has had continuing relevance for centuries of Jewish history (Rydelnik, *The Messianic Hope*, 104–08).

31:18-20. Jeremiah ended this section by recording the grief, shame, and contrition **Ephraim** (Israel) will express when she is **restored** to the Lord. Though she had behaved like an **untrained calf** she will return to the Lord, repent, and be **instructed**. God in turn will **remember** Israel, because the Lord's **heart yearns for** His people (has great compassion) and will **have mercy on** them when Israel returns to their Father (cf. 31:9; Hs 2:16-23; Rm 11:28-29).

31:21-22. The imperatives in these verses show the urgency of Israel's preparation for return: **Set up**, **place**, **direct**, **return** (twice). God called on the captives to **set up . . . road marks** and **guideposts** as they traveled to Babylon and to remember the road they would take home. They would need this information during His promised restoration so they could return to their **cities** (see comments on 50:1).

This time of promised restoration will be so remarkable that it will be as if God will create **a new thing in the earth**. That new event is described proverbially by the clause, a **woman will encompass** ("encircle, surround") **a man**. Although this verse is obscure, the possible idea is that a woman will seek or court a man. In Jewish culture of the biblical period a woman would not court a man; but instead the brides were brought to their arranged husbands (cf. Gn 2:22; 24; 29:16-30). This encompassing would indicate something unusual. The woman here is Israel (Jr 31:21) who had been **faithless**, but in the future she will **return** to the Lord—God, her true Husband—and ask to be united with Him again, loving Him wholeheartedly (29:33). This verse is the basis for the Jewish practice of a bride walking around the groom seven times at a wedding ceremony.

b. The National Restoration of Judah (31:23-26)

When God restores Israel, He will also reverse the fortunes of **Judah**. Those living in **Judah** will **once again** invoke a blessing on the **abode of righteousness** (Jerusalem, cf. Is 1:21, 26) and the **holy hill** (temple) (cf. Pss 2:6; 43:3; Is 66:20). The land will be repopulated, and God will meet every need and **refresh everyone**. As throughout this oracle, Jeremiah is speaking of events and conditions in the last days, not just the return from Babylon.

Jeremiah received this revelation (Jr 30:3-26) in a dream from the Lord, so he wrote, **At this I**

awoke (Dn 10:9; Zch 4:1). Jeremiah's **sleep was pleasant** because the truth he received from the Lord was a comforting preview of the future hope of his people.

c. The New Covenant (31:27-40)

Jeremiah used the Hebrew phrase "Behold, days are coming" to introduce the three sections of this unit (31:27, 31, 38).

The phrase "Behold, days are coming" (*hinneh yamim ba'im*) is used 15 times in his book. It is used in a negative sense seven times, and refers then to the coming destruction of Judah and surrounding nations. Some of the negative occurrences have eschatological implications (cf. 7:32; 9:25; 19:6; 48:12; 49:2; 51:47, 52). The final nine occurrences of this phrase are eschatological, pointing to a future period of blessing for Israel when (1) the nation will be restored to the land (cf. comments on 16:14-15; 23:7-8; 30:3); (2) the righteous Branch of David will be ruling over a united monarchy (23:5-6; 33:14-15); (3) the nation will be experiencing peace and prosperity in the land (vv. 27-28; 33:14, 16); (4) the new covenant with its cleansing from sin will be in effect (vv. 31-34), and (5) the city of Jerusalem will be rebuilt as a holy city that will never again be destroyed (vv. 38-40). These promises transcend anything that Israel has experienced throughout her long history. They will find their ultimate fulfillment only in the millennial age when the messianic kingdom is established, when God will fulfill all the promises He made to Israel and Judah (33:14).

31:27-30. In chap. 31, the three occurrences of the phrase **Behold, days are coming** introduce three aspects of the Lord's new relationship with His people in the new covenant (vv. 27, 31, 38). First, God vowed to provide a new beginning for His covenant people, Israel. **Behold the days are coming** in the future messianic kingdom when God will **sow** the nations of **Israel** and **Judah** with **man** and **beast** (Ezk 36:8-11; Hs 1:11-23). Jeremiah used agricultural and architectural metaphors to illustrate God's work of blessing and prosperity (cf. Jr 1:10). God had judged Judah for her sin and brought **disaster**, but He will reverse that judgment **to build and to plant**.

God's work for the nation will silence a proverb that was common in Jeremiah's day (cf. the comments on Ezk 18:2-4). Those facing judgment by the Babylonians felt they were being unfairly punished by God for their ancestors' sins. Though the **fathers [had] eaten sour grapes**, it was the children who had their **teeth . . . set on edge**. This proverb would be false **in those days** because God's justice will guarantee that each guilty person will **die for his own iniquity**.

31:31-37. Second, **days are coming** when God would **make a new covenant** with His people, the **house of Israel** (the northern kingdom) and the **house of Judah** (the southern kingdom). One aspect of this covenant is that it was **new**, and **not like the covenant** God made with **their fathers** at the time of the exodus from **the land of Egypt**, because that covenant had been broken by the people (cf. 11:1-8). This earlier covenant was the Mosaic (or Sinai) covenant contained in the books of Exodus, Leviticus, Numbers, and Deuteronomy (Ex 19:1–31:18; 34:1-27). Twice God had announced a series of punishments or "curses" that would be invoked on those who violated His law given at Sinai (Lv 26:1-46; Dt 28:1-68). The final judgment would be a physical deportation from the land of Israel.

The new covenant is related to the major covenants God made with Israel in the OT, and it was foreshadowed in the Abrahamic covenant. God promised that in the seed of Abraham "all the families of the earth will be blessed," which is a reference to the coming Messiah (Gn 12:3; 22:18). The opening verse of the NT identifies Jesus as the descendant of Abraham (Mt 1:1) who was the blessing to the whole world. The new covenant fulfilled the Mosaic covenant, because Jesus the Messiah kept the law perfectly, fulfilling all its requirements. He was the ultimate, final Passover Lamb (1Co 5:7) and Atonement (2Co 5:17; 1Jn 2:1-2). The Davidic covenant (2Sm 7:8-17) has far-reaching implications of establishing a dynasty in David's line that would have an eternal house (descendants), throne (dynasty), and kingdom (land). The Davidic covenant looks forward to a descendant of David who would bring peace and justice to God's people through His reign. This Son of David is the Messiah Jesus. The new covenant is linked to the Davidic covenant with the promise of the eternality of the Jewish people (Jr 31:35-37).

God had set a holy standard of conduct before the people, but because of their sinful hearts they could not keep those standards. A change was needed; **days are coming** when the temporary Mosaic covenant would be replaced by a permanent **new covenant**.

This **new covenant** will involve an internalization of His law. He will put (**write**) His **law within them** and **on their heart**, not just on stones, like the Mosaic covenant (Ex 34:1). People will not remind one another to **know the Lord**. They will already **all know** Him, because they have been forgiven (cf. Is 11:9; Hab 2:14) so God will include them in His new covenant community. God's new covenant will give Israel the inner ability to obey His righteous standards and thus to enjoy His blessings.

Ezekiel indicated that this change will result from God's bestowal of the Holy Spirit on these believers (cf. Ezk 36:24-32). In OT times the Holy Spirit did not universally indwell all believers. Thus one different aspect of the new covenant is the indwelling of the Holy Spirit in *all* the members of God's covenant community (Jr 31:33; Rm 8:9).

The new covenant will be God's final provision for sin. The sins of the people under the old covenant were temporarily covered by the continual offering of sacrifices according to the Sinai covenant (Ex 24:8; Lv 17:11; Heb 9:1-22). However, as part of the new covenant God will **forgive** Israel's **iniquity** and remember their sins **no more**. God cannot overlook sin, and the Mosaic sacrificial system was set up to temporarily deal with sin. His righteousness demanded a payment for sin. Under the new covenant, the penalty for sin would be paid for by His Suffering Servant, the Messiah (cf. Is 53:4-6; Mt 5:17; Jn 19:30).

The Lord Jesus announced the new covenant in the Upper Room at His last Passover (the Lord's Supper). He indicated that it would be inaugurated through the shedding of His blood (cf. Mt 26:27-28; Lk 22:20). Forgiveness of sin would be part of the new covenant because God provided Messiah Jesus as the perfect sacrifice to pay the penalty for sin once for all (2Co 5:17; Rm 6:10; Heb 7:27; 9:12; 10:10; 1Pt 3:18). The new covenant was promised to Israel and Judah and actually initiated with the faithful remnant of Israel embodied by the Jewish followers of Jesus. However, the new covenant's benefits have a broader scope than Israel alone. The spiritual aspects of this new covenant are available to all people, whether Jewish or Gentile, who put their faith in the Messiah Jesus (1Co 11:23-26; 2Co 3:6).

To underscore Israel's permanence in relation to the new covenant, God compared her existence to the heavens and the earth (Jr 31:35-37). As God had appointed the **sun for light by day** and the **moon and stars for light by night** (Gn 1:14-19), so He had appointed **Israel** as His chosen **nation** . . . **forever**. Just as it is impossible to stop the natural **fixed order** of sun, moon, and stars, neither is it possible to make **Israel** . . . **cease from being a nation**. The power God displayed in creating the universe was the power that He exercises in preserving Israel as a nation. Throughout history people have tried in vain to destroy Israel, but none have succeeded—and none ever will. Those who claim that the Church replaces Israel in God's program, or who claim that the NT teaches this, fail to come to grips with promises such as these.

Not only will the Jewish people survive as a distinct people, they will be **a nation before** the Lord **forever** (Jr 31:36). He will never stop loving His chosen people; only if the **heavens above** could **be measured** and the **foundations of the earth** could be **searched out** (which is as impossible as pulling the moon and sun out of the sky), only then will the **offspring of Israel** be **cast off** by God for **all that they have done** (Rm 11:1-2, 28). In other words, God will always be faithful to His chosen people.

The new covenant was made with Israel (Jr 31:31, 33; Lk 22:1-20) just as the Mosaic covenant had been (Jr 31:32). Ultimately the new covenant will find its complete fulfillment during the millennium when Israel is restored to her God under King Messiah. Though the ultimate fulfillment of this covenant awaits the millennial reign of Christ, the Church today is participating in some of the spiritual benefits of the new covenant. The covenant was inaugurated at Christ's sacrifice (Mt 26:27-28; Lk 22:20) with the faithful remnant of Israel, His Jewish disciples. After the resurrection and the birth of the Church at Pentecost, many Gentiles came to faith in Christ. The Church, by her union with Christ, is sharing in many of the spiritual blessings promised to Israel (cf. Rm 11:11-24; Eph 2:11-22) through the new covenant (2Co 3:6; Heb 8:6-13; 9:15; 12:22-24).

Though the Church's participation in the new covenant is real, it is not the ultimate fulfillment of God's promise. That all believers today, Jewish and Gentile, enjoy the spiritual blessings of the new covenant (forgiveness of sins by faith in Jesus and the indwelling Holy Spirit) does not mean that God is finished with His plan for the Jewish people. Scripture clearly says **days are coming** when all the spiritual and physical blessings promised to Israel will be realized by her. That still awaits the day when Israel will acknowledge her sin and turn to her Messiah for forgiveness (Zch 12:10–13:1) when "all Israel will be saved" (see comments on Rm 11:25-27). The new covenant, made possible by the blood of Messiah, brought redemption to the world and will ultimately bring unique blessing to Israel.

31:38-40. Verse 38 includes the third use of the phrase **behold, days are coming** (cf. vv. 27, 31). In the future, God will establish a new **city** for His people. Jerusalem, the city that symbolizes God's relationship with His people, was destroyed by Babylon. But even before that destruction, God promised that the **city will be rebuilt**.

The **Tower of Hananel** was at the northeast corner of Jerusalem (cf. Neh 3:1; 12:39; Zch 14:10), and the **Corner Gate** was probably at the northwest corner of the city (cf. 2Kg 14:13; 2Ch 26:9; Zch 14:10). Thus the northern wall will be restored. The locations of the **hill** of **Gareb** and **Goah** are unknown, but since Jr 31:38 describes the northern boundary and 31:40 describes the southern and eastern boundaries it may be assumed that **Gareb** and **Goah** detail the western boundary of the city. The southwestern and southern boundary will be the valley in which **dead bodies** and **ashes** are thrown. This is the Hinnom Valley (cf. 7:30-34; 19:1-6). The eastern boundary is the **fields as far as the brook Kidron**. This boundary would extend to the corner of the **Horse Gate** on the southeast tip of the city, where the Kidron Valley and Hinnom Valley unite. These geographic locations give an outline of Jerusalem.

God described two characteristics of this new city. First, it will be **holy to the Lord** (cf. Zch 14:20-21). The city and its inhabitants will be set apart to God who will dwell in her midst (Ezk 48:35). Second, the city will **not be plucked up or overthrown anymore forever**. The ravages of war will never happen this new city. These verses were not fulfilled after the Babylonian captivity ended. The postexilic period provided clear evidence that holiness was not a primary characteristic of the people in Jerusalem and Judah (Mal 1:6-14; Lk 13:34), so the city was destroyed again in AD 70 by the Romans. Furthermore, war has ravaged Jerusalem from ancient times up until the present political turmoil. Therefore the city awaits the coming of her King Messiah to bring the peace that the prophets predicted. These promises await their future fulfillment during the millennium (Jr 31:31-40) when Israel will know, "I have loved you with an everlasting love; Therefore I have drawn you with lovingkindness" (31:3-4; Is 11:9).

3. The Restoration of Israel and Judah Illustrated (32:1-44)

Although Israel's ultimate restoration will come in the Messianic age (31:31-40), the captivity in Babylon would be for only 70 years (25:11-12; 2Ch 36:20-21). God promised that afterward the Jewish people would return to their land. This section illustrates the restoration of the Jewish people to their land.

a. The Illustration: Buy a Field in Anathoth (32:1-12)

(1) Jeremiah's Circumstances (32:1-5)

32:1-2. Jeremiah's message was given in the **tenth year of Zedekiah**, which was also the **eighteenth year of Nebuchadnezzar**. The time frame of this prophecy was given because of its significance to the message. The **tenth year of Zedekiah** ended on October 17, 587 BC (using the Jewish calendrical reckoning of Tishri-to-Tishri comprising a year) while the **eighteenth year of Nebuchadnezzar** began on April 23, 587 BC (using Babylonian reckoning of a Nisan-to-Nisan year), so this prophecy occurred sometime between April 23 and October 17, 587 BC. Jerusalem was under siege from Babylon from January 15, 588 BC, until July 18, 586 BC. When this message was given, **Babylon was besieging Jerusalem** and **Jeremiah the prophet was shut up** under arrest in the **house of the king of Judah**.

32:3-5. Zedekiah imprisoned Jeremiah for the prophet's messages, namely: (1) that God would give Jerusalem **into the hand of the king of Babylon**, (2) that **Zedekiah** would **not escape out of the hand of the Chaldeans**, and (3) any attempt to oppose the Babylonians would **not succeed**. These negative, defeatist statements were demoralizing to the nation and insulting to the king, who was trying to withstand Babylon's assault.

(2) The Purchase of the Field at Anathoth (32:6-12)

32:6-9. God told Jeremiah of an impending visit by his cousin **Hanamel the son of Shallum** and gave him an unusual assignment. This Shallum, Jeremiah's **uncle**, was a servant in the temple and was carried into exile (1Ch 9:19); he is not the royal Shallum, also known by the name Jehoahaz (1Ch 3:15). Hanamel visited Jeremiah in prison and asked Jeremiah to **buy** his **field at Anathoth** because Jeremiah had the **right of redemption** to **buy it**. The Mosaic law called for a person to redeem (purchase) the property of a relative who was forced to sell; this law kept property in the family (Lv. 25:23-28; Ru 4:1-6).

Hanamel's motives for selling the land are not given, but to purchase land in Anathoth that was already under Babylonian control would appear to be foolish. Who would buy a parcel of land that was already in enemy hands? God told Jeremiah in advance that Hanamel would come so Jeremiah would recognize God's hand in the request and not dismiss this seeming foolishness. However, buying a field prior to going into captivity indicates a hope of return.

When Hanamel came, Jeremiah **bought the field** for **seventeen shekels of silver** (about seven ounces). Ordinarily this would have been a small price for a field (cf. Gn 23:12-16). But the size of the field is unknown.

32:10-12. Following the legal practice of the day, Jeremiah **signed and sealed the deed** and **called in witnesses** and **weighed . . . the silver**. Two copies of the deed of purchase were made, a **sealed copy** and **open copy**. One was sealed by being bound with a piece of cord with Jeremiah's official seal stamped into a lump of clay placed over the string. The other copy remained unsealed so it could later be examined. Jeremiah handed both copies of the deed to **Baruch**, Jeremiah's scribe and friend (cf. 36:4, 8, 26). This was a public action **in the sight of Hanamel**, and **in the sight of the witness who signed the deed**, and **before all the Jews** who were **sitting in the court of the guard**, the area where Jeremiah was imprisoned (v. 2).

b. The Explanation of the Purchase (32:13-15)

32:13-15. Jeremiah **commanded Baruch** to take both **deeds** and put them in an **earthenware jar** for preservation. The documents had to last a **long time** in storage while the people were in exile. This object lesson was to show that **houses, fields, and vineyards** would again be **bought** by the people of Israel in **this land**. The people would return from exile in Babylon.

c. The Prayer of Jeremiah (32:16-25)

(1) His Praise for God's Greatness (32:16-23)

32:16-19. As he prayed, Jeremiah focused on the incomparable greatness and majesty of God's character. God's creation of the **heavens and the earth** proved that **nothing is too difficult for** the Lord (31:27). He is omnipotent, and He is also a God of love and justice. He **shows lovingkindness** (*chesed*; cf. 9:24; 31:3) to **thousands**, countless generations; but He also punishes **iniquity** (cf. Ex 20:5; 34:7; Nm 14:18; Dt 5:9-10). In God's omniscience He gives to **everyone according to his ways** (according to their behavior). Jeremiah worships God as **great and mighty** (Dt 10:17; Neh 9:32), **the Lord of hosts** (the name of God indicating His power, righteousness and covenant keeping, used hundreds of times in the OT, and dozens of times by Jeremiah; see 1Sm 17:45; 2Sm 5:10; Ps 89:8; Is 54:5; Jr 5:14; 50:34). Since nothing escapes His **eyes** He can justly reward everyone according to his conduct, **the fruit of his deeds**.

32:20-23. God's character was evident in His deeds throughout Israel's history, briefly recounted in this passage: From God's **signs and wonders** (cf. Dt 4:34; 26:8; 29:3; 34:11) during the exodus, to the disobedience of Israel when they took possession of the **land** He promised, to the **calamity** that was about to occur (cf. Lv 26:14-39; Dt 28:15-68).

(2) His Puzzlement over God's Promise (32:24-25)

32:24-25. After proclaiming God's mighty character and deeds, Jeremiah expressed his confusion at God's workings. In light of vv. 32:17-23 it seems unreasonable to believe that Jeremiah doubted God's ability to restore His people. Probably Jeremiah was expressing in vv. 24-25 his bewilderment over how God would accomplish this restoration rather than doubting if God would accomplish it.

Babylon's **siege ramps** had already **reached the city**. Jerusalem's fate was sealed; she would be **given** over to **the Chaldeans**, and the people to **the sword, famine**, and **pestilence** (cf. v. 36 and see comments on 14:12.) Everything that God had foretold through His prophets had **come to pass**. Yet as the army of Babylon stood poised to reduce Jerusalem to rubble, God had commanded Jeremiah to **buy a field** and **call in witnesses**, although **the city** was doomed (vv. 6-12). Jeremiah did not understand how God's promised restoration related to Judah's present calamity.

d. The Answer of the Lord (32:26-44)

(1) The City Will Be Destroyed (32:26-35)

32:26-29. God answered Jeremiah by first reminding him of His identity and power: **Behold, I am the Lord . . . is anything too difficult for Me?** (v. 17; Gn 18:14; Lk 1:34-37). Jeremiah could depend on God's word even if he did not understand how it would be accomplished. **Nebuchadnezzar** would destroy Jerusalem. He would set it on **fire and burn it** down (cf. Jr 21:10; 34:2, 22; 37:8, 10; 38:18, 23) because of the people's worship of **other gods** (cf. 19:13).

32:30-35. Doing only evil had characterized both **Israel** and **Judah . . . from their youth**. They provoked God to **anger by the work of their hands**, practicing idolatry. Spiritually they turned their backs on God and refused to listen or respond to discipline. Everyone was guilty: their **kings, leaders, priests, prophets, men of Judah, inhabitants of Jerusalem** (2:26). They **turned their back** to God, despite His repeated lessons **again and again**. The temple was defiled with **detestable things** (7:30; Ezk 8:3-16), and the **valley of Ben-hinnom** had become the offering place of child sacrifice to **Molech** (cf. comments on Jr 7:31-32; 19:5-6), an act so abominable it had never **entered** the **mind** of God (cf. comments on 7:30-31). Jerusalem would fall to Babylon because of her sin.

(2) The City Will Be Restored (32:36-44)

32:36-44. Jerusalem was **given into the hand of the king of Babylon by sword, famine and by pestilence** (32:24; see comments on 14:12). Yet that catastrophic event did not signal the end of God's chosen people. God offered hope in the midst of despair. First, He promised to **gather them** (cf. Ezk 37:1-14). God will regather His people from **all the lands** where they had been in exile and **will bring them back** to the land of Israel where they will **dwell in safety** (cf. Jr 31:1-17). They will have **one heart** to **fear** the Lord. Second, He promised an **everlasting covenant**, the new covenant (cf. 31:31-34; Ezk 36:24-32). It was called **everlasting** (*'olam*) to stress its duration. Not only will the people of Israel be restored to their land, but also they will be restored to their God. They will be His people and He will be their God (see comments on Jr 30:22), and they will never **turn away** from Him. With singleness of heart His people will follow the Lord, and He will never stop doing **all the good** He promised to them.

Just as God had been faithful to His word in bringing **great disaster** on Israel because of her sin (Dt 28:15-68), so He will also be faithful in providing the **good** He had promised them (Dt 30:1-10). Thus Jeremiah's purchase of the field (Jr 32:1-15) was a symbolic act to show that people **will buy fields for money** throughout Israel, from **Benjamin** and **Judah** to the **hill country** to the **Negev**, because God will **restore their fortunes** (cf. 30:18; 33:11, 26; Dt 30:3).

4. The Restoration of Israel and Judah Reaffirmed (33:1-26)

"The Book of Consolation" concludes in chap. 33, which is structurally and chronologically related to chap. 32. In chap. 33:1-13, Jeremiah continued relaying God's promise of blessing, even as the Lord reaffirmed both the coming destruction and the future restoration of Jerusalem. God then reaffirmed His covenants with David and with the Levitical priests (33:14-26).

a. The Coming Judgment and Future Restoration (33:1-13)

(1) The Judgment (33:1-5)

33:1-3. While he was **still confined** in the guardhouse (cf. 32:2), **the word of the LORD** came to Jeremiah the second time with a message similar to the first he received while in custody (chap. 32). God again reminded Jeremiah of who He was, stressing both His power and His character as **the LORD** who **made the earth** (cf. 32:17). This emphasized His covenant-keeping faithfulness to Israel by stating that the **LORD is His name**, it is the **LORD** who created the earth, and He is able to **answer** when called upon (cf. 32:18; Ex 3:13-15).

Jeremiah did not understand how God could restore a nation that was destined for doom (cf. Jr 32:24-25), so God challenged the prophet to call to Him for understanding. God promised to **answer** by revealing **great and mighty things**. The word for **mighty** (*b'surot*) means "something that is made impenetrable by fortifying it or enclosing it." It is used to describe heavily fortified cities (cf. Nm 13:28; Dt 3:5; 28:52; Ezk 21:20). God's plans for the future are inscrutable to ordinary people. Only God can unlock the secrets of the future, and He offered this knowledge to Jeremiah. God would share with Jeremiah information the prophet did not know or understand about Israel's future. Likewise, God wants us to come to Him for understanding and insight. All true wisdom ultimately begins with Him (Pr 1:7) and in Christ "are hidden all the treasures of wisdom and knowledge" (Col 2:3).

33:4-5. As Babylon's siege wore away at Jerusalem's outer resistance, the defenders of Jerusalem used **houses** and the royal palaces to provide wood and stone to strengthen the walls **against the siege ramps** to prevent **the sword** of Babylon's soldiers from making a breach in the walls and entering the city. God revealed that all these defensive plans would fail because of His **anger and . . . wrath**. God would hide His **face from this city**, refusing to deliver it from this destruction **because of all their wickedness** (cf. 18:17; Ezk 4:1-3). Jerusalem had to be destroyed because of **all their wickedness**.

(2) The Restoration (33:6-13)

33:6-9. The key to understanding God's seemingly contradictory prophecies of judgment and blessing is to realize that the judgment was to be only temporary. After the time of judgment God will, in days to come, bring **health and healing** to His city and His people with abundant **peace and truth**.

God spoke to Jeremiah about three elements of this blessing. First, the blessing will involve a restoration to the land (cf. 31:8-11; 32:37). God will bring both **Judah** and **Israel** back from captivity, and **restore** (*shuv*, "return") their **fortunes** (*shavuth*, "captivity" or "captives"). They will be rebuilt, reestablished. Second, the blessing will involve a restoration to the Lord (cf. 31:31-34; 32:33-40). God will **cleanse** the people from **all their iniquity** and **pardon** them of their transgressions. Third, the blessing will involve a restoration to a special place of honor among the nations (cf. 31:10-14; Dt 28:13). Jerusalem will bring renown, **joy**, **praise**, and **glory** to God **before all the nations of the earth**. Nations will be in awe and will tremble as they marvel at the **good** and **peace** God will lavish on His people (Jr 33:6, 9). The fulfillment of this prophecy did not occur following the exile and awaits an eschatological realization.

33:10-13. God drew two pictures that contrasted Israel's present judgment and her future blessing. Each picture began with similar phrases, including the words **Thus says the LORD**, **again**, and **in this place**, and the theme of various **cities** being a **waste** (vv. 10, 12).

God emphasized that this is what **the LORD** (or **LORD of hosts**) says. In each picture the scene in Jeremiah's day was similar (vv. 10, 12). Jerusalem was a desolate **waste, without man or beast** (cf. 32:45). Though the siege was still in progress, the fall of Jerusalem was so sure that God pictured it as if it had already happened. However, these events are yet in the future, when King Messiah reigns over His people, who will be cleansed from all their iniquity (v. 8).

At this point the two pictures changed. First, God illustrated the **joy** and **gladness** that will again return to **Judah** and **Jerusalem** (vv. 10-11). Next, He illustrated the peace and prosperity of the people, where **flocks . . . pass under the hands** of good shepherds, throughout all of Israel from the **hill country** to the **lowland** to the **Negev** in the south, to **Benjamin**, **Jerusalem**, and **Judah** (vv. 12-13; 17:26). The streets **of Jerusalem** that were **desolate** after its destruction by Babylon (cf. Lm 1:1-4) will again be filled with the **voice of joy and . . . gladness**. This joyful sound will be typified by the voices of a **bride** and **bridegroom** in a wedding ceremony (cf. Jr 7:34; 16:9; 25:10) and the voices of worshipers who bring a **thank offering into the house of the LORD** (cf. Ps 100:1-2, 4; Jr 17:26). The song to be sung by the worshipers, **Give thanks to the LORD of hosts, For the LORD is good**, recorded by Jeremiah, resembled the refrain of several psalms (cf. Pss 100:4-5; 106:1; 107:1; 136:1-3). Joy will come when God restores Judah's fortunes (cf. Jr 30:18; 32:44; 33:26; Dt 30:3).

Throughout the land **flocks will again pass under the hands of the one who numbers them**, as a shepherd counts his sheep to be sure none is absent. Return of flocks of sheep points to a time of prosperity. Possibly Jeremiah was using shepherd and sheep in a metaphorical sense to refer to the leaders of Israel and the people. He had already compared the leaders to shepherds (cf. comments on 3:15) and the restored nation to a regathered flock (cf. 23:3; 31:10). Ultimately the Lord is the Shepherd of Israel and will care for His flock (Ps 80:1; Ec 12:11; Ezk 34:11-31; Jn 10:11; Heb 13:20; 1Pt 5:4).

b. The Covenants with David and the Levitical Priests (33:14-26)

Jeremiah had also used this imagery of future blessing to introduce his message on the "righteous Branch" of David (23:1-6; 33:14-26).

(1) The Covenants (33:14-18)

The second section of this chapter is introduced with the phrase "Behold, the days are coming" (*hinneh yamim ba'im*, cf. comments on 31:27) when God would "fulfill the good word . . . concerning . . . Israel and . . . Judah." Although the monarchy and the priesthood were suspended during the exile, Jeremiah proclaimed there would be both an eternal Davidic kingship and an eternal Levitical priesthood (vv. 17-18) in the coming days. However, the fulfillment was not realized at the return from Babylon (Ezk 1:8; 2:2, 40-54; 8:15-20). The "good word," a phrase that captures the entire breadth of the glorious promises made to both parts of the nation (16:14-15; 23:3-6; 29:10-14; 31:1-14, 27-40; 32:37-44; Hs 1:10-11; 2:14-23; Am 9:11-15; Mc 7:18-20; Zph 3:10, 14-17; Zch 8:3-8, 10:6, 14:9-20) will be fulfilled in the Messianic Age.

33:14-16. The first aspect of this fulfillment will be the restoration of the monarchy (cf. 23:5). The **righteous Branch of David** (cf. 23:5-6; 33:15; Is 11:1-4) will rule as King over the nation. This was a prophecy about Jesus Christ who descended from the line of David and was promised David's throne (cf. Mt 1:1; Lk 1:31-33). His reign is characterized by **justice and righteousness** and extends to the whole **earth**.

The second aspect of this fulfillment will be the restoration of **Jerusalem** as God's dwelling place. The city that was about to be destroyed by Babylon (Jr 33:4-5) will, in the coming days, **dwell in safety**, and **she will be called: the LORD is our righteousness**. This verse is similar to 23:6, but here a significant change gives it a new meaning. In 23:6 Jeremiah pictured the safety of Israel and Judah through the ministry of the Messiah who was called "The LORD Our Righteousness." However, by changing "Israel" to "Jerusalem" and by changing the pronoun "He" to "she," Jeremiah here applied the title, **the LORD Our Righteousness**, to the city of Jerusalem instead of to the Messiah. Under the kingship of Messiah, Jerusalem will take on the same holy characteristics as the Lord who will dwell in her (cf. Ezk 48:35).

It is significant that Jeremiah singled out the royal (Jr 33:15) and religious (v. 16) aspects of God's restoration. Both were vital to Israel's existence as God's covenant community. With the certain destruction by Babylon, the people would be carried into exile and the promised land reduced to rubble, and all God's covenants with His people seemed to be at the point of annulment. The series of messages to Jeremiah (vv. 17-26) confirms that the ancient covenant is secure, based on the character God.

33:17-18. To stress the importance of both priesthood and king, God reiterated His covenants with the line of David and with the Levitical priests. The first covenant mentioned was God's covenant with David (cf. 2Sm 7:8-16; 1Ch 17:4-14). God vowed that **David shall never lack a man to sit on the throne of the house of Israel**. Some have felt that this promise failed because the monarchy ended in 586 BC when Jerusalem fell. However, God did not promise an *unbroken* monarchy but an unbroken line of descendants from David who would be qualified to sit on that throne when it was reestablished. David's line would not fail before the righteous Branch of David came to claim His throne (cf. Lk 1:31-33). The genealogies of Matthew and Luke show that this promise was fulfilled, as Messiah Jesus was able to trace both His legal line through Joseph and His physical line through Mary back to David (Mt 1:1-16; Lk 3:23-31).

The second covenant mentioned was God's covenant with the **Levitical priests**. This covenant was God's promise that the Levites would **never lack a man** to stand before Him to **offer burnt offerings . . . grain offerings**, and **sacrifices**. Again the promise was not that the sacrifices would continue unabated, because they did cease in 586 BC and were not resumed till 537 BC (cf. Ezr 3:1-6). The promise here was that the Levitical priesthood would not be extinguished. God was referring back to the promise He made to Phinehas (Nm 25:12-13). Although the Messiah Jesus, our Redeemer King Priest who ever lives to make intercession, is our high priest, this prophecy is not about Him (Heb 7:24-25). Certainly, neither the monarchy nor the priesthood would ever be abolished. Messiah Jesus will reign as King from the line of David (2Sm 7:16; Ps 89:34-37; Jr 33:17, 20-22; Lk 1:32-33) and as High Priest. However, He is fulfilling the office of high priest, not from the Levitical priesthood, but as a priest in the line of Melchizedek; a change in law, from the Sinai covenant to the new covenant, leads to a change in high priesthood (Gn 14:18-20; Ps 110:4; Heb 5:5-6; 6:20; 7:1-28). However, in the messianic kingdom, there will be a messianic temple with offerings and sacrifices, and at that time, Levitical priests will continue to minister there under the high priesthood of the Lord Jesus (see Ezk 43:19; 44:15-19 and comments there).

(2) The Confirmation of God's Covenant Promises (33:19-26)

Going into exile would cause the people to doubt their future and even God's faithfulness to His promises. In this section, Jeremiah records reassurance from the Lord.

God gave two assurances that He would keep His covenant promises. Each assurance began with the same introductory phrase, "The word of the LORD came to Jeremiah" (33:19, 23), and each used God's "covenant for day and . . . night" to illustrate the permanence of these institutions (33:20, 25; cf. 31:35-37).

33:19-22. Only if man could break God's **covenant for the day and . . . covenant for the night** (cf. Gn. 1:14-19) could God's **covenant[s] . . . with David** and **with the Levitical priests** be broken. That is, God's covenants with them were as fixed as the natural order in the universe. They could not be overthrown by mere mortals. The word for "covenant" (*berit*) referred to a treaty or agreement made between individuals or parties by which they bound themselves to a specific relationship or course of action. A covenant could be conditioned on the behavior of both parties, or unconditional, based on the behavior of one party. The covenants to Abraham, David, and the Levitical priesthood were unconditional covenants, assured by the actions of God alone.

God had promised to preserve the kingly line of **David** (2Sm 7:8-16) and priestly line of Phinehas (Nm 25:12-13), and He would not break His oath. Indeed, God promised to bless both lines of the descendants of **David** and **the Levites**, and both would become as countless as **the host of heaven** (the stars) and **the sand of the sea**.

33:23-26. God's second promise was to **Jeremiah** because of the doubt and reproach raised against him by **this people**, a phrase used to refer only to Israel and/or Judah. Some people in the nation claimed that God had so **rejected** the **two families** of Israel and Judah that He would no longer regard them **as a nation**. They felt that Israel's and Judah's sin, and coming exile, had led God to invalidate His covenant promises.

God responded to this argument by reaffirming His commitment to His covenants. The covenants with Abraham and David were not conditioned on people's obedience but on God's character (cf. comments on the unconditional nature of these covenants at 22:6-10). They were as sure as His **covenant for day and night** and as immutable as **the fixed patterns of heaven and earth**. Only if these natural laws could be repealed would God **reject** the **descendants of Jacob and David**. The reference to **Abraham, Isaac, and Jacob** is God's unconditional covenant with Abraham and the patriarchs regarding His selection of Israel as the chosen people (cf. Gn 12:1-3; 15:7-21; 17:1-8; 26:1-6; 28:10-15). God was bound to His promises and He would **restore** the nation's **fortunes** (cf. Jr 30:18; 32:44; 33:11; Dt 30:3) and have **mercy on them**. The greatest argument for the future restoration of Israel as a nation is the character of God. He made a series of covenants with the patriarchs, David, and the Levites; His character demands that He will preserve Israel and ultimately fulfill these promises to the Jewish people (Rm 11:1-6, 28-29).

D. Present Catastrophe of Judah (34:1–45:5)

After describing the future hope of Judah (chaps. 30–33), Jeremiah returned to their present judgment. The destruction he had been predicting (chaps. 2–29) would now occur. The theme of judgment that began in chaps. 26–29 is taken up again in chaps. 34–36. The prophet was clear about the coming judgment (chaps. 2–29 and chaps. 34–45), but used a central part of his message in this book to confirm the Lord's mercy and faithfulness (chaps. 30–33).

1. Before the Fall of Jerusalem (34:1–36:32)

A detailed eyewitness account of the events that occurred during and after Jerusalem's fall to Babylon is presented in chronological order in chaps. 37–45. However, Jeremiah introduces those events with a record of life in Jerusalem immediately prior to its fall, to show the necessity of God's judgment.

a. The Inconsistency of the People (34:1-22)

(1) The Warning to Zedekiah of His Exile (34:1-7)

34:1-3. When **Nebuchadnezzar** and all **his army . . . were fighting against Jerusalem**, God gave **Jeremiah** a message for King **Zedekiah**. This message was that Zedekiah's rebellion against Babylon would not succeed. God had already determined to give Jerusalem **into the hand of the king of Babylon**, who would **burn** it (cf. 33: 22; 32:29; 37:8, 10; 38:18, 23). Though Zedekiah would try to flee, he would **not escape**. Instead he would **see the king of Babylon** and **speak** with him **eye to eye** and be judged for his rebellion. Zedekiah would be taken captive to **Babylon** as punishment for his rebellion. Everything Jeremiah predicted came to pass (cf. 39:4-7; 52:7-11).

34:4-5. Because of his rebellion **Zedekiah** could have been executed by Nebuchadnezzar, but God promised that he would **not die by the sword**. Rather, he would **die in peace** and have a funeral befitting a king (in contrast with Jehoiakim; cf. 22:18-19; 36:27-31). With **spices . . . burned** is not a reference to cremation, which was not practiced by the Jewish people, but the custom of burning spices (incense) at royal funerals (cf. 2Ch 16:14; 21:19). The lament **Alas, lord!** is equivalent to "Alas, our Majesty!" It is not giving qualities of deity to the king since Israel did not view their kings as gods.

34:6-7. Jeremiah delivered his message to King Zedekiah **when the army . . . of Babylon** relentlessly continued its attack **against Jerusalem** and the only **remaining** fortified cities **of Judah**. The guard cities of **Lachish**, 27 miles southwest of Jerusalem, and **Azekah**, 18 miles southwest of Jerusalem, fell in 587 BC.

(2) The Warning to the People for Enslaving Their Countrymen (34:8-22)

34:8-11. Jeremiah highlighted the specific sin of keeping Jewish slaves. Perhaps in a desperate attempt to win God's favor during Babylon's siege of Jerusalem, **Zedekiah had made a covenant with all the people** . . . to **release** their Jewish slaves because the law commanded that **no one should keep** . . . **a Jew, his brother, in bondage** (cf. Ex 21:2-11; Lv 25:39-55; Dt 15:12-18).

The slaves' freedom, however, was short-lived. All those who released their slaves **afterward** . . . **turned around and took back the male** . . . **and the female servants** and enslaved them again. The slave owners changed their minds when the Babylonians broke off their siege of Jerusalem to repel an attack by the Egyptians. The people hoped for an Egyptian victory, which would end the Babylonian threat. But after so much destruction from the siege, slaves would be needed to rebuild the cities and towns. So the people reneged on their promise to obey God when it seemed that life would return to normal (cf. Jr 37:4-13).

34:12-16. God rebuked the people for their inconsistency by reminding them of their history. He had **made a covenant** with their **forefathers** when He freed them from Egyptian **bondage**. The law required that every **seven years** all **Hebrew** slaves were to go **free**. No Israelite was to be forced into permanent bondage again. Unfortunately the people **did not obey** God's Word. Because of Babylon's attack, the people finally repented and did what was right by granting freedom to their countrymen, but it was an insincere obedience. When they no longer felt under threat, they no longer felt the need to obey the Lord, and so they **profaned** God's **name**. They **made a covenant before** God **in the house which is called by** His **name**, the temple, and they broke that covenant, treating His name as unholy—with irreverence and contempt.

34:17-20. God's penalty matched their sin. By revoking their covenant the people had not proclaimed **release** for those Israelites who were wrongfully enslaved. Therefore, God would give them **release** to die by the **sword**, **pestilence**, and **famine** (cf. comments on 14:12).

In making their **covenant** in the temple (cf. v. 15) the people had **cut the calf in two**, and **passed between its parts** to signify their commitment to the covenant. By walking through the parts of the animal they were symbolizing the judgment that would befall them if they violated the agreement. God promised to treat those who broke the covenant like the calf they had slaughtered for the covenant. All who made the agreement would be given **into the hand of their enemies** and their **dead bodies** would be **food for the birds** . . . **and beasts** (cf. 7:33; 15:3; 16:4; 19:7).

Significantly when God made His covenant with Abraham, the patriarch did not pass between the parts of the animal. Only God passed between the parts, symbolized by the blazing torch (Gn 15:4-18, especially v. 17). The Abrahamic covenant rested on God's character, not on man's obedience.

34:21-22. Zedekiah and **his officials** should have been models of godly leadership, but they were as godless as the people. Though the Babylonians had **gone away** from Jerusalem, God would **command** them to come **back to this city**. The siege would resume until the Babylonians would take Jerusalem and **burn it** down (cf. v. 2). The other **cities of Judah** would be devastated, and the whole country would be a **desolation without inhabitant**.

b. The Consistency of the Rechabites: An Object Lesson to Judah (35:1-19)

(1) The Fidelity of the Rechabites (35:1-11)

35:1-5. This prophecy was given during the reign of **Jehoiakim** (609–598 BC), at least 11 years earlier than the prophecies in chap. 34. Jeremiah placed the chapter here to contrast the faithfulness of the Rechabite people with the unfaithful Judeans. The **Rechabites** were a nomadic clan (vv. 7-10) descended from Jonadab [or Jehonadab] son of Rechab (v. 6), who assisted Jehu in exterminating Baal worship from Israel (2Kg 10:15-27). They were related to the Kenites (1Ch 2:54-55) who descended from Moses' father-in-law, Jethro (Jdg 1:16). Jonadab chose to live as a nomad, not a city dweller, and his lifestyle became the norm for his clan (Jr 35:6-10). Rechabites dwelt in tents in the Negev (Jdg 1:16; 1Sm 15:6), but they were forced to move to Jerusalem when Nebuchadnezzar threatened Judah in 598 BC (Jr 35:11).

Jeremiah invited the **Rechabites**, including **Jaazaniah**, for a meeting in **the house of the Lord** in the **chamber of** . . . **Hanan** . . . **the man of God**, a term usually used of a prophet (cf. 1Kg 12:22; 1Kg 1:9-13; 4:21-22). These rooms surrounded the temple court and were used for meetings, storage, and as priests' residences (1Kg 6:5; 1Ch 28:12; 2Ch 31:11; Neh 13:7-9). The room occupied a prominent position, **near the chamber of the officials** and over the room of **Maaseiah** . . . **the doorkeeper**. This was evidently a high position because doorkeepers were singled out by the Babylonians for judgment along with the chief priests (cf. 2Kg 25:18-21; Jr 52:24-27).

Jeremiah brought the nomadic Rechabites to this serious meeting with high-level Jerusalemites. He offered hospitality with **pitchers full of wine and cups**, and invited them to **drink wine**.

35:6-11. As Jeremiah knew, the Rechabites would **not drink wine** because the founder of the Rechabites, **Jonadab the son of Rechab** had prohibited it. He **commanded** his descendants: **You shall not drink wine, you or your sons, forever**. Nor were they allowed to **build a house, sow seed**, or **plant a vineyard**. They were not to live as farmers or in the city; they were to live **in tents** as nomads.

Jonadab's descendants, and their **wives, sons** and **daughters**, had **obeyed the voice of Jonadab, the son of Rechab . . . in all that he commanded**. (vv. 8-10). Only the Babylonian war had driven them to Jerusalem.

(2) The Example of the Rechabites (35:12-17)

35:12-17. The Rechabites were an object lesson to Judah. They consistently **obeyed their father's command**, in sharp contrast with the people of Judah who had consistently disobeyed God their Father (cf. 31:9). The Rechabites were a reminder of Judah's sin. God vowed to bring **on Judah . . . all the disaster [He had] pronounced against them**. This disaster could refer to either (1) the curses of the covenant (cf. Lv 26:14-39; Dt 28:15-68) or, more probably, (2) the fall of Judah and Jerusalem predicted by Jeremiah (cf. Jr 4:20; 6:19; 11:11-12; 17:18). Judah would be punished because she **did not listen** to God's words and **did not answer** God's summons.

(3) The Reward of the Rechabites (35:18-19)

35:18-19. In contrast to faithless Judah, the Rechabites had faithfully **obeyed the command** of their forefather **Jonadab**. God rewarded their faithfulness by assuring them they would **not lack a man to stand before** the Lord **always**. The word "always" should be understood in context. Here "always" does not mean necessarily forever into eternity, but has a limited duration of their service in the temple. The promise was given to the Rechabites prior to the destruction of the temple and fall of Jerusalem, indicating they would return to Jerusalem with the Jewish people after the exile and take up their worship of the Lord in the temple (Neh 3:14). They apparently continued their worship in the temple until the Romans destroyed it in AD 70.

"To stand before" was used of those who served in a variety of ways: as prophets (Jr 15:19; 1Kg 17:1), as officials who served the king (1Kg 10:8), and of priests in the temple (Dt 4:10; 10:8; 2Ch 29:11). It was these people of Israel who stood before the Lord at the tabernacle and the temple (cf. Lv 9:5; Dt 4:10; Jr 7:10). The Lord promised that the line of the Rechabites would always have descendants who would be able to worship the Lord. The promise pointed to a continuing line of people who followed God, rather than a specific office of ministry for Him. Although the Rechabites are not specifically mentioned in Ezekiel's description of the millennial temple, perhaps they too will be part of the worship in that future temple, along with the Levitical priests (see 33:17-18; Ezk 43:18-19; 44:15-19).

God is always looking for individuals whose lives are characterized by faithfulness. Such people will experience God's blessing even in the midst of trials and will always have opportunity to serve Him.

c. Jehoiakim's Scroll-Burning (36:1-32)

(1) The Writing of the Scroll (36:1-7)

36:1-3. The events of this chapter began in the **fourth year** of King **Jehoiakim** (605–604 BC; cf. 25:1). This is just prior to Judah becoming a vassal to Babylon (2Kg 24:1) and Babylon taking the best of the young men captives (Dn 1:1-4). God commanded **Jeremiah** to **take a scroll and write on it all the words** God gave him about **Israel, Judah**, and . . . **all the nations** from the **day I first spoke to you . . . even to this day**. God **first spoke** to him in **the days of Josiah** (627 BC; cf. Jr 1:2; 25:3). This was the first formal compilation of Jeremiah's prophecies (25:13). At least two additional stages of compilation are mentioned in the book (cf. v. 32; 51:64).

One purpose for recording these prophecies was so they could be read aloud to the people. The hope was that **the house of Judah** would **hear all the calamity** God would **bring on them** and **turn from his evil way** and God would **forgive their iniquity and their sin**.

36:4-7. Jeremiah called Baruch, his scribe (cf. 32:12-16; 36:26), and dictated to him **all the words of the Lord**. It is not known whether Jeremiah recited all the prophecies from memory or if he read them from scrolls on which he had recorded them earlier. Either method allows for God's superintendence.

Jeremiah was **restricted** and could not **go into the house of the Lord**, possibly because of his earlier unpopular Temple Address there (cf. 7:1-15; 26:1-19) or because of his message about the broken jar and Pashhur's attack (cf. 19:1–20:6). So Jeremiah **commanded Baruch** to go to the temple in his place **on a fast day** when people would be assembled there. Prior to the fall of Jerusalem (586 BC) fast days were not specified (other than Yom Kippur, Lv 23:26-32) but were called in times of emergency (cf. Jr 36:9; 2Ch. 20:3; Jl 1:14; 2:15). Only after the fall of Jerusalem were regular fast days instituted (Zch 7:3, 5; 8:19). Jeremiah hoped that as Baruch read the scroll **everyone [would] turn from his evil way**.

(2) The Reading of the Scroll (36:8-19)

36:8-10. Some time elapsed before a national emergency arose that prompted **all the people** to proclaim **a fast before the Lord**. The scroll was written in Jehoiakim's fourth year (v. 1), but it was not read until the **fifth year**, in the **ninth month** (December), a possible gap of several months. (For a detailed discussion of the chronological issues see Edwin R. Thiele, *The Mysterious Numbers of the Hebrew Kings*, rev. ed. [Grand Rapids, MI: Zondervan, 1983]; and Richard A. Parker and Waldo H. Dubberstein, *Babylonian Chronology: 626 BC–AD 75* [Providence, RI: Brown University Press, 1956]).

The date was significant because the *Babylonian Chronicles* (cf. 27:1-7) report that, at the same time, Nebuchadnezzar was in Judah collecting "vast tribute" from those nations he had conquered. In the same month the fast was called, Nebuchadnezzar captured the city of Ashkelon and plundered it. It is possible that the fast was called to plead for deliverance from Babylon's harsh hand.

Baruch read from the book the words of Jeremiah in the **chamber of Gemariah** that was in the **upper court** of the temple (cf. v. 10) at the entrance of the **New Gate**. It seems Baruch stood at the door of Germariah's room so that what he read could be heard by all the assembled people in the temple courtyard. This was the first of three readings that day (vv. 10, 15, 21). Because of the repeated readings, it is likely that only portions of the scroll were read each time.

36:11-19. Gemariah's son **Micaiah . . . heard all the words of the Lord from the book**. He went to the **king's house** in the **scribe's chamber** to report the contents of the scroll to the **all the officials**, including **Delaiah** and **Elnathan the son of Achbor**, who urged Jehoiakim not to burn Jeremiah's scroll (v. 25). However, Elnathan had earlier led an expedition to Egypt to extradite the righteous prophet Uriah back to Jerusalem to be executed.

When **Micaiah** finished his report, **Baruch** was summoned to appear before them and **read** the scroll to them. The officials **turned in fear to one another** when they heard the message of the scroll, and knew they must **report all these words to the king**. They asked if **Baruch** wrote **all these words** at Jeremiah's **dictation**.

To protect them from the king, the officials warned Baruch and Jeremiah: **hide** and **do not let anyone know where you are**. Jehoiakim's prior reaction against Uriah the prophet showed the wisdom of this advice (cf. 26:20-23).

(3) The Burning of the Scroll (36:20-26)

36:20-22. The **scroll** was placed in the **chamber of Elishama**, the scribe, while the officials **reported all the words to the king** in court. **Jehudi** was sent to retrieve scroll, and he **read it to the king** and his **officials**.

The events took place in the **ninth month** (between November 24 and December 23, 604 BC). Since it was cold in Jerusalem, Jehoiakim was in his **winter house** (Am 3:15), probably facing south to catch the winter sun. Further, he had a **fire burning in the brazier**, a small stove, for warmth.

36:23-26. Hebrew scrolls are written in vertical columns. After **Jehudi had read three or four columns**, Jehoiakim interrupted him and **cut** those columns off the scroll with a **scribe's knife**, then threw those pieces into the **fire . . . in the brazier**. What a contrast with his godly father Josiah's (cf. 2Kg 22:11-13) responsive behavior when he found the scroll of the Lord. Instead, Jehoiakim burned the scroll column by column as it was read to him **until all the scroll was consumed in the fire . . . in the brazier**.

This was shocking behavior. **Yet** the **king** and all his **servants, who heard all these words were not afraid** of God's words of judgment. Neither did they **rend their garments** in grief and repentance for their sins enumerated in the scroll. Instead Jehoiakim ordered the immediate arrest of **Baruch** and **Jeremiah**. However, **the Lord hid them** and kept them safe from the king.

(4) The Rewriting of the Scroll (36:27-32)

36:27-31. A scroll can be burned, but the Word of God cannot be destroyed. Since Jehoiakim **burned the** first **scroll**, God told Jeremiah to write on **another scroll** all the **words that were on the first scroll**. Because **Jehoiakim** had burned the scroll and refused to believe God's warning about the king of Babylon, God vowed to judge him. First, no descendant of his would permanently sit on **the throne of David**. Though his son, Jehoiachin, did follow him to the throne (cf. 2Kg 24:8-17), he was deposed by

Nebuchadnezzar after only three months. No other descendant of Jehoiakim ascended the throne (see comments on Jr 22:24-30). Second, Jehoiakim would not receive a proper burial (cf. 22:18-19). Instead **his dead body** would be **cast out** and left unburied, exposed to the elements. Third, Jehoiakim's **descendants and his servants** would be punished for their **iniquity**. God would bring on **them** and **Jerusalem** and **Judah** every **calamity** that He had **declared** . . . because **they did not listen**.

36:32. Jeremiah obeyed God's command exactly. He **took another scroll**, and **Baruch wrote** . . . **at the dictation of Jeremiah** on the new scroll **all the words** of the **burned** scroll. Plus Jeremiah, according to the instruction of the Lord, added many **similar words**, most likely the contents of chap. 36, including the judgment on Jehoiakim. This verse used the word **scroll** (*megillah* "a scroll") and **book** (*sapher,* "writing," "written document," "decree"—not a square bound book with pages) interchangeably. Ancient scrolls were made of tanned leather or papyrus sewn together in long sheets and rolled scrolls.

2. During the Fall of Jerusalem (37:1–39:18)

The events of chaps. 37–39 are arranged chronologically. They record Jerusalem's final days before the fall, and trace Jeremiah's life and ministry during the final siege and fall of Jerusalem. The events foretold in Jeremiah's messages and recorded on the scroll begin to occur.

a. Jeremiah's Message to Zedekiah about Egypt (37:1-10)

37:1-2. The section focuses on **Zedekiah**, the last king of Judah, who was placed on the throne as a vassal king by **Nebuchadnezzar** (cf. 2Kg 24:15-17). From the king to the common people, no one **listened to the words of the Lord** given by **Jeremiah.**

37:3-10. Although Zedekiah did not listen to the words of the Lord, he asked Jeremiah to **pray to the Lord** for Judah. Jeremiah was **not yet** . . . **in the prison**, and Babylon, **the Chaldeans**, had just lifted her siege of Jerusalem to defend herself from **Pharaoh's army** marching **from Egypt** as Judah's ally. Perhaps Zedekiah hoped that Jeremiah's prayers would induce God to grant a victory to the Egyptians and force Babylon out of Judah (cf. 21:1-7 for a similar request).

God's answer was bad news for Zedekiah. Pharaoh's army that had marched out to give **assistance** to Judah would be crushed by Babylon and forced to **return to** . . . **Egypt**. Then the **Chaldeans** would return and **fight against** Jerusalem, **capture it** and **burn it** down (cf. 21:10; 32:29; 34:2, 22; 37:10; 38:18, 23). Those who hoped for a Babylonian withdrawal were deceiving themselves. Even if **only wounded men** were in Nebuchadnezzar's army, they would **rise up and burn** Jerusalem (cf. v. 8).

b. Jeremiah's Imprisonment (37:11–38:28)

(1) Jeremiah's Arrest and Confinement in a Dungeon (37:11-16)

37:11-16. When the Babylonian army withdrew to fight the Egyptians, they **lifted the siege from Jerusalem**, and the city had a time of relative calm. Jeremiah used this pause in fighting to leave the city for a short journey (perhaps 10 to 15 miles or so, depending on the exact destination), to his home in the **land of Benjamin** (cf. 1:1). The purpose of his trip was to **take possession of some property** belonging to his family, either to secure some land or to divide up some land for sale to others. Apparently Jeremiah had purchased the field earlier without ever leaving the premises of the court of the guard (32:1-15). Now with the siege lifted, he went **out from Jerusalem** to care for the **property**.

On his way out of Jerusalem, **at the Gate of Benjamin** (38:7; Zch 14:10), the northeast city gate toward the territory of Benjamin, the **captain of the guard** at that gate **arrested Jeremiah** and charged him with deserting to the **Chaldeans**, a logical accusation since many people from Judah had defected (Jr 38:19; 39:9; 52:15), and Jeremiah constantly foretold Babylonian victory (21:9). Jeremiah called the charge **a lie**, but the captain, **Irijah**, **arrested** him anyway. Jeremiah was beaten and put into **jail** in the **house of Jonathan the scribe**. He was put in a **dungeon** (lit., "in the house of the cistern, in the vaulted rooms"). This was probably a broken or dry cistern made into a **prison** where Jeremiah **stayed many days**.

(2) Jeremiah's First Meeting with Zedekiah and Transfer to the Courtyard of the Guard (37:17-21)

37:17-20. The Babylonian army returned to Jerusalem and renewed the siege of the city, as the Lord said (vv. 9-10). Zedekiah **took** Jeremiah **out** . . . **secretly** because of Jeremiah's unpopularity with the people (cf. 26:10-11; 37:11-13; 38:4) and brought him to the **palace**. The resumption of the Babylonian siege was crushing, so Zedekiah asked for a **word from the Lord**. Jeremiah gave him the same message as before: **You will be given into the hand of the king of Babylon!** (21:7; 32:4; 34:3).

Jeremiah used his audience with Zedekiah to plead his innocence. He asked how he had **sinned against** the king or his **servants** or **this people** that he should be put **in prison**. Other prophets had prophesied lies, declaring the Babylonians would **not come against . . . this land**; Jeremiah was jailed for telling the truth. He petitioned Zedekiah to **not make** him **return** to the dungeon to **die there**.

37:21. Zedekiah granted Jeremiah's request and had him transferred from the cistern to the **court of the guardhouse** in the royal palace (cf. 32:2) and arranged for Jeremiah to be given **bread daily . . . until all the bread in the city was gone** (cf. 52:6). Being imprisoned in the guardhouse of the palace assured Jeremiah of food during the siege, while many others in Jerusalem died of starvation. This is an example of how "God causes all things to work together for good to those who love Him" (Rm 8:28).

(3) Jeremiah's Confinement in a Cistern (38:1-6)

38:1-3. Confinement in the courtyard of the guard (37:21) gave Jeremiah some freedom to speak **to all the people** (cf. 32:1-2, 6). He used this time to deliver God's message to any who would listen. His message was overheard by four high-ranking officials: **Shephatiah** son of Mattan (not mentioned elsewhere), **Gedaliah** son of Pashhur (possibly a son of the Pashhur who beat Jeremiah, 20:1-3), **Jucal** son of Shelemiah (sent by Zedekiah to inquire about the lifting of Babylon's siege, 37:3), and **Pashhur** son of Malchijah (sent by Zedekiah to inquire about Babylon's initial attack on Jerusalem, 21:1-2). These four powerful officials **heard the words** Jeremiah was **speaking to all the people.**

Jeremiah's message (summarized in 38:2-3) was the same one that Jeremiah gave before (21:3-10). Those who stayed **in** Jerusalem would **die by** the **sword**, **famine**, or **pestilence** (cf. comments on 14:12). Only those who went **out to the Chaldeans** would **stay alive**. Jerusalem's only hope was to surrender. Any thought of withstanding Babylon's siege was futile since the Lord had said the **city will certainly be given into the hand of the army of the king of Babylon**.

38:4-6. The **officials** went to **the king** and demanded Jeremiah be **put to death** for **discouraging** the **men of war** and **all the people**. These officials did not believe the word of the Lord, but thought Jeremiah was **seeking . . .** the **harm** of the people and the city. Zedekiah's weak leadership was most evident in his response to these officials. He forsook his promise to protect Jeremiah (37:18-21) and handed him over to those who sought his life. Saying, **Behold, he is in your hands**, Zedekiah abdicated his authority concerning Jeremiah, and maintained that he could **do nothing**. Zedekiah was a political puppet, incapable of making strong, independent decisions. He was controlled either by Nebuchadnezzar (cf. 2Kg 24:17) or by the city officials who urged him to rebel against Babylon and then influenced his decisions (Jr 27:12-15; 38:5, 19, 24-28).

The officials took Jeremiah from the royal guardhouse (37:21) and **cast** him into the **cistern of Malchijah**, in the courtyard of the guard (cf. 2:13; 37:16). This cistern was so deep that they had to lower Jeremiah **down with ropes**. It had **no water** in it, probably because of the prolonged drought (cf. 14:1-4), but there was **mud** that collected in the bottom of the pit. **Jeremiah** then **sank** down into the mud, an even worse condition than the dungeon-prison in Jonathan's house (37:15). Had the water or mud been deeper he would have drowned or suffocated, and death by starvation was likely. Perhaps people threw stones at Jeremiah in the cistern, hoping to kill him outright or to knock him unconscious so he would sink into the mud and die (Lm 3:52-54).

(4) Jeremiah's Rescue from the Cistern (38:7-13)

38:7-9. Many of Jeremiah's countrymen wanted him killed because they hated his message of the coming fall of Jerusalem and exile to Babylon. The only official who cared enough to intercede on his behalf was **Ebed-melech** (lit., "servant of the king") **the Ethiopian**. He was a **eunuch**. The word (*saris*) did not always mean castrated, but often was used in the sense of "officer" or "court official."

Ebed-melech went to the **Gate of Benjamin** (cf. 20:2; 37:13) where the **king was sitting**, perhaps conducting royal business. He described Jeremiah's circumstances, and reported that other officials had **acted wickedly** by throwing Jeremiah into a cistern where he would starve to death. Evidently Zedekiah had not known the officials' specific plan to kill Jeremiah or else he had not believed that they would carry it out. But now he knew Jeremiah's death was imminent.

38:10-13. Zedekiah ordered **Ebed-melech** to rescue **Jeremiah . . . from the cistern** before he died. He gave him **thirty men** to pull Jeremiah from the pit and to defend the rescue party. After being hauled up by ropes, with **rags** protecting his **armpits**, Jeremiah was again put in the **court of the guardhouse** (cf. 37:21).

(5) Jeremiah's Second Meeting with Zedekiah (38:14-28)

38:14-16. Again **Zedekiah sent** for **Jeremiah** to meet him at the **third entrance** to the temple. This entrance, not mentioned elsewhere, may refer to a private entrance that connected the king's palace with the temple. Zedekiah told the prophet to **not hide anything from** him.

Jeremiah voiced two objections. First, if he answered with a message the king did not want to hear he had no guarantee that the king would not **put [him] to death**. Second, any counsel Jeremiah gave would be wasted because the king would **not listen** to him. Zedekiah answered the first objection but not the second. He promised **in secret** that he would not put Jeremiah **to death** or **give** him **over** to men **seeking** his **life**; but the king made no promise to heed Jeremiah's message.

38:17-23. Jeremiah's message was unchanged (cf. 21:1-10; 37:17; 38:1-3). If Zedekiah would surrender to the Babylonians he would **live**, the city would **not be burned** down, and his household would **survive**. However, if he would not surrender, Zedekiah would **not escape** but would be seized by **the king of Babylon** (cf. 39:5-7; 52:8-11) and the **city** would be handed **over to the Chaldeans** who would **burn it** (cf. 21:10; 32:29; 34:2, 22; 37:8, 10; 38:23).

Zedekiah refused to heed Jeremiah's message because he had a **dread** of **the Jews** who had already **gone over to the Chaldeans**. He believed if he went to Babylon he would be handed over to these Judahites who would **abuse** him for his past acts of cruelty and bad leadership. Jeremiah assured Zedekiah that this would not happen. He begged him to listen: **Please obey the Lord**, that **you may live**. Then Jeremiah detailed the horrible results of **refusing to go out**. Zedekiah would suffer the very ridicule and humiliation he sought to avoid. The **women** from his **palace** would be given to the **officers of the king of Babylon** to be raped. The women would mock Zedekiah's weak leadership for following the advice of his **close friends**. Zedekiah would be **misled and overpowered**, his **feet** would sink **in the mire** of a dungeon, and his friends will have **turned back** from him. If Zedekiah refused to surrender to Babylon he would see his **wives and . . . sons** being led away (cf. 39:6), he would **not escape**, and Jerusalem would be **burned** (cf. v. 18).

38:24-28. Zedekiah rejected Jeremiah's advice. Such a bold step was beyond the ability of this spineless monarch. Instead he warned Jeremiah not to let anyone **know about these words**; their conversation needed to be kept secret for the sake of the king's reputation and Jeremiah's life. If word got out, the officials would try to kill Jeremiah. Palace spies were everywhere, so Zedekiah gave Jeremiah an alibi in case he was questioned. If the officials asked Jeremiah what he said to the king and what the king said to him, he was to tell them that he was pleading with Zedekiah not to send him back to the dungeon in Jonathan's house (cf. 37:15-16, 20). Jeremiah had indeed made such a request during his first meeting Zedekiah, so this would be an accurate reply.

Zedekiah's caution was well founded because the officials did hear about the meeting and **questioned** Jeremiah, and he **reported to them** as **the king had commanded**. His answer ended their questions, but he remained in the court of the guardhouse as a political prisoner until **Jerusalem was captured** by Nebuchadnezzar.

c. Jerusalem's Destruction (39:1-18)

Chapters 39-45 give the most detailed account in the OT of the fall of Jerusalem to Babylon, and the circumstances of the Jewish people who were not taken captive.

(1) The Fate of the Jews (39:1-10)

39:1-4. In one sense, chap. 39 is a climax to God's messages of judgment against Jerusalem. Jeremiah provided a detailed account of how **Jerusalem was captured**.

The final assault began in the **ninth year of Zedekiah king of Judah** in the **tenth month**. This event was so traumatic that it was recorded three other times in the OT, even noting the day of the month (cf. 2Kg 25:1; Jr 52:4; Ezk 24:1-2). The siege lasted over 30 months. Using our modern calendar, the siege began on January 15, 588 BC. Jerusalem fell in the **eleventh year of Zedekiah**, specifically the **ninth day** of the **fourth month**, a day of mourning in the Jewish calendar to the present time, Tisah b'Av (ninth of Av, August 14, 586 BC).

After the 30-month siege by the Babylonians, **the city wall was breached**. The **officials of . . . Babylon** entered the city and **sat down at the Middle Gate** to establish their control over the city and to judge those taken captive (cf.

comments on Jr 38:7; Ezk 11:1). One of the officials overseeing the siege was **Nergal-sar-ezer Samgar-nebu** (cf. Jr 39:13), Nebuchadnezzar's son-in-law. He ascended Babylon's throne after the death of Nebuchadnezzar's son (560 BC). So the officials who oversaw the capture of Jerusalem were of the highest rank.

When King **Zedekiah** and his military commanders (**men of war**), saw that the city had fallen, they **fled** toward the **Arabah**, the Jordan Valley.

39:5-7. Escape was impossible, as Jeremiah had foretold (38:18). **Zedekiah** was captured by the **army of the Chaldeans** on the **plains of Jericho**, in the Jordan Valley, about 14 miles east of Jerusalem. He was taken north to **Nebuchadnezzar** in the Babylonian military headquarters at the city of **Riblah in . . . Hamath**. **Riblah** was a key city in the Beqa Valley, north of Damascus (2Kg 23:29-35; 25:6, 20, 21; Jr 52:10, and Hamath was a political territory in ancient Syria (2Sm 8:9-10; 2Kg 14:28, 17:24), part of modern Lebanon and Syria. The king of Babylon had established military headquarters there to direct the siege of Judah (2Kg 25:20-21; Jr 52:10). There Nebuchadnezzar **passed sentence** on Zedekiah for rebelling against Babylon. First, Zedekiah was forced to watch as the Babylonians slaughtered his **sons . . . before his eyes** and killed all the **nobles of Judah**. Then, to seal this sight of horror in Zedekiah's mind forever, Nebuchadnezzar **blinded Zedekiah's eyes**. Finally he **bound** Zedekiah with **fetters** (shackles) **of bronze** to drag him in humiliation to **Babylon**. Zedekiah was shamed more than he even feared (cf. 38:17-23) because he had ignored the warnings of the Lord.

39:8-10. Jerusalem suffered the exact fate Jeremiah predicted . The Babylonians **burned with fire** the magnificent **king's palace** and the **houses of the people** (cf. 21:10; 22:6-7; 32:29; 34:2, 22; 37:8-10; 38:18, 23). The soldiers also **broke down the walls of Jerusalem** so the city would remain defenseless (cf. Lm 2:8-9; Neh 1:3). **Nebuzaradan**, captain of the bodyguard, **carried . . . into exile** everyone who was still alive in the city (cf. Jr 13:19; 15:2; Ezk 5:8-12), to join the people who had **gone over** earlier (cf. Jr 21:8-9; 38:1-4, 17-23). Only the very **poorest people . . .** were **left behind in the land** to insure stability and productivity; they were given **vineyards and fields** to keep them alive.

(2) The Fate of Jeremiah (39:11-18)

39:11-14. Nebuchadnezzar had apparently heard of Jeremiah, either through the letters the prophet had sent to Babylon (cf. chap. 29) or through the testimony of those who had defected to the Babylonians (21:8-9; 38:1-3). **Nebuchadnezzar . . . gave orders** for his soldiers to take Jeremiah and **look after him**. They were not to harm Jeremiah but were to do for him whatever he desired. Jeremiah was released from the **court of the guardhouse** (cf. 38:28). Apparently Jeremiah was moved from the guardhouse with the captives to Ramah, five miles north of Jerusalem (31:15; 40:1), but Nebuchadnezzar arranged for him to be released and not returned to the guardhouse. Instead, Jeremiah was **entrusted** to **Gedaliah**, the son of Ahikam and grandson of Shaphan, the scribe in the reign of Josiah (2 Kg 25:22-25; Jr 39:14; 40:5-16; 41:1-18). Nebuchadnezzar appointed Gedaliah as governor of those who remained in the land (40:7, cf. 41:12 about the murder of Gedaliah). So Jeremiah **stayed among the people** of Jerusalem who were not sent to exile in Babylon.

39:15-18. While Jeremiah was **confined in the court of the guardhouse**, before the city fell, God gave him a message for **Ebed-melech** (cf. 38:7-13). God's words against Jerusalem would be fulfilled **before** Ebed-Melech's eyes **on that day**. God promised that when Jerusalem fell He would **rescue** Ebed-melech so that he would not **fall by the sword**, or be executed with all the other officials (cf. v. 6; 52:10, 24-27). Ebed-melech would escape because he had **trusted in** God by helping Jeremiah when he secured the prophet's release from the cistern (cf. 38:7-13).

3. After the Fall of Jerusalem (40:1–45:5)

It seems the fall of Jerusalem would have taught Judah a permanent lesson. She would have learned to listen to and obey the word of God through Jeremiah. However, by recording the events that happened after the fall of the city, Jeremiah demonstrated that the basic character of the people who remained in the land was unchanged. They still refused to trust the Lord or the word of His prophet (cf. Ezk 33:23-29).

a. Jeremiah's Ministry to the Remnant in Judah (40:1–42:22)

(1) The Governorship of Gedaliah (40:1-12)

40:1-6. After Jeremiah was **released** from **Ramah** where he had been taken **bound in chains** with the other captives, **Nebuzaradan**, the Babylonian **captain of the bodyguard**, said he was aware of Jeremiah's prophecies, that **the Lord . . . God promised this calamity** because the people had **sinned** and **did not listen**.

However, Nebuzaradan was **freeing** Jeremiah **from** his **chains** and would **look after** him (cf. 39:12), because he was innocent in Judah's revolt against Babylon.

Jeremiah was free to go, and **the whole land** was **before** him (Gn 13:9). Jeremiah was free to choose; he could go to Babylon with the other captives or stay anywhere in Judah. However, if he did stay in Judah, Nebuzaradan suggested that he go **to Gedaliah** and live with him. Governor Gedaliah, whom Nebuchadnezzar **appointed over the cities of Judah**, could offer both the protection and the physical provisions that Jeremiah would need. To start Jeremiah on his new life of freedom and for the three-mile journey from Ramah to **Mizpah**, the administrative center for Judah after the destruction of Jerusalem, Nebuzaradan gave him **a ration and a gift**.

40:7-12. As often in war, scattered remnants of the army often still remained deployed under **commanders of the forces** in **the field** after the surrender of the main body of troops. The main forces of Judah, located in Jerusalem, Lachish, and Azekah, had been crushed; but groups of army officers and their men were still scattered in the open country. When these soldiers heard that **Gedaliah** was now governor over the land they came to him at **Mizpah**. Two of the leaders were worthy of special notice because of subsequent events (v. 8). **Ishmael the son of Nethaniah** (vv. 14-15) was from the royal family of David (cf. 41:1; 2Kg 25:25) and had served as one of King Zedekiah's officers. **Johanan** was one of two sons of Kareah (cf. vv. 13-16).

These commanders wanted to know what would happen if they would lay down their arms and surrender. Gedaliah reassured them if they served **the king of Babylon** it would **go well** with them. Gedaliah promised to **stand for**, or represent, them before the Babylonians while they concentrated on harvesting the **wine**, **summer fruit**, and olive **oil**. They would be free to live in the **cities** they had **taken over**.

The news of Gedaliah's appointment not only reached the scattered bands of Judah's resistance fighters, but it also reached the **Jews** who had fled to **Moab**, **Ammon**, **Edom**, and all the **other countries**. These refugees **returned** to the land to resettle it, and helped in harvesting the **wine** and **summer fruit in great abundance** (cf. v. 10).

Judah's prospects looked bright. Peace and stability were returning to the land. The warring factions had submitted to Gedaliah's rule, and some refugees had returned.

(2) The Assassination of Gedaliah (40:13–41:15)

40:13-16. But despite the calm, forces of intrigue and rebellion were churning. News of danger was brought by **Johanan the son of Kareah** (cf. 31:8) and the field **commanders of the forces**. They reported to **Gedaliah** a plot by **Baalis king** of the Ammonites to have **Ishmael son of Nethaniah** (v. 8) kill Gedaliah. The motive for this assassination was woven into the relationship between Judah and Ammon and the political fabric of the area under Babylonian threat. Both nations were vassals to Babylon and had participated in a secret meeting of nations in 593 BC to evaluate their prospects of uniting in rebellion against Babylon (cf. 27:1-11). Although that meeting did not produce any definite action, Egypt's new Pharaoh (Hophra) persuaded Judah, Ammon, and Tyre to revolt against Babylon in 588 BC.

Nebuchadnezzar had to decide which nation to attack first, and God directed him to Judah instead of to Ammon (cf. Ezk 21:18-23). Judah and Ammon were still allies when Jerusalem fell, and Zedekiah was probably heading for Ammon when he was captured (Jr 39:4-5). Despite the alliance of Judah and Ammon, they were not friends but allied because of strategy. Ammon rejoiced over Jerusalem's fall because she knew that if Nebuchadnezzar committed his army against Jerusalem he would not be able to attack Ammon (cf. 49:1-6; Ezk 25:1-7).

Thus Gedaliah's commitment to Babylon was unsettling to Ammon. If Judah did submit to Babylon, then after Nebuchadnezzar finished his siege of Tyre (cf. Ezk 29:17-18) he would probably attack Ammon. But a destabilized Judah could force Nebuchadnezzar to commit large numbers of troops there to maintain order, which would improve Ammon's chances for survival. So it was to Ammon's advantage to replace pro-Babylonian Gedaliah with an anti-Babylonian leader like Ishmael.

Unfortunately **Gedaliah . . . did not believe** these officers. **Johanan . . . spoke secretly** with **Gedaliah** and offered to **kill Ishmael** to protect the governor for the good of Judah. Gedaliah ordered Johanan not to **do this thing**; Gedaliah thought the whole report was a **lie about Ishmael**. Gedaliah was an honorable man who made a fatal mistake when he misjudged Ishmael's character.

41:1-3. Ishmael . . . came to **Gedaliah** with **ten men** for a supposedly peaceful meeting, **eating bread together**. Then Ishmael and his cohorts **struck down Gedaliah** and also killed **all the Jews who were with him**, as well as the **Chaldeans . . . who . . . were men of war** there (cf. 2Kg 25:25). The killings occurred in the **seventh month** (late September/early October) Though the month was given, the year was not, so the exact dating of the assassination is uncertain. It would be difficult for all of these events to have occurred in 586 BC because the army of Babylon was still in Jerusalem as late as August 17th of that year (Jr 52:12). This would have allowed the Babylonians less than two months to deport the people, establish a government, allot the land, and withdraw the main body of their forces. So the assassination must have happened in a later year. Jeremiah records a little-known deportation in 583–582 BC (cf. 52:30), without giving the details of the event. Perhaps this Babylonian deportation was to restore order after the assassination of the governor and the Jewish migration to Egypt. If these events are related, then the **seventh month** when Gedaliah was assassinated began on October 4, 583 BC.

41:4-9. The assassinations probably took place in the evening. The plot had gone so well that **the next day** no one **knew about it**. The next day **eighty men**, a large caravan, were going to Jerusalem in mourning (with **beards shaved . . . clothes torn**, cf. 16:6), from **Shechem**, **Shiloh**, and **Samaria**, three cities of the northern kingdom of Israel. Since these upright men were from the largely apostate northern kingdom, at least some of King Josiah's reforms (cf. 2Kg 23:15-20; 2Ch 34:33) had a lasting impact. They were carrying grain offerings and incense to **the house of the Lord**. Though the temple had been destroyed (cf. Jr 52:13, 17-23), people still worshiped at its site. These worshipers were traveling to Jerusalem to celebrate one of the three feasts held during the seventh month (Trumpets, the Day of Atonement, Booths; cf. Lv 23:23-44), yet were in mourning because of the destruction of the temple.

Ishmael . . . went out . . . to meet the pilgrims, **weeping as he went**. After feigning sympathy he invited them to **come to Gedaliah**. Certainly an offer to meet with the governor could not be refused, so they went together to Mizpah. Once **inside the city**, Ishmael and his band of cutthroats **slaughtered them**, and threw their bodies into **the cistern**. Though not specifically stated, the passage implies (Jr 41:8) that he intended to plunder his victims and seize their provisions. Certainly a caravan of 80 travelers would carry a large amount of food and money, plus the offerings for the temple. Ten of the 80 managed to bargain for their lives by announcing that additional supplies of **wheat** and **barley**, **oil** and **honey** were **hidden in the field**. If he would spare them, they would show him the location of this cache. Ishmael's greed prompted him not to kill them.

Jeremiah explained the historical significance of the site where the slaughter occurred (v. 9): The **cistern** in which the bodies of the men and Gedaliah were cast had been constructed nearly 200 years earlier by **King Asa**. It served as part of the defense of Judah by King Asa's men against King **Baasha** of the northern kingdom, in the war between Judah and Israel (cf. 1Kg 15:16-22). The cistern that had once helped preserve life was now **filled . . . with the slain**.

41:10-15. Ishmael had killed only a specific group living in Mizpah (v. 2), but he **took captive** all the rest, **the remnant**, who lived there. These included the **king's daughters** and **all the people who were left in Mizpah** who been **put under the charge of Gedaliah**. Jeremiah was probably among the captives (cf. 40:6). The group set out from Mizpah to go to **Ammon**, Ishmael's ally (40:14).

When **Johanan the son of Kareah** and the military **commanders** and troops heard about **all the evil that Ishmael . . . had done**, they set off **to fight** Ishmael. The troops caught up with the slower group of captives near the **great pool . . . in Gibeon** (2Sm 2:12-16). Those taken captive were **glad** when they spotted their rescuers, and escaped from Ishmael. However, **Ishmael** and **eight men** fled to **Ammon**.

(3) The Leadership of Johanan (41:16–42:22)

41:16-18. Johanan and **the commanders** took **all the remnant** they had rescued from Ishmael. This group included **soldiers**, **women**, **children**, and **eunuchs**. But instead of returning to Mizpah they went on. Their first place of rest was at **Geruth Chimham** near **Bethlehem**, 13 miles from **Gibeon**. The group was on its way to **Egypt** to escape the Babylonians because they were afraid that Babylon would retaliate for the death of **Gedaliah**.

42:1-6. Before going on, **all the commanders**, including both **Johanan** and **Jezaniah** (called

"Azariah" in 43:2), and **all the people** decided to seek the Lord's guidance. They asked Jeremiah to **pray for** them **to the LORD.** They wanted God to tell them where they should go and what they should do. They had already decided to flee Israel, and they seemed to want God's approval for their plan to escape to Egypt (v. 14; 43:7).

When speaking to Jeremiah they referred to the Lord as **your God** (vv. 2-3), as if they thought of the Lord as more of Jeremiah's God than their own. Jeremiah agreed to pray for them, but corrected their thinking by referring to **the LORD** as **your God**, indicating that He was their God as well. He said he would pray and tell them the whole **answer**, while they vowed to act in accordance with whatever God commanded, **whether it is pleasant or unpleasant**. After watching God destroy their nation because of disobedience they were careful to agree that they would obey the Lord.

42:7-12. Jeremiah prayed for the people, and then **ten days** later God answered. Jeremiah told them, if they would **stay in this land**, God promised to **build** them **up** and **plant** them. They should **not be afraid** of the Babylonians because the Lord was **with** them to **save** and **deliver them**. God would cause Nebuchadnezzar to **have compassion** (*raham*, "show tender concern") on them, a characteristic not associated with the Babylonians (cf. 6:23; 21:7). If the people submitted to the Babylonians, God promised that Nebuchadnezzar would **restore** them to their land.

42:13-18. Similar to the blessings and curses of Dt 28, Jeremiah followed his list of blessings for obedience with a list of judgments for disobedience. **But if** the people refused to **stay in this land** and did **not listen to the voice of the LORD** by going to **Egypt** . . . **then** they would experience God's judgment for violating their oath (Jr 42:5-6).

Their desire to move to Egypt was understandable, considering their expectation that they would no longer **see war** or **hear** the **trumpet** announcing an impending attack (cf. 4:5, 19-21; 6:1). Also, in Egypt they would escape the famine (cf. Lm 1:11; 5:6, 9) of the siege of Jerusalem and would no longer **hunger for bread**.

Despite this logic, Jeremiah warned that if they disobeyed the Lord and settled in Egypt, they would die by the **sword**, **famine**, or **pestilence** (cf. Jr 14:12; 42:22). God's wrath would be poured out on them **when** they entered **Egypt**, just as it was **poured out on** . . . **Jerusalem**. Like Jerusalem, they would become a **curse**, an **object of horror**, and a **reproach** (cf. 18:16; 24:9; 29:18; 44:12). The very dangers they wanted to avoid would overtake them, and they would never see Judah again.

42:19-22. Jeremiah repeated God's word to the **remnant of Judah**, **The LORD has spoken to you** . . . **do not to go into Egypt!** God's will was clear. For though they had vowed to do everything God said (v. 6), when His word finally came, they refused to obey and stay in Judah as He commanded. Thus, Jeremiah warned them, the only thing they could be certain was that they would **die by the sword**, **famine**, and **pestilence** (v. 17) if they went to Egypt **to reside**. Jeremiah was forced by the disobedient remnant to go down to Egypt with them (43:6), and the tradition is that Jeremiah died in Egypt.

b. Jeremiah's Ministry to the Remnant in Egypt (43:1–44:30)

(1) The Remnant's Flight to Egypt (43:1-7)

43:1-3. The true character of the remnant surfaced in their response to the Lord's message. In spite of Jeremiah's previous vindication as God's prophet, they refused to believe him.

Immediately after Jeremiah finished speaking, both **Azariah** (called "Jezaniah" in 42:1) and **Johanan**, along with **all the arrogant men**, accused Jeremiah of **telling a lie**. They accused **Baruch**, Jeremiah's secretary, confidant, and companion, of inciting Jeremiah to join a conspiracy to hand these former rebels **over into the hand of the Chaldeans**, who would then kill them or **exile [them] to Babylon**.

43:4-7. But the group did not return to Mizpah, they marched south toward Egypt (41:17). There was total disobedience: **Johanan** and **all the commanders** and **all the people, did not obey the voice of the LORD to stay in the land of Judah**. As leader, **Johanan** . . . **took the entire remnant of Judah** . . . **together with Jeremiah** . . . **and Baruch** . . . **and they entered the land of Egypt**. They settled in **Tahpanhes**, a fortress city on the eastern delta border of Lower (northern) Egypt.

(2) The Prophecy of Nebuchadnezzar's Invasion of Egypt (43:8-13)

43:8-13. As some of the Jewish travelers watched, Jeremiah performed another symbolic act to teach them a lesson from the Lord (cf. 13:1-11). The Lord told him to **take some large stones** and bury them in **mortar** under the **brick terrace** (the pavement) that covered the large courtyard at the **entrance of Pharaoh's palace** in Tahpanhes. Since Pharaoh's main residence at this time was at Elephantine in southern Egypt, the "palace" mentioned by Jeremiah was probably a government building that served as Pharaoh's residence when he visited the city of Tahpanhes. Excavations at Tahpanhes have uncovered a wide pavement at the northern entrance to the fortress.

Jeremiah's buried stones were to mark the spot where **Nebuchadnezzar** would **set his throne** when the Lord brought him to **strike the land of Egypt**. The specters of **death** . . . **captivity**, and the **sword**, which these exiles were fleeing (cf. 42:13-17), would follow them into Egypt. God would use Nebuchadnezzar to **set fire to the temples of the gods of Egypt** and take the gods **captive**. Nebuchadnezzar would **wrap himself with the land of Egypt**, as a **shepherd wraps himself with his garment**. Nebuchadnezzar would **shatter the obelisks of Heliopolis**, a center for Egyptian sun god worship with many **obelisks** and **temples**, all to be demolished by the Babylonians.

Because the *Babylonian Chronicles* (cf. 27:1-7) that have been discovered go only through 594 BC, there is a lack of extrabiblical detail on the invasion of Egypt. However, one fragmentary text has been found that implies an invasion of Egypt by Nebuchadnezzar in 568–567 BC. This would harmonize well with the prophecy of Nebuchadnezzar's invasion of Egypt in Ezk 29:19. That prophecy, given on April 26, 571 BC, indicated that the invasion was still future. Therefore Nebuchadnezzar's attack on Egypt probably occurred sometime between 571 and 567 BC.

(3) The Warning of God's Judgment (44:1-30)

44:1-10. God's word came to Jeremiah a second time while he was in Egypt (cf. 43:8). This time it concerned **all the Jews** who were **living in** . . . **Egypt**. It applied to those in northern Egypt, which included the cities of **Migdol**, **Tahpanhes**, and **Memphis**; and it extended south to **Pathros**, in southern Egypt. The message was for all the Jews throughout Egypt.

God reminded them of the disaster He brought against **Jerusalem** and all **cities of Judah**. Their **ruins** stood as testimonies to God's judgment on their **wickedness**, especially in provoking the Lord to anger by **continuing to burn sacrifices** to **other gods**.

Though God had repeatedly warned the people through His **servants the prophets** to turn from their **wickedness, they did not listen**. God's **wrath** then raged against Judah and Jerusalem, so they were **a ruin and a desolation**. Instead of learning from the recent events of Jerusalem's judgment for idolatry, these Jews who had escaped to Egypt were **burning sacrifices to other gods in the land of Egypt**. They were in danger of becoming an object of **curse** and **reproach** (cf. 24:9) for their idolatry. It was as though they had **forgotten the wickedness** (repeated no less than five times in v. 9) that both they and their ancestors had committed and the resulting judgment of God. They had not **become contrite** before God nor **feared** Him, nor **walked in** His law, which was clearly **set before** them and their ancestors. How quickly they had forgotten God's Word!

44:11-14. God would **set** His **face against** them to bring disaster on the remnant in Egypt for their sin, just as He had on **all Judah**. This **remnant** that had **set their mind** on entering **Egypt** would perish there by **sword** and **famine** (cf. 42:22). This judgment would include nearly everyone, **small and great**. Those living in Egypt would experience the same judgments God used when He **punished Jerusalem**—the **sword**, **famine**, and **pestilence**. Though these fugitives hoped to return home someday, they would not. All those who had fled to Egypt in violation of God's command would die there, except for a **few refugees** whom God would allow to return.

44:15-19. The people totally rejected Jeremiah's message. Whole families, **men** and **their wives**, were **burning sacrifices to other gods**. They said, **We are not going to listen**, and refused to repent. Instead of obeying every word that came from the mouth of the Lord (cf. Dt 8:3), they said they would **carry out every word that has proceeded from** their own **mouths**. They would continue **burning sacrifices** to the **queen of heaven** (see comments about this idolatrous worship at Jr 7:18). The widespread nature of that pagan practice of offering incense sacrifices to this goddess is evident because it was done by the people, their ancestors (**forefathers**), their **kings**, and their **princes** in Judah and Jerusalem.

In an ironic reversal of truth, the people blamed their difficulties on their failure to continue these pagan rituals. They said that as long as they sacrificed to the **queen of heaven** (see comments on 7:18), they had **plenty of food** and **no misfortune**. They said that when they **stopped burning sacrifices to the queen**

of heaven, they **lacked everything** and began perishing by **sword** and **famine**. They were lying to themselves, for just the opposite would have been true had they followed God's directions (cf. chap. 14; Hs 2:5-9; Am 4:4-12). Faithfulness and obedience to God brought blessing, while unfaithfulness and disobedience to God brought cursing (Lv 26:1-45; Dt 28).

44:20-23. Jeremiah responded to **all the people**, especially to the ones who **were giving him such an answer**. He reminded them **the Lord** did **remember** their **smoking sacrifices**. When He was no **longer able to endure** their sin, He judged the people, and the land became an object of cursing and a desolate waste. **Because** of their **evil** sacrifices Judah was under judgment—the worship of false gods had assured her doom and had not protected her in any way. This failure to acknowledge and follow the Lord had produced **calamity** in Judah. That same judgment would fall on them in Egypt for their sacrifices to the queen of heaven.

44:24-28. Jeremiah spoke to **all the people, including all the women** concerning their vow to continue worshiping the **queen of heaven** with incense **sacrifices** and **drink offerings** (v. 17). Since they were so determined to pursue their idolatry, God sarcastically told them to **go ahead** with the **vows** they had made to this false goddess. But as they worshiped her they were also to hear God's message of judgment. The Lord took a solemn oath, swearing by His **great name** that none of the Judahites living anywhere in Egypt would ever again invoke His **name** or swear by Him in an oath. His judgment would pursue them until all were destroyed. God was **watching over them for harm and not for good**. Only a very few would survive to return to Judah. Then they would know **whose word will stand, Mine or theirs**, a direct rebuke at their vow to the queen of heaven and their claim that idolatry brought prosperity (vv. 17-18).

44:29-30. God then gave **a sign** to show that His **words** would **surely stand** against the idolatrous Jews in Egypt. The sign was that **Pharaoh Hophra** would be handed over to **his enemies . . . just as . . . Zedekiah** was handed over to **Nebuchadnezzar**. According to the ancient Greek historian Herodotus (fifth century BC), Hophra was killed by his rivals in 570 BC (Herodotus 2. 161-3, 169), only a short time after Jeremiah gave this prophecy. Despite all God had done to vindicate His messages from Jeremiah, the people still refused to believe. The issue was not one of needing more evidence, divine miracles, or compelling messages, but a question of faith. "And without faith it is impossible to please Him" (Heb 11:6; cf. Gn 15:6).

c. Jeremiah's Ministry to Baruch (45:1-5)

45:1-3. This chapter fits chronologically between 36:8 and 36:9, in the **fourth year of Jehoiakim** (605–604 BC) after **Baruch** had **written down** at **Jeremiah's dictation** God's message on a scroll (cf. 36:1-8). Jeremiah likely placed this out of chronological order for the benefit of exilic readers. Having seen the judgment of the exile, the prophet wanted to emphasize the response that God desired from the godly remnant in difficult times. It uses Baruch's discouragement and the exhortation to faith to be a model for all of the godly remnant who were disheartened. Baruch was discouraged by the message of judgment, saying, **Ah, woe is me!** He felt that God had added **sorrow** to his **pain**. Much as Jeremiah felt earlier (cf. 8:21–9:2; 14:17-18; 15:10, 15-18), Baruch was worn out with **groaning** and could find **no rest**.

45:4-5. God responded with a message to encourage Baruch's faith in the midst of judgment. The Lord would indeed **bring disaster** and **uproot** what He had **planted** (cf. 1:10). Baruch's discouragement came because the realities of judgment clashed with his personal aspirations of **seeking great things**. The Lord reminded him that instead of groaning because God did not provide all he wanted, Baruch should have been thankful that God would **give** him his **life,** despite the disaster happening all around. His contemporary Habakkuk should have been his model of faith in the midst of judgment (cf. Hab 3:16-19).

In the midst of disaster or national judgment, a godly person should have his hope fixed firmly on the Lord. We too can choose to be bitter because God has withheld what we expected, or we can choose to be thankful because God has supplied what we need, and protected us beyond our own limited vision.

III. Prophecies Concerning Nations (46:1–51:64)

Jeremiah had been commissioned as a prophet to the nations who would come against Judah and Jerusalem (cf. 1:5; 46:1). Before addressing those nations, he first prophesied concerning the nation of Judah (chaps. 2–45), showing what the nations would do to her because, despite being God's covenant people, Judah had sinned against the Lord God of Israel. The nations, who rose up against Judah and were rife with their own sin and idolatry, did not escape the Lord's judgment in Jeremiah's prophetic voice. Jeremiah had already declared God's sovereignty over the nations (27:1-5), so in chaps. 46–51 he described, in poetic form, the coming judgment on the nations, including Egypt (chap. 46) and Babylon (chaps. 50–51).

A. Prophecy against Egypt (46:1-28)

Egypt was the first nation selected for judgment. She was Judah's ineffective ally who had encouraged Judah's revolt against Babylon. However, when Judah needed Egypt's military support for defense against Babylon, Egypt abandoned Judah (cf. 37:4-10; Ezk 29:6-7).

1. Egypt to Be Defeated at Carchemish (46:1-12)

46:1-6. Jeremiah's message was directed against the army of **Pharaoh Neco**, who killed King Josiah of Judah in 609 BC (2Kg 23:29). Jeremiah penned his prophecy after Egypt's army was defeated at **Carchemish** (in what is now southern central Turkey). This was the only major city on the upper Euphrates and was the key to Syria on the East and the passageway to the Euphrates. After the fall of the Assyrian Empire, Carchemish was the strategic battleground between Egypt and Babylon for control of the area. When **Babylon defeated** Egypt at Carchemish, it signaled the end of Egyptian military supremacy in the region. The victorious battle took place in 605 BC, the **fourth year of Jehoiakim**.

God gave a sarcastic message to the army of Egypt. They were to prepare their **shield[s]** and march out for battle against the Babylonians, to **harness the horses** and have the troops **stand with helmets on** ready to fight. Their **spears** and **scale-armor** were to be ready for battle. Although Egypt was famous for the finest horses, Babylon's swift attack left **terror . . . on every side** as their warriors were defeated, fleeing in panic and confusion. The retreating Egyptian soldiers obstructed their own retreat, so the **swift** were not able to flee nor were the **mighty** able to escape. Babylon overtook the Egyptians and destroyed them. *The Babylonian Chronicles* (see comments on 43:8-13) confirm this picture of hopeless confusion and defeat. The Egyptian army "withdrew" before the Babylonians, but the Babylonians "overtook and defeated them so that not a single man escaped to his own country" (Donald J. Wiseman, *Chronicle of Chaldean Kings [626-556 BC] in the British Museum* [London: Trustees of the British Museum, 1956], 67-69). The Babylonian defeat of Egypt at Carchemish was one of the most decisive battles in the ancient world, and it ended mighty Egypt's position as a world power.

46:7-8. God sarcastically asked **who** this nation was that was trying to rise **like the Nile** with its surging waters that overflowed its banks and inundated the country with life-giving rich soil. Likewise Egypt planned to **rise like the Nile** and conquer the world. The **surge** of Egypt's armies with her horses and charioteers would resemble the rushing of a mighty river. In prophetic judgment God would **rise and cover that land** of Egypt, and He would **destroy the city** and **its inhabitants**.

46:9-10. Egypt's army contained mercenary soldiers from **Ethiopia** and **Put** (modern-day Libya) who carried shields as infantrymen, and **Lydians** (inhabitants of the west coast of Asia Minor) who were archers (they **bend the bow**). Ezekiel named these same groups of mercenaries (Ezk 30:5). Though Egypt amassed a mighty army, the day of battle belonged **to the Lord God of hosts**, as a day of His **vengeance** on Egypt. It would be a **slaughter for the Lord God of hosts**. Only then would His **sword** of judgment be satisfied. God compared this slaughter to the offering of a sacrifice (Is 34:4-5; Zph 1:7-8) as He destroyed the Egyptians at Carchemish, **in the land of the north by the river Euphrates**.

46:11-12. Even if the Egyptians went to **Gilead** to get **balm** for their wounds (8:22), their remedies would be in **vain** because God would permit **no healing** for them. The surrounding **nations** would hear of Egypt's **shame** as her **cry of distress** and pain filled the **earth**. In the panic of war, the mighty warriors would stumble over one another (cf. v. 6) and fall **down together** in defeat.

2. Egypt to Be Invaded and Exiled (46:13-26)

46:13-17. Nebuchadnezzar defeated the Egyptians at Carchemish, the key city in modern Turkey, in 605 BC, but he did not invade Egypt until approximately 571–567 BC (see comments on 43:8-13). In this undated prophecy (vv. 13-26) God supplied additional details of the **coming of Nebuchadnezzar** to **smite the land of Egypt**. The warning of Nebuchadnezzar's approach was to be sounded in **Migdol**, **Memphis**, and **Tahpanhes** in northern Egypt (cf. 44:1). Nebuchadnezzar's forces were told to **take [their] stand** and **get**...

ready for battle. Babylon and Egypt would fight in the area where the refugees of Judah had settled against God's will after Gedaliah's murder (chap. 43).

Jeremiah asked why Egypt's **mighty ones** had **become prostrate**, or "laid low" (v. 15). There is a textual issue here. The Septuagint reads, "Wherefore has Apis fled. . . ?" (Septuagint/LXX 26:15; the LXX has rearranged the order of several chapters in Jeremiah so that 46:15 in Hebrew is 26:15 in the Septuagint; cf. "The Book of Jeremiah and the Septuagint" in Introduction to Jeremiah). The Septuagint has divided the Hebrew verb for "laid low" (*nishap*) into two words (*nas khaf*, "Apis has fled," a reference to Apis, the bull god of Egypt. The defeat of a people was often symbolized by the defeat of their god (cf. Is 46:1-2; Jr 50:2; 51:44). If the Septuagint reading is accepted, then Jeremiah was pointing to the inability of Egypt's god Apis to protect them from the judgment of the Lord. However, the Masoretic Text of Jr 46:15, **Why have your mighty ones become prostrate?** (laid low) seems to fit the context of the defeat of Egypt by the Babylonians (46:13) better. The point is the Lord God will be victorious, either over the Egyptian bull god Apis, or over the Egyptian army's mighty warriors.

The text answers the question about the warriors. They could not stand because God had **thrust them down**. As the mercenary army **stumbled** over one another in their effort to flee from Egypt they decided to **get up . . . and go back** home to their **own people** and their **native land** to escape the **sword of the oppressor**. Pharaoh Hophra had made bold claims about his ability to defeat the Babylonians, but these vanquished soldiers realized now that **Pharaoh king of Egypt** was only a **big noise** who could not deliver victory.

Pharaoh Hophra (44:30) had already **let the appointed time pass** to defeat Babylon. After being defeated at Carchemish, the Egyptians might have had the opportunity for a comeback victory over Babylon. Nebuchadnezzar did not follow up his triumph by invading Egypt right away; instead he returned to Babylon because of his father's death. Pharaoh did not press this advantage to defend or fortify Egypt, so when Nebuchadnezzar returned to battle, Egypt was defeated by the Nile.

46:18-19. The eternal God proclaimed the certainty of coming judgment on Egypt. He swore by His own self (**As I live**; cf. Gn 22:16), announcing His sovereignty (**declares the King**; cf. Jr 8:19; 10:7, 10; 48:15; 51:57; Pss 10:16; 47:7; Is 43:15) and identifying the scope of His authority (**Lord of hosts**, used about 80 times in Jeremiah; cf. 2Sm 5:10; Is 14:27; 54:5; Jr 5:14).

God was sending **one** to Egypt (i.e., Nebuchadnezzar) who towered above all others just as Mount **Tabor** stood out **among the mountains**. This one would rise as impressively as Mount **Carmel** does **by the sea**. The Egyptians were to **make [their] baggage ready for exile** (cf. Ezk 29:9-16) because Nebuchadnezzar would attack **Memphis** (cf. Jr 46:14) and leave it a **desolation** without **inhabitants**.

46:20-24. Jeremiah described Egypt's doom with clear word pictures. First, he compared Egypt to a **pretty heifer**. This metaphor is especially striking since Apis, one of Egypt's gods, was a bull. However, a **horsefly . . . from the north** (Babylon) **is coming** (repeated twice), to bite her. Second, he compared the **mercenaries** (vv. 9, 16) in the **midst** of Egypt's soldiers to **fattened calves** who would turn and flee when the day of disaster came. Third, Jeremiah compared Egypt to a fleeing **serpent**. She could do little more than hiss at her enemy as she slithered away to avoid the axes of these mighty **woodcutters** who had come to chop down **her forest**. Fourth, he compared the size of Babylon's invading army to a swarm of **locusts** that were too numerous to be counted. The point of the image was the same: **Egypt** would be **put to shame** (vv. 12, 24) because God had **given** her **over** to the **people of the north**, to Babylon.

46:25-26. Neither the gods nor the kings of Egypt would be spared from the judgment of God. He would **punish Amon of Thebes** in southern Egypt (Ezk 30:14-16). Amon (Amun-Ra) was the chief god of Egypt during much of its history. Amon was god of air, wind, fertility, and later the sun, creator of all things. God's judgment began in the north (Pr 46:14, 19) and would extend to the south. It would encompass all **her gods** and **kings, even Pharaoh** and all who **trust in him**. They would be handed over to **Nebuchadnezzar** (cf. Ezk 29:17-20).

However, Egypt's destruction would not be permanent. God promised that **afterwards . . .** Egypt would be **inhabited as in the days of old**. This could refer to the return of Egypt's exiles from Babylon (cf. v. 19; Ezk 29:10-16). However, the association of Egypt's fortunes with the still-future restoration of Israel (Jr 46:27-28) and the future focus in some of Jeremiah's other prophecies to the nations (cf. 48:47; 49:39) suggests that the fulfillment would come during the millennial reign of the Messiah when Egypt would again be in her land and would join Israel in the worship of the God of Israel (see comments on 50:1; Is 19:24-25).

3. Israel to Be Regathered (46:27-28)

46:27-28. In contrast to the judgment on Egypt and her false gods, the Lord interjected a word of comfort for Israel. Although Judah and Jerusalem would be punished for their sin, God wanted them to have hope. Thus, after describing the judgment of Egypt, the Lord comforted His own people: **O Jacob My servant, do not fear nor be dismayed**. Israel could rejoice because God promised to **save** her and **return** her people from **captivity**. Israel could look forward to a time when she would enjoy peace and security, **with no one making [Jacob] tremble**. Though she went into exile, God vowed that He would **make a full end of all the nations** where He had driven Israel; but he would **not make a full end of** her. The Lord would **correct** her **properly** and punish her for her sins, but Jacob would be preserved. A remnant would survive to receive God's blessings again (cf. 31:1-6).

B. Prophecy against Philistia 47:1-7

47:1. The **Philistines** were one of Israel's most ancient and persistent enemies (Jos 13:2-3; Jdg 3:31; 13:1), but the Lord would judge them for their sin.

The Philistines occupied the coastal plain of Judah. Whenever they were strong, they tried to expand from the coast into the hill country of Judah. These attempts at expansion were opposed throughout Israel's history: during the period of the Judges (Jdg 3:31; 13-16), by Samuel (1Sm 7:2-17), by Saul (1Sm 13:1–14:23; 17–18; 28:1-4; 29:1-2, 11; 31:1-10), and by David (2Sm 5:17-25). David finally subdued the Philistines (2Sm 8:1), and they remained a vassal of Israel through the reign of Solomon. During the time of the divided monarchy the balance of power shifted back and forth. Judah was in control during the reigns of Jehoshaphat (2Ch 17:10-11) and Uzziah, but Philistia regained dominion during the reigns of Jehoram (2Ch 21:16-17) and Ahaz (2Ch 28:16-18).

Jeremiah's message was delivered **before Pharaoh conquered Gaza**. The exact date for this event is uncertain but the two most likely times were either 609 BC when Pharaoh Neco marched north through Judah to meet the Babylonians (2Kg 23:29-30), or 601 BC when Neco defeated the armies of Babylon.

47:2-7. The Babylonians were depicted as **waters** rising **from the north** to become an **overflowing torrent** that would sweep away the Philistines. The Philistines would **cry out** in anguish as the swirl of **galloping hoofs** and enemy **chariots** rushed through the land. The people would be so overcome by fear that **fathers** would not even turn back to help their **children**. Their allies, **Tyre and Sidon**, would not be able to help them (cf. Ezk 27–28).

The Philistines (*philisti*, meaning "to wander, immigrants") were one of the groups of sea peoples who made their way in ancient times to the coast of Canaan (see the map "The World of Jeremiah and Ezekiel," in the Introduction). They were the **remnant** people **of the coastland of Caphtor**, the ancient name for Crete (Am 9:7; Zph 2:5). When they settled the coastal plain of Judah they formed a coalition of five major cities, the Philistine pentapolis (cf. Jos 13:3; 1Sm 6:4, 18): Gaza, Ashkelon, Ashdod, Gath, and Ekron. **Gaza** was attacked by the Egyptians (cf. Jr 47:1), and **Ashkelon** was later destroyed by Nebuchadnezzar 604 BC (v. 1; cf. comments on 36:9). Archaeological evidence of layers of ash, broken pottery, and human remains reveals the destruction of Ashkelon at that time. As a result of their destruction, the people of Gaza and Ashkelon would shave their heads (thus their **baldness**) and **gash** themselves in grief (cf. comments on 16:6). The **sword of the Lord** would strike in judgment until **Ashkelon** and the **seacoast** were destroyed (cf. Ezk 25:15-17; Is 14:28-32).

"Philistia" or "Philistine" is the basis for the Latin term *Palestina*, from which the English word "Palestine" derives. Since this word is so common on Bible maps and resources, it is puzzling that the word "Palestine" cannot be found in the Bible. After the Romans crushed the Second Jewish Revolt (AD 135), they sent a message to the Mediterranean world ("Never revolt against Rome!") and made an example of Judah by bringing about many changes, three of them deserving special attention. First, Rome changed the name of Jerusalem to *Aelia Capitolina* (in honor of the Emperor Hadrian, whose family name was "Aeila"). Second, they banned all Jewish people from the city on pain of death. Finally, Rome changed the name of the country to *Syria-Palestina*, after the ancient Philistine coastal region. The Roman goal was to wipe the names of Israel and Judah off the face of the earth and from all of history. *Syria-Palestina* (Palestine) became the official name of the region on maps, documents, and scholarly works handed down from the Romans to the Byzantines, through the Middle Ages, even into the Reformation and Enlightenment eras, and into modern times as well. Although the name "Palestine" is never used in the Bible for the land of Israel or Judea, since the Roman period it has often been used as a synonym for the region. Because the term has once again taken on a political undertone, it might be best to use the more biblically accurate term (cf. 3:18-19; 16:18) to refer to the promised land: the land of Israel.

C. Prophecy against Moab (48:1-47)

Moab is the ancient name of the mountainous country alongside much of the eastern shore of the Dead Sea, (now modern Jordan). It was separated from Edom on the south by the Zered River and from Ammon on the north by the Arnon River. Moabites were descendants of Lot (Gn 19:37). Much of the imagery used by Jeremiah for Moab is also used by Isaiah (Is 16:6-12). Moab was a frequent enemy of God's people, from the time of the conquest (Nm 22–24) throughout the days of the kings (2Ch 20). The judgment of Moab is often pictured in terms of vineyards, wine, and drunkenness—a fitting image since Moab was famous for its vineyards (Jr 48:11-12; 26; 32–33; Is 16:8-10).

Nebo, Kiriathaim, Heshbon, and several other cities mentioned in this chapter are referred to in *The Mesha Stele*, also known as the *Moabite Stone*, a black basalt stele (an inscribed or carved stone for commemorative purposes), four feet by two feet, written about 840 BC as a memorial of Mesha, king of Moab (2Kg 3:3-10). This stele was discovered in what is now Jordan in 1868, and is kept in the British Museum. It records Mesha's victories over "Omri king of Israel" (1Kg 16:23-28) and "his son" (his descendants, 2Kg 3:4), who had been "oppressing" Moab. The Mesha Stele bears the earliest known extrabiblical reference to the Hebrew name of God, *YHWH*, as well as a reference to "the house of David."

1. Moab's Land to Be Destroyed (48:1-10)

48:1-5. The Lord's judgment against **Moab** is frequently mentioned in Scripture (Is 15:1–16:14; Ezk 25:8-11; Am 2:1-3; Zph 2:8-11). In this section God's judgment will result in **devastation and great destruction!** Moab is described as **broken**. The initial oracle describes Nebuchadnezzar's advance against Moab.

Nebo is the name of the mountain from which Moses viewed the promised land and died (cf. Dt 32:48-50), as well as a Moabite city located southwest of Heshbon (Nm 32:3; Is 15:2). Since it **has been destroyed** this indicates that the **Nebo** here is the city. The phrase **has been** is a Hebrew prophetic perfect verb, indicating that the prophecy was so certain, it was if it had already occurred). The city of **Kiriathaim** was also inhabited by the tribe of Reuben (Jos 13:19) and later captured by Moab and would be **captured** again.

Heshbon was a region about 35 miles east of Jerusalem, northeast of the northern tip of the Dead Sea (Nm 1:26; Dt 2:24). As part of the conquest of the land, Heshbon was allotted to the tribe of Reuben (Nm 32:37; Jos 13:17) but assigned as a Levitical town to Gad since it was on the border of Gad (Jos 13:26; 21:39). It would suffer **calamity**.

The city of **Madmen** (*mad-mane'*, "dunghill") would be silenced by God in His judgment. The **outcry** from **Horonaim** (cf. 2Sm 13:34) would be, **Devastation and great destruction!** In summary Moab was **broken**, and her children would be crying in **distress**. The fugitives of Moab who fled up to **Luhith** and **Horonaim** (locations unknown) wept bitterly at the **destruction**.

48:6-10. The Moabites would **flee** for their lives to escape the coming judgment. They would become like a **juniper** bush in the wilderness (17:6), a short shrub that barely survived the harsh habitat. Because Moab had trusted in her **achievements** and **treasures**, she would be judged and **captured**. **Chemosh** (Jdg 11:24; 2Kg 23:13) was the chief god of Moab. Although little is known about the worship practices, he was associated with the control of the planets and stars. Chemosh is called "the detestable idol of Moab" (1Kg 11:7). Solomon built a sanctuary to Chemosh on the Mount of Olives (1Kg 11: 7, 33) that was maintained until the reforms of Josiah (2Kg 23:13). Thus, the worship of Chemosh was a part of the religious life of Israel for nearly 400 years (cf. 1Kg 11:7). The **priests** of Chemosh and the **princes** of Moab would be defeated and **go off into exile** (cf. 49:3).

A **destroyer** would come on every city. The **valley** could refer to the many valleys of hilly Moab, or it could refer to the Jordan Valley on Moab's western border. The **plateau** was the Transjordan highland where most of the cities of Moab were located. Moab would **be destroyed**.

The meaning of the Hebrew statement behind the English translation, **Give wings to Moab** (47:9) is uncertain. Some see a root from Ugaritic for the word (*tseets*) and translate it as "salt" (NIV); some, relying on the LXX, amend the text and translate it as "gravestone" (NET Bible). The NASB and ESV translate it as "wings," deriving the translation from an Aramaic root. Abu Walid and most medieval Jewish commentaries support the translation as "wings," as does the verb in the second part of the verse ("flee"), which makes it the more likely meaning. Thus, Moab will be given **wings** so she could **flee away**, leaving her **cities** as **a desolation** and **without inhabitants**. Moab's destruction was so certain that God said anyone who was lax in performing His work of judgment would be **cursed**.

2. Moab's Complacency to Be Shattered (48:11-17)

48:11-13. Protected by natural boundaries between the Dead Sea on the west and the desert to the east, Moab had a history of relative peace. She had been **at ease** from her **youth**. Jeremiah compared her to **wine** left on its **dregs** (lit., "his flavor has stayed in him") that had **not been emptied from vessel to vessel**. This was a picture of a people who had lived undisturbed and not **gone into exile**.

The Lord declared that **the days are coming** (cf. comments on 31:27) when He would arouse Moab from her complacency by sending **those** who would **tip** . . . and **empty** the **jars**. At that time **Moab** would be ashamed of **Chemosh** (cf. v. 7) just as **Israel** was ashamed of **Bethel**, one of the two cities in the northern kingdom where Jeroboam set up the golden calf worship following the secession of Israel from Judah (cf. 1Kg 12:26-30). Israel found out too late that her trust in the false god at Bethel could not prevent her destruction and deportation. Moab would learn the same lesson about Chemosh.

48:14-17. Moab felt confident in her **warriors** who were **valiant** in battle, yet they would go down in the **slaughter**. The image of slaughter is drawn from the slaughter of sacrificial animals (Is 34:6). Moab's calamity was declared by **the King** . . . **the LORD of Hosts** (Jr 46:18) and would come **soon** and **swiftly**. Jeremiah called for those nations surrounding Moab to **mourn** for that nation at the time of its destruction, because **the mighty scepter** and **staff** (signifying rule and identity) had been **broken** (Gn 49:10; Ps 2:9; Ezk 19:11, 14).

3. Moab's Cities to Experience Catastrophe (48:18-27)

48:18-25. The mighty city of **Dibon** would be humbled and **come down** because **the destroyer of Moab** would **come up against** her. Dibon was built on two hills, 13 miles east of the Dead Sea near the Arnon River. It was here the *Moabite Stone* was found (cf. the introduction to chap. 48). Those living in the remote city of **Aroer** were to stand by the road and ask the people fleeing **what has happened**. They would **wail and cry out** when they learned **Moab has been destroyed.**

Jeremiah listed the cities of Moab on the Transjordan plateau that would be destroyed from north to south. Though the exact location of some is not certain, many of them have been identified. By naming these 11 cities Jeremiah showed that all the towns of Moab, both far and near, would be destroyed. **Bozrah** here is probably the same as Bezer, the city of refuge (Dt 4:40-43). It may be represented today by Qusur Bashair, some 15 miles Southeast of Dibon (*International Standard Bible Encyclopedia,* 1939). This is not the same city as Bozrah in Edom (cf. Jr 49:7).

Jeremiah used two symbols of strength and military power to show that Moab's might would be broken. First, Moab's **horn** would be cut off (cf. 1Sm 2:1, 10; Pss 75:4-5; 89:17, 24; Mc 4:13; Zch 1:19-21). Second, Moab's **arm** would be broken (Dt 4:34; 11:2; Ps 77:15; Ezk 30:20-26). In Scripture the most common figurative use of **horn** is taken from the image of battling animals. Horns were emblems of power, dominion, glory, and fierceness, being the chief means of attack and defense for the horned animals such as oxen or rams. Horns represented power or strength of individuals or nations (Dt 33:17; 1Sm 2:1, 10; 1Kg 22:11; Ps 75:4; Jr 48:25). The figure of an **arm** likewise represented personal power, often in terms of strength in battle (Ps 10:15; Ezk 30:21). It is also used of the omnipotence of God (Ex 15:16; Pss 89:13; 98:1; 77:15; Is 40:10; 53:1).

48:26-27. Jeremiah pictured Moab's impending doom for being **arrogant toward the LORD** as a **drunk** (cf. 25:15-29). Moab would now **wallow in his vomit** and become a **laughingstock**. Moab had mocked and scorned **Israel** with contempt, as toward one **caught among thieves**. Now Moab would experience the same scorn directed at her.

4. Moab's Pride to Cease (48:28-39)

48:28-30. Moab would be forced to abandon his **cities** and dwell **among the crags**, to hide like **dove[s]** that nest inside a **chasm** from the invaders who sought their lives. Moab's main characteristic was **pride** (he is **very proud**; cf. Is 16:6). The physical security and history of relative peace had fed **his arrogance** (Jr 48:11-12). Unfortunately his insolence and **boasts** were **futile** and **accomplished nothing** in preventing destruction.

48:31-33. Yet God expressed compassion for Moab. He would **cry out** and **moan** for **Kir-heres**, another of her chief cities (cf. Is 16:7, 11). Jeremiah pictured the Lord weeping along with the city of **Jazer** for the **vine of Sibmah**, an area covered with vineyards, which would be destroyed. The country of Moab was known for its vineyards (Jr 48:11-12), and Jeremiah pictured Moab as a vineyard that would be destroyed. The **tendrils** of her branches **reached to** the **sea**, a picture of Moab's wide political and economic influence beyond the Dead Sea. Now the **destroyer** had **fallen** on her **grape harvest**. Moab's civilization and population would be ruined. The vineyards, the **fruitful field**, would be devoid of **gladness**, and the flow of **wine** would **cease from the wine presses**. When destruction came there would be **shouting** (cf. vv. 3-5), but it would not be **shouts of joy** like those heard at the pressing of grapes.

48:34-39. The **outcry** of Moab at this destruction would be heard in all its cities, extending from **Heshbon** in the north to the **waters of Nimrim** in the southern part of the country. God would put an end to **the one who offers sacrifice** at Moab's many **high place[s]** . . . **who burns incense to his gods.**

Although the judgment of Moab is just, the Lord's **heart wails for Moab** and **the men of Kir-heres** (cf. 49: 31), like the sound of **flutes** played by mourners at funerals (Mt 9:22-23). Moab would lose her wealth, and the people would be in mourning with **every head** shaved **bald** . . . and **beard cut**, many wearing **sackcloth** (47:5). The Lord had **broken Moab like an undesirable vessel** (vv. 4, 12; 22:28). The once-proud country was to **become a laughingstock** and an **object of terror** to the surrounding nations (cf. 24:9).

5. Moab's Destruction to Be Complete (48:40-47)

48:40-44. Moab's enemies would **fly swiftly** like an **eagle** spreading its **wings** over Moab to seize her. The Moabite city of **Kerioth** would be **captured**, and their **mighty men** (cf. v. 14) would be as fearful as a **woman in labor** (cf. 49:24; 50:43). Jeremiah repeated parts of vv. 40-41 in 49:22 in his message to Edom.

The Lord told Moab exactly why she **will be destroyed**. Destruction would come because Moab was **arrogant toward the Lord**. None would escape: those who would try to flee God's **terror** would **fall into a pit**; anyone who **climbs up out of the pit** would be **caught in the snare** (cf. Am 5:18-20). All in Moab would take part in **the year of their punishment**.

48:45-47. This section on Moab's judgment is a quote from an old Heshbon song (cf. Nm 21:27-29). Balaam's oracles against Moab would soon be fulfilled. The **fugitives** who had escaped the destruction stood **without strength** because God's **fire** of judgment had gone out into all Moab to burn those who had been boasters. Now the nation was destroyed, **the people of Chemosh have perished**. The Lord's judgment was upon Moab because of their enmity toward Judah (cf. Ezk 25:8-10). Yet God still offered hope to Moab. He vowed to **restore the fortunes of Moab in the latter days**. The phrase "the latter days" places this restoration during the millennial reign of Christ (cf. Dt 4:30; Jr 49:39; Dn 2:28; 10:14).

D. Prophecy against Ammon (49:1-6)

The Ammonites were descendants of Lot (Gn 19:38) and lived east of the Jordan River, north of Moab. Their capital was Rabbah, modern Amman, Jordan. The Ammonites were frequent enemies, and poor allies to Israel. In the days of Moses and Joshua they hindered the Jewish people from entering Israel and supported Balak in his plan to curse them (Dt 23:4), then during the reign of Jehoiakim they raided Judah (2Kg 24:2). Later they allied with Judah against Babylon during Judah's final revolt, yet were a driving force for the assassination of Gedaliah for their own advantage (Jr 40:13-14). When Jewish people returned after the captivity, Ammonites hindered the rebuilding of Jerusalem (Neh 4:7).

49:1-3. The judgment on **Ammon** is introduced by a series of rhetorical questions of reproach focusing on Ammon's sin. The northern kingdom of Israel had been taken captive in 722 BC, and Ammon, assuming Israel had **no sons** or **heirs** who would return to the land, seized Israel's territory of **Gad** just east of the Jordan River and north of the Dead Sea.

The Lord announced that **days** were **coming** (cf. comments on 31:27) when an enemy would attack Ammon's capital city of **Rabbah**, and it would become **a desolate heap**. Then **Israel will take possession** and repossess the land taken from them by Ammon.

Heshbon, on the border between Moab and Ammon, was controlled by different countries at different periods of time (cf. Jdg 11:12, 26; Jr 48:34, 45). The **Ai** mentioned in v. 2 was not the Ai in Israel (cf. Jos 7:2). It was a city in Ammon whose location is not known today. The people of **Rabbah** would put on **sackcloth** (see comments on Jr 4:8) and **lament** (cf. 48:37). Molech, also known as **Malcam** (which could be translated "their king") was the national god of Ammon and would **go into exile** together with his followers, **priests** and **princes** (cf. 48:7).

49:4-6. Ammon's sin, like Moab's, was pride (cf. 48:29). Ammon was **boastful** of her **valleys** that were so fruitful. She trusted in her **treasures** and felt secure enough to question who would have the courage to **come against** her (cf. Ezk 21:18-23). But God's judgment would shatter Ammon's confidence and pride when He brought His **terror** on her. Those who had been boasting of their security would be **driven out**, and no leader would be found to **gather the fugitives**. Yet in His grace God vowed that **afterward** He would **restore the fortunes** (captivity) of the Ammonites, just as He promised Moab (cf. Jr 48:47; 49:39).

E. Prophecy against Edom (49:7-22)

The country of Edom was south of Moab and southeast of the Dead Sea, stretching toward the Gulf of Aqaba. Edomites were the descendants of Esau (Gn 25:1-34; 36:1-19). It had a long history of conflict with Judah so that Edom came to symbolize all the heathen nations that sought Judah's harm (cf. Jr 9:25-26; 25:17-26; Ezk 35; 36:5; Ob 15-16). Much of the imagery Jeremiah used to describe Edom parallels that used by Obadiah, whose prophecies were directed specifically at Edom.

49:7-13. The association of **wisdom** with the men of **Teman** (v. 7) is ancient (cf. Jb 2:11), and all of Edom was known for its wise men (cf. Ob 8). **Teman** was in central Edom. The district was named after Teman, the grandson of Esau, the son of his firstborn, Eliphaz (Gn 36:11; 1Ch 1:36). The area was associated with Bozrah (cf. Jr 49:13; Am 1:12), the capital of Edom in the days of Jeremiah (cf. Jr 49:13).

Dedan (v. 8), a city in the northern part of the Arabian peninsula southeast of Edom, was known for its trading (cf. 25:23; Ezk 25:13). The Dedanites living in Edom were warned to **flee away** and **turn back** from the disaster God was about to bring on **Esau**, the name of their progenitor being used by metonymy for the nation. Two images were used to show the thoroughness of God's judgment. His judgment would be more thorough than **grape gatherers** who at least leave a few grapes on the vine as **gleanings** when they are done (Jr 49:9; cf. Ob 5c; Dt 24:21). God's judgment would also be more thorough than **thieves** by **night** who steal only **until they** have **enough** (cf. Ob 5). In contrast, after God's judgment **Esau** (Edom) would be **stripped bare** of her population (Jr 49:10) and have no **hiding places**. Only the helpless **orphans** and **widows** would be kept alive (v. 11).

Judgment against Edom is mentioned more frequently than against any other foreign nation (Is 11:14; 34:5-17; 63:1-6; Lm 4:21-22; Jl 3:19; Am 1:11-12; 9:11-12; Mal 1:4). Edom's primary sin was its prideful, unrelenting and violent hatred of Israel and rejoicing over Israel's misfortunes (Ob 3, 10-14). If nations unrelated to Judah were to **drink the cup** of the wrath of God (Jr 49:12) and be punished for their mistreatment of her, then nations closely related to Judah deserved greater condemnation (cf. 25:15-29; Ob 10).

The seriousness of this judgment is highlighted because God had **sworn by** Himself that He would enact this judgment (v. 13; cf. 22:5; 51:14; Gn 22:16; Is 45:23). This **Bozrah** is the ancient city of Jobab, one of the early Edomite kings (Gn 36:33). It is often mentioned by the prophets (Is 34:6; Jr 49:13; Am 1:12; Mc 2:12). It lies in the mountain district of Petra, 20 miles southeast of the Dead Sea and was the capital of Edom (not the same as the Bozrah in Moab, Jr 48:24). Falling under God's judgment, it would become an **object of horror** and **ruin** (cf. 24:9; Is 63:1-6).

49:14-18. Borrowing language from international diplomacy, Jeremiah pictured God sending an **envoy** to His allies **among the nations** asking them to **gather** and **rise up for battle** against Edom (cf. Ob 1). The Lord would make Edom **small among the nations** and **despised** by all (cf. Ob 2). Edom's pride in her strong natural defenses made her feel secure, but no topography could protect Edom from invaders sent by God. He would bring her down (cf. Ob 4) from her **clefts of the rock**, and people would be horrified at her condition (cf. Jr 24:9; 49:13). Edom would be destroyed as completely as **Sodom and Gomorrah** (cf. 50:40) so that **no one will live there**.

49:19-22. God is pictured as fierce as a **lion** when He rose up to **make** Edom **run away** from its land. No one would be able to challenge God:

For who is like Me (Ex 15:11; Is 46:8-9) **and who will summon Me . . . who then is the shepherd . . . who can stand against Me?** Jeremiah laid out the **plan of the LORD** against **Edom**. He would **drag** away the young of **the flock** and destroy the **pasture** of Edom. The cry of destruction would carry to the **Red** (Reed) **Sea**—the site of God's first destruction of a nation that threatened His chosen people (cf. Ex 14:21-31). Jeremiah repeated (with slight modifications) his message concerning Edom to his message about Babylon (compare Jr 49:19-21 and 50:44-46).

Jeremiah used images here earlier applied to Moab (48:40-41) for Edom. The **noise** of Edom's **downfall** would shake the earth. God indicated that like an **eagle** He would swoop down in judgment upon **Bozrah**. The **hearts** of the warriors on which **Edom** depended would be as afraid as the heart of a **woman in labor** (cf. 48:41; 49:24; 50:43). They would not be able to stop God's destruction.

Notably, Jeremiah offered no future blessing for Edom. Unlike Egypt, Moab, and Ammon (cf. 46:26; 48:47; 49:6), Edom was given no promise of future restoration. Her wickedness toward Israel, especially Edom's assistance in the Babylonian destruction of Jerusalem, precluded future blessing (Ps 137:7; Is 34:5-8; 63:1-4; Lm 4:21-22; Ezk 25:13-14; Am 1:11-12; Ob 10). Amos predicted that Israel will "possess the remnant of Edom" (Am 9:12) indicating that in the messianic kingdom, the faithful remnant of Edom will not have a distinct national area but will become a possession of the land of Israel.

F. Prophecy against Damascus (49:23-27)

49:23-27. Damascus was the ancient capital of Aram (modern Syria) and is the oldest continually inhabited city in the world. Damascus is located 70 miles northeast of the Sea of Galilee on a natural highway from east to west, making it a center of commerce (Ezk 27:18). Three major caravan routes passed through Damascus heading southwest to Israel and Egypt, south to Edom and the Red Sea, and east to Babylon and Mesopotamia. Damascus is mentioned in Scripture in connection with Abraham, first in the rescue of Lot (Gn 14:15), and second in connection with Abraham's faithful servant Eleazar who was from Damascus (Gn 15:2). From the reign of David to its fall to Assyria in 732 BC (2Kg 16:7-9), Damascus was in conflict with Israel. When Babylon conquered Assyria, Damascus was also carried away into exile (605 BC).

When the trade route cities of **Hamath**, 115 miles north of Damascus, and **Arpad**, 95 miles north of Hamath, heard the **bad news** of the fall of Damascus, they were **disheartened** and could not **be calmed** (Is 10:9). These smaller fortified cities had their own kings and local gods, and were fearful that if Damascus fell, there was no hope for them.

Damascus's pain was like that of a woman in childbirth (cf. Jr 4:31; 13:21; 22:23), as her **young men** and the **men of war** died (would be **silenced**) in **her streets**. As he did to other cities, Nebuchadnezzar burned the **wall of Damascus** (cf. Am 1:4; Jr 32:29; 38:23; 43:12). God vowed to consume the **fortified towers of Ben-hadad**, the name of the dynasty that ruled in Damascus ("Ben-hadad" means "son of the god Hadad") in the ninth and eighth centuries BC (cf. 1Kg 15:18, 20; 20:1-34; 2Kg 6:24; 8:7; 13:3, 24).

G. Prophecy against Kedar and Hazor (49:28-33)

Kedar was a nomadic tribe in the north Arabian desert, descendants of Ishmael (cf. Gn 25:13) known for their archery skills (Is 21:16-17), sheep herding (Is 60:7; Jr 49:28-29), extensive trade (Ezk 27:21), and warlike nature (Ps 120:5-6). The kingdoms of Hazor (not the Hazor in northern Israel) were a district of villages in the Arabian desert, not yet located. It is a general term designating several nomadic tribes in northern Arabia (Jos 15:23-25). Arab tribes sometimes served the Babylonians as mercenaries. The *Babylonian Chronicles* (cf. Jr 43:8) record Nebuchadnezzar's campaigns against Arab tribes in 599 BC. The exact reason for God's judgment on these desert people is not specified, but as Huey observes, "Perhaps the purpose for including these relatively insignificant peoples was to show that no one, however unimportant by our standards, would escape God's judgment" (F. B. Huey, Jr., *Jeremiah, Lamentations,* NAC, ed. E. Ray Clendenen [Nashville, TN: B&H Publishing Group, 1993], 405).

49:28-29. God summoned Nebuchadnezzar to attack **Kedar**, destroying their **tents**, **flocks**, and **camels** (Sg 1:5), causing **terror on every side** (Jr 6:25; 20:3, 10; 46:5).

49:30-33. The people of **Hazor** were warned to **flee** and hide from **Nebuchadnezzar king of Babylon**. These Arabian people felt so secure in their remote desert location that they had **no gates or bars** to protect against attack. The inhabitants would **scatter to the all the winds**, and the city would become a **haunt of jackals**

(cf. 9:11; 10:22; 51:37). These metaphors of desolation are also used to describe Jerusalem (9:11) and the cities of Judah (10:22).

H. Prophecy against Elam (49:34-39)

49:34-39. The people of **Elam** were descendants of Shem (Gn 10:22; Ezk 4:9). **Elam** was east of Babylon in the lower Tigris River Valley (modern Iran). Their capital was Shusan (Susa) (Neh 1:1; Est 1:2; Dn 8:2). Elamites were skilled archers (cf. Is 22:6), and fought for control of Mesopotamia against the Babylonians, Assyrians, and Persians.

This prophecy was given **at the beginning of the reign of Zedekiah** (597 BC). God would **break the bow of Elam**, their most notable skill, and the **finest of their might** (cf. Is 22:6). Her invaders would come from all directions (the **four winds** and the **four ends of heaven**) and would **scatter them to all these winds**.

Though there is some evidence that Nebuchadnezzar defeated the Elamites about 596 BC, their subjugation at that time did not fulfill this message. Elam became a central part of the Persian Empire that later conquered Babylon (cf. Dn 8:2). Jeremiah's statement about Elam's destruction seems to take on eschatological dimensions as God said He would **set My throne in Elam** to supervise her destruction. These events were to happen **in the last days** (cf. Jr 23:20). Yet Elam's destruction will not be total because God **will restore the fortunes of Elam** (cf. 48:47; 49:6).

I. Prophecy against Babylon (50:1–51:64)

1. The Announcement of Judgment (50:1-10)

50:1-3. The time of fulfillment for Jeremiah's prophecies of the judgments of Babylon and the restoration of Israel is a matter of controversy. Some have suggested that all the future events in the book of Jeremiah, spoken of as "days are coming" (see comments on 16:14 and 31:27-40), were fulfilled when the Jewish people returned from Babylon in 539 BC. However, for a number of reasons, it seems better to understand these as eschatological, end-time, events.

(1) The return is to be from "all the countries where He had banished them" not just from Babylon. This return will be so spectacular it will overshadow in importance the return from Egyptian captivity (16:14-15; 23:7-8; 29:14; 32:37; Is 43:5-7; Ezk 34:13-14; 37:21). (2) When the Jewish people return, they will be transformed spiritually, cleansed of all iniquity and idolatry (Jr 3:15-18; 31:14; 33:6-11; 50:4-5). Sadly, this was not the spiritual condition of the Jewish people when they returned from Babylon. Throughout their post-Babylonian history, Jewish people have wandered from the Lord. The spiritual transformation of Israel will only occur in the future, when the nation will turn and recognize Jesus as Messiah (Zch 12:10). (3) In the future Israel will "dwell securely" because the land of Israel will be in complete peace, "never to be overthrown again" (Jr 23:6; 31:40; 33:16; 46:27-28). However, when the Jewish people returned from Babylon, they were met with immediate and violent opposition by the Samaritans living in the land (Neh 4:1-8; 6:1-9). That opposition was just the beginning of conflict. Since the return from Babylon, Israel has never enjoyed a time of genuine security. After the captivity they lived under the domination of the Greeks and Romans, then were expelled from the land (AD 70) and suffered persecution (from the Crusades to the Inquisition to the Holocaust) up to the present time. Although the modern state of Israel provides a homeland for the Jewish people, since its founding in 1948 Israel has not had a single year of peace and has been under constant threat of war and annihilation. Only when the Messiah Jesus rules from Jerusalem will the nation be guaranteed to live in safety and "not be plucked up or overthrown anymore forever." (4) In the future Israel will be ruled by King Messiah, the Son of David, the Righteous Branch (Jr 23:5-6; 30:8-11; 33:14-17). He will establish righteousness in the people and security in the land. This certainly did not occur at the return from Babylon, but awaits fulfillment after the time of Jacob's distress, when all Israel will be saved (Rm 11:26-27; Is 59:20). (5) The destruction of Babylon described does not fit the historical events of the period. The prophet foretold that Babylon would be destroyed in a cataclysmic way (Jr 50:29–51:64). But when Babylon fell to the Medes, it was not by violent attack but rather peaceful takeover. The events described here certainly are yet future.

The Lord commanded **Jeremiah** to **declare**, **proclaim** (twice), **lift up a standard**, and **not conceal** the public humiliation of **Babylon**. She would be **captured**. **Bel**, her protecting god (also known as **Marduk**) was the supreme deity of Babylon (cf. 51:44; Is 46:1). He was their god of thunder, fertility, and power, but he would be **shattered** and **put to shame** (cf. Jr 46:24). Shattering the chief pagan god points to the God of Israel as the one and only true God (Jdg 16:23-31;

1Sm 5:1-7). The repetition of these phrases underscores the doom of these pagan idols (cf. Is 44:9-20).

Babylon would be destroyed by a nation from **the north** (cf. Jr 50:9). Many see this as a reference to Babylon's fall to the Medo-Persian Empire, but several points do not fit historically. First, the Persians were from the east of Babylon, not from the north. Second, when Cyrus took Babylon he did not **make her land an object of horror** or destroy the city. Several times Jeremiah emphasized that Babylon would be uninhabited (cf. 50:39b-40; 51:29, 37, 43, 62). Yet Cyrus spared the city and made it one of the ruling centers for the Persian Empire. He appointed Daniel to a key administrative position there (cf. Dn 5:30; 6:1-3). Third, no one fled the city when it fell to Medo-Persia. In fact, Daniel, who had access to Jeremiah's prophecies (cf. Dn 9:1-2), remained in the city during and after its fall (cf. Dn 5:28, 30-31; 6:1-3). Fourth, the promise that **in those days and at that time . . . the sons of Israel . . . and the sons of Judah** would again unite as a nation, return to **Zion**, and bind themselves to God in an **everlasting covenant** (cf. Jr 31:31; 32:40) was not fulfilled when Babylon fell in 539 BC. Jeremiah's prophecy looked beyond the ancient destruction of Babylon to a future, eschatological devastation that will reverse the fortunes of Israel and Judah. The future destruction of Babylon will be the climax of God's judgment on the Gentile powers that have oppressed His people, and it will open the way for the fulfilling of God's promises to Israel. Scripture elsewhere points to this still future rebuilding of Israel and destruction of Babylon (cf. Zch 5:5-11; Rv 17–18). The ancient city of Babylon, which has fallen into ruin over the centuries, will be rebuilt prior to the coming of the antichrist only to be destroyed at the end of the tribulation before Messiah returns to establish His millennial reign.

50:4-5. In those days and at that time, the Jewish people, **Israel** and **Judah**, will return to the Lord, **weeping** in repentance (3:21-22; 31:9; Zch 12:10), and it **will be the LORD their God** whom **they will seek**. These events will take place following the future tribulation period (Jr 30:7) when Israel will turn and recognize Jesus at Messiah (Zch 12:10) and all Israel will be saved. The **everlasting covenant** refers to the new covenant (Jr 31:31ff.; Ps 84:5). At that time, Israel will return to **Zion** to **join themselves to the LORD** and enjoy the blessings of the messianic kingdom (cf. comments v. 1).

50:6-10. These verses are an editorial comment on the restoration of Israel and Judah. They will need to be restored because they have been **lost sheep**, led **astray** by false **shepherds**, wandering over **mountain** and **hill** (cf. 23:1-2; Ezk 36:5-6). They **have forgotten their resting place** in the Lord (Jr 50:19-20). They have been **devoured** by their enemies because they **sinned against the LORD . . . the habitation of righteousness . . . the hope of their fathers** (14:8, 22).

Their **adversaries** justified their attacks on the Jewish people by saying, **We are not guilty**, since the Jewish people deserve to be attacked—**they have sinned against the LORD**. This is a line of anti-Semitic logic that has been used by the Babylonians, the Crusaders, the Inquisition, and the Nazis—and that continues today against Jewish people and the nation of Israel.

2. The Fall of Babylon (50:11-16)

50:11-13. Babylon was judged **because** she was **glad** and **jubilant** when they **pillage[d]** Judah. God will judge any nation that rejoices, frolicking like a **heifer** and neighing like **stallions**, when it **pillage[s]** His **heritage** (whether it be the land of Israel, Ex 15:17; Jr 3:18; 12:14, or the people of Israel, Dt 9:26, 29; 10:16). The Lord vowed to disgrace Babylon by making it a **wilderness**, **completely desolate**, and a horror to all who pass by (cf. Lm 2:15).

50:14-16. Babylon will fall in **battle** because **she has sinned against the LORD**. The battle was graphically pictured with the enemy archers taking their positions around the city and shooting **arrows** at Babylon's defenders. When the city finally surrenders, her **pillars** and **walls** will be **torn down** and God's **vengeance** (used twice for emphasis) will be poured out. She would suffer what she had **done to others**. Again, this scene was not fulfilled when Cyrus the Mede conquered Babylon in 539 BC, taking the city without drastic warfare. This fall of Babylon awaits a future fulfillment at the end of days (vv. 1-3).

3. The Restoration of Israel (50:17-20)

50:17-20. Israel, here both the northern and southern kingdoms, had become like a **scattered flock** (vv. 6-7). The northern kingdom had been conquered by **Assyria** in 722 BC, and the southern kingdom was crushed by **Babylon** in 586 BC. The Lord vowed to restore His people, and **punish** the kings of **Babylon** and **Assyria** for their destruction of His people. He will **bring Israel back**

to her land. Once again, the Mediterranean summit of **Carmel** and the fertile plains of **Bashan** east of the Sea of Galilee will belong to Israel, as will the hills of **Ephraim** and **Gilead** on the western and eastern banks of the Jordan River. These blessings are eschatological and will occur **in those days and at that time** (see comments on v. 1). These blessings are not just geographic, but they include a spiritual renewal. Though some will search for **the iniquity of Israel**, it cannot be found for **there will be none**. Israel's guilt and the sins of Judah **will not be found** because God will **pardon** His **remnant** (31:31-34).

4. The Attack on Babylon (50:21-40)

50:21-28. Using two wordplays, God ordered the attack on the land of **Merathaim** and on the people in **Pekod. Merathaim** was the region of *Mat Marratim* in southern Babylon where the Tigris and Euphrates Rivers enter the Persian Gulf. However, the word in Hebrew (*meratayim*) means "double rebellion." **Pekod** referred to an Aramean tribe (called the *Pequdu*) in southern Babylon on the east bank of the Tigris River; but the word in Hebrew (*peqod*) means "to punish" or "punishment," creating a play on words. Thus God was saying He would attack the land of double rebellion and inflict His punishment on it.

The **noise of battle** signaled the **great destruction** of Babylon. Like a **hammer**, Babylon had been shattering **the whole earth**, but now she would be **broken**. God spoke of Himself as a hunter who had set a **snare** and **caught** Babylon, because she had engaged **in conflict with the Lord**. To battle against Zion is to battle with the Lord, as the Psalmist says: "Your enemies . . . hate You . . . and make plans against Your people and conspire together against Your treasured ones" (Ps 83:2-3; Gn 12:3; 2Kg 19:21-22). The fall of Babylon will be reported by the **refugees** who will **declare in Zion** that Babylon's destruction was the **vengeance of the Lord our God** as **vengeance for His temple** (Jr 52:13).

50:29-32. Many archers were summoned to **encamp against** Babylon to ensure that no one would escape, and to **repay her according to her work**. Judgment fell on Babylon because she had **become arrogant against the Lord . . . the Holy One of Israel** (regarding Damascus, cf. 49:26). **The arrogant one** would **stumble and fall** with no one to help as the Lord's judgment **set fire** to her **cities** and **environs** (cf. 15:14; Lm 4:11; Am 1:4, 7, 10, 12, 14; 2:2, 5).

50:33-34. The people of **Israel** and **Judah** were being **oppressed** and **held captive** by enemies who refused to **let them go**, a phrase reminiscent of Pharaoh's response to Moses (Ex 5–10). Their release here is not just the return from Babylon, but an end-time deliverance (Jr 31:11; Is 63:1; see comments on v. 1).

Their Redeemer is strong, the Lord of hosts is His name who will **plead their case** (Mc 7:9) and **bring rest to the earth** (Is 2:4; 11:9). As Feinberg points out, "Few nations have ever realized that God is the Kinsman-Redeemer of Israel (50:34). The OT gave specific instructions for the kinsman redeemer, the male relative who had the responsibility to act to protect a relative from physical or financial danger (Gn 48:16; Ex 6:6; Lv 27:9-25, 47-55; Nm 5:8, 35:9-34). This is the background of Boaz's purchase of the field from Naomi and marriage to Ruth, Naomi's widowed daughter-in-law in the Book of Ruth. The Kinsman-Redeemer is voluntarily committed to champion Israel's cause. He brings peace to His own but unrest to His oppressors" (Charles L. Feinberg, *Jeremiah: A Commentary* [Grand Rapids, MI: Zondervan, 1982], 322).

50:35-38. The "turmoil" their Redeemer will bring on **Babylon** (v. 34) is the **sword** (*hereb*), used five times in this section, followed by the pronouncement of a drought (*horeb*). This two-pronged judgment, a wordplay in Hebrew, will devastate the **land of idols** and the people who acted like lunatics in worship of **idols** (25:16).

50:39-40. The great Babylon will become desolate, a home for **desert creatures . . . jackals** (9:11; 10:22; 49:33; 51:37) and **ostriches**. After its destruction Babylon **will never again be inhabited** (cf. comments v. 3). Her desolation will be as complete as God's overthrow of **Sodom and Gomorrah** (49:18; Gn 19:24-25). This prediction awaits end-time fulfillment, since Babylon has been inhabited throughout history.

5. The Anguish of Babylon (50:41-46)

50:41-46. The Lord applied the same words of judgment for Babylon as He had for Jerusalem (cf. 6:22-24). Verses 44-46 are almost verbatim the judgment expressed against Edom (49:19-21). Here the judgment is applied to Babylon.

6. God's Vengeance against Babylon (51:1-14)

51:1-10. The Lord will **arouse . . . a destroyer** against **Babylon** and **Leb-kamai**. The expression "Leb-kamai" means "heart of my adversaries" but it is an *atbash* (see comments on 25:26) for Chaldea. The consonants for "heart of my adversary," when reversed in the Hebrew alphabet, spell "Chaldea." **Foreigners** sent by God to devastate **Babylon** will completely destroy **her army**.

The destruction of Babylon was a sign that **neither Israel nor Judah** had been **forsaken** by their **God**. He would destroy Babylon so that Israel and Judah would be free to return home (cf. 50:33-34). God called to His people to **flee** from Babylon to avoid being **destroyed** (cf. 50:8; Rv 18:4). Babylon had been the Lord's **golden cup** (Jr 51:7) of judgment **intoxicating all the earth** (cf. 25:15-29; Rv 17:3-4; 18:6), and she too will be **broken**. As she suddenly falls, her allies will try to find **balm for her pain** (cf. Jr 8:22; 46:11); but she will **not** be **healed** so her allies will desert her to avoid the effects of her judgment. God's people, knowing **the Lord** has **brought about** their **vindication** (51:5; 50:28, 34; Pss 9:1-6; 35:27; Is 54:17) by judging Babylon, will raise a song of praise **in Zion** to **recount . . . the work of the Lord** (cf. Jr 23:5-6; 50:28; Is 40:9).

51:11-14. Jeremiah described in familiar terms the preparations of the armies poised to attack Babylon (cf. 46:4, 9; 50:2). The attackers were, in a limited sense, the **kings of the Medes** (v. 28) when they conquered Babylon (539 BC; cf. Dn 5:31). This could indicate that one of the future kings who will invade Babylon during the tribulation period will come from the area controlled by the Medes (what is today northern Iran; cf. comments Jr 50:1-5). God will summon this army to take **vengeance** (v. 11; cf. 46:10; 50:15, 28, 34; 51:6, 36) on Babylon for her having destroyed His **temple** (cf. 50:28).

God will carry out His purpose to destroy the Babylonians **who dwell by many waters**, that is, near the Euphrates River, because He has **sworn by Himself** to do it (cf. 44:26; 49:13). The Lord has personally assured **victory over** Babylon.

7. God's Sovereignty over Babylon (51:15-26)

51:15-19. Babylon's downfall is guaranteed by the **Maker of all**, the **Lord of hosts** (v. 19). Jeremiah stressed God's sovereignty and power, and His relationship with **Jacob . . . His inheritance** in language that is virtually synonymous with 10:12-16 (cf. comments there).

51:20-26. Babylon was God's **war-club**, to shatter (*napas*, "to shatter to pieces") other nations (50:23). The phrase **I shatter** is used nine times in vv. 20-23 indicating the extent to which God had used Babylon for judgment. Now, however, the Lord will **repay Babylon** for the evil they had **done in Zion**. Babylon is called a **destroying mountain**; but it will become a **burnt out mountain**, like an extinct volcano, made **desolate forever** by God's judgment.

8. The Summons to the Nations against Babylon (51:27-33)

51:27-33. God summoned the **nations** for the third time (cf. 50:2; 51:12) calling them to lift up their **signal** banner and rally their troops against Babylon. The nations set apart for this task include the **Medes**, as well as the **kingdoms of Ararat** (present-day Armenia), **Minni** (an area in western Iran), and **Ashkenaz** (northwestern Iran, near Turkey). The people in all three areas were warlike.

These invaders will be appointed to accomplish **the purposes of the Lord against Babylon** and make Babylon **a desolation without inhabitants**. Since this has not yet transpired, this desolation will be an end-time event (48:9; 51:29, 37; cf. comments on 50:3). Instead of offering resistance, the warriors of Babylon will stop fighting and withdraw to their **strongholds** for protection. The city will be **captured**, with every escape route and hiding place burned. Even the **fords**, ferries, or bridges, and **marshes** on the Euphrates surrounding the city of Babylon will be set ablaze preventing escape. Ancient Babylon had an extensive and well-known messenger network. These couriers will run the message from one to **another . . . to tell the king** that his whole **city**, from **end to end**, has been **captured**.

God compared **Babylon** to a **threshing floor** being prepared for use. At threshing time, the ground would be **stamped firm** to make it ready to use for threshing and winnowing grain. Likewise Babylon has been prepared for judgment, and would be stamped down, like the threshing floor awaiting the work of **harvest**, a familiar image of destruction (Is 27:12; Jl 3:13; Mc 4:12-13).

9. God's Revenge on Babylon (51:34-44)

51:34-36. Zion complained that the **violence** she suffered at the hands of **Babylon** should be repaid. **Nebuchadnezzar** had **devoured** and **crushed** Jerusalem. Her complaint would be answered by the Lord, who would **plead** her case and **exact full vengeance** (Ps 140:12; Mc 7:9; cf. comments on Jr 50:33-34).

Babylon, built on the alluvial plain of the Euphrates, was famous for her extensive fountains and irrigated city gardens. In judgment, God would **dry up** the **sea** (lit., "broad river") and **make her fountain dry**.

51:37-44. God answered Zion's question (v. 35) by declaring that He will make Babylon **a**

heap of ruins and **a haunt of jackals** (cf. 50:39-40), a place where no one lives (cf. comments on 50:3). She will be **an object of . . . hissing** (cf. comments on 24:9). The Babylonians were fierce like **young lions** (cf. 2:15), and God will prepare a **banquet** for them to make them **drunk** (25:15-16, 26). As they drink from His cup of judgment they will **sleep** and never wake up (cf. v. 57). The Babylonians are also compared to **lambs** (cf. 50:45) being led to the slaughter.

Sheshak (or Sheshach) was an *atbash* for "Babylon" (see comments on "Sheshach" in 25:26; cf. 51:1). Babylon will be **captured** and destroyed. She will be **engulfed** as if the **sea** had risen over her. Her **cities** will become desolate (cf. comments on 50:3) like a **desert**.

Babylon was famous for its main god, Bel, and for its impressive walls. God will punish **Bel** (cf. 50:2) by making him spew out the wealth he had swallowed. The **wall of Babylon** was a double wall. The inner wall was 21 feet thick and wide enough for several chariots to race across the top side by side. It was separated from the outer wall by a 23-foot dry moat. Yet, **even the wall of Babylon has fallen down!**

10. The Warning to the Remnant in Babylon (51:45-48)

51:45-48. God ordered His people to **come forth** from Babylon to **save** themselves and escape God's judgment. They were not to be **afraid** of the many reports of victory or **violence**. Instead they were to remain confident that the **days are coming** when God would **punish . . . Babylon**. At that time **heaven and earth . . .** will **shout for joy over** God's victory. This was not fulfilled at the return from Babylon authorized by Cyrus (539 BC), but refers to Israel's great end-of-days regathering from worldwide dispersion. (see comments on 16:14, 31:27-40; 50:1; Rv 18:20).

11. The Certainty of Babylon's Fall (51:49-53)

51:49-50. God had ordained that **Babylon** must **fall** because she was responsible **for the slain of Israel**. God promised Abraham that those who cursed him would themselves be cursed (Gn 12:2-3). This assurance is applied to **Babylon**. When the Israelites escape from the future destruction of Babylon they should **depart . . . not stay**. Instead they should **remember the Lord** and think on **Jerusalem** (Pss 84:5; 137:5). Babylon's destruction will be the catalyst God uses to bring the Jewish people home to their land. Babylon had a Jewish community from the OT period until the mid-1950s. After the birth of the modern state of Israel however, anti-Semitism became so intense in Iraq that virtually the whole Jewish population fled to the new state of Israel to save their lives. Persecution in modern Babylon was certainly a catalyst to bring Jewish people back to the land of Israel. The flight of the Jewish people from Iraq to Israel may be the fulfillment of this prophecy, escaping before the eschatological judgment of Babylon.

51:51-53. As the remnant in exile thought of Jerusalem, they were **ashamed** and **disgrace[d]** because they heard that **aliens** had entered the **holy places** of the temple. God comforted these exiles by assuring them that **days are coming** when He will **punish** (destroy) Babylon's **idols** (cf. vv. 44, 47). No matter how she would **fortify her . . . stronghold**, God still vowed to send **destroyers** (cf. v. 48) against her.

12. God's Repayment of Babylon (51:54-58)

51:54-58. An **outcry . . . of great destruction** will be heard from the land of Babylon, because **the Lord is going to destroy Babylon**. Her own **loud noise** of political power and world significance will **vanish** because **the Lord is a God of recompense, He will fully repay** (cf. 46:10; 50:15, 28; 51:6, 11, 36). Every class of officials in Babylon will become **drunk** on God's wine of judgment (cf. 25:15-29; 51:7-8); they will **sleep and not wake up** (cf. v. 39). Again such wholesale destruction of Babylon's leaders and warriors did not occur when Babylon fell to Medo-Persia (cf. Dn 5:29-6:2). It still awaits God's future fulfillment in the tribulation (cf. Jr 50:1-3).

Since God had already announced that **the broad wall of Babylon will be completely razed** and her **gates . . . set on fire** (cf. 50:15; 51:30, 44; Hab 2:13), any **toil** expended to prevent His judgment is **for nothing**, only creating fuel for the **fire**.

13. Seraiah's Symbolic Mission (51:59-64)

51:59. The capstone of Jeremiah's oracle against Babylon was a message to **Seraiah**, a staff officer to king **Zedekiah**. Seraiah went to Babylon with Zedekiah **in the fourth year of his reign** (594–593 BC). William Shea offers strong evidence that Nebuchadnezzar summoned all his vassal kings to Babylon in 594 BC to ensure their loyalty after an attempted revolt less than a year earlier. Shea believes that this gathering was recorded in Dn 3 (William H. Shea, "Daniel 3: Extra-Biblical Texts and the Convocation on the Plain of Dura," *Andrews University Seminary*

Studies 20 [Spring 1982]: 29-52). Whatever the cause, Zedekiah was forced to make an official trip to Babylon, and brought along Baruch's brother, Seraiah.

51:60-64. Jeremiah **wrote . . . a single scroll** of all the prophecies of **calamity . . . concerning Babylon**. Probably this was the information recorded in chaps. 50–51 of Jeremiah. He gave the scroll to Seraiah with specific instruction. First, he was to **read all these words aloud** when he got to Babylon. Second, he was to proclaim to his audience this message: **You, O Lord, have promised concerning this place . . . perpetual desolation**. Third, as a visual lesson of God's intention, Seraiah was to **tie a stone** to the scroll and **throw it into the . . . Euphrates**. Finally, as the scroll and stone sank beneath the water, Seraiah was to announce that, like the scroll, Babylon would **sink down** and not rise **because of the calamity** the Lord would **bring upon her** (cf. Rv 18:21; Jr 50:1-3).

The chapter closes with the sentence: **Thus far are the words of Jeremiah** (v. 64). J. Ludbom has pointed out that this phrase forms an inclusio with 1:1, as the book begins with the phrase, "The words of Jeremiah." The inclusio gives a suggestion of unity to the entire book (J. Ludbom, *Jeremiah: A Study in Ancient Hebrew Rhetoric,* SBLDS 18 [Missoula, MT: Scholars, 1975], 25). The sentence makes it clear that the rest of the book is the addition of an unidentified editor who later added chap. 52 to the already compiled work of the prophet Jeremiah. Whoever the editor was (many suggest Baruch), the Holy Spirit guided the editor to include chap. 52 as a fitting ending to the book.

IV. Conclusion: Historical Supplement (52:1-34)

Chapter 52 was written sometime after 561 BC, when King Jehoiachin was released from prison in Babylon (v. 31). It is nearly identical to 2Kg 24:18–25:30. Much of the material is parallel to information in Jr 39, and it serves as a historical supplement to the book of Jeremiah.

It shows that Jeremiah's words of judgment against Jerusalem had been fulfilled and that his words about Judah's release from the exile were about to be fulfilled. This final chapter served to vindicate the prophet and encourage the remnant still in captivity. It likewise serves as an encouragement for readers to believe that all the prophecies of the Lord will ultimately be fulfilled by Him.

A. The Fate of Jerusalem (52:1-23)

1. The Fall of Zedekiah (52:1-11)

52:1-11. This is a brief history of **Zedekiah**, Judah's final king. It is nearly identical to 2Kg 24:18–25:7, as well as Jr 39:1-7 (cf. comments on 39:1-7).

2. The Destruction of the City (52:12-16)

52:12-16. The fall and burning of Jerusalem was described earlier (chap. 39), but this passage focuses more on the looting and burning of the temple. By the **tenth day** of the fifth month, which was the **nineteenth year of King Nebuchadnezzar** (August 17, 586 BC), Jerusalem had been cleared of rebels and sacked by the Babylonians. At that time, **Nebuzaradan the captain of the bodyguard . . . came to Jerusalem**. He was in charge of the final events in Jerusalem and **he burned the house of the Lord**, as well as **every large house** in the city as Jeremiah had predicted (cf. 22:7). Those who survived the siege and had been civic leaders were **carried away into exile**. Only the **poorest** people were left behind.

There is a minor issue about the date in this passage, because 2Kg 25:8 indicates that **Nebuzaradan** came on "the seventh day of the fifth month," instead of the **tenth day**. Two possible answers have been suggested. Perhaps there was a scribal error in copying the text. However, there is no textual or manuscript evidence to support this position. The preferable understanding is that "the seventh" was the day Nebuzaradan **came to Jerusalem** (2Kg 25:8), entered the temple and removed the articles, then set fire to the temple on the ninth day, and **the tenth day** he **burned the house of the Lord** and continued burning the city. The Jewish remembrance of the burning of the temple is the fast of the ninth day of the month of Av (*Tisha b'Av*), a date that falls in late July to early August on the modern calendar.

3. The Destruction of the Temple (52:17-23)

52:17-23. Jeremiah's conflict with the false prophet Hananiah (27:16–28:17) is the background for this passage. That passage contains Jeremiah's prediction that the temple vessels would go and remain in Babylon (27:19-22) and the account of Hananiah predicting that the temple vessels would be restored to Israel in peace (28:3), in opposition to what Jeremiah had foretold. At that time Jeremiah said, "when the word of the prophet comes to pass, then that prophet will be known as one whom the Lord has truly sent" (28:9). This account is included at the end of the book as an affirmation of Jeremiah's authenticity as a prophet and the truth of his entire prophetic work. The details of this chapter prove the accuracy of Jeremiah's words. Everything from the temple was carried away to Babylon. The inventory is given in detail: the **bronze pillars**, the **firepans**, the **bowls** of **fine gold** and **fine silver**, the bronze **pomegranates**. This was such an extensive undertaking that the writer detailed the size of the bronze pieces that were removed and the number of pomegranates carried away (50:21-23). These treasures were all removed for transport to Babylon before the temple was burned.

B. The Fate of Certain Individuals (52:24-34)

1. The Fate of Those in Jerusalem During Its Fall (52:24-27)

52:24-27. All of Jerusalem's leaders were rounded up by the **captain of the guard**. These included **Seraiah the chief priest**, who was grandson of Hilkiah, the high priest in King Josiah's time (1Ch 6:13-15) (not the brother of Baruch; cf. Jr 32:12; 51:59), **Zephaniah**, who was the priest next in rank (cf. 29:25-29; 37:3), and the **three officers**, doorkeepers who were responsible for keeping order in the **temple**. Also captured were the **official[s]** in charge of the **men of war**, **seven of the king's advisers**, and so on. The list indicates that **Nebuzaradan** took all the leaders of Jerusalem (spiritual, civil, and military) to **Riblah**, where Nebuchadnezzar's field headquarters was located (v. 9). All these leaders of Jerusalem were **struck down**, or executed. Then **Judah was led away into exile from its land**.

2. The Fate of the Exiles (52:28-30)

52:28-30. This account of the fall of Jerusalem is not included in the 2Kg 25 account. It was added here to show that other groups of exiles were taken to Babylon. The dates given for the deportations (Jr 52:28-29) do not correspond with the dates of the two deportations given in 2Kg 24:12-14; 25:8-12. Two possible solutions to this difficulty have been advanced.

First, some suggest the deportations in 2 Kings and Jeremiah refer to the same events and should be harmonized. This is usually done by assuming that the writer of 2 Kings used a non-accession year method of dating the kings of Babylon, while Jeremiah employed an accession year method in Jr 52:28-30. In ancient times, the Israelite system for counting the dates of a king's reign would include the first year ascended to the throne as the first year of the reign. Alternatively, the Babylonian system did not include the accession year in counting the years of a reign and instead counted the second year as the first. Since 1 and 2 Kings was likely written in Babylon, the author used the Babylonian method while Jeremiah always used the Israelite system (see comments at Dn 1:1 and also John Bright, *A History of Israel*, 3rd ed. [Philadelphia: Westminster Press, 1981], 326 n. 45).

Second, others suggest the first two deportations listed in Jr 52:28-30 were not the same as those in 2 Kings but were minor ones preceding the major deportations associated with Nebuchadnezzar's capture of Jerusalem in 597 and 586 BC. Two arguments make this second view the more likely view. First, the years given (the seventh and 18th years of Nebuchadnezzar) are each one year earlier than the years given in 2 Kings for the two major assaults on Jerusalem by Babylon (the eighth year, 2Kg 24:12-14; and 19th year, 2Kg 25:8-12 of Nebuchadnezzar). Second, the numbers of captives who were exiled in these deportations mentioned in Jeremiah do not correspond with the numbers taken during the 597 and 586 BC deportations as delineated in 2 Kings. In 597 BC about 10,000 people were taken (2Kg 24:14), but here Jeremiah (Jr 52:28) mentioned only 3,023. In 586 BC Nebuchadnezzar deported "the rest of the people who were left in the city and the deserters who had deserted to the king of Babylon and the rest of the people" (2Kg 25:11). The figure in Jeremiah Jr 52:29 of just 832 seems far too low to correspond to this final deportation. So according to this second view it seems reasonable to assume that these two deportations (vv. 28-29) are secondary deportations. The writer included them (along with a third minor deportation mentioned in v. 30) to show the full extent of Babylon's destruction of Judah. (See Alberto R. Green, "The Chronology of the Last Days of Judah: Two Apparent Discrepancies," *Journal of Biblical Literature* 101 [1982]: 57-73.)

The third deportation mentioned by Jeremiah perhaps corresponds with Nebuchadnezzar's return to the land after Gedaliah's assassination (cf. chap. 41). Certainly such a threat to Babylon's control over Judah did not go unnoticed. Perhaps Nebuchadnezzar sent a force to restore order and to remove anyone suspected of promoting rebellion. The small number of 745 Jews would support the limited size of this action. The dates of these three deportations (based on a Tishri calendar, counting the New Year from Rosh Hashanah, Feast of Trumpets in the Fall) mentioned in vv. 28-30 were then (1) Nebuchadnezzar's seventh year (598 BC), (2) his 18th year (587 BC), and (3) his 23rd year (582 BC).

3. The Fate of Jehoiachin (52:31-34)

52:31-34. These verses are also found in 2Kg 25:27-30, with minor variations. In the **thirty-seventh year** of **Jehoiachin**'s exile (561–560 BC) Evil-merodach (*Awl-marduk*, "man of Marduk," god of Babylon) became king of Babylon. As part of the festivities at the end of his accession year he released **Jehoiachin . . . out of prison** on the 25th day of the 12th month (March 21, 560 BC). From that day until the day he died, he received a **regular allowance and had his meals in the king's presence**, that is, he was cared for by the provision of the king of Babylon.

The book ends with a thread of hope. Just as Jeremiah's prophecies of destruction had come true, now his prophecies of future blessing were beginning. Jehoiachin's circumstances gave hope to the exiles that God's promised blessing and restoration for Israel would be fulfilled.

The Lord will always keep His word. He will do exactly what He has promised and He is always righteous. If we believe this, our lives will be characterized by joy in the Lord and a sense of obedience and expectancy, no matter what our circumstances. We, like the remnant of Judah, are awaiting the coming of our King Messiah to fulfill all the good words He has promised.

BIBLIOGRAPHY

Allen, Leslie C. *Jeremiah*. Louisville, KY: Westminster John Knox Press, 2008.

Archer, Gleason Jr. *A Survey of Old Testament Introduction*. Chicago: Moody Publishers, 2007.

Bright, John. *A History of Israel*, 3rd ed. Philadelphia: Westminster Press, 1981.

Brown, Michael. *Jeremiah*. Expositors Bible Commentary, rev. ed. Grand Rapids, MI: Zondervan, 2010.

Bullock, C. Hassell. *An Introduction to the Old Testament Prophetic Books*. Chicago: Moody Press, 1996.

Elwell, Walter. "Inheritance," in *The Evangelical Dictionary of Biblical Theology*, 374. Grand Rapids, MI: Baker, 1996.

Feinberg, Charles L. *Jeremiah: A Commentary*. Grand Rapids, MI: Zondervan, 1982.

Freeman, H. *Jeremiah*. London: Soncino Press, 1949.

Green, Alberto R. "The Chronology of the Last Days of Judah: Two Apparent Discrepancies." *Journal of Biblical Literature* 101 (1982): 57-73.

Harrison, R. K. *Jeremiah and Lamentations*. The Tyndale Old Testament Commentaries. Downers Grove, IL: InterVarsity, 1973.

Huey, F. B. Jr., *Jeremiah, Lamentations*. The New American Commentary, edited by E. Ray Clenden. Nashville, TN: B&H Publishing Group, 1993.

Jensen, Irving L. *Jeremiah and Lamentations*. Everyman's Bible Commentary. Chicago: Moody, 1974.

Kaiser, W. C. Jr. *The Messiah in the Old Testament*. Grand Rapids, MI: Zondervan, 1994.

Kidner, Derek. *The Message of Jeremiah*. The Bible Speaks Today, ed. J. A. Moyter. Downers Grove, IL. InterVarsity, 1987.

Kinsler, F. Ross. *Inductive Study of the Book of Jeremiah*. South Pasadena, CA: William Carey Library, 1971.

Ludbom, J. *Jeremiah: A Study in Ancient Hebrew Rhetoric*. Society of Biblical Literature Dissertation Series 18. Missoula, MT: Scholars, 1975.

Mackay, John L. *Jeremiah*. A Mentor Commentary. Fearn, Rose-shire, Scotland: Mentor, 2004.

Parker, Richard A. and Waldo H. Dubberstein. *Babylonian Chronology: 626 BC–AD 75*. Providence, RI: Brown University Press, 1956.

Rydelnik, Michael. *The Messianic Hope: Is the Hebrew Bible Really Messianic?* Nashville: B&H, 2010.

Ryken, Philip Graham. *Jeremiah and Lamentations*. Preaching the Word, ed., R. Kent Hughes. Wheaton, IL: Crossway, 2001.

Shea, William H. "Daniel 3: Extra-Biblical Texts and the Convocation on the Plain of Dura." *Andrews University Seminary Studies* 20 (Spring 1982): 29-52.

Thiele, Edwin R. *The Mysterious Numbers of the Hebrew Kings*, rev. ed. Grand Rapids, MI: Zondervan, 1983.

Thompson, J. A. *The Book of Jeremiah*. The New International Commentary on the Old Testament, ed. Robert L. Hubbard. Grand Rapids, MI: Eerdmans, 1980.

Wiseman, Donald J. *Chronicle of Chaldean Kings [626-556 BC] in the British Museum*. London: Trustees of the British Museum, 1956.

● ● ● ●

LAMENTATIONS

Charles Dyer with Eva Rydelnik

INTRODUCTION

In Christian Bibles, Lamentations follows Jeremiah, as the messages are directly connected. In the Jewish Bible, Lamentations is one of the "Five Scrolls" (*megillot*), read in synagogues on various Jewish holy days. Lamentations is read in the synagogue yearly on the Ninth of Av (*Tisha b'Av*), the day of fasting set aside to mourn the destructions of the first and second temples. The other scrolls are Esther, read on Purim; Song of Songs, read on Sabbath during the intermediate days of Passover; Ruth, read on the second morning of the Feast of Weeks (*Shavuot*); and Ecclesiastes, read on Sabbath during the intermediate days of Tabernacles (*Sukkoth*). Together these books/scrolls form part of the third section of the Hebrew Bible, the *Ketuvim*, ("the Writings"). When Lamentations is read in the synagogue, after the final verse (5:22) then verse 5:21 is repeated, so that the reading may close with a focus of hope in God: "Restore us to You, O Lord, that we may be restored; Renew our days as of old."

In Hebrew the title is taken from the book's first word, *'ekah*, which is best translated "Alas" rather than "How." It is a cry of grief (2Sm 1:19; Jr 1:19). The Talmudic writers called the book by the name *Kinot*, (*Bava Batra* 14b), meaning "lamentations, dirges, or elegies." This title derives from the book being a cry of grief over the destruction of Jerusalem and sorrow for the Jewish people who had been taken into captivity. The Septuagint translates the rabbinic title into the Greek for "lamentations" (*thrēnoi*). This title was carried over to the Latin Vulgate, as the "The Lamentations of Jeremiah" and from there into the English Bibles as Lamentations.

Author. The book does not specifically name Jeremiah as its author, but Jewish and Church traditions unanimously attribute the work to him. The Septuagint translation introduces the book, "And it came to pass, after Israel was taken captive, and Jerusalem made desolate, that Jeremiah sat weeping, and lamented with this lamentation over Jerusalem, and he said . . ." Also, the ancient rabbinic tradition, (i.e., Babylonian Talmud, *Bava Batra* 15a, as well as early Christian tradition (i.e., Latin Vulgate) attribute the book to Jeremiah. The internal evidence also points to Jeremiah as author, as the books of Jeremiah and Lamentations show a strong link. In both books, the writer's eyes flowed with tears (Jr 9:1, 18; Lm 1:16; 2:11), and he claimed to be an eyewitness of Jerusalem's siege and fall to Babylon (Jr 19:9; Lm 2:20; 4:10).

Date. The book was composed within a brief period of time after the fall of Jerusalem (586 BC; cf. 1:1-11) and before Jeremiah was taken to Egypt (583-582 BC, cf. Jr 43:1-7). The vivid descriptions and deep emotions argue for a composition immediately after the events occurred, possibly in late 586 or early 585 BC.

Recipients. Jeremiah directed this message to the survivors of Judah after the fall of Jerusalem, including those taken into captivity to Babylon, those who remained in the land of Judah, and those who had fled to Egypt. All these individuals experienced the Lord's ongoing judgment. Lamentations reminded them to maintain hope in God because "The Lord's lovingkindnesses indeed never cease, For His compassions never fail. They are new every morning; great is [His] faithfulness" (Lm 3:22-23).

Theme and Purpose. There are two themes running together: the judgment of God and the faithfulness of God. Both call for hope in the Lord and obedience to Him.

The purpose of the book is to express grief over the fall of Jerusalem and confidence in the faithfulness of God. All the tragedy Jerusalem experienced had been predicted almost 900 years earlier when God warned of the fearful consequences of disobedience (Lv 26; Dt 28). Lamentations is a record of those consequences.

Yet this judgment makes the book of Lamentations a book of hope for Israel because it records God's faithfulness in discharging every aspect of the covenant. Israel was punished for disobedience, but not destroyed. The same covenant that promised judgment for disobedience also promised restoration for repentance (Dt 30:1-10). Jeremiah's message to Judah was for the nation to turn back to the Lord and "hope in Him" (Lm 3:24)

There are several key words in the book. "Zion" (15 times) and "Jerusalem" (seven times) are used synonymously to identify the Jewish people or the city. Zion or Jerusalem is connected to "the daughter of" frequently to denote the people. "Desolate" (seven times) emphasizes the grief of loss, and "hope" (five times) emphasizes the positive expectation that the God of the covenant gave His people.

Background. From 588 to 586 BC the army of Nebuchadnezzar, king of Babylon, besieged Jerusalem. The long siege ended abruptly in July 586 BC when the walls were breached, the temple burned, and Judea was taken into exile (events detailed in the book of Jeremiah). Lamentations is a mournful postscript to the book of Jeremiah. In five funeral dirges, or laments, the prophet Jeremiah grieves over the fate of Jerusalem because of her sin (1:8). The book of Lamentations goes beyond grief to provide a theological explanation of the fall of Jerusalem and offers instruction and hope in the faithfulness of the Lord.

The genre of Lamentations is poetry. Each chapter is a solemn elegy, lament, or song of mourning, written in acrostic form, as described in the following paragraph (cf. Ps 119). The purpose of the acrostic in Lamentations is perhaps twofold: first, to make the content easy to remember and second, to emphasize the extent (i.e., from A to Z) of the consequences of sin.

Lamentations has three structural markers. First, the book is written as a series of five laments, that is, as a funeral poem or dirge recited as if someone had just died (cf. 2Sm 1:17-27). Second, each of the chapters has an acrostic, a form in which the first word of each line or verse, when taken in order, follows the sequence of the 22 letters of the Hebrew alphabet. Third, the book has a definite structural balance. Chapters 1 and 5 are parallel, focusing on the people, and chaps. 2 and 4 are parallel, focusing on the Lord. Chapter 3 is the pivot for the book, focusing on hope in the Lord and a declaration of His lovingkindness in the midst of affliction.

OUTLINE

I. First Lament: Jerusalem's Desolation Because of Her Sin (1:1-22)
   A. Jeremiah's Lament Over Jerusalem's Desolation (1:1-11)
   B. Jerusalem's Plea for Mercy (1:12-19)
   C. Jerusalem's Prayer to the Lord (1:20-22)
II. Second Lament: The Lord's Punishment of Jerusalem's Sin (2:1-22)
   A. The Lord's Anger at Jerusalem's Sin (2:1-10)
   B. Jeremiah's Grief Over Jerusalem's Sin (2:11-19)
   C. Jerusalem's Plea for the Lord's Mercy (2:20-22)
III. Third Lament: Jeremiah's Response to Jerusalem's Desolation (3:1-66)
   A. Jeremiah's Afflictions by the Lord (3:1-18)
   B. Jeremiah's Hope in the Lord (3:19-40)
   C. Jeremiah's Prayer to the Lord (3:41-66)
IV. Fourth Lament: The Lord's Wrath Poured Out on Jerusalem (4:1-22)
   A. The Contrast of Zion Before and After the Siege (4:1-11)
   B. The Causes of the Siege of Zion (4:12-20)
   C. The Call for Vindication Against Edom, Enemy of Zion (4:21-22)
V. Fifth Lament: The Remnant of Jerusalem's Response (5:1-22)
   A. The Remnant's Prayer for the Lord to Remember Zion (5:1-18)
   B. The Remnant's Prayer for the Lord to Restore Zion (5:19-22)

COMMENTARY ON LAMENTATIONS

I. First Lament: Jerusalem's Desolation Because of Her Sin (1:1-22)

The first lament establishes one of the themes of the book—the consequences and sorrow of sin. The people of Judah had turned from the protective care of her God to pursue foreign alliances and lifeless idols. Now Zion "weeps bitterly," is in mourning, and has "gone into exile" because of her sin. There is "none to comfort her" (vv. 2, 9, 16-17, 21). Two perspectives are presented in this lament. First, the prophet's perspective is from the outside looking in (vv. 1-11). The second perspective is of Jerusalem personified, calling for mercy from those who pass by (vv. 12-19). The lament closes with personified Jerusalem turning to God in prayer (vv. 29-22).

A. Jeremiah's Lament Over Jerusalem's Desolation (1:1-11)

Jeremiah's first words, "How lonely sits the city," express his deep sorrow for the fall of Zion. As Jeremiah surveyed the destruction of the thriving city, the lament begins: "How" (*'ekah),* better translated "alas," a word of lament (1:1; 2:1; 4:1), is an exclamation often associated with grief and mourning (cf. Is 1:21, 2:2; Jr 48:17). The first paragraph (Lm 1:1-7) vividly describes the extent of Zion's destruction, and the second (vv. 8-11) explains the cause for her destruction.

1:1-2. Jerusalem had experienced catastrophic devastation and three significant changes. (cf. Introduction: Background in Jeremiah). First, her population was devastated: **How lonely sits the city that was full of people!** Second, her economic position was bankrupt. The city that once been **great among the nations** was reduced to the status of a **widow**. Widowhood is used throughout the OT to depict poverty, destitution, and despair (cf. Ex 22:22; Dt 10:18; 24:19-21; 26:13; 27:19; Is 1:17). Third, her social position was that of a slave. The **princess** . . . has now become a **forced laborer**. The city that used to rule other nations was now taken in slavery to Babylon.

Her emotional condition was complete sorrow, weeping **bitterly in the night**. She has turned from the Lord and there was **none to comfort her**. Her **lovers**, a term that refers to her spiritual adultery (idolatry) and her **friends**, meaning political allies, had become her **enemies**.

1:3-4. Judah has gone into exile to Babylon (cf. Introduction: Background in Jeremiah). The **roads of Zion are in mourning**, implying that there were so few citizens left that the roads were largely unused, and **gates are desolate** because the temple is destroyed and worship at the appointed feasts is impossible.

1:5. The contrast is stark between Zion's slavery and **grief**, and her enemies who **have become her masters** and now **prosper**, a word meaning "at ease" or "at rest."

This crucial text explains the cause of her grief and exile: **For the Lord has caused her grief because of the multitude of her transgressions**. The destruction of Jerusalem and being **captives** to her **adversary** Babylon was the Lord's judgment for Israel's sin (cf. vv. 8, 9, 14, 18, 20).

1:6. Daughter of Zion personified the city and her people, the name being used for Jerusalem throughout Lamentations, Jeremiah, and the Prophets (cf. 2:1, 4:22; Is 1:8; Jr 4:31; Mc 4:8). Jeremiah 1:4-6 emphasizes the religious desolation in Jerusalem after its temple was destroyed, as were its associated sacrifices and feasts, all of which symbolized God's presence and fellowship with His people.

The word **Zion** (vv. 4, 6) referred originally to the mountain on which the City of David was built (cf. 2Sm 5:7; 1Kg 8:1). Later the temple was built on Mount Moriah (2Ch 3:1; 5:2), and it became Mount Zion (Pss 20:2; 48:2; 78:68-69). "Zion" eventually was applied to the entire city of Jerusalem, which included the City of David, the Temple Mount, and the western hill on which the city later expanded (Jr 51:35). **Zion** is often associated with God's dwelling place, whether the temple proper or the city where the temple was located. "Remembering Zion" is a central aspect of Jewish liturgy and hope (Ps 137:5), and modern Zionism continues to emphasize the centrality of Israel and Jerusalem to the Jewish people as their historic national homeland.

1:7. The phrase **Jerusalem remembers** indicates the mental anguish that accompanied the physical suffering. Jerusalem remembered **all her precious things** (cf. v. 11), probably a reference to the temple treasures rather than personal wealth. The Babylonians stripped the temple of all its priceless ornamentation. Her **adversaries** saw and **mocked** her **ruin**

(*mishbath*), used only here in the Scriptures, and better translated "annihilation."

1:8-9. After describing the catastrophe (vv. 1-7) Jeremiah explained the cause of it (vv. 8-11). Jerusalem's destruction was not an action of a heartless God against an innocent people. She brought her destruction upon herself because **Jerusalem sinned greatly**. Jerusalem was personified here as an **unclean** woman, a term for ceremonial impurity (Lv 15:16-24) that renders a person unfit to worship in the temple. Israel's idol worship was spiritual adultery against the Lord; He saw **her nakedness** and the **uncleanness . . . in her skirts**, referring to sexual immorality, and in this context is linked to spiritual unfaithfulness. When Judah turned to idolatry, **she did not consider her future** nor did she give a thought to the consequences of her actions. Instead she had **fallen astonishingly**, the astonishment stemming from the assumption by the nation Judah that the Lord would protect it.

1:10-11. Jerusalem reaped two results from her sin. First, the temple was desecrated and the **precious things** (cf. v. 7) were taken by the **nations**, by pagans who were forbidden to **enter** into **her sanctuary**. The people had failed to trust in the God of the sanctuary; instead they had falsely relied on the building for their security (cf. Jr. 7:2-15; 26:2-11; 1Sm 4:1-11). Second, because of her sin, Jerusalem suffered a famine—they were **seeking bread** and selling **precious things for food** (cf. Lm 1:19; 2:20; 4:10).

B. Jerusalem's Plea for Mercy (1:12-19)

This lament now changes focus from the outside looking in, to the inside looking out. First, Jerusalem asks people who pass by (vv. 12-19) to see her desolation and pity her. Next, she calls on the Lord from a faint heart (vv. 20-22).

1:12-15. Jerusalem asks: **Is it nothing to all you who pass this way?** She wanted someone to stop and take note of her condition. First, she focused on God's judgment that was **severely dealt out** upon her (vv. 12-17). Then she explained that the Lord's judgment was deserved: "For I have rebelled against His command" (vv. 18-19).

Jerusalem's destruction was not a chance occurrence; it was a direct result of God's judgment. Thus, the destruction of Jerusalem was that **which the Lord inflicted** (cf. 2:1-8; 4:11; 5:20). God's judgment is described with four metaphors. First, it was like **fire**, which He sent down into the **bones** of Jerusalem (v. 13a), a vivid image of the destructive fire that burned into the inner recesses of the city. Second, it was like a **net spread for [her] feet** (v. 13b), a picture of being taken captive by a hunter. Third, His judgment was like wearing **the yoke . . . upon my neck** (v. 14). A yoke tied two draft animals together for pulling heavy loads. The heavy wooden crossbeam of the yoke referred metaphorically to slavery or to a burden or hardship someone had to bear (cf. Lv 26:13; Is 9:4; Jr 27:1-11). Jerusalem's **transgressions** produced the yoke of judgment, which **bound** her to captivity. Fourth, God's judgment was like the treading of grapes (Lm 1:15), a common metaphor of God's judgment (Is 63:2-3; Jl 3:13; Rv 19:15). **The Lord** would **crush** Jerusalem's **young men . . . in a wine press** as well as the **virgin daughter of Judah**, that is, the people of Jerusalem could not withstand His judgment (cf. Lm 2:2-5).

1:16-17. Jerusalem would **weep** tears that **run down [like] water** for all she was experiencing, and her **comforter** was **far** away. **Zion stretches out her hands** for mercy, but **there is no one to comfort** her (cf. vv. 9, 21). Lack of comfort is a major theme in this chapter (cf. vv. 2, 9, 16, 17, 21). The city was destitute and despised. The emphasis is on the source of judgment—**The Lord has commanded**. The people are identified as **Jacob**, another name for Israel. All of his neighbors to whom he had turned for aid were now **his adversaries** (cf. v. 2). Jerusalem had become **unclean** (*niddh*), referring to ceremonial impurity (cf. Lv 15:19-20; Ezk 18:6). Again, ritual impurity serves as a metaphor for Israel's idolatry, her spiritual adultery (cf. v. 8).

1:18-19. Zion declares **the Lord is righteous**; His judgments are justifiable discipline because **I have rebelled against His command**. God is not the author of moral evil nor is He a supreme sadist who delights in inflicting punishment on others (cf. Ezk 33:11; 2Pt 3:9). But He is a just judge (He **is righteous**) and will not allow sin to continue unchecked. Sin exacts a horrible price from those who enjoy its temporary pleasures, leading to great pain. Hence, Jerusalem cries, **behold my pain**. Jerusalem was paying the price for her rebellion: betrayal by **lovers**, death by starvation, and **captivity** (cf. Lm 1:3). Judah's confession of guilt acknowledged that a righteous God brought judgment upon an unrighteous people as discipline.

C. Jerusalem's Prayer to the Lord (1:20-22)

This first lament ends with Jerusalem shifting her focus. Jerusalem called for mercy from those passing by (vv. 12-19) but found none. Now she turned her cry to the Lord.

1:20-22. Jerusalem calls, **See, O Lord** and then describes her **distress**. While Nebuchadnezzar's army attacked Jerusalem, those who tried to escape the siege were killed by **the sword**. But for those who remained in the city (**in the house**), it was **like death**, dying of starvation and plague.

Jerusalem called on God to see Babylon's **wickedness** and judge these enemies, calling on Him to **bring the day which You have proclaimed**. The **day** was the "day of the Lord," which the prophets foretold against the enemies of Jerusalem (Is 13:6; Ezk 30:3; Jl 1:15). This was the time when God's judgment would extend to all the earth to avenge injustice and bring about the age of righteousness that had been promised.

Jerusalem wanted God to judge the sins of her enemies as He had judged her sins: **deal with them as You have dealt with me** (Lm 4:21-22). This did not happen at that time, but God said He would judge all nations in the still-future tribulation period (cf. Is 62:8–63:6; Ezk 38-39; Jl 3:1-3, 9-21; Ob 15-21; Mc 7:8-13; Zch 14:1-9; Mt 25:31-46; Rv 16:12-16; 19:19-21).

II. Second Lament: The Lord's Punishment of Jerusalem's Sin (2:1-22)

The focus moves from the personified city of Jerusalem to the punishment God inflicted on the city. First, the Lord's anger is depicted (vv. 1-10), followed by Jeremiah's grief as he wept over the destruction of his beloved city, including his call for the people to repent (vv. 11-19), and finally the people's response and Jeremiah's prayer for mercy (vv. 20-22).

A. The Lord's Anger at Jerusalem's Sin (2:1-10)

The second lament began by focusing on the real cause for Jerusalem's calamity. God was the One who destroyed Jerusalem in righteous judgment. The words depict an image of the Lord personally overseeing the dismantling of the city: "He" and "His" are used more than 25 times to indicate the Lord's participation. The verb "swallowed up" (*bala*, "to engulf completely") was used four times (vv. 2, 5 [twice], 8) to picture the fire of God's judgment engulfing the city. Other vivid terms are: "cast from heaven" (v. 1), "thrown down" (v. 2), "cut off" (v. 3), "burned" (v. 3), "destroy/ed" (vv. 5, 6, 8), "violently treated" (v. 6), "abandoned" (v. 7), "destroyed and broken" (v. 9). These words describe the havoc and disaster in Jerusalem, but recognize that the Lord was the one responsible for the rubble.

2:1-5. God's **anger** (vv. 1 [twice], 3; cf. 1:12; 2:6, 21-22; 3:43, 66; 4:11) and **wrath** (2:4; 3:1; 4:11) were directed against the strongholds of the **daughter of Judah** (v. 2). The **daughter of Judah** refers specifically to the people and city of Jerusalem (1:15; 2:5) as do the parallel phrases **daughter of Zion** (1:6; 2:1, 4, 8, 10, 13, 18; 4:22) and daughter of Jerusalem (vv. 13, 15). These words referred to the physical dwellings, **habitations** (2:2), **palaces** (vv. 5, 7), and **strongholds** (vv. 2, 5). They also included the leadership, **kingdom**, and **princes** (v. 2). Thus, God brought down **all the habitations of Jacob** (v. 2). King Zedekiah and the royal family were ousted from their positions of leadership. The phrase to **cut off all the strength** (lit., "every horn") **of Israel** (v. 3) probably referred to the royal family, the Davidic dynasty, which was reaching its end. A "horn" was a common metaphor for power and pride (cf. Pss 75:10; 132:17; Jr 48:25). Thus, God removed all those to whom the people looked for guidance and leadership.

His right hand (v. 4) is a symbol of divine power (cf. Ex 15:6, 12). The intensity of destruction by the Lord seemed like a **fire** (vv. 3-4) and like an **adversary** or **enemy** (vv. 4-5), bringing about **mourning and moaning** (v. 5) among the people of Judah.

2:6-7. God's anger was directed specifically against His temple: He **violently treated** His **tabernacle**. The **tabernacle** is the temple (cf. Ps 27:4-5), **His appointed meeting place** (Ex 25:22; Ps 74:4). With the judgment on Jerusalem, God **violently** destroyed the temple just as a farmer would tear down a temporary **garden booth** (hut) built for shade. Without the temple, religious observance **in Zion (The appointed feast and sabbath**, cf. Ex 3:15) would be **forgotten** (v. 6) because **the Lord** had **rejected His altar** and **abandoned His sanctuary** (v. 7). The Lord had **delivered** the whole city (**walls of her palaces**) into the **hand of the enemy**. The **noise** in the **house of the Lord** was not the joyous sound of temple worship, but the enemy's shouts of victory (v. 7).

2:8-9. The Lord's destruction was **determined** ("calculated") and **not restrained**. It was computed with the precision of a builder's measuring **line**. Jerusalem was **destroy[ed]**, and there was **lament** from her **rampart** and **wall[s]** to her **gates**. Just as the physical protective walls around Jerusalem were destroyed, so was her leadership devastated. The **king and her princes** (cf. v. 2) were exiled **among the nations**. The destruction of the temple meant there was no need for priests (v. 6) and **the law is no more** (v. 9). The law was not ended, but it could no longer be kept without the temple in which to offer sacrifices. The **prophets** had been so corrupted by charlatans (cf. Jr 23:9-32; 28; Ezk 13) that they had no **vision** or communication **from the LORD** (Lm 2:14). Thus, every group charged by God to lead the people—the king, the priests, and the prophets—was affected by Jerusalem's fall.

2:10. The people mourned their loss of leadership, **the elders** along with **the virgins**, meaning that everyone—young and old and all in between—was grief stricken. In sorrow and anguish they sat **on the ground**, **silent**, with **dust on their heads**, in **sackcloth**, with their heads **bowed . . . to the ground** (cf. Gn 37:34; Jb 2:12-13; Neh 9:1); these were typical Jewish mourning practices at the loss of loved ones.

B. Jeremiah's Grief Over Jerusalem's Sin (2:11-19)

Jeremiah, known as "the weeping prophet," wept in anguish as an eyewitness to the "destruction." The causes of his tears are sketched here in five portraits.

2:11-12. The first portrait highlighted the starvation that devastated Jerusalem during the siege, especially the suffering of the children. Jeremiah wept so much his **eyes** failed **because of tears**, a picture of prolonged emotional distress. His **spirit** was **greatly troubled** and his **eyes** blinded by tears. (cf. 3:48-49). His **heart** (lit., "liver") was **poured out on the earth**, meaning that he was fully drained emotionally. His heart broke as he described **little ones and infants**, fainting and starving **in the streets** (cf. v. 19). They asked for food as their lives ebbed away in **their mothers' bosom**. Parents who loved their children could not provide even the necessities of life.

2:13. The second portrait was of a man trying desperately to offer comfort to a grieving friend. The city's hopeless condition prompted Jeremiah to address Jerusalem directly: **How shall I admonish you?** Sadly her **ruin** and brokenness were so severe, **as vast as the sea**, that there was nothing to be done to **heal** the **virgin daughter of Zion**. Only the Lord our Healer (Ex 15:26) could restore Jerusalem.

2:14. The third portrait was of false **prophets** who hastened rather than prevented Jerusalem's downfall. Their **false and foolish** messages had not **exposed** or rebuked **iniquity**. God had warned Jerusalem that sin would lead to captivity. The prophets should have announced this impending disaster and exhorted the people to repent; instead they predicted peace and prosperity. Jeremiah and Ezekiel were true prophets of God, who were persecuted for their faithful messages (cf. Jr 28:1-4, 10-11; 29:29-32). Jerusalem chose to ignore the true prophets' warnings and to listen to **false and misleading** lies of the false prophets, which could not deliver them from **captivity**.

2:15-17. The fourth portrait pictured the victorious enemy mocking the vanquished people. **Jerusalem**, once known as **the perfection of beauty** and a **joy to all the earth** (Pss 50:2, 48:2), was now the object of hissing and derision. God caused her **enemy to rejoice** in their victory (cf. Lm 3:46).

Jerusalem was reminded not to believe the boasts of the enemy, but to know that God was in control. It was not her enemies who gained the victory for themselves: **The LORD has done what He purposed** to the city. The enemies of Jerusalem were victorious, and could **rejoice over** her, only because God had **exalted** their **might** and given them the victory. God **accomplished His word** (cf. Dt 28:64-68; Lv 24:14-17; 2Kg 24:1-5), and had **thrown** the Jewish people **down** (overthrown) **without sparing** (cf. Lm 2:2, 21; 3:43) because of the sins of His people.

2:18-19. The fifth portrait is of the remnant of people, the **daughter of Zion** crying out **to the Lord** with tears **like a river day and night**. To **pour out your heart like water** is an expression of deepest, sincere prayer. The people were to unleash their innermost thoughts and emotions in prayer to God (cf. Pss 42:4; 62:8; 142:2).

There is a similarity between Jeremiah's exhortation to the remnant and his own response (cf. Lm 2:11). In both cases (1) they were weeping and in torment, (2) they poured out their feelings in prayer to God, and (3) the focus of their grief was the heartrending scene of starving children. Jeremiah ended the expression of his personal grief by calling on Jerusalem to respond to her calamity (vv. 12-19) as he had: **Arise**, cry aloud in the night; **Pour out your heart**; **Lift up your hands to Him**.

C. Jerusalem's Plea for the Lord's Mercy (2:20-22)

2:20(a-b). The lament now transforms into a prayer of direct address to the Lord. In a cry of pain and horror, the city called on God to **look** and think about her calamity. Starvation was everywhere during the siege, leading to appalling self-preservation. Some **women** became cannibals and ate **their offspring**, the children they cared for. Moses had predicted this horror when he warned Israel of the consequences of disobedience to God's law (cf. Lv 26:27-29; Dt 28:53-57). This reprehensible practice surfaced only during the most desperate times (cf. 2Kg 6:24-31).

2:20c-21b. Priest and prophet were **slain** inside the temple **sanctuary** as the Babylonian army rushed in for the conquest. No one was spared: corpses of the elderly and children, **young and old**, lay unburied **on the ground in the streets**, with **virgins**, unmarried girls, and **young men**. When Babylon finally did break through Jerusalem's defenses, its soldiers were furious because Jerusalem had kept them at bay for 30 months. They made no distinction between age and sex; the bloodthirsty Babylonians butchered uncounted thousands.

2:21c-22. The ultimate Judge is again brought to mind (v. 17). The Lord **[You, Your]** was the One wielding the sword of punishment in the hand of the Babylonians. They prevailed only because He let them prevail **in the day of the LORD's anger**. God had warned Israel that He would do so if she disobeyed Him (Lv 26:14-39; Dt 28:15-68) and He faithfully carried out His word. Those whom He had loved, whom He **bore and reared**, were now **annihilated**.

III. Third Lament: Jeremiah's Response to Jerusalem's Desolation (3:1-66)

The third lament is the heart of Jeremiah's short book. This chapter gives the book a positive framework around which the other chapters revolve. The black velvet of sin and suffering in chaps. 1–2 and 4–5 serves as a fitting backdrop to display the sparkling brilliance of God's loyal love in chap. 3.

This chapter differs markedly from the first two. Instead of 22 verses it has 66—three verses for each letter of the Hebrew alphabet, instead of one verse per Hebrew letter. It also begins without the familiar "How" (*'ekah, perhaps* better translated "Alas") that stands guard over chaps. 1, 2, and 4 (1:1, 2:1; 4:1). Instead, a first-person narrative unfolds as Jeremiah describes his reaction to the suffering he has experienced. He uses his own experience as representative of many of the sufferings Israel endured at the fall of Jerusalem.

The chapter is divided into three sections. First, it describes Jeremiah's afflictions during Jerusalem's fall (vv. 1-18). Then it reveals Jeremiah's knowledge of God's ways, in the midst of affliction, which produced hope in Him (vv. 19-40). Finally, it includes Jeremiah's prayer to God for deliverance, restoration, and vindication (vv. 41-66).

A. Jeremiah's Afflictions by the Lord (3:1-18)

3:1-9. Jeremiah is Judah's representative: **I am the man who has seen affliction**. He then identifies the source of the affliction as **the rod of His** (the Lord's) **wrath** (v. 1; cf. 2:2, 4; 4:11). God had **driven** him and **made** him **walk in darkness** instead of light. The Lord had **turned His hand repeatedly all the day** against him (v. 3) (cf. 1Sm 5:6; Jb 19:21). The physical suffering was matched by inner **bitterness** (Lm 3:5, 15). He could see no way out, lamenting that God **shuts out** [Jeremiah's] **prayer** and has blocked his ways of escape (3:8, 9). Jeremiah was broken in body and spirit.

3:10-18. Jeremiah described his difficult circumstance of falling under the rod of God's wrath (v. 1) as ambush attacks (cf. Jr 11 and 26). He pictured this as falling prey to **a bear lying in wait** or **a lion in secret places**, leaving him **torn to pieces** (Lm 3:10, 11). Jeremiah, a representative of the people of Israel, was a **target** for the Lord's **arrows** of punishment (vv. 12-13). He had no comfort from his **people**; instead, he was **a laughingstock** and endured **mocking** by them (v. 14; Jr 20:7).

Jeremiah foretold that Jerusalem would be fed with **wormwood**, a bitter plant symbolizing hardship; and that they would drink poisonous water (cf. Jr 23:15). Here Jeremiah was **filled . . . with bitterness** and **drunk with wormwood** (Lm 3:15) and without **peace**, **happiness**, **strength**, or **hope** (vv. 17-18).

B. Jeremiah's Hope in the Lord (3:19-40)

3:19-24. Jeremiah's condition was parallel to Judah's. His outward **affliction** (v. 19a; cf. vv. 1-4) and inward **bitterness** (v. 19b; cf. vv. 5, 13, 15) pushed him toward despair—he was **bowed down** (v. 20). However, his hope was sustained by recalling (**surely my soul remembers**) God's loyal covenant love and His deep compassion for His people. There are two possible interpretations of v. 22 based on the textual variants. The Masoretic text has a first person plural verb of the Hebrew verb for "complete" (*tamam*) yielding the translation "Because of the LORD's faithful love we do not perish" (HCSB and similarly, KJV, NKJV, NIV). However, the various ancient texts (LXX, Syriac, Aramaic) have an alternate reading with a third person plural verb of the same Hebrew verb, yielding the translation **the Lord's lovingkindnesses indeed never cease** (NASB and similarly, ESV, RSV, NET). This variant reading is preferred because of the strong external support and the internal evidence of the synonymous parallel statement that follows, **for His compassions never fail**.

The Lord was punishing Judah for her sin, but He did not reject her as His covenant people. The word **lovingkindnesses** is *chesed*, a word describing God's special characteristic of "loyal love" to those with whom He is in a covenant relationship (Dt 7:9, 12). Further, God's "loyal love" is frequently linked with His forgiveness and mercy (Ex 34:6-7; Ps 103:4). Despite the Lord's judgment, which resulted in sorrowful conditions, God would never abandon the people whom He had chosen. The covenant He made with Abraham (Gn 12:3) and confirmed with Isaac and Jacob (Gn 26:1-5; 28:4) was an unconditional, unbreakable covenant (Jr 31:35-37). The Sinai covenant made with Israel (Dt 28) had not been abrogated. In fact, God's loyal love could be seen in His faithfulness in carrying out the consequences (curses) of the Sinai covenant. He had promised judgment for disobedience, while at the same time preserving a remnant of the people. This judgment on Jerusalem itself testified to God's faithfulness and was proof that He had not abandoned His people. God's never failing **compassions** (His gentle feeling of concern for those who belonged to Him) were still evident.

Could Judah push God so far that He would finally abandon her forever? Was God's supply of loyal love and compassion limited? Jeremiah's answer was, "No!" God's **lovingkindnesses** are **new every morning** (Lm 3:23). God offered a fresh supply of loyal love every day to His covenant people, based on His character and covenant keeping faithfulness to Israel. He was faithful to discipline them for their sin because of His great love for them. He had not abandoned them or terminated His relationship with them despite their sin, and those who repented of their sin experienced His love, even in the midst of judgment. For Jeremiah and the faithful remnant living through the days of judgment, God's presence and comfort were **new every morning**. Today those who love the Lord Jesus, but are going through difficult times, can daily experience the love and faithfulness of God's presence and care by trusting Him, spending time in prayer, reading Scriptures, and staying in the fellowship of others who love and serve the Lord. Much like the manna in the wilderness, the faithful supply of God's love could not be exhausted. This truth caused Jeremiah to call out in praise, **Great is Your faithfulness** (v. 23). Because of this, Jeremiah resolved to **wait for** God to act and bring about restoration and blessing. He could trust God despite his circumstances because he understood the inexhaustible supply of God's loyal love.

3:25-40. The God who brought the curses of Dt 28 would also bring about the restoration promised in Dt 30. In the meantime, God's people needed to develop the proper attitude toward their afflictions. Jeremiah wrote seven principles about the nature of Israel's affliction: (1) Affliction should be patiently endured (**wait**) (v. 25) with **hope** (v. 29) in God's **salvation**, that is, ultimate restoration (vv. 25-30). (2) Affliction is not **forever** and is tempered by God's **compassion** and love (vv. 31-32). (3) God does not delight in affliction, nor does He **afflict willingly**, that is, He is not capricious in judgment and when He does judge it is with reluctance (v. 33). (4) If affliction comes because of injustice, God sees it and does not approve of it (vv. 34-36). (5) Affliction is always in relationship to God's sovereignty; nothing can occur unless He **has commanded it** (vv. 37-38; cf. Jb 2:10). (6) Affliction ultimately came upon the nation because of Judah's **sins**, as all have sinned, fallen short of God's holy standard, and have no grounds for complaint (Lm 3:39; Is 59:2, 64:6). (7) Affliction should accomplish the greater good of calling people to **return to the Lord** (Lm 3:40).

Jeremiah was able to place his (and Israel's) affliction in proper perspective by remembering how it related to God's character and His covenant with Israel. Judah's afflictions were not cruel acts of a capricious God who delighted in inflicting pain on helpless people. Rather, the afflictions came from a compassionate but just God who was being faithful to His covenant. He did not enjoy making others suffer, but He ordained the afflictions as a temporary means to force Judah back to Him. So Jeremiah ended this section by exhorting the people, **let us examine and probe our ways, and let us return to the Lord** (v. 40).

C. Jeremiah's Prayer (3:41-66)

3:41-47. This prayer, **we lift up our heart and hands Toward God in heaven** (v. 41), flows out of the exhortation to "return to the LORD" (v. 40). This section is written in the plural (**we, us, our**), showing Jeremiah's identification with the people. As God rescued Jeremiah and judged his enemies, so He would rescue Judah and judge her enemies if she would call on Him. Judah should confess that she had **transgressed** (*pasha*, to cross the line, to break away from righteous authority, to apostatize), and **rebelled** (*marah*, to be rebellious against, to provoke with sinful behavior; this term is often used of Israel during the wilderness wanderings) thus turning back to the Lord (v. 42).

All the sufferings include Jerusalem being **slain** (v. 43), **no prayer** answered (v. 44), seen as **refuse** or garbage among **the peoples** (v. 45), mocked, feeling panic (vv. 46-47), experiencing **devastation** and **destruction** (v. 47). All of these stemmed from her disobedience to God. When Judah would realize the awful consequences of her sin, she would finally admit her guilt.

3:48-51. Here Jeremiah abruptly shifted from the plural ("we") to the singular ("my"). It is a transition from the people's confession (vv. 41-47) to his own example (vv. 52-66).

As the people confessed their sin and waited for God to respond, so Jeremiah continued to weep (cf. 2:11) and would pray **until the LORD looks down and sees from heaven** (v. 50). God promised to restore Israel when she called on Him from her captivity (Dt 30:2-3). So Jeremiah vowed to continue calling for God's restoration of His people until the event actually happened. This is an excellent example for God's people to pray continually and not lose heart.

3:52-55. Jeremiah's ministry during Judah's final days created many **enemies** (v. 52). The people from his own hometown plotted to kill him (Jr 11:18-23), and the temple leadership called for his death (Jr 26:7-9). He was beaten and thrown into prison as a traitor (Jr 37:11-16), and later near the end of Nebuchadnezzar's siege, left to starve to death in a muddy cistern (**pit**, Jr 38:1-6).

3:56-58. Jeremiah's **cry for help** from the pit was answered: **You drew near when I called on You**. God rescued him from certain death in the muddy cistern (Jr 38:7-13). So Jeremiah was a living example to Judah of God's loyal love and faithfulness (Lm 3:22-23). God did deliver (**redeemed**) when he called on Him for help.

3:59-66. Jeremiah called on God to vindicate him (**Judge my case**). This was fulfilled historically when Nebuchadnezzar entered Jerusalem. The leaders responsible for rejecting and persecuting Jeremiah for his message from the Lord were punished by Babylon (Jr 39:4-7; 52:7-11, 24-27). The parallel to Jerusalem was obvious. She too, was persecuted by her enemies (Lm 3:46-47); but she could be confident that God would vindicate her before her enemies if she would turn to Him. The Lord promised to **recompense them** and **destroy them from under the heavens**.

IV. Fourth Lament: The Lord's Wrath Poured Out on Jerusalem (4:1-22)

Chapter 4 parallels the judgment discussed in chap. 2. After describing the response of an individual (Jeremiah) in the midst of judgment (chap. 3), Jeremiah returned to a scene of calamity in Jerusalem. He contrasted the conditions in Jerusalem before and after the siege (4:1-11), explained the causes for the siege, (4:12-20), and gave a call for vindication for Zion (4:21-22).

A. The Contrast of Zion Before and After the Siege (4:1-11)

4:1-2. The opening exclamation, **How** ("Alas" cf. 1:1; 2:1), points to Zion's tragic situation. **Zion**, or Jerusalem, whose **precious sons**, the inhabitants, were compared to **pure gold** and **sacred stones**, are now **changed**. They have lost their luster (social rank and influence) and been scattered at the **corner of every street**. The Jewish people were now **regarded as earthen jars**. Clay was common material used in Israelite pottery. These **earthen jars** were abundant and inexpensive. If one broke, it was thrown out and a new one replaced it. Similarly the people of Jerusalem, God's precious people, had seemingly become worthless.

4:3-4. Loathsome animals were used in contrast and comparison to some of the desperate mothers of Jerusalem during the siege. First, **jackals** were associated with areas of desolation and destruction (cf. Is 35:7; Jr 9:11; 10:22; 49:33; 51:37; Mal 1:3); yet, in contrast, even jackals **nurse their young**. But the children of the people of Jerusalem were starving, so weak that they could not nurse. Thus **the tongue of the infant** cleaved **to the roof of its mouth**. Second, **ostriches** are known proverbially for the neglect of their young, abandoning their eggs in the sand (cf. Jb 39:14-18). Similarly, Jeremiah laments that the **daughter of my people**, those who lived in Jerusalem, were **cruel** as **ostriches** because of the conditions associated with the siege. The **little ones ask for bread**, but no one takes care of them or **breaks it for them** (cf. Lm 2:19).

4:5. Wealth was no protection against the sufferings under siege. People who once had the finest foods, **delicacies**, and wore the finest **purple** garments (purple was the color of royalty because purple dye was so rare and expensive to produce) were now **desolate in the streets**. They would **embrace** (*chabaq*, to embrace or fold, implying a fondness or affection) the **ash pits** (*ashpoth*, refuse heap, ash pit or dung hill). Their situation was so destitute even the garbage dump was desirable to them. Rather than dressing in the finest clothing, enjoying the richest foods, they were scavenging in the dumps for food and perhaps applying the ashes as medication to their wretched bodies (cf. Jb 2:8).

4:6. This section of the lament concludes with Jerusalem compared to **Sodom**. But her punishment for **iniquity** was worse than Sodom's because (1) Jerusalem's punishment was prolonged under siege, while Sodom was **overthrown . . . in a moment**; and (2) Jerusalem's destruction came despite assistance from an ally, Egypt, while Sodom had no assistance (**no hands were turned toward her**).

4:7-9. Jeremiah's second stanza (vv. 7-11) paralleled his first (vv. 1-6), but the illustrations here are both heightened and narrowed for effect. The "sons of Zion" (v. 2) are now called the **consecrated ones**, people set apart, notionally devoted to the Lord. The leaders of the city suffered the same fate as everyone else. Their beauty is described in the most glowing terms (cf. Sg 5:10, 14) (**purer**, **whiter**, **ruddy** [tan]), polished); their fine complexions and healthy bodies did not escape the ravages of the siege. They became dirty, sickly, and emaciated with hunger—**blacker than soot**, **shriveled**, **withered**, **like wood**—in stark contrast to their early description (cf. 5:10). It would be better to die a quick death by the **sword** than a slow painful death by **hunger**.

4:10-11. The horror of maternal cannibalism is the lowest point of the siege. The gnawing pangs of hunger (cf. 1:11, 19) finally drove **compassionate women** to cook and eat their own children (**boiled . . . they became food**) (cf. comments on 2:20).

Jeremiah concluded this second stanza by again pointing to **the Lord** as the source of Zion's punishment (cf. 1:12-17; 2:1-8; 5:20). Jerusalem was experiencing God's **wrath** (cf. 2:2, 4; 3:1) and **fierce anger** (cf. 1:12; 2:3, 6) for her sin. God's judgment was like a **fire in Zion** (cf. 2:3) that **consumed** the entire city down to the **foundations**. God's people cannot take their own sin lightly.

B. The Causes of the Siege of Zion (4:12-20)

4:12. Jerusalem was such a mighty fortress, a walled city of strong **gates** on a hill, that she had seemed unassailable. On a few occasions previously, the city had been entered by invading armies (cf. 1Kg 14:25-28; 2Kg 14:13-14; 2Ch 21:16-17). But its defenses had been rebuilt and strengthened (cf. 2Ch 32:2-5; 33:14), and a water supply into the city was established with the digging of Hezekiah's tunnel (cf. 2Ch 32:30). So, by Jeremiah's time, even **the kings of the earth**, the foreign nations, considered the city impregnable. Yet God kindled a fire in Zion and consumed its foundations (Lm 2:3).

4:13-16. One cause of Jerusalem's fall was **the sins of her prophets and the iniquities of her priests**. The spiritual leaders had become corrupt. Instead of promoting righteousness and stressing faithfulness to God's covenant, these men had **shed . . . the blood of the righteous**, and therefore were **defiled with blood**. They were so polluted with sin that they were treated like people who had been defiled by touching corpses, and therefore shunned as **unclean** (Lv 19:11). They were forced out of the covenant community and **fled and wandered** (cf. Lv 13:45-46). God's judgment upon them for leading the people into sin was that He **scattered** them among the nations. The MT has third person plural verbs in the phrases **they did not honor . . . they did not favor** (Lm 4:16). However, the LXX and all the majority of the variant readings have third person singular verbs "He did not honor . . . He did not favor." This is probably the correct reading, indicating that the Lord who had **scattered** them did **not continue to regard** the wicked **priests** and **elders**. The MT probably reflects an intentional scribal change to avoid the appearance that God has disfavored the priests and elders.

4:17-19. The second cause of the fall was the futility of foreign alliances. Instead of trusting in God, the Jewish leaders had turned to Egypt for protection from Babylon. They looked for help from **a nation that could not save**. Both Jeremiah and Ezekiel had warned against trusting in Egypt for protection (Jr 37:6-10; Ezk 29:6-7). That false hope of military assistance from Egypt brought only bitter grief when the **end had come**. Babylon's armies **hunted our steps** and **were swifter than the eagles**, and those who tried to escape to the **mountains** or **the wilderness** were pursued, chased, and caught in ambush (cf. Hab 1:8).

4:20. The third cause of Jerusalem's fall was the failure of Zedekiah, Judah's king. He had opposed Jeremiah's message from the Lord (Jr 32:1-5) and followed the false prophets. Zedekiah was the **LORD's anointed**. The word **anointed** (*mashiach*) was used of the kings of Israel because oil was poured on their heads to indicate that they were set apart for their task by God (cf. 1Sm 10:1; 16:1; 1Kg 1:39-45; 2Kg 11:12). When Jerusalem fell, Zedekiah tried to escape (Jr 39:2-7), but he was **captured** by the enemy's **pits** (traps). His children were also captured and killed before his eyes, then he was blinded and carried away in chains to Babylon. King Zedekiah, to whom Jerusalem looked for security (**Under his shadow We shall live among the nations**), was powerless to protect her.

C. The Call for Vindication Against Edom, Enemy of Zion (4:21-22)

4:21-22. Because of God's covenant with Israel (Dt 28–30) the people could hope for vindication. The last two verses in chap. 4 draw a contrast between Israel and her enemy, Edom, and promise judgment on the enemies of Zion.

Edom is the epitome of Israel's enemies. She seems to have taken an active role in promoting Jerusalem's fall to Babylon and rejoiced to see it fall (Ps 137:7). Nevertheless, God's judgment of them (cf. Jr 49:7-22; Ezk 25:12-14; 35) was on the way (**the cup will come around to you,** cf. Lm 1:21-22). Drinking from a cup pictured judgment (cf. Jr 25:15-28). Edom's crimes against Jacob (Dt 23:7) represented the actions of all the nations that profited at Jerusalem's expense. God had noted their actions, and would punish those nations for their sin, exactly as He had said He would do (Dt 30:7). Just as God judged Jerusalem for her sin in Jeremiah's day, so one day He would also judge Edom (and, by extension, all Gentile nations) for their sins. Jerusalem could look forward to restoration, but **Edom** could only expect judgment (cf. Ob 4, 15-18, 20-21).

V. Fifth Lament: The Remnant of Jerusalem's Response (5:1-22)

The prophet's final lament breaks the earlier pattern in two ways: first, the acrostic pattern is *not* used; and second, it is more of a prayer than a lament. Chapters 1, 2, and 3 close in prayer (1:20-22; 2:20-22; 3:55-66), but no prayer is included in chap. 4. Perhaps chap. 5 functions as the closing prayer for chap. 4, as well as the concluding prayer for the whole book. The remnant, the Jewish people who were faithful to the God of Israel, called on Him to restore both the land and people of Israel, as well as to bring the blessings of the covenant (Dt 30:1-10).

A. The Remnant's Prayer for the Lord to Remember Zion (5:1-18)

5:1. The remnant cried to God to **remember** what they had suffered, **what has befallen**, and look at their **reproach** and disgrace (cf. 3:34-36). The call was not just for God to **see** what had happened (for He sees everything, cf. Pr 15:3). The prayer was for Him to help Jerusalem.

5:2-4. Written in the first person plural (*we, us, our*), Jeremiah's words record the people's description (vv. 2-10) of their suffering under Babylonian occupation (cf. Jr 40:10; 41:3; Ezk 35:10). The land of Israel was the **inheritance** the Lord had given the Jewish people (Ex 15:17; Nm 34:1-2; Dt 25:19; Jr 3:18). Now it had been parceled out to cruel **strangers** and **aliens**. The Jewish people as a whole were oppressed and brought to the social and economic level of **orphans** and **widows** (cf. Lm 1:1), even having to pay for the most basic necessities like **drinking water** and **wood** for cooking and heat. Judah was the vanquished enemy, and Babylon her cruel overlord (cf. Hab 1:6-11).

5:5. Babylon's rule over Judah was severe, **at** their **necks**. Both in Judah and in Babylon the Jews were **worn out** and found **no rest** from their pursuers (cf. Dt 28:65-67; Ezk 5:2, 12).

5:6-8. Tragically, Judah had **submitted to Egypt and Assyria to get enough bread**. The words translated **submitted to** (*natannu yad*) literally mean "to give the hand to" or "to shake hands," a phrase used of establishing a pact or treaty (cf. 2Kg 10:15). It often referred to one group surrendering or submitting to a more powerful group in a treaty (1Ch 29:24; 2Ch 30:8; Jr 50:15). Judah had pledged her allegiance both to Egypt and Assyria in her history, for the sake of national security (cf. Ezk 16:26-28; 23:12, 21). Judah's past leaders, their **fathers**, had shifted their allegiances between countries instead of trusting in the Lord. Therefore, although they had **sinned** and died and were **no more**, their survivors bore the punishment for the previous generation's **iniquities**. The present generation, however, did not claim to be suffering unjustly (cf. Lm 5:16); they saw their punishment as a logical conclusion to their ancestors' folly. Their forefathers' alliances with godless nations were bearing bitter fruit. The servants of Nebuchadnezzar were the oppressors of Judah (**slaves rule over us**), and **there** was **no one to deliver** them.

5:9-10. People had to **risk** their **lives** to survive. Leaving the city meant going to the **wilderness** to buy **bread** (food), where they were attacked by robbers carrying a **sword**. Their **skin** was feverish, **hot as an oven**. High fever and dry skin (**the burning heat of famine**) is a common side effect of starvation (cf. 3:4, 4:8).

5:11-13. Here Jeremiah's text switches from the first person ("we," "our") to the third person ("they," "their"). Having first identified with the general conditions of the sufferings of the Jewish people (vv. 2-10), he now presents specific groups within society to highlight their condition (vv. 11-12). No element of society escaped the hammer of judgment.

First **the women in Zion** (adults, probably wives) and **the virgins**, (sexually pure, unmarried young women), of the **cities of Judah** suffered the horrors of foreign occupation. They were **ravished,** mercilessly raped by the sadistic soldiers (v. 11). Second, the leadership, young (**princes**) and old (**elders**), were humiliated (**not respected**), tortured (**hung by their hands**), and executed publicly (v. 12). Third, the **young men** (young adults) and **youths** (boys) were enslaved to hard labor. Because of the shortage of domestic animals in Judah (probably because most had been eaten during the 30-month siege), young men and boys were forced to perform work usually done by animals: **at the grinding mill** (as Samson also had been forced to do; cf. Jdg 16:21) and carrying heavy **loads of wood**. Those who were Judah's hope had been reduced to the status of slaves (Lm 5:13).

5:14-15. Wisdom, justice, and happiness had departed from the city. The **elders** sat at the city **gate** to wisely settle disputes and administer justice (Jos 20:4; Ru 4:1-2, 11). Now they were **gone**. The joyful **music** (cf. Ps 95:1-2) of the **young men** had **ceased**. There was no **joy** in their **hearts**, and their **dancing** was **turned into mourning**, just as Jeremiah had foretold (Jr 25:10-11).

5:16. The crown, the glory and majesty of the Davidic line, had **fallen** (1:1, 2:15, cf. Is 28:1, 3; Jr 13:13-19). For Judah, the fall of the Davidic line had more far-reaching implications than it would for other peoples. The messianic hope was anchored in the Davidic covenant (2Sm 7:16). Realizing the seriousness of their transgression, they confessed their guilt: **Woe to us, for we have sinned!**

5:17-18. Because of all the judgment, their hearts were **faint**, sick with sorrow (Is 1:5); their **eyes** were **dim** from constant weeping (cf. Lm 2:11; 3:48-49). The focus of their grief was **Mount Zion**, the glory of Israel (2:1), which lay **desolate** ("deserted," "a horror," "appalling"). The once regal, thriving city, His appointed meeting place (1:1, 4; 2:6, 15), was a ruin, inhabited by **foxes**.

B. The Remnant's Prayer for the Lord to Restore Zion (5:19-22)

5:19. After describing her condition (vv. 1-18), Jeremiah recorded how Judah concluded her prayer by calling on God to act (vv. 19-22). She called on God because of His eternal sovereignty: **You, O Lord, rule forever; Your throne is from generation to generation** (cf. Ps 102:12). Zion's suffering was not because the gods of Babylon were stronger than the God of Israel. The God of Israel was the only true God, and He had caused her calamity (cf. Lm 1:12-17; 2:1-8; 4:11). Yet God, who brought about her destruction, alone had the power to bring about her restoration—if He chose to do so.

5:20. The knowledge of God's ability to restore the nation prompted the people to ask two questions, parallel in Hebrew poetic form. Why had the Lord forgotten, and why had He forsaken Judah? To **forget** about Judah would be to **forsake** her to her present condition of suffering. Note that **forget** used here is the opposite of "remember" in v. 1. God cannot *forget* anything. This figure of speech means "to forsake" or "abandon" the people as though He has forgotten them. The people were asking God why He had abandoned them for so long. Significantly, Moses employed the figure of God remembering His covenant if His people would confess their sin (Lv 26:40-42). So the people of Judah were calling on God, asking Him to remember His covenant promise (2 Ch 7:14; Jr 31:17-18).

5:21-22. The prayer implores God, **Restore us to You, O Lord, that we may be restored**; or "Turn us back to Yourself, that we may return to You" (cf. Jr 31:18). The Lord is the initiator of revival and restoration. The people wanted to be restored to the blessings of relationship to the Lord and of God's covenant, which included being returned to the land of Israel (Lv 26:40-45; Dt 3:1-10). Their ultimate hope for restoration was God's faithfulness to His covenant promises. In Scripture, the expectation of the restoration of Israel was always eschatological and messianic. In Dt 4:30 the return from dispersion is said to take place "in the latter days." In the

Prophets, Israel's restoration would begin with their return to the Lord when they would "seek the LORD their God and David their king; and they will come trembling to the LORD and to His goodness in the last days" (Hs 3:5).

After the final note of hope and confidence in future restoration, the closing verse speaks of God potentially rejecting and being **angry** with Israel. This concluding verse was so distressing to ancient rabbis, that in order not to end on this dire phrase, they established the custom to repeat the previous verse (Lm 5:21) at the conclusion of any public reading of Lamentations. Thus, the book would conclude with a statement of confidence and hope: **Restore us to You, O LORD, that we may be restored**.

The troubling phrase is: **Unless** God had **utterly rejected** the nation and seems to indicate that it would be possible for God to reject Israel. However, God vowed never to reject His people (Rm 11:1). No matter what the outward circumstances or depth of the national sin, the Lord will keep His covenants with His chosen people (Lv 26:44; Gn 12:1-2; 2Sm 7:16; Jr 31:31-37; Rm 11:28-29).

Thus, the message of book of Lamentations is of God's love and faithfulness. Despite severe suffering because of her sin, Judah had not been abandoned as a nation. God was still sovereign, and His covenant with Israel was still operative despite her disobedience. "The Lord's lovingkindnesses indeed never cease, For His compassions never fail. They are new every morning; Great is Your faithfulness" (Lm 3:22). The hope for the nation was that if she would call on God and confess her sin, the Lord would protect her during her captivity (3:21-30) and would ultimately restore her as a nation to covenant blessing under the leadership of King Messiah ruling on David's throne (v. 19).

BIBLIOGRAPHY

Berlin, Adele. *Lamentations: A Commentary.* Old Testament Library. Louisville, KY: Westminster John Knox, 2002.

Cohen, Abraham. *The Five Megilloth.* London: Soncino Press, 1946.

Dobbs-Allsopp, F. *Lamentations.* Louisville, KY: Westminster John Knox, 2002.

Ellson, Henry. "Lamentations." In *Expositor's Bible Commentary*, edited by Frank E. Gabelein. Grand Rapids, MI: Eerdmans, 1986.

Garrett, Duane, Paul R. House, and David Hubbard. *Song of Songs and Lamentations.* Word Biblical Commentary, vol. 23B. Nashville: Thomas Nelson, 2004.

Harrison, R. K. *Jeremiah and Lamentations: An Introduction and Commentary.* Tyndale Old Testament Commentaries. Downers Grove, IL: InterVarsity, 1973.

Hillers, Delbert R. *Lamentations.* The Anchor Bible, rev. ed. Garden City, NY: Doubleday & Co., 1992.

Huey, F. B. Jr. *Jeremiah and Lamentations.* The New American Commentary. Nashville: Broadman Press, 1993.

Ironside, H. A. *Jeremiah: Prophecy & Lamentations.* New York: Loizeaux Brothers, 1950.

Jensen, Irving L. *Jeremiah and Lamentations.* Everyman's Bible Commentary. Chicago: Moody, 1974.

Kaiser, Walter C. Jr. *A Biblical Approach to Personal Suffering.* Chicago: Moody, 1982.

Provan, Iain. *Lamentations.* New Century Bible Commentary. Grand Rapids, MI: Eerdmans, 1991.

Ryken, Philip. *Jeremiah and Lamentations.* Wheaton, IL: Crossway Books, 2001.

EZEKIEL

Charles H. Dyer with Eva Rydelnik

INTRODUCTION

The message of Ezekiel was given after the first exiles had been taken captive from Judah to Babylon (597 BC, 2Kg 24:12-16) and continued to the destruction of Jerusalem by Nebuchadnezzar (586 BC, cf. Ezk 33:21; Jr 39:1; 2Kg 25:1-12). While Ezekiel was proclaiming the word of the Lord to the captives in Babylon, Daniel was serving the royal court of Nebuchadnezzar, and Jeremiah was ministering in Jerusalem under siege. For further details of Judah's history in Ezekiel's time see the Introduction to Jeremiah.

Author. The author is "Ezekiel the priest, the son of Buzi" (1:3). Like Jeremiah (Jr 1:1) and Zechariah (Zch 1:1; Neh 12:4, 16), Ezekiel was also a priest. They were the only prophet-priests, and all three prophesied during the exilic or postexilic periods. Although he was from a priestly family and knowledgeable about priestly duties and temple details, nothing is recorded about his service as a priest.

The name Ezekiel means "God will strengthen" or "God will harden." His name indicates his character and task because when the Lord called him to be a prophet, He told Ezekiel the people would not heed His message. However, the Lord would give Ezekiel "a forehead harder than flint" in order to carry God's word to a resistant people (3:4-11).

The internal evidence of Ezekiel's authorship is strong. The autobiographical style of the book and the frequent first-person pronouns identify him as the writer. "I," "me," and "my" are in almost every chapter of the book (cf. 2:1-10).

Ezekiel's ministry began "in the thirtieth year" (1:1), probably a reference to his age. Thus he was commissioned as a prophet at the same age he became qualified to enter the priesthood (cf. Nm 4:3). Based on this, he was born in 627 BC. He was deported to Babylon with King Jehoiachin (1:2; 33:21) in the eighth year of Nebuchadnezzar (597 BC; cf. 2Kg 24:14) and ministered to the exiles in Babylon before and after the fall of Jerusalem.

Ezekiel lived with a group of captives in the Babylonian city of Tel-abib on the Chebar River (3:15). The location of the settlement is unknown, but the Chebar River has been identified with the Grand Canal in Babylon, perhaps where the captives mourned for fallen Jerusalem (Ps 137:1).

In Babylon he lived in his own house (8:1) where the exiled elders of Israel came to speak with him (3:24; 8:1; 14:1; 20:1). Ezekiel had a beloved wife, but apparently no children. During his ministry, his wife died, but the Lord forbade him to mourn. Her death and his handling of grief were a sign to the exiles (24:15-17). Many events in the prophet's life were object lessons to Israel from the Lord (e.g., 3:24-26; 4:12; 5:1; 24:27). He apparently died in Babylon among the captives, but no details are known.

Date. Ezekiel began prophesying in the "fifth year of Jehoiachin's exile" (593 BC; 1:2), with his last dated prophecy being "in the twenty-seventh year, in the first month, on the first of the month" (March 26, 571 BC; 29:17). So Ezekiel's prophetic activity spanned at least 22 years (age 30 to 52; 593–571 BC). For the book's many chronological notations see Introduction: Structure and Style.

Until the 20th century, few Bible scholars questioned the unity, authorship, or date of Ezekiel. Yet, when some critical scholars questioned the historicity of the Babylonian destruction of Judah, they dismissed Ezekiel entirely. Contemporary archaeology and biblical studies, however, have corroborated the events of Ezekiel.

Other critics suggest the book is postexilic, written about 400 BC by an unknown redactor. They deny Ezekiel's authorship for three main reasons. First, they doubt a prophet would give such harsh messages of judgment along with words of comfort. However, most OT prophets spoke both judgment and comfort. Second, they allege that Ezekiel has an Israelite viewpoint, rather than a Babylonian perspective. This is not problematic because Ezekiel and his readers were Israelites in exile. Third, these critics suggest the message of Ezekiel is drawn from fictional accounts and fanciful stories. This rationalistic presupposition denies both the history of Babylon and the supernatural quality of God's revelation (for more detailed responses to these critics, see Gleason L Archer, Jr., *A Survey of Old Testament Introduction*, rev. ed. [Chicago: Moody, 1996], 410-413; and John B. Taylor, *Ezekiel: An Introduction and Commentary*, TOTC, ed. D. J. Wiseman [Grand Rapids, MI: Eerdmans, 1969], 13-20).

Ezekiel was consistently included in the Hebrew canon, although there was rabbinic controversy concerning the millennial sacrifices in Ezekiel in contrast to the Mosaic law (Nm 28:11; Ezk 46:6). The rabbis struggled with this issue (*b. Sab.* 13b) and decided that this controversy would await clarification until the days of the Messiah *(Seder Olam 26; Rashi; Radak).* In the Hebrew canon, Ezekiel follows Isaiah and Jeremiah among the Major Prophets. In the Greek canon, which the English arrangement follows, Ezekiel was placed after Lamentations, since that small book by Jeremiah, Ezekiel's contemporary, shares a similar message.

Recipients. Ezekiel lived among the Jewish exiles in Babylon and proclaimed God's message to them (2:3; 3:1). He warned the captives not to believe the false prophets who denied God's coming judgment of Jerusalem and called them to repent and turn back to the Lord. His prophecies of judgment to the Gentile nations served as a message of hope for the Jewish people, reminding them of God's faithfulness to avenge His people. His message of the millennial kingdom was a beacon of hope for captives, awaiting the King Messiah.

Structure and Style. The book of Ezekiel has several major structural and stylistic characteristics.

1. The book has a chronological arrangement, evident from the dates of the messages (1:2; 8:1; 20:1; 24:1; 29:1, 17; 30:20; 31:1; 32:1, 17; 33:21; 40:1). The "year of the exile" indicates the year that began with King Jehoiachin's exile (597 BC, 2Kg 24:8). The majority of Ezekiel's prophecies are arranged chronologically, starting with "the fifth year" of the exile, (592 BC, Ezk 1:2) and ending with "the twenty-fifth year of our exile," (40:1, 573 BC).

The only chronological exceptions are the prophecies introduced in 29:1, 17. These two variations may be explained because they are grouped topically as part of the prophecies against Egypt (chaps. 29–32). Ezekiel is the only Major Prophet with such a precise chronological arrangement, although the Minor Prophets Haggai and Zechariah have a similar arrangement.

2. Ezekiel also has structural balance, with a distinct order and harmony throughout. The book begins with Ezekiel's call to ministry (chaps. 1–3). The first major section focuses on the judgment of Judah (chaps. 4–24), while the last section addresses the restoration of Judah (chaps. 33–48). These two extremely opposite perspectives are divided by a section dealing with God's judgment on the nations for their treatment of Israel and Judah (chaps. 25–32).

3. The book uses several literary devices. Ezekiel used more symbols, allegories, and object lessons than any other prophet. He presented God's messages in dramatic and forceful ways to compel Israel to respond. He used proverbs (12:22-23; 16:44; 18:2-3), visions (chaps. 1–3; 8–11; 37; 40–48), parables (chaps. 17; 24:1-14), symbolic actions (chaps. 4–5; 12; 24:15-27), and allegories (chaps. 16–17).

Themes. *Glory of the Lord.* The glory of the Lord is a major theme in the book, and it is presented in visions unique to Ezekiel. He focused on the glory and character of the Lord, beginning with the vision of God's glory when he was commissioned, and continued to refer to the glory of the Lord throughout, concluding with "The LORD is there." (1:28; 3:12, 23; 8:4; 9:3; 10:4, 18-19; 11:22-23; 39:11, 21; 43:2-5; 44:4; 48:35). He showed the glory of the Lord departing from the temple in judgment (9:3; 10:4, 18-19; 11:22-25) and the return of His glory at the end of days in the millennial temple (43:1-5).

Son of Man. Ezekiel is called "son of man" 94 times by the Lord (e.g., 2:1; 3:1; 4:1; 5). This expression indicated Ezekiel's mission and status as a representative of humanity, and the distance between humanity and God. In Scripture "son" often goes beyond a physical descendant to denote association or identification. This title highlights Ezekiel's role and task.

Ezekiel's "son of man" is distinct from Daniel's use, which is a messianic title (Dn 7:13; 8:17). The phrase "son of man" is used 85 times in the NT, primarily in the Gospels, almost always by Jesus referring to Himself (e.g., Mt 8:20; 11:19; 12:8; Rv 1:13) When Messiah Jesus used the title "Son of Man," He was referring to Daniel's messianic use as prophecy of the One who would be "given dominion, Glory and a kingdom" (Dn 7:13-14; Mk 14:62; Rv 1:7).

For the sake of His name. The book also emphasizes the consistent character of the Lord, which caused God to act in judgment as He did. God declared 15 times that He had behaved "for the sake of His name" to keep His name from being profaned (e.g., 20:9, 14, 22, 39, 44; 36:20-23 [twice in 23]; 39:7 [twice], 25; 43:7-8).

Know that I am the Lord. Moreover, God said He had acted so that the people would "know that I am the Lord." This phrase is used over 60 times in the book (e.g., 6:7, 10, 13-14; 7:4; 39:22) to stress His identity as the covenant-keeping One. He always acts to make Himself known.

The Lord God. Ezekiel used the identification "the Lord God" (*Adonai Yahweh*) 217 times. Elsewhere in the OT the phrase occurs only 103 times. This name stresses both God's sovereign authority and His covenant-keeping faithfulness (Otto Eissfeldt, "'adhon," *Theological Dictionary of the Old Testament*. ed. G. Johannes Botterweck and Helmer Ringgren, trans. John T. Willis [Grand Rapids, MI: Eerdmans, 1974], 1:62-63).

Judgment and hope. In light of God's consistent character, the book includes the themes of both judgment and hope. Ezekiel was commissioned to deliver a message of judgment (chaps. 2–3) and declared judgment to those who lived in iniquity and continued in false hope (37:11). On the other hand, Ezekiel later was recommissioned to give a message of deliverance and hope, based on God's faithfulness to His covenants and mercy to those who would turn to Him (chap. 33).

The messianic theme is not as prominent in Ezekiel as in Jeremiah or Isaiah. However, there are strong messianic aspects to the book. The Messiah is presented as (1) a sprig from the line of David (17:22); an allusion to Is 11:1; (2) the future rightful King (Ezk 21:26, 27; cf. Gn 49:10; Rv 5:5); (3) the horn the Lord will cause to sprout, an intertextual link to the Davidic promise in Ps 132:17; (4) the True Shepherd who will restore Israel (Ezk 34:11-31; cf. Jr 23:5-6; Jn 10:1-10); and (5) the King Messiah and Son of David who will reign over the messianic kingdom from Jerusalem (Ezk 37:15-28).

The book of Ezekiel begins with the prophet's call to ministry, in which he has a vision of divine glory (chaps. 1–3). The first half of the book focuses on God's coming judgment of Judah for their iniquity and call for repentance (chaps. 4–24). The next section is prophecies of God's judgment of the Gentile nations for their treatment of the Jewish people (chaps. 25–32). The book closes with the regathering of the Jewish people to Israel, their rebirth, and details of the coming millennial kingdom and the messianic reign in a restored Jerusalem (chaps. 33–48).

OUTLINE

I. Prophetic Call to Ministry (1:1–3:27)
  A. Call from Priest to Prophet (1:1-3)
  B. Visions of the Throne of the Lord (1:4–2:7)
    1. Vision of the Four Living Beings (1:4-14)
    2. The Vision of the Four Wheels (1:15-21)
    3. The Vision of the Expanse (1:22-25)
    4. The Vision of the Throne (1:26-28)
    5. The Task for Ezekiel, the Son of Man (2:1-7)
  C. Message for Ministry (2:8–3:11)
    1. The Vision of the Scroll (2:8–3:3)
    2. The Delivery of God's Word to Rebellious Israel (3:4-11)
  D. Motivation for Ministry (3:12-27)
    1. Ezekiel Led by the Spirit (3:12-15)

2. Ezekiel Appointed as a Watchman for the House of Israel (3:16-21)
3. Ezekiel's Physical Restraints by the Lord (3:22-27)

II. Exilic Judgment of Judah (4:1–24:27)
- A. Necessity of Judah's Judgment (4:1–11:25)
  1. Four Signs of Coming Judgment on Jerusalem (4:1–5:17)
     - a. Sign of the Brick (4:1-3)
     - b. Sign of Ezekiel's Lying on His Sides (4:4-8)
     - c. Sign of the Unclean Food (4:9-17)
     - d. Sign of Ezekiel's Shaved Head and Divided Hair (5:1-17)
  2. Messages of Coming Judgment (6:1–7:27)
     - a. Message: Idolatry, the Cause of Judgment (6:1-14)
     - b. Message on the Nature of Judgment (7:1-27)
  3. Vision of Coming Judgment (8:1–11:25)
     - a. Vision of the Wickedness in the Temple (8:1-18)
     - b. Vision of the Slaughter in Jerusalem (9:1-11)
     - c. Vision of the Departure of God's Glory from the Temple (10:1-22)
     - d. Judgment on Jerusalem's Rulers (11:1-25)
- B. Futility of Judah's False Optimism (12:1–19:14)
  1. Two Signs of Impending Captivity (12:1-20)
     - a. Sign of the Baggage and the Hole in the Wall (12:1-16)
     - b. Sign of Trembling While Eating and Drinking (12:17-20)
  2. Five Messages on the Certainty of Judgment (12:21–14:23)
     - a. First Certainty of Judgment Message: Correcting the Proverb About Visions (12:21-25)
     - b. Second Certainty of Judgment Message: Correcting the Proverb About Delay (12:26-28)
     - c. Third Certainty of Judgment Message: Against False Prophets and Prophetesses (13:1-23)
     - d. Fourth Certainty of Judgment Message: Condemnation of Idolatry (14:1-11)
     - e. Fifth Certainty of Judgment Message: Unavailing Prayer of Noah, Daniel, and Job (14:12-23).
  3. Three Parables on Judgment (15:1–17:24)
     - a. Parable of the Fruitless Vine (15:1-8)
     - b. Parables of Unfaithful Jerusalem (16:1-63)
       - (1) Parable of the Rescued Infant Who Became the Adulterous Wife (16:1-43)
       - (2) The Parable of the Sisters: Jerusalem, Sodom, and Samaria (16:44-59)
       - (3) The Faithfulness of God and the Everlasting Covenant (16:60-63)
     - c. Parable of the Two Eagles (17:1-24)
  4. Message on Individual Responsibility (18:1-32)
  5. Parable of Lamentation for Israel's Final Kings (19:1-14)
- C. History of Judah's Iniquity (20:1–24:27)
  1. Message of Israel's Past Rebellion and Restoration (20:1-49)
     - a. Israel's Past Rebellion (20:1-32)
     - b. Israel's Future Restoration (20:33-44)
     - c. Parable of the Forest Fire (20:45-49)
  2. Four Messages of the Sword (21:1-32)
     - a. The Sword Drawn (21:1-7)
     - b. The Sword Sharpened (21:8-17)
     - c. The Sword Directed Toward Jerusalem (21:18-27).
     - d. The Sword Directed Toward Ammon (21:28-32)
  3. Three Messages on the Defilement and Judgment of Jerusalem (22:1-31)
     - a. Cause of Jerusalem's Judgment (22:1-16)
     - b. Means of Judgment (22:17-22)

c. Recipients of Judgment (22:23-31)
4. Parable of the Two Adulterous Sisters: Oholah and Oholibah (23:1-49)
a. Infidelity of the Sisters: Oholah and Oholibah (23:1-21)
b. Punishment of the Sisters (23:22-35)
c. Conclusion of the Message to Oholah and Oholibah (23:36-49)
5. Parable of the Boiling Pot (24:1-14)
6. Sign of the Death of Ezekiel's Wife (24:15-27)

III. Ultimate Judgment on Gentile Nations (25:1–32:32)
A. Judgment on Ammon (25:1-7)
B. Judgment on Moab (25:8-11)
C. Judgment on Edom (25:12-14)
D. Judgment on Philistia (25:15-17)
E. Judgment on Tyre (26:1–28:19)
1. Destruction of Tyre: Oracle One (26:1-21)
2. Dirge Over Tyre: Oracle Two (27:1-36)
3. Downfall of Leader of Tyre: Oracle Three (28:1-10)
4. Downfall of Power behind King of Tyre: Oracle Four (28:11-19)
F. Judgment on Sidon (28:20-26)
G. Judgment on Egypt (29:1–32:32)
1. Sin of Egypt (29:1-16)
2. Defeat of Egypt by Babylon (29:17-21)
3. Destruction of Egypt and Her Allies (30:1-19)
4. Scattering of Egypt (30:20-26)
5. Allegory of Assyria and the Fall of Pharaoh King of Egypt (31:1-18)
a. Allegory of Assyria as a Cedar Tree (31:1-9)
b. Downfall of Assyria (31:10-14)
c. Descent of Assyria into the Grave (31:15-18)
6. Lament for Pharaoh (32:1-16)
7. Descent of Egypt into Sheol (32:17-32)

IV. Eschatological Blessings for Israel (33:1–48:35)
A. New Life for Israel (33:1–39:29)
1. Ezekiel Is Reappointed as a Watchman (33:1-33)
a. Ezekiel's Duties as a Watchman (33:1-20)
b. The Opening of Ezekiel's Mouth (33:21-33)
2. Present False Shepherds Contrasted with the Future True Shepherd of Israel (34:1-31)
a. Present False Shepherds of Israel (34:1-10)
b. Future True Shepherd of Israel (34:11-31)
3. Edom, the Enemy of Israel, Destroyed (35:1-15)
4. The People of Israel Blessed (36:1-38)
a. Israel's Mountains Will Prosper (36:1-15)
b. Israel's People to Be Regathered (36:16-38)
5. Nation of Israel Restored (37:1-28)
a. Vision of the Dry Bones (37:1-14)
b. Sign of the Two Sticks—Israel United (37:15-28)
6. Prophecy of Attack and Defeat of Gog (38:1–39:29)
a. Invasion of Israel by Gog (38:1-16)
b. Judgment of Gog by God (38:17–39:29)
(1) Defeat of Gog (38:17–39:8)
(2) Aftermath of the Defeat of Gog (39:9-20).
(3) Effects of the Lord's Defeat of Gog on Israel (39:21-29)
B. New Order for Israel (40:1–48:35)
1. A New Temple (40:1–43:27)
a. Introduction to the Vision of the Temple (40:1-4)

b. Outer Court of the Temple (40:5-27)
c. Inner Court of the Temple (40:28-47)
d. The Temple Building (40:48–41:26)
e. Chambers in the Inner Court of the Temple (42:1-14)
f. Outer Walls of the Temple (42:15-20)
g. Return of the Lord's Glory (43:1-12)
h. Altar of Burnt Offering (43:13-27)

2. A New Service of Worship (44:1–46:24)
a. The Temple Ministers (44:1-31)
b. Land Allotment for the Temple and Priests (45:1-8)
c. Warning to Jewish Leaders Living in Babylon (45:9-12)
d. Offerings in the Temple (45:13–46:24)

3. A New Land (47:1–48:35)
a. The River from the Temple (47:1-12)
b. Boundaries of the Land (47:13-23)
c. Division of the Land (48:1-29)
d. Gates of the City (48:30-35)

COMMENTARY ON EZEKIEL

I. Prophetic Call to Ministry (1:1–3:27)

God's commission of Ezekiel is the longest prophetic call in the Bible. Like Moses (Ex 3:1-10), Jeremiah (Jr 1:1-10), and Isaiah (Is 6:1-10), Ezekiel was called and prepared for his ministry by a supernatural encounter with the holiness of the Lord.

A. Call from Priest to Prophet (1:1-3)

1:1-2. Ezekiel was called as a prophet **in the thirtieth year**, probably a reference to his age. Ezekiel was a priest (cf. v. 3), and 30 was the age he would enter the Lord's priestly service (Nm 4:3). The vision came **On the fifth of the month in the fifth year of King Jehoiachin's exile**, (Tamuz 5/July 31, 593 BC, 2Kg 24:8-17).

Ezekiel had been taken into captivity with King Jehoiachin (March 597 BC, 2Kg 24:12-15), and settled **among the exiles** of Judah by the **river Chebar**, off the Euphrates River. There **the heavens were opened and** Ezekiel **saw visions of God** (cf. Ezk 1:4–2:7). God's messages to Ezekiel were often in the form of visions (cf. 8:1; 9:1; 10:1; 11:24; 12:27; 37:1, 11; 40:1; 43:1-3).

1:3. That the word of the LORD **came expressly to Ezekiel** indicates the exactness and seriousness of his call. Ezekiel was a **priest**, and was given the additional ministry of prophet. Ezekiel's mandate for his ministry was by **the hand of the LORD**, signifying the powerful call of divine revelation, a phrase repeated six times in the book (3:14, 22; 8:1; 33:22; 37:1; 40:1).

B. Visions of the Throne of the Lord (1:4–2:7)

This section describes Ezekiel's vision of God's holiness (1:4-28) in detail and his specific call (2:1-7).

1. Vision of the Four Living Beings (1:4-14)

1:4. This vision of God (cf. v. 1) was shown to Ezekiel first: **As I looked, behold** (cf. v. 5) **a storm wind . . . a great cloud . . . with fire flashing . . . continually** and **bright light**. This was a storm-like manifestation of the Lord. There was **something like glowing metal in the midst of the fire**, a word used only twice in the OT, both times describing God's glowing splendor (cf. v. 27; 8:2).

1:5. The **figures resembling four living beings** are later identified as cherubim (cf. 10:1). Angels in this category have special access to God (cf. 28:14, 16) and serve as guardians of His holiness and His throne chariot (Gn 3:22-24). On the ark of the covenant, gold images of cherubim, with outstretched wings, guarded the mercy seat where the glory of the Lord was enthroned (Ex 25:17-22; Nm 7:89; 1Sm 4:4; 2Sm 6:2, Pss 80:1; 99:1; Is 37:16). Since the earthly tabernacle and temple were a copy of the heavenly reality (Heb 8:5), Ezekiel's vision was a glimpse of the actual throne chariot of God borne by cherubim.

These **figures** had the **appearance** or likeness of **human form**. The terms "resembling" "appeared," and "were like" are used in Ezk 12 times to emphasize that the descriptions are impressionistic because the vision is so difficult to describe (cf. vv. 5, 10, 16, 22, 26; 2:8; 8:2; 10:1; 10:10, 21-22; 23:15).

1:6-7. The angelic beings had human form but should not be mistaken for mortals. Each of the four living beings had **four faces** and **four wings**, enabling them to move in all directions as needed. Their **legs were straight**, implying they were standing upright. Their **feet were like a calf's hoof**, perhaps indicating agility (Ps 29:6; Mal 4:2), and were like **burnished bronze**, seeming highly polished and not like ordinary animal hooves.

1:8-9. They had **wings** on **four sides**, as well as **human hands**, giving them both supernatural and natural characteristics. Two of the four **wings** of each one were outstretched so that **their wings touched one another**, forming a connecting square. Having **faces** on four sides of their heads, they could simultaneously see in all directions. They were able to travel **straight** in any direction and could change direction but **did not turn**, indicating the supernatural movement.

1:10. The front of each cherub was the **face of a man**, and on the right side was the **face of a lion**. The left side was the **face of a bull**, and the **face of an eagle** was apparently in the back (cf. Rv 4:7). Perhaps these images represent intelligence, courage, strength, and speed.

1:11. Two of the four **wings** on each cherub were **spread out above**, and were **touching** a wing of a cherub on either side, forming a square with a cherub at each corner. The other **two** wings on each cherub were **covering their bodies** in reverence as they served the Lord in His holy presence (cf. 1:23; Is 6:1-3).

1:12. The cherubim always moved **straight forward**, so they could go in any direction **without turning**. Their movement was directed by **the spirit** (e.g., Gn 1:2; 6:3; Ex 31:3; Ps 139:7), a reference to the Holy Spirit of God's guidance of these beings (cf. Ezk 1:20; Ex 13:21-22; Nm 9:15-23; Mt 4:1).

1:13-14. In the midst of **the living beings** was **something . . . like burning coals of fire . . . like torches**. This image of **lightening . . . flashing from the fire** and the urgency of the cherubim running **to and fro like bolts of lightning** indicate the power and urgency of God's message.

2. The Vision of the Four Wheels (1:15-21)

Following the description of the living beings is the vision of the wheels, one of the most familiar, but enigmatic, images in Ezekiel. This is a description of the throne chariot (cf. v. 26) of God Almighty with its awesome wheels (vv. 15-18) and cherubim/living beings (vv. 19-21).

1:15-17. The second part of the vision, concerning the wheels, is introduced with **I looked** (cf. v. 4). On the **earth** beside **each** of the **living beings** was a **wheel** of **sparkling beryl**, a transparent golden green gemstone. **One wheel** was **within another** so they could move in **four directions without turning as they moved** (v. 7).

1:18. The **rims** of the wheels were **lofty** and **awesome**, tall, and terrifying in appearance (cf. v. 5). This majestic quality was intensified by the **rims** being **full of eyes** all around. This indicates the divine omniscience of the all-seeing Lord God, who rides on this throne chariot (cf. 2Ch 16.9; Pr 15:3).

1:19-21. The **living beings** and the **wheels** were connected in movement (cf. v. 12), because **the spirit of the living creatures was in the wheels**. The **wheels** were an extension of the cherubim beneath the Almighty seated on His throne chariot. As He directed the cherubim, the wheels responded and the chariot would go in any direction.

3. The Vision of the Expanse (1:22-25)

1:22-23. There was a covering **over the heads** of the **living beings . . . something** (cf. comments on v. 5) **like an expanse**, which separated the **beings** from the glory of the Lord (cf. Gn 1:6-7). The **expanse** had the **awesome gleam of crystal**, a shining brilliance John used to describe the throne of the Lord—as "clear as crystal" (Rv 4:6). The outstretched wings of the cherubim joined together, **covering** their bodies in reverence (cf. Ezk 1:11).

1:24-25. When the wings of the cherubim moved, the sound was like **abundant waters**, as intense as the voice of **the Almighty** (*shaddai*). It was the **sound of tumult like . . . an army camp**, with many soldiers marching in rank. This was similar to thunder, which sometimes is heard at God's presence (cf. 43:2; Jb 37:4-5; 40:9; Pss 18:13; 104:7). When the cherubim **stood still**, they **dropped their wings** (vv. 24-25). The **voice from above the expanse** over the heads of the cherubim was the voice of the Lord (cf. v. 28).

4. The Vision of the Throne (1:26-28)

1:26. Above the **expanse** was **something resembling** (cf. comments on v. 5) a **throne**. It looked like **lapis lazuli** ("sapphire"), a costly azure-blue gemstone. Seated on this shining blue throne was **a figure with the appearance of a man**.

1:27-28. His body looked **like glowing metal**

and **something like fire**, surrounded by a **radiance**, like the **appearance of the rainbow**. This dazzling image of the beauty of the Lord is described by the apostle John in his vision of God's heavenly throne (Rv 4:3).

This figure is identified as having the **appearance of the likeness of the glory of the Lord**. Therefore, Ezekiel responded in worship and awe. He **fell on** his **face** (cf. Ezk 3:23; Gn 17:3) and heard **a voice speaking**. This should always be a believer's attitude toward the Lord when considering His glory and majesty.

Ezekiel did not see the Lord God Himself (cf. Gn 16:13; Ex 3:6; 33:20; Jdg 13:22; Jn 1:18), but certain manifestations. It was an indescribable likeness of Him or a theophany (cf. comments on Ezk 1:5; 8:2), symbolically communicating the revelation of the glory, power, and majesty of the Lord (cf. Ex 40:34; Is 6:3). The Lord's **glory** is a key idea in Ezekiel (see Introduction: Themes).

5. The Task for Ezekiel, the Son of Man (2:1-7)

As God spoke (1:28), He empowered Ezekiel (2:1-2), explained Ezekiel's mission (2:3-5), and challenged him to be fearless, despite difficulty (2: 6-7).

2:1-2. God called Ezekiel **Son of man**, (see Introduction: Themes). God told Ezekiel to **stand** so He could **speak with** him. Then the Holy **Spirit** empowered Ezekiel to obey. In the OT period, the Holy Spirit did not permanently indwell believers as He does in the church age (Rm 8:9). Instead, He temporarily indwelt selected individuals for specific divine service (cf. Ezk 3:24; Ex 31:1-11; 1Sm 10:9-11; Ps 51:11).

2:3-4. Ezekiel needed supernatural power to carry God's message to a resistant audience, the **sons of Israel . . . a rebellious people** who were **stubborn and obstinate** (cf. 3:7). "Rebellious" occurs eight times in chaps. 2 and 3 (2:2, 4, 6, 8; 3:9, 26, 27), and seven times elsewhere in Ezekiel (12:2, 3, 9, 25; 17:12; 24:3; 44:6). This description emphasizes that the Jewish people were determined in their disobedience to the Lord, but also that their God was determined in His faithfulness to them, sending His messenger to declare His word to them. The message from the **Lord God** (see Introduction: Themes) was to the Jewish people who had already gone into Babylonian exile.

2:5. Ezekiel had to deliver God's message, **whether they listen or not** (cf. 2:5, 7; 3:11). Israel is called **a rebellious house** in Ezekiel 12 times (2:5-6, 8; 3:9; 26–27; 12:3, 9, 25; 17:12; 24:3) to underscore their defiance against God. Despite their attitude, by Ezekiel's message they would **know that a prophet has been among them**.

2:6-7. The Lord told Ezekiel three times **neither fear them nor fear their words**. Ezekiel needed this encouragement because opposition was certain and the task was difficult. It would be like working among **thistles and thorns** and as dangerous as sitting **on scorpions**. Even so, Ezekiel was to **neither fear** their **words** nor their **presence**. God again commanded Ezekiel to **speak My words . . . whether they listen or not** (cf. 2:4, 3:11).

God's encouragement to Ezekiel to be fearless in his task was a bridge between the vision when he was called to ministry (1:4–2:7) and the message of his ministry (2:8–3:11).

C. The Message for Ministry (2:8–3:11)

1. The Vision of the Scroll (2:8–3:3)

2:8. In contrast to Israel's **rebellious** attitude toward God and His word (vv. 3, 5), Ezekiel was obedient to **listen to what** the Lord was **speaking** to him and to **Open** his **mouth and eat** what God was **giving** him. He was to internalize the word of the Lord and live by it (Dt 8:3; Mt 4:4).

2:9-10. A **hand** gave Ezekiel **a scroll**. The hand was possibly the hand of a cherub (cf. 1:8), but the One speaking was the Lord (cf. vv. 7-8). The scroll had writing on the **front and back**, unusual since most scrolls were written on only one side. Writing on both sides shows the intensity of warning and severity of judgment (cf. Zch 5:3; Rv 5:1). The double-sided message was of **lamentations, mourning and woe**. This summarizes the judgment messages of Ezekiel (Ezk 4–32).

3:1-3. God repeated the command to **eat this scroll** (cf. 2:8) and **speak to the house of Israel**. Ezekiel **opened** his **mouth**, and the Lord **fed** him the **scroll**. Although the message of judgment was woeful (cf. 2:10), the scroll tasted as **sweet as honey** because it was God's word (cf. Ps 19:10; Jr 15:16; Rv 10:9-11).

2. The Delivery of God's Word to Rebellious Israel (3:4-11)

3:4. Ezekiel was commanded to **go** to **the house of Israel**. The phrase **house of Israel**, or a variation, is used more than a hundred times to identify the Jewish people as a whole, both Israel and Judah, in the land of Israel or in exile (cf. 2:5; 6:11; 8:11-12). God said **speak . . . My words to them**.

3:5-6. Ezekiel was **sent to a people** who understood his language. There was no barrier for his message to the Jewish people in Babylonian exile who **should listen** to Ezekiel's message.

3:7. Although there was no language or cultural barrier, **yet the house of Israel** would **not . . . listen** to Ezekiel because they were **not willing to listen** to the Lord. Their sin extended to the **whole house of Israel**. This does not imply that every Israelite rejected God, for Habakkuk, Jeremiah, Ezekiel, and Daniel were all ministering faithfully during these years. A faithful remnant of Israel heeded their message. This general description of **stubborn and obstinate** refers to all parts of Israel without distinction (from the priests and leaders to the common person) rather than every individual Israelite without exception.

3:8-9. The Lord prepared Ezekiel for his difficult task by making the prophet's **face as hard as their faces**. The word for **hard** (*hazaq*) is the root of Ezekiel's name (*y'khezqel*) and means "God will strengthen" or "God will harden." This is a play on words because the people were hardened in their obstinacy, but Ezekiel was made hard/strong for his prophetic mission. Ezekiel's name was a reminder of God's faithfulness and the source of his strength to meet the hardest opposition.

God would also make Ezekiel's **forehead . . . harder than flint** (cf. Jos 5:2-3). The hard stone used to make knives and tools showed Ezekiel's determination to deliver God's message. God commanded Ezekiel **not [to] be afraid of them or be dismayed before them** (cf. Ezk 2:6-7; Jr 1:17). Though opposition was certain, Ezekiel had nothing to fear because God would enable him to meet the resistance of the **rebellious house** (cf. Ezk 2:5).

3:10-11. God commanded Ezekiel to **take into your heart all**—to listen carefully to **all my words**. Ezekiel was identified with the Jewish people in exile as the **sons of your people**. However, the prophet heard and obeyed God's word, although the exiles did not. Ezekiel announced **thus says the Lord God** and was responsible to proclaim God's word **whether they [would] listen or not** (cf. 2:5, 7).

D. The Motivation for Ministry (3:12-27)

Seeing the vision of God's glory gave Ezekiel perspective for his task (1:4–2:7). God provided the message of His word (2:8–3:11), and the hand of the Lord empowered him for the ministry (1:3). This section shows Ezekiel being guided by the Spirit to his place of ministry (3:12-15) and appointed as God's watchman to Israel (3:16-21), with certain restraints (3:22-27).

1. Ezekiel Led by the Spirit (3:12-15)

3:12-14a. The **Spirit** (cf. 2:2) **lifted** Ezekiel **up**, and he heard the **rumbling sound** (cf. 1:24) of the praise **Blessed be the glory of the LORD in His place** and the **sound of** the **wings of the living beings** (cf. 1:15). Several times the Holy Spirit transported Ezekiel in a vision, not physically, to give him instruction (cf. 8:3; 11:1; 24; 37:1; 43:5).

3:14b-15. As Ezekiel understood God by consuming His words (cf. 2:8–3:4) and seeing the vision of His presence (1:22-28; 3:12-13) he felt, as God did toward Israel's sin, **embittered in . . . rage**.

Ezekiel was guided by **the hand of the LORD . . . strong** on him. This picture of God's power and authority to direct appears in Ezekiel seven times (1:3; 3:14, 22; 8:1; 33:22; 37:1; 40:1), and about 90 times in the OT. This does not mean the Lord has actual hands, but it is a figure of speech for God's guidance.

Ezekiel was directed by **the Spirit** to go to **the exiles . . . at Tel-abib**, the Jewish area in Babylon on the **river Chebar** (cf. 1:1). He **sat** there for **seven days**, but he did not deliver a message. His presence caused **consternation**, as the exiles wondered what he would say.

2. Ezekiel Appointed as a Watchman for the House of Israel (3:16-21)

3:16-17. After **seven days** of silence, **the word of the LORD** appointed Ezekiel **a watchman to the house of Israel**. Watchmen were stationed on city walls, hilltops, or watchtowers to warn of approaching enemies or any impending danger (e.g., 2Sm 18:24-25; 2Kgs 9:17; Is 62:6-7; Jr 4:5; 6:1). **Watchman** is often a term used for God's prophets (e.g., Is 56:10; 62:6-7; Jr 6:17; Hs 9:8).

3:18. As God's watchman, Ezekiel was responsible for sounding God's warning of impending judgment to the house of Israel. He was to **warn** both **the wicked** (vv. 18-19) and "the righteous" (vv. 20-21).

3:19. A wicked person would surely **die** unless he turned from his **wicked way**. Those who refused to heed God's warnings to repent would **die in [their] iniquity**. Ezekiel obeyed God by warning the wicked. Ezekiel was not responsible if they did **not turn from [their] wickedness** in response to his message.

3:20-21. A **righteous man** was required to continue faithfully in righteousness, heeding the prophet's warnings, rather than slipping into sin. So he also needed to be **warned** to prevent his turning from his righteousness and committing **iniquity**, for which he would then **die**.

Ezekiel was not accountable for the response to his message but was only accountable to obey God by delivering His message. People who refused to heed his warning had only themselves to blame. If Ezekiel did not deliver the message: **his blood I will require at your hand** (vv. 18, 20); if he did deliver God's word: **you have delivered yourself** (vv. 19, 21).

3. Ezekiel's Physical Restraints by the Lord (3:22-27)

3:22-23. The **hand of the LORD** directed Ezekiel to the **plain** where God would **speak to** him. Here Ezekiel saw **the glory of the LORD** (cf. 1:28) for the second time. Again he responded in reverence and **fell on** his **face**.

3:24. The Spirit again **entered** Ezekiel and made him **stand** up (cf. comments on 2:2), giving him instructions and strength for his ministry.

Along with his specific message from the Lord, Ezekiel was given specific restrictions in communicating God's message. First, he was to **shut** himself **up in** his **house**. He should stay at home. He was not a prisoner, but his field of ministry was confined to his house, with limited contact with the community (cf. 5:2; 12:3). Instead of his going out, the leaders came to him at his house to receive God's word (cf. 8:1; 14:1; 20:1).

3:25. Ezekiel had to stay at home for his own protection, or the people would **put ropes on** him and **bind** him. If he would **go out among** the people at this point, his message would be rejected and his opponents might attack him.

3:26. The second restriction concerned his ability to talk. God would **make** Ezekiel's **tongue stick to the roof** of his mouth so that he would be **mute** and not speak **rebukes** to them. Ezekiel experienced temporary dumbness so that he could not speak to the people. This muteness, however, was not continuous (v. 27) or permanent (33:22). He would speak only when and what God directed.

3:27. There is no contradiction between Ezekiel's commission as a watchman (vv. 16-21) and his prohibition against speaking to the people (v. 26). Ezekiel only spoke God's message and at God's time. God told him: **But when I speak to you, I will open your mouth**. When he was silent, it was because God had not spoken. When he spoke, it was because God had given him a message: **Thus says the Lord GOD** (cf. 2:4).

A person's reception or rejection of Ezekiel's message was a reflection of his openness to God (cf. Ex 16:8; 1Sm 8:7). The section closes, **He who hears, let him hear; and he who refuses, let him refuse**. This is similar to Messiah Jesus' words: "He who has ears, let him hear" (Mt 11:15; 13:9, 43; Mk 4:9, 23; Lk 8:8; 14:35; Rv 2:7).

II. Exilic Judgment of Judah (4:1–24:27)

The book opens with Ezekiel's dramatic call to ministry by the vision of God's glory. He was given the task of watchman for Israel to proclaim God's message of impending judgment to resistant Israel (chaps. 1–3). This first half of the book of Ezekiel is the prophet's message of God's coming judgment of Judah (chaps. 4–24). Ezekiel was to explain to the Jewish people already in Babylonian captivity the causes and details of God's impending judgment on Jerusalem for her sin (chaps. 4–11), warn the exiles against false hope of victory over Babylon (chaps. 12–19), and review the history of Judah's iniquity (chaps. 20–24).

A. Necessity of Judah's Judgment (4:1–11:25)

As a watchmen Ezekiel had to confront Israel with her sin and warn her of impending judgment (cf. 3:17) He used dramatic signs (chaps. 4–5), sermons (chaps. 6–7), and visions (chaps. 8–11).

1. Four Signs of Coming Judgment on Jerusalem (4:1–5:17)

While confined to his home (cf. 3:24), Ezekiel delivered God's message of the coming siege of Jerusalem, enacted in four dramatic signs.

a. Sign of the Brick (4:1-3)

4:1. For the first sign, Ezekiel was to get a **brick** and **inscribe** on it the familiar outline of **Jerusalem**. Soft clay tablets were commonly used in Babylon for writing, and bricks were common building materials.

4:2. After drawing the image of Jerusalem, Ezekiel was to **lay siege** against the Jerusalem image on the brick to demonstrate the city's future. Ezekiel was to attack this Jerusalem image with a **siege wall ... a ramp ... camps ... battering rams**. This depicted upcoming events during the Babylonian siege of Jerusalem (cf. 2Kg 25:1; Jr 24:1; 52:4). Ezekiel was called to ministry in 593 BC (cf. 1:2), and these signs were probably enacted a short time afterward. If so, these warning signs were given about seven years prior to the fall of Jerusalem in 586 BC.

4:3. Finally, Ezekiel **set ... up** against the Jerusalem image **an iron plate ... as an iron wall**. The **iron plate** was the iron griddle commonly used for making bread. The description of it as an **iron wall** showed the inescapable Babylonian siege wall against Jerusalem. Ezekiel was commanded to **set your face toward it** (Jerusalem) to show God's inescapable judgment. This phrase, **set your face**, is used of judgment 14 times by Ezekiel (4:3, 7; 6:2; 13:17; 14:8; 15:7 [twice]; 20:46; 21:2; 25:2; 28:21; 29:2; 35:2; 38:2). Jerusalem had no hope of escaping God's judgment by defeating Babylon. Ezekiel's role-play with the brick was for **a sign to the house of Israel** (cf. 12:6, 11; 24:24-27; Is 8:18; 20:3).

b. Sign of Ezekiel's Lying on His Sides (4:4-8)

4:4-5. God used Ezekiel's posture as a second sign. Ezekiel was to **lie** on his **left side** to emphasize the **iniquity of the house of Israel**, the northern kingdom (since Judah is mentioned separately, v. 6). His actions would not **bear** their iniquity but highlight the nation's sin (taking the Hb. literally as "lift up" not **bear**). He was to lie there for **three hundred and ninety days, corresponding to the years of their iniquity**. The **three hundred and ninety** may refer to the years of golden calf worship initiated by Jeroboam in the northern kingdom, which continued until the fall of Jerusalem (975–586 BC; 1Kg 12:20-33).

4:6. After remaining on his left side, he was to **lie down a second time**, now on his **right side**, and lift up or highlight **the iniquity of the house of Judah** (the southern kingdom) for **forty days**. The **forty** likely refers to the years of Judah's idol worship and iniquity during Manasseh's wicked reign (697–643 BC; 1Kg 21:10-16; 23:26, 27).

Ezekiel did not remain in this position 24 hours a day, because the very next sign (Ezk 4:9-17) includes some other actions that required Ezekiel to move around. He probably remained in this position for a portion of each day as a sign of the sin of Israel and Judah.

4:7. Ezekiel was commanded **set your face** (cf. v. 3) **toward the siege of Jerusalem**. He was to have his **arm** bared, illustrating military readiness.

4:8. To symbolize the confinement the Jewish people would suffer during the Babylonian siege, God had Ezekiel **put ropes on** so he could not **turn from one side to the other**. Apparently Ezekiel was tied up only during the time each day when he lay on his side, but moved around at other times **until** he had **completed** the role-play of the **days** of siege.

c. Sign of the Unclean Food (4:9-17)

4:9-10. The severity of the siege of Jerusalem is Ezekiel's third role-play sign. He had to put **wheat, barley, beans, lentils, millet and spelt** into **one vessel** and **make them into bread**. These are common food grains in Israel (cf. 2Sm 17:27-29) but would usually be cooked separately and not mixed together. However, food was so scarce during the siege that several grains had to be combined to have enough for one loaf. Ezekiel had to **eat** this bread during the **three hundred and ninety days** he was lying on his left **side**. He was to weigh out just **twenty shekels** (about eight ounces) of this bread to eat each day for his ration.

4:11. His daily **water** ration was only a **sixth . . . of a hin** (20 ounces). These meager rations predicted the famine conditions during the siege of Jerusalem (cf. vv. 16-17).

4:12-13. Most repulsive to Ezekiel was the command to bake this **barley cake**, which included the other grains as well (cf. v. 9), using **human dung** for fuel. The Mosaic law gave specific instructions for the disposal of human excrement, and using human excrement for any purpose is a violation of Torah (cf. Dt 23:12-14). However, siege conditions in Jerusalem would destroy most trees, camels, cattle, and donkeys, so there would be no wood or animal dung for cooking fuel. Ezekiel was to **eat** the **barley cake** (bread) . . . **in their sight**, as a sign that they would **eat their bread unclean**, in violation of God's dietary laws, when the Lord would **banish** them **among the nations** (Gentiles).

4:14. Ezekiel begged God not to ask him to violate His law, **Ah, Lord GOD! Behold, I have never been defiled** . . . [or eaten] **any unclean meat**. As a devout Jew, Ezekiel had always kept God's dietary and purity laws (cf. 1:3; Lv 22:8; Dt 14). Therefore, he begged for mercy not to be required to break God's law.

4:15. God mercifully answered Ezekiel's plea, saying, **I will give you cow's dung in place of human dung** . . . to **prepare your bread** so he would not be defiled. Ezekiel was willing to face the rejection of his message without fear (2:1-7), the mental anguish of muteness without complaint (3:26-17), and suffer the physical pain of lying on his side for a year without lament (vv. 1-8), but he pled for mercy not to violate the God's law.

4:16-17. God broke **the staff of bread in Jerusalem**, meaning He destroyed the food supply during the Babylonian siege, so the people would **eat bread by weight and with anxiety** (cf. 12:19; Lm 1:11; 2:11-12, 19) and **drink water by measure and in horror** (Lm 4:4-5, 9). Both food and water would be rationed, just as Ezekiel had modeled (cf. Ezk 4:10-11). Jerusalemites would **waste away**, or starve to death, (cf. Lm 4:8-9) because of **their iniquity**.

d. Sign of Ezekiel's Shaved Head and Divided Hair (5:1-17)

5:1. God commanded Ezekiel to shave his **head** and **beard** with a **sharp sword** like a **barber's razor**. Using a **sword** for a **razor** prefigured military assault. The book of Ezekiel uses **sword** 80 times to describe military attack (e.g., 6:11; 25:13). Moreover, shaving one's head and beard was a sign of mourning (cf. 7:18; Jb 1, 20; Is 15:2-3; Jr 7:29; 48:37) and humiliation (2Sm 10:4-5; Is 7:20), emotions appropriate for defeat. He was to collect the hair, put it on **scales for weighing**, and **divide the hair** to be used as a sign.

5:2. God commanded Ezekiel to take **one third** of his hair to the **center of the city** to **burn** it there; **one third** he was to strike with the **sword**; and **one third** he was to **scatter to the wind**. These actions illustrated what would happen to the inhabitants of Jerusalem when the city would fall to Babylon: a third of the people would die by the sword; a third would perish when the city burned; and another third would be exiled.

5:3-4. A **few** strands of hair remained after the burning, striking, and scattering. Ezekiel was to **bind** these in the **edges of** his **robes** to represent God's preservation of a remnant in the midst of judgment. Even the few hairs were not safe, however, because God commanded Ezekiel to toss **some of them** in the **fire**, depicting the suffering and death awaiting even the remnant. This judgment was for **all the house of Israel**.

5:5. The Lord highlighted the city He chose (Dt 12:5; 2Ch 6:6; Ps 132:13) and loves (Ps 87:2) above all others, saying, **This is Jerusalem; I have set her at the center of the nations** (cf. Ezk 38:12). Jerusalem's unique importance to God is not a simple geographic location, although in the Middle Ages both Rabbinic and Christian literature and maps oriented the whole world toward Jerusalem. The Lord was highlighting Jerusalem's historical and redemptive position (cf. Is 2:1-4; Mc 4:1-3). Jerusalem was the recipient of God's word, the dwelling place of His glory, and the object of His love (Ps 48:2; Neh 1:9; Zch 8:2; Mt 23:37).

5:6-7. Tragically, in spite of this exalted position, Israel **rebelled** (cf. 2:3) against God's **ordinances**, acting **more wickedly** than the Gentile **nations . . . which surround** her.

5:8. Because the people of Jerusalem rejected God's love and laws, He emphatically stated His decision: **thus says the Lord God, 'Behold, I, even I, am against you'** (cf. 13:8; 21:3; 26:3; 28:22; 29:3, 10; 30:22; 34:10; 35:3; 39:11). She would be judged **in the sight of the nations**. God's judgment, the destruction of Jerusalem, would be a public event.

5:9-10. Because of all Jerusalem's **abominations** (ritual uncleanness and moral impurity) something would happen that had never been **done** or would ever happen **again** in Israel. The famine would be so severe that **fathers will eat their sons . . . and sons will eat their fathers**. Because of the extreme famine conditions, some people would resort to cannibalism rather than starve. This horror had been predicted in the law prior to the conquest of the promised land and settlement of Jerusalem (Dt 28:53-57; Lv 26:29). During the siege some parents killed their healthy children for food (2Kg 6:28-29; Lm 2:20; 4:10). Apparently adults were consumed for food as well, however, it is not clear how they died (Jr 19:9). This abhorrent behavior added to their sin, and God would **execute judgments** on them and **scatter** them **to every wind**, meaning expel them from the land in every direction.

5:11-12. Because they had **defiled My sanctuary** the temple, with **detestable idols and . . . abominations**, the Lord would **withdraw** His presence from them (cf. chap. 10) and judge them without **pity**, using the full fury of the four judgments: **plague**, **famine**, **sword**, and **scatter**[ing] (cf. 7:15-16; 14:21; Lv 26:25-26; Dt 32:23-25; Jr 14:11, 22; 24:10). Jerusalem, the object of God's unique favor, would soon become the object of His unique judgment.

5:13. God's judgment would last until the fury of His **wrath** was **appeased**. The emphasis is on the divine source of each judgment: **I, the Lord, have spoken** . . . (vv. 13, 15, 17). God's judgment would continue until He had poured out His **wrath upon them.**

5:14-15. God's judgment on Jerusalem would be humiliating. She would be **a desolation and a reproach among the nations** (cf. Lm 2:15). Yet those ridiculing nations would be horrified at what was happening to Jerusalem, and the carnage in the city would be a **warning** to them.

5:16-17. When the divine judgment of **deadly arrows of famine . . . wild beasts . . . plague**, and the **sword** would (cf. vv. 11-12) fall, God declared that it would demonstrate that **I, the LORD, have spoken**.

2. Messages of Coming Judgment (6:1–7:27)

Following his four dramatic signs (chaps. 4–5), Ezekiel delivered two sermons, both beginning with the phrase "The word of the LORD came to me" (6:1, 7:1). The first message concerned the cause for judgment, Israel's idolatry (chap. 6). The second message depicted the nature of Israel's judgment (chap. 7).

a. Message: Idolatry, the Cause of Judgment (6:1-14)

6:1-3. God commanded Ezekiel to **set** his **face** (cf. 4:3) against **the mountains of Israel** . . . **hills** . . . **ravines** . . . **and the valleys**. This was judgment on the Jewish people, not the geography, for engaging in pagan worship at shrines throughout Israel (cf. 2Kg 21:2-6, 10-15; Jr 2:20-28; 17:1-3; 32:35). Instead of being faithful to worship the Lord in His temple in Jerusalem, the Jewish people followed the pagan practices of the Gentiles and set up pagan shrines throughout the land. Consequently God would **bring a sword** of judgment (cf. Ezk 11:8; 14:17; 29:8; 33:2) to destroy Israel's **high places** of pagan worship.

6:4-5. Both the false places of worship and the worshipers would be destroyed. God would make the **slain** worshipers **fall in front** of their **idols**.

6:6-7. God told Ezekiel that when the people saw the **slain**, then they would **know that I am the LORD**. This key phrase **know that I am the LORD** occurs more than 60 times in Ezekiel (e.g., vv. 7, 10, 13, 14; 7:4; 27; 11:10; 25:17; 39:22) and refers to God's design in judgment. God intended Israel to see His predictions of judgment fulfilled so Israel would recognize the God who made them come to pass.

6:8. God would judge the wicked, but He would **leave a remnant** because of His faithfulness to His chosen people (cf. 5:3-5; 12:16; Gn 12:1-3; Jr 31:31-40). Not all the Jewish people would be destroyed. Some would escape the **sword** when Israel was **scattered** among the **countries**.

6:9-10. The Jewish people who **escape** and live **among the nations** will **remember** God's character and how the Lord had **been hurt** by Israel's **adulterous hearts** when they **turned away** from God. **Adulterous** hearts refers to the spiritual immorality of idol worship, an act of unfaithfulness parallel to marital infidelity. They would also remember God's faithfulness and **know** . . . **I am the LORD** who always does what He promises, even **inflict this disaster** for judgment for disobedience. They would know God never speaks **in vain**.

6:11-12. Because **of all the evil abominations** Ezekiel is to **clap** his **hands** . . . **stamp** his **foot**, (cf. Jb 27:23; Lm 2:15; Ezk 21:14, 17; 22:13; 25:6; Nah 3:19) and **say, Alas!** in derision. Destruction would be by the **sword, famine and plague**—a summary of the judgment announced by Ezekiel's fourth sign (cf. Ezk 5:11-12). Those in Jerusalem who escaped one calamity would only find another waiting to strike them as God fulfilled His **wrath on them**.

6:13. The message of judgment on the Jewish people who engaged in pagan worship (cf. vv. 1-7) is repeated in graphic summary. **Then you will know that I am the Lord, when their slain are among their idols around their altars, on every high hill** . . . **under every green tree** . . . **every leafy oak**. Often altars of the high places were built among stately trees, which represented growth, fertility, and the habitation of spirits (cf. Hs 4:13). God had given His people a land rich with natural resources, but the people defiled His land and used it to offer **soothing aroma** (incense) **to all their idols**.

6:14. God would strike their **habitations** with judgment, making them **more desolate** than the **wilderness toward Diblah**. Although the exact location is unknown, the point is clear: judgment on Israel's idolatry would make the land a ruin. The result of judgment will be the acknowledgment of God's supreme authority: **thus they will know that I am the LORD** (cf. vv. 7, 10, 14).

b. Message on the Nature of Judgment (7:1-27)

7:1-2. The emphasis on **the word of the LORD** (cf. 6:1) in this message is the culmination of judgment: **An end! The end is coming on the four corners of the land**. The word **end** is used five times in this message (vv. 2 [twice], 3, 6 [twice]), predicting the judgment on **the four corners of the land** and indicating that no part of Israel or Judah would escape God's judgment.

7:3-4. The emphasis is on the holiness and wrath of God. The people would realize that God, being righteous, would punish sin. God vowed to **send My anger against** Israel because of her **abominations** (cf. 5:8). God would judge **according to your ways** (cf. vv. 4, 8-9, 27) without **pity**. Being judged on the basis of ways/conduct is mentioned 41 times in Ezekiel (e.g., vv. 8, 9, 27; 9:10; 16:43; 22:31). God would hold them accountable for their wicked actions. Then Israel would **know that I am the LORD** (cf. 6:7).

7:5-6. The **Lord GOD** gave a shout of warning: **A disaster, unique disaster** . . . (twice for emphasis) **behold it is coming**. The Hebrew phrases are short, staccato, and emphatic. The words **coming** or **has come** occur six times in vv. 5-7. This is urgent news of immediate certainty.

7:7. Jerusalem's coming **doom** was certain: **the day is near**. There would be **tumult** (confusion, panic) **rather than** the **joyful shouting** associated with pagan worship **on the mountains** (cf. 6:1-5).

7:8-9. God would **pour out** His **wrath** of judgment (9:8; 14:19; 20:8, 13, 21; 22:31; 30:15; 36:18). The destruction would come as predicted, so those affected **will know that I, the LORD**, had done the **smiting**. This is a variation of the other statements about knowing the Lord as a result of prophecies of judgment against Israel being fulfilled (cf. 6:7).

7:10-11. Behold, the day! Judgment was imminent, for **the rod** (or branch) **has budded, arrogance has blossomed**. The almond tree is the first tree to bloom in Israel (Jr 1:1-12). Just as the budding of the almond branch indicated spring, so the sin of the people signaled God's coming judgment. Israel's **violence** had **blossomed** and grown into a **rod of wickedness**.

7:12-13. Judgment was imminent: **The time has come, the day has arrived** (cf. vv. 5-7, 10). God's **wrath** was against **all their multitude**, and the nation's economy would collapse. After Jerusalem fell, nothing of value would remain, so neither the **buyer** would **rejoice** nor the **seller mourn** over business deals. The judgment could not be **averted** by any means.

7:14. Even sounding **the trumpet** to make **everything ready** for war would be a useless defense against God's **wrath**.

7:15-16. Israel would have no defense and no escape from the wrath of the Lord's judgment by **sword**, **plague**, and **famine** (cf. 5:12). People who **escape** to the **field** would be hunted down and killed by the **sword**. Those who sought protection within the city walls faced **plague** and **famine** (cf. Jr 14:18). The few **survivors** will hide in the **mountains** . . . **mourning** . . . **each over his own iniquity**, recognizing their sin and God's just judgment.

7:17-18. God's judgment will cause everyone to become weak with fear. Their **hands will hang limp** and **knees will become like water** (cf. 21:7). They will act like mourners dressed in **sackcloth** . . . **shuddering** . . . overwhelmed with **shame** (for their sin) . . . cutting their hair in grief, causing **baldness** (Gn 37:34; 1Sm 3:31; Jb 16:15; Is 58:5; Jr 6:26).

7:19. They will **fling their silver into the streets and their gold will become** . . . **abhorrent** because it could not **deliver them in the day of the wrath of the LORD**, nor could it **fill their stomachs**. Their gold and silver idols (cf. Jr 10:1-10) were useless. They could not defend them against God's judgment or stop the famine. The idols were thrown into the street because idolatry had **become** . . . **abhorrent**. The word **abhorrent** (*niddah*) is used of ceremonial impurity (Lv 15:19-33; Nm 19:13-21). The people would feel revulsion toward their idolatry, which was the cause of their **iniquity** and **stumbling**.

7:20. The Lord's house, **the beauty of His ornaments**, had been **transformed** by the **images** of their **abominations** and . . . **detestable things**. Idolatry was rampant during the siege of Jerusalem. After the Babylonian captivity idolatry would become **an abhorrent thing to them**. Jewish history has shown that after the return from Babylon, idolatry was no longer practiced in Israel.

7:21-22. The Jewish people wrongly believed that, because the ark of the covenant was in the temple, Jerusalem was safe from destruction (cf. 1Sm 4-7). Yet God would give His temple **into the hands of the foreigners as plunder** to **spoil** and **profane My secret place**, the Holy of Holies (Jr 52:17-23). Israel's sin was so serious that not even the temple would escape God's judgment (Mc 3:12).

7:23-24. God's command to **Make the chain** previews the people of Jerusalem being taken captive in chains by cruel Babylon, the **worst of the nations**, (cf. 28:7; Jr 6:23; Hab 1:5-11). God **will bring** Babylon to **possess** everything. Israel's confidence (**pride**) in her **strong ones**, her soldiers, and pagan **holy places** would prove useless.

7:25-26. The people will respond to the **disaster** with **anguish** and a futile search for **peace, but there will be none**. No sooner would one catastrophe befall than **rumor** would come of another on the way. The people would seek a word from God, **a vision** from **a prophet** . . . **priest**, and **elders**, but He would not respond because they had rejected God's word already given by His prophets.

7:27. Hearing the message of judgment, **the king** (Jehoiachin), who was already in

Babylonian captivity (cf. 1:2), would **mourn**. The **prince** (Zedekiah, cf. comments on 12:8-11), would be **clothed with horror**, and **the people . . . will tremble**. There would be no direction from the Lord, or leadership from the monarchy, leaving the people terrified. The Lord would **deal with them according to their conduct**. The Lord is not random in His judgment, but after He gave repeated warning to repent, His wrath will fall based on the **conduct** of the people. This standard of judgment is mentioned five times in chap. 7 (vv. 3-4, 8-9, 27) and reiterated throughout the book (cf. 9:10; 11:21; 16:43; 18:30). The judgments were based on the behavior of the people and designed to make them **know that I am the Lord** (cf. 6:7).

3. Vision of Coming Judgment (8:1–11:25)

Since his call to ministry, Ezekiel had received a vision of God's glory (chaps. 1–3), had acted out four signs (chaps. 4–5), and had given two messages on judgment (chaps. 6–7). Now he is given a vision, with four parts focusing on judgment: (1) the wickedness of the people in the temple, chap. 8; (2) the slaughter of the people of Jerusalem, chap. 9; (3) the departure of the glory of the Lord from the temple, chap. 10; (4) and judgment on evil rulers as the glory of the Lord departed, chap. 11.

As Ezekiel was transported in a vision to Jerusalem (cf. 3:14; 11:1, 24; 37:1; 43:5) his body remained in Babylon. The elders seated before him did not see the vision of God, which Ezekiel later described to them (11:24-25).

a. Vision of the Wickedness in the Temple (8:1-18)

8:1. The vision occurred **in the sixth year** (of Jehoiachin's exile, cf. 1:2) in **the sixth month on the fifth day** (Elul 5/September 17, 592 BC). This was exactly 14 months after Ezekiel's first vision (1:1-2).

Ezekiel was **sitting in** his **house with the elders of Judah**. Although Ezekiel's ministry beyond his house was limited (cf. 3:24), the elders of the community could come to his house, where they received Ezekiel's message. The expression **the hand of the Lord God fell on** him (cf. 1:3; 3:14, 22) indicates direction from God, not that He has a literal hand (cf. 8:3).

8:2. Ezekiel saw a **likeness as the appearance of a man** (lit., *fire*). The figure seems to be more than an angelic being, but rather like a manifestation of God (cf. 1:26). From His **loins** (waist) down He was like **fire**, and above his waist His **appearance** was as bright as **glowing metal** (cf. 1:4). Ezekiel did not say that he saw God, but described the **likeness as the appearance** of the supernatural being, which was "the glory of God" (v. 4; cf. comments on 1:5; 1:26-27).

8:3. The **Spirit lifted** Ezekiel **up** (cf. 3:14; 11:1, 24; 37:1; 43:5) **between earth and heaven** and transported him in **visions** to **Jerusalem**, to the **entrance of the north gate of the inner court** of the temple. Here he saw **the seat of the idol of jealousy**. This idol was an insult to God, who was righteously provoked **to jealousy** because of this pagan god receiving worship that was due Him alone (Ex 20:4; cf. Dt 4:23-24).

8:4-6. While Ezekiel was looking at the idol of jealousy, **the glory of the God of Israel** (cf. 1:28; see Introduction: Themes), which he had seen on **the plain**, (cf. 3:23) asked him a rhetorical question: **Do you see what they are doing, the great abominations which the house of Israel are committing** . . . that will drive God **far from My sanctuary?** God will not share His glory with an idol (cf. Is 42:8). As horrible as was the **idol of jealousy**, Ezekiel would **see still greater abominations** (cf. Ezk 8:13, 15).

8:7-9. Then God **brought** Ezekiel **to the entrance of the court** of the temple, probably the inner court, where he saw **a hole in the wall**, and the **entrance** where he saw **the wicked abominations** being committed there.

8:10. Ezekiel **entered** and saw **every form of creeping things and beasts and detestable things . . . the idols of the house of Israel . . . carved on the wall**. This is an unveiled presentation of God's view of idolatry (Rm 1:21-23).

8:11. In the room stood **seventy elders of the house of Israel**. These were the leaders of Israel (cf. Nm 11:16-17) who should have prevented sin, not perpetuated paganism by offering incense in their **censer** to the idol of jealousy. The presence of **Jaazaniah the son of Shaphan** is noteworthy because everyone else in Shapan's family had remained faithful to the Lord (cf. Jr 26:24; 39:14; 40:5).

8:12-13. God told Ezekiel these **elders of the house of Israel** sought to justify their sin by saying **The Lord does not see us; the Lord has forsaken the land**. They thought the sins they were **committing in the dark** were unseen by God. They imagined God had abandoned them in time of trouble (cf. 9:9). They rationalized worshiping other gods for their protection.

The people's progression of idolatry went from open worship on the mountains' high places to idolatry in the temple. Yet this was not the full extent of Israel's wickedness. Ezekiel would **see still greater abominations** (cf. vv. 6, 15).

8:14-15. God brought Ezekiel **to the entrance of the [north] gate** of the **Lord's house**, the outer court of the temple, where he saw **women . . . weeping for Tammuz**. Worship of Tammuz, a Babylonian agricultural fertility god involved beseeching him for rain with weeping and gross acts of immorality. These women of Israel had replaced the worship of the Giver of rain (Lv 26:4; Dt 11:14) with debased paganism. Yet Ezekiel was to **see still greater abominations** (cf. vv. 6, 13).

8:16. Then God **brought** Ezekiel **into the inner court of the LORD's house . . . at the entrance to the temple . . . between the porch and the altar**, the area near the bronze altar on which sacrifices were offered (cf. 1Kg 6:2-3). Here the priests of Israel should have offered sacrifices and cried out to God for mercy (cf. Jl 2:17). Instead, Ezekiel saw **about twenty-five men with their backs to the temple of the LORD and their faces toward the east . . . prostrating themselves . . . toward the sun**. These **men**, probably priests since they were in the temple, had literally turned their backs on the Lord and were worshiping the sun (Dt 4:19).

8:17 The **house of Judah** had **commit**[ted] **the abominations** . . . which **filled the land with violence**—cruelty, corruption, mistreatment of widows and orphans, and immorality. These practices **provoked** God to anger and would bring His judgment (cf. Ex 22:21-22; Is 1:17; 10:1-2; Jr 5:26-29; 22:3).

The expression **putting the twig to their nose** is probably an idiom meaning "to sneer" at someone, or it could be part of ceremonial nature worship. Whichever, the gesture was a gross insult to God.

8:18. God's response to these abominations was resolute: **I indeed will deal** [with them] **in wrath** and . . . **have no pity nor . . . spare**. God would not listen to a last-minute **cry in My ears with a loud voice**. Certainly, God hears all things. However, because of their abominable sin, He would not respond to their voice and spare them.

b. Vision of the Slaughter in Jerusalem (9:1-11)

The second part of this vision is the carrying out of God's judgment on Jerusalem for the wickedness described in chap. 8.

9:1. The Lord **cried out . . . with a loud voice** (cf. 19:19, Ps 29:3-5), indicating urgency, and the opposite of the ineffectual plea of the people (cf. Ezk 8:18). **Draw near, O executioners of the city**, literally "those who punish."

9:2. Then **six men came from the direction of the upper gate which faces north**, (cf. 8:3) the direction from where the Babylonians would invade Jerusalem (cf. Jr 1:14). The area where the worship of the idol of jealousy had taken place. They **each** had **his shattering weapon in his hand**, probably a club or a battle-ax.

Distinct from the group was a seventh figure, **a certain man** who wore **linen** clothing, suggesting dignity and purity (cf. Dn 10:5; 12:6-7). His work of marking the righteous (those who shared God's view of sin) for preservation (Ezk 9:4) suggests He was perhaps the "angel of the LORD," the pre-incarnate Messiah (e.g., Gn 16:7-14; 22:11-15; 31:11-13; Jd 2:1-3). He carried a **writing case**, literally, a "case for the scribe" that held reed pens and an inkhorn. He **stood beside the bronze altar**, the symbol of God's righteousness requirement of sacrifice (Lv 1).

9:3-4. Now **the glory of . . . God** began to move away from the **temple**. From the **threshold of the temple** He gave instruction to the **man clothed in linen. Go through . . . Jerusalem** and **mark**, with the tools in the writing case, **on the foreheads of the men who sigh and groan over all the abominations . . . being committed**. As in Elijah's day, there was a faithful remnant in Judah who had "not bowed the knee to Baal" (cf. 1Kg 19:18). God knew those who had remained faithful to Him, and He would spare their lives when He judged the nation through the Babylonians. This is similar to applying blood to the doorposts at Passover to be spared from death (Ex 12:23) and the seal on the 144,000 faithful witnesses in the tribulations (cf. Rv 7:3-4).

9:5-7. The **others**, the six men, were commanded to **go through the city . . . and strike** those without the mark. But they were not to **touch any man** . . . who had **the mark** made by the man in linen. But everyone who did not have a mark from the scribe was to be destroyed without exception—**do not . . . pity and do not spare**. Judgment was to be **started with the elders** in **the temple** (cf. 1Pt 4:17) who had turned their backs on God (cf. Ezk 8:16) and had led the people astray. Their dead bodies would **defile the temple**, but the temple had already been defiled with their idolatrous practices of the wicked. The Babylonians did this exactly because they "had no compassion on young man or virgin, old man or infirm" (cf. 2Ch 36:17-20).

9:8. Grief stricken, Ezekiel **fell on** his **face** and cried, **Alas, Lord God! Are You destroying the whole remnant of Israel**? Like Abraham, Moses, and Amos, Ezekiel loved the Jewish people despite their sin (cf. 11:13; Gn 18:20-33; Ex 32:11-14; Am 7:1-9).

9:9-10. God explained the **iniquity of . . . Israel and Judah** was **very, very great** (doubled for emphasis) and **filled with blood** (cf. 8:17) and **full of perversion**. They wrongly thought, **the Lord has forsaken** them and **does not see**, (cf. 8:12). However, He corrected them: **My eye** does see and would have **no pity** on their wicked **conduct**, which would bring judgment **upon their heads** (cf. 7:4, 9; 8:18; 24:14).

9:11. The **man clothed in linen . . . reported . . . I have done just as You have commanded me** (cf. v. 4). He had marked the righteous for protection, because each person's destiny is determined by his relationship with the Lord.

c. Vision of the Departure of God's Glory from the Temple (10:1-22)

This vision continues the departure of the Lord from His temple, a process begun in 9:3. God is too holy to share His dwelling place with idolatry. The images of the Lord are similar to those in chap. 1.

10:1- 2. The **man clothed in linen** is told to take . . . **coals of fire** (1:13, cf. Is 6:6) . . . **and scatter them over the city**. God would use the burning coals of judgment to purify Jerusalem (Neh 11:1; Is 52:1).

10:3-5. God's departure from Jerusalem is in stages (cf. vv. 18-19). Now **the glory of the Lord went up . . . to the threshold of the temple** (cf. 9:3). The image of the cherubim is similar to the vision in chap. 1.

10:6-7. The **man clothed in linen** who had marked the righteous for protection now received **fire** from a **cherubim . . . and went out** to bring judgment on Jerusalem (e.g., Jr 4:4; 11:14-17; 15:14; 17:4; 21:12; 2Kg 25:8-9).

10:8-13. More detail is given about **cherubim** and the **wheels** (cf. 1:15-21): **their whole body . . . backs . . . hands . . . wings** and . . . **wheels** were **full of eyes**. This probably represents divine omniscience. They are like the four creatures John saw surrounding God's throne and covered with eyes (Rv 4:8).

10:14. Here the faces of the beings are of a **cherub . . .** a **man . . .** a **lion**, and an **eagle** The face of the bull is replaced by a **cherub** (cf. 1:10), without further physical description. Some have suggested that this is a scribal error, copying "cherub" for "bull," but there is no textual support for this. More likely, the face of a bull was the normal understanding of the image of a cherub because in the ancient Mesopotamian empire of Akkadia the *kuribu* (cognate term for Hb. *cherub*) were portrayed as bulls.

10:15-17, 20-22. The description of the cherubim similar to that in chap. 1.

10:18-19. The departure of the **glory** of God is presented in stages. The Lord was resolved to depart from the temple, for He would not share His dwelling place with idols that had polluted His sanctuary. Then the cherubim rose up (v. 15). God moved from the Holy of Holies to the **threshold of the temple** (cf. 9:3), while the cherubim remained on the "right side of the temple" (v. 3). The Lord went up and sat (figuratively, because the Lord God does not have a literal physical body) on the throne (10:4). Finally, the Lord with His throne chariot and the cherubim **departed from the threshold of the temple**. After **they stood still at the entrance of the east gate** (vv. 18-19) . . . **the Glory of the God of Israel hovered** before leaving (v. 19).

d. Judgment on Jerusalem's Rulers (11:1-25)

The account of the "twenty-five" wicked "men" underscores the need for judgment (11:1-21).

11:1. While God's glory hovered in departure, **the Spirit lifted** Ezekiel (cf. 3:8, 14; 11:24; 37:1; 43:5) and took him to the **east gate** of **the Lord's house** facing the Mount of Olives. At the entrance to the gate were **twenty-five men**, probably not the same twenty-five who were worshiping the sun at the temple. They are at a different location, the **east gate**, not the inner court (8:16), and were not serving as priests. Furthermore, this was **Jaazaniah** son of **Azzur**, rather than the son of Shaphan (cf. 8:11).

11:2-4. Instead of being righteous leaders, these men would **devise iniquity and give evil advice** to Jerusalem. Using a proverb, **Is not the time near to build houses? This city is the pot and we are the flesh**, they encouraged the Jerusalemites to build houses, a sign of peace and safety (28:26), and forget the prophet's predictions of the coming Babylonian invasion. They said Jerusalem was like a pot on the fire that would keep the meat **(flesh)** from burning, so the people were safe. God said this was **evil advice**. Because of this false optimism, and ignoring the word of the Lord concerning judgment, God told Ezekiel to **prophesy against them** (twice for emphasis).

11:5-7. The Lord knew their **thoughts**. He replied with an altered imagery of the meat and the pot to foretell judgment. The righteous men who had been **slain in this city** had been Jerusalem's hope to turn the city back to the Lord. The city was the **pot**, but it was surrounded by the fires of judgment of the coming Babylonian attack.

11:8-12. They **feared a sword** (an attack), but for their evil God would bring His **sword** upon them in judgment (cf. 6:3). The people would be driven **out of the . . . city**, and God's **sword** would begin at the **border of Israel**. This was fulfilled literally when the captives of Jerusalem were deported or killed at the border city of Riblah, Nebuchadnezzar's siege headquarters near Syria (cf. 2Kg 25:18-21; Jr 52:8-11, 24-27). When this happened, then they would **know that I am the Lord**.

11:13. When **Pelatiah**, one of the 25 men who had given evil advice (cf. v. 1) **died**, it foreshadowed the judgment that would soon destroy all of Jerusalem and confirmed the prophet's message. Again, Ezekiel **cried out, . . . Alas, Lord God!** a plea for God's mercy not to **bring the remnant of Israel to a complete end** (cf. 9:8).

11:14-15. God's response to Ezekiel was twofold, one of personal and then of national encouragement. It is the first promise of restoration in Ezekiel. Although natural disasters and military calamity would result in the death of the righteous along with the wicked, a righteous remnant would remain.

First, He showed Ezekiel that those already in exile in Babylon would be preserved. They were his **brothers . . . relatives . . . fellow exiles**, not just his physical relatives, but also the Jewish people.

Second, God reminded Ezekiel of Jerusalem's need for judgment, and the justice of God. Those still in Jerusalem thought the people in exile (whom God had just said were the true remnant) were **far from the Lord**, just because they were outside the land of Israel. God had given Israel the land (Gn 12:7; 15:18; Dt 34:4), but He had also said He would remove them from it for disobedience (Dt 28:36, 64-68). Being outside Israel did not mean God had forgotten His promises. He would always preserve a remnant (Ezk 6:8; 12:16; Jr 31:35-37).

11:16. The faithful remnant in Babylon, although away from the temple in Jerusalem, (which would soon be destroyed) had the Lord for **a sanctuary for them . . . in the countries where they had gone**. The Lord was accessible to faithful Jews wherever they were geographically.

11:17. Even with judgment looming and the glory of the Lord departing from the temple, there was yet a future for Israel nationally. God promised, **I will gather you from . . . the countries among which you have been scattered, and I will give you the land of Israel**. The remnant of Israel could look forward to a national restoration to the promised land. A partial restoration took place after the Babylonian captivity (cf. Ezra and Nehemiah), but there will be a greater restoration in the future. This promise goes beyond the return from Babylon. It points to the new covenant and a future gathering of Israel at the end of days (cf. 36:24-38; 37:11-28; Jr 16:14-16; Is 11:11). The events described here are kingdom events, e.g., purification from sin and perfect obedience, neither of which happened at the return from Babylon. Israel's future return will be accompanied by spiritual renewal.

11:18-20. When the Jewish people come back to the land at the end of days, **they will remove all its detestable things and all . . . abominations** (cf. v. 21). The land will be purged of idolatry, and the people purified to the Lord. He will **give them one heart and put a new spirit within them . . . and give them a heart of flesh**. This is a picture of the new covenant described by Jeremiah (cf. comments on Jr 31:31-34), not anything that occurred at the return from Babylon. God's purpose in giving Israel **one heart** and a **new spirit** is so they will **walk in My statues and keep My ordinances**.

The Jewish people are always His people, whether in faith or disbelief, obedient or in sin (cf. Rm 11:1, 27-28). Though Hosea described a time when God called Israel "not My people" (Hs 1:9), that is not to say God fully cast off Israel. As Hosea said, for "the Lord loves the sons of Israel though they turn to other gods" (Hs 3:1). For a fuller discussion of Israel's status in unbelief, see Hs 3:1-5. When the Jewish people are faithful to the Lord, however, they will have a spiritual experience that matches their national relationship with the Lord and **they will be My people, and I shall be their God** (cf. Ezk 14:11; 36:28; 37:23, 27; Hs 2:23).

The new covenant (cf. Jr 31:31) was inaugurated with the death and resurrection of Messiah Jesus (cf. Mt 26:28; Mk 14:24; Lk 22:20; Heb 8:6-13; 9:15; 10:14-16; 12:24). But the ultimate fulfillment of physical and spiritual blessings awaits Israel's national recognition of her

Messiah Jesus when they call upon Him at His return (cf. Zch 12:10). The Church today is participating in the spiritual aspects (not the physical or national benefits) of the new covenant, having been grafted into the new covenant (see comments at Rm 11:17-24). By faith in Jesus all who believe in Him are redeemed and indwelt by His Spirit (Rm 8:9), but these blessings to the Church (made up of both non-Jewish and Jewish believers in Messiah Jesus, Eph 2:11-22) have not superseded God's promises to Israel (Rm 11:27-29).

11:21-22. After the confirmation of the hope of the new covenant, the focus is redirected to the glory of God departing from the temple. Those in Jerusalem **whose hearts go after their detestable things and abominations** (cf. v. 18) would be judged for their **conduct** (cf. comments on 7:27). The abominable acts of Israel caused God's Spirit to depart (chaps. 8–11), beginning with **the cherubim lift[ing] up their wings . . . and the glory of the God of Israel hover[ing] over them**. Soon God's glory would leave completely.

11:23. As the **glory of the LORD** (cf. 1:28) left Jerusalem it lingered and then **went up from the midst the city and stood over the mountain . . . east of the city**, the Mount of Olives. This departure signaled Jerusalem's doom. The city would be devoid of God's blessing, but Ezekiel predicted a return of the departed glory via the Mount of Olives (cf. 43:1-3). At His triumphal entry, Jesus retraced this route as if to indicate the glory of the Lord returning (Lk 19:29-40).

11:24-25. Ezekiel's vision ended as it began as **the Spirit lifted** (cf. 3:14; 8:3; 11:1; 37:1; 43:5) him **up** and carried him back **to the exiles in Chaldea**. As the vision **left** him he told the exiles **all the things that the LORD had shown** him.

B. Futility of Judah's False Optimism (12:1–19:14)

Although Ezekiel had shown through signs, sermons, and visions (chaps. 4–11) the necessity of Jerusalem's judgment, the people refused to believe him. Therefore (in chaps. 12–19) the Lord gave Ezekiel a new series of 11 signs and messages to show Jerusalem it had no hope of escape from judgment.

The phrase, "The word of the LORD came to me," introduces 10 of the 11 messages in this section (12:1, 17, 21; 13:1; 14:2, 12; 15:1; 16:1; 17:1; 18:1). The phrase emphasizes the importance of the message. Only the final message, a lament (19:1), begins without this phrase, because it sums up the whole section.

1. Two Signs of Impending Captivity (12:1-20)

a. Sign of the Baggage and the Hole in the Wall (12:1-16)

The Babylonian takeover of Judah was progressive. The first deportation had occurred in 597 BC during the reign of Jehoiachin, when Ezekiel was carried into exile. Ezekiel gave his action signs to the Jewish exiles in Babylon, confirming the coming fall of Jerusalem. Following a long siege, Jerusalem fell in 586 BC. Ezekiel gave this message to his fellow exiles in Babylon to portray what would happen in Jerusalem.

12:1-2. Because of the people's unbelief, Ezekiel gave two more action messages. He said, They **have eyes to see but do not see, ears to hear but do not hear; for they are a rebellious house** (cf. 2:5-8; 12:2, 3, 9). Israel's blindness and deafness were willful disobedience and disbelief (cf. Dt 29:1-4; Is 6:9-10; Jr 5:21; Mt 13:13-15; Ac 28:26-28). Even those already in captivity could not believe Jerusalem would fall.

12:3-4. The first sign had two aspects: baggage (vv. 3-4) and a hole and blindfold (vv. 5-7). Ezekiel, in Babylon, acted out a scene that would occur in Jerusalem. He packed his **baggage for exile . . . in their sight**. This phrase is repeated seven times in this section (vv. 3 [twice], 4 [twice], 5, 6, 7). God wanted them to see what He was going to do and to understand that Jerusalem would fall and everyone in the city would go into captivity. Ezekiel was to **bring** the **baggage out by day** . . . then **go out at evening** as a role-play "as a sign to the house of Israel" of people going into exile.

12:5-7. The second aspect predicting the coming exile included **a hole** and blindfold, which followed immediately, at evening in their sight (cf. v. 3). Ezekiel had to **dig a hole through the wall** and take his **baggage on** his **shoulder . . . in the dark**. Then he was to **cover** his **face**, blindfold himself, so that he could **not see the land**, as a **sign to the house of Israel**. The people would be carried to Babylon and never again see their land. The Babylonian captivity lasted 70 years, so few people who went into captivity lived to return to Israel (cf. Jr 25:8-11; 2Ch 36:20-21). Of course, by the time the book of Ezekiel was completed, the captivity had already begun. The original readers would see that Ezekiel had predicted their exile, though they had not believed him. They themselves, would never see their land again.

12:8-11. The Lord explained that this **burden** (message) concerned King Zedekiah, the

prince in Jerusalem, as well as the whole **house of Israel**. Ezekiel often called the kings of Judah **prince**, meaning "leader," not the son of the king (cf. 7:27; 21:25; 34:24; 37:25). Ezekiel's actions were a **sign** to the people already in captivity and the king that the nation would certainly **go into exile, into captivity**.

12:12-16. The sign of the hole in the wall (v. 5) previewed **the prince['s]** (Zedekiah's) attempted escape from Jerusalem **in the dark . . . through the wall**. He would be caught in God's **snare**, and Nebuchadnezzar would **bring him to Babylon**, but **he will not see it** and he will **die there**. This was dramatically and precisely fulfilled in 586 BC. After a failed escape attempt from Jerusalem, Zedekiah was captured by Babylonian troops, his sons were killed before his eyes, then he was blinded by Nebuchadnezzar and carried off to Babylon where he eventually died in prison (cf. 2Kg 25:1-7; Jr 52:4-11).

Judah would fall to Babylon, but a **few** Jerusalemites (cf. Ezk 6:8) would be spared from the **sword . . . famine** and . . . **pestilence** to be scattered **among the nations**, so that they **may know that I am the Lord**.

b. Sign of Trembling While Eating and Drinking (12:17-20)

12:17-20. In this simple sign, Ezekiel was to **eat . . . bread** (his meals) **with trembling and drink . . . water with quivering and anxiety**. Ezekiel's actions represented the daily terror **the inhabitants of Jerusalem** would experience in the siege and famine (cf. 4:16). God had **stripped** the land of **its fullness**, and His judgment fell because of their **violence**, cruelty, and injustice (cf. 7:23; 8:17). God's purpose: so they would **know that I am the Lord** (cf. 6:7).

2. Five Messages on the Certainty of Judgment (12:21-14:23)

After his dramatic role-plays, Ezekiel gave a series of five messages (12:21-25; 12:26-28; 13; 14:1-11, 12-23) followed by two signs of exile and trembling (12:1-20). Judgment was certain, and there was no hope for rescue from the Babylonians.

a. First Certainty of Judgment Message: Correcting the Proverb About Visions (12:21-25)

12:21-23. The Lord asked Ezekiel about a popular **proverb . . . concerning the land of Israel . . . the days are long and every vision fails**. That is, time is going by (**the days are long**), but the message of the prophets (**the vision**) never comes true (**fails**). Instead, God would **make this proverb cease**. When they saw the judgment, they would say, **The days draw near** and the **fulfillment of every vision** has come about.

12:24-25. Every hopeful **vision** and **flattering divination** that said Jerusalem would never fall was the message of false prophets. They contradicted the judgment prophecies of God's true messengers, in both Jerusalem (cf. Jr 28:1-4) and Babylon (cf. Jr 29:1, 8-9). Judgment was imminent; God would **perform** His word (cf. Ezk 12:28).

b. Second Certainty of Judgment Message: Correcting the Proverb About Delay (12:26-28)

12:26-28. The first proverb (vv. 21-25) doubted the fact of God's judgment. This proverb said judgment was just not imminent: **the vision that he sees is for many years from now, and he prophesies of times far off**. Even those Israelites who believed the message of the prophets thought the prophecies would not happen until the distant future. However God said, **None of My words will be delayed any longer**. The judgment spoken of by the prophets was about to happen. Certainly, whatever the Lord speaks, **will be performed**.

c. Third Certainty of Judgment Message: Against False Prophets and Prophetesses (13:1-23)

In his third message Ezekiel denounced the false prophets (vv. 1-16) and the prophetesses (see vv. 17-23) who were responsible for the people's false hope, leading them away from God. Ezekiel first condemned their sin and then pronounced judgment.

13:1-3. The source of the message of the false **prophets** was **their own inspiration** (cf. v. 17), not from the Lord. God declared **Woe** to the foolish prophets who got their message from their **own spirit**, yet truly had **seen nothing**. **Woe**, in the Scriptures means "alas" or "how tragic."

13:4. Their message was not only false, it was also dangerous. The false prophets were like **foxes among ruins**. Instead of preventing destruction, they promoted disaster, toppling the stones and living as scavengers off the lies they told.

13:5. The false prophets had **not gone up** to **build** the breaks in the **wall**. Israel's moral walls were ready to collapse, but the false prophets did not **stand in the battle** to defend the people.

13:6-9. Although the false prophets claimed to represent God, He had **not sent them**. In fact because of their **false** words and **lying divination[s]**, He was **against** them.

The false prophets would be excluded from the community of Israel. First, they would **have no place in the council** of God's people; they would no longer have a leadership role. Second, they would not be **written down in the register of the house of Israel**; they would be forgotten (cf. Ezr 2:62). Third, the false prophets would never again **enter the land of Israel**; they would die in captivity.

13:10-12. Judgment on the false prophets was **definitely because** they **misled My people** Israel saying, **Peace! when there [was] no peace** (cf. 13:16; Jr 6:14; 8:11; 23:17; Mc 3:5). Although the people were disobedient, God still identified them as **My people** (cf. 13:9, 10, 18, 19, 21, 23; 14:8, 9). God faithfully loves His chosen people, even in the midst of discipline. They are always beloved because of His faithful love and covenant with them (Rm 11:28).

The deceptive ministry of the false prophets was like a damaged wall covered with **whitewash**. Instead of calling Israel's attention to the serious cracks in its moral foundation (cf. 13:5), these prophets were applying **plaster** to hide the cracks. The false prophets were compounding Israel's difficulties by hiding problems that needed to be corrected. When flooding rain... hailstones... violent wind are sent by the Lord, He will tear down the wall... plastered over by the false prophets.

13:13-16. The **violent wind** of God's **wrath** of **rain and hailstones** would lay **bare the wall** and its **foundation** (cf. v. 11) and the false prophets would be **gone**, for they said **peace for her when there is no peace**.

13:17-19. Ezekiel was told, **set your face** (cf. 4:3) against the false prophetesses, **the daughters of your people** who were **prophesying from their own inspiration** (cf. v. 2). True prophetesses ministered in both Old and New Testament times (Ex 15:20; Jdg 4:4-5; 2Kg 22:14; Ac 21:8-9). However, these false prophetesses were mediums or sorceresses.

The Lord said, **Woe to the women** [the false prophetesses], as He had to the false prophets (cf. v. 3). They would **sew magic bands on all wrists** and made **veils** to fit people of **every stature** to deceive the people. Scripture strictly forbids occult practices (cf. Lv 19:26, 31; Dt 18:10-14). By their occultism these false prophetesses would **hunt down the lives of My people** or **preserve the lives of others** for their own evil purpose. They used their evil practices in matters of life and death.

By their false teaching and occult practices these women ensnared people who were looking for powerful answers, but rejected the message of the Lord's prophets. For **handfuls of barley and fragments of bread**, probably in payment for divination since food is better than gold in time of famine, these women **profaned** the Lord **to** His **people**. They sought to exercise diabolical power to **put to death some**... and **to keep others alive who should not live**. God was clear: these prophetesses were **lying to My people** (cf. v. 9).

13:20-21. God was **against** their **magic bands**, which they used to **hunt lives** (cf. vv. 18), preventing people from believing the Lord. He would **tear** off their **magic bands**... and **tear off** their **veils** and **deliver** His **people from** their **hands**. These women would be exposed as sorceresses, and people would **no longer** be entrapped (**be in your hands**). Instead they would **know that I am the Lord** (cf. 6:7).

13:22-23. The prophetesses had **disheartened the righteous** with their lies and encouraged the **wicked not to turn from his wicked way**. God would judge the prophetesses and **deliver My people out of your hand**. He would end **false visions** and **divination** (cf. Dt 18:10) from Israel and save His people from their terrible deception. Likewise, today followers of the Lord should never consult mediums or fortunetellers or dabble in the occult. These are sinful practices, and their answers are never from God.

d. Fourth Certainty of Judgment Message: Condemnation of Idolatry (14:1-11)

14:1-3. Though Ezekiel was still confined to his house (3:24) **some elders** of Israel went to see Ezekiel to seek a message from him (cf. 8:1).

God revealed to Ezekiel the spiritual condition of these elders. They had **set up their idols in their hearts** and put **stumbling block[s] of their iniquity** before their faces (cf. 7:19; 14:3-4, 7; 18:30; 44:12). They followed the teaching of the false prophets and prophetesses. The Lord did not want to be **consulted**, a technical term for seeking an oracle from a prophet (cf. 2Kg 1:6; 3:11; 8:8), by these hypocritical elders who had **idols in their hearts**. God knew they worshiped idols, and they did not sincerely want to hear from Him.

14:4-5. However, God would **answer** them because He wanted to **lay hold of** ("capture") **the hearts** of those who are **estranged** from Him because of **their idols**.

14:6. Therefore, His urgent message was **Repent and turn away from your idols and turn your faces away from all your abominations**. Before judgment fell, God called for repentance. God constantly calls sinners back to His love.

14:7-8. The warning against idolatry applied to the **house of Israel** (cf. vv. 3, 7) as well as to **immigrants** (*ger*, "alien"). The law of Moses required these non-Jews **who stay[ed] in Israel** to obey the laws of God, since they functioned as part of the community of Israel (cf. 47:22-23; Lv 16:29-30; 17:12-16; 18:26; Nm 15:13-16; Is 56:3-8).

If an Israelite or an immigrant who **separates himself** (apostatized), then dared to **inquire** of the Lord, He **will . . . answer** but not the way the apostate expected. God would respond in judgment and would **set** His **face against that man** (cf. 4:3). God would **make him a sign and a proverb** (cf. 23:10; Jb 17:6; 30:9; Ps 44:14; Jr 24:9; Jl 2:17), so people would know about him and use his name as a bad example (e.g., calling a person who commits treason "Benedict Arnold") and **cut him off from among My people** (cf. 13:9).

14:9-11. In the phrase **but if the prophet is prevailed upon to speak**, the word **prevailed** is better translated with a negative connotation such as "enticed" or "seduced." It probably refers to a false prophet who could be bribed into giving a message (cf. Ex 22:16; 2Sm 3:25; 1Kg 22:19-23; Jr 20:7).

Both the false prophet . . . and the inquirer **will bear the punishment of their iniquity**. The goal is for **the house of Israel** to **no longer stray from Me and no longer defile themselves with all their transgressions**. Then **they will be My people, and I shall be their God** (cf. comments on 11:20; 36:28; 37:23, 27; Hs 2:23).

e. Fifth Certainty of Judgment Message: Unavailing Prayer of Noah, Daniel, and Job (14:12-23).

14:12-20. If a **country sins** against God so He stretches out His **hand against it**, the judgment might come by **famine** (v. 13), **beasts** (v. 15), **sword** (v. 17), and/or **plague** (v. 21; cf. 5:17). Judgment is so certain that even though these righteous men **Noah, Daniel and Job** pray for it, they could **deliver only themselves** (cf. Jr 15:1; Gn 15:6). **They alone would be delivered, but the country would be desolate**.

These three men are strong examples of faith in the Scriptures (Gn 6-9; Jb 1; Dn 6:3). Ezekiel's spelling of **Daniel** (in Hb.) differs slightly from the usual spelling of the prophet Daniel. Such a minor difference in name spelling is common (cf. "Azariah" = "Uzziah," 2Kg 15:1; 2Ch 26:1; "Jehoram" = "Joram," 2Kg 3:1; 8:16; "Coniah" = "Jechoniah" Jr 22:24; 24:1). The alternative spelling of his name is inconsequential.

14:21. With the general principle established, namely, that in a wicked society the prayers of righteous people will result only in their own deliverance and not that of the broader community, Ezekiel applied it to Jerusalem. If those righteous men, Daniel, Job, and Noah, could not save a wicked land, how could Jerusalem hope to escape without righteous leadership? God would send His **four severe judgments against Jerusalem: sword, famine, wild beasts and plague** (cf. 5:17).

14:22-23. After the judgments, **survivors** of the siege of Jerusalem **will be left** and **brought** to Babylon. God's justice would be vindicated, and Ezekiel **will be comforted**. Ezekiel had been brokenhearted over Jerusalem, but when he sees the wicked **conduct and actions** of these survivors it will confirm that God's judgment of Jerusalem was **not done in vain, whatever I did to it** (cf. Gn 18:25).

3. Three Parables on Judgment (15:1–17:24)

After his two signs (12:1-20) and five messages (12:21–14:23) regarding impending judgment, Ezekiel gave three parables (chaps. 15–17) to show there was no possibility of deliverance.

a. Parable of the Fruitless Vine (15:1-8)

15:1-5. In this parable the grape **vine** illustrates Israel's condition. Grape vines cannot be used to build anything, not even a **peg** to **hang any vessel**. Furthermore, even if the branches are used for **fuel** and the middle is **charred**, it cannot be **made into anything**. Israel is often pictured as a vine, but she had not produced the spiritual fruit God intended (cf. Ps 80:8-18; Is 5:1-7; Jr 2:21; Hs 10:1).

15:6. Just as the **wood of the vine** is used for **fire for fuel**, so God has **given up the inhabitants of Jerusalem**.

15:7-8. God's judgment was certain: I will **set My face against them** (for emphasis twice; cf. 4:3). Jerusalem had surrendered to Babylon in 597 BC and escaped total destruction. However, God would bring Babylon back to finish the judgment in 586 BC. Although they had **come out of the fire** of 597 BC, the fire would **yet . . . consume** them in 586 BC. There was no cause for optimism. God would **make the land desolate, because they acted unfaithfully** to Him.

b. Parables of Unfaithful Jerusalem (16:1-63)

(1) Parable of the Rescued Infant Who Became the Adulterous Wife (16:1-43)

In this extended parable, Jerusalem is portrayed as an abandoned infant who is rescued by the Lord, betrothed to Him, but then becomes an unfaithful wife (cf. Hs 1–2; Jr 2; Is 1:21; 50:1). First her sin is described (vv. 3-34), then her punishment (vv. 35-53), and finally her restoration (vv. 53-63). The parable is spoken to Jerusalem as the representative of the Jewish people, and may also be understood as a chronological illustration of Israel's history.

16:1-3. Jerusalem is depicted as an unwanted child from **the land of the Canaanite**, whose **father was an Amorite and . . . mother a Hittite** (cf. v. 45). The Amorites were a large tribal group living in Canaan prior to the conquest. Their name is sometimes a synonym with Canaanite (Gn 10:16; 48:22; Jos 5:1; 10:5; Jdg 1:34-36). The Hittites were another people living in Canaan prior to the conquest who had frequent interaction with Israel (cf. Gn 15:20; 23:10-20; Nm 13:29; Jdg 3:5; 1Sm 26:6; 1Kg 10:29). This is not the literal genealogy of Abraham or a specific individual from Jerusalem. Rather, it is a moral genealogy of the Jewish people. The pagan occupants of the land should have been driven out at the conquest to protect Israel from adopting their pagan worship. However, Israel failed to expel them and instead adopted their pagan **abominations**, behaving as if they were the spiritual children of Canaan (cf. Ex 23:23-24; Dt 12:30; Nm 33:55; 1Kg 11:1-8).

16:4-5. Jerusalem is represented as an abandoned infant. In biblical times, after the **navel cord** was cut, a newborn was then **washed** and **rubbed with salt** to clean and dry the skin. Then the infant was **wrapped** in cloth for warmth. But these things were not done for Jerusalem. No one looked on her with **pity** or had **compassion**. Instead the baby was **thrown out into the open field**, for she was **abhorred**. The cruel practice of infanticide was prevalent in the ancient world. It was a common pagan practice to leave unwanted children in fields or by the side of the road to die. It was less sophisticated than modern abortion, but it had the same result and wide social approval.

16:6-7. As the Lord **passed by** He **saw** the newborn, still unwashed from its birth, **squirming in [her] blood**. He did not leave her to die; He said **Live!** God's basic desire for all people, proclaimed in one word, is **Live!** Historically, this parable mirrors God's choice of Abraham (Gn 12:1-3; Dt 6:6-8).

The Lord made the child grow. She became **numerous**, literally "a myriad," which may refer to the patriarchal period when Israel increased from a few in number to a multitude who left Egypt (cf. Ex 12:37-38; Ac 7:14). She grew naturally like **plants of the field** (i.e., "grew like a weed"). When she **grew up** to the age of sexual maturity, the **age for fine ornaments**, her **breasts . . . formed and . . . hair . . . grown**, she was still **naked and bare**, in a destitute state, as Israel was in the wilderness.

16:8. God again **passed by** and noticed she was **at the time for love**, that is, of marriageable age. God then entered into a **covenant** of marriage with her. He **spread** His **skirt over** her and **covered [her] nakedness**. He **swore to** her and **entered into a covenant**, and she **became Mine**. The symbolic act of a man spreading his skirt (lower part of his garment) over a marriageable woman signified protection and betrothal (cf. Ru 3:9). God pledged His fidelity to the Jewish people, as represented by Jerusalem, and took her as His own. He chose her because He loved her, not because of any individual qualities that drew her to Him (Dt. 7:6-9). This could refer to the giving of the Sinai covenant (cf. Jr 2:2; 3:1; Hs 2:2-23; Mal 2:14).

16:9-14. God **bathed** and **anointed** her **with oil**, then clothed her in splendor: **embroidered** dress, **porpoise skin** sandals, **fine linen** and **silk**, **bracelets**, a **necklace**, a **ring**, and a **beautiful crown on** her **head**. This passage describes in figurative fashion all of God's provision for Israel when He chose her and made Jerusalem the nation's capital.

Jerusalem also was given the choicest foods: **fine flour**, **honey**, and olive **oil**. Everything she could possibly need or want, her gracious, generous "Husband" lavished on her. She was **exceedingly beautiful and advanced to royalty** and became famous throughout the **nations**. Her **beauty . . . was perfect** because of the **splendor** of the Lord that He **bestowed on** her. Historically, this suggests that under God's blessing during the reigns of David and Solomon Jerusalem became a magnificent city and Israel a powerful nation (cf. 1Kg 10:4-5).

16:15-16. Sadly, Jerusalem turned from the Lord to focus on herself, and she **trusted in** her **beauty and played the harlot** because of her **fame**. Jerusalem forgot the One who had rescued her and cared for her. She turned away from the Lord and worshiped other gods (cf. Dt 6:10-12; 8:11-20). Beginning in Solomon's reign (1Kg 11:7-13, 970 BC) until Jerusalem fell to Nebuchadnezzar (586 BC), Israel and Judah constantly turned from God to idols. Despite brief times of revival, their direction was downward to iniquity.

16:17-19. The people of Jerusalem **took** every blessing God had given them and used them to **play the harlot** and worship the idols in high places. She **took** all the **beautiful** things given to her by God (vv. 9-14) and corrupted them with idol worship (vv. 17-22). She even used His **gold** and His **silver** to make pagan worship symbols—**male images** (phallic symbols). They took the **incense** and **fine flour** God gave them to **offer before** the idols.

16:20-21. Worst of all, they **took** the children **borne to Me and sacrificed them to idols . . . you slaughtered My children and offered them up to idols**. God called these innocent children His children. The abomination involved sacrificing **sons and daughters** alive, placing them in the red-hot altar to Molech, and burning them alive in the Kidron Valley (cf. 2Kg 21:6; Jr 7:30-32; 19:4-5; 32:35). The altars built to honor Molech were small or large iron stoves, ornamented with the hands and arms of Molech. When the altars were heated red hot, children would be placed in those hands and burned alive as an offering to Molech, an act called "passing through the fire" (cf. 23:26-39). Child sacrifice is so abhorrent to the Lord, it is specifically forbidden (Lv 18:21; 20:2-5; Dt 12:31; 18:10).

16:22. Jerusalem could fall into these wicked practices because she **did not remember** the Lord had rescued her in **the days of [her] youth**.

16:23-26. The Lord cried to Jerusalem for her wickedness: **Woe, woe to you!** (twice for emphasis, cf. 13:3, 18; 24:6, 9; 34:2). The people had built **a shrine and . . . a high place in every square . . . at the top of every street** (cf. v. 31), and it was filled with pagan altars. Her worship of idols is graphically portrayed as a once-beautiful woman, now a prostitute, who would **spread [her] legs to every passer-by**.

16:27. So God **stretched out** His **hand against** her and allowed her enemies who **hate[d]** her to **diminish [her] rations**, referring to the sacking of Jerusalem. Yet Jerusalem did not change her evil behavior. Even the pagan **Philistines** who plundered Israel (2Ch 21:16-17) were **ashamed** of Jerusalem's **lewd conduct**.

16:28-29. Jerusalem's **harlotry** included following the gods of the Egyptians (v. 26) . . . **Assyrians** (v. 28) . . . and **Chaldea** (Babylon, v. 29), but her lust (pagan worship) was **not satisfied**. Mentioning these nations implies not only Jerusalem's worship of their gods, but also her depending on foreign military alliances instead of trusting the Lord.

16:30. The heart of the Jewish people was **languishing** (sick or weak), which motivated them to abandon God and multiply evil. Jerusalem behaved like a **bold-faced** (shameless) **harlot**.

16:31-34. Yet she did not behave like a typical **harlot** who took money for sexual acts. Jerusalem bribed her **lovers** to come to her for **harlotries**. Because **you give money and no money is given to you**, she was **different** (lit., "the reverse") **from** prostitutes to whom **men give gifts**—she gave **gifts to all** her **lovers to bribe them**. Her wickedness was worse than adultery and ordinary prostitution.

16:35-37. Jerusalem had degenerated from beautiful royalty (cf. v. 13) to a detestable harlot (vv. 35, 36). Her sins were summarized: **detestable idols**, sacrifice of **sons . . . to idols**, multiple **lovers**.

16:38-39. So God would **judge** her **like women who commit adultery or shed blood**. God would use her **lovers** (the pagan nations) to destroy her. They would **tear down** the **shrines**, **strip** her of her **clothing . . . and . . . leave** her . . . **naked**. This parallels the punishment prescribed for a woman caught in adultery (cf. Gn 38:24; Lv 20:10; Dt 22:21-24). Jerusalem would again be as defenseless before her enemies as she had been when she was an infant rescued by the Lord (cf. vv. 4-8).

16:40-41. God had said that if a city in Israel practiced idolatry its people were to be killed by the sword and the city was to be burned (cf. Dt 13:15-16). God would cause a sword to fall on Jerusalem at the hands of the Babylonians (cf. Ezk 23:47). After Jerusalem's fall Babylon would **burn** her **houses** and **execute** the Lord's **judgments** on it. God's judgment on Jerusalem would finally stop her from **playing the harlot**.

16:42. After her destruction God would **calm** His **fury**. God's jealous anger is not petty or vindictive. Instead it is an essential display of His absolute holiness (cf. Ex 20:1-3; Is 6:3; 42:8; 45:5-7)

16:43. The root of Jerusalem's sin was her failure to remember **the days of** her **youth** (cf. vv. 22, 61, 63). All her beauty and success were from the Lord's gracious favor. Turning from Him, she cut herself off from the source of blessing. Worse, she betrayed and angered the One who loved her and had raised her to greatness. He wanted only to bless her.

(2) Parable of the Sisters: Jerusalem, Sodom, and Samaria (16:44-59)

The first parable of Jerusalem is the story of Jerusalem as an adulterous wife (vv. 1-43). The second parable is an analogy of Jerusalem and the wicked sisters Samaria, and Sodom (vv. 44-59). If Jerusalem's depraved sisters were judged for their sin, how could Jerusalem, who was even more wicked, hope to escape?

16:44-45. This proverb **like mother, like daughter** is applied to Jerusalem. Her actions (that of her citizens) were characteristic of her family heritage. Her **mother** had **loathed** her husband and her children. Ezekiel repeated the ancestral background of Jerusalem for emphasis. Jewish Jerusalem behaved just like the city's past pagan residents (cf. comments on v. 3).

16:46-48. In this family story Samaria, to the **north**, and Sodom, to the **south**, are Jerusalem's sisters. The **daughters** are residents of the cities. Both cities were known for their wickedness. Yet, Jerusalem **acted more corruptly in all** her **conduct**.

16:49-50. The guilt of **Sodom** was twofold. First, she had **abundant food**, but did **not help the poor and needy**. Second, the Sodomites **committed abominations**, referring, at least in part, to their sexual misbehavior **before** the Lord (cf. Gn 19:4-5; Lv 18:22-23; Rm 1:18-22). Thus Sodom is often mentioned as an example of depravity (e.g., Dt. 29:23; 32:32; Is 1:9-10; 3:9; Jr 23:4; Lm 4:6; Mt 10:15; 11:23-24). Therefore, God removed Sodom and **her** daughters (surrounding areas) in the famous judgment of fire and brimstone (cf. Gn 19:23-25).

16:51-52. The sin of **Samaria** was syncretistic worship after Solomon's kingdom was divided (930 BC). Jeroboam set up gold calf altars in Dan and Bethel combining paganism and biblical worship (1Kg 12:25-33; Hs 8:5; Am 8:14). Yet, **Samaria did not commit half** of Jerusalem's **sins**. Under God's judgment, Assyria destroyed Samaria and the northern kingdom fell (721 BC, 2Kg 17). But Jerusalem's sins were such a **disgrace** that she **acted more abominably** than they, so in comparison Sodom and Samaria would **appear righteous**.

16:53. Having announced judgment on Jerusalem for her sin, the LORD indicated there was yet hope. The Lord will **restore** the **captivity** of **Sodom** . . . **Samaria** . . . and Jerusalem. There will be a national restoration of these cities in the millennial kingdom, with Jerusalem in the forefront (cf. chaps. 33–48).

16:54-58. Jerusalem would **feel ashamed** of her sin. In the **day of** her **pride**, when Jerusalem was deep in sin, she would not let the word **Sodom** be **heard from** her **lips**. However, once Jerusalem's **wickedness was uncovered**, she became the **reproach** of her pagan neighbors, **Edom** (cf. 2Kg 8:20-22; 2Ch 28:17; Ob) and **the Philistines** (Jos 13:2; Jdg 13:1; 1Sm 4:2; 14–17). Jerusalem would be restored, but she would first have to bear the **penalty of** her **abominations**.

16:59. God's faithfulness to His covenants concludes the parable. Jerusalem had **despised the oath** by **breaking the covenant** with spiritual adultery (cf. vv. 15-43). This was the Mosaic covenant, the only covenant Israel entered into through an oath (cf. Ex 24:7-8; Dt 28:14-68; 29:10-21). The nation, represented by Jerusalem, had broken that covenant and would suffer the consequences of being dispersed from the land, exactly as described in the covenantal agreement (Dt 28).

(3) The Faithfulness of God and the Everlasting Covenant (16:60-63)

16:60. Despite Israel's failure to be faithful to Him, **nevertheless** the Lord will faithfully **remember** His **covenant** He made with her **in the days of [her] youth**. This is the unconditional Abrahamic covenant (Gn 12:1-3; 17:7, 13, 19; 1Ch 16:17; Ps 105:10). Then He would establish the **everlasting covenant**, the new covenant (Jr 31:31-34; Ezk 11:18-20, 36:26-28, 37:26-28). The unfaithfulness of people does not change the faithfulness of God (cf. Lv 26:42-45; 2Tm 2:13; Rm 11:29).

16:61-63. When God establishes the new covenant Jerusalem will **remember** and **be ashamed** of her sinful past. Then Jerusalem will be restored and even the **sisters** Sodom and Samaria **shall know that I am the LORD . . . when I have forgiven you for all that you have done**.

c. Parable of the Two Eagles (17:1-24)

Chapter 16 presented the theological background for Jerusalem's condition. Chapter 17 is a parable with a more political perspective. For the history of the events, see 2Kgs 24:8-20; 2Ch 36:9-13; Jr 37; 52:1-7.

17:1-2. God commanded Ezekiel to tell **a riddle** and **parable** to **the house of Israel**. A **riddle** in Hebrew is an enigmatic saying that teaches a lesson and often requires explanation (e.g., Jdg 14:12-19). A **parable** is a story that teaches a lesson. Here the story with explanation is presented in cycles (Ezk 17:3-10; 11-21), and concluded with an epilogue of hope (vv. 22-24).

17:3-4, 11-12. First, came the riddle of the **eagle** and **the cedar**. The eagle pictured the beauty and power of Babylon (v. 12), and Lebanon (v. 3) stood for **Jerusalem** (v. 12). The eagle had gone to **Lebanon** and **plucked off the top of the cedar** tree and replanted the bough in a **land of merchants . . . city of traders** (Babylon). Nebuchadnezzar **came to Jerusalem** and **took its king** (v. 12), the **top** shoot of the tree, and her **princes and brought them to . . . Babylon** and replanted the shoot there (cf. 2Kg 24:8-16). This referred to Nebuchadnezzar's attack on Jerusalem (597 BC) when he deposed King Jehoiachin and took him prisoner to Babylon (2Kg 23–24).

17:5-6, 13-14. Yet **he** (the eagle i.e., Nebuchadnezzar) did not destroy the land completely, but **took some of the seed of the land and . . . planted it in fertile soil** so that **it sprouted** (v. 6) into a **spreading vine**. Nebuchadnezzar weakened Jerusalem, but he did not destroy it at that time. Instead he set up Zedekiah as a vassal king (**planted . . . in fertile soil**). Jerusalem's military might was gone, but as long as Israel was **in subjection** to Nebuchadnezzar, her people could continue to live in peace. The eagle took Zedekiah, a member of the **royal family**, and put **him under oath** (v. 13) to be loyal to Babylon. Though he **took away** into exile **the mighty of the land** (cf. 2Kg 24:14) and Judah was **in subjection**, she could **continue** as long as she kept her treaty/**covenant** with Nebuchadnezzar.

17:7-8, 15. This parable is of the second eagle and the vine. **Another . . . eagle** similar to the first, came along and the **vine** was encouraged **toward him**. This new eagle was **Egypt** (v. 15), which influenced Zedekiah to **rebel** against Babylon. Judah sent envoys to **Egypt**, seeking **horses** and **troops** from the Egyptians (v. 15). When Ezekiel spoke this prophecy (592–91 BC; 8:1; 20:1) Zedekiah's final revolt had not yet happened (588 BC), so Ezekiel predicted Zedekiah's revolt about three years before it happened.

17:9-10, 16-21. The consequences for Jerusalem, the vine (v. 8), would be disastrous. Babylon would **pull up its roots** and **cut off its fruit**, and Jerusalem would **completely wither** because Jerusalem **despised** the **oath** (cf. Jr 27). Zedekiah would **die in Babylon** because **Pharaoh . . . will not help him in the war**. God would spread His **net** and **snare** over Zedekiah to bring him to **Babylon** with **his troops**, and Jerusalem would **fall by the sword**, and the **survivors** would be **scattered** (cf. 2Kg 24).

17:22-23. The parable of the eagles ends with a Messianic promise, using similar imagery but in a new way. In the future, the **Lord God** will **take a sprig from the lofty top of the cedar and . . . plant it on a high . . . mountain of Israel**. The Jewish people will not be destroyed because God will restore them to their land in the end times. The transplanting of the **young twig a tender one** has messianic implications (Ps 89; Is 11:1; Jr 23:5-6; 33:14-16; Zch 3:8; 6:12-13). The Messiah is called a shoot from the root of Jesse, King David's father. This is the One whom God would establish as King over Israel. When He reigns as a **stately cedar**, He will meet all the needs of His kingdom (i.e., He will **bear fruit**) and provide protection for all. **Birds** (nations) **of every kind will . . . nest in the shade of its branches** (Mt 13:31-32), indicating that His reign will have a worldwide scope. The **mountain of Israel** refers to Mount Zion and the temple, where Messiah Jesus will reign as King (cf. Ezk 20:40; Ps 2:6; Mc 4:1-3). When the Messiah reigns from Mount Zion, all the trees of the field (the nations) will know that I am the Lord (cf. Is 56:7; Is 11:1-9).

17:24. God has a plan for all nations. The Lord has the right to **bring down . . . and dry up** world powers, but His plan for the nations will be fulfilled in the restoration of Israel under the reign of King Messiah. Then all the nations of the earth will know **I am the Lord; I have spoken, and I will perform it.**

This prophecy (vv. 22-24) was not fulfilled when the Jewish people returned to Israel after the Babylonian captivity (cf. 11:17). The fulfillment awaits God's establishment of Israel in the millennium under the Messiah Jesus. At that time God's kingdom will encompass the entire world (cf. Dn 2:44-45; Zch 14:3-4, 16-17; Hab 2:14).

4. Message on Individual Responsibility (18:1-32)

Having shown the justice of God's judgment on the nation in the three previous parables, Ezekiel next demonstrated that individuals in Judah are not victims of their parents' bad behavior but that they share responsibility for judgment because of their own sins.

18:1-4. A familiar proverb is again used (cf. 12:21-28) to correct Israel's wrong ideas: **The fathers eat the sour grapes, But the children's**

teeth are set on edge (cf. Jr 31:29-30). This proverb replaces personal responsibility with blame, i.e., "What is happening to us is not our fault! We are suffering because someone else sinned." People were accusing God of punishing them unjustly (cf. v. 25).

This proverb may have arisen from a misunderstanding of the consequences of sin. The Lord visits "the iniquity of the father on the children, on the third and the fourth generations of those who hate Me" (cf. Ex 20:5; 34:7; Dt 5:9). The point is that the wicked behavior of one generation has ongoing consequences to the next. It does not mean one person is punished for the sin of another. Everyone is personally responsible to God for his or her sins. **All souls are mine** said God, and **The soul who sins will die** (cf. v. 20).

18:5-18. The example of three generations illustrates God's point. First, God gave the example of the "righteous" father who "practices justice" (vv. 5-9); second, the "violent son" of that righteous father (vv. 10-13); and third, the righteous son of a violent father (vv. 14-18). Each case described the individual's actions and God's response.

18:5-9. In the example of the first generation was the **righteous** man who **practices justice** (toward his fellow man) **and righteousness** (toward God). He did not worship **idols** (cf. 8:12; 16:24-25, 31, 39; 18:15; 22:9). He kept himself morally pure; he did not **defile his neighbor's wife** by committing adultery with her (Ex 20:14; Lv 20:10). He maintained personal purity by not having intercourse with his wife during her **menstrual period** (forbidden according to Lv 18:19). He did not **oppress anyone**. He was concerned for social justice (cf. Dt 24:13-15). He did **not commit robbery** (Ex 20:15) or even **lend money on interest** (Dt 23:19-20). He gave food **to the hungry** and **clothing** to the needy (Dt 15:7). He kept away from **iniquity** and executed **true justice**. He was a sterling example of righteousness, obeying the **statutes** and **ordinances** of the Lord. As a result, God announced that **he is righteous and will surely live**.

18:10-13. In the example of the second generation was the righteous man's **violent son who sheds blood**. He was the wicked opposite of his father in every detail (**defiles his neighbor's wife, oppresses the poor and needy, commits robbery,** worships **idols, lends money on interest**). **He will not live! He has committed all these abominations** . . . **his blood will be on his own head**. Despite having a righteous father, the wicked son is responsible for his own behavior.

18:14-18. In the example of the third generation was the **son** of the violent man **who has observed all his father's sins** but **does not do likewise**. Instead, this man followed in the righteous path of his grandfather (cf. vv. 6-9). He **executes** God's **ordinances** and **walks in** His **statutes; he will not die for his father's inequity, he will surely live**.

18:19-20. Each person is responsible for his own behavior. **The person who sins will die. The son will not bear the punishment for the father's iniquity** (see comments at vv. 1-4). The **righteousness of the righteous will be upon himself** and the **wickedness of the wicked will be upon himself**. The proverb about the father's eating sour grapes (v. 2) was completely false. When the people were judged it was not for someone in the past generation who sinned, but because the people in the present generation were sinful.

18:21-23. God called the nation to turn back to Him and escape judgment. If the **wicked man turns from all his sins** and keeps God's decrees **he shall** . . . **live** (cf. 14:6; Pr 28:13). The phrase **turns from** means to "repent" (cf. Ezk 14:6). The Lord takes no **pleasure in the death of the wicked** (v. 32; 33:11). He wants people to **turn from** their wicked **ways and live**.

18:24. But God does not simply excuse the sins of someone who has been walking in **righteousness** and then **turns away** to **iniquity**. **He will die**. None of the righteous things he has done **will be remembered**. Righteousness must be consistent, not random.

18:25-28. A person who once followed God's law but who later turned to idolatry or immorality was no longer righteous. His past righteousness would not negate his present sins. But when this formerly **righteous** person, who became wicked, repents and **turns away from his wickedness** . . . **and practices justice** . . . **he will save his life**. God is willing to forgive and receive the repentant individual.

18:29-32. Israel charged God with unrighteousness, but God responded with a challenge: **Is it not your ways that are not right?** (cf. Jb 40:8). God reminded Israel of the responsibility of individual behavior: **I will judge you** . . . **each according to his conduct**. This is a call to **repent** and **turn away from** . . . **transgressions**. Then God would give them a **new heart** and a **new spirit** (cf. Ezk 11:19; 36:26; Jr 31:31-34) in right relationship with Him. He repeated, **I have no pleasure in the death** of the wicked (Ezk 18:23; 33:11) and declared, **Therefore, repent and live**. Despite God's compassion on the wicked and His call to repent, He also decrees the death of the wicked and holds those who fail to repent accountable. In this God is glorified as the Just Judge of all the earth.

5. Parable of Lamentation for Israel's Final Kings (19:1-14)

The section on the futility of false optimism (spanning chaps. 12–19) concludes with a lament or funeral poem/song over Israel's final kings. This is the first (19:1-14) of five laments in Ezekiel. Three others are for Tyre (cf. 26:17-18; 27:1-36; 28:12-19), and a fourth is for Egypt (32:1-16).

19:1-2. This was a **lamentation for the princes of Israel**, the last four kings reigning in Jerusalem (cf. comments on 7:27; 12:8-11). The dirge was not over one individual. It was sung for the "demise" of the Davidic dynasty just prior to the fall of Jerusalem. It opens with the image of **lions**, which are common representations of the Davidic dynasty and Jerusalem (e.g., Gn 49:9; 1Kg 10:19-20; Is 29:1; Rv 5:5). The **mother lioness** is the nation of Israel who **reared her cubs** (that is, from whom came these kings).

19:3-4. The first of the lion **cubs** was Jehoahaz, the wicked son of good king Josiah (2Kg 23:24-32, reigned 609 BC). He **learned to tear his prey** and **devoured men**, doing evil in the sight of the Lord. During his three-month reign, he made a reputation for cruelty, and **nations heard about him**. He was **captured** and deposed by Pharaoh Neco II, who **brought him with hooks**, probably literal hooks in his nose attached to a rope-leash, and paraded as a conquest trophy to **Egypt**, where he died in captivity (cf. 2Kg 23:31-34; Jr 22:11-12).

19:5. The next **of her cubs** who was king of Judah was Jehoiakim (reigned 609–598 BC). Judah's **hope was lost** under his pro-Egyptian rule. He is not highlighted in this lament. The lioness then **took another of her cubs and made him a young lion**—a ruler. This was Jehoiachin (2Kg 24:8-17; 2Ch 36:8-10).

19:6-9. Jehoiachin's wicked rule (598–597 BC) was cruel. He **learned to tear his prey** . . . and **devoured men** (cf. v. 3). He **destroyed** Judah's **fortified towers** and **laid waste** Judah's **cities**. His corrupt reign **appalled** his citizens. Then **nations**, Babylon and her allies, **set against him** and caught Jehoiachin. The captured king was brought **to the king of Babylon** . . . **in hunting nets**, a description which conjures the image of hunting animals by spreading nets over a pit. Parading prize captives as wild animals was a common practice. Jehoiachin was imprisoned for 37 years Although released by Nebuchadnezzar's successor, Jehoiachin never returned to Judah, the land he had ravaged by his irresponsibility (2Kg 24:8-17; 25:27-30; Jr 52:31-34). So **his voice would be heard no more** . . . in **Israel**.

19:10-11. The lament changes from the image of lions to **a vine**, a frequent figure of Israel (cf. Is 5:1-7; Ezk 15; 17:5-10; Mt 21:33-41). Zedekiah, Israel's final king (ruled 597–586 BC), is the prince addressed here. The **mother**, Israel, was **like a vine**. In her past glory, Israel was **fruitful**, prospering under the blessing of God by **abundant waters** (Dt 8:7-8). She was **full of branches** producing many rulers. Her branches were **fit for scepters of rulers** and **raised above the clouds**, showing the grandeur of the Davidic dynasty.

19:12. But now the vine **was plucked up in fury** and **cast down. Its strong branch was torn off**. An **east wind** (Babylon, from the east) decimated the vine, the land of Israel, and the Davidic kings. Its **strong branch**, the king, was **torn off**, so the nation **withered** and **fire consumed it**.

19:13-14. In judgment, God uprooted the nation, deporting her to Babylon: **now it is planted in the wilderness, in a dry and thirsty land**. After Zedekiah was overthrown the Davidic line of kings ended, and **there [was] not in it a strong branch, a scepter to rule** in Judah. Zedekiah was the last king from the Davidic dynasty until Messiah Jesus came, just as the prophets foretold (Gn 49:10; Dn 9:26; Lk 1:30-33). Not until Jesus returns will a son of David sit on a throne in Jerusalem to reign as Israel's king (cf. Dn 2:44; Is 52:1-10; Jr 23:3-8).

C. History of Judah's Iniquity (20:1–24:27)

This review of Judah's history of iniquity demonstrates Israel's continuing pattern of sin. Chapter 19 showed that the end of the Davidic line was certain. What follows are further messages of judgment: a review of Israel's history (chap. 20); the sword that would strike Jerusalem (chap. 21); prophecies of judgment on Jerusalem for specific sins (chap. 22); and a comparison of the northern kingdom (Oholah/Samaria) and the southern kingdom (Oholibah/Judah), highlighting Judah's greater corruptions (chap. 23). It ends with the parable of the boiling pot and the example of Ezekiel's grief over the fall of Jerusalem (chap. 24).

1. Message of Israel's Past Rebellion and Restoration (20:1-49)

a. Israel's Past Rebellion (20:1-32)

20:1-3. This is the third dated prophecy of Ezekiel (cf. 1:2; 8:1), about 11 months after the previous recorded date (cf. 8:1). The date emphasizes its importance: The **seventh year**, in the **fifth month** on the **tenth** day, in the seventh year of Jehoiachin's exile (10th of Av, August 14, 591 BC). The message was given when **certain of the elders of Israel came to inquire of the Lord** (cf. 8:1; 14:1). This is a technical term for seeking an oracle from God, but He refused to respond to their request: **I will not be inquired of by you** (cf. comments on 14:3). The answer God gave was not a response to their question.

20:4. God asked Ezekiel, **Will you judge them?** (expressed twice for emphasis). In Hebrew it is not so much of a question as a command to "Arraign these people!" (cf. 22:2). God commanded Ezekiel to review Israel's history to make **them know the abominations of their fathers** as the basis for making a judgment. Ezekiel was to act as the prosecuting attorney and judge (cf. 22:2b), and he presented the evidence of Israel's sin in overview: (1) God's choice of Israel and deliverance from Egypt (20:1-9); (2) the people's movements from Mt. Sinai to Kadesh-barnea (20:10-17); (3) their wilderness wanderings (20:18-26); and (4) their idolatry after entering the land of Israel (20:27-31).

20:5-6. The history of Israel begins with the Abrahamic covenant: **On the day** God **chose Israel** to be His people (cf. Gn 12:1-3; 15; 17:1-8) and **swore to the descendants of . . . Jacob** (Gn. 26:2-5; 28:1-14).

God made Himself **known to them in . . . Egypt** to Moses at the burning bush: **I am the Lord your God** (cf. Ex 3:1-10). While in Egyptian slavery, God swore **to bring them out from . . . Egypt into a land that I had selected for them . . .** a land **flowing with milk and honey**, a fruitful land (cf. Ex 3:8; Lv 20:24; Nm 13:27; Jr 11:5), **the glory of all lands**. Israel is God's chosen land for His chosen people (cf. Dt 7:6-11; 8:7-10; 12:5-11; Jr 3:19).

20:7-8. God loved them (cf. Dt 7:6-9) and asked Israel to **cast away . . . the idols of Egypt**. The book of Exodus did not detail Israel's religious life in Egypt, but this verse indicates they had taken on the paganism of Egypt while living there 400 years. Even Moses failed to keep the most basic command to obey the Abrahamic covenant and circumcise his sons as commanded by God (cf. Gn 17:10-14; Ex 4:24-25).

But Israel **rebelled against** God's command. They did not **listen** to Him or **cast away the detestable things . . .** or **forsake the idols of Egypt** (cf. Ezk 23:3; Jos 24:14). Even in Egypt Israel deserved judgment but was spared from God's **wrath** and given an opportunity to believe and obey by His Passover deliverance (cf. Ex 12:13).

20:9. God's faithfulness to Israel was, and is, based on His grace, mercy, and His zeal to safeguard His own reputation, **for the sake of My name** (cf. vv. 14, 22; 36:21; Dt 7: 6-9; Is 37:35; 43:25). The **name of** God expresses His character; His reputation among the godless nations was at stake in His covenant faithfulness toward His people (cf. Ezk 36:20-23; Ps 23:3; Is 48:9-11). The Lord would not allow His name to be **profaned** (ridiculed, treated as less than holy) **in the sight of the nations** by failing to care for His people (cf. Nm 14:15-16), so He took them out of . . . Egypt.

20:10-12. When they left Egypt, God **brought them into the wilderness** where He **gave them My statutes and . . . ordinances** at Sinai (cf. Ex 19–34). God gave His **sabbaths** as the **sign** of the Mosaic covenant (cf. Ex 31:13-17). These elders listening to Ezekiel were reminded of the purpose of the statutes. First, **if a man observes them, he will live** (cf. Lv 18:4-5), that is, have a right relationship with the Lord. Second they would **know**, in an intimate, personal way **that I am the Lord who sanctifies them** (cf. Ex 31:13; Lv 20:8). This is not works righteousness. Obedience to the law must be motivated by faith (cf. Gn 15:6), not empty ritualism (cf. Is 1:11; Am 4:21-24).

20:13. Rather than keep God's commandments, **the house of Israel rebelled against** Him even **in the wilderness** (cf. Nm 10:11–14:35) and continued in idolatry (Ezk 20:16). They did **not walk in** God's **statutes** and they **greatly profaned** the **sabbaths**. Since the Sabbath was one of the primary signs of the Mosaic covenant (cf. Ex 31:13-17; Is 56:1-8), observance of the Sabbath was an outward sign of inward devotion to the Lord. Failure to keep the Sabbath was one of the causes of God's judgment and the 70-year captivity (22:8, 26; 23:38; 44:24; 45:17; 46:3; Jr 17:19-27; 25:8-11; Neh 13:17-18).

20:14-17. For their disobedience in the wilderness, the people deserved to die, but for **the sake of [His] name** (vv. 9, 14, 22) God spared them. There was specific judgment against the generation who doubted God at Kadesh and believed the evil report of the 10 spies (Nm 13–14). They were not brought **into the land** of promise, but their children born in the wilderness entered the land along with Joshua and Caleb (Nm 14:30-31).

20:18-22. God repeated His offer of blessing and His call to **their children in the wilderness** to obey: **Do not . . . defile yourselves with . . . idols**. Instead He required them to recognize that **I am the Lord your God** (18:19, 20)**; walk in My statutes . . . sanctify My sabbaths. But** the second generation **rebelled** as their parents did. Yet God preserved them, acting in mercy **for the sake of My name** (vv. 21b-22; cf. 20: 9, 14).

20:23-24. God did not destroy them for their sin, but He **swore to them** (cf. Dt 28) that if they sinned, he **would scatter them among the nations** (Dt 28:64-68).

20:25-26. If they chose to disobey God He would abandon them to their sin and its consequences. He gave them (over to) **statutes that were not good** and **ordinances by which they could not live**. Some have suggested this is a reference to the Mosaic law being too hard to keep. However, this view should be rejected because it lowers the intrinsic quality of the Mosaic law as an expression of God's righteousness found in Scripture. The NT declares that God's law is "holy, righteous, and good" (Rm 7:12), and even sinners must "agree that the law is good" (Rm 7:16; 1Tm 1:8). Further, God said the one who keeps His law will live (cf. Ezk 20:11; Lv 18:4-5). It is better to see these **statutes** and **ordinances** as commandments of the pagan religions that Israel followed. Once the people rejected God's law, they turned to pagan religions, and the Lord gave them over to those practices, until the time of judgment fell. They became **unclean** by observing the ordinances of paganism, such as the sacrifice of **their firstborn** (cf. Ezk 16:20). God's giving over of the people to sin was His judicial act. Because they refused to follow His righteous ways, God would abandon them to the consequences of their actions (cf. Rm 1:24-28; 2Th 2:11-12).

20:27-29. When God brought the people into **the land which I swore to give to them** (cf. Gn 12:1-7; Ex 33:1-3; Dt 34:4), they still **blasphemed Me by acting treacherously against Me**. Sin is very personal to the Lord. They adopted Canaanite religion and **offered . . . their sacrifices** to idols on **every high hill** and under **every leafy tree** (6:14).

20:30-32. The **house of Israel** worshiped **detestable things** and defiled themselves **after the manner** of their ancestors, with idolatry and child sacrifice, causing their children to **pass through the fire** (cf. comments on 16:20). Therefore God would **not be inquired of by** these elders (v. 3). This review of Israel's history proved Israel wanted to **be like the nations . . . serving** idols/gods of **wood and stone.**

b. Israel's Future Restoration (20:33-44)

20:33-34. Despite their past failures, the **Lord God** would make Himself known to Israel **with a mighty hand and with an outstretched arm**, and even with **wrath poured out**. This recalls God's deliverance of Israel in the past (cf. Ex 6:6; 32:11; Dt 4:34-35; 5:15; 7:19; 11:2; Ps 136:10-12). He would faithfully continue to be **king over** Israel (e.g., Ps 145:1; Is 32:22). God would **bring** the Jewish people **out** from all the **lands where you [were] scattered**. This likely refers not to the return from Babylon because of the universal scope of the return. Therefore it predicts the worldwide regathering of the Jewish people to Israel before the future tribulation.

20:35-36. After their return to the land of Israel, God will drive some of those who returned out to **the wilderness**, where God's **judgment** would begin. This wilderness judgment refers specifically to the events in the period before the return of the Messiah, commonly called the tribulation. Revelation 12:14 describes the woman, Israel, fleeing to the wilderness in the second half of the tribulation. There will be a purging process as in the **wilderness** wanderings when Israel left **Egypt**.

20:37. God would discipline those who had rebelled, using His **rod** to correct His people. Through this process, the Shepherd of Israel (cf. Gn 48:15; Ps 23:1; 80:1; Mt 2:6; Heb 13:20) **will bring you [Israel] into the bond of the covenant**. This is not the Mosaic covenant, which Israel had broken and invalidated by her unbelief (cf. Ezk 16:59; Jr 31:31-32). This is the new covenant, an everlasting covenant, enacted to restore Israel to the Lord (cf. Ezk 16:60; Jr 31:31-33). The new covenant was inaugurated with the death and resurrection of Messiah Jesus (cf. Lk 22:20), but awaits its fulfillment when He returns and fulfills all the promises to faithful Israel. On the relationship of the new covenant to the other covenants, see comments on Jr 31:31-37.

20:38. At that future time, God will **purge** those **rebels** who do not belong to Him. Those who **transgress against** the Lord would not **enter the land of Israel**, just as the generation who left Egypt did not enter the promised land because of their disbelief (Nm 14:32-33). These events were not fulfilled in the Babylonian exile. Those who returned were not the purified nation that this passage describes. God's process of purification means only those faithful to Him will enjoy the covenant of blessing.

20:39. Using irony, God said for now, **Go serve . . . idols**; this was Israel's current spiritual condition. **But later**, at the end of days, the nation will **surely listen to** the Lord and honor **My holy name** (39:7; 43:7).

20:40-41. Then on the Lord's **holy mountain . . . the high mountain of Israel**, the temple mount (Pss 2:6; 3:4; 15:1; Is 11:9; 56:7; 57:13; 65:11; Ob 16; Zph 3:11), the **whole house of Israel** will **serve** the Lord **in the land** of Israel. He will **accept** the people, and **seek** their **contributions and . . . gifts** (cf. 40:38-43) because they would be offered from a pure heart (cf. Ps 24:4-6). God will **prove** Himself **holy among you in the sight of the nations**.

Israel had profaned her God, turning away from Him to idolatry. In the future, however, the nation will set God apart so all the nations will sense God's holiness (Is 56:1-8). This did not happen at the return from Babylon, and it is not happening now through the Church. These events are future, when Israel recognizes Jesus as Messiah (Zch 12:10), and all Israel will be saved (Rm 11:26-27).

20:42-44. God's restoration of Israel has two key changes: First, there will be a true recognition of God. Israel will **know that I am the Lord**. The nation will **know** Him in a personal intimate way, as He revealed Himself by covenant to Abraham (Gn 15:1-18), to David (2Sm 7:8-24), and in the new covenant (Jr 31:31-34). The Lord will keep His word **for My name's sake** to demonstrate His covenant loyalty in fulfilling His promises and for His honor (cf. Ezk 20:5-9; 36:21; Rm 11:27). Second, this knowledge of God is a result of repentance when Israel comes to the Lord. She will **remember** the **ways** she had **defiled** herself and will **loathe** herself for all the **evil** she has done (cf. Ezk 6:9; 16:61; Zch 12:10ff.). The shame Israel should have felt when she sinned in the past will finally be manifested when God restores her in the future.

That God will bring about these conditions in the future and is not producing them in the present era through the Church derives from His sovereign purposes for Israel the nation. God formed Israel to mediate His name to the world (Ex 19:6; Is 43:7; 44:23; 60:7, 13, 21; Ezk 39:13; Zch 2:5). Israel fulfills this mission almost exclusively as God reveals Himself to the world through her display of holiness (Dt 4:5-6; 26:18-19). He also reveals Himself through His historical acts with Israel as a nation, including judging the people (Dt 29:24-25; Ezk 5:8, 13; 6:14; 7:9; 12:15-17; 15:7; 21:5; 39:21-24) and rescuing and restoring them (Ex 6:7; 7:5; 14:4, 18; Jos 2:10; Pss 67:1-2, 7; 102:13-15; Is 49:26; 52:7-10; 55:3-5; Ezk 36:22-36; 39:27). Even Israel's failure did not cancel this purpose, her failure being foreknown by God (Dt 29:4; Is 29:10; Ps 69:22-23; Is 42:16-19; 43:8-13, 22-28). But failure and judgment are not the end of Israel's story. God also promised to restore the nation and cause her to fulfill His purpose for her (Lv 26:43-44; Is 11:11-12; 48:9; Jr 30:3, 10, 11; 31:8; Ezk 20:33-44; 34:11-16; Am 9:11-15), after which time she will radiate God's glory to the world. Robert L. Saucy ("Is Christ the Fulfillment of National Israel's Prophecies? Yes and No!" unpublished paper presented at the Evangelical Theological Society Annual Meeting, November 2010, 17) writes:

> These prophecies of Israel's restoration and fulfillment of purpose refer to the same Israel who had a history of disobedience. It is the blind and deaf disobedient servant to which the spiritual transformation and restoration as a nation are promised again and again in Isaiah, not a new spiritual Israel [that is, the Church]. According to Ezekiel it is the Israel that God brought out of the land of Egypt and who had profaned the Lord's name by their disobedience (20:9, 13, 16, 21-22) that is going to be renewed and restored through a new purging even as their fathers were judged in the wilderness (20:34-44).
>
> It is Israel as a *nation*, and not . . . people gathered from all nations as is the church today. In connection with the promise of a new covenant, the Lord declared that only if the fixed orders of nature ceased would "the offspring of Israel also . . . cease from being a *nation* before Me forever" (Jer. 31:35-36, emphasis added). It is as a nation among nations that Israel will become a blessing to other nations that they might receive the same salvation and become God's people alongside of it (see Is. 19:23-25).

The Church does not fulfill Israel's promises related to the manifestation of the kingdom of God. Saucy argues, "As a spiritual community of God's people, the church cannot manifest a paradigm of the kingdom of God before the nations as is prophesied through the theocracy of Israel, where all of the structures of human society are ruled by God and there is no Caesar governing the people along with Christ, as is true during this age of the church" (Saucy, 18). The prophecies regarding Israel's restoration include an incomparable display of God's power and glory, something not seen in the demonstration of the present manifestation of the kingdom in the Church. "Israel's witness to the nations was to be primarily through God's historical actions in restoring and blessing that nation before the eyes of the world. Freed from the persecution and oppression of the nations, the spiritually transformed Israel would live in their land in God's peace and prosperity, exalted among the nations who look to the God of Israel for the same blessing" (Saucy, 19). But the Church witnesses through its suffering (Jn 15:18-21; Ac 9:15; 1Pt 4:12-19), and at the end of the age, the Church wanes in its influence (see Mt 24:10-12, 37-39) and evil becomes pervasive (2Th 2:3-12; Rv 19:17-19). These points illustrate that the Church is not the means whereby these purposes of God will be realized. The restoration of Israel in the future is what Ezekiel pictures.

c. Parable of the Forest Fire (20:45-49)

20:45-46. After an overview of Israel's past and future, Ezekiel focused on the imminent judgment for sin. Ezekiel was told to **set your face** (cf. 4:3) in judgment against three areas. **Teman**, a poetic term for "south" as well as the proper name of a city in Edom, to Judah's south (cf. Am 1:12; Jr 49:7). The **south** is the **Negev**, the southern region of Israel.

20:47. Although Babylon's army could come from the north (cf. 9:1-2) and the focus of their attack was on Judah, their invasion would cover the **whole** land **south to north** (cf. 21:4). God was going to devastate Judah by **fire**, a phrase often used of judgment and invasion (cf. 15:7; Is 10:16-19; Jr 15:14; 17:4, 27; 21:14). No one would escape. **It will consume every green tree . . . as well as every dry tree.**

20:48-49. The people mocked Ezekiel, saying he was just **speaking in parables**, and they refused to understand them. But God said, **all flesh will see that I, the LORD have kindled** the fire and **it shall not be quenched**. The upcoming sword judgments (chap. 21) are inevitable.

2. Four Messages of the Sword (21:1-32)

Because the people mocked Ezekiel's message about the fire (20:45-49), God gave him four specific messages of coming judgment by the sword, a term used 15 times in this chapter to emphasize the violent form His judgment would take against the people.

a. The Sword Drawn (21:1-7)

21:1-2. Ezekiel was to **set** his **face** (cf. 4:3) **toward Jerusalem**, **speak against** the **sanctuaries** (the temple), and **prophesy against the land of Israel**. God was against (cf. 5:8) His land, His Holy City, and His dwelling place. The Lord emphasized His relationship and ownership.

21:3-5. Although Babylon was the immediate instrument of judgment, God was clearly behind this judgment: **I will draw My sword** (vv. 3, 5) and **I will cut off**. In the course of war . . . both the **righteous and the wicked** would die. Just as a forest fire burns both the dry and the green trees, so judgment would be indiscriminate. War and natural disaster sweep away everyone in their path, the guilty as well as the innocent (cf. Lk 13:1-4). Scripture teaches that each individual is responsible for his own righteousness or wickedness before the Lord (cf. comments on chap. 18), but it does not promise that the righteous will supernaturally escape disaster. Ezekiel stressed the extent of the coming judgment, **against all flesh from south to north** (cf. 20:47). When judgment came, then the people would **know that . . . the LORD** had **drawn My sword** (cf. v. 3).

21:6-7. Ezekiel was brokenhearted about their sin and the coming judgment (cf. 9:8; 11:13). God commanded him to show his **breaking heart and bitter grief** by groaning **in their sight**—he was to "cry out and wail" (v. 12). So when the people ask **Why do you groan?** Ezekiel was to explain to them it was **because of the news** that the fall of Jerusalem was coming. The awful realization of their judgment would be devastating. **Every spirit will faint** (cf. 7:17). Yet there was no doubt: **Behold, it comes and it will happen, declares the Lord GOD.**

b. The Sword Sharpened (21:8-17)

21:8-10. God's drawn **sword** was **sharpened** (vv. 9, 10, 11) and **polished** (vv. 9, 10) to move fast and **flash like lightening** (vv. 10, 15) ready for the **slaughter** of His judgment. This song to the sword of judgment shifts to the image of a **rod** that will fall in judgment **on every tree** (cf. comments on 20:47).

The term **rod** (*shevet*) simply means a stick. One use for it is the scepter of a king (cf. Gn 49:9-10), used like a shepherd's rod to rule and direct his people. Thus, Ezekiel was saying that the people had rejected God's rod of rulership, so now He would use the sword over them instead. But seeing the rod as a scepter and referring to God's rulership seems foreign to this passage. Another usage of the word "rod" is a rod of discipline, in the way that a shepherd uses a rod to discipline the flock (cf. Ps 23:4; Pr 10:13, 13:24; 23:13). Hence, it frequently refers to God's chastisement (2Sm 7:14, Jb 9:34; 21:9). This makes sense in context. Israel had despised God's earlier attempts to use a rod to correct her, so God would now use a sword.

21:11-12. The **polished** sword is given to the **slayer** to execute judgment on God's **people** and . . . **against all the officials of Israel**. Because of the number of slain, God told Ezekiel to **Cry out and wail** (cf. v. 6) and **strike your thigh** in grief. The leaders had rejected God's leadership, and they would be removed from leadership.

21:13. This would be a time of **testing**. The **rod** (*septer*) **which despises will be no more** (cf. v. 10). This is somewhat obscure because the object of the statement is unclear. However it seems to point to the interruption of the Davidic line, which came because the officials had rejected living in righteousness under Davidic leadership. So it would **be no more** until the coming of Messiah (cf. Gn 49:10).

21:14-17. Here the work of the sword is stressed. Both Ezekiel, the **son of man** (20:14), and the **Lord** (20:17) would **clap** their **hands** in judgment, a phrase that bookends this section (vv. 14, 17; cf. 6:11; 22:13). The **sword** would strike repeatedly, which is the sense of the phrase **let the sword be doubled the third time**, so that the people's **hearts may melt** (cf. v. 7) in fear. Swift judgment would come from the **glittering**, highly polished, **sword** . . . striking quickly **like lightening** (cf. 20:10) from all sides (**to the right** . . . **to the left**) as it relentlessly pursued the people. It would stop only when God would **clap My hands together** and **appease My wrath**.

c. The Sword Directed Toward Jerusalem (21:18-27)

21:18-19. Although unaware of it, Nebuchadnezzar was directed by the Lord to overthrow Jerusalem. God told Ezekiel to mark out **two ways** (routes) for the **sword of the king of Babylon**. Ezekiel was to **make a signpost** . . . **at the** . . . **way to the city** of Jerusalem. This seems to be a symbolic act, rather than posting a literal sign, or drawing the route Nebuchadnezzar would take regarding the attack on Jerusalem.

In 588 BC three vassal states were seeking independence from Babylon: Tyre (north of Israel along the Mediterranean coast), Ammon (east of the Dead Sea) and Judah. Nebuchadnezzar led his forces north and west from Babylon along the Euphrates River to quell the rebellions.

21:20-23. At **Rabbah** (north of Damascus) Nebuchadnezzar came to a **parting of the way** and had to decide which nation he would attack first to control the rebellion and which route to take. Nebuchadnezzar used common practices of Babylonian **divination** to determine his course of action: **shakes the arrows**, similar to drawing straws; consulting his **household idols**, the portable images (cf. Gn 31:19; Hs 3:4) of the family gods, and examining the **liver** of a sacrificed animals. By themselves these practices could do nothing, but God worked through them to accomplish His plan: into Nebuchadnezzar's **right hand** would come the lot for **Jerusalem**. That would be the signpost (the route) they would take **to set battering rams against the gates** . . . **to build a siege wall** against Jerusalem.

21:24-26. Israel's leaders had made the **iniquity** . . . **transgressions** . . . and **sins** of the nation **to be remembered** . . . **uncovered** . . . and **appear**, so they would be taken captive, **seized with the hand**. King Zedekiah, the **wicked one, the prince of Israel** (cf. 12:8-11), would be stripped of authority (his **turban** and **crown** symbolize royalty and will be removed). Nebuchadnezzar would take the king captive, **abase** that which is **high,** and **exalt** the **low**, leaving only the poorest people in the land (2Kg 25:4-12).

21:27. With the deportation of Zedekiah, Davidic kingship ended in Israel. The triple use of **a ruin** stressed that Israel's throne was to be absolutely desolate. It will not be restored **until He comes whose right it is**, and the Lord **will give it to Him**. This prophecy of the restoration of the Davidic kingship is a deliberate reference to Gn 49:10. Although the NASB takes the word "Shiloh" in Gn 49:10 as a proper name, it is better understood as "He whose right it is" (HCSB; see comments on Gn 49:10 for the reasons that this is a preferable reading.) Ezekiel 21:27 uses the same words in Hebrew, the difference being that Gn 49:10 has them in a contracted form, while Ezkekiel has them in an expanded form. Regardless, Ezekiel is referring to the prediction of the Messiah in the Torah. Jerusalem would fall and Zedekiah would be taken away, but God has a faithful long-range plan. The line of David would be restored when Messiah, the righteous God-appointed King, came.

Between the time of Zedekiah and Jesus, Israel did not have a Davidic king. There were no valid claims to the throne until Jesus rode into Jerusalem on a donkey to present Himself as Messiah King. Only after His resurrection did His faithful disciples recognize Him (cf. Zch 9:9; Mt 21:1-11; Rv 5:5; 19:11-16; 20:4). One day, the Messiah will return in victory, be recognized by the nation of Israel, and reign from His throne in a restored Jerusalem as King of Israel.

d. The Sword Directed Toward Ammon (21:28-32)

21:28. The judgment of **Ammon** concludes the sword oracles. Ammon, part of modern Jordan whose capital is named for this ancient kingdom, was a pagan nation whose deity was "the detestable Molech" (1Kg 11:7; Ezk 16:20-21), the god of child sacrifice (Lv 18:21). They were perpetual enemies of Israel (cf. Dt 23:3-4; Jdg 3:13, 10:6–11:28; 1Sm 11:1-11; 2Kg 24:1-2; 2Ch 20:1-23). Both Ammon and Judah became vassals to Babylon (Jr 27:1-7). When Nebuchadnezzar attacked Jerusalem, Ammon's destruction was delayed (cf. Ezk 21:18-23). After Jerusalem's fall, the Ammonites organized a coup that caused the death of Gedaliah, the Babylonian appointed Jewish governor of Judah (cf. Jr 40:13–41:10), hoping to keep Babylon's army focused on Judah.

21:29-32. Despite Ammon's **false visions** of security, her **day** of judgment **has come . . . the time of the punishment of the end**. God's **indignation** against Ammon's personal wickedness (cf. 1Kg 11:7) and their enmity toward Judah (cf. Am 1:13-15; Zph 2:8-11) would cause Him to hand Ammon over to **brutal men**, the Babylonians who were **skilled in destruction**. They would be **fuel for the fire** of God's wrath in their own land. Ammon is at the head of the list of seven nations to be judged for their mistreatment of Israel (cf. 25:1-7).

3. Three Messages on the Defilement and Judgment of Jerusalem (22:1-31)

a. Cause of Jerusalem's Judgment (22:1-16)

22:1-2. The opening of this section is another legal indictment against Jerusalem (see comments on 20:4).

22:3-5. There are two charges against Jerusalem: First, **shedding blood** (repeated seven times in this message, vv. 2-4, 6, 9, 12-13, 27) underscores Jerusalem's sin of extreme violence (cf. 7:23; 8:17; 12:19). Second, is the **defilement** by worshiping **idols**, a frequent charge against Israel (e.g., 5:11; 8:10; 14:3). These two sins violated the Mosaic law concerning Israel's relationship with man and God (cf. Dt 6:5-9; Lv 19:9-18). When judgment came, nations **near and . . . far** would **mock** Jerusalem, who had considered herself beyond the reach of judgment.

22:6-12. The **rulers of Israel** led the country into violating the Mosaic law (e.g., Ex 20:1-17) in many categories: disrespecting **father and mother** (Ezk 22:7); breaking **My sabbaths** and apostasy (vv. 8-9); sexual immorality/**lewdness** (vv. 10-11); coveting/financial corruption—**injured your neighbors for gain by oppression** (v. 12) The root cause: **you have forgotten Me** (cf. 23:35; Is 17:10).

22:13-14. Because of their **dishonest gain** and **bloodshed**, God would **smite** ("clap") His **hand** (cf. 6:11; 21:14, 17) in judgment. The question, **Can your heart endure?** demands a negative response. Jerusalem's courage would fail.

22:15-16. God would **scatter** them **among the nations** for their disobedience, as the law demanded (cf. Lv 26:27-39; Dt 28:64-68). Israel did **profane** (defiled) God's law (cf. Ezk 22:6-2), now she would **profane** herself **in the sight of the nations** (cf. v. 8). In exile, she would understand the character of the God she had scorned and forgotten: **you will know that I am the Lord.**

b. Means of Judgment (22:17-22)

22:17-18. The smelting furnace is the next image of judgment. Dross is the scum of impurity that forms on the surface of molten metal when it is refined. Israel had become like the **dross** of **bronze . . . tin . . . iron and lead** to the Lord. Because of her sin, Israel needed purification (cf. Ps 119:119; Pr 25:4-5; Is 48:9-11).

22:19-22. Just as metals are melted in a refiner's furnace, God would **gather** the people in the **midst of Jerusalem**. The city became the crucible as the **fire** of God's **wrath** melted her as **silver** (cf. Is 1:22, 25; 48:10; Jr 6:27-30). God's judgment would force the people to acknowledge Him: **and you will know that I, the Lord, have poured out My wrath on you.**

c. The Recipients of Judgment (22:23-31)

Here the recipients of the judgment are divided into groups: "prophets" (22:25, 28), "priests" (23:26), "princes" (23:27), and "people of the land" (22:29).

22:23-24. The physical **land** literally suffered the consequences of the people's sin. God promised the blessing of rain for obedience (cf. Dt 28:12), but the consequence of sin would be drought (cf. Dt 28:23-24). The land had not been

cleansed, a term for ceremonial purification, or **rained on** because of God's **indignation**.

22:25. The **conspiracy** of false teaching by **prophets** was **like a roaring lion** (cf. 19:1-19; 1Pt 5:8) that **devoured lives**, destroying the people with their corrupt teaching (cf. Ezk 13:18). They had **taken treasure and precious things**, a term Jeremiah used for temple articles (cf. Jr 20:5), for their own use, and they caused the deaths of many men, resulting in many widows in the community (Ezk 22:8; Ex 22:22; Dt 10:18; Is 10:1-2).

22:26-27. Judah's **priests** did **violence to My law** and **profaned My holy things** (cf. v. 25; Zph 3:4). They **made no distinction between the holy and the profane**, the main duty of the priests (Ezk 44:23; Lv 10:10-22; 11:47; 20:25; Jr 2:8). They ignored God's **sabbaths** (Ezk 20:16, 21, 24), the sign of the Mosaic covenant between God and Israel (Ex 31:13). Instead of lovingly shepherding the people (cf. Ezk 34:5), they were **like wolves . . . shedding blood . . . destroying lives . . .** for **dishonest gain**.

22:28. The **prophets**, who should teach God's truth, instead taught **false visions** and covered their **divining lies** as **whitewash** covers a broken wall (cf. 13:8-16). They declared, **Thus says the Lord GOD, when the LORD has not spoken**.

22:29 Iniquity characterized the whole society from the civil and spiritual leadership down to the **people of the land** (*am ha'aretz*), a term meaning the common man. Virtually the entire populace was involved in **oppression** and **robbery** and they **wronged** the **poor**, **needy** and **sojourner** (cf. 21:6-12).

22:30-31. God wanted faithful followers. He searched **for a man** in **the land**, to **build up the wall** (cf. 13:5; Ps 106:23) and **stand in the gap** to obey Him and defend His honor. Yet He **found no one** (cf. Gn 18:23-33). Consequently, they would be **consumed . . . with the fire of My wrath** (cf. Ezk 21:31). Israel had brought judgment **upon their heads**, according to their sinful behavior (cf. 7:3).

4. Parable of the Two Adulterous Sisters: Oholah and Oholibah (23:1-49)

a. Infidelity of the Sisters: Oholah and Oholibah (23:1-21)

23:1-3. This is a parable similar to the story of Sodom and Samaria, the sisters of Jerusalem, (16:44-59). Here **two women** (sisters) shared the same moral degradation of being a **harlot in Egypt** from their **youth**. The emphasis in this parable is on the political alliances with pagan powers, while the earlier parable of the sisters (chap. 16) was about idolatry.

23:4. The older sister was **Oholah**, (*"her tent"*), who represented **Samaria**, and the northern kingdom of Israel; and the younger was **Oholibah**, (*"my tent is in her"*) who represented **Jerusalem** and the southern kingdom of Judah. The word "tent" was often used of the tabernacle, God's sanctuary (cf. Ex 29:4, 10-11, 30). The name **Oholah** connotes that the sanctuary associated with this sister was of her own making, since corrupted worship of the Lord was established in the northern kingdom by Jeroboam when the kingdom divided in 931 BC. By contrast, the name **Oholibah** connotes that God's true sanctuary was in her midst, in the temple in Jerusalem. Both kingdoms belonged to the Lord **they became Mine** and . . . had **sons and daughters**.

23:5. The sin of **Oholah**/Samaria was reliance on the **Assyrians**. Israel had a long relationship with Assyria. Jehu (841–814 BC) allied Israel with Assyria and submitted himself as a vassal (2Kg 10:32-34). Menahem (752–742 BC) paid tribute to Assyria (2Kg 15:19-20). The prophet Hosea (760–720 BC) rebuked Israel for her dependence on Assyria instead of on the Lord (cf. Hs 5:13-14; 7:11; 8:9; 12:1). Hoshea was on the throne when the northern kingdom fell to Assyria (2Kg 17:3-4) in 721 BC. Samaria did not trust the Lord for protection or stay faithful to Him but instead made an alliance ("played the harlot") with Assyria, leading to her downfall.

23:6-10. Oholah was attracted to the rich **purple** clothing and **desirable** appearance of the powerful Assyrian **officials**; she **lusted** after all their **idols** and **defiled herself**. God gave Israel, the northern kingdom, over to her **lovers**, the Assyrians, for whom she **lusted**, and Assyria **took** Israel's **sons** and **daughters** captive to Assyria and killed many of the people **with the sword** (cf. 2Kg 17; 721 BC).

23:11-13. Jerusalem saw God's judgment on Oholah (Samaria), and it should have been a warning, yet **Oholibah** was **more corrupt** than her **sister**. Even after Israel's captivity to Assyria, Judah's King Ahaz (2Kg 16:1-20, 735–716 BC) sought an alliance (**lusted after**) with the **Assyrians**, refusing Isaiah's message (cf. Is 7:7-9).

23:14. When Judah became a vassal state to Egypt (2Kg 23:29-37) she wanted out of that political oppression. Instead of turning to the Lord, **she increased her harlotries** and made an alliance with the **Chaldeans** (Babylonians). She began worshiping Babylonian gods, which were often **portrayed on** a **wall** (cf. Jr 22:14; Ezk 8:10).

23:15-16. Jerusalem was attracted to their military might, their **belts**, and **turbans**. She **lusted after** the **Babylonians** for military protection, and **sent messengers** to them asking for aid.

23:17-18. When the **Babylonians came** they did not give the help Jerusalem expected. Instead they **defiled her**, and she **became disgusted** with them. In turn, God became **disgusted** with Jerusalem's lustful behavior as He had with Samaria **her sister**.

23:19-21. Jerusalem **multiplied her harlotries, remembering** the pagan practices of the **days of her youth . . . in . . . Egypt** (vv. 3, 19, 21). Ezekiel presented a graphic picture of her **lewdness** to clearly portray their spiritual degradation. Judah **lusted after** them, for their political alliance (2Kg 24:1; 25:1; Jr 37:5-8) and followed their pagan religious practices.

b. Punishment of the Sisters (23:22-35)

Ezekiel gave four oracles of judgment against the sisters, beginning with the phrase, **Thus says the Lord God** (vv. 22, 28, 32, 35). The focus of the judgments is on **Oholibah**, Jerusalem.

23:22-26. *First Oracle of Punishment: The Attack of the Lovers.* God would **arouse** (to wake up, to incite) Jerusalem's allies/**lovers against** her **from every side**. The combined army of the Babylonians and her allies **Pekod**, **Shoa**, and **Koa** (small Aramean tribes in eastern Babylonia), along with **all the Assyrians**, would **come against** Jerusalem. The highest command of **governors . . . officials . . . men of renown . . . riding on horses** would carry out an intense military campaign: **weapons**, **chariots**, war **wagons**, **buckler**, **shield**, and **helmet** to deliver the Lord's **judgment**. His **wrath** would be delivered by the cruel hand of Babylonia's gruesome **customs**: they would cut off **your nose and . . . ears**. Even **survivors** of battle would **fall by the sword . . .** or **be consumed by the fire**. Everything of beauty and value they would **strip** away.

23:27. The Babylonian captivity would cure Judah's **lewdness and . . . harlotry**. She would no longer seek pagan idols or alliances or **remember Egypt** for help.

23:28-31. *Second Oracle of Punishment: Given Into the Hand of Your Enemy.* This oracle is similar to the first (cf. vv. 22-27), but adds: Babylon would **deal with you in hatred** and **leave** Jerusalem **naked and bare**. All this would **be done to you** because she **played the harlot with the nations** and **you have defiled yourself with their idols** (cf. 6:9).

23:32-34. *Third Oracle of Punishment: The Cup of God's Judgment.* This is a poetic oracle of certain doom on Jerusalem. The symbol of a **cup** of judgment is frequently used in Scripture (e.g., Ps 75:8; Is 51:17-23; Jr 25:15-19; Hab 2:16). This cup is large, **deep and wide . . .** and **contains much**. The contents are **sorrow**, **horror**, and **desolation**. Jerusalem was certain to **drink it and drain it**, for her judgment would be extensive.

23:35. *Fourth Oracle of Punishment: The Reasons for Judgment.* This final oracle presents the main reason for the judgments. God said they had **forgotten Me** (cf. 22:12). The importance of remembering the Lord's faithfulness is a key theme in Scripture (e.g., Ex 13:3; Dt. 4:9-10; 8:2; Ps 77:11). God reminded Jerusalem she had **cast Me behind your back** (cf. Jr 32:33) forgetting Him, so she must **bear** the **punishment** for her **lewdness** (cf. Ezk 23:8, 27, 44).

c. Conclusion of the Message to Oholah and Oholibah (23:36-49)

23:36-39. The conclusion is a summary of their **abominations**. The lowest point of their unfaithfulness to the Lord beyond their spiritual **adultery** and the **blood . . . on their hands** was sacrificing their **sons, whom they bore to Me** to the **idols**. The Lord considered their children His children. The altars built to honor Molech were little more than stoves that would be heated to red-hot temperatures. They also had carved in their lids the hands and arms of Molech. When the altars were heated, children would be placed in those hands and burned alive, an act called "passing through the fire" (cf. 16:20-21; Jr 7:31). Heartlessly, **on the same day** they **slaughtered their children** they would enter the temple and defile **My sanctuary** with their corrupt worship. Their wicked presence **profaned My sabbaths.**

23:40-41. Their failure to trust God in every area of life was expressed in spiritual adultery and political alliances with pagan nations: **they have sent for men . . . from afar**. Both sisters prepared themselves (**bathed**, **painted** their **eyes**, **decorated** themselves with **ornaments**) to entice foreign nations into alliances, which were forbidden by God (cf. Dt 17:14-20). They prepared a **table** that should have been used for God's **incense** and His **oil**, but instead offered to their lovers.

23:42-44. This is a vivid picture of **Oholah** and **Oholibah, the lewd women**, (symbolizing

Israel and Judah), preparing themselves for the **men** as they **put** on **bracelets** and **crowns** until they were **worn out by adulteries**.

23:45. The **righteous men** who would **judge them** were like Ezekiel, who would pronounce **judgment** on them. The judgment for adultery was death, usually by stoning (cf. Lv 20:10, 27). Adultery is not a casual, private sin. It has the serious consequences of **shed blood** because such a **woman** destroys lives and **blood is on their hands** (cf. Pr 6:24-26; 9:18; 23:27-28). Thus, Israel and Judah's spiritual adultery from the Lord was reprehensible and would bring judgment.

23:46-47. They would be given over to **terror and plunder** . . . and be stoned with **stones** . . . **cut . . . down** with **swords** . . . their children killed . . . and **their houses** would be burned **with fire**. These events describe the plunder and destruction of Jerusalem by the Babylonians.

23:48-49. God would make **lewdness cease from the land** (cf. v. 27) after they bore the **penalty of worshiping . . . idols; thus you will know that I am the Lord God**.

5. Parable of the Boiling Pot (24:1-14)

The third series of judgments on Judah (cf. chaps. 4–11; 12–19; 20–24) concludes in chap. 24 with two additional messages of the inevitability of God's wrath.

24:1-2. The specific day of calamity was the **ninth year** . . . **tenth month** . . . **tenth** day since King Jehoiachin's exile (10 Tevet/January 15, 588 BC). The **king of Babylon** besieged **Jerusalem this very day**. This was the exact day Ezekiel had been pointing to for over four years and is significantly mentioned elsewhere in Scriptures (2Kg 25:1; Jr 39:1; 52:4).

24:3-5. In this **parable** the **rebellious house** of Israel (cf. 3:9) is described as being inside a cooking **pot**. This was similar to Ezekiel's earlier message to the leaders who thought they would be safe in the city (chap. 11). The people of Jerusalem who were spared the initial deportation to Babylon (2Kg 24) thought the worst was over and that they were safe in Jerusalem. However, even the **choicest of the flock** were not safe. The **pot** would **boil vigorously** and **bones** would **seethe in it**. All would be destroyed.

24:6. The parable was explained using two similar statements: **Therefore, thus says the Lord God, Woe to the bloody city** (vv. 6-8, 9-14), a statement of their sad future and of the cause for their judgment (cf. 22:1-16). In this parable, Jerusalem is like a **rust**-encrusted cooking pot, a reference to the iniquity of the people. The rust had **not gone out of it**, but surfaced during cooking. Her corruption could not be hidden.

People in Jerusalem had felt secure from Babylon's onslaught inside the walled city. But when the city fell they would be taken **out of it piece after piece**, like removing every piece of meat from a pot **without making a choice**. That is, every inhabitant without exception would be removed from the city for exile.

24:7-8. Jerusalem would be judged, **For her blood is in her midst**. The city was guilty of bloodshed (cf. 22:1-6). The Lord said Jerusalem had shed innocent blood, and the evidence was in plain sight, openly displayed as **she placed it on the bare rock**. That blood was crying out, figuratively speaking, for vengeance. **She did not pour it on the ground to cover it with dust** (Gn 4:10; Lv 17:13-14; Jb 16:18; Is 26:21). Because Jerusalem had openly shed the blood of others, God's **wrath** would **come up to take vengeance**, and He would openly shed her blood **on the bare rock**.

24:9-10. This statement of judgment begins: **Woe to the bloody city!** continuing the image of the pot around which God would **make the pile** (of wood for the fire) **great**. The **flesh** in the pot was to be cooked **well** and the **bones** to **be burned**. This forecast the burning of Jerusalem by Babylon.

24:11-12. Finally the pot would be **empty**, that is, Jerusalem would be without its inhabitants. It would be placed on the **coals** (suffer judgment) until **its filthiness** was **melted** and its **rust** burned away. The city would be destroyed and her citizens carried away to remove its iniquity.

24:13-14. God **would have cleansed** His people from their sin, but they refused to repent and obey. Therefore the people and the city would experience the purifying work of God's **wrath**. He would **act** and **not relent** or have **pity** or **be sorry**. They would be judged **according to your ways and . . . deeds**. God's mercy prompts Him to withhold judgment as long as possible to enable people to repent (Rm 2:4-5), but He does not wait indefinitely. God will eventually and inevitably punish wickedness: **I will judge you**.

6. Sign of the Death of Ezekiel's Wife (24:15-27)

24:15-19. Ezekiel's personal sad experience was a lesson to the Israelites already in captivity who were watching the fate of Jerusalem (cf. 2Kg 24:1-5). Ezekiel was given **the word of the Lord** that the sign of the tragic death of his beloved wife, **the desire of [his] eyes**, would be an act of

God and a sign to the nation. It would be natural to mourn, but God told Ezekiel not to **mourn** or **weep**. He was to **groan silently** and not follow the customary practices of **mourning for the dead** (cf. Jr 16:5-7). In the **morning** Ezekiel told the people what God said, and **in the evening** his **wife died**. The next day when his wife was buried, he obeyed as God **commanded**—not to mourn. The people were shocked at his lack of grief and asked **what these things . . . mean**.

24:20-21. Ezekiel explained to the **house of Israel** that the death of his wife symbolized the coming destruction of God's **sanctuary** in Jerusalem, **the pride of your power, the desire of your eyes and the delight of your soul** (cf. v. 25). Solomon's temple was the most beautiful building in the ancient world, and the most sacred because the Spirit of the Lord dwelt in the Holy of Holies. The loss of this magnificent structure was incomprehensible for the Jewish people. Plus, the children who they thought were safe in Jerusalem would **fall by the sword**. This was crushing news.

24:22-24. Ezekiel commanded his fellow exiles in Babylon to **do as I have done** when my wife died. When they heard of the fall of Jerusalem, Ezekiel ordered them, **You will not mourn and you will not weep**. Not because they were not sad, but because the magnitude of the destruction would render grief inadequate. They would **rot** (or better "pine away" or "be left to waste away") in their **iniquities** and **groan to one another** when they understood that the consequence of their sin was the fall of Jerusalem. Finally they **will know that I am the Lord God**.

24:25-27. The catastrophic loss of Jerusalem, **their stronghold**, including the temple, which was **the joy of their pride, the desire of their eyes** (cf. v. 21), along with the slaughter of their **heart's delight, their sons and their daughters**, would change Ezekiel's ministry to the exiles. When the news of Jerusalem's fall reached the exiles, **on that day** the prophet's **mouth** would **be opened**. He would be **mute no longer**. Ezekiel had been commanded to remain silent before his fellow exiles, except to pronounce the prophecies God gave him (cf. 3:25-27). Now that his words against Jerusalem had been fulfilled, his selected muteness would end (cf. 33:21-22). He would have a ministry to those **who escaped** death, those who would be brought to Babylon after Jerusalem fell. He was a **sign to them, and they will know that I am the Lord**.

III. Ultimate Judgment on Gentile Nations (25:1–32:32)

The Lord's judgment began with Israel (chaps. 4–24), but it would extend to seven nations surrounding Israel (chaps. 25–32). If God would not spare His own people because of their sin, He certainly would not spare the sinful pagan nations who had afflicted His chosen people. Each prophecy ends with "Thus you will know that I am the Lord."

The basis of God's judgment on the nations is the Abrahamic covenant (cf. Gn 12:1–3). Those who bless the Jewish people, the descendants of Abraham, will be blessed; and those who curse (abuse, mistreat, or rejoice over the calamity of) the Jewish people will be judged. God loves and cares for the Jewish people whether they are obedient or disobedient. The spiritual condition of the Jewish people is no excuse for anti-Semitism.

These first four prophecies (against Ammon, Moab, Edom, and Philistia) each cited the sin that prompted God's judgment and then described that judgment. This follows the *because-therefore* pattern. *Because* these nations had sinned against God by vindictive jealousy and hatred toward God's people, *therefore* God would punish them (25:3).

As Feinberg observes, the nations of the earth refused to learn that God meant every word of the Abrahamic covenant of Gn 12:1-3, 7. "No nation under heaven could touch Israel for ill without bringing down upon them the wrath of Almighty God. The pages of history are strewn with the wreckage of nations who, though great in the eyes and councils of the world, incurred the just wrath of an outraged God. While God reserved the right to judge His chosen people for their sins, He also reserved the right to judge those who spitefully treat the Jews, and thus bring reproach on the One who made an everlasting covenant with Israel" (Charles Lee Feinberg, *The Prophecy of Ezekiel: The Glory of the Lord* [Chicago: Moody, 1969], 146).

A. Judgment on Ammon (25:1-7)

25:1-2. The Lord commanded Ezekiel to **set your face** (cf. 4:3) **toward . . . Ammon**. Judgment had already been pronounced on Ammon and is reiterated here among the seven nations (see details about Ammon at 21:28-32).

25:3-6. Ammon was under judgment **because** she rejoiced over Judah's fall to Babylon. Ammon mocked, saying, **Aha!** an exclamation of malicious joy (v. 3; cf. 26:2; 36:2; Ps 35:21-25) **against**

My sanctuary . . . the land of Israel . . . against the house of Judah. When Jerusalem fell and **Judah** went into **exile**, Ammon gloated. The Ammonites **clapped** their **hands** and **rejoiced with all the scorn of your soul against the land of Israel** (v. 6). Ammon's attitude about Israel and the fall of Jerusalem would cause God to give them **to the sons of the east for a possession** (v. 4). This nomadic people from the Transjordan would conquer Ammon and make Ammon's capital, **Rabbah**, a **pasture for camels** and a **resting place for flocks** (v. 5). This is a phrase often used to describe destroyed cities (cf. Is 34:13-15; Zph 2:13-15).

25:7. Therefore Ammon's hatred of Israel caused the Lord to **stretch out** His **hand against** Ammon, causing that nation to be **spoil to the nations, cut . . . off** from the peoples, and to **perish** from the **lands**. Ammon's adversarial relationship to Israel prompted this response from God: **I will destroy you. Thus you will know that I am the Lord.**

B. Judgment on Moab (25:8-11)

25:8. The kingdom of **Moab** was east of the Dead Sea, in the southern region of modern Jordan. It was a perpetual enemy of Israel from the time of the exodus when Balak, king of Moab, hired Balaam to curse Israel (cf. Nm 22–24). In the period of the Judges, Israel was oppressed by Eglon, king of Moab (Jdg 3:12-30), and Moab frequently attacked Israel throughout the monarchy (cf. 1Sm 14:47; 2Sm 8:2; 2Kgs 3:4-27; 13:20; 24:2; 2Ch 20:1-23). **Seir**, a mountain range on Edom's border was a synonym for Edom (cf. 2Ch 20:10; Nm 20:14-21). Moab and Edom (cf. Ezk 25:12-14) shared the sin of envy and contempt for the people of God.

Moab's greatest sin was failure to recognize Israel's position in God's plan. **Because** Moab mocked, **Behold, the house of Judah is like all the nations** it denied God's promises to and His unique relationship with Israel. Moab repudiated Judah's central position among nations, and thereby profaned God's name. Moab's sin was exemplified by Balak's plan to hire Balaam to curse Israel (Nm 22:1–25:9) and led eventually to Moab's gloating over the fall of Jerusalem (cf. Jr 48:27).

The sin of Moab is still prominent today. When nations, theologians, or people in general deny Israel's uniqueness as God's chosen people, and the nation of Israel as His unique land (cf. Lv 25:23; Pss 10:18; 78:54; Zch 9:16) they are guilty of this grievous sin of Moab. To say the Jewish people and the nation of Israel **is like all the nations** still denies God's promises and plans for Israel—His covenant people and His holy land.

25:9. Since Moab treated Judah with contempt, **therefore** God would **deprive the flank of Moab**, their important defense cities and considered the **glory of the land**. Thus, Moab would be exposed to invasion and her key cities would fall. Mentioned are **Beth-jeshimoth**, which guarded the plains of Moab on the Jordan River, **Baal-meon**, and **Kiriathaim**, which protected Moab atop the Medeba Plateau.

These cities are also mentioned in the *Mesha Stele* or the Moabite Stone. This four-foot black basal memorial stone (c. 850 BC), a ninth-century BC memorial stone, was found in 1868. It chronicles the reign of King Mesha of Moab, including Moab's battle with Israel (2Kg 3:4-17). The Moabite Stone is a significant archaeological find because it confirms OT events and geographic locations.

25:10-11. Like **Ammon**, Moab would be conquered by the **sons of the east** (cf. v. 4) and would **not be remembered among the nations**, losing its place of power and significance. God would cause Moab to **know that I am the Lord**.

C. Judgment on Edom (25:12-14)

25:12. This is Ezekiel's first prophecy against **Edom** (cf. chap. 35). Edom was a kingdom east of the Dead Sea, south of Moab, extending to the Gulf of Aqaba in modern Jordan. The Edomites were descendants of Esau, Jacob's brother, a man who did not value the Lord (Gn 25:25-30; 36:1-8; Heb 12:16). Ezekiel was not the only prophet to denounce Edom (see Ezk 25:12-14; 35; Is 34; Jr 49). Obadiah did so as well. At the time of the exodus Edom initiated the hostility with Israel by refusing to allow Israel to cross her territory in peace (cf. Nm 20:14-21). Enmity continued throughout Israel's history (cf. 1Sm 14:47; 2Sm 8:13-14; 1Kg 9:26-28; 11:14-18; 2Kg 14:7; Is 34:5-7; Jr 49:7-22; Am 1:11-12; Ob).

Judgment would fall **because Edom [had] acted against the house of Judah**. The phrase **by taking vengeance**, literally "revenge with revenge," means an unabated revenge. Edom bears **grievous guilt** because they **avenged themselves** on God's people. When Judah revolted against Babylon (588 BC) Edom sided with Babylon, aided Nebuchadnezzar's assaults on Judah, and rejoiced at Jerusalem's fall. Furthermore, Edom refused to give refuge to the Jewish people who escaped the siege of Jerusalem (cf. Ps 137:7; Jr 49:7-22; Ob 9-14).

25:13-14. Because Edom had a perpetual hatred of Israel and had aided in Judah's destruction (cf. 35:15; 36:5), **therefore** God would **stretch out My hand against Edom** . . . from **Teman** in the north . . . **to Dedan** in the south. God would **lay My vengeance on Edom by the hand of my people Israel**. The Lord personalized His participation in the judgment of Edom and assigned the Jewish people as agents of His wrath.

Edom was conquered by the Nabateans, the nomadic people who controlled the region from the Red Sea to the Euphrates River during the intertestamental period. Later, the Edomites, also known as the Idumeans, moved west to the Negev. Later (126 BC) they were forced to convert to Judaism by John Hyrcanus, a Jewish ruler, and descendant of Mattathias Hasmon, who initiated the Maccabean revolt (Josephus, *Ant.*, 13.9). Although Edom lost its national identity and significance after the Roman period, the wrathful judgment described by Ezekiel does yet not seem to be fulfilled. But it will happen at the end of days when the Messiah will bring His judgment on the archenemy of the Jewish people (cf. Is 63:1-6). When God will "execute great vengeance . . . they will know that I am the LORD" (Ezk 25:17). The Edomites, presented here as the epitome of Israel's enemies (cf. 35:5), are no longer a distinctive people today. Nevertheless, the people that occupy their territory continue to mistreat the people of Israel even as the original Edomites did. Hence, this end-of-days judgment will fall upon the people in Edom in that day. God knows who His enemies are and will ultimately defeat them.

D. Judgment on Philistia (25:15-17)

25:15. The **Philistines** were a prominent seafaring military people who inhabited Philistia, the southern Mediterranean seacoast west of Judah. From the time of the conquest, the Philistines were Israel's enemies (Jdg 3:1-4, 31). They launched attacks from their five major cities: Ashdod, Gaza, Ashkelon, Gath, and Ekron. Goliath was their most famous warrior, but even after his defeat by David, the Philistines continued to battle Israel (cf. 1Sm 7:2-17; 13:1–14:23; 28:1-4; 29:1-2, 11; 31:1-3, 7-10; 2Sm 5:17-25; 8:1; 2Ch 21:16-17; 28:16-18).

Philistia was under God's judgment **because** they had **taken vengeance with scorn** and tried to **destroy** God's chosen people and dispossess Israel of their promised land.

25:16-17. Therefore God would destroy her. He would **stretch out** His **hand** against the Philistines, a powerful image of God's judgment (cf. Ex 3:20; 7:4, 5). He would **cut off** the **Cherethites** (synonym for the Philistines, cf. 1Sm 30:14; 2Sm 8:18; Zph 2:5). The Philistines had planned to destroy God's people, but He would **destroy** even their **remnant** along the **seacoast**. So the Lord will **execute great vengeance** on them.

By the intertestamental period, the Philistines were no longer a political entity. However, their name continued to be associated with the southern coast of Israel, and their five major cities continued to be significant. After the Roman conquest of Israel (AD 70–135), to humiliate the Jews and attempt to wipe Jewish identity off the map of history, the Romans changed the name of the land from Judea to *Palaestina* (in Latin, translated Palestine in English) after Israel's ancient enemy, the Philistines. Palestine became so closely associated with the biblical land of Canaan, Israel, and Judah, that many Biblical resources, theologians, and maps still identify those regions as Palestine and go so far as to speak of "Abraham's journey to Palestine" or "Palestine in the time of Jesus." The Bible never uses the word Palestine to identify Israel or Judah.

The fulfillment of the destruction of the Philistines will come at the end of days (cf. Is 11:14; Ob 19; Zph 2:4-7) when the Lord defeats all His enemies (cf. comments on Ezk 25:13-14). The Philistines are no longer a distinctive people today. However, the people that will occupy their territory at the end of days will continue the same hostility to the people of Israel that the original Philistines practiced. Hence, this end-of-days judgment will fall upon the people in the area of the Philistines in that day. This nation that had tried to destroy God's people will understand God's true character and **they will know that I am the LORD** (cf. vv. 7, 11) **when I lay My vengeance on them.**

E. Judgment on Tyre (26:1–28:19)

Ezekiel's four short prophecies against the nations east and west of Israel (chap. 25) are followed by a long prophecy against Tyre. This ancient Phoenician city-state, on the shore of the Mediterranean north of Israel, was famous for its merchants and sea trade (cf. 27:3; Is 23). David formed a mercantile alliance with Hiram, king of Tyre, who supplied materials and craftsmen for the temple (cf. 2Sm 5:11; 1Kgs 5:1; 7:13; 2Ch 2:3). Later Tyre became infamous for its idolatry (cf. Is 23:17; Mt 11:21-22).

There are four separate oracles against Tyre, each beginning with the phrase, "The word of the LORD came to me" (26:1; 27:1; 28:1, 11).

1. Destruction of Tyre: Oracle One (26:1-21)

26:1-2. This prophecy was given **on the first of the month** in the **eleventh year** of Jehoiakim's exile (586/587 BC). Ezekiel did not state which month, since Jerusalem fell to Babylon July 18, 586 BC. Possibly Ezekiel's prophecy against Tyre was prompted by Jerusalem's impending fall.

The prophecy follows the *because-therefore* format (cf. 25:1-4, 6-7, 9-9, 12-13). Tyre's judgment was **because** of her sin of greedy rejoicing **concerning** the fall of **Jerusalem** saying, **Aha, the gateway . . . is broken; it has opened to me. I shall be filled**. Jerusalem and Tyre had vied for the lucrative trade routes between Egypt and Mesopotamia. Tyre dominated the sea routes, while Jerusalem controlled the caravan routes. Without Jerusalem controlling the overland caravan routes, more products would be shipped by sea—to Tyre's commercial advantage.

26:3-5. God said **therefore . . . behold, I am against you, O Tyre**. The Lord would **bring up many nations against you, as the sea brings up its waves**. Tyre was wealthy because of her seagoing economy. So the image of a violent storm at sea describes God's judgment. As **waves** crash, so God would **destroy the walls** and **break down her towers**. He would **scrape her debris** to **make her a bare rock . . . a place for . . . spreading . . . nets**. This major city of commerce would become a smooth, barren rock where fishermen laid out their nets to dry to prevent them from rotting. Her great wealth would be given as **spoil for the nations**.

26:6. The main city of Tyre was on the shore, but it included outlying areas of settlement further in on the **mainland** and a community on an island about a half-mile off the coast. These **daughters**, surrounding towns, would be **slain by the sword**, along with the citizens of the central city of Tyre.

26:7-11. The second **thus says the Lord GOD** identifies **Nebuchadnezzar** as Tyre's attacker. After defeating Jerusalem, Nebuchadnezzar laid siege to Tyre for 13 years with **horses, chariots, cavalry and a great army**. Tyre withstood the **blow of** the **battering rams** of long siege because Tyre's navy was able to supply the city. Ultimately, Babylon destroyed all settlements on the mainland: **with the hoofs of his horses he will trample all your streets**, but the island stronghold survived.

26:12-14. During the intertestamental period, Alexander the Great devastated the island settlement of Tyre when it refused to submit to him on his march to Egypt (332 BC). He built a one-and-one-half mile long causeway from the mainland to the island fortress. He used the **stones, timbers**, and **debris** from the rubble left from Nebuchadnezzar's destruction of the old mainland city to do so, throwing them **into the water** (see Zch 9:3-4) just as Ezekiel prophesied here. Island Tyre ceased to be a trade city but did become a **place for the spreading of nets**. By NT times, Tyre recovered from Nebuchadnezzar's and Alexander's onslaughts (cf. Mt 15:21) but was no longer a major power on the Mediterranean. Modern Tyre in Lebanon is a medium-sized city near to, but smaller than, the ancient site. No city has been built over the ruins of ancient Tyre, in fulfillment of this prophecy.

26:15. Thus says the Lord GOD to Tyre begins the third section of this prophecy. Tyre's neighbors, the **coastlands**, would **shake . . .** tremble . . . and be appalled when she fell. The destruction of the premier port in the ancient world would have economic repercussions throughout the region.

26:16-18. All the **princes** of the **sea** coast who had depended on Tyre's commerce would **clothe themselves** in mourning (cf. Jb 2:11-13). Tyre's allies sang a **lamentation**, a funeral lament (cf. 19:1), for the **renowned city . . . mighty on the sea** because they were **terrified at your passing**. If this could happen to Tyre, no one was safe.

26:19. Poetically, Tyre, the important seafaring merchant city, would sink like a great ship. **Thus says the Lord GOD** to Tyre when He makes the great seaport a **desolate city, covere[d]** over by **great waters** (cf. v. 3). Seafaring ancient Tyre would drown in the sea, and all traces of this city would be lost (cf. 27:26-35; see comments on vv. 12-14).

26:20-21. To **go down to the pit** is figurative for death and the grave (Pr 1:12; Is 14:15, 19; 38:18). Tyre's dreadful end, **like the ancient waste places**, is contrasted to the **glory in the land of the living**. Life in the region would thrive after Tyre was forgotten. She would **never be found again**. For an in-depth discussion of the destruction of Tyre, see Feinberg, *The Prophecy of Ezekiel*, 147–48.

2. Dirge Over Tyre: Oracle Two (27:1-36)

Ezekiel's second oracle ("the word of the LORD") against Tyre was an expanded lamentation over Tyre (cf. 26:17-18). The lament is in three stanzas: the first (vv. 1-9), in poetry, describes Tyre's former glory as a beautiful ship; the second (vv. 10-25) gives Tyre's many trading partners; the third (vv. 26-36) describes Tyre's destruction as a catastrophic shipwreck.

27:1-7. The first stanza compares **Tyre** a **merchant** city **at the entrance to the sea**, to one of her ships. Tyre is **perfect in beauty** with **planks** made of costly **fir** from **Senir** (Mount Hermon) and the **mast** of **cedar from Lebanon**, prized for her tall, strong trees (1Kg 4:33; 5:6); **oaks from Bashan** (east of Galilee, famous for its oak forests, Is 2:13) **made** the **oars**; the deck was ornamented with **ivory** on expensive **boxwood**; the **sail** was **of fine embroidered linen from Egypt**; and its **awning** was of expensive **blue and purple**, the most expensive dyes in the ancient word. This was an accurate image of the ornate ships that were the hallmark of Tyre's merchant fleet.

27:8-9. The crewmen of the ship were the best on the Phoenician coast from prominent Mediterranean ports of **Sidon** (an ancient city on the Mediterranean coast about 25 miles north of Tyre), **Arvad** (a small island city in the Mediterranean Sea off the coast of Syria and 200 miles north of Tyre), and **Gebal** (a city in Phoenicia on the Mediterranean coast, 70 miles north of Tyre). The earliest Phoenician ships each had 50 oarsmen and were swift. The later commercial ships were much longer and had a crew of up to 200 with two or three banks of oars on each side. There were **wise men** as **pilots** and for **repairing your seams** in the sails during the voyage. The ship of Tyre was prepared to **deal in . . . merchandise** without even having to put into port for repairs.

27:10-25. The second stanza describes the military and commercial activity of Tyre.

27:10-11. Soldiers hailed from **Persia** (modern Iran), **Lud** (north Africa), and **Put** (Libya) in Tyre's mercenary **army**, along with soldiers from **Arvad** (a small Phoenician island-city in the Mediterranean Sea off the coast of Syria and 200 miles north of Tyre; cf. v. 8) and the **Gammadim** (lit., "valorous one"). These **men of war** protected the **towers** and **walls** and **perfected** Tyre's **beauty** by their defense of the city and their own impressive appearance.

27:12-25. Tyre's commercial network extended across the ancient world. Tyre's **customer[s]** around the Mediterranean were: **Tarshish** (Spain), **Javan** and **Vedan** (Greece), **Tubal** and **Meshech**, **Beth-togarmah** (Eastern Turkey), **Judah** and **Israel**, **Aram**, **Damascus**, and **Helbon** (Syria). Her **customers** from **Arabia** included **Dedan**, **Uzal** (Yemen), **Kedar**, **Sheba**, and **Raamah**. Many cities from Mesopotamia also **traded** with her: **Haran**, **Canneh**, **Eden**, **Asshur**, and **Chilmad**. She traded **an abundance** of **all kinds** of **goods**: metals, precious jewels, expensive materials (vv. 12, 13, 15, 16, 18, 22, 24), military supplies (vv. 14, 19, 20), livestock, and foodstuffs (vv. 17, 19, 21). If there was anything to be traded or transported, it was carried by the ships of Tyre's commercial empire—**filled** and **very glorious in the heart of the seas.**

27:26-36. The lament concludes (vv. 26-36) with the image of the ship's catastrophic wreck.

27:26-29 Tyre's great ship is **broken . . . in the heart of the seas** (cf. v. 34). The **east wind** has the dual image of a storm wind sinking a ship and of the Babylonian invaders coming from the east (cf. 19:12).

27:30-32. Her seamen and her commercial partners would **cry bitterly** at the loss of Tyre. They would **cast dust on their heads**, roll in **ashes**, and observe all the mourning practices—wearing **sackcloth**, weeping, and asking, **Who is like Tyre**?

27:33-36. Tyre's commercial empire had **satisfied many peoples** and **enriched . . . kings**. Her downfall would affect **all the . . . coastlands**. Her trading partners would be bankrupt, and **kings** would be **horribly afraid**. If the great city of Tyre could be destroyed by the Babylonians, they had no hope of escape. The **merchants** would **hiss** in shock at Tyre's demise. They could not believe Tyre would **cease to be forever**.

3. Downfall of Leader of Tyre: Oracle Three (28:1-10)

28:1-5. The third message against Tyre is directed to the **leader** (or ruler) **of Tyre**. This proud king evaluated his skillful leadership and economic success and proclaimed **I am a god, I sit in the seat of gods in the heart of the seas.** The underlying sin of Tyre's king was his claim to be divine (cf. vv. 6, 9). God confronted this blasphemous claim: **yet you are a man and not God** (cf. v. 9). The Lord presented a series of rhetorical statements, saying **Behold you are wiser than Daniel**, referring to the prophet Daniel (cf. 14:14, 20), who had a reputation for his wisdom and righteousness in the courts of Nebuchadnezzar (cf. Dn 1:19-20; 2:46-49). The king thought that there was **no secret** to **match** his **great wisdom** through which he thought he had increased his **riches** (cf. Ezk 28:4, 5). His **heart** was **lifted**

up (had grown proud) because of his national success and his **riches**.

28:6-8. Because the king **made** his **heart** proud . . . **Therefore** God would bring **strangers**, that is, Babylon (cf. 26:7-11; Jr 27:1-3), **the most ruthless of the nations** (cf. Ezk 23:22-27; 30:11), to judge Tyre's leader. Unimpressed with his **wisdom**, Babylon would **defile** his **splendor** and **bring** him **down to the pit** (cf. 26:20).

28:9-10. He would not be able to say **I am a god** in the **presence of** his **slayer**. He would not have a peaceful royal death, but would die in shame like a barbarian—**die the death of the uncircumcised** (cf. 32:30; 1Sm 17:26, 36). He claimed to be a god but would suffer an ignoble death as the lowest mortal **by the hand of strangers**.

4. Downfall of Power behind King of Tyre: Oracle Four (28:11-19)

The final prophecy against Tyre was a "lamentation" concerning the "king of Tyre." God rebuked the ruler for claiming to be a god though he was just a man (vv. 1-10). This "lamentation" over the "king of Tyre" shifts from addressing the actual king (vv. 1-10) to describing the power behind his throne (vv. 11-19). This is evident in that Ezekiel's description uses terms that could not apply to the human ruler of Tyre or to any mortal man. For example he is said to have "the seal of perfection" (v. 12) and to have been "in Eden" (v. 13). He is called "the anointed cherub" (an angelic being) who was "on the holy mountain of God" and "walked in the midst of the stones of fire" (v. 14). He is also said to have been directly "created" by God (v. 15), and to have been "blameless" until "unrighteousness was found" in him. These descriptions cannot be explained as some kind of "Semitic" or "ancient Near Eastern hyperbole." Therefore, in this section, the prophet was not speaking to the literal king of Tyre but to the supernatural being who empowered the literal king, namely, Satan. This idea is supported by the book of Daniel, which also links angels and demons to the principalities they influence (Dn 10:12-14).

28:11-19. This **king** had **the seal of perfection**, was full of **wisdom** and **perfect in beauty** in the garden of **Eden** (v. 13), had been the **anointed cherub** (v. 14a), had possessed free access to the **holy mountain of God** (v. 14b), and had been **blameless** (sinless) from the time he was **created** (v. 15) **until unrighteousness was found in you** (v. 15). Finally he was overcome by pride (**heart was lifted up**) and **corrupted** so that God **cast** him . . . **to the ground** (v. 17; cf. Is 14:3-21).

This **anointed cherub** is best understood to be Satan, and this passage reveals events in Eden before the fall. Ezekiel described this being as God originally created him (Ezk 28:12-15a). Satan was in the garden of Eden (Gn 3:1-7). He had access to God's presence (Ezk 28:14-15; Jb 1:6-12), and Satan's chief sin was pride (1Tm 3:6), leading to his downfall (**you will cease to be forever**, Ezk 28:19).

Here Ezekiel presented an overview of the fall of Satan as a single act, but other passages reveal that it occurred in stages. Satan's initial judgment was his expulsion from the position of God's anointed cherub before His throne. God later expelled him from the mountain of God (heaven; cf. vv. 14, 16). Satan was cast from God's presence in heaven (cf. Lk 10:18) but was still allowed access to God (cf. Jb 1:6-12; Zch 3:1-2). In the tribulation Satan will be cast from heaven and restricted to the earth (Rv 12:7-13). In the millennium he will be in the bottomless pit (Rv 20:1-3), and after his brief release at the end of the millennium (Rv 20:7-9) he will be cast into the lake of fire forever (Rv 20:10). Thus, all of Satan's judgments are in view here, in compressed form.

F. Judgment on Sidon (28:20-26)

28:20-23. Ezekiel is told to **Set your face** (cf. 6:2) **toward Sidon**. This city-state, often associated with the more prominent Tyre, was located 25 miles north of Tyre on the Mediterranean (cf. Jr 25:22; 47:4; Jr 3:4; Zch 9:2; Lk 6:17; 10:13-14). God was **against** . . . **Sidon**. It would be judged with **pestilence** and **sword**.

28:24. Sidon was under judgment for her wicked influence on the **house of Israel**, which had been like the pain of **a prickling brier or a** . . . **thorn** (cf. 1Kg 18–19). The sin of Baal worship entered Israel through Jezebel, the daughter of the king of Sidon (1Kg 16:31), who married Israel's King Ahab (874–853 BC) and corrupted Israel and Judah until the Babylonian captivity.

28:25-26. God will reveal His holiness by His faithfulness to Israel. God would **manifest** His **holiness** (cf. 20:41; 28:22, 25; 36:23; 38:16; 39:27) by gathering **the house of Israel from the peoples among whom they are scattered**. Israel would be judged for her sin, but God will never abandon her. She is unique among all nations because God had established His everlasting, unconditional covenant with her. God will **execute judgments upon all** nations **who scorn** Israel. The promises made to Abraham, Isaac, and Jacob (Gn 13:14-17; 15:17-21; 17:21; 35:11-13) concerning blessing and the land of Israel have not been revoked. Israel **will live in** her own **land**, because God has given it to **Jacob** (cf. Ezk 37:25; Gn 28:10-13; 35:9-12; Pss 46:4-11; 105:8-11).

After the Babylonian captivity, many Jewish people returned to Israel (cf. Neh 1:3; 7:1-59). Although the walls and temple were rebuilt, the Jewish people did not **live** . . . **securely**. They were expelled from their homeland in AD 70 by the Romans. Since 1948 Israel has been a modern Jewish state, but the land is under constant threat of war. In the future, when she is restored to her land, Israel will enjoy God's blessings, including security and prosperity, when God judges all the nations who **scorn** her. This promise, made through Ezekiel, awaits fulfillment in the millennial kingdom. When God finally punishes Israel's enemies and blesses His chosen people, the nation will recognize Jesus as Messiah (Zch 12:10) and **they will know that I am the Lord their God**.

G. Judgment on Egypt (29:1–32:32)

Egypt is the focus of Ezekiel's seventh and final prophecy against the nations. Like the message against Tyre, it is a series of seven oracles. While the judgment against Tyre is directed at its commercial identity, the judgment against Egypt focuses on its military power. Each of these messages against Egypt and its Pharaoh begins with the phrase, "The word of the Lord came to me" (29:1, 17; 30:1, 20; 31:1; 32:1, 17). Six of these oracles are dated (except 30:1) and only one (29:17) is out of chronological sequence, indicating the historical accuracy with which this prophecy was recorded. These were not mere random recollections, but a dated record of these oracles against Israel's ancient foe.

Egypt and Israel have a long history, beginning with Abraham and the patriarchs (Gn 12:10-20; 46–52). After the exodus, Egypt was often in conflict with Israel (except for a short peace during Solomon's reign). Israel sometimes made military alliances with Egypt, always with disastrous consequences (cf. 2Kg 18:21; Is 36:6; Jr 37:1-10).

1. Sin of Egypt (29:1-16)

The prophecy against the sin of Egypt has three sections, each closing with the phrase, used about 20 times in Ezekiel, "then they will know that I am the Lord" (vv. 6, 9, 16).

29:1-3a. This prophecy was given almost a year after the siege of Jerusalem began (cf. 24:1-2; 2Kg 25:1), in **the tenth year** (of Jehoiachin's exile), **in the tenth month on the twelfth of the month** (12 Tevet/January 7, 587 BC), seven months before Jerusalem's fall (2Kg 25:3-8).

The prophecy is against **Pharaoh king of Egypt** . . . **against all Egypt**. This was Pharaoh Hophra (589–570 BC; Jr 44:30) the grandson of Pharaoh Neco, who killed godly Josiah at Megiddo (cf. 2Ch 35:20-27). Pharaoh Hophra's promise of military allegiance prompted Judah to rebel against Babylon, instigating Nebuchadnezzar's siege of Jerusalem (cf. Jr 37:1-10).

29:3b-6a. Pharaoh is compared to a **great monster** (Hb. *tannim*) in the **rivers** (often translated "Nile"; cf. v. 3; 30:12; Gn. 41:1; Ex 2:3, 5; 4:9; 7:15) of Egypt. *Tannim* is translated to describe a variety of reptiles (Gn 1:21; Ex 7:9-10; Dt 32:33). The reference here is probably to the crocodile, which was abundant along the Nile. The Egyptian god Sobek was a crocodile, symbolizing Egypt's strength, ferocity, and control of the Nile. Pharaoh was a god-king to the Egyptians and would be judged for his arrogance in saying, **My Nile is mine, and I myself have made it** (cf. Ezk 29:9).

God's judgment on Egypt is presented with images of capturing a crocodile. He would **put hooks in your jaws** . . . and **bring you up out of the midst of your rivers** (the Nile), away from safety and protection. Pharaoh would be left in **the wilderness** . . . in the **open field** to be **food to the beasts** . . . and **birds**, despite Egypt's great strength. **Then all the inhabitants of Egypt will know that I am the Lord.**

29:6b-9a. The second section of this prophecy deals with Egypt's sins of treachery against Israel. Depending on Egypt (cf. Jr 37:4-8) always brought disaster for Israel. It was like leaning on a **staff made of reed to the house of Israel** (2Kg 18:21; Is 36:6), which did not provide support but only **broke and tore all their hands**, leaving them weak with fear and making **their loins quake**.

Therefore, because of Egypt's false promises of support for Israel, the **Lord God** would **bring upon** Egypt the **sword** of judgment (cf. 6:3), and the **land of Egypt** would **become a desolation and waste. Then they will know that I am the Lord.**

29:9b-13. Because of Egypt's arrogance in saying **The Nile is mine, and I have made it** (cf. v. 3), **therefore** God was **against** her and her Nile (rivers, cf. v. 3). The extent of judgment was on all Egypt from **Migdol** (in the north) **to Syene** (in the south) **and even to** . . . **Ethiopia** in the east.

The devastation of Egypt would last for **forty years**. Egypt would be attacked by Babylon (vv. 17-21; cf. Jr 43:8-13; 46:1-25), and God would **scatter** Egypt among **the nations**. Although no archeological evidence has yet confirmed an Egyptian judgment as described here, it is unwise to dismiss a clear statement of Scripture on the basis of incomplete archaeological data. Perhaps it awaits future fulfillment.

29:14-16. When Egypt would **return** it would be the **lowest of the kingdoms**, nothing compared to its former greatness. Egypt would **never again** be the **confidence of the house of Israel**. Egypt's political weakness would be a continual object lesson to Israel, **bringing to mind**, causing Israel to remember the sin of depending on **Egypt** instead of the Lord for safety. **Then they will know that I am the Lord God.**

2. Defeat of Egypt by Babylon (29:17-21)

29:17-18. This second prophecy against Egypt came in the **twenty-seventh year**, of Jehoiachin's exile, the **first month** on the **first** day (1 Nissan/ April 26, 571 BC). It is the latest dated prophecy in the book Ezekiel, but is recorded out of chronological sequence. It is probably recorded here to draw attention to the logical progression of Egypt's judgment by **Nebuchadnezzar king of Babylon** (vv. 1-16).

This prophecy begins with a review of Nebuchadnezzar's 13-year siege of **Tyre** (585–572 BC). **Every head was made bald and every shoulder was rubbed bare** by the prolonged wearing of helmets and carrying materials for the siege works. Nebuchadnezzar **had no wages from Tyre for the labor . . . he had performed against it**. Evidently Tyre shipped off her wealth before she surrendered. Thus, Nebuchadnezzar found meager spoils of war for his long siege.

29:19-20. Therefore, the Lord was going to **give the land of Egypt to Nebuchadnezzar** as a source of **wealth and . . . spoil and . . . plunder** as **wages for his army**. Prompted by economic necessity, as well as political expediency against a rival military power, Babylon attacked Egypt. Yet God was the force behind Babylon's attack on Egypt: **I have given him** (Nebuchadnezzar) **the land of Egypt for his labor which he performed, because they** (the Babylonian army) **acted for Me.**

29:21. A promise to the exiles in Babylon concludes this prophecy against Egypt. **On that day** is an eschatological marker. In the future, God would **make a horn sprout for the house of Israel**. It looks to the future when the Lord will restore Israel to her land and judge the nations around her. The growth of a **horn** indicates a rise in power or strength (cf. 1Sm 2:1; 2Sm 22:3; 1Kg 22:11; Pss 18:2; 89:17; Jr 48:25). The idea was applied in an ultimate sense to the strength of the Messiah who would deliver Israel (cf. Ps 132:17; Lk 1:69). There would be a blessing on the nation of Israel after the judgment of Egypt, perhaps looking to the end times when Messiah will judge the nations, including Egypt, and restore Israel (Jl 3:19-21; Mc 7:7-20). At that time Egypt will come to know the Lord, and there will be a highway uniting Egypt, Assyria and Israel (cf. Is 19:19-25).

Although this broader section of Ezekiel has not had a messianic focus, the Messiah is a constant theme in Scripture. The prophets at times will insert a prophetic statement that depends upon and presupposes the concept of the Messiah. Moreover, the mixed metaphor of the words **horn** (*keren*) and **sprout** (*tsemach*) found here occur in only one other text, Ps 132:17. According to Daniel Block, this verse in which "Yahweh promises to 'cause a horn to sprout for David' . . . provides the basis for the long-standing messianic interpretation" of Ezk 29:21 (Daniel I. Block, "Bringing Back David: Ezekiel's Messianic Hope," *The Lord's Anointed: Interpretation of Old Testament Messianic Texts*, ed. Philip E. Satterthwaite, Richard S. Hess, and Gordon J. Wenham [Grand Rapids, MI: Baker, 1995], 169). This promise, then, is a direct messianic prediction of the future Davidic Messiah.

Now God said He would **open** Ezekiel's **mouth in their midst**. This cannot refer to the ending of Ezekiel's divine muteness (cf. 3:26). That had already ended in the 12th year of Jehoiachin's exile (cf. 33:21-22; 585 BC), and this prophecy came in the 27th year (v. 17; 571 BC) 14 years later. Rather, when the exiles saw the fulfillment of Ezekiel's prophecies concerning Egypt's fall to Babylon, his message would become clear to them. The exiles would recognize God's character as He faithfully accomplished His promises of divine judgment, as well as the certainty of future hope and blessing for Israel. **Then they will know that I am the Lord.**

3. Destruction of Egypt and Her Allies (30:1-19)

This third prophecy is the only undated one of the seven oracles against Egypt, perhaps because it is a summary prophecy. Nebuchadnezzar is mentioned as the instrument of judgment (v. 10). It is subdivided into four sections, each beginning, "Thus says the Lord GOD" (vv. 2, 6, 10, 13).

30:1-4. The opening section is a lament over the destruction of Egypt: **Wail, Alas for the day!** Though judgment is certain, Ezekiel, like the other prophets (e.g., 6:11; 9:8; 11:13; Jr 30:7; Am 5:18), was not heartless, vindictive, or gleeful in his pronouncement. He viewed the days of reckoning with mourning.

This prophecy looks forward to **the day**! **For the day is near, even the day of the LORD is near**. The **day of the LORD** (mentioned four times in vv. 2, 3) is frequently a reference to God's eschatological judgment of the earth, when the nations will be judged and Israel fully restored (cf. Is 13:6-16, 9; 34:8; Jl 1:15; 2:1, 11; 3:14; Am 5:18, 20, Ob 15; Zph 1:7, 14; Zch 14:1, Mal 4:1-6; 1Th 5:2; 2Th 2:2; 2Pt 3:10). However, it can also refer to God's temporal judgments (Lm 2:21-22), even as Judah and Israel had experienced God's temporal judgment when punished for their sins (Ezk 7:1-14). This is the more likely case here with God's day of judgment falling on Egypt with Nebuchadnezzar's conquest. Nevertheless, this historical judgment foreshadows the future day of the Lord when God will judge the nations for the mistreatment of Israel (Gn 12:3).

It will be a **day of clouds, a time of doom for the nations**, expanding the judgment beyond Egypt. **Clouds** when connected to the day of the Lord often pictured doom (cf. Ezk 30:18; 32:7-8; 34:12; Jl 2:2; Zph 1:14-15). The **sword** of judgment that had been drawn against Israel (cf. Ezk 21:1-17) **will come upon Egypt**. Egypt's people would be **slain**, her **wealth** taken away, and the **foundations** of her society and power **torn down**.

30:5. Ethiopia, adjoining Egypt on the south, **Put** (Libya), **Lud** (northern Africa, cf. 27:10), and all **Arabia** were allies and mercenaries in Egypt's army **in league** with them (Jr 46:8-9, 20-21). Thus, they will all **fall . . . by the sword** along with Egypt.

30:6-9. All **those who support Egypt will fall . . . by the sword**. Throughout the land, from **Migdol to Syene** (the northern and southern extremities of Egypt; cf. 29:10) the lands and cities would be **desolate**.

On that day, (cf. vv. 2, 3, 9), the Lord would **set a fire in Egypt** and send **messengers . . . in ships to frighten . . . Ethiopia**, and it would cause **anguish** for the certainty of the judgment: **for behold it comes**! Although these nations will not become followers of the one true God, **they will know that I am the LORD** (v. 8), and they will acknowledge that the God of Israel had predicted their destruction.

30:10-12. The **hordes** (multitude) **of Egypt** are mentioned repeatedly in chaps. 30–32, to emphasize Egypt's political power (cf. vv. 10, 15; 31:2, 18; 32:12, 16, 18, 20, 24, 25, 26, 31, 32). Egypt's power would **cease** by the Lord's judgment through the **hand of Nebuchadnezzar** and his **ruthless** army (cf. 23:24-27; 28:7; 32:12). Babylon's attack is carefully explained as coming at the plan of the Lord: **I will** (three times in these two verses). Babylon was the tool God used to accomplish His judgment. The complex **Nile canals** irrigation system was a key to Egypt's prosperity. It required constant upkeep. As a result of war the river would be neglected, **dry** up, and the **land** become **desolate . . . by the hand of strangers** (7:21; 11:9; 28:7, 10; 30:12).

30:13-19. No major city there would escape God's wrath. He would **destroy the idols** and **. . . the images . . . from Memphis** (cf. v. 16), an important worship center with numerous temples (15 miles south of modern Cairo). He would judge **Pathros** in southern Egypt; **Zoan** (Rameses) in northeast Egypt (cf. Ex 1:11); **Thebes**, capital of Upper Egypt, present-day Luxor (cf. Jr 46:25); **Sin** (Pelusium), a fortress in the eastern Nile delta; **On** (Heliopolis) city of the sun, 6 miles from modern Cairo (cf. Jr 43:13); **Pi-beseth** near Goshen, 40 miles northeast of modern Cairo (cf. Gn 45:10); **Tehaphnehes**, the location of one of Pharaoh's palaces (cf. Jr 2:16; 43:9; 43:7-8) on the Suez delta. God will **break . . . the yoke bars**, the oppressive power of Egypt, and make the **pride of her power** cease. A **cloud** of judgment **will cover her** (cf. Ezk 30:3; 32:7-8; 34:12; Jl 2:2; Zph 1:15). The people would **go into captivity** when God would **execute judgments on Egypt**. As before (vv. 18-19), **they will know I am the LORD**, meaning acknowledge His prediction of their destruction.

4. Scattering of Egypt (30:20-26)

30:20. The fourth of seven prophecies against Egypt was given in the **eleventh year** (of Jehoiachin's exile) in the **first month** on the **seventh** day (7 Nissan/April 29, 587 BC), almost four months after Ezekiel's first prophecy against Egypt (29:1). The first prophecy indicated the time when Egypt failed Israel as an ally against Babylon (cf. Jr 37:4-5). The fourth prophecy was recorded after God's judgment of Egypt by the Babylonians: **I have broken the arm of Pharaoh king of Egypt**. Possibly the time between the first and fourth prophecies against Egypt was approximately the length of time the siege on Jerusalem was lifted as Babylon repositioned its army against Egypt.

30:21-23. Here the image of Egypt shifts from a crocodile (cf. 29:3-7) to a person who was injured in combat. Nebuchadnezzar broke the **arm** of Egypt, so it was unable to defend itself. Egypt's arm, its strength, was not even **bound up for healing** so that it could again **be strong to hold the sword**. God would **break . . . both the strong and the** (already) **broken** of Egypt's arms, and **the sword** will **fall from his hand**. It would have no power to defend itself.

30:24-26. At the same time the Lord was destroying the power of Egypt, He would **strengthen the arms of the king of Babylon** and **put My sword in his hand** to be the agent to **break the arms of Pharaoh**, who would **groan** in defeat.

Nebuchadnezzar's attack on Egypt would succeed (cf. 29:1-20), then God would **scatter the Egyptians among the nations** (a fact stated twice for emphasis; vv. 23, 26; cf. 29:12). Egypt would follow Judah into exile. **Then they will know that I am the Lord** (cf. vv. 25, 26).

5. Allegory of Assyria and the Fall of Pharaoh King of Egypt (31:1-18)

a. Allegory of Assyria as a Cedar Tree (31:1-9)

31:1-2. The message, in allegorical form, was given to **Pharaoh king of Egypt** in the **eleventh year** (of Jehoiachin's exile), in **the third month, on the first** day (1 Sevan/June 21, 587 BC), less than two months after the previous prophecy (30:20-26). Pharaoh Hophra was confident of Egypt's power and thought there was no one compared to his **greatness**.

31:3-7. Egypt is challenged to **Behold, Assyria** and learn from that example. Assyria would have had great significance to Egypt for two reasons. First, Assyria had attacked Egypt and destroyed the capital of Thebes (633 BC; cf. Nah 3:8-10). Assyria could be compared with Egypt in military might. Second, Egypt would have been aware that Assyria had been destroyed by Babylon. Now using Assyria as an example, Ezekiel prophesied the same fate for Egypt.

Assyria is compared to a **cedar in Lebanon**, the stateliest tree in the region (cf. Jdg 9:15; 1Kg 4:33; 5:6, 8; 2Kg 14:9; Ezr 3:7; Ps 92:12; 104:16). At the apex of her power Assyria dominated the Middle East, towering like a cedar higher than all the **trees of the field**. The key cities of Assyria were situated at or near the Tigris River and the **waters made** the nation **grow**. **All the birds of the heavens . . . and . . . all the beasts**, that is all the surrounding nations, found protection (**lived under its shade**; cf. Ezk 30:6, 12, 17).

31:8-9. Using hyperbole, Ezekiel stressed Assyria's grandeur: **The cedars in God's garden** (Eden, cf. 28:13) could not **compare with** its **beauty. All the trees of Eden . . . were jealous of it**. The fall of Assyria was the perfect example to show Egypt the effects of God's judgment.

b. Downfall of Assyria (31:10-14)

31:10-11. Because . . . its heart is haughty Assyria was judged for its pride, as were Judah (16:56), Tyre (27:3; 28:2), and Egypt (30:6). **Therefore** the Lord would **give** Assyria **into the hand of a despot** (lit., "mighty one") **of the nations** for its **wickedness**. Nineveh, the capital of Assyria, fell to Nabopolassar, Nebuchadnezzar's father, in 612 BC. The rest of the Assyrian army was crushed by Nebuchadnezzar in 609 BC.

31:12. The **alien tyrants of the nations**, Babylon, (cf. 28:7, 30:11; 32:12) had **cut . . . down** the mighty tree of Assyria and its **branches have fallen**. Then those who had sought protection under Assyria's **shade** (cf. vv. 6, 17), her allies, **left** her. The ruin of Assyria was an object lesson to other nations, especially Egypt.

31:13-14. Now Assyria is a **ruin . . . they have all been given over to death**, destined to **go down to the pit** (death and the grave; cf. 26:20-21). Assyria's fall is as an object lesson to other nations (**all the birds . . . all the beasts . . . all the trees**), especially to Egypt.

c. Descent of Assyria into the Grave (31:15-18)

31:15-16. On the day of Assyria's fall, **when it went down to Sheol**, the Lord **caused lamentations**, the nations mourned her destruction. The Tigris and Euphrates rivers were the heart of the Assyrian empire. God **closed** all the waters of Assyria, the **deep** (subterranean waters) and **held back its rivers**. Southwest of Assyria, **Lebanon** mourned, and **all the trees of the field wilted** (v. 15). The **nations** were alarmed (**quake**) that a power as strong and mighty as Assyria could ever **fall** (v. 16).

31:17-18. Egypt was Assyria's chief ally prior to Assyria's fall to Babylon. Ezekiel drove home the point of the Assyria story, rephrasing the opening question (cf. vv. 2, 18): Which of the **trees of Eden** can be compared with you in **glory and greatness**? Only mighty Assyria was similar to Egypt, and Assyria had fallen. Likewise, Egypt's end would be one of shame like that **of the uncircumcised** (cf. 28:10; 32:19), who were **slain by the sword** and buried without proper respect. For emphasis Ezekiel repeated the point: **So is Pharaoh and all his hordes** (cf. 30:10).

6. Lament for Pharaoh (32:1-16)

32:1-2a. In the **twelfth year** (of Jehoiachin's exile), in the **twelfth month** on the **first** day (1 Adar/March 3, 585 BC), **the word of the Lord came** to Ezekiel, and he gave his sixth prophecy against Egypt. The fall of Egypt was now so certain that Ezekiel was told to **take up a lamentation** (funeral dirge) concerning **Pharaoh king of Egypt**. Ezekiel had already written laments for Judah (chap. 19), the city of Tyre (26:17-18; 27), and the king of Tyre (28:12-19). The lament for Egypt is in three parts (vv. 2b, 3-10, 11-16).

32:2b. Pharaoh Hophra had **compared** himself to both a **young lion of the nations** and **the monster** (large crocodile; cf. notes on 29:3) **in the seas** (cf. 29:2-5). The **monster** had **muddied . . . and fouled** up the placid water of the **rivers** (Nile). The political actions of Pharaoh were disturbing the international waters as he vied with Babylon for power.

32:3-5. Using the picture of the crocodile, **Thus says the Lord God, Now I will spread my net over you**. God would lead **a company of many** of Pharaoh's enemies on a crocodile hunt, and they will **lift you up in My net** (cf. 29:3-5). Pharaoh would be trapped by his enemies and removed from power. God would **cast** Pharaoh **on the open field** (the surface of the ground, v. 4) where his body would be food for **the birds** and . . . **the beasts** (cf. 29:5-6).

32:6-8. The **land** would **drink the discharge of your blood** and God would **extinguish** him, snuff him out like a candle. Pharaoh was worshiped as the son of Ra, the Egyptian sun god, but the Lord would **darken** the heavenly lights **over** him and **set darkness** on Egypt (v. 8). The references to **blood** and **darkness** are allusions to God's plague judgments of blood and darkness on Egypt at the time of the exodus (cf. Ex 7:19; 10:21-23).

32:9-10. The **destruction** of Egypt would **trouble the hearts of many peoples** (cf. 26:16-18; 27:35; 28:19). As God revealed His power in judgment on Egypt, kings would **be horribly afraid** when they saw God **brandish My sword before them**. Whenever major world powers fall, lesser nations **tremble every moment** for fear of their own future. If mighty Egypt could be destroyed, no one was safe.

32:11-12. This third section of the lament changes from the figurative language of the crocodile to a direct description of Egypt's fall to Babylon. The **sword of the king of Babylon will come upon** Egypt. Pharaoh's army, **Egypt and all its hordes** (cf. 30:10), would be crushed by the **tyrants of the nations** (cf. 29:17-21; 30:10-12, 24).

32:13. Judgment would strike both **beasts** and **man**. Figuratively, Pharaoh had muddied the waters with his international intrigue (cf. v. 2). Literally, the Nile was **muddy** through the daily activities of man and **beasts**.

32:14-16. After Egypt's judgment, **Then** God would make the **waters settle** because there would be no activity to disturb the water. The **rivers** would **run like oil**, smooth and undisturbed, because the land would be **destitute** of inhabitants. When God made the **land of Egypt a desolation . . . then they shall know that I am the Lord**. This **lamentation** (vv. 12-16) would be a **chant** of the surrounding **daughters of the nations . . . Over Egypt and over all her hordes** (cf. 30:10, 15; 31:1; 32:18).

7. Descent of Egypt into Sheol (32:17-32)

32:17-18. This is the last of Ezekiel's seven prophecies against Egypt, and his final oracle against a foreign nation. It came in the **twelfth year** (of Jehoiachin's exile) on the **fifteenth** day of the month (Adar 15/March 17, 585 BC). The month was not named, but it is often assumed to be the same month as the previous prophecy (v. 1), exactly two weeks after the preceding message (cf. v. 1). Ezekiel is told to **wail for the hordes of Egypt**, who were assigned to Sheol, **the nether world** (cf. 31:15), with **the daughters of the powerful nations** surrounding Egypt, **those who go down to the pit**, Sheol (cf. 26:18-21). God's word of judgment was so sure that Egypt's appointment to the grave was already made.

32:19-21. This lament opens with the derisive question: **Whom do you surpass in beauty?** Despite Egypt's beauty and power, it was told, **Go down and make your bed with the uncircumcised.** Egypt's pride would be shattered when her people were destroyed. She would be forced to take her place in death with "the uncircumcised." This word **uncircumcised** is used 10 times in this chapter (cf. vv. 19, 21, 24, 25, 26, 27, 28, 29, 30, 32) to describe a pagan's death of shame and defeat by the **sword** (cf. comments on 28:10). The language is poetic, and Ezekiel's purpose was not to give a precise description of the afterlife. However, this passage confirms there is individual conscience existence and identity after death when the nations **from the midst of Sheol** taunt them.

32:22-23. In Sheol, Egypt would join **Assyria** (cf. chap. 31) and **all her company**. The descriptions of the nations in this section (vv. 22-32) are similar: **All of them are slain, fallen by the sword** (vv. 22, 23, 34, 25, 26, 28, 29, 30, 31, 32), and lie with the uncircumcised (cf. v. 19).

32:24-25. Elam, the warlike nation east of Babylon (cf. Gn 14:1-17), had been subdued by Assyria and conquered by Nebuchadnezzar (cf. Jr 49:34-39). They were already in the **grave**.

32:26-28. Meshech and **Tubal** (cf. 27:13) were probably in what is now northeastern Turkey. They were Gog's allies (chaps. 38–39). They carried on a long battle with the Assyrians for control of the southern Black Sea region. These are especially wicked warriors who **instilled their terror** in the area. They would not even be buried beside the **heroes** (cf. 30:10) **of the uncircumcised** (cf. v. 19), but their **iniquity rested on their bones**.

32:29. Edom had already received notice of God's judgment (cf. 25:12-14). Her **kings** and **princes** would be **slain by the sword** and, as with the **uncircumcised**, awaiting Egypt's arrival.

32:30. The final group named included the **chiefs of the north** and **all the Sidonians**, (cf. 28:21) the Phoenician city-states. The mighty maritime powers would suffer the same **disgrace**. Their past exploits could not save them from **the pit** of death (cf. 26:20-21).

32:32. Although the Lord **instilled a terror** of Pharaoh in the **land of the living**, he did not learn to fear the Lord, and he and **all his hordes** (cf. 30:10) went **down among the uncircumcised** (cf. v. 19), separated from the Lord for eternity.

IV. Eschatological Blessings for Israel (33:1–48:35)

The restoration and blessing of Israel culminates the book of Ezekiel. After announcing judgment on Israel for her sins (chaps. 25–32) and judgment on the Gentile nations for their iniquity (chaps. 25–32), the book concludes by focusing on the promised restoration of Israel (chaps. 33–48). God is always faithful to His Word. He made a covenant with His chosen people Israel, and He will fulfill His promises to her. There will be new life for Israel under the leadership of her true Shepherd, the Messiah, and the final defeat of her enemies (chaps. 33–39), along with a new worship order for Israel in the messianic kingdom, at the messianic temple in the land of Israel (chaps. 40–48).

A. New Life for Israel (33:1–39:29)

Prior to the fall of Jerusalem, warnings of judgment dominated Ezekiel's oracles, with glimmers of hope. After the fall the pattern is reversed, with Ezekiel's messages focusing on the future hope, with a few judgment warnings. The only date in these chapters is the day the news of the fall of Jerusalem reached the exiles (33:21; 5 Sivan/January 9, 585 BC).

In the future, the false leaders will be replaced with a true Shepherd who will guide the people (chap. 34). The external enemies of Israel will be judged (chap. 35). The people will be restored both to the land and to their God (chaps. 36–37), and their security will be guaranteed by God Himself (chaps. 38–39).

1. Ezekiel Is Reappointed as a Watchman (33:1-33)

a. Ezekiel's Duties as a Watchman (33:1-20)

33:1-3. Ezekiel was given a renewed call to **speak to the sons of your people** and function as a **watchman** (cf. 3:16-17). Before highlighting the message of hope, God reminded the prophet and the **people** of their responsibilities. When anyone **sees the sword coming**, if he **blows on the trumpet and warns the people**, he has carried out his responsibility.

33:4-5. If anyone **hears . . . the trumpet** and **does not take** the **warning**, he is responsible for the consequences, **his blood will be on his own head**. If he had **take[n]** the **warning**, he would have been **delivered**.

33:6-9. If a **watchman** saw the **sword coming**, but failed to **blow the trumpet** warning of danger, and the people were captured, then the **blood** of those killed would be required **from the watchman's hand** by the Lord. The ineffective watchman would be held guilty. This message parallels the message about the question of responsibility and God's justice in chap. 18 (see comments on chap. 18). God appointed Ezekiel as **a watchman for the house of Israel**.

33:10. Rather than blaming their fathers (18:2) or God (18:19, 25) for their situation, at last the exiles took responsibility for their iniquity: **Surely our transgressions and our sins are upon us**. They realize their sins: **we are rotting away in them; how then can we survive?** (lit., "live").

33:11. God answered by reminding Israel of His character: **I take no pleasure in the death of the wicked, but rather that the wicked turn**

from his way and live (cf. 18:23, 32). He gave a clear call for personal action, **Turn back, turn back from your evil ways! Why . . . will you die, O house of Israel?**

33:12-13. A person's destiny is always decided on the basis of his faith, the legitimacy of which is expressed in his behavior (cf. Jms 2:14-26; Gn 15:6). A person who claims to be **righteous**, but **commits iniquity** has demonstrated his lack of righteousness and **he will die.**

33:14-16. But when a **wicked** person **turns from his sin and practices justice and righteousness**, his behavior has demonstrated a change of relationship with God and **he shall surely live; he shall not die.**

33:17-20. Ezekiel's **fellow citizens** had no basis for accusing the **Lord** of not being **right**. There are no grounds for accusing the Lord of injustice: **O house of Israel, I will judge each of you according to his ways**. God's judgment of an individual's **ways** was reckoned on their obedience to Him, based on personal faith, not outward ritual (see comments on 20:10-12).

b. The Opening of Ezekiel's Mouth (33:21-33)

33:21-22. Jerusalem fell, and the temple was burned on 9 Av/August 14, 586 BC (2Kg 25:8). It took several months to travel from Jerusalem to Babylon (Ezr 7:8-9), so **in the twelfth year of our exile, on the fifth of the tenth month** (5 Sivan/ January 19, 585 BC, news reached the **refugees from Jerusalem** in Babylon, **The city has been taken**. In the **evening, before** the news arrived, **the refugees** came to speak with Ezekiel, and the Lord **opened** the prophet's **mouth**. The selective muteness imposed by God for seven years, allowing Ezekiel to speak only God's judgments, was now lifted (cf. 3:26-27; 24:27), and he **was no longer speechless**.

33:23-24. Two groups are addressed by the **word of the Lord** in the conclusion of this chapter: the Jewish people who remained in Israel (vv. 23-29) and the Jewish people in the Babylonian exile (vv. 30-33).

First were those Jewish people who had escaped death in Jerusalem and **who live in** those **waste places in the land of Israel** and who refused to acknowledge God's judgment. They used God's promise to **Abraham** (Gn 12:1-7) as their justification to remain in the land. If the **one** man, Abraham, had a right to the land, certainly, they reasoned, the **many** Israelites remaining there had a right to it.

33:25. Although the promises to Abraham were unconditional, God is righteous to judge His people for their sin, and the Babylonian exile was His judgment. This was explained in the conditions of the Mosaic covenant, made 800 years earlier (Dt 28). God gave the land to Abraham unconditionally (Gn 12:1-3; 15:15-21), however, the enjoyment of and security in the land was predicated on obedience. The people who were claiming their right to remain in the land based on the promise to Abraham failed to realize that Abraham believed God and it was counted to him as righteousness (Gn 15:6), while they remained in unbelief and wickedness. They ate **meat with the blood in it** (cf. Lv 17:10-14), worshiped **idols** (Ex 20:4-6), and **shed blood** (cf. Ex 20:1-3). The right to possess the land depended on spiritual obedience, so the Lord twice asked: **Should you then possess the land?** (vv. 25, 26).

33:26-27. They were committing **abominations** while proclaiming their right to **possess the land** and would not be able to **rely on** their own **sword** for self-defense. Soon they would experience the pains of judgment. Those in Jerusalem's ruins, **waste places**, would **fall by the sword**; those who fled to the **open field** would be eaten by wild **beasts**; and those who hid in **strongholds** and **caves** would die of **pestilence**.

33:28-29. Those were the same judgments the people of Jerusalem had experienced earlier (cf. 5:17; 14:21). Then **they will know that I am the Lord** when God's judgment makes the **land** of Judah and Israel a **desolation** and a **waste**.

33:30. Ezekiel's message to **fellow citizens** in Babylonian exile had a mixed reception. There were some who were faithful to the Lord and recognized Ezekiel as a prophet. But the majority of the exiles, although interested in Ezekiel, did not obey Ezekiel's message. They would **talk about** Ezekiel **by the walls and in the doorways** and frequently gathered to **hear what the message is which comes forth from the Lord**—without changing their behavior.

33:31-32. Although they would come and **sit before** Ezekiel to **hear** his **words . . . they [did] not do them** (cf. Jms 1:22-25). Instead they followed their own **lustful desires**. His message to these exiles was as attractive as a **sensual song** sung with a **beautiful voice**. They liked to **hear [his] words but they [did] not practice them**.

33:33. But a day would come when everything Ezekiel said **comes to pass . . . then they will know that a prophet has been in their midst**. When their day of accountability came, those who heard the word would be forced to acknowledge the truth of Ezekiel's prophetic message.

2. Present False Shepherds Contrasted with the Future True Shepherd of Israel (34:1-31)

a. Present False Shepherds of Israel (34:1-10)

34:1-3. The **LORD** commanded Ezekiel to **prophesy against the shepherds of Israel**. The prophets and priests of Israel were often called shepherds (cf. Ps 78:70-72; Is 44:28; 63:11; Jr 23:1-4; 25:34-38). Their job was to be strong, caring leaders who protected Israel as a shepherd guards his flock. This section itemizes the sins of the false shepherds (Ezk 34:1-6), followed by the pronouncement of judgment (vv. 7-10).

Their first sin was economic exploitation, putting their own interests above those of the people. **Woe** to the **shepherds of Israel** who had been **feeding themselves**, when they should have been feeding **the flock**. Israel's corrupt leaders had committed "white collar crime," collecting money for themselves instead of properly using it to care for the people. To these false shepherds, the flock was a source of wealth to be exploited rather than a trust to be protected: **You eat the fat** and use the **wool**, **you slaughtered the fat sheep without feeding the flock**.

34:4. Their second sin was cruelty to the people. These false shepherds had not **healed** sheep who were **diseased** or injured (**broken**) nor brought back the **scattered** or **sought for the lost** sheep. They did not take care of the physical and spiritual needs of the people. Instead they treated the people with **severity** and **dominated** them. They ruled . . . harshly, brutally, and selfishly.

34:5-6. The third sin was their failure to protect the people from danger. The shepherds' lack of care for the people caused them to be **scattered** (repeated three times in two verses) and become **food for every beast** (enemy). Israel's leaders had allowed the nation to fall into sin. Consequently Israel was overtaken by the Assyrians (721 BC) and the Babylonians (586 BC), who had scattered Israel and Judah among the nations. Even worse, the spiritual leaders had become false prophets, so there was **no one to search or seek** for the flock and lead them back to the Lord.

34:7-8. These false **shepherds** are reminded, with an oath, **as I live**, the rightful owner of flock is **the Lord GOD**, who calls these sheep **My flock** or My sheep 13 times in vv. 7-31. God still called the Jewish people My sheep even though they were disobedient and even under His judgment. The Jewish people are always the apple of His eye and beloved for the sake of the forefathers (cf. Dt 7:6-9; 32:9-10; 33:27; Mc 7:18-20; Zch 2:8; Rm 11:28-29; see comments on 20:42-44 for God's faithfulness to Israel and His purpose for providing a future restoration for her).

34:9-10. Because these shepherds had neglected their responsibility, the sheep were in danger, so God said **I am against the shepherds, and I will demand My sheep from them** (cf. comments on vv. 7-8). The false shepherds would be judged for their actions. They would **cease from feeding sheep** . . . and **not feed themselves anymore**. Now God **will deliver My flock from their mouth, so that they** (the people/sheep) **will not be food for them** (the false shepherds). Because the false shepherds had brought Israel to ruin, God Himself would intercede and rescue His people as the true Shepherd of Israel, as described in the next section (vv. 11-31).

b. Future True Shepherd of Israel (34:11-31)

In contrast to false shepherds, God would care for His flock (vv. 11-16), judge between His sheep (vv. 17-22), and set His Shepherd, the Messiah to care for them (vv. 23-31).

34:11-14. The **Lord GOD** Himself **will search for My sheep and seek them out**. The flock was scattered because of cruel, indifferent shepherds (vv. 2-6), but they would be rescued and restored by the Lord, the Great Shepherd. God would intervene personally on Israel's behalf and **care for My sheep**, highlighting God as owner and loving caregiver of the flock of Israel.

God would rescue and **deliver [Israel] from all the places** . . . **they were scattered** . . . **I will bring them out from the peoples and gather them from the countries and bring them to their own land**. The regathering will be from worldwide dispersion back to **their own land**. God will provide a **good pasture** for them by **streams** . . . **on the mountains of Israel** (cf. Ps 23). This prophecy was not fulfilled when the Jewish exiles returned to Israel after the Babylonian captivity. They returned to Israel, but faced immediate opposition as they worked to rebuild the temple and Jerusalem, as recorded in Ezra and Nehemiah. Furthermore, the future return is from many countries, not just Babylon. Since AD 70, Jewish people have been scattered around the world, and the 1948 revival of the State of Israel brought Jewish people back from everywhere. Even so, that is not the return in peace and rest pictured here. This still awaits future fulfillment in the millennium.

34:15-16. God's shepherding care is a dynamic contrast to the treatment by the false shepherds (cf. v. 10). He will **lead them to rest . . . seek the lost, bring back the scattered, bind up the broken and strengthen the sick**. The false shepherds, now portrayed as the **fat and the strong** sheep who had abused the flock (cf. vv. 1-10, 22-20) would face **judgment**. This prophecy was not fulfilled with the return from Babylon because: (1) the return here is from worldwide dispersion; (2) when Israel returned after the exile they did not fully know the Lord as this passage describes; and (3) the returned exiles did not experience the peace and rest this passage describes.

34:17-19. God will care for His **flock** by judging **between one sheep and another, between the rams** (male sheep) and **the male goats** on the basis of their faith, as demonstrated by their behavior. The false leaders oppressed the people by using the **good pasture** for themselves, and destroying the rest (**tread down**). They would **drink the clear waters**, then **foul** them by trampling the stream.

34:20-22. These **fat sheep**, the wicked leaders, would be judged for brutalizing the **lean sheep**, the innocent **weak** people. So God would deliver **My flock** (cf. vv. 7-8) by judging between **one sheep and another**.

34:23-24. God will then **set over** His flock **one shepherd** (cf. Ec 12:11). The Lord God is identified as the Shepherd of Israel (cf. Gn 48:15; 49:24; Ps 23; Ec 12:11; Jr 31:10; Mt 2:6). He will **set over** Israel **My servant David** to care for Israel. Although some suggest this is the resurrected King David, **My servant David** is better understood as David's greater Son, the Messiah. Jesus identified Himself as the Good Shepherd (cf. Jn 10:11-18). This Shepherd will be from the line of David, but will be fully divine (cf. Pss 2:1-6; 89:4, 20, 29; Jr 23:5-6; Lk 1:69), not a resurrected David. The term "Son of David" is used 20 times in the NT as a messianic title (e.g., Mt 1:1; 9:27; 15:22; 20:30-31; 21:9, 15; 22:42; Lk 1:32; 18:39; Rm 1:3; 2Tm 2:8). As Feinberg points out: "The verb 'set up' (v. 23) does not imply the resurrection of David himself, but the appointment of Another (cf. the language of II Sam. 7:12 for the same verb; see Jr. 23:5; 30:9; Hosea 3:5—in the last two referenced He is already called David)" (Feinberg, *Prophecy of Ezekiel*, 198).

34:24. This shepherd David will be the **prince among them** (34:24 [twice]; 37:25; 44:3). In Hebrew the word *nasi*, translated **prince**, is literally "ruler," and does not mean "the son of a king" as it is commonly understood in English. *Nasi* is often synonymous with *melech*, "king" (e.g., 1Sm 9:16; 2Sm 3:38; Ezk 12:10, 12; for an in-depth study cf. E. A. Speiser, "Background and Function of the Biblical *Nasi*," *CBQ* 25 [1963]: 111–17). In place of the false shepherds, God will install the Messiah as the King and true Shepherd to tend His sheep.

34:25-26. The Lord will **make a covenant of peace** with the Jewish people under the kingship of Messiah. The **peace** will be more than an absence of war or temporary armistice. The word *shalom* means whole or complete. Therefore, it refers to the nation coming into a whole or right relationship with the Lord and the realization of all the blessings of the new covenant (cf. Jr 31:31-34). The elimination of **harmful beasts** will be fulfilled in the messianic kingdom (cf. Is 11:6-9). God will make the **places around My hill** (Mount Zion, Pss 2:6; 48:1, 2) **a blessing** to surrounding nations (cf. Zch 8:13). The peace that Israel has always longed for, which the Lord has promised in the Messianic Age (Is 11:1-9), will be experienced when the land is blessed with showers **in their season . . . showers of blessing**, just as He promised to provide rain as a reward for obedience (cf. Dt 11:14; 28:12).

34:27-28. The land will be fruitful when the **tree . . . will yield its fruit and the earth . . . . its increase** (cf. Lv 26:5; Am 9:13). The Lord will remove every harmful element from the land, and they will **be secure on their land** (Is 32:18) from every threat and **know that I am the Lord**, recognizing God has **delivered them**. Israel will be **delivered . . . from the hand of those who enslaved them**. They will **no longer be a prey to the nations** who are described as **the beasts of the earth** (cf. Dn 7). The Jewish people **will** live **securely** in their land, and **no one will make them afraid**.

34:29. The Lord will **establish for them a renowned planting place**, a homeland of significance, peace, and security, characterized elsewhere as under the leadership of the Messiah (cf. Is 4:2; 60:21; 61:3). They will be safe from beasts and **famine**—such threats being typically associated with judgment and war (cf. Ezk 5:17; 14:21; Dt 32:24; Jr 16:4; Rv 6:8)—as well as safe from the **insults of the nations**. All false accusations, slander, mockery, and anti-Semitic remarks will be silenced.

34:30-31. In the millennial kingdom, under the leadership of the Good Shepherd, Son of David, peace at last will be a reality for Israel and the Jewish people, and **they will know that I, the LORD their God, am with them, and that they, the house of Israel, are My people** (vv. 27, 30, 31; Lv 26:11-12). God will restore Israel because of His faithful love for them and their unique relationship to Him. Israel will know they are **My sheep, the sheep of My pasture, you are men, and I am your God** (cf. vv. 7-8; Ps 100:3).

3. Edom, the Enemy of Israel, Destroyed (35:1-15)

This is Ezekiel's second prophecy (cf. comments on 25:12-14) against Edom. Here the nation is identified by its common synonym, Mount Seir, a mountain range south of the Dead Sea. Because of Edom's long enmity toward Israel, it became the prototype of all Israel's later foes. The judgment on Edom represents God's judgment on all nations based on any nation's treatment of Israel (cf. Gn 12:3). The prophecy against Edom is in three parts, each ending with Ezekiel's hallmark expression, "Then you [they] will know that I am the LORD" (Ezk 35:4, 9, 15).

35:1-4. God proclaimed inescapable judgment on **Mount Seir**, saying, **I am against you** and would **stretch out My hand against you** (cf. 25:13; 35:3; Ex 3:20) and make Edom a **desolation** (cf. Ezk 35:3, 4, 7, 9, 14, 15) and a **waste**.

35:5-6. The judgment on Edom follows the **because** . . . **therefore** format (cf. 25:1-17; 35:10-11). **Because** of Edom's **everlasting enmity** against Israel, **therefore** God swears by Himself (**as I live**) to underscore the certainty of Edom's **desolation** (cf. comments on 25:12).

Because of this **everlasting enmity**, Edom had **delivered** the Israelites over to the **sword at the time of their calamity**, when Babylon attacked Jerusalem. Edom was an ally of Nebuchadnezzar **therefore**, for this hatred and cruelty, Edom will be judged (cf. 25:12; 36:5; Ps 137:7; Ob 10, 14).

Edom's judgment would parallel her iniquity. Because Edom had assisted in Israel's bloodshed, God would give Edom over **to bloodshed** (four times in v. 6). The principle here is Edom will experience bloodshed because they had not hated bloodshed. The whole country—mountains . . . hills . . . valleys . . . and ravines—will be filled with those slain.

35:7-9. Mount Seir will become a **waste** place, filled with its **slain**. Edom will be an **everlasting desolation**. These images of battle await an end-time fulfillment when Messiah will judge the enemies of Israel (cf. Zch 14). However in the messianic kingdom, all nations will be brought under the dominion of Messiah, and even a remnant of Edom will be subject to the Lord (cf. vv. 14-15; Am 9:12).

35:10. Edom is under judgment because when Israel fell, Edom wanted to make the **two lands**, Israel and Judah, **mine, and** . . . **possess them**. Edom failed to realize **the LORD was there** in the land of Israel with His people Israel. Israel is uniquely the Lord's land (Lv 25:23; Pss 10:16; 78:54; Ezk 25:8; 36:20; Zch 9:16). Although Israel and Judah were judged for their sin, God never abrogated the promises made to Abraham, Isaac, Jacob, and their descendants (cf. Gn. 12:1-7; 26:3-5; 35:11-12). Edom was trying to usurp Israel's title deed to the land, which had been guaranteed by God to Israel forever. This is a good attitude-check for the 21st century as well—when we think of Israel, we should remember, "the Lord is there."

35:11. The judgment on Edom was based on Edom's behavior toward Israel: **therefore** . . . **I will deal with you according to your anger** . . . **envy** . . . **because of your hatred against** the Jewish people. Through judgment, God would **make Myself known among them** (the Jewish people) **when I judge you** (Edom).

35:12-13. Edom had dared to plot against God's chosen people, and God had **heard all your revilings** ("contempt," "blasphemy") **spoken against the mountains of Israel**. However, Edom was not showing contempt *only* for Israel. God said, **you have spoken arrogantly against Me and have multiplied your words against Me; I have heard it**. Whenever anyone speaks against, persecutes, plots evil against, or demeans Israel and the Jewish people, that person is actually speaking against the God of Israel (cf. Ps 83; Jr 48:26, 42). Even if these malicious statements are made against Israel when she is being disobedient to the Lord, it does not justify anti-Semitism. The proper attitude is to pray for the Jewish people to return to the Lord their God, but never to side with Israel's enemies in attacking or castigating the nation. This is because the enemies of Israel are actually the enemies of the God of Israel (Ps 83). Followers of Jesus must never join the enemies of God in persecuting His people, nor stand idly by when observing the anti-Semitism of others. Rather, followers of Jesus must stand with the Lord in the defense of His beloved chosen people. It is up to the Lord to judge. His followers should be careful to leave any correction in His hands and never become arrogant toward Israel (cf. Rm 11:17-20).

35:14-15. The time when **all the earth rejoices** is in the millennial kingdom (cf. Is 44:23; 55:12), then Edom will be made a **desolation** as an object lesson for all nations. When God restores Israel in the future, He will judge the nations of the world and the individual within those nations, based on their treatment of Israel (cf. Mt 25:31-46). In her boast against God, Edom rejoiced when **the house of Israel . . . was desolate**. Likewise God will make **a desolation** of **Mount Seir, and all Edom, all of it**. Edom's treatment of Israel determined her fate: **Then they will know that I am the Lord**.

4. The People of Israel Blessed (36:1-38)

This section about blessing on Israel (35:12; 36:1), makes a dramatic contrast to the focus on judgment on Edom (chap. 35). The chapter is united by its images of mountains. The mountains of Israel represent the whole nation, just as Mount Seir represents Edom. When God intervenes on Israel's behalf, the "mountains" of Israel's enemies will be judged, but the "mountains of Israel" will be blessed.

The first section of the prophecy (vv. 1-15) uses the *because-therefore* format to compare the judgment on the nations for their treatment of Israel with Israel's restoration. The second section of the prophecy (vv. 16-38) focuses specifically on the blessing on the people of Israel.

a. Israel's Mountains Will Prosper (36:1-15)

36:1-2. The **mountains of Israel** represent the people not just the geography. **Because** the **enemy** of Israel had **spoken against** Israel, and claimed **the everlasting heights** of Israel, even Mount Zion, as their own, judgment was certain. The term **everlasting heights** points to Israel's eternal land grant by God, and His future plans for His land (cf. v. 5; Gn 12:1-3; 17:8; 48:4). Some have challenged the eternal nature of the land grant, but see the comments on Jr 7:1-15, particularly 7:7, for support for the eternality of God's gift of the land to Israel.

36:3-4. Therefore God promised to punish Israel's enemies, **the nations which are round about** Israel, for their evil actions against her **mountains**, **hills**, **ravines**, and **valleys**: they had **crushed**, slandered with **talk** and **whispering**, and made Israel a **prey and a derision**, attacking and mocking her.

36:5-7. Their wicked behavior against Israel ignited God's **fire of My jealousy** ([twice], vv. 5, 6) against all enemies of Israel, **rest of the nations**, and **all Edom**, who had **appropriated My land for themselves** with **joy** and **scorn**.

God's concern for His people is seen in His **jealousy** for her. This is a reflection of God's love, and generally refers to His exclusive covenant relationship with Israel (Ex 20:5; Ezk 36:6; 39:25; Nah 1:2; Zch 1:14; 8:2). The Lord is jealous for His Holy Name, His people, and His land, and will ultimately act in their defense (cf. Ezk 39:25; Nah 1:2; Zch 1:14-17; 8:2-3). The Lord was personally insulted by the derision of the nations against Israel, which He identified as **My land** (Ezk 36:5). **Therefore** God swore by keeping His covenant to Israel (cf. 20:5, 15, 23; 47:14) that the **nations** (v. 5, 7) who had **insult[ed]** Israel (v. 6) will also **endure . . . . insults**, the consequences of God's judgment.

36:8-11. An immediate contrast is presented between the judgment on Israel's enemies and the restoration and blessing on Israel: **But you, O mountains of Israel**. In a reversal of the catastrophe that God had earlier called against the mountains of Israel in judgment for sin (6:1-7), the restored Israel will be productive, **branches** will **bear . . . fruit**, and fields will be **cultivated**. The population will **multiply**, **cities will be inhabited**, and **waste places will be rebuilt**.

36:12. There will be permanent peace for **My people Israel**, highlighting the Lord's relationship with His people. They will experience the blessing of the land of Israel being **their inheritance** (cf. comments on vv. 1-2), and they will never again be bereaved of their **children**. God will restore the land so it can provide for the restored Jewish people. This will take place when Israel possesses her land during Messiah's millennial reign.

36:13-15. Because of the past wars and famine in the land, Gentile nations said Israel was a **devourer of men**, often **bereaved** of her children. God would remove Israel's reproach. The **insults** and **disgrace** Israel had suffered by the **nations** (vv. 3-6, 15) will cease when God judges Israel's enemies and blesses her, so she will not **stumble any longer**. Israel will be given her position of blessing among the nations, recognized as God's chosen people (cf. Dt 28:13; Zch 8:13, 20-23).

b. Israel's People to Be Regathered (36:16-38)

Ezekiel reviewed Israel's sinful past (vv. 16-21), then discussed the nation's future restoration in three sections, each beginning "Thus says the Lord God" (vv. 22, 33, 37).

36:16-19. Before explaining Israel's future cleansing, Ezekiel reminded the exiles **when the house of Israel was living in their own land**, their sin had led to God's judgment. They **defiled it** by their **ways** and their **deeds**. Their wicked behavior was like **the uncleanness of a woman in her impurity**, the menstrual cycle that made a woman ceremonially unclean (cf. Lv 15:19-23). Similarly, the land had been **defiled** by **blood** offered in sacrifice to **idols** (cf. Ezk 33:25).

Therefore God **poured** out His **wrath** on them and **scattered** and **dispersed** the Jewish people **throughout the lands**. His judgment was based on **their ways and their deeds**.

36:20-21. Where they lived in exile among the **nations**, Israel's behavior profaned God's reputation, and He had **concern for [His] holy name** (cf. comments on 20:9; 36:22-13). The Gentiles said, **these are the people of the Lord, yet they have come out of His land** (cf. v. 5). Gentile nations viewed the sovereign God through the actions of His people Israel, and **His holy name had been profaned**. They thought God had failed to keep His people in His land, so His name/reputation, was insulted.

36:22-23. Therefore the Lord said **to the house of Israel** He was going to take action, **not for your sake . . . but for My holy name** (cf. 20:9). Although Israel had no intrinsic merit that prompted God to act on her behalf, yet He would **vindicate the holiness of [His] great name** (cf. 20:9, 41-44; 28:22, 25; 38:16; 39:27). He would restore Israel to her own land because His character was at stake. God had shown His justice when He punished Israel for her sin. He will show His grace and faithfulness when He restores her and fulfills His covenant promises. **Then the nations** (Gentiles) **will know that I am the Lord . . . when I prove Myself holy among you** (Israel) **in their sight**.

36:24. God will prove Himself holy when He gathers Israel **from . . . the lands** of their dispersion and brings them back to their **own land**. He will first restore the nation physically and geographically (v. 24), and then spiritually (vv. 25-28). The vision of the dry bones (chap. 37) expands the sequence of restoration.

This return to the land goes beyond the return from Babylon because the future regathering will be not just from Babylon but also **from all the lands** where the Jewish people have been scattered.

36:25. God promised, **I will sprinkle clean water on you, and you will be clean; I will cleanse you from all your filthiness and from all your idols**. This is reference to the Mosaic sprinkling or washing with water as part of the Levitical sacrifices. It indicates cleansing from ceremonial defilement (cf. Lv 15:21-22; Nm 19:17-19). Since Israel's sin was like the ceremonial impurity of menstruation (Ezk 36:17) her cleansing was compared to the ceremonial act of purification. This purification will occur in the coming Messianic Age. God will purify Israel from her sins, and this cleansing will be followed by the impartation of new life.

36:26-28. God will give the purified Israel a **new heart and . . . a new spirit**. In place of a **heart of stone** He will give Israel a **heart of flesh** (cf. 11:19; 18:31), not hardened toward the Lord, but alive in Him. With God's **Spirit** indwelling them (cf. 37:14), they will be motivated to **walk in** (obey) His **statutes** and **observe** (keep) His **ordinances** (cf. 37:24).

God's restoration will not be simply an undoing of Israel's sin to bring her to a state of neutrality. Rather it will be the implanting of a new nature in the Jewish people, making them righteous. This is an application of the new covenant introduced by Jeremiah (cf. Jr 31:31-33) and initiated by the Lord Jesus with Israel through His disciples (Mt 26:26-32; Lk 22:14-20). Since the initiation of the new covenant at the death and resurrection of the Lord Jesus, any individual who trusts Jesus as his or her Savior can experience the spiritual aspects of the new covenant. However, in the future all Israel (all the Jewish people living at the time of the tribulation), when they call upon the Lord to save them and recognize Jesus as He returns, (Zch 12:10) will be saved and become partakers of the new covenant (cf. Rm 11:26). Implanting God's Spirit in believing Israelites will produce a new spiritual relationship between Israel and her God. The Lord established a unique relationship with the Jewish people as His chosen people at the call of Abraham, a relationship based on God's faithfulness to them, regardless of Israel's obedience and spiritual condition (cf. Gn 12:1-3; Dt 7:6-8). However, in the future all Israel will recognize Jesus as the Messiah, and their spiritual condition will match their national status: then **you will be My people, and I will be your God** (cf. Ezk 11:20; 14:11; 37:23, 27).

36:29-30. Moreover, in the kingdom, God will extend all His graciousness to His people to provide bountiful provision in the land, including **grain** . . . **fruit**, and crops of the **field** (cf. 34:27) without **famine** (cf. 34:29), so Israel will never again be a **disgrace** . . . **among the nations**.

36: 31-32 In the midst of blessing, **then** Israel will **remember** her former **evil ways** and wicked **deeds**, and she will realize how gracious the Lord is to her. In fact she will **loathe** herself because of her **iniquities** and **abominations** and will understand that God was **not doing this for your** (Israel's) **sake**, but to magnify His own name.

36:33-36. On the day when God will **cleanse** Israel from all her **iniquities**, the land will be transformed to become like the **garden of Eden**. Israel's formerly ruined cities will be **fortified and inhabited**. Israel will become an object lesson of God's grace to the world. Israel's neighbors will be forced to acknowledge God's sovereign power in restoring His people: they **will know that I, the Lord, have rebuilt the ruined places and planted that which was desolate**. The restoration of Israel will be a testimony to God's covenant-keeping character: **I, the Lord, have spoken and will do it**.

36:37-38. God will **increase** the population of Israel **like a flock**, a sign of God's blessing (cf. Gn 12:2; 15:1-6; 1Sm 1:5-6, 2:1-11; Zch 8:4-5). Ezekiel, a priest, compared Israel's population growth to the numerous flocks for **sacrifices** gathered for **Jerusalem['s]** . . . **appointed feasts**. Comparing the population to festival offerings suggested times of spiritual obedience and blessing. Then the formerly **waste cities** will be **filled with flocks of men**. At this time of great blessing, **Then they will know that I am the Lord**.

5. Nation of Israel Restored (37:1-28)

The Lord's promise of restoration is dramatically depicted in this vision of the dry bones, perhaps the most familiar passage in Ezekiel. After the destruction of Jerusalem, the Jewish people were in despair (cf. v. 11), hopelessly bereft of their land, their king, and their temple, scattered in exile. At this point God gave this astonishing message concerning Israel's future physical return to the land and spiritual restoration to the Lord (vv. 1-14), as well as the reunification of the divided kingdom (vv. 15-28).

a. Vision of the Dry Bones (37:1-14)

This prophecy emphasizes God's sovereign power and ability to fulfill His promises of restoring His people to His land. The Lord gave this vision to Ezekiel (vv. 1-10), and then He interpreted it (vv. 11-14).

37:1-3. The **hand of the Lord** brought Ezekiel **by the Spirit** (cf. 3:14; 8:3; 11:1, 24; 43:5) to a **valley** . . . **full of bones** which were . . . **very dry**. These **many** human bones had been lying **on the surface of the valley** for so long they were dried out by the sun.

The Lord asked Ezekiel, **Son of man, can these bones live?** Ezekiel answered with reverence, deferring to the Lord's knowledge: **O Lord God, You know**. Only God can give life to the dead.

37:4-8. God directed Ezekiel to **prophesy over these bones**. Then the bones came **rattling** together, forming skeletons. They were covered with **sinews, flesh** and **skin**, but were still lifeless bodies, because **there was no breath in them**. God gave life to the bones, but the restoration of life to the dry bones came in stages. As Ezekiel was giving this prophecy the "bones came together" (v. 7). The scattered bones become whole skeletons, but they were not yet alive.

37:9-10. God's promised restoration, to the **slain** (scattered, hopeless lifeless) nation of Israel would come about when He would give them the **breath** of life. The Hebrew *ruah* is translated **breath** (v. 5 and 30 other places) as well as "Spirit of the Lord" (cf. 11:5) and "spirit" (cf. v. 14; Gn 1:2; 3:8; 6:3 and 70 other places) and could also be translated "wind" (cf. Ezk 1:4 and 90 other places). The meaning of this frequently used word, whether translated "breath," "wind," "spirit" or "Spirit" is determined by the context. Thus, in the vision, the dead come to life and are given "breath." Nevertheless, in this vision the dry bones coming to life represent Israel's national resurrection, an event that could not occur apart from the work of the Spirit of God. Therefore, the breath is symbolic of the work of the Spirit (cf. v. 14).

The absence of **breath** in the bodies indicates that the Jewish people will be returned to their homeland in lifeless bodies, spiritually dead, prior to the nation coming to know the Messiah. This return seems to look beyond the return from Babylon to the end times. At that time the Jewish people will return to Israel from around the world (cf. 11:17; 17:22-24), yet the nation will be in unbelief in the land in the end times when all the nations declare war against Israel (cf. 20:33-38; 36:24-25; see comments at Zch 12:1-14; 14:2). At that desperate hour when the Jewish people recognize Messiah Jesus (Zch 12:10) He will rescue them from the hand of the nations (cf. Is 63:1-6; Zch 13:8-9; 14:3-11). Then, when Israel comes to know their Messiah, the

Lord will cause **breath** to enter them, and they will come **to life** as an **exceedingly great army**, or strength, of people.

37:11-13. The Lord explained the vision: the **bones are the whole house of Israel**. The Jewish people in exile thought, **Our bones are dried up and our hope has perished**. **We are completely cut off**. The vision of the dry bones signified Israel's future national and spiritual restoration. Israel's new life depended on God's power, not outward circumstances: **I will open your graves**. This is not about the literal resurrection of dead people, but of the restoration of the nation of Israel to their land and to their God when they felt all hope was dead. God identified the Jewish people, while in unbelief, as **My people**, whom He **will bring** . . . **into the land of Israel**. When Israel is returned to their land and rescued from their enemies at their most desperate hour (cf. Is 63:1-6; Zch 12:1-3; 13:8-9; 14:2-11; Jl 3:9-14), then they will turn to the Messiah Jesus (cf. Zch 12:10) and **Then you will know that I am the Lord**.

37:14. When God restores Israel nationally, He will subsequently renew them spiritually: **I will put My Spirit within you and you will come to life**. This is the Holy Spirit, promised in Israel's new covenant (cf. 36:24-28; Jr 31:31-34) and spoken of by Jesus to Nicodemus (cf. Jn 3:1-21). Today the vast majority of Jewish people do not recognize Jesus as their Messiah. They have not yet had the Spirit of God "blown into them." The reconnecting of the dry bones may find an initial fulfillment in the reconstitution of the modern state of Israel. Jewish people are being regathered from around the world to their ancient homeland. As yet, however, they are spiritually dead. But when the nation turns and recognizes Jesus as Messiah, they will **come to life**. Shortly thereafter Jesus will establish His messianic kingdom. Then Jews from around the world will come to Israel and live peacefully in their **own land** under the kingdom rule of Messiah (Jr 31:33, 33:14-16; Mt 24:30-31). See comments on Mt 23:37-39 and Ac 3:19-21 for an explanation of the salvation of Israel as a precursor to the millennial kingdom.

b. Sign of the Two Sticks—Israel United (37:15-28)

Following the vision of restoration of the dry bones is the second sign of hope of God's reunification of the nation of Israel. First the sign was given (35: 15-17), then explained (35:18-28).

37:15-17. This is Ezekiel's last object lesson (cf. 4:1, 3, 9; 5:1). Here **the Lord** commanded him to **take** . . . **one stick and write on it, 'For Judah and** . . . **the sons of Israel'** and a second stick and **write on it, 'For Joseph, the stick of Ephraim.'** Then Ezekiel was to **join them** . . . **into one stick**.

Under King David and Solomon, Israel was one nation, but after the death of Solomon (931 BC) the nation divided into the northern kingdom of Israel with ten tribes ruled by a non-Davidic king (1Kg 11:26; 12:25-33), and the southern kingdom of Judah consisting of two tribes (Judah and Benjamin) ruled by the descendants of David (cf. 1Kg 12:20-24). **Ephraim**, one of the sons, had a large tribal land allotment in the north so the northern kingdom is sometimes identified by his name (e.g., Hs 5:3, 5, 11-14). About 200 years after the division of the kingdom, Israel was taken into captivity by Assyria (721 BC). Judah remained until it fell to Babylon (586 BC). Here the Lord gives hope of a restored, united Davidic kingdom.

37:18-21. The Lord explained the lesson. This would be a future event, **when the sons of your people** ask **what you mean**, God will give the answer. He emphasized His role in the restorations: **I will take** . . . **I will put** . . . **they will be one in My hand**. The Lord Himself will unite **Ephraim** and **Judah** into **one in My hand**. God will **gather them from every side and bring them into to their own land**.

37:22. God **will make them one nation in the land** with **one king**, and they **will** . . . **no longer be divided into two kingdoms** (cf. Hs 1:11). The uniting of the sticks pictured God's restoring and reuniting His people **in the land** as a single nation.

37:23. At that time the nation will **no longer defile themselves with their idols**. They will be transformed because the Lord will **deliver them** from the places where they **sinned** and **cleanse** them, not just wash away dirt, but also make them morally pure (cf. 20:42-44). Then **they will be My people, and I will be their God** (cf. 11:20; 14:11; 36:28; 37:27). This spiritual rejuvenation and reunification will occur in the millennial kingdom.

37:24. The reunited kingdom will be ruled over by **My servant David** as **king over them** (see comments on 34:23-24) and as their **one shepherd** (cf. 34:23).

37:25-28. The key idea of this passage is that the blessings will last forever. The Jewish people **will live on the land that I gave to Jacob My servant** (cf. 28:25). There are several aspects of the eternal quality of God's blessing: the Jewish people will inhabit their land **forever** (v. 25); the kingship of Messiah, David's Son is **forever** (v. 25); the **covenant of peace** (cf. 36:15; 34:25; Is 54:10; Jr 31:31-34) is **everlasting** (Ezk 37:26; cf. 16:60); God's **sanctuary** will be **in their midst forever** (vv. 26, 28). This prophecy concludes with the promise of God's presence: **My dwelling place also will be with them; and I will be their God, and they will be My people**. Israel's restored relationship with their God and the literal structure of the **sanctuary in their midst** will be a testimony to **the nations** (the Gentiles) who **will know** (cf. 36:23; 38:16, 23; 39:7) **that I am the LORD who sanctifies Israel** (cf. Lv 22:32). This **sanctuary** that will be **in their midst forever** is described in detail in Ezk 40–43.

6. Prophecy of Attack and Defeat of Gog (38:1–39:29)

After foretelling the regathering of the Jewish people to their land (chap. 36), Ezekiel told of yet a future, and final, attack on Israel from which they will be rescued by the returning messianic King (chaps. 38–39). This attack by Gog will occur after the Jewish people are resettled in their land (38:8b) and living in peace (38:8c), although not yet knowing the Messiah (since they will come to the Lord after He delivers them from attack). It culminates in the Lord's victory over Israel's enemy and Israel recognizing Jesus as their Messiah (39:22). Ultimately Gog will be judged.

a. Invasion of Israel by Gog (38:1-16)

38:1-3. The Lord told Ezekiel to **set your face** (v. 2; cf. 4:7, 6:2), a phrase of determined judgment, **toward Gog of the land of Magog, the prince of Rosh, Meshech and Tubal**. The identification of **Rosh** is essential. This is a *transliteration*, not a *translation*, of the Hebrew word *rosh* which simply means "head" or "chief." It should not be taken as the proper name of a nation. **Rosh** never appears as a nation in any other biblical list of place names, while all the other names in chaps. 38–39 are well attested (cf. Gn 10:1-7; 1Ch 1:5-7; Ezk 27:13-24; 32:26). The clear evidence of Scripture is that the phrase translated by the NASB as **the prince of Rosh, Meshech and Tubal** (*nasi rosh meshach*) should be translated as Gog the . . . "chief prince of Meshech and Tubal" (HCSB, NIV, KJV, ESV, JPS).

The land of **Magog** was probably the nation from which the Scythians descended. **Meshech** and **Tubal** and Gomer were in eastern Asia Minor. **Gog** is mentioned only here and in Rv 20:8 and is of/in **Magog**.

38:4. God will judge this pagan nation (vv. 1-3), but He will use Gog to accomplish His plans concerning Israel, just has the Lord had used Assyria and Babylon in the past. The Lord will **turn** Gog **about** to head in the direction He has determined. The Lord is completely in control of all world events, as indicated by His providence over these battles against His people Israel.

38:5-6. These nations were well known in the biblical period: **Persia** (Iran), **Ethopia** and **Put** (Libya), **Beth-togarmah** in modern Syria. Additionally, Magog, Meshech, Tubal, and **Gomer** were in areas that are now modern Turkey, Armenia, Azerbaijan, and Georgia. They were part of the former Soviet Union, but are now independent nations. Because of the similarity of the sounds of Rosh and Meshech to Russia and Moscow and Tubal to Tobolsk, some interpreters, especially during the Cold War period, inaccurately identified Israel's attackers with the USSR. The interpretation was based more on headlines and hysterics than hermeneutics and history.

All of the countries mentioned here by Ezekiel are today Muslim countries. Assuming their spiritual allegiance does not change, the future invasion of Israel by these nations will not be a Russian invasion, but an Islamic invasion. The coordination of attack on Israel will not come from Moscow, but from the leadership of these Muslim governments.

38:7-9. The time of the attack is described in eschatological terms, **after many days . . . in the latter years**. This attack will occur in the end times. This attack will be against **Israel**, whose people will be **gathered from many nations** and will be **living securely** back in the land of Israel. Gog and his allies will go against Israel in massive strength, advancing like a **storm** and a **cloud** (cf. v. 16).

No past historical event or political alignment matches this prophecy. It is set **in the latter years** so it awaits a future fulfillment. Some think this attack on Israel should be identified with the attack of Gog and Magog at the end of the millennium (Rv 20:7-9), but this identification has several flaws. The first is a chronological consideration. Why would the people remain on earth after the battle to burn the weapons of war for seven years (Ezk 39:9-10) instead of entering immediately into eternity (Rv 21:1-4)? The results of Ezekiel's battle do not coincide with the events following the battle in Rv 20. Why bury the dead for seven months after the battle (Ezk 39:12-13) when the next prophetic event is the resurrection of the unsaved dead (Rv 20:11-13)? The events after each battle are so different that two separate battles must be assumed, both involving Gog as Israel's enemy.

The second flaw concerns the results of this battle. The effect on the people is different. In Ezekiel the battle is the catalyst God will use to draw Israel to Himself (cf. Ezk 39:7, 22-29) and to end Israel's dispersion among the nations. In contrast, in Rv 20 the battle will occur after Israel has been faithful to her God and has enjoyed His blessings for a thousand years (Rv 20:1-7).

Others have suggested the battle of Ezk 38–39 is at the beginning of the millennium. This also seems extremely doubtful. Everyone who enters the millennium will have faith in Messiah Jesus. The surviving Jewish people will have recognized the Messiah at the end of the tribulation when they call on Him to return (Zch 12:10); and the Gentiles will have demonstrated their faith in Christ by protecting God's chosen people during the tribulation (cf. Mt 25:31-46). So everyone who enters the millennial kingdom will be a believer in Jesus Messiah (Jn 3:3). Furthermore, at the beginning of the millennium all weapons of war will be destroyed (Mc 4:1-4). Thus it would be improbable for a war to occur when all unsaved warriors have been eliminated and all weapons destroyed.

Thus, it seems best to place Ezekiel's battle of Gog in the tribulation period. The attack will come when the Jewish people are living at peace in the land of Israel (Ezk 38:8, 11). Although they are in the land, the Jewish people will not have yet recognized that Jesus is the Messiah (39:22, 29). This peace will be the result of the covenant with the antichrist made at the beginning of Daniel's seventh week (Dn 9:27a). However, at the midpoint of the tribulation, that covenant will be broken by the antichrist. Then Israel will suffer tremendous persecution (see comments on Dn 9:27b; Mt 24:15-22).

So most likely the Islamic invasion, the battle described by Ezekiel, will begin just prior to the antichrist breaking his covenant with Israel. The defeat of these nations will free the future world ruler from maintaining a military alliance with Israel. If the battle occurs at this point, it will provide the time needed to bury the dead (Ezk 39:12-13) and to burn the weapons of war (Ezk 39:9-10)—namely, during the remainder of the great tribulation and perhaps into the initial months of the millennial kingdom following Jesus' second coming. Ezekiel was describing a battle that will involve Israel's surrounding neighbors, near and far, who sense their opportunity to attack when Israel feels secure and who have the false confidence of a covenant with the antichrist. Ezekiel first presented the invasion by Gog and his allies (vv. 1-16) and then described the judgment of Gog and his allies (38:17–39:29).

38:10-13. Gog will **devise an evil plan**, and . . . will say, **I will go up against** Israel who will be living in peace, **securely** with **no bars or gates**. The Jewish people will be back in their land, living as a political entity, **gathered from the nations** and at peace in the Middle East. Israel's importance geographically, politically, and economically is described as **the center of the world** (cf. comments on 5:5). These events are focused around Israel (cf. Zch 12:1-3).

38:14-15. On that day . . . in the last days (vv. 14, 16, 18) are eschatological terms for the end times, and indicate the time of Gog's attack is against **My people Israel** (vv. 14, 16) when they are living securely. Although at this point Israel is a nation without faith in Messiah Jesus, they are still designated by God as **My people**. Whether the Jewish people are living in disbelief and rebellion or in repentance and obedience, they are still beloved by God and remain His chosen people. Gog's attack will come from all sides, **the remote parts of the north**, with his **mighty army** of allies.

38:16. They will advance against **My people Israel like a cloud to cover the land** (cf. v. 9). Gog's attack will be against **My land**. Israel is identified as belonging not simply to the Jewish people but to the Lord Himself (cf. 36:5; Is 14:25; Jr 2:7, 3:18). Gog's powerful army will overrun Israel as completely as a cloud casts a shadow over the land below.

This attack will be another means of God's displaying to the nations His holy character and sovereign power, **so that the nations may know Me when I am sanctified through you before their eyes, O Gog** (cf. Ezk 20:41; 28:22, 25; 36:23; 39:27). As a result of Gog's unsuccessful attack, Israel will be delivered and God glorified.

b. Judgment of Gog by God (38:17–39:29)

(1) Defeat of Gog (38:17–39:8)

38:17. The **Lord God** will crush Gog's attack. The question, **Are you the one of whom I spoke**

in former days through My servants the prophets of Israel? is not a direct quote of any specific prophet. It is, however, a general reference to what earlier prophets said of the coming invasion of Israel in the last days (cf. Jl 3:9-14; Zph 3:15-20).

38:18-20. When the army **comes against . . . Israel**, God's **fury will mount up in . . . anger . . . zeal . . . and blazing wrath** against them. He will cause a **great earthquake in . . . Israel** that will interrupt Gog's invasion plans. This natural disaster will cause **fish . . . birds . . . beasts . . . and all the men** . . . to **shake at** God's **presence**, and it will spread fear and disarray throughout the invading armies. God will call for a sword against Gog on all My mountains.

38:21. In the confusion **every man's sword will be against his brother**. As in the days of Jehoshaphat, the enemies of Israel will destroy themselves (cf. 2Ch 20:22-25).

38:22-23. God will **enter into judgment** against the enemies of Israel with additional meteorological catastrophes, including **torrential rain . . . hailstones. . . fire and brimstone**. This is similar to the Lord's actions on behalf of Israel in the days of Joshua (cf. Jos 10:7-11). Through these events, God will **magnify . . . sanctify . . . and make** Himself **known in the sight of many nations; and they will know that I am the Lord**.

39:1-4. Ezekiel is again told to **prophesy against Gog** (cf. 38:2). Deliver the message of the **Lord God**, that He is **against . . . Gog**, chief **prince** (cf. comments on 38:2) of **Meshech and Tubal**. God will disable their **left** . . . and **right hand** and strike them down **on the mountains of Israel**. This once-mighty army will then be **food . . . to every kind of predatory bird and beast of the field**.

39:5-7. Not only will the enemy armies die on Israel's **open field** in battle, God will also judge their homelands: **I will send fire upon Magog and those who inhabit the coastlands**. Sending fire indicates destruction and military devastation (30:8, 14, 16; Hs 8:14; Am 1:4, 7, 10, 14; 2:2, 5). The nation that initiated the invasion will be destroyed. The **coastlands**, (cf. 26:15, 18; 27:3, 6-7, 15, 35) indicate the farthest reaches of the known world. Through all these events God will **make known** His **holy name** (twice for emphasis in v. 7) . . . **in the midst of . . . Israel** and the nations will see that that He is **the Holy One in Israel**.

39:8. All of these events are certain: **"Behold, it is coming and it shall be done," declares the Lord God**. Despite modern skepticism, mockery of the Scriptures, or disputed geopolitical current events, the Lord will fulfill His word: **That is the day of which I have spoken**.

(2) Aftermath of the Defeat of Gog (39:9-20)

39:9-10. At the end of the great battle, **those who inhabit the cities of Israel** will gather up the **weapons and burn them**. Those who will come to plunder Israel (38:12) will themselves be plundered. Israelites will use the weapons of the fallen army for fuel throughout the remainder of the tribulation period and into the beginning of the millennium, **for seven years**. Israel will burn those weapons for fuel and not cut down trees **from the forests**. The repetition of the number **seven—seven years** for burning the weapons and "seven months" for burying the dead (vv. 9, 12, 14)—signifies the finality of this great battle against God's people and suggests the size of the invading armies (cf. comments regarding the time of this event on 38:7-9).

39:11-16. Gog will have **a burial ground there in Israel**. The burials will take place in **the valley of those who pass by east of the sea**, meaning the burial will be on the east side of the Dead Sea, what was Moab in Ezekiel's day and Jordan today. Yet the burial will be reckoned as "in Israel" because Israel controlled that area during some periods of her history, and it was part of the land grant to Abraham. Israel will inhabit it in the future (cf. 2Sm 8:2; Ps 60:8; Gn 15:18). Even in the midst of post-war clean up, in these events the Lord says He will **glorify Myself**.

Some of **the people of the land**, the Jewish people, will be **set apart** to be sure all the bones are picked up and buried and the graves marked so the ground will be cleansed. They will make their **search** at the end of the **seven months**. The number of corpses will be so great it will **block** the way of travelers. The name of the valley will be changed to **the valley of Hamon-gog**, meaning "the Valley of the hordes of Gog," because of the enormous size of the graveyard of Gog.

39:17-20. Another result of Gog's defeat will be a great sacrificial feast for the wild animals, introduced in v. 4. **Every kind of bird and . . . beast** was called to **assemble** . . . to the **great sacrifice on the mountains of Israel**. They were to **eat** slain **men of war** as if they were . . . **rams, lambs, goats and bulls of . . . Bashan**, the area east and northeast of the Sea of Galilee which was known for its fertile land and fat cows (cf. Am 4:1). God will reverse the roles of animals and people. Usually people slaughtered and ate sacrificed animals. Here, however, the men of Gog's armies will be sacrifices to be eaten by animals. God identifies the slain of Gog as **My sacrifice which I am going to sacrifice for you**. The wild birds and animals will be **glutted** with Gog's slain military **horses**, **charioteers**, and **men of war**.

(3) Effects of the Lord's Defeat of Gog on Israel (39:21-29)

39:21. There are several results of this battle. First, God says He will **set My glory among the nations**. His honor and visible presence will be recognized when He delivers Israel by defeating Gog (cf. 1:28).

39:22-24. Second, Israel will turn back to her God and **know that I am the Lord their God from that day onward** (cf. v. 7). The Lord's stunning defeat of Gog will force Israel to acknowledge His power forever and never again stray from Him (cf. 37:24-28).

39:25-27. Third, God will restore all Israel back to the land from her final dispersion. God will **restore . . . Jacob and have mercy on the whole house of Israel**. Although God judged Israel for her sin, He always loves His people and has a heart of compassion for them (e.g., Ps 102:13; Is 14:1-2; 49:13-16). Many Jewish people will be living in their homeland of Israel when the events in these chapters occur, and some Jewish people will still be living around the world. Now God will **bring them back from the peoples and gather them from the lands of their enemies**. God will be **sanctified through them in the sight of many nations** (cf. Ezk 20:41; 28:22, 25; 36:23; 38:16).

39:28-29. Fourth, the ultimate result of the battle with Gog will be Israel's national repentance and spiritual restoration. At that time **they will know that I am the Lord their God**. Although God had scattered His people **into exile** in the past, He will gather them **to their own land**, and he will **leave none of them** outside the land of Israel **any longer**.

The Lord will **not hide My face from them**. Instead He will pour out His **Spirit on the house of Israel** when they recognize Jesus as Messiah (cf. 36:25-28; 37:14; Jr 31:31-34; Jl 2:28-32; Zch 12:10).

B. New Order for Israel (40:1–48:35)

When Messiah returns to rescue His people Israel and defeat her enemy, Gog (chap. 39), the Lord will establish a new order of worship in the restored Israel. A new temple will be built as a sign of God's presence among His people (chaps. 40–43), and a new service of worship will be established so the people will have access to the Lord their God (chaps. 44–46), and a new division of the land will be made for the people (chaps. 47–48).

1. A New Temple (40:1–43:27)

God had promised to set His sanctuary in the midst of His people forever (37:26-28), and the plans for this new temple are given in detail. Three basic interpretations exist of chaps. 40–43. (1) Ezekiel predicted a rebuilding of Solomon's temple immediately after the Babylonian captivity. (2) Ezekiel was speaking of the temple in a figurative sense, prophesying about the Church, and did not have a literal temple in mind. (3) Ezekiel spoke of a still-future literal temple to be built during the millennial kingdom.

The first view, of a Solomomic post-Babylonian captivity temple, must be eliminated. Ezekiel's specifications do not coincide with Solomon's temple, nor were they used by the remnant returning from Babylon. The temple built at the return from Babylon was not of Solomonic grandeur (Ezr 3:12-13; Hg 2:3). If this temple was built in the time of Ezra, Ezekiel would have been mistaken when he wrote; no prophet speaking under God's authority ever uttered a false prediction (Dt 18:21-22; Mt 5:17-18).

The second view of the temple as an allegory representing the Church must also be discounted. Support for this interpretation is drawn from Jesus' statements that He is the true temple (see Jn 2:18-21), and the Church with Him constitutes the temple in the present era (see 1Co 3:16; 6:19; 2Co 6:16-18; Eph 2:21-22; 1Pt 2:5; Rv 3:12; 11:1-2). Gregory K. Beale, a leading proponent of this view, observes that Ezk 11:16 indicates that the temple took on a less architectural sense during the exile, and this provides warrant for Paul to say that the Church is the fulfillment of the eschatological temple (Gregory K. Beale, "Eden, the Temple, and the Church's Mission In the New Creation," *JETS* 48 [March 2005], 19-24; see also, in much more detail, Beale's *The Temple and the Church's Mission: A Biblical Theology of the Dwelling Place of God*, NSBT [Downers Grove, IL: InterVarsity, 2004]). Among other things, Beale maintains that a literal future temple would detract from Jesus being the ultimate temple.

In response, first, it is not inappropriate to say that the Church is the temple—the place where God intersects with the world—*in the present era*. Clearly it is. But this fact by itself does not inform regarding the possibility that there might also be a future literal kingdom. Regarding Jesus' ultimate fulfillment of the features of the temple, this also does not preclude the possibility of a literal, eschatological temple. Robert L. Saucy notes that Jesus is the great Prophet (Heb 1:1-2), but He has given the gift of prophecy and prophets to the Church (1Co 12:10, 18; Eph 4:11), yet in a way that does not eclipse Him and His work. He is also the great High Priest (Heb 2:17; 4:14; 7:26-27; 9:24-28; 10:11-14), but the Church is a priesthood called to function as priests through Christ (1Pt 2:5, 9; Rm 15:16). Jesus is the great King (Lk 1:32-33; Rv 11:15; 19:16), but believers also function as kings (2Tm 2:12; Rv 1:6; 5:10; 20:4, 6 ("Is Christ the Fulfillment of National Israel's Prophecies? Yes and No!" Unpublished paper presented at the Evangelical Theological Society Annual Meeting in November, 2010, 9). What this suggests is that Jesus can assign a function He fulfills to other agents (in the case of the present discussion, the future temple) without in any manner overshadowing His accomplishments.

Second, the observation that Ezk 11:16 sets the stage for a non-architectural temple fails on the rebuilding of a literal temple by the Jewish people following the exile. That God could and did connect with the exiles in Babylon does not preclude the rebuilding of a physical temple following their return. What this suggests is that the Church could be the temple in a spiritual sense during the current era without eliminating the possibility of a literal temple in the future.

Third, some have pointed out that there are remarkable parallels between Ezekiel and Moses. Both received a call from God that they were reluctant to fulfill. Both had visionary experiences of God's glory. And both mediated legislation regarding the place God would intersect with Israel (Moses for the tabernacle; Ezekiel for the future temple) and the sacrifices associated with them. If God gave Moses instructions about a literal tabernacle and then a temple that came to architectural fruition, it is possible that what Ezekiel was shown will have a similar literal fulfillment. This observation is bolstered by the mention of a future, millennial temple by other prophets along with Ezekiel (see Is 2:3; 60:13; Dn 9:24; Jl 3:18; Hg 2:7, 9).

Finally, it is admittedly tricky to build an argument on "what the original readers or hearers would have understood." Having said that, it is hard (not impossible) to believe that the original readers or hearers of this prophetic book would have understood the minute details associated with the dimensions and furnishings of this temple in a spiritual, non-physical way. If the temple's features were intended symbolically, neither the prophet nor God gives any clues as to what they symbolized. Rather, there are parallels with the details of the design of the tabernacle and then the Solomonic and postexilic temples following it, and these were physical structures.

The view adopted for this commentary is that Ezekiel predicted a literal, physical, millennial temple. The detailed description of the millennial temple is important. First, the temple was the visible symbol of God's presence among His people. The prelude to Israel's judgment began when God's glory departed from Solomon's temple (Ezk 8-11). This was followed by Nebuchadnezzar's destruction of it. Although the temple was rebuilt, the presence of the Lord did not reside in the Holy of Holies. That temple was destroyed by the Romans, just as Messiah Jesus has predicted (Mt 24:2; Mk 13:2). A high point of Israel's restoration as a nation will come when God's glory reenters the new temple in Jerusalem (Ezk 43:1-5).

Second, the new temple will become the visible reminder of Israel's relationship to God through His new covenant. Since God gave detailed instructions for building the tabernacle to accompany His inauguration of the Mosaic covenant (cf. Ex 25-40), it is not unusual that He would also supply detailed plans for His new center of worship, to accompany the full implementation of the new covenant. This temple will be the focal point for the visible manifestation of Israel's new relationship with her God.

a. Introduction to the Vision of the Temple (40:1-4)

40:1-2. This final vision was given to Ezekiel in the **twenty-fifth year of . . . exile, at the beginning of the year, on the tenth of the month**, **in the fourteenth year** after the **city was taken**, in the fall of Jerusalem. The Jewish religious calendar marked the **beginning of the year** as Nissan (April/May at Passover; Ex 12:1-2) or later using the civil or regnal year as Tishri (October/November). So the date would be 573 BC, either April 28 or October 22. God took Ezekiel back to **the land of Israel** in a **vision** (cf. Ezk 8:1-3) and brought him to **a very high mountain . . . to the south there was a structure like a city**.

The mountain was probably Mount Zion (17:22; 20:40; Is 2:2; Mc 4:1; Zch 14:10), which is north of the city (cf. Ps 48:1-2).

40:3-4. In visions (cf. 1:1; 8:3; 40:2) Ezekiel was taken to the future temple by **a man whose appearance was like**... **bronze**, indicating this was an angelic being (cf. 8:2). He had **a line of flax and a measuring rod in his hand**, implements used by builders. The **line of flax** was a lightweight rope used for longer measurements and the **rod**, a wooden pole, for shorter measurements. Ezekiel was instructed by the **man** to **give attention** to all he was **going to show** him, so the prophet could **Declare to the house of Israel all that** he saw. This was a precise, important message specifically for the Jewish people.

b. Outer Court of the Temple (40:5-27)

40:5. There was a **wall on the outside of the temple** (*bayit*, lit., "house") **all around**, separating the sacred from the secular. The man measured it with a **measuring rod of six cubits,**... **a cubit and a handbreath**. A common cubit was about 18 inches long, but the one used by the angel was a long cubit, about 21 inches long. Ezekiel is specifically using the more ancient standards of cubic measurement (2Ch 3:3) for the new community. The length of the rod was six of the ancient cubits or about 10 ½ feet long. The wall surrounding the temple was 10 ½ feet thick and 10 ½ feet high. Since the wall was not high enough to provide security from attack, its purpose was separation of the holy from the profane (cf. 42:20).

40:6-16 Ezekiel **went** into the outer court through the **gate** facing **east**, the most important gate (cf. comments on 44:1-3). It is described in detail, with exact measurements, its **steps**... **threshold** ... **guardrooms** ... **porch** ... **facing inward** ... **pillars** toward the temple ... with **palm tree ornaments** along the projecting walls. Palm tree designs also decorated Solomon's temple (1Kg 6:29, 32, 35).

40:17-19. The angelic being **brought** Ezekiel **into the outer court**, where he saw **a pavement made for the court**, and **thirty chambers faced the pavement** ... **all around the court**. These rooms were probably spaced evenly along the north, east, and south walls of the temple (see sketch "The Millennial Temple" on p. 1266). They may have been used for the people celebrating the feasts (cf. Jr 35:2). The distance from the inside of the **lower gate** (i.e., the east gate) to the outside of the **inner court** (i.e., to the threshold of the gate leading to the inner court) was **a hundred cubits** (175 feet).

40:20-27. Ezekiel was then led to the **north** gate (vv. 20-23) and to the **south** gate (vv. 24-27). The design and dimensions of both gates were identical to those of the gate facing **east**, demonstrating the symmetry of the temple design. (vv. 6-19).

c. Inner Court of the Temple (40:28-47)

40:28-37. After measuring the outer court the angel measured the **inner court**, through the **south gate**. This **gate** had the **same measurements** as the other gates (vv. 28-31; 32-34; 35-37). The measurements were the same for the **guardrooms**... **pillars**... **porches**... **windows** ... **palm tree ornaments** (41:18). However, the **porches all around** were reversed on these gates, allowing them also to face **toward the outer court** (see sketch "The Millennial Temple" on p. 1266).

40:38-43. A **chamber** was located by the **side** of the inner **gates** where the person offering sacrifice could **rinse** and prepare the **burnt offering**. **Four tables** were set on **each** side of the gate, eight tables in all, to prepare the **slaughter** for **burnt offering and the sacrifice**. Restored sacrifice is a key function of the millennial temple.

The institution of animal sacrifice in the millennial temple has raised questions because Jesus' death on the cross is the ultimate and final sacrifice for sin (Heb 10:10). Some suggest the sacrifices in the millennial temple might be symbolic and not actual animal sacrifices. It is argued by objectors that since these sacrifices revert back to the Levitical sacrificial system they seem out of place after the sacrifice of Jesus. An understanding of the proper function of these sacrifices clears up the confusion and objections. First, Levitical animal sacrifices never took away sin; only the sacrifice of Christ can do that (Heb 10:1-4, 10). Under the Levitical system, in OT times, Israelites were saved by grace through faith, as was Abraham (Gn 15:6). Each person had to offer the proper sacrifice as an expression of his genuine faith (Is 1:10-18), and the sacrifices served to restore a believer's fellowship with God. Sacrifices offered without faith were useless (e.g., Is 1:11-17; Am 5:21-24). Second, even after the Church began, Jewish believers did not hesitate to take part in the temple worship (Ac 2:46; 3:1; 5:42) and even to offer sacrifices (Ac 21:26). They understood the new covenant had been instituted with the death and resurrection of Messiah and memorialized with the Lord's Supper (cf. Lk 22:14-20; 24:13-35). Yet they continued to worship in the temple, fully aware of the final sacrifice of the Lord Jesus, until it was destroyed by the Romans (AD 70).

Before the coming of the Messiah, the Levitical sacrifices were central to Israel's worship of God. After the death and resurrection of Messiah, the Church was born and a new economy or dispensation began. Gentiles no longer had to become part of the commonwealth of Israel to know the God of Israel (Eph 3:3-6; Rm 11:11-24; Ac 15). The Levitical sacrificial system, which foreshadowed the coming sacrifice of Christ (Heb 10:1-18), ended. During the present Church Age, the memorial Lord's Supper is celebrated by followers of Messiah looking back to His death and resurrection and forward to His coming again (Lk 22:19; 1Co 11:23, 26; 2Tm 2:8).

At Messiah's second coming, Israel will again assume her central role in God's kingdom program. The Lord's Supper will no longer be observed because Christ will have returned. As Ezekiel prophesied, animal sacrifices will be offered in the millennial temple as memorials or object lessons of the supreme sacrifice made by the Lamb of God (Jn 1:29; Rv 5:12). Several passages refer to a sacrificial system in the millennium (Is 56:7; 66:20-23; Jr 33:18; Zch 14:16-21; Mal 3:3-4). The sacrifice of these animals will be vivid and necessary reminders of the Messiah's suffering and death, especially since death will be uncommon in the millennial kingdom (Is 11:6-10; 65:20).

Although there are some similarities between the millennial temple worship and the Levitical system, they are not identical. For example: in Ezekiel, Shavuot (Feast of Weeks/Pentecost) is not mentioned perhaps because it was fulfilled with the beginning of the Church (Ac 2). There is no ark of the covenant in Ezekiel's temple because Messiah is the final offering for sin (1Jn 1:2), and there is no high priest mentioned, for Messiah is the great high priest (Heb 4:14).

40:44-47. Not only will there be rooms to prepare the millennial sacrifices, there will also be **chambers for the singers** . . . and for the **priests who keep charge of the temple** . . . and **keep charge of the altar** (see sketch "The Millennial Temple" below). These priests will be **sons of Zadok** (cf. 43:19; 44:15; 48:11), continuing the priestly line from Solomon's day (1Kg 1:26-27). Specifying the sons of Zadok links the prophecy to the ancient priestly family line.

d. The Temple Building (40:48–41:26)

40:48–41:4 From the inner court, Ezekiel was "brought" to the "porch of the temple to" describe it in detail (see sketch "The Millennial Temple" below). The measurements of the "porch of" the "temple," although similar to Solomon's temple, were slightly larger (cf. 1Kg 6:3). A "stairway" led up to the portico and pillars and into the "nave," or great hall of the temple.

Each "doorway" is narrower than the one before it. Possibly this reflects God's restricting people's access into His holy presence. Ezekiel entered the outer sanctuary but not the "most holy place." Instead, the angel went into the

The Millennial Temple

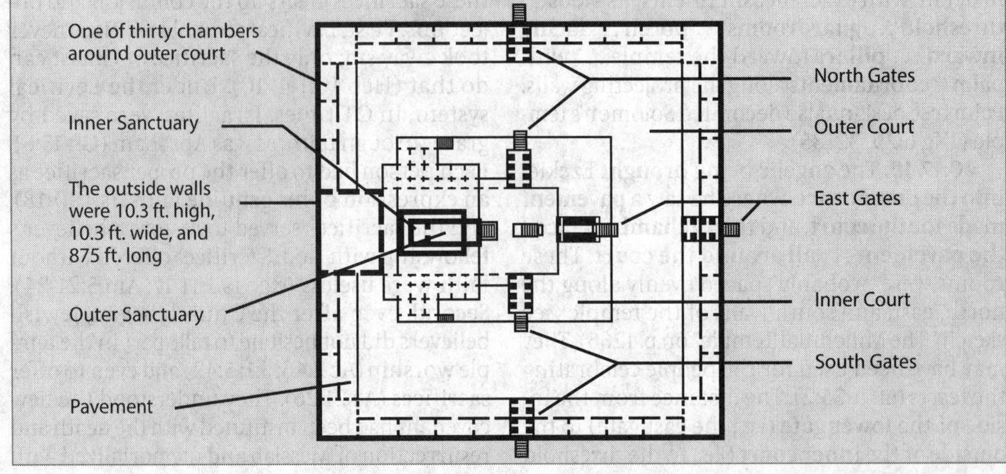

"temple" to measure it. As a priest (Ezk 1:3), Ezekiel was allowed into the outer sanctuary, but was barred from the most holy place (cf. Lv 16; Heb 9:6-7).

41:5-11. Surrounding the temple were **side chambers** built **three stories** high, **one above another** . . . **thirty** rooms **in each story**. These rooms got **wider** with **each successive story**. These 90 rooms were probably storerooms for the temple equipment and storage chambers for the people's tithes and offerings (cf. Mal 3:8-10). These rooms were similar to those in Solomon's temple (cf. 1Kg 6:5-10).

41:12-15. Ezekiel recorded the overall dimensions of the temple **building**. It was **a hundred cubits long**, and the width of the front of the temple and adjoining courtyard was 100 cubits, about 175 feet (vv. 13-14). A cubit represented the length of a forearm, from elbow to fingertips. So it varied by person and among ancient civilizations, anywhere from 17.5 to 21 inches. While 18 inches is commonly used for conversions, the context of Ezekiel uses a long cubit, "a cubit and a handbreadth," or 21 inches (40:5; see comment there).

Immediately west of the temple was a structure described as **the building that was in front of the separate area** facing the temple courtyard on the **west** side (v. 12). It measured a width of **seventy cubits** (122.5 feet) and a length of **ninety cubits** (157.5 feet). The function of this building, however, is not explained.

41:16-20. The interior of the temple building was surrounded by **latticed windows** and **paneled with wood**. It was decorated with **cherubim** and **palm trees** carved into the wood. `Each **cherub** had **two faces** . . . **a man's face** . . . **and a young lion's face** (cf. 1:10; 10:14). Perhaps **cherubim** represent the guardians of God's dwelling place (cf. 1:4-28; 10), and the **palm trees** (40:16; 41:25-26; 1Kg 6:29) represent the fruitfulness and blessing provided by God.

41:21-22. The only furniture described in the temple is the **altar** of **wood**, three cubits by two cubits (5 ¼ feet by 3 ½ feet), called **the table that is before the LORD**. There was a large altar outside the temple proper for sacrifice (cf. 43:13-17), and this smaller one just outside the most holy place. If it served the same purpose as the furnishing in Solomon's temple it would hold the bread of the Presence (Ex 25:30; Lv 24:5-9) or perhaps be the altar of incense (cf. Ex 25:23; 30:1-2). However, Ezekiel does not indicate the purpose of this **altar** . . . **of wood**.

41:23-26. The main area of the temple, the **nave and the sanctuary** . . . **each** had a **double door** that led to the outer sanctuary of the temple and to the Holy of Holies. This was something like a bifold door, made of **two swinging leaves**. As with the temple, the doors to the outer sanctuary had **cherubim** and **palm trees** . . . **carved** on them (cf. vv. 16-20).

e. Chambers in the Inner Court of the Temple (42:1-14)

42:1-12. Then the angelic being **brought** Ezekiel to the **outer court** to see several **chamber[s]** for use by the priests **opposite the separate area** (cf. v. 2). This complex of rooms **three stories** high was connected with the inner court with entrances from the outer court. There were two buildings on the **north** side with a common corridor 10 cubits wide (17 ½ feet). An identical group of rooms was on the temple's **south** side. Similar rooms are not described in Solomon's temple (1Kg 6).

42:13-14. The **north** and the **south chambers** were **holy chambers**. They were used by the **priests who are near to the LORD** as a room where they could **eat the most holy things**. According to the Mosaic law the priests received a portion of certain offerings (Lv 2:3; 6:16, 26-30; 7:7-10). This is a similar provision for the millennial priesthood. These chambers will also serve as dressing rooms and storage rooms for the **holy** . . . **garments** the priests wore. Mosaic law specified garments to be worn by the priests when ministering before the Lord (Ex 39:1-31; 40:12-16; Lv 8:1-13). This room will serve a similar purpose in the millennial temple.

f. Outer Walls of the Temple (42:15-20)

42:15-20. After the measuring of the **inner house**, the external dimensions of the temple were **measured** . . . **all around**. The complex was a square measuring 500 cubits (875 feet) on each side. The total area of this temple complex was 765,625 square feet—larger than 13 football fields. This is much larger than the area of Solomon's and Zerubbabel's temples. Around the temple on all **four sides** will be a **wall** . . . to **divide between the holy and the profane** (cf. 40:5).

g. Return of the Lord's Glory (43:1-12)

43:1-4. Earlier Ezekiel had seen the glory of the Lord departing (11:22-23). Now, he saw **the glory of the God of Israel** returning **by the way of the gate facing** . . . **east**, to dwell once again in His temple with His people. The temple had been prepared for the Lord's return, and the real significance of the millennial age rests on

His presence. **His voice was like the sound of many waters** (cf. Rv 1:15; 14:2) indicating His power and majesty.

43:5. Then **the Spirit lifted** Ezekiel **up** (cf. 3:14; 8:3; 11:1, 24; 37:1) and **brought** him into the **inner court** in front of the temple and **the glory of the LORD filled the house** (the temple). Throughout the book it is clear the glory of the Lord was active (3:23; 9:3; 10:4, 18) but here the Lord is manifest specifically in the temple where He will reside during the millennial kingdom.

43:6-8. Now Ezekiel **heard one speaking to [him] from the house** (the temple). This speaker was distinct from Ezekiel's angelic guide who was still **standing beside [him]**. The **one speaking** from the temple was the Lord Himself. He is identified by the personal pronouns: **this is the place of My throne** (cf. Is 6:1; Jr 3:17) **and the place of the soles of My feet** (cf. 1Ch 28:2; Pss 99:5; 132:7; Is 60:13), **where I will dwell among the sons of Israel forever** (Ezk 43:7, 9; Ps 132:13-14). Using these anthropomorphic images, the Lord declared this temple to be His earthly dwelling place among His people, until the establishment of the new heaven and the new earth (cf. Rv 21:22). Israel would never **again defile** His **holy name** (cf. Ezk 20:39; 39:7) by the **harlotry** of idol worship, spiritual adultery, and religious prostitution in the temple (2Kg 23:4-20).

43:9. Israel will never again defile the temple area with graves of **the corpses of their kings**. Some of the royal sepulchers of the 14 kings of Judah were separated from the temple by only a wall (2Kg 23:30). Although the glory of the Lord had departed from the temple in Ezekiel's day (cf. Ezk 10:18), God promised that in the future, **I will dwell among them forever**.

43:10-12. The angelic being (cf. 40:3) told Ezekiel to **describe the temple to the house of Israel** so Israel would be **ashamed of their iniquities**. A clear vision of God's future plan would remind them of the sins that had led to the destruction of the temple by Babylon. Then they would be motivated to return to God and rebuild the temple—faithfully according to His exact measure, plan, and **whole design**.

The **entire area on the top of the mountain ... shall be most holy**; the whole area of the temple was sacred (cf. 41:4; 45:3; 48:12). The **law of the house**, the temple, included all of the details of the design given in chaps. 40–42.

h. Altar of Burnt Offering (43:13-27)

Daily services will begin when the millennial temple is built and the glory of the Lord returns there. Just as the building had specific measurements, Ezekiel was given a specific description of the altar (vv. 13-17) and regulations for consecrating it (vv. 18-27).

43:13-17. The **altar** will be in front of the temple (40:47), and the **measurements of the altar** in long cubits (cf. 40:4) are larger (17 ½ feet) than those of the altar in the Solomonic temple, which was about 15 feet using the standard cubit (2Ch 3:3; 4:1). The altar was to be **twelve cubits** square (about 21 feet) with **four horns**, which was typical of Israel's altars (cf. Ex 29:12; Ps 118:27). It would be reached by a flight of **steps** that **face the east**. Although such steps were forbidden in the Levitical temple (Ex 20:26), they are required in the millennial altar because of the height of the altar. This altar is for animal sacrifice (cf. comments regarding millennial animal sacrifice on Ezk 40:38-43).

43:18-26. The consecration of this altar will take place in a ceremony lasting **seven days**, and must be performed by the **Levitical priest** from the family of **Zadok** (cf. 40:46; comments on 44:15-19). This consecration service will be similar in some ways to the services followed by Moses (Ex 40:10, 29) and Solomon (2Ch 7:8-9) to sanctify the tabernacle and the temple. There will be seven days of offering sacrificial animals **without blemish**—of bulls, goats, and rams as **burnt** offerings (Ex 29:18) and **sin** offerings (Lv 4) to **make atonement for the altar and purify it**, and thus **consecrate it**. The **priests shall throw salt on them** (Lv 2:13) as a sign of the covenant of God.

43:27. From **the eighth day and onward** the priests will present the people's **burnt offerings ... and ... peace offerings** on the altar. This process will mark the full resumption of God's fellowship with His people, as then God will accept them. These sacrifices will remind the Israelites of the atonement Messiah Jesus provided to give access to the Father (Heb 10:19-25).

Many questions arise related to the efficacy of these millennial sacrifices in the face of Jesus' atoning death. Critics of the view espoused in this commentary argue that a return to such sacrifices would be needless or blasphemous, and would detract from the work of Christ (see comments introducing chaps. 40–48). Of the various offerings in chaps. 40–48 (the burnt offering, 45:15, 17, 20; the grain offering, 42:14; 44:29; the peace offering, 43:27; the sin offering, 40:39; 42:13; and the reparation offering, 40:39; 44:29), only the burnt offerings were said to atone for the sins of people (see 45:15, 20). The altar could be "atoned" for as well (vv. 20, 26), but there the sense of the verb "atone" carries the common nuance of "wiping" or "cleansing," and refers to the purification of the altar so it is fit for use before God. For the relationship between animal sacrifices in the law of Moses and salvation in the OT, see comments on Heb 10:1-18.

Some of those who assert that there will be a millennial temple maintain that the sacrifices that take place there will be largely commemorative of the perfect work of Jesus, much as the celebration of the Lord's Table is today (see comments on 1Co 11:23-26; and for more on the efficacy of the millennial sacrifices, see comments on Ezk 43:13-17). The early Christians apparently had no problem with going to, worshiping in, and sacrificing at the temple for years following the death and resurrection of the Lord (see Lk 24:53; Ac 3:1; 21:26). They could hardly be accused of distracting or detracting from Jesus' work. This view is possibly the correct one, but nowhere does Ezekiel make it explicit that the atoning sacrifices in Ezk 45:15 are memorial sacrifices. Instead it appears that they have some level of atoning significance (see 45:15).

Several observations may help in getting at Ezekiel's meaning in its canonical context. The obvious differences between Ezekiel's description and the Mosaic covenant indicate that this is not simply a return to the Mosaic covenant. Some of these differences include: The priests were to wear splendid clothes, including dyed cloth of some sort and fine linen with gold threads (Ex 28), while the priests in Ezekiel's temple were to wear plain linen (Ezr 44:17-19). In the Mosaic covenant, the tabernacle (and later the temple) contained the ark of the covenant, the lampstand, the anointing oil, and the table of the bread of the Presence (see Ex 25), but all of these are missing from the future temple. According to Nm 28:11, the new moon offerings included two bulls, one ram, and seven male lambs, but the book of Ezekiel records one bull, six sheep, and one ram (Ezk 46:6-7). Plainly, Ezekiel is not recording a mere revival of the law of Moses.

Perhaps the best explanation of the sacrifices in chap. 45 is to be found in its parallels with the animal sacrifices for atonement in the law. There are several items to consider.

First, sacrifices, and any deed prescribed by the law, were repugnant to God without the proper attitude. These sacrifices did not save the individual, even if he or she were sincere, since the ceremonial aspects of the law saved no one (see Rm 3:20). But when one trusted in the God of Israel as Abraham did (Gn 15:6), that believer was counted righteous. The offerings of sacrifices were to flow from the life of one rightly related to God by faith, but were not the means of that saving relationship. God said that *He* would cleanse the believing offerer from his sin when he brought the required sacrifices. Yet, without the heart attitude of trust and repentance (see "humbling one's soul"—or better "*afflicting* one's soul"—in Lv 16:29, 31), the sacrifices meant nothing at best, and at worst were repugnant to God (see Pss 40:6-10; 51:10-18; Is 1:11-15; Mc 6:6-8). The one who offered the sacrifice did not thereby earn God's favor.

Second, the saved OT believer needed periodic cleansing from sin, just as a NT believer does, and God determined in the OT that the means for this cleansing was through the believer making animal sacrifices. Those sacrifices offered by one who believed resulted in forgiveness by God (see Lv 1:4; 4:26-31; 16:20-22; 17:11; see also, for the general idea of forgiveness without the explicit mention of sacrifices, Pss 25, 32, 51, 103, 130; Is 1:18; Ezk 18:22).

Third, Heb 10 indicates that sacrifices "can never . . . make perfect" (Heb 10:1), do not cleanse from the consciousness of sin (Heb 10:2), and can never "take away sins" (Heb 10:4, 11). Only the sacrificial death of the Messiah can do this (Heb 10:10-12). Yet Lv 1:4; 4:26-31; 16:20-22, and other passages assign an "atoning" result to sacrifices. How can this be? The answer comes by recognizing that atonement functioned on two levels—the subjective human level and the objective divine level. The OT believer who offered sacrifices or celebrated the Day of Atonement had every reason to feel forgiven subjectively. His sins were "covered," but they were not exactly "expiated." However, on the objective, Godward side of it, full forgiveness was not objectively obtained until the death of Jesus.

Fourth, for the OT believer, the outworking of faith included the offering of sacrifices in reliance upon God, who said that the believing offerer would be forgiven. John S. Feinberg writes,

> "Performing substitutionary and expiatory sacrifices seems to be more involved with cleansing the sin of a believer than with bringing a person to salvation. Job, when he

offered a sacrifice for cleansing (Job 42:7-9), was obviously saved at the time he gave the sacrifice.... A comparison of sanctification in the Old and New Testaments would show that when the NT believer sins, in order to restore fellowship with the Lord [note, restore *fellowship*, not *salvation*] he must receive cleansing from the sin. In order to continue to grow, he must confess his sin in faith, believing that on the basis of Christ's sacrifice God will cleanse him from sin (1Jn 1:9). The OT believer also confessed his sin, but in addition, he brought in faith a sacrifice, believing that God had revealed that sin would be handled in that way. Before Christ's sacrifice, the public offering had to accompany the repentance of the believer. Once the all-sufficient sacrifice of Christ had been made, the repentant believer need not give another sacrifice to have cleansing" (John S. Feinberger, "Salvation in the Old Testament," in *Tradition and Testament: Essays in Honor of Charles Lee Feinberg*, ed. John S. Feinberg and Paul D. Feinberg [Chicago: Moody, 1981], 69–70).

Rather than the act of offering a sacrifice saving an OT believer, it functioned to impress upon him his profound need for something (or Someone) else to atone for his sin.

Fifth, another prominent feature of animal sacrifices in both the OT and NT was the ritual and physical purification they brought (see Heb 9:13, they "sanctify for the cleansing of the flesh," i.e., one's body, not one's fallen nature). Specifically, being cleansed by water mixed with the ashes of the red heifer would ceremonially cleanse one's physical body if he had contacted a corpse (see Nm 19:13, 20). Otherwise the physical filth remained, one was excluded from the company of his fellow Jews and could not participate in worship, and its corrupting effect continued. But this was a ceremonial cleansing only, not a saving one (see Rm 3:20—no one is saved by the works of the law).

Finally, in attempting to apply this to Ezk 45:15, it would be difficult to assign a different meaning to the word "atonement" from what is implied in other OT uses (see Lv 1:4; 4:26-31; 16:20-22; 17:11) and in light of Heb 9:13 and 10:4, 11. Namely, for the Jewish believer alive during the millennial kingdom, salvation is by faith in the finished work of Christ. The sacrifices performed in faith at that time will provide a subjective experience of forgiveness for sins, a forgiveness ultimately purchased by the death of Christ, and will provide cleansing, whereby fellowship—not salvation—with God is restored, much as the OT sacrifices did for one who had the faith of Abraham.

2. A New Service of Worship (44:1–46:24)

Following the descriptions of the millennial temple and the altar, the Lord described the holy standards in Israel's future worship and He challenged the people in exile to reevaluate their present worship practices (chap. 44). He described the millennial allotment of land (45:1-12) and gave details about the millennial offerings (45:13–46:24).

a. The Temple Ministers (44:1-31)

44:1-2. Ezekiel was led out of the inner court to the **gate... which faces east; and it was shut**. This outer gate of the **sanctuary** opened toward the Kidron Valley and the Mount of Olives. Ezekiel had just seen the Lord enter it on His return to His temple from this direction (43:1-4). God's presence had sanctified the gate. Therefore, **This gate shall be shut; it shall not be opened, and no one shall enter by it, for the Lord God of Israel has entered by it; therefore it shall be shut** (declared twice for emphases). No one will be allowed to tread through the gate which God Himself had entered.

Some mystery and superstition have arisen from this passage. The "Golden Gate" of the present walls of Jerusalem has been identified as this gate. However, this sealed eastern gate is not Ezekiel's gate because it is a much later gate. The current wall was built in the seventh century AD on ancient foundations and then repaired by the sultan, Suleiman (AD 1520–1566). Based on this Ezekiel text, there is a Jewish tradition that Messiah will enter Jerusalem via the eastern gate, so Suleiman sealed this gate and built a Muslim cemetery in front of it to keep Messiah out of Jerusalem. Furthermore, the dimensions of the present "Golden Gate" do not correspond with Ezekiel's gate. This gate in Jerusalem's ancient walls is a beautiful gate, and a good reminder that Messiah will return. It is just not the gate spoken of by Ezekiel.

44:3. Only **the prince... shall sit in** the gate and be allowed to **enter by way of the porch of the gate and... go out... the same way**. Although the gate will be shut, the area of the gate will be used by the **prince** (Hb. word *nasi* would be best translated "leader" cf. 34:23-24). This leader will **sit** in the gate, a place of rendering judgments or settling affairs (cf. Jos 20:4; Ru 4:1). Some suggest this **prince** is the Messiah. However, evidence is to the contrary. This prince/leader is not the Messiah because this leader made a sin offering for himself (cf. Ezk 45:22), an act that would be unnecessary for the sinless Messiah (cf. Heb 4:15). Further, this prince/leader has natural children (Ezk 46:16), another impossibility for the God-Man, Messiah Jesus. He will have a special portion of the land allotted to him (cf. 45:7-8; 46:18; 48:21-22), whereas all the land belongs to King Messiah. Although some have suggested this prince is a resurrected David, there is little in the text to corroborate this idea. More likely, this prince will be Messiah's representative in a unique sense, and will have the privilege to **eat bread before the LORD**, possibly referring to the fellowship offerings that the worshipers will eat after offering them to the Lord (cf. Lv 7:15-21).

44:4-5. Ezekiel was brought back . . . **by way of the north gate**, the gate most often used by Ezekiel in this vision and the one designated for use by the priests who have charge of the temple (40:44-45), to the **front of the house**, the temple.

Here Ezekiel saw **the glory of the LORD** as it **filled the house of the LORD** (cf. comments on 1:28) and his response was the response of everyone who sees the Lord: he **fell on** his **face** in worship and awe. The **LORD said** to Ezekiel to pay careful attention, **mark well** (lit., "set your heart on" used twice) His instruction **concerning all** (used three times) **the statutes** . . . **laws** . . . **entrance** . . . and **exits of the sanctuary**.

44:6. In the past Israel failed to take the worship and service of the Lord seriously. The Lord gave specific instructions to correct **rebellious ones** of **the house of Israel** (cf. 2:5-6, 8; 3:9, 26-27; 12:3, 9, 25; 17:12; 24:3). The **Lord GOD** (cf. comments on the significance 2:3-4) declared, **Enough of all your abominations**, thus highlighting the sins involving His temple, and demanded holiness from His people and respect for His sanctuary.

44:7-9. One of Israel's sins regarding the temple was allowing pagans, **foreigners, uncircumcised in heart and uncircumcised in flesh** into **My sanctuary**. This does not mean non-Jews were excluded from sincerely worshiping the God of Israel with the people of Israel (Nm 9:14; 15:14-16; Is 56:7). Israel's **abominations** included bringing pagans who did not worship the God of Israel into the temple and even giving them **charge of** the **sanctuary**. When the Jewish people returned from Babylonian captivity the leadership was vigilant not to allow pagans to participate in temple worship (cf. Ezr 4:1-3; Neh 13:1-9; Ac 21:27-32).

44:10. The **Levites** were the descendants of Levi, one of Jacob's 12 sons (Gn 29:34). Moses and Aaron were Levites, (cf. Ex 2:1–4:14). After the exodus, the Levites were responsible for caring for, and service in, the sanctuary (Nm 3:1-28; 1Ch 23:24-32). Aaron and his sons were given the duty of priests (Ex 28:1). All priests were Levites, but not all Levites were priests. During the monarchy, especially in the decades prior to the fall of Jerusalem, **the Levites** . . . **went far from** the Lord, **went astray** with Israel worshiping **idols** (e.g., 1Kg 18; Jr 2:8; 5:3; Ezk 22:26), and led the nation away from God. They deserved **punishment for their iniquity**.

44:11-14. The Levites should have been spiritual leaders for the **house** of Israel, but instead they **became a stumbling block of iniquity**. So in the future not all of them will **serve as a priest** . . . **nor come near to any of** God's **holy things**. **Yet**, in the kingdom they will be allowed to serve as gatekeepers, **to keep charge of the house**, the temple buildings, and do **all its service**, such as slayers of the sacrifices, and assisting worshipers.

44:15-16. The **Levitical priests, the sons of Zadok**, remained faithful to the Lord, when many of the Levites **went astray**. **Zadok** was appointed chief priest during Solomon's reign (cf. 1Kg 1:32-35; 2:26-27, 35) and His **sons** became one branch of the Levitical priesthood. So in the kingdom, they are to **offer** sacrifices, and they alone **shall enter My sanctuary**, and **minister** there.

44:17-19. Several regulations and functions of the Zadokite priests were similar to the Mosaic laws governing the priests. The priestly garments were to be made of **linen**, the primary clothing of the priests (cf. Ex 28:39-41), rather than the more common fabric made of wool. Linen is lighter than wool, and the priests were not allowed to wear **anything which makes them sweat**. Before the priests could **go out** . . . **into the outer court to the people**, they needed to change from the **garments** they wore while **ministering**. The Levitical concept of transmitting **holiness** was that contact with holy objects temporarily set that person apart to be subject to its restriction and disqualified from the ordinary tasks of life (cf. Ex 29:37; 30:29; Lv 6:11, 27). However Haggai demonstrated that such holy objects only consecrate that which they have touched and nothing else (Hg 2:12). Thus holiness could be transferred to the third party (although defilement could be spread). The Zadokites' clothing change demonstrated to the people the distinction between the holy and the ordinary (common or profane) and would keep the common people from the responsibilities of the priesthood.

44:20-23. Every aspect of life was specified for these priests. They must not **shave their heads** or **let their locks grow long**. Completely shaving one's head or letting one's hair go unkempt were signs of mourning (cf. Lv 10:6; 21:5, 10). They were not allowed to **drink wine when they enter[ed] the inner court**, that is, when ministering, lest they become drunk and not perform their duties properly (cf. Lv 10:8-9). Also restrictions were placed on whom they could marry (cf. Lv 21:7, 13-15). These restrictions and actions were designed to **teach My people the difference between the holy and the profane ... to discern between the unclean and the clean**.

44:24. The priests were to settle **a dispute** and to **judge it according to** God's **ordinances** (cf. 2Ch 19:8-11). They were to be examples in keeping God's **laws ... statutes ...** and all of His **appointed feasts and sanctify My sabbaths**. In the Kingdom everyone who follows the Lord will keep these appointed feasts (Lv 23:2, 4, 44).

44:25-27. The priests were to avoid ritual defilement by not going near a **dead person** (cf. Lv 21:1-4), unless a close relative, but then the priest would have to wait **seven days** and then offer a **sin offering** for himself before reentering the temple service. Although death will be uncommon during the millennium (cf. Is 65:20), provision was made for those instances when it will occur.

44:28. The Lord Himself is the **inheritance** of the priests (cf. Nm 18:20; Dt 10:9), so they would not be given land in Israel except the allotment surrounding the temple (cf. Ezk 45:4). They would have no other **possession in Israel**—because the Lord is **their possession** (Jos 13:14, 33; 18:7).

44:29-31. God will take care of those who minister before Him (cf. Dt 18:1-5). Their food will come from the **grain** and meat from the **sin** and **guilt** offerings, along with the **first fruits** and **dough** offered by the people in temple sacrifice. This would be a provision for the priests who received it as their allotment, and a **blessing** for the people. The reasons they will be blessed are manifold: in giving, they are being obedient to the Lord, they are being sacrificial, and they are providing for those who minister to relieve the ministers of concern for earning their own food. This blessing of provision is available today as believers support those who serve the Lord vocationally.

b. Land Allotment for the Temple and Priests (45:1-8)

45:1-4. The Lord gave specific instruction about the division of the land in Israel. There is to be a land **allotment to the Lord, a holy portion of the land**. This sacred district is **25,000 cubits** (about 8.3 miles) long and **20,000** cubits (about 6.6miles) wide (cf. 40:5 concerning cubits). Within this area will be the **sanctuary** (temple) complex described in chaps. 40–43.

This rectangle of land will be divided into two equal portions, each about 8.3 miles long and about 3.3 miles wide. The first portion will be allotted to the **priests ...** for their **houses** and **a holy place for the sanctuary**.

45:5-6. Another portion will be allotted to the **Levites** who serve in the temple as **their possession cities to dwell in**. Instead of being scattered throughout Israel, as they were in the biblical period of Joshua (Jos 21:1-42), the priests and Levites will reside near their place of ministry.

Jerusalem, **the city**, will be **5,000 cubits wide** (about 1.7 miles) and **25,000 cubits long** (about 8.5 miles), adjoining the **holy portion**. This area will include the urban area, grazing land, and farmland (cf. Ezk 48:15-18).

The entire square of land, about 8.5 miles on each side, will be located at the present site of Jerusalem. A band of land will extend from Jerusalem to the east and west. The holy city will be for the **whole house of Israel**, all the Jewish people, whether they live there or not. Although all Israel will not necessarily live there, Jerusalem will be their undisputed capital and their central area of worship.

45:7-8. The prince (cf. comments on 44:1-3) will have the land **adjacent to the holy allotment and the property of the city**. This strip of land will extend on the **east** to the Jordan River and on the **west** to the Mediterranean Sea, an area easily visualized in modern Israel. Thus, the prince will have easy access to the future sanctuary.

c. Warning to Jewish Leaders Living in Babylon (45:9-12)

45:9-12. This section shifts back to the Lord's admonition to the captives living in Babylon.

These **princes** (leaders, cf. 44:3) **of Israel**, living in Babylonian exile, were admonished to repent: **Enough . . . put away violence and destruction** (cf. 44:6). They must not disregard the rights of those they were to protect (cf. 19:1-9; 22:25; 34:1-10). They must **practice justice and righteousness**, as exemplified by interpersonal relationships and just commerce. The passage is a detailed description of accurate weights and measures: correct **balances** for weight, an accurate **ephah** (bushel) for dry goods, and **bath** (six gallons) for liquid measurements. From the **standard** of the large **homer** (fifty gallons or six bushels) down to the tiny **gerahs** (Israel's smallest unit of weight, just sixteen barley grains), God always demands honesty at every level (Lv 19:35-37; Dt 25:13-16; Pr 11:1; 16:11; 20:10; Mc 6:10-12).

d. Offerings in the Temple (45:13–46:24)

After the admonishment of the Jewish leaders in Babylon to be honest in weights and measures, the focus returns to the millennial temple, where the future prince will use just weights to receive and offer gifts to God (45:13-17). This mention of offerings includes a brief description of the future sacrificial system (45:18–46:24), then a return to the subject of the division of the land.

45:13-17. The prescribed portion to be given for an **offering** is to be proportionate to each individual's financial circumstance, as it was in the law (cf. Lv 5). They are each to give a **sixth of an ephah from a homer of wheat** . . . and **barley**, and a **portion of** (olive) **oil** (cf. vv. 9-12). They are also to offer **one sheep from each flock of two hundred**. The grains and animals were to be used **for a grain offering, for a burnt offering and for peace offerings, to make atonement for them**. This tithe or tax will be required of all the people for use by the **prince in Israel** (see comments on 44:1-3). As the people's representative, he will collect their gifts and use them to maintain the temple sacrifices, including **burnt offerings, the grain offerings and the drink offerings, at the feasts, on the new moons and on the sabbaths, at all the appointed feasts of the house of Israel** (cf. comments on 40:38-43).

45:18-25. There are several calendars of Israel's annual festivals (Ex 23:14-17; 34:18-24; Lv 23:1-44; Nm 28:11-31; 29:1-39; Dt 16:1-17), however, Ezekiel's list of festivals does not exactly parallel any of them. The millennial festivals will include sacrifices to **cleanse the sanctuary** on the **first** day of **the first of the month** (vv. 18-20), as well as sacrifices for the **Passover**, **feast of . . . unleavened bread** (vv. 21-24), and the **seven days of the feast** of Booths on the **seventh month, on the fifteenth day** (v. 25). If someone sins unintentionally, **goes astray or is naive**, a second purification will be offered on the seventh day of the month (v. 20). This offering and ceremonial cleansing possibly will replace the Day of Atonement on the seventh month (Lv 23:26-32). The **prince** will **provide for himself and all the people . . . a bull for a sin offering**, indicating he is an important person, but he is not the sinless Messiah (Ezk 45:22-24).

Ezekiel's omission of Israel's other national feasts, the Feast of Pentecost, the Feast of Trumpets, and the Day of Atonement, is a puzzle. There are two possible explanations for the differences.

First, perhaps the omissions signaled a change in God's program for Israel. The inauguration of the new covenant and the fulfillment of Israel's kingdom promises may render those three feasts (Pentecost, Trumpets and Day of Atonement) unnecessary. Thus only three of the six annual feasts under the Levitical system (cf. Lv 23:4-44) will be followed, two feasts celebrating national redemption (Passover and Unleavened Bread combined as one feast, as was the custom by the NT period), which will point back to Messiah's death, and the Feast of Booths (Tabernacles), which will symbolize the Lord dwelling with His people (see comments at Zch 14:16-19).

Second, and perhaps more likely, Ezekiel's list is a *merism*, a literary structure that mentions the first and the last in a sequence to include everything in between. By naming the first of Israel's appointed feasts (Passover and Unleavened Bread) and the last one (Booths), Ezekiel could be implying that all Israel's feasts would be reinstituted.

46:1-11. The **Lord** gave specific directions about the daily worship as well. The **gate of the inner court facing east** will be closed the **six working days** of the week, but **opened on the sabbath day** and on the **day of the new moon**. The **prince** will be allowed to **stand by the post of the gate** during these days when the sacrifice he brought on behalf of the people will be offered (cf. 44:3). He will also provide the sacrifices for the people on the **sabbaths** and **new moons** as well as on the major feast days.

The worshipers at the temple are given instructions about how to assemble before the Lord at the **appointed feasts**. There is no entrance to the temple on the west, and the east gate will be permanently shut (cf. 44:1-2). To avoid turmoil, the worshipers will follow predesignated routes in the temple so that whoever enters by the **north** gate to worship is to go out the **south** gate, and whoever enters by the **south** gate is to go out the **north** gate. God is a God of order, and He wants orderliness to prevail in worship.

46:12-15. When **the prince** (see comments on 44:1-3) makes a **freewill offering to the LORD** . . . the **gate facing east** is to be **opened for him**. The regulation concerning the closing of the east gate to the inner court (cf. 44:1-2) will be suspended for this special offering. But after the prince leaves, the **gate shall be shut after he goes out**. The **morning** sacrifice is mentioned, but the evening sacrifice (cf. Ex 29:38-41; Nm 28:3-4) is not mentioned. Ezekiel was giving only the highlights of the sacrificial system and assumed that his readers would apply the same regulations to the evening sacrifice, although no explanation of the omission is given.

46:16. The **prince** can give a **gift out of his inheritance to any of his sons**, and it will be **their possession by inheritance**. This is another confirmation that the **prince** is not the Messiah since he is a human being who fathers children, and not the divine Messiah Jesus (cf. comments on 44:1-3).

46:17. The **year of liberty** is probably a reference to the year of Jubilee on the Levitical calendar. Every 50 years property in Israel that had been sold or given outside the family was to revert to its original owners (see comments on Lv 25:8-15). A gift made to a servant will not be permanent to future generations of his family, but **it shall be his until the year of liberty; then it shall return to the prince. His inheritance shall be only his sons**. The land belongs to God and He will apportion it to Israel, by tribal units, as His stewards. This regulation assures that no one individual will gain permanent control of the land, nor will it be lost to its rightful owners.

46:18. The prince will **not take** any land outside his allotted inheritance from the people's inheritance. In contrast with evil princes in Ezekiel's day (45:8-9), the godly prince will not oppress the people or take their property, **so that My people will not be scattered, anyone from his possession**.

46:19-24. Next the angelic guide brought Ezekiel into **holy chambers** where the **priests shall boil the guilt offering and the sin offering and . . . bake the grain offering**. The food is to prepared within the temple area and not taken **out . . . to transmit holiness to the people** (cf. comments on Hg 2:12). This is the kitchen of the temple complex, the area that **faced north . . . at the extreme rear toward the west**, where the priests will prepare food from the sacrifices. When the people offer fellowship offerings to the Lord, they will be allowed to eat part of the sacrifice in a fellowship meal (cf. Lv 7:15-18). Evidently at these **four corners of the court** the priests will cook the food used in the sacrifices. Thus, activities in the temple will include fellowship meals as well as sacrificial worship.

3. A New Land (47:1–48:35)

a. The River from the Temple (47:1-12)

During the millennium there will be a change in the topography of Israel when the millennial temple will be the source of life-giving "water." There is nothing in the passage to suggest anything other than a literal river, even though many think this refers only symbolically to the blessings that flow from God's presence. The inclusion of details such as the "fishermen" (v. 10) and the salty "swamps" and "marshes" (v. 11) indicate realism, not allegory. These details become meaningless if the passage is only symbolic of spiritual blessing. In the millennium this river will be another visible reminder of God's presence and blessing, as the prophets foretold (cf. vv. 1-2; Jl 3:18; Zch 14:8).

47:1-2. Ezekiel was **brought . . . back** to the entrance of the **door of the house** (temple). There he saw **water flowing from under the threshold** of the **house toward the east**. This stream, flowing out from God's presence, went eastward and passed **south of the altar**. Ezekiel left the temple complex through the **north gate** and saw the water . . . **trickling** out of the temple on the **south side** into the Kidron Valley. According to Zechariah, the water flowing from Jerusalem will divide into two branches, with half flowing east toward the Dead Sea and half flowing west toward the Mediterranean (Zch 14:8). Ezekiel followed only the branch that went toward the east.

47:3-6. The angelic **man went out toward the east** and **measured** the **water**. He **led** Ezekiel **through the water** and measured it becoming deeper and deeper. After **a thousand cubits** (1,750 feet or ⅓ mile) the water . . . was **ankle** deep; in another **thousand cubits** the river was **knee** deep. The angel measured another **thousand cubits** (now a mile from the temple), and the water reached Ezekiel's **loins**. A fourth measurement of **a thousand cubits** farther to the east revealed that the water had risen and was deep enough to **swim** in and so deep that it was too wide to cross, it **could not be forded**. The trickle that flowed from the temple had now become a powerful river.

47:7-8. On the **bank** of this river were **very many trees** on both sides. This river will begin at the temple and flow toward the **eastern region**, continuing into the **Arabah . . . toward the** (Dead) **sea**. The Arabah is the Jordan Valley running south from the Sea of Galilee to the Dead Sea and ultimately to the Gulf of Aqaba at the far northern end of the Red Sea. The Dead Sea is the lowest and saltiest body of water on earth, six times saltier than the oceans, and consequently cannot sustain life, but this will be changed in the millennium. As this river enters the Dead Sea, the salt **waters** will **become fresh**, truly a miracle of God. This now-lifeless body of water will then support life.

47:9-10. Plants and fish will thrive, **so everything will live where the river goes**. Now the salt and mineral content of the Dead Sea is so intense no fish can survive there, but in the future **fishermen will stand** on its shores from **En Gedi** to **Eneglaim**, oases areas near the Dead Sea (Jos 15:62; 1Sm 23:29; Sg 1:14), **spreading** their fishing **nets**. They will catch many **kinds** of fish, **like the fish of the Great Sea** (the Mediterranean).

47:11-12. Although the Dead Sea will become fresh, the swamps and marshes around it **will not become fresh; they will be left for salt** to supply this essential mineral for the needs of the people and the animals in Israel.

There will be **all kinds of trees** on the riverbanks of this freshwater sea. Their **leaves will not wither and their fruit will not fail**. They will bear fruit year-round. They will be watered **from the sanctuary**, so the trees will provide **fruit** for **food**, and their **leaves** will be medicinal, providing **healing**. It is likely they will have divinely supernatural medicinal qualities so that people will live long in the millennium (cf. Is 65:20).

b. Boundaries of the Land (47:13-23)

47:13-14. The land of Israel was given by God to Abraham and his descendants (Gn 13:14-17; 15:17-21). During the millennial kingdom the land will be divided **among the twelve tribes of Israel** (cf. Nm 34; Jos 13). The Levites will not have a portion in the land, but instead be given territory in the sacred district (cf. Ezk 45:4), and **Joseph shall have two portions**, one for Ephraim and Manasseh (Gn 48:17-20; Ezk 48:4-5). It was given to the Jewish people as an unconditional covenant promise that will never be rescinded. Israel's experience of blessing in the land was conditioned on her obedience to the law of Moses (Dt 28), and disobedience to the Lord had serious consequences. When Israel recognizes the Messiah and begins to experience the fullness of the blessings of the new covenant during the Messianic kingdom, she will be restored to her place of blessing in the land (cf. Ezk 36–37). **For I swore to give it to your forefathers** (cf. Gn 12:1; 15:9-21; 26:2-4; 28:13-15), **and this land shall fall to you as an inheritance**.

47:15-17. The **boundary of the land on the north** will run east from the **Great Sea**, the Mediterranean, starting somewhere north of Tyre and Sidon by the **Hethlon** road past Lebo-**Hamath** to **Hazar-enan** at the border of **Damascus**. So the northern border will stretch east from the Mediterranean Sea north to include what was then the northern border of Syria.

47:18. The **east side** of Israel will extend between **Hauran** and **Damascus**. The edge of Israel's territory will arch back from Hazar-enan along the southern border of Syria till it reaches the Jordan River south of the Sea of Galilee. From there it will go along the Jordan between **Gilead and the land of Israel**. The eastern border here **shall be the Jordan** river to the **eastern sea**, the Dead Sea. (See the map of "The Tribes of Israel in the Millennial Kingdom" on p. 1276).

47:19. The **south side** will extend from **Tamar** to the waters of **Meribath-kadesh** to the **brook of Egypt** (Wadi el-Arish, the wadi of Egypt, Nm 34:5) toward the **Great Sea** (Mediterranean Sea). Kadesh-barnea is the more familiar name of **Meribath-kadesh**, a district about 50 miles south of Beersheba. It is the area from which the 12 spies departed to investigate the promised land after the exodus. It was the border marker into the land of Israel at that point (Nm 13:25-26; 27:14; 34:4). The **brook of Egypt** is not the Nile river, because the Jewish people did not enter the promised land when they crossed the Nile at the exodus, but the spies crossed this brook when they went from Kadesh-barnea to spy out the land. The **brook *of* Egypt** ("of Egypt" is not in the Hb. but has been erroneously supplied by translators) is the Wadi el-Arish, a deeply cut streambed on the northeast side of the Sinai Peninsula that flows toward the northwest into the Mediterranean. It is about 50 miles south of Gaza and marked the southernmost extremity of Solomon's kingdom (1Kg 8:65).

The Tribes of Israel in the Millennial Kingdom

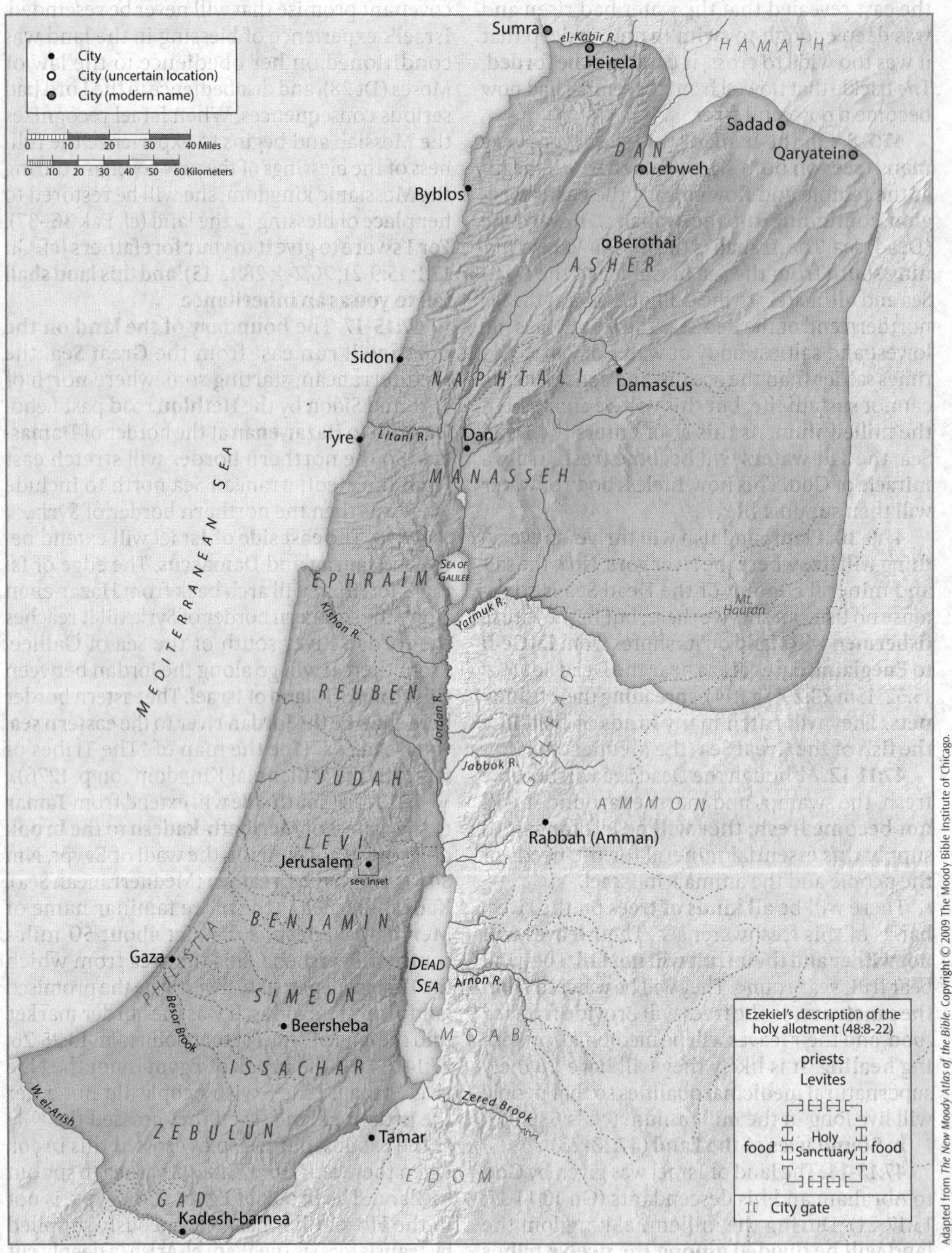

47:20. The **west side** boundary will be **the Great Sea** from the **south border** to **Lebo-hamath**. The western border of Israel is the Mediterranean, from the shoreline of the Wadi el-Arish in the south to the point opposite **Lebo-hamath** in the north, an ancient city in Syria, beyond Damascus (cf. vv. 15-17).

47:21-23. The land will be divided among **the tribes of Israel** . . . **by lot for an inheritance**. There is also a stipulation for allotting land to resident **aliens** who want to associate with Israel. When these resident aliens have lived in the land, stayed in **your midst**, and had **sons** as part of the community, **they shall be to you as the native-born among the sons of Israel** and be given an inheritance within the tribe where they lived.

Though foreigners had always been allowed to live in Israel (cf. Lv 24:22; Nm 15:29), in the millennium they will be given other privileges previously limited to Israelites (cf. Is 56:3-8). Though the millennial age will be a time of blessing for Jewish followers of Messiah, Gentile followers of Messiah will also enjoy God's blessing (cf. Is 9:2; Lk 2:32; Mt 25:31-46).

c. Division of the Land (48:1-29)

The division of the land is not exactly the same as in Joshua's time (Jos 13–22). In the millennium the allotments will extend across the land in parallel tracts from east to west, and there will be no tribal allotment east of the Jordan. About a fifth of the whole land, in the center, is an allotment as a sacred area designated to Jerusalem, the sanctuary, and the prince. This allotment to the Lord will cause each tribe to have only about two-thirds of the territory given them under Joshua.

48:1-7. The division of the land into portions is described **from the northern extremity** to south, with the tribal allotment described **from east to west**: **Dan** . . . **Asher** . . . **Naphtali** . . . **Manasseh** . . . **Ephraim** . . . **Reuben** . . . **Judah**.

48:8-10. Next to the **border of Judah**, in the central part of the land, will be the **allotment** for the **Lord**. This **holy allotment** will have **the sanctuary** . . . in the **middle** and the land will be **for the priests**. The size (cf. comments on 45:1-8) is **25,000 cubits in length** by **10,000** cubits **in width**. Since the sacred district area is given as 20,000 cubits wide in chap. 45, this may refer to a subdivision of the allotment for the sanctuary, or perhaps it is a scribal error; the LXX reads "20,000."

48:11-14. The **priests**, the **sons of Zadok** (cf. 44:15), and the **Levites** will have property in this **holy** district and must **not sell or exchange any of it**, . . . **for it is holy to the Lord**.

48:15-20. Surrounding Jerusalem will be open land for **common** use, an area of **4,500 cubits** (7,875 feet, about 1 ½ miles) on each side. There will be **open spaces** of land **250 cubits** (437 ½ feet) wide, and an area **10,000 cubits** (3.3 miles) long that will serve as pasture and farmland to produce **food** for the **city**. These areas must be **set apart** alongside the **holy allotment**.

48:21-22. Some of the central area around the **holy allotment** of the land is **for the prince** (see comments on 44:1-3). The **holy allotment and the sanctuary** will be in the **middle** of the land (cf. vv. 8-10). There will be **property of the Levites**, and of Jerusalem (**the city**) but **everything between** . . . **Judah** and **Benjamin** will be for **the prince**.

48:23-29. The remainder of the land will be divided among the **rest of the tribes** continuing from north to south: **Benjamin** . . . **Simeon** . . . **Issachar** . . . **Zebulun** . . . **Gad**.

d. Gates of the City (48:30-35)

48:30-31. After describing the city, the holy allotment and the land division, the book closes with a description of the gates, the **exits of the city**. Millennial Jerusalem will be enclosed with a wall and have 12 **gates**, three on each side, each one **named for** one of the 12 **tribes of Israel**, from the 12 sons of Jacob (cf. Gn 48). These names will also appear on the gates in the new Jerusalem (cf. Rv 21:10-12). The description confirms the significant role Jewish tribal identity will have in the kingdom. Each side of Jerusalem is **4,500 cubits** long (7,875 feet, about 1½ miles; Ezk 48:30, 32, 34) with **three gates** on each side. The **three gates toward the north** are **Reuben**, **Judah**, and **Levi** (cf. Gn 29:31-35).

48:32. The three gates on the **east side** are **Joseph** (cf. Gn 48:1), **Benjamin** (cf. Gn 30:22-24; 35:16-18), and **Dan** (cf. Gn 30:4-6). In the division of the land under Joshua, Joseph was given tribal identity through his sons Manasseh and Ephraim (Jos 16:1–17:18). Because Levi has a gate, the tribes of Manasseh and Ephraim are represented by their father, Joseph.

48:33. The gates on the **south side** are **Simeon**, **Issachar**, and **Zebulun** (cf. Gn 29:33; 30:17-20).

48:34. The gates on the **west side** are **Gad**, **Asher** (cf. Gn 30:9-13), and **Naphtali** (cf. Gn 30:7-8).

48:35. After describing the millennial Jerusalem and the new order of worship (chaps. 40–48), Ezekiel concluded with the most important aspect of the millennial city of Jerusalem, the glorious presence of the Lord. The glory of God had departed from Jerusalem as a prelude to its judgment (cf. chaps. 10–11). In the future, all Israel will recognize Jesus as their King Messiah (Zch 12:10; Rm 11:25-27) and will enjoy the Lord's holy presence in the Messianic Age, worshiping Him forever. Jerusalem ("City of Peace," Gn 3:18) has many identifying names in the Scriptures (e.g., Pss 48:2; 87:2; Is 1:26; 60:14; 62:4; Jr 2:17; 33:16; Zch 8:3), but in the kingdom, it will have a new name. The Lord will return to dwell in Jerusalem with His people, and **The name of the city from that day shall be, The Lord is there**. The name *"Yahweh-Shammah"* is a Hebrew wordplay on *Yerushalayim* (Jerusalem). The names sound similar, but *"Yahweh-Shammah"* represents the true character of Jerusalem's restored relationship of the Lord with His people.

The book of Ezekiel opened with a dazzling vision of divine glory (chaps. 1–3). In light of the holiness of the Lord, Ezekiel prophesied the necessity of judgment against Judah and Jerusalem for their disobedience (chaps. 4–24). Then he announced the judgment on the Gentile nations for their moral corruption and international intrigues against God's chosen people (chaps. 25–32). God's faithfulness to His unconditional covenant with Abraham and the promise of the new covenant are brought into clear focus in Ezekiel's message of the blessings and restoration of Israel (chaps. 33–39). Finally Ezekiel presented the glory and majesty of the Lord God's sovereign rule and His absolute holiness in the details of the millennial kingdom, the temple, and new Jerusalem (chaps. 40–48).

The eschatological emphasis of the prophet anticipates God's future work in world events and His faithfulness to His people Israel. Moreover, it challenges every person who loves the Lord to greater personal holiness and obedience to the King Messiah, who will one day rule from His throne in Jerusalem. The city will then be known as *Adonai Shammah*, "The Lord Is There!"

BIBLIOGRAPHY

Alexander, Ralph. *Ezekiel.* Everyman's Bible Commentary. Chicago: Moody, 1976.

_______. "Ezekiel." In *The Expositor's Bible Commentary*, vol. 7, edited by Tremper Longman III and David Garland, 641–924. Grand Rapids, MI: Zondervan, 2010.

Block, Daniel. *The Book of Ezekiel, Chapters 1-24.* The New International Commentary on the Old Testament. Edited by Robert L. Hubbard, Jr. Grand Rapids, MI: Eerdmans, 1997.

_______. *The Book of Ezekiel, Chapters 25-48.* The New International Commentary on the Old Testament. Edited by Robert L. Hubbard, Jr. Grand Rapids, MI: Eerdmans, 1997.

Carpenter, Eugene and David L. Thompson. *Ezekiel, Daniel.* Cornerstone Biblical Commentary. Edited by Philip W. Comfort. Carol Stream, IL: Tyndale, 2010.

Cooke, G. A. *A Critical and Exegetical Commentary on the Book of Ezekiel.* The International Critical Commentary. Edinburgh: T. & T. Clark, 1936.

Cooper, LaMar Eugene. *Ezekiel.* The New American Commentary. Edited by E. Ray Clendenen. Nashville: Broadman & Holman, 1994.

Eichrodt, Walther. *Ezekiel.* The Old Testament Library. Philadelphia: Westminster, 1970.

Eisemann, Moshe. *Yechezkel/Ezekiel.* The Artscroll Tanach Series. Brooklyn, NY: Mesorah Publications, 1988.

Feinberg, Charles Lee. *The Prophecy of Ezekiel: The Glory of the Lord.* Chicago: Moody, 1969.

Fisch, S. *Ezekiel.* London: Soncino Press, 1950.

Freeman, Hobart E. *An Introduction to the Old Testament Prophets.* Chicago: Moody, 1968.

Rooker, Mark F. *Ezekiel.* Holman Old Testament Commentary, vol. 17. Edited by Max Anders. Nashville: Broadman & Holman, 2006.

Schmitt, John W. and J. Carl Laney *Messiah's Coming Temple: Ezekiel's Prophetic Vision of the Future Temple.* Grand Rapids, MI: Kregel, 1997.

Taylor, John B. *Ezekiel: An Introduction & Commentary.* Tyndale Old Testament Commentaries. Edited by D. J. Wiseman. Grand Rapids, MI: Eerdmans, 1969.

Tuell, Steven. *Ezekiel.* New International Bible Commentary. Edited by Robert L. Hubbard, Jr. and Robert K. Johnston. Peabody, MA: Hendrickson, 2009.

Wevers, John W. *Ezekiel.* The Century Bible Commentary. Grand Rapids, MI: Eerdmans, 1969.

DANIEL

MICHAEL RYDELNIK

INTRODUCTION

The book of Daniel is set during the Babylonian captivity. The book opens after King Nebuchadnezzar's first siege of Judah (605 BC) when he brought Daniel and his friends to Babylon along with other captives of the Judean nobility. Nebuchadnezzar assaulted Judah again in 597 BC and brought 10,000 captives back to Babylon. In 586 BC he once again besieged Jerusalem, but this time destroyed the city and the holy temple and exiled the people of Judah to Babylon. Daniel's ministry began with the arrival of the first Jewish captives in Babylon (605 BC), extended throughout the Babylonian captivity (539 BC; see Dn 1:21), and concluded sometime after the third year of the Medo-Persian king Cyrus the Great (537/536 BC; see Dn 10:1).

Author. The critical view of the book of Daniel is that it was written by a second-century BC Jewish author who chose to use the name of the prophet Daniel as a pseudonym. This naturalistic perspective denies the possibility of authentic foretelling. Since the book contains many precise predictions of events in the second century BC, critics think that it must have been penned after that time by someone other than Daniel to appear to be predictive.

The traditional view maintains that Daniel the prophet did indeed write this book. Internal testimony supports this claim. In the text itself, several times Daniel claimed to have written visions (8:2; 9:2, 20; 12:5). Passages containing third-person references to Daniel do not dismiss the fact of his authorship, since other biblical authors at times speak of themselves in the third person (for example, Moses in the Pentateuch). Moreover, God speaks of Himself in the third person (Ex 20:2, 7). Other ancient authors, such as Julius Caesar in *The Gallic Wars* and Xenophon in *Anabasis,* refer to themselves in the third person. The prophet Ezekiel refers to the prophet Daniel (Ezk 14:14, 20; 28:3) as well. Jesus Christ also attributes authorship of the book to Daniel (Mt 24:15).

Date. The critical view maintains a date of 165 BC in the Maccabean period, primarily because of the precise prophecies related to that time period. It views the historical sections as mere fiction, written much later than when the events allegedly transpired. R. K. Harrison points out that this critical approach became the standard understanding of the book so that "no scholar of general liberal background who wished to preserve his academic reputation either dared or desired to challenge the current critical trend" (R. K. Harrison, *Introduction to the Old Testament*, [Grand Rapids, MI: Eerdmans, 1969], 1111).

The traditional view asserts that the book was written just after the end of the Babylonian captivity in the late sixth century BC. It holds that the book contains a factual recounting of events from the life of Daniel as well as supernatural predictions of events that took place during the intertestamental period and other prophecies that have yet to be fulfilled.

The traditional understanding is supported by *manuscript evidence*. Fragments from the book of Daniel were found among the Dead Sea Scrolls—this would be unexpected if the work had just been written. *Linguistic evidence* also supports the early date. For example, the use of Aramaic in Daniel appears to fit a fifth- to sixth-century BC date because it is parallel to the Aramaic of Ezra, the Elephantine Papyri, and other secular works of that same period. The use of Persian loanwords would not discredit the traditional view since Daniel's final composition would have taken place in the Persian period. It is not surprising to find Greek words in Daniel since the Greek language had already begun to spread even prior to the conquests of Alexander the Great. *Historical evidence* also supports the early date. For example, Daniel accurately described Belshazzar as coregent with another king (Nabonidus) (cf. Dn 5:7, 16, 29), a fact that was lost until modern times. It appears that the late date view is driven by a categorical rejection of supernatural prophecy and not by objective evidence.

Some have argued that because the Jewish canon of the Hebrew Bible places Daniel in the Writings, Daniel must have a later date (165 BC). This wrongly assumes that the Hebrew canon developed progressively and that the Writings were the last section. An argument against this assumption is that an early book like Ruth, most likely written in the preexilic period, was also included in the Writings. It is wrong to view the canon as having a haphazard or progressive arrangement. Rather, it was formed with literary purpose and structure. Therefore, Daniel is not in the Writings because of a late date but because of its contents. It follows Esther and precedes Ezra/Nehemiah (in the Jewish canon) because the narratives of Daniel fit within the same time period as the events of these other books. Also, Daniel was one of the wise men of Babylon and Persia, so it made sense for those who ordered the canon to include his book in the section of the Bible that contained wisdom literature. Regardless, the LXX and Josephus (*Contra Apion* I, 38–39) both place Daniel among the Prophets, which most English versions follow. Since Josephus preceded the Masoretic division of the Bible by several centuries, its placement in the Writings has no bearing on its date.

Purpose and Theme. The theme of the book of Daniel is the hope of the people of God during the times of the Gentiles. The phrase, "the times of the Gentiles," used by Jesus (Lk 21:24), refers to the time period when the Jewish people lived under ungodly, Gentile, world dominion, between the Babylonian captivity and the Messiah Jesus' return. The hope that the book promotes is that at all times "the Most High God is ruler over the realm of mankind" (Dn 5:21). The book's purpose was to exhort Israel to be faithful to the sovereign God of Israel during the times of the Gentiles. Daniel accomplishes this by recounting examples of godly trust and pagan arrogance, as well as predictions of God's ultimate victory.

The genre of Daniel is narrative, defined as "the recounting of events for the purpose of instruction." This narrative contains history, prophecy, and apocalyptic visions. Apocalyptic literature refers to revelation by God given through visions and symbols with a message of eschatological (end-time) triumph. Although Daniel contains apocalyptic elements, it is not an apocalyptic book. Rather it is a narrative with apocalyptic visions included.

Some have noted that the book of Daniel contains both history (chaps. 1–6) and prophecy (chaps. 7–12) and divide the book accordingly. However, a better way to view the structure of the book is based on the two languages it uses: Dn 1:1-21 (Hebrew); Dn 2:1–7:28 (Aramaic); and Dn 8:1–12:13 (Hebrew). The Hebrew sections pertain primarily to the people of Israel, while the Aramaic part, using the international language of that time, demonstrates God's dominion over all the Gentile nations. (See the chart "Structure of the Book of Daniel.")

Background. The covenantal background of Daniel relates to God's unconditional promises to Abraham, Isaac, and Jacob and their descendants (Gn 12:1-7; 13:14-15; 15:18; 17:7-8; 26:2-3; 28:13; 35:12; 1Ch 16:16; 2Ch 20:6-7). When God added the Mosaic law, He expanded the land promises made to the patriarchs with a land covenant that promised the people of Israel material blessing in the land of Israel if they obeyed the law (Dt 28:1-14). However, if Israel disobeyed, God promised that He would discipline the nation. If they still disobeyed, God promised to drive them from the land of Israel into captivity (cf. Dt 28-30, especially 28:63-68). Despite the discipline of dispersion, God swore that He would never break his promises to Israel (Dt 4:31). Further, He promised that in the last days He would give Israel a circumcised heart and regather the Jewish people from all the lands in which they were scattered (Dt 4:30; 30:1-10).

The events in the book of Daniel occurred during the dispersion of the Jewish people to Babylon, and many of the prophecies pertain to their ultimate regathering at the end of days.

Contribution. Daniel's book establishes the validity of predictive prophecy and lays the foundation for understanding end-times prophecy as well as the book of Revelation in the

NT. But, most important, it emphasizes that the Lord God has dominion over all the kingdoms of the earth, even in evil days when wicked empires rule the world. Two key words in the book are *king* (used 183 times) and *kingdom* (used 55 times). Above all, Daniel teaches that the God of Israel is the Sovereign of the universe, "For His dominion is an everlasting dominion, and His kingdom endures from generation to generation" (Dn 4:34).

Structure of the Book of Daniel

History: 1:1 – 6:28

The *Godly Person* in the Times of the Gentiles 1:1 – 2:3	*God's Sovereignty* over the Times of the Gentiles 2:4 – 7:28	*God's People Israel* in the Times of the Gentiles 8:1 – 12:13
HEBREW	ARAMAIC	HEBREW

Prophecy: 7:1 – 12:13

OUTLINE

I. The Godly Remnant in the Times of the Gentiles (1:1-21; in Hebrew)
- A. Daniel and His Friends in the Babylonian Captivity (1:1-7)
- B. Daniel and the King's Food (1:8-16)
- C. Daniel and the Lord's Reward (1:17-21)

II. God's Sovereignty over the Times of the Gentiles (2:1–7:28; in Aramaic)
- A. Nebuchadnezzar's Dream and the Wise Men of Babylon (2:1-49)
  1. The King's Disturbance (2:1-3)
  2. The Wise Men's Difficulty (2:4-11)
  3. The King's Decree (2:12-13)
  4. Daniel's Delay (2:14-16)
  5. Daniel's Prayer and Praise (2:17-24)
  6. Daniel's Revelation and Interpretation before the King (2:25-45)
  7. The King's Response to the Dream and its Interpretation (2:46-49)
- B. Daniel's Friends and the Fiery Furnace (3:1-30)
  1. The King's Demand to Worship the Statue (3:1-7)
  2. The Young Men's Refusal to Worship the Statue (3:8-23)
  3. The Lord's Deliverance from the Fiery Furnace (3:24-27)
  4. The King's Recognition of the God of Israel (3:28-30)
- C. Nebuchadnezzar's Pride, Madness, and Repentance (4:1-37)
  1. The Prologue: A Declaration of Praise (4:1-3)
  2. The Story: A Dream Comes to Pass (4:4-34a)
     - a. The King's Dream (4:4-18)
     - b. Daniel's Interpretation (4:19-27)
     - c. The Dream's Fulfillment (4:28-34a)
  3. The Epilogue: A Declaration of Sovereignty (4:34b-37)
- D. Belshazzar's Feast and the Writing on the Wall (5:1-31)
  1. The Feast of the King (5:1-4)

2. The Writing on the Wall (5:5-9)
3. The Advice of the Queen (5:10-12)
4. The Meeting with Daniel (5:13-29)
5. The Fall of Babylon (5:30-31)

E. Daniel in the Lions' Den (6:1-28)
1. The Plot against Daniel (6:1-9)
2. The Prosecution of Daniel (6:10-14)
3. The Punishment of Daniel (6:15-18)
4. The Protection of Daniel (6:19-24)
5. The Praise of Daniel's God (6:25-27)
6. The Prosperity of Daniel (6:28)

F. Daniel's Vision of the Four Beasts, the Ancient of Days and the Son of Man (7:1-28)
1. Daniel's Vision (7:1-14)
2. The Angel's Interpretation (7:15-28)

III. God's People Israel in the Times of the Gentiles (8:1–12:13; in Hebrew)

A. Daniel's Vision of the Ram and the Male Goat (8:1-27)
1. The Vision of the Ram and the Goat (8:1-14)
2. The Interpretation of the Vision (8:15-27)

B. Daniel's Prayer and Vision of the Seventy Weeks (9:1-27)
1. Daniel's Prayer of Contrition (9:1-19)
2. Daniel's Vision of the Seventy Weeks (9:20-27)

C. Daniel and His Final Vision (10:1–12:13)
1. Daniel's Reception of the Vision (10:1–11:1)
   a. The Setting of the Vision (10:1-3)
   b. The Messenger of the Vision (10:4-9)
   c. The Hindrances to the Vision (10:10-13)
   d. The Purposes of the Angelic Visit (10:14–11:1)
2. The Angel's Explanation of the Vision of Persia, Greece, and the False Messiah (11:2–12:3)
   a. The Predictions of the Persian to the Maccabean Periods (11:2-35)
      (1) The Predictions about the Persian Kings (11:2)
      (2) The Predictions about Alexander the Great (11:3-4)
      (3) The Predictions of the Hellenistic Period (11:5-35)
         (a) The Period of the First Seleucids and Ptolemies (11:5-6)
         (b) The Period of Ptolemy III (11:7-9)
         (c) The Period of Antiochus III (11:10-19)
         (d) The Period of Seleucus IV (11:20)
         (e) The Period of Antiochus IV (11:21-35)
   b. The Predictions of the End of Days (11:36-45)
   c. The Comfort of the Chosen People (12:1-3)
3. The Angel's Final Instructions to Daniel Concerning His Prophecies (12:4-13)
   a. The Sealing of the Book (12:4)
   b. The Time of the End (12:5-13)

COMMENTARY ON DANIEL

I. The Godly Remnant in the Times of the Gentiles (1:1-21; in Hebrew)

The first chapter of Daniel serves as an introduction to the entire book, identifying its setting, Babylon, and the main characters of the narrative, particularly Daniel. Since the book is designed to urge Israel to remain faithful to God despite living under ungodly, Gentile, world dominion, the first chapter demonstrates how faithfulness is to be maintained. Daniel and his friends represent Israel's faithful remnant that remain true to the Lord despite the pressures of a pagan society.

A. Daniel and His Friends in the Babylonian Captivity (1:1-7)

1:1. While Daniel records that these events took place **in the third year of the reign Jehoiakim**, Jeremiah writes that it was in the fourth year (Jr 25:1, 9; 46:1). Most likely Daniel used the Babylonian system, which did not count a king's year of accession to the throne, while Jeremiah used the Israelite system of counting, which did include the accession year, thus making it the fourth year. The events took place during the accession year of Nebuchadnezzar (whose name means *O god Nabu, protect my son*), king of Babylon (605–562 BC), apparently when he was still coregent with his father and just after his victory in the battle of Carchemish (605 BC, on the modern border of northwest Syria and southeast Turkey). This battle established the Babylonian Empire's dominance and ended the Assyrian Empire's role as a world power.

1:2. Although Nebuchadnezzar viewed his defeat of Judah as a victory for his gods, Daniel recognized that it was **the Lord** who **gave Jehoiakim king of Judah** over to the Babylonians (cf. 2Ch 36:5-6). The secular ancient historian Berosus (Hellenistic-era Babylonian writer, third century BC) mentioned these events when he wrote that Nebuchadnezzar conquered Hatti-land (meaning Syro-Palestine). After this initial conquest of Judah, Nebuchadnezzar would take more captives in 597 BC and then destroy Jerusalem and exile Judah to Babylon in 586 BC.

The Babylonian captivity fulfilled the covenant God had made with Israel when they were about to enter their land (Dt 28–30). In it, God promised that if Israel obeyed His commandments, He would bless them in the land of Israel. However, if they disobeyed, God assured Israel that He would discipline them with expulsion from the land. Just as Moses had foretold (Dt 31:29), Israel and Judah, for the most part, disobeyed the law, engaging in idolatry (Jr 7:30-31; 16:18), and neglecting the Sabbath and sabbatical years (Jr 34:12-22). So the Lord expelled the northern tribes of Israel from the land by the hand of the Assyrians (721 BC) and the southern tribes of Judah to Babylon.

At the time of Nebuchadnezzar's first invasion, the king took **vessels of the house of God** (Dn 1:2; 2Ch 36:7) fulfilling what Isaiah had predicted when Hezekiah had shown the temple treasures to the Babylonian king a century before (cf. Is 39:2, 6). Nebuchadnezzar brought these to **the land of Shinar**, using the old word for Babylon as an allusion to the rebellious behavior surrounding the original building of the city and tower of Babel (Babylon) in Genesis (Gn 11:1-9).

1:3-5. The king ordered that some of the nobility of Judah be brought to Babylon to be trained so they could serve as leaders when Nebuchadnezzar would take all of Judah captive. **Ashpenaz**, described as **chief of his officials**, literally means "chief of the eunuchs." Since by this time the word had come to mean "royal official," most likely Ashpenaz was not a eunuch, nor did he make Daniel and his friends literal eunuchs.

Although Daniel and his friends were called **youths**, the Hebrew word literally means "children" or "boys." Here it probably refers to teenagers of around age fifteen. The Judean captives were to learn **the literature and language of the Chaldeans**, a reference to an ancient university-style education in Sumerian, Akkadian, and Aramaic. At that time, Babylon was the most cosmopolitan city and the seat of academia in the known world. They were also to be given **the king's choice food** and **wine**, indicating their privileged status as counselors in training, despite being captives.

1:6-7. To assimilate the Judean captives, **the commander of the officials assigned new names to them; and to Daniel** ("God is My Judge") **he assigned . . . Belteshazzar** ("Bel Protect Him")**, to Hananiah** ("God Has Been Gracious") **Shadrach** ("The Command of Aku"), **to Mishael** ("Who Is What God Is?") **Meshach** ("Who Is What Aku Is?") **and to Azariah** ("The LORD Has Helped"), **Abed-nego** ("Servant of Nebo"). These new Chaldean names replaced their Hebrew names, exchanging those that referred to the true God of Israel with others that referred to the false gods of Babylon.

B. Daniel and the King's Food (1:8-16)

1:8. Daniel made up his mind that he would be faithful to God's law even in a foreign land. **Made up his mind** literally means, "set upon his heart" and refers to a deep inner resolve. Daniel decided **that he would not defile himself** with meat from the king's table because the Babylonian diet at that time included nonkosher meat such as horseflesh and pork. With regard to **the wine**, Daniel would not want to drink what had been offered to Babylonian gods as a libation. So he asked Ashpenaz for permission to abstain from the royal diet so **that he might not defile himself**.

1:9-10. God gave Daniel **favor and compassion** with Ashpenaz, indicating that it was not merely Daniel's winsome personality but divine intervention. Nevertheless, the Babylonian official risked his own life if Daniel and his friends were to look **more haggard** (lit., "thin") than the other captives because of their diet. In that culture, appearing thin was a sign of illness, not health. If the four young Jewish captives were deemed ill because of mistreatment by Ashpenaz, Nebuchadnezzar would likely kill him, since the king was notorious for decreeing death for those who displeased him (2:12; 3:13-15).

1:11-14. Daniel demonstrated his wisdom by asking **the overseer** (better translated "guardian," since he was there to protect and provide care for the youths) **whom** Ashpenaz had assigned to them if they could eat a diet of **vegetables** and **water** for a trial period of **ten days**. The word for **vegetables** refers to that which grows from seed and would include vegetables, fruits, and grains. The guardian agreed to the experiment, after which he would observe **the appearance** of the youths compared to those **eating the king's choice food**.

1:15-16. At the end of ten days Daniel and his friends looked **fatter** (i.e., healthier) but this is not a biblical endorsement of vegetarianism (cf. Gn 9:3). Rather, God in His providence made them healthy and strong so they could remain faithful to the Lord. Since they were fit, they were allowed to continue their diet.

C. Daniel and the Lord's Reward (1:17-21)

1:17. Daniel and his friends received several rewards for their faithfulness to God. First, they were granted superior wisdom. All gifts come from God but **these four youths** received a special endowment of **knowledge** (referring to academic skill) and **intelligence** (meaning "good sense"). Additionally, **Daniel even understood all kinds of visions and dreams**, a point included to show Daniel's prophetic ability and superior gifting as well as to prepare the reader for the events in the next chapter and the rest of the book.

1:18-19. As a second reward for their faithfulness, God granted Daniel and his friends special service to the king. At the end of their education, King Nebuchadnezzar **talked with them** and found them superior to all the other recent graduates of the King's academy. As a result, **they entered the king's personal service** at the king's court.

1:20-21. God gave yet a third reward for faithfulness to Daniel and his friends—a successful ministry. This is evident in that the king found their counsel significantly superior (**ten times better**) to that of the wise men of Babylon.

Throughout the book of Daniel, there occur six different expressions for the king's counselors. The first two, used here, are **magicians and conjurers**. The word *magician* comes from a root that means "engraver" and refers to those who engraved Babylonian religious activities and astrological movements of the stars onto clay tablets. The word *conjurer* refers to those who used spells and incantations to communicate with the spirit world. No wonder then that Daniel and his friends, by avoiding such occult practices and instead seeking wisdom from the true God, were wiser than the king's pagan counselors.

Daniel's successful ministry is also evident in the length of his service. He lived to see the end of the exile, serving the Babylonian kings until **the first year of Cyrus the king** (539 BC) of Persia. Once the Persian Empire conquered the Babylonians, Daniel continued as a counselor to the Persian king (cf. 10:1; 536 BC), resulting in more than 70 years of service.

In 1924, in an event made famous by the 1981 movie *Chariots of Fire*, Olympic runner Eric Liddell sat out a race because of his convictions as a follower of Jesus Christ. Later on, as he prepared to run the 400-meter race, a man slipped him a note that contained the words of 1Sm 2:30, "Those who honor Me I will honor." Liddell won the gold medal and broke the world record for that race at that time. As it was true for Liddell, for Daniel and his friends, and for the faithful remnant of Israel, it will be true for any follower of Christ—the Lord will honor those who honor Him.

II. God's Sovereignty over the Times of the Gentiles (2:1–7:28; in Aramaic)

Having portrayed Daniel and his friends as models of the way the godly remnant is to live in the times of the Gentiles (Dn 1:21), the book of Daniel next addresses (in chaps. 2–7) God's continued ultimate rule over the world despite Gentile world dominion. Since chaps. 2–7 pertain to God's revelation about the Gentile nations, they were written in Aramaic, the international language in those days. The structure of this section is chiastic (A B C C' B' A') with chaps. 2 and 7 each referring to the four kingdoms of this world, chaps. 3 and 6 dealing with persecution by Gentile kings, and chaps.

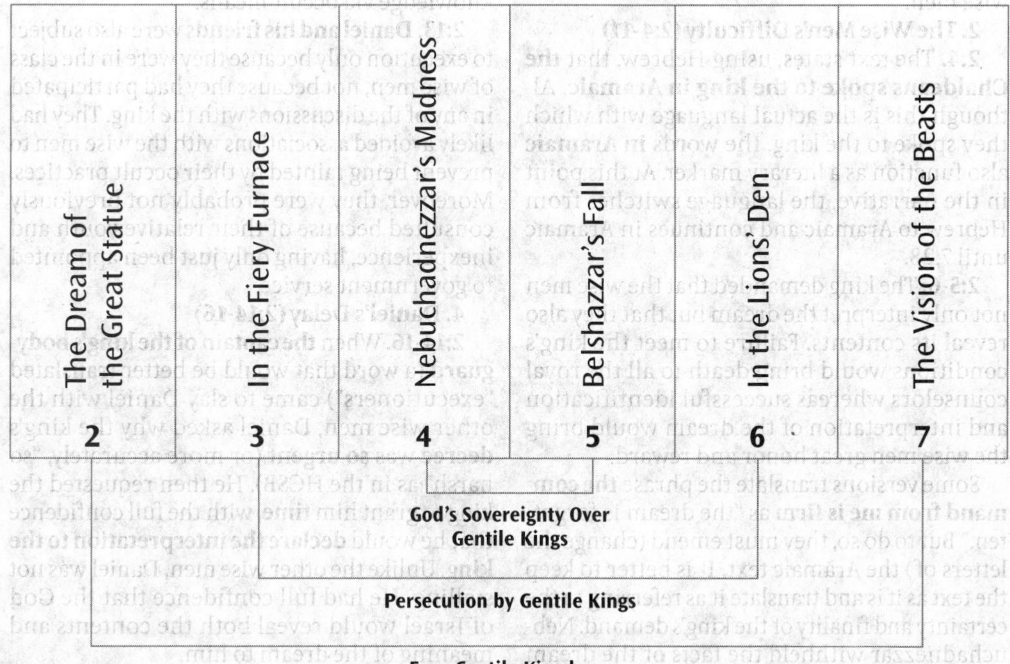

4 and 5 containing God's special revelation to pagan kings.

Chapter 2 tells the story of King Nebuchadnezzar's disturbing dream of a **great statue** (2:31) and Daniel's revelation and interpretation of it. In so doing, it reveals the empires that would dominate Israel and the world during the times of the Gentiles. The primary message of chap. 2 is that the God of Israel is greater than the greatest of men.

A. Nebuchadnezzar's Dream and the Wise Men of Babylon (2:1-49)

1. The King's Disturbance (2:1-3)

2:1. The chapter opens with King Nebuchadnezzar having had troubling **dreams**, and therefore he called upon his wise men to interpret them for him. Since it is later revealed in the chapter that there was only one dream, the plural used here indicates that the king had a recurring dream. Since Nebuchadnezzar considered the dreams significant, he was **troubled** by them and could not sleep.

The events of Dn 2 took place **in the second year of** Nebuchadnezzar's **reign**, which would appear to be a historical contradiction in that Daniel's three-year training program (1:5) began in Nebuchadnezzar's first year (1:1). The problem is resolved if, as is likely, Daniel was using Babylonian reckoning: Daniel would have arrived as a captive and entered his first year of training during the year reckoned as Nebuchadnezzar's accession year (605–604 BC); Daniel's second year of training would have been during the year reckoned as the first year of Nebuchadnezzar's reign (604–603 BC); Daniel's third and final year of training would have been during the year reckoned as the second of Nebuchadnezzar's kingship (603–602 BC). Therefore, the king sought interpretation of his dreams in 602 BC, shortly after Daniel had completed his three-year education.

2:2-3. As a result of the king's disturbing dreams he called for the court wise men to interpret for him. (For the meaning of **magicians** and **conjurers**, see notes on 1:20-21.) The Hebrew word used for **sorcerers** comes from the Akkadian word meaning "practitioners of sorcery or witchcraft." The word **Chaldeans** is both a general ethnic term for the Babylonian people and a specific term for priests who served as astrologers, soothsayers, and wise men in the king's government. It is used in the secondary sense here, referring to the king's astrologers/ wise men.

2. The Wise Men's Difficulty (2:4-11)

2:4. The text states, using Hebrew, that **the Chaldeans spoke to the king in Aramaic**. Although this is the actual language with which they spoke to the king, the words **in Aramaic** also function as a literary marker. At this point in the narrative, the language switches from Hebrew to Aramaic and continues in Aramaic until 7:28.

2:5-6. The king demanded that the wise men not only interpret the dream but that they also reveal its contents. Failure to meet the king's conditions would bring death to all the royal counselors whereas successful identification and interpretation of the dream would bring the wise men great honor and reward.

Some versions translate the phrase **the command from me is firm** as "the dream is forgotten." But to do so, they must emend (change the letters of) the Aramaic text. It is better to keep the text as it is and translate it as referring to the certainty and finality of the king's demand. Nebuchadnezzar withheld the facts of the dream not because he could not remember them, but because he wanted to test his wise men.

2:7-10. The wise men repeated their request for the king to reveal the dream to them. Yet the king was skeptical of his royal counselors—he sensed that they claimed supernatural knowledge without supernatural ability. Thus, Nebuchadnezzar demanded that they disclose what could only be known by supernatural revelation. The counselors insisted that this sort of request was unprecedented and that **not a man on earth** could provide such knowledge. Their objection provides a narrative introduction for Daniel's entrance into the story as the man who could and would receive supernatural revelation directly from God and thereby disclose and interpret the dream.

2:11. The wise men admitted that what the king wanted could only be obtained through the **gods** whose **dwelling place is not with mortal flesh**. This is a candid confession that despite all their incantations, magic, and astrology, they were not capable of receiving supernatural revelation.

3. The King's Decree (2:12-13)

2:12. The king became indignant and very furious at the failure of his counselors to identify his dream. The words **wise men** are used as a general term for all the king's counselors who, except for the Jewish captives, gained their knowledge via occult means.

2:13. Daniel and his friends were also subject to execution only because they were in the class of wise men, not because they had participated in any of the discussions with the king. They had likely avoided associations with the wise men to prevent being tainted by their occult practices. Moreover, they were probably not previously consulted because of their relative youth and inexperience, having only just been appointed to government service.

4. Daniel's Delay (2:14-16)

2:14-16. When **the captain of the king's bodyguard** (a word that would be better translated "executioners") came to slay Daniel with the other wise men, Daniel asked why the king's **decree** was **so urgent** (or more accurately, "so harsh" as in the HCSB). He then requested the king to grant him **time**, with the full confidence that he would **declare the interpretation to the king**. Unlike the other wise men, Daniel was not stalling. He had full confidence that the God of Israel would reveal both the contents and meaning of the dream to him.

5. Daniel's Prayer and Praise (2:17-24)

2:17-19. Daniel informed his Jewish companions of his need, and then together they sought help from the true **God of heaven**. The title **God of heaven** is used four times in this chapter (2:18, 19, 37, 44) and nowhere else in the book. It is a fairly common name for the God of Israel in the postexilic writings (Ezr 1:2; 5:11-12; 6:9-10; 7:12, 21, 23; Neh 1:4-5; 2:4, 20) although it is not limited to this period (cf. Gn 24:3, 7; Jnh 1:9). This chapter uses this title to emphasize that only the God of heaven is omniscient (cf. Dn 2:20-22) and capable of revealing **this mystery** even as the pagan wise men recognized (2:10-11). Moreover, Babylonians worshiped the luminaries but the God of Israel was over all of them, hence called the **God of heaven**. The word **mystery** refers to a secret that can only be known by divine revelation. In response to their prayers, the dream **was revealed to Daniel.**

2:20-23. When God revealed the king's dreams, Daniel "blessed the God of heaven" (v. 19). Daniel's song of praise emphasizes that God is sovereign over the political affairs of humanity because **He** controls **the times and the epochs** and **removes kings and establishes kings** (v. 21). Moreover, Daniel recognizes that God alone can give revelation by giving **wisdom to wise men** and by revealing **profound** (lit., "deep")

and hidden things, even the king's mysterious dream. Daniel was careful to **give thanks and praise** the **God of** his **fathers**, recognizing that the ability to interpret dreams did not generate from within himself but rather his **wisdom and power** came as a gracious gift from God.

The point of the first half of chap. 2 is that the God of Israel is greater in wisdom than the greatest of men, since He was able to reveal the king's dream, with its sovereign plan for the nations, to His servant Daniel. The God of heaven is vastly superior to all the great Babylonian Empire's false gods, who were not able to reveal the king's dream to all the wise men of Babylon.

2:24. With his knowledge from God, Daniel showed his compassion for his pagan colleagues, telling the executioner not to **destroy the wise men of Babylon**. He also told the king's executioner that he would **declare the interpretation**, and by implication, the contents of the dream to the king.

6. Daniel's Revelation and Interpretation before the King (2:25-45)

2:25-27. Having been brought to the king and asked if he was able **to make known . . . the dream . . . and its interpretation**, Daniel asserted that no pagan soothsayer could **declare it**. The word translated **diviners** contains the idea of "cutting" or "determining" and refers to a person who is able to determine another's fate.

2:28. Daniel attributed revelation to God alone, who is able to reveal mysteries. His statement that God has revealed **what will take place in the latter days** indicates that the king's dream would find its complete fulfillment only in the end times.

2:29-30. Daniel gave glory to God, who alone is omniscient. Thus, He **reveals mysteries** and can disclose **what will take place** in advance. Daniel was also self aware, recognizing that he was merely an instrument of God, not someone with more wisdom than **any other living man**.

2:31-45. Daniel described the king's dream of **a single great statue** (2:31-34), consisting of several parts. Each part was made of different elements and represented a different empire in historical succession. **The head of that statue was made of fine gold** (2:32a) and represented the kingdom of Babylon (605–539 BC) (2:37-38). **Its breast and its arms** were **silver** (2:32b) and symbolized the Medo-Persian Empire (539–331 BC) (2:39a). **Its belly and thighs** were **bronze** (2:32c) and stood for the Greek Empire (331–146 BC) (2:39b). The **legs** were **iron** (2:33a) and referred to the Roman Empire (146 BC–AD 476 in the West and 1453 in the East) (2:40). The feet were mixed of **iron** and **clay** (2:33b) and represented a yet future continuation or revival of Rome (2:41). It will divide into ten parts but with less cohesion than the original Roman Empire (2:42-43). The material of each section of the statue decreases in value but increases in strength. The decreased value may refer to the decline of morality or lessening political influence with each succeeding kingdom. The increased strength of the metals refers to the harsher domination each successive kingdom would impose. Daniel also described a **stone . . . cut out without hands** which would shatter the statue (2:34). It represents a final kingdom that would grow into **a great mountain and fill the whole earth**—this is the kingdom of God (2:35, cf. v. 44-45).

Critical scholars, primarily because of their denial of predictive prophecy, divide the four kingdoms into Babylon, Media, Persia, and Greece (alleging that the book Daniel was written in 165 BC so it could not have foreseen the Roman Empire). This interpretation is doubtful because of its historically inaccurate division of the Medo-Persian Empire into two separate empires, a division that is rejected even within the book of Daniel itself (cf. 8:20 where the lopsided ram represents the unified Medo-Persian Empire).

A select few interpreters, while maintaining a sixth-century date for the book of Daniel, hold an alternative view that the four kingdoms are to be identified as the Assyrian, Median, Medo-Persian, and Greek Empires (cf. John H. Walton, "The Four Kingdoms of Daniel," *Journal of the Evangelical Theological Society* 29.1 [Mar 1986]: 25–36). This is certainly incorrect in that Daniel tells Nebuchadnezzar, king of Babylon and founder of the Babylonian Empire, that he represents the first kingdom (**you are the head of gold**) (2:38). Moreover, to justify this alternative view, Assyria and Babylon must be conflated into one empire. But the book of Daniel ignores Assyria and treats Babylon as the first kingdom of the times of the Gentiles.

Most interpreters who accept the reality of predictive prophecy view the four kingdoms as Babylon, Medo-Persia, Greece, and Rome. Rome is then conquered by the kingdom of God. In seeing the fourth kingdom as Rome, these interpreters assert different opinions about the meaning of the stone. Some view it as a spiritual kingdom, embodied in the Church, which gradually conquered the Roman Empire. Others view it as a future, earthly kingdom, to be established when Messiah Jesus returns and institutes His physical rule that will fill **the whole earth** (2:35) and **never be destroyed** (2:44). According to this view, the Roman Empire will continue to exist until the end of days. According to some, the Roman Empire continues through its persistent influence in Western Civilization, existing until the end of days and the establishment of the kingdom of God. A more likely explanation is to recognize a prophetic gap, beginning with the fall of the Roman Empire (Rome I) and lasting through the establishment of a revived Roman Empire at the end of days (Rome II). The leader of this kingdom will be the little horn of Dn 7:8, 24-25. The destruction of this last phase of the Roman Empire will come with the establishment of the kingdom of God.

The evidence that there will be a literal, earthly, end-of-days kingdom of God and not merely the Church spiritually overtaking human governments is, (1) that all the previous kingdoms depicted in the statue were earthly; (2) that there was no coalition of conquered kings or kingdoms as described in 2:41-42 in the Roman Empire at the Messiah's first advent as would be required if the Church were the kingdom; (3) that the stone, which represents the kingdom of God, destroys earthly kingdoms, yet the Lord Jesus did not do this at His first advent; (4) that the advent of the kingdom of God is described as a sudden overturn of earthly kingdoms, not the gradual transformation through the influence of the Church, and (5) that this vision is parallel to the four beasts described in chap. 7. All agree that in chap. 7 the kingdom arrives with the return of Jesus the Messiah—so should it be the same with the coming of the kingdom of God here in chap. 2 (cf. Stephen R. Miller, *Daniel*, NAC, edited by E. Ray Clendenen [Nashville: Broadman and Holman, 2003], 100-101).

Daniel's second chapter demonstrates that the God of Israel is greater than the greatest of men. In 2:1-24, it shows that He is greater in wisdom than all. In the second half of the chapter (2:25-45) it emphasizes that the God of Israel is greater in power than all the great earthly kings and kingdoms. In the end, God will establish His kingdom that will never be shaken.

7. The King's Response to the Dream and its Interpretation (2:46-49)

2:46-47. The king's initial response was to give **homage to Daniel**, but he also recognized that God was the source of Daniel's supernatural knowledge. Although King Nebuchadnezzar gave honor to the Lord as one of many gods, even as **God of gods** and **Lord of kings**, he did not yet recognize the God of Israel as the one and only true God. He merely included the God of Israel in his pantheon of gods.

2:48-49. The ending note that the king **appointed Shadrach, Meshach and Abed-nego over the administration of the province of Babylon** provides the setting for the events that will be described in the following chapter.

Even as Daniel previously praised the God of heaven upon the revelation of the dream (2:20-23), so the king also responded to Daniel's revelation of his dream with an outburst of praise to God (2:47). Worship should be the response of any follower of the Messiah Jesus when encountering God's supernatural revelation in His Word, the Bible. Daniel expresses it well: "Let the name of God be blessed forever and ever, for wisdom and power belong to Him" (2:20).

B. Daniel's Friends and the Fiery Furnace (3:1-30)

The events of Dn 3 probably took place shortly after Daniel explained the king's dream (cf. Dn 2) although some have estimated that it could have been 10 or even 20 years later. Babylonian records indicate that there was a revolt against Nebuchadnezzar during the tenth year of his reign, and so this may have led to the king's desire for the loyalty test described here. The purpose of this chapter was to give the faithful remnant of Israel a model of standing firm for the God of Israel in the face of pagan Gentile oppression.

1. The King's Demand to Worship the Statue (3:1-7)

3:1. Nebuchadnezzar **made an image of gold**, much like a colossus, not of solid gold but more probably overlaid with it. Most likely, this statue reflects the king's desire to have an actual replica of the image he saw in his dream (cf. 2:31-33). In that image only the head representing Babylon was made of gold. Therefore, the king had a statue built covered entirely in gold so as to negate the earlier message of a temporary Babylonian Empire. Since a size of 90 feet high and nine feet wide (the equivalent dimensions of a **height** of **sixty cubits and** a **width** of **six cubits**) would make a grotesque distortion of a human body, it is more likely this was an image placed on a large pedestal.

The location of the statue was **on the plain of Dura**, a site that has not been conclusively identified. It was not in the city of Babylon but on a plain somewhere in the province. Perhaps Daniel was not involved in the events here since he remained in the capital city "at the king's court" (2:49) while other officials, including his three friends Shadrach, Meshach and Abednego, were called to Dura to show their loyalty. No doubt, had Daniel been there, he too would have refused to bow to the image.

3:2-3. Nebuchadnezzar . . . sent word to assemble all the officials of the realm **to come to the dedication of the image**. Seven offices are mentioned specifically, but the exact meaning of each position is unclear other than that they are listed in descending order of rank. The use of the Persian loanword for **satraps** does not necessarily imply an anachronism since Persian inscriptions have been discovered from the neo-Babylonian era. Moreover, by the time Daniel completed this book, the Persian period had already begun so it would not be surprising for him to use Persian words.

3:4-5. Upon hearing the music, all present were **to fall down and worship the golden image**. Six specific instruments are mentioned, three of which (**lyre**, **psaltery**, and **bagpipe**) are the only Greek loanwords in Daniel. This also should not imply a date for Daniel in the later Greek period because even Assyrian inscriptions, predating the Babylonian period, refer to Greek instruments and musicians (Gleason Archer, "Daniel," EBC, edited by Frank E. Gabelein [Grand Rapids, MI: Zondervan, 1985], 21).

Although some conjecture that the image was of Nebuchadnezzar himself, this is unlikely because the Babylonians did not believe their king was divine. More likely, the image was of a Babylonian god, perhaps Nebuchadnezzar's patron Nabu or the chief Babylonian god Marduk. Despite ancient paganism tending to tolerate a panoply of gods, here Nebuchadnezzar made this demand for worship of his god as a form of a loyalty oath to him personally.

3:6-7. Those failing to worship the image would be incinerated in **a furnace of blazing fire**, a punishment that Nebuchadnezzar had also used on two Judean false prophets, Zedekiah and Ahab (Jr 29:22). This was a normal Babylonian penalty as seen in the Code of Hammurabi, Sections 25, 110 and 157. Perhaps this furnace was built to smelt the gold for the image Nebuchadnezzar had made. The king's threat was sufficient to make all the officials present there, except the three Jewish young men, worship **the golden image**.

2. The Young Men's Refusal to Worship the Statue (3:8-23)

3:8-12. When Shadrach, Meshach, and Abednego refused to worship the false god, **certain Chaldeans** maliciously **brought charges** to the king. The word **Chaldeans** is both a general ethnic term for the Babylonian people and a specific term for priests who served as astrologers, soothsayers, and wise men in the king's government. It is used in the secondary sense here, referring to the king's astrologers and wise men. Likely these were the governmental officials who had been summoned to the plain of Dura.

Their motive in denouncing the three faithful Jewish men was not devotion to the king's demand but a hatred for the Jewish people. They sought to accuse **the Jews** (3:8) and they referred to **certain Jews whom you have appointed** (3:12). Were it not hatred for God's chosen people, their accusation would have been about some royal officials without mention of their ethnicity. Hatred of the Jewish people has been a persistent sin in the Bible from Pharaoh to Haman. It reflects a hatred of the God of Israel and is expressed through oppression and even attempts at genocide of His people (Ps 83:2-5). By saying that these Jewish men did **not serve your gods or worship the golden image**, the wise men were accusing them of disloyalty, another anti-Jewish slur, which persists to this day.

3:13-18. The enraged king offered Daniel's friends a second chance to worship the idol, but they persistently refused. They were confident that the true God was **able to deliver** them **from the furnace of blazing fire**. The Aramaic imperfect verb *yesezib* ("He can deliver, rescue") in this context indicates possibility and not certainty. They were saying that God may deliver them or He may choose not to rescue. It was His choice. Their faith was not limited to belief in a miracle but also included trust in God's sovereignty. They asserted that if God chose not to deliver them from this punishment but would allow them to become martyrs for Him, they would still refuse to serve the king's **gods or worship the golden image**. This is one of the strongest statements of faith in the entire Bible. They trusted the Lord to decide their destiny while still being faithful to Him.

3:19-23. The infuriated king gave **orders to heat the furnace seven times more than it was usually heated**, an idiom for "as hot as possible." When the appointed guards cast Shadrach, Meshach and Abed-nego into the furnace, the heat was so intense that its flames **slew those men who carried** God's three faithful servants to the furnace. This indicates that there was no naturalistic explanation for the survival of the three.

The ancient furnace was shaped like an old-fashioned milk bottle and built on a small hill or mound with openings at the top and side. The ore to be smelted would be dropped in a large opening at the top and wood or charcoal would be inserted in a smaller hole on the side, at ground level, to heat the furnace. There would have been two other small holes at ground level in which to insert pipes connected to a large bellows to raise the temperature of the fire. (Archer, "Daniel," 56). Some have estimated that this furnace could reach a temperature of 1,800 degrees fahrenheit (Miller, *Daniel,* 115, 122). Most likely this furnace was used to smelt the gold ore and bricks for Nebuchadnezzar's statue. Thus, the three men **fell into the midst of the furnace** (3:23) from the top and the king was able to see into the furnace (3:24-25) from its side opening.

3. The Lord's Deliverance from the Fiery Furnace (3:24-27)

3:24-25. When the king looked into the furnace, he **was astounded** to see **four men . . . walking about** in the furnace, and the **fourth** looked **like a son of the gods**. This may have been an angel or even more likely, the Angel of the Lord, meaning a pre-incarnate appearance of the Messiah. Nevertheless, it is doubtful that a pagan king would have understood this. Rather, his statement is indicative of the glorious appearance of the deliverer whom he saw. The faithful reader is to understand who was in the furnace even though the pagan king did not.

3:26-27. Having called the men out of the furnace, Nebuchadnezzar and all his government officials saw that **the fire had no effect on** their **bodies.** Not only did the fire fail to burn their hair and clothing, they did not even have **the smell of fire** on them. Hebrews 11:34 cites this miracle of faith, referring to those who "quenched the power of fire."

4. The King's Recognition of the God of Israel (3:28-30)

3:28-30. King Nebuchadnezzar continued on his odyssey of faith, begun in Dn 2. There he learned that the Lord is a true God, powerful enough to reveal secret dreams and to control the destinies of nations. In a sense, he recognized the God of Israel as a part of the panoply of gods. However, in Dn 3, Nebuchadnezzar learned that Shadrach, Meshach, and Abed-nego were "servants of the Most High God" (3:26), indicating that he saw the God of Israel as the one who is greater than all other gods. Even so, he remained a polytheist, believing in many gods. Despite Nebuchadnezzar's praise of **the God of Shadrach, Meshach and Abed-nego** for His deliverance and the king's prohibition against saying **anything offensive against** the God of Israel (3:28-29), he still had not come to a full knowledge of the one and only true God.

The three young men remained faithful to the true God despite intense pressure to acquiesce to idolatry. They experienced the promise of Is 43:2: "When you walk through the fire, you will not be scorched, nor will the flame burn you." Thus, they became a model to the faithful remnant of Israel in the times of the Gentiles as well as to any person today who has become a follower of the Lord Jesus. Despite living in a pressure-packed society that consistently invites disloyalty to the Lord, His followers can be assured of His presence in the midst of the fire. God is fully capable of supernatural deliverance from the intense heat of pressure or to bring His faithful ones safely home to Him.

C. Nebuchadnezzar's Pride, Madness, and Repentance (4:1-37)

1. The Prologue: A Declaration of Praise (4:1-3)

4:1-3. The text does not indicate when the events of Dn 4 took place nor is it significant to the interpretation of the passage. Nevertheless, King Nebuchadnezzar most likely had his dream (see v. 5) about ten years before the end of his 43-year reign. Then, God in His grace allowed the king one year to repent followed by seven years of madness. Once he came to his senses, the king lived approximately two to three years before dying in 562 BC.

Daniel has included this chapter as a formal letter sent by Nebuchadnezzar himself to his empire. No doubt, the king did indeed write the letter, but it is Daniel, as author of the book, who chose to include it. It would be unlikely that the king would switch from writing about himself in the first person (4:1-27, 34-37). Yet Daniel, as the author of the book and personal confidante of the king, was uniquely aware of the king's experience. Therefore, he most likely wrote the section that speaks of the king in the third person (vv. 28-33) and records his time of mental illness. The chapter is structured in three sections: (1) a *prologue* in which the king praises the true God (4:1-3); (2) a *narrative body* (4:4-34a), which recounts (a) the king's dream, (b) Daniel's interpretation, (c) the king's illness and repentance; and (3) an *epilogue* in which the king declares his own recognition of the sovereignty of the true God (4:34b-37). Of course, the chapter is written from the perspective of the king looking back at **the signs and wonders which the Most High God** had done for him (4:2). Therefore, this prologue reflects what the king had already come to understand by the end of the chapter—that God's **kingdom is an everlasting kingdom and His dominion is from generation to generation.**

2. The Story: A Dream Comes to Pass (4:4-34a)

4:4-34a. The story covers a period of eight years, beginning with the dream, the year afterward, and then the seven-year period of mental illness.

a. The King's Dream (4:4-18)

4:4-7. King Nebuchadnezzar once again had recurring dreams that alarmed him. Therefore, he called the four classes of wise men to interpret his dream (for the meaning of **magicians** and **conjurers**, see the comments at 1:20-21, for **Chaldeans** see 2:2-3 and for **diviners** see 2:27). Unlike the dream of Dn 2, the king **related the dream to them** but similarly **they could not make its interpretation known** to him.

4:8. Daniel finally came before the king—perhaps he was away from the palace when the previous wise men appeared before the king or maybe he was only brought to deal with problems beyond the ability of the ordinary wise men. No matter, the king recognized that **a spirit of the holy gods** was in Daniel. This translation reflects the perspective of a pagan king but since the king is relating this from the perspective of a chastened king who knows that God alone can reveal what is hidden, it might be better to translate the phrase "the spirit of the Holy God is in him."

Beginning in this verse and throughout the chapter, Daniel is most frequently called by his Babylonian name **Belteshazzar**, likely because it was written from the perspective of the Babylonian king, not a Hebrew exile.

4:9-13. Nebuchadnezzar related his dream to Daniel, describing what he saw as **a tree . . . great** and which **grew large and became strong And its height reached to the sky**, a figure for an exceptionally tall tree. A similar expression was used in Gn 11:4 for the tower of the city of Babylon, the top of which was to reach "into heaven." The tree provided **food** and shelter for all the **creatures** of the earth. The king also saw an angel, here called a **watcher, a holy one**.

4:14-18. The angel in the king's dream announced that the tree would be cut down but that **the stump with its roots** would remain **in the ground**, indicating the continuation of life. The stump was to have **a band of iron and bronze around it**, indicating the protection of the stump. The tree plainly represents a man (the king) because the angel declared that **his mind** would **be changed from that of a man** to that of **a beast's** for **seven periods of time** or for seven years.

b. Daniel's Interpretation (4:19-27)

4:19. Daniel **was appalled for a while** and **his thoughts alarmed him** upon hearing the dream because he understood its meaning. As a loyal servant of the king, Daniel was alarmed about the dreadful discipline that would befall the king.

4:20-26. The **tree** represented King Nebuchadnezzar who would be given a mental illness that would cause him to live outdoors like **the beasts of the field** and feed on **grass . . . like cattle** for seven years. This would last until King Nebuchadnezzar repented of his pride and **recognize[d] that the Most High is ruler over the realm of mankind and bestows it on whomever He wishes.** Rather than taking credit for his own accomplishments, the king needed to recognize God's sovereignty in placing him in his position. When the king would acknowledge that **it is Heaven that rules**, God would restore his sanity and realm to him. This is the only place in the OT where **Heaven** is a metonymy for God. This usage became commonplace in intertestamental literature, the NT, and Rabbinic literature.

4:27. Daniel advised the king to repent with the hope that this might stay God's discipline. To do so, the king was to separate himself from his sins **by doing righteousness**. Some have understood the Aramaic word for "righteousness" as a reference to giving charity. In post-biblical Hebrew and Aramaic this word does indeed begin to include "giving charity" within its range of meaning. However, this use in the book of Daniel would be too early for that definition and would merely mean "justice." Rather than calling for good deeds as a means of salvation or even of staying temporal judgment, Daniel exhorted the king to acknowledge God's rulership by faith, and having done so, to **break** with his **sins** and live in conformity to God's righteous (or just) standard.

c. The Dream's Fulfillment (4:28-34a)

4:28-30. One year later, Daniel's predictions were fulfilled. Nebuchadnezzar, who had no fewer than three palaces in the city of Babylon, was **walking on the roof** of one of them. Seeing the magnificent city, he was overcome with its grandeur and became consumed with pride. He called the city **Babylon the great**, a phrase echoed in Rv 17:5 and 18:2.

According to Herodotus (a Greek historian who died c. 425 BC), Babylon was the most glorious city of the ancient world. He recorded that Babylon's outer walls alone were 56 miles long, 80 feet wide and 320 feet high. Nebuchadnezzar was a great builder and expanded the city to six square miles. He also beautified it with magnificent buildings, temples, and palaces. Within the city there were some 53 temples to various gods, many containing massive gold statues. The main sacred procession street passed from the famed Ishtar Gate to the Temple of Marduk, with its adjacent *ziggurat* rising 288 feet into the sky. A 400-foot bridge spanned the Euphrates River and united the eastern and western halves of the city. On the northwest corner of the king's primary palace sat one of the Seven Wonders of the World, the famed Hanging Gardens of Babylon. Built on terraces, it more properly should be called overhanging gardens. Whether the ancient historian exaggerated or gave a precise depiction, the city of Babylon was indeed the largest, most populated, and greatest city in the known world at that time. Perhaps it was on the roof of the Hanging Gardens with a view of his glorious city that Nebuchadnezzar became filled with pride.

The king's overwhelming pride is evident in his exclamation: **Is this not Babylon the great, which I *myself* have built . . . by the might of *my* power and for the glory of *my* majesty?** (italics added, v. 30). Note Nebuchadnezzar's emphasis on himself and his failure to give God the credit and the glory for giving all of this to him. Many years later, Paul would upbraid the Corinthians for their pride by asking, "What do you have that you did not receive? And if you did receive it, why do you boast as if you had not received it?" (1Co 4:7). Herein lies the problem with pride: it takes credit for what God alone has done.

4:31. After a year of patience (4:28), God enacted His discipline at the very instant that Nebuchadnezzar had become fully consumed with his pride, even **while the word was in the king's mouth**. As evidence that God alone is the source of human accomplishment and authority, Nebuchadnezzar's **sovereignty** was taken away and the king descended into the abyss of mental illness.

4:32-33. Nebuchadnezzar was driven to live with **the beasts of the field**, apparently suffering from boanthropy, a rare mental illness in which people believe they actually are cattle. Hence, he began **eating grass like cattle, and his body was drenched with the dew**. One modern case of boanthropy resulted in the patient growing long matted hair and thickened fingernails, much like Nebuchadnezzar, whose hair grew **like eagles' feathers and his nails like birds' claws** (Harrison, *Introduction to the Old Testament*, 1116–17).

Critics contend that secular history has no record of Nebuchadnezzar's mental illness, thereby challenging the historicity of this account. However, it is questionable as to whether an ancient Near Eastern despot would place his bout with insanity into official court records. Moreover, Eusebius, the church historian (d. AD 339), citing Abydenus, a third-century BC Greek historian, referred to a time, late in Nebuchadnezzar's life when he was "possessed by a god" (Praeparatio Evangelica IX, 41, cited by Leon Wood, *A Commentary on Daniel* [Grand Rapids, MI: Zondervan, 1973], 121–22), a possible secular reference to the events of Dn 4. Also, third-century BC historian Berosus possibly referred to these events when he spoke of an illness that befell Nebuchadnezzar just prior to his death (Wood, *Daniel*, 122).

Critics have questioned whether the Babylonian Empire could function while mental illness incapacitated its king. Yet, excellent administrative leadership, such as provided by Daniel, would certainly have kept the kingdom intact.

4:34a. The nature of boanthropy is not such that the sufferer cannot reason or understand what has befallen him. So, it was possible for the king to realize that his own pride had caused his insanity and therefore, repent. Hence, when **Nebuchadnezzar raised** his **eyes toward heaven**

in repentance for his pride and acknowledged the Most High God, his sanity returned to him fully and instantly.

3. The Epilogue: A Declaration of Sovereignty (4:34b-37)

4:34b-35. As an epilogue to the narrative, Nebuchadnezzar glorified God, using words that describe not only his own realization but summarize the theme of the book of Daniel: He recognized God's **everlasting dominion**, His eternal **kingdom**, and His sovereignty over all **the inhabitants of the earth**.

4:36-37. Having repented, Nebuchadnezzar finds his sanity returned, and the Lord also restored his **majesty** and **sovereignty** over Babylon. The very last sentence of the chapter summarizes the message of this story: God **is able to humble those who walk in pride**. Although some have disputed that the pagan King Nebuchadnezzar actually did come to a saving knowledge of the true God, it appears that he did. In his 40-year journey of faith, Nebuchadnezzar accepted the God of Israel into the panoply of gods (2:47), recognized Israel's God as the Most High God (3:26), and ultimately repented of his pride and submitted to the God of Israel's sovereignty over the world and his own life (4:34-37). Therefore, near the end of his life, Nebuchadnezzar experienced salvation when he came to know and follow the God of Israel.

Too often, people take credit for their own skills, status, or success. It would be wise to learn the lesson of Nebuchadnezzar and acknowledge that all these come from the Sovereign of the universe, not ourselves.

D. Belshazzar's Feast and the Writing on the Wall (5:1-31)

The developments in Dn 5 took place some 23 years after the events in the previous chapter. Nebuchadnezzar had died in 562 BC, shortly after his time of insanity and subsequent repentance. After his death, a series of intrigues and assassinations resulted in several obscure kings ruling Babylon until Nabonidus took the throne (556–539 BC). Earlier critics questioned the historicity of Belshazzar, since he was unknown in secular documents. However, beginning in 1914, 37 separate archival texts have been discovered, documenting the existence of Belshazzar as crown prince. Discovered ancient texts also confirm that Nabonidus spent much of his reign in Arabia, leaving Belshazzar in Babylon, to rule the empire as coregent.

1. The Feast of the King (5:1-4)

5:1. Belshazzar the king held a great feast for a thousand of his nobles most likely to bolster the morale of the nobility after Nabonidus had experienced a crushing defeat at the hands of the Persians. Ancient Greek historians Herodotus and Xenophon confirm that Babylon fell while a great feast was in progress (5:30). Excavations in Babylon have uncovered a large throne room that could have easily accommodated one thousand nobles.

5:2-4. While feasting, Belshazzar **gave orders to bring the gold and silver vessels** which had been **taken out of the temple** 47 years earlier. By drinking libations to Babylonian gods with vessels devoted to the true God of Israel, Belshazzar was acting in an unusually aggressive and blasphemous way. **Nebuchadnezzar** was called Belshazzar's **father**, even though Nabonidus was his father. Most likely, Belshazzar's father, Nabonidus, married Nebuchadnezzar's daughter to establish his own claim to the throne of Babylon, making Nebuchadnezzar the grandfather of Belshazzar. The Aramaic word translated "father" could refer to a grandfather, ancestor, or even a predecessor to a king without any lineal tie whatsoever.

2. The Writing on the Wall (5:5-9)

5:5. It was precisely at that moment, when the king and his nobles were mocking the God of Israel, that **the fingers of a man's hand emerged and began writing . . . on the plaster of the wall**. This was not a vision merely seen by Belshazzar alone but a miracle seen by all present. Even afterward, the wise men called to interpret could still see the words written on the plaster wall. According to the archaeologist who excavated Babylon, the Babylonian throne room (see 5:1) had walls covered with white gypsum (or plaster), fitting the description contained in Daniel (cf. Robert Koldeway, *The Excavations at Babylon*, [London: Macmillan, 1914], 104).

5:6-7. The writing on the wall so terrified Belshazzar that **his hip joints went slack and his knees began knocking together**. Therefore, he **called** for the wise men and offered great honor if any of them could interpret the words on the wall. He even proposed to make the successful wise man **third ruler in the kingdom**, after Nabonidus and Belshazzar.

5:8-9. None of the **wise men** could **read the inscription or make known its interpretation**, following the pattern of the book (cf. 2:3-13, 4:7). Consistently, the wise men of Babylon were incapable of interpreting God's messages—only Daniel, God's prophet, was capable of doing so (1:17).

3. The Advice of the Queen (5:10-12)

5:10. The queen who **entered the banquet hall** was the Queen Mother, not the wife of King Belshazzar since all his wives were already present with him (cf. 5:3).

5:11-12. Daniel was approximately 80 years old at this point and was either retired or forgotten. The Queen Mother, who was the daughter of Nebuchadnezzar, remembered Daniel's **extraordinary spirit** and his abilities to interpret **dreams**, explain **enigmas**, and solve **difficult problems** during her father's reign. Therefore, she advised her son to call Daniel to **declare the interpretation** of the writing on the wall.

4. The Meeting with Daniel (5:13-29)

When Daniel was brought before the king, he did not demonstrate the same level of respect that he had consistently shown to Nebuchadnezzar. Instead, he rebuked Belshazzar for his brazen attitude and failure to learn from Nebuchadnezzar. Rather than remembering the lesson of humility before the God of Israel that his father had learned, Belshazzar had brazenly mocked the true God.

5:13-17. Upon hearing the king's offer to honor him and make him **the third ruler in the kingdom**, Daniel refused to accept any gift, telling the king to **give** his **rewards to someone else**. This was not because Daniel was rude or arrogant but rather indignant at the king's disregard for Nebuchadnezzar's lesson of humility before God and his blasphemous use of the temple vessels.

5:18-24. Writers of historical narrative frequently communicate the essential message of a text through dialogue. In this case, Daniel's words served as a rebuke for Belshazzar for his failure to learn from the experience of Nebuchadnezzar (as described in Dn 4). Daniel reviewed for Belshazzar that **the Most High God** had **granted sovereignty** to **Nebuchadnezzar**, Belshazzar's predecessor. Also, that God had humbled Nebuchadnezzar when **his spirit became . . . proud** by afflicting him with boanthropy **until he recognized** the sovereignty of the God of Israel. Daniel reprimanded Belshazzar because he had not **humbled** his **heart, even though** he **knew all this**. According to ancient Babylonian texts, Belshazzar had served in the government of King Neriglissar (who ruled Babylon from 560–556 BC) in 560 BC indicating that he had been old enough to be aware of the events at the end of Nebuchadnezzar's life. Instead of learning to submit to the Almighty, he used the temple vessels to blaspheme God and so **exalted** himself **against the Lord of heaven**. The specific sins Daniel cited were pride, blasphemy, idolatry, and failure to glorify the true God. For this reason, the **inscription was written** on the wall with a message of judgment and doom.

5:25-29. The three words on the wall were Aramaic as follows: **MENE** (numbered), **TEKEL** (weighed) and **UPHARSIN** (divided). They indicated that Belshazzar's days were numbered and his kingdom would come to an end, that his reign had been weighed and **found deficient**, and that Babylon would be **divided** among **the Medes and Persians.**

Although the third word was written on the wall in the plural form **(UPHARSIN)**, Daniel explained its meaning by using the singular form (**PERES**). The prediction that Belshazzar's **kingdom has been divided** does not indicate that the Babylonian Empire would be divided equally by two kingdoms (**Medes and Persians**) but rather that Babylon would be destroyed or dissolved and taken over by the Medo-Persian Empire. The third word on the wall (**UPHARSIN**) has the same letters as the Aramaic word for "Persian," and was used as a play on words, indicating that the kingdom would fall to a Persian army.

5. The Fall of Babylon (5:30-31)

5:30. Having lost a brief skirmish outside the walls of Babylon, Belshazzar had retreated to the city and made light of the coming Persian siege. The Babylonians had 20 years of provisions, and the city was a seemingly impregnable fortress. Nevertheless, Darius diverted the waters of the Euphrates and entered below the water gates. He took the city **that same night** without a battle and killed Belshazzar. Xenophon noted that the city fell while the Babylonians were in the midst of a drunken feast. The kingdom of Babylon fell just as foretold by Daniel in his interpretation of Nebuchadnezzar's dream of the statue (2:39). The head of gold (Babylon) had fallen and was replaced by the chest and arms of silver (Medo-Persia) (2:40).

5:31. The identity of **Darius the Mede** who **received the kingdom at about the age of sixty-two** is uncertain. Some believe that he was Gubaru, the governor of Babylon (cf. J. C. Whitcomb, Jr., *Darius the Mede* [Grand Rapids, MI: Baker, 1959]). and called **Darius** because it was not a personal name but an honorific title, meaning "royal one" (Archer, "Daniel," 76–77). Others maintain that **Darius the Mede** was an alternate title for the Persian emperor, Cyrus the Great, also viewing the word **Darius** not as a name but as a royal title (J. M. Bulman, "The Identification of Darius the Mede," *WTJ* 35 [1973]: 247-67). Both of these identifications are possible, but there is no conclusive evidence for either. Regardless, Darius the Mede was not a fictional character but an actual historical figure.

God did not intend for Nebuchadnezzar alone to learn to honor the true Lord of heaven (cf. Dn 4:37). He also expected Nebuchadnezzar's descendants to glorify Him as well. Unlike Belshazzar, who ignored the humbling of his predecessor, followers of Messiah today must learn the lesson of humility, exalting the Lord above all in their lives and recognizing His granting of every good gift.

E. Daniel in the Lions' Den (6:1-28)

In one of the most well-known stories in the book, Daniel was cast into the lion's den for his faith. Since Daniel was about 15 in 605 BC, when the Babylonians brought him as a captive to Babylon, and since the events in Dn 6 most likely took place in the second or third year after the Medo-Persian conquest of Babylon in 539 BC, Daniel would have been approximately 82 years old when he was cast into the lions' den (see the chart, after the comments on 6:28, on Daniel's age throughout the events in the book). He was an old man, not a teenager, as is often pictured in Bible storybooks and sermons.

1. The Plot against Daniel (6:1-9)

6:1. Darius began organizing the newly conquered Babylonian Empire and immediately decided **to appoint 120 satraps over the kingdom**. According to Herodotus, there were 20 satrapies in the Medo-Persian Empire (3.89-94), while the book of Esther records that the Persian Empire had 127 provinces (Est 1:1; 8:9). It can be assumed that the **120 satraps** identified here are not to be understood as one satrap for each particular section of the entire empire, but rather lower officials who helped rule over the entire empire or just over that part of the empire that was formerly Babylonian.

6:2. The king appointed **three commissioners** over the 120 satraps, to assure that the 120 government officials would properly collect taxes without any embezzlement or corruption. For the three administrative leaders, the king needed men with trustworthy reputations and so chose **Daniel** as one. He must have heard of Daniel's reputation or perhaps he may have been aware of Daniel's interpretation of the writing on the wall on the night Babylon fell.

6:3. Quickly, Daniel **began distinguishing himself** as a superlative administrator because of his **extraordinary spirit**, a phrase previously used to describe him (5:12). Therefore, **the king planned to appoint him over the entire kingdom** as prime minister.

6:4-5. The king's choice of Daniel created jealousy in the other court officials and they wished to denounce Daniel. Since Daniel was both diligent and honest in his work, **the commissioners and satraps** could not find any **negligence or corruption . . . in him**. Therefore, they sought to create a law sure to contradict Daniel's faith in order to entrap him.

6:6-7. When these corrupt officials approached the king, they falsely claimed that **all** government officials supported the proposal that for 30 days **anyone who makes a petition to any god or man besides** the **king** would **be cast into the lions' den**. By agreeing to this law, Darius had not claimed deity but rather adopted the role of a priestly mediator. His goal was to unite the Babylonian realm under the authority of the new Persian Empire.

6:8-9. The irrevocability of **the law of the Medes and Persians** is confirmed elsewhere in Scripture (Est 1:19; 8:8) and secular literature (Diodorus of Sicily, XVII:30).

2. The Prosecution of Daniel (6:10-14)

6:10-11. Even though the law prohibiting prayer had gone into effect, Daniel still prayed with his **windows open toward Jerusalem**. Jewish people in exile always pray toward Jerusalem—even today—just as Solomon had directed in his prayer of dedication for the temple (1Kg 8:44-49). Daniel prayed **three times a day** either because this was his own personal devotional habit or perhaps because the Jewish custom of morning, afternoon, and evening prayers had already been established. Daniel prayed not out of rebellion to the king but out of obedience to the greater command of God. As the apostles would later say, "We must obey God rather than men" (Ac 5:29). So great was Daniel's reputation for spiritual commitment that even his enemies knew that he would obey God rather than the king's edict.

6:12-14. The conspirators reminded the king of his injunction and notified him of Daniel's behavior. As a result, the king **was deeply distressed** at hearing of Daniel's disobedience, not because Daniel had defied him, but because the king now understood that the true purpose of the law was to entrap Daniel. As a result, the king was **exerting himself** to find a way **to rescue** Daniel—but he was trapped by his own law and could not deliver Daniel.

3. The Punishment of Daniel (6:15-18)

6:15-16. Since **the law of the Medes and the Persians** could not be overturned, Daniel was thrown **into the lions' den** as punishment. The Persians used mutilation by lions as one of several brutal forms of execution. The king hoped that the **God whom** Daniel **constantly serve[d]** would **deliver** him.

6:17-18. The word for **den** could also be translated "pit." Daniel was cast into a pit over which **a stone was brought** and **the king sealed it with his own signet ring** and the **rings of his nobles**. The king then **spent the night fasting** without **entertainment**, presumably praying to his own gods for Daniel.

4. The Protection of Daniel (6:19-24)

6:19-23. Early the next morning, when the king came to inquire of Daniel's condition, Daniel told the king that **God sent his angel and shut the lions' mouths**. God uses angels to accomplish his purposes, including protection of His people (Ps 34:7; 91:11; Heb 1:14). He did so for Daniel's three friends in the furnace many years before this incident (3:25). As on that occasion, this may have been not merely an angel but the Angel of the Lord (i.e., a pre-incarnate appearance of the Messiah) who rescued Daniel.

Daniel was not claiming perfection in declaring that he **was found innocent before** God. Rather, Daniel claimed that his allegiance to God, even above the king, made him guiltless in this matter. Nevertheless, it was not Daniel's works that brought him deliverance from God but his faith, **because he had trusted in his God**.

6:24. The king punished those **who had maliciously accused Daniel** by casting them into the lions' den with **their children and their wives.** Although executing family members is exceptionally cruel, according to Herodotus, this was a common Persian practice (*Histories*, 3.119).

5. The Praise of Daniel's God (6:25-27)

6:25-27. Just as King Nebuchadnezzar did before him (4:2), so Darius issued a decree to **all the peoples, nations and men of every language** (cf. 4:2) declaring praise to the God of Daniel. Darius recognized the greatness of God: that **He is the living God**, eternal, sovereign and powerful, and able to rescue His people, even as He **delivered Daniel from the power of the lions**. Nevertheless, it is unlikely that Darius came to a saving faith at this point but instead accepted the God of Israel into the panoply of gods.

6. The Prosperity of Daniel (6:28)

6:28. Now secured as prime minister, Daniel continued his government service **in the reign of Darius and . . . of Cyrus the Persian**. Although some have maintained that the citation of both kings would indicate that Darius could only be identified with Gubaru and not as Cyrus the Persian (cf. 5:31), it is possible to translate this verse as "during the reign of Darius, *even* Cyrus the Persian." This translation could be understood as a biblical historical notation, clearly identifying "Darius the Mede" as an alternate name for Cyrus. Once again the identification of Darius the Mede is inconclusive.

Daniel's Ages

(All approximate based on the conjecture that Daniel was about 15 when taken captive to Babylon)

AGE	DESCRIPTION OF EVENTS	YEAR & REFERENCE
15	when brought to Babylon	(605 BC, Dn 1)
18	when called to interpret Nebuchadnezzar's dream	(602 BC, Dn 2)
50	when called to interpret Nebuchadnezzar's vision	(570 BC, Dn 4)
67	when dreaming of the four beasts	(553 BC, Dn 7)
70	when receiving the vision of the ram, the goat, and the horns	(550 BC, Dn 8)
81	when called to interpret the writing on the wall	(539 BC, Dn 5)
81	when visited by Gabriel with the message of 70 weeks	(539 BC, Dn 9)
82	when cast into the lions' den	(538 BC, Dn 6)
83	when receiving the vision of future events	(537 BC, Dn 10-12)

Pressure to deny the Lord still exists for those who want to live for Him. Resistance to those forces can present terrifying results—loss of jobs, relationships, or in some parts of the world, life itself. Nevertheless, Daniel's trust in the Lord to deliver him (6:23) is a model for living in a pressurized world. Hebrews 11:33 says that by faith, some, like Daniel, even "shut the mouths of lions." When the strains and pressures of life cause fear of contemporary lion pits, just as in Daniel's life, faith is the key to commitment and deliverance.

F. Daniel's Vision of the Four Beasts, the Ancient of Days and the Son of Man (7:1-28)

Daniel 7 is one of the most important chapters in the whole OT. Located at the center of the book of Daniel, it is an essential guide to biblical prophecy. Moreover, the vision of the Son of Man is the centerpiece of OT revelation concerning the Messiah.

The King's dream of the statue in chap. 2 and Daniel's vision in chap. 7 form a parenthesis (or an *inclusio*) for the Aramaic section of Daniel. Written as a parallel, the two chapters should be interpreted in light of each other (see the chart comparing the two visions near the comments on chap. 7). One reason for repeating the similar information in these two chapters is that they offer differing perspectives on the same material. Chapter 2 presents the world kingdoms from a Gentile perspective, with the use of glittering metals to show the grandeur and glory of the world kingdoms. Chapter 7 views the Gentile empires from the perspective of the Jewish people, envisioning them as violent and destructive beasts. Another reason for the repetition of the content in these two visions is to confirm the certainty of the predictions. As Joseph said, Pharaoh's dreams were repeated because "the matter is determined by God, and God will quickly bring it about" (Gn 41:32).

The vision was included in the book to give hope to Israel in captivity, informing the nation that life in the times of the Gentiles would get worse for God's covenant people, but ultimately the messianic kingdom would be established.

1. Daniel's Vision (7:1-14)

7:1. Daniel received this vision **in the first year of Belshazzar**, the Babylonian king who was overthrown in Dn 5, who became coregent with Nabonidus in 553 BC. Assuming Daniel was about 15 in 605 BC when he was exiled to Babylon, he would have received this vision when he was approximately 67 years old. The events described in this chapter preceded those of Dn 5 but were placed here at the end of the Aramaic section to form a literary *inclusio* with chap. 2.

7:2. The four winds of heaven were stirring up the great sea refers to the convulsions of the Gentile nations in the times of the Gentiles. The chapter later indicates that the sea represents "the earth" (7:17) from which the four kingdoms arise. Moreover, "the sea" is frequently symbolic of Gentile humanity in other biblical passages (Is 17:12-13; 57:20; Rv 13:1, 11; 17:1, 15).

7:3. The **four great beasts** represent the four nations (7:17) previously identified in the vision of the statue in Dn 2 (cf. 2:31-45). Here animals are used as symbols because images from the animal kingdom, even today, commonly represent nations. These four beasts are increasingly violent, perhaps indicating the growing moral degeneracy of the respective kingdoms they represent.

7:4. The **lion** with **wings of an eagle** represents the Babylonian Empire. The winged lion was a fitting symbol because some biblical passages represent Nebuchadnezzar as a lion (Jr 4:7; 49:19, 22; 50:17, 44) and others as an eagle (Jr 49:22; Lm 4:19; Ezk 17:3; Hab 1:8). The Babylonian Empire used lions to represent itself, and statues with winged lions were common there. The famous Ishtar gate of Babylon was decorated with lions. Perhaps the plucked-off wings represent Nebuchadnezzar's madness and the lion standing **on two feet like a man** and receiving **a human mind** indicates his restoration.

7:5. The lopsided **bear** with **three ribs . . . in its mouth** represents the Medo-Persian Empire and its three main conquests: Babylon (539 BC); Lydia (546 BC); and Egypt (525 BC). Its lopsided nature expresses the Persian dominance in this joint empire. Some have argued that the bear represents the Median Empire alone and not the combined Medo-Persian (cf. C. Marvin Pate and Calvin Haines, *Doomsday Delusions* [Downers Grove, IL: InterVarsity, 1995], 65; also Walton, "The Four Kingdoms of Daniel," 30–31). This is highly unlikely in that, at no time after the fall of the Neo-Babylonian Empire, did the Median empire exist as separate and distinct from the Persian empire. Moreover, the book of Daniel never views the kingdom of the Medes and the Persians as two distinct empires but consistently links them together (for example, in 8:20, the two-horned ram "represents the kings of Media and Persia," and 6:8, 15 refers to "the law of the Medes and Persians"). It would be decidedly inconsistent of Daniel to link the two empires as one in these other chaps. but view them as separate kingdoms in chaps. 2 and 7. Finally, the text of Daniel identified the successor kingdom to the Babylonians, not as the Medes, but as the Medo-Persians, when Daniel told Belshazzar, "your kingdom has been divided and given over to the Medes and Persians" (5:28). Although critical scholars and a few evangelicals have interpreted the second kingdom as just referring to the Medes alone, the overwhelming history of interpretation within both the Church and Judaism, have identified the second kingdom as Medo-Persia.

7:6. The flying **leopard** represents the Greek Empire. Its **four wings** refer to the great speed of Alexander's conquests and its **four heads** represent the four principle sections of the empire: Greece and Macedonia, Thrace and Asia Minor, Syria and Babylon, and Egypt and Israel. Some have identified the leopard as Persia, stating that "the brilliant, swift-moving armies of Cyrus defeated the ponderous, bearlike Median empire" (Pate and Haines, *Doomsday Delusions*, 66–67; Walton, "The Four Kingdoms of Daniel," 31). This view fails in that the second empire is identified throughout Daniel as the united Medo-Persian Empire (see the comments on 7:5), so this third beast must represent the kingdom of Greece. Additionally, the use of a leopard is more appropriate as a symbol for Greece than Persia in that Alexander conquered the known world in just 10 years. Cyrus, however, took approximately 30 years to complete his conquests and never did conquer Greece. That was left to his son, Cambyses II, who conquered Egypt, Nubia, and Cyrenaica after Cyrus's death. Additionally, in light of the next chapter plainly stating that Alexander's kingdom would be divided into four (8:21-22), the four heads of this beast more suitably represent the division of Alexander's Greek Empire among four generals and in four sections rather than four Persian kings (Cyrus, Artaxerxes, Xerxes, and Darius III Codomannus).

7:7. The **fourth beast**, characterized as **dreadful and terrifying**, represents the Roman Empire. This beast is only described by its external appearance in a limited way (**large iron teeth**) but more so by its fearful character. That **it devoured and crushed and trampled** points to Rome's conquests. This beast **was different** from the previous three because it was more powerful and had a longer dominion. Also, with regard to this beast, it appears that there will be a yet future or revived Roman Empire with **ten horns**, perhaps representing the ten parts of this future kingdom, much in the same way that the statue had ten toes (2:41-43). **Horns** commonly represent kings or kingdoms in Scripture (Ps 132:17; Zch 1:18; Rv 13:1; 17:12) as the angel's later interpretation plainly indicates (Dn 7:24).

As discussed in the comments at 2:31-45, the fourth kingdom continues to the end of days, when it is replaced ultimately by the kingdom of God. To explain this, some affirm that the Roman Empire has continued through its persistent influence in Western civilization, and thus will exist until the end of days and the establishment of the kingdom of God. A more likely explanation is to recognize a prophetic gap, beginning with the fall of the Roman Empire (Rome I) and lasting through the establishment of a revived Roman Empire at the end of days (Rome II).

Some have objected that it is more suitable to identify the fourth kingdom with Greece rather than Rome, with its ten horns representing the 10 independent states in the third century BC descended from the initial four divisions of Alexander's empire: Ptolemaic Egypt, Seleucia, Macedon, Pergamum, Pontus, Bithynia, Cappadocia, Armenia, Parthia, and Bactria. (Pate and Haines, *Doomsday Delusions*, 68–69; Walton, "The Four Kingdoms of Daniel," 31–33). However, in light of the above arguments for taking the second kingdom as Medo-Persia (see the comments on 7:5) and the third as Greece (see the comments on 7:6), it seems essential to view this fourth kingdom as Rome. Moreover, this kingdom "will devour the whole earth" (7:23), a more appropriate description of Rome than Greece. Additionally, in both chaps. 2 and 7, the fourth kingdom is said to be displaced by the kingdom of God (2:34-35, 44-45; 7:26-27). But the Greeks were displaced as a world power by Rome and not by the kingdom of God, making this proposed interpretation unlikely. Finally, Daniel's precise prophecies of Greece (8:8, 22; 11:3-4) do not view the Greek Empire as dividing into 10 kingdoms but into four and then focus on just two of them, the Seleucid and Ptolemaic kingdoms (11:5-35). This makes it unlikely that Daniel has the 10 successor kingdoms to the quadripartite kingdoms of Greece in view here.

7:8. Another horn, a little one represents a king from the fourth kingdom who starts small in power but becomes dominant. It appears that this king takes power gradually sometime yet in the future, in the revived Roman Empire. He extends his authority over **three of the first horns** by pulling them out **by the roots**, indicating conquest over three of the 10 fellow kings. Since the future kingdom of God destroys the little horn and replaces his fourth kingdom, the little horn's defeat of the three kings is yet future. It does not refer to Antiochus the Great and Antiochus Epiphanes' defeat of Cappadocia, Armenia, and Parthia (so Walton, "The Four Kingdoms of Daniel," 33–34). This interpretation requires the conflation of the little horn into two kings (Antiochus the Great and Antiochus IV Epiphanes), but the text describes the little horn as just one king (7:24).

The little horn's **eyes like . . . a man** indicates its shrewdness, and its **mouth uttering great boasts** points to its blasphemous boasting against God (7:25). This little horn is not to be identified as a Roman or Greek king from the past, but he is a future world ruler. Scripture calls him "the prince who is to come" (9:26), the king who "will do as he pleases" (11:36), "the man of lawlessness," "the son of destruction," (2Th 2:3), "the beast," (Rv 13:1-10), and "antichrist" (1Jn 2:18).

7:9-10. Daniel then saw God as **the Ancient of Days** (referring to His eternal nature) in blazing glory, taking His throne as judge, even as **the court** of heaven (v. 10) was convened in the presence of **myriads upon myriads** of angels. **His vesture** (clothing) **was like white snow**, indicating His holiness and moral purity (Is 1:18; Rv 1:14). His **hair** was **like pure wool**, symbolic of old age, an apt description for the eternal God. God's **throne was ablaze with flames**, indicating God's just judgment. That the throne had fiery wheels describes it as a chariot (cf. Ezk 1, 10), a common description of the thrones of both kings and gods in the ancient Near East. The **river of fire . . . flowing** from the throne demonstrates that God's wrathful judgment would be poured out upon the wicked. An innumerable number of angelic beings **were attending Him**, ready to do God's bidding. The entire scene is of the righteous Judge sitting in judgment in the **court** of heaven, with **the books . . . opened** (Ex 32:32; Dn 12:1; Lk 10:20; Rv 20:12), in which every human thought, word, or deed was recorded. Although all will stand in judgment before the Ancient of Days, the emphasis here is to promise God's righteous and wrathful judgment on the little horn and his kingdom described in the previous verses.

7:11-12. The destruction of **the beast** by **burning fire** refers to end of the fourth kingdom, the revived Roman Empire, with the return of the Messiah and the coming of His kingdom. The **rest of the beasts** would maintain some continuity even when the fourth beast has its dominance. But **the** fourth **beast**, and whatever remained of the other three beasts that preceded it, will be destroyed by **burning fire** of judgment when the Messiah comes and establishes His kingdom.

7:13-14. Having defeated and destroyed the four kingdoms of the times of the Gentiles, **the Ancient of Days** granted **One like a Son of Man** to receive **a kingdom** in which **all the peoples, nations, and men of every language might serve Him**. Although some have maintained that the Son of Man is the archangel Michael or even just a collective personification of the "saints of the

Comparison of Daniel 2 and 7

VISION	STATUE	FOUR BEASTS
CHAPTER	Two	Seven
BABYLON	Head of Gold	Winged Lion
MEDO-PERSIA	Chest and Arms of Silver	Lopsided Bear
GREECE	Belly and Thighs of Bronze	Four-Headed, Four-Winged Leopard
ROME I	Legs of Iron	The Terrifying Beast
ROME II	Feet of Iron and Clay/Ten Toes	Ten Horns on the Terrifying Beast
THE FUTURE FALSE MESSIAH		The Little Horn
GOD'S KINGDOM	The Stone Cut without Hands	The Son of Man Given the Kingdom

Highest One" (7:18), this one is none other than the divine Messiah Himself. Jesus understood it to be a messianic title (see the comments on Mt 8:18-22; Mk 14:61-62) and used it to speak of Himself. The high priest considered Jesus' usage of the title to be blasphemy (Mk 14:64), demonstrating that it was a term for deity. Later Rabbis saw it as one of the names of the Messiah (*b. Sanhedrin* 98a). The phrase **Son of Man** is used of the Messiah because He will fulfill the destiny of humanity (Ps 8; Heb 2:5-18) while at the same time being deity.

2. The Angel's Interpretation (7:15-28)

7:15-16. Alarmed by the ferocious animals in the vision, Daniel asked **one of those who were standing by**, most likely one of the myriads of angels he had seen, for help in understanding the vision. The rest of the chapter contains the angel's interpretation of Daniel's vision.

7:17-18. Having identified the four beasts as the four kingdoms, the angel indicates that **the saints of the Highest One will receive the kingdom**. Perhaps **the saints of the Highest One** refers to the faithful of all ages, but more likely it is a reference to Israel, describing the nation when it turns in faith to their Messiah Jesus (Zch 12:10; Rm 11:26). The literal covenant people will **receive the kingdom**, emphasizing that Messiah's final kingdom will be "a literal, earthly kingdom, replacing the previous empires of men" (Archer, "Daniel," 93).

7:19-24a. After Daniel requested a more in-depth interpretation of the fourth beast (7:19-22), the angel explained that the fourth kingdom, in its future state, **will devour the whole earth**, depicting world domination. The identity of the **ten kings** might not be literal but rather a figure for completeness. In light of the literal nature of the numbers in this chapter (four kingdoms, the four successor kingdoms of Greece) and the number ten's linkage with the ten toes in the dream of the great statue (2:40-43), more likely this refers to an empire with a literal confederation of **ten kings** (Rv 17:12-13).

7:24b-26. Another king, the antichrist (cf. 7:7-8), described in the vision as the little horn, will arise and take control of this last human empire by **subdu[ing] three kings**. He will be characterized by blasphemy (**speak[ing] out against the Most High**), anti-Semitism (**wear[ing] down the saints of the Highest One**), religious corruption (**he will intend to make alterations in times and in law**). His oppressive rule will last for **a time, times, and half a time**, three and one-half years, or the second half of the future tribulation (cf. Rv 7:14). Some consider that this was fulfilled when Antiochus oppressed the Jewish people from 167–164 BC. This is unlikely since that period was for only three years and not three and one-half. Since this has not yet been fulfilled, it is better to view this oppression as still future. When the heavenly **court will sit for judgment**, the antichrist **will be taken away** and **destroyed forever**.

7:27-28. The Son of Man will take His throne and rule over His **everlasting kingdom**. Then **the people of the saints of the Highest One**, namely the believing remnant of Israel, will receive this kingdom under the authority of their Messiah, the Son of Man.

Daniel was terrified as he reflected on the powerful and cruel nations that will govern the world during the times of the Gentiles. Followers of Messiah today also gasp at the totalitarian governments in various parts of the world and the persistent oppression of the Jewish people and believers in Jesus. Yet Daniel's hope as described in this chapter is still available, namely, the coming of the Son of Man in glory to establish His kingdom on earth. While great nations will arise in wickedness, the kingdom of God will be established in righteousness. With this message, the section of Daniel (chaps. 2–7) about God's sovereignty over the times of the Gentiles ends.

III. God's People Israel in the Times of the Gentiles (8:1–12:13; in Hebrew)

Having shown God's ultimate authority even when it appears that ungodly nations control the world, the book returns to the Hebrew language in Dn 8:1–12:13, and it now turns to describing God's people of Israel during the times of the Gentiles.

A. Daniel's Vision of the Ram and the Male Goat (8:1-27)

Daniel 8 does not reiterate the message about all four great kingdoms and their end-time significance (as in Dn 2 and 7). Rather, this vision predicts events about the second and third world empires and focuses on events that would take place from the sixth through the second centuries BC.

1. The Vision of the Ram and the Goat (8:1-14)

8:1. Daniel received this **vision** in **the third year of the reign Belshazzar the king** who became coregent with Nabonidus in 553 BC. Assuming Daniel was about 15 in 605 BC when he was exiled to Babylon, he would have received this vision in 550 BC when he was approximately 70 years old. Although the events in this chapter precede those described in Dn 5, they are included here because of the literary focus on Israel in the times of the Gentiles.

8:2-4. Daniel's vision places him in **Susa . . . beside the Ulai Canal**, a location not under Babylonian control but which would become the future capital of Persia. As in the previous chapter, Daniel sees a vision of animals that stand for world empires. First, he saw **a ram**, representing the Medo-Persian Empire (8:20). It **had two horns**, to represent the two nations in this confederated empire. **One was longer than the other, with the longer one coming up last**, signifying the dominant status of Persia in the empire even though it originally was the weaker kingdom. The ram in this text is comparable to the chest and arms of silver in the vision of the statue (2:32, 39) and the lopsided bear in the vision of the four beasts (7:5).

8:5. Daniel also saw **a male goat**, representing the Greek Empire with a **conspicuous horn** representing Alexander the Great (8:21). It came **from the west**, crossing **the surface of the whole earth without touching the ground**, referring to Alexander's speedy conquest of the entire Near East in only three years. The male goat, in this vision, represents the same kingdom as the belly and thighs of bronze in the vision of the statue (2:32, 39) and the four-winged and four-headed leopard in the vision of the four beasts (7:6).

8:6-7. The goat **struck the ram and shattered his two horns** indicating the Greek Empire's crushing defeat of Medo-Persia (331 BC).

8:8. Although **the male goat magnified himself**, at the height of his power, **the large horn was broken**, referring to Alexander's sudden death at the peak of his greatness (323 BC). The **four conspicuous horns** that replaced him describe Alexander's four generals (Cassander over Macedon and Greece, Lysimichus over Thrace and Asia Minor, Seleucus over Syria and Babylon, Ptolemy over Egypt) that divided the Hellenistic Empire.

8:9-12. As opposed to the little horn that would come from the fourth kingdom (Rome) described in Dn 7:8, a different **small horn** emerged out of one of the four kingdoms that divided the Greek Empire. This one was Antiochus IV Epiphanes (175–163 BC), ruler of the Seleucid dynasty, who conquered surrounding areas to **the south** and to **the east** but especially dominated **the Beautiful Land** of Israel. He **caused some of the host and some of the stars to fall . . . and . . .** [he] **trampled them**. The depiction of the host and stars provides a symbolic reference to the Jewish people (cf. Gn 22:17; 37:9). His trampling of the stars refers to Antiochus's brutal persecution of the Jewish people from 170–164 BC. Antiochus blasphemously presented himself as **equal with the Commander of the host**, God Himself (also called the "Prince of princes" in 8:25). He also stopped **regular sacrifice** and defiled God's **sanctuary**, the holy temple in Jerusalem (167 BC) by offering a swine to the pagan god Zeus on the altar in the holy of holies. He would **prosper**, but only temporarily.

8:13-14. An angel announced that the time of Antiochus's defilement of Israel would only be for **2,300 evenings and mornings**. This is a reference either to the 2,300 full days from Antiochus's appointment of the murderer Menelaus as high priest (171 BC) to the rededication of the temple under Judah Maccabee (164 BC) or to a total of 1,150 morning and 1,150 evening sacrifices from the defiling of the temple (167 BC) to its rededication (164 BC). In either case, Antiochus's defilement would last only until the temple would be rededicated by Judah Maccabee, an event still celebrated by Jewish people today during the festival of *Chanukah* (English, "dedication") (cf. Jn 10:22-23).

2. The Interpretation of the Vision (8:15-27)

8:15-16. Daniel did not understand the vision and so received the interpretation from the angel **Gabriel**, only one of two good angels (along with Michael) who are named in Scripture. Gabriel would also give the message of Daniel's 70 weeks (9:24-27) and announce the birth of John to Zechariah (Lk 1:19) and the birth of the Messiah Jesus to Mary (Lk 1:26).

8:17-22. Gabriel addressed Daniel as **son of man**, but does not use the Hebrew equivalent of the Aramaic title given to the Messiah (7:13). Rather this phrase emphasizes the human weakness and mortality of Daniel. Gabriel also indicated that the vision referred **to the time of the end** (vv. 17, 19). This might seem unexpected since the events predicted all took place between the sixth and second centuries BC and do not appear to be end-time events. But chap. 7 and 8 were intentionally placed next to each other and both mention a little horn. In this way, the author established a deliberate typological relationship—Dn 7 referring to the end-time antichrist and Dn 8 referring to the second-century BC Antiochus IV Epiphanes. While a different character, Antiochus is similar and deliberately presented as a type of the future antichrist. Readers through the ages would identify him as the little horn of Dn 8 but also recognize that he would typify the end-time antichrist. So, although Dn 8 directly referred to Antiochus, this vision pertains to the end-times as a type deliberately intended by the author of Daniel. Gabriel interpreted Daniel's vision of the beasts as explained above, to refer to the Medo-Persian and Greek Empires as well as the fourfold division of Alexander's empire.

8:23-25. After his summary explanation of Daniel's vision, Gabriel expanded his description of Antiochus. He would rise treacherously, being **skilled in intrigue**, taking the throne through deceit against the rightful heir, his nephew Demetrius. His great **power** would not be his own but have a satanic source. This demonic power would enable him to **destroy to an extraordinary degree**, devastating the land of Israel and the Jewish people. This power will cause him to **prosper and perform his will**, defeating **mighty** rulers and generals and destroying many of God's **holy people** Israel. Additionally, this king will **magnify himself** enough to oppose God, **the Prince of princes**. Nevertheless, he will ultimately and suddenly be **broken** and not by **human agency**, but rather by God. This refers to his death not through assassination or battle but by God. According to *1 Macc* 6:8-16, Antiochus IV died of sorrow and sadness in Babylon after being defeated in the battle of Elymais and also receiving word that his forces had been crushed in the land of Israel.

8:26-27. Gabriel instructed Daniel to *seal up the vision* (not to **keep the vision secret** as in the NASB). This sealing was not to hide its meaning from the faithful readers of Scripture but to secure it for safekeeping into the distant future. The predictions would need to be read for many years because the vision **pertains to many days in the future**, both the time of Antiochus, which would be some 400 years after the vision, and the time of the antichrist, which is yet future and typified by Antiochus. **Astounded at the vision**, Daniel went back to serving the king in Babylon, where he was physically present at the time of the vision.

The message of Dn 8 to the faithful of Israel was that God would indeed allow Gentile nations to be instruments of discipline of His chosen people. Nevertheless, God promised that He would also deliver them from the oppression of these Gentile nations. Followers of Messiah Jesus ought to remember this lesson, never siding with the anti-Semitism of the nations but always with the Lord, in His love and protection of His people.

B. Daniel's Prayer and Vision of the Seventy Weeks (9:1-27)

1. Daniel's Prayer of Contrition (9:1-19)

9:1. Daniel received this vision in **the first year of Darius** which was 539/538 BC. If Daniel was approximately 15 when he went into captivity, he would have been around 81 years

Antiochus IV as a Type of the Antichrist

Antiochus (8:9) and **antichrist** (7:8) are symbolized by horns that were "little" or "small" at the beginning.
Antiochus was a "stern-faced king" (8:23), and **antichrist** will have an "imposing" look (7:20).
Antiochus was "a master of intrigue" (8:23), and **antichrist's** brilliance is suggested by the "eyes" of the horn (7:8, 20).
Antiochus had great power (8:24); **antichrist** will have even greater power (11:39; 2Th 2:9; Rv 13:7-8).
Antiochus was energized by Satan (8:24); **antichrist** also will be empowered by Satan (2Th 2:9; Rv 13:2).
Antiochus destroyed thousands (8:24); **antichrist** will destroy more (Rv 13:15; 16:13-16).
Antiochus prospered for a short time (8:24); **antichrist** also will prosper for a brief period (11:36; Rv 13:7).
Antiochus persecuted the Jewish people (8:24); **antichrist** will also persecute (7:21, 25; Rv 12:13).
Antiochus was a deceiver (8:25); **antichrist** will be a master deceiver (2Th 2:9; Rv 13:4, 14; 19:20).
Antiochus was proud (8:25); **antichrist** will be a megalomaniac (7:8, 11, 20, 25; Rv 13:5).
Antiochus blasphemed God (8:25); **antichrist** will also blaspheme God (7:25; 11:36).
Antiochus was not killed by human hands (8:25), nor will the **antichrist** be (2Th 2:8; Rv 19:19-20).

old at the time of the vision. That Darius was called **the son of Ahasuerus** is not an anachronistic reference to Xerxes (485–465 BC), the later Persian king mentioned in the book of Esther (Est 1:1). The name Ahasuerus was most likely a Persian royal title rather than a personal name and refers to an ancestor of Cyrus the Great or Governor Gubaru (cf. comments on 5:31).

9:2. Although the book of **Jeremiah the prophet** was completed only a generation before the events described in Dn 9, Daniel already recognized it as Scripture, or **the word of the Lord**. Jeremiah predicted that **the desolations of Jerusalem** would last for **seventy years** (Jr 25:11-13; 29:10), so Daniel calculated that since the first captives had been taken to Babylon in 605 BC, at this time, some 67 years later, the 70 years were nearly complete.

9:3. Daniel's **prayer** was with **fasting, sackcloth and ashes**, three customary ways to express contrition (Ezr 8:23; Neh 9:1; Est 4:1, 3, 16; Jb 2:12; Jnh 3:5-6).

9:4-19. Daniel prayed to the **Lord** his God (the Hebrew name Yahweh is translated Lord in English). This name of God is used seven times in Daniel but only in this chapter (9:2, 4, 8, 10, 13, 14 [twice], 20). Since Daniel's prayer emphasized God's faithfulness, it was appropriate to use the name Yahweh because it is associated with the covenant-keeping nature of the God of Israel (Ex 6:2-8). Daniel's prayer of contrition begins with *worship* of the covenant-keeping God (9:4), continues with *confession* of Israel's sin (9:5-14), and concludes with a strong *plea* for the Lord to deliver Israel from captivity (9:15-19). The author included this prayer not as a mere record of the humble prayer of the godly Daniel, but also as a model prayer for Israel in the times of the Gentiles and for contemporary believers to follow.

9:4. *Worship.* Daniel began his prayer by addressing God as **Lord** (*Adonai*, meaning "Master" or "Sovereign One"), glorifying Him as **great and awesome**. The word **great** refers to God's grandeur and importance while **awesome** comes from the verb "to fear," indicating God is the one to be feared. Moreover, Daniel recognized the Lord as one **who keeps His covenant**, a reference to the Abrahamic covenant in which God promised to preserve the Jewish people and provide them with a land (Gn 12:1-7; 15:18-21). Daniel acknowledges God as one who keeps **lovingkindness**, a word describing God's special characteristic of "loyal love" to those with whom He is in a covenant relationship (Dt 7:9, 12). Moreover, God's "loyal love" is frequently linked with His forgiveness and mercy (Ex 34:6-7; Ps 103:4). The covenantal and merciful aspects of God's love are prominent in this passage. Finally, these gracious benefits are for **those who love Him and keep His commandments**.

9:5-14. *Confession.* Although always faithful and obedient to the Lord, Daniel confessed the sins of the nation, notably including his own, showing his identification with the guilt of his own people.

9:5-6. Daniel began his confession of sin, specifying the nature of Judah's waywardness by citing six different characteristics of disobedience to God. (1) Daniel admitted that all Israel had **sinned**, a word that means "to miss the mark" (Jdg 20:16) of God's righteous standard. (2) Also, they had **committed iniquity**, a word that refers to being twisted or bent and indicates that they had behaved perversely or crookedly. (3) Daniel recognized that Israel had **acted wickedly**, meaning they had committed crimes against people and God. (4) Daniel said they had **rebelled**, using a word emphasizing the wickedness of knowingly disobeying God and defying Him. (5) He confessed that they were guilty of **turning aside**, a verb that refers to apostasy from God. They had done so by abandoning God's **commandments**, as found in the Mosaic law. This apostasy was the underlying problem, causing the above-mentioned sinful behaviors. (6) Additionally, Daniel confessed that the entire nation, from royalty to commoners, had **not listened** to the exhortations of God's prophets, whom God had sent as covenant enforcers, reminding them to obey the law.

9:7-8. Having confessed Israel's sins, Daniel moved to describing the consequences of those sins. He does this by contrasting God and Israel. **Righteousness** belongs to the **Lord**, meaning that God is holy in completely adhering to His own just standards. In contrast, Israel was characterized by **open shame** (vv. 7 and 8) for departing from God's holy and just requirements. While shame in English is generally an inner quality, the Hebrew word indicates public disgrace. All classes of Judah experienced disgrace by their public dispersion among the nations.

9:9. In the center of this confession, Daniel identified the sole hope upon which he and the rest of Judah could depend, namely, that while rebellion belonged to Judah, **to the Lord our God belong compassion and forgiveness**. The Hebrew word for God's **compassion** is rarely used of humanity and commonly used of God. It refers to the deep, tender love and pity that a parent feels for a child (Ps 103:13) which God in His sovereignty chooses to bestow. The word for **forgiveness** is used solely of God, never being used of human forgiveness. It refers to the pardon that God alone can provide to those who rebel against Him. Both words are plural, intensifying the expression of the depth of God's pity and pardon.

9:10-14. Daniel's confession identified the nature and consequences of Judah's disobedience as well as their only hope. Daniel also cited God's absolute justice in His discipline of Judah. God was righteous in His judgment because Israel had disregarded **the prophets** and disobeyed the **law**. As a result, God sent the nation into exile, in fulfillment of His **oath** . . . **written in the law of Moses** (Lv 26:27-33; Dt 28:63-68). The great **calamity** that befell Judah and Jerusalem was in direct fulfillment to the warnings found in the law, that if Israel failed to obey God's commandments, eventually God would "scatter [them] among all peoples, from one end of the earth to the other end of the earth" (Dt 28:64). In contemplating Judah's dispersion, Daniel expressed no bitterness toward God for their suffering, noting that **the Lord our God is righteous with respect to all His deeds which He has done**.

9:15-18. *Plea.* Daniel concluded his prayer with a plea for God to forgive and restore Judah and Jerusalem. His plaintive request is based on God's reputation and His merciful character but not on any merit found in Israel. At the outset of His plea (v. 15), Daniel reminded God of the exodus, when God had established Himself as the faithful God of the covenant, who remembered Israel and brought them **out of the land of Egypt with a mighty hand**. At that time, God had **made a name for** Himself among the nations as the God of Israel. Israel often appealed to God's reputation as the nation's Redeemer when calling upon Him to show mercy and compassion (cf. Ex 32:11-14; Nm 14:11-19). Daniel appealed to God to **turn away** His **anger** and His **wrath** from **Jerusalem** and His **holy mountain** (v. 16). Evoking the Aaronic benediction (Nm 6:24-26), he begged the **Lord**, **let Your face shine on Your desolate sanctuary** (v. 17). Despite God's justice in sending Israel into exile, Daniel pleaded with God not on the basis of Israel's **merits** but on God's **great compassion** (v. 18). God's forgiveness and restoration was not derived to be from human works but God's grace alone.

9:19. With heightened and growing passion, Daniel begged God to act. Repeating the vocative, **O Lord**, three times, Daniel importuned God to **hear**, **forgive**, **listen and take action**. Ultimately, Daniel's plea for the Lord to act without **delay** was based on Jerusalem (**Your city**) and Israel (**Your people**) being called by His **name**. Once again, God's reputation was the basis of Daniel's plea for the restoration of the Jewish people to their land.

2. Daniel's Vision of the Seventy Weeks (9:20-27)

9:20-23. While Daniel was still praying, the angel **Gabriel** appeared for a second time in the book of Daniel (8:16). Here he is called a **man**, not an angel, because he appeared in human form. He arrived at **about the time** when **the evening offering** would have been offered had the temple still stood, or between 3 and 4 p.m. Gabriel came immediately in response to Daniel's fervent and humble prayer because God **highly esteemed** Daniel.

9:24. The vision Gabriel recounted referred to a sum total of **seventy weeks**, which some

Daniel's Vision of the 70 Weeks

Israel's Sabbatical Violations	Israel's Captivity	Israel's Prophetic Destiny
70 Weeks of Years 70 x 7 = 490 Years (Lv 26:34-35, 43; 2Ch 36:21)	70 Years (Jr 25:11; 29:10)	70 Weeks of Years 70 x 7 = 490 Years (Dn 9:24-27)

Israel's Past

Daniel's Day
Dn 9:1-2

Israel's Future

Daniel's prayer looked backward

Daniel's vision looked forward

have interpreted as a symbolic number. However, in the context, at the opening of the chapter, Daniel recognized that the 70-year captivity referred to literal time (9:2). Therefore, it is more likely that the 70 weeks also refer to a literal number.

The word **weeks** in Hebrew refers to a unit of seven, or a heptad, with its meaning determined by the context. Sometimes it refers to a period of seven days but here it denotes a period of seven years. The reasons for this are (1) that in this context Daniel was concerned with years not days (9:2); (2) that in the Hebrew of Dn 10:2-3, Daniel specified that he was fasting for "three weeks of days" [literal translation] to distinguish from the weeks of years described in the previous paragraph (9:24-27); (3) that the broken covenant of the 70th week leaves three and one-half periods of desolation and destruction, and this amount of time is described as three and one-half years in parallel passages (7:25; 12:7; Rv 12:14).

Why did the message of the angel, pertaining to 490 future years, come when Daniel was pondering the end of the 70-year captivity? Judah's captivity lasted 70 years because the nation had failed to keep the sabbatical rest of the land 70 times (Lv 26:34-35, 43). Thus, 70 years of captivity provided the land with the 70 Sabbatical rests it had missed (2Ch 36:21). Therefore, the context of Daniel's considerations was not merely the 70-year captivity but the cause of that length of time, namely, 70 weeks of years (i.e., 490 years) when the land had not experienced its rest. While Daniel's prayer was focused on the past period of 70 weeks of years and the end of the 70-year captivity, the angel came with a message about the future, also about a period of 70 weeks of years. (See the chart "Daniel's Vision of the 70 Weeks.")

By the completion of the 490-year period, six objectives would be accomplished in a comprehensive way. The first three objectives pertain to dealing with sin: first, finishing **transgression** refers to bringing an end to Israel's history of rebellion against God; making **an end of sin** brings it to a halt by final judgment; and making **atonement for iniquity** refers to the Messiah's once for all death for sin. The final three relate to consummating prophetic events by bringing in a kingdom of **everlasting righteousness**, fulfilling all **vision and prophecy**, and setting apart **the most holy place** (lit., *the holy of holies*), referring to a yet future, literal, millennial temple (cf. Ezk. 40–48). All six of the purposes will be fulfilled completely for Israel by the time of the return of the Messiah and the establishment of the messianic kingdom.

9:25. The first part of the prophecy predicts that from a particular future starting point until the coming of the **Messiah the Prince**, there would be 69 weeks of years. The Hebrew word *mashiach* (**Messiah**) is commonly and accurately translated as "anointed." It is used 39 times in the Hebrew Bible, generally with another noun, such as "the anointed priest." The word also has a technical meaning, commonly translated as "the Messiah" and defined by W. H. Rose as "a future royal figure sent by God who will bring salvation to God's people and the world and establish a kingdom characterized by features such as peace and justice" (W. H. Rose, "Messiah," in *Dictionary of the Old Testament: Pentateuch*, edited by T. Desmond Alexander and David W. Baker [Downers Grove, IL: InterVarsity, 2003], 566). Although some believe that the term did not develop this technical meaning until after the close of the OT canon, this is not so. Besides its specialized usage here and in 9:26, there are at least 10 other OT passages that use the technical term "Messiah" (1Sm 2:10, 35; 2Sm 22:51; 23:1; Pss 2:2; 20:6; 28:8; 84:9; 89:51; Hab 3:13; see Michael Rydelnik, *The Messianic Hope: Is the Old Testament Really Messianic?* [Nashville: B&H Publishers, 2010], 2–3). Here the Messiah has the additional title, "the Prince." The Hebrew word means "ruler" or "leader" and derives from the idea of "one who goes before."

Some have argued (Pate and Haines, *Doomsday Delusions*, 73) that the word "anointed" cannot have a technical messianic sense in this context since it lacks the definite article. They have also maintained that the word "anointed" is more suitable for describing a priest (Lv 4:3). Furthermore, they assert that the word "prince" is also used of a priest (Neh 11:11; Jr 20:1). Thus, they conclude that this verse refers to Joshua, son of Jehozadak, the high priest after the captivity.

However, in Hebrew, proper nouns, names, or titles such as "Anointed One" or "Messiah" need not have the article. Furthermore, the Hebrew word *mashiach* was not used of a high priest "beyond the Mosaic period and whenever it was used it was always clarified by juxtaposition with the word 'priest'" (J. Paul Tanner, "Is Daniel's Seventy-Weeks Prophecy Messianic? Part 2" *BibSac* 166 [July–Sept 2009], 323)—like "the anointed priest." And while the word "prince" may be used of a priest, it is a rare usage (only three of 43 times). In fact, it is used in a prediction of the coming Messiah in Is 55:4. For these reasons, throughout the history of interpretation, overwhelmingly, the Church has understood "*mashiach nagid*" to refer to the Messiah the Prince. Ancient Judaism also understood this passage as messianic. According to the Talmud (AD sixth-century rabbinic writing), when, in the first century BC, Jonathon ben Uzziel wanted to write a Targum (paraphrastic commentary) on the Writings (including Daniel), it was said that the Bat Kol (voice of heaven) stopped him, because Daniel contained the fixed date of Messiah's coming (Megillah 3a). Although this is merely a legendary account, it demonstrates that ancient Rabbis interpreted Dn 9:24-27 as of the Messiah. It seems that only tendentious interpretation, seeking to avoid the messianic understanding, explains it otherwise.

The starting point of the prophecy is **from the issuing of a decree to restore and rebuild Jerusalem**. Some scholars who seek to minimize the messianic predictions of the OT maintain that the word "decree" is literally "word" and therefore refers to Jeremiah's prophetic word (Jr 30:18-22; 31:38-40) issued in 587 BC about Jerusalem's restoration (Pate and Haines, *Doomsday Delusion*, 72–73). This would see the fulfillment in 538 BC with Joshua the high priest under Zerubbabel. However, the Hebrew word for "decree" is *debar*, which means "a word" or "thing." In this context, it is used in the general sense of a word from a king, i.e., **a decree**, and in no way requires the interpretation of a "word" from the Lord or a prophet. Second, the passages cited from Jeremiah do not refer to the return from captivity but are eschatological, looking forward to the end-time restoration of Israel. Third, it is entirely arbitrary to choose 587 BC as the date that Jeremiah gave his oracle. In fact, even if Dn 9:25 referred to Jeremiah's prophetic word, the dating in Jr 29:1-3 indicates that the year was 597 BC, making the proposed fulfillment ten years late. Finally, at the outset of this chapter, it is clear that Daniel does not have these verses from Jeremiah in view but rather, Jr 25:11-13; 29:10, which speak of a 70-year, not a 49-year captivity.

Among those who interpret this passage as referring to Messiah, some identify this with Cyrus's decree allowing the captives to return (2Ch 36:22-23; Ezr 1:1-3) in 539/538 BC and interpret the 69 weeks of years symbolically. Thus, the period of time from the decree until the coming of the Messiah is merely described as a symbolic length of time. Three factors make this interpretation especially problematic. First, Cyrus's decree was for the captives to return to the Holy Land from Persia, not for the restoration of Jerusalem. Second, Daniel understands Jeremiah's prediction of the 70 years of captivity to be literal years and so calls into doubt treating these numbers symbolically. Third, there would be no significance to this prediction since any amount of time could be used to fulfill it.

Others suggest that the starting point is Artaxerxes' first decree in 457 BC (Ezr 7:11-26) and calculate that the 69 weeks (483 years) were fulfilled at Jesus' baptism, when He began His public ministry. However, this particular decree only provided a call for more exiles to return, the restoration of the temple's utensils, and permission to appoint civil leaders (Ezk 7:11-26). It did not include the most essential element mentioned here, namely, a decree for the restoration and rebuilding of Jerusalem.

The most likely starting point was Artaxerxes' second decree in 444 BC, authorizing Nehemiah to rebuild the walls of Jerusalem (Neh 2:1-8). This decree fits the requirement of the prediction since it was indeed for the restoration of Jerusalem. Moreover, the restoration was carried out **in times of distress** just as Daniel predicted (v. 25) and Nehemiah described (Neh 4:1–6:14).

The calculation of the prophecy is as follows: There will be a period of **seven weeks** of years (49 years) followed by **sixty-two weeks** of years (434 years), making a total of 69 weeks of years or 483 years from the decree until the coming of **Messiah the Prince**. The seven-week period (49 years) most likely pertains to the time it actually took from the issuing of the decree until the restoration of Jerusalem. The total of 483 years (69 weeks) should be calculated as specific biblical/prophetic years of 360 days each. The starting point of the prophecy would have begun on Nisan 1 (March 5), 444 BC, followed by 69 weeks of 360 day years or 173,880 days, and culminated on Nisan 10 (March 30), AD 33, the date of Jesus the Messiah's triumphal entry (Lk 19:28-40) (cf. Harold W. Hoehner, "Daniel's Seventy Weeks and New Testament Chronology," in *Chronological Aspects of the Life of Christ* [Grand Rapids, MI: Zondervan, 1977], 115–139).

Those who seek to reject the messianic interpretation deny that the **seven weeks** and the **62 weeks** are consecutive, totaling 69 weeks of years. Rather, they maintain that a Hebrew disjunctive accent mark (called an *athnach*) requires the two periods to be concurrent. Then, they date the beginning of the 62 weeks in 605 BC and see its fulfillment 434 years (62 x 7) later in 171 BC when Onias III, the high priest was murdered (Pate and Haines, *Doomsday Delusions*, 73).

In response, it seems that they build far too much on an extremely small accent. First, the Hebrew accents were added quite late—AD 800–1000—and were not part of the inspired Hebrew text. Second, the ancient versions (LXX, Theodotion, Symmachus, the Peshitta, Syriac, Vulgate) do not reflect the disjunctive accent found in the Hebrew text but treat the seven- and 62-week periods as a single period of 69 weeks. Third, although the scribes who added the accents and vowels faithfully followed Jewish tradition, it is likely that in the Rabbinic and Church Fathers eras (second-third centuries AD), polemical interaction between Christians and Jews over the messiahship of Jesus led to the adaptation of the Jewish understanding of messianic texts such as this one. It is likely that, at that time, Jewish interpreters added the disjunctive accent to avoid the identification of Jesus as Messiah the Prince. Several centuries later, Jewish scribes, seeking to consolidate the Hebrew text, incorporated the accent as the tradition that they received into the Hebrew Bible as it stands now (Roger T. Beckwith, "Daniel 9 and the Date of Messiah's Coming in Essene, Hellenistic, Pharisaic, Zealot and Early Christian Computation," *Revue de Qumrani* 10 [1979–81]: 541); Rydelnik, *The Messianic Hope*, 35-36). Thus, it is better to view, with all the ancient versions, the seven- and 62-week periods as one single 69-week period. The reason the 69 weeks were divided into two continuous periods was to recognize the purpose of the original decree (**to restore and rebuild Jerusalem**) and identify the completion of the rebuilding of Jerusalem at the end of the seven weeks of years.

9:26. The second feature of the prophecy is to predict several events that would follow the seven weeks and the **sixty-two weeks** (or the total of 69 weeks). First, **the Messiah** would **be cut off**, a prediction of the death of the Messiah. Thus, the book of Daniel, written in the sixth century BC, contains predictions not only of the precise date of the Messiah's coming (9:25) but also of the Messiah's death sometime before the destruction of Jerusalem in AD 70. This was fulfilled when Jesus the Messiah was crucified in AD 33 (AD 30 according to some interpreters, a date, however, that does not easily fit the historical conditions at the time of Jesus' death). Second, **the people of the prince who is to come** would **destroy the city** of Jerusalem and the second temple. **The prince who is to come** is distinct from **Messiah the Prince** but instead is a reference to the future ruler described as the little horn in Dn 7, also known as the beast or the antichrist. He, himself, will not be the one who destroys Jerusalem and the temple, but rather it is his people who will do it. Since previously Daniel (cf. 7:7-8) viewed this ruler as coming from the fourth major world power, or Rome, this prophecy predicts that the Romans would destroy Jerusalem, as they did in AD 70. Third, there appears to be a significant time gap from the end of the 69th week to the beginning of the 70th week, as is common in prophecy. The beginning of the 70th week is yet future.

9:27. The third part of the prophecy is the prediction of the final seven-year period, or the 70th week, which will begin when **he** (the coming prince or the antichrist) **will make a firm covenant** of peace **with the many** in the leadership of Israel. Although some consider this prince to be Christ, establishing the new covenant and ending the OT sacrificial system, it is inconceivable that Messiah would be the one who would commit the abomination of desolation. Therefore, he is more accurately identified as the antichrist, who will desecrate the future temple and stop worship in it. This covenant is yet future and will mark the beginning of a time of oppression of the Jewish people called "the time of Jacob's distress" (Jr 30:7) or the tribulation period (Mt 24:29; Mk 13:24). **In the middle of the week**, or after the first three and one-half years, the antichrist will break his covenant with Israel, leading to a time of unprecedented persecution of the Jewish people (Mt 24:21; Mk 13:19) as well as followers of Jesus (Rv 7:14) that will last for another three and one-half years (Dn 7:25; Rv 11:2-3; 12:14; 13:5).

When the antichrist breaks his covenant, he will also **put a stop to sacrifice** in the yet-to-be rebuilt temple (Dn 7:25). In desecrating the temple and declaring himself to be God (2Th 2:4; Rv 13:5-7), he is said to be one who comes **on the wing of abominations** and **makes desolate** (or as the one who commits "the abomination of desolation" (see the comments on Mt 24:15 for evidence supporting the as-yet future fulfillment of the abomination, and the unlikely fulfillment either under Antiochus or in 70 AD). The Antichrist's oppression and abominations will continue until God's decree of a **complete destruction . . . is poured out on the one who makes desolate** (11:45; Rv 19:20).

A few evangelicals have identified the coming Prince, not as the antichrist but Antiochus Epiphanes, leaving open the possibility that there would be multiple fulfillments of the same prediction, including Titus in AD 70 and the future antichrist (Pate and Haines, *Doomsday Delusion,* 74–75). However, this contradicts a basic interpretive rule that any biblical text has only one intended meaning. Second, when Jesus spoke of "the abomination of desolation" after the time of Antiochus, he viewed it as yet future (Mt 24:15). Finally, although Antiochus did indeed desecrate the second temple as a prefiguration of the future antichrist (Dn 11:31), in this verse it speaks of a desecration after the destruction of the second temple (9:26). Therefore, this indicates that the **one who makes desolate** will do so in a yet future temple, not the one that Antiochus defiled and Titus destroyed. Finally, the figure here is linked to the little horn of chap. 7. In Dn 9:27, this **one who makes desolate** breaks his covenant in the middle of the 70th week, leading to three and one-half years before the **decreed** final judgment is poured out on him. In Dn 7:25, the little horn carries out his oppression of Israel for three and one-half years. Significantly, after the judgment of the little horn, his dominion will be destroyed (7:26) and replaced by the messianic kingdom (7:27), an event not yet fulfilled in the defeats of Antiochus or Titus. Thus, identifying the **one who makes desolate** with Antiochus does not fit the context and literary evidence of the book of Daniel.

Daniel's concern at the outset of the chapter was God's restoration of the people of Israel to the land of Israel after 70 years of captivity. But God's concern was not with the past or present but with the future. Therefore, he sent an angel with a message about His prophetic program for Israel, including the Messiah's advent, death, return, and the restoration of Israel. Much like Daniel, followers of Messiah can become frustrated at the decay, desecration and corruption of contemporary society and long for God to take action immediately. Nevertheless, those who have trusted in Jesus can be encouraged that God has the big picture in view and that He will certainly fulfill His prophetic calendar and establish His kingdom on earth.

C. Daniel and His Final Vision (10:1–12:13)

The last three chapters of Daniel form a single unit, containing Daniel's final vision. Daniel 10:1–11:1 contains the description of Daniel's reception of the vision, 11:2–12:3 includes the angel's explanation of the vision, and 12:4-13 marks the angel's final instructions to Daniel regarding his prophecies. The entire three-chapter section was designed to give the faithful remnant of Israel hope and confidence during the times of the Gentiles.

1. Daniel's Reception of the Vision (10:1–11:1)

Daniel 10 functions as a prologue to the detailed vision explained in the next chapter. Although merely an introduction, it contains "important facts relative to angels and demons and their respective interests in the people and work of God" (Wood, *Daniel,* 264).

a. The Setting of the Vision (10:1-3)

10:1. Daniel received this vision **in the third year of Cyrus**, which was in 536 BC. Assuming Daniel was about 15 when taken captive (605 BC) he was approximately 84 years old at the time of this vision. The vision was about a **great conflict** in the future, described in Dn 11:2–12:3.

10:2. Possibly, Daniel **had been mourning** because of the poor conditions of the returned captives. The Samaritans were opposing reconstruction of the temple and the work had been stopped (Ezr 4:5, 24). Daniel's mourning period was **for three entire weeks**. The Hebrew text contains the words "weeks of days" to distinguish it from the weeks of years in the paragraph immediately preceding this one (9:24-27).

10:3. Daniel engaged in a partial fast, rejecting **tasty** (or rich) **food** such as **meat or wine**, recalling his decision as young man not to eat from the king's table (1:8-16). At this time, it was not because the food had been offered to the gods but as a spiritual discipline to intensify his prayers.

b. The Messenger of the Vision (10:4-9)

10:4. Daniel **was by the bank of the great river . . . the Tigris**, some 20 miles from Babylon when he received the heavenly messenger. At his advanced age of 84, Daniel had not made the difficult and demanding journey to Israel with the other Jewish returnees but instead remained in government service in Babylon.

10:5-6. Daniel saw an angel in the form of **a certain man** with a glorious appearance. This was not the pre-incarnate Messiah (despite his similarity with Christ's appearance in Rv 1:12-16) because the Messiah would not need help from the angel Michael, as this angel did.

10:7-9. The Hebrew for **I, Daniel, alone saw the vision** is emphatic: *"I saw, I, Daniel, I alone."* His companions sensed a powerful and terrifying presence but saw nothing, so they ran and hid (cf. Ac 9:3-7).

c. The Hindrances to the Vision (10:10-13)

10:10-13. As the vision came to Daniel, he was weakened and fell **into a deep sleep** (10:9). Therefore, the angel strengthened and informed Daniel that God had heard him **from the first day** of the three weeks of prayer and had immediately sent the angel to answer him. Some interpreters have identified the angel as Gabriel, an unlikely conclusion since the text does not identify him as such. The angel had only arrived after **twenty-one days** because **the prince of the kingdom of Persia** had withstood him. The Persian prince had to be supernatural to oppose this angel and evil to oppose God's purposes. Therefore, he was a demonic spirit seeking to influence Persia's political affairs and oppose God's purposes. Other biblical passages also teach of unseen spiritual forces influencing principalities and world powers (Ezk 28:11-19; 2Co 10:3-4; Eph 6:12). The angel was able to prevail over the demon associated with Persia only when the angel **Michael, one of the chief princes, came to help** him. Michael (whose name means "who is like God?") is the guardian angel of Israel (cf. Dn 10:21; 12:1; Rv 12:7) and designated an archangel in the NT (Jd 9).

d. The Purposes of the Angelic Visit (10:14–11:1)

10:14. The angel revealed that the first purpose of the vision was to reveal what would happen to Israel **in the latter days**. Although many of the predictions in Dn 11 pertain to events in the intertestamental period, they shift dramatically (11:36–12:3) to events related to the return of Christ. Even those fulfilled earlier, such as the abominations of Antiochus IV, have a deliberate typological significance to point to the last days.

10:15-19. The angel's second purpose in coming was to strengthen Daniel. Although Daniel was in **anguish** because of the vision and without **strength**, twice the angel **strengthened** him, first by his touch (10:18) and second with his words of encouragement (10:19).

10:20-21. As the angel prepared once again to **fight against the prince of Persia**, he informed Daniel that afterward he would also take up the battle against **the prince of Greece**, the demonic power seeking to control the Greek Empire and oppose God's purposes for that nation and Israel. This is an allusion to the prediction that Greece would follow Persia as the next major world power (8:4-8, 20-22). The angel's third and final purpose was to reveal **what is inscribed in the writing of truth**, a reference not to a particular earthly book but rather to God's heavenly decrees regarding the future of the nations of the world.

11:1. Although the linen-clothed angel visited Daniel "in the third year of Cyrus king of Persia" (10:1), he revealed to Daniel that he had arisen as an **encouragement and a protection** for Michael in the first year of **Darius the Mede**. Whether Darius the Mede is used as the alternate name for Cyrus or as the title of Gubaru (see the discussion at 5:31), the angel's point was that he had begun his work of encouragement and protection of Michael not when he brought word of the vision but two years earlier, in the year Cyrus began his reign (539 BC). God is concerned for and active in the political affairs of humanity and in the protection of the Jewish people.

2. The Angel's Explanation of the Vision of Persia, Greece, and the False Messiah (11:2–12:3)

Daniel 11 contains some of the most precise predictions in the entire Bible, so much so that it has led many scholars to claim that it was written as a pseudo-prophecy after the events actually took place. But if God is omniscient, knowing the end from the beginning (Is 46:10), and capable of foretelling future events, then there is no problem with predictive prophecy. The first part of the chapter predicts events in political history from Daniel's time (536 BC) until the Maccabean period (164 BC) (11:2-35). The second section of the vision contains end-time predictions of the antichrist, the tribulation, and the resurrection of humanity (11:36–12:3).

a. The Predictions of the Persian to the Maccabean Periods (11:2-35)

(1) The Predictions about the Persian Kings (11:2)

11:2. The angel predicted that there would be **three more kings . . . in Persia**, namely Cambyses (530–522 BC), Pseudo-Smerdis (522 BC), and Darius I Hystaspes (522–486 BC). Xerxes I would be the **fourth** king with **far more riches** than the others.

(2) The Predictions about Alexander the Great (11:3-4)

11:3-4. The **mighty king** predicted was Alexander the Great (336–323 BC) and, as prophesied, his kingdom was **parceled out toward the four points of the compass**, referring to the division of his empire between his four generals, rather than **his own descendants** (cf. comments on Dn 8:8).

(3) The Predictions of the Hellenistic Period (11:5-35)

These verses contain predictions covering approximately 160 years, from 323 BC to 164 BC. The predictions are limited to the Ptolemaic and the Seleucid Hellenistic kingdoms rather than all four divisions of Alexander's empire, because these two alone relate to Israel (10:14).

(a) The Period of the First Seleucids and Ptolemies (11:5-6)

11:5. The king of the South is Ptolemy I Soter (323–285 BC) of Egypt, who was outstripped by **one of his princes**, Seleucus I Nicator (311–280 BC). Seleucus I had abandoned Ptolemy I to become ruler of Babylonia, Media, and Syria, and establish the Seleucid kingdom, which surpassed in greatness that of Ptolemy's Egypt.

11:6. Tensions between the Ptolemaic and Seleucid kingdoms would continue. **The king of the South**, Ptolemy II Philadelphus (285–246 BC) would make **an alliance** with **the king of the North**, Antiochus II Theos (261–246 BC), sealing the **arrangement** by giving his **daughter**, the Ptolemaic princess Berenice, to marry Antiochus. Yet the agreement would not continue nor would Berenice **retain her position of power**, as Antiochus's former wife Laodice would murder Antiochus, Berenice, and their child.

(b) The Period of Ptolemy III (11:7-9)

11:7-9. One of Berenice's family members (lit., "a shoot from her roots"), her brother Ptolemy III Euergetes (246–221 BC) would avenge her murder by storming Antioch, **the fortress of the king of the North**, Seleucus II Callinicus (246–226 BC), and killing Laodice. Ptolemy III would even seize Seleucid **gods** and valuables and bring them back **to Egypt**.

(c) The Period of Antiochus III (11:10-19)

11:10. The **sons** of Seleucus II, Seleucus III Ceraunus (226–223 BC) and Antiochus III (223–187 BC) would **wage war up to** the Ptolemaic **fortress** Raphia in southern Israel.

11:11-12. The king of the South, Ptolemy IV Philopator (221–203 BC) of Egypt would counter-attack **the king of the North**, Antiochus III (219–218 BC). Although both would command large armies, the result would be a great victory for the Ptolemies. As a result of his success, Ptolemy IV's **heart** would become **lifted up** (arrogant) and slaughter **tens of thousands** of Seleucid troops. Nevertheless, he would not be able to maintain his dominance over the Seleucid kingdom.

11:13-15. Fifteen years later, **the king of the North**, Antiochus III, would raise an even greater army and attack the Ptolemies in Phoenicia and Israel. Antiochus III would receive support from Jewish rebels (here called **violent ones among your people**) and some Ptolemies against **the king of the South**, Ptolemy V Epiphanes (203–181 BC). Antiochus III's forces would win a resounding victory, even capturing the **well-fortified city** of Sidon (199–198 BC).

11:16-17. Antiochus III would make **the Beautiful Land** of Israel a possession of the Seleucid kingdom in 198 BC and force a peace agreement on the Ptolemies. Antiochus III would give his **daughter** Cleopatra to Ptolemy V as a wife, hoping to control the Ptolemaic kingdom through her. This failed because Cleopatra helped her Ptolemaic husband and did **not take a stand** with or support her father, Antiochus III.

11:18-19. Antiochus III would then **turn his face to the coastlands** around the Mediterranean Sea but would be defeated by the Roman **commander** Lucius Cornelius Scipio at Thermopylae (191 BC) and then Magnesia (190 BC). This would force Antiochus to focus on his own country where he would **stumble and fall and be found no more**. Antiochus tried to pillage the temple of Zeus in Elymais and was killed by a mob that was defending the temple.

(d) The Period of Seleucus IV (11:20)

11:20. The king who would arise **in his place** was Seleucus IV Philopator (187–175 BC) who would send **an oppressor**, his tax collector Heliodorus to the temple in Jerusalem (**the Jewel of his kingdom**), to collect money with which to pay the heavy indemnity he owed to Rome. After his short reign, Seleucus IV was killed **not in anger nor in battle** but by poison from his tax collector.

(e) The Period of Antiochus IV (11:21-35)

This longer section predicted the rise and reign of the despicable king Antiochus IV Epiphanes (175–163 BC), who was previously predicted as the little horn in 8:9-12, 23-25 (cf. the comments there). He is emphasized in this section for two reasons: First, he would have a terrible and oppressive effect on the Jewish people. Second, his reign is designed as a pattern of the future world ruler who would also oppress the Jewish people, namely, the antichrist.

11:21. Antiochus IV was not directly in line to be king but would nevertheless **seize the kingdom by intrigue**, while the rightful heir, Demetrius, was held in Rome. The prediction called him **a despicable person** because of his hatred of the Jewish people, his attempt to destroy Judaism, his desecration of the temple, and megalomania, calling himself by the divine title *Epiphanes* (Manifest One, Illustrious One). People of that time also called him *Epimanes* (madman).

11:22. Despite Ptolemy VI Philometor (181–146 BC) attacking with **overflowing forces**, Antiochus IV would be able to defeat them and also to depose **the prince of the covenant**, the Jewish high priest Onias III.

11:23-24. Antiochus IV would **gain power** by sharing the wealth of his conquests, distributing **plunder, booty and possessions** to his followers.

11:25-26. Referring back to the war with Ptolemy VI (11:22), the vision predicted that not only would the power of Antiochus IV defeat Ptolemy VI, but also that **schemes . . . against him** (Ptolemy VI) by his own followers would cause **his army** to be destroyed.

11:27-28. After the defeat of Ptolemy VI, Ptolemy VII took control of Egypt. Then, **both kings**, Antiochus IV and Ptolemy VI, would meet and **speak lies to each other at the same table**, to plot Ptolemy VI's restoration to the throne. After initial limited success, in **the end**, they would fail. Then, Antiochus IV, having plundered Egypt, would return to his land, with **his heart . . . set against the holy covenant**. En route home, he would attack Israel, kill 80,000 Jewish men, women, and children, and plunder the holy temple (169 BC).

11:29-30. Antiochus IV would launch another attack against Egypt but this time, **ships of Kittim** (cf. Nm 24:24), the Roman fleet led by Gaius Popilius Laenas, would force him to withdraw in humiliation.

11:31-32. Antiochus IV would once again attack Israel (167 BC) while returning to Syria, this time desecrating **the sanctuary** in Jerusalem. Antiochus would prefigure the future antichrist's actions (9:27; 12:11) by doing **away with the regular sacrifice** and committing **the abomination of desolation**, dedicating the holy temple to Zeus and offering a pig on its altar. In response, **the people who know their God will display strength and take action**, a prediction of the Maccabean revolt (cf. comments on 8:13-14).

11:33-35. The Maccabees would experience suffering in their battle with Antiochus—some would die **by sword and by flame**, while others would experience **captivity** and **plunder** (cf. Heb 11:35-38). The phrase **the end time** literally reads "time of the end" and refers to the end of Antiochus's oppression of the Jewish people, not to the end of days. At that time, the Maccabees would defeat Antiochus, rededicate the holy temple in Jerusalem, and establish the festival of Chanukah (Dedication), which the Lord Jesus celebrated (Jn 10:22) and Jewish people still observe today.

b. The Predictions of the End of Days (11:36-45)

At this point, the predictions shift away from Antiochus IV and begin to focus on the end of days. The king now in view (11:36-45) is the future antichrist, already identified as the little horn (cf. 7:8, 20) and "the prince who is to come" (9:26). Since there is no clear-cut change in 11:36, some have seen this as a continuation of the description of Antiochus. There are several reasons to see a different, end-times king in view here. First, the actions predicted of this king cannot be attributed historically to Antiochus IV. There is no evidence that Antiochus exalted and magnified "himself above every god" (v. 36), or that he showed "no regard for the gods of his fathers" (v. 37), or honored "a god whom his fathers did not know" (v. 38). Antiochus minted coins with the inscription, "King Antiochus, God Manifest" and with an image of Zeus or Apollo on the reverse side. Additionally, Antiochus was generally devoted to the Greek gods, and he specifically erected a statue of Zeus and required sacrifices to be made to it. He also advocated the worship of Dionysius in Jerusalem (*2 Macc* 6:7). Second, Antiochus IV is considered a king of the North (11:26-28), but the king in view here will be opposed both by a king of the North and South (11:40). Third, the author has already established a clear cut type/antitype relationship between Antiochus and the antichrist, calling them both "little horns" in adjoining visions. (In Dn 7 the little horn is the antichrist, and in Dn 8 the little horn is Antiochus IV—see notes on 8:17-22 and the chart on Antiochus IV on p. 1302; see also Andrew E. Steinmann, "Is the Antichrist in Daniel 11?" *BibSac* 162 [April–June 2005], 195–209.)

11:36-39. This is a description of the future antichrist. He will be authoritarian (he **will do as he pleases**), self-exalting (**he will exalt and magnify himself**), blasphemous (he **will speak monstrous things against the God of gods**), temporarily successful (**he will prosper until the indignation is finished**), irreligious (**he will show no regard for the gods of his fathers**), opposed to Christ (will show no regard **for the desire of women**, a reference the longing of Jewish women to give birth to the Messiah), warlike (**he will honor a god of fortresses**), and manipulative (**he will give great honor to those who acknowledge him . . . parcel[ing] out land for a price**, lit., "as a reward").

11:40-44. During the great tribulation, the antichrist will engage in world war. Attacked in a pincer movement from both the North and the South, he will still be successful, entering **countries** and conquering them. **He will also enter** Israel, **the Beautiful Land**, ignoring some nations that are in alliance with him but conquering others, including **Egypt**, Libya, and Sudan (NASB **Ethiopians** but literally "Cushites" referring to Sudan). **Rumors** of nations from **the East and from the North** coming to attack **will** both **disturb** and infuriate him, leading him to pursue a course of genocidal war against his enemies, especially **many** of the Jewish people (cf. Zch 13:8-9).

11:45. The antichrist will establish his military capital in Israel, pitching **the tents of his royal pavilion between the** Mediterranean Sea and the city of Jerusalem, situated on **the beautiful Holy Mountain**. There the nations of the earth will gather (Zch 14:2) at Mount Megiddo to begin the campaign of Armageddon (Rv 16:13-16). At that time, when the nation of Israel calls on the Messiah Jesus, He will return (Mt 23:37-39) to deliver them, and the antichrist **will come to his end, and no one will help him.**

c. The Comfort of the Chosen People (12:1-3)

12:1. At that time refers to the events predicted in the previous paragraph (11:36-45), which details the antichrist's furious attempt "to destroy and annihilate" the Jewish people (11:44). Then, the archangel **Michael . . . who stands guard over** the Jewish **people, will arise** to their defense (cf. comments on 10:12-13; Rv 12:7). This will be necessary because the great tribulation (the second half of Daniel's 70th week, Dn 9:27) will be **a time of** unprecedented **distress . . . since there was a nation**. Messiah Jesus Himself alluded to 12:1 when He said, "For then there will be a great tribulation, such as has not occurred since the beginning of the world until now, nor ever will" (Mt 24:21; see the comments there). Despite the horrific nature of the persecution of Israel, the result will be that the surviving remnant of the Jewish nation will turn in faith to their Messiah Jesus (Zch 12:10; Rm 11:25-27) and He will deliver them. These Jewish people who **will be rescued** are called those **found written in the book**, a reference to the heavenly book of life in which the names of the elect are listed (Ps 69:28; Php 4:3; Rv 13:8, 17:8, 20:15). This metaphor is derived from the ancient practice of keeping books with the names of a town's citizens written in them.

12:2. Following Israel's deliverance, there will be a resurrection of **those who sleep in the dust**, **sleep** being used as a metaphor for death. This verse does not imply any kind of soul sleep before the resurrection since the faithful go to be with God instantly upon dying (2Co 5:8; Php 1:21-23) and the faithless go to a place of suffering also immediately upon dying (Lk 16:22-23). The word **sleep** is used as a metaphor to emphasize the temporary state of death before being physically awakened at the resurrection (cf. Jn 11:11-15). All the dead will be raised, some **to everlasting life** and **others to disgrace and everlasting contempt**. Although telescoped together here (as is common in prophecy), the resurrection of the faithful and the unfaithful will be separated by the 1,000-year messianic kingdom (see the comments on Rv 20:4-6). Daniel 12:2 contains the clearest statement of resurrection in the OT, but by no means is it the only one (cf. Jb 19:25-27; Is 26:19).

12:3. Those who have insight refers to those with the wisdom to turn in faith to the Messiah Jesus and as a result, they will **lead . . . many** others to faith and thereby **to righteousness.**

3. The Angel's Final Instructions to Daniel Concerning His Prophecies (12:4-13)

This last section of Daniel's final vision functions as a conclusion to the vision and the entire book. Here the interpreting angel gave Daniel final directions for his book.

a. The Sealing of the Book (12:4)

12:4. Although it is possible that Daniel was told to **conceal these words** of the vision, a better rendering of the Hebrew is to "close up the words" **and seal up the book**, a reference to preservation of the text of Daniel **until the end of time** (or better, "the time of the end"). Preserving Daniel's prophecy was necessary because in the end of days, **many will go back and forth**, not a reference to air travel but to seeking for answers that will be found in the book of Daniel. Moreover, in that day, **knowledge will increase**, not referring to the growth of general knowledge or science in the last days, but to understanding of Daniel's prophecies, as the fulfillments of his predictions are recognized.

b. The Time of the End (12:5-13)

12:5-7. Daniel saw **two others**, meaning angels, who served as witnesses for the oath of the linen-dressed angel (10:5), two being the minimum number of witnesses necessary for an oath (Dt 19:15). One of the witnessing angels asked **how long will it be until the end** of the predicted time of distress. The angel **dressed in linen** answered that the time of the great tribulation (the second half of Daniel's 70th week) **would be for a time, times, and half a time**, or three and one-half years (Dn 7:25; Rv 12:7). By the end of the great tribulation, **the power of the holy people** Israel would be shattered, causing them to turn in faith to their long-rejected Messiah, Jesus (Zch 12:10). At that time, He will return and deliver them (Zch 14:1-21) and **all these events will be completed**.

12:8-10. Daniel's statement that he **heard but could not understand** was not that he did not comprehend that his prophecy was about the end of days but rather he did not understand how these events would precisely happen. Daniel was told to **go** on his **way** and not worry about these matters because **these words are concealed** (or better, "closed") **and sealed up until the end time** (or better, "the time of the end"). This means that they would not be fully recognized until their fulfillment at the end of days. At that time, the wicked will fail to **understand** their situation, **but those have insight will understand** the fulfillment of Daniel's words and turn in faith to the God of Israel and His Messiah Jesus. They will receive this insight as a result of the Holy Spirit sovereignly drawing them.

12:11-12. Two periods of time were revealed to Daniel. First, from the middle of the tribulation when the antichrist stops **regular sacrifice** and commits **the abomination of desolation** until the end, **there will be 1,290 days**. The great tribulation is said to be three and one-half years (12:7) or 1,260 days (Rv 12:6; 13:5). Here it is 30 days longer, probably to include time for the judgment of the nations (Mt 25:31-46). Second, a blessing awaits **he who... attains to the 1,335 days**, a period that includes not only the 30 days for judging the nations but an additional 45 days, perhaps to establish the government of the messianic kingdom. Those who enter that kingdom are said to be **blessed** because they will be part of the most glorious world, governed by its greatest king, the Lord Jesus Himself (Archer, "Daniel," 156–157).

12:13. The angel told Daniel that he was to **go** his **way**, a phrase used in 12:9, meaning to continue in unconcerned fashion, **to the end** of his life, at which point he would **rest**, a euphemism used for death. Yet, he was given the hope that he too would **rise** from the dead **at the end of the age** (12:2).

Thus, the book of Daniel ends with the hope that the times of the Gentiles will not be forever and Israel will not be eternally oppressed. Rather, its message is that God is in control of all time and will place His King on the eternal throne. All readers of this book, from Daniel's day until the present, if they have trusted in God's Messiah, Jesus, have ultimate and eternal hope. The content of that hope is that God is still the Sovereign of the universe and He will surely establish His righteous rule over the world through His divine messianic King, Jesus.

BIBLIOGRAPHY

Archer, Gleason L. "Daniel." In *The Expositor's Bible Commentary*, vol. 7, edited by Frank E. Gabelein. Grand Rapids, MI: Zondervan, 1985.

Baldwin, Joyce G. *Daniel: An Introduction and Commentary*, Tyndale Old Testament Commentaries, edited by D. J. Wiseman. Downers Grove, IL: InterVarsity, 1978.

Culver, Robert Duncan. *The Earthly Reign of Our Lord with His People*, 4th edition. Rushford, MN: Vinegar Hill Press, 1999.

Feinberg, Paul D. "An Exegetical and Theological Study of Daniel 9:24-27." In *Tradition and Testament*, edited by John S. Feinberg and Paul D. Feinberg, 189–220. Chicago: Moody, 1981.

Goldingay, John. *Daniel*, Word Biblical Commentary, edited by David A. Hubbard and Glenn W. Barker. Dallas, TX: Word, 1989.

Goldwurm, Rabbi Hersh. *Daniel: A New Translation with a Commentary Anthologized from Talmudic, Midrashic and Rabbinic Sources*, 2nd ed. Brooklyn, NY: Mesorah Publications, Ltd., 1980.

Hoehner, Harold W. "Daniel's Seventy Weeks and New Testament Chronology." In *Chronological Aspects of the Life of Christ*. Grand Rapids, MI: Zondervan, 1977.

Longman, III, Tremper. *The NIV Application Commentary: Daniel*. Grand Rapids, MI: Zondervan, 1999.

Lucas, Ernest C. *Daniel*. Apollos Old Testament Commentary, edited by David W. Baker and Gordon J. Wenham. Downers Grove, IL: InterVarsity, 2002.

Miller, Stephen R. *Daniel*. New American Commentary, edited by E. Ray Clendenen. Nashville: Broadman & Holman, 2003.

Shepherd, Michael B. *Daniel in the Context of the Hebrew Bible*. New York: Peter Lang, 2009.

Steinmann, Andrew E. "Is the Antichrist in Daniel 11?" *Bibliotheca Sacra*, 162:646 (April–June 2005), 195–209.

Tanner, J. Paul. "The Literary Structure of the Book of Daniel." *Bibliotheca Sacra*, 160:639 (July–Sept 2003), 269–82.

______. "Is Daniel's Seventy-Weeks Prophecy Messianic? Part 1." *Bibliotheca Sacra*, 166:662 (April–June 2009), 181–200.

______. "Is Daniel's Seventy-Weeks Prophecy Messianic? Part 2." *Bibliotheca Sacra*, 166:663 (July–Sept 2009), 319–35.

Wallace, Ronald S. *The Message of Daniel: The Lord is King*. The Bible Speaks Today, edited by J. A. Motyer. Downers Grove, IL: InterVarsity, 1979.

Waltke, Bruce. "The Date of the Book of Daniel." *Bibliotheca Sacra*, 133 (Oct-Dec 1976): 319–29.

Walvoord, John F. *Daniel*. The John Walvoord Prophecy Commentaries, edited by Charles H. Dyer and Philip E. Rawley. Chicago: Moody, 2012.

Wood, Leon. *A Commentary on Daniel*. Grand Rapids, MI: Zondervan, 1973.

Young, E. J. *The Prophecy of Daniel*. Grand Rapids, MI: Eerdmans, 1949.

● ● ● ●

HOSEA

JOHN K. GOODRICH

INTRODUCTION

Author and Date. Although other men in the OT have the name "Hosea," nothing is known of this prophet besides what is recorded in this book. Hosea, the son of Beeri, was a contemporary of Micah and Isaiah. According to the superscription (1:1) his prophetic ministry coincided with the reigns of several Israelite and Judean kings (Uzziah, Jeroboam II, Jotham, Ahaz, Hezekiah), spanning about 30 years (c. 755–722 BC) until the northern kingdom of Israel was besieged by Assyria (2Kg 17:1-6).

Recipients. Though Hosea brought some charges against Judah, his ministry was directed primarily toward Israel. The deteriorating political and economic climate of the northern kingdom—referred to throughout as Israel, Ephraim, and Samaria—is often apparent, as God's judgment of Israel's apostasy began to take effect and the prosperity of the nation progressively waned. Chief among Israel's sins was the nation's religious and political unfaithfulness. Seeking economic and political security, the Israelites participated in idolatry (particularly Baal worship) and made ill-advised treaties with foreign powers, thus demonstrating their lack of trust in and exclusive devotion to the Lord. To illustrate the heinousness of Israel's apostasy the metaphor of marital infidelity is employed throughout the book and in a particularly vivid way in the life of Hosea himself.

Themes. Hosea's prophecy stands at the head of the Book of the Twelve, and deservedly so. In its literary sophistication and theological significance Hosea is unsurpassed by the other Minor Prophets. Employed throughout the book are many metaphors and wordplays that expose both the utter rebelliousness of humanity and God's unwavering righteousness. Still, Hosea's frequent announcements of the Lord's retributive wrath are often immediately followed by promises of God's restorative mercy. Hosea then is a book with profound theological insights, exhibiting not only God's grief over the sin of His people but also His redemption of His beloved.

Hosea's ministry was ultimately unsuccessful. The sins with which Hosea charged Israel are those for which Israel was eventually sent into exile (2Kg 17:7-23). Yet God's sovereign control over Israel's future was never out of sight. Israel's defeat at the hands of the Assyrians was entirely a divine sentence that the nation faced strictly because God willed it to be. Even as He sought to discipline His wayward people, God always had their restoration in view. And inasmuch as God demanded genuine and heartfelt devotion from His people, covenant obedience—observance of the Mosaic law—remained the quintessential expression of Israel's love for and faithfulness toward God.

The structure of Hosea's prophecy is difficult to discern. Though the argumentation of chaps. 1–3 (which clearly stand apart from chaps. 4–14) is relatively easy to follow, this is not the case for the latter part of the book. Commentators disagree on how to outline chaps. 4–14, as Hosea includes very few structural markers in the text. The preferred way of outlining Hosea, therefore, is by way of the prophet's thematic use of cycles of judgment and restoration. Hosea employed six such cycles throughout, three in chaps. 1–3 and three in chaps. 4–14.

OUTLINE

I. Superscription (1:1)
II. Hosea's Marriage and Family (1:2–3:5)
   A. First Cycle of Judgment and Restoration Emphasizing the Children as Signs (1:2–2:1)
   B. Second Cycle of Judgment and Restoration Emphasizing the Unfaithful Wife (2:2-23)
   C. Third Cycle of Judgment and Restoration Emphasizing the Faithful Husband (3:1-5)
III. Hosea's Prophetic Oracles (4:1–14:8)
   A. Fourth Cycle of Judgment and Restoration Emphasizing Israel's Unfaithfulness (4:1–6:3)
   B. Fifth Cycle of Judgment and Restoration Emphasizing Israel's Discipline (6:4–11:11)
   C. Sixth Cycle of Judgment and Restoration Emphasizing God's Faithfulness (11:12–14:8)
IV. Postscript (14:9)

COMMENTARY ON HOSEA

I. Superscription (1:1)

1:1. The opening verse announces the book's revelatory nature and Hosea's prophetic role. **The word of the LORD which came** is a common OT idiom indicating God's communication with and through a Hebrew prophet (Jl 1:1; Mc 1:1; Zph 1:1). The name **Hosea** means "salvation of the Lord." The names of the Judean and Israelite kings reveal the historical setting of Hosea's ministry. Though the reigns of **Uzziah** (792–740 BC) and **Jeroboam** II (793–753 BC) were contemporaneous, curiously the Israelite counterparts to the Judean kings **Jotham**, **Ahaz**, and **Hezekiah** are not included, perhaps because Hosea did not recognize the legitimacy of Jeroboam's successors.

II. Hosea's Marriage and Family (1:2–3:5)

A. First Cycle of Judgment and Restoration Emphasizing the Children as Signs (1:2–2:1)

1:2-3a. Hosea's message was not only conveyed through utterances, but personified through his marriage to **a wife of harlotry** and the birth of their **children**. Hosea's relationship with his family was intended to illustrate God's troubled relationship with the Israelites (**the land**), His covenant people who through idolatry were guilty of spiritual infidelity. The noun *zenunim* ("promiscuity") denotes both Gomer's character and her profession (prostitute). Interpreters debate whether **Gomer** was sexually promiscuous before or only after her marriage to Hosea. Since the Lord's instructions suggest that Hosea was already aware of Gomer's promiscuity, and it is nearly impossible to explain how Hosea would have otherwise been able to identify a chaste woman having only tendencies toward infidelity, it seems most likely that when they married, Gomer had already had extramarital sexual encounters, and was probably practicing prostitution.

1:3b-5. The names of Hosea's three children announce God's coming judgment and restoration on Israel. **Jezreel** alludes to the town and valley bearing that name located between Galilee and Samaria, a region well known for violence. **The bloodshed of Jezreel**, then, refers to Jehu's destruction of Omri's dynasty at that site (2Kg 9:1–10:11). Since Jehu's campaign came at the Lord's direction, God's judgment on **the house of Jehu** and **the kingdom of the house of Israel** is not in response to the king's bloodshed at Jezreel, but in resemblance of it. The verb *paqad*, though often translated "punish," here means "visit or bring": "And I will *bring* the bloodshed of Jezreel upon the house of Jehu" (Duane A. Garrett, *Hosea, Joel*, NAC [Nashville: Broadman & Holman, 1997], 57). In other words Jehu's dynasty, which proved no more faithful than those whom Jehu had destroyed, would in **a little while** meet the same fate, along with the entire kingdom (2Kg 15:10).

1:6-7. Lo-ruhamah ("no mercy") reiterates God's forthcoming judgment on Israel at the hands of Assyria. The Lord's withholding of

compassion (*racham*) and refusal to **forgive** (*nasa*) Israel's sin is consistent with His character. For though the Lord is a "compassionate" (*rachum*) God who "forgives" (*nasa*) sin (Ex 34:6-7), "He will by no means leave the guilty unpunished, visiting the iniquity of fathers on the children and on the grandchildren to the third and fourth generations" (Ex 34:7). Conversely God's mercy toward **Judah** sustained the nation against the threats of Assyria, and miraculously this came about apart from military might (2Kg 19:32-36; Is 36–37).

1:8-9. Lo-ammi (not My people) signifies Israel's estrangement from God. Though most translations insert **your God** at the end of v. 9, they are not in the Hebrew. **I am not** might therefore be a negation of YHWH ("I am"), God's covenant name; thus while Israel became the Lord's people at the establishment of the Mosaic covenant (Ex 6:7; Lv 26:12) and continued to be so, there is a sense in which Israel's apostasy during these days put her in a similar category as the Gentile nations who would face God's judgment.

1:10–2:1. Immediately after God warned of Israel's coming discipline, He abruptly forecasted the judgment's total reversal. In keeping with the Abrahamic covenant, God reassured Israel of the innumerability of Abraham's progeny (Gn 22:17; 32:12), implying the nation's eventual reinstatement. This is made explicit by contrasting God's rejection of the Israelites with their inevitable restoration as **sons of the living God**. Although Paul applied this promise (with Hs 2:23) to Gentiles in Rm 9:25-26, it is a mistake to see Paul as transferring the promises made to Israel to the Church as if the Church is "the new Israel." If Israel, during Hosea's day, temporarily had a status similar to Gentiles because of their sin, then it is appropriate to apply these verses to Gentiles as well, without saying the Church replaces Israel.

The promises from Hosea spoke directly of Israel. They will be fulfilled at the end of days when God will reconcile Israel with Judah to Himself (Rm 11:25-26), creating a (re)unified nation with a single Davidic leader (Hs 3:5). Nevertheless, Hosea's words are also suitable as a description of what God is currently doing among the Gentiles. Therefore, Paul was merely applying a principle of election, that God has taken some Gentiles, who were not God's people, and by election made them into His people and placed them into the Church. That Paul did not see the Gentiles as replacing Israel is evident in the very next verses in Romans (Rm 9:27-29), where he cited Is 10:22-23 as proof that God will also choose a remnant of the sons of Israel to be saved at the end of days.

The expressions **go up from the land** and **Jezreel** ("God sows") are agricultural puns signifying the nation's prosperity (cf. 2:23). On account of God's restorative mercy, Israel will cease to be typified by the names of Hosea's children, "Lo-Ammi" and "Lo-Ruhamah," and will be redesignated **Ammi** ("My people") and **Ruhamah** ("My beloved").

B. Second Cycle of Judgment and Restoration Emphasizing the Unfaithful Wife (2:2-23)

Hosea's relationship with Gomer is recast and developed in chap. 2 as an allegory of God's punishment of Israel's infidelity. Although the metaphor extends for nearly half the chapter, Hosea and his family are basically absent from the discourse; their relationship provides only a paradigm for God's relationship with Israel.

2:2a. The command to **contend** may depict a legal proceeding. The charge probably signifies the people's need to rebuke their political and religious leaders (**your mother**). God's repudiation of His marriage to Israel does not suggest that the relationship has been completely severed since as the passage develops He will seek to bring them to repentance (2:7).

2:2b-3. God's repudiation began by calling Israelites to abandon their adulterous ways. The **face** and **breasts** symbolize sexuality; together they represent the entirety of the woman. Because adultery in Israel was a crime deserving of execution (Lv 20:10; Dt 22:22), shaming an adulteress by stripping her (a common ancient Near Eastern practice) may be a prelude to her stoning (Ezk 16:39-40). Israel's refusal to repent will reap nakedness and bareness (**wilderness . . . desert land**), representing humiliation, starvation by famine, and expulsion by exile.

2:4-5. God will withhold **compassion** from all Israel because as **children of harlotry** (1:2) each was tainted and followed in the unfaithfulness of their "mother," the nation's leaders. **Bread . . . water . . . wool . . . flax . . . oil**, and **drink** were Israel's prostitute "wages" (2:12) and represent the basic necessities of ancient life, which the Israelites foolishly supposed were supplied by other deities they worshiped (e.g., "Baal," 2:8).

2:6-8. Verse 6 introduces a series of **therefore** clauses (also in vv. 9, 14) describing God's judgment of Israel's disobedience. God sought to win the nation back by various means of discipline: (1) establishing a barrier (2:6-8); (2) withdrawing provisions (2:9-13); (3) seducing them (2:14-23). First God placed a restrictive barrier around Israel. Thorny **hedge[s]** and **wall[s]** were used in antiquity to direct human and animal traffic (Jb 3:23; 19:8; Pr 15:19; Lm 3:7, 9) and to provide protection. Historically God used Assyria to prevent Israel's access to idolatrous temples and ultimately to discredit Baal, the Canaanite deity mistaken as the source of Israel's prosperity. God's plan was to frustrate Israel so the nation might return to its **first husband** and true provider.

2:9-13. Because Israel failed to recognize God as the source of their blessings, God planned to withdraw His gifts and provisions. Material losses were in keeping with the covenant curses God had warned would be issued for disobedience (Lv 26:14-39; Dt 28:15-68). By stripping away the nation's possessions before its **lovers**, and even allowing **beasts** to **devour** them, God would humiliate Israel and expose the poverty and powerlessness of idols. God would also remove Israel's religious festivals. Though the nation worshiped idols, apparently it had not completely forsaken its religious rites. Israel's cultic calendar was observed with rejoicing and formed part of the nation's collective identity. Its removal, therefore, was cause for remorse. Moreover, God will **punish her for** (lit., "bring upon her"; cf. 1:4) the nation's idolatry. By burning incense to **the Baals** (various Canaanite deities) and thereby seeking their favor, Israel was acting like a woman who adorns herself with sensuous attire to seduce another man.

2:14. Following God's foretelling of His punishment of Israel's unfaithfulness, the Lord announced His plan to restore the nation to its previous state of privilege. God's promise to **allure** Israel, to **bring her into the wilderness and speak kindly to her**, perpetuates the courtship metaphor. Although in v. 3 the "wilderness" represents the nation's bareness as a result of judgment, here it alludes to the Egyptian desert where God established the Mosaic covenant. The imagery in v. 14 then is reminiscent of the exodus, recalling God's original betrothal to Israel and the intimacy experienced between the nation and its God (Jr 2:2).

2:15. The imagery here is reminiscent of Joshua's conquest of Canaan. Israel's **vineyards** represent the inheritance the nation received when they initially inhabited Canaan (Dt 6:11), would forfeit due to covenant disobedience (Dt 28:30, 39), and would regain when God brought the nation back from exile. **The valley of Achor** (*akor*, "trouble") was probably one of the entrances leading into the central hill country 15 miles east of Jerusalem at the northwest end of the Dead Sea. It was where the Israelites executed Achan and his household following Israel's defeat at the battle of Ai as a result of Achan's sin (Jos 7:24-26). Although Israel experienced this troublesome route when originally entering the promised land, God promised **a door of hope** for Israel's reentrance. Israel would respond (*anah*) to God at her restoration as she did when the nation responded (also *anah*) affirmatively to the terms of the covenant at Sinai (see Ex 24:3).

2:16-17. God's restoration of Israel would involve three promises that will be fulfilled **in that day**: (1) reconciliation with God (v. 16), (2) security from enemies (v. 18), and (3) abundance of resources (v. 21). In ancient Israel the Hebrew terms *ishi* ("my husband") and *baali* ("my master") were probably interchangeable when used by a woman with reference to her spouse. But at Israel's reinstatement God will forbid his bride from calling Him **Baali**, since some in Israel were apparently using the designation syncretically—referring to God as if He were merely a Canaanite deity, a *Baal*. Moreover, the invocation of the Baals will be terminated in Israel.

2:18. Israel's restoration will also bring about universal harmony. Just as **beasts** would destroy Israel's vines (v. 12), so in its restoration Israel will live peaceably with all wild animals. And though Israel would be defeated by other nations (1:5), at their restoration God's people will be made to **lie down in safety** from all foreign enemies, a chief covenantal blessing (Lv 26:6), one that will ultimately be fulfilled under the Messiah, the Son of David (see 1Ch 17:9-10). The three classes of animals mentioned are exactly those from Gn 1:26-30, while the **bow**, **sword**, and **war** were mentioned by Hosea in 1:7. In the messianic kingdom, Israel would be at peace with the entire creation: animals and humanity.

2:19-20. God again portrayed Israel's restoration as a betrothal, three times employing the verb *aras* ("to **betroth**"). The passage follows the betrothal rite of ancient Israel wherein the groom gave gifts to the bride's family to compensate for their loss of labor. The gift guaranteed the bridegroom's right to the marriage, so that "[a]cceptance of the gift or payment was tantamount to marriage under the law" (Victor H. Matthews, "Family Relationships," in *Dictionary of the Old Testament Pentateuch*, edited by T. Desmond Alexander and David W. Baker [Downers Grove, IL: InterVarsity, 2003], 295). The gifts God would give at Israel's betrothal would be distinctive. The Hebrew prefix *be*, translated **in** by most versions and appearing five times here, indicates that **righteousness** . . . **justice** . . . **lovingkindness** . . . **compassion**, and **faithfulness** were all given by God as the bride-price. These gifts, being divine attributes, function as God's pledge of Himself to Israel. Through them, God reestablishes His relationship with Israel and enables them to **know** Him intimately once more.

2:21-23. God's blessings toward Israel will also include an abundant agricultural provision. God is shown here not only to be sovereign over the forces of nature, but also (in contrast to Baal) Israel's true purveyor of produce and life. God promises to supply (the sense of **respond** here) for Israel in abundance, and to do so He need only speak. God's reinstatement of Israel will culminate in the reversal of those judgments associated with the names of Hosea's three children and previewed in 1:4, 7, 10. Here, as at 1:4, **Jezreel** ("God sows") represents Israel, though now rather than signifying the nation's destruction, the name signifies Israel's prosperity and repopulation, as God promises then to **sow her for Myself in the land**. Further, God will once again show **compassion** to the nation who previously **had not obtained compassion**, and He will accept as His **people** those He once considered **not My People**. In response Israel will declare that the Lord is indeed their **God**. As Garrett remarks, "To affirm that Yahweh is their God is to confess that he is their Savior, to submit to him as their only King, to worship him as the One who alone is worthy, and to awaken the truth that they had once rejected" (Garrett, *Hosea, Joel*, 96).

C. Third Cycle of Judgment and Restoration Emphasizing the Faithful Husband (3:1-5)

3:1. God's reinstatement of Israel is illustrated by Hosea's reconciliation with Gomer, though here she remains unnamed. Hosea's reconciliation with Gomer assumes that the two experienced a separation (judgment) in their relationship similar to the rupture described previously between God and Israel (2:2-23). Parallels between 3:1 and 1:2 are also clear. The "man" who loves the wife, in light of the Hebrew word meaning "lover" or "paramour," is probably not **her husband**, as rendered by some translations, but "another man" (ESV) with whom she commits adultery. The Hebrew word translated **yet** (*wa*) in the NASB has an explanatory rather than contrastive sense: the woman is loved by another man thus is an adulteress. Such a reading eliminates redundancy (i.e., Hosea loving Gomer, who is loved by Hosea) and creates closer parallelism between 3:1a and 3:1b: Hosea is to love a woman who is loved by another man, just as **the LORD loves the sons of Israel, though they turn to other gods**. **Raisin cakes** might have had cultic, perhaps even idolatrous, significance (2Sm 3:16). Hosea's **love** for Gomer was patterned after God's love for Israel: "It is not selfish, remorseful, or a begrudged requirement, but an excited giving of one's self to people who do not deserve to be loved" (Gary V. Smith, *Hosea, Amos, Micah*, NIVAC [Grand Rapids, MI: Zondervan], 2001).

3:2. Hosea paid a significant price in exchange for Gomer, though the specifics of the payment and the reason Gomer had to be purchased remain unclear. Perhaps as a result of Gomer's temporary abandonment by Hosea, she acquired significant debt or gave herself up to slavery. Hosea, therefore, either settled her debts or purchased her from her master. The payment was made in cash (**fifteen shekels of silver**) and goods (**barley**). The modern equivalent of **a homer and a half of barley** has been estimated to be between 300 and 400 liters. The value of 15 shekels is difficult to determine because shekels are used here as a weight of measure. However, because the approximate value of an ancient Hebrew slave was 30 shekels of silver (Ex 21:32), the payment in silver was probably worth the same amount as the barley. At any rate, Gomer's purchase price was somewhat steep, indicating Gomer's (and Israel's) great value to her husband.

3:3-4. The marital dynamics described in v. 3 are patterned after God's probationary relationship with Israel in v. 4 (**for**). Though Hosea intended again to cohabit with Gomer and the latter would cease committing harlotry, the two were to remain celibate **for many days**. This would serve as a purification period, whereby Gomer's sexual abstinence would cleanse her from previous immorality. By analogy, Israel was to be without those important political leaders (**king or prince**), the temple (**sacrifice or sacred pillar**), and priestly paraphernalia (**ephod or household idols**) that had been corrupted and thus previously hindered the nation. Israel's lack of governmental leadership and temple worship suggests a period of foreign rule and perhaps exile.

3:5. Following Israel's probationary period (**afterward**), Israel will be fully reinstated as God's people. At that time the nation will repent and will actively pursue **the LORD** and **David their king** (Dt 4:25-30). The mention of **David** is not a reference to a resurrected King David but rather to the future messianic Son of David predicted in the Davidic covenant (2Sm 7:12-16; 1Ch 17:11-14; Am 9:11-14). The nation will have the appropriate disposition toward God and the Messiah King, and fully return in faith, being fearful of His judgments and yet awestruck by **His goodness**.

III. Hosea's Prophetic Oracles (4:1–14:8)

A. Fourth Cycle of Judgment and Restoration Emphasizing Israel's Unfaithfulness (4:1–6:3)

4:1-3. Chapter 4 records God's charge of covenant unfaithfulness against Israel. Hosea imagined himself serving as an accuser in a legal proceeding between two parties. The prophet began by gaining Israel's attention and announcing that God had a **case** (a legal term, constituting a legal indictment) **against** them. In a sense, this whole section (4:1–14:8) presents God's indictment of Israel for sin. The summary of that indictment, found in this verse, is that the Israelites lacked the appropriate disposition toward God and behaved immorally toward one another. **Faithfulness . . . kindness**, and **knowledge of God** indicate devotion to the Lord and the covenant, while the five vices listed in v. 2 (**swearing, deception, murder, stealing and adultery**) are covenant prohibitions taken directly from the Ten Commandments (Ex 20:7, 13-16). The consequences (**therefore**) of Israel's covenant infidelity are covenant curses (Lv 26:4-45; Dt 28), which would affect the prosperity of **the land** as well as its human and non-human inhabitants.

4:4-6. Although v. 4 is difficult to understand, it appears that the object of God's accusation turned from the entire nation to **the priest**. Priests were Israel's spiritual leaders and teachers, but they had neglected their responsibility to educate the nation with the **knowledge** of God as revealed through the **law** (Jr 2:8). According to Dearman, "'Knowledge' in this sense refers to apprehension of and fidelity to divine instruction, the maintenance of the covenant ethos" (J. Andrew Dearman, *The Book of Hosea*, NICOT [Grand Rapids, MI: Eerdmans, 2010], 148). As a result of these priestly failures, God pronounced judgment on the priesthood and the entire nation.

4:7-8. The Levitical priesthood would multiply during times of prosperity. But, counterintuitively, the numerical growth of priests (probably witnessed during the reign of Jeroboam II) resulted in widespread spiritual laxity. Therefore rather than granting priests privileged status (**glory**) in Israel, Hosea prophesied that the priesthood would be maligned (would experience **shame**) for its sin. The image of devouring **sin** is an allusion to the priestly right of eating the sacrifices brought by the people. But rather than simply consuming sin offerings, the priests were indulging in sin itself.

4:9-11. The expression **like people, like priest** indicates that God would **punish** Israel's priesthood and bring on it the very injustices they issued to the Israelites. The activities of eating and committing harlotry probably have cultic resonances here, especially given the religious context of prostitution in vv. 13-14. Thus the priests would neither be able to satisfy their appetites nor multiply their offspring because of their failure to guard their relationship with the Lord. **Harlotry, wine and new wine** may imply a festival celebration. The proverb in v. 11 affirms that both sexual impropriety and excessive alcohol consumption impair the heart, the seat of one's mental and volitional faculties.

4:12-13a. Hosea proceeded to mock those Israelites who sought guidance from handcrafted objects (i.e., idols; cf. Is 44:9-17; Jr 10:1-16). The **spirit of harlotry** refers both literally to Israel's sexual promiscuity and metaphorically to their spiritual infidelity. Pagan worship often occurred on tree-covered **hills** (2Ch 28:4; Jr 2:20; 3:6; 17:2; Ezk 6:13), where shade was plentiful and pleasurable for the worshipers.

4:13b-14. Both married and unmarried women were prostituting themselves at the hilltop altars. However, God would withhold individual judgment on the women of Israel because Israel's men were also indulging in sacred prostitution. Therefore in a final proverbial statement God declared that He would bring ruin on all Israel for their sexual promiscuity and rejection of spiritual discernment (cf. vv. 1, 6, 11).

4:15. Assuming the spiritual waywardness of **Israel**, Hosea turned his attention to **Judah** and gave three consecutive prohibitions: the nation must (1) resist Israel's negative influence, (2) avoid **Gilgal** and **Beth-aven** (Bethel) because of their religious apostasy (Am 4:4; 5:5), and (3) refrain from taking an **oath** in the Lord's name because of the hypocrisy of outward devotion while practicing idolatry.

4:16-18. The hopeless state of Israel's spirituality was seen in their rebellion, idolatry, and moral laxity. In contrast to **a lamb** that follows without resistance (Is 53:7), Israel was a **stubborn heifer**. Here and in the remainder of the book the tribe of **Ephraim** refers metonymically, i.e., the part for the whole, in this case one tribe for the entire northern kingdom. Since Israel was **joined** as a slave **to idols**, Hosea's audience must leave Israel to their own devices. Drunkenness that leads to sex is again underscored as characteristic of the Israelites.

4:19. The wind is depicted as an agent of affliction, perhaps causing a draught in the land. The people would then suffer shame when they realized the foreign gods they were worshiping could not come to their aid.

5:1-2. An alternative reading proposed for the initial clause of v. 2 (**the revolters have gone deep in depravity**) is "a pit they have dug at Shittim." This translation (variations of which are adopted by the NRSV and the NLT) creates an exact parallelism between v. 1a and vv. 1b-2: three calls for the attention of the nation's leaders (**priests . . . house of Israel . . . house of the king**) are followed by an announcement of their **judgment**; then three charges against the places where those leaders performed injustices (**a snare at Mizpah . . . a net . . . on Tabor**, and "a pit . . . at Shittim") are followed by a second announcement of judgment (**chastise**). Mizpah was located in Benjamin, a territory that Hosea warned of judgment (5:8). Shittim, about 15 miles southwest of Jericho, was near Baal-peor, a place that Hosea was charging with sin (9:10). Not much is known about Tabor, though as a mountain it may have been the home of an idolatrous shrine.

5:3-4. The initial clause of v. 3 uses a literary exchange (A-B-A′-B′: **Ephraim . . . Israel . . . Ephraim . . . Israel**), the repetition emphasizing God's identification and awareness of the northern kingdom's disobedience. Like so many modern believers, there were some in Israel who foolishly hoped God had overlooked their sin. But though the Lord "knew" Israel, the nation did **not know** God. Knowledge of God is not merely cognitive; it is also relational and includes covenantal obedience (4:6). Thus the unrighteous **deeds** of Israel reveal their faithlessness (**a spirit of harlotry**) to the Lord, and their impenitence prevents reconciliation.

5:5-6. Hosea attributed Israel's disobedience to the **pride** (*gaon*, "arrogance") of their leaders, which had led the nation to follow its own iniquitous way. But as surely as "pride goes before destruction" (Pr 16:18), so Israel and Judah (despite the warning in Hs 4:15-19) will **stumble** and collapse as a result of their sin. They will then sacrifice **their flocks and herds** in the desperate attempt to placate **the Lord**, as they would Baal. Even so it will be too late, for God will have already **withdrawn from them**.

5:7. Israel's bearing of **illegitimate** (lit., "foreign") **children** is another metaphor for their spiritual adultery, their idolatry. To deal **treacherously against** God is to break the covenant (6:7). The **new moon** devouring Israel and their land is a reference to the approaching day of the Lord (see the comments on Jl 2:10-11), the time when God would purify the land and judge Israel's sins by sending the nation into exile. Although the day of the Lord here refers to the nation's coming temporal judgment of exile, it foreshadows the latter day judgment of the people and land of Israel prior to the Messiah's return.

5:8. A number of the descriptions in vv. 8-15 can be attributed to the Syro-Ephraimite War with Tiglath-pileser III (745–727 BC). The **horn** (*shophar*) and **trumpet** were used as military signals. Just as Hosea warned of judgment at three locations in 5:1-2, so he does here, for **Gibeah**, **Ramah**, and **Beth-aven**. These Benjamite towns, aligned vertically directly north of Jerusalem and between Judah and Ephraim, were about to suffer attack from an unnamed enemy.

5:9-10. The **desolation** of Israel was a curse for covenant disobedience (Dt 29:27; 2Kg 22:19). Isaiah linked such desolation with the day of the Lord (Is 13:9), the time of God's judgment and exile of Israel (see 5:7). Those who stole land (**who move a boundary**) were also cursed under the law (Dt 19:14; 27:17), and Judah's leaders were apparently committing comparable crimes. Thus both Ephraim and Judah deserved a flood of divine **wrath**.

5:11-12. Being **oppressed** and **crushed** by foreign powers was another curse for covenant disobedience (Dt 28:33). The **command** Israel followed was not God's law, but a foreign policy, probably the financial tribute demanded of Assyria when Israel became its client state (2Kg 15:19-20). God's destruction of Israel and **Judah** would then be **like a moth** to a garment or **rottenness** to wood or bones (Jb 13:28; Is 40:20).

5:13-15. Ephraim and **Judah** eventually observed the dire nature of their political and economic condition, if not also the gravity of their moral and spiritual perversion. Israel therefore sent embassies with tributes to **Jareb**, probably a title for the king of Assyria meaning "the great king," in exchange for aid (10:6). Since this occurred numerous times, the occasion in 5:13 is undeterminable. But despite Israel's political ploy, the cure for their ailment could not be supplied by a human king, for God was the one inflicting the wounds, **like a lion** against which there could be no defense (Dt 32:39). Moreover, God, the true King, alone possesses the ability to remedy sin and restore His covenant people. But God would withhold His presence and mercy from Israel until the nation's **affliction** caused them to repent and once again to **seek** after Him **earnestly**.

6:1-2. In view of God's temporary departure from Israel, Hosea exhorted the nation to repent and **return** to the Lord. The verbs **torn**, **heal**, and **wounded** echo their use or that of similar words in 5:13-15. Revival after **two** or three **days** indicates God's ability to reverse Israel's fortunes after just a short time (Ezk 37:1-14). Acknowledging God's role in their afflictions, Hosea confidently affirmed God's commitment to heal and restore His broken people if they would humble themselves before Him.

6:3. As noted earlier (5:4), to **know** God is relational, and Hosea called for the nation to **press on to know** Him. God's **going forth** to save and restore Israel was **as certain** as the coming of **the dawn** and seasonal **rain**, which were reversals of the judgments brought about by the new moon (5:7) and droughts (2:9; 4:3).

B. Fifth Cycle of Judgment and Restoration Emphasizing Israel's Discipline (6:4–11:11)

6:4-5. God responded to the repentance of Israel and Judah in frustration by questioning their sincerity. Their track record shows their lack of fidelity—it had appeared and then subsided **like a morning cloud** and **the dew**. Consequently God used **the prophets** to pronounce judgment on them.

6:6. Though **offerings** and sacrifices functioned as the outward expression of the Jewish faith, God stated that covenant **loyalty** (*chesed*, "kindness") and obedience (*daath*, lit., **knowledge**) are the true hallmarks of spirituality, not liturgy (1Sm 15:22; Mk 12:33). Yet Israel and Judah continued to disobey the covenant.

6:7-9. Hosea illustrated the ongoing covenant disobedience of Israel (esp. their leaders) and the disintegration of society, this time in discrete locales. **Adam** probably refers to the city of that name situated in the Jordan Valley about 18 miles northwest of Jericho. The region of **Gilead**, located east of the Jordan River, was famous for indecent behavior (Gn 31:25-26; 32; Jdg 11). **Shechem**, located in the hill country about 38 miles north of Jerusalem, was the northern kingdom's first capital (1Kg 12:1, 25). Tracks of blood and homicidal **priests** suggest that the people were committing violent crimes, which often occurred during travel (Lk 10:30).

6:10-11a. Verse 10 summarizes Israel's immorality, linking promiscuity with impurity (5:3). The **harvest appointed for** Judah is a declaration of judgment. Judah had followed right in Israel's footsteps.

6:11b–7:2. As many scholars suggest, 6:11b belongs with 7:1. The parallelism shows this to be correct: **when I restore . . . when I . . . heal**; **the iniquity of Ephraim . . . the evil deeds of Samaria**. God depicts His people as if they were pillaging His home (4:2; 6:9). Of course their sins must be **uncovered** before His people are restored. But Israel is ever forgetful that the Lord remembered their sins (5:3). In fact evil **deeds** surrounded the nation so that their sins were all that God saw.

7:3-7. This is an obscure passage that, by curiously mixing the images of baking and political deceit, probably describes the assassination of Israelite kings (2Kg 15). The unspecified subjects of v. 3 are probably two-faced political leaders of Israel who simultaneously pleased and plotted against the monarch; they joined the king in debauchery, and yet stabbed him in the back. This political scheming is compared to **the baker** (**king**) who sleeps **all night** (being consumed with **wickedness**) and thus fails **to stir up the fire** and knead his **dough**, so by morning the leaven (evil) spreads and the oven's **fire** (plotter's **anger**) rages uncontrollably. **The day of our king** (v. 5) is a royal celebration, perhaps a birthday or coronation, when **princes** drank till they **became sick** (or poisoned). When the king **stretched out his hand** to confront his plotters (perhaps for poisoning his princes), they merely mocked him. Though this is a strangely constructed metaphor, its point remains clear: because the king failed to respond to his plotters and to call on the Lord, wickedness would spread throughout the kingdom and he would eventually be overthrown.

7:8-10. Israel's assimilation with foreign **nations** was religious, political, and cultural. Israel is therefore compared to an unturned **cake** (reminiscent of the baking metaphor in vv. 3-7), because its leaders have neglected the responsibility of preserving the particularity of the nation. These **strangers** were consuming Israel like food, robbing the nation of its wealth (2Kg 15:20) and its religious and cultural identity. Israel's integration process was by no means immediate; it came about slowly and unwittingly, like **gray hairs**. Verse 10a repeats 5:5a. Israel's **pride** is their finding security in political alliances, one of their foremost sins. When Israel's trust remained in their diplomacy, it was impossible for the nation to trust God and repent.

7:11-12. Israel was as foolish and senseless (*ayin leb*, "without heart") as **a silly dove** that had left its home and could not find its way back. So it was with Israel when they made alliances with other nations (**Egypt** and **Assyria**) and failed to trust in the Lord. But much like a bird captured in a **net** and pulled back **down** to earth, Israel would be restrained from finding outside help (2:6-7). Israel's negotiations would fail and their diplomats would bring back the bad news to the community.

7:13-16. These four verses function as a single unit, bookended with general and specific declarations of judgment (vv. 13a-b, 16c). The themes of rebellion deserving of penalty (vv. 13a-b, 14, 16) and grace without repentance (vv. 13c, 15) are repeated throughout. Verses 13a and v. 13b parallel one another and emphasize God's judgment (**woe . . . destruction**) of Israel's disobedience (**strayed rebelled**). The **lies** spoken **against** God were probably spiritual in nature, and perhaps referred to Israel's syncretism and idolatry. Verse 14 forms a chiasm with Israel's abandonment of God bracketing the nation's shortcomings. Israel's remorse was supposed to be **from their heart**, and indeed wholehearted (Jl 2:12-13). To **wail on their beds** might suggest remorse without turning completely from sexual sins. Their assembling **for the sake of grain and new wine** indicates the observance of cultic, idolatrous practices. Training and strengthening Israel's **arms** is a military reference, and probably indicates God's empowering of and fighting for Israel in battle. When Israel did turn, it was not to God in repentance, but to idols, diplomacy, and other means of support. A **deceitful bow** was one that did not work correctly (Ps 78:57). In such cases the weapon, far from being helpful, became potentially dangerous to its user. Similarly Israel's leaders worked not for God but against Him. **The insolence of their tongue**, a possible reference to their illegitimate treaties, would cause God to slay Israel's **princes**. Then the Israelites themselves would be the subject of **derision in the land of Egypt**. Though some Israelites fled from the Assyrians into Egypt, Hosea often used Egypt to represent Assyria, whose exile of Israel is portrayed as a reversal of the exodus (8:13; 9:3, 6; 11:5, 11).

8:1. The trumpet (*shophar*) was used to signal danger (5:8), and here the danger (**the enemy**) is represented as **an eagle** roaming over Israel (**the house of the Lord**). Since Hosea alludes elsewhere to the exodus, the portrayal of Israel's **enemy** as an eagle may be an echo and indeed a reversal of the depiction of God as an eagle supporting Israel during their escape from Egypt (Ex 19:4; Dt 32:11). God Himself caused the attack on Israel because of the nation's violation of the Mosaic covenant.

8:2-3. Though many in Israel undoubtedly cried out to God for help while under the impression that their relationship with the Lord was still intact, their faith was fickle and insincere (7:14). God promised temporal **good** to Israel in return for obedience (Nm 10:29; Dt 30:15), but their breach of the covenant was a rejection of God's gifts and the cause of His temporary rejection of them.

8:4a. Hosea was not repudiating the monarchy in general, but only those rulers appointed illegitimately without divine approval (**not by Me**). **Know** is relational, so the complaint is that the appointees were strangers to God.

8:4b-6. The idolatry of Israel is a key theme in the book. **Idols** were worshiped to bring about material blessing for the worshiper, but in fact Israel's idolatry only incurred God's wrath. Verses 4b and 6b are parallel (**they have made idols . . . cut off**; **a craftsman made it . . . broken to pieces**) and bookend the passage. The **calf** idol of Samaria represents Baal and probably refers to the calf idol Jeroboam erected at Bethel (1Kg 12:28-29; cf. Hs 10:5-6). The incident is also reminiscent of the golden calf erected at Sinai (Ex 32). Just as Aaron ground the Sinai calf to powder (Ex 32:20), so God would break Samaria's idol to bits. That the man-made idols cannot be divine is a common prophetic announcement (Is 41:6-20; Jr 10:1-5).

8:7. This verse contains two analogies. The first employs the truism "you reap what you sow" to show how Israel's disobedience would bring about a storm, representing God's judgment through both hazardous climate and a foreign army (Jr 4:13; Am 1:14). The second analogy is similar, for it describes at once the barrenness of Israel's land and the inevitable consumption of their harvest by **strangers**, if it had produced crops. The irony of both metaphors is unmistakable: though the nation entreated Baal for abundance and security, it received infertility and political turmoil instead.

8:8-10. The verb "swallow" figuratively depicts Israel's assimilation with **the nations** (7:8). The expression **a vessel in which no one delights** is apparently a stock phrase indicating ordinariness and disposability, and is an insult to persons once held in honor (Jr 22:28). This charge is given to Israel as a result of their alliance with Assyria, since Israel had agreed to pay tribute (**hire allies**) to the Assyrian king so he would not wage war on the Israelites. Israel's alliance is likened to prostitution, which will be punished as God "gathers" (*qabats*) Israel, an expression implying judgment (see 9:6 for the same word), and as God eliminates the nation's leadership ("kings and princes").

8:11-13. The **altars** erected by Israel were intended to atone **for** their **sin**, but ironically they caused rather than removed sin. How Israel managed to use sacrifice to make matters worse is not clear. Perhaps this means that worshipers remained unrepentant, using the sacrificial system as a means of easy grace, or perhaps their religious practices had become contaminated by syncretism. Whatever the reason, they were unfamiliar with the Mosaic law (**My law**), and they treated sacrifices as mere ritual rather than as relational. Yet God delights in obedience, not sacrifice (1Sm 15:22; Hs 6:6), in sincere devotion rather than in superficial religious performance. Before God gave Israel the land, He called the nation to love Him with all their heart, soul, and might, and to demonstrate their love for Him by obeying His commandments and keeping the covenant (Dt. 6:5, 17). Therefore, when the Israelites participated in religious ceremonies without first observing the more fundamental aspects of loving and obeying the Lord, God rightfully rejected their sacrifices. In fact, rather than forgiving and forgetting Israel's transgressions (Ps 103:3-4), God held Israel responsible for their **iniquity** by reversing the exodus and sending the nation into exile (7:16).

8:14. Israel's **fortified cities** illustrate the nation's reliance on military might and failure to trust in God (Israel had **forgotten his Maker**), as did Israel's construction of **palaces** (if by **palaces** Hosea had in view something like the fortresses comparable to Herod's future residence at Masada). Nevertheless all of Israel's defenses could not withstand the attack (**fire**) that God would allow to overtake the nation. God always finds a way to pierce those very things people trust in the most.

9:1-2. When God gave Israel a harvest, the nation would celebrate (Jl 2:23-24). But here Hosea admonished Israel for even considering such festivities (Hs 9:5), for the nation had prostituted itself to idols in pursuit of a bountiful harvest (**earnings**). But in judgment God would withhold blessing so that Israel's **threshing floor and wine press** will not be able to satisfy the nation.

9:3-4. God's judgment will also result in the reversal of the exodus (**return to Egypt**, including the oppression and hardship that was associated with their time there) and Israel's exile to **Assyria**. There the nation would become **defiled** by **unclean food** (**bread** contaminated by death), which will feed them while in exile but will be of no use in worship. They will not be allowed to reenter the land (here called the **house of the Lord**).

9:5-6. Which **festival** Hosea had in view is not known, but it could be the Feast of Booths, which is associated with the harvest and twice was called **the feast of the Lord** (Lv 23:39, 41). This festival would not be celebrated since Israel **will go** into exile. Verse 6 has numerous allusions to the exodus, which Hosea declared will be reversed so that the Israelites will be buried by **Memphis** (Egyptians). **Treasures of silver** alludes to Israel's "plunder[ing] the Egyptians" (Ex 12:35-36), while **tents** recall the nation's lodging in the wilderness. Neither will be of use or value in Israel's exile.

9:7-9. The prophets were charged with madness in the OT and NT (1Sm 10:11; 2Co 5:13). Here Hosea sarcastically acknowledged the charge, for if Hosea was insane (**a fool**), it was only because Israel's sin had made him so! As **a watchman** over Israel, the prophet identified the nation's sin and warned them of impending danger (2Sm 18:24-29). In this sense the prophet brought not salvation, but judgment, resulting in **hostility** within Israel (**the house of his God**). The **depravity . . . of Gibeah**, situated about five miles north of Jerusalem, probably referred to the rape and murder of the Levite's concubine in Jdg 19.

9:10. The horticultural metaphors in v. 10a recall the exodus and express God's delight in discovering Israel's **forefathers** in no less than the infertile **wilderness**. However, the delectability of Israel quickly faded when certain Israelites were enticed by cult prostitutes at **Baal-peor** (Nm 25:1-11; Dt 4:3-4; Ps 106:28-39). By referring to Baal-peor, Hosea demonstrated the early arrival of apostasy in Israel (before they even entered the land of Israel) and likened that episode to their current apostasy.

9:11-12. Ephraim's **glory** is God Himself who will **fly away** and **depart** from Israel. God's departure will result in the Israelites' infertility and premature death (Dt 28:18, 22). Though hyperbole, the curse anticipates the difficulty of reproduction and the abbreviated lifespan of those Israelites going into exile.

9:13-14. Tyre and Israel had certain advantages (**planted in a pleasant meadow**), which were being revoked. Tyre, located about 100 miles northwest of Jerusalem on the coast of the Mediterranean, fell to the Assyrians in 722 BC, and the same would happen to Israel when the nation's **children** would die in battle. Though the nation used the sacrificial system to entreat God for gifts and blessing, God cursed Israel with infertility. As Ephraim was Joseph's second son, the curse reversed Jacob's blessing of Joseph's descendants (Gn 49:22-25).

9:15. Gilgal, immediately north of Jericho, was guilty of every Israelite sin (4:15; 12:11) and here represents all of Israel (**all their princes**). Since Gilgal is where Saul was crowned king (1Sm 11:15), the city probably symbolized Israel's rejection of God and vice versa. Thus God's hatred of Gilgal implies His general disdain for the entire nation. **I will love them no more** portrays Israel as an abandoned adulteress.

9:16-17. The withered **root** and fruitlessness of Israel indicates biological infertility (**bear children . . . the precious ones of their womb**), though famine may also be implied. Strikingly God is the agent of judgment who will **slay** Israel's children and **cast them away** from the land as **wanderers** in exile.

10:1-2. The OT frequently compares Israel to a vineyard (e.g., Is 5:1-7), and here the metaphor picks up Hosea's frequent vegetation theme. Though translations often render the verb *baqaq* positively ("to be **luxuriant**"), it is better understood negatively ("to cause to degenerate" as in the alternate reading in the NASB footnote, "Israel is a *degenerate* vine"), just as **for himself** negatively portrays Israel's intentions. The **fruit** of such a **vine** is consistent with Israel's own **heart**. Thus while God granted Israel conditions sufficient to produce abundantly, the nation bore only idolatry (**altars** and **pillars**). For the Israelites to **bear their guilt** meant they would be judged for their sin.

10:3-4. Hosea attributed speech to Israel in v. 3 in which the nation rejected its **king**. Israel's king was supposed to be God's regent; by extension rejection of the king was rejection of God Himself. Together with the vineyard metaphor, this description is analogous to Jesus' parable of the tenants ("vine-growers," Mk 12:1-11). Israel's failure to **revere** God was essentially a breach of the covenant to which the nation was giving only lip service. **Judgment** will therefore ensue as Israel was abandoned like a wretched vineyard (**field**).

10:5-6. Verse 5 illustrates the extent of the idolatry in **Beth-aven** ("house of wickedness"), another name for Bethel, by portraying those who once revered the calf idol as continuing to grieve its departure (8:6). Ironically Israel's political corruption eventually led to the removal of their idolatry through the purging that resulted from judgment. Israel realized God's punitive hand at work here, for the nation was **seized with shame** as a result of sin and judgment.

10:7-8. The judgment of Beth-aven (in the region of **Samaria**) is further elaborated as the nation and its **king** are said to be **cut off** and quickly run off like a small **stick** (perhaps better translated "foam") **on the surface of the water**. Moreover Beth-aven's **high places** of idolatry will be **destroyed** and buried by **mountains** and **hills**, which may symbolize an enemy nation (e.g., Is 42:15), namely Assyria.

10:9-10. Gibeah was mentioned earlier as a site of past sin (9:9) and forthcoming conflict (5:8). Its reference here combines both senses as Israel was indicted for sin and assured of their imminent defeat at the hands of **the peoples** (Assyria). The phrase **sons of iniquity** probably means "sons of violence." Israel's two sins (**double guilt**) are left undefined, but may refer to Gibeah's past sins or Israel's trust in both idols and armies.

10:11-13a. Here Hosea introduced another agricultural metaphor. The comparison of Israel (**Ephraim/Jacob**) to **a trained heifer** wearing God's **yoke** indicates the nation's initial readiness to obey the covenant. Having entered into a relationship with God, Israel was instructed to **sow** (obey) the seeds that would produce **righteousness**, and thus **reap** God's **kindness** (blessing). Instead the nation had **plowed wickedness** and **reaped injustice** against God and their own people.

10:13b-15. One of Israel's primary covenantal offenses is their having trusted in their military powers rather than in their God. The nation's **numerous warriors** would be defeated, its impressive **fortresses . . . destroyed**, and its **king** removed by God through the Assyrians. **Shalman** may be Shalmaneser III, the ninth-century Assyrian king. **Beth-arbel** may be modern Irbid, a city near the Sea of Galilee. The **battle** there, which included the murder of women and **children**, is not reported elsewhere in the OT.

11:1-2. The reference to Israel as a youth describes its nonfamilial status during the Egyptian captivity. At the exodus, however, Israel became God's firstborn son/heir (Ex 4:22-23), demonstrating His love (election) of the nation. In Hs 11:1 God is the One who called Israel as sons but in 11:2, Hosea cites Israel's history of resistance to God. He sent them prophets, and **the more they** (the prophets) **called them, the more they** (Israel) **went from them** (the prophets) and pursued false gods (**the Baals**). Thus even though God redeemed Israel from captivity and made them His son, the nation pursued Baals and idols.

Matthew used Hs 11:1 typologically to describe Jesus' childhood retreat to and return from Egypt (Mt 2:14-15). While it could be that Matthew was attempting to identify a simple correspondence between the infancies of Israel and Jesus, there may be more significance to Matthew's use of this passage than simply correspondence. In Nm 23:22-24 (the second Balaam oracle) and 24:5-9 (the third Balaam oracle) Moses established that Israel was a type of the future Messiah, with one point of similarity being that both Israel and her future King would come out of Egypt. Matthew may have cited Hs 11:1, a passage about Israel coming out of Egypt, with the perspective that this is typologically true of the Messiah, a point already established in the Pentateuch. Although Hosea's words refer directly to Israel, the previously established type may have enabled Matthew to cite it legitimately of Jesus the Messiah (cf. Michael Rydelnik, *The Messianic Hope: Is the Hebrew Bible Really Messianic?* [Nashville: Broadman & Holman, 2010], 99–104).

11:3-4. God's redemption (**yoke**) of Israel, the giving of the law (**taught**), and His provisions (**led** and **fed**) for them during their desert wanderings demonstrated His father-like **love** for the nation. But God's efforts went unappreciated as Israel failed to acknowledge God's grace and to reciprocate His covenant loyalty.

11:5-6. Because of Israel's disobedience and failure to repent in Hosea's day (**they refused to return**), God would punish Israel by sending the nation back into captivity, this time in **Assyria**. The **sword** represents the military forces that would **demolish** Israel's cities.

11:7-9. The Hebrew word translated **bent** (*tala*, lit., "to hang upon") indicates determination or pinning one's hopes on something. Hosea described Israel as determined to remain disobedient. Therefore when the nation called out to God (the **One on high**), He would not respond. But ignoring and surrendering Israel was not easy for the Lord, for as a compassionate father His **heart** remained with His wayward children. Even though God does not actually question His own decision-making, here Hosea used human terms to describe God's emotions in continuing to love Israel. The cities of **Admah** and **Zeoboiim** were neighbors of Sodom and Gomorrah (Gn 14:2, 8) and represent human depravity.

Although Israel's sin made the nation deserving of complete destruction in the manner of Sodom and Gomorrah, God chose not to repeat (**again**) the corporate death sentence exacted at Sodom. God's righteousness demands that sin be punished, but in His **compassions** God can choose to limit the extent of his **anger** and **wrath**.

11:10-11. God's compassion will be displayed in the return of His people from exile in **Assyria**, an event typologically resembling God's rescue of Israel from **Egypt** during the exodus. At that time Israel will follow (**walk after**) God in humility (**trembling like birds** and **doves**) as He leads them out of captivity with the ferocity of a **lion**. Hosea's prophecy of Israel's return from exile is thought by some to have been fulfilled through the events reported in Ezra and Nehemiah.

However, others see three reasons indicating that this refers to Israel's eschatological restoration. First, Hosea speaks of a return from the **west**, south (**Egypt**), and the north (**Assyria**), indicating an international regathering to the land of Israel, not just from Assyria. Second, since the prophet sees a permanent settlement in the land (**I will settle them in their houses**) he is not likely speaking of the return from captivity, which did not result in permanent settlement. Third, the nation's humble (**trembling**) **walk after the LORD** indicates a spiritual transformation that did not take place at the return from captivity but will be true in the last days (cf. 3:4-5). Hence, these verses presumably refer to God's restoration of Israel in the last days, when the nation trusts in Jesus as their Messiah and they become God's faithful people in the millennial kingdom (see Hs 3:4-5 and comments there).

C. Sixth Cycle of Judgment and Restoration Emphasizing God's Faithfulness (11:12–14:8)

11:12–12:1. Israel's deception is mentioned several times in the book (7:3; 10:13). The precise nature of Israel's **lies** is not specified, but they are probably related to the nation's waywardness and idolatry. Such covenant infidelity was characteristic of Israel's behavior and contrasted with God's faithfulness. Israel was also further charged with shepherding the **wind**, an impossibility, which illustrates Israel's foolishness. No one can corral the wind, and efforts to do so are pointless. Israel's folly is also compared to pursuing the **east wind**, which would normally be avoided because of the desert's severe dry heat. Such folly is exhibited in Israel's treaties with and tributes to **Assyria** and **Egypt**, both of whom would turn on Israel.

12:2-6. Judah was also charged with sin (cf. 11:12), for which Hosea declared that the people would be punished. Hosea then recited several incidences in the life of the patriarch **Jacob** to draw a comparison with Judah: Jacob's grabbing of Esau's **heel** at birth (Gn 25:26); Jacob's wrestling with the **angel** at Peniel (Gn 32:28); Jacob's weeping at his reunion with Esau (Gn 33:4); Jacob's encountering God at **Bethel** (Gn 28:11-22). These allusions to the shortcomings and eventual blessings of Jacob are recalled to show how the Israelites could also overcome their disobedience and receive God's blessing if only they would repent, keep the covenant, and patiently hope in God.

12:7-9. The sin of Israel was also apparent in the nation's attaining of possessions. Like an oppressive **merchant**, some in Israel had acquired **wealth** through immoral and unjust means. Furthermore those immoral persons believed themselves to be without **iniquity**. Therefore the God who rescued them from **Egypt** and gave them the promised land was prepared to reverse the exodus by sending them back to the wilderness to **live in tents**, as they did during the Feast of Booths (Lv 23:33-43).

12:10-11. Though God's judgment in v. 9 seems quite harsh, Hosea reminded Israel that for some time God had been warning the nation of His coming retribution. These warnings had come through **the prophets**—including Hosea—even if mediated through strange **visions** and **parables**. The esoteric nature of prophecy was then exhibited through Hosea's reindictment of **Gilead** and **Gilgal**, two cities apparently well known for sin (see the comments on 6:8; 9:6) and destined for destruction.

12:12-14. Hosea introduced two more examples from Israel's early history to illustrate how the nation must now proceed: **Jacob** shepherding for two terms in exchange for a **wife** (or wives) in **Aram** (Gn 27:43–29:30); Moses (**a prophet**) shepherding **Israel** out of **Egypt** through the exodus. The brevity of the accounts, together with the inexact and inexplicit nature of their parallels, causes Hosea's purpose for including the narratives difficult to discern. The point to be illustrated is probably that, just as both Jacob and Moses labored to possess and protect a precious person/people in troubled times, so God was presently using **a prophet** (Hosea) to shepherd Israel during a turbulent period in the nation's history. The Israelites had therefore better heed the prophet's warnings! In significant contrast to those earlier events, however, God had no immediate plans to remove His people from either their current or impending hardships. Instead, God would **leave His bloodguilt on** Israel, for they had **provoked** Him **to bitter anger**.

13:1-3. The judgment of Israel stated in 12:14 is expanded in chap. 13, with the opening three verses recounting the past, present, and future of **Ephraim**. Though Ephraim by metonymy often represents the northern kingdom of Israel, here it refers to the tribe of Ephraim, though by extension it too represents all Israel.

The historical occasion behind v. 1 remains unclear, but Ephraim's initial esteem (**exalted**) among the tribes and subsequent apostasy (worshiping **Baal**) is apparent. Ephraim's **sin** and idolatry increased until the present time (**now**). Hosea exposed the folly of worshiping man-made objects (8:5-6) and may have been comparing Ephraim's idolatry to the golden calf incident at Sinai (Ex 32; 1Kg 12:20-33). Israel's future then was as fleeting as a **morning cloud** and as **dew**, **chaff**, and **smoke**, for God would suspend His covenant with the nation and punish them by removing them from the land through the Assyrian exile.

13:4-6. Hosea again recounted Israel's history in Egypt, where God called the nation into relationship with Him and became Israel's **savior**. The Lord's prohibition against "knowing" (*yada*) other gods is an allusion to the first commandment (Ex 20:3; Dt 5:7), though slightly modified to underscore the intimacy of the marital bond (**know**) between the Lord and Israel. The verb *yada* is then reemployed in v. 5 to reemphasize the intimacy with which God **cared for** (or "knew," as in NASB footnote) Israel **in the wilderness** by providing for His people. But despite God's warnings, Israel took the Lord's provisions for granted and **forgot** Him (Dt 8:11-14).

13:7-8. Israel's forgetfulness and ingratitude would cause God to judge the nation, like a **wild beast** ambushing its prey. A variety of similes used here portray the suddenness (**lie in wait**) and violence (**tear open** and **devour**) of God's coming wrath. The image of God as Israel's wilderness savior in vv. 4-5 contrasts here with God as their predator.

13:9. The form of the Hebrew verb *shachath* used here should be translated "it has destroyed you," the implied subject being the wrath of God described in vv. 7-8. Though God is Israel's "helper," the nation aligns itself **against** Him and thus reaps **destruction**.

13:10-11. The **king, judges, and princes** were all powerful political figures. The rhetorical question in v. 10 implies either that Israel currently had no ruler or that the government was ineffective. **In all your cities** implies the need for an attacking army to conquer a nation city by city. The Israelites' request for a **king and princes** demonstrates their desperation for centralized, human leadership and perhaps their lack of trust in God's rule (1Sm 8:4-20). But the monarchy was in God's complete control; He installs and removes kings at will (Dn 4:17, 25, 32; 5:21).

13:12-13. Israel's sinfulness and folly are portrayed here by the metaphor of **childbirth**. The description of Israel's **iniquity** as **bound up** and **stored up** implies the nation's retention of sin and refusal to repent. But the one who retains sin, Hosea suggested, is as foolish as a baby who refuses to exit **the womb** during labor and chooses death over life. Hosea's point is that as God's judgment approaches, Israel must rid itself of sin and thereby avoid God's wrath.

13:14a. Although many versions (such as the NASB) translate the opening two statements of v. 14 as questions, they are better interpreted as declarations: God will indeed **ransom** and **redeem** Israel from **death**. Although many individual Israelites would die in and as a result of the exile, death in this context refers primarily to God's suspension of His covenantal blessings to Israel and the removal of the nation from the land (see Lv 18:5, where "live" refers to God's provision of covenantal blessings). Thus, the two declarations lead into two rhetorical questions where the pain and fear of **Death** and **Sheol** (the afterlife) are taunted. That is because they posed no permanent threat to Israel since God would reverse His judgment on the nation and bring them out of exile in Assyria. Ultimately, at the end of days, God will bring Israel back from worldwide dispersion. Paul quoted a version of Hs 13:14a in 1Co 15:55 to highlight the defeat of physical and eschatological death through Jesus Christ's resurrection.

13:14b-16. The removal of God's **compassion** implies the exacting of His judgment, which had to occur before He would ransom the nation. Flourishing Israel was to be devastated by a desert **wind** (12:1), which would dry up the nation's water supply and agricultural resources. The **east wind** also represents the invasion of Assyria, which would **plunder** Israel's **treasury** and violently murder its **pregnant women** and children (9:12).

14:1-3. Hosea's final words to Israel begin with a call to **return** to God. Repentance was the primary condition on which God would forgive and restore Israel. Therefore Hosea instructed Israel how to be reconciled with God, giving the nation the very **words** to pray. First, the prayer has an appeal to God for His forgiveness and acceptance. Then being pardoned, Israel was to "repay" God with prayers and praise (**the fruit of our lips**). Second, the prayer contains Israel's admission to misplaced faith in political alliances (**Assyria**), military might (**horses**), and idols (**Our god**). Third, the prayer includes an affirmation of God's **mercy** toward fatherless orphans like Israel.

Hosea made no mention of Israel's need to make sin offerings to receive forgiveness. There are a couple of reasonable explanations for this. First, God was more concerned in the immediate with Israel's contrition and covenantal faithfulness, since these, and not the sacrificial system, were the conditions for Israel's restoration from the very beginning (Dt 30:2; see the comments on Hs 6:6; 8:11-13). In fact, animal sacrifices could not actually atone for sin, as the NT would later reveal (Rm 3:25; Heb 10:1-14), and without repentance every Israelite would remain liable to judgment (Rm 2:5). Second, Israel's sacrificial system itself had been corrupted. Without prior repentance, the further misuse of sacrifices would only increase sin (Hs 8:11). And even once Israel had repented, God probably desired that Israel undergo a probationary period without the privilege of offering sacrifices in order to purify it, as He did for other aspects of Israelite life following the exile (see the comments on 2:16; 3:4).

14:4. In response to Israel's contrition, God promised to **heal** and **love** the nation without their sin causing any hindrance to the relationship (2:13-23). Characterizing Israel's **apostasy** as in need of healing suggests that the nation's waywardness was caused by an underlying spiritual condition requiring divine restoration. Though Hosea did not mention it explicitly here, in the new covenant God will finally remedy this ailment by giving believers a new heart of flesh through the Holy Spirit (Ezk 36:27).

14:5-7. Dew often reflects refreshment in a dry land (see Ps 133:3), the blossoming of lilies and olive trees signifies the future **beauty** of restored Israel, and roots connote security. Sprouting **shoots**, blossoming vines, and living in the **shadow** signify the new growth and splendor (**renown**) Israel will experience in its restoration. Israel's pleasant **fragrance**, along with many of the earlier images, may portray Israel as a bride being united with a spouse (Sg 4:8-15; 5:5). **Lebanon** (northern Galilee) is mentioned three times because this region was well known for its fertile soil and fragrance.

14:8. In His final statement God expressed His desire for Israel to move beyond idolatry once and for all. God had said all He can on the subject; now He was simply waiting and watching for Israel to obey. Further, God made His rightful claim on Israel: It is the Lord, not Baal, who answers and watches over Israel, and it is He who like a tree gives them **fruit**.

IV. Postscript (14:9)

14:9. Hosea's postscript begins with a riddle that appropriately characterizes the entire book. The point of the puzzle is not that the **wise** person will **understand** these prophecies, but that those who **know** them are in fact wise. Knowledge is further clarified to mean not merely comprehension but also, as throughout the book, compliance with and relation to God. True wisdom, then, is **righteous** living in accord with God's **ways**, while folly results in transgressing and stumbling.

The message of Hosea is the story of God's jealous and yet unrelenting love for His wayward bride. A people chosen by grace and redeemed from slavery to serve the only true God, Israel failed to remain faithful to her Husband when she pursued other lovers by trusting in idols and foreign powers. God therefore promised to suspend His covenant blessings to Israel by sending the nation into exile so they would repent and appreciate God's incomparable love when He graciously accepted them back again. In this light, the message of Hosea prefigures the gospel: Only by God's grace through the work of Jesus Christ can wayward humanity be redeemed from the power of sin and death and be forever reconciled to its Creator. As Ortlund says, "The gospel is not an imperialistic human philosophy making overrated universal claims; the gospel sounds the voice of our Husband who has proven his love for us and who calls for our undivided love in return" (Raymond C. Ortlund, *God's Unfaithful Wife: A Biblical Theology of Spiritual Adultery*, New Studies in Biblical Theology [Downers Grove, IL: InterVarsity, 2002], 173). Indeed, even as readers of Hosea repeatedly encounter God's jealousy and judgment, they are always reminded of the Lord's merciful salvation available to all who will return to their faithful and forgiving God.

BIBLIOGRAPHY

Andersen, Francis I. *Hosea: A New Translation with Introduction and Commentary*. Vol. 24 of The Anchor Bible. Garden City, NY: Doubleday & Co., 1980.

Dearman, J. Andrew. *The Book of Hosea*. New International Commentary on the Old Testament. Grand Rapids, MI: Eerdmans, 2010.

Garrett, Duane A. *Hosea, Joel*. New American Commentary. Nashville: Broadman & Holman, 1997.

Macintosh, A. A. *A Critical and Exegetical Commentary on Hosea*. International Critical Commentary. Edinburgh: T&T Clark, 1997.

Matthews, Victor H. "Family Relationships." In *Dictionary of the Old Testament Pentateuch*, edited by T. Desmond Alexander and David W. Baker, 291–299. Downers Grove, IL: InterVarsity, 2003.

Ortlund, Raymond C. *God's Unfaithful Wife: A Biblical Theology of Spiritual Adultery*. New Studies in Biblical Theology. Downers Grove, IL: InterVarsity, 2002.

Rydelnik, Michael. *The Messianic Hope: Is the Hebrew Bible Really Messianic?* Nashville: Broadman & Holman, 2010.

Silva, Charles H. "The Literary Structure of Hosea 1–3." *Bibliotheca Sacra* 164 (2007): 181–97.

———. "The Literary Structure of Hosea 4–8." *Bibliotheca Sacra* 164 (2007): 291–306.

———. "The Literary Structure of Hosea 9–14." *Bibliotheca Sacra* 164 (2007): 435–53.

Smith, Gary V. *Hosea, Amos, Micah*. NIV Application Commentary. Grand Rapids, MI: Zondervan, 2001.

Stuart, Douglas. *Hosea–Jonah*. Word Biblical Commentary. Waco, TX: Word, 1987.

● ● ● ●

JOEL

MICHAEL RYDELNIK

INTRODUCTION

Author. Joel, whose name (*yoel*) means "Yahweh is God," is the author of this book (1:1). Although Joel is a common name in the OT, nothing is known of this Joel, except that he is the son of Pethuel. It is likely that Joel ministered in Jerusalem because he addressed his message to the priests and elders (1:2, 14; 2:16), and he referred to Judah, Jerusalem, and the temple (cf. 1:2, 9, 13-14, 16; 2:1, 14-15, 17, 23, 32; 3:1-8, 12, 14, 17-21). His authorship is corroborated in the NT (cf. Ac 2:16).

Joel's place among the OT Minor Prophets (called the Twelve in Hebrew) has never been seriously questioned. Joel's text in the Masoretic Text is clean and straightforward, with few textual variants and none that alter the overall message of the book. Joel is written in Hebrew poetry, like the Psalms. The language is rich in imagery, parallelism, and emotion.

Date. Because no specific dates appear in the text, the date of the book has been debated. Three possible dates are frequently proposed:

Early Preexilic Date. Some see Joel as early preexilic (ninth century BC) because Hosea and Amos are early preexilic prophets and Joel is placed between them in the Hebrew canon. Joel's references to Tyre, Sidon, Philistia, Egypt, and Edom as enemies of Judah (3:4, 19) seem to indicate an earlier date, prior to the Babylonian threat. Finally, because Joel seems to emphasize elder and priestly rule rather than a strong monarchy (1:2; 2:16; 1:9,13; 2:17) some suggest he wrote in the period of Jehoash, when the boy king was under the tutelage of the elders (835 BC; cf. 2Kg 11:1–12:21). These arguments, however, are not indisputable. The canonical position of the book is not absolutely conclusive for chronology. Also, the prophets delivered oracles against the nations mentioned, even during the Babylonian threat (cf. Jr 46–47; Ezk 27–30; Zph 2:4-7). Finally, the prophets mention elders and priests, even in periods of a strong monarchy (e.g., Is 3:14).

Postexilic Date. An alternative view dates Joel after the return from Babylonian captivity (539 BC). As support, some identify the temple Joel mentions as the postexilic sanctuary built by Zerubbabel (1:9, 13; 2:17). They also suggest that the emphasis on elder leadership (1:2; 2:16) indicates the lack of monarchy after the return from Babylon. Finally they maintain Joel's interactions with other prophets (cf. Jl 2:3 and Ezk 36:35; Jl 2:10 and Ezk 32:7; Jl 2:27-28 and Ezk 39:28-39) as evidence of the later date. However, there is no evidence that the temple is Zerubbabel's. Further, elders held powerful roles in the leadership of Judah even during the monarchy prior to the exile (cf. 2Kg 23:1; Jr 26:17). Finally, it is difficult to determine which prophet is quoting whom in closely dated literary references or parallels.

Late Preexilic Date. Dating Joel from the late preexilic period prior to the Babylonian captivity (597–587 BC) seems to have the greatest support from the text. The gathering of the nations against Judah and scattering of God's people (3:1-3) would refer to the Babylonian invasion of 587 BC, when 10,000 of Judah's finest men were deported (cf. 2Kg 24:10-16; Dn 1:1). There is no reason to question Joel's reference being to Solomon's temple (1:9, 13; 2:17) prior to the Babylonian destruction. The judgment passages are looking toward the soon coming final destruction of Jerusalem in 586 BC (cf. 2Kg 25:1-21; Jl 1:15, 2:1-11). Furthermore, Joel's prophecy of the "day of the LORD" (cf. Introduction: Theme) is parallel to other prophetic descriptions of the Babylonian destruction of Jerusalem (e.g., Jr 5:17; Lm 1:12; 2:1; Ezk 7:19; 13:5; Zph 2:2-3). Joel's mention of the slave trade with the Greeks (3:6), which flourished in the seventh and early sixth centuries, is historically linked to the late preexilic period (cf. Ezk 27:13). Thus, from the internal evidence it seems best to date the message of Joel from the late preexilic period, just prior to the Babylonian destruction of Jerusalem.

Regardless of the date of Joel, the book's message remains. Indeed, "most of what Joel has to teach we can grasp without the precise knowledge of his times . . ." (David Allan Hubbard, *Joel and Amos*, TOTC [Downers Grove, IL: InterVarsity, 1989], 23).

Recipients. The original recipients of Joel's message were the inhabitants of Judah just prior to the Babylonian invasion of Jerusalem. The message is especially to the faithful remnant of Israel, those who were open to the message of the prophet.

Purpose. The message of Joel is a call for repentance in light of the coming day of the Lord (Jl 3:1). However, the message and purpose of Joel pertain beyond preexilic Israel to all generations of God's people who await the Lord's return. The basis for Joel's call to repentance is the "gracious and compassionate" character of the Lord, who is "abounding in lovingkindness" (2:13). Joel demonstrates that salvation will come for Zion (3:17). The emphasis on Zion (2:1, 15, 23, 32; 3:17, 21) links the day of the Lord to the messianic kingdom, when Messiah Jesus will rule on David's throne in Jerusalem (cf. 2Sm 7:16; Is 9:6-7).

Theme. The "day of the LORD" is the key theological idea in Joel (mentioned five times: 1:15; 2:1, 11, 31; 3:14) as well as an important theme in the OT prophets. The phrases "that day" or "the great day" may be synonymous expressions (cf. Is 13:6, 9; Jr 46:10; Ezk 13:5; 30:3; Am 5:18-20; Ob 15; Zph 1:7, 14; Mal 4:5).

In the OT, the phrase may mean a particular temporal judgment: e.g., the Assyrian invasion of the northern kingdom (e.g., Am 5:18, 20) or the Babylonian invasion of Judah (e.g., Ezk 13:5). However, it frequently refers to a future end-time period of eschatological judgment (e.g., Is 13:6-13). The eschatological day of the Lord follows the evening and morning of the Jewish reckoning of a day, with two aspects: (1) the darkness of the Great Tribulation of the Lord's judgment (e.g., Is 2:12-19; 4:1; Mal 4:5) followed by (2) the light of blessing with the return of Messiah and His reign in the millennium (e.g., Jl 3:17-21; Is 4:2; 19:23-25).

OUTLINE

I. The Plague of Locusts (1:1-20)
   A. Call to Mourn in Light of the Coming Invasion (1:1-12)
      1. The Judgment Will Be Unique (1:1-3)
      2. The Judgment Will Be Complete (1:4-12)
   B. Call to Repentance in Light of the Coming Judgment (1:13-20)
      1. Way of Repentance: Priests Are to Mourn and Call a Solemn Assembly (1:13-14)
      2. Reason for Repentance: The Day of the Lord Is Near (1:15-20)
II. The Day of the Lord (2:1-32)
   A. Evening of the Day of the Lord: Judgment of Israel (2:1-17)
      1. Fierceness of the Lord's Army (2:1-11)
      2. Call for Repentance (2:12-17)
         a. Repentance Must Be Genuine (2:12-14)
         b. Repentance Must Include the Whole Nation of Israel (2:15-17)
   B. Morning of the Day of the Lord: Restoration of Israel (2:18-32)
      1. The Lord Is Zealous and Merciful (2:18)
      2. The Lord Will Respond to Repentance and Restore the Land (2:19-27)
      3. The Lord Will Provide Spiritual Renewal (2:28-32)
III. The Judgment of the Nations (3:1-21)
   A. The Lord Will Judge the Nations for Their Mistreatment of Israel (3:1-15)
   B. The Lord Is a Refuge for His People (3:16-17)
   C. The Lord Will Bless Judah and Jerusalem Forever (3:18-21)

COMMENTARY ON JOEL

I. The Plague of Locusts (1:1-20)

The book opens with a description of a recent locust plague that was characterized as a judgment by God. The prophet's purpose was to use this temporal judgment to prefigure the future "day of the LORD."

A. Call to Mourn in Light of the Coming Invasion (1:1-12)

1. The Judgment Will Be Unique (1:1-3)

1:1. The opening phrase **the word of the LORD that came to Joel**, indicates the prophetic nature of the message, a frequent formula in the prophets (e.g., Jr 1:2; Ezk 1:3; Hs 1:1).

1:2-3. The command to **hear** God's message is to the **elders** (the leaders of Judah) and **inhabitants of the land** of Judah. The rhetorical question, "**has anything like this** (this locust plague) **happened** before?" requires a "No" response. Its uniqueness, like the events of the exodus, should cause them to **tell** it to their **sons**, who should likewise tell **the next generation** (cf. Ex 10:2; Ps 78:4).

2. The Judgment Will Be Complete (1:4-12)

A destructive locust swarm was a familiar event in the Middle East, but it was a specific reminder of God's judgment on the Egyptians at the time of the exodus (Ex 10:1-20). Now, however, this locust swarm was in Israel, and the judgment was against God's people.

1:4-7. In describing the judgment of the **locust** invasion, the prophet first emphasized its complete destruction. The **gnawing, swarming, creeping**, and **stripping locust** (v. 4) may describe one species of locust in various stages of development or four different kinds. Regardless, they bring complete devastation as they move across the landscape, devouring every plant in their path. The call to the **drunkards** and **wine drinkers** (v. 5) may suggest that self-indulgence is disastrous. However, the emphasis is that they are to **wail** because the source of their **sweet wine** will be **cut off**, as all the vineyards have been destroyed. Likewise, ultimately everything we depend on, apart from the Lord, will not survive His judgment.

Joel described the insects poetically, as if they were a nation and not a swarm of insects (cf. Pr 30:25-26). They are **mighty and without number**, like the locust plague at the exodus (cf. Ex 10:4-6; Ps 105:34). They destroy like a **lion/lioness** who devours with **teeth/fangs**, leaving the landscape an agricultural wasteland. The image of locust as destroyers is even more graphic in the NT (cf. Rv 9:8). Identifying Israel as **my vine**, Joel used a metaphor that Isaiah used (Is 5:1-7; 27:2-6). The pronouns **my vine** and **my fig tree**, used here and throughout the book, indicate the Lord's personal relationship with His people (cf. 1:6, 13-14; 2:13-14, 17-18, 23, 26-27; 3:2-5, 17). These plants will be **stripped . . . bare**, so that they are left **white**, without even any bark remaining.

1:8-12. Having described the complete destruction of the locust plague, the prophet next emphasized the complete sorrow associated with the judgment. The people of Judah are called to **wail** as a **virgin** mourning the death of her **bridegroom** (v. 8), an expression of profound grief at the death of her husband who had died during the engagement period, since she is still a **virgin**. Additionally, **the priests** were to **mourn** (v. 9) because the locusts had destroyed the vineyards and without a grape harvest **the house of the LORD** would be without **grain** and **drink offering** (cf. Ex 29:38-42; Lv 23:13). Finally, the **farmers** and **vinedressers** (v. 11) were to **be ashamed** and **wail** because the **field [was] ruined**. This would cause the **land** to mourn, personifying the effect of the devastation (cf. Jr 23:10; Hs 4:3). There was total devastation: **field**, **land**, **grain**, **new** (grapes) **wine**, (olive) **oil**, **fig** trees, **pomegranate**, (date) **palm**, **apple** (lit., "apricot"), **all the trees . . . dry up** (v. 12). "Grain, new wine, and oil" are frequently used together to epitomize the fruitfulness of the land of Israel (cf. 2:19; Dt 7:13; 11:14; 2Ch 31:5; Neh 10:39). There was a drought along with the locust invasion so the prophet poetically stated that not only did the plants dry up, but also **rejoicing dries up from the sons of men**.

B. Call to Repentance in Light of the Coming Judgment (1:13-20)

1. Way of Repentance: Priests are to Mourn and Call a Solemn Assembly (1:13-14)

1:13-14. To **gird . . . with sackcloth** is a sign of mourning or repentance (e.g., Gn 37:34; 2Sm 3:31; Est 4:1; Is 37:1). The **priests**, as spiritual leaders, should be the first to grieve, **lament**, and **wail** for the judgment. They could not even offer the required **grain offering and the drink offering** (cf. 1:9) because the locust had destroyed the grain and grapes. Their personal relationship with the Lord is evident in that He is called **my**

God . . . your God (cf. note on 1:4-7). Not only are the priests to mourn, they are to **consecrate** (set apart) **a fast** and **a solemn assembly** to **cry out to the LORD** for mercy. Fasting was required on the Day of Atonement (cf. Lv 16:29, 31) and often during times of calamity (e.g., Jdg 20:26; 2Sm 12:16; Est 4:16; Jr 14:12). It was time for all **the elders** and **all the inhabitants of the land** to gather in the temple, **the house of the LORD your God**.

2. Reason for Repentance: The Day of the Lord Is Near (1:15-20)

Introducing the key idea of the day of the Lord (cf. Introduction: Theme), this section gives a detailed description of the aftermath of the locust plague, and introduces the idea of the day as judgment.

1:15. They are to cry out in horror, **Alas for the day!** This phrase is used to describe the locust plague as a judgment and, as such, it foreshadows the eschatological day of the Lord ("the time of Jacob's distress" [Jr. 30:7] and the day of the Lord's judgment on the nations [Ezk 30:7]) described in chaps. 2 and 3. **For the day of the LORD is near**, and it will be a time of **destruction from the Almighty** (cf. Is 13:6).

1:16-18. The plague results in the cutting off of their **food** supply and of their **gladness and joy . . . seeds shrivel** (dry up), **storehouses are desolate, the barns are torn down, for the grain is dried up**. Furthermore, **beasts** (cattle and livestock) and **sheep** would find **no pasture** and would **suffer**. Drought, as well as the devouring locusts, was destroying all food supply.

1:19-20. Judah should respond with a personal plea for mercy: **To You, O LORD, I cry** (cf. 2:32; Pss 28:1; 30:8). God's coming discipline of Judah is presented as **fire** and **flame**, a common image of judgment (e.g., 2Kg 8:12; 13:3-7; 25:8-9; Jr 4:4; 15:14; 17:27; Ezk 5:4; 15:6-7; Am 1:4, 7, 10). Just as the Lord is the source of the judgment, He is also the sole source of help. Even **beasts** (livestock and wild animals) would **pant for [Him]** (i.e., for Him to provide water) when **the water brooks are dried up**.

II. The Day of the Lord (2:1-32)

Taking a late preexilic date (see Introduction: Date) has caused some to conclude that the invasion prophesied here refers to the coming Babylonian invasion. However, the earthly and celestial upheavals (2:10-11) and incomparable nature of the judgment (2:2) more likely point to the eschatological day of the Lord. That Joel is part of the Twelve Prophets, a work compiled in the postexilic period, indicates that the prophecy was not yet considered fulfilled but seen as pointing to events in the future.

Like a "day" in the Bible, the day of the Lord would have two components, evening and morning. The evening would consist of judgment and is described in Jl 2:1-17. The day would consist of blessing, and is described in 2:18-32.

A. Evening of the Day of the Lord: Judgment of Israel (2:1-17)

1. Fierceness of the Lord's Army (2:1-11)

The invading force depicted here uses terms that might describe locusts, but the images seem to be of a literal army. This depiction links the eschatological judgment to the temporal judgment of locusts described in chap. 1.

2:1. The suddenness of judgment called for repentance. Hence, the command to **blow a trumpet** means to **sound an alarm** because of unexpected judgment (cf. Jr 4:5-6; Ezk 33:2-6) that should have made **all the inhabitants of the land tremble**. Each time the phrase **the day of the LORD is . . . near** is used, it refers to sudden and terrifying judgment (cf. Jl 1:15; 3:14; Is 13:6; Ezk 30:3; Zph 1:7, 14). The focal point of the judgment will be **in Zion**, a place name synonymous with Jerusalem (cf. 2:15; 3:17; 1Kg 8:1; Ps 2:6).

2:2. The judgment will not only be sudden but also horrific, **a day of darkness and gloom** (cf. Is 5:30; 8:22; 50:3; Jr 2:6, 31; Ezk 34:12; Am 3:6; 5:18-20). The words **clouds and thick darkness** evoke OT images of God's presence (Ex 20:18; Ps 17:2) and judgment (Jr 13:16; Zph 1:15). That judgment is expressed through an overwhelming, unparalleled military presence as pervasive as **the dawn** spreading **over the mountains**. The judgment again is described as unique: **There has never been anything like it, nor will there be again after it** (cf. Jl 1:2).

2:3. The invaders sent to judge Zion are described as coming as **fire . . . before them and behind them**, thereby alluding to the Lord's fire of judgment (e.g., Pss 50:3; 97:3; Is 66:15). The contrast of the condition of the **land** before and after judgment is like the difference between **the garden of Eden** and a **desolate wilderness** like Sodom after its destruction (cf. Gn 2:8, 15; 13:10).

2:4-5. The coming judgment will be as swift as **war horses** (cf. Jb 39:19-20; Jr 51:27) and as destructive as military **chariots**. This agile military force is able to traverse **mountains** as quickly as a **fire** consumes **stubble**. They are a **mighty** (meaning "vast in number and strength") **people arranged for battle**.

2:6-9. Everyone in the path of this army will be **in anguish**, and their **faces** will **turn pale**. The phrase **before them** is literally "before Him," indicating that the Lord is the power behind the army. These soldiers on their orderly march are compared to a swarm of locusts, who do not **break ranks** in their **rush on the city**, methodically stripping every leaf in their path. Nothing can stand in the way of this conquering force.

2:10-11. Literally, before Him (cf. 2:6 comment), identified as **the LORD** (2:11), the **earth quakes** (cf. 68:8; 77:18; Is 24:18-20; Jr 4:23-24), the **heavens tremble** (cf. Jl 3:16; Is 13:13), and the **sun**, **moon**, and **stars** will grow dark (cf. Is 13:10; Ezk 32:7; Zch 14:6-7). The Lord Himself will command **His army** (cf. Jdg 5:4; Pss 18:7; 77:18; Is 13:13; Jl 3:16) on **the day of the LORD**, making the day **great and very awesome**, just as He Himself is (cf. 2:31; Dt 7:21; Neh 1:5; 4:14; Ps 99:2; Dn 9:4).

2. Call for Repentance (2:12-17)

a. Repentance Must Be Genuine (2:12-14)

2:12-13. The Lord desires a relationship with His people. **Yet even now** He invites repentance, that none should perish (Ezk 18:23; 1Tm 2:3-4; 2Pt 3:9). **Return to Me** is a powerful call to a restored relationship (v. 12). The requirement is genuine faith with **all your heart**, not with false humility. They were to **rend [their] heart and not [their] garments** as a sign of genuine mourning for sin (cf. Pss 34:18; 51:17; Is 57:15), and not just perform the external actions of grief, like the tearing of garments, as was customary (e.g., Gn 37:34; 2Sm 1:11; Jb 1:20). The Lord wanted true repentance, indicated by **fasting** (cf. comments on 1:13-14), **weeping and mourning**.

The call to **return to the LORD your God** (v. 13) is a plea for the restoration of personal relationship. To **return** is the key OT phrase for "repentance" for sin (e.g., Dt. 30:2; 1Sm 7:3; Is 55:7; Hs 6:1). The Lord calls for repentance because **He is gracious and compassionate, slow to anger, abounding in lovingkindness** (cf. Ex 34:6-7).

2:14. The question, **who knows?** reflects the Lord's sovereign will. It leaves the possibility that after repentance the Lord could **turn and relent** concerning His plan for judgment, and He would **leave a blessing behind Him**. The offer is genuine, but is based on the requirement of repentance.

b. Repentance Must Include the Whole Nation of Israel (2:15-17)

2:15-16. Here the command to **blow a trumpet** is not a military alarm, but a call to **proclaim a solemn assembly** (e.g., Lv 23:24; 25:9; Nm 10:10; Jos 6:4-5; Pss 47:5; 81:3). This **fast** is urgent for all levels of their society, **the people . . . elders** . . . the **children** . . . the **infants** . . . **bridegroom[s]**, and **bride[s]**.

2:17. The **priests, the LORD's ministers**, and leaders are to **weep** in the temple **between the porch and the altar**. They are to plead for the **LORD** to **spare** His **people** Israel, who are His **inheritance** (cf. 3:2; Ex 19:5; Dt 7:6; 9:29; 32:9; Pss 94:14; 106:4-5). Otherwise, God's name could become **a byword** (derogatory proverb) among the Gentile **nations**, maligning His character in failing to keep His covenants (cf. Ex 32:11-14; Nm 14:13; Dt 9:28; Jos 7:9).

B. Morning on the Day of the Lord: Restoration of Israel (2:18-32)

Joel's emphasis on the day of the Lord includes a morning aspect, the restoration of Israel. The prophets generally present the Lord's restoration of His people following their discipline (e.g., Is 40:1-2; 49:14-16).

1. The Lord Is Zealous and Merciful (2:18)

2:18. The section opens with the promise **the LORD will be zealous** (cf. Ex 20:5 and Dt 4:5) **for His land and will have pity on His people**. The Lord identified the people of Israel as **His people** and the land of Israel as **His land**, indicating His faithful covenant relationship with them (cf. Gn 12:1-3). The word **zealous** depicts the righteous, jealous ardor a husband would have for his wife, indicating God's zeal for Israel. The word pity describes an emotional feeling that causes sparing from difficulty, indicating that God would come to Israel's aid if they would turn to Him.

2. The Lord Will Respond to Repentance and Restore the Land (2:19-27)

2:19. The restoration of Israel follows their judgment. After the evening darkness will come the blessing of morning light, expressing both aspects of the day of the Lord. He will restore the blessings, including **grain, new wine and oil**. In the future, Israel will **never again** be **a reproach among the nations**, a promise not yet fulfilled with the advent of the modern state of Israel.

2:20. Along with blessing Israel, God will judge the **northern army**. The enemies of Israel most frequently came from the north, i.e., Assyria and Babylon. These northern enemies were presented as the final end-times enemy of Israel (cf. Ezk 38-39; Dn 11:40; Zch 14:2). This enemy will be driven to **a parched and desolate land**, the Negev Desert and into the **eastern** and **western sea**, i.e., the Dead and the Mediterranean seas. At the end of battle the **stench** of the multitude of slain will be apparent.

2:21-22. The **land** and the **beasts** are told, **do not fear** but **rejoice and be glad**. Here Joel describes the blessing associated with the Jewish people's eschatological return to their land. As elsewhere in the prophets, the blessing on the land is synonymous with the **great things** the Lord has done for His people, indicating that more than agricultural blessing is in view (cf. Is 54:4; Jr 30:10; Zph 3:16, 17).

2:23. A clue to this greater blessing described here is in the phrase **the early rain for your vindication**. At issue is whether the Hebrew phrase *hamoreh litsdaqah,* should be translated as "early rain for your vindication" (as in the NASB and various other English translations) or as "the teacher of/for righteousness." The basis for translating this as **early rain for your vindication** is that the word *moreh* is found in the second half of the verse where it does indeed mean **the early rain**. But, for several reasons, the use of the word "rain" (*moreh)* in the second half of the verse does not compel translating it that way in the first part. (1) Even though *moreh* is indeed used in the second half of the verse to mean rain, it is an extremely unusual form—the normal form would be *yoreh.* (2) It seems that the author is using a deliberate play on words, indicating that when the teacher (*hamoreh)* came, so would the early rain (*moreh).* (3) Translating the word *litsdaqah* as "vindication" is virtually impossible. It is a moral/ethical term meaning "righteousness" and cannot describe rain.

The more likely translation should be "the teacher of/for righteousness," for several reasons. First, the word *moreh* in the singular form is used eight times in the OT and is translated "teacher" in all cases (cf. 2:23; 2Kg 17:28; 2Ch 15:3; Jb 36:22; Is 30:20 [2 times]; Hab 2:18, 2:19). Further, it is translated as "teacher" in several ancient texts (the Vulgate, the Targum, the Greek Symmachus and the DSS). Second, Joel's use of the definite article with "the teacher" (*hamoreh*) indicates that it is speaking of a particular person. Third, the pairing of "the teacher" with the word "righteousness" and with the preposition "to" or "for" indicates that this teacher personifies righteousness.

Hence, Jl 2:23 indicates that the blessings described here will occur when God the Father will send the Messiah, "the Teacher of Righteousness" to the people of **Zion**, who should **rejoice . . . and be glad**. At the same time, God will send blessing to Israel in the form of the early (fall) and latter (spring) rains. Isaiah provides a parallel idea, predicting an eschatological Teacher who will guide Israel (cf. Is 30:20), and when He comes, God will send rain (Is 30:23). For a complete discussion, see Walter C. Kaiser, Jr., *The Messiah in the Old Testament* (Grand Rapids, MI: Zondervan, 1994), 139–42, 172–73.

Jesus called Himself Teacher (Mt 10:25; 26:18; Jn 13:13), as did His followers (Mk 4:38; 9:38; 10:35) and opponents (Mt 9:11; 12:38; 22:16). Of the 90 times Jesus was addressed directly in the gospels, 60 times He was called "Teacher."

2:24-25. The blessings will include **threshing floors . . . full of grain** and **vats** overflowing **with the new wine and** (olive) **oil**. The future blessing of the Lord will **make up to you for the years** destroyed by the **great army** that the Lord sent in judgment.

2:26-27. The result will be **plenty to eat**, and they will **praise the name of the Lord [their] God Who has dealt wondrously** with His people as He did at the deliverance from Egypt (cf. Ex 7:3). The assurance that they **will never be put to shame** (twice for emphasis) awaits fulfillment in the millennial kingdom (cf. Is 45:17; 49:23). The purpose of the restoration is that they **will know that [God is] in the midst of Israel** (cf. Ex 6:7; Dt 5:6; Is 43:3; Ezk 20:5), that He is their **God**, and that **there is no other.**

3. The Lord Will Provide Spiritual Renewal (2:28-32)

2:28-32. After this indicates events in the distant future. This prophecy relates not to the return from the Babylonian captivity but to the eschatological day of the Lord (Ac 2:17 renders it "and it shall be in the last days . . ."). There are three characteristics of the eschatological renewal promised here. First, there will be an outpouring of God's Spirit on Israel (vv. 28-29). This will come upon their **sons**, **daughters**, **old** and **young men**, and **male and female servants** so that they all will **prophecy** and have prophetic **dreams**. This will be a change from a limited office of prophet to a wide range of people who will have the Spirit of the Lord and will fulfill Moses' hope for Israel (cf. Nm 11:29).

Second, there will be supernatural phenomena in the skies: These cosmic wonders will include **wonders in the sky and on the earth**, **blood**, **fire**, and **smoke**, the **sun** and the **moon** darkened at the time of the **great and awesome day of the Lord** (vv. 30-31). Such events are often associated with the future tribulation (cf. Is

13:9-10; 34:4; Mt 24:29; Rv 6:12; 8:8-9; 9:1-19; 4:14-20; 16:4, 8-9).

Third, there will be great deliverance at that time for **whoever calls on the name of the Lord**. This seems to be an invitation to escape the wrath of God spoken of at the start of the chapter (cf. Jl 2:1-11). The prophet promises **escape** for those **on Mount Zion and in Jerusalem** (cf. Rv 14:1-5) and seems to refer to the eschatological deliverance, both physical and spiritual, of Israel at the return of Christ (Zch 12:10; 14:3-5; Rm 11:26-27).

At question is why Peter used this passage when explaining the disciples' supernatural gift of speaking in unlearned foreign languages (Ac 2:14-21). Some have maintained that Peter viewed the events at Pentecost as being fulfilled directly. Hence, Joel's predictions, while originally about God's promises to Israel, find their fulfillment in the Church. Others have maintained that Peter viewed Jl 2 as partially fulfilled at Pentecost (or perhaps inaugurated) but will indeed be completely fulfilled for Israel at the end of days. Both of these views seem problematic in that the events described in Acts do not match Joel's prediction. In Acts, the disciples spoke in unlearned foreign languages (2:6), but Joel predicted visions and dreams. Further, Acts does not indicate that there were any cosmic wonders or signs in the sky. Therefore, it is more likely that Peter cited Joel as a form of applicational fulfillment. This refers to finding a principle in Joel and applying it to the situation at Pentecost. At Pentecost, it was thought that the disciples were drunk (Ac 2:13). Therefore, Peter cited the principle from Joel that when the Holy Spirit falls, remarkable signs would follow. Thus, the disciples' supernatural gifts should not be attributed to drunkenness but to the Holy Spirit. For a full discussion of NT use of the OT and the principle of applicational fulfillment, see Michael Rydelnik, *The Messianic Hope: Is the Hebrew Bible Really Messianic?* (Nashville: B&H Academic, 2010), 95–111, esp. 104–08.

III. The Judgment of the Nations (3:1-21)

Chapter 3 moves from the more general context of judgment to details of judgment on specific Gentile nations for their mistreatment of Israel. The chapter concludes with a promise of deliverance and blessing for Israel.

A. The Lord Will Judge the Nations for Their Mistreatment of Israel (3:1-15)

In this opening section, seven times the Lord identifies the people of Israel and the land of Israel as "My" (3:2-5) indicating His personal relationship with them (cf. 2:7).

3:1. In those days and at that time indicates an eschatological period when the Lord will **restore the fortunes of Judah and Jerusalem,** initiating that blessing by judging Israel's enemies. God will gather **all the** Gentile **nations,** who have oppressed God's people, Israel (cf. Pss 83:1-12; 110:6; Is 66:18; Jr 25:32; Ezk 39:21; Mc 4:11-12) to Jerusalem. As the final part of the campaign of Armageddon (cf. Rv 16:16), they will have besieged the city and been defeated by Messiah (Zch 14:2-4). Afterwards, the Lord will judge the nations in the **valley of Jehoshaphat** (lit. "Yahweh Judges" cf. 3:12), not a place name but a descriptive title for the Kidron Valley, east of Jerusalem. There God will judge the Gentile nations for their treatment of the Lord Jesus' Jewish brothers during the tribulation ("these brothers of mine" cf. Mt 25:31-46, esp. v. 40). The "sheep" in the parable of the sheep and the goats are those who, as an expression of their faith in Jesus, aided the Jewish people and the "goats" are those who lacked faith and therefore harmed them (Mt 25:41-46).

3:2-3. In response, the Lord Himself will **enter into judgment with them . . . on behalf of My people and My inheritance Israel** (cf. comments on 2:17; Dt. 32:9; 1Kg 8:53; Ps 94:14; Jr 10:16). The sins of the Gentile nations are identified as having **scattered** the Jewish people **among the nations** and **divided up My land** and **cast lots for My people** by selling the children into slavery (cf. 3:6).

3:4-5. God's future judgment of Israel's enemies is presented through the impending judgment of **Tyre, Sidon and all the regions of Philistia,** areas that range from the northern to the southern coastline of Israel. God rhetorically asked these nations, in courtroom style, if they believed they were **rendering** Him **a recompense** (i.e., "giving Me what I deserve") by their treatment of Israel. He pronounced judgment upon them **swiftly and speedily . . . return your recompense on your head.** They will be judged for the theft of His **precious treasures**, the wealth of Israel, which they took to their own pagan temples.

3:6-8. They were also guilty of selling **the sons of Judah and Jerusalem** as slaves **to the Greeks**. In a stroke of justice in kind ("an eye for an eye," Lv 24:19-21) God declared He would sell their children into slavery. Some have suggested that this was literally fulfilled by Artaxerxes III in

345 BC and Alexander the Great in 332 BC who took the children of Tyre and Sidon captive as slaves. This is unlikely, since these nations are mentioned here merely as representatives of all the Gentile nations that will gather against Israel at the end of days. These verses describe the judgment of the nations when the Lord vindicates His people (Gn 12:3; Pss 43 and 54). It will certainly occur because **the Lord has spoken**.

3:9-10. The **nations** are called to **prepare a war**, summoning **soldiers** to **draw near** and commanding them to **beat** their **plowshares into swords** and their **pruning hooks into spears** to prepare for the battle in the valley of Jehoshaphat (cf. 3:2ff.). This call to war is prior to the future of everlasting peace (Is 2:4; Mc 4:3). Before there can be everlasting peace, there must be ultimate judgment of the enemies of Israel, who are the enemies of the Lord (cf. Ps 83).

3:11. Further, **all** the **surrounding nations** are beckoned to engage in the battle (cf. 3:2; Ezk 38-39; Rv 16:12-16). To match the massive array of military power assembled against the Lord, Joel called for God to **Bring down, O Lord, Your mighty ones**, an army of angels to battle His enemies (cf. Ezk 38–39; Rv 19).

3:12. The phrase, **let the nations be aroused** summons the nations to do their worst, yet they will be no match for God and His mighty ones (Mc 4:11–5:1; Rv 19:11-19). They are to assemble in **the valley of Jehoshaphat**, the "valley of Yahweh's judgment," where the Lord will **sit to judge** them (cf. 3:2). Charles Feinberg noted that, although the nations gathered in the valley of Jehoshaphat "in the white heat of wrath against Israel," it is there that "they will meet the blessed King of Israel, their Protector through the ages, and their Champion in their darkest and blackest hour, the Lord Jesus Christ, who will sit ready to judge once and for all the accumulated sins of the nations against Israel" (Charles Lee Feinberg, *Joel, Amos, Obadiah* [New York: ABMJ, 1948], 35).

3:13-15. This is the **harvest** of judgment on the nations that are **ripe** and ready for the **sickle** and **wine press. The vats overflow** because their **wickedness is great** and now ready for reaping in the day of the Lord (cf. Jr 25:12-25; Rv 14:18-19). There will be **multitudes, multitudes** gathered to face Him **in the valley of decision**. At that time **the sun and moon grow dark and the stars lose their brightness** (cf. Jl 2:10; Is 24:21-23), indicating that the heavens themselves will feel the force of the Lord's judgment.

B. The Lord Is a Refuge for His People (3:16-17)

The closing section of Joel highlights two important themes: First, that the Lord's salvation and blessing will come from Zion (cf. Gn 14; 2Sm 7), and second, that the Lord is present in Zion (cf. Pss 48; 133).

3:16. The Lord is the mighty lion of Judah and like a lion He will judge and destroy His enemies (Jr 25:30; Rv 5:5). **The Lord roars . . . and utters His voice**, making **the heavens and the earth tremble** (cf. 2:10). He **utters His voice** from **Zion** and **Jerusalem** (cf. Am 1:2), His royal city (cf. Ps 48:2).

3:17. Israel will take refuge in the Lord because they will **know that [He is] the Lord [their] God**. This is the centerpiece of His taking up residence **in Zion . . . so Jerusalem will be holy** (Is 11; Zch 14:20-21). In the future, **strangers**, those who do not worship the Lord, **will pass through it no more** (cf. Is 35:8-10; 52:1; Nah 1:15; Zch 14:20-21).

C. The Lord Will Bless Judah and Jerusalem Forever (3:18-21)

3:18. In that Day, in the millennial kingdom (the Messianic Age), the blessings of Jerusalem are for the land and the people who will enjoy the land. The **mountains** dripping **with sweet wine** and **the hills** flowing **with milk** go beyond even the blessing mentioned at the exodus (Ex 3:8; 13:5; 33:3; Lv 20:24; Dt 6:3; Is 55:1). Furthermore, **all the brooks of Judah will flow with water**—the rains will be plentiful (cf. Jl 2:23) as a sign of God's blessing (cf. Dt 28:12).

Significantly, Ezekiel also speaks of the time when **a spring will go out from the house of the Lord**. During the Messianic Age there will be a stream of water flowing south from the temple toward the Dead Sea, growing deeper until the Dead Sea itself becomes fresh water, and along its banks will be all kinds of fruitful trees (cf. Ezk 47:1-12; Rv 22:1-22). The **valley of Shittim** (Acacia trees) is the streambed west of the Jordan where waters from Jerusalem are carried down the Jordan Valley to the Dead Sea.

3:19. In stark contrast to the Lord's blessings on Israel, the perpetual enemies of God, personified by two of Israel's most notorious enemies, **Egypt . . . and Edom** (e.g., 1Kg 14:25-26; 2Kg 23:29-34; Is 34:5-17; Ezk 25:12-14) **will become a waste** and a **desolate wilderness**. The cause of their judgment is clear: for **the violence done to the sons of Judah, in whose land they have shed**

innocent blood. The judgment on Egypt and Edom is a fulfillment of God's covenant with Abraham (cf. Gn 12:3).

3:20. At this time of final blessing, **Judah will be inhabited forever and Jerusalem for all generations** in fulfillment of God's promises (Gn 12:1-3; 15:1-5; 17:1-8; 2Sm 7:16; Ps 105:8-13; Jr 33:24-26).

3:21. The book ends with a summary statement of two ideas. First, the Lord will **avenge their blood** (cf. Rv 6:10-11). No enemy of Israel will escape the judgment of the Lord. Second, God's ultimate protection of Israel is certain because He perpetually **dwells in Zion** as King of kings and Lord of lords (cf. Pss 48:2; 87:2; Rv 19:16).

Thus Joel's prophecy, focusing on the day of the Lord, foresees not only the coming judgment of Israel for her unfaithfulness (1:1–2:11), but also Israel's deliverance and restoration, when the nation turns and trusts in the Lord (cf. 2:12-32; 3:18-21; Rm 11:26-27). Moreover, it predicts the Lord's judgment of the nations for their enmity toward Israel (see 3:1-15) **for the LORD dwells in Zion** (3:21; cf. 2:27; 3:17).

BIBLIOGRAPHY

Achtemeier, Elizabeth. *Minor Prophets I.* The New International Bible Commentary. Vol. 17, edited by Robert L. Hubbard, Jr., and Robert K. Johnston. Peabody: Hendrickson, 1996.

Allen, Leslie C. *The Books of Joel, Obadiah, Jonah, and Micah.* The New International Commentary on the Old Testament, edited by R. K. Harrison. Grand Rapids, MI: Eerdmans, 1976.

Barton, John. *Joel and Obadiah.* The Old Testament Library, edited by James L. Mays, Carol A. Newsom, and David L. Peterson. Louisville: Westminster John Knox, 2001.

Boice, James Montgomery. *The Minor Prophets* (2 volumes). Grand Rapids, MI: Baker, 2006.

Dillard, Raymond Bryan. "Joel." In *The Minor Prophets: An Exegetical and Expository Commentary*, edited by Thomas Edward McComiskey. Grand Rapids, MI: Baker, 2009.

Feinberg, Charles Lee. *Joel, Amos, Obadiah.* New York: ABMJ, 1948.

________. *The Minor Prophets.* Chicago: Moody, 1990.

Hubbard, David Allan. *Joel and Amos.* The Tyndale Old Testament Commentaries. Vol. 22b, edited by D. J. Wiseman. Downers Grove, IL: InterVarsity, 1989.

Patterson, Richard D. *Joel.* The Expositor's Bible Commentary. Vol. 7, edited by Frank E. Gabelein. Grand Rapids, MI: Zondervan, 1985.

AMOS

JOHN A. JELINEK

INTRODUCTION

Author. The title of the book comes from its human author whose name means "burden bearer" or "load carrier." Amos is not mentioned in other biblical books or in any inscription archaeologists have uncovered. Amos was a shepherd (*noqed*) or sheep breeder, and he described himself as a herdsman (*boqer*; 7:14). He possibly owned or managed large herds and may have been in charge of shepherds, though the terms used do not necessarily suggest this. Amos described himself as a grower of sycamore figs (7:14), a variety of the mulberry family, producing fig-like fruit.

Amos's authorship is supported by the claim of the book (1:1; 7:14), by the pastoral language (7:1-4, 14-15), and by the contents demonstrating his knowledge of an outdoor lifestyle (3:4-5, 12; 5:8-9; 9:9). Amaziah's suggestion that he "flee away to the land of Judah" (7:12) implies that he was from Judah.

Date. An older contemporary of Hosea and Isaiah, Amos was active during the reigns of both Jeroboam II (793–753 BC, in Israel) and Uzziah (790–739 BC, in Judah). Most scholars date Amos's ministry toward the end of this period; however, since Jotham was coregent with Uzziah during the latter part of his reign (2Kg 15:5; 2Ch 26:21), a date between 760 and 755 BC is likely more accurate.

During Jeroboam's reign, Egypt, Assyria, and Babylon were relatively weak. Aram, Israel's nearest enemy, had been brought under subjection for a time (2Kg 14:25-28). Adad-Nirari III of Assyria completed a successful conquest of Damascus in 802 BC, but he did not extend his influence over Israel. These factors helped forge a time of economic development in Israel.

Amos ministered two years before the earthquake (1:1), joining Zechariah, who mentioned an earthquake during the reign of Uzziah (Zch 14:5). Josephus related that an earthquake occurred when Uzziah entered the temple and was struck with leprosy (2Ch 26:16-20; Josephus, *Ant.* 9.10.4). Excavations at Hazor and Samaria point to evidence of a violent earthquake in Israel about 760 BC (Philip J. King, *Amos, Hosea, Micah—An Archaeological Commentary* [Philadelphia: Westminster Press, 1988], 21). A 760 BC date may account for his omission of the name of King Jotham, a coregent with Uzziah from 750 to 739 BC. Amos was a contemporary of the other eighth-century prophets: Jonah, Hosea, Isaiah, and Micah.

Recipients. Amos wrote his book just after Israel had attained its greatest power and prosperity under Jeroboam II (793–753 BC), and had at last triumphed over the Syrians. Jeroboam extended his borders beyond those achieved by Solomon, conquering Ammon, Moab, Damascus, and Jordan. With prosperity came pride and idolatry. The rich gained extravagance through exploitation of the poor. Idolatrous shrines arose in Gilgal, Dan, and Beersheba, with Baal worship in Bethel. Amos directed his message against Bethel's priest and prophets (1Kg 12:27-33).

Judah and Israel's commerce thrived (Am 8:5), an upper class emerged (4:1-3), and expensive homes were built (3:15; 5:11). The rich enjoyed an indulgent lifestyle (6:1-6), while the poor became targets for legal and economic exploitation (2:6-7; 5:7, 10-13). Contrary to Mosaic law, slavery for debt was easily accepted (2:6; 8:6). Standards of morality had sunk to a low (2:7). Formal "religion" thrived as people participated in yearly festivals (4:4; 5:5; 8:3, 10) offering their sacrifices enthusiastically (4:5; 5:21-23). Believing that God was with them, they considered themselves immune to disaster (5:14, 18-20; 6:1-3; 9:10). Yet inconsistent with their professed belief, they worshiped pagan deities along with the Lord.

Israel was successful because Aram and Philistia, Israel's traditional enemies, lacked the military might to challenge her. Assyria was dealing with its own internal problems at this time. In this season of prosperity, likely in the midst of the New Year feast at the central shrine of Bethel, Amos appeared to disturb Israel's complacency.

Purpose and Themes. As one of the 12 Minor Prophets, Amos belongs to the early era of the prophets. Recent studies tracking common themes and warnings of the Minor Prophets indicate that this collection of books needs to be viewed as a whole. One Jewish tradition holds that these 12 are arranged chronologically with the first six books coming from the eighth century, the next three from the seventh century, and the final three dating to the postexilic period. Amos would belong to this early era. Amos provides background for understanding the spiritual state of affairs in Israel while reinforcing the law's warnings concerning sanctifying the presence of the Lord in His land. Amos's prophecy exhibits a remarkable correspondence to the Torah, which suggests that there was an authoritative body of law that Amos identified as the "law of the LORD" (2:4).

Amos is tightly written poetry, often with three word-units to the line (this brevity is typical of earlier Hebrew poetry). Most of what is not strictly poetry (lacking clear rhythm or exhibiting weak parallelism) shows care in its composition. Features that contribute to this impression include alliteration (e.g., 5:4-6; 6:13-14; 9:14); puns (e.g., 8:1-2; 9:14); chiasm (e.g., 5:4-6a and all of 5:1-17); unexpected words (e.g., "sins are great" 5:12); and graphic word pictures (5:19).

By genre, Amos is a prophetic book containing oracles (speeches originating from God and delivered on His behalf). Prophets predating the exile used more judgment oracles, and the exilic prophets used more salvation oracles. Amos contains hymns (1:2; 4:13; 5:8-9), visions (7:1-9; 8:1-3; 9:1-4), narrative (7:10-17), and a disputation speech (rhetorical questions arguing a case, 3:3-6), all typical of prophetic communication styles.

One way to view the structure of the book is to identify its common elements in their contribution to the book. After an introduction indicating Amos's call, the book includes eight judgment speeches/oracles against nations (1:3–2:16). Then follow three "hear this" oracles describing the reasons for the judgment (3:1–5:17) and two woe oracles (5:18–6:14). Then Amos added four visions to show how bad the future judgment will be (7:1–8:3) and a final "hear this" oracle for those who "trample the needy" (8:4-14). The book concludes with a final vision of the restoration of the fallen house of David (9:11-15).

OUTLINE

I. Introduction: The Call of Amos (1:1-2)
II. Body: The Message of Judgment (1:3–9:10)
  A. The Oracles of Judgment (1:3–2:16)
    1. The Oracle against Syria (1:3-5)
    2. The Oracle against Philistia (1:6-8)
    3. The Oracle against Tyre (1:9-10)
    4. The Oracle against Edom (1:11-12)
    5. The Oracle against Ammon (1:13-15)
    6. The Oracle against Moab (2:1-3)
    7. The Oracle against Judah (2:4-5)
    8. The Oracle against Israel (2:6-16)
  B. The Reasons for Israel's Judgment (3:1–6:14)
    1. Israel's Oppression of Others Despite Their Own Privileged Position (3:1-15)
    2. Israel's Economic Exploitation of the Poor (4:1-13)
    3. Israel's Stubborn Refusal to Repent (5:1-17)
    4. Israel's Hypocritical Worship (5:18-27)

5. Israel's Comfortable Complacency Despite Warnings of Judgment (6:1-14)

C. The Results of Judgment (7:1–9:10)

1. The Vision of the Locust Swarm (7:1-3)
2. The Vision of a Fire (7:4-6)
3. The Vision of the Plumb Line (7:7-17)
4. The Vision of the Basket of Summer Fruit (8:1-14)
5. The Vision of the Lord beside the Altar (9:1-10)

III. Conclusion: The Restoration of the Davidic House (9:11-15)

COMMENTARY ON AMOS

I. Introduction: The Call of Amos (1:1-2)

1:1. Amos was from **among the sheepherders** of **Tekoa**, ten miles south of Jerusalem in Judah. Amos may have been a prosperous and influential Judahite, but there is no indication that he was a priest or had any connection with the ruling classes in Judah. Amos's rural background had a profound effect on him and his writing (cf. 1:2; 2:9; 3:4-5; 5:19-20, 24; 6:12; 7:1-6; 8:1; 9:3-15).

Amos's visions became prophecies concerning Israel during the reigns of **Uzziah** (790–739 BC) in Judah and **Jeroboam** II (793–753 BC) in Israel **two years before the earthquake**. Earthquakes were associated with the Lord's appearances as a warrior (cf. Jdg 5:4; 2Sm 22:8; Ps 77:18; Is 13:13) so Amos's use of an earthquake here could signal the Lord's approach. Amos lived in a day of relative political stability, material prosperity, and geographical expansion for Israel and Judah (cf. 1:6; 6:2, 13; 2Kgs 14:23-29). Uzziah and Jeroboam II were competent kings, and their respective kingdoms enjoyed peace. Aramea, whose borders were about 60 miles northwest of the Sea of Galilee, had not recovered from its defeat by Adad-Nirari III of Assyria in 802 BC, and Assyria's power peaked later under Tiglath-pileser III (745–727 BC).

1:2. As a lion announcing attack (3:4), **the LORD roars**, announcing his judgment on Israel. "The LORD" is the emphatic first word in the Hebrew sentence; usually a verb comes first. God had been Israel's shepherd. As such, He was supposed to care for them. Amos used a shepherd's fear of a lion attack to focus Israel's attention on her peril. All the land would mourn, from **the shepherds' pasture grounds** in the lowland to **the summit of** the **Carmel** mountain range. God promised to discipline His people if they proved unfaithful to His Mosaic covenant (Dt 28:20-24).

II. Body: The Message of Judgment (1:3–9:10)

A. The Oracles of Judgment (1:3–2:16)

The order of the oracles contributes to the impact Amos intended. Foreign nations precede the nearer relatives of the Israelites, with Judah as her closest kin. In Amos's rhetoric of entrapment, Israel felt "a noose of judgment" tighten round her own throat. From the distant city of Damascus, Amos moved in ever-tightening circles toward Israel. Israel likely approved the denunciation of her heathen neighbors and applauded God's indictment of Judah because of their historical animosities. Then, the northern kingdom of Israel would be shocked to find itself in the center of judgment.

1. The Oracle against Syria (1:3-5)

1:3-4. Damascus, capital of ancient Syria, received judgment for their abuse of **Gilead** (cf. 2Kg 8:12-29). Aramean centers of power and pagan worship were destroyed by Tiglath-pileser III between 734 and 732 BC. The saying **for three transgressions of . . . and for four** is Amos's trademark expression (see vv. 6, 9, 11, 13; 2:1, 4, 6) meaning "for numerous sins" (cf. Jb 5:19). Three transgressions represent fullness, and the fourth suggests an overflow of them (poetically symbolizing completeness). Comparing parallels in Proverbs using a "three, even four" numerical pattern (see Pr 30:15-16, 18-19), one expects to find four specific sins in each oracle. Yet after specifying one or two sins, Amos frequently broke off the presentation of a list, announced judgment, and indicted another nation—as the target of God's anger lay elsewhere.

Transgressions (*pishe*, "rebellion against a covenantal oath") signifies that these sins were against God. For each of Israel's enemies Amos cited only the transgression making judgment inevitable. **Fire** is used in all but the last oracle

Amos's Oracles of Judgment Encircle Israel (1:3–2:16)

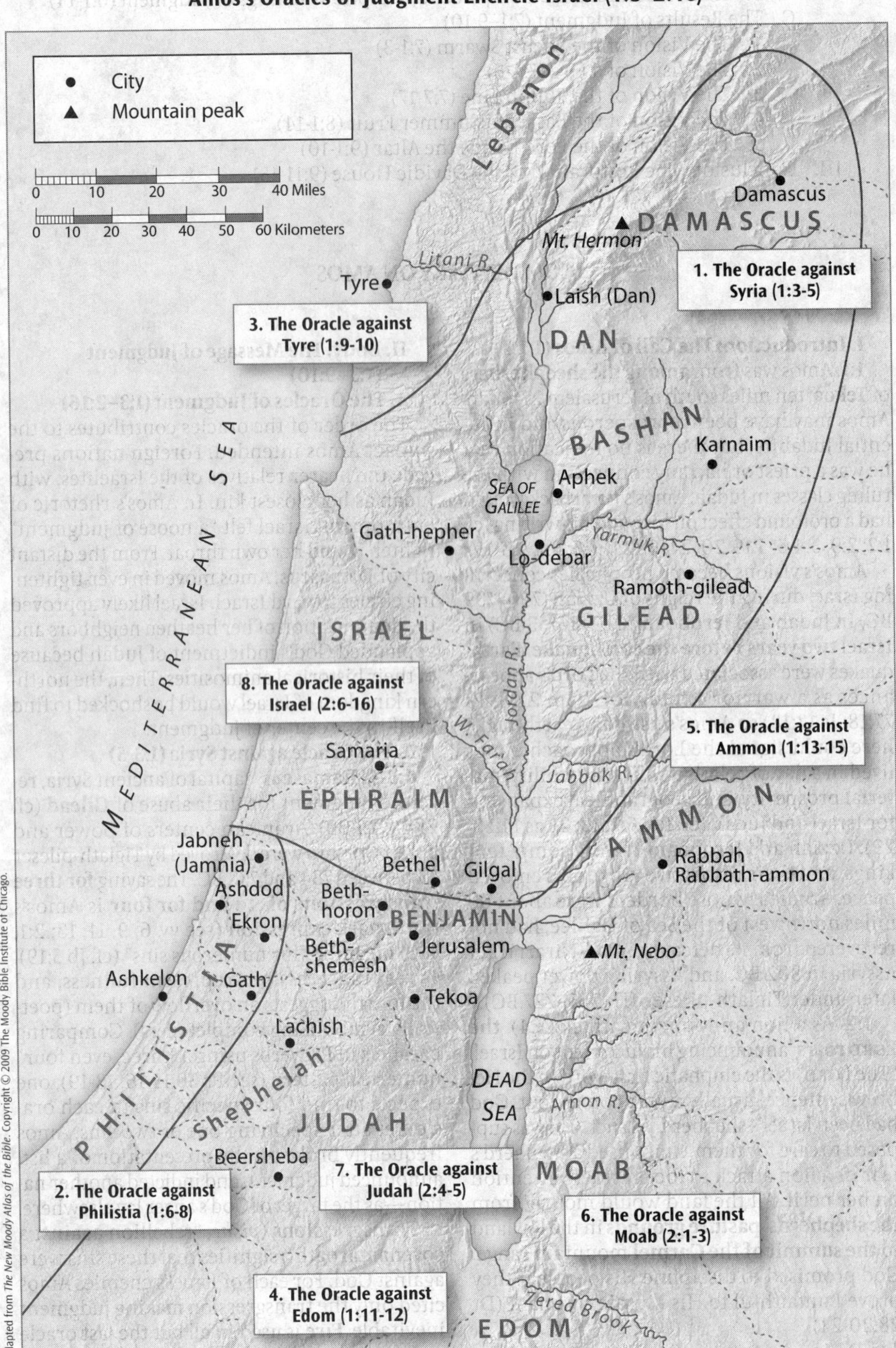

to symbolize the destructive power of a military leader (cf. Nm 21:27-30). **Hazael**, the founder of the Syrian dynasty (841–806 BC) and **Ben-hadad**, his son, repeatedly invaded Israel between 842 and 802 BC. Israel had suffered greatly during battles with the Syrians (they were also known as the Arameans), especially in the Transjordan (cf. 2Kg 8:7-12; 10:32-33).

1:5. The **gate bar of Damascus** symbolized the breach of the city's last defense. **Aven** means "wickedness" and may refer to Baalbek or the Biq'ah Valley in Lebanon. Baal(im) means "Lord" or "God" in ancient Canaanite. Baalbek was probably named after Baal-Biq'ah, the west Semitic weather god and "lord of the plains" of Lebanon who was worshiped there. **Beth-eden** ("house of pleasure") refers to the royal house (Bit-Adini, on the Euphrates River). God had originally brought the Arameans to their place in the land from **Kir** (Kerak in what is now modern Jordan, 9:7); now He will reverse their lot and send them back! The Assyrians killed King Rezin in 732 and exiled the Arameans to Kir.

2. The Oracle against Philistia (1:6-8)

1:6-8. The Philistines were a non-Semitic people who came to the land of Israel from the Aegean (possibly Crete, c. the 12th century BC). The Philistines' control of iron supplies and their tight political organization of cities made them Israel's rival for centuries. **Gaza**, a chief city of Philistia (an Egyptian garrison town) received the Lord's judgment because of their having **deported an entire population** (or people "at peace," *shelema*) **to Edom** as slaves (cf. Jl 3:4-8). During Jehoram's reign (852–841 BC), the Philistines and Arabs plundered the temple and sold the people into slavery (2Ch 21:16-17). The divine image assured human dignity (Gn 1:26-27), yet the Philistines treated people as commodities for profit. The Lord vowed to destroy the Philistine power centers (**citadels**, Am 1:7) leaving no surviving **remnant** (v. 8). Four of the five major cities of Philistia are indicted, except Gath, a town that had already fallen (cf. 6:2; 2Kg 12:17).

The **Lord God** ("Sovereign Lord," a title that occurs 19 times in Amos and five times in the other Minor Prophets; cf. Ob 1; Mc 1:2; Hab 3:19; Zph 1:7; Mal 1:6) vowed to cut off **the remnant of the Philistines**. Uzziah and Hezekiah invaded Philistia (2Ch 26:6), and a succession of Assyrian conquerors captured these towns (Daniel D. Luckenbill, *The Annals of Sennacherib, Oriental Institute Publications* [Chicago: University of Chicago Press, 1924], 2:31-32). During the Maccabean period (169–134 BC) the Philistines passed out of existence.

3. The Oracle against Tyre (1:9-10)

1:9-10. Tyre (on the coast of the Mediterranean, north of Israel, a colony of Sidon, modern Sur), the leading city of Phoenicia, also had **delivered up an entire population** in slavery to **Edom,** breaking the **covenant of brotherhood**. This is the sole explicit reference to slave trade by Tyre in Scripture, though Ezk 27–28 alludes to Tyre's trade practices. Since Israel was the injured partner, the pact between Solomon and Hiram (1Kg 5:1-12) or later relations established through Ahab and Jezebel are in view (1Kg 16:29-31). Where two or more rulers relate as equals, treaty language referred to partners as "brother." Alexander the Great destroyed Tyre in 332 BC (cf. Ezk 26–28), and Phoenicia never revived as a major power, fulfilling this prophecy.

4. The Oracle against Edom (1:11-12)

1:11-12. Edom, a people descended from Esau and Israel's bitterest enemy whose territory was south and east of the Dead Sea, had exhibited hostility toward Israel their **brother** (cf. Gn 25:29-30). Historically (Nm 20:14-18), Moses was rebuffed with the threat of the **sword** when he sought Israel's safe passage through Edom's territory. God put fear of Israel into Edom as they entered the land (Dt 2:2-4) and Obadiah warned Edom not to gloat over Judah's captivity (Ob 10-12). God sent armies to destroy Edom's southern region with its central cities (Am 1:12). Southern Edom, **Teman**, was occupied by Esau's descendants (Temanites) southeast of the Dead Sea. Fulfilling this prophecy, **Bozrah** (modern Busayra, Jordan), a northern city, was subjugated by the Assyrians (eighth century BC) and later by the Nabateans (fourth century BC).

5. The Oracle against Ammon (1:13-15)

1:13-15. The army of **Ammon**, which was the region east of the Jordan River (the Ammonite people being Lot's descendants, Gn 19:30-38), brutally attacked Israel, killing the **pregnant women** living in Gilead (west of Ammon), **to enlarge their borders** to the west. **Gilead,** an eponym of the Gileadites, grandson of Manasseh, was a fertile, mountainous region, northeast of the Dead Sea allotted to Reuben, Gad, and Manasseh. Gilead extended from the southern end of the Sea of Galilee to the northern end of the Dead Sea (the modern kingdom of Jordan). The **Lord** would destroy the capital city of the Ammonites, and take their **king** and his **princes**

into captivity. **Rabbah** (modern Amman), the capital, and Ammon's walled cities would fall in battle to Assyria (eighth century BC), Nebuchadnezzar (586 BC) and later to Antiochus III (c. 218 BC).

6. The Oracle against Moab (2:1-3)

2:1-3. Ammon and **Moab**, descendants of the daughters of Lot, sinned by burning the **bones of the king of Edom** (King Mesha). A peaceful burial ("gathered to one's fathers") was sacred, and burning human remains indicated a desire to destroy the peace of a man for eternity. Such treatment of a corpse reflected a lack of respect for man created in God's image. While other oracles highlight crimes against God's covenant people, an aspect of Torah transcended Israel in obligation (see Rm 1:18ff.). The Noahic covenant provides background for the Lord's indictment (cf. Gn 9:5-7; Is 24:5). **Kerioth** (or Hezron) was a major city in Moab. As a result of their desecrations the **Lord** would destroy the leaders of Moab in the tumult of battle under Nebuchadnezzar in 598 BC.

7. The Oracle against Judah (2:4-5)

2:4-5. In Amos's case against Judah, the multiple **transgressions of Judah** are an elaboration of one sin: they **rejected the law of the Lord** by disobeying His statutes. They followed false gods. In Amos's rhetoric of entrapment, Israel would presume Judah, as the seventh nation listed, to be the focus of Amos's oracles. Judah's sin, lack of covenant faithfulness to her Lord, makes it the worst nation thus far in the list, and seemingly appropriate for a climactic pronouncement. However, Amos was not finished with his oracles, and an even stronger pronouncement was made concerning Israel.

God treated Judah with the same justice granted Israel's neighbor nations. Judah's failure to obey the Mosaic covenant stemmed from their listening to false prophets and worshiping idols (*kazib*, **lies**, e.g., 2Kg 18:4-6; 21:11); these were evidences of their apostasy. God would destroy Judah and Jerusalem by **fire** through Nebuchadnezzar's attack in 586 BC (cf. 2Kg 25:1-12)

8. The Oracle against Israel (2:6-16)

2:6-8. Israel was God's target all along, as the length of this oracle indicates. Using the second person ("you") rather than the third ("they") in 2:10 suggests that Amos delivered these oracles orally to Israel prior to their inclusion in this book. Those who **sell the righteous** are the creditors. The poor or **needy** were victims of the dishonest legal and economic practices in Israel (cf. 5:10-12). Seven sins were charged (five in vv. 6-8; two in v. 12) to Israel's account. This oracle follows the same structure and formulas as the preceding oracles, yet the accusation and judgment are more detailed. Israel took advantage of **righteous** and **needy** people for material advantage, selling them into debtor's slavery (cf. 2Kg 4:1-7). Those seven sins included the following:

The *first sin* for which Israel was indicted involved taking bribes for as little money as what a **pair of sandals** cost, in exchange for a man's life. Israel should have been generous toward the poor (Dt 15:7-11), but their sin devalued human life.

The *second sin* was legal corruption. Moses had called for impartiality (cf. Ex 23:4; Dt 16:19), but Israel's courts sided with creditors against debtors (Am 2:7). Oppressors were so greedy that they would **pant after the very dust** that the poor threw on their heads in mourning.

Israel's *third sin* (2:7b) was that fathers and sons were having sexual intercourse with the **same girl**. This may have been with temple prostitutes, concubines, or female relatives (cf. Ex 21:7-11; Lv 18:8, 15). Whichever, their behavior showed contempt for God's **holy name** (cf. Ex 3:13-15; cf. Lv 18:6-18; 20:11).

Amos renounced a *fourth sin* (2:8). The Israelites failed to return **garments taken as pledges** for debts. Creditors could take a garment as collateral toward debt (Dt 24:17), but were to return it to the owner before nightfall (Ex 22:26-27). Perpetrators took these garments before pagan altars at feasts honoring whatever god they worshiped.

The *fifth sin* related to idolatry among the Israelites (2:8; cf. v. 4). They used the **wine** that they had received as fines extracted from the poor to honor heathen gods.

2:9-10. Other nations under God's judgment had not enjoyed Israel's special blessings. Yet in spite of God's destroying the **Amorite before them** in the land, Israel had breached the covenant. Enemies who had been as strong and tall as **cedars** or **oaks** (cf. Nm. 13:28-33; Dt 1:26-28), the Lord destroyed completely, from their **fruit above** to their **root below**. The Amorites, the most formidable of the Canaanites, represented all the displaced Canaanites (cf. Gn 15:16). The defeat of these powerful enemies demonstrated God's love for His people. God reminded Israel that He had redeemed them from Egypt and had **led** them safely through the **wilderness forty**

years. He had preserved them so they could **take possession of the land of the Amorite**. By shifting to the second person (**you**, v. 10), Amos strengthened the force of God's appeal by making it more direct.

2:11-12. God had raised up spiritual leaders in the land: **prophets** and **Nazirites** from among the Israelites' sons (Dt 18:15-18). Prophets relayed God's messages to them, and Nazirites were ordinary citizens who dedicated themselves completely to the Lord by vow and restraint. The order of blessings is arranged to highlight the exodus, the central of the three blessings mentioned and the most important event in Israel's history.

Israel's *sixth* and *seventh sins* highlighted her ungrateful response to His grace. Israel encouraged Nazirites to **drink wine** and **commanded** the prophets to stop prophesying!

2:13-16. Burdened by the sinfulness of His people, the Lord was like a **wagon . . . weighted down** to capacity. Alternately, Amos pictured Israel being crushed by God like any object under the wheels of a heavily laden cart. The Lord was to Israel like a cart loaded with **sheaves** at harvest, creaking beneath a load of sin and oppression and hastening the day when He would bear Israel's sins no longer.

In previous oracles Amos likened God's judgment to fire. Here he described God's wrath coming on Israel with seven images of panic in battle (v. 14) as a parallel to the previous sevenfold description of Israel's sins (2:6-12). *First,* **the swift** will not escape. *Second,* **the stalwart** (*chazaq*), a term used of God's own strength or the strength of a military force, will have his strength fail. *Third,* the warrior, or *gibbor* ("hero"), a common term for a **mighty man**, will lose his life. *Fourth,* the archer **who grasps the bow** would find no place for his feet. *Fifth* and *sixth,* those **swift of foot**, along with the horsemen, will not be able to save their own lives. *Seventh,* when the **LORD** intervenes, **even the bravest among the warriors will flee naked**, a sign of shame and defeat on the field of battle. Running provided no escape, resistance left no place to stand, and no leader could deliver his people from the onslaught of the enemy. Past heroes had routed the Canaanites, but here the leaders will be unable to deliver even themselves.

B. The Reasons for Israel's Judgment (3:1–6:14)

In the next three chapters Amos focused his attention on Israel's rejection of God's Word and how this led to the corruption of her life. God measured their faithfulness in the treatment of their fellow man, not in glorious homes or in stately liturgy. In five messages in four chapters (chaps. 3–6) Amos explained the reasons for God's judgment. Appeals for repentance occur within each message. The first three messages begin with the words "Hear this" (3:1; 4:1; 5:1), and the last two begin with the Hebrew word hoy, translated "Alas" (5:18) and "Woe" (6:1).

1. Israel's Oppression of Others Despite Their Own Privileged Position (3:1-15)

3:1-2. Amos summoned Israel to **hear** the first reason that God would judge them. It was because they had oppressed others in spite of a privileged relationship with Him. He initially addressed this message to both Israel and Judah, **the entire family**, but later he focused his warning mainly on Israel (vv. 9, 12). Israel's unique relationship with God required a unique discipline.

God spoke directly as Amos moved from the second person (**which the LORD has spoken**, 3:1) to the first person singular (**you only have I chosen**, 3:2). **You only** alluded to the special privilege of covenant that God made with the Israelites at Mount Sinai (Ex 19:3-6). God's sovereign and elective choice for blessing (spiritual privilege), however, required stern measures for disobedience (greater accountability). God had **chosen** (or "known," *yada'*; cf. Jr. 1:5) Israel and had revealed Himself to Israel as to no other people.

3:3-8. Amos asked seven intensifying questions in vv. 3-6 to convey the certainty of God's intervention, suggesting that everyone knows that certain causes inevitably produce certain effects. The questions in vv. 3-5 expect a negative answer, and the questions in v. 6 expect a positive answer. Verses 7-8 draw the conclusion that prophets speak when God has made His will clear.

The question, **Do two men walk together unless they have made an appointment?** suggests that Israel and God are not walking on the same path together. They could not travel together toward God's intended destination for the nation unless they did so on terms of the covenant bond between them (cf. v. 2). Amos's remaining questions show how an unjust action (sin) leads to a just effect (God's discipline). Just as a **lion** does not roar if he has no reason to, when he **has no prey**, so also the Lord is not coming to Israel without cause. Similarly, a **bird** will not **fall into a trap on the ground** with nothing as

bait for it. Trumpets blown in cities cause the people to **tremble** in fear of impending danger. Even so, when **calamity** happens to a city, the **Lord** Himself has **done it**.

This ominous progression, to the point where God Himself initiates human calamity, brought Amos to his statement on the need to speak: **Who can but prophesy? God does nothing** to His people unless He first warns them through **secret counsel** to one of His prophets (vv. 7-8; cf. Jr 23:18, 22). Obviously God does many things without giving a particular revelation to His people. Yet as only imbeciles ignore the roar of a lion, so only a fool ignores God's word. Amos must prophesy or incur the wrath of *the* Lion.

3:9-10. Israel would experience unparalleled oppression from God because of her ignorance of how to **do what is right**. Because of the **tumults within her**, Amos called for witnesses to **proclaim on the citadels** (i.e., the people living in them) **in Ashdod** in Philistia and to those in **Egypt** to bear witness against Israel. Moses' law required two witnesses in cases involving the death penalty (Dt 17:6). Israel's sin resulted in an inability to **do what is right** (*n kohah*, "straightness"). Israel's sin hid the straight path from them.

3:11-15. An **enemy** was headed for Israel. The judgment would come in three waves (vv. 11, 12, 13-15). In the *first wave*, an enemy would surround the **land** of Israel to destroy and loot its impressive citadels (Assyria did this in 722 BC). The *second wave* would leave only a small remnant of the people surviving, similar to when a shepherd **snatches** a remaining fragment of a sheep from the mouth of an attacking wild animal to prove that he had not stolen the sheep (cf. Ex 22:10-13). The judgment would be similar to someone stealing everything in a house and the owner being able to retain only a piece of his **bed**. An enemy would steal away the people, and few would escape. A **shepherd** represented God in Israel (e.g., Ps 23:1), the One who rescues His people, but when God visited to judge, all such symbols of comfort were reversed.

In the *third wave*, God would destroy both the pagan altars that Jeroboam I had erected at Bethel and her people who worshiped there (cf. 1Kg 12:26-30). **Altars** at **Bethel** and Dan had supplanted the temple in Jerusalem for those who lived in Israel in the north. Judah, however, continued to worship at Jerusalem. Bethel's altar was Israel's most popular religious center. The **horns** of this altar, symbolic of the strength of its deity (or mercy for refuge) would be **cut off** and would fall to the ground, showing their god's impotence (1Kg 1:50). God would destroy **winter** and **summer** homes of royal families, indicating a thorough invasion. Some embellished their **great houses** with expensive **ivory** decorations (cf. Ps 45:8).

2. Israel's Economic Exploitation of the Poor (4:1-13)

4:1-3. A command to **hear this word**, addressed to the women of Samaria, presented the second reason Israel would be judged—their economic exploitation of the poor and needy. Addressing the wealthy Samaritan women as **cows of Bashan**, God condemned them for taking advantage of the poor and the lifestyle that fostered it. Bashan, a luxuriant region east and northeast of the Sea of Galilee, had plentiful cattle fodder (cf. Ps 22:12; Jr 50:19). These women, along with their **husbands**, were oppressing the poor to provide luxury for themselves. Reversing divinely ordained roles, they ordered their husbands to wait on them (cf. Is 32:9-13). This warning was so serious that seven times Amos asserted **declares the Lord** (vv. 3, 5, 6, 8, 9, 10, 11), thereby expressing the divine authority of his message against them.

God had **sworn by His holiness** to bring judgment in harmony with that holiness. Judgment would cart them off as butchers carry beef (**with meat hooks**) and as fishermen carry **fish**. Assyrian reliefs show captive people led by a rope attached to a ring in the jaw or lip (W. King, *Annals of the Kings of Assyria* [London: British Museum, 1902], 116–20, 125–26). An enemy would carry the bodies of these women **through breaches in** Samaria's **walls** toward **Harmon** (Mount Hermon, north of Bashan) in the deportation to Assyria.

4:4-5. Exacerbating the economic exploitation of the needy was Israel's pretense of spirituality. Amos sarcastically condemned the sin of religious hypocrisy in Israel by inviting the people to **enter Bethel** (meaning "the house of God"), not to worship, but to **transgress** (the law)! This parodied the summons of Israel's priests to come to the sanctuary to worship (cf. Pss 95:6; 96:8-9). **Gilgal** (from *galal*, "to roll"), another Israelite worship center where exiles entered the land erecting memorial stones (Jos 4:20-24), was a place of pilgrimage and **sacrifices** (cf. Hs 4:15; 9:15). At Gilgal, God had removed the reproach of Egypt from His people (cf. Jos 5:9), but now their transgressions were multiplying their sinfulness.

God mockingly urged Israel: **bring your sacrifices every morning** and **your tithes every three days** (not three years as the law required; Dt 14:28-29). Though Israelites were careful to worship regularly, Israel's empty and insincere ritual demeaned God's worth. **Thank offering[s]**, offered to celebrate peace with God (Lv 7:11-16), were actually rebellious acts. Passion for outward religious activity is not the same as worshiping God, and the rote discharge of religious activity is an insult to Him.

4:6-11. Israel should have recognized God's warnings as covenant curses from Deuteronomy but the nation ignored them. Famine (**cleanness of teeth** because there was no food to cause discoloration and decay) and drought came (Dt 28:17, 48), expressing God's displeasure (cf. 1Kg 8:37). God **withheld the rain** when it was needed most, three months before their harvest (Am 4:7-8; cf. Dt 28:22-24). Sirocco winds, plant diseases, and insects blighted their gardens, vineyards, and fruit trees (Am 4:9; cf. Dt 28:18, 22, 38-40). Wars had brought various plagues, and many Israelite soldiers died (Am 4:10; cf. 1Kg 8:33, 37). God was judging them as He formerly had plagued the Egyptians. The stench of dead bodies sent a divine message (cf. Dt 28:21-22, 28).

Conquest of key cities did not stir the Israelites to repentance (Am 4:11; cf. Dt 28:62). Comparing these overthrown cities to **Sodom and Gomorrah**, Amos indicated complete destruction (cf. Is 1:9; Jr 50:40). God had rescued His people **like a firebrand snatched from a blaze**, as He had formerly extracted Lot from Sodom (Gn 19). He sometimes ordains suffering so people will return to Him (cf. Heb 12:6), but God repeatedly lamented over Israel: **Yet you have not returned to Me** (Am 4:6, 8, 9, 10, 11).

4:12-13. God spoke bluntly: Israel should **prepare to meet** Him as they would prepare to encounter an enemy in battle (cf. Ex 19:10-19). The words **prepare** and **meet** indicate a confrontation with Israel's most formidable opponent imaginable: **The LORD God of hosts** (Am 4:13). He is the one who **forms mountains and creates the** intangible **wind**, knows people's **thoughts**, turns **dawn into darkness**, and steps on the hills of Israel like a giant approaching Samaria.

3. Israel's Stubborn Refusal to Repent (5:1-17)

Besides oppression of the innocent (3:1-15) and exploitation of the poor (4:1-13), the third reason God would judge Israel was that the nation had stubbornly refused to repent when warned.

A Possible Chiastic Approach to Amos 5:1-17

A A dirge and a description of certain judgment (5:1-3)
- **B** A call for individuals to repent (5:4-6)
  - **C** An accusation of legal injustice (5:7)
    - **D** A portrait of a sovereign God behind judgment (5:8-9)
  - **C'** An accusation of legal injustice (5:10-13)
- **B'** A call for individuals to repent (5:14-15)

A' A dirge and a description of certain judgment (5:16-17)

5:1-2. As in the two previous oracles (3:1; 4:1), but here using a chiastic structure (see chart above), Amos began with the word **hear**, this time summoning Israel to listen to a **dirge** taken up on her behalf. Heightening the tragedy, Amos proclaimed death for **virgin** daughter **Israel**, who could not be raised to continue the family line. Prophets used dirges to foretell the death of a city, people, or nation (e.g., Jr 7:29; Ezk 26:17-18). Amos thus foretold Israel's death at the height of her prosperity—an experience akin to reading one's own obituary. **Fallen**, in such funeral songs, usually meant "fallen in battle" (2Sm 1:19; 3:34; Lm 2:21). No one came to her aid (cf. Jdg 6:13; 2Kg 21:14), and she lay **neglected** in her land, dispossessed where she should have found an inheritance.

5:3. A city that sent **a thousand** soldiers against her enemies would see only **a hundred** survive. Smaller towns would be destroyed by 90 percent. The last 20 years of Israel's northern kingdom saw the nation's domestic policies in ruins, with successive political coups (cf. 2Kg 15-17) until 722 BC when Sargon II of Assyria deported the remnant of the population.

5:4-5. Given this grim prospect, Amos issued a call for individual repentance. In Genesis, **Bethel** is associated with Jacob, making it significant to a nation that had taken Jacob's new name as theirs. Jacob came to Bethel twice, meeting God. In the national consciousness of Israel, at Bethel, God revealed Himself. Amos, however, warned the nation, **do not resort to Bethel** but **seek** God and **live**. The life-giving presence of the Lord is found not in a place, but in a vital relationship. In effect, Israel was honoring Bethel as a talisman for power.

Gilgal, about 25 miles northeast of Jerusalem near Jericho, was the site of the first national encampment under Joshua (Jos 4:19). Saul was confirmed in his kingship there (1Sm 11:14-15), and Israel was loyal to Saul's house. Amos spoke of Gilgal going into **captivity** (cf. Am 5:27). Gilgal historically received an inheritance and a promise, yet God was preparing to banish its inhabitants! At **Beersheba** (about 50 miles southwest of Jerusalem), all three patriarchs were assured of God's redeeming presence (Gn 21:31; 26:23; 46:1-4). Amos averred that though Israel might seek God's companionship for blessing at Beersheba, those who would **cross over** would find futility. Sacred places did not make Israel legitimate partakers of God's promises.

5:6. Though judgment and death were inevitable for the nation as a whole, individuals could still **seek the Lord** and **live**. The Lord invited the Israelites to seek Him so they might live (see also vv. 4, 14-15). Otherwise God's judgment would **break forth like a fire** and consume the **house of Joseph** (Ephraim, Joseph's son, Israel's main tribe).

5:7. One reason for Israel's judgment was that they turned sweet **justice** into bitter **wormwood**. Wormwood is also associated with poison. In Israel's contempt for what was right (cf. Pr 1:3; 2:9; Is 1:21), the judicial system should have functioned like medicine: healing wrongs and delivering the oppressed. But Israel had turned it into poison.

5:8-9. Since the Lord made the **Pleiades** (traditionally understood in the ancient world as a grouping of seven stars in the constellation Taurus) **and Orion**, He could certainly bring His will to pass on earth. Pleiades rose before daybreak portending the onset of spring, and Orion rose after sunset signaling the onset of winter. God controls daily cycles and seasons, brings light out of darkness, and **darkens day into night**. He who **calls for the waters of the sea** to form clouds that empty them on the land could easily change Israel's fate from prosperity to adversity. Israel's pagan neighbors attributed such activities to their idols, but the Lord is the only God who **flashes forth** like lightning from heaven, striking strong oppressors and bringing an end to their fortresses.

5:10-13. Israel reviled anyone who reproved them and sought neither a just verdict in the **gate** (where city elders sat) nor a truthful witness. Israel came to Bethel (v. 5) and departed (vv. 10-12) unchanged. They participated in the rites, they sang, they left, and nothing had changed. Justice was still bitter (vv. 7a, 12c, the poor were denied justice in the gate), and the righteous man was still overthrown (vv. 7b, 12b, they were distressing the righteous by accepting **bribes**).

The rich in Israel viewed the **poor** as there merely to be exploited. More important than serving God, they **exact[ed] tribute** and weighed the **bribes** in their hand. The Bethel of Jacob in Genesis was to be a place where Israel could come under the transforming influence of the God of Jacob. Instead, the nation, by continuing in sin, had revealed that its motivation in coming was personal profit. The **prudent person** never voiced an opinion that went against profit because it was **an evil time**. To this situation, God proclaimed His just retribution of exile.

5:14-15. Amos urged Israel to **seek good** rather than evil so they could **live** (cf. vv. 4-6). Establishing a just society (**in the gate**) gives substance to an otherwise intangible confession of God. God defends and does not prosecute those who bear this fruit. Repentance creates the conditions that make it viable **(perhaps)** for God to bless.

5:16-17. Amos's second dirge described the certainty of Israel's judgment in familiar Passover allusions. God would now pass through the midst of His people in judgment (cf. Ex 12:12) resulting in **wailing in all the plazas** of Israel. Everyone would lament conditions of divine judgment, not just the **professional mourners**, but even the poor outlying **farmer** who would have to bury his oppressors. **Vineyards**, often places of joy and merriment, would be full of mourning and wailing.

4. Israel's Hypocritical Worship (5:18-27)

Amos's lament began with "alas" (*hoy*, "woe"), in contrast with the first three in this section that began with the word "hear" (3:1; 4:1; 5:1). This lament focuses on Israel's insincere worship as the fourth reason for future judgment.

5:18. The opening word **alas** (*hoy*, "woe"), suggests impending doom for the one who eagerly anticipated **the day of the Lord**. Earlier prophets heralded a day when God would conquer Israel's enemies and establish His rule over the world (e.g., Is 24:21-23; Jl 3:18-21; for a fuller treatment of **the day of the Lord** see the comments on Jl 2:28–3:21). Israel sought such a divine blessing, but Amos foretold a time of **darkness and not light**, when God would fight against Israel, not for her. In the near future, the

day of the Lord meant impending judgment on the nation of Israel via Assyrian attack. This does not, however, give a complete picture of the day of the Lord, which is also characterized by eschatological judgment on the nations and a pouring out of divine blessing upon God's people (cf. Is 4:2-6; 30:26; Hs 2:18-23; Jl 3:9-21; Am 9:11-15; Mc 4:6-8; Zph 2:7; Zch 14:6-9).

5:19. The coming day of the Lord meant inescapable tragedy for Israel. Thinking they had escaped one enemy (**flees from a lion**), they would face another (**a bear meets him**). Assuming security in their homeland (**goes home**), deadly judgment would overtake them (**a snake bites him**; cf. 9:3). To escape from any one terror would be considered a miracle, yet each one turns out to be no escape at all!

5:20-22. The coming day of the Lord would be characterized by **darkness instead of light** and **gloom**, not joy (cf. Jl 2:1-2, 10-11). A brighter day of the Lord was also coming (Am 9:11-15), but first will come a dark day to purify the nation. Thus Israel had half of the picture. God commanded the Israelites to observe several feasts and one fast each year, likely the **festivals** in view (v. 21). Yet God rejected their **solemn assemblies** because they were going through the motions of worship. The threefold **I hate**, **I reject**, and **nor do I delight** emphasize how much God detests such worship. Israel "hated" justice (v. 10); the Lord "hates" (v. 21) hypocritical worship. God would not accept (lit., "smell") an offering's sweet savor or take any notice of any of their offerings (cf. 4:4-5). In God's plan, worship must further the development of spiritual character and be accompanied by justice, or it is merely empty emotions. God requires justice in our person-to-person relationships.

5:23-24. In contrast to vv. 21-22 (which use plural pronouns), vv. 23 and 24 use a singular pronoun **your**, indicating a call for *individuals* to repent. *Negatively*, their celebrations in songs must cease as so much **noise** in God's ears. He would not listen, shutting His ears as well as His nostrils. *Positively*, the Lord wanted **justice** and **righteousness** (cf. Mc 6:8) rather than religiosity and external rituals. Token practices of justice and righteousness do not honor God.

5:25-26. The Lord asked if Israel *really* presented their **sacrifices** to Him sincerely when they were in the **wilderness for forty years**. Hypocritical worship marked them from the beginning (e.g., Ex 32). In the wilderness Israel had carried shrines of **Sikkuth your king** (Am 5:26; Sakkut, the Assyrian war god), perhaps unauthorized shrines honoring Yahweh or other deities (cf. Ac 7:42-43). **Kiyyun, your images**, refers to the Assyrian astral deity also known as Kaiwan (Saturn). Amos ridiculed these gods by substituting the vowels of the Hebrew word for "abomination" (*shiqqus*) into their names. The Lord was to be Israel's King (cf. Dt 33:5; Ps 10:16). Now, heading into exile, they must bear the burden of the idol they have created (since Sikkuth could not "bear" them up). **The star of your gods** [or god] refers to the planet Saturn, represented by Kiyyun.

5:27. Because of this hypocritical worship, God promised that the Israelites would **go into exile beyond Damascus** (cf. 4:3). Exile meant more than the ruin of defeat and capture; it meant being removed from the land God sanctified.

5. Israel's Comfortable Complacency Despite Warnings of Judgment (6:1-14)

Opening the fifth lament in this section with the word *hoy* (alas, woe), Amos cited Israel's living at ease and comfort, choosing to ignore or disbelieve the prophet's warnings, as the fifth reason that the nation would be judged.

6:1. Amos began this message announcing a coming **woe** (*hoy*; cf. 5:18), warning those living in comfortable affluence in Israel that God's hand would bring destruction upon them. Those who felt **at ease in Zion** and **secure** in Samaria were susceptible to complacent attitudes because of their belief in Jerusalem's invincibility. Samaria, likewise, stood on a high hill (**the mountain of Samaria**) that was easily defensible. These **distinguished men** regarded Israel, and Judah, as the **foremost of nations** of the day.

6:2-3. Israel's leaders were unconcerned with military conquests of nations lesser than themselves. Amos challenged them to visit other cities that had once considered themselves great. **Calneh** and **Hamath** were city-states in northern Aram overrun by Shalmaneser III of Assyria in 854–846 BC. **Gath** had been a notable city in Philistia, but fell before Hazael of Aram in 815 BC and again to Uzziah of Judah in 760 BC. Other cities had the sense to know that they were in trouble; yet those dwelling in Samaria lacked any sense of impending **calamity**. Unrepentant hearts hastened the day of terror (or **seat of violence**); refusing to acknowledge their sins. They imagined that they were putting off the day, whereas in reality they were bringing it near.

6:4-6. The affluence of Samaritan leaders promoted a false sense of security that insulated them from their real situation. Those who **recline on beds of ivory** also ate the best, most tender meat obtainable. **Calves from the midst of the stall** refers to animals specially restrained for fattening. Archaeologists have uncovered these stalls with their hitching posts in Megiddo and Beersheba. In the everyday life of commoners, eating meat was a luxury few common Israelites would have enjoyed regularly.

They imitated King **David** and improvised songs, but *exalted themselves rather than praising God*. They consumed **wine** by the bowlful rather than in cups and they would **anoint** their bodies with the **finest of oils** to preserve physical appearances. Their preoccupation with personal leisure diluted their ability to discern and mourn the coming **ruin of Joseph**, a reference to the coming destruction and exile. **Joseph** is used here for the northern kingdom of Israel since Joseph's two sons were Ephraim and Manasseh.

6:7-8. Their complacency made them first in line to **go into exile**. Their **banqueting** would cease; they would sprawl on soft couches no longer. God placed high value on having the right priorities in the stewardship of His resources. Thus the **Lord God** vowed the complete devastation of Samaria. He had **sworn by Himself** (by His own life or *nephesh;* cf. 4:2; 8:7) to exile Israel. Because God can swear by no one greater than Himself (cf. Heb 6:13-14) this expression emphasized the certainty of what was sworn. The **arrogance of Jacob** probably refers to the city of Samaria. The **citadels** were a mark of this arrogant confidence God despised.

6:9-11. God's judgment would be such that if **ten men** took refuge in **one house**, they could not preserve their lives. Survivors, understanding that judgment proceeded from God, would not allow the Lord's **name** to be mentioned lest that act draw His attention and result in their deaths. God would command the utter destruction of all houses in Samaria, both **great** and **small**, and the houses of the rich and poor would perish with them.

6:12-14. Amos posed absurd questions to prompt agreement with God's judgments. Injustice is as absurd as horses running on rocky crags or oxen plowing rocks. Israel's leaders had sown injustice where righteousness was expected. The result was that their decisions killed the poor as surely as though they had given them **poison**. Humanity's sin causes people to boast in *nothing*. Many felt confident because Jeroboam II recaptured territory Israel had formerly surrendered to Aram (cf. 2Kg 14:25), including the town of **Lodebar** east of the Jordan River (cf. 2Sm 9:4; 17:27). Yet Amos made light of this feat, purposefully mispronouncing the city "Lo-dabar," meaning "not a thing."

Israel boasted that they had **taken** the stronghold of **Karnaim** (lit., "a pair of horns," about 20 miles east of the Dead Sea) by their own strength. In God's scheme, however, Karnaim was insignificant. The **Lord God of Hosts** announced that He was raising **up a nation against** the **house of Israel**. God would prove His strength, and Israel would fall to an oppressor (Assyria) who would **afflict** them from **Hamath** (north) to the **brook of the Arabah** (south, the Dead Sea).

C. The Results of Judgment (7:1–9:10)

The last section of Amos has five visions, depicting what the results of God's judgment will look like. These visions also balance God's retributive justice with His compassion. God's holiness requires that justice be satisfied when His law is violated, yet He is compassionate for the sake of mercy toward the repentant.

The first four visions have the same introductory formula ("Thus the Lord God showed me," 7:1; 7:4; 7:7; 8:1) while the first two visions have a common structure: An introductory formula, a description, Amos's intercession for Israel, and God's decision. The historical incident at the temple at Bethel (7:10-17) suggests that Amos was at Bethel when he originally gave these messages (although that does not indicate when or where he wrote this book).

1. The Vision of the Locust Swarm (7:1-3)

7:1-2. God showed Amos a **locust-swarm** He was forming **after the king's mowing** (a taxation feeding the king's house and animals; cf. Dt 28:38-42) . . . **eating the vegetation of the land**. Thus the people's food (**the spring crop**) was under threat, leaving little provision until the fall harvest. Amos prayed and asked the sovereign Lord to **pardon** . . . **Jacob** (Israel) for Israel's covenant unfaithfulness, as a **small** nation could not survive such devastating judgment. God viewed Israel as **small**, in contrast to those in Israel who believed it was strong and invincible (cf. Am 6:1-3, 8, 13).

7:3. God's response to Amos was immediate and gracious. The **Lord** relented on this judgment (**changed His mind about this**). Fervent prayers of righteous individuals, like Amos, can alter the events of history (cf. Jms 5:13-18). Although Amos used an anthropomorphism (**the Lord changed His mind**) for the sake of his readers' understanding, this should not be taken literally (see Nm 23:19; Is 41:21-29). Rather, this may be understood in harmony with other declarations made by God (e.g., Is 46:8-11 where God connects His ability to know the future with His own deity) as a consistent application of His justice. When a person repents, God does not change but He relates to him in accordance with His unchanging nature, for His nature allows Him to exercise grace to repentant sinners as He wills. Similarly, when one is unrepentant, God acts in accord with His unchanging justice or his mercy and hardens whomever He wills.

2. The Vision of a Fire (7:4-6)

7:4-6. In his second vision the **Lord God** showed Amos a vision of a great **fire** that consumed all the **farm land** in Israel. Unlike the fire that consumed the capital cities in chaps. 1 and 2, Amos saw a scorching heat wave that resulted in a drought. The **great deep** refers to subterranean waters that feed springs (cf. Gn 1:2; 7:11; 8:2; 49:25). Great heat with consequent drought was another divine consequence for covenantal unfaithfulness (Dt 28:22). Amos interceded, using virtually the same prayer as Am 7:2, and again the Lord relented.

3. The Vision of the Plumb Line (7:7-17)

7:7-9. Amos's third vision does not depict an event and its outcome; instead it presents an image. **The Lord** asked Amos to identify the **plumb line** in the vision. A plumb line was a string with a weight on the end used to determine if a vertical structure like a wall or foundation was completely straight. Since God was the One testing, the standard He used is true; the Lord was about to test Israel by the standard of the covenant. The Lord announced that intercession would not avail; He would **spare them no longer**. The nation was so far out of plumb that God would tear it down. God would use the **sword** (cf. Dt 32:42) to destroy the **high places** and the temple **sanctuaries**. Amos may have used **Isaac** simply as a synonym for "Jacob" and "Israel," or it may reflect the veneration for the patriarch Isaac that Israel displayed in making pilgrimages south to Beersheba (cf. Am 5:5; 8:14), Isaac's birthplace.

7:10-11. The event described here followed and grew out of the preceding visions in general, and the vision of the plumb line in particular, specifying an example of God's plumb line proving someone to be crooked. Key words occur in the visions and the event at Bethel but not elsewhere in Amos (e.g., "Isaac," vv. 9, 16, and "sanctuary," vv. 9, 13). Amos's placement of this event here anticipates the overall rejection of God's Word in Israel.

Amaziah, an apostate priest who served at Bethel, considered Amos's prophesies treasonous. So he sent a message to **Jeroboam** (II), in which he charged Amos with conspiring against the king **in the midst of** Jeroboam's kingdom. Amaziah held Amos in suspicion on two counts: By what authority could he proclaim visions about a future destruction of Israel's worship centers and the royal family? Does he not prophesy for personal profit? Amaziah gave a fair assessment of Amos's words (cf. vv. 8-9 with v. 11), and personalized the danger of Amos to the king, thereby inciting him to action.

7:12-13. Amaziah approached Amos, telling him to move back to Judah and to earn his living there (cf. 1:1). By referring to Amos as a **seer** (a term for a prophet; cf. 1Sm 9:9; 2Sm 24:11), Amaziah was disparaging Amos's visions. Telling him to **eat bread** in Judah, he hinted that Amos get a job **prophesying** in Judah (cf. Ezk 13:17-20) rather than Bethel, as it was the king's **sanctuary** and a royal residence.

7:14-15. Amos responded that he was not a **prophet** by his own choosing or by birth. It was common and expected for sons to follow in their father's line of work. Amos had not been trained in one of the schools of the prophets (cf. 2Kg 2:1-15; 4:1). He earned his living as a **herdsman** and a **grower of sycamore figs** (see Introduction). God often calls people from their present work into His service. Amos 7:15 repeats the words **the Lord** for emphasis. Amos left his former occupation to obey a divine calling (**the Lord took me**).

7:16-17. Amos announced **the word of the Lord** for Amaziah. Because he had forbade Amos to **prophesy against Israel**, his wife would become a **harlot in the city** of Bethel. For a priest's wife to turn to harlotry would be publicly humiliating, since priests were forbidden to marry such women (Lv 21:7, 14). **Sons** and **daughters** falling **by the sword** implied the end of Amaziah's family line. The text records no fulfillment of it, but as a prophet, Amos foretold that Amaziah's property would go to the Assyrians in the future, as he would die in a pagan (**unclean**) land.

4. The Vision of the Basket of Summer Fruit (8:1-14)

8:1-3. In the fourth vision of this section, Amos revealed that the **Lord God** showed him a **basket of summer fruit**. Amos's first three visions, culminating with the vision of the plumb line, showed that judgment was deeply deserved. Amaziah's response to Amos's preaching exposed the fraud of the spiritual headship of Israel as the warning from God was rejected. This vision of the **basket of summer fruit** showed the time was ripe (impending) for executing judgment. Like the fruit in the basket, Israel would be consumed soon. This vision gave rise to the prophetic oracles that follow (vv. 4-6, 7-10, 11-14), explaining the nature of the imminent judgment.

A wordplay exists in 8:2 between the word for **summer fruit** (*qayis*) and the word for **the end** (*qes*). Amos saw a basket of *qayis*. God replied, "Yes, the *qes* has come." Palace singers (who had been composing royal songs, 6:5) will **turn to wailing** as **corpses** cover the land (8:3). So many bodies will result from the enemy's slaughter that the living would dispose of them **in silence**. Like so much rotten fruit, dead Israelites would be **cast . . . forth**.

8:4-6. Judgment was imminent because of Israel's oppressions, which **trample the needy** and crush them (cf. 4:1). Amos exposed Israel's motivation: **to do away with the humble of the land**. Their religious hypocrisy was evident in their resenting worship on **the new moon** and **the sabbath**, which kept them from going back to the work of cheating (making **the bushel smaller and the shekel bigger**). Merchants defied the law and tampered with the scales (e.g., Lv 19:35-36).

8:7. Amos described more fully the predicted wailing and silence in Israel (cf. v. 3) that would take place when the imminent judgment arrived. Again Amos said that the **Lord has sworn** (cf. 4:2; 6:8) indicating the certainty of coming judgment. The **pride of Jacob** refers to Israel's arrogance (cf. 6:8). Some see a reference to God Himself (cf. 1Sm 15:29), but this is unlikely since the force is greater when it refers to the unchanging nature of Israel's pride (J. A. Motyer, *The Day of the Lion: The Message of Amos* [Downers Grove, IL: InterVarsity, 1974], 179).

8:8-10. These sins would cause the land to quake from the Lord's approach. The judgment would be cosmic in scope and accompanied by national mourning. Perhaps a literal earthquake did occur, though likely trembling with fear is also in view. The waves of terror and destruction would be like the rising and falling of the **Nile** River.

In that (unnaturally bad) **day**, God would send darkness over the land (eclipses had occurred previously in 784 and 763 BC), so even the **sun** will go into mourning with the rest of creation. Joyous festivals will turn into mourning ceremonies. People will wear **sackcloth** and shave their heads (**baldness**) as signs of grief. **Mourning** the death of an **only son** meant extinguishing hope for the future through the provision for one's old age. The end of that day would be **bitter** indeed. This prediction saw the **day** as the coming Assyrian conquest but was intended to foreshadow the eschatological day of the Lord (cf. comments on 5:18).

8:11-14. The few remaining Israelites would be silent as they disposed of the corpses of their fellows (cf. v. 3), but God would also be silent, withholding words from His people. This **famine** of the nourishment and refreshment God's Word provides would send people to **stagger from sea to sea**. It is better to be without food than without a word from God. The people **will go to and fro to seek the word of the Lord**, but to no avail. Even those capable of great endurance in quests (**beautiful virgins and the young men**) will give up from exhaustion. Israel rejected the Lord's words to them (2:11-12; 7:10-13), so He would not send further revelation to them. Apostate Israelites who swore in the name of pagan deities would **fall and not rise again** because their idols would not uplift them. Amos described the prominent idol (Asherah; cf. Jdg 6:25; 2Kg 23:4) as **the guilt of Samaria**. From **Dan** (north) to **Beersheba** (south), Israelites would seek some word from their gods and find none.

5. The Vision of the Lord beside the Altar (9:1-10)

9:1. Amos's final vision differs from the preceding four. In this one Amos played no active part in the vision, but he saw the **Lord standing beside the altar** (at Bethel). The Lord commanded that some unidentified person should **smite the capitals** that supported the roof of the temple so that its foundation stones would **shake** and the structure would fall down (cf. Jdg 16:29-30; Is 6:4). The Lord would **slay . . . with the sword** any priests and worshipers who survived the temple collapse. No one would **escape** with his life.

9:2-4. Even if they tried to **dig into Sheol** (here, the earth) or **ascend to heaven** (cf. Ps 139:7-8) God's **hand** was there to **bring them down**. If neither heights nor depths can separate people from the love of God (Rm 8:38-39), neither can they hide them from God's wrath, whether hiding on Mount **Carmel** (the highest elevation in Israel), or on the **floor of the sea**. The Lord seeks out the guilty and sends His agents, even if that is a **serpent** in the sea (cf. Am 5:19; Jb 26:12-13). Those who would try to escape His judgment by going **into captivity** the Lord would **slay** with the **sword**. Normally God watched over His people for their good, but here He promised to set His **eyes against them for evil** (that is, "misfortune," "calamity" in the form of destruction as judgment against their sins).

9:5-6. Amos presented God's character in an inclusio: **The Lord God of hosts** who would judge the Israelites is the One of whom Amos concluded, **The Lord is His name**. Israel's sovereign Lord controls and leads armies, both heavenly and earthly. By His touch the **land . . . melts** like ice when a human finger presses on it. He alters the course of earthly matters to rise and fall, to ebb and flow, like the waters of the **Nile of Egypt**. His control of heavenly issues is seen in that His **upper chambers in the heavens** (His dwelling) are as a **vaulted dome over the earth** and He manages the rain that **pours . . . out on the face of the earth**. The word vault is difficult. A vaulted dome is foreign to the architecture of the period, and it may better refer to something bound together or clustered. Although God did indeed create a round earth, this verse should not be used to support that idea.

9:7-10. God asked Israel if she was any different from those nations whose fates He orchestrated. **Ethiopia** (Cushites) was a remote people, on the edge of the earth from an ancient Near Easterner's perspective, yet God watched over them. He had separated the **Philistines from Caphtor** (Crete; cf. Dt 2:23) and the **Arameans** (Syrians) **from Kir** in Mesopotamia (cf. Am 1:5). Though they were Israel's enemies, God had been gracious to them as He had been to Israel. Israel considered herself superior, but she was no less accountable than these nations. Referring to the pagan nations again at the end of the book, Amos came full circle (cf. 1:1-15) as the Lord's sovereignty brackets this prophecy like bookends.

While the Lord looked over **all** earth's kingdoms, His eyes were on **the sinful kingdom** to **destroy it**. Israel would reap God's justice for any other sinful nation (9:8; cf. 3:1-2). Yet He promised not to **totally destroy the house of Jacob**, because of His covenant (cf. 5:4-6, 14-15, 23-24; see also the comments on Rm 8:28-29). God sifted all Israelites **as grain** in a sieve, separating the people deserving judgment from the righteous. The righteous person would slip through, but God would retain the unrighteous for judgment. God determines just how much sinfulness makes His punishment inevitable. None who claimed that they would escape that **calamity** could escape the Lord's **sword**!

III. Conclusion: The Restoration of the Davidic House (9:11-15)

God's judgment, however fierce, does not destroy without purpose. God stands boldly against the sinful nation that presumes on His grace. One's past relationship with God is not license for sin. The Lord knows His own and separates out a faithful remnant for His purposes, as this final section of the book makes clear.

9:11-12. Amos's warnings of divine wrath are also balanced with the prospect of the eventual triumph of God's kingdom. The relationship that God created with His people has a future, and His people will be vindicated at the end of time. Like other eighth-century prophets to Israel and Judah, Amos found reason to hope (e.g., Is 40-66; Hs 1:10-11, 14-23; Mc 2:12-13).

In that day God will miraculously intervene and also restore **the fallen booth** (dynasty) **of David** that had suffered some destruction (9:11). David's "tent" had suffered major damage because of the division of the nation into two parts (Israel in the north, Judah in the south), though it had not yet collapsed. In the future God would **rebuild it as in the days of old**, with a descendant of David ruling over a united kingdom (Jr 30:3-10; Ezk 37:15-28; Hs 3:4-5). This restoration will follow in the millennium after the judgments of the tribulation. Some may regard this statement as a postexilic insertion into the text after David's house had fallen, but this final oracle is genuinely from Amos and is a prophetic restoration of David's house even before it fell. It reflects both eighth-century terminology and eschatology that had been held long prior to his day by orthodox Israelites (J. D. W. Watts, *Vision and Prophecy in Amos*, CBC [Cambridge: Cambridge University Press, 1975], 25–26)

Other **nations** will participate in the blessings on the house of David, and Israel will be a source of blessing to them. What follows is a transparent allusion to Nm 24:17-19, which speaks of the day when the Messiah the star from Jacob comes, and Edom will become the possession of Israel. Therefore Amos stated that Israel will **possess the remnant of Edom**. The Edomites, who had formerly been implacable enemies (cf. Ob 19), here represent all of Israel's enemies. **All the nations** associated with the **name** of the **Lord** will also enjoy His lordship as the One **who does this**. This use of parallelism explains the LXX translation of this text. Just as Edom is parallel to the nations, so the LXX paraphrastically translates Edom as "Adam" or "mankind," indicating the same point as the Masoretic Text, that the nations will all know the Lord in the messianic kingdom. Additionally, in Ac 15:16-18, James quoted the LXX of Am 9:11-12, making the same point about the Gentiles.

James's citation of this passage at the Jerusalem council (cf. Ac 15:11-18) does not indicate that this prophecy is fulfilled in the Church. The phrase **in that day** clearly puts the fulfillment at the end of days, with the establishment of the Messiah's kingdom. More likely, James used this text to make an application of a principle. Thus, the words of Amos agree with the situation in the early Church. James's point is that even as Gentiles will know the Lord in the messianic kingdom without converting to Judaism, so also, Gentiles in the Church Age can become followers of Israel's Messiah *as Gentiles* without first converting to Judaism (also see the comments on Ac 15:16-21).

In Am 9:12, Amos spoke of Israel possessing the remnant of Edom, forming a canonical link with the next book of the 12 Minor Prophets. In that one, Obadiah picked up the same theme and promised that at the end of days Israel "will possess the mountain of Esau" (Ob 18-19).

9:13-15. The blessings of the millennial Davidic kingdom include the restoration of the land. The land will be so fertile that farmers planting seed for the next harvest will push reapers of the same fields to finish their work so they can plant the next crop. The **mountains** will be full of fruitful grapevines described as dripping with **sweet** (the best) **wine**. All the **hills will be dissolved** in the sense of flowing down with abundant produce. In the Messiah's kingdom (cf. Is 65:17-25), the curse that afflicts creation (Rm 8:20-21) is lifted and the productivity of the land returns when Satan is banished (Rv 20:1-3).

Israel will return to the land and **rebuild the ruined cities and live in them**. They will enjoy security, abundant food, and blessings possible only in peacetime (cf. Lv 26:6; Dt 28:6). Israel will put roots down in the promised land, never to leave it again (Mc 4:4-7; Zch 14:11). Nothing in Israel's historical restoration after exile fulfilled the promises given here. These promises are yet to be fulfilled in the millennium when Jesus Christ, David's descendent, rules from Jerusalem.

Thus Amos concluded his book of judgment with an emphasis on future hope for Israel. Even though the overall message of Amos's book was judgment for disobedience, there was ultimate hope that one day the house of David would be restored, leading to the full restoration of the people of Israel. The central implication is that Israel's entire hope rests on the coming of the future Son of David, the Messiah of Israel, identified in the NT as Jesus of Nazareth.

BIBLIOGRAPHY

Chisholm, Robert B., Jr. *Handbook on the Prophets*. Grand Rapids, MI: Baker, 2002.

Dyer, Charles H., and Eugene H. Merrill. *The Old Testament Explorer*. Nashville: Word Publishing, 2001.

Feinberg, Charles L. *The Minor Prophets*. Chicago: Moody, 1990.

Finley, Thomas J. *Joel, Amos, Obadiah*. The Wycliffe Exegetical Commentary. Chicago: Moody, 1990.

Hubbard, David A. *Joel and Amos*. Tyndale Old Testament Commentaries. Downers Grove, IL: InterVarsity, 1989.

McComiskey, Thomas Edward. "Amos." In *Daniel-Minor Prophets*. Vol. 7 of The Expositor's Bible Commentary. Edited by Frank E. Gaebelein and Richard P. Polcyn. Grand Rapids, MI: Zondervan, 1985.

Motyer, J. A. *The Day of the Lion: The Message of Amos*. Downers Grove, IL: InterVarsity, 1974.

Smith, G. *Amos: A Commentary*. Grand Rapids, MI: Zondervan, 1989.

Watts, J. D. W. *Vision and Prophecy in Amos*. The Cambridge Bible Commentary. Cambridge: Cambridge University Press, 1975.

● ● ● ●

OBADIAH

STEVEN H. SANCHEZ

INTRODUCTION

Obadiah, the shortest Old Testament book, highlights God's judgment of His enemies. It reveals a God who provides protection and vindication for His people, Israel, and promises to punish their enemy, Edom. The Edomites' name comes from their ancestor Esau, who was given the name "Edom" ("red") because he traded his birthright for some red stew (Gn 25:30). The Edomites occupied territory on the eastern side of the Dead Sea. Frequently aggressive towards Israel, Edom was the repeated subject of prophetic rebuke (Pss 83:6; 137:7; Is 11:14; 21:11-12; Jr 25:21; 34:5-8; 49:7-22; Lm 4:21; Ezk 25:12-14; 35:1-15; Jl 3:19; Am 1:11-12; Ml 1:2-5).

Author. The name Obadiah means "servant of Yah[weh]," (the LORD) and he may be one of several Obadiahs mentioned in the Bible (1Kg 18:3-16; 1Ch 3:21; 7:3; 8:38; 9:16; 9:44; 12:9; 27:19; 2Ch 17:7; 34:12; Ezr 8:9; Neh 10:5; 12:25). Tradition identifies him as Ahab's godly servant (1 Kg 18).

Date. Possible dates for this book include the ninth century BC during the reign of Jehoram, a son of Ahab (852-841 BC); at the end of the eighth century BC, during the reign of Ahaz (735-715); or the beginning of the sixth century, just after the fall of Jerusalem in 586 BC.

While many argue that only the fall of Jerusalem could have inspired such a scathing prophecy, the multiple invasions of Judah could also qualify as sufficient cause for this prophecy.

Three arguments support dating Obadiah before the fall of Jerusalem. First, Jeremiah seems to be aware of Obadiah and used his ideas prior to captivity (cf. Ob 1-2 with Jr 49:14-15; Ob 5 with Jr 49:9; Ob 6 with Jr 49:10).

Second, vv. 12-18 warn Edom against future aggression, indicating that both Judah and Edom existed after the message was given. This could not be the case after the destruction of Jerusalem because Edom fell in 553 BC, before the Jewish people returned to Jerusalem in 539 BC.

Third, it is likely the northern kingdom, Israel, was not dwelling in Ephraim and Samaria when Obadiah prophesied because v. 19 promises a restoration in the future. The only time Israel was not present in this region and city was after Shalmaneser V destroyed the northern kingdom in 722 BC. Therefore, the date of Obadiah is most likely (but not certainly) during the co-regency of Judah's King Ahaz (735-715) and his son Hezekiah (729-686).

Purposes. The purposes of the book are threefold. Primarily, it is designed to comfort Judah, showing that God will defend them and defeat their enemies. To Edom, and other nations, it is a warning that God will punish them for aggression against Israel. For all believers, it provides consolation in learning that God will defend His people.

Themes. The Lord's power to judge His enemies is a major theme of this book. Although many passages describe God as kind, loving, merciful, generous, patient, understanding, and forgiving (e.g., Ex 34:6; Ps 103:8), He also hates sin and judges those who oppose Him (e.g., Ex 34:14; Dt 4:24). The Bible presents a holistic view of God as both just and loving. God uses this message to comfort godly sufferers throughout the ages, reminding them of His power to crush their oppressors.

Another theme is God's commitment to defend His people Israel. He has bound Himself to Israel by covenant and He will keep His promise to protect them (Gn 12:3; Zch 2:8).

Background. The Edomites had a history of conflict with Israel. The first of twin boys born to Isaac and Rebecca, Esau (Edom) sold his birthright to his brother Jacob, gave up the privileges of the firstborn (Gn 25:31), and later lost his father's blessing to Jacob (Gn 27:5-10). Although Esau initially plotted revenge, eventually his anger subsided (Gn 27:41-43; 33:4, 9, 11, 12-14). Centuries later, however, after the exodus from Egypt, Esau's descendants, the Edomites, refused Israel safe passage through their territory (Nm 20:18; Jdg 11:17).

Under Saul, the relationship between Israel and Edom was fractious (1Sm 14:47). David (ca. 1010-971) exerted control with devastating consequences for Edom (2Sm 8:13-14; 1Ch 18:12). Solomon included Edom in Israel's sphere of influence, but eventually a native ruler, Hadad, rebelled against him (1Kg 11:14). Many of the kings of Judah, including Jehoshaphat (2Kg 3:9; 2Ch 20:1, 2, 10), Jehoram (2Kg 8:20; 2Ch 21:8-16), and Ahaz (2Kg 16:6; 2Ch 28:17), struggled to keep Edom under control. The Edomites supported Babylon in the fall of Jerusalem in 586 BC (Lm 4:18-22; Ezk 25:12-14; 35:1-15), thereby becoming emblematic of Israel's enemies.

OUTLINE

I. The Title of the Book (1a)
II. God's Declaration of the Punishment of Edom (1b-9)
III. God's Justification of the Punishment of Edom (10-11)
IV. God's Warning to Edom against Future Aggression (12-14)
V. God's Judgment of Edom in the Future Day of the Lord (15-21)

COMMENTARY ON OBADIAH

I. The Title of the Book (1a)

1a. Obadiah's message is a **vision,** describing how God spoke to the prophet (cf. Nm 12:6-8). The opening words, **Thus says the Lord God,** establishes the authority of Obadiah's message—it is from God Himself. **Concerning Edom** indicates it is about Edom and perhaps even meant for Edom to read. The opening phrase likely functions as a subtitle (cf. Jr 49:7).

II. God's Declaration of the Punishment of Edom (1b-9)

A. The Coming Punishment (1b)

1b. The prophetic message begins with God's declaration that Edom's judgment is imminent. Obadiah heard **a report from the Lord,** reflecting the prophet's testimony that God had spoken to him. That an **envoy has been sent among the nations** implies that Edom will receive this word from God too (cf. Jr 49:14). With the exhortation to **Arise**, God calls the armies of heaven to **battle** against Edom.

B. The Coming Humiliation (2-3)

2-3. The aim of this divine campaign of judgment is to humble Edom (v. 2). God says **I will make you small among the nations**, promising to reduce Edom to nothing. The parallel statement, **you are greatly despised,** indicates both the explanation and certainty of judgment.

The Edomites believed themselves to be secure against attack (v.3). This **arrogance of . . . heart has deceived** them into believing they were invulnerable. Their position **in the clefts of the rock** suggests their natural defenses gave them the illusion of security. The Nabateans would later use the Edomite region to build Petra in the rocky canyons. The Edomites trusted in themselves, asking rhetorically, **Who will bring me down to earth?**

C. A Comprehensive Punishment (4-9)

4. The prophet further depicts Edom's complete judgment, describing the nation as an **eagle** with its **nest among the stars**, that is, high in the mountains. But even from there, God will bring Edom down. The repetition of the phrase **declares the Lord** reminds the people that it is Israel's God who will humiliate Edom.

5-9. God illustrates the severity of impending devastation by comparing it to **thieves**. Even a thief does not take everything in a robbery (v. 5), but God will thoroughly ransack Edom (v. 6). Edom's full destruction is indicated by the exclamation, **O how you will be ruined!** (v. 5). This suggests the prophet's relief and, by extension, the satisfaction of all who have suffered indignities at the hand of the wicked (cf. Rv 19:1-4).

Obadiah reinforces his point with the image of **grape gatherers** (v. 5), who always intentionally leave some fruit on the vines for the poor to glean (Lv 19:10; Dt 23:22; 24:21; Ru 2:2-3). In contrast, when God "harvests Edom" nothing will remain of their **hidden treasures**.

The prophet uses the name **Esau** for the first time in v. 6 (also vv. 8 and 9), hinting at the ancestral relationship between Esau and Jacob (cf. v. 10). This is to remind the Edomites of Jacob's privileged covenantal position versus Esau's unfortunate status.

Edom will also suffer a reversal of fortune when her allies turn on her (v. 7). These forces now **will send** [the Edomites] **forth to the border.** Nations with whom Edom had peace treaties, who shared **bread** together, their friends, will **ambush** and displace them.

The parenthetical interjection **there is no understanding in him** suggests the surprising nature of Edom's destruction, heightening their humiliation. Expecting that Edom will not believe Him, God asks, **Will I not on that day** do it?, implying "Yes, I certainly will."

III. God's Justification of the Punishment of Edom (10-11)

Having described the humiliating future judgment of Edom, God now justifies His actions as a legal case, giving the bill of particulars against Edom.

A. Edom's Violence against Judah (10)

10. The first charge is **violence to your brother Jacob.** Edom's guilt was compounded because Esau and Jacob were brothers. Relatives should not treat each other as Edom acted toward Judah. The consequence of this **violence** will be **shame**.

B. Edom's Indifference to Judah's Distress (11)

11. The second charge is that Edom **stood aloof** as Judah's enemies pillaged God's people, acting as one of Judah's enemies and failing to come to Judah's aid. Instead of defending a brother nation, Edom watched as **strangers carried off** Judah's **wealth, and foreigners entered his gate and cast lots for Jerusalem.** These enemies were the Arameans and Philistines (2Kg 16:5; 2Ch 28:5, 17-18), who invaded Judah at the same time they invaded the northern kingdom. Edom's passivity while Judah suffered identified Edom as an enemy.

IV. God's Warning to Edom against Future Aggression (12-14)

God will judge Edom for her history of hostility toward Judah. Here God warns Edom against any future aggression against Judah.

A. Do Not Celebrate Judah's Suffering (12)

12. God's first warning was that Edom should not **gloat** or **rejoice** at Judah's future **distress.** Yet Edom failed to heed this when Babylon conquered Judah (cf. Ezk 35:1-15, esp. v. 15).

B. Do Not Participate in War against Judah (13-14)

13-14. God's second warning was that Edom should not use **the day of** Judah's **disaster** as a pretext for invasion. The image of Edomites **enter**[ing] **the gate** and **loot**[ing] Judah's **wealth** indicates active participation in attacks against Judah. In an attempt to humiliate the fleeing Judahites, Edom might be tempted to **cut down their fugitives**, capture others, and **imprison their survivors.** Yet, Edom ignored this warning and urged the Babylonians to destroy Jerusalem (Ps 137:7).

V. God's Judgment of Edom in the Future Day of the Lord (15-21)

The **day of the LORD** refers to a period of time at the end of days when God will render judgment on those who reject Him (see the comments at Zch 14:1-2 and the introduction to Joel). Citing this **day** serves as a reminder that God does not always judge sin immediately. However, God will ultimately provide deliverance for the oppressed, and He will punish all oppressors.

A. The Judgment and Eradication of Edom (15-16)

15-16. Why should Edom heed God's warnings? **For the day of the LORD draws near on all the nations.** The time is coming when God will judge all nations, not just Edom. The principle of retribution, **as you have done, it will be done to you,** will be enforced (cf. Mt 5:7; 26:52; Jms 2:13). Edom is compared to a person who became drunk in God's house, presumably rejoicing over Judah's humiliation and the temple's desecration (God's **holy mountain**). In normal drunken revelry, the drinking comes to an end, but in a startling reversal, all the nations, including Edom, will be forced to **drink** a cup of judgment **continually**. They will be forced to **drink and swallow** until they become so incapacitated that it will be **as if they had never existed.**

B. The Deliverance and Glory for Israel (17-21)

17-18. The Lord will use a divine reversal to grant Israel deliverance in the very place desecrated by their enemies (v. 17). **Zion** refers to the temple mount (Is 18:7), indicated by the parallelism with verse 16. The temple **will be holy**—sanctified by its deliverance. As a result, **the house of Jacob will possess** what was previously taken.

This divine reversal continues with Israel becoming the instrument of judgment (v. 18). Using the ancestral names **Jacob** and **Joseph**, to represent Israel, God declares the nation will become **a fire . . . and a flame**, consuming their enemies **as stubble**. As when flame burns stubble, so **there will be no survivor of the house of Esau.** The assertion, **for the LORD has spoken**, confirms that this will take place with certainty. Although the Edomites disappeared from history much earlier, this passage depicts the final battle, when Israel will be granted a great victory from their messianic King (cf. Zch 12:6 and comments there). Edom is used as an archetype of the nations gathered against Jerusalem during the last battle (cf. Am 9:12).

19-21. These events will affect Israel's future borders (vv. 19-20). Those who live in the Negev, the region south of Judah, will take possession of Edom, the **mountain of Esau** (cf. 2Ch 20:10). The inhabitants of the **Shephelah** (the hill country of western Israel) will take the Philistine Plain (modern-day Gaza Strip). Judah will also branch into **Ephraim** and **Samaria**. Israel's territory at the end of days will increase dramatically in fulfillment of the Abrahamic covenant (Gn 12; 15; Is 27:12-13; Ezk 36:33; Am 9:14-15)

Although some prophets foretold the partial regathering of the Jewish people while still in unbelief as a precursor to end-time events (cf. Ezk 37 and comments there), other prophets also predicted that once Israel believes in the Messiah Jesus at the end of the tribulation, the Lord would fully restore all the remaining Jewish exiles to the land. Obadiah's promise of restoration refers to this full regathering at the end of the tribulation. He predicts that someday, Israel's exiles will be restored to the land of the **Canaanites** as far as **Zarephath** or modern Sidon on the Mediterranean Sea.

Exiles of Jerusalem who are in Sepharad will once again **possess the cities of the Negev.** Possible locations for Sepharad include modern-day Turkey, Greece, or Spain. This return is from afar, not just from Babylon. When the Jewish people believe in Jesus as their Messiah and Deliverer, He will bring them back. They will travel great distances to return to their promised homeland, and their borders will be larger than present-day Israel. In that day, **deliverers** will become the judges of Edom's land (**the mountain of Esau**), perhaps a reference to earthly rulers from Israel, serving under the Messiah in the messianic kingdom.

Finally, Israel will **ascend Mount Zion to judge the mountain of Esau** (v. 21). Judah's enemies, Edom included, will be punished, and the world will know for certain that **the kingdom will be the LORD's** (v. 21; for the concept of "Kingdom of the LORD" see the comments on Mt 3:1-4; 13:1-17).

This theme finds its ultimate fulfillment in the future work of Jesus the Messiah, who, during His ministry on earth, reminded His followers that He would return to judge and rule the nations (Mt 19:28; 25:31–33; John 5:24-29).

This will be a day of salvation for Israel and all those who trust in Him (Zch 12), and a day of destruction for those who will not (Rv 19:11-16).

BIBLIOGRAPHY

Allen, Leslie C. *The Books of Joel, Obadiah, Jonah, and Micah*. NICOT. Grand Rapids, MI: Eerdmans, 1976.

Armerding, Carl E. "Obadiah," *The Expositor's Bible Commentary*, ed. Frank E. Gaebelein. Vol 7. Grand Rapids: Zondervan, 1985.

Baker, David W. Joel, *Obadiah, Malachi*, The NIV Application Commentary. Grand Rapids, MI: Zondervan, 2006.

Boice, James Montgomery. *The Minor Prophets*. Grand Rapids, MI: Zondervan, 1983.

Chisholm, Robert B., Jr. *Handbook on the Prophets*. Grand Rapids, MI: Baker, 2002.

Feinberg, Charles L. *The Minor Prophets*. Chicago: Moody, 1976.

Finley, Thomas John. Joel, Amos, Obadiah. Chicago: Moody, 1990.

Neihaus, Jeffrey J. "Obadiah," *The Minor Prophets: An Exegetical and Expository Commentary*. Ed. Thomas J. McComisky. Vol. 2. Grand Rapids, MI: Baker, 1992.

● ● ● ●

JONAH

BILL THRASHER

INTRODUCTION

Author. The book does not explicitly state its author; however, the traditional view is that it was Jonah, the son of Amittai. He was a prophet from Gath-Hepher in Zebulun, which is north of Nazareth in Galilee. His only other recorded prophecy in Scripture was the prediction of the extension of Israel's borders under Jeroboam II (2Kg 14:25). He lived near the end of Elisha's ministry and was a contemporary of Hosea and Amos. In this book, which is largely narrative, there is only one verse of prophetic warning (Jnh 3:4). However, the life and ministry of Jonah can be seen as predictive and typical prophecy.

There is no conclusive reason to deny Jonah's authorship of this book that bears his name. The second chapter is in the first person, and the other chapters written in the third person do not rule out his authorship. Moses (Ex 6:27; 7:1, 20; 11:3; Nm 12:1-8); Samuel (1Sm 12:1); Isaiah (Is 38:1; 39:5); and Daniel (Dn 1:1-17) sometimes wrote in the third person.

Date. Jonah was probably written between 800 and 750 BC, most likely in the late 760s before Israel was conquered by Assyria in 722 BC. Objections to an early date usually come from those who view the book as fictional, and these objections have been adequately answered.

1. Jonah 3:3 does not have to be interpreted as Nineveh having previously been conquered but simply that it was great in Jonah's day.
2. The Aramaisms—the influence of Aramaic words on the Hebrew of Jonah—do not necessarily indicate a late date, as they can be seen even in Jonah's day.
3. The universalistic concern of God for all nations was not only a postexilic idea; it also can be seen throughout the OT (Gn 12:3).
4. Referring to the King of Assyria in the unusual way as the "king of Nineveh" does not necessarily point to a later writer unfamiliar with the correct terminology of Jonah's day. Whereas Nineveh was not yet the capital of Assyria, it was still a key city, and there is evidence of a royal residence in Nineveh both before and after Jonah's day.

Themes. Jonah's experience can be compared with that of the nation of Israel—both were to be witnesses to the world, and both were disobedient. Both were disciplined by God but also preserved by Him—Jonah in the fish and Israel among the nations in centuries of dispersion and anti-Semitism. They will also be preserved in the future tribulation. As Jonah was saved and brought back to the land when he cried out to God, so will Israel be saved and brought back to their land (Dt 4:29, 31-33; Mt 24:31).

The nation was also guilty of Jonah's sin. They had been loved greatly by God and were to share this love with the world. The way to preserve one's security is not to keep God to oneself. Jonah needed to learn that the Lord was the "God of Gentiles also" (Rm 3:29).

The book opens and closes with God speaking (Jnh 1:1; 4:11). He is the main character of this book and of the entire Bible. Too many people focus on the great fish that swallowed Jonah and miss the great God. He is sovereign over His creation and over the nations of the world. He is also gracious and merciful as shown to the sailors, Jonah, and Nineveh. He has a merciful love for all people and desires them to come to repentance (2Pt 3:9).

Background. Jeroboam II (782–753 BC) was the king of Israel when Jonah prophesied. He was the greatest and longest reigning king of the northern kingdom. His domain was almost as extensive as David's.

In Assyria, Adad-nirari III reigned from 810–783 BC and was succeeded by three of his sons: Shalmaneser IV (782–773 BC), Ashur-dan III (773–756 BC), and Ashur-nirari V (755–745 BC). The latter was succeeded by Tiglath-pileser III (745–727 BC). The "king of Nineveh" was probably Ashur-dan III (cf. Jnh 3:3).

Assyria was a hated and cruel nation. To bless them was to curse Israel in Jonah's mind. Their power had subsided during the time of Jeroboam II, but their reputation lingered, and the prophecies of Hosea (11:5) and Amos (5:27) were, no doubt, a concern to Jonah. Nineveh was not yet the capital, but it was a great city (1:2; 3:2-3). Assyria did conquer Israel in 722 BC and was itself conquered by Babylon in 612 BC.

There is no indication in the text itself that the book is either an allegory or a parable. The following evidences point to its being taken as historical.

1. Jonah was seen as a historical person (2Kg 14:25).
2. Jewish tradition accepted this book as historical (Josephus, Antiquities IX, 10:2 and the apocryphal Book of Tobit 14:4ff.).
3. Christ's reference to Jonah can be seen in Mt 12:39-41; 16:4, and Lk 11:29-32. Jonah's experience in the fish is seen as a sign of Christ's death and resurrection (Mt 12:39-40; 16:4; Lk 11:29-32), and the response of Nineveh to Jonah's preaching was a rebuke to the unbelieving Jews of Christ's day (Mt 12:41; Lk 11:32).

The miracles in the book are no reason to doubt its historicity. The sovereign and omnipotent God can perform great signs and wonders. These miracles include:

1. The calming of the sea (1:15)
2. The appointment of the fish for the preservation of Jonah (1:17)
3. The deliverance of Jonah from the fish to the land (2:10)
4. The repentance of Nineveh (3)
5. The appointments of the plant, worm, and east wind (4:6-8)
6. God's self-revelation to Jonah

OUTLINE

- I. Jonah's Disobedience (1:1-17)
  - A. Jonah's Commission by the Lord (1:1-2)
  - B. Jonah's Flight from the Lord (1:3)
  - C. The Lord's Displeasure with Jonah (1:4-6)
  - D. Jonah's Confession to the Lord (1:7-10)
  - E. The Lord's Discipline of Jonah (1:11-17)
- II. Jonah's Prayer (2:1-10)
  - A. Jonah's Description of God's Deliverance (2:1-2)
  - B. Jonah's Testimony of God's Deliverance (2:3-7)
  - C. Jonah's Praise for God's Deliverance (2:8-9)
  - D. Jonah's Restoration to the Land (2:10)
- III. Jonah's Preaching (3:1-10)
  - A. Jonah's Re-commission (3:1-2)
  - B. Jonah's Obedience (3:3-4)
  - C. Nineveh's Repentance (3:5-9)
  - D. God's Response (3:10)
- IV. Jonah's Lesson (4:1-11)
  - A. Jonah's Despair (4:1-4)
  - B. God's Appointments (4:5-8)
  - C. God's Rebuke of Jonah (4:9-11)

COMMENTARY ON JONAH

I. Jonah's Disobedience (1:1-17)

A. Jonah's Commission by the Lord (1:1-2)

1:1-2. The opening verse introduces the two main characters of the book, the Lord, and Jonah, whose name means "dove." It is the only book to begin in this way. The exact manner of how God's communication came is not given, but that it came from the Lord to Jonah is certain. All that is known of Jonah, outside of this book, appears in 2Kg 14:25, and nothing else is known about his father, Amittai, except that his name means "truth." The two commands, **Go to Nineveh . . . and cry against it** (v. 2), give clear direction and will be repeated in 3:2. Nineveh was called great because of its size and importance. It was originally built by Nimrod (Gn 10:11) and was located on the eastern bank of the Tigris River over 500 miles from Israel in modern-day Iraq. Some have estimated that this would be a month's journey by land at the pace of 18 to 20 miles per day.

Yahweh is the Judge of all the nations. His wrath is His righteous reaction to sin and His determination to punish it. Jonah's communication involved warning of God's judgment and giving an opportunity for repentance (cf. Jnh 3:4).

B. Jonah's Flight from the Lord (1:3)

1:3. While some have identified Tarshish with Carthage in North Africa, it is most commonly connected with a city in southern Spain. Instead of going 500 miles northeast to Nineveh, he went to Joppa (modern Jaffa), the nearest Mediterranean seaport, about 35 miles from Samaria, and traveled 2,000 miles west to Tarshish.

Although none can escape God's presence (Ps 139:7-12), Jonah was fleeing from the land of His manifest presence and offering his resignation from God's service. The reason for this appears in Jnh 4:2: there Jonah's deep hatred for the cruel and idolatrous nation of Assyria (cf. Nah 3:1, 4) is contrasted with God's compassion for them. Jonah was obedient to deliver the message of blessing to Israel of expanding its borders (2Kg 14:25), but not a message that could bless his enemies. There is a danger of loving one's people more than God. The only way to love God's people truly is to obey God fully (1Jn 5:1).

C. The Lord's Displeasure with Jonah (1:4-6)

1:4-6. The Lord was at work in the midst of the disobedience of His servant. The wind and the sea were obedient to His purposes (v. 4). In light of the ship's attempt to return to land (v. 13), the storm evidently happened soon after the departure. The sudden storm (v. 5) had the feel of something divine. In that polytheistic culture the fearful sailors called out for assistance from their gods with the hope that one of them might be able to help. There is a difference between calling out for help and calling out in repentance. So severe was the storm that the experienced sailors sought to lighten the ship (cf. Ac 27:18-19). Jonah, out of exhaustion and maybe even depression, was fast asleep. This was a far different sleep from our sinless Lord's on the Sea of Galilee (Mk 4:37-39). The heathen sea captain had to instruct the Hebrew prophet to pray (v. 6), just as in the NT exhortation to awaken from the sleep of disobedience while the world perishes (cf. Rm 13:11). If the rebellious prophet did indeed pray for deliverance from the storm, the prayer was not answered at this time.

D. Jonah's Confession to the Lord (1:7-10)

1:7-10. Finding no help from their prayer meeting, the sailors tried to find the cause of the divine wrath that they sensed behind the storm. Casting lots was a widely used practice in the ancient Near East, and here the purpose was to determine which mate needed to confess his offense to his god. (For the use of this method, see Jos 7:14-18; 18:10; 1Sm 10:20-21; Pr 16:33; Ac 1:24-26.) Some suggest that the practice was like drawing straws out of a container, and others suggest it was more like rolling dice using stones or pebbles. Whatever the case, Jonah won the lottery. He was the first one chosen to confess his offenses. With their lives in grave danger (v. 8), the sailors commanded Jonah to immediately confess and then quickly asked him five questions about his background and reason for this calamity. They desired to know his personal information to learn more about his God. Jonah provided the answers (v. 9)—first his ethnic identity as a **Hebrew** and then his confession of faith. While he was not living consistently with his profession, he feared (unlike their fear in vv. 5, 10) or worshiped the **Lord**. Jonah then described the God of Israel as no mere local deity but **the Lord God of heaven** who is the Creator and Lord of all creation (v. 9). The frightened sailors reminded the prophet of how unthinkable it is to try to run from the One who created and controls everything (v. 10).

E. The Lord's Discipline of Jonah (1:11-17)

1:11-17. The sailor's question concerned how to appease the anger of Jonah's God. It reflected no knowledge of the need for repentance—or of the righteous and loving God of Israel. They showed no knowledge of a God who disciplines His people out of love. Jonah's conscience was guilty (v. 12), and he desired to accept his punishment. While some have noted his nobility in being willing to die to save others, it may be simply that he preferred death over obeying God's desire to bless Nineveh. Jonah certainly cannot be compared to an innocent Christ who took our guilt to save His enemies. The hero in this book is the Lord—not Jonah.

The sailors' frantic activity (v. 13) shows that self-made solutions do not work (cf. Pr 21:30). Their reluctance to follow Jonah's advice may reflect a fear of his God and some concern for human life—even more than Jonah had for Nineveh. In v. 14, the sailors, who had previously prayed to their god (v. 5), now prayed to Jonah's God. They realized that Jonah had not been tried by a human court and proven guilty. They feared God's wrath and did not desire to perish if they executed Jonah. Their respect for God's prophet was even greater than what Israel had for the prophets at times (cf. Mt 23:34-36).

The sailors affirmed their action was only carrying out God's pleasure as reflected by the storm and the casting of lots. As a result of their tossing Jonah into the sea, the storm abated (v. 15), thereby fulfilling the prophet's words (v. 12). Note that the wind and the sea obeyed God (cf. Lk 8:24) even if the prophet did not. The "fear" of v. 16 included some reverence for Jonah's God. It probably fell short of Jonah's confession (v. 9) but advanced beyond their previous fear (vv. 5, 10). While the exact nature of their sacrifices to the Lord is not explained, the text reveals that the sailors made vows promising more sacrifices in the future.

The Lord manifested His complete control of His creation by appointing a **fish** to rescue the disobedient prophet (v. 17). Other divine appointments followed (4:6, 7, 8) that revealed the gracious Lord as the hero of the story. While the Hebrew word for **fish** allows for a whale and there has been much research of the physical characteristics of sea creatures capable of swallowing a man, there is no need to speculate or seek a natural explanation. It was probably a miracle—no problem since it was an appointment by a sovereign and all-powerful God. The three days and three nights represent a literal span of time (cf. 3:3), but according to the Hebrew reckoning of time part of a day or night can be rendered as a whole day. Therefore, the time span is not required to be 72 hours (see Est 4:16; 5:1; and comments on Mt 12:38-45). Our Lord referred to Jonah's situation as an illustration of His death and resurrection (see Mt 12:40). Just as Jonah's three-day burial in the fish followed by restoration of the Ninevites functioned as a sign, so the Messiah's three days in the tomb would function as a sign to Israel and the world.

II. Jonah's Prayer (2:1-10)

A. Jonah's Description of God's Deliverance (2:1-2)

2:1-2. The scene shifts from the sailors and the ship to only Jonah, the fish, and God (v. 1). Before, Jonah had been asked by pagans to pray (1:6), but his prayer came from his own volition. He, like the sailors, prayed to the Lord (1:14), but unlike them he prayed to **the Lord his God**. He, like the prodigal son, was returning to his Father (cf. Lk 15:18). His prayer is a psalm of thanksgiving for the deliverance from the fish. Jonah's mind was full of Scripture (v. 2; cf. Ps 18:6; 111:5; 120:1), and he used it to cry out to God. **Sheol** here refers to the abode of the dead, and the **depth of Sheol** refers to his near-death experience. It is parallel with **my distress** (cf. Ps 30:3). The Lord **answered** his call and **heard** his cry. To "hear" means "to respond to one's cry for help," in this case by delivering Jonah from drowning. The mercy he experienced was the mercy he had to preach to Nineveh.

B. Jonah's Testimony of God's Deliverance (2:3-7)

2:3-7. Even though the sailors had thrown him into the sea (1:15), Jonah saw God's sovereign hand behind their action. In the same way, he saw God in charge of the sea (**Your breakers and billows**). Jonah's discipline for insisting on his own way was to experience despair from being out of God's **sight** (v. 4), which here means out of His favor. However, his faith had not failed (cf. Lk 22:32) as he voiced his hope of praying to the God who had manifested His special presence in the temple in Jerusalem. Jonah's very life was threatened as he was swept under the waters of the waves and engulfed in seaweed (v. 5). The **roots** or foundations **of the**

mountains (v. 6) were understood to be in the depths of the earth under the sea. Jonah saw himself descending into his grave. He further described his despair as being in the tomb of the sea with no chance of escape back to dry land because he was locked behind the **bars** of the earth.

This is yet another of the "But God" passages (cf. Gn 8:1; 50:20; Ps 49:15; Ac 2:24; 10:40; 13:30; Rm 5:8; 2Co 7:6; Eph 2:4; Php 2:27) that are so prominent and encouraging in Scripture. The Lord miraculously delivered him from death through the appointed fish. At the brink of death, this OT prodigal son remembered the Lord by acting on his knowledge and calling to God. The reference to the temple in Jnh 2:7 may be a reference to the temple in Jerusalem, but more likely is His heavenly abode (cf. Ps 11:4).

C. Jonah's Praise for God's Deliverance (2:8-9)

2:8-9. Jonah declared his covenant loyalty to Yahweh (cf. Ps 31:6) by noting the emptiness and worthlessness of any substitute **vain idols** (cf. Ps 127:1-2). Those who regard idols abandon their loyalty to Yahweh. The emphasis here appears to be on abandoning their source of confidence—the true Lord—and not experiencing His faithfulness or covenant loyalty. For this reason, idolatry leads to multiplied sorrows (Ps 16:4). Just as God's deliverance of the sailors led them to sacrifice and vow to the Lord (Jnh 1:16), so it led Jonah to promise to give a sacrifice (v. 9). His vow is evidently a promise to continually thank God. The vow may have included his pledge to live up to his role as a prophet.

Since repentance is not a single act but rather involves both a continual change in attitudes and actions, the rest of the book indicates that Jonah had not reached complete repentance. The mercy that he had been shown was to be available to Nineveh. **Salvation**—both physical and spiritual deliverance—is from the sovereign and gracious Lord (cf. Ps 3:8, Ac 4:12). He had physically delivered the sailors in chap. 1, Jonah in chap. 2, and will deliver Nineveh in chap. 3.

D. Jonah's Restoration to the Land (2:10)

2:10. This verse resumes the narrative from 1:17. The deliverance from drowning through the fish reached its climax in Jonah's being delivered back to the land—probably the land of Israel. What the sailors were unable to do (1:13), God did. The omnipotent God, who sent the storm (1:4), caused the lot to fall on Jonah (1:7), calmed the sea (1:15), and appointed the fish to swallow Jonah (1:17), also completed His deliverance of the prophet.

III. Jonah's Preaching (3:1-10)

A. Jonah's Re-commission (3:1-2)

3:1-2. The commission is restated (cf. 1:1) and without a rebuke—showing that God is gracious in offering a second chance. While such grace is to be received with gratitude—as with Peter after his denial (Jn 21:15-17) and John Mark after his desertion (2Tm 4:11)—it is not to be presumed upon. Some disobedience does not result in a second chance (cf. 1Kg 13:26; Nm 20:12; Heb 9:27). God graciously repeated the command to make the over 500-mile trip to Nineveh (v. 2). This great city (cf. 1:2) had over 1,500 towers and an inner and outer wall. The inner wall was over 100 feet tall and wide enough for three chariots to ride abreast. Care was to be given to proclaim God's word precisely. If Satan could not block the message, he would seek to pervert it.

B. Jonah's Obedience (3:3-4)

3:3-4. Unlike in his previous response (1:3), Jonah obeyed God's word. Nineveh is described as "an exceedingly great city" which literally reads, "a great city to God." It was great in God's estimation, which probably underscored His love for the people of this great city (cf. 4:11). The phrase "three days' walk" has been much discussed as to whether it is referring to the city's circumference or diameter. The circumference of the greater metropolitan area, which included the surrounding lands, has been estimated at 55 to 60 miles, while the diameter of Nineveh proper was considerably smaller. However, the three days' walk may be referring to the time necessary for Jonah to accomplish his preaching mission, which would include visits with dignitaries and ministry stops. On the first day of his mission, Jonah proclaimed his prediction of coming judgment: **Yet forty days and Nineveh will be overthrown** (v. 4). This was not all that Jonah proclaimed but rather was a summary of his prophetic message. He probably spoke in Aramaic, the language of the populace. The word **overthrown** was used of the destruction of Sodom and Gomorrah (Gn 19:25). While some see this as only a prediction of doom, the sending of a prophet and the delay of 40 days seems to indicate that "unless you repent" is understood as part of this prediction of judgment (cf. Jr 18:7-8). While some have noted that Jonah's credentials of being delivered from the fish gave him an unusual hearing, what brings repentance is God's Word. It is as a prophet that Jonah was a sign to the Ninevites.

C. Nineveh's Repentance (3:5-9)

3:5-9. The response to Jonah's preaching is the greatest miracle in the book. They believed God, "Elohim," and as outward evidence proclaimed a fast and put on sackcloth—a coarse, dark cloth made from goat or camel's hair—as a symbol of sorrow and repentance. Was this the greatest revival in history or only a desire to be spared from judgment? It was clearly a response to God's word and a contrast to the ways Israel had treated the prophets on many occasions and to Jonah's initial response to God's message. God did respond to Nineveh by relenting, and He does not respond to hypocrisy. Jesus did term it "repentance" (Lk 11:32; Mt 12:41), and used it as an example for Israel's leaders.

The **king of Nineveh** refers to the ruling monarch (v. 6). His identity was either Adad-nirari III (810–783 BC) or more probably Ashurdan III (773–756 BC). The latter did reign in a turbulent time that included a solar eclipse and political threats, which may have readied his heart for this prophetic word. The text identifies his fourfold response: he arose from the throne, removed his royal attire, put on sackcloth to identify with the common people, and sat in ashes—a sign of helplessness and despair (cf. Jb 2:8; Mc 1:10). The king's personal response is followed by his official decree—all Ninevites were to observe a complete fast of food and water (v. 7). Domesticated animals were included in the fast, which appears unusual but was not unknown in the ancient Near East and can be found in Persian records. All creation is affected by man's sin (cf. Rm 8:20, 22; Jl 1:18-20) and is not outside the sphere of God's compassion (Jnh 4:11). Their inclusion underscores the utter desperation of the decree. It was mandated that both man and animal were to wear sackcloth (3:5) and **call on God earnestly** (lit., "with strength"), meaning "with sincerity" (v. 8). The last part of the decree was to turn from his **wicked way** and from **violence**. The Hebrew word for wickedness refers to moral depravity while the word for **violence** does not refer to natural catastrophes or justifiable force but rather to morally depraved and oppressive force. Nineveh was known for cruel practices, especially to prisoners of war. As the sailors had hoped to be spared from judgment (1:6), the king of Nineveh expressed his similar hope (v. 9) (cf. Jl 2:12-14). Even a cruel nation that had oppressed God's people can be spared from deserved judgment if its people repent.

D. God's Response (3:10)

3:10. God's character is unchanging (Jms 1:17), but He does make changes to His plan of action as He deals with men (cf. Jr 18:7-8). Later, Nineveh did return to its wickedness and destroyed Israel in 722 BC, and was itself destroyed in 612 BC. However, this judgment was delayed 150 years. Later generations are responsible for their own repentance. God's promise to bless repentance is not to be interpreted as if the accomplishment of God's sovereign plan is ever in question (Jb 42:2; Eph 1:11).

Some theologians, known as "open theists" have argued that God's relenting **concerning the calamity which He had declared He would bring upon them**, supports the idea that God changes His mind based on the actions of humanity. But the Bible is plain that God knows and declares "the end from the beginning" (Is 46:10). God affirms that He is sovereign over the future, asserting "My purpose will be established, and I will accomplish all My good pleasure . . . Truly I have spoken; truly I will bring it to pass. I have planned it, surely I will do it" (Is 46:10-11). As stated above, God's warning through Jonah came with an implicit condition: that the judgment would happen *unless they repented*. When Nineveh repented, God did not bring the judgment to pass. Certainly, it appeared obvious, even to Jonah (Jnh 4:2) that "it was God's intent all along to show mercy to the Ninevites, knowing that the *stated prediction* of judgment would elicit their repentance so that God could then display his *originally intended mercy*" (Bruce Ware, *Their God is Too Small* [Wheaton, IL: Crossway, 2003], 40).

IV. Jonah's Lesson (4:1-11)

A. Jonah's Despair (4:1-4)

4:1-4. What pleased God (3:10) **greatly displeased** Jonah in that he considered God's action wrong and evil. That God's wrath had been averted by His merciful response to Nineveh's repentance made Jonah angry. He sank into self-pity because God had not served Jonah's self-interest. Unlike his prayer in chap. 2, this prayer is a self-centered complaint to God full of "I" and "me" (v. 2). He cited his reason for fleeing as a dread of the success of his ministry. He did not want Nineveh to experience the very same mercy of God shown to him (chap. 2).

While he had obeyed God (3:1-3), it obviously was not in a spirit of submission. His begrudging attitude toward the Ninevites brings to memory the forgiven debtor who did not extend the same grace (see Mt 18:21-35) and the elder brother's attitude toward the prodigal son (see Lk 15:25-30). Jonah's mention of God's **gracious** character refers to His favor that He extends to the undeserving. The adjectival form occurs 13 times in the OT and 11 of these are a conjunction with *raham* (compassion). It always refers to God. His **compassionate** character refers to His tender and merciful affection, like that of a mother's love toward her nursing baby. **Slow to anger** underscores God's patience, while the word **lovingkindness** refers to God's unfailing and loyal love that has a special connection to Israel but extends to the whole world (Ru 1:8; 2Sm 15:19-20; Pss 33:5; 117:1; 119:64). (For other verses with these attributes, see Ex 34:6-7; Nm 14:18; 2Ch 30:9; Neh 9:17; Pss 86:5; 103:8; 145:8; Jl 2:13; Nah 1:3.)

In Jnh 1:12, Jonah resigned himself to being thrown overboard, but then he praised God in chap. 2 for sparing his life. He now expressed his preference for dying rather than being restored to serving a merciful God (v. 3). While Moses (Nm 11:15) and Elijah (1Kg 19:4) reached this point of despair under the burden of their ministries, Jonah's despair was unique. Death can be gain for the believer (Php 1:21), but it is not to be sought in rebellion to God. Mercifully for Jonah, God did not answer his prayer. Rather, God responded in great kindness and tenderness rather than with a blasting rebuke (v. 4). He asked Jonah to ponder and reflect on whether he had **good reason to be angry**. In so doing, God invited him to judge himself (cf. Gn 4:6). There is no merit in being angry at the advancement of God's cause, the glorification of His name, and that in which the angels rejoice (Lk 15:10).

B. God's Appointments (4:5-8)

4:5-8. Jonah would have entered the city from the west and would have been sitting east of it in his temporary shelter. This shelter was probably made of stone with tree branches for its roof or possibly even a shelter of stone that lacked a roof. While some see these verses as a flashback to vv. 1-4, they can be seen as his response to God's question in v. 4. Jonah went out to see what would happen after the 40 days. As he fixated upon "his" way of protecting Israel—his enemy's downfall—he sat in hope for Nineveh's return to wickedness that would result in their judgment. He was looking for circumstances to change, but God was seeking to elicit a change in him.

While the identity of the plant (v. 6)—possibly a caster-oil plant with large leaves—has sparked much discussion and even a bitter controversy in church history between Jerome and Augustine who disagreed on the kind of plant, what is emphasized here is its appointment by God who enabled its rapid growth. The word for **discomfort** (*ra'ah*) is a general word in Hebrew, used in a variety of ways. In 3:8, it is translated wicked and refers to moral evil. In 3:10 it is translated calamity and refers to the disaster of judgment that God would bring. Here (v. 6) it means distress or misery. The author is using a deliberate word play. The plant was designed not only **to deliver him from his discomfort** but also to deliver Jonah from his wicked attitude. As Nineveh's repentance shielded it from eternal calamity, so now the plant shielded Jonah from the bitter heat of possibly as much as 110 degrees. Jonah's extreme happiness (lit., rejoiced with great rejoicing) was over his personal comfort, and his displeasure and anger (v. 1) was over what brought great joy to God. The God who appointed the fish (1:17) and the plant (v. 6) also showed His sovereignty over His creation by appointing a worm (v. 7) and a scorching east wind (v. 8). All of God's creation followed God's sovereign appointment but His prophet, who refused the initial appointment to preach and even resented the success of His second appointment.

The worm, possibly a black caterpillar, destroyed the plant. The east wind (cf. Ezk 17:10) created a discomfort that caused Jonah to repeat his request for death (Ezk 4:3). This kind of wind causes a dramatic rise in temperature, and the LXX calls it a "scorcher." God's hand is evident in both the rapid growth and quick destruction of the plant.

C. God's Rebuke of Jonah (4:9-11)

4:9-11. God's unanswered question of v. 4 is repeated in v. 9, and Jonah emphatically answered that he did **have good reason to be angry, even to death**. His passion overruled his reason and his conscience. Jonah's attitude gave rise to another question that provided the reason behind God's appointments of the plant, worm, and east wind. While emphasizing Jonah's self-centered **compassion** (meaning "pity") on a temporal plant (cf. v. 2), which was wholly a gift of His grace (v. 10), God asked, "**Should I**

not have compassion (pity) **on Nineveh**?" which was filled with eternal beings whom God loved (v. 11). Self-preoccupation such as Jonah's can be blinding as it leads to valuing personal and temporal comfort over God's will and the souls of men. The 120,000 **who [did] not know the difference between their right and left hand** (v. 11) may refer to the children of the city. In light of the word for **persons** (v. 11), a reference to people in general, it more likely refers to the whole city that was as morally and ethically undiscerning as children. In either case, was it right to be angry that the plant was destroyed and that the precious people of Nineveh were not? Even the animals (cf. 3:7-8; 4:11) were more valuable than the plant.

God's question ends the book in order to help readers learn from Jonah's lesson about God's character. He is sovereign, righteous, gracious, and merciful; He desires that His people obey Him and not put limits on His love. God is kind to evil and ungrateful humanity (Lk 6:35) and patiently desires repentance (2Pt 3:9). Selfish agendas and wrong priorities are to be repented of, for only the pure in heart can spiritually discern the character of God.

BIBLIOGRAPHY

Allen, Leslie C. *The Books of Joel, Obadiah, Jonah, and Micah*. The New International Commentary on the Old Testament. Grand Rapids, MI: Eerdmans, 1976.

Beyer, Bryan, and John Walton. *Obadiah, Jonah*. The Bible Study Commentary. Grand Rapids, MI: Zondervan, 1988.

Chisholm Jr., Robert B. *Handbook on the Prophets*. Grand Rapids, MI: Baker Academic, 2002.

Cohen, A. "Jonah." In *The Twelve Prophets*, edited by S. Goldman. London: The Soncino Press, 1957.

Feinberg, Charles L. The Minor Prophets. Chicago: Moody, 1976.

Gaebelein, Frank E. *Four Minor Prophets: Obadiah, Jonah, Habakkuk, and Haggai*. Chicago: Moody, 1977.

Hannah, John D. "Jonah." In vol. 1 of *The Bible Knowledge Commentary*, edited by John F. Walvoord and Roy B. Zuck. Wheaton, IL: Victor Books, 1985.

Keil, C. F. "Jonah." In vol. 10 of *Commentary on the Old Testament in Ten Volumes*, reprint. Grand Rapids, MI: Eerdmans, 1982.

Kohlenberger, John R. III. *Jonah-Nahum*. Everyman's Bible Commentary. Chicago: Moody, 1984.

Livingston, G. Herbert. "Jonah." In *The Wycliffe Bible Commentary: The Old Testament*. Chicago: Moody, 1962.

Page, Frank S. "Jonah." In vol. 19B *The New American Commentary*. Nashville: Broadman Press, 1995.

Price, Brynmor F, and Eugene A. Nida. *A Handbook on Jonah*. New York: United Bible Society, 1978.

Price, Brynmor F, and Eugene Nida. *Translator's Guide to the Book of Jonah*. Stuttgart: United Bible Society, 1978.

Pusey, E. B. Vol. 1 of *The Minor Prophets: A Commentary*. Grand Rapids, MI: Baker, 1970.

Stuart, Douglas. "Hosea–Jonah." In vol. 31 of *Word Biblical Commentary*. Dallas: Word Books, 1987.

Walton, John, Victor Matthews, and Mark W. Chavalas. *The IVP Bible Background Commentary: Old Testament*. Downers Grove, IL: InterVarsity, 2000.

Ware, Bruce. *Their God is Too Small*. Wheaton, IL: Crossway, 2003.

●●●●

MICAH

DANIEL GREEN

INTRODUCTION

Author. The author of the book was Micah, a prophet God called to pronounce judgment on Israel. His hometown, Moresheth, was likely Moresheth Gath, in the fertile hills southwest of Jerusalem, between the Dead Sea and Mediterranean Sea. His name means "who is like Yahweh?" Although less prominent than his contemporary Isaiah, he was mentioned in Jr 26:18-19 for his effective preaching. Nothing else is known of him except what is revealed in the biblical text.

Date and Background. Micah prophesied during the reigns of Jotham (742–735 BC), Ahaz (735–715 BC), and Hezekiah (715–686 BC). During this period Assyria, under Tiglath-pileser III, began to dominate the region. Resistance was futile as Samaria, the capital of the northern kingdom, fell in 722 BC. The southern kingdom was overrun as well and heavy fines were levied, although Hezekiah (and Jerusalem) were spared. At the time the prophecy was given, Israel was enjoying considerable economic prosperity, which led to "a selfish materialism, a complacent approach to religion as a means of achieving human desires, and disintegration of personal and social values" (Leslie Allen, *Joel, Obadiah, Jonah, and Micah* [Grand Rapids, MI: Eerdmans, 1976], 240). The book is prophetic in tone and often employs poetry to communicate its message.

Purpose. The purpose of the book is to demonstrate that true faith results in social justice and practical holiness, with a view toward the ultimate reign of Messiah on the earth. The emphasis on social justice is evident in the censure of unlawful seizure of fields (2:1-2), theft (2:2), exploitation of women and children (2:9), corrupt leadership (3:1-9), unethical business practices (6:10-12), violence (7:2), and bribery (7:3). Nevertheless a better future is foreseen when such sin will be banished as Messiah is born to reign righteously over Israel (4:1-8, 5:2-5a, 7:7-20).

Structure. The book is clearly divided into three messages that follow the superscription (1:1). The divisions begin with the words "hear, oh peoples" (1:2), and "hear now" (3:1; 6:1). The messages say that judgment will come (1:2–2:13), blessing will follow judgment (3:1–5:15), and blessing will surpass judgment (6:1–7:20).

OUTLINE

I. Superscription (1:1)
II. Message One: Judgment Will Come (1:2–2:13)
- A. Sins Against God (1:1-16)
- B. Sins Against Men (2:1-13)

III. Message Two: Blessing Will Follow Judgment (3:1–5:15)
- A. The Rebuke of Israel's Leaders (3:1-12)
- B. The Future Blessing of Jerusalem (4:1–5:1)
- C. The Coming of Messiah (5:2-15)

IV. Message Three: Blessing Will Surpass Judgment (6:1–7:20)

A. God's Ethical Standards (6:1-8)
B. Rebuke for Poor Business Ethics (6:9-16)
C. Rebuke for Poor Interpersonal Ethics (7:1-6)
D. Hope for Messianic Compassion (7:7-20)

COMMENTARY ON MICAH

I. Superscription (1:1)

1:1. This verse provides introductory background for the three messages of the book. **The word of the LORD** (Hb. *Yahweh*) refers to the prophecy that came from the God of Israel, and emphasizes His faithfulness to covenantal promises. It was given to Micah to be delivered to three kings of Israel (see Introduction). It concerned the impending judgment of Samaria and Jerusalem, the capital cities of the northern and southern kingdoms, respectively.

II. Message One: Judgment Will Come (1:2–2:13)

A. Sins Against God (1:1-16)

1:2a. The command to listen (3:1, 6:1) is directed to the world. The phrases **hear, O peoples** and **listen, O earth** are set in synonymous parallel. They are identical in meaning, summoning all the people, without exception, to pay attention. It is best to see the nations not as recipients of the prophesied judgments, but as witnesses to what God was about to do among His own chosen people.

1:2b-3. Lord GOD (Hb. *Adonai Yahweh*) emphasizes the supreme might of God who dwells in heaven, His holy temple. He was about to issue an indictment (Dt 31:19-21) against His unholy people. God would come down from heaven to trample on the **high places** of pagan idolatry (1Kg 12:31-32; Ezk 20:27-32) that His people had built. While the phrase may include geographical mountains, it is best taken as the cultic shrines located on them (Bruce K. Waltke, *A Commentary on Micah* [Grand Rapids, MI: Eerdmans, 2007], 48).

1:4. Micah employed hyperbolic language to emphasize the catastrophic results of God's visitation. He used the words **mountains** and **valleys** as a merism, a figure of speech marking opposite extremes to indicate that everything in Israel would be affected. **Wax** (Pss 68:1-2; 97:5-6) and cascading **water** describe both the geological and sociopolitical instability that would ensue.

1:5-7. Rebellion (Hb. *pesha*, to transgress) and **sins** (Hb. *chattaah*, to miss the mark, sin; Jdg 20:16) describe attitudes and actions that are contrary to God's holy standards. These words are often coupled in Micah (1:5; 3:8; 6:7; 7:18). The rhetorical questions (v. 5) indict the religious centers of Samaria and Jerusalem as the most sinful places in their respective kingdoms. No stone would be left unturned in the destruction of the former, and her foundations would be razed. In the process, all the accoutrements of pagan worship would be destroyed. The clever play on words in v. 7b means that the silver and gold from the idols of Israel (Dt 7:25), here depicted as a harlot, would be harvested from its burning buildings by another religious harlot, Assyria. Believers should realize that any idols in their own lives are most displeasing to God and should rid themselves of them. Fame, food, money, power, sex, and sports are all potential false gods.

1:8-9. Micah would prophesy **barefoot and naked** as a sign of his utter spiritual humiliation, just as Isaiah did (Is 32:11). A **lament** was mournful wailing over sin that was often accompanied by fasting (Jnh 1:13; Zch 7:5). His would be like that of a howling jackal which, along with the ostrich, lived in places made uninhabitable by the judgment of God (Is 13:20-22). It was too late for the southern kingdom to repent as the enemy hordes were certain to ravage the country. The Assyrian commander Sennacherib destroyed 46 cities of Judah before he stopped short of Jerusalem in 701 BC.

1:10-12. A number of skillful word plays are employed here to signal the destruction of southern cities: (1) **Beth-le-aphrah** (possibly an alternative name for Ophrah, about 12 miles northwest of Jerusalem, the name meaning "House of Dust") **roll yourself in the dust** (*aphrah*), a sign of deep grief; (2) **Tell it** (*nagad*) **not in Gath** (which means "the place of telling," i.e., the city of Gath, southwest of Jerusalem); (3) "abandon, oh dweller of the beautiful place

(**Shaphir**) in shameful nakedness"; (4) "do not go forth (*yatsa'*) you who dwell in 'Go Forth'" (*tsa'anan*, **Zaanan**, along the southern coast); (5) "from the house of protection (**Beth-ezel**) he will withdraw support"; and (6) "because the inhabitant of **Maroth** (sounds like *mara*, meaning 'bitterness' in Hb.) has become weak."

1:13-16. Lachish (30 miles southwest of Jerusalem), which sounds like the Hebrew word (*racash*) for "gathering," would gather its fine chariot horses for a hasty retreat from Sennacherib. He would later decorate his walls in Assyria with the finery that he pillaged from the rebellious city that had led Israel into sin. **Moresheth-gath** brings to mind the betrothal of a bride (Hb. *meoreset*, betrothal gifts) with the accompanying gifts being given instead to the invaders. **Achzib** (sounds like the Hebrew for "deception") would not be able to provide the expected resistance to the invaders. **Mareshah**, which sounds like the Hebrew word *yarash* (possess) would be possessed. **The glory of Israel** refers either to the people in general or its children (Hs 9:11-13). All would flee in shame to **Adullam**, 12 miles south of Bethlehem, to which David had once run for his life (1Sm 22:1). They would shave their heads as they mourned their sins (Is 15:2).

B. Sins Against Men (2:1-13)

2:1-3. Woe would come on those who had lain awake at night thinking of strategies for defrauding fellow Israelites (Pr 4:16). They had abused power, coveting and seizing the precious inherited land and houses of the poor (1Kg 21:1-15). God would therefore visit the family of oppressors with **calamity**. Their strutting would be stopped, and they would find no way of escape.

2:4-5. People would taunt these evildoers and would mockingly "lament a lament of lamentation" (literal translation). God's principle of an eye for an eye (Ex 21:24) would play out as the land grabbers would have their own lands taken from them. These would be given to **apostate**, hostile Assyrians who cared nothing for the God of Israel. The enemy who would control the land would not be **stretching [out] a measuring line**, that is, survey the land to establish rightful ownership. In a similar way, God will not overlook the sins of believers today, who cheat the poor of their precious assets through bogus monetary schemes, or who see to the eviction of such people from public housing so as to build fabulously profitable high-rise condominiums on the sites. They will surely reap what they sow (Gl 6:7).

2:6-7. These verses contain the words of false prophets who understandably resented Micah's preaching and tried to get him to follow their own practice of not preaching against sin. It is possible that the Hebrew word *sug* translated in the NASB as **turned back** might be translated as "overtake," and may refer to the consequences of sin that the false prophets believed would not befall them ("disgrace will not overtake us" [ESV, NIV]). But *sug* usually means "to turn away" or "to turn back" (Jr 38:22; 46; Is 42:17; Zph 1:6) and more likely is understood here as the embarrassment of the false prophets, which would not cease until Micah stopped contradicting them. They were losing face. Micah defended the character of God, and His right to judge them, by asserting these truths. (1) His Spirit had shown great patience. (2) He could not justly be accused of any wrong. (3) His words always led to blessing for those who applied them in leading a righteous lifestyle. These were truths that the false teachers were not willing to hear or preach.

2:8-9. God viewed Israel's unethical actions as the aggression of an enemy. The false prophets illegally seized the clothing of unsuspecting travelers and war veterans who were perhaps debilitated due to wounds or weariness. Unrepresented widows were driven from their homes, depriving them of their meager pleasures. Their children suffered likewise. **My splendor** means the glory of God, which would not be manifested in the land due to the disobedience of Israel's leaders.

2:10-11. Micah uses a play on words to depict the coming judgment. The rebellion of v. 8 ("My people have arisen as an enemy") is associated with their displacement (**arise and go** to exile). Their filthy idolatry would be the motivation for God to drive them from the restful conditions that they enjoyed in the land. The prophet denounced the gullibility of the people who were willing to follow false teachers (those who were aimless [walked **after wind**], who told **falsehood** and **lies**, v. 11), no matter how absurd their messages might be.

2:12-13. Despite the certainty of the coming judgment, there was still hope for Israel. In the future God would reassemble Israel and bring her en masse back to the land. The noise of so many people would be like a huge herd of sheep. Their king, the Lord, would break down all barriers to their return. The word "breaker" (Hb. *parats*, Ex 19:22, 24; 2Sm 6:8) should be

Southern Cities of Micah's Prophecies

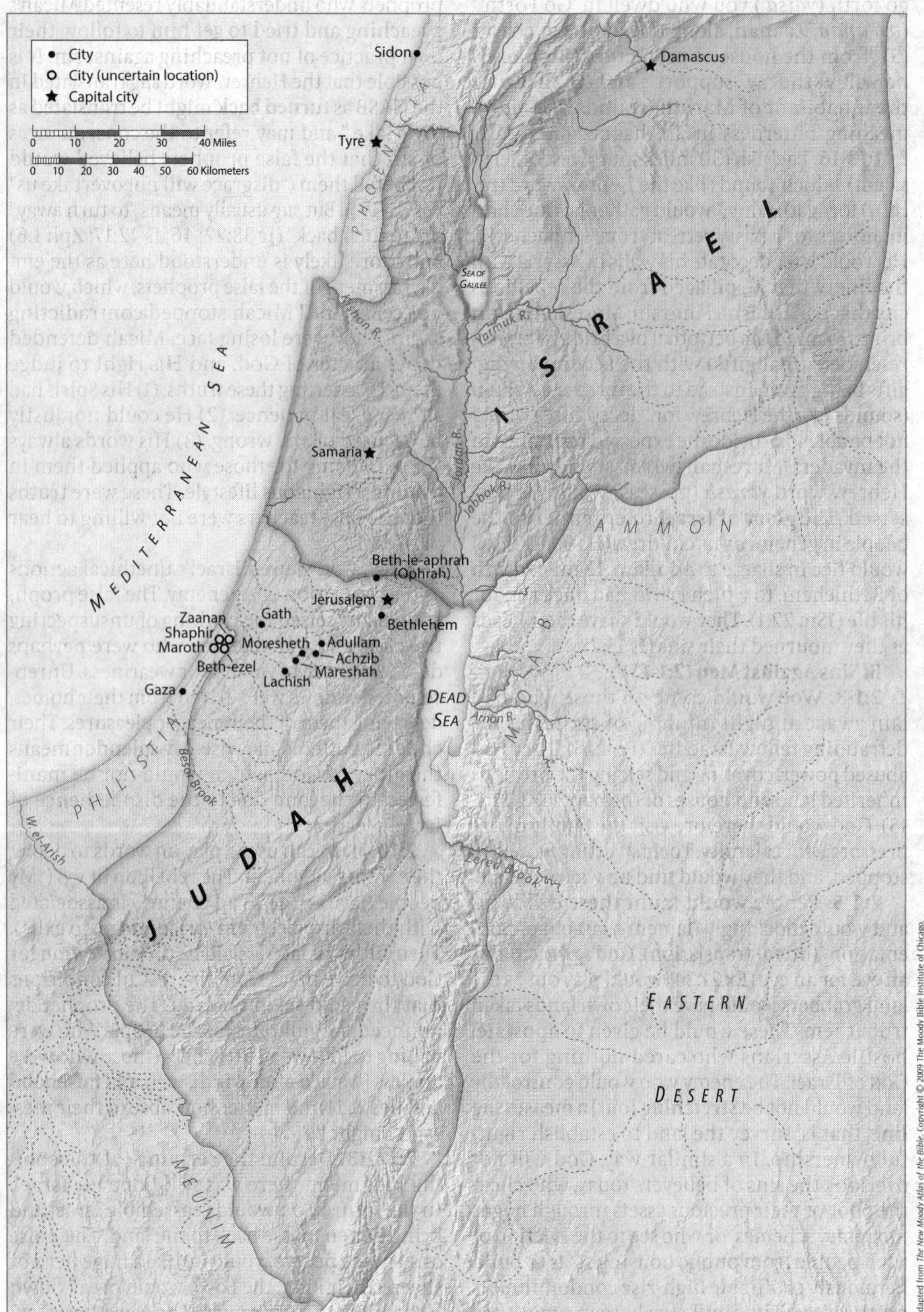

interpreted as a substantival participle, referring to the Messiah. He is the same person as the "king" and the "lord" and will lead the return of His people to the land. While some scholars understand this prophesy to have been fulfilled when the people were released by Cyrus the Persian in 539 BC, it is best, considering the context, to take it as a reference to the Messianic reign in the millennial kingdom (Mc 5:2-5a).

III. Message Two: Blessing Will Follow Judgment (3:1–5:15)

A. The Rebuke of Israel's Leaders (3:1-12)

3:1-4. Hear now (see 1:2; 6:1) marks the beginning of the second message, which is addressed to unjust leaders, beginning with political rulers. Micah describes their love for evil and hatred for good under the extended metaphor of slaughtering an animal. Their destructive treatment resembled skinning dead animals and chopping them up for the cooking pot (vv. 2-3). This oppression would result in God turning a deaf ear to the leaders when they later cried for help. The shining or hiding of God's face (v. 4) in Scripture stands for His blessing or the withholding thereof (Nm 6:24-26; Is 59:2). Leaders of churches and other Christian organizations should be careful not to exploit people in order to achieve selfish personal or professional goals.

3:5-7. Next in line for rebuke were the religious officials. The prophets led the flock astray through their partiality. They preached sweet messages of assurance to those who filled their bellies, but delivered highly threatening messages to those who did not (Jr 5:14-15). The judgment of their ministries was likened to the setting of the sun. Darkness would replace light, and there would be no more messages for them to preach. God would shut their mouths.

3:8. In contrast, Micah was filled with the power of God's mighty Spirit. This empowered him to call boldly for justice and courageously denounce the rebellion of the southern and northern kingdoms, **Jacob** and **Israel**, respectively. Believers need to depend on the Spirit to speak without fear to the various cultures of the world that have long since departed from God's will.

3:9-12. These verses address a spectrum of ungodly leaders. The rulers of both the northern and southern kingdoms had perverted God's standards of justice. They had rendered the smooth road to social justice impassable. **Who build Zion with bloodshed** (v. 10) refers to the characteristic violence and intimidation by which they governed. Financial gain was the main motive for their teaching (Ex 23:8; Pr 17:23). Yet they were self-deluded, believing that God would protect them from all threats (v. 11). But this was not so. The foundations of the buildings in Jerusalem would be torn up like sod turned by the plow, and the temple and its mount would be made desolate (v. 12). Christian leaders today should examine their motives for teaching the Word of God (1Pt 5:2), and those serving in the political realm should govern by God's principles.

B. The Future Blessing of Jerusalem (4:1–5:1)

4:1-2. Although judgment would come upon Israel prior to the exile, the distant future would still be bright. The Lord would initiate a grand era of peace. The temple mount, to be desolated by the Babylonians under Nebuchadnezzar, would come to worldwide prominence in the millennial kingdom (Is 2:1-4). Unprecedented interest in the worship of the true God will exist. The crooked paths of the rulers of Micah's day (Mc 3:9) will give way to God's justice. The exclusive worship of Yahweh will prevail as **the word of the Lord from Jerusalem** went out.

4:3-4. The Lord will govern the world justly (through the One to be revealed in 5:2-5a). All the nations will submit to Him and enjoy a time of universal peace. The **fig tree** and **vine** represent the broad individual prosperity that will exist at that time.

4:5. This verse looks forward. Although religious compromise presently reigned in their country, it would not always be so. Instead, they would live faithfully by God's strength in the future (Jos 21:45).

4:6-8. Early in the millennium Jewish believers, who make up the faithful remnant of Israel, will regather in Jerusalem (Is 56:1-8). **Tower of the flock** (v. 8) identifies Jerusalem, populated by the faithful remnant, with a tower in an open field near Jerusalem where Jacob pitched his tent after Rachel's death in childbirth (Gn 35:16-21). Terrible suffering would give way to joyous celebration in the land. The conditions of this prophecy were not met in the return of the Israelites to the land after the Babylonian exile. They did not, at that time, become a strong nation (v. 7) nor were they restored to their former dominion (v. 8). The prophecy will come to pass after the great tribulation and the second coming of Christ (Zch 14:1-11). Jerusalem will then be returned to its former glory.

4:9-10. The cry of lamentation bemoaned the loss of leadership, which would vanish from Judah, leaving it without guidance (Pr 11:14; 15:22). The people will be led through fields on their way to Babylon. Hope remained, though, as a rescue would one day bring them back to their homeland.

4:11–5:1. The scene shifts to the more remote future here, to another siege on Jerusalem. The nations will assemble for the campaign of Armageddon, intent on resisting the Messiah and destroying His people. Instead, they will be destroyed (Ps 2:1-12; Zch 14:1-3; Rv 19:11-19). The word **gather** is a double entendre. While the nations will be intent on gathering to destroy Jerusalem, God will in fact be gathering them for the figurative threshing floor (Robert Chisholm, *Interpreting the Minor Prophets* [Grand Rapids, MI: Zondervan, 1990], 148). The prophecy (Mc 5:1) looks back briefly to the preexilic siege and the smiting of Zedekiah by the Babylonians (2Kg 25:1-7). Christ has at no time been smitten in a military encounter with enemy troops. Thus, it represents Micah's encouragement to Jerusalem to resist Nebuchadnezzar, an effort that ultimately proved futile.

C. The Coming of Messiah (5:2-15)

5:2. This verse returns to the future and forms one of the most remarkable prophecies in the Bible. In contrast to the fall of the eminent city of Jerusalem is set the glory of little known **Bethlehem** ("house of bread"). The added description of **Ephrathah**, by which it was first known (Gn 35:19), distinguished it from Bethlehem of Zebulun (Jos 19:15). **Too little to be among the clans of Judah** is explained by its omission from the list of more prominent cities in Judah (Jos 15:21-63; Neh 11:25-36). Its significance would be as the birthplace of the Messiah. The temporal nouns when used alone can speak of eternity. **From long ago** (Hb. *qarem*) refers to God as eternal in Dt 33:27 (translated "eternal") and Hab 1:12 (translated "everlasting"). **Eternity** (Hb. *olam*) refers to the eternality of God in Gn 21:33 (translated "Everlasting"). The two words when used together as in Pr 8:22-23 ("of old," Pr 8:22, and "from everlasting," Pr 8:23), denote eternity past. In both Pr 8 and Mc 5:2 they are placed together to emphasize Messiah's coming from and existence in eternity past, not merely the antiquity of His ancestral roots as a descendant of David. The Talmudic idea of a preexistent Messiah is based on this passage. The use of the plural **goings forth** indicates that Messiah made multiple appearances since eternity past. This fits well with the appearances of the Angel of the Lord (i.e., theophanies; in Ex 23:20-23; 32:34 with 33:14-15; Is 63:9). The one Micah described had been active in the world for centuries before his writing, yet would be born as a human being centuries thereafter. He would be fully divine, yet would be born of a woman (Mt 2:1-12). Thus the Messiah of Israel would be a God-Man and their ruler. Micah made this prediction more than eight centuries before its fulfillment.

5:3. Give them up anticipates God sending the nation into exile. A debate over the meaning of **she who is in labor** yields three common interpretations of the phrase. (1) It refers to Israel being regathered to the land after the Babylonian exile. (2) It refers to the virgin Mary who gives birth to Jesus who gathers His people to the promised land after the second coming. (3) It refers to Israel as metaphorically giving birth with the same result. If this last view is correct, then the events of the two advents of Christ are brought together in 5:2-3 without reference to the time between them (Is 9:6-7). This view is consistent with Mc 4:9-10 and is to be preferred. **The remainder of His brethren** refers to a believing remnant to be identified at the time of Christ's second coming.

5:4-5a. The Messiah would be endued with the power of God as David His ancestor had been (1Sm 5:2), and God's majesty would be evident in His rule. Israel would remain securely in the land during His universal reign (Ps 2:7-8; 72:8; Mal 1:11-14).

5:5b-6. The shepherd would protect Israel during this time by raising up numerous faithful leaders. Assyria and Nimrod (a synonym for Assyria) seems to be used figuratively here for all of the nation's future enemies.

5:7-9. The future faithful remnant of Israel would bring spiritual refreshment and insight to the whole world, like **dew** (v. 7). As God sent the dew upon the ground, so they would be used instrumentally to bring knowledge of Him to the inhabitants of the millennial kingdom. They would also wield military might when necessary (vv. 8-9), thus destroying their enemies. The metaphor of a **lion** indicates fierce and intimidating power.

5:10-14. The Lord Himself would purify the people of Israel. The words translated **cut off** (vv. 10, 11, 12, 13), **destroy** (vv. 10, 14), **tear down**

(v. 11), and **root out** (v. 14) suggest strong disciplinary action. He would purge the nation of its dependence on military might (Dt 17:16) and idols. These idols were carved with human hands and then vested with supernatural power in the minds of the people. The images were related to the worship of the pagan god Baal and his female counterpart Asherah. This purging will apparently take place at the second coming to prepare the nation for the millennium.

5:15. Rebellious enemies of God and His people would not be spared at this time. He would pour out wrath on them (Ps 2:1-12; Is 63:1-6). They would not raise their heads again in rebellion until the end of the 1,000 years (Rv 20:7-10).

IV. Message Three: Blessing Will Surpass Judgment (6:1–7:20)

This last message continues to critique the attitudes and actions of God's people, but it also offers more hope than the first two addresses. Poor ethics and idolatry continue to be impugned, but the correction yields, finally, to blessed assurance in the grace of God.

A. God's Ethical Standards (6:1-8)

6:1. This verse introduces a courtroom metaphor that pictures God challenging Israel to defend its actions before the mountains, which are a personified jury. They represent the people of the world who had witnessed Israel's actions against Him. Mountains also appeared this way in secular treaties in the ancient Near East and thus give solemnity to the proceedings (Chisholm, *Interpreting the Minor Prophets*, 153).

6:2. God took the part of the plaintiff issuing an indictment. He called on the witnesses (the mountains) to hear His complaint against Israel so as to make a decision as to its innocence or guilt.

6:3-5. Israel was put on the witness stand here, being addressed with rhetorical questions. God challenged the rebellious nation to justify its recalcitrance. How had God **wearied** Israel? The point of the question was to challenge any impatience that they had with Him. They had no ground for this feeling since God is always good and never blameworthy (Nah 1:7; Jms 1:13-17). God made His case by recalling His past faithfulness, beginning with His miraculous deliverance of Israel from Egypt (Ex 5–15), and continuing with His determined blessing of the people in the face of pagan opposition (Nm 22–24). In the former, an oft-cited act of might, He provided the necessary leadership and, in the latter, frustrated ungodly leaders who wished to harm His people. The words from **Shittim to Gilgal** recall His continued faithfulness in guiding the people through the wilderness and across the Jordan River (Jos 3:1; 4:18-19). **Gilgal** was the base of operations for the attack on Jericho. This had all been a demonstration of God's **righteousness**, evidence that His people were ignoring at that time. In difficult times, God's people need to remember what He has done for them and acknowledge His faithfulness in some way (Jos 4:7) perhaps in a journal, photograph, or blog. These can be used as reminders when doubts arise.

6:6-8. At this point, Micah speaks of himself. The above demonstration of God's righteousness formed the basis for His demands of moral righteousness from his people. They had been hypocritical, executing the offerings that God commanded (Lv 1–8) without the proper preparation of heart. The point is most certainly not that God did not value animal sacrifices but rather that the sacrifices needed to be offered sincerely as part of a whole life given to God (Jr 17:24-26). Bruce Waltke (*A Commentary on Micah*, 391) addresses this critical relationship: "The prophets did not repudiate sacrifice, but subordinated it to ethics (1Sm 15:22-23; Is 1:12-20; Am 5:21-27)." Israelites were to demonstrate the reality of their faith by both sacred ritual and love for their fellow men. Even if they had given their firstborn sons on the altars of sacrifice (a hyperbole) it would not have been sufficient to mask their inconsistency elsewhere. The often-quoted v. 8 seems to form a sort of summary of the law (Mk 12:29-31). God wanted Israel to manifest three characteristics: (1) **justice** (Hb. *mishphat*, the moral rectitude of God that His people may also possess, Ps 106:3) in dealings with other human beings (Jms 1:27–2:13; Gl 6:9-10); (2) **kindness** ("loyal love," Hb. *chesed*, absolute faithfulness to covenantal relationships) for the community of believers that God had called to Himself; and (3) **humility** (Hb. *sane*, modest reserve before God) and contrition in their relationship with Him. Christian social action must begin with a proper understanding of God, who is righteous. Some in the contemporary church have minimized doctrinal orthodoxy in their admirable concern for social justice, resulting in a weakening of sound theology. Evangelicals, on the other hand, have held tenaciously to basic doctrine, while sometimes being unconcerned with the social implications of their faith. Believers should understand that to walk with the righteous God of the Bible requires both.

B. Rebuke for Poor Business Ethics (6:9-16)

6:9-12. Micah called on the people to pay attention to God's accusations concerning their dishonest business dealings. Instead of taking God casually, they were to **fear** His name (v. 9), that is, revere His person, a practice of all wise people (Pr 9:10; 15:33). The rendering of the term **tribe** (NASB) is difficult. It may be better to translate it "rod" (ESV, NIV) as the context is one of God's displeasure. Thus, God personifies and addresses the rod of discipline and warns that should Judah not repent of their practices, He would use that rod to chasten them. They had gotten rich dishonestly by delivering **a short measure** (v. 10) (lit., "not delivering a full ephah," approximately a bushel) for the money and using inaccurate weights on manipulated scales (v. 11; see Lv 19:35-36; Am 8:5-6). They had also resorted to lies and intimidation. Modern believers should realize that the workplace is often a more telling test of character than a church service.

6:13-15. God would strike them with his rod (Heb 12:5-12), changing their health to sickness and their security to insecurity. What they tried to put in safekeeping would be lost and nothing they had would satisfy. Their fields and vineyards would not produce. In short, their ill-gotten gain would vanish.

6:16. This verse helps explain the demise of their ethics. They had essentially left their faith, adopting the practices of pagans. The Omride dynasty had produced Ahab who, under the influence of his Sidonian wife Jezebel, brought full-fledged Baal worship to Israel. The spirit of Omri still lived on after 150 years. God would eventually give them up to the humiliation of the Babylonian captivity (Ps 137:1-3; Lm 2:10-17).

C. Rebuke for Poor Interpersonal Ethics (7:1-6)

7:1. Woe was the mournful cry of the prophet over the spiritual destitution that he witnessed in the land (Jb 10:15; Mt 23:13-39). Fruit is commonly used in Scripture as a metaphor for character (Mt 7:15-22; Gl 5:22-23). Lack of good fruit brings rebuke by God (Is 5:1-7). Micah was shaken by the spiritual barrenness of his country. He likened himself to one working in a vineyard that had not produced. There was not even enough fruit to fill his stomach, let alone a marketable crop.

7:2. Micah wrote hyperbolically about Israel. It seemed like every single good and upright person had become corrupt. He pictured them lying in wait to commit wicked deeds against their countrymen (Pr 1:10-19).

7:3-4. The **prince**, **judge**, and a **great man** should have led the country toward righteousness. Instead, they were so skilled in evil as to be called ambidextrous in the performance of it (**both hands**), and their relationships were characterized by intrigue. Then, as now, power spoke more loudly than conscience. They manipulated the system toward their desired end. Their actions were as injurious to the nation as **briars** and **thorn hedges**. The phrase **the day**... (v. 4c) introduces a break in the flow of the passage and may be best translated "the day of your watchers, the day of visitation, has come." God appointed Micah and other prophets (watchers) to warn Israel about spiritual pitfalls (Ezk 3:17) but they would not listen (Jr 6:17). Consequently, He would visit them with the judgment of exile in Babylon. Christians in high places should flee corruption and, instead, use their influence in ways that please the Lord.

7:5-6. Micah returned to his previous theme of national treachery. It ran so deeply that no relationship was unaffected. Not a neighbor, a close friend, or even a wife (she **who lies in your bosom**) could be trusted. There was no safe haven. Even the most closely related persons in a family were suspect.

D. Hope for Messianic Compassion (7:7-20)

7:7-8. Micah served as an example to the nation here. The situation was grim but he still hoped in God's mercy. He would continue to pray to God to save him and his country. Although the northern and southern kingdoms would fall, the people and the nation would be restored in the future. The words **do not rejoice over me** (v. 8) are a polemic against Israel's enemies. The victory these nations enjoyed would not be final. Micah and his people would survive, and thrive again when Messiah's kingdom comes to the earth.

7:9. A stunning contrast is present in this verse in which Micah serves as a representative of the Jewish people. The one who is indignant with Micah's (and Israel's) sin is the same one who pleads the prophet's case. God would pour out wrath against the people for their sin. Jerusalem would be besieged, and they would go into exile. Nevertheless, as they acknowledged their sins before Him, He would faithfully lead them back to Himself.

7:10-13. In the future, Israel's mockers would be brought into submission according to the prayers of His people (Ps 79:10-13). When the millennium begins, Israel's borders will be expanded and walls will be built not around her cities (Zch 2:4-5) but around her prosperous vineyards (John Martin, "Micah," in *The Bible Knowledge Commentary: Old Testament*, eds. John F. Walvoord and Roy B. Zuck [Wheaton, IL: Victor Books, 1985], 1490). Just before the beginning of this period, God will humble Israel's Gentile enemies (Mt 25:31-46).

7:14. Who speaks here? Is it the congregation of Israel, God, or the author of the book? It is probably Micah who appeals to God to lead His flock like a good shepherd (He is the shepherd in 2:12 and 5:4), directing them to blessing with His rod. The flow of the argument is that although God will judge Israel with exile, there would be a future restoration (vv. 9-13). Micah appeals to God, in v. 14, to faithfully bring about that restoration. They were His special possession. Micah longed for **the days of old** (v. 20) when they had inhabited a terrain of alternating woodlands and fertile pastures, safe from their enemies. **Bashan** and **Gilead** were regions on the east side of the Jordan river.

7:15-17. God's response to Micah's plea in v. 14 came in a promise to do a miracle like the Exodus on their behalf. A **hand on their mouth** indicated shock or awe (Is 52:15). In the future, the nations of the world will be stunned by Israel's recovery and will flee like frightened reptiles. They will greatly fear Israel, even as they did her God. **Lick the dust** may be intended to call to mind God's promise to eventually crush Satan (Gn 3:15) who always opposes His will.

7:18-20. Micah closes his book with praise to God for a number of His attributes that benefited **the remnant**, that is, the faithful among Israel. He acknowledged Him as unique (Ex 15:11), forgiving, relenting of anger, and immutable in His love for them. In addition, He was compassionate and protective. The beautiful metaphor of v. 19b pictures God casting their sins into a deep sea, far from His sight. The phrase **you will cast all their sins into the depths of the sea** is the basis for the Jewish custom of Tashlich (which means "you will cast"), when Jewish people cast bread into a body of water on Rosh Hashanah to symbolize God's removal of sin. His last words recall the unconditional covenant with Abraham (Gn 12:1-3; 15:12-21; 17:1-8). Although God would chasten them for their sins, He would never cast them away. A kingdom will one day come upon the earth in which all the promises to the patriarchs will be fulfilled (Is 2:1-4; 9:1-7; 11:1-10; 35:1-10). The nation of Israel has a bright physical and spiritual future to which she may look forward. God's faithfulness to Israel is a reminder for contemporary believers that they should exult in the astoundingly faithful nature of God who watches over them with loving discipline and grants forgiveness freely and fully to those who seek it.

BIBLIOGRAPHY

Allen, Leslie. *Joel, Obadiah, Jonah, and Micah*. Grand Rapids, MI: Eerdmans, 1976.

Barker, Kenneth, and Waylon Bailey. *Micah, Nahum, Habakkuk, Zephaniah*. Nashville: Broadman & Holman, 1998.

Chisholm, Robert. *Interpreting the Minor Prophets*. Grand Rapids, MI: Zondervan, 1990.

________. "A Theology of the Minor Prophets" in *A Biblical Theology of the Old Testament*, edited by Roy Zuck, 397-434. Chicago: Moody, 1991.

Feinberg, Charles. *The Minor Prophets*. Chicago: Moody, 1976.

McComiskey, Thomas. "Micah" in *The Expositor's Bible Commentary*, vol. 12, edited by Frank E. Gaebelein, 395-445. Grand Rapids, MI: Zondervan, 1985.

Smith, Gary V. *NIV Application Commentary: Hosea, Amos, Micah*. Grand Rapids, MI: Zondervan, 2001.

Smith, Ralph L. *Micah–Malachi*. Waco: Word Books, 1984.

Waltke, Bruce. *A Commentary on Micah*. Grand Rapids, MI: Eerdmans, 2007.

●●●●

NAHUM

MICHAEL J. BOYLE

INTRODUCTION

Author. Nahum is one of the Twelve Prophets (Minor Prophets) as well as part of the entire section of the Prophets. The author of this book is "Nahum" (Hb. *nachum*; 1:1), and his name means "comfort" or "consolation." The meaning of this prophet's name is appropriate for his ministry to Judah because he brings words of comfort and promise that God remembers His people and is caring for them by judging Nineveh. Additionally, his name reminds Nineveh that they have no "*nachum*," no comfort, nor any "comforters" (Hb. *menachamim* from root *n-ch-m*) in their judgment (3:7).

Nahum does not appear anywhere else in the Bible. Other OT names that are from the same Hebrew root of Nahum are Nehemiah ("Yahweh comforts"), Nehum ("comfort," Neh 7:7), Nahamani ("merciful," Neh 7:7), Naham ("comfort," 1Ch 4:19), Tanhumeth ("consolation," Jr 40:8), and Menahum ("comforter," 2Kg 15:14).

Nahum is called "the Elkoshite," that is, he is from Elkosh. Several sites have been suggested for Elkosh in Assyria, Galilee, and Judah, but no consensus has emerged for the actual location of Elkosh.

Nahum has always been placed among the Prophets in both the Jewish canon (The Twelve in the Latter Prophets) and Christian canon (Minor Prophets or the prophetic books). As the prophets continued to bring words to Judah to repent and turn from their sin and back to the Lord, the kings and people for the most part refused. Even after the defeat and capture of the northern kingdom of Israel, the nation of Judah was primarily led by wicked and evil kings. Nahum offered the southern kingdom of Judah the hope of being delivered from the power of Assyria. He spoke in the same vein as the other prophets sent to Judah: God judges those who sin and His prophecies are true and will be fulfilled. Even as Judah watched the fulfillment of this judgment of Nineveh, the Lord's warnings through Nahum's prophecy did not bring them to repentance.

Date. Nahum 3:8 mentions the fall of Thebes ("No-amon"). This occurred in 663 BC. The fall of Nineveh prophesied in the book of Nahum occurred in 612 BC. Therefore, the prophecy was delivered and the book written sometime between 663 BC and 612 BC. The book identifies Nineveh at its height of power. Under the final years of the reign of Ashurbanipal (638–633 BC), Assyria was weakening and rapidly declined after his death in 633 BC. This narrows the period for writing the book to sometime between 663 and 639 BC. Walter A. Maier further dates the book between 663 and 654 BC because Thebes was rebuilt in 654 BC (Walter A. Maier, *The Book of Nahum*, Thornapple Commentaries [Grand Rapids, MI: Baker, 1980], 36).

Recipients. Although Nahum addressed his message against Nineveh, this must not be confused with the people for whom the book was ultimately written. The prophet's words were addressed to Judah as a message of comfort, because during the time when Nahum's prophecies were being delivered and written down, Judah was experiencing domination and oppression under the Assyrian Empire.

Theme. The theme of Nahum is found in the opening line of the book as "the oracle of Nineveh." The term "oracle" (Hb. *massa*) can be translated "burden" (from Hb. root *n-s-'*, "lift, carry, take"). The prophetic word that Nahum must carry certainly brings a weighty and burdensome message for Nineveh. As Nineveh's brutal atrocities against nations multiplied, including the defeat of Israel and the subjugation of Judah, the "avenging" and 'wrathful" God (1:2) promised to judge and destroy this wicked and rebellious empire. For God, the guilty will not go unpunished (v. 3). Alongside this judgment, Nahum weaves words of hope, promise, and refuge for Judah. The defeat of Nineveh will provide freedom and peace for Judah.

Purpose. The purpose of Nahum is to announce the fall and destruction of Nineveh and to offer comfort and consolation to Judah that God is in control and will remain faithful to His promises. Those promises are for a complete freedom from Nineveh forever (1:13, 15b), a reinvigorating practice of worship (v. 15a), and the restoring of Israel's splendor (2:2) through the Messiah.

The book of Nahum does not exhibit any one clear literary structure on which all scholars agree. The themes and development of those themes are clear enough to see, but not an exact structure. Waylon Bailey has identified a structure built around the kind of language that Nahum uses in each chapter: "Chapter 1 uses hymnic and oracular language to describe the character of God. Chapter 2 uses oracular and battle description language to announce the Lord's judgment on Nineveh. Chapter 3 uses the language of funeral woes and dirges along with historical comparison to pronounce death on Assyria" (Waylon Bailey, *Micah, Nahum, Habakkuk, Zephaniah: An Exegetical and Theological Exposition of Holy Scripture,* NAC [Nashville: Broadman & Holman, 1998], 151).

Contribution. The book of Nahum makes a significant contribution to the rest of the Bible by clarifying God's perspective on wicked rulers and empires and the way He intends to deal with them. God's people know that God is slow to anger and great in power (1:3; cf. Ex 34:6-7; Ps 103:8), but they are told that God in His time is an avenging and wrathful God (Nah 1:2). When the wicked prosper and expand in their power and influence, God is not blind to their crimes and brutality. The Lord will judge and destroy the wicked. He will wipe away their name, destroy their false religions, and put them in a grave because of the contemptible way they have treated people, nations, and God Himself (1:14). God is sovereign and in control of all things that happen in this world (cf. 1:1-14).

Background. The book of Nahum is a prophecy against Nineveh. About 75 years before the events recorded in Nahum, the prophet Jonah was used by God to have a powerful ministry in that great city of the Assyrian Empire. But the results of Jonah's preaching evidently wore off, and Nineveh slipped back into her former brutal, godless ways and once again faced the judgment of God.

Nineveh is first mentioned in the Bible when Nimrod, the son of Cush, built Nineveh (Gn 10:8-11). At the time of Nahum's writing, Assyria had extended its power into Israel and Egypt and by then had afflicted Israel for many years. Tiglath-Pileser III (745–727 BC) invaded Israel during the reign of Menahem (752–742 BC) and extracted tribute (2Kg 15:19-22). In 731 BC, King Ahaz of Judah (732–715 BC) became a vassal of King Tiglath-Pileser (2Kg 16:7-9). Shalamaneser V (727–722 BC) defeated the northern kingdom of Israel in 722 BC (2Kg 18:9-10). In 701 BC, Sennacharib (704–681 BC) invaded the southern kingdom of Judah conquering cities and threatened Jerusalem during Hezekiah's reign (728–687 BC; 2Kg 18:13–19:37). The Lord afflicted rebellious Judah by the army of Assyria, which resulted in the capture of King Manasseh (687–642 BC) because of his evil (2Ch 33:10-11). Ashurbanipal (669–633 BC) defeated Thebes in 663 BC. The Babylonians and Medes had an alliance that brought the siege and defeat of Nineveh in 612 BC. Nineveh was the capital of the Assyrian Empire and was one of the most brutal, powerful, and idolatrous empires in the ancient world (Nah 1:14; 3:1, 4).

Like other prophets, Nahum uses an oracular style with majestic poetry combining simile, metaphor, rhetorical questions, irony, assonance, alliteration, repetition, use of synonyms, and abrupt changes of person and number. In Richard Patterson's estimation, "Nahum was the poet laureate among the Minor Prophets" (Richard D. Patterson, *Nahum*, WEC [Chicago: Moody, 1991], 10).

OUTLINE

I. Title of the Book of Nahum (1:1)
II. Certainty of God's Destruction of Nineveh (1:2-15)
  A. The Theophonic Power of God to Judge His Enemies (1:2-8)

B. The Prediction of the Complete End of Nineveh (1:9-11)
C. The Promise to Judah (1:12-15)
III. Description of God's Destruction of Nineveh (2:1-13)
A. The Capture of Nineveh (2:1-7)
B. The Plunder of Nineveh (2:8-10)
C. The Humiliation of Nineveh (2:11-13)
IV. Completeness of God's Destruction of Nineveh (3:1-19)
A. Reasons for God's Judgment of Nineveh (3:1-4)
B. Disgrace of the Destruction of Nineveh (3:5-7)
C. Defeat of Nineveh Is the Same as the Defeat of Thebes (3:8-15a)
D. Total Internal Collapse of Nineveh (3:15b-19)

COMMENTARY ON NAHUM

I. Title of the Book of Nahum (1:1)

1:1. Nahum is **the oracle of Nineveh**, which signifies that this will be a weighty message upon the capital of Assyria. And this book is **the vision** received by the prophet, a divine communication by God to **Nahum the Elkoshite**.

II. Certainty of God's Destruction of Nineveh (1:2-15)

God has the power to judge Nineveh and to bring a complete destruction upon the Assyrians. This destruction of Nineveh provides the framework for the promise to Judah of its freedom from Assyrian power.

A. The Theophonic Power of God to Judge His Enemies (1:2-8)

1:2-3a. A theophany is an appearance of God to man. In this theophany God appears as a storm sweeping through His creation. He is introduced as **God** (used once in the book), which signifies that He is the mighty One with great strength, and He **is the Lord** (v. 2a), Yahweh (Hb. *yhwh*), the personal name of God and the One who has made a covenant with His people (*yhwh* is used 11 times in the book (vv. 2 [3 times], 3 [twice], 7, 9, 12, 14, 2:2, 13; see also 2:13; 3:5; and comments there). God will judge sin because He is **jealous** and **is avenging and wrathful** because He has a zeal for His honor and His people (v. 2b). **Wrathful** means that God reserves wrath for His enemies, and this implies that they will receive it. As a word to encourage God's people, the Lord is described as **slow to anger and great in power**. He will certainly punish **the guilty** (v. 3a).

1:3b-5. As the theophany appeared, God descended as a great storm from the heavens. The power of God came in the **whirlwind** of a **storm** and **His feet** stirred up the **clouds** as **dust** (v. 3b). This powerful storm of God reminds His people of the waters of the Red Sea that the Lord "swept . . . back by a strong east wind all night" (Ex 14:21-22)—God **rebuke[d] the sea and [made] it dry** and **[dried] up all the rivers**. Just as God had "great power" over the Egyptians in the exodus (Ex 14:31), He had power over the surrounding areas of Judah that Nineveh currently controlled: **Bashan**, a fruitful land east of the Jordan River, **Carmel**, a mountain in the northern kingdom with gardens and fertile land, and **Lebanon**, the region along the northern border of Israel with its wooded forests (v. 4). These fertile and productive lands will be withered by the Lord. God in this powerful theophany transforms the mountains, hills, and the whole earth. In fact, this avenging powerful work of God affects **all the inhabitants of the world** (v. 5).

1:6. Answering the question of who can stand before God, the prophet stated that no one, not even Nineveh, can **stand before His indignation** and none **can endure His burning anger**. God's fiery **wrath** will consume and devour everything in its path and break down every walled fortification of **rocks**.

1:7. The Lord's people are reminded that **the Lord is good**. He will provide a **stronghold**, a place of safety and protection **in the day of** their **trouble**. And God has a personal knowledge of His people who flee to Him for protection: **He knows those who take refuge in Him**.

1:8. The contrast for those facing the judgment of God is that they will face **an overflowing flood** of judgment that **will make a complete end of** a city like Nineveh and bring about death for His enemies.

B. The Prediction of the Complete End of Nineveh (1:9-11)

1:9-10. After demonstrating His power to judge, God addressed the one to be judged, which more than likely here refers to Nineveh. There is nothing that this city or nation can **devise**, imagine, or plan **against the LORD** because the Lord will terminate their plan and devastate their city. The **distress** they plan will not **rise up twice**, meaning that they will not be given a second chance (v. 9). Like **thorns** they cannot be untangled, they cannot sober up from their **drunken** state, and they cannot be rehydrated from their **withered** condition. As a result, they will be devoured and destroyed (v. 10).

1:11. This city or nation is identified as the **one** who sent out **a wicked counselor** and who **plotted evil against the LORD**. This ambassador of evil is identified with Assyria and King Sennacharib and his brutality against Judah (see 2Kg 18:13, 26–19:37).

C. The Promise to Judah (1:12-15)

1:12-13. The LORD assured Judah that even though Nineveh is powerful with its large army, Nineveh will be **cut off** and destroyed (v. 12a). Then He promised His people that soon their oppression will end and the Lord **will break** into pieces the iron rod of Nineveh. The Lord will give Judah freedom by **tear[ing] off** the **shackles** of Nineveh (vv. 12b-13).

1:14. The promise given to Judah is certain because **the LORD . . . issued a command**, giving His word concerning Nineveh's certain judgment. There will be an end to Nineveh's **name**. Their **idol[s]**, **image[s]** and temples will be eliminated and destroyed. The reason for this total destruction is because God considered Nineveh **contemptible**. He deemed it so because of the city's disregard of God's sovereignty as "the LORD of hosts" (2:13; 3:5; see comments there) and its ruthless treatment of people (3:1).

1:15. The coming judgment of Nineveh led Nahum to declare, **Behold**—an admonition to pay attention. Nahum's admonition and commands are spoken as if the destruction of Nineveh had already occurred, although it was yet to happen in the future. From **the mountains** surrounding Judah came an **announce[ment]** of **good news**. Assyria had been destroyed, and these words brought hope and **peace** (Hb. *shalom*) to God's people. This peace provided a renewed worship for Judah and a rest from war. Judah is commanded to once again engage in their full worship of the Lord by **celebrat[ing]** their **feasts** and **pay[ing]** their **vows**. And the nation of Israel is promised that Nineveh will **never again** attack or subjugate Judah because they will be **completely** destroyed.

III. Description of God's Destruction of Nineveh (2:1-13)

Nahum envisioned an aerial view of the destruction of Nineveh. From a distance, the advancing army would come to assault Nineveh, overcome the Assyrian army, and capture the city. Then in the selfsame Assyrian pattern of warfare, the victorious army would plunder the wealth and treasure of Nineveh. Finally, the city would be humiliated by the taunt of Nahum and the words of the Lord of hosts.

A. The Capture of Nineveh (2:1-7)

2:1. Nineveh will be scattered by **the one who scatters**. This speaks of the Lord who will scatter and destroy Nineveh, and it may also refer to Babylon and the Medes when they **come up against** Nineveh and defeat her. For this battle, the Ninevites are commanded to stand on the walls of the **fortress**, to keep an eye on the **road[s]** leading to the city, and to **strengthen** their **back[s]**, which can mean "stand strong" or it may indicate that one should "put on armor and be courageous." These commands are not words of encouragement or hope but are intended as irony that taunts the Ninevites in their futile efforts to avoid defeat.

2:2. When the Lord defeats Nineveh, it will be because He intends to **restore the splendor**, majesty, pride, and exaltation **of Jacob** (perhaps a reference to the southern kingdom of Judah) **like the** former **splendor of Israel** (perhaps a reference to the northern kingdom of Israel) before it was defeated and scattered in 722 BC by Assyria. With Nineveh's defeat, Judah is envisioned as being restored to enjoy renewed peace, freedom, and prosperity in the land. With the plural use of **them** and **their**, this also envisions a promise for both Judah and Israel of future exaltation in the millennial kingdom that will be established by the Messiah. This future exaltation and splendor of Israel is set in contrast to the **devastators** or plunderers who will take everything from Nineveh and destroy their fertile land.

2:3-4. Now Nahum writes in the historical present tense. The assaulting army approaches from a distance and is made up of warriors dressed in **scarlet** battle garb and carrying **red** shields. The **red** could be a rubbed on red color, the copper color of a shield, or blood signifying a battle-experienced army. Its warriors ride in **chariots** of **steel** that glisten in the sun. When the troops are mustered and prepared for battle, soldiers shake their spears when they attack (v. 3). When they break through the city walls, the **chariots race madly** and **rush wildly** through **the streets** and town **squares**, creating chaos, confusion, and disorder. They are moving with such quickness and speed that they are like **flashes** of **lightning** (v. 4).

2:5. The Ninevites attempt to resist the onslaught, with their king recalling his military and community leaders to defend the city. But they are so disoriented and confused that their efforts resemble someone **stumbl[ing]** in their attempt to **march**. However, they are able to **hurry** and get to the **wall**; yet already **the mantelet is set up** outside, a defensive large shield or portable shelter that protects those besieging the city from rocks or other debris the Ninevites throw down at the invading soldiers (cf. Ps 140:7).

2:6. Nahum prophesied that the fall of Nineveh will be from the flooding of **rivers** that damage and destroy the palace (cf. 1:8; 2:8). "Diodorus wrote that in the third year of the siege heavy rains caused a nearby river to flood part of the city and break part of the walls . . . . Xenophon referred to terrifying thunder (presumably with a storm) associated with the city's capture" (Elliot E. Johnson, "Nahum," in *BKCOT*, ed. John F. Walvoord and Roy B. Zuck [Wheaton, IL: Victor Books, 1985], 1495). This historical record attests to the fulfillment of Nahum's prophecy.

2:7. The Lord has determined and **fixed** the certainty of Nineveh's defeat. This will occur when the city **is stripped** of all her possessions and **is carried away** into captivity. The leaders and servants of the city, likened to **handmaids**, will weep and grieve their losses.

B. The Plunder of Nineveh (2:8-10)

2:8-9. Nineveh had been a reservoir of the spoils and possessions from other conquered nations. Now, In fear of dying, the people of Nineveh are **fleeing** the city and a cry goes out, **Stop, stop, but no one turns back** (v. 8). Another cry is heard by the attackers, **Plunder the silver! Plunder the gold!** Indeed, for the attackers, **there is no limit to the treasure** and **wealth** of Nineveh (v. 9). The Babylonian Chronicle, a clay tablet inscribed with cuneiform, describes the spoils taken in the sacking of Nineveh as "a quantity beyond counting" (Hermann J. Austel, "Nahum," *BCB*, ed. Walter A. Elwell [Grand Rapids, MI: Baker, 1989], 663).

2:10. When the plundering is complete, the chants arise: "Nineveh **is emptied**! Nineveh **is desolate and** lies **wast[ed]**! The Ninevites are completely crushed with **melting hearts**, **knocking knees**, **pale faces**, and a trembling of fear throughout the **whole body**.

C. The Humiliation of Nineveh (2:11-13)

2:11-12. In response to the pending capture, plundering, and evacuation of Nineveh, Nahum offered a taunt or song of mockery over the defeated city of Nineveh. Nahum asked, **Where is the den of the lions**? The lion's den provides a **feeding place** for **the young lions** and is the place that the lion family can **prowl** about where no one can **disturb them** (v. 11). This imagery of **the lion** evokes the way the kings of Nineveh portrayed themselves in reliefs of lions depicted on palace walls and elsewhere throughout the city. For Nineveh, the great **den** is the palace, and the **lion**, **lioness[es]**, and **cub[s]** are the king, queen (and concubines), and their offspring. Now the city is bereft of its lions. Nineveh's brutality is described as being like a **lion**, **kill[ing]** its **prey** and tearing its **flesh** (v. 12). Nineveh exhibited a cruel, ruthless, vicious, ferocious, and inhuman conquest of people and nations (cf. Erika Bleibtreu, "Grisly Assyrian Record of Torture and Death," *BAR* 17, no. 1 [January/February 1991]: 52–61, 75).

2:13. Pay attention! The One leading the charge of the army of God, **the LORD of hosts** (Hb. *yhwh tseba'ot*; also in 3:5), here makes His first declaration against Nineveh. He **declares** that He is **against** Nineveh, and as a result He will destroy its army, kill the royal family, free their captives, and silence their **voice** in Judah and in this world (cf. 2Kg 18:17, 28).

IV. Completeness of God's Destruction of Nineveh (3:1-19)

Nahum has traced the certainty and description of Nineveh's destruction. He concludes that the city's destruction will be complete. Nineveh is a nation deserving of God's judgment and will be disgraced by nations, defeated like Thebes, and abandoned by its leaders.

A. Reasons for God's Judgment of Nineveh (3:1-4)

3:1. Woe is an interjection of lamentation. In the prophets, it often involves "negative warnings or threats of God's physical chastisement" (Carl Philip Weber, "hoy," in TWOT, vol. 1, ed. R. Laird Harris, Gleason L. Archer, Jr., and Bruce K. Waltke [Chicago: Moody, 1999], 212). The first reason for God's judgment is the warlike nature of Nineveh. The **city** is described as bloodthirsty with war and death. It is **completely full of lies**, dealing in treachery, robbery, and deception. Nineveh was a city of **pillage** and plundering, where owners were parted from their property and the city's enemies were brutally killed.

3:2-3. Nineveh's warlike nature will ultimately lead to its defeat, a downfall described as a battle. The great city's fall will begin with the crack **of the whip**, the rumbling **of the** chariots, the **horses** kicking up the dust, and the **chariots** flying through the air over the corpses and debris on the ground (v. 2). The battle will escalate with **horsemen charging**, wielding **swords**, thrusting **spears**, and killing many. There will be **a mass of corpses**, **countless dead bodies**, and the attackers will **stumble over the dead bodies** (v. 3)!

3:4. The phrase **all because of** introduces the second reason for Nineveh's destruction—she led people into false and faithless religion. Called the **charming one**, Nineveh played **the harlot** and led people away from the truth. She enticed them into Nineveh's **sorceries** and witchcraft and betrayed **nations** and **families** by forcing upon them her wicked culture and lifestyle. Nineveh engaged in black magic by using unholy means to deny the sovereignty of God and thereby attempted to determine the future for its own benefit. Through its **harlotries**, Nineveh attracted and enticed the nations, and through her sorceries and witchcraft she enslaved the nations.

B. Disgrace of the Destruction of Nineveh (3:5-7)

3:5-6. The LORD of hosts (Hb. *yhwh tseba'ot*) here makes another declaration **against** Nineveh (cf. 2:13). His actions against Nineveh will demonstrate the **disgrace**, humiliation, shame, degradation, and ignominy that Nineveh deserves.

3:7. When people see the destruction of Nineveh, they will step back and shout, **Nineveh is devastated**! And with two questions the Lord assured Nineveh that no one **will grieve for her** and no **comforters** (Hb. *menachamim* from root *n-ch-m*) will be found for the city. The Hebrew word for comfort is *nachum*. The Lord had promised the people of Judah comfort through Nahum, yet there is no "*nachum*" for Nineveh (see "Author" in Introduction).

C. Defeat of Nineveh Is the Same as the Defeat of Thebes (3:8-15a)

3:8-10. No-amon is the city of Thebes in Egypt. It was conquered by Assyria in 663 BC. Thebes was on **the Nile** River with canals and channels throughout the city. The city's shoreline provided a water **wall** for defense and protection. Thebes' allies were **Ethiopia** (southernmost region in modern Egypt and northern Sudan, not the modern Ethiopia), **Egypt**, **Put** (northern Africa, roughly in modern Libya), and **Lubim** (northern Africa west of Egypt in modern Libya; v. 9). **Yet** even with these powerful allies, Thebes **became an exile** and **went into captivity**. Her infants were killed, and her men of leadership and the military were sold and bound as slaves (v. 10).

3:11-15a. The text shifts to the future tense, describing the defeat Nineveh will face. Like Thebes, Nineveh **will become drunk** with her own pride and arrogance (v. 11). When her attackers come, there will be no help or **refuge** (Hb. *ma'oz*, used of God in Ps. 31:2, 4; 37:39, Nah 1:7). Nineveh's defenses and **fortifications** will be like **ripe fruit**. When Nineveh is **shaken**, she will fall into the hands of her attackers like a **ripe fig** that **fall[s] into** a hungry person's **mouth** (v. 12). **Behold** ("take note") that the men and troops of the city will abandon their responsibilities, and the **gates** of the city will be **opened wide**, allowing her **enemies** to enter (v. 13). Commands will be shouted to the Ninevites to **draw . . . water** to put out the fires as well as to **strengthen** the crumbling **fortifications**! They will strengthen the fortifications by making **brick[s]** with the **clay . . . mortar . . .** and **mold[s]** (v. 14). Nevertheless, the people will be killed by **fire** and **sword** and will be completely destroyed and devastated (v. 15a).

D. Total Internal Collapse of Nineveh (3:15b-19)

3:15b. It is unclear whether Nahum is telling those who attack Nineveh to **multiply** themselves or if this is directed to the Ninevites. If the command is directed to the Ninevites, the prophet is using irony. Nineveh cannot increase and multiply its troops because of the internal collapse of leadership. If the command is directed to the attackers, it assures them that they will overwhelm Nineveh and be victorious. However, in light of Nahum's previous use of irony (see 2:1) and the internal collapse of military and community leaders, more likely Nahum is taunting the Ninevites by telling them to **multiply** themselves. In either case, the outcome is the same—Nineveh will be destroyed. In these verses, the NASB identifies **the creeping locust** as the caterpillar stage of the locust and **the swarming locust** as the flying locust.

3:16-18. Nineveh's final defeat will be the internal collapse of the nation. Its leaders will fail in their responsibilities and abandon the city (cf. v. 13). The merchants who have multiplied **more than the stars of heaven** with the city's growing economy will flee the city with their profits (v. 16). The **guardsmen** (the meaning of the word is uncertain) and **marshals** (city officials) will wait for the right cue, and then they too will **flee** the city, and no one **know[s] where they** will go (v. 17). Even the leaders, ironically called **shepherds**, who are supposed to lead, teach, and care for the people, will be **sleeping** (a dereliction of duty). This "oracle of Nineveh" (1:1) is finally addressed to the **king of Assyria**. He will be abandoned by all his leaders and rulers. The **people** will have **scattered** and left the city. And the king will be told, **there is no one to regather** the beaten, broken, and scattered people of Nineveh (v. 18).

3:19. In Nineveh's complete defeat, **there is no relief**, no cure, no respect, and no help. No one will come to their aid because Nineveh brought so much **evil** to this world.

The book of Nahum demonstrates the certainty of God's judgment of evil and wicked nations that ruthlessly and treacherously oppress people, especially God's people Israel. These nations will face the vengeance of God and find no comfort. Yet for the people of God who suffer and are oppressed, they are promised hope, help, and comfort as they wait for the Lord's vengeance. Nahum echoes the words of Moses "Be strong and courageous, do not be afraid or tremble at them, for the LORD your God is the one who goes with you. He will not fail you or forsake you" (Dt 31:6).

BIBLIOGRAPHY

Armeding, Carl E. *Nahum.* The Expositor's Bible Commentary, vol. 8., rev. ed. Edited by Tremper Longman III and David E. Garland. Grand Rapids, MI: Zondervan, 2008.

Austel, Hermann J. "Nahum." *The Baker Commentary on the Bible.* Edited by Walter A. Elwell. Grand Rapids, MI: Baker, 1989.

Baker, David W. *Nahum, Habakkuk, and Zephaniah: An Introduction and Commentary.* Tyndale Old Testament Commentaries. Downers Grove, IL: InterVarsity, 1989.

Barker, Kenneth L., and Waylon Bailey. *Micah, Nahum, Habakkuk, Zephaniah: An Exegetical and Theological Exposition of Holy Scripture.* New American Commentary. Nashville: Broadman & Holman, 1998.

Bleibtreu, Erika. "Grisly Assyrian Record of Torture and Death." *Biblical Archaeology Review* 17, no. 1 (January/February 1991): 52–61, 75.

Cathcart, Kevin J. *Nahum in the Light of Northwest Semitic.* Biblica et orientalia. Rome: Biblical Institute Press, 1973.

Freeman, Hobart E. *Introduction to the Old Testament Prophets.* Chicago: Moody, 1981.

Johnson, Elliott E., *Nahum.* The Bible Knowledge Commentary, Old Testament. Edited by John F. Walvoord and Roy B. Zuck. Wheaton, IL. Victor Books, 1985.

Longman, Tremper, III. "Nahum." *The Minor Prophets: An Exegetical and Expository Commentary.* Vol. 2. Edited by Thomas Edward McComiskey. Grand Rapids, MI: Baker, 1993.

Maier, Walter A. *The Book of Nahum: A Commentary.* Thornapple Commentaries. Grand Rapids, MI: Baker, 1980.

O'Brien, Julia M. *Nahum, Habakkuk, Zephaniah, Haggai, Zechariah, Malachi.* Abingdon Old Testament Commentaries. Nashville: Abingdon, 2004.

Patterson, Richard D. *Nahum, Habakkuk, Zephaniah.* Wycliffe Exegetical Commentary. Chicago: Moody, 1991.

Roberts, J. J. M. *Nahum, Habakkuk, and Zephaniah: A Commentary.* Old Testament Library. Louisville: Westminster/John Knox, 1991.

Robertson, O. Palmer. *The Books of Nahum, Habakkuk, and Zephaniah.* New International Commentary on the Old Testament. Edited by R. K. Harrison and Robert L. Hubbard Jr. Grand Rapids, MI: Eerdmans, 1990.

Smith, Ralph L. *Micah–Malachi.* Word Biblical Themes. Dallas: Word, 1990.

Weber, Carl Philip. "Hoy." In *Theological Wordbook of the Old Testament,* edited by R. Laird Harris, Gleason L. Archer Jr., and Bruce K. Waltke. Chicago: Moody, 1999, 212.

● ● ● ●

HABAKKUK

MICHAEL RYDELNIK

INTRODUCTION

Author. Habakkuk is identified by the text as the author of the book (1:1). Little is known of Habakkuk's life other than his identification as a prophet. The final verse of the book is directed to the "choir director, on my stringed instruments," suggesting that Habakkuk may have been a Levitical musician (3:19). The Septuagint (the second-century BC Greek translation of the Hebrew Bible) includes an addition to the book of Daniel, the apocryphal *Bel and the Dragon*, mentioning Habakkuk as "the son of Jeshua of the tribe of Levi." It then goes on to record a legend about him that is pure fantasy.

The name Habakkuk means "to embrace/embracer" or "to fold the hands," perhaps indicating his love for the Lord, as exemplified in his bold interactions with Him. Luther suggested that Habakkuk offered a comforting message to his people. Jerome proposed that the name indicates Habakkuk's embracing the problem of divine justice. Perhaps Habakkuk's ultimate confidence in the Lord despite all circumstances is the Lord's embrace of the prophet with His comfort.

Date. The content of the book indicates Habakkuk's message was given shortly before the Babylonian invasion of Judah (605 BC; 2Kg 24:1), when God proclaimed the horrific news to Habakkuk that He was raising up the Chaldeans in judgment on Judah (1:6). "Chaldean" and "Babylonian" are synonymous for this commentary. Habakkuk was a contemporary of Jeremiah and Ezekiel, and he shared a similar prophetic message of Babylon's coming invasion.

Nabopolassar's son, Nebuchadnezzar, defeated the Egyptians and Assyrians at the battle of Carchemish in 605 BC, but the first captives from Judah were not taken until later in Jehoiakim's reign (2Kg 24:1; Dn 1:1-7). Since Hab 1:5-11 reflects Judah's awareness of the Babylonians' cruelty and power without a direct assault on Judah having taken place, the most likely date for the book is in the years just prior to 605 BC.

After the death of King Josiah (640–609 BC), his spiritual reforms quickly crumbled. Habakkuk gave his message during the reign of King Jehoiakim (609–598 BC; cf. 2Kg 23:36–24:7; 2Ch 36:5-8), when the moral character of Judah was "violence," "iniquity," and "wickedness" and the judgment of the Lord was on the horizon (Hab 1:2-4).

Recipients. Rather than a typical prophetic oracle of judgment, the book is a record of Habakkuk's struggle with God's justice in light of His announcement of coming judgment by the Babylonians. The audience seems to have been the righteous remnant of Judah, and the message was recorded to encourage them to remain faithful during days of judgment ahead (2:4). The message of Habakkuk continues to be a source of hope for faithful believers whenever they are facing difficult days.

Themes. Like Job, the book of Habakkuk deals with a troubling issue of the goodness of God in the face of evil. In particular Habakkuk asks, "how can a righteous God use the more wicked to judge the less wicked—and how should believers respond when He does?" This tension becomes more acute when God has determined that repentance and faith may delay His judgment, but cannot stop it (see 2Kg 22; 23:24-27). This means the experience of God's discipline *precedes* His deliverance.

The answer to Habakkuk's question hinges on the depth and purity of faith (see Hab 2:4), with close ties to an understanding of God's corrective discipline toward those in whom He delights (Pr 3:11-12; Heb 12:4-11) and His ultimate judgment of those He uses to correct His people (see Jr 50–51). The book has links to the covenant stipulations of Dt 32 and the expressed faith, historical setting, and eschatological foreshadowing of Ps 18. In an honest journey from complaint and doubt to resolution, faith, and praise, Habakkuk shows that God's justice ultimately prevails so that, above all, He can be trusted.

The book includes several significant theological themes:

God's Sovereignty. The Lord is eternal (Hab 1:12), and His word is certain (2:6). Ultimately all the people in the whole world will recognize Him (2:14). He alone is in control of all events in the world (3:2-15).

God's Justice. The Lord is holy (1:12) and will not overlook wickedness (1:13), even though the timing of His actions may surprise us (2:3).

God's Requirement of Faith. Even in the face of seeming injustice and oncoming evil, the righteous must live by faith in God. The Lord is already at work, and the faithful must wait for His appointed time when His salvation will be revealed to the whole world (2:4). This faithful attitude is possible only because the Lord is our strength (3:19).

God's Provision of Salvation. The theme of God's salvation is traced in the closing chapter of the book (3:8, 13, 18). It is linked with the work of the Messiah, God's anointed (3:13).

Background. Since ancient times, Habakkuk has been grouped in the Jewish canon as part of the "Book of the Twelve." In the Hebrew Bible, the last 12 books were written on one scroll and considered one book. These short prophetic books are commonly known as the Minor Prophets, in what Christians refer to as the Old Testament. Habakkuk and the other books in this unit are not minor in importance. They are designated "Minor Prophets" because they are much smaller than the longer prophetic books designated the Major Prophets (e.g., Isaiah, Jeremiah, Ezekiel, Daniel).

The book of Nahum, just before Habakkuk in the OT, focuses on the northern kingdom of Israel and her enemy Assyria, who would take Israel captive in 721 BC. Nahum closes with the destruction of Assyria, a nation God judged for her treatment of His people. The book of Habakkuk, in turn, focuses on the southern kingdom of Judah and her enemy Babylon, whom God would use to discipline His people, and whom He would then likewise judge. The book following Habakkuk, Zephaniah, focuses on "the day of the Lord" when the whole earth will be filled with the knowledge of the Lord as the waters cover the sea (2:14). Habakkuk's acceptance in both the Jewish and Christian canon was historically unquestioned, and there is no record of dispute about it in ancient writings.

An incomplete commentary on Habakkuk was found among the Dead Sea Scrolls. This was a significant find, indicating the antiquity and importance of the text. However, recent criticism of Habakkuk has arisen from this Qumran discovery. That commentary covers chaps. 1 and 2, although chap. 3 is absent. This has caused some modern scholars to be critical of the book, suggesting it was incomplete at the time the Dead Sea community was writing their commentary—giving Habakkuk a post-Babylonian captivity date. However, this is an argument from silence. The absence from the Qumran commentary of chap. 3 more likely indicates that the commentary was unfinished. This is especially probable because the manuscript itself has space for a column of text that was never written. The omission of the third chapter from the Qumran manuscript does not seriously call into question the authenticity or preexilic date of Habakkuk.

OUTLINE

I. Habakkuk's Problem of Doubt (1:1–2:20)
  A. The First Dialogue: Regarding Judah's Iniquity (1:1-11)
    1. Habakkuk's Complaint: Why Do You Allow Iniquity to Continue among Your People? (1:1-4)
    2. The Lord's Reply: I Will Judge the Iniquity of My People (1:5-11)
  B. The Second Dialogue: Regarding Perceived Injustice (1:12–2:20)
    1. Habakkuk's Protest: How Can a Righteous God Use a Nation More Wicked than Judah as an Instrument of Judgment? (1:12–2:1)
    2. The Lord's Reply: The Righteous Live by Faith in God's Justice because God Will Judge the Babylonians (2:2-20)

II. Habakkuk's Prayer of Faith (3:1-19)
 A. Praising God for His Past Deliverance of Israel (3:1-7)
 B. Praising God for His Power in Bringing Salvation (3:8-15)
 C. Praising God with Determination in Every Circumstance (3:16-19)

COMMENTARY ON HABAKKUK

I. Habakkuk's Problem of Doubt (1:1–2:20)

The book opens with a dialogue between Habakkuk and the Lord in two sections. Each is a complaint by the prophet followed by the Lord's answer.

A. The First Dialogue: Regarding Judah's Iniquity (1:1-11)

1. Habakkuk's Complaint: Why Do You Allow Iniquity to Continue among Your People? (1:1-4)

1:1. The book is an **oracle**, a message from the Lord, which Habakkuk saw, or was given. Oracles were often judgments against Gentile nations (e.g., Is 13:1; 15:1; 17:1). In a bitter irony, this oracle is God's judgment, not against Gentiles, but against Judah (Hab 1:2-17).

1:2-3. Habakkuk's question, **How long, O LORD, will I call for help, and You will not hear?** emphasizes the continual nature of Habakkuk's complaint and the apparent lack of response on God's part. This does not mean the Lord is unable to **hear**, or is deaf, to Habakkuk's words. The Lord does see, **hear**, and know everything all the time. The problem for Habakkuk is God's lack of action in light of his **call for help**.

The number and repetition of words used (e.g., **violence** . . . **iniquity** . . . **wickedness, destruction** . . . **strife** . . . **contention**) indicate Judah's wicked condition during the reign of King Jehoiakim (609–598 BC), just prior to the Babylonian captivity.

1:4. God's **law** (i.e., all utterances of His truth and will) is **ignored** ("paralyzed"; the nation was numb to God's teaching). The **wicked surround the righteous**, and **therefore justice comes out perverted** ("to bend or twist"). God's truth and will are distorted, misrepresented, or misused. Whenever the wicked overcome the righteous, the righteous suffer (cf. Is 5:20; Ps 11:3).

2. The Lord's Reply: I Will Judge the Iniquity of My People (1:5-11)

1:5. God gave a shocking answer to Habakkuk—He would deal with Judah's iniquity, but in a way that would cause him to be **astonished** and **wonder** ("to be amazed, stunned, dumbfounded"). The idea is so unprecedented that **You would not believe if you were told**. The pronoun "you" is plural in Hebrew, indicating the message is for the whole nation, not just for Habakkuk.

1:6-8. The shocking reply is **behold, I am raising up the Chaldeans** as instruments of God's judgment. Babylon was the greatest military power at that time: **fierce**, **dreaded**, and **feared**. Babylon's army moved on **horses** . . . **swifter than leopards** and the **eagle**, and they were **keener** (more eager) to attack than **wolves**.

1:9-10. The phrase **their horde of faces moves forward**, (lit., "toward the east wind,") is poetic description of the military taking **captives like sand**, the way sand is moved in a windstorm. Mighty Babylon had the military strength to **mock at kings and rulers** (reminiscent of Ps 2:4), yet soon God would be the One mocking them.

1:11. The description of Judah's impending doom is countered with the description of the Babylonians' paganism. The phrase **whose strength is their god** indicates Babylon's confidence in their own power. A nation of people who basically worshiped themselves was being used by God to judge the nation He called to worship Him, the God of Israel. Yet, Babylon would **be held guilty** for their failure to recognize the God of Israel.

B. The Second Dialogue: Regarding Perceived Injustice (1:12–2:20)

The problem of God using the wicked nation of Babylon to punish the wickedness of Judah, His own people, is the key theological question of the book.

1. Habakkuk's Protest: How Can a Righteous God Use a Nation More Wicked Than Judah as an Instrument of Judgment? (1:12–2:1)

1:12. Habakkuk began his response by acknowledging the eternal character of God. **Are You not from everlasting, O LORD, My God, My Holy One?** This intensely personal plea was an appeal to God's eternal holiness, power, sovereignty, and covenant loyalty. The prophet knew that God supports and defends the righteous (Ps 34:19; 103:6; 146:8-9) and would never utterly forsake His people (Gn 12:3; Jr 31:35). Habakkuk affirmed God's faithfulness to preserve a remnant of His people, saying, **we will not die**. Yet Habakkuk recognized that God, identified as **O Rock** (cf. Dt 32:4; Ps 18:2), had appointed Babylon as His agent of judgment **to correct** Judah (cf. Is 7:18-20; 44:28–45:1).

1:13. Still the question is: How can God, who is faithful to His covenant, use the pagan and vastly more wicked Babylonians to judge and correct when He cannot **approve evil** or **look on wickedness with favo**r? Clearly, God will never condone evil or wickedness (Pss 5:4; 34:16, 21; Pr 15:26), yet how could He use wicked Babylon against Judah? Habakkuk was wrestling with the complex truth that God uses even the wickedness of man to accomplish His own purposes (Pr 16:4).

This verse is frequently, though incorrectly, cited to explain how the Father turned from the Son at the crucifixion. It is suggested that when Jesus bore the sin of the world the eternal fellowship between the Father and the Son was broken. Jesus' death on the cross did not separate Him from the Father. The Godhead is an eternal, inseparable, mysterious union. The death of the Messiah provided the necessary eternal sacrifice for sin. However, it does not mean that God cannot look upon evil (or how could He look at all the earth?), but rather that He does not approve evil.

Habakkuk posed here the central question of the book: **Why are You silent when the wicked swallow up those more righteous than they?** It seemed contrary to God's character to use the more wicked, Babylon, to punish the less wicked, Judah (cf. Jb 19:7).

1:14-17. Babylon's taking their enemies captive is described by a fishing metaphor: men are **like the fish of the sea**, and the Babylonians **bring . . . them up with a hook** and **drag them away with their net**. Babylon's victims were helpless. Babylon worshiped its military might, offering **sacrifice** and **incense to their fishing net** (cf. v. 11). The question is, will they constantly fill and **empty their net and continually slay nations without sparing** those nations? The coming judgment by Babylon seems inescapable and ruthless.

2:1. Having asked this central question of the Lord, Habakkuk presented himself as a sentry posted on a city wall waiting to **see what He will speak to me, and how I may reply when I am reproved**. Habakkuk yearned for God to explain what he had failed to understand and awaited a response (cf. Ps 50:15; 91:15; Jr 33:3). He was not anticipating a reprimand from God for his questions, but rather a genuine corrective response (cf. Pr 3:11; 12:1; 15:31).

2. The Lord's Reply: The Righteous Live by Faith in God's Justice because God Will Judge the Babylonians (2:2-20)

The Lord's answer to Habakkuk was twofold: He would judge the Babylonians for their destruction of Judah, therefore, the righteous must trust God's actions and timing in judging the wicked.

2:2-3. Habakkuk was instructed to **record** God's answer **on tablets**, an echo of the giving of the law written on tablets of stone (see Ex 24:12; 31:18; 32:16). **Record[ing]** the message on stone resulted in a permanent but portable message that a messenger could deliver—**the one who reads it may run**. The message was to encourage the faithful of Judah that **the vision** of the events was **yet for the appointed time**, but it would **certainly come** and **will not delay**. Babylon did capture Jerusalem, and seemed for a while to be an unconquerable world ruler. Yet within 70 years Babylon would fall to the Medo-Persians, just as God foretold. The Lord's word is always fulfilled, but often in unexpected ways (cf. Ps 90:4; 2Pt 3:9; Rv 22:20). This verse is quoted in the NT to encourage followers of Messiah to remain faithful to Him until the Lord Jesus returns (Heb 10:37).

2:4. This is the key verse in Habakkuk, which contrasts the difference between the **proud** Babylonians who had made "their strength . . . their god" (1:11) and the **righteous** attitude of the faithful remnant of Israel who **will live by faith**.

The indictment against Babylon is addressed to **the proud one**, the leader of Babylon, Nebuchadnezzar, as representative of the nation. He (**his soul**) was **not right within him** because he trusted in his strength as his god (1:11).

This **proud one** is contrasted with the **righteous** person who **will live by his faith**. This familiar verse appears three times in the NT (Rm 1:17; Gl 3:11; Heb 10:38), yet the emphasis of the verse is somewhat unclear. The Hebrew word *'emunah*, can mean either "faith" or "faithfulness," as well as carry the emphasis of "integrity." The question then becomes, do the righteous live by God's faithfulness to them or by their faithfulness to God?

Throughout the Scriptures, a right relationship with the Lord is based on personal faith in Him (cf. Gn 15:6; Rm 1:17; Gl 3:11; Heb 10:38), because the Lord is faithful (e.g., Ps 36:5; 86:15; 145:13). Thus these ideas are more similar than they are different. One who has faith in God will also live in faithfulness to Him. Likely, the author intended both ideas in this verse.

All this makes it difficult to understand why Paul cited it in support of a *person* having *faith* in order to be saved. The noun *'emunah* would even be considered a work (faithfulness, constancy). Another difficulty rests in the slight ambiguity of the Hebrew. The suffixed pronoun **his** (or "its") most likely refers to a person who is righteous, but possibly refers to God's steadfastness or fidelity, or, even less likely, to the trustworthiness of the vision God gave to Habakkuk (see Hab 2:2, 3). But the closest antecedent is the one who is righteous, making it the likely choice.

A solution to its meaning here and in Paul's letters may be found in similar uses of the word righteous (*tsedeqah*) and the verb "believe" (*'aman*, a cognate of the noun faith or "faithfulness," *'emunah*, used here by Habakkuk) in Gn 15:6 ("Then he *believed* in the LORD; and He reckoned it to him as *righteousness*"—italics added). It is likely that Habakkuk had in mind the Genesis passage, and that he was encouraging his people to have the kind of faith Abraham had—a faith that was grounded in God's promises (see Hab 3:1-19 and comments there), in spite of delays in their fulfillment. A considerable amount of time would elapse for God's promises to be fulfilled for Abraham. His trust would need to be firm, steady (*'emunah*). Likewise Habakkuk would have to wait a long time for God to judge Babylon and rescue His people (see 2:3 and 3:16 for the concept of waiting, though the two words are different). The prophet urged the righteous to be steadfast, firm, and faithful (live by his faith, *'emunah*) in his reliance upon God's promises—even over the long period of time it would take to rescue His people (see especially 3:16-19).

2:5. In contrast to the righteous, the Babylonians were **haughty**, foolishly proud, and seemingly unaware that **wine betrays** them. It drove their appetite for conquest. Like **Sheol** and **death**, they were **never satisfied** in the pursuit of **peoples** to conquer. (See Pr 4:17 for affirmation of misuse of alcohol as giving rise to violence.)

2:6-8. Babylon's judgment is outlined in poetic detail in a song of five stanzas, each beginning with **Woe**, a word in Hebrew that means "alas for you" or "how tragic for you" (vv. 6-20). **Woe**, used frequently by the prophets, and 14 times in the Minor Prophets, is an interjection of distress pronounced in the face of disaster or coming judgment (e.g., Is 3:11; 5:11; 10:5). The first **Woe** is for Babylon's oppressive financial practices. It is introduced as part of the **taunt-song[s]** (i.e., **mockery and insinuations**) sung by the conquered nations against Babylon for its corrupt financial oppression and because it **looted many nations**. Those debtors would become **creditors**, and the Babylonians would be plundered as a recompense for the **bloodshed and violence** they inflicted (Is 13:17; Jr 50:37b; Dn 5:25-31).

2:9-11. The second **Woe** is for Babylon's unjust **gain**, which established Babylon's false security. It is against **him who gets evil gain for his house to put his nest on high** (a likely tie to the mention of eagles at 1:8b; see also Jb 39:27), supposing he will be **delivered from the hand of calamity**. The eagle's nest was considered secure from the reach of enemies, so the Babylonians, who were great builders, thought their empire was unassailable. However, by **cutting off many peoples** through war and cruelty, they were **sinning against** themselves. The **stone** and **the rafter** of the house, built in a lofty place by the cruel conquest of others, will **cry out** and **answer** in judgment against him.

2:12-13. The third **Woe** is for Babylon's brutality. The Babylonian empire (**city**) was built on **bloodshed** and **violence**. Yet their **toil** for military superiority was in vain, because **the LORD of hosts** (denoting God's sovereign might, cf. 1Sm 15:2; Ps 46:6-7, 9-11) had decreed Babylon's fall. The nation's pursuit of conquest was nothing more than a **toil for fire** (i.e., their victories would be obliterated by God's burning judgment). Babylon's judgment is an example of every nation's futile efforts (**grow weary for nothing**) if they are not serving the Lord.

2:14. Instead of the world being dazzled by the power of Babylon, in the future everyone will know the Lord, **For the earth will be filled with the knowledge of the glory of the LORD as the waters cover the sea**. In the Messianic Age, God's great glory will fill the whole earth, just as the oceans are filled with water (cf. Nm 14:21; Pss 22:27; 72:19; Is 6:3; 11:9; Jr 31:34).

2:15-17. The fourth **Woe** is for Babylon's inhumanity to their neighbors, the surrounding nations. Babylon deceived its **neighbors** with alcohol, described as **venom** (anger or rage). They were motivated by anger to deceive and control the surrounding nations. Just as a wicked man will get a woman drunk to take sexual advantage of her, Babylon took immoral advantage of its neighbors **to look on their nakedness** ("naked sexual parts"; cf. Gn 9:20-22). In a perfect example of justice, the Babylonians would soon **drink and expose [their] own nakedness** (lit., "show yourself uncircumcised"). Referring to the Babylonians as "uncircumcised" emphasized their godless condition (e.g., Gn 34:4; Jdg 14:3; 1Sm 17:36).

The judgment on Babylon is from the **cup in the LORD's right hand**, a symbol of divine retribution (cf. Is 51:17-23; Jr 25:15-17; Lm 4:21; Rv 14:10; 16:19). Judgment would fall for the **violence done to Lebanon**. Perhaps **Lebanon** is a synecdoche for Israel, as it is elsewhere (cf. 2Kg 14:9; Jr 22:6, 23), and **the town** likely refers to Jerusalem. Or the judgment may be for Babylon's actual wanton **devastation** of Lebanon's **beasts** and **land**. But the worst sin was the **human bloodshed**.

2:18-19. The fifth and final **Woe** is for Babylon's idolatry. It begins with the question, **What profit is the idol**? The Hebrew means "nonentity" and indicates a worthless thing (cf. Ex 20:4-15; Ps 115:4-8; Is 41:29; 4:9; Jr 10:15). An idol's **maker trusts in his own handiwork when he fashions speechless idols**. These idols are in pronounced contrast to the Lord God, who speaks with thunder (Ex 19:19), who commands and it stands fast, and who "fashions the hearts of all men [and] understands all their works" (Ps 33:9, 15).

That contrast leads to a final **Woe** directed to those who foolishly say **to a piece of wood, "Awake!" To a mute stone, "Arise!"** and who cover an idol **with gold and silver** yet **there is no breath at all inside it**. Their craftsmen may call them gods, but they are lifeless, in stark contrast to the Lord, who breathed life into humanity (Gn 2:7). When He merely blows on godless nations "the storm carries them away like stubble" (Is 40:24).

2:20. The pronouncement of Babylon's judgment ends with a call to worship the Lord: **But the LORD is in His holy temple** declares that the Lord is the one true God who dwells, not only among His people on Mt. Zion, but over all from His throne in heaven. The only appropriate response is for **all the earth** (i.e., all people everywhere) to **be silent** (in awestruck reverence) **before Him**. The demand was true then, but one day it will be literally fulfilled in Messiah's presence (cf. 2:14; Ps 18:46-50; Php 2:9-10).

II. Habakkuk's Prayer of Faith (3:1-19)

After two dialogues with God about the problem of evil, Habakkuk still did not fully understand. Therefore he concluded the book with a prayer expressing his trust in the Lord, despite his doubts and difficulties. The prayer is in the form of a psalm (chap. 3): it is poetic in meter, has a heading (as do many of the psalms, v. 1, cf. Ps 4:6; 54), and includes the musical/literary notation *selah* (Hab 3:3, 9, 13, 19).

The prayer/psalm of obedience has three sections: first, praise for the Lord's powerful deliverance in the past, recalling the events of the exodus (vv. 1-7); second, some rhetorical questions focusing on the purposes of the Lord's actions to bring salvation (vv. 8-15); third, a statement of trust in God's plan while waiting for deliverance (vv. 16-19).

A. Praising God for His Past Deliverance of Israel (3:1-7)

This sections recalls God's faithful and powerful deliverance of His people from Egypt at the time of the exodus.

3:1. A **Shigionoth** is a musical notation meaning an energetic, passionate song with rapid changes of rhythm (cf. Ps 7:1).

3:2. The prayer opens by reviewing God's work in the past (**I have heard the report**), and continues with a review of the events at the exodus. It also predicts that God will once again powerfully deliver His people (see Pss 18; 144:5-8; Is 64:1-3 for similar uses of deliverance imagery). While some have understood these images as primarily focused on the Lord's impending dealings with Judah and Babylon, the perspective of history demonstrates that this vision (cf. also 2:3) was not fulfilled then. Rather, it will yet be fulfilled in the Lord's final, eschatological judgment.

This recollection is characterized by **fear** of the Lord. It contains the only petitions in Habakkuk's prayer: that God would **revive [His] work** (accomplish Your promises), provide understanding (**make it known**), and **in wrath remember mercy** in the midst of the coming judgment.

3:3-4. Habakkuk borrows imagery from Israel's history, starting with the exodus. **God comes from Teman** (with the connection to **Mount Paran**), which is a broad geographical region south of Judah including Sinai (Nm 13:3, 26: Dt 32:2) and therefore a reminder for Israel of its deliverance from Egypt (including the giving of the law).

Selah is a musical notation, meaning "pause," "lift up," or "exalt." The three uses of *selah* in this chapter (Hab 3:3, 9, 13) are its only occurrences outside the book of Psalms (where it appears 71 times).

God's **splendor covers the heavens**, and **radiance . . . like the sunlight** is a poetic description of God's glory at Sinai and elsewhere (e.g., Ex 19:16; 20:18; Dt. 33:2; Jdg 5:4-5; Ps 18:7-15).

3:5. Elements of divine punishment like **pestilence and plague** appear in several OT books and call to mind God's judgment on Pharaoh at the exodus (cf. Ex 7:14–12:30).

3:6-7. The geologic turmoils of **mountains . . . shattered** and **ancient hills collapsed** are similar to those associated with God's descent to Sinai when He gave the law (see Ex 19:18; Ps 18:7). In response to God's mighty acts of deliverance, the **nations**, specifically the nomadic desert tribes of **Cushan** and **Midian** (Nm 31; Jdg 7), were **startled** (cf. Jos 2:10-11; 9:9-10).

B. Praising God for His Power in Bringing Salvation (3:8-15)

3:8. This section (vv. 8-15) opens with rhetorical questions concerning the results of God's actions. The **Lord** was not raging or angry **against the rivers**, referring to the Nile when He changed it to blood (Ex 7:20-24), or the Jordan when He stopped its flow (Jos 3:15-17). Neither was He filled with **wrath against the sea** when He parted the Red Sea (Ex 15:14-16; Jos 2:9-10). Through these actions He, expressed here picturesquely, **rode** on His **horses** and **chariots of salvation** to defend His people Israel and make Himself known (Dt. 32:39-43).

3:9. God is presented as a warrior, whose **bow was made bare**, meaning pulled from its sheath ready for war. The phrase **rods of chastisement were sworn** is obscure, with dozens of potential translations for just three words in Hebrew. Perhaps the best understanding is, "God had enlisted weapons and pledged them on oath for the destruction of his enemies" (O. Palmer Robertson, *The Books of Nahum, Habakkuk, and Zephaniah*, NICOT [Grand Rapids, MI: Eerdmans, 1990], 234).

3:10-15. In this section various aspects of nature are personified in their reaction to the power of the Lord. To begin (v. 10), the **mountains quaked** in response to God's power, as recorded at Sinai (Ex 19:18; Ps 114:4, 6-7) and torrential rains (**downpour of waters**) **swept by**, causing floods (Gn 7:11, 19-20). The **deep**, a synonym for the seas or oceans, **uttered forth its voice**; it had loud crashing waves in the midst of a storm, and **lifted high its hands** (waves) in response to His command (cf. Ps 77:15-17, 19).

Next, the prophet recalled the episode at Gibeon (cf. Jos 10:12-13) when, by a miracle of God, the **sun and moon stood in their places** (the heavens). Military images again illustrated God's power: **light of Your arrows** and **Your gleaming spear**. In comparison to His brightness, the **sun and moon . . . went away**—were no longer visible (v. 11).

God appeared as a warrior who **marched through the earth** with **indignation** and **anger** to express His wrath against pagan **nations** who assaulted His people (v. 12). It is the Lord who executes judgment: **You trampled**, literally "threshed" even as cut grain is separated from the stalks by driving a wooden sledge fitted with sharp teeth over it. This is a frequent image of judgment (cf. Am 1:3; Jb 41:30; Is 41:15).

The prophet declared God's purposes in His actions and His displays of power. First the Lord **went forth for the salvation of [His] people** (v. 13), the Jewish people. He would deliver them from the oppression of the nations (cf. v. 12). Second, He is described as going out **For the salvation of Your anointed** (v. 13), a term used in the OT, not for the nation of Israel, but for specific individuals. Priests and kings were anointed for God's service (cf. Ex 29:29; 1Kg 1:34), but the English translation of the Hebrew term *masiach* (Messiah) applies to the Messiah Himself in this context (Ps 2:2; Dn 9:26).

When the Lord comes in judgment, He will strike **the head of the house of evil**, which, in addition to the immediate context, is an allusion to the promise of the Messiah's ultimate victory over Satan (Gn 3:15). This depiction, in military terms, shows God inflicting a mortal wound (**from thigh to neck**) on the enemies of Israel who over the years devoured **the oppressed in secret**, by using stealth to gain an advantage (Ex 14:1-9; 2Sm 15:1-12; 2Kg 6:8-20; Ps 10:5-11). God preserved the Jewish people from total destruction by the Egyptians and Babylonians, and they survived. Through them the Messiah would come to bring salvation to the world (cf. Mt 1:1; 2Tm 2:8).

Finally (v. 15), in an *inclusio* with v. 3, the exodus is again recalled, reminding God's people that just as the Lord **trampled** the Egyptian chariots with His own **horses** while the Red Sea surged with chaos and death (Ex 15:21), so He will defeat the Babylonian army and later ultimately bring salvation through Messiah, who will strike the **head** of Satan.

C. Praising God with Determination in Every Circumstance (3:16-19)

Despite God's past faithfulness and certainty of future salvation, Habakkuk faced one of the most fundamental and challenging questions in a believer's experience: "Am I willing to trust God—even if it means facing trouble experiencing His deliverance?"

3:16. Facing the certainty of coming destruction by Babylon, Habakkuk experienced fear that penetrated his **inward parts**. He was physically shaken by the dreadful events ahead. His **lips quivered**, he was on the brink of tears, and he felt weak as if **decay** was entering **[his] bones**. Even in the midst of this emotional and physical anguish, he realized there was nothing to be done. The prophet knew that before God carried out the deliverance for Judah, he would have to wait **eagerly**, literally "rest" before the Lord (cf. Ps 37:7; Is 46:10), while waiting for the **day of distress** when the Babylonians would **invade**.

3:17. Habakkuk knew the coming invasion would lead to devastation and starvation. He outlined the loss of major sources of food in a brief sketch: **fig** would **not blossom**; no grapes **on the vines**; **olive** crop and grain in the **fields** would produce no food; even the **flock[s]** of sheep and goats, as well as **cattle**, would die—**be cut off**. Nothing would be left.

3:18. But in a remarkable statement of faith and trust, Habakkuk pledged to **exult in the Lord** and **rejoice in the God of my salvation**. This is a personal statement of relationship and confidence in the Lord, expressed in the parallel ideas of exulting (cf. Pss 18:7; 68:4; 149:5; Zph 3:14) and rejoicing (cf. Pss 9:14; 30:1; 31:7; 40:16). These emotions are not centered on circumstances but, on the contrary, they are focused on the Lord, who is the source of his salvation and strength. No matter what the circumstances, the prophet was determined to trust in God and rejoice in the midst of whatever the Lord allowed to come. He was fully confident in God's ability to move His people through judgment to deliverance.

3:19. The antithesis of the Babylonians (whose strength is their god, 1:11b), Habakkuk affirmed **the Lord God is my strength** (cf. Ex. 15:2; Pss 28:7; 18:21; 118:14). He depicted God's delivered people as a **hind** (deer) that securely climbs and lives in mountainous terrain (i.e., **high places**—see Dt 32:13; Ps 18:33).

The final musical movement ends with an indication the psalm was to be sung and accompanied by **stringed instruments**.

This remarkable encounter between Habakkuk and the Lord concludes with a lesson as relevant today as it was two-and-a-half millennia ago when the Babylonians were on the brink of capturing Jerusalem. Habakkuk is a model of righteousness for today, as a man who loved the Lord and was willing to seek to understand His ways—yet also willing to trust and rejoice in God's salvation, even when His plans seemed beyond comprehension. Those who love the Lord may still be facing incomprehensible difficulties, but should not be overwhelmed by them. Those who live by faith will remain loyal to Him despite circumstances. Remembering that God is the salvation and strength of His people (Hab 3:18-19) will produce rejoicing in the Lord and confidence in the Lord's ultimate good plan. He will vindicate His followers at the return of the Messiah Jesus, when the earth will be filled with the knowledge of the Lord as the waters cover the sea (2:14).

BIBLIOGRAPHY

Armerding, Carl E. "Habakkuk." In *Daniel–Minor Prophets*. Vol. 7 of The Expositor's Bible Commentary, edited by Frank E. Gaebelein and Richard P. Polcyn. Grand Rapids, MI: Zondervan, 1985.

Barker, Kenneth L. *Micah, Nahum, Habakkuk, Zephaniah*. New American Commentary. Nashville: Broadman & Holman, 1998.

Boice, James Montgomery. *The Minor Prophets*, 2 vols. Grand Rapids, MI: Baker, 2006.

Bruce, F. F. "Habakkuk." In *The Minor Prophets*, edited by Thomas E. McComiskey, 831–896. Grand Rapids, MI: Baker, 2009.

Bruckner, James. *Jonah, Nahum, Habakkuk, Zephaniah.* The NIV Application Commentary. Grand Rapids, MI: Zondervan, 2004.

Chisholm, Robert B., Jr. *Handbook on the Prophets.* Grand Rapids, MI: Baker, 2002.

———. "A Theology of the Minor Prophets." In *A Biblical Theology of the Old Testament*, edited by Roy B. Zuck, 397–433. Chicago: Moody, 1991.

Feinberg, Charles. *The Minor Prophets.* Chicago: Moody, 1990.

Hill, Andrew E., et al. *Minor Prophets: Hosea through Malachi.* Cornerstone Biblical Commentary. Carol Stream, IL: Tyndale, 2008.

Kaiser, Walter C., Jr. *Toward an Old Testament Theology.* Grand Rapids, MI: Zondervan, 1978.

Prior, David. *The Message of Joel, Micah, and Habakkuk.* The Bible Speaks Today. Downers Grove, IL: InterVarsity, 1999.

Robertson, O. Palmer. *The Books of Nahum, Habakkuk, and Zephaniah.* New International Commentary on the Old Testament. Grand Rapids, MI: Eerdmans, 1990.

● ● ● ●

ZEPHANIAH

WALTER WHITE, JR.

INTRODUCTION

Author. Little is known about the author Zephaniah, except what is provided in the opening verse of the book. His name means "Yahweh has hidden," or "Yahweh sheltered or stored up." Unlike any of the preceding prophets, Zephaniah's genealogy is traced through four generations, including "Hezekiah" (1:1; cf. Hs 1:1; Jl 1:1; Zch 1:1). Although there is no proof that this Hezekiah was the renowned king of Judah, this unusual genealogical structure, by comparison to other genealogies, seems to be intentional, perhaps to reveal Zephaniah's kinship to the royal family (C. F. Pfeiffer, "Zephaniah," *New Bible Dictionary*, ed. I. Howard Marshall, A. R. Millard, J. I. Packer, and Donald J. Wiseman [Leicester, England; Downers Grove, IL: InterVarsity, 1996], 1268–69). The name of Zephaniah's father, "Cushi" (1:1) means "black" or "Cushite," sometimes describing someone of Ethiopian or Nubian (African) descent, but not necessarily. The name is also found in Jr 36:14. But there is insufficient evidence to make any firm conclusions about his ethnicity or heritage (for a full discussion of this issue, see Walter A. McCray, *The Presence of Blacks in the Bible: Discovering the Black and African Identity of Biblical Persons and Nations*, vols. 1 and 2 [Calumet City, IL: Urban Ministries, Inc., 1995] and William McKissic, *Beyond Roots: In Search of Blacks in the Bible* [New Jersey: Renaissance Productions, Inc., 1990]).

Date. The superscription (1:1) makes it clear that Zephaniah prophesied during the days of Josiah (640–609 BC). However, whether Zephaniah's ministry occurred prior to or after Josiah's reforms is disputed. The traditional view is that Zephaniah ministered in the early part of Josiah's reign. Thus, the descriptions of idolatry (1:4-5, 8-9; 3:1, 3, 7) are included because Josiah's reforms had not yet taken place. The alternate view places Zephaniah's proclamations in the latter part of Josiah's reign and presumes that Josiah's initial reforms had failed, with Judah reverting to its idolatry. This alternative view is often predicated on the extensive parallelism with Deuteronomy (Zph 1:13, 15, 17; 2:2, 5, 7, 11; 3:5, 19-20), incorrectly alleged to have been written in the Josianic era in support of his reforms. In defense of the traditional view, Zephaniah did not refer to any of Josiah's reforms. Certainly, this would be expected if he were calling them back to the most recent standard from which they had fallen.

Theme and Purpose. The theme of the book of Zephaniah is the "day of the LORD" (1:7, 8, 14, 18; 2:2, 3). The phrase, "the day of the LORD," also used by the prophet Joel (Jl 2:1-11; see the comments there), refers to a period characterized by gloom, darkness, and judgment and followed by prosperity, restoration, and blessing. Occasionally, the phrase is used in the OT in reference to judgment that had already transpired before the biblical writers wrote their books, or to imminent judgment. However, most often future climactic judgment involving the whole earth, including Israel, is in view. The purpose of Zephaniah is to warn Judah and Jerusalem of the imminent judgment and devastation coming upon them because of their rebellion and disobedience. This is designed to indicate future cataclysmic judgment and to exhort Israel to hope and trust in the Lord because of His promise of future restoration, healing, and blessings for the faithful remnant of Israel (Zph 1:2–2:7; 3:12-18).

Zephaniah is apocalyptic literature. This type of literature is defined as "a special kind of literature used to reveal mysteries about heaven and earth, humankind and God, angels and demons, and the world to come" ("Zephaniah," *Nelson's*

New Illustrated Bible Dictionary, ed. Herbert Lockyer, Sr., F. F. Bruce, R. K. Harrison, Ronald F. Youngblood, and Kermit Eckelbarger [Nashville: Thomas Nelson, Inc., 1986], 71). Zephaniah speaks a great deal about judgment, salvation, and instruction, using striking imagery to enhance communication.

Contribution. Zephaniah teaches that the Lord is sovereign over all the nations of the world and that He holds them accountable for their sin and rejection of His will. He also teaches that God will punish His covenant people Israel when they choose to live like those who do not know Him. Finally, although His holiness demands that He address sin in the lives of His chosen people, ultimately He will fulfill all of His covenant promises to Israel so that they can love and live with Him in joy, peace, and freedom forever.

The book of Zephaniah occupies the ninth place among the larger group of the 12 Minor Prophets. In all cases, it follows Habakkuk and precedes Haggai. With Zephaniah's theme of "the day of the LORD," it is fitting that it follows Habakkuk, the final chapter of which is a description of events of that day. As Zephaniah ends with promises of restoration that go far beyond the return from Babylon to the Messianic Age, it is fitting that it is followed by Haggai, which attempts to show that the return from Babylon did not fulfill the promises of the Messianic Age.

The book consists of three chapters constituting 53 verses. The introduction is relatively brief and includes a longer-than-usual genealogy. Similar to Micah, it opens with a mass judgment on the entire world (1:2–2:15). In chap. 3, Zephaniah further describes the sins of Jerusalem and the punishment that is coming in spite of God's appeal to repent. However, the promise is given that for those who continue to wait for the Lord in faith, He will bring complete restoration and freedom from guilt to the believing remnant (3:1-20).

Background. The historical setting for Zephaniah's ministry is the reign of "Josiah son of Amon, king of Judah" (1:1). King Josiah ruled in Judah between 640 and 609 BC. Politically, Assyria had risen to power under the leadership of three of its most cruel and aggressive kings, Sennacherib, Esarhaddon, and Ashurbanipal. For more than half of the seventh century BC, Israel was under its grip as well. Assyria dominated Israel during the reigns of both of Josiah's grandfather, Manasseh (696–642 BC), and his father, Amon (642–640 BC), until the empire crumbled in 626 BC. This control also meant that the deities of Assyria exercised spiritual influence over Israel as well. King Manasseh, and then his son Amon, caused Judah to depart from the Lord for more than 50 years, so that the nation embraced pagan worship of heavenly deities, Baal and Molech, and even the offering of child sacrifices (see 1Kg 11:7; 2Kg 21:1-9, 16; 23:10). It was against such idolatry, Baal worship, temple prostitution, and syncretism (1:4-5), that Zephaniah warned Judah of the Lord's impending judgment against their rebellion (1:4-6).

As the Assyrian Empire began to weaken with the death of the last Assyrian ruler, Ashurbanipal, in approximately 626 BC, it became possible for Josiah to advance his reforms in Judah (621 BC). In all probability, this also set the stage for the rise of the Babylonians during the period of 625 to 562 BC (Ralph L. Smith, *Micah-Malachi*, WBC [Dallas: Word, 2002], 120–124)

OUTLINE

- I. Introduction to Zephaniah (1:1)
  - A. Source of His Message (1:1a)
  - B. Setting of His Ministry (1:1b-c)
- II. Promise of Future Judgment (1:2–3:8)
  - A. Coming Judgment upon the Entire Earth (1:2-3)
  - B. Coming Judgment upon Judah and Jerusalem (1:4-18)
  - C. Coming Judgment upon the Enemies of Judah (2:1-15)
  - D. Coming Judgment upon Jerusalem (3:1-8)
- III. Promise of Future Restoration (to Righteousness) (3:9-20)
  - A. Purification of the Nations (3:9-10)
  - B. Restoration of Israel (3:11-20)

COMMENTARY ON ZEPHANIAH

I. Introduction to Zephaniah (1:1)

A. Source of His Message (1:1a)

1:1a. The introductory phrase, **The word of the LORD which came**, points back to the use of this phase by several other prophets to introduce their message (e.g., Jr 1:1; Hs 1:1; Jl 1:1; Jnh 1:1; Hg 1:1; Mal 1:1). The use of the Hebrew word *hayah*, translated "came," underscores the source from which the word or message originated. Here the emphasis is that the message given **to Zephaniah** did not originate with him, but had the Lord as its source. Thus, Zephaniah introduced his message by pointing out that his message came to him from **the LORD**, and thus carried His full authority.

B. Setting of His Ministry (1:1b-c)

1:1b-c. These opening words relate Zephaniah's unusually long genealogy (see Introduction: Author). Although the reason for this lengthy genealogy is not explicit, it is possible that, in addition to tracing Zephaniah's lineage to the royal family, the names were mentioned simply because of their meanings. It is noteworthy that God appears in each of them. **Zephaniah** means "whom the LORD hid"; **Gedaliah** means "whom the LORD made great"; **Amariah**, "whom the LORD promised"; and **Hezekiah**, "whom the LORD strengthened." Only the name of Zephaniah's father, "Cushi," abandons this format (see Introduction: Author for a discussion of this name).

The opening lines also present the historical/political/religious setting of Zephaniah's ministry: **in the days of Josiah son of Amon, king of Judah** (2Kg 23–24; see Introduction: Background for more information). Zephaniah, much like his contemporary Jeremiah, proclaimed God's impending judgment upon Judah and Jerusalem because of their idolatry and rejection of the Lord as their God. His ministry likely overlapped with the prophets Nahum and Habakkuk.

II. Promise of Future Judgment (1:2–3:8)

Beginning in v. 2 and throughout the rest of the book, Zephaniah delineates the central theme of his message, namely, the "day of the LORD" (e.g., 1:7, 8, 14, 18; 2:2, 3). He is not the first of the prophets to use this expression, but being familiar with their message, he used their terms: "Be silent before the Sovereign LORD," "the day of the LORD is near," and "the LORD has prepared a sacrifice" (See Zph 1:7; cf. Hab 2:20; Jl 1:15; Is 34:6). Moreover, Zephaniah makes reference to "the day of the LORD" 23 times in his book, using this phrase more than any other prophet (Larry L. Walker, "Zephaniah," in *Daniel-Malachi*, vol. 8 of EBC, rev. ed., ed. Tremper Longman III and David E. Garland [Grand Rapids, MI, 2008], 665).

"The day of the LORD" is used here to describe intermediate judgments that would be exercised against Judah by the surrounding nations. These judgments foreshadowed a greater fulfillment at the end of the age. Indeed, if the full impact of historical, grammatical, and rhetorical methodology is followed, one must conclude the scenes and allusions Zephaniah described drive toward a greater, eschatological fulfillment. Ultimately, "the day of the LORD" is the eschatological time of God's judgment and restoration (See Jl 3:1-21 and comments there). Just as the Scriptures depict a "day" with two parts, evening and morning (Gn 1:5; 8, 13, 19, 23, 31), so the "day of the LORD" has two parts: an evening, which is the time of dark judgment known as the tribulation period, followed by the bright day, which is the one-thousand-year reign of Messiah Jesus on this earth. Therefore, Zephaniah's view of the "day of the LORD" included both a period of severe judgment against sin and the restoration and blessing to the faithful remnant (2:3; 3:12-20).

A. Coming Judgment upon the Entire Earth (1:2-3)

In this section, Zephaniah described the "day of the LORD" in terms of the wrath of God against the sin and rebellion of both the nations and His own covenant people in Judah because of their disobedience, rejection of Him, and idolatry.

1:2. Beginning abruptly, without any transition from v. 1, God **declares** that He **will completely remove all things from the face of the earth**. **Remove** is used in the intensified form in v. 2 (*'asop 'asep*, "utterly sweep away," ESV; "destroy," NET; "completely sweep away," HCSB), and twice more in the simple form in v. 3 (*'asep* by itself). These words of destruction refer to literal coming destruction. The repetition of **remove** intensifies its force and portrays not only the certainty of God's outpouring of judgment (note the future force of the *'asep* verb, translated correctly as **I will** . . . **I will** . . . **I will**) but the cataclysmic scope of His wrath upon the **earth** (David J. Clark and Howard Hatton, *A Translator's Handbook on the Book of Zephaniah,* UBS Handbook Series [New York: United Bible Societies, 1989], 145–147). The universal scope of this judgment indicates that this "day of the LORD" refers not to the Babylonian destruction of Jerusalem but to an eschatological judgment of the whole earth. Yet, in 1:4–2:3, it appears that Zephaniah does describe the Babylonian devastation and he calls it "the day of the LORD." Some have suggested that all references to "the day of the LORD," even the one describing universal judgment (vv. 2-3), refer to events in the sixth century BC, albeit hyperbolically. Others suggest that the events described in 1:4–2:3 are not references to a historical event at all, but to the eschatological "day of the LORD." Perhaps the best solution is to recognize that the "day of the LORD" described in 1:2-3 is indeed the universal end-of-days judgment by the Lord. At the same time the judgment in 1:4–2:3 does describe a historical judgment that also foreshadows the end-of-days judgment.

1:3. Zephaniah describes in detail that which was only described in summary in v. 2, namely, God's actions to **remove** completely or utterly sweep across **the earth**. This is a reverse parallel to Gn 1–2, where Moses describes in detail God's activity in creation in Gn 1, and then briefly summarizes God's activity in Gn 2. The list of entities slated for destruction is **man**, **beast**, **birds**, and **fish**, just the opposite order of the original creation (see Gn 1) and a judgment that surpasses the devastation of the flood. In this judgment even the fish would come under the judgment of the Lord. (Clark and Hatton, *A Translator's Handbook on the Book of Zephaniah*, 147; Gn 1:20-28; see the comments on Rm 8:20-21, where Paul described the curse due to the fall and its future reversal).

Moreover, humanity is singled out with the Lord's certain warning that He **will cut off man from the face of the earth**. The Hebrew construction of the verb "to cut off" includes the idea of causation, indicating that God will cause the creation to be ruined, destroyed, or cut down (Francis Brown, Samuel Rolles Driver, and Charles Augustus Briggs, *Enhanced Brown-Driver-Briggs Hebrew and English Lexicon*, electronic ed. [Oak Harbor, WA: Logos Research Systems, 2000]); (cf. 1:4). In fact, the Lord states this twice (vv. 3, 4) leaving little doubt that God is behind this impending judgment of catastrophic proportions and He will do it (Thomas L. Constable, *Expository Notes on the Bible* [Galaxie Software, 2003]).

B. Coming Judgment upon Judah and Jerusalem (1:4-18)

In this section, Zephaniah's message moves from the announcement of worldwide judgment to a warning of the Lord's terrifying judgment to come upon Judah and Jerusalem at the hands of the Babylonians. His message of castigation and the promise of severe judgment upon Judah and Jerusalem begin in 1:4-18 and are later resumed in 3:1-7.

1:4-6. Although the entire world would come under His judgment, God is seen here to narrow His focus on the men and women in Judah and Jerusalem. This community had pledged its devotion to the Lord (Jos 24:16-25) but, having failed, would be judged now. The evil of kings Manasseh and Amon had seduced the people of Judah and they had become an overtly idolatrous community, a **remnant of Baal** (the Canaanite deity of fertility) worshippers (1Kg 16:29-33; 18:19-40; Hs 9:10) and those who **swear by Milcom** (another name for the Ammonite deity Molech or Moloch, 2Kg 23:13; Jr 49:1, 3, a sun god associated with human sacrifice). Among them too were those who were engaging in a form of syncretistic worship, bowing down to **the LORD and yet** making oaths **by Milcom** (v. 5). There were those as well who had **turned back from following the LORD**, and sadly had not **sought the LORD or inquired of Him** (v. 6). Consequently, God declared to the people of Judah and of Jerusalem, **I will stretch out My hands** not to help or rescue them, but in judgment **against Judah and . . . all the inhabitants of Jerusalem** (v. 4) to cut them off (lit., "to sever, remove," the same verb used for the cutting off and discarding of foreskin at the time of circumcision; cf. Ex 4:25) (Constable, *Expository Notes*; Brown, Driver, and Briggs, *Enhanced BDB*, 503).

In this next section (1:7-18), the focus of Zephaniah's proclamation narrowed to **the inhabitants of Jerusalem** (v. 4). Previously, he had not specifically mentioned "the day of the LORD." But the core of his message is the imminent judgment and wrath of God against the rebellion and rejection of the Lord among the nations and among His people Judah.

1:7-9. Zephaniah began the announcement regarding **the day** with the imperative **be silent** ("Hush!" "Quiet!" "Silence!"; see Jdg 3:19; Am 6:10; Zch 2:17; Heb 2:20) **before the Lord GOD! For the day of the LORD is near**. On this appointed time, **the LORD has prepared** ("appointed," "established"), not a feast, but a **sacrifice** (v. 8) designed to punish **the princes**. They had denied the Lord through their pagan attire (related to their inclination to embrace foreign practices and make alliances with the godless nations; see 1:4-5) and through their jumping over **the temple threshold** (out of a fear of demons). This superstitious practice was likely connected to the incident when the Canaanite god, Dagon, fell in the presence of the ark in the temple, and the arms and head were found lying on the threshold of the temple (1Sm 5:1-5).

1:10-11. On that day, referring to "the day of the LORD," there will be in the city of Jerusalem a **cry** of great distress **from the Fish Gate** (a gate on the northern wall of Jerusalem; v. 10; cf. 2Ch 33:14; Neh 3:3; 12:39) and **a wail** from the nearby **Second Quarter** (2Ch 34:22), a section of the city. In that day, the judgment sent by the Lord will bring such pain and anguish that the screams, cries, and howling will be heard throughout the city. Even the merchants who perceive themselves secure will not escape (v. 11; cf. Jms 5:1).

1:12-13. Next, the Lord is portrayed as One going through the streets of **Jerusalem with lamps** in search of **the men who are stagnant in spirit** that He might **punish** them. The phrase **stagnant in spirit** is literally "thick in their sediment" and derives from an expression about wine that fermented too long so that it became thick or syrupy, and thus unpalatable. It indicates men who have become spiritually stuck, unmoved, unconcerned, and unaffected by the circumstances surrounding them. These say in their hearts, even as people say today, that **the LORD will not do good or evil**, meaning that God does not care what people do or how they live (Dt 29:19; Jb 15:31; Ps 30:6; Is 28:15; 31:1; Jr 17:5; 23:17; Am 6:1, 3). But the Lord did care, and judgment would come so that their wealth would be plundered and they would not enjoy the homes and vineyards they had made for themselves (v. 13).

1:14-16. Next Zephaniah gave a description of that dreadful and terrifying **great day of the LORD**. By twice announcing that it was **near** (v. 14), and in fact, that it was **coming . . . quickly**, he indicated that it would arrive with great speed and with tremendous intensity and force.

1:17-18. The pain and distress that would come on that day would cause men to **walk like the blind**, groping and staggering (v. 17). Their sin and hardening against the Lord would cause God to have **their blood . . . poured out** as indiscriminately as **dust and their flesh** (their corpses) to be piled as **dung** (animal waste) in the streets. Wealth and position would not be able to buy an exemption from **the LORD's wrath** against the sin of the people He so jealously loves (v. 18).

C. Coming Judgment upon the Enemies of Judah (2:1-15)

2:1-3. Few things so powerfully demonstrate God's sovereign rule over the earth as His ability to bring the nations of the world into accountability (Ps 33:10; Is 13:3-5; 45:1-5; Jr 51:20; Dn 4:3, 17, 35). But prior to describing this end-of-days judgment, God calls Israel to return to Him. At the outset, Zephaniah exhorted the people of Judah to **gather yourselves together, yes, gather** (v. 1). Although this could be a call to collective repentance, it could also be a call to return to the land of Israel prior to the eschatological "day of the LORD." The word used for "gather" (*qashash*) is used only here in Zephaniah, but two other synonyms for "gather" (*'asaph*, 3:8, 18; and *qabats*, 3:19, 20) are also used in the book. Since both of these uses refer to a physical and literal gathering, it is also likely that in this context the word should be taken literally as well. Thus, it refers to the Lord literally regathering Judah back to the land prior to the "day of the LORD," the seven-year tribulation period (Dn 9:27). The nation would be returned to the land of Israel **before the decree** (of judgment) **takes effect** (v. 2). Here is the evident mercy of God, even in the face of certain dreadful judgment.

Zephaniah pronounced God's judgment against many of the hostile nations that surrounded Israel—they too would be devastated in the eschatological "day of the LORD." However, before the Lord addressed these nations, in view of Judah's imminent and certain judgment, Zephaniah appealed to Judah to **seek the LORD** (v. 3) in humility, so that possibly they **will be hidden in the day of the LORD's anger**. Although the decision to punish cannot be averted, mindful of His covenant with Israel and His "chesed" (His steadfast, covenantal love), God offered mercy through forgiveness and providential care amid their suffering (See 2:7, 9; Neh 9:27-28; Ps 25:6; Is 30:18-26; Ezk 39:25-29).

2:4-15. In these verses several nations are identified and slated for destruction in the "day of the LORD" (vv. 4-7). Some were close by, such as Philistia, Moab, and Ammon (vv. 5-8), while others were far away, like Cush and Assyria (vv. 9-15). Nonetheless, the nations included here were major enemies to King Josiah and Judah either because of their proximity and/or because of their historical ominous relationship with the Israelites (cf. Jdg 3:12-14; 1Sm 31:1-7; 1Ch 18-19; Kenneth L. Barker, *Micah, Nahum, Habakkuk, Zephaniah*, NAC, vol. 20 [Nashville: Broadman & Holman, 1999], 453).

2:4-7. The first nation that will be judged is Philistia, in the western part of the land of Israel. From south to north, Zephaniah named four of the five Philistine cities, likely excluding Gath because it had already become subject to Judah (2Kg 18:8; 2Ch 26:6). As a result of this judgment, the seacoast was to become pasture for Judah (Zph 2:6). Thus, the Lord would settle **the remnant of... Judah** throughout the promised land (2:7).

2:8-15. Next the Lord foretold the judgment of Moab and Ammon, east of Israel, whose destiny would be like Sodom and Gomorrah, a perpetual desolation (2:9). God will judge them because they were **arrogant against the people of the LORD of hosts** (2:10; See Nm 22; 24:17; Jdg 3:12, 10:7; 1Sm 11:1-5; 2Sm 12:26-31; Is 25:10-11; Jr 48:29-30). In much the same way, the apostle Paul warned Gentile Christians against becoming arrogant toward believing and unbelieving Israel (Rm 11:18-20). As Charles Feinberg says, "The nations are exceedingly dull in learning how greatly they displease the Lord when they deal in pride against the nation whom He has chosen as His medium for world-wide blessing" (Charles Lee Feinberg, *Habakkuk, Zephaniah, Haggai, Malachi*, The Major Messages of the Minor Prophets Series [New York: American Board of Missions to the Jews, 1951], 57). After this judgment, the prophet foretold conditions in the millennial kingdom when the Lord will end all false worship and all **nations will bow down to Him** (2:11).

D. Coming Judgment upon Jerusalem (3:1-8)

Having condemned the surrounding nations (2:1-15), Zephaniah creates a stunning effect by shifting to the judgment of the city of Jerusalem (3:1-8), the same literary technique that the prophet Amos used (Am 1:3–2:16; Barker, *Micah, Nahum, Habakkuk, Zephaniah*, 471–473; Smith, *Micah-Malachi*, 137).

3:1-2. With the opening word **Woe**, Zephaniah used this onomatopoeic expression to call attention to an event of profound pain, calamity, and disaster. Here, it introduces God's impending judgment against rebellious Jerusalem as it did against sinful Philistia (2:5). Although the city is not identified by name, Zephaniah speaks of a location that has a sanctuary (3:4) and the Lord present within it (3:5). Hence, the prophet is describing Jerusalem as **the tyrannical city**, made so by rejecting God's word (**heeded no voice... accepted no instruction**) and refusing to exercise faith in God (**did not trust in the LORD... did not draw near to her God**).

3:3-5. Besides the people, the prophet indicted the city's leaders because of their unrighteous and faithless example, beginning with the civil rulers and then moving to the spiritual leaders. The **princes** cared little for the people, but devoured them like lions (v. 3) and the **judges** behaved like ravenous wolves administering justice to their own benefit (v. 4). The **prophets** were **reckless** and **treacherous**, while the **priests... profaned the sanctuary** and did **violence to the law**, making no distinction between what is holy and what is secular (v. 5; Smith, *Micah-Malachi*, 138; Clark and Hatton, *A Translators Handbook on the Book of Zephaniah*, 185–187).

In contrast, in v. 5, the Lord is righteous within her (Jerusalem). Consequently, He has not done nor will He do injustice. In spite of the people's rebellion and disobedience, the Lord has been faithful to His covenant to provide justice and righteousness. Nevertheless, **the unjust** remained without **shame** for their rebellious deeds (v. 5).

3:6-7. Having described Jerusalem's rebellion, the Lord alerted the city of the potential danger of ignoring Him. Therefore, the Lord reminded them that He judged and even destroyed nations in the past so that **their cities** were **laid waste... without an inhabitant** (v. 6). It was His desire that, having witnessed God's power and judgment on other rebellious peoples, Judah would have come to fear Him, accept His instruction and obey Him, **so** that their **dwelling will not be cut off** (v. 7; see Am 2:9; Mc 6:5). Sadly, they did not learn from the Lord but rather became all the more **eager to corrupt all their deeds**.

3:8. In the final verse of the judgment section, the prophet returned to the beginning. Even as he began with a prediction of universal judgment (1:2-3), so he once again predicted that God will judge **all the earth**. At the end of the future tribulation, the Lord will **gather nations** and **assemble kingdoms** against Jerusalem (see Zch 12:2-9 and 14:1-2 and the comments there) for the campaign of Armageddon (Rv 16:14-16). It is during this time of Jacob's distress (Jr 30:6) that God will purge Israel and bring them back to Himself.

III. Promise of Future Restoration (to Righteousness) (3:9-20)

This last section has a dramatic transition, from judgment (the evening portion of "the day of the LORD") to blessing (the morning portion of "the day of the LORD"). The goodness and grace of God will be poured out on the Gentile nations and upon His people Israel when He effects an unparalleled transformation within them.

A. Purification of the Nations (3:9-10)

3:9-10. The God of Israel is the God of all the earth. Thus, He promised that after He gathers the nations for judgment, those who call on His name will be transformed and He **will give to the peoples purified lips** (v. 9). Words are a reflection of the inner person (Mt 12:33-37), hence the image of purification of speech (Is 6:5-7). In that day, the nations will come from distant lands ("from beyond the rivers of Cush," Zph 3:10, HCSB), to worship the Lord in Jerusalem (see Zch 14:16-19 and comments there).

B. Restoration of Israel (3:11-20)

What follows is the depiction of restored Israel in the future messianic kingdom. Having purged Israel during the tribulation, the Lord foretold the many benefits that would come to penitent Israel.

3:11-13. The first benefit God promised is the purification of Israel. God promised that **in that day**, the beginning of the millennial kingdom, He would remove Israel's shame for their past evil deeds (v. 11). Not only would He purge them of sin, but He would also remove the **proud, exulting ones** who led Israel astray. The nation will become **humble and lowly**, finding **refuge in the name of the LORD** (v. 12). This **remnant of Israel** will be utterly transformed, doing **no wrong** and exhibiting transformed speech (v. 13), even as the nations were promised (v. 9).

3:14-17. The second benefit God promised is the joy that Israel will experience. Calling upon Jerusalem to **shout for joy** (v. 14), the Lord gave three reasons for their exultation. First, God has acquitted them, taking away His judgments (v. 15a). Second, He has delivered them from their enemies (v. 15b). Third, and most important, their longed-for King Messiah, the Lord, will be ruling in their **midst** (v. 15c). Obviously this reflects that day during the tribulation period when Israel as a nation has turned in faith to Jesus as Messiah (see the comments on Zch 12:10; Mt 23:39; Ac 3:19; Rm 11:25-27). As a result, the nation will **not be afraid** or despairing (**let your hands fall limp**; v. 16). They need not do so because **the LORD . . . in [their] midst** will protect them (as **a victorious warrior**), rejoice over them (**He will exult over you with joy**), and love them (**He will be quiet in His love**) (v. 17).

3:18-20. The third benefit God promised is the regathering of Israel. Although God would have regathered some of Israel before the "day of the LORD" (see 2:1), many Jewish people will still be scattered in exile when Messiah Jesus returns. Thus He will **gather** them so that they no will longer need to grieve about being unable to celebrate the biblical feasts (Lv 23) far from Jerusalem (Zph 3:18). God promises to **gather . . . outcast** Israel (v. 19), at which time He will transform them from **shame** to **praise and renown in all the earth**. Thus, all the covenant promises made to the patriarchs would be fulfilled.

Some object that these verses merely describe the restoration from exile when Israel returned from Babylon in 539 BC. However, this description goes far beyond the events of those days. Certainly, when the people returned from exile, all Israel did not know the Lord, nor were all the captives restored physically to the land, nor did the nation become a reason for praise in all the earth. These verses anticipate their fulfillment in the millennial kingdom. At best, the prophets used the return from Babylon as a mere foreshadowing of the future Messianic Age when the Lord would be faithful to keep His covenant with Israel literally and completely. The prophet Zephaniah, by focusing on "the day of the LORD," continually forced the reader to look for that day when Israel comes to know her Messiah, and He will fulfill every promise He made to the nation.

BIBLIOGRAPHY

Bailey, Waylon. "Zephaniah." In *Micah, Nahum, Habakkuk, Zephaniah*, edited by Kenneth L. Barker and Waylon Bailey. The New American Commentary. Nashville: Broadman & Holman, 1999.

Baker, David W. *Nahum, Habakkuk and Zephaniah: An Introduction and Commentary*. Tyndale Old Testament Commentary. Leicester, England, and Downers Grove, IL: InterVarsity, 1988.

Bruckner, James. *Jonah, Nahum, Habakkuk, Zephaniah*. The NIV Application Commentary. Grand Rapids, MI: Zondervan, 2010.

Hannah, John D. "Zephaniah." In *The Bible Knowledge Commentary*, vol. 1, edited by John F. Walvoord and Roy B. Zuck. Wheaton, IL: Victor Books, 1985.

Feinberg, Charles Lee. *Habakkuk, Zephaniah, Haggai and Malachi*. The Major Messages of the Minor Prophets Series. New York: American Board of Missions to the Jews, 1951.

Keil, Carl Friedrich. *The Twelve Minor Prophets*, 2 vols. Translated by James Martin. Biblical Commentary on the Old Testament. Reprint, Grand Rapids, MI: Eerdmans, 1949.

Motyer, J. Alec. "Zephaniah." In *The Minor Prophets: An Exegetical and Expositional Commentary*, 3 vols., edited by Thomas Edward McComiskey. Grand Rapids, MI: Baker Books, 1992, 1993, and 1998.

Patterson, Richard D. Nahum, *Habakkuk, Zephaniah: An Exegetical Commentary*. Peabody, MA: Biblical Studies Press, 2003.

Robertson, O. Palmer. *The Books of Nahum, Habakkuk, and Zephaniah*. The New International Commentary on the Old Testament. Grand Rapids, MI: Eerdmans, 1994.

Smith, J. M. *Zephaniah and Nahum, a Critical and Exegetical Commentary*. Edinburgh: T. & T. Clark, 1911.

Walker, Larry L. "Zephaniah." In *Daniel-Malachi*. Vol. 8 of Expositor's Bible Commentary, revised edition, edited by Tremper Longman, III, and David E. Garland. Grand Rapids, MI: Zondervan, 2008.

HAGGAI

MICHAEL RYDELNIK

INTRODUCTION

Author. The book is named "Haggai" after the prophet whose messages are compiled within it. His name means "my festal one," so it is commonly conjectured that he was born on a festival. Another explanation links his name to the book's message, anticipating the restoration of the festivals in the soon-to-be-rebuilt temple.

The book of Ezra mentions the prophet Haggai's message and work and links these to the prophet Zechariah, whose book follows Haggai's in the canon (Ezr 5:1-2). The authorship of Haggai has been attributed to the prophet although it is possible that an editor compiled Haggai's prophetic messages. Nevertheless, it is still correct to consider Haggai the author, since the messages are indeed his.

Date. The book of Haggai states that the messages were given "in the second year of Darius the king" (1:1; cf. also 1:15, 2:10). Scholarly consensus affirms that Haggai's four messages were proclaimed between August and December 520 BC. The book itself must have been compiled some time after those dates.

Place in the Canon. Haggai is the first of the last three books of the twelve Minor Prophets (i.e., Haggai, Zechariah, and Malachi). All three are postexilic and together they provide the explanation for the great issue of their day: the relationship of the Messiah to the return. The people anticipated, based on 2Sm 7, that if they built the temple, the Messiah would come. Haggai's message was to exhort the people of Judah to rebuild God's sanctuary and prepare for the Messiah's coming. Although he does not record the full response of the people, both Zechariah and Malachi do: they show that the people still did not believe and obey God fully. Therefore, Israel would still have to wait for their Messiah. All three of these books were placed in the canon to keep the postexilic Israelite community focused on the future, when the Messiah would come.

Theme and Purpose. The theme of Haggai is Judah's need to renew their walk with the Lord by rebuilding the temple and worshiping the Lord in purity. The purpose was to force Israel to confront their spiritual indifference and renew their spiritual commitment so that they might once again receive God's blessing. In essence, Haggai called upon the Jewish people to abandon their spiritual failures so that God would grant them success.

Background. The book of Haggai is set in the postexilic period, approximately 20 years after the restoration from the Babylonian captivity. Judah had gone into captivity in Babylon in three stages. In 605 BC, King Nebuchadnezzar of Babylon had besieged Judah and brought captives from the Judean nobility to exile in Babylon (cf. Dn 1:1-3, 2Kg 24:1-4; 2Ch 36:6-7, 10). Then, Nebuchadnezzar again assaulted Judah in 597 BC and brought 10,000 captives back to Babylon (2Kg 24:10-14). In 586 BC he besieged Jerusalem, this time destroying the city and the holy temple and exiling most of the people of Judah to Babylon (2Kg 25:1-12).

In 539 BC, Cyrus the Great of Persia conquered Babylon and adopted a more generous attitude, allowing exiled captives to return to their native lands. Thus, Cyrus, in 538 BC, decreed that the people of Judah could return to Israel and rebuild their holy temple (Ezr 1:4; 6:2-5). Immediately, some 50,000 Judean captives returned to their homeland (Ezr 2:64-65). In the seventh month of their first year back, those who returned restored the altar and began offering sacrifices (Ezr 3:1-3). The following year (537 BC), they laid the foundation and began to rebuild the temple (Ezr 3:8-13). Almost immediately afterward, the foreigners who had come to live in the land during the exile opposed the work on the temple. This discouraged those who returned, and they abandoned the rebuilding of the temple. This is where matters stood when the book of Haggai opens. The book addresses the small remnant of Judah who had returned and rebuilt their homes, but had failed to rebuild the temple. Thus, they did not succeed in fulfilling their actual purpose in returning (Ezr 1:2).

Structure. The book is composed of four addresses by the prophet Haggai (1:1-15; 2:1-9; 2:10-19; 2:20-23), of which the first has two sections (1:1-11 and 1:12-15). Each message is marked by its date and by the expression "the word of the LORD came" (to the prophet). The first and third messages address the disobedience of those who returned in not rebuilding the temple, while the second and fourth messages look forward to the day God will shake the nations and establish His kingdom on earth.

Contribution. Although Haggai lacks the poetic heights of other prophets like Isaiah, it has a clear, concise message from God, proclaiming "thus says the Lord" (or similar expressions) 26 times in its two short chapters. Readers from ancient days until today are reminded of the crucial need to make the Lord their priority and to live holy lives in order to receive God's blessing. Ultimately, the book reminds readers that God's glory would be revealed through the coming of the Messiah (2:7) who will fulfill the promises to David (2Sm 7) and restore the Davidic house (2:20-23).

OUTLINE

I. Message One: The Call to Rebuild the Temple (1:1-15)
   A. The Prophet's Exhortation to Reorder Priorities (1:1-11)
      1. The Prophet's Address to the Leaders (1:1)
      2. The Prophet's Rebuke for Inverted Priorities (1:2-8)
      3. The Prophet's Evidence of God's Disfavor (1:9-11)
   B. The People's Response of Renewed Priorities (1:12-15)
      1. The People Responded to the Lord with Obedience (1:12)
      2. The Lord Responded to the People with Encouragement (1:13)
      3. The People Worked on the Temple with Zeal (1:14-15)

II. Message Two: The Call to Renewed Perspective (2:1-9)
   A. The Discouragement of Comparison (2:1-3)
   B. The Encouragement of God (2:4-9)

III. Message Three: The Call for Spiritual Purity (2:10-19)
   A. The Need for Purity (2:10-14)
   B. The Discipline for Impurity (2:15-17)
   C. The Promise of Blessing (2:18-19)

IV. Message Four: The Hope of a Messianic Promise (2:20-23)
   A. The Coming of the Messianic Age (2:20-22)
   B. The Coming of the Messianic King (2:23)

COMMENTARY ON HAGGAI

I. Message One: The Call to Rebuild the Temple (1:1-15)

Haggai's first message has two sections: the first is an exhortation for the people to put God first by rebuilding the temple (1:1-11) and the second is a word of encouragement for the people's response to the prophet's exhortation (1:12-15).

A. The Prophet's Exhortation to Reorder Priorities (1:1-11)

1. The Prophet's Address to the Leaders (1:1)

1:1. Each of the four messages, including this first one, begins with a date. The first message was **in the second year of Darius** Hystaspes (who reigned 521–486 BC). Later, when work on rebuilding the temple had begun and local residents had objected to it, Darius researched the archives of Persia, discovered Cyrus's original decree for Judah to rebuild, and reaffirmed it (Ezr 6:1-12). Marking the date by a Gentile king was a reminder that Israel, though back in the land, was still in the times of the Gentiles (cf. the Introduction to Daniel and the comments on Dn 2:1-49 and 7:1-28). The date, **the first day of the sixth month** (August 29, 520 BC), was on the monthly new moon when crowds of Jewish people gathered for worship. The **word of the Lord** was given through **the prophet Haggai** to the leaders of those who returned. The civil leader was **Zerubbabel** (a name which means "seed of Babylon"), also known as Sheshbazzar (Ezr 1:8; 5:14, 16), who had been appointed by Cyrus (Ezr 5:14). The religious leader was **Joshua . . . the high priest**, whose ancestor, **Jehozadak**, had been high priest at the time of the exile (1Ch 6:15). These two leaders were linked here and in Ezr 5:1-2 and Zch 3–4.

2. The Prophet's Rebuke for Inverted Priorities (1:2-8)

1:2-4. At the outset, Haggai's message identified how Israel disobeyed God with their inverted priorities. He gave this message from **the Lord of Hosts**, a title for God that is used 14 times in this short book. The postexilic prophets (Haggai, Zechariah, and Malachi) used this title nearly 100 times, accounting for approximately one-third of all uses in the Hebrew Bible. It is better translated "the Lord of armies," identifying the God of Israel as the commander of the armies of heaven, an important reminder when Israel had no earthly army. The message was to **this people** (as opposed to the more common "My people"), showing God's displeasure with Israel. The first aspect of their inverted priorities was *delay*. Although it had been 16 years since they abandoned work on the temple, they still procrastinated, saying, **The time has not come** (v. 2) for construction to begin again. Israel's inverted priorities were also seen in their *selfishness*. Although the temple remained **desolate**, those who returned were living in **paneled houses** (v. 4). According to Ezra (Ezr 3:7), those who returned had obtained lumber from Lebanon to rebuild the temple. Once the project had been abandoned, there is no record of what happened to that lumber. Yet those who returned were living in paneled houses, which would be unusually expensive in ancient Israel. Perhaps they had used the lumber that had been imported for the temple on their own homes.

1:5-7. Not only had the people been disobedient, God reminded them that they also had become dissatisfied. Twice telling those who returned to **consider** their **ways** (lit., "Set your ways upon your hearts," vv. 5, 7; cf. 2:15, 18), they were called to recognize that despite all their selfishness, they never had enough drink, or clothing, or wages (v. 6). Only when they put God first would He then provide personal satisfaction and material necessities (cf. the comments on Mt 6:33).

1:8. At the heart of this rebuke, the Lord called Israel to change their ways by gathering supplies to **rebuild the temple**. Thus, God would be **pleased** (a word used of acceptable sacrifices in Lv 1:4; 23:27; Dt 33:10-11) and **glorified** (meaning, "to bring Him honor" by rightfully putting Him first).

3. The Prophet's Evidence of God's Disfavor (1:9-11)

1:9. Having rebuked them for their inverted priorities, the prophet showed the evidence of God's disfavor. Israel had expected a good return for their labors, but God, as a discipline, withheld their crops, saying that He blew **it** all away in His displeasure.

1:10-11. Recalling the covenant warning that disobedience would bring discipline upon the land (see Lv 26:19-20; Dt 28:23-24), God sent drought, even withholding the dew that watered the land in summer (vv. 9-10a). This in turn caused famine (v. 10b), demonstrating that God was withholding blessing on **all the labor of [their] hands** (v. 11).

B. The People's Response of Renewed Priorities (1:12-15)

Upon hearing the prophet's message from God, the people took immediate and dramatic corrective action. It is appropriate, but unusual, for people to respond so quickly to God's Word.

1. The People Responded to the Lord with Obedience (1:12)

1:12. Following their political leader **Zerubbabel**, and their spiritual leader **Joshua . . . the high priest, with all the remnant of the people, obeyed the voice of the Lord their God**. Identifying those who returned as the remnant alludes to Isaiah's prediction that a **remnant** would return to the land (Is 6:11-13, 7:3; the name of Isaiah's son, Shear Jashub, means "a remnant will return"). Although the word "remnant" can be a technical term for the spiritually faithful few of Israel, here it refers to the small portion of the nation that actually returned from exile. Now leaders and people all responded by **obey[ing]** God's Word through His prophet and they **showed reverence** (lit., "feared") for the Lord. The fear of the Lord has two aspects: positively, it regards God with awe, devotion, and reverence, while negatively, it views with apprehension God's displeasure and loving discipline.

2. The Lord Responded to the People with Encouragement (1:13)

1:13. Upon seeing the nation's response, the prophet came as a **messenger of the Lord** (the only place where the word **messenger**, normally used of angels, is used in reference to a prophet). God told them, **I am with you**. This recalled God's promise to the remnant in Isaiah, "Do not fear, for I am with you" (Is 43:5). God was present with them, empowering them to do His work.

3. The People Worked on the Temple with Zeal (1:14-15)

1:14-15. God's presence became evident in that He **stirred up the spirit[s]** of both leaders and people so that they zealously **worked on the house of the Lord**. Although it took some weeks to gather supplies and make plans, 23 days after the original prophetic message, **on the twenty-fourth day of the sixth month** (September 21, 520 BC), they began to rebuild the temple. At the outset, the prophet's message was about "this people" (1:2) but once they began to obey, the prophet described the Lord as **their God** (v. 12, 14), emphasizing His relationship to His people.

II. Message Two: The Call to Renewed Perspective (2:1-9)

While Haggai's first message served to correct the disordered priorities of those who returned, the second address dealt with their discouraged perspective. Seeing that their rebuilt temple would be inferior to Solomon's, the people might have abandoned their reconstruction work. Therefore, the Lord gave Haggai a message of encouragement for them to persist in working.

A. The Discouragement of Comparison (2:1-3)

2:1-2. The second message was proclaimed **on the twenty-first of the seventh month** (October 17, 520 BC), nearly one month after they had begun rebuilding. This was the last day of the Feast of Booths (Ex 23:16; Lv 23:39-44; Nm 29:12-38), also known as Hoshanah Rabbah, the great day of the feast (cf. Jn 7:37), when the people would have gathered for a grand harvest festival. However, the combination of the famine and the slow progress on the smaller temple would have made the celebration feel like a Thanksgiving dinner without a turkey. With discouragement rampant, the prophet offered an encouraging **word of the Lord**.

2:3. Sixteen years earlier, during the first attempt to rebuild the temple, those who returned looked at the foundation they had laid, and those present, "who had seen the first temple, wept" (Ezr 3:10-13) at its inferiority to Solomon's magnificent sanctuary. Now, as the rubble was removed and the foundation restored, the people became discouraged once again. The first temple's **former glory** made this one seem **like nothing in comparison**.

B. The Encouragement of God (2:4-9)

Those who returned were discouraged because their perspective was skewed. Therefore, God provided comfort by directing them to the present, the past, and the future.

2:4. God's first encouragement pertained to the situation the people were in at that time. The command **take courage** was repeated three times for emphasis, using the same terminology as when commanding the conquest of the promised land (Dt 31:6; Jos 1:6, 7, 9, 18). Additionally, He ordered all of them to continue to **work** at their building project. Similarly, David commissioned his son Solomon to build the temple, exhorting him, "Be courageous and act" (1Ch 28:10).

2:5. God's second encouragement reminded the Jewish returnees of the past. Just as God had promised to be with them when they left Egypt (Ex 29:45; 33:12-14), so God's **Spirit** was still **abiding in [their] midst**. They were not to fear, because the same promise of God's presence that He had made at the exodus remained true at the return from exile.

2:6-9. The third encouragement looked to the future when God would take what seemed to be an inferior temple and **fill** it **with glory** (v. 7). The Jewish people who returned were encouraged to know that God would begin to act **in a little while** (v. 6), meaning imminently (at any moment) not immediately (in the next moment). When God glorifies the temple, He will once again **shake the heavens and the earth, the sea also and the dry land** (v. 6). The Lord had done this previously when He had parted the Red Sea

(Ex 14:21-22) and gave the Sinai covenant (Ex 19:16-20) and He will shake the world once again in the future. The writer of Hebrews, quoting Hg 2:6-7, interpreted this as occurring at the end of days, when God will establish His kingdom on earth (cf. comments on Heb 12:26-28).

God promised that He would **shake all the nations**, and then "the desire of all nations shall come" (KJV) to the temple and **fill** it **with glory** (v. 7). Past interpreters identified "the desire of all nations" as a person, the Messiah, the One who is precious and desired by all the nations (KJV, NKJV, NIV). Current interpreters, for the most part, view this as the treasures of the nations coming into the temple to fill it with wealth and glory at the end of days (NASV, ESV, HCSB, NET). At issue is the singular noun, translated as "desire" or "treasure." While the singular lends itself to the "Desired One" interpretation, it is also possibly a singular form with a collective sense, yielding the idea of "treasures."

Evidence for the "treasures" view is threefold. First, grammatically, the verb "will come" is a third person plural, yielding the meaning, "they will come with treasures." Second, inner biblical support is found in the parallel promise of Is 60:5: "The wealth of the nations will come" to Jerusalem in the end of days. However, the word for "wealth" in Isaiah is different from that in Hg 2:7. Third, the context supports it by speaking of **silver . . . and the gold** (v. 8).

Alternatively, there is support for taking the verse messianically as well. First, the messianic view has text critical support. The singular noun, without changing the consonants but only the vowels, could become plural, the very way the LXX understood it. The addition of vowels to the Hebrew text was quite late—between the eighth and tenth centuries AD. If the better reading is as a plural, it would be viewed appropriately as a plural of majesty with a plural verb, and would be translated, "the Desire of all nations shall come." Second, the messianic view is supported by lexical evidence in that the same plural Hebrew word is used in this way of other individuals like Daniel (Dn 9:23; 10:11, 19). Moreover, whether in a singular or plural form, the word is used frequently to refer to individual people (Gn 27:15; 1Sm 9:20; Ezk 24:16). Third, the messianic view is supported by its long history, being held by both ancient Jewish and Christian interpreters.

Herbert Wolf has suggested that this was deliberately ambiguous, allowing for both ideas (Herbert Wolf, "'The Desire of All Nations' in Haggai 2:7: Messianic or Not?" [JETS 19, 1976]: 97–102). Thus, when the Messiah, or Desire of the nations, would come, the temple would be filled with the wealth of the nations.

Although the "deliberately ambiguous" view has the benefit of blending both alternatives, it is unlikely that this is what the prophet had in mind. Rather, the inner biblical reference in Mal 3:1 supports the messianic interpretation. There, using a similar idea, it prophesies that "the Lord, whom you seek, will suddenly come to His temple." The prophet Zechariah also had an expectation of the Messiah coming to the eschatological temple (Zch 6:11-15).

The end-of-days fulfillment of this prophecy was foreshadowed when the Messiah Jesus came to the temple and His presence filled it with glory. However, literal fulfillment of this verse awaits the future messianic kingdom, when the millennial temple will be glorified by the presence of the Messiah Himself, reigning over Israel and the world. Then **the latter glory of this house will be greater than the former** (v. 9). It will be a place of **peace**, not turmoil, when the Prince of Peace reigns over the world (Is 9:6-7).

III. Message Three: The Call for Spiritual Purity (2:10-19)

2:10. The third message, given on **the twenty-fourth of the ninth month** (December 18, 520 BC), three months after the reconstruction of the temple had begun, addressed the situation as it was before they began building. It affirmed the need for internal spiritual reality, not mere outward ritual conformity.

A. The Need for Purity (2:10-14)

2:11-13. Haggai began by asking **the priests for a ruling** on the laws concerning consecration and defilement (v. 11). This was their role as interpreters of God's law (cf. Dt 17:9-10), contrasted with prophets, whose job it was to exhort faithfulness to the law. The first question asked whether there was secondary consecration. According to the law, when a priest carried **meat** consecrated as a sacrifice **in the fold of his garment**, the priest would be ritually consecrated by touching the sacrificial meat (Lv 6:27). The question, based on this, was whether the garment could spread holiness to any **other food** by mere touch, to which **the priests answered, "No"** (v. 12). The second question was whether ritual defilement **from a corpse** could be spread to these other elements merely by touch (cf. Nm 19:11-13 and the comments there), to which **the priests answered** affirmatively. These questions proved that ritual defilement could be transferred to consecrated objects but that holiness was not transferable, much like disease, which can be infectious, whereas health is not contagious.

2:14. The prophet moved from interpretation to application. His questions were not some abstract, hypothetical discussion. Rather, they were designed to teach a lesson about the nation's sin in failing to rebuild the temple. Once again, God speaks of Israel as **this people** (1:2), showing His displeasure with their past behavior. All their sacrifices offered on the altar while there was no temple (Ezr 3:1-6) failed to consecrate the people. Instead, their offerings had become **unclean** because of their sin of abandoning temple reconstruction. All their sacrifices were defiled because they reflected mere ritual conformity to the law instead of true faith and obedience to God. The Pentateuch had given Abraham as an example of faith leading to obedience. It says that Abraham "believed in the LORD; and He reckoned it to him as righteousness" (Gn 15:6). As a result of his faith, Abraham was also considered obedient to the law even before God gave it to Moses. God said "Abraham obeyed Me and kept My charge, My commandments, My statutes and My laws" (Gn 26:5). The point of the law itself was that only faith could produce genuine obedience. The converse was also true: the lack of faith defiled mere formal obedience. The same is true for believers today: religious ritual without authentic faith defiles those acts of devotion. In contrast, a life of faith will consecrate rituals and transform them into holy worship.

B. The Discipline for Impurity (2:15-17)

2:15. The prophet began to address the response of the Lord to their renewed obedience by telling them to **consider** (lit., "set upon your hearts," cf. 1:5, 7, 2:18) what the Lord would do for them **from this day onward** (lit., "upward"). The difficulty with this expression is that in what follows immediately, God reminds the nation of the past, not the future. This has led some to translate "upward" as "backward," a possible but unlikely translation, in light of its use for looking forward in 2:18. It seems more likely that the words about the past that follow immediately are a parenthetical discussion of God's discipline of the nation before they began to build (**before one stone was placed on another**). Then, in 2:18, the prophet returned to the same phrase ("consider from this day onward") to complete what he had begun to say about the effect on the Lord of their renewed obedience.

2:16-17. The parenthetical note about the past reminded them of the lack of return for all their labors (v. 16; cf. 1:9-11). Moreover, what little they did grow, God **smote** with a **blasting wind** and **mildew**, just as the law foretold if Israel were to disobey (cf. Dt 28:22; note that the same Hebrew word for "blasting wind" in Hg 2:17 is translated "blight" in Dt 28:22). God also sent **hail** to destroy their crops, a sign of judgment (cf. Ex 9:25; Is 28:2; 30:30).

C. The Promise of Blessing (2:18-19)

2:18. Returning to what he began to say in 2:15, the prophet urges the nation to **consider**, since **on this day**, they had completed restoration of the temple's foundation. Although the NASB translates the phrase, **the temple of the LORD was *founded*** (italics added), the Hebrew word for **founded**, *yusad*, can be translated "repaired," "restored," or "rebuilt" (as in 2Ch 24:27; 2Kg 12:12; cf. Anthony Gelston, "The Foundations of the Second Temple," *Vetus Testamentum* 16:2 [April, 1966]: 232–35). In obedience, they had begun work and now rededicated the restored foundation.

2:19. The prophet asks, **Is the seed still in the barn?** rhetorically. The entire nation knew the answer, that all the seed had been planted by December for their winter crops. Yet, the seed had not yet **borne fruit**. At this point, God promised that He would **bless** them with a large crop because of their renewed obedience.

IV. Message Four: The Hope of a Messianic Promise (2:20-23)

A. The Coming of the Messianic Age (2:20-22)

2:20-21. The fourth and final message came on the same day as the third message (**the twenty-fourth day of the month**, December 18, 530 BC, v. 20) and was directed to **Zerubbabel** (v. 21). Not only was he governor of Judah but he also was a descendant of David and the one through whom the royal Davidic line would continue. This message was designed to remind readers of the coming Messiah and His kingdom, and thereby give end-time hope. Just as predicted previously (2:6-7), the Lord promised **to shake the heavens and the earth** (v. 21), indicating the upheavals that will take place in the last battle.

2:22. The prophet used God's victories for Israel in the past to picture His future triumph (v. 22). At that time, God **will overthrow** the earthly nations and powers that are in revolt against Him. This is the same word used of God's "overthrow" of Sodom and Gomorrah (cf. Dt 29:23, English versions; 29:22 in the Hebrew text; Is 13:19). The promise to **overthrow the chariots . . . riders . . . and the horses** reflects Moses' song after the exodus and the drowning of the Egyptian army in the Red Sea (Ex 15:4). Also, the prediction that God's enemies would destroy themselves by turning **the sword** on one another reminds of Gideon's defeat of the Midianites (Jdg 7:22).

B. The Coming of the Messianic King (2:23)

2:23. Although some commentators believe that the referent of this promise is solely the historical figure Zerubbabel, this is unlikely. Rather, it addresses Zerubbabel as the prototype of the Messiah. First, considering the eschatological language used in this section ("shake the heavens and the earth" (v. 21) **on that day**) the passage addresses the end of days and not the postexilic period when Zerubabbel lived. Second, the predictions of this passage were not fulfilled in the days when Zerubbabel was governor of Judea—kingdoms and armies were not overthrown as they will be in the end of days when Messiah comes (Zch 12:6-9; 14:1-7). Third, two of the three titles used are used of the Messiah ("Servant"—Is 42:1; 49:5; 50:10; 52:13; "chosen"—Is 42:1). The question remains: Why then is Zerubbabel addressed by name? The answer is that as the key royal descendant of the House of David, Zerubbabel, is the link to the Davidic covenant. It is through his seed that the promise of Messiah will be fulfilled. Thus, he is addressed as the prototype of the future messianic king. Other prophets used this same literary device, speaking of the Messiah but using the name of David as the one to whom the promise was given (cf. Jr 30:9; Ezk 34:24; 37:24-25; Hs 3:5).

With the Davidic covenant, God had promised David that he would have a descendant who would have an eternal house, kingdom, and throne (see the comments on 2Sm 7:12-16). However, with the Babylonian exile, God seemed to have spurned the Davidic covenant, casting David's crown into the dust and overturning his throne (Ps 89:39, 44). Just before the exile, God cursed one of the last Davidic kings, Coniah, describing him as a signet ring whom God would cast off (Jr 22:24). Therefore, Haggai's promise, ostensibly to Zerubbabel, but actually to the Messiah, affirmed the restoration of the Davidic promise.

Zerubbabel represents the future Messiah who would fulfill the Davidic covenant. God used three messianic terms of him. First, God speaks of the Messiah as **My servant**, a word used for the messianic Servant of the Lord (Is 42:1; 49:5; 50:10; 52:13). Second, He calls Him, **a signet ring**, seemingly undoing the curse on Coniah, the signet ring that was cast away. Moreover, ancient kings protected signet rings because they represented the king's identity and authority. Therefore, they wore and guarded the ring as that which was most valuable to them. Calling the Messiah "a signet ring," represents His position as most precious to the Lord. Third, the Lord declares that He has **chosen** Him, just as the Servant of the Lord was called God's "chosen one" (Is 42:1) who would fulfill all the promises of the messianic King.

The Book of Haggai ends on this promise, reminding the faithful remnant of Israel that God would indeed fulfill His unbreakable covenant with David by sending the future Son of David and by establishing His house, kingdom, and throne forever. Thus, the book that began with such a negative message of correction ends with the hope of the coming Messiah.

BIBLIOGRAPHY

Alden, Robert L. "Haggai." Vol. 7 of *The Expositor's Bible Commentary*, edited by Frank E. Gaebelein, 569–91. Grand Rapids, MI: Zondervan, 1985.

Baldwin, Joyce G. *Haggai, Zechariah, Malachi: An Introduction and Commentary*, Tyndale Old Testament Commentaries, edited by D. J. Wiseman. Downers Grove, IL: InterVarsity, 1972.

Chisholm, Robert B. Jr. *Interpreting the Minor Prophets*. Grand Rapids, MI: Zondervan, 1990.

Feinberg, Charles L. *The Minor Prophets*. Chicago: Moody, 1990.

Merrill, Eugene H. *An Exegetical Commentary: Haggai, Zechariah, Malachi*. Chicago: Moody, 1994.

Motyer, J. Alec. "Haggai." Vol. 3 of *The Minor Prophets: An Exegetical and Expository Commentary*, edited by Thomas Edward McComiskey, 963–1002. Grand Rapids, MI: Baker, 1998.

Taylor, Richard A. "Haggai." In *Haggai, Malachi*, New American Commentary, edited by E. Ray Clendenen, 21–201. Nashville: Broadman & Holman, 2004.

Verhoef, Pieter A. *The Books of Haggai and Malachi*, New International Commentary on the Old Testament, edited by R. K. Harrison. Grand Rapids, MI: Eerdmans, 1987.

Wolf, Herbert. *Haggai–Malachi: Rededication and Renewal*. Chicago: Moody, 1976.

● ● ● ●

ZECHARIAH

MICHAEL RYDELNIK

INTRODUCTION

Author. The book of Zechariah contains the prophetic messages of Zechariah (lit., "The LORD Remembers"), the son of Berechiah, grandson of Iddo (concerning the alleged contradiction with Ezr 5:1; 6:14, see comments on Zch 1:1). Zechariah was not only a prophet but also a priest (Neh 12:4, 16). Since he was called young man (Zch 2:4), it is possible that he had just attained adulthood when he began his prophetic ministry.

Modern biblical criticism challenges the unity of Zechariah. Initially, this was an attempt to defend the accuracy of Mt 27:9, which gives a loose rendering of Zch 11:12-13 and attributes the quotation to Jeremiah. Hence, some scholars, without any substantiation, believed that Jeremiah wrote Zch 9–14 in the preexilic period. (Regarding Matthew's citation of Jeremiah, see comments on 11:12-14.) Later critics also disputed the unity of Zechariah but rather saw chaps. 9–14 as an addition, compiled several hundred years after Zechariah's ministry in the third century BC.

Two primary arguments are raised against Zechariah being the author of the entire book: (1) alleged differences in wording and style between chaps. 1–8 and 9–14; and (2) alleged anachronistic references to historical events that occurred many years after Zechariah's ministry.

As to the first argument, George L. Robinson responded that there is "no mode of reasoning so treacherous as that from language and style" (George L. Robinson, "The Book of Zechariah" in ISBE, ed. James Orr, John L. Nuelson, and Edgar Young Mullins [Peabody, MA: Hendrickson], V:3139). Even so, possible variations in style between the two major parts of Zechariah could result from being written at different periods in the prophet's life and also from differences in genre.

Beyond the alleged differences, there are substantial similarities in language and style. For example, Barker suggests the following words and expressions found in both sections of the book: (1) the same Hebrew phrase appears in 7:14 (translated as "that no one went back and forth") and 9:8 (translated as "him who passes by and returns") but is found nowhere else in the Hebrew Bible; (2) the phrase "declares the Lord" appears 13 times in the first part of the book (1:3, 4, 16; 2:5, 6a, 6b, 10; 3:9, 10; 5:4; 8:6, 11, 17) and seven times in the second part (10:12; 11:6; 12:1, 4; 13:2, 7, 8); (3) the name "the LORD of hosts" is repeatedly used in both sections of Zechariah (1:3, 4, 6, 12, 14, 16, 17; 2:8, 9, 11; 3:7, 9, 10; 4:6, 9; 5:4; 6:12, 15; 7:3, 4, 9, 12, 13; 8:1, 2, 3, 4, 6, 7, 9, 11, 14, 18, 19, 20, 22, 23; 9:15; 10:3; 12:5; 13:2, 7; 14:16, 17, 21); (4) the Hebrew verb *yshv* (to dwell, inhabit) is used in both sections (2:4; 7:7; 12:6; 14:10) (cf. Kenneth L. Barker. "Zechariah," EBC, ed. Frank E. Gaebelein [Grand Rapids, MI: Zondervan, 1985], 7:596).

Brevard C. Childs defended the canonical unity of the book and argued that both sections rely heavily on themes from the Major Prophets. The congruent elements between chaps. 1–8 and 9–14 include: (1) a new Jerusalem protected by the Lord (2:5 / 9:8; 11:14); (2) return of the land to Eden-like fertility (8:12 / 14:8); (3) restoration of the relationship between Israel and the LORD (using covenant terminology, 8:8 / 13:9); (4) the prediction of the pouring out of a curse on the land (5:3) and the prediction of the removal of the curse (14:11); (5) God's judgment on the nations (1:18-21 / 14:12-15); (6) the conversion of the nations and their worship of the Lord (2:11; 8:20, 22 / 14:6, 16; (7) the regathering of the exiles of Israel (8:7-8 / 10:9-11); (8) changes in worship rites at the coming of the new age (8:18-19 / 14:20; (9) the outpouring of God's Spirit at the end of the age (4:6 / 12:10); (10) the purging of the land of those who swear falsely (5:3-4 / 13:3); (10) the Messiah who triumphs by humility, not power (3:8; 4:6 / 9:10) (Brevard C. Childs, *Introduction to the Old Testament as Scripture* [Philadelphia: Fortress Press, 1979], 482–83). Additional congruent elements are: (11) joy at the coming of the King (2:10 / 9:9); (12) the need for repentance and cleansing from sin (1:4; 3:4, 9; 9:7 / 12:10; 13:1, 9); (13) Jerusalem's ultimate exaltation (1:21; 2:11 / 12:3-9; 14:12-19); and (14) the Messiah presented as the coming King of Israel (6:12-13 / 9:9).

The second argument against Zechariah's authorship (that the prophet refers to events yet in the future) is only problematic to those who deny supernatural revelation and future prediction. Thus, for example, the prediction of Greece in 9:13 is reasonable if the omniscient Lord could reveal this to Zechariah even as He revealed the coming of the Messiah to him (3:8-10; 6:9-15; 9:9; 11:4-14; 12:10; 13:7-9). Therefore, there is substantial evidence that Zechariah is indeed the author of the entire book attributed to him.

Date. The messages in chaps. 1–8 have dates ranging from 520–518 BC and were generally simultaneous with Haggai's prophetic ministry. Chapters 9–14 are undated and were likely written much later in the prophet's ministry. Bullock suggests that since Zechariah was a young man in the first eight chapters, it is likely that he was still alive when Greece began to be dominant over Persia after the battles of Marathon (490 BC, on the coast northeast of Athens) and Salamis (480 BC, between Athens and Corinth). Transitions in the times of the Gentiles (cf. Introduction to Daniel) called for prophetic insight to comfort the people of Israel. So he suggests that the oracles in chaps. 9–14 are to be dated "in the early decades of the fifth century B.C." (C. Hassell Bullock, *An Introduction to the Old Testament Prophets* [Chicago: Moody, 1986], 316–17).

Nevertheless, dating the visions and oracles of Zechariah do not date the book. It is not as if the prophet kept a daily journal that was ultimately published as one volume. Rather, near the end of his prophetic ministry, the prophet composed a book using selected visions and oracles from both his early and later messages. The unified work, using many themes of the earlier prophets, is likely dated in the early fifth century BC, not long after the prophet's final oracles.

Theme and Purpose. Robinson describes Zechariah as "the most Messianic, the most truly apocalyptic and eschatological, of all the writings of the OT" (Robinson, "The Book of Zechariah," V:3136). Thus, the theme of the book is the redemption and restoration of Israel and the world through the messianic King. The book's purpose was to encourage spiritual renewal in Israel and confidence in the faithful remnant by revealing the messianic hope and God's ultimate plan for the future.

Perhaps the best description of the book's genre is George Eldon Ladd's term, "prophetic apocalyptic" (George Eldon Ladd, "Why Not Prophetic-Apocalyptic?" *Journal of Biblical Literature* 76 [1957]: 192-200). Clearly Zechariah uses the distinctive elements of classical prophecy, including both an emphasis on ethical behavior and the expectation of the kingdom of God to be established on earth as part of the day of the Lord. Additionally, Zechariah includes apocalyptic revelation by God given through visions and symbols with a message of eschatological (end-time) triumph.

Meredith G. Kline has proposed a bifold framework for the book of Zechariah ("The Structure of the Book of Zechariah," *Journal of the Evangelical Theological Society* 34/2 [June 1991], 179–93) as follows: The book of Zechariah divides into two major panels with 6:9-15 forming a primary hinge between them. Each panel also is divided by a secondary hinge. The first panel, focusing on the night visions, extends from 1:1 to 6:8, with a hinge at 3:1-10, and the second panel, emphasizing prophetic burdens (or oracles), extends from 7:1 to 14:21 with a hinge at 11:1-17.

Zechariah's purpose in using this structure was to draw attention to the hinges as the central message of the book. Significantly, the major hinge (6:9-15) is a prediction of the Messiah uniting the offices of King and Priest. The first minor hinge (3:1-10) is a prediction of the Messiah bringing cleansing from sin to Israel, emphasizing His work as Priest. The second minor hinge (11:1-17) is a prediction of Israel's rejection of the true shepherd, a term used of kings, emphasizing the Messiah's royal office. Significantly, each hinge uses a role-play to teach about the Messiah's offices: (1) the cleansing of Joshua as a picture of the Priestly Messiah's cleansing of Israel at the end of days (3:1-10); (2) the crowning of Joshua as Priest and King as a symbol of Messiah uniting the offices of Priest and King (6:9-15); and (3) the rejection of Zechariah as a symbol of Israel's rejection of the Messiah, the true King (11:1-17). The hinges are designed to draw the reader to the main point of the book, the revelation of the Messiah, who will both cleanse and deliver Israel. The chart below depicts the bifold structure of Zechariah.

Contribution. The book of Zechariah makes several significant contributions to the Bible, foremost being the revelation of the Messiah. David Baron says of the messianic theme, "Indeed it seems to be the special aim and mission of Zechariah to condense and concentrate in small compass, and in his own peculiar terse style, almost all that has been revealed to the 'former prophets' about the person and mission of Messiah—about His Divine and yet truly human character, and of His sufferings and of the glory that should follow" (David Baron, *Commentary on Zechariah: His Visions and Prophecies* [London: Morgan and Scott, 1918], 5–6). Thus, Zechariah reveals that Messiah will cleanse Israel at the end of days (3:8-10; 13:1); Messiah will unite the offices of Priest and King (6:12-13); Messiah, although a king, will arrive humbly, riding a donkey (9:9-10); Messiah will be rejected by His own people (11:4-14); Messiah will be recognized as the rejected shepherd and ultimately welcomed by Israel (12:10); and Messiah will be pierced prior to the scattering of His people (13:7-9).

Additionally, the book of Zechariah provides details concerning the end of days. This includes: the final siege of Jerusalem (12:1-3; 14:1-2); the Lord's deliverance of His city and people (14:3-4); the judgment of the nations (1:21; 12:9; 14:3); the repentance and restoration of Israel (12:10; 13:8-9); the leadership of Israel among the nations in the messianic kingdom (8:23); and the redemption of Gentile nations and their worship of Israel's Messiah in the messianic kingdom (8:20-23; 14:16-19).

Ultimately, the book reveals much about the nature of the living God. He is omniscient, knowing the future regarding the nations (9:13) and the coming of the Messiah. The Lord is faithful, remembering His covenant promises to Israel (8:8; 13:9). Finally, the book reveals God to be the sovereign Lord of history, bringing to pass all that He decreed and establishing a righteous kingdom over Israel and the world.

Background. The prophecies of the book of Zechariah are from the postexilic period, beginning approximately 16 years after the restoration from the Babylonian captivity. (For background on the captivity, see Introduction to Daniel. For background on the postexilic period, see Introductions to Ezra and Haggai.)

At the opening of Zechariah's book, Judah was experiencing political peace (1:11) but

The Structure of Zechariah

NIGHT VISIONS					BURDENS			
Introduction: A Call to Repentance	The Rider on the Red Horse (1:7-17) Four Horns and Four Craftsmen (1:18-21) The Measuring Line (2:1-13)	The Messianic Priest (The Cleansing of Joshua) Secondary Hinge	The Lampstand and the Two Olive Trees (4:1-14) The Flying Scroll and the Woman in the Basket (5:1-11) The Four Chariots (6:1-8)	The Messianic Priest-King (The Crowning of Joshua)	Introduction: A Call to Righteousness	The Coming of Israel's True King	The Messianic King (The Rejection of Zechariah) Secondary Hinge	The Restoration of Israel by the True King
1:1 1:6	1:7 2:13	3:1 3:10	4:1 6:8	6:9 6:15	7:1 8:23	9:1 10:12	11:1 11:17	12:1 14:21
PANEL ONE				Primary Hinge	PANEL TWO			

national despair. The temple was still not built (Hg 1:2-4), the walls of Jerusalem were in ruins (Neh 2:17), and the people were facing adversity, including both poverty (Hg 1:6) and drought (Hg 1:11). By the time the book was compiled (early fifth century BC, cf. comments on Date), the Persian Empire was fading and the Greek Empire was ascendant, causing uneasiness among the returned captives. Therefore, Zechariah was called to give the returned Judahites hope for the present in light of the Lord's promises to them for the future.

OUTLINE

- I. The Night Visions of Zechariah (1:1–6:8)
  - A. The Introduction to the Night Visions: A Call to Repentance (1:1-6)
  - B. The Declaration of the Night Visions: The Comfort of Israel (1:7–6:8)
    - 1. The First Set of Night Visions (1:7–2:13)
      - a. The Rider on the Red Horse (1:7-17)
      - b. The Four Horns and Four Craftsmen (1:18-21)
      - c. The Man with a Measuring Line (2:1-13)
    - 2. The Hinge in the Night Visions (The Messianic Priest) (3:1-10)
      - a. The Cleansing of Joshua by the Angel of the Lord (3:1-5)
      - b. The Cleansing of Israel by the Messianic Priest (3:6-10)
    - 3. The Second Set of Night Visions (4:1–6:8)
      - a. The Lamp Stand and the Two Olive Trees (4:1-14)
      - b. The Flying Scroll and the Woman in the Bushel Basket (5:1-11)
      - c. The Four Chariots (6:1-8)
- II. The Central Hinge: The Messianic Priest King (6:9-15)
  - A. The Crowning of Joshua as a Symbol of the Messiah (6:9-11)
  - B. The Uniting of Priest and Kingship by the Messiah (6:12-15)
- III. The Burdens of Zechariah (7:1–14:21)
  - A. The Introduction to the Burdens: A Call to Righteousness (7:1–8:23)
    - 1. The Questions Concerning Fasting (7:1-3)
    - 2. The Answers Concerning Fasting (7:4–8:23)
      - a. Concerning Repentance and Ritual (7:4-7)
      - b. Concerning Righteousness and Religion (7:8-14)
      - c. Concerning Restoration and Rejection (8:1-17)
      - d. Concerning Rejoicing and Remorse (8:18-23)
  - B. The Declaration of the Burdens: The Coming of the Messiah (9:1–14:21)
    - 1. The First Burden: The Coming of Israel's True King (9:1–10:12)
      - a. The Judgment of the Nations (9:1-8)
      - b. The Coming of the Messiah (9:9-10)
      - c. The Deliverance of Israel (9:11–10:12)
    - 2. The Hinge in the Burdens: The Rejected Messianic King (11:1-17)
      - a. The True Shepherd (11:1-14)
        - (1) The Consequences of Rejecting the True Shepherd (11:1-3)
        - (2) The Depiction of Rejecting the True Shepherd (11:4-14)
      - b. The False Shepherd (11:15-17)
    - 3. The Second Burden: The Restoration of Israel by the True King (12:1–14:21)
      - a. Oracle: A Description of Jerusalem's Future Deliverance (12:1–13:6)
      - b. Poem: A Survey of Israel's Destiny (13:7-9)
      - c. Oracle: A Description of Jerusalem's Future Renovation (14:1-21)

COMMENTARY ON ZECHARIAH

I. The Night Visions of Zechariah (1:1–6:8)

The first major panel records the night visions of Zechariah. The first paragraph (1:1-6) is an introduction to the panel followed by the night visions (1:7–6:8). In the middle of the six night visions, Joshua the high priest is cleansed of filthy garments (3:1-10), a role-play that functions as a hinge in this section and represents the future priestly work of the Messiah. The message of the night visions, God's comfort of Israel, places its central idea in the hinge—that comfort finds its source in the priestly work of the Messiah, cleansing Israel from sin. The hinge (3:1-10) also links the promises of deliverance and restoration (1:7–2:13) with the promises of empowerment and enablement (4:1–6:8), demonstrating that ultimate deliverance will come only with cleansing from sin and that empowerment will follow that cleansing.

A. The Introduction to the Night Visions: A Call to Repentance (1:1-6)

1:1. Zechariah's first message, received in **the eighth month of the second year of Darius** Hystaspes (521–486 BC, cf. Ezr 4:5, 24; 5:5-7; 6:1, 12, 15) or October/November, 520 BC, some 2–3 months after Haggai's first message (cf. commentary on Hg 1:1) functions as the introduction to night visions. Dating it by the reign of a Gentile king indicates that Israel was still in the times of the Gentiles (Dn 2:7; Lk 21:24). Called **the word of the Lord**, the technical term for prophetic revelation, the message came to **Zechariah the prophet**. When using this phrase in the rest of the book, the author uses the first person (to me, Zch 4:8, 6:9, 7:4, 8:18) but here the name of the prophet since it stands at the head of the book. Called **the son of Berechiah, the son of Iddo**, this identification is alleged to contradict Ezr 5:1 and 6:14, where he is simply called **the son of Iddo**. Rather than a contradiction, it is more likely that the book of Zechariah names both father and grandfather, while Ezra names only the more famous grandfather, who was head of a priestly family (Neh 12:12-16). This is plausible, as the Hebrew word "son" can mean son, grandson, or descendant (e.g., 2Ch 22:9).

1:2-3. God is said to be **very angry** with Israel's ancestors (1:2). Zechariah used an intense word (*qatsuph*) for **angry** (used in Dt 1:34; 2Kg 5:11; Is 57:16-17; 64:5; Est 1:12; 2:21) and places it in an emphatic position with a redoubling (lit., "angry with anger"), making it better translated "furious" or "wrathful." In light of this, the Lord invites the returned exiles to **return** to Him. This is the Hebrew word for "repent" and literally means "to turn around." If they repent of the sins of their fathers, the Lord would **return** to them, restoring His favor.

1:4-6. Having invited them to repent, the Lord warned the Jewish people not to resist His offer as their **fathers** did (1:4). **The former prophets**, a reference to the preexilic prophets, had called Israel to repent of their **evil ways . . . but they did not listen**. The quotation from the prophets is not direct but rather a summary (cf. Mt 2:23) of their messages (cf. Is 55:6-7; Jr 3:12; Hs 7:10; Jl 2:12-13; Am 5:4-6). Although their fathers and the former prophets had died (Zch 1:5), God's **words** of warning ultimately did **overtake** the Jewish people, and they were sent into exile (1:6). As a result, some of the returned exiles **repented** (lit., "turned," as used in 1:3), recognizing God's justice in disciplining Israel. This introductory warning establishes the context for the entire book: God would bring the blessings of the messianic kingdom when Israel would turn to Him in obedience and righteousness (cf. 3:7; 6:15; 7:9-14; 8:14-17).

B. The Declaration of the Night Visions: The Comfort of Israel (1:7-6:8)

Having introduced the first panel, Zechariah began to reveal the night visions he had received. This major panel contains six night visions, three visions on either side of a hinge describing the cleansing of Joshua the High Priest, a messianic prediction of the priestly Messiah's cleansing of Israel (for the significance of this hinge, see Introduction).

1. The First Set of Night Visions (1:7–2:13)

a. The Rider on the Red Horse (1:7-17)

1:7. All six visions were received **on the twenty-fourth day of the eleventh month . . . in the second year of Darius**, or on February 15, 519 BC, some three months after Zechariah's first message and two months after Haggai's last messages (Hg 2:10, 20). Although the visions were received on that date, the book of Zechariah was written many years later. Zechariah included this record of the visions to give hope and comfort to the exiles who had returned.

1:8-11. All the visions came on one **night**, this first one depicting a rider **on a red horse** in the midst of a grove of **myrtle trees** in front of other riders on **red, sorrel and white horses**. The rider on the red horse is **the angel of the LORD** (1:9, 11), a phrase found over 50 times in the OT. In some cases, it appears to refer to the Lord spatially present in a particular time and place (cf. Gn 18:1-15, where the leader of the three angelic visitors is identified as the Lord while the other two are merely angels; Gn 48:15-16, where the angel that led Jacob is used synonymously with God; and Ex 3:1-22, where the angel of the Lord appeared to Moses in Ex 3:2 but is identified as the Lord who is present in the burning bush throughout the chapter, also see Ex 23:2-23; 32:34; 33:14; Jdg 13:1-25; Is 63:9).

Since those who saw the angel of the Lord actually saw God (cf. Jdg 13:22), many interpreters have correctly recognized that these were preincarnate appearances of the Messiah Jesus. Here, the angel of the Lord is to be distinguished from the interpreting angel (Zch 1:9, 13-14, 19; 2:3; 4:1, 4-5; 5:5, 10; 6:4-5). The other riders were angelic beings, returned from patrolling the earth (1:10). The horses' colors may be significant: **red**, perhaps representing blood and judgment (cf. Is 63:1-6 where red represents the blood of the nations under judgment by the Messiah); **white,** triumph and glory (cf. Rv 19:11-14 where the white horse represents the glorious and triumphant return of Jesus); and **sorrel**, although not identified elsewhere in Scripture, since it is better translated as "variegated," this horse might represent a combination of judgment and triumph.

The identification of the **myrtle trees** is not explicit in the text. Since the myrtle is one of the special shrubs depicting the redeemed land of Israel in the future kingdom (Is 41:19; 55:13) some have proposed correctly that here they represent the nation Israel (Charles L. Feinberg, *God Remembers: A Study of the Book of Zechariah* [New York: ABMJ, 1965], 27; H. C. Leupold, *Exposition of Zechariah* [Grand Rapids, MI: Baker, 1971], 33; Merrill F. Unger, *Zechariah: Prophet of Messiah's Glory* [Grand Rapids, MI: Zondervan, 1963], 27–28). Positioned in a **ravine**, they would represent Israel in a lowly, oppressed place. The riders reported that they **patrolled the earth** and found it **peaceful and quiet**, a negative quality because Israel had hoped that the LORD would soon shake the earth (Hg 2:21-22), overthrow kingdoms, and deliver them from the oppression of the nations.

1:12-17. The following paragraph presents the meaning of the vision and reflects God's compassion for oppressed Israel. When the angel of the Lord prayed for compassion after **seventy years** of captivity (1:12; cf. 7:5; Jr 25:11-12; 29:10; 2Ch 36:21; Ezr 1:1; Dn 9:2), the LORD responded with **gracious** (lit., "good") and **comforting words** (Zch 1:13). These included that He was **jealous for . . . Zion** (1:14). God's jealousy is part of the biblical idiom of love and generally refers to God's exclusive covenant relationship with Israel. God demands Israel's absolute love and devotion as a result of His jealousy.

As comfort, God promised ultimately to deliver His nation from oppression (2Kg 19:31; Is 26:11; Ezk 39:25), to express His great anger at the nations for doing far worse to Judah than He wanted (Zch 1:15), and to offer eschatological promises. These include that He would **return to Jerusalem** (1:16a), rebuild His **house**, and grow (the **measuring line**, like a tape measure, indicating increase in size, 1:16b) and prosper Israel, when **the LORD will again . . . choose Jerusalem** (1:17).

Although some see this fulfilled in the postexilic period with the building of the second temple, since the glory and presence of God did not return to the rebuilt temple (as predicted in Ezk 43:4) and since the description depicts the composite eschatological description of Jerusalem from the Prophets, it is more likely an eschatological prediction. Thus the **return to Jerusalem** more likely refers to the literal coming of the Messiah (even as Zch 12:10 indicates; cf. Mt 23:37-39) when He will be literally present in the city (Ezk 48:35; Is 2:1-4; 4:2-6; 9:7; 11:9-10); the rebuilt house finds its fulfillment in the future millennial temple (Zch 1:16b; cf. 6:13; Ezk 40–48); the expansion of Jerusalem points to its end-of-days rebuilding and expansion (Jr 31:38-40; Is 60:4-9; Zch 9:17); and the comfort of Jerusalem predicts the messianic future (Is 14:1).

b. The Four Horns and Four Craftsmen (1:18-21)

1:18-19. The second vision describes **four horns** (1:18) and **four craftsmen** (1:20). The word **horn** generally refers to strength and power, but may refer to a king or kingdom (Ps 132:17; Dn 7:7; Rv 13:1; 17:12). Here it represents four kingdoms that **have scattered Judah, Israel and Jerusalem** (Zch 1:19). Since these visions all have an eschatological framework, they refer to the same four empires Daniel predicted (for evidence supporting the following interpretation, cf. comments in Dn 2 and 7): Babylon, Medo-Persia, Greece, and Rome (with Rome either being revived at the end of days or represented as continuing through Western civilization until the end of days).

1:20-21. The **four craftsmen** represent those empires that God used to judge those who **scattered Judah**. In turn, therefore, they are, Medo-Persia that defeated Babylon, Greece that conquered Persia, Rome that overcame Greece, and finally, the kingdom of Messiah that will overcome the end-of-days Rome (cf. Dn 2:34, 44-45 and comments there).

c. The Man with a Measuring Line (2:1-13)

2:1-5. The third night vision depicts a man with **a measuring line** (2:1) going out **to measure Jerusalem** (2:2). The tape measure (cf. 1:16) represents Jerusalem's increase in size. As the interpreting angel was leaving, another rushed **to meet him** (2:3) with a message for the **young man**, namely Zechariah (2:4), who would in turn give it to the people. Jerusalem would one day have so many people and cattle living beyond its boundaries that it would be like a city without walls. There is no historical record of this occurring in the past, so it has either been fulfilled figuratively in the expansion of the Church, or it will yet be fulfilled literally in the eschatological kingdom.

Charles Feinberg fervently responds to the figurative interpretation: "What baseless and unfounded hermeneutical alchemy is this which will take all the prophecies of judgment upon Israel at their face value, to be understood literally, but will transmute into indistinctness any blessing or promise of future glory for the same people?" (Feinberg, *God Remembers*, 45). It is best, then, to see the future restoration of Jerusalem in the literal messianic kingdom. At that time, the LORD will protect Jerusalem, like **a wall of fire** around the city and will restore **the glory** of Jerusalem by being **in her midst** (Ezk 43:1-7). In support of this understanding, other prophets also link the eschatological expansion and prosperity of Jerusalem to the future literal reign of Messiah in that city (Is 9:7; 11:1-10).

2:6-9. The next section gives a further expansion of the meaning of the vision. The glory of the future is seen in three addresses. The first exhortation is *to the dispersed of Israel* (2:6-9), here called **Zion**. They are to **flee from the land of the north** (2:6), specifically named as Babylon (2:7). Since the exile was already completed and this dispersion is presented as worldwide (**four winds of the heavens**), this is an eschatological call to flee dispersion. As Merrill says, the prophets "knew of a dispersion far more serious and widespread than anything known in biblical times, a dispersion nonetheless couched in terms of a Babylonian exile (cf. Deut. 28:64; 30:1-4; Isa. 40–55; Ezek. 12:15-16; Mic. 4:10)." (See Eugene H. Merrill, *An Exegetical Commentary: Haggai, Zechariah, Malachi* [Chicago: Moody, 1994], 119–20.) God declares that **after glory He has sent me** (Zch 2:8a).

This surprising construction can be taken in two ways. First, some have viewed the pronoun "me" as referring to the prophet Zechariah himself saying that God had sent him to pursue God's glory. The problem is that the prophet is not identified as the speaker here. Second, since the text does identify the speaker as the LORD Himself, others have viewed the pronoun "me" as a reference "to the messianic Servant-Messenger, the Angel of the Lord" (Barker, "Zechariah," 618). This is similar to the first-person construction in 12:10, where the Lord is speaking but plainly is referring to the Messiah. Therefore, the Messiah will be sent to pursue God's glory in judging the nations (2:9) for their wicked treatment of Israel, **the apple of** God's **eye** (2:8b; Dt 32:10). As Feinberg states, "God's cause and glory are inseparably linked with the fortunes of His people. The humiliation and subjugation of Israel by the nations must be avenged by the One who is dishonored in their dejected condition" (Feinberg, *God Remembers*, 49).

2:10-12. The second address is *to Jerusalem*, here called **daughter of Zion**. The city will be glorified in the messianic kingdom by the presence of the LORD, in the person of the Messiah, dwelling in the **midst** of it (Zch 2:10). Jerusalem's divine glory will be evident in the millennium, when Gentile **nations will join themselves to the LORD** and Israel as whole will believe **that the LORD of hosts** sent the Messiah Jesus to them (2:11). Some interpreters hold that the inclusion of the Gentile nations here indicates that the Church will be prominent in the kingdom with all people being one in Christ. This eliminates Israel's future place of prominence as described in this passage. Yet the prophets in general (Is 2:4; 19:23-25) and Zechariah in particular (Zch 8:23; 14:16-19) foresaw that people from the Gentile nations would also become believers in the days prior to the return of the Messiah and then share in the messianic kingdom. Nevertheless, this passage as well as others (8:23; 14:16-19) indicates that regenerated Israel will be central in God's kingdom plan. Then God will make the land of Israel into a **holy land** (this is the only passage in which this title is used in Scripture for Israel; Ps 78:54 is translated "holy land" by the NASB, but it is literally "holy border"), choosing Jerusalem again as His city even as He did in the past (Dt 12:11; 2Sm 5:6-7; Ps 48:1-3, 8).

2:13. The third address is *to all flesh.* When Israel believes in Messiah Jesus and He returns, all humanity will **be silent** before the Lord. They will submit because He has been **aroused** (awakened, incited to activity) leaving **His holy habitation** (the heavenly realms) to descend to His holy land (2:12), His earthly dwelling place. This is not merely a "spiritual" descent of God to vindicate and help His people. The context places the event described in the messianic era at the end of days. When the Lord comes to deliver His people, other prophets recognize that He will do so with the literal return of the Messiah (cf. Is 59:20; Rm 11:26-27; Mc 2:12-13; 5:4).

2. The Hinge in the Night Visions (The Messianic Priest) (3:1-10)

The panel with the night visions has a literary hinge in its midst, with three visions on either side of it. This hinge, linked to the primary hinge depicting Messiah as King and Priest, here pictures the cleansing of Joshua the high priest and reveals the Messiah's priestly role, cleansing Israel at the end of days. Thus, immediately after the night visions that promise the messianic deliverance of Israel, the hinge focuses on the essential need for that deliverance to begin—Israel must turn in faith to the Messiah and experience His purification from sin.

a. The Cleansing of Joshua by the Angel of the Lord (3:1-5)

3:1-3. Zechariah was shown a vision of **Joshua** ("Jeshua" in Ezr 2:2; Neh 7:7) **the high priest** performing his priestly duties (Dt 10:8; Jdg 20:28; 2Ch 29:11; Ezk 44:15) **before** the divine **angel of the Lord**. Suddenly, **Satan** (lit., the Accuser; Jb 1:6-12; 2:1-7; Rv 12:10) appeared **at his right hand**, the place of accusation in a courtroom (Ps 109:6) **to accuse him** (Zch 3:1). **The Lord** rebuked Satan (two times for emphasis), calling Joshua **a brand plucked from the fire**, meaning one who is still useful and not to be consumed or destroyed (3:2). As background, Zechariah explained that Joshua was wearing **filthy garments**, the Hebrew literally referring to excrement-covered clothing (3:3). In this vision, Joshua represents the people of Israel (cf. 3:8-9) in all their sinfulness.

3:4-5. The angel of the Lord directed the angels around Joshua to **remove the filthy garments**, indicating that God had cleansed him from **iniquity** (3:4), and to replace them with festive clothing and a clean turban (3:5), showing that God had made him fit to serve as high priest once again (Ex 28:36).

b. The Cleansing of Israel by the Messianic Priest (3:6-10)

3:6-7. With the vision described, what follows explains its significance (3:6-10). To begin with, **the angel of the Lord** exhorts Joshua to keep His requirement—he is personally to **walk** faithfully in God's ways and professionally to serve as priest. Then he would be granted leadership as high priest (**govern My house**) and have **free access** to God, even as the angels (**these who are standing here**) do.

3:8-9. Besides the significance to Joshua personally, there is prophetic significance to Israel as well. **Joshua** and his fellow priests functioned as a **symbol**, the Hebrew word signifying "a sign with prophetic significance; a prophetic portent" (1Kg 13:3, 5; 2Ch 32:24, 31; Is 8:18; 20:3; Ezk 12:6, 11; 24:24, 27). These priests point forward to the day when God's **servant the Branch**, a linking of two messianic titles (Is 11:1; 42:1; 49:6; 50:10; 52:13; Ps 132:17; Jr 23:5-6; 33:15; cf. comments on Zch 6:12-13), brings deliverance to Israel (3:8). He is also called by the messianic title **stone** (v. 9; cf. Ps 118:22; Is 28:16), described as having **seven eyes**, indicating omniscience, and coming to **remove the iniquity of that land in one day**. Although some wrongly identify this day as Good Friday, the prophecy is actually pointing to the eschatological day (note the use **in that day**, Zch 3:10) at the return of Jesus when Israel finally recognizes Him as their Messiah (12:10) and a fount for cleansing the nation is opened (13:1; cf. comments on Mt 23:37-39; Rm 11:25-27). Thus, Joshua, cleansed of filthy rags and restored to service as a priest, symbolizes the future cleansing of Israel from their sin by Messiah and their restoration by Him to their status as a nation of priests.

3:10. Israel, cleansed from sin, will enter the messianic kingdom, where sitting **under his vine and under his fig tree** represents divine favor, prosperity, and peace. At that time, paradise lost will become paradise regained.

3. The Second Set of Night Visions (4:1–6:8)

Having introduced the night visions (1:1-6), the prophet has also revealed the first three visions about the comfort and deliverance of Israel (1:7–2:13), placed a hinge about the priestly work of the future Messiah (3:1-10), and will now complete the revelation of the remaining three night visions describing the empowering and enablement of Israel (4:1–6:8). Both the comfort and the empowering of Israel are possible through the spiritually cleansing work of Messiah.

a. The Lamp Stand and the Two Olive Trees (4:1-14)

4:1-5. The next night vision is described in vv. 1-5 and then explained in vv. 6-14. In the vision, Zechariah saw **a lampstand all of gold**, a seven-branched menorah, similar but not identical to the one in the tabernacle (Ex 25:31-37). Above it was a bowl serving as a reservoir for oil with seven pipes (a better translation than **spouts**) leading to each one of the lamps on the menorah (Zch 4:2). Additionally, there were two olive trees on either side of the menorah (4:3) with golden pipes conducting golden oil directly from the trees to the reservoir (4:12). While this depiction seems impossible, it is a vision, not an actually engineered menorah, that the angel needed to explain (4:4-5).

4:6-10. The angel gave Zechariah a message for Zerubbabel, a descendant of King David, the head of the Davidic house and the governor, explaining the essential meaning of the vision in summary form: God's work would be done **not by might** (strong or firm, used of all kinds of human resources including wealth or physical strength (Gn 34:29; Ps 84:7; Ec 10:10) **nor by power** (human strength, Jdg 16:5; Is 44:12), **but by** God's **Spirit** (Zch 4:6). His point was that Zerubbabel would overcome the **great mountain**, or obstacle before him and turn it into **a plain** (4:7), referring to the completion of the construction of the temple (4:9). Despite the **small** beginnings of the temple (4:10), there would ultimately be shouts of **Grace, grace to it**, meaning, "Lovely, how lovely it is!" (4:7). Also, God, in His omniscience (**seven . . . eyes**), will see the temple and approve (4:10). Although the message to Zerubbabel, as an event in space and time, was given in 520 BC, the book of Zechariah was written many years later, after the completion of the second temple. Thus, Zechariah's prediction had come true already, and readers of the text would have been aware of the near-term fulfillment of this prediction, giving them confidence in the eschatological fulfillment to which the rest of the prophecy points.

4:11-14. Zechariah still did not understand the significance of the **two olive trees**, so he inquired of their meaning (4:11). They represented **two anointed ones** (lit., "sons of oil"), meaning the high priestly office (then represented by Joshua) and the royal office (then represented by Zerubbabel). By ministering before **the Lord of the whole earth** (4:14), they were empowered by Him and transmitted that spiritual power to the menorah (lampstand). Since the seven-branched menorah was and remains the symbol of Israel, and since Israel was to be the light to all the peoples (Is 58:8-10), it is likely that the menorah represents Israel at the end of days, when it has come to faith in Messiah. Thus, the believing community of Israel would rebuild the temple and fulfill their function as the light to the nations.

Although this vision gave encouragement to the people of the sixth century BC, Zechariah's use of the title **the Lord of the whole earth** links this vision to an ultimate eschatological fulfillment in the messianic kingdom. Citing its use in Mc 4:13 (see also the context of Mc 4:1-12), Unger correctly states that the title "describes Messiah as King-Priest, putting down His enemies and reigning over the entire world during the kingdom age" (Unger, *Zechariah: Prophet of Messiah's Glory*, 81). The major hinge of the book will reveal that these two offices will be united by the future messianic King-Priest, who will build the messianic temple (Zch 6:12-13). Thus, the vision of the lampstand gave encouragement to the original readers about recently fulfilled predictions and simultaneously pointed to the future, when Messiah would unite the offices of king and priest, build the eschatological temple, and make Israel the light to the nations.

The book of Revelation speaks of the two witnesses of the tribulation period, using terms from Zch 4, calling them "two olive trees" and "two lampstands" (Rv 11:4). It is unlikely that John intended to identify the two witnesses as the fulfillment of Zch 4, since there is only one lampstand in Zch 4 and two in Rv 11. Rather, he was alluding to the message of Zch 4, that these two witnesses would also have a Spirit-empowered ministry at the end of days.

b. The Flying Scroll and the Woman in the Bushel Basket (5:1-11)

Although most interpreters see two separate visions in this chapter, the consistent introductory patterns of the visions argue against this. In each of the visions, except for the one that allegedly begins in 5:5, there is the introductory formula, "I saw and behold" (1:8; 1:18; 2:1; 4:2; 5:1; 6:1). Since this is lacking in 5:5, it indicates that chap. 5 is "a compound vision of a flying scroll and a flying ephah" (Kline, "The Structure of the Book of Zechariah," 186). Just as the previous vision revealed that God's Spirit will empower redeemed Israel in the future, this vision shows that at that time, God will also forcefully and finally deal with sin.

5:1-4. This vision depicts the LORD's promise to deal with sin at the end of days. To begin, it identifies sin as disobedience to the law. The **flying scroll** is huge, 30 by 15 feet (**twenty cubits** by **ten cubits**) and represents the Torah, or the law of Moses (5:2). The symbolism is plain since the law was always written on a scroll, and this one in particular has allusions to two of the Ten Commandments written on it. It reminds readers of **the curse** for disobedience **that is going forth over the whole land** of Israel (cf. Lv 26; Dt 28:15-68). As with the tablets of the law, there is writing on both sides (Zch 5:3), promising the purging of **everyone who steals** (5:3) and **everyone who swears falsely by** God's **name** (5:4). These two sins represent disobedience of the two sides of the tablets of the law—stealing, (an offense against other people and breaking the eighth commandment), and swearing (a sin against God and breaking the third commandment). No one who commits these sins, or other violations of the law, will escape this judgment (**enter the house . . . spend the night . . . and consume it**, v. 4).

5:5-11. With the evil in the land identified, the second part of the vision identifies how God will ultimately punish it. Zechariah next saw an **ephah**, or a bushel basket (5:5-6), with **a woman sitting inside** (5:7) representing **Wickedness** (5:8). Two other women, angelic beings with **wings**, fly off (5:9), carrying her to **the land of Shinar** or Babylon, the center of all wickedness. The use of the old word **Shinar** for Babylon is an allusion to the rebellious behavior surrounding the original building of the city and tower of Babel (lit., "Babylon") (Gn 11:1-9). Also, Judah was sent into exile in Shinar (Babylon) for disobedience to the law (see Dn 1:2 and comments there). This vision depicts the end of days when God will purge Israel of rebels (Ezk 20:34-38) and destroy Babylon, the capital of all wickedness (Jr 50–51; Rv 17–18, especially 18:2-3).

While some interpreters understand the vision as depicting the past exile to Babylon, it is better viewed as an eschatological prediction. All the other night visions look forward, not backwards. Moreover, the woman, representing wickedness, is not being brought to **a temple** nor is she being placed on **her own pedestal** (as the NASB translates it). Rather, she is being brought to a "residence" or a dwelling place for sin, and she is being put "in her own place." It is extremely unlikely that God's angels would establish a temple of wickedness and honor "wickedness" by placing it on a pedestal. Thus, the NIV more accurately translates this as the angels taking the basket with wickedness "to the country of Babylonia to build a *house* for it. When it is ready, the basket will be set there *in its place*."

Hence the passage foretells that Israel's wickedness will be sent to its ultimate abode in Babylon. Other prophets had already foretold that Babylon, with all its wickedness, would be destroyed (cf. Jr 50–51 and comments there). As Feinberg notes, the placing of the woman in her own place (Zch 5:11) indicates "a permanent settling of sin" (Feinberg, *God Remembers*, 92). Joyce Baldwin also recognizes that "the removal of Wickedness to Babylon is in preparation for the final onslaught between good and evil" (Joyce Baldwin, *Haggai, Zechariah, Malachi: An Introduction and Commentary*, TOTC, ed. D. J. Wiseman [Downers Grove, IL: InterVarsity, 1972], 130). With sin removed, the land of Israel will live up to its previous description as the holy land (2:12).

c. The Four Chariots (6:1-8)

The last of the night visions pertains to the LORD's final judgment of the nations. It is similar to the first night vision, in which riders on horses patrolled the earth, providing reconnaissance. In this vision, chariots with horses now patrol the earth to carry out judgment. This vision fits with the two that preceded it by detailing events at the end of days: redeemed Israel will be empowered (4:1-14), her sin will be removed (5:1-11), and the nations that had oppressed her will be judged (6:1-8). In later passages, the book will also deal with the ultimate judgment of the nations (cf. 12:1-2; 14:3-4).

6:1-3. At the outset, Zechariah described the vision he saw. **Four chariots** proceeded from between two **bronze mountains** (6:1), which some have identified as Mount Zion and the Mount of Olives. This is unlikely for three reasons: first, this is merely a vision; second, the mountains are made of bronze; and third, the chariots go forth from **the Lord of all the earth** (6:5). It is more likely that they are symbolic, functioning as mountain gateposts outside the divine throne room, similar to the bronze pillars outside the Solomonic temple (1Kg 7:15-22). The four chariots had different colored horses (Zch 6:2-3), each with possible, but not certain, symbolic significance. The **red horses** may represent war (cf. 1:8; Is 63:1-6; Rv 6:4), the **black,** famine and death (Rv 6:5-6), and the **white,** triumph (Zch 1:8; Rv 19:11-14). The significance of the **dappled** horse is unclear, but Unger has proposed plague and judgment (cf. Rv 6:8; Unger, *Zechariah: Prophet of Messiah's Glory*, 103). This last one is uncertain since the color described in Zechariah is dappled but the color of the horse in Rv 6:8 is pale.

6:4-6. The interpreting angel explained that the chariots represent **the four spirits of heaven**, or angelic beings, sent forth after standing before the throne of God (6:4-5). Clearly, **the black horses** proceed **to the north** while the **dappled** proceed **to the south**. The **white** horses are said to follow the black ones, but with a slight emendation (*'aharehem*, **after them**, to *'ahare hayyam,* "after the sea") the phrase would be an idiom for "to the west," a far more likely scenario. The direction of the red horses is not mentioned. This could be because they were held back in reserve or perhaps, in light of the directions of the other three, it can be assumed that the red horses went to the east. Another possibility may be, as Baldwin suggests, that the syntactic awkwardness of the Hebrew text in v. 6 (lit., "which in it") indicates that a phrase about the red horses moving east has been accidentally lost in the transmission of the text (Baldwin, *Haggai, Zechariah, Malachi*, 131).

6:7-8. Although only the dappled horses were called **strong** (6:3), the description of **the strong ones** going out **to patrol the earth** (6:7) likely refers to all four chariots. Those going to the north have, in the literal translation, "caused My (God's) Spirit to be at rest" **in the land of the north**, meaning that God's wrath has been appeased. This refers to the eschatological judgment that will be brought to Babylon (cf. 5:5-11), at which time all the other horses will have judged the earth as well.

II. The Central Hinge: The Messianic Priest King (6:9-15)

Having completed the first panel of the book emphasizing the night visions, Zechariah presents the primary hinge of the book. It involves a role-play by Joshua the High Priest, emphasizing the unification of the offices of priest and king in the future Messiah. The significance of the location of this symbolic ceremony is that the role-play follows the eschatological judgment of the Gentile nations (6:1-8), indicating that the symbolism will be fulfilled only after the end-time judgment of the world. This central hinge links the night visions (1:1–6:8), emphasizing the comfort of Israel, and the burdens (7:1–14:21), emphasizing the coming of the King Messiah. Thus this hinge reminds readers that Israel's comfort is only found in the Priest-King Messiah, and when Israel trusts in Him, He will come to their eschatological deliverance.

The two secondary hinges in the midst of the two panels also use symbolic role-plays to present the Messiah, the first highlighting His priestly role (3:1-10) and the second, His royal role as the rejected King of Israel (11:4-14). These two depictions are then united in the major hinge of the book (6:9-15), presenting the Messiah as the one who unifies the offices of king and priest. The significance of this unification is that the law made it clear that there was a distinction between Israel's three theocratic offices, king, prophet, and priest (Dt 17:14–18:22). Moreover, there was serious divine discipline when Uzziah usurped the office of priest by offering incense in the temple (2Ch 26:16-21). Nevertheless, the psalmist had already predicted that when the Messiah came He would be a king/priest "according to the order of Melchizedek" (Ps 110:4). Joshua's role-play in this central hinge clearly points to the Messiah, who alone would unite these offices.

A. The Crowning of Joshua as a Symbol of the Messiah (6:9-11)

6:9-10. The crowning of Joshua is a ceremony designed to symbolize the future work of the Messiah. At the outset, Zechariah was to receive **an offering** from a delegation of men from the exile (6:9-10).

6:11. Afterwards, Zechariah was to use the **silver and gold** of the offering to make a **crown**. The word for **crown** is plural, leading to three possible interpretations. (1) Some have speculated that Zechariah was to make two crowns, one for the head of Joshua and the other for Zerubbabel. The difficulty is that Zerubbabel is not found in this passage and the prophet is directed to place the crowns only on the head of Joshua. (2) Some interpreters translate the word **crown** as a plural of majesty (NASB, **an ornate**

crown). While possible, the context does not seem to emphasize a magnificent crown. (3) The best possibility is that it refers to a composite crown of two parts, one representing the royal office and the second, the priestly office. This fits the context since the ceremony was to symbolize the unification of the offices of priest and king in one person, the Messiah (6:13).

B. The Uniting of Priest and Kingship by the Messiah (6:12-15)

6:12-13. Having crowned Joshua with the composite crown in a symbolic ceremony, the prophet declared the meaning of this action. The designation **a man whose name is Branch** (6:12), a messianic title, indicates that the passage is not about Joshua but his symbolic representation of the Messiah. The term "Branch" is from the root word meaning "sprout," "growth," or "branch." A Phoenician inscription (third century BC) uses the phrase "righteous branch" for the rightful heir to the throne. When used this way it refers to a son or scion of a king (Walter Kaiser, "Branch," *Theological Wordbook of the Old Testament*, edited by R. Laird Harris, Gleason Archer, Bruce Waltke [Chicago: Moody, 1980], 769). It was previously used in Zechariah of the Messiah (3:8) and is used explicitly of the Messiah in Jeremiah, where God promises to "raise up for David a righteous Branch" who "will reign as king" (Jr 23:5) and "execute justice and righteousness on the earth" (Jr 33:15). The future Messiah would both **build the temple of the Lord** and also **sit and rule on His throne** (6:13), indicating His unification of the previously separate offices of priest and king. The Messiah, as King-Priest (Ps 110:4), will make **peace . . . between the two offices** (Zch 6:13). This does not suggest that antagonism existed previously between these two offices. Rather, as mentioned above, these two offices were clearly distinct and separate. Hence, this verse is using the word "peace" in its most basic Hebrew idea, that of wholeness or completion: The Messiah will unite priesthood and kingship, making the separate offices whole. The temple He will build refers to the millennial temple (cf. Is 2:2-4; 56:6-7; Ezk 40–48 and comments there).

6:14-15. The composite crown was to be placed **in the temple** as **a reminder** of the future Messiah (6:14). The son of Zephaniah, host of the delegation of exiles, previously called Josiah (6:10), is now given the honor of a new name, **Hen** ("grace," v. 14). It also reminded Israel of the need to **completely obey the Lord** (6:15) by faith, just as the new covenant promised they would at the end of days (Dt 4:30; 30:6-8; Jr 31:31-34; Ezk 36:26-28). At that time, **those who are far off** (meaning the Gentile nations, cf. Zch 2:11; 8:22; Is 2:2-4; 56:6-7) **will come and build the temple of the Lord** by contributing their wealth to the project (Is 60:1-7).

III. The Burdens of Zechariah (7:1–14:21)

Having completed the primary hinge between the two major panels, Zechariah opens the second panel of his book as he did the first panel—with an introduction (7:1–8:23). Afterward he will present two sets of burdens (9:1–10:12 and 12:1–14:21), divided by a hinge emphasizing the Messianic King (11:1-17). The hinge is essential to linking these two major panels. The first panel emphasizes the comfort that the Lord will grant Israel at the end of days, while the second one presents the details of the events at the end of days. Both the comfort of Israel and the contents of the last events find their focus in the central person of the hinge—the messianic King-Priest who will restore Israel at the end of days.

A. The Introduction to the Burdens: A Call to Righteousness (7:1–8:23)

Having returned from captivity, postexilic Jewish people might have considered their restoration to the land as the final fulfillment of God's promises. Therefore, this section is designed to correct that misunderstanding. As John Sailhamer states, the point of this introductory section "is that those who returned to Jerusalem in Zechariah's day and their leaders (e.g., Zerubbabel and Joshua) were not to be understood as the final fulfillment of God's promises. A future fulfillment yet awaited them" (John H. Sailhamer, *NIV Compact Bible Commentary* [Grand Rapids, MI: Zondervan, 1994], 434). Introducing this idea prepares the way for the main point of the burdens that follow—that Israel will experience God's blessings in the eschatological, messianic era.

1. The Questions Concerning Fasting (7:1-3)

7:1. This message is dated **in the fourth year of King Darius . . . on the fourth day of the ninth month**, corresponding to December 7, 518 BC. Since the book was written some thirty years later, Zechariah included this to remind them that the promises had not yet been fulfilled.

7:2-3. A delegation came to Zechariah and the other priests, seeking divine guidance. They asked if they were to continue to fast and mourn

in the fifth month, a reference to the Ninth of Av, the fast day held on the anniversary of the temple's destruction. The return to Zion (536 BC) and the rebuilding of the temple (begun 520 BC), had led them to wonder whether the prophets' promises were now fulfilled.

2. The Answers Concerning Fasting (7:4–8:23)

The prophet's answers were designed to show that those who had returned from exile were just as sinful as those who had gone into exile. Thus, the time of full spiritual *and* geographical restoration had not yet truly begun but would still come at the end of days. This section with the answer to the delegation is divided into four messages, each beginning with the phrase, "Then the word of the LORD came" (7:4, 8; 8:1, 18).

a. Concerning Repentance and Ritual (7:4-7)

7:4-6. God's first response through Zechariah (7:4), offered in a series of rhetorical questions, was that God wanted repentance, not ritual. Those who fasted, on the **fifth** month, (to mourn the temple's destruction), and the **seventh month**, (to mourn the assassination of Gedaliah, cf. comments on 8:18-19), were acting selfishly, merely showing their religiosity. Their mourning was not penitent but only benefitted themselves (7:5), even as they would **eat and drink** for themselves (7:6).

7:7. The returned exiles were fasting not out of a heart of sincere repentance but merely external religious rites. Their ritualized fasts were as problematic as the ones prior to the exile, when **Jerusalem** and Judah had been **inhabited and prosperous**. The **former prophets** had previously addressed this problem (cf. Is 1:11-17; 58:3-8; Hs 6:6; Jr 14:10-12). By ignoring the exhortations of the former prophets, those who returned proved they were just as sinful as their ancestors who had gone into exile.

b. Concerning Righteousness and Religion (7:8-14)

In the second message, God also demanded true righteousness and not merely outward religion. The prophet's words in this section, while referring to the preexilic community, were also implicitly relevant for those of the postexilic era who had already returned.

7:8-10. Both before and after the exile, God expected His people not merely to practice religion (i.e., observing fasts) but also to exhibit righteous behavior: They were to **dispense true justice** (a judge's obligation to decide cases with equity and fairness) **and practice kindness** (treating others with consideration and mercy where no obligation exists to do so) **and compassion** (feelings of mercy for the helpless) (7:9). God demanded that they treat the weakest segments of society, **the widow** (the word refers not merely to a woman who has lost her husband but has also been left with no means of financial support) **or the orphan, the stranger or the poor** (those lacking standing or legal rights), with fairness and kindness—**not oppress[ing]** them (abusing power, taking advantage) or **devis[ing] evil** (unjust injuring) against them (7:10).

7:11-14. Before the exile, the people of Judah **refused to pay attention** to the Lord's demands through **the former prophets** for righteous behavior (7:11-12; cf. Is 1:17; 56:1; Jr 7:6; 22:3; Mc 6:8; Am 5:21-24). Since they hardened **their hearts like flint** (Zch 7:12) and **would not listen** (7:13) in fulfillment of the law's warnings, God sent Judah into exile (Dt 28:64-65). They were **scattered ... among all the nations** so that **the pleasant land** of Israel became **desolate** (Zch 7:14; cf. Lv 26:32-33). Zechariah's aim was not merely to point backwards to the previous generation's sin and discipline, but to warn the new generation that had returned from exile. If they also ignored the words of the prophets, God would also be deaf to their prayers (Zch 7:13), scatter them (7:14a), and once again, make the land of Israel desolate (7:14b).

c. Concerning Restoration and Rejection (8:1-17)

The third message in response to the delegation points to the future fulfillment of God's promises to Israel. The return from captivity was not the fulfillment of the promises. Rather, the restoration of Israel would take place in the distant future when God would restore, rather than reject, them.

8:1-8. Reiterating God's words from 1:14, the Lord once again declared His love for Israel and His determination to judge the nations with **wrath** (8:2; cf. comments on 1:14). Although some see God's promise of restoration as having been fulfilled historically at the return from captivity, for several reasons it is better to see these predictions fulfilled in the eschatological messianic kingdom.

First, as in 1:12-17, the depiction of Jerusalem fits more with the depiction of the millennial kingdom in prophetic literature (see comments on 1:12-17). Second, the terminology used in 8:3 (the Lord promised to **return to Zion and** to **dwell in the midst of Jerusalem**) points to an eschatological fulfillment. The term "Zion" is generally used eschatologically in prophetic literature, and the Hebrew word for "dwell" (*sakan*) connotes permanent residence (Merrill, *An Exegetical Commentary: Haggai, Zechariah, Malachi*, 221). Obviously the Lord did not take up permanent residence in Jerusalem at the return from captivity nor has He yet done so. Third, it would require a serious dilution of the promises to consider them fulfilled at the return from captivity. One would be hard pressed to see Jerusalem as having already become a **City of Truth,** a **Holy Mountain** (8:3), or a place of complete security (8:4-5). The regathering described in 8:7-8 is universal and not merely from Babylon. Moreover, although idolatry did cease with the return from Babylon, Israel did not become a complete people of truth and righteousness at that time or ever since.

The depiction of the messianic kingdom is glorious. Then, the Lord will be *present* **in the midst of Jerusalem** (8:3a), which other biblical passages associate with the Messiah reigning there (Ps 2:6; Is 9:7; Zch 9:9-10). He will also *purify* Jerusalem, as seen in the new names that the city and temple mount will be given, **the City of Truth** and **the Holy Mountain** (8:3b). **Old men and old women** as well as **boys and girls**, the most defenseless elements of society, will be safe on the streets of Jerusalem, demonstrating God's future *protection* of His people (8:4-5). Finally, God's *people* will be restored. From a human perspective, a future eschatological restoration of the Jewish people from a worldwide dispersion might seem **too difficult** for God to effect (8:6). Nevertheless, God will bring the Jewish people back from the **east** and the **west** (8:7), indicating a worldwide restoration, from far more places than Babylon. In that day, not only will they be physically restored to the land of Israel, but they will also be spiritually transformed. Israel will become God's people in the fullest sense—He **will be their God in truth and righteousness** (8:8).

8:9-17. The prophet moved from the vision of the future to an exhortation for his own day. The promise of restoration was to affect the behavior of the returned Jewish people at that time. Described as those who listened **to these words from the mouth of the prophets** Haggai and Zechariah, the people were to be encouraged (lit., **be strong**) in the work of rebuilding the temple (8:9). As a motivation to finish their task, Zechariah reminded them of their previous poverty (**no wage**) and distress (**no peace**) when they had failed to complete the temple prior to 520 BC (8:10; cf. Hg 1:6-11 and comments there). God promised that if they would now be faithful in building in their own day, the land would again be fruitful, there would be adequate rain, and **the remnant** would **inherit all these** blessings (Zch 8:12). Instead of being an example of God's **curse among the nations**, Israel would become an example of God's **blessing** (8:13).

Using the exhortation, **do not fear**, two more times (8:13, 15), the prophet exhorts Israel to persist. Not only were they to complete the temple but to practice righteous behavior. Since God had **purposed . . . to do good to Jerusalem** at that time (8:15), they were to become honest men and women. Since God is truth, He hates all forms of dishonesty (8:17). Therefore, the returned remnant was to **speak the truth** and **judge with truth** (8:16), to forego **evil** plans and reject **perjury** (lit., false oaths).

d. Concerning Rejoicing and Remorse (8:18-23)

8:18-19. The prophet's fourth message in response to the delegation returned to the question of fasting and also again pointed to the ultimate future kingdom fulfillment of God's promises to Israel, as indicated by 8:20-23. God promised that the sorrow of Israel's captivity would be turned to joy at the end of days. At that time, Israel would experience three great reversals. First, God promised that Israel's fast days would become feast days in the messianic kingdom. **The fast of the fourth** month, commemorating the breaching of the walls of Jerusalem (Jr 39:2; 52:6-7), **the fast of the fifth** month, mourning the destruction of the temple (Jr 52:12-13; 2Kg 25:8-9), **the fast of the seventh** month, remembering the assassination of Gedaliah (Jr 41:1; 2Kg 25:25-26), and **the fast of the tenth** month, recalling the beginning of the siege of Jerusalem (Jr 39:1; 2Ki 25:1), will all **become . . . cheerful feasts** in the future (Zch 8:19).

The prophet views this future transformation as one that will come about for Israel. The prophets only understood God's promises to Israel as referring to literal ethnic Israel and never expected those promises to be fulfilled figuratively in the Church. Obviously, Israel's fast days did not come to an end with the return to Zion, and they continue to be observed even at present. The prophet Isaiah likewise envisioned the messianic era when the Lord would transform sorrow and mourning to joy and gladness

(Is 61:2-3; 65:18-19). Zechariah therefore likely foresaw the same period of time as Isaiah, when fasting will be replaced with feasting in the days of Messiah's millennial reign.

8:20-23. The second reversal will be that instead of Israel being dispersed among the nations, in the kingdom the **peoples will come** to Jerusalem **to seek the LORD of Hosts** (8:21). The third reversal will be the most remarkable—instead of Israel's sin leading people away from the God of Israel (Rm 3:24), their faith in Messiah and spiritual transformation will lead the nations to Him. Thus, the Gentile nations will seek God's **favor** in **Jerusalem** (Zch 8:22). Zechariah foresees that **ten men from all the nations will grasp the garment of a Jew saying, "Let us go with you, for we have heard that God is with you."** The phrase **ten men** is not to be taken literally but indicates a large number (Gn 31:7; Lv 26:26; Nm 14:22; 1Sm 1:8; Neh 4:12). The word **garment** literally means "corner" or "wing" and likely refers to the fringes worn by Jewish men on the corners of their garments (cf. Nm 15:38; Dt 22:12). In the millennial kingdom, when all Israel will know the Lord completely (Zch 12:10; 13:1; Rm 11:26-27), the nations will follow Jewish people to the Lord because they will realize that **God is with** Israel. The Scriptures indicate that Israel will know the Lord in this way in the last days, when they trust in Jesus as the Messiah (Jr 30:9; Ezk 34:23-24; 37:24-25; Hs 3:5). Thus, the nations will recognize God's presence in Israel in the person of the Messiah of Israel, Jesus.

B. The Declaration of the Burdens: The Coming of the Messiah (9:1–14:21)

The introduction to the burdens (7:1–8:23) served to tell the Jewish people of Zechariah's day that the return from Babylon did not fulfill the prophetic promises of Israel's restoration. Rather, Israel was to continue to look to the end of days for those promises to be fulfilled. Having established an end-of-days perspective, the prophet turned to the declaration of two separate oracles (9:1–10:12 and 12:1–14:21) concerning the events that will take place at that time, with an emphasis on the Messiah's central role in the future. These two oracles of Israel's future Messianic King are divided by a hinge passage (11:1-17), describing Israel's unexpected rejection of the Messianic King.

1. The First Burden: The Coming of Israel's True King (9:1–10:12)

9:1a. The prophet declares his first **burden** (9:1; cf. 12:1), a term used for a prophet's message (2Kg 9:25; Is 13:1; Hab 1:1). The noun is derived from the verb, "to lift up" or "to bear a burden" and indicates a weight on the prophet. It emphasizes the prophet's constraint or compulsion in needing to give this message (see Baldwin, *Haggai, Zechariah, Malachi*, 162–63). The burden can contain both judgment and blessing, as do these two found in Zechariah. Significantly, this first burden includes a description of two future kings, Alexander the Great (Zch 9:1-8) and the Messianic King (9:9-10).

a. The Judgment of the Nations (9:1-8)

9:1b-7. The burden begins by describing the future judgment of the nations north and west of Judah finding fulfillment at the hands of Alexander the Great (333–332 BC). Although God uses human instruments, He is the real judge, thus, **the eyes of men . . . are toward the LORD** (9:1), recognizing His actions. The judgment will begin at **the land of Hadrach**, a region of Syria extending from Aleppo in the north to Damascus in the south. **Damascus**, the capital of Syria, is the focal point (or **resting place**) of the message of judgment (9:1; Alexander subdued these regions in 333 BC). Alexander's conquests moved from **Hamath**, north of Damascus, southwest to **Tyre and Sidon** in Lebanon (9:2-3). The prophet predicted the destruction of Tyre, describing how the Lord would **cast her wealth into the sea**, a prophecy realized when Alexander constructed a causeway built to reach the seemingly impregnable island city (9:4; cf. Ezk 26:3-14; 28:20-24). Alexander's conquests in fulfillment of this prophecy moved southward to the Philistine cities of **Ashkelon**, **Gaza**, **Ekron**, and **Ashdod** (accomplished in 332 BC). The few Philistines who remained would not maintain a distinct ethnic identity but would intermarry, becoming **a mongrel** (lit., bastard) people, so that God **will cut off the pride of the Philistines** (Zch 9:6). Afterwards, the prophet foresees the distant future, that these mongrel Philistines will also come to know the true God. At that time, they will **be a remnant for our God** and also be absorbed among the faithful of Israel, so that they will become **like a clan in Judah** (9:7). Although they will know the God of Israel, they will not become part of Israel. They will be **like a Jebusite**, a people that David conquered but whom he allowed to keep their distinct identity—much like Araunah who knew the God of Israel but remained known as a Jebusite (2Sm 24:18-24).

9:8. Although the Lord warned that He would judge the nations, He also promised to **camp**

around [His] **house** "as a guard" (ESV), indicating that He would protect Jerusalem and its temple from Alexander. Both the Jewish historian Josephus and rabbinic literature relate a story, with fantastic elements, of Alexander bowing to the high priest and deciding not to destroy Jerusalem, having previously seen the priest in a dream (Josephus, *Ant.* 11.8 [304-305, 313-339]; *Lev. Rab.* 13:5; *b. Yoma* 69a). According to the legend, when Alexander turned his attention to Jerusalem, the city, in sheer terror, prepared to offer him a warm welcome in hopes of avoiding destruction at the Macedonian's hand. The high priest Jaddus went out to meet him, showed him Dn 8:21, and claimed that Alexander was the one about whom Daniel spoke and that Alexander would succeed in subduing the Persians as Dn 8 said. Although the legendary aspects are certainly questionable, there is no denying that Alexander spared Jerusalem and established a good relationship with the Jewish people of Judah. God's deliverance in the days of Alexander foreshadows His protection of Israel in the end of days, when **no oppressor will pass over them anymore**. What was true then remains true today—God will use human agents to judge this world and to protect His people.

b. The Coming of the Messiah (9:9-10)

In contrast to Alexander the Great, who would function as an agent of judgment, the prophet also foretold another king who would come afterward as an agent of salvation.

9:9. Here is a direct prediction of the future Messiah. The prophecy begins with an exhortation directed at the **daughter of Zion** and the **daughter of Jerusalem**, both poetic terms describing God's fatherhood over Zion and Jerusalem. The names "Zion" and "Jerusalem" are used as a synecdoche, the capital city representing the entire Jewish nation. The word **rejoice** literally means "to twirl," and the word **shout** is used of war cries (Jos 6:10) or loud shouting (Mc 4:9). All the Jewish people are exhorted to rejoice in the most exuberant way or "to whoop it up." The reason for this great joy is the coming of the Messianic King. He is righteous (**just**) and brings deliverance (**endowed with salvation**). As opposed to Alexander's arrogance, this King is **humble** and comes in peace, riding a **donkey** rather than a warhorse. This verse was literally fulfilled on Palm Sunday when Jesus of Nazareth entered Jerusalem on a foal of a donkey (Mt 21:1-11; Mk 11:1-10; Lk 19:29-38; Jn 12:12-19). Ancient rabbis used this verse to explain the seemingly different pictures of the Messiah. Rather than seeing one Messiah with two comings, they saw two possible scenarios of Messiah's arrival: if Israel was unworthy, Messiah would come on a donkey; if worthy, then on a white horse (*b. San* 98b). Furthermore, they used this verse to show that Israel's messianic expectations were not fulfilled by Hezekiah, a view held by some ancient rabbis, since Zechariah still expected the Messiah after Hezekiah's days (*San* 99a).

9:10. This is a classic example of a telescoped prophecy, with the previous verse finding its fulfillment in the first coming of the Messiah, and this verse, after a large gap in time, awaiting future fulfillment with the return of the Messiah Jesus and the establishment of His earthly kingdom. When He returns, the Messiah Jesus will destroy the implements of war and **speak peace to the nations**. Moreover, He will establish His just rule from **the River to the ends of the earth**, a merism for the whole world.

c. The Deliverance of Israel (9:11–10:12)

Having set forth God's judgment of the nations surrounding Israel at the hands of Alexander the Great, the prophet follows with an extended description of God's eschatological deliverance of Israel at the second advent of Jesus the Messiah, offering five specific promises from God to Israel.

9:11-13. To begin, *the Lord promised to preserve Israel* because of **the blood of My covenant with you** (9:11a), a reference to the unconditional covenant God ratified with Abraham (and his descendants) by blood (Gn 15:9-12, 18-21). God will set Israel free from **the waterless pit** of dispersion (Zch 9:11b) so they could **return to the stronghold** (9:12), likely a reference to the land of Israel. He promised to **restore** to Israel **double** of what the nation had lost (9:12) and foretold a military victory against **Greece** (9:13). Although some see this as a prediction of the victory of the Maccabees over Antiochus and the Seleucid Greek empire (164 BC) it more likely predicts the great end-times victories the Lord will grant Israel over the nations. Merrill argues for this eschatological understanding by citing the holy war language used in the paragraph and the phrase "in that day" (9:16), used in Zechariah (2:11; 3:10; 12:3, 4, 6, 7, 9, 11; 13:1, 2, 4; 14:4, 6, 8, 9, 13, 20, 21) and the other prophets (Is 10:20; 19:24-27; 52:6; Jr 49:26; Hs 2:16; Am 9:11) to indicate eschatological events (Merrill, *An Exegetical Commentary: Haggai, Zechariah, Malachi*, 261–64).

9:14-17. *The Lord also promised to protect Israel in battle.* He is seen as hovering **over** His people while they fight. This same imagery appears on ancient Assyrian bas-reliefs of the Assyrian god Assur hovering protectively over his armies (Unger, *Zechariah: Prophet of Messiah's Glory*, 168). Although some believe that God alone fighting for His people will accomplish Israel's deliverance, these verses (and 12:6-8) indicate that Israel will participate with God in the last battle, with actual warfare carried out by Israel, empowered by the Lord. Here God is also anthropomorphized as a warrior, shooting arrows **like lightning**, blowing a **trumpet** in battle, and marching to war (9:14). As a result of God's defense, Israel is depicted as achieving a great military victory—**they will devour and trample** their enemies, producing so much blood as to fill a **sacrificial basin** drenching **the corners of the altar** (9:15; cf. Lv 4:7). God will deliver His people **in that day** (Zch 9:16a), a phrase that emphasizes eschatological fulfillment. At the end of days, God will make Israel sparkle like jewels in **a crown** (9:16b). The outcome of the battle makes the prophet exclaim of God, "how great is His goodness, and how great is His beauty" (9:17, ESV) [the third person pronouns in Hebrew are singular and refer to God (as in the ESV) not Israel (as in the NASB)]. In His goodness the Lord will give **grain** and **new wine**, indicating prosperity.

10:1. *Further, the Lord promised to provide for Israel in the messianic kingdom.* God would send **the spring rain** in response to Israel's prayer, bringing agricultural blessing to the people.

10:2-5. *Additionally, the Lord promised to purify Israel.* At the outset, the prophet described Israel's need for purification—their dependence on false household idols, called **teraphim,** (cf. Gn 31:19) and trust in **diviners** (cf. Dt 18:10-12) who offer **lying visions** and **false dreams** (Zch 10:2a). God holds the leaders of Israel responsible for the people's spiritual wanderings with **no shepherd** (10:2b), a metaphor used for leaders but specifically of kings (cf. Is 44:28; Jr 23:2-4). Therefore, God will **punish** Israel's kings (here called **male goats**) while making the lost sheep like a **majestic horse in battle** (Zch 10:3).

Using the third-person singular (him) pronoun in v. 4, its antecedent is Judah in v. 3. Since him in v. 4 refers to an entire Jewish tribe, the singular him is a collective pronoun and the NASB appropriately translates it **them**. The prophet foretold that **the cornerstone**, **the tent peg**, and the battle bow would come **from them**, the tribe of Judah. The ancient rabbinic Targum correctly understood these to be figures for the King Messiah, coming from Judah. As cornerstone, He would be the foundation upon which Israel would find stability (Is 28:16); as tent peg, He would secure Israel to Himself; and as the battle bow, He would bring the strength of military victory. Some see the fourth figure, **every ruler**, as yet another reference to the Messiah. This is unlikely for two reasons. First, the term for **ruler** is not the word for king, but rather "dictator" or "oppressor" (cf. Ex 3:7; Zch 9:8). Second, the words "every oppressor together" indicate that more than one dictator is in view. Feinberg understands, "the cornerstone, the nail, and the battle bow of the Messiah, while the second clause, presents the result of His activities. Because the Messiah intervenes in the manner to be noted, every oppressor will depart from Judah. Cause and effect are clearly stated" (Feinberg, *God Remembers*, 185).

The point in this verse is that as a result of Messiah's coming, **every ruler** (v. 4; or better, "every oppressor") will depart from Judah, leaving the nation with the godly leadership of King Messiah (10:4). He will transform the nation into **mighty men**, granting them great military victories because **the Lord will be with them** (10:5). Israel will fight under the banner of the Messiah Jesus. He will lead them in battle, and He will grant their victory (see comments on 9:14-17).

10:6-12. *Finally, the Lord promised to regather Israel.* In response to those who see this as merely predicting a restoration from Babylon, Walter Kaiser has made three arguments to support an end-time restoration of the Jewish people to the land of Israel. First, Zechariah made this prediction of regathering *after* the return from Babylon, and hence was not referring to that but to restoration of the Jewish people to the land in the future. Second, those returning to the land will comprise both **the house of Judah** and **the house of Joseph**. Since the northern ten tribes contained Ephraim and Manasseh, sometimes the kingdom of Israel was called Ephraim (cf. Is 7:1-17). Here Zechariah calls that land by the name of Ephraim and Manasseh's father, Joseph, referring to the northern kingdom. The unification of the land is not what happened with the return from Babylon when just the southern kingdom of Judah returned. Rather, it indicates a return of both the southern and northern kingdoms, an eschatological reunification of both Judah and Israel (Zch 10:6-7). Third, God promised to restore His people, not from Babylon, but from far countries, naming **Egypt** and **Assyria**, the southern and northern empires, as representative of the worldwide dispersion of the Jewish people (10:9-10; Walter C. Kaiser, Jr. "The Land of Israel and the Future Return [Zechariah 10:6-12]" in *Israel: The Land and the People* [Grand Rapids, MI: Kregel, 1998], 213–18). Zechariah's point in this paragraph is that the Lord promised that, at the end of days, when the Jewish people **remember** the Lord and trust in the Messiah (10:9a), God **will whistle for them** (10:8) and **bring them back** to their land (10:9-10). Not only will God physically restore the Jewish people to the land, but He will also spiritually restore them (**and in His name they will walk**; 10:12).

2. The Hinge in the Burdens: The Rejected Messianic King (11:1-17)

Zechariah 11 functions as a hinge within the second major panel of the book (see comments on 3:1-10 and 6:9-15; cf. "Introduction: Structure"). Chapter 10 contains extraordinary promises of blessings when Messiah comes to deliver the people. The hinge (11:1-17) explains why those promised blessings had not yet begun: Israel rejected their Messianic King. Chapter 11 has a twofold structure: (1) the prophet's role-play depicting Israel's rejection of the true Shepherd (11:1-14); and (2) the prophet's role-play depicting God's rejection of a future false shepherd (11:15-17).

a. The True Shepherd (11:1-14)

This section about the true shepherd has two paragraphs. The first predicts the future judgment of Israel (11:1-3) and the second describes the reason for that judgment: Israel's rejection of the Messiah (11:4-14).

(1) The Consequences of Rejecting the True Shepherd (11:1-3)

11:1-3. In poetic form, the prophet predicted the coming judgment of Israel using the image of a forest **fire** destroying the land. Beginning with the destruction of **Lebanon** in the northwest (11:1), followed by the devastation of **Bashan** in the northeast (11:2), and moving to the south along the **Jordan** (11:3), the entire land, and by implication, its people, is pictured in ruined condition. This judgment is a consequence of the event described in the next paragraph—Israel's rejection of the true Shepherd, the messianic King (cf. Lk 19:41-44). The prediction was fulfilled when the Roman generals Vespasian and Titus destroyed the land of Israel during the first Jewish revolt (AD 68–73; see description of events of AD 70 in introductory comments on Mt 24).

(2) The Depiction of Rejecting the True Shepherd (11:4-14)

The Lord directed Zechariah to "pasture the flock," leading some to conclude that these verses describe Israel's rejection of the prophet Zechariah and his ministry. However, that this is about the rejection of the Messiah and not the prophet is evident in the following: (1) Zechariah is merely role-playing as the true shepherd just as he also plays the role of the false shepherd in 11:15-17. It is plain that he cannot be both the true and the false shepherd. (2) Role-plays are common in the book of Zechariah. Previously, in hinge passages, Joshua and his fellow priests represented Israel (3:1-10), and Joshua played the role of the Priestly Messiah (6:9-15). (3) Only the Lord's Messiah is represented as the Good Shepherd (Ezk 34:22-24). (4) The actions taken by the true shepherd (annihilating the three shepherds, Zch 11:8; breaking the staff of Favor, 11:10) require more authority than Zechariah would take to himself—he is representing someone with far more sovereignty than he possessed.

11:4-7. The work of the True Shepherd was to **pasture the flock doomed to slaughter** (11:4). Israel will experience sorrowful judgment because of the rejection of the True Shepherd. Thus, the Gentile nations, **those who buy them** and **slay them** (11:5) will take advantage of them. At the same time, Israel's own rulers, **their own shepherds**, will abandon them and **have no pity on them** (11:5). Israel's ultimate doom is that God Himself will **no longer have pity** on them, allowing the land to fall, either by internecine conflict or by the Roman king (11:6). Nevertheless, the True Shepherd **pastured** the doomed **flock**, particularly **the afflicted of the flock**, graciously. This refers to the Messiah Jesus' earthly ministry and the gentle care He provided for the poor and downcast of Israel (cf. Mt 9:35-38; Jn 10:11-18). He did so with **two staffs**, one representing God's **Favor** for Israel and the other representing God's provision of **Union** (Zch 11:7), keeping Israel distinct and intact as a people, from the time of their rejection of the Messiah Jesus, throughout the nation's dispersion after AD 70, and until the national Jewish recognition of Him as the true Messiah (12:10).

11:8. From 11:8-14, the text's focus becomes Israel's rejection of the True Shepherd. Here, Zechariah, in his Messianic role-play, gives his first response to this rejection—he cut off **three shepherds**. There are some forty different interpretations suggested for this phrase, none completely satisfying. Perhaps the best is as a reference to the end of the three leadership offices in Israel, prophet, priest and king/civil magistrate, at the time of the Roman destruction of Jerusalem. Likely, **one month** indicates that this would happen over a brief time span.

11:9-11. A further response to rejecting the Messiah would be His withdrawal of favor from Israel, allowing **what is to die** to die by famine or pestilence, "what is to be cut off" to die by violence, and some even to die by civil strife (11:9; civil unrest did erupt at the start of the revolt against Rome in AD 66; cf. Josephus, *War*, 2.17.4-6 [321-429]). He would break the staff of **Favor** as a sign of the breaking of a **covenant**, not the Abrahamic covenant made with the Jewish people but the covenant God providentially **made with all the peoples** of the world to restrain them from oppressing Israel (11:10). He would no longer restrain the nations, and they would painfully persecute Israel. Thus, with the staff of **Favor** broken, God would temporarily change Israel's most favored status, and Rome would devastate the land in AD 70. Only the **afflicted of the flock**, the faithful remnant, would understand that these sorrowful events were under God's sovereign authority (11:11).

11:12-14. In climactic fashion, Zechariah describes the reason for Israel's loss of favor. The role-playing prophet, as Messiah, asks Israel to evaluate His ministry to them. They respond by valuing Him with **thirty shekels of silver** (11:12), the compensation paid for a gored slave (Ex 21:32). That price was to be cast **to the potter** (Zch 11:13), one of the lowest of the laboring classes. All this describes Israel's despising and rejecting the Messiah sent to them (cf. Is 53:3). These events were literally fulfilled and recorded in Matthew's gospel (Mt 26:14-16; 27:3-10).

According to Mt 27:9, Judas' betrayal fulfilled the words of Jeremiah, not Zechariah. Solutions to this problem have included the following: (1) Matthew had a memory lapse and cited the wrong prophet. (2) A later copyist changed the citation from Zechariah to Jeremiah by mistake. (3) Matthew was citing a passage in Jeremiah that was deleted from later versions of Jeremiah. (4) Matthew was making a composite citation of Old Testament texts from Jr 19:6, 11; 32:6-8 and Zch 11:4-14, identifying it as coming from Jeremiah because he was the more significant prophet. (5) Matthew's citation is to the Prophets in general while specifically quoting from Zch 11. This is the most likely solution since the Talmud states that, in the past, Jeremiah stood at the head of the Prophets section of the Hebrew Bible (Baba Bathra 14b; for another approach, however, see comments on Mt 27:3-10). As such, the entire section could be named for him, even as Jesus cites the Psalms, the first book of the Writings, as standing for the whole section (Lk 24:44).

As a consequence of Israel's rejection, the Messiah breaks the **second staff, Union**, destroying the unity of the Jewish people (Zch 11:14). In Israel's devastating defeat by Rome in AD 70, factionalism and party strife were major factors.

b. The False Shepherd (11:15-17)

11:15-17. In contrast to Israel's rejection of the True Shepherd, the following paragraph describes God's rejection of the false shepherd. Just as Zechariah played the role of the True Shepherd, now he is to play the role of **a foolish shepherd**. This one will be wicked, **not car[ing] for the perishing** and taking advantage of the flock. The chapter begins and ends with a poem of judgment, thereby forming an inclusio. This poem describes the judgment of the foolish shepherd. **His arm**, representing strength, and **his right eye**, representing intelligence, will be destroyed. The foolish shepherd has been wrongly identified with Herod the Great, Simon Bar Kokhba (a messianic claimant and the leader of the second Jewish revolt against Rome, AD 132-135), or false religious leaders and others. Since he is completely antithetical to the True Shepherd he is probably the depiction of a future false Messiah, also known as the little horn (cf. Dn 7:8-12; 24-26), the man of lawlessness (2Th 2:3), the Antichrist (1Jn 2:18), and the Beast (Rv 13:1-10), whom God will ultimately destroy.

3. The Second Burden: The Restoration of Israel by the True King (12:1–14:21)

The second and final prophetic burden (see comments on 9:1) predicts the events at the end of days, when Messiah returns to deliver Israel and establish His kingdom on earth. The eschatological emphasis is evident in two ways: first, in the identification of the subject, concerning

Israel (12:1), not Judah, and looking forward to restoration of the entire nation, not merely the Judahites who returned from Babylon; second, in the repeated use of the eschatological phrase "in that day" (12:3, 4, 6, 8, 9, 10, 11; 13:1; 14:2, 4, 8, 10, 11, 12, 14, 16, 17, 21), indicating that these events point to the distant future, not Zechariah's own day.

The burden has three sections: (1) a prophetic oracle emphasizing God's eschatological deliverance of Israel; (2) a poetic survey of Israel's destiny (13:7-9); and (3) a prophetic oracle of God's end-days deliverance of Israel, emphasizing the renovation of Jerusalem (14:1-21).

a. Oracle: A Description of Jerusalem's Future Deliverance (12:1–13:6)

12:1. The burden begins with a poetic introduction describing **the Lord** as the omnipotent creator of **the heavens**, **the earth**, and **man**. This is to establish the credibility of the message in two ways. First, God's omnipotence validates His ability to foretell the future. Second, God's creation confirms God's ability to remake the world as predicted in chap. 14.

After the introductory poem (12:1), the burden describes the events of the last days, particularly the campaign of Armageddon (Rv 16:13-16). The nations will muster in the Jezreel Valley in front of Mt. Megiddo and make their way to Jerusalem.

12:2-3. The prophet provides several characteristics of the last battle. First, *it will be a time of deliverance for Israel* (12:2-9). At the outset, the nations will besiege Jerusalem. Their attempt to destroy Jerusalem will cause them to be destroyed as the Lord makes Jerusalem **a cup that causes reeling** (12:2) and **a heavy stone** for them (12:3). The imagery is Jerusalem as a cup of wine that will make the nations stagger in drunkenness (cf. Ps 60:5 [Hb.]; 60:3 [Eng.]) and a rock so heavy that it will cause injury to the nations that try to lift it.

12:4-9. In response to the siege of the nations, the Lord will liberate Jerusalem through divine sabotage of the nations (12:4). God will strike every **horse** and **rider with madness** and **blindness**. These military descriptions do not require that the last-days battle include cavalry as opposed to modern military hardware. Rather, the prophet uses military imagery from his own days, as he understood it. That is not to say that these depictions are not real, rather, that the prophet likely could not comprehend or reveal a depiction of a modern military. Therefore, the oracle is depicting real warfare, and all the events described throughout are indeed real and literal.

The Lord will also liberate Jerusalem through divine enablement of the Jewish people (12:5-9). Thus God will cause the leaders (so HCSB, not **clans** as in the NASB) of Judah to draw encouragement from God's support of the Jerusalemites in battle. God will enable Israel by giving divine success to the leaders of Judah as they defend themselves from an attempted genocide (12:6-7), devastating their foes as a **firepot** does to a woodpile and a **torch among sheaves** (12:6). As a result, they will be as successful as **the house of David** and the **inhabitants of Jerusalem** (12:7). God's enablement of Israel will also include His divine strengthening of **the inhabitants of Jerusalem** (12:8), making even those who stumble from weakness to fight **like** King **David** and making the **house of David** as powerful as **the angel of the Lord**. Finally, God's enablement of Israel will result in a divine slaughter of all the armies of the nations that came against Jerusalem (12:9). The emphasis of this description is that Israel will fight powerfully, but its strength and success will actually come from the Lord of armies.

A second characteristic found in this general description of the last battle is that *it will be a time of repentance for Israel* (12:10-14). At the climax of the campaign of Armageddon, Israel will turn to the Messiah Jesus in mourning, calling for His deliverance. The text moves from physical (12:1-9) to spiritual deliverance (12:10-14).

12:10-14. God's **Spirit** will be poured out, conveying **grace** to Israel's leadership (**the house of David**) and populace (**the inhabitants of Jerusalem**) and thereby enabling them to offer **supplication**. The support for seeing this as referring to God's Spirit rather than a mere disposition (i.e., "spirit") is found in the many parallel passages that identify Israel's end-times repentance as a work of God's Spirit (Is 44:1-5; 59:20-21; Jr 31:31-34; Ezk 36:24-29; 39:25-29).

As a result of this divine enablement, Israel will respond with faith. The words **look on** are the same as used in Nm 21:9, when Israel looked upon the bronze serpent in faith to receive healing.

The object of their look of faith is the Lord (YHWH) Himself (**Me**)—the One **they have pierced**. Some take this piercing figuratively since it seems impossible for God to be physically pierced. Nevertheless, since all other uses of the verb "pierce" refer to literal piercing (Nm

25:8; Jdg 9:54; 1Sm 31:4; Is 13:15; Jr 37:10; 51:4; Zch 13:3), it is better to take this verse literally as well. As such it refers to the piercing of a representative of God, namely, the incarnate Messiah. The Talmud also interprets this as "the slaying of the Messiah" (*b. Sukkah* 52a, cf. *j. Sukkah* 52a) as does the New Testament (Jn 19:37). Moshe Alshech, a 16th-century Jewish biblical commentator provides this remarkable comment:

> I will do yet a third thing, and that is, that they shall look unto Me, for they shall lift up their eyes unto Me in perfect repentance, when they see Him whom they pierced, that is, Messiah, the Son of Joseph; for our Rabbis, of blessed memory, have said that He will take upon Himself all the guilt of Israel, and shall then be slain in the war to make an atonement in such manner that it shall be accounted as if Israel had pierced Him, for on account of their sin He has died; and, therefore, in order that it may be reckoned to them as a perfect atonement, they will repent and look to the blessed One, saying that there is none beside Him to forgive those that mourn on account of Him who died for their sin: this is the meaning of "'they shall look upon Me'" (Cited by Baron, *Commentary on Zechariah: His Visions and Prophecies*, 442).

About the human responsibility for piercing the Messiah, Kaiser wisely warns: "This is not to add fuel to the fires of those who have castigated our Jewish neighbors by the stigma of being 'Christ killers.' That slur is as unfair as it is untrue! In fact, the Messiah was put to death by the Jews *and the Romans* [italics his]. It is also true that He was put to death for the sins of all the world. So caution must be exercised in this area when describing the roles that were carried out by the first-century participants in the death of Christ" (Walter C. Kaiser Jr., *The Messiah in the Old Testament* [Grand Rapids, MI: Zondervan, 1994], 223). These verses do indicate that at their end-time repentance, Jewish people will recognize that their ancestors were participants in the conspiracy against the Messiah, not that they acted alone or were perpetually guilty (cf. Ac 4:27-28 and comments there).

Along with exercising faith, Israel **will mourn for Him** and **weep bitterly over Him** in repentance. The shift from **Me** to **Him** is striking. However, this does not indicate a new person being brought into the picture. Rather, Hebrew poetry and prophecy sometimes transitions from one person to another (Wilhelm Gesenius, E. Kautzsch, and A. E. Cowley, *Gesenius' Hebrew Grammar*, edited by E. Kautzsch, 2nd English ed., Revised in Accordance with the Twenty-Eighth German Edition [1909] by A. E. Crowley [Oxford: Clarendon Press, 1910, 16th impression, 1982], 462) for emphasis (Jb 33:28; Is 22:19; Lm 3:1). Moreover, it reflects differing points of view. From God's perspective, Israel looks to **Me**; From Israel's, they mourn for **Him**.

There are four components to Israel's repentance. First, Israel's repentance will be intense, mourning as for the loss of **an only son** (Gn 22:2). Israel's intense sorrow is also compared to **the mourning of Hadadrimmon in the plain of Megiddo** (Zch 12:11), a reference to the great grief at the untimely death of good King Josiah (2Ch 35:20-27).

Second, Israel's repentance will be for their past rejection of Jesus. Recognizing their millennia of rejecting Jesus as the Messiah, virtually all the Jewish people around the world will repent of this sin. The lament in Is 53:1-9, expressing sorrow for failing to recognize Messiah, articulates a fitting expression for Israel's mourning at the end of days.

Third, Israel's repentance will be national. This is not to say that their mourning will be collective, since **every family** will mourn **by itself**, indicating personal repentance. Yet it also begins with the royal house (**the house of David**, 12:12a), and includes the prophetic order (**the house of Nathan**, the prophet from the time of David, 12:12b), and the order of priests (**the house of Levi**, 12:13a) and Levites (**the Shimeites**, 12:13b; Ex 6:16-17; Nm 3:17-18; 1Ch 6:1-3). This literary expression indicates that the leadership of Israel will all repent. This will spread to **all the families** (Zch 12:14), to all the Jewish people, in Israel and around the world, who will finally turn to their Messiah.

Finally, Israel's repentance will be in the future. It is possible for Jewish people to recognize Jesus as the Messiah now. However, this ethnic repentance is eschatological. Drawing from other biblical passages, it is possible to locate Israel's turn to the Messiah in a sequence of end-time events. God foretold that there would be a future tribulation, a time of Jacob's distress (Jr 30:7) when Israel will experience God's rod of discipline (Ezk 20:34-38). As a result, Israel will repent, and call for the Messiah Jesus to return to save them (Zch 12:10-12) in fulfillment of Jesus' words that He would not return until Israel welcomed Him back as Messiah (see comments on Mt 23:37-39). Having turned to Him in faith, "all Israel will be saved" (see comments on Rm 11:26), followed by the second coming of the Messiah Jesus and His establishment of the earthly millennial kingdom.

Besides being a time of deliverance (Zch 12:1-9) and repentance (12:10-14), the third characteristic found in this general description of the last battle is that *it will be a time of cleansing for Israel* (13:1-6).

13:1. Now that Israel has looked upon the Messiah with faith and repented of the years of rejection, the Lord will open **a fountain** to cleanse the nation of **sin and . . . impurity** (cf. Ezk 36:25-28; Jr 31:34). The word **sin** means "to miss the mark" (Jdg 20:16) of God's righteous standard and refers to personal wrongdoing. The word **impurity** is rooted in the ritual defilement that comes from menstruation (Lv 12:5; 15:19-20, 26). The metaphorical sense, when describing sin, means "filthiness" or "that which is abhorred," and is applied to Israel's most wicked sins (Ezr 9:11; 2Ch 29:5). Zechariah wrote of this earlier (Zch 3:1-10), when Joshua the High Priest was cleansed of filthy robes as a symbol of Messiah's end-time cleansing of Israel (see comments there).

13:2-6. While the people are forgiven of their sin, the land will be purged of wrongdoing. The Lord will remove both idolatry (13:2a) and false prophets (13:2b-6). In obedience to the Torah (cf. Dt 13:6-9), parents will even **pierce** their own children for having been false prophets (Zch 13:3). The false prophets will be so ashamed of themselves that they will deny that they had claimed to be prophets (13:4-6).

b. Poem: A Survey of Israel's Destiny (13:7-9)

In the middle of the burden, there is a brief poetic interlude, describing the major events of Israel's future. The poem is not chronological with the events described in the previous paragraph. Rather, it takes up a discussion of the rejected True Shepherd, last seen in 11:4-14. This poem follows here in order to contrast the previously described false prophets and their self piercing (13:6) with the future true Prophet, the shepherd of Israel, who would also experience piercing. However, His piercing would be redemptive and not self-inflicted.

13:7a. As the prophet looks into Israel's future, he begins by describing the death of the Messiah. Using a personified **sword** as a metonymy of cause (**sword**) for effect (piercing), it predicts the death of the rejected True Shepherd (cf. 11:4-14). This is a literal piercing because it is contrasted with the literal self-inflicted piercings of the false prophets (13:6). Moreover, it is a description of the same person recognized as the Pierced One (12:10). The masculine imperative **strike** indicates that God is the sovereign agent in the death of the Messiah (cf. Is 53:10). The Lord also calls the Shepherd **My Associate**, a term Baldwin defines as one "who stands next to me" (Baldwin, *Haggai, Zechariah, Malachi*, 197–98). It is used to describe a relative, friend, or neighbor—essentially an equal (Lv 5:21; 18:20; 19:11, 15, 17; 24:19; 25:14, 17), giving an OT hint of the Messiah's deity (see comments on Mt 26:30-35).

13:7b. The prophet also foresees the dispersion of Israel. The striking of the True Shepherd will cause **the sheep** to **be scattered**. This is a prediction of the dispersion of the Jewish people around the world for nearly two thousand years. The gospels view the scattering of the disciples on the night of Jesus' betrayal as the inauguration of the dispersion (Mt 26:31-32; Mk 14:27-28).

13:8-9. Since this poem is about Israel's destiny, there is no mention of the Church. Rather, the prophet looks forward to the distant future, describing the tribulation or time of Jacob's trouble. Israel will have three distinct experiences at that time: (1) Israel will experience persecution, so that **two parts** or ⅔ of the population **in all the land** of Israel **will be cut off** (13:8). As tragic as this is, it is limited in number because God will have previously sent much of the Jewish population of the land of Israel into the wilderness (cf. Ezk 20:35-36; Rv 12:13-16). (2) Israel will experience purification. The persecution they undergo will **refine them as silver is refined**, causing them to **call on** the Lord's **name** in faith and repentance (Zch 13:9a), trusting in Jesus as their Messiah, even as the oracle previously described (12:10). As a result, (3) Israel will experience restoration. When they call on the LORD, He **will answer them**, calling them **My people**, and **they will say, The LORD is my God** (13:9b). At that time, Israel will know the Lord and receive all the kingdom benefits God had promised in the Abrahamic covenant. This verse indicates that Israel's repentance takes place during the tribulation period and precedes the second coming of Christ (see comments on Mt 23:37-39).

c. Oracle: A Description of Jerusalem's Future Renovation (14:1-21)

The final burden resumes, taking up further predictions of the end of days, as was described in 12:1–13:6. Since Hebrew prophecy is frequently cyclical, these are not to be viewed as following the previous predictions chronologically. Rather, this part of the oracle takes up what was previously described from another perspective, emphasizing the renovation of Jerusalem in the day of the Lord.

14:1-2. What follows is a description of the day of the Lord, the eschatological period of time of God's judgment and restoration (See Jl 3:1-21 and comments there). Just as the Scriptures depict a "day" with two parts, evening and morning (Gn 1:5, 8, 13, 19, 23, 31), so the day of the Lord has two parts: evening, which is the time of judgment or the tribulation period, followed by day, which is the one-thousand-year reign of Messiah Jesus on this earth. This chapter begins with a snapshot of the "evening" portion of the day of the Lord (Zch 14:1-2), depicting *the future devastation of Jerusalem*. At that time, **all the nations** will gather **against Jerusalem** (see comments on 12:2-9), capture the city, plunder the homes, rape the women, and exile half of the survivors (14:2). God declares His own sovereignty over these terrible events, stating **I will gather all the nations**. Israel is to remember that as devastating as these events will be, God is directing them for an ultimately good purpose. This is a good reminder for any believer enduring difficulties today.

14:3-5. Having described the city's future devastation, the prophet next predicts *the future deliverance of Jerusalem* (14:3-21), including seven distinct promises. First, God promised to rescue the Jewish people in Jerusalem (14:3-5). In response to the repentance of the nation and their turn in faith to Jesus the Messiah (cf. 12:10-14), the Lord declares that He will **fight against those nations** (14:3). He will break the siege by descending physically, in the person of the Messiah Jesus, so that **His feet will stand on the Mount of Olives** (14:4; cf. Rv 19:11-16). For several reasons, this is not merely a figurative description of the Lord providentially coming to Israel's defense but rather the literal return of the Lord Jesus, the Messiah. The term "feet" seems to indicate the LORD will be literally present in Jerusalem, so much so that the Mount of Olives is literally split in two. Other prophetic passages seem to indicate the LORD's literal presence with Israel at the end of days, leading the people in battle (cf. Is 63:1-6 with Rv 14:14-19 and 19:11-16; Mc 2:12-13). Also, the apostles were promised that the Lord Jesus Himself would descend upon the Mount of Olives when He returns to restore the kingdom to Israel (Ac 1:11).

The mountain will split and provide a way of escape for the trapped Jerusalemites (Zch 14:5a). Then the incarnate Messiah **will come** to do battle, along with an army of **holy ones** (14:5b). This could refer to angels or perhaps to previously raptured believers, returning with their Lord to defend Israel. At Jesus' ascension from the Mount of Olives, the angels promised He would return "in just the same way as you have watched Him go into heaven" (Ac 1:11), likely referring to this passage.

14:6-8. Second, God promised to remake the areas around Jerusalem. There will be cosmic changes (14:6-7), as other Scriptures also foretell (Is 13:9-10; Jl 2:31; 3:15; Am 5:18; Mt 24:29-30; Rv 6:12-14; 8:8-12; 9:1-18; 14:4-20; 16:4, 8-9). The water sources will also be transformed (Zch 14:8), with a river of **living waters** flowing **out of Jerusalem** to **the eastern sea** (the Dead Sea) and **the western sea** (the Mediterranean Sea), thereby irrigating the land year round and ending all droughts (14:8). Ezekiel also predicted the revitalization of the Dead Sea in the messianic kingdom (Ezk 47:8-12).

14:9. Third, God promised to reign over the world from Jerusalem. He **will be king over all the earth**, not just the land of Israel, for all the nations will have to come to Jerusalem to worship Him (14:16-18). This will finally end all idolatry, since He **will be the only** God and **His name** the only one worshipped.

14:10-11. Fourth, God promised to renovate the topography of Jerusalem. The land around Jerusalem, both north (**Geba**) and south (**Rimmon**) will be flattened while Jerusalem, including all its landmarks, will be elevated, indicating its greater prominence. Once and for all, political issues that vex contemporary society will be resolved. Jerusalem will be recognized as the capital of Israel, and the people who live there **will dwell in security**.

14:12-15. Fifth, God promised to repay the oppressors of Jerusalem. The nations that came against Jerusalem will be judged with both **plague** (14:12, 15) and **panic** (14:13). They will also surrender their **wealth** to Judah (14:14). These things will occur at the culmination of the battle of Armageddon (Is 11:4; 63:1-6; Rv 14:19-20; 19:15, 21) when the Lord finally devastates and defeats those nations.

14:16-19. Sixth, God promised to require universal worship in Jerusalem. Many Gentiles from other nations of the world will embrace Messiah Jesus during the tribulation and will not be destroyed by Him when He returns. The nations that are spared this judgment (cf. Mt 25:34-40 and comments there) will be made to show their continued allegiance to the LORD by going **up from year to year to worship the King**, the Messiah Jesus. They will also be expected **to celebrate the Feast of Booths** (Zch 14:16; Lv 23:40; Dt 16:14-15), a feast of ingathering and dwelling in booths. It will be the required festival of the messianic kingdom because "it will celebrate the gathering of the nations to the Lord and especially His tabernacling among them" (Feinberg, *God Remembers,* 261).

As the millennial kingdom progresses, however, many will not embrace King Messiah by faith (see Rv 20:7-10 and comments there), and will not obey Him. Failure to **worship the King** at the Feast of Booths will make God withhold rain (Zch 14:17). Zechariah described this act of judgment as a **plague** (14:18), so that once more Egypt will come under God's judgment should they fail to obey God (14:19). That there will exist nations that could potentially rebel and thus face judgment, and that they will also need rain, demonstrates that Zechariah is describing the messianic kingdom (or millennium), not the eternal state (compare with the conditions described in Rv 21–22).

14:20-21. Finally, God promised to realize total holiness in Jerusalem. The word **HOLY** means "set apart" or "separate" and refers to what is distinct from what is common or profane. This is a description of the messianic millennial kingdom, in which there will be some rebellion in the end (Rv 20:7ff.), not the new heavens and the new earth in which there will no longer be any rebellion against the Lord (Rv 21:27). Nevertheless, in the messianic kingdom, the fear of God will be so pervasive and ordinary that even **the bells on the horses** will be inscribed with **HOLY TO THE LORD,** words previously found only on the mitre of the High Priest (Ex 28:36). Then even **the cooking pots** will be considered holy, or set apart for God's service (Zch 14:20). There will no longer be a division between the sacred and the profane—everything will be sacred. Even the holy sacrifices will be cooked in ordinary cooking pots, as they will be holy too (for discussion of sacrifices in the millennial temple, see comments on Ezk 40:38-43). Most important, all people who worship the King will be holy—**there will no longer be a Canaanite**, or unclean people, **in the house of the LORD** "for the earth will be full of the knowledge of the LORD as the waters cover the sea" (Is 11:9; Hab 2:14).

As Israel looked at their circumstances with despair, frustrated by their failure to rebuild the temple, distraught at their own disobedience to the Torah, and despondent with their grinding poverty and drought, the book of Zechariah brought hope that God would once more renew His people and remake Jerusalem. Thus, it would motivate them to trust and obey God until that day should come. The same is true for contemporary readers—frustrated by failure, distraught at disobedience, despondent with difficulties—the book brings hope for the future and motivates trust and obedience today. Especially in the last climactic burden (12:1–14:21), but throughout, the book reminds readers that the Messianic King, the Lord Jesus, will come again and establish a righteous kingdom for all the earth, with Jerusalem at its center. Then "the kingdom of the world [will] become the kingdom of our Lord and His Messiah; and He will reign forever and ever" (Rv 11:15).

BIBLIOGRAPHY

Baldwin, Joyce. *Haggai, Zechariah, Malachi: An Introduction and Commentary.* Tyndale Old Testament Commentaries. Edited by D. J. Wiseman. Downers Grove, IL: InterVarsity, 1972.

Barker, Kenneth L. "Zechariah" in *The Expositor's Bible Commentary.* Edited by Frank E. Gabelein. Grand Rapids, MI: Zondervan, 1985.

Baron, David. *Commentary on Zechariah: His Visions and Prophecies.* London: Morgan and Scott, 1918.

Bultema, Harry. *Zechariah: A Brief Commentary*. Translated by Ralph Vunderink. Grand Rapids, MI: Grace Publications, 1987.

Cashdan, Eli. "Zechariah" in *The Twelve Prophets*, The Soncino Books of the Bible. Edited by A. Cohen. London: Soncino Press, 1957.

Chisholm, Robert B. Jr. *Interpreting the Minor Prophets.* Grand Rapids, MI: Zondervan, 1990.

Feinberg, Charles L. *God Remembers: A Study of the Book of Zechariah.* New York: ABMJ, 1965.

Kaiser, Walter C., Jr. *The Messiah in the Old Testament.* Grand Rapids, MI: Zondervan, 1994.

Kimchi, David and Alexander McCaul. *Rabbi David Kimchi's Commentary upon the Prophecies of Zechariah.* Translated and with notes by Alexander McCaul. London: James Duncan, 1837.

Merrill, Eugene H. *An Exegetical Commentary: Haggai, Zechariah, Malachi.* Chicago: Moody, 1994.

McComiskey, Thomas E. "Zechariah" in *The Minor Prophets: An Exegetical and Expository Commentary,* vol. 3. Edited by Thomas Edward McComiskey. Grand Rapids, MI: Baker, 1998.

Smith, Ralph L. *Micah-Malachi.* Word Biblical Commentary. Edited by David A. Hubbard and Glenn W. Barker. Waco, TX: Word Books, 1984.

Unger, Merrill F. *Zechariah: Prophet of Messiah's Glory.* Grand Rapids, MI: Zondervan, 1963.

MALACHI

MICHAEL RYDELNIK

INTRODUCTION

Author. Malachi is the last of the Twelve Prophets (Minor Prophets) as well as the entire section of the Prophets. Likely, the author's name, "Malachi," means "my messenger" or "my angel." Most traditional Jewish sources speculate that Malachi was a member of the Great Synagogue along with Haggai and Zechariah. But Targum Jonathan, an early Jewish paraphrase (followed by Jerome and the medieval Jewish interpreter Rashi), saw "Malachi" as a title, adding the phrase, "who is Ezra the Scribe" after the word "Malachi."

Support for taking "Malachi" as a title is that there is no personal information about the prophet. However, little or nothing is known about other prophets as well (e.g., Obadiah and Habakkuk). Since the book follows the pattern of other prophets, whose names are found in the opening of their works, it seems most likely that it refers to an actual prophet named Malachi.

Date. The book contains no dates but it is believed to be postexilic largely from its canonical context, immediately following the postexilic books of Haggai and Zechariah. Internal evidence associates Malachi with conditions in that period, including the use of the term "governor" (1:8; Hg 1:1, 14; 2:2, 21), the references to intermarriage with foreign wives (Mal 2:11; Ezr 9–10; Neh 13:23-27), and the failure to pay tithes (Mal 3:8-10; Neh 13:10-14). Malachi implies that people gave offerings to their governor (Mal 1:8), a practice that Nehemiah flatly rejected (Neh 5:14, 18), indicating that the book was not written during Nehemiah's administration. Therefore, Malachi wrote in the mid-fifth century BC, either before or after Nehemiah's first term as governor.

Theme. The theme of Malachi is that the God of Israel loves the people of Israel (Mal 1:2) and they are to live in faithful obedience to Him. Simply put, the book of Malachi is about how to behave in light of God's love.

The book is structured as a series of six disputations between the Lord and His people. Although other prophets used disputation as a literary device (e.g., Mc 2:6-11), Malachi is unique in structuring his entire book around it. The first disputation, regarding God's love for Israel, functions as an introduction and establishes the book's theme. The rest of the disputations present God's rebuke of Israel for failing to live in light of His love. The book concludes with an exhortation based on God's promise to restore Israel at the end of days.

Purpose. The book's purpose is to motivate Israel's faithful obedience to the Lord by reassuring them of God's love and reminding them that His promises would be fulfilled by the Messiah in the eschatological day of the Lord (Mal 3:1-4; 4:4-6). Malachi intended to exhort the people to faithfulness in their own day in anticipation of God fulfilling His promises in the last days.

Although Malachi uses an oracular or sermonic style, as found in other OT prophets, his use of quotations, questions, and arguments gives it a distinctive style. Although Malachi does not use poetry, he does employ elevated language, which Herbert Wolf describes as "lofty prose" (Herbert Wolf, *Haggai–Malachi: Rededication and Renewal* [Chicago: Moody, 1976], 59). The use of the phrase "says the Lord of Hosts" 20 times in 55 verses emphasizes the prophetic nature of the book, indicating that the prophet's message was from God Himself.

Contribution. A significant contribution of Malachi to the rest of the Bible is in guiding the interpretation of previous prophetic books. Although early readers may have taken the Major Prophets' prophecies of the restoration to the land of Israel as being fulfilled in the returns under Zerubbabel, Ezra, and Nehemiah, Malachi reminds Bible readers that those actually will not be fulfilled until the end of days. The future promises will be fulfilled in the great and terrible day of the LORD (4:5) when the sun of righteousness will arise with healing in its wings (4:2).

Background. The book's historical setting is after Israel's partial return from captivity under Cyrus (539 BC; cf. Introduction to Haggai) and the rebuilding of the temple (515 BC). In the seventh year of King Artaxerxes (458 BC), Ezra the scribe returned with another group of exiles to the land of Israel. Ezra brought funds to engage in temple worship (Ezr 7:15-17), instructed the people in the law of Moses (Ezr 7:10), and instituted reforms to prohibit intermarriage with Gentile women (Ezr 9–10).

In Artaxerxes' 20th year (445 BC), Nehemiah was made governor and allowed to lead the people in rebuilding the walls of Jerusalem. Having completed the task in 52 days (Neh 6:15), Nehemiah instituted reforms, including protection of the poor (Neh 5:2-13), rejection of intermarriage, Sabbath observance, and material support for the temple and priests (Neh 10:28-39). Nehemiah then returned to Persia in service of the king (Neh 13:6), and while he was away, the people broke virtually all their commitments (Neh 13:7-13). Some time later, Nehemiah returned for a second stint as governor and reestablished the previously instituted reforms (Neh 13:7-31).

As the final book of the Twelve, Malachi continues the eschatological emphases of both Haggai and Zechariah. Just as both Haggai and Zechariah conclude with eschatological/messianic promises (Hg 2:23; Zch 12–14), so Malachi continues this theme. His message is to look for Elijah to return to announce "the great and terrible day of the LORD" (Mal 4:5).

As the last book in the section of the Hebrew Bible called the Prophets, Malachi plays a role in the final canonical shape of the Hebrew Bible. John Sailhamer has observed a discernible strategy. The last paragraphs of both the Law (Dt 34:9-12) and the Prophets (Mal 4:4-6) predict the coming of a prophet who will announce the messianic kingdom. At the same time, the first paragraphs of the Prophets (Jos 1:1-9) and the Writings (Ps 1) call for meditating on the law of God, day and night. Thus, the final canonical shape of the OT functions as a call to look for the Messiah in the Word of God, while, at the same time, exhorting faithfulness to God's Word until He comes (John H. Sailhamer, *Introduction to Old Testament Theology* [Grand Rapids, MI: Zondervan, 1995], 239–52).

OUTLINE

I. Introduction: God's Love for Israel (1:1-5)
II. Body: God's Disputations with Israel (1:6–4:3)
- A. God's Rebuke of the Priests for Failed Spiritual Leadership (1:6–2:9)
  - 1. For Blemished Sacrifices (1:6-14)
  - 2. For Corrupted Teaching (2:1-9)
- B. God's Rebuke of the People for Marital Unfaithfulness (2:10-16)
- C. God's Affirmation of His Justice Seen in Coming Judgment (2:17–3:6)
- D. God's Rebuke of the Nation for Failing to Tithe (3:7-12)
- E. God's Affirmation of the Value of Serving Him (3:13–4:3)
  - 1. The Complaint of the Wicked (3:13-15)
  - 2. The Answer of the Faithful (3:16-18)
  - 3. The Judgment of God (4:1-3)

III. Conclusion: God's Restoration of Israel (4:4-6)

COMMENTARY ON MALACHI

I. Introduction: God's Love for Israel (1:1-5)

The opening paragraph of Malachi functions as an introduction to the entire book. It establishes the theme of God's love for Israel. In the rest of the book, God will direct Israel to live in light of that love.

1:1. The prophet Malachi calls his message a "burden" (**oracle**) (see comments on Zch 9:1a) conveying urgency, constraint, or compulsion. Malachi's message is **the word of the LORD** and he must proclaim it.

1:2a-b. God makes the unconditional statement, **I have loved you**. "Love" reflects covenantal terminology, not meaning "affection," but rather the unconditional choice of Israel (cf. Dt 7:7-8). Israel responded by asking **how**, or, "Oh, really!" Perhaps their less glorious rebuilt temple (Hg 2:3), the agricultural difficulties they had faced (Hg 1:11), and/or the hostility of their neighbors (Neh 6:1-14) had caused them to doubt God's love.

1:2c-5. God responds by comparing His relationships with **Jacob** and **Esau**. Since **Esau** was **Jacob's brother** (1:2c), they had deserved equal treatment. Yet God **hated Esau** (1:3), referring to God's active rejection of Esau. **Hated** in this verses does not mean "loved less" (see comments on Rm 9:13).

The differing way God treated the two nations' lands proved His choice of Jacob (and the Jewish people) and rejection of Esau (and those descended from him, the Edomites). Israel's sins caused God to exile them, but He allowed them to return and rebuild. Edom's sins caused God to bring the Nabateans (around 500 BC) who drove out the Edomites and made their land **a desolation** (Mal 1:3). Edom could boast that they would **return and build** their nation, but God would not allow it. Although Israel was a holy land (Zch 2:12; Ps 78:54), Edom would forever be considered a **wicked territory** and a **people toward whom the LORD is indignant** (1:4). Israel would ultimately recognize God's love and **magnify** Him above (not **beyond**) **the border of Israel**, recognizing His gracious treatment of their land and people.

II. Body: God's Disputations with Israel (1:6–4:3)

With the keynote idea that God still loves Israel established, the prophet turns to the body of his message, namely, a series of disputations demonstrating Israel's unfaithfulness despite that love. Covering all of Israelite society, the message reminds readers that God's love should motivate covenantal loyalty. The first group Malachi addressed was the failed priesthood.

A. God's Rebuke of the Priests for Failed Spiritual Leadership (1:6–2:9)

Malachi confronted the priests for failing in two primary roles of ministry: as intermediaries before God (1:6-14) and teaching God's Word to the people (2:1-9).

1. For Blemished Sacrifices (1:6-14)

1:6. Once again entering into a disputation, God charged the priests with dishonoring Him. The priests failed to live up to the basic standards of human relationships, wherein **a son honors his father, and a servant his master**. Instead, Israel's priests despised God's **name**, meaning they showed contempt for God's person and character. The Hebrew word translated "despise" means "to accord little worth" or "to show utter contempt." It was used to describe the rejected Messiah (Is 49:7; 53:3) and even the "despicable" king, Antiochus (Dn 11:21). Nevertheless, the priests feigned ignorance, asking, "How so?"

1:7-8a. The Lord presented His proof—they allowed the offering of **defiled food** (lit., "bread," used of sacrificial offerings, Lv 21:6) on the Lord's **table**, a synonym for the altar and an allusion to covenantal meals (Ex 24:1). By allowing imperfect animals (**blind**, **lame**, **sick**, Mal 1:7-8) to be sacrificed, they blatantly disobeyed the law (cf. Dt 15:21; note that the word translated "serious" in Dt 15:21 is literally "evil," the same word used in Mal 1:8 to describe priestly behavior) and showed their contempt for the Lord.

1:8b-10. The Lord then gave four ways that the priests treated Him contemptibly (1:8-14). First, they failed to understand God's standard of excellence (1:8b-10). To prove this, the Lord compared their deplorable offerings to food they would offer a **governor**. He would not receive them (1:8b), yet they offered imperfect sacrifices to the Lord of the universe, whose perfection, glory, and standards were infinitely higher. These sacrifices could not be used to obtain an audience with God (lit., "will you not seek God's face?" not the NASB's **entreat God's favor**) or cause Him to be **gracious** (1:9). God preferred that someone would **shut the gates** of the temple rather than have priests **uselessly kindle fire** and offer defiled sacrifices on the altar.

1:11. Second, Israel's priests believed God needed Israel to worship Him. The Lord reminded the priests that one day, **from the rising of the sun even to its setting**, God's name would be **great among the nations** (cf. Is 2:2-4) of the whole world. This would not take place in their own day, but in the last days, even as revealed in Zch 14:16-23, the previous chapter in the book of the Twelve Prophets.

1:12-13a. Third, the priests failed to understand the great privilege of worship. They were profaning God's name, treating it as if it were common or ordinary, by causing **the table of the Lord** to be **defiled** (or better, "desecrated," v. 12). Also, they sniffed at the **tiresome** nature (lit., what a hardship," cf. Ex 18:8; Nm 20:14; Lm 3:5; Neh 9:32) of worship, treating the reverence of God as a chore instead of recognizing that it was a privilege (Mal 1:13a).

1:13b-14. Finally, the priests tried to swindle God. First, they gave sacrifices that were **taken by robbery**. This would be like a bank robber giving a tithe of stolen money—God could not accept this. Second, they kept the male animal that they had previously vowed to give as a sacrifice, instead offering **a blemished animal** (1:14). But they could not fool God—He is **a great King** who demanded that the priests of Israel should fear Him even as, at the end of days, all the nations would.

2. For Corrupted Teaching (2:1-9)

Not only did the priests fail as mediators (1:6-14), they did not fulfill God's expectations as messengers either (2:1-9).

2:1-3. The rebuke of the priests' failure as teachers begins with a decree of discipline against them. There is no **commandment** to the priests here (2:1), but rather the word means "decree, admonition, resolution" (cf. Nah 1:14). Since the priests failed to **honor** God's **name**, God would undo their service. First, He promised to *distort* their work, turning their priestly blessings into curses (Mal 2:2). Second, God would *deny* their work. When a priest would lift his arm to bless, God would **rebuke** it (2:3a). According to the Masoretic Text, God would rebuke their "seed," referring either to the discipline of their **offspring** (NASB, ESV; "descendants" NIV, HCSB) or their grain (NJPS). By reading the consonants with other vowels, the LXX understood the word to be "arm," referring to the priestly action of blessing. This makes sense in the context—the previous verse spoke of priestly blessing. Third, God would *dishonor* their work by **spread**[ing] **refuse on** their **faces** (2:3b). **Refuse** refers to the offal, or the unclean waste products of sacrificial animals, which was to be burned outside the camp (Lv 1:17; 16:27). God would treat the priests as unclean, deserving of being placed outside the camp.

2:4-7. Moving from His decree of discipline, God then described the covenant responsibilities of faithful priests. God expected the priests to respond to their discipline so that the covenant with Levi would continue (2:4). No specific covenant with Levi is mentioned in the Pentateuch. Malachi likely referred to the covenant God made with Phineas (2:5a; Nm 25:11-13; note similarity of terms like "covenant of peace") as applying to all Levitical priests (cf. Dt 33:8-11).

God's covenant **of life and peace** was made with Phineas because he **revered** God (Mal 2:5; Nm 25:1-9; Ps 106:28-31), taught **true instruction** (lit., "Torah," law, Mal 2:6a), and walked with God **in peace and uprightness** (2:6b). This set the standard for any priest—so that any priest was expected to **preserve knowledge** and function as a **messenger of the Lord** (2:7). **Messenger** is the same word as Malachi's name. Here is the only place that the OT uses it of priests, while Hg 1:13 is the only one to use it of prophets. Malachi also uses the word for the forerunner of the Messiah (Mal 3:1a) and the Messiah Himself (3:1b).

2:8-9. Malachi now delineates the failure of the priests. In contrast to Phineas, they have failed as a source of instruction (2:7) but instead have **caused many to stumble by the instruction** (2:8). The principle way they did this was by failing in their judicial responsibilities (Dt 17:9-11) by **showing partiality** (Mal 2:9). Malachi's rebuke of the priests should be remembered by pastors and elders who are also called upon to lead their people in undefiled worship and sound instruction.

B. God's Rebuke of the People for Marital Unfaithfulness (2:10-16)

Not surprisingly, the general population, following the pattern of the spiritual leaders, failed to keep covenant with God. This became apparent in their marriages, which is the subject of the next disputation.

2:10-12. Emphasizing that God is the Father and Creator of Israel (Dt 32:6; Is 63:16; 64:8), Malachi chided Israel for dealing **treacherously**, a word frequently used for breaking covenant (Ps 78:57; Is 24:16), particularly the marriage covenant (Jr 3:20). This profaned the Abrahamic **covenant** (Mal 2:10), which made Israel distinct as a people. The first way they were unfaithful was in their selection of pagan foreign women as wives. The issue was not that they married non-Jews (cf. Boaz's marriage to Ruth, Ru 4:13), but that these women followed other gods (Mal 2:11). As a result, these Jewish husbands followed their wives' idolatry and **profaned the sanctuary**. Men who committed the sin of marrying pagans and worshiping their gods would be **cut**

off from the community of Israel (excommunication) "even though" (NIV) they might bring **an offering** to the temple (2:12).

2:13-16. The second way Israel behaved treacherously was by divorcing their wives in order to marry pagan women (2:14). These actions caused the Lord to break fellowship with them, **no longer regard[ing]** their offerings or showing them **favor** (2:13). Frequently considered unintelligible, v. 15 contains the reason for God's anger. There are four basic interpretations on the meaning of v. 15:

(1) It refers to Abraham taking Hagar ("what did that one [i.e., Abraham] do while he was seeking a godly offspring?" NASB). (2) It refers to the original marriages of those who were divorcing their wives ("Did He not make [you] one [with your wives], and a remnant of that Spirit-created unity [still] belongs to that relationship?"). (3) It refers to God's creation of Adam and Eve as a monogamous couple (Gn 2:24, "Why did God make for them only one partner, although He had a remainder of the Spirit to create other wives for Adam?"). (4) It refers to God's original creation of marriage with Adam and Eve as one flesh (Gn 2:24; "Has not [the LORD] made them one? In flesh and spirit they are His"; NIV. This requires emending one vowel in the word *se'er* ["remnant"] to *se'ar* ["flesh"]). The first view seems unacceptable since it arbitrarily brings Abraham into this context. The second requires far too many glosses to derive the meaning from the actual words of the text. The third makes sense only if the issue were polygamy, not divorce. The fourth view makes the most sense because it explains God's reason for expecting couples to stay married—they are permanently one in flesh and spirit. Although emending a vowel is required, the vowels were not part of the original Hebrew Bible but were added in the medieval period.

The question then becomes, "Why did God create marriage to be a permanent relationship?" The rest of the verse answers, "He was **seeking a godly offspring**" (Mal 2:15b). God intended couples to stay together for life because this was the best environment to raise a godly family. Therefore, the Lord was angry with men for divorcing their wives, disrupting marriage as God intended it to be. Concluding that He **hate[s] divorce** (in Hebrew, the Lord speaks of Himself in the third person), God exhorts Israel's men to **take heed to [their] spirit[s]** and end their treacherous behavior toward their Jewish wives.

C. God's Affirmation of His Justice Seen in Coming Judgment (2:17–3:6)

2:17. The next disputation revolved around God's justice. As justification for their misbehavior in marriage and divorce, Israel claimed that God had failed them by allowing evil all around them. Therefore, Israel **wearied the LORD**, complaining that He approved of evil and was uncaring about justice—so why should they care about obedience to Him?

3:1. The LORD responded by promising that judgment and, with it, justice would come. The first aspect of that promise is the prediction of the coming of two different messengers. The first one, **My messenger** (a play on words of the prophet's name), refers to Elijah (4:5) who is to announce the coming of the Messiah (Is 40:3-5). The NT quotes this verse of John the Baptist (see comments on Mt 11:10), who functioned in the role of Elijah at Messiah's first coming, though he was not literally Elijah (Jn 1:21; see comments on Mt 11:13-15). Ultimately, Elijah will literally fulfill this prediction when Messiah returns (Mt 17:11). For those who recognized that John came in the spirit and power of Elijah (Lk 1:17) and were willing to accept him in Elijah's role, John functioned in Elijah's role as forerunner of the Messiah (Mt 11:9-13).

The second messenger, called **the messenger of the covenant**, was the Lord (the Hb. word *ha'adon* when used with the definite article always refers to the divine Lord), whom the Jewish people were seeking. The Lord is called the "messenger" or "angel," reminiscent of the angel of the covenant who led Israel in the wilderness, within whom the LORD placed His own name (Ex 23:20-23; 33:14-15), and who was present in all Israel's afflictions (Is 63:9). Elsewhere, this angel is referred to as the Angel of the LORD, a preincarnate appearance of the divine Lord (Gn 18:1, 22; Ex 3:2-4; Jdg 6:12; 13:2-23; see comments on theophanies at Mc 5:2). Therefore, this angel or messenger is a reference to the Messiah. The covenant spoken of is the Abrahamic covenant, because when Messiah returns at the consummation, all its aspects will be fulfilled. Although Jesus came to the temple many times during His earthly life and ministry, this predicts His coming to the eschatological temple (cf. Zch 6:11-15), because He will arrive in judgment.

3:2-4. Having told those who doubted God's justice that the Messiah would indeed come, Malachi also reminded them that judgment would fall not just on their enemies but on them as well. No one can **endure the day of His coming**. When Messiah comes in judgment, He will purify all, from the **sons of Levi** to all **Judah and Jerusalem**.

3:5-6. When judgment comes, it will fall on all covenant breakers (3:5). But God's promise to Israel will keep them from being destroyed. Those crying out for justice must remember that based on God's justice, Israel should be **consumed** (3:6)—utterly destroyed in judgment. But though they break His covenant, He will never break His promise. God's unchanging faithfulness will cause Him to preserve and purify His people.

D. God's Rebuke of the Nation for Failing to Tithe (3:7-12)

3:7. The next disputation pertained to Israel's disobedience of the law. Having accused God of being unjust by tolerating evil, the nation felt justified in their breaking of the law. Although the nation had disobeyed since **the days of** [their] **fathers**, God graciously offered them restoration if they would **return** (or repent). The people responded by asking, **how shall we return?** (3:7). They were not asking how to repent but rather, "How can we repent if we do not know how we have sinned?"

3:8-9. Therefore, the Lord gave a specific example of their disobedience—their failure to give **tithes and offerings**. The word "offerings" (*terumah*) likely links this to the temple tithe for the priests (Nm 18: 8-32). Their sin was tantamount to **robbing** God.

3:10-12. Challenging their faith, God called upon them to **test** Him. If they would give, He promised to **pour out** . . . **blessing** so that they would not have blight but rather an abundance of crops. This would produce a great testimony to the surrounding **nations**—in seeing their abundance, the nations would recognize God's **blessing** on Israel.

Three questions are frequently raised regarding the application of this passage today. First, does God require "storehouse" giving, or giving only to one's local congregation? The NT shows believers giving to other congregations (1Co 16:1-2; 2Co 8:1-5), indicating that giving cannot be restricted to one's church, and additional giving to other ministries is certainly a good use of money. Second, is tithing (giving 10 percent) still required? Since Paul writes that each believer should give "as he has purposed in his heart" (2Co 9:7) and on the basis of how God has prospered him (1Co 16:2), it appears that 10 percent is not required. However, for believers having experienced God's grace in the Messiah Jesus, it also seems that 10 percent would be a good starting point for giving, though more affluent believers should regularly give a much higher percent. Finally, will giving result in material benefits? The promise of agricultural blessing is directed to Israel based on their obedience to the law (cf. Dt 28:1-14), a promise tied only to those living under the Mosaic covenant (i.e., it is not guaranteed to those living under the "new covenant"). However, the NT indicates that believers who give generously, sacrificially, and with cheerful hearts will experience *spiritual* blessings (2Co 9:7-11).

E. God's Affirmation of the Value of Serving Him (3:13–4:3)

1. The Complaint of the Wicked (3:13-15)

3:13-14. The final dispute between God and Israel concerns the value of serving Him. Since Israel had questioned God's justice and love, they also questioned the usefulness of serving God. The people spoke (the Hb. Niphal stem indicates a grumbling to one another) against God, using **arrogant** (lit., "strong") **words** (3:13). The same Hebrew word was used of Pharaoh's *hard* heart (Ex 4:21; 7:13; 7:22; 8:19; 9:12; 9:35; 10:20; 10:27; 11:10) and indicates the rebelliousness of the people. They expressed their attitude by declaring God's service to be **vain** ("worthless," "futile," "to no avail") and without **profit**. This last word is taken from the weaver's trade and refers to the piece of cloth cut from the loom, hence they asked, "Where is our *cut* now that we have **kept His charge** (obeyed God) and **walked in mourning** (practiced repentance) before God?" (Mal 3:14).

3:15. The evidence they cited for their opinion was that the **arrogant** wicked were happy (**blessed**), prosperous (**built up**), and unpunished (**test God and escape**) (3:15).

2. The Answer of the Faithful (3:16-18)

3:16. Rather than God answering these rebellious charges, it was **those who feared the LORD** (meaning those who genuinely revered Him) who responded. Even as the arrogant spread discouragement to each other (3:14), so the faithful also **spoke to one another** with encouragement (3:16).

3:17-18. They reminded each other that God would remember the faithful (with His book of remembrance, cf. Est 6:1-2); receive them as His **own possession** (a phrase used of Israel, Ex 19:5-6); and forgive their sin (**spare them**) (Mal 3:17). In the last day, when God judges the world, He will distinguish between His righteous servants and the wicked (3:18). The great value of serving God will be evident only to those who keep the ultimate rather than the immediate in view.

3. The Judgment of God (4:1-3)

4:1. Malachi spoke of the future day of the Lord, the eschatological time of God's judgment and restoration (See Jl 3:1-21 and comments there). The day of the LORD has two parts: evening, which is the time of judgment or the tribulation period, followed by day, which is the one-thousand-year reign of Messiah Jesus on this earth. Malachi here describes the "evening" portion as an intense (**burning like a furnace**), destructive (**every evildoer will be chaff**), and complete (**leav[ing] them neither root nor branch**) judgment of the wicked.

4:2-3. When God judges the world, He will also remember those who feared Him. Contrasting the blazing heat that will burn the wicked, God promises the faithful that the **sun of righteousness** will arise, bringing its warm rays of **healing in its wings** (4:2). This is often considered a messianic verse. Yet in light of the feminine forms (*she* will arise with healing in *her* wings) and the association with kingdom conditions (Is 35:6; 60:1-3; Hs 14:4-7; Am 9:13-15; Zph 3:19-20), it is better to see it using the healing warmth of the sun as a picture of God's comfort of the righteous in the morning portion of the day of the LORD. Not only will God heal the faithful, He will grant them vindication, so that they **tread down the wicked** in the day of the Lord.

III. Conclusion: God's Restoration of Israel (4:4-6)

The conclusion of the book does not follow the disputation model of the other sections. Rather it contains an exhortation and a reminder.

4:4. The exhortation is to **remember the law of Moses**, a reference to the laws God gave Israel at Mount **Horeb** (an alternate name for Mount Sinai; cf. Ex 3:1; 19:18-25; 24:16-18; Dt 30:10). Having returned from captivity, the nation was to remember that the Torah remained their constitution and law while they awaited the day of the LORD.

4:5-6. The reminder is to continue to look for the arrival of Elijah. Just as Moses was linked to Mount Horeb, so was the great prophet Elijah, who fled and heard the gentle whisper of God there (1Kg 19:8-14). Even as Moses represented the Law, so Elijah represented the Prophets, significant since the Hebrew Scriptures were sometimes called "the Law and the Prophets" (Mt 7:12; 22:40; Ac 13:15; Rm 3:21).

Previously, Malachi had foretold the coming of "My Messenger" to prepare the way for Messiah (Mal 3:1); now he is explicitly named as Elijah. God will send him **before the coming of the great and terrible day of the LORD** (4:5; cf. Jl 2:11ff.), perhaps to function as one of the two witnesses before the return of the Messiah (Rv 11:3-13). He will **restore** (lit., "turn," the same word used in Mal 3:7 for repentance) **the hearts of the fathers to their children and the hearts of the children to their fathers** (4:6). Rather than seeing this as merely addressing familial reconciliation, Malachi's use of the word for repentance makes it more likely to refer to the turning of the Jewish people in the latter days to the same faith as the patriarchs (Jn 8:56), **their fathers**. At that time, the nation will turn to their Messiah Jesus and be fully reconciled to their God (see the comments on Zch 12:10; 13:1; Rm 11:25-27). Israel's end-of-days repentance will cause God not to **smite the land** (of Israel) with a curse—rather He will rejuvenate it (Is 35:1-2).

God's faithful love for Israel is unchanging, just as His love for all who trust in the Messiah Jesus is immutable (Rm 8:38-39). The God who urged Israel, through His prophet Malachi, to live faithfully in light of that love, calls all His people to do the same, even as we await the return of the Messiah.

BIBLIOGRAPHY

Alden, Robert L. "Malachi." In *The Expositor's Bible Commentary*, edited by Frank E. Gaebelein. Grand Rapids, MI: Zondervan, 1985.

Baldwin, Joyce M. *Haggai, Zechariah, Malachi: An Introduction and Commentary*. Tyndale Old Testament Commentaries. Edited by D. J. Wiseman. Downers Grove, IL: InterVarsity, 1972.

Blaising, Craig A. "Malachi." In *The Bible Knowledge Commentary: Old Testament*, edited by John F. Walvoord and Roy B. Zuck. Colorado Springs: David C. Cook Publishers, 1985.

Chisholm Jr., Robert B. *Interpreting the Minor Prophets*. Grand Rapids, MI: Zondervan, 1990.

Clendenen, E. Ray. "Malachi." In *Haggai-Malachi,* The New American Commentary, edited by E. Ray Clendenen. Nashville: Broadman & Holman, 2004.

Feinberg, Charles L. *The Minor Prophets.* Chicago: Moody, 1990.

Kaiser Jr., Walter C. *Malachi: God's Unchanging Love.* Grand Rapids, MI: Baker, 1984.

Merrill, Eugene H. *An Exegetical Commentary: Haggai, Zechariah, Malachi.* Chicago: Moody, 1994.

Smith, Ralph L. *Micah–Malachi.* Word Biblical Commentary. Edited by David A. Hubbard and Glenn W. Barker. Waco, TX: Word Books, 1984.

Stuart, Douglas. "Malachi." In *The Minor Prophets: An Exegetical and Expository Commentary,* vol. 3, edited by Thomas Edward McComiskey. Grand Rapids, MI: Baker, 1998.

Verhoef, Pieter A. *The Books of Haggai and Malachi.* New International Commentary on the Old Testament. Edited by R. K. Harrison. Grand Rapids, MI: Eerdmans, 1987.

Wolf, Herbert. *Haggai–Malachi: Rededication and Renewal.* Chicago: Moody, 1976.

● ● ● ●

THE NEW TESTAMENT

MATTHEW

MICHAEL G. VANLANINGHAM

INTRODUCTION

Author. The Gospel of Matthew is an anonymous work, but ancient church tradition universally supports Matthean authorship of this Gospel. Papias (early second-century church leader from what is now Turkey, though he is dependent upon an earlier source), Pantaenus (d. c. AD 200, theologian who taught in Alexandria), Tertullian (c. AD 160–220, apologist from northeast Africa), Irenaeus (d. c. AD 202, church leader from Western Europe), Origen (c. AD 185–254, a scholar who died in Caesarea by the Sea), Eusebius (c. AD 263–339, a church leader and "father of church history" from Caesarea by the Sea), Jerome (c. AD 347–420, a priest and scholar from southeastern Europe), and Augustine (AD 354–430, a scholar from North Africa who also lived in Rome and Milan) say so. A major concern is the "Papias Fragment" in which he made the cryptic statement, "Matthew put together the oracles of the Lord in the Hebrew language." (Similar statements are made by Pantaenus, Irenaeus, and Origen, but they may depend upon Papias's comments). No consensus exists regarding what this statement means, but Matthew gives little evidence of being translated from a Semitic language into Greek. It may mean that Matthew wrote sayings of Jesus in Hebrew or Aramaic and later incorporated them into the Greek Gospel of Matthew (for the details on this view, cf. Daniel B. Wallace, "Matthew: Introduction, Argument, and Outline," at http://bible.org/seriespage/matthew-introduction-argument-and-outline, accessed September 8, 2009). It is also possible that Papias was wrong regarding an initial Semitic work by Matthew, and that Matthew wrote in Greek the gospel extant today. The key is to recognize that these ancient writers ascribe to Matthew some sort of work about Jesus' life.

Recipients. Nothing is known of the recipients of the gospel. The best suggestions range from Jewish believers still engaged with, or who had broken from, the synagogue system in Capernaum, Caesarea by the Sea, or Syrian Antioch. Because of the strongly Jewish flavor of the book, it is unlikely that it was written primarily to Gentiles. There was a vibrant Jewish and Gentile Christian community in Antioch, one that took seriously the urgency of the Great Commission. It is possible that Matthew wrote his gospel with this group in mind, but there is no way to know for sure.

Date. Matthew's gospel is dated by most scholars as coming from the late first century, partly on the assumption that it depends on Mark's gospel for much of its contents (see the "Excursus" below), and therefore had to be written after Mark. It is possible that Matthew wrote after the fall of Jerusalem (Mt 22:7; 24:1). His references to the Church (16:18; 18:17), to the other nation that will possess the kingdom (21:43), and his refined Christology are sometimes invoked as support for a late date of Matthew. But there is a great deal of evidence in Matthew that supports a pre-70 date (on AD 70, see the comments introducing Matthew 24). He referred often to the Sadducees (3:7; 16:1-12; 22:23, 34), although they fade from significance after AD 70. Jerusalem was the center of Jewish opposition to the movement Jesus started, but after 70 that center shifted to Jamnia (western Israel). The destruction of Jerusalem in AD 70 did not come about in the manner presented in Mt 24, making it likely that it was written before that war. Matthew recorded Jesus as enjoining, "leave your offering there before the altar" (5:23-24), which he probably would not have done if no altar remained after AD 70. A similar point could be made related to swearing "by the gold of the temple" (23:16-22) and paying the temple tax (17:24-27) if the temple had been destroyed. These observations are not absolutely conclusive, but taken together support the likelihood that Matthew was written before AD 70, perhaps between the early 40s to mid 60s. For the evidence for a pre-70 composition of Matthew, see Robert H. Gundry, *Matthew*, 1982, 602–6.

Purpose. It would have been helpful if Matthew wrote, "I'm writing this book for this reason: . . ." But he did not, and the gospel is complex enough that it is folly to suggest a single purpose for it. The purpose of Matthew's gospel appears to be at least partially apologetic. He seems to build a case for Jesus of Nazareth being the One who fulfilled the OT prophecies about the Messiah, the Son of David, King of the Jews, Immanuel, and the King of the world. Matthew also wrote to explain why the Jewish Messiah was rejected by the Jewish leadership and crucified by the Romans. The "mystery form" of the kingdom (chap. 13) may have been presented by Matthew to explain why the kingdom had not yet come in its fullest form, even though the King had been present. These themes may have been intended by the evangelist to help his messianic community interact intelligently with antagonistic members of the "synagogue down the street." That Gentiles are presented favorably (especially 2:1; 15:21; 28:18-20) is often cited by scholars who maintain that Matthew's purpose was to motivate his audience, primarily Jewish believers, to begin to fulfill the Great Commission. Finally, Matthew's gospel contains a considerable amount of instruction both on what it means to be a follower ("disciple") of Jesus, and the consequences of not embracing Him as King of kings.

Excursus: Gospel Critical Studies.

Matthew, Mark, and Luke are called "the Synoptic Gospels" since they present a similar narrative on Jesus' life ("synoptic" is derived from a Greek term that means "sharing or presenting a common view"). The Synoptic Gospels have a remarkable agreement on wording, content, and order of events. This agreement has puzzled scholars for centuries, and how to account for it forms the basis of what is called the "Synoptic Problem" or "Gospel Critical Studies." Three related disciplines have developed in an attempt to account for the similarities between the Synoptic Gospels: Source criticism, Form criticism, and Redaction criticism.

Source Criticism. This discipline attempts to determine the relationship between the Synoptic Gospels by identifying the written traditions that lie behind them. Source critics seek to determine what information the gospel writers received from the church, and what those individual writers may have added to what they received to fit their editorial, theological, and practical purposes. Gospel critical scholars look at the similarities between the Gospels and conclude that the agreements stem from some kind of literary dependence between them. Matthew, Mark, and Luke have considerable overlap (e.g., Mt 12:9-14 // Mk 3:1-6 // Lk 6:6-11). Most argue that Mark was the Gospel written first, and that Matthew and Luke utilized Mark when they wrote their own gospels. Hence there are similarities between all three. Sometimes, however, Matthew and Luke agree in wording that is not contained in Mark (e.g., Mt 13:16-17 // Lk 10:23-24). To account for these agreements between Matthew and Luke against Mark, source critics postulate that there was another source besides Mark that Matthew and Luke both used. That source is called "Q" (an abbreviation for the German term *Quelle*, "source"), and is theorized to have been a list of sayings by Jesus. However, there is no extant Q. It is a hypothetical source proposed by scholars to explain Matthew and Luke's agreements against Mark. The proposed dependence of Matthew and Luke upon Mark and Q is called "The Two-Source Theory." But sometimes Matthew and Luke contain material unique to their own gospels (for Matthew, see 19:10-12; for Luke, see 17:27-30). In these cases, scholars hypothesize that Matthew used a source (or many sources) unique to him, called the "M" source(s) not shared by Luke, and Luke's unique content is derived from a hypothetical source called "L." The proposal that Matthew and Luke used Mark, Q, M, and L, is called "The Four-Source Theory." Many recent source critics reject the idea of the Four-Source Theory, though it was popular during the first quarter of the 20th century.

Source criticism can help one see the similarities between the Gospels and may give an indication of the individual emphasis of each gospel writer. Many evangelical scholars adopt the assumptions and engage in the practice of source criticism. But in the hands of more critical scholars, source criticism tends to diminish the credibility of Matthew, Mark, and Luke as independent witnesses and historians. The

Two-Source Theory has come under attack for being illogical. For example, as it was mentioned above, source critics assert that Mark was written before Matthew and Luke, and that Matthew and Luke depend on Mark. They also point out (rightly) that Luke agrees with Mark's order of events when Matthew departs from Mark's order, and Matthew agrees with Mark's order when Luke departs from it. Thus, they argue, Mark was written first. But it is possible that Mark's gospel was written after Matthew and Luke, and depended upon both. When Matthew and Luke departed from each other, Mark may have chosen on one occasion to follow Matthew, on another to follow Luke. In addition, the fact that the Two-Source Theory requires an as-yet undiscovered hypothetical source called Q renders it hard (not impossible) to believe.

Form Criticism. This discipline seeks to determine the shape and content of oral traditions that circulated in the early church before they were written down. One of the goals of form critics is to provide a description of what the early church was like based upon what they believe can be determined about it from the oral traditions used by the gospel writers. Form criticism also seeks to categorize the kinds of features found in the Gospels, labeling some of its contents as "logia" (proverbial, prophetic, or "I am" sayings of Jesus in which He makes some statement of His identity), "pronouncement stories" (a short narrative that climaxes in Jesus making a profound statement on some topic), "parables," and "miracle stories" (stories that include supernatural acts by Jesus). As an example of the methodology of form critics, they will look at a "miracle story" and postulate that the early church formulated this story to help it compete with miracle-working characters in Greco-Roman religions called *theios aner*.

Form criticism is grounded in several assumptions. First, the Gospels were not the work of one person. The stories in the Gospels evolved as they circulated throughout Christian communities, who adjusted them and embellished them to meet their own situational needs. Second, the stories about Jesus circulated for at least 20 years in oral form and in independent units. These units were retained or discarded based upon their helpfulness for the localized church. Third, Mark and Q (and perhaps M and L as well) were the first written records of these diverse oral traditions. Matthew and Luke depend upon these two (or four) sources. Fourth, the sayings of Jesus are authentic only if they differ from the kinds of things said either in early (intertestamental) Judaism or in the early church, if they have multiple independent sources that attest to their authenticity, and if the sayings fit well with other sayings thought to be authentic.

There are numerous dangers with form criticism. First, because it assumes the validity of the Two- (or Four-) Source Theory, it inherits the weaknesses of that approach to the Synoptic Gospels. Second, the more radical forms of Form Criticism (i.e., as espoused and practiced by non-evangelicals) tend to de-historicize Jesus and make Him an invention of the early church. Critical scholars say that the picture of Jesus in the Gospels largely does not square with the Jesus "of history." Third, form criticism denies the presence of eyewitnesses and the biographical interest of the early church. If stories and sayings were fabricated and circulated in Christian communities, eyewitnesses to the events may well have challenged the validity of those inventions. Even Paul was careful to distinguish between what Jesus taught about divorce and what he taught (1Co 7:10, 12). If the more radical form critics are right, Paul would never have made such a distinction. Finally, so little is known about the first 30 years of the early church that the assumptions and conclusions of form critics rest upon speculation and subjective opinions.

Redaction Criticism. "Redaction" is drawn from the German term *Redakteur*, which means "editor." Redaction criticism is the discipline that seeks to discover the editorial emphasis of each gospel writer. This emphasis is discerned by seeing how a writer adjusted the contents of the stories and sayings he received from the church, and how he arranged them into his larger narrative framework. Rather than seeking to determine how the contents of the Gospels were shaped by the early church (one of the goals of form criticism), redaction criticism seeks to determine the distinctive contributions by Matthew, Mark, and Luke by noting their differences from each other.

For example, Matthew arranges Jesus' temptations in this order: bread, pinnacle of the temple, worship Satan (Mt 4:1-11). Luke's order is bread, worship Satan, pinnacle of the temple (Lk 4:1-13). Why this change in the order? Matthew probably gives the more strictly chronological account (see his temporal marker "then" in Mt

4:5), and Luke has chosen to order the temptations to fit his emphasis on the temple. His gospel begins with the temple (Lk 1:8) and ends with the temple (Lk 24:53) and generally gives the temple a more prominent place than Matthew or Mark do.

Redaction criticism may have more to offer than source or form criticism, for it is demonstrable that one gospel writer draws attention to certain things that are not emphasized by the others, and vice versa. But it is better to say that their editorial work highlighted certain aspects of events that really happened, rather than to say that they adjusted the information they received from the church to fit their own theological purposes. For example, Matthew notes the exception clause regarding divorce because of adultery (Mt 19:9; see the comments there), a clause absent from Mark (Mk 10:11) and Luke (Lk 16:18) (see the comments there). Rather than say that Matthew added this material, or "changed Mark" (a phrase seen often in the commentaries of Two-Source scholars), it is preferable to maintain that Jesus really said "except for adultery," and to propose why Matthew included it to suit his purposes, and why Mark and Luke omitted it to suit theirs.

There are several dangers associated with the more radical and critical approaches to redaction criticism (drawn from Robert L. Thomas, "Redaction Criticism," *The Jesus Crisis*, 255-57). First, it inherits the weaknesses of the Two- and Four-Source Theories upon which it depends. Second, redaction criticism does not deal adequately with its chronological, evidential, and ethical questions. Chronologically, redaction critics maintain that the tradition about Jesus circulated through and was formed by the early church (Form Criticism), but that after this it was fashioned and shaped by the Evangelists—all in a span of 30–40 years. In a day when communications moved slowly, this is nigh unto impossible. Evidentially, form criticism does not deal adequately with the fact that there were eyewitnesses still alive whose word would challenge the "artistry" of the Evangelists. Ethically, the more radical redaction critics maintain that the Evangelists ascribed words and deeds to Jesus that did not originate with Him. Christianity is the mother of high morality and makes it somewhat unlikely that the writers would have done this.

So how does one account for the similarities and differences in the Gospels? The similarities are explained by recognizing that Jesus was an itinerant teacher. It was common for Jewish itinerant teachers to present much of the same material in the various places where they traveled. If Jesus gave the Sermon on the Mount once, He probably gave it a dozen times in various locations to various crowds. The disciples, of course, would have heard it almost every time. When they wrote their Gospels as eyewitnesses (Matthew) or as church historians using primary sources (Mark and Luke), there would understandably be considerable similarity in the words they ascribed to Jesus. The differences in wording can be accounted for as they individually emphasized certain things Jesus said in any one setting. What He taught about divorce (Mt 19:3-12) can be read slowly in about 60 seconds. But He almost certainly took considerably longer to interact with the Pharisees, and later His disciples, on the topic. Matthew thus chose to emphasize one aspect of that much longer discussion, Mark and Luke others. The differences in the order or location of events can also be explained by Jesus' travels. In Matthew's gospel, Jesus taught the Lord's Prayer (Mt 6:9-13) in Galilee early in His ministry (cf. Mt 4:23), but Luke (Lk 11:2-4) places it during Jesus' trek from Galilee to Jerusalem much later, perhaps in Samaria (cf. Lk 9:51-52), possibly even in Bethany in the vicinity of Jerusalem (Lk 10:38-42, if Mary and Martha are the sisters from Bethany—a fair assumption). So which is it? Did Jesus teach the Lord's Prayer in Galilee or much further south? Critical scholars maintain that this difference in location signals historical inaccuracies in the Synoptic Gospels. But as an itinerant teacher, He probably taught about prayer in *both* Galilee (the episode Matthew records) *and* elsewhere (Luke's episode), just as any good traveling preacher does today, and did in Jesus' day.

For evangelical discussions sympathetic to source, form, and redaction criticism, cf. the articles by Scot McKnight, Darrell L. Bock, and Grant R. Osborne, respectively, in *New Testament Criticism and Interpretation*, ed. David Alan Black and David S. Dockery (Grand Rapids, MI: Zondervan, 1991). For an interesting interaction between evangelicals who differ on these disciplines, see Robert L. Thomas, ed., *Three Views on the Origins of the Synoptic Gospels* (Grand Rapids, MI: Kregel, 2002). For a capable critique of Gospel critical studies, see Robert L. Thomas and F. David Farnell, eds., *The Jesus Crisis: The Inroads of Historical Criticism*

Into Evangelical Scholarship (Grand Rapids, MI: Kregel, 1998), and Eta Linnemann, *Is There a Synoptic Problem? Rethinking the Literary Dependence of the First Three Gospels*, trans. Robert W. Yarbrough (Grand Rapids, MI: Baker, 1992).

OUTLINE

I. The Introduction to the King-Messiah (1:1–4:11)
   A. The King-Messiah's Background (1:1–3:12)
      1. The Messiah's Ancestry (1:1-17)
      2. The Messiah's Birth (1:18-25)
      3. The Messiah's Fulfillment of the OT (2:1-23)
         a. The Birth in Bethlehem (2:1-12)
         b. The Flight to Egypt (2:13-15)
         c. The Murder of Babies (2:16-18)
         d. The Disdain Because of His Hometown (2:19-23)
      4. The Messiah's Forerunner (3:1-12)
   B. The King-Messiah's Preparation for Ministry (3:13–4:11)
      1. The Messiah's Baptism (3:13-17)
      2. The Messiah's Test (4:1-11)
II. The Authority of the King-Messiah (4:12–11:1)
   A. The Setting for the Expression of the Messiah's Authority (4:12-25)
      1. The Messiah's Relocation to Galilee (4:12-16)
      2. The Messiah's Initial Followers (4:17-25)
   B. The Messiah's Teaching Demonstrated His Authority: The Sermon on the Mount (5:1–7:29)
   C. The Messiah's Miracles Demonstrated His Authority (8:1–9:34)
   D. The Messiah's Disciples Functioned with His Authority (9:35–11:1)
III. The Reactions to the King-Messiah (11:2–12:50)
   A. John Was Confused (11:2-15)
   B. The Masses Were Unresponsive (11:16-24)
   C. The Downhearted Were Encouraged (11:25-30)
   D. The Leaders Were Antagonistic (12:1-50)
      1. Regarding Sabbath Practices (12:1-21)
      2. Regarding Exorcisms (12:22-37)
      3. Regarding Signs (12:38-45)
   E. Family Ties Were Narrowed (12:46-50)
IV. The Kingdom and the King-Messiah in the Present Era (13:1-52)
   A. The Parable of the Sower and the Soils (13:1-23)
   B. The Parable of the Wheat and Tares (13:24-30; cf. 36-43)
   C. The Parable of the Mustard Seed (13:31-32)
   D. The Parable of the Leaven (13:33)
   E. The Reason for the Parables (13:34-35)
   F. The Parable of the Wheat and Tares, cont. (13:36-43; cf. 13:24-30)
   G. The Parables of the Buried Treasure and Pearl of Great Price (13:44-46)
   H. The Parable of the Dragnet (13:47-50)
   I. The Parables Gave New Revelation about the King and Kingdom (13:51-52)
V. The Withdrawal, Help, and Opposition of the King-Messiah: Four Cycles (13:53–16:28)
   A. Cycle #1: The Ministry in Nazareth (13:53–14:12)
      1. Jesus Withdrew: To Nazareth (13:53)
      2. Jesus Helped: By Teaching in the Synagogue (13:54)
      3. Jesus Faced Opposition: From His Kin and King Herod (13:55–14:12)
   B. Cycle #2: Feeding the Five Thousand at Bethsaida (14:13–15:20)
      1. Jesus Withdrew: To a Secluded Spot (14:13)

2. Jesus Helped: By Feeding the Multitude and Stilling a Storm (14:14-36)
3. Jesus Faced Opposition: From Pharisees and Scribes Over Oral Traditions (15:1-20)

C. Cycle #3: Tyre and Sidon and Feeding the Four Thousand (15:21–16:4c)
1. Jesus Withdrew: To the Region of Tyre and Sidon (15:21)
2. Jesus Helped: By Assisting the Canaanite Woman and Feeding Many (15:22-39)
3. Jesus Faced Opposition: From the Pharisees and Sadducees Who Wanted a Sign (16:1-4c)

D. Cycle #4: The Leaven of the Pharisees and Teaching the Disciples (16:4d–16:28)
1. Jesus Withdrew: To the Other Side of the Sea (16:4d)
2. Jesus Helped: By Teaching His Disciples (16:5-20)
3. Jesus Faced Opposition: From Disciples Who Did Not Understand (16:21-27)

VI. The Foretaste of the Glory of the King-Messiah: The Transfiguration (16:28–17:8)

VII. The Model of Humble Service Provided by the King-Messiah (17:9-27)

A. The Messiah Was Willing to Suffer (17:9-13)
B. The Messiah Was Willing to Help the Dull (17:14-20)
C. The Messiah Was Submissive (17:22-27)
1. Prepared to Die (17:22-23)
2. Prepared to Pay a Tax (17:24-27)

VIII. The Ethics of the Leaders Chosen by the King-Messiah (18:1–19:12)

A. Humility: Necessary to Enter and Serve in the Kingdom (18:1-6)
B. Personal Purity: Avoid Harming Self and Others (18:7-14)
C. Corporate Purity: Conduct Church Discipline (18:15-20)
D. Forgiveness: Remember How Much God Forgives (18:21-35)
E. Divorce: Avoid It (19:1-12)

IX. The Citizens of the Kingdom and the King-Messiah (19:13–20:34)

To Be a Citizen of the Kingdom, One Must . . .

A. Be Childlike to Be in It (19:13-15)
B. Depend on God to Enter It (19:16-30)
C. Not Be Shocked at Those Whom God Excludes (20:1-16)
D. Yield to the Messiah the Desire for Prominence (20:17-34)
1. Jesus Was Willing to Die (20:17-19)
2. The Leaders of the Disciples Were Required to Serve (20:20-28)
3. Jesus Was Willing to Serve (20:29-34)

X. The Rejection of the King-Messiah (21:1–23:39)

A. The Messiah Offered Himself to the People (21:1-11)
B. The Messiah Confronted the Corruption of the Priests (21:12-17)
C. The Messiah Foretold the Judgment Against the Nation (21:18-22)
D. The Messiah Exposed the Cowardice of the Leaders (21:23-27)
E. The Messiah Presented Parables about the Consequences of Their Rejection (21:28–22:14)
F. The Messiah Escaped Their Traps (22:15-46)
G. The Messiah Condemned the Leaders (23:1-39)
1. The Leaders Craved Acclaim (23:1-12)
2. The Leaders Corrupted the People through Their Hypocrisy (23:13-36)
3. The Leaders Faced Judgment (23:37-39)

XI. The Future Coming of the King-Messiah (24:1–25:46)

A. The Beginning of the Great Tribulation (24:1-14)
B. The Middle and End of the Great Tribulation: The Abomination of Desolation (24:15-28)
C. The Second Coming (24:29-35)
D. Instruction Urging Readiness for the Day of the Lord (24:36–25:30)
E. The Judgment Following the Second Coming (25:31-46)

XII. The Death of the King-Messiah (26:1–27:66)

A. The Hateful Plot Against Jesus (26:1-5)
B. The Act of Kindness for Jesus (26:6-13)
C. The Plans Judas Formed (26:14-16)
D. The Objective of Jesus' Death: Inauguration of the New Covenant (26:17-29)
E. The Boast of Jesus' Disciples (26:30-35)
F. The Anguish in Gethsemane (26:36-46)
G. The Incarceration at Gethsemane (26:47-56)
H. The Jewish Phase of Jesus' Trial (26:57-68)
I. The Denials by Peter (26:69-75)
J. The Remorse of Judas (27:1-10)
K. The Roman Phase of Jesus' Trial (27:11-26)
L. The Ridicule and Torture of Jesus (27:27-32)
M. The Crucifixion of Jesus (27:33-37)
N. The Cruelty Against Jesus (27:38-44)
O. The Death of Jesus (27:45-56)
P. The Burial of Jesus (27:57-61)
Q. The Securing of Jesus' Tomb (27:62-66)

XIII. The Resurrection of the King-Messiah (28:1-20)
A. The Angel Announced the Resurrection (28:1-8)
B. Jesus Announced the Resurrection (28:9-10)
C. The Guards Were Bribed to Lie about the Resurrection (28:11-15)
D. The Disciples Saw Jesus in His Resurrection (28:16-17)
E. The Great Commission Flows from the Authority of the Resurrected One (28:18-20)

COMMENTARY ON MATTHEW

I. The Introduction to the King-Messiah (1:1–4:11)

A. The King-Messiah's Background (1:1–3:12)

1. The Messiah's Ancestry (1:1-17)

1:1. Matthew introduced his gospel by emphasizing the legal right of Jesus of Nazareth to be the king of the Jews and of the entire world. Matthew included Jesus' genealogy to argue for the validity of His claim to David's throne. As the creation accounts began with the phrase **record of the genealogy** (LXX Gn 2:4; 5:1), Matthew's description here of the fulfillment of God's plan begins with the same phrase, suggesting that He was beginning the "new creation" (2Co 5:17). In Christ's humanity, He was legally a son of David and was a rightful heir to the Davidic throne (2Sm 7:12-13).

1:3-6. What is the connection between **Tamar**, **Rahab**, **Ruth,** and **Bathsheba**? Women were not usually included in Jewish genealogies (though cf. 1Ch 2). It is impossible to be certain, but perhaps the best view is that all four had unusual marriages through which God brought much good. He did the same through the unusual circumstances of the virgin birth. **Tamar**, **Rahab**, and **Ruth** were Gentiles, and **Bathsheba** was married to a Gentile. This may suggest Matthew's desire to indicate to his audience that Gentiles not only had a role in the ancestry of the Messiah, but should benefit from the sacrificial death of the Messiah as well (Mt 28:18-20).

1:11. Jeconiah (*aka* Jehoiachin) is Joseph's ancestor in the line of David through Solomon. Second Samuel 7:12-17 unconditionally promises the perpetuity of the Davidic kingdom through Solomon (vv. 12-13). But Jeconiah, who was in that line, was so wicked that God cursed him, not allowing his descendants to be king (Jr 22:30). This posed a dilemma. How can both the promise and curse be fulfilled? The answer is, "Through the virgin birth." Joseph was legally in that line through David, Solomon, and even Jeconiah. But Jesus is not a *physical* son of Joseph, and so dodges the curse while still fulfilling the legal requirement of being a son of David. Jesus, through Joseph, is in the *legal* line to David and Solomon without being under the *physical* curse.

1:17. Matthew structured the genealogy in three groups of 14 names, possibly to indicate that the Davidic kingdom dismantled in the exile would be restored by King Jesus. The importance of the number **fourteen** is unclear, but the name "David" (Hb. *dwd*) adds up to 14 on the basis of Hebrew numerology (4 ["D"] + 6 ["W"] + 4 ["D"]), and since there were three letters, this may account for three sets of 14. But Matthew left no clues for the significance in his thinking of this arrangement. This is not a pure genealogical record, but makes a theological statement about Jesus as son of David. In order to get 14-14-14, David should be counted only once, but Jeconiah twice (because of the break ending v. 11 and introducing v. 12, where Jeconiah is viewed both as the last of the kings of Judah before the exile, and the first of the kings of Judah during the exile).

2. The Messiah's Birth (1:18-25)

1:18-21. Jewish marriage practices had the groom taking the initiative in approaching the father of the prospective bride. If the bride's father agreed to the marriage, the groom paid a price called a *mohar*, a sort of reverse dowry that compensated the bride's family for any financial loss they might incur without her help in the family business. The couple exchanged vows and was considered legally married. Dissolution of the marriage during betrothal required formal divorce. The couple did not cohabit for a year while the groom prepared living quarters, often attached to his father's house. After the year the groom and his friends would surprise the bride and her family, the wedding feast would begin, further vows would be exchanged, and the marriage consummated. It was during the year of betrothal that Mary's pregnancy was discovered. Marriage would have been a tacit admission by Joseph that the child was his, possibly something intolerable to this **righteous man**. But he was kind as well, and intended to divorce her **secretly** by writing a bill of divorcement in the presence of two or three witnesses rather than suing Mary and her family to recoup the *mohar* and to make a case for his innocence. It required angelic intervention to change Joseph's mind.

1:22-23. How Matthew views the connection between Is 7:14 and the birth of Jesus is debated. Possibly Isaiah's words were fulfilled in the eighth century BC, with Jesus not so much "fulfilling" Isaiah, but Matthew "filling Isaiah full" of new meaning. Another view is that Isaiah's prophecy had multiple fulfillments—one in the day of Ahaz and one in Jesus' day. The preferable understanding is to see the prophecy as a direct prediction with an unvarnished fulfillment in the virgin birth. The meaning of **Virgin** (Gk. *parthenos* in Matthew and in the LXX at Is 7:14; *almah* in Hb.) is debated. *Almah* usually means "a young woman who is not sexually active" (Gn 24:43; Ex 2:8; possibly Ps 68:25 [ET; MT and LXX, 67:26]; Sg 1:3; 6:8; probably Pr 30:19). *Parthenos* meant "a young woman," usually one who is presumed to be sexually inexperienced (though see LXX Gn 34:3, where it probably means simply "girl"). Only in Gn 24:43 and Is 7:14 does *parthenos* translate *almah*, and in Gn 24:43 it designates a young woman with no sexual experience. The one(s) who translated Isaiah into Greek for the LXX had other words available for "young woman of marriageable age who is having or who is about to have sexual relations" (e.g., *neanis* which could mean "maiden" or "young married woman," or *kore*, "bride," "young wife," "concubine"), and apparently understood *almah* in Is 7 as referring to sexual inexperience. This weighs against the understanding that Isaiah was referring to his own or another's wife on the verge of conception.

The structure of the words addressed to Judah (Is 7:1–9:7) and Israel (Is 9:8–11:16) are parallel, and contain the following features: the parallels mean that Is 7:1–9:7 should be read as a unit, and indicates that the promised Immanuel (Is 7:14) will possess the land (Is 8:8), defeat all enemies (8:10), and appear in Galilee as a light to the Gentiles (Is 9:1-2; see Mt 4:15-16), and will be seen as divine, ruling forever on David's throne (Is 9:6-7). Matthew saw these themes directly fulfilled in the birth of Jesus (for the details, see

Feature	Text for Judah	Text for Israel
Opportunity to repent before wrath comes	Is 7:1-17	Is 9:8–10:4
Assyria will invade	Is 7:18–8:8	Is 10:5-15
Enemies destroyed and a faithful remnant preserved	Is 8:9-22	Is 10:16-34
A glorious kingdom ruled by a Son of David	Is 9:1-7	Is 11:1-16

D. A. Carson, "Matthew," In *Matthew, Mark, Luke* of EBC, ed. Frank E. Gaebelein [Grand Rapids, MI: Zondervan, 1984], 78–81).

1:24-25. Joseph complied with the angel's message and married Mary, apparently without any wedding celebration. To safeguard the integrity of the virgin birth, Joseph **kept** Mary **a virgin** until after the birth. While Mary is commendable for her role in Jesus' birth, Joseph is similarly impressive. He was ethically upright, compassionate toward the woman he intended to divorce, and was in control of his libido enough to abstain from relations until after the birth. Joseph is the forgotten hero of Christmas!

3. The Messiah's Fulfillment of the OT (2:1-23)

a. The Birth in Bethlehem (2:1-12)

2:1. Bethlehem was about six miles southwest of Jerusalem. **Herod the king** was the ruthless and paranoid puppet ruler under Rome. His atrocities included killing three sons, a wife, and her mother to protect his regime. There is no secular record of what happened in Bethlehem, but it is perfectly in keeping with his paranoia to slaughter these children. The **magi** remain enigmatic figures, but were probably wise men specializing in astronomy and astrology. In the Greco-Roman world they purportedly predicted the ascendancy of great leaders (Astyages of Media in the sixth century BC; Alexander the Great, and Augustus). **From the east** could be Egypt, but was more likely Babylonia, where a large and influential group of Jews still lived in exile. It is remotely possible that these magi were familiar with the prophecies of Daniel and that these, in association with the star, would have caused them to come to the Holy Land.

2:2. A **star** could signal the birth of powerful men. In Jewish tradition a new star appeared following the birth of Abraham, and the Messiah is associated with a star (Nm 24:17; Rv 22:16). What was this star? Jupiter and Saturn were aligned in Pisces in 7 BC, but such planetary alignments were never called "stars." Halley's Comet was visible in 12 BC but this is certainly too early. That this star appeared (2:7) suggests it had not been documented previously, and 2:9 implies that this star *moved around*, supporting a supernatural origin, and may parallel the pillar of fire that led the Hebrews in the wilderness.

2:3-6. These verses indicate that neither the magi nor Herod knew what Scripture said regarding the location of Messiah's birth. Matthew cites Mc 5:2, where he only appears to contradict Micah's words. Micah emphasizes what made Bethlehem great, the birth of the Messiah, and Matthew asserts that Bethlehem consequently was not unimportant. Matthew may have related the episode of Jesus' birth in **BETHLEHEM** to make His connection with King David clearer. Though Jesus grew up in Nazareth, not Bethlehem, His birthplace links Him with David, a fact that would have carried some apologetic clout for those who might doubt the legitimacy of His descent from David.

2:7-12. Herod's deception about worshiping the King of the Jews was consistent with what is known about his *modus operandi*. Matthew's reference to **gold, frankincense, and myrrh** may intend to establish a parallel with Solomon, a son of David, to whom similar gifts were given (1Kg 10:1-2; 2Ch 9:23-24; Sg 3:6).

b. The Flight to Egypt (2:13-15)

2:15. The exact day of Herod the Great's death is not known, but Josephus says it happened after a lunar eclipse on March 12-13, 4 BC, and before the Passover on April 11, 4 BC. Matthew's use of Hs 11:1 (**OUT OF EGYPT I CALLED MY SON**) is puzzling. In its OT context, Hosea is looking backward—but not entirely. Hosea 11:9-11 contains the promise of a future restoration of the Jewish people after all their exiles. Hosea 3:4-5 indicates that Hosea knows about the future Son of David, and that He will be involved in the restoration of the nation and people. God had the power and ability to protect His people once in Egypt and brought her out from Egypt (Hs 11:1); He will protect His people and someday restore them (Hs 11:9-11). He will do this with the Son of David (Hs 3:5). Where does Jesus fit in? Jesus is the typological fulfillment of Israel, seen in that God protected both the Hebrews and Jesus in Egypt. The future restoration promised through the Son of David in Hs 3:5 and 11:9-10 will be accomplished through Jesus Christ. Just as the Jews were brought out of Egypt, and that was a proof that they would one day be restored, so Jesus being protected in and brought out of Egypt signals the commencement of Israel's restoration. Israel's full restoration will come only at Jesus' second coming when He will free Israel from Gentile oppression (called "the times of the Gentiles" in Lk 21:24), following their faith in Him (cf. the comments on Mt 23:38-39 and Rm 11:20-27).

c. The Murder of Babies (2:16-18)

2:16-18. Herod discovers that he was duped by the magi, and cruelly has the baby boys in

Bethlehem killed. Good estimates are that about 20 children were killed **two years old and under**, their ages specified to provide Herod a margin of error.

How does Matthew use Jr 31:15 (**RAMAH**)? Jeremiah indicated that the tears associated with exile (Jr 31:15) would end. Matthew has already made the exile a turning point in his thought (Mt 1:11-12), for during the exile the Davidic line was dethroned. The tears in Jeremiah's day caused by the exile find a parallel in the tears of the mothers of Bethlehem. The exile is nearly over, the heir to David's throne has come, and the true Son will introduce a new covenant (Jr 31:31ff.; Mt 26:28) promised by Jeremiah. See the comments on Jr 31:15.

d. The Disdain Because of His Hometown (2:19-23)

2:19-22. Herod's kingdom was divided among his sons Philip, Antipas, and Archelaus. Archelaus ruled Judea proper, Samaria, and Idumea. He was more debauched than the others, his nine-year reign marked by immorality, brutality, and tyranny. Matters got so bad that there were complaints lodged in Rome against him by a deputation of Jews and Samaritans. Augustus summoned him to Rome, fired him, and exiled him to Gaul in AD 6. God warned Joseph about Archelaus, and when the family left Egypt, they went into the region of Galilee and lived in Nazareth, under the control of Herod Antipas.

2:23. He shall be called a Nazarene has no clear OT source. **Nazarene** apparently was a term of scorn in the first century (Jn 1:45-46; Ac 24:5), and Matthew appears to indicate that the OT prophets foretold that the Messiah would be despised (cf. Ps 22:1, 6-8, 13; 69:8, 20-21; Is 49:7; 53:2-3; and see Mt 8:20; 11:19; 15:7-8).

4. The Messiah's Forerunner (3:1-12)

3:1-4. Matthew shifts his narrative about 30 years into the future to the start of Jesus' ministry. John the Baptist's attire (3:4) is strikingly similar to Elijah's (2Kg 1:8), and Matthew makes that connection explicit (Mt 11:14; see Lk 1:17). Matthew thus consistently uses the phrase **kingdom of heaven**, not "kingdom of God" as in the other gospels, probably because his Jewish audience might have been offended at the excessive and overly-familiar use of God's name. What is the **kingdom of heaven**? In Luke's gospel, the initial announcements of the kingdom were made to Mary regarding her Son, of whom the angel Gabriel says, "God will give Him the throne of His father David; and He will reign over the house of Jacob forever, and His kingdom will have no end" (Lk 1:32-33). Gabriel appeared to reiterate the Davidic covenant found in 2Sm 7, in which God promised David a son who would rule and reign over His kingdom Israel forever. Of importance are the verbal parallels between Lk 1:32-33 and 2Sm 7:13-16 (both passages referring to and using the words "son," "house," "kingdom," "throne," and "forever"), which indicate that Jesus has come, among other things, to fulfill the role as the ultimate Son of David. These points suggest that the gospel writers had an apologetic purpose, to argue for Jesus fulfilling the promises regarding David's seed ruling over David's kingdom. It makes the best sense to see this kingdom as the same one promised in the Hebrew Scriptures. It is a literal geopolitical kingdom in which there was a ruling king, replete with authority that is exercised over a literal people and a literal land. Matthew calls it the **kingdom of heaven** *not because it exists only in heaven*, but because it will come *to earth from heaven*.

3:5-12. The connection between the baptism administered by John and the confession given by those baptized is disputed. The preposition **for** (*eis*) in the phrase **for repentance** (v. 11) can carry the nuance "because of" or "on the basis of" (see Mt 10:41, where the phrase "in [*eis*] the name of a prophet" could be translated "on the basis of the name of a prophet" or "because one is called a prophet"), so that the baptism in water by John is "because of" or "on the basis of" the prior repentance of the people. John's blistering words for **the Pharisees and Sadducees** (v. 7) indicate that there was an element among those who came whose actions were hypocritical. **We have Abraham for our father** (v. 9) indicates that their ethnic and religious background was presumptuous and gave them false security. To be **children to Abraham** was wrongly restricted to Jewish people in their thinking, and would depend upon one's repentance (a change of mind regarding one's sins). True repentance was to be demonstrated by the production of **good fruit** (v. 10), the absence of which negated the baptism and showed the repentance to be spurious. For Matthew, it is **good fruit** that provides the evidence that one is in right standing with God (i.e., "saved"), not the supposed presence of life without good fruit (Mt 7:16-20; 13:3-9; 18-23).

John declares that the baptism Jesus will bring will be **with the Holy Spirit and fire** (v. 11). Jesus is the "baptizer" and the Spirit is the element into which the believer is baptized (Mk 1:8; Lk 3:16; Jn 1:33; Ac 1:5; 11:16, and even 1Co 12:13). The Spirit does not do the baptizing. **With the Holy Spirit and fire** indicates that everyone will experience *both* aspects of this baptism, either a baptism in the Spirit that is a "refining fire" (strengthening through trials or growth in sanctification; see Zch 13:9; Rm 8:12-14; 1Pt 1:7) for those who embrace Christ, or for those who do not embrace the Messiah, a "fiery judgment" (Gn 19:24; Ps 21:9; Ezk 22:20; 2Th 1:7-8; Heb 10:27) eternal in duration.

B. The King-Messiah's Preparation for Ministry (3:13–4:11)

1. The Messiah's Baptism (3:13-17)

3:13-14. John's reluctance to baptize Jesus is understandable. John's baptism was in response to one's confession of sins, was preparatory for the One who would dispense the fiery Spirit baptism, and was enacted in anticipation of the coming kingdom. Jesus was sinless, was ready to dispense the eschatological baptism, and was the King who was present. How could *John* baptize *Him*? Jesus' baptism, however, was important for establishing His identification with John, the coming kingdom John preached, and those who had undergone John's baptism in preparation for that kingdom.

3:15-17. In the baptism of Jesus, both Jesus and John cooperate **to fulfill all righteousness** (v. 15). **This is My beloved Son** (v. 17) (citing Ps 2:7) is from a psalm loaded with messianic freight, and **in whom I am well-pleased** (citing Is 42:1) is about the call of the Suffering Servant. In Is 42:1, God says, "I have put My Spirit upon Him." This finds a parallel in Mt 3:16 with the words **Spirit . . . descending . . . on Him**. How does all this fit together? Jesus entreated John to baptize Him so that together they might do all that God required (**righteousness**) of Jesus as He fulfilled Scripture when He embarked on His messianic suffering-servant ministry for which God gave Him a visible manifestation of the Holy Spirit who came upon Him. The Spirit **descending as a dove** probably does not refer to creation (Gen 1:2 where the Spirit hovered dove-like) nor to Noah's dove (Gn 8:8-12). It seems to be simply a visual manifestation apparently seen only by Jesus and John (Mt 3:16; Jn 1:32-33), intended to convey God's approval of His Son as He embarked on His ministry.

2. The Messiah's Test (4:1-11)

With His baptism, the first of two prerequisites for Jesus beginning His ministry was over. The second involved His testing. At His baptism, God identified Jesus as His Son. In the first two temptations, the Devil attacks Him on precisely His divine Sonship.

4:1-2. There are a number of parallels between Jesus' temptations and the testing of Israel in the wilderness (Dt 8:2). Israel was led by the Spirit (Neh 9:20) as was Jesus (Mt 4:1). Moses fasted for 40 days (Ex 34:28; Dt 9:9) and later Elijah did as well (1Kg 19:8). Matthew may allude to these possibly to indicate that Jesus was the supreme prophet or the "new Moses."

4:3-4. The first temptation may have been designed to influence Jesus to act independently of God by using His own powers to alleviate His hunger. But Jesus responded by citing Dt 8:3, which is in a context of God humbling Israel, evaluating the people's obedience, determining if they would depend on Him, disciplining them as a father disciplines a son (Dt 8:3-5). Where Israel failed, Jesus was faithful.

4:5-7. In the second temptation, the Devil cited Scripture about God's promises to protect His people (Ps 91:11-12). Either physically or in a vision, Jesus was taken to the temple probably because it symbolized God's intense care for His people (Ps 18:6; 48:9; 65:4), the very point of this temptation. Jesus responded with another reference to Deuteronomy (6:16), where Moses warned the people not to test God as they had when they sought to force Him to give them water (Ex 17:1-7). While God promises to protect His children, they must not coerce Him to do so, which would be tantamount to turning Him into their slave. Jesus' response does not indicate that this temptation was to dupe Jesus into a spectacular display so that people would forcibly make Him king and cause Him to bypass the cross.

4:8-10. The third temptation may also have been a visionary experience. What the Devil offered Jesus, the Father had already promised Him, namely world dominion (Nm 24:15-19; Ps 2:7-8; Dn 7:13-14). Jesus cited Dt 6:13, a verse found in the context of warnings about idolatry on the eve of the Hebrews entering the Holy Land. Failure to worship God alone would result in decisive judgment (Dt 6:14-15), and had Jesus succumbed to the temptation to worship the Devil, He would have faced God's wrath and forfeited His saving role.

4:11. Unlike Israel in the wilderness, Jesus did not fail when He was tested. When the Devil left him, angels came **to minister to** [lit., "to serve"]

Him—possibly indicating that they brought food since a forty-day fast would have left Him precariously weak.

There are practical lessons suggested by this episode. First, Jesus drew upon Scripture to resist the attacks of the Devil. How can Christians hope to fare very well against Satan if they have little knowledge of the Word (Eph 6:17)? Second, the Devil quoted Scripture, but did so out of context. Psalm 91:11-12 is about His protection in the vicissitudes of life, not in presumptuous and impetuous actions chosen in foolishness. God's people must not only be able to quote Scripture, but will need to know what it means in its context. Third, eventually God met all of Jesus' needs, and as His children wait humbly for Him to act, He will never let them down.

II. The Authority of the King-Messiah (4:12–11:1)

A. The Setting for the Expression of the Messiah's Authority (4:12-25)

1. The Messiah's Relocation to Galilee (4:12-16)

4:12-16. Jesus shifted His base of operations back to Galilee in the north, probably because of the threat posed by Herod Antipas who incarcerated John the Baptist. It was also a logical place for Jesus to begin the more aggressive phase of His ministry. Galilee was open, densely populated, and laced with roads that fostered its bustling commerce. Matthew indicates that Jesus' relocation fulfilled Is 9:1-2. This prophecy, connected with the birth of the Child in Is 9:6-7, refers not to the restoration of the tribes of Zebulun and Naphtali after the exile but to the ultimate restoration of Israel in messianic days, aspects of which were beginning during Jesus' ministry.

2. The Messiah's Initial Followers (4:17-25)

4:17. Repent means "to change one's mind (about the seriousness of one's sins) and behavior." It does not carry the primary sense of sorrow over sin, nor is it usually understood in the Gospels strictly as a mental adjustment. When John the Baptist preached repentance, he expected it to be accompanied by a change in behavior (Mt 3:7-10; see Lk 3:8-14).

4:18-22. It is unclear what other exposure to Jesus **Peter** and **Andrew** might have had before this call, but it is likely that there was some. **Fishers of men**, in contrast to their previous vocation, suggests that their role would be to help win people to the movement started by the Lord. Their response was immediate, but while Peter and Andrew **left their nets**, **James** and **John** left **their father**, implying a deeper sacrifice.

4:23-25. Matthew 4:23 has a virtual twin in Mt 9:35, with minor differences depicted by the bold font in the chart below.

This feature, called an *inclusio*, implies that Matthew intended the material between 4:23 and 9:35 to be read as a thematic whole. That primary theme is Jesus' authority. In 4:23a, b, c, Jesus exercised His prophetic authority by His teaching and preaching. A grand example of this was the Sermon on the Mount, chapters 5–6–7 (see especially 7:29). In 4:23d-24, Matthew reported that He showed His authority as He healed the people (see 8:9; 9:6, 8; 10:1), a theme developed through the nine miracles in chaps. 8 and 9.

B. The Messiah's Teaching Demonstrated His Authority: The Sermon on the Mount (5:1–7:29)

The Sermon on the Mount is probably the most famous of all the teachings of Christ, but it is difficult to determine exactly what its purpose is. The approach here is that the sermon is Jesus' teaching about how those who repented in preparation for the coming of the kingdom should live as they await its coming.

5:1-6. The purpose of the Beatitudes is to present the virtues that should characterize those who are ready for the kingdom and to assure them of blessing and reward when it comes. Verses 1-6 express the blessedness of one who is rightly related to God and vv. 7-12 the blessedness of one who is rightly related to people. In the most basic sense, **blessed** means "deep joy," usually flowing from knowing one has received divine favor. **Poor in spirit** (v. 3) may include an economic component, but the focus here seems to be on recognition of one's spiritual bankruptcy; those who have nothing of their

4:23	9:35
Jesus was going throughout **all Galilee**, teaching in their synagogues and proclaiming the gospel of the kingdom, and healing every kind of disease and every kind of sickness **among the people**.	Jesus was going through **all the cities and villages**, teaching in their synagogues and proclaiming the gospel of the kingdom, and healing every kind of disease and every kind of sickness.

own to offer God have the kingdom. Those who **mourn** (v. 4) look primarily at the sadness often experienced in this evil, difficult era while anticipating the kingdom. The promise is that **they shall be comforted**, the passive voice referring to what God will do for them. For the idea of **gentle** (v. 5), see Ps 37:9-11 where the "gentle" rely on God to reverse their fortunes. On thirsting **for righteousness** (v. 6), see Mt 5:20.

5:7-9. Social relationships are the focus of these beatitudes. Being **merciful** (v. 7) embraces both forgiveness for those who are guilty and compassion for the suffering; **they shall receive mercy** does not indicate that God's mercy toward us is contingent upon us showing mercy to others. Mercy cannot be merited (for a fuller explanation of this, see the comments on 18:31-35). The **pure in heart** (v. 8) refers to those who are morally unstained, clean, and free from duplicity or filth in their relationships with others. **Peacemakers** (v. 9) are **sons of God** because, like God, they pursue reconciliation with others, just as God has extended Himself to reconcile people to Himself.

5:10-12. Verse 10 parallels v. 3, both concluding with the same promise. Verses 11-12 serve as an expansion of v. 10. Persecution can come from living **for the sake of** (*heneken*) **righteousness**. But in v. 11, Jesus says that persecution can come **because of** (or "for the sake of," also *heneken*) **Me**. This particular righteousness for which one might be persecuted is a righteousness based upon and found in Jesus.

5:13-16. The **salt** and **light** figures make it clear that Jesus intended His people to influence the world. The main point of the **salt** in this text is not to create thirst or serve as a preservative against the moral decay of the world, but to improve taste, to make the world a better place. A **lamp** provides light precisely so that one can see in the darkness, and it is nonsense to conceal it. The citizens of the kingdom *are* light, and they must shine and not conceal that light. The result is the enhancement of God's reputation in the world, not the aggrandizement of the lamp.

5:17-19. The flow of thought is not completely clear, but the idea of **good works** in v. 16 might summon notions of keeping the Law as fulfilled by Christ. The phrase **Law or the Prophets** occurs in 7:12 where the golden rule appears to satisfy the requirements of the Law (the Pentateuch, Mt 12:5) and Prophets (the rest of the OT, Lk 16:29, 31). Matthew indicates that Jesus does **fulfill** the OT, using "fulfill" 15 times for bringing about what was forecast in the OT (e.g., 1:22; 2:15, 17; 8:17; 26:56). The Law or the Prophets remain relevant **until all is accomplished** (v. 18), the precise idea probably being that the OT serves as a beacon shining upon Jesus as the one who provides the fulfillment of messianic promises. From this standpoint all of the Law and each of the prophets are valid forever (**until heaven and earth pass away**, possibly at the conclusion of the millennial kingdom) as they all point toward Christ. This includes not only the Ten Commandments but all 613 of them, even the ritual and civil aspects of the Law (**not the smallest letter or stroke shall pass from the Law**, v. 18; not even **the least of these commandments** will pass away, v. 19). The religious leaders would hardly have dismissed even the least of these commandments, but they certainly would not have taught that they pointed to *Jesus of Nazareth* as the One who fulfilled them. However, vv. 17-18 do not require the people of God to perform the Law today, but to promote the ongoing validity of the OT as a signpost identifying Jesus of Nazareth as the Messiah. Only where the NT reiterates the OT commands are believers to keep the Law; but then it becomes "the Law-as-fulfilled-in-Jesus," also known in the NT as the "law of Christ" (1Co 9:21; Gl 6:2), but is no longer the Law of Moses (cf. Rm 3:31; 8:4). **Then** (v. 19) introduces a conclusion Jesus draws from the previous verses. Those who minimize the importance of the OT as an apologetic for Jesus being the Messiah will face loss of rewards in the kingdom.

5:20. For I say to you introduces an additional thought to that of one's rank within the kingdom—namely, the circumstances under which one might be excluded from the kingdom altogether. **Righteousness** in Matthew generally has two connotations: ethical behavior in keeping with the teachings of Jesus (Mt 5:10, 20; 6:1), and a rather Pauline understanding of righteousness as a pure, holy, and innocent status before God that He imparts to followers of Jesus. This finds support in Mt 5:6, where those prepared for the kingdom hunger and thirst for righteousness, and they are promised that "they will be satisfied"—a divine passive, so that *God* is the one who fills them full of righteousness. This makes it unlikely that the context allows for 5:20 to be understood as a proof text for works righteousness. See further the comments on 7:21-23.

The fundamental problem with the Pharisees was that at the core of their righteousness was keeping the law or their own oral traditions, but they excluded Jesus. The scribes and Pharisees would probably not have objected to the righteousness Jesus presented in 5:21-48, except that He claimed to be its authoritative source and that His teaching superseded the OT. The righteousness one needed to **enter the kingdom of heaven** came as a gift from God to the spiritually bankrupt and is found only in connection with Christ.

5:21-48. As is the case with much of Matthew, it is hard to figure out exactly the purpose of the six "antitheses" in these verses. The view adopted here is that He was presenting new revelation alongside the OT based upon His prophetic authority. Moses prophesied that a great prophet would arise in the future (Dt 18:15, 18; cf. Dt 34:10-12 for the implication that the coming of this great prophet was still future), and the NT writers see this fulfilled by Jesus (Ac 3:20-23). While Jesus is more than a prophet, He functions in the role of a prophet, calling the people back to faithfulness to God.

5:21-26. Jesus cited the sixth commandment regarding murder (Ex 20:13) but equated the guilt of an emotion with the act of murder, something not found in the sixth commandment itself. He could do this because of His prophetic authority as the law's fulfiller. In v. 22 there is probably not an escalation in the venues of judgment, but **court**, **supreme court**, and **fiery hell** represent the certainty of accountability for anger expressed in a way that shames a neighbor. The main point of vv. 23-25 is that the followers of Christ are to seek reconciliation as swiftly as possible when one has harmed another out of anger.

5:27-30. Jesus cited the seventh commandment regarding adultery (Ex 20:14). Again, He connected inner motive with outward act. When Jesus said, **but I say to you**, He was not giving material derived from the commandment, but altogether new revelation that complemented the law. **With lust for her** could also be translated "in order to cause her to lust" for him. Either way, the attitude of lust is the problem here. Verses 29-30 indicate that His followers must take radical steps to conquer moral sins. Gouging out the eye or cutting off the hand are surely hyperbolic statements but suggest extreme measures to avoid sexual sins. On being thrown **into hell**, see the comments on 18:7-10.

5:31-32. Jesus cited Dt 24:1, 3 regarding the regulation of divorce. If lust in the heart is spiritually tantamount to adultery, then divorce without biblical warrant is full-fledged adultery. Technically, divorce was not commanded in Dt 24:1; what was commanded was the need to give a certificate of divorce, and divorce was permitted only **for the reason of unchastity**. See the comments on 19:1-9. What Jesus taught here went beyond Moses, who permitted divorce if a certificate were provided. But Jesus emphasized the gravity of the consequences for one who executed an improper divorce and for one who marries an improperly divorced person.

5:33-37. Jesus' instructions regarding vows were drawn probably from several passages, for there is no single OT verse that says this precisely (see Lv 19:12; Nm 30:3; Dt 23:21; Ps 56:12). To make a vow involved the pledge to do something, to call upon God to witness the discharge of the action, and to punish if it were not carried out. The OT did not forbid the trading of vows, but it did regulate the practice. Today one might say, "I swear on the soul of my grandmother" to do this or that, and in Jesus' day people might swear by the gold in the temple or any number of other revered things. This sounds solemn enough, but such vows were used occasionally by the unscrupulous to conceal the intention to never keep their promise. Jesus dismissed the practice altogether, demanding absolute truthfulness instead. Scripture says that God swears by Himself (Heb 6:13), and that Paul also made a vow (Ac 18:18), suggesting that making vows is permissible on earnest occasions (such as weddings or giving testimony in court).

5:38-42. Jesus may have alluded to several OT texts (Ex 21:24; Lv 24:20; Dt 19:21) regarding acts of retaliation. Dt 19:18 indicates that the "law of the tooth" (*lex talionis*) was a guideline for the civil authorities and did not approve private retribution. It was possible that many applied it wrongly for personal revenge, but Jesus forbade the practice for his followers. Not only should they not retaliate, they should be willing to surrender what was theirs to avoid taking revenge (**turn the other** [cheek] . . . **let him have your coat also** . . . **go with him two** [miles], and **give** and lend to those who ask; see 1Co 6:7).

5:43-48. In the last of the six antitheses, Jesus enjoins love in keeping with Lv 19:18, but goes beyond that command by insisting on loving one's enemies (contrast *1QS* 1:4, 10). Jesus' followers are to **pray for those who persecute** them (see 1Th 5:17), because to do so is so like God who provides the necessities of life for all, even those who hate Him. There is no reward in loving only those who love us, for even the tax collectors and Gentiles—both despised by many of the Jewish people—show the same love (the verb is *agapao*) for each other. Verse 48 must be read in its context. **Perfect** might be translated better as "mature." Jesus expects His followers to show the same kind of mature love for everyone, those who are pleasant and difficult, as God shows to them, especially by joyfully meeting their daily needs.

Jesus emphasized the need for virtue in Mt 5. Starting in Mt 6 he discussed the proper motives for living virtuously. A. B. Bruce ("Matthew," *The Expositor's Greek Testament, The Synoptic Gospels*, ed. W. Robertson Nicole [Grand Rapids, MI: Eerdmans], 116) points out that in chap. 5 Jesus encouraged His followers to show their good works when they are tempted to hide them, and in chap. 6 to hide their good works when they are tempted to show them.

6:1. Righteousness has an ethical sense of giving (6:2-4), praying (6:5-15), and fasting (6:16-18). For those who follow Jesus' teaching there is the promise of **reward**, a theme that dominates the chapter (6:1, 4, 6, 18). Those rewards may include God's approval (1Co 4:5; Mt 25:21) and perhaps the opportunity to serve Him in a grand way when the kingdom comes (Lk 19:17).

6:2-4. One needed to avoid hypocrisy when fasting. **Sound a trumpet** suggests "calling attention to one's self" at the start of a fast. People were **hypocrites** if they fasted purportedly to please God but actually to **be honored** (lit., "glorified") by others, or if they gave to help others when they intended to "help themselves" by inflating their reputation. Giving was to be done **in secret** (not letting the **left hand know what** the **right hand is doing**), and God would "pay back" the one who gives in this manner. It is a mistake to restrict God's reimbursement to money.

6:5-8. Hypocrisy in prayer was also forbidden. The **synagogues** and **street corners** include every indoor and outdoor public place where one might pray to impress others. Impressing others would be the only reward, but God is unimpressed. When public or corporate prayer is motivated by narcissism it is wrong.

Meaningless repetition was a characteristic of the prayers of some Gentiles (1Kg 18:26; perhaps Ac 19:34). God already knows the needs of His children and delights to meet them. Mindless repetition is unnecessary.

6:9-10. Pray, then, in this way (ESV, "like this") indicates that this prayer provides a pattern to follow rather than a prayer to recite (though see Lk 11:2). Verses 9-10 focus upon matters related to God's program, while vv. 11-13 focus upon people's needs. **Father** probably reflects an Aramaic word *Abba*, which was used both during childhood and adulthood and could be used for respected men outside of one's family. "Daddy" is not quite the best English equivalent. This intimate **Father** is also **in heaven**, emphasizing His transcendence and divinity. **Hallowed** is not a call to worship but is an imperative of request or entreaty for God to cause His **name** (His "fame") to be revered. The **kingdom** has present manifestations (see Mt 13) and a future cataclysmic coming (Mt 22:1-14; 25:31-46); this petition may incorporate both a request for more people to experience the present form of the kingdom (i.e., find salvation) and for the kingdom to come soon in its full eschatological form.

6:11-13. Daily bread probably means "bread for the coming day." On forgiveness, see 6:14-15. **Temptation** refers to solicitations to moral infractions, and **Do not lead us into temptation** is informed by the second positive part—**deliver** ["rescue"] **us from evil** or better "the evil one." It is the Devil, not God (Jms 1:13), who initiates the temptation, but God rescues us from his evil designs.

6:14-15. Jesus expands on the theme of forgiveness in v. 12 (see the comments on 18:31-35). It is possible that He means, "If you do not forgive others, God will not forgive you," but this runs contrary to the very idea of forgiveness, which by definition cannot be earned. It is better to see it as indicating that one's capacity for forgiving others is tied to the receipt of forgiveness from God. If one does not or cannot forgive others, it may indicate that he has not yet received forgiveness, so that forgiving others becomes an evidence of one's forgiveness before God.

6:16-18. Jesus forbids ostentation related to fasting. To **anoint your head** was a common practice in which oil laced with aromatic spices was applied to the hair or beard during times of celebration or when honoring someone (Lk 7:46; Jn 12:3). Jesus' point is that, out of humility, one is to conceal his serious spiritual activity, even to the extent of "putting on a happy face," and God will reward him.

6:19-21. Just as Jesus' followers should not crave earthly acclaim (6:1-18), they should not crave earthly things (6:19-34). Jesus does not forbid the accumulation of wealth, but He does command that it not be treasured because it can be lost. Storing up **treasures in heaven** in context may be fostered by the spiritual disciplines of giving, praying, and fasting—performed with the right attitudes and in the right way.

6:22-23. People fix their heart on where their treasure is (vv. 19-21); so they fix their eyes on what they desire most (vv. 22-23) (for both, see Ps 119:10, 18). The **clear eye** probably parallels the heart set on heavenly treasure. Just as a healthy eye gives light to the body, so wholehearted fidelity to God gives meaning and light to one's life. Unbridled lust for material things can cloud one's spiritual sight; obsession with earthly things obscures one's sunny view of God.

6:24. A misplaced heart and a clouded eye lead to a misaligned will that tries to serve two irreconcilably different masters. One could not have served Franklin Delano Roosevelt and Adolph Hitler at the same time. Eventually a person would default to serving one or the other, and that is the case with **God** and **wealth** (*mamo nai, mamonai,* "mammon," "worldly things").

6:25-30. Materialism beguiles one of heavenly treasure, obscures spiritual sight, and enslaves to something other than God (vv. 19-24). **For this reason** (v. 25) the followers of Christ must not permit themselves to be obsessed with worldly goods. **Do not be worried** is an imperative verb which means "to have anxiety based upon perceived or real impending misfortune" (see also Php 4:6). God gives the greater gifts (**life** and one's **body**) and will supply the lesser ones (**food, clothing**). The Father **feeds** the birds (v. 26); but He hardly ever makes worms rain from the sky into opened beaks. They work for their food, but He providentially puts worms where the birds peck. His children are more precious to Him than birds; they can count on Him to provide food, clothing, and shelter, usually through their work (which He also provides). By **being worried** (v. 27) one cannot add a **single hour** (literally "one cubit") to one's life span, which is sometimes described in units of measured distances. Wild flowers usually grow only for a few weeks in Israel because it is so arid, but God dresses them with splendor (vv. 28-30). The materials to make dyes were difficult to obtain and yielded mediocre results. Even Solomon could not clothe himself in garments as brilliantly colored as the **lilies of the field**. Such vegetation, however, was disposable, used for tinder to light the fire in a home's oven. God can be trusted to clothe the follower of Jesus, whom He values more than dried grass.

6:31-32. For the second time Jesus forbids fixating on things. Such obsession characterizes the **Gentiles**—probably a reference to those outside the covenant community of God who, as a result, do not know God's provision.

6:33. The **kingdom** includes both a future cataclysmic coming and present effects (see the commentary on Mt 13). To **seek first His kingdom** involves not only being prepared for its future coming but also incarnating its values and glorifying its King in the present time. **His righteousness** (see 6:1) surely includes what He demands of His children ethically (see the connection of **kingdom** and ethical **righteousness** in Rm 14:17). **All these things** include the basic essentials of life. There is no guarantee that God provides luxury items when people claim them or visualize their reception. The main point of 6:33 is that God so demands His people's undivided attention that He promises to provide their necessities so that they will not worry about them and can fully concentrate on Him.

6:34. In the phrase **tomorrow will care** [lit., "will worry"] **for itself**, Jesus probably personifies **tomorrow** as owning its own anxieties. It is folly to wrest what belongs to "Mr. Tomorrow" and make it one's own today. Instead, when tomorrow comes, it will have **enough trouble of its own**, but God will enable the believer to handle those troubles then (6:25).

7:1-2. Jesus has been discussing His disciples' motivation. Here He begins to discuss His disciples' relationships with others, especially those who are antagonistic to His message. **Do not judge** does not mean that believers are to suspend all discernment. In 7:6 determining the identity of the "dogs" and "swine," as well as false prophets (v. 15), is impossible without critical thinking. **Judge** means "harsh, destructive criticism." If a person sets himself up as judge, it implies that he has a broader knowledge of God's Word and standards and a higher degree of being able to live it. The harsh, strict standards by which they criticize others will be the same standard by which God will hold them accountable.

7:3-5. Judgmentalism (7:1-2) can easily lead to fault-finding (7:3-5). When people are critical of others without recognizing their own faults, they have the satisfaction of self-righteousness without the rigors of self-improvement. One is a

hypocrite who uses an apparent act of kindness (removing a speck) to inflate his own ego. Before presuming to help others, one must undergo some self-discipline and yield to the discipline of the Lord (Ps 51:10-13).

7:6. If one is not to be judgmental, neither is one to be completely blind to others' faults. **Dogs** and **swine** were considered unclean animals by the Jews. The **holy** thing and the **pearls**, given the context of vv. 3-5, may be the correction a disciple might give to someone who needs it, after the disciple has removed the log from his own eye.

7:7-11. When seeking to remove the speck from someone's eye (vv. 3-5), or trying to discern when to refrain from casting pearls (v. 6), one must pray for wisdom and discernment. Verse 8 does is not guarantee that every persistent prayer will be answered the way one prefers. The context (vv. 6-11) suggests that God is generous when His people ask for discernment when "casting pearls before swine." Three analogies indicate He will gladly provide discernment. First, many desert rocks had roughly the same color and shape as loaves of bread, but no father would substitute a rock if a child asked for bread (v. 9). Second, snakes were considered unclean for eating (Lv 11:12) but like fish had scales. A snake filet might resemble a fish filet, but no father would deliberately trick a child with something that would defile him (v. 10). Third, as parents give gifts to their children, similarly God will give wisdom in knowing how to act toward those who are resistant (v. 11).

7:12. This is arguably the most famous verse in all Scripture. God is gracious in response to prayer for discernment (vv. 6-11), so God's people should be gracious in how they treat others (v. 12). The guideline is to treat others the way one wishes to be treated. Such an approach summarizes and fulfills the 39 books of the Hebrew canon (the **Law and the Prophets**) and puts in pithy form the command, "love your neighbor as yourself" (Lv 19:18; Mt 22:39; Rm 13:8-9).

7:13-14. Verse 12 concludes the Sermon on the Mount. What follows in vv. 13-27 are four warnings Jesus gives to His audience about applying the sermon. The first warning (vv. 13-14) is a caution to the lost about where they are headed. The verb **enter** (v. 13) has no grammatical object, but v. 14 indicates that *eternal* **life** is the destination and should probably be understood here. The **narrow gate**, **small gate** and **narrow way** are harder to **find** than the **wide** ones and must be sought deliberately, or people will not escape destruction. The **narrow way** that **leads to life** is found only by faith in the death and resurrection of Jesus Christ (Jn 14:6; Ac 4:12). **Destruction** means "a loss that produces utter ruin, perishing," and here refers to loss of eternal life.

7:15-20. This is the second warning, cautioning His followers about "pretenders." Perhaps the connection here with vv. 13-14 is that false prophets prevent others from entering the narrow gate because they beckon people to the broad gate. Verses 16-20 tell of their deeds, vv. 21-23 of their words.

False prophets (v. 15) are **ravenous wolves** who look like the sheep but will devour God's flock for their devious ends. Not all who claim to be a part of the covenant community are. Jesus teaches that there are wolves in sheep's clothing, houses that look similar but have different foundations, tares that resemble wheat (13:24), wise and foolish virgins (25:1-13), and good and bad slaves (25:14-30). **Fruits** refer to the actions of false prophets, and while their deeds might temporarily conceal who they really are, eventually their actions will betray them (vv. 16-18). A false prophet does evil deeds and teaches rotten doctrine just as surely as a bad plant produces correspondingly bad fruit

7:21-23. This is the third warning, directed at those who claim to be a part of Jesus' community but who are not. No one is allowed admission into the kingdom on the basis of the good deeds he has performed, no matter how spectacular they might be (**prophesy**, **cast out demons**, **perform many miracles**). Entering the kingdom only happens when one has the kind of righteousness grounded in Christ that surpasses the Pharisees' (5:10-11, 20); when, like a little child, one depends on the Lord for entrance (18:3); when one recognizes that entering is possible only as God effects it (19:16-17, 23-26); and when one enters only through Jesus (and the religious leaders hindered people from doing this, 23:13). **I never knew you** has the sense, "I do not recognize you as one of my people," and their alleged good deeds He views as **LAWLESSNESS**.

7:24-27. The last of the four warnings, this one is about acting upon the words of Jesus. Just as there are wolves among the sheep (7:15-23) and tares among the wheat (13:24-30) until the end, so do the houses of the wise and foolish stand side by side until the Son of Man comes to judge and take His throne. The **house** is a person who has heard Jesus' words; the **rock** represents the teachings of Jesus that, as one does them, result in withstanding the storm, whether it be eschatological judgment (Is 29:6; 30:30; Ezk 13:10-16; 38:22) or life's trials.

7:28-29. The **scribes** were virtually walking footnotes who derived their authority by citing other famous rabbis. By contrast Jesus taught with His own **authority**, functioning as a prophet, giving new revelation from God. Jesus' authority continues into the next several chapters of Matthew (see 8:9, 27; 9:6, 8; 10:1), serving to tie the Sermon on the Mount where He displayed His authority through His teaching with chaps. 8–10 where He displayed His authority through His miracle-working ministry.

C. The Messiah's Miracles Demonstrated His Authority (8:1–9:34)

Matthew 11:4-5 is a key for understanding chaps. 8 and 9. The miracles not only show Jesus' compassion but also confirm His messianic authority. Matthew 11:6 ("And blessed is he who does not take offense at Me") is equally important as it serves to connect the narratives about the miracles in Mt 8 and 9 with the dialogue in these chapters. Donald A. Hagner (*Matthew 1-13*, WBC [Dallas: Word Books, 1993], 196) points out that Jesus confronted several groups whose response to Him was either appropriate or deficient (see 8:10; 8:26-27; 9:8; 9:3, 11; 9:33-34). Those who are blessed are those who do not stumble over Jesus; they or their loved ones usually receive healing. But those who stumble over Him face dire consequences (8:11-12).

8:1-4. Leprosy was a term applied to skin diseases such as eczema, psoriasis, possibly seborrhea, not Hansen's Disease (or modern leprosy). Leprosy rendered one a social outcast (Lv 13:45-46), ritually impure (Lv 13:3-30), and was thought to be a sign of judgment (2Ch 26:20; Nm 12:9-12). When Jesus **touched him**, He was formally violating Lv 5:3; but the Law was to benefit people (Mk 2:27), and to help someone was no real infringement of the Law. In the next miracle He heals with a word without touching the sick one. Perhaps Jesus knew that this leper needed caring physical contact, something denied him during his illness. The healed leper was to **show** [himself] **to the priest** and offer the prescribed sacrifices in obedience to Lv 14:1-33. For Mt 8:4, see the comments on 9:27-31.

8:5-13. Capernaum was the center of Jesus' Galilean ministry (cf. 4:13). The centurion in a Roman legion would be roughly somewhere between a high-ranking noncommissioned officer and a captain in the modern army. He oversaw 100 soldiers, with each legion having 60 groups of 100 when fully staffed. This **centurion** was courteous in not insisting that Jesus **come under** [his] **roof**, as Jewish people often refused to enter the homes of Gentiles to avoid becoming ritually impure. The centurion's **faith** was bolstered by his own military context. He was given authority and exercised it over his troops. Jesus had authority over all diseases and the evil spirits that sometimes inflict them. Jesus had not seen faith like this "even in Israel"—the *birthplace* of faith in God. Those who will **come from east and west** are probably Gentiles like the centurion and not scattered Jews. Those with faith will **recline . . . in the kingdom of heaven**, which is likened to a wedding feast (Is 25:6; Mt 25:10; Lk 14:15; Rv 19:7-10). The **sons of the kingdom** refer to the Jewish people who simply assumed their inclusion in the messianic kingdom (see *m. Sanh.* 10:1) and who even viewed themselves as God's agents in judging the nations (*2 Bar* 72:6; *T. Abr.* 13:6). Jesus makes it clear that without faith in Him they would be excluded from the kingdom. The **outer darkness** (Mt 22:13; 25:30) and **weeping and gnashing of teeth** (13:42, 50; 22:13; 24:51; 25:30) are metaphors for the experience of God's judgment reserved for unbelievers. Some scholars view those in the **outer darkness** as believers excluded from the celebrative aspects of the kingdom because they failed to live for God (the view of Zane C. Hodges, *Grace in Eclipse: A Study on Eternal Rewards* [Dallas: Redención Viva, 1985], 83-95). This view is impossible, however, in light of 13:42, 50, where tares—who are labeled "sons of the evil one" in 13:38, bad fish in 13:48, and called "wicked," not righteous, in 13:49—experience this judgment.

8:14-17. Peter's **mother-in-law** was healed so thoroughly that she had no residual effects, evident in that she **waited on Him**. The citation of Is 53:4 has engendered considerable discussion. Does the atonement guarantee healing for Christians? The answer is, "Yes, but. . ." Believers are guaranteed the resurrection body in the atonement also (Rm 6:4-10), but there is no indication that they will receive it prior to the rapture of the Church, at which time—and not before—God frees His child from all physical *and spiritual* ills. Matthew cites Is 53 as *initial* proof that Jesus was filling the role of the Suffering Servant, with the fuller, more climactic fulfillment coming at His crucifixion and experienced by the Church at the rapture.

8:18-22. It is possible that Jesus' departure to the east side of the Sea of Galilee prompted some to pursue remaining with Him. **Teacher** is used in Matthew by people who did not actually believe in Jesus (12:38; 19:16; 22:16, 24, 36). **Scribe**(s) is used 23 times in Matthew, each time negatively except 23:2-3. **Son of Man** is used in contexts that either emphasize His earthly ministry and divine authority (9:6; 12:8; 19:28) or His suffering and death (8:20; 17:12, 22; 20:18). Daniel 7:13-14 uses it in an eschatological context for the One who establishes the kingdom on earth (see Mt 24:27-39). Jesus emphasized not only His divine authority but also His humility. Only one who is divine could inaugurate the kingdom and reconcile God and humankind. **Nowhere to lay His head** testifies of the rigors of Jesus' itinerate ministry. Following Jesus would be a challenge for the scribe, for the disciples (who leave their homes in 8:23 for the east side of the Sea of Galilee), and for anyone.

Bury my father probably includes both the funeral and the months of mourning that traditionally followed. Burial of one's father was so important that other religious observances could be suspended (e.g., saying daily prayers, study of the Torah), but following the Messiah was the highest priority. The **dead** burying the **dead** probably means, "Let those who are dead to the call of the kingdom bury those who are physically dead."

8:23-27. The Sea of Galilee (a fresh-water lake) is rimmed by hills and valleys that can funnel high winds that can whip up whitecaps abruptly. These violent waves, however, do not fully subside for 24–48 hours, making this miracle remarkable (**it became perfectly calm**) when the winds instantly abated and the water became glassy. Matthew may have drawn a parallel with Israel's deliverance at the Red Sea in Ex 14 (the people cried out for deliverance beside the water, had fear, were rescued by God, and as a result, had faith in God and Moses). Jesus is the "New Moses" and more—Jesus **rebuked** the winds and waves and they obeyed, but Moses was silent.

8:28-34. The country of the Gadarenes is difficult to locate with certainty, and a number of textual variants are connected with the name ("Gergasenes?" "Gerasenes?"). It is probably the general area of Gadara, a city about five miles southeast of the Sea of Galilee. Its influence extended to that sea, including the town now called Kursi. The topography there fits Matthew's description, with fertile but steep slopes that plummet into the sea.

What business do we have with each other? is an OT phrase (2Sm 16:10; 1Kg 17:18; 2Kg 3:13) that always indicates hostility. **Torment us before the time**: Demons will be tortured forever in judgment (Jd 6; Rv 20:10; *1 Enoch* 16:1; *Jub* 10:8-9; *T. Levi* 18:12; *1QS* 3:24-25; 4:18-20). Jesus, because He is the **Son of God**, will mete out this punishment at the appointed time, but the Gadarean episode is a foreshadowing of that future judgment.

The presence of **swine** makes it likely that this was a Gentile region, and the city of Gadara was in the Gentile province of the Decapolis. It is not clear why the demons wanted Jesus to send them into the herd, though 12:43-45 implies that demons seek hosts to wreak their destructive work. Jesus permits them, but the situation does not unfold as they anticipated. The drowning may have occurred to show the demons' colossal power versus the superior power of Jesus or possibly as a sign of their future judgment. Mark 5:13 says there were 2,000 pigs, and as any hog farmer will attest, they are uncooperative creatures.

It is also unclear why the townspeople **implored Him to leave**. They appear to be worried about further financial loss, and the identity of Jesus as well as the deliverance of the demoniacs was inconsequential to them, suggesting that their priorities were skewed. The proper response, in spite of their loss, would have been to welcome Christ, thank Him for delivering the possessed men, and help to spread His fame in the region (see Mk 5:18-20).

9:1-8. Matthew continues to emphasize the theme of authority (9:6, 8) and the reaction of various groups to His miracles. The **paralytic** needed physical healing, but his greater need was spiritual. The reaction to Jesus' pronouncement of forgiveness is understandable in light of the OT texts that ascribe the prerogative only to God (Is 43:25; 44:22). **Blasphemes** (v. 3) means "to speak against someone," "to harm one's reputation." When a person claimed to have divine privileges, it diminished God's unique and exalted place by suggesting that a mere human could share His attributes. It was not just uttering a theological lie. The healing confirmed that Jesus was not blaspheming, that He did have the divine authority to forgive sins. Miracles in the Gospels and Acts frequently occur to substantiate those whom God used to initiate a new movement and to validate new revelation.

9:9. The call of **Matthew** took place in Capernaum, and it is likely that he was willing to follow so readily because of observing these miracles. As a **tax collector**, Matthew's job may have been to work a tollbooth for people traveling to or from the regions under Herod Antipas (Galilee) and Philip the Tetrarch (Gaulinitis, northeast of the Sea of Galilee, roughly the same as the modern Golan Heights). Tax collectors usually contracted with Roman authorities to gather a set amount of tax revenue each year, and as long as that quota was met, those authorities were satisfied. They made a profit by overcharging people, and their assistance rendered to Rome as well as their contacts with Gentiles resulted in Jewish people despising them.

9:10-13. Sinners refers to those who, at best, were irreligious, and at worst reputed violators of the Law. The question posed by the Pharisees in v. 11 is more of an accusation than a request for information. They disapproved of Jesus' interaction with such known sinners for He was allowing Himself to be defiled by their company, and perhaps charged Him with "guilt by association." The words **healthy** and **righteous** should be understood as ironic, for Jesus saw the Pharisees as being neither (cf. 5:20), though these words summarized their estimation of their own condition. Jesus cites Hs 6:6 in v. 13. Neither Hosea nor Jesus should be understood as dismissing sacrifices, for God desired them; but He desired **COMPASSION** (mercy) more. The Pharisees were in the same category as the apostates of Hosea's day for they neither showed compassion toward the outcasts Jesus was reaching nor joy at their repentance. Many believers today fall into this trap as they pompously isolate themselves from the world, when God desires them to extend His love even to those on the fringes of society.

9:14-17. It is likely that John the Baptist was imprisoned by Herod Antipas by this time (see 14:1-12). The **disciples of John** had ascetic tendencies as did John and, on the topic of fasting, were in agreement with the **Pharisees.** Jesus' disciples did not fast since it was inappropriate for them to do so—the **bridegroom** (Jesus) was still present, a cause for celebration. The guests at a wedding feast freely enjoyed themselves. Later, when He was gone, His disciples would fast.

The connection of vv. 16-17 with what precedes is unclear. Perhaps by these images He (and Matthew) meant that His presence (vv. 14-15) entailed the rise of a new spirituality that could not simply be added onto Judaism as most were practicing it. Those, like John's disciples and the Pharisees, could not maintain their traditional ways and add "a little bit of Jesus" to them. There is considerable continuity between the Hebrew Scriptures and the ministry of Jesus of Nazareth, but the religious system of Israel could not be just slightly amended without disastrous results (**a worse tear results . . . the wine pours out and the wineskins are ruined**). Jesus' point is not so much that Judaism and Christianity, respectively, are ruined by trying to combine them, as if they are both perfectly fine when unmixed. Instead, He proposed that catastrophe follows such an attempt, namely the forfeiture of salvation found only in Him.

9:18-19. The four miracles in 9:18-34 may provide concrete examples of individuals coming wholly to Jesus for their "preservation" (9:17), as well as providing substantiation that Jesus is the Messiah (see 11:4-6).

The typical **synagogue official** would have been similar to an administrative elder or executive pastor. He did relatively little of the preaching, but recruited those who did and otherwise oversaw the affairs of a synagogue. These officials were usually prominent in their communities.

9:20-22. Why did Matthew intertwine the miracle of the official's daughter and the woman with the hemorrhage? There are few clues, but both episodes emphasize Jesus' compassion (see 9:36) and His ability to deliver against all human expectations and perceived time constraints (the daughter was already dead by the time Jesus got to the official's home in all three gospels [Mk 5:35; Lk 8:49]; the woman had been ill for 12 years). God can work on behalf of His children even when they think enough time has passed to make it impossible for Him to do so.

The **hemorrhage** was due to some uterine disorder, and this sort of illness had serious social and spiritual implications (Lv 15:19-25; see also Ezk 36:17; CD 4.12-5:17; 11QTemple 48:15-17; Josephus, *War* 5.227; *m. Nidda*; *m. Zabim* 4:1). The **fringe of His cloak** may have been the tassels that were worn on the four corners of one's garments to remind a person of the Law (Nm 15:38-41; Dt 22:12). It is possible that the sick woman did not approach Jesus directly because of the shame of her condition. **Made you well** is literally "saved you." When Paul uses the verb it usually means "being rescued" from the eternal consequences of sin, and Matthew uses it this way (1:21; 10:22; 16:25; 18:11; 19:25); but here it may mean little more than God delivering her from her physical condition.

9:23-26. At the official's home, a **crowd in noisy disorder** had gathered, probably consisting of musicians, professional mourners, and friends bringing food and condolences (2Ch 35:25; Jr 9:17-22; 16:7; Ezk 24:17, 22; Hs 9:4; Ec 12:5; Am 5:16). The job of the professionals was to express grief for the family, the louder the better. Even a poor family was expected to hire two flute players and one wailing woman (*m. Ketub* 4:4). The crowd **began laughing at Him** when He said the girl was just asleep. They may have felt disdain for Him as they knew she was dead and perhaps Jesus did not yet know it, or because they assumed that even this great Healer could not raise one from the dead. But "sleep" was an apt description of her condition; when people sleep they awaken from that temporary condition. Because of Jesus' authority, her state of death was rendered temporary. This was also the first time in Matthew's Gospel that Jesus raised one from the dead, and this was important for substantiating His messianic identity (Mt 11:5).

9:27-31. This is the first explicit mention of healing the blind in Matthew. According to the OT, messianic days would be accompanied by sight being restored (Is 29:18; 35:5; 42:7). The miracle lent weight to the claim that Jesus was the Messiah (Mt 11:5), and the blind men recognized Him as such, calling Him by the messianic title **Son of David** (9:27; see Matt 1:1) and even **Lord** (9:28). Josephus (*Ant.* 8.42-49) ascribes great healing prowess to Solomon, David's son, which may account for the title here.

As in the case of the woman with the hemorrhage (9:22), the key for the blind men being healed was their faith. Apparently, Jesus wanted to avoid the sensationalism this miracle might produce, and **sternly warned them** against announcing it. There was the risk that the crowds would foment rebellion against Rome utilizing Jesus as the messianic liberator and cause Him to bypass the cross. The men, however, could not contain themselves.

9:32-34. Matthew says that the **demon was cast out** of the mute man in contrast to the other miracles where he wrote that people were "healed." The exorcism provided the setting for the accusation of the Pharisees that Jesus conspired with **the ruler of the demons** to help this man (see 10:25; 12:24). The accusation was public, given in response to the musings of the crowd, and signals open and explicit opposition by the Pharisees for the first time in Matthew. The opposition grew considerably more intense from that point on.

D. The Messiah's Disciples Functioned with His Authority (9:35–11:1)

9:35-38. On 9:35 and its broader contextual connections, see the comments on 4:23-25. **The harvest** refers to the extensive needs of the distressed and downcast people of Israel, who were like **sheep without a shepherd**, a phrase that had messianic associations (Ezk 34:5, 23). Jesus commanded the disciples to pray that God would raise up and send out workers—and then Jesus enlisted the disciples to do what He urged them to pray about. God's people must always pray—but there comes a time when effort must be coupled with entreaty.

10:1-4. The *inclusio* of 4:23 and 9:35 finds a continuation in 10:1, where the words that conclude 4:23 and 9:35 occur again. Chapter 10 is the second major discourse in Matthew and continues the theme of Jesus' **authority** (10:1). This is a precursor of the Great Commission in Mt 28:18-20. For a detailed discussion of the twelve disciples, see John MacArthur, "Matthew 8-15," MNTC (Chicago: Moody, 1987), 129-182.

10:5-6. These verses specify the "target audience" of the disciples. They were not to go to the **Gentiles** or to the **Samaritans**, though no reason is given for the restriction to **the lost sheep of the house of Israel**. Perhaps the best reason is that it was expedient to go to those with whom the disciples shared a common set of values and beliefs. There would be time for a ministry to the Samaritans and Gentiles later (10:18). The Jewish national rejection of Messiah had not yet taken place (Mt 12:14, 24); only afterward could the message be taken to the Gentiles (cf. Rm 11:11).

10:7-8. Here, Jesus instructs the Twelve about some of the ministry activities they would perform. No nature miracles are mentioned, and, as Craig Blomberg points out, the curing of each of these kinds of maladies occurred in the book of Acts (3:1-10; 8:7, 13; 9:32-43; 14:8-10; 19:13-16; 20:7-12) except for lepers (*Matthew*, NAC [Nashville: Broadman & Holman, 1992], 171).

10:9-10. Jesus also instructed them regarding their belongings while engaged in this work. There is a harmonization problem between Matthew and Mark. In Matthew, Jesus forbids taking sandals and a staff (with other items). In Mk 6:8-9, Jesus allows them. The best solution is that Jesus allowed only one pair of sandals and one staff in keeping with Mark, but not two. That Jesus, in Matthew, says "shake the dust off your feet" (10:14) and not "off your sandals" does not prove they lacked sandals. Mark 6:11 says "shake the dust off the soles of your feet," but those feet had sandals. Given the harsh terrain of the land of Israel, walking for any distance without shod feet would be impossible, and theirs was to be a traveling ministry (see the verbs for going, entering, and leaving in vv. 5-15). If the disciples had sandals when they began their travels, then they probably also had one tunic and one staff but should not **acquire** more. By being lightly equipped they would not be hampered by the weight of transporting extra supplies and would experience and demonstrate God's provision. Accusations of greed would also not stick to them.

10:11-14. The instruction to **stay at** a **house until you leave** would help the disciples not waste time finding better accommodations, nor perplex an initial host. **Peace** was often associated with the arrival of the Messianic Age (Is 9:6; 52:7; Mc 5:5; Nah 1:15; Zch 9:10); if a **house is worthy** probably means "they welcome you and your message," then they would have the kind of peace that will characterize the kingdom and avoid the judgment for those who do not embrace the gospel (Mt 10:15). Jewish people who traveled through Gentile regions would **shake the dust off** their **feet** (v. 14), for unholy places might make one unclean or one could track defilement into Jewish districts (cf. *m. Ohal.* 2:3). For the disciples to do this as a testimony against *Jewish* homes was to insinuate that they might someday be judged by God just as the Gentiles would be.

10:16-20. Verses 16-20 present the likelihood of more active opposition, and may have been given by Jesus in preparation for what would happen to them further in the future. These kinds of persecution happened in the book of Acts.

Sheep and **doves** are both victims of predators with few defenses, and the metaphors suggest that the disciples were to be transparent and vulnerable to people to serve them, but they were also to be wise **as serpents** (or "snakes"), which have a knack for self-preservation. The disciples were not to be unduly naïve, resulting in perpetual victimization. The **courts** (v. 17), refer to judicial actions against the disciples. Though they would encounter overwhelming obstacles, they nevertheless must provide **a testimony** (lit., "witness") to their abusers. The promise of vv. 19-20 was intended chiefly for the disciples, and in Acts they speak in crisis situations while "filled with the Holy Spirit" (Ac 4:8; 7:55; 13:9). The promise that their words **will be given** to them by **the Spirit** reflects a prophetic experience that is not guaranteed to every believer.

10:21-22. The **one who has endured**, based on vv. 21-22, is the one who continues his witness in the midst of furious antagonism. The **end** sometimes refers to the last days (e.g., 1Co 1:8; Rv 2:26), but it often carries a less technical sense of "the end (of a period of time)" (Lk 1:33; 1Co 10:11; 2Co 3:13; 1Pt 4:7). In v. 21, **death** due to persecution makes it likely that the **end** here is the end of life, whether from persecution or other causes. **Saved** refers to spiritual deliverance, and perseverance is the evidence from which one can infer that a person is saved (Col 1:22-23; Heb 3:5-6, 14; and see the comments on Mt 13:18-23). Perseverance, however, is not the cause of salvation.

10:23. Does the phrase **you will not finish** ["going through" is not found in the Gk.] **the cities of Israel** reassure persecuted disciples that they will always have places of refuge in Israel despite widespread persecution? Or does it mean that the mission to Israel will not be completed even at the second coming? The two views are not mutually exclusive, for to say one is surely to suggest the other. Matthew 10:11-15 places this statement in the broader framework of the Church's mission to Israel. But the explanatory **for** linking the desperate flight from one town to the next in 23a and b with "finishing the cities" in 23c supports the first view. **Until the Son of Man comes** is similarly difficult. It may be a reference to His "coming" to the Father at His ascension or to His eschatological second coming. But a satisfying option is that it is a reference to Jesus' "coming" in judgment in AD 70. In 16:27 and 26:64, the coming of the Son of Man is associated with judgment. In addition, the persecution of His followers is depicted as taking place early on, during the period before relations with the synagogue were curtailed (10:17), making it likely that Jesus is referring narrowly to the experience of His disciples following the resurrection. This does not exclude the need for the ongoing mission to Israel today, however.

10:24-31. For **Beelzebul**, see the comments on 12:22-24. As 10:16-25 indicates, there will be intense opposition to believers, especially those involved in evangelistic efforts. **Fear** would be a normal reaction, so Jesus encourages them three times not to **fear** (vv. 26, 28, 31), and gives them truths that might assuage it. Verse 26 contains the first truth, promising that the identity of Jesus and the disciples will finally be revealed in the day of judgment if not before; they are not of Satan, but of God, and eventually even their persecutors would see that. Therefore, they were to be bold about what He told them in **darkness** and **whispered** in their **ear**, probably figures for the private instruction Jesus gave the twelve in contrast to the open proclamation coming later (v. 27).

The second truth is that their fear of God must supersede fear of opposition so that their mission would continue (v. 28). The third truth emphasized God's sovereign awareness of their distress and His care for them. If God cares about even the little things (**sparrows**; the number of the **hairs of your head**), why should they fear people?

10:32-33. Therefore introduces an inference from what precedes. If Jesus' followers do not fear people in a paralyzing sense, then they will confess Him. The meaning of Jesus denying a person probably refers to being deprived of salvation (cf. 10:22). Will Jesus deny Peter before the Father (see 26:70, 72)? This is unlikely. The tense of the verb **denies** indicates that if a person's life could be defined or summarized as a whole by the words, "He denied Me," then that person can expect to be denied by Jesus. But that label does not fit Peter's life. He surely denied Christ, but he repeatedly "confessed Christ" (Jn 21:15-17) thereafter. Jesus is not warning about an occasional lapse in one's witness that is otherwise found in a life punctuated by outspoken identification with Him.

10:34-39. Jesus must be confessed before people, even if His witnesses experience contention and martyrdom. **I did not come to bring peace** refers to dissension that they, and all His people, would experience because of their loyalty to Jesus. Eventually there will be peace on earth for His gospel is one of peace, but in the meantime even family members may be set at odds with one another. Breaking with one's family because of Jesus (v. 37) is to take up the **cross** and "lose one's life" in this world (vv. 38-39). It was common for a criminal to carry both the crosspiece of his crucifix and a plaque that delineated his crimes. Jesus probably meant that following Him could lead to such severe persecution that crucifixion might result. Verse 39 could be paraphrased, "He whose life pleases only himself will miss eternal life, and he whose life is lived for Me even to the point of death will find that eternal life awaits him."

10:40-42. What if a person is not a missionary? There are other ways to help the cause. Those who contribute even in small ways (giving **a cup of cold water to drink** to a weary, hot, roaming minister—probably what is meant by **little ones**) will share in the reward of those who are on the front lines.

11:1. To teach and preach are the same words found in the *inclusio* of 4:23 and 9:35. In 10:1, the mention of healing every kind of disease and every kind of sickness provided a continuation of the theme of Jesus' authority; in 11:1, the teaching aspect of His work continues.

III. The Reactions to the King-Messiah (11:2–12:50)

A. John Was Confused (11:2-15)

Matthew 11:2 provides a transition with John the Baptist inquiring about **the works of Christ**. Chapters 4–10 emphasized the authority of Christ based upon His teaching and healing ministry, and beginning in chap. 11 the main theme revolves around how one should respond to Jesus.

11:2-6. See 14:3 for John's imprisonment. John's question (v. 3) is understandable in light of his own prophesying about the Messiah coming with judgment (3:7-12), but there was little judgment so far in His ministry. In addition, most of the Jewish people anticipated a Messiah who would come as a great warrior king like David to free Israel from her oppressors (c. 164 BC, the SibOr 3:652-656; c. 63-48 BC, PssSol 17:1-4, 21-25, 30-32, 35-37, 45-46). Jesus' answer (vv. 4-5) draws heavily upon messianic texts from Isaiah (26:19; 29:18; 35:5-6; 42:7, 18; 61:1) as proof that He was **the Expected One**.

11:7-11. Jesus defended John's ministry. **A reed shaken by the wind** would have been a common sight along the Jordan where John baptized; but people did not go out to see just something commonplace or even something with worldly splendor (**soft clothing** belonged to the rich and powerful). John was **more than a prophet** (v. 9) from the standpoint that he was the one chosen to prepare the way for the Messiah (citing Ex 23:20 and Mal 3:1). John was greater than all from the standpoint that he was the one who would point to Christ more clearly than anyone else. But even those **least in the kingdom of**

heaven are greater than John, probably because those who are citizens of the messianic kingdom and who look back to the cross can give a more profound explanation of Jesus than John could.

11:12. Verse 12 is puzzling, but it probably should read, "The kingdom has violence done to it, and violent men are seeking to seize it." The verb **suffers violence** could be middle voice ("The kingdom is forcefully advancing itself" or something like it) but is probably a true passive judging from the parallel expression **violent men take it** ["violently seize" it] **by force**. The verse indicates the spiritual battle the opponents were waging against John and later Jesus as these opponents discouraged people from following them.

11:13-15. John himself is Elijah (v. 14), but not in the literal sense of Elijah descending to earth from heaven. Luke 1:17 says John came "in the spirit and power of Elijah," not unlike Elisha. God gave three orders to Elijah toward the end of his ministry (1Kg 19:15-16), only one completed by him before his ascension (1Kg 19:19), the others being accomplished by Elisha "in the spirit and power of Elijah" (2Kg 8:7-8; 9:1-3). At the transfiguration, it was not John the Baptist and Moses who joined Christ but Elijah and Moses.

B. The Masses Were Unresponsive (11:16-24)

11:16-19. In this little analogy, Jesus is symbolized by the children playing the flute for other children who refused to dance (cf. 11:19, where "playing the flute" corresponds to Jesus' "eating and drinking") and John is symbolized by the children who sang mournfully but other children did not mourn (cf. 11:18, where "singing a dirge" corresponds to John's refusal to eat or drink). **This generation** disregarded John and Jesus—John because of his asceticism and Jesus because of His "excessiveness." Both Jesus and John taught with **wisdom**, each in his own unique but complementary way, but the people found both repugnant. The **wisdom** John and Jesus voiced, however, was **vindicated by her deeds**; i.e., the works of John and Jesus (see 11:2) exonerated them from unwarranted accusations and showed the validity of the wisdom they articulated.

11:20-24. Woe refers to a condition of deep destitution, suffering, or pain. **Chorazin**, **Bethsaida**, and **Capernaum** were within about five miles of each other around the north end of the Sea of Galilee. In spite of the innumerable miracles Jesus performed there, as well as the amount of teaching, their reaction, based on these verses, was one of unbelief. Miracles do not always promote faith in unbelievers. **Tyre and Sidon** were Gentile cities north of Israel on the Mediterranean Sea, and **Sodom** needs no comment. Verses 21 and 23 give indirect evidence for Jesus' omniscience, for He knew what *might have happened* in these corrupt cities if He had done the kinds of miracles there that He performed in Galilee. Notably, today Chorazin, Bethsaida, and Capernaum are just ruins, but other cities in the region (Svat *aka* Safed, probably the "city set on a hill"; Magdala *aka* Migdal; Tiberias) are still bustling towns. When Jesus pronounces a woe, ruin is the result.

C. The Downhearted Were Encouraged (11:25-30)

11:25-27. Lord of heaven and earth expresses God's sovereignty and indicates that even the dissension that surrounded Jesus was part of His sovereign plan. He **revealed** spiritual truths about Jesus and the kingdom to **infants** (those who are of no account in the world's opinion) but hid them **from the wise and intelligent** (see 1Co 1:26-29). Both groups witnessed the same miracles and heard the same Teacher, but God gave special insight to those who welcomed Christ, and it pleased Him to do so (v. 26). Those who were sympathetic to Christ were the ones **to whom the Son wills to reveal** these realities, for He is the only one capable of adequately mediating knowledge of God to humankind.

11:28-30 The promise of **rest** was tied especially to the promises about the Son of David, the Messiah, providing security for the house of Israel (see Jr 23:5; 33:15-16; Ezk 34:15, 23-25; Am 9:11-15). That rest is found only in Jesus, and has eternal implications (Heb 4:1-11). The people were **weary and heavy-laden** because the excesses of the traditions of the Pharisees marginalized those who were spiritually "sick" (Mt 9:12) and even on the Sabbath left people hungry, maimed, and demon possessed (12:1-24). The religious leaders laid heavy burdens upon the people without providing any help (23:4) or showing mercy (9:13; 12:7; 23:23). On the other hand, Jesus' **burden is light** but not necessarily effortless. Anyone who has tried to embody the ethic of the Sermon on the Mount knows the requirements are agonizingly difficult. But they are **easy** and **light** in contrast to the heavy burdens of the Pharisees precisely because He is **gentle and humble in heart** and, as the Suffering Servant, bears His people's sins (Is 53:11-12). He does not break off a battered reed, nor snuff out the spark from a smoldering wick (Mt 12:20)—that is, He *helps* those who are demoralized. Jesus says, "**Come to Me**," and those who do find a challenging yoke, but also a compassionate Savior who encourages, loves, forgives, restores, strengthens, and saves (for this interpretation, see Jon Laansma, *I Will Give You Rest: The Rest Motif in the New Testament with Special Reference to Mt 11 and Heb 3-4*, Wissenschaftliche Untersuchungen zum Neuen Testament, Series 2 [Tübingen: Mohr Dieback Siebeck, 1997], 238-50). Rabbinic literature speaks of taking on the yoke of the Torah or the yoke of the commandments, meaning "adopting Torah," including the performance of Rabbinic instruction as a lifestyle. Jesus is contrasting following Him, which is light, with following Rabbinic Torah, which is burdensome (Mt 23:4). Perhaps the more severe expressions of Christianity have strayed from the kind of discipleship He offers.

D. The Leaders Were Antagonistic (12:1-50)

1. Regarding Sabbath Practices (12:1-21)

12:1-8. At that time provides a chronological connection with the events of chaps. 10–11. Thematically the connection may involve prime examples of the rest that Jesus provides in contrast to the heavy burdens of the religious leaders.

The **Sabbath** is mentioned here in Matthew for the first time, and chap. 12 begins a recurring theme of Sabbath controversies. One of the reasons was that during and after the exile (around 440 BC), Pharisaic Judaism began to develop rules that augmented biblical Sabbath law in order to "build a fence around the Law" (*m. Aboth* 1:1) so that one would not inadvertently violate it. Those additional rules are not found in the Hebrew Scriptures. Carrying a burden on the Sabbath was forbidden (Jr 17:21-24), but the later authorities felt the need to be more explicit about identifying what a burden was. They formulated dozens of rules so people would avoid carrying a burden on the Sabbath (a tailor could not carry around a needle stuck into his coat; one could not carry enough ink with which to write two letters of the alphabet, etc.). So, according to these traditions, when the disciples were picking **the heads of grain** off the stalks, they were guilty of reaping and of preparing food for consumption on the Sabbath, both banned under Pharisaic traditions.

What David did (vv. 3-4) is recorded in 1Sm 21:1-6. The **consecrated bread** was 12 loaves of bread placed on a special table in the tabernacle and later the temple, symbolizing God's presence with the tribes of Israel. Only the priests could eat these loaves (Ex 25:30; Lv 24:5-9), but David was no priest. Jesus' point is that the OT did not condemn David for his action. If the written Law could be suspended for David without consequence, then oral traditions could be suspended for Jesus and His followers. The rigidity of the Pharisees' interpretation of the Law was not in accord with Scripture itself and it could not explain the incident with David.

Even the priests **break the Sabbath and are innocent** (v. 5). On the Sabbath priests changed the consecrated bread (Lv 24:8) and offered double the number of animals for the burnt offering (Nm 28:9-10). If priests "broke" the Sabbath for the sake of the temple, and if Jesus is greater than the temple (v. 6), then He could "break" the Sabbath as well. The authority of the temple laws shielded the priests from guilt; the authority of Jesus shields His disciples from guilt. The Pharisees needed not only to keep the Law but to be compassionate (v. 7, see 9:13; Hs 6:6), a trait that many of them lacked as seen in their attitudes on this occasion. **For the Son of Man is Lord** ["boss"] **of the Sabbath** (v. 8) not only sums up Messiah's supremacy over the temple in v. 7, but also serves as the ground for the innocence of Jesus and the disciples. Jesus has the unequivocal authority to determine how to apply the Sabbath.

12:9-14. To heal on the Sabbath was to work. It was laid down in their oral tradition that only if life was in actual danger could one provide medical attention (*m. Yoma* 8:6; *m. Shabbat* 22:6), and then steps could be taken only to keep the sufferer from getting worse, not to improve his condition. **Withered** means "dried up, shriveled, lifeless."

In v. 11, the main question was simply whether the Sabbath was a day for doing beneficial activity or not. Judging from Ex 23:12, it was. Jesus' point was that if it were permissible to help an animal on the Sabbath, it was certainly permissible to help a person.

The man's hand **was restored to normal**—its shriveled, shrunken condition was reversed, perhaps expanding and becoming muscular before their eyes. The Pharisees' anger came because He rejected their view of the Sabbath and exposed their inconsistency; they were willing to help an animal on the Sabbath but not a person.

His mercy, His easy yoke, and light burden were highlighted in contrast to the heavy burden of the Pharisees.

12:15-21. Matthew 12 is thematically linked to Is 42:1-3, a passage viewed as messianic (see Tg. *Is* 42:1, and W. D. Davies and Dale C. Allison (*A Critical and Exegetical Commentary on the Gospel According to Saint Matthew*, ICC [Edinburgh: T. & T. Clark, 1991], 322-24). Those connections include: (1) the Spirit (Is 42:1; Mt 12:18) as the agent of Jesus' miracles and the focal point of the blasphemy of the Spirit in 12:24; (2) The double mention of Gentiles (Is 42:1, 3; Mt 12:18, 21), which fits with Matthew's and Jesus' emphasis on the gospel going to the Gentiles; (3) Is 42:2, which says that people did not **HEAR HIS VOICE IN THE STREETS**, a feature that corresponds with Mt 12:16, where Jesus told people to keep quiet about healing them, and (4) the mention of the **BATTERED REED** and **SMOLDERING WICK** (Is 42:3), which corresponds to His kindness in healing so many (Mt 12:15). Jesus was fulfilling the role of the prophesied Suffering Servant.

2. Regarding Exorcisms (12:22-37)

12:22-24. In the wake of the healing of the blind man, the crowds begin to wonder if Jesus was the **Son of David**. The syntax, however, indicates that the question was asked with some doubt. The **Pharisees** countered that idea by claiming connivance between Jesus and **Beelzebul the ruler of the demons**. **Beelzebul** may have come from the Hebrew wo*alzebub* ("lord of the flies," with "flies" serving as a euphemism for "manure"), a mocking takeoff of *Ba'alzebul* this should read *Ba'alzebul* ("Prince Baal"), a pagan deity (see 2Kg 1:2-3, 16). It was clearly intended by the Pharisees pejoratively, along with **ruler of the demons**, for the Devil.

12:25-30. These verses presuppose that Satan also has a well-organized kingdom. The reference to a kingdom, a city, and a house shows that in large or small organizations, internal division wreaks havoc. Jesus responded to their accusation with three arguments. (1) He showed the absurdity of their view. **How then will his kingdom stand?** (v. 26). It made no sense for the Devil to give a person power if that power was used to ransack his own kingdom. (2) He showed the inconsistency of their view. **Your sons** were the disciples of the Pharisees (i.e., other Pharisees), and Pharisees sometimes engaged in exorcisms. But exorcisms by Jesus and exorcisms by the Pharisees were assigned by them to two different sources (Beelzebul and the Spirit of God, respectively). Jesus rightly brands this as inconsistent. (3) He showed what was actually taking place through the exorcisms (vv. 28-29). **The kingdom of God has come upon you** suggests that with the presence of the King some effects of the kingdom were also present, including exorcising demons. The connection between vv. 28 and 29 is that Jesus was not part of Satan's kingdom. Rather, He was successfully attacking Satan's kingdom, called the **strong man's house**. **His property** was the people under Satan's sway. Verse 30 unpacks the consequences of Jesus' battle with Satan. There could be no middle ground: one was, and is, either on God's side with Christ or on Satan's side.

12:31-32. In v. 31, Jesus stopped explaining and started warning. On **blasphemy**, see 9:3. Most scholars agree that the **blasphemy against the** Holy **Spirit** refers to attributing the miracles Jesus performed through the power of the Spirit to the evil one. The title **Son of Man** was used in contexts that emphasized His humility associated with the incarnation (see 8:20). Perhaps speaking against the **Son of Man** was pardonable because Jesus' identity was veiled. Someone might reject His words but eventually be forgiven if the person accepted the evidence of His miracles performed through the Spirit. But if *that* evidence was rejected, then there was no other evidential "safety net" that could keep one from falling into spiritual ruin.

It is unlikely that this sin can be committed today, for conditions are different; Jesus is not physically present performing miracles, validating His identity as the Son of Man and Son of God. Some aver that unbelief is the unpardonable sin. However, every person who trusts Christ is pardoned for the sin of unbelief. If one dies in a state of unbelief, that sin is not so much unpardon*able* as it is unpardon*ed*. Other texts (Heb 6:4-6; 10:27-29; 1Jn 5:16) are cited as references to the unpardonable sin. However, those texts seem to describe individuals who were outwardly and superficially sympathetic to faith in Jesus, but then apostatized, showing that they were never saved. Those situations are different from Mt 12.

This sin **shall not be forgiven him, either in this age or in the age to come**. Those who committed the sin in Jesus' day were beyond salvation. The **age to come** is not "heaven" or "purgatory," but is the messianic kingdom on earth when Jesus once again will be physically present performing miracles. Some will reject Him then also (Rv

20:7-10). The conditions will exist for this sin to be committed again without hope of forgiveness.

12:33-37. The Pharisees' evil words (v. 24) originated from the evil that **fills the heart** (v. 34). **Make the tree** (v. 33) refers to arboriculture, developing and cultivating trees to produce the desired fruit. If the fruit is bad, the tree is defective. The Pharisees' reaction (their "fruit") to Jesus' ministry indicated that their heart was faulty. They would be held accountable in the judgment for **every careless** ("worthless," "useless," "unproductive") **word**. No one is "justified by words." But good words (**good treasure**) demonstrate that one has a good heart, which, in context, means acknowledging that what Jesus says about Himself is true. Words dismissing Jesus demonstrate an evil heart that will result in condemnation.

3. Regarding Signs (12:38-45)

12:38-42. The irony of v. 38 is that His earlier miracles led the Pharisees to accuse Jesus of working with the Devil, yet they wanted more miracles. **Sign** means "an unusual act with special meaning," and here carries the nuance of a miraculous act. The **scribes and Pharisees** were looking for such an astounding display of power that all reservations about Jesus could be dismissed. Perhaps if Ursa Major (the Big Bear constellation) would run across the sky and bite Orion's belt—*then* they could believe. The THREE DAYS AND THREE NIGHTS causes some concern since Jesus only spent Friday and Saturday night in the tomb. But Jewish people regarded even a part of a day as "a day and a night" (see 1Sm 30:12-13; 2Ch 10:5, 12; Est 4:16; 5:1). The Gentile **men of Nineveh** and **the Queen of the South** (1Kg 10:1; 2Ch 9:1) make unusual protagonists in Jesus' rebuke, but they are commendable inasmuch as they responded appropriately to those with considerably less authority than Jesus.

12:43-45. The key to understanding this brief allegory is in v. 45c, d. **This evil generation** is used in both vv. 39 and 45, linking the two warnings together. Jesus' ministry brought profound benefits for many (12:15), but most remained either noncommittal or hostile toward Him. As a result, they were worse off (**the last state of that man becomes worse than the first**) because eventually God would judge them for their antipathy.

E. Family Ties Were Narrowed (12:46-50)

12:46-50. The point of this paragraph is to encourage people to follow Jesus even in the general environment of animosity. **Brothers** cannot refer to Joseph's sons through a previous marriage to someone other than Mary; this would make Joseph's oldest son the legal heir to David's throne, not Jesus. Jesus has to be Joseph's legal first-born to qualify for the throne. Jesus is not undermining the importance of blood ties, but being a follower of Jesus supersedes family commitment, and those who follow are adopted into a new family with God as their Father (Rm 8:15-17). On doing **the will of My Father**, see the comments on 7:21-23.

IV. The Kingdom and the King-Messiah in the Present Era (13:1-52)

A. The Parable of the Sower and the Soils (13:1-23)

In many ways chap. 12 is the watershed chapter of Matthew. There the leaders formally rejected Jesus and committed the unpardonable sin. They rejected the King. In light of this, what happens to the kingdom He offered? Jesus answered that question in Mt 13 with eight parables about the nature of the kingdom in light of the nation's rejection of the King.

"Parable" could be defined many ways, but the working definition here is that it is a true-to-life story designed for teaching some specific spiritual truth usually pertaining to the King, the kingdom of God, or the citizens of the kingdom.

13:1-9. See 13:18-23 below. Often seeds would be scattered on the ground from leather pouches as a farmer walked the field. Sometimes the fields were plowed, then seed scattered, and fields plowed again. In the parable, some seed **fell beside the road** (v. 4) where footpaths often bordered the fields. There were **rocky places** just below the surface of the soil in many areas. The plant could grow, but eventually withered under the sun because it did not get the moisture or nutrients it needed. **Thorns** often grow when no other plants will. In the rugged terrain of Israel, they can take over an area so the crops are **choked. Let him hear** (v. 9) served as both a warning and an invitation by Jesus to His hearers to exercise their minds to grasp the spiritual significance of this and the other public parables.

13:10-17. Up to this point in Jesus' ministry He had not once taught the crowds in parables. This is why the disciples questioned Him about it (v. 10). He teaches the crowds predominantly in parables throughout the remainder of Matthew's gospel. Verses 10-17 explain why. The disciples have the privilege of knowing the **mysteries of the kingdom of heaven**, but not all do. "Mystery" means "a secret" or "that which is hidden," the contents usually revealed to a select group. Here it refers to truth Jesus was revealing about the **kingdom of heaven** for the first time (for "kingdom of heaven, see 3:1-4). In the OT prophecies, the kingdom would come to earth in a cataclysmic, civilization-shattering way, accompanied with judgment of the nations and the restoration of Israel (see Is 2; Dn 2, 7; Zch 14). But with the rejection of the King, Jesus reveals new aspects of the kingdom not forecast by the OT. George Eldon Ladd (*The Presence of the Future: The Eschatology of Biblical Realism* [Grand Rapids, MI: Eerdmans, 1974], 225), wrote, "The new truth, now given to men by revelation in the person and mission of Jesus, is that *the Kingdom which is to come finally in apocalyptic power, as foreseen by Daniel, has in fact entered into the world in advance in a hidden form to work secretly within and among men*" (italics Ladd's). In the end, the kingdom will come in all its outward power at Jesus' second coming, but in the wake of the nation rejecting the King, the "mystery form" of the kingdom is at work in the world initially.

The parables were designed to reveal truth to the privileged few, including the disciples, but to conceal it from the spiritually dull (vv. 12-13)—especially the religious leaders and opponents of Jesus seen in Mt 12. The parables thus have a dual function, the key being God's elective purposes. However, as in much of Scripture, divine election and human responsibility are not mutually exclusive; the spiritual receptivity of the hearer plays a role in this, and if one did not persist in rejecting Jesus, he or she could later embrace Him. The citation from Is 6:9-10 (vv. 14-15), spoken by God through the prophet, was for Isaiah's contemporaries, and addressed their spiritual unresponsiveness. That citation served as an analogy for the Jewish rejection of Jesus.

13:18-23. In the parable, the **seed** represented **the word of the kingdom** (v. 19), and Jesus was the sower. The seed **sown beside the road** was those who heard the word about the kingdom but who did not understand it (13:9), and Satan (symbolized by the birds in v. 4) hindered their understanding of the truth (see 2Co 4:3-4). The **seed sown on the rocky places** represented one who was superficial, lacking the ability to follow through, especially **when . . . persecution arises** (vv. 20-21). The seed among **thorns** (v. 22) represented the person distracted by material concerns (worry, wealth) that **choke the word** (see 1Tm 6:10). The **good soil** receives and understands the word being spread by the King and produces a bountiful crop (see Mt 13:12).

A crucial question emerges: Which of these four is "saved?" All agree the first is not. All agree that the fourth is. The other two may have been saved since they seemed to have "life," but this is unlikely, for several reasons. First, none of the first three produced fruit, so the fourth seed was in a distinct category. Second, John's and Jesus' teaching suggested that avoiding judgment was not dependent upon the apparent presence of life but upon the production of good fruit (Mt 3:10; 7:19). Third, in Mt 10:22, 32-33, Jesus said that endurance *during times of persecution* were indications that one was truly saved, but the second seed sown in rocky soil falls away when persecution arose, making it likely that the second seed (and probably the third) was not saved.

What is the point of this parable? Prophecies of the kingdom in the OT did not envision this kind of "coming" of the kingdom quietly and spiritually into the hearts of people as they responded correctly to the Word. None of this precludes the climactic coming of the kingdom in the future at the second coming of Christ.

B. The Parable of the Wheat and Tares (13:24-30; cf. 13:36-43)

13:24-30. For the interpretation of this parable, see the comments below on 13:36-43. The second parable is about one of the mysteries of the kingdom. It reveals how, during the present age before its climactic coming, the kingdom contains diabolical counterfeits, something not seen in the OT concept of the coming kingdom from which all enemies of God are removed.

C. The Parable of the Mustard Seed (13:31-32)

13:31-32. In later rabbinic thought, the **mustard seed** was proverbial for smallness (*m. Niddah* 5:2). It was the smallest seed regularly cultivated in Israel. In a single season modern mustard bushes can grow in excess of ten feet tall. The point of the parable is that *in the OT* gradual growth was not part of the coming of the kingdom. However, this newly revealed truth about the kingdom, the "mystery form" of the kingdom during this present era, does grow gradually into a large entity. This gradual growth does not preclude a future coming that is sudden, enormous, and earthshaking. The **BIRDS** may refer to malevolent elements found in its mystery form, but birds do not always represent evil in Scripture (see Mt 6:26), and may be a feature in the parable simply to indicate the large size of the bush.

D. The Parable of the Leaven (13:33)

13:33. Bread was usually baked using a piece of dough with active yeast in it from a previous batch of dough. **Leaven** sometimes refers to corrupting influences (Mt 16:6; 1Co 5:6), but not always (Lv 7:13; 23:15-18). Here the **leaven** probably has much the same function as the mustard seed, indicating small origins with gradual growth that permeates a much larger entity such as the world. The **leaven** in this parable infuses **three pecks**, a huge amount enough for 100-150 people. Jesus' small band would have a gradual but wide effect upon the world, then subsequently the kingdom would come in full force.

E. The Reason for the Parables (13:34-35)

13:34-35. Psalm 78:1-2 is cited in v. 35. It was written by Asaph, poet and prophet under David and Solomon. Psalm 78 is an extended review of the history of the Jewish people from the patriarchs through David's time. The main theme in the psalm is God's faithfulness despite the people's disobedience. Asaph calls his psalm a "parable" and "dark sayings" (78:2), probably indicating that he was drawing insights from historic events not usually seen in them. Asaph wrote the psalm to instruct his own and following generations. When Matthew says Jesus taught in **parables** it was **to fulfill** typologically what Asaph had done, i.e., presenting new insights about the kingdom of God that would come in spite of the people's unfaithfulness.

F. The Parable of the Wheat and Tares, cont. (13:36-43; cf. 13:24-30)

13:36-43. In v. 36 Jesus withdrew from the boat (13:2) and the crowds, and continued instructing the disciples in parables privately. He explained the referents of the elements of the parable of the wheat and the tares. The **good seed** is **the sons of the kingdom** placed in the **world** by Jesus. **The devil** places **the tares** in the **field**, i.e., **sons of the evil one** in the **world**. **Tares** bore a strong resemblance to wheat and could not be distinguished from it until a crop matured. This **enemy** places counterfeits of **the sons of the kingdom** (true followers of Jesus) in the world to hinder the spread of the mystery form of the kingdom during the present age. In the future when the kingdom fully comes the **Son of Man** will remove these fakes from the kingdom (**stumbling blocks, and those who commit lawlessness**) and judge them. The moment Jesus returns to earth at the second coming the kingdom arrives as well, but there is a short period of time in which Jesus judges those not aligned with Him (1,335 days, Dn 12:12; see the comments there). At the end of that period of judgment, **the sons of the evil one** are removed from the kingdom and experience **weeping and gnashing of teeth**—a favorite expression of Jesus for eschatological judgment (Mt 8:5-13 and see the comments there; also 13:50; 22:13; 24:51; 25:30). At that time, finally, **THE RIGHTEOUS** will share and enjoy the glory of God with Him in His kingdom.

G. The Parables of the Buried Treasure and Pearl of Great Price (13:44-46)

13:44-46. The parables of the treasure and the pearl emphasize the great worth of the mystery form of the kingdom. Jewish prophetic thought did not view the kingdom as something as inconspicuous as a buried box of valuables or a priceless pearl that one might providentially stumble across. It was to come powerfully and openly from God alone at the end of the age. Jesus tells us virtually nothing about the situation surrounding the **treasure** and the ethics of the man who obtains it; these do not fit His purpose. The point seems to be that while the kingdom is not physically resplendent, it is nevertheless priceless and one *must* obtain it at all costs. **Pearls** were more highly prized in the ancient world than today (see Jb 28:18; 1Tm 2:9; Rv 17:4; 18:12, 16). This mystery form of the kingdom is worth obtaining, no matter the cost.

H. The Parable of the Dragnet (13:47-50)

13:47-50. Not unlike the parable of the wheat and tares, the parable of the dragnet indicates that the mystery form of the kingdom encompasses good and evil components, and only the final "sweep of the net" sorts them out. That the righteous are not mentioned indicates the emphasis of this parable. Jesus is concerned with the final removal of evil, when the net is full at the end of the fishing. This is not about church discipline. The focus here is on the state of the kingdom when the final judgment occurs. Initially it includes both the righteous and the wicked, but an infallible sorting out will certainly take place so that only the righteous remain. For v. 50, cf. the comments on 8:5-13.

I. The Parables Gave New Revelation about the King and Kingdom (13:51-52)

13:51-52. The **scribe** probably refers to disciples who will teach other disciples. The **head of a household** in Jesus' teaching was one who dispensed items for others (20:1-16; 21:33-43). The **treasure** sometimes referred to what one produces from one's heart (12:35). So the disciple-scribes must teach **things new and old** for others. This has special relevance for the Twelve, but the entire Church is included since it is founded upon their teaching. **Things new and old** indicates Jesus taught new truth about the mysteries of the kingdom, but old truth clearly seen in the OT as well, and that His followers must teach both. He taught what is found in the OT about the coming of the kingdom—future separation and judgment and the enormity of the kingdom. But there is also new material in this chapter, the mysteries of the kingdom, which included small beginnings, gradual growth, permeation, and the mixture of good and bad elements. The followers of Jesus are to teach the old and the new.

V. The Withdrawal, Help, and Opposition of the King-Messiah: Four Cycles (13:53–16:28)

A. Cycle #1: The Ministry in Nazareth (13:53–14:12)

1. Jesus Withdrew: To Nazareth (13:53)

13:53-58. This section is the first of four cycles with parallel structure that run through Mt 16:28. Matthew 13:53-58 presents all the elements of each section. Matthew's structure continues to show the ongoing kindness of Jesus in the face of mounting opposition. See the table "Parallel Cycles in Matthew 13:53–16:28" below.

2. Jesus Helped: By Teaching in the Synagogue (13:54)

It is not clear what **His hometown** (v. 54) is. In 14:13 Jesus enters a boat, supporting the possibility that it is Capernaum. But more than likely it is Nazareth, and Matthew omits the return to Capernaum. He **began teaching them in their synagogue**. This would, under normal circumstances, be a blessing for these people. But their hard-heartedness left them without benefit from His teaching.

3. Jesus Faced Opposition: From His Kin and King Herod (13:55–14:12)

The residents of Nazareth fixated upon His humble beginnings, and failed to be led past these by His powerful ministry and thereby grasp who He truly was (vv. 55-56). The proverb **A prophet is not without honor except in his hometown and in his own household** (v. 57) is similar in force to the modern adage, "Familiarity breeds contempt." The relationship of the paucity of **miracles** and **their unbelief** is not that their lack of faith hampered Jesus' power. **He did not do many miracles there** because they did not bring their sick to Him at all, precisely because they did not believe in Him.

14:1-2. One of the themes of chap. 13 was the gradual growth of the mystery form of the kingdom (13:31-33) in spite of mounting opposition to Jesus by the religious leaders (chap. 12) and others (13:53-58). Here the governing authorities opposed Him, namely **Herod the tetrarch** (b. 20 BC). This was Herod Antipas, one of Herod the Great's sons, who ruled from 4 BC until AD 39 over the region of Galilee and Perea, where John the Baptist and Jesus ministered. It is the same Herod who assisted Pilate in the trial of Jesus (Lk 23:6-12). **John the Baptist . . . risen from the dead** was probably a reflection of superstition and not reflective of a well-rounded theology of resurrection. Jesus and John both preached the kingdom of heaven, which may have led Antipas to this conclusion.

14:3-5. The date of John's imprisonment is unknown, but it is mentioned in 4:12 and 11:2. It was occasioned by John's denunciation of Antipas, who around AD 29 became attracted to and eventually married the wife of his half brother, Herod Philip. Her name was **Herodias**, and she was also Antipas's niece, the daughter of another half brother, Aristobulus. She insisted that Antipas divorce his Nabatean wife, daughter of the king of Petra, Aretes IV, an act that was both a breach of a political alliance and a personal affront. Hostilities arose between them, and eventually Aretes started a war that led to Antipas's downfall in AD 36.

The Law forbade a man marrying his brother's wife (Lv 18:16; 20:21) unless the brother died childless (Dt 25:5). Herod Philip was alive and

Parallel Cycles in Matthew 13:53–16:28

	He Withdrew	He Helped	He was Opposed
Cycle #1	13:53	13:54	13:55–14:12
Cycle #2	14:13	14:14-36	15:1-20
Cycle #3	15:21	15:22-39	16:1-4c
Cycle #4	16:4d	16:5-20	16:21-28

had a daughter, Salome. John challenged Antipas's marriage to Herodias on these grounds.

14:6-12. Matthew omits the unseemly details (cf. Mk 6:14-29). Salome was probably 12–14 years of age, akin to an 18–22 year old today. It was culturally acceptable in Roman settings for a young woman, even a princess, to dance in such an audience. Antipas was **grieved** (v. 9), perhaps because he found John interesting (Mk 6:20), perhaps because he did not want John executed this way. According to Josephus (*Ant.*, 18.119), John was executed at Machaerus, Antipas's fortress east of the Dead Sea. After his disciples buried the body, they **went and reported to Jesus**, possibly to warn Him (see his withdrawal in v. 13; also 2:22; 4:12) or possibly to look to Him to take up John's mantle.

B. Cycle #2: Feeding the Five Thousand at Bethsaida (14:13–15:20)

1. Jesus Withdrew: To a Secluded Spot (14:13)

14:13. Beginning in 14:13, Matthew presents the second cycle of withdrawal (14:13), helping people (14:14-36), and opposition (15:1-20). See the table at 13:53 entitled "Parallel Cycles in Matthew 13:53–16:28."

2. Jesus Helped: By Feeding the Multitude and Stilling a Storm (14:14-36)

14:14-21. The site of the feeding of the five thousand is unknown, but may have been in the vicinity of Bethsaida on the northeast shore of the Sea of Galilee (cf. Mk 6:45). The traditional site of Tabgah on the northwest shore is unlikely because of v. 34, for Gennesaret is located close to it and would not accommodate the long boat ride. The numbers of the **five loaves and two fish** (v. 17) are probably not symbolic but serve to show the scant resources despite which Jesus was able to help the crowd. Matthew gives few clues explaining why he recorded the process of distributing the food (**took the five loaves . . . looking up . . . blessed the food . . . breaking the loaves**, and giving them **to the disciples**); these things were so often done at a typical meal that they would not have been included, except Matthew probably intends to link them to other miraculous feedings (e.g., through Moses, Exodus 16; Elijah, 1Kg 17:8-16, and Elisha, 2Kg 4:1-7, 42-44). Matthew also may be forecasting the Lord's table (Mt 26:26). There also He took bread, blessed it, and gave it to the disciples (same words both passages). Perhaps the point is that the ultimate and wildly abundant provision for Israel (the **twelve full baskets** are probably symbolic) will no longer be found in the one who brought the Law nor in the prophets, but in Jesus.

14:22-33. Once again, Matthew gives no clues regarding Jesus' actions in sending away the disciples, dismissing the crowds, and finding solitude to pray. In the stilling of the storm in 8:23-27, the main threat to the disciples was the waves, which were on the verge of swamping the boat. Here it is a **contrary** wind that hindered their progress (v. 24). **The fourth watch of the night** (v. 25) would have been between 3:00 and 6:00 a.m., probably closer to the latter since there was apparently just enough light for the disciples to see Jesus, though not to recognize Him. The disciples thought they saw a **ghost** (v. 26; Gk. *phantasma*)—people with corporeal bodies could not do what they saw Jesus doing. When Jesus said **it is I**, the Gk. words are *ego eimi*, a phrase used in Isaiah 40–50 (LXX) by God when He alone claims to have the power to rescue His people (cf. Is 41:10; 43:1-2, 10; 45:22; 46:4; 48:17). Is 41:10 says, "Do not fear ["fear" here is *phobou*; in Mt 14:27, *phobeisthe*—same word, different person and mood], for I am with you; Do not anxiously look about you, for I am [ego eimi] your God. . . . Surely I will uphold you with My righteous right hand." Peter's ability to walk on the water (vv. 28-29) was contingent upon Jesus' identity as **God's Son**. As long as Peter focused in faith upon Jesus, the authoritative Son, he could walk on water as Jesus did. Matthew indicates that when Jesus' followers rely upon Him and do not **doubt**, they will be able to do remarkable things on the basis of His strength (opening the kingdom, 16:19; "moving mountains," 17:20; reaching the nations, 28:18-20). When Peter "anxiously looked about him" (Is 41:10) at the waves he needed Jesus to stretch out His **hand** (v. 31). In other OT passages, God is the one who rescues His people from the sea (Ex 14:10–15:21; Ps 107:23-32; Jnh 1:4–2:10). Jesus took that prerogative for Himself and intimated that He was fulfilling this divine role. On the disciples' exclamation **You are certainly God's Son!** see the comments on 16:14-17.

14:34-36. Gennesaret (modern Nof Ginosar) is on the NW side of the Sea of Galilee, about three miles southwest of Capernaum. See 9:20 for the woman being healed by touching His cloak.

David Turner (*Matthew*, BECNT [Grand Rapids, MI: Baker, 2008], 376) offers a helpful summary of the significance of chap. 14. "Looking back on Matt. 14, one can conclude that in the midst of growing opposition, the authority of the kingdom is also growing [as assured in the parables of chap. 13] through the miracles and through the weak but genuine and maturing faith of the disciples."

3. Jesus Faced Opposition: From Pharisees and Scribes Over Oral Traditions (15:1-20)

Matthew 15:1-20 continues the second cycle by presenting the heightened opposition of the **Pharisees and scribes . . . from Jerusalem** (v. 1) (see the comments on 14:13, and the table at 13:53, "Parallel Cycles in Matthew 13:53–16:28"). The flow of Matthew's argument may include the theme of ritual defilement. External incidental contact with unclean things (sick people, 14:34-36; bread "defiled" by unclean hands, 15:1-20) does not defile a person, but what comes out of the heart does.

15:1-9. The **Pharisees and scribes . . . from Jerusalem** probably denote an official party that has come to engage in a theological investigation of the popular Teacher who staunchly opposed some from their sect (12:38). The **tradition of the elders** (v. 2) refers to the "fence around the Law" put in place by the ancient Jewish scribes (see the comments on 12:1-8 on the Sabbath). Jesus' disciples did **not wash their hands when they eat bread**. The Pharisees and scribes believed that hands could become ritually unclean by a host of ways. That impurity could be transferred to food when someone held it while eating. Defiled food would then make unclean the entire person, and those who were serious about their status before God would hardly allow this (cf. John Nolland, *The Gospel of Matthew: A Commentary on the Greek Text*, NIGTC [Grand Rapids, MI: Eerdmans, 2005], 611–15 for the details and bibliography; cf. also *m. Yadaim* for the need for washing hands). However, there was nothing quite like this in the Law for anyone other than priests or community leaders on special occasions (Ex 30:17-21; Dt 21:1-9), or if one had a bodily discharge (Lv 15:11). Jesus' answer (v. 3) confronted the leaders with an accusation similar to the one they levied against Him and the disciples; when the disciples did not wash, they appeared to dismiss the Pharisees' **tradition**, but when the Pharisees kept their own traditions they would sometimes **transgress the commandment of God**, the more serious of the two shortcomings. Jesus illustrated this with reference to the fifth commandment (Ex 20:12; Dt 5:16; Ex 21:17). The phrase **has been given to God** (v. 5) reflects a tradition called *korban* (cf. Mk 7:11), "a gift" pledged to God, no longer allowed to be used in common affairs. One could make a vow to turn over all his assets to the temple upon his death but retain use of them until then. However, these assets could not be transferred to others nor used to benefit anyone else (the poor; one's family) since they belonged to God (Blomberg, *Matthew*, 238). **Invalidated** (v. 6) means "to disregard or refuse the authority or power of something," in this case **the word of God** which must have sole authority for the life of God's children. Religious traditions often do not supplement Scripture; they supplant Scripture.

Jesus cited Is 29:13 (vv. 7-9) which addressed Jerusalem (called "Ariel" in Is 29:1, 2, 7) with God's plans to deliver her from the Assyrians (Is 29:1-8). In spite of what He would do, the city would continue to worship Him in a perfunctory manner, as they had always done (their reverence for Me consists of tradition learned by rote, 29:13), with their hearts far from Him. Jesus makes a typological connection between the people's reaction to the Word of God given through Isaiah and the people's reaction in Jesus' day to the Word of God given through Him. The worship of those who substitute human religious traditions for the Word is **VAIN** ("to accomplish nothing," "to have no result," "to be as though nothing has happened")—no good comes of it unless it conforms to the Word and flows from a warm heart.

15:10-11. So serious was the Pharisaic neglect of Scripture that Jesus initiated an opportunity to teach the **crowd**. Verses 17-20 develop v. 11. What one ate was important in the OT and could result in one being unclean (see the context of Lv 11:24, 39-40). **Defile** means "to be profane, ritually unacceptable to God." Jesus indicates that food was morally neutral (Mk 7:19); the problem was not what one ate but what one did. The more fundamental purpose of Jesus was not so much to show that food laws were obsolete as much as that other matters deserved a higher priority. Matthew 15:11 with Mk 7:19 sounded the death knell of dietary laws for the Church, but it was not Jesus' primary purpose here.

15:12-14. Jesus ascribed the Pharisees' taking offense to their being plants **which My heavenly Father did not plant**. This alludes to Is 60:21; 61:3, where restored Israel is right with God on the basis of His gracious action. The Pharisees were not the recipients of God's restorative work, now manifested in Jesus. As a result, they would be **uprooted** (judged) and resist Jesus' ministry. That God did not plant them, and that Jesus told Peter, "Leave them!" (NET) is reminiscent of the parable of the wheat and the tares. The landowner lets both grow together until the harvest when they are separated and the tares (sons of the evil one, 13:38) are judged (13:30, 40-41). The Pharisees were **blind guides** in that they were blind to the true intent and "weightier matters" of the Law, as well as to their own unenviable condition, and could not be counted on to lead others safely in spiritual matters.

15:15-20. Jesus commanded the crowd to hear and understand (v. 10), suggesting that He anticipated the difficulty of His instruction. The disciples had a private audience with Jesus and received further instruction. For the comments on 15:16-19, see above on 15:10-11. **To eat with unwashed hands** (v. 20) forms an *inclusio* with the phrase "they do not wash their hands" in v. 2. This signals that Jesus' main point in the discussion was to deal with the sub-biblical oral traditions of the Pharisees, which often obscured the true requirements of the Law.

C. Cycle #3: Tyre and Sidon and Feeding the Four Thousand (15:21–16:4c)

1. Jesus Withdrew: To the Region of Tyre and Sidon (15:21)

15:21. This begins the third cycle of Matthew's "He withdrew, He helped, He was opposed" structure running through 16:28 (see the table at 13:53-58, "Parallel Cycles in Matthew 13:53–16:28"). **The district of Tyre and Sidon** provides an important geographical note. Both cities were on the Mediterranean coast, Tyre being about 30 miles northwest of Capernaum, Sidon about 25 miles north of Tyre, and both in the Roman province of Syria. **The district** suggests that Jesus may not have gone all the way to the cities, so that the farthest north He traveled may have been to the district of Caesarea Philippi (16:13).

2. Jesus Helped: By Assisting the Canaanite Woman and Feeding Many (15:22-39)

15:22-28. The **Canaanite woman** (v. 22) makes an unlikely heroine, as Canaanites were the indigenous people almost displaced by the Hebrews and their perpetual enemies (Jos 3:10; Jdg 1:1). How she addressed Jesus, however, sounded very Jewish (see the plea of the blind men in Mt 9:27-28 and 20:30-31) and indicates well-rounded knowledge of His mission and power. Once again the disciples show how calloused they were (see 14:15), and Jesus seemed ready to dismiss her (**I was sent only to . . . Israel**, vv. 23c-24). When she became more insistent (v. 25), He gave a further explanation in v. 26. The **children's bread** is probably a metaphor for the covenant blessings intended for the Jewish people, and **dogs** a reference to Gentiles as those outside of the covenant community of Israel. Her response in v. 27 indicated a surprising level of insight regarding the relationship of the Jewish people's covenant blessings and the benefits they provide for Gentiles (see Gn 12:3; Rm 11:17-18; Eph 2:11-22). The salvation-historical priority of Jesus was to reach the Jewish people, but as the Great Commission (Mt 28:18-20) indicates, even Gentiles benefit from the Jewish Messiah.

15:29-31. It is not clear where this episode takes place. **By the Sea of Galilee** is probably on the southeastern shore in the Gentile region of Decapolis (see Mk 7:31), a fact bolstered by the boat ride into the Jewish region of Magadan (v. 39), probably Magdala, on the northwest shore of the Sea. The textual clues in Matthew do not make this reconstruction certain, however. Like Moses, Jesus went **up on the mountain** and healed a number of the Gentiles there. The crumbs that blessed the Canaanite woman are now applied to a much wider group, indicating Jesus' intent to broaden His ministry to encompass Gentiles.

15:32-39. The similarities with the feeding of the 5,000 in Mt 14:15ff. are obvious, but there are differences. Here Jesus was probably in a Gentile region with Gentile people, He went up on a mountain, the crowd was with Him three days, Jesus initiated this feeding, the amount of the provisions and leftovers differ, and the size of the crowd is smaller. The point of this miracle may be to indicate that Jesus would include Gentiles in the scope of His ministry and that they would participate in the great messianic banquet that described the kingdom, along with the Jewish people. Carson ("Matthew," 358) explains the unbelief of the disciples in light of Jn 6:26. There Jesus rebuked the crowds for following Him in order to receive nothing more than food. It is possible that the disciples thought He might not feed a crowd again because of that previous episode. In addition, this second feeding miracle parallels the two feeding miracles prompted by Moses (Ex 16; Nm 11), suggesting that Jesus was the new Moses. It is impossible to determine if the **seven large baskets** are symbolic, as Matthew does not give any helpful clues.

3. Jesus Faced Opposition: From the Pharisees and Sadducees Who Wanted a Sign (16:1-4c)

16:1-4. It is not easy to determine the flow of the argument here. Matthew may have included 16:1-4 to demonstrate the stark contrast between the (probably) Gentile recipients of blessings in 15:21-38 who also received remarkable signs and the complete blindness of the religious leaders.

The Pharisees and Sadducees were hostile sects but united in their opposition of Jesus. On the **sign from heaven** (v. 1) and **the sign of Jonah** (v. 4), see 12:38-40. These religious leaders could forecast the weather, which is always difficult because conditions change so quickly. But in spite of the indisputable miracles Jesus performed, they could not comprehend that they were **the signs of the** (messianic) **times**.

D. Cycle #4: The Leaven of the Pharisees and Teaching the Disciples (16:4d–16:28)

1. Jesus Withdrew: To the Other Side of the Sea (16:4d)

16:4d. And He left them and went away begins the fourth cycle involving Jesus withdrawing, helping someone, and then being opposed. See the table at 13:53-58 above, "Parallel Cycles in Matthew 13:53–16:28").

2. Jesus Helped: By Teaching His Disciples (16:5-20)

16:5-6. Mark 8:22 notes that Jesus and the disciples came to Bethsaida, on the northeast shore of the Sea of Galilee, at the conclusion of the boat trip. Matthew 16:5 makes it sound as if the disciples traveled without Jesus, while 14:13 and 15:39 sound as if Jesus sailed without them. Unless the text is clear that they traveled separately (cf. 14:22), the assumption must be that they were together. The focus here is upon the disciples whose negligence in bringing bread (v. 5) becomes the point of the episode.

The **leaven of the Pharisees and Sadducees** (v. 6) is explained in v. 12 as the teaching of the Pharisees and Sadducees. A small amount of dough with active yeast could make a large batch of unleavened dough rise. **Leaven** sometimes, though not always, refers to evil influences (Lk 12:1; 1Co 5:6-8). The metaphoric reference to leaven stands for the poisonous influence of the religious leaders who sought to turn the people against Jesus. According to 27:20-26, they were successful.

16:7-12. Verse 7 indicates that the disciples did not understand Jesus. They may have thought He was warning them not to buy bread from the leaders (v. 6). Their preoccupation was with their lack of bread and presumably the hardship that might bring, whereas Jesus' concern was with more potent issues. The disciples' anxiety about food was unfounded in light of the care and the power of Jesus, who recounts the two feeding miracles as a reminder of both. The disciples are still **men of little faith** (v. 8). Jesus will provide the mundane things needed for survival. What the disciples—then and now—needed to **watch out and beware of** (v. 6) was not the lack of physical provisions but the subtle permeation and influence of false teaching, hypocrisy (Pharisees; cf. 23:13, 15), and unbelief (Sadducees; cf. 22:23).

16:13. The disciples demonstrated a considerable lack of spiritual insight in 16:1-12, but in 16:13-20 God overcame that through the revelation given to Peter. **Caesarea Philippi** was about 25 miles north of the Sea of Galilee. The city, originally called Paneas, was given by Caesar Augustus to Herod the Great in 20 BC, and Herod promptly built a temple in honor of Augustus on the site. Herod then gave it to his son, Philip the tetrarch, who renamed it "Caesarea Philippi" in honor of Augustus, adding Philip's name to it in order to distinguish this city from Caesarea by the sea. Philip also kept a palace there. A large spring was there, one of the main sources of the Jordan River, and a shrine to the god Pan. It was a thoroughly pagan, Roman place, and the promise of an unstoppable Church flew in the face of the assumed powers that were represented there. On the title **Son of Man**, see the comments on 8:18-22.

16:14-17. The common denominator between **John the Baptist**, **Elijah**, and **Jeremiah** was that they were all prophets calling the people to return to covenant faithfulness. **Elijah** performed miracles (1Kg 17), and there were great prophetic hopes attached to him as the forerunner of the Messiah (Mal 4:5-6; Mt 11:7-15). That Jesus' ministry might be confused with his was understandable. **Jeremiah** and **the prophets** prophesied judgment, as did Jesus (cf. 11:20ff.; 21:33ff.). **The Christ** (v. 16) is a title, not a proper name, and means "one who is anointed." In the LXX *christos* is used for the Hebrew *masiah*, "anointed," for priests (Lv 4:5, 16; 6:22 [LXX 6:15]) and kings (e.g., 2Sm 23:1), including the future great Davidic king, the Messiah (PssSol 17:32; 18:5; *2 Bar* 29:3; 30:1; 27:2; *4 Ezra* 12:32). Matthew uses the word **Christ** elsewhere in narrative sections of his gospel (1:1, 16, 17, 18; 2:4; 11:2), but the disciples use it for the first time here. **Living God** is used in Jos 3:10; Jr 10:10; Dn 6:20, 26, for God's power and uniqueness in contrast to false gods like Pan. As the **Son of the living God**, Jesus can guarantee that the gates of Hades (see the comments below) will not prevail over the Church. "Son of God" occurs in 4:3, 6, and figures prominently in 14:33 ("You are certainly God's Son!"), where Jesus rescues Peter and the disciples from the sea, a prerogative reserved only for God in the OT (Ex 14:10–15:21; Ps 107:23-32; Jnh 1:4–2:10).

The response of Jesus is enigmatic (v. 17). In 14:33 the disciples recognized that Jesus was God's Son. Why did He claim divine revelation for Peter's confession when the disciples seem to have understood this previously? Perhaps the best answer is to understand that in 14:33 the disciples ascribe divinity to Him as they witnessed His God-like power over natural forces. That episode surely led them to a budding perception of Jesus' deity. But in 16:16, Peter connects Jesus' divine identification with the concept of the coming Messiah, who, with a few noteworthy exceptions, was not viewed as divine in the OT or Early Judaism (for a human Messiah, see 1QS 9:11; CD 12:23; 4QPBless 3f; *b. Ber.* 56b; *b. Suk.* 52a; *4 Ezra* 7:28; *b. Sanh.* 99a; for the exceptions, see the LXX of Dn 7:13; *b. Hag.* 14a; *b. Sanh.* 38b). Peter's insight that connected these two facts came from God, not his own ingenuity.

16:18. Jesus assigns Simon a new name, **Peter**, just as God did with Abraham. In both cases the new name shows how the individual will function in God's plans (Abraham becomes the "father of many," Gn 17:1-8, and **Peter** the "foundation stone") as He creates a new people (the Jewish people in Abraham's case, the Church in Peter's). The identification of **this rock** is interpreted variously as Peter's faith, Peter's confession, Peter's preaching office, the truth shown to Peter, the 12 disciples, Jesus Himself, Jesus' teaching, and even God Himself. Most of the variety stems from the bitter antagonism between interpreters from markedly different backgrounds. Many take exception to identifying Peter as the **rock**, but some of the reason for that is grounded in saying too much about Peter (e.g., that he was the first pope). But Peter is the focus in the verses before and after v. 18. Eph 2:20 and Rv 21:14 speak of the 12 apostles as foundational for the Church, a fact supporting that Peter was part of the foundation, but was not the sole foundation *vis-à-vis* the other apostles. And it was Peter who, using the **keys of the kingdom**, opened the kingdom for the Jewish people (Ac 2), the Samaritans (Ac 8), and the Gentiles (Ac 10), so that Jesus' prophecy about Peter seems to have actually come true in that he does function as the foundation of the Church. On this much most recent commentators, even from highly diverse religious persuasions, agree. However, doctrines related to apostolic succession or the infallibility of the Church cannot be substantiated from this, nor any other, text.

The gates of Hades probably means "death" (see Jb 38:17; Ps 9:13; 107:18; Is 38:10). As Son of the living God Jesus guarantees that the power of death would neither conquer nor imprison (as **gates** can incarcerate) the Church. In Matthew, there was much opposition to Christ, and the church being "killed" was quite possible. And Jesus in the next section (Mt 16:21) would talk about His own death.

16:19. Precisely how Peter functions as the rock is explained in v. 19. On **keys**, see Rv 1:18; 3:7; 9:1-6; 20:1-3. **The keys of the kingdom of heaven** probably refers to Peter's and the apostles' authority to admit people into the blessings of the kingdom, for **keys** often were used by the stewards who supervised one's household to dispense provisions for those who needed them (Is 22:15, 22; see Lk 11:52 where the "key of knowledge" related to entering the kingdom). The **keys** relate specifically to **bind[ing]** and **loos[ing]**. As Peter and the apostles preached in various areas—as they wielded the **keys of the kingdom** and Jesus built His Church—people would be loosed from their sins (forgiven) as they responded correctly to their gospel message (Ac 2:14-39; 3:11-26), or bound in their sins (remain unforgiven) if they did not (Ac 4:11-12; 8:20-23; 13:4-12, 44-52; 18:5-10). The verb construction **shall have been bound**, **shall have been loosed** (*estai dedemenon, estai lelumenon*, future perfect periphrastics) probably does not indicate that heaven made the determination of who is bound or loosed before Peter, though the concept is theologically sound. Instead, it probably accentuates the permanent divine agreement between Peter and heaven on the matter. To paraphrase: "Peter, when, in the future, you bind or loose people, be assured that unquestionably they will remain bound or loosed in heaven as well."

16:20. Jesus **warned the disciples** to remain silent about this discussion, probably to avoid misunderstanding in the throng that followed Him and would have forcefully made Him king with very little encouragement, but also perhaps to avoid aggravating the religious leaders further.

3. Jesus Faced Opposition: From Disciples Who Did Not Understand (16:21-27)

16:21-22. The disciples did not yet adequately understand the more serious implications of Jesus' divine Messiahship. **The elders and chief priests and scribes** is an apt summary of those included in the Sanhedrin, the ruling religious body. Jesus alluded cryptically to His death before this (9:15; 10:38; 12:40), but this was the first time He did so explicitly with the disciples (see Mk 8:32). Peter demonstrated that he still had a lot to learn about Jesus' Messiahship.

16:23. Get behind Me, Satan! reflects Jesus' words at the conclusion of the temptation (4:10). There the Devil sought to keep Jesus off the cross by soliciting Him to sin, rendering Him unfit to be a sacrifice. Peter unwittingly played the same role, becoming a **stumbling block** (lit., "a trap," but metaphorically "a situation or person that causes another to sin") for Jesus. Peter was **setting** his **mind on man's** interests. The typical Jewish expectation was that the Messiah would provide enormous political, economic, and spiritual relief for the Jewish people (cf. PssSol 17), but a dead Messiah could hardly do any of that.

16:24-27. On this section, see the comments on 10:34-39. Verse 24 is explained by vv. 25, 26, and 27. If one **gains the whole world and forfeits his soul** ("life"), this is pointless, for one would not be able to enjoy all that he acquired. Nothing can be given **in exchange** for one's **soul**. Therefore, if one wishes to preserve his life, paradoxically it must be given up to follow Christ. Verse 27 gives another motivation for following Jesus. At the second coming, Jesus **WILL THEN REPAY EVERY MAN ACCORDING TO HIS DEEDS**—especially those, in context, related to following Him (v. 24; see also Jn 5:28-29; 6:28-29).

VI. The Foretaste of the Glory of the King-Messiah: The Transfiguration (16:28–17:8)

16:28. The Son of Man coming in His kingdom has been interpreted as the transfiguration, the resurrection, the destruction of Jerusalem in AD 70, and the full-orbed establishment of the kingdom (i.e., assuming that the Church = the kingdom). The more defensible view is that v. 28 refers to all indicators of Christ's kingly authority and judgment, including the transfiguration, His resurrection, the spread of the Church, and the judgment of Jerusalem. If 16:28 is about the kingly authority of Jesus that has residual effects, then the transfiguration alone is not the best referent. This view fits well with the idea of judgment in v. 27, with the transfiguration that follows immediately in chap. 17, and with some of the disciples who would **not taste death**, which seems to require a lengthier span of time than the six days that passed before the transfiguration (17:1). In addition, Judas is an example of one who did **taste death** and missed the resurrection, Pentecost, the Church's growth, and AD 70.

17:1. Jesus provided a powerful experience for the three "inner circle" disciples, perhaps to offset the distressing mention of His impending death (16:21; 17:22). Exodus 24:9-18 provides a typological background for this episode (six days, Ex 24:16; three associates, Ex 24:9; a mountain covered by a cloud, Ex 24:12, 15; the glory, Ex 24:17, and God's voice, Ex 24:16; 25:1). Matthew's point in presenting these features of what transpired may be to build a case for Jesus being the new Moses, the new leader of God's people. Mt. Tabor is the traditional **high mountain**, but Mt. Hermon (30 miles north of Capernaum), which rose to over 9,200 feet, is a better option, though the precise location is unknown. Lk 9:28 says the transfiguration took place some (lit., "about," "approximately") eight days later, but Matthew gives the more precise chronology.

17:2-3. Transfigured (*metamorphoo*, "to transform, change in form," here "a change that is outwardly visible") is further described by the remainder of the verse. The appearance of **Moses and Elijah** was probably to indicate the superiority of Jesus over these two prominent OT characters.

17:4-8. Peter offered to build three **tabernacles** (better "shelters" or "booths"—usually temporary dwellings made of animal skins supported by poles and secured with rope and stakes), perhaps to commemorate the event. But Peter's intent to honor Moses and Elijah, as well as Jesus, brought a correction from God (v. 5), who clearly put the priority upon His Son.

VII. The Model of Humble Service Provided by the King-Messiah (17:9-27)

A. The Messiah Was Willing to Suffer (17:9-13)

17:9-13. This was the last time Jesus commanded His followers to remain silent about His power (8:4; 9:30; 12:16; 16:20; see the comments on 9:27-31). The connection between vv. 9 and 10 centers on the relationship of Elijah to the death of Jesus. Mk 9:11-12 suggests that their confusion resulted from being unable to harmonize the promise that Elijah **will restore all things** with Jesus' forecast of His own death. If Elijah would lead the Jewish people in revival and spiritual restoration, then why would any revived and restored Jewish person kill the Messiah? The scribes were right about Elijah's coming (v. 11), but failed to connect John's ministry to what was promised of Elijah's (Mal 4:5; Lk 1:17; see the comments on Mt 11:13-15). John did prepare the people for Jesus' coming, but was killed nevertheless (v. 12); the same fate could well await the Messiah, Jesus.

B. The Messiah Was Willing to Help the Dull (17:14-20)

17:14-20. The thematic connections between this episode and the ones surrounding it are not clear. Jesus' references to His death (17:9, 12, 22-23) are followed by miracles (17:14-21, 24-27), indicating that He was nevertheless the divine Messiah. Davies and Allison (*The Gospel According to St. Matthew*, 2:728) point out the primary thrust of these verses, which is seen in the repetition of various words for "faith" (**unbelieving**, *apistos*, v. 17; **littleness of faith**, *oligopistia*, v. 20, and **faith**, *pistis*, v. 20) and "power" (*edynasthesan*, [not] "to be able," translated **could [not]** in v. 16; *edynethemen*, [not] "to be able," translated **could [not]**, and *adynatesei*, "to be unable," translated **impossible**, v. 20). God's merciful power, which He makes available to His people as they serve others, is conditioned upon their reliance on Him. **Lunatic** (v. 15) means "to be moonstruck," i.e., adversely affected by the supposed supernatural powers of the moon, but here refers to something akin to epilepsy.

The disciples' inability to heal (v. 16) is surprising in light of 10:1-8, but in keeping with their stumbling progress. Jesus' rebuke (v. 17) was directed primarily against the disciples, but **generation** broadens the scope to include the others who were there. The disciples failed **because of the littleness** (better "poverty") **of** their **faith**, which may consist of understanding God's vast power but not relying adequately upon Him; poor faith is faith mixed with a portion of doubt (see 8:26). The extreme condition of the boy, the pressure from the father and perhaps the crowd, the absence of Jesus and the three prominent disciples—these may have contributed to their lack of faith. **Nothing will be impossible to you** is clearly hyperbolic, and it is imperative to recognize that faith is not a shamanistic spell that compels God to give health and wealth to His children. The context is that of power *in ministry* that comes in outrageous reliance upon God, and **faith** includes not only belief in God's ability to act but reverent dependence upon Him that does not mandate how He should respond.

As a side note, Lk 9:28 says that Jesus went up on the mountain prior to His transfiguration to pray, and Mk 9:29 emphasized the need for prayer (as does Mt 17:21—a verse not found in the best manuscripts). Perhaps one of the reasons Jesus was able to exorcise this pernicious demon, aside from His divine power, was because of His life of prayer. Significant times of prayer precede remarkable accomplishments in ministry.

C. The Messiah Was Submissive (17:22-27)

1. Prepared to Die (17:22-23)

17:22-23. The trek to Caesarea Philippi and back was finished. The mention of **Galilee** anticipates 17:24 and 19:1, where Jesus leaves never to return. The verb **delivered** is used for Judas's betrayal of Jesus (26:15, 16, 21, 23, 24, 25, 45, 46, 48), and this is the first time Jesus mentioned it (though cf. 10:4). **Deeply grieved** indicates that the disciples only heard **they will kill Him** and not the glorious final outcome **raised on the third day**. They were beginning to comprehend the dark day that awaited them, and no longer chastised Jesus for speaking of it.

2. Prepared to Pay a Tax (17:24-27)

17:24-27. The **two-drachma tax** (v. 24) was the temple tax used to support the sacrificial system in Jerusalem. According to the Mishnah (*m. Shek.* 1:1), the tax was a fixed amount seen as equivalent to two days' wages, to be paid annually in the month of Adar (February-March) by all adult Jewish males over 20 years of age. The question posed to Peter indicates some concern regarding Jesus' practice on this matter. Jesus used the opportunity to make a strong Christological point (vv. 25-26); as God's Son, the Son of the King, Jesus would be exempt from paying this tax, just as **kings of the earth** exempted their own **sons**. Jesus, however, surrendered His right to the exemption to avoid undue offense, and miraculously provided the resources for Peter to pay the tax for both of them, suggesting that Peter is among "God's sons" because of his connection with Jesus. Once again Matthew shows his readers Jesus' humility in paying a tax for His Father's house from which He was exempt, and in His perfect willingness to provide for Peter's needs.

VIII. The Ethics of the Leaders Chosen by the King-Messiah (18:1–19:12)

A. Humility: Necessary to Enter and Serve in the Kingdom (18:1-6)

18:1-6. The question, **Who then is greatest in the kingdom of heaven?** may have arisen because of the mention of Jesus' death. Which of them would be leader in His absence? On **the kingdom of heaven**, see 3:1-4. Jesus' answer focused not on rank, but on the more critical issue of how to enter the kingdom—that is, by being **converted** ("change one's ways, to turn to God") and becoming **like children**. This comparison could be understood several ways, but the key is being **humble** (v. 4), explained further in v. 6 as believing **in Me**. Entering the kingdom is the prospect only for those who humbly trust in Jesus for salvation (see the comments on 7:21-23 for entering the kingdom). In v. 4, Jesus returned to the initial topic of being great in the kingdom. Humility was needed to enter the kingdom and to be great in it, for the leaders of His community are to be its servants (20:24-28) willing to care even for the insignificant (a **child**, v. 5). **Whoever causes** [a Christian]... **to stumble** ("spiritual harm") will be held accountable for it (v. 6).

B. Personal Purity: Avoid Harming Self and Others (18:7-14)

18:7-10. Jesus does not say why **it is inevitable that stumbling blocks come** (v. 7), but later He indicates that evil thrives before it is expunged (24:6). Verse 7 indicates both God's providential superintendence of **stumbling blocks** and human responsibility for them. In v. 8, Jesus warns that His followers could cause themselves spiritual harm by their own imprudent behavior. The OT forbade self-mutilation (Dt 14:1; 1Kg 18:28; Zch 13:6), and Jesus surely did not mean this verse to be applied literally. His point is that dealing with sin requires severe steps.

Fiery hell (v. 9) is literally "Gehenna of fire." For the history of Gehenna, aka the Hinnom Valley on the southwest end of Jerusalem, see 2Kg 16:3; 21:6; 23:10; 2Ch 33:6. Under King Josiah, the valley became Jerusalem's city dump where fires constantly burned to reduce volume and speed putrefaction. It was a graphic representation of hell. According to this context, some of the characteristics of being saved include being dependent upon God and believing in Jesus (see comments above). But if one harms and despises His followers (vv. 2-10) and does not deal severely with his own sin, he shows an affinity with the world that indicates he might be unsaved and condemned (destined for **fiery hell**). The main point of v. 10 is that believers are important to God, and if angels who serve them (Heb 1:14) observe one of **these little ones** receiving harsh treatment, God will "find out about it" from them and neither He nor they will approve.

18:12-14. See Lk 15:3-7. The point here, however, is that God goes to great pains to redeem His people and to keep them in His love. The followers of Jesus should show the same kind of pastoral concern for each other that God demonstrates.

C. Corporate Purity: Conduct Church Discipline (18:15-20)

18:15-20. This passage indicates how a wayward sheep is brought back to the fold. The first step (v. 15) involves a caring, private admonition of the sinful disciple. To the verb **sins** some ancient mss add "against you" (reflected in the KJV; NKJV; ESV; RSV), but scribes tended to add material, supporting the shorter and more encompassing reading. **Show** is literally "to rebuke," or "to convince a person of his wrongdoing." This reproof is to be conducted **in private**; slander and gossip have no place in Jesus' community. **You have won** ["to gain," "prevent the loss of"] **your brother** presents the goal of the process. These steps must be conducted with family-like kindness (**brother** is used twice). Those who relish church discipline are precisely the ones who should not engage in it.

The second step (v. 16) involves the enlistment of **TWO OR THREE WITNESSES** (see Dt 19:15). These additional participants probably did not observe the initial sin. The need for privacy would be reduced if they had. Their role is to accompany the original witness to lend weight to the gravity of the situation, and perhaps to certify to the church that restoration was being conducted correctly.

The third step (v. 17) involves telling **the church**, presumably so that the entire church becomes involved in the effort to restore. If this attempt fails, then the offending party is to be treated **as a Gentile and a tax collector**. Jewish people kept their interaction with Gentiles and tax collectors to a bare minimum. While Jesus accepted Gentiles and tax collectors, an unrepentant believer who has been taken through the three steps of church discipline should not be accepted back into the church. In the phrase

let him be to you, **you** is singular, not plural. Jesus was personalizing the instruction, making the responsibility for restoration and discipline binding upon every individual in Jesus' community (not just the leaders!).

For v. 18, see 16:19. Here, however, it is the entire community that participates in the binding and loosing, not just Peter. In this context it deals less with salvational forgiveness of sins and more with the restoration (being **loosed**) of one who is already saved. The **two** who **agree** (v. 19) refers to the same two or three witnesses of v. 16 and the **two or three** . . . **gathered** (v. 20). Their agreement probably relates to the need to tell the entire church. **On earth** and **in heaven** (v. 19) parallel the similar phrases in v. 18. **Anything that they may ask** *must* be governed by the context as a promise related to church discipline, and surely includes asking for God's providential guidance through these steps. **Anything** literally is "any matter" or "any affair," i.e., any circumstance requiring church discipline. In v. 20 Jesus promised to be present with His people when they engage in restoration, just as He does in 28:20. The church needs reassurance of His presence and authority not only in the daunting task of evangelism, but also in the distressing task of church discipline.

D. Forgiveness: Remember How Much God Forgives (18:21-35)

18:21-22. Peter's question flows from the implications of church discipline in vv. 15-20. There are petty offenses not worthy of church discipline for which forgiveness is appropriate. **Seventy times seven** (NASB; KJV; RSV; NLT) is literally "seventy-seven" times (so NRSV; NIV; NET), indicating that no restriction should be placed on the number of times forgiveness is offered.

18:23-27. On the **kingdom of heaven** (v. 23), see the comments on 3:1-4. The talent (v. 24) (*talanton*) was the largest denomination of money in the Roman world, and **ten thousand talents** was the largest number employed in that day. In modern currency, the spending power could easily be several billion dollars. The slave made a promise he could not possibly keep (v. 26). Driven by his **compassion,** the king no longer counted the loan against the slave (v. 27) and acted as if the loan had never been made. There were no further consequences, no further punishment, and complete release from the obligation.

18:28-30. What follows in vv. 28 mirrors vv. 24-27, except the amount of money and response of the unforgiving slave differ. The denarius was a Roman silver coin, worth one day's wage for a common laborer. The second slave owed the first about 100 days' wages. This is not a trifling amount, but 100 denarii is minute in comparison to the 10,000 talents.

18:31-35. There are two options regarding the main point of the parable. The first is that certain results should be present if one has been forgiven, and the absence of the results indicates that the person did not receive forgiveness from God. In Lk 7:36-50, the sinful woman was saved by her faith (Lk 7:50), her many sins forgiven (Lk 7:47). She responded by expressing her great love to Jesus (Lk 7:47). The implication is that if she had not been forgiven, she would not have shown her love, a proper response to receiving forgiveness. Conversely, the unforgiving slave gives evidence of never actually receiving his king's forgiveness, for if he had, a reasonable response would have been forgiveness of the other slave. As a result, the king rescinds the forgiving of the debt, and increases the severity of the punishment (**torturers**, not simply "jailers," NIV; TNIV; KJV; ESV; HCSB), a reference to judgment and eternal condemnation.

Another approach is that the parable is a warning to those who have "entered the kingdom of heaven" as children who trust Jesus (see 18:1-6 above) and who are brothers in the fullest sense (18:21), saved individuals who have received the gracious forgiveness of God (18:27, 32-33). But they choose to be unforgiving of others. As a result, God turns those saved individuals over to **torturers**, probably discipline from God in this life, until they learn to forgive. While the first view is unobjectionable, the second has better contextual support mentioned above.

The details of the parable must not be forced to "walk on all fours." God is not so capricious as to change His mind about forgiving people. Verse 34 cannot be invoked as a support for purgatory; if anything, it supports the idea of the eternal duration of hell since the slave would never have paid off the debt and been released. The essential lesson is this, and only this: In this life God will severely discipline those whom He has forgiven but then refuse to forgive others.

E. Divorce: Avoid It (19:1-12)

19:1-2. The connection between chaps. 18 and 19 may be on the need for forgiveness, not only in general relationships with others, but especially in marriage where unfaithfulness and divorce may occur.

19:3. The test was designed to trick Jesus into being at odds with Moses or into infuriating those who held contrary views. **For any reason at all** (see Dt 24:1-4) reflects the more popular view of divorce championed by the famous rabbi Hillel (d. AD 20, leader of the Sanhedrin during the reign of Herod the Great), who taught that one could divorce his wife for any reason, including burning dinner or being unpleasant (*m. Git.* 9:10; see also Josephus, *Ant.*, 4.253; *Life* 426; *Sir* 25:26). Rabbi Shammai (Hillel's contemporary) had a much narrower view, permitting divorce only for "indecency," probably lewdness or promiscuity short of actual intercourse.

19:4-6. Jesus cited Gn 1:27 (v. 4); God did not create many women for Adam, nor many men for Eve. God brought one man and one woman together in an intense sharing of a common life which included sexual union (**JOINED TO HIS WIFE . . . BECOME ONE FLESH**, Gn 2:24) and which superseded all other familial bonds (**SHALL LEAVE HIS FATHER AND MOTHER**). Serial monogamy was not, and is not, God's design.

19:7-8. The Pharisees returned to the question about Dt 24:1-4. They believed that **Moses** required divorce, but Jesus corrected them. Moses **permitted** divorce **because of your hardness of heart**, a reference to unfaithfulness by a spouse. The only command in Dt 24 comes in v. 4 (see the comments there). Divorce is therefore "never to be thought of as a God-ordained, morally neutral option but as evidence of sin, of hardness of heart" (Carson, "Matthew," 412-13). **From the beginning** (see Mt 19:4) indicates that God's foundational purpose for marriage was that it be permanent between one man and one woman, and that purpose is not trumped by the allowance for divorce in Dt 24 when there is moral failure.

19:9. The verse probably does not mean "Whoever divorces his wife, *even for immorality*, and marries another, commits adultery." If Jesus forbade all divorce for all reasons, it is highly unlikely that Paul would have allowed divorce for abandonment by an unbelieving spouse (1Co 7:12-16), and v. 9 would be placed at loggerheads with 5:32 where Jesus clearly permits divorce. **Immorality** (*porneia*) is sometimes interpreted as "an incestuous marriage" (forbidden in Lv 18:6-18) on the basis of its use in 1Co 5:1. But in that context an incestuous *affair* is meant, not a marriage, and the word elsewhere means "sexual sin," referring to prostitution, premarital and extramarital sex (1Co 6:13, 18; Eph 5:3; 1Th 4:3), and sometimes adultery (*Sir* 23:23), depending on the context. Incest is also unlikely because 19:6 says that God joined together the man and woman, which would not be true if the marriage were contrary to the Law. Nor does **immorality** mean "unfaithfulness during betrothal," for which divorce was the approved action (1:18-19). Jesus spoke of a consummated marriage in 19:5-6 (one flesh), but the marriage was not consummated during betrothal. The exception clause may modify only **whoever divorces his wife**, allowing divorce but forbidding remarriage. However, it is hard to see how divorce could constitute **adultery** without a subsequent one-flesh remarriage, and remarriage following divorce was assumed (see *m. Git.* 9:3). Jesus appears to permit divorce and remarriage without either being a sin if one's spouse was unfaithful. In addition, the **adultery** could be forgiven (see David's case, 2Sm 12:13; also 1Co 6:9-10), but this must not be used to rationalize it, and forgiveness never precludes serious consequences.

19:10-12. Jesus' approach to the permanency of marriage and the restrictions on divorce elicited a strong reaction from the disciples. He is much more narrow than Hillel, but in line with Shammai's view of marriage and divorce. However, Shammai's view was probably virtually abandoned in Jesus' day, making the contrast between Jesus' approach and the popular one all the more startling.

IX. The Citizens of the Kingdom and the King-Messiah (19:13–20:34)

To Be a Citizen of the Kingdom, One Must . . .

A. Be Childlike to Be in It (19:13-15)

19:13-15. Matthew may have recorded this episode to emphasize the sanctity of the family, the heart of it being marriage and children.

B. Depend on God to Enter It (19:16-30)

19:16-22. This episode shows the kinds of attitudes that do not characterize the childlikeness approved in 19:13-15. **What good thing** (v. 16) is contrasted with the **One who is good** (v. 17), suggesting that obtaining **eternal life** is dependent upon God rather than one's deeds. Verse 17a is literally, "Why are you asking Me about *a good thing* [that you would do]?" He made this theme explicit in 19:26, namely, that one's entrance into the kingdom is the result of God's work, not a result of one's deeds. **Keep the commandments** is puzzling in light of the strong grace context, but Jesus played the works card to challenge the man's assumption that he, by his deeds, could obtain eternal life. Jesus included Lv 19:18 (v. 19) on loving one's neighbor, a critical observation for understanding what followed. The young man may have made money his idol, but Jesus gave no hint of this. Instead He focused on his failure to keep the very laws he claimed to have kept. Jesus commanded him to **sell** everything and **give to the poor** (v. 21), an application of Lv 19:18 for this man. Jesus called his bluff and proved that he had not and would not do what he claimed to have done. He even revealed an awareness of his own deficiency in keeping the law (v. 20).

19:23-26. The disciples were astonished because (v. 25) in Early Judaism wealth was an indication of God's favor, since it was believed that God would surely not endow a sinner with wealth. Hence if it were hard for a rich man to get into the kingdom, how could anyone else hope to do so? Jesus responded by saying it is ultimately God's work (for more on entering the kingdom, see the comments on 7:21-23).

19:27-30. In contrast to the rich young ruler, the twelve left the little they had to follow Jesus. How would that benefit them? **Regeneration** (v. 28) is used again in the NT only in Ti 3:5 where it refers to the regenerating work of the Spirit for the believer. But here it refers to the future renewal of the earth when the curse is lifted (Rm 8:18-25) during the "new age," the millennial kingdom, when Jesus comes to reign upon the earth. The disciples will judge **the twelve tribes of Israel**. This is a significant promise because it shows that the disciples were not only the foundation of the Church (Eph 2:20-22) but also the leaders of the remnant of Israel (Rm 11:1-6). Jewish believers have this unique status as members both of the Church and Israel. This promise was probably made only to the twelve as a unique group, but the NT indicates that all believers will participate with Christ in His judgment of the earth (Mt 25:21; Rm 16:20; 1Co 6:2; Rv 2:26-27; 3:21). The promise of v. 29 is not a literal one, since one cannot have 100 literal mothers! God is no man's debtor: if Jesus' disciples were shunned by family members, they would find within the messianic community a hundred surrogate loved ones, in addition to eternal life. The **first will be last; and the last, first** provides both reassurance and a warning. The statement in context states that God's grace extends to those who approach God in childlike trust (vv. 13-15). God will incorporate and advance them in the kingdom instead of those who enjoy power and prominence like the rich young ruler, which provides the warning in these verses. The same phrase is found in 20:16, giving a slightly different look at God's grace there, namely that He is remarkably gracious and does the unexpected for His people.

C. Not Be Shocked at Those Whom God Excludes (20:1-16)

20:1-2. There is a clear structure in 19:30-20:16. It begins with the saying, "But many who are first will be last, and the last first" (19:30). Then, in the parable, often called Parable of the Gracious Landowner, during the morning hours workers are *hired* from first to last (20:1-7), but in the evening, workers are *paid* from last to first (20:8-15). Verse 16 inverts the clauses in 19:30. The reversal theme from 19:23-30 continues. (See David Turner, *Matthew*, 478.)

20:3-7. The **third**, **sixth**, **ninth**, and **eleventh** hours were approximately 9:00 a.m., 12:00 noon, 3:00 p.m., and 5:00 p.m., and assume a twelve-hour workday. Jesus did not explain why the **landowner** returned throughout the day, and probably nothing should be read into this (perhaps he was disorganized; the harvest was urgent). Similarly, the workers hired at the end of the day were probably not the reputed worst workers (v. 6), but rather simply had not found work.

20:8-16. Temporary laborers were usually paid each **evening** (v. 8) (Lv 19:13; Dt 24:15). Those who worked longer but were paid a single denarius **grumbled at the landowner** (v. 11) since, by human reckoning, they deserved more than those who came later, though they were paid appropriately (20:2). But this is the point of the parable. It is not primarily about deathbed conversions, disciples who joined Jesus after the initial twelve, the Gentiles being included in the people of God after the Jewish people, the need for not seeing rewards in the kingdom as an entitlement. These points are not clearly evident in the parable. What is clear is that God exercises His freedom to give kingdom blessings graciously to whom He chooses, and that may cause shock when He reverses human expectations.

D. Yield to the Messiah the Desire for Prominence (20:17-34)

1. Jesus Was Willing to Die (20:17-19)

20:17-19. It is possible that 20:17-19 looks back to the Parable of the Gracious Landowner and presents the basis on which even late-comers can be part of the kingdom—through God's grace effected in the death of Christ. This is the third time Jesus mentioned His death to the disciples (16:21-23; 17:22-23). **To go up to Jerusalem** (vv. 17-18) was a topographical expression, as the city is about 2,500 feet above sea level. Jesus and the disciples were headed to Jerusalem to celebrate the Passover, as were thousands of others, for the Law required three pilgrimages each year for Jewish men in celebration of certain holy days (Ex 23:14-17). On **Son of Man**, see 8:18-22. This prediction, unlike the others, included the condemnation by the leaders, and the mocking, scourging, and crucifixion by the **Gentiles**. Although the Church has historically held the Jewish people responsible for the death of Jesus, obviously Jesus includes Gentiles as responsible parties in this conspiracy of guilt (see Ac 4:27-28). It is the **Son of Man**, the Son of David, the divine Son of God, who would voluntarily undergo such treatment to save others. His humility would contrast starkly with the arrogance of the sons of Zebedee in the following section.

2. The Leaders of the Disciples Were Required to Serve (20:20-28)

20:20-23. These verses function as the bridge connecting 20:1-18 with 20:29-34. God will give rewards on the basis of His grace (vv. 1-16) through the death of His Son (vv. 17-19); all jockeying for rewards and status are misdirected in light of what God alone has determined and in light of Jesus' example.

The **sons of Zebedee** (v. 20) were James and John (4:21). The only other place in Matthew's gospel where a mother directs a request to Jesus for a child is in 15:22. The Canaanite woman's request was granted on the basis of her sheer desperation and faith, in contrast to the denied request voiced by Mrs. Zebedee. **Sit one on Your right and . . . left** (v. 21) was an appeal for the brothers to acquire a high rank in the kingdom, even to direct the other disciples. Jesus already promised that the twelve would reign in the kingdom with Him (19:28), but James and John wanted a guarantee that they would be the first among equals. **To drink the cup** (v. 22) was an idiom for "undergoing God's wrath" (Pss 11:6; 75:7-9; Is 51:17, 22; Jr 25:15, 17, 27-28; 49:12; Lm 4:21; 16:19; 18:6), but here probably means "to undergo intense suffering" since they were not the objects of wrath. **We are able** is ironic, for neither brother stayed awake in Gethsemane while Jesus prayed for the "cup" to pass from Him (Mt 26:37-46). **Prepared** (v. 23) refers to the preordained plan of God who sovereignly governs all things, including His determination regarding a disciple's position in the kingdom. James was martyred in Ac 12:2; John suffered, but apparently was not a martyr (cf. Jn 21:20-23; Rv 1:9).

20:24-28. Matthew does not say why the **ten became indignant**, but possibly because they were afraid they would lose their own prominence in the kingdom, or become subservient to James and John. They forgot the childlikeness enjoined by Christ in 18:4. The **rulers of the Gentiles** (v. 25) were counter-examples; **lord it over them** means "to have mastery" (Mk 10:42; 1Pt 5:3), sometimes "to bring into subjection, gain dominance" (Ac 19:16), usually with a sense of heavy-handedness. **Shall be your servant** (or "helper," v. 26), **shall be your slave** (v. 27) give the positive values, all too frequently ignored in some ecclesiastical settings. It is true that a leader serves his organization by exercising authority and influence. But the true **servant** leader—one who satisfies Jesus' job description—occasionally gets his hands dirty in the process of helping those who cannot reciprocate. Jesus Himself **did not come to be served**, and provides the supreme example of servant leadership. **Ransom** means "the money paid to obtain the freedom of a slave." Jesus' sacrifice frees those who trust Him from the tyranny of sin, personified as a slave master in Rm 6:1-14. **For** (*anti*, meaning both "in exchange for" and "in the place of") points to a person who receives a benefit because of some kind of exchange or substitution. At the cross, Jesus took the penalty of the sins of His people upon Himself, dying in their place as their substitute, and in exchange gives them eternal life. How the **many** (*pollon*) are ransomed is specified in 26:28 (My blood . . . poured out for many [*pollon*] for forgiveness of sins), where the wine symbolized His blood soon to be shed on the cross. **Many** indicates that the benefits of Jesus' death are applied only to those who trust Him as Savior (see Rm 5:18, where all men refers only to those who receive grace and the gift of righteousness in Christ, Rm 5:17). Matthew 20:28 is cited often in support of the doctrine of particular redemption.

3. Jesus Was Willing to Serve (20:29-34)

20:29-34. In 9:27, at the beginning of Jesus' ministry before He faced opposition, two blind men cried out using the same words as in 20:30 (with **Lord** being textually suspect in v. 30). This episode is near the end of His ministry after rejection and opposition. "So despite being rejected, Jesus' charity remains the same throughout. His difficulties do not cancel His compassion" (Davies and Allison, *The Gospel According to Saint Matthew*, 109). In addition, Jesus demonstrates His ongoing role as a servant leader.

Matthew and Mark (10:46) state that this miracle happened as Jesus left Jericho, Luke (18:35ff.) while entering. There is not a good explanation for this (see the major commentaries for the options), but Luke's account is the least precise (literally, When Jesus was near Jericho, Lk 18:35), and may indicate a compressed account in order to accommodate the Zaccheus narrative. Matthew relates that there were two blind men, Mark and Luke only one. Matthew may have referred to both men in order to draw the parallels between them and the other two blind men in 9:27 (cf. above on 20:29-34). But there are no formal contradictions in the three accounts.

For **Son of David**, and the other details of the healing, see 9:27-31. Jesus possessed great authority; He was the messianic leader; He was no doubt preoccupied with what awaited Him in Jerusalem. But, unlike the **crowd**, He took the time to show **compassion** (v. 34) as the model servant-leader for these blind men, and by doing this instructed His disciples.

X. The Rejection of the King-Messiah (21:1–23:39)

A. The Messiah Offered Himself to the People (21:1-11)

21:1-3. The theme of Jesus' royal identification ("Son of David," 20:30-31) continues in chapter 21 (He is "King," v. 5; "Son of David," vv. 9, 15). In spite of all that will happen to Him in Jerusalem, Jesus was still the King of the Jews.

Bethphage was probably on the eastern slope of the Mount of Olives. The Mount is an eschatologically important location (e.g., Zch 14:4; Ac 1:9-11) and historically important as the place from which the glory of the Lord departed from Israel (Ezk 9:3; 10:4, 18-19; 11:22-23). Jesus' triumphal entry roughly retraced this route as if to say, "The glory has returned!"

21:4-9. Verse 5 is drawn from Is 62:11 and Zch 9:9, both from eschatological contexts about the deliverer rescuing Israel. **The crowd spread their coats** (v. 8) as a symbolic act. As their coats were under His feet, so they pledged to submit to their King. The **branches from the trees** were reminiscent of the celebration when Judas Maccabeus liberated Israel from Antiochus Epiphanes IV in 164 BC (*1Mac* 10:7; *2Mac* 13:51), suggesting that the crowd expected a similar military emancipation through Jesus. **Hosanna** (v. 9) is probably a term of praise (see Lk 19:37-38), with their wish that their praise be heard in heaven (**in the highest**). The crowd shouted Ps 118:26 (cited also in Mt 23:39). The heart of Ps 118 is God's deliverance of His people (vv. 13-14) who cry out to Him (vv. 15-21). The deliverance would come through the rejected stone (v. 22), the **ONE WHO COMES IN THE NAME OF THE LORD** (v. 26), the Messiah.

21:10-11. This is the prophet may reflect an inadequate view of the residents of Jerusalem regarding Jesus, but Matthew offers no appraisal of their view. But Jesus did function as a prophet in this context.

B. The Messiah Confronted the Corruption of the Priests (21:12-17)

21:12. The priests and people **were buying and selling in the temple**, probably a reference to the purchase of animals for sacrifice (for **doves**, see Lv 5:7). The **money changers** were necessary since many pilgrims would have brought foreign coins embossed with pagan images, and these were not to be used to pay the temple tax. Jesus' primary concern appeared to be with the misuse of the temple and not with the leadership swindling the pilgrims. **MY HOUSE SHALL BE CALLED A HOUSE OF PRAYER** (v. 13), from Is 56:7, looks forward to a time when God-fearing Gentiles will be welcome in the temple (Is 56:3-8). **ROBBERS'** [better "revolutionists'"] **DEN** (or "cave") alludes to Jr 7:11. In Jeremiah's day, those who were disobedient to God viewed the temple as a magic charm that would spare them from His retribution. In Jesus' day, the priests disregarded God's desires for the temple, rendering them rebels against Him. Yet they functioned as if there would be no repercussions for their apathy.

Jesus' act was considered insidious. His measures shut down the normal sacrifices probably for the rest of a busy day close to Passover. At Jesus' trial, His action against the temple, and the authority with which He claimed to perform it (21:23), were the primary charges raised against Him (26:61; see also 27:40). No mere mortal had the right to do such things.

21:14-17. Perhaps to show one of the proper functions of the temple, Jesus healed **the blind and the lame**, probably in the outer Court of the

Gentiles since the physically challenged were not admitted into the inner courts (Lv 21:18-19). The question voiced by **the chief priests and the scribes** (see 16:21) in v. 16 was a veiled mandate for Jesus to silence the children. He cited Ps 8:2, in which God ordained the children's praise to nullify the opposition of His enemies. God was doing that in Jesus' setting through these children. Jesus implicitly placed these leaders among God's enemies. When Jesus left the temple and went to **Bethany**, about two miles southeast of Jerusalem on the eastern slope of the Mount of Olives, He stayed probably with Lazarus (Jn 12:1).

C. The Messiah Foretold the Judgment Against the Nation (21:18-22)

21:18-22. The withering of the fig tree comes between two sections that speak of opposition by the leaders in the temple (21:12-17 and 21:23), and, for reasons presented below, was probably a symbolic act portending God's judgment because of their obstinacy. **In the morning** (v. 18) signifies Monday of Passion Week, the next morning after the triumphal entry on Sunday. Usually when fig trees are in leaf, they have fruit. Figs were used as a metaphor for the Jewish people (Jr 24:5, 8; 29:17; Hs 9:10), and the image of withered trees represented God's judgment (Is 34:4; Jr 8:13; Hs 2:12; Jl 1:7; Mc 7:1). In Matthew, good fruit (righteous living) was the evidence of a right relationship with God, and absence of fruit made one liable to judgment (see comments on 3:5-12). The Jewish leaders were obligated to render the good fruit of Israel to God but failed to do so (see the comments on 21:33-46). As the fig tree advertised fruit but provided none for Jesus, so the Jewish leaders advertised spiritual fruit from Israel but actually offered none to God.

Verses 20-22 must also be read in this context of judgment. For the promise related to faith and prayer, see 17:14-21. The twelve apparently did not throw mountains around, but their prayers did result in the advancement of the Church against an otherwise insurmountable "mountain" of antagonism (Ac 1:14; 4:31-33; 8:15; 10:9; 13:2-3).

D. The Messiah Exposed the Cowardice of the Leaders (21:23-27)

21:23-27. Matthew does not note it, but Mk 11:27 ("they came again to Jerusalem" suggesting the start of a new day) and Lk 20:1 ("on one of the days" similarly indicating another day) indicate that 21:23 took place on the day after the events of Mt 21:18-22 which transpired on Monday (see the comments on Mt 21:18-22). Matthew 21:23 introduces the events on Tuesday of Passion Week. The question about His **authority** to do **these things** related to the cleansing of the temple. However Jesus answered would be problematic. If He claimed only human authority, He would leave Himself vulnerable to the charge of sinful action against the temple. But if He claimed divine authority, He might be open to the charge of blasphemy by claiming divine prerogatives. So, He responded with a question about their view of the **source** of John's **baptism** (vv. 24-25a). Jesus' question sounds evasive, but if they answered His question correctly then they would be answering their own. John the Baptist was a prophet sent by God, and he testified regarding Jesus (3:11-14). The religious leaders should have believed John and embraced Jesus, but their failure to do so gave their real estimation of John. They feared **the people** (v. 26), who saw John's ministry as legitimate, so to avoid infuriating the crowds they feigned ignorance. By doing this, however, they implied that they were not fit to lead the Jewish people, for one of their main jobs was to determine who posed a spiritual threat, or who was actually sent from God.

E. The Messiah Presented Parables about the Consequences of Their Rejection (21:28–22:14)

21:28-32. The purpose of the Parable of the Two Sons was to expose the leaders' deficient view of John and ultimately Jesus. The vineyard owner represents God, the first son the known sinners who, before John started his ministry, were disobedient to God but repented under John. The second son represents the religious leaders who claimed to be obedient. Yet when John came, they refused to believe the message God sent through him (cf. vv. 25, 32). Verse 32 indicates a twofold rejection of John by the leaders, in the initial stages of his work (**John came to you**) and later when John's ministry had an impact on sinners (**afterward** the leaders persisted in their unbelief). **Before you** (v. 31) may reiterate the theme of the reversal of human expectations but may actually mean that the leaders would not get into the kingdom at all because of their opposition of Jesus (7:21-23; 23:13).

21:33-41. This parable continues the attack against the religious leaders. The **landowner** is God, the **VINEYARD** is Israel (cf. Is 5:1-7; Jr 2:21;

Hs 10:1), the **vine-growers** are the leaders of Israel, the fruit they raised is what they owed God (a righteous life; see Mt 3:8-10; 7:16-20; 12:33; 13:23). The rejection of the landowner's slaves represents the rejection of the prophets by the Jewish religious leaders (see 21:45), and the rejection of the son was the rejection of Jesus. Verse 33 suggests that considerable effort was expended developing this vineyard, reflective of God's creation and care of Israel. The landowner sought **to receive his produce** (v. 34), a percentage of the yield divided with those who farmed it. The mistreatment of the slaves (vv. 35-36) shows the continuity between previous generations of religious leaders who abused God's prophets and the leaders of Jesus' day—a point that becomes explicit in 23:29-36. The phrase **they said among themselves** (v. 38) has an earlier parallel in v. 25 (reasoning among themselves), making explicit the connection between the farmers and the religious leaders. The deeds of the farmers were so outrageous that they would not get away with them. The landowner will punish the thugs and replace them with farmers **who will pay him** (v. 41). The verb **pay** (*apodidomi*) is used in 22:21 (translated "render" in the phrase "Render . . . to God the things that are God's"). The religious leaders had not given God what was due Him, namely the kind of lives He required them to live, nor had they led Israel to bear the kind of spiritual fruit He sought.

21:42-44. Jesus cited Ps 118:22, which is found in a context that defines who the true followers of God are, namely those who trust in the Lord for their deliverance (Ps 118:15-21). Their deliverance comes through **THE STONE WHICH THE BUILDERS REJECTED** (Ps 118:22), the blessed one who comes in the name of the Lord (v. 26; see the comments on 21:9). Verse 43 is often cited in support of the idea that the Church replaces Israel in God's program. But in the phrase **the kingdom of God will be taken away from you**, the antecedent of **you** in v. 43 is not Israel but the religious leaders (v. 45), and in the parable it is the farmers, not the vineyard. The supervision of **the kingdom** would **be given to a people producing the fruit of it**, a reference to the apostles who would lead the faithful remnant of Israel (cf. 19:28). The word **people** [lit., "nation," *ethnos*] in the singular as it is here was used often in the LXX for the Jewish people rightly related to God (e.g., Gn 12:2; Ex 19:6; Dt 4:6; Mc 4:7; Zph 2:9), with the plural often referring to Gentile nations (Lv 26:45; 1Sm 8:20; Ps 2:8; Is 2:4). In v. 44, Jesus indicated that if one fell on the **stone**, the stone won, and if the **stone** fell on a person, the **stone** won. No matter what, the **stone** wins (see Is 8:14-15; Dn 2:44-47). One had better not reject the **stone** (21:42).

21:45-46. The religious leaders understood Jesus correctly. Yet, in spite of the fate of the wicked farmers in the parable, they **sought to seize Him** and ignored the consequences.

22:1-14. Again indicates that Jesus continued addressing the theme of the removal of the kingdom from the Jewish leaders. For **the kingdom of heaven** (v. 2), see the comments on 3:1-4 and 13:10-17. The **kingdom** is often likened to a wedding feast (Mt 8:11-12; Rv 21:2, 7-9). The king **sent out his slaves** (v. 3), a reference to the prophets and John the Baptist. The verb **call** in this context means "to invite," and does not mean "to experience the effectual call of God for salvation" as it does frequently in Paul (see Rm 8:28-30). Often in ancient times an initial notification of such a gala would be followed by the formal summons when preparations were complete. This was the second call. **They were unwilling to come** indicates that they were reneging on an assumed previous agreement, not unlike the second son in 21:30 and the evil farmers in 21:35-36. In his rage, the king **set their city on fire** (v. 7), prophetic of what happened to Jerusalem in AD 70 (cf. Josephus, *War*, 6.403-422). **Worthy** (v. 8) is the same word John the Baptist used when he addressed the Pharisees in 3:8 (bear fruit in keeping with ["worthy of"] repentance); the parable was directed mainly to those leaders who never repented.

Verses 9-10 are sometimes interpreted as presenting a transition from God's focus upon Israel to a predominantly Gentile Church. But as in 21:33, it is the religious leaders who are confronted with this parable, who snub the king, and who will be judged. The king's slaves went to the roads on the outskirts of town and invited everyone (vv. 9-10). The fringe people in the parable parallel the first son (21:29) and the good farmers (21:41, 43) who, late in the day, do God's will. The leaders parallel the second son (21:30) and the wicked farmers. They early on appear to fulfill their obligations but ultimately refuse to do so and, in the case of the farmers, will suffer the consequences. The ones who accepted the invitation later are the Jewish riffraff (21:31-32) who will be included in the kingdom while the respectable leaders are turned away. In this parable, Jesus reiterated the reversal principle (see 19:30–20:16).

On the inclusion of the **evil** guest (v. 10) **not dressed in wedding clothes** (vv. 11-12), see the comments on 13:24-30, 36-43, and 47-50. The fate of this man is similar to that of the false prophets in 7:15-23. The lack of appropriate **wedding clothes** may depict his failure to meet the requirements for entering the kingdom (see the comments on 5:20; 7:21; 18:3-4, 6; 19:23-24).

The parable concludes with a foreboding note (vv. 11-13). This describes the judgment following the second coming, when the unprepared guest is thrown **into the outer darkness** where there is **weeping and gnashing of teeth** (v. 13). In support of this as a reference to eternal punishment of unbelievers, not the regret of carnal Christians excluded from the happy aspects of the kingdom, see the comments on 8:5-13. **Few are chosen** (*eklektos*, i.e., "elect," "chosen" for salvation; cf. Rm 8:33; Col 3:12; 2Tm 2:10) (v. 14) indicates that God chooses those who will be in the kingdom. But His sovereign choice is surely compatible with the decisions people make (like ignoring God, v. 5), but here, and in all of Scripture, the impetus is grounded in God's sovereign plan.

F. The Messiah Escaped Their Traps (22:15-46)

22:15-22. This section reiterates 21:41, 43, about rendering to God what He requires. The **trap** (v. 15) was brilliant. Whatever Jesus said would get Him in trouble. Rome might see Him as an insurrectionist and punish Him if He disallowed paying taxes. But with an affirmative answer He might infuriate the Jewish people, for paying taxes was an agonizing reminder of their subjugation. The **Herodians** (v. 16) were aristocratic Jews in league with Rome, intent on the perpetuation of their privileged status and despised by their fellow Jews. Normally the Pharisees would not have sought any accordance with them, but if Jesus disparaged paying taxes, the **Herodians** would report it to the Roman authorities. The flattery (v. 16) was designed to embolden Jesus to say something against Rome. The **poll-tax** was a Roman tax upon personal property and agricultural products and probably amounted to about one day's wage each year. The **likeness** (v. 20) on the front of the coin, assuming it was a Roman denarius, would be the image of Emperor Tiberius with a wreath on his head, with the **inscription** "*TI CAESAR DIVI AUG F AUGUSTUS*" ("*Tiberius Caesar Augustus, Son of the Divine Augustus*"). On the back was the abbreviation "*PONTIF MAXIM*," or "*High Priest*" of the ancient Roman religions, with a picture of a seated woman ("peace" personified). It was clearly an idolatrous coin, deifying Caesar. The coin had Caesar's image on it, suggesting that he "owned" it and that it should be given back to him in the appropriate tax amounts. **Render** (v. 21) was used in 21:41, translated pay. Jesus' point there and here was that the Jewish leaders in particular failed to **render** to God what He required, namely, spiritual lives expended for Him and His glory, and the kind of leadership that would result in similar fruit from the entire nation.

22:23-33. On that day was still Tuesday of Passion Week (cf. the comments on 21:23-27). **Sadducees** did not believe either in a disembodied existence after death nor in the resurrection, so their question was not intellectually honest. They cited Dt 25:5 (v. 24) concerning Levirate marriage (see the comments on Dt 25:5-10). The Sadducees set up a scenario that was designed to make Jesus look either completely arbitrary (how could He pick one out of the seven when **they all had married her** [lit., "had her" in a conjugal way] in this life? v. 28), or to trick Him in to conceding that resurrection was an impossible doctrine, thereby alienating the Pharisees who cherished the belief. But the Sadducees were **mistaken** about the resurrection (v. 29). They assumed wrongly that Jesus believed it would be the continuation of a bodily existence like the present life, where marriage, intercourse, and procreation would continue. Jesus corrects them, saying that **in the resurrection** (v. 30) there will be no marriage (for which having children was a crucial component; Gn 1:28), for people will be **like angels in heaven**, that is, they will live forever. Hence procreation to perpetuate the race will be unnecessary. Note that He did *not* say that people *become* angels. Jesus responded further by citing Ex 3:6, which indicated that **ABRAHAM**, **ISAAC**, and **JACOB** were still alive as disembodied souls and eventually would be resurrected. God's covenantal promises to the patriarchs were largely unrealized at the time of their deaths, so their eventual resurrection is necessary for God to fulfill those promises (for these points and many more, see N. T. Wright, *The Resurrection of the Son of God* [Minneapolis: Fortress, 2003], 416-29).

22:34-40. The **Pharisees** once again went on the offensive. The responsibilities of a pharisaic **lawyer** (v. 35; synonymous with "scribe," Mk

12:28, and "teacher of the law," Lk 5:17) included studying the Law to derive legal principles from it, teaching it, and administering the Law as a counselor and judge in local courts (see Geza Vermes et al., ed., *The History of the Jewish People in the Age of Jesus Christ [175 BC–AD 135]* [Edinburgh: T. & T. Clark, 1987], 330). **Testing him** once again indicates the diabolical intent of the question, this time posed by one with impressive biblical savvy. The test may consist in duping Him into demeaning some aspects of the Law in favor of others, or in expressing a firm opinion on the **great commandment** when the very question was hotly debated (see Hagner, *Matthew 14-28*, 646 for the evidence). He cited Dt 6:5 and Lv 19:18 (vv. 37-40). **HEART . . . SOUL . . . MIND** indicate that love for God is to come from every facet of one's constitution. It is unlikely that the Pharisees would have taken exception to this part of His answer. **YOU SHALL LOVE YOUR NEIGHBOR** means taking delight in meeting the needs of others. Sometimes the phrase **AS YOURSELF** is used to prove the need for cultivating a positive self-image before being able to love others. But Moses and Jesus assume self-love as the basis for the comparison of loving one's neighbor. When one is cold, he puts on a sweater; when he is hungry, he eats. As one happily meets his own needs, i.e., "loves himself," he should similarly meet the needs of his neighbor. These two great commandments are not mutually exclusive, for if one loves God he will love what God loves, and God loves people (cf. Mt 25:31-46; 1Jn 4:20).

22:41-46. Jesus went on the offensive here. He tested their understanding of the Messiah, perhaps to expose their superficiality, but perhaps also to help them understand more completely who He was. The stock answer to the question, "Who is the Messiah?" was "**The son of David.**" But the answer is deficient. Jesus cited Ps 110:1 (in v. 44) as proof that the Messiah was more than a human descendant of David. In Hebrew, the first occurrence of **LORD** (the Hebrew word often transliterated *YHWH* or *Yahweh*) is a clear reference to God, but the second occurrence is a different word (*'adoni*), usually referring to human authorities (e.g., Gn 18:12; 40:1; but cf. Jos 5:14; Jdg 6:13, where it is used for the angel of the Lord). However, the LXX (the Greek translation of the Hebrew Scriptures, ca. 200 BC) uses the same word (*kyrios*) for both God and for David's **Lord**, suggesting that the translators saw *'adoni* as a reference to a divine being. Furthermore, the word **ENEMIES** is used seven times in Psalms, six of them for God's enemies, not those of a human ruler (8:2; 21:8; 66:3; 74:23; 89:10, 51; 92:9 twice). When footstool (Hebrew and LXX in Ps 110:1; **BENEATH YOUR FEET** in Mt 22:44) is used elsewhere in the OT (1Ch 28:2; Ps 99:5; 132:7; Is 66:1; Lm 2:1), it is God's footstool. These points together suggest that while the Messiah was not less than the son of David, He was much more than that (for more details, cf. Barry C. Davis, "Is Psalm 110 a Messianic Psalm?" *BibSac* 157 [April-June, 2000]: 162-63). In verse 43, Jesus asked the question, "If the Messiah is David's son, then how can David call Him 'Lord'?" In v. 45, the flip side is asked: "If David called the Messiah 'Lord,' then how can He be David's son?" The answer to both questions is that the Messiah has dual natures and dual paternity. As a result of the incarnation, Jesus is fully human, and descended from David, and He is also fully God, and therefore, He is David's Lord.

G. The Messiah Condemned the Leaders (23:1-39)

Jesus excoriates the Pharisees in Mt 23, but He was not alone in doing so. Others within Judaism were critical of Pharisaism. For example, in *m. Sotah* 22b, seven different kinds of Pharisees are discussed, six of which are portrayed negatively. They are: (1) The "shoulder" Pharisee wore his good deeds on his shoulder so everyone could see them. (2) The "wait a little" Pharisee always found an excuse for putting off a good deed. (3) The "bruised" Pharisee shut his eyes to avoid seeing a woman and knocked into walls, bruising himself. (4) The "humpbacked" Pharisee always walked bent double, in false humility. (5) The "ever reckoning" Pharisee was always counting up the numbers of his good deeds. (6) The "fearful" Pharisee always quaked in fear of the wrath of God. (7) The "God-loving" Pharisee was a copy of Abraham who lived in faith and charity. What Jesus does here is akin to other in-house criticism by some Jewish people against other Jewish people.

1. The Leaders Craved Acclaim (23:1-12)

23:1-12. Chapter 23 is a separate discourse, serving as an apt conclusion to Jesus' running dispute with the religious leaders. In vv. 1-12 Jesus **spoke to the crowds and to His disciples** about the improper actions of the **scribes and the Pharisees**, especially related to their thirst for acclaim. In vv. 13-36, He pronounced seven "woes" upon them (23:13, 15, 16, 23, 25, 27, 29) because of their hypocrisy and corrupt influence upon the people. And in vv. 37-39, He expressed a lament regarding the desolation that will come upon Israel. Verse 39 does, however, conclude with a note of hope.

In light of Jesus' positive injunction in v. 3a, the **chair of Moses** probably does not refer to the leaders' role as teachers of the Law. It probably reflects Moses' role as a judge for the Hebrews (Ex 18:13, Moses sat to judge the people), a role that was largely delegated to faithful leaders (Ex 18:21-27). Moses commanded the people to **do** [same word in the LXX as in Mt 23:3] according to the terms of the verdict handed down by a judge, usually a priest or another notable leader, and to be careful to **observe** that decision (Dt 17:8-10). **Scribes** often filled the role of judges in their towns (cf. *Sir* 38:33—39:11). When they rendered a judicial verdict, they sat in a special chair in the synagogue to do so (a "chair of Moses" was found in the ruins of several synagogues, including Chorazin). Jesus taught that those verdicts were binding. But His followers were not to **do according to their deeds**, that is, imitate their religious practices. For the **heavy burdens** (v. 4), cf. 11:28-30. **Phylacteries** (v. 5) were small leather containers worn on the arm or forehead as an application of Ex 13:9 and Dt 6:8; 11:18; the **tassels** were worn on the corners of their clothes to remind the Jewish people to obey the Law (Nm 15:38-40), but many religious leaders enlarged them simply to impress others. The **place of honor at banquets** (v. 6) was always the seat closest to the host and signaled the importance of the guest. **Chief seats in the synagogues** were usually on a raised platform close to where the Scriptures were read. The **respectful greetings** (lit., "a greeting that reflected homage or acclaim"; cf. Lk 1:28-29) (v. 7) often followed a set formula with the one of lower status saluting the superior. **Rabbi** was a transliteration of a Hebrew word that meant "my teacher" or "my master," carrying considerably more prestige than "reverend." Verses 8-12 indicate that Jesus' followers were to eschew such titles. **One is your Teacher** (v. 8) refers to Jesus, as in v. 10. The authority possessed by contemporary ministers is derived from Jesus, and humility dictates that they be cautious about self-aggrandizement, **for . . . you are all brothers** (there is equality among God's people). **Father** (v. 9) was used for great leaders and for respected elderly male acquaintances. **Leaders** (v. 10) means "a guide, instructor," perhaps "mentor." On vv. 11-12, see the comments on 20:26-28 and Jms 4:10, respectively. In light of these verses, it seems inappropriate for church leaders to *oblige* others to call them by these honorific titles ("Reverend," "Doctor," "Father," "Bishop," even "Pastor").

2. The Leaders Corrupted the People through Their Hypocrisy (23:13-36)

23:13-15. Woe is an exclamation that approximates "How sad!" or "Alas!" because of coming distress. As such it is a statement of lament but it also entails the future judgment of these leaders. The word **hypocrites** was used for the work of an actor. But here it means "pretending to be what you are not." Jesus' opponents put on a facade of pious conduct (though it really was not all that pious, v. 23) that cloaked a fundamental failure to do God's will sincerely, all to enhance their reputation. Judgment would come on them because, by their opposition to Jesus (9:33-34; 11:19; 12:23-24; 21:15), they kept people from entering the **kingdom** (cf. the comments on 7:21-23). The better manuscripts omit v. 14, which was probably borrowed by some impulsive scribe from Mk 12:40 or Lk 20:47 for harmonization purposes. **Proselyte** usually referred to a Gentile who fully converted to Judaism. A **son of hell** here probably means "a follower (of Pharisaism) destined for hell" because, like the Pharisees, the proselyte is unwilling to welcome Jesus as the Messiah.

23:16-22. In these verses, Jesus attacked those who drew distinctions between binding and nonbinding oaths. In 5:33-37, Jesus' teaching focused on the avoidance of volunteering oaths, while here it is on the question of how binding certain oaths were. The leaders were **blind guides** (v. 16) (see the comments on 15:12-14). The verb **swears** means "to promise a course of action by calling upon an important entity (God, or "the soul of my mother") to witness it and to punish if it does not come about." Someone spared no expense to give **gold** items, or the offerings on the altar, to the temple. Thus they were *korban*, wholly dedicated to the Lord's use. On the other hand, some of the Jewish people and the leaders may have viewed the **temple** and **altar** as the more constant and less dramatic components of worship. If this reflects their thinking (and it is impossible to say with any certainty that it does), what they failed to grasp was that the **gold** was dedicated to the Lord (**sanctified**) *precisely because of its connection with the temple*, otherwise it would be no more important than any other gold. The **altar** made the mundane things on it extraordinary. Jesus evened out the prominence of the entities used in making oaths. By doing this, He removed the loophole whereby one might renege on an oath simply because it did not invoke something foremost in their estimation. He went further, emphasizing that because the **altar**, **temple**, and **heaven** all pertain to God, then making an oath in reference to any of them was tantamount to invoking God. Therefore, all oaths are binding.

23:23-24. The Law commanded that virtually everything be tithed to support the Levites (Lv 27:30-33; Nm 18:21-32; Dt 12:5-19; 14:22-29), and the Pharisees included even **mint and dill and cummin**. But they neglected the more serious aspects of the Law (**justice**, **mercy**, **faithfulness**; cf. Mc 6:8). Jesus graphically and proverbially makes the same point in v. 24. Some would pour wine through a strainer to avoid accidentally ingesting an unclean **gnat** (Lv 11:23, 41), a minor infraction of the Law compared to swallowing **a camel** (also an unclean animal; Lv 11:4). Jesus' followers need to guard against being fixated on gnats (like not smoking, drinking, dancing) to the neglect of bigger issues (like controlling lust or curbing materialism).

23:25-26. The cup and **the dish** are metaphorical for the religious leaders who presented the image of well-scrubbed piety that concealed **robbery** ("the strong craving to obtain things, even by violent or deceptive means") and **self-indulgence** ("lack of self-control," used in 1Co 7:5 for sexual excess).

23:27-28. The metaphor changes in vv. 27-28, but the point is much the same as in vv. 25-26. A **tomb** might be attractive when painted, but that did not change what was inside. For **hypocrites**, cf. 23:13-15. Jesus drew attention to the irony of the religious leaders who claimed to keep the Law but, because of their inattentiveness to the more important aspects of the Law, were actually engaged in **lawlessness**.

23:29-33. The figure of **tombs** was applied in a different way in these verses. Jesus' point may be that the leaders were proud of their forebearers and of their connection with them, and yet did not want to identify with their abuse of the prophets (v. 31). Nevertheless, these leaders were planning His death, an act that forged a strong link to their murderous progenitors. Verse 32 puts in narrative form the parabolic prophecy of 21:35-39.

23:34-36. Therefore, to facilitate the leaders' filling up the measure of the guilt of their fathers (v. 32), Jesus will send them Christian **prophets**, **wise men and scribes** whom they will persecute. Like the generation exiled in Babylon, the Jewish leaders not only were accountable for their own sinfulness, but rode a wave of evil created by those who preceded them who killed Abel (Gn 4:8-10) and Zechariah, and they would experience the full expression of God's wrath, which had been building through the years. **Abel** and **Zechariah** are mentioned by Jesus because they encompass the entire Hebrew canon (Genesis being the first, 2 Chronicles being the last book in the Hebrew order of the OT). **Berechiah** is probably a scribal error here but found also in two ancient Jewish texts (*Tg. Lam.* 2:20; *Midr. Eccles.* 3:16), and Jerome (*Comm. in Matt.* 4.23.35–6) mentions a book called "The Gospel of the Nazarenes" (which may have been the Gospel of Matthew, but there is no certainty of this) that has "Jehoiadah" instead of "Berechiah," in keeping with the details of 2Ch 24:20-22.

3. The Leaders Faced Judgment (23:37-39)

23:37-39. Jesus reiterated the fate awaiting the Jewish people because of the disobedience of the leaders. Judgment, however, is not the last word, for Jesus will come again to a repentant people. At some time in the future, as a virtual prerequisite for the second coming, the Jewish people will recognize that Jesus of Nazareth is their Messiah, and will express a Ps 118:26-like confession. Only then will He come (cf. also Ac 3:19-20) and be seen by them in fulfillment of Zch 12:10. Cf. the comments on Mt 21:4-9 for the significance of Ps 118:26.

XI. The Future Coming of the King-Messiah (24:1–25:46)

The Olivet Discourse. There are several different approaches to this often disagreed upon discourse. Preterists (from the Latin "praeteritus," "that which has passed," "bygone events") maintain that these chapters were fulfilled in AD 70, with Jesus' second coming being a coming only to Israel (not for the whole world) *in judgment*. But the view is extremely unlikely. David Turner (*Matthew*, 584) writes, "One difficulty with preterism is its truncation of Jesus's eschatology, which brings the reign of heaven to earth (6:10) and renews the world (19:28). If all this has already occurred, one wonders at the underwhelming denouement of the glorious future promised by the biblical prophets, John, and Jesus himself. It is very doubtful that the global language of Mt 24 (e.g., 24:3, 7, 14, 21-22,

27, 30-31, 40-41; see also 25:31-32) can be satisfactorily explained by a local event in 70 CE, as significant as that event was. . . ."

Partial preterists see the structure of Mt 24 in a number of ways. One view is that 24:4-25 (or 28) is about AD 70, and 24:26 (or 29; or 36) is about the second coming of Christ. But Jesus weaves the mention of His coming into this whole section (cf. v. 14, where the end should probably be connected with His coming on the strength of v. 3; cf. also vv. 27, 30), and the extreme conditions of vv. 21-22 make it unlikely that AD 70 are in view.

Another approach held by some futurists is that vv. 4-28 refers to hardships throughout the Church Age, as do vv. 32-35, with AD 70 a notable example of them in vv. 15-20. This period is then followed by the second coming, seen in vv. 29-31. But this view requires the reader to shift his historical and chronological understanding from the expanse of the entire Church Age (vv. 4-13), back to AD 70 (vv. 15-20), then to the second coming (vv. 21-22), then back to AD 70 (vv. 23-28), then to the second coming again (vv. 29ff.), then to the entire Church Age yet again (vv. 32-35), though "this generation" in v. 34 refers to the generation of Jesus' day that experienced AD 70. How vv. 32-35 can refer to the entire Church Age but "this generation" in v. 34 only to Jesus' contemporaries is not made completely clear. All of this chronological shifting is expecting a lot, perhaps too much, of Jesus' hearers and Matthew's readers.

An attractive alternative is offered by other futurists. They maintain that the events associated with AD 70 serve as an attesting sign that some day the events of the great tribulation will also take place, followed by the second coming. Verses 32-33 indicate that vv. 4-31 are the signs about the end of the age and the second coming but do not actually include those end time events. "This generation" (v. 34), many of those alive in Jesus' day, will see all the events associated with AD 70, and that guarantees that there will be a tribulation period followed by the *Parousia* in the future. But this view falls prey to the objections leveled against the preterist views.

Still other futurists maintain that Mt 24 has a dual fulfillment, so that it speaks both of the events of AD 70 and of the second coming. But neither Jesus nor Matthew give any clear clues that this is the case, and without them it is difficult to conclude that the original hearers or readers would have understood that this one text presented twofold layers.

The approach adopted here is to view Mt 24–25 from a consistently futurist and pretribulational position. The first question in 24:3c, **When will these things happen?** (24:3c), is answered second by Jesus in 24:36-44, and His answer describes the surprise commencement of the day of the Lord (also known as "the great tribulation" [Dn 12:1; Mt 24:21] and "the time of Jacob's trouble [Jr 30:7]) which is initiated by the rapture of the Church. The second question in 24:3d, **what will be the sign of Your coming, and of the end of the age?**, is answered first in 24:4-35, in which Jesus describes the various signs that arise during the day of the Lord. The various time references move back and forth during the seven-year tribulation period (v. 14 mentions the end of the tribulation; v. 15 describes events occurring in the middle of it; vv. 29-31 the end and the second coming; vv. 32-35 the entire tribulation period and the second coming; vv. 36-44 the startling commencement of the tribulation, including the rapture). This is a common dispensational interpretation, and for the best defense of it, see John F. Hart, "Should Pretribulationists Reconsider the Rapture in Matthew 24:36-44?", *Journal of the Grace Evangelical Society* 20 (Spring 2007), 51-75.

The weakness of this approach is that it does not adequately account for 23:38, where Jesus is surely referring to AD 70. It also requires that the first question of 24:3 receives an answer that is about an eschatological molestation of Jerusalem and the temple and not about its destruction in AD 70. Another weakness is that it sees "this generation" in v. 34 as a reference to people other than those alive in Jesus' day who saw the events of AD 70. See the comments below for the responses to these issues. There are other weaknesses as well, but overall the consistently futurist view handles the text less awkwardly at key points than the other approaches.

Since AD 70 figures prominently in how some interpret Mt 24–25, a brief review of the revolt is in order. The Jewish people had endured religious insults and monetary pilfering under corrupt Roman governors for some time, and when they reacted negatively to it Rome countered brutally. Governor Gessius Florus killed over 3,000 people, and Jewish zealots wrested control of Jerusalem away from the Romans in an effort to inspire its inhabitants to join in their revolt. Nero dispatched General Vespasian to deal with the uprising which had spread into Galilee in the north. But in June, 68, Nero committed suicide to avoid being assassinated by subordinates. In the ensuing year, Servius Sulpicius Galba and Marcus Salvius Otho successively took the throne and were promptly terminated. Vitellius (Aulus Vitellius Germanicus) took the throne but lost the support of the Roman army. The eastern Roman legions backed Vespasian as the new emperor, who abruptly departed for Egypt in late 69 and orchestrated the demise of Vitellius from there. Vespasian left his son, Titus, about 30 at the time, in charge of subduing Jerusalem, which was finally accomplished in September, 70, after a seven-month siege that left the temple burned, much of the city destroyed, and a majority of the populace of Jerusalem dead because of starvation.

A. The Beginning of the Great Tribulation (24:1-14)

24:1-2. Matthew 23 is a stand-alone discourse because, as with the other discourses, when Jesus concluded it Matthew recorded that He departed from the place the discourse was given (cf. 8:1; 11:1; 13:53; 19:1; and 24:1). But 24:1-2 are closely connected thematically to 23:37-39, describing further the desolation of Jerusalem. **Going away** indicates that at the end of Tuesday of Passion Week, Jesus returned to Bethany with His disciples. The slope of the Mount of Olives affords a panoramic view of the Temple Mount and engendered the disciples' observation (v. 1). **Not one stone here will be left upon another** may refer to the destruction of Jerusalem and the temple in AD 70, but the events described by Jesus in vv. 4-28 do not fit what is known of those days. Cf. the comments on vv. 15-16. If Matthew's gospel was written before AD 70, and the evidence indicates that it was, then a reasonable understanding of v. 2 is that He was referring to the trauma that would be incurred by the Holy City during the future tribulation period (cf. Mc 4:11–5:1; Zch 12:1-3; 14:1-2). This well-known end-times event would have been readily familiar to Matthew's readers and Jesus' disciples, but the same cannot be said for AD 70 as it had not yet occurred.

24:3. It is likely that the disciples' questions do not have AD 70 in mind. **When will these things happen?** (answered in vv. 36-44) should be understood in light of the dual-sided question, **What will be the sign of Your coming, and of the end of the age?** (answered in vv. 4-35). The twelve apparently envisioned a connection between "when" these things happen and the sign(s) that culminate in the end, which makes it somewhat difficult to see AD 70 as playing much of a role in His answer. The syntax of the question, **What will be the sign of Your coming, and of the end of the age?** suggests that the disciples inquired about a **sign** that forecast both the **coming** of Jesus and the **end of the age**, two matters that are distinct, closely-related, but not identical (see Daniel B. Wallace, *Granville Sharp's Canon and Its Kin: Semantics and Significance* [Studies in Biblical Greek] [New York: Peter Lang, 2009], 185–93). For **the sign**, see the comments on 24:30. **Your coming** (*parousias*, from which the word *Parousia*, a technical term for Christ's second coming, is derived) signals that the disciples finally grasped, at least to some extent, that Jesus was leaving (16:21; 17:9, 12, 22-23; 20:17-19; 21:38-39), and that His return would involve cataclysmic events.

24:4-8. Beginning in v. 4 and running through v. 35, Jesus answers the question in 24:3 regarding the sign of His coming and the end of the age (see the recurrence of sign in v. 30). He gave several signs, not just one, indicating that His answer to their question was somewhat unexpected. Verses 4-14 summarize the entirety of the tribulation period including its end (v. 14). The events of vv. 4-8 are part of the seal judgments early in the tribulation. See the comments on Rv 6:9-11. **I am the Christ** (v. 5) is often viewed as a reference to the presence of messianic claimants before AD 70, the most likely candidates being Judas of Galilee (Ac 5:37), Theudas, who led a short-lived revolt c. AD 43-46 (Ac 5:36; Josephus, *Ant.* 20.97-98), an unknown Egyptian (Ac 21:38), Simon bar Giora, a leader of one Jewish faction at AD 70 (Josephus, *War*, 2.521-522; 7.26-32), Menahem, another leader in the war c. AD 70 (Josephus, *War*, 2.433-448). But there is no clear indication that any of them applied the title to himself, as v. 5 requires, until Simon bar Kokhba at the time of the second revolt (c. AD 132–135). It is preferable to see Jesus referring to a phenomenon during the great tribulation (cf. the comments on Rv 6:2). For vv. 6-7, see Rv 6:4-6 for these same events being part of the seal judgments during the tribulation. **That is not yet the end** (v. 6) and **the beginning of birth pangs** (v. 8) are cited in support the view that this part of the discourse is about the trials of the Church Age, or events culminating in AD 70, and not the *Parousia*. Perhaps more likely is that they refer to events early in the tribulation period (the seal judgments), and indicate that other eschatological events with greater severity will follow them before the end. **Birth pangs** is a technical expression for the upheaval associated with the day of the Lord (Is 13:8; 26:17; 66:7-8; Jr 4:31; 6:24; 22:23; 30:5-7; 48:41; Hs 13:13 Mc 4:9-10; 1QH 3:7-10; *1 Enoch* 62:4; 1Th 5:3; Rv 12:2), and their **beginning** more easily supports the idea of events early during those end-times woes than they do a reference to AD 70 or the span of the Church Age. **These things** picks up these things in v. 3.

24:9-14. The events in this paragraph describe conditions that arise later in the tribulation period, with **then** (v. 9) signaling this transition. **The one who endures . . . will be saved** (v. 13) is found verbatim in 10:22. See the comments there. **And then the end will come** (v. 14), in connection with **Your coming** in v. 3, must refer to the end of the age, which makes it difficult to understand vv. 9-14 as referring to conditions around AD 70 when the gospel can hardly be said to have been **preached in the whole world . . . to all the nations** (though cf. Rm 10:18 and the comments there).

B. The Middle and End of the Great Tribulation: The Abomination of Desolation (24:15-28)

24:15-16. Verse 15 shifts from the end of the tribulation described in v. 14 to consider one of the key signs in the middle of the tribulation period, namely, **THE ABOMINATION OF DESOLATION**. It is mentioned in Dn 9:24-27; 11:31; 12:11; see the comments there. According to Daniel, the **abomination** takes place half-way through the 70th week of Daniel. The **abomination of desolation** should not be associated with the destruction of the temple in AD 70, for a number of reasons. The **abomination of desolation** in Mt 24:15 seems to take people by surprise, but there was no surprise when the Romans came under General Titus, who laid siege to the city for seven months before its fall in September, AD 70. In 24:16, the people could flee, but could not with Titus since the Romans built a siege wall all the way around Jerusalem's walls to prevent this. In addition, the siege left enormous numbers of the residents of Jerusalem dead or severely weakened, and when the Romans finally took the city, there was virtually no one who fled. According to Mt 24, the temple will be desecrated. However, with Titus, in AD 70, it was destroyed before it could be desecrated (though the Roman soldiers raised their ensigns in the temple, sacrificed to their gods, and sang in honor of Titus. Cf. Josephus, *War,* 6.316). In short, if Jesus is giving a prophecy of AD 70, He was wrong about much of what actually happened—which is somewhat problematic for one's Christology. **Let the reader understand** was probably a comment made by Jesus rather than an editorial aside by Matthew, challenging His followers to read Daniel 9 in light of His reference to it here. **Flee to the mountains** (v. 16) is also unlikely to refer to AD 70, since the Judean mountains were crawling with the soldiers from four Roman legions.

24:17-20. Verses 17-18 indicate that people should flee without giving any thought to getting things from their homes. During the **winter** (v. 20), roads were wet, muddy, and could be extremely hard to travel on. On the **Sabbath**, they might be more reluctant to flee as it would violate the command to rest, or they might not find much help along the way.

24:21-22. This is probably a reference to the future tribulation period, and not to AD 70. As bad as the Jewish war with Rome was, it does not match the severity of the language Jesus employed here. The phrase **unless those days had been cut short** means that God would not allow the days to go on for an undetermined time. This shows He is sovereign over the length of the great tribulation. **Elect** (v. 22; cf. also 24:24, 31) is often applied to Christians (cf. Rm 8:33; Col 3:12), and it is usually assumed that the word here refers to believers. At this point in the Olivet Discourse, the apostles function as representatives of the nation of Israel, not necessarily the Church (see Bruce A. Ware, "Is the Church in View in Matthew 24-25?", *BibSac* April-June 1981, 158-172), and, more precisely, as the leaders of the remnant of Israel during the tribulation. David K. Lowery ("A Theology of Matthew," in *A Biblical Theology of the New Testament*, Roy B. Zuck and Darrell L. Bock, eds. [Chicago: Moody, 1994], 44, 60) points out that Jesus' disciples serve as a model of future disciples in 10:17-22, where they and the subsequent disciples whom they represent will suffer for their testimony, and in 10:23, where their mission to reach Israel will be continued by others after them. It is plausible that the disciples here serve as a model of the experience of future Jewish believers and those who lead them during the tribulation. Furthermore, Dn 9:24, which introduces the abomination of desolation prophecy, says, "Seventy weeks have been decreed for your people and your holy city. . . .", indicating that Dn 9 was intended for, and was primarily about, the Jewish people. Jesus' reference to Daniel in Mt

24 probably carries over the same focus, so that at least in 24:4-15 the experience of believing Israel during the tribulation is in view here, not that of the Church, while the experience of the Church is found in 24:36.

24:23-28. The main difference between this warning (v. 23) and the one in 24:4-5, 11, is that here the claim to be the messiah is made by one on behalf of another. False leaders arise calling attention to themselves in the earlier section, but here they garner support from many others. In contrast to Jesus, the false messiahs and false prophets will freely work miracles to promote themselves (v. 24), whereas Jesus insisted on secrecy about most of His acts. On the miracles of the antichrist, cf. 2Th 2:8-9; Rv 13:13. Unlike the first advent, the second will be as sudden and unmistakable as a flash of lightning (vv. 26-27). All doubt will vanish, and all false messiahs will be unmasked. No one will have to say, "Look here, look there." These verses make the preterist position (that Jesus' second coming to judge Israel happened in AD 70) more difficult to defend. Verse 28 is puzzling, but by this Jesus may mean that in the same way vultures inevitably find carrion, so also it is inevitable that everyone alive in those days will see the second coming.

C. The Second Coming (24:29-35)

24:29-31. It is possible that there is a gap between v. 28 and v. 29 to accommodate enough time for AD 70 to transpire and the Church Age to run its course before the second coming. "Prophetic foreshortening" is a phenomenon found in biblical prophecy where eschatological events are presented as if happening one immediately after another when in fact there may be centuries between them (cf. Is 9:6a,b, with 9:6c; Dn 9:24-25, with 9:26-27). If there is such a gap here, that would fit nicely with the unknowability of the time of the *Parousia*. If vv. 4-28 are about events surrounding AD 70 (the preterist and partial-preterist view) or about the entire Church Age (some futurists) followed by a time gap after which the events of vv. 29 transpire, then no one could know when He will come. The main problem with this understanding is that it seriously minimizes the force of the phrase **immediately after the tribulation of those days**. Jesus gives a clear chronological marker that does not easily allow for prophetic foreshortening here, and **immediately** connects the temporal proximity of the signs of the tribulation to the second coming. The darkening of the heavenly bodies (v. 29) signals the arrival of the day of the Lord, the great tribulation. For other passages that refer to cosmic disturbances at the end of the tribulation, cf. Ezk 32:7; Jl 2:31; 3:15; Rv 6:1-14. The two occurrences of **then** (v. 30) make it likely that the **sign** is distinct from, and chronologically follows, the phenomena in the sky (v. 29) and is distinct from but immediately precedes the coming of the Son of Man mentioned in the last half of v. 30. The word **sign** (see 24:3d) could be translated "ensign, standard, flag." When ancient Israel's troops were mustered, a ram's horn was blown (note the **TRUMPET** in 24:31; cf. Ex 19:16) and an ensign with a crosspiece at the top was raised, to which an animal (usually a snake) was affixed. There is an end-times context in Is 11:10-16, where God raises His flag as He begins His campaign to crush Israel's enemies and regather His people to their land. The **sign of the Son of Man**, then, is some kind of visible militaristic portent that indicates the commencement of Jesus' campaign. The appearance of this **sign** causes the **tribes of the earth** to **mourn**, an allusion to both Dn 7:13 and Zch 12:10 but with world-wide application. Sometimes v. 31 is interpreted as a reference to a posttribulational rapture, and while possible, it is unlikely that this is the case. The phrase **WILL GATHER** (*episynago*) is used in the LXX in Ps 105:47 (English translations 106:47) and 147:2 (English translations 146:2) for the regathering of the Jewish people to the Holy Land following God rescuing them (also the point of the sounding of the trumpet in Is 27:13, cited by Matthew in v. 31). In the OT, this regathering was not a "rapture" in which God's people would receive their resurrected, glorified bodies but appears to be an event experienced in natural bodies in which God gathers them into the millennial kingdom.

24:32-35. All these things (vv. 33, 34) refers to the signs mentioned in vv. 4-31. When these signs begin to come to pass, the people alive at that time can be assured that they will see His second coming as well. **All these things** (plural adjective and pronoun; see "these things" in 24:3c) is distinct from **He** [or "it"—probably the *Parousia*] **is** [the verb is third person singular] **near**, so that the *Parousia* is not included in **all these things**. **This generation** (v. 34) is almost universally taken as a reference to the people alive in Jesus' day, and **generation** usually means this in Matthew (cf. 11:16; 12:41; 17:17). However, this is often assumed rather than argued, and the context of v. 34 points in another direction. The **generation** in v. 34 will pass away only after **all these things take place**. **All these things** probably include the world-wide preaching of the gospel message followed by the end (v. 14), the future abomination of desolation (vv. 15), the unparalleled world-wide tribulation for which God limits the days (vv. 21-22), the increase of false messiahs (vv. 24), followed immediately by cosmic upheaval (v. 29), the militaristic sign of Jesus' coming (v. 30), and then, presumably, His second coming which follows hard on the heels of these signs (v. 30; probably v. 33). The near-demonstrative pronoun **this** often refers to that which is near in the mind of the writer or speaker (cf. Daniel B. Wallace, *Greek Grammar Beyond the Basics: An Exegetical Syntax of the New Testament* [Grand Rapids, MI: Zondervan, 1996], 325), and to assign to **this generation** the referent "those living in the disciples' day who survive until AD 70" is somewhat ungainly in light of the contextually-immediate discussion of the events associated with the end (especially vv. 30-31, **all these things** in vv. 33 and 34). Another interpretation which understands the meaning of **generation** as "family" or "race" ("this family—the Jewish people—will not pass away," even though it might seem like they will because of the severity of the tribulation) is an unlikely sense based on Jesus' and Matthew's other uses.

D. Instruction Urging Readiness for the Day of the Lord (24:36–25:30)

24:36-41. These verses answer the first question in 24:3c, "When will these things happen?" **But** (v. 36) is actually two words, "but concerning" (*peri de*; see the ESV), and frequently indicates a move to a new thought (Mt 22:31; Mk 12:26; 13:32; Ac 21:25; 1Co 7:1; 8:1; 12:1; 16:1, 12; 1Th 4:9, 13; 5:1). In this case the shift is away from the discussion of Jesus' coming during **those days** (note the plural; see vv. 19, 22, 29) at the end of the tribulation (vv. 29-31) to the suddenness of the *beginning* of the day of the Lord (**that day**, v. 36—note the singular) including the rapture of the Church which commences it. **Of that day** [the day of the Lord; 1Th 5:4] **and hour** [used for end-time woes in Jn 16:21-22; Rv 3:10] **no one knows** is highly problematic for every eschatological school, for Jesus claims that one can know that His coming is near based upon observable signs (24:4-35, especially vv. 29-35), and yet says that no one can know **that day and hour** (vv. 36, 39, 42, 43, 44, 50 twice; 25:13) (for the issue, see Douglas J. Moo, "The Case for the Posttribulation Rapture Position," in Gleason L. Archer, Jr., Paul D. Feinberg, Douglas J. Moo, and Richard R. Reiter, *The Rapture: Pre-, Mid-, or Post-tribulational?* [Grand Rapids, MI: Baker, 1984], 209). The problem stems from the failure to note that the events of vv. 29-35 and vv. 36-44 are different events. The second coming will be recognizable (v. 33), but the beginning of the day of the Lord will be a complete surprise unknown to all (v. 36) (Robert L. Thomas, "Imminence in the NT, Especially Paul's Thessalonian Epistles," *The Master's Seminary Journal* 13 [Fall 2002], 193; Hart, "Should Pretribulationists Reconsider the Rapture in Matthew 24:36-44? Part 1 of 3," 71-74). Similarly intriguing is that Jesus claims to have no knowledge of the time of His own second coming, leading some to question His omniscience. It is important to remember that Jesus had both a human and a divine nature. In His humanity, He grew tired, hungered, and could be tempted – and apparently could choose to be ignorant of things not necessary or profitable for Him or others to know. Robert H. Gundry (*Matthew: A Commentary on His Literary and Theological Art* [Grand Rapids, MI: Eerdmans, 1982], 492) notes, "Theologically we may say that just as Jesus did not exercise his omnipotence except to further the kingdom . . . , so he did not exercise his omniscience except to further the kingdom. To have known and made known the exact time of his coming [better, the beginning of the day of the Lord and the rapture of the Church] would have damaged the work of the kingdom by encouraging carelessness during the interim." On this occasion, Jesus chose not to "access" knowledge about the timing of the *Parousia*, something He could have done through His divinity. The analogy with **Noah** (vv. 37-39) is detrimental for a preterist view of the discourse, for the flood, like the *Parousia*, had world-wide effects and did not just affect the Holy Land. It will be "business as usual" in the world when Jesus returns, suggesting similar conditions **before the flood** and before the start of the day of the Lord (the tribulation), and the pretribulational rapture which designates its inception (v. 38; see the comments on 1Th 5:1-3). **They did not understand** (lit., "know," v. 39) reflects the surprise coming of the day of the Lord (v. 36). **The flood came and took them all away** (v. 39) does not refer to Noah and his family being taken away safely by the ark. The plural pronouns and verbs in these verses relate to those who perished in the flood. In addition, Matthew's **the flood came and took** [*airo*] **them all way** (v. 39) in Lk 17:27 is the flood came and destroyed them all, indicating that the rapture (whether pre- or post-tribulational) is not in view in v. 39. The verb **will be taken** (*paralambano*) in vv. 40-41 can have sinister overtones in Matthew (27:27; cf. also Jn 19:16). But it also has a positive sense, "to receive to one's self, to take to safety" (Mt 1:20, 24; 2:13, 14, 20, 21), and in Jn 14:3 it is used in reference to the rapture of the Church. These points support the idea that the man and woman who are **taken** in vv. 40 and 41 are raptured out of the world before the start of the tribulation, just as Noah was taken out of harm's way before the coming of the flood. The verb **will be left** (*aphiemi*) (vv. 40, 41), when used in reference to people in Matthew's gospel, connotes abandonment (e.g., 4:11, 22; 8:15; 13:36; 19:29; 22:22, 25; 26:56), and in Jn 14:18 Jesus uses the verb to promise that He will never "abandon" believers. The man and woman who are **left** will face God's wrath in the tribulation, just as those left on the earth in Noah's day underwent God's judgment in the flood. The separating of the righteous and unrighteous for judgment is a theme seen elsewhere in Matthew (cf. 8:12; 13:39-43, 49-50; 24:48-51; 25:30, 41-46). This passage, in connection with the transition in v. 36 (see the comments there) does not readily support the concept of a post-tribulational rapture (for a helpful treatment of the analogy of the flood and its relationship to the rapture and the tribulation, see John F. Hart, "Should Pretribulationists Reconsider the Rapture in Matthew 24:36-44? Part 2 of 3," 45-63; and Hart, "Should Pretribulationists Reconsider the Rapture in Matthew 24:36-44? Part 3 of 3," 43-49).

24:42-44. The suddenness and unexpectedness of the day of the Lord, and the need to be ready for it, is the focus of this and the remaining sections. Since no one knows during what **time of the night** (literally what "watch" of the night) a **thief** might strike, constant vigilance is required. Similarly, the start of the day of the Lord will be completely unexpected, as indicated by vv. 36-39 (see the comments there). For the imagery of a **thief** in connection with the rapture, see 1Th 5:2, 4; 2Pt 3:10; Rv 3:3; 16:15. To be **on the alert** (*gregoreo*, vv. 42, 43) refers to living in a way that pleases the Lord at all times so that there is no shame when He comes for the Church (1Jn 2:28). See the comments on 24:45-47 regarding the characteristics of being **alert**. A homeowner suffers loss when a thief burglarizes his home. The follower of Christ who does not live for Him will suffer loss of rewards when He comes unexpectedly (see the comments on 1Co 3:10-17). Being **on the alert** also means living differently from the behavior of those in the world (for the verb, see 1Th 5:6, 10; for the behavior, see 1Th 5:4-8).

24:45-47. Jesus spends the rest of the discourse describing what being on the alert (vv. 42, 43) for the coming of the Lord looks like. The **slave** in this parable (vv. 45-47) is the head over all the other domestics. Some think this might limit the parable to church leaders, but the application is wider. Readiness involves being **faithful and sensible** in one's interaction with others. Readiness means being kind to others (**give them their food**). There are rewards for caring for others. One is **blessed** (v. 46; see the definition at 5:1-6), and is given an enlarged capacity to serve Him (v. 47). The Parable of the Talents (25:14-30) unpacks the latter point.

24:48-51. The Parable of the Unrighteous Slave typifies the lack of readiness for the rapture. The wicked servant uses the Master's delay to abuse his fellow servants and carouse. **Beat his fellow slaves and eat and drink with drunkards** suggests that the evil slave begins to act as if he were his own master and could abuse the other slaves as many masters did. But he was not a master, and he would be held accountable for his actions. So, here is the flip side of being ready for the *Parousia*—being sure to avoid mistreating others. On v. 51, cf. the comments on 8:5-13.

25:1-4. Then (v. 1) looks back to the conditions associated with that day and hour in 24:36. The phrase **the kingdom of heaven will be comparable to** (*homoiothesetai he basileia ton ouranon*) is similar to 13:24 (*homoiothe he basileia ton ouranon*) which refers to the "mysteries of the kingdom" during the present age (see the comments on 13:10-17). Michael J. Wilkins writes, "This indicates that this parable (and the next) points explicitly to conditions during this age, the age in which the kingdom operates in a 'mystery' manner" (*Matthew*, NIVAC [Grand Rapids, MI: Zondervan, 2004], 804), suggesting that the Parable of the Wise and Foolish Virgins relates to the theme of readiness for the beginning of the day of the Lord and the rapture of the Church. The virgins, unlike the wicked slave (24:48), had no prior knowledge of a delay. These virgins assembled near the groom's home to which the wedding party would venture after the groom collected the bride (see the comments on 1:18-21). **For** (v. 3) explains what constituted the foolishness of the five. The **oil** could stand for numerous things, but because the main point of the parable is readiness, it is unnecessary to be specific. The key is not what the oil is but the lack of readiness in the form of insufficient foresight by the foolish virgins (cf. vv. 10, 13 with 24:42, 44, 50-51).

25:5-13. The **bridegroom** is Jesus, the delay is the time between the ascension and His coming, the wise and foolish virgins are true or false disciples, and the exclusion of the foolish virgins from the wedding feast represents the judgment of unbelievers on earth during the day of the Lord, while believers participate in the heavenly "marriage supper of the Lamb" (Rv 19:7-10; see the comments there) following the rapture, and later in the millennial kingdom on earth. **They all got drowsy and began to sleep** (v. 5) does not mean that even the wise virgins had some moral lapse or that they had all died. Their sleeping simply functions to indicate the length of the delay. For the **shout** (v. 6), see also 1Th 4:16. **All those virgins rose** (v. 7) likewise does not depict the resurrection of dead believers, nor do vv. 8ff. indicate that people will have a second chance to enter the kingdom after their resurrection. The phrase **those who were ready** (v. 10) reveals the main point of the parable, namely, that here readiness is preparedness *before He returns*. One cannot leave "getting ready" to the last minute. If one seeks to get ready while He is coming, it is too late (similarly 22:11-14; and see the comments on 23:39). The coming of the Lord in the rapture and the start of the day of the Lord will be completely unexpected, and unless one is prepared before that time, he will face the hardship of the tribulation period (vv. 11-12). See the comments on 7:21-23, where, like the unwise virgins, false teachers say, "Lord, Lord," Jesus responds with "I do not know you" and exclusion from the kingdom also occurs. Those excluded from the kingdom are those who failed to prepare for His coming well in advance of it. **Then** (v. 13) should be translated "therefore," and introduces the application Jesus intends His followers to grasp from the parable. The verb **be on the alert** means "to be alert, watchful" as it does in 24:42, 43. For **the day** and **the hour**, see the comments on 24:36. Both passages encourage spiritual vigilance to be ready for Christ's coming.

25:14-18. The word **for** (v. 14) introduces an expansion on the concept of readiness found in 24:36–25:13. Being ready for the return of the Lord at the rapture means being industrious for Him. The **man** in the parable represents Jesus, the **journey** is His absence during the Church Age, the productive **slaves** represent faithful disciples who are ready, and the third slave an unfaithful (false) disciple. A talent (Gk. *talanta*) was the largest denomination of money in the Greco-Roman world and is estimated to be worth as much as 6,000 days' wages, or about 20 years of income for an average laborer. Each slave was given a different amount, **each according to his own ability**, but the same expectation appeared to go with each: Gain something for the master while he was gone. The **talents** are often identified as the gospel, the Word of God, one's spiritual gifts, or stewardship of "time, talent, and treasure." None of these work especially well in the parable (Did the first slave gain five more gospels? Did the second slave gain two more spiritual gifts?). In light of the reward consisting in greater responsibility (vv. 21, 23), the **talents** should be understood in the most general terms, such as a disciple's fulfillment of his or her responsibilities, whatever they might be. The third slave (v. 18) **hid his master's money** by burying it, which was not a bad measure in those days to ensure security. As a result, however, he **gained** nothing for the master, in contrast to the other two slaves (vv. 16, 17).

25:19-23. After a long time (v. 19) indicates a delay in the start of the day of the Lord and the rapture. **Settled accounts** refers to the judgment following the rapture, perhaps at the *bema* seat judgment (see 1Co 3:10-17; Rm 14:10-12). The two slaves were given differing amounts and their returns reflected that. But the master said identical words to both **(You were faithful with a few things, I will put you in charge of many things; enter into the joy of your master**, vv. 21 and 23) in connection with the reward, which included a slice of the master's own **joy**. This implies that whatever level of abilities Jesus has given, His followers will be held responsible for faithfully making gains corresponding to the amount entrusted to them – no more, no less. Scripture is muted about future rewards, but this parable suggests they involve enlarged opportunities to serve Him when the millennial kingdom is established and to experience **the joy of** the **master** as it is done. But it also ties those rewards to what the believer does presently, during the time the Master is away. While works will not save a person, one must never think that works are inconsequential.

25:24-25. These verses provide the motivation for the third slave's inappropriate actions. **I knew you to be a hard man** is not repeated by the master when he reiterates the slaves comments in v. 26, and this may be part of the point of the parable. Nothing in the master's interaction before this suggested that he was **hard** ("harsh," "severe," "demanding," possibly "violent").

25:26-28. But (v. 26) indicates a contrast between the treatment of the other two slaves and this one. **Lazy** means "being timid about or shrinking from accomplishing a task." The knowledge of his master's characteristics should have motivated the slave to be industrious for him. Assuming that the reaping and sowing are fittingly applied to Jesus, the sense may be that He looks for returns on work which He has not performed. Granting that a believer's fruitfulness for Jesus is a mark of His power and grace ("by the grace of God I am what I am," says Paul in 1Co 15:10a), nevertheless this fruitfulness is a result of the believer's work for Him as well ("I labored even more than all of them," 1Co 15:10c), and from the work of His followers He expects returns for Himself.

25:29-30. For begins to explain the main principle of the parable. The two faithful slaves are in the category of those who make gains for the master (**everyone who has** [made gains]) and thus, they **shall be given more** (probably more "rewards" consisting in responsibility and joy). But the evil slave is in a completely different category, being **one who does not have** anything for the Lord. **Even what he does have** does not suggest that the third slave had either fruit for the Lord or rewards, but that whatever he appeared to have was forfeited by his inactivity (cf. also 7:21-23, where the alleged good deeds of false teachers are regarded by Jesus as "lawlessness"). It is true that the third slave is counted among the slaves (v. 14), but he cannot be understood to portray a true but perhaps carnal follower of Christ, especially in light of v. 30 (for which see the comments on 8:5-13). He is a counterfeit disciple, one who never actually knew Him. In Matthew's gospel one finds true and false prophets, sheep and wolves in sheep's clothing, houses built on sand and houses built on rock, wheat and tares, wise and foolish virgins, righteous and unrighteous servants; not all who are associated with Jesus are true disciples.

E. The Judgment Following the Second Coming (25:31-46)

25:31-33. Matthew 24:36–25:30 is about His people being ready for the rapture and day of the Lord. In 25:31, the scene shifts to the judgment that will take place after the tribulation, following His second coming, when He begins to reign in His earthly kingdom (**when the Son of Man comes in His glory . . . then He will sit on His glorious throne**, v. 31). **All the nations** (v. 32) indicates that Jews and Gentiles alike are included and that this is a universal judgment.

25:34-40. The altruistic actions are done by the sheep who are called **righteous** in vv. 37, 46 (see the comments on 5:20). This text is sometimes seen as a support for works salvation, but several factors weigh against this. First, it is out of step with the rest of the NT. Second, it is the **righteous** who do these deeds. There is no indication that they are righteous because they do righteous deeds. Third, these sheep will be in the kingdom, for which see the comments on 7:21-23. Fourth, the sheep are called **blessed** (v. 34), and while there is nothing in the immediate context that develops the concept, see 5:3, 5, 10; 11:6; 13:16 and the comments there, which indicates that those who are poor in spirit and hunger and thirst for righteousness are **blessed** (see the comments on 5:3, 5, 10; 11:6; 13:16). Fifth, the righteous sheep **inherit the kingdom prepared for** them **from the foundation of the world**. Their inclusion in the kingdom cannot be contingent upon their works, for that destiny was settled before doing any works. Finally, the sheep were surprised regarding the reasons for their admission into the kingdom (i.e., good deeds; vv. 37ff.). This indicates they were not doing them in an attempt to gain admission into the kingdom. The implication from the passage is that while the good deeds do not produce righteousness, those who are righteous do good deeds. Conversely, the lack of good deeds indicates that one is among the goats. **You did it to one of these brothers of Mine** (v. 40) indicates that Jesus had in mind especially Jewish believers who suffer persecution during the tribulation and who receive help from Gentile believers at that time. It is good and proper that believers should be involved in prison ministries, but it must be noted that v. 40 indicates that these acts of kindness are rendered especially (not exclusively) to the Jewish followers of Jesus (see Gl 6:10). On vv. 34-40, D. A. Carson ("Matthew," 520) writes, "Good deeds done to Jesus' followers, even the least of them, are not only works of compassion and morality but reflect where people stand in relation to the kingdom and to Jesus himself. Jesus identifies himself with the fate of his followers and makes compassion for them equivalent to compassion for himself . . . ."

25:41-46. Those who are not true followers of Jesus will not show kindness to believers (whether they are Jewish or Gentile believers), and will also thereby indicate that they have no connection with Him (cf. 1Jn 3:14-15; 4:7-14). The goats are destined for **eternal fire which has been prepared for the devil and his angels**, but which is also enlarged to accept all who are apart from Jesus (Rv 12:9-12; 20:11-15).

In the Parable of the Sheep and Goats, Jesus reiterated the themes from the previous three parables but applies those themes to the demonstration of righteousness and being prepared for the kingdom during the tribulation. One shows he is destined for the kingdom by being kind to others, as the sheep were here. In 25:1-13, being ready meant one must be ready before He returns, and the sheep had a lifestyle of care demonstrated over some time even during the tribulation. In 25:14-30, the labor of the good slaves, like the assistance rendered by the sheep, was ultimately for the Lord. "Readiness" is the key to the Olivet Discourse, and Jesus provided concrete examples of readiness so that His followers would not be left in the dark.

XII. The Death of the King-Messiah (26:1–27:66)

A. The Hateful Plot Against Jesus (26:1-5)

26:1-2. As He was leaving the Mount of Olives, Jesus gave clear instruction about His impending death. The One who will judge will Himself be judged. He mentioned His impending crucifixion (cf. 20:19), suggesting that He knew exactly what was going on. He was no victim (in the truest sense) in what would transpire. **After two days the Passover is coming** (v. 2) indicates that Matthew is narrating events from late Tuesday afternoon or early evening that, in Jewish reckoning, would have been the start of Wednesday. Note the deliberate effort on Jesus' part to tie His death to the celebration of the Passover (see the comments on Ex 12–13). He is the Lamb of God that takes away the sins of the world (Jn 1:29). For a harmonization of the various chronological problems associated with the timing of events around Good Friday, see Carson, "Matthew," 528-32.

26:3-5. Jesus' teaching became so caustic against the leaders that they saw the need to kill Him. **The high priest** (v. 3) was appointed by the Romans to four-year terms, and one of his primary responsibilities, for which he also utilized his family, was to direct the affairs of the temple. The temple cleansing was a frontal attack against them. **Caiaphas** (a name that means "Inquisitor") was appointed by procurator Valerius Gratus and held the position from AD 18–36, a much longer tenure than traditionally was allowed, attesting to his political finesse. His father-in-law Annas served before him and continued to wield considerable authority (cf. Lk 3:2; Jn 11:47-53; 18:13-24). Their plot would not be carried out until after **the festival** (v. 5), the weeklong celebration of Passover and the Feast of Unleavened Bread. By then the pilgrims, who were enthusiastic about Jesus, would have returned to their homes.

B. The Act of Kindness for Jesus (26:6-13)

26:6-13. The episode at Bethany is a remarkably tender demonstration sandwiched between the most reprehensible deeds. The **alabaster vial** (v. 7) was probably a fine, translucent white gypsum bottle. **Costly perfume** was typically made by combining exotic oils and extracts of various spices and flowers. Mark 14:5 and Jn 12:5 indicate that it was worth about 300 denarii, or about 300 days' wages. The disciples reacted so strongly (vv. 8-9) because, during Passover, it was customary for affluent Jews to offer financial help to the poor. The perfume could have been sold for that. But Jesus defended the woman (vv. 10-13), saying that her act would serve **to prepare Me for burial** (v. 12). When a rich person died the body was doused in perfume then wrapped in a burial shroud. More spices were placed in its folds, not to mummify the body but to cut the odors of decomposition for tombs were not airtight. However, crucified criminals did not receive such treatment. After a body was left to putrefy on a cross, it was usually cast into the city dump, in Jerusalem's case the Hinnom Valley on the southeast edge of Jerusalem, and received no burial at all. What this woman did honored Jesus and gave Him burial preparations that, under normal circumstances, He otherwise would not have received.

C. The Plans Judas Formed (26:14-16)

26:14-16. These verses contain the one event Matthew recorded that took place on Wednesday of Passion Week. Judas's motivation remains one of the biggest enigmas in NT studies. Perhaps Judas wanted to betray Jesus in order to hasten

His establishment of the kingdom, and the disciples' privilege in it, as well as the overthrow of Rome. But there is not a whisper of this in the Gospels. The best evidence is that he was greedy (see the comments on Jn 12:4-6) and betrayed Jesus for the money. Matthew makes more of the **thirty pieces of silver** (v. 15) in 27:9-10.

D. The Objective of Jesus' Death: Inauguration of the New Covenant (26:17-29)

26:17-19. Verse 17 introduces Thursday of Passion Week. It was customary for the citizens of Jerusalem to provide accommodations for the Passover pilgrims (many of them family and friends). It cannot be known if Jesus made some previous arrangements with this man who would become His host for Passover or if this was an exercise of His divine omniscience. Mark 14:13 and Lk 22:10 both mention that this man would be carrying a pitcher of water. It was typically woman's work, so he would have been easy to spot. **My time is near** (v. 18) notes again the theme of Jesus' death, His knowledge and God's sovereignty over it, and its connection here with the Passover celebration.

26:20-25. That Jesus knew what was in Judas' heart but never let on to the other disciples is a remarkable testimony to His patience and self-control. Judas was assigned the place of honor closest to Jesus during their celebration (v. 23). Verse 24 presents the mysterious balance between divine sovereignty and human responsibility. Cf. also Ac 2:23-24; 4:27-28. God determined the time and circumstances of Jesus' death, and brought them about through the sinful actions of Judas. But this neither absolved Judas of guilt nor placed upon God the moral culpability of Judas's treachery.

26:26-29. For the treatment of the Lord's Table in the other gospels, see the comments on Mk 14:22-25; Lk 22:17-20; and 1Co 11:23-26. Jesus altered the traditional celebration of Passover so that it would commemorate His death. **This is My body** (v. 26) was a metaphor, not unlike the metaphors by which He likened Himself to a vine, a shepherd, or a door. The text gives no hint of any miraculous transformation as they ate the bread. As a Passover meal, it included many symbolic elements. The unleavened bread represented the haste to depart from Egypt, and the bitter herbs represented the bitterness of slavery. When these elements were discussed and consumed in the traditional Passover meal, there was no expectation that they would be mystically transformed. In the same way, when Jesus held up the elements and declared they were His body and blood, no listener would have expected it to refer to a mystical transformation. Rather, they would have understood it to mean a symbolic representation of Jesus' body and blood.

The Mishnah, which is the recorded traditions of the Jewish people collected around AD 200, prescribes how Passover should be observed (though there is no way to be certain that it reflects how it was practiced in Jesus' day). See specifically *m. Pesach.* 10. They enjoyed four cups of wine at different points in the Passover meal, corresponding to the four promises of God in Ex 6:6-7. Jesus may have introduced the Lord's Table after the third cup, called "the cup of redemption." **This is My blood of the covenant** parallels Ex 24:8: Behold the blood of the covenant [LXX *to haima tes diathekes*], which the LORD has made with you in accordance with all these words. When God made the covenant of Law with the Jewish people, the blood of bulls was used to institute it (Ex 24:5-6). But in Mt 26:28, Jesus said, **for this is *My* blood of the covenant** [*to haima* mou *tes diathekes*, emphasis added]. The wine is a symbol of His shed blood through which He inaugurated the new covenant, a covenant forecast in the OT. God would transform the hearts of His new covenant community, forgive their sin (Jr 31:31-34), and give them the Spirit (Ezk 36:25-27). See the comments on Jr 31:31-34 and Heb 8–9. The Lord's Table is also a symbol of the messianic kingdom, which is compared to a great feast (v. 29) (see 8:11; 22:2; 25:10; Is 25:6-10; Rv 19:7-9). While the disciples would engage repeatedly in the Lord's Table, Jesus would not again until He joins them in the consummated kingdom. The Lord's Table is a profound memorial (not "just" a memorial!), and conveys sanctifying (not saving) grace, strengthening the believer who reflects upon the tortured body and spilled blood of the Son of God.

E. The Boast of Jesus' Disciples (26:30-35)

26:30-35. Judas took the steps to betray Him apparently when they left the upper room for the Mount of Olives (v. 30). Jesus predicted that the disciples would flee from Him at His arrest (v. 31), and cited the messianic passage Zch 13:7, which prophesied their dispersion (for the details, see Craig Blomberg, "Matthew," 91-93). In contrast to the evil shepherds in Zch 13:1-6, the "Good Shepherd" would be struck down. God calls that Shepherd "My Associate," a word used for one's blood relatives, for those who shared ancestral ties or ethnic background (Lv 6:2; 18:20; 19:11, 15, 17; 24:19; 25:14, 15, 17). This suggests that the **SHEPHERD** is more than a mere mortal but God's equal. Jesus reassured them that He would **go ahead of** them into **Galilee,** where they would again regroup after being scattered and once again be with Jesus.

F. The Anguish in Gethsemane (26:36-46)

26:36-46. Gethsemane (v. 36), which means "olive press," was located in the Kidron Valley at the foot of the western slope of the Mount of Olives. Above it was the Temple Mount. John 18:1-2 indicates that Jesus spent time there occasionally with His disciples, perhaps debriefing at the conclusion of the stressful days of Passion Week. Judas knew the place, and this may explain how he found Him. The word **cup** is sometimes a metaphor for God's judgment in the OT (cf. Ps 11:6; Is 51:22). But why did Jesus request to not undergo His ordeal when He knew He would die that way (20:19)? Matthew does not say. He was not close to dying in Gethsemane because of the stress, as some teach, and knew that He would die of crucifixion (26:2). The phrase **to the point of death** (v. 38) very likely means something like, "I am so sad, I feel like dying." A more likely possibility is that before Gethsemane, in His humanity, He did not fully comprehend the extreme entailments of His death. God may have given Him an exhaustive view of what was before Him so that His sacrificial death could be fully obedient and fully voluntary. To go blindfolded is to go as a victim, not a gracious, obedient volunteer. In Gethsemane the blindfold came off. It was when Jesus saw the full force of His suffering that He exercised full obedience, offered with full freedom, with full knowledge, with full willingness (credit Jonathan Edwards, in his sermon "Christ's Agony," for these ideas). See the comments on Heb 5:7-10. In His human nature, He recoiled from the prospect and prayed for deliverance from it. But since God the Son came to do the will of God the Father, He obeyed His Father.

When He found the three sleeping (v. 40), He addressed **Peter** in light of his boast in v. 33, but the verbs in vv. 40-41 are second person plural and include James and John. The **temptation** (v. 41) probably related to denying Him. He wanted the disciples to escape when His captors came (cf. Jn 18:8), but denying Him was unacceptable (cf. the comments on 10:32-33). **The spirit** probably refers to the immaterial part of one's nature favorably disposed to God when the Holy Spirit influences it (Ac 17:16; 1Co 7:34). **The flesh** probably refers to the immaterial part of man typified by human weakness and values (see, e.g., Rm 7:5 and the comments there), and **is weak** when it comes to doing what is right. On three occasions Jesus found Peter and the others sleeping, and Matthew probably intends his readers to connect Peter's threefold denial to that. Peter serves as a warning about the dangers of prayerlessness in the lives of Jesus' followers. In contrast, Jesus' second and third times of prayer (vv. 42, 44) reflected a deeper resolve to obey His Father's will regardless of the extreme test that was coming.

G. The Incarceration at Gethsemane (26:47-56)

26:47-50. Judas (v. 47) came with **a large crowd with swords and clubs**. Jn 18:3 says that a "cohort"—about 600 Roman soldiers when full—was sent "from the chief priests and Pharisees" presumably with Pilate's approval, and included some Jewish officials (v. 51). A cohort was garrisoned in the Antonia Fortress adjacent to the temple complex, making their dispatch to Gethsemane uncomplicated. The **sign** of a **kiss**, and the greeting (vv. 48-49) were necessary because many of the soldiers would have been unfamiliar with Jesus. Judas may have gone ahead of the larger group to give them the cues. The betrayal in Gethsemane afforded the Jewish leaders an ideal opportunity to apprehend Jesus sooner than they planned but without Jerusalem knowing it (26:3-5, 14-16). **Friend** means "companion," though not always with a sense of warmth, or "comrade." John 18:3 says that they came "with lanterns and torches," making it likely that Jesus could see their approach from a distance. He showed remarkable courage. A twenty-minute walk up the Mount of Olives, a couple miles down the opposite slope, and He would have been in the Judean wilderness with a good possibility of escape.

26:51-54. John 18:10 names Peter as the disciple who cut off the ear of the **slave of the high priest** (v. 51) and names the slave (Malchus). Only Luke (22:51) records that Jesus healed the slave. **All those who take up the sword shall perish by the sword** (v. 52) is less a slogan supporting pacifism than it is a proverbial statement about how violence in a fallen world tends to breed more violence. If Peter had persisted in his fierce reaction, the soldiers would have killed him. Verse 53 indicates, among other things, that Jesus did not need Peter's help. **Twelve** full Roman **legions** would have contained 72,000 soldiers. **Angels**

will participate in eschatological events (13:41; 24:31), but Jesus, who here functioned as the sovereign director of this sad scene, kept them off stage. It is difficult to say which **Scriptures** were being **fulfilled** (vv. 54, 56) by Jesus' ordeal, but cf. Zch 13:7 in Mt 26:31; Ps 22:1 in Mt 27:46; Is 52:13–53:12 (especially Is 53:9, 12 in Mt 27:38, 57-61).

26:55-56. Jesus rebuked the soldiers and Jewish officials (v. 55). He taught openly in the **temple,** implying that He had nothing to hide. The leaders did not move to incarcerate Jesus during Passion Week (**I used to sit in the temple teaching and you did not seize Me**, v. 55), adopting that strategy to avoid incensing the people who favored Jesus. But in the privacy of Gethsemane there was no longer any need to restrain themselves. They accosted Him as if He were a terrorist (a better translation than the word **robber**) though He was not, and came blanketed by darkness to conceal their obscene conspiracy from the masses. Ironically, they were the ones guilty of duplicitous behavior. But their conduct did **fulfill the Scriptures** (v. 56), and Jesus was clearly aware of God's supervision of these events.

H. The Jewish Phase of Jesus' Trial (26:57-68)

26:57-58. On **Caiaphas**, cf. 26:3-5. **Scribes and elders** refer to the makeup of the Sanhedrin—71 men from both the Pharisees and Sadducees. The Romans recognized it as a self-governing body with judicial and religious authority over Judea under the leadership of the high priest. The Mishnah tractate *m. Sanhedrin* 4:1 forbade trying such a case at night, but the Mishnah was codified later than these events and it does not necessarily reflect the protocol from Jesus' day. Additionally, **the courtyard of the high priest** was an equally bizarre place to conduct such a trial. According to the record left in the Mishnah 200 years later, capital cases could be tried only within the confines of the temple complex (*m. Sanhedrin* 11:2). Such irregularities show the leaders' rush to judgment against Jesus.

26:59-64. Note that **false testimony** (v. 59) was a violation of the Law (Ex 20:16) and one who gave it was to be severely punished (Dt 19:16-19). The testimony eventually given misrepresented Jesus' statement, **I am able to destroy the temple of God and to rebuild it in three days** (v. 61) (reflected in Jn 2:18-22; see the comments there). On the cleansing of the temple and its significance for His trial, cf. the comments on Mt 21:10-13. **Jesus kept silent** (v. 63; cf. also 27:12-14) while being questioned for at least two reasons: First, it showed his willingness to die in fulfillment of Is 53:7. Second, Jesus was brilliant, as demonstrated by His skill in debating His opponents (Mt 22:15-46). If He would have spoken in His own defense, He could have procured His own acquittal. The only times He spoke were to answer questions related to His identity (**Tell us whether You are the Christ, the Son of God**, v. 63; Are you the King of the Jews?, 27:11). For Him to remain silent on these questions would have been to deny Himself. **You have said it yourself** (v. 64; cf. 26:25; 27:11) was an affirmative response to Caiaphas, and the reaction of the members of the Sanhedrin indicated that they took it that way. Many critical scholars deny that Jesus ever actually claimed to be the Messiah, the Son of God, but Matthew indicates otherwise. For the force of Dn 7:13-14, see the comments there.

26:65-68. When **the high priest tore his robes** (v. 65), he violated Lv 21:10. This act by Caiaphas was apparently intended to incite the Sanhedrin against Jesus even more. On the verb **blasphemed**, see the comments on 9:1-8. Blasphemy was considered a capital offense in the OT, deserving stoning (Lv 24:16). Once again, *m. Sanhedrin* 4:1, written much later, required that the rights of the one being tried be protected, and the authorities were supposed to safeguard the presumption of innocence until proven guilty. His "trial" was a mockery of justice.

I. The Denials by Peter (26:69-75)

26:69-75. See the comments in 10:32-33 for the relationship between "denying Christ" and Peter's denials. Jesus predicted that both Judas (Mt 26:25) and Peter (Mt 26:34) would deny Him. Matthew says that both were overcome by remorse. The main difference between the two, aside from Judas being an unbeliever (Jn 6:64, 70-71)—an important distinction—is that Jesus prayed for Peter (Lk 22:31-32), just as He does for all His true followers (Rm 8:34) who are thereby kept forever in God's love. **The way you talk gives you away** (v. 73) reflects Peter's Galilean accent, which led **the bystanders** to connect him with Jesus. The denials were solemnized with **an oath** (v. 72), cursing and swearing (v. 74). On oaths, see the comments on 5:33-37 and 23:16-22. **To curse** means "to invoke God to bring harm upon one's self if what he said were not true, or if he failed to do what he promised." When Peter **wept bitterly**, some of the anguish may have stemmed from the prospect of God afflicting him for making these false statements.

J. The Remorse of Judas (27:1-10)

27:1-2. When morning came introduces the final part of the all-night phase of Jesus' trial. **Conferred together** reflects the Sanhedrin's deliberations regarding how to enlist Pilate's assistance to execute Jesus. "Blasphemy" was not a charge for which the Roman government would have executed someone. **Pilate** was a prefect (a military leader) who received his appointment in AD 26 from Sejanus, the powerful leader of the Praetorian Guard in Rome. Sejanus was both a friend of Emperor Tiberius and a known hater of the Jewish people, and Pilate probably was influenced by his anti-Semitism. Pilate's tenure was immediately beset with problems. He brought into Jerusalem army flags embossed with the emperor's figure, infuriating the Jewish leaders as it bordered on idolatry. Later he confiscated money from the temple treasury to build an aqueduct into Jerusalem, and when a crowd protested, he had soldiers, disguised among the crowd, club many of them to death. After his brutal suppression of the followers and leaders of a (supposed) Samaritan prophet, he was dismissed from his post and sent home to Rome in late AD 36 or early 37. By all accounts, he felt nothing but repugnance for the Jewish people.

27:3-10. On the basis of pure chronology, Judas probably acted after Pilate's decision, but Matthew may have included it here to contrast Judas and Peter. Judas **felt remorse** (*metamelomai*), but did not sincerely repent. In contrast, Peter did indeed repent, and his restoration to Jesus and the leadership of the early church demonstrated his genuineness. Judas may have sought forgiveness from the **chief priests and elders** (v. 3), but their response indicated that they had no more interest in the one who betrayed Jesus. See the comments on Ac 1:18-19 for the harmonization of the accounts of Judas's suicide. The use of funds gained illicitly could not be used to benefit the temple (v. 6; cf. Dt 23:18). The leaders once again "strained out a gnat" in their caution to use Judas's blood money correctly, but "swallowed a camel" by orchestrating Jesus' death. They bought an unclean piece of property in the Hinnom Valley, according to tradition, where those who died while visiting Jerusalem could be buried. Matthew spliced together several OT passages in vv. 9-10, but which ones, and the point he makes with them, is not altogether clear (see the comments in the relevant OT passages). For the view that Zch 11:4-14 is a direct messianic prophecy, see the comments there. Both Zechariah (out of anger) and Judas (out of despair) threw the money into the temple. Jeremiah bought a field (Jr 32:6-9) as a prophetic sign that God would judge, then restore, the nation (Jr 32:23-36). Long before Zch 11, Jeremiah used the metaphor of a potter for God's right to judge Judah (Jr 18:2, 9-12; 19:2-13) in part because of atrocities done in the Hinnom Valley (called "Topheth" in Jr 19:6, 14). As in Jeremiah's day, the leaders preferred to buy an unclean field in the Hinnom Valley rather than embrace the Son of God, an atrocity for which God would judge them. Matthew referred to **Jeremiah** (v. 9) probably because Matthew's immediate intent was to show that the purchase of the Potter's Field fulfilled prophecy, and possibly because Jeremiah was the more prominent prophet who originated the potter imagery long before Zechariah mentioned it.

K. The Roman Phase of Jesus' Trial (27:11-26)

27:11-14. The governor questioned Him. In provinces like Judea the governors investigated charges and tried cases by themselves without juries in a procedure called *cognitio extra ordinem*. Hence Pilate acted alone. According to custom, the governor would sit on the tribunal seat (*bema*) to try the case (cf. Bruce Corley, "Trial of Jesus," in *Dictionary of Jesus and the Gospels*, eds. Joel B. Green and Scot McKnight [Downers Grove, IL: InterVarsity, 1992], 852-53).

Are You the King of the Jews? (v. 11) was the charge submitted by the Sanhedrin. They shifted the charge from "blasphemy" to "sedition." Only Caesar was king. The charge amounted to sedition, a crime that would deserve the death penalty. But the Romans would not have executed someone over a religious dispute. So the Sanhedrin adjusted the charge against Jesus, hoping to manipulate Pilate into executing Him. For Jesus' silence (v. 14), see 26:59-64.

27:15-23. According to the Mishnah (*m. Pesach.* 8:6), it was customary for amnesty to be granted a prisoner at Passover. In an attempt to remove from himself the responsibility for dealing with Jesus, Pilate sought to get rid of Jesus through this *privilegium paschale*. But this backfired. Matthew called **Barabbas** a **notorious prisoner** (v. 16; see also Mk 15:7; Lk 23:19; Jn 18:40). **Envy** (v. 18) indicates that the leaders were threatened by Jesus' miraculous power and charisma, and sought to get rid of Him though they had no legal grounds for doing so. Pilate understood this, and was apparently hoping that the crowds, which so enthusiastically received Jesus earlier in the week, would prevail over the leaders and insist on Jesus' release. Once again, his plan backfired. The warning from Pilate's Gentile wife (v. 19) heightened her husband's guilt.

27:24-26. Pilate **washed his hands** (v. 24), indicating that he would not be liable for whatever happened to Jesus. His act, however, does not absolve him of his guilt. It was Pilate's job to investigate the charges, try the accused, render a verdict, and ensure that justice was accomplished. He was grossly irresponsible and therefore, guilty (cf. Ac 4:27). Romans often scourged criminals as part of the execution and this treatment of Jesus (v. 26) was undoubtedly gruesome. They used the dreaded *flagellum* whip, consisting in leather strips braided with sharp pieces of bone and metal. Scourging could tear the flesh down to arteries and veins, and even internal organs (Eusebius, *Eccl. Hist.* 4.15.3-5; Josephus, *War,* 2.611-612). It was not unusual for one to die while being scourged. **All the people** (v. 25) describes only the mob, not all Jewish people. The phrase **and on our children** can no more bring perpetual guilt on all the Jewish people for Jesus' death than can Pilate's hand washing absolve his guilt. Human culpability for Jesus' death rests upon the Jews and Gentiles, then, at that time, who conspired against Him (cf. Mk 10:33-34; Ac 4:27-28), not upon all Jewish people forever.

L. The Ridicule and Torture of Jesus (27:27-32)

27:27-32. A **Roman cohort** (v. 27) had 600 soldiers when full, which was unlikely inasmuch as the Holy Land was more or less at peace during this time. Nevertheless, there would have been a large gathering of men who mocked Jesus. The color **scarlet** (v. 28; "purple" in Mk 15:20, 17; Jn 19:2, 5) could be a sign of wealth, though the same word was used for the color of a soldier's tunic (the likely meaning of **robe**). The **crown of thorns** may have been a parody of the images of the emperors who were often depicted in art and on coins with rays of light emanating from their heads. **Reed** was often used for the material to make the shaft of an arrow or a stake for supporting vines. Following this abuse, they **led Him away to crucify Him** (v. 31). In a typical crucifixion, the execution squad consisted of four soldiers. They marched the condemned to the site, forcing him to carry the crosspiece (*patibulum*) to which he would be nailed. The scourging left Jesus so weakened that **a man of Cyrene**, a city in northeastern Africa, **named Simon** (v. 32) was drafted to help him carry the crosspiece.

M. The Crucifixion of Jesus (27:33-37)

27:33-37. Golgotha (v. 33) means "skull," and "Calvary" comes from the Latin word *calvaria*, also meaning "skull." Both the reason for its name and its location are uncertain, but the Church of the Holy Sepulchre commemorates the most likely place. **Golgotha** was outside the northern wall, probably alongside a busy road (Mt 27:39) near the city (Jn 19:20). **Wine mixed with gall** (v. 34) was offered to Jesus before the crucifixion by the soldiers, as Jesus' friends were not close by (27:55). Mark uses the word "myrrh" to describe the ingredient (Mk 15:23), and Matthew uses **gall** to describe the taste and provide a link with Ps 69:21. The blood loss from scourging resulted in severe dehydration not unlike profuse perspiration, and intense thirst was the result. Offering the **wine** appeared on the surface as an act of kindness, but He was mercilessly taunted since it was undrinkable. In addition, on the basis of the use of the same word (LXX *chole*) in Ps 68:22 [English 69:21] and Jr 8:14, this drink may have been poisonous. The soldiers' duty required them to remain at the site until those crucified had expired, and that could take days. It is possible that they offered Jesus this poisoned wine to hasten His death. Casting lots for the clothing of the condemned (v. 35) was customary, providing partial compensation for the soldiers due to the repulsiveness and length of their assignment (cf. also Ps 22:18). **They began to keep watch over Him there** (v. 36) because part of their duty was to ward off any rescue attempts by the associates of the crucified and to verify when death occurred. The inscription (v. 37) reflected the charge levied against Jesus by the Jewish leaders.

N. The Cruelty Against Jesus (27:38-44)

27:38-44. Robbers (v. 38) means "insurrectionists," "revolutionaries," a capital offense in Roman law—mere banditry was not. While there are no linguistic connections with it, Matthew may have presented this detail to forge a connection with Is 53:12. Three groups deride Jesus, each challenging Him to **come down from the cross** (vv. 40, 42, suggested in v. 43). The derision Jesus underwent had a typological connection with Ps 22:7-8. The words **If You are the Son of God** are found verbatim in Jesus' temptation (Mt 4:3, 6), and may hint at the diabolical source of the words of those who mocked Him. This may have been the Devil's last attempt to keep Him from fulfilling His role as the unblemished sacrificial lamb. The references to Jesus destroying **the temple** (v. 40), being the **Son of God** (vv. 40, 43), and being **King of Israel** (v. 42) reflect the accusations leveled against Him during the various phases of His trial (see 26:61, 63-64, and 27:11 respectively). Ironically, they spoke the truth about Him as the King and the Son of God, and even as the one who would destroy the temple, a feat He would accomplish in AD 70. The connection with Ps 22:8 becomes stronger in v. 46 (see comments below).

O. The Death of Jesus (27:45-56)

27:45-50. The sixth hour . . . until the ninth hour (v. 45) was noon to 3:00 p.m. **Darkness** sometimes suggested God's judgment (Ex 10:22; Jl 2:2, 31; Am 8:9), and its presence here shows the upheaval in creation that took place when God poured out His wrath upon His Son who was dying as a sacrifice. Jesus' cry (v. 46) was a citation of Ps 22:1, and by citing it Jesus was probably calling attention to His fulfillment of all that is contained in Ps 22:1-18, and not strictly 22:1 alone. This is supported by Matthew noting several connections with Ps 22 in the immediate context (Ps 22:7, 16 in Mt 27:39; Ps 22:8 in Mt 27:43; Ps 22:18 in Mt 27:35). Jesus' cry, **ELI, ELI (MY GOD, MY GOD)** was mistaken as a cry **for Elijah** (v. 47). The **drink** He was given (v. 48), judging from vv. 47 and 49, was, once again, not an act of compassion but of mockery. The **sour wine** (usually wine mixed with vinegar, a common drink of soldiers) was administered to improve His enunciation and enhance their sadistic amusement. Matthew probably intended his readers to view this in connection with Ps 69:21b. **And Jesus cried out again with a loud voice, and yielded up His spirit** [or "gave up breath"] (v. 50). That He still had **a loud voice** is remarkable, for people who died of crucifixion usually did so in such a weakened condition that they had no voice left. **Yielded up** is an active-voice verb, putting into grammatical form Jesus' sovereignty over His own death and the voluntary surrender of His life. **His spirit** is ambiguous, and could refer either to Jesus' immaterial nature (His "soul" or "spirit," but probably not "the Holy Spirit"), His "life," or His "breath" ("spirit" and "breath" employ the same word, *pneuma*, in Gk.). However it is understood, life went out of His body.

27:51-56. Matthew gives no clues regarding the significance of the tearing of the **veil of the temple** (v. 51). However, many of Matthew's fulfillment verses (e.g., 5:17-20; 11:11-13), including those related to the new covenant (26:26-29), suggest that it served as a sign of the obsolescence of the Mosaic covenant's sacrificial system and the free access of humankind to God through Jesus' blood. The earthquake and cracking of rocks also sometimes functioned as a display of God's coming in the OT (Jdg 5:4; Ps 18:6-8; 77:18), frequently associated with judgment (Is 5:25; 24:17-18; 29:6; Ezk 38:19) or great tragedy (1Sm 14:15). **Bodies of the saints who had fallen asleep** (on "sleep," see 1Th 4:13-18) **were raised** (vv. 52-53) but only **after His resurrection**. Matthew may have included this occurrence here, rather than in chap. 28, to connect it to the other effects of Jesus' death mentioned in 27:51 and to avoid distracting from the more important narrative elements about the resurrection in chap. 28. It is impossible to say from Matthew's account if the **saints** were resuscitated and subsequently died or actually received their glorified resurrection bodies and somehow ascended into heaven with Jesus. Matthew may have referred to this episode to ground the resurrection of OT and NT saints in the death and resurrection of Jesus. **The Son of God!** (v. 54) was the title used to ridicule Jesus in vv. 40, 43, but here was spoken with sincerity by the **centurion** (see 8:5-13), his rank lending credibility to his observation. The mention of **many women** (v. 55) provides continuity with 27:61 and 28:1. For a suggestion on how to harmonize 27:56 with Mk 15:40-41 and Jn 19:25, cf. Carson, "Matthew," 583.

P. The Burial of Jesus (27:57-61)

27:57-61. Arimathea (v. 57) was located at the site of modern Ramathain, about 20 miles east of modern Jaffa. **Joseph** is known only from the other gospels (Mk 15:43; Lk 23:51; Jn 19:38). Usually the body of one who was crucified was left on the cross as a graphic warning to any who would challenge Rome. That **Pilate** allowed Joseph to take Jesus' body (vv. 57-58) was another indication that **Pilate** believed Jesus was innocent. Joseph laid Jesus' body **in his own new tomb** (v. 60). It was expensive to fashion a tomb, and only the rich had them (providing the fulfillment of Is 53:9). A **large** disc-shaped **stone** usually sat in an inclined groove at the mouth of the tomb, making it easy to roll the stone into place but difficult to move it from the opening. The mention of the two Marys (v. 61) adds credence to their testimony of the empty tomb, and a note of pathos as they grieved for their fallen Master.

Q. The Securing of Jesus' Tomb (27:62-66)

27:62-66. The day after the preparation (v. 62) was Saturday, the "preparation day" being Friday before sundown during which Sabbath preparations were made. **The Pharisees** (vv. 62-64) may have been thinking of Jesus' words concerning the sign of Jonah (Mt 12:38-42, see the comments there). Debate exists regarding the nature of the **guard** to which Pilate refers (v. 65). He may have granted permission for the leaders to use the Jewish temple guard for this duty or approved the use of a contingent of Roman soldiers, the more likely possibility because of the following. The soldiers went to the Jewish leaders after the resurrection, possibly because they feared Pilate, and these leaders promised to protect them if Pilate found out about the missing body (28:14). This would not have been necessary if they were the temple guard, making it more likely that they were Roman. The **seal on the stone** (v. 66) was not placed there to make the tomb air tight, but to warn those who came to the tomb that the seal could only be broken, and the stone moved, by the Roman authorities. All others who would seek to do so would bring upon themselves the wrath of Rome.

XIII. The Resurrection of the King-Messiah (28:1-20)

A. The Angel Announced the Resurrection (28:1-8)

28:1-8. After the Sabbath (v. 1) was early Sunday morning. For "three days and three nights," see the comments on 12:38-42. Matthew did not explain why **Mary Magdalene** and **Mary** came to the tomb, but it was probably to anoint Jesus' body further (Mk 16:1), augmenting what Joseph did (Jn 19:39-40). It is not clear if the women felt the **earthquake** (v. 2), but the narrative seems to indicate that they were close by when the angel arrived and the soldiers **became like dead men** (vv. 3-5), implying that the women did feel it. An empty tomb may have meant several things, so the angel explained the reason for the missing body: **He has risen, just as He said. Galilee** was considered the "last stop" in Israel before entering Gentile lands (Is 9:1; Mt 4:15). It is significant that Jesus would give the Great Commission, targeting "all the nations," to His disciples there. For the best harmonization of all the resurrection appearances of Jesus, see Murray J. Harris, *Raised Immortal: Resurrection and Immortality in the New Testament*, (n.p.: Marshall Morgan & Scott, 1983), 69-71.

B. Jesus Announced the Resurrection (28:9-10)

28:9-10. When the women encountered Jesus, they **took hold of His feet**, indicating, among other things, that Jesus was raised bodily and was no ghost. **My brethren** (v. 10) probably encompassed more than the eleven remaining disciples, and may accommodate those who had doubts in v. 17.

C. The Guards Were Bribed to Lie about the Resurrection (28:11-15)

28:11-15. That the guards told the Jewish leaders **all that had happened** (v. 11) heightened the guilt of those leaders, who bribed the soldiers to lie (vv. 12-13). Moreover, it was not even a good lie, for if the soldiers had actually been asleep, how would they have known that the disciples stole His body? It defies credence to argue that the disciples, who hid during Jesus' execution, marshaled enough courage to raid a tomb sealed with a Roman brand, guarded by Roman soldiers. **This story was widely spread among the Jews, and is to this day** (v. 15). Justin Martyr (in *Dialogue with Trypho*, 108, c. AD 155, a Christian response to Jewish objections to Christianity), Tertullian (in *De Spectactulis* 30, c. AD 200, a treatise warning Christians not to attend gladiatorial games), and *Toledoth Yeshu* (an anti-Christian Jewish work extant from AD 826 but existing much earlier) refer to the claim that Jesus' disciples stole His body.

D. The Disciples Saw Jesus in His Resurrection (28:16-17)

28:16-17. No certainty exists regarding the **mountain** in **Galilee** where Jesus met **the eleven disciples** (v. 16). On **some were doubtful**, cf. vv. 9-10 above. Their doubts may have been allayed by the actual appearance of Jesus (v. 18).

E. The Great Commission Flows from the Authority of the Resurrected One (28:18-20)

28:18-20. The word **all** occurs in each of Matthew's last three verses, indicating the comprehensive nature of the scope of Jesus' power and His ongoing mission. As the Second Person of the Godhead, Jesus always possessed **all authority** (v. 18), but at the resurrection God vindicated Jesus and demonstrated that Jesus' claims were true (e.g., He had authority to forgive sins, 9:6, and judge the world, 26:63-64). **Therefore** (v. 19) indicates that the sole ground for the disciples' success is His authority. The only imperative in the verse is **make disciples**, whereas the other verbs, **go**, **baptizing**, and **teaching** are adverbial participles. **Go**, however, should not be understood in a temporal sense ("When you go") as some have argued. In Greek, when an aorist adverbial participle precedes an aorist imperative (command) verb, the participle usually takes on the force of a command as well (see Mt 9:13; 11:4; 17:27). **Go** becomes a virtual second command along with **make disciples** (see Constantine R. Campbell, *Basics of Verbal Aspect in Biblical Greek* [Grand Rapids, MI: Zondervan, 2008], 126-27; Wallace, *Greek Grammar*, 642, 645; K. L. McKay, *A New Syntax of the Verb in New Testament Greek: An Aspectual Approach*, Studies in Biblical Greek vol. 5, ed. D. A. Carson [New York: Peter Lang, 1994], 82-84). The disciples must **go** *and* **make disciples**. **Make disciples** means "to become a follower, a pupil, an apprentice" of Jesus, including doing what He teaches and furthering His cause. The verb here has a slightly causative force: "Urge them to become disciples." **All the nations** encompasses the Gentile world as well as Israel. The verb **baptizing** means "to dip" or "immerse." Cf. the comments on Rm 6:2-4. **Name** is a singular noun (not "names"), giving an implicit witness to the tri-unity of God. None of the baptisms in Acts utilizes the Trinitarian formula (cf. Ac 2:38; 8:16; 10:48; 19:5) perhaps because Jesus was not imparting a baptismal *formula* at all. He was describing Christian baptism as demonstrating belief in the triune God as its fundamental referent. John's baptism referred instead to repentance for the forgiveness of sins. **Teaching** (v. 20) is a present participle that, along with the present participle **baptizing**, gives the primary means whereby Jesus' followers **make disciples**. Jesus is so intent on the members of His redeemed community fulfilling the Great Commission that He promised to be with them, in all His authority, as they go and make disciples.

Conclusion

How does one sum up the content and implications of Matthew's Gospel? Darrell Bock provides some helpful words. "Although Jesus did point out the way to God and urged disciples to have integrity and show love even to those who hated, that character was to be the product of a life resting in the divine hope and promise that Jesus brought. Jesus' ministry was about the new era that he inaugurated along with the opportunity for forgiveness and enablement that he represented and supplied. That ministry compelled a choice. Had the new era come? Was the unique anointed one present? If he was, then embracing him and his message becomes an imperative from God. Death's inability to hold Jesus and devour him showed the way to the answer. The Synoptics together are telling us that anyone with ears to hear and eyes to see should use them to find forgiveness in Jesus and enter into his promise. They also tell us that having responded, we should stay the course until he completes what he started, no matter how rough the world's rejection of him becomes" (*Jesus According to Scripture: Restoring the Portrait from the Gospels* [Grand Rapids, MI: Baker, 2002], 405).

BIBLIOGRAPHY

Broadus, John A. *Commentary on the Gospel of Matthew*. Valley Forge: Judson, 1886.

Bruce, A. B. "Matthew." In *The Synoptic Gospels*. Vol. 7 of The Expositor's Greek New Testament, edited by W. Robertson Nicole, 61–340. Grand Rapids, MI: Eerdmans, 1951.

Blomberg, Craig L. *Matthew*. In The New American Commentary. Nashville: Broadman & Holman, 1992.

Carson, D. A. "Matthew." In *Matthew, Mark, Luke*. Vol. 8 of The Expositor's Bible Commentary, edited by Frank E. Gaebelein, 3–599. Grand Rapids, MI: Zondervan, 1984.

France, R. T. *The Gospel of Matthew*. In New International Commentary on the New Testament. Grand Rapids, MI: Eerdmans, 2007.

MacArthur, John. *Matthew 1-7, Matthew 8-15, Matthew 16-23*, and *Matthew 24-28*. In The MacArthur New Testament Commentary. Chicago: Moody, 1985, 1987, 1988, 1989.

Morris, Leon. *The Gospel According to Matthew*. In Pillar Commentary. Grand Rapids, MI: Eerdmans, 1992.

Turner, David L. *Matthew*. In Baker Exegetical Commentary on the New Testament. Grand Rapids, MI: Baker, 2008.

Wilkins, Michael J. *The NIV Application Commentary: Matthew*. Grand Rapids, MI: Zondervan, 2004.

● ● ● ●

MARK

LOU BARBIERI

INTRODUCTION

Author. Although none of the gospels names its author, each has had a fairly consistent testimony in church history. That John Mark is the author of the second gospel is the consistent widespread traditional view. Papias gives the first witness to Mark's authorship of the second gospel. Justin Martyr, Irenaeus, Clement of Rome, and Ignatius, as well as others, agree. The internal evidence for authorship is extremely weak. There is a brief incident in 14:50-52 that might refer to the author. In the confusion over Jesus' arrest in Gethsemane, a young man, grabbed by one of the soldiers, ran away into the night leaving behind the sheet that had been wrapped around his body. No other gospels record this. It is possible that the young man could have been Mark, and this was his way of saying he was there.

Ten references to Mark occur in the NT (Ac 12:12, 25; 13:5, 13; 15:37, 39; Col 4:10; Phm 24; 1Pt 5:13; and 2Tm 4:11). The Jerusalem church met in his home so perhaps he came from a wealthy family (cf. Ac 12:12). When Paul and Barnabas went to Antioch for ministry, they brought Mark along (cf. Ac 12:25). He accompanied them as a "helper" on their first missionary journey (cf. Ac 13:5), but left in the middle of the trip and returned home (cf. Ac 13:13). This became the focus of controversy when the second missionary journey began (cf. Ac 15:37-39). As a result, Barnabas took Mark and went to Cyprus; Paul took Silas and headed overland for Asia Minor. That Mark became an effective servant cannot be denied. Mark was with Paul in Rome when the apostle wrote Colossians (cf. Col 4:10) and Philemon (cf. Phm 24) and also with Peter in "Babylon," when 1 Peter was written (cf. 1Pt 5:13). Paul made a concluding admission concerning Mark when he told Timothy, "Pick up Mark and bring him with you, for he is useful to me for service" (cf. 2 Tm 4:11).

Although Mark was the writer of the second gospel, there is good indication the person behind the book was Simon Peter. That a relationship existed between the two is verified both outside and inside this gospel. Outside the gospel: (1) Papias commented: "Mark, having become the interpreter of Peter, wrote down accurately whatever he remembered of the things said and done by the Lord, but not however in order" (Cited by Eusebius, *Hist. Eccl.* III.xxxix.15). (2) Peter said Mark was with him in "Babylon" (cf. 1Pt 5:13). (3) The second gospel covers the same material mentioned in Peter's report to the church at Jerusalem (cf. Ac 10:34-43). (4) Peter was aware of his imminent death and declared he was taking steps to ensure his brethren would be able to remember what he had taught (cf. 2Pt 1:13-15). Was Peter filling Mark's mind with stories from Jesus' life so he could write them down? Internal evidence also points to a relationship between Peter and Mark: (1) The second gospel basically begins with Peter's call to follow the Lord. (2) The second gospel clearly has an eyewitness behind it. The stories concerning Jesus appear in the present tense, which pictures them as actually occurring. There are about 150 historic presents in this gospel compared with 78 in Matthew and only four in Luke. (3) The second gospel relates a number of facts about Peter not found in the other gospels, and some favorable details about Peter are omitted (cf. 1:36; 11:21; 13:3; 16:7). (4) This gospel gives special attention to the ministry of Jesus in Galilee, especially Capernaum, the place of Peter's residence.

Date. Dates for the writing of the second gospel range from AD 44 to 75. Documentary theories on the writings of the Synoptic Gospels require that Mark be the earliest of the gospels (for the issues related to gospel critical studies, see the introduction to the commentary on Matthew). There has been a tendency in recent scholarship to date the writing of all the NT books earlier than previously thought. Part of the reason for this is that the destruction of Jerusalem (in AD 70) is never mentioned in the New Testament. That fact would have been extremely significant in a number of the gospel stories, and, if it had indeed occurred, surely one or more of the gospel writers would have mentioned it. A quote from Irenaeus must be evaluated when considering Mark's date: "Matthew also issued a written gospel among the Hebrews in their own dialect, while Peter and Paul were preaching in Rome, and laying the foundation of the church. After their departure, Mark, the disciple and interpreter of Peter, did also hand down to us in writing what had been preached by Peter" (*Against Heresies*, III, i, 1). The word "departure" is the word *exodus*, used in Scripture for physical death (cf. Lk 9:51). If that was what Irenaeus was communicating, the second gospel could not have been written until after Peter's death. According to Eusebius, Mark wrote the gospel based on Peter's lectures on the life of Jesus in Rome and was approved by Peter. Mark's gospel was circulated privately while Peter lived, and then Mark published it after Peter's death. In what year did Peter die? Tradition states Peter died under the persecutions of Nero, which began in AD 64. Many believe that Peter's death may have occurred around AD 66 or 67. After his death, there was a desire to commit to writing Peter's stories concerning Jesus. Mark was the natural choice to pen the account. Not only that, but the Holy Spirit moved him along (cf. 2Pt 1:21) to communicate the stories without errors. The actual writing probably took place in AD 67 or 68.

Recipients. Mark seems to have written the second gospel for a Gentile audience, and in particular he may have had Romans in view. Several factors point to this conclusion.

1. The second gospel has the fewest quotes and allusions (63) to the OT of all the gospels. A Gentile reader would not have been interested in or familiar with its contents.

2. Mark interprets the Aramaic words found in the gospel. For example the cry of Jesus from the cross, "Eloi, Eloi, lama sabachthani?" is translated "My God, My God, why have you forsaken Me?" (cf. 15:34).

3. Mark explains geographical locations in connection with his stories. The location of the Mount of Olives "opposite the temple" is spelled out in 13:3.

4. There are no references in Mark to the Jewish law. There were so many items of importance to Jewish people that related to the law, yet Mark never mentions them.

5. Mark explains Jewish customs. "Jews do not eat unless they carefully wash their hands" (cf. 7:3). Such a custom would have been known and practiced by Jews (cf. 14:12 and 15:42).

6. Mark presents Jesus as the mighty worker, a man who conquers by doing. Romans were concerned with a person's production, not his words. The effective service of Jesus was of greater significance than His lineage or claims.

Although there is no direct reference to a city in the gospel, tradition says Mark wrote this book from Rome. Several lines of evidence support this contention.

1. Mark used a number of Latin words, even though there were Greek equivalents: cf. two lepta (12:42), "modius" for bushel (4:21), "speculator" for executioner (6:27), "census" for tribute (12:14), the "Praetorium" for the palace (15:16), and "centurion" for centurion (15:39, 44, 45).

2. Roman divisions of time are used in this gospel, four "watches" in the night, whereas in Jewish reckoning there were only three.

3. Mark referred to Alexander and Rufus (15:21), sons of Simon of Cyrene, the one who carried Jesus' cross. They were personal acquaintances of the author and his readers. Paul referred to a "Rufus" and called him "a choice man in the Lord" (cf. Rm. 16:13). That these two men named Rufus are the same individual may have some warrant.

Purpose. The occasion prompting the writing of this gospel is not known. The compulsion of the Holy Spirit working in Mark's life is paramount. But after Peter's death there was a desire within the church at Rome to have his great teachings written down. Mark was the natural choice to do the job. Peter had spent time preparing him for the task (cf. 2Pt 1:13-15).

Several outstanding characteristics are apparent in Mark. First, the second gospel is the gospel of action. Events in this gospel move rapidly. About two of every three verses begin with the word "and," a device for action. This is further seen in a key word in the gospel: "straightway" or "immediately."

Second, Mark pictures Jesus as the Servant of the Lord, the reason such a stress was placed on immediacy of action. When considering a servant, one is primarily interested in his service. Jesus' servitude is emphasized in the key verse in Mark: "For even the Son of Man did not come to be served, but to serve, and to give His life a ransom for many" (10:45).

Third, this gospel emphasizes Jesus' miracles. This reflects the servant character of the Lord, for as a servant His miracles are prominent. However, only two miracles are unique to the second gospel: the healing of the deaf and dumb man (7:31-37) and the healing of the blind man at Bethsaida (8:22-26).

Fourth, Mark emphasized common, familiar aspects of life. He gave attention to such ordinary features as boating and fishing, animals, clothing, housing, coins, and divisions of time.

Fifth, Mark is the gospel of vivid detail. Special attention is given to such particulars as the looks and gestures of the Lord (3:5; 10:16). In the story of the feeding of the five thousand men, only Mark's account gives the vivid detail of "green" grass (6:39).

Background. Where does the material written by Mark end? The options are the gospel ends at 16:8, at 16:20, or that another ending should be added either after 16:8 or 16:20. Additional material may have become lost over the centuries, but it was part of the early texts.

The evidence to support the ending of the gospel of Mark comes down to the question, "Which is the best Greek text?" The issue revolves around whether one considers the majority of the manuscript evidence to be what supports one's conclusion or whether one regards certain ancient texts as a better and more faithful rendering of the original Greek. The majority of the manuscripts support the reading of Mark's gospel through 16:20. The older manuscripts (e.g., Vaticanus and Sinaiticus, both fourth century) support the shorter ending at v. 8.

Some internal arguments may be hard to follow unless one has competent ability in the original language. The vocabulary and theology of vv. 9-20 are quite different from the earlier portions of the gospel. It seems that the internal evidence substantiates the claim that Mark's manuscript should conclude at v. 8. If the gospel does end at v. 8, how can the addition of vv. 9-20 be explained? Certainly it would not have simply been lost. The gospel of Mark was probably written on a scroll, and the conclusion of the gospel would have been rolled up on the inside. It was more common for the first portion to be removed for some reason or simply become worn out through use. Perhaps over the decades, as the gospel was copied, it was felt that the ending at v. 8 was much too abrupt and not an appropriate conclusion. The most common suggestion has been that Aristion, a disciple of the apostle John, made the addition, perhaps even under the authority of John. Some, while recognizing that vv. 9-20 are not Markan, nevertheless conclude that they are a part of the manuscript in the same sense that Deuteronomy 34, concerning the death of Moses, and Joshua 24, concerning Joshua's death, were added. Do vv. 9-20 fit the same criteria? Some believe they do. Perhaps Mark himself intended to add to the manuscript but may have died before he could do so. The problem of the ending of Mark's gospel probably will not be solved as long as people live in physical bodies on this earth.

OUTLINE

I. The Introduction of the Servant of the Lord (1:1-13)
  A. By Proclamation (1:1-8)
  B. By Identification (1:9)
  C. By Authentication (1:10-11)
  D. By Temptation (1:12-13)
II. The Presentation of the Servant of the Lord (1:14–3:5)
  A. By Direct Testimony (1:14-15)
  B. By Personal Enlistment (1:16-20)
  C. By Demonstrating Authority (1:21–3:5)
    1. Over Demonic Forces (1:21-28)
    2. Over Disease (1:29-34)

3. Over Personal Direction (1:35-39)
4. Over Leprosy (1:40-45)
5. Over Forgiveness of Sins (2:1-12)
6. Over Men (2:13-14)
7. Over Traditions (2:15-22)
8. Over the Sabbath (2:23–3:5)
   a. Sabbath Issue Questioned (2:23-28)
   b. Sabbath Miracle Performed (3:1-5)

III. The Opposition to the Servant of the Lord (3:6–8:26)
   A. The Pharisees' Conclusion (3:6)
   B. The Multitude's Confusion (3:7-12)
   C. The Servant's Decision (3:13-19)
   D. His Family's Intervention (3:20-21)
   E. The "Official" Conclusion (3:22–4:34)
      1. The Accusation (3:22)
      2. The Denial (3:23-30)
      3. The Ramifications (3:31-35)
      4. The Instruction (4:1-34)
         a. A Parable Taught (4:1-12)
         b. A Parable Explained (4:13-20)
         c. Further Parabolic Instruction (4:21-34)
   F. The Servant's Authentication in Spite of Opposition (4:35–5:43)
      1. To the Apostles (4:35-41)
      2. To the Region of Decapolis (5:1-20)
      3. To the "Religious" Leaders (5:21-43)
         a. The Request (5:21-24)
         b. The Interruption (5:25-34)
         c. The Fulfillment (5:35-43)
   G. The Rejection of Nazareth (6:1-6)
   H. The Ministry to Combat Opposition (6:7-13)
   I. The Civil Ruler's Opposition (6:14-29)
      1. The Fear of Herod (6:14-16)
      2. The Actions of Herod (6:17-29)
   J. The Servant's Instruction in View of Opposition (6:30-56)
      1. The Intended Retreat (6:30-32)
      2. The Actual Reality (6:33-44)
      3. The Authenticating Signs (6:45-56)
         a. Walking on the Water (6:45-52)
         b. Healings at Gennesaret (6:53-56)
   K. The Pharisees' Continued Opposition (7:1-23)
      1. The "Violation" Stated (7:1-5)
      2. The Servant's Explanation (7:6-13)
      3. The Servant's Warning (7:14-23)
   L. The Servant's Retreat from Opposition (7:24–8:9)
      1. To the Region of Tyre (7:24-30)
      2. To the Region of Decapolis (7:31–8:9)
         a. Healing of the Deaf Man (7:31-37)
         b. Feeding of the 4,000 (8:1-9)
   M. The Pharisees' Final Demand (8:10-21)
      1. The Demand (8:10-11)
      2. The Servant's Explanation (8:12-13)
      3. The Servant's Warning (8:14-21)
   N. A Concluding Miracle (8:22-26)

IV. The Instruction of the Servant of the Lord (8:27–10:52)

A. Instruction Concerning His Person (8:27-30)
B. Instruction Concerning His Program (8:31–9:13)
1. His Coming Death (8:31-33)
2. His Requirement for Followers (8:34-38)
3. His Coming Kingdom Pictured (9:1-10)
4. His Relationship to Elijah (9:11-13)
C. Instruction Concerning the Impossible (9:14-29)
D. Instruction Concerning His Upcoming Death (9:30-32)
E. Instruction Concerning Pride (9:33-37)
F. Instruction Concerning Partisan Spirit (9:38-50)
G. Instruction Concerning Divorce (10:1-12)
H. Instruction Concerning Faith (10:13-22)
1. Faith as a Child (10:13-16)
2. Faith for Eternal Life (10:17-22)
I. Instruction Concerning Wealth (10:23-31)
J. Instruction Concerning His Near Future (10:32-34)
K. Instructions Concerning Positions in the Kingdom (10:35-45)
L. Instruction Concerning Faith (10:46-52)
V. The Rejection of the Servant of the Lord (11:1–15:47)
A. The Presentation of the Servant (11:1-26)
1. The Triumphal Entry (11:1-11)
2. The Judgment Announced (11:12-14)
3. The Cleansing of the Temple (11:15-19)
4. The Judgment Fulfilled (11:20-26)
B. The Controversies with the Servant (11:27–12:40)
1. With the Religious Leaders (11:27–12:12)
a. The Question of Authority (11:27-33)
b. The Parable for Instruction (12:1-11)
c. The Leaders' Response (12:12)
2. With the Pharisees and Herodians (12:13-17)
3. With the Sadducees (12:18-27)
4. With the Scribes (12:28-34)
5. The Response of the Servant (12:35-44)
a. The Question of Challenge (12:35-37)
b. The Warning (12:38-40)
c. The Proper Illustration (12:41-44)
C. The Predictions of the Servant (13:1-37)
1. The Questions of the Disciples (13:1-4)
2. The Response of the Servant (13:5-37)
a. Coming Tribulation (13:5-23)
i. The First Half of the Tribulation (13:5-13)
ii. The Second Half of the Tribulation (13:14-23)
b. Coming Triumph (13:24-27)
i. Return of the King (13:24-26)
ii. Regathering of Believers (13:27)
c. Concluding Teaching (13:28-37)
i. The Fig Tree (13:28-32)
ii. The Steward (13:33-37)
D. The Preparatory Events Surrounding the Servant (14:1-42)
1. The Plot of the Leaders (14:1-2)
2. The Anointing by Mary (14:3-9)
3. The Agreement with Judas (14:10-11)
4. The Passover Meal (14:12-26)
a. Preparation (14:12-16)

b. Participation (14:17-21)
c. Initiation (14:22-26)
5. The Prediction of Denial (14:27-31)
6. The Garden of Gethsemane (14:32-42)
E. The Arrest and Trials of the Servant (14:43–15:20)
1. Arrest in Gethsemane (14:43-52)
2. Trial before the Council (14:53-65)
3. Prediction of Denial Fulfilled (14:66-72)
4. Second Trial before the Council (15:1)
5. Trial before Pilate (15:2-15)
6. Mocking before the Roman Soldiers (15:16-20)
F. The Crucifixion of the Servant (15:21-32)
G. The Death of the Servant (15:33-41)
H. The Burial of the Servant (15:42-47)
VI. The Resurrection of the Servant of the Lord (16:1-20)
A. The Revelation of the Women (16:1-8)
B. The Appearances of the Servant (16:9-14)
1. To Mary (16:9-11)
2. To Two Disciples (16:12-13)
3. To the Eleven (16:14)
C. The Commission of the Servant (16:15-18)
D. The Ascension of the Servant (16:19-20)

COMMENTARY ON MARK

I. The Introduction of the Servant of the Lord (1:1-13)

A. By Proclamation (1:1-8)

1:1. Mark's **gospel** begins with **Jesus Christ, the Son of God**. He is fully sinless man and fully God.

1:2-8. Jesus was preceded by His ambassador as prophesied. **Isaiah** is named (v. 2) but see also Mal 3:1. Together they present three factors: the herald, the Lord, and the wilderness. The coming of John and Jesus to the wilderness is fulfillment of the promised salvation of which Isaiah spoke. John's messenger role prepared the way, linking his ministry to the prophetic emphasis. He preached **a baptism of repentance for the forgiveness of sins** (v. 4). Ritual cleansings were prescribed by the law and were commonly practiced, but a one-time baptism was unknown in early (intertestamental) Judaism except for Gentiles converting to Judaism. The noun **baptism** means "the act of immersing" or "dipping" (it does not *mean* "an identification with"), and here indicates that one has repented and been spiritually cleansed in preparation for the coming of the Messiah and the kingdom He would bring. Those who came in saving faith (see the comments on Mt 3:5-12) received **forgiveness of sins**. John's ministry created excitement as **all the country of Judea** was coming and submitting to baptism (v. 5). He dressed as a prophet (clothed in **camel's hair** with **a leather belt around his waist**.) His wilderness diet was **locusts** (the insect or the fruit of the carob tree) and **wild honey** (v.6). This was not the totality of his diet, but it demonstrated a simple lifestyle. His preaching pointed to someone far greater than himself. John baptized **with water** but the One coming would baptize **with the Holy Spirit** (v. 8; see the comments on 1Co 12:12-13).

B. By Identification (1:9)

1:9. Jesus came from **Nazareth** to the Jordan where John baptized Him. Total immersion was the common Jewish method of ritual cleansing, and was likely the form of baptism John conducted. Jesus was identifying Himself with His forerunner and his message of repentance in preparation for the coming Messiah.

C. By Authentication (1:10-11) (see also the comments on Mt 3:15-16)

1:10-11. As Jesus came out of the water **immediately** the heavens were opened and the Spirit, **like a dove**, descended on Him. The opening of the heavens is significant. God had not spoken through any prophet for centuries. The Father declared: **You are My beloved Son, in You I am well pleased**, which reflects both Psalm 2:7 and Isaiah 42:1. All three members of the Godhead, Father, Son, and Holy Spirit, are present at the same time.

D. By Temptation (1:12-13)

1:12-13. The temptation is connected with the preceding by **immediately**. Jesus was **impelled** (a strong word, "to drive") into the wilderness by **the Spirit.** This was part of God's will, for Jesus was there for **forty days**. He was **tempted by Satan** and was **with the wild beasts**, which stresses the hostile environment. The number **forty** is used in Scripture of a time of testing (cf. Dt 8:2; Nm 13:25, 14:33-34). **Satan** means "an adversary" or "opponent." The specifics of Satan's temptations are not given, but when they were complete, the angels ministered to Him with sustenance and encouragement.

II. The Presentation of the Servant of the Lord (1:14–3:5)

A. By Direct Testimony (1:14-15) (see also the comments on Mt 14:1-12)

1:14. Jesus' ministry began when John was taken into custody. No details about the arrest are given here (cf. 6:14-29). With John's removal Jesus began to preach the **gospel of God** in the region of **Galilee**.

1:15. The gospel began with the declaration **the time is fulfilled, and the kingdom of God is at hand**. Israel knew of the coming Messiah who would reign on David's throne. But the idea of repentance and believing in the gospel implied there was a question concerning the institution of the kingdom. The nation needed to turn from its confidence in a physical relationship to Abraham and believe the good news concerning Jesus. Although there are two aspects in repentance, there is only one act. As one turns from one position, one immediately turns to the second.

B. By Personal Enlistment (1:16-20)

1:16-18. Jesus encountered brothers, **Simon and Andrew**, employing their trade. He said: **Follow Me, and I will make you become fishers of men**. It was not uncommon for men to follow a learned rabbi for instruction. Jesus was choosing followers for a far greater task than any ever attempted.

1:19-20. James and **John**, possibly fishing partners with Peter and Andrew (cf. Lk 5:7), were enlisted to follow Jesus, departing so quickly they left their **father Zebedee in the boat**. Jesus' sovereign authority and the radical obedience of these men are obvious.

C. By Demonstrating Authority (1:21–3:5)

As Jesus began His ministry, everyone was asking, "Does He have the power to accomplish what He promises?" In this section, Jesus shows the extent of His authority over both the physical and spiritual realms.

1. Over Demonic Forces (1:21-28)

1:21-22. Capernaum was located on the northern shore of the Sea of Galilee. On the **Sabbath** Jesus **entered the synagogue and began to teach**. Those hearing Him were astonished for He taught with His own inherent authority (*exousia*) as opposed to contemporaries who usually cited the noted rabbis to substantiate their own teaching.

1:23-28. A man with **an unclean spirit** reacted to Jesus' authoritative teaching. His speech reflected significant knowledge. First, the demon knew **Jesus of Nazareth** and that Jesus would one day be his Destroyer/Judge. **"Have You come to destroy us?"** he asked. The men in the synagogue were amazed at Jesus' teaching, but the demon knew His presence spelled his ultimate destruction. Jesus rebuked the demon, **"Be quiet and come out of him!"** Jesus has authority to silence all creatures and direct their movements. Leaving the man, the demon threw him to the ground, causing him to go **into convulsions**. The people were **all amazed** that Jesus taught with His own authority and that **even the unclean spirits . . . obey**[ed] **Him**. That **the news about Him** spread is not surprising.

2. Over Disease (1:29-34) (see also the comments on Mt 8:14-17)

1:29-31. They left the synagogue and entered the house of Simon Peter and Andrew. There Peter's **mother-in-law was lying sick with a fever**. Learning of the illness, Jesus healed her, and she began to wait on those who had come from the synagogue.

1:32-34. When the Sabbath ended, crowds appeared outside the house. Reports of His healings had rapidly spread. Many brought ill or demon-possessed acquaintances. **The whole city had gathered at the door** is probably hyperbole. Jesus **healed many** and demon-possessed individuals were set free. Physical disease and demonic possession are clearly distinguished, with Jesus' authority demonstrated over both.

3. Over Personal Direction (1:35-39)

1:35-39. After a strenuous day, **in the early morning** Jesus went to a place to be alone to pray. The content of His prayer is not revealed. Peter and his companions **searched** (lit., "hunted") until they found Him. **Everyone is looking for You**, they said. Their goal was to bring Jesus back to Capernaum to continue His healing ministry. But Jesus' primary ministry was not to provide physical healing but spiritual salvation. His authority enabled Him to direct His own steps. Therefore He instructed the disciples, telling them that they needed to go to other towns that He might **preach there also**. They traveled **throughout all Galilee** preaching and casting out demons to demonstrate His authority.

4. Over Leprosy (1:40-45) (see also the comments on Mt 8:2-4)

1:40-42. A leper came, falling before Jesus, and beseeched Him to be made clean. Leprosy was a diagnosed skin condition that caused ceremonial uncleanness. It is not the same as modern leprosy, known as Hansen's Disease. Because of ritual uncleanness, a leper could not move freely through society. That this leper came to Jesus was a bold move on his part, yet he was certain of Jesus' power to heal him. Jesus was **moved with compassion** and performed an unheard of act by touching him. His words, **I am willing; be cleansed**, imply a radical healing took place. This miracle had never been observed in the lifetime of anyone present. The OT records two individuals healed of leprosy: Moses' sister Miriam (cf. Nm 12) and the Syrian Naaman (cf. 2Kg 5). But Scripture instructs a person cleansed of leprosy to offer appropriate sacrifices (cf. Lv 14:1-32).

1:43-45. Jesus gave a stern warning to the healed leper sending him away: **See that you say nothing to anyone; but go, show yourself to the priest**. It was important that this man go to Jerusalem and follow the cleansing Moses commanded (Lv 14:1-33). His action would bear testimony to the religious leaders that something unique was happening in their midst necessitating a complete investigation. One can only speculate about the commotion when this man showed up in the temple claiming to have been cleansed from leprosy. The man departed and began to tell others of his cleansing. This is not to say he did not also present himself to the priests. But he was so excited about his cleansing he wanted to tell others. The crowds so mobbed Jesus He **could no longer publicly enter a city**. He stayed in **unpopulated areas**, but people continued **coming to Him from everywhere**.

5. Over Forgiveness of Sins (2:1-12) (see also the comments on Mt 9:1-8)

2:1-2. Jesus returned to Capernaum, probably to Peter's home, but so many **were gathered together** it was impossible to enter. Jesus sat and spoke the Word of God to those who would listen.

2:3-7. Four men came carrying a paralyzed man on a pallet, but entrance was impossible. They climbed to the roof, dug through the thatch, and lowered their friend down, still on his pallet. As Jesus saw **their faith**, He said to the paralytic, **Son, your sins are forgiven**. Evidently the physical infirmity that brought about his paralysis was connected with sin. This man's sins were at that very moment permanently forgiven. The scribes, however, concluded Jesus' statement was blasphemy because only God can forgive sin. If Jesus was speaking the truth, He would have to be God. Their logic is correct, but they failed to accept the possibility Jesus could be God. Yet Jesus knew what they were thinking.

2:8-12. His question exposed their thoughts. They were the sinful ones in this story, for they had come with the specific purpose of finding accusations to destroy Him. The discussion revolved around two statements, both easily stated. But it would be easier to say, **Your sins are forgiven**, because who could determine whether it had actually occurred. But if one says, **Get up, and pick up your pallet and walk**, and the person fails to move, the speaker is clearly an imposter. Therefore, Jesus told the paralytic to get up, pick up his pallet, and walk. If he remained prostrate, Jesus would be proven a fake, and neither statement would have validity. Such a blasphemer would be worthy of death. The paralytic responded **immediately**, obeying Jesus' command. The result was amazement and the people glorified God: **We have never seen anything like this**. Jesus' miraculous work was far beyond their comprehension, demonstrating His authority.

6. Over Men (2:13-14) (see also the comments on Mt 9:9, particularly for the description of tax gatherers)

2:13-14. Jesus went along the shore of the Sea of Galilee with multitudes thronging about Him. He **was teaching** everywhere He went. **Levi, the son of Alphaeus**, was sitting in his **tax booth**, and Jesus said to him, **Follow Me!** He immediately rose, left a corrupt but lucrative profession, and followed Jesus. He became known as Matthew (cf. Mt 9:9; 10:3). Whether he changed his name or had been given both names cannot be determined.

7. Over Traditions (2:15-22) (see also the comments on Mt 9:14-17)

2:15-17. When Levi decided to follow Jesus he gave a farewell dinner for his friends to introduce them to Jesus (cf. Lk 5:29-39; and see also the comments on Mt 9:10-13). Jesus **was reclining** at dinner with many **tax collectors and sinners**, Levi's friends, along with His disciples. Some were observing this banquet, but were not participating in the meal. They would never have broken bread with individuals who failed to keep the law and their traditions. They questioned, if Jesus was indeed a holy man, why would he be eating with such people? They interrogated the disciples, but when Jesus learned of the discussion, He responded with a proverb that it is not those who are healthy who need a physician, but those who are sick. Jesus was not interested in dealing with people like these scribes who considered themselves righteous, not sinners in need of repentance (cf. Mk 1:15). Jesus wanted to reach those who acknowledged their sinfulness and were willing to turn from it.

2:18-22. Some of John's disciples and Pharisees asked Jesus about fasting, their common practice. The Mosaic law required fasting only on the Day of Atonement (cf. Lv 16:29-34; 23:26-32; Nm 29:7-11), but by the first century, its practice in Judaism had increased to twice a week. Why did Jesus' disciples not fast? His response came from a custom of the time and a metaphor that John the Baptist had used (cf. Jn 3:29). When celebrating at a wedding, did the associates of the bridegroom fast? Jesus was picturing Himself as a bridegroom at a feast, but He indicated this joyous situation would change. A time would come when He would be **taken away from them** (cf. Is 53:8), and **in that day** they would fast. Two parables provide additional information to the question of v. 18. First, one would not patch an old garment with new cloth, for if the repaired garment were washed, the patch would shrink and pull away, resulting in a **worse tear**. The second parable related to wineskins. The fermentation process produces expansion. New wineskins have elasticity and are able to stretch. But once stretched, they cannot expand further. If one fills old wineskins with new wine, the skins will burst and the wine will be lost. Jesus was teaching He had not come merely to reform Judaism but to present previously unrevealed truths.

8. Over the Sabbath (2:23–3:5)

a. Sabbath Issue Questioned (2:23-28) (see also the comments on Mt 12:1-8)

2:23-24. They passed **through the grainfields on the Sabbath**. Jesus' disciples began to pluck some of the grain and eat it. The corners of fields were left for the poor to gather, and anyone could go into a field and take what he could eat (cf. Dt 23:24-25). The Pharisees were not questioning the legality of their eating, but they were questioning the disciples' actions on the Sabbath. Their argument was that picking the grain constituted harvesting, rubbing the kernels of grain between their palms was threshing, and blowing away the chaff was winnowing. The disciples were working on the Sabbath, and that was not lawful (cf. Ex 34:21).

2:25-28. Jesus' defense of the disciples' actions came from Scripture. He recalled David's flight from Saul (cf. 1Sm 21:1-6) when David and his companions became hungry. The comparison is between David and his men and the greater Son of David and His disciples. David came to the tabernacle asking the priest for food. The only thing available was bread from the table in the holy place meant for the priests (cf. Ex 25:23-30). Nevertheless, that bread was given to David and his companions. Why? Because the human need for food transcended the law. It is noted that this occurred **in the time of Abiathar**. The high priest actually was Ahimelech, Abiathar's father, but Abiathar became a more prominent figure in Israel's history. This was the customary Jewish way of placing a historical event into an OT time frame. Jesus concluded: **The Sabbath was made for man, and not man for the Sabbath**. The religious leaders had made the Sabbath into something far less than God intended. Sabbath rest was to be a blessing to people, not a curse. As Lord, He can command what should transpire on any given day.

b. Sabbath Miracle Performed (3:1-5) (see also the comments on Mt 12:9-14)

3:1-5. Jesus entered the synagogue, probably in Capernaum, and saw a man **whose hand was withered**. People with physical impairments were usually ostracized from the community since deformity was viewed as an indication of some terrible sin. That this man was conspicuously seated in the synagogue suggests he was a "plant." **They were watching** Jesus, hoping He would try to heal this man so they could accuse Him. Jesus was never concerned by men's threats. If something should be done, He would do it, regardless of the outcome. He called forth the man, turned to His accusers, and asked a significant question: **Is it lawful to do good or to do harm on the Sabbath, to save a life or to kill?** These religious leaders should have known what was right and what was wrong, but **they kept silent**. It is ironic that religious leaders, who should be interested in doing what was right, were in the process of doing harm on the Sabbath. They were plotting how they might kill Jesus. Jesus looked at these accusers **with anger**, for the hardness of their hearts brought Him continual grief. He said, "**Stretch out your hand.**" As the man obeyed, healing was instantaneous and complete. Jesus did not violate the Sabbath. He had not even touched the man, but simply spoke words. His accusers were left with no accusations, but Jesus' authority was clearly seen.

III. The Opposition to the Servant of the Lord (3:6–8:26)

The Servant of Jehovah had been presented working in various areas to demonstrate His authority. But would the people accept His authority? A developing negative conclusion is now presented, for opposition to the Servant of the Lord was growing.

A. The Pharisees' Conclusion (3:6)

3:6. One would think the religious leaders would fall at Jesus' feet in worship, but the opposite occurred. The Pharisees went out and **began conspiring** with the **Herodians** about **how they might destroy Him**. They not only failed to do good on the Sabbath, but they actively plotted how they might do away with Jesus. The combination of Pharisees and Herodians was unusual, for the Herodians championed the political status quo under the Romans, while the Pharisees longed for the coming of the Messiah to remove Roman domination. How was it possible for such a group to join with Pharisees, the conservative purists? Their mutual suspicion of Jesus drew together these two antagonistic groups in a bizarre alliance.

B. The Multitude's Confusion (3:7-12)

3:7-12. Jesus departed from Capernaum and with His disciples **withdrew to the sea**. Wherever Jesus went, multitudes followed. People from **Galilee**, **Judea**, **Jerusalem**, and **Idumea** (Edom) appeared. People from the eastern side of the **Jordan** and **Tyre and Sidon** in the north were now following Jesus. They heard about **all that He was doing** and wondered if He could be the promised Messiah. They were confused because the religious leaders failed to recognize Him. Jesus instructed His disciples to keep a boat ready for a quick departure should the crowd press too strongly. As Jesus healed many, news of His ability spread. People with many afflictions pressed in, seeking **to touch Him**, anticipating healing. In addition to those with physical infirmities, people possessed with unclean spirits were also coming. The spirits knew Jesus (cf. 1:23-26) and they cried out, **You are the Son of God!** The religious leaders failed to understand Jesus, but demons clearly understood. Demonic testimony might confuse people, so Jesus commanded them to keep quiet.

C. The Servant's Decision (3:13-19)

3:13-15. Jesus **went up** one of the Galilean mountains and **summoned those whom He Himself wanted** to follow Him. This handpicked group was chosen to **be with Him** so **He could send them out to preach**. Twelve disciples communicating the same message could cover a larger area and speak to more people. He also encouraged them **to cast out the demons**, demonstrating **authority**. Only God has greater authority than demonic forces.

3:16-19. The twelve "apostles" appear in three additional passages (cf. Mt 10:2-5; Lk 6:14-16; and Ac 1:13). Simon, a fisherman, was named **Peter** at his first meeting with Jesus (cf. Jn 1:42). "Peter" means "a rock" in Greek, which is what he became in the early church. **James** and **John**, sons of Zebedee, appear next. Jesus gave these two the nickname **Boanerges**, which means "Sons of Thunder." Why this is recorded here is not clear (cf. Lk 9:54; Mk 9:38), but it may be included to explain what kind of men Jesus called as His disciples, including thunderous men like James and John. Possibly Mark was making a more precise identification of these two men since **James** (literally "Jacob") and **John** were common Jewish names. **Andrew**, a fisherman with his brother Peter, was one of two apostles with Greek names. **Philip**, the other disciple with a Greek name, was from Bethsaida, Peter and Andrew's town. When Jesus called Philip, he recruited Nathaniel (cf. Jn 1:43-47). **Bartholomew**, connected here with Philip, could be the same person. **Matthew**, Levi the tax collector (cf. Mk 2:14), means "the gift of God." **Thomas**, Didymus, "the twin," (cf. Jn 11:16), is known as "doubting" Thomas. He wanted to be certain Jesus had risen from the dead (cf. Jn 20:25). It is rarely mentioned he courageously said, "Let us also go, so that we may die with Him" (cf. Jn 11:16). **James, the son of Alphaeus**, an inconspicuous scriptural figure, is possibly "James, the less" (cf. Mk 15:40), meaning "short." **Thaddaeus** might be "Judas the son of James," or "Judas not Iscariot." Perhaps Jesus' betrayal by Judas Iscariot produced the name change. **Simon the Zealot** is then named. Some texts translate "Zealot" as "the Canaanean." The term however has nothing to do with ethnic (Canaanite) or geographic (Cana) origins. It was used of Jewish extremists organized for overthrowing the Roman government by violent rebellion, even advocating murder when necessary to advance their cause. The final apostle is **Judas Iscariot**, who betrayed Jesus. "Iscariot" (Hb. *ish-keristra*) means "a man of Kerioth," a town in southern Judea. If that is correct, Judas was the only non-Galilean apostle.

D. His Family's Intervention (3:20-21)

3:20-21. Jesus **came home**, implying He returned to Peter's house in Capernaum (cf. 1:29). Again a **crowd gathered**, making it impossible for Jesus to eat. He was completely occupied with ministry needs. **His own people** may refer to extended family members who lived nearby. They were concerned for Him and the family's reputation so they went **to take custody of Him** saying, **He has lost his senses.**

E. The "Official" Conclusion (3:22–4:34)

1. The Accusation (3:22)

3:22. Jesus' claims required investigation. Scribes came from Jerusalem to examine His actions and teaching. They concluded Jesus was **possessed by Beelzebul**, the Baal worshiped at Ekron centuries earlier. This meant Jesus was demonically possessed and His power was Satanic.

2. The Denial (3:23-30) (see also the comments on Mt 12:22-32)

3:23-30. Jesus engaged the scribes and **began speaking to them in parables** (for a definition of "parable," see the comments introducing Mt 13). Jesus rarely defended Himself, but the charge that He was empowered by Satan had to be addressed. He responded, **How can Satan cast out Satan?** If Satan was casting out Satan, would his kingdom not be **divided against itself**? Jesus carried the analogy of kingdom division further: **If a house is divided against itself, that house will not be able to stand.** If a "house" (family) was divided against itself, it would not remain powerful for long. In conclusion Jesus applied everything He had said to Satan, who was not in the process of being defeated. His kingdom was powerful and his demons active. No one could enter a strong man's home and take away his property unless he could first bind the strong man. Only then could the intruder **plunder** the home. If Jesus was casting out Satan's demons, does that not imply He had greater power and authority than Satan? **Truly I say to you** means Jesus was saying something of great importance. All acknowledged sin will be forgiven man, even **blasphemies** against Jesus Himself. But blasphemy **against the Holy Spirit** would never be forgiven, for it is **an eternal sin**. Religious leaders should have recognized God's power at work. They might have misunderstood Jesus, but not the divine power He was demonstrating. Their conclusion was Jesus had **an unclean spirit** and His power was Satanic. It was not too late to change their minds. But if they failed to change, their sin would have serious personal and national consequences. It would lead to the rejection of their King and the postponement of His kingdom.

3. The Ramifications (3:31-35) (see also the comments on Mt 12:46-50)

3:31-35. Suddenly **His mother and His brothers arrived**. "His own people" (cf. v. 21) may have voiced their concern over Jesus' behavior to Mary. She and her unnamed sons **sent word** to Jesus when they could not enter the crowded building. Learning of the situation, Jesus said, **Who are My mother and My brothers?** The implication of this rhetorical question was not to repudiate family values that God established at creation. Their interruption implied they had a claim on Him taking precedence over other matters. Jesus said, **whoever does the will of God, he is My brother and sister and mother**. He was asserting physical relationships were not the proper access to Him. Obediently doing the Father's will gives evidence one is properly related to Jesus.

4. The Instruction (4:1-34) (see also the comments on Mt 13:1-23)

a. A Parable Taught (4:1-12)

4:1-2. Jesus continued teaching, but the multitude was so great he could not communicate effectively. He **got into a boat** (cf. 3:9), and from the sea He taught in parables to those gathered on the shore.

4:3-9. Possibly at the moment He said **Listen**! He pointed to someone in an adjacent field doing what He was describing. As seed is sown, it falls on different soils. Seed falling on **the road** becomes food for birds. Seeds falling

on the rocky ground might immediately spring up. But with shallow soil, the sun dries them out and the plants quickly wither. Seed falling **among the thorns** would be choked, resulting in no crop. Some seeds, however, fell into **good soil** and **yielded a crop** in varying amounts. Jesus encouraged the multitude to listen carefully to His words. They heard with their ears, but understanding occurs in the heart.

4:10-12. Getting away from the multitude, His followers and **the twelve** asked **Him about the parables**. Jesus indicated He told parables to reveal truth to His followers. They were being given **the mystery of the kingdom of God**. "Mystery" implies a previously unrevealed truth now revealed so the instructed may know. It is known because God chooses to reveal it. The promised Davidic kingdom was not a mystery. But not everything about that kingdom program was revealed in the OT. Jesus communicated new things to His disciples. Parabolic teaching carried an aspect of judgment. This may seem harsh, but the historical context gives clues to understanding. The crowds, especially the religious leaders, had heard Jesus teach. Instead of responding in faith, they were rejecting Him, concluding He worked by Satan's power (cf. 3:22-30). Such individuals would not receive further truth. But they could still come in saving faith to Jesus.

b. A Parable Explained (4:13-20)

4:13-20. Jesus knew they did not understand. If they could not understand simple parables, how would they understand more complicated ones? The sower was explained as one sowing **the word**. The emphasis is on the four kinds of soils, not the sower. The word sown **beside the road** fell on unprepared individuals, and Satan snatched it away. The word sown **on the rocky places** represented individuals who received the word with joy, recognizing it as truth. But the reception was superficial and change did not follow. Seeds germinate because there is life in the seed. But persecution's impact is similar to hot sun on rootless plants. A third response occurred as seed was **sown among the thorns**. There was a response, but thorns choked out the truth and no fruit developed. Thorns that arise include **the worries of the world, and the deceitfulness of riches, and the desires for other things**. Finally some seed fell into prepared hearts producing fruit: thirtyfold, sixtyfold, and a hundredfold. Although one cannot be dogmatic, if genuine conversion results in a changed life that produces fruit (cf. Mt 7:16, 20; Lk 3:8), perhaps only this fourth response indicates genuine salvation. The first three responses produced no fruit indicating there was no permanent change. But the purpose of this parable is not to elaborate on genuine conversion versus reformation. The parable is explaining why individuals responded as they did to Jesus.

c. Further Parabolic Instruction (4:21-34)

4:21-25. Jesus continued using common objects. One does not light **a lamp** and place it under **a basket** or **bed.** That would diminish the light or possibly extinguish it. It is placed on a lamp stand so light fills the room. The gospel is not to be kept secret either. A person is judged by the light he receives, so one should be careful **what** he listens to. God gives additional revelation to individuals who respond positively to light. Those who turn from the truth may find that truth **taken away from** [them].

4:26-29. God's rule is **like a man who casts seed upon the soil**. After sowing he **goes to bed at night and gets up by day**. A farmer learns patience, for how seeds sprout he **does not know**. He cannot give life to the seed, but his job is to sow it. The crop arrives in stages: **first the blade, then the head, then the mature grain in the head**. The harvest comes through God's marvelous provision, not through man's efforts. So is the coming of this mystery form of God's kingdom during the present age, prior to its climactic future arrival.

4:30-32. The kingdom of God is pictured **like a mustard seed**, their smallest known seed. Though tiny when sown, it becomes a large plant, often more than ten feet tall. The emphasis is the contrast between its beginning and ending size. When grown, it can sustain **THE BIRDS OF THE AIR** on its branches, holding their nests **UNDER ITS SHADE**. Jesus was teaching that God's kingdom would begin small but would grow large in number (see also the comments on Mt 13:31-32).

4:32-34. Jesus taught many parables and communicated truth as His hearers **were able to hear** it, but **He was explaining** everything privately to the disciples. Thus, the purpose of parables was fulfilled: Truth was revealed to His followers but concealed from rejecting individuals (cf. Mt 13:10, 36).

F. The Servant's Authentication in Spite of Opposition (4:35–5:43)

1. To the Apostles (4:35-41) (see also the comments on Mt 8:23-27)

4:35-36. After a day of ministry, Jesus said, **Let us go over to the other side**, a five-mile trip to a region where Jesus was unknown. The disciples had a boat ready (cf. 3:9) so they departed quickly. **Other boats** were with them, but what happened to them is not revealed.

4:37-38. They departed in clear weather, but **a fierce gale of wind** arose and **waves were breaking** over the bow. Jesus' interaction with the multitudes had resulted in physical exhaustion. He boarded the boat, retreated to the stern, and quickly fell asleep. The disciples roused Him crying that they were **perishing**. Jesus' presence in the boat did not prevent the difficult situation. Nor did His sleep indicate a lack of care for His followers. Rather, that the omniscient Son of God directed them into the boat, knowing a storm was coming, indicates that Jesus intended to use the storm to teach His disciples.

4:39-41. Jesus **rebuked the wind** (**Hush**) commanding it be quiet. To the sea He said **be still** (literally "be muzzled"). It was as though He were placing His hand over the sea. Immediately **it became perfectly calm.** Jesus did not stop with the physical elements. The greatest danger was the disciples' unbelief. He rebuked them: **Why are you afraid?** After months following Jesus, why did they not have greater faith? Now they were **very much afraid**. Their reverential awe was far greater than their fear of the storm. They were standing in the presence of divine power. They had never seen physical elements respond to a human's command. Jesus' point was to use the calming of the storm to reveal how powerful He really was, even to reveal His deity.

2. To the Region of Decapolis (5:1-20) (see also the comments on Mt 8:28-34)

5:1-5. Jesus and the disciples arrived in **the country of the Gerasenes**, a region largely populated by Gentiles. A demon-possessed man who was dwelling among the tombs met them. His demonic strength kept anyone from being able to bind him, but by **night and day** his shrieks were heard as he gashed **himself with stones**.

5:6-10. The man **bowed down before** [Jesus] The demon cried out, **What business do we have with each other**? He knew Jesus as the **Son of the Most High God**. He continued, **I implore You by God, do not torment me!** He understood he was a creature under Jesus' authority and that his ultimate end was separation from God. Jesus actually initiated the encounter. **He had been saying to him, "Come out of the man, you unclean spirit!"** Jesus asked the demon his name. **My name is Legion; for we are many**, he replied. A Roman legion's maximum strength was six thousand men. The demon continued begging Jesus not to send them out of the region. They needed to possess something or they would be forced into the Abyss (cf. Lk 8:31).

5:11-13. A large herd of swine was feeding nearby. Since demons are unclean spirits and pigs unclean animals, they probably thought their request would be favorably received. When given permission they entered the swine and the herd **rushed down the steep bank into the sea** and drowned. The herd numbered about two thousand pigs.

5:14-17. The herdsmen realized they were in trouble. The pigs had been entrusted to them. How would they explain the loss? They **reported** what happened and many came out to see for themselves. They were surprised to see Jesus and the formerly demon-possessed man sitting quietly fully clothed. The story of the swine was repeated many times. The impact on the pigs seems to have been of greater concern than the impact on the man. One would expect great joy over the healing of this poor man. Instead they asked Jesus **to leave their region**, perhaps because they feared His ongoing presence might bring additional financial loss.

5:18-20. As Jesus was departing, the delivered man wanted to go with Jesus and become a disciple. The greater need for this man was to return to his home and report **what great things** God had done for him. He could now return to his estranged family with a testimony of God's work in his life. He did become a great testifier for Jesus in the region of the **Decapolis**. He faithfully proclaimed his testimony and **everyone was amazed**.

3. To the "Religious" Leaders (5:21-43) (see also the comments on Mt 9:18-26)

a. The Request (5:21-24)

5:21-24. As Jesus arrived on the west side **a large crown gathered** welcoming Him. A synagogue official, **Jairus**, approached Him. Synagogue officials were responsible for the administrative details of the synagogue, such as determining who would pray and read Scripture in services. This position was looked on with honor. Jairus **fell at His feet** begging for help. His little girl was near death. If Jesus would **come and lay** [His] **hands on her** she would be healed. Jairus had observed this before (cf. 3:1). Jesus departed with Jairus with **a large crowd** following.

b. The Interruption (5:25-34)

5:25-29. A woman who had **a hemorrhage for twelve years** was in the crowd. The nature of her illness made her ceremonially unclean (cf. Lv 15:25). She **had endured much at the hands of many physicians**, and spent all her money, but had grown worse. Because of her condition, she did not directly confront Jesus. Her plan was to come up behind Jesus and **touch His garments** (perhaps a reference to the ceremonial fringes that were part of the shawls worn by Jewish men). The Lord rewarded her faith. When she touched His garments, the hemorrhaging stopped. She knew she had been **healed of her affliction** through the object of faith, Jesus.

5:30-34. Jesus sensed **power** had gone out from Him. Stopping, He asked, **Who touched My garments?** The question was almost humorous. Surely the disciples thought, "Lord, everyone is touching You." But Jesus wanted **the woman who had done this** to come forward to clarify what had happened. She approached in fear, **fell down** in worship, **and told Him the whole truth**. Jesus called her **Daughter** implying a special relationship had started between them. She was now viewed as one of His children. He said, **your faith has made you well; Go in peace, and be healed of your affliction.** This woman received physical and spiritual healing. When anyone comes to faith in Christ, peace is established between that person and God (cf. Rm 5:1).

c. The Fulfillment (5:35-43)

5:35-37. A group arrived from Jairus's house with sad news. His daughter had died and he should not **trouble the Teacher anymore**. Nothing could be done. Jesus ignored their words but gave two present-tense commands to Jairus: **Do not be afraid**, and **only believe**, or "keep on believing." If Jesus could heal Jairus's daughter of illness, could He not also do something about her death? Jesus took along Peter, James, and John to observe the miracle, possibly as part of the special training these three in His innermost circle should receive.

5:38-40a. At Jairus's home, an assembled group was **weeping and wailing**. Jesus told them to stop, for the **child has not died, but is asleep**. By this figure Jesus taught death is a temporary condition, much like sleep. The crowd's repeated laughter indicated that most of these people were insincere. They were simply there to do a job.

5:40b-43. Jesus took Jairus, his wife, and his three companions into the room where He took the girl **by the hand**. He said to her in Aramaic, **Talitha kum!** which means, "Little girl, I say to you, arise!" "Talitha" might have been an affectionate term for "girl." The phrase, **I say to you**, shows Jesus' authority. Someday He will call all people from the grave (cf. Jn 5:28-29). The girl arose and began to walk around. The age of the girl, 12 years, and the length of time the woman suffered the physical infirmity are the same. The notation of 12 years probably emphasizes the difference between the woman and the girl. The former had 12 years of misery, the latter 12 years of happy childhood. The occupants of the room **were completely astounded**, but Jesus issued two directives. First, He ordered them to not make known what had happened, for that might attract additional people for the wrong reasons. His second directive displayed His compassion for the little girl. He encouraged her parents to give her something to eat.

G. The Rejection of Nazareth (6:1-6) (see also the comments on Mt 13:54-58)

6:1-3. Jesus left Capernaum accompanied by His disciples and came to Nazareth, His hometown. As a rabbi with a growing reputation, Jesus would have been asked to speak in the synagogue on the Sabbath. Those who listened **were astonished**, marveling at His **wisdom** and wondering about its source. They also wondered about the **miracles** He was performing. They had seen Him work with wood as their **carpenter** for many years. They acknowledged He was **the son of Mary**, and His brothers **James**, **Joses**, **Judas**, and **Simon** are mentioned along with unnamed sisters. These people were saying, "We know this Jesus. He is common. He is one of us." They stumbled over Him and failed to follow Him.

6:4-6. Tragically, even His own family disbelieved Jesus' Messianic claims (cf. Jn 7:1-5). Yet some of His family later became His followers. James became the leader of the church in Jerusalem, according to Ac 15:13, and was the author of the epistle that bears his name. James's brother wrote the book of Jude (see Jd 1). Since Nazareth did not believe in Him, He only healed **a few sick people** who came to Him. Their unbelief caused Jesus to wonder (cf. Mt 8:10). He left Nazareth and traveled around the villages of Galilee teaching.

H. The Ministry to Combat Opposition (6:7-13) (see also the comments on Mt 10:1-14)

6:7-11. The time arrived for the apostles to begin their ministries. Jesus sent them out **in pairs**, giving them **authority over the unclean**

spirits, which demonstrated God's authority. They were told to **take nothing for their journey, except a mere staff**, to secure no food or a traveling bag, or take **money in their belt**. They could **wear sandals** but should not bring an extra pair or take a second tunic. No elaborate preparations should be made, for He would provide for them. In every town they were to secure lodging and remain in that home until their ministry concluded. Rejection should not surprise them. Their message concerning Jesus would undoubtedly find opposition. But they should **shake the dust off the soles of** [their] **feet**, demonstrating that they did not take the rejection of the message of Jesus personally. The people were not rejecting the messengers but the One who sent them, Jesus.

6:12-13. The disciples **went out and preached** the same message as John the Baptist and Jesus, a message of repentance. Their hearers were steeped in traditions, and they needed to look to the true understanding of God's wishes for mankind. They demonstrated their authority by **casting out** demons and anointing many sick people with oil, bringing healing.

I. The Civil Rulers' Opposition (6:14-29) (see also the comments on Mt 14:3-12)

1. The Fear of Herod (6:14-16)

6:14-15. News of the Twelve's ministry reached Herod, a son of Herod the Great named Antipas, who ruled Galilee and Perea. As Jesus was becoming better known, some were saying He was **John the Baptist**, risen from the dead. Others suggested He was **Elijah**, or a prophet **like one of the prophets of old**.

6:16. Herod concluded Jesus was John the Baptist, risen from the dead, because he had issued the order to behead John.

2. The Actions of Herod (6:17-29)

6:17-20. John had been preaching against Herod's marital situation. On a trip to Rome, Herod had stayed with a half brother, Philip, who was married to Herodias. Though he was married, Herod fell in love with his sister-in-law and persuaded her to return with him to Israel. They divorced their spouses and married, totally contrary to Mosaic law. John the Baptist fearlessly denounced them, for the Mosaic law applied equally to all in Israel, even rulers. Herodias became so angry with John she **wanted to put him to death**. But Herod had locked him in prison thinking he could silence his preaching. Herod was actually **afraid** of John for he was a **righteous and holy man**. He enjoyed **listening to him**, but was confused by John's words. He did not want to recognize his own sin and repent.

6:21-29. Herod was hosting his birthday party with **his lords and military commanders and the leading men of Galilee** present. During the party, **the daughter of Herodias** (Salome) danced for the guests. No Jewish mother would have encouraged her daughter to dance before a group of men. Salome's dance greatly **pleased Herod and his dinner guests**, prompting him to say, **Ask me for whatever you want and I will give it to you**. He even promised her **up to half of my kingdom**. This hyperbolic statement meant he wanted to be very extravagant in his dealings with her. Salome asked her mother what she should ask for. Herodias responded, encouraging her to ask for **the head of John the Baptist**. Salome returned to the king and asked for John's head **on a platter**. This saddened the king, for he did not want to kill him, and he realized his wife had tricked him. Since he had taken an oath, he sent **an executioner** who carried out the sentence. The head of John the Baptist was brought to the girl and she brought it to Herodias. Some of John's disciples buried his decapitated body and reported the news to Jesus (cf. Mt 14:12).

J. The Servant's Instruction in View of Opposition (6:30-56) (see also the comments on Mt 14:13-21)

1. The Intended Retreat (6:30-32)

The apostles **gathered together with Jesus** and reported what they had accomplished. Jesus realized they needed to get away, for people were **coming and going** and **they did not even have time to eat**. They departed by boat to go to **a secluded place** to talk without interruption.

2. The Actual Reality (6:33-44)

6:33-36. However many people went around the shore on foot, arriving before Jesus and the disciples. The news spread that Jesus was back, and a large crowd was waiting on the shore. Jesus viewed the crowd as an opportunity for ministry. **He felt compassion for them** viewing them as **sheep without a shepherd**. Therefore he taught them throughout most of the day. As it grew late the disciples suggested that He send the people into surrounding villages to secure food.

6:37-44. Jesus' answer probably startled the disciples: **You give them *something* to eat!** Philip's calculation (cf. Jn 6:7) was two hundred denarii (about eight months of labor) would be necessary to provide **something** for each person. Jesus encouraged them to see **how many loaves** of bread they had. Their search produced five loaves and two fish. The assembled crowd reclined by groups on the **green grass** and in **groups of hundreds and of fifties**. Jesus **took the five loaves and the two fish**, blessed them, and began to break them into baskets given to the disciples. These were served to the crowd, but the miracle occurred in Jesus' hands as He multiplied the food. The disciples however were the ones who brought the food to the people. They would continue to serve their Lord in years to come, but their supply and strength for ministry would always come from the Lord Himself. **All ate and were satisfied**. When the meal was over **twelve . . . baskets** of leftovers were gathered. The number fed was 5,000 men, but women and children were also present (cf. Mt 14:21).

3. The Authenticating Signs (6:45-56) (see also the comments on Mt 14:22-36)

a. Walking on the Water (6:45-52)

6:45-46. Following the miracle, Jesus sent His disciples **ahead of Him . . . to Bethsaida**, on the northeastern side of the Sea of Galilee. Jesus dispersed the multitude and departed to a **mountain to pray**.

6:47-50a. When evening came, the boat with the disciples was **in the middle of the sea**. They were **straining at the oars** because a northerly wind was driving them off course. **About the fourth watch of the night** (3:00 to 6:00 a.m.), Jesus decided to join them on the sea. The One who had created water could walk on it. **He intended to pass by them**. The verb **to pass by** (*parerchomai*) is used in the Septuagint for appearances of Jehovah (cf. Ex 33:19, 22; 34:6; 1Kg 19:11), commonly called theophanies, when God was described as "passing by" an OT character. Jesus' deity is indicated by the use of the verb in this passage. The disciples **all saw Him** and were frightened, thinking He **was a ghost**.

6:50b-52. But Jesus spoke to them. **Take courage; it is I, do not be afraid**. "It is I" (lit., "I am"), could have been an echo of the OT formula of God's self-revelation, "I am who I am" (cf. Ex 3:14). When Jesus **got into the boat**, the wind immediately stopped. The disciples **were utterly astonished** because they failed to gain **insight from the incident of the loaves**. Indeed, their hearts were **hardened**. These miracles coming in close proximity should have reminded them that Jesus is the Son of God who has power over creation. He can create food; He can walk on water.

b. Healings at Gennesaret (6:53-56)

6:53-56. Many scholars believe the storm drove them off course and they landed at **Gennesaret** on the northwest corner of the sea. It would not prove to be a place of solitude, as the people there **recognized** Jesus. Some of these people might have been at the recent feeding of the 5,000. They brought to Jesus **those who were sick**. Many were seeking to touch **the** ceremonial **fringe of his cloak**, perhaps a result of the healing of the woman with the issue of blood (cf. 5:25). Those who **touched** His cloak in faith were healed.

K. The Pharisees' Continued Opposition (7:1-23) (see also the comments on Mt 15:1-20)

1. The "Violation" Stated (7:1-5)

7:1-2. Pharisees and scribes **had come from Jerusalem** to investigate Jesus. **Scribes** were professional students who defended scriptural and traditional law. They would be quick to point out violations of the law or traditions. They had seen unnamed disciples **eating their bread with impure hands.**

7:3-5. Impure hands meant "unwashed" hands, an issue of ceremonial washings extremely important to Pharisees. They would not eat a meal until they carefully washed. This was a tradition passed down by Jewish elders, not part of the law. This practice was followed with things like **washing of cups and pitchers and copper pots**. Jesus was asked, **Why do Your disciples not walk according to the tradition of the elders**? See the comments on Mt 12:1-8 for a discussion of oral traditions of the Jewish leaders. As the head of the group, Jesus was being held responsible for their actions.

2. The Servant's Explanation (7:6-13)

7:6-7. Jesus took the offensive using scriptural arguments. He said Isaiah rightly called these individuals **hypocrites**. As in Isaiah's day, they were seeking to honor God with their lips, but their hearts were far from Him (cf. the comments on Is 29:13). Jesus' reference to Isaiah indicates that the opposition He faced from the Jewish leaders was a pattern that was not new.

7:8-13. They were substituting the ideas of men for clearly stated doctrines. They were neglecting **the commandment of God** and holding **to the traditions of men**. See the comments on Mt 12:1-8 for a discussion of oral traditions of the Jewish leaders, and Mt 15:1-9 for Matthew's version of this episode. The fifth commandment, **HONOR YOUR FATHER AND YOUR MOTHER**

(cf. Ex 20:12), is used to illustrate. The religious leaders had avoided this commandment by saying a possession was **Corban**, or **given to God**. One's parents could not benefit from that thing, so it would be easy to deprive them of possible aid. The possession devoted to God would still be retained by the individual. By making a vow (cf. Nm 30:1-2), they could set aside a clear commandment of God. They were therefore **invalidating the word of God** through their traditions.

3. The Servant's Warning (7:14-23)

7:14-16. Jesus turned to the issue of the true source of defilement. Nothing entering from the outside defiles a person, but it starts within and proceeds outward. This contradicted the rabbinic view then current, but it is a biblical view of defilement (cf. Jr 17:9-10; Ec 9:3).

7:17-23. Cf. the comments on Mt 15:10-11. Jesus left the multitude and probably entered Peter's house in Capernaum. The disciples **questioned Him about the parable** just presented. Jesus rebuked them: **Are you so lacking in understanding also?** The religious teachers were teaching that people were defiled because something unclean contacted their bodies. Jesus said that things coming into the body never touch the heart, but go into the stomach and finally are eliminated. Food never touches the heart, the true source of defilement. Jesus' words did not formally end Levitical distinctions between clean and unclean animals. Jesus was explaining the true source of defilement. Evil comes out of the heart. **Evil thoughts** are pictured in the twelve following words in the text. The first six are plural; the last six singular. The plural nouns describe various wicked acts: **fornications**, **thefts**, **murders**, **adulteries**, **deeds of coveting**, and **wickedness**. The six singular nouns picture internal attitudes: **deceit**, **sensuality**, **envy**, **slander**, **pride**, and **foolishness**. All these proceed from within and cause defilement. Jesus pointed out the hypocrisy of the religious leaders and clarified the true source of defilement.

L. The Servant's Retreat from Opposition (7:24–8:9)

1. To the Region of Tyre (7:24-30) (see also the comments on Mt 15:22-28)

7:24-30. From Capernaum, Jesus went away to Tyre and Sidon, attempting to keep His location secret. Word of His arrival circulated and a **Gentile** woman **of the Syrophoenician** people (not **race** as in the NASB, a term that identifies people by biological characteristics whereas the Greek word describes people by their descent) with a demon-possessed daughter sought Him out. She **fell at His feet** and kept asking Jesus **to cast the demon out of her daughter**. He responded that He could not **take the children's bread and throw it to the dogs**. Jesus was not equating Gentiles with dogs as the Pharisees might have done. His point was to compare the position of privilege of the Jewish people as God's covenant people (in this analogy, the "children") with the relative lack of privilege of the Gentiles ("the dogs," not having the same benefits as the children). The woman saw herself as one of the canines in the room. She addressed Jesus as **Lord**, reminding Him that even the puppies were able to catch scraps falling off the table around the children. She was only asking for a small blessing, and her answer demonstrated true humility. When she arrived home she found her daughter released from the demon.

2. To the Region of Decapolis (7:31–8:9)

a. Healing of the Deaf Man (7:31-37)

7:31. Jesus left Tyre, **and came through Sidon to the Sea of Galilee, within the region of Decapolis**, a journey of some miles. He was avoiding the northern shore of the Sea of Galilee, the multitudes seeking miracles, and the religious leaders with their controversies.

7:32-35. In Decapolis **one who was deaf and spoke with difficulty** was brought to Him. They asked Jesus **to lay His hand on him** to bring about his healing (cf. 6:5). Jesus took the man away from the multitude. He **put His fingers into his ears**, spat on the ground, and touched the man's tongue. These acts communicated to the man that He was about to do something to affect his ears and tongue. He looked up to heaven, showing help was coming from above. With **a deep sigh**, Jesus spoke to the man: **Ephphatha!** (Aramaic meaning "Be opened!"). The deaf man's ears were opened and he began **speaking plainly**. Jesus not only healed his deafness but also his speech.

7:36-37. Jesus ordered that the details of this miracle not be broadcast, but this kind of news was hard to keep quiet. The people **were utterly astonished**, saying Jesus had **done all things well**. Jesus was able to make deaf people hear and dumb people speak.

b. Feeding of the 4,000 (8:1-9) (see also the comments on Mt 15:32-39)

8:1-3. There was again need for food for a large crowd. Jesus said to His disciples, **I feel compassion for the people**. Some had been listening to His teaching for three days. Many had come from great distances, and He did not want to send them away hungry.

8:4-9. The disciples' comments seem surprising since they had seen Jesus feed 5,000 men, plus women and children (cf. 6:30-44). Some believe this story is a distortion of that miracle, but evidence requires this miracle to be unique (cf. 8:19-20, where Jesus' mention of both miracles in the same context supports a distinction between them). Jesus did not rebuke them for their failure to remember, but asked them to gather the food they possessed. This clearly fixed in their minds the inadequacy of their supply, for they found only seven loaves of bread.

Jesus told **the people to sit down on the ground**. Taking **the seven loaves**, He gave thanks and gave it to the disciples to distribute. Again the multiplication occurred in the hands of the Creator, but the disciples served the food. **A few small fish** were also served and **they ate and were satisfied**. **Seven large baskets**, baskets capable of holding a man (cf. Ac 9:25), were gathered. On this occasion about 4,000 were fed before Jesus **sent them away**.

M. The Pharisees' Final Demand (8:10-21)
(see also the comments on Mt 16:1-12)

1. The Demand (8:10-11)

8:10-11. Jesus and the disciples crossed the sea to **Dalmanutha**, possibly near modern-day Tiberias. They were met by Pharisees, who were **seeking from Him a sign from heaven, to test Him**. They wanted a miraculous display to prove His claims. The religious leaders were saying they rejected all His previous miracles. They were hoping for a public failure that would discredit Him.

2. The Servant's Explanation (8:12-13)

8:12-13. Jesus sighed **deeply in His spirit** and asked: **Why does this generation seek for a sign?** They should have accepted the miracles of Jesus and not have looked for something spectacular. No sign would be given now. Jesus and the disciples simply departed for **the other side** of the lake.

3. The Servant's Warning (8:14-21)

8:14-16. In their haste the disciples failed to take provisions, and they only had **one loaf** of bread. Jesus gave a solemn warning: **Watch out! Beware of the leaven of the Pharisees and the leaven of Herod**. Leaven, yeast, combined with flour, permeates the whole loaf. Jesus was warning the disciples about the sin of the **Pharisees** (cf. 8:11) and **Herod**. The former were noted for their hypocrisy, and the latter represented a worldly group with an intense interest in political power. However, the disciples completely missed Jesus' intention. When He mentioned "leaven," they began to discuss their failure to bring bread.

8:17-21. Jesus clarified He was not merely talking about bread. That they had failed to bring bread was irrelevant. He said, **Do you not yet see or understand? Do you have a hardened heart?** He quoted Ezekiel, who lived among rebellious people, without eyes to see or ears to hear (cf. Ezk 12:2). This description should not have characterized the Twelve, although Jesus had said (cf. Mk 4:11) this would be true of the crowds. His disciples should have seen and heard. He reminded them of the feeding of the 5,000 (cf. 6:33-44) when they picked up twelve small baskets of leftovers, and the feeding of 4,000 men (cf. 8:1-9) when they collected seven large baskets. They recalled the facts from each miracle, but they did not understand their significance. Jesus concluded: **Do you not yet understand?**

N. A Concluding Miracle (8:22-26)

8:22-24. They came to Bethsaida, near the area where the feeding of the 5,000 had occurred. When Jesus was recognized, **they brought a blind man** asking for His touch, thinking that would bring healing (cf. 1:41; 5:41; 6:5; 7:32). Jesus led the man **out of the village** to get with him alone. He spit on the man's eyes, laid His hands on him (cf. 7:31-37), and asked, **Do you see anything?** He responded, **I see men, for I see them like trees, walking around**. Since he recognized trees and men, he must have had sight previously, though it is possible that the upright nature of both trees and men that he had previously experienced with his other senses may have prompted his comparison.

8:25-26. Jesus laid hands on the man's eyes a second time. The man looked **intently** and **was restored**, seeing everything clearly. This unique miracle occurred in stages. Did Jesus not have the necessary power to heal this man with one touch? Yes, but since the miracle occurred in stages initiated by Jesus, there must be a reason. Perhaps through the two stages Jesus was showing the disciples that their faith and knowledge of the person of Jesus was becoming clearer all the time, as this man's sight. It is also possible that Jesus performed two distinct miracles, the first being the man's ability to see, and the second his comprehension of what he saw. Jesus sent the man to his home for a testimony, not back to Bethsaida.

IV. The Instruction of the Servant of the Lord (8:27–10:52)

A. Instruction Concerning His Person (8:27-30) (see also the comments on Mt 16:13-20)

8:27-28. Jesus and His disciples headed for **Caesarea Philippi**, twenty-five miles north of the Sea of Galilee. As they traveled Jesus questioned them: **Who do people say that I am?** The disciples responded as before (cf. 6:14-16): **John the Baptist . . . Elijah . . . one of the prophets**, all flattering suggestions.

8:29-30. Jesus questioned them specifically: **But who do you say that I am?** Peter answered for the group saying: **You are the Christ**, the anointed One by God, the Messiah. The great blessing on Peter (cf. the comments on Mt 16:17-18) is not recorded here. Jesus warned the disciples to tell no one about this disclosure. The concept of the Messiah had become quite distorted in Israel, differing from OT predictions. The concept of a suffering Messiah who would redeem His people had virtually been lost, being replaced with a political emphasis. Until He could explain the true concept, the disciples were to say nothing. The true concept would clearly explain His death and resurrection.

B. Instruction Concerning His Program (8:31–9:13) (see also the comments on Mt 16:21–17:13)

1. His Coming Death (8:31-33) (see also the comments on Mt 16:21-26)

8:31-32a. Following the testimony concerning His person as Messiah, Jesus **began to teach** His disciples of His coming death, this first of three such predictions in this gospel (cf. 9:31; 10:33-34). The **Son of Man** must suffer many things and be killed (cf. Is 52:13–53:12). He would **be rejected by the elders and the chief priests and the scribes**, the Sanhedrin, the group that would ultimately have to officially condemn the Son of Man. But after three days Jesus would **rise again**. Jesus **plainly** stated the matter of His coming death.

8:32b-33. This revelation was not in keeping with the disciples' understanding of Messiah's actions. It is not surprising that Peter took Jesus **aside and began to rebuke Him**. His understandable reaction is nevertheless presumptuous. Jesus could not allow Peter's words and actions to stand. He turned and looked at all the disciples, who probably were in agreement with Peter's rebuke. He said to Peter, **Get behind Me, Satan**. Peter and Satan were not the same individual. Jesus' rebuke does not indicate that Peter was demon possessed but rather that he was acting as Satan's spokesman at this moment. He was encouraging Jesus to follow the route Satan suggested earlier: that He could have the glory without the cross (cf. Mt 4:8-9). Peter's mind was set on man's interests, not on God's.

2. His Requirement for Followers (8:34-38)

8:34. Jesus **summoned the crowd** and said: **If anyone wishes to come after Me, he must deny himself, and take up his cross and follow Me**. Denying self does not mean a denial of one's personality, but a denial of self-centeredness and placing Jesus on the throne of one's life. Taking up one's cross was not a Jewish metaphor, but a common figure to the readers. A condemned criminal often carried the crosspiece of his cross, if not the entire cross, to his place of execution, showing Rome had authority over him. When a disciple takes up his cross in a decisive act, he is acknowledging Christ's authority over his life. When the disciple follows Him, His will is revealed daily, and the disciple continues to follow.

8:35-38. Four statements elaborate on Jesus' words, each beginning with the preposition, **for**. Who would not wish to save his life? Yet, if one seeks the wrong things, he will lose it. If one loses his life for the cause of Christ and the **gospel**, he will save it. One who understands the person of Jesus Christ and the need of the lost will live his life to proclaim the good news. In a rhetorical question Jesus asked: **For what does it profit a man to gain the whole world, and forfeit his soul?** There is much to be gained in this world, but what if a person should gain everything the world has to offer? How much could he take with him beyond the grave? A second rhetorical question follows: **For what will a man give in exchange for his soul?** There is nothing one can give in exchange for his soul. In a final statement Jesus reflected on His return to this earth in power and glory as Judge. People who have not committed themselves to Jesus as Savior are classic examples of those who live in an **adulterous and sinful generation**. Therefore when He comes in the glory of the Father with the holy angels to exercise judgment, they will be denied admission to the millennial kingdom.

3. His Coming Kingdom Pictured (9:1-10) (see also the comments on Mt 17:1-13)

9:1-4. Jesus mentioned His glorious return and that some standing there would not die until they saw the kingdom of God come in power. **Six days later** He took Peter, James, and John to **a high mountain**, probably Mount Hermon, where He **was transfigured before them** (cf. v. 1). "Transfigured" is similar to the English "metamorphosis," a change from within. **His garments became radiant and exceedingly white**, purer than any **launderer** could achieve. **Elijah** and **Moses** were there **talking with Jesus** about His departure (cf. Lk 9:31), or death. Elijah and Moses represent the Prophets and the Law.

9:5-6. Peter reacted: **Rabbi, it is good for us to be here; let us make three tabernacles, one for You, and one for Moses, and one for Elijah.** Peter thought this was the fulfillment of the Feast of Tabernacles (cf. Zch 14:16), which recalled Israel's wilderness wanderings followed by blessing in the land, picturing millennial glory. Peter thought the kingdom had come, but he really **did not know what to answer** and was **terrified**.

9:7-8. A voice said: **This is My beloved Son, listen to Him!** (cf. 1:11). **Listen to Him** connects Jesus with "the Prophet" promised in Dt 18. Moses and Elijah disappeared; Jesus is the final form of God's revelation (cf. Heb 1:1-2a). How was this a taste of the kingdom (cf. v. 1)? First, it occurred on earth, where Jesus will reign. Second, Jesus was glorified, as He will be then. Third, all necessary kingdom people are represented: saints in physical bodies (the three disciples), saints who experience death and resurrection (Moses), and saints who will not die but be translated to heaven (Elijah).

9:9-10. Coming down from the mountain, Jesus told the disciples **not to relate to anyone what they had seen** until the **Son of Man rose from the dead**. They continued to discuss **what rising from the dead meant**. Messiah's death and resurrection were not yet clear to them.

4. His Relationship to Elijah (9:11-13) (see also the comments on Mt 17:10-13)

9:11. Elijah's appearance prompted their question. Did Elijah's presence on the mount satisfy prophecies concerning his coming (cf. Mal 4:5-6)? **Why is it that the scribes say that Elijah must come first?**

9:12-13. Jesus affirmed Elijah must prepare the way for Messiah (Mal 4:5-6). They misunderstood, however, that Messiah would be **treated with contempt**. Elijah had come, but His predicted suffering was necessary (cf. Pss 22:1-18; 69:1-21; Is 52:13-53:12). John the Baptist's ministry fulfilled the prophecy if the nation believed (cf. Mt 11:14). The appearance of two witnesses (cf. Rv 11:3-12) will complete the prophecy before Jesus' second coming.

C. Instruction Concerning the Impossible (9:14-29) (see also the comments on Mt 17:14-21)

9:14-16. Returning from the mountain, Jesus and the three discovered the nine disciples arguing with scribes over their failure to exorcise a demon (v. 18). The crowd **began running up to greet Him**, so He inquired about the discussion.

9:17-19. One responded to Jesus that he was looking for him, but encountering the nine disciples, sought their help. His demon-possessed son was mute, possibly also deaf (cf. v. 25.) The demon would seize the boy, slamming him to the ground. He would foam at the mouth, grind his teeth, and stiffen his body. Although the disciples had been given authority over demons (cf. 6:7), they could do nothing. Jesus, probably addressing the nine disciples, called them an **unbelieving generation** and commanded, **Bring him to Me!**

9:20-24. The demon threw the boy **into a convulsion**, and he fell to the ground **rolling around and foaming at the mouth**. Jesus asked how long he had been like this. The father responded, **From childhood**, adding the demon often tried to throw the boy **into the fire and into the water** to destroy him. Finally he said, **But if You can do anything, take pity on us and help us!** Jesus replied: **If You can? All things are possible to him who believes.** The father cried, **I do believe; help my unbelief.** While he believed, faith is never perfect. Unbelief always potentially exists.

9:25-27. Jesus **rebuked the unclean spirit**: **come out** of the boy and **do not enter him again**. The father had to be encouraged. His son was set free, and he would never be possessed again. The demon threw the boy into **terrible convulsions** and he fell down. Some thought he had died, but Jesus **took him by the hand and raised him** (cf. 5:41).

9:28-29. In a house the disciples questioned Jesus: **Why could we not drive it out?** Apparently they had previously been successful (cf. Lk 10:17). Jesus said, **This kind cannot come out by anything but prayer**. Some manuscripts add "and fasting," probably added later to support asceticism. Exorcising a demon was not automatic based on past performance. Even for the disciples who had been granted authority over demons in Jesus' name, prayerful dependence on God's power was required.

D. Instruction Concerning His Upcoming Death (9:30-32)

9:30-31. Jesus and His disciples **began to go through Galilee**, arriving in Capernaum (v. 33). **He was teaching** that He was about **to be delivered into the hands of men** (cf. Ac 2:23) who would kill Him, but He would **rise three days later** (cf. 8:31).

9:32. The disciples **did not understand**. They were not anticipating a dying Messiah but were also **afraid to ask** for clarification. Perhaps Jesus' previous rebuke of Peter (cf. 8:33) prompted their silence. Jesus' words had a devastating effect on their hope of His reign.

E. Instruction Concerning Pride (9:33-37) (see also the comments on Mt 18:1-5)

9:33-34. Jesus asked the disciples what they had been **discussing**. They became silent, for they had been discussing which one of them was the greatest. Perhaps the selection of the three to accompany Jesus to the transfiguration fueled their competitive fires.

9:35-37. Jesus began to discuss positions of authority (cf. 10:43; Mt 23:8; Lk 22:24). **If anyone wants to be first, he shall be last of all and servant of all**. Kingdom positions are determined by willingness to serve. He sat **a child** in their midst. **Whoever receives one child like this in My name receives Me; and whoever receives Me does not receive Me, but Him who sent Me**. Kingdom positions are also based on acceptance of others. Key marks of Jesus' servants are humility and service.

F. Instruction Concerning Partisan Spirit (9:38-50) (see also the comments on Mt 18:7-14)

9:38. John recalled an incident when the disciples observed an outsider casting out demons in Jesus' name. They **tried to prevent him because he was not following us**. This is an illustration of narrow exclusivism and an attempt to divert Jesus' attention from the embarrassing discussion. The disciples could not exorcise a demon (cf. 9:14), but they were preventing someone who was doing so.

9:39-41. Jesus said they should not have hindered the individual. One cannot perform mighty works in His name, and then speak evil of Him. **For he who is not against us is for us**, (cf. Mt 12:30). There is no neutrality with the person of Jesus. Giving **a cup of water** to someone in His name, a hospitable and humble act, could produce a reward. Such behavior should be typical of genuine followers of Jesus.

9:42-43. He continued with instructions concerning offending others. Surely the man casting out demons was offended by their rebuke. It would be better for one to have a **millstone hung around his neck** and be **cast into the sea** than to cause someone to stumble. **Little ones** is probably an affectionate label Jesus used to refer to anyone who follows Him, whether young or old. If one's hand causes stumbling, it would be better to enter life crippled than have two hands and **go into hell, into the unquenchable fire**.

9:44-48. Reference to the foot and eye logically follows. It would be better **to enter life** without a foot or an eye than, having two feet and two eyes, **be cast into hell**. Jesus was not teaching mutilation. One could remove a hand, foot, or eye and still be a terrible sinner. He was pointing out that sin originates in the heart (cf. 7:18-23), not in bodily parts. Gouging out the eye or cutting off the hand and foot are surely hyperbolic statements, but suggest extreme measures to avoid sin. Hell (*ge-Henna,* Hb. for the Valley of Hinnom) is a real place. Hinnom was Jerusalem's garbage dump (cf. 2Kg 23:10) where its refuse was deposited and burned; the part not on fire was usually infested with worms. Isaiah 66:24 pictures eternal torment as external (fire) and internal (worms). The eternal separation of the wicked from God is clearly presented in v. 48. Verses 44 and 46 are not in the better manuscripts, probably inserted for emphasis.

9:49-50. Fire in the phrase **salted with fire** is probably not the fire of judgment as it is in vv. 43 and 48. **Salted with fire** appears to be parallel with being salted in v. 50, and there it seems to be a good thing. **Fire** in vv. 49-50 may refer to the refining and purifying that will take place as His followers are persecuted, and they will be persecuted because they are different from the unsalted world. Even though their salty distinctiveness will attract opposition, they are nevertheless to **have salt in** [themselves] (maintain their unique flavor, i.e., their counter-cultural values and influence in the world, as in Mt 5:13-16). Though they can expect antagonism from the world, they must **be at peace with one another**. Discussing who was greatest (cf. Mk 9:33) was inappropriate in light of Jesus' command to be at peace. They should not be clamoring for positions and promoting themselves.

G. Instruction Concerning Divorce (10:1-12) (see also the comments on Mt 19:1-9)

10:1-2. Jesus crossed **the Jordan; crowds gathered**, and He taught them. **Some Pharisees** asked **whether it was lawful for a man to divorce a wife**. Divorce was considered a gift from God, but denied to Gentiles.

10:3-9. Jesus asked what their authority Moses would say. They responded, **Moses permitted a man to write a certificate of divorce and send her away** (cf. Dt 24:1-4). This safeguard protected wives, since written charges were required. Jesus did not deny Moses permitted divorce, but said it was because of their **hardness of heart**. Jesus referred to creation when God initiated marriage. **GOD MADE THEM MALE AND FEMALE** (cf. Gn 1:27). **FOR THIS REASON A MAN SHALL LEAVE HIS FATHER AND MOTHER, THE TWO SHALL BECOME ONE FLESH.** (cf. Gn 2:24). Physical oneness produces a union unlike any other on earth. Only death terminates this union (though see the comments on Mt 19:9). **What therefore God has joined together, let no man separate**. People are not to **separate** the lifelong commitment God established.

10:10-12. No discussion followed between Jesus and the Pharisees, for His teaching was clear. But later the disciples **began questioning Him**. Jesus clarified when a man **divorces his wife and marries another**, he **commits adultery against her**. Some believe exceptions could be adultery (cf. Mt 19:9) and/or desertion (cf. 1Co 7:15); see the comments there. The same applies if a woman divorces her husband and marries another. Divorce initiated by women was uncommon among Jews, though Herodias had divorced Philip to marry Antipas (see the comments on Mk 6:17-20; Mt 14:3-5).

H. Instruction Concerning Faith (10:13-22)

1. Faith as a Child (10:13-16)

10:13. Parents arrived **bringing children** so Jesus **might touch them**, showing Jesus' growing respect. The disciples **rebuked them**, sensing Jesus was moving with purpose toward Jerusalem (cf. Lk 9:51), where He would be crucified. They thought His time could be better spent with adults.

10:14-16. Jesus issued two commands: to allow the children to come, and to stop hindering them from doing so. He said, **the kingdom of God belongs to such as these**. "Kingdom of God," refers to God's rule over one's life. Unless one receives God's rule with a childlike faith and dependence upon God, he will never enter His kingdom. Jesus took the children in His arms and blessed them (cf. Gn 48:8-20).

2. Faith for Eternal Life (10:17-22) (see also the comments on Mt 19:16-23)

10:17-19. A man knelt before Jesus asking: **Good Teacher, what shall I do to inherit eternal life?** (cf. Jn 6:28). His identification, "Good Teacher," used a word rabbis refused to apply to humans. Jesus responded: **Why do you call Me good?** He was not denying He was good, but was helping the man understand with whom he was speaking. Did he truly recognize Jesus as God? If so, was he open to Jesus' words? Jesus recalled five commandments the man knew (cf. Ex 20:12-16): murder, adultery, stealing, bearing false witness, and honoring one's parents. Jesus omitted covetousness, though some believe **Do not defraud** was synonymous. Others believe Jesus omitted covetousness because that was the man's problem.

10:20-22. He replied, **I have kept all these things from my youth up**. He believed from his youth he had kept these commandments. However, he sensed something was missing (cf. Mt 19:20). Jesus issued two commands: He was to sell his possessions, giving the proceeds to the poor, and come follow Him. The man's countenance fell and he left grieving for he **owned much property**. He had done everything, but he treasured his possessions more.

I. Instruction Concerning Wealth (10:23-31) (see also the comments on Mt 19:24-30)

10:23-25. Jesus commented, **How hard it will be for those who are wealthy to enter the kingdom of God**. The disciples were amazed. If the wealthy could not enter the kingdom, who could? Jesus' hyperbole about a camel going through a needle's eye was well-known. Jesus was speaking about literal camels and needles, but suggestions have been given to accomplish this feat.

10:26-27. The disciples understood: **Then who can be saved?** Jesus said men find some things impossible, but with God **all things are possible** (cf. Gn 18:14), indicating that one's entrance into the kingdom and eternal life are dependent upon God, not human effort.

10:28-31. Peter reminded Jesus the disciples had **left everything** to follow Him. He was saying, "What's in it for us?" Jesus said those who have left valued assets and relationships for the Lord's sake (cf. 8:35) will be recompensed **a hundred times as much . . . in the present age**. There will be other possessions and houses, brothers and sisters and mothers in fellow believers. There will be persecutions, but also rewards and **in the age to come, eternal life**. Many, like the rich man, appear to be prominent, but will ultimately be last (actually, not admitted at all). Those with more humble positions, like the disciples, will someday find themselves first (cf. Mt 19:30; 20:16; Lk 13:30).

J. Instruction Concerning His Near Future (10:32-34) (see also the comments on Mt 20:17-19)

10:32-34. The purposefulness of Jesus' walk (cf. Lk 9:51) amazed the disciples, but a sense of foreboding was developing because of opposition. He said for the third time (cf. 8:31; 9:31) that He would **be delivered to the chief priests and the scribes**, and condemned **to death** (cf. 14:55-64). They could not execute anyone, but would deliver Jesus to the Gentiles (cf. 15:1) for the crucifixion. They would **mock Him** (cf. 15:16-18), **spit on Him** (cf. 15:19), **scourge Him** (cf. 15:15), and **kill Him** (cf. 15:24, 37). After **three days** He would **rise** from the dead (cf. 16:1). Jesus and the gospel writer did not present the Jewish people as solely guilty for the death of Jesus—rather, human responsibility for the crucifixion was a conspiracy of guilt between the Jewish leaders and Gentile rulers and soldiers, permitted by the sovereign plan of God (cf. Ac 2:23; 4:27-28).

K. Instructions Concerning Positions in the Kingdom (10:35-45) (see also the comments on Mt 20:20-28)

10:35-36. James and John asked Jesus to grant an unspecified request. He refused to commit Himself, but asked them to be specific.

10:37-40. They wanted privileged places at His right and left hands in His coming kingdom. Had Jesus not just announced He was going to Jerusalem to die? Their request resurfaced the issue of greatness (cf. 9:33ff.), which Jesus had already settled. He asked if they were **able to drink the cup** He would drink and be **baptized with the baptism** with which He would be baptized. The **cup** pictures divine judgment on human sin (cf. Ps 75:8; Is 51:17-23; Jr 25:15-28, 49:12, 51:7; Lm 4:21-22; Ezk 23:31-34; Hab 2:16; Zch. 12:2). Sharing one's cup meant sharing an experience. To be immersed in water implies becoming overwhelmed by the water. Jesus was about to experience betrayal and death. His question asks if they were ready to follow in His footsteps and also experience death. They responded **We are able**. Jesus said they would share His suffering: James through martyrdom (cf. Ac 12:2), John through persecution and exile (cf. Rv 1:9). However, granting kingdom positions was not His to give, but was His Heavenly Father's.

10:41-45. When the others learned about this discussion, they became **indignant with James and John**. Another discussion on servanthood followed (cf. 9:35-37). Jesus explained Gentile rulers loved to exercise authority over people. His followers must not do that. One wanting to be great must become a **servant**; one wanting to be first, a **slave**. Jesus humbled Himself, taking on the role of a servant, when He came to earth and veiled His deity. He came not **to be served, but to serve** and give His life **a ransom** (cf. Is 53:11), the price to free a captive or a slave. Jesus gave Himself **for** ("in the place of") **many**, the single life benefiting the many. The debt of sin owed by the sinner was owed to God, not to Satan (cf. Rm 3:23-26). Jesus' followers must reflect His humility.

L. Instruction Concerning Faith (10:46-52) (see also the comments on Mt 20:29-34)

10:46-49. In Jericho **Bartimaeus** sat beside the road asking for alms. When he learned Jesus was passing by, he cried out, **Jesus, Son of David, have mercy on me!** Jesus did not object to this Messianic title. Many rebuked Bartimaeus, **telling him to be quiet**. He paid no attention, but continued crying out for mercy using the title Son of David. Jesus commanded him to come forward.

10:50-52. Casting aside his cloak, which may have held his collected alms, he **jumped up** approaching Jesus. He asked Bartimaeus what he wanted of Him. He called Jesus **Rabboni**, "My Master" (cf. Jn 20:16), and asked for his sight. This was not unreasonable. The Messiah would give sight to the blind (cf. Is 61:1). Jesus said, **Go; your faith has made you well**. As with the woman with the hemorrhage (cf. 5:34) and others, faith produced healing and a changed spiritual condition. Bartimaeus was restored and **began following** Jesus, unlike the rich young man (cf. 10:22). He may have followed Him to Jerusalem where he would have given an offering for his healing.

V. The Rejection of the Servant of the Lord (11:1–15:47)

A. The Presentation of the Servant (11:1-26) (see also the comments on Mt 21:1-22)

1. The Triumphal Entry (11:1-11)

11:1-3. Coming from Jericho, Jesus entered **Bethany** on the Mount of Olives. He sent two disciples to nearby **Bethphage** to **find a colt tied**. If questioned about their actions, they should say, **The Lord has need of it**.

11:4-6. They found the colt, though challenges came from **bystanders** (cf. Lk 19:33). After speaking Jesus' words, the disciples received permission to take the animal.

11:7-11. They brought the colt to Jesus, and He rode it into Jerusalem. Accompanying pilgrims removed their coats and spread them in the road with **leafy branches** from trees as a gesture of respect. They began crying **Hosanna!** a Hebrew word meaning "Save us now!" (cf. Ps 118:25-26, a Psalm of Ascent sung by pilgrims). They shouted, **BLESSED IS HE WHO COMES IN THE NAME OF THE LORD** and **Blessed is the coming kingdom of our father David**. Jesus' actions had a Messianic intent, showing fulfillment of Zch 9:9. Jesus entered the temple, probably the Court of the Gentiles, and returned to Bethany.

2. The Judgment Announced (11:12-14)

11:12-14. On the next day, Jesus headed for Jerusalem. **He became hungry**, but spied **a fig tree in leaf** with no fruit on it. He said, **May no one ever eat fruit from you again!** The disciples later called Jesus' words a curse (cf. v. 21). Although **it was not the season for figs** (v. 13), by the time a fig tree is in leaf, it should have fruit on it, even if it is unripe. Hence, this fig tree, despite its leaves, was actually barren. Jesus was demonstrating the danger of spiritual hypocrisy as evident in the temple leaders: all the trappings of religion (leaves), without true transformation (no fruit).

3. The Cleansing of the Temple (11:15-19)

11:15-16. They **entered the temple**, and Jesus **began to drive out those who were buying and selling** (cf. Jn 2:13-16, which occurred earlier). Jesus dealt with **money changers** and those **selling doves**. Their exorbitant prices were not in keeping with the spirit of the temple. Jesus also stopped those carrying **merchandise through the temple**, using it for shortcuts.

11:17-19. The temple was to be a house of prayer **FOR ALL THE NATIONS** (cf. Is 56:6-7). They had turned it into **A ROBBERS' DEN** (cf. Jr 7:11), making what should have been a place for prayer and worship, a place of merchandise. When **the chief priests and the scribes heard** what Jesus was doing, they recognized He was claiming greater authority than the high priest. But they **were afraid of Him** because of the multitude who viewed Jesus as Messiah. To keep their power the chief priests and scribes had to destroy Jesus. That evening Jesus and the disciples returned to Bethany.

4. The Judgment Fulfilled (11:20-26)

11:20-21. On Tuesday morning, Jesus and His disciples passed the fig tree now withered from the roots up. No one would ever eat its fruit again (cf. v. 14). Peter said, **Rabbi, look, the fig tree which You cursed has withered**.

11:22-26. Jesus encouraged the disciples, **Have faith in God**. Besides the lesson of spiritual hypocrisy, Jesus used the cursed fig tree for a second lesson, specifically, on the power of faith. The key to this teaching is the object of faith. The focus of faith must be on the sovereign Lord, not on faith itself. Since He was standing on the Mount of Olives, Jesus' hyperbole becomes clear. He was referring to that mountain and the Dead Sea, visible fifteen miles away, when He said the person of faith could say **to this mountain, 'Be taken up and cast into the sea.'** A "mountain" pictured an obstacle in one's path (cf. Zch 4:7). Prayer can remove great obstacles. Therefore He said, **all things for which you pray and ask, believe that you have received them, and they will be granted you**. But everything must be right with the Heavenly Father, which includes a forgiving spirit. Problems between individuals must be confronted and forgiveness sought. Verse 26 is not in the best manuscripts, but is the logical outcome of v. 25 (cf. Mt 6:15).

B. The Controversies with the Servant (11:27–12:40)

1. With the Religious Leaders (11:27–12:12)

a. The Question of Authority (11:27-33) (see also the comments on Mt 21:23-27)

11:27-30. Members of the Sanhedrin, guardians of Israel's religious life, confronted Jesus in the temple: **By what authority are You doing these things?** They were referring to His triumphal entry and the cleansing of the temple. Also they asked, **Who gave You this authority to do these things?** Jesus countered with one question, which if they would answer, He would answer their questions: **Was the baptism of John from heaven, or from men?** Jewish people revered God's name and did not want to use it in vain; therefore, "heaven" became a euphemism for God. Jesus' question was basically, "Was John's authority from God or men?"

11:31-33. The religious leaders realized Jesus had them in a quandary. If they answered John's authority was from God, He would say, **Then why did you not believe him?** But if they answered from men, **they were afraid of the people**, for they considered John a prophet. A crowd had gathered so they responded, **We do not know**. Since they refused to answer, Jesus refused to reveal His authority, which came from God directly and not any man. This would be objectionable to Jewish people in that it was thought that only Moses received authority directly from God. All other authority was passed down from one authority to the next (cf. *Pirke Avot* 1:1 in the Mishnah). Therefore, Jesus' authority, which came directly from the Father, identified Him as "the prophet like" Moses (Dt 18:15-19).

b. The Parable for Instruction (12:1-11) (see also the comments on Mt 21:33-46)

12:1-8. Jesus spoke in **parables**, but only one is recorded. Why only one is given is not explained. A man planted a vineyard, doing everything necessary to make it productive. He rented it to caretakers and departed. At harvest, he sent a slave to **receive some of the produce**. But they **beat him and sent him away empty-handed**. He sent **another slave** but he was physically abused. A third slave sent was killed. Jesus added, **and so with many others**. Finally the owner's **beloved son** was sent. The renters said, **This is the heir; come, let us kill him**, thinking by eliminating him, the field would be theirs. The murdered son's body was discarded, thrown over the vineyard's wall.

12:9-11. Jesus asked the leaders what they thought the owner would do. They responded that he would come and **destroy the vine-growers**, and give the vineyard to others (cf. Mt 21:41). An immediate application is made using Psalm 118:22. The imagery changes to a **STONE WHICH THE BUILDERS REJECTED**, which becomes **THE CHIEF CORNER STONE**. Jesus continued: **THIS CAME ABOUT FROM THE LORD, AND IT IS MARVELOUS IN OUR EYES**. This was God's plan and the application was clear. The vineyard was Israel and the religious leaders the caretakers who had poorly treated God's servants and would reject and participate in killing the beloved Son, Jesus. At question is the identity of the "others" to whom the vineyard would be given. Although some see in this the church replacing Israel, the parable is addressing the religious leaders of Israel. Jesus is saying that the rejection of the Messiah will lead to a change of leadership over Israel (the vineyard) from the Sanhedrin to the faithful remnant of Israel (cf. Rm 11:1-6), the Jewish followers of Jesus the Messiah.

c. The Leaders' Response (12:12)

12:12. The religious leaders understood Jesus spoke **against them** and wanted to seize Him. They feared the people who a few days before were shouting "Hosanna!" in His honor. What would happen if Jesus were suddenly removed? They **left Him and went away**.

2. With the Pharisees and Herodians (12:13-17) (see also the comments on Mt 22:15-22)

12:13-15a. Some **Pharisees and Herodians** approached Jesus **to trap Him in a statement**. These two groups were usually opponents: the Herodians were always for the political status quo and were sympathetic to the Romans, while the Pharisees looked forward to the coming of Messiah to remove Roman oppression (see comments at 3:6). They said flattering things about Jesus: He was truthful deferring to no one, He was not partial to any, and He taught the way of God in truth. They asked, **Is it lawful to pay a poll-tax to Caesar, or not?**

12:15b-17. Jesus knew they were hypocrites, seemingly asking a sincere question, but wanting to trap Him. He requested a denarius, the small Roman coin that paid the questionable poll-tax. He asked, **Whose likeness and inscription is this?** The reigning Roman Emperor was Tiberius Caesar. They replied, **Caesar's**. Jesus said they should pay **to Caesar the things that are Caesar's**. Since they were using Roman coins, they were under Rome's authority and were benefiting from it. But Jesus added, render **to God the things that are God's**. God's authority must be acknowledged. The people **were amazed** having never heard anything like this. Jesus was teaching the principle of obedience to governmental authority so long it does not force disobedience to God, found elsewhere in the NT (Ac 5:29; Rm 13:1-7; 1Pt 2:13-14).

3. With the Sadducees (12:18-27) (see also the comments on Mt 22:23-33)

12:18-23. The Sadducees, the "religious aristocrats" of Judaism, next questioned Jesus. They acknowledged only the book of the Law (the five books of Moses), rigorously opposing Pharisaic traditions. While the Pharisees believed in the resurrection from the dead, the Sadducees denied it, claiming that this doctrine was not found in the Law. These Sadducees spoke to Jesus of levirate marriage (cf. Dt 25:5-10). If a man died with no male heir, his brother was to marry the widow. If they produced a male child, that child would be named for the dead brother, keeping his name in the family inheritance. They speculated about a family of **seven brothers**, the first of whom died, leaving no offspring. The second brother married the widow, but he too died, leaving no offspring. This happened to all seven brothers, and finally the women died. Whether this story was true or one adapted from Tobit (cf. *Tb* 3:8) cannot be proven. They asked, in the resurrection, **which one's wife will she be?** Since they denied the resurrection, this was clearly a ridiculous illustration. They were picturing resurrection life as an elevation of the pleasures enjoyed on earth, the sexual relationship of husbands and wives being one.

12:24-27. Jesus said they were wrong. They did not understand **the Scriptures, or the power of God**. God is able to raise the dead, and resurrection life will be different from what is presently known. Marriage will not be necessary because, after the resurrection, humans will be **like angels in heaven**, who do not die. Since they never die, reproduction is unnecessary. They truly did not understand the resurrection. Jesus defended the doctrine of resurrection using the Law, the Sadducean source of authority, citing God's conversation with Moses at the burning bush (cf. Ex 3:6). God said, **I AM THE GOD OF ABRAHAM, AND THE GOD OF ISAAC, AND THE GOD OF JACOB**. If the Sadducees were correct, those men were dead and gone when God spoke. He should have said, "I **was** the God." But they were alive, and he was still their God. The Sadducees were **greatly mistaken**.

4. With the Scribes (12:28-34) (see also the comments on Mt 22:34-40)

12:28. One of the scribes recognized Jesus **answered them well**. He asked, **What commandment is the foremost of all?** Religious leaders had discovered 613 commandments in the Law, 365 negative and 248 positive. Many of the commandments had champions who argued for their validity as the greatest. Which one was greatest?

12:29-31. Jesus answered the foremost was the one recited every day: **HEAR, O ISRAEL! THE LORD OUR GOD IS ONE LORD** (cf. Dt 6:4). A person should love the Lord with his heart, soul, mind, and strength. But Jesus added: **YOU SHALL LOVE YOUR NEIGHBOR AS YOURSELF** (cf. Lv 19:18). Some streams of first-century Judaism (e.g., the zealots) taught that one should love his neighbor and hate his enemy (cf. Mt 5:43). Jesus taught that "neighbor" meant anyone in need (cf. Lk 10:29-37). Uniting love for God and neighbor is truly the greatest commandment.

12:32-34. The scribe said Jesus was correct. He repeated His words, substituting pronouns for God's name. To love God and one's neighbor was more important **than all burnt offerings and sacrifices**. Jesus responded, **You are not far from the kingdom of God**. Here was a Pharisee who understood the true intent of the law and was close to believing in Jesus. Realizing they were about to lose one of their own, His opponents stopped asking questions.

5. The Response of the Servant (12:35-44)

a. The Question of Challenge (12:35-37) (see also the comments on Mt 22:41-46)

12:35-37. Jesus asked a question concerning the person of the Messiah. How could the scribes say **the Christ** (Gk. for the Messiah) was **the son of David?** Jews knew the Messiah had to come from David (cf. Is 9:2-7; 11:1-9; Jr 23:5ff.; 30:9; Hs 3:5; Am 9:11). But the teaching about Messiah had degenerated into the one-dimensional view of an earthly deliverer coming to overthrow Israel's enemies. The Messiah was also to be a divine spiritual deliverer. Jesus quoted Psalm 110 where David declared: **THE LORD** [*Yahweh*] **SAID TO MY LORD** [*Adonai*], **'SIT AT MY RIGHT HAND, UNTIL I PUT YOUR ENEMIES BENEATH YOUR FEET.'** *Yahweh* tells *Adoni* He is to sit at His right hand, the place of honor while waiting for God to subjugate His enemies. David was calling the Messiah "Lord." Robert Alden notes, "The vowels in the Hebrew expression for 'my lord,' which the Jewish scribes put in, indicate a human title, but the inspired consonantal text would allow either a human or divine title" (*Psalms: Songs of Discipleship*, [Chicago: Moody, 1976], 31-32). Moreover, even the word commonly understood as a human title, *Adoni*, is occasionally used of God in the OT (Jos 5:14; Jdg 6:13). It is evident from this context that Jesus understood the word translated "Lord" as a reference to the Messiah and to be a divine appellation. His point is that if the Messiah is God, He must be more than a mere man coming in David's line to overthrow enemies. **The large crowd** enjoyed the way Jesus confounded the religious leaders. It was doubtful they fully understood, but they knew He was teaching with authority.

b. The Warning (12:38-40)

12:38-40. Jesus warned them about the scribes' actions. (See Matthew 23 for His complete indictment.) They loved receiving

respectful greetings in the market places and wanted the **chief seats in the synagogues**, those closest to the biblical scrolls. They cherished **places of honor at banquets** (cf. Lk 14:8). Their worst behavior was taking advantage of the weakest links of society, especially widows. They spoke **long prayers**, giving an appearance of piety, but inside their concerns were about position, power, and money. They would receive a greater judgment. Jesus' indictment did not pertain to all scribes and Pharisees but rather to the religious hypocrites among them. Even the Talmud, reflecting the view of Rabbinic Judaism, cited seven categories of scribes and Pharisees and found six of them to be hypocritical and quite in line with Jesus' description of them (cf. *b. Sotah 22b*; *J. Berakhot 14b*).

c. The Proper Illustration (12:41-44)

12:41-42. Jesus **sat down opposite the treasury** in the Court of the Women. Into marked receptacles worshippers placed offerings, and Jesus was observing their giving. Rich people were contributing large sums. **A poor widow** offered **two small copper coins**, two leptas, the smallest in circulation, worth $1/64^{th}$ of a denarius. This was the amount that the Temple authorities gave to the poor so they could obtain bread for the day. If she planned to give this back to God, it seems reasonable that she could have kept one, at least to obtain half of a food allotment.

12:43-44. Jesus told His disciples this widow had contributed **more than all** the others, not more in quantity, for some gifts were large. The others gave from their surplus; but this woman gave sacrificially, since she contributed **all she owned**. As she departed, she had nothing to purchase food until she found work or until God provided. But she believed God would sustain her. The amount of the gift one gives is not the greatest significance. Commitment of heart and sacrifice mean more to God.

C. The Predictions of the Servant (13:1-37)

1. The Questions of the Disciples (13:1-4)
(see also the introductory material on the Olivet Discourse and the comments on Mt 24:1-3)

13:1-2. As Jesus left the temple, a disciple noted the marvelous **stones** and **buildings** of the complex. Jesus' words of coming destruction (cf. Mt 23:38-39) precipitated his remarks. He responded, **Not one stone will be left upon another which will not be torn down.** This hyperbole pictures massive coming destruction. The Roman legion in AD 70 utterly destroyed the temple and Jerusalem. For an understanding that does not see AD 70 in the Olivet Discourse, see the material introducing the comments on Mt 24, as well as those on 24:1-2.

13:3-4. As they rested on the Mount of Olives, Jerusalem must have been beautiful with the sun setting behind the city. The disciples asked Jesus when **these things** would occur and what would be **the sign** of their fulfillment. Their questions prompted Jesus' longest sermon in this gospel (cf. Mt 24–25; Lk 21:5-36). Their questions related to the temple and end-time events leading to Messiah's kingdom, not questions concerning the church, which is never mentioned in this gospel (though, for a different approach, see the comments on Mt 24–25).

2. The Response of the Servant (13:5-37)

a. Coming Tribulation (13:5-23)

i. The First Half of the Tribulation (13:5-13)
(see also the comments on Mt 24:4-14)

13:5-8. Jesus warned the disciples of deceivers who **will come** in His name, each one even declaring that he is the Messiah. There will be **wars and rumors of wars** and **earthquakes**, and **famines. These things are merely the beginning of birth pangs**. Jesus was picturing the coming of the end of days with the birth of a child. A woman's labor can extend for some time before the birth.

13:9-13. Jesus' warnings were for the disciples and future generations. There would be religious persecution and political oppression. They would be brought before **courts** and into **synagogues** because of their testimony for Jesus. **The gospel must first be preached to all the nations** during the tribulation. When brought before officials, believers need **not worry beforehand** concerning what to say. The Holy Spirit will speak for them. Persecution could arise within a family or among friends. Jesus said, **You will be hated by all**, but **the one who endures to the end . . . will be saved**. In this context the **end** is the end of the tribulation (though, for a different approach, see the comments on Mt 10:22). Those living to that point will experience deliverance, for believers in Jesus will enter His kingdom as physical subjects.

ii. The Second Half of the Tribulation (13:14-23) (see also the comments on Mt 24:15-28)

13:14-18. The sign indicating the middle of the tribulation is **the ABOMINATION OF DESOLATION** (cf. the comments on Dn 9:24-27). An

abomination was any detestable object in the OT usually connected with idolatry. This abomination will stand **where it should not be**, in the temple (cf. Mt 24:15). A coming world dictator will make a covenant with Israel (cf. Dn 9:27) starting Daniel's 70th "week." Halfway through the seven years his true character will emerge. He will demand everyone worship him (cf. the comments on 2Th 2:3-4). Those in Judea should **flee to the mountains**. One **on the housetop** should not go into the house for anything. One **in the field** should not attempt to retrieve his cloak. Circumstances will be difficult, and they should pray it might not happen in **winter** when travel will be difficult.

13:19-23. The following days will produce **a time of tribulation such as has not occurred since the beginning of the creation**. Unless the Lord terminated the time, **no life** would survive. But for the sake of God's chosen (i.e., individuals from all races who will come to faith following the rapture), those days will end (cf. 13:13). False messiahs would arise, but Jesus warned, **Do not believe him**, even if he produces **signs and wonders** (cf. Dt 13:1-3). Jesus' warnings should enable believers to respond properly.

b. Coming Triumph (13:24-27) (see also the comments on Mt 24:29-31)

i. Return of the King (13:24-26)

13:24-26. After the tribulation, disturbances will affect the sun, moon, and stars (cf. Is 13:9; Ezk 32:7; Jl 2:1; Am 8:9; and Zph 1:14-16). This could imply physical forces will be subject to new dynamics resulting from the tribulation's natural calamities. This climaxes in the return of the Son of Man **COMING IN CLOUDS with great power and glory**.

ii. Regathering of Believers (13:27)

13:27. When Jesus returns, He will send His angels to **gather together His elect from the four winds**, those who became believers during the tribulation (cf. v. 13). OT saints will probably be resurrected at this time (cf. Dn. 12:2, 13) as well as tribulation martyrs. These are gathered to enter the millennial kingdom Jesus will inaugurate.

c. Concluding Teaching (13:28-37)

i. The Fig Tree (13:28-32) (see also the comments on Mt 24:32-35)

13:28-29. Jesus concluded with two parables (see the comments on 3:23). When a fig tree's branches became tender and leaves appeared, it would soon be summer. Jesus declared, **when you see these things happening, recognize that He is near, right at the door**. People hearing Jesus did not see all these things. That is why Jesus' prophecies were not completely fulfilled in Jerusalem's AD 70 destruction.

13:30-32. The generation seeing all these things **will not pass away** until all has been fulfilled. A future generation will see the culmination of God's plan. Only the Father knows when this will come to pass. Neither the angels nor Jesus in His incarnate state know that time. For the significance of the prophetic timing of **But of that day or hour no one knows** (v. 32), see the comments on Mt 24:36.

ii. The Steward (13:33-37)

13:33-37. Since no one knows the time, all are admonished: **Take heed, keep on the alert**. A second parable spoke of a man who departed **on a journey**. His slaves were given responsibilities in his absence. Whenever he returned, the doorkeeper should be awake to welcome him, demonstrating his faithfulness. Jesus' admonitions were given to all: **Be on the alert!** Expectancy should characterize every believer's life.

D. The Preparatory Events Surrounding the Servant (14:1-42)

1. The Plot of the Leaders (14:1-2) (see also the comments on Mt 26:3-5)

14:1-2. Passover annually recalled Israel's deliverance from Egypt, and **Unleavened Bread** their quick departure (cf. Ex 23:14-17, 34:23; Dt 16:16). **The chief priests and the scribes were seeking** a way to seize Jesus and **kill Him**. Recent events and intense debates convinced them Jesus must be destroyed. The most propitious time would not be during the festival. The huge crowds, including many Galileans, might provoke unwanted riots.

2. The Anointing by Mary (14:3-9) (see also the comments on Mt 26:6-13)

14:3-5. As Jesus ate in **the home of Simon the leper**, a woman (cf. Jn 12:1-3), entered with an expensive vial of **pure nard**, aromatic oil from India. She poured the contents over Jesus' head. Some disciples responded with indignation, the most vocal being Judas Iscariot (cf. Jn 12:4). He believed the perfume had been **wasted**, for its value was **over three hundred denarii**, a worker's pay for an entire year. The perfume should have been sold **and the money given to the poor**, a generous deed expected during Passover (cf. Jn 14:20). In light of Judas's character, his real concerns were selfish (cf. Jn 12:6). They **were scolding** her, a word used of the snorting of horses.

14:6-9. Jesus said to leave her alone. They would always have the poor around to whom they could minister (cf. Dt 15:11), but He would not always be with them. She anointed His body for burial. Perhaps as she listened at Jesus' feet (cf. Lk 10:39), she truly understood He was about to die. **Wherever the gospel is preached in the whole world** this gracious act would be remembered. That happens whenever this Scripture is read.

3. The Agreement with Judas (14:10-11) (see also the comments on Mt 26:14-16)

14:10-11. This wasteful act was in Judas's thinking as he **went off to the chief priests** to negotiate Jesus' betrayal. More than this act was involved, however, because Satan entered into Judas (cf. Lk 22:3). Jesus' goals were clearly spiritual, and Judas's hopes of power were crushed. He rationalized he could at least come out with monetary gain. The authorities were delighted and **promised to give him money**, thirty pieces of silver (cf. Mt 26:15), the price of a slave (cf. Ex 21:32; Zch 11:12). Thus, Judas began seeking **an opportune time** to betray Jesus.

4. The Passover Meal (14:12-26)

a. Preparation (14:12-16) (see also the comments on Mt 26:17-19)

14:12-16. Jesus and His disciples stayed in Bethany, but the Passover lamb had to be eaten in Jerusalem. The disciples asked Jesus where they should make preparations for the meal. Two disciples (cf. Lk 22:8) were sent to Jerusalem and told to look for **a man . . . carrying a pitcher of water**. Some think this was a prearranged sign, but it could have been a reflection of Jesus' omniscience. The disciples were to follow him to a home and say to the owner: **The Teacher says, 'Where is My guest room in which I may eat the Passover with My disciples?' A large upper room furnished and ready** was where the meal was prepared. They found everything as Jesus said.

b. Participation (14:17-21) (see also the comments on Mt 26:20-25)

14:17-18. Jesus came **with the Twelve** to the upper room. This meal was normally eaten between 6 p.m. and midnight. As they were eating, Jesus made a shocking announcement: one eating with them would betray Him.

14:19-21. Each disciple said, **Surely not I?** The identity of the betrayer was not revealed. If the disciples had known Judas's intentions, they would never have let him leave the room (cf. Jn 13:27-30). The betrayer was one who dipped with Him in the bowl (cf. Ps 41:9), probably a reference to sharing the bitter herbs. It was a treacherous act to eat with someone and then betray him. The Son of Man would accomplish God's will. Jesus' death was under God's providence, planned before creation. But Judas also acted freely as a morally responsible individual. **It would have been good for that man if he had not been born**. Judas would suffer the consequences of his unbelief.

c. Initiation (14:22-26) (see also the comments on Mt 26:26-29)

14:22-24. As they ate, Jesus **took some** (unleavened) **bread** (or Matzah) and after a blessing, **broke it and gave it to them**, saying, **Take it; this is My body**. The bread had not become His body, but the bread represented His body. He followed with **a cup**, probably the third cup, the "cup of blessing." He gave thanks, **gave it to them; and they all drank**. He said, **This is My blood of the covenant, which is poured out for many**. The wine represented His blood. The word **covenant** spoke of an arrangement made by one party, God Himself, and it had been sealed by Jesus' blood. In light of all the symbolic foods eaten at a Passover meal, Jesus' disciples would not have taken His words about the bread and wine literally.

14:25-26. Jesus said He would **never again drink of the fruit of the vine until that day** when He would drink it in **the kingdom of God**, an anticipation of His coming earthly kingdom. Ending the meal, they sang **a hymn**, probably from Pss 115–118 and then started walking to **the Mount of Olives** heading to Bethany.

5. The Prediction of Denial (14:27-31) (see also the comments on Mt 26:30-35)

14:27-28. Jesus said the disciples would **all fall away** that evening (cf. Zch 13:7). However His death was not the end, for He was going to rise. Then He would meet them in Galilee.

14:29-31. Peter reacted strongly to Jesus' words. It was inconceivable he would forsake his Lord. Others might fall away, but Peter insisted that he never would. Jesus responded, **before a rooster crows twice** Peter would deny Him **three times** (cf. 14:72). Yet Peter insisted he would never forsake his Lord, and all the disciples agreed.

6. The Garden of Gethsemane (14:32-42) (see also the comments on Mt 26:36-46)

14:32-34. Jesus and the Eleven came to **Gethsemane**, a place well known to them. Eight disciples were told to stay behind, but **Peter**

and James and John continued on with Jesus (cf. 5:35-43; 9:2-9). In His hour of need, Jesus desired the companionship of these three. He **began to be very distressed** and His soul was **deeply grieved to the point of death**. The cross was drawing near, and the enormity of bearing the sin of the world was pressing on Him. The disciples were to **remain** and **keep watch**.

14:35-38. Jesus began to pray that **if it were possible, the hour might pass Him by. Abba!** is an affectionate Aramaic word like the English "Dad" or "Pa." This term showed the intimacy of the relationship between the Father and Jesus. He asked that the **cup** might be removed. The **cup** was a picture of death and judgment falling on Jesus as He bore sin. There would be a sense of separation between Jesus and the Father, and He did not look forward to that. He submitted to the Father's will: **not what I will, but what You will**. Returning to the three, He **found them sleeping**. His statement, **Could you not keep watch for one hour?** might indicate the length of His prayer. He encouraged them to continue **watching and praying**.

14:39-42. Jesus prayed the same words as before. Returning, He found the disciples sleeping. When awakened they did not know how to respond (cf. 9:6). The details of Jesus' third period of prayer (cf. Mt 26:44) are not given, but Jesus returned again and said, **Are you still sleeping and resting?** He had prayed **the hour** might pass (cf. v. 35), but the time had come. He was about to be **betrayed into the hands of sinners**. The betrayer (cf. vv. 18-21) was outside the garden, and they would meet momentarily.

E. The Arrest and Trials of the Servant (14:43–15:20)

1. Arrest in Gethsemane (14:43-52) (see also the comments on Mt 26:47-56)

14:43-46. Judas arrived with an armed crowd. That Judas is called **one of the twelve** shows the horror of his deed. Roman soldiers were the ones legally carrying **swords**, those with **clubs** were part of the temple guard, representing **the chief priests and the scribes and the elders**. Roman soldiers were present to preclude resistance. Pupils often greeted rabbis with a kiss, and that was the chosen **signal**. The one Judas kissed should be lead **away under guard**. They **laid hands on Him, and seized Him**, with no resistance from Jesus.

14:47-49. One of the disciples, probably Peter (cf. v. 29; Jn 18:10), drew a sword in defense. Striking **the slave of the high priest**, he cut off his ear. Jesus immediately stopped this defense but asked why they had come **with swords and clubs** in the middle of the night as though He were **a robber**? Throughout the past week He had been daily **in the temple teaching**. Why had they not seized Him then? He understood His arrest occurred **to fulfill the Scriptures** (cf. Is 53; Zch 13:7).

14:50-52. When Jesus was arrested, the disciples **all left Him and fled**. However, one did not flee. A certain **young man** was following, wearing nothing but **a linen sheet over his naked body**. This unidentified young man was probably Mark himself. He was showing he was present at this event. He was seized, but **pulled free** of the garment **and escaped naked**.

2. Trial before the council (14:53-65) (see also the comments on Mt 26:57-68)

14:53-54. Jesus was taken to the house of the high priest, Caiaphas. The Sanhedrin (**the chief priests and the elders and the scribes**) had to be awakened. These 71 men were the supreme ruling body in Israel. Peter followed **at a distance**, entering the courtyard and **warming himself by the fire** with those who had arrested Jesus.

14:55-59. The Council began seeking testimony to convict Jesus. They could not execute anyone (cf. Jn 18:31), but their recommendations to Roman officials were considered. They could not find evidence, though **many were giving false testimony** and **their testimony was not consistent**. Mosaic law required at least two agreeing witnesses (cf. Dt 17:6; 19:15). Some heard Jesus say, **I will destroy this temple made with hands, and in three days I will build another made without hands**. Jesus never said He would harm the physical temple, but was speaking about His own body (cf. Jn 2:21).

14:60-65. Caiaphas finally questioned Jesus: "Surely you are going to answer these accusations, are you not?" He was tempting Jesus to say something that might be used against Him. Jesus **kept silent**, for no charges had been specified. Caiaphas asked a second question: **Are You the Christ, the Son of the Blessed One?** He used the euphemism, "Blessed One," for God. Jesus' answer was clear: **I am** (cf. Ex 3:14). Jesus continued, those hearing Him would one day see Him as **THE SON OF MAN SITTING AT THE RIGHT HAND OF POWER**. They also would see Him **COMING WITH THE CLOUDS OF HEAVEN**. They were judging Him, but one day He would judge them. The high priest tore his garments, an act forbidden by law (cf. Lv 10:6; 21:10). He declared all had **heard the blasphemy**, the penalty for which was death (cf. Lv 24:15-16). They **all condemned Him**. Taking the law into their own hands, they treated Jesus as a criminal. They **spit at Him**, demonstrating contempt, blindfolded Him, **beat Him with their fists**, and asked Him to prophesy. If He was the Messiah, He would know who struck Him. This was a crude misrepresentation of Is 11:2-4, that the Messiah would not judge by what He saw or make decisions by what He heard. Jesus was entrusted to the **officer**s who arrested Him, who also treated Him unworthily, slapping Him with their hands.

3. Prediction of Denial Fulfilled (14:66-72) (see also the comments on Mt 26:69-75)

14:66-72. While Jesus was before the Sanhedrin, Peter was undergoing a trial in the courtyard (cf. v. 54). A **servant-girl** saw Peter. **You also were with Jesus the Nazarene**. Peter stated he did not know what she was talking about. The same girl again said, **This is one of them!** Again he denied it, but his speech betrayed him. A bystander said, **Surely you are one of them, for you are a Galilean too**. He had to do something drastic. He **began to curse and swear**. This does not mean Peter used profanity; rather he placed himself under an oath. He said he did not know **this man**, deliberately avoiding the name "Jesus," denying his Lord. Immediately **a rooster crowed a second time**. **Peter remembered** the Lord's words (cf. v. 30) and **began to weep**.

4. Second Trial before the Council (15:1) (see also the comments on Mt 27:1-2)

15:1. Early in the morning the Sanhedrin assembled. Night trials were illegal, but after sunrise they formalized their conclusions. The Romans would never execute Jesus for blasphemy, so the charge was changed to treason (cf. Lk 23:2) and Jesus was led to Pilate.

5. Trial before Pilate (15:2-15) (see also the comments on Mt 27:3-26)

15:2-5. Pilate, the fifth procurator appointed by Caesar, began reigning in AD 26. He questioned Jesus concerning His being King of the Jews. Jesus' answer, **It is as you say**, has been understood two ways. Some say Jesus was noncommittal: "You say that, not I." Others believe He answered emphatically: "You said it!" The chief priests **began to accuse** Jesus of treason, but He gave no defense (cf. 14:60). Although encouraged to speak, Jesus remained silent, rare action by one condemned.

15:6-11. A Roman custom designed to win over the Jewish people was the release of a requested prisoner during the feast. **Barabbas** was a well-known insurrectionist who had committed murder. Pilate expected Jesus to be the choice. He had seen through the chief priests, knowing Jesus had been delivered because of their envy. But he did not count on their influence on the crowd. In light of the early morning hour (15:1), it is likely that this was not a random crowd but a group the chief priests specially gathered to support their wishes concerning Jesus. They began asking for Barabbas.

15:12-15. Pilate asked what he should do with their **King** when He should have ordered Jesus' release. They answered: **Crucify Him!** He asked regarding what evil Jesus had done since He found no fault in Him. They shouted louder, **Crucify Him!** He gave in, releasing Barabbas. Jesus was subjected to a brutal beating using a leather whip studded with pieces of bone, lead, or brass, and delivered up **to be crucified**.

6. Mocking before the Roman Soldiers (15:16-20) (see also the comments on Mt 27:27-32)

15:16-20. Jesus was taken into the **Praetorium**, the governor's residence. The **cohort**, possibly as many as 600 men, mocked Jesus, dressing Him in purple and placing **a crown of thorns** on His head. They cried, **Hail, King of the Jews!** They beat Him about His head **with a reed** and spat on Him. They bowed, mocking Him, not only because of His kingship claim but also because of their hatred for the Jews. They removed the cloak, restored His garments, and **led Him out** for crucifixion.

F. The Crucifixion of the Servant (15:21-32) (see also the comments on Mt 27:33-44)

15:21. A condemned prisoner carried his cross to the place of execution. It is not surprising that Jesus' beating left Him unable to bear His own cross, so **Simon of Cyrene** was **pressed into service**.

15:22-26. Jesus was **brought** to a well-known place called **Golgotha**, or **Place of a Skull**. The English word "Calvary" comes from the Latin word for skull, *calvaria*. Perhaps the rock there looked like a skull or maybe, as the site of crucifixions, it was associated with skulls. They offered Jesus wine mixed with myrrh to help His pain, but He refused it. All the details of crucifixion are not given here. Victims were stripped and their arms were tied or nailed to the crosspiece. It was fitted onto a post embedded in the ground. Death came through dehydration or asphyxiation as victims found breathing difficult.

The soldiers **divided up His garments among themselves, casting lots** to determine their take (cf. Ps 22:18). Jesus was crucified about 9:00 a.m. (**the third hour**) although Jn 19:14 places the crucifixion at the sixth hour. Most likely, Mark used Jewish time reckoning (third hour = 9:00 a.m.) while John used Roman time reckoning (sixth hour = 9:00 a.m.). A placard placed on the cross listed the crimes that prompted the execution. Judging from the reports of all four gospels, the inscription probably read, "This is Jesus of Nazareth, the King of the Jews."

15:27-28. Jesus was crucified with **two robbers**, probably insurrectionists associated with Barabbas. The better manuscripts do not include v. 28, a verse probably added to show these events fulfilled OT prophecy.

15:29-32. Passersby shouted abuses against Jesus, ridiculing Him. The claim He was going **to destroy the temple and rebuild it in three days** was recalled (cf. 14:58-59). They challenged Him to come down from the cross, a virtual impossibility. The leaders who condemned Jesus came to make sure the execution was completed. They said Jesus had supposedly saved others but could not save Himself. If He had saved Himself, all of mankind would have been lost. If Jesus would come down from the cross, they would **see and believe!** That is highly unlikely. They were convinced Jesus was unworthy of their worship. The two crucified with Jesus reproached Him, but later one asked to be remembered when Jesus came into His kingdom (cf. Lk 23:39-43).

G. The Death of the Servant (15:33-41) (see also the comments on Mt 27:45-56)

15:33-37. From noon until 3:00 PM, **darkness fell over the whole land**, an indication of God's judgment. In fulfillment of prophecy, Jesus cried: **Eloi, Eloi, lama sabachthani?** an Aramaic expression: **My God, My God, why have You forsaken Me?** (cf. Ps 22:1). Jesus sensed the Father's abandonment as He bore the world's sin. Bystanders said, **He is calling for Elijah**. A sponge, filled with **sour wine**, was offered to Jesus. They waited to see if Elijah would come.

15:37-39. Jesus **uttered a loud cry** (cf. Jn 19:30), **and breathed His last**. When He died, **the veil of the temple was torn in two from top to bottom**, something humanly impossible, thus inaugurating access for mankind into God's presence through His blood (cf. Heb 10:19-20). **The centurion** said: **Truly this man was the Son of God!** Whether he believed Jesus was "the" Son of God or was acknowledging an extraordinary death cannot be determined from this text. Compared to other statements in this context, he seems to have been affirming Jesus' deity.

15:40-41. Some of the last witnesses of Jesus' death were women **looking on from a distance**. **Mary Magdalene, and Mary the mother of James the less and Joses, and Salome** had assisted Jesus during His ministry (cf. Lk 8:1-3), which freed Him from routine chores.

H. The Burial of the Servant (15:42-47) (see also the comments on Mt 27:57-66)

15:42-45. Jesus died on the **preparation day**, a Greek term for "Friday." Removal of His body from the cross and its entombment needed to occur quickly, for Sabbath began at sundown (cf. Dt 21:22-23). **A prominent member of the Council**, Joseph of Arimathea, **was waiting for the kingdom of God** (cf. Jn 19:38; Lk 23:51). He boldly went to Pilate and asked for Jesus' body, marking him as a disciple of Jesus. Pilate wondered if Jesus was dead, since crucified men could linger for days. When the centurion affirmed Jesus' death, Pilate **granted the body to Joseph**. Allowing the body to be properly buried, rather than dumped into an unmarked grave or the city dump, might have been Pilate's final attempt to get back at the Jews. Whatever Pilate's reason, Joseph's burial of Jesus in his own tomb fulfilled Isaiah's prediction that the Servant would be "with a rich man in His death" (Is 53:9).

15:46-47. Joseph purchased items and secured help to bury Jesus' body (cf. Jn 19:39-40), which was washed, wrapped in a **linen cloth**, and laid **in a tomb**. A stone was rolled against the entrance to keep out wild animals and grave robbers. The two Marys observed the burial. They knew exactly where Jesus was buried, and would return to this location.

VI. The Resurrection of the Servant of the Lord (16:1-20)

A. The Revelation of the Women (16:1-8) (see also the comments on Mt 28:1-8)

16:1-4. Sabbath was a time of inactivity. When it ended, the two Marys and Salome (cf. 15:40) bought aromatic oils, which were poured on grave wrappings to counteract the odors of decaying flesh. They arrived at the tomb shortly after sunrise on Sunday. Remembering the large stone covering the entrance, they wondered, **Who will roll away the stone for us from the entrance of the tomb?** They were not aware of extra precautions taken by the Jewish leaders, including the sealing of the tomb (cf. Mt 27:62-66). They were surprised to see the **extremely large** stone removed and the tomb open.

16:5-8. They saw **a young man . . . wearing a white robe**, an angel (cf. Mt 28:2-5) who told them not to be amazed. He knew they were looking for **Jesus the Nazarene**, who had died, but was raised. He pointed to where the body had laid. The women were instructed to go and **tell His disciples and Peter**, words of reassurance for Peter. Although he had denied his Lord, he was forgiven and still considered part of the apostolic band. All the disciples fled, but they were still "His disciples." Jesus was going into Galilee, where they would see Him (cf. 14:28). The women **fled from the tomb**, and **trembling and astonishment** gripped them. **They said nothing to anyone, for they were afraid**. The full ramification of the announcement was not understood.

B. The Appearances of the Servant (16:9-14)
(see also the comments on Lk 24:13-15)

Bible scholars do not agree on this gospel's ending. Verses 9-20 are not found in two manuscripts that, according to many, are among the most important, but they are found in the majority of inferior NT manuscripts. Some manuscripts add verses after v. 8, some after v. 20. There is no clear manuscript evidence to support the inclusion of these verses. Since these verses are questioned, it would not be wise to base any doctrine or experience on a verse found only in this section. Nevertheless, in what follows, these verses will be discussed and suggestions given to the various problems.

1. To Mary (16:9-11)

16:9-11. Jesus **first appeared to Mary Magdalene, from whom He had cast out seven demons**. After the meeting, Mary reported to Jesus' followers who were still **mourning and weeping**. When they learned Jesus was alive and Mary had seen Him, **they refused to believe it**. This could reflect their culture, for a woman's testimony was not highly regarded.

2. To Two Disciples (16:12-13)

16:12-13. Jesus later appeared **in a different form** to two disciples **on their way to the country** (cf. Lk 24:13-35). That He appeared in "a different form" could mean they did not recognize Him when He first appeared. When they reported the Lord had appeared to them, they too were met with unbelief. The idea of a resurrected Jesus had not worked its way into every disciple's heart.

3. To the Eleven (16:14)

16:14. Jesus **appeared to the eleven . . . as they were reclining at the table. He reproached them for their unbelief and hardness of heart**. Had He not said He would rise from the dead? They should have believed the reports coming from faithful followers.

C. The Commission of the Servant (16:15-18)

16:15-18. Jesus commanded His disciples: **Go into all the world and preach the gospel to all creation** (cf. Mt 28:19-20) and in response many would believe. In the early church belief in Jesus was immediately followed by baptism. Believing and being baptized, linked by a single Greek article, demonstrate an inward act in the heart followed by a public profession of that faith. New Testament writers assumed under normal circumstances believers in Jesus would be baptized. That baptism is not a requirement for salvation is demonstrated by the second half of the verse, which declares the one who disbelieves is condemned. As the disciples proclaimed the gospel, **signs** would accompany them (the apostles and not all believers in general, cf. Ac 2:43; 2Co 1:12) demonstrating their authenticity. In His name they would **cast out demons** (cf. Mk 6:7; Lk 10:1-20) demonstrating the messenger had greater power than Satan. They would **speak with new tongues**. This ability (to speak in earthly foreign languages not previously learned) occurred on the Day of Pentecost (cf. Ac 2:1-12) and was repeated later in the church (cf. Ac 10:46, 19:6; 1Co 12:10). Two signs have caused difficulties. It may be best to understand the first two as conditional clauses, in this manner: if anyone is compelled to pick up serpents, or is required to drink deadly poison, he shall not be hurt. There are no illustrations of either of these in the NT. However, Paul did not suffer after inadvertently picking up and being bitten by a snake (Ac 28:3-5). Finally they would **lay hands on the sick**, and they would **recover** (cf. Ac 9:12; 28:8; Jms 5:14), signs carried out throughout the book of Acts.

D. The Ascension of the Servant (16:19-20)

16:19-20. When Jesus finished His post-resurrection ministry, **He was received up into heaven**, which the disciples witnessed. That He **sat down at the right hand of God** must be accepted by faith. The ascension was a fulfillment of Ps 110:1, which Jesus mentioned earlier (cf. Mk 12:13, 36). On the Day of Pentecost Peter quoted that passage, saying Jesus had been exalted to the Father's right hand in heaven (cf. Ac 2:33-36). Jesus said He would be seated at the right hand of God (cf. Mk 14:62). It is not surprising when Jesus ascended, He sat down at God's right hand, the place of privilege and authority. From this position He entered a new work in heaven, His work on earth was completed. He continues to work on earth today through His followers, who **went out and preached everywhere**. The Lord also confirmed their testimony **by the signs that followed**. Many signs were prevalent in the church's early days, but as time passed they diminished (cf. Heb 2:3-4). Although spectacular signs have diminished, the testimony has continued throughout the world and people believe in the Servant of the Lord, the One who came not to be served but to serve and to give His life a ransom for many.

BIBLIOGRAPHY

Barnhouse, Donald Grey. *Mark: The Servant Gospel.* Wheaton, IL: Victor, 1988.

Cole, R. Alan. *The Gospel According to Mark.* Tyndale New Testament Commentary. Leicester, U.K.: Inter-Varsity, 1989.

Earle, Ralph. *Mark: The Gospel of Action.* Chicago: Moody, 1970.

Grassmick, John D. "Mark." In *The Bible Knowledge Commentary*, edited by John F. Walvoord and Roy B. Zuck. Wheaton, IL: Victor, 1983.

Henriksen, William. *Exposition of the Gospel According to Mark.* Grand Rapids, MI: Baker, 1975.

Hiebert, D. Edmond. *Mark: A Portrait of the Servant.* Chicago: Moody, 1974.

Hughes, R. Kent. *Mark,* 2 vols. Westchester, IL: Crossway, 1989.

Ironside, H. A. *Expository Notes on the Gospel of Mark.* Neptune, NJ: Loizeaux Bros., 1948.

Kelly, William. *An Exposition of the Gospel of Mark,* reprint. Sunbury, PA: Believershelf, 1971.

Lane, William L. *The Gospel of Mark.* New International Commentary on the New Testament. Grand Rapids, MI: Eerdmans, 1974.

Martin, Ralph. *Mark: Evangelist and Theologian.* Grand Rapids, MI: Zondervan, 1973.

Morgan, G. Campbell. *The Gospel According to Mark.* Old Tappan, NJ: Revell, 1927.

Pentecost, J. Dwight. *The Words and Works of Jesus Christ.* Grand Rapids, MI: Zondervan, 1981.

Ryle, John Charles. *Expository Thoughts on the Gospels: St. Mark,* reprint. Greenwood, SC: The Attic, 1973.

Scroggie, W. Graham. *The Gospel of Mark.* Grand Rapids, MI: Zondervan, 1979.

Swete, Henry Barclay. *The Gospel According to St. Mark.* Grand Rapids, MI: Eerdmans, 1956. Reprinted as *Commentary on Mark.* Grand Rapids, MI: Kregel, 1977.

Wiersbe, Warren W. *Be Diligent.* Wheaton, IL: Victor, 1987.

Wuest, Kenneth S. *Mark in the Greek New Testament.* Grand Rapids, MI: Eerdmans, 1950.

● ● ● ●

LUKE

KEVIN D. ZUBER

INTRODUCTION

Author. The Gospel of Luke is technically anonymous. The idea that Luke is the author turns upon several converging lines of evidence.

The name "Luke" appears three times in the NT: 2Tm 4:11; Phm 24; Col 4:14. Luke was an associate of the apostle Paul and was a physician. In Col 4 he is mentioned separately from those "of the circumcision" (see 4:10-11). The tradition of the church holds that Luke was a Gentile.

The man who wrote the gospel also wrote the book of Acts (see Ac 1:1-3), and he was a traveling companion of Paul (see the "we" passages (Ac 16:10-17; 20:5-15; 21:1-18; 27:1–28:16). The account of the institution of the ordinance of communion (Lk 22:19, 20) is similar to Paul's (1Co 11:23-25), supporting the traditional view of the author of the third gospel. He appears to have a special interest in Jesus' healing ministry (compare Lk 4:38 to Mt 8:14 and Mk 1:30), and the language of Luke/Acts is that of someone educated and familiar with the Septuagint (the ancient Gk. translation of the Hebrew Scriptures). Of Paul's coworkers Luke best fits the profile of the author of Luke/Acts.

Early church fathers such as Irenaeus (c. 185, *Against Heresies*, III.i.1); Tertullian (c. 200, *Against Marcion*, IV.ii); Origen (c. AD 230, in Eusebius *Ecclesiastical History*, IV.xxv.3-6); and Jerome (c. AD 400, *De Viris Illustribus* VIII) consistently attribute the third Gospel to Luke. The *Muratorian Canon* (c. AD 180) attributes "The third book of the gospel" to "Luke, that physician" (cf. Walter L. Leifeld, "Luke," EBC, ed. Frank E. Gaebelein [Grand Rapids, MI: Zondervan, 1984], 8:799; Darrell L. Bock, *Luke: 1:1-9:50*, BECNT [Grand Rapids, MI: Baker, 1994], 5).

Date. There is no mention of the destruction of Jerusalem by the Romans (AD 70) in either Luke or Acts. If Luke and Acts were written at approximately the same time it probably would have been no later than Paul's first Roman imprisonment (ca. AD 60–63). The book does not mention the persecution of Nero (AD 64), nor does it mention the martyrdom of James (AD 62). At the outset of his gospel Luke admitted that he used sources (since he himself was not an eyewitness to the events in the gospel). He may have used the Gospel of Mark (written as early as the AD 50s). From these considerations a composition date of AD 60–61 is most likely.

Purpose. Luke's purpose in writing his gospel was (see the Prologue 1:1-4): (1) to provide an "orderly account" of the events of the life of Christ; (2) to show how those events "connect" to the church; (3) to spread the saving truth about the Lord Jesus Christ to *all* nations (cf. 24:47).

Themes. Bock notes, "Four issues were particularly problematic in the church of Luke's time" (Bock, *Luke*, 1, 2). (1) Gentile inclusion in salvation; (2) the largely negative response to Jesus by the Jewish nation; (3) how "the person and teaching of a crucified Jesus fits into God's plan" (Bock, *Luke*, 2); (4) what are believers in this new community (disciples who follow Jesus) to be? "Luke-Acts says Jesus is Lord of all, so salvation can go to all" (Bock, *Luke*, 3). The major theme of Luke's gospel, however, revolves around a simple question, "Who is Jesus?" Nearly every strand of the narrative is related to this question and its vitally important answer—Jesus is the Messiah (Christ).

OUTLINE

- I. Luke's Prologue (1:1-4)
  - A. Luke's Motive and Method (1:1-3a)
  - B. Luke's Reader(s) (1:3b)
  - C. Luke's Purpose (1:4)
- II. The Birth and Childhood Narratives (1:5–2:52)
  - A. Announcement of the Birth of the Forerunner (1:5-25)
    - 1. Introduction of a Faithful Couple: Zacharias and Elizabeth (1:5-7)
      - a. A Despotic Ruler (1:5a)
      - b. A "Priestly" Couple (1:5b)
      - c. A Righteous and Blameless Couple (1:6)
      - d. A Barren Couple (1:7)
    - 2. An Angelic Announcement (1:8-23)
      - a. Zacharias's Priestly Service Interrupted (1:8-12)
      - b. The Angel's Message Delivered (1:13-17)
      - c. Zacharias's Doubt; Angel's Reassurance and (Mild) Rebuke (1:18-20)
      - d. The People Waiting and Wondering (1:21-23)
    - 3. Elizabeth's Joy (1:24-25)
  - B. Announcement of the Birth of Jesus (1:26-38)
    - 1. Time, Agent, Location, and Recipient of the Announcement (1:26-27)
    - 2. Greeting, Reaction, and Assurance (1:28-30)
    - 3. The Message Is about Jesus Christ (1:31-33)
    - 4. Mary's Reaction, Angel's Explanation, Mary's Submission (1:34-38)
  - C. Mary's Visit to Elizabeth (1:39-56)
  - D. John the Baptist: the Birth and the *Benedictus* (1:57-80)
    - 1. Birth and Naming of John by Elizabeth (1:57-66)
    - 2. The *Benedictus* of Zacharias (1:67-80)
  - E. Birth of Jesus; Visitations of Angels and Shepherds (2:1-20)
    - 1. Birth of Jesus (2:1-7)
    - 2. Visitation of the Angels to the Shepherds (2:8-14)
    - 3. Visitation of the Shepherds (2:15-20)
  - F. Scene at the Circumcision of Jesus (2:21-39)
  - G. Boyhood of Jesus (2:40-52)
- III. Transition to Ministry (3:1–4:13)
  - A. Preparation by the Forerunner: John the Baptist (3:1-20)
  - B. Preparation of Jesus (3:21–4:13)
- IV. The Great Galilean Ministry (4:14–9:62)
  - A. Jesus in Galilee and the Synagogue in Nazareth (4:14-30)
    - 1. Jesus in Galilee (4:14-15)
    - 2. Jesus in the Synagogue in Nazareth (4:16-30)
  - B. Jesus' Ministry Is Powerful (4:31-44; 5:12-26)
  - C. Jesus Calling His First Disciples (5:1-11; 27-28; 6:12-16)
    - 1. Jesus Called Simon (Peter), James and John, Levi (Matthew) (5:1-11, 27-28)
    - 2. Jesus Called the Twelve to Be Apostles (6:12-16)
  - D. Jesus' Ministry Was Contrary to Expectation (5:29–6:11)
  - E. Jesus' Teaching Was Contrary to Expectation (6:17-49)
    - 1. Sermon on the Level Place (6:17-38)
    - 2. Three Warnings for Disciples (6:39-49)
  - F. "Who Is Jesus?" His Identity Revealed (7:1–8:3)
    - 1. Jesus Healed the Centurion's Servant (7:1-10)
    - 2. Jesus Healed a Widow's Son (7:11-17)
    - 3. Three Episodes Concerning John the Baptist (7:18-35)
      - a. John's Questions about Jesus Are Asked and Answered (7:18-23)

- b. Jesus' Praise of John (7:24-30)
- c. Jesus' Rebuke of that Generation (7:31-35)

4. Jesus: At Dinner and Anointed; Parable of the Two Debtors (7:36-50)
5. Jesus Is Ministered to by Certain Women (8:1-3)

G. Jesus' Teaching in Parables (8:4-21)
1. Parable of the Soils (8:4-15)
2. Parable of the Lamp (8:16-18)
3. Jesus' True Family (8:19-21)

H. Jesus: the Master (8:22-56)
1. Jesus Stilled the Storm (8:22-25)
2. Jesus Cast Demons Out of a Man and Into Swine (8:26-39)
3. Jesus Healed Woman with Hemorrhages; Raised Little Girl from the Dead (8:40-56)

I. Jesus' Disciples (9:1-62)
1. Mission of the Twelve: A Mission for Disciples (9:1-10a)
2. A Lesson for Disciples: Feeding Five Thousand (9:10b-17)
3. A Disciple's Confession (9:18-22)
4. On Discipleship: Definition, Motivation, and Expectation of a True Disciple (9:23-27)
5. Transfiguration: An Event and Word to Assure the Disciples (9:28-36)
6. Healing a Demon-Possessed Son: A Test for Disciples (9:37-42)
7. Four Failures of Jesus' Disciples (9:43-56)
8. Three Failures of Discipleship (9:57-62)

V. Journey to Jerusalem (10:1–19:27)

A. More on Missions; More on Discipleship (10:1-24)
1. The Mission of the Seventy (10:1-16)
2. Two Lessons on Discipleship (10:17-24)
   - a. Joys of Being a Disciple (10:17-20)
   - b. Blessings of Being a "Knowing" Disciple (10:21-24)

B. Lawyer with Questions; Parable of the Good Samaritan (10:25-37)
1. The Lawyer's Questions (10:25-29)
2. The Good Samaritan (10:30-37)

C. Martha and Mary (10:38-42)

D. Teaching on Prayer (11:1-13)

E. A Series of Conflicts (11:14-54)
1. The Question of Jesus' Power (11:14-36)
   - a. Satan or God? (11:14-23)
   - b. Four Explanations (11:24-36)
2. Jesus, a Pharisee, and the Discourse of Woes (11:37-54)

F. Jesus Warns His Disciples (12:1-21)
1. Warning about Hypocrisy (12:1-3)
2. Warning about the Fear of Man (12: 4-7)
3. Warning about Confessing and Denying (12:8-12)
4. Warning about Worldliness—the Parable of the Rich Fool (12:13-21)

G. Lessons on the "Eternal Perspective" (12:22-48)
1. Do Not Worry (12:22-34)
2. Be Ready, Be Faithful (12:35-48)

H. Six Serious Matters for Disciples to Consider (12:49–13:9)

I. Six Features of Jesus' Ministry (13:10-35)

J. Jesus at Dinner with a Pharisee (14:1-24)

K. Jesus' Teaching on Discipleship (14:25-35)

L. Three Parables of "Lost and Found" (15:1-32)
1. Setting of the Parables (15:1-2)
2. Parable of the Lost Sheep (15:3-7)

3. Parable of the Lost Coin (15:8-10)
4. Parable of the Lost Son (15:11-32)
    a. The First Son (15:12-24)
    b. The Gracious Father (15:20b-24)
    c. The Second Son (15:25-30)
    d. The Gracious Father (15:31-32)

M. Parables and Teaching for Disciples and Pharisees (16:1-31)
1. Parable of the Dishonest Manager (16:1-9)
2. Teaching about Faithfulness in Service (16:10-13)
3. Corrections for the Pharisees (16:14-18)
4. Parable of the Rich Man and Lazarus (16:19-31)

N. Jesus Warning, Teaching, Healing (17:1-19)
1. Sayings for Disciples (17:1-10)
2. Healings of the Ten Lepers (17:11-19)

O. Jesus' Teaching on the Kingdom and the Second Coming (17:20-37)
1. The Pharisees' Question (17:20-21)
2. The Instruction to the Disciples (17:22-37)

P. Two Parables Concerning Prayer and Righteousness (18:1-14)
1. The Widow and the Judge (18:1-8)
2. The Pharisee and the Tax-Collector (18:9-14)

Q. Jesus Meets Children, a Wealthy Ruler, a Blind Man, and Zaccheus (18:15-30; 18:35–19:10)

R. Jesus Foretold His Death and Resurrection (18:31-34)

S. The Parable of the Ten Minas (19:11-27)

VI. Ministry in Jerusalem (19:28–21:38)

A. Triumphal Entry (19:29-44)
1. Preparations for the Entry (19:29-34)
2. The Event Itself (19:35-40)
3. Jesus' Lament Over the City (19:41-44)

B. Jesus and the Religious Leaders (19:45–21:4)
1. How the Conflict Began (19:45-48)
2. How the Conflict Continued (20:1–21:4)

C. Jesus' Teaching about the Tribulation and the Second Coming (21:5-38)
1. The Disciples' Questions (21:5-7)
    a. Exchange that Prompted the Questions (21:5-6)
    b. The Two Questions (21:7)
2. Jesus' Answers to the Questions: The Tribulation (21:8-24)
    a. Warning to Be Wary about Signs (21:8-11)
    b. Warning and Encouragement Regarding Persecution (21:12-19)
    c. Warning about Jerusalem (21:20-24)
3. Jesus' Answers to the Questions: The Second Coming (21:25-36)
    a. Times of Upheaval (21:25-26)
    b. The Coming Itself (21:27)
    c. A Word of Encouragement to Be Hopeful (21:28)
    d. Words of Warning to Be Alert and Expectant (21:29-36)
4. Summary of the Temple Ministry (21:37-38)

VII. The Passion and the Resurrection (22:1–24:53)

A. Plot to Murder Jesus (22:1-6)
1. The Plotters (22:1-2)
2. The Traitor (22:3-6)

B. Upper Room (22:7-38)
1. Preparations for Passover (22:7-13)
2. Institution of the Lord's Supper (22:14-20)
3. Four Post-Supper Conversations (22:21-38)
    a. The Betrayer Announced (22:21-23)

b. Debate Over Who Is the Greatest (22:24-30)
c. Jesus Predicts Peter's Denials (22:31-34)
d. Jesus Attempted to Prepare His Men for the Coming Conflict (22:35-38)

C. Three Heartbreaking Scenes (22:39-62)
1. Prayer in Gethsemane (22:39-46)
2. Arrest in the Garden (22:47-53)
3. Denial in a Courtyard (22:54-62)

D. Four Unjust Trials (22:63–23:25)
1. Jesus before the Sanhedrin (22:63-71)
2. Jesus before Pilate the First Time (23:1-7)
3. Jesus before Herod (23:8-12)
4. Jesus before Pilate the Second Time (23:13-25)

E. Crucifixion and Burial (23:26-56)
1. The Cross (23:26-49)
a. On the Way to the Cross (23:26-32)
b. Crucifixion (23:33-38)
c. Conversation with Criminals (23:39-43)
d. The Conclusion of Jesus' Passion (23:44-49)
2. The Tomb (23:50-56)

F. Resurrection, Commission, Ascension (24:1-53)
1. Resurrection (24:1-46)
a. At the Tomb (24:1-12)
b. On the Road to Emmaus (24:13-32)
c. With the Disciples in Jerusalem (24:33-46)
2. Commission (24:47-49)
3. Ascension (24:50-53)

COMMENTARY ON LUKE

I. Luke's Prologue (1:1-4)

This "prologue" is one long, complicated sentence. A prologue is typical in ancient literary pieces, but Luke's is atypically brief and quite "formal." There is a balance to this prologue: "a protasis in 1:1-2 ['in as much as' or '*since*'] in which Luke announced his motivation for writing this gospel and an apodosis in 1:3-4 ['it seemed good to me also']" or *therefore* (Bock, *Luke,* 51) in which he explained his purpose for writing.

A. Luke's Motive and Method (1:1-3a)

1:1-3a. Luke noted that there were other accounts—both written and oral. While he made no negative judgment about these accounts, it may be assumed that he thought (1) they were perhaps a bit fragmentary (since **many have undertaken** the task to tell the story); (2) since they were from **eyewitnesses** and therefore most likely being passed on through oral tradition, they needed to be written down; (3) they were perhaps in danger of being lost; (4) each of these other accounts was incomplete standing alone—one account that collected all the information needed to be compiled. Luke proposed to **compile an account** of his own and **write it out** in a careful and orderly way. He wanted to provide his reader(s) a clear and complete record of the **things accomplished among us**. He was referring, of course, to the events of Jesus' life. The term **accomplished** could be translated "fulfilled" and suggests that the events of Jesus' life are the fulfillment of God's OT promises.

Luke related that he had **investigated everything carefully**, that is, he had gone back to **the beginning**, he had checked the sources, and perhaps he even consulted with the **eyewitnesses**. What Luke recorded in the birth narratives is unique to his gospel, information that only those who were there would know. Luke may have spoken to Jesus' immediate family (even Mary herself). The detailed content of the birth narratives makes this possibility plausible.

B. Luke's Reader(s) (1:3b)

1:3b. Many ancient literary works had prologues and were addressed to important personages, so Luke addressed his work to **Theophilus**—"Lover of God." This was a name "used by both Greeks and Jews" making it difficult to establish the person's ethnic identity (Bock, *Luke*, 64), but most likely he was a Gentile. Some have suggested this was a generic title, a way for Luke to address any interested but anonymous reader, or "symbolic of 'pious Christians'" (Bock, *Luke*, 63). However, the direct address—**you**—makes it more probable that the one addressed was a specific individual. Some have suggested that he was a Gentile who had already "been taught" (1:4) some truth about Jesus and was perhaps already a Christian. Others have proposed that "been taught" here means merely that this man had "heard about" Jesus, and Luke was attempting to bring him to faith in Jesus. **Most excellent** was an honorific title for a Roman official (as Paul called the Roman governors in Ac 23:26; 24:3; 26:25), so perhaps Theophilus was a Roman official who had heard about this new faith but did not yet believe.

Theophilus would be the prototype of the larger audience, so that the Greco-Roman world would hear of the Son of Man. In any case, Luke's intent was to explain to **Theophilus** how he, as a Gentile, fit into the larger narrative of Jesus and His fulfillment of God's plan of salvation. Luke had the wider Gentile world in mind as he wrote. He wanted all the nations to know that Jesus Christ, "the Son of Man, had come to seek and to save the lost" (Lk 19:10). Some suggest that Theophilus was Luke's patron, who supported him so Luke could do his research and write his book. However, Bock notes, "there is no clear way to determine this point" (Bock, *Luke*, 63).

C. Luke's Purpose (1:4)

1:4. Luke explained that he undertook this task **so that you may know the exact truth** about the life of Jesus—the events and His teaching. Luke was not suggesting that the other gospels had been deficient in any way. His objective was comprehensive precision. The matters at hand—the birth, the life, the teaching, the death, the resurrection of Jesus Christ—are so eternally vital that Luke wanted to make sure his readers **know the exact truth**.

II. The Birth and Childhood Narratives (1:5–2:52)

A. Announcement of the Birth of the Forerunner (1:5-25)

Luke began his gospel with the story of the forerunner—John the Baptist. In a sense this takes the reader back to the end of the OT and ties the story of Jesus to the messianic expectation of the OT (cf. Is 40:1-3; Mal 4:5-6).

1. Introduction of a Faithful Couple: Zacharias and Elizabeth (1:5-7)

a. A Despotic Ruler (1:5a)

1:5a. By starting with a reference to **Herod** the Great, **king of Judea**, Luke tied the events of his narrative to the narrative of the wider world (cf. 2:1-2; 3:1). Luke was not just trying to provide a chronology of the events he recorded, but he also was saying in effect, "The matters of which I am writing have a place in the larger narrative of world history." John the Baptist and Jesus of Nazareth were born in turbulent times—times not necessarily favorable to those who sought to live a life faithful to the God of the Scriptures. Nevertheless, even in such times, God was working out His purposes through His faithful people.

b. A "Priestly" Couple (1:5b)

1:5b. Zacharias ("The Lord has remembered") was identified as **a priest**—he was **of the division of Abijah** (cf. 1Ch 24:4-19, esp. 24:10). At this time the temple priesthood was made up of 24 divisions—16 from Eleazar (Aaron's oldest surviving son; cf. Ex 28:1 and Lv 10) and eight from Ithamar (cf. 1Ch 24:4). Each division was named for one of the descendants of these sons of Aaron (cf. 1Ch 24:7-18), and **Abijah** appears as eighth in the list. Each division would serve "in the temple service for a week at a time, twice a year" (Robert H. Stein, *Luke*, NAC [Nashville: Broadman & Holman, 1992], 73). **Zacharias** was descended from a long line of godly priest-servants (cf. Neh 12:4). Likewise, his wife **Elizabeth** ("God is an [my] oath" meaning "as God is reliable, so is my oath") was **from the daughters of Aaron**. Thus both husband and wife had "priestly credentials." It was quite common for a priest to marry a young lady from the line of Aaron. Leviticus (21:7, 14) specifies that a priest's wife must be a virgin. Since both Zacharias and Elizabeth were from the line of Aaron they would have expected from birth to be servants in Israel.

c. A Righteous and Blameless Couple (1:6)

1:6. The couple was described as **righteous in the sight of God**—or "justified" (perhaps an echo of Paul's theology; cf. Rm 3–4)—or simply, this couple lived rightly, openly, and visibly, before God and men. They were **walking** (living) **blamelessly in all the commandments and requirements of the Lord**. Luke was not suggesting that they were sinless but they had a deep inner piety that manifested itself in outward behavior. They lived by the requirements of the law not to *get right*(eous) with God but because they were, in His sight (by faith Rm 3:28) *already right*(eous). The word **blameless** actually comes at the end of the verse ("requirements of the Lord—blameless") and is emphatic.

d. A Barren Couple (1:7)

1:7. The significance of the statement **they had no child because Elizabeth was barren** was something Luke's readers in that day would have instantly understood. This was a personal tragedy (see the stories of Sarah and Rachel in Genesis and Hannah in 1Sm 1). Fertility was understood as a blessing (see Dt 7:14; Ps 113:9)—barrenness was the opposite. Since **they were both advanced in years** it seemed the prospects of children and family life were now past for this faithful couple. However this condition set the stage for God to intervene. In the OT there were a number of births only God could accomplish—e.g., Isaac and Samuel. God often waited to do His work when human ability and temporal possibility were exhausted. Nevertheless, this godly couple remained faithful and obedient to the Lord, they continued to serve (see Lk 1:8), and apparently they prayed (see 1:13). Zacharias and Elizabeth were just two, quite normal, common people who, like many others in the biblical narrative, are outstanding examples of faithfulness.

2. An Angelic Announcement (1:8-23)

a. Zacharias's Priestly Service Interrupted (1:8-12)

1:8-10. Now it happened ("It came to pass") was an obvious way to advance the story. Zacharias continued to go about his regular duties **performing his priestly service before God** according to the regular schedule (1:8). Luke noted that at this time Zacharias was given a special opportunity (1:9-10). Due to the large number of priests serving in that day (as many as 18,000), not every priest could expect to serve in the inner chamber of the temple itself. The honor of this service was determined by lot twice each day, at sunrise and sunset. A priest would consider it the high point of his career, and it was never conferred twice on any one man. It was at this time, in the service of a humble priest offering the daily incense in the temple, which had been done day-in-day-out for decades, that God chose to break His silence and advance His program of salvation.

1:11-12. While he was engaged in this special service, an angel appeared to Zacharias (1:11). The detail that the angel was **standing to the right of the altar of incense** was something only Zacharias himself would have known, an indication of the care and detail of Luke's research. Perhaps the angel stood there as an answer to Zacharias's prayer. The **altar of incense** was one of the furnishings of the temple symbolizing the prayers of the people. Zacharias was **troubled**, and **fear gripped him** (1:12), an appropriate and reasonable response. The appearance of an angel was as unexpected in Zacharias's day as it would be today.

b. The Angel's Message Delivered (1:13-17)

1:13-14. The angel's message to Zacharias had six parts: (1) a word to calm him, **do not be afraid**; (2) a word to encourage him, **your petition has been heard**; (3) a word of joyful news, **Elizabeth will bear you a son**; (4) a word to instruct him, **you will give him the name John**; (5) a word about his personal joy, **you will have joy and gladness**; (6) a word about the joy for many outside his family, **many will rejoice at his birth**. It would have been clear to Zacharias that this birth was significant beyond being the end Elizabeth's barrenness.

1:15-17. The message of the angel about John himself (1:15) indicated three particulars: The angel indicated that John (1) would be great, (2) would drink no wine, and (3) would be filled with the Holy Spirit. In short, John would be a unique figure—unmistakably devoted to a unique and powerful ministry for the Lord. The angel's message about John's ministry in 1:16-17 indicated five facts about John's ministry: Note facts #1 and #4 are related; facts #2 and #5 are the same; fact #3 is at the center and is a key "salvation historical" fact that said in effect, "Get ready! God is about to once again take up His program with the nation and advance His plan of salvation." (1) John's ministry will **turn many . . . back to the Lord** (1:16)—it will be a ministry of leading people to repentance. (2) John **will go as a *forerunner* before Him** (1:17a, emphasis added)—it will be a ministry of preparation for the Messiah. (3) John will serve **in the spirit and power of Elijah** (1:17b)—it will be a ministry of power and prophetic fulfillment. John will (4) **TURN THE HEARTS OF THE FATHERS** . . . and **the disobedient** . . . (1:17c; cf. Mal 4:6)—it will be a ministry of "reconciliation between families that occurs through the ministry of reform" (Bock, *Luke*, 88). (5) John will **make ready a people prepared for the Lord** (Lk 1:17; cf. 2Sm 7:24)—it will be a ministry of preparation of the people to respond to the "Lord's way of salvation" (Bock, *Luke*, 91). Thus the angel indicated John's ministry would be empowered by God, undertaken in behalf of others, and focused on Christ—a pattern for all Christian service.

c. Zacharias's Doubt; Angel's Reassurance and (Mild) Rebuke (1:18-20)

1:18-20. Zacharias's doubt was not serious but was notable in contrast to Mary's humble acceptance and instant submission (cf. 1:26-38). Those who enjoy the Lord's promises most assuredly are those who take Him at His Word most readily. The angel was **Gabriel** (cf. Dn 8:16; 9:21). Zacharias was assured that Gabriel knew whereof he spoke since he was one **who stands in the presence of God** (Lk 1:19a) and such announcements were apparently his special ministry. Zacharias ought to have been focusing on the divine "promise" of the message, not the human "problems" of the message. For his doubt Zacharias would be **silent and unable to speak** until the promise was fulfilled. This would serve both as a sign of the angel's verity and a rebuke for Zacharias's incredulity.

d. The People Waiting and Wondering (1:21-23)

1:21-23. The delay caused by the extended conversation between the angel and Zacharias began to cause some mild concern among the worshipers and Zacharias's priestly colleagues who were waiting for him to reappear after making the prescribed offerings (1:21). It was customary for the priest to emerge and pronounce a blessing on the people. To their astonishment when he did appear he was **unable to speak** (1:22a). By some means it was conveyed to them that he had **seen a vision** (1:22b). Zacharias, no doubt, desired to relate his marvelous experience, but in spite of his attempts to communicate he **remained mute** (1:22c). After serving the rest of his priestly duties Zacharias **went back home** (1:23).

3. Elizabeth's Joy (1:24-25)

1:24-25. With delicate simplicity Luke recorded that, indeed, **Elizabeth his wife became pregnant** (1:24). There was no supernatural "divine intervention" in this instance. Presumably, the pregnancy occurred in the normal course of human life and family. Nevertheless, Elizabeth clearly understood that this pregnancy was a favor (grace) from the Lord—**the Lord has . . . looked with favor upon me** (1:25a). No reason is given for Elizabeth secluding herself. It might have been that, fearing a miscarriage, wishing to avoid the incredulity of friends and family, or some other anomaly, she wanted the pregnancy to develop sufficiently before she announced the good news. Luke's point in this account was that the outworking of God's purposes are not usually seen among the powerful in the world, or among the societal "movers and shakers." They transpire and are observed at the level of the humble, the personal, and the private, among the faithful, the weak, the base, and the foolish (cf. 1Co 1:26-28) who simply serve, obey, and trust in God.

B. Announcement of the Birth of Jesus (1:26-38)

1. Time, Agent, Location, and Recipient of the Announcement (1:26-27)

1:26-27. The announcement came in the **sixth month** (1:26) of Elizabeth's pregnancy. The agent was that same **Gabriel** (cf. 1:19a), and the location was **a city in Galilee . . . Nazareth** (1:26). The region was "not notable." The city (*polis*) was actually more of a rural village, and the best estimate of Nazareth's population at that time is that it had no more than 400 people. Like the recipient herself (Mary), the location is humble and obscure, contrary to expectation. The most astonishing and world-altering event in human history, the incarnation of the Son of God, was going to happen, not in a great city or region of power, but in the obscure and humble locations of Nazareth and Bethlehem. The recipient is identified by name—**Mary** (1:27c). Her name meant something like "excellence." The order of the information given about Mary is peculiar. Typically her name would be given first, then her associations, then the more personal details. However, Luke identified her first as a **virgin** (mentioned twice; the Gk. term *parthenos* is unambiguous, meaning that she had never had sexual relations) who was **engaged** (better "betrothed") to a man named **Joseph**. Luke, unlike Matthew (Mt 1:22-23), does not refer to the prophecy of Is 7:14, but the point is unmistakable—the impending birth was something only God could accomplish and it would be in fulfillment of Messianic prophecy. Her betrothed is identified as one of the **descendants of David**.

2. Greeting, Reaction, and Assurance (1:28-30)

1:28-30. The angel began with two alliterative terms (*chaire, kecharitomene*), **Greetings, favored**

one—literally, "Grace to you, graced one." She was assured **the Lord** (*Kyrios*) **is with you**. This note is actually rich with significance—**with *you*** is emphatic. Mary's reaction, in contrast to that of Zacharias, was not fear but thoughtful questioning. She **kept pondering what kind of salutation this was**, trying to think about the import of the words themselves, mulling them over. The angel's **Do not be afraid, Mary** (1:30) is literally, "Stop being afraid." His words **you have found favor with God** convey no mere pleasant sentiment—they indicated a divine intention to use this "favored one" in some important way.

3. The Message Is about Jesus Christ (1:31-33)

1:31-33. The angel's message began with revealing the virgin birth and the name of the Child—**you shall name Him Jesus** (1:31). The transcendent significance of the Child was related: His person—**He will be great** (1:32a); His relation to God—**He will be called the Son of the Most High** (1:32b; a way of saying He is the "Son of God"), and His purpose—**the Lord God** (Yahweh of the OT) **will give Him the throne of His father David** (1:32c). This child will be the fulfillment of the Davidic covenant promises (1:33; cf. 2Sm 7) and the OT promises of the literal earthly kingdom for the nation of Israel (see also the comments on Mt 3:1-4).

4. Mary's Reaction, Angel's Explanation, Mary's Submission (1:34-38)

1:34-38. While the angel had been relating the transcendent significance of this child, Mary had been stuck on the first point—the matter of her pregnancy! Unlike Zacharias's, Mary's response was not an expression of disbelief but only a question of process—**How can this be**? (1:34). The angel's explanation was delicate, simple, and effective. The child will be the offspring of this young woman and the **power of the Most High** (1:35). This indicates He will be (fully) man and **the Son of** (fully) **God** (1:35c). **Holy Child** (1:35) indicates, among other things, that this child would not possess a sin nature and was holy from the moment of conception. To encourage her, the angel told Mary of Elizabeth's pregnancy (1:36) and reassured her that **nothing will be impossible with God** (1:37). Mary's humble submission (1:38) indicates the reason she was chosen for this tremendous honor.

C. Mary's Visit to Elizabeth (1:39-56)

1:39-45. To confirm the word of the angel (cf. 1:36) Mary immediately went to visit Elizabeth (1:39-40). Upon hearing Mary's greeting, Elizabeth and her unborn child experienced the movement of the Spirit (1:41, 44b; see comments on v. 67), prompting Elizabeth to pronounce a blessing on Mary (1:42-45). This blessing indicated that Elizabeth understood the tremendous honor that had been conferred upon Mary and the significance of her child—namely, that He was her **Lord** (1:43b), indicating that Elizabeth understood this child to be the Messiah (cf. Bock, *Luke*, 137). Elizabeth also blessed Mary for her faith in the angel's message (1:45).

1:46-56. Mary's response to this confirmation of the angel's word prompted a song of praise (1:46-55) known as *"The Magnificat"* (after the first word of this song in the Latin version). The song begins with a "Word of Praise" (1:46-47), continues with the "Cause for Praise" (1:48-49a), and centers on the "Object of Praise" (1:49b-55)—namely, the **Mighty One** (1:49a), the One whose name is **holy** (1:49b)—the God of the OT covenant promises. The song itself is filled with OT allusions (e.g., compare 1:46 with 1Sm 2:1; 1:47 with Ps 35:9; 1:52 with Job 5:11; 1:55 with Gn 17:19) and praises God for His mercy (1:50; cf. Ps 103:17; 54), His power (Lk 1:51), His justice and equity (1:52-53; cf. Ps 107:9), and mostly for His covenant faithfulness (Lk 1:54-55). For Mary the greatest significance of this impending birth was that God was about to fulfill His covenant promises to **Abraham and his descendents forever** (1:55).

D. John the Baptist: the Birth and the *Benedictus* (1:57-80)

1. Birth and Naming of John by Elizabeth (1:57-66)

1:57-66. The birth of John (1:57-58) was recognized by Elizabeth's family and friends as a display of unusual **mercy** to her from the Lord. In accord with the custom of naming a child on the day of his circumcision (cf. Lv 12:1-3) and following the angel's instructions (cf. Lk 1:13) Elizabeth named her son **John** (1:60b) instead of **Zacharias** after his father (as the relatives wanted to do, 1:59). Still pressing their case, the relatives inquired from Zacharias (that they **made signs** to him would suggest he was not only mute but deaf as well, 1:62), and to their surprise he confirmed in writing that the child was to be called **John** (1:63). Zacharias had turned from skeptic to believer, and thus he instantly regained his powers of speech and began **to speak in praise of God** (1:64). The first reaction of the people was **fear** (1:65a) because the whole event was awe-inspiring. Then the news of the event spread to the whole region (**the hill country of Judea** 1:65b) because the event was remarkable. Finally the people wondered about this child because it was clear that **the hand of the Lord was certainly with him** (1:66)—he was extraordinary.

2. The *Benedictus* of Zacharias (1:67-80)

1:67-79. With his restored powers of speech, and being **filled with the Holy Spirit** (a manifestation that in Luke's writings always comes before a person speaks in some revelatory way; cf. Andreas J Kostenberger, "What Does It Mean to Be Filled with the Spirit: A Biblical Investigation," *JETS* 2 [1997], 229-40), Zacharias immediately turned to praising God. This song—a work of poetry—was intended to be the answer to the people's question in 1:66—**What will this child turn out to be?** The song, drawn mostly from quotations and allusions of the OT (e.g., 1:68 with 1Kg 1:48 Ps 41:13; 72:18; 1:69 with 1Sm 2:1, 10; Ps 18:2; 89:17; 1:71 with Ps 106:10; 1:73 with Gn 22:16; 1:78 with Mal 4:2; 1:79 with Is 9:2), is called the *Benedictus* (after the first word of Lk 1:68 in the Latin version). In one long sentence (1:68-75) Zacharias praised God for His work of fulfilling His covenant promises to David (1:69) and to Abraham (1:73). This work of "covenant fulfillment" was to be accomplished by the One whom John would one day announce and introduce to the world—this child (**you, child** 1:76). In the rest of the song (1:77-79) Zacharias highlighted the ministry of the coming One in terms of salvation, forgiveness, mercy, guidance, and peace.

1:80. The astonishing beginning of John's life was followed by many years of normal growth and development—physical and spiritual (1:80a). While he did develop his calling outside first-century Judaism's normal paths of instruction (1:80b), it is doubtful that John joined one of the desert sects of his day. While there were superficial similarities between John the Baptist and such groups as the Essenes and the so-called Qumran community (such as ascetic practices, the importance of baptism, and an eschatological message; cf. Stein, *Luke*, 129), John's ministry was much different. His ministry was personal and independent (he was not part of a group). His baptism was unique—an expression of repentance (cf. 3:8) and an initiation into the Messianic community (not a system for ritual cleansing and personal sanctification). His message was about the coming Messiah and the salvation He would bring (cf. 3:6; not about the coming apocalyptic victory of the "sons of light").

E. Birth of Jesus; Visitations of Angels and Shepherds (2:1-20)

1. Birth of Jesus (2:1-7)

2:1-3. Once again, Luke tied his history of Jesus to the history of the wider world (2:1). The time and nature of this **census** is uncertain, as is the exact reason for Joseph to be registered in **his own city** (2:3). **Caesar Augustus**, whose name was actually Octavian, was the great nephew of Julius Caesar. He ruled Rome for 41 years and was the emperor behind *Pax Romana* (Peace of Rome). Although shrewd and ruthless in his rise to power, he was wise and even benevolent in his actual reign. He accepted the (semi-divine) title of "Augustus" in 27 BC (which marked the beginning of his reign and of emperor worship). He died in AD 14 and was succeeded by his stepson Tiberius (see 3:1).

While **Quirinius** (2:2) may be a name obscure to us (aside from this reference) he was a well-known figure of the era. He was mentioned in Josephus (*Antiquities* 17.13.5 paragraph 355) and was a military man as well as **governor of Syria** (a much wider area than the present day country).

Apparently Caesar Augustus had ordered a number of regular and special censuses during his reign, so this is not out of the ordinary. The purpose of the census was to get an accurate record of a region's population for taxation purposes, and that seems to be the reason Joseph considered it necessary to travel to the hometown of his clan—Bethlehem. The problem is trying to fit Luke's census with those of the day (according to the extrabiblical records). In brief, we know of a census conducted by Quirinius in AD 6 (cf. Ac 5:37), but that does not seem fit with this census. Furthermore, the most likely time for Jesus' birth (all things considered) is between 4 and 6 BC—but Quirinius was governor of Syria much later than that. While more than a few commentators have offered possible solutions, some have simply suggested that Quirinius was governor of Syria twice, so there may have been a census before the (recorded) one that occurred in AD 6. Others have noted that the word **first** in Lk 2:2 (**This was the first census taken**) could be understood as "before," or "prior to"—hence, Luke is saying this census was before the (more famous one) conducted by Quirinius. All in all, the scene here is quite believable, and we can assume that the problems could be worked out if we had more specific information. There is no reason to doubt Luke's accuracy (see Bock, *Luke*, 903-09).

2:4-6. For Luke the important point was that this decree, in some sense, required Joseph and Mary—**who was engaged to him, and was with child** (2:5) to travel to the city of his heritage—**Bethlehem, because he was of the house and family of David** (2:4). (The note that the couple was only **engaged** is subtle but clear—this child is not Joseph's—this birth will be a virgin birth). Luke did not mention Mc 5:2, but his readers (as many readers today) would already have known the name of the town and the significance of its association with David. They would have understood that a pagan emperor's decree (that moved an empire) was the means of a sovereign God to accomplish His perfect plan (by moving an obscure young couple to an obscure town to fulfill biblical prophecy).

2:7. With a surprising reserve and simplicity—given the expectations created in the first chapter—Luke described the birth of Jesus Christ—**And she gave birth to her firstborn son** (2:7a). The description—**wrapped Him in cloths** (2:7b)—depicted the normal procedure for newborns, who were bound in cloths to straighten their limbs, an act thought to help promote the health and strength of an infant's limbs. However, the detail—**and laid Him in a manger** (2:7c)—described an act that was completely contrary to expectation and seemingly utterly absurd! Tradition and familiarity with the story has removed the absurdity for many readers. Yet the idea that a young mother—even an inexperienced one—would place her newborn in an animal feeding trough is to be understood as entirely incongruous. The explanation—**there was no room for them in the inn** (2:7d)—tells the reader why there was a manger present, but it does not take away the inappropriateness of using it as a crib for a newborn. The scene is one of abject humility—of utter condescension. It is contrary to expectation so far as the arrival of the Messiah is concerned. Luke is letting the reader know from this beginning, this Messiah will surprise you; this Messiah will do the unexpected.

Inn (*katalyma*) is better translated "guest room in a private home" (cf. Lk 22:11, where the same word is used; see Lk 10:34, where a different word, *pandocheion*, is used for an "inn"). The home, probably belonging to a relative, where Mary and Joseph would have stayed, was full, so they sought refuge and privacy either in an animal room adjacent to the home (analogous to an attached garage), or in a nearby cave used for housing animals. In either case, the idea of the holy family being turned away from an inn so Jesus would be born in a stable is probably not quite accurate.

2. Visitation of the Angels to the Shepherds (2:8-14)

2:8-14. In keeping with the theme of events that are "contrary to expectation" Luke recorded that the first persons to hear the "good news" of this birth were shepherds. Tradition has led many to think of this announcement as quite fitting, but in reality shepherds were the least likely persons to receive such a glorious announcement. Shepherds, especially those charged with the night watch, were among the most socially undesirable classes. They were considered disreputable and unclean, and they represented "the outcasts and sinners for whom Jesus came" (cf. Stein, *Luke*, 108). The glorious appearing of the (at first, single) angel was meant to impress these lowly shepherds with the glorious truth in the words—**for today in the city of David there has been born for you a Savior, who is Christ the Lord** (2:11). The three titles—**Savior**, **Christ**, **Lord**—appear in this combination only here in the NT, and they highlight His mission, His royalty, and His authority. The sign—the description of the circumstances of the child—would have made locating the babe rather easy; the song of the angels (**a multitude of the heavenly host**, 2:13-14) would have made locating the child rather urgent.

3. Visitation of the Shepherds (2:15-20)

2:15-20. Luke emphasized that the shepherds went in haste to find the child (2:15, 16). The scene of the shepherds' visitation of the infant Jesus highlighted two themes that run throughout Luke's Gospel: First, this Messiah will not come, or serve, or engage in His calling in a way that is "expected" by the religious establishment, but He will be recognized by the humble, the outcast, and the socially marginalized; second, this Messiah will cause people to "wonder," to be "amazed"—here by the manner of His coming, later by His teaching and His ministry (cf. 2:33, 47, 48; 4:22; 5:9; 8:25; 9:43-45; 11:14; 20:26; 24:12, 41). Luke noted that **Mary treasured all these things** and continued to think about them (2:19; cf. 2:51). No doubt it was Mary's recollection of these events that informed Luke's narrative.

F. Scene at the Circumcision of Jesus (2:21-39)

2:21-24. Luke depicted Joseph and Mary as dutifully fulfilling the laws concerning **circumcision** (2:21; cf. Lv 12:3) and **purification** (after giving birth) (2:22; cf. Lv 12:1-8) and presentation (of the **firstborn**) (2:23-24; Ex 13:2, 12). Mary's sacrifice of **A PAIR OF TURTLEDOVES OR TWO YOUNG PIGEONS** (2:24; cf. Lv 12:8) indicated that the couple was not wealthy.

2:25-39. The performance of these required rituals set up two encounters in the **temple**. The first encounter was with a man named **Simeon** (2:25-35). Simeon was described as **righteous and devout** (2:25) and one to whom the Spirit of God had given a promise that he would live to see **the Lord's Christ** (2:26). Upon seeing the child he recognized the fulfillment of that promise (2:29) and of the Lord's promise of salvation for **all peoples** (2:31)—both Gentiles and **Your people Israel** (2:32). Simeon had an ominous warning about this child as well—His life would be a challenge to the nation of Israel and would bring sorrow to Mary (2:34-35). The second encounter was with **a prophetess** named **Anna**. She was described as an elderly but devout worshipper. As with Simeon, when she saw the child she recognized that in Him was the fulfillment of the promise for **all those who were looking for the redemption of Jerusalem** (2:38).

G. Boyhood of Jesus (2:40-52)

2:40-52. In this, the only account in the gospels of Jesus' boyhood, Luke described a time when the family visited Jerusalem for Passover (2:41). After the celebration Jesus was not found with the caravan heading back to Nazareth (2:43-44). When Joseph and Mary returned to the city and found Jesus, He was in the temple discussing spiritual matters with the teachers (and amazing them with His understanding 2:46-47). When His parents found Him, His mother chided Him, **Your father and I have been anxiously looking for You**. But His explanation—**I had to be in My Father's house** (2:49)—indicated that He was well aware of His own identity at an early age, and of the identity of His true Father, the Lord God. Other than this instance of "divine precociousness" Luke indicated that Jesus' growth and development were completely normal, except for the **grace** (2:40b) and **favor** (2:52) He enjoyed from God.

III. Transition to Ministry (3:1–4:13)

A. Preparation by the Forerunner: John the Baptist (3:1-20) (see also the comments on Mt 3:1-13)

3:1-20. Luke began the description of John's ministry by identifying the political and religious leaders of the day (3:1-2), once again tying the history of Jesus to the history of the wider world. John is identified as the **son of Zacharias** (3:2)—the same person from the earlier narrative (cf. 1:5-24, 57-80). He is the one to whom **the word of God came**, identifying him as a prophet. John is also identified by his message of **baptism of repentance** (3:3) and as the fulfillment of the prophecy of **Isaiah** (3:4-6; Is 40:3-5). His message was geared to the people who came to hear him. To the curious (Lk 3:7), to the presumptuous (3:8), and to the complacent (3:9) he preached a message of warning and repentance. To those who did repent (crowds, tax collectors, and soldiers who said **what shall we do**? in 3:10, 12, 14a), he gave practical advice to show the **fruits** of **repentance** (3:8). To those looking for the Messiah he pointed away from himself to One who was **mightier than** he was (3:16). John's ministry aroused the opposition of Herod, who had him imprisoned (3:18-20). John the Baptist epitomized faithful preaching, Christ focused ministry, and boldness in the face of opposition.

B. Preparation of Jesus (3:21–4:13) (see also the comments on Mt 3:13-17)

3:21–4:13. The baptism (3:21-22) of Jesus assured Him of the approval of His Father and the empowerment of the Holy Spirit. While Matthew's genealogy established Jesus' legitimate right to rule on David's throne, being the royal line through Joseph—Solomon—David, Luke's genealogy (3:23-38) of Jesus proved His birthright (probably the legal blood line through Mary, through Nathan; 3:31b). Thus Jesus had both the prophetic and legal right to the Davidic promises. Furthermore, Luke's genealogy tied Jesus solidly to the family of man, Adam (3:8), since Luke traced the genealogy to Adam, in contrast to Matthew who goes only so far as Abraham. This was to emphasize the universal relevance of Jesus for the entire race. The temptation (4:1-13) proved His sinlessness and His power over Satan. The three temptations (in different order from that of Matthew, cf. Mt 4:1-11) were: (1) Serve Yourself (Lk 4:3-4); (2) Honor Yourself (4:5-8); (3) Be spectacular (be presumptuous and prove

Your self-importance; 4:9-12). Jesus countered each temptation with an appeal to Scripture (cf. Dt 8:3; 6:13; 6:16). These events proved Jesus was the right man, with the appropriate background, with the proper credentials, and with the desirable experience for the ministry He was about to begin. On the temptation, see also the comments on Mt 4:1-11.

IV. The Great Galilean Ministry (4:14–9:62)

A. Jesus in Galilee and the Synagogue in Nazareth (4:14-30)

1. Jesus in Galilee (4:14-15)

4:14-15. Luke introduced the great Galilean ministry of Jesus by identifying five general features of this period: (1) the location of this ministry was **Galilee** (4:14a); (2) the power for this ministry was **the Spirit** (4:14b); (3) the impact of this ministry was extensive—**news about Him spread** (4:14c); (4) the practice of this ministry was **teaching in their synagogues** (4:15a); (5) the reception of this ministry was generally popular—He **was praised by all** (4:15b).

2. Jesus in the Synagogue in Nazareth (4:16-30)

4:16-19. Jesus' experience in His hometown of **Nazareth** (4:16) was in stark contrast to the last of the general features of His ministry just mentioned (4:15b). As was His pattern He took the opportunity to teach in the synagogue. His reading was from the scroll of Isaiah and the text was Is 61:1. This was a recognized messianic text and spoke of the Spirit-empowered Servant of the Lord (cf. Is 42:1-4; 49:1-6; 50:4-9; 52:13–53:12); His power was from the Spirit of the Lord, His ministry was preaching the gospel, His audience was the poor, the captive, the blind and the oppressed. His message was good news, release, recovery of sight, and freedom. In His reading of the text Jesus stopped after reading the first line of Is 61:2—**To proclaim the favorable year of the Lord** (Lk 4:19).

4:20-21. Luke's description masterfully conveyed the tension of the scene: Jesus closed the book, sat down, and calmly but firmly informed the group, **Today this Scripture has been fulfilled in your hearing** (4:21b). Note two key points: the place where Jesus stopped reading is significant—the rest of the verse in Is 61:2 describes the events that will take place at Jesus' second coming, namely judgment and full-orbed restoration of Israel (thus, had He read the whole verse He could not have said that text was fulfilled!) Also, by stopping and applying the first part of the text to Himself (in His first coming) He is, in effect, claiming that He Himself will fulfill the rest of the verse (in His second coming). Here Jesus was making an unmistakable claim to be the Messiah. At the outset of His public ministry He answered the question "Who is Jesus?"—He is the Messiah!

4:22-30. Jesus might have legitimately expected that the application of this verse to Himself would be a cause for praise and rejoicing (as His impending birth had been for Mary and Zacharias). But He was well aware that His present ministry would not be universally well received even by the citizens of His hometown (4:22b). He quoted a proverb, **Physician heal yourself**. The proverb means, "Do yourself a favor—perform a miracle right here, right now, like the one you performed in Capernaum, so we can see clear proof that you are the One who fulfills this verse!" He also cited two OT examples of "prophetic rejection" that exposed their resistance and precipitated their rejection of Him (4:23-27). Even though the people of Nazareth wanted to kill Him, Jesus escaped and relocated the base of His ministry to Capernaum (4:29-30, 31) with occasional visits to synagogues in Judea (4:44).

B. Jesus' Ministry Is Powerful (4:31-44; 5:12-26)

4:31-44. Jesus' ministry at this time was characterized by (1) powerful, authoritative preaching (4:31-32), (2) demonstrations of power over the demonic forces (4:33-37; 41), and (3) demonstrations of power over disease (4:38-40; for the healing of Peter's mother-in-law, see the comments on Mt 8:14-17).

5:12-16. Two special instances of His power over disease are recorded in the healing of a leper (5:12-16) and healing of a paralytic (5:17-26). In the first instance Jesus was confronted with a man **covered with leprosy** (5:12; this was likely not the disease known as "Hansen's Disease" today but one of a multitude of skin rashes and diseases prevalent in that day). This condition would have provoked general revulsion and would have rendered the man ceremonially unclean, excluding him from society and from worship in the temple. The man's plaintive cry—**Lord, if You are willing, You can make me clean** (5:12c) did not imply that he thought Jesus might be unwilling. Rather, it demonstrated he indeed believed Jesus had the authority

(**Lord**), the inclination (**if You are willing**), and the power (**You can make me clean**). Jesus' response confirmed the leper's faith in Him: (1) He touched him—an act of incredible compassion (the man may not have been touched by another human hand in years); (2) He spoke to him—**I am willing** (5:13b); (3) He healed him—**immediately the leprosy left him** (5:13c). Jesus' instructions to the man were probably intended to prove Jesus' deference to the law (5:14) and to forestall the kind of publicity that only served to confuse and confound His ministry (see also the comments on Mt 8:1-4).

5:17-26. The second special example of power over disease—the healing of the paralytic (5:17-26; see also the comments on Mt 9:1-8)—occurred at a time when, as Jesus was teaching (Luke informs us) He also had **power. . . to perform healing** (5:17c). This note is likely simply meant to remind the reader that healing power was a mark of His "messianic credentials"; cf. 4:18; Is 61:1. While He was teaching, several men brought a paralyzed man on a bed or cot. As the size of the crowd prevented them from getting to Jesus (Lk 5:18-19a), they made a hole in the roof of the room where Jesus was and deposited the man **in front of Jesus** (5:19b). On this occasion Jesus took the opportunity not only to demonstrate His power over disease but also to confirm His authority to forgive sin. Instead of immediately doing what the paralyzed men and his friends wanted, Jesus, **seeing their faith** (5:20a, seeing they believed He had the power and authority to heal), said to the paralyzed man, **Friend, your sins are forgiven you** (this need not suggest that the man's disease was caused by sin). This declaration provoked a reaction in the hearts (they **began to reason**) of the Pharisees in the crowd (5:21a). For them such a claim amounted to blasphemy because **God alone** can forgive sins (5:21b). Jesus offered a reasonable challenge to the "reasoning" of the Pharisees: to say **Your sins have been forgiven you** is just as easy to say as **Get up and walk** (5:23). The unexpressed point Jesus was making is if One can say to a paralytic "Get up and walk" and he does get up and he walks, that says something about the power and authority of that One—both to heal *and* to forgive sins. Jesus then explicitly claimed the authority to forgive sins (5:24a) by healing the paralytic (5:24b-25). The effect on the crowd provoked astonishment, fear, and praise (5:26).

C. Jesus Calling His First Disciples (5:1-11; 27-28; 6:12-16)

1. Jesus Called Simon (Peter), James and John, Levi (Matthew) (5:1-11, 27-28)

5:1-11. Jesus continued His teaching ministry in Galilee, right on the shore of the lake (5:1). It was at this time that Jesus met Simon (Peter), possibly because Jesus used Peter's boat as a preaching platform (5:3). When Jesus challenged Simon to continue fishing, even after an unproductive night (5:4-5a), it was a test to see if Simon understood who this man was. Verse 5 contains a fair amount of irony. Simon was the fisherman and knew fishing during the day would be pointless (fish feed on the insects that come out at night when it is cooler, and when it is darker so that they are less likely to be seen and eaten by other predatory fish). After all, Simon was the fish expert; Jesus was just a carpenter. What does He know about fish? But Simon complied, and his compliance led to a miraculous catch (5:6-7). Immediately Simon knew who Jesus was. Peter called him **Lord** (5:8a). Peter's reaction was not a command for Jesus to go away but an expression of his own unworthiness (5:8b). Far from disqualifying Peter, his recognition of Jesus' worthiness and his own sinfulness is precisely what made him an ideal candidate to be a disciple. Jesus reassured Peter and gave him a new assignment (5:10b), as He did with James and John (5:10a), so that they **left everything and followed Him** (5:11). The point here is starkly simple: a disciple is one who sets everything else aside (literally if necessary) and follows Jesus. In addition, if Jesus could make Simon successful at something Simon knew was impossible (fishing during the day), then there was an implicit encouragement for Simon that Jesus could also make him successful at **catching men** (v. 10).

5:27-28. The calling of Levi (Matthew) followed the same pattern: Levi was identified as a tax collector at work (5:27a). Nevertheless, Jesus called him—**Follow Me** (5:27b), and he did just that (5:28). His response was immediate and complete.

2. Jesus Called the Twelve to Be Apostles (6:12-16)

6:12-16. The calling of the first disciples was given greater significance by Jesus' identifying them as **apostles** (6:13)—ones sent out with a unique authority in Jesus' ministry and in the history of the church. These men were from all walks of life, from various social and economic backgrounds, and from different hometowns. Yet they had at least one thing in common—they were devoted to Jesus and the work He had called them to do.

D. Jesus' Ministry Was Contrary to Expectation (5:29–6:11)

5:29–6:11. Luke recorded several scenes of Jesus' unconventional ministry (see also the comments on Mt 9:10-13). First, he recorded that Jesus ate with sinners (5:29)—despite the opposition it provoked (5:30). He did so because He saw His ministry as that of a physician who needed to have contact with the sick (5:31) and because he saw Himself as a prophet/evangelist calling **sinners to repentance** (5:32). A second unconventional feature of Jesus' ministry (see also the comments on Mt 9:14-17) was that he did not teach His disciples to fast (5:33). Jesus explained that this time in His ministry was not the time for fasting (5:34-35). He also explained that His ministry was not just a "patch on the old" but something entirely new, so old forms of "piety" were not appropriate (5:36-39). A third unconventional feature of Jesus' ministry was that He did not require the disciples to conform to the legalistic practices of the Pharisees (6:1-5). Finally, Jesus healed on the Sabbath (6:6-11)—even though this provoked the opposition of the Pharisees (6:11)—because it demonstrated Jesus' priority of life over legalism.

E. Jesus' Teaching Was Contrary to Expectation (6:17-49)

1. Sermon on the Level Place (6:17-38)

6:17-38. In this section Luke presented his version of the Sermon on the Mount (see the comments on Mt 5–7). Matthew placed this event on a mountain (Mt 5:1), but Luke put it on a level place. Some see this as a contradiction, but likely it was a level place on the top of a mountain. Three groups of people were present: a **large crowd of His disciples** (6:17b), a **great throng of people** (6:17c), many of whom had come to be healed (6:18-19), and the Twelve. Nevertheless, Jesus' teaching was directed at the Twelve (6:20a). In the first section, the so-called "Beatitudes" (6:20b-23; *makarios* means "blessed," or "happy"; see the comments on Mt 5:1-6) and the "woes" (20:24-26), Jesus presented attitudes and values for His disciples that were contrary to expectation. Jesus' disciples should consider themselves "blessed" in situations that would otherwise produce sorrow (poverty, loss, persecution), for they knew that in the end they would have a **reward** in heaven. Likewise, they needed to be wary of situations that produce temporal and temporary comfort, ease, and popularity. In the second section (6:27-38; see also the comments on Mt 5:43-48) Jesus laid down some "rules for living as disciples": disciples must love, do good to, pray for, be generous toward, and be merciful and non-judgmental toward unbelievers. Such contrary-to-expectation living (1) contrasts with how unbelievers act (6:32-34), (2) conforms to the nature of **your Father** (6:35-36), and (3) is the way to be rewarded (6:37-38).

2. Three Warnings for Disciples (6:39-49) (see also the comments on Mt 6:1-6; 7:7-27)

6:39-49. In concluding His instruction to the disciples, Jesus gave them three principled warnings using multiple illustrations. First, He warned against "spiritual pride" using illustrations of the "blind leading the blind" (6:39), a pupil and his teacher (6:40), and a ludicrous picture of a man with a log in his eye attempting to help a man with a speck in his eye (6:41-42). Second, He warned against "inconsistent living" (living "bad" and trying to produce "good") using illustrations of two types of trees (6:43) and of various types of fruit-bearing plants (figs, grapes) (6:44). "Good" only comes from "good." Third, He warned against "spiritual presumption" (6:46) using the illustration of houses: those "founded well" last, but those "founded poorly" do not (6:47-49). Disciples must not presume that a superficial relationship with Jesus will stand in times of distress.

F. "Who Is Jesus?" His Identity Revealed (7:1–8:3)

In the next section Luke drew together several events and encounters along with examples of Jesus' teaching to address the question of Jesus' identity further. Luke contrasted those who identified Jesus with those who failed to do so. The action took place in **Capernaum** (7:1).

1. Jesus Healed the Centurion's Servant (7:1-10) (see also the comments on Mt 8:5-13)

7:1-10. In this account of a healing the unexpected element is the centurion himself. This man—a Gentile (likely a Roman) was a centurion—a leader of soldiers (7:8a). A centurion had to be a tough, fair, and authoritative figure. This particular centurion was depicted as a loving master who was concerned about his sick slave (7:2), and was a **worthy** man, esteemed by the Jewish people under his jurisdiction (7:4), a man civil—even cordial—to the Jewish nation (**he**

loves our nation 7:5a), and a generous man (he **built us our synagogue** 7:5b). There is possibly an implicit fulfillment of Gn 12:3 here. Because the soldier was kind to the Jewish people, he himself received a blessing from the Lord. Furthermore, even though he apparently had never seen but had only heard of Jesus, he sent for Him to **come and save the life of his slave** (Lk 7:3b). Despite his own authority, the centurion was deferential, not considering himself worthy of a personal visit from the Master (7:6, 7). He displayed a great faith and an understanding of Jesus' authority and power (7:8b). For this he not only received an answer to his request—His servant was healed (7:10)—but Jesus commended him for his faith (7:9). Jesus is thus seen as One with authority, compassion, and power to heal—all qualities of the Messiah (cf. Is 61:1; cf. Lk 7:18-23).

2. Jesus Healed a Widow's Son (7:11-17)

7:11-17. As Jesus and His disciples traveled to a village called Nain (with a large crowd in tow, 7:11) they encountered another large crowd (7:12c) accompanying a funeral already underway (7:12a). The circumstances were doubly tragic—the deceased was the only son of a widow (7:12b). This meant the widow was completely destitute—no husband and no son meant no foreseeable means of support. Looking beyond the crowds, the sorrowful event, and the hopelessness of the circumstances, Jesus **saw her**. He **felt compassion for her**, and He spoke to her (7:13a)—no doubt this was a breach in the decorum of the sad situation. But His words were even more out of keeping with the event—He **said to her, Do not weep** (lit., "stop weeping" 7:13b). Then He stopped the procession altogether (7:14a). Jesus had happened upon this funeral, and He took the initiative to reverse the entire circumstance. He addressed the young man and commanded him to **arise** (7:14b). When Jesus returned the young man back to his mother, the crowd reacted with fear and praise. The estimate of the crowd was not complete—this man was not merely a **great prophet** through whom God had **visited His people** (7:16)—He was fully divine, the Son of God, the One with authority and power to raise the dead.

3. Three Episodes Concerning John the Baptist (7:18-35) (see also the comments on Mt 11:2-19)

The last reference to John the Baptist was in 3:20, which notes that Herod (Antipas) had "locked John up in prison." Apparently, from prison John had heard about Jesus' ministry—**about all these things** (7:18).

a. John's Questions about Jesus Are Asked and Answered (7:18-23)

7:18-23. These questions do not necessarily indicate that John was having a "crisis of faith" or had begun to doubt Jesus. He did have questions, and he logically and properly sent his disciples to Jesus to get the answers. It seems that while he was sitting in prison John wanted reassurance. (Perhaps he was thinking of the prophecy that the Messiah would "set the captives free"; Is 61:1), and he knew Jesus was the only One who could do it. As the disciples of John arrived at the place where Jesus was, it just so happened that **At that very time** (Lk 7:21a) Jesus was healing people and casting out demons. Jesus told John's disciples to report what they witnessed (7:22a) (e.g., **the BLIND RECEIVE SIGHT**, cf. Lk 4:18 and Is 61:1; 29:18; **the lame walk**, cf. Lk 5:17-26 and Is 35:6; diseases are cured Lk 5:12-16; 17:11-19 and 2Kg 5:1-19; **the deaf hear** Lk 11:14 and Is 29:18; 35:5; 42:18; **the POOR HAVE THE GOSPEL PREACHED TO THEM**, cf. Lk 4:18 and Is 35:5; 61:1. Note that Jesus did not mention the OT Scripture (Is 61:1) about setting the captives free at this juncture!). These were things the Messiah was expected to do and proved He was indeed **the Expected One** (Lk 7:19, 20).

b. Jesus' Praise of John (7:24-30) (see also the comments on Mt 11:7-15)

7:24-30. Jesus used this occasion to offer some words in praise of John. Jesus asked the crowds three versions of the rhetorical question, **What did you go out into the wilderness to see?** (7:24, 25, 26). A **reed shaken by the wind** was something pliable and bendable—John was not fickle or vacillating. A **man dressed in soft clothing** was someone refined who lived in comfort in **royal palaces** (7:25b)—John was tough and lived in the desert. So the answer to the first two questions was "No!" But John was a **prophet** and **more than a prophet** (7:26)—he was the forerunner to the Messiah (7:27). John was great because of his humility (cf. Jn 3:30) and because he fulfilled his mission for the Messiah—he pointed men and women to Messiah Jesus. Jesus' estimate of John was well received by the common folk (7:29) but rejected by the religious leadership (7:30).

c. Jesus' Rebuke of that Generation (7:31-35) (see also the comments on Mt 11:16-19)

7:31-35. Jesus' rebuke was directed at the religious leadership that had rejected John (7:31). His point was that neither John's asceticism and stern message of the need for repentance nor Jesus' message of healing and hope (His welcoming of sinners) was satisfactory to the self-appointed arbiters of "taste" and "wisdom." The leaders were like "petulant children" who refused to play when John and Jesus did not play what they wanted (cf. Liefeld, "Luke," 8:901).

4. Jesus: At Dinner and Anointed; Parable of the Two Debtors (7:36-50)

7:36-39. The contrast between the common Jewish people who accepted Jesus and the leadership who rejected Him was starkly drawn in an encounter between Jesus and **one of the Pharisees** (7:36a). Jesus had accepted an invitation to dine with a Pharisee, and while He was eating (**reclined at the table** 7:36b) a woman, identified only as **a sinner** (7:37a), came to the house. It was not unusual to have uninvited guests standing at the perimeter of the banquet table, perhaps seeking to be noticed or to be offered some portions of the dinner. This woman, however, had come with a bottle of perfumed oil (7:37b) with only one purpose: to honor Jesus. Luke described her movements in meticulous detail to highlight the effect on the dinner party. Her actions of devotion (**weeping**—lit., "bursting into tears"—and positioned at His feet, **wiping** His feet with her hair, **kissing His feet and anointing them with the perfume** 7:38) were heedless of all propriety—they were actions of uninhibited affection toward Jesus. The Pharisee's reaction was one of judgmental disgust. He (and no doubt others) thought to himself (7:39a) that if Jesus were indeed a prophet he would know what sort of woman (**she is a sinner**) was touching Him (7:39b) and that He would have refused her devotion and put a stop to this display.

7:40-50. Jesus responded to this unexpressed criticism with a parable, virtually asking the Pharisee, named **Simon**, permission to tell it (7:40). The parable involved **a moneylender** with **two debtors** (7:41a) One owed a considerable sum—a debt it might have taken years to pay back; the other owed a lesser some—a debt that might have taken weeks to pay back (7:41b). Graciously the lender forgave both men. Jesus' question to Simon was **which of them will love him more**? (7:42). When Simon had given the obviously correct answer—the one forgiven more loved more (7:43)—Jesus applied the parable to the current situation. Jesus acknowledged that the woman had shown great love toward Him while Simon had shown little respect for Him (7:44-46). She had been extravagant in her love—Simon had failed even at common courtesies. Her devotion was an evidence of her love, which was the outworking of her gratitude for being forgiven. When Jesus said to her, **Your sins have been forgiven** (7:48), He was not suggesting she had earned forgiveness by her actions, but that her actions were the loving evidence that she had been forgiven. To the consternation of the dinner party (7:49), Jesus pronounced forgiveness and confirmed her salvation (7:50).

5. Jesus Is Ministered to by Certain Women (8:1-3)

8:1-3. Jesus' mission involved much traveling and preaching (8:1a, b) (cf. Lk 4:18; Is 61:1), being diligent in His calling and assisted by the Twelve (Lk 8:1c). In all of this activity, several women supported Him (8:2-3). Women were held in rather low esteem in that day, but Jesus loved and sought out those who were outcast and downtrodden by the culture. Although He did not appoint women to positions of leadership or as His apostles, He treated women with respect and esteem, and they showed their appreciation by supporting His mission (8:3c).

G. Jesus' Teaching in Parables (8:4-21)

8:4-21. In Luke's gospel these two parables have specific application to the teaching of Jesus. Those who acknowledge and receive Him are the good soil—they "see and understand," and they "take care how they listen" to Him.

1. Parable of the Soils (8:4-15) (see also the comments on Mt 13:1-23)

8:4-10. The parable is divided into three sections: the parable itself (8:4-8); the disciples' question about Jesus' reason for teaching in parables (8:9-10); and the explanation of the parable (8:11-15). The parable itself is straightforward. A sower sowing seed would have been a common sight to Jesus' hearers (8:5a). Some seed fell **beside the road** (8:5b) on the edges of the footpaths where it was **trampled under foot** (8:5c), hence, ruined. This seed would also be exposed and therefore easily picked off by the **birds of the air** (8:5d). Some seed was sown (unknowingly by the sower) **on rocky soil** (8:6a) that was merely a thin layer of dirt over bedrock. Such soil had no depth to retain water, and plants that germinated there would perish from lack of **moisture** (8:6b). Some seed fell **among the thorns** (8:7a). This was soil that had (again, unbeknownst to the sower) the seeds of weeds already mixed into it. Since the weeds were more aggressive they **grew up** with the good seed but eventually **choked it out** (8:7b). Finally, some seed **fell into the good soil** (8:8a); this seed thrived and **produced a crop** (8:8b)—the only seed to do so—and it was an abundant crop.

Jesus admonished His hearers to really listen to His teaching—**He who has ears to hear, let him hear** (8:8c). This may have prompted the disciples' twofold question: One, what did the parable mean? (the answer was to come in the final section), and two, (implied) why did Jesus speak in parables? (cf. Mt 13:10-17). Jesus answered in effect that His parables made it possible for the "fruitful hearted" (cf. Lk 8:8) and the "illuminated heart" (cf. 8:16) to really hear and understand while making it impossible for the "hard hearted," the "distracted heart" (cf. 8:5-7), and the "careless heart (cf. 8:18) to "see, hear, or **understand**."

8:11-15. In His explanation of the parable Jesus made it clear that the seed was **the word of God** (8:11). The various soils represented various types of human hearts. In the Bible the "heart" is understood as the seat of human thinking as well as emotions (cf. Jr 17:9-10; Mt 9:4; 15:18). The problem with the first type of soil/heart was its hardness, which left it vulnerable to the influences and deceptions of Satan (Lk 8:12). The problem with the second type of soil/heart was that these people liked what they heard in the Word and responded to it for a time. However, they were shallow and there was no depth of root, so trials and temptations caused them to wither. The third type of soil/heart was "mixed" with **worries and riches and pleasures of this life** (8:14b). Whereas the demise of the seed in the case of the second soil/heart was somewhat sudden, the failure here was gradual. The good seed was **choked** out by **worries**—the cares of everyday life; **riches**—the goods of this life; and **pleasures**—not just sensuous pleasures, but the amusements of this mundane and temporal world. It was not necessarily the "big issues" that choked out the good seed but the life of the "everyday" that slowly overtook the heart and left no room for the more serious issues—eternal and spiritual matters—that had to do with Christ and sin and salvation. Only one type of soil/heart (8:15a) was a **good heart** (8:15b), and only such hearts **hold** [the Word] **fast, and bear fruit with perseverance** (8:15c). The bearing of fruit is the marker of the good soil and the evidence of genuine life (see also the comments on Mt 13:18-23).

2. Parable of the Lamp (8:16-18)

8:16-18. Using the metaphor of a lamp, Jesus revealed three qualities of His teaching: (1) it was itself fully visible and illuminating (of the heart/soil) (8:16), (2) it exposed what was hidden (it will expose what sort of "soil" one's heart is) (8:17), (3) it is to be heeded (8:18).

3. Jesus' True Family (8:19-21) (see also the comments on Mt 12:46-50)

8:19-21. Luke briefly noted that Jesus' family, while not neglected, was not favored over others. Rather, He gave His preference and attention to those who heard and recognized **the word of God** (8:21) in His teaching and obeyed it.

H. Jesus: the Master (8:22-56)

In the next section Luke depicted Jesus as the Master, highlighting His power and authority. Jesus demonstrated His power over nature in the stilling of the storm (8:22-25); His power over the supernatural when He cast the demons out of the Gerasene demoniac (8:26-39); His power over disease in the healing of the woman with the hemorrhage (8:43-48); and His power over death in raising Jarius's daughter (8:40-42, 49-56). The theme of "fear" was prominent in these events. Jesus inspired "fear" when He displayed His power over the natural (8:25) and supernatural (8:37). He quelled "fear" with His healing power (8:47, 50).

1. Jesus Stilled the Storm (8:22-25) (see also the comments on Mt 8:23-27)

8:22-25. Jesus and the disciples often moved from place to place in small boats, which had been familiar to them as fishermen. The scene depicted here was mundane and commonplace (8:22), and the sailing was serene enough that Jesus quickly **fell asleep** (8:23a). Soon, however (as was not uncommon on the lake), a **fierce gale** arose (8:23b), and the boat was in danger of capsizing (8:23c). Amazingly, Jesus was still asleep and these experienced—but terrified—fishermen frantically awakened Him (8:24a). Their panicky address to Him—**Master, Master** (8:24b)—was one that Luke probably intentionally recorded to highlight the reality of His person, a reality He was about to prove. He was indeed the Master! Upon rising He **rebuked the wind and the surging waves** (8:24c), and they simply **stopped** (8:24d). The unnatural calm and His gentle rebuke to them—**Where is your faith?** (8:25a)—unnerved them more than the natural wind and waves. They were **fearful and amazed** (8:25b). While their own question was for them a genuine one (8:25c), in Luke's account it was rhetorical—He was the Master, and the Lord.

2. Jesus Cast Demons Out of a Man and Into Swine (8:26-39) (see also the comments on Mt 8:28-34)

8:26-39. The eventful boat ride ended at a place Luke identified as **the country of the Gerasenes** (8:26). The exact location is disputed. Likely, this was in the Decapolis, a community of 10 Roman cities, nine of which were on the eastern side of the Jordan River. That this was a Gentile area explains the presence of the swineherds who appear later in the narrative. There Jesus and the disciples immediately encountered a man whose spiritual condition was dire—**possessed with demons**, whose physical condition was destitute (he had no clothes), and whose social condition left him isolated—no house, living **in the tombs** (8:27). Upon seeing Jesus, the man cried out, addressing Jesus in terms that indicated His divine Sonship and majesty, and begging Jesus not to **torment** him (8:28). These statements were actually the voices of the demons, who had abused the man for some time (8:29). The man was actually possessed by many demons—**Legion** (8:30). Apparently not wanting to be disembodied—a prelude to ultimate punishment in the **abyss** (8:31)—but nevertheless knowing they were powerless to resist His command to leave the man (8:29), the demons requested to be cast into a herd of **swine** (8:32a). When Jesus had permitted it (8:32b) they entered the swine, and the maddened animals rushed into the lake and drowned (8:33). News of the event spread rapidly (8:34). Rather than marveling at the liberation and restoration of the now demon-delivered man (8:36), whom they surely all knew well (8:35b), the residents were fearful and requested that Jesus **leave** their country (8:37). These people were among the many who "saw but did not see, nor did they understand." In one last scene, Luke described how the demon-delivered man requested to go with Jesus (8:38). He was denied, but he was given the task of spreading the message of the **great things** God had done for him (8:39). It was important that a witness to the Lord remain even in this country that had turned Jesus away.

3. Jesus Healed Woman with Hemorrhages; Raised Little Girl from the Dead (8:40-56) (see also the comments on Mt 9:18-26)

8:40-42. In the next account Luke actually recorded two healings—one "unintentional" and one plainly "intentional." Upon His return to Capernaum Jesus was welcomed (in contrast to the Gerasenes, 8:37) and was confronted by a man named Jairus (8:41a), **an official of the synagogue** (8:41b) and the father of an only **daughter**, who was 12 years old and dying (8:42a). He was desperate to have Jesus come and heal her (8:41c). Jesus agreed to this request, but the ever-present crowds blocked His progress on the way (8:42c).

8:43-48. In this throng was a woman who had been hemorrhaging for 12 years (the exact age of the dying little girl) (8:43), leaving her weak and ritually unclean (cf. Lv 15:19-25; see also Ezk 36:17; CD 4.12-5:17; 11QTemple 48:15-17; Josephus, *War* 5.227; *m. Nidda*; *m. Zabim* 4:1). Luke recorded that she **could not be healed** (8:43d; Mark added that she had spent all her money on physicians who not only did not help her but actually made things worse, Mk 5:26—a detail Dr. Luke left out!). Her plan was to touch His garment (cf. Mt 9:21) believing that in doing so she would be cured. This was a bold act—she risked rejection or worse. Her act could be considered an assault because she was unclean, and might render Him and others unclean. Nevertheless, she surreptitiously **came up behind** (Lk 8:44a) and without His notice **touched the fringe of His cloak** (8:44b). The fringe may have been the tassels worn on the four corners of one's garments to remind a person of the law (Nm 15:38-41; Dt 22:12). Luke wanted his readers to understand that there was no natural way Jesus could have perceived this woman's act. She was healed **immediately** (Lk 8:44c). Just as immediately, Jesus was aware that He had been touched, not just by the press of the crowd (8:45), but in such a way that healing **power had gone out** of Him (8:46b). His insistence, **Someone did touch Me** (8:46a), convinced the woman to admit what she had done (8:47a). In her fear (and perhaps shame) she confessed her act, explained why she had done it (8:47b), and reported her healing (8:47c). By compelling her to make a public confession Jesus actually completed her restoration for now she could freely associate with her fellows who would know that her uncleanness was ended. Jesus' blessing—the only place where He addressed anyone as **Daughter** (8:48)—assured her that because her faith in Him was genuine, her healing by Him was complete.

8:49-56. During this time Jarius had been waiting for Jesus to come to his house to heal his daughter. However, the sad report arrived that the daughter had died (8:49). Before Jarius could react to the news he was reassured and encouraged by Jesus—**Do not be afraid . . . only believe, and she will be made well** (8:50). While the delay with the woman may have annoyed Jarius, now her healing by Jesus was an encouragement to him. Jesus' parting words to her about faith and healing were exactly what Jarius needed at that moment—faith (believe) in Jesus leads to being "made well." Although Jesus was a "passive participant" in the healing of the woman, here He took control. "The timing may not have been what Jarius desired, but the events were still in [Jesus'] control" (Bock, *Luke*, 806). Jesus took only His inner circle of disciples—Peter, James, and John (those who were privileged to see the special demonstrations of His power, who would later understand what this power meant) and the girl's parents into the room (8:51). He rebuked the "professional mourners" (8:52a) and commanded them to **Stop weeping** (8:52b) as He explained that she was not dead but only sleeping (8:52c). The "laughter" of this crowd showed their disingenuousness—they were insincere mourners at best. Jesus tenderly took the child's hand and spoke softly to her—**Child arise!** (8:54). Jesus had been close to uncleanness when the woman touched Him. Now He deliberately touched a dead body, but His touch cleansed and healed. Again the healing was "immediate"—**her spirit returned** (8:55a; cf. 1Kg 17:21-22). She had indeed died, and then she **got up immediately** (Lk 8:55a). In a touch of realism, Luke recorded Jesus' instructions that she should be given something to eat (8:55b). When Jesus returned the girl to her amazed—and no doubt grateful—parents, He instructed them not to spread the news of this event around (8:56). Perhaps this was to help avoid the sensationalism that might have led the people in a frenzy to make Him king prematurely.

I. Jesus' Disciples (9:1-62)

In the next several sections the focus in Luke's account is on the disciples and issues of discipleship.

1. Mission of the Twelve: A Mission for Disciples (9:1-10a) (see also the comments on Mt 10:1-18)

9:1-5. Although there are noticeable differences between Luke's accounts and those of Matthew (cf. Mt 10:1-14; 14:1-14) and Mark (cf. Mk 6:7-16; 30-34), none of these discrepancies is serious enough to doubt the basic credibility of the narrative. Jesus clearly headed this mission: (1) He called, empowered, and authorized it (Lk 9:1); (2) He set the task—to cast out demons, to heal, and to preach (9:1b-2); (3) He controlled the message—**proclaim the kingdom** (9:2); (4) He delimited the provisions for the mission (9:3)—this was to be no pleasure trip but a working journey—they were to travel light; (5) He instructed them on the procedures of the mission (9:4)—they were not to seek their own comfort or be concerned about their own popularity—they were not to play favorites for personal favors; (6) He dictated the terms of the mission (9:5)—they were not to stop and debate the message—they were not to seek revenge for petty slights, but they were to keep moving.

9:6-10a. The disciples' responsibility was to follow Jesus' orders. They were obedient and so fulfilled the mission (9:6). Herod was **perplexed** (9:7b) by the mission, indicating that it was having an impact. Luke recorded how Herod reacted to the events—**all that was happening** (9:7a). The strange rumors about Jesus that Herod heard were apparently also heard by the disciples (9:8; cf. 9:19), indicating that they were widely known. These rumors—especially those that suggested that John had risen from the dead—were particularly disconcerting to Herod, for he had had John beheaded and now, it seemed, another like him had already come in his place (9:9a). The note that Herod **kept trying to see Him** (9:9b) was an ominous foreshadowing of Jesus' trial before Herod (cf. 23:8-12). Finally, the disciples were successful in this mission (9:10a). When they returned the notoriety of their mission created a large interest in Jesus Himself.

2. A Lesson for Disciples: Feeding Five Thousand (9:10b-17) (see also the comments on Mt 14:13-21)

9:10b-17. The interest created by the mission of the Twelve resulted in large crowds following Jesus and the disciples, even as far as **Bethsaida** (9:10b). Jesus welcomed them, continuing to do as He had been doing—teach and heal (9:11). The presence of the crowd set the stage for an opportunity for Jesus to challenge His disciples to rest in their confidence in Him. Late in the day it became obvious that the crowds needed to be dispersed so they could find food and shelter (9:12). When the disciples urged Jesus to send the crowds away—an eminently practical suggestion—Jesus challenged the disciples: **you give them something to eat** (9:13).

The disciples, looking to their own resources, quite rightly observed that the few provisions they could muster were woefully inadequate (9:13). Jesus did not dispute this conclusion but instructed the disciples to have the crowd sit down in an orderly fashion (9:14), and they did so (9:15). This crowd numbering **about five thousand men** meant there were many thousands more counting women and children. Luke managed to build tension into his narrative by relating the details of Jesus' deliberate actions. He **took** the few provisions, looked up to heaven, blessed them, and broke them. He **kept giving** them—the ongoing action is the climax—to the disciples (9:16). It was the disciples who distributed the provisions, just as Jesus had commanded them, to the people. The lesson, intended primarily for the disciples, was, "Do not look to your own resources but look to and trust in Jesus' ability to use whatever resources you have to meet the needs of others" (see Stein, *Luke*, 272). The full satisfaction of the people and the excess abundance were residual reminders of Jesus' messianic power (cf. Ps 105:40; Jl 2:26).

3. A Disciple's Confession (9:18-22) (see also the comments on Mt 16:13-20)

9:18-20. In Luke's account this great confession of Peter happened during (or just after) a time of prayer (9:18). Jesus asked a preliminary question to set up the question He really wanted to ask: **Who do the people say that I am?** (9:18b). Once again (as Herod had learned, see 9:7-10) the rumors about Jesus ranged from the ludicrous (**John the Baptist**) to the hopeful (**Elijah**; this is understandable in the light of the prophecy of Mal 4:5) to the improbable (**one of the prophets** returned to life) (Lk 9:19). These answers do indicate that the people recognized in Jesus a "transcendent presence," but they were wide of the mark, as the disciples knew. Jesus' direct question, **But who do you** (emphatically spoken) **say that I am?** (9:20a) received a direct and swift answer from Peter—**The Christ of God** (9:20b). Luke intended this confession to be taken at face value as the conclusion of one—a close and trusted disciple—who was in a position to know whereof he spoke. Jesus was indeed the Christ. The confusion of the people would explain to Theophilus and to Luke's readers why so many who saw Jesus did not believe in Him while the disciples were so confident in their convictions about Him. They were in the place to know (and the account of the transfiguration that follows reinforces that point).

9:21-22. Surprisingly, Jesus immediately instructed the disciples **not to tell this to anyone** (9:21). The reason for this may have been that such information could be badly used either by Jesus' friends or His enemies, but the main reason for this instruction is explained in the next verse. If the disciples were to announce the Messiah had come, the people may have anticipated the political, warrior Messiah and have obstructed or misunderstood Jesus' ministry as the suffering servant.

It was at this crucial point Jesus made the first of several predictions of His passion (9:22; cf. 9:44-45). He told the disciples that He **must suffer many things** (9:22a). "He *must* suffer. Suffering for Him was no accident, but a compelling divine necessity. The cross was His vocation" (Leon Morris, *The Gospel According to Luke*, TNTC [Grand Rapids, MI: Eerdmans, 1974], 169), and He must not be prevented from accomplishing the work there—the very work He had come to do.

4. On Discipleship: Definition, Motivation, and Expectation of a True Disciple (9:23-27) (see also the comments on Mt 16:24-27)

9:23. These episodes about discipleship were placed around other events in the life of Christ, in which Jesus was directing more and more of His ministry toward the disciples. In light of the impending turn toward Jerusalem (cf. 9:51) and then just after that turn, Jesus took the opportunity to instruct His disciples (9:23a) on the meaning of following Him.

The definition of a true disciple may be understood in four terms: the disciple must have *desire*—**If anyone wishes to come after Me** (9:23b), must practice *denial*—**he must deny himself** (9:23c), must show *dedication*—**and take up his cross** (an act of submission; "the fundamental idea is of submission to another"; Bock, *Luke*, 853) **daily** (9:23d), and must accept *direction*—**and follow Me** (9:23e). The basic requirement of a disciple is to "follow Jesus."

9:24-26. The motivation of a true disciple can be found in three principles: (1) the principle of the reversal of ultimate commitments—disciples live not for their own sakes but Christ's—**for My sake** (9:24); (2) the principle of the apparently disproportionate exchange—"This verse is essentially a proverb" (Stein, *Luke*, 279)—a disciple gives up the world (if necessary) for Christ (9:25); (3) the principle of reciprocal repudiation—a disciple knows that being ashamed of Christ will bring shame by Christ—that is, Christ **will be ashamed of him** at Christ's return (such a person will prove not to be a true disciple and be lost) (9:26). True discipleship requires utter selfless commitment to Christ, repudiation of the world for Christ, and unflagging loyalty to Christ.

9:27. The expectation of a true disciple is life in Christ. When Jesus said there were some who would **not taste death** (9:27) He had in mind those disciples who were about to witness the transfiguration. (For more on the theme of discipleship see 9:57-62.)

5. Transfiguration: An Event and Word to Assure the Disciples (9:28-36) (see also the comments on Mt 17:1-8)

The transfiguration might well be considered the Father's answer to the question Jesus had posed to the disciples ("But who do you say that I am?" cf. 9:20). The Father's answer was the best informed and most precise of all! The event and the confirmation of Jesus' identity were intended to fortify the disciples' convictions about Jesus. This event was also meant to give encouragement to Jesus just as a major transition point in His ministry—the "journey to Jerusalem" (cf. 9:51)—was about to begin.

9:28-29a. Luke recorded that the events took place **eight days after** the events of Peter's confession and Jesus' instruction following that dramatic declaration (9:28). The apparent discrepancy with Mark (Mk 9:2, "six days") was due to different ways of reckoning days. Perhaps Mark counted only the days "in between" the events and Luke counted those days but also the day of Peter's confession and the day on which the transfiguration occurred. The point of the note (which is actually only to say "about eight days," NIV) is to tie Peter's confession (Lk 9:20) to the transfiguration (cf. Stein, *Luke*, 283). For this occasion Jesus took Peter, James, and John (as He had done at the home of Jarius, cf. 8:51). Their part was to observe and record this transcendent event (cf. 2Pt 1:16-18). There was no indication of which mountain was chosen for this happening. The traditional site of Mt. Tabor is unlikely because of its distance from the events at Caesarea Philippi. Mt. Hermon is more likely since it was a tall mountain and close to Caesarea Philippi. The initial reason for this interlude was prayer (Lk 9:28b-29a).

9:29b-31. Luke omitted the word "transfigured" (cf. Mt 17:2; Mk 9:2) and simply, if enigmatically, described the alteration in Jesus' appearance—**His face became different** (lit., "other") and **His clothing became white and gleaming** (Lk 9:29). The image was reminiscent of Moses' face as described in Ex 34:29-35: "Moses' face shone." The term **gleaming** appears only here in the NT and has the idea of "emitting light," probably indicating that it was Jesus' body that was "shining" and not a change in the clothing. The whole scene was one of otherworldly, transcendent, "Majestic" (cf. 2Pt 1:17) glory. Instantly, (**behold**) two attendants appeared with Jesus, identified as **Moses and Elijah** (Lk 9:30b). Likely these two represented the Law and the Prophets—indicating that Jesus was the continuation of the salvation-historical program revealed in the OT. That they came to His transfiguration demonstrated His superiority over them—He was the fulfillment of what they had prophesied. Their conversation focused on His coming Passion—His death, burial and resurrection—to which Luke cryptically referred as **His departure** ("exodus" 9:31b) that He would soon **accomplish at Jerusalem** (9:31c). "Fulfillment is the key theme of this verse. The events discussed are part of God's plan, which will come to pass" (Bock, *Luke*, 869).

9:32-33. At this time the earthly observers, **Peter and his companions** (9:32a), who had been asleep (9:32b), were aroused and became **fully awake** (9:32c). They saw Jesus' glory and then two men (9:32d). They had been brought to the mountain for this event, and they had nearly missed it. The overwhelming splendor of the event and the heady privilege of seeing Moses and Elijah prompted Peter to speak—but he did so without thinking (**not realizing what he was saying**, 9:33c). His first expression was not inappropriate even if it was rather feeble: **Master, it is good for us to be here** (9:33a). Surely this was one of the most memorable events of Peter's life, and it was well beyond "good." His proposal to build three booths (tabernacles, 9:33b) was singularly inappropriate for three reasons: one, by suggesting **three tabernacles** he was essentially putting Moses and Elijah on par with Jesus (ignoring that only Jesus was transfigured); two, the suggestion of tabernacles indicated that Peter wanted to make the "mountaintop moment" last (but such moments are given not to divert one from service but to prepare one for service; and to "stay on the mountain" would make an end out of a means); three, this was not the fulfillment of the OT prophetic word—this was not the kingdom, and this was not the end of Jesus' sojourn.

9:34-35. Before Peter could finish his inappropriate suggestions a heavenly interruption set him right. First, **a cloud** appeared (9:34). The suddenness of the cloud's appearance and the reaction of Peter and his companions signified that this was no ordinary cloud. It was none other than the outward manifestation of the divine presence (cf. Ex 16:10; 19:9; 1Kg 8:10-11). The **voice** that **came** from the cloud (Lk 9:35a) was unmistakably that of God the Father (since He identified Jesus as **My Son**, 9:35b). His designation of Jesus was intended to eliminate all speculation and provide rock-solid assurance of His person—He is **My Chosen One** (9:35c). Here the Father Himself confirmed what Mary and Zacharias had testified, what Jesus had claimed in the synagogue in Nazareth, and what Peter himself had so recently confessed: Jesus is the Promised One, the Messiah, and the Son of God. The Father's final command—**listen to Him!** (9:35d) had a double meaning: first, "Peter, stop talking and listen!" and in a wider sense, "Listen to the Word of Jesus." There is probably a subtle allusion here to Dt 18:15. Jesus is the prophet like Moses, the prophet regarding whom God through Moses commanded, "You shall listen to him" (Dt 18:15c; cf. also Ac 3:22 which indicates that Jesus was the fulfillment of this prophecy).

9:36. The dramatic scene ended with Jesus standing alone (9:36a). The mysterious nature of this event—understanding it would only be possible after the Passion of Jesus—caused them to keep **silent** about it (9:36b) for the time being.

6. Healing a Demon-Possessed Son: A Test for Disciples (9:37-42) (see also the comments on Mt 17:14-20)

9:37-40. Jesus had no sooner descended from the Mount of Transfiguration (9:37a) than He was confronted with several situations that demonstrated the disciples' lack of faith, their slowness to learn, their pride, and their intolerance. The first situation involved a father and his **boy** possessed by a demon **(a spirit seizes him)** (9:38, 39). The picture Luke drew was chaotic. A large crowd (9:37b), apparently attempting to gain Jesus' attention, was hindering a distraught father from making his appeal to Jesus. He had to shout over the crowd (9:38a), "begging" Jesus to help (9:38b), and he was describing his son's sorry condition (9:39). Furthermore, he was lamenting the disciples' failure to deal with the demon (9:40).

9:41-42. Jesus expressed His exasperation as an aside, that is, it was addressed to no one in particular and to the entire group in general: **You unbelieving and perverted generation** (9:41a). Having just come from the wonderful experience on the mountain to this chaos was a trial to Him, and He longed to be finished with His earthly mission—**how long shall I be with you and put up with you?** (9:41b). No sense of personal pettiness was expressed, but there was, no doubt, exasperation with His disciples' failure to help the man, weariness with His spiritual opposition (the demons), and grief for the plight of the man and his son. Nevertheless, He was instantly ready to serve—**Bring your son here** (9:41c). Jesus' power was evident in His rebuke of the demon (an obviously powerful demon by the demonstration that he made before he left the boy, 9:42a). Jesus showed His compassion by the way He gave the son back to the father (9:42b).

7. Four Failures of Jesus' Disciples (9:43-56) (see also the comments on Mt 17:22-23)

9:43-45. The effect of the exorcism on the crowd—amazement (9:43a) and marveling—(9:43b) seemed to have little effect on Jesus, who turned His attention to the disciples (9:43c). In four brief scenes Luke recorded failures of Jesus' disciples. First, even when He tried to get them to pay attention—**Let these words sink into your ears** (9:44a)—offering yet another prediction of His coming Passion (9:44; cf. 9:21-22), they failed to understand. In this instance, however, Luke recorded that **it was concealed from them** (9:45). This was a divine concealment. Had they understood what Jesus was telling them they may have lost all motivation, or they may have tried to take steps to prevent it. *After* all these things happened they would recall these predictions, and they would then understand that His death was no accident and He was always in control.

9:46-48. In the second of these four scenes of failure Luke recorded an argument between the disciples over **which of them might be the greatest** (9:46; see also the comments on Mt 18:1-5). Besides being particularly inappropriate right after Jesus had predicted His own suffering and death, their behavior displayed an appalling lack of humility and an unsavory exhibition of hubris. Jesus—**knowing** not just the content of the argument but **what they were thinking in their heart** (9:47a)—confronted this outrageousness by taking a **child** and standing him **by his side** (9:47b). His point here was not "disciples are to be as this child" but "disciples are to receive this child," that is, to serve and honor this child (9:48a). Jesus' point was that disciples must not be too proud and self-important to refuse to act as a "servant to a child." He concluded this lesson with the principle of reversal: the way to greatness in God's economy is to be the least important in this present economy (9:48b).

9:49-50. In the third scene of disciple failures Luke recorded that an indignant disciple, **John** (9:49a), reported to Jesus that someone (not of the immediate group) was casting out demons **in** [Jesus'] **name** (9:49b). With apparently no sense of irony that this unnamed individual was apparently able to accomplish what Jesus' own disciples had recently failed to do (cf. 9:40)—and that it was inherently a good thing to cast out demons, regardless of who was doing it—John informed Jesus, **we tried to prevent him** (9:49c), all because he was not one of them. The failure here was obvious. To stop the doing of good in order to preserve that work for the "right people" is not merely inefficient, it is misguided. Jesus corrected John and explained, **he who is not against you is for you** (9:50). If the ministry is good and right and true, the work should be encouraged not hindered, regardless of who gets the credit.

9:51-56. The fourth and final scene of disciple failure happened in Samaria. In this instance, as Jesus was beginning His journey to Jerusalem (9:51), He sent some of His disciples ahead to a village in Samaria **to make arrangements for Him** (9:52) to engage in ministry there. Jesus was on His way to Jerusalem, so the Samaritans (the longtime antagonists of the Jews) were not helpful, nor were they receptive to the idea of His visit (9:53). The first inclination of James and John for this affront was excessive retaliation, to say the least. They wanted to call down **fire . . . from heaven** (9:54). Jesus' rebuke was swift and pointed—"This is not the way His followers behave" (Morris, *Luke*, 179). This sort of retaliation was exactly the opposite of the spirit and intent of Jesus' mission. The lesson for these disciples was this: those who reject Christ are not the enemy. They are the mission field.

8. Three Failures of Discipleship (9:57-62)
(see also the comments on Mt 8:18-22)

9:57-62. These verses are addressed to potential disciples. In each instance the term "follow" is prominent. Three would-be disciples encountered Jesus. In the first encounter the would-be disciple made a rash commitment (9:57) but was reminded of the cost. Following Jesus meant having **nowhere to lay** one's head (9:58). Those who follow Jesus may not enjoy the comforts of home in this life. In the second encounter, the would-be disciple is called by Jesus—**Follow Me** (9:59a), but he revealed his misplaced priorities. The request for a delay to **bury my father** (9:59b) did not mean he needed to attend a funeral but that he needed to wait until his father died (perhaps to collect an inheritance), or perhaps to engage in a customarily protracted time of mourning. This explains Jesus' response (9:60a). He was not making a callous demand of a grieving son but calling on this man to forsake any potential personal benefit and to put eternal loyalties and commitments above all other—even family—loyalties and temporal commitments (9:60b). In the third encounter the would-be disciple apparently just wanted to **say goodbye** to his family (9:61b). Jesus knew, however, that were the man to go home the strength of his commitment to **follow** the **Lord** (9:61a) would weaken and that he would be drawn back by the bonds of family love. Using the image of a plowman, Jesus admonished this would-be disciple to see that a plowman **after putting his hand to the plow** cannot **look back** (9:61c) and make a straight furrow. So a disciple cannot be "looking back" (to his or her old life, old friends, old habits) and be committed to Christ.

V. Journey to Jerusalem (10:1–19:27)

A. More on Missions; More on Discipleship (10:1-24)

This section continues the emphasis on discipleship—emphasizing the requirements, meaning, and practice of discipleship.

1. The Mission of the Seventy (10:1-16)

10:1-16. The mission of the seventy was similar to that of the mission of the Twelve (see 9:1-6). (There is a discrepancy with this number in several important Gk. manuscripts. Some have "seventy" and others have "seventy-two." Either reading may be correct. There is no substantive difference for the meaning of the text with either reading).

Jesus was clearly in charge: He assembled the **seventy** (10:1), motivated them (10:2), and warned them of the dangers (10:3). As they were few in numbers their dependence on the **Lord of the harvest** (10:2b) was all the more acute. He instructed them to travel light for the journey (10:4), to seek peace with the people they met (10:5-6), not to seek personal advantages on the way (10:7), to accept whatever provisions were available (10:8), to offer their services freely and fully to all (10:9), and to eschew retaliation if rejected (10:10-11). They were to know that ultimate justice would befall their opponents (10:12), so they could leave the matter of judgment in the hands of the Lord. Jesus offered an aside to these instructions—a pronouncement of woe on the cities of Chorazin, Bethsaida (10:13), and Capernaum (10:15) for their lack of response to His ministry and message. It should have been a chilling warning of the inevitability of the judgment of the Lord—to which the cities of Sodom (10:12) and Tyre and Sidon (10:13) could attest. The time to heed the message of Jesus' messengers is immediate because they speak for Him (10:16). And those who speak for Jesus must not take rebuff personally—the rejecters are rejecting Christ (10:16). This mission was a foretaste of future gospel proclamation (cf. 24:46-48; Acts 1:8).

2. Two Lessons on Discipleship (10:17-24)

Those disciples involved in the mission were not mere spectators of Jesus' mission but participants—and they could expect the joys and blessings of being in His service.

a. Joys of Being a Disciple (10:17-20)

10:17-20. The seventy returned and reported their experiences **with joy** (10:17). They knew the joy of spiritual accomplishment (10:17a) since they had completed the task given to them. They knew the joy of spiritual victory (10:17b). Demons had apparently been cast out in the name of Jesus—**Your name** (10:17c). Jesus' response to this news is interesting, as He added a detail to their report of which they would have been unaware. While they were engaged in the mission Jesus saw **Satan fall from heaven** (10:18). The picture here is metaphorical: as the mission had spread, the influence of the enemy had diminished. "In that gospel triumph Satan had suffered a notable defeat" (Morris, *Luke*, 185). Furthermore, they had experienced the joy of spiritual protection and confidence (10:19). "The disciples are secure in God's hands" (Bock, *Luke*, 1008) (e.g., Dn 3:16-18); but mostly, they had come to a greater assurance of the joy of their own salvation (Lk 10:20).

b. Blessings of Being a "Knowing" Disciple (10:21-24)

10:21-24. In an expression of joy and praise that sprung from His deep relationship with **the Holy Spirit** (10:21a) Jesus turned to His **Father, Lord of heaven and earth** (10:21b) to praise Him for the gracious revelation of His plans and purposes—**these things** (10:21b). The Father had not given His revelation to the **wise and intelligent** (to such persons these things were **hidden**) but to **infants** (10:21c). Jesus rejoiced that His disciples "knew things." They "knew" about the Son (10:22); they "knew" about things that **many prophets and kings** (10:24) had wanted to know. This "knowing" had come to them by the Father because it pleased Him to do so (10:21d) and they were blessed in it (10:23).

B. A Lawyer with Questions; Parable of the Good Samaritan (10:25-37)

1. The Lawyer's Questions (10:25-29)

10:25-29. Luke provided no background for this exchange. Apparently Jesus was teaching in a public setting when **a lawyer** (10:25a) (a scribe schooled in the law of Moses) asked Jesus a question, attempting to find a flaw in Jesus' teaching (**put Him to the test**, 10:25a). While the question itself is a good one—**what shall I do to inherit eternal life?** (10:25b), clearly he "was thinking of some sort of salvation by works and had no understanding of divine grace" (Morris, *Luke*, 187). Jesus' question in response was not intended to be evasive—**What is written in the Law?** (10:26a)—but meant to limit the discussion so as to eliminate from the outset fruitless exchanges and debates involving human speculations (cf. Ti 3:9). In His next question—**How does it read to you?**—Jesus was not asking for the lawyer's own relativistic take on the law but was conducting a counter-test. There was a right and a wrong answer to this question. When the lawyer quoted Dt. 6:5 ("love the LORD your God") and Lv 19:18 ("love your neighbor as yourself") (both cited in Lk 10:27), Jesus acknowledged that he had **answered correctly** (10:28a). However, Jesus' quotation of Lv 18:5—**DO THIS AND YOU WILL LIVE** (Lk 10:28b)—brought home the devastating point that perfect obedience to the law was not possible. At this point the lawyer should have realized the inherent error of "works righteousness" implied in his opening question. The lawyer was not ready to give up and so **wishing to justify himself** (10:29a) he evasively asked another question—**And who is my neighbor?** (10:29b). The lawyer was attempting to "limit the commandment" so as to make it possible for him to obey it sufficiently enough to merit eternal life. **To justify** may carry the same sense of "justification" in Paul's writings since Luke was one of Paul's missionary companions and would be steeped in the apostle's theology. Jesus exposed the fallacy of this tactic, and He answered the lawyers' question in the parable of the Good Samaritan.

2. The Good Samaritan (10:30-37)

Several important features of this parable (mostly lost on those who are familiar with its traditional title, if not its specific contents) would have been "contrary to expectation" for the initial audience. The setting (on the road traveling away from Jerusalem to Jericho), the indifferent characters (a priest and a Levite), and especially the hero of the story—a Samaritan—were all contrary to the expectations of a Jewish audience. Such a morality tale would be expected to have the characters moving toward Jerusalem, the initial audience would have expected that the respected religious leaders would be the heroes and the despised Samaritan a scoundrel.

10:30-37. The scene Jesus drew was credible—the 17-mile road between Jerusalem and Jericho (10:30a) had a reputation as a dangerous road (Josephus, *Jewish War*, 4.8.3. §474)—and it was tragic. A man was set upon by **robbers** and beaten and left **half dead** (10:30c). The appearance **by chance** of **a priest** (10:31) offered a ray of hope into this awful scene, but alas the priest **passed by** the broken figure. Perhaps he had concluded that the man was already dead and did not want to risk ceremonial defilement. Likewise a **Levite** (one who assisted priests in the affairs of their ministry) passed by the man (10:32). Depicting these religious authorities as callous and unfeeling would no doubt have scandalized the audience. They would have bristled at the notion that these respected authorities could be so unsympathetic. However, the appearance of the **Samaritan**, cast in the role of hero would have perplexed Jesus' audience even more. The Samaritans and Jews despised each other (for the reasons for the hatred, see comments on John 4:4-6). Although the hatred ran both ways, Jewish people thought "such people were unclean and were to be avoided" (cf. Bock, *Luke*, 1031). "Jesus' introduction of the Samaritan was thus devastating" (Morris, *Luke*, 189-90). The actions of the Samaritan were compassionate, selfless, and costly (Lk 10:33-35). (None of the elements of this parable is to be taken allegorically.)

Jesus concluded with a final question to the lawyer, one that he could not evade (10:36). The point of Jesus' parable (in answer to the lawyer's question, 10:29c) was this: anyone in need is my neighbor, anyone who helps another in need is my neighbor, and anyone who helps me is my neighbor. Jesus indicated that one's neighbor was anyone in need that an individual could help, and that the help that should be rendered must be lavish and extensive if one wishes "to justify himself" before God as this lawyer did. But the man would not be capable of always fulfilling the law at the level required, and would not be able to "justify himself" by keeping it. When it comes to works righteousness, God is a maximalist with respect to obeying the law. A minimalist approach, as assumed by the lawyer, is unacceptable to Him. For this reason, because of humankind's inability to live the law, justification must be by grace through faith.

C. Martha and Mary (10:38-42)

10:38-42. A brief scene involving two sisters—Mary and Martha—provided the setting for another lesson on discipleship. Since Luke simply mentioned **a village**, he probably assumed the reader would be familiar enough with the story to know that the village was Bethany and that these two women were sisters to Lazarus (see Jn 11:1). Jesus arrived at the home of Martha, and she **welcomed Him into her home** (Lk 10:38). Her sister Mary took the opportunity to sit **at the Lord's feet** (10:39) to listen to His teaching, while Martha herself was busy with the **preparations** and formalities associated with the visit of an important person like Jesus (10:40a). Martha appealed to her guest Jesus, asking Him to direct Mary to assist her. The Lord's response was gentle (**Martha, Martha**—"My dear, dear Martha" 10:41a), but pointed. In a mild rebuke to Martha for her concern for **so many things** (10:41b), so many trivial things, Jesus informed Martha that Mary had chosen what was most important—listening to the Lord (10:42). Jesus' point was that the mere formalities of a relationship with Jesus—things like serving the Lord dinner, or meeting Him in a social setting—must never take the place of a vital and personal relationship with the Lord. Mere social contact (with Jesus or other disciples in church) cannot replace serious attention to His teaching.

D. Teaching on Prayer (11:1-13)

11:1-4. Luke included a brief section on prayer (parallel to the more extended teaching as recorded by Matthew (Mt 6:9-15 in the Sermon on the Mount; see the comments there). Jesus taught the importance of prayer by His own example (**Jesus was praying**, Lk 11:1). He also taught His disciples a model prayer (11:2a), indicating that this was not a prayer to be repeated but a paradigm to be followed when praying.

The prayer included: (1) address to the **Father** (11:2b)—to address the Father as such was prayer with assurance and respect; (2) petition for the Father's name to be **hallowed** (11:2c)—that His name would be honored; (3) petition for the **kingdom** to **come** (11:2d)—that the final rule and authority of God would be recognized and actualized on earth; (4) petition for **daily bread** (11:3)—that all the promised provisions of the Lord for physical life would be forthcoming (a confession of creaturely dependence); (5) petition for God to **forgive** (11:4a)—that the promised provisions for spiritual life would be forthcoming (a confession of spiritual dependence); (6) promise of forgiveness to others (11:4b; see also the comments on Mt 6:14-15 and 18:31-35)—a recognition of the need for humility before others; (7) petition for protection from temptation (11:4c)—a confession of spiritual reliance.

11:5-13. Jesus followed this instruction on prayer with a parable on prayer and a principle about prayer. The parable taught the need for persistence in prayer (11:5-8). The principle taught the need for confidence in prayer (11:9-13). The verbs in the rhythmic **ask** . . . **seek** . . . **knock** are present imperatives—"keep asking, keep seeking, keep knocking." The confidence of a believer is to be like that of a child with a loving parent. It is an honor to the parent that a child asks and expects to receive what is needed. God is honored by the requests of childlike believers. And of course, their needs are supplied through the means of prayer.

E. A Series of Conflicts (11:14-54)

While on the journey to Jerusalem Jesus was involved in a series of conflicts. Luke recorded these conflicts not only to illustrate Jesus' person but also to prove His power and authority. Ability and authority are often best demonstrated when they are challenged.

1. The Question of Jesus' Power (11:14-36)

In essence, in this episode Jesus was challenged as to the source of His power. Ludicrously, His opponents suggested He was in league with Satan.

a. Satan or God? (11:14-23) (see also the comments on Mt 12:22-37)

11:14-16. Here a miracle of healing and exorcism was not the climax but the setup for the ensuing conflict. A man was possessed by a demon, which caused him to be mute (Mt 12:22 indicates he was blind as well), and Jesus marvelously delivered him. While the crowds were **amazed** (Lk 11:14), the opposition was unimpressed. They charged Jesus with being empowered by **Beelzebul** (a derisive pun on Baal-zebub, a Canaanite god. Beelzebul means "lord of the flies," i.e., a pile of dung) (11:15). Jesus was challenged to prove Himself by producing a **sign from heaven** (11:16)—a rather ironic challenge in the light of the miracle that had just occurred.

11:17-23. Jesus' **knew their thoughts** (11:17a), that is, He knew and understood their motives for the charges and the challenges, and His response was devastatingly simple. He pointed out that their reasoning was illogical (11:17b-18), inconsistent (11:19), and based upon faulty perception (11:20). His short parable about **a strong man** (Satan, 11:21) and a **stronger** man (Jesus Himself, 11:22) employed simple and unassailable logic. The parable demonstrated that the struggle on the spiritual level of existence (Satan and his forces vs. the power of God, of Christ, and the Holy Spirit) is subject to the same rules and principles as temporal conflicts—the stronger force wins (cf. 1Jn 4:4). He concluded with a warning to the opposition (Lk 11:23) that effectively turned the tables on them. It was they, not He, who were in alliance with Satan, and the proof of their demonic alliance was their opposition to Jesus. Neutrality regarding Jesus Christ is impossible.

b. Four Explanations (11:24-36)

11:24-36. To prove that His power came from God and that He served God, Jesus gave four explanations about spiritual matters. First, the truth about unclean spirits is that they work together (11:24-26)—the lesson here is "partial reformation" is inadequate. Second, true joy does not come from merely acknowledging Jesus but from obeying God (11:27-28). Third, the truth about signs is that they can be missed (11:29-32)—the lesson here is that the "sign giver" is more important than the signs themselves. Fourth, the truth about light is that without a "clear eye" the light does no good (11:33-36)—the lesson here is one must have "open eyes" (faith) to "see" that Jesus is the power, the sign, and the light from God. Anyone who fails to "see the light" is thereby shown to be **full of darkness** (11:34; see also the comments on Mt 6:22-23).

2. Jesus, a Pharisee, and the Discourse of Woes (11:37-54)

11:37-38. Following the short discourse on the light, Luke recorded an instance of one who was "in darkness." A Pharisee had invited Jesus to lunch (11:37a), and in spite of the (possible) disingenuousness of this invitation, Jesus accepted (11:37b). It is doubtful that the Pharisee wanted to learn from Jesus—more likely he was looking for an opportunity to criticize Him; "Jesus was being watched" (Bock, *Luke*, 1111). Upon the instant of Jesus' reclining at the meal, the Pharisee observed an offense—Jesus had failed to be **ceremonially washed** for the meal according to the tradition of the Pharisees (11:38). This was not a washing for hygiene but a ceremonial ritual of external and self-congratulatory piety required by tradition but not by the law of Moses.

11:39-41. Jesus' rebuke to the Pharisee was as swift as the Pharisee's observation of Jesus' supposed offense. He first pointed out their failure, namely, their hypocrisy of overly scrupulous concern for the external cleansing of objects and utensils (11:39a) while demonstrating a complete disregard for their internal impurities (11:39b). He also pointed out the cause of their failure: He called them **foolish ones** (11:40a)—which in OT terms meant they were "blind to God" and had failed "to respond to God's will or his way" (Bock, *Luke*, 1113). He finally pointed to the cure for their failure: they needed to cultivate the inner virtues—love, generosity, humility. Only these would render them truly clean before God (11:41).

11:42-44. From this particular lesson to a single Pharisee, Jesus turned to a "Discourse of Woes" pronounced upon the Pharisees as a group (see also the comments on Mt 23:1-36). The word "woe" used here is not so much of a curse as a lament. A paraphrase that expresses the meaning of "woe to you" is "how sad for you." The first woe was pronounced against "selective obedience" and the neglect of the commands of true piety (11:42). The practice Jesus had in mind was "overly scrupulous tithing." Their failure was the neglect of **justice and the love of God**, while the solution was finding and maintaining a proper balance. The second woe was for pride (11:43). The third was for deceptive and deadly false teaching (11:44). The overall theme of these first three woes was the sin of hypocrisy.

11:45-52. The recitation of the woes was disrupted by a lawyer, objecting that Jesus' indictments were too broad and insulting to the lawyers—the experts in the law (11:45). Jesus then directed the following woes to the lawyers **as well** (11:46). The fourth woe was pronounced upon the lawyers because, instead of expounding the law so as to enhance a man's relationship with God, they added **burdens** (extra stipulations and commandments) to the law, burdens that neither the average man, nor even they, could **bear** or keep adequately (11:46). The fifth woe accused them of falsely honoring the **prophets** (11:47a, 48b). Their honor of the prophets was mere formalism—the homage to mere ciphers of the prophets as symbols without honoring the substance of the prophets, namely their message of the wisdom of God. In reality, they had the same attitude toward the prophets as their **fathers**—who **killed** the prophets (11:47b-48a). Jesus explained that the prophets were not only God's messengers but—in demonstration of **the wisdom of God** 11:49a)—the act of sending prophets, who were then rejected, served to prove who was and who was not a true follower of God (11:49-51). The sixth woe was for the lawyers' failure to use the **key of knowledge** (11:52)—a euphemism for the law itself—to open up a way for men to know God. Instead they used it to keep men from knowing God.

11:53-54. The "Discourse of Woes" against the **scribes and the Pharisees** (11:53a) solidified their opposition against Jesus, and they responded with increasing hostility toward Him, more pointed questioning of Him, and by **plotting against Him** (11:53b-54).

F. Jesus Warns His Disciples (12:1-21)

In the light of the opposition to Jesus and in the face of Jesus' rising popularity, Jesus had some pointed teaching for His disciples—four warnings.

1. Warning about Hypocrisy (12:1-3)

12:1-3. Jesus first warned His disciples about the **leaven of the Pharisees** (12:2a)—the pervasive sin of the "externally religious," namely, hypocrisy. The "hypocrite" in Greek was originally one who "acted" a part, assumed a "mask" (as in a play or at the theater). The religious hypocrite merely played the part of a religious man, but there was no reality, no relationship with God in and from the heart. Jesus explained, by means of two proverbs, that hypocrisy is a shortsighted practice because what is hidden will eventually be exposed (12:2) and because what is whispered will eventually be made public (12:3). In short, nothing remains hidden or secret forever. One day, hypocrisy will be exposed for what it is—a sham (cf. Rm 2:16; cf. Ps 139:12).

2. Warning about the Fear of Man (12: 4-7)

12: 4-7. Jesus next warned His disciples (**My friends**, 12:4) about the danger of the fear of man. This is a danger to which disciples are often exposed and may result in a denial of the faith or a failure to maintain expressed convictions. Pressure often causes people to "go along to get along." In the opening contrast (12:4-5) Jesus took the issue right to the extreme to make His point. People ought not to be feared, for the worst they can do is **kill the body** (12:4). But God is to be feared because He can kill and **cast into hell** (12:5). The point being made must not be lost by the extreme comparison—Jesus is not threatening His friends with hell. The point is, men have limited capacity for either helping or hurting us while God has unlimited capacity for judging or blessing. Accordingly, disciples should concern themselves with seeking the good will of God before being concerned about seeking the good will of men. Jesus softened the contrast with a word of comfort: the one who fears God will find a God who cares for His own (12:6-7). Two illustrations make Jesus' point. God's care for sparrows ought to assure us that He cares for us (12:6-7), and God's knowledge of us—some of which is quite trivial, like the number of hairs on our heads—should assure us that He knows and cares about all our non-trivial concerns (12:7; see also the comments on Mt 10:24-31).

3. Warning about Confessing and Denying (12:8-12) (see also the comments on Mt 10:32-33)

12:8-12. The third warning is the solution to hypocrisy and fear of man. Jesus demanded that His friends **confess** Him **before men** (12:8). To confess is more than just a "cold recitation of words" but it is an active acknowledgment—by life and word—that "Jesus is Lord" of one's life. Three reasons are offered to encourage disciples to confess Christ: one, there is "the principle of reciprocity"—that is, if we desire Christ to confess us (acknowledge us as rightfully belonging in heaven—**before the angels** 12:8b) we must confess Him before men (12:8-9). Two, there is the problem of blasphemy against the Holy Spirit (12:10). This appears to be a case of willfully denying the revealed truth about Christ—that is, unbelief. A "permanent rejection" (cf. Bock, *Luke*, 1143) of the Spirit-revealed truth will not be—indeed cannot be—forgiven. Third, Jesus encouraged His friends to confess Him before men by reminding them of the promise of the Holy Spirit (12:11-12). When accused and threatened for commitment to Christ, there is no need to worry or fret about how to respond. This is so because Jesus promised that **in that very hour** (12:12) the strengthening provision of the Spirit would provide ability to offer a bold and clear witness.

This promised provision is "for that very hour," not for the prior imaginings of what one could or one would say in that hour. The promise here is not for some supernatural or revelatory information but more likely a promise to bring to mind at the appropriate time those truths one has learned by the normal means (Bible reading, study, listening to the Word preached). The same expression—"do not worry"—is used in 12:22, and the promise there is not for "supernatural provisions" but a promise of sufficient material provisions supplied, again most likely by the usual means (employment, God's abundant creation, the generosity of others). These promises are not for unusually gifted or especially spiritual persons but for all disciples who put their trust in the Lord.

4. Warning about Worldliness—the Parable of the Rich Fool (12:13-21)

Finally, Jesus offered His friends a warning about worldliness—an overweening concern for the things of this world and this life.

12:13-15. The account began with an "impertinent request" from a man in the crowd for Jesus to be an arbiter in a dispute (apparently) over an inheritance (12:13). Jesus immediately rejected the suggestion that He become involved in a family dispute (12:14). However, this exchange prompted Jesus to address a more serious concern—a problem that lay at the heart of the dispute (and, no doubt, in the hearts of both disputants). The problem was greed (12:15a), which at root is but one expression of a deeper pathology, worldliness. Jesus explained that greed—the inordinate desire for "more"—is pointless because life does not consist of an abundance of **possessions** (12:15b). That is, life is to be about more than the "stuff" accumulated in this temporal existence. There is another, transcendent existence that the "stuff" of this life is to serve. The "stuff" of this life must never become an end in itself.

12:16-20b. Jesus illustrated this principle with a devastatingly simple and true-to-life parable. A rich man found his land so productive he could not store all the crops (12:16-17). Apparently it never occurred to him to give the excess away to others who might be in need. He was so self absorbed that he consulted only with himself on how to address this "problem" (12:17,

19a). After making provision for himself (12:18), and after congratulating himself (12:19b), he made plans for himself to enjoy his excess fortune for **many years** (12:19). However, God, the One to whom he had given no thought at all, now took notice of him. **But God said** (12:20a) abruptly changes the rosy picture of temporal ease. God called the man a **fool** (12:20b)—which indeed he was for he had actually made no provision for his **soul**!

12:20c-21. The phrase **your soul is required of you** (12:20c) is literally "they demand your soul from you" but is a substitute for the divine passive . . . and means his soul was demanded (*apaitousin*, from the verb *aiteo*, "to ask, to demand") by God (Stein, *Luke*, 352). His life was not his own but a gift, something entrusted to him by God, and now at his death he was required to give an accounting to God for his life (cf. Bock, *Luke*, 1153). However, when that accounting was given, while he left many provisions behind, he had no provisions, or treasure, with God (20:21). "The really stupid thing was the rich man's easy assurance that the future was in his control" (Morris, *Luke*, 213). The rich man's purely temporal perspective left him with no provision for eternity. The mere possession of wealth does not guarantee favor with God (cf. Jms 1:9-11; 5:1-6), much less assure one of salvation. "Wealth's only legacy is its fleeting nature (Lk 6:24-25). Only wealth handled with generosity meets with God's approval" (Bock, *Luke*, 1155).

G. Lessons on the "Eternal Perspective" (12:22-48)

1. Do Not Worry (12:22-34) (see also the comments on Mt 6:25-34)

12:22. The parable of the rich fool—the man who had many temporal provisions but none for eternity—led Jesus (**For this reason**) to some instruction for **His disciples** (12:22a) on the need to develop the "eternal perspective."

Jesus first addressed the disciples with a simple but powerful command. "The catchword that unites this section is the word 'worry' which occurs in 12:22, 25, 26. (The synonym *meteorizo* in 12:29 is also translated 'worry.')" (Stein, *Luke*, 353-54). **Do not worry** (12:22) is literally "stop being worried" and is an imperative, a command; the converse, "be content" is also implied (cf. Php 4:11-12; 1Tm 6:6-8).

12:23-34. Jesus next addressed the concerns that made the command necessary. They are the basic needs of life, the concerns of "daily existence," of **life** itself—food and clothing. In essence Jesus listed the reasons one should not worry: One, it shows a lack of the proper perspective on life (12:23). Two, it is unnecessary, as demonstrated by the birds, which do not cultivate crops or store them in barns, yet they are fed (12:24), and by the lilies, which do not gather the materials or spin yarns for clothing, yet they are more gloriously clothed than Solomon (12:27). Three, worry is pointless. It cannot add any time to one's life and is a waste of the time one does have (12:25-26). Four, it shows a lack of faith (12:28c). Five, it is what unbelievers do and is a poor testimony before them (12:30). In sum, worrying is a failure of faith.

The solutions to worry are: One, disciples are to know that they have a heavenly **Father** (12:30b). Two, disciples are to **seek His kingdom** (12:31a), that is, be about the work of living for and seeking souls for His kingdom. Three, disciples are to **not be afraid** (12:32a) and instead are to be resting in the assurances of **your Father** (12:32b). Four, disciples are to divest themselves of "temporal possessions" (12:33), while investing in eternal things (e.g., one's own soul, cf. 12:19-21).

2. Be Ready, Be Faithful (12:35-48)

12:35-38. Continuing on the same theme, Jesus encouraged His disciples to readiness and faithfulness. To these ends He offered three illustrations: In the first illustration disciples are to be like men **dressed in readiness** with lighted lamps prepared for the "master's" return (12:35, 36). The duty of the master's men is to wait (12:36); their responsibility is to be alert (12:37a); their challenge is they do not know the hour he is coming (12:38); the reward they will receive is "blessing" and "table fellowship" with the master (12:37).

12:39-40. The second illustration encouraging readiness pictured a homeowner and a thief (12:39-40). Without spelling the details, apparently, a thief had broken in to the house of the homeowner. Jesus' commonsense observation was that if the homeowner had known the time the thief was coming he would have prevented the break-in. This is an admonition for constant readiness, since disciples do not know the time of the return of **the Son of Man** (12:40).

12:41-46. The third illustration encouraging readiness was prompted by a question from Peter that amounted to "Who is this teaching for?" (12:41). Jesus did not answer Peter directly (which is to say the teaching is for anyone who understands and applies it), but Jesus introduced a parable by means of a question: **Who then is the faithful and sensible steward**? (12:42; see also the comments on Mt 24:45-51). The positive answer to this question is, the faithful steward is the one who is given a task (12:42b), who performs the task (12:43b), and who is therefore blessed by the master (12:43a). The reward Jesus mentioned here—**put him in charge of all his possessions** (12:44)—is a hyperbolic expression meant to say that the reward will be far greater than the challenges and hazards encountered in his temporal service. "The reward is a more permanent form of service . . ." (Bock, *Luke*, 1180). The Lord's reward for a job well done is more work. The negative answer to the question is, the unfaithful and foolish slave is the one who assumes the master's delay will continue indefinitely, who chooses **to eat and drink and get drunk** (12:45; "Such behavior recalls the fool of 12:19" [Stein, *Luke*, 361]), who will be shocked by the master's return, and who will be severely punished (12:46; cf. Ex 29:17).

12:47-48. Jesus next pictured two cases of "unprepared" slaves. The willfully unprepared slave will be punished with **many lashes** (12:47), but the ignorantly unprepared slave will receive a lighter punishment (12:48a). Jesus was not here introducing several "classes" of Christians (e.g., genuine, committed ones; "carnal" ones; spurious, false, mere "professing" ones). The issue here is not soteriology (salvation) but "faithfulness." The parable assumes those in view are simply stewards and slaves of a master and they are either faithful or they are not. Jesus was not giving the disciples a way to "test" their genuineness or to assure themselves of salvation or eternal rewards. In the parable the master will return, and Jesus' disciples must live with the expectation that He too will return. If they live with that expectation they will be found faithful—and that faithfulness will be rewarded. If they live with callous disregard they will be found unfaithful—and that will be punished. The point of the parable is not to provide the hearer with a catalogue of rewards and punishments, or to draw conclusions about the relationship of the slaves to master or disciples to Jesus but to encourage faithfulness. Furthermore, as the parable concludes, the principle is that the more one knows, the greater his or her responsibility. "We are all accountable" (Morris, *Luke*, 219). Verse 48 indicates that there will be varying degrees of both responsibility and reward based on one's inherent gifts and abilities.

H. Six Serious Matters for Disciples to Consider (12:49–13:9)

12:49-12:59. In light of the eternal perspective and the ministry and responsibility to which the disciples were called, Jesus, in quick succession, presented six matters for the disciples to consider.

1. They needed to consider the judgment to come. First, He mentioned the judgment He would render—**to cast fire** (12:49), and then He referred to the judgment that He Himself would suffer—**a baptism to undergo** (12:50). Jesus tied the two events together because the latter, His suffering on the cross, is the only way for men and women to escape the former (1Th 5:9). "Jesus' commitment to God's will was total. He was completely governed by the desire to complete his baptism, even though it meant suffering death in Jerusalem (Lk 13:32–33)" (Stein, *Luke*, 365).

2. The disciples needed to know the **division** that serving Jesus would bring (12:51-53; cf. Mc 7:6). "With Jesus' arrival comes a period of decision and crisis for people and between people" (Bock, *Luke*, 1192). This division will reach to the most intimate levels—even among families.

3. They needed to be discerning about the nature of the times (12:54-56). The time for repentance was running out. They were hypocrites who could discern the weather but claimed to be unable to discern the meaning of Jesus' ministry—**this present time** (12:56).

4. They needed to **settle** (temporal) accounts quickly (12:57-59). The point here appears to be that disciples must not be found fussing over temporal matters when the Lord returns. Disciples should do whatever it takes to avoid spending their last dime or last hour before the Lord returns dealing with merely temporal concerns. "Because of the arrival of God's kingdom (12:53–56), it [was] time to get one's life in order and be reconciled to God (12:58)" (Stein, *Luke*, 367). In short, they were to get things settled with the earthly judges so they could prepare to face the heavenly One.

13:1-9. 5. They needed to **repent**—turn to God because of the uncertainty of life (13:1-5). Jesus' teaching prompted a few in the crowd to report to Him an incident in which **Pilate** ruthlessly executed some **Galileans**, apparently as they were in the act of offering **sacrifices**. "They were killed as they were sacrificing" (Stein, *Luke*, 370).

No known incident fits the exact picture indicated here (cf. Bock, *Luke*, 1205). Jesus did not take the occasion to excoriate Pilate, or offer a defense of God in the face of evil, or even to propose an explanation of why such tragedies happen at all. He rejected the idea that the deaths of these unfortunates were because (as many might suppose) they were especially notorious sinners. They were no more and no less sinful than anyone else. Jesus unnervingly affirmed that "the threat of a tragic end [was] present for all" (Bock, *Luke*, 1206). He even added another tragic, and in this case seemingly even more inexplicable, incident of calamitous death (13:4) to reinforce the point that His hearers should not waste time seeking to fathom the exigencies of (apparently capricious) events. Rather, they—as sinners themselves—should **repent** before God and be prepared for the eternity that looms after this unpredictable and often tragic existence. "The issue is not when death will happen or why, but avoiding a terminal fate with even greater consequences" (Bock, *Luke*, 1206).

6. Finally, they needed to produce **fruit** (show evidence of the working of God in their lives) soon (13:6-9; cf. Mc 7:1). The key to the point of this parable is not that the owner wanted to cut down the fruitless tree, but rather the advice of the vineyard-keeper to wait and give it a chance—with some care and tending—to produce fruit. Jesus' hearers are warned that as of yet they have no fruit—but the Lord is longsuffering. Still, without fruit they can anticipate only judgment. The **fig tree** was often used as a symbol for the nation of Israel (cf. Mt 21:19; Mk 11:14), so there may be an application to that nation and to individuals who were fruitless (cf. Stein, *Luke*, 371). "Literally the parable's ending is open ended, awaiting an appropriate response by those it represents" (Bock, *Luke*, 1210).

I. Six Features of Jesus' Ministry (13:10-35)

13:10-35. Luke used this juncture to exhibit six features of Jesus' ministry: (1) Jesus showed compassion by healing a woman on the **Sabbath** (13:10-13; for background on the Sabbath controversies, see the comments on Mt 12:1-14). (2) He dealt with opposition by facing down His critics (13:14-17). (3) He provided instruction in two parables that revealed the nature of the kingdom (13:18-21—when it comes the kingdom will be "extensive" and "pervasive"; see also the comments on Mt 13:31-33). (4) He gave a strong admonition to **strive to enter** the **narrow** way—that is come into a relationship with God through faith and trust Him alone (13:22-30; see also the comments on Mt 7:13-14). (5) He showed resolution to press on to **Jerusalem** to fulfill His mission (13:31-33). (6) He demonstrated His affection for the inhabitants of Jerusalem in His lamentation over **the city** (13:34-35; see also the comments on Mt 23:37-39). Here again, Luke mentioned that Jesus was on His way to **Jerusalem** (13:22).

J. Jesus at Dinner with a Pharisee (14:1-24)

14:1-6. Jesus did not refrain from meeting and even dining with His opponents. He used these opportunities to rebuke and instruct them. On this occasion Luke recorded Jesus' attendance at a **Sabbath** dinner with **one of the leaders of the Pharisees** (14:1), "a synagogue head (8:41) or a higher official" (Bock, *Luke*, 1255). More than likely, **a man suffering from dropsy** (14:2; "'dropsy' is literally *hydropikos*, probably edema in which various parts of the body become filled with fluid"; Stein, *Luke*, 386) was present for the purpose of testing Jesus. Luke notes He was under the scrutiny of the opposition—**they were watching Him closely** (14:1). "The term means 'to watch lurkingly'" (Bock, *Luke*, 1256), no doubt to find some cause to accuse Him of some infraction of their traditions. Jesus challenged His opposition with a question: "Is it lawful to heal on the Sabbath or not?" (14:3; cf. 6:9; 13:16). Their silence allowed Him to proceed to heal the man. Jesus healed him with three actions: **He took hold** . . . He **healed him** . . . He **sent him away** (14:4), thus the miracle was firm, full, and final. Jesus concluded this encounter with an illustration of simple, commonsense kindness and humanitarianism (14:5) that made the unarguable (14:6) point that even Sabbath observance was subordinate to compassion.

14:7-15. Jesus then took the occasion to teach on humility (14:7-11), a quality apparently lacking in the other guests, and hospitality (14:12-14), a quality apparently lacking in his hosts. The simple principle behind both pericopes is that a concern for others should supersede a concern for oneself. Once again, Jesus taught His disciples to consider the eternal perspective. His disciples must wait to be **exalted** (cf. 14:11), and they must be generous and considerate of others in this life, expecting to be repaid **at the resurrection** (14:14).

14:16-17. Jesus followed this teaching with a parable about a **big dinner** (14:16-24). Apparently, Jesus' teaching had had an effect on the guests—but not the effect He desired. In response to Jesus' words a man cried, **Blessed is everyone who will eat bread in the kingdom of God** (14:15). It is unclear if the man meant the "bread of Jesus' teaching" (which he should have meant) or the physical bread of this Jewish (Sabbath) dinner (which he probably meant). This man was expressing the common assumption that only the Jews—the pious Jews—would be in the kingdom enjoying this feast. In response Jesus told this parable of a man who prepared a dinner and invited guests (14:16-17). Stein notes, "It was customary to extend two invitations. The first (as here v. 16) was to 'make reservations' and the second (cf. v. 17) to announce that the banquet was beginning" (Stein, *Luke*, 393).

14:18-24. Apparently, many of these invitees had accepted the first invitation, but they began to make excuses, and the excuses were superficial, insincere, and even insulting (14:18-20). "Such excuses are lame, even insulting, in light of the occasion and their previous willingness to come" (Bock, *Luke*, 1273). The man was angered by this disrespect, and in response he sent his slave to invite the **poor**, **crippled**, **blind**, **lame** (14:21). Even then there was still room, and so the man sent his slave out beyond the confines of his neighborhood. "To find these outcasts and afflicted takes effort, and so the servant searches the city" (Bock, *Luke*, 1275). There was still room, and so the slave was sent to the **highways and along the hedges** that lined the fields, and travelers were compelled—irresistibly drawn in to the feast (14:22-23), while the first invitees were shut out (14:24). The meaning and application of the parable became dramatically clear when Jesus revealed that He had been speaking of **my dinner** (14:24). In this parable Jesus made it clear that his hosts—the leaders of the nation—had in effect declined His invitation (to believe in Him) and that others (the Gentiles) would be invited to take their places. "The rejection of Jesus and the kingdom by official Judaism (14:24) precipitated the inclusion of Israel's outcasts (4:18; 7:22) and the Gentiles (Acts 13:47–48; 18:6; 28:25–28). The great reversal had taken place" (Stein, *Luke*, 394; cf. Bock, *Luke*, 1277).

K. Jesus' Teaching on Discipleship (14:25-35)

14:25-35. Even though large crowds followed Jesus (14:25), Jesus' attention was on His own disciples. "Jesus wants those who are contemplating a relationship with Him to know what it means" (Bock, *Luke*, 1283). In His teaching to them He instilled several principles of true discipleship. The principle of "first loyalty" (14:26) is that devotion to Jesus must take precedence over all others. Jesus' saying that His disciples are to **hate** their own relatives probably has the idea of "in comparison to their overriding devotion to Christ." "Discipleship is fundamentally a call to allegiance. Jesus is to have first place over all, including family" (Bock, *Luke*, 1284). Next is the principle of "cross bearing" (14:27). A disciple must be willing to suffer (see also the comments on Mt 10:34-38). This is complete commitment to Christ that sets aside all personal ambition and gives oneself to the third principle, "counting the cost" (14:28-32). One must plan ahead and serve Christ prudently. Jesus illustrated this principle using the example of the "imprudent builder" (14:28-30) who began but could not complete his project, and by the example of the "prudent king" (14:31-32) who came to terms with an enemy he could not defeat. Next is the principle of "sacrifice" (14:33). The disciple must be willing to give up all temporal goods in service to Christ. The principle of "being salt" (14:34-35a) reveals that disciples are to have an "influence" on the world and not the other way around. Finally, the principle of "hearing with one's ears" (14:35b) indicates that disciples are to do more than "hear Jesus' words." They are to follow through on these principles in their daily lives.

L. Three Parables of "Lost and Found" (15:1-32)

In this chapter Luke recorded three parables. One of them—the Prodigal Son—is among the best known and most beloved of all Jesus' parables. The primary point of the parables, usually neglected in popular lessons on them, is that the religious leaders should not have been criticizing Jesus for seeking tax collectors and sinners (15:1; note how this verse introduces all three parables). God rejoices when such are "found," and the sour attitude of the Pharisees and the scribes is condemned (as seen in the interaction between the father and the older brother in 15:25-32, *which makes up nearly half of the parable*, another point frequently neglected). A secondary, though admittedly important, theme of all three parables is that God rejoices when repentant sinners turn to Him and are "found." "The way to God is through repentance. God's arms are open to the person who will seek Him on His terms. God's arms close around the child ready to run to Him and receive what He offers"

(Bock, *Luke*, 1295). Another theme is the joy that comes when that which is lost is found.

1. Setting of the Parables (15:1-2)

15:1-2. The setting in which Jesus spoke these parables is important to the point of the parables. **The tax collectors and the sinners**, the ostracized, and the outcast, were coming to hear Jesus (15:1), and He received them. This provoked **the Pharisees and the scribes** who criticized Jesus for these associations. The parables explained why Jesus welcomed and fellowshipped with such people. The fourfold pattern—an item is lost, a search is made, the item is found, rejoicing follows—appears in each of the parables. This pattern is the pattern of salvation—sinners are lost, they are sought by Christ (cf. 19:10), they are found by God, rejoicing follows. Only in the parable of the Prodigal Son is the human responsibility to repent presented.

2. Parable of the Lost Sheep (15:3-7)

15:3-4. The parable of the lost sheep is best known for the numbers involved. Jesus put the hypothetical situation before His listeners. He imagined a man with **a hundred sheep—ninety-nine** were with him safe and secure while **one** has become **lost** (15:4a). In real life, the risk of leaving the ninety-nine in **open pasture** (lit., "wilderness") would probably have been too great to **go after the one which is lost** (15:4b). Yet the caring shepherd did just that. He searched for the lost sheep until he found it (15:4c).

15:5-7. The tender picture of a shepherd carrying the sheep across **his shoulders** (15:5) would have heightened the point: the shepherd is the one who pursued, found, and retrieved the sheep. The initiative (of seeking) and the accomplishment (of finding) belong to the shepherd. When the sheep was found there was great joy. The picture of rejoicing—calling the neighbors, rejoicing over one lost, but found, sheep is to be understood as hyperbole. While an actual circumstance like this would surely be a cause for joy and relief (for the shepherd anyway), it is unlikely that the picture Jesus was describing would actually happen. The "over-the-top" reaction of the shepherd (15:6) is meant to contrast with the attitude of the Pharisees and scribes toward the tax collectors and sinners who have come to hear Jesus. They should at least have been supportive—if not ecstatic—when sinners showed an interest in the things of the Lord. They were however as unmoved as this shepherd was overjoyed. Jesus made the point: **heaven** (a metonymy for God) is much more like the overly ecstatic shepherd when sinners come to repentance (15:7) and unlike the critical Pharisees.

3. Parable of the Lost Coin (15:8-10)

15:8-10. The second parable is remarkably simple and reiterates the same basic point as the first: something lost (a coin) was diligently searched for and ultimately found, to the great joy of the finder. As with the parable of the lost sheep, the reaction of the woman who found her coin—calling neighbors and friends—is not true to life. It is an exaggeration. However, it is meant to make the point that there is extravagant joy **in the presence of the angels** (15:10 indicating God Himself) when sinners repent. Both of these parables teach that it is God who takes the initiative to seek the lost (cf. 19:10), as demonstrated by the controversial actions of Jesus who sought the social and spiritual rejects.

4. Parable of the Lost Son (15:11-32)

15:11. This parable appears only in Luke's gospel and is acknowledged by many as a masterpiece of storytelling. While it is often known as the parable of the Prodigal Son, note that Jesus began the parable with the mention of **two sons** (15:11), with the older brother playing as vital a role in the parable as the younger.

a. The First Son (15:12-24)

15:12-20a. The younger of the man's sons exhibited a foolish rebellion (15:12-13). He selfishly requested his inheritance, showing himself as disrespectful and uncharitable In effect, when the young man asked for his inheritance he was betraying a materialistic, selfish impulse at best, and at worst was saying to his father, "I wish you were already dead." When the young man received his inheritance (15:12) he imprudently departed, and then he sinfully squandered his money (15:13). The young man found himself in an inevitable destitution (15:14-16). He was struck by poverty (15:14), thrown into virtual slavery (15:15a), and experienced hunger and estrangement (15:16-17), probably for the first time in his life. From the nadir of this condition the young man took the steps necessary for his restoration (15:17-20a). He **came to his senses** (15:17), that is, he became aware that his own foolishness and sinfulness had brought him to this destitution. He realized he needed to make a full confession (15:18, 21), and he had to own up to the condition of his heart and the consequences of his actions. He exhibited genuine humility when he concluded that he was unworthy to be called a son and was willing to accept the status of hired man (15:19). Finally, he took the necessary action to follow through in deed from the intentions of his heart—**he got up and came to his father** (15:20a).

b. The Gracious Father (15:20b-24)

15:20b-24. The note that **his father saw him** (15:20b) while the young man was still far off may indicate that the father was looking for the son, though the text does not say this and the point should not be pressed. The father's reaction, like the response of the shepherd to finding the lost sheep and of the woman upon finding the lost coin, was "exaggerated" (15:20c). "There can be no doubt that in the father's welcome of the younger son Jesus is teaching that the heavenly Father welcomes returning sinners" (Morris, *Luke,* 243). The father's compassion for his returning son would not permit him to accept the terms offered by the Prodigal. The father did not even allow his son to get so far as to propose becoming like one of the **hired men** (15:19b)—nothing short of full restoration would do. The son was clothed (15:22) and his return was celebrated (15:23). The father's justification for this celebration revealed the severity of the son's condition before his repentance (**was dead . . . was lost**) and the complete restoration of his condition since his repentance (**has come to life . . . has been found**) (15:24). The father's statement made the application of the parable clear: Sinners are dead and lost, but they can come to life and can be found if they return to the Father.

c. The Second Son (15:25-30)

In a sense the parable was complete, having made, for the third time, the point made in the first two parables of this chapter—God finds and receives lost sinners who repent and return to Him. But the attitude of the Pharisees (15:2) needed to be addressed directly. It is clear that the older brother represented the scribes and Pharisees. It is this half of the parable that is most pertinent to the context of 15:1, and in which the primary point of the parable is found.

15:25-30. When the older brother was made aware that his younger brother had returned and that a celebration was underway to welcome him back (15:25-27) he became angry and resentful (15:28a). His complaint **I have never neglected a command of yours** (arguably not true) (15:29) echoed the attitude of the legalistic Pharisees. His accusations against his brother were uncharitable (and untrue—there is no mention of **prostitutes** [15:30b] in the earlier narrative about the younger son). His unwillingness to be forgiving was in stark contrast to the attitude of the father. And his attitudes were not significantly different from those of his younger brother's. The older brother would have liked **a young goat** so that he could **be merry with** his **friends** (v. 29), that is, to enjoy material goods from his father without his father's company. The two were not so different after all!

d. The Gracious Father (15:31-32)

15:31-32. Again, the father was the picture of graciousness and forbearance. His pleas to the older son, reiterating his earlier words about the younger son's pre- and post-repentant states were largely lost on the bitter and resentful older son. No conclusion to this exchange between the father and this older son is given. Jesus allowed the Pharisees to write their own conclusion: They could continue to resent that Jesus welcomed tax collectors and sinners (cf. 15:2), or they could drop their bitterness and join the celebration as repentant sinners themselves. Perhaps an application from these parables is that God's people should weigh carefully their own attitudes toward those on the fringes of society—and consider more deliberate attempts to reach them as Jesus did, and for which He was criticized. We should also be slow to criticize or question the motives of those who are seeking to minister to social and spiritual outcasts (such as drug addicts, homosexuals, prostitutes, or criminals). The last verse summarizes the point of all three parables—what was lost has been found.

M. Parables and Teaching for Disciples and Pharisees (16:1-31)

In this chapter Jesus challenged His disciples and the Pharisees about temporal values and worldly ways of thinking. The relation of the teaching here to the previous chapter is unclear. "The material in this chapter is for the most part unique to Luke" and it "deals with the common theme of possessions" (Stein, *Luke*, 411). Both the disciples and the Pharisees needed to understand that the values, principles, and standards of the world—the "ways of thinking" that enable one to get along in this life—are incommensurate for one who serves God, and God will judge those who do not serve Him.

1. Parable of the Dishonest Manager (16:1-9)

16:1-9. In an enigmatic parable Jesus taught the disciples that they needed to be wise in the use of temporal positions, possessions, and power. Jesus pictured a discredited manager who was about to be fired by his employer

(16:1-3). This dishonest manager shrewdly used his position to secure his future—at his employer's expense—by discounting the outstanding accounts of his master's debtors (16:4-7). Surprisingly, the master **praised** this man, not for his dishonesty, but for his shrewdness (16:8). Jesus also commended the man, not for his dishonest dealings, but for his foresight and shrewdness (16:9). "He is commended for acting and preparing himself for the judgment awaiting him. He is commended essentially for being a shrewd scoundrel and taking care of his future" (Stein, *Luke,* 412). The master did not like it, but he had to give the "shrewd manager" his due—the master had been outwitted! Jesus was not encouraging His disciples to be dishonest, but to be shrewd—and that not about temporal matters like this scoundrel, but with respect to eternal matters (cf. 12:33). Our temporal wealth should be used for treasure in heaven.

2. Teaching about Faithfulness in Service (16:10-13)

16:10-13. Still addressing the disciples, Jesus articulated two principles (loosely related to the previous parable) about service. First, the principle of "faithfulness"—**He who is faithful in a very little thing** can be trusted with **much** (that is, many more and larger things). Thus disciples are to be faithful (exhibiting honesty and integrity) in temporal things (like money) if they want to be trusted in more important (spiritual and eternal) matters. (16:10-12). The second principle concerns masters: It is impossible to **serve two masters**. Therefore, disciples need to serve God (out of love and loyalty to Him) and not wealth, that is, they must not serve merely to get paid or because they want to get rich (16:13).

3. Corrections for the Pharisees (16:14-18)

16:14-18. Jesus commended faithfulness for His disciples in contrast to the greed of the Pharisees—**lovers of money** (16:14). The Pharisees were given several (somewhat disparate) correctives to their way of thinking: What they valued was not what God valued (16:15). The law was not what they thought it was (16:16), and as an example of that, their views on divorce were judged by Jesus to be deficient (16:18).

4. Parable of the Rich Man and Lazarus (16:19-31)

It seems best to understand this as a type of parable or a parable-like story (cf. Bock, *Luke,* 1363). Some argue that several of the features of this story are not typical of a parable: It is not actually identified as a parable. Unlike in other parables, one of the characters is named. Lazarus was a fairly common name, meaning "God helps" (see comment on 16:20). This is not the Lazarus of Jn 11. Unlike other parables, it is not an illustration that could be observed in the course of everyday life (e.g., a sower sowing, a woman cleaning her home). It portrays the afterlife in untypical ways (i.e., there's no judgment or banquet), cf. Bock, *Luke,* 1362-63. However, "to call this account parabolic is not entirely incorrect" (Bock, *Luke,* 1363). Considering the lack of clear corroborating passages in Scripture, it is highly speculative to suggest this story describes either Hades (the abode of the dead, in the LXX *Sheol*) or the relative arrangement of the compartments of the afterlife for the righteous and unrighteous dead. In other NT uses (Mt 11:23; 16:18; Rv 20:13-14) Hades is understood as a real but otherwise shadowy place for the wicked dead until the time of judgment, and there are no indications that people there can see, much less communicate, with the righteous dead. Bock is probably correct to suggest that "the conversations are simply part of the story's literary means to depict the great chasm in the afterlife between the righteous in Paradise and those in Hades" (Bock, *Luke,* 1363).

16:19-25. The skewed values and thinking of the Pharisees and the foolishness of all who live without a thought for eternity are exposed by this parable. Jesus began by describing the temporal conditions, the life circumstances, of two men: one was rich and lived an opulent life (16:19); the other was not just poor but destitute and diseased (16:20-21). Even though they lived in proximity—the poor man at the rich man's **gate** (16:20b) living off the scraps **from the rich man's table** (16:21)—their lives could not have been more disparate. Upon his death the **poor man named Lazarus** (16:20a; the one "helped by God") is taken by angels to **Abraham's bosom** (16:22), a place of comfort and blessing. Upon his death the rich man is confined to **Hades** (16:23). Their circumstances are completely reversed. The rich man first asked for relief but was informed that this was impossible (16:24, 26) because there was a **great chasm fixed** between them. **Chasm** is a term found only here and describes an "unbridgeable space." "The theological passive that such a place 'has been fixed' asserts that God has set up the afterlife in such a way that the righteous and the unrighteous do not mix . . . the image is strong and suggests that how we respond in this life is decisive for where we reside in the next" (Bock, *Luke*, 1373). The rich man's torment increased knowing that he could have elevated Lazarus in life (and perhaps himself in death) had he been more concerned about the injustice of their temporal circumstances (16:25). Now it is too late for him.

16:26-31. The rich man then turned to thoughts about those whom he had left behind. Showing that he was still thinking like the worldly man he was, he asked that someone might return to warn his brethren about his fate (16:27-28). Surely, he reasoned, **if someone goes to them from the dead, they will repent!** (16:30)—evidences and human reason would certainly bring his brethren around. But he was informed that, in effect, the warning was already available in the Scriptures (**They have Moses and the Prophets**, 16:29) and that additional warnings—even by someone rising from the dead—would prove ineffective. The point of the parable is clear: a set of values and a perspective on life that considers only the temporal, the worldly, and the "present life" is inadequate and will prove to be foolish in the light of eternity. The rich man did not go to Hades/hell because he was rich. He went there because his life and hope were devoted to his earthly riches, which he never used to "lay up treasure in heaven." He put his own earthly ease before his concern for others, which indicated that his heart was not right with God! The parable also indicates that even the most extreme miracles (**if someone rises from the dead**, v. 31) will not be sufficient to engender faith or repentance in those who observe them.

N. Jesus Warning, Teaching, Healing (17:1-19)

1. Sayings for Disciples (17:1-10)

17:1-10. To prepare His disciples for the ministry they will undertake for Him, Jesus warned them about **stumbling blocks** (17:1-3a)—people and things that cause His disciples to sin. These stumbling blocks are **inevitable** (17:1a), will be judged severely (17:1b-2), and should be avoided (17:3a). Furthermore, Jesus taught them to be prepared to rebuke and forgive those who stumble (sin) and repent (17:3b-4). Additionally, Jesus taught them about faith (17:5-6): it is not the size or amount of faith but the object of faith that gives faith its power. Finally, Jesus taught them to be prepared to be **a slave** (17:7-10)—completely at the Master's disposal.

2. Healings of the Ten Lepers (17:11-19)

17:11-19. Luke again (for the third time cf. 9:51; 13:22) mentioned that Jesus was **on the way to Jerusalem** (17:11). On the way he was confronted by ten lepers (17:12). He did not immediately heal them but sent them **to the priests** (17:13) an act that would be appropriate for one who was healed from leprosy (cf. Lv 13:2, 3; 14:2-32), and on the way **they were cleansed** (Lk 17:14). However, only one (**and he was a Samaritan**, 17:16—a people who were, in the prevailing view of the Jews of the pharisaical type, not acceptable to God) turned to glorify God, to acknowledge that Jesus had healed him, and to give thanks to Jesus (17:15). Jesus commended his **faith** (17:19). The principle here is that even those in low religious standing (as the Samaritans were, in the opinion of the Jewish people in Jesus' day) were able to acknowledge and believe in Jesus. But the religious leaders of Israel, who should have been most sympathetic to Jesus and His teaching, were unwilling to embrace Him.

O. Jesus' Teaching on the Kingdom and the Second Coming (17:20-37)

1. The Pharisees' Question (17:20-21)

17:20-21. The Pharisees—apparently in yet another attempt to trip up Jesus—had asked about the **coming** of the **kingdom** (17:20a). Jesus' answer did not cast doubt on the fact of the coming of the kingdom, but His answer corrected two popular notions. First, the kingdom was not coming in such a way that it could be predicted (**with signs**) (17:20). Second, the kingdom would not come in exactly the way men expected it would (17:21).

2. The Instruction to the Disciples (17:22-37) (see also the comments on Matthew 24-25)

17:22-37. The question and answer about the kingdom led to Jesus' more detailed instruction about the kingdom for the benefit of His disciples (17:22a). Jesus instructed them about the kingdom in four areas. First, as to the timing of the coming of the kingdom, there will be a longing for the **days of the Son of Man** (17:22) as well as false sightings of the Son of Man (17:23). Yet, there will be no missing Him when He does appear (17:24), and He will not appear until after the cross (17:25). Second, Jesus instructed them about the earthly conditions when the kingdom comes. It will be a time like the days of Noah (17:26-27; see also the comments on Mt 24:37-39) and the days of Lot (17:28-30), meaning that life will proceed in a normal, even mundane way until a time of sudden and unexpected catastrophe. Third, Jesus taught them about the urgency related to the coming of the kingdom (17:31-33). It is a time not to look back or hesitate. This is a description of the second half of the tribulation period (cf. Dn 9:24; Rv 19:11; Mt 24:29-44), and it applies to the nation of Israel. Finally, Jesus revealed that the purpose of the coming of the kingdom (Lk 17:34-37) would be judgment.

P. Two Parables Concerning Prayer and Righteousness (18:1-14)

1. The Widow and the Judge (18:1-8)

18:1-3. This episode begins a bit differently in that the application of the parable about to be told appears as the introduction of the parable. In light of the troubles of life and the difficulties encountered because of their service to Christ, the disciples needed **to pray and not to lose heart** (18:1). The note about praying here makes it clear that the actions of the widow in the parable to follow are to be understood as lessons on prayer, not legal advice! Specifically, disciples are to pray for the Lord's return and not grow weary in those prayers! The persons in the parable are a **judge** (18:2) who lived **in a certain city** and a **widow** (18:3) in the same city. Jesus described the judge (18:2) as one **who did not fear God**. "This describes the judge's lack of the most fundamental requirement in life, reverence toward God (cf. Pr 9:10)" (Stein, *Luke,* 444). Furthermore this judge **did not respect man**. "This judge did not care what people thought. This judge was not the type to be moved out of compassion" (Bock, *Luke,* 1448). In these respects he was completely unlike God (and Jesus' hearers may have wondered where this comparison was headed). The woman is noted for her persistence—**she kept coming to him** and her insistence—**Give me legal protection** (18:3).

18:4-5. The widow came day after day to register her legal claim. At first the judge resisted—**he was unwilling** to give her legal protection (18:4a). He was probably waiting for a bribe, which she could not pay. But after a time he relented—**I will give her legal protection** (18:5b). He explained (to no one in particular) it was not because he feared God, which he did not, and not because he respected man, which he did not, but only because by her coming she had worn him out (18:5). She had so badgered him that he gave her what she wanted only to get relief from her pestering. "The words 'wear me out' (*hypopiazei me*) are difficult to translate, for they literally mean 'strike under the eye, give a black eye' [BAGD, 858; TDNT 9:50 n. 88]" (Leifeld, "Luke," 1000; cf. Bock, *Luke*, 1449). This seems to be a figurative expression for "wear one down emotionally."

18:6-8. Jesus then explained—**And the Lord said** (18:6)—in a "lesser to greater" type of argument, that if such an unlikable, irascible, ignoble judge can be moved to do the right thing by the persistence of a lowly widow (who means nothing to this judge), what will the good, loving, kind, and righteous God do for His elect ("chosen ones"), His own people, when they **cry to Him day and night** (18:7b) (continually, without ceasing)? "As in 16:1-8, Jesus used a less-than-noble character as an illustration (cf. also Mt 13:44: 25:1-13) . . . If the unjust judge finally granted the persistent widow's request, how much more will a just God hear and grant the petitions of his followers who pray to him day and night" (Stein, *Luke*, 444). The answer is He will not **delay long** to answer their cries (Lk 18:7c). He will **bring about justice** (18:7a), and He will answer them **quickly** (18:8). The promise here is not necessarily for speedy, but for timely answers to prayer.

In this parable Jesus taught that God need not be badgered by prayer but that those who pray, His own elect, should do so consistently (18:1), persistently (18:5), and expectantly. For those who pray this way answers will come—maybe not as soon as they want or expect, but when they come they will be understood as having come "right on time."

2. The Pharisee and the Tax-Collector (18:9-14)

18:9-12. Luke introduced the next episode with the term **parable** (18:9) and again provided the reader with the application in the introduction. Possibly this lesson was prompted by an incident Jesus actually witnessed in the temple and related in this parabolic form. Jesus identified two men praying in the temple (18:10). One was a self-righteous **Pharisee** (18:11). His prayer was filled with contempt for others (18:11) and self-congratulation (18:12). His prayer reflected the typical attitude of the self-righteous Pharisees who thought they could be in a right standing before God (that is, "justified"), by such fastidious acts as fasting and tithing (18:12). The other man was a **tax collector** (18:10). Tax-collectors were typically Jews who served the Romans by collecting taxes for them. They were viewed as collaborators and were ostracized. Often they were unscrupulous and greedy and took advantage of their fellow Jews by overtaxing them and keeping the takings. Roman authorities typically contracted with individuals to collect taxes. As long as the Roman quota was met, the Romans were happy. For a tax collector to make a profit, however, required systematic overcharging of those who were taxed, as the Romans did not share a percentage of the fees with the tax collectors.

18:13-14. The people looked at the tax collectors both as traitors and as thieves. For Jesus to use such a person as the "hero" of a parable would have been a surprising twist indeed. This tax collector's demeanor conveyed his sense of unworthiness (18:13a), in that he stood **some distance away** from the temple proper. He showed utter self-abasement before God—**unwilling to lift up his eyes to heaven**. He displayed a distressed and penitent attitude by his act of **beating his breast**, and his prayer was a cry for mercy from a repentant heart (18:13b). He entreated God to **be merciful** to him. **Merciful** (*hilaskomai*) was used in the LXX to translate verbs related to atonement for sins, and here means "to be gracious because of some sacrifice." This publican was completely dependent on God for establishing a right relationship with Him, in contrast to the Pharisee in the parable. Jesus' shocking conclusion was that the humble man, the tax collector, was **justified** (considered righteous in the eyes of God) rather than the proud man (18:14). The lesson was clear: only those who come to God with authentic humility can expect to find God favorable. This parable is one of the most significant lessons on the crucial truth of justification (cf. Rm 3:21-28). The tax-collector was declared righteous on the basis of his repentant faith.

Q. Jesus Meets Children, a Wealthy Ruler, a Blind Man, and Zaccheus (18:15-30; 18:35–19:10)

18:15-17. Jesus' first meeting with the **children** demonstrated His approachability and illustrated the type of faith needed to approach Him (18:15-17). This does not mean one must be credulous (like a child who will believe anything), but one must trust in Jesus implicitly—as a child would trust a parent or other responsible adult. Such a child does not ask for an adult's credentials or inquire into his or her parents' qualifications—he or she just recognizes the authority and ability of the parent intuitively.

18:18-27. Jesus' next meeting with **a ruler** demonstrated that, while He could be approached, this approach had to be with the right understanding (18:18a; the designation "rich young ruler" is arrived at by combining all three synoptic gospel accounts of the meeting—see Mt 19:22, Mk 10:22, and here, the only account where he is identified as **a ruler**). The response of Jesus to the ruler's greeting—**Why do you call me good? No one is good except God** (Lk 18:19)—was not a denial by Jesus of His own deity, but a question designed to expose the ruler's superficiality. The man had a superficial understanding of "goodness," and therefore a superficial understanding of God. As the conversation continued he showed a superficial understanding of the law (18:20-21). Finally, he proved to have a superficial understanding of Jesus, for he failed to demonstrate humility before Jesus or a willingness to follow Jesus, because that meant giving up the comforts and securities he possessed in this life (18:23; see also the comments on Mt 19:16-30). Even though there are many explanations for the saying Jesus quoted in 18:25—**For it is easier for a camel to go through the eye of a needle**—in the end it seems that it is a hyperbolic expression. As such the meaning is fairly plain—it is very difficult for those who are rich by the temporal standards of the world to give up those riches for the sake of the kingdom. This saying perplexed some of Jesus' followers. It was assumed that the rich had advantages not only for this life but also for the next. Riches were considered a sign of God's blessing and favor. Jesus' words seemed to belie that assumption. Jesus answered that even in such cases only the grace and power of God can break the hold of temporal riches (18:27) (cf. Stein, *Luke*, 459).

18:28-30. This discussion of riches prompted Peter to remind Jesus of all that he and the others had given up to follow Him (18:28). Jesus assured Peter and the others that such sacrifices would not go unrewarded (28:28-30).

18:31-34. See page 1588.

18:35-43. Jesus' next meeting with the blind man on the Jericho road (18:35; see also the comments on Mt 20:29-34) demonstrated that Jesus was indeed the Messiah—the **Son of David** (18:38b, 39b) and that He would show compassion (as it was predicted for the Messiah, see Lk 4:18; Is 61:1).

19:1-10. Jesus' last meeting with Zaccheus in Jericho (19:1) demonstrated that Jesus had indeed come "to seek and save the lost" (cf. 19:10). One might consider Zaccheus an unlikely candidate for Jesus' attention—he was a tax collector (see 18:10 above) and he was rich (19:2b). With this description no doubt Luke intended that the reader recall the incident with the rich young ruler at this point (cf. 18:23-24). He also was **small in stature** (19:3b; he would have been easy to overlook). Nevertheless, Zaccheus had the desire and determination to see Jesus (19:3a, 4). Jesus saw not only the figure in the sycamore tree but also the desire of the man's heart. He spoke to him and invited Himself to Zaccheus's **house** (19:5-6). Despite Jesus' reception of sinners rankling some (19:7), it was soon clear that Zaccheus had been changed by this encounter with the Messiah. He resolved to give to the poor and make restitution to those whom he had defrauded (19:8). This quick, decisive reversal of attitude toward wealth—a willingness to spend it not in a shrewd, worldly way but to spend it with eternal life in view (cf. 16:9) (in contrast to the reticence of the ruler, cf. 18:18; in contrast to the life of the rich man, cf. 16:19) made it clear that **salvation** had **come to** Zaccheus's **house** (19:9).

R. Jesus Foretold His Death and Resurrection (18:31-34) (see also the comments on Mt 20:17-19)

18:31-34. This was the third prediction by Jesus of His coming passion (cf. 9:22; 43b-45). He made the prediction to the disciples in particular (18:31a) and with a precision that made it unmistakable (18:31b-33). Yet the disciples failed to understand (18:34). Luke's purpose for including these predictions was to prove that Jesus was in control—His death was no miscalculation or accident of history.

19:1-10. See p. 1587.

S. The Parable of the Ten Minas (19:11-27) (see also the comments on Mt 25:14-30)

19:11-27. This parable taught a concluding lesson (at the end of the journey to Jerusalem, 19:11) on the proper attitude toward one's temporal resources in light of eternity. There are two parts to this parable: Part one concerned a **nobleman** who departed to a **distant country to receive a kingdom . . . and then return** (19:12). The citizens, however, sent a delegation saying, **We do not want this man to reign over us** (19:14). At the end of the parable it was revealed that these rebellious citizens—called **enemies** of the Master/king (19:27a)—would be destroyed (19:27b). The picture is, of course, that of the Lord Jesus Christ who would depart (after the resurrection) but will return to establish His kingdom. The rebels needed to be warned: "There is no neutral position in relationship to Jesus" (Bock, *Luke,* 1543).

Part two of the parable concerned the charge the Master left with His slaves. Ten slaves were each given a mina (a unit of money worth about one-sixtieth of a talent, or about three months' wages) and charged to **do business** with this money—invest it (19:13b). Upon his return, the master looked for an accounting. With two of the slaves the accounting was good. Each man had made money by his investments (19:16, 18), and each was commended (19:17, 19) and given greater opportunity for service. Thus far this parable illustrated the principles Jesus had taught on earlier occasions (cf. 12:34-48;16:10-12). A third slave is called **Another** (*heteros*), a word that means "another of a completely different sort." This slave had not invested the money. He had for fear of the Master hidden it away and intended only to return it to the Master (19:20-21). This provoked a scathing rebuke from the Master (19:22-23) and the loss of the man's mina (19:24). He proved to be a faithless slave unworthy of any opportunity to serve the Master (see also the comments on Mt 25:29-30). The lesson once again was that (while Jesus is away) His disciples are to use the goods of this world and the opportunities to serve Him to accomplish spiritual goals.

VI. Ministry in Jerusalem (19:28–21:38)

19:28. This is a transitional verse that marks the end of the journey to Jerusalem that began at 9:51 and the beginning of the next phase of Jesus' earthly ministry. Jesus had a complex relationship with Jerusalem and its inhabitants. His fame had obviously spread to the populace of the city (cf. 19:37b), but just as obviously they had little genuine understanding of His mission.

A. Triumphal Entry (19:29-44)

The triumphal entry was "an event of outstanding significance" (William Hendriksen, *Exposition of the Gospel of Luke*, [Grand Rapids, MI: Baker, 1978], 872). Actually, Luke recorded only the approach to the city (cf. 19:37) and not the actual entry.

1. Preparations for the Entry (19:29-34) (see also the comments on Mt 21:1-6)

19:29-34. The preparations were made as Jesus approached **Bethphage** (exact location unknown) **and Bethany** (19:29a) on the eastern side of the Mount of Olives (itself just east of the city.) Luke recorded: Jesus' instructions (19:29b-31), the disciples' compliance (19:32), and the acquiescence of those who owned the colt that Jesus said would be ready for Him (19:33-34). The entire picture seems to indicate, not "prophetic insight" or "divine omniscience," but that Jesus, by means not revealed, had made prior arrangements with the colt's owners to have the animal in readiness. That the owners so freely allowed the colt to be taken seems to suggest this was a prearranged rendezvous. Also, the instructions Jesus gave included a mix of precise and vague terms (19:30-31), and this semi-cryptic conversation is repeated exactly in the actual event of retrieving the animals (19:33). This all looks very much like a preplanned event. Luke's point in this account seems to be that Jesus took the initiative and that He was fully in control of the event. Furthermore, by this arrangement He was giving evidence of His own messianic consciousness. He knew what He was doing, and what He was doing was fulfilling prophecy. Specifically He was consciously fulfilling the prophecy of Zch 9:9 (see the comments there) much as He had done in Lk 4:16-21 when He was consciously fulfilling the prophecy of Is 61:1-2a. He was announcing Himself as the Messiah.

2. The Event Itself (19:35-40)

19:35-40. All of the details of this event (see the commentary on Mt 21:1-9)—Jesus on a colt (19:35), the coats strewn on the road (19:36), the words used by the shouting crowds (19:37-38), indicated the messianic presence. Luke alone used the title **King** (19:38a) to alert his audience to the "regal figure" of Jesus and to highlight (for Gentiles who may not have been as cognizant of OT messianic imagery) that as Jesus entered the city He presented Himself "as the king who brings the nation's eschatological hope" (Bock, *Luke*, 1559). However, even as the crowds were expecting eschatological triumph (over the Romans), Jesus was about to bring the eschatological judgment on sin—at the cross (cf. Dn 9:24a, "to make an end of sin, to make atonement for iniquity"; see the comments there). The rebuke of the Pharisees (Lk 19:39) demonstrated that they understood the implicit (messianic) claim that was being made in this event. Jesus' response (19:40; cf. Hab 2:11) indicated that this claim could not be denied.

3. Jesus' Lament over the City (19:41-44)

19:41-44. Luke recorded Jesus' reaction upon seeing the city. The expression **wept over it** (19:41) fails to convey the depth of emotion—Jesus "burst into tears" (cf. Jr 8:18-21; 9:1). He saw . . . He wept . . . He said. He entered as the King but turned immediately to His role as prophet and again (cf. Lk 13:34-35) pronounced judgment on the city (19:44-45). This judgment was fulfilled in AD 70 (Lk 21:10-28 describes events at the end of days; for the historical background of AD 70, see the comments introducing the Olivet Discourse in Mt 24–25). In spite of the apparent recognition of Him, He knew these things had **been hidden from** their **eyes** (19:42b). Their own preconceptions and self-generated expectations about who the Messiah would be and what he would do prevented them from seeing the Messiah in Jesus and kept them from recognizing **the time of your visitation** (19:44c).

The judgment of Jerusalem clarifies two issues regarding the history of anti-Semitism: First, the judgment was caused by the Jewish leadership's *rejection* of Jesus as Messiah, not for being uniquely and perpetually guilty of crucifying Jesus. This contradicts the historic "Christ-killer" accusation against the Jewish people. Second, the judgment was fulfilled by the devastating events of the destruction of Jerusalem in AD 70, not through the oppression of the Jewish people in their perpetual wanderings and persecutions. Beginning with Justin Martyr (who wrote of the Jewish people "tribulations were justly imposed on you, for you have murdered the Just One," *Dialogue with Trypho*, 16), the church has frequently leveled both these false charges against the Jewish people, misunderstanding the clear teaching of Lk 19:41-44.

B. Jesus and the Religious Leaders (19:45–21:4)

1. How the Conflict Began (19:45-48) (see also the comments on Mt 21:12-13)

19:45-48. Soon after the events of the triumphal entry Jesus embarked on a course of action that brought Him into conflict with the religious leadership of the nation. He **entered the temple** and drove out those who had perverted the place of prayer and worship into a commercial enterprise (19:45-46). He taught in the temple, and His popularity provoked the opposition of the **chief priests and the scribes** (19:47-48).

2. How the Conflict Continued (20:1–21:4)

20:1-8. The opposition to Jesus took the first available opportunity to question His teaching and authority (20:1-2; see also the comments on Mt 21:23-27). Jesus countered this inquiry with one of His own about John the Baptist (20:3-4).

Jesus knew that the leaders had not believed in John but He, and they also, knew the people regarded John as a prophet of God (20:6). They could not openly deny John, but they refused to acknowledge him (20:7). Jesus therefore refused to answer their question about His authority. Yet in effect He had answered it, for His authority came from the same God and Father who had commissioned John.

20:9-18. Jesus followed this encounter with a parable about a vineyard owner and some renters who refused to honor the vineyard owner's representatives when he sent them to receive his payment (see also the comments on Mt 21:33-46). The wicked renters mistreated and killed the owner's men and finally mistreated and killed the owner's son (20:9-16). Afterward, the owner himself destroyed them and gave **the vineyard to others** (20:16a). The religious leaders understood immediately that they were being cast as the wicked renters (cf. 20:19) and rejected the story—**May it never be**! (20:16b). It appears from the context and the reaction of the religious leaders that Jesus meant them—those leaders had been rejected. Jesus was not making an application to the nation of Israel (and notions of "replacement theology" are not indicated by this parable and its application. See Anthony J. Saldarini, *Matthew's Christian-Jewish Community* [Chicago: University of Chicago Press, 1994], 59 commenting on Mt 21:43). But Jesus drove home the point that these leaders, in rejecting Him, had rejected the **CHIEF CORNER stone** (20:17)—in effect, the Messiah (cf. Ps 118:22).

20:19-26. The conflict continued with questions from the religious leaders designed to trap Him in a contradiction or to get Him to say something that would diminish His popularity. The first question was about paying taxes (20:21-22; see also the comments on Mt 22:15-22). Jesus' answer made it clear that paying taxes (**to Caesar** or any human government) did not indicate divided loyalty. Rather paying taxes and devoting oneself to God were both expressions of submission to God (cf. Rm 13:1-7).

20:27-40. Next the Sadducees, who did not believe in the supernatural afterlife, presented Jesus with a ludicrous hypothetical scenario about a woman who successively (according to the law) married seven brothers (one after the other as each died) (20:27-31; see also the comments on Mt 22:23-33). Their question was, "In the afterlife, **which one's wife will she be?**" (20:33). Jesus' answer was simply to point out that the conditions of that life will be completely different from conditions in this life so far as marriage is concerned (20:34-36). Then He turned their reasoning back on them by pointing out that the very Scriptures they honored spoke of **the Lord THE GOD OF ABRAHAM . . . ISAAC, AND . . . JACOB** (20:37b; cf. Ex 3:6). The way Scripture spoke of the patriarchs indicated that they were still living years after they had passed from the scene. This proved **He is not the God of the dead but of the living** (Lk 20:38), and thus these patriarchs could look forward to the resurrection (cf. Dn 12:2).

20:41-47. At this point Jesus turned the tables on the opposition, and He asked them a question (see also the comments on Mt 22:41-46). In Psalm 110 David, clearly in reference to the Messiah (Christ), calls the Messiah **MY LORD** (20:42; Ps 110:1). Jesus' question to the religious leaders was, "How is it that David calls the Messiah—one who is David's descendant—**MY LORD**?" Of course, the leaders had no answer, but Jesus knew that the One who was the "child born" descendant of Abraham and David humanly speaking was also the preexistent "son who was given" (cf. Is 9:6). This made it possible for the Messiah to be both David's descendant and divine Lord. Jesus then warned his disciples about the duplicity and hypocrisy of the scribes (Lk 20:45-47; see also the comments on Mt 23:1-36) and contrasted that with the lesson of the widow's humble gift (21:1-4).

21:1-4. Apparently, Jesus noticed a **poor widow** who put **two small copper coins** into one of the several chests designed to receive such offerings. "These coins (*lepta*) were the smallest coins in use" (Stein, *Luke*, 509), and the smallest denomination acceptable as a gift. No one else was paying her any attention because what she would give would be inconsequential and unworthy of notice compared to the grand gifts of others. But Jesus noticed and commented the others gave **out of their surplus** (21:4a)—that is, they gave what they could easily spare. However, she gave **out of her poverty** (21:4b)—that is, she gave what she could not really spare. She gave **all that she had to live on**. She gave sacrificially. The actions of this poor widow are not to be seen as a "requirement" to get right with God. One does not earn a right standing with God by giving—sacrificially or otherwise. But these are the actions of one who is right with God. They prove one's standing with God.

C. Jesus' Teaching about the Tribulation and the Second Coming (21:5-38)

In the context of this conflict with the religious leaders (on the same day, see 20:1) Luke included Jesus' teaching to the disciples about the second coming. Much of this discourse is prophetic and refers to the time of the tribulation (see commentary on Mt 24–25) and the second coming of Jesus.

1. The Disciples' Questions (21:5-7)

a. Exchange that Prompted the Questions (21:5-6) (see also the comments on Mt 24:1-2)

21:5-6. During a lull in the back-and-forth with the opposition, the disciples took time to admire the striking beauty of the temple (21:5). The temple itself was adorned with beautiful white marble stones (Josephus, *Wars*, 5.5.6). The massive foundational stones, some of them 30 feet long and still in place today, would have been impressive. The decorations, contributed by wealthy worshipers (**votive gifts**, 21:5b), would have made the temple a place of unusual opulence—something quite beyond what the disciples would have seen anywhere else. The admiration of the disciples was soon broken by Jesus' stark prediction that one day this structure, as massive and as beautiful as it was, would be utterly destroyed—not **one stone** left **upon another** (21:6). (It may be that this prophecy was fulfilled in 70 AD when the Romans sacked Jerusalem in the Jewish revolt (Lk 19:41-44), but the content and context of the discourse to follow would suggest that this was an eschatological prediction (cf. Bock, *Luke*, 1663; but see the interpretive options for the Olivet Discourse in the introductory comments before Mt 24:1).

b. The Two Questions (21:7) (see also the comments on Mt 24:3)

21:7. The unexpected and stunning nature of Jesus' prophecy about the temple would have impressed the disciples. "The disciples recogniz[ed] the importance of Jesus' reply and ask[ed] Him, as Teacher (*didaskale*) when 'these things' will be" (Bock, *Luke*, 1663). Note that there were *two* questions the disciples asked—**when**? (21:7a) . . and **what** sign? (21:7b). In effect, Jesus answered the first question in the discourse itself and warned them not to attempt to focus and rely on any "one sign."

2. Jesus' Answers to the Questions: The Tribulation (21:8-24)

Jesus did not discount the value or relevance of "predictive prophecy" but addressed the disciples' questions with a series of "warnings" and "words" of instruction.

a. Warning to Be Wary about Signs (21:8-11) (see also the comments on Mt 24:4-8)

Jesus began by turning to the question about **the sign** (21:7b). In effect, He warned about the relative predictive value of the signs—that is, the disciples must be wary about the use of the signs—do not be **misled** (21:8a). He warned them about the coming of "phony prophets" (**will come in My name**), "false Christs" (**I am He**), and "deceitful date-setters" (**the time is near**) (21:8b). Even "catastrophic" events (**wars and disturbances** 2:9b, 10a; **earthquakes** . . . **plagues** . . . **famines** . . . **terrors** . . . **signs from heaven** [such as eclipses] 2:10b-11), must not cause them to follow the false alarmists (2:8c) or to lose heart (2:9a). These things will continue to happen **but the end** is not **immediately** (21:9c)—that is, He has not yet come. The events Jesus was describing here are the events of the first half of the tribulation (cf. Jr 30:7; Jl 2; Rv 6–19) and are thus the events that *lead up to*, but are not the second coming itself.

b. Warning and Encouragement Regarding Persecution (21:12-19) (see also the comments on Mt 24:9-14)

21:12-19. Here Jesus offered the disciples not only a word about the nature of the tribulation but also some practical instruction about persecution. First, disciples were to expect persecution from the world (21:12a, b, 17a). Second, they should recognize the opportunity for a witness (12:13) for **My name's sake** (21:12c, 17b). Third, disciples should be determined to endure persecution (21:14a; **make up your minds**). Finally, they must expect the promise of preservation and endurance from the Lord (21:18-19).

c. Warning about Jerusalem (21:20-24) (see also the comments on Mt 24:15-28)

21:20-21. The tribulation will be a time of unprecedented persecution and hardship for the Jewish people and nation of Israel (21:23b; cf. Jr 30:7). The height of persecution will come with a siege of Jerusalem (Lk 21:20a; Zch 12:1-9). The description here and in parallel texts on this point in prophetic history (cf. Mt 24:4-31) make it unlikely that this is a description of the destruction of Jerusalem by the Romans in AD 70 (for more evidence on this understanding, cf. the comments introducing Mt 24, and on Mt 24:15-16). This siege will be a prelude to the city's **desolation** (Lk 21:20b; cf. Mt. 24:15). "The abomination of desolation" is the center point of the tribulation period (cf. the comments on Dn 9:24-27).

21:22-24. The note that these things will happen **so that all things which are written will be fulfilled** (21:22b) indicates that Jesus expected the OT prophecies concerning the end times to be literally fulfilled. The uniquely Lukan phrase **times of the Gentiles** (21:24b) (cf. Bock, *Luke*, 1680) covers the time when Israel lives under ungodly Gentile rule, from the beginning of the Babylonian captivity (c. 586 BC; cf. 2Kg 25), through the era of the postexilic return, the era of the NT, the era of the Church until the second coming, and the ensuing restoration of the Davidic kingdom (cf. Zch 14:9). Some maintain that the events referred to in Lk 21:24 should be restricted to the destruction of Jerusalem in AD 70, and that Luke's version of the Olivet Discourse was altogether fulfilled when Rome destroyed Jerusalem. For a criticism of this view, see the comments introducing Mt 24. Finally, there is the note that the city will be **trampled under foot . . . until the times of the Gentiles are fulfilled** (21:24b), which again covers the time from the fall of Jerusalem to Babylon in 586 BC until the restoration of the kingdom during the millennium following Christ's second coming (cf. Rv 20:1-6).

3. Jesus' Answers to the Questions: The Second Coming (21:25-36)

Jesus finally turned to the matter of His second coming (cf. Mt. 24:3b).

a. Times of Upheaval (21:25-26) (see also the comments on Mt 24:29)

21:25-26. Jesus described the days prior to the second coming itself as days of upheaval—cosmic, 21:25a, 26b (cf. Jl 2:30-31; Ac 2:19-20a); international, Lk 21:25b; terrestrial, 21:25c; and social, 21:26a (cf. Rv 15-19). "Humans will be overcome by fear" (Bock, *Luke*, 1683).

b. The Coming Itself (21:27) (see also the comments on Mt 24:30-31)

21:27. At this time of unprecedented upheaval the **SON OF MAN** (21:27a; cf. the comments on Dn 7:13) will return. He will return in the same way as the disciples will see Him ascend into heaven (cf. Ac 1:11b and the comments there)—physically, and in **A CLOUD** (21:27b; cf. Ac 1:11a). He will return **with power and great glory** (Lk 21:27c; Zch 14:4-6; Rv 19:11-16).

c. A Word of Encouragement to Be Hopeful (21:28)

21:28. Jesus offered a word of encouragement to those who will survive the upheavals of the tribulation and are awaiting the return of their Lord. "Redemption here is used in a broad sense, not deliverance from the penalty of sin but deliverance from a fallen world" (Bock, *Luke*, 1687). Jesus' return will mark the ultimate victory over the forces of the world and Satan.

d. Words of Warning to Be Alert and Expectant (21:29-36) (see also the comments on Mt 24:32-35)

21:29-33. Jesus followed up His discourse with some words of warning and admonition. The parable of the fig tree essentially warned the disciples that once the events Jesus has just described begin to unfold they will continue unabated to the conclusion—the second coming—He has just described. The note about **this generation** (21:32a) is best taken to refer to the generation that is alive when these events begin to unfold (not to the generation to whom Jesus was speaking; similarly, see the comments on Mt 24:34). Jesus' point is, "When the signs come, they will proceed quickly; they will not drag on for generations. It will happen within a generation" (Bock, *Luke*, 1692). Jesus' strong assurance of the veracity of His words—**My words will not pass away** (21:33b)—is also a bold claim to ultimate authority.

21:34-36. Jesus concluded His discourse with a warning to be expectant and to live expectantly—**Be on guard** (21:34)—**keep on the alert** (21:36). In essence, He was teaching His disciples that the way to endure the day-to-day trials of life, as well as the times of peculiar stress and even persecution, is to live with the expectation of the Lord's return—to "keep seeking the things above," to "set your mind on the things above," and keep living for the Lord's return (cf. Col 3:1-4).

4. Summary of the Temple Ministry (21:37-38)

21:37-38. Luke added a note at the end of this section to inform the reader of the situation in which Jesus found Himself during these days of opposition and teaching. Although Jesus' teaching in the temple was popular, this only increased the intensity of the opposition against Him. While He was teaching the crowds in the temple **during the day** He was relatively safe, but in the **evening**, when the crowds went home, He found it necessary to retire to the safety of the mount that is called **Olivet** (Mount of Olives).

VII. The Passion and The Resurrection (22:1–24:53)

A. Plot to Murder Jesus (22:1-6) (see also the comments on Mt 26:1-5, 14-16)

Having noted that Jesus found it necessary to spend His nights at this time outside the city on the Mount of Olives, Luke made explicit the reason for these movements.

1. The Plotters (22:1-2)

22:1-2. Luke noted the time when the plotters began to get serious about their work—it was **Passover** (22:1). Luke was alerting his non-Jewish audience that this was a time of unique significance—the time of the sacrifice of the paschal lamb (cf. Ex 12:1-27; Lk 22:7). The plotters are, in effect, preparing the sacrifice of the "Lamb of God who takes away the sin of the world" (cf. Jn 1:29). The plotters are identified as **chief priests** and **scribes** (Lk 22:2a)—they were more on the political side of Jesus' opposition. Apparently, they wanted to get rid of Jesus before the crowds of Passover worshipers entered the city. They feared He would find even greater popularity with the crowds who came into the city from around the nation (22:2c) so they coldly and deliberately determined to **put Him to death** (22:2b).

2. The Traitor (22:3-6)

22:3-6. Luke immediately stated that **Judas** (**Iscariot** was his family name) was motivated and animated by **Satan** (22:3a). This was by no means an effort to exonerate Judas, but was meant to highlight that one facet of the opposition to Jesus was supernatural, spiritual, and satanic—alongside the human designs of Judas and the religious leaders. The note that Judas had been one **of the twelve** (22:3b) made this act the more unfathomable and heinous. How Judas knew that the plotters would receive him (22:4a), accept his offer to **betray Him** (22:4b), and pay him for this act (22:5) is not made clear. While the exchange of money might seem to indicate a motive of greed, in reality, Judas' act was utterly irrational and inexplicable, as is unbelief itself. Judas' plan was to seek a suitable time and opportunity to betray Him—a time when Jesus was isolated from the protection of the **crowd** (22:6).

B. The Upper Room (22:7-38)

With the plot hanging over Jesus' head, the scene in the upper room had a melancholy aspect to it from the start. Throughout Luke's description there is a "sense of the significant" in every scene.

1. Preparations for Passover (22:7-13) (see also the comments on Mt 26:17-19)

22:7-13. The note about the feast of **Unleavened Bread** and the sacrifice of the **Passover lamb** (22:7) would have added to the significance and solemnity of these preparations for the reader who was aware that Jesus Himself is "our Passover" (cf. 1Co 5:7). Jesus Himself knew this was His last Passover and these were His last hours. The Passover had to be eaten within the walls of the city (cf. Lk 2:41; 2Ch 35:16-19; *Jub* 49:15-16; cf. Stein, *Luke*, 538), so He needed to make arrangements other than His retreat to the Mount of Olives. Luke alone noted the names of the two disciples charged with the preparations for this Passover—**Peter and John** (Lk 22:8a). The preparations would have involved "seeing the lamb was roasted ... and preparing all the side dishes and wine" (Stein, *Luke*, 538), and yet the only question from the disciples was, **Where?** (22:9b). The details in Jesus' response indicate that this was a prearranged meeting (22:10) and the room had already been secured (22:11-12). The disciples found that everything was **just as He had told them** (22:13). Jesus was thus presented as an observant Jew, performing all the responsibilities of piety as described by the law. It also showed that Jesus was in control of the situation—an emphasis that will be true even through His arrest and trials. (On the question of the chronology of the Passover accounts see Thomas and Gundry, *Harmony of the Gospels*, 320–23).

2. Institution of the Lord's Supper (22:14-20) (see also the comments on Mt 26:20-29)

22:14. Luke's introduction to the scene of the last supper—**When the hour had come** (22:14a)—continued "the sense of the significant." This was "the hour" not just of the start of the Passover celebration, but the hour that actually began the passion of Christ. However, the scene opened with no hint of all that was to come. Jesus **reclined** at the table (22:14b) and **the apostles with Him** (22:14c), enjoying the meal and each other's company.

22:15-20. Into this idyllic scene Jesus introduced an ominous note, one He had attempted to convey to the disciples previously (cf. Lk 9:22)—His impending suffering (22:15b). In addition, He announced He would not eat another Passover with them **until it is fulfilled in the kingdom of God** (22:16). It was in the light of the cross (His suffering) and the hope of His future reign (**until the kingdom of God comes**; 22:18b) that Jesus instituted the celebration of "the bread and the cup." Using items left over from the Passover meal, Jesus took the elements of bread and wine and re-signified them as **My**

body (22:19b) and **My blood** (22:20c). As the bread was given (22:19a) and the wine **poured out** (22:20b) so His body was given and His life poured out. Jesus viewed His death as sacrificial and vicarious—His body was **given *for you*** (22:19a), His blood **poured out *for you*** (22:20b; emphasis added). The actions He prescribed—eating and drinking—indicated the disciples, by partaking of these elements, were signifying their faith in Him and their trust in the death He was about to suffer. "Here is not only deep theological truth but great love" (Bock, *Luke*, 1725). Jesus' command, **Do this in remembrance of Me** (22:22:19c), was meant to remember His Person, His work on the cross, and that He is coming again—we are "proclaiming His death until He returns" (1Co 11:26).

3. Four Post-Supper Conversations (22:21-38)

The disciples were given no time to reflect on the significance of the ceremony that Jesus had just instituted because the events of that night moved inexorably, allowing little time to reflect or think.

a. The Betrayer Announced (22:21-23) (see also the comments on Mt 26:21-24)

22:21-23. In the first post-supper conversation, Jesus announced that He would be **betrayed** (22:22). Although the reader already knew this, it was a shock to the disciples. Even more outrageous was that the betrayal (22:21b; lit., "is in the process of betraying") was already underway. Next, Jesus explained that this treachery was not unexpected but was a part of the way that had **been determined** (22:22a) as part of the divine plan (cf. Ps 41:9; 55:12-14; Ac 2:23). Nevertheless, He indicated that the traitor would still be culpable for his crime (Lk 22:22b). This conversation concluded with the disciples speculating on who the culprit might be (22:23).

b. Debate Over Who Is the Greatest (22:24-30)

22:24-30. Whatever angst the disciples felt over the revelation that Jesus was about to be betrayed soon left them, and, in the second post-supper conversation, they began a silly argument over which of them would be regarded as the **greatest** (22:24). It was an evidence of Jesus' selflessness and patience that He did not rebuke them for their truly amazing indifference to Him and His impending passion, but instead He used the occasion to teach them yet another serious lesson on service. True greatness, He taught, is not in having others serve you (22:25), but the greatest is the one who **serves**. Jesus pointed to Himself as the supreme example (22:27). Still, He gave them an encouraging promise and assured them that their service and sacrifice would not go unrewarded (22:28-30).

c. Jesus Predicts Peter's Denials (22:31-34)

22:31-34. In the third post-supper conversation Jesus revealed to Peter that he would deny Him. The conversation began with Jesus reassuring Peter that while Satan had asked to **sift** Peter **like wheat** (22:31)—that is, to test him severely, nevertheless, He, Jesus, had **prayed** for Peter, specifically that his **faith may not fail** (22:32a). Jesus' words indicated that Peter would not be completely unscathed by this Satanic attack, but that he would be **turned again** (22:32b; i.e., repentant) and that he could look forward to being again in a place where he could **strengthen** the others (22:32c). Peter's response showed that he had no inkling of the danger he was in, and that he was overconfident in his own ability to keep himself faithful. His boast—**I am ready** (22:33)—would in short order be proven empty, sadly, as Jesus' sobering prediction of Peter's denial would be fulfilled (22:34).

d. Jesus Attempted to Prepare His Men for the Coming Conflict (22:35-38)

22:35-38. In the final post-supper conversation Jesus once again attempted to prepare His disciples for the conflict that was just ahead of them. He first reminded them that He had not previously sent them out unprepared (22:35). Now, speaking metaphorically (using the items of **money belt**, **bag**, and **sword** as non-literal expressions of "being prepared"), they were called to prepare themselves (22:36) because He was going to be **NUMBERED WITH TRANSGRESSORS** (22:37b). What He was about to undergo was to be considered a **fulfillment** of what was **written** (predicted in the OT) (22:37). Nevertheless they were to be ready for His absence. The disciples did not understand Jesus' point, or the nature of the conflict to come, and they produced two actual swords (22:38a). Jesus' words, **It is enough** (22:38b), may be understood not as a commentary on the number of weapons but as an expression of mild frustration over the disciples' misunderstanding (cf. Stein, *Luke*, 555). But **enough** means "to be sufficient, suitable in number or amount." The disciples had two swords after accompanying Jesus for nearly three years. If He objected to the possession of weapons as a general rule, the disciples would not have had them so late in their association with Jesus in His ministry. **It is enough** more than likely indicates that Jesus did not object to the means for self-defense.

C. Three Heartbreaking Scenes (22:39-62)

Even with the institution of the Lord's Supper and the post-supper conversations, the disciples had not realized the deep significance of the events of the night thus far. Moreover, nothing in the movement of Jesus out of the city would have alerted them to the shattering experiences that were soon to follow. Luke noted that it was **His custom** (22:39; cf. 21:37) to leave the city at night for the refuge of the Mount of Olives. In three emotionally fraught scenes, the disciples' world was turned upside down.

1. Prayer in Gethsemane (22:39-46) (see also the comments on Mt 26:30-46)

22:39-40. Upon reaching the western slope of the **Mount**, identified by Luke only as **the place** (22:40a, identified in the other gospels as "Gethsemane," which means "olive press," Mt 26:36; Mk 14:32), Jesus admonished His disciples to **pray** (lit., "keep praying") **that you may not enter into temptation** (Lk 22:40b). The events to follow would test the disciples' trust and commitment to Jesus. They needed the strength that only divine assistance could provide. Tellingly, Jesus' response to an impending crisis was prayer (cf. Bock, *Luke*, 1763). Even as He was facing the monumental challenge of His passion, He was concerned for His men. Luke did not record that Jesus took Peter, James, and John with Him inside the garden to pray (cf. Mt 26:37).

22:41. Luke recorded Jesus' actions with a simplicity that still conveyed the depth of significance of the scene. First, Jesus **withdrew . . . about a stone's throw** (22:41a) or simply "not far away." The term **withdrew** (*apospao*, "tear away") is stronger than simply "went away"—it adds a note of emotion (cf. Ac 21:1). Second, He **knelt down** (Lk 22:41b); again, the action is more vivid than simply the act of "kneeling." The parallel accounts (cf. Mt 26:39; Mk 14:35) say He "fell down," in the sense "He dropped to His knees." Finally, He began **to pray** (22:41c), indicating that He gave voice to the sentiments of His heart.

22:42-44. There are four parts to Jesus' prayer: First, He acknowledged the Father's ability to hear and to answer—**if You are willing** (22:42b). Second, He communicated His petition—**remove this cup from Me** (22:42c). Jesus was not asking to be released from the purpose for which He had come, but He was voicing the perfectly understandable desire to avoid the suffering He was about to face. Third, He expressed His submission—**yet not My will, but Yours be done** (22:42d). This was no mere resignation but an active submission, a giving of Himself to the Father's purpose and will. Fourth, He conveyed His fervency (22:44b). So intense was this act of prayer that Luke recorded that He was **in agony** (22:44a), that is, He was physically affected—so much so that **His sweat became like drops of blood** (22:44c). This may be an instance (noted only by Luke the physician) of *hematridrosis*—a condition that occurs when one is under great stress. However, Luke said Jesus' perspiration was **like** blood, using a comparative particle (*hosei*). The phrase probably indicates simply a comparison, meant to indicate the intensity of Jesus' effort; it produced profuse or dripping sweat. The intensity of the prayer affected Him spiritually as well, so much so that an **angel from heaven** (22:43) arrived to strengthen Him (perhaps with encouraging words; cf. Dn 9:3, 23). This is another detail found only in Luke's account.

22:45-46. As the mysterious scene began with Jesus' concern for His disciples, so it concluded with that concern. Jesus returned to find the disciples asleep. Luke noted that the sleep was **from sorrow** (22:45), which may indicate that they were aware of His struggles in, and the intensity of, His prayers. Nevertheless, He rebuked them for their inattention and warned them of the danger at hand (22:46). Although Jesus understood the gravity of the moment, the disciples did not. Yet in a short time they would.

2. Arrest in the Garden (22:47-53) (see also the comments on Mt 26:47-56)

22:47-51. Luke's account indicates the swift and confusing rush of events. From the secluded scene of prayer, the action moved to the chaotic events of arrest and trial. Luke's account of the arrest is the shortest of the gospel writers. Even while Jesus was **still speaking** (22:47a), a crowd of **chief priests and officers of the temple and elders** (22:52a) led by Judas the traitor (22:47b) approached Him **to kiss Him**. The **kiss** (22:47c; Luke did not record the act of the kiss itself) was no doubt the signal to the officers that He was the One to be arrested (cf. Mt 26:48-49; Mk 14:44). But the familiarity and (false) affection of the act made the betrayal that much more heinous. Jesus' rebuke to Judas (Lk 22:48) was blunt and withering—no question that this was the despicable act of a traitor. This word from Jesus may have been the first indication to the disciples of what was actually happening, and it prompted an inept and futile response (22:49). The impetuous act of **one of them** (22:50a; Peter, cf. Jn 18:10), slicing off the ear of a servant of the high priest (Lk 22:50b), indicated the continued misunderstanding of the disciples (cf. 22:38). The swift rebuke of Jesus—**Stop! No more of this** and His compassionate act of healing the man's **ear** (22:51, the last miracle of Jesus' ministry) contrasted with the militant actions and harsh intentions of His accusers.

22:52-53. Jesus' rebuke to the religious leaders was condemning and revealing. As if this healing was not enough of an implied rebuke, Jesus noted that their method (**with swords and clubs**), their manner (**as you would against a robber**, 22:52), their choice of location, and their timing (not in the temple and at **this hour**, 22:53) of this arrest all indicated something of their real motivation and intentions. Bluntly, He attributed their act to **the power of darkness,** namely, Satan (cf. Col 1:13).

3. Denial in a Courtyard (22:54-62) (see also the comments on Mt 26:69-75)

22:54-55. As the sweep of events moved on, Luke recorded that Jesus was taken to the **house of the high priest** (22:54a). Before the trial itself Luke (as did the other three gospel writers) recorded Peter's denial. It is a testimony to the veracity of the gospel writers that they faithfully recorded the failure of one of the "pillars of the church" (cf. Gl 2:9). The events of the scene are almost painful to read, and they unfolded slowly over the course of Jesus' trial. First, Peter's **following at a distance** (22:54) is noted. It is doubtful that any spiritual significance is to be attached to that note. He simply lagged behind the arresting party. Next, Peter's presence at a small fire with a group of the locals is mentioned (22:55). Again, this is merely a factual statement meant to set up the three identifications that follow.

22:56-60a. Three separate people identified Peter, likely because he had sat with them for perhaps two or three hours, outside the high priest's house. First a mere **servant-girl**, after **looking** at him **intently** (22:56b; this probably was meant to convey that Peter was trying to conceal himself in the dim glow of the firelight), identified him as one who **was with Him too** (22:56c). Peter's denial was swift and terse (22:57). Second, **a little later** (22:58a) another man placed Peter with Jesus' disciples—**You are one of them too!** (22:58b). Again, Peter's denial was swift, but now a bit more emphatic—**Man, I am not!** (22:58c). Then, after **about an hour** (22:59a) yet another man more insistently began to affirm that **certainly** Peter **was with Him**, and he asserted that Peter was Galilean to back up his identification (22:59b). The rising conviction of his accusers was met by the rising intensity of Peter's denials. Therefore, he responded with his most vehement denial—**Man, I do not know what you are talking about** (22:60a; Luke omitted Peter's cursing, cf. Mk 14:71). The scene was distressing, but it was about to grow even more intense.

22:60b-62. While the words of denial were being spoken, Peter heard the crow of a rooster (22:60b). At that instant, **the Lord turned and looked at Peter** (22:61a). One can only imagine the searing pain of conscience that swept over Peter at that moment as Peter recalled Jesus' words (cf. 22:34) spoken only hours before (22:61b). **He went out and wept bitterly** (22:62); "The effect on Peter was shattering" (Morris, *Luke*, 316). As difficult as this scene is to read, it serves not only to reassure readers of the veracity and accuracy of the narrative as a whole. It also served to teach that restoration, even after the most egregious failures, is possible. The gospel writer spared no one's reputation so as to tell the story completely and faithfully.

D. Four Unjust Trials (22:63–23:25)

The identity of Jesus is the main theme of the trials, as it is of the historical narrative as well. Luke kept asking and answering, who is Jesus? Ironically, in these accounts the interrogators are the ones who speak the truth about Jesus. Although Luke does not highlight it, evidently the accounts themselves demonstrate that there were a number of illegalities about these trials. Luke left it to the reader to see and come to the appropriate conclusion that Jesus was unjustly charged and executed.

1. Jesus before the Sanhedrin (22:63-71)

22:63-64. Apparently there was some sort of illegal pre-trial hearing that Luke did not record (cf. Mt 26:59-68; Mk 14:55-65). Holding Jesus at the high priest's house had been illegal, as was the beating that followed. The abuse Jesus suffered involved both psychological (**mocking**) and physical abuse (**beating**, Lk 22:63), as well as a cruel game—they blindfolded Him, struck Him, and then taunted Him to identify the attacker (22:64). Luke added the emphatic explanation—they were **blaspheming** (22:65). All of this had been predicted by Jesus (cf. 9:22, 44), showing that in spite of the appearances, through all the abuse, Jesus was in control, and all of it was according to the divine plan (cf. Mt 26:53-54).

22:65-67. As the trial itself got underway, Luke noted who was attending. The **Council of elders** (22:66a) is probably a synonym for the Sanhedrin (cf. Acts 22:5). Among those sitting in judgment were some of those who had been in the garden to arrest Jesus—**scribes** and **chief priests** (Lk 22:66)—so much for a fair trial! There followed a series of questions from the council and Jesus' response. The first question—**If You are the Christ, tell us** (22:67a) was completely disingenuous. Everything Jesus did, His healings and His teachings, from His affirmation in Nazareth (cf. 4:21) up to the healing of the servant's ear just hours earlier, had proven that He was the Messiah. His first response exposed their dishonesty—**If I tell you, you will not believe** (22:67b). Jesus' point was that neither "evidence" nor "reason" would change their minds because they were already convinced that Jesus was *not* the Messiah.

22:68-71. Jesus also exposed their prejudice by pointing out that "dialogue" with them was useless because they would refuse to answer Him honestly (22:68). However, even in the face of their dishonesty and bias (and knowing how His answer would be twisted by them) He answered honestly and more completely than they expected. In effect He told them, "Yes, I am the Messiah and one day I will prove it to your satisfaction and chagrin." He quoted a portion of Ps 110:1 and applied the messianic title **Son of Man** (cf. Dn 7:13-14) to Himself. This prompted the council to ask an even more inflammatory question—**Are You the Son of God, then?** (Lk 22:70a). Jesus' ready and confident answer was in effect, "Yes, I am the Son of God." (**Yes, I am** is literally "You say that I am"; both expressions convey the same idea.) Luke recorded this to convey that Jesus did not hesitate to affirm His messiahship and His deity, truths that Luke had been affirming throughout his narrative (cf. 1:32-35; 3:22; 4:3, 9, 41; 8:28; 9:35; cf. Ac 9:20; 13:33). The reaction of the council was swift and definitive. "As far as Jesus' opponents were concerned, their purpose . . . had now been accomplished" (Stein, *Luke*, 571).

2. Jesus before Pilate the First Time (23:1-7)
(see also the comments on Mt 27:11-14)

23:1-2. However, while the council had the verdict they wanted, they did not have the authority to carry out the death sentence they wanted. For that they needed another charge, one that would stand before Pilate, the Roman governor (23:1). Therefore, Jesus' accusers would change their strategy before Pilate. Rather than question Jesus, they attempted to bring three accusations against Him. One accusation was that He was **misleading our nation** (23:2a)—a sort of general charge of stirring up insurrectionist sentiments. A second accusation was that He was encouraging insubordination to the Roman authorities, at just the point that mattered most to those authorities—the paying of **taxes** (23:2b). (That this charge was patently false would have been clear to anyone; cf. 20:20-26). The third accusation was that Jesus was calling Himself **Christ, a King** (23:2c). This last accusation revealed that Jewish people considered any claim to be the Messiah as a claim to be king, no doubt reflecting their expectations of the literal fulfillment of the promises of the Davidic covenant (cf. 2Sm 7; Ps 89). From this charge, they also wanted Pilate to conclude that Jesus intended to foment a literal (armed and military) rebellion against Rome.

23:3-4. It was this last charge that interested Pilate and so he followed it up with a direct question to Jesus—**Are You the King of the Jews?** (23:3a). Jesus' answer was likewise direct. **It is as you say** (23:3b; see Jn 18:33-37 for a fuller reply). In spite of what appeared to be an admission of guilt, Pilate rendered his verdict—**I find no guilt in this man** (23:4).

23:5-7. The accusers were not so easily dissuaded and sought to press the first charge (insurrection) that Pilate had apparently ignored (22:5). However, upon their mentioning of Galilee, Pilate saw a possible opening to avoid further involvement in the matter. He would refer Jesus to Herod (Antipas, ruler of Galilee who had also ordered John the Baptist's execution, cf. 13:31) who happened to be visiting Jerusalem for Passover.

3. Jesus before Herod (23:8-12)

23:8-12. The account of Jesus before Herod is unique to Luke (cf. Ac 4:27-28). This was a meeting that was long overdue (Lk 23:8b). Herod had wanted to see Jesus **to see some sign**, that is some miracle, **performed by Him** (23:8c). The expression is a clue to Herod's mindset—Jesus was considered to be a "performer" who could put on a good show; Herod had no deeper interests. As Herod was an insincere inquirer (23:9a), Jesus felt no inclination to dignify the proceedings with any answers (23:9b; cf. Is 53:7). This is not the silence of one "Jesus meek and mild," but the silence of a superior not condescending to lower Himself to the childish level of this shallow knave. Once again, it is an example that through it all Jesus was in control. However, His accusers were again vehemently pressing their case (Lk 23:10). Luke's description of their behavior is emphatic. Herod's contemptuous and juvenile mockery (23:11a) of Jesus only served to reinforce the picture of Herod as a superficial and foolish character who, in the presence of the Son of God, can only think of coarse jests and mocking contempt. He made no verdict and sent Jesus back to Pilate (23:11b) "The really frightening thing about the incident [is that] with the Son of God before him Herod could only jest" (Morris, *Luke*, 321). Luke noted that their mutual hostility toward Jesus turned the hostility between Pilate and Herod to friendship (23:12)—a twisted and corrupt basis for becoming **friends**.

4. Jesus before Pilate the Second Time (23:13-25) (see also the comments on Mt 27:15-26)

23:13-17. Since Herod had not relieved him of the responsibility of dealing with Jesus, Pilate once again found himself before the Jewish religious authorities (23:13). The scene unfolded in three parts: First, Pilate rendered his (what he thought would be the final) verdict. Again, in Luke's narrative an unbeliever stated the truth—**I have found no guilt in this man** (23:14b). The charges against Jesus were, indeed, groundless—He was simply an innocent man—and this was the opinion of Herod as well (23:15) who, like Pilate, had the authority to execute Jesus. Still, to appease the leaders and the crowd, Pilate decided to (unjustly) **punish Him**, but then to **release** Him (23:16). In a parenthetical note, Luke informed the reader that, not only had he found Jesus innocent but Pilate also was using a recognized custom, an act of clemency, to **release** Jesus (23:17; this verse is not found in a few of the oldest Gk. mss).

23:18-25. In the second part of this scene, the crowds (**they**, 23:18a), no doubt prompted by the religious leaders, expressed their displeasure with Pilate's verdict and demanded not only that Jesus be taken away (23:18b) and crucified (23:21), but also (in a tragic irony) that a genuine insurrectionist, **Barabbas** (23:18c-19), be released instead. The scene shifted back and forth—Pilate reiterating his verdict of Jesus' innocence and his intent to release Jesus (23:20, 22), and the crowds increasingly insistent on his death (23:21, 23). In the final, tragic scene of this trial a pliable Pilate capitulated to the will of the people—he condemned Jesus (23:24) and released the insurrectionist (23:25). Why did the crowd prefer the insurrectionist? That his insurrection was mentioned twice would indicate that that is what they wanted—they were rejecting Jesus as Messiah who came to save sinners (cf. 19:10) and not to throw off the yoke of Rome.

E. Crucifixion and Burial (23:26-56)

Luke related the crucifixion and burial with a studied simplicity. There is no attempt to draw out the pathos of the scene, there is no melodramatic description, (cf. Stein, *Luke*, 588), and there is no theological explanation of the events—no "theory of the atonement" (see Is 53). There is only the record of the events, which is designed to keep to Luke's main theme—answering the question "Who is Jesus?"

1. The Cross (23:26-49)

a. On the Way to the Cross (23:26-32) (see also the comments on Mt 27:31-34)

23:26-27. In Luke's account, the narrative of the way to the cross is taken up with the people encountered on the way. The first person is **a man, Simon of Cyrene** (23:26a). Normally criminals were forced to carry their own cross to the place of execution. However, the beatings and extended trials caused Jesus to be too weak to perform this task, and so Simon was forced (only Luke uses the forceful term **seized**) to carry the cross (23:26b). Simon, probably a Jew from North Africa (Cyrene), was visiting Jerusalem for the Passover and may have become a follower of Jesus (cf. Mk 15:21). Luke noted **a large crowd** (Lk 23:27a) of people following Jesus to His execution. Luke's description of the crowd was ambiguous. Sometimes the crowd seemed to be with Jesus, but at other times (as during the recent trials) they were with the opposition. Once again the crowd displayed its ambivalence toward Jesus, following more out of curiosity than concern. Next came a brief encounter between Jesus and some **women**, the professional mourners (23:27b) (not those who had followed Jesus during His ministry) who were dutifully, if somewhat mechanically, performing their duties. Even in His weakened condition Jesus took the opportunity to offer a word of warning to these women and the crowd.

23:28-32. First, instead of expressing appreciation for their sentiments on His behalf, He surprisingly admonished them to direct their lamentations, not for Him, but for themselves and their children. For rejecting Him they will all face a judgment (23:28). Second, He offered a prophetic word on the tragedy about to befall them. The **days are coming** (23:29a), He said, when conditions would be so bad that those without children would be the most **blessed** (23:29a, b), certainly a stark and disturbing thought for these women. Furthermore, in those days men would prefer being covered with earth—i.e., death—rather than face the judgment that was about to befall them (23:30). Jesus quoted Hs 10:8 and Is 2:19, both contexts that speak of judgment. Finally He offered a proverb (Lk 23:31) that said in effect, if this travesty—a condemnation of the innocent (**when the tree is green**)—can happen then how much more likely will be the judgment on the guilty (when the wood is **dry**)? The overall point Jesus was making is this: the citizens needed to wake up and realize that by this rejection of the Messiah they were in danger of judgment. Indeed, that judgment fell in AD 70.

Luke added a brief note about the two criminals who **were being led away** with Jesus (23:32) in order to provide a setting for the conversation that took place during the crucifixion.

b. Crucifixion (23:33-38) (see also the comments on Mt 27:35-44)

23:33. The place of the crucifixion was not only a place of shame (with criminals, 23:33b), but even its name—**the place called The Skull** (23:33a) was foreboding. It may have resembled a human skull ("Calvary" is a transliteration of the Latin word *calvaria*, which means "skull"; "Golgotha" is the Aramaic equivalent) or it may have been a place associated with skulls, that is, a place of death—executions and graves.

23:34a, b. The first of three statements from the cross (as recorded by Luke) was a word of forgiveness (23:34). If Jesus' prophetic retort to the professional mourners seemed a bit discordant (one would think He would appreciate the gesture), this word of forgiveness is completely unexpected (in an entirely different way). When one might expect Him to be reasserting His innocence (which in a way He does here), He rather prayed a prayer for forgiveness for His executioners—**Father, forgive them** (23:34a). Jesus was not suggesting that ignorance is an excuse for sin (23:34b); he was being gracious. He was practicing what He taught (cf. 6:27-28), and He was fulfilling prophecy (cf. Is 53:12).

23:34c-38. The activity around the cross involved the soldiers playing games of chance with His **garments** as the prize (23:34c; cf. Ps 22:18) and several groups of people mocking and berating Him. Once again, even in the cruel derision and contempt of the **people** (Lk 23:35a), **rulers** (23:35b), and **soldiers** (23:36a), Luke managed to have the opponents of Jesus speak the truth about Him. Unknowingly they were confirming that He is the One who can save others (23:35c; 37b; cf. 19:10) *not by saving* Himself but by *giving* Himself. "[T]he saving nature of Jesus' ministry is referred to four times in the space of five verses" (23:35-39; Stein, *Luke* 590). He is **the Christ of God, His chosen One** (23:35d), He is **the king of the Jews** (23:37a, 38). All of this mockery *was fulfilling* the prophetic word of Ps 22 (cf. Ps 22:6-18) and thus is itself confirmation that Jesus was the Messiah. Luke expected his readers to understand that these mockers were correct in their mockery and chiding because unwittingly they confirmed the Christology that he had related in the previous 22 chapters: He is the Christ/Messiah (cf. Lk 1:32-33; 2:11, 26; 4:41; 9:20), He is the King of the Jews (cf. 1:32-33; 2:4; 18:38-39; 19:38), and He is the Savior (cf. 1:47, 69, 77; 2:11; 19:10).

c. Conversation with Criminals (23:39-43)

23:39-43. Luke's account of the conversation with the two criminals is unique to his gospel. With Matthew (Mt 27:44) and Mark (Mk 15:32), Luke noted the abuse that Jesus received from the criminals, but unlike the others he recorded that while the abuse came from one of the criminals (Lk 23:39a) the other criminal defended Jesus. Once again the facts of Jesus' person and mission (that He was **the Christ** and had come to save others) were put into the mouth of Jesus' antagonists through the first criminal's rant (23:39b). The second criminal responded in three ways. First, he rebuked the mocking criminal, acknowledging the justice of their punishment (23:40-41a). Second, he defended Jesus, acknowledging the Lord's innocence (23:41b). Third, he made a request of Jesus, demonstrating his faith. In the simple request, **Jesus, remember me when You come in Your kingdom** (23:42), the criminal affirmed his belief that Jesus was the Messiah and the King of the Jews, since he expected Jesus to have a kingdom, and that He could save him—**remember me**. As a result, the criminal received a promise—**Today, you shall be with Me in Paradise** (heaven; Rv 2:7) (23:43b). This was the second of the sayings of Jesus from the cross as recorded by Luke.

d. The Conclusion of Jesus' Passion (23:44-49) (see also the comments on Mt 27:45-56)

23:44-46. The **sixth hour . . . until the ninth hour** (23:44) would have been noon to three o'clock in the afternoon. The supernatural darkness (23:44-45a; there is no hint of an eclipse or other natural phenomenon) indicated that an event of cosmic significance was happening. The rending of the veil in the holy place of the temple was another supernatural indication that the way into the presence of God was now accomplished by Jesus' sacrifice (cf. the comments on Mt 27:51; cf. Heb 10:19-20). The third word of Jesus from the cross (as recorded by Luke) and the final cry of Jesus, committing Himself into His Fathers' hands, quotes Ps 31:5. In that psalm a righteous man pleads for a rescue from his enemies but nevertheless commits himself in trust to the LORD. "Jesus' remarks are an expression of righteous faith . . . Jesus is the righteous sufferer *par excellence*." Bock suggests that in this expression of "his trust that God will care for him . . . Jesus is expressing his trust that God will "resurrect him" (Bock, *Luke*, 1862). And as in Jn 19:30—"It is finished!"—Jesus was affirming that He had accomplished the sacrificial atonement for sins, that work for which He had been born (cf. Lk 1:77; 2:29-32). "Thus after finishing his mission, Jesus committed himself into his Father's hands and breathed his last. No one took his life from him. He gave it freely (cf. Jn 10:18)" (Stein, *Luke*, 597). Of course, this does not imply the silly notion that Jesus "committed suicide" but that He freely submitted Himself to the Father's purpose for His incarnation (cf. Mt 1:21; Jn 1:29; Gl 1:4) and offered Himself willingly as a sacrifice.

23:47-49. Luke recorded three reactions to Jesus' death: The first was the confession of the centurion that **this man was innocent** (23:47). This is significant because any centurion would have been a man of utmost integrity whose word was to be accepted as completely unbiased and true. Also, he would have been the man in charge for this execution (he was in a position to know the man he was executing). Finally, he was a Gentile, so his testimony would have had great weight with Luke's readership. Furthermore, this is the same testimony as that of the criminal. Thus from both sides of the "law" came the same conclusion—Jesus was innocent. The second reaction was that of the crowd, which was remorse (23:48). The fickle crowd that had cried for His death, that had gathered for the **spectacle** of it all, those people, after they witnessed all the events, were **beating their breasts** (23:48c; Luke alone recorded this act of communal contrition). The final reaction to Jesus' death was on the part of the friends (**acquaintances**), and faithful women who had followed Him from Galilee (23:49). They were vigilant. They **were standing at a distance** and waited for the opportunity to serve Jesus one final time.

2. The Tomb (23:50-56) (see also the comments on Mt 27:57-66)

As with the account of the crucifixion, the account of the burial is related simply and without a melodramatic flourish.

23:50-52. First, a good man made a bold request. In a short space, Luke related several key facts about this man: his name was **Joseph** (23:50a; a common name then as now), he was **a member of the Council** (23:50b; which meant that this request may have put him at odds with those who had opposed Jesus), and he was a man of quality (**a good and righteous man**, 23:50c), meaning a man of integrity. As proof, it is related that he **had not consented to their plan and action** (23:51a)—that is, he had not approved or participated in the unjust trials or false accusations against Jesus. Additionally, he was from a town called **Arimathea**, a city of Judea (23:51b), and he was **waiting for the kingdom of God** (23:51c)—that is, he was looking for the Messiah. He also was a bold man, asking Pilate for **the body of Jesus** (23:52). For Joseph to identify himself as sympathetic to Jesus—if not as actually one of His followers—right after Jesus had been executed would have required courage.

23:53-56. Next, Luke recorded a considerate and sympathetic burial (23:53). The whole scene conveyed a sense of deep respect and loving care for Jesus. "The reader is to note the respect shown to Jesus and the effort made to give Him care" (Bock, *Luke*, 1878). Finally, there was a hasty internment. The notes regarding the **preparation day** and the onset of **the Sabbath** (23:54) conveyed that the normal preparations for burial had to be curtailed. The women (cf. 23:49) made sure they knew where the tomb was (23:55) so that they could return there after preparing **spices and perfumes** (23:56) to complete the rituals of burial.

F. Resurrection, Commission, Ascension (24:1-53)

In Luke's account the events surrounding the resurrection all occurred on the same day, and all of them in, or around, Jerusalem (cf. Stein, *Luke*, 602).

1. Resurrection (24:1-46)

a. At the Tomb (24:1-12) (see also the comments on Mt 28:1-8)

24:1-3. Luke assumed the reader would understand that it was the women who came to the tomb (**they came**; cf. 23:49, 55) to complete the burial rituals for Jesus (24:1). Note that Luke recorded that women were the first to learn of the resurrection. That it was **on the first day of the week** and **at early dawn** (24:1a) accords with the accounts of the other gospels. Luke had not previously mentioned **the stone**, which was now **rolled away** (24:2). On entering the tomb, the women did not find **the body of the Lord Jesus** (24:3). Luke's emphasis was on the absence of the "body"—it was a "bodily resurrection." Furthermore, the fuller identification, "Lord Jesus," conveyed something of the import of the resurrection—it proved His claim to lordship (cf. Ac 22:22-36; Eph 1:20-21).

24:4-5a. Two men appeared (24:4a; only Luke mentioned both, one of whom was the only speaker, hence Mark's one man, Mk 16:5, and Matthew's one angel, Mt 28:2-3, 5). They were clearly angels, as revealed by the suddenness of their appearance, the description of their clothing (Lk 24:4b), and the insight they were able to give to the women (cf. 24:5-6). This was later made explicit in v. 23. This manifestation of angelic glory was startling and caused the women look away in fear (24:5a).

24:5b-8. The message of the angels was stunning. First, there was a question: **Why do you seek the living One among the dead?** (24:5b), which came as a mild rebuke. Before the women could protest (it was after all quite reasonable for them to be at the tomb looking for Jesus' body) the angel added: **He is not here, but He has risen** (24:6a). This was quickly followed by an explanation (24:6b-7), emphasizing the "divine necessity" of the events that had led to this moment (24:7, **must be**). In effect, the angel was saying to the women, "You should have expected all these events—the passion, the cross, and the resurrection—because this is what Jesus was telling you all along." Luke noted that they **remembered His words** (24:8). It was not the evidence of their own eyes—an empty tomb—or even the words of angels, that convinced them. Rather, it was the memory of the Word that Jesus taught and now confirmed by His resurrection that brought them to realize that He had **risen**!

24:9-12. The women immediately returned to the city and **reported all these things** to the disciples (24:9). Including the names of some of the women (24:10) is yet another example of how Luke gave prominence to the role of women in the gospel narrative. The report of the women did not receive immediate acceptance (24:11) but prompted Peter to go out to the tomb in haste; he **ran to the tomb** (24:12a). While he saw the evidences of the empty tomb and the linen wrappings—and he was impressed (**marveling**)—the impression from what Luke wrote was that Peter did not yet believe (24:12b).

b. On the Road to Emmaus (24:13-32)

The account of the appearance of the risen Jesus to the two on the road to Emmaus is unique to Luke's gospel.

24:13-14. The **two** discussing **all these things** are identified only as being **of them** (24:13a) that is, of the number of the disciples (not of the Eleven but of **the rest** 24:9c). They were on **that very day** (24:13b), that is, the day of the resurrection, traveling to Emmaus, a village **about seven miles** [west] **from Jerusalem** (24:13c). That distance might take them half a day to travel and afforded them several hours of conversation on the way. They were probably headed home (cf. Bock, *Luke*, 1907), talking about **all these things** that had occurred, (24:14; "these things" and related phrases are key terms in this account) concerning Jesus' passion and death.

24:15-17a. It is immediately apparent that the One who joined the two travelers was Jesus (24:15), but they **were prevented from recognizing Him** (24:16). The passive "were kept from recognizing" is a "divine passive, that is, *God kept them from recognizing Jesus*" (Stein, *Luke*, 610). His question amounted to, "What were you just talking about?" (24:17a).

24:17b-19a. The question posed by the One stopped them in their tracks (**they stood still**). So direct a question caused them to think of why "these things" had been the topic of their conversation—and that made them sad (**looking sad**) (24:17b). Cleopas—the only one of the two to be named—answered with a mild edge of incredulity—**Are You the only one . . . unaware of the things**, the recent events in the city? (24:18). Incredulous, these men were amazed that He could have missed so shocking an event as Jesus' death. The stranger pressed His question—**What things?** (24:19a).

24:19b-24. Luke took this occasion to rehearse the narrative one more time—giving a historical summary. He took care to include all the most relevant facts about Jesus—His identity: **Jesus the Nazarene** (24:19b); His calling: **a prophet** (24:19c); His work: **mighty in deed and word** (24:19d); His reputation: **in the sight of God and all the people** (24:19e); His rejection: **the chief priests and our rulers delivered Him** (24:20a); His death: **the sentence of death, and crucified Him** (24:20b); and their disappointment over what they thought was His mission (which it was): **He who was going to redeem Israel** (24:21a). In addition, they related the recent events: it was the third day since **these things** (24:21b), and they had received a report from the women about the empty tomb not containing Jesus' body, and a visitation of angels **who said that He was alive** (24:22-23). Furthermore some of the leaders had checked out the tomb, but **Him they did not see** (24:24). This mere historical account was complete, but by itself it was not convincing.

24:25-27. Surprisingly, at this point, Jesus, still hidden to their eyes, rebuked them for their silly unbelief (**O foolish men . . . slow of heart to believe**) (24:25a). They should have understood this "history" in the light of the "predictions" of the Scriptures (24:25b). He pointed out that all of **these things** (24:26) were **necessary**, and He thus patiently took them through the whole of the Scriptures (**Moses and with all the prophets**, 24:27a) and explained **the things** (the theology) about Him and His messianic mission that they should have understood. Had they understood messianic prophecy, it would have explained all "these things" to them. The key point Jesus made here was that the OT Scriptures foretold the coming of the Messiah, including two events: a suffering (the first coming) and an entering into glory (a second coming; cf. 21:27).

24:28-32. This discourse must have taken some time, for by its conclusion the party was at the village **where they were going** (24:28a). The two extended an invitation to the stranger, and it was readily accepted (24:28b-29). It was at this dinner, specifically when He prayed for and began to distribute the bread (24:30), that **their eyes were opened and they recognized Him** (24:31). **Were opened** is another divine passive, cf. 24:16; Stein, *Luke*, 613). The supernatural obscurity was replaced by supernatural illumination (perhaps a way for Luke to explain why some come to faith and others do not). The term **recognized** is the same term used in 1:4 with respect to "knowing (*epignos*) the certainty of the things" taught (Stein, *Luke*, 613).

The impact of this encounter on the two was profound—from "foolish" hearts of unbelief (cf. 24:25) to **burning hearts** of understanding and faith (24:32).

c. With the Disciples in Jerusalem (24:33-46)

24:33-35. Even though the two had just come from Jerusalem, and the hour was late (cf. 24:29b), they returned **that very hour** (24:33a) to the city, found the Eleven, and reported their encounter to the others (24:33b). Once there, they were informed that **the Lord has really risen** (24:34a), confirmed by an appearance to Peter (**Simon**; 24:34b). The two then corroborated this news, as they related their own encounter with Jesus.

24:36-37. While they were busy trying to convince themselves of the truth of the resurrection **He Himself stood in their midst** (24:36a). Luke did not explain how Jesus did this or speculate on the nature of Jesus' resurrection body and its capacities. Ironically, here were the disciples trying to convince each other of the truth of Jesus' resurrection, but when He actually arrived, they were **startled and frightened** (24:37a). Luke related that they thought **they were seeing a spirit** (24:37b). With all the appearances and evidences they were still not convinced of the resurrection. Now, even the presence of the risen Lord Jesus was not enough to overcome their fears and rationalistic thinking.

24:38-43. Again, with a slightly ironic tone, Luke related how Jesus first questioned them: **Why are you troubled, and why do doubts arise in your hearts?** (24:38). The thrust of these questions was, "Do you not believe your own eyes? Do you not trust your own reason?" Of course, the point was they did not, nor should they. Second, Jesus challenged them: **See My hands and My feet** (24:39a). The thrust of this challenge was, "Do you not trust your own senses?" And they had to admit that they did not, for **they still could not believe it because of their joy** (24:41a). Luke was emphasizing that this was a bodily resurrection. The proof was Jesus could show **His hands and His feet** (24:40) and even eat some **fish** (24:41b-43), something impossible for a "spirit" (a mere ghost).

24:44-46. But these are not the things that lead to faith in the resurrection. As it was with the women who first confronted the empty tomb, for the disciples real belief came through Jesus' Word. He left off with the physical proofs and evidences and began to speak to the disciples, as He had done for the two on the road to Emmaus, about how the Scriptures prophesied of Him (24:44). Using the tripartite division of the Hebrew Bible, **the Law of Moses and the Prophets and the Psalms** (the first book in the writings), Jesus showed how the Hebrew Scriptures predicted that **Christ** (the Messiah) **would suffer and rise again** (24:46). As A. T. Robertson said, "Jesus found himself in the Old Testament, a thing that some modern scholars do not seem to be able to do" (A. T. Robertson, *Word Pictures in the New Testament,* Vol. 2. [Nashville: Broadman & Holman, 1930], 294). It was through the Scriptures (not reasons or evidences) that Jesus **opened their minds to understand the Scriptures** (24:45) and thus to understand that what He—the Messiah—had suffered and how He had been raised was all according to the divine plan of redemption.

2. Commission (24:47-49)

24:47-49. In this short discourse, Jesus turned quickly to the message that must be preached in light of the truth of His person and work. The content of the message would be about sin—the need for **repentance** from it and **forgiveness** for it (24:47a). This was to be proclaimed **in His Name** (24:47b), that is, on the basis of His divine person and authority (cf. Ac 2:38; 3:6, 16; 4:7) they are to preach His death and atonement for sin. The venue for this message was to be the world—**to all the nations** (Lk 24:47c). While Ac 2:38 connects baptism to forgiveness (though see the comments there), Luke made no such association here (writing **repentance for forgiveness of sins** without baptism), suggesting that the key is repentance and not baptism. The means of this gospel message would be human witnesses to the truth (24:48). The power for this message would be **the promise of My Father** (which is the Spirit, cf. the comments on Ac 1:4-5, 8), for which they would have to wait (see chaps. 1 and 2 of Luke's second volume, the book of Acts.

3. Ascension (24:50-53)

This gospel concludes with an abbreviated account of the ascension (24:50-53). The ascension was necessary for the next phase of the plan of redemption to begin; (cf. Ac 1 for a fuller account of the events and significance of the ascension).

Luke certainly fulfilled his purpose giving the church a portrait of Jesus that, while parallel to Matthew's and Mark's, in key ways provided unique and vital information about Him so that we "may know the exact truth about the things" (1:4) concerning Jesus Christ.

BIBLIOGRAPHY

Bock, Darrell L. *Luke 1:1–9:50.* Baker Exegetical Commentary of the New Testament. Grand Rapids, MI: Baker, 1994.

__________. *Luke 9:51–24:53.* Baker Exegetical Commentary of the New Testament. Grand Rapids, MI: Baker, 1996.

Craddock, Fred B. *Luke.* Minneapolis: John Knox Press, 1990.

Green, Joel B. *The Gospel of Luke.* New International Commentary on the New Testament. Grand Rapids, MI: Eerdmans, 1997.

Hendriksen, William. *Exposition of the Gospel of Luke.* Grand Rapids, MI: Baker, 1978.

Leifeld, Walter L. "Luke." In *Expositors Bible Commentary,* vol. 8, edited by Frank E. Gaebelein. Grand Rapids, MI: Zondervan, 1984.

Morris, Leon. *The Gospel According to Luke.* Tyndale New Testament Commentaries. Grand Rapids, MI: Eerdmans, 1974.

Stein, Robert H. *Luke.* New American Commentary. Nashville: Broadman & Holman, 1992.

JOHN

JOHN F. HART

INTRODUCTION

Author. The Gospel of John is greatly beloved—probably because the author presents so clearly Jesus' promise of eternal life for those who simply believe in Him.

Internal Evidence. The unnamed author was an eyewitness of Christ (1:14; 19:35; 21:24) and has identified himself as "the disciple whom Jesus loved" (13:23; 21:7, 20). He was also one of the 12 apostles (Mt 10:2). On several occasions, the author is shown closely associated with Peter (20:2-8; 21:7), as the apostle John is in the Synoptics and Acts (Mt 17:1; Ac 3:1-4). In addition, the similarities with Revelation, written by John, reinforce the strong case made for the traditional view that the apostle John wrote the book.

External Evidence. The early church father Irenaeus (d. AD 200) claimed that John wrote the Fourth Gospel after he was released from prison on the island of Patmos (Rv 1:9) and lived in Ephesus. Irenaeus also wrote that he personally learned this information from the aged Polycarp, bishop of Smyrna (d. AD 155), who in turn was discipled by the apostle John.

Date. A first-century date for the writing of John has been confirmed by the 1920 discovery of the Greek ms fragment of John known as P 52, written c. AD 125. The original must have been penned much earlier, perhaps c. AD 80–90. This date is strongly supported by patristic testimony. However, Jn 5:2 states, "By the Sheep Gate in Jerusalem there *is* [present tense] a pool" (HCSB, italics added). This may point to a date even before the Roman destruction of Jerusalem (AD 70).

Recipients. The readers were likely non-Christians whom John hoped to win to faith (20:31). Many Semitic (Hebrew) expressions are given a Greek equivalent (e.g., Jn 1:38, 41), suggesting the readers were Greek-speaking. Sometimes Jewish concepts are left unexplained (e.g., "the Lamb of God," 1:29). The natural conclusion is that John was writing to Greek-speaking, Jewish non-Christians living outside Israel, perhaps in Ephesus.

Purpose and Theme. Faith in Christ for eternal life is central to John's gospel, as his purpose statement reflects (20:30-31). The verb "believe" (*pisteuo*) is used about 100 times, with numerous synonyms of and symbols for "believe" such as "receive" (1:11), "know" (4:42; 6:69), "come to" (5:40; 6:35), "behold" (6:40), and "eat" and "drink" (6:54). Various other synonymous constructions include "believe in" (*pisteuo eis*) and "believe that" (*pisteuo hoti*). In the NT, the Fourth Gospel also presents the most extensive testimony that Jesus is the divine Son of God and prophesied Messiah.

While the Synoptic Gospels (Matthew, Mark,

A Few Facts about the Apostle John

- John's father was Zebedee, and his older brother was James (Mt 4:21).
- Because of their fiery tempers, Jesus named John and James, "sons of thunder" (Mk 3:17).
- John worked in his father's fishing business (Mk 1:19–20) and had Peter as a partner (Lk 5:10).
- John was the only disciple to witness the death of Jesus (Jn 19:26).
- While on the cross, Jesus told John to care for His mother after His death (Jn 19:26).
- John was the first of the disciples to see the empty tomb (Jn 20:1-3).
- John was a leader with Peter in the early church (Ac 3–4; 8:14-17, 25; Gl 2:9).
- His long life was prophesied by Jesus (Jn 21:20-23).
- John lived into his 90s, wrote the book of Revelation, and was the last apostle to die.

Luke) contain much parallel material, over 90 percent of John is unique. Unlike the Synoptics', John's unique content (e.g., woman at the well, Nicodemus) was designed primarily for evangelism (20:30-31). In the OT, God demonstrated perfection and completeness by mentioning a number plus one (Ps 62:11; Pr 6:16; Dn 3:24-25; Mc 5:5). Three Synoptic Gospels plus one (John) implies a complete but not exhaustive revelation of Christ. See also the sidebar, "A Comparison of the Synoptics and John."

Background. The discovery of the Dead Sea Scrolls in 1948 proved that most of John's concepts derive from Judaism, not Hellenism. Characteristics of John include stark contrasts (e.g., light/darkness, life/death), symbolism, and irony (see commentary throughout).

The term "the Jews" is recurrent in John and refers to (1) the Jewish people in general (e.g., 18:33); (2) the hostile Jewish people in Jerusalem (e.g., 11:54); or (3) the hostile Jewish leaders in Jerusalem (most references). The negative references have sometimes resulted in a charge of anti-Semitism. However, some passages use the term in a positive (8:31; 11:45; 12:11) or neutral way (3:1). Even when John presented the Jews negatively, the viewpoint is no more severe than similar denunciations of Israel by the OT prophets, who like John, were themselves Jewish.

After the prologue (chap. 1), chaps. 2–12 feature seven major signs that prove Jesus' messianic identity (see comment on 2:11). After describing Christ's farewell instructions to His disciples (chaps. 13–17) and His crucifixion (chaps. 18–19), John presented the climactic eighth sign (a number + 1; see above)—Christ's resurrection (20:1-29; cf. 2:18-22). This account is immediately followed by John's purpose statement (20:30-31). A final epilogue balances the prologue and completes the book (21:1-25).

A Comparison of the Synoptics and John

Synoptics	John
Focus on Galilee	Focus on Judea
Numerous parables	Few parables
Theme of "the kingdom of God"	Only one use of "kingdom of God"
Genealogies of Jesus	No genealogy but the eternal origin of Jesus
Few "I am" claims	Seven "I am" claims
No uses of "truly, truly . . ."	Twenty-five uses of "truly, truly . . ."
Sixteen references to "the Jews"	Seventy-one references to "the Jews"
Mentions only the Feast of Passover at Christ's death	Mentions three or four Passovers, the Feasts of Booths (7:2) and Dedication (10:22)

OUTLINE

I. Prologue (1:1-18)
II. Public Ministry: Miraculous Signs of Jesus' Identity (1:19–12:50)
  A. Preliminary Events to Jesus' Ministry (1:19-51)
    1. Testimony of John the Baptist (1:19-34)
    2. First Disciples (1:35-51)
  B. Premature Reception of Jesus' Ministry (2:1–4:54)
    1. Wedding at Cana (2:1-11)
    2. Temple Cleansing (2:12-25)
    3. Dialogue with Nicodemus (3:1-21)
    4. Additional Testimony of John (3:22-36)
    5. Samaritan Woman (4:1-42)
    6. Official's Son Healed (4:43-54)
  C. Progressive Rejection of Jesus' Ministry (5:1–12:50)
    1. Events at the Unnamed Feast (Healing of the Lame Man) (5:1-47)
    2. Events Near the Passover (6:1-71)
      a. Feeding of the 5,000 (6:1-14)
      b. Walking on Water (6:15-21)
      c. Bread of Life Message (6:22-71)
    3. Events at the Feast of Booths (7:1–8:59)

a. Preparation and Teachings at the Feast (7:1-44)
b. The Pharisees' Council (7:45-52)
c. Woman Caught in Adultery (7:53–8:11)
d. Light of the World Message (8:12-59)
4. Healing of the Blind Man (9:1-40)
5. The Good Shepherd Message (10:1-21)
6. Events at the Feast of Dedication (10:22-42)
7. Events at the Final Passover (11:1–12:50)
a. Raising of Lazarus (11:1-54)
b. Anointing of Jesus' Feet (12:1-11)
c. Presentation of the Messiah-King (12:12-19)
d. Gentile Openness and Israel's Blindness (12:20-50)
III. Private Ministry: Farewell Instructions to Jesus' Disciples (13:1–17:26)
A. Washing the Disciples' Feet (13:1-20)
B. Identifying His Betrayer (13:21-30)
C. Revealing His Departure (13:31–14:31)
D. Abiding in the Vine (15:1-17)
E. Ministering in the World (15:18–16:33)
F. Praying for All Believers (17:1-26)
IV. Passion Ministry: Sacrificial Nature of Jesus' Death (18:1–20:31)
A. Betrayal and Arrest (18:1-11)
B. Interrogation and Trial (18:12–19:16)
C. Crucifixion and Burial (19:17-42)
D. Resurrection and Appearances (20:1-29)
E. Purpose Statement (20:30-31)
V. Epilogue (21:1-25)
A. The Great Catch of Fish (21:1-14)
B. Future Roles of Peter and John (21:15-23)
C. Final Attestation to Truth (21:24-25)

COMMENTARY ON JOHN

I. Prologue (1:1-18)

The prologue introduces the Fourth Gospel by demonstrating the supremacy of Jesus as the unique One who should be believed. He is the Word (vv. 1, 14), true Light (v. 9), One and Only Son (vv. 14, 18, HCSB), Lamb of God (vv. 29, 36), Rabbi or Teacher (vv. 38, 49), Messiah (vv. 20, 25, 41), Son of God (vv. 34, 49), King of Israel (v. 49), and Son of Man (v. 51).

1:1. In the beginning (cf. Gn 1:1) **was the Word** (*logos*) already in existence in eternity past. John took the OT concepts of God's spoken word and applied them to Jesus. The parallels between Gn 1 and Jn 1 demonstrate that the concept behind the "Word" in Jn 1 is drawn from the OT. God's Word creates all life (Gn 1:11, 20, 26), and Jesus has the right to give eternal life (Jn 6:27; 10:28). God sends out His word, and it always accomplishes His will (Is 55:11), just as Jesus was sent out and accomplished the Father's will (Jn 4:34; 6:38). God's word in the OT is His divine self-expression (Ps 138:2). So Jesus is the divine self-expression of God. Since **the Word was with God** before all else existed, He had intimate companionship with the Father. This points to separate persons in the Godhead (the Trinity). Yet, since **the Word was God**, everything that God was in essence, the Word was also. This indicates the deity of Christ—a major theme of the Fourth Gospel.

1:2. Verse 2 subtly repeats v. 1. The Greek phrase **was . . . with** [*pros*] **God** places a stress on the loving companionship that has always existed between Jesus and the Father (another theme in John). As v. 3 implies, before what happened **in the beginning**, God was all that there was— and the Word was there personally with God.

1:3-4. The Word created **all things**—material and immaterial (e.g., angels). While the Father initiated creation, **through Him** confirms that

Jesus was the direct agent of creation (cf. Rm 11:36; Col 1:16; Heb 1:2). John rephrased the thought of v. 3a in 3b to confirm the all-inclusive nature of Christ's creative work. Since **in Him was life** (v. 4; cf. 14:6), all life derived from and is given by Jesus (5:21; 10:28; 17:2). The life that was in Jesus was to be a **Light** for people. In Scripture, light (a thematic word in this gospel) is the place of security and deliverance (Ps 27:1; Ac 13:47), and a figure for holiness, revelation, and truth (1Jn 1:5).

1:5. John stressed the ongoing reality that **the Light shines** [pres. tense] **in the darkness**. A spiritual battle exists between good and evil, God and Satan. All darkness (e.g., Satan, Judas, the unbelieving Jews) opposed Jesus. In His sacrificial death for sin, He gained the victory over darkness (cf. 19:30). Therefore, **the darkness did not comprehend** the light. Since the Greek word "comprehend" (*katalambano*) means "overtake" in a similar statement in 12:35 ("so that darkness will not *overtake* you"), it is best taken that way in 1:5 (i.e., the darkness "did not *overcome*" the light; NET, ESV).

1:6-8. The great forerunner to the Messiah is now introduced. As was the case with OT prophets, John was **sent from God**. That God "sent" **John** the Baptist begins the missionary outlook of the book. **Witness**, which appears for the first time (v. 7), fits into this theme of mission. John's witness, like the testimony of the book itself (20:31-32), existed **so that all might believe** in Christ. This marks the first of nearly 100 uses of "believe" (*pisteuo*) in the book. To "believe" (*pisteuo*) means "to have confidence in" or "be fully persuaded about" (Ac 28:24; Rm 4:20-21). Even though John the Baptist never did any miracles (10:41), the fact that **he came to testify about the Light** (v. 8) gives the explanation for his greatness.

1:9-10. Coming into the world refers to Christ's incarnation (cf. 6:14; 9:39; 11:27; 12:46; 16:28). This phrase does not describe when or in what sense Jesus **enlightens every man**. The primary point of the phrase is to describe who Jesus is. "The true light that gives light to every man was coming into the world" (NIV; cf. ESV, NET). Since Jesus is Creator (vv. 3-4), He has given a measure of light to everyone through general revelation and an inner moral law (Rm 1:18-32; 2:14-15; Leon Morris, *The Gospel of John*, NICNT [Grand Rapids, MI: Eerdmans, 1995], 84). Alternately, He may bring objective revelation to all, forcing people to accept or reject Him (D. A. Carson, *The Gospel According to John*, PNC [Grand Rapids, MI: Eerdmans, 1991], 124). **The world was made through Him** (v. 10), including plants and animals. However, in John "world" (*kosmos*, a thematic word, used 78 times in John, 15 times in the Synoptics) primarily refers to people (e.g., Jn 3:16-17, 19), and **the world did not know Him** means that most people did not believe in Christ (17:3). The first two references to *kosmos* in this verse are neutral (cf. 17:24; 21:25), but more often *kosmos* carries negative overtones (third reference). The "world" is in need of forgiveness (1:29), a Savior (4:42), and eternal life (6:33; 8:12). It hates God (17:25) and Jesus (7:7) as well as believers (15:18, 19), and is ruled by Satan (14:30; 16:11). While believers are in the physical world (13:1; 17:11), they are separated out of the evil world system by their faith in Christ (17:6, 17).

1:11-13. Through the incarnation, Jesus **came to His own** nation and land (in Gk. "own" is neuter pl.). Ironically, the Jewish people, **who were His own** (Gk. masculine pl.) people, refused to accept their own Messiah. **As many as** (v. 12) stipulates a universal promise extending beyond the Jewish people. The promise is to all who have **received** [*lambano*, "welcome, take"] **Him**. "Receive Him" is parallel to **believe in His name**, showing the terms "receive" and "believe" are essentially synonymous (cf. 12:48; 13:20; 17:8). This is the first of over 35 uses of the phrase "believe in" (*pisteuo eis*)—a special Johannine construction that always means genuine faith (3:16, 18, 36; 6:40; 11:25). Becoming a child of God results in a spiritual "birth" produced by God's Spirit (cf. 3:3-8; 1Pt 1:3, 23; 1Jn 5:1, 4) unlike human birth (v. 13). Spiritual birth is **not of blood**, i.e., it is not the result of human descent. Neither is it **of the will of the flesh**, as if human desires can bring it about. **Nor** is spiritual birth **of the will of man** (Gk. "male, husband"), negating any pride of males in producing children as was common in Jewish culture (and in most cultures). Contrary to anything innate, spiritual birth is an act **of God**.

1:14. John 1:1-13 and v. 18 focus on the deity of Christ; vv. 14-17 outline the humanity of Christ. **The Word became flesh**, i.e., He became fully human. The Word **dwelt** or "tabernacled" (*skenoo*) on earth. God's **glory**, resident in the OT tabernacle, now became resident in Jesus as God's NT temple (cf. 2:19-21). This begins John's theme that Jesus has fulfilled the OT system of worship (cf. 4:21). **Glory** draws on the images of the OT when God manifested Himself to Israel

(Ex 16:10; 24:15-17; 33:22), but also encompasses Christ's incarnation, miracles (Jn 2:11; 11:4, 40), and death, resurrection, and ascension (12:16; 13:31-32; 17:1). The phrase **only begotten** (*monogene*) is used for the first of four times in John (1:18; 3:16, 18). NIV, NET, and HCSB translate this word, "one and only," because it looks at the uniqueness of the Son, not at a "birth." Isaac is called Abraham's "only begotten son" (Heb 11:17), but was neither Abraham's only nor first-born son, though he was certainly Abraham's "one-of-a-kind" or unique son. **Full of grace and truth** is to be understood in light of the incarnation ("the Word became flesh"). See v. 17.

1:15-16. Next to Jesus, John the Baptist as the forerunner of the Messiah is the apostle's chief example of one who boldly **testified** to the truth (see comment on 2:23). Like an OT prophet, John **cried out** in giving his message. Jesus was born after John the Baptist (**He who comes after me**). But Christ was superior to John (**has a higher rank than I**) on the grounds that He is eternally preexistent (**for He existed before me**). In light of the words **His fullness** (v. 16), the phrase **grace upon grace** means a maximized grace or "one gracious gift after another" (NET).

1:17. As did Paul (Rm 5:20; 6:14), John made a contrast between the **law** and Moses (not Judaism), and **grace** and Jesus Christ. **Grace** (used in John only in vv. 14, 16, 17) **and truth** may recall the OT concept of "lovingkindness [Hb. *chesed*] and truth [Hb. *emet*]" (Ex 34:6; 33:13, 18-19) and point to God's covenant faithfulness to Israel. Moses was the indirect source of law; Jesus was the source of all grace, even God's grace shown to Israel (cf. Ex. 34:6-7). (Note the preexistence of Christ in Jn 1:15). So ultimately, grace and truth were mediated (**were realized**, lit., "came") **through Jesus Christ** in both the OT and NT.

1:18. No one has seen God at any time (cf. 1Tm 6:16), though people have received partial revelations of Him in the person of the preincarnate Christ (e.g., Abraham, Gn 18:1; Moses, Ex 33:18-23). **The only begotten God**, "the only God" (ESV), or "the only one, himself God" (NET) reads a different set of Greek mss as opposed to "the One and Only Son" (HSCB, TNIV). The latter is more Johannine (cf. 3:16, 18), though many scholars think the antiquity of the manuscripts and the difficulty of the reading (a scribe probably would not have changed "Son" to "God") support the NASB translation. **In the bosom of the Father** is an idiom denoting the extreme intimacy that Jesus had with God the Father (cf. 13:23). Other versions translate the phrase "in closest relationship/fellowship with" (TNIV, NET), or "near/close to the Father's heart" (NLTse, NJB, NRSV).

II. Public Ministry: Miraculous Signs of Jesus' Identity (1:19–12:50)

The first major unit of John centers on the public ministry of Jesus with seven sign-miracles performed by Him (eight signs including Jesus' resurrection; see chart at 2:1) that identify Him as the Christ. Verses 19-51 offer four witnesses (John the Baptist, Andrew, Philip, Nathaniel) to the truth presented in the Prologue: Jesus is the Messiah, the Son of God who is fully God come in human form.

A. Preliminary Events to Jesus' Ministry (1:19-51)

1. Testimony of John the Baptist (1:19-34)

1:19-20. The Jews sent to John the Baptist **priests and Levites from Jerusalem to ask him** about his identity. The "Jews" refers here to the Jewish authorities (cf. v. 24). Behind the question **Who are you?** is the thought that John the Baptist might be the coming Messiah (cf. Lk 3:15). The forerunner vigorously denied it (v. 20). **Christ** is the Greek term corresponding to the Hebrew and Aramaic word "Messiah." Both terms mean "anointed one."

1:21-23. Judaism had diverse opinions about what great leaders were promised in the OT to deliver Israel. **Elijah** was prophesied to return in the end times (Mal 4:5; Mt 17:11; Lk 1:17). Also, there was an eschatological **Prophet** (cf. Jn 1:45; 6:14; 7:40) predicted to be like Moses (Dt 18:15, 18). Peter and Stephen claimed this prophet was Jesus (Ac 3:22; 7:37), and while He certainly functioned in a way befitting a prophet, He was also much more.

1:23. John the Baptist (v. 23) literally preached **IN THE WILDERNESS** as Is 40:3 indicated (cf. Mt 3:2-3; Mk 1:3-4; Lk 3:3-4). By calling for repentance, he was preparing the people's hearts (**MAKE STRAIGHT THE WAY**) to receive Christ by faith (cf. Ac 19:4). Of the four Gospels, only John's does not mention the word "repent" or "repentance."

1:24-25. That these men had been sent **from the Pharisees** contrasts radically with those sent from God, i.e., John the Baptist and Jesus Himself (cf. vv. 6, 19, 22, 33). The Pharisees (about 6,000 at the time) were laymen (not priests) who zealously followed the Mosaic law but added many extrabiblical traditions to it. As the largest Jewish religious-political party, they exercised considerable influence. While the Jewish people highly esteemed them, Jesus often unmasked their hypocrisy (cf. Mt 23:1-36). This is not surprising since even later rabbinic authorities, having sprung from Pharisaism, also criticize their hypocrisy (Babylonian Talmud *Sotah* 22b). John's **baptizing** ministry (v. 25) grew out of the OT emphasis on symbolic cleansing with water (Lv 13–17; Nm 19; Ps 51:2, 7; Is 4:4). The form of the question presupposes that the Jewish leaders thought of baptism as a mark of the coming Messiah.

1:26-28. Among you stands One whom you do not know implies the Messiah could be easily overlooked (Is 53:2) and potentially rejected (v. 10). John acknowledged his unworthiness to serve Christ even as a slave who loosens the straps of another's **sandal**. The location of **Bethany beyond the Jordan** (3:26; 10:40) is uncertain, though it may be the area northwest of the Sea of Galilee where there was a considerable amount of water that served as the headwaters of the Jordan River. The Latinized form of the name of this region was "Batanaea." At any rate, it is to be distinguished from the Bethany near Jerusalem (11:1). "Beyond the Jordan" recalls the time when Israel was positioned to conquer the promised land (Nm 22:1; Dt 3:20; Jos 1:14-15; 22). Israel is now positioned to be led by Jesus, the new Joshua.

1:29. Chronologically, **the next day** sets up a sequence of an entire week (cf. vv. 29, 35, 43; and "the third day" in 2:1). By referring to Jesus as **the Lamb of God** (cf. v. 36), John the Baptist alluded to the fulfillment of OT sacrificial imagery (Gn 22:8; Is 53:7, 12; 1Pt 1:19; Rv 5:12), especially the Passover lamb (Jn 19:36; Ex 12:1-13; 1Co 5:7). The substitutionary death of Christ **takes away the sin of the** whole **world**, including all Gentiles—a shocking revelation to the Jewish readers.

1:30. For the third time (cf. vv. 15, 27), the Baptizer confirmed that the Messiah would appear **after** him. The reason He **has a higher rank than** the forerunner is that **He existed before** John. Since John the Baptist was born before Jesus (Lk 1:26-31), this can only refer to the eternality (and therefore the deity) of Jesus—a theme in harmony with the purpose of chap. 1.

1:31. Unlike the Synoptics', the Fourth Gospel's record of John the Baptist downplays the role of his baptism (see comment on v. 22). Instead, the focus is on the forerunner's testimony to Jesus' true identity. As everyone else, John **did not recognize** Jesus as the Messiah at first. In the dialogues with the Jewish interviewers (vv. 19-27), he had offered very little information about his own identity. John's role was that Jesus **might be manifested to Israel** as their Messiah.

1:32-33. The Spirit's descent on Christ took place at the baptism of Jesus (not mentioned in John). The significance of the event was that the Spirit **remained upon** Christ. The wording recalls Isaiah's prophecies where the Spirit rests on the Messiah (11:1-2; 42:1; 61:1). The Messiah had to be revealed to John (v. 33) from the Father (**He who sent me**) by means of **the Spirit descending and remaining upon** Jesus. This Jesus would be **the One who baptizes in the Holy Spirit** (see the comments on 1Co 12:13). This is the only mention in John of the baptism of the Holy Spirit (Mt 3:11; Mk 1:8; Lk 3:16).

1:34. The title **Son of God** is reserved in the Fourth Gospel for Jesus alone, implies His deity, and is roughly synonymous to "Christ" (11:27; 20:30-31). It finds its background in the Davidic covenant (2Sm 7:14; Ps 2:7; see the comments there) where God promised an unending reign for His chosen King-Son (cf. v. 49). Jewish people rightly understood Jesus' claim to being the Son of God as a claim to be being equal with God (5:18).

2. First Disciples (1:35-51)

1:35-37. For **the next day**, see v. 29. Jesus' first **disciples** were originally disciples of John the Baptist. As such they had faith in the One true God of Israel. They now understood that Jesus is the Messiah they had believed would come to Israel (cf. 6:37). That **John was standing** (v. 36) while Jesus **walked** intimates that the movement of God was shifting to Jesus (Edwin A. Blum, "John," BKCNT [Wheaton: Victor, 1983], 275). For **Lamb of God**, see v. 29. **Two** of the forerunner's **disciples . . . followed Jesus** (v. 37). In the Jewish culture, discipleship entailed physically following one's teacher or rabbi to receive training.

1:38. Since Jesus **turned and saw** the two disciples **following** Him, they could not follow Him secretly (see the theme of the secret disciple at 2:24-25). Jesus asked them **What do you seek?** Jesus' question was designed to draw out their commitment. What were they hoping to gain in life by following Christ? They asked, **Where are You staying?** The thought of "staying" (*meno*, "abide") with Jesus prepares the reader for the intimate relationship of abiding in Jesus, the True Vine (15:1-17).

1:39. Come, and you will see invited the disciples to investigate Jesus further, a pattern of evangelism and discipleship that should be imitated. Although it is often assumed, the text does not directly state that they stayed overnight. A debate exists over whether John used Roman or Jewish reckoning of time (the Synoptics use the Jewish system). By Roman reckoning, the **tenth hour** would be 10:00 a.m. (HCSB). The time indications in 4:6 and 19:14 best fit the Jewish system, making the "tenth hour" 4:00 p.m. (NET, TNIV, NLTse, TEV).

1:40-42. Only **one of the two** who **followed** Jesus is mentioned (cf. v. 37), **Andrew, Simon Peter's brother**. The other is unnamed, but is likely the apostle John (see Introduction: Author). Andrew, who **found first his own brother** (v. 41), became one who brought others to Christ (cf. 6:8-9; 12:22). Andrew's confession (**We have found the Messiah**, v. 41) is the first direct declaration in John that Jesus is the Christ. For **Messiah** and **Christ**, see 1:20. In the OT, God changed the name of an individual to mark out his divine calling (e.g., Abraham, Gn 17:5; Jacob, Gn 32:28). Jesus renamed Peter as **Cephas** (v. 42), an Aramaic word meaning "stone." Peter would become a solid leader in the early church, despite his denials at the trials of Jesus.

1:43-44. On **the next day**, see v. 29. Since Jesus **purposed to go into Galilee**, He found another disciple originally from Galilee. **Philip**, the fourth disciple to follow Jesus, was from **Bethsaida** (cf. 12:21), a village on the northeast shore of the Sea of Galilee. **Andrew and Peter** (v. 44) were also from Bethsaida. Bethsaida (meaning "house of fish") was the scene of the feeding of the 5,000 (Lk 9:10-17) and the healing of a blind man (Mk 8:22-26). By this time, however, all three had taken up residence in Capernaum (Mk 1:21, 29).

1:45-46. Philip found Nathanael (21:2), probably the disciple named Bartholomew in other accounts (Mt 10:3; Mk 3:18; Lk 6:14; Ac 1:13). **We have found Him** begins Philip's personal testimony. Personal witness brings people to Christ. Philip mentioned **Him of whom Moses in the Law and also the Prophets wrote**, i.e., the Messiah (see comment on 1:22). The "Law and the Prophets" was a common title for the whole OT (Mt 7:12; 22:40; Lk 16:16). Nathanael questioned whether **any good thing** could **come out of Nazareth**, so insignificant it was not even mentioned in the OT (cf. 7:52). Philip responded simply, **Come and see**, imitating Jesus' own methods (v. 39; cf. 4:29).

1:47. Nathanael was a regenerate man of OT faith. Otherwise, Jesus could not have said of him that he was an **Israelite indeed** (cf. Rm 2:29) and that **no deceit** could be found in him. This faith would soon include a belief in Jesus as the Messiah (v. 49). Jesus made a wordplay on the name "Israel," the new name given to Jacob, the patriarch of the Jews (Gn 27:35; 31:26). Nathanael exemplified Jacob's faith rather than his deceit (Heb 11:21).

1:48. Nathaniel's question **How do You know me?** begins the Johannine theme of the Lord's supernatural knowledge of people and events (2:24-25; 5:42; 6:15, 64; 13:1, 3, 11; 18:4; 19:28; 21:17). **Before Philip called** Nathanael and without being physically present, Jesus miraculously **saw** Nathanael **under the fig tree**. Jesus' divine awareness of Nathanael's heart brought about immediate faith in Jesus as Israel's Messiah. In the OT, the fig tree symbolized peace and safety brought by the messianic kingdom (Mc 4:4; Zch 3:10). In addition, "being under the fig tree" is a rabbinic figure of speech for studying the Torah (Bab Talmud Erubin 54a, also Midrash Ecclesiastes 5:11 and Midrash Song 6:2; cf. Jerome H. Neyrey, *The Gospel of John,* NCBC [Cambridge: Cambridge University Press, 2006], 58). Perhaps Nathanael was busy studying his Torah when Jesus saw him.

1:49. Nathanael addressed Jesus first as **Rabbi** or teacher, then as **the Son of God** (see v. 34), and third as **King of Israel**. As King of Israel, Jesus will sit on the throne of David in the coming millennial kingdom (2Sm 7:12-16; Ezk 37:21-28). In contrast to Nathanael's sincere confession, the Jewish people will falsely claim Jesus as King during the last week of His life (Jn 12:13), and the Romans will crucify Him for claiming to be King of the Jews (19:3, 14-21).

1:50. Jesus praised the simplicity of Nathanael's faith. The new disciple believed merely because Jesus, without being present, **saw** him **under the fig tree**. The phrase **You will see greater things** is both a prophecy and a promise, and refers to Jesus' sign-miracles (2:1–12:50), especially the resurrection (2:18-22). The fulfillment began at the wedding of Cana (2:1-11).

1:51. Truly, truly ("I tell all of you the solemn truth," NET) is found 25 times in John, never in the Synoptics. It is always spoken by Christ and introduces an earnest announcement that stresses His unique authority. The Greek word for "truly" is *amen,* from which we get the English word "amen" (cf. Jesus as the authoritative "Amen" in Rv 3:14). The Greek for **you** in v. 51

now becomes plural, addressing the group. The disciples **will see** "previews" of the coming kingdom (cf. Mt 16:28–17:8). See comment on 2:11. The **heavens opened** refers to a new phase in revelation (e.g., Is 64:1; Ezk 1:1; Mt 3:16; Rv 4:1; 19:11). Like Jacob's ladder that mediated between heaven and earth (see the comments on Gn 28:12, 16), Jesus will be humanity's access to God and God's communication with humanity (Jn 14:6; 10:9). **Son of Man** is a messianic title of One (Jesus) who exhibits both human and divine characteristics and receives an eternal, earthly kingdom (Ps 8:4-5; Dn 7:13-14).

B. Premature Reception of Jesus' Ministry (2:1–4:54)

1. Wedding at Cana (2:1-11)

Jesus traveled to Cana of Galilee with Mary, His mother, and His disciples. Jewish weddings were filled with festivity and occasionally lasted a week.

2:1-2. The **third day** is marked from the time Jesus found Philip (1:43; see comment on 1:29). **Cana** was about eight miles north of Nazareth, the home of Jesus and Mary. For the first time, Jesus is said to have **disciples** (never called "apostles" in John). Mary, **the mother of Jesus** (never identified by name in John), was fully aware by faith that her Son was the Messiah (Lk 1:26-56; 2:1-51). Apparently Mary thought the time for Jesus to reveal His identity had come. Since she gave directions to the servants (v. 5), she must have had some official responsibilities.

2:3. Mary told Jesus, **They have no** [more] **wine.** A failure of this kind was a serious offense against Jewish standards of hospitality. Mary's request implied that she anticipated a miracle.

2:4-5. In the Jewish culture, **woman** was a respectful address (cf. 4:21; 19:26). Yet by asking, **What does that have to do with us?** Jesus distanced Himself from His earthly mother (cf. Mk 1:24; 5:7). The reference to Jesus' **hour** or "time" (see also comment on 4:21) is not found in the Synoptics but is frequent in John. At first, His hour had not yet come (2:4; 7:6, 8, 30; 8:20), but later it had come (12:23; 13:1; 16:32; 17:1). The term refers to the glory displayed in Jesus' death and resurrection. Since in v. 4 it had **not yet come**, the Lord was fully aware of its divine timing. This timing was set by the sovereign plan of the Father (12:27). Mary instructed the servants, **Whatever He says to you, do it**. This must also be our response to His will.

2:6-7. Symbolically, **six** may well represent the imperfection or insufficiency of Judaism (Andrew T. Lincoln, *The Gospel According to Saint John,* [Peabody, MA: Hendrickson, 2005], 129; Andreas J. Köstenberger, *John,* BECNT [Grand Rapids, MI: Baker, 2004], 96) and characterizes the **Jewish** legalistic **custom of purification** (cf. Mt. 15:1-2). Yet it is impossible to be certain that John intended such a symbolic use of the number "six." Such washings were for religious, not hygienic, purposes. The six **stone waterpots** holding **twenty or thirty gallons each** totaled 120 to 180 gallons. At Jesus' directions, the servants were to **fill the** large **waterpots with water**. That the servants **filled them up to the brim** expresses the overabundance of joy (wine) that comes through the Messiah (cf. 1:17).

2:8-10. In obedience to Mary's advice and Jesus' instructions, the servants were to **draw** from the waterpots **some** water-turned-to-wine and take **it to the headwaiter**. Culturally, the poorer wine was served last when the sensibilities of the guests had become dull. To the headwaiter's surprise (v. 9), he now tasted a wine that was far better than the bridegroom had been serving to this point. Jesus contradicted what **every man** does (v. 10) and corrected a conventional but unethical social custom.

2:11. This was the very first **of** the **signs** or miracles **Jesus did** and it **manifested His glory** (an attribute of God). The divine glory and presence that first dwelt in the OT tabernacle (1:14) was now residing in the person of Jesus. But the greatest display of glory, ironically, was yet to come in the humiliation and suffering of the cross (7:39; 12:16; 13:31, 32; 17:1). A "sign" (*semeion*), a special word in John (the Synoptics use *dynamis*, "power," for Jesus' miracles), is a miracle designed to attest to the authority of a messenger and the validity of His message. The Evangelist recorded these signs to bring about faith in Christ (20:31-32). The words **His**

The Eight Signs in John

1. Turning water to wine (2:1-11)
2. Healing of the nobleman's son (4:46-54)
3. Healing of the lame man (5:1-15)
4. Feeding of the 5,000 (6:1-15)
5. Walking on water (6:16-21)
6. Healing of the blind man (9:1-41)
7. Raising of Lazarus (11:1-44)
8. Christ's resurrection (2:18-22; 20:1-29)

disciples believed in Him show that at the earliest contacts with Jesus (cf. 3:24 with Mt 4:12, 17; Mk 1:14-15), His disciples (excluding Judas, Jn 6:70-71) had saving faith. A Jewish wedding symbolized the messianic kingdom (Is 54:1-8; 62:1-5; Mt 8:11; 22:2; Rv 19:7, 9), and the wine symbolized the joy and blessings of that kingdom (Is 25:6; Jr 31:12; Jl 2:19; 3:18; Mt 26:29). The water-to-wine miracle also revealed Jesus as the Creator (Jn 1:3, 10) and the Giver of Life (1:4; 4:14), and that He would be the One to provide the abundant fertility that would yield much wine (joy and celebration) in the millennial kingdom (see Am 9:13-15).

2. Temple Cleansing (2:12-25)

The temple cleansing reveals that Jesus is the "temple" of the New Era. The miracle of the new wine (2:1-11) was semiprivate; the cleansing of the temple was the first public presentation to Israel that Jesus is the Messiah.

2:12. Jesus **went down** from the mountains of Cana to **Capernaum**, some 16 miles NE of Cana. The author's comment is brief since the Fourth Gospel is more interested in Jesus' activities in Jerusalem. **His mother and His brothers** are mentioned (cf. Mt 13:55; Mk 6:3), but not Joseph, who apparently died before Christ's public ministry. Although His brothers witnessed this miracle, they did not believe (cf. Jn 7:5). Since the Passover was near (cf. v. 13), they stayed only **a few days** in Capernaum.

2:13-14. This is the first of three explicit references to the **Passover** in John (though the feast mentioned in 5:1 is probably also a Passover), marking perhaps as many as three-and-one-half years of Jesus' ministry (see comments on 5:1). The Synoptics refer to a second cleansing of the temple during the last week of Jesus' life (Mt 21:12-13; Mk 11:15-17; Lk 19:45-46). The Greek for **temple** (*hieron*) designates the temple complex that included the large Court of the Gentiles where the **money changers** were **seated**. Money changers exacted a fee to exchange Roman and Galilean coins for acceptable temple coinage. Jewish worshipers could then pay the temple tax and purchase animals for sacrifice.

2:15. Jesus viewed this commerce inside the temple complex as a sacrilege since it exploited the poor to gain funds to beautify the temple, and it disrupted Gentile worship in the court of the Gentiles, their only place to worship (Köstenberger, *John*, 106). So He **drove** the merchants **all out of the temple**, including the animals. He also **overturned** the **tables** of the money changers, symbolically cleansing the temple. This act fulfilled Malachi's prophecy of the sudden entrance of the Messiah into the temple to purify the nation (Mal 3:1-3). It also may have served as a symbolic act of judgment against the leaders who had allowed the corruption to go so far (see the comments on Mt 21:12).

2:16-18. Jesus' command **stop making My Father's house a place of business** alluded to Zch 14:20-21. Zechariah described the messianic kingdom as one in which there would be no "merchants" in the temple (see NASB footnote at Zch 14:21). "My Father's house" set forth a clear messianic claim, as the quote (v. 17) from Ps 69:9 proves. For **His disciples remembered**, see v. 22. In Ps 69, David's passion for the temple typifies the greater **ZEAL** that the Messiah would have for protecting the sanctity of God's **house**. Jesus' actions invoked the anger of the **Jews** (v. 18)—the first note of antagonism toward Jesus in John. The **Jews** (the religious leaders of the temple) demanded an attesting **sign** (see comment on 2:11) by which He could validate His authority in having committed such a subversive act. Their question was understandable. No Jewish man would dare to do what Jesus did. But He was not simply a man.

2:19-22. As God's foremost Prophet, Jesus predicted His own death (**Destroy this temple**) and the precise timing of His resurrection (**in three days**). The words **I will raise it up** present Jesus as the divine agent of His own resurrection. The **temple** (*naos*, "sanctuary," vv. 19, 20, 21) refers to the Most Holy place where God's presence lived in the OT, not the entire temple complex. The sanctuary (*naos*) construction was completed in 18/17 BC. **It took forty-six years to build this temple** (v. 20) means "this sanctuary has been built (completed) for forty-six years" (i.e., AD 20–30). This helps date the crucifixion of Christ three years later in AD 33. Because Jesus **was speaking of the temple** (*naos*) that was **His body** (v. 21), the glory that resided in the OT sanctuary now resided in Jesus (cf. 1:14). Prompted by His resurrection to reflect on OT messianic prophecy, **His disciples remembered** (v. 22) these prophecies in Zch 14 and Ps 69 (see 2:16-18 above) and linked them to **the word which Jesus had spoken** about His death and resurrection (raising the "temple" in three days).

2:23-25. The **Passover** included the Passover itself (one day) followed by seven days for the

Feast of Unleavened Bread. Some understand **many believed in His name** to be inauthentic faith because (1) faith based on miracles (the **signs which He was doing**) is insufficient, and (2) Jesus **was not entrusting Himself to them** (v. 24). But John declared that Jesus' signs were intended to bring about faith (20:31-32). Also, the apostle used a Greek phrase (**believed in His name**) that clearly speaks of genuine faith (cf. Jn 1:12; 3:18; cf. 20:31). That Jesus **was not entrusting Himself to them** means that Jesus considered these new believers not yet prepared for further disclosures of spiritual truth. This begins John's theme of the "secret disciple" (cf. 19:38-39). John's declaration that **He Himself knew what was in man** (v. 25) underlines the Lord's divine knowledge of people (see comments on 1:48). To demonstrate that knowledge of humanity, three interviews follow, with Nicodemus, a Jewish leader, the Samaritan woman, and a Gentile nobleman. In each one, Jesus demonstrated His supernatural understanding of their inner thoughts and needs. With Nicodemus, a scholar, Jesus saw his need for a faith that was not merely intellectual. With the woman, He saw a need for moral transformation. With the nobleman, He perceived the man's need for a physical healing of his son.

3. Dialogue with Nicodemus (3:1-21)

Believers are fond of the encounter of Jesus with Nicodemus because it reveals the wonderful truth of being "born again" (or better, "born from above").

3:1. There was a man ties directly to chap. 2. Jesus "knew what was in man" (2:25), so He knew what was in Nicodemus. On the **Pharisees**, see comment on 1:24. As **a ruler of the Jews**, Nicodemus was a member of the Sanhedrin (on the Sanhedrin, see comments on 11:47). Joseph of Arimathea, Nicodemus's friend (cf. 19:38-39), was also on this council (Mk 15:43).

3:2. Although Nicodemus had not yet believed in Christ, he was moving toward faith. His remark **We know that You have come from God** reflects the growing conviction of sincere seekers among the Jews. Many eventually came to faith (12:42). Jesus' role as a **teacher** contrasted with Nicodemus's limitations as a teacher among the Jewish people (v. 10).

3:3-4. For **truly, truly**, see comments on 1:51. One needed more than the recognition that God was with Jesus (v. 2). The Pharisee needed a spiritual birth—to be "born from above." The word translated "again" (*anothen*) can also mean "from above," and this is the preferable understanding here. Jesus spoke of a spiritual birth "from above," but Nicodemus misunderstood this to be a physical rebirth ("born again"). The gospel of John records numerous misunderstandings of Jesus.

3:5. In the phrase **born of water and the Spirit,** "water" cannot refer to Christian baptism, as this would have been meaningless to Nicodemus at this point in salvation history. It also does not mean that baptism is necessary for eternal life since this would contradict the single requirement of faith for eternal life in John (1:12; 3:16, 36; 8:24; 20:31; see the comments on 1Pt 3:21). **Water** (v. 5) probably does not refer to human birth, being born through the amniotic fluids associated with birth, for there is no indication that the ancient world thought of birth in such terms. The better understanding is that Jesus alludes to Ezk 36:25-27, a passage that refers to God providing spiritual cleansing ("I will sprinkle clean water on you") and giving His Spirit. And this is a "new covenant" passage, one with which Nicodemus should have been familiar (hence Jesus' reproof in Jn 3:10). To see [or **enter**, v. 5] **the kingdom of God** means to live in the future millennial kingdom on earth (Rv 20:1-6), and afterward, to live the eternal life that was received in this earthly life. For **kingdom of God**, see v. 3 and the comments on Mt 3:1-4.

3:6-8. Like original creation that can only bear after its kind (Gn 1:11-12, 24-25), whatever **is born of the flesh is flesh**. So only the **Spirit** can produce a spiritual birth. Jesus illustrated this concept with the **wind**. We do not doubt the reality of the wind (**you hear the sound of it**) even though it is invisible and mysterious. The Spirit's work of new birth is also invisible and mysterious but must be readily accepted like the wind.

3:9-10. Since **Nicodemus** became a disciple who at first failed to verbally testify of Christ (see comment on 19:38-40), his last words with Jesus are recorded in v. 9. John did not include his response. Jesus rebuked Nicodemus for not knowing the OT Scriptures that teach the necessity of a new birth by the Spirit (e.g., 1Sm 10:9; Ezk 11:19; 36:25-27; Jr 31:33).

3:11-12. We speak could refer to (1) Jesus only (the editorial "we"); (2) Jesus and the OT prophets; or (3) the Trinity (best option). All of the persons of the Trinity **know and testify of**

what they **have seen**. But the Jewish leaders did **not accept** this **testimony**. Jesus had explained spiritual events (new birth, the Spirit's work) that take place on earth (**earthly things**) and Nicodemus did **not believe** them. If Jesus spoke of unseen things in heaven (**heavenly things**), this would not change.

3:13-14. To speak to people about things in heaven (v. 12), one would need to have **ascended into heaven**, or be from there and have **descended from heaven**. The **Son of Man** (see comment on 1:51) has done the latter. **Moses lifted up** (v. 14) a bronze snake on a pole when God judged Israel **in the wilderness** with venomous snakes (Nm 21:4-9). God healed instantly anyone who simply looked at the snake (Nm 21:9). The instrument of judgment and death (the snake) became the means of life. So it is with the Christ lifted up on the cross, the instrument of His death. One "look" of faith in Christ immediately heals and brings eternal life. This is the first of three **lifted up** sayings in John (8:28; 12:32). Jesus being "lifted up" refers both physically to the cross, and spiritually to His exaltation/glorification through His death (cf. 8:28; 12:32-34).

3:15. The phrase **eternal life** appears here for the first time of 17 times in John—four times more often than any other NT book. But the word "life" appears frequently by itself when it means "eternal" life. Some interpreters understand Jesus' words to stop at v. 15 (cf. NET, NIV, NABRE), with 3:16 being comments provided by John and not Jesus. It is true that in 3:16ff. the third person, not the first person, predominates. But Jesus referred to Himself in the third person in 3:13-15. Why would this not continue in 3:16-18? Elsewhere in John, Jesus referred to Himself in the third person within a first-person discourse (5:19-30). A more natural break starts at v. 22, not v. 16 (cf. ESV, HCSB, NIV, CEB).

3:16. John 3:16 is perhaps the most well-known verse in the NT. **God so loved the world** includes all people, not just believers. God's love is not sentimentality. "Loved" is an aorist tense, and traditionally is viewed as referring to the cross. It also anticipates the next phrase, **that He gave His only begotten Son**. God's love is linked to His giving of Christ to die for sins (Gl 2:20; Eph 5:2, 25). For **only begotten Son,** see comment on 1:14. For **believes in**, see comment on 1:12. **Whoever believes in Him** is better translated "all who believe" or "everyone who believes," so that the death of Christ is for the purpose of providing escape from destruction and eternal life for believers. **Perish** contrasts with "eternal life" and involves an eternal conscious punishment (cf. Mk 9:42-48; Rv 14:9-11). Those who believe in Christ **have** (present tense) **eternal life** now, even while on earth.

3:17. The words **God did not send the Son into the world to judge the world** repeat v. 16 negatively: the Father's heart is not predisposed initially to condemnation (cf. 1Jn 4:14; 2Co 5:19). The Son was "sent" by the Father (Jn 5:36; 6:57; 17:21; 20:21), a concept found about 40 times in John. Being sent by the Father marks out mission as a central focus of Christ. **Saved** or "salvation" is not a common term in John (used seven times).

3:18. One's eternal destiny is determined on earth, not in heaven. Anyone **who believes in** Jesus **is not judged** or condemned in the future judgment. Anyone **who does not believe has been judged already**, here and now. The future judgment confirms but does not determine one's eternal destiny. For **only begotten**, see comment on 1:14.

3:19-21. Jesus is **the Light** that **has come into the world** (cf. 1:4-9). **Darkness** is the place of hiding where evil deeds are done, either by non-Christians or disobedient Christians. Light is the place of openness and exposure. The unbeliever certainly **hates the Light** and totally avoids it. But even sinning Christians must see that they are, from God's perspective, hating the light (cf. Jms 4:4) when they persist in their sins. They, too, do **not come to the Light** [a different concept from "coming" to or believing in Christ for eternal life] **for fear that** their **deeds will be exposed** and reproved (cf. 1Jn 1:6). For some time, King David hid his sins after he committed adultery and murder (see comments on Pss 32 and 51). Once a non-Christian comes to faith, he or she can be instead one **who practices the truth** and then **comes to the Light** (i.e., openly identifies with the truth) for fellowship with Christ (1Jn 1:7, 9). Only an obedient Christian can have **his deeds** become evident or **manifested as having been wrought** [produced] **in God**.

4. Additional Testimony of John (3:22-36)

Nicodemus who never told us of his response to Jesus' message (see comments on 2:23-25; 3:9-10) was now contrasted with John the Baptist, the bold witness.

3:22-24. The time reference, **after these things**, is nonspecific, but the events took place before John's imprisonment (cf. v. 24). John was imprisoned before Jesus began His public (Galilean) ministry (Mt 4:12-13,17; Mk 1:14-15). Part of making disciples is **spending time with them**, as Jesus did. Jesus and the forerunner carried on parallel **baptizing** ministries (cf. 4:2), giving rise to the issue of vv. 25-26. Only John's gospel mentions that Jesus was baptizing. The exact locations of **Aenon** and **Salim** are not known, despite the clue that **there was much water there**. They may have been located on the Jordan River forming the eastern boundary of Samaria. It is possible that Jesus' effective ministry in John 4 in Sychar, a Samaritan city, may be because of the precursory work of John in the same vicinity. Christian baptism is distinct from John's baptism (Ac 19:3-5) since it was not given until after the resurrection (Mt 28:18-20). Christian water baptism is designed to be a symbolic representation of what God has done for the believer in uniting him with Christ (see the comments on Rm 6:3-4; 1Co 12:13), but John's baptism is a symbol indicating repentance and spiritual cleansing in preparation for the coming of the kingdom of God.

3:25-26. A debate between **John's disciples** and an unidentified **Jew** regarding **purification** brought the group to the Baptist. Whether their motives (**they came**) were pure or tainted by jealousy or other sins, the resulting remark to John the Baptist was an enticement to compare his ministry with Jesus': **He . . . to whom you have testified . . . all are coming to Him**. Comparisons with others are unwise (2Co 10:12).

3:27-28. The Baptizer's answer to his disciples (v. 26) generalizes a truth applicable to all, particularly to ministry: **A man can receive nothing unless it has been given him from heaven**. Most directly, it applies to Christ's gathering of disciples (6:37, 39). John's own disciples could testify to his avowal that he was only the predecessor to the Messiah (see 1:15, 20, 23). For **Christ**, see comment on 1:20.

3:29-30. John likened Jesus to a **bridegroom** (cf. Mk 2:19; Mt 25:6) at a wedding. John's role was like **the friend of the bridegroom** (the "best man"). He **stands** next to the groom and **rejoices greatly** on hearing the groom's **voice** as he pledges his commitment to the bride (cf. 2Co 11:2; Rv 21:9). Recognizing his God-given role, John humbly remarked of Jesus, **He must increase**. John also realized that his ministry would not continue the same; he **must** actually **decrease**.

3:31-33. The NASB (contra HCSB, ESV) rightly continues the quotation of the forerunner through v. 36. Because Jesus **comes from above**, He is therefore **above all** other teachers of truth. Other religious leaders are **of the earth** and are earthly (imperfect, limited) in their teaching. Since He has been in the presence of the Father (1:1), Christ can testify of **what He has seen and heard** (v. 32). The words **has set his seal to this** (v. 33) mean "has confirmed clearly" (NET) **that God is true**.

3:34-36. Since God **gives the Spirit without measure** to the Son, Jesus will fulfill all of God's intentions for the Messiah. The Father's love-gift of **all things** (v. 35) to the Son gives Christ the right to grant eternal life. Eternal life begins now, as is evident in the present tense, **has eternal life** (v. 36; cf. v. 16). **Does not obey the Son** contrasts with "believe," and refers to disobeying the command to believe in Christ (12:36, 50; Ac 16:31). The **wrath of God** is presently on the unbeliever (Rm 1:18) and **abides on** (remains on) him as long as he refuses to believe.

5. Samaritan Woman (4:1-42)

Like the story of Nicodemus (3:1-21), the narrative of Jesus' conversation with the woman at the well is treasured as a wonderful example of an evangelistic encounter.

4:1-3. The narrative begins by describing the historical circumstances that led Jesus to leave Judea. **The Lord knew that the Pharisees** had received reports that He was **making and baptizing more disciples than John**. The forerunner's words were being fulfilled (cf. 3:30). The Fourth Gospel downplays water baptism (cf. 1:6, 31) by noting that **Jesus Himself was not baptizing, but His disciples were** (v. 2). Since the precise occasion for His death had not yet come (cf. 2:4), Jesus chose to avoid controversy with the Pharisees in Jerusalem. So He **went away again into Galilee** (v. 3).

4:4-6. The historic tensions between Jewish people and Samaritans usually (but not always) caused Jewish people to avoid traveling straight north through Samaria to Galilee. Instead they would circle around Samaria to the east, into Perea and the Decapolis east of the Jordan. Jews and Samaritans despised each other (cf. 4:9; 8:48). The reason for this hatred, from the Jewish perspective, was manifold. First, Samaritans were of mixed heritage with Gentiles, yet they claimed to be the "true" recipients of the Abrahamic promises. Second, they had violently opposed Cyrus's restoration of the Jewish people to the land of Israel. Third, the Samaritans had built their own counterfeit temple on Mt. Gerizim and adopted their own priesthood and sacrificial system, all independent of the Jewish people. Fourth, during the Seleucid king Antiochus IV's religious persecution of the Jewish people (167 BC), the Samaritans allied with the pagan attack on Judaism. In retaliation, Jewish leader John Hyrcanus (reigned 134–104 BC) destroyed the Samaritan temple. Clearly, the hatred ran both ways between these two people groups.

But Jesus **had to** [*edei*, "it was necessary"] **pass through Samaria**. By divine obligation, Jesus violated social, cultural, and religious conventions to demonstrate God's love for an outcast people. Jesus stopped at **Sychar** (v. 5), where **Jacob's well** was located (v. 6). Now after 1,800 years, Jacob's well was still productive. Jesus was **wearied from His journey** (showing He was fully human) and sat down **by the well** at the **sixth hour** (noontime; see comment on 1:39).

4:7-8. It was customary in Jewish culture for women to draw water (Ex 2:16) and do it in the evening (Gn 24:11). That this immoral **woman of Samaria** came **to draw water** at noon by herself may suggest her intention to maintain anonymity. Jesus, now without His disciples (v. 8), initiated the conversation, opening with a question. Believers must take the initiative in evangelistic conversations, and questions are often the place to begin. The **disciples** were **to buy food** (v. 8; cf. the cost of discipleship in Lk 14:26-33), in contrast to the woman who will be offered the free gift of "living water" (eternal life, v. 10).

4:9. The Samaritan woman was amazed that Jesus spoke to her since (1) in that culture men did not talk to women, especially unknown women; and (2) **Jews have no dealings with Samaritans** (a comment by John and not the woman). Tradition taught that taking a drink from a vessel handled by a Samaritan woman would make Jesus ceremonially unclean. In reality, the water Jesus wanted to give the woman would make her spiritually and eternally clean.

4:10. Jesus gave the woman three conditions for gaining "living water": she needed to (1) know the free **gift** of eternal life that **God** gives; (2) know the identity of Jesus, the One who gives this gift on behalf of God; and (3) to ask Jesus for it (i.e., to believe in him). That Jesus claims to be the source of living water indicates that he viewed Himself as the God of the OT and the Messiah (Ps 36:9; Jr 2:13; 17:13).

4:11-12. Nicodemus and the woman both confused spiritual truths with physical realities. How could this unknown Jewish man be **greater than** their patriarch **Jacob** (v. 12)? And how could the water-gift He gives be greater than the **well** Jacob gave that watered even **his cattle**? The woman's questions reflect her skepticism (the Greek construction of the question **You are not greater than our father Jacob, are you?** anticipates a negative response). Like so many others, the woman did not recognize who Jesus was (1:10, 26, 31, 33).

4:13-14. Jesus contrasted the temporal satisfaction of physical water that needs to be drunk repeatedly with the permanent, eternal satisfaction of the **water** He will give (v. 14). The one who drinks just once of the water (i.e., believes) Jesus gives will **never thirst** again because it **will become in him a** perpetual **well** (*pege*, an active "spring") **of water springing up to eternal life**. The Greek word, "springing up" (*hallomai*), is used of the lame "leaping" after being healed (Ac 3:8; 14:10).

4:15-16. The woman asked for **this water, so** that she would **not be thirsty nor come all the way** to the well **to draw** water again. The woman's request was more to gain earthly contentment and convenience than eternal life (cf. 6:34). She had knowledge of the coming Messiah (vv. 25, 29). Jesus' response (v. 16), **Go, call your husband**, is designed ultimately to lead her to identify Him as the Messiah (cf. v. 39).

4:17-18. The woman's reply **I have no husband** both revealed and concealed truth. Jesus complimented the woman for telling the truth, but at the same time uncovered her immorality. Over her adult life, she was married to and divorced from **five** different **husbands** (v. 18). Presently, she was committing adultery with a sixth man **not** her **husband**. Little more is made of her sin in the narrative.

4:19-20. I perceive that You are a prophet marks an advance in the woman's perception of Jesus. His knowledge of her marital status illustrated His prophetic abilities. It also suggests that what follows is not an attempt to change the subject. Instead, the woman wondered if this newly discovered prophet could solve an age-long dispute between Samaritans and Jews on the place of worship (v. 20). Was it **this mountain**, Mt. Gerizim, or was it **Jerusalem**?

4:21-22. On **woman**, see 2:4. If the woman considered Jesus a prophet (v. 19), she must have also **believe**[d] His prophecy about future worship. The phrase **an hour is coming** is used seven times in John (4:21, 23; 5:25, 28; 16:2, 25, 32) and here refers to the time beginning with His death and resurrection. For similar expressions, "My hour," see comments on 2:4; for "His hour," see comments on 7:30; 8:20; and 13:1. Soon **the Father** would be worshiped in any location, not just Jerusalem. The Samaritans (**you** is pl. in Gk., v. 22) worshiped in ignorance. The true message (as found in the Scriptures) and Provider (Messiah) of **salvation** comes **from the Jews**, not the Samaritans. Nevertheless, the provision of salvation would encompass all people who had faith in the Jewish Messiah, including the Samaritans.

4:23-24. Jesus, the Prophet, also predicted that the time for this transformation of worship was **now**. **True worshipers** are defined as those who **will worship the Father in spirit and truth**. **In spirit** does not mean "with enthusiasm" or "with spiritual gifts." In v. 24, Jesus explained that **God is spirit**. To worship **in spirit and truth** means, among other things, to worship *with God in one's life*, to worship as one in whom God, who is a spirit, dwells. **In truth** indicates the full revelation now given through Christ (1:14, 17). **The Father seeks** (cf. v. 27) this kind of worshiper. Our worship (v. 24) must correspond to the nature of God: **God is spirit** and we **must worship in spirit and truth**.

4:25-26. The woman believed in a coming **Messiah** or **Christ** (see comment on 1:20) who would **declare all things** to them. Since Jesus had already exposed her past (v. 29) and had prophesied a radical change in worship (v. 23), her hopes ran high that He might be the Messiah. **I who speak to you am He** (v. 26) means, lit., "I am—the one who speaks to you" (there is no predicate or "He" in the Gk.). The statement is similar to Jesus' "I am" claims in John. See comments on 6:35, 8:24, and 8:58. "I am" recalls the name of the self-existent God of the OT (Ex. 3:14-15; Is 41:4; 43:10, 13) and implies Jesus' deity.

4:27. The **disciples**, influenced by the attitudes toward women in first-century Judaism, **were amazed that He had been speaking with a woman**. Their surprise might have been eliminated if they had not refused to communicate with Him (**no one said**). The answer to **What do You seek?** was that Jesus was seeking exactly what the Father was seeking (v. 23): true worshipers.

4:28-30. In the joy of her discovery, she **left her waterpot** to go **into the city**. That Jesus **told** her **all the things that** she had **done** (v. 29) was for the Samaritans the supernatural knowledge of the coming Messiah (v. 25). Her hesitancy (**this is not the Christ, is it?**) was because she needed to be cautious as a woman "teaching" men. By her testimony, the Samaritans started **coming to Him** (v. 30), both physically and spiritually.

4:31-33. The **disciples** were focused on physical needs (**Rabbi, eat**), while Jesus was concerned for spiritual needs. **I have food to eat that you do not know about** exposed their ignorance of His true inner sustenance (Mt 4:4). That is not to say that Jesus did not need to eat. Jesus was willing to forgo food for a time to engage in what truly energized and strengthened Him, namely ministry. The disciples still did not know the Lord intimately (cf. Jn 14:9). They again misunderstood Jesus' attempt to communicate spiritual truth by means of physical analogies.

4:34-35. The disciples' confusion presented the opportunity for Jesus to teach them. His spiritual **food** was **to do the will of** the One **who sent** Him (5:30; 6:38-40; 8:29) **and to accomplish His work** (9:4; 17:4). **There are yet four months** may be a proverb or used literally of the time of the year (December, before the harvest of winter crops in April). His followers must **look** at the masses of people (viz., the Samaritans coming, v. 30) as **fields** that are **white** (ripe) **for harvest**.

4:36-38. Even now (**already**), ahead of time, on earth, the disciple who leads others to faith in Christ **is receiving wages**, rewards, or blessings. "Wages" (*misthos*) is the same word translated as (future) "reward" (Mt 5:12; 6:1-2; 10:41-42). Paul's identical teaching on future rewards (1Co 3:6-15) originated with the Lord. Sowing and reaping are both necessary for a spiritual harvest. So the planter and the harvester can **rejoice together** without jealousy and competition. **Others have labored** may refer to the OT prophets and John the Baptist, who ministered in Samaria previously (cf. 3:23).

4:39-40. From that city (Sychar, v. 5) specifies **many of the Samaritans** who **believed in Him**. When Philip later visited the area (Ac 8), many more Samaritans believed, likely because of the impact made by John the Baptist and Jesus before him. When a pastor enjoys great success, he and his congregation need to recognize that much of the credit is due to those who came before him and prayed and worked.

In contrast to Nicodemus (see comment on 3:9), the Samaritan woman boldly testified about Christ. With divine omniscience, Jesus had described **all the things that** the woman had **done**. At the request of the **Samaritans** (v. 40), Jesus stayed **two days** in Sychar. Perhaps He stayed at the Samaritan woman's home (cf. Ac 16:14-15).

4:41-42. The wisdom of Jesus' decision to stay in Sychar became evident: **Many more believed because of His word**. God's Word is the stimulus to faith (Rm 10:17; Gl 3:2, 5). The woman's reward (cf. v. 36) was to hear from those to whom she witnessed, now witnesses of their own faith. To **believe** in Christ is to **know that this One is indeed the Savior of the world**. The words "Savior of the world" include Gentiles.

6. Official's Son Healed (4:43-54)

4:43-45. After Jesus' successful two-day ministry among the Samaritans, He continued on to His original destination (v. 3), **Galilee**, about a three-day walk from Sychar. In contrast to the response of Samaria (v. 44), Jesus **testified that a prophet** (cf. v. 19) **has no honor in his own country**, in His case Galilee and Judea (cf. 1:11, 46). **The Galileans received Him** (v. 45) as a wonderful healer (but not with saving faith; a Greek word for "receive" is used here that is different from what is used in 1:12) because they had personally **seen all the things** (the miracles, 2:23) **that He did in Jerusalem at the** Passover **feast**.

4:46. Jesus went **again to Cana**. By this time, the townspeople would have learned how **He had made the water** into **wine** (2:1-11). The **royal official** was probably a high-ranking civil or military officer (he had slaves, v. 51) under Herod Antipas (4 BC–AD 39), tetrarch over Galilee. The healing of the centurion's servant in Mt 8:5-13 and its parallels represents a different incident. Since the officer was likely a Gentile, John presented the movement of Jesus' message to a Jew (chap. 3), then to a Samaritan (chap. 4), and finally to a Gentile (cf. Acts 1:8), signifying the relevance of the message and ministry of Jesus for all people groups. His **son was sick at Capernaum** with a severe fever (v. 52), so the official traveled 20 miles to Cana to seek Jesus' help.

4:47-48. The official implored Jesus **to come down and heal his son; for he was** near **death**. While signs are designed to lead to faith (2:11, 23; 7:31; 20:31-32), requiring that God provide signs before one believes is reprehensible. It makes God into one's slave, rather than making God into one's Lord. **Unless you people** [Gk. pl.] **see signs and wonders, you simply will not believe** (v. 48) confronted the reluctance on the part of the official (**Jesus said to him**) and the Galilean Jews to believe that He was the Christ.

4:49-50. The **official** was not dissuaded by Jesus' challenge but repeated his request for help. His petition was answered in a way that demanded faith. **Go; your son lives** (v. 50) was both a prophecy (vv. 19, 44) and a healing. "Your son lives" is reminiscent of the prophet Elijah, who pronounced the healing of the son of the woman from Zarephath (1Kg 17:23). But Jesus, as the greater prophet, healed the official's son without even being personally present. The essence of faith is to believe **the word that Jesus spoke**—the very thing the official did. His faith was evident in that he **started off** to Capernaum.

4:51-53. The father did not have to reach Capernaum (about 18 to 20 miles from Cana) to learn the news of his son's health. On his way **down** from Cana (a drop of 1,300 ft.), **his slaves met him, saying that his son was living**. To confirm that this was not mere coincidence (v. 52), **he inquired of them the hour when** his son **began to get better**. He learned that it was the previous day at 1:00 p.m. (**the seventh hour**) that **the fever left him**. For "the seventh hour," see comment on 1:39. Convinced (v. 53) that Jesus had healed his son at that precise time, **he himself believed and his whole household**, which included the now healed son. It was common in the NT era for whole households to come to faith together (cf. Ac 11:14; 16:31; 18:8). Since the word "life" appears three times in the narrative (vv. 50, 51, 53), the miracle points to Jesus as the messianic source of all life (1:4).

4:54. The healing of the official's son was not the second sign Jesus did (cf. 2:23; 3:2; 4:45) but the second sign **when He had come out of Judea into Galilee**. The narrative brings the reader full circle back to Cana (2:11; 4:46).

C. Progressive Rejection of Jesus' Ministry (5:1-12:50)

In chaps. 5–12, John described how Jesus as Messiah is Lord of the Sabbath and fulfills the imagery of the Jewish feasts such as Passover and Booths. With opposition growing against Him (cf. 5:16, 18), it was as if Jesus was being put on trial and needed to produce witnesses in His defense (5:31-36; 8:13-17). The signs provided that testimony. Ironically, it was His opponents who were put on trial by Jesus.

1. Events at the Unnamed Feast (Healing of the Lame Man) (5:1-47)

5:1. The **feast** to which John alludes is not identified except that it fell on a Sabbath (v. 9). It is impossible to be sure, but more than likely it was a Passover. Since all males were commanded to attend three feasts at the temple each year—Passover, Pentecost, and Booths (Ex 24:13-17; Dt 16:16)—**Jesus went up to Jerusalem**.

5:2-3a. The present tense in the phrase **there is in Jerusalem** helps identify the date of writing before AD 70 and the destruction of Jerusalem (see Introduction: Date). If the composition of the Fourth Gospel was after that date, the **sheep gate** would have been destroyed and the author would have used the past tense ("there *was* in Jerusalem a sheep gate"). The **sheep gate** (cf. "door of the sheep," 10:7) and **Bethesda** ("house of mercy") probably have spiritual, symbolic significance. The pool was on the northeast side of Jerusalem. It consisted of two trapezoid-shaped pools surrounded by covered walkways (**porticoes**) on four sides and a fifth separating the pools.

5:3b-4. Verses 3b-4 are not found in some important, early mss. Yet Morris writes (*John*, 267-68), "there is no reason for doubting that it explains the presence of the people (cf. v. 7)," i.e., why a multitude of the sick and crippled came regularly to the pool. Against including these verses, the external evidence clearly supports the omission. Much from these verses is repeated in v. 7, which does not need vv. 3b-4. And the omission is the harder reading, for it is unlikely that a scribe would remove these verses if they were originally in the text. Surely they were added to explain why people gathered there.

On the other hand, in support of including vv. 3b-4, first, Tertullian (AD 200) gives evidence of having known the verse. This means its inclusion in the mss can be dated just as early as P66 and P75 (around AD 200 and 400, respectively). Second, v. 7 cannot be understood easily if vv. 3b-4 are absent. Much is left unexplained. Third, it is highly likely that the verses were deleted because a scribe thought it reflected a pagan superstition. In the first century, the Greek god of healing, Asclepius, became associated with this place, and a scribe after this date may have removed the verses to avoid confusion or syncretism. Raymond Brown notes, "This ancient gloss, however, may well reflect with accuracy a popular tradition about the pool" (*John*, 207). On the balance, vv. 3b-4 were probably not written by John. In the OT, the **angel of the Lord** (v. 4) was the preincarnate Christ. Apparently on rare occasions, the angel of the Lord **stirred up the water** to heal graciously the first one who entered. John has already contrasted the role of angels with that of Jesus (1:51). Now *the* Angel of the Lord (Jesus) was personally present to heal just one.

5:5-7. Out of a multitude of ill people (v. 3), Jesus chose one who was ill for **thirty-eight years**. The number recalls Israel's wanderings in the wilderness for 38 years (Dt 2:14). Jesus **knew** (v. 6) by His supernatural knowledge (cf. 1:47; 2:25; 4:39) **that he had already been a long time in that condition**. Jesus' question **Do you wish to get well?** reveals the complete inability of the man to be healed. The question was also intended to prepare the man's heart for faith; instead he complained. Since he was paralyzed, the sick man could not move quickly enough to get **into the pool** himself (v. 7), and had no one to put him in **when the water** was **stirred up**.

5:8-9. The healing was completed with the words **Get up** (rise up, *egeiro*) a term used of resurrection. In the following dialogue, Jesus will use this word of His life-giving power in the last day (v. 21). But the Lord also commanded, **pick up your pallet and walk**. Though no faith was expressed (the man did not even know who it was who healed him), the healing was instantaneous (v. 9). In the Synoptics, faith led to one's healing (e.g., Mt 8:5-13; 9:2-7, 20-22, 27-29; 15:22-28; Mk 9:17-27). But Jesus' three miraculous healings recorded in John (here; 4:46-54; 9:1-38) were noted by John to lead his readers to faith (cf. 21:30-31). The current narrative demonstrates that not all miracles will bring about faith in their recipients. It also indicates that the Son shows grace to those who do not deserve it. The comment, **Now it was the Sabbath on that day**, prepares the readers for the following controversy.

5:10-11. Since the paralytic was also Jewish, the term **Jews** must refer to the Jewish leaders (see Introduction). Carrying items such as a bedroll was **not permissible** on the Sabbath because it violated Jewish traditions added to the Mosaic law. Thirty-nine types of work are described in the Mishnah that violated the Sabbath, such as tying and untying a knot (cf. *m. Sabb.* 7:2). When questioned, the healed man replied (v. 11) that the One who had **made** him **well was the** same **one who said to** him, **Pick up your pallet and walk**. It appears that the man was seeking to shift the blame for his supposed violation of the Sabbath from himself to Jesus, so that his comment in v. 11 was designed to get Jesus in trouble and sidestep their reproof.

5:12-14. When questioned further, the healed man could not identify Jesus by name (v. 13). The man was so focused on his new condition, and apparently so devoid of gratitude, that he was not aware that **Jesus had slipped away** through the **crowd** to avoid publicity (cf. 6:15). But later, **Jesus found him in the temple** complex (cf. 9:35) just south of the pool of Bethesda. **Do not sin anymore** indicates that the man's illness may have been the result of some unidentified sin 38 years before (cf. 9:2-3). Jesus knew his past life (cf. 4:39). Another **worse** physical disease or even physical death (cf. Pr 2:18; 11:19) might result if he engaged in a life of sin.

5:15-16. The man . . . told the Jews that it was Jesus. When these verses are taken with v. 11, it appears that the healed man continued his attempt to alleviate himself of the guilt of violating the Sabbath and place it fully upon Jesus. It is unlikely that the healed man came to faith (cf. 11:45-46). As a result of his report, the Jewish leaders **were persecuting Jesus** [i.e., slandering Him as a law-breaker], not because He did this healing on the Sabbath but **because He was doing these things** (pl.) repeatedly **on the Sabbath**.

5:17-18. The Sabbath commemorated God's work in creation (Gn 2:2-3; Ex 20:8-11) and in redemption (Dt 5:15). For Jesus to say that **My Father is working until now** [e.g., babies are born on the Sabbath; He sustains the universe on the Sabbath], **and I Myself am working** implied that He, like His Father who is the Creator-Redeemer, is the source of all life and salvation. The words **were seeking all the more** (v. 18) show that the Jewish authorities were plotting **to kill Him** even before this attempt (cf. Mk 3:6). The plots to kill Jesus are frequently mentioned in John (7:1, 19, 25, 30; 8:37, 40; 10:39; 11:8). The charge was not only Sabbath violation. Jesus **was calling God His own Father, making Himself equal with God**—one of the clearest claims to deity in John.

5:19. John began a long response by Jesus, divided into two sections: Jesus' equality with but subordination to the Father (vv. 19-30), and Jesus' witnesses that testify to His authority. Although Jesus is equal in essence to the Father, nothing He does is independent of the Father's initiative. For Jesus to do **something He sees the Father doing** affirms their unique, intimate relationship (1:1; 17:5). **Whatever the Father does, these things the Son also does in like manner**, accurately imitating the Father's will and working in perfect unity. John's purpose is to present a high Christology here. Some understand this section as a model for the Christian life—that one should see where God is at work and then join Him there in it. But John's purpose is clearly Christological—to prove that the Son shares the Father's divine authority (vv. 22-23).

5:20-21. The Father loves the Son. In 3:35 ("the Father loves the Son"), "loves" is the Greek verb *agapao*, but in 5:20 ("the Father loves the Son"), "loves" is a different verb, *phileo*. The two words in John's gospel are essentially synonyms (though *phileo* can mean "to kiss" in *Koine* Greek), and neither here nor elsewhere can be pressed to show a distinction in meaning—a fact that has considerable implications for Peter's interaction regarding his love for Jesus in 21:15-17. Elsewhere in John, the love of the Father for the Son is always the Greek word *agapao* (cf. 3:35; 10:17; 15:9; 17:24). The Father's love causes Him to show Christ **all things that He Himself is doing**. The **greater works** are the right given to the Son to raise **the dead** (v. 21) and give **life to whom He wishes**, i.e., to those who believe.

5:22-23. As in the OT, the Father gives life and raises the dead. So He has the right to judge. Since the Father has given to the Son the right to raise the dead, **He has** also **given all judgment to the Son**. This shows the persons of the Trinity are distinct while perfectly united. **All** people must **honor** (v. 23) or worship **the Son even as they honor the Father**, substantiating Christ's divine authority along with God the Father's.

5:24-25. To have eternal life, one must believe in the God **who sent** Christ. Islam rejects this God, and Judaism's view of Him is culpably insufficient. **Has eternal life** and **has passed out of death into life** communicate the immediacy of this divine transaction (see comment on 3:36). For **does not come into judgment**, see comments on 3:18. For **an hour is coming and now is** (v. 25), see comments on 4:21, 23. **The dead** who **hear the voice of the Son of God** and **live** are spiritually dead nonbelievers (Eph 2:1, 5; Col 2:13) who come to faith (**hear**, v. 25) and receive eternal life now. They, and those who have believed and who have died, will participate in the future resurrection (see the comments on v. 28).

5:26-27. Just as the Father has life in Himself begins another comparison in which Jesus claims to be the source of life (cf. 1:3-4; 14:6). **Even so** completes the comparison. Like the Father, Jesus has authority over life as well as over the Sabbath (cf. vv. 17-18). For all eternity past, the Father **gave to the Son also to have life in Himself**. Jesus' **authority to execute judgment** is **because He is the Son of Man** (v. 27). Man will be equitably judged by Jesus not primarily as the Son of God but as the Son of Man (cf. 1:51; Dn 7:13-14).

5:28-29. An hour is coming refers to the future resurrection (**all who are in the tombs . . . will come forth**). In this passage, all Christians are considered to be **those who did the good deeds** (v. 29), namely, they exercised faith in Jesus (see the contrast between believing and disobeying in 3:36), and they will go **to a resurrection of life**. But all who fail to believe are also viewed from the perspective of eternity. Even though those who reject Christ may do many commendable things, those deeds are not oriented toward the glory of God and are not done in the power of the Holy Spirit. Those who do not embrace Christ are viewed as **those who committed the evil deeds** and go **to a resurrection of judgment**.

5:30-32. For **I can do nothing on My own initiative**, see v. 19. If Jesus judges only on what He hears from the Father, His **judgment** will be **just** (righteous) since God is just. The Son does **not seek** His **own will** (4:34; 6:38; 7:28; 8:29). He knows perfectly and seeks continually the Father's will. In the Mosaic law, proper court procedure required two or more witnesses (Dt 17:6; 19:15; Nm 35:30). In submission to the law, Jesus agreed that His **testimony** alone (v. 31) could not be verified as **true** in a human court. But He was trusting **another**, the Father, to bring **testimony** to Him (v. 32).

5:33-34. For **You have sent to John**, see comments on 1:19-28. Jesus acknowledged that **John** the Baptist had **testified to the truth** of His identity as the Messiah. But the authoritative testimony He received was not a human testimony (v. 34). Christ needed to **say these things** about the Father's true testimony (v. 32) **so that** those listening to Jesus (and the readers of John) **may be saved**.

5:35-36. John was a **lamp**, fulfilling the prophecy of the "lamp" that was to prepare for the Messiah (Ps. 132:17). While he was preaching (**shining**), the Jewish people **were willing to rejoice for a while**, hoping he would bring in a messianic ruler who would establish the kingdom and overthrow Rome. But the **greater** testimony to which Jesus appealed was **the very works** (pl., His teachings, miracles, and later His death and resurrection), **which the Father** had **given** Him **to accomplish** (cf. 4:34; 17:4).

Five Witnesses to Jesus in John 5

- John the Baptist (v. 33)
- Jesus' own works (v. 36)
- the Father (v. 37)
- the Scriptures (v. 39)
- Moses (v. 46)

5:37-38. The **Father** had **testified** in the OT Scriptures (cf. v. 39), by a voice from heaven at the baptism of Jesus (Mt 3:17; Mk 1:11), and by the descent of the Spirit like a dove on Christ (Jn 1:32-33). Yet these Jewish leaders (vv. 16, 18) had **neither heard His voice** spiritually **at any time nor seen His form** (i.e., nature) by faith, as proven in their failure to believe in the Son (v. 38).

5:39-40. The Pharisees held that those ignorant of the law were accursed (7:49). So they searched **the Scriptures because** they thought that in the mere knowledge of Scripture they had **eternal life**. Blinded by their self-righteousness, they missed the true Messiah about whom the Scriptures prophesied. This failure meant they were **unwilling to come to** Christ for eternal **life**, not merely that they were ignorant of the truth.

5:41-42. I do not receive glory from men corrects the opponents' assumption that Jesus was disappointed that they did not give Him honor. Christ abandoned all self-righteousness and sought **glory** (see comments on 1:14; 2:11) from God, not from people. "Glory" carries slightly different emphases in John. Here, "glory" means "praise," "honor," or "recognition." The Pharisees sought admiration from their contemporaries by their knowledge of Torah. At the incarnation, Jesus willingly set aside His divine glory (17:5; see comment on Php 2:7). Now on earth, Jesus sought honor from God by His complete humiliation and obedience to the Father's will (Jn 17:4). Contrary to sincere faith in Christ, religious systems surreptitiously promote seeking honor from contemporaries (cf. v. 44; Mt 6:5, 16; 23:5). Seeking honor from people and **love** for **God** (v. 42) are mutually exclusive.

5:43-44. In My Father's name means Jesus was God's supreme representative. The foremost act of love for God (v. 42) is to **receive** the representative He sent. **If another comes in his own name, you will receive him** may refer to the future Jewish reception of the beast (Dn 9:27; Rv 13:1-8) or the False Prophet (Rv 13:11-17), or even Simon bar Kokhba, who led the second revolt against Rome in AD 132–135. Seeking **glory from one another** seriously hinders faith in Christ (cf. Jn 12:42-43). For faith in Christ, one needs to seek after **the glory** [i.e., glorification/

resurrection; cf. Rm 5:2; 8:21] **that is from the one and only God**.

5:45-47. In the future judgment, Christ does not need to bring a judgment against the Jewish leaders. **Moses** (i.e., the first five books of Scripture that he wrote) **in whom** they had **set** their **hope** for eternal life (v. 39) would testify to their guilt in failing to recognize Jesus as the Messiah he predicted. Moses frequently prophesied of the Messiah (cf. Gn 3:15; 49:10; Ex 12:21; Nm 24:17; Dt 18:15; cf. also Jn 1:45; 3:14; 8:56). Anyone who **believed** in the Scriptures **Moses** wrote (and therefore believed in the Lord) would have believed in Jesus as the Messiah (v. 46; see comment on 6:37).

2. Events Near the Passover (6:1-71)

In Jn 6, Jesus fed the 5,000, calmed the storm on the Sea of Galilee, and in Capernaum explained the meaning of the feeding miracle. The feeding of the 5,000 is the only miracle recorded in all four Gospels. The events took place about half a year after those of chap. 5, in spring, just before the Passover (v. 4). Jesus had just claimed that Moses spoke of Him (5:39, 46-47). In the following events, John showed how Jesus illustrated this claim. As in chap. 5, where a healing led to a discourse by Jesus on His true identity as the life-giver, (5:21, 24, 26), so the feeding miracle of chap. 6 led to a discourse on Jesus' identity as the bread of life.

a. Feeding of the 5,000 (6:1-14)

6:1-2. The time reference, **after these things**, is vague but provides for Jesus' unidentified movement from Jerusalem (chap. 5) to Galilee. **The other side of the Sea of Galilee** refers to the eastern shore. Only John identified the Sea of Galilee as also the Sea of **Tiberias** (cf. 21:1) after the major town on the southwestern shore. Jesus went to the eastern side to get some rest (Mk 6:30-32) and to avoid Herod Antipas, who had just killed John the Baptist (Lk 9:7-10). The miraculous **signs** (v. 2) that Jesus did for **those who were sick** drew a large, curious crowd of followers.

6:3-4. Mountain may refer to the sloping hills (cf. "went down" in v. 16) of the Golan Heights. As was common for rabbis, Jesus **sat down with His disciples**, probably to teach (Mt 5:1; 13:2; Mk 4:1; 9:35), the common rabbinic posture for instruction. This **Passover** (v. 4) would have been one year before Jesus' crucifixion. The Passover commemorated the deliverance of Israel from the Egyptians through Moses (cf. v. 32), and messianic hopes ran high during this festival.

6:5-7. Jesus addressed Philip concerning **where** to **buy bread** since he was originally a local resident (1:44). The question was designed as a **test** (v. 6). Since God had provided manna for His people in the wilderness, Philip should have known that the Messiah would do the same for the multitude. Jesus did not feed the 5,000 based on a last-minute expedient, but **He Himself knew** ahead of time **what He was intending to do**. A denarius (a silver coin) was worth a day's pay, and 200 denarii (v. 7) were worth about eight months of wages. Philip's answer established the fact that a human solution was impossible.

6:8-9. According to Mk 6:38, Jesus had instructed the disciples to determine how many loaves were available. **Andrew, Simon Peter's brother** (like Philip, both were from Bethsaida, 1:44), mentioned **a lad** there (v. 9) **who has five barley loaves and two fish**. While Jesus could have supplied food from nothing, He chose to multiply the barley loaves of the young boy (the loaves are identified as barley only in John), purposefully replicating a miracle done by the prophet Elisha (2Kg 4:42-44). The prophet Elisha fed 100 men with 20 barley loaves and verified he was sent by God. Jesus demonstrated by the feeding miracle that He is *the* Prophet sent from God (see the comments on Dt 34:10-12).

6:10-11. The springtime of the Passover season (v. 4) produced plenty of **grass in the place**. As the Good Shepherd, Jesus led His Jewish lost sheep (cf. 10:1-16; Mt 10:6) to lush pasture. The number, **about five thousand** (the number is rounded off), was the count of the adult men (Mt 14:21 mentions women and children). The total number of people may have been 15,000 or even 20,000. Before distributing the bread and fish (v. 11), Jesus gave **thanks** for the food (cf. v. 23).

6:12-13. Christ always supplies an overabundance for our needs. The people **were** all **filled** and there were many **leftover** pieces. "Leftover" is the Greek word *perisseuo*, lit., "abundance" (cf. v. 13; 10:10). Since John favors symbolism, the **twelve baskets** (v. 13) may symbolize the Messiah's sufficiency for the twelve tribes of Israel. Only the leftover bread is mentioned since that alone relates to the bread of life teaching that follows (vv. 32-58).

6:14-15. Moses fed the Israelites in the wilderness with manna from heaven. **When the people saw the sign** (see comment on 2:11), **which** Jesus **had performed**, it reminded them of Dt 18:18, "I will raise up for them a prophet like you [Moses]." In disregard for the spiritual, they sought a political solution, deciding to **take** Christ **by force to make Him king** (v. 15)—a point not mentioned in the Synoptic parallels. Resisting the temptation for recognition and power, Jesus **withdrew again to the mountain by Himself alone**.

b. Walking on Water (6:15-21)

6:16-17. Although John did not specifically call Jesus' walking on water a sign, there is little doubt he presented it as such. According to the Synoptics, Jesus had instructed the disciples to sail ahead of Him to Capernaum while He spent time praying (Mt 14:22-23; Mk 6:45-46). So **when evening came**, the disciples set out on their trip (four to five miles). **It had already become dark** (v. 17) pictures the physical environment. But with the added phrase, **and Jesus had not yet come to them**, the clause "may also be symbol-laden: as in 3:2; 13:30, the darkness of night and the absence of Jesus are powerfully linked" (Carson, *John*, 274).

6:18-19. The Sea of Galilee is well known for its sudden storms. Cooler Mediterranean winds from the west get funneled through several valleys that descend to the lake, often colliding with hotter inland air, resulting in strong winds. As the winds increased, the disciples found that they had only rowed **about three or four miles** (v. 19), to the middle of the lake (Mk 6:47). The storm did not terrify them. But **they saw Jesus walking on the sea and drawing near to the boat; and they were frightened**, thinking they were seeing a ghost (Mk 6:49). John did not call Jesus' walking on the water a "sign" (see comment on 2:11). Instead, it was a private manifestation of His messianic glory to His disciples.

6:20-21. Jesus' walking on water is united with His unique claim to deity, **It is I** (lit., "I am"). See comments on v. 35 and 8:58. In the OT, the sea often represented anarchy and disorder. It was God who brought it under control (cf. Jnh 1:4-15; Pss 65:5-7; 93:1-4). Since they were in the middle of the lake, the words **immediately the boat was at the land to which they were going** carry a supernatural sense.

c. Bread of Life Message (6:22-71)

6:22-24. The disciples' willing reception of Jesus (v. 21; cf. 1:11-12) contrasted with the response of **the crowd that stood on the other** [eastern] **side of the sea** (cf. vv. 26, 36, 41-42, 52), across the lake from Tiberias. They eventually discovered the disciples had left for Capernaum (on the northwest shore of the lake) without Jesus. But they also determined that Jesus was not in the area. The crowd had dwindled enough by now (Jesus had dismissed them; Mt 14:22; Mk 6:45) that they could all fit in the **small boats** that came **from Tiberias** on the southwest shore of the lake (vv. 23-24). They **came to Capernaum seeking Jesus**, and apparently all crowded into the synagogue at Capernaum (v. 59). The archaeological discovery in 1976 of a contemporary synagogue at Gamla (10 miles east of Capernaum) indicates it held about 300 people. The synagogue at Capernaum may have been a similar size.

6:25-27. Since Jesus had not taken a boat and could not have traveled on foot to Capernaum that quickly, the people knew something unusual had happened. Their question **when did You get here?** expressed their confusion. Jesus did not explain when He arrived but addressed their motive in seeking Him (v. 26). It was not **because** they **saw signs**, which could lead them to faith (20:31-32), **but because** they **ate** food and **were filled**. Two kinds of food must be distinguished (v. 27): **food which perishes** and **food which endures to eternal life**. Jews would recall that the manna given by Moses in the wilderness lasted only a day (Ex 16:19-21). For **set His seal**, see comment on 3:33. God's seal on Christ is the Spirit (Jn 1:32-33; 3:34; Ac 10:38).

6:28-29. The command to "work" for eternal food (v. 27) prompted the question **What shall we do, so that we may work the works of God?** Jesus redefined the "works of God" (pl.) as the **work of God** (sg.): to **believe in** the Son (v. 29). By this wordplay on "work," Christ declared that eternal life is really not gained by works (Eph 2:8-9; Rm 4:4; Ti 3:5). Even the manna that Moses gave the Israelites was so that they might learn not to live by physical bread alone but also spiritual bread (Dt 8:3).

6:30-31. The crowd at Capernaum consisted of skeptics who had seen Jesus' previous signs (v. 2) and the feeding miracle, and others who had not seen the feeding miracle (cf. those in the boats from Tiberias, vv. 23-24). Together they asked, **What then do You do for a sign so that we may . . . believe You?** In their thinking, if Jesus were the Prophet like Moses, then His miracles would be superior. Jesus provided one meal for 5,000 on a grassy hillside; Moses fed a nation **manna** (v. 31) in the wilderness for forty years. Jesus used earthly fish and bread, but Moses **GAVE THEM BREAD OUT OF HEAVEN TO EAT** (a quote from Ps 78:24). Later rabbis also saw a link between Moses feeding Israel manna in the wilderness with the future Messiah, as seen in the Midrash (the ancient rabbinic exposition of the Bible). "As the first redeemer (Moses) was, so shall the latter Redeemer (Messiah) be.... As the former redeemer caused manna to descend ... so will the latter Redeemer cause manna to descend" (Ecclesiastes Rabbah 1:9).

6:32-33. The bread given by Moses in the wilderness was temporal. In that sense, it was not **the bread out of heaven**. Instead, it was **My Father**, Jesus said, who was giving them the **true** heavenly **bread**. "True" means spiritual and eternal as opposed to temporal and physical. The feeding miracle pointed to Jesus, the true **bread of God** (v. 33). This Bread is far superior because it **gives** eternal **life to the world**, not just temporal life to the Jews.

6:34-36. The woman from Sychar mistakenly asked for a continual supply of physical water (4:15). Similarly, these listeners requested never-ending physical bread (**always give us this bread**). Verse 35 (**I am the bread of life**) contains the first of seven "I am" statements in John (but cf. v. 20; 4:26). **Will not hunger** and **will never thirst** are emphatic in Greek and demonstrate that eternal life is a permanent possession. In v. 30, the Jews told Jesus that if they saw a sign, they would believe. Jesus contradicted this (v. 36), explaining that they had **seen** Him and His signs but still did **not believe**.

6:37. All that the Father gives to the Son **will come to** Him (i.e., believe). Similar statements are mentioned frequently in John (6:39; 10:29; 17:2, 6, 9, 24; 18:9). The "giving" could refer to a divine election that precedes the "coming" (cf. Eph 1:3-6) or to the certain reception of Jesus by those who genuinely seek the One True God (cf. "if you believed Moses, you would believe Me," Jn 5:46; cf. also 1:35-51; 5:24, 38; 10:27-29). **Will certainly not cast out** is clarified in the following verses. **Cast out** (two words in Greek, the first from the verb *ekballo*, "I throw out," and the second an adverb *ekso*, "outside") does not refer to how Jesus will receive people, but how He will keep people who have believed in Him. Though the blind man was cast out of the synagogue (*ekballo* and *ekso* also, 9:34), he will always be "in" Christ.

Jesus' Seven "I Am" Claims

"I am the bread of life" (6:35, 48, 51).

"I am the light of the world" (8:12; 9:5).

"I am the door" (10:7, 9).

"I am the good shepherd" (10:11, 14).

"I am the resurrection and the life" (11:25).

"I am the way, the truth, and the life" (14:6).

"I am the true vine" (15:1).

6:38-40. Christ's purpose in coming to earth was to do **the will of** the Father **who sent** Him (4:34; 5:30; 8:29). On the basis of His perfect obedience to the Father, Jesus promised (v. 39) that **all that He has given Me I lose nothing, but raise it up on the last day**. The "last day" refers to the resurrection and final judgment. Verse 40 emphatically repeats v. 39. No clearer verses can be found that affirm the ultimate safekeeping of the believer. Our eternal security depends on Jesus fulfilling **the will** of the **Father**, which He will never fail to do.

6:41-42. Grumbling is reminiscent of Israel's rebellion in the wilderness (Ex 16:2, 7-9, 12). **The Jews** stumbled over Jesus' claim to be **the bread that came down out of heaven**. "Came down" is the language of incarnation (Jn 1:14; Gl 4:4; Php 2:7-8). Their familiarity with Jesus' human lineage like His **father and mother** (cf. Mk 6:3; Lk 4:22) prevented them from seeing His true nature as God come in human flesh (cf. 1:14).

6:43-44. The crowd of skeptics grumbled against the assertion that Jesus had come down from heaven and that people were coming to Him because the Father "gave them to" Jesus (v. 37). Jesus both rebuked their complaining and corrected their ignorance. **No one** could come to Him **unless the Father who sent** Christ **draws** that person. Left to oneself, no one would ever seek God or Christ (see the comments on Rm 1:18-23 and 3:9-18). God provided that everyone who hears the message of Christ should be drawn (12:32), but that drawing does not last forever (cf. 12:40).

6:45-46. Jesus confirmed the universal drawing of God (cf. 12:32) by a quote from the writing of **the prophets**. Isaiah 54:13 declared that in the millennial kingdom, people will **ALL BE TAUGHT** by **GOD** (Is 2:3; Mc 4:2). "Taught" clarifies how God "draws" people (v. 44). But it is not enough to be drawn or taught by God. **Everyone who has heard and** has actually **learned from the Father comes to** or believes in Jesus. Those who have "learned from the Father" will be given to the Son (v. 37). Because of a switch from the first person to the third person, v. 46 is regarded by the NET as a parenthetical note by John. But Jesus may use the third person of Himself (cf. Jn 5:19; 10:11; 17:1-2) here to explain that He is the only One who has learned from the Father by actually seeing Him.

6:47-48. Truly, truly alerts the listener to the significance of what follows. The one who does nothing more than believes **has eternal life**. In radical contrast, every other religion requires some works to gain eternal life or reach the "ultimate," whatever it might be. Christ's claim **I am the bread of life** (v. 48; cf. vv. 35, 51) uses one of the most basic sources of nourishment to express metaphorically His role in sustaining everlasting life.

6:49-51. By referring to **your fathers**, Jesus identified His opponents with the rebellious Israelites who **ate the manna in the wilderness**, and **died**. For the first time of several in the chapter (vv. 50-54, 56-58), Jesus mentioned directly that one must **eat of** this bread (v. 50). To **eat** this **bread** is a metaphor for believing in Christ, since this thought is the central concern in the chapter (vv. 29-30, 35-36, 40, 47, 64, 69). Just as one takes in bread for physical life, one must "take in" Christ by faith for eternal life. One who eats **living bread** (v. 51) will **live forever**. The bread is now defined as His "flesh" or body that He will voluntarily offer (**I will give**) on the cross to bring salvation for everyone (**for the life of the world**). Since neither wine nor the cup is mentioned (Mt 26:27; 1Co 10:16; 11:26-28), there is no clear allusion to the Lord's Supper.

6:52-53. Jesus' analogy of eating His flesh was purposeful. Eating someone's flesh is abhorrent. Likewise, sinful humanity is repulsed by the need to believe in Christ. Misunderstanding Jesus again (cf. v. 34), the unbelieving Jews question, **How can this man give us His flesh to eat?** To the need to **eat the flesh of the Son of Man** (v. 53), Jesus added an additional revolting image, the command to **drink His blood**. With the imagery of "eating" and "drinking," Christ helped communicate the need to assimilate by faith Christ's death for one's self.

6:54-56. The phrase **He who eats My flesh and drinks My blood** cannot refer to the Eucharist or the Lord's Supper since John (1) paid very little attention to sacraments (the Lord's Supper is never mentioned in the book); (2) made faith alone the means by which one **has eternal life**; and (3) showed that interpreting Jesus literally and physically (as in a sacramental view) is a misunderstanding (a common literary feature in John). For **true**, see v. 32. As with food that our body completely absorbs, one who by faith **eats** Christ's **flesh and drinks** His **blood abides in** Christ, **and** Christ abides **in him**. "Abiding" in Christ in v. 56 involves an ongoing fellowship with Jesus that begins at the moment of faith. But as 15:1-11 will show, "abiding" in Christ requires ongoing obedience (15:10). So 15:4 will give the command to remain or continue in this fellowship with Christ.

6:57-59. This is the only place in the Bible that God is called **the living Father**. The Son draws His life from the Father (**I live because of the Father**). Similarly, the believer's eternal life is dependent on the Son (**so he who eats Me, he also will live because of Me**). Verse 58 restates v. 49. **Not as the fathers ate and died** contrasts with Jesus' reference to the "living Father." John informed us (v. 59) that Jesus' message on the Bread of Life took place **in the synagogue** at **Capernaum**. Adult men competent in the OT Scriptures could speak in the synagogue service (Lk 4:16; Ac 13:15, 42; 17:2).

6:60-61. Many of Christ's **disciples** found it difficult to accept the teaching that one needed to eat Jesus' flesh and drink His blood (i.e., believe in Christ) to gain eternal life. "Listen" (**Who can listen to it?**) is better rendered "accept" (NIV, HCSB). **Jesus** (v. 61) was supernaturally **conscious** (Gk. "knew within Himself") **that** many of **His disciples grumbled** at His claims. **Stumble** (*skandalizo*) means "that which causes an obstacle" to faith, "that which shocks or causes anger." The cross (cf. v. 51) is the primary offense to man's persistence in self-righteousness (1Co 1:23; Gl 5:11).

6:62-63. What then if you see the Son of Man ascending implies the crucifixion (cf. v. 61) and resurrection through which the ascension is accomplished will be more difficult to believe. **Where He was before** is part of the offense since it teaches Christ's preexistence (cf. 1:1). **The Spirit** is the One **who gives** eternal **life**. The **flesh** (human nature associated with sin and self-righteousness) **profits nothing** as it relates to the attainment of eternal life, or even in evaluating who Jesus is. The truth about Jesus' death by crucifixion seems unthinkable from a human perspective ("the flesh"). But the Spirit works through Jesus' **words**, not fleshly reasoning.

6:64-65. Without pointing out individuals, Jesus told His disciples, **There are some of you who do not believe**. In His omniscience (cf. v. 61; also 1:47; 2:24-25; 6:15), **Jesus knew** the ones **who did not believe**. The parallel words **and who it was that would betray Him** identify Judas as an unbeliever (cf. 6:71; 13:11). The words **no one can come to Me unless it has been granted him** (v. 65) show again the divine side of human faith. Unless God brings about faith in the heart of a person, he or she will not believe. In salvation, God is the "prime mover" (i.e., "drawing," v. 44).

6:66-67. Many of Christ's **disciples withdrew** and stopped following Him as their Teacher/ Rabbi (i.e., stopped traveling with Him and learning His teachings). Jesus' total disciples may not have been a large group (for an estimate of the total crowd, see 6:22-24). These followers were not rejecting the conditions of discipleship but the condition of eternal life as found exclusively in Christ (vv. 30, 35-36, 40, 47, 64, 69). But Judas continued as a disciple (vv. 70-71), yet also never believed. Although Jesus questioned (v. 67) **the twelve** (including Judas), this does not imply that all His other disciples left. His question called for a confession of faith from His closest followers.

6:68-69. Peter's spontaneity results in testimony. **Lord, to whom shall we go?** rightly assesses the exclusive role of Christ in receiving eternal life (cf. 14:6). **You** alone ("alone" is implied in the context) **have words** that lead to **eternal life**. Peter announced as the representative for the others (v. 69), **We have believed and have come to know that You are the Holy One of God**. For "know" as a synonym for "believe," see 4:42. Faith in Christ for these eleven disciples began at least as early as 2:11.

6:70-71. Peter thought that all twelve disciples had believed ("we have believed," v. 69). Jesus corrected him, **Did I Myself not choose you, the twelve, and yet one of you is a devil** [or just possibly "the Devil"]**?** Jesus stated that among the twelve (not among the disciples who left), there was one controlled by the **Devil**, or Satan. This is the first mention of **Judas** (v. 71), identified as the **son of Simon Iscariot**, and thereby distinguished from another apostle (Lk 16:16) and Jesus' half brother (Mt 13:55). Since both Judas and his father, Simon, are called **Iscariot**, "Judas" may be a Greek transliteration of the Hebrew for "man of Kerioth" (Jos 15:25), the town from which they came (Carson, *John*, 304).

3. Events at the Feast of Booths (7:1–8:59)

a. Preparation and Teachings at the Feast (7:1-44)

7:1-2. After these things marks about six months since the Passover (6:4). Jesus stayed in Galilee because **in Judea** the Jewish authorities **were seeking to kill Him** (cf. vv. 19-20, 25, 30, 32, 44). The Jewish **Feast of Booths** (v. 2), also called the Feast of Tabernacles, Tents, or Ingathering, was celebrated by building leafy tents in which Jewish families camped out in fields or on rooftops. It was an eight-day celebration in the autumn after harvest (Sept. or Oct.) in remembrance of when Israel lived in tents during their wanderings in the wilderness (Lv 23:33-43).

7:3-5. Jesus had four half-brothers (Mt 13:55; Mk 6:3). Some or all of **His brothers** (Jn 2:12) instructed Him to **go into Judea, so that** His **disciples also** might **see** the **works** He was **doing**. Their worldly suggestion (v. 4) placed before Jesus the temptation to seek **to be known publicly** for personal gain—a temptation He overcame (v. 10). If He claimed to be the Messiah, in their opinion He should now **show** Himself **to the world**. John's explanatory comment (v. 5) reveals that **not even His** own **brothers were believing in Him** (cf. 1:11). His brothers did not come to faith until after the resurrection (Ac 1:14).

7:6-7. Jesus was conscious of right timing. His words **My time is not yet here** (and v. 8; see comment on 2:4) reflect His concern as to when and how He will present Himself as Messiah. It was to lead to His death, not His fame. **Your time is always opportune** means Jesus' brothers could go to the feast anytime without threats on their lives. The unbelievers of the world practice evil, and love others who do the same. But the world **hates** Jesus **because** He testifies **that its deeds are evil**.

7:8-9. Although debated, the better mss contain "yet" (omitted in the NASB) and read, **I do not *yet* go up to this feast** (v. 8; NKJV, HCSB, NIV). Jewish men were required by the Mosaic law to attend the feast (Ex 23:17; 34:23; Dt 16:16). Jesus would not have left the impression of violating the law. "Go up" has a double sense in that the same Greek word is used of Jesus' ascension (Jn 3:13; 6:62; 20:17). It was not Jesus' time to go up (i.e., "to ascend"—Jerusalem is 2,500 feet above sea level, and one went topographically "up" to get to it) to the feast; but it also was not the time for His death, resurrection, and ascension (7:30). For a few more days, Jesus **stayed in Galilee** to avoid a premature death.

7:10-11. Jesus waited until **His brothers had gone up to the feast**. Afterward, **He Himself also went up . . . in secret**, successfully triumphing over the satanic temptation to seek human glory (cf. v. 4). The wisdom of choosing initially to remain obscure is confirmed by the fact that the Jewish authorities (v. 11) **were seeking Him at the feast** so they might kill Him (cf. v. 1).

7:12-13. The reference to **much grumbling** indicates that unbelief had divided the people (cf. 6:41, 61) and recalls the feast's theme of Israel's wilderness wandering during which the people also grumbled because of their lack of faith (Ex 15:24; 16:2; Nm 14:2; see comments on 7:1-2). **Some were** judging Him to be a **good man**, though not necessarily the Messiah. **Others were saying** that **He leads the people astray**—a charge punishable by death (Dt 13:9-10). **No one was speaking openly of Him for fear of the Jews** (v. 13). As this statement implies, "grumbling" (v. 12) also carries overtones of suppressed conversation. Any favorable opinions about Jesus expressed openly might bring reprisal.

7:14-15. Jesus chose **the midst of the feast** to be the opportune time (cf. v. 6) to go **into the temple**, and to begin **to teach**. The Jewish leaders **were astonished** that Jesus had such a thorough grasp of Scripture (**How has this man become learned . . . ?**), since He had not been **educated** formally under a rabbi according to tradition (cf. Ac 4:13).

7:16-17. The Jews reasoned that Jesus' teaching must be His own. Jesus countered, **My teaching is not Mine, but His who sent Me**. This fact could be confirmed. **If anyone is willing to do** the Father's **will** (v. 17), i.e., believe in Christ for eternal life (6:40a), **he will know of the teaching, whether it is of God or whether I speak from Myself**. Faith authenticates and internalizes God's testimony (1Jn 5:10). The Word, when it is believed, is a life-giving seed (1Pt 1:23), bringing assurance through the Holy Spirit that God's promises are true (cf. Heb 11:1).

7:18-20. He who speaks from himself (such as a false messiah) **seeks his own** honor. **He who is seeking the glory of the One who sent Him** refers to Jesus Himself and His heaven-to-earth mission. **He is true, and there is no unrighteousness in Him** is a claim by Jesus to sinlessness in character and motive. In contrast to Jesus' righteousness, **none** of the Jewish authorities kept the **Law** (v. 19). But neither does anyone (Rm 3:19-20). The attempt **to kill** (murder) Jesus (cf. v. 1) was in actuality a violation of the sixth Commandment (Ex 20:13). Instead of recognizing the Father speaking through His Son, **the crowd** (v. 20) absurdly accused Jesus of **demon** possession (cf. Jn 8:48; 10:20; Mt 12:24).

7:21-22. I did one deed (lit., "work," a synonym for "miracle," cf. 10:25, 32, 37-38) refers to the Sabbath healing of the paralytic (5:1-9). Jesus did other miracles (2:23; 3:2; 7:31). But this healing was thought to violate the law against work on the **Sabbath**. Yet to fulfill the law, the Jews themselves "worked" on the Sabbath whenever they circumcised (mostly male children on the eighth day, Lv 12:3). Hence if they were consistent, they would not have condemned Jesus for "working" on the Sabbath.

7:23-24. Jesus reasoned that it was contradictory to show concern on the Sabbath for one part of the body (**circumcision**) but show no concern for the whole body of one in need (**I made an entire man well**). Blinded by their traditions, Christ's opponents were judging Him (v. 24) by what "appeared" to them as right (**according to appearance**), but was not a **righteous judgment**.

7:25-27. The residents of **Jerusalem** knew the authorities planned to kill Jesus (cf. vv. 1, 20) but were confused. Jesus was **speaking publicly** (v. 26), but the rulers did not confront Him. Could it be that they had changed their minds and now secretly thought that He was the Christ? Little did they know that some **rulers** like Nicodemus and Joseph of Arimathea (cf. 12:42; 19:38-39) **really** did **know that** Jesus was **the Christ**. But the crowds reasoned self-assuredly, **We know where this man is from; but whenever the Christ may come, no one knows where He is from**. See v. 42 for another view of the Messiah's origin.

7:28-29. The Lord's reply may be sarcastic as if to say, "So you think that **you both know Me and know where I am from**?" Jesus repeated previously mentioned descriptions of His identity: (1) He did **not come of** Himself but by the Father's authority; (2) the One **who sent** Jesus **is true**, but they did **not know** Him; and (3) Jesus knew the Father, **because** He was **from** the Father (1:1, 18), **and He sent** Him.

7:30-31. Most of the crowd joined with the rulers in **seeking to** seize the Lord, yet they could not. John described both human (6:15; 10:39) and divine means (7:30, 44; 8:20) that prevented Jesus from being arrested. For **His hour**, see comments on 2:4 and 4:21. The same phrase "His hour had not yet come" appears in 8:20; in 13:1, the phrase "His hour had come" makes a thematic transition to the "hour" of Jesus' death. The people expected the Messiah to work miracles like Moses (cf. Ex 4:21 with Dt 18:15, 18). Therefore, because of the signs (Jn 20:31-32), **many of the crowd believed in Him**. John used his special phrase, "believe in (Him)," to designate their saving faith (see comment on 1:12).

7:32. The **chief priests** (almost all from the party of the Sadducees) mentioned with the **Pharisees** implies that a meeting of the Sanhedrin had taken place (for "Sanhedrin," see comment on 11:47). The chief priests took on a more prominent role at the crucifixion (18:3, 35; 19:6, 15, 21). For "Pharisees," see comment on 1:24. The **officers** who were **sent** were temple police.

7:33-34. The new believers had reasoned, "When the Christ [Messiah] comes, He will not perform more signs than those which this man has, will He?" (v. 31). But they were wrong! The greatest miracle—His death and resurrection—was yet to come (**then I go to Him who sent Me**). After the resurrection, the Son would return to His Father. **You will seek Me** (v. 34; cf. 7:36; 8:21; 13:33) **and will not find Me** refers either to (1) the empty tomb, or (2) the constant search of Israel for the Messiah after rejecting Jesus.

7:35-36. Christ's opponents misconstrued His words (vv. 34, 36) as His intent to go on a mission to the Greek-speaking Jewish people throughout the Roman Empire (**the Dispersion among the Greeks**). While they thought this was improbable, Jesus indeed had such a mission in mind. After His resurrection (v. 33), His message would go to both Jews and Gentiles throughout the Roman Empire.

7:37. According to the Talmud, (*Sukk.* 4.9), each day during the Feast of Booths (v. 2), a priest would carry water from the spring-fed Pool of Siloam to the temple and pour it out on the altar in expectation of the coming Messiah (cf. Zch 14:16-19). Jesus proclaimed, **If anyone is thirsty, let him come to Me and drink**, i.e., a figurative expression for "let him believe in Me" (v. 38). Jesus was declaring that He was the true springwater in the temple, which brings eternal life (cf. Is 12:3; 55:1). Also, Booths (Tabernacles) celebrated the supply of water given through the rock Moses struck in the wilderness. Jesus fulfilled the imagery of this Rock that provided life-giving water (1Co 10:4). In essence, Jesus claimed to fulfill what the Feast of Booths signified.

7:38-39. The Feast of Booths was the most joyous of Israel's festivals. The citation from Scripture summarizes several messianic verses (e.g., Is 44:3; 55:1; 58:11; Zch 14:8). **He who believes in Me** may be taken with the preceding verse (cf. NET, NLT, TEV), leading to a Christological interpretation of the phrase **from his** [i.e., His] **innermost being will flow rivers of living water.** Christ is the overflowing source of joyous, living water (eternal life). More likely, the verse teaches that the believer will experience great joy internally in receiving eternal life and **the Spirit** (v. 39). This matches Jesus' earlier remark to the Samaritan woman, "the water that I will give him will become in him a well of water springing up to eternal life" (4:14). For "living water," cf. 4:10.

7:40-42. John recorded the mixed viewpoints concerning the Messiah. (1) Some thought that Jesus was **the Prophet** (Dt 18:15) but not the Messiah (see comment on 1:21; 6:14). (2) **Others were saying, "This is the Christ"** (v. 41). These were believers (cf. 11:27; 20:32). (3) Some felt that the birthplace of the Messiah could not be known (cf. v. 27). (4) While others (v. 42) held that He would be **from Bethlehem**, since **David** was from Bethlehem.

7:43-44. It is not surprising that **a division occurred in the crowd because of** Christ. Jesus still divides people today. On the desire of the Jewish leaders to **seize** Jesus (v. 44), see vv. 30, 32.

b. The Pharisees' Council (7:45-52)

7:45-46. The officers or temple guards sent by the **chief priests and Pharisees** returned empty-handed to the council meeting (the Sanhedrin, v. 32). An explanation was in order. **Why did you not bring Him?**, the Jewish leaders asked. The temple guards replied (v. 46), **Never has a man spoken the way this man speaks.** Their response acknowledged that Jesus was a man, but also someone greater than other men (cf. 1:1, 18).

7:47-49. The Pharisees criticized the officers. **You have not also been led astray, have you?** The irony is that the Pharisees are the ones who are the most led astray. **No one of the rulers or Pharisees has believed in Him, has he?** Nicodemus's reaction (cf. v. 50) suggests that he was one of the rulers who had believed in Christ, and others soon would (12:42). But as an intimidated disciple at this point, he did not confess his faith outright (cf. 3:9; 19:38). With a prideful superiority and lack of compassion, the Pharisees condemned the **crowd** as ignorant and **accursed.**

7:50-51. John used **Nicodemus**, not mentioned since 3:1-9, as an example of growing faith. Previously, he had visited Jesus secretly, at night. Now he was mildly defending Jesus publicly by questioning the legal procedures the Jewish leaders were taking. **Our Law does not judge a man unless it first hears from him and knows what**

he is doing, does it? The question implied his companions were not thoroughly investigating the situation as the law required (Dt 1:16-17; 17:2-5; 19:15-19). The Pharisees had just judged the crowds as ignorant of the law. Ironically, Nicodemus called them to account for missing one of its elementary requirements: fairness ("judges shall investigate thoroughly," Dt 19:18).

7:52. The Pharisees resorted to ridicule. **You are not also from Galilee, are you?** exposes their prejudice. They thought that **no prophet** came from despised **Galilee**. But Jonah (2Kg 14:25) and Nahum (Nah 1:1) came from Galilee. Even more ironic, the prophecy of Is 9:1-2 (quoted in Mt 4:12-16) prophesied that the Messiah would arise in Galilee and "bring light to the Gentiles."

c. Woman Caught in Adultery (7:53–8:11)

7:53-8:2. Based on what is thought to be the most reliable mss, the majority of scholars, including evangelicals, believe that the adulterous woman narrative (7:53–8:11) is not part of the original text. Support for its inclusion includes the following. First, about 1,350 continuous-text mss of John contain the narrative. Second, the story fits the context well. A woman was brought to Jesus in the temple. The only appropriate location for this event would be the Court of Women, the location described in 8:20. Since the Feast of Booths was now over (7:37, 53), **everyone went** from living in tents (see comment on 7:1-2) **to his home** [lit., "house"], supporting the legitimacy of 7:53 as part of this episode. In characteristic irony over against the Council's claim that no prophet comes from Galilee (v. 52), John noted that Jesus **went to the Mount of Olives** (8:1). It was at the Mount of Olives that Jesus, the greatest prophet of all, would soon give the greatest prophecy of the NT apart from the book of Revelation (Mt 24–25; Mk 13; Lk 21). **Early in the morning** (v. 2; *orthros*, "at dawn, daybreak") symbolically (cf. 21:4) depicts the breaking in of moral light in the person of Jesus (see comment on 7:52) who, in 8:12, is the "light of the world." This carries on the light/darkness theme of John. In contrast to "everyone [who] went to his house" (7:53), Jesus went **into the temple**, His Father's house (cf. 2:16, where Jesus called the temple His Father's house).

Against the inclusion of this episode are several factors. First, it does not fit as well in the context as it is often argued. In 7:52, the Pharisees disputed His claim to be a prophet because of His Galilean origins, and Jesus' statement in 8:12 serves as a response to their argument. In this case the episode is an unnecessary intrusion into the text. Second, the symbolic connection between Jesus coming "at dawn" into the temple (8:2) with Him dawning as "the light of the world" (8:12) is not clearly borne out in the text. Third, the style and vocabulary are atypical of John's writing (for the details, see Daniel B. Wallace, "Reconsidering 'The Story of Jesus and the Adulteress Reconsidered,'" *NTS* 39 [1993]: 290-296). Fourth, at this time, the Jewish people did not have the autonomy to execute people on their own authority. Rome was the final arbiter and probably would not have permitted this. Stephen's stoning was mob action, not judicial, but this episode does not have the "mob action" feel associated with Stephen's murder. This makes it unlikely that the episode is historically accurate. Fifth, Jesus words in 8:12 about being the Light of the world are more likely to have been said on the last day of the Feast of Booths (7:37). On that day, there was always a huge torch ceremony on the Temple Mount, as a symbol of the Messiah being the One who would bring light to the world.

Finally, the external ms evidence is strongly in favor of the omission of the episode. Virtually all Alexandrian mss, considered by the majority of scholars to be the oldest and least corrupt mss, omit it, and virtually all Byzantine mss, viewed by the majority of scholars as much later and generally more corrupt, include it. But even when they include it, the episode also "floats around" in various locations in the various mss. This indicates great doubt about its inclusion even among the mss that contain it.

While the preponderance of evidence is against its inclusion, the evidence is not airtight, and since this episode is loved by those who cherish John's gospel, a commentary on it is provided here.

8:3-5. Since Jesus was being contested as a teacher of the law, **scribes** who were interpreters of the law came with the **Pharisees**. Together they **brought** to Jesus **a woman caught in adultery . . . in the very act** (v. 4). In light of the fact that the man involved was not brought, the Jewish leaders revealed their malicious intent and their disregard for fairness required by the law (cf. 7:50-51). According to the **Law** of Moses (v. 5), all adulterers (male or female) were to be put to death by stoning (Lv 20:10; Dt 22:22), not just **such women**.

8:6-7. The scribes and Pharisees were **testing** Jesus. If Jesus called for her stoning as an adulteress, this would put Him in defiance of the Roman government's sole authority to try capital cases and carry out executions. (cf. 18:31).

If He chose to free her, He would be disobeying the Mosaic law. After Jesus **stooped down and with His finger wrote** something **on the ground**, He **straightened up** (v. 7) to say, "Let the witness **who is without sin . . . be the first to throw a stone at her**," as the law commanded (Dt 17:7). But the law also required that any witness guilty of malicious intent was to be stoned to death instead (Dt 19:16-19).

8:8-9. What Jesus wrote is not identified. More important is that Jesus **stooped down and wrote** with His finger (v. 6) and that He wrote twice (v. 8). God came down at Mt. Sinai (Ex 19:11, 20) and wrote the Ten Commandments twice with His finger (Ex 31:18; 34:1, 4; Dt 9:10). Jesus, by writing twice with His finger, was revealing symbolically that He was here fulfilling the same role God the Father fulfilled for Israel as the giver of the law (Jn 1:1; 5:18; 8:58; 20:28). Then **they began to** leave (v. 9), **beginning with the older ones**, the ones whose conscience weighed on them longer.

8:10-11. According to the law, a person could be put to death only with two or more witnesses (8:17; Dt 17:6; 19:15). But now there were no witnesses to **condemn** her to be stoned to death. Jesus could fully obey the Mosaic law in releasing the woman since there were no witnesses (v. 11): **I do not condemn you, either**. As in this case, forgiveness always precedes the command to **sin no more**, and forms its greatest motivation.

d. Light of the World Message (8:12-59)

8:12. Jesus again spoke to them refers to the Pharisees (8:3, 7). During the Feast of Booths, large menorahs lit up the temple complex, commemorating the fire that guided the Israelites during the wilderness wanderings (Nm 9:15-23) and anticipating the Messiah who would bring light to nations. After seven days of dramatic illumination in the temple, Jesus declared, **I am the Light of the world** (1:4-5, 9; cf. "Jesus' Seven 'I Am' Claims" at 6:35). If one believes in Christ and then **follows** Him (cf. 8:31), he or she **will not walk in the darkness** (1Jn 1:5-10).

8:13-14. The law called for multiple witnesses to the truth (v. 17). But a single testimony was not necessarily false. So Jesus claimed (v. 14), **My testimony is true, for I know where I came from and where I am going.** His heavenly origin, mission in the world, and return to the Father validated His testimony. But the Pharisees did not acknowledge His glorious origin or ultimate destiny.

8:15-16. Jesus criticized the Pharisees for evaluating His claims **according to the flesh**, i.e., according to human values. His response, **I am not judging anyone**, seems to contradict other statements He made (5:22, 27; 9:39). But here He meant that judgment was not the primary purpose of His first coming (3:16-17). Yet rejecting His claims invited His and His Father's judgment (**I am not alone in it**, v. 16). Like the law (v. 17), two Witnesses—Jesus and the Father—will testify and execute the final judgment.

8:17-18. In saying **your law** (cf. 10:34; 18:31), Jesus was distancing Himself from the law since He would replace the Mosaic law (cf. 1:17; 7:19) with the new covenant (Mt 26:28; Mk 14:24; Lk 22:20). The Pharisees agreed that **the testimony of two men** was **true** (Dt 17:6; 19:15; Nm 35:30). So Jesus offered two Witnesses (v. 18), Himself and the Father—far greater than any human witnesses.

8:19-20. The question of the Jewish leaders, "Where is Your Father?" exposed a serious spiritual problem: they did not know the Father. "If you knew Me, you would know My Father also" asserts that a true knowledge of God comes through a personal knowledge of the Son. According to v. 20, Jesus' "Light of the world" message (v. 12) took place in or near (NIV, NET) the treasury (cf. Mk 12:41-42; Lk 21:1-2), where the Court of Women was located. (See chart, "The Temple Area.") The Court of Women was the temple area in which all Jews including women (but no Gentiles) could

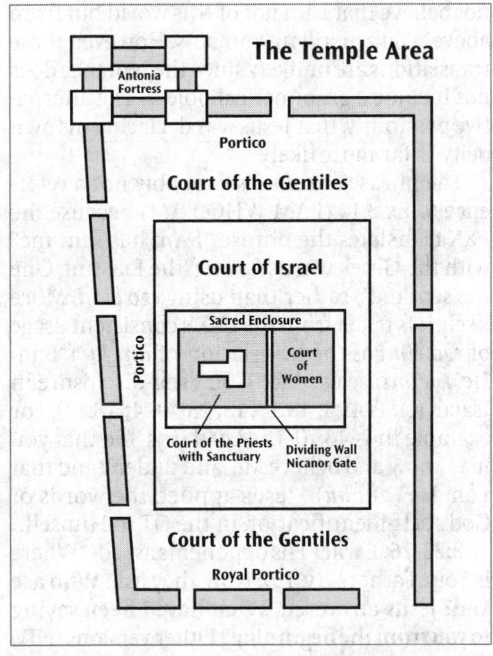

gather. It was also called the treasury because in this court there were 13 offerings boxes, each shaped like a trumpet (*m. Seqal.* 6.5). For **His hour had not yet come**, see 7:30.

8:21. For the third time in John, Jesus explained He was going away (7:33; 8:14, 21). After Jesus' death, these same Jewish leaders **will seek** for Him (see comment on 7:34). But they **will die in** their **sin** and come into eternal judgment. One has only until death to believe in Christ for eternal life (Heb 9:27).

8:22-23. The Jewish questioners rightly understood Jesus to be alluding to His death, but thought that He might **kill Himself**. Ironically, Jesus would not commit suicide but would willingly give up His life (10:11, 15, 18). Their origin explained their discrepancies with Jesus (v. 23): **from below** versus **from above**, and **of this world** (the natural, sinful, human realm) versus **not of this world**, but sent from the Father.

8:24. Twice in this verse, the Lord stated that those who remain in unbelief **will die in** their **sins**. For the unbeliever, nothing changes when he dies; he remains a sinner for eternity. The words **I am He** (*ego eimi*; "I Am") contain terms peculiar to the Fourth Gospel and significant to Jesus' explicit self-declaration of deity (see comments on vv. 28, 58). Some have objected that the phrase *ego eimi* is not referring to deity but has an implicit completion, such as, "if you do not believe I am who I claim to be" or "if you do not believe that I am not of this world but from above" you are still in your sins. However, these translations are unlikely since the sentence does not include a grammatical object. The alternative possibility, that Jesus was declaring his own deity, is far more likely.

The phrase *ego eimi* is probably not a reference to Ex 3:14 (I AM WHO I AM) because the LXX translates the phrase "I Am has sent me" with the Greek words *ho on* ("the Existing One has sent me") rather than using *ego eimi*. More likely it is taken from the LXX's consistent usage of *ego eimi* as the translation of *ani hu* ("I am He"), a phrase used for God's self-disclosure in Isaiah (cf. Is 41:4; 43:10, 13, 25; 46:4; 48:12). For example in Is 43:10, the Lord says, "So that you may know and believe Me, and understand that I am He (*ani hu*)." Jesus applied the words of God's self-identification in the OT to Himself.

8:25-26. Earlier His opponents asked, "Where is Your Father?" (v. 19). Now they ask, **Who are You?** Jesus answered, **What have I been saying to you from the beginning?** Other versions (NIV, ESV, HCSB) translate this as a declaration: "Just what I have been claiming all along." The phrase **to speak and to judge** (v. 26) is best translated as a hendiadys, "I have many things to speak in judgment concerning you."

8:27-28. While Jesus' claims were enigmatic, the Jewish leaders should have comprehended them. Instead, **they did not realize that He had been speaking to them about the Father** who sent Him (v. 26). **When you lift up the Son of Man** (v. 28) presents another prophecy of His death on the cross. For "lifted up," see comment on 3:14. Again, Jesus made an **I am** statement without a predicate (**He** is not in the Gk.). See comment on 4:26; 8:24. For **I do nothing on My own initiative**, see comment on 5:19, 30.

8:29-30. God never **left** Jesus **alone** because Jesus **always** did **the things that** were **pleasing** to the Father (4:34; 5:30; 6:38-40). Once again, Christ's sinlessness is implied (vv. 7, 46; cf. 2Co 5:21; Heb 4:15). The words of Jesus (**As He spoke these things**) led **many** Jewish people (v. 30) **to believe in Him** (*pisteuo eis*, John's unique phrase for genuine faith; 1:12; 3:16, 18, 36; 6:40; 11:25, 26).

8:31-32. Because of vv. 33-59, some think that the ones who believed (vv. 30-31) did not have true faith. But one must distinguish between the new believers and the crowd at large. John interjected that Jesus' words were spoken only to **those Jews who had believed Him** (v. 31), not the resistant crowd in vv. 33-59. Eternal life is by faith alone, but being true **disciples** requires Christians to **continue** or "abide" in Christ's teachings (see comments on 6:66; 15:1-5). As believers obey (v. 32), they **will know the truth** experientially, and this **truth will make** them **free**. This freedom concerns sanctification, not justification (cf. 17:17, 19). This liberation is not an intellectual accomplishment but a God-empowered freedom from sin, realized through an ongoing faith relationship with Jesus (v. 36).

8:33. They does not find its antecedent in vv. 30-32 but in the "they" of the preceding passage (vv. 19, 25, 27), the wider audience of unbelieving Jews (vv. 13, 22). Many Jews relied on their physical descent from **Abraham**. Despite the nation's domination by Babylon, Persia, Greece, and Rome, the Jewish people thought of themselves as a free people, both politically and spiritually. But Jesus was speaking spiritually of freedom from sin.

8:34-36. Since **everyone**, apart from Christ, **commits sin** (Rm 3:10-19, 23), everyone is a **slave**

of sin (2Pt 2:19; Rm 6:16, 20). Jesus illustrated this idea with an example from real life. Since a **slave** can be sold by his owner to another family, he **does not remain in the** household **forever** (v. 35). But a **son does**. Since Jesus is **the Son** of God, He can make one **free** (v. 36) in its true spiritual sense (**free indeed**), both from sin's penalty (justification) and sin's power (sanctification).

8:37-38. Jesus agreed to their claim that they were **Abraham's** physical **descendants**. But they lacked Abraham's faith (cf. Rm 4:12, 16). Instead, they were seeking **to kill** Jesus (see comment on 5:18). Christ's **word** [had] **no place in** their spiritually rebellious hearts. He spoke **the things which** He had heard, but also had **seen** (v. 38) while **with** the **Father** (before His incarnation). Correspondingly, they did **the things which** they **heard from** their **father** (the devil, v. 44).

8:39-40. In light of Jesus' reference to "your father" (v. 38), the Jewish leaders replied, **Abraham is our father**. In Jewish tradition, a "child" was considered metaphorically to be anyone who imitated another (cf. 1Pt 3:6). Jesus argued that **Abraham's** true spiritual **children** would not be **seeking to kill** Him (v. 40; cf. v. 37). Jesus' point appears to be that when Abraham heard truth from God, he embraced it. But the religious leaders, who heard God's truth through Jesus, rejected it, even to the point of seeking to kill the Son.

8:41. Again (cf. v. 38), Christ spoke of **your father** without clarification (which awaits v. 44). That **we were not born of fornication** may be (1) a denial that they were illegitimate children of Abraham, or (2) a defamatory remark about Jesus' birth. The "we" is emphatic in Greek and favors the second option (see comment on v. 48).

8:42-43. Since Jesus was the revelation of God, **if God were** their **Father**, they **would love** Jesus, the One who had **come from God**. Christ gave a further motive for loving Him: **I have not even come on My own initiative, but He sent Me**. To love Jesus was to love the Father who sent Him. Like these Jewish leaders, if people do not respond to Christ, they **cannot hear** and spiritually understand His **word** (v. 43).

8:44. Spiritually, one has either God or **the devil** as a Father. The devil **was a murderer from the beginning** of history. Satan incited Cain to kill his brother (Gn 4:8; 1Jn 3:12). More to the point, in the garden of Eden his lie (Gn 3:4-5) brought death to the whole human race (Rm 5:12). So Satan is **the father** (creator) **of lies**.

8:45-47. The minds of these Jewish leaders were so deceived that **the truth** was impossible for them to **believe**. Jesus spoke only the truth. **Which one of you convicts Me of sin?** He asked (v. 46). No sin or falsehood can be found in Christ. Since the one **who is of God hears the words of God** (v. 47), the resistance of the Jewish leaders proved they had failed as the leaders of Israel and were **not of God**. As Paul wrote, "a natural man [non-Christian] does not accept the things of the Spirit of God . . . he cannot understand them" (1Co 2:14).

8:48. Rather than answering Jesus' questions, Jesus' opponents responded again with disparagement, calling Jesus a **Samaritan** and declaring He had **a demon** (i.e., was insane, 10:20; cf. also 7:20; 8:52). The Jewish leaders associated Jesus with the Samaritans, who were regarded as illegitimate Jews (cf. v. 41). For "Samaritan," see comment on 4:4. In their opinion, Jesus should be put to death for blasphemy against God (10:33, 36; Mt 9:3; 26:65). But in claiming Jesus had a demon, the Jewish leaders ironically committed blasphemy against the Holy Spirit (Mt 12:31; Mk 3:28-29).

8:49-51. After denying the charge of being demon-possessed, Jesus explained that He gave **honor** to His **Father**. But they were actually dishonoring the One (Jesus) who gave honor to the Father. Was this not contradictory? Christ was not seeking glory for Himself (v. 50). Yet, **there is One who seeks** Christ's glory, **and** He **judges** on Christ's behalf. With strong emotion (**truly, truly**), Jesus asserted (v. 51) that **anyone** who **keeps** His **word** (i.e., believes) **will never see** eternal **death**.

8:52-53. Misunderstanding Christ again, the Jewish opponents reasoned that **Abraham** and the **prophets** had died. So how could Jesus promise anyone **he will never taste of** [or experience] **death**? Jesus could not be greater than Abraham or the prophets, they reasoned (v. 53). Here another Johannine irony surfaces (cf. 4:12). Jesus was not just greater than Abraham and the prophets. He was their God!

8:54-55. Jesus denied that His claims were self-glorifying and pointed out their hypocrisy. **It is My Father who glorifies Me, of whom you say, 'He is our God.'** The clause (v. 55) **you have not come to know** [*ginosko*] **Him, but I know** [*oida*] **Him** uses two different Greek words for "know." The first typically implies acquired knowledge; the second refers to knowledge without detailing how it was acquired. They had failed to gain true knowledge of the Father, but Christ already and always knew Him, probably because of His intimate fellowship with Him (cf. 1:18).

8:56-57. Abraham rejoiced at God's promise that he would see the **day** of the Messiah. This took place when Abraham received the promise that through his offspring (i.e., the Messiah, Gl 3:16) "all the families of the earth will be blessed" (Gn 12:3; 17:17; 22:18). Then when Isaac was born 25 years later, Abraham **saw** Messiah, in that he anticipated the fulfillment of covenantal promise and looked for the coming of the Messiah **and was glad**. Abraham also witnessed, through the binding of Isaac, a foreshadowing of the death and resurrection of Christ (Heb 11:19).

8:58-59. The remark **before Abraham was born, I am** (not "I was"; *ego eimi*) makes a claim to deity and eternality (see comments on 4:26 and 8:24). The reaction of the Jewish leaders verifies that Jesus made a claim to deity. They **picked up stones to throw at Him** (v. 59), but **Jesus hid Himself**. Spiritually, the Jewish leadership was blind, and His departure from the temple pictured God's OT glory departing from the temple (Ezk 10–11).

4. Healing of the Blind Man (9:1-40)

The preceding claim of Jesus to be the "light of the world" (8:12) is elaborated symbolically in the narrative of the blind man (cf. v. 5). Although the blind man had lived in darkness, his healing by Jesus made him able to see the light.

9:1-2. Jesus left the temple (8:59) and **as He passed by, He saw a man blind from birth** (cf. v. 12). Healing the blind was a characteristic sign of the Messiah (Mt 11:5; Lk 7:22). The disciples' question (v. 2) **who sinned, this man or his parents . . . ?** shows they had adopted the mistaken theology that all illness was the result of personal sin or parental sin. A similar erroneous concept is found in the law of karma as taught in many Eastern religions. Nevertheless, the man's physical blindness did picture every person's spiritual blindness from birth (2Co 4:4).

9:3-5. The Lord corrected the disciples, establishing the truth that many disabilities are not the result of sin. In the sovereign plan of God, the man's blindness allowed for **the works of God** to **be displayed in him**. This display of God's works has been multiplied as millions have read this story through the centuries. **Night is coming when no one can work** (v. 4) refers to the time of the crucifixion, when the disciples will be scattered and Christ will neither teach nor do miracles. This is supported by Jesus' remark **While I am in the world, I am the Light of the world** (v. 5).

9:6-7. In preparation for the healing, Jesus **spat on the ground, and made clay of the spittle, and applied the clay to** the blind man's **eyes**. The making of clay (*pelos*) is central to the narrative (vv. 6, 11, 14-15). By putting **the clay** on **his eyes**, Christ symbolically claimed to be God the Potter (cf. Rm 9:21; cf. Jb 10:9; 33:6) who makes the seeing and the blind (Ex 4:11). Jesus previously presented Himself as the life-giving waters symbolized in **the pool of Siloam** (v. 7; see comment on 7:37). In addition, just as the man would cleanse his eyes in the Pool of Siloam (which means "Sent"), so also people will find spiritual cleansing and "sight" in the One who was sent (4:34; 5:23, 37; 7:28; 8:26). This miracle was an enacted symbol of Jesus' saving mission.

9:8-9. The confusion over the identity of the blind **beggar** parallels the confusion of the crowds over the identity of Jesus. To identify himself (v. 9), the blind man **kept saying, I am the one** [*ego eimi*], the exact Greek phrase Jesus used (8:58) to identify Himself. If the listeners correctly recognized the blind man, they would open the door to see accurately the "I Am" who heals spiritual blindness.

9:10-12. If this was the former blind man, his sight demanded an explanation. The facts were straightforward (v. 11). The blind man knew the person who healed him was **called Jesus**, and that He **made clay, and anointed** his **eyes**. Then Jesus told him, **Go to Siloam and wash**. When he obeyed **and washed**, he **received** his **sight**. Few things are more convincing than a simple testimony of our personal encounter with Christ. Since he was blind at the time, the former blind man when questioned (v. 12) did not know where Jesus had gone.

9:13-14. Because of the unusual nature of the case, those acquainted with the beggar (v. 9) led him to **the Pharisees** (for Pharisees, see comment on 1:24). First, the blind man appeared before the Pharisees (vv. 13-17). Then his parents were interviewed (vv. 18-23). Finally, the blind man was questioned a second time (vv. 24-34). As in 5:9, John reported that the healing was done on the **Sabbath** (v. 14). In Jewish tradition, both healing one whose life was not threatened (*m. Yoma* 8:6) and kneading dough (*m. Sabb.* 7:2), and by analogy making **clay** were forbidden on the Sabbath.

9:15-17. Although **the Pharisees** would have been told the situation, they personally questioned the former blind man themselves, **asking him again how he received his sight**. They used the information gained from him to judge Jesus (v. 16): **This man is not from God, because He does not keep the Sabbath**. Like the people's split over the healed man (cf. vv. 8-9), there was **a division among** the Pharisees over Jesus (7:12, 40-44; 10:20-21). But the debate served to advance the blind man's understanding of his Healer. When asked (v. 17), he became convinced that Jesus was **a prophet**.

9:18-19. Rather than believe that Jesus was from God and had healed the blind man, the Pharisees doubted that the man **had been blind** at all **and had received** his **sight**. This was the case only **until they called** in his **parents** and **questioned them**. The questions (v. 19) reflected a hope on the part of the Pharisees that the situation was a case of mistaken identity. To discredit the healing was to discredit the character and identity of Jesus.

9:20-21. His parents answered by rehearsing the basic facts. He was their **son**, and **he was born blind**. But they avoided giving an answer (v. 21) to how he was healed and who healed him. Their suggestion was to ask their son since he was surely old enough to give a responsible answer. **He is of age** suggests the son could be as early as thirteen and need not be older than his late teens or early twenties.

9:22-23. The parents eluded answering (cf. v. 21) because **the Jews** [i.e., the Pharisees] **had already agreed that if anyone confessed** Jesus **to be Christ, he was to be put out of the synagogue**. (For "Christ," see comment on 1:20.) To be expelled from the synagogue (v. 22; 12:42; 16:2) would have resulted in serious social and economic consequences. Although there is no extrabiblical evidence that an official Jewish ban against those confessing Christ was established at this time, the severe persecution of Christians in the rest of the NT (e.g., the book of Acts) supports the apostle's interpretive remark.

9:24-25. The Pharisees interrogated the former blind man **a second time**, calling on him to **give glory to God**. This OT idiom means, "as God is your witness, tell the truth" (Jos 7:19; 1Sm 6:5). With the words **we know that this man is a sinner** the Pharisees attempted to coerce him to change his testimony. Instead (v. 25), he boldly confessed the **one thing** he did **know, that though** he **was blind, now** he could see.

9:26-27. The Pharisees had finally come to believe that the blind man was healed (cf. v. 18). But they still held that anyone who broke the Sabbath was a sinner (v. 24). The former blind man became irritated, having to reply to questions that had already been answered. Sarcastically he asked (v. 27), **Why do you want to hear it again? You do not want to become His disciples too, do you?**

9:28-29. The healed man had confronted the Pharisees' resistance to truth. So the Jews resorted to ridicule. **You are His disciple**, they contended. As would happen with Caiaphas (11:49-52), the Pharisees unknowingly foretold what the healed man would become (v. 38). On their part, they claimed to be **disciples of Moses** and to lack knowledge of Jesus' earthly identity. Misunderstanding His earthly identity (cf. 7:41-42; Mt 2:5-6; Lk 2:15) made them ignorant of His heavenly origin as well.

9:30-33. The Jewish leadership should have marveled at Jesus' healing of the blind man. Instead, the blind man marveled at the Pharisees' ignorance of the Healer's origin. He reasoned with sound OT theology. **God does not hear** the prayers of **sinners** (v. 31). He only hears **God-fearing** people who do **His will** (Pss 66:18; 145:19; Pr 28:9). He also reasoned from OT history that no one ever **opened the eyes of a person born blind** (v. 32). No known biblical or extrabiblical Jewish sources record the healing of a blind man. This was a power associated only with the coming Messiah (Is 29:18; 35:5; 42:7, 18; 61:1). The healed man concluded (v. 33) that Jesus could do nothing on His own initiative—the very affirmation Jesus Himself made (Jn 5:19, 30; 8:28).

9:34. You were born entirely in sins picks up and intensifies the prejudicial Jewish perspective that Jesus refuted (vv. 2-3). In light of v. 22, **they put him out** refers to expulsion from the synagogue.

9:35-36. Jesus sought out the healed man (cf. the Good Shepherd described in 10:1-16) and asked, **Do you believe in the Son of Man?** For "Son of Man" as a messianic title, see comment on 1:51; cf. also 12:34 and Dn 7:13-14. Since the man was blind when he left Jesus to wash in Siloam, he had not yet seen Christ. He was willing to believe in Messiah (v. 36) if he only knew who He was (cf. 4:10).

9:37-38. You have . . . seen Him pointed to Jesus as the One who healed the man's blindness. For the second time in John, Jesus revealed His messianic identity to an individual (cf. the Samaritan woman, 4:26): **He is the one who is talking with you**. The man's knowledge of Jesus progressed from a man (v. 11), a prophet (v. 17), one from God (v. 33), and finally the Son of Man to be believed (v. 38) and **worshiped** like God Himself (cf. 4:21-24).

9:39-41. The **judgment** that Jesus brought **into this world** was the condemnation of sin that would lead people to faith. This judgment was **so that those who do not see may see**, i.e., the spiritually blind may believe and gain spiritual sight. The antithesis is **that those who see may become blind**, i.e., the self-righteous who "see" may become hardened (cf. 12:39-40). Jesus conceded that the Pharisees did "see" to a degree (vv. 40-41) since He had clearly revealed Himself as Messiah to them. **If** they **were** totally **blind**, they **would have no sin** of rejecting Him. But they insisted, **We see**. Therefore, Jesus declared that their **sin** of rejecting Christ remained. The Jewish leaders had greater accountability because of their privileged position as the leaders of the chosen people, to whom God's revelation had been entrusted (Rm 3:1).

5. The Good Shepherd Message (10:1-21)

Although the events of chap. 10 occurred almost three months after chap. 9 (cf. 7:2, 37, associated with the Feast of Booths in the fall; the Feast of Dedication in 10:22 was held in December), John joined the narratives of the chapters without a break (cf. the reference to the blind man in 10:21). Chapter 10 comprises an extended metaphor comparing Jesus and His followers to a shepherd and his sheep.

10:1. For **truly, truly**, see comments on 1:51. The Pharisees (cf. 9:40) are the false shepherds (leaders) of Israel (cf. Ezk 34:1-10; Jr 23:1-4). A Jewish family could have several flocks in one sheepfold and assign a gatekeeper for nighttime to guard the single opening. The shepherd would **enter by the door into the fold of the sheep** to get his particular flock out for grazing. **A thief** needed to sneak over the stonewall enclosure to steal sheep.

10:2-3. In the OT, a shepherd was an image of an ideal leader and king. God was the supreme Shepherd (Ps 80:1; Is 40:10-11) and the Messiah was a King-Shepherd (Ezk 34:23-24; 37:24; Jr 23:1-5; Mt 2:6). Jesus, as Shepherd, **enters by the door**, i.e., He is the legitimate shepherd, and He fulfills messianic prophecy. Just as the best man stands with the bridegroom (Jn 3:29), so the words, **To him the doorkeeper opens** (v. 3), may depict John the Baptist's role as forerunner to Jesus (1:6-8). But most interpreters hold that the "doorkeeper" should not be given any symbolic significance. The sheepfold represents Israel (cf. v. 16). **The sheep**, those who have believed in the One true God of Israel, recognize the **voice** of Jesus to be the true Messiah (cf. 5:37-38, 46-47; 8:47). The "leading out" means, within the metaphor, that the shepherd takes them out to find food and water. On the spiritual side of the metaphor, it means Jesus provides spiritual sustenance for His sheep.

10:4-6. Shepherds in Israel would lead their sheep (**he goes ahead of them**) rather than drive them. The sheep responded only to the voice of their shepherd. They would not follow a stranger's voice (v. 5), much as the blind man refused to be convinced against Jesus by the Pharisees. Jesus spoke **this figure of speech** to the Pharisees (v. 6), but **they did not understand** because of their blindness (9:40-41). They thought that they were the true sheep of God.

10:7-8. Since the Pharisees did not understand Jesus' parable (v. 6), He changed the imagery slightly (vv. 7-10). In vv. 1-6, Jesus was the Shepherd. Here Jesus claimed, **I am the door** or gate **of the sheep**. (See "Jesus' Seven 'I Am' Claims" at 6:35.) The sheepfold represents all who have eternal life. Jesus is the only means ("door") by which one can enter the sheepfold, i.e., have eternal life (vv. 9-10; 14:6). There were many true prophets in the OT. So **all who came before Me are thieves and robbers** refers to those false leaders (including the Pharisees) and messiahs who claimed to be the way to God. God's **sheep** (true OT believers) **did not hear them**.

10:9-10. The words **if anyone** establish that faith in Jesus is available to all. In the simile, **he will be saved** means delivered from thieves and wild animals, but pictures eternal life (cf. v. 10). **Will go in and out** (a merism) together with **find pasture** describes complete provision and security in all of life (cf. 4:14; 6:35). Contrary to **the thief**, Christ **came that** believers **may have** eternal **life**, both now and in the world to come. Eternal life is not a static quality. Once received, it can be enriched through obedience so that it may be experienced **abundantly** (cf. 2Pt 1:11). **The thief** who **comes only to steal and kill and destroy** is not Satan, as commonly thought, but refers to the false teachers who predated Jesus and who led Israel at this time (v. 8).

10:11-13. I am the good shepherd begins a third illustration (the fourth of the seven "I am" statements). Jesus is the good shepherd because He **lays down His life** voluntarily **for the sheep** (vv. 15, 17-18; 15:13). While the thief is devious in his concern only for himself (not the sheep), the **hired hand** (v. 12) is disinterested and self-preserving since he **is not the owner of the sheep**. "Owner" hints at the purchase Christ will make with His blood to redeem the sheep (1Co 6:20; 7:23). The hireling is driven by fear **and is not concerned about the sheep** (v. 13); the Shepherd is compelled by love for them.

10:14-15. As **the good shepherd**, Jesus enters into a reciprocal, intimate relationship with His sheep (**I know My own and My own know Me**). Amazingly, this relationship is as personal and intimate as the relationship shared by **the Father** and Son (v. 15). The Shepherd's death **for the sheep** is a substitutionary death, one life for another (2Co 5:21; 1Pt 2:24; 3:18). This is supported by the Greek word "for" (*hyper*), which carries the notion in this context that the death of Jesus was "for our sakes" as well as "in our place."

10:16-17. Other sheep, which are not of this fold (Israel) refers to Gentiles who will come to faith in Christ and form **one** new **flock with one shepherd** (Gl 3:28; Col 3:11). The universal outlook of John (1:9, 29; 3:16-17; 4:42; 6:33, 51; 8:12; 9:5; 12:47) supports this interpretation. This passage directly states that **the Father loves** the Son (v. 17). Just as the Father's love for the Son results in the Father's "giving" to the Son (3:35; 17:24), so the Son's love for the world results in His "giving" to the world (3:16; Gl 2:20; Eph 5:2).

10:18. I lay My life **down on My own initiative** (v. 18) repeats vv. 11, 15, 17. Since Jesus was without sin (8:46; 14:30; 2Co 5:21), if Jesus had not voluntarily chosen to die, He would have never died at all. He also declared He had the **authority to take** His life **up again** by initiating His own resurrection according to the command of the Father. According to this verse, Jesus had the authority to resurrect Himself from the dead, something that would be impossible for a mere human. The Father (Ac 2:32; 4:10; Rm 10:9) and the Son (Jn 2:19) were both active in the death and resurrection of Jesus.

10:19-21. On two other occasions (7:43; 9:16), a **division** took place over Christ's teachings. And on two other occasions (7:20; 8:48, 52), the Jews said He had a **demon** (v. 20). Those who were favorably disposed to Jesus reasoned that even a demon in a possessed person could not **open the eyes of the blind** (the blind man of 9:1-41). To "have a demon" (v. 20; also 7:20; 8:48-49, 52) is synonymous with being "demon-possessed" (v. 21).

6. Events at the Feast of Dedication (10:22-42)

10:22-23. The **Feast of the Dedication** (modern "Chanukah," Hb. for "dedication") was an eight-day festival held on Kislev 25 on the Hebrew calendar—the month of Kislev is comparable to December in the western calendar. It celebrated the restoration of the temple (165 BC) after its desecration by the Syrian king Antiochus Epiphanes. Symbolically, Jesus is the One who restores the true temple of God and is true Leader (Shepherd) over Israel. The date was probably December 18, AD 32, roughly three-and-a-half months before Jesus' crucifixion. The **portico of Solomon** ran along the eastern wall of the temple complex.

10:24. The words **gathered around Him** literally mean "surrounded" Him (NET, NKV, HCSB). The question of the Jewish leaders, **If You are the Christ, tell us plainly**, veiled their real attempt to gain further evidence of blasphemy against Jesus (cf. 8:25). For "Christ," see comment on 1:20.

10:25-26. I told you, and you do not believe shows that Jesus had not hidden from them His true identity. The root problem was an unwillingness to believe. **The works** or sign-miracles gave clear evidence that He was the Messiah. **You do not believe because you are not of My sheep** (v. 26) may refer to Jesus' rejection of them as not among the elect. More likely, Jesus was speaking of their present condition (cf. His later appeal to them to believe, vv. 37-38; cf. 8:47).

10:27-28. These rulers should not think they sincerely want to believe in the Messiah. Those who wanted to believe in the Messiah were **sheep** who **hear** the true Messiah's **voice** (Jesus) and **follow** Him (i.e., believe). He gives His sheep **eternal life** (v. 28) because of their faith. Christ's sheep **will never perish** (emphatic in Gk.). The Good Shepherd does not lose *any* of His sheep. **No one will snatch them out of My hand** underscores the power of the Shepherd apart from any conduct of the sheep.

10:29-30. For **My Father, who has given them to Me**, see comment on 6:37. **No one is able to snatch** (*harpazo*, the same word in v. 12) the sheep **out of the** Son's (v. 28) or **the Father's hand**. This united security points to a unity between the Father and the Son: **I and the Father are one** (v. 30). The word "one" is neuter, not masculine, confirming that the Father and Son are one in nature and purpose, not one in identity. In other words, Jesus is fully divine, but He is a divine Person distinct from God the Father.

10:31-32. The Jewish authorities argued that Jesus was vague about His identity (v. 24). But now they **picked up stones again** (cf. 8:59) **to stone Him** for blasphemy, as the law instructed (Lv 24:16). Jesus questioned His opponents about their charges. Of all the wonderful miracles He had shown them, **for which of them** were they **stoning** Him? This sarcasm was designed to shake them from their evil prejudgment.

10:33. This is the first time in John the Jews charged Jesus directly with **blasphemy**. They accused Him of being **a man** who made Himself **out to be God**. Ironically, Jesus was claiming that He was the second member of the Godhead who became a man (1:14; Gl 4:4; Php 2:6-7; 1Tm 3:16).

10:34-36. In His defense, Jesus quoted from Ps 82:6, **written in** the **Law**. Here "Law" refers to the entire OT (cf. Jn 1:45; 12:34; 15:25; Mt 7:12; Rm 3:21). Jesus' argument is as follows. In Ps 82:6, even sinful Israelite leaders were given the title **gods** since they had the divine responsibility to speak the word of God and carry out justice under God. There is no error in Scripture (**Scripture cannot be broken**). Therefore, how much more should the Christ, **sanctified and sent into the world** (v. 36) on a divine mission to speak the word of God as the incarnate Word of God (1:1, 14) and to carry out justice (5:22, 27, 30), be rightly called the divine (sinless) "Son of God?"

10:37-38. Jesus set before the Jewish leaders His **works** or miracles as proof of His unity with the Father (v. 30). He challenged them, saying, **If I do not do the works of My Father, do not believe Me**. But if He did do them (v. 38), even though they stumbled over His claims, they were obligated to **believe the works** were from God. Then faith in Christ might follow faith in the miracles (cf. Nicodemus, 3:2).

10:39-42. They were seeking again to seize Him repeats a familiar theme of Jewish opposition that began early in Christ's ministry (5:18; 7:1, 19, 25, 30; 8:37, 40; 11:8). Behind the words **He eluded their grasp** is God's sovereign timing of Jesus' death. But the apostle may also imply an unspecified miracle (cf. 6:21; 8:59; 21:6). Jesus (v. 40) went away (cf. 11:54; 12:36) **beyond the Jordan** (see comment on 1:28) to Perea (the east side of the Jordan river) to finalize His public ministry in the location He first began (**where John was first baptizing**). The location prompted people to recall the forerunner's testimony of Christ (v. 41), and **many believed in Him there**. Like the book of Acts, the success of Christ's message took place as He moved away from Jerusalem.

7. Events at the Final Passover (11:1–12:50)

a. Raising of Lazarus (11:1-54)

The events of chap. 11 occur sometime between the Feast of Dedication (December) and the crucifixion (April). Although Jesus raised others to life (a widow's son, Lk 7:11-17; Jairus's daughter, Mt 9:18, 23-25), the raising of Lazarus became the last and most dramatic sign-miracle Jesus performed before His own death and resurrection.

11:1-2. Lazarus, not to be confused with the Lazarus in the story of Lk 16:19-26, is mentioned only in John. **Bethany** (not the Bethany of 1:28) was two miles east of Jerusalem (v. 18) and near the Mt. of Olives (Mk 11:1). The parenthetical remark (v. 2) may anticipate 12:1-8 or may assume that the readers were familiar through early Christian teaching with **the Mary who anointed** Jesus' feet (e.g., Mk 14:3-9; cf. Lk 10:38-42).

11:3-4. The sisters knew of the Lord's love for Lazarus, so they **sent word to Him** of their brother's sickness. Those who carried the message are not identified. Jesus responded (v. 4), **This sickness is not to end in death**. Instead, the situation was **so that the Son of God may be glorified by it** (cf. 9:3). Ironically, Jesus would not only be honored in this miraculous healing (v. 40). He would also be glorified by His crucifixion that resulted in part from raising Lazarus (cf. 11:47-53) whereby He aroused the paranoia of the religious leaders.

11:5-6. In the narrative, Jesus' love for Lazarus is highlighted (vv. 3, 5, 36), but is also expressed for his sisters. **Martha** is given prominence, probably because she was the oldest or because she speaks first in vv. 20ff. On hearing about Lazarus's sickness (v. 6), Jesus purposefully **stayed two days longer in the place where He was**, a response that must have seemed uncompassionate. This was not to bring on Lazarus's death. Lazarus died by the time word reached Jesus of his sickness (vv. 11, 14).

11:7-8. Two days after receiving the message of Lazarus's sickness (v. 6), Jesus decided to return to Bethany in **Judea**, a more dangerous area than Perea (see comment on 10:40). Jesus' delay did not lead to Lazarus' death; He knew already that Lazarus was dead (v. 14). By delaying two days, the miracle was all the more undeniable. In light of 10:31, 39, the disciples' reaction is humanly realistic. They said (v. 8), **Rabbi, the Jews were just now seeking to stone You** (cf. 5:18; 7:1, 19, 25, 30; 8:37, 40; 10:39). So they wondered why He intended to go there again.

11:9-10. There was only a limited time to accomplish the Father's will (cf. 9:4). Work was done in the 12 hours of daylight, and when it became dark the work stopped. But it was unwise to cease labor while it was still light. The "daylight" during which Jesus ministered had not yet run out, and it would be wrong for Him to stop prematurely. Hence His determination to continue ministering, in this case to Lazarus and his family, in spite of the risks. Verse 10 is difficult, but Jesus appears to have meant that eventually His time for ministry will run out and He will face "the night" of His betrayal and crucifixion, a time of great distress for Him that parallels when one walks around at night without light available to him (the sense of **the light is not in him**). Jesus comforted His disciples by asserting that His ministry was not yet over, but reaffirmed that it would be some day.

11:11-13. Proceeding to Judea presented potential dangers (v. 8). The words **our friend Lazarus** added incentive for the disciples to join Jesus in the trip. But when Jesus referred to Lazarus as having **fallen asleep**, the disciples again misunderstood Jesus (v. 12). "Sleep" was a common enough metaphor for death in the OT (1Kg 2:10; 11:43; Dn 12:2). Nevertheless, the disciples **thought that He was speaking of literal sleep** (v. 13), and this was a good sign of Lazarus's recovery.

11:14-16. The confusion of the disciples called for a forthright reply: **Lazarus is dead, and I am glad for your sakes that I was not there** (vv. 14-15). Why was Christ glad? Eleven disciples had already believed that Jesus was the Christ (2:11; 6:69). Now that Lazarus was dead, the Lord was able to resurrect him and strengthen the disciples' faith that He is the "resurrection and life" (v. 25). In the NT, only John mentioned **Thomas** (v. 16) as also **Didymus** (meaning "twin," 20:24; 21:2) and gave him a significant role. Thomas's pronouncement **Let us also go, so that we may die with Him** is ironic in that ultimately the disciples and every believer must die with Christ spiritually (Rm 6:6, 8; Col 2:20; 2Tm 2:11).

11:17-19. When Jesus arrived outside the village, **He** heard what He already knew (vv. 11-14)—**that** Lazarus **had already been in the tomb four days**. It is possible that John noted the **four days** to emphasize that in Israel's climate decomposition would have already begun. Even the most petty, resistant fault finder would be challenged by Jesus, the resurrection and the life, who could raise a dead person to new life even after his body had begun to decay in the grave. This may explain why Jesus waited two more days in Perea (v. 6). There would then be no question that Lazarus was dead. For his readers outside Palestine, John mentioned (v. 18) that **Bethany** was only **about two miles** away from Jerusalem. Therefore, **many of the Jews** (v. 19) could make the trip from Jerusalem and the surrounding areas, and they came to comfort **Martha and Mary** in their loss. These probably consisted of friends and relatives of the family who helped bury Lazarus (v. 34).

11:20-22. Luke's portrayal of Martha and Mary (10:38-42) agrees with the picture John gives. **Martha** was a woman of action. So **when she heard that Jesus was** near Bethany, she **went to meet Him**. Mary was more patient. She **stayed at the house** and waited for Christ to come. Martha believed Jesus would have healed His friend Lazarus if He had been in Bethany (v. 21). In v. 22, she also expressed a confidence that Jesus could resurrect her brother if He asked the Father for it (**Even now I know that whatever You ask of God, God will give You**); cf. vv. 41-42.

11:23-24. Martha's expressed confidence (v. 22) was an indirect request, and Jesus answered it. **Your brother will rise again**. To this promise, Martha responded with a marvelous statement of her faith. **I know that he will rise again in the resurrection on the last day**. Martha knew assuredly that her brother would be resurrected to life, according to OT teaching (Jb 19:25-27; Ps 17:15; Is 26:19; Dn 12:2). We too can have this assurance about the resurrection of other believers.

11:25-27. Jesus did not merely have the power to resurrect. His claim **I am the resurrection and the life** makes Him the very source of resurrection and all life. (See "Jesus' Seven 'I Am' Claims" at 6:35.) **Everyone who lives** (v. 26) refers to one's physical life since it is followed by **and believes in Me**. Only in this life does one have the chance to believe in Christ (Heb 9:27). **Believe this** parallels "believes in Me" (vv. 25, 26). Believing the NT truths about Christ should not be distinguished from "believing (or trusting) in" the person of Christ. Martha's confession (v. 27) **You are the Christ, the Son of God** anticipates John's purpose statement (20:31). Taken together, to believe that Jesus is "the Christ, the Son of God" means to believe that He is *my* resurrection and eternal life.

11:28-29. At the close of their conversation, Jesus asked Martha to go and tell **Mary her sister**

to come to Him. Since Martha spoke to her sister **secretly**, she probably understood that Jesus wanted a private conversation with Mary. **The Teacher** was a title used for Jesus as a Jewish rabbi (cf. 1:38; 3:2; 20:16), but is not used of Him outside the Gospels. The role of the Teacher after Pentecost is taken up by the Spirit (14:26; 15:26). That Mary **got up quickly** (v. 29) and came to Jesus demonstrates her respect and faith.

11:30-31. Probably to avoid the crowds, Jesus remained outside of Bethany. So that Mary would know where to find Him, He stayed **in the place where Martha met Him**. The comforters (v. 31) who had come to console Mary and Martha **followed** Mary as she went to meet Jesus. These Jewish friends thought Mary **was going to the tomb to weep there**. Jewish mourners commonly grieved at the tomb of their dead.

11:32-35. Mary was regularly found at the **feet** of Jesus (11:2; 12:3; Lk 10:39). Martha primarily needed teaching (cf. "Teacher," v. 28), but Mary needed compassion. Mary repeated the same words spoken earlier by Martha (v. 21), implying the sisters discussed the situation. But unlike with Martha, emotions had overtaken Mary (see the different Greek words for weeping in vv. 33 and 35). When Jesus saw Mary and the others crying (*klaio*, "to wail"; v. 33), He **was deeply moved in spirit** [*embrimaomai*, "be indignant, angered"] **and was troubled.**

The question arises, "At whom or what was Jesus angered?" The best clues are found in the reference to "the Jews" (probably prominent Jewish leaders) in v. 19 who came to console Mary and Martha, and who appeared to have deep unbelief in God's power, even in the presence of Jesus, as expressed by their mourning (vv. 30-32). Unbelief is seen in v. 37 as well, and to this Jesus had a similar reaction as v. 33. This situation also angered Him in v. 38, where the same word is used as in v. 32 ("deeply moved," *embrimaomai*). Jesus' anger appears to be directed at their lack of faith in what God could do, especially through Jesus. This so moved the Lord that He **wept** at their unbelief. Note that two significant examples of Jesus weeping (this and Lk 19:41) were in response to the unbelief of the Jewish people.

11:36-37. Jesus' show of emotion was cause for division among the mourners (cf. 7:43-44; 9:16; 10:19-21). Some took it as evidence of **how** much **He loved** Lazarus. But others (v. 37) questioned Jesus' power or willingness to heal. They reasoned that if He healed a blind man, He should have been able to prevent Lazarus **also from dying** (a less difficult miracle in their estimation). This doubt led to pronounced unbelief in vv. 45-46.

11:38-40. Jesus was **again** ... **deeply moved within** (lit., "angered"; the same Greek verb in v. 33), this time because of the unbelief of the crowd. Tombs were commonly hewn vertically or horizontally out of rock, making a **cave**. A large, round **stone** covered the entrance. The command to **remove the stone** called for faith (v. 39). **Martha** objected that **there** would **be a stench** now that Lazarus was **dead four days** (cf. v. 17) and decomposition had set in. Jesus answered Martha, but spoke to all (v. 40): **Did I not say to you** [pl.] **that if you believe, you will see the glory of God?** Jesus previously spoke these words to His disciples and the messengers sent from the two sisters (vv. 3-4). These words would have been communicated to Mary and Martha on the messengers' return.

11:41-42. Jesus then prayed publicly to the Father. **I thank You** recalls Jesus' habit of gratitude in prayer (cf. 6:11, 23). Christ offered a previous (unspoken or unrecorded) petition to the Father to raise Lazarus, evident in the words **You have heard Me**. Also, **You always hear Me** (v. 42) shows that by His inviolate union with the Father, every prayer He prayed was answered, though not always affirmatively (as in Jesus' prayer in the garden of Gethsemane). Before it happened, Christ expressed absolute certainty that He would raise Lazarus.

11:43-44. Jesus **cried out with a loud voice**, audibly illustrating divine power (cf. Rv 1:15; 14:2). Like the Good Shepherd who calls His own sheep by name (10:3), Christ called for **Lazarus** personally to **come forth**. Part of the miracle may have been that Lazarus was able to walk despite being **bound hand and foot with wrappings** (v. 44). Jesus commanded the people, **unbind him, and let him go.**

11:45-46. As a result of Jesus' miraculous resurrection of Lazarus, **many of the Jews** ... **believed in Him** and gained eternal life. John's positive use of "Jews" in this verse demonstrates he was not anti-Semitic. For this group of Jews who are separate from the religious leaders (v. 46), see vv. 18-19, 32-33, 35-36. Before Lazarus's resurrection, some doubted Jesus' ability to do miracles (v. 37). Now in contrast to those who believed (v. 46), **some of them** (apparently those who did not believe) **went to the Pharisees**, who were known to be seeking to kill Jesus (5:18; 7:19, 25; 8:37, 40).

11:47-48. Some of **the chief priests and the Pharisees** were members of the Jerusalem **council** called the Sanhedrin. The Sanhedrin was composed of 71 men and exercised authority over all religious practices in Israel. The members of the council did not deny that Jesus was **performing many signs**. But they felt that if He were allowed to continue unabated (v. 48) the Romans would consider the masses who came to **believe in Him** as an insurrection. Then the Romans would respond by destroying their **place** (the temple or their own positions of prominence) **and** their **nation**.

11:49-50. Caiaphas ruled as **high priest** in AD 18–36 (for more on Caiaphas, see the comments on Mt 26:3-5). He was irritated by the indecision of the council and recommended (v. 50) that **one man**, Jesus, **die** in place of **the people**, rather than all the Jewish people dying at the hands of the Romans. Although Caiaphas's design was political prudence, he unwittingly expressed the very intent of God's sacrifice of His Son: the substitution of the life of one man, Jesus, for the sins of all people. Ironically, even though the Jews crucified Christ to prevent the nation's demise, the Romans destroyed Jerusalem and the temple in AD 70.

11:51-53. It was not merely **on his own initiative** that Caiaphas made his pronouncement. Caiaphas unwittingly **prophesied** because he was **high priest that year**. Caiaphas's prophecy did not make him a prophet nor is it ever recorded that he prophesied again. In his governing authority as high priest (cf. Rm 13:1), he was unconsciously and providentially used by God. "That year" refers to the year of Christ's death. But where Caiaphas thought of Christ's death as only for His own people, God's purpose was **not for the** Jewish **nation only** but for Gentiles as well (cf. Jn 10:16). In God's plan, Jews and Gentiles who will believe will be gathered **together into one** group or body (cf. Eph 2:11-22) because they are all **children of God** by faith alone (cf. Jn 1:12). At this meeting, weeks before the crucifixion, the Jewish leaders had already **planned together to kill** Jesus.

11:54. Once again, Jesus took precautions against an early death by refraining to **walk publicly among the Jews** (cf. 10:40; 12:36). Instead, He stayed out in **the country near the wilderness**, which would have provided some protection. **Ephraim** is usually identified with a town located 12 to 15 miles northeast of Jerusalem.

11:55-57. This was the final **Passover** in the life of Christ, during which He would be crucified. **Many** who lived at a distance took the trip **to Jerusalem** early to **purify themselves** (cf. 2:6; 18:28). On various occasions in the OT, the LORD gave instructions to consecrate oneself for worship (Gn 35:2; Ex 19:10, 11), and this was applied to the Passover (2Ch 30:16-20). But instead of consecration (v. 56), the people were caught up in conversation and curiosity. The decision of the council led to a warrant for Jesus' arrest. Word was spread throughout the crowds (v. 57) so that **if anyone knew where He was, he was to report it**. But the actual arrest would not come until a week or more later.

b. Anointing of Jesus' Feet (12:1-11)

Chapter 12 begins the final week of Jesus' life and climaxes His public ministry. Mary's anointing of Jesus is also recorded in Mt 26:6-13 and Mk 14:3-9 (see the comments there). The story in Luke 7:36-50 is not the same event.

12:1-3. It was just **six days before the Passover** (i.e., Saturday), presumably in the evening after the Sabbath was over. For **Bethany**, see comment on 11:1. True to her character (v. 2; see comment on 11:20) **Martha was serving** (*diakoneo*). The same Greek word will be used shortly of "serving" Christ by following Him (v. 26). Lazarus was **reclining at the table with** Jesus. The custom was to lie on one's side on a low couch or on the floor with the head at a low table and feet pointing away (see comment on 13:23). Mary (v. 3) poured a large amount (Gk., *litra*, a Roman **pound**, about 12 ounces) of **very costly perfume** over Jesus' feet and in a supremely humble act **wiped His feet with her hair**. In ordinary burials, ointment masked the odor of decomposition. So anointing Jesus' feet prophesied Jesus' coming death. Since wiping off the ointment would never be done at an ordinary burial, this act may prophesy His rising incorrupt (note both the anointing and wiping in 11:2).

12:4-5. Mary's supreme act of devotion is set in contrast to **Judas Iscariot**, the one **who was** consciously **intending to betray** Jesus. Although debated, this contrast may imply Mary consciously anointed Jesus for His coming death. Judas asked (v. 5) **why** the **perfume was not sold for three hundred denarii**, the equivalent of about an average year's wages, **and given to poor people**. In the Synoptics, other disciples joined in Judas's indignation at the expensive waste of perfume (Mt 26:8; Mk 14:4).

12:6. Judas disguised his thievery by implying that **he was concerned about the poor**. The

Eleven trusted Judas with **the money box** containing the financial contributions of those who gave to Jesus' ministry (Mt 27:55; Lk 8:3). If the perfume had been sold and entrusted to Judas, he would have had more money from which **to pilfer**.

12:7-8. Verse 7 could read, "Leave her alone. She has kept it [not **so that she may keep it**] for the day of my burial" (NET). This act of anointing perfume as burial preparation indicates that Mary was probably one of only a few who realized Christ was soon to die (cf. Mt 26:12; Mk 14:8). Jesus' words (v. 8) **You** [pl.] **always have the poor with you** have been true for 2,000 years. Charitable opportunities will never cease until Christ returns. **But you do not always have Me** referred to His death just six days away.

12:9. Jesus' fame could not prevent curiosity seekers. **The large crowd of the Jews** (in this case the general populace, not the rulers) who came to Jerusalem for the Passover (11:55) also came to Bethany to see Jesus. But they wanted to see the resurrected **Lazarus** too.

12:10-11. One sin leads to another. Not only did **the chief priests** plot to kill Jesus, they now **planned to put Lazarus to death also**. Lazarus stood as a living testimony of Christ's messianic power, and He had to be eliminated also. Too many Jews **were going away and were believing in Jesus**. "Going away" could mean the Jews were "deserting" the Jewish leaders (HCSB) or that the Jewish people were "going over to" Jesus (NIV).

c. Presentation of the Messiah-King (12:12-19)

The event described in 12:12-19 is traditionally known as the triumphant entry (Palm Sunday in Christian history) and is found in all four Gospels (Mt 21:1-11; Mk 11:1-10; Lk 19:28-40; see the comments there). The attention aroused by the resurrection of Lazarus (chap. 11) intensified the celebration.

12:12-13. On the next day identifies the day as the Sunday before the Passover **feast** and Jesus' death. The palm **branches** the crowd waved to greet Jesus entering Jerusalem symbolized the victory or triumph of the Messiah-King. **Hosanna!** is a Hebrew term meaning "Save [us] now!" but came to be used as an expression of praise. The people cried out words from Ps 118, a psalm sung at the Passover meal. Their shouts that Jesus was the **King of Israel** (cf. 1:49) showed that they understood the psalm to speak of the Messiah.

12:14-15. Unfortunately, many in the crowd thought of Jesus only as a political deliverer and not a spiritual Savior. Instead of riding in on a horse like a warrior, Jesus chose a donkey—a burden-bearing animal. OT prophecy had identified the Messiah-King (Zch 9:9; see the comments there) as coming to the **DAUGHTER OF ZION** (v. 15; a common OT idiom for the people of Jerusalem) **SEATED ON A DONKEY'S COLT**. The donkey was also a symbol of peace and humility (2Sm 19:26).

12:16. Although well taught by Jesus, the **disciples** still **did not** fully **understand** the OT prophecies about the Messiah. After the resurrection, **when Jesus was glorified** (cf. 7:39), the resurrected Lord taught them the messianic significance of the Hebrew Scriptures (see Lk 24:25-27, 44-46). Moreover, afterward the Holy Spirit assisted them to recall the details of Jesus' life and to match them with the OT prophecies that **were written of Him** (Jn 16:13-14).

12:17-18. The people who were with Him when He called Lazarus out of the tomb are distinguished from the crowd in v. 18. Most of the former group witnessed the resurrection of Lazarus and **continued to testify about** Jesus and this miracle. **The people** who **went and met Him** had not witnessed the miracle but went to meet Jesus **because they heard** how Jesus had resurrected Lazarus.

12:19. Jesus' popularity provoked the Pharisees to criticize each other. **You . . . are not doing any good; look, the world has gone after Him**. Though they meant a multitude of Jews were turning to Jesus, John saw an ironic "fulfillment" in the Greeks (likely Gentile God-fearers in Jerusalem to celebrate the feast) who came to see Jesus (v. 20).

d. Gentile Openness and Israel's Blindness (12:20-50)

The coming of the Greeks (i.e., Gentiles) to Jesus marks the climax of Jesus' ministry to the Jews, and closes the first major section of the Fourth Gospel (1:19-12:50), which dealt primarily with Jesus' public ministry of performing miracles and teaching the people. John shortly would concentrate on Jesus' private ministry to the disciples in the upper room (chaps. 13–17).

12:20-22. Along with the Jews traveling from Galilee to Jerusalem **were some Greeks**—Gentiles who abandoned paganism in favor of believing in the God of Israel ("God-fearers"). It is unlikely that they submitted to circumcision (as proselytes) because they would then have been fully accepted as Jews and not called Greeks.

These Greeks **came** first **to Philip**, probably because he had a Greek name and because he was from **Bethsaida** of Galilee. They may have come from the Gentile territory of the Decapolis, named for its ten Gentile cities, which lay east and south of Galilee. These Greeks wanted **to see** Jesus. For John, "seeing" Jesus often pictured faith (1:39, 46; 4:29; 8:56; 9:39). **Philip** told **Andrew**, and together they came to Jesus. Philip and Andrew were known to bring people to Jesus (cf. 1:41, 45).

12:23-24. Up to this point in the Fourth Gospel, Jesus' "hour" was said to be future. Now the "hour" is said to have arrived. At the height of Jewish rejection of Jesus, Gentiles were seeking Him. The coming of the Greeks was a sign that **the hour** of Jesus' death had now **come** (cf. 7:33-35)—possibly because finally, at this point, the door was cracked open a bit for the inclusion of the Gentiles, something not seen clearly in John's gospel prior to this. For "hour," see comments on 2:4 and 4:21. Through His death and resurrection, Jesus would **be glorified**. For **truly, truly** (v. 24), see comments on 1:51. Jesus likened His death to the paradox that **a grain of wheat** is unable to produce life unless it first **dies** (i.e., is buried in the ground as if it had no life). When it "dies," a great harvest comes from its "death."

12:25-26. Jesus applied to His followers the principle of dying to self. Anyone who lived life for himself (**loves his life**) destroyed the potential of his earthly life for eternal reward (cf. Mt 16:24-27; Mk 8:34-38; Lk 9:23-26). But if he **hates his life in this world**, i.e., rejects self-centered choices, his life will be rewarded in eternity. **If anyone serves Me, he must follow Me** (v. 26) shows that following Christ includes service. Moreover, to serve the Lord Jesus, the disciple must walk closely and attend to Him, so that wherever Jesus leads, there His **servant will be also**. The rewards God's servants will receive include commendation and **honor** from the Father (Mt 25:21, 23), resulting in leadership responsibilities in the world to come (Lk 12:44; 19:17; Rv 2:26, 27).

12:27-28. Much like during His later agony in the garden (Mt 26:38; Mk 14:34), Jesus' heart became **troubled** as He contemplated taking on the sin of humanity at the cross. Jesus could have prayed for the Father to **save** Him **from** the **hour** of His death. But that would be contrary to His whole mission in the world. So He prayed instead (v. 28) for the Father to be glorified. This is the last of three occasions in the life of Christ that **a voice came out of heaven** (Mt 3:17; 17:5) through which the Father expressed His satisfaction with the Son.

12:29-30. Some in **the crowd** were unprepared to receive revelation and thought only that **it had thundered**. Others thought of some spiritual reality behind the voice, supposing that **an angel** had **spoken** something to Christ. But as Jesus explained, the **voice** did **not come for** His **sake, but for** the sake of the people. He needed no proof that the Father would glorify Him (v. 28). But the Father graciously provided to the crowd further confirmation of Jesus' authority and Sonship. Yet they missed its significance.

12:31. Beside forgiveness, the cross (implied in the word **now**) accomplished the **judgment** of the **world** and the defeat of Satan, **the ruler of this world** (cf. 14:30; 16:11; Eph 2:2; 2Co 4:4). Satan was **cast out** at the cross. This was not spatial, as if the Devil were driven out of heaven (cf. Rv 12:10). Instead, his power was permanently broken and his destiny was fixed. His complete destruction awaits Christ's return (Rv 20:10).

12:32-33. The thought that Christ **will draw all men to** Himself could mean He will draw all groups of people (not necessarily every single person), as opposed to only Jewish people. The reference to the Greeks (v. 20) may support this. But to the contrary, John has shown a universal perspective throughout his book (1:29; 3:16, 17; 4:42; 6:33, 51) and "all [people]" is usually all-inclusive (1:7, 9; 2:24; 5:23, 28; 10:29; 17:2). Everyone who hears the message of the cross will be "drawn" to, or brought closer to, the Savior by that message. But this is no promise of a universal salvation. John and Jesus have made it clear that one must believe (cf. 3:16). **Lifted up** (v. 32; cf. 3:14; 8:28) refers to the method of Jesus' death (i.e., crucifixion), as is confirmed by the words **He was saying this to indicate the kind of death by which He was to die**. "Lifted up" also depicts the glory that would come to Christ by His death (12:23; 13:31-32; 17:1).

12:34. The crowd understood the **Law** to say that when the Messiah came, He was **to remain** alive **forever** as their King. The "Law" here probably means the entire OT as in 10:34. Many OT passages indicated that the Messiah's reign would be forever (2Sm 7:13; Ps 89:35-37; Is 9:7; Dn 7:13-14).

12:35-36. Jesus indirectly answered their question (v. 34) by referring to Himself as **the Light** that is among them a little while longer. The Jewish people needed to **walk while** they had

the Light so that darkness (spiritual blindness) would **not overtake** them. Verse 36 defines "walk in the light" as **believe in the Light** and the **sons of Light** as believers. That Jesus **went away and hid Himself from them** (cf. 10:40; 11:54) anticipates symbolically the blindness that is about to come on Israel for their unbelief (vv. 37-40).

12:37-38. Jesus **had performed so many signs**, but the majority did not find the miracles convincing. As a result, the people **were not believing in** Jesus. John cited (v. 38) a well-known messianic passage about God's Suffering Servant (Is 53:1) as now fulfilled in Christ. The **ARM OF THE LORD** is a figure of speech for God's power, displayed in Jesus' sign-miracles (v. 37). The rhetorical questions of the OT prophecy suggest that only a remnant in Israel would believe the message of the Messiah.

12:39-40. Israel's refusal to believe (v. 37) finally led to hardening (**they could not believe** any longer; but see v. 42). Corporately, Israel became **BLINDED** (v. 40) by God as a judgment for their unbelief (see the comments on Rm 11:11-24), even as all people are blinded by unbelief (1Co 2:14; 2Co 4:4). As with Isaiah's ministry (Is 6:9-11), Jesus' teaching resulted in desensitizing the Jewish people rather than leading them to faith. These are hard verses and will challenge one's theology: in v. 36, Jesus commanded the Jewish people to believe. They were thus morally responsible for believing. Verses 37-38 say they did not believe, committing the sin of unbelief. Verses 39-40 say *why* they do not believe—because God **HARDENED THEIR HEART** (see the comments on Rm 9:14-18) so that Israel might not **BE CONVERTED** from sin and unbelief and God **HEAL THEM**. The interchange between divine sovereignty over sin (in this case unbelief) and human responsibility is mystifying, but one does not cancel out the other. Both doctrines are equally true, and one passage may well emphasize one over the other. Here John emphasized God's sovereignty over their unbelief, but in other places their moral responsibility is foremost. For the relationship between God's sovereignty and human sin, see the comments on Rm 9:22-23, and the comments introducing Rm 9:30.

12:41. When Isaiah **saw His glory, and he spoke of Him**, the prophet was referring to Yahweh, the God of the OT (Is 6:3). But John revealed that the glory of Yahweh was also the glory of the preincarnate Christ (cf. 1:1, 14; 8:58; 10:30; 20:28). This is confirmed by the personal pronoun in v. 42, "many . . . believed in *Him*" (italics added).

12:42-43. Nevertheless, despite the blindness that came on Israel, **many even of the rulers** (not just of the crowd) **believed in Him**. The "rulers" were members of the Sanhedrin. Nicodemus and Joseph of Arimathea are two of the rulers identified in John as believing in Jesus as the Messiah (3:1; 19:38-39). In this early stage of their new faith, these rulers **were not confessing** Christ publicly for fear of being excluded from the **synagogue** (cf. 9:22). Their love for human **approval** (v. 43) subverted their witness. For the theme of the "secret disciple," see 19:38-40.

12:44-46. In the following verses, Jesus gave the final teaching of His public ministry. Although it is not clear when or where Jesus delivered these words, they are placed here as the culmination of Jesus' proclamation to Israel. Afterward, the book will shift to the private ministry of the Messiah to His disciples (Jn 13–17). **Jesus cried out** shows the importance of these teachings. **He who believes . . . does not believe in Me** means "does not believe *only* in Me." The unity of the Son and the Father is repeated three times in these verses. The second is expressed in v. 45: **He who sees Me sees the One who sent Me**. Jesus is the perfect revelation and expression of God (1:18; 14:9). Jesus (v. 46) as the **Light** of the **world** (1:4-9; 3:19-21; 8:12; 12:35) and the need to **believe in** Him are themes John accentuated elsewhere in the book (see Introduction: Purpose and Theme).

12:47-48. Judgment (3:17-19; 5:22-30; 16:8, 11) and the words of Jesus (4:41, 50; 5:24; 6:63, 68; 14:23; 15:7) are also major themes in John. All future judgment has been given to Jesus (5:22, 27). But Jesus' purpose in coming to the world was not to **judge** it at that time, but instead **to save the world** (3:17; 8:15). Final judgment is self-imposed and fixed in this life by a person's response to the gospel message (3:18; 5:24; 12:48). Therefore, if anyone (v. 48) **does not receive** Jesus' **sayings**, His word **will judge him at the last day** (the final judgment; cf. 6:39-40). Jesus' "words" tie into His identity as the Word (1:1, 14).

12:49-50. Jesus made it clear repeatedly that He **did not speak** by His own authority or **initiative** (5:30; 8:28, 42; 12:49; 14:10). So his message about eternal life is the Father's message as well. **His commandment is eternal life** (v. 50) means that God commands everyone to believe, and believing leads to eternal life. It is thoroughly appropriate that Jesus' public ministry in the

Fourth Gospel ended with a comment about the need for faith in the Messiah.

III. Private Ministry: Farewell Instructions to Jesus' Disciples (13:1–17:26)

The farewell remarks of Jesus comprise the second major unit in John. These private instructions to His disciples began in an upper room. But at 14:31, Jesus and the eleven remaining disciples left the upper room and wandered through the streets of Jerusalem where Jesus continued to instruct them and to pray. Finally, at 17:26, they left Jerusalem and crossed the Kidron Valley.

A. Washing the Disciples' Feet (13:1-20)

13:1. Of the three Passovers cited in John, this **Feast of the Passover** is the only one recorded in the Synoptics. **Jesus** was fully aware that the time of His death had come (cf. 12:23). His disciples were not. **He loved** His disciples, even Judas, **to the end** (*telos*)—to the cross where He cried, "It is finished" (*teleo*, 19:30). Up to this point in John, it was said that his hour had not yet come (2:4; 7:30; 8:20). Now it is said that **His hour had come**, i.e., the time of His death, resurrection, and ascension as described in the words, to **depart out of this world to the Father**.

13:2-5. The idea of betraying Jesus was not an original thought of Judas; **the devil** had **already put** the notion **into** his faithless **heart** (cf. 6:71; 12:4). Once again (cf. v. 1), Jesus had a complete self-awareness of His universal authority (cf. Mt 28:18), His origin, and His destiny (v. 3). That **He had come forth from God** was symbolized as He **laid aside His garments** to take the role of a servant (v. 4). In Israel, one's feet became dirty as one walked from place to place. Washing the feet of a guest was a common courtesy provided by a host but performed by a household servant, and never by the head of the home. Jesus became His disciples' servant, breaching social customs. Instead of saying that Jesus "took off" and then "put on," John said He **laid aside** (*tithemi*, v. 4) and "took up" (*lambano*, 13:12) His garments—words used earlier for His death (10:17-18).

13:6-8. Some of the disciples submitted as Jesus washed their feet. But when Jesus **came to Simon Peter**, he questioned the Lord's lowly act. Jesus knew Peter's limited understanding (**you do not realize now**, v. 7). The meaning of the foot washing would become clear **hereafter**, i.e., after the upper room teachings and/or after the resurrection. Peter still resisted (v. 8), using a strong negative in Greek: **Never shall You wash my feet!** Jesus replied that if Peter refused to have his feet washed by Him, then he could **have no part with** the Messiah. Ongoing partnership or fellowship with Jesus is conditioned on the recurrent cleansing of the believer as he confesses his sins (1Jn 1:9).

13:9-11. In Peter's enthusiasm to be in companionship with his Lord, he asked Jesus to wash his whole body. Jesus' instructions to Peter about two distinct cleansings must not be overlooked. **He who has bathed** [*louo*] **needs only to wash** [*nipto*] **his feet**, because he **is completely clean** (v. 10). The bath represents the complete, unrepeatable cleansing of new birth; the washing of the feet pictures the repeated cleansing needed for intimacy with Christ after salvation (cf. 15:14). This intimacy requires walking in the light and confessing sins (see 1Jn 1:6-9). The apostle interpreted Jesus' words (v. 11), **you are clean, but not all of you**, to single out Judas. Since Judas had not believed, he was not clean, i.e., regenerated.

13:12-15. For Jesus to have **taken up His garments** again forecasted His glorification at the resurrection. After a rhetorical question to gain their attention, Christ reasoned that He was rightfully above them. They themselves called Him **Teacher and Lord** (v. 13), terms relevant for ongoing discipleship. Since a servant is not above his master (Mt 10:24), the disciples needed to humble themselves like their Teacher and serve others. To **wash one another's feet** (v. 14) included laying down their lives for their brothers or sisters (10:11, 14, 17; 15:13; 1Jn 3:16). Foot washing is not set down as an ordinance but as an **example** (v. 15) of all forms of humble service modeled by the Lord's foot washing (cf. 1Tm 5:10).

13:16-17. Since a **slave** is never more privileged than the **master** who owns him, and an ambassador is never more important **than the one who sent him**, so logic must compel the disciples to humble themselves in lowly service as their Master had done in washing their feet. The "one who is sent" (*apostolos*, lit., "apostle") hints at the apostolic mission of the Eleven. The disciples must **know these things** (v. 17) Jesus had spoken before they could obey them. Knowledge is a prerequisite to obedience. But being **blessed** or spiritually happy is conditioned on obeying Christ's call to servanthood.

13:18. I do not speak of all of you refers to Judas. Jesus knew all about the **ones** He had **chosen**, including Judas. He was not caught by surprise at Judas's betrayal. "Chosen" does not refer here to election for salvation, but to the choosing of His twelve disciples (cf. 6:70). The selection of the disciples resulted in Ps 41:9 being **fulfilled**. In the psalm, David's close friend Ahithophel (**He who eats My bread**) betrayed David (**lifted up his heel** is a cultural sign for contempt). Later Ahithophel hung himself (2Sm 16:20-22; 17:23), foreshadowing how Judas would betray the Greater David (Messiah) and later hang himself (Mt 27:5; Ac 1:18).

13:19-20. Jesus declared that the prophecy about Judas was designed to increase the faith of the disciples in Jesus' divine status, sovereignty, and omniscience once it was fulfilled. For **believe that I am He**, see comments on 4:26 and 8:28. Taking the gospel to the world was in the Lord's heart. The disciples must be sent to carry out the task. But the one who is sent is nothing (**whomever I send**, v. 20). The authority rests in the Lord who sends them. Therefore, anyone **who receives** a person sent by Christ receives Christ Himself (cf. 1:12) and the Father as well.

B. Identifying His Betrayer (13:21-30)

13:21-22. For the third time, the sinless Jesus was **troubled in spirit** (cf. 11:33; 12:27). Although Christ had previously hinted that He would be betrayed (6:64, 71; 13:11), He now directly **testified** that the betrayer would be **one of** the Twelve. By pointing out that the disciples were **at a loss to know of which one He was speaking** (v. 22), John again underlined the ignorance of the disciples. Judas must have insincerely joined in the interchange that followed (cf. Mt 26:22; Mk 14:19; Lk 22:23).

13:23-25. The beloved disciple, presumably John (see Introduction: Author), **was reclining on Jesus' bosom**, or chest, not only because of the cultural style of eating (see comment on 12:2) but also because this was a Passover meal where reclining to the left was part of the ceremony. This is the first of five times the author identified himself as the disciple **whom Jesus loved** (19:26; 20:2; 21:7, 20). Each reference occurred within the events of Jesus' death and resurrection. Jesus was flanked by Judas and John (both honored positions), but John was between Jesus and **Peter** (v. 24). So Peter prompted John to ask Jesus for the identity of the traitor. In this reclined position, **leaning back thus** (v. 25), John could speak to Jesus.

13:26-27. Jesus revealed the identity of the traitor to John alone (see comment on 21:20). For a person to **dip** a **morsel and give it to** another was a sign of friendship and honor. Judas's heinous character was his own responsibility. Calling him **the son of Simon Iscariot** showed that he was an ordinary human person. But **after** Judas ate **the morsel**, **Satan then entered into him** (v. 27). As the bread entered Judas, so did the Devil. Jesus, in full control of the moment, precipitated the betrayal Himself by releasing Judas to **do quickly** his dastardly deed.

13:28-30. Surprisingly, **no one** understood **for what purpose** Jesus told Judas to carry out his activities quickly. Judas had been entrusted with the funds given to the disciples for their traveling ministry or for the needy they encountered (cf. 12:6). So the disciples thought (v. 29) Judas was sent out to **buy** some **things** needed for the Passover **feast**, or to **give something to the poor**. Nighttime almsgivings were part of Passover. After Judas **went out** (v. 30), the author remarked climactically, **it was night**—darkness had descended both literally and symbolically. Though John did not record it, sometime after Judas left Jesus introduced the institution of the Lord's Supper (Mt 26:26-29; Mk 14:22-25; Lk 22:15-20).

C. Revealing His Departure (13:31–14:31)

13:31-32. Again Jesus' knowledge of the precise time of His death is revealed: **Now is the Son of Man glorified**. This is the first of 23 uses of the verb, "glorify" (*doxazo*) in the Fourth Gospel (14 uses in the Synoptics). Sometimes it refers to building one's own status (8:54; cf. 5:41, 42; 8:50); the enhancement of God's reputation by Jesus (12:28; 14:13) or the believer (15:8; 21:19); or the enhancement of Jesus' reputation by accomplishing God's work (11:4; 17:4; cf. 2:11). Here it refers to Jesus' death, resurrection, and ascension by which He will receive an exalted status from God (11:4; 12:16, 23; 13:31, 32; 17:5). Jesus' miracles manifested His glory (2:11). But it was in supreme weakness—His death on the cross—that His glory was most displayed. **God** was **glorified in** Jesus (v. 32), and reciprocally **God will also glorify** Jesus **in Himself**. Since Christ's death was within hours from that moment, the crucifixion would **glorify** Jesus **immediately**.

13:33. A Jewish teacher called his disciples **little children**. This is the only time Christ used this address in all the Gospels. John later adopted the term (1Jn 2:1, 12, 28). Jesus told the Jewish authorities (Jn 7:34; 8:21), **Where I am going** [the cross, the ascension] **you cannot come**. Now He was telling His disciples the same (but see 14:3).

13:34-35. Love for others was commanded in

the OT (Lv 19:18, 34; Dt 10:19). The love Jesus commanded was **new** since it called His followers not merely to love but to love sacrificially even as Jesus loved them. Paul referred to this one aspect of the law as the law of Christ (1Co 9:21; Gl 6:2). Since love is one of the primary marks of discipleship, others **will know** (identify) Jesus' **disciples** by their **love for one another**.

13:36-38. When Peter questioned where Jesus was going, Christ promised Peter **you cannot** [*ou dynasai*, lit., "are not able to"] **follow Me now** [to the cross] **but you will follow later**, i.e., to his own death. Peter impetuously boasted that he would willingly **lay down** his life for the Lord. According to Mk 14:31, all the disciples made the same claim. Ironically, it would be Jesus who would die for Peter. Then Peter would follow Jesus (but not **right now**) to his death (Jn 21:18-19). A strutting, crowing **rooster** fits Peter's boastful claim and forms a prophetic rebuke. Peter gave no response to the prediction and did not speak again in the narrative until his denial (18:17).

14:1. The thought of Jesus' betrayal and departure (13:21-38) would have greatly disheartened the disciples. To console them, Jesus instructed, **Do not let your** [pl.] **heart be troubled**. The disciples could calm their hearts by faith [**believe in God** and **believe also in Me**]. The two occurrences of the verb "believe" are spelled the same (*pisteuete* in both), but that spelling could make either or both verbs a statement of fact (an indicative mood verb, "You do believe"), or a command (an imperative mood verb, "Believe!"), or a combination of the two (one could be a statement and the other a command). The first phrase could also be a question ("Do you believe in God?"). It is a complicated issue. The NET Bible (p. 2073 n. 8) is most likely correct in its reasoning: "[Jesus] is about to undergo rejection by his own people as their Messiah. The disciples' faith in him as Messiah and Lord would be cast into extreme doubt by these events, which the author makes clear were not at this time foreseen by the disciples. After the resurrection it is this identification between Jesus and the Father that needs to be reaffirmed (cf. Jn 20:24-29). Thus it seems best to take the first *pisteuete* [transliteration added] as indicative and the second as imperative, producing the translation "You believe in God; believe also in me."

14:2-4. Jesus' teaching about His **Father's house** with **many dwelling places** evokes the image of a first-century wealthy home with beautiful additions. Jesus would not **go** to **prepare a place** for His disciples unless He would also **come again and receive** them to Himself (v. 3). This "coming" is the pretribulation rapture (see the comments on Mt 24:36-44; 1Th 4:13-17) rather than the second coming since at the latter Jesus returns to stay on earth (Zch 14:3-4; Mt 24:29-31; Rv 19:11-21). This is Jesus' second revelation about the rapture (Mt 24:36-44 was a few days earlier, probably on Tuesday of Passion Week). Jesus deeply desires us to be with Him **where** He is (cf. 1Th 4:17). The disciples **know the way** (v. 4) Jesus will take to the Father's house. He has told them repeatedly of the cross.

14:5-6. Thomas questioned Jesus' logic. **Lord . . . how do we know the way?** Jesus affirmed (v. 6) their faith with the sixth **I am** claim in John. He is not one way but **the way** to God. He is not only true. He is **the truth**. Truth is embodied in Christ, and so is eternal **life** (1:4). **No one comes to the Father** for eternal life or for Christian living except first by way of faith in Christ.

14:7. Although born again (2:11; 14:10-11), the Eleven had not begun true intimacy with Christ. They lacked a more complete understanding of who He was. That He was the only way or access to the Father (v. 6) escaped their thinking so far. **If** they (**you** is pl. in Gk.) **had known** Christ intimately (cf. Php 3:10), they would have known the Father intimately as well. But they had not (v. 9). **From now on** references that moment forward. Through the farewell instructions (chaps. 13–17), they could gain an intimate knowledge (**know**) and full spiritual vision (**have seen**) of the Father.

14:8-9. Philip, in his request **show us the Father**, demonstrated the very unfamiliarity with the Father Jesus had just mentioned. Jesus had spent three years with the disciples (v. 9) and yet they had **not come to know** Him fully (v. 9). To "know" or "see" Christ (**He who has seen Me**) is to recognize God Himself fully (**has seen the Father**). God the Father is completely revealed in Jesus the Son, but Jesus Christ, the Son of God, is distinct from God the Father in terms of their respective personhood. For this important point, see the comments on 1:1, 18. This claim of Jesus is nothing less than a stupendous declaration of deity, leading to the NT teaching of the Trinity.

14:10-11. Jesus is **in the Father, and the Father is in** Jesus—a holy, eternal fellowship and unity in the Godhead. The **words** that Jesus **speak**[s] are never on His **own initiative**, independent of the Father. **The Father abiding in** Christ **does His works.** The mutual indwelling of the Father and the Son stresses inseparability, yet maintains a distinction within the Trinity. If the disciples **believe because of** Jesus' **works themselves**, they would see the truth of this abiding relationship between the Father and the Son.

14:12. What are the **greater works** Jesus says believers will do? These greater works were made possible **because** Jesus went **to the Father**, i.e., after His ascension when the Holy Spirit was given. The "greater works" took place at Pentecost and ever since when people are brought to faith in Christ.

14:13-14. The promise that the disciples will do greater works than Jesus was now directly linked to their prayers in His Name. **Whatever you ask** (*aiteo*, a request from an inferior to a superior) begins the subject of prayer for the first time in the upper room teaching (15:7, 16; 16:23-24, 26). It also instructs Christians for the first time that prayer is to be made through Christ (**in My name**) to the Father (15:16; 16:23-24, 26). Prayer in Jesus' name suggests that the one who offers it understands that Jesus is the sole mediator between the one who prays and the Father (v. 6). The prayer is made for Jesus' sake, not primarily for personal benefit (cf. Ps 25:11). So we can ask in prayer as if Jesus were asking it. This implies that our prayers must be designed according to His will, character, and purpose (1Jn 5:14-15). But **if you ask Me** (v. 14) authorizes prayers also made to the Son of God (cf. Ac 7:59; 2Co 12:8). The promise **I will do it** must be harmonized with other conditions for prayer (e.g., Ps 66:18; Jms 4:3; 1Pt 3:7; 1Jn 5:14-15).

14:15-17. To **keep** Jesus' **commandments** is a test of devotion to Him. The coming of **another Helper** (*parakletos*; v. 16), i.e., the Spirit at Pentecost, implies that Jesus Himself is a *parakletos*. This Greek word is used five times in the NT, all by John (14:16, 26; 15:26; 16:7; 1Jn 2:1). The various functions of the *parakletos* in these contexts make it difficult to translate with a single term. The word often means "one who helps, by consoling, encouraging, or mediating on behalf of" another (L&N, 1:141). Most translations capture something of its meaning (cf. "Helper," ESV, NKJV; "Counselor" NIV, HCSB; "Advocate," NET, NRSV; "Companion," CEB; though in its use in 1Jn 2:1 it means "advocate" in a legal sense). The Spirit is **with** the believer **forever**, securing his salvation. Just as Christ embodies the truth (14:6), the Spirit is **the Spirit** who promotes and spreads **truth**. Like Christ (1:10-11), **the world cannot receive** the Spirit either. By saying that the Spirit **abides with you**, Jesus depicted the relationship of the Spirit in the OT with OT saints, i.e., the Spirit was "with" them. But at that time the Spirit did not reside within them as He does following Pentecost (when He **will be in** them).

14:18-19. Christ would **not leave** His disciples permanently **as orphans**, i.e., helpless. He promised to **come** to them during the 40 days after His resurrection (16:16-24), and later through the coming Holy Spirit. After His death, **the world** would **no longer see** Christ (v. 19), but the Eleven, and other disciples, would. The resurrection appearances were only to believers (cf. 1Co 15:6). His resurrection (**because I live**) is the guarantee of our resurrection (**you will live also**).

14:20-21. The words **you in Me, and I in you** speak of the believer's ongoing intimacy with Christ, maintained by obedience (v. 21; cf. 15:1-11). Verse 21 returns to the love-theme of v. 15 and connects it to the mutual indwelling of Jesus and the believer in v. 20. It is not merely the one who **has** the **commandments**, but the one who also **keeps them** who is identified as **the one who loves Me** (cf. v. 15). "The one who loves Me" is broader than just the Eleven. Jesus promised **to disclose** more and more of His heart to each believer who loves Him by his obedience (see the comment on 2:23).

14:22-23. This is the only time that **Judas** (but **not** the betrayer, Judas **Iscariot**), one of the Twelve, speaks in the Gospels. He may be Thaddaeus of the Synoptics (Mt 10:3; Mk 3:18). Judas asked why the Lord was **going to disclose** Himself to the disciples **and not to the world.** Judas thought of the Messiah setting up His earthly kingdom publicly. To Judas's question, Jesus restated His previous teaching (v. 23) that the full experience of His and His Father's love required obedience to His word. Then the Son and the Father would **make** their **abode** (their home) in the obedient follower. Jesus' self-disclosure would come through the gift of the Spirit and the abiding or friendship relationship explained further in chap. 15.

14:24. The Lord then declared the reverse of v. 23: **He who does not love Me does not keep My words**. The reference to Jesus' "words" (pl.) recalls His commandments (v. 21), and is now identified as **the word** [sg.] **which you hear**. One cannot claim obedience to Christ's word without keeping all of His individual commands and teachings, especially the instructions to love one another (13:34, 35).

14:25-26. These things I have spoken to you (14:25; 15:11; 16:1, 4, 25, 33) refers to the teachings Jesus gave while **abiding with** the apostles in the upper room. Jesus also promised (v. 26) that **the Holy Spirit** would **teach** the apostles (including Paul) **all things** (the rest of the NT). "Helper" (Gk. masculine) and "He" (Gk. masculine) suggest the Spirit is a person. The Spirit would guide the memory (**bring to your remembrance all that I said**) of the apostles as they wrote down the teachings of Christ (cf. 2:17-22; 12:16; 20:9). "I have spoken to you" and "bring to remembrance all that I said" limit the specific promise of this verse to the apostles. The result is the completeness and inerrancy of the NT record of Jesus.

14:27-28. Jesus pledged to give the disciples His **peace**, far superior to the deficient and fleeting peace the **world gives**. The disciples are again informed of the Lord's departure and promised return (v. 28). The disciples should **have rejoiced because** Jesus was going **to the Father**, instead of selfishly desiring that He stay. In their essence and nature, Christ and the Father are equal (10:30) while also being distinct Persons. But in Christ's incarnation and humanity, **the Father is greater than** the Son in function, not in possessing a superior essence. Both the Father and the Son are equally divine, though distinct in their personhood. But **the Father is greater than** the Son from the standpoint that Jesus submitted to and obeyed the Father, and came to do His will. In this Christ submitted fully to Him.

14:29-31. Christ had predicted His death and resurrection (13:31-32) **so that when it** happened, the disciples would **believe**. Fulfilled prophecy builds faith. Satan, **the ruler of the world**, holds control over the minds and hearts of the unbelievers (8:44; cf. Lk 4:6; Eph 2:2; 6:11-12; 1Jn 5:19). Although believers have divine protection (Jn 17:15), they are tempted by Satan (2Co 2:11; Eph 4:7; 1Pt 5:8). But the Devil was defeated at the cross and will ultimately be destroyed (see the comment on 12:31). Jesus said he was soon **coming** (cf. 12:31; 16:11), i.e., in Judas (cf. 13:27), in the garden to betray Him. As the sinless Messiah (8:46; Heb 4:15; 1Jn 3:5), Jesus could declare **he** [Satan] **has nothing in Me** (i.e., no sin through which to gain control). To the end that **the world may know that** Christ loves **the Father**, He did all things **exactly as the Father commanded** Him, including the crucifixion and all the events leading to it. With the command **let us go from here**, the disciples left the upper room. At 18:1, they would leave the city.

D. Abiding in the Vine (15:1-17)

15:1-2. Israel was God's unfaithful vine (Is 5:1-7; Ezk 17:5-10; Mt 21:33-41). But Jesus is the **true** and faithful **vine** and the **Father is the vinedresser**. See "Jesus' Seven 'I Am' Claims" at 6:35. Two views predominate the identification of the various elements of the extended metaphor.

First, both the fruitless branch and the fruitful branch refer to true believers. This view is supported by the phrase **every branch in Me**, which refers to genuine believers. Elsewhere in the NT, nonbelievers are never said to be "in Me (Christ)" in any sense of the term. "In Me" in John denotes ongoing fellowship and is not identical with "in Christ" in Paul's epistles. The verb translated **takes away** can just as easily be translated "lifts up," denoting the Vinedresser's action in stimulating growth in a fruitless branch (God helping a fruitless believer to produce fruit). In the viticulture of Israel, late fall was the season for removing dead branches (v. 6). The springtime (the time of the upper room message and Jesus' death) was the season to "lift up" fruitless branches from the ground to encourage productivity. The fruitful branch (i.e., a fruitful believer) receives pruning (divine discipline) so that it might be even more fruitful.

A second approach understands the metaphors this way. There are two different kinds of branches here, one that is fruitless, is taken away (*airo* is used frequently with this sense in John's gospel; cf. 2:16; 11:39, 41; 17:5; 20:1, 2, 13, 15), is thrown away, dries up, and is burned (v. 6). The fruitless branch represents one who, like Judas, is associated with Jesus (**in Me**), but who had no true connection with Him and thus no fruit. The other category is one that bears fruit, receives pruning, abides, and bears more fruit (vv. 2, 4-5), and represents the true believer. This view is supported by the common meaning of *airo*, and the contrast between the two kinds of branches. Under the first view, the two branches receive the same treatment, namely nurturing so that fruitfulness might result. But Jesus seems to intend a contrast between them, punctuated by the discarding and burning of the fruitless branch. Finally, in v. 16, Jesus chose the disciples to bear fruit, suggesting that if there is no fruit, then they were not chosen (in a salvific, elective sense) by Him, and thus would face judgment (burning).

The majority of scholars favor the second view, but both views share the common concern of the need to maintain intimacy with Christ (to abide in Him) and to produce fruit in keeping with that relationship.

15:3-5. "Clean" (*katharos*) is a related Greek word to "prune" (*kathairo*) in v. 2. **Because of the word which** Jesus had **spoken to** them that night, the eleven disciples were "cleansed" or "pruned" for sacrificial service (13:12-17). **Abide in Me** (v. 4) sets the necessary condition for fruit-bearing and the vital union in which Christ lives dynamically in the believer (cf. Eph 3:17). Just as a **branch cannot bear fruit** in and **of itself unless it abides in the vine, so neither can** believers bear fruit **unless** they **abide in** (remain intimate with) Christ.

15:5-6. Christ is **the vine**, the life source, and believers **are the branches**, the place where fruit is produced. Before Christ abides in the believer, the believer must **abide in** Christ. Followers of Jesus are not commanded to bear fruit but to abide. The believer who does not abide is **thrown away as a branch and dries up** (v. 6). According to the first view mentioned above under 15:1-2, the passage is parabolic, involving symbolism (cf. "*as* a branch"). So **fire** and **burned** are not references to hell. They symbolize (1) the uselessness of these branches (Mt 5:13); and/or (2) divine discipline now and reproof at the future evaluation of believers (1Co 3:13-15; 1Jn 2:28). According to the second view, the fruitless branches represent unbelievers who never abided in Christ, never produced fruit, and who are taken away from the vine and burned (i.e., will face God's eternal judgment in hell). But this second view is unlikely since in the analogy, there is no such thing as a branch that has never been joined to the vine. "Branches" that have never had life in the vine are non-existent and can never be "burned."

15:7-8. If . . . My words abide in you adds another qualification for abiding: the need to internalize Christ's teachings (cf. Col 3:16). Then believers can **ask whatever** they **wish**, and their prayer is answered because they will be praying according to God's will. Some believers lack fruit (vv. 2, 6) and are not "disciples" in the fullest sense (see comment on 8:31). When believers **bear much fruit** (v. 8), they **prove** to others that they are His **disciples**. Love is this proof (13:34-35; 15:12-13, 17).

15:9. Just as the Father has loved Me remarkably parallels the Son's love for the disciples with the Father's love for the Son. "Abiding in Me" is now defined as abiding **in My love** (cf. Jd 21; Rv 2:4). "Abiding" is a love relationship with Jesus.

15:10-11. The construction of this particular conditional statement (a third class condition using *ean*, "if," plus an aorist subjunctive verb, "keep") projects the action as hypothetical, as something to consider, without actually making a statement about the reality or degree of likelihood of its fulfillment. The idea is, "When people keep my commandments, they abide in My love." **My commandments** refers to the new teachings of Christ in the NT, especially the command to love sacrificially (cf. Mt 5:21-48; see comment on 13:34). Believers cannot have Christ abiding in them without having His joy abiding in them as well (v. 11). As they abide, their **joy may be made full**. But as abiding can be lost, so can joy.

15:12-13. The command to love requires a supernatural component to fulfill, requires faith, and is more a choice than an emotion (for a definition of "love," see the comments on 1Co 13:1-3). The priority for believers is to **love one another** first, since every believer is part of the family of God. Love may involve reproof (Gl 6:1-2). No love will ever be **greater** than when someone **lay**[s] **down his life for his friends**. Jesus was applying this principle foremost to His own death, but secondarily to all His followers (cf. 1Jn 3:16).

15:14-15. You are My friends parallels abiding in Christ since both result in intimacy (friendship). This friendship is conditioned on obedience as is demonstrated in the words **if you do what I command you**. Here the conditional statement indicates that if one is obedient to Jesus' commands, it is correct to infer that such a person is Jesus' friend. James informed us that Abraham's works (not merely his faith), flowing out of his righteous standing before God by faith, made him a friend of God (Jms 2:22-23). **No longer** marks a dispensational change from the OT where the believer was treated like a servant (cf. Gl 4:1-5). New revelation (**all things that I have heard from My Father**) disclosed in Christ's farewell teachings **have** now been **made known to** His disciples. See comments on 2:23 and 14:21.

15:16-17. I chose you does refer both to election to salvation for the eleven disciples and to Jesus' choice of them to be His apostles (Lk 6:13; Ac 1:2) and carry out the Great Commission (Mt 28:18-20). They were **appointed** to **go and bear fruit**—a love (cf. v. 17) that brings others to Christ (cf. Ac 2:41-47; 4:32-35). This **fruit would remain** because salvation is a permanent gift. **Whatever you ask** may specify asking for all that is necessary to win people to Christ. For **ask of the Father in my name**, see the comment on 14:13.

E. Ministering in the World (15:18–16:33)

15:18-19. Since the disciples are chosen to "go and bear fruit" (v. 17) in the world, they must be warned of the opposition they will face. The **world**, the evil spiritual order controlled by Satan (12:31; 14:30; 16:11), **hates** believers because they are identified with Jesus and **it has hated** Him **before it hated** any disciple of Christ. In saying this, Jesus called all believers to persecution with Him. The Eleven (and by application, all believers) have been chosen **out of the world** for a mission as Christ's apostles (v. 16; 6:70; 13:18; Lk 16:13; Ac 1:2, 24). The world's hatred is to be expected.

15:20-21. Jesus called the apostles to **remember the word** He had **said** to them about a **slave** not being **greater than his master** (13:16). The disciple will be treated like his master. Negatively, **if they persecuted** the Master, **they will also persecute** the disciple. Positively, **if they kept** the master's **word**, they will keep the disciple's word **also**, since the disciple will teach exactly what his master taught. Rejection of Christ's followers (v. 21) reveals that such people **do not know the One who sent** the Messiah.

15:22-23. If the Messiah **had not come** to the Jewish people and **spoken to them**, revealing the nature of God, they could have continued unchallenged to claim their faith in God. But with the appearance of Jesus, it became evident that they were guilty of the sin of rejecting God because they rejected Jesus. **They** now had **no excuse for their sin** of rejecting their Messiah. **He who** rejects and therefore **hates** Jesus (v. 23) unconsciously rejects and **hates** God the **Father also**.

15:24-25. If Jesus **had not done among them the works which no one else did, they would not have sin**. The latter phrase means the Jewish people would not have the specific sin of rejecting their Messiah. Because of Jesus' words (v. 22) and **works**, the nation's abandonment of their Messiah was inexcusable. The miracles of Jesus, **which no one else did**, were unmatched by even the prophets (cf. 7:31; 9:32). For **written in their Law** as the whole OT, see comment on 10:34. Jesus cited Ps 69 as messianically fulfilled (cf. 2:17). David, who is hated for no sin of his own, represents the sinless Messiah who is hated **WITHOUT A CAUSE**.

15:26-27. As the disciples went into the world to testify, the world would respond with hatred, not friendship (vv. 18-25). Jesus was now promising the assistance of the Spirit in their testimony. For **Helper**, see comment on 14:16. Jesus said that He **will send** the Spirit **from the Father**. The **Spirit of truth** (see comment on 14:17) is essential for witness. Jesus promised the Eleven (v. 27), **you will testify also, because you have been with Me from the beginning**. A condition for apostolic witness was having been with Jesus from the time when John the Baptist was still free and active in his ministry, a time that overlapped with Jesus briefly (Ac 1:21-22). In Acts, Christ continued His ministry through the presence of the Spirit's testimony in the Church.

16:1. These things I have spoken to you (see comment on 14:25) picks up the forewarnings about persecution (15:18-21). Without Christ's warnings, the disciples may not have been **kept from stumbling** (*skandalizo,* a failure of faith causing one to discontinue being a disciple; cf. 6:61).

16:2-3. Two kinds of persecution are predicted: being expelled **from the synagogue** (cf. 9:22; 12:42) and being martyred. Perpetrators will reach the height of deception when they kill Christ's disciples and **think that** they are **offering service to God** (cf. Ac 7:58-60). Such persecutions (**These things**, v. 3) arise from an ignorance of both the **Father** and the Son.

16:4-5. The coming time of persecution (v. 2) is now called **their** [the persecutors'] **hour**. The term implies the illusion of victory the persecutors will have over the disciples and is set in irony to Jesus' "hour" (see comments on 2:4 and 4:21), the ultimate victory of the cross. **At the beginning** of His ministry, the Lord was personally with His disciples and received the brunt of maltreatment. After His death and resurrection, Jesus was **going to** the Father (v. 5) and would no longer be on earth to help. **None of you asks Me** forms an apparent contradiction with 13:36 and 14:5, but there the questions of Peter and Thomas were superficial and not pursued.

16:6-7. Sorrow had **filled** the **heart** of Jesus' disciples over His departure. But His departure would be to their **advantage** (v. 7). The advantage may include: (1) without His departure, there is no death of Christ to cover sin; (2) the omnipresent ministry of the Spirit will be greater than the bodily presence of Christ; or (3) Christ's departure will usher in the ministries of the Spirit (worldwide mission, baptism of the Spirit, etc.) and result in a fully spiritual experience (cf. 7:37-39).

16:8-11. When the Spirit **comes** He will reside in believers. His ministry to **convict** [expose and prove wrong] **the world** will be mediated through them (Mt 5:13-14) and the NT Scriptures. The Spirit proves the world wrong concerning: (1) **sin** (v. 9). The Spirit will expose the world's guilt both for putting Jesus to death and for sin in general. This is necessary **because they do not believe in Me**. Unbelief is the primary sin of the world, and leads to all other sin; (2) **righteousness** (v. 10). The death and resurrection of Christ (**because I go to the Father**) proves the Savior's righteousness and establishes the world's false "religious" righteousness; (3) **judgment** (v. 11). On the cross **the ruler of this world has been judged** (see comment on 12:31). If the world's ruler has been judged, the world is also implicated in judgment.

16:12-13. Although Jesus desired to say **many more things** to the disciples, He refrained from revealing truths they could not **bear** or understand before the gift of the Spirit. The Spirit is subordinate to the Son as the Son is to the Father. So the Spirit **will not speak on His own initiative**. He speaks only what **He hears** from Christ (v. 13). The Spirit **will disclose** to the apostles **what is to come**. This could refer to prophecy (e.g., Christ reveals the book of Revelation; Rv 1:1) or to all NT truth.

16:14-15. The Spirit **will** always **glorify** the Son, not Himself. Ministries that overemphasize the Spirit more than Christ are inappropriate. The Spirit will also **take** the truth that belongs to Jesus and **disclose it to** the disciples. The three persons of the Trinity share truth equally. So, **all things that the Father has** belong to Christ (v. 15), and the Spirit **takes** from Christ and imparts truth to us through the apostles' writings (cf. 17:10).

16:16. In vv. 7-15, He taught that the Spirit would be their Advocate during His absence. Now in vv. 16-24, Jesus returned to the subject of the sorrow the disciples would have when He was gone (vv. 5-6). It was within hours (**a little while**; 13:33; 14:19) that Christ would die and the apostles would **no longer see** Him. Then **again a little while**, and they would **see** Jesus—a reference to the resurrection, not the second coming.

16:17-18. Some of His disciples were confused about His remark (v. 16) that in **a little while** they would **not see** Him, but then **again a little while** they would see Him. They were also puzzled about His earlier statement that He was soon to **go to the Father** (v. 10; cf. 14:2-3, 28). **So they were saying** (v. 18) suggests a private discussion ensued and that Jesus' teachings on that night were not an uninterrupted sermon.

16:19-20. Jesus knew hints at the Lord's supernatural knowledge (2:24-25; 13:1, 11; 19:28) as is implied in the rhetorical question that follows, **Are you deliberating together about this ...?** In v. 20, Jesus answered His own question. **Truly, truly** (see comment on 1:51) introduced a seriousness in Jesus' announcement. In drastic contrast to the disciples' coming sorrow over Jesus' upcoming crucifixion (v. 20), the **world will rejoice** with a sinful joy. This corrupt joy reveals the depravity of the human heart. But the **grief** of the Eleven will be short-lived and **will be turned into** long-lasting **joy** by the resurrection.

16:21-22. A short parable that the Lord gave illustrated the emotional changes that would come to the disciples. The OT pictured the age that leads to the Messiah (both first and second coming) as the pain of a **woman** who **is in labor**. The words **her hour has come** parallel Jesus' statements about His "hour" (2:4; 13:1). Like a woman's **joy** when her **child has been born**, the disciples' **heart**[s] **will rejoice** at Messiah's resurrection (v. 22). That **no one will take your joy away** points to the indisputable evidence that will confirm the Lord's resurrection.

16:23-24. In that day you will not question Me looks to the time after the resurrection when Jesus' death will be understood. For **ask the Father for anything in My name**, see the comment on 14:13. **Until now** (v. 24) designates the NT era when believers pray in Jesus' name. Prayer is not restricted to praise or thanksgiving. Jesus repeatedly taught that believers can **ask** and they will **receive** (cf. Mt 7:7-8). Answered prayer results in **joy** being **made full**.

16:25-28. Coherent prayers could not be offered in Jesus' name (v. 24) if the disciples lacked understanding. Jesus had been speaking **in figurative language** (e.g., the woman in labor, v. 22; the vine and branches, 15:1-8). However, after the resurrection (**an hour is coming**), He would **tell** them **plainly of the Father** (cf. Lk 24:27; Ac 1:3). For the sixth time that evening (v. 26), Jesus taught the disciples to **ask in My name** (Jn 14:13-14; 15:16; 16:23-24, 26; see the comment on 14:13). Jesus did not need to **request of the Father on** the disciples' **behalf**. The Father was already well disposed toward them (v. 26; **the Father Himself loves you**). God loves everyone (3:16). But here the Father's love is dependent on the believer's love for Him (**because you have loved Me**). This expresses the deeper intimacy that the Father has with obedient believers (see comment on

14:21-22). Just as our love for our enemies (Mt 5:44) will differ from our love for an obedient child, so the Father has a special love for the believer. Jesus summarized His entire mission (v. 28) by describing His divine origin (**I came forth from the Father**), His incarnation (**and have come into the world**), His death and resurrection (**I am leaving the world again**), and His ascension (**and going to the Father**).

16:29-30. Jesus spoke of a future day when His words would become clear (v. 25). How little the disciples truly understood will be exposed in the coming hours when they would all fall away (v. 31; Mk 14:27, 50). Yet they claimed, **Lo** [behold, look]**, now you are speaking plainly . . . Now we know . . . we believe that You came from God** (v. 30). The disciples thought the time for clear understanding had just begun, and they confessed their "confident" faith in Jesus' heavenly origin. But their faith was soon to be shaken. Jesus needed to confront their overconfidence.

16:31-33. Christ recognized the disciples' self-assurance in His question **Do you now believe?** Instead of their acting in faith (v. 32), He predicted that they would all **be scattered** in fear (cf. Zch 13:7; Mt 26:31) and would **leave** Him **alone** to be arrested and crucified without human support. Only the **Father** would be **with** Him. Jesus' words that evening (**in Me you may have peace**, v. 33) would lead the disciples to peace when they returned to abiding in Him (Jn 15:1-11). This peace will be possible despite future **tribulation**. Christ's promise **I have overcome the world** will lead the disciples to **take courage**. The final words of Jesus to His disciples end on a note of victory (cf. Rm 8:37-38; 1Co 15:54-57).

F. Praying for All Believers (17:1-26)

The verses of chap. 17 comprise the longest prayer of Jesus in Scripture, sometimes called Christ's High Priestly Prayer. Jesus first prayed for Himself (vv. 1-5), then for his disciples (vv. 6-19), and last for all believers (vv. 20-26).

17:1-3. Jesus began His prayer by **lifting up His eyes to heaven**, a common Jewish custom suggesting His confidence in the Father (cf. 11:41; Mk 7:34). His first request was for the Father to **glorify** His Son (see comment on 13:31). This was not self-seeking since its purpose was **that the Son may glorify** the Father in return. Jesus received delegated **authority over** all people (v. 2), including authority to **give eternal life** and to judge (5:27). For **all whom You have given Him,** see vv. 6, 9, 24 and comments on 6:37, 39. **Eternal life** is defined as coming (by faith) to **know** personally both **the only true God, and Jesus Christ**.

17:4-5. Jesus **glorified** God in that He **accomplished the work** (the earthly ministry) God gave Him **to do**. The verb "glorify" in these verses means "to manifest the splendid greatness of another," in this case God and Christ. This work was finalized on the cross when Jesus cried, "It is finished" (19:30). The request for the Father to glorify the Son (v. 1) is repeated in v. 5. Since this glory will be equal to **the glory** that Jesus **had with** God **before the world was** created (cf. 1:1-3), Jesus' resurrection and ascension (exaltation) are included in the "work." "Glory" and "glorify" in vv. 1-5 carry slightly different nuances. (1) The Son is to be glorified in His "hour," i.e., the cross and resurrection (v. 1). (2) The cross/resurrection would glorify the Father in that it would complete the Son's authority to give eternal life to all who believe (v. 2). (3) The Son has glorified the Father on earth by His works (v. 4). (4) The Son will be glorified in heaven together with the Father in the ascension and eternity future (v. 17:5a). (5) The future glory of the Son will equal the glory He had with the Father in eternity past (17:5b).

17:6-8. To manifest God's **name** means to reveal His character and attributes. The disciples (and all believers) are given as a gift from the Father to the Son (cf. v. 2) and spiritually taken **out of the world**. This expresses the divine side of salvation. The disciples also responded by faith (**they have kept Your word**), the human side. Their faith included the understanding that **everything** the Father had **given** the Son (v. 7) originally belonged to the Father. Jesus' additional words underscored the disciples' faith (v. 8): **they received . . . and truly understood . . . and they believed**.

17:9-11. In vv. 9-11, Jesus prayed for His disciples. **I ask on their behalf** points primarily to the Eleven (cf. vv. 6, 8). What belonged to the Father is now in the omnipotent care of the Son (**those whom You have given Me**; cf. v. 2). The shared divine status of the Father and the Son is conveyed in the statement **all things that are Mine are Yours, and Yours are Mine** (v. 10). After Jesus' departure, the unity of the apostles would be under attack. So Jesus prayed, **keep them in Your name** (v. 11). A person's name represented his character. For the Father to "keep" the apostles in His name meant that He would maintain among them the whole truth His Son had revealed about the Father (cf.

v. 6). The outcome would be a complete unity among the Eleven (**that they may be one**). This unity among the apostles is modeled on the impeccable unity of the Father and the Son (**even as We are**), and evidences itself in the harmony of NT Scriptures.

17:12-13. Your name which You have given Me is another of Christ's astounding claims. The name given to Jesus is "I AM" (see comment on 8:24, 58). By identifying Himself as "I AM," Jesus revealed Himself with the Father's own name. Like the term "sons of light" (12:36), **son of perdition** means "belonging to" destruction, not predestined to hell. **That the Scripture would be fulfilled** alludes to Ps 41:9 (cf. Jn 13:18). Judas fulfilled at least three OT prophecies (Ps 69:25; 109:8; cf. Ac 1:20). In v. 12, Jesus had spoken of the time He "was with them" on earth. **But now I come to You** (v. 13) is set in contrast to v. 12. The statement is not a reference to Jesus' coming to the Father in prayer but to His future ascension (vv. 11, 12).

17:14-16. The communication to the disciples is now complete (**I have given them Your word**). Jesus reminded the Father that **the world has hated** His disciples because of their identity with their Savior. But instead of asking the Father to **take them out of the world** (v. 15), Christ asked Him to **keep them from the evil one** (vv. 11, 15). This phrase could be translated, "keep them from evil." But Johannine usage strongly favors "evil *one*," i.e., Satan (1Jn 2:13, 14; 3:12; 5:18, 19). Paul also mentioned this protection (1Co 10:13; 2Co 12:9). Verse 16 repeats v. 14b, showing that our new relationship to Christ is the foundation for His request for our protection. For more on v. 15a and its implications for Rv 3:10, see the comment on Rv 3:10.

17:17. Sanctify means to "set apart" for God's use which, according to v. 18, is the mission to the world. All sin involves being deceived in some regard. Sanctification or growth in holiness (Rm 6:22; 1Th 4:3) includes the process of replacing lies with truth. God's **word is** the source of this **truth**. Scripture is not just "true," as if there were another standard to which the Bible rightly conforms. All Scripture is "God-breathed" (see comment on 2Tm 3:16) and therefore is the source of truth, just as Jesus is truth (14:6).

17:18-19. Sanctification (v. 17) is not isolation from but mission to the world. Just as the Father **sent** Christ **into the world**, so too Christ has sent His disciples **into the world** (cf. 15:6; Mt 28:18-20). Jesus prayed, **For their sakes I sanctify Myself**, signifying how He has set apart Himself to the Father's will (i.e., to go to the cross in fulfillment of Jesus' mission). There is nothing commanded of the Christian, even being **sanctified in truth**, that Christ has not first modeled.

17:20-21. Christ prayed for **those also who** would **believe in** Him **through** the disciples' **word**—their preaching and writing of Scripture. His prayer was specifically for the unity of all believers (**that they may all be one**; v. 21; cf. v. 11). The prayer is answered foremost through Spirit baptism in which every believer is placed into the one body of Christ (cf. 10:16; 1Co 12:13; Rm 12:5; Gl 3:28; Eph 4:4). Elsewhere believers are commanded to live out this integral unity (13:34-35; Rm 12:16; 1Co 1:10).

17:22-23. Jesus prayed for a unity parallel to that between the Father and the Son (**that they may be one, just as We are one**). The full answer to Jesus' prayer will not come until heaven, when all believers are **perfected in unity** (v. 23). But to maintain that His prayer has not been answered is to suggest that He has failed in His mission or that His prayer was not in accordance with the Father's sovereign will. It is better to argue that there is fundamental unity among all believers in the key points of the Christian faith (for example, the authority of Scripture; salvation by grace through faith; the deity of Christ; the triunity of God; the resurrection of Christ, and the second coming), while the details are clearly disputed. The problem arises, however, when believers become divisive about the secondary issues. In order to reach **the world**, Christians are to practice their positional unity in Christ (see comments on vv. 11, 21). There is no more shocking truth about believers than that God has **loved them even as** He has **loved** His own Son.

17:24. For the fifth time, Jesus addressed God as **Father**. For **they . . . whom You have given Me** (cf. v. 2). As a direct result of Jesus' prayer, every believer will **be with** Christ in heaven **where** He will be (cf. 14:2-3).

17:25-26. Despite knowing the unjust treatment ahead, Jesus called God loving (v. 24) and **righteous**. This came about only because Jesus had **known** the Father. That Jesus **will make** [future tense] the Father **known** (v. 26) points to the role of the Holy Spirit after Pentecost (14:26; 16:13-14). The result will be that love will dominate the lives of the disciples (**the love with which You loved Me may be in them**) and Christ will abide **in them** (cf. 15:1-11).

IV. Passion Ministry: Sacrificial Nature of Jesus' Death (18:1–20:31)

So as not to distract from his presentation of Jesus' matchless resolve as the Son of God to go to the cross, John left out details of Jesus' agony in Gethsemane (for which see the comments on Mt 26:30-46; Mk 14:26-42; Lk 22:39-46). He also included more detail concerning the trial before Pilate. For example, Jesus and Pilate dialog in John (Jn 18:33-38; 19:9-11), but in the Synoptics Jesus is portrayed as silent (Mt 27:14; Mk 15:5; Lk 23:9). John also cited the fulfillment of several messianic prophecies (Jn 19:24, 28, 36, 37).

A. Betrayal and Arrest (18:1-11)

18:1. John's words **He went forth with His disciples** are best understood as their departure from Jerusalem, not from the upper room (cf. 14:31). They proceeded across the **ravine of the Kidron** on the east side of Jerusalem, and to a **garden** or grove of olive trees called Gethsemane (cf. the comments on Mt 26:36; Mk 14:32), which means "olive press," at the foot of the Mount of Olives. The preincarnate Christ entered the garden of Eden to fellowship with people (Gn 3:8). Now he entered a garden leading to His death and resurrection (Jn 19:41; 20:15) so as to restore this lost fellowship.

18:2-3. Judas easily found the garden because he **knew the place**. In fact, **Jesus had often met there with His disciples**, perhaps for prayer. The Gentile **Roman cohort** (v. 3) was a detachment of 600 men, but the full number may not have been deployed. Contrary to religious custom, Jewish **officers** willingly joined the Gentile soldiers (see also Mt 26:51). The **lanterns and torches** were for the nighttime search, and the **weapons** were in anticipation of serious resistance.

18:4-6. Jesus, even though He knew **all the things that were coming upon** Him, did not retreat from the impending dangers. Instead, He **went forth** to meet His enemies. By asking **Whom do you seek?** and gaining the reply **Jesus the Nazarene** (v. 5), Christ effectively prepared for His disciples' release. His reply **I am He** ("He" is not in the Gk.) recalls Jesus' use of the same term to claim deity (see comments on 4:26; 6:35; 8:58). Precisely **when He said to them, I am He** (v. 6), His opponents **fell to the ground**. The collapse of the soldiers came in reaction to a small taste of the divine power of Jesus. If He had chosen to do so, He could have exercised this divine power sufficiently to escape His arrest and crucifixion. But he withheld this power and thereby demonstrated that He was going to the cross willingly (10:17-18).

18:7-9. A second time, Jesus asked, **Whom do you seek?** leading to the second **I am He** testimony from Jesus (vv. 5, 8) and a third by John (v. 6). With these words, Jesus both interceded for His disciples (cf. His prayer in chap. 17) and acted as their substitute (cf. His death in chap. 19). Since they sought only "Jesus the Nazarene," He could request, **So if you seek Me, let these go their way** (v. 8). Verse 8 indicates that it was Jesus' wish that the disciples *not* stay with Him throughout His ordeal, so that their abandonment of Him was not the moral or spiritual failure it is sometimes made out to be. The denial of Peter, however, was inappropriate. The phrase **to fulfill the word** (v. 9) is used by the author elsewhere of OT Scripture (12:38; 13:18; 15:25; 19:24, 36). But here Jesus' words spoken earlier (17:12) are given a fulfillment, placing Jesus' words on a level with Scripture.

18:10-11. True to his character revealed elsewhere (13:8, 37; 21:7; Mt 16:22), Peter impulsively drew his short sword (*machaira*), probably hidden under his clothes, and **struck the high priest's slave**, cutting **off his right ear**. These details, including John's knowledge that **the slave's name was Malchus**, suggest John personally knew the high priest and his slave (cf. v. 15). Contrary to Peter's misunderstanding (v. 11), Jesus must drink **the cup which the Father** had given Him (a metaphor for His crucifixion).

B. Interrogation and Trial (18:12–19:16)

18:12-14. The first phase of the six-phase trial of Jesus took place at night. Jesus was **bound** and led **to Annas first** (v. 13). Except for Peter and John, the disciples had all scattered (16:32; Mt 25:56). Annas reigned as high priest from AD 6–15. But he continued to influence the subsequent high priests. **Caiaphas**, his son-in-law, **was high priest** from AD 18–36. **That year** refers to the prophesied year of Christ's death (Dn 9:24-26). Since Caiaphas foresaw the prudence of **one man** dying **on behalf of the people** (v. 14; cf. 11:49-52), God sovereignly placed him in the position of high priest (cf. Rm 13:1) during the year foreordained for Christ's death.

18:15-16. In the trial narrative, only two disciples are mentioned: **Peter** and **another disciple**—probably John. He was **known to the high priest** (mentioned twice; vv. 15, 16), Annas. John's father, Zebedee, seemed to have been affluent (e.g., he had servants, Mk 1:20). This may have brought John into contact with Annas and

Caiaphas since they were also wealthy. So John freely **entered with Jesus into the court of** Annas, but had to negotiate for Peter's admittance (v. 16).

18:17-18. Peter's first temptation to deny Christ came through the least likely source—a **slave-girl**. She asked if Peter was one of Jesus' **disciples**. Her question anticipated a negative answer (**You are not . . . are you?**) and tempted Peter all the more to deny it. Peter feared being identified as a disciple of Jesus in front of **the slaves and the officers** there (v. 18). John's comment that **it was cold** marks out both the physical and the spiritual climate.

18:19-21. The interrogation before **the high priest**, Annas, was an unofficial pretrial. In hopes of finding blame, Annas questioned **Jesus about His disciples** to discern if there were sufficient numbers for a charge of insurrection. He also questioned Him **about His teaching** in hopes of finding grounds for blasphemy. Jesus replied that He had no secret plans or hidden teachings. With the words **I spoke nothing in secret** (v. 20), Jesus identified Himself with the God of the OT (Is 45:19; 48:16). Additionally (v. 21), the information about His teachings that Annas sought was readily available from those who had **heard** what Jesus taught.

18:22-24. Besides the illegal nature of the preliminary investigation, **one of the officers standing nearby** Annas unjustly **struck Jesus**. The officer's actions and his question **Is that the way You answer the high priest?** show his obsequious respect for the high priest. Jesus responded by calling for witnesses as the law required (8:17; Dt 17:6; 19:15) to **testify of the wrong** He had allegedly done. With this point, John wrote (v. 24) that **Annas sent** Jesus still **bound to Caiaphas the high priest**. Both Annas and Caiaphas are called high priest in John (vv. 13, 15, 16, 22, 24, 26; cf. Lk 3:2) even though Annas no longer had legal authority (see vv. 13-14).

18:25-27. Annas was fearful of the threat posed by the disciples, while ironically **Peter** was nearby denying Christ. According to the Synoptics, **they said to him** included the servant girl who kept the door (v. 17; Mk 14:69), another servant girl (Mt 26:71), and another unidentified person (Lk 22:58). Others may have joined in the question **You are not also one of His disciples, are you?** For a second time, Peter denied Christ. When **a relative of the one whose ear Peter cut off** was sure he saw Peter in the garden with Jesus, **Peter then denied it** a third time. Just then a **rooster crowed**, fulfilling Jesus' earlier prophecy (Jn 13:38). Jesus would have six phases in His trial and would be faithful in each; Peter had three tests and failed in each.

18:28-29. The Jewish leaders led Jesus to the **Praetorium** (the governor's palace) **early** in the morning. **They themselves** went into the courtyard but not into the palace **so that they would not be** ceremonially **defiled**. While their bodies were not defiled, their hearts were. The Passover meal itself was now ended (13:1-2). The words **eat the Passover** do not refer to the actual Passover meal itself, which Jesus and all the Jewish people had already consumed. "Passover" can include not only the memorial meal, but also the week of celebration that followed it called "the Feast of Unleavened Bread" (see Nm 28:16-19; Lk 22:1). The religious leaders would not enter Pilate's residence so as to avoid making themselves ritually unclean. By keeping themselves ritually clean they could celebrate and serve during the Feast of Unleavened Bread, which followed the Passover celebration. Some maintain that Jesus had a meal *before* the Passover meal, but that is not the case. **Pilate**, governor of Judea in AD 26–36, **went out to** the Jewish leaders to receive their charges against Christ. For more on Pilate, see the comments on Mt 27:1-2.

18:30-32. Since the Jewish leaders hated Pilate for his cruelty, they responded contemptuously, evading a direct answer to Pilate's request for official charges against Christ. If the Jewish leaders charged Jesus with blasphemy (cf. 10:33, 36), Pilate would be unconcerned. His reply showed this to be true (v. 31): **judge Him** yourself **according to your law**. But the Sanhedrin had no power to put Jesus to death without official Roman approval. If the Jewish leadership put Him to death themselves, He would be stoned to death according to the law of Moses (Lv 24:16). This act would be considered mob action and would be illegal under Roman law. But in order **to fulfill** Jesus' own prophecy (v. 32; cf. 3:14; 8:28; 12:32, 33) **signifying by what kind of death He was about to die**, Jesus had to be crucified under Roman jurisprudence.

18:33-34. Pilate likely had been informed that Jesus claimed to be the King of Jews. If this were political, the emperor would hold Pilate responsible. So he reentered **the Praetorium, and** asked **Jesus** directly, **Are You the King of the Jews?** If Pilate's question of "king" was from his own political vantage point (**Are you saying this on your own initiative . . .?**, v. 34), Jesus' answer would be "No." But if the Jews were the source of the question, Jesus indeed was the King of the Jews.

18:35-37. Ultimately, Pilate was uninterested in Jewish debates about their "king." **The chief priests** had **delivered** Jesus to him. So it was necessary for him to ask Jesus **what** He had **done** to receive these charges. This afforded Christ the opportunity to define His **kingdom** (v. 36). Its origin and principles were **not of this** evil **world** system (*kosmos*). Otherwise, His **servants would be** leading an insurrection. Pilate replied (v. 37), **So You are a king?** The governor was looking for the truth and Jesus confirmed it—He was a king. The reason He came to earth was **to testify to the truth**. All those under the influence of **truth** would respond to Jesus' teaching.

18:38-40. Overlooking Jesus, the Truth (14:6), Pilate asked sarcastically, **What is truth?** and **went out again to the Jews**. **What is truth?** is typically viewed as a profound theological or philosophical question, but Pilate was simply asking a rhetorical question about the truth related to the case against Jesus, and could be translated, "What is the truth?" Although he now told them, **I find no guilt in Him** (the first of three times; cf. 19:4, 6), he would soon sidestep the truth about Christ's innocence. For a Roman governor's role in such a case, see the comments on Mt 27:11-14. Pilate is sometimes accused of being indecisive because he went back and forth between Jesus and the religious leaders several times. That is not the case. He was simply doing his job of gathering facts to help him render a verdict. There is yet no clear extrabiblical evidence for the **custom** of pardon at the **Passover** (v. 39; but see *m. Pesach* 8:6, and the comments on Mt 27:15-23). But the Synoptics support that this was Pilate's practice (Mt 27:15; Mk 15:6). **Barabbas** (v. 40) was a known insurrectionist and murderer (Mk 15:7; Lk 23:19). The word for **robber** can also mean "revolutionary" (NET, HCSB). Barabbas, Aramaic for "son of abbey (father)," was released while Jesus, the true Son of the Father, was crucified.

19:1-3. In hopes of gaining the crowd's sympathy and Jesus' release, **Pilate** ordered that Jesus be **scourged**, unknowingly fulfilling messianic prophecy (cf. Is 50:6; 53:5). A Roman whip was made by attaching pieces of metal to three leather straps. Scourging could repeatedly rip the victim's flesh, causing death. A **crown of thorns** (v. 2) was placed on Jesus' **head**, and **a purple robe** was thrown on Him, mocking His claim to be the King of the Jews. With the injurious thorns and the **slaps in the face** (v. 3), Jesus' face would have been bloody and disfigured (cf. Is 52:14; 53:2, 3).

19:4-5. For the second time (cf. 18:38), Pilate announced that he had found **no guilt in** Christ. Bringing Jesus out **wearing the crown of thorns and the purple robe** (v. 5) was Pilate's desperate plan to humiliate Jesus and, he hoped, to change the crowd's intentions. Pilate's proclamation **Behold, the Man!** mocked Jesus as a pathetic representation of mankind. But in recording this statement, John hoped that all readers would look carefully at (behold) the One who has taken on human flesh (1:9, 14) and has represented mankind in His sacrificial death.

19:6-7. Undeterred, the Jewish authorities callously **cried out**, **Crucify** Him, **crucify** Him! For the third time (cf. 18:38; 19:4) Pilate insisted, **I find no guilt in Him**. Pilate's third reiteration of Jesus' innocence indicates one of the Fourth Gospel's emphases—that Jesus was innocent of the charges levied against Him. The Romans permitted its conquered provinces to exercise their own religious laws. So the Jewish leaders (v. 7) insisted on Jesus' death because He violated their law against blasphemy (Lv 24:16) by making **Himself out to be the Son of God** in equality with God (cf. 5:18), and Pilate crucified Jesus because he wanted to get out from under the pressure of the Jewish leaders and to save his own position. Yet it was Pilate's responsibility to ensure justice in this case, and his opinion that he found **no guilt in Him** (v. 6) obligated him to release Jesus (see also the comments on 19:14-16).

19:8-9. Driven by pagan Roman beliefs (cf. Ac 14:11), Pilate became **even more afraid** when he heard that Jesus might be a god come to earth. His wife's fearful dream added to his worries (cf. Mt 27:19). He again took Jesus **into the Praetorium** (v. 9; the Fortress of Antonia at the northwest corner of the Temple Mount) and asked him privately, **Where are You from?** The governor knew his earthly origin was Galilee (Lk 23:6-7). Was He a god come from heaven? **Jesus gave him no answer**, fulfilling messianic prophecy (Is 53:7).

19:10-12. Aggravated by Jesus' silence, Pilate boastfully threatened, **Do You not know that . . . I have authority to crucify You?** But Pilate (v. 11) had **no** earthly **authority** to sentence Jesus to crucifixion **unless it had been given** to him **from above** (cf. Pr 8:15; Rm 13:1). Pilate wished to release Jesus. **For this reason**, his guilt was less than the one **who delivered** Jesus to Pilate. The reference is to the powerful high priest, Caiaphas, who sent Jesus to Pilate to be condemned (Jn 18:30, 35). Therefore, the high priest had **the greater sin** because the greater the knowledge, the greater the culpability. Nevertheless, greater sin indicates lesser sin. It is incorrect to exonerate Pilate and not include him among those guilty for the death of Jesus (cf. Ac 4:27-28). Finally, the crowd confronted Pilate's inclination to release Jesus because he saw no guilt in Him (v. 12). **If you release this Man, you are no friend of Caesar**.

19:13. To make the proceedings official, Pilate **sat down on the judgment seat**, a raised platform for rendering judicial decisions. The platform was located at **The** Stone **Pavement** (cf. ESV, NIV). Now at the "Stone Pathway," many will stumble over the Messiah, the "stone of stumbling" (Is 8:14; Rm 9:33; 1Pt 2:8).

19:14-16. The **day of preparation for the Passover** means the day before the Sabbath (Friday) of Passover week (cf. 19:31), and the Sabbath started at sundown. Fridays were called " preparation day," for the Jewish people would use Friday before sundown to prepare for the Sabbath. John noted that **it was** now **about the sixth hour** (noon). At the time the Lamb of God (cf. 1:29) was about to be sacrificed, Jewish tradition suggests the priests began to slaughter the Passover lambs in the temple. During the time of Jesus' ministry, Jewish people calculated Nissan 14, the date of the Passover (Lv 23:5), in two different ways. Jesus, His disciples, and the Pharisees followed the Galileans method in which the day was from sunrise to sunrise.

In the year of Jesus' crucifixion, Nissan 14 began for them on Thursday morning, and they celebrated the Passover meal early Thursday evening. The Sadducees calculated the day from sunset to sunset. Nissan 14 began at Thursday's sunset, and the Passover lamb was sacrificed Friday afternoon. Their Passover meal was eaten before the sunset that evening. The Synoptics are written with the first method in view; John was written from the viewpoint of the second method. This explains why Jesus celebrated the Passover on Thursday evening (Jn 13:1-2), but He was crucified Friday while the Passover lamb was being slain in the temple in anticipation of the Passover meal.

To Pilate's announcement **Behold, your King!** John recorded three stark replies to take Christ **away** and **crucify Him** (v. 15). Pilate mocked them in return. **Shall I crucify your King?** The same Jews who accused Jesus of blasphemy, now themselves blasphemed, claiming **Caesar** to be their only king. Pilate succumbed to the Jewish leaders' demand (v. 16) and the crucifixion began. Pilate's action was completely irresponsible. It was his job as governor to ensure that justice prevailed, but he abdicated his duty and allowed the Roman soldiers under his authority to crucify Jesus (see v. 23) to appease the Jewish leaders.

C. Crucifixion and Burial (19:17-42)

19:17-18. As was traditional for Roman crucifixions, Jesus carried **His own cross** (i.e., the crossbeam). The Synoptics record that Simon of Cyrene (a city in northeastern Africa) was soon conscripted to carry Jesus' cross for Him (Mt 27:32; Mk 15:21; Lk 23:26). The destination was **called the Place of a Skull**. "Calvary" derives from the Latin word *calvaria* for skull. Today, the pristine garden called Gordon's Calvary (also known as the "Garden Tomb") outside the old city of Jerusalem is often identified as the location of Jesus' crucifixion and tomb. But there is considerable historical and archeological evidence for locating Calvary at the Church of the Holy Sepulcher, and virtually none for the Garden Tomb. To add to the insult against Jesus, **two other men** (v. 18), both criminals (Lk 23:33), were crucified on **either side** of Jesus. One of them came to faith (Lk 23:39-43).

19:19-22. Pilate also wrote an inscription that was intended to ridicule the Jewish people and Jesus but inadvertently publicized the truth: **JESUS THE NAZARENE, THE KING OF THE JEWS**. Numerous **Jews** (v. 20) passing by **read this inscription**. This was possible because **the place where Jesus was crucified was** on a public roadway **near the city**. This testimony of Jesus' identity was far-reaching since it was written in the three principal languages (**Hebrew** or Aramaic, **Latin**, and **Greek**) read by Jews and Romans (Gentiles). The Jewish leadership (v. 21) vehemently objected to Pilate's wording, insisting that he write only **that He said, I am King of the Jews**. This protest aroused Pilate's obstinacy. His response (v. 22), **What I have written I have written**, means in modern terms "Take it or leave it!"

19:23-25a. The **soldiers** who **had crucified Jesus** divided His **outer garments and made four parts, a part to every soldier**. Apparently four soldiers carried out the crucifixion—a detail John alone recorded. The **tunic** or undergarment, however, was **seamless, woven in one piece**. Since the OT high priest may have worn a seamless garment (Josephus, *Ant.* 3.161-62), some have seen this as symbolic of Christ's high priestly ministry on the cross. The soldiers chose to divide Jesus' clothing and keep the seamless garment as one piece and **cast lots for it** instead (v. 24). As such, they unwittingly fulfilled two statements in Ps 22:18, **THEY DIVIDED . . . THEY CAST LOTS.**

19:25b-27. Four women, not three, were **standing by the cross**. It is unlikely that **His mother's sister** is to be identified with **Mary the wife of Clopas**, making Mary the name of both the mother of Jesus and her sister. For **Mary Magdalene**, see comments on 20:1; Lk 8:2. The sister of Jesus' mother may be the same as "the mother of the sons of Zebedee" in Mt 27:56, making Jesus' mother John's aunt. If so, it is quite natural for Jesus to instruct John, **the disciple whom He loved** (v. 26; see Introduction: Author), to care for His mother. For **Woman** as a polite address, see 2:4. John obeyed the Lord's instructions immediately (**from that hour**, v. 27).

19:28-30. Only John recorded that **to fulfill the Scripture**, Jesus cried, **I am thirsty**. He was physically thirsty (Pss 22:15; 69:21). Profuse bleeding, like profuse perspiration, dehydrates the body and causes intense thirst. **Hyssop** (v. 29) was used in the Passover (Ex 12:22) to spread the blood of the lambs on the doorposts, and may underscore Jesus as the true Passover Lamb. Jesus had earlier refused a pain-killing wine-myrrh mixture (cf. Mk 15:23; but see also the comments on Mt 27:33-37), but now took the simple **sour wine** (v. 30). His final announcement in John, **It is finished!** confirmed that the atonement had now been completed. Since He Himself **gave up His spirit**, Christ fulfilled His prophecy that no one would take His life from Him (Jn 10:11, 15, 17, 18).

19:31. For the **day of preparation**, see comment on 19:14. Crucifixion was often prolonged for days as the crucified person excruciatingly pushed upward on his nailed feet to relieve his outstretched arms and prevent asphyxiation. Breaking the **legs** of the victim hastened death.

19:32-34. That the soldiers **broke the legs** of the two men who were **crucified** along with Jesus sets in contrast Christ's unique death. The soldiers observed (v. 33) that Christ **was already dead**, and therefore did not need to **break His legs** to hasten His death. To be absolutely sure, **one of the soldiers pierced His side with a spear** (v. 34). The **blood and water** that **came out** indicated that Jesus' heart no longer functioned. John may have included these details for symbolic purposes too. The water flowing from Christ's side symbolized the promise of the Spirit prophesied in 7:37-39, and the blood recalled the sacrifice of the Passover lamb. According to later rabbinic tradition (see *m. Pesahim* 5:3, 5), blood from a sacrificed animal was required to run freely from its body at the time of death. Another tradition required the priest to pierce the heart of the animal and thereby cause it to bleed to death (see *m. Tamid* 4:2; for these references, see NET note on Jn 19:34). It is possible that what John recorded here reflects an early form of these traditions.

19:35-37. At the climax of the death of Christ, John interjected a personal testimony to the **truth** of his report (cf. 20:31-32). The readers are addressed with the words **so that you** [emphatic in Greek] **also may believe**. As further proof of the truth of Christ's death, John cited the fulfillment of two messianic prophecies (v. 36). First, Scripture predicted that the Messiah's bones would not be **BROKEN** (Ps 34:20), as typified in the Passover lamb (Ex 12:46; Nm 9:12). Second (v. 37), Israel will one day call for the Messiah to return to them and they will see Him as the One who was pierced. Thus, Zch 12:10 indicates that the Messiah, at His first coming, would be pierced. But at His second coming, **THEY SHALL LOOK ON HIM** in faith **WHOM THEY PIERCED** (cf. the quote of Zch 12:10 in Rv 1:7, and the comments on Zch 12:10).

19:38-40. Joseph of Arimathea, mentioned in all four Gospels (Mt 27:57; Mk 15:43; Lk 23:50-51) was a **secret disciple** (see comments on Jn 3:9; 7:47-51; 12:42-43). **Fear of the** Jewish leadership had previously prevented him from boldly confessing his faith, though he did not stay that way for long. Joseph began to conquer this fear ("he gathered up courage," Mk 14:43) when he **asked Pilate that he might take away the body of Jesus**. The association of **Nicodemus** (v. 39) with Joseph implies that Nicodemus was also a secret disciple—but now took a bold, open stand before Pilate. The reminder that Nicodemus was the one **who had first come to** Jesus **by night** underscores the hidden nature of his faith. His faith did, however, lead him now to act openly with Joseph against the sentiment of his fellow Sanhedrin members. Nicodemus brought **myrrh** for simple embalming and **aloes** for perfume. The **hundred pounds** (*litra*) is better translated "seventy-five pounds" (ESV, NIV), as a Roman *litra* was about 12 oz, not 16.

19:41-42. Joseph of Arimathea was the wealthy owner (Mt 27:57, 60) of a **new tomb in which no one had yet been laid**. This demonstrates that after the resurrection, Jesus' body could not be mistaken for another lying in the same tomb. Christ's burial fulfilled prophecy: "They intended to bury him [the Messiah] with criminals, but he ended up in a rich man's tomb" (NET, Is 53:9). For the **day of preparation** (v. 42), see comment on v. 14.

D. Resurrection and Appearances (20:1-29)

John's account of the resurrection is the most extensive of the four Gospels, with specific details of the empty tomb. First, Mary Magdalene, Peter, and John confirmed Jesus' resurrection (vv. 1-18). Then Jesus appeared to the disciples (except Thomas) in a closed room (vv. 19-23). Finally, Jesus appeared again to the disciples and affirmed to Thomas evidence of His resurrection (vv. 24-29).

20:1. Mary Magdalene was first introduced as one who looked on at the crucifixion (19:25). Jesus had delivered her from severe demon possession, and she followed Jesus, serving and supporting His ministry (Mt 27:55; Lk 8:1-3). On arrival at the tomb, Mary unexpectedly found the large round **stone** at the tomb's entrance had been rolled **away**.

20:2-3. Mary **ran** to find **Peter** and John, **the other disciple whom Jesus loved** (see Introduction: Author; cf. 18:15-16; 19:26; 21:7, 20). The explanation of her flight is that she saw an angel inside the tomb (Mk 16:5) and that she suspected the Jewish authorities (**they**) had **taken** Jesus' body **away**. Mary's wording, **we do not know**, shows John's awareness of the other women with Mary (cf. Mt 28:1; Mk 16:1; Lk 24:10). Based on Mary's word, **Peter and the other disciple** (v. 3) proceeded to the empty **tomb**.

20:4-5. As Peter and John ran to the tomb, John (**the other disciple**; cf. v. 2) **ran ahead faster** and was the **first** to arrive. He stooped down (the opening of a rock tomb was usually low) and looked inside (v. 5). When **he saw the linen wrappings lying there**, something prevented him from entering—perhaps respect or fear of ceremonial defilement associated with contacting a corpse. But Peter did not share this hesitancy.

20:6-7. Since John waited for Peter's arrival before entering the grave, Peter could be assured that when **he saw the linen wrappings lying there**, they were not repositioned by John. John's delay provided for two authentic witnesses to the wrappings of the empty tomb. In contrast to the grave wrappings that bound Lazarus (11:44), Jesus' **face-cloth which had been on His head** (v. 7) was lying separately, **rolled up in a place by itself**. Though it is impossible to say with any certainty, Jesus may have passed through the wrappings and left them right where He had lain. This orderly arrangement is evidence of resurrection, not robbery, and the separate face cloth makes it difficult to believe that a shroud that supposedly survived from Jesus' burial is genuine.

20:8-10. John, **the other disciple** (cf. v. 2), entered the tomb after Peter—then **saw and believed** Jesus had risen from the dead. The eleven disciples (**they**) had failed until now to **understand the** [OT] **Scripture, that** the Messiah **must rise again from the dead** (v. 9). Later, Peter preached that Ps 16:10 had prophesied the resurrection (Ac 2:24-28). Since Peter and John **went away again to their own homes** (v. 10), John would have announced Christ's resurrection to Jesus' mother, Mary, who was now staying at his home (Jn 19:27). Since all the disciples except Judas Iscariot were from Galilee, the disciples' homes in Jerusalem may have been temporary lodgings with family or friends for the Passover.

20:11-13. Jesus' first resurrection appearance was to a woman, Mary Magdalene. This (1) confirms the historicity of the resurrection (no first-century writer would have created a narrative with a woman in such a critical role unless it actually transpired this way), and (2) highlights the importance of women in Jesus' ministry. Mary (see v. 1) returned but remained **outside the tomb weeping** (*klaio,* lit., "wailing"). Still crying, she **looked into the tomb; and she saw two angels in white**. The presence of angels alone should have alerted Mary that Jesus' body was not stolen and something supernatural had taken place. That the angels were seated **where the body of Jesus had been lying** also testified to His resurrection. The angels did not explain to Mary that Jesus was raised (v. 13). They simply asked, **Woman, why are you weeping?** as if to suggest that there was really no reason for sorrow. Mary answered the angels, explaining her theory that the body was stolen. Mary's sorrow, soon turned to joy, would fulfill the promise Jesus gave the disciples in 16:20-22.

20:14-16. When Mary **turned around**, she did not recognize the One standing behind her. For **Woman** (v. 15), see comment on 2:4. Jesus repeated the question spoken by the angels (v.

13) but added **Whom are you seeking?** Mary thought the voice was that of **the gardener**. Perhaps he had placed the body elsewhere. But when Jesus affectionately called her by name (v. 16), she knew it was Jesus. Although she had often called Him Lord (vv. 2, 13, 18), she addressed Him as **Rabboni** (only elsewhere in Mk 10:51), which means **Teacher**. "Teacher" is the most common form of address for Jesus in the Gospels, but is never used of Him after the ascension (cf. 11:28).

20:17-18. Mary was **clinging to** Jesus, holding on to her earthly relationship with Christ. Some see in v. 17 a mystical demand that Mary not touch Christ because of His alleged descent to hell and that He had not yet been in His Father's presence. The simpler and more likely explanation is that Mary was fervently clinging to Jesus. Therefore, Jesus encouraged her to let go of Him because He was not leaving just yet (**Stop clinging to Me, for I have not yet ascended to the Father**). He would be with them for a while longer, 40 more days before His ascension, and there would be more time for meaningful interaction later. Then through the Spirit after His ascension, He would be with them forever. Instead of clinging to Him, Jesus wanted Mary to go to the disciples and tell them what she saw and what He said. Mary was instructed to tell the disciples, **I** will soon **ascend to My Father and your Father, and My God and your God**. The first phrase focused on Jesus' own unique relationship with the Father (**My Father . . . My God**). At the same time, the second phrase (**your Father . . . your God**) drew the disciples into a similar closeness to the Father that Jesus Himself had. This is also marked out by Jesus' reference to His disciples as **My brethren**.

20:19-20. It was Sunday **evening** of resurrection day. The disciples were still in **fear** of the Jewish authorities and made sure the **doors were shut** (NIV, ESV, "locked") **where** they gathered. For **fear of the Jews**, see 7:13; 12:42-43; 19:38. Miraculously, **Jesus came and stood in their midst**. Jesus' address, **Peace be with you**, was a normal Hebrew greeting. At the sight of **His** imprinted **hands and His** scarred **side**, the disciples **rejoiced** (v. 20), fulfilling Jesus' promise given in the upper room (16:20-22).

20:21-23. With a second pronouncement of peace (cf. 14:27; 16:33), Jesus commissioned His disciples as His witnesses (4:38; 13:20; Lk 24:46-49; Mt 28:18-20): **as the Father has sent Me**, **I also send you**. When Jesus **breathed on** His disciples (v. 22), He symbolized the coming gift of the Spirit received at Pentecost. When Jesus **breathed** ("on" is not included in the sense of the word) and said **Receive the Holy Spirit** He was probably acting in a symbolic way. It is unlikely that He gave, and the disciples received, the Spirit at this time. Jesus said earlier that the Spirit would not come to them until He left them (Jn 7:39; 16:7), and even immediately prior to His ascension He instructed them to wait for the Spirit's coming (Ac 1:4, 5, 8).

Before Jesus died, the bread and the cup shared at the Passover-Communion celebration was done in anticipation of the actual giving of His body and blood. Likewise the act of Jesus breathing coupled with the command to receive the Spirit anticipated the Spirit coming at Pentecost. "Breath" and "Spirit" are the same word in Greek (*pneuma*), and Jesus' breath probably symbolized His future sending of the Spirit following His ascension. It is unlikely that the disciples "received" or were "indwelt" by the Spirit at this time and then "baptized" in the Spirit as an experience subsequent to that at Pentecost. With this anticipatory commissioning came the authority of the apostles (and any believer) to announce to one who believes that **their sins have been forgiven** (v. 23) or to the one who does not believe that their sins **have been retained** (unforgiven).

20:24-25. Thomas was not with the **twelve** (now eleven since Judas Iscariot committed suicide; Mt 27:5). **Didymus** (mentioned three times, only by John, 11:16; 20:24; 21:2) means "the twin." Perhaps John personally knew Thomas's twin. Thomas's unbelief was inexorable. He rejected the testimony of the women and all the other disciples who had **seen the Lord** (v. 25). Thomas insisted that he would not believe unless he personally **put** his **finger into the place of the nails, and put** his **hand into** Jesus' **side**.

20:26-27. After eight days, i.e., the Sunday a week after the resurrection, Jesus appeared to **His disciples** and **Thomas**. The circumstances duplicated His previous appearance (vv. 19-23) when the **doors** had **been shut**. The disciples still lacked the boldness they would receive at Pentecost. Thomas must have been shocked to hear Jesus tell him the same words (v. 27; cf. 25) he had told the other disciples about handling His **hands** and His **side**.

20:28-29. John's writing reaches a climax with Thomas's confession **My Lord and my God!** No greater affirmation of faith can be found than this announcement on the lips of

Thomas. With it, John reiterated the theme of the deity of Christ provided in his introduction (1:1, 14, 18). **Because you have seen Me, have you believed?** (v. 29) is better expressed as a statement ("because you have seen Me, you have believed"; NKJV, NIV). Jesus affirmed Thomas's designation that He is fully divine, just as God the Father is, and called **blessed** those future believers who will not see the resurrected Lord but will yet believe.

E. Purpose Statement (20:30-31)

20:30-31. The apostle's purpose for his book is evangelistic. Since **many other signs** (for "sign," see comment on 2:11) were done by Christ yet were **not written in this book**, John carefully selected his content for evangelism, especially among the Jewish people. To **believe that Jesus is the Christ, the Son of God** (these titles indicate His humanity, royalty, and deity, see also comments on 1:20, 34) means to be fully convinced that Jesus alone provides eternal life and resurrection (cf. comment on 11:25-27). Locating the purpose statement here rather than at the end of the book highlights Jesus' blessing on those who believe in His death/resurrection apart from physical sight (v. 30). It also demonstrates that the resurrection is the greatest sign of the book.

V. Epilogue (21:1-25)

In the Epilogue, the author challenged his readers who have believed to join in the mission of Christ to the world.

A. The Great Catch of Fish (21:1-14)

21:1-3. After these things is indefinite chronologically (cf. 20:26). An angel had told the disciples to meet Jesus in Galilee (Mt 28:7). Their fishing expedition recalls the only other events in John's gospel that took place at the **Sea of Tiberias**, namely the feeding of the 5,000 (Jn 6:10-14). On that occasion, Jesus taught that no one could come to Him unless the Father draws (*helko*) him (6:44; cf. 12:32). In 21:6 and 11, *helko* is used of the disciples drawing in their fishing net. The fishing expedition illustrates how Jesus will draw people to Himself through the mission of His followers. Early Christian readers would have detected in this story parallels with Lk 5:1-11. The **sons of Zebedee** are James and John (Mt 4:21), fishing partners with Peter (Lk 5:10).

21:4-5. Jesus appeared as **the day was now breaking.** Jesus manifested Himself (vv. 1, 14) in light to the disciples by His word. First, He spoke to them, addressing them as **Children**. Jesus had entered with them into a discipleship relationship in which He was their "father" (cf. 1Jn 2:18). His question (v. 5) **you do not have any fish, do you?** implied He had divine foreknowledge of the answer (cf. v. 17).

21:6-7. The supernatural catch is the only recorded miracle of Jesus after His resurrection. His promise **you will find a catch** was sufficient for the disciples to obey. Their obedience was rewarded with so many fish that **they were not able to haul** the net **in**. Like Thomas (20:28), John identified Jesus as **Lord**. Peter, after his denial of the Lord, reverted to his occupation prior to being called as a fisher of men. This miracle was designed to remind the disciples of their initial call to be fishers of men, a call associated with another enormous catch of fish in Lk 5:1-10. This miracle reiterated that call. The phrase **he put his outer garment on (for he was stripped for work)**, (the words **for work** are not in Greek) could be translated, "he tucked in his outer garment (for he had nothing on underneath it)" (NET). It is improbable that one who worked so frequently around water would put on his outer garment to dive into the sea and swim to shore. "Put on" (Gk., *diazonnumi*) can mean "tying up one's clothing around oneself," and "stripped" (Gk., *gymnos*) could mean "to wear nothing else underneath one's outer garment."

21:8-11. The **charcoal fire** (v. 9; a word only used elsewhere in 18:18) recalls Peter's denial of Christ, which took place at a similar fire in the courtyard of the high priest. Perhaps the impending restoration of Peter at this charcoal fire was designed to impress upon him the seriousness of his denial at the earlier fire, and of the depth of Jesus' forgiveness. Peter's leadership was evident in that **he drew the net to land**. The number **a hundred and fifty-three** is unusual. John provided no indication that the number is a symbol. However, such an exact number verifies the eyewitness character of the author John (a fisherman by trade).

21:12-14. For the disciples to eat with Jesus was a strong verification of His resurrection (Ac 10:41). **Jesus** also **took the bread and gave it to them** along with **the fish**, reminding them of the Bread of Life message and the feeding of the multitude (Jn 6:11). This too confirmed their certainty of who He was. The author designated this as the **third time that Jesus was manifested**. In accord with the Jewish law that two or three witnesses establish the truth (cf. 8:17), John presented three accounts of Jesus' resurrection appearances. But later many different appearances took place (1Co 15:5-8).

B. Future Roles of Peter and John (21:15-23)

21:15-17. The following threefold exchange between Christ and Peter paralleled the apostle's threefold denial of Christ (18:17, 25, 27). Twice Christ asked Peter if he loved Him (*agapao*). Twice Peter affirmed his love using another Greek word (*phileo*; see the discussion on the two words at 5:20-21). In the last significant conversation between Peter and Jesus before the crucifixion, Jesus nuanced *agapao* as "laying down one's life" (13:15-23). He also called on his followers to love (*agapao*) one another "even as I have loved you" (13:34; cf. 15:13, 12, 17), referring to the love by which He would lay down His life. *Phileo* and *agapao* probably do not differ in meaning in this context (i.e., *phileo* does not refer to some "superficial, inferior love" since the word is used for the Father's love for the Son in 5:20-21, and *agapao* can be used for frivolously craving the acclaim of people in 12:43). In John's gospel they both mean "love." They may, however, have slightly different references, *agapao* referring to an aspect of love that includes sacrifice, an aspect not associated with *phileo* in John's gospel. In other words, John may have noted Jesus' use of *agapao* to elicit from Peter a commitment to the kind of self-sacrificing love Jesus modeled and demanded from his disciples as seen in the previous uses of *agapao*.

The question, "**Do you love Me more than these** disciples love Me?" corresponds to Peter's boastful promise to love Jesus so much he would lay down his life for Him, even if the other disciples do not (13:37; Mk 14:29). Jesus was asking Peter if he would still claim what he did previously—that He would lay down his life for His Lord. Remembering his denials in the courtyard, Peter was hesitant to make that promise again. **Tend My lambs** and **Shepherd My sheep** (v. 16) evoke Jesus' teaching on laying down His life for the sheep (Jn 10:15, 17) and dovetail with the sacrificial nuance of *agape*. Peter replied in ignorance with *phileo* and not *agapao* because he had still not understood the sacrificial emphasis of *agape* love as Jesus had delineated it in the upper room. For **the third time** (v. 17), Jesus asked, **Do you love Me?** now using Peter's own word for love (*phileo*) in hopes that Peter would be shaken from his misunderstanding and recall Jesus' original call to self-sacrificial *agape*. Instead, **Peter was grieved because** Jesus had questioned him three times.

The threefold pattern of questions and answers recalls Peter's three denials predicted by the Lord in 13:38 and fulfilled in 18:15-27. It is impossible to be certain, but Peter's distress may have been due to his awareness of the parallel between Jesus' third question and Peter's three denials. Jesus' use of *phileo* in this third question may also include probing Peter for his affection for Jesus when none was evident during his denials. So perhaps *agapao* in the first two questions asked by Jesus is to explore Peter's willingness to sacrifice himself for Jesus and His people, while the use of *phileo* in His third question was designed to compel Peter to reflect on his lack of affection for Jesus evident during the denials. It was this third interrogation by the Lord that so pained Peter. But it is impossible to be certain of this.

21:18-19. Jesus now predicted that Peter would lay down his life just as Christ did. Peter will **stretch out** his **hands**, a term that suggests crucifixion. **Signifying by what kind of death he would glorify God** parallels other statements that speak of Christ's crucifixion (12:33; 18:32). Others would **gird** Peter (NET, HCSB, "tie you up") for his death. Despite the prospect of suffering, Christ commanded Peter, **Follow Me!** (cf. 1:43; 12:26).

21:20-22. In **turning around** to see **the disciple whom Jesus loved**, Peter physically and spiritually took his eyes off Christ. John, however, was **following** Jesus (**them** is not in the Greek). Would Peter? Peter's question **Lord, and what about this man?** revealed Peter's struggle with Christ's will for his life. When other believers appear more prosperous in ministry or life, the Lord's disciple must keep a focus on Christ's command, **Follow Me!**

21:23. A misinterpretation of Jesus' words was spread **among the brethren** that John **would not die** (cf. Mt 28:11-15). By quoting the exact words of Jesus again (cf. v. 22), John stressed the imminence of the Lord's return. While Jesus prophesied His any-moment return in rapture (see comment on 14:3; see also the comments on Mt 24:36-41), this could not take place until after certain prophesied events such as His own death and resurrection, the giving of the Spirit (Ac 2), the first widespread preaching of the gospel (Ac 1:8), and Peter's death in old age (Jn 21:18-19). By the time the Fourth Gospel was written (late AD 60s or 80s; see Introduction: Date), these had been accomplished so that Jesus could come in rapture before or after John died.

C. Final Attestation to Truth (21:24-25)

21:24-25. In his final words, the author maintained that he **wrote these things** as a **testimony** that **is true**. When John said **we know**, he probably referred to himself (as suggested by **I suppose**). There is no fully exhaustive account of Jesus' life. If such a "Bible" **were written in detail**, then **the world itself** could **not contain** all **the books that would be written** – clearly a hyperbole. But in his book the Evangelist set out to prove that Jesus was the Redeemer who would grant forgiveness to those who believed in Him, and he included abundant evidence that Jesus is indeed the Messiah, the Son of God.

BIBLIOGRAPHY

Blum, Edwin A. "John." In *The Bible Knowledge Commentary, New Testament,* edited by John Walvoord and Roy Zuck, 267–348. Wheaton, IL: Victor, 1983.

Beasley-Murray, George R. *John.* Word Biblical Commentary. Edited by David A. Hubbard. Waco, TX: Word Books, 1987.

Bruce, F. F. *Gospel of John.* Grand Rapids, MI: Eerdmans, 1983, 1994.

Carson, D. A. *The Gospel According to John.* Pillar New Testament Commentary. Grand Rapids, MI: Eerdmans, 1991.

Keener, Craig S. *The Gospel of John: A Commentary.* Peabody, MA: Hendrickson, 2003.

Köestenberger, Andreas J. *John.* Baker Exegetical Commentary on the New Testament. Grand Rapids, MI: Baker, 2004.

Laney, J. Carl. *John.* Moody Gospel Commentary. Chicago: Moody, 1992.

Lincoln, Andrew T. *The Gospel According to Saint John.* Peabody, MA: Hendrickson, 2005.

Morris, Leon. *The Gospel of John.* New International Commentary on the New Testament. Grand Rapids, MI: Eerdmans, 1995.

Michaels, J. Ramsey. *John.* New International Bible Commentary. Edited by W. Ward Gasque. Peabody, MA: Hendrickson, 1988–1999.

Neyrey, Jerome H. *The Gospel of John.* New Cambridge Bible Commentary. Cambridge: Cambridge University Press, 2006.

Tenney, Merrill C. "John." In *The Expositor's Bible Commentary.* Grand Rapids, MI: Zondervan, 1981.

● ● ● ●

ACTS

WILLIAM H. MARTY

INTRODUCTION

Acts is the second volume of Luke's two-part narrative of the origins of Christianity. In Acts, Luke has continued the exciting story of Christianity by recording what the followers of Jesus did after His death, resurrection, and ascension. Under the sovereign leading of the Holy Spirit, the church expanded from Jerusalem to Rome and advanced from a movement in Israel alone to a faith for the whole world. Though Peter was the primary agent in the growth of the Jewish faith movement, he also initiated the witness to the Gentiles. After Paul's miraculous conversion, he successfully took the gospel to both Jewish people and Gentiles in Asia Minor and Europe.

The title *Acts* is the translation of the Greek term *praxeis*. In secular Greek, the word *praxeis* was used to summarize the heroic accomplishments of great individuals. In the book of Acts Luke focused on Peter and Paul, the pillars of the Jewish and Gentile church, respectively.

Author. The traditional view that Luke wrote both the third gospel and the book of Acts is supported unanimously by the external testimony of the ante-Nicene church fathers: Irenaeus (second century, c. 202), Tertullian (c. 160–c. 220), Clement of Alexandria (c. 150–c. 215), and Origen (185–254), indicating that Lukan authorship was established early in the history of the church. Plus Luke has been identified as the author in the Muratorian Canon, the earliest list of the NT books, c. AD 175) (Simon J. Kistemaker, *Acts:* NTC [Grand Rapids, MI: Baker, 1990], 20).

In addition to the external evidence, the internal evidence points to Luke as the author. First, the author was a traveling companion of Paul. He used the first-person plural pronoun "we" in 16:10-17; 20:5-21:18; and 27:1–28:16. Second, though another person could have written other parts of Acts, the similarity of content and style suggests that the entire book was written by the same person. Third, the mention of Theophilus in Lk 1:3 and Ac 1:1 connects both books with the same author. Both books emphasize how God is working out His divine plan of redemption, the role of the Holy Spirit in the life of Christ and the growth of the church, and the universal impact of the ministry of Christ and the message of the church. Last, the description of illnesses and the use of medical terminology point to a physician as the author (see 4:10; 28:6). From Col 4:14, we know that Luke was a doctor. It is reasonable to conclude that Luke penned both the third gospel and the book of Acts.

From the prologue to the third gospel, we know that Luke was a competent historian (Lk 1:1-4; see the comments there). His intent was to provide Theophilus with an accurate and reliable account of the life of Christ and the origin of the church. In both books, we have factual history, not fiction about Christ and the church.

Date. The last reference to Paul in Acts indicates that he was under house arrest (28:20). This suggests the earliest possible date for the writing of the book is AD 62, since that was the year Paul was released from house arrest. The latest possible date for the book is AD 70. That is the year the Romans destroyed Jerusalem (for this, see the comments introducing Mt 24). If Luke's gospel and Acts were written afterward, then Jesus' prediction of the destruction of Jerusalem (Lk 19–20) would be history, not prophecy. In addition, some events recorded in Acts took place in Jerusalem, making it highly improbable that Luke would not have mentioned the destruction of the city. The book does not mention Nero's burning of Rome (AD 65), the persecution of Christians (AD 65), or Paul's execution (c. AD 68). The evidence supports an early date c. AD 62–64.

Recipients. The third gospel and Acts are addressed or perhaps dedicated to Theophilus (1:1). In the prologue to his gospel, Luke referred to him as "most excellent Theophilus" (1:3). This title suggests that Theophilus was a government official because Luke used it with reference to Felix (23:26; 24:3) and Festus (26:25), both Roman governors.

Theophilus was probably a Gentile believer, though it is impossible to be certain of his identity or spiritual status. A considerable amount of scholarly opinion views Theophilus as Luke's patron or sponsor, underwriting Luke's expenses so Luke could research and write the gospel and Acts. It was written in "Theophilus's honor," but would be distributed to the church at large. Another possibility, with equal merit, is that Theophilus was a Gentile seeker, that the book was written to honor him but truly designed for the Greco-Roman world. What is certain is that Luke wanted to provide Theophilus with an accurate historical account of the life of Christ and the early church (Lk 1:4). Luke's purpose was apparently to assure Theophilus, a Gentile, that it was by divine design the church was not limited to Jewish people but was indeed a faith for the whole world. The church, which began in an exclusively Jewish context, was actually the fulfillment of God's redemptive purposes for all nations. For this purpose Luke certainly intended Acts for a larger audience.

Purpose. Luke stated his purpose for writing in the prologue to his gospel. He wrote to assure Theophilus of the truth of the teachings of Christianity (Lk 1:4). We can only speculate what Theophilus had been taught and why Luke believed he needed additional information about the life of Christ and the growth of the church. Luke was probably writing to defend the truth and integrity of the Christian faith, not for Theophilus alone, but also, the group he represented, the Greco-Roman world. From the contents of Acts, it appears that Luke masterfully wove together four purposes in writing the book.

Historical Purpose: The first followers of Jesus were Jews, and the first church was Jewish. It was, however, always God's intention to save people from every nation. Luke explained how following Christ, which was at first exclusively Jewish, became a universal faith. After His ascension Jesus sent the Holy Spirit to empower His followers to witness in Jerusalem, Judea, and Samaria, and the entire world. In his account of the supernatural growth of the church, Luke showed how His first followers, under the sovereign direction of the Holy Spirit, courageously proclaimed the gospel from Jerusalem to Rome. He emphasized that the gospel of salvation is for all people—Jews and Gentiles, men and women, rich and poor, rulers and slaves. As John Stott put it, "Jesus is the Savior of the world; nobody is beyond the embrace of his love" (*The Message of Acts*, BST [Downers Grove, IL: InterVarsity, 1990], 31).

Critical scholars have questioned the historical reliability of Acts. Some claim that Luke created some of the stories in Acts, and others have charged that Luke was not a competent historian. The evidence, however, supports Luke's accuracy as a historian and the historical reliability of Acts. In the prologue to his gospel (Lk 1:1-4), Luke stated his purpose was to give a reliable historical account. Since Luke and Acts are two volumes of a single work, we can assume Luke's methodology would apply to Acts as well. Luke was a physician (Col 4:10), which means he was educated. The Greek in Luke and Acts reflects the style of an educated and cultured person. It is unlikely that a physician, who was trained to be careful in his practice, would be careless in writing a history of Christ and the church.

Luke was a traveling companion of Paul, as revealed by the use of "we" in the accounts of Paul's journeys (see 16:10-17; 20:5–21:18; 27:1–28:16). This means that Luke was an eyewitness to some of the events he recorded, plus his association with Paul would have given him the opportunity to interview Paul for additional information. The similarity of writing style suggests a single author wrote the entire book.

Luke was familiar with the land of Israel, and indications are that he personally traveled in the land of Israel conducting research for both Luke and Acts. Both books indicate an intimate familiarity with geography and customs.

Apologetic (Political) Purpose: Luke was somewhat of a political apologist. Initially the new faith community was considered part of Judaism, and therefore its legal status was protected in the Roman Empire. As the church grew, Luke wanted to assure the Romans they had nothing to fear from the new movement. They were not insurrectionists stirring up anti-Roman sentiment. This may explain in part why Luke dedicated the gospel and Acts to Theophilus, who was apparently a government official. He wanted to assure Theophilus that Christianity was not a subversive movement threatening to overthrow Roman rule.

In his accounts of the verdicts of Roman administrators, Luke defended the legal status of Christianity (*religio licita*). When charged with violating Roman law Luke emphasized that Roman authorities concluded Christians were not guilty of civil disobedience. Gallio, the proconsul or governor of Achaia, warned some Jewish opponents that the Romans were not interested in matters of Jewish law. Since Paul and his companions had not broken Roman law, Gallio refused to hear any complaints against Paul, and threw his accusers out of court (Ac 18:12-17). Paul successfully refuted the charges of Tertullus, an attorney hired by Jewish leaders to prosecute their complaints against Paul (Ac 24:1-27). After Agrippa, a Jewish king, heard Paul's defense he concluded Paul could have been released if he had not appealed to Caesar (Ac 26:1-32). Luke gave indirect evidence that Christianity was not a subversive movement by recording the conversion of several Roman officials. Cornelius, a centurion (Ac 10); Sergius Paulus, a proconsul/governor of Cyprus (Ac 13); and the father of Publius, the leading official on the island of Malta (Ac 27) all become believers.

Biographical Purpose: A close examination of the book reveals that Luke compared Paul to Peter to prove that Paul's apostleship was legitimate. As did Peter, Paul healed a handicapped man (cf. 3:1-8; 14:8-10). Both men rebuked a magician (cf. 8:9-24; 13:6-12). Both raised a believer from the dead (cf. 9:36-41; 20:7-10). God directed Peter to Cornelius in a vision (10:9-23), and He led Paul to Macedonia in a vision (16:6-10). God miraculously released both men from prison (cf. 12:3-19; 16:9-34). Luke did not invent the parallels between the ministries of Peter and Paul, but he did deliberately identify them as evidence that Paul's apostleship was by divine appointment. God supernaturally worked through Paul, the apostle to the Gentiles, in the same way he worked through Peter, the apostle to the Jewish people (see Gl 2:6-8).

Theological Purpose: Luke provided his readers with a theological explanation of how the Holy Spirit worked in the birth, and through the work, of the church. All four of these purposes work together to support the truth and integrity of the faith.

Contribution. Acts is the third longest book in the NT. Together Luke and Acts comprise almost one-third of the NT, exceeding the writings of both Paul and John in size.

The book is the second volume in a two-part work. Originally the gospel of Luke and Acts were a series, but they were separated near the end of the first century when John was placed after the Synoptic Gospels. As a sequel to the Gospel of Luke, Acts reveals how the resurrected and ascended Lord continued to advance the kingdom through Spirit-filled witnesses.

Acts introduces us to Paul, who would be almost a complete stranger if we did not have his story in the book, and provides helpful background information for locating Paul's epistles in their historical context.

Luke also explained how a movement, which had its origins in Judaism, fulfilled the divine mandate to take the gospel to the nations, creating an ethnically diverse universal church.

Geography is a crucial element of the story of the church (1:8). In 1:1 through 6:7, Luke described the birth and growth of the church in Jerusalem. He explained the church's witness in Judea and Samaria in 6:8 through 9:31. In 9:32 through 28:31 Luke vindicated Paul's ministry to the Gentiles and highlighted Paul's missionary journeys and the events that took Paul to Jerusalem, the capital of Judaism, and Rome, the capital of paganism.

In addition to geography, Luke gave numerical summaries at crucial stages of the growth of Christianity (see 2:41, 47; 6:7; 9:31; 12:24; 16:5; 19:20). The summaries emphasize that the growth of the church was nothing less than supernatural. At the beginning of Acts, the followers of Jesus in Jerusalem numbered 120 (1:15), but when Luke completed his account there were thousands of believers throughout the Roman Empire, and though Paul was a prisoner, the gospel was not chained. Paul boldly proclaimed the gospel of the kingdom in the capital of the empire (28:30-31).

An important question remains for the student of Acts: "How does one know what is perpetually normative and binding from the book of Acts for the church and Christians?" Many believers look to the book of Acts to undergird such practices as baptism by immersion for believers, but deny that other practices found in Acts are binding, such as speaking in tongues. What hermeneutical warrant is there for making such distinctions? It is difficult to answer this question to everyone's satisfaction, but three questions can help to substantiate whether or not a practice is *prescribed* in Acts rather than simply *described*.

First, is an action taught or commanded by a major character in Acts? In the case of baptism, the answer is "Yes" (see 2:38; 22:16; and the virtual command in 10:48). In the case of speaking in tongues, the answer is "No." Individuals are never coached or commanded to speak in tongues.

Second, is there a consistent pattern in Acts that suggests that it was Luke's intention to prescribe an action? As it relates to baptism, the consistent pattern is that individuals believed and were baptized as believers. But there is not a clear pattern related to speaking in tongues. In Ac 2, the phenomenon included tongues of fire and the sound of a wind, but these are missing from the other occurrences of tongues in Acts. In Ac 2, there is no mention of the laying on of hands as in 8:17 or 19:6, and in 10:46 the gift of tongues came upon those at the moment they believed, while in Ac 2, 8, and 19, it came upon those who had been believers for a while. In Ac 8, the gift came upon those who had already been baptized, but in Ac 10 it came to those who had not been. There is no clear pattern associated with tongues in Acts, making it difficult (not impossible!) to defend the concept that Acts presents tongues as binding for the church.

Third, does the remainder of the NT provide justification for behavior found in Acts? For example, believer's baptism is taught elsewhere (e.g., Rm 6:3-4; Col 2:9-12; Gl 3:27; 1Pt 3:21), but so is speaking in tongues (1Co 12-14), though 1Co 13:8-13 makes it difficult to think that tongues has not ceased (see the comments there). Another example of a practice in Acts, the elder-ruled form of church government, may be justified by Paul's instruction to the Ephesian elders in Ac 20:17-35, but it is bolstered considerably by explicit instruction from the pastoral epistles (1Tm 3:1-7; Ti 1:5-9).

The same three questions can be applied to any practice in Acts. Does Ac 1 teach that church leaders should be chosen by drawing lots? Does Ac 4–5 teach a socialist economic model for the church? Does Ac 9 teach that a believer should expect revelatory guidance to identify his ministry for the Lord? The three questions help to determine whether a practice is intended by Luke to be normative for the church. For a helpful discussion on this question, see Walter L. Liefeld, *Interpreting the Book of Acts,* Guides to New Testament Exegesis (Grand Rapids, MI: Baker, 1995), 113–127, though Liefeld does not specify the three questions suggested here.

OUTLINE

- I. The Establishment of the Church: Jerusalem (1:1–6:7)
  - A. The Introduction to Luke's Book about the Mission (1:1-2)
  - B. The Means of Preparing the Disciples for the Mission (1:3-26)
  - C. The Initiation of the Mission (2:1-47)
    - 1. The Power of Pentecost (2:1-13)
      - a. The Coming of the Spirit (2:1-4)
      - b. The Reaction of the Crowd (2:5-13)
    - 2. The Proclamation of Pentecost (2:14-47)
      - a. The Reference to Joel (2:14-21)
      - b. The Reference to Christ (2:22-36)
        - (1) His Life of Power (2:22)
        - (2) His Death and Resurrection (2:23-32)
        - (3) His Exaltation (2:33-36)
      - c. The Reaction of the Crowd (2:37)
      - d. The Appeal of Peter (2:38-40)
      - e. The Salvation and Fellowship of Three Thousand (2:41-47)
  - D. Difficulties for the Mission (3:1–6:7)
    - 1. External Persecution: Arrest of Peter and John (3:1–4:31)
      - a. The Ministry of Healing (3:1-11)
      - b. The Message of Peter (3:12-26)
      - c. The Menace of the Sanhedrin (4:1-31)
    - 2. Internal Corruption: Deception of Ananias and Sapphira (5:1-11)

3. External Persecution: Arrest of the Apostles (5:12-42)
4. Internal Strife: Neglect of the Hellenistic Widows (6:1-7)

II. The Extension of the Church: Judea and Samaria (6:8–9:31)
  A. Stephen: Witness to the Jews (6:8–8:3)
    1. The Seizure of Stephen (6:8–7:1)
      a. The Context of Stephen's Life (6:8-10)
      b. The Charge Brought against Stephen (6:11–7:1)
    2. The Sermon of Stephen (7:2-53)
      a. The Breadth of God's Revelation (7:2-8)
      b. The Rejection of God's Messengers (7:9-53)
    3. The Stoning of Stephen (7:54–8:3)
      a. The Sight He Saw (7:54-56)
      b. The Suffering He Experienced (7:57-58)
      c. The Steadfastness He Displayed (7:59–8:3)
  B. Philip: Witness to the Samaritans (8:4-40)
    1. In the City of Samaria (8:4-25)
      a. Philip's Preaching and Power (8:4-8)
      b. The Samaritan's and Simon's Reaction (8:9-13)
      c. The Coming of the Apostles (8:14-25)
    2. On the Chariot with the Eunuch (8:26-40)
  C. Saul: Witness to the Gentiles (9:1-31)
    1. His Malice against the Christians (9:1-2)
    2. His Meeting with the Lord (9:3-7)
    3. His Future Ministry for the Lord (9:8-31)

III. The Expansion of the Church: To the Roman Empire (9:32–28:31)
  A. The Mission through Peter to the Gentiles (9:32–11:18)
    1. In the Miracles for Aeneas and Dorcas (9:32-43)
    2. In the Salvation of Cornelius and His Family (10:1–11:18)
      a. A Vision to Motivate Peter (10:1-33)
      b. A Message to Reach Cornelius (10:34-42)
        (1) Introduction of the Message (10:34-35)
        (2) The Body of the Message (10:36-42)
      c. The Conclusion of the Message: The Need for Faith (10:43)
      d. The Results of the Message (10:44–11:18)
        (1) The Salvation of Cornelius's Household (10:44-48)
        (2) The Controversy among Jewish Believers (11:1-18)
  B. To Antioch (11:19–12:25)
    1. The Mission through Barnabas and Saul at Antioch (11:19-30)
    2. The Fruitfulness of the Gospel in Antioch (11:19-24)
    3. The Recruitment of Saul by Barnabas (11:25-26)
    4. The Concern for the Disadvantaged in Judea (11:27-30)
    5. The Persecution of Believers in Judea (12:1-25)
      a. Through Prayer: Peter Was Rescued (12:1-19)
      b. Through Retribution: Herod Agrippa I Was Struck Dead (12:20-25)
  C. To Asia Minor: The First Missionary Journey (13:1–15:35)
    1. The Circuit of Proclamation (13:1–14:28)
      a. The Commissioning of Saul and Barnabas (13:1-3)
      b. The Journey by Saul (Paul) and Barnabas (13:4–14:28)
        (1) Antioch to Seleucia to Salamis on Cyprus (13:4-12)
          (a) The Opposition by Elymas (13:4-8)
          (b) The Blinding of Elymas (13:9-12)
        (2) Paphos to Perga in Pamphylia (13:13)
        (3) Perga to Pisidian Antioch (13:14-50)
          (a) Paul's Message in Antioch (13:14-41)

            (b) Reaction to the Message in Antioch (13:42-50)
        (4) Antioch to Iconium: Mixed Reactions (13:51–14:5)
        (5) Iconium to Lystra (14:6-20a)
            (a) A Case of Mistaken Identities (14:6-18)
            (b) Opponents from Iconium and Antioch (14:19-20a)
        (6) Lystra to Derbe: A Favorable Reaction (14:20b-21a)
        (7) Backtracking: Derbe Back through Lystra, Iconium, and Pisidian Antioch to Perga (14:21b-23)
        (8) Perga to Attalia to Syrian Antioch: The Conclusion of the First Missionary Journey (14:24-28)
    2. The Council of Confirmation (15:1-35)
        a. The Issue at Stake (15:1-6)
        b. The Speeches (15:7-21)
            (1) Peter: Declaration of the Facts (15:7-11)
            (2) Barnabas and Paul: Authentication of the Facts (15:12)
            (3) James: Correlation with the Prophets (15:13-21)
        c. The Letter to Gentile Churches (15:22-35)
D. To the Aegean Area: The Second Missionary Journey (15:36–18:22)
    1. The Selection of the Team (15:36–16:3)
    2. The Leading into Europe (16:4-10)
    3. The Witness at Philippi (16:11-40)
    4. The Witness at Thessalonica (17:1-9)
    5. The Witness at Berea (17:10-15)
    6. The Witness at Athens (17:15-34)
    7. The Witness at Corinth (18:1-17)
    8. The Return to Antioch (18:18-22)
E. To Asia and Greece: The Third Missionary Journey (18:23–21:16)
    1. Witness through Paul at Galatia and Phrygia (18:23)
    2. Witness through Apollos in Ephesus and Corinth (18:24-28)
    3. Witness through Paul in Ephesus and En Route to Jerusalem (19:1–21:16)
        a. In Ephesus (19:1-41)
            (1) Witness to the Disciples of John (19:1-7)
            (2) Witness to a Larger Audience (19:8-41)
        b. In Macedonia, Greece, and Asia (20:1-5)
        c. In Troas (20:6-12)
        d. In Miletus (20:13-38)
        e. In Tyre and Caesarea (21:1-14)
            (1) Tyre (21:1-6)
            (2) In Caesarea and to Jerusalem (21:7-16)
F. To Rome: Paul a Prisoner (21:17–28:31)
    1. His Witness in Jerusalem (21:17–23:30)
        a. Before Imprisonment (21:17-30)
            (1) Paul's Meeting with Jewish Believers and Their Proposal (21:17-25)
            (2) The Jewish Leaders' Charge against and Seizure of Paul (21:26-30)
        b. After Imprisonment (21:31–23:30)
            (1) His Arrest and Request to Address the Jews (21:31-40)
            (2) His Address before the Crowd (22:1-21)
            (3) His Claim of Roman Citizenship (22:22-29)
            (4) His Appearance before the Sanhedrin (22:30–23:9)
                (a) His Incident with the High Priest (22:30–23:5)
                (b) His Incitement of Pharisees and Sadducees (23:6-9)
            (5) The Conspiracy to Take His Life (23:10-30)
    2. His Witness in Caesarea by the Sea (23:31–26:32)
        a. Paul's Arrival and Assignment of Quarters (23:31-35)

b. Paul's Defense before Felix the Governor (24:1-21)
  (1) The Accusation by the Jewish Leaders (24:1-9)
  (2) The Answer by Paul (24:10-21)
c. Paul's Later Experience with Felix the Governor (24:22-27)
d. Paul's Defense before Festus the Governor (25:1-12)
e. Paul's Defense before Herod Agrippa II the King (25:13–26:32)
  (1) Prelude to the Defense (25:13-27)
  (2) Particulars of the Defense (26:1-29)
  (3) Result of the Defense: A Declaration of Paul's Innocence (26:30-32)

3. His Witness En Route to Rome (27:1–28:15)
  a. Aboard Ship (27:1-44)
  b. At Malta and Again En Route to Rome (28:1-15)
4. His Witness in Rome (28:16-31)
  a. The Setting for It (28:16-22)
  b. The Substance of It (28:23)
  c. The Sequel to It (28:24-31)
    (1) In Regard to the Need for a Decision (28:24-27)
    (2) In Regard to Paul's Audience (28:28)
    (3) In Regard to Time (28:30)
    (4) In Regard to Emphasis (28:31)

COMMENTARY ON ACTS

I. The Establishment of the Church: Jerusalem (1:1–6:7)

A. The Introduction to Luke's Book about the Mission (1:1-2)

Luke introduces the major themes of the book—the resurrection as the non-negotiable message of Jesus' witnesses, the mandate to witness to the ends of the earth, the strategy for the growth of the church under the sovereign direction and power of the Holy Spirit, and the obedience of the witnesses to the instructions of the Lord. Jesus gave the apostles the divine strategy for advancing the kingdom of God.

1:1-2. Luke's reference to **the first account I composed** connects Acts with the third gospel. Like the Gospel of Luke, Acts is addressed to Theophilus (cf. Lk 1:3), whose name means "lover of God." Some have suggested this is a spiritual title for all believers, whom Jesus called friends in the upper room discourse (see Jn 15:14). The title "most excellent," (Lk 1:3), however, may identify Theophilus as a government official (see Ac 23:26; 24:3; 26:25) who may have served as Luke's patron, underwriting his expenses while he researched and wrote his gospel and its sequel. Another possibility is that he was a Roman official who had made inquiries about this new faith and therefore was the receptor of the book written to defend the faith for the Greco-Roman world. **All that Jesus began to do and teach** refers to Jesus' actions and ministry recorded in Luke's gospel. After His resurrection, Jesus continued His earthly ministry by instructing His apostles **by the Holy Spirit**. "By the Spirit" refers not to the delivery of the instruction by Jesus to the disciples in the power of the Holy Spirit, but anticipates Jesus' promise of the Holy Spirit to empower His followers in their witness to the world.

B. The Means of Preparing the Disciples for the Mission (1:3-26)

1:3. Luke focused on two important truths Jesus emphasized in His teaching prior to His ascension. First, after His suffering, Jesus appeared to His disciples and gave them **many convincing proofs** that He was alive. **Convincing proofs** (*tekmerion*) is used only here in the NT and means "that which causes something to be confirmed or verified in a decisive way" (see BDAG, 994; L&N, 1:339). It refers to evidence that is so credible it could be used in an official trial. **Over a period of forty days** means that Jesus appeared on multiple occasions to His followers and not merely once or twice. Because the message of the resurrection is crucial to the "gospel," it was absolutely essential for Jesus to convince His followers that He is alive.

Second, during His earthly life, the theme of the kingdom of God dominated Jesus' teaching. Now, in preparation for taking the gospel to the world, Jesus again taught about the kingdom. The kingdom of God theme brackets the book of Acts. The book opens with Jesus teaching about the kingdom in the city of Jerusalem (1:3) and ends with Paul teaching about the kingdom of God in the city of Rome (28:31). For an explanation of "the kingdom of God," see the comments on Mt 3:1-4).

Christians debate the exact time of the inauguration and fulfillment of the kingdom. The gospels, especially Mark, make it clear that Jesus inaugurated the kingdom (Mk 1:15; and see the comments on Mt 13:10-17); however, the complete establishment of the kingdom is future. If the messianic kingdom were only a spiritual kingdom equated with the church, it seems strange that Peter would continue to emphasize Israel's hope for a future literal and geo-political kingdom in his preaching to the Jewish people (see the comments on 1:6 and 3:19-21).

1:4-6. Though Jerusalem was a place of danger, Jesus commanded His followers to stay in the city to wait for the Spirit whom God had promised (cf. Jl 2:28-32; Ezk 36:24-28) and Jesus had taught them that they would receive (Jn 14:16-17). For the phrase **baptized with** [better "in"] **the Holy Spirit**, see the comments on Mt 3:5-12; 1Co 12:12-13

The apostles asked, **Lord, is it at this time You are restoring the kingdom to Israel?** The apostles naturally interpreted Jesus' teaching as referring to the full and immediate establishment of the messianic kingdom for Israel, promised for the Jewish people in the Hebrew Scriptures (see Is 2:2-4; Jr 31:27-34; Am 9:11-15). The disciples correctly understood that the promises made to Israel about the restoration of the kingdom under the Messiah were not fulfilled in the fullest sense by the church. For the relationship of the church to the kingdom of God in the present era (before the second coming of Christ), see the comments on Mt 13:10-17.

1:7-8. Nothing in Jesus' answer suggests that the disciples' question was in error, other than their fixation on the time of the restoration. Israel would have a full restoration under the Messiah. But Jesus did not specify when this would happen, and instead presented the mission that must preoccupy His disciples before the kingdom is established.

Some believe that the promises in the OT to Israel about restoration to the land have been fulfilled in Christ for the church. Therefore they interpret Jesus'words as a rebuke for the apostles for misunderstanding the nature, the extent, and the timing of the kingdom. In contrast others believe that Israel will be literally restored to the land during the future millennial (thousand-year) reign of Christ on earth. According to this interpretation, Jesus did not rebuke the apostles for anticipating a literal kingdom but rather for their desire to know **times or epochs.** This view is more plausible since Jesus did not actually deny that there would be a future kingdom for Israel. Rather He maintained that the disciples just could not know when it would come. Moreover, this view is supported by Peter's continuing expectation for a future "restoration of all things" at the second coming of Christ (cf. 3:19-21).

As further clarification of their kingdom mission, Jesus promised His followers the gift of the Spirit. The promise confirmed Jesus' previous promise in Jn 14:16, 25. Its fulfillment would provide the witnesses supernatural power for proclaiming the gospel.

Jesus enlarged the vision of His followers by removing all geographical boundaries for ministry. Instead of waiting for the nations to come to Jerusalem (see Is 2:2; 51:11; Mc 4:1-2), Jesus commissioned His followers to go to the nations. Like the ripples that widen from the place where a stone is tossed into a pond, the gospel will radiate from its origination in Jerusalem to Judea and Samaria, and ultimately to the ends of the earth. In the context of the book of Acts, the ends of the earth may be a reference to Rome, though it should not be restricted to it.

1:9-14. After commissioning the apostles, Jesus ascended to heaven enveloped in a cloud. God guided Israel in the wilderness and hovered above the tabernacle in a cloud, and when he revealed His deity at the transfiguration, Jesus was surrounded by a cloud. It was appropriate then for Jesus to return to heaven in a cloud, symbolizing the presence of God. The bewildered apostles responded like a convention of stargazers until two angels appeared and promised them that Jesus would return in the same way. This promise (v. 11) is pivotal for a proper understanding of the second coming. Preterists believe that the second coming has already taken place in AD 70. According to this view, Jesus' return to earth was not physical but rather a return in judgment against Israel and Jerusalem (see the comments introducing Mt 24–25). In light of Ac 1:11, however, the preterist view is untenable. Jesus will descend visibly, physically, and literally to the Mount of Olives, parallel to how He ascended (see the comments on Zch 14:1-5). The ascension gives assurance of God's approval of Christ's life and work and the certainty of His second coming.

As the Lord had commanded (cf. 1:4), the apostles courageously and obediently returned to Jerusalem. In Jerusalem they gathered in an upper room, probably in the home of Mary (see Ac 12:12, though it is impossible to be certain). It is unlikely that this was the same room used by Jesus and the disciples on the night He was betrayed. Different words are used for that location (in Mk 14:15 and Lk 22:11-12). Both men and women prayed. Luke gave two essentials for effective prayer. **These all with one mind were continually devoting themselves to prayer**. They prayed with "with one mind and purpose" (*homothymadon*) (BDAG, 706), and they were "devoted to" (*proskartereo*, "to persist in some activity, to be busily engaged in" something) (see BDAG, 880) prayer. They were united and prayed constantly. This kind of devotion to prayer indicated total confidence the Lord would soon send the Spirit and they would become His witnesses.

1:15-20. Peter emerged as the leader of the early believers, who numbered 120. His short speech contained two important points. He recognized that even the tragic events surrounding Christ's betrayal and arrest were a fulfillment of Scripture (v. 16). He affirmed the inspiration of the OT, **the Scripture . . . which the Holy Spirit foretold by the mouth of David**. He alluded to the Psalms to explain Judas' betrayal of Christ (1:20) and the need for a replacement (vv. 21-22). Peter combined quotations from two Psalms with a change in wording to make specific application to Judas (Ps 69:25 and Ps 109:8 in v. 20). He took the curse pronounced on David's enemies, applied it to Judas (Ps 69:25), and combined this with Psalm 109:8, a Psalm that condemns the wicked who had betrayed David. Possibly, he did not mean that these passages were direct predictions of Judas; rather, that the curses of the wicked described in these passages merely applied to Judas, a wicked man. (See Michael Rydelnik, *The Messianic Hope: Is the Hebrew Bible Really Messianic?* [Nashville: B&H Publishers, 2010], 95–111 for the four ways the NT uses the OT, especially pp. 104–08 for an explanation of "applicational fulfillment.")

Luke's account of Judas's death (vv. 18-19) raises two apparent contradictions about how Judas died and who bought the "Field of Blood." Matthew recorded that Judas hanged himself (Mt 27:5), and Luke wrote that Judas fell forward and his body burst open (Ac 1:18). The simplest explanation is that after Judas hanged himself, the rope or the branch broke and his body, which may have become bloated from the searing heat in the Middle East, broke open when he hit the ground. More significant is the reason for Matthew's and Luke's different presentations. For Matthew, writing to a Jewish audience, both committing suicide and hanging on a tree would depict Judas as someone who was accursed (Dt 21:23). In the Greco-Roman world, committing suicide would be considered an honorable way of showing remorse. Thus, Luke emphasized the mutilation of Judas's body—something that would be considered a curse in that culture. Although the events in the two accounts can and should be harmonized, it is essential to note that both authors sought to demonstrate that Judas fell under God's curse for his betrayal of the Messiah.

Matthew said that the chief priests bought the field (Mt 27:6-7) and Luke that Judas bought it (Ac 1:18). However, it is not a contradiction to state that Judas bought the field since it was purchased with the money that had been given to him by the chief priests. The field is called "Hakeldama" (Aramaic), "Field of Blood" (v. 19) because the chief priests purchased it with the money they had paid Judas to betray Jesus and because Judas committed suicide in the same field.

1:21-22. Because Jesus had promised the Twelve that they would rule over the twelve tribes of Israel (Mt 19:28; Lk 22:28-30), Peter recommended a replacement for Judas. In his recommendation of a replacement for Judas, Peter gave the basic qualification and work of an apostle. First, one qualification included an association with Jesus from His baptism to His ascension. Second, Peter stated that the primary work of an apostle was to witness to Christ's resurrection (1:21-22).

1:23-26. Two candidates met the criteria—**Joseph**, who was also called **Barsabbas** (Hb.) or **Justus** (Lat.), and **Matthias**. They prayed, acknowledging that God knew their hearts (their desire to do His will), and asked Him to reveal His will. The casting of lots is an OT method for determining God's will (cf. Ex 28:30, Dt 33:8, Ezr 2:63). The principle is stated in Pr 16:33: "The lot is cast into the lap, but its every decision is from the LORD." The lot identified God's choice of Matthias to replace Judas. Some have charged that the choice of Matthias was wrong because they used an OT method for determining God's will. Those who hold this view claim that Paul is the twelfth apostle. Nothing in the text, however, suggests that God disapproved of the choice of Matthias. In fact, Luke referred to this group as the Twelve in 2:14 and 6:2. Moreover, it is likely that the Twelve were apostles to Israel and thus they would one day rule over Israel. Paul was an apostle to the uncircumcised, or Gentiles, and as such was not one of the Twelve (cf. Richard N. Longenecker, "The Acts of the Apostles," in *John, Acts,* EBC, ed. Frank E.Gaebelein [Grand Rapids, MI: Zondervan, 1981], 265).

The promise of the Spirit, the commission for believers to become witnesses to all the world, and the choice of a replacement for Judas set the stage for Jesus to continue His supernatural work in the lives of those who believe in Him. Only one element was missing—the Holy Spirit.

C. The Initiation of the Mission (2:1-47)

1. The Power of Pentecost (2:1-13)

a. The Coming of the Spirit (2:1-4)

Acts 2 can be divided into four sections: (1) the gift of the Spirit (1-13), (2) Peter's message explaining the phenomenon of the gift of the Spirit (14-36), (3) the response to Peter's message (37-41), and (4) the description of the early church (42-47).

Approximately six weeks after His resurrection and only days after His ascension, the exalted Lord Jesus fulfilled His promise to supernaturally empower His disciples by pouring out the Holy Spirit on them.

2:1. Pentecost means "fiftieth" because the Feast was on the 50th day after the Feast of First Fruits (Lv 23:16). It was originally one of three harvest festivals, but in early (intertestamental) Judaism it was commemorated as the anniversary of the giving of the law at Mount Sinai because it was thought that God gave the law to Israel 50 days after the exodus. Pentecost would come in May or June on our calendar. It is possible that God gave the Holy Spirit on Pentecost to contrast with the law. The law was an external means of restraining Israel from sin, but in the new era of the church, the Holy Spirit would provide internal power for believers to live righteously (Jr 31:33; Ezk 36:26-27).

2:2-3. The initial giving of the Spirit was accompanied by the phenomena of powerful wind and flashes of fire. The wind symbolized the power of the Lord (cf. the appearance of the Lord to Elijah in 1Kg 19:11) and the fire His presence (cf. the appearance of the Lord to Elijah and Moses in 1Kg 19:12 and Ex 3:2). Luke's statement that the Spirit **rested on each one of them** is significant: every believer (men and women) was filled with the Spirit; no one was excluded (see 1Co 12:7). Plus, in contrast to the selective and temporary giving of the Spirit in the OT era (See Samson, Jdg 14:19, 16:20; Saul, 1Sm 10:10, 16:14), in the NT era the Spirit is a permanent gift (Jn 14:16).

2:4. The internal and invisible gift of the Spirit was manifested by the external and visible phenomenon of speaking in tongues.

In the OT era, the gift of the Spirit was often corroborated by prophetic proclamations (e.g., Eldad and Medad, Nm 11:26-29; Saul, 1Sm 10:6-12), but after the ministry of Malachi, the spirit of prophecy ceased (for support, see *1 Macc* 9:27; *4 Ezra* 14:44; Josephus, *Against Apion* 1.41). The Jews expected, however, with the coming of the messianic age, God would once again give His Spirit and people would prophesy (Jl 2:28-32; Ezk 36:25-27). That hope was realized on the day of Pentecost, but the prophecy was of a special type. They **began to speak with other tongues** (*heterais glossais*).

To understand this phenomenon it is necessary to answer four questions:

First, did the disciples speak a foreign language, or did they speak in a language they knew but the hearers heard it in their own language? Judging from the infinitive **to speak** (*lalein*) in 2:4, the disciples spoke in other languages. In addition, the audience did not receive a special capacity from the Spirit to understand the language spoken by the disciples in their own languages.

Second, was it a foreign language or ecstatic speech? More than likely, it was an earthly foreign language not learned formally by the disciples. In 2:6, 8 the word "language" is the Greek word *dialektos,* which means "the language of a nation or region" and not an ecstatic utterance (BDAG, 232). Plus, the list of fifteen ethnic regions in vv. 7-11 suggests foreign languages.

Third, what was the purpose of the phenomenon? In Acts, speaking in tongues was a "sign" indicating the beginning of a new era in God's program of redemption. It was not confirmation to new believers that they had received the gift of the Spirit. In v. 16, Peter said the gift fulfilled what was predicted by the prophet Joel (Jl 2:28-32). For a fuller discussion of the purpose and nature of speaking in tongues, see the comments introducing the commentary on 1Co 14:1.

Fourth, is speaking in tongues a normative experience for all believers or a unique phenomenon related to the birth and growth of the early church? The evidence supports the latter. The phenomenon is mentioned explicitly only three times in Acts (among the Jewish people in 2:4, among the Gentiles in 10:45-46, and among the disciples of John in 19:6). The Samaritans (Ac 8) and Paul (Ac 9) may have spoken in tongues after they received the Spirit, but it is not stated. In reporting dozens of other conversion experiences, Luke did not mention speaking in tongues. Furthermore, none of the major characters in Acts commanded or instructed others on how or whether they should speak in tongues (which is not the case for many practices in Acts, e.g., baptism). This fact supports the idea that Luke did not intend speaking in tongues to be understood as normative or binding upon the church perpetually. Instead, Acts simply recorded what did happen, not what should happen consistently. The phenomenon of tongues, like many of the experiences in Acts, is a unique event, signaling the beginning of the era of the Spirit who has come to empower believers to take the gospel to all nations.

b. The Reaction of the Crowd (2:5-13)

2:5-13. Some were amazed because they heard them speaking in their own language. Others, unable to grasp what has happened, concluded they were drunk. The Spirit, who had seized control of the witnesses, made them appear as if they were drunk—not in control of their own actions. Apparently when the disciples spoke in tongues they spoke known languages, but when the listeners heard them speaking a language that was not their own, they assumed wrongly that those disciples were intoxicated.

2. The Proclamation of Pentecost (2:14-47)

a. The Reference to Joel (2:14-21)

2:14-21. Starting in 2:14, Peter explained how the gift fulfilled prophecy, and then he gave evidence that Jesus is Lord and Christ.

Peter addressed his countrymen (Jews), and refuted the charge of drunkenness. The Jewish day began at 6 a.m.; the third hour was 9 a.m. Only a hard-core alcoholic could get drunk by 9 a.m.

From Peter's perspective, the gift of the Spirit fulfilled the promise of Jl 2:28-32 (see the comments there). Though debatable, it seems best to interpret the day of Pentecost as only a partial fulfillment of Joel's prophecy—an "already, not yet" kind of fulfillment. The division between the "already" and "not yet" comes between vv. 18 and 19. The gift of the Spirit marked the beginning of the Holy Spirit's work, but not the complete fulfillment of the events at the day of the Lord. For an explanation of the phrase **BEFORE THE GREAT AND GLORIOUS DAY OF THE LORD**, see the comments on Jl 2:30-31. Peter anticipated the fulfillment of all of God's promises to Israel when Christ returns from heaven (cf. 3:20-21). Another possibility is to recognize that Jl 2:28-32 predicts the Holy Spirit's work in the events of the future tribulation period, while Ac 2:14-21 merely applies them to the Spirit's work. The application would be that just as many unusual signs would follow the Holy Spirit's powerful work at the end of days, so here at the birth of the church, the unusual and demonstrative work of the Spirit was evident in the apostles' speaking in tongues.

b. The Reference to Christ (2:22-36)

(1) His Life of Power (2:22)

2:22. His miraculous works proved Jesus is the Messiah. Peter used three different terms to describe Jesus' works. The word **miracles** identifies the supernatural element of Jesus' works; **wonders** describes the effect of the miracle on the witnesses; and **signs** indicates the purpose of the miracle. It is significant that no one protested Peter's statement, since many of those present had been eyewitnesses to Jesus' miraculous works. During his earthly life, Jesus used His divine power to authenticate His messianic claims by healing the sick, restoring sight to the blind, casting out demons, and even raising the dead. If Jesus' miracles had been suspect, someone would have challenged Peter's claim about Jesus' works.

(2) His Death and Resurrection (2:23-32)

2:23. The crucifixion was not an accident. Christ was put to death according to **the predetermined plan and foreknowledge of God**. **Plan** (*boule*) refers to God's unchangeable purpose when used in reference to His will (BAGD, 182;

see Heb 6:17). Yet Peter implicated both Jews and Gentiles in Christ's death. Longenecker states that nowhere in the NT is the paradox of Christian history put more sharply than in the death of Jesus. Though the crucifixion was determined by God's purpose and foreknowledge, it was executed through the instrumentality of wicked men exercising their free will (Longenecker, "Acts," 207). The Bible teaches but does not explain the paradox of God's sovereignty and human freedom.

2:24-28. In spite of the intentions of godless men, God raised Jesus from the dead. It was impossible for death to hold Him. Moreover, His resurrection fulfilled the prediction in David's prophetic Word. Peter quoted Ps 16:8-11, and in particular, **Because You will not abandon my soul to Hades, Nor allow Your Holy One to undergo decay** (2:27). There David declared his confidence in his own resurrection because he knew that God would not allow His "Holy One," the future Messiah, to decay in the grave. Psalm 16 uses first-person pronouns throughout except for Ps 16:10b, where the only non-first-person construction is found ("Holy One," not "me"), suggesting that both David and Peter saw in Ps 16 a reference to the resurrection of someone other than David and in whom David placed the hope of his own resurrection.

2:29-32. The passage must refer to someone other than David because he is buried in Jerusalem. Peter called David a prophet because he confidently predicted God would fulfill His promise that one of his descendants would rise from the dead and also rule forever (Ps 132:11-12; cf. 2Sm 7:12-13). In addition to Scriptural evidence for the resurrection, Peter gave personal evidence. **We are all witnesses**, he said. In 2:31, Peter reiterated themes from 2:27, but in v. 31, Ps 16:10a is now applied to Jesus in His resurrection rather than to David's confidence in the "Holy One" for his own resurrection. But if David's hope of resurrection was founded upon the resurrection of the Holy One, then what can be said of David's future resurrection can be applied to the Holy One Himself.

(3) His Exaltation (2:33-36)

2:33-36. The exaltation proved Jesus is the Messiah.

2:33. The authority for Jesus to send the promised Holy Spirit derived from the exaltation. Christ always possessed the rights of divine authority, but in His exaltation He received the right to exercise the power and authority of His deity.

2:34-35. Peter again quoted from David for scriptural support. The point from Ps 110:1 is that Jesus, not David, is the one seated at the right hand of God, a position of unique honor and authority. Some maintain that Peter's citation of Ps 110:1 indicates that Jesus is already ruling upon the throne of David. But Peter did not cite Ps 110:2, which makes explicit the exercise of Messiah's *future* lordly rule upon the earth. Peter cited the psalm to support Jesus' exalted status as Messiah, not to express a particular function of the Messiah (such as ruling on the throne of David) during the present age.

2:36. Verse 36 is the high point of Peter's sermon. Jesus' miraculous works, His resurrection, and His exaltation indicate overwhelmingly that He is both **Lord** (a common title for God and applied to Jesus in Acts; see 4:33; 8:16; 15:11; 16:31; 21:13; 28:31) and **Christ** (the Messiah, the "Anointed One" who rescues Israel and all humankind). This was a shocking conclusion for his Jewish audience, who did not comprehend the triunity of God. Peter's conclusion reflects the high Christology of the early church, which believed that Jesus was God because of the historical evidence. Their Christology was based on personal conviction of what they knew was true, not wishful thinking.

c. The Reaction of the Crowd (2:37)

2:37. It is not surprising that Peter's audience experienced emotional trauma. The expression **pierced to the heart** is used figuratively for the feeling of sharp pain due to anxiety or remorse (BDAG, 415). They were not merely intellectually convinced, but spiritually convicted of their dilemma.

d. The Appeal of Peter (2:38-40)

2:38. Peter's answer to the anguished question of his countrymen is good news, yet raises some controversial issues about the relation of repentance, forgiveness, and baptism. The Jews were familiar with John's message emphasizing repentance and baptism (see the comments on Mt 3:5-12). On the imperative verb **repent**, Louw and Nida write, "Though in English a focal component of repent is the sorrow or contrition that a person experiences because of sin, the emphasis [in the Gk. words "to repent" and "repentance"] seems to be more specifically the total change, both in thought and behavior, with respect to how one should both think and act. Whether the focus is upon attitude or behavior varies somewhat in different contexts" (L&N, 509). Peter was calling the hearers to change their minds about their participation in and approval of the crucifixion of Jesus. Darrell Bock notes that repentance and faith are two sides of the same coin. One cannot turn to Christ in faith for forgiveness without also turning away from reliance upon something else. He proposes, however, that there is a distinction between faith and repentance: "Repentance stresses the starting point of the need for forgiveness, whereas faith is the resulting trust and understanding that this forgiveness comes from God, the one turned to for the gift (Acts 20:21)" (*Acts*, BECNT [Grand Rapids, MI: Baker, 2007], 142). Peter introduced two new elements. First, he said baptism must now be **in the name of Jesus**. This means a commitment to and identification with Jesus as Lord and Christ. For an explanation for why the name of the triune God is not used in the baptismal formula here, see the comments on Mt 28:18-20. Second, he promised them the **gift of the Holy Spirit**. This is the Spirit Himself, as in 2:33 ("the promise of the Holy Spirit" is the Spirit Himself), and not the "gifts" that the Spirit gives to believers.

Some believe that both repentance and baptism are required for the forgiveness of sins (baptismal regeneration). This view, however, is inconsistent with the overall teaching of Scripture. In addition, in Lk 24:47; Ac 3:19; 10:43; 13:38, and 26:18, **forgiveness** (*aphesis*, the same Gk. word translated with "forgiveness" in each verse) is promised *without baptism* to those who respond appropriately (i.e., with faith or repentance). The grammatical construction of the sentence does not support the idea that baptism is essential for salvation. The command to **repent** is plural ("all of you repent") as is the word **your** in **for the forgiveness of your sins**, forging a close connection between repentance and forgiveness. On the other hand, the command **be baptized** is a third person *singular* verb, implying that baptism is not directly connected to forgiveness. As in 10:47-48 and 16:33, baptism is the appropriate response for those who have found salvation in Christ, but it is not the *means* effecting that salvation.

Others believe in a second work of the Spirit after conversion, usually signified by speaking in tongues. The context, however, suggests the reception of the Spirit is a one-time experience. No mention is made about the 3,000 who believed speaking in tongues (though admittedly this is an argument from silence—but sometimes the silence is *deafening*), nor is the laying on of hands mentioned as the means for conveying the Spirit as a gift to others, nor for enabling others to speak in tongues.

Clearly, the apostles were believers prior to their reception of the Holy Spirit at Pentecost. Nevertheless, this does not teach that all believers must receive the Holy Spirit subsequent to their salvation experience. Rather, the described events demonstrate the transition from the way the Holy Spirit worked in the OT, to the Spirit's work in the NT church. In the OT, the Holy Spirit came upon some believers to empower them for a limited time to accomplish a specific task. In the NT, the Holy Spirit permanently indwells all believers (Jn 14:16-17). The falling of the Holy Spirit on the apostles marked the transition to the new way the Holy Spirit would work.

The three elements of the conversion experience are repentance (implying also faith), baptism, and the gift of the Spirit. If a person will turn from sin in faith and repentance (essential and internal) and be baptized (nonessential and external), God will forgive his sin and he will receive the gift of the Holy Spirit.

2:39. The expression **for all who are far off** could refer to either Jews of the Diaspora or Gentiles. The former seems more likely in view of Peter's restricted understanding of God's redemptive program prior to the vision leading him to Cornelius. But, at the time of writing, Luke may have understood it as a prediction of the proclamation of the gospel to the Gentiles without limitation to any ethnic group.

The statement, **as many as the Lord our God will call to himself**, refers to God's electing purposes, whereby people are drawn to Christ for salvation. In his prophecy, Joel promised salvation to "everyone who calls on the name of the Lord" (Ac 2:21); Peter was indicating that God is sovereign over the call to salvation.

2:40. The recorded message is only a summary of what Peter said. Peter's primary concern was the imminent judgment of the day of the Lord. If Peter's listeners wanted to escape destruction of that **perverse generation** they had to acknowledge Jesus as Lord and Christ (Messiah). The description of his present generation as **perverse** means that they were morally and ethically corrupt (see BDAG, 930).

e. The Salvation and Fellowship of Three Thousand (2:41-47)

2:41. The response was amazing. Three thousand believed and were baptized. Those who believed did not start a new sect but were added to the 120. The growth from 120 to 3,000 was nothing less than supernatural. Baptism was not a foreign concept for Jewish people. By the first century, the prescribed ritual washings in the law (Lv 8:6; 15:31-33) had led to an elaborate system of ritual baths for Jewish people. Thus, John the Baptist's baptism of repentance was understood and accepted by the many Jewish people who went out to the wilderness to hear John preach (Mt 4:25). Peter's command for them to repent and be baptized would have been understood as an outward sign of their repentance from sin and commencement of following Jesus.

In 2:41-42, Luke gave a concise, vivid description of community life in the first followers of Jesus. These first believers rightly saw themselves as the faithful remnant of Israel. Unbeknownst to them at this point, they were also part of something entirely new—a supernatural community bonded together by their common faith in Jesus Christ, their unselfish love for one another, and their determination to proclaim the gospel. It would take the ministry of the apostles (Eph 3:5a), Paul (Eph 3:5b-6) and the Jerusalem Council (Ac 15) to reveal that this was the beginning of the universal church, the one new man composed of Jews and Gentiles (cf. Eph 2:11-22; 3:1-13 and comments there).

2:42. Devoting (*proskartereo*) means "exerting great effort to persist in doing something." It indicates action that is continuous and habitual. Luke uses the term in 1:14 to describe the "devotion" of the 120 to prayer and in 6:4 to refer to the apostles' devotion to prayer and ministry of the word. What were the early believers devoted to? What were their priorities?

The **apostles' teaching** identifies material that the church considered authoritative because it was taught by the apostles. The content undoubtedly focused on the life and teaching of Jesus Christ, especially the redemptive aspects of His life, death, and resurrection.

Fellowship (*koinonia*) refers to intimate, not casual, community spirit. Christian fellowship includes a relationship with the Father, Son, and Holy Spirit, and a horizontal relationship with other believers. The latter was Luke's focus here in Ac 2. The definite article suggests that the first believers formed a distinct and identifiable group. Their fellowship included two activities.

Breaking of bread was more than a meal to satisfy the pangs of hunger. It was an occasion for intimate fellowship. It probably included both the Lord's Supper and a common meal (2:46, 20:7, 1Co 10:16). At the meal they celebrated their communion with one another. At the Lord's Table they celebrated their communion with the risen Christ.

Prayer is plural and suggests corporate prayer. The early church realized their need for God's ongoing help and the importance of praise and devoted themselves to prayer.

2:43. Wonders and signs gave evidence God was at work in the church. While miracles in Acts did provide deliverance for those who were sick, equally important was their confirmation of the gospel message given through the apostles and the other members of Christ's body (14:3). For the most part, signs and wonders took place through the hands of the apostles (2:43; 3:16; 5:12; 15:12; 19:11-12), a fitting fact since the NT identifies performing signs and wonders as authentication of true apostle (2Co 12:12; Heb 2:3-4). The only exceptions in Acts are Stephen (6:8) and Philip (8:6), who, having had the apostles lay hands on them (6:5-6), functioned as apostolic legates (or representatives) and thereby performed signs and wonders.

2:44-45. Their spiritual unity was manifested in voluntary, compassionate sharing. This was not socialism or communism. The purpose was to meet needs and not redistribute wealth.

2:46. The early believers considered themselves part of the faithful remnant in Israel, so they continued to worship in the temple. They also met in individual homes in a more informal setting.

2:47. At this point the church was not threatened by persecution or disrupted by internal problems. Internally there was a spirit of rejoicing and generosity. Externally they enjoyed popularity and respect from the people. **And the Lord was adding to their number**. Their growth was supernatural and rapid. Christ had promised, "I will build my church . . ." (Mt 16:18), and He kept His promise. Luke concluded his description of the founding of the church on a note of triumph.

D. Difficulties for the Mission (3:1–6:7)

1. External Persecution: Arrest of Peter and John (3:1–4:31)

a. The Ministry of Healing (3:1-11)

This extended section deals with the healing of a lame beggar, and both the positive and negative responses to this miracle. Like Jesus before them, the apostles had power to work miracles to authenticate their message. There was however a significant difference. Christ healed by His own authority. Peter and others healed "in the name of Jesus." Their power was not their own, it came from the resurrected Lord.

The pattern of events in Ac 3 is similar to Ac 2. A miraculous event captured the attention of the people; then Peter capitalized on the excitement to proclaim that Jesus is the Servant of the Lord. The result, however, was different. Instead of seeing remorse and repentance, the church came under attack because of the message of the resurrection.

3:1-3. As did all godly Jews, Peter and John went to the temple to pray. The **ninth hour** is 3:00 p.m. and is the second of three daily prayer times. They met a man who was physically challenged from birth. Because he was lame, he was not allowed to enter the temple area; so he sat at the entrance of the temple by the **gate . . . called Beautiful** begging for a handout. It is not easy to identify this gate. Luke may have given the name "Beautiful" to the Nicanor Gate, which provided an entrance from outside the temple complex into the Court of the Gentiles and the Court of Women. Because it was considered an act of piety to give to the poor, the disabled man had strategically located himself in direct view of those coming to the temple to worship.

3:4-7. When Peter made eye contact, the man expected to receive a coin but was initially disappointed. Peter's response was classic: "Silver or gold have I none; but such as I have give I thee" (KJV). Peter gave him a greater gift. **In the name of Jesus Christ the Nazarene** he healed him. The healing was instantaneous and complete. The expression **in the name of** stands for more than someone acting as the representative of another person. The name of Jesus identified the person of Jesus, who healed the man. Peter was only the agent, not the source of the power. The point of the healing was primarily evidential. Jesus was not dead; He is alive.

3:8. The man's jubilant response was normal, not excessive. His leaping and praising God provided a dramatic illustration of what Israel could experience if they would recognize Jesus as Messiah. Isaiah had predicted that with the coming of the messianic age "the lame will leap like deer" (35:6).

3:9-11. The miracle was public not private. There is no doubt about the healing, and it has the effect of attracting a large crowd of unbelieving Jews.

b. The Message of Peter (3:12-26)

In 3:12-26, Luke has provided an explanation of the source of the power exhibited in the miraculous healing. As he did on the day of Pentecost, Peter seized the opportunity to proclaim that Jesus is God's glorified Servant. The "servant" theme brackets Peter's message (3:13, 26). The background for the "servant" theme comes from the servant songs in Isaiah (Is 40–53). F. F. Bruce observes that no passage of OT prophecy has made a greater impact on NT thought and language than the servant passages of Isaiah (*The Book of Acts*, NICNT [Grand Rapids, MI: Eerdmans, 1979], 89).

3:12-15. Peter addressed his countrymen and quickly dispelled any misconceptions that the man was healed by his personal power. Peter emphasized the tragedy of Israel's rejection of Jesus, who was the fulfillment of God's promises to His people.

By mentioning **the God of Abraham, Isaac and Jacob** (v. 13), Peter identified himself with his people. That God **has glorified His servant Jesus** is a reference to the resurrection and ascension. The crucifixion was a travesty of justice. The Jewish leadership and their mob ruled in favor of a violent criminal and insisted on the crucifixion of **the Holy and Righteous One**. These two titles were used for God in the OT (Lv 11:44-45; 19:2) and also for the Messiah. David wrote in Ps 16:10, "Nor will You allow Your Holy One to undergo decay" (cf. Ac 2:27). The prophets identified the Messiah as "righteous." Isaiah said, "By His knowledge the Righteous One, My Servant, will justify (declare righteous) the many" (Is 53:11; see also Is 32:1; Zch 9:9). In addition to these two titles from the Old Testament, Peter introduced a new title, **Prince of life** (cf. 5:31). The term **Prince** (*archegos*) can also mean "Author" in the sense of source of life (Heb 2:10; BDAG, 138-39). It is valid to say that Jesus is both the leader of life and the source of life.

3:16-18. Peter took no credit for the healing. After the resurrection, Jesus' name possessed the same power as the name of God. The lame man's spiritual condition prior to the healing is not stated in the text. His healing was not a result of his faith, and in fact he did not even expect to be healed. The primary function of miracles in Acts is Christological—to prove that Jesus was alive and thus Israel's promised Messiah.

The primary theme of 3:17-23 is the need for repentance by the Jewish people. Peter acknowledged that the crowd and their leaders had acted in ignorance in insisting the Romans crucify Christ (3:17). This admission does not mean they were not responsible for their actions. Peter distinguished here between "sins of ignorance" and "intentional sins," a distinction that his listeners would understand. Under the law, atonement was available for sins committed "in error" (a better translation than sins committed "unintentionally") on the basis of human weakness (including, for example, lying, theft, and fraud; Nm 15:24, Lv 6:1-7) but not the sin of deliberate, calculated rebellion against God (Nm 15:30-36), a type of sin called "the blasphemy of the Holy Spirit" in the NT.

Though their actions fulfilled prophecy about the suffering Messiah (3:18), their ignorance was no longer excusable. Peter challenged his countrymen to "repent," which requires a change of mind involving the intellect, emotions, and will. He was insisting that they change their mind about Jesus. Instead of dismissing Him as a false prophet, they needed to believe on Him as Messiah, God's anointed Servant.

3:19-21. Peter made two promises—personal forgiveness of sins and national restoration. **Wiped away** means "to remove completely." In ancient writing ink could be removed before it dried on papyrus by wiping it off with a damp cloth. The imagery implies that when God forgives sins, He also removes the stain of sin.

Times of refreshing and **restoration of all things** are not found in any other NT passages and suggest that Peter was thinking of the spiritual and national restoration of Israel. Cognate verbs of the noun **restoration** are used in the LXX for the eschatological restoration of Israel as a national entity (Jr 15:19; 16:15; Ezk 16:55; Hs 11:11) (Longenecker, "Acts", 297). Though Christ had taught his followers more about the kingdom of God in the 40 days between His resurrection and ascension, Peter and the apostles still anticipated a literal, geo-political messianic kingdom that would be inaugurated with the visible return of Christ to earth. Peter's expectation favored a literal kingdom for regenerated Israel with Messiah Jesus ruling on the throne of David over them and the world. According to Peter, this offer was for Israel and will be fulfilled whenever the nation turns in faith to Jesus as their Messiah and Lord (cf. comments at Zch 12:10; Mt 23:37-39; Rm 11:25-27).

3:22-23. Peter also warned of the consequences of continued unbelief. The quote in v. 22 is from Dt 18:15, to which Peter added Lv 23:29-30. Deuteronomy contains the promise and warning of rejecting the prophet like Moses, who is identified as Jesus of Nazareth both here and in Ac 7:37. Jesus was more than *the* prophet foretold by Moses, but in much of His earthly ministry He functioned prophetically as Moses did, providing prophetic revelation, communing with God, and performing miracles (see Dt 34:10-12). The Leviticus passage warns that those who refuse to observe the Day of Atonement will be "completely cut off" from Israel. Like OT apostates, those who reject Israel's Messiah will be banned from the community of God's people.

3:24-26. Peter concluded with an appeal to Israel's national heritage. Any movement that could not show its continuity with Israel's prophetic heritage stood little chance of success. Thus, Peter appealed to the voice of prophecy to convince his Jewish countrymen that Jesus is God's promised Servant. He referred first to Samuel and all the other prophets. Peter's words, **all the prophets who have spoken, from Samuel and his successors onward, also announced these days**, indicate that from Samuel, the first prophet, and all the prophets onward, their focus was the revelation of the Messiah. This is similar to the later rabbinic dictum, "All the prophets prophesied only with reference to the days of Messiah" (*Berakot* 34b).

Next, Peter reminded his countrymen of God's promise to bless Abraham (personal), to make him into a great nation (national), and to bring a blessing to all mankind through him (universal) (see Gn 12:1-3). The term **SEED** is singular, indicating that Jesus is the ultimate seed of Abraham and fulfills God's promise to the patriarch. Peter reminded his Jewish audience that God sent His Servant first to them. Though God's plan of redemption included Gentiles, God gave the Jewish people priority as recipients of His grace (see comments at Rm 1:16).

The healing of the lame man and the ensuing sermon is a model of the early proclamation of the gospel to the Jewish people. According to Longenecker, "Luke seems to have included it as an example of how the early congregation in Jerusalem proclaimed the message of Jesus to the people of Israel as a whole" (Longenecker, "Acts", 296). The message emphasizes Jesus as the resurrected and exalted Lord and Messiah, and as such, He has become the direct source of divine power. The most important point in this story is not the physical healing of the lame man but the source of the power that brought the healing. Luke's purpose was to give evidence that Jesus is Israel's Messiah and Lord, not to provide a paradigm for a healing ministry. This view is supported in Ac 4 when the lame man was the material witness before the Sanhedrin that he was healed in the "name of Jesus," proving that Jesus is alive, not dead, and that He is indeed God's glorified Servant and Savior.

This emphasis on the power and authority of Jesus continues in Ac 4:1-31. While Peter and John were still speaking, the religious leaders arrived and arrested them because of their teaching about the resurrection. Though Peter and John were only fishermen, they were filled with the Holy Spirit and inspired by the certainty of the resurrection. They would not and could not be intimidated by the most powerful religious leaders in Israel. Peter answered the charges of the Sanhedrin with a message claiming Jesus is the "cornerstone/capstone" of God's plan of redemption.

c. The Menace of the Sanhedrin (4:1-31)

4:1-3. Luke's presentation of the formal persecution of the church in the wake of the miracle in chap. 3 begins in 4:1-4 with the arrest of Peter and John. The arresting contingent included **the priests and the captain of the temple guard and the Sadducees**. All were Jewish, not Roman, and had authority in matters related to the temple. The Sadducees were rationalists (see Jn 11:49), and did not believe in a resurrection. Their rejection of the hope of a resurrection was the motivation for the arrest. Peter and John were held overnight because there was not enough time for a trial before sunset.

4:4. Luke gave a numerical summary of the growth of the church at this point to emphasize its remarkable growth in spite of the hostility of the religious leaders. The 5,000 (total) included only men and not women and children (contrary to the translation of the TNIV). The total was obviously more (see Longenecker, "Acts", 287, for a defense of the size of the church in relation to the population of Jerusalem in the first century).

4:5-6. Acts 4:5-12 presents the details of the trial of the two apostles. Peter and John were interrogated by the Sanhedrin, which was Israel's "Supreme Court." The membership totaled 71 (70 members plus the high priest). The Sanhedrin included "rulers" or "high priests," "elders," and "scribes" (teachers of the law).

Annas was not the actual high priest but the father-in-law of Caiaphas, the ruling high priest. For more on Caiaphas and Annas, see the comments on Mt 26:3-5. The identity of John and Alexander are unknown.

4:7. The authorities did not deny the healing. Their question was by whose authority the healing took place.

4:8-12. Peter's courage was rather remarkable considering his background (fisherman) and his audience (the most intellectual and powerful in Israel). His courage came from the Holy Spirit (4:8). He made two startling points. The first was about the miracle. The man was healed in the name of Jesus Christ, who is alive, not dead. The second was his message that Jesus, "the rejected stone," is the "cornerstone" (NASV) or "capstone" (NIV). Peter quoted Ps 118:22 because of its messianic significance. It is now recognized that the book of Psalms was collected after Israel's exile. In the post-exilic period, the central figure of the Psalms, the Davidic king, was no longer on the throne. In light of this recognition, Brevard Childs insightfully asks, "Indeed, at the time of the final redaction, when the institution of kingship had long since been destroyed, what earthly king would have come to mind other than God's Messiah?" (*Introduction to the Old Testament as Scripture* [Philadelphia: Fortress, 1979], 516). Thus, Sailhamer says of the cornerstone described in Ps 118:22, "He is the Blessed One who comes in the name of the Lord [v. 26a]. Though the psalm itself does not identify who this One is, the larger context within Psalms makes it clear that he is the Promised Seed of the house of David, the Messiah. It is for this reason that this psalm is frequently alluded to in the NT" [Mt 21:42; Mk 12:10-11; Lk 20:17; Ac 4:11; Eph 2:20; 1Pt 2:7] (John H. Sailhamer, *The NIV Compact Bible Commentary* [Grand Rapids, MI: Zondervan, 1994], 342). The implication is obvious; the Jewish leadership had rejected Jesus, who is the indispensable One in God's kingdom program. It is useless to look for salvation in someone else.

4:13. In 4:13-22, Luke recorded the judicial decision of the Sanhedrin as it related to the work and message of the two apostles. The Sanhedrin were astonished by the courage of two unschooled and ordinary men. It was obvious the men were followers of Jesus, who also courageously defied their own nation's leaders.

4:14. Three men, not two, were present at the hearing before the Sanhedrin. Because of the presence of the healed man, the religious authorities could not refute Peter and John. The people of Jerusalem knew that they had performed a miracle (4:15-22).

4:15-22. They could threaten, but not silence them. Peter and John objected to the imposed restriction for two reasons. They were ultimately accountable to God not men. They were compelled to testify about what they had witnessed.

The Sanhedrin were forced to release Peter and John because they could not deny the lame man had been healed in the name of Jesus. The people were convinced and praised God for the miraculous healing. The mention that the man **was more than forty years old** and had been lame all of his life highlights the power of the miracle. **Miracle** (v. 22) is better translated "sign." The healing is a "sign" pointing to the awesome power of Jesus to heal physically and ultimately to save spiritually.

4:23. In 4:23-31, Luke showed how the church responded to the threats of the Sanhedrin. They prayed! In their prayer, the Jewish believers addressed God as Sovereign Lord (**O Lord**; *despota*, a word that signifies one who has complete power and authority over others under him, emphasizing God's sovereignty). The prayer in these verses reflected their conviction of God's sovereignty in five areas:

4:24. The Lord is sovereign over creation. He is the creator of everything that exists. He was with them and would give them the courage to overcome all opposition.

4:25-26. The Lord is sovereign over the hostility of evil men who oppose the kingdom of God. Recalling what David said in Ps 2:1, 2, they realized that throughout history whenever the kingdom of God had threatened the kingdom of man, the kings of earth had made a futile attempt to defy God. In the end God would prevail, and His kingdom would be established.

4:27-28. The Lord is sovereign over the conspiracy against Christ and His crucifixion. They understood the crucifixion of Jesus was according to the preordained plan of God. These verses are significant in that they demonstrate the falsity of the classical Christ-killer charge against the Jewish people. For centuries Christendom has alleged that only Jewish people and all Jewish people are guilty, for all time, of killing Christ. However, this prayer indicates that there was a conspiracy of guilt, including a Jewish king (**Herod**), a Roman governor (**Pontius Pilate**), some **Gentiles** (Roman soldiers), and some Jewish people composed of the Sanhedrin and the mob (**the peoples of Israel**). Moreover, these people, though fully responsible for their evil deeds, acted under the sovereign plan of God, doing what His **hand and . . . purpose predestined to occur**.

4:29-30. The Lord is sovereign over the believers' supernatural courage and power to heal. The miraculous healings were signs to validate their message and ministry.

4:31. The Lord is sovereign over filling them with the Holy Spirit. God answered their prayer and gave them a fresh filling of the Holy Spirit. They continued to proclaim the Word of God with uncommon courage.

4:32-35. In this brief paragraph, Luke delineated one of the effects of the Holy Spirit's power in the early church. There was not only remarkable courage to testify regarding the identity of Jesus and to perform miracles to validate what they said about Him, but the Spirit also produced a remarkable unity and love in the church that resulted in a generous sharing of their resources. The sharing was voluntary not compulsory, being compelled by love not law (note Peter's question to Annanias, "While it remained unsold did it not remain your own? And after it was sold, was it not under your control?" (Ac 5:4). It is charity of the heart. The expression, **and lay them at the apostles' feet**, means they placed their resources under the control of the apostles.

4:36-37. Luke focused on Joseph, nicknamed Barnabas, which means **Son of Encouragement**, and presented three characteristics of Barnabas. First, he was a Levite, the tribe that assisted the priests in their service in the temple (see Nm 3:5-14). Second, he was from Cyprus, so he was a Hellenist rather than a Jew from the land of Israel. He returned to Cyprus with Paul on the first missionary journey. Third, he was affluent enough to own property, which he sold and gave to the church.

2. Internal Corruption: Deception of Ananias and Sapphira (5:1-11)

The dishonesty and death of Ananias and Sapphira is a vivid and ugly contrast with the generosity and integrity of Barnabas. The sin of Ananias and Sapphira is similar to the sin of Achan (cf. Jos 7:25). F. F. Bruce says that in both the OT and NT narratives an act of deceit interrupts the victorious progress of the people of God (*Acts*, 110). Bruce also identifies the linguistic connection between the two passages. He notes that the word translated **kept back** (*enosphisato*, "to skim off the top" or "embezzle") in 5:2 is the same word used in the LXX in Jos 7:1 where it says, "The sons of Israel . . . took" for their own use (*enosphisanto*) some of the things under the ban which had been set aside strictly for God (Bruce, *Acts*, 110). In the same way that Achan's sin had disastrous implications for all Israel, so the early church's unity and care was put in peril because of the sin of Ananias and Sapphira. Although God does not always treat dishonesty and embezzling with a death penalty (Achan) or by striking someone dead (Ananias and Sapphira), He acted thus in both of these cases at the outset of Israel's history in the land and the beginning of the church to demonstrate the severity with which He takes these sins.

5:1-2. Perhaps motivated by the example of Barnabas, Ananias and Sapphira sold property, but instead of giving it all to the church as promised, Ananias **kept back** some of the money with his wife's full knowledge.

5:3-4. The Holy Spirit made Peter aware of their dishonesty supernaturally. Though Ananias had lied to the church, in v. 3 Peter charged him with lying to the Holy Spirit, and in v. 4 to God. The theological implication of Peter's charge is that God dwells in the corporate church through individual believers filled with the Spirit. Ananias was not filled with the Spirit but with Satan. The verb **filled** (*eplerosen*) has reference to the idea of control or influence. It is the same verb used in Eph 5:18, "be filled with the Spirit." Ananias was influenced by Satan rather than by the Spirit. The sin of greed apparently gave Satan an opportunity to influence Ananias. Luke did hang the responsibility also upon Ananias in 5:4, and the influence of the devil did not absolve him of the culpability for this act, which was a sin against the fellowship and care of the church.

5:5-6. When his sin was exposed, Ananias collapsed and died. His death was divine judgment, not psychological trauma. The verb translated **breathed his last** is used only in the context where someone is struck down by divine judgment (cf. Ac 5:5, 10; see 12:23 where God struck down Herod because he accepted worship as a god) (Longenecker, "Acts," 314). Because of the rapid decomposition in the heat, the body was removed quickly for burial.

5:7-10. A short time later Peter confronted Sapphira, who was unaware of her husband's death. Peter asked her if what they had given was the amount they had gained. As did her husband, she lied and collapsed at Peter's feet. Like that of her husband, her body is quickly removed for burial.

5:11. What is the impact of the divine judgment on Ananias and Sapphira? Luke said **great fear came over the whole church**. For the first time in Acts, Luke used the term **church** (*ekklesia*), which typically, in secular Greek, refers to an assembly of people. This early in Luke's history it probably did not have the full-blown technical sense it would have, e.g., in 20:28. **Fear** is not so much an emotional response as it is awe or respect for the Lord, though an element of psychological fear is undoubtedly present in this situation. This incident stands as a frightening warning against sin in *and against* the body of Christ. Though this is a unique example of God dealing severely and suddenly with believers, the judgment on Ananias and Sapphira shows how seriously God takes sin. The Lord wants believers to honor and serve Him in truth and with integrity, and failure to do so can disrupt the flow of harmony and care He intends for the church (see Eph 4:25-28).

3. External Persecution: Arrest of the Apostles (5:12-42)

This passage presents the third element in the external-internal opposition cycle during the early part of the book of Acts: External Opposition (the arrest of Peter and John in the wake of the healing of the lame man in Acts 3–4)—Internal Opposition (the episode involving Ananias and Sapphira). External Opposition (persecution because of the jealousy of the Sadducees in this passage)—Internal Opposition (the problem with the neglect of the Hellenistic Jewish widows in Ac 6).

The miraculous events related to Ananias and Sapphira produced fear among those both inside and outside of the church (5:11). That fear led many to respect the apostles and others in the church (the topic of 5:12-16), but not all were so favorably impressed (the topic of 5:17). Initially, the Sadducees tried to silence Peter and John by intimidation (Ac 4). They then made a bolder move by ordering all the apostles arrested. Though they intended to execute the apostles, Gamaliel argued for a more reasonable response. The Sanhedrin did not kill the apostles, but they ordered them flogged.

5:12. God continued to confirm the ministry of the apostles by signs and wonders. The believers met at "Solomon's portico," an area east of the Court of the Gentiles. Because they were Jews, it was reasonable for them to continue worshipping in the temple.

5:13-14. The phrase, **none of the rest,** could refer to either believers or unbelievers. The contrast with "people" in the second half of the verse supports the view they were believers who were apprehensive about associating with apostles because of the judgment on Ananias and Sapphira and the warning from the Sanhedrin. Luke, however, pointed out that, although some were cautious and apprehensive, the Lord continued to grow His church as both men and women were added.

5:15-16. According to his pattern of writing, Luke moved from a general description of events to a specific example. He focused on Peter's power to heal through the example of his shadow passing over those who were sick and demon possessed. In the ancient world, people thought that a person's shadow was an extension of the person. If one's shadow touched a corpse, that person would be as unclean as if he actually touched the corpse (for the details, see Craig S. Keener, *The IVP Bible Background Commentary: NT* [Downers Grove, IL: InterVarsity, 1993], 335). Though the people's expectations may have been based in part on superstition, God worked through this means to authenticate Peter's apostolic ministry. This miracle of healing through indirect contact with Peter had parallels to the miracles of healing done by touching the edge of Jesus' cloak (Mt 9:2) and Paul's aprons and handkerchiefs (Ac 19:11-12). This correlation is one of several intentional parallels in Acts among the ministries of Peter, Paul, and Jesus. Luke's objective, among other things, was to authenticate both Peter and Paul as true apostles.

5:17-18. The second arrest of the apostles was inevitable because they publicly defied the Sanhedrin. Some critics have contended that this is a second account of the same historical event when the apostles were arrested and tried before the Sanhedrin (cf. 4:1-31 for the first account). More accurate is that the two arrests actually occurred, reflecting an aspect of Jewish law at that time. Jewish law required that

> [I]n non-capital cases the common people—as distinguished from those with rabbinic training, who, presumably, would know the law—had to be given a legal admonition before witnesses and could only be punished for an offense when they relapsed into a crime after due warning. Acts 4:1ff., therefore, presents the Sanhedrin as judging that the apostles were 'unschooled, ordinary men' (v. 13) and tells how they were given a legal warning not to speak anymore in the name of Jesus (v. 17). But Acts 5:17 tells how the Sanhedrin reminded the apostles of its first warning (v. 28) and turned them over to be flogged because they had persisted in their 'sectarian' ways (v. 40). (Longenecker, "Acts," 300)

Because of the emphasis on the resurrection in their preaching, it is not surprising that when the apostles won the favor of the people, the Sadducees were filled with jealously. Jealousy is "intense envy over the successes of another" more capable than one's self, and often includes the sense of fear at being displaced by someone else in the affections or esteem of those important to a person. The apostles were popular, and the Sadducees were not.

5:19-26. Luke reported they were released by an **angel of the Lord**. It is ironic that God sent an angel to release the apostles since the Sadducees did not believe in angels. Also, they had been placed in a public jail. Therefore, everyone knew they had escaped.

The angel had a twofold task. First, the angel released the apostles. How the angel opened the doors without attracting the attention of the guards was part of the miracle. Second, the angel instructed them to continue to preach **the whole** (not just a *part*) **message of this Life**. In 4:15, Peter referred to Jesus as the "Prince (Author) of Life," so **Life** here is the new and everlasting life that comes from Jesus Christ. In obedience to the divine command, the apostles returned to the temple and continued teaching (imperfect tense) new life in Christ as the people arrived for morning prayers.

It is impossible to miss the humor of this incident. When the Sanhedrin reassembled the next day for the trial of the apostles, they were shocked by the report of the guards that there had been a "breakout" at the city jail. The guards arrested the apostles again, but avoided any kind of violence because they feared a violent reaction from the people.

5:27-28. The seating arrangement of the Sanhedrin at the trial was designed to intimidate the accused. The members sat in a semicircle with the accused in the center facing them. The High Priest reminded the apostles of the previously established restriction, and leveled two charges against the apostles. First, he accused them of filling **Jerusalem with your teaching**. They had publicly proclaimed Christ in defiance of the strict orders of the Sanhedrin. Second, he said that they intended **to bring this man's blood upon us.** In spite of the obvious facts, the Sanhedrin refused to accept responsibility for their part in the crucifixion of Christ.

5:29-32. The apostles' determination to obey God rather than man placed the Sanhedrin in a predicament. Because the Sanhedrin claimed they were committed to obeying God (see 5:29 and 5:32b), they did not want to be perceived as opposing the Lord. Luke recorded three key points of Peter's message to the Sanhedrin. (1) Peter implicated the leadership in the killing of Jesus by hanging Him on a **cross** (lit., "wood," or perhaps "tree"; this may be a veiled allusion to Dt 21:23 and the idea Paul made explicit in Gl 3:13; see the comments there). (2) In contrast to the human opinion about Jesus, God had vindicated Him by exalting Him to His right hand (the highest place of honor). Because of His position as "Prince" or "Leader," Jesus could grant repentance and forgiveness to Israel. Like God, the Savior of His people in the OT era, Jesus was now the Savior of Israel, but they needed to repent to receive forgiveness for their sins. As Bock says, "It is not the apostles who need to obey God, but the leadership" (Bock, *Acts*, 248). (3) The apostles were eyewitnesses of Christ's death and resurrection and so was the Holy Spirit, who empowered the witnesses to testify about Christ.

5:33-39. Gamaliel was formerly a pupil of Hillel, who died in AD 20 and was leader of the Sanhedrin during the reign of Herod the Great. Gamaliel was one of the most respected Pharisaic leaders of his time. The second-century compendium of Jewish law called the Mishnah says of him, "Since Rabban Gamaliel the elder died there has been no more reverence for the law; and purity and abstinence died out at the same time" (*Sotah* 9:15). Paul stated in Ac 22:3 that Gamaliel was once his teacher. As was typical of the Pharisees, Gamaliel believed that God is in control of everything happening, but he also believed in free will. He cautioned the Sanhedrin against exercising their free will in opposition to God's will. Perhaps he was thinking of a passage like 2Ch 13:12, "Do not fight against the LORD God of your fathers, for you will not succeed."

Gamaliel summarized the story of two revolts against the Romans that ultimately had failed. The identity of **Theudas** is uncertain, and poses a serious historical problem. There was a Theudas who led a short-lived revolt c. AD 43–46 (Josephus, *Ant.* 20.97-98), but this was too late for Gamaliel's speech, which occurred at least several years before this revolt. Luke's Gamaliel placed **Theudas** before **Judas**, and it may be possible that a Theudas otherwise not known to us was in Luke's mind, or that Josephus may have been wrong, or even that "Theudas" may be another form of the man's given name (possibly "Theodotus," "Theodorus," or "Theodotion," each a popular Gk. name among some of the Jewish people) (for the details, see Colin J. Hemer, *The Book of Acts in the Setting of Hellenistic History* [Winona Lake, IN: Eisenbrauns, 2001], 162 n. 5). If Theudas preceded Judas chronologically as Gamaliel indicated, then both of these men may have participated in revolts after the death of Herod the Great. That was a period of enormous unrest when other revolts are known to have occurred. One of them took place under **Judas**, who led his revolt during **the days of the census** (probably AD 6/7). It is obvious these revolts were not of God. Gamaliel, however, was not so certain about Christianity.

The greater question concerns Gamaliel's advice. Was he right in stating that if Christianity was a movement of God, the Sanhedrin would not be able to stop it? And if it was not of God, then would it not succeed? Gamaliel was both right and wrong. He was certainly right in arguing that if God was with this new movement, even the Romans would not be able to control it. In addition, history shows a movement can succeed through human effort and determination without divine intervention. From Luke's perspective, however, of the advance of the church in Acts, Gamaliel was right. The church advanced from Jerusalem to Rome. It could not be stopped because it was a movement of God.

5:40-42. The Sanhedrin ordered the disciples flogged and commanded them not to speak in Jesus' name. Jewish flogging was done with leather whips. They gave 13 lashes on the chest and 26 on the back for a total of 39 lashes (40 minus one). Though the Sanhedrin attempted to prevent the witnesses from testifying that

Jesus is Israel's Messiah, in the end they were powerless to stop them.

4. Internal Strife: Neglect of the Hellenistic Widows (6:1-7)

The final threat Luke described in this section was apparently the result of an administrative oversight. A group of widows in the church were neglected in the daily distribution of food. No one would criticize the church if this had only been the inability of the church to keep up with explosive growth, but the cause of the problem was deeper. It was cultural discrimination, potentially dividing the church into Hellenistic Jewish and Hebraic Jewish factions.

6:1. Luke introduced the problem in 6:1. Members of the church in Jerusalem were both **Hellenistic Jews** and **native Hebrews** (Hebraic Jews). The evidence regarding the characteristics of the Hellenistic Jews is diverse and it is impossible to be dogmatic about who they were. The best indicators are that they may have been from outside of Judea, spoke and understood only Greek as their native tongue, and may have viewed the law and the temple as somewhat less central to their faith than their Hebraic counterparts. The word **Hellenistic Jews** is also used in 9:29, which indicates that they were zealous for Judaism in their opposition to Paul. Hebraic Jews spoke Hebrew, though many would have known Greek as the *lingua franca* of the day, and probably to a greater degree resisted Greek culture. The Hellenistic Jews complained their widows were being neglected in the daily distribution of food. The problem in part was the result of explosive growth: **the disciples were increasing in number**.

6:2-4. The twelve wisely anticipated that if they focused their attention on this problem it could distract them from their primary ministry of prayer and teaching the Word. They recommended the church select seven men to oversee the care of widows. Though this passage does not specifically establish the office of deacon in the early church, the term "deacon" is related to the noun serving (*diakonia*) in v. 1 and the verb **to serve** (*diakoneo*) in v. 2.

The solution was not imposed on the church by the apostles. Rather they asked all of the disciples to choose seven reputable men whose character was known by others. Though serving widows might seem like a mundane task, those chosen should be **full of the Spirit and of wisdom**. This means they should be obedient to the Spirit's leading and of sufficient experience and knowledge to make decisions consistent with the will of God.

6:5-7. Judging from the names of those chosen, the proto-deacons were Hellenistic rather Hebraic Jews. Since the church had neglected the Hellenistic Jewish widows, they intentionally put Hellenistic Jews in charge of the ministry. Luke introduced **Stephen**, who became a key figure in proclaiming Christ to the Sanhedrin (chap. 7) and **Philip**, who was instrumental in taking the gospel to the Samaritans (chap. 8).

The decision by the larger group was confirmed by the apostles through prayer and the symbolic laying on of hands. Stephen and Philip were already Spirit-filled and men of wisdom. The laying on of hands indicated that the apostles commissioned them as their representatives in this ministry to the widows. Furthermore, as apostolic representatives, both Stephen and Philip functioned as apostolic legates in preaching the gospel and thereby were able to perform signs and wonders (6:8; 8:6).

From the church's handling of this problem, three helpful principles can be discerned: (1) Rapid growth will challenge the resources of the church, and the church should be ready and willing to reorganize to meet needs. (2) Neglect of the needy for any reason is unacceptable in the church. Faith in Christ transcends all ethnic and cultural differences. (3) In ministry, church leaders should focus on the priorities of prayer and teaching the Word.

Luke summarized the first section (panel) of his story of the church by focusing on the church's remarkable growth. The message (Word of God) continued its successful march outward from Jerusalem; God multiplied the disciples in Jerusalem; and a notable number of priests became obedient to the faith. The explanation for the amazing birth and growth of the church is that Christ is alive and that He has poured out the Holy Spirit on His followers exactly as He had promised.

II. The Extension of the Church: Judea and Samaria (6:8–9:31)

A. Stephen: Witness to the Jews (6:8–8:3)

1. The Seizure of Stephen (6:8–7:1)

a. The Context of Stephen's Life (6:8-10)

This section (6:8–9:31) introduces a new unit (panel) in the story of the church. Luke turned the inspired spotlight on three men: Stephen, Philip, and Paul. In preparation for the universal mission of the church, each of these men witnessed to a different ethnic group of people: Stephen to Hellenistic Jews, Philip to Samaritans, and Paul was divinely chosen and commissioned to take the gospel to Gentiles.

Because the believers were determined to obey God rather than men, it was inevitable that one of Christ's followers would pay the ultimate price for his devotion. Stephen became the first martyr of the church. To understand the rage that drove the Sanhedrin to stone Stephen, it is necessary to identify the traditional beliefs that preserved Judaism. There are three: land, law, and temple. First, the Jewish leadership correctly believed that God had promised Abraham and his descendants a country to call their own (Gn 12:1-3). The problem was thinking that God could only actively work in this land. Second, while they correctly understood God had given Israel the law through Moses, the leadership were confused about themselves being the guardians of the law. Third, they correctly believed in the sanctity of the temple as the dwelling place of God. However they were mistaken in believing that His presence in the temple guaranteed blessing and protection. In his speech, Stephen challenged their mistaken ideas about the land, the law, and the temple, and charged them with rejecting their own Messiah Jesus.

6:8. Stephen was full of **grace and power**. The combination seems paradoxical, yet the two are related. Grace and power are divine provisions that gave Stephen an attractiveness of character and strength of spirit. As one popular preacher has stated, Stephen was "tender yet tough." He demonstrated his power in miracles. It is significant for the widespread development of the church that God worked miraculously through Stephen, a Hellenistic Jew, in the same way as He did through the apostles, Hebraic Jews. He could do so because the apostles had laid their hands on him (6:5), so he functioned as an apostolic representative.

6:9-10. Yet, in spite of his gracious character and powerful ministry, Stephen faced fierce opposition from **the Synagogue of the Freedmen**. The Synagogue of the Freedmen consisted of Jews from foreign countries who were formerly slaves, but had gained their freedom and organized a synagogue in Jerusalem. Although it is not stated, they were most likely offended by Stephen's outspoken faith in Jesus as Israel's Messiah, so they challenged him publicly. However, they were frustrated by Stephen's **wisdom and the Spirit**. His arguments made sense, and the Spirit convicted them that his message about the Messiah was true.

b. The Charge Brought against Stephen (6:11–7:1)

6:11-12. These Freedmen convinced some of their sympathizers to accuse Stephen, charging him with blasphemy against Moses and God, both capital offenses (Ex 22:28; Lv 24:11-16). Stephen was brought forcibly before the Sanhedrin.

6:13-14. The specific charges were somewhat of a misrepresentation of what Jesus had said about the temple and the law, though He warned about the end of both. It is impossible to know if the accusations were related to anything specific because the witnesses were persuaded to testify against Stephen.

6:15–7:1. Stephen's face had the countenance of an angel, meaning he had the appearance of one who stands in the presence of the Lord. In response to the question of the high priest (7:1), Stephen gave a panorama of Jewish history challenging the overconfident beliefs of his countrymen on matters concerning (1) the land, (2) the law, and (3) the temple. Their overconfidence was rooted in their mistaken notion that possession of all three blessings, legitimately promised to Israel in the OT, indicated that God's favor rested upon them at that time regardless of their sinful actions and attitudes, especially against their Messiah and His people. Stephen focused on Abraham and Joseph to refute the misconception that Israel's presence in the promised land was evidence of God's favor.

2. The Sermon of Stephen (7:2-53)

a. The Breadth of God's Revelation (7:2-8)

7:2-8. God called Abraham and promised to give him the land while he was still in Mesopotamia. In his lifetime Abraham never received a foot of the promised land, yet he believed God. Abraham again demonstrated remarkable faith when he continued to believe God, who said his descendants would be slaves for 400 years before they inherited the land. God confirmed His covenant with Abraham with the rite of circumcision. Stephen's point was that God blessed Abraham because he believed and obeyed, not because he had dwelt in the land.

b. The Rejection of God's Messengers (7:9-53)

7:9-16. Like Abraham, Joseph was honored by God when he was in another country. Because of jealousy, Joseph's brothers sold him into slavery, yet God blessed him in Egypt. He was elevated as a ruler over all of Egypt by Pharaoh.

When a famine threatened their survival in the promised land, Jacob sent his sons to buy grain in Egypt. However, they did not learn that Joseph was their brother until their second visit. Without being dogmatic, it is possible Stephen was implying a foreshadowing of Israel's recognition of Jesus as Messiah when He comes a second time. Like Joseph's brothers who did not learn of his identity the first time they came to Egypt but did in their second meeting, Israel did not recognize Jesus at His first coming but will at His second coming.

Stephen's point was that the land was not a "magical kingdom" on earth. Geography does not determine God's blessing, but rather faith and obedience.

7:17-29. In this section Stephen responded to misunderstandings about the law and Moses. This was not a self-defense but a spiritual indictment of these leaders of his countrymen. Stephen reminded the Sanhedrin that when they were slaves in Egypt, the Lord raised up Moses to rescue them; but they rejected him as ruler and judge (7:27-29, 35). Though Moses was born in perilous times, he was no ordinary child. He was highly favored by God, who providentially made it possible for Moses to live in the palace and receive an Egyptian education.

Moses, however, was forced to flee to Midian when he killed an Egyptian who was abusing a son of Israel. He also attempted to mediate between two Israelites who were fighting with one another. Instead of thanking Moses, the one who was abusing his neighbor rejected him and asked sarcastically, **WHO MADE YOU A RULER AND JUDGE OVER US?** (7:27). When the man rebuked Moses by asking if Moses intended to kill him as he had killed the Egyptian, Moses realized that the people would not accept his leadership, and he fled to Midian.

7:30-35. In Midian, not the promised land, the Lord appeared to Moses. He came as a theophany (a visible manifestation of God) in a burning bush, and identified himself as the God of Israel's patriarchs (cf. Ex 3:1-6). He ordered Moses to return to Egypt, to the same people who had rejected him as their deliverer.

Twice Stephen referred to the appearance of the Lord as an **ANGEL** (7:30, 35). The reference, however, was most likely to the visible appearance of the Lord in an angel-like form. The Jewish tradition that the law was mediated through angels (Bock, *Acts,* 295) is confirmed elsewhere in the NT in Heb 2:2 and Gl 3:19.

7:36-38. Even after God confirmed Moses as a prophet through miraculous signs, their ancestors refused to obey him. Though he did not make the point directly, Stephen quoted Dt 18:15 to imply a comparison between Moses and Jesus. Jesus was the prophet like Moses whom God promised to send to Israel; just as their ancestors rejected Moses, the current leadership rejected Jesus, the second Moses. Yet like Moses who returned from a 40-year sojourn in the wilderness to rescue his people, so Jesus will return a second time to rescue Israel. The phrase **the congregation in the wilderness** does not use the word *ekklesia* (church, congregation, assembly) in the technical sense of the church, as if the church existed in the OT. Note for example the very same word (*ekklesia*)is used in a non-technical sense for an unruly mob (Ac 19:32), clearly not meaning the church. In Stephen's speech the word was merely used as a reference to the *assembly* of Israel when wandering in the wilderness.

7:39-43. Contrary to their opinion of themselves as the true guardians of the Torah, they actually had a history of rebellion against God. They made a golden calf and sacrificed to other gods like **MOLOCH** and **ROMPHA**. As did their forefathers who had rejected Moses, the Jewish leadership of Stephen's day had rejected the Messiah of Israel, who was their deliverer and prophet.

7:44-50. Stephen gave a short review of events leading to the building of the temple. God gave Moses instructions for building the tabernacle ("tent of meeting," Ex 27:21) in the wilderness. David found favor with the Lord, but he was not permitted to build a dwelling place for God. Instead, David's son Solomon built a **house** for God. Though Solomon's temple was magnificent, he knew God does not dwell in man-made houses (1Kg 8:27). Quoting Is 66:2, Stephen declared that all of creation is the temple of God. The physical structure in Jerusalem did not limit the work of God to Israel.

7:51-53. Stephen's speech was a courageous challenge to Israel's leaders. He accused them of being like all unregenerate people, **stiff-necked**, unable to turn their heads to see a different point of view, and no better than **uncircumcised** Gentiles. He called them **uncircumcised in heart and ears** (v. 51) to contrast with their physical circumcision. Literal circumcision was designed to motivate its recipients to have sincere faith or "spiritual circumcision." This was the same challenge that Jeremiah made to

Israel (Jr 4:4; 9:25). Their being **uncircumcised in heart** meant their relationship with God did not reflect any spiritual life. Had they been spiritually alive they would have recognized Jesus as the Messiah. Instead, as their ancestors who persecuted the prophets, they betrayed and murdered the **Righteous One** (v. 52). The title "Righteous One" is messianic (Is 53:11) and emphasizes Jesus' innocence and the seriousness of their crime. This is not an affirmation of the church's long-held Christ-killer charge against the Jewish people as a whole, but rather to identify the Sanhedrin's role (with the Gentiles) in the conspiracy against Jesus (see comments at 4:27-28).

Stephen's final statement was an extremely bold declaration. Contrary to the charges that he was a renegade Jew, Stephen accused the Sanhedrin of disobedience to the law, the same charge that it made against him (see 6:13).

3. The Stoning of Stephen (7:54–8:3)

a. The Sight He Saw (7:54-56)

7:54. The action of the Sanhedrin resembled a lynch mob. They became furious because Stephen's message stabbed them in the heart. **Gnashing their teeth** indicates an intense rage.

7:55-56. Luke affirmed Stephen's testimony by noting that he was **full of the Holy Spirit**. God vindicated Stephen by allowing him to glimpse His glory, and see **Jesus standing at the right hand of God**. Jesus' position at the right hand of God placed Him in a place of divine authority, and the title **Son of Man** confirmed Jesus had received sovereign and eternal power over all the kingdoms of the earth (see Dn 7:13-14). So even though the Sanhedrin condemned Stephen, mostly as an angry mob rather than as an official judicial body, Jesus stood as Stephen's divine advocate. The Sanhedrin judged Stephen guilty; Jesus, the divine judge, stood to declare him innocent and the Sanhedrin guilty. That Jesus was standing rather than seated at God's right hand (cf. Eph 1:20) may be of some pastoral significance. Jesus was standing to welcome Stephen into heaven. Though the idea may somewhat lessen the fear of death, the judicial interpretation should be considered primary.

b. The Suffering He Experienced (7:57-58)

7:57-58. Their body language indicated the Sanhedrin were blinded and driven by uncontrollable rage. Most likely those people in the galley observing the trial intervened at this point and formed a lynch mob. They dragged Stephen outside the city and executed him by stoning, which was the penalty for blasphemy (Lv 24:14; Dt 17:5-7). Luke introduced Saul, who became a major player in the story of the early church, by noting that he was present supporting Stephen's executioners.

c. The Steadfastness He Displayed (7:59–8:3)

7:59-60. Stephen became the first martyr of the church. Though he experienced a horrible death, Luke said that he **fell asleep**. "Sleep" is the common euphemism for the death of a believer and always includes the hope of resurrection (cf. 1Th 4:13-18). Though he was stoned and not crucified, the manner of Stephen's death paralleled that of the Lord:

Words of Stephen and Jesus Compared

Stephen	Jesus
Lord Jesus, receive my spirit	Father, into Your hands I commit My spirit (Lk 23:46)
Lord, do not hold this sin against them	Father, forgive them; for they do not know what they are doing (Lk 23:34)
Having said this, he fell asleep	Having said this, He breathed His last (Lk 23:46)

These parallels indicate Jesus' ongoing work through the church (Ac 1:1), suggesting that Luke's gospel is about what Jesus started, and Acts is about what He continued to do—and seen specifically in the martyrdom of Stephen.

8:1a. Luke again brought Saul into focus before concluding the story of Stephen. Stephen's speech convinced him that these followers of the Messiah Jesus were a threat to traditional Judaism and needed to be stopped at all costs. Stephen's speech enraged his hearers because it challenged the central tenets of first-century Judaism, it identified a Messiah rejected by the Sanhedrin, and it threatened the authority of Judaism's leadership. Therefore, they attacked the Jewish followers of Jesus with zeal. The persecution scattered believers, but like seed tossed in the wind they grew and multiplied. Wherever they went, they preached the Word. The Holy Spirit led Philip to Samaria and to Gaza. The outburst of hostility prompted followers of Jesus to seek safety in remote areas.

8:1b-2. Most of the Jewish believers were forced to leave Jerusalem **except the apostles**. Luke did not say why the apostles were excepted.

It could be that public opinion of them was so high that to drive them out would have created a bigger headache for the Jewish leadership than leaving them alone, or perhaps they stayed to care for those believers who still remained in Jerusalem. Possibly they did not leave because they were not Hellenistic Jews. Though they faced persecution by the Sanhedrin, **devout men** honored Stephen by burying his battered body.

8:3. Saul realized that established Judaism was threatened by this new faith so the new faith (messianic Judaism, *aka* Christianity) needed to be resisted. Luke portrayed him as a wild beast. The word **ravaging** is used of a wild beast tearing a carcass to shreds (John B. Polhill, NAC [Nashville: Broadman Press, 1992], *Acts*, 212). Saul was brutal and cruel. Even women did not escape his vicious assault on the church.

Philip's ministry in Samaria marked an important advance in the church. Though largely oblivious to its responsibility for a worldwide ministry, the church was being compelled, under God's providential hand by which the church was scattered, to fulfill the great commission.

Jews and Samarians despised one another. The hostility originated from the Assyrian conquest of Samaria in 722 BC and the Assyrian policy of relocating conquered peoples. They deported Jews from the Northern Kingdom and imported Gentiles into the area. The Samaritans were the descendants of the mixed marriages between Jews and Gentiles. The hostility between these two groups intensified through the years. The Samaritans built a rival temple on Mount Gerizim, developed their own form of worship, and even had their own slightly emended form of the Pentateuch. Thus the racial tension was compounded by a religious schism. John Hyrcranus (d. 104 BC), one of the Maccabean leaders, fueled the schism by destroying the Samaritan temple in 127 BC.

B. Philip: Witness to the Samaritans (8:4-40)

1. In the City of Samaria (8:4-25)

a. Philip's Preaching and Power (8:4-8)

8:4-5. Luke recorded only the theme of Philip's preaching—Messiah. The point is crucial. Philip did not change the message for the Samaritans, and he appealed for them to become followers of Jesus, not to convert to Judaism.

8:6-8. Philip, though not an apostle, had power to work miracles. This was unusual but likely possible because the apostles had laid hands on him (6:5) and now, as Stephen, he functioned as an apostolic representative. The miracles authenticated his message to the Samaritans, a new ethnic group in the story of Acts that received the gospel. The description of Philip's ministry ended on a positive note, **so there was much rejoicing**. Polhill notes the importance of Luke's statement. "The gospel is a great equalizer. In the gospel there are no 'half-breeds,' no physical rejects, no places for human prejudices. There is acceptance for all, joy for all, 'great joy for all the people' (Luke 2:10)" (Polhill, *Acts,* 215).

b. The Samaritan's and Simon's Reaction (8:9-13)

8:9-13. Men like **Simon** were common in the ancient world. Astrologers, soothsayers, and magicians exerted great influence on people and earned a comfortable living. Simon had impressed people with magical powers, and claimed that he was **someone great**. His magic was effective. The Samaritans regarded him as the **Great Power of God**, which meant he was the channel of divine power and not necessarily God himself. His self-promoting egotism sharply contrasted with Philip, who preached Christ. It is unclear why Luke included this episode. What purpose does it serve in his book? Perhaps the point was to emphasize the superiority of the power of Philip, or that while Simon appeared to endeavor to glorify himself, Philip's intent was to glorify only Jesus.

The Samaritans, men and women, believed and were baptized. Simon also believed and was baptized. At this point in the account, there is no reason to think that Simon's faith was suspect, though he did seem more interested in Philip's power than the person of Jesus.

c. The Coming of the Apostles (8:14-25)

8:14-17. When the church in Jerusalem heard of the response of the Samaritans to **the word of God**, they sent Peter and John to investigate. Note that Luke identified Philip's preaching as **the word of God**. Philip was not an apostle. He was a Hellenistic Jew, but his message was **the word of God**.

Peter and John discovered that, though many Samaritans had believed, they had not received the Spirit. They prayed and these new converts received the Spirit through the laying on of hands. There is no indication that two-stage conversion is normative or perpetually the pattern for the church throughout all time. It was a historically exceptional situation for the purpose of establishing unity between Jewish and Samaritan believers. The Samaritans received the promised Spirit at the hands of the apostles subsequent to Philip's evangelizing and their trusting in Christ for salvation. The final blessings of conversion, however, did not come through Philip but through Peter and John. This had the effect of bringing the Samaritan believers under the apostolic umbrella and ensured the unity of the church. Otherwise the Samaritans may have remained a splinter group because of their historical animosity toward the Jewish people.

Verse 17 does not state explicitly that the Samaritans spoke in tongues, but there was some outward manifestation of the reception of the Spirit, and it is reasonable to think that tongues was the indication. Rather than establishing a post-conversion baptism of the Spirit with tongues as the proof of it, the manifestation of the Spirit in the Samaritans served to indicate to the Jewish apostolic church that the Samaritans were now included in the body of Christ.

This was the second occasion Peter was instrumental in the growth of the church (2:14-41; cf. Mt 16:16-20). As he had ministered to his Jewish countrymen on the day of Pentecost, he now opened the door of faith to the Samaritans.

8:18-25. Simon was intrigued by what had happened and made the foolish mistake of trying to buy the Spirit. The term "simony" comes from his misguided attempt to purchase the gift of the Spirit. His request revealed two major misconceptions. First, he mistakenly assumed the Holy Spirit was a gift that could be purchased. Second, he thought the Spirit was a power that could be manipulated. The Spirit is a gift God gives to true believers, and the Spirit is a person, not a power to exploit for selfish purposes.

Peter's stern denunciation of Simon raises questions about the genuineness of Simon's faith: **May your silver perish with you**. The term "perish" sometimes means "eternal destruction" (cf. Jn 3:16). Several factors suggest Simon's faith was spurious. First, his interest in the Spirit was purely selfish. He wanted the power for profit. Second, Peter's admonition for Simon to repent (v. 22) was usually addressed to unbelievers. Third, the description of Simon in 8:23 as being **in the gall of bitterness and in the bondage of iniquity** is a better description of an unbeliever than a believer. Fourth, though Luke said Simon believed, he never said Simon received the Spirit.

2. On the Chariot with the Eunuch (8:26-40)

8:26. An angel of the Lord directed Philip to go to Gaza, south of Jerusalem. The reference to an angel confirms that God was guiding Philip and the program of building the church (cf. 5:19; 10:3; 12:7, 23; 27:23).

8:27-28. Philip obeyed and met an **Ethiopian eunuch**, who was an official of Queen Candace. Men who supervised harems and served as treasurers were often physically altered. This raises questions about his participation in Judaism, but Is 56:3-5 says that God graciously offers salvation to all, even the eunuch. It is also possible that he was not a physical eunuch since the term came to mean "government official" even for those who were not literally eunuchs. He was probably at least a Gentile proselyte to Judaism judging from his visit to Jerusalem and reading Isaiah, so his conversion did not exactly mark an extension of the gospel to Gentiles, which Luke reserved for Cornelius in Ac 10. It does reflect the ever-widening movement of the gospel from indigenous Jewish people (Ac 2), to Hellenistic Jews in Stephen's ministry (6:8-9), to Samaritans with Philip's ministry (8:5), to this Gentile proselyte to Judaism. The Ethiopian official was probably returning home from the Feast of Pentecost.

8:29. The Spirit ordered Philip to join the eunuch in his chariot. Philip discovered he was reading from the prophet Isaiah but did not understand the passage. He became the official's guide for interpreting Isaiah.

8:32-35. The passage is from Is 53:7-8, which compares the Suffering Servant to a sacrificial lamb, whose life was taken from him in unjust judgment. The passage was confusing for the eunuch. He wanted to know if Isaiah was speaking about himself or someone else. Philip explained the passage is about Jesus, and focused witness on the person of Christ. Explaining one of the most clear and compelling OT messianic predictions, Philip identified Jesus as the referent who was sacrificed for sin.

8:36-38. When they come to water, the eunuch asked if he could be baptized. Though there is a textual question about v. 37, it shows that as a proselyte to Judaism, the eunuch must have understood ritual immersion as an initiatory rite. If the verse was added, it indicates that the early church saw immersion as an initiatory rite, functioning as a confession of faith (see Bock, *Acts*, 345, 348).

The eunuch stopped his chariot, and both of the men entered the water for baptism, which was most likely by immersion. The baptism here would be the same as in the rest of Acts, identifying the baptized as a follower of Jesus.

8:39. The Spirit of the Lord **snatched Philip away** in a manner similar to the translation of Elijah (2Kg 2:16), though the text does not state the Spirit transported Philip bodily to **Azotus**. The eunuch did not search for Philip as the prophets searched for Elijah. Instead he continued his journey with **rejoicing**, because of his new relationship with God through Christ.

8:40. Philip continued preaching "the good news" from Azotus (35 miles west of Jerusalem) to Caesarea (on the coast, a distance of 55 miles).

The story of Philip and the eunuch is highly significant for Luke's account of the growth of the church. His conversion represented a further advance of the gospel geographically and ethnically. The church was moving out from Jerusalem, south and west. Though he was originally probably a proselyte to Judaism, the eunuch continued his journey to his country as follower of Christ. Some traditions teach that the eunuch was from Ethiopia and started the church in that country.

C. Saul: Witness to the Gentiles (9:1-31)

1. His Malice against the Christians (9:1-2)

Stephen's message had convinced Saul that the new faith was a threat to Judaism. From his perspective the followers of Christ were apostate Jews who threatened to corrupt Judaism. With the zeal of a fanatic, he devoted himself to stopping this new faith. The fervor of his religious fanaticism is seen in his request to the Sanhedrin to extradite and punish believers who had sought safety in Damascus.

9:1-2. The brutal execution of Stephen did not satisfy Saul's hatred of Christ's disciples. He was still on a rampage, **breathing threats and murder**. His goal was the execution of all Jewish believers in Jesus. Like a bounty hunter, he asked for official authority from the Sanhedrin in Jerusalem to travel to Damascus to arrest believers and bring them to Jerusalem for trial. The reason he needed permission from the Sanhedrin for actions in Damascus was related to the political control in Damascus. The city was not under the Roman empire but the Parthian. The Parthians had delegated all matters pertaining to Jews in their empire to the authority of the Sanhedrin in Jerusalem. Thus, Saul needed to receive letters from the Sanhedrin authorizing him to take action against what they perceived as a corruption of Judaism. The reference to believers in Damascus, Syria, indicates the new messianic faith had spread beyond the boundaries of the land of Israel. The designation of believers as belonging to **the Way** referred to a distinctive moral and spiritual way of life. Significantly, this is in contrast to Jewish "halacha," a Hebrew term meaning "the way of walking," used of rabbinic explanations and applications of Mosaic law. Instead of following "halacha," these believers follow the way of the Messiah.

2. His Meeting with the Lord (9:3-7)

9:3-4. While traveling to Damascus, Saul was stopped by a blinding light and fell to the ground. According to Ac 26:13, the light was more brilliant than the sun, and its brilliance engulfed not only Saul but also those traveling with him.

Saul heard a voice asking, **why are you persecuting Me?** The wording of the question is surprising. Saul's attacks were on followers of Jesus, but the Lord asked, **why are you persecuting Me?** To persecute Jesus-followers is to persecute Jesus. Though the idea was probably not in Paul's mind at the time, it is possible this revelation was the origin of Paul's favorite theological metaphor for the church, "the body of Christ" (cf. Eph 1:22-23; Col 1:18).

9:5. Saul responded, **Who are You, Lord?** Saul's question indicates that he did not know to whom he was speaking. The word "Lord" both in Hebrew and Greek just means "sir." If he knew it was the Lord Jesus, then he would not have had to ask who he was and it would have been unnecessary for the Lord to state **I am Jesus whom you are persecuting**. This answer must have struck like a lightning bolt in Saul's heart. In a brief moment, he realized that everything he believed about Jesus and His followers was wrong. If Jesus was alive, and He obviously was (and is), then He must be Israel's Messiah, and Saul himself was in the wrong, not the followers of Jesus.

9:6. Saul needed time to reflect on what had happened, so the Lord instructed him to go into Damascus where he would receive further instructions.

9:7. Luke inserted a parenthetical comment about Paul's traveling companions (*aner*, **men**). They also heard the voice but did not understand it (cf. Ac 22:9), but they witnessed that something happened to Saul on the road to Damascus.

3. His Future Ministry for the Lord (9:8-31)

9:8-9. Saul's companions escorted him to Damascus. He remained blinded for three days during which time he fasted and undoubtedly reflected thoughtfully on his condition. Saul's blindness was designed to demonstrate his own spiritual condition—he was spiritually blind.

9:10-12. The Lord spoke to Ananias **in a vision**, a common way of communicating unusual information in Acts (cf. 10:1-3 [Cornelius]; 10:9-23 [Peter]; 16:9-10 [Paul]. In each of these situations God gave instructions that were unexpected and required courageous obedience. Ananias was specifically told to go to a house on a **street called Straight** where he would find Saul, who was **praying** and had also seen a vision about the restoration of **his sight**.

9:13-14. It is not surprising that Ananias protested. He had heard about Saul's persecution of the Lord's **saints**. We find here for the first time in Acts the designation of believers as **saints,** those who are set apart for the name of Christ (v. 13; cf. 26:10). Though the term is used only one other time in Acts, Paul used it frequently in his epistles to identify Christians (e.g. Rm 1:7).

9:15-16. The Lord assured Ananias that Saul was about to become a different man. Longenecker explains the dramatic changes that would occur in Saul: (1) instead of a persecutor he would become the Lord's **chosen instrument**; (2) instead of concern for Israel alone his mission would be both to Gentiles and Jews; and (3) instead of personal prominence and glory, he would experience the same kind of suffering he had inflicted on others (see Longenecker, "Acts," 373).

9:17-31. Ananias obeyed. God restored Saul's sight and gave him the gift of the Spirit through the laying on of hands. This was the moment Saul became a true follower of Jesus, with the **scales** falling **from his eyes** as symbols of his new understanding and faith. Although Ananias had called him **brother Saul** (9:17), this was not because Saul was already a believer but because Annanias addressed him as a fellow Jew (Rm 9:3). Saul was immediately **baptized** and regained his strength.

The giving of the Spirit to Saul through an intermediary was not programmatic for all believers in Acts. The epistles teach the Spirit is given when a person believes (see the comments on 1Co 12:7, 13; Gl 3:2; 4:6). This was a non-normative experience to provide evidence to Ananias that Saul was a true believer because he had received the Holy Spirit. No mention was made of speaking in tongues, so even if the phenomenon was present, Luke did not consider it crucial to Saul's conversion experience.

Saul immediately proclaimed that Jesus is the Son of God. Those who knew how viciously he had persecuted Christians were amazed that he now was arguing that Jesus is Israel's Messiah. The expression **was strengthened** means more effective in his witness and not physically strong. He was so effective in proving that Jesus is the Messiah his opponents were totally perplexed.

Unable to refute his arguments, the Jewish leadership in Damascus plotted to kill him. Saul had come to Damascus as a champion and defender of Judaism; now he was forced to sneak out of the city like a fugitive. In 2Co 11:32-33, Paul listed his escape from Damascus in a basket last in a long list of hardships.

Saul returned to Jerusalem, but the church was understandably afraid and refused to accept him until Barnabas assured them of his conversion experience.

As in Damascus, Saul boldly proclaimed the name of Jesus, but again faced fanatical opposition. When the Jerusalem believers found out about the threat on Saul's life they sent him to Tarsus where he would remain until Barnabas recruited him for help with the ministry at Antioch in Syria.

Luke concluded the account of Saul's conversion with a positive report of the growth of the church. The church experienced peace and strength. Living in the fear of the Lord, not the fear of persecution, the church was encouraged by the Holy Spirit and continued to increase.

Luke gave three accounts of Paul's conversion experience (chaps. 9, 22, 26), which indicates that from Luke's perspective it was the most important event in the development of the early church. In contrast to Peter who was a Jew from Israel, Paul was a Hellenistic Jew. He was trained as a rabbi and knew the OT, but he also spoke Greek and understood the Greek culture. He was the ideal person to take the gospel to the Gentiles. On his missionary journeys Paul would later take the gospel to Jews and Gentiles throughout the Roman Empire.

But Paul was not one of the Twelve, so he was continually forced to defend his apostleship. Because of the controversy over Paul's calling as the apostle to the Gentiles, God used Peter to initially open the door of ministry to Gentiles, which was Luke's focus in the next phase of his story. This also fulfilled Jesus' promise to give Peter the keys of the kingdom (Mt 16:16-18). Peter first preached to Jews (Ac 2), he welcomed the Samaritans into the church through the laying on of his hands (Ac 8:14-17), and then he would unlock the door to the Gentiles when he preached to Cornelius and his household (Ac 10).

III. The Expansion of the Church: To the Roman Empire (9:32–28:31)

A. The Mission through Peter to the Gentiles (9:32–11:18)

1. In the Miracles for Aeneas and Dorcas (9:32-43)

Luke explained how God breaks through the barrier of prejudice and prepares His witnesses to take the gospel to the world. He focused initially on Peter, who opened the door of faith to the Gentiles, and then on Paul, who became the apostle to the Gentiles. Both were ideally suited for their particular ministries. Peter was one of the Twelve and had credibility with the Jewish congregation. Thus his ministry to Gentiles would be less controversial than Paul's. Paul, on the other hand, was a Hellenistic Jew and more open-minded and qualified for ministry to Gentiles. Peter opened the door for ministry to Gentiles and Paul walked through it. The ministry of Peter in Lydda and Joppa showed Peter's apostolic authority to move further away from exclusive Jewish outreach and toward a proclamation to all people groups.

9:32-42. In Lydda, Peter healed Aeneas, and in Joppa he raised Tabitha (also known as "Dorcas") from the dead. The miracles gave evidence that the power of the gospel is not in bondage to geography, and these miracles served to establish the authority of Peter as an apostle to open the door of the gospel to the Gentiles.

9:43. Luke pointed out that while Peter was in Joppa he stayed at the house of Simon, a tanner. A pious Jew would have never stayed in the house of a tanner because the handling of dead animals would have ceremonially defiled the person. It is possible that Peter's willingness to stay with Simon showed that a change was taking place in Peter's thinking. He was gaining freedom from long-standing Jewish ceremonial traditions, thus freeing him to respond to the call to minister to Cornelius, a Gentile. The text, however, does not make Peter's change of heart explicit until he experienced the vision.

2. In the Salvation of Cornelius and His Family (10:1–11:18)

a. A Vision to Motivate Peter (10:1-33)

The conversion of Cornelius, who was a God-fearer and not a full proselyte to Judaism, became a new paradigm for the church. Peter's witness to Cornelius and his family gave legitimacy to ministry directly to Gentiles, and their reception of the Holy Spirit showed that Gentiles could become followers of Jesus without first converting to Judaism.

10:1. Cornelius, a Roman **centurion**, was stationed at **Caesarea**, a massive seaport on the Mediterranean Sea. Herod the Great had built the seaport and named it after Julius Caesar. The Romans made Caesarea their administrative capital of Judea. As a centurion, Cornelius commanded a military unit of 100 men (a "century"). Centurions were carefully selected because the century was the basic combat unit in the Roman army. Cornelius would have been a man of good character and courage and capable of leading men in battle.

10:2. Though a Gentile, Cornelius was a man of God. He was called **devout**, which meant that both he and his family honored God. Second, he was a God-fearer. The term was used to identify someone who believed in God and accepted the moral and ethical teachings of Judaism, but was not a full proselyte. Though respected by the Jews, Cornelius would still have been considered a Gentile. That he **gave many alms to the Jewish people** reflects the Lukan perspective that godly Gentiles love and bless the Jewish people (cf. Lk 7:1-10, esp. v. 5; Gn 12:3). As a man of prayer, he **prayed to God continually**. For Luke prayer was a primary characteristic of devotion. Cornelius was not only an exceptional Roman officer, he was also an exceptional man of God. Judging from 11:14, as devout a man as he was, he was not "saved" in an OT or NT sense and needed to trust Christ to be saved.

10:3-6. During the time of the afternoon prayers, the Lord spoke to Cornelius through an angel and instructed him to send for Peter. Though surprised by the appearance of an angel, he did not question the heavenly messenger. In fact, he showed respect for the angel by calling him "Lord."

10:7-8. Though Cornelius was more accustomed to giving orders than taking them, he obeyed the angel's instructions and sent two of his servants to Joppa.

10:9. The scene shifted to Peter who also had a vision while praying. Noon was not the time for scheduled prayer, and we are not told why Peter was praying at noon. He climbed the staircase on the outside of the house to the **housetop** to pray privately.

10:10-16. Since it was about noon, he was also **hungry**. He slipped into a **trance** (Gk. *ekstasis*), and saw a sheet-like object descend from heaven. He heard a voice, **Get up, Peter, kill and eat!** Peter was hungry, but the command was both shocking and offensive. Some of the animals were clean but others were unclean according to the categories of the Mosaic law (Lv 11). Peter protested, but the Lord reprimanded him. God, who gave the law, declared all the animals in the vision clean. The command was repeated **three times** to confirm that Peter had not misunderstood. He was **perplexed**, not knowing the meaning of the vision and the divine command.

The vision was not about food laws but God's attitude toward people. At the house of Cornelius, Peter interpreted the vision (see 10:28). It signaled the arrival of a new era in which spiritual barriers that had previously separated Jews and Gentiles were now eliminated. Without the vision it is unlikely that Peter would have met with the messengers from Cornelius and gone with them to Caesarea. In a vision that lasted only minutes Peter determined to obey God even if it was contrary to many of the biases he had held for a lifetime.

10:17-30. The meeting between Peter and Cornelius showed the extent of the ethnic barriers between Jews and Gentiles. Note the following: (1) The messengers from Cornelius stood outside the outer courtyard until Peter invited them into the house (10:17; 23). (2) Cornelius, knowing that Peter was Jewish, fell down in deference to him (10:25). (3) Peter declared that Jewish people do not normally associate with Gentiles, but that God had shown him that he should not consider any person unclean (10:28). (4) Peter explained to Cornelius why he responded to his request (10:28b-29).

10:30-33. Because of the angelic visitor, Cornelius was certain their meeting was by divine design. Gathering in the presence of the Lord with Peter the Jewish apostle speaking, Cornelius the Gentile Roman and his family were ready and eager to hear Peter's message.

b. A Message to Reach Cornelius (10:34-42)

Peter's message can be outlined in three sections as follows:

(1) Introduction of the Message (10:34-35)

10:34-35. Because of the vision, Peter realized that God does not discriminate against people because of their ethnicity. This is not a new revelation—God's love for the nations is taught in the Hebrew Bible as well. The Abrahamic covenant was given to provide ultimate blessing to the nations (Gn 22:18); the prophet Jonah was sent to preach repentance to the wicked and rebellious people of Nineveh (Jnh 1:2); and God used Elisha to heal the Syrian officer Naaman (2Kg 5:14). The new discovery related to Peter's new understanding, not God's previous revelation.

These verses are often claimed to show that God will save people who fear Him and do what is right even if they do not believe in Jesus. If that were the case, then why was Peter directed by the Lord to preach Jesus to Cornelius? The answer is that despite his devotion, Cornelius was not yet saved. In Ac 11:13-14, the angel is said to have directed Cornelius to send for Peter that he might "speak words to you by which you will be saved." The point of Ac 10:34-35 is not that fearing God and doing good apart from faith in Jesus is salvific. Rather that, regardless of nationality, those who seek God are welcomed by Him and so God will, in His sovereignty, extend greater light to such people.

(2) The Body of the Message (10:36-42)

The body of Peter's message can be summarized by noting three points. In 10:36-39a, Peter rehearsed the bare facts of the life and ministry of Jesus the Messiah. In 10:39b, Peter voiced the violent reaction of the Jewish leaders against Jesus' ministry and His crucifixion. In 10:40-43a, he emphasized the resurrection and that there were witnesses to it to whom was entrusted the proclamation of these mighty acts.

10:36-39a. By tradition, Peter was the source of Mark's gospel—and, significantly, this sermon follows the same outline as Mark.

10:39b-42. Peter began by announcing good news to Cornelius, the preaching of **peace through Jesus Christ**. In this context the gospel is good news because the promise for the forgiveness of sins through faith in Jesus Christ is for everyone—both Jews and Gentiles. His message then included the baptism of John (10:37), Christ's ministry and works (10:38), Christ's death (10:39), Christ's resurrection (10:40a), His appearance to His chosen witnesses (10:40a-41), and Christ's commissioning of His witnesses (10:42). These actions by God were not a novelty,

Peter's Sermon to a Roman Household	Mark's Gospel to the Romans
Introduction 10:36-37 • Prophetic Message 10:36 • John the Baptist 10:37	Introduction 1:1-8 • Prophetic Message 1:1-3 • John the Baptist 1:4-8
Public Ministry 10:38 • Baptism by John • Anointed by the Spirit • Doing Good	Public Ministry 1:9–10:52 • Baptism by John 1:9 • Anointed by the Spirit 1:10 • Doing Good 1:11–10:52
Passion Ministry 10:39-42 • Death of Jesus 10:39 • Resurrection of Jesus 10:40 • Appearances to Witnesses 10:41 • Commissioning of the Disciples 10:42	Passion Ministry 11:1–16:20 • Death of Jesus 11:1–15:47 • Resurrection of Jesus 16:1-8 • Appearances to Witnesses 16:9-13 • Commissioning of the Disciples 16:14-20

for they had their foundation in the Hebrew Scriptures (10:43a). The barrier of the law that separated Jew and Gentile was not a new development, it was anticipated by the prophets, though Peter did not refer to a specific passage.

c. The Conclusion of the Message: The Need for Faith (10:43)

10:43. Peter ended his message by saying that **everyone** who believes in Jesus **receives forgiveness of sins**. As Peter was speaking the events of the day of Pentecost were repeated, but this time served to bless *Gentile* people.

d. The Results of the Message (10:44–11:18)

(1) The Salvation of Cornelius's Household (10:44-48)

10:44. Peter's preaching was interrupted by the pouring out of the Holy Spirit on the Gentiles who heard and believed the gospel

10:45. As at Pentecost, the Jews who were present were amazed, this time not because of the falling of the Holy Spirit in power, but because the Spirit had been given to the Gentiles. The giving of the Spirit directly to Gentiles was evidence that Gentiles did not need to convert to Judaism in order to become followers of Israel's Messiah.

10:46a. That those who received the Spirit were **speaking with tongues** as the Jewish people had on the day of Pentecost was evidence to Peter's Jewish companions that God's plan of salvation included Gentiles.

10:46b-47. As he did on the day of Pentecost, Peter took advantage of the situation to explain the unexpected pouring out of the Holy Spirit on Gentiles. He said now that the Gentiles had received the baptism of the Spirit, they could be **baptized** with **water** in the name of Jesus. For the early church the outward act of water baptism was evidence of the inner work of the Spirit in the conversion experience.

10:48. He ordered the Gentile converts to be **baptized in the name of Jesus Christ**. They did not convert to Judaism but became followers of Jesus Christ. At this point, Gentiles were united with Jewish believers by their faith in the Messiah.

Acts 10 is rightly called "The Gentile Pentecost." Luke drew close parallels between the coming of the Spirit on the day of Pentecost and the conversion of Cornelius. Both groups had the Spirit "fall" on them (10:44; 11:15—mentioned in reference to the experience in Ac 2); both spoke in tongues (10:46; 2:4); both in Ac 2 and 10 the tongues were "heard" (2:6; 10:46); and both "spoke the great things of God" (10:46, "exalting God" [*megalunonton ton Theon*]; 2:11, "great things of God" [*megaleia tou Theou*). What these parallels suggest is that Luke forged a direct connection between what the Jewish people experienced on the day of Pentecost and what the Gentiles experienced in Caesarea. The experience, and Luke's record of it, was necessary to prove to the early (Jewish) church that the Gentiles could also be included in the people of God.

(2) The Controversy among Jewish Believers (11:1-18)

11:1-3. The conversion of Cornelius and his household did not go unnoticed by the Jewish believers in Jerusalem. The circumcision group criticized Peter because he associated with Gentiles (**uncircumcised men**) and baptized Cornelius without having him circumcised first.

Peter gave a twofold defense of his ministry to Cornelius.

11:4-14. He recounted the **vision** of the **sheet** and insisted that meeting with Cornelius was by sovereign arrangement.

11:15-17. He said that the coming of the Holy Spirit on the Gentiles confirmed the legitimacy of his ministry. The Holy Spirit fell on the Gentiles in the same way as He did on the Jewish believers **at the beginning**, a reference to the beginning of the church. This demonstrated that the universal church began at Pentecost in Ac 2, not with Abraham or Adam.

11:18. The Jewish believers in Jerusalem accepted Peter's explanation and confirmed the admission of **Gentiles** to the universal church apart from any allegiance to Judaism.

At an earlier time, Peter declared that Jesus is the Messiah and the Son of God. Christ predicted he would use Peter to build the church (Mt 16:17-19). As Christ predicted, Peter was instrumental in a foundational ministry to Jews (Ac 2), Samaritans (Ac 8), and now Gentiles (Ac 10). The conversion of Cornelius and his household showed how the door of faith was opened to Gentiles and became the basis for Paul's ministry to Gentiles. God-fearers like Cornelius became the nucleus of the Christian church in the cities where Paul preached the gospel.

B. To Antioch (11:19–12:25)

1. The Mission through Barnabas and Saul at Antioch (11:19-30)

Once the Jerusalem church officially recognized the conversion of Cornelius apart from the need to become Jewish, the church was prepared for a universal mission to the Gentiles; however, two barriers still stood in the way: location and persecution. Luke described in Acts 11:19–12:25 how God helped the church to overcome both.

This passage focuses on the three events that established Antioch rather than Jerusalem as the missionary center for the early church.

2. The Fruitfulness of the Gospel in Antioch (11:19-24)

11:19-21. Luke gave a summary of the activity of the believers who were scattered by persecution after the death of Stephen. Some preached to Jews, but others took a courageous step and crossed ethnic and cultural boundaries. They preached to Greeks and established a church in Antioch.

The hand of the Lord refers to the power of God, which is the primary reason large numbers of Greeks responded in faith.

11:22-26. The Jerusalem church sent Barnabas to Antioch to investigate the Gentile church. Barnabas lived up to his name, which means "son of encouragement." He encouraged the new converts to remain wholeheartedly devoted to the Lord. He is described as a **good man, and full of the Holy Spirit and of faith** (v. 24). **Good** means he was of wholesome character, which could be true of anyone, but Barnabas was also filled with the Spirit and a man of faith. The Spirit gave him power and the ability to overcome challenges that would defeat others. Even larger numbers were brought to the Lord (Jesus).

3. The Recruitment of Saul by Barnabas (11:25-26)

Because of the explosive growth of the church in Antioch, Barnabas needed help, but instead of returning to Jerusalem, Barnabas went to Tarsus and brought Paul to Antioch. The two taught for a year in Antioch. They undoubtedly explained how Jesus fulfilled the promises of the OT Scriptures.

Believers were first called "Christians" at Antioch (11:26). The term Christian is a combination of *Christ-* and the suffix *-iani*, which means a "follower of" or "a miniature replication of." A Christian then is a follower of Christ or a "miniature Christ." The word is used only three times in the NT, and in all three occasions it appears in a pejorative sense. In Ac 26:28 Agrippa mocked Paul by asking if he were trying to make him one of these lowly Christians. In 1Pt 4:16, Peter called those who were reviled for the name of Christ (1Pt 4:14) those who suffered as "Christians," likely using the derisive term used of them. It seems that here in 11:26 the term has a similar pejorative nuance since in the book of Acts the disciples called themselves adherents of the Way (cf. 9:1-2). This slur ultimately became an honorific title. Apparently, when Christianity spread into areas that were predominately Gentile rather than Jewish, the term "disciple" was dropped because the concept of discipleship was primarily Jewish rather than Gentile.

4. The Concern for the Disadvantaged in Judea (11:27-30)

11:27. Jewish believers who were prophets came from Jerusalem to Antioch. As did OT prophets, they received and proclaimed direct revelation from God, including the prediction of upcoming events. But in this context at least, unlike OT prophets, they did not predict apocalyptic-type events related to God's unfolding plans in the remote future. Instead here they predicted events that would occur in the near future, such as Agabus, who predicted a severe famine. The Roman historian Suetonius who died in the mid-130s AD (*Lives of the Emperors: Claudius* 18.2) spoke of widespread famine in the Mediterranean world due to drought throughout the reign of Claudius (AD 41–54), and Josephus (*Ant.* 20.5 [lines 51-52]) noted a more localized famine during the years AD 46–47. It is possible that the latter is the famine Agabus warned about (cf. the discussion by Hemer, 164–165). Periodic local famines were common in different parts of the Roman Empire. For the relationship of Agabus's prophecy about famine with Gl 2:1-10, see the comments there. Luke's focus, however, was not the natural disaster itself but the prophecy about the famine. The revelation was given at Antioch rather than Jerusalem and helped establish the legitimacy of the Gentile ministry at Antioch.

11:28-30. The shift from Jerusalem to Antioch received additional confirmation in the church's response to Agabus' prophecy. The church collected funds and appointed Barnabas and Saul to take the gifts to Jerusalem (Gl 2:1). Thus Antioch showed continued respect for the Jewish church and anticipated the request made by the pillars of the Jerusalem church that Paul, as apostle to the Gentiles, always remember "the poor" (Gl 2:10), an ancient name (Evionim, the Poor) given to the Jewish believers of Jerusalem.

5. The Persecution of Believers in Judea (12:1-25)

a. Through Prayer: Peter was Rescued (12:1-19)

Even though Antioch had become the center for the church's universal mission, the events in this chapter confirmed that God had not abandoned the Jewish people. As Longenecker says, "Before Luke turns to his portrayal of the Christian mission to the Gentile world, he takes the opportunity of presenting two further glimpses of God's working on behalf of the believers in Jerusalem . . . Luke seems desirous of making the point that, though he is about to portray the advances of the gospel within the Gentile world, it should not be assumed that God was finished with Jerusalem Christianity or that His activity in the Jewish world was finished. Divine activity on behalf of the Gentiles . . . does not mean divine inactivity on behalf of Jewish Christians or unconcern for Jews—which is a heresy that has often afflicted Gentile Christians and resulted in horrendous calamities" (Longenecker, "Acts," 405–06). Therefore, in this chapter, James died as a martyr, but Peter was miraculously released from prison. Herod Agrippa I could stop the advance of the church. For a sacrilegious act of self-glorification, God took his life.

Unlike his grandfather, Herod the Great, who was despised by the Jews, Herod Agrippa I was popular and attempted to appease both the Romans and the Jews. Consistent with his policy of appeasement rather than justice, he ordered James executed and Peter arrested.

One of the great mysteries of the Christian faith is why God delivers some believers from danger and death and not others. Herod's execution of James and the miraculous release of Peter give a vivid illustration of the "mystery of God's sovereignty."

12:1-2. James was the first apostle to meet a martyr's death. He was the brother of John. They were the sons of Zebedee (Mt 4:21) and infamous for their fiery personalities (Lk 10:54). Perhaps politically rather than religiously motivated, Herod went on a rampage against the church. The literal expression reads "laid violent hands on some." His intention was to do evil to Christians. James was **put to death with a sword** (beheaded).

12:3-4. Because Peter was a leader in the church, Herod knew that the Jewish leaders would savor his death. He ordered him arrested, intending to hold a public trial and execution after Passover.

12:5. The church prayed fervently. We cannot know exactly how they prayed since later in the account it was obvious the church did not expect Peter's release (12:14-16).

12:6-16. While Peter was sleeping, an angel appeared in his cell. Peter's chains fell off, and the angel escorted him past the guards, through locked gates, and out of the prison. At first Peter thought his experience was a vision, but once he was on the street, he realized he had actually been rescued. It has been argued that since the word "angel" literally means messenger, in this instance a human messenger and not a heavenly being led Peter to freedom. This view fails because of the supernatural light that shone at the angel's appearance (no doubt leading Peter to believe this was a vision (v. 7), the supernatural way the chains fell from Peter (v. 7), and the miraculous opening of the gates as they left the prison (v. 10). This was a heavenly being sent to minister to Peter (Heb 1:14).

The angel departed, and Peter went to the house where the believers were praying. He knocked on the door, and Rhoda answered. She recognized Peter, but the others thought she was **out of** her **mind**. When she insisted and Peter kept knocking they answered the door and were amazed. After explaining how the Lord delivered him, Peter told them to inform James (the brother of the Lord) about his release, and left Jerusalem. Either sometime previously or at this point, James had become the leader of the Jerusalem assembly. Peter, who had functioned in this role at the birth of the church, recognized James' leadership here. This foreshadowed the role James would play as leader of the Jerusalem council where Peter merely served as a witness (Ac 15).

12:17-19. The escape was a mystery to the guards. Herod questioned them and ordered them **led away** for execution. Guards were held accountable for the security of prisoners, and sometimes would commit suicide to avoid execution if a prisoner escaped (See 16:27, the Philippian jailer).

b. Through Retribution: Herod Agrippa I Was Struck Dead (12:20-25)

12:20-23. In contrast to Peter's dramatic release, Luke described Herod's disastrous end. The historical situation is described well by Bock *(Acts*, 430): "Herod is caught in a dispute with Tyre and Sidon over the provision of food. These two Phoenician cities need food and commerce from the region and have engaged in trade over a long period . . . Herod can control where the commerce goes, and so, if he uses another port, such as Berytus (Beirut) or Caesarea, it could hurt Tyre and Sidon financially and possibly in terms of provision as well." Apparently Herod became infuriated with the cities, and representatives from them came to Herod at Caesarea to fix things. Once an accord was reached, perhaps in connection with Herod's celebration of Caesar Claudius's birthday, Herod sought to celebrate with a speech, the reactions to which both Luke and Josephus (*Ant.* 19.8.2 [lines 343-350]) attested. Those reactions included the people praising him as a god. This type of flattery was often heaped on rulers and dignitaries among the Gentiles; the Jews, however, reserved this honor for God. But Herod did not refuse their praise. In fact he seemed to delight in it. The Lord ordered an angel to judge him, and he died from some kind of painful and horrible intestinal disease (**eaten by worms**). **Died** is literally "breathed his last" (cf. 5:5), and was used for divine judgment.

12:24. Though Herod attempted to eliminate the church's leaders, in the end, he was eliminated. His death made it possible for the Word of God to continue its advance.

God's sovereignty is a mystery. James was executed, but Peter was miraculously released. Why God did not intervene to rescue James is a mystery that defies finite understanding. The mystery continues today. We still do not understand why God delivers some believers from danger and even death, but not others. Christians who suffer and die, sometimes as martyrs, are not notorious sinners. They are godly and love the Lord, yet the Lord allows the enemies of Christianity to persecute them. In many places in the world today, Christians suffer and die for their faith. Stott, however, has reminded us that the victory of tyrants is temporary. He said, "Tyrants may be permitted for a time to boast and bluster, oppressing the church and hindering the spread of the gospel but they will not last. In the end their empire will be broken and their power abased" (*Acts*, 213).

We do not know what would have happened to Peter if the church had not prayed. We are not even certain that they were praying for his release, since they seem to have been embarrassingly surprised when he suddenly appeared at the house where they were meeting. Like God's sovereignty, prayer is also somewhat of a mystery. Scripture makes it clear that we ought to pray and that prayer does make a difference. God answers prayer. But contrary to what some believe and teach, we do not need to have a gigantic measure of faith, only enough to believe that God will hear us and answer according to His sovereign and unalterable purposes.

In 12:25–13:3, the church at Antioch fulfilled Jesus' mandate to take the gospel to the world by commissioning two Jewish men, Paul and Barnabas, as the first missionaries to the Gentiles.

12:25. Luke continued the narrative from 11:30. Barnabas and Saul returned to Antioch after delivering aid to the church in Jerusalem. They brought Barnabas' cousin, John Mark, with them. This introduction of John Mark to the narrative prepares the reader for the role he would play on the first journey.

C. To Asia Minor: The First Missionary Journey (13:1–15:35)

1. The Circuit of Proclamation (13:1–14:28)

a. The Commissioning of Saul and Barnabas (13:1-3)

The elimination of Herod's threat freed the church for its first missionary endeavor. The reason the first Gentile mission began in Antioch and not Jerusalem had nothing to do with anti-Gentile bigotry in Jerusalem. Initially, the gospel spread from Jerusalem to Antioch, so it was Hellenistic Jews who intentionally reached out to other Hellenistic Jews of Antioch (Ac 11:19). The Antiochene church was initially composed of Hellenistic Jews (Ac 11:20-21). Additionally, the Jerusalem church heard of the ministry in Antioch, sent Barnabas to investigate, and granted their approval of the church at Antioch through Barnabas (Ac 11:22-24). Ultimately, the primary teachers at Antioch were Saul and Barnabas, both Jews (Ac 11:25-26). The reason the mission began in Antioch was that at this point Saul was ministering in Antioch and he was God's chosen vessel to be the apostle to the uncircumcised. Therefore, God sovereignly directed the Antiochene church to send these two Jewish men, Saul and Barnabas, to reach the Gentiles. Under the direction of the Holy Spirit,

Paul's First Missionary Journey

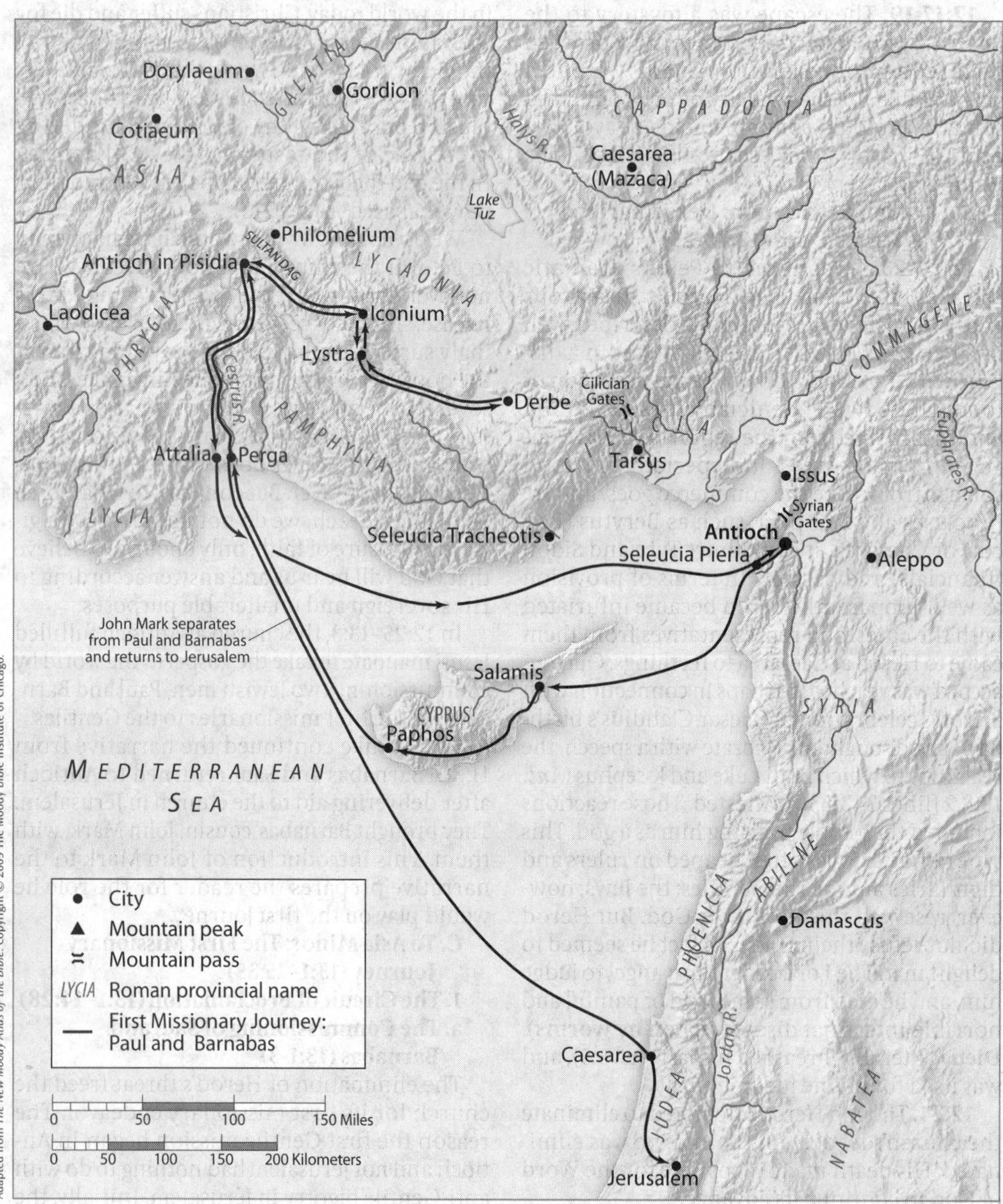

the church commissioned the missionaries, and they sailed for Cyprus, the homeland of Barnabas. When they set out for Galatia, Mark left the team and returned to Jerusalem. Paul and Barnabas made a circuit in Galatia preaching the gospel in four strategic cities—Antioch in Pisidia, Iconium, Lystra, and Derbe. On their return to Antioch, they reported how God opened the door of faith to the Gentiles.

13:1. The presence of both prophets and teachers is evidence God had blessed the church at Antioch with gifted men. The text here does not suggest a distinction in the ministry of prophets and teachers, but generally in the NT, prophets carry on an itinerant ministry and the teachers instruct believers in the local church. For other features related to those who were prophets, see the comments introducing 1Co 14.

The names of the men listed show the universal impact of the gospel. **Barnabas** was Jewish and from Cyprus; **Lucius** was from Cyrene in North Africa; **Simeon** (Niger) was Jewish with a Roman name; **Manaen** was a member of the upper class with connections to Herod; and **Saul** was a Jew from Tarsus, who trained under the great Rabbi Gamaliel (regarding whom, see the comments on 5:33-39).

13:2-3. The commissioning of the missionaries took place while the church was worshiping and **fasting**. The Holy Spirit gave divine authorization for the first missionary journey by directing the church to **set apart** (dedicate) Barnabas and Saul for the first missionary journey.

The church recognized the divine commission of Barnabas and Saul by the "laying on of hands" (for which, see the comments on 6:5-6). After more fasting and prayer, the men were sent out under the authority of the church.

The description of the commissioning of the missionaries suggests a twofold responsibility for the church—worship and mission. Both are essential. The church should meet to worship and also to witness to the world.

b. The Journey by Saul (Paul) and Barnabas (13:4–14:28)

(1) Antioch to Seleucia to Salamis on Cyprus (13:4-12)

(a) The Opposition by Elymas (13:4-8)

In 13:4–14:28, Luke presented the circuit the missionaries travelled, starting with Paphos in 13:4-12.

13:4-5. The missionary team went first to **Cyprus**, the home of Barnabas (cf. Ac 4:36). They began their ministry in Salamis on the east of the island in **synagogues**, which were logical places for explaining how Jesus fulfilled OT messianic promises.

13:6-8. From Salamis, they traveled about 90 miles west to **Paphos**, the capital of Cyprus. At Paphos they encountered **Bar-Jesus** who was described as a Jewish **magician** and **false prophet**. His name meant "son of Jesus," which is ironic because he opposed the servants of Jesus. It is also ironical that **Sergius Paulus**, who was a Gentile and **proconsul** (governor), summoned Barnabas and Paul so he could hear the Word of God from them (which is probably why Luke labeled him as **a man of intelligence**, v. 7), but Elymas (the Gk. name for Bar-Jesus) tried to keep Sergius Paulus from coming to faith. Elymas, who was the personal magician of the proconsul, realized that if Sergius Paulus trusted Christ, he would be unemployed.

(b) The Blinding of Elymas (13:9-12)

13:9-11. Luke noted Saul's name change. Now that he was ministering in a Gentile cultural context, Saul assumed his Greek name, "Paul." It is also significant that Paul was **filled with the Holy Spirit**, an indication that his ministry was divinely approved and inspired.

Paul announced judgmental blindness on Elymas, who was full of deceit and treachery. He was a **son of the devil**, an **enemy of all righteousness**, and attempted to pervert the truth. Paul announced temporary, not permanent, judicial blindness on Elymas.

13:12. In contrast to the blinding of Elymas, a Jew, Sergius Paulus, a Gentile, came to faith not because of the judgment on Elymas but because of the teaching of the Lord. The blinding of Elymas and the conversion of Sergius Paulus demonstrated the beginnings of the change that would happen in the early church—Israel would more and more reject the gospel, while Gentiles would be increasingly receptive. Paul noted later in Rm 11 that the Jewish people were hardened by God to allow time for the gospel to be taken to the Gentile world, and the Gentiles would be the ones more inclined initially to embrace Messiah Jesus (cf. the comments on Rm 11:11-24). Paul's experience here at Paphos foreshadowed what he would experience throughout his life in ministry to Jews and Gentiles. His gospel message would largely be rejected by Jews but accepted by Gentiles. From a theological perspective this event provided the historical background for Paul's discussion of Jewish unbelief in Rm 9–11. There Paul answered the question about Gentile responsiveness to the gospel and Jewish unbelief. Did it mean that God's plan of redemption for the Jewish people had failed? The answer is an emphatic, "No!" Rather, Paul explained, Jewish unbelief opened the door of faith to the Gentiles. Nevertheless, the temporary blinding of Elymas cannot be cited to support the teaching that the church has replaced Israel in God's program. See the comments on Rm 11:25-32.

This act of judgment was similar to Peter's announcement of judgment on Simon Magus (Ac 8), a comparison that functions to confirm the legitimacy of Paul's apostleship. Like Peter, who was one of the Twelve and an apostle to the Jews, Paul had the same apostolic authority as an apostle to the Gentiles.

(2) Paphos to Perga in Pamphylia (13:13)

13:13. When they arrived at the port town of Perga, John Mark returned to Jerusalem (cf. 11:30). Numerous reasons have been suggested for Mark's returning to Jerusalem. Most likely he was overwhelmed with the rigors of the ministry this missionary team was involved in, rather than that some fundamental doctrinal rift developed between John Mark and his veteran colleagues.

(3) Perga to Pisidian Antioch (13:14-50)

(a) Paul's Message in Antioch (13:14-41)

13:14-15. At Antioch, Paul established a pattern for ministry by preaching first to Jews and then to Gentiles. Paul followed this strategy in every city with a sizeable Jewish population. In Philippi, according to 16:13, it seems Paul was seeking a "place of prayer," probably for Jewish people. So even in Philippi he sought out Jewish people first.

After reading from **the Law and the Prophets**, the elders of the synagogue asked Paul and Barnabas to speak. It was customary to read from two sections of the OT—**the Law and the Prophets**, and then give an interpretation. The elders apparently considered Paul and Barnabas qualified to explain the Scriptures, so although they were visitors, they were asked to speak. Paul seized the opportunity to explain how the promises of God to Israel were fulfilled in Christ.

Paul's message spanned the historical preparations God had made to prepare the Jewish people for the coming of their Messiah (13:16-22), and what actually transpired when Jesus arrived (13:23-37). Paul concluded this review of the historical facts related to Jesus by challenging his listeners to trust in Jesus for the forgiveness of sins (13:38-41).

13:16. He addressed both Jews and God-fearers, Gentiles who believed in God but were not converts to Judaism. The primary theme was suggested in 13:39: justification by faith, not by keeping the Law of Moses.

13:17-41. In his message, Paul gave a brief survey of Israel's history from the exodus (Moses) to the united kingdom (David). His main purpose in 13:17-23 was to connect Christ to David: **From the descendants of this man, according to the promise, God has brought to Israel a Savior, Jesus** (13:23). When David desired to build a house for God, Nathan the prophet promised David an eternal dynasty (see the comments on 2Sm 7:6-16 for the Davidic covenant). Paul identified Jesus as the promised seed of David.

Paul leaped from David to John the Baptist in 13:24-25. His main point here was to emphasize that John was not the Messiah, but that his mission was to prepare the nation for the coming of the Messiah. John was regarded favorably by most of the Jewish people, and his purpose here may have been to connect Jesus with the Baptist in an attempt to incline the listeners favorably to Him.

In 13:26-30, Paul said that though the Scriptures were read in the synagogues, Israel's leadership did not understand the message of the prophets and they condemned the Savior though He was innocent. In contrast to how the Jewish leaders and Pilate condemned and conspired to kill Jesus, God raised Him from the dead, and His followers were witnesses of His resurrection.

In 13:31-37 Paul appealed to three OT texts to prove Christ's resurrection. Psalm 2 is a royal Psalm, and v. 7 makes an intimate connection between the Messiah and God. He is God's Son. Paul alluded to Is 55:3 in v. 34, and he informed his audience that the promises made to David had been given to them through Jesus who had been raised from the dead. As did Peter in his speech in Ac 2, Paul quoted Ps 16:10, and insisted that David could not have been speaking of himself since his tomb was in Jerusalem. Paul's appeal to these texts was not arbitrary. First, as a postexilic collection, the Psalms in general, and the royal Psalms in particular, pointed forward to the future royal son of David, the Messiah. Thus, just as Paul explained, in Ps 2 God was not addressing David, but rather called the Messiah His Son. In the same way, Ps 16:10 predicts that some future individual would not experience decay in the grave, referring not to David but rather the future Davidic Messiah. This is all in accord with the Davidic covenant (2Sm 7:12-16), in which God mercifully promised David (Is 55:3) a future descendant, the Messiah, who would have an eternal house, throne, and kingdom.

Paul's main point is in 13:38-39. Forgiveness and justification are through faith in Jesus and not by the keeping of the **Law of Moses**. Both forgiveness and justification have a forensic sense. **Forgiveness** means that the legal penalty for one's sins is cancelled, and justification means that a person is declared right with God. Paul insisted it is only through faith in Jesus' atoning death and resurrection that God grants complete forgiveness and declares a person totally righteous.

This text seems to fly in the face of the "New Perspective on Paul." Proponents of the New Perspective argue that Paul's problem with Judaism was the use of the law as a barrier to keep themselves separate from Gentiles and that Jews did not believe the law was a means to gain status with God. But it is the use of the law for justification that Paul refuted in his message. For more on the "New Perspective on Paul," see the Introduction to the book of Romans.

Paul concluded his message in 13:40-41 with a stern warning of judgment for rejecting Christ. Using a quote from Hab 1:5, he compared his audience to the Israelites who were destroyed during the Babylonian exile. The present generation of Jewish people would also experience judgment if they refused to believe that God is working through Jesus Christ. The key idea in the comparison is God's work. In the context of Acts, God's work included the atoning death and resurrection of Jesus Christ and Christ's work of building the church through Spirit-inspired witnesses.

(b) Reaction to the Message in Antioch (13:42-50)

13:42-43. In the response to Paul's message, some begged Paul to speak again the following Sabbath, and many Jews and converts to Judaism even began spending time with Paul and Barnabas. They were urged to continue to rely on God's grace and not revert to living by the law of Moses.

13:44-45. When Paul spoke the next Sabbath, the events of Paphos were repeated. When the Jewish leaders saw the favorable response of many in the audience they were **filled with jealousy** and began to slander ("blaspheme") Paul.

13:46-48. Paul and Barnabas rebuked the opposition while saying it was necessary for the gospel to be preached to the Jewish community **first** because the gospel had primary relevance to the Jewish people (Jn 4:22; and comments at Rm 1:16). Nevertheless, Paul declared two consequences of their rejecting his message. One, they had judged themselves **unworthy of eternal life**. Here and in v. 48 are the only references in Acts where the content of **SALVATION** is described as the hope of eternal life. Two, Paul stated that rejection by the Jewish people justified his ministry to the **Gentiles**. Some have interpreted this as a transfer of Paul's ministry and message away from the Jewish people to exclusive proclamation to Gentiles. However, in the very next city (Iconium, 14:1-2), he went to Jewish people first once again. Much earlier, the prophet Isaiah had predicted the worldwide relevance of the ministry of God's Servant (Is 49:6; 42:6). The quote from Isaiah (v. 41) indicates that Jesus is God's anointed Servant.

13:48-49. In contrast to the Jews, Gentiles rejoiced and those who were **appointed to eternal life believed**. As God chose Israel as His special people, He now sovereignly granted eternal life to Gentiles. In addition, Luke indicated that no one can save himself; people are saved only because of God's gracious choice. Opposition could not stop **the word of the Lord**; the gospel made an impact upon the entire region. Luke referred to the message as **the word of the Lord** (vv. 48-49) not to describe the apostolic preaching as Scripture but to indicate that their message was from God. As Paul stated in Gl 1 the gospel is not a message he created but one he received from God.

13:50. The response of the Gentiles led to even greater opposition. Some Jewish people incited upper class women (probably Gentiles) and the Gentile leaders of the city to persecute Paul and Barnabas, who were forced to leave the district.

(4) Antioch to Iconium: Mixed Reactions (13:51–14:5)

13:51-52. With a symbolic act of judgment, Paul and Barnabas **shook off the dust of their feet** and traveled to Iconium, 90 miles southeast of Pisidian Antioch.

Like the apostles who rejoiced when flogged by the Sanhedrin (cf. Ac 5:40-42), the disciples were filled with joy and the Holy Spirit. Joy and courage to boldly proclaim the Word of God in the face of persecution were evidences of the Holy Spirit in Acts.

14:1-2. At Iconium the divided response and hostility of some Jewish people at Paphos and Pisidian Antioch were repeated. When the missionaries spoke in the synagogue, a large number of both **Jews and Greeks** believed. But some unbelieving Jewish people **stirred up** the minds of the Gentiles, turning them against Paul and Barnabas. The word translated by the NASB as **embittered** is literally "to cause someone to think badly about another, *make angry, embitter*" (BDAG, 502). Paul and Barnabas were so effective in convincing Jews and Greeks of the truth of their message that Jews sought the help of Gentiles to stop the missionaries.

14:3-7. Though the missionaries authenticated their message with **signs and wonders**, the people were still divided. Some believed the slander of the Jews, but others sided with the apostles. Luke called both Barnabas and Paul **apostles**, an extension of the ministry of an apostle beyond the Twelve.

(5) Iconium to Lystra (14:6-20a)

(a) A Case of Mistaken Identities (14:6-18)

When both Gentiles and Jews attempted to stone the missionaries, Paul and Barnabas fled further southeast to the region of **Lycaonia**, and the cities of Lystra and Derbe.

14:8-10. At **Lystra** Luke provided an example of how Paul preached to Gentiles who did not know the OT. As Peter had healed a handicapped man (Ac 3), Paul healed a man who was physically challenged from birth. Luke's purpose was to authenticate Paul's apostleship to the Gentiles by showing that God was working in Paul's ministry to the Gentiles with the same power that he worked in Peter's ministry among the Jewish people. The difference between this account and Peter's healing of the handicapped man is that Paul saw the man had **faith to be made well**. Though not stated, his physical healing was a picture of spiritual salvation.

14:11-13. The superstitious Gentiles mistakenly believed that Barnabas and Paul were the gods **Zeus** and **Hermes**. According to the local legend these gods had visited the region and blessed those who extended them hospitality but destroyed the homes of those who would not welcome them. Not wanting to risk judgment, the local temple priest brought sacrifices to worship them.

14:14-15. Barnabas and Paul vehemently protested. They did not attempt to exploit the Lycaonians as itinerant sages might have done. Instead Paul seized the opportunity to tell the Lycaonians about God. Luke gave only a summary of Paul's message. Paul took a different tack in preaching to Gentiles from what he did in preaching to Jews. He contextualized his message, but he did not change the essential content of his **gospel** message.

Paul called his message the **gospel**, the announcement of good news. The message of the pagan world was "bad news." People lived in fear of fate and the fickleness of their gods. No one could know for sure what his or her eternal destiny would be, or even if there was life after death. Men and women were powerless to deliver themselves from the sinful tendencies of their fallen humanity. To helpless and hopeless pagans, the gospel is "good news."

Because God is the creator of everything, Paul appealed for Lycaonians to repent, "to turn" from idolatry to faith in the only living God (cf. 1Th 1:19). Paul's argument was from nature. It was not theological (Romans) or scriptural (Antioch) or philosophical (Athens).

14:16-17. Paul attempted to present a plan of salvation based on progressive revelation. The statement that in the past **He permitted all nations to go their own ways** does not mean that after God made the heavens and earth He abandoned His creation, or that He did not constantly exercise His providential and sovereign control. Paul's point seems to indicate that God had not previously provided direct revelation of Himself to nations other than Israel, and had not called them to live under a specially revealed law similar to the law of Moses. He did, however, provide for them "general revelation," proof of Himself in creation, as demonstrated by His provisions specified in v. 17. God has consistently provided evidence of His existence through His providential goodness by sustaining life. He gives to all men **rains**, **fruitful seasons**, and **food**. For a similar argument see Rm 1:18-32 and the comments there.

14:18. Paul's message did not dissuade the Lycaonians from worshipping the missionaries as gods.

Paul made it clear that the people of Lystra had to choose. His presentation did not contain a hint of relativism. There is only one living God who is the creator of everything. To worship any other god is idolatry; the Lycaonians needed to repent. Had Paul been able to continue, he undoubtedly would have stated that Jesus Christ is the culmination of redemptive history, though he would have arrived at that conclusion differently from how he did at Antioch preaching to Jews.

(b) Opponents from Iconium and Antioch (14:19-20a)

14:19-20a. Resembling a lynch mob, some Jewish people came from both Antioch and Iconium and stoned Paul. The wording of the text suggests that Paul was only unconscious and not killed, though the mob thought he was dead.

(6) Lystra to Derbe: A Favorable Reaction (14:20b-21a)

14:20b. Paul was no coward. After he regained consciousness, he went back into the city for the night. The next day he and Barnabas left for Derbe, which was about 60 miles away. Paul was not only courageous, he was also tough.

14:21. Luke gave only a capsule summary of Paul's ministry in Derbe. He preached "the good news" and won a large number of **disciples**.

(7) Backtracking: Derbe Back through Lystra, Iconium, and Pisidian Antioch to Perga (14:21b-23)

The missionaries retraced their steps going to Lystra, Iconium, and Antioch in Pisidia.

14:22-23. Paul and Barnabas were **strengthening** and **encouraging** the new converts. Paul was brutally honest. He warned that following Christ would not be easy. Believers should expect verbal abuse and physical persecution (**tribulations**), but he encouraged them to be faithful. In 2Tm 3:12 Paul wrote, "In fact, everyone who wants to live a godly life in Christ Jesus will be persecuted."

They appointed elders, the spiritual leaders in the early church. 1 Timothy 3 and Ti 1 give their qualifications. After committing the new believers to the Lord by prayer and fasting, they traveled through Pisidia, preached the word in Perga, and sailed from Attalia to Antioch in Syria.

(8) Perga to Attalia to Syrian Antioch: The Conclusion of the First Missionary Journey (14:24-28)

14:24-28. Their work was complete because independent churches had been established. They gave God the credit for what they accomplished and were particularly surprised at how God had **opened a door of faith to the Gentiles**.

Some of the more significant features of the first missionary journey encompassed the inclusion of Gentiles in the people of God. Almost by accident, the missionaries discovered God's plan of redemption included Gentiles as well as Jews. Because the Holy Spirit directed the church to commission Paul and Barnabas, it was God himself who authorized the new missionary strategy of preaching the gospel to Gentiles, enabling them to come to Christ independent of Judaism—a policy that would be challenged and resolved at the Jerusalem Council.

2. The Council of Confirmation (15:1-35)

a. The Issue at Stake (15:1-6)

15:1-4. As a result of the first missionary journey, the conversion of Gentiles alarmed a group of Jewish traditionalists who insisted on circumcision as an essential part of maintaining one's salvation experience. The issue was not about Gentile participation in the covenant people of God.

When a group of these traditionalists came from Judea to Antioch teaching that circumcision was essential for salvation, Paul and Barnabas correctly viewed this as a threat to God's grace. After a heated debate with the protestors, Paul and Barnabas traveled to Jerusalem and requested that the church resolve the issue. The meeting on this issue was called "the Jerusalem Council." Luke's account of this extremely important council explains how the early church resolved the issue of the law for Gentile believers. There is an enormous debate regarding the relationship of the Jerusalem Council with the timing of the writing of Paul's letter to the Galatians. It is not clear if Galatians was written before or after the Council. For these issues, see "Date" in the Introduction to Galatians. It is most likely that Galatians was written just prior to the Jerusalem council because Paul would likely have cited the decision of the council had it already happened.

15:5-6. Some men refers to those who belonged to "the party of the Pharisees" (cf. 15:5). It is not clear who these people **from Judea** were. They were Jewish people who may have been believing emissaries from the Jerusalem church who misrepresented the opinion of the apostles and the elders (vv. 5, 6), or they may have been false teachers with a Jewish background. However they are identified, they insisted that Gentile believers be circumcised and keep the other aspects of the law as befitting a member of God's covenant people. They insisted that every Gentile become a Jew in order to be right with God. Because circumcision was the physical sign for identifying a person as a member of Israel (see Gn 17), the practice became the linchpin for adherence to the law of Moses. These Jews who advocated Gentile conversion to Judaism and obedience to the law were later rebuked as legalists in the epistle to the Galatians. **Dissension and debate** (v. 2) indicate that this was an enormously controversial issue, especially in light of Paul and Barnabas's practice of not requiring circumcision and law-keeping for those Gentiles already won to Christ. Paul's opponents understood Paul to be bringing a message that seemed to tell new followers of the Jewish Messiah that they need not obey God's laws.

Paul's concern was not primarily pragmatic, that adding circumcision to the gospel would hinder the success of the gospel. Rather, his concern was theological, that adding circumcision as a requirement would be adding works to the message of grace. Forcing Gentiles to submit to the law would distort the gospel of God's grace into a message of grace mixed with works. Paul and Barnabas protested this teaching and were appointed with a delegation to go to Jerusalem to resolve the controversy. The controversy broached in 15:1 is expanded in v. 5 and addressed beginning in v. 7. **Some of the sect of the Pharisees** (v. 5) are identified as believers.

b. The Speeches (15:7-21)

(1) Peter: Declaration of the Facts (15:7-11)

15:7-11. In the report on his ministry to Cornelius (vv. 7-11), Peter identified the heart of the issue. Salvation is by grace made available through the work of **the Lord Jesus**, not through the works of the law (v. 11). Even the Gentiles, as seen in the case of Cornelius, received the Lord by faith, received the Spirit, spoke in tongues, and were baptized. How could anyone think that they were not genuinely right with God, even apart from the works required by the law of Moses?

(2) Barnabas and Paul: Authentication of the Facts (15:12)

15:12. Barnabas and Paul reported on their ministry to Gentiles, giving a supernatural perspective. God confirmed their ministry among the Gentiles with miraculous **signs and wonders**, just as He had through Peter with Cornelius's household. See v. 8, which implies the miraculous manifestation of the giving of the Spirit to the Gentiles "just as He also did to us" (in Ac 2).

(3) James: Correlation with the Prophets (15:13-21)

15:13-21. James related the issue to God's comprehensive plan of redemption with a quotation from Am 9:11-15. James did, however, refer to **the Prophets** (v.15), and while he cited only Am 9, other passages from the prophets forecast the inclusion of Gentiles *as Gentiles* (not "as Jews") among God's people (e.g., Is 2:2; 45:20-23; Jr 12:15-16; Hs 3:4-5; Zch 2:11; 8:22; and see Paul's citations of other texts on the theme of the inclusion of Gentiles in Rm 15:8-13; see the comments there). The rebuilding of David's dynasty refers to the promises God made to David (2Sm 7) and to Abraham (Gn 12:1-3), promises that had an initial, partial fulfillment in the wake of the death, resurrection, and ascension of Jesus, and the spread of the gospel, all of which signaled the presence of "messianic days." James's citation of Amos is primarily about the inclusion of Gentiles among the people of God without their having to become Jewish, not about the restoration of David's kingdom in and through the church (as covenant theologians argue). Robert L. Saucy (*The Case for Progressive Dispensationalism: The Interface Between Dispensational and Non-Dispensational Theology* [Grand Rapids, MI: Zondervan, 1993], 79) writes, "Amos looked forward to the times of the Messiah, which included the salvation of Gentiles without their becoming part of Israel. These times have arrived with Jesus, and the new work of God indicates that salvation is going out to the gentiles apart from keeping the law." Amos had prophesied the future salvation of Gentiles as part of God's program of redemption. God's plan is for **THE REST OF MANKIND** to **SEEK**, not only for Jews.

James's perspective drew less upon the practical experiences reported by Peter, Paul, and Barnabas and more upon the teaching of the OT prophets. If God's redemptive purposes included Gentiles, then the Jewish believers should not have erected barriers to their inclusion among God's covenant people. He recommended that the council reject the view of the legalists and not impose the law on Gentiles.

c. The Letter to Gentile Churches (15:22-35)

15:22-35. James also recommended the council send a letter to the Gentiles asking them to refrain from practices especially offensive to Jews (15:2-21). The council asked Gentiles to **abstain from** (1) **things sacrificed to idols**; (2) **fornication**; and (3) eating meat that has been **strangled** or has large amounts of **blood** in it.

The request for Gentile abstinence raises questions about the nature of these restrictions. Were the restrictions essentially a reiteration of the ceremonial aspects of the law of Moses? If they were, then the council was contradicting its decision not to impose the law on Gentiles. The best solution is to relate the restrictions to the cultic worship in pagan temples where worshipers would strangle animals, cut their jugular veins to drink their blood, eat the meat that had been offered to idols and conclude with temple prostitution. This interpretation is consistent with Paul's teaching to the Corinthians about participating in idol worship (1 Co 10:14-22). The intent was to prevent the syncretism of paganism and the new faith. Although Gentiles did not need to convert to Judaism, they were required to leave pagan idol worship (cf. 1Th 1:9). This would preserve the testimony of the church among Jewish people, where the Torah and its strict prescriptions against idolatry are "read in the synagogues every Sabbath" (15:21).

The decision was important for three reasons. First, by not requiring Gentiles to convert to Judaism it protected the doctrine of salvation by grace through faith alone. Second, it preserved the purity of the church so that paganism would not be blended with the true faith. Third, the messianic faith, by not tolerating idolatry, set an important precedent of maintaining the messianic faith's testimony before Jewish people.

The wisdom of the decision was reflected in the response of the Gentile church at Antioch. When Paul and Barnabas, along with two respected men from the Jerusalem church, Judas and Silas, read the letter to the church at Antioch, the believers rejoiced. The potentially divisive issue of the law had been officially resolved and unity was preserved.

Judas and Silas ministered to the Gentile church with a message that strengthened them in their faith, and then they returned to Jerusalem (v. 34 is omitted in many manuscripts). Paul and Barnabas remained in Antioch teaching **the word of the Lord.** The two continued their ministry among Gentiles unhindered by the dispute over the law of Moses.

D. To the Aegean Area: The Second Missionary Journey (15:36–18:22)

1. The Selection of the Team (15:36–16:3)

15:36–16:3. Paul and Barnabas decided to revisit the churches started on the first journey, but they disagreed on whether or not to take John Mark. Perhaps, because they were cousins, Barnabas wanted to take him. This is perfectly in keeping with Barnabas's nature as "the son of encouragement," that he would want to afford John Mark another opportunity. But Paul objected. The mention that Mark had deserted them on the first journey supports Paul's view. This was a serious disagreement and not merely a difference of opinion. The expression **sharp disagreement** (*paroxysmos*) means "a state of irritation expressed in argument" (BDAG, 780). Both men vigorously defended their positions, leading to a separation of Paul and Barnabas. As promised in Rm 8:28, God brought good out of this disagreement. There were now two strong missionary teams instead of one!

Though Barnabas and Mark are not mentioned again in the book of Acts, Paul later spoke positively of Barnabas (1Co 9:6, Col 4:10), and also of Mark (2Tm 4:11).

The circumcision of Timothy (16:1-3) showed that the decision of the Jerusalem council was limited to Gentiles not being circumcised, not Jews. Timothy's mother was Jewish, so Timothy should have been circumcised as an outward sign of the Abrahamic covenant (Gn 17:9-14). By requiring Timothy to submit to circumcision, Paul avoided offending Jews for the purpose of ministry and recognized the continuation of the Abrahamic covenant for Jewish believers.

Paul's action here seems to contradict his position in Gl 2:3-5. He adamantly refused to allow for the circumcision of Titus; however, these two situations are different. Timothy was a Jew, but Gl 2:3 describes Titus as a Greek. So he was a Gentile, for whom circumcision would have been inappropriate and brought into question justification by faith alone. Paul had Timothy circumcised not as a precondition for salvation but as an outward sign of the Abrahamic covenant. Paul would never compromise the gospel, but he did compromise on lifestyle issues for the sake of effectiveness in ministry. Paul was willing to become all things to all men in order that he might win some (1Co 9:9-23). Moreover, Paul would have expected a Jewish believer like Timothy to maintain the outward sign of God's covenant relationship with Israel.

Paul continued his ministry of strengthening the churches by informing believers in Derbe and Lystra of the decision of the Jerusalem council. The wisdom of the council's decision about the law of Moses and Paul's decision to circumcise Timothy were reinforced in the positive response of the churches and their growth.

2. The Leading into Europe (16:4-10)

16:4-5. In the first journey, Luke focused on the Lord's sovereignty in opening the door of faith to a new group of people—the Gentiles. In

Paul's Second Missionary Journey

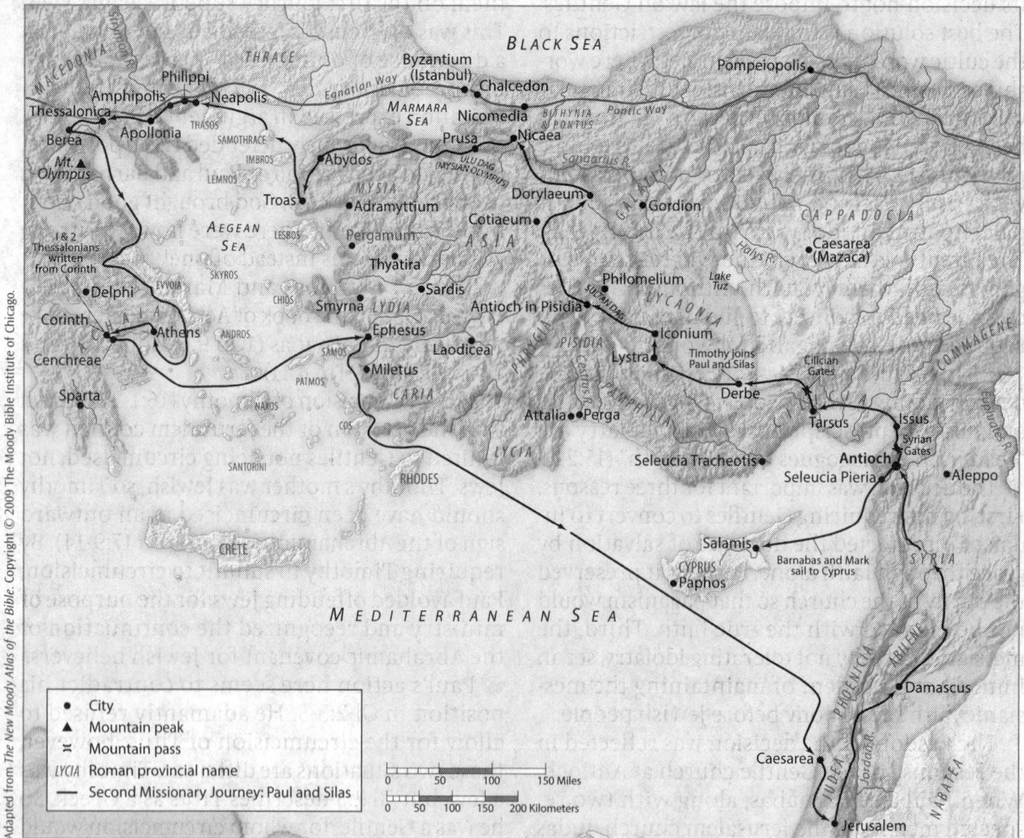

his account of the second (AD 51–52) and third (AD 53–56) missionary journeys, Luke showed the sovereignty of the Spirit in directing Paul and his companions into new geographical locations. Note that Luke did not make a sharp distinction between the second and third journeys. He began his account of the third journey almost incidentally in 18:23.

Acts 16:6-10 explains how Paul and his companions decided to preach the gospel in Macedonia. This was one of Paul's most strategic decisions because it resulted in the spread of the church westward to the continent of Europe.

16:6. Paul intended to minister in Asia, probably Ephesus after he revisited the churches planted on the first journey in Phrygia and Galatia, but **the Holy Spirit** prevented Paul and his companions from entering Asia. Luke did not tell us how, but it is obvious that He had a different plan for the missionaries.

16:7-8. Instead of turning back, Paul turned north, but again **the Spirit of Jesus** prevented him from entering Bithynia. Paul turned west and traveled through Mysia to Troas. The change from Holy Spirit to the Spirit of Jesus reflects the early church's understanding of the deity of Jesus. Troas was located on the northwestern coast of Asia Minor or what is now part of Turkey. It was a coastal city and a departure point for Greece.

16:9-10. At Troas, in a vision, Paul saw a man of Macedonia summoning him to come to Macedonia. Paul could not have anticipated the importance of his response to the Macedonian vision. The vision marked a major turning point in the history of the church. Paul's obedient response to God's call caused the gospel to move westward and so to bridge two continents, Asia and Europe, positioning the new faith to become universal.

Longenecker reminds that the believer's response to the call of God is never a trivial matter. "Indeed as in this instance, great issues and untold blessings may depend on it" ("Acts," 458).

It may be to go across the street, across the country, or around the world. The eternal destinies of men and women may depend on our openness and willingness to obey the Spirit's promptings and move out of our comfort zones.

3. The Witness at Philippi (16:11-40)

In 16:11-40, Luke recorded that Paul began his Aegean campaign in Philippi, a strategic city on Egnatian Way (a major east-west road in the Roman Empire).

16:11-15. The missionaries sailed from Troas to **Samothrace** (an island approximately halfway to Neapolis) and then to **Neapolis** (a seaport 10 miles from Philippi). At some point, Luke joined Paul and Silas, which is indicated by the plural pronoun **we**.

Philippi was named after Philip II, father of Alexander the Great, in about 356 BC, and had developed into a major city in the province of Macedonia. Under Roman rule it was a senatorial rather than imperial province, so the city had elected magistrates (see vv. 20, 22, 35-38).

On the Sabbath, the missionaries went to **a place of prayer**. Apparently the Jewish community was small, and there was only a place of prayer rather than a synagogue (some think the place of prayer was in a synagogue). Women were present for prayer. Though participation in worship was limited, women were permitted to pray. While Paul was speaking to the women, the Lord opened the heart of Lydia to respond to the gospel. Lydia is identified as a businesswoman from Thyatira who sold **purple fabrics**, which was the color of royalty and the rich. Purple cloth was extremely expensive because of the difficulty of producing the dye, which was made from mollusks (shellfish). Her name indicates she was a Gentile, so she was most likely a God-fearer (a Gentile who believed in God and followed the moral and ethical teachings of Judaism but was not a full convert). She was apparently single, perhaps a widow, since she was the head of her household, and they followed her lead in responding to the gospel. The evidence that Lydia's conversion was genuine was her offer of hospitality to the apostolic band. As did Peter (see 10:48), Paul and his companions stayed in the home of a Gentile convert.

16:16-18. On a subsequent Sabbath, Paul was confronted by a slave girl with **a spirit of divination**. **A spirit of divination** (lit., a "spirit of python," *pythona*) means "demon possessed." The "python" was a mythical serpent or dragon that guarded the Delphic oracle. The "python" was supposedly killed by Apollo, but according to the legend "the spirit of the python" lived on, enabling those it possessed the ability to predict the future. The girl was not only demon possessed, she was a slave and exploited by her owners for profit.

Following Paul and his companions she repeatedly identified them as **bond-servants of the Most High God**. Paul objected for two reasons. First, though her statement was true, in a polytheistic culture it did not mean she recognized them as messengers of the only true God. Second, Paul did not want anyone to think that he was complicit in her magical or demonic powers.

Her constant tirade **annoyed** Paul, so he used his apostolic authority to deliver the girl from demon possession. He did this **in the name of Jesus**, giving evidence of the superiority of Jesus over demonic powers. She was delivered from the demonization, but her conversion was implied though not explicitly mentioned in the text.

16:19-24. Her owners were not happy about her conversion because it meant a loss of income. They seized Paul and Silas and accused them of disturbing the peace. The meaning of the charge about the violation of Roman customs (v. 21) is not clear. It was undoubtedly related to the loss of income and probably the fact that the religion of Rome was inclusive in contrast to Christianity, which is exclusive. If Paul and Silas were allowed to continue their ministry, it could affect the economy of Philippi and Rome's policy of religious toleration.

The magistrates arrested and punished Paul and Silas without a fair trial. They were flogged with rods (not the harsher whips with pieces of bone or metal) and imprisoned. The punishment would have involved being publicly stripped and caned. Under Roman law, however, Roman citizens were not to be beaten or whipped (see Cicero, *In Verrem* 5.62). It is unclear why Paul did not here invoke this privilege since he was a Roman citizen by birth, but it is possible that he may not have been given the chance.

16:25-26. In the middle of the night (**about midnight**) while Paul and Silas were praying and singing, they were miraculously set free. Instead of sending an angel as He did to free Peter, God used an earthquake. Though an earthquake is a natural phenomenon, God was the efficient cause behind the event.

16:27-30. The earthquake woke the jailer; and when he saw the prison doors were open, he assumed the prisoners had escaped. Since he was responsible for the security of the prisoners, he prepared to take his own life rather than risk execution. It was Roman law to execute the guard who allowed a prisoner to escape.

The jailer could not have been more surprised by what he discovered. Instead of escaping as the apostles did in Ac 5 and 12, Paul, Silas, and all the other prisoners stayed put. Seeing that the jailer was about to take his life, Paul **cried out with a loud voice, saying, "Do not harm yourself for we are all here!"**

The jailer fell on his knees before Paul and Silas in fear, not worship. He called them **Sirs** (lit., "lords"), concluding they were undoubtedly divine men. The question he asked was not to save his life, **Sirs, what must I do to be saved?** He already knew the prisoners had not escaped. Most likely he heard enough of the gospel message from the disruptive but accurate words of the slave girl (Longenecker, "Acts," 465), or perhaps from the missionaries following their incarceration, to recognize his spiritual need.

16:31. His cry for salvation (16:30) and Paul's quick and concise answer captured the essence of the proper response to the gospel: **Believe in the Lord Jesus, and you will be saved, you and your household**. Paul urged the jailer to place his complete dependence upon the Lord Jesus for deliverance from the consequences of his sin. **And your household** does not mean that when he gets saved his household is automatically saved. The statement means that if he believed, and if his whole household believed, they would all be saved.

16:32-34. The jailer's household was saved because they also believed, suggesting that his **household** consisted of those who were of sufficient age to exercise faith in Christ, and that infants were not among those baptized. All were immediately baptized after they believed. Though baptism does not save, it symbolizes cleansing from sin and is a further step of submission to the Lord. Luke presented twofold evidence of the authenticity of their faith. One, they opened their home to Paul and Silas. Two, they experienced the gift of joy; they **rejoiced greatly**.

16:35-40. The officials wanted to get Paul and Silas out of town quickly and quietly since the officials themselves had violated Roman law by arresting and punishing them without a trial. Paul, however, was not willing to allow these administrators to simply dismiss the issue. Since they had been publicly punished, Paul used the leverage of his Roman citizenship to force the officials to admit publicly that they had misused their authority.

Paul did not use his citizenship to "get even." He forced the officials to admit their error to protect the new faith from becoming an unauthorized or unfavorable religious movement. Paul also met with the believers at Lydia's house to encourage them before leaving. He probably assured them that the officials would not punish them because of their faith in Christ.

The converts at Philippi were all completely different. Lydia was a successful businesswoman. The demon-possessed girl was a slave being exploited for profit. The Philippian jailer was a cog in the Roman machinery, afraid of losing his life. The conversion of these three individuals from culturally and economically diverse backgrounds is a testimony to the universal appeal and power of the gospel.

In this current time of social and ethnic diversity, believers also need to set an example of the power of Christ to unite rather than divide people by proclaiming the gospel to all people.

Luke, in 17:1-9, has given us only a brief summary of Paul's ministry in Thessalonica. Paul attempted to minister in the synagogue, but was forced to flee to Berea because of Jewish opposition. The courage Paul and his team showed was remarkable. After enduring the abuse in Philippi, they then walked about 70 miles to Thessalonica to continue their missionary endeavors, but with the wounds on their bodies not yet healed from the beating.

4. The Witness at Thessalonica (17:1-9)

17:1. From Philippi, Paul traveled along the Egnatian Way to **Thessalonica**. It was a free city with its own elected officials (v. 6) and the capital of Macedonia. The city was founded by Cassander, one of the rulers of Macedon after Alexander the Great's death, in 315 BC and named after his wife, daughter of Philip II and half-sister of Alexander the Great. At the time of Paul's visit, the population may have been as high as 100,000.

Paul considered Thessalonica a strategic location for preaching the gospel. The "good news" could spread east and west on the Egnatian Way, plus the synagogue in the city provided a point of contact for explaining how Christ's life, death, and resurrection fulfilled Scripture.

17:2-3. Paul followed his personal strategy (**custom**) for ministry by going first to the synagogue. Though he had faced opposition from his Jewish countrymen on the first missionary journey, Paul remained committed to the strategy of proclaiming the gospel first to the Jews and then to the Gentiles (cf. comments at 13:46-48 and Rm 1:16). It was a wise strategy. His most effective ministry would have come from sharing the gospel with those whose backgrounds included knowledge of the Hebrew Scriptures and the concept of the Messiah, namely Jewish people and Gentile God-fearers.

Paul appealed to the OT to support his message that Jesus is the Messiah. It is not clear whether the reference to three Sabbaths means that Paul was only in Thessalonica for three weeks or that his ministry in the synagogue was for three consecutive weeks. The fruit of his ministry suggests the latter, so that he conducted his outreach even after the three weeks in the synagogue ceased. In either case he was obviously in the city long enough to organize a church.

Luke did not explain how Paul made his case, but his summary of Paul's preaching gives us the core message of the early church. First, Jesus' suffering and death was not a tragic and unexpected turn of events. The OT predicted both the suffering and resurrection of the Messiah. Second, this Jesus who rose from the dead is Israel's promised Messiah.

17:4. Though some Jews believed, Paul's greatest success was with Gentiles. Among the converts were **a number of the leading women**, most likely the wives of some of the city officials.

17:5-7. Some Jewish leaders became jealous. They resented that Paul persuaded Jewish people, Gentiles, and even women to become believers. They incited a mob that went to Jason's house in search of Paul and his companions. Unable to find Paul, they dragged Jason and other new believers before the city officials.

The charges were serious. One, they accused them of political agitation. Upsetting **the world** is hyperbole, but it does suggest that this new faith made a significant impact on the Roman Empire. Perhaps they had heard reports about Paul's arrest at Philippi. Two, they were defying Caesar's decrees by claiming that Christ is a king. Claiming that Jesus is an emperor rivaling Caesar was a capital offense. If the apostles had proclaimed Christ as king, they were talking about a different kind of kingdom. We know from the epistles to the Thessalonians that Paul emphasized Jesus' second coming. Perhaps he had spoken about the future messianic kingdom. The charges were civil and political rather than religious because the Jewish leaders knew that the Romans would ignore religious issues but take strong action against anyone causing a civil disturbance or advocating a revolt.

17:8-9. The agitators were successful. The city officials required **Jason and the others** to post bail (**pledge**). **Jason** was apparently a leader in the Thessalonian synagogue who trusted Christ under Paul's ministry. He was probably affluent since his house was substantial enough to host the congregation and house Paul and his team, and **Jason** more than likely became the leader of the church after Paul left. The traditional view is that "the bond" was collateral guaranteeing Paul would not return to Thessalonica during the administration of the current officials, but it is equally possible that **Jason** and the other members of the newly founded congregation (**they**, indicating others than strictly Paul) were also implicated in the unrest and posted a bond for themselves. The bail bond may have been the satanic barrier that Paul said prevented from him from returning to Thessalonica (see 1Th 2:17-18).

Paul's ministry at Thessalonica emphasized that Paul based his message that Jesus was the Messiah on the OT and presented the evidence in a logical and persuasive format. He did not attempt to manipulate or trick people to become believers, as he explained in 1Th 2:1-4.

5. The Witness at Berea (17:10-15)

17:10. To avoid further trouble, the believers sent Paul and Silas to Berea under the cover of darkness. When Paul arrived in Berea, which was about 45 miles southwest of Thessalonica, he went immediately to the synagogue.

17:11. Paul could not have known that the Bereans would become a model for how to study the Bible. Luke gave a threefold description of the Bereans' response to Paul's preaching. First, they approached Paul's teaching with some open-mindedness. The expression **more noble-minded** than the Thessalonians means that the Bereans were objective in their evaluation of Paul's message. They judged his message by the standard of Scripture rather than their preconceived prejudices. Second, they also received the Scriptures **with great eagerness**. They had an appetite to learn. Finally, they examined **the Scriptures daily, to see whether these things**

were so. They carefully evaluated Paul's message to determine for themselves if it was true.

17:12-15. The response was similar to what happened in Thessalonica. Many, including, women and men of high social and political standing, believed.

But not everyone was pleased about Paul's preaching the gospel. When the same Jewish leaders from Thessalonica discovered that Paul was preaching **the word of God** in Berea, they took action to stop him. Luke's reference to the Scriptures (v. 11) and to Paul's message as **the word of God** confirmed that the gospel had a divine origin (cf. 13:5; 15:35; 16:32). Paul made the same claim in defending his gospel to the Galatians. The gospel was not his own creation; he received it directly from the Lord (Gl 1:11-17).

The Jewish opponents from Thessalonica incited opposition, forcing Paul to go to Athens, leaving Silas and Timothy behind in Berea. It is not clear whether Paul took a ship to Athens, which was the normal means of travel in and out of that city, or went overland.

6. The Witness at Athens (17:16-34)

At Athens Paul faced the blind wisdom of pagan philosophers. Paul was alone but not intimidated because he was zealous for the honor of God and confident of the power of his gospel message.

17:16. Paul's first observation was distressing. **Being provoked** is the verb *paroxuno*, "greatly disturbed." suggests that Paul was incited to jealousy for the Lord because of the pervasiveness of idolatry. Instead of worshiping the Lord as the only true God, the Athenians were bowing down to lifeless idols. It was this inward anger that motivated Paul to proclaim Christ.

17:17. He preached in the synagogue and the marketplace to anyone who would listen. It is obvious that Paul believed that Jesus Christ was unique and that those who worshiped other gods needed to turn to the living God.

17:18. Paul confronted two of the more popular philosophies in the Roman Empire, Epicureanism and Stoicism. The Epicureans believed in pursuing a life free from pain. They held to the existence of the gods, but thought that the gods were completely detached from humanity, as any interaction with people would disturb them and, true to Epicurean doctrine, the gods had a blessed and undisturbed existence. Epicureans believed the soul was material, though composed of finer atoms than the body, and would deteriorate upon death. There was thus no room for the theory of an afterlife. Because they prized an imperturbable life, they rejected the idea that one could anger the gods or face punishment or judgment from them since those concepts would disturb one's thoughts and disrupt life—which explains their strong reaction to Paul's mention of the resurrection and future judgment. It is misleading to call them hedonists in the modern sense. Their concept of pleasure involved avoidance of disturbances in life rather than crass self-indulgence. The pursuits of wanton amusements could be counterproductive to a happy life (for a summary of Epicureanism as it intersected with Ac 17, see N. Clayton Croy, "Hellenistic Philosophies and the Preaching of the Resurrection [Acts 17:18, 32]," *Novum Testamentum* 39 [1997], 21–39). The founder of Stoicism was Zeno (342–270 B.C., from Cyprus). Stoics believed that God permeated all things, and that what was rational in humankind was the manifestation of God. Theologically they would be considered pantheists. According to Stoics, Reason or the Logos controlled the universe, but people were responsible for their voluntary actions. They rejected the Epicurean philosophy of pleasure and instead stressed virtue.

17:18. After **conversing** with Paul, the Epicureans and Stoics concluded he was a **babbler** and **proclaimer of strange deities**. **Babbler** refers to someone who picks up bits and pieces of information and then proclaims them as if he were an expert on the topic (Bock, *Acts*, 561–62). The charge Paul was a teacher **of strange deities** meant he was talking about gods they did not understand.

17:19-21. They took Paul to the **Areopagus**, the place where the Athenians discussed ideas of mutual interest. He was not arrested, but given the opportunity to give them more information about what he believed. Luke did not specify what caught their interest. He said only that from their perspective it was a **new teaching** and **strange things**. Luke's editorial comment in v. 21 implies the Athenians wasted a lot of time in useless discussions about irrelevant issues.

17:22-23. Paul's introductory comment that the Athenians were **very religious** was a commendation rather than a criticism, since he hoped to convince his audience to listen to his message. He connected with the Athenians by referring to an altar erected **TO AN UNKNOWN GOD**. It is probable there was more than one altar to an unknown god in Athens, but Paul influenced his audience with this comment to have them focus on one God by referring to only one altar (Bock, *Acts*, 565). Paul proceeded to make known the god they worshiped but by their own admission did not know.

17:24-26. Paul began with creation. God is the creator of everything that exists and is transcendent (17:24-25). He does not dwell in man-made temples and is independent. He is the source and sustainer of life (17:26-29). Paul alluded to Adam as the single source of humanity in the statement, **He made from one man every nation of mankind**. Because He is creator, God is sovereign. He controls history (or possibly seasons) and national boundaries (**appointed times, and the boundaries of their habitation**). Genesis 10–11 may have been the OT background for Paul's comment, but he did not explicitly cite it since it would have minimal significance for Greek philosophers.

17:27-31. In v. 27 Paul revealed the point of his observations about God in vv. 23-26. As the sovereign creator, God intends for men and women to seek him. The verbs **grope** and **find** are in the optative mood, which suggests finding God through human effort is only a remote possibility. The word picture suggested by **grope** is a blind man fumbling around to find his way (Bock, *Acts*, 567). This implies that, though God is near, it is highly unlikely the Athenians would find Him because their strategy was flawed. While a considerable amount about God can be apprehended from an objective consideration of creation (cf. the comments on Rm 1:18-32), Paul would make it clear that full comprehension of God requires the augmenting truth of the gospel, the proper response of repentance, and recognition of the validity of the resurrection and authority of Jesus Christ (cf. Paul's concluding words in vv. 30-31). Without these additional elements, God will not be found.

The statement **in Him** (God) **we live and move and exist** (v. 28) probably comes from the Greek poet Epimenides (philosopher, poet, and seer from Crete, c. 600 BC), in a poem entitled *Cretica*. The same poem is quoted in Ti 1:12. The reference to **children of God** is an allusion to a statement by another Stoic poet, Aratus. This is not pantheism. Paul argued that if men and women are living beings made in the image of God, then God is a living being. He is not a man-made object of wood or stone (v. 29). These two references to Greek poets do not mean Paul endorsed their view of God, but he had no qualms about using pagan poets to support his argument if some of what they had written coincided with revealed truth.

Having established common ground with the Athenians, Paul stressed the need for them to repent in view of coming judgment. **Therefore having overlooked the times of ignorance** (v. 30) does not mean ignorance is excusable. God's mercy was the reason that in the past He did not usually pass judgment *in this life* on mankind even though they deserved it. In other words, He did not always bring temporal destruction upon an idolatrous people as an act of judgment for their sin. Now, however, because they knew about God, they could not plead ignorance. If they refused to repent, they would suffer eternal punishment. In speaking to Gentiles, the call to repent means to turn from lifeless idols to faith in the living God (1Th 1:9). Polhill writes, "The times of forbearance had now ended because their ignorance had now ended. Now they knew the one true God through Paul's proclamation. He was no longer an 'unknown God'; and should they continue in their false worship and fail to acknowledge his sole lordship of heaven and earth, their sin would no longer be a sin of ignorance but a high-handed sin" (*Acts*, 376).

Paul did not mention Jesus Christ by name, but declared the resurrection proved He has the authority to judge. Though Paul did not give the exact time of judgment, it is on a **fixed day,** meaning it is certain. That Jesus will judge the world **in righteousness** means that his judgment will be just.

17:32-34. The response was divided. Most ridiculed the idea of **resurrection**, but a few became believers. The prevailing view of death among the Greeks was either the complete extinction of the body and soul or a temporal survival of the soul after death. Neither the Epicureans nor the Stoics believed in immortality, thus they not only rejected Paul's message but also mocked (**sneer**) him. For more on the common Greco-Roman view of death, see the comments at 1Co 15:12.

Paul's ministry, however, was not a complete failure—**some men joined him and believed** (v. 34). Luke identified two of the believers by name, Dionysius the Aeropagite and a woman named Damaris. Nothing for certain is known about these two individuals. Providing the names of two individuals gives credibility to Luke's account and is consistent with Luke's emphasis on the place of women in the life of Jesus and the early church.

Some have criticized Paul for his ministry at Athens. They appeal to 1Co 1:18-25 and claim Paul confessed he made a mistake. He focused on natural theology and Greek philosophy, not special revelation and the cross. This evaluation is too harsh. Some did become believers. Those who refused to believe rejected Paul and his statement about the resurrection not because he erred in attempting to contextualize his message.

Two truths emerge from Paul's ministry at Athens. First, Paul believed in the uniqueness of Christ and the gospel. People will not find Christ by following their felt needs. They will "grope" in darkness. People will find Christ only in the "gospel." Second, not only here but also in other locations where Luke has given us a summary of Paul's preaching, it is plain that he contextualized his message to reach his audience. Paul did not water down or corrupt the gospel, but he did attempt to proclaim the good news in the cultural and historical context of the people he wanted to bring to Christ. His refusal to dilute his message is seen in vv. 30-31. Paul must have known that his words would be a direct affront to the Epicureans who denied eternal life and future judgment, and to the Stoics who denied the transcendence of God. Contextualization is important in spreading the gospel, but doctrinal truth must not be sacrificed upon the altar of cultural relevance.

When he left Athens, Paul went to Corinth, 40 miles west of Athens. Corinth's location on the narrow isthmus that connected the mainland with the south caused it to be "the marketplace of Greece." Paul's ministry in Corinth extended from the spring of 50 AD to the fall of 52, and the mention of Gallio in 18:12-17 helps to provide one of the clearest and most unassailable historical markers for the whole book of Acts (see the comments below).

7. The Witness at Corinth (18:1-17)

18:1. Corinth was infamous for more than its commerce. It was a city of great wickedness. The Acropolis, a high hill about a mile from the city center, dominated Corinth, and the temple of Aphrodite had been built on the Acrocorinth. At one time a thousand cultic priestesses served in the temple as sacred prostitutes and came into the city in the evening to sell sexual services. This was not the case of "New Corinth," Corinth as it existed in Paul's day, though it was morally corrupt for numerous other reasons during the first century (see the Introduction to the commentary on 1 Corinthians). Barclay quotes a Greek proverb that reads, "Not every man can afford a journey to Corinth" (William Barclay, *The Acts of the Apostles* [*Daily Study Bible*], Philadelphia: Westminster, 1955, 145). Yet in Corinth, Paul witnessesd the triumph of God's grace over greed and lust. For more on the background and location of Corinth, see the "The City of Corinth" in the Introduction to the commentary on 1 Corinthians.

18:2-3. Paul sometimes worked as a tent-maker to support himself (1Th 2:9), so it is not surprising that he met **Aquila** and **Priscilla**, who were also Jewish and **tent-makers**. They had been forced to leave Rome because of the edict of Claudius, issued in AD 49, expelling all Jews (whether believers or not) from Rome for causing a civil disturbance because of their dispute about Jesus.

18:4-6. Paul began his ministry in the synagogue proclaiming the gospel first to his own people. When Silas and Timothy arrived with support from the Macedonian churches Paul was able to **devot[e]** himself full time to ministry. Paul also wrote 1 Thessalonians in response to the report Timothy brought about the new church (see the Introduction to 1 Thessalonians, and the comments on 1Th 3:6).

Intense opposition forced Paul to abandon his ministry in the synagogue. In a symbolic gesture, Paul **shook** the dust off his clothes. This was a common practice among the Jews who, when returning to their home from a journey, would often knock dust off their sandals and clothes. They did this to remove any "unclean" substances that might have been picked up in Gentile lands so as to avoid rendering their homes or villages ritually impure. Paul declared the Jews were responsible for their own fate: **Your blood be upon your own heads!** (cf. Ezk 3:14-21). Their opposition justified his ministry to Gentiles (but see the comments on Rm 11:13-14).

18:7-8. Instead of leaving Corinth, Paul relocated his ministry to the house of **Titius Justus**, a god-fearer. He made his home available for Paul to continue his ministry. God honored Paul's courage and persistence. **Crispus**, the synagogue ruler, and his household were among **many of the Corinthians** who believed and were baptized.

18:9-11. Paul was human, not a superhero. In Corinth, he was almost overcome with fear. In his Epistle to the Corinthians, Paul wrote, "I was with you in a weakness and in fear and in much trembling" (1Co 2:3). The Lord spoke to Paul in a vision and made two promises. He promised him divine protection: **I am with you.** Paul would not be beaten as he was at Philippi. **I have many people in this city** is a promise that Christ would bring people to salvation. Paul obeyed. He preached the Word of God in Corinth for 18 months, longer than in any other city on his second journey.

18:12-13. Some Jewish opponents from the synagogue attempted to disrupt Paul's ministry by charging that he was violating the law. He was arraigned before the **proconsul Gallio** and brought before **the judgment seat** (*bema*) for a hearing. The Gallio episode provides one of the strongest chronological markers for students of Acts, and lends credibility to Luke's accuracy as an historian. Gallio, born in southern Spain, was governor of Achaia for about 18 months around AD 51–52. He was the brother of the famous statesman and philosopher Seneca, and was in his own right a highly respected legal expert. His decision was both enormously important for the spread of Christianity and respected in secular political realms. The **judgment seat** was an elevated platform in the market at Corinth used for public hearings. It was where a political or judicial leader would sit to render a verdict in a case he had overseen.

The charge was apparently religious in nature. In the statement, **this man persuades** [better "seduces," "misleads," LSJ, 115] **men to worship God contrary to the law**, the word **law** probably refers to the law of Moses, since, if Paul were accused or guilty of violating Roman law, Gallio would not have refused to act on the accusation as he did here.

18:14-15. Gallio's decision was extremely significant. He concluded the complaint was religious and not political, and ruled the charges were unwarranted. What Paul was doing was not a **wrong** ("a felony") or a **vicious crime** ("a political misdemeanor"; for these definitions, see Bruce W. Winter, *After Paul Left Corinth: The Influence of Secular Ethics and Social Change* [Grand Rapids, MI: Eerdmans, 2001], 279).

Though Judaism enjoyed legal status under Roman law, Rome had not made a decision about this new faith that was springing from Judaism. The Roman policy toward Judaism was to afford the Jewish people considerable autonomy, something the Jews insisted upon to avoid Roman interference. Gallio acted on the basis of this policy in this situation. Gallio's decision emphasized that he, and thus Rome, would view nascent Christianity as a subset of Judaism. Consequently, any disputes between Jewish unbelievers and Jewish or Gentile believers should be handled as an internal dispute between the two factions; Rome would not become involved.

18:16-17. He ordered the crowd to disperse. Angered by Gallio's decision, the Jewish opposition resorted to violence. They assaulted **Sosthenes**. He may have been the believing Sosthenes in 1Co 1:1, but it was a common name so it may not have been the same man. It is impossible to say exactly who beat him and why. If this Sosthenes was a believer, then he could have recently become a believer in Jesus, and the Jewish opponents were taking out on him their frustration. Or, it could be that Sosthenes, the new leader of the synagogue who took the place of Crispus following his faith in Christ (cf. v. 8), was spearheading the case against Paul and failed so miserably that his Jewish fellows roughed him up in frustration. Or it could be that he was beaten by Gentiles who, emboldened by Gallio's anti-Jewish act, took advantage of the opportunity to vent their hatred. That Gallio was hateful of Jews is known from secular history, and it is possible that this motivated him to ignore the beating of Sosthenes, perhaps by Gentiles. But certainty is impossible. Gallio ignored the violence, which is somewhat surprising since the Romans were concerned about maintaining peace.

Christ said in Jn 10:16 that he had other sheep. Paul's strategy confirmed God's sovereign plan to use the unbelief of Israel for the salvation of Gentiles.

Longenecker says that Gallio's decision was profound ("Acts," 486). It is additional evidence that this new faith in Jesus was not a subversive movement, and his judicial decision set an important precedent for the church to freely proclaim the gospel and expand without fearing Roman opposition.

Ephesus was the sixth major city that Paul visited in the area surrounding the Aegean Sea. But before he began an extended ministry in Ephesus, Paul returned to Antioch, and while he was in Antioch, Luke shifted his account back to Ephesus. Apollos came to Ephesus and preached in the synagogue, but he was deficient in his understanding of the gift and ministry of the Spirit. After further instruction by Priscilla and Aquila, Apollos left Ephesus for ministry in Achaia. Apollos's lack of knowledge of the Spirit linked this account with Paul's encounter with the disciples of John (19:1-7).

8. The Return to Antioch (18:18-22)

18:18. While it is impossible to be certain regarding the details and motivation, Paul had apparently taken a temporary vow, possibly a Nazirite vow (see Nm 6:1-21) as a symbolic act of his ongoing service to God and for Israel, even while he evangelized in predominantly Gentile regions. Usually the Nazirite vow was taken within the city of Jerusalem, but was allowed elsewhere if the individual subsequently went to Jerusalem (see *m. Nazir* 1:1–9:5). For the period of the vow, he did not cut his hair, did not drink wine or anything made from the fruit of the vine, and did not touch anything that was dead (cf. Nm 6:1-21). Now that he was at the end of the vow, he got his hair cut at Cenchrea, close to Athens, before leaving for Jerusalem to offer his hair and the prescribed sacrifices on the altar in the temple. Making the sacrifices would also be a way of thanking God for the spiritual victories of God's grace while at Corinth. Though now a follower of Christ, Paul did not see this as contradicting his Jewish identity, and he never abandoned his Jewish cultural and religious practices (cf. Ac 28:17).

18:19-22. On the way to Jerusalem, Paul stopped briefly in Ephesus. After making his case for Christianity in the synagogue, he left for Antioch via Caesarea and Jerusalem, but he promised to return **if God wills**. Luke's account of Paul's travels demonstrates that he was a Spirit-filled man who made his plans but always submitted his plans and their timing to God's will.

E. To Asia and Greece: The Third Missionary Journey (18:23–21:16)

1. Witness through Paul at Galatia and Phrygia (18:23)

18:23. Without much fanfare, Ac 18:23 marks the beginning of Paul's third missionary journey, a journey of over 1,500 miles and about four years. Paul took a route through the regions of Galatia and Phyrgia to strengthen those who had become disciples on the first missionary journey. While Paul was ministering to believers in those regions, God used Apollos to prepare for Paul's work in Ephesus.

2. Witness through Apollos in Ephesus and Corinth (18:24-28)

18:24-25. Apollos was from Alexandria, a city that was highly regarded as an educational center. That helps explain why he was well educated (**eloquent**), including a strong biblical background (**mighty in the Scriptures**). The expression **fervent in spirit** (v. 25) is ambiguous. If the phrase **being acquainted only with the baptism of John** means that Apollos was ignorant of the coming and baptism of the Spirit (not a certainty given the contents of the passage), then it is unlikely that **fervent in spirit** refers to the Holy Spirit. More than likely, it describes Apollos's heartfelt enthusiasm about his work. He was not guilty of teaching error but was merely lacking in knowledge of the full details of the events associated with Pentecost. Since he taught **accurately the things concerning Jesus** and spoke out "boldly in the synagogue" (v. 26), it is unlikely that he was an unbeliever. It seems reasonable to think that he was saved in an OT sense, or more precisely, a "pre-Pentecost" sense, and that Luke included the episode about him, and about the 12 disciples of John in chap. 19, to indicate that believers caught up in this transitional matrix between the era of law and the age of grace would embrace their Messiah Jesus when they heard of Him and then receive the full new covenant blessings promised to those who had faith in the Messiah. His knowledge appears to have been deficient in matters related to the coming of the Spirit at Pentecost and the baptism of the Spirit associated with it, not the details of Jesus' ministry and death. After all, he **had been instructed in the way of the Lord** and **was speaking and teaching accurately the things concerning Jesus**. What happened with Apollos and the disciples of John may have been replicated in numerous other settings, though there are no other indications of this in Acts.

18:26-28. After hearing him speak, Priscilla and Aquila recognized his deficiency but also his potential. Not wanting to embarrass him, they privately informed him of **the way of God more accurately**, providing him with the complete story of the Messiah, which undoubtedly included the gift of the Spirit. Luke again took the opportunity to emphasize the role of women in the early church by listing Priscilla first. She may have been the primary instructor of Apollos. But even if she were, there is no clear indication that Luke was using her as a paradigm for women having the freedom to teach men in a corporate church setting. The instruction to Apollos was not conducted in a church setting, and the word **explained** (*ektithemi*, "to convey information by careful elaboration" [BDAG,

310], "to lay out something"), used also in 11:4 and 28:23, does not carry an authoritative or exhortational sense befitting the kind of teaching that was to typify church settings (see the comments on 1Tm 2:12).

Once he had a complete grasp of all that Jesus had done, Apollos became an even more effective apologist. The "brothers" encouraged him to go to Achaia, where he instilled greater confidence in believers and was even more effective in convincing Jewish people that Jesus is Israel's Messiah. It was probably on this occasion that Apollos spent time in Corinth, in the region of Achaia (see the comments on 1Co 3:5ff.).

3. Witness through Paul in Ephesus and En Route to Jerusalem (19:1–21:16)

a. In Ephesus (19:1-41)

(1) Witness to the Disciples of John (19:1-7)

As Luke often did in Acts, he gave a general or introductory account and then a specific situation to develop the same theme. So instead of continuing with the story of Apollos, Luke returned to his main character, the apostle Paul, and his encounter with a group of John's disciples. As was likely the case with Apollos, they had not received the gift of the Spirit, so Paul used his apostolic authority to baptize them in the name of Jesus and to give them the gift of the Spirit.

19:1-3. When Paul met John's disciples, he asked them if they received the Holy Spirit when they believed. Here the aorist participle **when you believed** (*pisteusantes*) indicates action simultaneous with the aorist main verb **did you receive**. Usually an aorist participle, when the word order situates it before the main verb of the sentence, refers to action before the action of the main verb. But when it comes after the main verb, it usually indicates action simultaneous to the action of the main verb (as in Eph 1:20; 5:26; Col 2:13; 1Tm 1:12; see Stanley E. Porter, *Verbal Aspect in the Greek of the New Testament, with Reference to Tense and Mood*, vol. 2 of SBG [New York: Lang, 1989], 381–384). The manner in which Paul phrased his question implies that he understood that the Spirit is normally given at the time of faith in Jesus and not subsequent to it. These men had apparently responded to John's call for repentance and baptism to prepare for the coming of the Messiah, but they were unaware that the gift of the Spirit had been given. Like Apollos, they were transitional believers (see the comments on 18:24-28).

Were these disciples believers? Some say "No," and base this upon the absence of the article before the word "disciples" in v. 1. Yet the word "some" does not indicate "some unsaved disciples," but is used to distinguish true disciples from other true disciples (cf. 9:10; 12:1; 16:1, 9, 14, 16; 18:24; and Mt 16:28). These 12 had undergone John's baptism, which was "in reference to forgiveness" (see the comments on Mt 3:5-12), suggesting that they were saved at that point in an OT sense, or, more precisely, in a "John the Baptist" sense. They apparently were deficient in the details related to the ministry, death, and resurrection of Jesus, as well as those related to Pentecost, all of which happened after John's ministry ceased. They apparently did not know that the Messiah had come, that He was Jesus of Nazareth. Furthermore, the phrase **we have not even heard whether there is a Holy Spirit** probably refers to their ignorance of the events of Pentecost and the outpouring of the Spirit (even John had taught about the Spirit in Mt 3:11, and the Jewish people in the OT knew about the Holy Spirit; cf. e.g., Zch 4:6). It is impossible to be certain, but these, like Apollos, were probably believers in an OT sense, and by relating their story, Luke indicated that there were pockets of people who were saved as OT believers but who had not yet heard of the full facts and blessings of salvation in Messiah Jesus. They too embraced Jesus by faith and received all the benefits of the new covenant.

19:4-7. Paul acted to complete their faith by baptizing them in the name of Jesus, and God gave them the gift of the Spirit when Paul laid his hands on them. The men prophesied and spoke in tongues as evidence they had received the Holy Spirit. There did seem to be a short period of time between their reception of Jesus and their reception of the Holy Spirit. This unusual event (cf. 1Co 12:13) likely occurred to prevent a schism within the faith. Had an apostle not laid hands on them to receive the Spirit, they may have considered themselves an even more ancient body of believers than the church. They might have formed a separate community of faith and failed to come under the authority of the apostles and to recognize that they were part of the universal body of Messiah.

The phenomenon parallels the experience of the Jews who believed at Pentecost, the Samaritans, and the Gentiles in the house of Cornelius. This group of disciples served as an exemplar of yet another group, those saved in an OT sense but who had not heard the full story of Jesus.

Now that all of these representative groups had received the Spirit, there was no further reference to speaking in tongues in Acts. It is reasonable to conclude that speaking in tongues was designed in part as a means to prove to the early church that the gospel had made inroads into these distinct and diverse groups (for other aspects of tongues, see the comments introducing 1Co 14). Since this had been established, there was little need for tongues to continue as a normative experience for the church.

The account was also another affirmation of Paul's apostleship. Like Peter, who was instrumental in mediating the Spirit to the Samaritans, Paul had apostolic authority to mediate the Spirit to John's disciples.

(2) Witness to a Larger Audience (19:8-41)

Paul's ministry in Ephesus involved more than the ministry to the disciples of John who were favorably inclined to his message. As God had given Paul victory at Corinth, the center of Gentile immorality, He gave him victory at Ephesus, the center of Gentile idolatry. Luke told the story in two contrasting scenes: (1) Paul's ministry in the synagogue and the lecture hall of Tyrannus (vv. 8-10); and (2) the power of Paul and the powerlessness of the Jewish exorcists (vv. 11-20).

19:8-9a. True to his strategy of going first to the Jews and then to the Gentiles, Paul began his ministry in the synagogue. He argued and attempted to persuade the Jewish people about the **kingdom of God** for three months. The message about the kingdom was the primary theme of Jesus' preaching (see the comments on Mt 3:1-4). Ministry in the synagogue, however, became impossible because **some were becoming hardened and disobedient**. **Hardened** (*skleryno*) carries the idea of "unyielding in resisting information" (BDAG, 930). This group of Jewish people was resistant to the gospel. They maligned Paul's message, **speaking evil of the Way**. The word **Way** describes the new way of following Jesus for Jewish people and the world (cf. comments at 9:1-2). Instead of leaving Ephesus, Paul relocated to the lecture hall of Tyrannus.

19:9b-10. The name Tyrannus may have come from a nickname for a philosopher who was a tyrant (an extremely hard teacher). Paul may have taught from the fifth to the tenth hour (11 a.m. until 4 p.m.) according to one Greek manuscript. If accurate, this was "siesta" time when all work stopped and people would be free to join Paul for his teaching. Luke was giving a picture of Paul, who was so devoted to Christ that he worked in the morning and preached in the afternoon.

God honored Paul's tireless effort. Luke said that in a two-year period **all who lived in Asia heard the word of the Lord, both Jews Greeks**. As a result of Paul's ministry in Ephesus, the churches at Colossae and Laodicea were started, and perhaps the other churches to which John referred in the book of Revelation.

19:11. The Lord confirmed Paul's ministry by empowering him to work **extraordinary** miracles. By using **extraordinary** (*tychousas*) to describe Paul's miracles Luke implied that they were exceptional in comparison even to the other miracles recorded in Acts. As an apostle of the Lord Jesus Christ, Paul was given power that was greater than the cultic magic connected with the worship of the goddess Artemis.

19:12. Like those who were healed indirectly by Peter's shadow (Ac 5:15), people were healed indirectly by contact with Paul's **handkerchiefs or aprons**. These were items Paul used in his work as a tentmaker. **Handkerchiefs** may refer to a sweatband worn around the head, and **aprons** to some kind of belt around the waist. Luke also made a clear distinction between diseases and exorcisms.

19:13-16. Impressed with Paul's power, a group of Jewish magicians attempted to use the name of the "Lord Jesus" as a magical formula. But they did not know the person of Christ, so they did not have the power of Christ. When they attempted to exorcise demons from a man, one of the demons rebuked them and the possessed man assaulted them. Not only were they badly beaten, but they were also humiliated, fleeing the **house naked and wounded**.

The incident contrasted Paul's power and apostleship with the impotent attempt of Jewish magicians to exploit the power of the resurrected Jesus. Paul was not another first-century itinerant charlatan; he was an apostle of the Lord Jesus Christ. Even the demon knew this: **I recognize Jesus, and I know about Paul, but who are you?** asked the demon.

19:17-20. The result of this abortive attempt to misuse the power of Jesus' name was similar to the story of Ananias and Sapphira, who were judged because of their "botched" attempt to commit fraud. When the news of what had happened became known to both Jews and Greeks, the superstitious pagans of Ephesus reacted as expected. They were overcome with fear and magnified the name of Jesus. This does not mean that they become believers, but merely that they held in awe a power that they did not understand.

Some, however, did become believers, and they gave tangible evidence of their faith by burning their books on magic. The 50,000 pieces of silver was a large sum of money—a "piece of silver" was approximately one day's wages. The burning of books on magic was costly and a powerful public statement of their conversion.

Luke's statement in v. 20 is crucial. Unlike the seven sons of Sceva, other first-century itinerant speakers, and unscrupulous ministers today who claim pseudo-miracles to fleece the gullible, God's power (*kratos*) at work in Paul to produce miracles was genuine. It was for the purpose of promoting the Word of God and not for financial gain to fund an extravagant lifestyle.

With the description of Paul's ministry in Ephesus, Luke concluded his account of the church's growth in strategic cities around the Aegean Sea. He has given a factual and graphic account of the entrance of the gospel into new regions. Though faced with opposition and persecution, the gospel was preached, people won to the faith, and churches established. Through providential circumstances and supernatural revelation, the Holy Spirit led and empowered Paul. Though much remained to be done, the evidence was overwhelming—the Lord Jesus was working through the church and especially through Paul, the apostle of God's grace and ambassador of Christ to the Gentiles.

The worship of idols is not new. The cult of Artemis flourished in the city of Ephesus, and the residents of Ephesus had built a magnificent temple to the goddess Artemis. According to legend, the image of Artemis fell from heaven on the location of the temple. In reality, the object that fell from the sky was most likely a meteorite that resembled a multi-breasted woman, but the superstitious Ephesians built a temple on the location to honor the goddess. It was believed that worshiping Artemis, the goddess of fertility, would bring good fortune, and pilgrims came to Ephesus from all parts of the vast Roman Empire.

As is often the case, religion became a guise for economic exploitation. A guild of silversmiths made small images of Artemis and sold the idols to pilgrims who came to worship the goddess.

Paul's ministry was so powerful that the gospel became a threat to the economic interests of the silversmiths. Demetrius, one of the silversmiths, organized a protest under the pretense of defending the honor of Artemis. When the protest escalated to a riot, the town clerk intervened, warning the protesters that they needed to follow the proper legal procedures if they wished to make charges against Paul and that they were the ones who risked committing a crime. His speech was persuasive, and he dismissed the crowd without further violence.

19:21. This verse reveals Paul's dream of reaching the world for Christ. Jerusalem was the capital of Judaism and Rome the capital of paganism. But preaching the gospel in these two strategic cities was not only Paul's plan, it was his divine destiny. **Spirit** (*pneuma*) is best interpreted as a reference to the Holy Spirit (see ESV; RSV; HCSB) rather than Paul's spirit (NET; NIV; TNIV). Paul made his plans but submitted them to confirmation by the Spirit. The word **must** suggests that Paul saw it as a moral necessity, as part of his fulfillment of God's choosing him for his apostolic office, to go to **Rome** (v. 21) and then continue on to Spain (cf. the Introduction to Romans, "Date" and "Recipients," and the comments on Rm 15:24-28).

19:22. In preparation for his return to Jerusalem, Paul sent Timothy and Erastus to Macedonia. They were apparently responsible for collecting the offering that Paul planned to take to Jerusalem (see the comments on 2Co 8:4; 9:1).

19:23. This theme of v. 23 suggests that the primary issue was not about Paul but rather the gospel, which Luke identified again as **the Way**, the "way of following Jesus" (cf. comments at 9:1-2), who is the way the truth and the life (cf. Jn 14:6).

19:24-27. Demetrius, who may have been a leader of the silversmiths, organized a protest (vv. 24-25). He and the other silversmiths made their living by selling small silver images of the temple (*naos*) of **Artemis** to pagan pilgrims (v. 24). **Artemis** (the Roman goddess Diana) was the goddess of fertility. The temple, one of the seven wonders of the ancient world, was first built in the sixth century BC. It was burned down by a young man, Herostratus, on the night Alexander the Great was born in 356 BC. With gifts received from all over the world, the temple was rebuilt with great glory and splendor, finally measuring 425 feet long, 220 feet wide, over 60 feet high and adorned with 127 marble columns. This temple also functioned as a bank. Merchants, kings, and whole cities would deposit their gold and silver there because its safety was guaranteed by the goddess Artemis herself. It was the largest building in the Greek world at that time. Today a lone pillar marks the location of this formerly magnificent structure. The temple attracted worshippers from all parts of the empire. Devotees of Artemis called her a god (*he Thea*; *ho Theos* was the typical Gk. word used by Christians for God), "savior," "lord." Extant prayers to her survive, calling upon her to give victory in athletic contests and to heal loved ones from their diseases. Worshipers bought the silver images, believing that the goddess would prosper them.

Demetrius made three charges that were all related to Christianity's threat to the economic interests of the silversmiths but cloaked in the pretext of defending the worship of Artemis. First, Christianity was a threat to their livelihood (v. 25). Their income depended on selling idols. Second, this man Paul had persuaded many, not only in Ephesus but also in all of Asia, that man-made gods were not gods at all (v. 26). Though not stated, Paul undoubtedly preached that they should turn from idols to worship the one true God. Third, not only was his preaching endangering the income of the silversmiths, but also Artemis might be dethroned (v. 27). The verb **dethroned** (*kathaireo*) means "to tear down" or "to conquer, destroy" (BDAG, 488). Christianity was a major, not a minor, threat to the worship of Artemis in Ephesus and the world.

19:28-29. The silversmiths erupted with rage and shouted out praise for Artemis. What was a small crowd grew to a large unruly mob that rushed into the amphitheater forcibly taking two of Paul's traveling companions with them. The amphitheater was huge, with a capacity of about 25,000, larger than most of the professional basketball arenas in America.

19:30-31. Unconcerned about his safety, Paul wanted to address the mob, but he was restrained by his disciples, and some of the **Asiarchs**. They were the leading men from the wealthy class who served one-year terms presiding over the affairs of the imperial cult and its temples. Their sympathy for Paul is surprising; perhaps as better-educated people, they were more broad-minded and did not see his message as a serious threat. The Asiarchs had authority over the theater, but could not control the mob. Instead, they tried to prevent Paul from endangering his life. Their concern for him indicates that Paul had been effective in influencing some of the higher social classes.

19:32-34. The mob became so fanatical and chaotic that many of them did not know why they were rioting (v. 32). **Alexander** (v. 33) is impossible to identify. **The Jews had put him forward**, perhaps as a new Jewish believer, to force him to tell the chaotic crowd what the meeting was about. More likely, he was probably a Jewish unbeliever who wanted to distinguish between Paul's messianism and their Judaism. Since Jewish people did not worship Artemis either, and since Paul was a Jew, Alexander may have been enlisted to try to distance the Jewish populace from Paul so the unbelieving Jewish people would not be persecuted by the Ephesian Gentiles when the Gentiles persecuted the Christians. It is impossible to say. But when the crowd realized that Alexander was Jewish, they exploded again in fervently shouting **Great is Artemis of the Ephesians!**

19:35-37. After about two hours of total confusion, the **town clerk** pleaded for law and order. The **town clerk** was the keeper of records, registrar, and accountant for temple funds. He was the highest civic official in the city, operating like a powerful city manager, and was the liaison to the Roman authorities. As a locally elected official, he would have been acutely aware of what was happening in the city as it related to the detrimental influence of Paul's work on the prosperity and popularity of Artemis's temple. His speech contained two important points. First, he reminded the Ephesians of the legend that they were guardians of the temple where Artemis' image fell from heaven. His argument was not based on evidence but the experience, faith, and devotion of the Ephesians. He emphasized that Paul and his companions had not committed a chargeable crime, and they had not actually robbed the temple or directly blasphemed the goddess.

19:38-41. Second, he charged that the action of Demetrius and the other silversmiths was illegal and that they could make charges in the courts if they wanted to pursue the matter (vv. 38-39). His plea to follow a legal course of action was motivated by fear of Roman intervention (v. 40) not because he was sympathetic with the Way (cf. comments at 9:1-2). Ephesus's status as a "free city" depended solely on the favor of Rome, and the clerk wanted to prevent the revoking of the city's privileges. His speech was persuasive, and he dismissed the assembly.

The riot at Ephesus focused on the powerful impact of the gospel on paganism. The transformation of believers was so radical that they abandoned their idolatrous lifestyle, without directly attacking the culture of idolatry. The speech of the town clerk exonerated the gospel, showing it as a legal movement within the Roman Empire. The new faith was not a violent movement attempting to overthrow Roman rule. In contrast to Jewish opposition, which was usually motivated by issues about the law, Gentile opposition was due to the threat to idolatry and economic interests.

b. In Macedonia, Greece, and Asia (20:1-5)

20:1-3. Paul traveled through Macedonia and Greece strengthening the Gentile churches, but he was forced to alter his traveling plans because of a threat to his life. Instead of sailing from Cenchrea for Syria, Paul went back through Macedonia and sailed from Philippi to Troas. In addition to danger from the Jews, Paul was carrying an offering for the churches in Judea (cf. Ro 15:25-27 and comments there), and the seaport at Cenchrea would have an easy place for Jews or thieves to attack Paul. Luke did not specify where Paul **spent three months** (v. 3), but it was probably Corinth, and it was probably during this time that he wrote his epistle to the Romans (see the "Introduction: Date and Recipients" for the commentary on Romans).

20:4-5. From the names of Paul's traveling companions, we can identify them as Greeks. They represented the Gentile churches that had contributed to the gift that Paul was taking to the Jewish believers in Jerusalem. Paul's traveling companions were representatives from the outlying, and principally Gentile, churches. Sopater (probably the same as Sosipater in Rm 16:21), Aristarchus (see Ac 19:29; 27:2; Col 4:10), and Secundus were from the churches in Macedonia. The churches in Asia were represented by Tychicus (Eph 6:21-22; Cl 4:7-8; 2Tm 4:12; Ti 3:12) and Trophimus (Ac 21:29; 2Tm 4:20). The Galatian churches sent along Gaius, who was probably from Derbe (Ac 14:20-21) (for these points, see F. F. Bruce, *The Book of Acts*, 382 and notes 16-20). They accompanied Paul probably to help protect him and to safeguard the delivery of this sizeable gift.

c. In Troas (20:6-12)

Paul's team went by ship to Troas, and Paul traveled by land to Philippi where Luke met him, and then they sailed to Troas. At Troas Paul celebrated the Feast of Unleavened Bread, where there was a small group of believers who may have needed encouragement (see Ac 16:40). Paul did not consider his faith in Jesus as contradicting his Jewish identity, and so he continued to observe Jewish practices.

20:6-12. In Acts 2:42-47 Luke had described the Jewish believers; here he described a Gentile congregation. Many see this as establishing a paradigm for Sunday worship (**the first day of the week**, v. 7). But Luke always used Jewish time, making it more likely that this meeting took place on the evening of the first day (note the **message** lasted **until midnight** [v. 7] and that there were **many lamps** in the room [v. 8]. Thus, they met on Saturday night (when the first day of the Jewish week began). They met in the evening because believers who were common laborers or slaves would not have had a day off and would have been required to work during the day. They shared a meal together, which included the celebration of the Lord's Table. The services were not regulated by time, so Paul preached until midnight because he planned to leave the next day. The church gathered in the upper room of a private home, and the lamps, used for lighting (v. 8), probably made the air stuffy and oppressive. As a result, **Eutychus** fell asleep and fell out of the third floor window and died (v. 9). The name "Eutychus" means "lucky one," and he was indeed fortunate. Paul's statement that his **life** ("soul," *psyche*) is still **in him** means that though the fall killed him, after Paul embraced him his life was restored (v. 10). In much the same way that God used Peter to raise Tabitha from the dead (9:36-43), God enabled Paul to restore the life of Eutychus. Paul extended his visit until daylight (v. 11) and left the church on an encouraging note: **They took the boy away alive, and were greatly comforted** (v. 12). The contrast is vivid. In many instances, both Jews and Gentiles were infuriated by Paul's ministry. At Lystra he was stoned. But to believers, especially Gentiles, Paul was welcomed and loved.

It is difficult to propose why Luke included this brief episode at the conclusion of his report of the third missionary journey. Bock proposes that this episode put Paul in good company, with Jesus who raised people from the dead (Lk 7:11-15; 8:49-56; Jn 11:38-44), with Elijah and Elisha (1Kg 17:19-22; 2Kg 4:34-35) (*Acts*, 620), and maybe Luke was trying to show that Paul, like them, had God's blessing. Perhaps Luke also included this to show that even though Paul was about to be arrested in Jerusalem, he was no criminal. On the contrary, God clearly used and approved of him.

d. In Miletus (20:13-38)

20:13-16. Luke and Paul's other traveling companions boarded a ship for **Assos**; Paul traveled by land. Luke did not explain why Paul chose to walk; it was perhaps for safety and time to reflect on what would lie ahead in his journey to Jerusalem and Rome. At Assos Paul rejoined his companions, and together they sailed for Mitylene and then to Chios and Samos. Each segment of the journey took a day, which was typical of ancient sea trips (Bock, *Acts*, 621). Paul took the ship from Chios to Samos, which did not stop at Ephesus, because he wanted to get to Jerusalem in time for the day of Pentecost. For these locations, see the map of the second and third missionary journeys.

Paul was a church planter with the heart of a pastor. He wanted people to come to saving faith in Christ, but he also wanted to develop believers who were biblically informed and fully devoted to Christ. For this task Paul was willing to sacrifice comfort and even risk his life teaching the Word of God and strengthening new converts.

From Miletus Paul summoned the elders from the church at Ephesus for his final message to them (Ac 20:17-38). His message to the Ephesian elders was unique because it was the only recorded speech in Acts directed to believers. His purpose was to prepare the church leadership for ministry in his absence. Paul was aware of the danger that lay ahead, but he was more concerned about the future of the church than his own personal safety. In his speech Paul reviewed the nature of his ministry at Ephesus and encouraged the elders to follow his example. They were to teach the word and protect the church from false teachers. He concluded with an emotional farewell informing the elders they would never see him again.

20:17-18a. After he arrived in Miletus, about 30 miles south of Ephesus, Paul summoned the elders to meet him at Miletus. It would take them about a day and a half to get to Miletus after they received the message from Paul.

The overall theme of Paul's instructions emphasized the need for elders to proclaim the whole counsel of God, to protect the church from false teachers and false doctrine, and to provide an example of humble service. Paul used himself and the ministry he provided in the past as an example of diligence and humility as he taught them the truth (20:18b-21). He also provided an example for them based upon his present motivation, which was to discharge every facet of his ministry no matter what the cost might be (20:22-24). Finally, in 20:28-31, he warned them about the need to be on the alert (v. 31) in the future to protect the flock, and he reminded them that he had warned them about the need to do this.

20:18b-19. In ministering to the Ephesians, Paul was transparent, setting an example for them to follow. He served humbly like a bond-servant. The word **humility** (v. 19) means "an attitude of deference, submission, and servility." Those who lead the church must be willing to sacrifice their reputations and agendas, and be willing regularly to get their hands dirty when serving their people. Augustine captured the greatness of humility when he said:

For those who would learn God's ways, humility is the first thing, humility is the second thing, humility is the third thing (Quoted in Kistemaker, *Acts*, 725).

Paul was both sensitive and compassionate. He shed tears when persecuted by his enemies (20:19) and when he agonized over the Ephesian converts (20:31).

20:20-21. Paul preached and taught boldly. With great courage and unwavering devotion, Paul proclaimed the gospel message publicly and privately (**from house to house**). His message was the same for both Jews and Greeks. He called on both to repent and put their faith in the Lord Jesus Christ. For Jews, this meant turning from seeking God's favor by keeping the law to recognizing Jesus as Messiah, and for Gentiles, it meant turning from the worship of idols to Christ for forgiveness of sins.

In 20:22-24, Paul also provided an example for them based on his present motivation, which was to discharge every facet of his ministry no matter what the cost might be (20:22-24). Paul's ministry was Spirit-directed and motivated by the grace of God.

20:22-23. He was **bound in spirit** to go to Jerusalem. **Spirit** could be either Paul's human spirit (an inner compulsion) or the Holy Spirit. The reference to the Holy Spirit in v. 23 favors Holy Spirit rather than Paul's spirit. Paul was not unaware of what he was about to experience. The Holy Spirit had warned him of imprisonment (**bonds**) and suffering (**afflictions**).

20:24. Self-preservation was not a high priority for Paul. He considered his life of little value in comparison to his responsibility to preach the gospel. Paul compared his ministry to a "race" (NASB **course,** *dromon*). Like an athlete focused on finishing the race, Paul was determined to finish his task (*diakonia,* **ministry**)—the proclamation of the "good news" of God's grace.

20:25-27. Paul turned his attention explicitly to the elders and gave them their marching orders as to how they should execute their ministry. Because Paul did not know exactly what would happen in the future, he told the elders they would never see him again. Paul did see the Ephesians again after he spent two years in Rome under house arrest; but at this point he did not know he would return to the area, so his concern was to prepare the elders for ministry in his absence.

Drawing on OT imagery of a watchman, Paul declared that he was **innocent of the blood of all men** (see Ezk 3:16-27). Because Paul had courageously proclaimed "the whole counsel of God," he did not bear any guilt for those who rejected or distorted the gospel. He had faithfully fulfilled his obligation.

In vv. 28-31, Paul compared the ministry of the elders to a shepherd responsible for protecting his flock. Sheep need shepherds. They need a shepherd to help them find water and pasture. Wolves were a constant threat to sheep, and because sheep are defenseless, they need a shepherd for protection.

20:28. Paul gave three reasons that the elders must be vigilant. First, they were appointed by the **Holy Spirit**. Paul did not explain how the Spirit revealed their appointment. Second, the church was God's. It did not belong to Paul or any other individual. Third, God **purchased** the church with **His own blood**, or better, "the blood of His own [Son]." Here "His own" refers to Jesus, not God the Father. It is possible that Jesus here was called God. He was called by the title *Theos* elsewhere in the NT (e.g., Jn 1:1, 18; Rm 9:5), but the NT writers were careful to avoid blending these unqualified statements of Jesus' deity with strictly human attributes (such as blood). One never finds, for example, statements like "the cross of God" or "God was crucified at Calvary," or "God died and rose again" (for a detailed discussion of this text, and for this understanding, see Murray J. Harris, *Jesus as God: The New Testament Use of* Theos *in Reference to Jesus* [Grand Rapids, MI: Baker, 1992], 137–141). And it is unlikely that the reference is to the blood of God the Father, who, as a spirit, does not have blood. Paul's point in making this statement may implicitly have reminded these elders that the church they oversaw belonged to God, not to them.

The word **overseers** (*episkopoi*) in secular Greek meant "[those who have] the responsibility of safeguarding or seeing to it that something is done in the correct way" and was adopted for use in the church to describe those who provided supervision and leadership (BDAG, 379). It is a virtual synonym for elders (*presbyteroi*, v. 17), which is literally "an older man," but had a specialized meaning that designated a church leader by his physical and spiritual maturity. These terms both signify the same office, namely that of "pastor." Though "pastor" (*poimen*) is not used in Ac 20, the related verb *poimaino* ("to shepherd") is found in v. 28. This suggests that those who are pastors are also elders and overseers in the church, and that pastor is not an office that differs from elder or overseer.

20:29-30. The elders have a twofold responsibility. They are to feed the sheep by teaching them the Word of God, and they are to protect the sheep from false teaching. The warning about false teachers is prophetic. The epistles reveal that false teachers were not always outsiders; often they were insiders (See 2Pt 2:1-3). False teachers are ruthless and pose a twofold danger. They will attempt to pervert the truth and persuade believers to follow them.

20:31. Paul's final exhortation was for vigilance (**be on the alert**). He reminded them of his example. Paul was both their teacher and pastor. For three years, he had constantly watched (**night and day**) over the flock at Ephesus, even shedding tears for them.

In the conclusion of his instructions to these men, Paul commited them to God and illustrated the nature of a servant's ministry from his own life once again (20:32-35).

20:32. Paul committed the elders to God's care. Though Paul would no longer be with them, they would not be alone. God would be with them, and by His grace they would receive their promised inheritance. **Inheritance** (*kleronomian*) is their eternal salvation that is safeguarded in heaven for believers (1Pt 1:4).

20:33-35. Paul was no greedy charlatan. He was a man of integrity with pure motives. Paul did not covet anyone's money (**silver and gold**) or possessions (**clothes**); rather while at Ephesus

Paul supported himself. At times, though not all the time, Paul worked as a tentmaker (Ac 18:2-3), and at other times Paul received support from the churches and devoted himself full time to ministry (Ac 18:5).

Paul was a model for helping the needy. In contrast to many of the itinerant speakers in the first century and televangelists in the 21st century, Paul's primary concern was for others, not himself. In caring for others Paul was following the instruction of the Lord Jesus who said, **It is more blessed to give than to receive**. This statement is not recorded in the Gospels, but is consistent with Jesus' teaching and ministry to the poor.

20:36-38. Before he departed, Paul knelt with the elders for prayer. The traditional posture for Jews was to stand with their hands lifted toward heaven (See 1Tm 2:8). Kneeling in this instance suggests a more personal and emotional farewell. Paul's announcement that they would never see him again brought tears and kisses. Obviously the elders loved Paul as a person and did not think of him as merely an austere apostle with divine authority. Kissing in this kind of situation was culturally appropriate and a sign of respect and regret they would never see the beloved apostle again. Though heartbroken, the elders escorted Paul to the ship.

Ministry is a serious responsibility. The church is God's flock, and leaders are called as shepherds. This role demands humility, integrity, devotion to teaching the Word of God, and protecting the sheep from false teachers (wolves). All of this would be impossible if it were not for the grace of God. Because of the Father's love and grace, God's Son shed His own blood for the church, and by His grace He will sustain those who faithfully shepherd the sheep.

e. In Tyre and Caesarea (21:1-14)

(1) Tyre (21:1-6)

In Ac 21, Luke continued his account of Paul's journey to Jerusalem and Rome (see 19:21). On the way, Paul visited believers at Tyre and Caesarea by the Sea. On both occasions, he was warned about the danger of going to Jerusalem, and his disciples attempted to dissuade him. But Paul was an apostle with a divine mission. He was ready to suffer and even to die for the Lord Jesus Christ.

21:1-3. Paul was not alone. **We** included Luke and others who were traveling with Paul. **We had parted from them** does not convey the emotional distress of leaving the Ephesian believers. The verb **parted** (*apospasthentas*) indicates it was a painful farewell. They sailed along the coast, stopping at Cos, Rhodes, and Patara. At Patara, Paul and his companions transferred to a larger ship that was sailing for Phoenicia. The ship made port at Tyre to unload cargo. See map on the opposite page.

21:4-6. Paul and his companions went ashore and spent seven days at Tyre. **Through the Spirit** the disciples warned Paul not to go to Jerusalem. The expression **through the Spirit** may refer either to the human spirit or the Holy Spirit. The latter is preferred because the knowledge of what awaited Paul required knowledge of the future. Also Agabus, who warned Paul in vv. 10-11, was called a prophet, suggesting he received revelation of Paul's future from the Spirit.

Some scholars maintain, on the basis of the two warnings "by the Spirit" that Paul received and ignored, that Paul viewed some prophecies as being of a lower level of authority than the message of OT prophets, and that some prophecies could be disregarded. But the text does not actually say, "Paul, the Spirit Himself says that you should not go to Jerusalem." **They kept telling Paul through the Spirit** could just as easily mean that through prophetic revelation they knew what awaited Paul, and because of their own love for him pled with him not to go—without the plea being part of the revelatory message. It is also argued that the prophecy of Agabus in Ac 21:11—that Jewish people would bind Paul—contained an error since it was the Romans who bound Paul instead (Ac 21:31-33). However, the Jews *were* the ones who initially seized Paul (Ac 21:30; note the shout, "Away with him!" in Ac 21:36, suggesting the Jewish people turned control of him over to the Romans), and when Paul recounted the episode in Ac 26:21, he said it was Jewish people who apprehended him. These points suggest that NT prophecy is every bit as potent as that of the OT, and that there is not some sort of second-tier type of prophecy resident in the church today that may be disregarded or fallible. Paul rightly did not regard 21:4, 10-13 as a prohibition from the Spirit but as a prediction, based upon the revelatory work of the Spirit, of what awaited him in Jerusalem. After prayer with the disciples and their families, Paul continued his journey to Jerusalem.

(2) In Caesarea and to Jerusalem (21:7-16)

21:7-14. On the trip to Caesarea, Paul stopped for a day at **Ptolemais** and greeted the believers

(v. 7). Luke did not explain how the church was established, but it probably came about through the preaching of the gospel by those scattered during the persecution after the martyrdom of Stephen (cf. 11:19-20). Paul stayed with **Philip the evangelist** and one of the seven chosen to supervise the distribution of food to the Hellenistic widows (cf. 6:1-7). Luke mentioned without comment that Philip had **four virgin daughters** who prophesy. His intention was perhaps to confirm that the gift of the Spirit had been given to both Jews and Gentiles and to men and women. **Agabus**, however, was the one who symbolically prophesied that Paul would be arrested and handed over to Gentiles in Jerusalem (vv. 10-14).

Again, Paul's companions responded according to human nature. They begged Paul not to go to Jerusalem. Paul understood Agabus's prophecy differently. He saw it as a prediction of what would happen and not as a prohibition (on Agabus, see also the comments above at 21:4-6). In fact Paul said that their pleading was **breaking** his **heart**, a vivid statement of an assault on Paul's determination to fulfill his mission. His friends resigned themselves to the will of God (**the will of the Lord be done**). Though they desired a different outcome, they recognized that Paul had to pursue God's will.

Was Paul acting in disobedience to the will of God by going to Jerusalem? Several points suggest that he was not. First, Paul himself sincerely believed that he was in God's will (see 20:22-24). Second, he was under the impression for a long time that he should go to Jerusalem (19:21; 20:3), so this was not a rash or sinful decision. Third, Paul was told that he would suffer greatly as he bore witness (9:15-16), so that suffering in Jerusalem would not be contrary to God's will for him. Fourth, God never told Paul not to go there, but rather warned him about what to expect (20:23). Finally, 23:11 implies that Paul had God's stamp of approval on what he did and said in Jerusalem. It is hard to conceive of

Paul's Third Missionary Journey

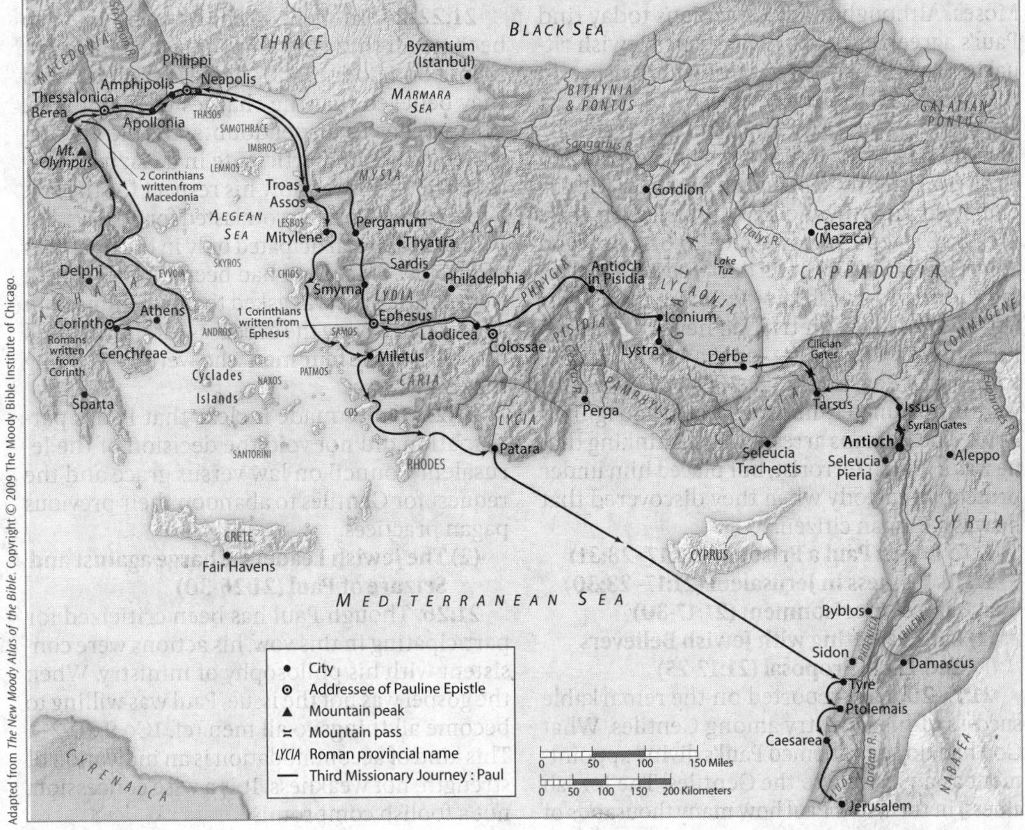

the mighty apostle consciously disobeying the leading of the Spirit if He did not want him in Jerusalem.

21:15-16. Some of the believers **from Caesarea** joined Paul and his companions for the overland trip to Jerusalem. They stayed at the house of **Mnason**, a Gentile convert from Cyprus, who would not object to hosting a group that included Gentiles.

Nothing could have been more definite than these two warnings, but like Christ on his final journey to Jerusalem, Paul knew what was ahead. Yet he did not allow the prospect of danger and suffering to prevent him from pursuing God's will. Sometimes in obedience to the will of God, believers may find it necessary to refuse the reasonable counsel of friends who mean well, but do not understand the compelling leading of God's Spirit.

When Paul arrived in Jerusalem, he reported to the Jewish congregation how God had blessed his ministry to the Gentiles. Though thankful for what God had done, the leaders informed Paul that his ministry among the Gentiles had raised suspicions about his loyalty to the law of Moses. Although many Christians today find Paul's agreement to participate in a Jewish ritual to prove his loyalty to the law surprising, in the context of the book of Acts, it makes perfect sense. He never considered faith in Jesus the Jewish Messiah as contrary to being Jewish, and so he consistently kept Jewish practices. He circumcised Timothy (Ac 16:3), took Jewish vows (Ac 18:18), kept Passover (Ac 20:6), observed Yom Kippur (Ac 27:9), and declared his absolute faithfulness to Jewish law (Ac 28:8) and customs (Ac 28:17). When on trial he never described himself as a Christian—only a Jew (Ac 21:39; 22:3) and a Pharisee (23:6; 26:5-6). His actions were unfortunately misinterpreted and ignited a riot. The Romans arrested Paul, thinking that he was a Jewish terrorist, but placed him under protective custody when they discovered that he was a Roman citizen.

F. To Rome: Paul a Prisoner (21:17–28:31)

1. His Witness in Jerusalem (21:17–23:30)

a. Before Imprisonment (21:17-30)

(1) Paul's Meeting with Jewish Believers and Their Proposal (21:17-25)

21:17-20. Paul reported on the remarkable success of his ministry among Gentiles. What God had done confirmed Paul's divine appointment as an apostle to the Gentiles. The Jewish elders, in turn, told Paul how many thousands of Jews had believed and were zealous for the law. Verse 17 says, **the brethren received us gladly**. It is likely that on this occasion Paul delivered the proceeds of the multichurch offering gathered from the predominantly Gentile congregations scattered throughout the Mediterranean world (see the comments on 1Co 16:1-3; Rm 15:26-27; 2Co 8-9; cf. also Ac 24:17). He arrived with an enormous relief fund for the poor and persecuted believers in Judea. No wonder he was **received gladly**!

21:21. Not everyone was enthusiastic about Paul's ministry among the Gentiles. Some spread rumors that he was teaching Jews to abandon the law of Moses. The charge was twofold. One, he was telling Jews they did not need to **circumcise their children**. God established circumcision as the physical sign of His covenant with Abraham (Gn 17). Two, he was saying that Jews did not need **to walk according to the customs.** In the book of Acts, Paul stated that he always observed Jewish customs. He only refused to impose these practices on Gentile believers, a decision confirmed by the Jerusalem Council (Ac 15).

21:22-24. In view of Paul's willingness to become all things to all people (see the comments on 1Co 9:19-23), the leaders indicated they believed that the charges were not true. Yet in order to dispel doubts, the elders suggested that Paul participate in a Nazirite **vow** (see Nm 6:1-21) to show his respect for the law. A temporary Nazirite vow lasted for 30 days, but Paul probably participated only in the final days of the vow. Since Paul had been ministering in Gentile areas, he was asked to **purify** himself in addition to paying the expenses for the required offerings of the **four men** who were completing the vow.

21:25. James made it clear that Paul's participation did not void the decision of the Jerusalem Council on law versus grace and the request for Gentiles to abandon their previous pagan practices.

(2) The Jewish Leaders' Charge against and Seizure of Paul (21:26-30)

21:26. Though Paul has been criticized for participating in this vow, his actions were consistent with his philosophy of ministry. When the gospel was not the issue, Paul was willing to become all things to all men (cf. 1Co 9:20-21). This kind of accommodation is an indication of strength, not weakness. It is a wise concession, not a foolish compromise.

Though Paul had hoped to avoid unnecessary controversy over his ministry to Gentiles by participating in a Nazirite **vow**, when he attempted to complete the vow his actions ignited a riot. The angry mob seized Paul and beat him. He would have been killed if the Romans had not intervened. After order was restored, Paul asked for permission to address his countrymen.

21:27-30. Jews from the province of Asia made two accusations against Paul. First, they claimed that he was teaching **all men everywhere** against the Jewish people, the law, and the temple. This was obviously an exaggeration and false. It was similar to the charge against Stephen, who was also accused of speaking against the law and the holy place. The law and the temple were the cultural and spiritual pillars of Judaism. Luke did not record the exact charges, but Paul's teaching was seen as a direct threat to traditional Judaism.

The second charge was also serious. They claimed Paul brought **Trophimus**, a Gentile, into the temple area. Gentiles were allowed only into the outer area that surrounded the inner courts of the temple. Inscriptions in Latin and Greek warned of the death penalty for any Gentile who trespassed. It is highly unlikely that Paul would have deliberately violated the sanctity of the temple, so the charge was a lie.

The irony of this turn of events was that Paul believed he was a faithful Jew and was attempting to convince his countrymen that Jesus is the fulfillment of their messianic hopes. For his effort he was falsely accused and his life threatened.

b. After Imprisonment (21:31–23:30)

(1) His Arrest and Request to Address the Jews (21:31-40)

21:31-33. It was reported to the Roman **commander** of the **cohort** (an officer in charge of a thousand soldiers) that a riot was taking place. Paul had been violently seized by some Jewish people in the temple area (21:30), and a mob scene was quickly forming. The **commander** acted quickly to restore order. He arrested Paul and ordered him bound with two chains because he thought Paul had instigated the riot. As Agabus had predicted, Jewish hostility led to the binding of Paul by Gentiles (21:11).

21:34-36. When the commander attempted to find out the cause of the riot, the Jewish opponents were so emotionally agitated that their answers were confusing. He ordered his soldiers to take Paul to the barracks for protection. The situation was again ironic. The Jewish people attempted to kill Paul, but he was rescued by the Romans. Paul's experience was somewhat similar to Christ's arrest and trials 30 years earlier when some Jewish people also shouted, "Away with him" (see Lk 23:18; Jn 19:15).

Paul's courage and commitment to Christ were evident in his defense. Instead of merely protesting his innocence, Paul seized the opportunity to give a testimony of his transformation by Jesus and his calling to the Gentiles.

21:37-40. When Paul asked, in Greek, for permission to speak, the commander was surprised, and concluded that Paul must be an Egyptian insurrectionist since Greek was commonly spoken in Egypt.

Though surprised, the tribune granted Paul's request, and Paul addressed the crowd in Hebrew. Many commentators think Luke used the word "Hebrew" to refer to Aramaic, the language in which Paul actually spoke, the common language of first-century Jewish people.

(2) His Address before the Crowd (22:1-21)

22:1-2. When Paul addressed the crowd in the Hebrew language, they become silent, seeing that he was one of them and not a Gentile.

22:3-5. Paul focused on his Jewish heritage, his transformation by the Messiah Jesus, and his calling as an apostle to the Gentiles. First, Paul referred to his heritage. He was born and raised in Tarsus, and was trained as a Pharisee by Gamaliel, one of the most renowned teachers of the school of Hillel (on Hillel's background, see the comments on Mt 19:3; for Gamaliel, see the comments on Ac 5:33-39). Paul was zealous for God, and had received official permission to arrest Jewish believers in Damascus and bring them back to Jerusalem for trial. Paul's point was that he was zealous for the law and had persecuted Jewish believers much as his countrymen were now persecuting him.

22:6-11. Paul also referred to his transformation by Jesus the Messiah. On the journey to Damascus, he was blinded by a brilliant light. He heard a voice saying, **Saul, Saul why are you persecuting me?** He discovered the heavenly messenger was **Jesus the Nazarene**, one of the common titles used by Jewish people to emphasize Jesus' human origin. Paul's use of the title here is evidence that the human Jesus is now the resurrected Lord and Messiah. The Lord informed Paul that he would find out what he had been appointed to do in Damascus. Those traveling with Paul knew something unusual had happened but did not understand the meaning of Paul's experience. They led Paul into the city.

22:12-16. Paul referred to his calling. He recounted how Ananias, a devout Jew who respected the law, was used by God to help restore his sight and informed him of his divine calling as a witness to all men. As one who personally saw the resurrected Lord, Paul met the qualifications for an apostle (cf. Ac 1:22, 1Co 9:1).

Because Paul expressed his faith by calling on the name of Jesus, he was instructed to submit to baptism as an outward sign of inward spiritual cleansing. In the early church baptism was symbolic and indispensable testimony of the conversion experience (see the comments on Rm 6:1-4; 1Pt 3:18-20); however, it is faith in Jesus and not baptism that saves (cf. Ac 16:31; Eph 2:8-9).

22:17-22. Paul provided new information about what happened when he returned to Jerusalem. As a faithful Jew, he went into the temple to pray (v. 17) and received divine guidance through a **trance** (*ekstasis*, from which the word "ecstasy" is derived). Paul's experience would resonate with Jews, who knew that God had sometimes spoken to the prophets through visions (cf. Is 6:1-13). His experience was also somewhat parallel to Peter's vision (Ac 10:10; 11:5, where *ekstasis* is also used).

Like those who were now Paul's accusers, Paul had once been an enemy of believers, but he had been wrong. The Lord warned Paul to leave Jerusalem (v. 18) because his own people would reject his testimony, though everyone knew of Paul's reputation as a persecutor of Jewish followers of Jesus (v. 19), and especially his role as a witness to the stoning of Stephen (v. 20). **Witness**, used here in reference to Stephen, may be the first use of the word *martus* in the full sense of a "martyr" in the Greek language—a witness who dies for his faith.

Instead the Lord dramatically reversed Paul's life and mission. He was commanded to go to the Gentiles (v. 21). This climactic point of Paul's testimony was more than his Jewish audience could tolerate. They exploded in anger and shouted that he did not deserve to live. Paul's statement infuriated them because they understood this as the reason that Paul had brought a Gentile into a forbidden area of the temple—the false charge they had brought against Paul.

(3) His Claim of Roman Citizenship (22:22-29)

22:22-24. Thinking that Paul had intentionally inflamed the crowd, the commander took measures to have Paul flogged with a whip, probably the *flagellum*, with pieces of bone and metal attached to the leather thongs (see the comments on Mt 27:24-26). This kind of flogging was used only on noncitizens since it could cripple or even kill the victim. It was thus completely improper to use it on Paul as a Roman citizen.

22:25-29. Rather than endure unnecessary punishment, Paul claimed his right as a **Roman** citizen. This shocked the commander, who revealed that he had to purchase his **citizenship** for a large sum of money. At various periods during the Roman Empire, it was possible to purchase citizenship, but it was very expensive and out of the question for most people. Paul, on the other hand, was born a Roman citizen. His status as a citizen immediately changed Paul's circumstances. The Romans now faced a serious problem, "How do we treat a Roman citizen who has been unjustly arrested?" Paul's appeal to his citizenship was not inconsistent with his willingness to suffer and die for his faith. In this particular situation, Paul saw the advantage of using his citizenship to proclaim the gospel and advance the kingdom. Paul probably did not realize that his citizenship would take him to Rome, but he at least knew that in his present circumstances it would give him an opportunity to witness to his own people.

Paul's defense emphasized several points. First, he was a faithful Jew, not an apostate. Second, the circumstances surrounding his faith in Jesus as Messiah were supernatural and were consistent with God's promises to Israel (cf. the comments on Rm 11:1-2). Third, his commission to the Gentiles was legitimatized by the Jewish rejection of the gospel and divine revelation.

As did his Lord and Stephen, Paul showed exceptional courage before the Sanhedrin, but instead of his being executed, the outcome was ironic. Paul was rescued by the Romans.

(4) His Appearance before the Sanhedrin (22:30–23:9)

(a) His Incident with the High Priest (22:30–23:5)

22:30. The commander was persistent because he was committed to upholding Roman law. He wanted to know **for certain** (the facts) why the Jews were violently opposed to Paul. The next day he ordered the Sanhedrin to convene and brought Paul before the chief priests and council (Sanhedrin).

23:1-2. Paul did not attempt to answer specific charges; instead he based his defense on his relationship with God. He had **a perfectly good conscience before God**. Paul was more concerned about how God would judge him than the Sanhedrin. Though he was a Jew who followed Jesus, he had done nothing to dishonor God.

His claim was inflammatory. The high priest thought Paul had committed blasphemy. He ordered him struck **on the mouth.**

23:3. Paul's response was surprising. He insulted the high priest calling him a **whitewashed wall.** The imagery comes from coating a decaying, crumbling wall (Ezk 13:10-16) with a veneer of whitewash to hide its true condition. Paul's implication could not have been clearer. The high priest dressed in priestly robes was a hypocrite. Jesus referred to Israel's religious leaders as whitewashed tombs (Mt 23:27).

23:4-5. It was against the law to curse God or the leader of God's people (Ex 22:28) as one of the bystanders reminded Paul. Paul's response was cryptic, **I was not aware, brethren, that he was high priest**. Paul even quoted Ex 22:28. This suggests Paul knew he was speaking to the high priest and the insult was intentional and ironic. Some have suggested Paul did not recognize the high priest for various reasons, but these seem improbable. Ananias, who was the high priest, was notorious as a glutton, thief, and conspirator with the Romans. Paul was sarcastically saying, "I did not realize such a man could become the high priest of Israel."

(b) His Incitement of Pharisees and Sadducees (23:6-9)

23:6-9. Paul did not wait for the high priest to respond. He went on the offensive. Realizing (**perceiving**) that both Pharisees and Sadducees were present, he instigated a volatile debate on the resurrection. Paul was a Pharisee and appealed to his hope for a resurrection. The Sadducees denied the resurrection. Luke also said the Sadducees denied angels and spirits (v. 8). This is somewhat of a problem since there is no other evidence the Sadducees did not believe in angels or spirits (see Bock, *Acts,* 671–72 for a discussion of the options).

The two Jewish sects became engaged in a bitter and violent argument. The Pharisees became Paul's advocates. Although they did not accept his claims that Jesus is alive, they said, **We find nothing wrong with this man**.

(5) The Conspiracy to Take His Life (23:10-30)

23:10. The commander rescued Paul for a third time. When the debate degenerated into physical violence, he ordered his men to take Paul to the barracks for safety. The mob was so violent it was apparently necessary for the soldiers to carry Paul to the safety of the barracks.

Proverbs 16:9 reads, "In his heart a man plans his course, the LORD determines his steps" (NIV 1984). Paul's situation was bleak. His fellow Jews wanted to kill him. The Romans thought he was a revolutionary and arrested him. He was the victim of lies and violence. His life was in jeopardy. There seemed hardly any chance that Paul's dream to witness in Rome would come true, yet the Lord remained sovereign.

23:11. In a theophany (a physical manifestation of God), the Lord reassured Paul that he made the right decision in coming to Jerusalem. He would have the opportunity to proclaim the gospel in Rome, the capital of the empire. He came to Paul at night. He stood by his side to assure him. He did not confront him face to face. Though Paul had every reason to be afraid, he was not a coward. The Lord told him to be courageous and confirmed that Paul's desire to proclaim the gospel in Jerusalem and in Rome (see 19:21) was His will and that it would come about. The promise in 23:11 dominates the narrative from this point on in Acts. Luke emphasized how the Lord worked providentially and supernaturally to protect Paul, His chosen servant, on his way to Rome.

23:12-15. A group of 40 Jews conspired to assassinate Paul. They made a suicidal oath vowing, essentially, "May God curse me if I fail to do this." Their **plot** was to ambush Paul in the narrow streets of Jerusalem. God, however, can and sometimes does frustrate the plans of evil men, and in this situation he providentially intervened through Paul's nephew.

23:16-22. Paul's nephew discovered the plot and told Paul. Though his discovery of the plot might seem as if it were "a stroke of good luck," it was the providence of the sovereign Lord in protecting Paul. Luke did not explain how Paul's nephew learned of the assassination plot, but he warned Paul, who asked one of the centurions to take his nephew to the commander. Paul's nephew informed the commander of the plot, and the commander cautioned Paul's nephew to keep their meeting a secret.

Paul's Journey to Rome

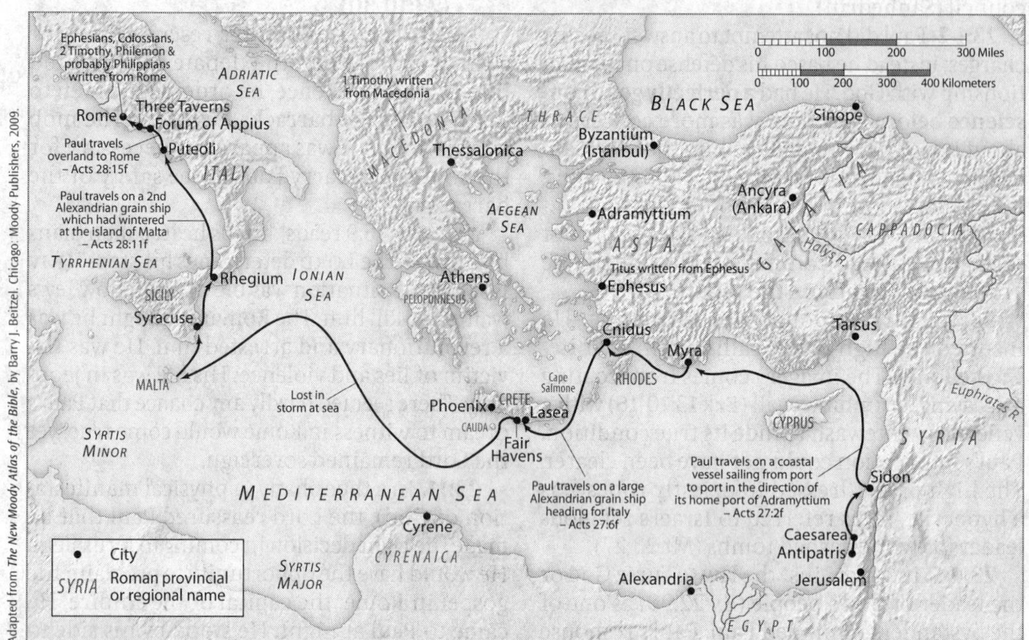

Adapted from *The New Moody Atlas of the Bible*, by Barry J. Beitzel. Chicago: Moody Publishers, 2009.

The contrast here is unbelievably ironic. Paul was threatened by his own people but protected by the Gentiles. These Jewish opponents were blinded and driven by fanatical zeal. The Roman commander, who was an unbeliever, was controlled and rational. This was high drama. The stakes could not have been higher. Paul's life was in danger. If Paul died, the new faith would receive a severe blow. If his enemies prevailed, Paul could be executed and Christianity declared an illegal religion by the Romans. But the Lord assured Paul of a different outcome (see 23:11).

After Paul's nephew informed the commander of the plot to assassinate Paul, the Romans took action to protect him. They organized a detachment of soldiers to transfer Paul to Caesarea, the center for Roman rule in Judea, where there was better security.

23:23-24. Because of the possibility of an ambush during the transfer from Jerusalem to Caesarea, a distance of 60 miles, the commander ordered a detachment of infantry, cavalry, and spearmen to escort Paul. He also ordered the transfer to take place at night for additional secrecy.

23:25. It is not known how Luke obtained his information, but he recorded a copy of the letter or at least part of it.

23:26. Claudius, the commander, wrote to Felix, who was the Roman military governor of Judea from AD 52 to 60. Antonius Felix (born probably before AD 10) was born as a slave, the son of Antonia Minor, who was the daughter of Marc Antony, and later received his freedom, probably from Emperor Claudius. He was a social outcast and obtained his position as procurator around AD 52, but only with considerable help from his influential older brother, Pallas, and a fair amount of underhandedness to oust his predecessor, Ventidius Cumanus. Felix was morally vile and cruel. The letter from Claudius the commander was to explain the reason he was transferring Paul to Caesarea rather than resolve the problem himself in Jerusalem.

23:27-30. Though the purpose was to explain the transfer of Paul, the letter was remarkably self-serving. Claudius was brazen in his attempt to make himself look good. The English text contains eight uses of the personal pronoun "I." The other important feature of the letter is that it exonerated Paul, a Roman citizen, of civil disobedience. The charges involved issues about Jewish, not Roman, law.

2. His Witness in Caesarea by the Sea (23:31–26:32)

a. Paul's Arrival and Assignment of Quarters (23:31-35)

23:31-35. The entire contingent of soldiers accompanied Paul to Antipatris, 25 miles southeast from Caesarea. The journey to Antipatris was the most dangerous part of the journey because the terrain was semi-mountainous and suited for an ambush. After Antipatris, the country was open and flat and less dangerous, so when they reached Antipatris, the infantry returned to Jerusalem. The soldiers delivered their prisoner to Felix, who decided to try the case even though Paul was from the province of Cilicia. This was somewhat unusual since cases were typically tried in the province of the accused. Plus, instead of receiving harsh confinement, Paul was basically under house arrest in Felix's official residence, the palace (**Praetorium**, the official abode of a governor) built by Herod the Great for himself about 75 years earlier. These developments were more than circumstantial. They revealed God's sovereign providence in fulfilling his promise to Paul that he would testify in Rome (cf. Ac 23:11).

At the time of Paul's hearing, Felix had been governor of Judea for five years. Though responsible to uphold Roman law, Felix was notorious as an inept and brutal ruler. Yet in his defense Paul boldly challenged Felix with the ethical demands of faith in Jesus Christ.

b. Paul's Defense before Felix the Governor (24:1-21)

(1) The Accusation by the Jewish Leaders (24:1-9)

24:1a. Chapter 24:1-8 continues Luke's narrative by summarizing the situation under which the charges against Paul were formed. The intensity of the opposition to Paul is reflected in the coming of the high priest, Ananias, to Caesarea and the hiring of a high-powered advocate to present the case against Paul.

24:1b-3. Tertullus's opening remarks were loaded with patronizing flattery. He praised Felix for his peaceful rule and reforms, hoping to influence the governor for a favorable decision. Civil unrest had actually become worse under Felix's rule.

24:4-6. Tertullus presented three charges against Paul. First, knowing that the Romans did not tolerate civil disorder, he said that Paul was a troublemaker, a **pest** or public nuisance. Second, he was the leader of a **sect of the Nazarenes**. Since the Romans had not yet distinguished Christianity from Judaism, which was a legal religion, Tertullus gave a cryptic description of this new faith in Jesus to raise Felix's suspicions about a new sect. Jesus was from Nazareth, so the description was accurate, but not one that would have been familiar to Felix, plus Paul was the ringleader of this seditious movement. Third, he accused Paul of defiling the temple. The Sadducees, who were collaborators with the Romans, were responsible for maintaining order in the temple. This is why they seized Paul—they were trying to keep peace, but Paul had ignited a riot. The charge was false but one that Tertullus hoped the Romans would act on. All three of these charges were cleverly designed. Under Gallio faith in Jesus was officially and legally viewed as a subset of Judaism, and as such Rome would not view it as illegal. But anything that disturbed the *pax Romana* ("peace established by Rome") was not going to be tolerated, and even a whiff of insurrection would arouse Rome's fury. Tertullus's charges minimized the religious dispute the Jewish leaders had with Paul, and emphasized the points about which the Romans would be most concerned.

24:7-9. Though Tertullus tried to frame the case to make it appear that Paul violated Roman law, he did not provide any solid evidence. This is perhaps the reason that he encouraged Felix to question Paul further and that all the Jewish opponents present joined in a verbal attack on Paul.

In his defense, Paul denied the charges, and claimed to be a Jew, whose hope was in God's promises to Israel. Though Felix knew that Paul was innocent, he ordered him held as a prisoner for two years but with limited freedom. Felix hoped that Paul would pay him a bribe, but he also talked with Paul about faith in Jesus. Paul used the opportunity to challenge Felix with the moral demands of following Christ.

(2) The Answer by Paul (24:10-21)

24:10-13. Paul claimed that the truth was that he had gone to Jerusalem to worship God, that he was not involved in civil disobedience, and that the Jews could not prove the charges against him.

24:14-16. He said he worshiped the same God as his accusers but **according to the Way** (cf. comments at 9:1-2), which his Jewish opponents claimed was a heretical sect. Paul contended that his new messianic Judaism, with Jesus at its core, was consistent with God's promises for Israel. Paul's point was that the dispute was religious and not political, and by emphasizing this he reflected Gallio's decision years before. As did his accusers, Paul believed in the law of Moses and the prophets and had the same hope in a resurrection of both the just and the unjust.

He had done his best to keep a clear conscience before God and men. Paul was not a renegade Jew, and he was not the ringleader of a subversive movement.

24:17-18. After his defense of the gospel, Paul defended himself. He had come to Jerusalem with an offering for the poor. Though a follower of Christ, Paul had not abandoned his Jewish heritage. He identified himself with the Jewish people by calling them **my nation**. He honored God by ritually purifying himself when he went into the temple.

24:19-21. Paul discredited his accusers by noting that they were not even present to defend their charges against him. The Jewish leaders had come from Jerusalem according to 24:1, but the actual Jews from Asia (v. 18), who had instigated the riot against Paul by accusing him of bringing a Gentile into the temple (21:27-28), were absent. Paul's only crime was that he believed in the resurrection. Such a belief was religious and not illegal according to Roman law or heretical according to Jewish hopes.

c. Paul's Later Experience with Felix the Governor (24:22-27)

24:22-23. Though Felix understood the basic facts about **the Way** (cf. comments at 9:1-2), he postponed his decision until Claudius Lysias, the commander who arrested Paul, came from Jerusalem. He ordered Paul placed under guard but with the privilege for his friends to visit and provide for his needs.

24:24. Because Felix's wife, Drusilla (born around AD 38), was nominally Jewish, Felix thought that perhaps she would be interested in what Paul had to say or at least she could give a more objective opinion about the controversy concerning the Way. She was the youngest daughter of Herod Agrippa I (the "Herod" of Ac 12 who killed James), and as a member of Herod's family probably knew more about this new movement than Felix.

24:25-26. Aware of Felix's reputation for immorality and corruption, Paul emphasized **righteousness, self-control, and the judgment to come** in his witness to the governor. These three terms focused on personal morality and not matters related to Felix's governorship. It is obvious from Felix's response that he was troubled by what Paul said. **Frightened** (v. 25) is the word *emphobos* rather than the more common *phobos*, and indicates a more intense emotional response. Instead of repenting, Felix dismissed Paul with the intent of meeting with him in the future. He was not, however, interested in more information but a bribe. Though illegal, Roman officials often accepted bribes from political prisoners.

24:27. Felix ignored justice and kept Paul confined for two years because he hoped to gain the support of the Jews. At the end of the two years of Paul's imprisonment, Festus replaced Felix as governor of Judea (c. AD 58). Felix was recalled to Rome to answer for his incompetent administration of the Region, but he was rescued from severe punishment by his brother Pallas. Nothing more is known of him following this point. Festus had the reputation of a more effective and just administrator; Luke, however, portrayed him as more interested in appeasing the Jewish leadership than administering justice. At first he resisted the Jewish leadership's request to return Paul to Jerusalem, but in the end he opted for patronizing expediency rather than political justice. He decided to return Paul to Jerusalem for a hearing before the Sanhedrin.

Paul knew that there were still plans to assassinate him, so he appealed to Caesar. This sort of appeal was a benefit of Roman citizenship. Any Roman citizen accused of a crime could appeal to be tried before Caesar himself. In appealing to Caesar, Paul's concern was about more than his personal fate; he was concerned about the freedom of the church to proclaim the gospel. If Paul would be exonerated, then the church would be exonerated.

d. Paul's Defense before Festus the Governor (25:1-12)

Though undoubtedly in circumstances different from what he had expected, Paul was now in a position to fulfill the second part of his dream—to preach the gospel in Rome. But before being transferred to Rome, Paul seized the opportunity to give his testimony to both Festus and Agrippa.

25:1-3. Luke recorded Paul's hearing before governor Festus in 25:1-12. When Festus, the new governor, traveled to Jerusalem, the foremost complaint of the religious leaders was about Paul. They asked Festus to transfer Paul to Jerusalem. Luke, however, revealed that their real motive was to ambush Paul.

25:4-5. Festus refused. He required the Jewish religious leaders to follow proper legal procedures and go to Caesarea to plead their case there against Paul.

25:6. As soon as Festus returned to Caesarea, he summoned Paul for a hearing. For the hearing he sat on a *bema*, a raised judgment seat where one in a position of judicial authority would sit to render his verdict in a court case he had overseen.

25:7-8. Paul's accusers surrounded him making numerous **serious charges**, which they could not prove. Paul denied that he had committed a crime against the law, the temple, or Caesar. He was an honorable Jew and Roman citizen. The charge about his loyalty to Caesar was perhaps the most serious. If Festus decided that Paul was a troublemaker, then he would move to prosecute him.

25:9. Instead of making a civil decision, Festus made a political one. He attempted to patronize the religious leadership by returning Paul to Jerusalem.

25:10-11. Paul protested. He claimed that he had not committed any crimes against the Jews. If he were a criminal, Paul was willing to accept even the death penalty, but if he were innocent, then he had the right to appeal to Caesar.

25:12. After conferring with his legal advisors, Festus honored Paul's request. More was at stake than Paul's well-being. Paul was concerned about protecting the legal status of the new movement, but his appeal was also motivated by his desire to proclaim the gospel in Rome. This latter motive is supported by the conclusion of Acts, which depicts Paul teaching about the kingdom of God unhindered (cf. 28:31).

e. Paul's Defense before Herod Agrippa II the King (25:13–26:32)

(1) Prelude to the Defense (25:13-27)

When Herod Agrippa II arrived with his sister Bernice to pay their respects to the new governor, Festus saw an opportunity to get his advice about Paul from two people who were more knowledgeable about Judaism. Agrippa II was the son of Herod Agrippa I (see Ac 12:1-23), and great grandson of Herod the Great. He ruled as tetrarch in Chalcis (modern northern Syria) beginning around AD 50, but eventually acquired Galilee and Jerusalem as well. He was well acquainted with Jewish customs so was occasionally consulted by the Romans, as was probably the case with Festus. Bernice was his sister, widowed when her second husband died in AD 48. After that she lived with Agrippa II, and though she denied an incestuous relationship, one probably existed.

25:13-16. Festus explained the problem that he inherited from Felix. When he was in Jerusalem, the Jewish leaders wanted Paul executed, but Roman law permitted the accused to meet face to face with his accusers.

25:17-19. Festus omitted details about the transfer of Paul to Caesarea. When Paul's accusers presented their case against Paul, Festus was surprised by the accusations. The dispute was about Judaism and a dead man named Jesus, whom Paul claimed is alive. The complaint was obviously religious and not civil in nature, charges that Festus could not judge.

25:20-22. When Festus decided to return Paul to Jerusalem for trial, Paul appealed to Caesar. Festus was now holding him in custody until he could be sent to Caesar. Agrippa was intrigued. He asked to hear the case, and the hearing was set for the next day.

25:23. The scene was one of contrast. Agrippa and Bernice came adorned in their purple robes of royalty and gold accompanied by a host of attendants. The military commanders were present, perhaps in full dress uniforms, and the prominent men of the city in their finest robes. The prisoner was brought in, perhaps in chains. Early descriptions of Paul portray him as short, coarse, and physically unimpressive.

25:24-27. Festus explained to Agrippa and the others present the reasons he needed their opinion about Paul's case. The Jewish religious leadership in Jerusalem and Caesarea had charged that Paul should be put to death, but Festus had not found sufficient evidence to support their accusation. Plus, Paul had made an appeal to Caesar, and Festus did not know what charges he should make against him. Festus admitted that Paul's case was absurd. He had already determined that the accusations were religious and not civil (cf. 25:19). Festus was probably concerned about his reputation. If he sent Paul to Caesar without credible charges, he would appear foolish.

(2) Particulars of the Defense (26:1-29)

26:1. Since Festus had asked for Agrippa's opinion, Agrippa was the one who granted Paul permission to speak. Paul **stretched out his hand** in respect for the king (Bruce, *Acts*, 496) as he began his **defense** (*apologeomai*, from which the word "apology" is derived).

26:2-3. Paul began by saying that he considered it a privilege to make his defense before Herod Agrippa II. Paul was not patronizing the king. The statement, **especially because you are an expert in all customs and questions among the Jews** is accurate because Agrippa was well informed about Jewish customs, and certainly more objective than the Sanhedrin to evaluate Paul's case.

Paul's defense followed a typical rhetorical form of prologue (vv. 2-3), narration (vv. 4-18), confirmation (vv. 19-20), refutation (v. 21), and concluding appeal (vv. 22-23) (Bock, *Acts*, 713). Though giving a formal defense, Paul focused his account on the resurrection (cf. v. 8 and v. 23).

26:4-8. Paul had been a Jew all of his life and was even a Pharisee, who lived according to the **strictest** demands of the law. Twice Paul identified himself with the Jews, **our fathers** (v. 6) and **our twelve tribes** (v. 7). Paul maintained he was thoroughly Jewish, and his hope in the resurrection was identical to the promise that God made to His chosen people.

26:9-11. Since he considered himself a faithful Jew, Paul formerly had felt obligated to oppose **the name of Jesus of Nazareth**. Paul referred to Jesus from the perspective of an unbelieving Jew. Before the Damascus road experience, Paul believed that Jesus was not Lord or Messiah; he was from the insignificant town of Nazareth. In Jerusalem, Paul had received authority from the chief priests to imprison Jewish believers, and he had voted for the death penalty for them. He had tried to force Jewish believers to **blasphem[y]** by apparently denying Jesus. He was so **enraged** against believers that he pursued them to cities outside of Israel.

26:12-15. But while on a mission to Damascus, he had an encounter that changed his life. He saw a light that was brighter than the sun and heard a voice that asked in Hebrew, **Saul, Saul, why are you persecuting me? The goads** are spikes on a pole or plank that is used to train and control an ox or horse to pull a cart. The imagery implies that resistance against Jesus is painful and useless. When Saul asked who was speaking to him, the Lord identified himself as **Jesus whom you are persecuting**. The implication could not be clearer. If Jesus were the one speaking to Saul, then Jesus must be alive, and if He were alive then what he claimed was obviously true. He is the Messiah.

26:16-18. Paul then explained his commission to be a witness to the Gentiles. Paul's mission was threefold: (1) to **open** the **eyes** of unbelievers, (2) to turn them from darkness to light, from Satan to God, and (3) to witness so that they could receive **forgiveness of sins** and an **inheritance** among those who had been **sanctified**. Sometimes the verb **sanctified** means "to be consecrated," "to be dedicated" to a certain task, "to be set apart for God," and can have the practical sense of growth in personal purity as a Christian set apart for God (see Jn 17:17; 2Tm 2:21). But often it is essentially synonymous with "being saved" (as in Ac 20:32; 1Co 1:2; 6:11), and this is the sense here. The effective cause of this supernatural transforming experience was **faith**. Of course, in describing his conversion experience in this manner, Paul hoped that both Festus and Agrippa would become convicted and repent.

26:19-21. Paul said that his Jewish opponents had tried to kill him because he was obedient to the heavenly vision. Paul gave a concise summary of his preaching. He challenged people to **repent** (lit., to change one's mind, and in the context of Acts, to specifically change one's mind about Jesus, cf. 3:13-19, especially, 3:19, and **turn to God** (based on the Heb. concept of repentance, meaning "to turn around toward God"), and perform **deeds appropriate to repentance** (the fruit of repentance being changed lives and accompanying good deeds). This is not salvation by works but a practical truth that a changed life is the inevitable result of genuine faith.

26:22-23. Paul insisted that his message was consistent with the promises of the prophets and Moses. There is little evidence that early (intertestamental) Judaism believed that the Messiah would suffer, die, and conquer death. Paul, however, though he did not cite specific texts, claimed that the OT predicted the concept of a suffering Messiah and the resurrection. Likely Paul had passages such as Is 52:13–53:12 and Ps 16:10 in mind. Jesus' correction of the thinking of the two men on the road to Emmaus supports Paul's understanding of the OT (cf. Lk 24:25-27).

26:24. Festus charged that Paul was so advanced in his training in Judaism that his thinking was ridiculous. The practical and rationalistic Romans did not believe in life after death. Longenecker has this insight about the timeless truth of Festus's charge: "Down through the ages Festus's response has been echoed by men and women too trapped by the natural to open to the supernatural, too confined by the 'practical' to care about life everlasting" (Longenecker, "Acts," 554).

26:25-27. Paul denied the charge of insanity, and appealed to Agrippa for support. He was sure that Agrippa had heard about the death and resurrection of Jesus. Plus, Agrippa must certainly have believed in the prophets. By asking Agrippa a direct question, Paul the prisoner, became Paul the persuader.

26:28. Paul's direct question upset Agrippa. Agrippa's response has been interpreted in a way that implies he was close to a decision: "Almost thou persuadest me to be a Christian" (KJV). His response was actually somewhat cynical: "Are you trying to convince me to become a Christian?" Agrippa was ridiculing Paul for thinking that he could convince him to become a Christian with such a brief argument (see comments about the word "Christian" at 11:26).

26:29. Paul's answer contained a bit of irony. He wished that all who were present would become like him, that is spiritually free but not a prisoner in chains.

(3) Result of the Defense: A Declaration of Paul's Innocence (26:30-32)

26:30-32. Agrippa, Festus, Bernice, and the others who were present left the room to discuss the case. All agreed that Paul had not committed a capital offense. Luke recorded the words of Agrippa to vindicate both Paul and Christianity of sedition.

Paul was God's attested servant (apostle). In his account of Paul's journey to Rome, Luke showed how the sovereign Lord providentially protected his chosen servant and those who were with Paul.

3. His Witness En Route to Rome (27:1–28:15)

a. Aboard Ship (27:1-44)

After the hearing before Festus and Agrippa, Paul was placed in the custody of a centurion and put on a ship sailing for Rome. The journey was uneventful until they attempted to sail from Fair Havens for a safer harbor for the winter; then the ship was caught in a powerful storm. When the crew gave up hope, Paul emerged as a courageous Christian and assured the crew no one would be lost. The ship foundered on a reef, but all on board made it safely to land on the island of Malta.

27:1-3. Under circumstances Paul could not have anticipated, he began his journey to Rome. When he was turned over to a centurion for transfer to Rome, God used two men to assure Paul of His sovereign control over the situation. The pronoun **we** indicates that Luke was with him.

Aristarchus, a believer from Thessalonica, also made the trip with Paul. In Col 4:10, Paul referred to Aristarchus as his "fellow prisoner," so he apparently traveled all the way to Rome with Paul. Neither Luke nor Aristarchus was given free passage, so they probably paid their own expenses. Plus, it was risky to associate with a prisoner, so both men were obviously dedicated to the Lord and to Paul.

Paul and other prisoners were placed in the custody of Julius, a centurion, who belonged to the Augustan (Imperial) Regiment, which was a special corps of men who acted as liaison officers between the Emperor and the provinces.

They sailed on a ship from **Adramyttium**, a seaport on the northeast shore of the Aegean Sea, near Troas. Instead of sailing directly across the Mediterranean Sea, they sailed north to **Sidon** to perhaps unload cargo and pick up supplies.

In the providence of God, the centurion charged with the security of the prisoners was gracious and not brutal. He allowed Paul to visit his friends who provided him with supplies for the voyage. Passengers and prisoners were responsible for their own supplies.

27:4-6. When they left Sidon the voyage became difficult. The strong winter **winds** made progress difficult, so they sailed north of Cyprus for protection from northwestern winds. After they passed Cilicia and Pamphylia, they sailed for Myra. When they reached Myra, the centurion transferred the prisoners to a ship from Alexandria that was sailing to Rome. The ship was probably carrying grain. Egypt was the breadbasket for Rome.

27:7-8. The voyage became increasingly difficult as they sailed west, but they finally reached **Fair Havens** on the island of Crete. Here there was debate and indecision.

27:9-12. Since so much time had been lost on the voyage to Fair Havens, sailing had become dangerous. The reference to **the fast** identified the time of the year. The **fast** was part of the Day of Atonement, so it was late September or October. Winter was approaching. Most sailing was discontinued from November to March.

Paul was an experienced traveler. He began to **admonish** the captain and the crew, "strongly recommending" they stay put for the winter and not attempt to reach another port. His counsel was ignored. The captain of the ship persuaded the centurion they should sail for another harbor for the **winter**. He recommended Phoenix, which has a protected harbor **facing southwest and northwest**. Its location would provide the ship with better protection than the harbor at Fair Havens.

27:13. When a light wind came up from the south, they weighed anchor to sail for Phoenix, keeping as close to the shoreline as possible.

27:14-15. The decision to leave port was a mistake. They had not sailed far when the ship was hit broadside with **a violent wind, called Euraquilo**. The wind was a dreaded "northeastern." Luke described it as **violent** (*typhonikos*, "typhonic") in force. It was so powerful, the sailors lost control of the ship and were **driven along** by the wind.

27:16-17. The wind drove the ship 25 miles south to the island of Clauda. On the southern side of the island they found enough **shelter** from the wind to secure the lifeboat that was towed behind the ship. The use of "we" suggests some of the passengers may have assisted the crew.

They also used rope cables to secure the hull of the ship. Polhill lists the four possible ways they may have used the cables to make the timbers of the ship more secure (*Acts*, 521, n. 23). One, they could have passed width-wise under the ship on the outside of the hull. Two, they could have run the cables length-wise around the length of the ship on the outside. Three, the cables could have run width-wise across the inside of the ship. Four, the cables could have run length-wise inside the hull from bow to stern.

The crew was working frantically to keep the ship from running **aground on the shallows of Syrtis**. The shallows were a series of deadly sandbars off the coast of North Africa infamous as a graveyard for vessels. The ship was about 400 miles from where they started (Bock, *Acts*, 735–36).

27:18-20. On the second day of the storm, they began to **jettison** cargo (probably some of the grain; cf. 27:38). When the storm continued into the third day, the crew became so desperate they threw **tackle** overboard. Luke did not specify what equipment was jettisoned. The purpose was to make the ship lighter, so it would ride higher and take on less water from the waves that were apparently crashing over the sides of the ship.

None of their efforts were successful. The storm continued its relentless assault on the ship. After several days without seeing the sun or stars, they lost all hope and resigned themselves to death at sea.

27:21-26. In this hopeless situation, Paul emerged as man of courage and common sense. Because the ship had been tossed around on the sea for several days, all on board had lost their appetite. No one appreciates someone who says, "I told you so," but that is exactly what Paul said, **Men, you ought to have followed my advice** . . .

He assured them no one would drown at sea. Paul was not a divine man who could control nature. The ship would be lost, but there would be no loss of life. How did Paul know this? An angelic messenger of God appeared to him. The angel assured Paul he would **stand before Caesar**, and because it was God's intention to protect Paul, He would also protect all of those who were with Paul. The angel's reassurance served as a promise to Paul that God would fulfill what He had previously revealed to Paul about testifying in both Jerusalem and Rome.

Paul urged the men to **keep up** their **courage**. That would take faith, the kind of faith Paul had in God and his Word. We do not know if any of the sailors or soldiers became believers, but it is reasonable to assume that some did.

Paul's speech of salvation ended with a second warning about the loss of the ship. He revealed exactly how the ship would wreck. It would **run aground on a certain island**. That was a remarkable prediction since in their present location hitting the island of Malta would be "like finding a needle in a haystack" (Bock, *Acts*, 738).

27:27-29. On the fourteenth night, the storm had driven the ship into the **Adriatic Sea** (sea of Adria—the body of water that forms the east coast of Italy). Polhill identifies this area as the Ionian sea and the north central Mediterranean sea between Greece and Italy, extending south to Crete and Malta (*Acts*, 524–25). The storm had driven the ship 475 miles from Clauda to Malta.

About midnight, the sailors sensed they were near land and began taking soundings. This would involve throwing a rope overboard with some kind of a weight on it. The depth of the first sounding was twenty fathoms (120 feet) and the second fifteen fathoms (90 feet). They were obviously nearing land. To keep the ship pointed in the direction of land, they dropped four anchors from the stern (the back of the boat) and **wished for daybreak**. They hoped that by the light of day they could determine their location.

27:30-32. The sailors had had enough. They decided to abandon ship in the lifeboat but under the pretense of putting out anchors from the bow (front) of the ship. Paul knew what they were doing and warned the centurion: **Unless these men remain in the ship, you yourselves cannot be saved**. Paul had been right so far, so the sailors cut the ropes to the lifeboat, allowing it to drift away from the ship.

27:33-34. Paul was not only a man of incredible faith but also of common sense. The men who had been struggling to save the ship had not eaten full meals, or meals at regular times, for 14 days. He urged all on board **to take some food** and assured them they would survive. The expression, **not a hair from the head of any of you will perish**, is a Hebrew idiom for being preserved without harm (see 1Sm 14:45).

Stott says that Paul's counsel shows him as a well-rounded Christian. "Here then are aspects of Paul's character which endear him to us as an integrated Christian, who combined spirituality with sanity, faith and works. He believed that God would keep his promises and had the courage to say grace in the presence of a crowd of hard-bitten pagans . . . What a man! He was a man of God and of action, a man of the Spirit and of common sense" (*Acts*, 392).

27:35-38. Paul encouraged the others to eat by first giving **thanks to God** and eating bread. This was not a communion meal. That would not give those on board the nourishment needed to survive the ship wreck. All 276 followed Paul's advice and ate. Ships like this could hold up to 600 people, so 276 was not a representative number (Bock, *Acts*, 740). Confident they would not perish, they lightened the ship even more by throwing the remaining grain overboard.

27:39-44. At first light the sailors spotted land and decided to beach the ship if possible. They cut the lines to the anchors, freed the rudders (most ships had a dual-paddle mechanism connected by a crossbar operated by a sailor for piloting a ship—but this was dismantled in the hope of the wind driving them shoreward), and hoisted the foresail (a small sail on the front of the boat) to guide the ship to land. But before they hit land, they hit a reef. The bow stuck on the reef, and the ship was pounded by the surf. Realizing that if the ship broke up, the prisoners might escape, the soldiers planned to kill them since they would be held accountable if they escaped.

The centurion intervened in order to save Paul. He ordered those who could to swim for shore and the rest to float to shore on planks and other debris from the ship. All made it safely to land.

b. At Malta and Again En Route to Rome (28:1-15)

After Paul's long interlude from the ministry, God resumed the powerful works through Paul that the apostle previously experienced, but which were put on hold during Paul's imprisonment in Caesarea by the Sea. These proved to be an enormous blessing to the people of Malta, and though the text does not say it, the miracles no doubt served to add great effectiveness to Paul's witness. An added effect was the aid received by the castaways that enabled them to continue their journey.

28:1. Once the crew and passengers reached shore, they discovered they were on the island of **Malta**, about 50 miles south of Sicily. Malta, 18 miles long and 8 miles wide, was first colonized by the Phoenicians around 1000 BC but captured by the Romans in 218 BC. The islanders, however, enjoyed a measure of local autonomy with their own elected governor.

28:2-3. Luke identified the islanders as **natives** (*barbaroi*, an onomatopoeic word from which is transliterated the Eng. word "barbarians"). This term does not mean they were savages. It means they could not speak Greek, and the language they did speak sounded like "bar-bar-bar-bar" to those who spoke Greek. They were, however, thoughtful and helpful. They built a fire for the waterlogged survivors, and Paul helped by gathering wood for fuel. However, as he was adding wood to the fire, the heat drove a **viper** out of the wood, and it struck Paul on the hand. The term (*echidna*) does not identify the species but usually refers to a poisonous viper (BDAG, 419). The observation that there are no poisonous snakes on Malta today does not undermine the integrity of Luke's account. There could have been poisonous snakes on Malta in the first century.

28:4-5. Thinking Paul would surely die, the islanders concluded he must have been a **murderer** and though he survived the shipwreck, he was now getting what he deserved. This is divine justice. The reference to **justice** (Greek, *dike*) is a reference to the Greek goddess "Justice," often depicted in Roman times as holding balanced scales, and is not the theoretical concept of justice, though that is a related idea. Paul, however, did not die. God had a plan for Paul, and the sovereign Lord protected his chosen servant.

28:6. When Paul did not die after a reasonable amount of time, the islanders **changed their minds** and foolishly decided Paul must be **a god**. Actually, he was under God's protection, miraculously keeping him from the deadly effects of the venom of the viper.

28:7-10. The **leading** (*protos*) **man** of the island was **Publius**. He extended hospitality to Paul and his companions (probably Luke and the other believers) for three days. Publius's father was sick with a fever and dysentery. "Malta fever" was a common disorder not limited to Malta alone and was caused by drinking the unsterilized milk of diseased goats (Longenecker, "Acts," 565). Paul cured Publius' father by praying for him and placing his hands on him. This is the only instance in Acts where healing is brought about by both prayer and the laying on of hands. As in numerous other instances in Acts, the miracle provided Paul an opportunity for greater ministry. It appears that Luke began to assist Paul by establishing a clinic for medical care rather than an extensive healing ministry. This is suggested in three ways: First, Luke used two different verbs to describe their work—*iasato* (from *iaomai*, "healed," v. 8) and *etherapeuonto* (from *therapeuo*, "to heal," or here in the passive, "getting cured," v. 9). In the first case the word would refer to miraculous healing and the second to curing by medical means. Second, the people expressed their gratitude to both Paul and Luke (**they also honored *us***, v. 10). Third, they honored them with **many marks of respect**, a phrase used of payment of professional fees, such as to a physician, just as Luke was.

After two years of the apostle's imprisonment, this was a reaffirmation that God was still with Paul. It is possible that the miracles gave Paul confirmation that he had made the right decision in appealing to Caesar. The islanders expressed their appreciation with gifts and adequate supplies for the final leg of the journey to Rome.

28:11. After three months on Malta, Paul and his companions were put on an **Alexandrian ship**, registered in Alexandria, Egypt. The ship's figurehead was twin gods. The **Twin Brothers**, Castor and Pollux, were thought to be the protectors of seamen (Polhill, *Acts*, 535). These two were the mythical sons of Zeus and a woman named Leda who was raped by Zeus. In Latin, they were called "the Gemini," and they came to be viewed as a philanthropic pair, especially favorably inclined to travelers and sailors.

28:12-13. They sailed from Malta to Syracuse on the island of Sicily and stayed there for three days. From Syracuse they sailed to Rhegium (on the far south "toe" of the "boot" of Italy) and then to **Puteoli**, both on the mainland of Italy.

28:14-15. Before going on to Rome, Paul was invited to stay with believers at Puteoli, 130 miles south of Rome. Paul and his companions accepted the invitation and stayed for seven days. The presence of a church in Puteoli shows the extent of the gospel impact. Paul had never been to Italy, so the church there was not started by him. Luke does not give the reason they stayed in Puteoli, but it was most likely for rest. The sea journey was over; they would walk the rest of the way to Rome.

After Paul left Puteoli, believers came from Rome and met him at the **Market** [Forum] **of Appius** and **Three Inns**. The Forum **of Appius** was 43 miles south of Rome and on the Appian Way, a major road leading straight to Rome. **Three Inns** was ten miles north of the Forum of Appius and 33 miles from Rome (Polhill, *Acts*, 537).

Paul was Luke's hero, yet he was still only a man. Even Paul must have been apprehensive as he neared Rome. What would happen to a Jewish tentmaker in the citadel of Roman imperial power? Luke said **he thanked God and took courage**. Something happened to encourage Paul's heart. What was it? It was the believers in Rome walking miles to meet Paul before he ever set foot in the city. Barclay says that Paul was encouraged because he realized he was not alone (*Acts*, 209).

4. His Witness in Rome (28:16-31)

a. The Setting for It (28:16-22)

God was with Paul when he arrived in Rome. Though a prisoner, he was treated with respect and granted limited freedom. Paul used his privileges to meet with his Jewish countrymen two times. The response was disappointing. In the first meeting they were neutral. They had not received any reports, either positive or negative, about Paul. They wanted to hear more about what he believed. In a second meeting, though some were persuaded that Jesus is the fulfillment of Israel's hopes, most refused to believe. Paul recognized their unbelief as the fulfillment of prophecy and justification for his mission to Gentiles. Acts ends as it began with the proclamation of the kingdom of God; however, the messenger was different. Instead of Jesus teaching His followers about the kingdom of God, Paul taught about the kingdom of God and the Lord Jesus Christ.

28:16. When Paul and his companions entered Rome, Paul was not brutalized by Roman guards.

He was chained to a guard but allowed to live in his private quarters. Paul had accomplished part of his mission. He was not treated like a revolutionary or considered a threat to Rome, nor was the Christian faith that Paul represented. The "we" sections end in v. 16 indicating that Luke likely left Paul at this point to serve as the apostle's emissary someplace (Col 4:10-15, esp. v. 14), not that he had abandoned him.

28:17-22. Paul did not wait long to summon his countrymen. After only three days he requested a meeting with **the leading men of the Jews. Leading men** refers to Jews of high social and religious standing. He began by assuring them he was not a criminal. Jews in Jerusalem had charged that Paul was opposed to the law of Moses, but he assured his countrymen he was not an enemy of his own people, and he was not against Jewish customs. From Paul's perspective, though he was a believer in Jesus as the Messiah of Israel, this certainly did not mean that he was no longer Jewish. However, because of the complaints of the Jewish religious leaders, Paul had been turned over to the Romans.

Paul recounted his interaction with the Roman authorities (Felix, Ac 24, and Festus and Herod Agrippa II, Ac 25). Those rulers wanted to release Paul after a hearing. They had not heard any evidence that convinced them Paul had violated Roman law. When Paul said **there was no ground for putting me to death** (v. 18), he revealed that Jerusalem's religious leaders wanted him executed, not merely punished or imprisoned. Paul was forced to appeal to Caesar because of their protests.

Paul assured the leaders he had nothing against his own people (v. 19). The Romans had nothing against Paul, and he had done nothing against his own people. He had no disagreement with his own people other than about their need to embrace Jesus as their Messiah (Stott, *Acts*, 398). Paul's purpose for calling the meeting was to get acquainted with the leaders and explain why he was a prisoner. He was bound with a chain because he believed **the hope of Israel**. This phrase refers to the hope that the Messiah would come and fulfill God's promises to Israel. Paul's point was that this hope for the Messiah had already been fulfilled with the coming of Jesus of Nazareth. Thus, he was imprisoned only for believing that Israel's hope had already come and not because he denied any essential tenet of Judaism.

Though they had not heard anything specifically about Paul, they had heard about the new faith, so they requested a second meeting to hear Paul's opinion on **this sect.** The use of the term **sect** (*hairesis*, from which "heresies" derives) means "a group that holds tenets distinctive to it, *sect, party, school faction*" (BDAG, 27). It is the Greek equivalent of the Hebrew word *minim, minut* (kind, species, heretic, heresy), which came to be used in Rabbinic literature for Jewish followers of Jesus. It implies they considered this new faith a movement within Judaism, but a movement that was dangerous and potentially promulgated error.

b. The Substance of It (28:23)

28:23. On the day of the scheduled meeting, an even greater number of Jews came to Paul's rented house. Paul explained how Jesus fulfilled Israel's hopes for the **kingdom of God**. He appealed to both **the Law of Moses and from the Prophets.** If he were to persuade Jews that Jesus was the fulfillment of Israel's messianic and kingdom expectations, it was essential for him to connect Jesus to the Hebrew Scriptures. It was an extended meeting. He spoke from morning until evening.

c. The Sequel to It (28:24-31)

(1) In Regard to the Need for a Decision (28:24-27)

Some were convinced, but most refuseed to believe. The divided response is typical of the Jewish response to the Christian message throughout the book of Acts (cf. 13:42-45; 17:1-5, 11-14; 19:8-10).

28:24-27. The Jews of Rome disagreed not only with Paul; they **did not agree with one another**, and begin leaving after Paul warned them of making the same mistake as their closed-minded ancestors. He quoted from Is 6:9-10 (vv. 26-27) where the inspired prophet warned his generation of divine retribution for rejecting his message. The context of the warning was the call of Isaiah to his prophetic ministry, when the Lord forewarned the prophet he would face stubborn resistance. Israel rejected the prophet's message because their heart **HAS BECOME DULL**. The word **DULL** (*epachynthe*) literally means "to make fat, well-nourished." The figurative meaning is "to make impervious or to make gross, dull" (BDAG, 790). The result was they could not **HEAR WITH THEIR EARS** or **SEE WITH THEIR EYES**. Paul told his countrymen they risked becoming like the Jewish people of Isaiah's generation who came under divine retribution for their deliberate rejection of God's message through the prophet. As did Isaiah, Paul had faithfully proclaimed the Word of the Lord; if they rejected it, they would come under the judgment of God. This meant they would pass a point where they would never be able to return to the Lord and be spiritually restored ("healed," v. 27).

(2) In Regard to Paul's Audience (28:28)

28:28-29. Paul said the refusal of the Jews to accept Paul's messages justified his turning **to the Gentiles** (v. 28). God's gracious plan of redemption cannot be frustrated even by the unbelief of His chosen people. Their unbelief gave Paul the opportunity to offer salvation to Gentiles. Paul developed the wisdom of God's plan of salvation further in Rm 11 (see the comments there). He said the response of the Gentiles to the gospel would make Israel jealous and lead eventually to the salvation of God's chosen people (Rm 11:11, 25-27). As Bock points out, Ac 28:28 does not state that God has permanently abandoned the Jewish nation, only that the gospel will be preached to the Gentiles and the Gentiles will respond, which means at the very least Gentiles will be more responsive initially than the Jewish people (*Acts*, 756–57). (The ms evidence does not favor including v. 29 in the original text. The information has already been given in v. 25, so nothing is lost by excluding the verse from the original text.)

(3) In Regard to Time (28:30)

28:30. That the Lord fulfilled His promise to protect Paul is seen in the unusual freedom he was granted as a prisoner. He was not restrained in a prison cell. For two years, he lived **in his own rented quarters** and was able to receive visitors. **All** included Jews and Gentiles. Luke did not explain how Paul could afford his own quarters. Most likely he paid the rent from the gifts of Christians, such as the Philippians. While a prisoner, Paul wrote to the Philippians and thanked them for their generous support (Php 4:15-20).

(4) In Regard to Emphasis (28:31)

28:31. Acts ends on a note of triumph. The Word of God was being proclaimed **with all openness** (boldness), **unhindered** in Rome, the capital of the empire. As Paul testified during his second imprisonment, the messenger may be chained but not the message (2Tm 2:9).

The book of Acts also ends as it began, with the proclamation of the kingdom of God. In Ac 1, the resurrected Lord taught His followers about the kingdom of God. The setting was Jerusalem. Thirty years later, Paul taught about the kingdom of God and the Lord Jesus Christ. The setting was different. Now, it was Rome. Jesus' witnesses did as He commanded. Filled with the Holy Spirit, they proclaimed the gospel in Jerusalem, Judea, and Samaria, and to the entire world.

Luke did not reveal what happened to Paul, indicating that the book was likely written before Paul's release. The circumstances of his imprisonment suggest he was innocent of the charges of sedition. He was not a zealous revolutionary. He was a devoted and courageous follower of the Lord Jesus Christ. Paul was Luke's personal hero but only because God was with him. Bock is correct. In reality "God is the hero of Acts . . ." (*Acts*, 760). The Lord Jesus Christ is building His church, and all the forces of hell cannot overpower it.

BIBLIOGRAPHY

Bock, Darrell L. *Acts.* Baker Exegetical Commentary on the New Testament. Grand Rapids, MI: Baker, 2007.

Bruce, F. F. *The Book of Acts.* The New International Commentary on the New Testament. Grand Rapids, MI: Eerdmans, 1979.

Hemer, Colin. *The Book of Acts in the Setting of Hellenistic History.* Winona Lake, IN: Eisenbraun's, 1990.

Kistemaker, Simon J. *Acts.* The New Testament Commentary. Grand Rapids, MI: Baker, 1990.

Liefeld, Walter L. *Interpreting the Book of Acts.* Guides to New Testament Exegesis. Grand Rapids, MI: Baker, 1995.

Longenecker, Richard N. "The Acts of the Apostles." In *John, Acts.* Vol. 9 of The Expositor's Bible Commentary. Edited by Frank E. Gaebelein. Grand Rapids, MI: Zondervan, 1981.

Polhill, John B. *Acts.* The New American Commentary. Nashville: Broadman Press, 1992.

Stott, John R. W. *The Message of Acts.* Edited by John R. W. Stott and J. A. Motyer. Downers Grove, IL: InterVarsity, 1990.

Witherington III, Ben. *The Acts of the Apostles: A Socio-Rhetorical Commentary.* Grand Rapids, MI: Eerdmans, 1998.

ROMANS

MICHAEL G. VANLANINGHAM

INTRODUCTION

Author. There are scholars who deny that the apostle Paul wrote all the letters ascribed to him, but virtually no one disputes that Romans was his letter. Pauline authorship of Romans has been affirmed by even the most critical scholars of the last 200 years.

Date. According to Rm 15, Paul's travel plans included three places: Jerusalem, Rome, and Spain (15:23-29). Paul explicitly mentioned his intent to go to Jerusalem to deposit the proceeds from the offering gathered by the Gentile churches in the Mediterranean world (Ac 19:21; 20:16; Rm 15:25-27), then to go to Rome (Ac 19:21; Rm 1:11-13; 15:24, 28), and then to Spain (Rm 15:24, 28). The Acts passages are found in the context of Paul's third missionary journey. He was probably in Greece when he wrote Romans (Ac 20:2-3), more than likely Corinth, which had been his base previously. Paul commends several who lived in or around Corinth, such as Phoebe who lived in Cenchrea, about seven miles southeast of Corinth (16:1), and Gaius (Rm 16:23; 1Co 1:14). These points suggest a Corinthian origination of the letter. It is intriguing to think of Paul walking through Corinth, observing the immorality there, then writing about the decadence of the world in Rm 1, or through the business quarter of Corinth where the famous Corinthian pottery was made, and writing about the potter and the clay in Rm 9:20-21. A good estimate for the date of the book is AD 57.

Recipients. Paul wrote the letter to the Christians in Rome. The population of the city in Paul's day is estimated at between one and four million. This imprecision is due in part to the large number of slaves in the city who were not included in the censuses. Possibly as much as 60 percent of the population was slaves, and when Paul begins with the words "Paul, a bond-servant of Christ Jesus," he would have established rapport immediately with a good number in the church who were surely slaves. The Jewish community in Rome may have been as large as 40,000, influential in the economy, and perhaps the politics and arts of the great city.

Those to whom Paul wrote were believers already. Although in the early chapters Paul explores the plight of humankind apart from Christ, he was probably not emphasizing these points to evangelize his readers. Rather, he wrote to those who were "the called of Jesus Christ . . . who are beloved of God in Rome, called as saints" (1:6-7), and his words were intended to influence true believers there.

There is debate over whether Paul wrote primarily to Gentile believers, Jewish believers, or to both. In some places he clearly addressed Gentiles in the church (1:5-6; 11:13; 15:7-9, 14-21); in others Jewish believers (2:17; 4:1; 6:14-15; 7:1, 4; and see the Jewish names in the list in 16:3, 7, 11). The most plausible view is that Paul wrote to both, and on occasion specifically addressed one group, then the other (1:7; 11:12-24; 14:1–15:13).

Purpose. Paul does not say explicitly why he wrote Romans, but there are hints. Serving as "bookends" for this epistle are almost identical verses, 1:5 and 16:26, where Paul says his apostolic commission (1:5) and the gospel (16:25-26) exist "to bring about the obedience of faith among all the Gentiles." This "bookending" suggests that Paul's purpose was to provide warrant for his mission to Spain and for the Roman Christians to support him. In addition, he desired to minister to them and with them (1:10-13), and to solicit support from them (15:24). But the closest we have to a purpose statement for the epistle is in 15:15-16, where Paul writes that his intent was to remind them of some truths. This reminder came with the backing of his own apostolic commission (15:15), which, he notes, was a commission to evangelize primarily the Gentiles (15:16-20). The apostle then presented his itinerary, which included a visit to Rome to seek their financial assistance to execute the commission to Spain (15:24, 26-29). So Paul's purpose may have been to help the church clarify her doctrine and instill in her a new sense of urgency about the need for evangelizing the lost. This would motivate the church in Rome to provide support for Paul's outreach to Spain.

How do the diverse elements of the epistle fit with this overarching purpose? Chapters 1–3 present humanity's desperate need for the gospel (1:16-17). Each one has sinned and stands under the condemnation of God as a result of it—and no one can change his status through his own efforts. Thankfully there is hope. It is grounded in God's provision of His own righteousness, given freely to those who trust in the atoning death of His Son (3:21-31). The patriarch Abraham illustrates the nature and importance of faith, in that he was saved by faith and not by works (chap. 4). Chapters 5–8 present the extraordinary results of being right with God, results that the non-Christian world needs and that the Christian world should broadcast. Chapters 9–11 deal with the problem of Israel. One might argue that if God made promises to Israel in the OT and broke them by focusing His plans on the Church, then how could He be counted on to fulfill His promises in Christ? If God could not be counted on to keep those promises, why bother to evangelize? Paul argues that God *was* keeping His promises to Israel just as He always had, and that He could be trusted to keep them in Christ as well. In chaps. 12–16, the main theme is that of church unity. A church gutted by strife would be ill-suited to sustain a missionary venture for very long. Paul's goal for their unity is that they might glorify God (spread His name and enhance His reputation), and he prays to that end (15:5-6).

Excursus: The New Perspective on Paul. As an important side note, since the late 1970s there has been a controversial approach to Paul's theology called "the New Perspective" on Paul. In a book entitled *Paul and Palestinian Judaism*, E. P. Sanders explores the relationship of Paul's theology to first-century Judaism. He maintains that there was a considerable amount of grace in Judaism because God chose Israel by His grace to be His covenant people—to be saved. They kept the law (*nomos* in Gk.) to "stay in" that relationship, but not to "get in." Sanders coined the phrase "covenantal nomism" (staying in the covenant by faithfully observing the *nomos*, the law) to describe this belief. He argues, somewhat surprisingly, that this is also *Paul's* view of salvation in Christ: Christians are saved on the basis of election, but they uphold that status by good works (a dubious understanding of Paul). So (says Sanders), why would Paul criticize Judaism for being legalistic when in fact it was not? Sanders says that Paul either misrepresented Judaism as being legalistic when it was not, in contrast to the traditional understanding of Paul, or that Paul faulted a form of Judaism that is no longer extant, which in any case the apostle believed was flawed because it excluded Christ. If Sanders is right, then a new interpretive grid is necessary to understand the apostle's criticism of Judaism. But Sanders does not propose what that new grid should be, and remains uncertain as to what exactly the apostle Paul was doing in his polemic against Judaism.

Into this vacuum stepped J. D. G. Dunn. Dunn was not satisfied with Sanders's assertion that Paul misrepresented Judaism or rejected it just because it omitted Christ. Dunn alleges that Paul viewed Judaism as being ethnically too narrow. The "works of the law" that Paul opposed (especially, but not only, circumcision, observance of holy days, and the dietary laws) were the identity markers for the Jewish people whereby they preserved their distinctiveness and privileged status as God's covenant people. Paul, according to Dunn, was actually opposing their covenantal nomism. When the apostle wrote, "by the works of the Law no flesh will be justified in His [God's] sight" (3:20, 28; cf. Gl 2:16; 3:2, 5, 10), he opposed these works of the law because with them the Jewish people perpetuated a sense of isolationism and elitism that excluded the Gentiles from the covenant people of God. With Christ came a shift in God's redemptive program. Salvation was no longer confined to those who practice the covenant identity markers (i.e., solely the Jewish people), but became open to all by faith. It is therefore wrong to require Gentiles to do these works to enter into the covenant community. For this reason, Paul opposed such elitism as well as the imposition of "works of the law" upon Gentile converts, a problem at the center of the theological storm in Galatians. But once again, Dunn, like Sanders, does not see the "works of the law" as entrance requirements or as legalistic acts.

A third major player in the New Perspective is N. T. Wright, whose approach to Paul parallels much of what is found in Dunn but arguably with more nuancing. Wright, like Dunn, is heavily indebted to Sanders, and argues that Paul's view of salvation is less about how to get in to the covenant faithfulness of God and more about the assurance of being in that covenant. In Wright's thinking, "justification" is about God's recognition of those who are in the covenant by His faithfulness and their assurance of this status, rather than about God's declaration of a sinner's righteousness in Christ and His effecting that status. "Righteousness" for Wright is about the acquittal of the sinner as a result of God's decision, rather than about the holiness of God being imputed to the sinner. "Works of the law" are about actions that one who is in the covenant by grace shows in response to that grace, rather than about attempts to establish a right standing with God through one's own efforts.

Sanders, Dunn, and Wright have been criticized on a number of grounds. First, Sanders is partly right but mainly wrong on his understanding of the extent of grace in first-century Judaism. A considerable amount of evidence has been gathered to indicate that Early Judaism was much more synergistic than Sanders recognizes, with some texts affirming God's grace but many affirming the need for obedience to the law for "staying in" salvation. Even in Sanders's view, works play a determinative role in the outcome of salvation.

Second, Dunn insists that Paul criticized the Jewish people for their "works of the law" that barred Gentiles from being part of the covenant people of God. But Paul repeatedly criticized the Jewish people not for their exclusivism, which was shattered by the coming of Christ, but for their failure to keep the law by doing its works, which led to their condemnation (2:2-3, 22-23, 25-27; 4:1-12).

Third, Wright's view inherits all the problems of Sanders's and Dunn's, and collapses under the weight of the passages in Romans that indicate that justification *does something to the sinner*. It cannot be seen simply as an expression of God's *recognition* that one is in the covenant people. Romans 5:1, for example, indicates that justification *produces* peace with God. Righteousness is indeed *imputed* to individuals who have trusted Christ. In Rm 4:7-8, Paul links imputed righteousness with "lawless deeds that have been forgiven, sins that have been covered, and sins that have not been taken into account by the Lord."

Finally, and more generally, salvation for the Jewish people and Gentiles alike was promised *not* through the Mosaic covenant (the law of Moses), but through the Abrahamic covenant. Covenantal nomism fails precisely because the Mosaic covenant could not be kept by the Jewish people nor by anyone else (see Dt 31:29), and because it was not designed to ensure salvation either in terms of getting in *or* staying in a right standing with God (cf. Rm 3:19-20; 4:15; 7:5; 8:3). The way both Jews and Gentiles find salvation is through receiving the blessings of the Abrahamic covenant, and that happens only through faith (Gn 15:6; Rm 4:13-17; Gl 3:6-14)—after the cross, faith *in Christ*. Works performed in compliance with the Mosaic covenant are inadequate to make one right with God, and this is the fatal flaw in Judaism that Paul addresses in Romans and Galatians.

OUTLINE

I. Sin: The Need for Being Right with God (1:1–3:20)
   A. The Impact of the Gospel (1:1-17)
   B. The Need for the Gospel (1:18–3:20)

II. Justification by Faith: The Means for Being Right with God (3:21–4:25)
   A. Righteousness Is Available from God (3:21-26)
   B. Righteousness Is Appropriated by Faith Alone (3:27–4:25)

III. Blessings: The Results of Being Right with God (5:1–8:39)
   A. Christians Can Boast in God (5:1-11)
   B. Christians Can Live a Life of Security (5:12-21)
   C. Christians Can Live a Life Free from the Absolute Domination of Sin (6:1–7:25)
   D. Christians Have Life in the Holy Spirit (8:1-39)

IV. Vindication: The Jewish People and the Problems with Being Right with God (9:1–11:36)
   A. God Has Not Broken His Word to Israel (9:1-29)
   B. God Has Not Cheated Israel (9:30–10:21)
   C. God Has Not Rejected Israel (11:1-10)
   D. Israel Is Not Lost Forever (11:11-36)
V. Application: The Implications of Being Right with God (12:1–15:33)
   A. The Implications for the Christian's Spiritual Commitment (12:1-2)
   B. The Implications for the Christian's Life in the Body of Christ (12:3-13)
   C. The Implications for the Christian's Life in Relation to the Secular World (12:14–13:14)
   D. The Implications for the Christian's Life in His Relationships with Weaker and Differing Christians (14:1–15:13)
   E. The Implications for the Support of Paul's Ministry (15:14-33)
VI. Paul's Concluding Mandates (16:1-27)
   A. Appreciate Christian Workers (16:1-16)
   B. Avoid Contentious People (16:17-20a)
   C. Be Encouraged by Christian Leaders (16:20b-23)
   D. Glorify God (16:25-27)

COMMENTARY ON ROMANS

I. Sin: The Need for Being Right with God (1:1–3:20)

A. The Impact of the Gospel (1:1-17)

1:1-3. Paul begins his letter with a brief summary of the gospel he proclaimed and the purpose of his apostolic ministry. **Called** refers to the effectual, divine calling as opposed to human self-appointment. An **apostle** was a special messenger whose task was to spread the **gospel** message that had continuity with the OT. As a **descendant of David**, Jesus Christ could lay claim to the throne of David. In the Davidic Covenant, God promised that a son of David would rule Israel forever and provide security for her (2 Sm 7:8-17; 1Ch 17:1-15). None of David's descendants qualified, but Mt 1:1 identifies who it is: "The record of the genealogy of Jesus the Messiah, *the son of David* . . ." (my emphasis).

1:4-5. Jesus was **declared the Son of God with power**. The resurrection signaled a change not in His essence but in His function and manifestation now as the "Son-of-God-with-Power" (Ps 2:7; Ac 13:33; Heb 5:5). Paul's apostleship existed to **bring about the obedience of faith**, which has an almost identical expression in 16:26. See "Purpose" in the introduction for the significance of the repetition.

1:6-7. These verses indicate that the readers were predominantly Gentile. More important than their ethnic background was their spiritual position, **the called of Jesus Christ**, **called as saints**, and **beloved of God.**

In this introduction, Paul presents his apostolic credentials and goals. He is the apostle appointed to take the gospel to the Gentile people so that they come to faith and begin to live like Christians to the glory of God. Our passion should parallel Paul's!

1:8-15. Paul gives the reason for his planned visit to Rome: **so that I may impart some spiritual gift to you, that you may be established** (v. 11), **so that I may obtain some fruit among you also, even as among the rest of the Gentiles** (v. 13), and **I am under obligation both to Greeks and to barbarians** . . . (v. 14). The **spiritual gift** is not specified. Paul would need to determine what kind of help they needed before he could specify what gift(s) he would use for their benefit. Verse 14 provides the basis for his strong desire to minister with the Romans. He **was under obligation** and **eager** to do so, reflecting God's sovereign plans for him (Ac 9:15; 22:21; 26:16-20; 1Co 9:16-23).

1:16-17. These verses are often seen as the theme verses for Romans, though they correspond better with chaps. 1–8 than 9–16. **For** (1:16) offers an explanation for Paul's eagerness to evangelize (1:15): **I am not ashamed of the gospel. For** (second occurrence in 1:16) gives the reason Paul is not ashamed: **it is the power of**

God. **Power** means "mighty potency; an effective, transforming force and ability." **Salvation** was a word used in Greco-Roman settings for an individual being rescued from some physical peril, perhaps from a burning house or from drowning. Here it is God's deliverance of sinners from the eternal consequences of sin. **Believes** was used most often for trust or reliance upon a person and what he says. Paul uses it for one's reliance upon Christ for salvation. **To the Jew first and also to the Greek** probably describes the good fit the gospel of Christ is for the Jewish people (see 1:2-3). While it is true that the gospel came first to and then through the Jewish people historically (see Jn 4:22), Paul's point here in vv. 16-17 seems to be theological (note the words "power," "salvation," "everyone who believes") rather than historical, and Rm 1:2-3 appears to show the special relevance of the gospel to the Jewish people because it has its roots in the Hebrew Scriptures.

For (1:17) explains *why* the gospel is the power of God (1:16): **in it the righteousness of God is revealed**. The phrase **righteousness of** [i.e., "that originates with"] **God** has become enormously controversial. Is this the covenant faithfulness of God? Is it God's act of announcing or undertaking the vindication of His people on the judgment day? No doubt it includes these elements. But these signal what God's righteousness *does* rather than *what it is*. A better view is that the **righteousness of God** is God's moral virtue and excellence that prompts Him to do all that He does, including (among other things) bringing people into a proper relationship with Him, but also judging people for their sin. God's moral virtue and excellence includes His justice that leads Him to judge sinners, but also His love that leads Him in Christ to redeem them. Paul's emphasis in this verse is on the latter. Paul will make it clear in 3:21-26 that the key is not found in securing one's own righteousness by keeping the law, but in God reckoning His own righteousness to those who have faith in His Son. This righteousness is **revealed** ("fully disclosed") **from faith to faith**. The latter phrase is difficult, and it is best not to be dogmatic. A parallel construction is found with "from" and "to" in 2Co 2:16 ("from death to death" and "from life to life"). There the phrases suggest that Paul's ministry resulted exclusively in death for the lost, and exclusively in life for believers. In Rm 1:17, the construction probably designates that faith in Christ is the only way one can receive God's righteousness.

Paul cites Hab 2:4 for support. It should be translated "The one who is righteous by faith will live (be saved)." He uses the same verse in Gl 3:11 where he cites it to support how one receives eternal life (not through works of the law).

B. The Need for the Gospel (1:18–3:20)

1:18. For explains why salvation is available only by faith (1:16-17). People are not able to establish a right standing before God because sin sabotages the attempt. Therefore a right standing before God comes only through reliance upon Christ. **Revealed** is the same word used in 1:17 for the manifestation of God's righteousness to those who believe. God's wrath is "fully disclosed" against humanity because all **suppress the truth in unrighteousness**. Paul introduces one reason for God condemning humankind. People possess some truth about Him but reject it.

1:19-20. Because launches the substantiation for Paul's claim that people suppress knowledge of God. This knowledge is **evident within them**. **For** (1:20) introduces the basis for that claim. Paul mentions a paradox when he says that God's **invisible attributes** are **clearly seen**. Creation displays God's power and deity, so that when people suppress knowledge about Him available through the created order **they are without excuse** when He judges them for it. *No one* ever responds correctly to the light of God in creation.

1:21-23. For continues the theme of people being without excuse, begun in 1:20. They choose not to **honor** and thank Him, and worship created things rather than the Creator. Three times Paul says people **exchanged** the truth of God for lies (1:23, 25, 26), and three times he says **God gave them over** (1:24, 26, 28) to practices that manifested His judgment against them in this life. As people reject God's standards and afflict themselves by their disobedience, their sin becomes their punishment.

1:24-25. Therefore provides a logical conclusion from the action of people in rejecting knowledge of God. **God gave them over** first to degrading religious practices (1:25). In various ways false religions cause their adherents to live in fear or engage in practices that cheapen their lives (**their bodies** are **dishonored**) and bring God's judgment.

1:26-27. People "exchanged the truth of God" for idols (1:25); **For this reason God gave them over**, this time to homosexual behavior. Some claim that Paul is saying that it is wrong only for those whom God did not create as homosexuals to engage in homosexual behavior (the underlying thought being that God has created some as homosexuals, a contention that is unsubstantiated in science or Scripture). Others argue that God is forbidding the ritual homosexuality practiced in Greco-Roman religions. The text says neither. The statement indicates that the homosexual behavior is a form of judgment against those who reject the knowledge of Him. If it is a form of His judgment, then the people of God must neither practice nor condone it.

1:28-32. People "exchanged" the natural function of the sexes (1:26) and abandoned knowledge about Him in creation (1:28); therefore, **God gave them over**, this time to social problems (unrighteousness, wickedness, greed) as a form of His judgment.

2:1-2. Therefore (v. 1) connects with the idea of God's judgment mentioned by Paul in 1:18-19, a judgment that encompasses all of humanity. **You have no excuse** (or "no defense") picks up the idea from 1:20, where people have no defense before God on the day of judgment, for everyone suppresses and rejects the knowledge of God they have from creation. God's judgment **rightly** (lit., "according to the truth") comes upon people. That is, it comes upon them "according to the truth," according to the facts of how they actually live.

2:3-5. Moral people are presumptuous in their thinking. They strive to live a principled life, do not (usually) act as those in Rm 1, and assume that God will overlook their occasional moral lapse because they really do strive to be good. They do not have as many practical manifestations of God's **judgment** in their lives as those who do not strive to be good, as seen in chap. 1. They mistake this lack of present judgment for God's approval, and as proof that they will escape His eschatological judgment. That God does not vent His wrath upon them to a great extent in this life is designed by Him to cause them to recognize His goodness and turn to Him (**repentance**). But if they do not repent, they will face **the righteous judgment of God** (v. 5).

2:6-11. Verse 6 continues the sentence Paul began in v. 5. God **WILL RENDER TO EACH PERSON ACCORDING TO HIS DEEDS** is a key for the rest of chap. 2. God judges based on how well one lives his moral code. The key is what one *does* in his or her life, not the honorable rules for living which one applauds. God will render **eternal life** (v. 7) or **wrath and indignation** (v. 8) based on how one acts.

This interpretation is shocking in light of Paul's consistent point that salvation is always and only by grace through faith in Christ (cf. 1:16-17; 3:21-26). Scholars debate whether Paul is speaking of true believers whose good works demonstrate their regeneration, and Paul surely held this belief (cf. Gl 5:16-19, 24; 6:8). But here Paul explained what is necessary to be right with God *apart from faith in Jesus*. There is no clear indication that Paul referred to believers in vv. 5-11, and he made it clear that people **do not obey the truth** (v. 8; cf. 1:18, where unbelievers "suppress the truth") and **obey unrighteousness** (cf. 1:29, where they are "filled with all unrighteousness"). All people sin and consequently deserve the wrath that awaits them. The phrases **to** (or of) **the Jew first and also to the Greek** (vv. 9, 10) indicate that there is essential equality between both people groups regarding both the prospects of judgment, or of salvation apart from faith in Christ. But there is a place of prominence for the Jewish people because of their special privilege in God's program, both as it relates to righteousness and to judgment (cf. the comments on 1:16, and Am 3:2; Lk 12:48).

2:12-13. For (v. 12) introduces Paul's explanation about God impartially judging all people on the basis of their deeds. Sinful actions make one liable to judgment, whether that one has the law or not (v. 13).

2:14-16. For (v. 14) signals that Paul gives the basis for maintaining that a Gentile without the law of Moses will perish in God's judgment. Based upon the natural circumstances of their birth, Gentiles do not have the law, but sometimes **do instinctively the things of the Law**, probably a reference to its moral requirements (e.g., loving one's neighbor; not bearing false witness) rather than the ceremonial aspects (sacrificing a red heifer). When those who do not have the law sometimes do some of the things prescribed by the law of Moses (**the work of the Law**, v. 15), they **are a law to themselves**, i.e., Gentiles indicate that they have their own moral code that overlaps with the law. God created humanity with a sense of right and wrong (cf. 1:32), and while Adam's fall damaged that, it did not erase it altogether. One's moral code may be as rudimentary as "treat everyone fairly" or "be nice to everyone." That moral code is an imperfect reflection of the morality God instilled in humankind, seen most clearly in the law. The problem is that *no one* lives up to whatever moral code he or his culture approves. As a result, **their conscience** bears **witness** to how well they have kept their own moral code, and will accuse or defend them on the day of judgment. Each one's conscience will say, "You kept your moral standards when you did this and this . . ." But the conscience will *also* say, "You broke it here and here and here!" God knows **the secrets of men**, i.e., what their conscience tells them, and He will use these accusatory thoughts as evidence for condemnation on the day of judgment.

Although Gentiles do not have the OT law, they are still sinners and will still face condemnation from God. There are some who claim that God would give eternal life to someone who never hears about Jesus, as long as that person responds correctly to the light of God in creation, is sincere in his own religion, and is kind to other people. But Paul indicates otherwise. Such a Gentile is still a sinner, even on the basis of his own moral norms, and as a sinner will experience God's judgment and wrath.

2:17-24. Paul begins to turn his attention to the sinfulness of those in covenant with God, the Jewish people. He noted the special privileges the Jewish people enjoyed (vv. 17-20), but also their failure to live up to their privileges. Paul's point is not that every single Jew has stolen or committed adultery, but rather that the Jewish people as a whole (and the whole consists in the individual parts) have acted with such sinfulness that they disqualified themselves from being used by God to enlighten the world. Worse yet, by their sinfulness, they served to **dishonor God** (v. 23). The same thing can be said about Gentiles who profess to be Christians, but live scandalous lives. They harm God's reputation now as much as unbelieving Jews did then.

2:25-29. Circumcision (v. 25) was viewed by later generations of the Jewish people as a virtual guarantee of eternal life (cf. the ancient rabbinic commentaries *Gen R.* 48 [30[a]]; *Exod R.* 19 [81[c]]; and Tanhuma B, *hayye Sarah* 60[b].8), and may have been in Paul's day as well. Sin in the life of a circumcised Jew canceled out the benefits of circumcision. Conversely, if a Gentile kept the law and did not sin, he would receive the benefits of the covenant people of God. Once again, Paul's point is that disobedience brings condemnation whether one is a Jew or not, and obedience without sin brings salvation (vv. 26-27). **For** (v. 28) begins an explanation as to why being circumcised does not guarantee salvation. Here only in chap. 2 does Paul refer to believers, in this case exclusively Jewish believers, and his point is to argue that being right with God comes as He performs spiritual surgery upon the heart, not as one complies with the letter of the law, by undergoing circumcision in the flesh (v. 29). Note that Paul is speaking only of true, believing Jews in these verses. Gentile believers are not in view, and the idea that Gentile Christians are the new Israel is foreign to this section.

3:1-2. If both Jews and Gentiles are in equal danger because of their sin, as Paul said in chap. 2, then what benefit is there in being Jewish? Paul concedes that the Jewish people do have an historical advantage over Gentiles. **They were entrusted with the oracles** [the Hebrew Scriptures] **of God** is one advantage Paul mentions (see 9:4-5 for others).

3:3-4. Paul was apparently seeking to correct the idea held by many that God promised to save virtually every Jewish person. In response, Paul wrote that God's promises include not only promises to save, but also to judge (cf. Dt 30:15-20; Jr 16:10-15). He cited Ps 51:4, David's confession of sin with Bathsheba, where David recognized that God was just to punish him for that sin. Whenever a sinner, whether Jewish or Gentile, stands in the courtroom of the Judge and pleads his case, the Judge will *always* be found to be in the right and will win the case. When the verb **ARE JUDGED** is in the middle voice as it is here, it often means "to go to court" or "to engage in a legal dispute," and is the likely meaning here (so NIV; HCSB).

3:5-7. Paul put another argument on the lips of an imaginary opponent, a rhetorical device called "diatribe" (v. 5; for other examples of diatribe, see e.g., 2:3; 3:1; 6:1-2, 15; 9:19; 11:1, 11): "My **unrighteousness** (moral corruption) demonstrates just how morally excellent and virtuous God really is. Therefore, a person might object that since my sinfulness does God a favor by making Him look so good, He is not unjust or unfair (the likely meaning of **unrighteous** in this phrase), and therefore will not condemn me!" However, if a Jewish person could use this argument, so could a Gentile, for their lives were arguably more corrupt, and could make God look better still. Therefore, it would be unfair of God to judge Gentiles (**the world**, v. 6). But the Jewish people *relished* the prospect of God judging the Gentile world (e.g., *Sir* 36:1-10), and would not have conceded this point to Paul.

3:8. Some accused Paul of teaching that one should sin more to give God a chance to bring greater glory to Himself by providing more grace to counteract it. See the comments related to this in 5:20–6:2. But this is a misrepresentation of Paul's views, and any Jewish antagonists who assigned this belief to Paul deserved the **condemnation** they received.

3:9-18. The question, **Are we** [the Jewish people] **better than they** [Gentiles]? probably looks back to the advantage of having the **oracles of God** in 3:2. The Jewish people had advantages, but without a proper response to them, they were no better off salvifically than Gentiles. Paul wove together several OT verses, cited loosely, to support the theme of humanity's universal plight. Verses 10-12 describe humanity's rejection of God (from Ps 14:1-3). **There is none who seeks for God** (v. 11) should be understood with its full force, and does not allow room for *anyone* to respond positively to the light of God in creation. If it were not for God seeking people, no one, left to their own motivation, would seek Him. Verses 13-14 describe the harm that comes from words, vv. 15-17 the harm that comes from actions. Paul loosely cites several OT passages (v. 13 = Ps 5:9; 140:3b; v. 14 = Ps 10:7) that indicate the comprehensiveness of humankind's spiritual disease. In vv. 15-18 he cited Is 59:7-8, written by Isaiah about the sin of the Jewish people (Is 58:1, 14), so that Paul, once again, included them in the world's troubles.

3:19-20. Whatever the Law says (v. 19) includes Gentiles, since all people are under some kind of moral code that they fail to keep adequately (cf. 2:12-16). Therefore, everyone is **accountable** ("subject to being prosecuted and found guilty") to God. The referent of **works of the Law** (v. 20) has become astonishingly controversial. See the summary and critique of Dunn in the "Excursus" following the introduction to Romans. **Works of the Law** refers to deeds the law requires in order for one to remain in a proper covenant relationship with God. Paul mentioned **works of the Law** again in 3:28, but in 3:27 he used the solitary noun "works", also used alone in 4:2, and the cognate verb "work" in 4:4, 5. **Works** without the phrase **of the Law** refers to general (religious) deeds anyone might do to enter into or maintain a right relationship with God, but **works of the Law** refers to the religious deeds from a Jewish vantage point, since their religious deeds were defined by the Mosaic law. Doing the law does not save a person, for one intent of the law was to inform Israel about what sin was (**through the Law comes the knowledge of sin**) so that she could avoid God's judgment and be used by Him to mediate His grace to the world. But the law of Moses was not designed *to save* per se. Salvation came through responding to God in faith in response to the promises He made in the Abrahamic Covenant (Gn 15:6), never through keeping the law of Moses (see the comments on Gl 3:6–4:7).

II. Justification by Faith: The Means for Being Right with God (3:21–4:25)

A. Righteousness Is Credited to Believers by God (3:21-26)

3:21-26. But now (v. 21) introduces a significant transition in the argument of Romans. After delineating the sorry spiritual condition of humankind, Paul began a discussion of how one can become right with God. The key is not found in securing one's own righteousness by keeping the law, but in God imputing and crediting His own righteousness (His own moral excellence and virtue; see the comments on "righteousness" in 1:17) to those who have faith in His Son.

But now carries a temporal sense, "But now, after the cross." For **the righteousness of God**, see 1:17. This **righteousness** has always been **apart from the Law** (cf. the example of Abraham in Rm 4, drawn from Gn 15). The Jewish people had misread the OT, wrongly prioritizing the law as the means for righteousness before God, and had neglected the importance of the Abrahamic Covenant for that. While this righteousness comes **apart from the Law**, it was **witnessed by the Law and the Prophets**; that is, the Hebrew Scriptures contain a predictive element pointing toward God's bestowal of His righteousness to those who have faith (see some of the verses Paul will refer to: Hab 2:4; Gn 15:6; Ps 32:1-2; and Jr 31:33-34; Ezk 36:25-27; Is 53:4-6). God's **righteousness** is **through faith in Jesus Christ** [lit., "faith/fullness *of* Jesus Christ"; Gk. *pisteos Iesou Christou*] (v. 22), which could mean either the believer's "faith in Jesus Christ" (objective genitive, the traditional view) or "the faithfulness of Jesus" in dying on the cross (subjective genitive). The second view is not objectionable, but it is not required by the syntax. The traditional view is preferable. Usually *pistis* (faith) refers to one's reliance upon another, and only when the context is explicit should the idea of "faithfulness" be ascribed to it. Also, several passages have a similar construction using the word "faith" followed by a member of the Godhead in the genitive case, where one's faith is directed toward the divine one, but not indicating the "faith of" the one who is divine (cf. Mk 11:22; Ac 3:16; Php 1:27; Col 2:12; 2Th 2:13; Jms 2:1; Rv 2:13). This suggests that the phrase **faith** of / in **Christ** should be understood as having Jesus as the object of faith. In addition, the strong contextual evidence supports the view that this refers to the believer's faith in Jesus Christ (Rm 3:22c, 26, 27, 28, and throughout chap. 4; Gl 2:16). **For all those who believe** is not a redundancy if "faith in Christ" is an objective genitive, for this phrase gives the additional point that individuals from all people groups (Jews and Gentiles, **for there is no distinction**) can be saved by faith. The lack of **distinction** relates not only to salvation by faith in Christ, but to the consequences of sin as well (v. 23). **Fall short** means "lack" (1Co 1:7; 8:8). The **glory of God** is sometimes connected by Paul both to God's revealed perfections and to His immortality (Rm 1:23; 2:7-10; 5:1-5; 1Tm 1:17), so that lacking **the glory of God** here probably refers to God's immortal splendor forfeited by Adam and his descendants because of sin. But according to Early (intertestamental) Judaism, Adam possessed a special glory of his own as one made in the image of God, a special glory that he lost at the fall (*Apoc. Mos.* 20:2; 21:2, 6; *2 Apoc. Bar.* 56:5-6; *Gen. Rab.* 12.6.1), and which God will restore to the righteous in the future (CD 3:20; 1QS 4:6-8, 14-15, 22-23; *4 Ezra* 2:39; 7:97-98; 8:51-52; *2 Apoc. Bar.* 51:3, 10; *1 Enoch* 108:12-15; Rm 8:30). The emphasis, however, is upon *God's* glory.

Being justified (v. 24) probably connects with v. 22b, and reiterates the bright side of the "no distinction" theme, while v. 23 looks at the dark side of it. The verb **justified** (*dikaioo*) was a judicial term for a judge declaring a person innocent of whatever charges were levied against him. A sinner is rightly charged with breaking God's law. When a sinner trusts Christ for salvation, God declares him or her not only innocent of that charge (i.e., He "justifies" them, *dikaioo*), but as having kept the standard because of the relationship that is established with Him through Christ (Rm 8:4; 2Co 5:21). By God's declaration, the sinner is "put right" with God and possesses the status of "righteousness" (*dikaiosune*, a cognate of *dikaioo*, "to justify") on the basis of the favorable verdict rendered by the divine Judge. This is no legal fiction as is sometimes argued. When a judge declares innocent an individual charged with a crime, that declaration has a profound impact upon the one who was charged. **Grace** denotes the character quality of benevolence that leads a benefactor to bestow a favor upon another. **Redemption** means "the act of setting one free by paying a ransom," used for paying a master the amount his slave was worth to purchase the slave's freedom. The blood of Jesus paid the ransom for believers (see the comments on Eph 1:7). **Propitiation** (v. 25) usually involved a sacrifice that averted the wrath of a divine being, but the word was also used in the LXX for the "mercy seat," the cover on the ark of the covenant onto which blood was sprinkled whereby sin was forgiven and wrath was turned away (cf. Lv 16:2, 13-15). Jesus' bloody cross, not the mercy seat, remains the place where God's wrath is appeased. **Faith** is "reliance upon a person, including what he says or does." One is justified by God when he or she relies upon Jesus Christ alone for the forgiveness of sins. Jesus died **to demonstrate** (or "prove") God's **righteousness** (see the comments on 1:17), which in vv. 25-26 refers more narrowly to His justice or fairness as part of His wider moral excellence. And it needed to be proven. If a judge did not condemn a guilty criminal but let him go free, or if he had the criminal's pet collie go to prison in his place, the judge would be unjust, unfair, unrighteous. But in the OT, God both forgave sinners and determined to have animals sacrificed for sins (Lv 16; cf. the comments on Heb 9:15; 10:4). God would be unjust for doing this, except the death of Jesus safeguarded **His righteousness**. In the death of Jesus, God vented His wrath against sin, keeping **His righteousness** intact, and God applied the atoning work of His Son to OT saints. On that basis they were forgiven and **His righteousness** was upheld. All this is not only true for OT saints, but is relevant **at the present time** (v. 26). The death of Jesus allows God to remain **just** and yet forgive sinners who have faith in Jesus today (He remains **just** and is **the justifier of the one who has faith in Jesus**).

B. Righteousness Is Appropriated by Faith Alone (3:27–4:25)

3:27-31. In these verses, Paul presents the principles that flow logically from 3:21-26, and in chap. 4 he illustrates the principles with the concrete example of Abraham. The table at the top of the next page presents the connections.

It makes sense that if justification is a gift that springs from God's grace (3:22-26), then **boasting** in one's own ability to obtain it or maintain it **is excluded** (v. 27). The word **law** is puzzling, but here probably has a metaphorical meaning ("base, norm, standard, principle"), and probably

The Principles	The Concrete Illustration of the Principles
3:27 Boasting is excluded	4:1-3 Abraham could not boast
3:28 Justification is by faith, not works	4:4-8 Abraham was justified by faith not works
3:29-30 God justifies all by faith	4:9-12 Abraham indicates God justifies all by faith
3:31 Faith "establishes" the law	4:13-25 Abraham's faith "established" the law

does not refer to the OT law. In vv. 29-30, Paul bolstered his argument about one way of salvation by referring to monotheism. If justification is available only through the Jewish law, then God is the God of the Jews only, and the Gentiles are excluded from a relationship with Him. Since salvation is by grace through faith, the question arises: "Does faith render the law purposeless?" (v. 31). What Paul means by **we establish the Law** is disputed, but it is possible that faith is the sole avenue whereby one is able to experience all of God's promised blessings, blessings to which the law bore witness (3:21) but which could not be obtained on the basis of keeping the law (cf. 3:19-20; 4:13-15). While faith establishes **the Law**, v. 31 cannot be cited to support the idea that the law is still binding since it is not nullified by faith. Rather, faith does not nullify the teaching of the Pentateuch but actually establishes the law's teaching, which includes justification by faith as evident in the law's teaching concerning Abraham (cf. Gn 15:6; Rm 4:1-22).

4:1-3. Beginning in 4:1, Paul presents Abraham as the illustration of the principle in 3:27 that faith eliminates boasting. The phrase **according to the flesh** (v. 1) refers to Abraham being the physical **forefather** of the Jewish people, and does not refer to what he discovered "in the realm of the flesh" regarding salvation. Paul refers several times to Gn 15:6 (Rm 4:9, 22) as he employs Abraham to illustrate the principles of 3:27-31. **CREDITED TO HIM** (v. 3) translates a Hebrew phrase (the verb *hashab* followed by the preposition *le*) that means "to assign something to a person for his benefit *that he does not possess*" (cf. Lv 7:18; Nm 18:27, 30; 2Sm 19:19 [MT 19:20]; Ps 106:31 [MT 106:30]). God reckoned to Abraham the status of **RIGHTEOUSNESS** ("moral excellence and virtue"; see the comments on 1:17) that made him acceptable to God. Faith is not a work that makes one right with God. Faith is reliance upon *another's work* (after the cross, the work of Christ), and is a gift from God (Ac 18:27; Eph 2:8; Php 1:29).

4:4-8. Here Paul explores the principle from 3:28 that justification is by faith. If salvation were given on the basis of works (v. 4), then it would be a **wage** one had earned that God was obligated to pay. But Paul made it clear earlier (3:24) that **righteousness** is **credited** as a gift (v. 5). Both Ps 32 and Gn 15 use the same Hebrew verb, *hashab,* translated differently by the NASB in these verses ("reckoned" in Gn 15:6; "impute" in Ps 32:2a). Paul used a rabbinic interpretive method (called *Gezerah Shevah*) that links verses sharing common words (here "reckon to") to demonstrate a general principle. If God credited Abraham with righteousness on the basis of his faith, then David must have had faith for God to "credit" or "reckon" him with righteousness as well. Paul cites Ps 32:1-2 to emphasize that the imputation of righteousness includes forgiveness of sins, a point not found explicitly in Gn 15:6.

4:9-12. Paul unpacks another principle presented in 3:29-30, that God justifies everyone (Jews and Gentiles) by faith (v. 9). Abraham was counted righteous while he was a "Gentile" (**uncircumcised**) (v. 10). **The sign of circumcision** (v. 11) is described further as **a seal** (proof or validation of something; 1Co 9:2) of Abraham's righteous status by **faith**. Abraham's faith preceded his circumcision (Gn 15:6 vs. Gn 17:9-14). Circumcision contributed nothing to his righteousness. Circumcision was a sign that God (apart from human effort) would fulfill His promise, that Abraham had faith in Him, and that God credited righteousness to Abraham on the basis of his faith. Because he was saved as a Gentile, Abraham is the spiritual father of believing Gentiles. But he is also the father of believing Jews (v. 12), for he was a circumcised believer.

4:13-17. In 3:31, Paul gave the principle that faith establishes the true teaching of the law (see the comments there), and illustrates it in 4:13-25. **Not through the Law** (v. 13c) is developed in vv. 14-17, and **the righteousness of faith** (v. 13d) is developed in vv. 18-25. The **promise to Abraham** (v. 13) (Gn 12:1-3) could never have been fulfilled if its fulfillment were **through** (by means of) doing **the Law** (v. 14). Everyone fails to obey the law, exposing oneself to God's wrath (v. 15). If obtaining the promises depended upon one's ability to keep the law, then the whole plan would be doomed. **Where there is no Law, there also is no violation** continues Paul's explanation regarding the reason that obtaining the promise is not through the law. His point here is similar to the one in 3:20 ("through the Law comes the knowledge of sin"). The purpose of the law is to define what constitutes a **violation** ("an intentional act of disobedience to a law or custom"), not to facilitate the fulfillment of God's promises. Paul did not mean that when there is no law there is no sin and no judgment (cf. the comments on 2:12-16; 5:13-14). His purpose here is to explain the function of the law, and its function puts it at odds with obtaining God's promise. **For this reason** (v. 16), **the promise** is realized **by faith . . . in accordance with grace** (see 3:21-26). **So that** gives the purpose for God's design that salvation be by grace through faith, not by obeying the law, namely, that the promise may be fulfilled with certainty for **all the descendants**, Jews and Gentiles alike. Verse 17 indicates that Abraham is both the father of one nation, the Jewish people, and the father of **MANY NATIONS** (citing Gn 17:5). Although this is stating that there is but one spiritual people of God, ethnic distinctions are not extinguished. The **God** in whom Abraham believed is described as One who **gives life to the dead**, probably a reference to Abraham's and Sarah's inability to reproduce, but may include a glance at the resurrection of the dead, especially Jesus' resurrection (v. 24). God **calls into being that which does not exist**, a reference to the great nation of Israel and its impact on the entire world, which was not yet a reality when God spoke the promises to Abraham.

4:18-25. Paul has established that obtaining the promise of God was "not through the Law" (v. 13c; cf. vv. 14-17). Next, he developed the idea that the promise comes through the "righteousness of faith" (v. 13d) in vv. 18-25, with the emphasis on "faith" in vv. 17-21, and "righteousness" in v. 22. **In hope against hope** (v. 18) means "Abraham had hope contrary to all human expectations." Verse 19 explains v. 18. **His own body . . . as good as dead** and **the deadness of Sarah's womb** recalls what Paul said about God **who gives life to the dead** in v. 17. One might argue with Paul and say that Abraham did waver in unbelief (v. 20). He did not waver, however, after God explicitly told him that Sarah would bear him a son (Gn 17:19). **Grew strong** would be translated better as "was strengthened." **And being fully assured** (v. 21) reflects Abraham's conviction that God was the kind of God who could bring about what He promised.

Beginning in v. 22, Paul explored Gn 15:6c on the theme of "righteousness." Cf. the comments on 4:3 for v. 22. In vv. 23-25 Paul showed how Abraham's experience was relevant to more than just him. Believers share in common with Abraham the reality of faith, the object of faith (God), and the futility of works of the law in order to be right with God. Christians **believe in Him who raised Jesus our Lord from the dead** just as Abraham had faith in God "who gives life to the dead" by reviving the bodies of Abraham and Sarah. **Raised because of our justification** means that without the resurrection, no one would know that Jesus' death paid for believers' **transgressions**, and that they now have **justification**.

III. Blessings: The Results of Being Right with God (5:1–8:39)

A. Christians Can Boast in God (5:1-11)

Paul's theme from 5:1–8:39 relates to the benefits that accrue to the believer who has been justified. This section fits with his overall purpose of seeking to motivate the believers in Rome to support his mission to Spain. Unbelievers possess none of these privileges, and the Roman believers should assist Paul in proclaiming them.

5:1-2. Therefore (v. 1) introduces an inference from 3:21–4:25 that the believer has **peace with God**. There is a textual problem related to the verb **have** (whether it is an indicative "we have" or a hortatory [commanding] subjunctive "let us have"), but it is probably indicative. Paul begins giving commands in Romans only in chap. 6 (for hortatory subjunctives applicable to believers, see Rm 13:13; 14:13, 19; there are 22 imperative verbs from chap. 6 onward), but none before (except the hortatory subjunctive in 3:8, which is put on the lips of one in error, and the imperative in 3:4, which is purely rhetorical). Rather than encouraging the believer to strive for **peace with God**, Paul continues his statement of doctrinal facts so prominent in the first half of Romans. God Himself has established peace with those He **justified**. For **the glory of God** (v. 2), cf. the comments on 3:23.

5:3-5. It is possible that Paul presupposes the need to have faith for this chain (perseverance, character, hope) to be complete, but he does not mention it here, and it should not be read into the text. His point seems to be that through **tribulations** *God* will produce in the Christian **perseverance, proven character** (v. 4) and **hope**, similar to Rm 8:29-30.

5:6-10. For (v. 6) introduces an explanation regarding how God poured out His love, through Christ's death. The difference between the **righteous man** and **the good man** (v. 7) is that the **good man** has done something tangibly beneficial for another. I might die for someone who has been good to me, but I probably would not die for one who I considered to be righteous, but who had done nothing for me. If God has done the "major" thing (sinners being **justified by His blood**, v. 9, parallel to **enemies** being **reconciled to God**, v. 10), the believer can count on Him to do the "minor" thing (save sinners **from** His **wrath**, v. 9, parallel to being **saved by His life**, v. 10).

5:11. Believers boast not only in the "hope of the glory of God" (v. 2) and in tribulations (v. 3), but **in God** Himself.

B. Christians Can Live a Life of Security (5:12-21)

The connection with what precedes is not clear, but Paul may be presenting the basis of the hope detailed in 5:1-11. The believer can have hope because Jesus has overturned the negative effects of Adam's fall.

5:12. Just as may find its conclusion in "even so" (*houtos kai*) in v. 18, but more likely it is found in **and so** (*kai houtos*) at the end of v. 12. "Original sin" is a term used to describe the idea that every person sinned in and with Adam, so that Adam's sin and guilt was our sin and guilt. But Paul is probably not teaching original sin in these verses, for several reasons. First, the phrase **because** [*eph' ho*] **all sinned** literally means "on the basis of which" and signals that everyone sins because the state of spiritual death, and physical death, entered the race through Adam's act. Second, the verb **sinned** *always* refers to an individual's conscious acts, never to sins committed without conscious choice or committed by proxy. Third, **sinned** is probably a "gnomic" aorist, describing a general truth about acts that typically take place, not acts that did take place in the past (see 2:12; 3:23, where **sinned** is also used, but has a gnomic sense).

5:13-14. In v. 13, Paul explains how one could commit a sin when there was no law of Moses yet in existence. Between Adam and Moses **sin was in the world** (v. 13), indicated by the fact that people died in the flood because of their conscious acts of sin (Gn 6:5). With the phrase **sin is not imputed when there is no law** Paul means much the same thing as in 3:20 and 4:15 (see the comments on 4:15). People commit acts of sin even when there is no clear violation of an explicit command, and will experience God's wrath (see the comments on 2:12-16). **Imputed** is a commercial term, and would be better translated "tallied," "accounted," or even "charged to one's account" (cf. Phm 18). The law makes sin an **offense** (better, a "transgression," same word as 4:15) (v. 14)—it intensifies sin and its consequence—but *the law does not create sin*. Sin found its origination in Adam, not in the law. The phrase **those who had not sinned in the likeness of the offense of Adam** indicates that Paul is not teaching "original sin" as it is typically conceived. Adam violated a clear command. Those between Adam and Moses did not. Therefore they did not sin in and with Adam. Theologically, a **type** is an OT person, object, or event that had a useful function in its own historical setting, but that also was designed by God to prefigure a greater, more spiritually potent situation or person. In this case, Adam was a "type" of Christ since he functions as the founder of the human race and his action had a profound influence upon it. Jesus, of course, is the superior "antitype" to Adam.

5:15-19. Here (vv. 15-17) Paul demonstrates the *differences* (**the free gift is not like the transgression**, v. 15) between Adam and Jesus. The differences lie in the effects of the acts of Adam vis-à-vis Jesus. In vv. 18-19, Paul demonstrates the *similarities* between Jesus and Adam, those similarities being found in the comprehensiveness of the consequences of the acts of the first and second Adam.

Paul teaches neither original sin nor the imputation of Christ's righteousness in these verses. He omits altogether *how* Adam's sin has corrupted humanity and *how* Christ's righteousness is applied to believers. His purpose is simply to state that Adam's sin *did* corrupt all those in him, and Christ's gift reverses that for those *in Him*, a point that serves as the ground of great boasting for believers.

5:20-21. When Paul refers to the law, he sees it as fulfilling a role of providing information regarding the identification of sin (cf. 3:20; 4:15; 5:13) that results in an intensification of sin, and this is probably the sense of **so that** knowledge of **transgression would increase** (cf. also

Gl 3:19). But in Rm 7:7-13, the presence of the law also brings about the quantitative increase of sin. Paul's point indicates that the law, given after the entrance of sin into humanity courtesy of Adam, did nothing to improve the situation. Only God's super-abounding **grace** proffers sufficient power to grant **eternal life** to those who believe.

C. Christians Can Live a Life Free from the Absolute Domination of Sin (6:1–7:25)

6:1-2. One might wrongly think that it is appropriate to continue to live in sin either so that God might be glorified as He causes grace to abound (5:20), or so that the believer might have a more profound experience of grace. Paul will demonstrate that while both are spiritually possible, both are morally irrational, for sin ruins a believer's life. **Died to sin** (v. 2) indicates that when Jesus died on the cross (cf. 6:10), the believer died with Him in a spiritual yet real sense (cf. the comments on Gl 2:19-20; Col 2:20; 3:1-3; 2Tm 2:11; 1Pt 2:24).

6:3-4. Into carries a referential sense, indicating that baptism is especially a baptism "with reference to" **Christ Jesus**, and even more narrowly is a reference to **His death**. Paul closely connects baptism with the salvation experience in v. 4, but it is not a cause of salvation. Baptism depicts that aspect of the Christian's conversion that unites him to Christ, especially to Christ in His death. It is the outward expression of saving faith and the solemn symbol of dying with Christ. This was brought about by God so that **we too might walk in newness of life** (v. 4; cf. 7:6, where the Spirit is said to bring about this "newness").

6:5-7. The **likeness of His death** indicates that the believer's experience of dying with Christ is not identical to His death. The believer did not die physically upon the cross, but the benefits of Christ's death are experienced when the believer trusts Christ. This union with Christ guarantees the believer **resurrection** with Him in the future. The **old self** (v. 6) is not a reference to the old sin nature, for Paul makes it clear in the passage that it is not a "nature" or part of the believer that is crucified, but the entire person. It is a reference to who the believer was in Adam, under the mastery of sin. That person **was crucified** with Jesus on His cross and no longer exists. The believer is now "in Christ," no longer "in Adam" under sin. **Body of sin** refers to the believer's body as owned, dominated, ruled by sin. **Done away with** means "rendered powerless." As a result, believers are no longer **slaves to sin**, for a dead slave is no longer a slave (v. 7).

6:8-10. The believer was united with Jesus in His death, a death undergone with reference to breaking the power of sin (**He died to sin**, v. 10). Jesus rose from the dead, and the believer is united with Him in that as well. If Jesus' condition is irreversible (Jesus **is never to die again; death no longer is master over Him**, v. 9), then the believer's condition is also irreversible. Sin is no longer the slave master over the believer.

6:11. Here, for the first time in Romans, Paul gives a true command, the first application of the entire book. **Consider** means "to count, compute, calculate, take into account, to make account of" something, and here means "a deliberate and sober judgment on the basis of the facts one has." The believer is not commanded to "put the old sin nature to death" as he is in Eph 4:22 and Col 3:9 (see the comments there), for this is done for him and her by God at the moment of conversion. Rather, believers are *commanded to understand these profound facts*, and failure to do so amounts to sin (cf. Jms 4:17).

6:12-14. Paul continues the application of these truths. **Sin** was personified previously as a slave master, but here as a king who **reigns** (v. 12). **Presenting** is used in the LXX for one serving a superior (1Kg 10:8; 2Kg 5:25; Pr 22:29). Christians are no longer in Adam, under the tyranny of sin as a slave master or a king, but instead are now in Christ, under the rule of God to whom allegiance is owed. Verse 14 is developed fully in chap. 7 (see the comments there).

6:15-20. Since the believer is **not under law**, one might think that he is free to live however he wishes. But to live for sin results **in death** (v. 16). Many believe that Paul refers here to eternal death, and that the one who professes to be a Christian but who lives in sin is no Christian at all. This is possible, but Paul seems to be less eschatologically oriented here than is sometimes thought. Paul goes back and forth between reviewing what a believer's experience was before conversion and how life is—or *should be*—after it. **Death** is the experience of the unsaved, but Paul's words contain an implicit warning for the believer as well. **Death** in this verse is something that can be experienced by a true believer, and produces not an eternity in hell for the believer but **impurity** (moral filth), and **lawlessness** (or anarchy) (v. 19) and shame (v. 21). While it is true that an unbeliever receives eternal condemnation for his sin, he also experiences these practical consequences in this life. But so does the believer, and that is precisely Paul's point here. It is morally foolish for a Christian to live in sin like an unbeliever, and the believer who does will receive the same kind of "death" in this life that an unbeliever receives, namely impurity, anarchy, and shame.

6:21-23. Benefit (v. 21) is literally "fruit" (cf. 7:4). Christians are rightly **ashamed** of the kinds of things they did as unbelievers. Therefore, why do them as believers? In v. 21, the **benefit** or fruit of a sinful non-Christian life was shame and **death**. But the fruit of God freeing a believer from sin is **sanctification** (the process of becoming more holy in this life) and finally **eternal life** (v. 22). When a person, whether a believer or an unbeliever, sins he earns and deserves **death**—the moral corruption and hardships that come in this life as specified by Paul in 6:19-21. In contrast to what one deserves, God freely gives **eternal life** to believers.

7:1-4. In Rm 7, Paul develops the theme introduced in 6:14 (see the comments there). Law, whether Mosaic or any other, has **jurisdiction** only over the living (v. 1). But Paul wrote that the believer died with Christ in reference to sin (6:2, 6, 8, 11; see the comments there). That death was also a death with reference to the law (vv. 2-4). Sometimes these verses are cited in defense of the concept that Paul says only death dissolves the marital bond, and that all divorce, for whatever reason, is wrong. It is possible that Rm 7:1-4 could be understood this way, but it is unlikely since Paul himself appears to allow for divorce (see the comments on 1Co 7:12-16), as does Jesus (see the comments on Mt 19:1-9). In addition, Paul was simply using marriage, the death of one's spouse, and divorce as an illustration of dying with Christ so that one is freed from sin. His intent was not to give binding instruction on divorce. To understand this text as representative of Paul's view of divorce is ill-advised.

7:5-6. These two verses forecast the rest of chaps. 7 and 8, and are crucial for the proper understanding of chap. 7 in particular. **Flesh** (v. 5) refers to a conglomeration of human traits that contribute to one's disposition to sin, also known as "the old sin nature." **Flesh** has this sense in its ensuing occurrences (7:14, 18, 25; 8:3 [first occurrence], 4, 5 [twice], 6, 7, 8, 9, probably 12 and 13), and in each of its uses in these verses refers to the unsaved, non-Christian state as suggested by its use in 7:5. Because 7:5-6 forecast the rest of chap. 7 and all of chap. 8, and because "flesh" in 7:5 refers to the unsaved condition, it is likely that "flesh" in the other occurrences of the word in chaps. 7 and 8 should be understood with a similar sense, unless the context clearly indicates otherwise (as noted below). **Sinful passions . . . aroused by the Law** is the topic developed in vv. 7-12. **Death** is the theme developed in vv. 14-25. **But now** (v. 6) refers to the present state of the believer who is no longer "in the flesh" (i.e., no longer in the unsaved condition) nor under the law because of dying with Christ. Christians now **serve** (better, "are enslaved to"; see 6:18, 22) righteousness **in the newness** (see 6:4) **of the Spirit**. The mention of life in the Spirit forecasts the theme of Rm 8.

7:7-13. Verses 5 and 6 do not indicate that the law is evil. The law informs about what sin is (v. 7), and this is valuable (cf. 3:20; 4:15; 5:20). Paul employs a rhetorical technique called "impersonation" (Gk. *prosopopoeia*) with which he steps into a role to make a point (similarly, cf. 1Co 13:1-3, 11-12). But identifying who Paul impersonates is a challenge, and there are several interpretive options. First, it is possible that Paul uses "I" to describe the experience of Adam, or, second, of Israel before receiving the law. Third, Paul may be saying that sin is so strong in the believer that Christians should expect moral failure and accept it as an inevitability. In this case Paul is remarkably pessimistic about the Christian life, and in light of Rm 6 and 8, this is an unlikely view. Fourth, Paul's "I" may refer to a believer who seeks to sanctify himself by keeping the law, an approach to the Christian life also doomed to fail. But sanctification is possible if the believer relies upon the power of the Spirit to defeat sin. Fifth, the preferable view adopted here and argued below is that Paul is describing the futile experience of an unbeliever who seeks to conquer the power of sin by keeping his moral standards in his own power. Paul's "I" is autobiographical, but represents the experience of all unsaved individuals who seek unsuccessfully to keep their moral code. For the Jewish people, that moral code is the law of Moses. For Gentiles, it is some other philosophy of life they or their culture adopts (e.g., the "rule of fair play"; the Golden Rule; "all things in moderation"). Paul wrote in 2:12-16 (see the comments there) that Gentiles have their own moral code but fail to live up to it. This failure reveals them as sinners for whom condemnation is appropriate. But in chap. 7 Paul discusses primarily the experience of the Jewish unbeliever (7:1, **I am speaking to those**

who know the law), but what he says is equally relevant for Gentile unbelievers who fail to keep their own moral standards.

It is fashionable to maintain that Paul's "I" is not autobiographical since he kept the law competently enough that his conscience did not bother him (it was "robust"; cf. Php 3:2-6), contrary to the "I" in this chapter. However, Paul's law-keeping was sometimes motivated by impure intentions (Gl 1:10), and his pre-conversion conscience was not as robust as sometimes thought (Ti 3:3-6).

The law is good (v. 7), but it is weak, and does not help one who is "in the flesh," i.e., an unbeliever (see the comments on 7:5) break the power of sin *in this life* (not the eternal state, in keeping with 6:14) (v. 8). **Sin**, here viewed as an anti-God force that dominates the unbeliever, leads one to rebel against God. **Apart from the Law sin is dead** does not mean that sin is non-existent. Rather, sin is always active, but it is hyperactive when the unregenerate human heart encounters God's law (**sin became alive**, v. 9; **sin deceived me** and **killed me**, v. 11). That sin was energized **when the commandment came** likely refers to a "moral awakening" when one begins to grasp fully the implications of his moral code and the consequences of failing to fulfill it (**sin became alive** [or "sprang to life"] **and I died**). For the kind of death Paul has in mind (i.e., moral corruption and frustration), see vv. 13-24. The law is good (v. 12), but sin is so strong that it can use the good law as a weapon to kill an unbelieving person (vv. 10-11, 13), for sin influences people to violate the law and bring upon themselves the moral and spiritual sentence of death.

7:14-25. Verses 14-25 develop the theme of death introduced in 7:5d. **Death** is mentioned twice in v. 13 and again in v. 24, forming an *inclusio* (brackets) on the whole paragraph, clarifying what Paul means by "death." As in 6:15-23 (see the comments there), **death** refers to "moral frustration and corruption," not the cessation of biological life nor spiritual or eternal separation from God.

Verses 7-13 are dominated by aorist tense verbs, traditionally understood as reflecting Paul's past experience before he knew the Lord. In vv. 14-25, on the other hand, Paul used predominantly present tense verbs, and these have sometimes been interpreted as a description of Paul's present experience as a believer. But it is better to understand the present tense verbs as indicating Paul's *emphasis* in this chapter. His main point is to explore the unbeliever's moral frustration and corruption due to sin and its consequences (called **death**, not "condemnation," in vv. 14-25), not how "the Law arouses sinful passions" (vv. 7-13). The present tense verbs in vv. 14-25 indicate this emphasis. This interpretation is supported by much of Rm 6, which explores freedom from sin and death (cf. the comments on 6:2-14), and Rm 8:1-13, which reiterates this theme.

When Paul says **I am of flesh** (v. 14; also **my flesh** in v. 18), it is extremely unlikely that he is referring to his *Christian* experience, for no Christian is "in the flesh" following conversion (cf. v. 5). **Sold in bondage to sin** is the experience of an unbeliever, for Christians are no longer enslaved to sin (cf. 6:7, 18, 22). This is an unbeliever enslaved to sin who, like Paul before his conversion, loved the law and strove to obey it, but was frustrated by his inability to do so (vv. 15-17). While Paul does have a category for "fleshly believers" (see the comments on 1Co 3:1-4), his use of "in the flesh" in Rm 7:5, and **flesh** in vv. 14, 18, indicates that he used **flesh** in a way that differs from 1Co 3. Here it delineates the unsaved condition ("while we were in the flesh" in 7:5 indicates that Paul believes Christians are no longer "in the flesh," indicated also by the "then-versus-now" contrast in 7:5, 6), but the use of "flesh" in 1Co 3:1-3 describes true believers who are acting like the unsaved.

The willing (v. 18) and **the good that I want** (v. 19; cf. v. 21) refer to the desire to keep the law (vv. 22-23). But Paul already argued that the believer has "died to the Law" (vv. 2-4), another point that supports a non-Christian referent for "I." It is sin in the unbeliever that keeps him from obedience and brings moral frustration (**death** in this passage). In v. 23, **law** does not refer to Mosaic law, but, as in 3:27, means "rule" or "principle." **Who will set me free** (or "rescue" me) cannot be the words of a believer who knows who his Deliverer is, nor is the future tense appropriate for one who is already freed in Christ. **This** (v. 24) probably modifies **body**, not **death**. Paul, playing the role of an unbeliever, mentioned his "members" (body parts) in v. 23, and there those members are dominated by sin and death. This **body** (the entire person, inside and out; cf. 6:6; 12:1) of **death** is a reference to the unbeliever aggravated by the tyranny of sin. Then, as if he could no longer stand to continue his role-playing, Paul erupts in praise to God who has provided Jesus to rescue people from their wretched unsaved state. Here Paul speaks as a Christian. He abandons the first person singular "I" for the second person plural **our**, indicating a momentary shift out of his non-Christian impersonation. But then he steps back into that role immediately and recaps his discussion in 7:25b, c.

D. Christians Have Life in the Holy Spirit (8:1-39)

8:1-4. Paul continues with another benefit of salvation by grace through faith. Those who believe in Christ have the unparalleled privilege of living life in the power of the Holy Spirit. The Spirit is mentioned only in 1:4, 2:29, 5:5, and 7:6, but is mentioned 19 times in chap. 8. **Therefore** (v. 1) probably introduces a logical conclusion based on what Paul wrote in chap. 7, especially 7:24. **Condemnation** includes both the idea of rendering a verdict of guilt and the punishment that follows. In the context of 7:14-25 and the moral frustration and corruption the non-Christian "I" experiences, and based on the pronouncement of being free of the terrors of the non-Christian life in 8:1-11, **condemnation** here especially focuses upon the believer's freedom from the crippling power of sin in this life. On the meaning of **law** in v. 2, cf. the comments on 3:27. Verse 3 provides a succinct summary of Rm 7 in which the main theme was the weakness of the law to help an unbeliever defeat sin's power. For the meaning of **flesh** here and in 8:4, 5 (twice), 6, 7, 8, 9, 12, 13, cf. the comments on 7:5. **Likeness of sinful flesh** masterfully links Jesus closely with humanity because of His incarnation, but maintains a distinction between His body and that of everyone else. He had real flesh, but it was not sinful flesh. **Condemned sin in the flesh** means that Jesus, through the medium of His sacrificed body, pronounced judgment on sin and broke its power. The law could only pronounce judgment but could not "execute" sin. **Might be fulfilled in us** (v. 4) indicates the purpose of Christ's death. While one is not made right with God by performing the law, Jesus' perfect keeping of the law is **fulfilled in us**, but the law is not "performed by us." Christians no longer **walk according to the flesh**, are no longer under the absolute control of the flesh (cf. the comments on 7:5, 14, 18). Those who walk according to the flesh in this verse are unbelievers, not carnal Christians.

8:5-11. These verses contrast the values and experience of unbelievers (**those who are according to the flesh**, v. 5—and for an explanation of the meaning of **flesh** as unbelievers, see the comments on 7:5; those who **set their minds on the things of the flesh**, vv. 5, 6; **those who are in the flesh**, v. 8) with Christians (those who are **according to the Spirit**, v. 5, with their **mind set on the Spirit**, v. 6). Christians experience **life and peace** (v. 6), the primary reference being to the experience of these blessings in this life, while those according to the flesh reap **death** (cf. the comments on 6:15). Verses 7-8 are key verses, along with Rm 3:9-20, for the doctrine of total depravity (man's inability to obey God and his antipathy toward Him). Paul does not refer to the category of "carnal Christian" in 8:5-8 (for this, see 1Co 3:1-4). Paul places all believers into the category of those who are **not in the flesh but in the Spirit**, since every believer is indwelt by the Spirit (v. 9). The believer is freed from the absolute power and penalty of sin, but sin still exercises dominion over the believer's body through death (v. 10). Here the word **dead** refers to the cessation of biological life, but does not carry the sense of "eternal spiritual death." **The spirit is alive** would be better translated "the Spirit is life," for **spirit** here is better understood as a reference to the Holy Spirit who is the hero of this passage, not the human spirit, and He *is life* (**is alive** is actually a noun, not an adjective or a verb). He is the living and life-giving Spirit, and though believers will die physically because they are physically fallen and sometimes sin, the Spirit nevertheless gives them eternal, resurrection life (v. 11). This is **because of righteousness**, meaning "because believers are righteous in Christ, they have the Spirit who is, and who gives, life."

8:12-13. Flesh in these two verses refers to a conglomeration of human traits that contribute to one's disposition to sin (cf. the comments on 7:5), the "old sin nature." The believer still has the flesh, though he is no longer "in the flesh" (7:5), just as he has a body descended from Adam though he is no longer "in Adam" (6:1-10). If a believer lives like a non-Christian, **according to the flesh**, i.e., fulfills the desires of the flesh (Gl 5:16), then he **must die** (experience moral frustration and corruption as in 6:15-23; 7:13-24, but probably not eternal spiritual death). **If by the Spirit . . . you will live** probably refers to the believer's experience of the abundant life by the believer *in this life*. Paul is describing the quality of a believer's life. If a Christian lives in the power of the Spirit and puts **to death the deeds of the body**, he will experience the abundant life now. But to the extent that a believer lives in sin (**according to the flesh**, i.e., "like an unbeliever"; on **flesh** see the comments on 7:5), he will experience lack of the abundant life, a "deadly life." If **live** refers to *eternal* life (and it is often understood this way), then 8:13c teaches salvation by works (namely, by **putting to death the deeds of the body**), which is an unlikely understanding of Paul in this paragraph. While he teaches that true salvation will bring a change in life (e.g., Rm 8:29; 1Co 16:22; Gl 5:18-25; Eph 2:10; Php 2:13; Ti 2:14), Paul's point in Rm 8 is more practical than eschatological. If a Christian lives like an unbeliever (**according to the flesh**), he will receive what an unbeliever receives *in this life*, namely moral corruption and frustration which Paul here calls "death." **By the Spirit** indicates that sanctification in the believer's life comes from dependence upon and cooperation with the Spirit, not through keeping the law.

8:14-17. Being led by the Spirit of God (v. 14), in connection with vv. 12-13, relates to the Spirit's influence in avoiding sin and putting to death the deeds of the body, not to knowing His will when making mundane decisions (e.g., buying a Ford vs. a Chevrolet). The double occurrence of **spirit** (v. 15) is best understood as a reference to the Holy Spirit in light of His work whereby believers are made God's sons and daughters in vv. 14, 23. The Spirit brings sonship, not dreaded bondage. **Abba** is often popularly glossed with "Daddy," but it is a term that could be used by adult men for older men they respected so that "Daddy" may carry more of a sense of childish informality than is warranted. In much the same way that wealthier Roman families had a male slave who chaperoned the family's boys (called a *paidagogos*), so also God gives His Spirit to lead (*ago*) His sons and to help them avoid trouble in the form of sin. The **Spirit testifies** *to* the believer's spirit that he belongs to God. It would be odd to say that the Holy Spirit testifies *with* the believer's spirit, as if the believer's spirit added anything to His testimony. As the believer studies the Word and sees his life transformed (cf. 8:13), the Spirit impresses upon his mind that he belongs to God. If believers are God's children, then they are His heirs (v. 17) and may inherit God Himself or what God has in store for them—or both. But the road to glory for Christians is the same one Jesus trod, and His road was marked by the suffering of self-sacrifice for the sake of others. Perhaps Paul had in mind the sacrifices the church in Rome might make in order for him to reach Spain with the gospel.

8:18-25. Paul continues both the theme of the futurity and the suffering associated with being God's heir. At the second coming, believers will see God's glory (v. 18) as they return with Jesus to earth, but also will have their own glory (v. 21), a glory that surely reflects the glory of Jesus, just as the moon's glory is found in its reflection of the light of the sun. Verses 19-21 are Paul's commentary on Gn 3. When Jesus returns to earth with His people, the curse will be lifted from the world. Inanimate creation is personified in this passage as looking forward to the restoration of creation. **Creation groans** (v. 22) probably refers to natural disasters in which human life and property are lost. **Suffers the pains of childbirth** (v. 22) indicates that the natural disasters are not permanent, and will not continue past the second coming. When calamities happen in the world, they remind the believer that these conditions are temporary, just as a woman's labor is temporary. Eventually the baby comes, and happiness ensues, and so it will be when the Lord returns.

Not only does creation groan (v. 22), but believers **groan within** themselves (v. 23) **having** (or "because they have") **the first fruits of the Spirit**. **First fruits** may have OT offering connotations (cf. Lv 23). The first fruits offering was to show one's trust in the Lord, that if He has provided early aspects of the harvest, He could be trusted for good provision later. God has given the Spirit to believers at the present time, establishing an unbreakable connection between the initial experience of salvation and its end in eternity. The Spirit is both the first installment of our salvation and the down payment of the pledge that guarantees the remaining stages of the work of God in our salvation. Because believers have the Spirit, they have a slender experience of what awaits them, and as a result, they groan. There is no good reason to think that believers' groanings are not audible. Many of God's children, when they encounter hardship, have uttered a groan and said, "How I wish Jesus would come back *right now*!" Unbelievers do not express such sentiments, and the fact that believers do should serve to remind them that their utopia is not found in this life. They groan while **waiting eagerly for** their **adoption as sons**. In v. 15 the adoption is seen as already accomplished, and it surely is, but the full consummation of it awaits the future (a classic text for the concept of "now and not yet").

Redemption of our body refers to the resurrection, when all sin, evil, and suffering are set aside. If the Christian adoption as sons and daughters of God is accomplished (v. 15) but is not now fully accomplished (v. 23), then **perseverance** in **hope** (confident expectation) is needed (vv. 24-25).

8:26-27. In the same way that hope sustains believers when they suffer, so also **the Spirit helps** their **weakness** when they pray (v. 26), the **weakness** being found in ignorance concerning how one ought to pray. **Groanings too deep for words** is an oxymoron, but describes the Spirit's "wordless prayer groaning" on behalf of God's children. **Too deep for words** means "unspoken," "unspeakable," "unuttered," "unutterable," but in any case these groans are inaudible and therefore do not refer to speaking in tongues. In addition, **the Spirit Himself** performs this intercessory ministry, but speaking in tongues involves the participation of the believer (cf. 1Co 14:14), and while not every believer speaks in tongues (1Co 12:30), *every believer* can be confident of this prayer ministry of the Spirit. If God knows every thought of every person, then He is quite capable of understanding the Spirit's prayers for His children (v. 27). **He** [the Spirit] **intercedes... according to the will of God** provides the basis for what Paul will say in v. 28. If the Spirit prays for believers, then God's loving purposes will come to them. Not only does the Spirit intercede, but the Son does as well (v. 34), and the intercessory work of two members of the Godhead are what guarantees that "nothing will separate us from the love of God," and that believers will never lose their salvation.

8:28-30. Believers do not always know how to pray (v. 26), but **we** do **know that God causes all things to work together for good** (v. 28). It is not clear what the subject of v. 28 is, for the subject is embedded in the third singular verb (either "He/it works together") and "all things" could remotely be the subject (see KJV; NET). But God should be understood as the subject in light of His active role in calling and saving His people (vv. 29-30). Because God is both sovereign and loving, **all things** should be understood comprehensively. Even the tragic circumstances that believers undergo are part of His loving design for their lives, for from them He brings **good** ("that which is morally, tangibly beneficial"). **To those who love God** is defined further by **to those who are called**, so that **those who love God** are not some group of super-believers, but is a category in which *all* believers are found. **His purpose** is explained in vv. 29-30. **Foreknew** (v. 29) means "to determine ahead of time to enter into a loving relationship with someone" (cf. Ac 2:23; Rm 11:2; 1Pt 1:2, 20). The functional opposite is found in Rm 11:2, where the verb "foreknow" is the opposite of "reject." If "reject" has an active sense in Rm 11:2, then its opposite (God's foreknowledge) is an active, determinative foreknowledge. In other words, His foreknowledge is not simply a prognostication (a bare, passive knowledge of what will happen next—for which see the human forecasting in Ac 26:5; 2Pt 3:17), but a *causative, determinative* foreknowing, where His foreknowledge *brings about* what is foreknown. **Predestined** means "to decide upon beforehand," "to predetermine." **Foreknew** emphasizes God's initial decision to embrace a specific believer, but **predestined** refers to the final eternal goal of His active foreknowledge, namely, believers being **conformed to the image of His Son** on their way to their eternal "destination" (as in "pre-destination"). Sanctification is missing from Paul's five-item list, but that is covered by the last half of v. 29. Being **conformed to the image of His Son** probably pertains not only to what will happen on the day of Christ's return but also what happens in the lengthy period before that return. **Firstborn** does not mean "first created" but rather "preeminent." The same term is used in the LXX for Israel being a preeminent nation, not the first nation God made (Ex 4:22), and for David, the preeminent king compared to all others, not the first king who ever lived (Ps 89:27). **Among many brethren** indicates that God's purpose (v. 28) includes a vast number finding redemption, the restoration of the human race through Jesus' work. There is, in this phrase, a brief reminder from Paul about the obligation the Romans have to promulgate the gospel, especially by helping him go to Spain (cf. "Purpose" in the introduction to Romans). **Called** (v. 30) refers to the effectual call of God. This call is the believer's experience of God's foreknown and predestined plan (cf. 1:1, 6, 7). For **justified**, cf. the note on 3:24. **Glorified** (to experience God's glory with Him forever) is in the aorist tense, as are the other four verbs, and the tense presents each action comprehensively, as a complete (not "completed"), undifferentiated whole, without regard to its internal workings or how it unfolds. In God's plan, He foreknew, predestined, called, justified, *and* glorified each believer. If God foreknows, predestines, calls, and justifies a believer, then it seems extremely unlikely that the believer might fail to be glorified as well.

8:31-39. The contents of Rm 8 indicate that **God is for us** (v. 31). **Who is against us** does not prove that the Christian has no enemies. Paul's point is that those enemies cannot successfully turn God against him or her. If God sacrificed **His own Son** (v. 32) to bring about salvation, then He can be counted on to provide everything else delineated in chap. 8, including eternal life. **Charge** (v. 33) is a judicial term used for asserting that one was guilty of a crime and liable to prosecution and punishment. God, however, has chosen believers (**God's elect**) in Christ, and no one can successfully cause Him to condemn them. For **justifies**, see the note on 3:24. **Jesus . . . died** (v. 34) for sins and took care of the sin problem, something no one could do for himself. He **was raised** from the dead, and having conquered sin and death, He provides eternal life for all who have faith in Him. He **is at the right hand of God**, indicating that He shares God's authority, and that no higher authority exists who can turn Him against His people. And Jesus **intercedes for us** so that Christians always remain in the Father's love. Verses 35-36 indicate that visible threats, including the prospect of death by persecution (**sword**), cannot separate the believer from God's love. On the contrary, in spite of these, the believer **overwhelmingly conquers** ("we are hyper-victors"). In vv. 38-39, invisible threats cannot tear the believer from God's love. Paul concludes the list with the phrase **nor any other created thing**, which includes both the devil *and* the believer. It is inconceivable that a true believer, who at times might not be able to keep his own shoe tied or balance his checkbook, could undo the eternal purposes of God that include His foreknowledge and their glorification. The believer is not nearly that powerful, nor the Spirit and the Savior so incompetent.

IV. Vindication: The Jewish People and the Problems with Being Right with God (9:1–11:36)

A. God Has Not Broken His Word to Israel (9:1-29)

God will never stop loving believers, and He will keep all His promises to them on the basis of their connection with Christ (Rm 8). But this is harder to assert in light of what might appear to be God's ceasing to love Israel and His reneging on OT promises to the Jewish people. In chaps. 9–11, Paul vindicates God's character, proving that God always keeps His promises, even to Israel, and could thus be counted on to keep His promises to believers.

9:1-5. Paul felt great anguish about the spiritual condition of his kinsmen. **Accursed** (*anathema*, v. 3) means "to be cursed," here referring to eschatological judgment. Many scholars argue that Rm 9 is about God's sovereign choice to utilize entire nations to fulfill His purposes in history. But this is unlikely in light of Paul's wish to trade places with his fellow Jews and suffer eternal cursing. The preferable understanding is that God's choices involve the election of individuals for eternal life or its opposite.

Some of the privileges in vv. 4-5 have future components as well as past ones. For example, Israel's **adoption as sons** is grounded in God's selection of Israel as the recipient of His covenant blessings (cf. Ex 4:22; Jr 31:9). But Israel's sonship also has a glorious future component for Jewish believers (see Is 43:6; 45:11; 63:16-17; 64:8-12; Hs 1:10; Mal 3:17, all in eschatological contexts). This suggests, among other things, that God is not finished with the Jewish people yet, the primary point of Rm 9, 10, and 11. The future implications of these blessings gave Paul hope that God had not broken off relations with Israel and would yet keep His promises—all of them—to the people. Verse 5 indicates that **Christ** shares the divine nature, was incarnate, is absolutely sovereign, but is also worthy of eternal acclamation (**blessed forever**). Paul's anguish stems from his awareness that the Jewish people were not (yet!) experiencing everything God promised them, including their own exalted Messiah. Each of the privileges in 9:4-5 belongs to Israel presently (note the present tense **are** in 9:4a), suggesting that these privileges have not been rescinded. Their experience of these blessings, however, is contingent upon faith in Christ.

9:6-13. Paul argued that God would keep His promises for "true" Israel. **They are not all Israel who are descended from Israel** (v. 6) is explained by vv. 7-13. The true Jewish people are Jews who are not mere descendants of Abraham but are rather his ethnic descendants *who were chosen by God to be recipients of His covenant blessings* including salvation. In v. 6, Paul does not have Gentile believers in view. He is concerned to demonstrate that what God was doing with Israel in Paul's day was what God had always done with the descendants of Abraham, and Gentile Christians are not in view. Paul's point is to indicate that "true Israel" consists of the ethnic descendants of Abraham who have embraced Christ, who are the "faithful remnant," who are a narrower subset of broader ethnic Israel. **THROUGH ISAAC YOUR DESCENDANTS WILL BE NAMED** (v. 7) cites Gn 21:12; see the note there. **The children of the promise** (v. 8) comprise the true Israel, the true offspring of Abraham, and those, like Isaac but not Ishmael, are chosen by God to be blessed. For v. 9, see the note on Gn 18:10. But Isaac and Ishmael had different mothers. Perhaps God discriminated between the two on that basis. Jacob and Esau, however, had the same mother and were conceived at the same time (vv. 10-11). **God's purpose according to His choice** (v. 11) is a prominent theme in chaps. 9 and 11 (see 9:15, 17, 18, 19-21, 22-24; 11:1-2, 4-6, 23, 28-29, 30-32), and indicates that salvation rests upon His sovereign purposes. Verse 12 cites Gn 25:23; see the note there. In the phrases **JACOB I LOVED, BUT ESAU I HATED** (Mal 1:2; see the comments), **HATED** sometimes means "loved less" (Lk 14:26), but that is not the case here. Malachi 1:2 indicates that it has a more active sense. God **hated** Esau by rejecting him, excluding him from the blessings of the Abrahamic Covenant. This is supported by Mal 1, where God deliberately cursed Esau and his descendants. God's love for Jacob was manifested in actively choosing him to receive the promised blessings (including salvation). Both Gn 25:23 and Mal 1:2 begin with God's choice of the individuals, not whole people groups descended from them, and indicate that Paul's topic was God's sovereign choice of individuals to include them in His covenant or to exclude them from it.

9:14-16. God's electing love (v. 13) is developed in these verses. The question, **There is no injustice** ["unfairness"] **with God, is there?** (v. 14) means that Paul saw no unfairness in God freely choosing those who are saved. God would be perfectly just to condemn every person and save no one. That He chooses to save some indicates His grace, not His unfairness. Verse 15 cites Ex 33:19 where God reveals to Moses one of His fundamental attributes: that He remains free to show His **MERCY** and **COMPASSION** to whomever He freely chooses. Thus **it** (the bestowing of His mercy and compassion) depends on **God who has mercy** (v. 16). God determines who will be saved. That was true with the immediate offspring of the patriarchs, and it was true with the Jewish people in Paul's day. God was doing with the Jewish people what He had always done, namely, sovereignly and graciously selecting some of the physical descendants of Abraham to be recipients of the blessings of the Abrahamic Covenant including salvation (as indicated by Isaac and Jacob) and rejecting others from it (illustrated by Ishmael and Esau), and this indicates that He continued to fulfill His promises to Israel.

9:17-18. Here Paul develops the concept implied by "Esau I hated" (v. 13), using the example of Pharaoh as his illustration. Seventeen times Exodus mentions Pharaoh's hard heart, the first two being ascribed to God's decision to harden him (Ex 4:21; 7:3). Only four times does the text say that Pharaoh hardened his own heart (Ex 7:4; 8:15, 32; 9:34), and one of those verses (8:15) says that "he hardened his heart . . . as the LORD had said," indicating that God was the impetus behind Pharaoh's hardness. God hardened Pharaoh **TO DEMONSTRATE MY POWER IN YOU, AND THAT MY NAME MIGHT BE PROCLAIMED THROUGHOUT THE WHOLE EARTH**, and because God smote the Egyptians with no less than ten plagues because of Pharaoh's obduracy, even the inhabitants of Jericho, forty years later, heard and recollected the reports of His power (Jos 2:9-11). By implication, the hardening of Israel resulted in the spread of the gospel into Gentile lands.

9:19-21. Verse 19 could be paraphrased this way: "How can God judge people for their sinfulness (like Pharaoh's or Israel's hard-heartedness)? Are they not doing what *He* has sovereignly willed them to do?" Paul never gave an answer to the question, but instead reproves the vexed or dismissive attitude with which it is asked. **Answers back** (v. 20) means "to criticize in return" or "to answer antagonistically," and is found in Lk 14:6, when the lawyers and Pharisees could not refute Jesus on the topic of healing on the Sabbath ("They could *make* no *reply* to this."). The apostle gave no answer because, in the final analysis, the mechanics of God's providence over sin is a mystery. The **lump** of clay (v. 21) refers metaphorically to all of humanity from which the **potter** (God) chooses to make a **vessel for honorable use** (in context, to receive His mercy and compassion) and another **for common use** (i.e., to be excluded from His mercy and compassion).

9:22-23. The syntax of these two verses is complex, but should probably be understood in this way: But if God endured with much longsuffering vessels of wrath prepared for destruction

- because He was willing to demonstrate His wrath, and
- to make His power known, and
- to make known the riches of His glory upon vessels of mercy, which He prepared beforehand for glory,

then what will you say to that? (Paul's sentence is incomplete; he never provided a "then" for the "if" that begins v. 22, so this last phrase is added to make the sentence grammatically complete.)

God is longsuffering (translated **patience** in v. 22) not to provide extra time for unbelievers to be saved, but, in keeping with Pharaoh's example, to afford God a greater opportunity to **demonstrate His wrath and to make His power known**, and thereby to bring glory to Himself as the holy one who will not tolerate sin. See v. 17 for use of the words **demonstrate** and **power** in connection with Pharaoh, who is the concrete illustration of the principles found in vv. 22-23. Ultimately the demonstration of His wrath and power upon vessels prepared for destruction is for the purpose of showing His profound grace toward those **He prepared beforehand for glory**. It is impossible to appreciate God's saving grace unless it is seen against the sobering backdrop of His judgment. **Prepared for destruction** could be translated "who prepare themselves for destruction," but it is preferable to see it as a true passive. While the agent of the preparation is not mentioned in v. 22, the context makes it clear that it is God (9:13, 15, 16, 18, 19-21). If Rm 9 emphasizes God's sovereign role in the condemnation of sinners, Rm 10 makes it clear that the individual is equally responsible for his own sins that result in condemnation.

The Bible teaches that the sovereignty of God extends even to sin, evil, and suffering in the world. God stood behind the hard-heartedness of Pharaoh and Israel's sin of unbelief, but in neither case was *He* to be held morally culpable for their sins. They bear the guilt of their rebellious actions. For a defensible, logical, non-contradictory discussion of the relationship of God's sovereignty and man's free will and moral responsibility, see John S. Feinberg, *No One Like Him* (Wheaton, IL: Crossway, 2001), 625-734. On a more popular level, cf. Wayne Grudem, *Systematic Theology* (Grand Rapids, MI: Zondervan, 1994), 315-354.

9:24-26. God not only chooses Jewish people to be saved, but also **Gentiles** (v. 24). Paul cited Hs 2:23 in 9:25, and Hs 1:10 in 9:26 (see the comments in Hosea). By analogy, Paul applied what is said of the restoration of apostate Jews to Gentiles. Paul used these verses to indicate that God was fashioning for Himself a single people, consisting of both Jews and Gentiles, reconciled to Him by the work of Christ. But the citation of verses from Hosea does not indicate that "the Church fulfills the promises made to Israel" or that "the Church is the new Israel," for Jewish believers like Paul were fulfilling Hosea's prophecy, and later Israel will be reconciled as a whole (cf. 11:25-26).

9:27-29. Paul returned to Israel's situation. In vv. 27-28, Paul cited Is 10:22-23 in which Isaiah emphasized that only a small remnant would be saved, a situation that was being fulfilled in Paul's day (9:6-13). Isaiah also noted that God judges **THOROUGHLY AND QUICKLY** (better "completely and finally") those who remain unrepentant. Paul cited Is 1:9, a verse indicating that God had preserved some who had not succumbed to apostasy and judgment. These OT verses support what Paul said in 9:6-23. God was keeping His promises to Israel, and was doing so in the same way that He had always done it—through the remnant of Israel, meaning God was selecting some, but not all, of the physical descendants of Abraham to be in a right covenantal standing with Him, including salvation.

B. God Has Not Cheated Israel (9:30–10:21)

Many believers are understandably troubled by Rm 9, but beginning in 9:30 and running throughout chap. 10, Paul developed a more familiar doctrine, that of man's responsibility. In chap. 9, Israel rejects Jesus because God hardened her. In chap. 10, Israel rejects Jesus because she has freely chosen to do so.

9:30–10:4. Gentiles . . . attained righteousness . . . which is by faith (v. 30) provides an illustration of 9:16. Israel, however, did not attain righteousness, for they were "pursuing the law *for* righteousness" (v. 31) (a better translation than **pursuing a law of righteousness**), and seeking righteousness by **works** and not by **faith** (vv. 31-32). Paul cited Is 28:16 in v. 33, and based on its use in 10:11, understood it messianically as a reference to Jesus. As in 9:3, Paul expressed his longing that his kinsmen find salvation in Christ (10:1), another indication that Paul was writing about God's choice of individuals to receive salvation, not His choice regarding what roles people groups would play in history. On 10:3, cf. the note on Php 3:2-12. **The end of the law** indicates that Jesus, by His death, brought the era of living under the law to a close. Just as the finish line is both the goal and the end of a race, Jesus is the goal of the law inasmuch as it anticipated and pointed toward Him, and He is the end of the law since He brings its era of governing life to a close (see the comments on Mt 5:17-19; Rm 3:21-26; Gl 3:10-4:11).

10:5-13. In v. 5, Paul alluded to Lv 18:5 (see the note there), and with it censures unbelieving Israel (see the similar point of allusions to Lv 18:5 in Neh 9:29; Ezk 18:9; 20:11). He indicates that if one insists on establishing his righteousness with God by keeping the law, then he will live (have eternal life) *only* if he actually keeps the law. But Paul already demonstrated the futility of this in chaps. 1–3. In vv. 6-8, Paul cited Dt 9:4 and 30:11-14, where Moses commanded the people to obey the Lord. As in Moses' day when God graciously took the initiative to make the law readily available to the Jewish people so they could obey it, so also in Paul's day He made the gospel accessible as well. Verses 9-10 are sometimes cited to support the idea that one must publicly and verbally confess Christ in order to be saved. Confessing is a result of true saving faith and an evidence of it (cf. 1Tm 6:12; Ti 1:16), and lack of confession may indicate lack of salvation. Much of the apostolic preaching included an emphasis on Christ's resurrection (cf. Ac 2:14-40; 3:12-26; 10:34-43; 13:16-41; 17:16-31), and it is faith *in a resurrected Christ* that saves one (**believe . . . that God raised Him**, v. 9). In vv. 11-13, Paul cited Is 28:16 again (cf. 9:33), and expanded on the implications of "whoever believes" in vv. 12-13. In v. 13, Paul cited Jl 2:32, emphasizing the universal availablility of the gospel.

10:14-17. These verses ask questions that ultimately receive an affirmative answer in v. 18 (**Indeed they have**). Regarding the need to get the gospel to the Jewish people, messengers have been recruited (v. 14c), sent out (v. 15a), the word of faith has been preached (v. 14b), the message has been heard (v. 14b, 17, 18), and the message has been understood (vv. 19-20). So, what is the problem? The problem is, they did not believe it (vv. 16-17). Paul's point is that God cannot be blamed for not doing enough to get the gospel to the Jewish people. The problem, at least in chap. 10, resides with Israel's refusal to believe the gospel. Romans 10:14-15 are often used as motivational verses to bolster world evangelization, but the context makes it clear that Paul had in mind the Jewish people, and that, even in his day, the gospel had made extensive inroads into Jewish communities throughout the Mediterranean world. But the mission to the Jewish people has not been completed.

10:18-21. In v. 18 Paul cited Ps 19:4 about how creation broadcasts God's majesty everywhere. Similarly, the gospel was disseminated widely enough among the Jewish people and the rest of the world that Paul could say it **HAS GONE OUT INTO ALL THE EARTH** and **TO THE ENDS OF THE WORLD** (v. 18). He maintained that Israel has known its content (vv. 16-18), and should have known of God's plan to distribute it widely among the nations and have them embrace it (vv. 19b-20). Paul cited Dt 32:21b (v. 19) to indicate that God determined to bring salvation to the Gentiles and thereby cause Israel to be jealous when He did it. He also cited Is 65:1 in 10:20, where Isaiah prophesied that God would turn the Jewish people to Himself once again along with Gentiles (Is 66:18-21), the inclusion of Gentile salvation being Paul's main point here. God was doing this in Paul's day with a few believing Jews and a host of Gentiles. In v. 21 the apostle cited Is 65:2 in reference to the many unbelievers in Israel. Is 65:2 emphasizes both Israel's obstinate refusal to embrace her Messiah and God's refusal to withdraw His gracious offer of deliverance.

C. God Has Not Rejected Israel (11:1-10)

In Rm 9, Paul introduced the themes of election of some of the offspring of Abraham to be His children of promise and the hardening of others. In chap. 10, he emphasized the need for faith in Christ. In chap. 11, Paul weaves together all of these themes, and argues that there is still a future for ethnic Israel in God's program.

11:1-6. One might think that Paul believed that God rejected Israel because of her disobedience and obstinacy, but that is a misunderstanding of what Paul was saying. Once again, answering an unseen objector, Paul twice states categorically that **God has not rejected His people** (vv. 1-2). He cites himself as the textbook example that God had not altogether and permanently rejected the Jewish people (v. 1). **Rejected** (v. 2) is the functional opposite of **foreknew**, and indicates that God's foreknowledge is not simple prognostication, but is active and brings about what is foreknown. Paul referred to the record of Elijah (citing 1Kg 19:10, 14, 18), who had an over-inflated view of his own importance and wrongly saw himself as the sole Jew still faithful to God (v. 3). But God spiritually preserved a faithful remnant of 7,000 (v. 4), just as He was doing with the faithful remnant of Jews in Paul's day and throughout the Church age. This preservation was accomplished on the basis of **God's gracious choice** (v. 5), not **on the basis of works** by the Jewish people (v. 6).

11:7-10. The majority of the Jewish people did not attain a right standing with God. Instead, they were hardened (v. 7; cf. also Rm 9:17-18). But the elect attained it on the basis of God's grace. As shocking as it sounds that God would harden some of His people, the Law, the Prophets, and the Writings—the three divisions of the Hebrew Scriptures—all contain passages that speak of God's periodic hardening of His people in the past, so that what was happening in Paul's day was no anomaly. **GOD GAVE THEM A SPIRIT OF STUPOR** (v. 8) is a citation of Is 29:10. **EYES TO SEE NOT . . . TO THIS VERY DAY** cites Dt 29:4. Verse 9 cites Ps 69:22-23. God was continuing to interact with the Jewish people in the same manner that He had always treated them, and by noting these precedents, Paul indicates that God had not broken His promises to Israel in Paul's day.

D. Israel Is Not Lost Forever (11:11-36)

11:11-16. Paul's readers might conclude from 11:1-10 that Israel has permanently fallen from God's ongoing program, but that is not what Paul meant. **Stumble** (v. 11) refers to Israel's temporary spiritual setback, but her condition was not a permanent **fall**. God's hardening of Israel, and Israel's refusal to believe in Jesus as their Messiah, was ordained by God to provide time for the spread of the gospel to the Gentiles (vv. 11, 12, 15). Just as God's fame spread as a result of Pharaoh's hardening (cf. the note on 9:17-18), so also His fame was spreading to the Gentiles in Paul's day because of Israel's rejection of the gospel. As Gentiles embrace the Jewish Messiah and receive the accompanying blessings, God's and Paul's aim thereby was **to make them** [the Jewish people] **jealous** (lit., "to provoke them to be envious" so that they will imitate the Gentiles). Paul was intensely burdened that the Jewish people come to Christ, for when they do, the world will erupt in spiritual vitality and life (vv. 12, 15; cf. Is 27:6). **Their rejection** and **their acceptance** (v. 15) may refer to God's temporary rejection and future acceptance of them, but in light of "their transgression" in vv. 11, 12 and Paul's assertion that God has not rejected them (11:1-2), the better understanding is that the phrases refer to Israel's rejection of God and what He had done through Christ. The phrase **life from the dead** (v. 15) may indicate that Israel's restoration, and the concomitant blessings for the world take place at the time of the general resurrection immediately prior to the eternal state. But similar phrases are found in 4:17 (God "gives life to the dead") and 6:13 ("present yourselves as those alive from the dead"), and suggests instead that Paul was simply stating the fact that Israel will enjoy spiritual life at a time in the future, with that time left undefined. Verse 16 provides further support for Paul's assertion that Israel will be restored in God's favor. The identification of the **the first piece of dough** and **lump** is debated, as is the referent of **the root** and **the branches**. On the basis of 11:28-29, **the first piece of dough** and **the root** probably refer to the Jewish patriarchs who were upheld by the covenant promises of God. The promises God made to them guarantee an ethnic people who will stand in right relationship with Him (cf. Gn 12:1-3). This happy prospect, however, awaits a future fulfillment.

11:17-24. Paul continued to employ the metaphor of a tree to Israel's spiritual condition and awaited restoration. The **branches** that **were broken off** (v. 17) refer to Jewish unbelievers, and it should be noted that these were not individuals who once were saved and then lost their salvation. While Paul's analogy has them **broken off** from the tree, in reality they were never part of the tree to start with. The **wild olive** branches refer to Gentile believers. The grafting refers to their salvation. The **rich root** refers to the covenant blessings of God promised to the patriarchs. Those blessings sustained and supported Abraham, Isaac, and Jacob, and those covenant promises gave rise to **the olive tree**. The cultivated olive tree branches that were not broken off refer to the Jewish people chosen by God to be the recipients of His covenant blessings, including salvation through faith in Christ. Gentile believers have become partakers **with them** of the spiritual aspects of the Abrahamic and new covenants. Because Gentile believers benefit from the Abrahamic covenant, anti-Semitism is ludicrous (v. 18). Many of the Jewish people would not partake of the covenant blessings of God, and many Gentiles would. But that did not mean that Gentile believers were intrinsically superior to the Jews (v. 19). Therefore, Paul warns Gentile believers not to **be arrogant toward** (v. 18) the Jewish people. A Gentile believer must never think, "I have been grafted into God's blessings, but most Jewish people have not been. Therefore, that means that I am superior, that God prefers me to them." The key to a right standing with God is not some modicum of ethnic or religious superiority, but **faith** (v. 20). **You stand by your faith** means "You stand *only* by your faith, nothing else!" But Paul makes it clear that if Gentiles do not come to God through faith in Christ, they will not be saved either (vv. 21-22), and if Jews begin to have faith in Christ, they will be saved (v. 23). Paul held out the joyful prospect that some day the Jewish people would come to Christ. God has engineered the peculiar process of Gentiles receiving Jewish spiritual blessings, called by Paul **grafted contrary to nature** (v. 24). That is, if an older cultivated olive tree was failing to produce decent olives, branches from a more productive tree could be grafted into the limbs or trunk of the older tree, and those branches would, in time, produce good olives. But *no one* would take the branches from a wild olive tree and graft them into a cultivated olive tree. Those wild branches would not produce the desired quality of olive. Yet this is what God has done with Gentile believers. Verses 17-24 do not mean that Gentile believers "become Jewish." While they enjoy the spiritual blessings of the Jewish people, they remain "wild olive branches." They do not transform into "cultivated branches."

11:25-27. A **mystery** (v. 25) could be a truth hinted at in the OT but fully revealed in the NT, or one altogether unknown in the OT and revealed in the NT. The latter is the sense here, for the OT speaks of an enormous number of Gentiles being included in the one people of God (cf. the notes on Is 2:2-4; 66:18-24), but the idea that those Gentiles are included prior to the wholesale restoration of Israel is not seen in the OT. **Partial hardening** means that a (majority) part of Israel were not saved based on God's sovereign choice, but a minority (the faithful remnant) like Paul believed. **Fullness of the Gentiles** refers to the "full number of Gentiles" whom God has determined to be saved prior to Him lifting the hardening from Israel. **All Israel will be saved** (v. 26) is the climax of all of Rm 9, 10, and 11. **All Israel**, according to the use of the phrase in the LXX, never referred to every single Jew (cf. 1Ch 19:17 where it refers only to soldiers; 1Sm 25:1, where it refers only to those who buried Samuel), and more than likely Paul does not mean that in the future every Jew will be saved. **All Israel** should probably be understood to refer to the vast majority of the ethnic people of Israel, Jews from every tribe and from every locale all over the world. For the timing of Israel's salvation, cf. the comments on Zch 12:10, Mt 23:37-39, and Ac 3:19, which indicate that Israel's salvation happens during the tribulation period—before, not during, the second coming—and is a necessary precursor for His return. In addition, **all Israel** never referred to every Jew from all time. When the phrase is used in the LXX, it refers to a representation of Jewish people *at a given point in time* (e.g., Nm 16:34; 1Ch 11:10; 15:25; 2Ch 10:3), and Paul's use of the phrase reflects the same understanding. At a specific point in time that was future to Paul (and to us), a colossal number of Jews from all wings of Judaism will turn to Christ. Paul is not referring to Jewish people who became believers throughout the church age and who are enfolded into the church, and in fact **Israel** does not refer to "the Church" comprised of Jews and Gentiles in Christ, though it is often understood that way. In 11:25, **Israel** clearly refers to the ethnic people of Israel, and there is no indication that Paul redefines the term in v. 26 to mean the Church. In addition, in v. 28, **they** has as its antecedent **all Israel** in v. 26, and in v. 28 the Church is not in view. Paul cited Is 59:20-21 in 11:26b, c, and 27a, and Is 27:9 in 11:27b to provide warrant for his confidence that in the future all Israel will be saved, and it is less likely that they present the time of this conversion. Some view these OT verses as an indication of the time of Israel's salvation (when the Deliverer comes from Zion—i.e., at the second coming), but it was already argued above that the salvation of all Israel must precede the second coming, so that Is 59:20-21 and 27:9 give the assurance from the OT that all Israel will be saved, rather than establishing the time when that salvation takes place. Israel's salvation is grounded in the death of Messiah Jesus at His *first* coming, not at His second.

11:28-32. In Paul's day, many of the Jewish people were **enemies** of the gospel, but **for the sake of the fathers** (because of the promises God made to Abraham, Isaac, and Jacob; cf. Gn 12:1-3; 15:6; 17:7-8), they remain God's chosen people and will someday be restored (v. 28). **The gifts and the calling of God** (v. 29) does not refer to the supposed permanency of miraculous spiritual gifts. In context, Paul was speaking of God's covenant promises that remain **irrevocable** (v. 29). In v. 30, Paul addressed Gentile believers. Because of the hardening of most of the Jewish people, the Gentiles are given the time and opportunity to embrace the gospel. Verse 31 indicates, once again, that the disobedience of the

Jewish people is not permanent. In the future, when a precise number of Gentiles are saved at a time known only to God, God will lift the hardening of Israel and show them **mercy** (v. 31). It is God's intention to show His grace and mercy. In order to do that, He **shuts up all in disobedience** (synonymous with "hardening") **so that He may show mercy to all**, to "all people groups (i.e., Jews and Gentiles) without distinction," not "all individuals without exception."

11:33-36. The doxology that closes this section extols God for His **riches**, possibly the riches of His mercy (v. 32), His **wisdom** (His impressive skills), and **knowledge** (perhaps His foreknowledge so prominent in chaps. 9–11). **His judgments** do not refer to the eschatological condemnation of the lost, but His deliberative processes. Verse 34 cites Is 40:13-14, and emphasizes the futility of fully knowing how or what God has determined, as well as His utter independence of man in executing His plans. Verse 35 cites Jb 41:3, indicating even here that one experiences the "riches" of God's mercy (11:32-33) on the basis of His grace, not through reciprocity whereby He gives grace to those who have earned it. **From Him** (v. 36) indicates that He is the source of all things in the universe. **Through Him** indicates that He is the agent through whom all things exist and come about. And **to Him** means that He is the goal of all that exists and happens in creation, all of which serves to bring Him **glory** (praise) **forever**.

V. Application: The Implications of Being Right with God (12:1–15:33)

A. The Implications for the Christian's Spiritual Commitment (12:1-2)

12:1-2. In chap. 12, Paul transitioned to a discussion of the practical implications of being right with God, starting with the proper response to God. In light of the **mercies of God** (v. 1) expounded in chaps. 1–11, Paul urged the believers in Rome to function as **living sacrifices**. **Present** ("to stand before another in order to serve him," cf. Rm 6:13) is a virtual command, the aorist tense indicating not a one-time dedication, but the completeness and comprehensiveness of placing oneself at God's disposal. Unlike dead animal sacrifices, Christians must live to serve God constantly. **Spiritual** (*logikos*, from which the Eng. word "logical" is derived) means "rational," "reasonable," "that which is carefully thought through." **Conformed** (v. 2) means "to be shaped by a pattern or mold," namely, the pattern or mold of **this world** (*aion*, "temporary era"). Rather than be shaped to look like the world, the Christian's **mind** is to be renewed in order to appreciate the importance and benefits of God's will as revealed in His Word.

B. The Implications for the Christian's Life in the Body of Christ (12:3-13)

12:3-8. Beginning in 12:3, Paul turned his attention to the social implications of being right with God. **Measure of faith** (v. 3) probably means "the *instrument* for measuring, namely saving faith." Every believer is saved by faith, and if each measures himself against that "yardstick" or "standard," conceit will vanish, and the diverse parts of the local body will work together more profitably for their mutual care (vv. 4-5). The body receives help especially as its members use their spiritual gifts (vv. 6-8). **Prophecy** (v. 6) was not "powerful preaching" or "convicting others of sin." A prophet was God's mouthpiece, His spokesperson who received direct revelation and spoke it with authority to His people (Ex 7:1-2; Dt 18:18, 20; Jr 23:16; for more on prophecy, cf. the comments on 1Co 12:10, and on 1Co 14 as a whole). The prophet is to prophesy "according to the standard of faith" (HCSB), or "in keeping with the Christian faith"—i.e., prophecies must not contradict previously revealed truth. **Service** (v. 7) refers to working in practical ways to assist believers. **Teaching** is the systematic impartation of knowledge or skill, in this case biblical truth. **Exhortation** (v. 8) carries the dual sense of "comforting" (cf. 2Co 1:3-7) and "urging one to live biblically" (Rm 12:1). **Giving** refers to the glad contribution of financial resources to the needs of Christians and the church without duplicitous motives (the meaning of **liberality**). The one **who leads** provides the oversight and direction for the church (cf. 1Tm 3:4-5, where the word is translated "manage"; and 1Tm 5:17, translated "rule"). **Diligence** means "eagerness, hard work, and speed." **Mercy** involves showing sympathy or kindness to those who suffer. For more on spiritual gifts, cf. the comments on 1Co 12–14.

12:9-13. While one should serve mainly in the area of his giftedness, sometimes he or she must help more broadly, and this passage explains how that must be done. An act of **love** (v. 9) can be hypocritical if it cloaks an attitude of reluctance or self-seeking. **Abhor** means "a strong feeling of revulsion or aversion." **Cling** means "to glue something together." **Devoted** (v. 10) means "to be tender and affectionate" to another, as if to a cherished family member (**brotherly love**, Gk. *philadelphia*). **Give preference**... **in honor** means "being eager to value or promote the reputation of another" ahead of oneself. Not **lagging behind** (v. 11) means "not being slack in accomplishing what is worthwhile." For **diligence**, see 12:8. **Fervent** means lit., "boiling, seething," but here connotes having eagerness and enthusiasm (cf. Ac 18:25). **In spirit** may refer to one's inner disposition, but probably refers to the genuine gusto that comes from the Holy Spirit. **Rejoicing in hope** (v. 12) indicates "rejoicing *because of* hope." **Contributing** (v. 13) is from the verb *koinoneo*, and means "to share"; in this context, sharing one's resources to help when others have serious needs.

C. The Implications for the Christian's Life in Relation to the Secular World (12:14–13:14)

12:14-21. Paul moved from discussing life in the body of Christ to how a believer should respond to unbelievers who persecute them. Most of these exhortations are applicable to Christian relationships as well. **Bless** (v. 14; cf. Mt 5:44) means "to call upon God to bestow His kindness" on someone, and **curse** is its opposite. Verse 15 cannot be restricted to interaction only with believers. Nothing forbids the Christian from celebrating (appropriately) or mourning with a non-Christian friend. In v. 16, Paul may be speaking of relationships between Christians, but **be of the same mind toward one another** could equally be a directive "to have something in common" with one's unbelieving friends. Paul had already forbade arrogance in Christian circles (cf. 12:3), and may be encouraging the Roman believers to avoid spiritual conceit toward their unbelieving acquaintances. **Respect what is right in the sight of all men** (v. 17b) indicates that believers should do and value the praiseworthy things unbelievers applaud (e.g., working hard; giving to the poor). Believers are actively to seek **peace with all men** (v. 18), though sometimes peace is not possible, for an unbeliever may not cooperate. Paul cited Dt 32:35 in v. 19, and ordered believers to let God take revenge on those who hurt them. Believers are to carry out the mandate of v. 20 (which cites Pr 25:21-22). The phrase **HEAP BURNING COALS ON HIS HEAD** is puzzling, but Pr 25 was probably referring to an ancient Egyptian practice of demonstrating regret or repentance by carrying a pan filled with burning coals. Whatever the case, Paul's words must be understood in a redemptive light in view of vv. 14, 17, 19, and 21.

13:1-7. Paul continued discussing how Christians should interact with the secular world, but his focus shifted here to relationships with the governing authorities. **Subjection** (v. 1; cf. Eph 5:22, 24; Ti 3:1-2) means "to align oneself under the authority" of another, but Paul's order is not to be obeyed blindly. The Bible is full of examples of God's people passively resisting religious or secular authorities when those leaders required people to violate clear biblical directives (e.g., Dn 3, 6). **For** introduces a reason for submitting to governing authorities: They are **established by God** (cf. Ac 17:24-26). Because God is sovereign, the governments that exist are there because He ordained their existence. But as in the case of His providence over sin, the governmental leaders are morally culpable for the sin, evil, and suffering they propagate, not God (cf. the comments on Rm 9:22-23). **Therefore** (v. 2), because God founds all nations with their governments, to actively **resist** a secular regime is to rebel against God and **receive condemnation**, possibly both God's disapproval and formal condemnation from the authorities (cf. vv. 4–5). **For** (v. 3) explains why condemnation comes upon rebels. The government should not be opposed, for it guards the safety and security of its citizens (vv. 3-4). **Bear the sword** (v. 4) may mean "to practice capital punishment," or it may mean nothing more than "to punish criminals." But if a government determines that the death sentence is appropriate, it appears from this passage that it has the right to carry it out. **For conscience' sake** (v. 5) means that if a Christian understands that God is behind the existence of one's government, then disobeying that government will result in a violation of one's conscience. **Render** (v. 7) is the same word used by Jesus in Mt 22:21.

13:8-14. Paul gave more general commands in this section, but his primary emphasis may still be how the Christian should act in the world. **Owe nothing to anyone** (v. 8) does not forbid taking or giving loans, for both the law and Jesus permitted it (Lv 25:35-36; Mt 5:42; Lk 6:35). Paul's point is that the believer has the constant obligation to show **love** to all, and this obligation never stops. The verb **love** means "to demonstrate warmth and affection, usually to those with whom one is closely related or associated." It also has the nuance of joyfully and enthusiastically meeting the needs of others (cf. the comments on 1Co 13:1-3), even one's enemies (Mt 5:44). Love fulfills **the law**. In vv. 9-10,

Paul describes what happens when believers love others, but he is not prescribing that they must keep the law (cf. Rm 7:1-4; 10:4). Though Abraham did not possess and consciously obey the law of Moses, nevertheless by having faith in God his life fulfilled the law's requirements (Gn 26:5; see the comments there), though he was not saved by fulfilling them (Gn 15:6). Paul's command to love is presented with urgency in light of the rapture of the Church (v. 11). **Sleep** refers to the spiritual stupor that a believer must avoid. Jesus will hold each Christian accountable for his spiritual condition. **The night** (v. 12) refers to this present spiritually darkened era. **The day** probably refers to the inbreaking of Jesus and the kingdom, perhaps to the "day of the Lord." **Armor of light** would provide both spiritual protection and illumination so that one's enemies can be observed and avoided. One of the enemies is the believer's own **flesh** (v. 14; for "the flesh," cf. the comments on Rm 7:5-6; 8:12-13). **Carousing** (v. 13) means "a rowdy gathering typified by drunkenness and illicit sex." **Sensuality** refers to a lifestyle without any moral restraints, usually involving sexual sins. **Put on** (v. 14) was often used for putting on clothes (Mk 5:15; Ac 12:21), and in much the same way, the believer is to take Christ with him wherever he goes, just as he does his own clothing.

D. The Implications for the Christian's Life in His Relationships with Weaker and Differing Christians (14:1–15:13)

14:1-3. Paul addressed "strife and jealousy" in 13:13. Here he addressed a specific concern that could cause strife. Paul presented what he wanted the Romans to do in vv. 1-3, and gave the theological warrant for it in vv. 4-9. The **weak** were Jewish believers who felt that eating meat offered to a false god was an act of idolatry, so they ate **vegetables only** (v. 2). Food was offered in honor of the gods, and surplus fare was sold to the markets to provide income for the priests and maintain the temples. Gentile believers had the conviction (**faith**) that it was permissible to eat this meat. Paul directed the stronger Gentile believers to fellowship with Jewish believers, but not to coerce them to adopt the stronger brother's position (v. 1). They were not to **regard** their Jewish counterparts **with contempt** ("to despise," "to hold a disdainful, harsh attitude of disapproval"). Jewish believers were likewise not to **judge** (here "to nurse an unfavorable opinion of another," "to criticize, find fault") their Gentile brothers, for God **accepted** them.

14:4-9. Here Paul gave the theological basis for the exhortations of vv. 1-3. **Judge** (v. 4) specifically addressed the Jewish believers who were judging Gentile believers for eating meat offered to idols (cf. "judge" in v. 3). The Gentile Christians were **the servant of another**, i.e., of God, not of their fellow Jews. Jewish believers, therefore, could not dictate to the Gentile believers what they must do. Scripture was silent on the issue, so **each person** had to **be fully convinced in his own mind** (v. 5), i.e., had to follow his own convictions about what to do. **Day** indicates that Jewish believers continued to celebrate the Sabbath and holy days, though they were no longer under obligation to the law to do so (cf. Rm 6:14-15; 7:1-3; 10:4). Gentiles felt no compulsion to observe them. Both options were acceptable. Each group sought to please God in what they did (v. 6), but ironically disparaged each other when their opinions differed. Verses 7-9 reminded the Jewish and Gentile believers in Rome that only Jesus, on the basis of His resurrection authority, had the right to prescribe how believers should behave when Scripture was silent on an issue. But when Scripture clearly bans an action, the church is obliged "to judge" those whose lives are scandalously sinful (cf. the comments on 1Co 5:1-5, 9-13).

14:10-12. Paul reiterated the directives from vv. 3-4 (cf. "judge" and "regard with contempt"). **Judgment seat** (*bema*) was the raised platform where secular authorities rendered verdicts in criminal cases (e.g., Mt 27:19; Jn 19:13; Ac 18:12; 25:6). It never refers to the place where awards were given to the victors in athletic contests. Rewards are given *following* the *bema* judgment and are dependent upon God's evaluation of the believer there, but the judgment and the giving of rewards are distinct both in terms of what transpires and the time at which they take place. There is, in fact, no mention of the assigning of eternal rewards in 14:10-12, only an accounting of each believer to God. Some day, possibly following the rapture of the church, each believer will give an account of his life to God (cf. the comments on 2Co 5:10 and 1Co 3:10-17). The implication is that believers should not denounce one another when their opinions differ. God can be trusted to deal with them if they have done something wrong, and it should be left to Him. This judgment does not pertain to a believer's eternal destiny, but it certainly will affect his rewards (see the comments on 1Co 4:1-5). **GIVE PRAISE** (*exomologeo*, v. 11) would be better translated "admit doing wrong" (cf. LXX 2Ch 6:24; Mt

3:6; Jms 5:16). Paul cited Is 45:23, which affirms that God alone judges on the last day.

14:13-23. In vv. 1-12, Paul addressed both the weak and strong, but here the stronger Gentile believers are primarily in view. The **stumbling block** (v. 13) is sometimes understood as the anger that the weaker brother feels when a stronger brother legitimately exercises his liberty. This is possible, but a better understanding is that the **stumbling block** is the pressure a Gentile believer puts on a Jewish believer to violate his standards and sin against his conscience (cf. vv. 22-23). In v. 14, Paul sided with the strong, but made it clear that the actions of the strong could harm the weak (Jewish believers) (v. 15). **Hurt** means "to be distressed, saddened," possibly even "outraged." **Destroy** (*apollumi*) here does not mean "to send one to hell for eternal ruin," for no believer could do this to another. It often means "to damage," "ruin," or "harm" (Mt 9:17; Lk 21:18; Jms 1:11), and when the stronger brother cajoles the weaker to violate his standards, the weaker brother is harmed.

Therefore (v. 16) introduces Paul's conclusion to vv. 14-15. It was a **good thing** for a Gentile Christian to eat meat, but if he insisted that a Jewish believer should eat contrary to the dictates of his conscience, then that **good thing** took an evil turn. The **kingdom of God** (v. 17) is manifested in and through the Church, but the Church cannot be equated with the kingdom. **Righteousness** has a horizontal, social sense, "upright actions." **Drinking** anticipates drinking wine in v. 21. Wine was used as libations in the temples, and Jewish believers refused to purchase and drink wine just as they did meat. **All things indeed are clean** (v. 20) indicates that Jewish and Gentile believers alike were allowed to eat meat, just as Paul did. In v. 22, Paul urged the stronger brothers not to bully the weak into doing something that would violate their conscience. **He who doubts is condemned** (v. 23; also v. 22) does not mean that God will send this Christian to hell. As in v. 22, the weaker brother's conscience will experience guilt because he or she ate **not from faith**, i.e., because the weak did not have the conviction that it was permissible to eat. If one engages in some practice not clearly forbidden by Scripture, no sin has been committed. But if a believer violates his conscience, *that* constitutes sin. God wants His people to have sensitive consciences in order to avoid sin (1Tm 1:5, 19; Heb 5:14).

15:1-6. In 14:1-12, Paul wrote about the need to avoid condemning other believers. In 14:13-23, he urged the believers in Rome not to impose their practices upon others when Scripture did not require it. And in 15:1-13, Paul advocated the need to imitate Jesus, who served others. Verses 1-2 were addressed to the stronger Gentile believers, who were not to impose their practices upon the Jewish believers. They were to follow the example of Jesus (v. 3) who **did not please Himself**. There has always been the tendency of God's people to insist on their rights to engage in activities—sometimes questionable activities—on the basis of Christian liberty. But the more virtuous approach proffered by Paul is the willingness to surrender those rights for the sake of unity. Paul cited Ps 69:9, where **YOU** refers to God and **ME** refers to Jesus. The rebellious acts (**REPROACHES**) of all humankind against God were laid upon Jesus at the cross in the supreme act of self-sacrifice as He died to atone for sins. The Roman believers were obligated to follow His example, and act in ways that were considerate of others. The Hebrew Scriptures exist in part **for our instruction** (v. 4), and as believers see examples of those in the past who did not live solely to please themselves, they receive motivation from Scripture to persevere in the present and gain confidence (**hope**) regarding the future. See the comments on 5:3-5. Paul then recorded a wish related to the unity he has urged in the preceding verses. Scripture provides perseverance and encouragement (v. 4), but ultimately these come from God (v. 5). The **perseverance and encouragement** relate especially to unity, which is indispensable if this church would be effective in glorifying (enhancing the reputation of) **the God and Father of our Lord Jesus Christ** (v. 6) in Rome and in the world. Church unity would enhance their evangelistic endeavors, and would give the church greater capacity and vitality in supporting Paul's missionary work (see "Purpose" in the introduction to Romans).

15:7-13. Accept one another (v. 7) is the same command with which Paul began this section of Romans (cf. 14:1), but here he referred to Jesus as the prime example of accepting those with whom there are pronounced differences (cf. 5:6-10). By His death, Jesus served the Jewish people **to confirm the promises given to the fathers** (v. 8; cf. the comments on Gn 12:1-3). Jesus' atoning death provides the only means for the Jewish people to experience the full blessings of the Abrahamic covenant (cf. Rm 4:13-17; 11:27-29;

Gl 3:1-18). But His death also served Gentiles by providing them an avenue (**mercy**) through which they would **glorify God** for their share in salvation (v. 9). Paul cited Ps 18:49 in v. 9, Dt 32:43 in v. 10, Ps 117:1 in v. 11, and Is 11:10 in v. 12 (cf. the comments on the respective OT verses). These verses have in common the prospect, observed in the OT, that Gentiles would come to know the Lord along with the Jewish people. Paul expressed another wish for the church in Rome (v. 13). The selfless work of Jesus provided the confident expectation (**hope**) expressed in vv. 7-13 that the Jewish people would receive all the covenant blessings and Gentiles would receive God's mercy and be numbered among His people who believe (though without "becoming Jewish"). **Joy** relates to the happy anticipation of seeing one's spiritual hopes fulfilled, and **peace** results when, **in believing** (trusting Him), one has assurance that He will accomplish His promises. The achievement of all God's purposes for the spiritual welfare of His children, including the unity of the church, comes from the **power of the Holy Spirit**. What a fitting closing to the apostle's discussion of Christian living and Christian liberty.

E. The Implications for the Support of Paul's Ministry (15:14-33)

15:14-21. Not only was Paul confident that the Spirit would cultivate the unity he encouraged in 14:1–15:13, he was also confident that the Roman Christians would cooperate with the Spirit in that process (v. 14), as they could **admonish one another**. But not only would the Spirit do His work and they would cooperate with Him, Paul also wrote to promote unity so that they would more effectively "glorify the God and Father of our Lord Jesus Christ" (15:6). Verses 15-16 provide the closest thing Paul gives for a purpose statement for this epistle. He wrote to remind them of numerous doctrinal truths, truths that motivated him to discharge **the grace that was given** to him **from God** related to his apostolic office. His call was to evangelize primarily the Gentiles (vv. 16-20) (cf. "Purpose" in the introduction to Romans). Romans 15:16-21 contains the most complete statement of Paul's "philosophy of ministry" for himself as an apostle. His focus was on reaching the Gentiles in order to present them as an offering to God. Isaiah 66:18-20 indicates that in the end times the Gentiles will stream to Jerusalem and the Lord, and it is possible that Paul saw his work as contributing to a preliminary manifestation of that end-time event. The **obedience of the Gentiles** (v. 18) parallels the statements of 1:5 and 16:26, and reflects both the purpose of Paul's work and the reason behind the letter to the Romans. Paul's effectiveness came through **what Christ** accomplished **through** him, and **in the power of the Spirit** as well, including **the power of signs and wonders** (cf. 2Co 12:12) that designated him as a true apostle. If part of the purpose of **signs and wonders** was to prove that one was an apostle, then it is unlikely that they would be commonplace among the people of God. While Jesus and the Spirit were at work in Paul and were the source of all his accomplishments, he nevertheless did his part by **fully** preaching **the gospel of Christ** (v. 19). There is a wonderful but mysterious connection between God's power that brings achievement and the willing work of His people, but Paul's words credit God for the fruit produced through his work. **Illyricum** occupied what is modern Croatia and Bosnia-Herzegovina. The book of Acts does not mention **Illyricum** explicitly, but Paul probably went there on his third missionary journey after leaving Ephesus (Ac 19) and before arriving in Greece (Ac 20:1-2). It formed the farthest northwest area Paul reached before going to Rome. In keeping with his call as apostle to the Gentiles, Paul sought to evangelize in previously unreached areas (v. 20), and justifies doing so with a citation from Is 52:15 regarding God's spread of the renown of the Suffering Servant among the nations.

15:22-29. Paul presented his travel and ministry intentions in this passage. He was prevented from coming to the Roman church probably because of the demands of his work (v. 22). Paul mentioned that he was prevented in 1:13 as well, a verse that connects directly with 15:22. It is remotely possible that 1:14–15:21 is a parenthetical aside. What an aside it is! More likely, Paul simply reiterated his plans to visit Rome. For his travel plans, cf. "Date" in the introduction to Romans. Paul's immediate plan was to deposit the collection he gathered from the predominantly Gentile churches founded on his missionary journeys, a task that had occupied him for almost 20 years (cf. Ac 11:27-30 with Gl 2:1-10, c. AD 37–38). It was right for these Gentile churches **to make** this material **contribution** (better, "to establish fellowship" with, v. 26) to the persecuted Jewish believers in Judea, for the Gentiles were **indebted to them** spiritually for having disseminated the gospel (v. 27). This debt remains true today and churches might apply Paul's point by remembering to give financial support to those who labor at bringing the Good News to Jewish people. He planned then to travel to Rome and to receive financial assistance from them to continue to Spain (v. 24; **to be helped** means "to provide practical assistance for one who must make a journey"). Romans is, among other things, a letter from a missionary seeking to raise support.

15:30-33. Paul had three prayer requests for the believers in Rome (v. 30). He asked that they pray that God would protect him from Jewish opponents who would harm him in Jerusalem (v. 31a). God did protect him, but perhaps not in a way Paul would have anticipated nor preferred (cf. Ac 21:27). His second request was that the collection would be favorably received by the believers in Judea (v. 31b). The only indication that it was is found in the cryptic statement of Ac 21:17, ". . . the brethren received us gladly." No wonder! Paul showed up with a crate full of relief funds for them. The third request was that he might get to visit the believers in Rome (v. 32; cf. Ac 28).

VI. Paul's Concluding Mandates (16:1-27)

A. Appreciate Christian Workers (16:1-16)

16:1-16. Tucked away in what seem to be "ancillary" verses concluding Romans are other exhortations that would strengthen the church so it could be more effective in its evangelism. The word **greet** (*aspazomai*) (v. 3) does not mean "to say hello." It means "to pay one's respects," "to salute" (Mk 9:15; for the noun, cf. Mt 23:7), and as an imperative verb, Paul expected the Roman believers to *do* this. Paul named 25 people (17 men; 8 women; two unnamed women, vv. 13, 15, and two households, vv. 10, 11). A possible common denominator for at least some of them was that they distinguished themselves in their service to the Lord and the church (cf. vv. 2, 3, 6, 7, 9, 12 twice). Paul urged the church to recognize and appreciate them for the work they did. How would Paul have known so many people from a church he had not yet visited? Under emperor Claudius, all the Jews, both believers and non-believers, were expelled from Rome around AD 49 (cf. Ac 18:2). It was under these conditions that he met Aquila and Priscilla in Corinth, and probably the others mentioned in chap. 16. One of the people the church should salute was **Phoebe** (v. 1), a resident of **Cenchrea**, about seven miles southeast of Corinth, but who was apparently on her way to Rome, possibly bearing Paul's letter. Paul called her a **servant** (*diakonos*, "deacon"?) and **helper** (v. 2), and some conclude from these labels that she was one of the pastors of the church. But this is unlikely. Paul was not discussing those in formal church offices, and *diakonos* often has the non-technical sense of "servant" (cf. Mt 20:26). But even if she were a "deacon" in the technical sense, deacons were not entrusted with the primary leading or teaching ministry of the church. **Helper** sometimes meant "ruler," "leader," "chief," but often meant "patron, one who supports another from his or her resources." The latter sense is preferable here, for it is unlikely that Paul would call anyone other than Jesus his ruler.

A similar issue relates to the woman **Junias** (v. 7) who was **outstanding among the apostles**. It is possible that **Junias** was an apostle just as Paul was, and exercised considerable authority, but the grammatical construction is against it. The phrase is made up of the word "esteemed" or "outstanding" (*episemos*) + the preposition *en*, "in" or "among" + a word in the dative case that has a person or a group as its referent, in this case "apostles." This construction was usually used in Greek for an individual or a group who was held in high regard by another group to which the esteemed person(s) did not belong. In other words, the best evidence suggests that the apostles thought very highly of both **Andronicus and Junias**, or that they were well known to the apostles, but neither were apostles.

B. Avoid Contentious People (16:17-20a)

16:17-20a. Paul addressed a final concern that could keep the church from being strong for supporting his venture to Spain. The Christians in Rome were to **turn away from** those who spread false teaching, from those who were enslaved to their own desires (vv. 17-18). Their teaching caused **dissensions** ("the division of a unified group into two or more discordant ones") and **hindrances** ("that which causes indignation and antagonism"). Paul was confident of their ongoing **obedience** to the truth (v. 19). It was God who established peace in the church (16:20), not Satan, who probably placed the dissenting teachers in proximity to the body to disrupt it. On the role of believers in judging angels, including Satan, see 1Co 6:3.

C. Be Encouraged by Christian Leaders (16:20b-23)

16:20b-23. That some of Paul's foremost assistants were thinking of the church in Rome might have been a great encouragement to the believers there. **Lucius** (v. 21) may have been the same Jewish believer as "Lucius the Cyrene" in Ac 13:1, but it is impossible to be certain. **Jason** may be the same individual who was converted under

Paul's ministry in Thessalonica, and who provided housing for Paul (Ac 17:5-9). **Sosipater** is possibly the same person called "Sopater" who accompanied Paul on his way to Jerusalem at the end of the third missionary journey (Ac 20:4). **Tertius** (v. 22) was Paul's amanuensis (secretary). He wrote down what Paul dictated to him. **Gaius** (v. 23) was possibly one of the first converts in Corinth (1Co 1:14) whom Paul baptized, and is probably a different person than the Gaius mentioned in Ac 19:29, who was from Ephesus, or 20:4, who was from Derbe. **Erastus** was apparently a high-ranking city official, and an inscription discovered in 1929 in Corinth refers to an Erastus who was the head of Corinth's city works. It is impossible to say that this is Paul's Erastus, but the name was relatively rare. **Quartus** is not mentioned elsewhere in the NT.

D. Glorify God (16:25-27)

16:25-27. Paul's doxology is long and meandering, but a good guess at its structure is suggested in the following paraphrase:

"(v. 25) Now to Him, (skip to v. 27) to the only wise God, be the glory forever through Jesus Christ. (Back to v. 25) He is the One who is able to establish you, and that establishing comes about through the gospel, namely, the gospel which coincides with my preaching about Jesus Christ. This gospel also coincides with the revelation of the mystery kept secret for long ages past. (v. 26) But this mystery has now been manifested. Furthermore, God not only establishes you according to my gospel (cf. v. 25), but (v. 27) also by the Scriptures of the prophets who gave their revelation as our eternal God commanded them. Those Scriptures of the prophets have been made known to all the nations to promote in them the obedience which saving faith produces. (Reiterating v. 27) To Him be the glory forever through Jesus Christ. Amen!"

The doxology appears to emphasize three points: First, the gospel has continuity with the Hebrew Scriptures, but it was not fully understood until God manifested it in the epoch-shifting life and death of Christ and the evangelizing work of Paul and the other evangelists. Second, it was this gospel that both strengthened believers and produced active faith among all the nations. Third, God brings glory to Himself forever through the gospel of Jesus Christ, which brings about such profound change and unveils His unparalleled greatness. For these reasons, the Romans should spread the gospel themselves and support Paul as he sought to do so in Spain. For the details on the contents of this doxology, consult the commentaries by Moo and Schreiner listed in the bibliography.

Paul concluded his letter by referring once again to the **obedience of faith** for **all the nations** (cf. the comments on 1:4-5 and "Purpose" in the introduction to Romans). The letter to the Romans has as one of its major themes the need for the church in Rome to engage in spreading the gospel, especially by supporting Paul's plans for Spain. Any church or believer today that has lost a sense of urgency and fervor for reaching lost people would do well to study this letter. Understanding the gospel as the power of God should serve to energize a passion for souls and a desire to glorify God.

BIBLIOGRAPHY

Bruce, F. F. *Romans*. Tyndale New Testament Commentaries. Downers Grove, IL: InterVarsity, 1998.

Cranfield, C. E. B. *Romans: A Shorter Commentary*. Grand Rapids, MI: Eerdmans, 1985.

Hendriksen, William. *Exposition of Paul's Epistle to the Romans*. New Testament Commentary. Grand Rapids, MI: Baker, 1981.

MacArthur, John. *Romans 1–8* and *Romans 9–16*. MacArthur New Testament Commentary. Chicago: Moody, 1991, 1994.

Moo, Douglas J. *The Epistle to the Romans*. New International Commentary on the New Testament. Grand Rapids, MI: Eerdmans, 1996.

Morris, Leon. *The Epistle to the Romans*. Pillar Commentaries. Grand Rapids, MI: Eerdmans, 1988.

Murray, John. *The Epistle to the Romans*. Grand Rapids, MI: Eerdmans, 1997.

Osborne, Grant R. *Romans*. InterVarsity Press New Testament Commentary. Downers Grove, IL: InterVarsity, 2004.

Schreiner, Thomas R. *Romans*. Baker Exegetical Commentary on the New Testament. Grand Rapids, MI: Baker, 1998.

Witherington III, Ben. *Paul's Letter to the Romans: A Socio-Rhetorical Commentary*. Grand Rapids, MI: Eerdmans, 2004.

● ● ● ●

1 CORINTHIANS

MICHAEL G. VANLANINGHAM

INTRODUCTION

Author. Virtually no one of any scholarly credibility disputes that Paul was the author of 1 Corinthians.

Date. For the account of Paul's initial contacts with Corinth during his second missionary journey (c. April AD 50–September AD 52), see the comments on Ac 18. When Paul began his third missionary journey (spanning c. late AD 52 or early 53 through May AD 57), he returned to Ephesus, where his ministry was profoundly effective, and where he stayed for almost three years (probably fall AD 53 to spring 55) (cf. Ac 18:18-23 for these points). It was during this time that he wrote 1 Corinthians, probably in AD 55.

Recipients. *1. The city of Corinth was new.* The most relevant history of the city dated back to 146 BC when Corinth was destroyed and its people sold into slavery by the Roman general Lucius Mummius Achaiacus after the city led an unsuccessful revolt against Rome. It was this "old Corinth" that may have had 1,000 temple prostitutes for the goddess Aphrodite, though Strabo (first-century AD Greek geographer and historian, originally from Turkey), who wrote about this feature of Corinth, is probably inaccurate on this point. For about a century Corinth was in ruins until Julius Caesar, in 46 BC, decided to rebuild the city as a retirement location for the veteran soldiers who had served him. Restoration began in 44 BC. Though it was culturally and geographically Greek, it became a formal Roman colony, and in 27 BC was named capital of the province of Achaia. Estimates for its population in the first century are 60,000–200,000, and there is no consensus on a more specific number.

2. The city of Corinth was wealthy. Because of its location on the Isthmus of Corinth (the thin strip of land connecting the Peloponnesian Peninsula to northern parts of Greece), it controlled land routes and was a double port serving ships on both the Corinthian Gulf to the west and the Saronic Gulf, part of the Aegean Sea, to the east. The Isthmus was narrow enough (about four miles) that boats were hauled on log rollers across it, a process considered less expensive and less dangerous than sailing around the Peloponnesus. Commerce and travel enriched the city. Important industries included bronze, tile, and pottery. Corinth presided over the Isthmian Games, an athletic spectacle surpassed only by the Olympic Games. These Isthmian Games took place every two years in honor of Poseidon, god of the seas, the patron god of Corinth, and included track, wrestling, boxing, and chariot races.

3. The city of Corinth was wicked. It was notorious for its immorality. In Hellenistic Greek, the verb *korinthiazomai* meant "to practice fornication," a *korinthiastes* was a whoremonger (LSJ, 981), and to employ the services of a "Corinthian girl" meant "to hire a prostitute." The best indication is that Paul's letter to the Romans was written from Corinth, and it is possible that the sexual vices he observed in the city prompted some of the content of Rm 1:18-32.

Purpose. Several situations prompted Paul to write this epistle. He wrote a letter to them earlier that needed clarification (5:9, 11). He received reports about various problems that harmed the church from "Chloe's people" who visited Paul in Ephesus from Corinth (regarding divisions, see 1:10-11; possibly 11:17-34 regarding abuses of the Lord's table; and the resurrection, chap. 15). And the Corinthians corresponded with him, inquiring about his thoughts on several topics (7:1, and perhaps 7:25; 8:1; 12:1; possibly 16:1 and 12). First Corinthians was written to address these issues.

If there is a single all-encompassing problem exhibited by the members of the Corinthian church discernible in this letter, it might be unbridled and arrogant self-promotion. The factions of chapters 1–4 appear to be motivated to secure their own disciples (cf. the "Excursus on chaps. 1–4" at 1:18). Paul reproved them in 5:2 for their arrogance that motivated them to harbor immorality in their church. They sued one another for their own gain (6:7-8) and insisted on their right to use prostitutes (6:12-13). Some were apparently pressuring others to conform to their belief that one should not marry, or should abstain from sexual relations in marriage (cf. 7:37-38). They defended their ongoing participation in sacred meals for the Greco-Roman gods without concern for the harm it might bring to others (8:9-13) or themselves (10:6-12). The women may have sought to diminish the men's divinely ordained authority over them, perhaps to enjoy more autonomy or prominence in the life of the church (11:2-16). Some of the Corinthians purposely excluded the poor from their banquet associated with communion so they could enjoy their own better food and drink (11:17-22). They used their spiritual gifts without love and without consideration for the edification of the church (chaps. 12–14). Their view of the resurrection justified a great deal of their questionable morality (6:14; 15:32-33). And they were not forthcoming in the collection for the poor in Jerusalem (cf. 16:1-3, and note that Paul had to address this again, *with two full chapters*, in 2Co 8–9). The Greco-Roman world of Paul's day was filled with orators (called "rhetors" in the technical literature) who promoted themselves (cf. the "Excursus on Chapters 1–4" before the comments on 1:18 below), and it was common for people to pursue their own social enhancement and physical gratification with whatever means available. When the Corinthians came to Christ through Paul's ministry, they dragged with them into their church many of the self-aggrandizing values of their pre-Christian lives, and those attitudes had taken root in their church. Before their church could make significant spiritual progress, the Corinthians had to learn to reject the values and priorities of their culture, and live to promote the betterment of others rather than themselves. In other words, their situation was not unlike ours.

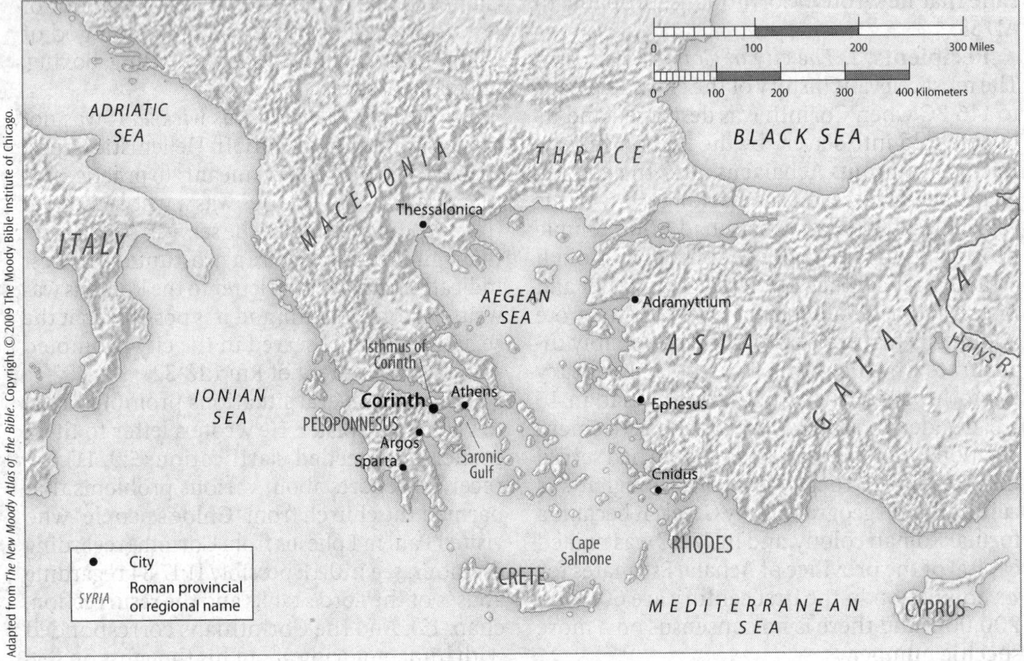

OUTLINE

- I. Paul's Introduction to the Letter (1:1-17)
  - A. Every Christian Belongs to God (1:1-3)
  - B. Every Christian Is Enriched by God (1:4-9)
  - C. Every Christian Possesses Christ (1:10-17)
- II. The First Problem: Divisions in the Church (1:18–4:21)
  - A. The First Exhortation: Do Not Divide the Divine Institution (1:18–2:5)
  - B. The Second Exhortation: Regard All Believers as Equals (2:6–3:4)
  - C. The Third Exhortation: View God as Preeminent in the Church (3:5–4:21)
- III. The Second Problem: Moral Flaws in the Church (5:1–6:20)
  - A. The First Exhortation: Practice Church Discipline (5:1-13)
  - B. The Second Exhortation: Avoid Lawsuits against Fellow Christians (6:1-11)
  - C. The Third Exhortation: Promote Personal Moral Integrity (6:12-20)
- IV. The Third Problem: Obligations and Value of Marriage (7:1-40)
  - A. The First Exhortation: View Marriage as Beneficial (7:1-7)
  - B. The Second Exhortation: Fulfill Your Marital Obligations (7:8-16)
  - C. The Third Exhortation: Develop Contentment with Present Marital Status (7:17-24)
  - D. The Fourth Exhortation: Emphasize the Benefits of Single Life (7:25-40)
- V. The Fourth Problem: Issues Related to Christian Liberty in Eating Food Offered to Idols (8:1–11:1)
  - A. The First Exhortation: Temper Christian Liberty with Love (8:1-13)
  - B. The Second Exhortation: Be Willing to Forego Christian Liberty (9:1-27)
  - C. The Third Exhortation: Limit Christian Liberty before God Disciplines (10:1-22)
  - D. The Fourth Exhortation: Adjust Behavior to Suit Various Settings (10:23–11:1)
- VI. The Fifth Problem: Chaos in Church Worship Services (11:2–14:40)
  - A. The First Exhortation: Maintain Sexual Distinctions (11:2-16)
  - B. The Second Exhortation: Correct the Abuses of Communion (11:17-34)
  - C. The Third Exhortation: Employ Spiritual Gifts Carefully (12:1–14:40)
- VII. The Sixth Problem: Denial of the Resurrection of the Dead (15:1-58)
  - A. The First Exhortation: Consider the Evidence for the Resurrection (15:1-11)
  - B. The Second Exhortation: Consider the Consequences of No Resurrection from the Dead (15:12-19)
  - C. The Third Exhortation: Consider the Centrality of the Resurrection in God's Program (15:20-28)
  - D. The Fourth Exhortation: Consider that the Christian Life Is Made Purposeful because of the Resurrection of the Dead (15:29-34)
  - E. The Fifth Exhortation: Consider the Majesty of the Resurrection Body (15:35-50)
  - F. The Sixth Exhortation: Consider the Miraculous Change Resulting in the Resurrection of the Dead (15:51-58)
- VIII. The Seventh Problem: The Collection for Poor Believers (16:1-4)
- IX. The Conclusion of the Epistle: Personal Remarks (16:5-24)

COMMENTARY ON 1 CORINTHIANS

I. Paul's Introduction to the Letter (1:1-17)

A. Every Christian Belongs to God (1:1-3)

1:1-3. Paul (v. 1) is universally seen as the author of this epistle, and only the most radical scholars deny this. **Called** refers to the urgent summons with which God appointed Paul with his apostolic office. **Sosthenes** is mentioned in Ac 18:17, where he is called "the leader of the synagogue," and may have either been a Jewish believer at that time, or became one later (cf. the comments there). **The church of God** (v. 2) should probably be understood as a genitive of possession. That the church belonged to Him may reflect Paul's discussion in chaps. 1–4, where he rebukes the factions some were forming around themselves to the exclusion of God. **Grace to you and peace** (v. 3) reflects a combination of greetings. The Greco-Roman world generally offered greetings of grace and the Jewish world offered greetings of peace, indicating Paul's uniting of both cultures as the Jewish apostle to the Gentiles. Through the cross, God has granted undeserved forgiveness (**grace**) as well as both personal wholeness and reconciliation to God (**peace**) by overcoming the spiritual enmity between humanity and God. Furthermore, the Corinthians also needed a serious dose of internal peace, which would come only as they appropriated God's grace (on grace as an ongoing power in the believer's life, see the comments on 1Co 15:10).

B. Every Christian Is Enriched by God (1:4-9)

1:4-9. Paul described the blessings that were possessed by all the believers in Corinth, not just a select few, and began even here to address the divisions in the church. **For the grace of God . . . given you** (v. 4) forms the basis for Paul's thankfulness for them. **Grace** here means "a favor," "being treated better than one deserves." **That** (v. 5) expands on the nature of the grace Paul mentioned in v. 4. **Enriched . . . in all speech and all knowledge** refers to the rich endowment of various kinds of spiritual gifts in the church. Paul's comment here may have a tinge of irony in light of the enormous problems generated by their gifts. **Even as the testimony . . . was confirmed in you** (v. 6) suggests that the spiritual gifts served to confirm the truth of the message concerning Christ. **The revelation of our Lord Jesus Christ** will take place at the rapture. **Confirm** ("complete legal security") and **blameless** ("being innocent of the accusation of committing a crime"; Col 1:22) were used in judicial contexts. This is probably a reference to believers' righteous standing before God **in the day of our Lord Jesus Christ**. In the OT (cf. Jl 2:31; 3:14; Zph 1:14-18), the "day of the Lord" was a time of eschatological upheaval and judgment. In the NT, it appears to follow the rapture of the church (cf. the comments on 1Th 4:13–5:11), and refers to a time from which the Church is delivered (1Co 5:5; 1Th 5:4-5, 9-10; Php 1:6). Paul called it **the day of our Lord Jesus Christ** possibly because the authority with which God will judge the world has been delegated to Jesus (2Th 1:7-10), and possibly because Jesus rescues His people from the tribulation period on that day.

C. Every Christian Possesses Christ (1:10-17)

1:10-17. Now *(de)* (v. 10) could be translated "but," and signals that the introduction is over, that Paul's discussion of the glorious benefits of being a believer is over, and that he will begin to address serious issues in the church. **Divisions** (*schisma*, from which the Eng. word "schism" is derived) means "dissension and division as a result of incompatible ambitions." Paul wants them to **be made complete**, a verb that meant "to adjust something so it is set in order." It was sometimes used for setting a broken bone, or even for reconciling political factions. Paul was informed about the strife there through **Chloe's people** (v. 11) of whom nothing is known—where they lived or what their social status was—but apparently they traveled to Ephesus and notified Paul of the problems in Corinth. **Quarrels** means "bitter, contentious discussions that resulted in divisions." Paul explained what contentions he meant in v. 12. It is not clear if some group was a follower of Paul, others of Apollos and Cephas, or if Paul used the names of these leaders instead of the names of those leading these factions in order to avoid giving them any publicity.

Most of what Paul wrote in the remainder of chaps. 1–4 is to correct this problem (cf. 3:5-9, 21-23). His basic point is that the entire church should enjoy all of God's remarkable servants and *glorify Him—not the servants*—for them. **I of Christ** was true of every Corinthian believer, but this group was sanctimonious, thinking of themselves as the only ones truly following Christ by not following human leaders or teachers. The problem seemed to be that some refused to submit to or profit from the benefits Paul, Cephas, or Apollos could provide, and refused to fellowship with those aligned with those leaders. **Has Christ been divided** (v. 13) could be paraphrased, "Has the resurrected and authoritative Christ, who belongs to all believers, been apportioned to only one group?" Paul worked to steer attention away from himself so that the allegiance of all would be given to Jesus. **Crispus** (v. 14), which means "curly," is probably the synagogue ruler converted early in Paul's Corinthian ministry (Ac 18:8). **Gaius** may be the same person mentioned in Rm 16:23. Romans was probably written from Corinth, and **Gaius** was renowned for his generous hospitality to

Paul and the believers in Corinth. **Stephanas** came from Corinth to Ephesus where Paul lived when he wrote 1 Corinthians, and may have reminded the apostle that Paul baptized him. That Paul was not sent **to baptize, but to preach the gospel** indicates that Christian baptism is not an essential, saving part of the gospel. **Cleverness of speech** (v. 17) is literally "wisdom of words," and with this phrase Paul launched his discussion against those who sought to win a following through their impressive verbal and intellectual skills (see the "Excursus on Chapters 1–4" below). **So that the cross of Christ would not be made void** indicates that Paul was convinced that people needed to embrace the cross on the basis of its own merits, and not because of the rhetorical cleverness and manipulative techniques with which many rhetoricians made their living. Paul's intent when he evangelized the Corinthians was that he would never eclipse the power or wisdom of the cross by his own brilliance, for doing so would cause it to become **void** ("to cause the power or significance of something to dwindle").

II. The First Problem: Divisions in the Church (1:18–4:21)

A. The First Exhortation: Do Not Divide the Divine Institution (1:18–2:5)

Excursus on Chapters 1–4

Considerable debate exists regarding the cultural background that evinced Paul's discussion in 1Co 1–4. It is possible that Paul was reacting to Jewish wisdom traditions, in which case some of the Cephas party may have campaigned for Moses and the law versus Christ and grace. Possibly Paul reacted to Gnosticism whereby some in the church boasted of their possession of spiritual knowledge vis-à-vis those without it, resulting in these cliques. A better explanation of the background of chaps. 1–4 is found in Greco-Roman rhetoric. "Rhetoric" is roughly synonymous with "sophistry," and "rhetors," those who taught rhetoric, is roughly synonymous with "sophists."

Success in political, religious, legal, and business settings demanded that one be trained in rhetorical skills. Sophists set up schools to teach rhetoric, which involved a combination of training in eloquence, argumentation, persuasive techniques, the development of vocal timbre, and even entertainment. Rhetors could establish these schools only if they were able to impress the citizens of a town, who would subsequently send their sons to them for training and pay considerable sums for the privilege. Those trained by a particular sophist became his "disciples" (*mathetes*, same word for the disciples in the gospels) and would typically imitate his master in a number of ways. A disciple was expected to defend and support his teacher against all others, and on occasion verbal and physical fights resulted between the proponents of competing sophists.

Paul's rebuke of the Corinthian factions involved several strategies. He denied that he was a sophist, seeking to impress people with his "cleverness of speech" (lit., "wisdom of words," 1:17) or "superiority of speech or of wisdom" (2:1)—terms often applied to Greco-Roman sophists—so they would follow and support him. As a result, they should not be overly zealous in backing their Christian heroes, which resulted in the church's disunity (4:6). He urged them to quit acting "like mere men" (3:3), like those in the secular world of Corinth, and to recognize that the Christian leaders were a gift for the entire church (not just parts of it; 3:21-32), that these heroes were nothing more than servants of God (4:1-5), and that God alone deserved the kind of zeal they gave to their mortal champions (3:6-9). For information on sophistry related to 1 Corinthians, cf. Bruce W. Winter, *After Paul Left Corinth: The Influence of Secular Ethics and Social Change* (Grand Rapids, MI: Eerdmans, 2001), 31–43; Idem, *Philo and Paul among the Sophists: Alexandrian and Corinthian Responses to a Julio-Claudian Movement* (Grand Rapids, MI: Eerdmans, 2002); Idem, "Rhetoric," in *A Dictionary of Paul and His Letters*, ed. Gerald F. Hawthorne *et al.* (Downers Grove, IL: InterVarsity, 1993), 820–822; Jeffrey S. Lamp, *First Corinthians 1–4 in Light of Jewish Wisdom Traditions: Christ, Wisdom and Spirituality*, SBEC (Lewiston: Mellen, 2000), 81–115; Duane Litfin, *St. Paul's Theology of Proclamation: 1 Corinthians 1–4 and Greco-Roman Rhetoric*, SNTMS (Cambridge: Cambridge, 1994), 109–243.

1:18-25. For (v. 18) develops Paul's explanation of the power of the cross (v. 17). **Foolishness** was sometimes used in secular Greek for what was insipid or dull, and even for the sluggishness of animals in winter. Crucifixion was viewed with universal disgust in the first century, and it was considered a faux pas to mention it in polite company. "Disgustingly stupid" gets at the sense of the word. Yet in this foolish cross is the **power of God**. **For** (v. 19) introduces a proof from Scripture to the effect that the cross is the power of God whereby He destroys the worldly wisdom of leaders. Isaiah 29:14 has eschatological and messianic overtones (cf. the use of "wondrously" in Is 29:14 in connection with the messianic prophecies of Is 9:6, "Wonderful Counselor"; 28:29) (see Roy E. Ciampa, and Brian S. Rosner, "1 Corinthians," in *Commentary on the New Testament Use of the Old Testament*, eds. G. K. Beale and D. A. Carson [Grand Rapids, MI: Baker, 2007], 697–98). The word **wisdom** (*sophia*) as a noun occurs 51 times in the NT, 28 times by Paul, 16 times (plus 10 uses of the cognate adjective *sophos*) in 1Co 1–4. Though this is debated, Paul seems to connect **WISDOM** with the rhetorical skill of sophists, which they employed to win a following. Some in the Corinthian church appeared to be using similar skills to advance themselves in the church. But Paul also employs **WISDOM** in reference to God, Jesus, and his own gospel message (e.g., 1:21, 24, 25, 30; 2:6, 7). "Impressive ability" is the sense of *sophia*, and this translation works well both in reference to secular wisdom (rhetorical skill) and God's wisdom.

Wise man (v. 20) is further defined by two terms, one for Jewish and the other for Greek wise men. **Scribe** is probably the Jewish legal expert who had expertise in the more technical aspects of the law and who taught the Pharisees especially. **Debater** (syzetetes) was often used for the professional debaters and quarrelers who were common among Greco-Roman sophists. God has turned their impressive abilities into foolishness. **For** (v. 21) introduces a detailed description about God making foolish the world's impressive abilities. **Since** explains why God made worldly wisdom foolish (because the world did not acknowledge Him), and the phrase **God was well-pleased . . . to save those who believe** presents how He made worldly wisdom foolish (through the foolishness of the gospel message). **For indeed** (v. 22) further expands upon the idea of how the world of unbelieving Jews and Gentiles acknowledged neither God nor His gospel. It is because **Jews ask for signs**. They believed that the arrival of the Messiah would be accompanied by signs and miracles and that He would do more spectacular works than even Moses did. Perhaps they were hoping for something like the constellation Ursa Major running to bite Orion on the leg, or the Big Dipper tilting the other way. They refused to recognize the signs Jesus performed, or to acknowledge the validity of the greatest sign, the resurrection. Jesus' death was **a stumbling block** for them (v. 23), for how could one who was crucified as a criminal be their Messiah? **Greeks search for wisdom** indicates why Greeks did not acknowledge God. A crucified carpenter is **foolishness** (v. 23), not impressive! **But** (v. 23), in contrast to what those in the world sought, Paul preached **Christ crucified** (v. 23). In His life, death, and resurrection is manifested **the power of God and the wisdom** [impressive ability] **of God**, against all human estimations. With **because** (v. 25), Paul confirmed that the gospel preached was the power and wisdom of God. C. K. Barrett writes, "What God has done in Christ crucified is a direct contradiction of human ideas of wisdom and power, yet it achieved what human wisdom and power fail to achieve. It does . . . deliver man from his bondage. . . ." (*The First Epistle to the Corinthians,* HNTC [New York: Harper & Row, 1968], 56).

1:26-31. For (v. 26) begins an illustration of God's powerful "foolishness" and "weakness" (v. 25) which are wiser and stronger than men. The very makeup of the Corinthian church, for whom God had done great things and through whom He was doing great things, is an indication of His power through those whom the world considers weak. Verses 27-28 indicate God's design, which is to **shame** ("to confuse," "to disgrace") **the wise** and strong by choosing, using, and blessing the weak and foolish **so that no man may boast before God** (v. 29; cf. v. 31). God alone gets the credit (v. 31). Part of the reason Paul emphasized this was to cause the Corinthian faction leaders to quit drawing attention to themselves as secular sophists did, and recognize the supremacy of God in the world and the church. They were joined to **Christ Jesus** (v. 30) **by His doing**, not through any impressive ability of their own. Because of that connection with Jesus, believers recognize in Him God's **wisdom**, His "impressive ability," and receive His **righteousness**, **sanctification**, **and redemption**. **Righteousness** (God's own moral excellence and virtue given to believers; see the comments on Rm 1:17; 3:21-31) comes to the believer because of being "in Christ." Many deny the concept of "imputed righteousness," and while Paul never used the exact term, he has a category for it (2Co 5:21; Php 3:9). **Sanctification** means "the status of being set apart and consecrated to God" with a life, it is hoped, of practical holiness that accompanies it. **Redemption** is "effecting the release of a slave or a prisoner of war by paying for that release." Theologically, it refers to the deliverance of sinners from sin's penalty and power by the blood of Jesus.

2:1-5. And (v. 1) takes up the thought of 1:18-25 that God's "weakness" is stronger than the world's strength. For **superiority of speech or of wisdom**, see "Excursus on Chapters 1–4" at 1:18. In vv. 2-5, Paul pointed out that his intent was to deliver the message of the gospel in a straightforward, unembellished way, and thereby he proved to be an anti-sophist. For **demonstration of the Spirit and of power**, see the note on 1:6. If he evangelized them using rhetorical techniques, they may have embraced Christ because of the techniques, not because of the wonder of the cross itself.

B. The Second Exhortation: Regard All Believers as Equals (2:6–3:4)

Paul's main point in this section emphasizes that all believers enjoy the illuminating work of the Spirit, to counter the boastful and elitist mentality of their cliques.

2:6-13. Yet (v. 6) corrects the possible misunderstanding that Paul was saying God had no wisdom at all (1:25). **Mature** refers to all believers, not to a few who are insightful. It is possible that by the word **mature** Paul means "mature or spiritual Christians" as opposed to carnal believers, but there are only two categories of people found in 2:1-14, namely those who are purely secular (**the rulers of this age**, v. 6; **the natural man**, v. 14), and those who are Christians (see the many first-person pronouns and verbs found here). In addition, it is highly unlikely that Paul would withhold spiritual truths related to Christ from immature believers. **Mature** here is the term he used for the category of all those who believe in Jesus Christ vis-à-vis the world. **Mystery** (v. 7) means "an undisclosed secret that has now been divulged." Often when Paul uses it in a theological sense, **mystery** refers to the contents of the gospel message forecast (**predestined**) in the OT but requiring historical fulfillment and the illuminating work of the Spirit to be fully understood. God did all this for **our glory**, to provide the profound salvific benefits that accrue to believers. While believers (the **mature**) grasped the wisdom of God in Christ, the Roman and Jewish rulers did not (vv. 6, 8), a situation foreseen by Isaiah (cf. Is 64:4 and 65:17 cited in 1Co 3:9). The Spirit knows all about God's plans in Christ and not only reveals their true significance to believers, but persuades them to embrace Him (vv. 10-12). The Spirit did not do this for the rulers, but they are still culpable for their actions (for the interchange between divine responsibility and God's sovereignty as it relates to sin, see the comments on Rm 9:22-23). This Spirit provides factual content (He helps believers know the full significance of the facts about Jesus) and the desire to act on those facts (to accept those things, unlike the natural man, v. 14). The difficult phrase **combining spiritual thoughts with spiritual words** (see the helpful summary by Archibald Robertson, and Alfred Plummer, *First Epistle of St. Paul to the Corinthians*, 2d ed. ICC [Edinburgh: T&T. Clark, 1914], 47) probably means something like "combining spiritual content (i.e., the message of the gospel) with spiritual (non-rhetorical) methods or forms for conveying it" (cf. Litfin, *St. Paul's Theology of Proclamation*, 218). Paul made it clear that his presentation of the gospel did not use worldly methods, but was straightforward, producing the intended spiritual results.

2:14-16. But (v. 14) signals a contrast between believers and the **natural man** (*psuchikos* here means "one whose mindset or behavior is natural, governed by purely human impulses" rather than by the Spirit). **Spiritually** refers to the help rendered by the Spirit. **Appraised** is "to make a decision based upon careful investigation." **Spiritual** (v. 15; "one who has and belongs to the Spirit") refers to every believer (see the comments on 2:6). Paul will begin to discuss a third category of individuals in 3:1, that of carnal believers. But here his point seems to be that *all believers* (**he who is spiritual**, v. 15), in contrast to unbelievers (the **natural man**, v. 14), have access to and the ability to comprehend the spiritual truth related to Christ because of the illuminating work of the Spirit for believers. **He himself is appraised by no one** means, most likely, that unbelievers do not have the capacity to understand adequately why believers think as they do. **The mind of Christ** (v. 16) in this context involves the knowledge concerning Christ, made known by the Spirit to believers, that Paul has emphasized (cf. 2:6-13; Is 40:13). Isaiah described God's inscrutable plans to rescue Israel through the Servant (Is 40:1-11, 15-17). The Corinthian cliques would be less problematic if they recognized that every believer receives these benefits from the Spirit.

3:1-4. Paul had to treat the Corinthians as if they did not have the mind of Christ (2:16) because of their carnality. **Spiritual men** (v. 1) are characterized by the Spirit, but Paul maintained that this church was conducting itself more like **men of flesh** (*sarkinos*), i.e., like unbelievers. Paul sometimes used **infants** in reference to unbelievers (Rm 2:20; Gl 4:3), but he qualifies the word with **in Christ** to indicate that he knew they were saved, though acting like unbelievers. **Milk** (v. 2) refers to the basic facts of the gospel that saved them. **Solid food** is probably the weightier implications of that same gospel, which would help them be less like the world and more united (cf. Php 2:5-11 where Jesus' sacrifice [the milk] is an example of serving others [solid food]). **Fleshly** (v. 3) means "to think or behave as an unregenerate person under the control of the sin nature," and is parallel to **walking like mere** (unsaved) **men**, a phrase Paul used to describe a purely secular mindset (Rm 3:5; 1Co 9:8; 15:32; Gl 1:1).

C. The Third Exhortation: View God as Preeminent in the Church (3:5–4:21)

3:5-9. Here Paul sought to temper their overinflated view of their church heroes. The key to the success of Apollos and Paul was **the Lord** who **gave opportunity to each one** (v. 5). Paul used the imperfect tense in the phrase, **was causing the growth** (v. 6), to emphasize God's role in their progress. But he also used aorist verbs (**planted**; **watered**) to understate the significance of the human servants, a point made explicit in v. 7. Paul and Apollos were **one** (v. 8), probably a reference to sharing the same level of relative (un)importance for the church's development. They have a similar status, but will receive distinct rewards (**reward** means "payment earned for work one has completed"). Serving God to gain eternal rewards is a legitimate motivation, and neither Jesus nor Paul discouraged it (Mt 5:12, 46; 6:1, 4; 1Co 9:17; Rv 22:12). Part of Paul's and Apollos's similar status (v. 8a) included them being **fellow workers** employed by God (not "they both work alongside God as He works"). God is the employer, the owner of the farm and the building.

3:10-15. Those who worked on constructing God's building (the church; v. 9) will be held accountable for it. Paul attributed his ministerial success to God's **grace** ("exceptional effect produced by [God's] generosity," roughly synonymous with God's power; cf. BDAG, 1080) (v. 10). A **master builder** (*architekton*) was both a building's designer and construction supervisor. Paul laid the right foundation, **Jesus Christ** (v. 11), but he warned the strident leaders at Corinth to be careful about how they built on it. **Gold, silver, precious stones** (v. 12) in the context of 1Co 1–4 refers to ministry that produces harmony. **Wood, hay, straw** refers to practices that lead to personal aggrandizement and widespread disunity. In **the day** of the Lord following the rapture of the Church, God will demonstrate that He is aware of those negative influences (v. 13) and will evaluate them negatively. **Fire** serves as a symbol of God's judgment that consumes what is not acceptable to Him (cf. Zch 13:9). Those whose toil resulted in strife **will be saved** (v. 15), but barely (**yet so as through fire** describing a narrow escape from some catastrophe). He or she **will suffer loss** of rewards. The **reward** (v. 14) probably includes expanded opportunities to serve Jesus with profound satisfaction in a glorious setting (His kingdom), and hearing the commendation, "Well done, good and faithful servant" (see the comments on Mt 25:21, 23; 1Co 4:5). Cf. the comments on Rm 14:10-12; 2Co 5:10, and James Rosscup, *Paul's Teaching on the Christian's Future Reward, with Special Reference to 1 Corinthians 3:10-17* [Unpublished Ph.D. Dissertation, University of Aberdeen, 1976], 464–465.

3:16-17. You are a temple (v. 16) is about the corporate church as the place where God and His **Spirit** dwelt, not vices that harm an individual Christian's body. Both occurrences of **destroy** (v. 17) mean "to cause harm," "to ruin," "to cause severe damage." If they damage the church by fomenting discord, God will damage them with rigorous discipline, though by this Paul does not mean that they will face eternal condemnation.

3:18-23. Wise in this age (v. 18) refers to the kind of impressive abilities that typified the sophists but which had no place in the church. To **become wise** in God's opinion required rejecting the brilliance applauded by the world and becoming foolish in the world's eyes. In v. 19, Paul cited Jb 5:13, which expresses the inevitability of God reversing the fortunes of the cunning (Jb 5:12) who seek their own advancement by oppressing the poor (Jb 5:15), similar to the Corinthians' situation. He cited Ps 94:11 (v. 20), which stresses God's judgment of the proud and wicked who crush His people (cf. Ps 94:2-7, 9-11). Likewise, the arrogant in Corinth will give an account of their troublemaking. One of the ironies in Corinth was that every believer could profit from each of the leaders whom God gave to bless the entire church (vv. 21, 22). All believers **belong to Christ** (v. 23), not to Paul, Apollos, or Cephas, and their allegiance should be directed to Him. But **Christ belongs to God**. Paul described Jesus' functional subordination to God, but his words do not mean that Jesus' nature was less than divine. Paul's point may be that Jesus humbly served God in dying on the cross, and He is a model for the Corinthians who apparently had little time for either humility or service.

4:1-5. Paul turned from the privilege each of the Corinthians had in all of their leaders to discussing how the leaders should be viewed by the church. They were **servants** ("helpers," "assistants") and **stewards** (slaves who had authority in their master's households) (v. 1), workers whose lower positions garnered little respect outside of their connection to their superiors. And this was Paul's point. The Corinthians mistook the slaves for the Master. **Trustworthy** means "one who is reliable" (v. 2). While accountable to the church (1Tm 5:19-20), the church leader is primarily accountable to God (1Co 4:3-4), and his job is to please Him, not to impress the churchgoers. Paul was reluctant to engage in too much self-evaluation because only God can know objectively how a minister is performing, though on occasion he analyzed his own performance and was **conscious of nothing against** himself (v. 4). The tendency of those who serve Christ is either to be too hard on themselves or too lenient, and surely both are problematic. A comprehensive and objective evaluation of one's own ministry, and certainly that of another's, should be left to **the Lord** in that future day (cf. the comments on 3:10-15). God will commend one who serves Him faithfully, in a way conducive to church unity. This commendation constitutes part of the believer's future rewards (see the comments on 3:14).

4:6-7. The party leaders in Corinth needed to listen less to their admirers, and their admirers needed to jettison their gratuitous zeal for their leaders. It is not at all clear what Paul meant by **what is written** (v. 6), but it may refer to what Scripture teaches about the need for humble servant leadership. No Corinthian party was superior to any other, at least not in God's estimation. These believers and their leaders were not the source of their own spiritual enrichment, and they had no reason to boast (v. 7).

4:8-13. Filled (v. 8) was a common term for the arrogant, and the wise man was thought to be as privileged as a king (for the ancient references, cf. David E. Garland, *1 Corinthians*, BECNT [Grand Rapids, MI: Baker, 2003], 137). **Kings** probably does not indicate that they thought their great wisdom and numerous spiritual blessings signaled that the kingdom had arrived for them. Paul's reaction to them in vv. 9-13 suggests that their problem was that they were "living like kings," at least in terms of their inflated self image and desire for followers, while he and the other apostles were treated like the world's riffraff (**scum** and **dregs**, v. 13). (Paul's statement gives an indirect indication that the Church is not the full-fledged kingdom of God in this age as many maintain. Believers will rule with Jesus in the future millennial kingdom [Rv 3:21], but Paul says here that they are not ruling now. Cf. also 15:50.) Christians must be humble servants, willing to get their hands dirty (**working with our own hands**, v. 12) for others, rather than seeking to build their own little kingdoms in the church and scrambling to win popularity contests in order to revel in their own importance. Furthermore, they need to be willing to be dismissed, or worse, assaulted by the world (vv. 12-13). Serious servant leadership is generally not glamorous.

4:14-21. Paul uses one more metaphor with the Corinthians (along with the metaphors of Paul being a field hand [3:6-9], builder [3:10-17], and household servant [4:1-5]). He likens himself to their **father** (vv. 14-15). **Tutors** (v. 15) means "chaperones." In wealthier Greco-Roman homes, a young adult male slave often accompanied the male children wherever they went to make sure they did not cause or encounter trouble. But Paul was more like their **father through the gospel**, and had the authority to push for change. Just as children tend to resemble their parents, so Paul urges them to follow his example (**be imitators of me**, v. 16). **For this reason** (v. 17)—so that they could better follow Paul's pattern—Paul **sent . . . Timothy** to them while Paul was in Ephesus (Ac 19:22), but apparently he had not yet arrived (1Co 16:10). Some had become smug thinking that they could further their own agendas without fear of recourse from Paul (v. 18). But he planned to visit them when God permitted, and when he did, he intended to find if the "wise" had any **power**, i.e., if they had accomplished anything worthwhile, or if they were just windbags (v. 19). Verse 20 does not mean that the Church equals the kingdom of God. The Church manifests some of the spiritual effects of the kingdom during the present era, but the kingdom awaits a climactic future arrival (cf. 1Co 6:9-10; 15:50; Gl 5:21;

Eph 5:5; Col 1:12-13; cf. Robert L. Saucy, *The Case for Progressive Dispensationalism: The Interface Between Dispensational and Non-Dispensational Theology* [Grand Rapids, MI: Zondervan, 1993], 106–110). One of those effects was the spiritual progress of Christians through the work of Paul and others, and which should have been evident in the ministries of the Corinthian leaders and their fans. Paul hoped that they might change their arrogant ways so that his visit might be less confrontational (v. 21).

III. The Second Problem: Moral Flaws in the Church (5:1–6:20)

A. The First Exhortation: Practice Church Discipline (5:1-13)

In chaps. 5 and 6, Paul responded to reports from Chloe's friends (1:11) or other visitors (16:17) about another problem, this time pertaining to arrogance and immorality in the church (chaps. 5–6).

5:1-2. Paul dealt with arrogance in 4:18-19, but here the arrogance manifested itself in their smug willingness to harbor immorality, specifically a man sleeping with his stepmother (5:2). **As does not exist** is not found in the original text, and instead supplying "as is not tolerated" better fits the evidence that this sin was known but not condoned in the ancient world. The law forbade this relationship (Lv 18:8; Am 2:7). The church had **become arrogant** (v. 2) by not dealing severely with this sin.

5:3-5. For (v. 3) begins an explanation of removing the immoral man. **Present in spirit** is probably a reference to Paul's own spirit rather than the Holy Spirit (v. 4 lit., is "when you and my spirit are assembled"). Paul was "backing them up" as an apostle, thinking of them, praying for them, wishing he could be there as they performed the discipline. **I have decided** (v. 5) is not in the Greek text, and "You should all decide . . ." fits better what Paul wanted them to do. **Deliver such a one to Satan** (v. 5) means "remove this man from the church and put him into Satan's realm, the world" (1Tm 1:20). **Flesh** in Paul often refers to the sin nature, which the believer still possesses (Rm 8:13; 13:14; Col 3:5; and see the comments on Rm 7:5-6). **The destruction of his flesh** probably refers to this man curbing his fulfillment of the desires of the flesh, thereby figuratively "destroying" the flesh, as a result of the discipline. Satan's role may be to inflame the man to sin even more, but in the end Paul hoped that he would burn out or become weary of sinning and repent. **So that his spirit may be saved** probably speaks of the immaterial part of a person that is favorably disposed toward God when made alive by the Spirit. **Satan** could not touch this man's redeemed **spirit** (Jn 10:28-29), but if he failed to repent it may indicate that he was not actually redeemed, and Paul does call him a "so-called brother" (v. 11). For **the day of the Lord Jesus**, see the comments on 1:8.

5:6-8. Paul picked up the theme of boasting from v. 2. **Leavens the whole lump** (v. 6) is similar to the proverb, "One bad apple can spoil the whole lot." The mention of **leaven** led Paul to compare the church to the celebration of Passover. The Hebrews would **clean out the old leaven** (v. 7; cf. Ex 12:15-19; 13:7) in preparation for the feast, and the Corinthians needed to "clean house" as well. **You are in fact unleavened** indicates that Paul viewed these Corinthians as truly born again, though their behavior sometimes brought doubt upon their true status. Verses 7-8 denote that, in Paul's analogy, the Passover celebration had already started and they were in danger of missing the feast. That is, if their community was infected with **the leaven of malice and wickedness**, they would forfeit their celebration of the Christian life and their delight in Him. Paul concludes his illustration by reminding them that **Christ our Passover also has been sacrificed**, a reminder of the pure and spotless lamb that was offered as the way of escape from the bondage of Egypt (Ex 12:1-13, 28-29). Just as the Israelites placed blood on the doorposts of their houses and God passed over judgment, so believers apply the blood of the sinless Messiah to their hearts by faith, and God passes over eternal judgment.

5:9-13. Regarding the **letter** in question, cf. the introduction to 1 Corinthians. They were not to associate with any **so-called** believer who was **immoral** (*pornos*, "one who engages in sexual immorality"), **covetous** ("those who would like to have more" and act unethically to get it), a **swindler** ("those who are ravenous" and extort to obtain something), a **reviler** ("those who speak rudely of others, who malign others' character"), or a **drunkard** (abuse of alcohol was a major social problem in the ancient world). **Associate** (v. 11) means "to join with others in shared social activities," and Paul defines this further as **not even to eat with such a one**. Church discipline is always intended to be redemptive and involves breaking fellowship—it is hoped for a short time!—with those involved in scandalous sin. **Do you not judge those who are within?** (v. 12) indicates that Paul expected them to be willing to **judge** these kinds of believers for these kinds of sins. For the relationship of church discipline to Jesus' command not to judge, see the comments on Mt 7:1-2. Excuses abound for not conducting church discipline, but ultimately, it can be an important tool in maintaining the purity and potency of the church.

B. The Second Exhortation: Avoid Lawsuits against Fellow Christians (6:1-11)

6:1-8. The Corinthians should judge an immoral believer but should not have the secular courts judge their petty litigations. **The saints will** participate with Jesus in the one-time judgment of **the** unbelieving **world** and the **angels** following the second coming (vv. 2-3; cf. Rv 2:26-27; 3:21; 20:4; Mt 19:28; Rm 16:20) which, in Paul's mind, makes them capable of settling their own legal disputes (a better translation than **law courts**, vv. 2, 4). The absence of any **wise man** (v. 5) who could settle disputes was proof that they did not have as much wisdom as they thought. The Corinthians should have been willing to be **wronged** and **defrauded** ("to be deprived of something through fraudulent means") in order to avoid besmirching the name of Christ by attacking a fellow believer in secular courts (vv. 7-8).

6:9-11. Here Paul developed the theme of believers' superiority over the secular legal authorities in judging their own affairs. **The unrighteous** (v. 9) refers to non-Christians who will not rule and reign with Christ in the millennial kingdom. Their characteristics are given in vv. 9-10, including those who are **effeminate** ("men who fill the sexual role of the female" in homosexual activity) and **homosexuals** (lit., "males who take other males to bed"; cf. Robert A. J. Gagnon, *The Bible and Homosexual Practice* [Nashville: Abingdon, 2001], 303–332). For **covetous**, **revilers**, **drunkards**, and **swindlers**, cf. the comments on 5:11 where they describe those who are saved but worthy of church discipline. **Such were some of you** indicates the unrighteousness that typified the Corinthians before they trusted Christ. Since they were no longer in the same category as the unrighteous, including unrighteous pagan judges, they were better suited to settle disputes between the righteous redeemed than the secular courts were. **You were washed** (v. 11) is a middle voice verb, here probably suggesting the enthusiastic consent of the Corinthian believers to undergo baptism. Baptism does not save an individual, but it serves as the profound sign of the prior work of God who cleanses one from the corruption of sin at the time of salvation (for the significance of baptism, see the comments on Rm 6:3-4). **Sanctified** here means "one who has the status of being separated from sin and set apart to God." Paul can speak of being **sanctified** in a practical sense in which the believer cooperates with the Spirit, separates himself from sin, and grows in personal holiness (see Rm 6:19, 22). But he can also speak of "positional" sanctification in which God separates the believing individual from sin unto Himself at the time of salvation (Rm 15:16; 1Co 1:2, 30). Because of the sorry spiritual condition of the Corinthian church (Paul next addressed their immorality in 6:12ff.!), **sanctified** here has the positional sense (note the "divine" passive voice—**were sanctified**, i.e., by God). Unlike the heathen judges, the Corinthians were set apart from evil unto God, and this makes them more capable of being in tune with Him so they can better settle their own disputes. **Justified** indicates the Corinthians were themselves declared righteous by God (see the comments on Rm 3:24 for the force of **justified**); this term also suggests that they were better able to reach righteous decisions in their legal wrangling than non-Christian judges. The appalling frequency in current society with which Christians sue other believers is an indication that Paul's injunction is either completely ignored or inappropriately domesticated.

C. The Third Exhortation: Promote Personal Moral Integrity (6:12-20)

6:12-20. Paul looked at one aspect of immorality as it affected the church in 5:1-13, and he looks at a different aspect here. **All things are lawful for me** (v. 12) probably reflects Paul's belief as one who was no longer under the constraints of the law (Rm 7:1-4), but was wrongly used by some of the Corinthians. The rich viewed their wealth as providing an opportunity for doing "all things that are lawful," especially satisfying one's culinary and sexual appetites. **Food is for the stomach . . . but God will do away with both of them** (v. 13) probably refers to death, though in the resurrection one will have both a stomach and the capacity to eat (cf. Lk 24:41-43). **The body is not for immorality**, even though in Paul's day much of the unbelieving Greco-Roman world thought it was. The financially elite commonly had banquets called *convivia* that included the services of prostitutes, and it was not unusual for a father to throw a party and hire a prostitute for his son when he turned 18 (a rite of passage called *toga virilis*) (cf. Winter, *After Paul Left Corinth*, 76–93). **The body** of a believer **is** intended **for** serving and enjoying **the Lord**. **Members** (v. 15) means "bodily appendages," "limbs," and suggests that Christians are His arms and legs (Rm 12:4-5; 1Co 12:12-14), i.e., they belong to *Him*. It is wrong to **take away the members** that belong to **Christ** and give them to a prostitute because that does the unthinkable. It involves Jesus in harlotry. Paul cited Gn 2:24 in v. 16, not to suggest that when one is involved sexually with a prostitute he is married to her. Paul's point is that the sexual relationship in marriage is a physical manifestation of the sharing of a common life. Having relations with a prostitute shares life with her rather than with the Lord, with whom one shares a spiritual bond (vv. 16-17). The believer must **flee** (*pheugete*, as in "fugitive") (v. 18) in the face of immorality. **The immoral man sins against his own body** should be understood in the context of Paul's statements that a believer's body is **for the Lord** (v. 13), that he is one of the **members of Christ** (v. 15a), and that he should not **take away the members of Christ** and give them to a prostitute (v. 15b). The **sin against** a believer's **own body** is keeping it from being available to Jesus for serving and glorifying Him, and giving it to a prostitute instead (so Gordon D. Fee, *The First Epistle to the Corinthians*, NICNT [Grand Rapids, MI: Eerdmans, 1987], 262–263). Paul's point in v. 19 is that believers belong to God who indwells them through the Spirit, just as the Greco-Roman gods owned and resided in their own temples. God "owns" believers. They are "bought and paid for" with the blood of Jesus (v. 20). He requires that each **glorify God** (live to enhance God's reputation in the world) in his physical **body**. Many today say that use of a prostitute constitutes evidence of not being saved, but Paul assumes the authenticity of the Corinthians' faith and so exhorts them based on their connection to Christ instead.

IV. The Third Problem: Obligations and Value of Marriage (7:1-40)

A. The First Exhortation: View Marriage as Beneficial (7:1-7)

7:1-7. Paul responded to their questions about marriage in chap. 7, but there is a thematic carryover from immorality in chap. 6. Marital relations can help one avoid immorality. Some of the Corinthians, however, favored asceticism over sexual fulfillment in marriage. The most likely reason for their ascetic leanings comes from hardships Paul mentioned in 7:26 (see the comments there). Times were hard enough for Christians that some thought marriage was inadvisable for the single, and sex too distracting from the Lord for the married. **It is good for a man not to touch a woman** (v. 1) was probably a Corinthian slogan because Paul did not condemn sex within marriage (7:2-6, 28, 36). He agreed with the slogan in part, but qualified it in v. 2. **To touch a woman** is a euphemism for sexual relations (Gn 20:6; Ru 2:9; Pr 6:29), in this context relations within marriage. **Have** (v. 2) is a euphemism for "have sex with" (Mk 6:18; Jn 4:18; 1Co 5:1; 7:29), and does not mean "to acquire" a wife. **Fulfill his duty to his wife** (v. 3) is remarkable because in that culture sexual satisfaction was considered the man's prerogative, not the woman's. But Paul insisted that each partner be available to the other, and neither was entitled consistently to deprive the other of conjugal rights (v. 4). Abstinence was appropriate for a temporary and mutually determined time to pray (or engage in any other spiritual discipline), but abstinence was not mandatory on those occasions (v. 6). Verse 7 refers to being content to be single, as Paul was. **Gift** is synonymous with **self-control** (v. 9), but can hardly be called a "spiritual gift." According to Paul, whatever a person's status, either contentedness to be single or being married, it is a gift from God.

B. The Second Exhortation: Fulfill Your Marital Obligations (7:8-16)

7:8-9. Paul expanded the theme of singleness introduced in v. 7. **Unmarried** (v. 8) refers to all categories of single people (divorced women and implicitly men in v. 11; those who were never married, or who were single again because of divorce or widowhood in vv. 32, 34), and Paul emphasized **widows** since there was considerable social pressure on them to remarry. Paul wished they would remain single (v. 9), but marriage was no sin, and Paul did encourage younger widows to remarry in 1Tm 5:14 if they could not control themselves. **To burn** is "the fire of inward lusts in conflict with conscience" (Frederic Louis Godet, *Commentary on First Corinthians* [Grand Rapids, MI: Kregel, 1977 reprint of the 1889 T&T. Clark Edition], 331). For those who are single, but not by choice, Paul would sympathize with their loneliness and sexual frustrations, and seek to reassure them that

God would provide the strength they needed to remain pure, and to find their joy in Him.

7:10-11. Paul turned his attention to Christian couples (v. 10). **Not I, but the Lord** points to Paul's awareness of Jesus' teaching on divorce (cf. the comments on Mt 5:32; 19:1-9) but in no way implies that the apostle's own words were not inspired or authoritative. It was unusual for a woman to **leave** ("divorce"; Lk 16:18) **her husband** (v. 10), but not unheard of (Mk 10:12). If a woman did divorce, she was required to remain single the rest of her life or until the death of her husband (Rm 7:1-4; 1Co 7:39), or be reconciled to him. Probably Paul required the same from the husband (v. 11).

7:12-16. In this paragraph Paul instructed believers not to divorce their unbelieving spouse (vv. 12-13). The believers in these mixed marriages probably came to faith after they were already married (cf. the comments on 7:39). Paul was not aware of any teaching on mixed marriages given by Jesus, but as an apostle inspired by God, Paul's words are binding (v. 12). **For** (v. 14) explains why the marriage should remain intact. **Sanctified through his wife** probably refers to the unbelieving spouse, and children, being "set apart" (**sanctified**) for special blessings from God, short of salvation, because of the tie with the believer. **Unclean** means "that which is not brought into contact with the divine" (BDAG, 34). However, if an unbelieving spouse physically and geographically (not just "emotionally") abandons the marriage, God no longer considers the believer married. Based on this principle, it is reasonable to allow divorce and remarriage for a Christian spouse who is abandoned by a believer as well. The verb **bondage** *(douloo)* was used widely in Paul's day as a metaphor for marriage (see Anthony C. Thiselton, *1 Corinthians: A Shorter Exegetical and Pastoral Commentary* [Grand Rapids, MI: Eerdmans, 2006], 303), so that not being in **bondage** was equivalent to being **free** (v. 39) as a virtual widow or widower. In this case, the believer who is abandoned is free to divorce and remarry. **But God has called us to peace** (v. 15) could be understood pessimistically ("Do not force an unbeliever to stay if he wants to leave. Divorce will bring peace."). Paul did permit divorce and remarriage if the unbeliever left (v. 15a, b, c), but his primary desire was for them to remain married, to live in **peace** with each other (v. 15d) (see vv. 10-13, 17, 20, 24, 27). Another reason to stay married (v. 16) was because the unbelieving spouse might come to trust Christ through the believer's influence.

C. The Third Exhortation: Develop Contentment with Present Marital Status (7:17-24)

7:17-24. The main point of vv. 18-23 is not remaining circumcised or enslaved, but remaining married. As in v. 15, they were to remain in whatever condition (married or single) God **called** them (see **called** in vv. 17, 18, 20, 21, 22, 24). When Paul wrote **he is not to become uncircumcised** (v. 18), he was probably referring to the minor surgery whereby a Jewish man who adopted Hellenistic values could reverse his circumcision to be more palatable to the Greco-Roman society. Paul's point was that if God called one as a Jew, he was to continue to be Jewish (albeit having trusted Christ), and if as a Gentile, he was to stay that way also. Paul qualified this directive, however, in v. 21, when he urged slaves to become free if they could, though that choice belonged to the master (cf. Murray J. Harris, *Slave of Christ: A New Testament Metaphor for Total Devotion to Christ*, NSBT [Downers Grove, IL: InterVarsity, 1999], 59–61). The command **Do not become slaves of men** (v. 23) disproves what critics say about the Bible condoning slavery.

D. The Fourth Exhortation: Emphasize the Benefits of Single Life (7:25-40)

7:25-31. Here Paul turned his attention to the needs of unmarried men and women (**virgins**, v. 25). On Paul's **opinion**, see the comments on 7:12. The **present distress** (v. 26) may refer to no less than three periods of acute grain shortage in the Mediterranean region from the mid AD 40s to early 50s, and more than one serious earthquake in AD 51 (for a detailed discussion of these conditions, see Winter, *After Paul Left Corinth*, 215–232). These conditions may have been the hardships that led some of the Corinthians to maintain that life was too difficult for the single to become encumbered with the obligations of caring for a spouse and children, and for the married to become distracted away from the Lord by sexual relations. **Wife** (*gune*, v. 27) can often mean simply "woman" (Mt 9:20, 22; 15:22, 28; Mk 14:3; 1Co 7:34), and, because Paul was writing to the unmarried in vv. 25-26 and 28, **bound to a** woman in this context refers to betrothal. **The time has been shortened** (v. 29) means that God will not permit the present age to continue forever. It will come to an end (v. 31), along with marriage (cf. the comments on Mt 22:30). **As though they had none** is Paul's way of urging those who are married to avoid being distracted from God by their spouse.

If married believers serve and nurture their spouse "as unto the Lord," then their focus remains on God while simultaneously caring for their spouse. Paul does not forbid the pursuits of vv. 29-31, but his words warn the Corinthians against becoming so involved in the affairs of life that they are swallowed up by them. It is permissible to marry, **weep**, **rejoice**, **buy**, and **use the world**, but not to the extent that they ensnare the believer.

7:32-35. Singleness is not only an advantage during hard times (v. 26), but it can help avoid worry. **The woman who is unmarried** (v. 34) includes widows and divorcees (cf. the comments on 7:8), with **the virgin** as the primary focus of these verses. It was not Paul's intent to deprive them of the opportunity to marry (v. 35), but to ensure complete **devotion to the Lord** (**devotion** is "single-minded focus upon and service for another").

7:36-38. These verses refer to a hypothetical situation in which a betrothed man was considering remaining single (so RSV; TNIV; NIV; ESV), not to a father who was debating marrying off his **daughter** (NASB). Several points support this view. First, **any man**, in the context of the instructions to those who are single in vv. 25-35, is probably someone who is unmarried. Second, **acting unbecomingly**, when used in the ancient world for relationships between men and women, overwhelmingly referred to sexual misconduct, making it unlikely that v. 36 refers to a father's deliberations. Third, the NASB's **if she is past her youth** is better translated "If he is sexually awakened" (RSV, "if his passions are strong"). The adjective *huperakmos*, translated wrongly by the NASB as **past her youth**, actually meant "sexually enlivened," or "to be sexually mature and feel the effects of it," and does not refer to old age in either gender. Consequently, fourth, the subject of the verb **is** in the phrase "if he *is* sexually enlivened" (once again, mistranslated by the NASB as **if she *is* past her youth**) should be understood as "he" and not "she." Paul was addressing the betrothed man in v. 36 (**he is acting . . . his virgin**) so that "he" is the more likely subject of "is" than "she." Fifth, **if it must be so**, if the betrothed man cannot control himself and sexual impropriety is imminent, then he should do what he **wishes**, and apparently what he **wishes** is to have sexual relations with his fiancée, for which marriage is a happy prerequisite. Sixth, **let her marry** is based on an inferior manuscript tradition, and the better reading is "let them marry" (RSV; TNIV; NIV; ESV). This fits the "betrothed young man" view better, as Paul might have written "let *her* marry" if he were addressing a father mulling over allowing his daughter to wed. Seventh, v. 37 reflects this man's resolve to remain single, a resolve not coerced by the anti-marriage advocates or by Paul (for the Greco-Roman background on this passage, see Winter, *After Paul Left Corinth*, 243–49). Eighth, **to keep his own virgin** was a phrase that meant "to safeguard a woman's virginity," and expresses the decision not to marry and have relations (cf. Fee, *1 Corinthians*, 353–54). The verb *gamizo* (NASB **gives . . . in marriage**) has a causative sense ("to give in marriage," "to have someone marry") elsewhere (Mt 24:38), but verbs with "*-izo*" endings were losing their causative force in Hellenistic Greek, and *gamizo* probably is synonymous with *gameo*, "to marry, take in marriage" (BDAG, 188).

7:39-40. Paul once again instructed widows here (cf. before, v. 8). A widow is free to remarry, but **only in the Lord** (v. 39), i.e., to another believer. This is the strongest NT verse supporting the idea that Christians should marry only other Christians. **She is happier if she remains as she is** for reasons given by Paul in vv. 26, 28, 32-35. On the gravity of Paul's **opinion** as a **Spirit**-inspired apostle, see the comments on 7:12.

V. The Fourth Problem: Issues Related to Christian Liberty in Eating Food Offered to Idols (8:1–11:1)

A. The First Exhortation: Temper Christian Liberty with Love (8:1-13)

8:1-3. Paul addressed another question from Corinth, namely, **the eating of things sacrificed to idols** (vv. 1, 4). Food offered to the gods often was eaten as a sacred meal in their honor. If one was invited to such a meal he was expected to go, and spiritual, social, and business ties were strengthened at these times. To decline such an invitation consistently was considered antisocial and could result in commercial suicide. It is understandable why the Corinthians would insist on continuing to go though they no longer worshiped those gods.

Paul's main concern was to steer the Corinthians away from idolatry, though they insisted on theological grounds that they had the freedom to go to the temples. In Rm 14–15, on the other hand, Paul confronted the divisions between Jewish and Gentile believers over eating kosher food (see the comments on Rm 14:1-9).

Verses 1 and 4 were probably Corinthian slogans with which Paul agrees in part. Their **knowledge** related to the recognition that gods do not exist, and they believed that it was no sin to eat a meal offered in honor of a non-god. True knowledge is tethered to **love** and does not lead to arrogance but to the edification of others (v. 1). Verse 3 implies that a believer's love for God is preceded by God's elective love for him, and both rule out any flirtation with idolatry.

8:4-6. The Corinthians understood rightly that the Triune God is the only true God and idols do not exist. But this did not mean that going to a temple and eating an idol's food was permissible. While idols do not exist (i.e., there is no such being named "Zeus"), false religions are promoted by demons, and to venture into a temple and eat a sacred meal in honor of a non-god nevertheless involved them in "partnering with demons" (cf. the comments on 10:20).

8:7-13. Some of the Gentile believers in Corinth still closely associated visiting a temple with the worship of idols, just as they did before their conversion. **Food will not commend us to God** (v. 8), but the thought requires serious caveats. Eating the food of idols was not a neutral activity; the **weak** could be led into idolatry by the influence of the knowledgeable ones (v. 10). Paul never urged the **weak** to become "strong" precisely because he approved of their weakness, which motivated them to stay away from idolatry. Ruin (v. 11, **ruined**) often means "to damage," "ruin," or "harm" (Mt 9:17; Lk 21:18; Jms 1:11), and in these chapters the ruin is reduced effectiveness in ministry (9:19-27), possible death as a disciplinary act from God (10:1-13), and partnering with demons (10:20) who oppose God. Harming one with a weak conscience was a **sin against Christ** (v. 12) inasmuch as it harmed a part of His body. **I will never eat meat again** refers to eating meat offered to idols, and is a different situation from eating non-kosher food (implied in 1Co 9:19-23 ; cf. Rm 14:14; Gl 2:11-14) which was permissible. Causing **my brother to stumble** (v. 13) does not mean annoying one who objects to the legitimate exercise of my Christian liberty. A weaker brother stumbles when he is influenced to violate his conscience by the direct or indirect inducement of another believer. Paul forbids this.

B. The Second Exhortation: Be Willing to Forego Christian Liberty (9:1-27)

9:1-7. Paul explored the need for the Corinthians to cease any activity that might be harmful to others (8:9-13), and he used himself as a prime example of that in chap. 9. Paul was an apostle (vv. 1-2), yet surrendered the privileges that an apostle deserved (vv. 4-6). **Have I not seen Jesus our Lord?** gives an important, though implicit, qualification of an apostle. Without a face-to-face encounter with Jesus, one could not be an apostle, a point that makes it difficult to believe that apostles are present in the Church today (see also the comments on 1Co 15:1-11). Verse 5 does not mean that Paul was married at the time he wrote 1 Corinthians (see 7:7-8), but it is possible he was a widower. Rabbis and Sanhedrin members were usually married, but it is not certain that Paul was either. Paul compared his right to support with a soldier, farmer, shepherd, and priest (cf. v. 13), each receiving provisions from his work (v. 7).

9:8-14. Paul used the **Law** (v. 8) to justify his right to receive support from his converts, not **human** arguments. Deuteronomy 25:4 (LXX) (v. 9) enforced kindness toward animals used for farming, but is found in a broader context dealing with benevolence to the poor or those who worked the fields (Dt. 24:19-22). Since Paul "planted" the church (1Co 3:6-9), he should enjoy some of the proceeds from it. **God** ***is*** **concerned about oxen**, but the main point in Deuteronomy, and with Paul, was receiving compensation for one's work. Paul expressed this concept explicitly in vv. 10-12a. Then, finally, in v. 12b (and v. 15), comes Paul's main point. He surrendered these privileges to avoid hindering the spread of the gospel. The Corinthians, however, had a more self-indulgent attitude. In addition, Paul referred to the priests who served in the temple (v. 13; cf. Nm 18:8-24). They kept a portion of the various sacrifices and offerings brought to the temple for their sustenance. Verse 14 is sometimes understood as enjoining a preacher to "practice what he preaches," but Paul's contention is that one who ministers the Word should be supported by those he serves. A church should remember that the pastors have the same goals for their income as they do (to provide for his family's needs, to prepare for emergencies, to establish financial security, to plan for retirement).

9:15-18. Paul would rather **die** than be counted among those who ministered just for the money (v. 15). The noun **boast** *(kauchema)* (vv. 15 and 16) has the connotation of "rejoicing" in 2Co 1:14; Gl 6:4; Php 1:26; 2:16; Heb 3:6. Paul's policy of ministering without compensation was the grounds for great delight. There is a sense in which he discharged that work because he was **under compulsion** (v. 16) from God to do it. But he was not under compulsion to do it for free. Verse 17 could be paraphrased, "If I volunteered to preach when I was not required to, then I might be extraordinary and should be rewarded for my preaching. But actually I was drafted by God against my will. I am His household slave and have no choice but to work for Him. There is no reward given under those circumstances." **What then** did Paul do that was worthy of **reward** (v. 18)? It was his **offer** of **the gospel without charge, so as not to make full use of my right in the gospel**. Robertson and Plummer wrote, "[It is as if Paul were saying] What is the pay that I get? Why the pleasure of refusing pay" (*1 Corinthians*, 190).

9:19-23. In vv. 19-22, Paul provided personal illustrations of 9:18 (he did not make full use of his rights). **Win** (v. 19) means "to acquire by investment or gain," and appears to be synonymous in this context with **save** (v. 22; cf. also 1Pt 3:1). **Jews** (v. 20) looks at Jewish people from the standpoint of their ethnicity, and **under the Law** from the standpoint of their religion. For **not being myself under the Law**, see the comments on Rm 6:14; 7:1-4. **Those . . . without law** (v. 21) refers to Gentiles. While Paul was no longer under the 613 commandments of Moses, he was under **the law of Christ** (v. 21) (cf. the comments on Gl 6:2). **The weak** (v. 22) were not weak Christians (cf. 8:9-13), but non-Christians (Rm 5:6), whether Jews or Gentiles, that Paul was trying to **win** to Christ just as in vv. 20-21. Paul practiced "contextualization," never changing the contents of the gospel but adapting its communication to the culture of his audience. This remains the model for missions and evangelism today. To **become a fellow partaker of** the gospel (v. 23) means that Paul did not want to be alone in possessing and enjoying the benefits of the gospel. He intended to take as many people as possible with him to heaven. **Fellow partaker** means "one who shares mutually with another a possession or relationship," with the emphasis on what both have in common. Paul did not mean that he hoped to obtain salvation by evangelizing people, which is salvation by works and an unlikely reading of this verse.

9:24-27. Paul sets up an analogy between the need for surrendering one's rights for the sake of others and athletic competition. Paul may have had in mind the Isthmian Games, held every third year in Corinth, second in prominence only to the Olympic Games in Athens. Contestants had to provide proof that they trained for ten months, had to exercise in the gymnasium for the 30 days before the games started, and only then could they compete. Only the winners received a reward, a **perishable wreath** (v. 25) which, in the first century, was made of celery and would wilt as soon as it was awarded. Paul never just ran laps or slapped at the air (v. 26). Everything he did was calculated to make gains for the gospel. The Greek word translated **discipline** (v. 27) means "to deliver a knock-out blow." **Make it my slave** may reflect the practice of the victor leading his beaten opponents around the arena amidst the applause of the spectators. Paul determined to subdue his **body** (who he was inside and out) to be most effective in serving the Lord. **So that . . . I myself will not be disqualified** does not mean that Paul feared losing his salvation if he did not adequately control himself. The disqualification here refers to forfeiting the chance to serve *effectively* in the great gospel mission. Effective service involves self-surrender, self-control, and self-sacrifice, and none of these typified the Corinthian believers. Self-indulgent Christians should not expect to be effective in serving the Lord.

C. The Third Exhortation: Limit Christian Liberty before God Disciplines (10:1-22)

10:1-5. For (v. 1) links Israel's disqualification to that mentioned in 9:24-27. **All** is used five times in vv. 1-4, stressing that every Jewish person participating in the exodus enjoyed its blessings. **Under the cloud** (Ex 13:21; 14:18, 24) and **through the sea** suggest supernatural guidance and deliverance. **Baptized into Moses** (v. 2), the **spiritual food** (v. 3; manna), and the **spiritual drink** (v. 4) parallel Christian baptism and the celebration of communion. God did these remarkable things for the Israelites, but His kindnesses were not a guarantee that He would refrain from disciplining them if they strayed. The scriptural record indicates that they did sin and He did discipline them. **Baptized** (v. 2) does not mean "to identify with," nor does it have a sacramental sense, because the Israelites remained dry when they crossed the Red Sea. Passing through the Red Sea was an indication of their dependence on Moses, just as Christian baptism points toward Jesus Christ as the one who saves (cf. the comments on Rm 6:2-4). Paul called this a "baptism" to enhance the parallel with the Corinthian church. **Spiritual**

(vv. 3-4) designates the origin of the **food** and **drink**, not its constitution. Water came from a **rock** at the beginning and end of the wilderness sojourn (Ex 17:6; Nm 20:1-13), though there is no mention that the rock moved. Paul was probably drawing attention to God's constant provision of water throughout their desert experience, which ultimately came from **Christ**. In Ex 17:5, God stood on the rock in front of Moses and Aaron at Horeb, and in Nm 20:6 the glory of the Lord appeared to them immediately prior to Moses striking the rock. Paul may have understood these as Christophanies, preincarnate OT appearances of Jesus. Both the Israelites and the Corinthians experienced deliverance through Jesus. **Nevertheless** (v. 5) introduces the "punch line." In spite of all that God did for them, the Israelites **were laid low in the wilderness**. Paul did not explore the issue of their eternal destiny. It is enough for him to say that the people of Israel who went too far in their behavior died due to God's retribution and, obviously, were disqualified from any opportunity to serve Him (cf. 9:24-27).

10:6-13. Now (v. 6) is literally "but," and demonstrates that Paul hoped for an outcome for the Corinthians different from that of the Hebrews. Paul cited four sinful events for which God chastised Israel: the idolatry with the golden calf (Ex 32:4-6) (v. 7), immorality with Moabite women (Nm 25:1-9) (v. 8), testing the Lord when the serpents attacked them (Nm 21:4-9) (v. 9), and grumbling in response to God's severe treatment of Korah (Nm 16:1-50, esp. 16:41) (v. 10). Numbers 25:9 says that 24,000 died in the plague, but Paul's number refers to those who died **in one day**, just as he wrote. **Instruction** (v. 11) means "an admonishment regarding the consequences of unwise or sinful actions." **The ends of the ages have come**, and God has typologically connected the ancient Hebrew Scriptures and the situation faced by the Corinthians as part of His sovereign plan. Because God has drawn these connections, the Corinthians might fall (v. 12) just as the Jewish people fell. The **temptation** (or possibly "test") facing the Corinthians (v. 13) involved returning to the temples in order to avoid the social, political, or financial ostracism that might result from refusing to go (cf. Garland, *1 Corinthians*, 357; 467–68). **God is faithful** to ensure that the tests He ordains are commensurate with the strength He provides to pass them. Note that the **escape** is not the complete removal of the test, but is the ability **to endure** it. The Corinthians would feel the ongoing pull to return to the temples, but God would help them to do what was right, which, in this context, is to **flee from idolatry** (v. 14).

10:14-22. Paul continued his warning by comparing the effects of communion and partaking of the sacrifices in the Jerusalem temple with the effects of a meal in honor of a Greco-Roman god. The elements of communion enhanced fellowship (**sharing**, *koinonia*) with Jesus (v. 16), and with other believers (v. 17), just as eating what was offered in the Jerusalem temple forged closer fellowship with God (**altar** is used as a metonymy for "God"; cf. Dt 14:22-27) (v. 18). Likewise, eating with pagan friends in the temple of a false god formed ties with them and it. Paul denied that these false gods actually existed (v. 19; cf. the comments on 8:4-6). But **demons** (v. 20) deceived worshipers into believing that the gods were real (see Dt 32:17). When these Christians went to the temples, they became **sharers** ("one who shares in some task or venture with another," "a partner") with **demons** (v. 20), perhaps by inadvertently promoting the worship of the false god, as the demons did, by their presence there. This was an act of idolatry. **Or** (v. 22) if one insisted on going to the temples, was that person trying to make God jealous? That will not work. For a husband to feel jealous about his wife, she has to have some sway over him, so that he would feel fear about being replaced in her affections by another. But Paul's point is that believers do not have that kind of influence over God, and when God becomes jealous because His people are spiritually adulterous, He punishes them (Dt 32:21-24). Paul's directives here dovetail well with the decisions of the Jerusalem Council and the letter sent in the wake of it (cf. Ac 15:23-29), which forbade idolatry for Gentile believers (including "things [including food] sacrificed to idols" and cultic sexual activity, Ac 15:29).

D. The Fourth Exhortation: Adjust Behavior to Suit Various Settings (10:23–11:1)

10:23-30. Here Paul wrote about the proper circumstances when meat offered to idols could be eaten. For v. 23, see the comments on 6:12-13. For v. 24, see the comments on 8:9-13. **For conscience' sake** (v. 25) refers to the believer's conscience, but in vv. 27-29 an unbeliever's conscience is in view ("If one of the *unbelievers* invites you," v. 27; v. 29 indicates that vv. 27-28 are about the unbeliever's conscience). In vv. 25-30, Paul gave four guidelines regulating the eating of meat offered to idols. First, a believer, in his own home (not in the temples; see the comments on 10:6-22 above), could eat meat sold in the markets (v. 25). If he did not know it had been offered, he should just eat it and not ask **questions** about it, for the Lord provided it (v. 26). Second, in v. 27, a believer could eat idol's meat in an unbeliever's home, but not in a temple. Third, in v. 28, if an unbeliever informed a believer that the meat was offered to an idol, the believer should abstain **for** the **sake** of the unbeliever's conscience. An unbeliever's conscience might be harmed or his spiritual progress impeded if he felt the Christian's quasi-idolatrous action justified his own, or if he felt the believer was hypocritical or lax on his belief in the existence of one true God. Fourth, if a Christian might be condemned (**judged**, perhaps as a hypocrite) by an unbeliever for eating, the believer should abstain (v. 29). In v. 30, Paul gives the reverse idea to the thought of v. 29: "If I give up my freedom to partake with thankfulness, I will not be slandered concerning that for which I give thanks." To summarize vv. 23-30, Paul maintains that a believer can eat meat offered to idols, though not in a temple. But if there was any chance anyone would be harmed by eating this food, the believer was to abstain—and thus Paul goes full circle back to chap. 8. For this approach to these verses, see Garland, *1 Corinthians*, 497–99.

10:31–11:1. To do something for **the glory of God** is to act in such a way that people see Him in action and that His reputation is enhanced (Mt 5:16). If the Corinthians acted more like Paul (11:1) around unbelievers (10:32), **many** more **may be saved** (v. 33). Sometimes believers insist on pastimes that may actually be contrary to the Word (risqué movies, using resources to pander to creature comforts and appetites) that may make them vulnerable to evil influences, and will make them so self-absorbed that they are ineffective in serving others.

VI. The Fifth Problem: Chaos in Church Worship Services (11:2–14:40)

A. The First Exhortation: Maintain Sexual Distinctions (11:2-16)

11:2-9. Starting in 11:2 and running through chap. 14, Paul began to address new concerns related to problems associated with their church gatherings. They could improve the extent to which they imitated Paul, but on the whole they embraced the **traditions** he taught them when he was in Corinth (v. 2). **But** (v. 3) signals their need to adjust yet another area of subpar performance. **Head** could refer to the extremity of almost any object, the physical head of a person, and the leader of a group. Some claim that it means "source" (cf. Catherine Kroeger, "Head," in *A Dictionary of Paul and His Letters*, ed. Gerald F. Hawthorne et al. [Downers Grove, IL: InterVarsity, 1993], 375–377; Berkley Mickelsen, and Alvera Mickelsen, "What Does *Kephale* Mean in the New Testament?" In *Women, Authority and the Bible*, ed. Alvera Mickelsen [Downers Grove, IL: InterVarsity, 1986], 97–110; Fee, *1 Corinthians*, 502–505), but there is no unequivocal use of the word with this sense in Greek, and it makes little sense in this passage. For example, in order to claim that "head" refers to "source," "head" must be assigned three different meanings in the same verse, so that Christ is the creating source of the biological and spiritual life of all people (**every man**), man is the substance from whom woman was fashioned by God, and God is the sending or incarnating source of Christ. This is semantically unlikely. It is better to understand **head** metaphorically as "one who has authority," "leader" (for these and other points, cf. the articles by Wayne Grudem: "Does *kephalē* ('Head') Mean 'Source' or 'Authority Over' in Greek Literature? A Survey of 2,336 Examples," *Trinity Journal* 6 NS [1985]: 38–59; "The Meaning of *kephalē*: A Response to Recent Studies," *Trinity Journal* 11 NS [1990]: 3–72; reprinted as an appendix to *Recovering Biblical Manhood and Womanhood*, ed. John Piper and Wayne Grudem [Wheaton, IL: Crossway, 1991] 425–468); "The Meaning of [*kephalē*] ["Head"]: An Evaluation of New Evidence, Real and Alleged," *Journal of the Evangelical Theological Society* [March 2001]: 25–65). **The man is the head of a woman** speaks of male leadership and female subordination, in this context, in the Church. **Man** and **woman** does not refer to "husband" and "wife" (contra the ESV). Paul is speaking of a corporate church setting (vv. 4-5), and husbands and wives do not originate from each other (vv. 8, 11). **God is the head of Christ** in that the Father exercises authority over the Son (cf. Jn 14:28), and the Son submits to and accomplishes the will of the Father (Jn 5:30; 6:38; Heb 10:9), while sharing all of the Father's divine attributes. Roman men covered their heads when they worshiped their gods, and for a Christian man to do so **disgraces his head** (Jesus), for it implicitly put Him in the same category with Roman idols. On **prophesying**, see the comments on 14:1-3. **But** (v. 5) introduces a discussion of how a woman should pray or prophesy in a church gathering. Respectable women covered their heads with a piece of their garment or a shawl in virtually all public settings, and it signaled that they were attached to a man (whether a husband, father, etc.), and were morally respectable. Like immodest clothing today, the lack of a covering announced a woman's willingness to entertain advances from men. To come to church in such a suggestive manner could sully (disgrace) **her head** (her male leaders) by causing them shame, just as a destructive teenager who harms others can cause his parents to feel shame. Why did these women remove their head coverings? Since Paul began this discussion with a reference to men's headship in the church, and since men were to worship with uncovered heads, it is possible that by removing their head coverings the women were seeking to establish equality with the men. But by doing this, they put themselves in the same category as **the woman whose head is shaved**, with one who earned a reputation for being immoral (for the ancient sources, see Garland, *1 Corinthians*, 521; Winter, *After Paul Left Corinth*, 128–29). **For** (v. 6) lends further support to the strong statement that an uncovered woman looked like an immoral woman. The husbands of adulterous women often had their wives' hair cropped. If the women wanted to remove their coverings to be more like the men, they ended up looking more like disreputable immoral women. They might as well go further, shave their heads, and settle the issue. But if they were not willing to go that far, then they should replace their coverings and act like respectable women. **For** (v. 7) launches the basis for the man being uncovered (vv. 4-5). Both Adam and Eve, as the representatives of the genders, were made in the image of God (Gn 1:26-27). The man, however, was assigned the task of cultivating and keeping (or better "worshiping and obeying" Him) (see comments at Gn 2:15), so that the man's task was specifically oriented toward God in a way that the woman's was not (Gn 2:18). She was created to help the man as he performed those tasks. The man is **the image and glory of God**, i.e., a man functions to serve God as His agent (His **image**) on earth, ruling and reigning over it with Him to bring Him honor (**glory**). "Honor" is probably the sense of **glory** here because in 11:14-15 "dishonor" is the opposite of "glory" (cf. Thomas R. Schreiner, "Head Coverings, Prophecies and the Trinity: 1 Corinthians 11:2-16," in *Recovering Biblical Manhood and Womanhood: A Response to Evangelical Feminism*, ed. John Piper and Wayne Grudem [Wheaton, IL: Crossway, 1991], 133). Since God has no superiors, the man, who represents Him, should therefore worship without a cultural sign of subordination, that is, without a head covering. **But the woman is the glory of man** indicates that a woman functions to assist the man and thereby honors him, and should have the sign of subordination (cf. v. 10). **For** (v. 8) introduces the first of two explanations as to why the woman is the glory of the man (v. 7). The *order* of creation—the man first, the woman second and derived from him—suggests that the man has priority in leadership (see also 1Ti 2:13). **For indeed** (v. 9) gives the second explanation, namely, the *purpose* of the genders. The **woman** was created **for the man's sake** (Gn 2:18), to come to his aid, not vice versa, suggesting also the priority of male leadership.

11:10-16. Therefore (v. 10) points back to the reasons Paul gave in vv. 6-9 for a woman to cover her head. The words "symbol of" are not found in the Greek, and to **have authority** over (the verb *echo*, "to have" + the noun *exousia*, "authority" + the preposition *epi*, "over") elsewhere means "to have control over" something (Mk 2:10; Lk 5:24; 19:17; Rv 11:6; 17:18; 16:9; 20:6). The phrase means that the woman is to exercise control over her physical head and keep it covered. **Because of the angels** is cryptic, but probably refers to angels who might be offended by the symbolically insubordinate act of the Corinthian women. Perhaps because of Satan's act of rebellion along with other angels, the good angels have become acutely interested in proper submission in the Church. It would be a mistake to think Paul saw women as unimportant in vv. 7-9, and he addressed that in vv. 11-12. Women need the men in the church, and men need the women. This is in keeping with the divine design of the human race by **the Lord** (Jesus, v. 11) and by **God** (v. 12).

Verse 13 introduces a new argument for women being covered, this one drawn from **nature** (v. 14). **Nature** probably means "the regular or established order of things" (BDAG, 1070) as reflected in cultural conventions. It was a **dishonor** for a man to have **long hair** in first-century Corinth. If a man had long hair, he was perceived negatively as attempting to feminize himself. It was expected that women would have long hair (vv. 5-6) (cf. Garland, *1 Corinthians*, 531, for the ancient sources). Long hair **is a glory to her** in that it is a mark of her respectability (see the comments on vv. 5-6) and femininity. Her hair **is given to her** by God as (not "instead of") **a** glorious **covering**, which was not intended for men. For a woman to reject this God-given sign of respectable femininity was to reject her identity and role as a Christian woman. Someone might object that long hair was not always a dishonor for men, as in the case of the Spartan warriors and Nazirites. But Paul was not writing to Spartans and Nazirites. In cultures where hair length is not tied to a specific gender, believers should embrace their culture's symbols of masculinity and femininity whatever they might be, and not blur or diminish them.

The question arises: "Should women who participate in a church setting be covered today?" The answer is "No, not unless one's culture expects it" (as in the case of the Amish and conservative Mennonite communities). Respectable women in the first-century Greco-Roman world were *always* covered in public, and they were to be covered in church as well. Today, if women should be covered in church, then to be consistent they should be covered at all times. How should the passage be applied in a setting where head coverings are not expected? Perhaps the most defensible application is that a woman should dress modestly to avoid the appearance of questionable morality, and in a feminine way as a demonstration of her deference to the male leadership of the church.

B. The Second Exhortation: Correct the Abuses of Communion (11:17-34)

11:17-22. From 11:17-34 Paul addressed a second problem associated with their church assemblies, namely abuses of the Lord's Table. **Divisions** (*schismata*, v. 18) means "dissension and division as a result of incompatible ambitions" (cf. 1:10). **Factions** (v. 19) means "the dividing of people into opposing groups." These problems with unity arose in God's providence so that the church could recognize the believers who promoted concord and who were thus worth following. **When** the church met **together** auspiciously for communion (v. 20), their behavior actually denied what the Lord's Table represented. They did indeed have a feast, but it could hardly be called communion. **For** (v. 21) justifies Paul's evaluation of their pseudo-communion in v. 20. **Each one takes his own supper first** . . . **hungry** . . . **drunk** (v. 21) may reflect a common Greco-Roman occurrence when dinner parties were held. Often the best food and drink were reserved for and consumed by the party's host and his high-ranking guests whom he was trying to impress for the sake of his own social enhancement, and the rest got inferior provisions. Furthermore, excessive drinking often followed the feasting (cf. Ben Witherington, *Conflict and Community in Corinth: A Socio-Rhetorical Commentary on 1 and 2 Corinthians* [Grand Rapids, MI: Eerdmans, 1995], 191–193; Thiselton, *1 Corinthians*, 890). The **hungry** in the Corinthian church were **those who have nothing** (v. 22), referring to the poor or perhaps the slaves who may have been detained in their duties and who found that there was no food for them when they arrived at the assembly because the others had eaten **first** (v. 21). A potluck associated with communion was not the place for gluttony, and the thoughtlessness exhibited against the poor was inexcusable (v. 22).

11:23-26. For (v. 23) explains why Paul could not **praise** them (v. 22). **From the Lord** indicates that Jesus originated the words Paul is about to cite, but whether they came by direct revelation to him or through Christian messengers is not clear. For vv. 23-25, see the comments on Mt 26:26-29, Mk 14:22-24, and Lk 22:19-20. **For** (v. 26) gives Paul's inference from the facts of communion. **Proclaim** . . . **until He comes** asserts that communion is an enacted proclamation of the atoning death of Jesus. Although believers must engage repeatedly in the Lord's Table, Jesus would not until He joins them in the consummated kingdom. The Lord's Table is a profound memorial (note not "just" a memorial!), and conveys sanctifying (not saving) grace, strengthening believers who reflect upon the tortured body and spilled blood of the Son of God.

11:27-34. Therefore (v. 27), because communion is such a profound ordinance, believers must be careful in how they approach it. The **unworthy manner** and being **guilty of the body and the blood of the Lord**, in this context, according to Thiselton (*1 Corinthians*, 890) is "the sin against Christ of *claiming identification with him* while using the celebration of the meal *as an occasion for social enjoyment or status enhancement without regard to what sharing in what the Lord's Supper proclaims*" (emphasis Thiselton's). **But** (v. 28), in order not to partake unworthily, one must examine himself to determine if he is entering into communion with the proper focus and intention. **For** (v. 29) strengthens Paul's admonition in v. 28 about self-examination. **Judgment** does not refer to eternal condemnation, for it is unlikely that Paul would understand that a blood-bought believer who inappropriately participated in communion would face eternal condemnation. Paul appears to think that there is a happier outcome than that for these believers (vv. 31-32). **The body** is a synecdoche (a part that stands for the whole) for the two elements of communion that are symbolic of "the body and blood" of Jesus offered in His death. **Body** probably does not refer to the church as the body of Christ because the nearest antecedent use of **body** in v. 27 refers to communion. Coming to communion with the proper aim, however, does not preclude caring for the members of Christ's body, the church. **For this reason** (v. 30), i.e., because some abused communion they drank **judgment** upon themselves, a **judgment** that included physical illness and death (for **sleep** as a euphemism for death, see 1Th 4:13-15). If one were careful to examine his motivation in gathering for communion and partook correctly, he **would not be judged** (v. 31; cf. also v. 28). **But** (v. 32) in the case of those who did not partake correctly and were **judged**, that judgment was different from that of the unbelieving world. God judges unbelievers for their sin even in this life (cf. the comments on Rm 1:24-32), and this leads to eternal condemnation as well. But when believers are "judged" by God in this life (evidenced by them becoming **weak**, **sick**, or dying, v. 30), His action is remedial and redemptive (**we are disciplined**), not purely punitive (**condemned**, as is the unbelievers' present and eschatological end). There were other places for satisfying one's hunger and seeking one's social delight or enhancement, but to do this at communion was wrong (vv. 33-34).

C. The Third Exhortation: Employ Spiritual Gifts Carefully (12:1–14:40)

12:1-3. Paul continued addressing problems in their church gatherings. **Spiritual gifts** (lit., "spirituals," *pneumatikon*, v. 1) means "that which pertains to, is caused by, or corresponds to the Spirit" (see BDAG, 837). The word is probably neuter ("spiritual things, activities") because Paul discussed gifts and their respective ministries. Unbelievers might say **Jesus is accursed** (v. 3), but the test of genuine Christianity is the sincere confession, **Jesus is Lord** not necessarily speaking in tongues. The confession is as much a *pneumatikon* as the exercise of the most miraculous spiritual gift.

12:4-11. All true Christians confess Jesus' lordship (v. 3), "but" (better than **now**) that does not mean that there are no distinctions between them. **Varieties** (vv. 5-6) means "that which is divided and distributed on the basis of certain implied distinctions or differences" (L&N, 1:567). **Gifts** (*charismaton*, v. 4) emphasizes God's gracious role in the assigning of these gifts, a point that might curtail the arrogance of some Corinthians regarding their gifts. A "spiritual gift" is a special ability (not just a ministry or function) God gives to believers to strengthen the church so that it accomplishes His will in the world. **Ministries** (v. 5) describes the tangible acts of service rendered to others as believers used their gifts. **Effects** (v. 6) means "the accomplishment of an act with an emphasis on the power to do it." All of the gifts, not just the miraculous ones, are graciously given, are intended to serve others, and are driven by divine power. Verses 4-6 reflect Paul's belief in the Trinity who are the source of all the gifts and the fruit of those gifts (**God . . . works all things**, v. 6). The Corinthians could not boast in their own abilities or productivity. **But** (v. 7) establishes the single intent of the gifts, **the common good** (13:1-7; 14:4, 6, 12, 17, 19, 26). The gifts are not designed primarily for one's own edification. Paul taught that **each** believer had a spiritual gift, called here the **manifestation** ("a detailed disclosure") **of the Spirit**. One of the ways the Holy Spirit makes Himself known is through believers using their spiritual gifts. **For** (v. 8) confirms v. 7. The **word of wisdom** may be the Spirit-revealed insight into God's redemptive program through Christ (cf. 1:30; 2:6-13). The **word of knowledge** may be a revelatory gift whereby one knew facts only through divine revelation, facts regarding the true nature of the world and spiritual truth (see the connections between **knowledge** and tongues, prophecy, and revelation in 13:2, 8-12; 14:6). Peter may have known of the deception of Ananias and Sapphira (Ac 5:1-11) by means of this gift. But not enough is known about these gifts to be certain of their characteristics (see Fee's comment on the **word of knowledge**, *1 Corinthians*, 593, as an illustration of the lack of certainty). **Faith** (v. 9) is an intense trust in Him to accomplish the impossible (cf. Mk 9:23; Mt 17:20; Ac 27:25; 1Co 13:2). The plural **gifts of healing** may indicate that there were different kinds of healings that different individuals could do at different times. **The effecting of miracles** (v. 10) probably overlaps with **healing**, and includes nature miracles and exorcisms. For **prophecy**, cf. the comments on 14:1-3. **The distinguishing of spirits** is the ability to determine if an utterance or miracle had demonic origins. For **kinds of tongues** cf. 14:1-3. On the **interpretation of tongues**, see 14:27. The **Spirit** gives gifts to **each** believer (v. 11) based on His sovereign determination (not on the believer's asking). Regarding the question of the permanence of the miraculous spiritual gifts, see the comments on 13:8-13.

12:12-13. On v. 12, see the comments on Rm 12:4-5. **For** (v. 13) describes how believers become part of the body. The phrase **by one Spirit . . . baptized** occurs in Mt 3:11; Mk 1:8; Lk 3:16; Jn 1:33; Ac 1:5; 11:16, where Jesus is the one doing the baptizing and the Spirit is the "element" into which Jesus immerses the believer, not the baptizer. **Baptized** is used metaphorically. As the believer is placed in water at baptism, so Jesus spiritually places the believer into the Spirit at the moment of conversion, causing the believer to be joined to the **one body** of Christ. The three occurrences of **all** in vv. 12-13 indicate that *every* believer has been **baptized** by Jesus in the Spirit. This verse makes the idea of a post-conversion baptism by the Spirit implausible. **Made to drink** refers to the indwelling of the Spirit, whose reception elsewhere is likened to the intake of water (Jn 14:13-14).

12:14-26. Each believer enters the body the same way (v. 13), but this does not preclude diversity (v. 14). The **foot** and the **ear** are not as adept as the **hand** or **eye**, but mobility and hearing are essential. One's hands and head are usually uncovered, but the **less honorable** parts (perhaps the trunk and thighs) receive the "honor" of being clothed, as are the **less presentable members** (perhaps one's private parts). Thomas writes, "Since the habit with the physical body is to take the 'behind-the-scenes' parts and devote special effort and attention to them, how much more should this be true in the spiritual body?" (Robert L. Thomas, *Understanding Spiritual Gifts: A Verse-by-Verse Study of 1 Corinthians 12–14,* 2nd ed. [Grand Rapids, MI: Kregel, 1999], 52). **God** honors even the members that others view as inferior (v. 24).

12:27-31. Now (v. 27) applies the analogy of the human body (vv. 14-26) to the body of Christ. All the gifts are necessary (vv. 14-26), but they are not all equally beneficial (vv. 28-31). **First . . . second . . . third** (v. 28) ranks the first three gifts according to their benefit to the church. **Apostles** were men who had some personal contact with Jesus, saw Him in His resurrection (1Co 9:1-2; Lk 24:48; Ac 1:8, 21-23), and were appointed by Him to their office. It was a group of undetermined size as indicated by the early church's struggle with false apostles (2Co 11:13), a struggle that would not have existed if one could say, "He is not one of the Twelve and therefore is not a true apostle." They carried enormous authority over the entire Church as opposed to having localized authority. Based on these qualifications, it is unlikely that they are present in the church today. Sometimes "apostle" is used in a non-technical sense for messengers or missionaries sent by churches (Php 2:25; 2Co 8:22-23), but this is not Paul's sense here. On **prophets**, cf. the comments on 14:1-3. **Teachers** grasp previously revealed truth (perhaps from the OT or from the apostles and prophets) and systematically impart knowledge of it to the church. **Then** indicates that Paul continued to rank the gifts, but the ranking becomes more generalized and shifts to functions rather than individuals. On **miracles**, see v. 10. On **healings**, see v. 9. **Helps** refers to different kinds of relief provided for those who suffer. **Administrations** means "the ability to lead," the capacity to accomplish scriptural goals through the assistance of others. On **kinds of tongues**, see the comments on 14:1-3. In vv. 29-30, Paul asked a series of rhetorical questions, each anticipating a negative response. *All* believers have been baptized by Jesus in the Spirit (v. 13), but not all speak with tongues (v. 30) so that tongues cannot be *the* sign of the baptism in the Spirit. **Earnestly desire** (v. 31a) is a command in light of 14:1, 12, but does not contradict vv. 11, 18. As a collective group they were to look for believers with high-ranking gifts (v. 28). If Paul were determining the individual value of love and gifts, love would win (v. 31b). Paul does, however, connect the two in chapter 13.

13:1-3. In vv. 1-3, Paul shows the necessity of love to make the employment of spiritual gifts constructive. **Tongues of . . . angels** is sometimes cited in support of tongues being a "heavenly language," but whenever angels are recorded as speaking, they use an earthly foreign language. **Love** is "a spontaneous inward affection of one person for another that manifests itself in an outgoing concern for the other and impels one to self-giving" (Joseph A. Fitzmyer, *First Corinthians: A New Translation with Introduction and Commentary,* AYB, vol. 32 [New Haven: Yale, 2008], 489).

13:4-7. Paul presented the characteristics of love in this paragraph. See the major commentaries for word studies on these characteristics.

13:8-12. Here Paul taught the permanence of love compared to spiritual gifts. For a discussion of **prophecy** and **tongues** (v. 8), see the comments on 14:1-3. **Knowledge** is the "word of knowledge" (12:8). **Will be done away** means "to be brought to an end," "to cease," "to be abolished," and is found in vv. 10 and 11 as well. **In part** (v. 9) indicates the incompleteness of the content or the comprehension of the gifts. **The perfect** (v. 10) could be the believer's death, the completion of the canon, or conditions following the second coming. A preferable view is "a relative state of maturity" for the Church. **The perfect** *(to teleion)* is used neither for death nor perfection following the second coming, and the Corinthians would not have understood it as a reference to the canon. Paul often used the word for relative maturity in contexts where it is contrasted with childishness or immaturity (1Co 2:6 with 3:1; 13:10 [perhaps]; 14:20; see especially Eph 4:13-14 in a context of spiritual gifts and the Church's maturity; cf. Heb 5:13-14) (Thomas, *Understanding Spiritual Gifts*, 123–32; F. David Farnell, "When Will the Gift of Prophecy Cease?" *BibSac* 150 (April-June 1993): 191–95). When the Church reached a point of relative maturity, **tongues**, **prophecy**, and **knowledge** ceased. Paul did not say precisely when this would happen, but Chrysostom (d. AD 407) and Augustine (d. AD 430) said the miraculous spiritual gifts had ceased, and around their time several important councils settled some critical issues for the Church. This may be the arrival of "relative maturity" for the Church, but this is purely conjectural. In v. 11 Paul compared the Church's maturation with his own. His childhood parallels the time when **the partial** exists (i.e., when **tongues**, **prophecy** and **knowledge** are present in the Church). **I did away with** is the same verb as in both vv. 8 and 10. **For** (v. 12) explains why the "childhood" things (the three gifts) are done away with. **Dimly** probably means "indistinctly, unclearly," and is synonymous with **the partial** (see v. 10). After the Church reaches its relative state of maturity, Paul anticipated that the understanding of the content of these gifts would be clearer. A **mirror** was made of highly polished brass and at best provided an imperfect reflection. **Face to face** is almost universally interpreted as "seeing God face to face" (Gn 32:30; Ex 33:11; Dt 5:4; 24:10; Jdg 6:22; Ezk 20:35). But God is not mentioned in v. 12, and Paul is continuing the metaphor of v. 12a into v. 12b, c, d. When one looks into a mirror he sees himself, not God, and in Paul's day one's reflection was blurred. Paul is saying that someday the image will be as clear as if one were actually looking at himself without a bad mirror. **Just as I also have been fully known** refers to knowing how one looks with the same accuracy that others know him, i.e., without a flawed reflection from an imperfect mirror, but it does not speak of God's knowledge of the believer. Exodus 33:11, a "face-to-face with God" passage, also speaks of friends speaking "face-to-face," and that is the sense of v. 12c, d. Some accuse this position of trivializing v. 12, but this is question-begging. It only trivializes it if one assumes that v. 12 is about "perfection," seeing God face-to-face, and the state following the *parousia*.

13:13. But introduces a contrast between the permanence of **faith**, **hope**, and **love** in v. 13, and the temporary nature of **tongues**, **prophecy**, and **knowledge** in v. 8. **But now** *(nuni de)* usually carries a temporal sense in Paul's letters (see the phrase in Rm 3:21; 6:22; 7:6, 17; 15:23, 25; 1Co 15:20; 2Co 8:22; Eph 2:13; Col 1:22; 3:8; Phm 9, 11; though 1Co 12:18 and 15:20 may be exceptions), **now** signifying the current Church Age (for a similar use of **now**, cf. Rm 11:30-31). **Faith, hope,** and **love abide** (they "remain," "stay") throughout the entire age in contrast to **tongues**, **prophecy**, and **knowledge**, which cease at some time during the Church Age. See the chart at the top of the following page for a graphic depiction of 13:10-13. **Love** is the greatest of the three virtues both from the standpoint that it is the most important for driving the use of gifts and from the standpoint that love for one another and for God lasts into eternity, while faith and hope are realized and will not.

14:1-3. Excursus on Prophecy and Speaking in Tongues. Chapter 14 deals with the inferiority of tongues, prized by the Corinthians, in comparison to prophecy. The gift of prophecy involved immediate divine inspiration of the spokesperson. The gift provided exhortation and encouragement (1Co 14:3), and shared elements in common with the gift of teaching. It incorporated prediction of the future into its function. It entailed a degree of authority that was less than that of the OT prophets and the NT apostles, but some kind of authority was inferred. A prophet could discern the validity of other prophecies, and had an ability

The Mature State (*to teleion*) of the Church

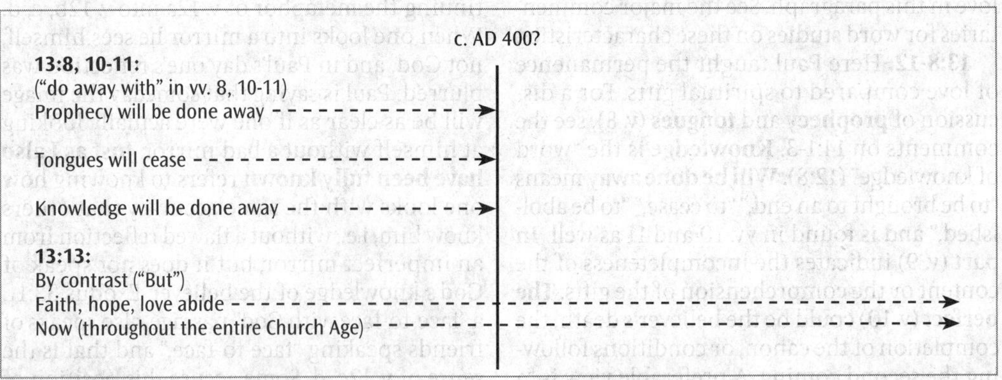

to perceive the thoughts and motives of other persons. Most often prophets were residents of a single locality, but some were also itinerant. Most NT prophecy was oral, but some was written. The gift of prophecy was temporary, and is probably no longer present in any kind of widespread sense in the Church today (see the comments on 13:8-13) (adapted with modifications from Robert L. Thomas, "Literary Genre and Hermeneutics of the Apocalypse," *The Master's Seminary Journal* 2 [Spring 1991]: 82–85). A growing number of scholars substantially redefine prophecy to include, first, a lower level of authority than OT prophets; second, fallible or erroneous messages, and third, an ongoing presence in the Church today (see D. A. Carson, *Showing the Spirit: A Theological Exposition of 1 Corinthians 12–14* [Grand Rapids, MI: Baker, 1987], esp. 91–100; Wayne Grudem, *The Gift of Prophecy in the New Testament and Today*, 2nd ed. [Wheaton: Crossway, 2000]).

In response to the first point, the evaluation of prophetic messages by other prophets in 1Co 14:29 is thought to indicate a lower level of inspiration or authority vis-à-vis the OT prophets and their messages. But even OT prophecies were evaluated (Dt 13:1-11; 18:22), so that the evaluation of NT prophets and prophecies does not support the idea of inferior level of authority. On the second assertion, it is argued that the prophecy of Agabus in Ac 21:11—that Jewish people would bind Paul—contained an error since it was the Romans who bound Paul instead (Ac 21:31-33). However, the Jews *were* the ones who initially seized Paul (Ac 21:30; note the shout, "Away with him!" in Ac 21:36, suggesting the Jewish people turned control of him over to the Romans), and when Paul recounted the episode in Ac 26:21, he said it was Jewish people who apprehended him. In response to the third point regarding the continuance of prophecy in the Church today, see the comments on 1Co 13:8-13. Interacting in any meaningful detail with these points is beyond the scope of this commentary, but see the important series of articles by F. David Farnell: "Prophecy Rediscovered? A Review of *The Gift of Prophecy in the New Testament and Today*," *BibSac* 149 (January-March, 1992): 83–96; "The Current Debate about New Testament Prophecy." *BibSac* 149 (July–September, 1992): 277–303; "The Gift of Prophecy in the Old and New Testaments." *BibSac* 149 (October–December, 1992): 387–410; "Does the New Testament Teach Two Prophetic Gifts?" *BibSac* 150 (January–March, 1993): 62–88; and "When Will the Gift of Prophecy Cease?" *BibSac* 150 (April–June 1993): 171–202.

Speaking in tongues was the supernatural ability to speak an earthly foreign language not learned by the speaker (Ac 2:7-12). It was apparently not a "heavenly prayer language" (see the comments on 13:1) nor "ecstatic speech." It had several functions, but not every function applies to every passage where speaking in tongues is mentioned. First, it was a means to draw attention as a kind of "pre-evangelistic" tool (Ac 2:13) to those who subsequently presented the gospel in Greek or Aramaic. Second, it served to validate the message of Christian evangelists, especially apostles (Ac 2:32-36; Rm 15:17-19; 2Co 12:12; Heb 2:3-4). Third, it functioned as evidence, especially to the apostles, that a new people group had received the Holy Spirit (probably Ac 8:15-17; 10:44-46, and see the explicit connection in Ac 11:15 between Cornelius's "Gentile Pentecost" and Pentecost in Ac 2; Ac 19:1-7). Fourth, it was a sign for unbelievers (see the comments on 1Co 14:20-22). Fifth, it produced personal edification (14:4). This is viewed by many as a positive result of tongues speaking, but in the context of chap. 14, it is a selfish misuse of a spiritual gift. Sixth, it provided edification for the entire church when it was translated (or "interpreted") (1Co 14:5, 26). Seventh, it was not the sign of the baptism of the Spirit (see the comments on 12:13, 30). Eighth, when speaking in tongues was interpreted, it was a virtual equivalent of prophecy. Ninth, speaking in tongues probably is no longer present in the Church in any sort of widespread sense.

Love (v. 1; see the definition of **love** in the comment on 1Co 13:1-3) is supremely important, but **spiritual gifts** are as well. Some gifts are more important than others, and Paul brought up prophecy as the most profitable gift generally available for the church at that time. **Desire earnestly spiritual gifts** must be read in light of 13:8-13 and the likelihood that the miraculous gifts have already ceased. **For** (v. 2) explains the superiority of prophecy over tongues. Speaking **to God** may not be as positive as it sounds. God gave the tongues message to the tongues speaker, and to speak the message back to God would be pointless and do little to profit the church. Even the speaker did not understand what he was saying. **Spirit** is probably shorthand for "spiritual gift" (see the same word—*pneuma*—in vv. 12, 14), giving the sense, "By means of his spiritual gift he speaks mysteries." Prophecy, however, produces **edification**, **exhortation**, and **consolation**, the purpose of spiritual gifts (cf. 14:4, 5, 12, 17, 19, 26, 31).

14:4-6. The tongues speaker **edifies himself** (v. 4). In light of the purpose of spiritual gifts being the edification of the church (14:4, 5, 6, 12, 14, 17, 19, 26), the edification of one's self is an inappropriate use of this or any other gift. **I wish that you all spoke in tongues** (v. 5) was a legitimate wish for the Corinthians (though cf. 12:30), but if the miraculous gifts have ceased, this wish cannot be applied today. **Tongues** was of little use for the church unless it was interpreted (or better "translated"), even if it were used by one with as much authority as an apostle (**if I come to you**), while other verbal gifts delivered in a group's vernacular language would be of great benefit. When speaking in tongues was interpreted, it had virtually the same force as prophecy.

14:7-12. Paul gave three analogies to illustrate the lack of value of uninterpreted tongues. If there is no distinguishable melody being played on a musical instrument (v. 7), if the trumpet does not sound the right notes to summon men to battle (v. 8), and if one cannot speak the foreign language of another, then nothing productive will transpire, and applied to tongues speaking, there will be no **edification of the church**, v. 12. The gift of tongues is not in view in vv. 10-11, where Paul referred to the difficulty of understanding a non-supernatural, earthly foreign language.

14:13-19. Since the "edification of the church" (v. 12) is the objective for all spiritual gifts, Paul commanded the tongues speakers to pray in their native language for someone to interpret their tongues messages (v. 13), so the verse could read, "Let he who speaks in a tongue pray that (some)one may interpret" (see 14:26-28). Paul explained why interpretation was important for tongues (**For**, v. 14). See the comments on **spirit** in 14:2 for **my spirit** (i.e., "my spiritual gift of tongues"). **But my mind is unfruitful** not in terms of personal edification (for which see 14:2, 4), but in terms of failing to produce fruit in others. **I will pray ... sing ... bless** (vv. 15-16) do not signal different gifts. This is still speaking in tongues, but employed in different modes. The **mind** is any verbal act accomplished with one's intellect and delivered in one's native language (see also **mind** in v. 19). Paul is not presenting two options—to pray or sing in tongues, or to pray or sing with the mind. Rather, he is stating what he would do consecutively. That is, if he prayed or sang in tongues, he would then also do so with his mind. This is supported by his point in v. 16—without translation there can be no affirmation of prayer or praise. **The ungifted** (v. 16) means "a person who has not acquired systematic information or expertise in some field of knowledge or activity—layman, ordinary person, amateur" (L&N, 1:329) and probably refers to believers who are ignorant of the charismatic gifts or possibly unbelievers. In light of vv. 23-24, **ungifted** probably refers to one who did not know the language used by the tongues speaker. Paul returned to a point he hammered repeatedly, namely, the need for the edification of others through all the gifts, including tongues (v. 17). Some claim that the purpose of speaking in tongues is to strengthen one's prayer life, aiding in communion with God. While it may be one of the benefits of the gift, Paul said its primary use lies in blessing others when it is translated. Paul spoke **in**

tongues more than you all possibly in his devotional life, but it is equally possible that **tongues** was indispensable for him in his missionary ventures, enabling him to converse and preach in an unfamiliar language (though there is no indication Paul did this in Acts, but Ac 2 leaves open the possibility). **That I may instruct others also** shows the need for helping others and not using one's spiritual gift in a self-centered manner.

14:20-25. Paul used Is 28:11-12 to describe further the ineffectiveness of uninterpreted tongues, this time with unbelievers. In Is 28:1-13, Israel is drunk with her own pride and power, and berates Isaiah for his wearisome message of judgment. They refused to listen to Isaiah's words, so God said they would hear foreign words from a foreign people who would conquer them. Sadly, even when the Assyrians destroyed Israel in 721 BC, the "stammering lips" with which the invaders spoke did not cause the Israelites to repent. The sign of the Assyrian language was indeed a sign, but it was a sign of judgment. Ciampa and Rosner ("1 Corinthians," 742) show how Paul applied Isaiah to the Corinthians. "Just as the experience in Is 28:11-12 did not result in the conversion of the hearers but instead expressed alienation between God and his people, so also Paul indicates that the use of tongues in the church will result not in the conversion of unbelievers but rather in their further alienation." Verse 22 is about **tongues** and **prophecy** in Isaiah's day, when the Assyrian tongue was a sign of impending judgment for the wicked, though they failed to repent. Isaiah's prophecies were intended for the godly remnant (Carson, *Showing the Spirit*, 115). Things were not much different for the Corinthians, as unbelievers who witnessed tongue-speaking in the Corinthian church would not be converted (**will they not say that you are mad?** v. 23). **But if all prophesy** (v. 24) in the language shared by the prophets and the unbelievers, prospects are considerably more optimistic (v. 25).

14:26-28. Paul began to regulate the use of tongues in the Corinthian church. Verse 26 gives evidence of a free-flowing church meeting with wide participation. The objective for all who shared was the **edification** of others. Only **two or at the most three** (v. 27) were allowed to speak in tongues, one after another, and it was necessary for someone to **interpret** ("to translate from one language to another," supporting the idea that tongues in 1Co 12–14 are earthly foreign languages) or else the tongues speakers could not speak. **Let him speak** [in tongues] **to himself and to God** (v. 28) assumes that the tongues speaker knew enough about the content of his tongues message to know if he was singing, praying, blessing, or giving thanks in the Spirit (vv. 14-16), and to the degree he understood, he was to meditate on that.

14:29-33a. Tongues speaking not only was regulated, but Paul also regulated how prophecy was delivered. The regulation includes several practices. First, the number of prophets who speak is limited (**two or three**, v. 29). Second, other prophets evaluated the message for its pure content (vv. 29, 32) (for evaluating prophets, cf. Dt 13:1-11; 18:22; Rm 12:6). Third, if a prophet was giving a revelation and another prophet received a message from God at that moment, the prophet who was speaking was to defer to the one who had the more up-to-date revelation (v. 30), presumably because God was giving him fresher, more relevant information. Fourth, prophecy, like tongues, needed to be presented in an orderly fashion because orderliness is God-like and brings glory to Him (v. 33a), and so **all may learn and all may be exhorted** (v. 31).

14:33b-40. In these verses Paul regulated how prophecies were to be evaluated by other prophets. **As in all the churches of the saints** serves as a fitting introduction to vv. 34-40 about what Paul expects in every church (**in the churches** occurring in vv. 33b and 34), and does not connect syntactically very well with the statement about God being an orderly God (He is orderly in and out of the church). **Keep silent** (v. 34) sounds unfairly restrictive, but Paul commanded silence of tongues speakers in the absence of interpreters (v. 28) and of prophets when a newer message was given to another (v. 30). The verb "to be silent" (*sigao*) is used in all three verses (vv. 28, 30, 34). He is not being as unfair to the women as he is sometimes made out to be. **The women** (*gune*) refers especially to wives (v. 35, "let them ask their own husbands *at home*"), but since Paul is discussing a corporate church meeting, unmarried women are included as well (see *gune* used for all the women in the church in 11:2-16). **They are not permitted to speak** should be understood in context, and the best view contextually is that the women were not permitted to join in the evaluation of prophetic utterances. Paul made it clear that women with the gift of prophecy could use it in church gatherings (11:5), and they may have assumed that they would have a role in the evaluation of prophetic utterances (vv. 29, 32). However, they were not permitted to do this, but were **to subject themselves**. These words sound belittling, but Paul also stated earlier that prophets are subject to other prophets (v. 32), so the women are not the only ones who had to submit. **The Law** Paul refers to is probably Gn 2:15-25 (drawn from the Pentateuch, the "book of the law"), a passage Paul referred to twice when he discussed the role of women in the church (cf. 1Co 11:8-9; 1Ti 2:13; see the comments on these verses). **If they desire to learn** [v. 35; cf. the same verb for "learn" in v. 31] **anything** about the nature of the prophecies, they were to **ask their own husbands at home**. For the restriction related to speaking **in church**, see the comments on v. 34. Verses 34-35 are found here or following v. 40 in many ancient manuscripts, and some argue that Paul did not write these verses at all (see Fee, *First Corinthians*, 699–711; Barrett, *First Epistle to the Corinthians*, 333). But no manuscripts lack vv. 34-35 altogether, and there are other ways to account for their placement in some (inferior) manuscripts after v. 40 (for a helpful summary of the text critical issue, see D. A. Carson, "'Silent in the Churches': On the Role of Women in 1 Corinthians 13:33b-36," in *Recovering Biblical Manhood and Womanhood*, ed. John Piper and Wayne Grudem [Wheaton, IL: Crossway, 1991], 141–144). The Corinthians had to do what all the churches were required to do (v. 36). They were not the source of the Word of God, as if they could set the standard for all others. Nor were they a one-of-a-kind church ("Has the Word **come to you only?**") that could do whatever they wanted. They had to embrace the same parameters that bound all the churches. **Do not forbid to speak in tongues** (v. 39) cannot be cited in support of the practice of tongues-speaking today. It had relevance for Paul's day, but if tongues, prophecy, and knowledge have ceased (see the comments on 13:8-13), then v. 39 is inapplicable for the modern church.

VII. The Sixth Problem: Denial of the Resurrection of the Dead (15:1-58)

A. The First Exhortation: Consider the Evidence for the Resurrection (15:1-11)

15:1-11. Paul did not explain how he knew of their questions regarding the resurrection, whether through the letter they wrote him (7:1) or reports from visitors (16:17). In vv. 1-11, Paul voiced the agreement he and the Corinthians shared on the resurrection of Jesus. The contents of **the gospel which I preached to you** (v. 1) are designated by four phrases introduced by **that** in vv. 3-5 (see below). The Corinthians believed Paul's gospel and were saved (**you received**; **you stand**; **you are saved**, vv. 1-2), though perseverance in saving faith (**hold fast**) is always necessary for final salvation (see the comments on Mt 10:21-22; Col 1:23; Heb 3:6, 14). But if Jesus were not raised from the dead then they **believed in vain** ("with no positive results," "to no avail"), that is, they are doomed, and their faith is grounded upon nothing (cf. v. 14). **What I also received** (v. 3) probably refers to the historical details of Christ's death and resurrection that Paul received from eyewitnesses, while Gl 1:11-12 refers to the theological implications of those facts revealed directly to Paul by Jesus on the Damascus road. Paul presented essentially two features related to the gospel. The first feature is that **Christ died for our sins**. Paul then supports this first feature with two lines of evidence. He cites biblical attestation (**according to the Scriptures**, possibly Is 53:6) and historical proof (**that He was buried**, v. 4a) supporting the fact of Messiah's *death*. The second feature of the gospel is that Christ **was raised** from the dead (v. 4b). The verb **was raised** is a perfect tense verb, used by Paul as a more emphatic or foregrounded tense to draw attention to what he considered the most important feature of the gospel as it related to the Corinthians' immediate need, i.e., the need to believe in resurrection. Paul then supports this second feature with two lines of evidence. Once again, he refers to biblical attestation (**according to the Scriptures**, v. 4c, possibly Ps 16:10; Is 53:10-11) and historical proof (**He appeared** to numerous followers, vv. 5-8), as evidence for the *resurrection* of the Messiah. It is impossible to say what Scriptures Paul had in mind when he wrote that Jesus was **raised on the third day according to the Scriptures**, but he may have been thinking of Jnh 1:17 (used in Mt 12:40) or Hs 6:2. Jesus **appeared to Cephas** according to Lk 24:24, 34, **then to the twelve** (v. 5) in Lk 24:33; Jn 20:19-23; Mt 28:16-20, and to **more than five hundred** (v. 6) probably in Lk 24:44-49. **James** (v. 7) was probably the Lord's half-brother, but no mention of this individual appearance is found outside of 1Co 15. **All the apostles** are difficult to identify, but may include Thomas who did not witness the initial appearances of the resurrected Jesus (Jn 20:26-29). Verse 8 describes the abnormal process by which Paul came to be saved and receive his apostolic appointment. **Untimely born** usually referred to "a birth that violates the normal period of gestation (whether induced as an abortion, or natural premature birth or miscarriage) . . ." (BDAG, 311), and probably depicts Jesus' abrupt and forcible enlistment of Paul. The disciples had three years of gradual training under Jesus, which Paul did not have. Paul viewed himself as fully within the apostolic ranks, but different from the rest and viewed himself as **the least** of them (v. 9) due to his persecution of believers. Verse 10 connects saving **grace** with "serving **grace**." **Grace** denotes the character quality of benevolence that leads a benefactor (in this case, God) to bestow a favor upon another. Salvation is not by good works, but salvation produces good works, the apostle Paul being a prime example of this. The word **grace** is used three different ways in v. 10. First, God's **grace** (kindness) made Paul what he was, the great apostolic representative of Jesus. Second, God's saving **grace** did not prove **vain** ("to be empty in the sense of lacking results"; cf. the same word in v. 14) in Paul. Rather enabling **grace**, third, empowered Paul to serve the Lord. Verse 11 is important for the entire chapter as it indicates that the Corinthians believed in the resurrection of Jesus and the basic facts of the gospel.

B. The Second Exhortation: Consider the Consequences of No Resurrection from the Dead (15:12-19)

In the Greco-Roman world, the concept of bodily resurrection was unknown. N. T. Wright (*The Resurrection of the Son of God* [Minneapolis: Fortress, 2003], 82) writes,

> Who were the dead thought to be, in the ancient pagan world? They were beings that had once been embodied human beings, but were now souls, shades, or *eidola* [phantoms]. Where were they? Most likely in Hades; possibly in the Isles of the Blessed, or Tartarus; just conceivably, reincarnated into a different body altogether. They might occasionally appear to living mortals; they might still be located somewhere in the vicinity of their tombs; but they were basically in a different world. . . . [For many] the soul was well rid of its body [because there was so much physical suffering without decent medical help]. . . . [S]ome kind of life might continue after death, but it was unlikely to be as rich and satisfying as the present one could be, at least in theory.

For the Greeks, death presented a problem for which there was no solution. The Corinthians came out of a cultural and religious environment for which resurrection was a complete novelty. No wonder they had a hard time grasping it. They believed in the immortality of the soul, but not the body, while the Christian hope is that of the immortality of both the immaterial (soul, spirit, mind) and material parts (the body) of one's constitution. For the nature of the resurrected body, cf. the comments on vv. 36-50 below.

15:12-19. In vv. 12-32, Paul presented a logical conclusion derived from Jesus' resurrection in vv. 1-11. If Jesus has risen from the dead, then all those in Him will as well. But it appears that it is precisely here where the Corinthians were "soft" in their doctrine of the resurrection, questioning the physical resurrection of Christians generally. So in vv. 12-19, Paul presented what would be the case if one denied that all those in Christ will rise as well. **There is no resurrection of the dead** (v. 12) speaks of the resurrection of believers, not the resurrection of Christ in which the Corinthians did believe. It is an absolute statement, but if Jesus rose from the dead, then it is possible that others might rise as well. Paul plays "Let's pretend" for a bit to show the error of their position. If no one in Christ is raised, then perhaps there is no such thing as resurrection at all, and maybe Jesus did not rise from the dead either (v. 13). But, as v. 11 indicates, the Corinthians would have rejected such a thought. Without the resurrection, **our preaching is vain** ("empty," "without results"; cf. v. 10), i.e., it will produce no fruit, and **faith also is vain**, i.e., will ultimately gain nothing (such as salvation; v. 17). Without the resurrection of Christ, Christianity is no more valid than any other religion, and Paul's message was false (v. 15). Verse 16 is a key to what precedes and what follows. Paul indicated that there is an indissoluble bond between Christ and His people regarding the resurrection. If no believers are resurrected, then their nonresurrection would be a proof that Jesus was not resurrected either. But if He was resurrected, they would be also. Verse 17 shows what would result if the Corinthians were right. They would not be saved, believers who died have **perished** ("suffered inestimable ruin" forever) (v. 18), and all Christians are pitiable for they have chosen a life of self-denial for no real lasting purpose (v. 19). N. T. Wright said, "The logic of it is simple, granted the close link throughout Scripture between sin and death: if God has overcome death in the resurrection of Jesus, then the power of sin is broken; but if he hasn't, it isn't" (*The Resurrection*, 332).

C. The Third Exhortation: Consider the Centrality of the Resurrection in God's Program (15:20-28)

15:20-28. While in vv. 12-19 Paul explored the logical entailments of denying that there is a general resurrection for believers, in vv. 20-28 he developed the logical entailments related to the truth of Jesus' resurrection, which has always been a central feature of God's program for humankind. The **first fruits** imagery (v. 20) is a reference to the initial offering of crops to the Lord in anticipation of a bountiful harvest that would follow (Ex 22:28; 23:19; 34:26; Lv 23:10-11; Nm 15:18-21). This is an illustration derived from the Festival of First Fruits, at the beginning of the counting of the omer on the day after Passover. The first fruits of the harvest were set aside for God in anticipation of the rest of the crop arriving. Jesus' resurrection is the first fruit in anticipation of His followers' resurrection. **First fruits** also sometimes has the nuance of a pledge or guarantee of something to follow. His resurrection prefigures and guarantees the resurrection of believers who **are asleep** (have died). Verses 21-22 explain what Paul meant by the **first fruits** imagery. Just as union with Adam resulted in death for the race, all those **in Christ** will participate in the resurrection.

All will be made alive does not teach universal salvation. The resurrection to blessed eternal life is only for **all *in Christ*** (v. 22, emphasis added) and **those who are Christ's** (v. 23). While every true believer will be resurrected (v. 22), they will not all be resurrected at the same time (v. 23). **Order** was sometimes used as a military term for a specific company, division, or class of soldiers, often arranged in an orderly fashion. The order of those resurrected is **Christ the first fruits**, followed sequentially (**then**, *epeita*; cf. 15:6, 7) and after a substantial amount of time (at least 2,000 years) by **those who are Christ's at His coming**. Some maintain that Paul's use of **coming** *(parousia)* describes a posttribulational rapture that takes place at the second coming following the tribulation. But *parousia* can mean "presence" (cf. 16:17, its only other use in 1 Corinthians), and its use in 1 Thessalonians is instructive. Thomas writes, "The complexity of the term *parousia* demands [at least in 1 Thessalonians] that it include an extended visit as well as the arrival initiating that visit. This is provided for adequately in the rarer meaning of *parousia*, 'presence' (cf. 1Co 16:17; 2Co 10:10; Php 2:12). Included in this visit is an evaluation of the saints (cf. [1Th] 2:19; 5:23), which is the aspect in view here in [1Th 3:13] . . . This judgment cannot be completely dissociated from Christ's coming in the air (4:15-17), because this advent marks its initiation. Yet it must be conceived of as a session in heaven in some measure separate from the arrival itself" (Robert L. Thomas, "1 Thessalonians," in EBC, ed. Frank E. Gaebelein [Grand Rapids, MI: Zondervan, 1978], 269). The use of *parousia* in 1Co 15:23 refers to the Lord's *presence (parousia)* with the Church in heaven prior to the second coming at the end of the tribulation, and supports a pretribulational view of the rapture.

Then (*eita*, see 15:5, 7; 1Tm 2:13;) (v. 24) also signals sequence after a lapse of time. Saucy (*Progressive Dispensationalism*, 281) writes that **the end** "is separated from the coming of Christ even as his coming is separated from his resurrection, as we see at the beginning of the sequence. If Paul had desired to say that the 'end' occurred at the coming of Christ, he could easily have used another adverb (*tote*, meaning 'at that time') for the second 'then'" (similarly Godet, *First Corinthians*, 785). Paul does not explicitly mention the millennial kingdom between the resurrection of believers and **the end** in this verse, but what he says allows for it, and the following verses are understood best within a premillennial framework. **The end** may refer to the resurrection of tribulation saints (cf. Rv 20:4c, d) or the resurrection of unbelievers for their final judgment (Rv 20:12; Jn 5:28-29; Ac 24:15), but **end** (*telos*) does not usually mean "the rest" (of those who are resurrected; cf. Murray J. Harris, *Raised Immortal: Resurrection and Immortality in the New Testament* [Basingstoke: Marshall Morgan & Stock, 1983], 175). Here it probably refers to the conclusion of the millennial **kingdom**.

In vv. 25 and 27, Paul cited Ps 8:4-6 to demonstrate how Jesus (all the third person pronouns in v. 25 refer to Jesus), with His people (note "who is man," Ps 8:4, a reference to humankind), fulfill God's purposes for the race by ruling and reigning together over all the earth in the kingdom. Paul also alluded to Ps 110:1, which in other passages appears to refer to Christ in His current exalted position in heaven (e.g., Ac 2:30-36), but here refers to what He will do in the future millennial kingdom. In support of this, the word **reign** (v. 25) describes a future function of Jesus in Lk 1:33; 19:14; Rv 11:15, 17, suggesting that the subduing of Jesus' enemies takes place in the future (see Rv 20:7-15) when the last **enemy**, **death**, **will be abolished** (v. 26), not during His present time in heaven (see Saucy, *Progressive Dispensationalism*, 282-288). The antecedents of the pronouns in vv. 27-28 are not completely clear, but the verses probably should be read this way: "For God has put all things in subjection under Jesus' feet. But when it [not "He"] says, 'All things are put in subjection,' it is evident that God is excepted who put all things in subjection to Jesus. When all things are subjected to God, then the Son Himself also will be subjected to the One who subjected all things to Jesus, so that God may be all in all." When Jesus hands the millennial kingdom over to God at the conclusion of His earthly messianic reign, this will signal the beginning of the eternal state, for which there will be no end. There will be a perfect merging of Jesus' earthly, Davidic, millennial throne with the eternal throne of God, so that God the Father and God the Son may be seen together as supreme (cf. Rv 22:3).

D. The Fourth Exhortation: Consider that the Christian Life Is Made Purposeful because of the Resurrection of the Dead (15:29-34)

15:29-34. There has been enough ink used to discuss the phrase **baptized for the dead** (v. 29) to actually immerse someone. Interpretations include believers being baptized for the benefit of unbaptized believers to ensure their final salvation, new converts who are baptized and take the place of believers who have died, or believers who become baptized for deceased Christians who were not baptized in order to testify for those dead believers that Christ had washed away their sins. The preferred view is espoused by G. G. Findlay ("1 Corinthians." In The Expositor's Greek Testament, ed. W. Robertson Nicoll, [Grand Rapids, MI: Eerdmans. 1979 reprint], 931): "Paul is referring rather to a much commoner, indeed a normal experience, that the death of Christians leads to the conversion of survivors, who in the first instance 'for the sake of the dead' (their beloved dead) and in the hope of re-union, turn to Christ—e.g., when a dying mother wins her son by the appeal 'Meet me in heaven!' Such appeals, and their frequent, salutary effect, give strong and touching evidence of *faith in the resurrection*" (emphasis Findlay's). **For** (i.e., **baptized *for* the dead**) means "for the sake of" fulfilling the wishes of the departed believer. Baptism is a solemn picture of conversion (cf. the comments on Rm 6:1-4). Those who became believers in the hope of being reunited with their Christian loved ones, and subsequently who underwent baptism, indicate their belief in the resurrection, for without it their hope could not come to fruition.

Verses 30-32 refer to Paul's ordeals endured during his missionary journeys. Such suffering is meaningless if the resurrection of Christ and His people is not true. On the **wild beasts at Ephesus** (v. 32), see the comments on 2Co 1:8-9. **Let us eat and drink for tomorrow we die** cites Is 22:13, which summarized the unrepentant Jewish people on the eve of their destruction by Assyria. Because they had no hope of a meaningful future, they chose to party. For the Corinthians, the lack of belief in the resurrection would cause them to find their ultimate fulfillment in the creature comforts of this life. In v. 33, Paul cited Menander (Greek comic playwright, d. 291 BC, this line from his play "Thaïs," no longer extant except for a few lines, but was apparently about courtesans and immorality) in v. 33. The **bad company** could be either the friends of the Corinthians who denied the resurrection, or "keeping the company" of bad doctrine. In either case, the denial of the future resurrection has a corrupting affect upon Christian morality. If one's body is destined for eternity and for a greater experience with the Lord, then the use of the body in the present should reflect that ultimate destiny. The future brings accountability as well (cf. 3:10-17; Rm 14:10-12). In addition, Paul specifically used the doctrine of the resurrection to correct their immorality in 6:14. Their thinking about the resurrection was muddled, as if they were in a drunken stupor (v. 34) (**become sober-minded**). **Some have no knowledge of** God's ability to raise the dead.

E. The Fifth Exhortation: Consider the Majesty of the Resurrection Body (15:35-50)

15:35-50. These verses provide answers to the two questions asked in v. 35. The first, **How are the dead raised?** is answered in vv. 36-41. The second, **With what kind of body do they come?** is answered in vv. 42-50.

You fool (v. 36) implies that Paul saw in the first question the assumption that the body would come from the grave in a state of putrefaction. It was foolish to think that way. Paul compared the natural body to a seed (vv. 36-37).

The believer's body is buried, with the prospect of resurrection, just as a seed is buried in anticipation of the plant that comes from it. One does not bury the plant, but a seed. There is continuity between the seed and the plant that comes from it, but the plant is different from the seed. So it is with the believer's natural body and resurrected body. This does not mean that the buried natural body has the "seeds" of the resurrection body in it, or that the natural body remains in the grave while the believer receives a second body at the resurrection. The same body comes to life, but it is transformed for the eternal state, according to God's design (v. 38). The resurrection body will have its own kind of beauty, just as the bodies of people and animals and the celestial bodies (**sun**, **moon**, **stars**, vv. 40-41) differ but all have splendor (v. 39).

Paul began to answer the second question in v. 35 related to the characteristics of the resurrected body. The **natural body** is **perishable**, **sown** (buried) **in dishonor** and **weakness** (vv. 42-44). The word **natural** *(psuchikon)* (v. 44) refers to the believer, inside and out with an emphasis on the outside (the sense of **body**, *soma*), considered from the perspective of existence in the natural world. The **spiritual body** does not mean that the resurrection body is composed of spirit. **Spiritual** (*pneumatikos*) describes a **body** that is "influenced and enlivened by the spirit," here probably the Holy Spirit-perfected human spirit of the believer following the resurrection. Harris (*Raised Immortal*, 121) comments on vv. 42-44: "Paul is saying, then, that in place of an earthly body that is always characterised by physical decay, indignity, and weakness, the resurrected believer will have a heavenly body that is incapable of deterioration, beautiful in form and appearance, and with limitless energy and perfect health. Once he experiences a resurrection transformation, man will know perennial rejuvenation, since he will have a perfect vehicle for God's deathless Spirit, a body that is invariably responsive to his transformed personality." **Adam** (v. 45) received life in a natural body as do all those in him. But there is also **the last Adam**, Jesus, who has a resurrected body perfectly suited for the eternal spiritual realm and who gives such resurrection life to His own. Verses 47-49 explain v. 46: Adam came first, was created from earth, had life suited only for the natural realm, and his body returned to the earth from which it was fashioned. Adam's descendants share the same kind of body with him. But Christ came after Adam, and in His resurrection had a body designed by and suited for heaven, and His people will share a similar resurrection body. Likewise believers have a natural body first, then followed by the reception of the resurrection body. **Flesh and blood cannot inherit the kingdom of God** (v. 50) does not mean that the resurrection body is non-corporeal, or that it has no continuity with the believer's natural, pre-resurrection body. Paul meant that mere mortals, with bodies designed only for the earthly realm and without the transformation of the resurrection, cannot **inherit the imperishable kingdom**. If the kingdom is a future inheritance for the saints, then the Church cannot be equated with the kingdom as most amillennialists maintain.

F. The Sixth Exhortation: Consider the Miraculous Change Resulting in the Resurrection of the Dead (15:51-58)

15:51-58. Paul indicated in vv. 36-50 that a believer's death would precede a believer's resurrection. Here he explains that some believers will be alive when the resurrection occurs, and he describes what their experience will be. **Mystery** refers to truth that was hidden but is now revealed, and the transformation of living and dead believers at the rapture of the Church is a doctrine not found in the OT. **Sleep** is a euphemism for death (see the comments on 1Th 4:13-15). **Changed** means "to cause a difference by altering the character or nature of something" (L&N, 1:590), and refers to the instantaneous (**in a moment, in the twinkling of an eye**, v. 52) transformation of both deceased and living believers at the resurrection (also known as the rapture).

The last trumpet is often associated with the trumpet of Mt 24:31 and the last trumpet judgment of Rv 11:15, which herald the second coming and the establishment of Jesus' kingdom on earth respectively. This, however, would place the rapture of the Church at the time of the second coming following the tribulation. But the rapture and second coming are distinct events, separated by the seven-year tribulation. This is supported by the differences between the two events. At the rapture, believers are removed from the earth, life on earth is otherwise normal, Jesus does not come with His heavenly armies, and believers return with Him to heaven (cf. 1Th 4:16-17; 5:3; Jn 14:2-3). But at the second coming, Jesus will come to His people on earth; there will be intense hardship on earth due to the seal, trumpet, and bowl judgments; He comes with

His armies for battle; and He remains on earth (Zch 14:4-5; Ac 1:11-12; Mt 24:30-31; 25:31-32; Rv 19:11-21). **The last trumpet** could be, instead, an allusion either to the Feast of Trumpets (Lv 23:24-25) that introduced a holy day of rest, or to the use of trumpets to summon people for a serious or celebrative assembly, or to a military use of trumpets as various signals. In the latter, the "first trumpet" would sound the call for soldiers to assemble for war, and the "last trumpet" signifies either the reassembly of troops at the conclusion of a battle or the dismissal of troops to return to their homes when a war was over (cf. Gerhard Friedrich, "[*salpigx*; *salpizo*, *salpistes*, "Trumpets"]," in *Theological Dictionary of the New Testament*, ed. Gerhard Friederich [Grand Rapids, MI: Eerdmans, 1971], 73–74, 78–81, 85–88; Renald E. Showers, *Maranatha, Our Lord, Come! A Definitive Study of the Rapture of the Church* [Bellmawr, NJ: The Friends of Israel Gospel Ministry, Inc., 1995], 259–269). It is impossible to be certain which sense Paul had in mind, but the more likely interpretation is the military one. The Corinthians may have understood the military sense more readily than the other views, and Paul did use a term common in military contexts, **order**, in v. 23 for the resurrection. **Must** (v. 53) indicates the necessity of resurrection for believers to live forever in the kingdom (v. 50). **Put on** (vv. 53-54) was a common term for getting dressed, and implies the corporeality of the raised body. It is invested with **immortality**, when **death** is utterly defeated for all believers. **DEATH IS SWALLOWED UP in victory** alludes to Is 25:8, where Isaiah prophesies that God will swallow up death when He comes to rescue His people. Verse 55 alludes to Hs 13:14, in which God tells death and Sheol to get ready to assist Him in the judgment of Ephraim. But in the resurrection, there will be no more judgment, grave, or death. The spiritual state of **death** (v. 56) produces both acts of **sin** and physical death. **Sin** is death's "stinger"—when it prompts people to **sin** the outcome of that is physical death, and in the case of unbelievers, eternal death as well. **The law** is the **power of sin** because **sin** incites rebellion against God when the unregenerate heart encounters **the law** (see the comments on Rm 7:7-12). When Jesus died on the cross for our sins (15:3), He received death's stinger, rendering death powerless. His people were removed from the regime of law, which is powerless to deliver from the domination of sin (Rm 6:14-15; 7:1-12), and were transferred into the realm of grace where divine power is available to give victory over the current domination and future condemnation of sin. For **toil** not being **vain** (v. 58), see the comments on vv. 29-34.

VIII. The Seventh Problem: The Collection for Poor Believers (16:1-4)

16:1-4. Paul concluded the discussion of the resurrection with encouragement related to "abounding in the work of the Lord" (15:58), and part of that work included the collection for poor believers. The **collection for the saints** (v. 1) occupied Paul's thinking for almost 20 years (assuming AD 38 as the date for Ac 11:27 and Gl 2:10 for his initial involvement in this relief effort, and AD 55 for the time of writing for 1 Corinthians), and next to his evangelistic work, was his highest priority. Their giving was to be systematic (**on the first day of every week**), was to involve every believer (**each one of you**), and was to be proportionate based upon what one earned (**as he may prosper**) (v. 2). The verse is less about gathering every week for worship than it is privately budgeting what to give. The phrase **each one of you** is literally "each one of you by himself," suggesting that this decision-making process takes place privately. There is no indication of a mandatory 10 percent tithe in these verses. For more on the Corinthians and giving, cf. the comments on 2Co 8–9. Paul wanted the collection to be completed before he arrived, perhaps so that they might give anonymously or freely, without a sense of coercion from Paul. They needed to select trustworthy people to transport the funds to Jerusalem because Paul intended to **spend the winter** with them (v. 6), and may have wished the money to be sent to Jerusalem sooner than he would have traveled there (vv. 3-4).

IX. The Conclusion of the Epistle: Personal Remarks (16:5-24)

16:5-12. For Paul's contacts with the Corinthians after 1 Corinthians, see the introduction to 2 Corinthians. Paul wrote 1 Corinthians from **Ephesus** (v. 8), and was planning to visit them in **Macedonia** during his third missionary journey. Paul sent **Timothy** to them from Ephesus (Ac 19:22; cf. 1Co 4:17), but apparently he had not yet arrived. Paul was concerned that **Timothy** might receive ill treatment from them inasmuch as he was going as Paul's representative to attempt to address some of the moral and doctrinal issues there.

16:13-18. Let all that you do be done in love (v. 14) was an enormously important exhortation for this church that was beset with self-centeredness and arrogance. For **love**, see the definition at 13:1-3. On **Stephanas** (v. 15), see the comments on 1:10-17. **First fruits of Achaia** indicates that **Stephanas** was one of the first converts from Corinth. For similar commands regarding the appropriate attitudes toward faithful Christian workers, see the comments on Rm 16:1-16. **Stephanas**, **Fortunatus**, and **Achaicus** visited Paul in Ephesus from Corinth and **supplied what was lacking on your part** (v. 17), explained in v. 18 as providing refreshment for Paul that the Corinthians, as a whole, could not supply because of their geographical separation from the apostle.

16:19-24. The churches of Asia would have included the Ephesian church, including **Aquila and Prisca** (short for "Priscilla") (v. 19). For this couple, see the comments on Ac 18:2-26 and Rm 16:3. **The church that is in their house** indicates that, at least in Ephesus, Christians usually gathered in small home groups, though this does not preclude the possibility of larger gatherings. And **the church** consists of people, not buildings. **Accursed** (*anathema*) v. 22) refers to eternal damnation, being eternally cursed (cf. Rm 9:3; Gl 1:8, 9). The meaning of **maranatha** is disputed. It is an Aramaic term, and if Paul wrote it as "maran atha," then it is a statement ("The Lord has come"). More likely he wrote "marana tha," and would be rendered as a wish, "Lord, please come!" (cf. the similar sense with Greek terms in Rv 22:20, and for the coming of grace in *Didache* 10:6). In spite of all the reproofs of the letter, Paul nevertheless loved them and made it clear to them here (v. 24). Forcefulness is sometimes necessary in ministry, but it should always be governed by love.

BIBLIOGRAPHY

Blomberg, Craig. *1 Corinthians*. The NIV Application Commentary. Grand Rapids, MI: Zondervan, 1995.

Findlay, G. G. "1 Corinthians." In *The Expositor's Greek Testament*, vol. 2, ed. W. Robertson Nicoll. Grand Rapids, MI: Eerdmans, 1979 reprint.

Garland, David E. *1 Corinthians*. Baker Exegetical Commentary on the New Testament. Grand Rapids, MI: Baker, 2003.

Godet, Frederic Louis. *Commentary on First Corinthians*. Grand Rapids, MI: Kregel, 1977 reprint of the 1889 T. & T. Clark edition.

Gromacki, Robert G. *Called to be Saints: An Exposition of 1 Corinthians*. Grand Rapids, MI: Baker, 1977.

Grosheide, F. W. *Commentary on the First Epistle to the Corinthians*, The New International Commentary on the New Testament. Grand Rapids, MI: Eerdmans, 1953.

Kistemaker, Simon J. *1 Corinthians*. The New Testament Commentary. Grand Rapids, MI: Baker, 1993.

Lenski, R. C. H. *The Interpretation of St. Paul's First and Second Epistles to the Corinthians*. Minneapolis: Augsburg, 1937 and 1963.

MacArthur, John. *1 Corinthians*. The MacArthur New Testament Commentary. Chicago: Moody, 1984.

Robertson, Archibald, and Alfred Plummer. *First Epistle of St. Paul to the Corinthians*, 2nd ed. The International Critical Commentary. Edinburgh: T. & T. Clark, 1914.

Thiselton, Anthony C. *The First Epistle to the Corinthians: A Commentary on the Greek Text*. The New International Greek Testament Commentary. Grand Rapids, MI: Eerdmans, 2000.

———. *1 Corinthians: A Shorter Exegetical and Pastoral Commentary*. Grand Rapids, MI: Eerdmans, 2006.

Witherington, Ben. *Conflict and Community in Corinth: A Socio-Rhetorical Commentary on 1 and 2 Corinthians*. Grand Rapids, MI: Eerdmans, 1995.

2 CORINTHIANS

DAVID WOODALL

INTRODUCTION

Author. Stylistic and theological considerations support the claim of Pauline authorship, and this claim is embraced by scholars of various theological persuasions.

There are several scholars who question the unity of the book—the idea that 2 Corinthians is a literary whole from beginning to end. (1) 2 Corinthians 2:14–7:4 is sometimes understood as a separate insertion (the account flows smoothly between 2:13 and 7:5), but 2:14 is best viewed as Paul's praise in the midst of hardship and a digression concerning the nature of new covenant ministry. (2) 2 Corinthians 6:14–7:1 is sometimes understood as a non-Pauline insertion, but it is best viewed as showing how the Corinthians could demonstrate their love for him. (3) Some think that chaps. 10–13 were written separately because the harsh tone of these chapters does not match the more irenic nature of chaps. 1–9. It is not impossible to postulate that Paul wrote chaps. 1–9 after the initial report from Titus and chaps. 10–13 a short time later after hearing about more difficulties, but there is no textual evidence that these sections were ever separated. This commentary will assume and argue for the essential unity of 2 Corinthians.

Background. The Corinthian correspondence must be understood in light of a historical background that includes three visits to Corinth, four letters to the church, and three travel plans (designated by letters below). Paul's initial visit to Corinth (**visit A**) during his second missionary journey lasted 18 months (Ac 18:1-18, fall of AD 50 to spring of AD 52). On his third missionary journey, Paul ministered in Ephesus for two years (Ac 19:8-10). During this time, Paul received both written and oral reports concerning problems in the Corinthian church. He responded by writing two letters, **Corinthians A** (mentioned in 1Co 5:9-11) and **B** (what we now know as 1 Corinthians), to address the issues. In **Corinthians B**, Paul announced his future travel plans (**travel plan A**): he would travel through Macedonia and then spend some time with them (see 1Co 16:5-9). This plan never materialized. Timothy informed Paul that opponents had infiltrated the church, and the problems were multiplying. This motivated Paul to change his plans and visit them immediately (**visit B**) with the hope of going on to Macedonia and returning to Corinth so that they might have the benefit of two visits (2Co 1:15-16, **travel plan B**). But **visit B** was a disaster—a painful visit (2Co 2:1) where Paul experienced personal attacks (2Co 2:5-10; 7:12) from the opponents while the church provided little support. Changing his plan again, Paul returned to Ephesus (**travel plan C**) defeated and discouraged.

From Ephesus, Paul wrote a severe letter to the Corinthians (**Corinthians C**, which is no longer available) and sent it via Titus. The purpose of this letter was to communicate his love for the Corinthians, to urge the people to repent, and to demand the punishment of the ringleader who had opposed Paul (2Co 2:3-4, 9; 7:8-12).

Desiring to know the Corinthian response to the letter, Paul traveled to Troas and eventually to Macedonia in search of Titus (2:12-13). When he finally found him, there was rejoicing (2:14). The ringleader had repented and most of the Corinthians were now favorable toward Paul (7:5-7, 11). Paul then wrote his fourth letter to the Corinthians—**Corinthians D**, our 2 Corinthians—around AD 55 in response to the news from Titus in anticipation of his third visit (12:14; 13:1, **visit C**). This visit was successful. Paul stayed in Corinth for three months (Ac 20:1-3) and wrote the book of Romans. This historical background illustrates that Paul never gave up on the people to whom he ministered.

Purpose. 2 Corinthians is a defense of Paul's apostolic ministry in light of the newly formed opposition against him. Paul wrote to the majority (2:6) to encourage them to show the genuineness of their faith by forgiving those who had repented, to separate from those who refused to repent, and to collect an offering for the poor Jewish believers in Jerusalem.

Paul also wrote to the minority who were still siding with the opponents to defend his apostleship and to urge them to repent. Three characteristics of the opponents are apparent in the letter. (1) Paul's response in 11:21b-22 indicates that they were Jews. (2) The church was giving them a hearing because they claimed to be Christians (10:7; 11:23), but Paul's response indicates that he questions that claim. They were preaching a different gospel (11:4) and were in fact servants of Satan (11:13-15). (3) They were Judaizers in the sense that they stressed keeping the Mosaic law as a condition of salvation or as a necessity for Christian fellowship (Murray J. Harris, *The Second Epistle to the Corinthians*, NIGTC [Grand Rapids, MI: Eerdmans, 2005] 77–87).

Throughout his ministry, Paul was concerned for the poverty-stricken Jewish Christians who lived in Jerusalem. While ministering in Antioch, Paul delivered a financial gift to them during a famine (Ac 11:27-30). He also promised the Jerusalem leaders that he would continue to remember the poor (a technical term for the Jewish believers in Jerusalem, Gl 2:9-10). As Paul established Gentile churches, he felt compelled to collect a massive offering for the poor Jewish believers in Jerusalem. He encouraged the Corinthians to be involved in this collection (1Co 16:1-4), but it was Titus who initiated it (2Co 8:6). Unfortunately, the collection stopped with the infiltration of the opponents. After delivering the severe letter (**Corinthians C,** not extant), Titus sensed that the time was right to revive the collection, and 2Co 8–9 is Paul's exhortation for the Corinthians to complete a generous collection before his arrival. Although Paul was genuinely concerned for the economic status of the Jewish believers and had a deep love for them, his main motivation for the collection was to establish fellowship between his Gentile converts and the Jewish followers of Jesus in Jerusalem (Rm 15:27). The collection was completed, delivered to Jerusalem, and accepted (Ac 21:17-20a).

OUTLINE

- I. Past Ministry in Corinth (1:1–7:16)
  - A. Greeting to the Corinthians (1:1-11)
    - 1. Introduction (1:1-2)
    - 2. Praise to God (1:3-7)
    - 3. Tribulation in Asia (1:8-11)
  - B. New Travel Plans (1:12–2:13)
    - 1. Integrity (1:12-22)
    - 2. Travel and Correspondence (1:23–2:4)
    - 3. Forgiveness (2:5-11)
    - 4. Travel to Troas (2:12-13)
  - C. Paul Defends His Ministry (2:14–7:4)
    - 1. The Sufficiency of Paul's Ministry (2:14–3:6)
    - 2. The Glory of New Covenant Ministry (3:7–4:6)
    - 3. Living and Dying with Jesus (4:7–5:10)
    - 4. The Ministry of Reconciliation (5:11–6:2)
    - 5. Paul's Integrity and Appeal (6:3-10)
    - 6. Separation from Unbelievers (6:14–7:1)
    - 7. Paul's Renewed Appeal (7:2-4)
  - D. Paul's Joy over Corinthian Repentance (7:5-16)
- II. Present Ministry in Corinth (8:1–9:15)
  - A. Complete the Collection (8:1-15)

B. Administer the Funds (8:16–9:5)
C. Reap the Benefits (9:6-15)
III. Future Visit to Corinth (10:1–13:14)
A. Paul Defends His Authority (10:1-18)
B. Paul Is Forced to Boast (11:1–12:13)
C. Paul Expresses Concern for the Corinthians (12:14-21)
D. Paul Gives a Final Warning (13:1-10)
E. Conclusion (13:11-14)

COMMENTARY ON 2 CORINTHIANS

I. Past Ministry in Corinth (1:1–7:16)

A. Greeting to the Corinthians (1:1-11)

1. Introduction (1:1-2)

In the typical format of an ancient letter, Paul identified both the author and recipients. Paul's apostolic ministry was based on the **will of God**, and this gave him unique authority. To reject the authority of Paul (as his opponents were doing), therefore, was to reject the authority of God. Along with **Timothy** (a co-sender of the letter), he sent this letter to the believers gathered throughout Corinth and Achaia.

2. Praise to God (1:3-7)

Instead of a typical thanksgiving, Paul praised God for comfort received during ongoing suffering. Paul's opponents questioned his apostleship because he suffered, but Paul argued that comfort in the midst of suffering—not the absence of suffering—is the mark of a true apostle. The key verb *parakaleo* (**comfort, comforts, are comforted**, four times in 1:3-7) and the action noun *paraklesis* (**comfort**, six times) refer to the action of consoling a person. Here the consoling comes from a relationship with God and those who have experienced His consoling ministry.

1:3-4. The reason Paul could praise God (the sense of **blessed**) during affliction is grounded in the character of God. He is (1) both God and Father to Jesus, (2) a compassionate Father during hardship, (3) the source of all genuine comfort, and (4) the actual comforter in time of need. There is also a purpose in suffering. After experiencing God's comfort, Christians are able to minister to those who are in affliction. To retreat into isolation during hardship is to reject God's purpose in the suffering.

1:5. Suffering is now defined as **the sufferings of Christ**. This does not refer to the hardships common to all humanity; this refers to the distress that results from serving Christ in a hostile environment. Paul was not implying that suffering atones for sin in any way. Why can Christians pass on to others the comfort they receive from God? As the suffering increases, it is matched by an increase in comfort.

1:6-7. Paul endured suffering for the spiritual **salvation** of the Corinthians. Paul's firm hope was that the Corinthians would reject his opponents and follow him in enduring hardship.

3. Tribulation in Asia (1:8-11)

1:8-9. Paul illustrated comfort in the midst of suffering by revealing the intense **affliction** he experienced **in Asia**. It was a unique burden so extreme that he could not continue in ministry. As a result of the affliction, he **despaired even of life**. The exact identity of the affliction is not stated. After an extended discussion, Harris concludes that the affliction was an intense flare-up of a chronic sickness (*Second Corinthians*, 164–182). Regardless of the exact nature of the affliction, the purpose was clear: trials come to keep Christians dependent on God.

1:10-11. Paul acknowledged God as the agent of this specific deliverance. Based on past experience, he boldly proclaimed that God would again **deliver** him from near-death experiences. This was quickly rephrased as a **hope** for deliverance conditioned on the **prayers** of the Corinthians. Christian prayers should not tell God what to do, but God does respond to prayer. As the Corinthians joined Paul in prayer, they could also join Paul in thanksgiving for deliverance.

B. New Travel Plans (1:12–2:13)

1. Integrity (1:12-22)

Some Corinthians believed that Paul's change in travel plans proved that he lacked integrity. But just as they trusted his word about Jesus Christ, they could trust his word about travel plans.

1:12. Paul's conscience bore witness to a consistent lifestyle that should be the motto of every minister. It was characterized by an openness (a better textual reading than **holiness**) and sincerity that finds its source in the grace of God rather than a worldly system.

1:13-14. Concerning Paul's previous letters, what they read and understood on the surface reflected Paul's intent. There was no hidden agenda reflecting an ulterior motive. Paul hoped that their current partial acknowledgment of his integrity would be a complete acknowledgment when they stood before Jesus. Paul hoped to acknowledge them fully as well.

1:15-16. Paul's initial plan was to travel from Ephesus to Macedonia and then to Corinth (1Co 16:2-8). This did not happen. Confident that the Corinthians would acknowledge his integrity, Paul then intended to travel from Ephesus to Corinth **first** on his way to Macedonia and then to retrace his steps back to Corinth where he would receive financial support for his journey to Judea. By two visits they would **twice receive** the **blessing** of his presence. This plan never materialized either, and Paul reverted to his original intention to travel to Macedonia first. This fluctuation, which said, "Yes," "No," "Yes" ("Yes, I'm coming to you from Ephesus through Macedonia," then, after circumstances required him to adjust the initial plan, "No, I'm not coming to you from Ephesus through Macedonia," then, when circumstances changed yet again, "Yes, I'm coming to you from Ephesus through Macedonia") generated criticism from the Corinthian opponents.

1:17. Paul identified and answered two questions framed by his opponents. (1) Was he fickle when devising these plans? No. (2) Did Paul change his plans on a whim with the result that he appeared to be saying "Yes" while meaning "No"? No.

1:18-20. In contrast to human deceitfulness, **God is faithful**. His messianic promises find fulfillment—their **yes**—in Christ, and Paul consistently proclaimed that people should say "Yes" to Christ. Paul was never duplicitous, saying one thing about the gospel while meaning another. **Silvanus** (Silas) and **Timothy** were witnesses of Paul's integrity. **Our Amen** is the Christian affirmation of Paul and the Corinthians that Christ is the fulfillment of God's promises. Since the Corinthians affirm this, they should certainly affirm the integrity of Paul's words concerning his relatively trivial travel plans. God is glorified by consistency, but duplicity is a denial of the gospel.

1:21-22. Paul's defense of his integrity concluded with the rehearsal of four things God has done for him. (1) God constantly confirms his relationship to Christ (**establishes us with you** means that the Corinthians share in this confirmation). (2) At his conversion, God metaphorically **anointed** him in the sense of assigning him to service, and (3) **sealed** him as His own by (4) giving him the Holy Spirit as a **pledge** of future blessings. Because all of this was true of Paul, it would have been inconsistent for him to be two-faced in the ministry. This fourfold work of God is continuously reproduced in the lives of all Christians, and it demands extreme integrity.

2. Travel and Correspondence (1:23–2:4)

1:23-24. After defending his integrity, Paul revealed his purpose for not returning to Corinth as planned: it was to **spare** them. He called on God to bear witness to this intent, and he staked his own **soul** on its truthfulness. From what did he intend to spare them? Perhaps Paul wanted to avoid an overly harsh rejoinder to their personal attack. Contrary to what some proclaimed, Paul was not a dictator in the realm of faith who delighted in harm (the Corinthians were **standing firm** in their trust in Christ anyway) but a coworker who delighted in joy. No minister enjoys inflicting pain on believers.

2:1-2. Verses 1-5 highlight the concept of pain in ministry: the pain of congregational rebellion and pastoral rebuke. Paul made up his mind not to make another visit that would be painful to the Corinthians. He did not want to inflict more pain on the very people (**the one whom I made sorrowful** is generic and does not refer to one specific individual) who should bring him joy. This does not mean, however, that we should make ministry decisions based on the avoidance of pain and the pursuit of happiness.

2:3-4. Instead of avoiding contact altogether, Paul decided to write a painful letter. The purpose of the change was: (1) to avoid the unnecessary pain of a sharp reprisal against them (Paul was confident that they would respond positively, making Paul's joy their joy) and (2) to communicate Paul's love. The faithful minister must never give up on people. Sin is addressed with **anguish** and **tears** out of **love**. This type of ministry changes lives.

3. Forgiveness (2:5-11)

Paul's tearful letter called for the discipline of an unnamed individual (**the offender** of 2Co

7:12) who had rejected his authority. This individual was probably not the incestuous man of 1Co 5:1. (1) The offense in 1Co 5 was sexual in nature; the offense here is a rejection of Paul's authority. (2) The offended group in 1Co 5 is the church as a whole; the offended person here is Paul himself (2Co 2:5).

2:5. Although the attack by this person against Paul was personal, the church had also experienced a certain degree of sorrow. There is no such thing as a private sin.

2:6-8. The **majority** of the church had enacted the discipline Paul desired, and the offender had repented (cf. 2Co 7:8-12). As a result, the **punishment** must stop and the overwhelming grief of the offender should be replaced with forgiveness, **comfort**, and **love** by the Corinthians. The goal of church discipline is always restoration.

2:9. Paul intended the request for discipline to be a **test** of the Corinthian's submission to his authority. By enacting the discipline, the majority became **obedient** and passed the test.

2:10-11. Now Paul was calling on them to forgive the repentant offender as Paul himself had already done. Paul was motivated to forgive (1) for the benefit of the Corinthian community, (2) for the approval of Christ whose **presence** is always near in discipline situations, and (3) a desire to stop the attack of Satan on the congregation. The enemy can use lack of forgiveness to destroy the church.

4. Travel to Troas (2:12-13)

After the painful visit and tearful letter, Paul left his ministry in Ephesus as a "depressed" minister (cf. 2Co 7:5-6) and traveled to **Troas**. Although he came to Troas with the expressed purpose of preaching the gospel concerning Christ and although the Lord provided an opportunity—a **door**—for success, Paul rejected the opportunity and left for **Macedonia**. The reason for this remarkable reversal was his distress over the situation in Corinth. No news from Titus was interpreted as bad news.

C. Paul Defends His Ministry (2:14–7:4)

The mention of Titus caused Paul to intentionally reflect on the comfort he received from God during this hardship. In what is often called a "great digression," Paul defended the genuineness of his ministry by reflecting extensively on the nature of new covenant ministry—a ministry that often involves suffering. When the travel narrative resumes in 7:5, the reader learns that God comforted Paul "by the coming of Titus" (7:6) and the Corinthian response to his ministry (7:7).

1. The Sufficiency of Paul's Ministry (2:14–3:6)

2:14. In the midst of suffering, Paul thanked God. The **triumph** recalls the triumphal victory parade sponsored by a Roman emperor for a general whose military accomplishments were truly extraordinary. The general's captured enemies were put on public display in front of the Roman populace. God had captured Paul on the road to Damascus and now was leading him **in** his ministry for **Christ**. In contrast to Corinthian triumphalism, Paul understood his suffering as the means that God uses to spread the **aroma** of the gospel.

2:15-16a. Because Paul's **fragrance** of suffering—reminiscent of OT sacrifices—reflects Christ's suffering, it separates humanity into two camps: those who embrace Paul's suffering and his message are genuine believers, but those who reject it **are perishing**. To reject Paul is to reject his gospel message and the triumph that comes only in Christ.

2:16b-17. Who is sufficient for the gospel ministry? In contrast to the newly arrived opponents who preached for the money, Paul is adequately equipped for this ministry because he preached (1) free of charge with pure (sincere) motives, (2) was commissioned **from God**, (3) was accountable **in the sight of God**, and (4) was in union with **Christ**.

3:1-3a. The opponents came with **letters of commendation**, but Paul seemed to commend himself (cf. 2Co 1:12; 2:17). Paul responded that (1) his previous statements were not from arrogance, and (2) he did not need official letters because the conversion of the Corinthians was his letter of commendation—a letter engraved on his heart, indicating the genuineness of his ministry (v. 2). This metaphorical letter is from **Christ** and serviced by Paul (v. 3a). It is superior because (1) it is internal rather than external, (2) seen by all rather than a few, and (3) authored by Christ rather than humans.

3:3b. The old covenant inaugurated by Moses was external—engraved **on tablets of stone** (Ex 31:18). In contrast, the OT prophets predicted a future new covenant inaugurated by Christ that would be internal—written by the Spirit on responsive **human hearts** (Jr 31:31-33; Ezk 11:19; 36:26-27). This prophetic promise found fulfillment when Jesus died (Lk 22:20) and the Spirit was poured out (Ac 2:1-21). The new covenant replaced the old. Corinthian conversions, therefore, were evidence of the Spirit's ministry through Paul.

3:4-6a. Such confidence before God (i.e., the adequacy of his ministry from God [2:16-17] and the evidence of adequacy in Corinthian conversions [3:1-3]) comes by means of Christ. Lest they misunderstand this confidence, Paul explained that his sufficiency for new covenant ministry came **from God**, not from himself.

3:6b. The current new covenant is now contrasted with the old covenant of the past. The **letter** refers to the law as chiseled in stone. This external code stated commandments but did not empower the hearer to obey. The result of disobedience was death for the rebellious (Ex 32:27-28). There was nothing wrong with the content of the OT law. It reflects the holy character of God, and most of the Ten Commandments are repeated in the NT. Here Paul stresses the inability of an external code to enable a person to keep it. The new covenant, however, is characterized by the inner work of the **Spirit,** which enables a person to do the will of God. The result of obedience is **life**. This letter/Spirit contrast should not be understood as pointing to a spiritual interpretation of the Bible over against a literal interpretation.

2. The Glory of New Covenant Ministry (3:7–4:6)

Based on a running explanation of Ex 34:29-35, Paul argued from lesser to greater for the permanence of the new covenant ministry.

3:7-8. Even though the old covenant resulted in **death** for the rebellious in Ex 32:27-28, it nevertheless possessed the glory of God—a glory that was evident in the glowing face of Moses (Ex 34:29). Israel in their rebellion could not gaze intently on this glory lest they be consumed. As an act of mercy, Moses veiled his face before Israel lest they die (the OT never mentions that the glory was **fading**; it was "a glory which was made ineffective" [NET] *by the veil*, cf. Scott Hafemann, *2 Corinthians* [NIVAC], Grand Rapids, MI: Zondervan, 2000, 144–163, and see the comments below on v. 13). Both covenants reflect the glory of God in equal degree, but their results are different: rebellious Israel died, but the believing Corinthians lived.

3:9-10. Rebellious Israel died because the law pronounced **condemnation** on sin (see the comments on Gl 3:10-14), and Israel was not able to keep all the law so as to avoid this condemnation (see Dt 29–31, Israel under the old covenant established a right relationship with God only by faith in God's promises that ultimately found fulfillment in the person of Christ). But the Corinthians lived because the Spirit brings and promotes **righteousness**. The glory of God, therefore, **abound**s in the new covenant because of its results. When compared in this way, it is clear that the old covenant ministry has come to an end. It has, by comparison to the new covenant, **no glory** at this time.

3:11. The very nature of the old covenant, which veiled the glory of God, revealed that it was temporary. The new covenant inaugurated by Christ replaced the old covenant and **remains** as a permanent covenant that manifests the unveiled glory of God.

3:12-13. The remainder of the chapter highlights the significance of Ex 34:29-35 for the Corinthians. Because Paul had this confident **hope** that the new covenant remains, he preached the gospel with a courageous **boldness**. This is in contrast to Moses who spoke through a veil to Israel. The purpose of the veil was to keep rebellious Israel from experiencing the **end** (*telos*, here refers to the consequence of destruction) that the unveiled glory of God would bring on "stiff-necked" people in a time of rebellion (Ex 34:33-35). The fact of a new covenant means that only those who embrace Paul's gospel can be saved. There is no separate way of salvation for the Jewish people.

3:14-16. Why then were so many Israelites rejecting Christ? Their **minds** continued to be hardened (see the comments on Rm 11:7-27). This is evident because the **veil** (which now was representing Israel's hardness) remained over their **heart** when **Moses** (i.e., the old covenant) was read (v. 15). The hardness is only removed when they embrace Christ as Savior. Just as Moses used to remove the veil to behold the glory of God (Ex 34:34), so Jewish people now have the veil of hardness removed when they repent and see the glory of God in the person of Jesus (v. 16). Moses was a paradigm for a **person** who **turns** in repentance **to the Lord** (a reference to God the Father in this quotation from Ex 34:34). Just as Moses removed the veil in the presence of God, so people throw off their hardness of heart when they turn to God.

3:17. By saying **the Lord is the Spirit**, Paul was not equating the Father and the Spirit as one person. He was explaining the significance of Ex 34:34 to NT believers. Moses uniquely turned to the Lord (Yahweh) in the tent of meeting;

but now NT believers turn to the Spirit in their conversion. The **liberty** that results is not an independence to do whatever one pleases, but rather is liberation from hardheartedness.

3:18. In contrast to Jewish unbelievers (3:14), all followers of Christ, Jewish or Gentile, now have an **unveiled face**—Paul's image for freedom from hardheartedness. Unlike rebellious Israel in the Exodus account, Christians can see God's glory and live. Those who intensely ponder this glory are continuously transformed (**from** the initial **glory** of their conversion **to** the final **glory** of the future) into the **image** of Christ who reveals the glory of God. This transformation comes from God who now works through **the Spirit**. Paul expected every true follower of Christ to experience an ever-increasing growth in godliness.

4:1-2. Because Paul had received this glorious new covenant **ministry** and because of the **mercy** God granted him during ministry, he refused to give up (cf. 4:16). Those who have a clear vision of the mercy of God in their lives and the glory of God manifested in Christ can persist in the gospel ministry during times of hardship. In response to his opponents, Paul defended his bold ministry by renouncing anything **hidden because** it is shameful. He did this negatively by rejecting deceit and misrepresentation of the OT and positively by a clear presentation of **truth** concerning Jesus.

4:3-4. If this truth is both glorious and clear, should not everyone respond to it? Unbelievers, however, are **blinded** by Satan lest they perceive the **light** that comes from the **gospel**. Although defeated on the cross (Co 2:15), Satan is referred to as **the god of this world** because he has limited dominion over unbelievers during **this** current age. Believers in this dispensation see the glory of God in Christ, who, as God's visible **image**, reflect His glory. Unbelievers can understand the clear presentation of the gospel, but in their blindness they evaluate it as foolishness (1Co 1:18; 2:14).

4:5-6. This explains why Paul preached the **Jesus** of history as the exalted **Lord** and why he served the Corinthians. Those who have been touched by the gospel realize that the gospel is not about them. **God**, who created **light** from **darkness** (Gn 1:3), confronted Paul with light on the road to Damascus (Ac 22:6-11) so that Paul clearly saw God's glory in Christ. Only through a work of God are people able to perceive **the glory of God** in the person **of Christ**.

3. Living and Dying with Jesus (4:7–5:10)

4:7. If the gospel ministry is so glorious, why did Paul suffer so much? The gospel about Christ is a valuable **treasure**, but it is communicated by human beings who are like fragile clay **vessels**. The divine intent of this contrast is that God's power might be manifested in human frailty. The true minister is one who is broken to the point where it is apparent that the transforming power of the gospel is from God.

4:8-9. The four sets of contrasts—all maximized by the phrase **in every way**—illustrate the connection between suffering in ministry and divine strength to overcome: (1) although **afflicted** (the verb is used of a crowd pressing against Jesus in Mk 3:9 and pictures being hard-pressed by opponents), never **crushed** in the sense of being backed into a corner with no escape; (2) although **perplexed** in the sense of being at a loss to know how to respond to a difficult situation (cf. Mk 6:20), "never a loser" (BDAG, 345); (3) although pursued by others, never **forsaken** by God; and (4) although **struck down** by physical abuse, never **destroyed** by physical death (cf. Paul's experience at Lystra in Ac 14:19-10).

4:10-12. These contrasts are paralleled to the life of Christ. The **dying of Jesus** refers to the constant hardships Jesus experienced, which were reproduced in the hardships of Paul. The purpose of the suffering is that the resurrection **life** imparted by **Jesus** might become a present reality in Paul's physical **body**. Paul was motivated to persevere in ministry—even though it meant suffering—because of Jesus (v. 11) and because it brought salvation to the Corinthians (**life in you**, v. 12).

4:13. Paul shared the **same** inclination to trust God during hard times as the author of Ps 116. Even when suffering brought the psalmist to the point of death (Ps 116:5, 8), he still believed in God even when he said, "I am greatly afflicted" (Ps 116:10). Faith leads to proclamation regardless of circumstances.

4:14-15. Paul also continued in ministry because he knew about the reality of a future glory. The resurrection of Jesus guarantees that Paul will be raised from the dead when Jesus returns (1Co 15:20, 23). When this happens, Paul will stand with the Corinthians in the presence of God. As a compassionate minister, Paul endured hardships for the sake of his people and for a higher purpose: the ever-increasing thanksgiving directed toward God that magnifies His glory after more people respond to the gospel.

4:16. Paul wasn't giving up on ministry. Instead he experienced that even **though** his **outer man** (that aspect of his current humanity that others saw) was being destroyed by suffering, his **inner man** (that aspect of his humanity that was planted at conversion and unseen by others) was constantly growing through the nourishment of the Holy Spirit.

4:17-18. This process of growth is further explained by contrasting the current suffering with the unimaginable production of **glory** that the suffering produces. The glory refers to the future blessings that culminate in the resurrection body but are experienced in part during this age. When a Christian understands this **eternal** and abundant glory, the present suffering is viewed as **momentary** and minimal in comparison. Paul can say this because he has a spiritual perspective on life: his focus is not on the **temporal** suffering and decay of the physical body (**the things** clearly **seen** with the physical senses); his focus is on the **eternal** glory (**the things not seen** with the physical senses).

5:1. The physical difficulties Paul faced in ministry and the ever-increasing possibility of his death did not lead to despair. He knew that in physical death—when the **house** is **torn down**—believers would have the certainty of a resurrection body (the future **building**) that comes **from God** and lasts forever. Paul reflected on three human states throughout this section: (1) the physical state of present existence illustrated as an **earthly tent**, (2) the intermediate state between death and the second coming when a believer is present with the Lord without a resurrection body (a state referred to as nakedness), and (3) the resurrection state that begins at the rapture of the Church when believers receive their resurrection body.

5:2-4. State 1 is characterized by the groaning that accompanies suffering. Paul was longing to be alive for the rapture, which ushers in state 3 without the experience of death (1Co 15:50-55). Believers at that time will be transformed from their mortal bodies to their resurrection bodies without the experience of death and state 2.

5:5. God gives the **Spirit** to believers at conversion. This Spirit is a guarantee that God works through suffering to prepare Christians for their resurrection body.

5:6-8. To be **at home in the body** (an idiom for being alive) is to be absent from the Lord. Paul was courageous in this state although at the time his relationship with the Lord was characterized by **faith** rather than **sight** (v. 7). But because he knew that **to be absent from the body** (an idiom for physical death) ushers one into the presence of the Lord in the intermediate state, he preferred to be with the Lord (v. 8). Paul was not suicidal or disparaging concerning the physical body; Paul remained hopeful in the face of death because it would inaugurate a new phase in his relationship with the Lord.

5:9-10. In anticipation of his future relationship with the Lord, Paul desired to please Christ in his present state. For Paul, this meant a continuation in ministry even through suffering. Paul was also motivated by the expectation that he and all Christians will **appear before** and be evaluated by **Christ**. This happens at the **judgment seat** (Gk. *bema*)—a word that referred to a raised platform where a judicial authority pronounced a verdict on the one standing before him (Jesus "stood before" Pilate while Pilate was "sitting on the judgment seat" [Mt 27:11-19], and Paul stood "before the judgment seat" of Gallio in Corinth [Ac 18:12-17]). The purpose of the evaluation is not to determine eternal destiny; the purpose is to identify the actions of the physical **body** and to evaluate them as **good** or **bad**. The reward for **good** works is praise (1Co 4:5); the reward for evil works is lack of praise (1Co 3:15).

4. The Ministry of Reconciliation (5:11–6:2)

5:11. Paul's motivation for his evangelistic ministry of persuading men, therefore, was his reverence for Christ and desire to have his works evaluated positively. This motivation was clear to God, and Paul hoped that the Corinthians would also share God's perspective.

5:12. Rather than having an inflated view of himself, Paul wrote concerning his motives so that the Corinthians might defend him against his opponents who prided themselves on outward **appearance** (thus rejecting Paul because of his suffering) rather than inward reality. The internal motivations of the **heart** are more significant than outward appearances.

5:13. The Corinthians responded to Paul differently: some incorrectly thought he was **beside [himself]**—out of his mind to put up with such suffering; others thought that his **mind** was **sound**. Regardless, Paul ministered for the sake of **God** and the Corinthians, not for himself.

5:14-15. Paul found a second motivation for ministry in **the love of Christ**, i.e., Christ's love for him. This love was manifested when Christ died as a substitute for the sins of those who believe in Him, and it leads to two conclusions: (1) the death of Christ to sin was the death of **all** Christians to sin (see the comments on Rm 6:1-7) and (2) this should motivate Christians to live for Christ (see the comments on Rm 6:11-14). The death of Christ is more than a fact to be believed; it demands a lifestyle that needs to be lived.

5:16-17. Paul described two consequences concerning the death of Christ. (1) His conversion experience gave him a new perspective on Christians and Christ. Gone were the days when Paul appraised them **according to the flesh**, from a human perspective. The death of Christ means that Christians are regarded as spiritual brothers and sisters rather than as just members of certain ethnic, social, or economic groups; Jesus is regarded as the Messiah rather than a messianic pretender. (2) The **old** era of the law ended with the death of Christ, and a **new** era in salvation history has arrived. When people become Christians, they are **in Christ** and view everything from a new perspective.

5:18-19. In this new period of salvation history, **God** was active **in** the life of **Christ** to reconcile humanity to **Himself**. "Reconciliation" is a key Pauline term. It is the activity of God that exchanges a broken relationship with humanity with a restored relationship through the work of Christ on the cross. Adam's sin broke humanity's perfect relationship with God and made humanity enemies with God (Rm 5:10). For Paul, humanity was so sinful that human beings could not reconcile themselves to God. But God Himself took the initiative in history to reconcile humanity through the death of Christ on the cross. This does not mean, however, that every human is automatically reconciled. The message must be proclaimed and received (Rm 5:11) by faith in Christ (Rm 5:1-2). Believers are free from the penalty of sin and their **trespasses** do not count **against them**. God gives reconciled believers the task of proclaiming the message of reconciliation.

5:20. As he was Christ's ambassador, Paul's appeal represented God's appeal. Paul's evangelistic plea was that unbelievers might **be reconciled to God** by embracing the gospel message (2Co 5:11). This plea was not directed toward the Corinthians, as the NASB **we beg you** implies (the pronoun **you** is not in the Gk. text); the audience is the unbelieving world.

5:21. The content of the appeal is clarified. Christ never committed **sin**, but He voluntarily became a **sin** offering (the likely sense of **to be sin on our behalf**) by bearing the penalty for sin as a substitute. He was punished for the sins of others. The purpose for his death was that those who believe might have a righteous standing before God. The sinless One died so that sinners might live.

6:1-2. The doctrinal section (5:11–6:2) concludes with a practical exhortation. Paul worked **together with** God to proclaim the message of reconciliation; the Corinthians embraced this message and benefited from a right relationship with God. As reconciled people, they must now reconcile with others—including Paul. **Grace**—specifically the new work that God has accomplished in Christ to bring about reconciliation and forgiveness of sins (5:18-19)—is received **in vain**, in a practical sense, when Christians do not live in harmony with their position in Christ. The reason for this action is grounded in the scriptural context of Is 49:8. Because God often breaks into history to help His people, the recipients should respond. Just as God had His **DAY** when He delivered Israel from their bondage in Babylon, so there was a **day** when the Corinthians were delivered from their bondage to sin. The stress on **now** refers to the new period of salvation history inaugurated by the death of Christ.

5. Paul's Integrity and Appeal (6:3-10)

6:3-4a. Paul made this exhortation as a man of integrity. His driving purpose in life was that no one would find fault with his gospel ministry because of an **offense** he committed. His life reflected his message. **As** a servant **of God**, Paul proved his integrity by **endurance** during suffering. This virtue applies to all the trials in the following list and is a crucial quality for every minister. Those committed to the gospel will stand firm during persecution.

6:4b-5. Paul listed his difficulties in three groups of three items: (1) general terms for hardships (**afflictions**, **hardships**, and **distresses**), (2) circumstances forced on Paul by others (**beatings**, **imprisonments**, and **tumults** or riots), and (3) hardships chosen by Paul for the sake of ministry (**labors**, **sleeplessness**, and **hunger**).

6:6-7. Paul commended himself through character qualities that manifest divine enablement: **purity**, **knowledge**, **patience**, **kindness**, and sincere **love** (which are fruit of the **Holy Spirit**), as well as truthful speech (which is an evidence of the **power of God**). Paul also received spiritual **weapons** from a righteous God both for offense (**the right hand**) and defense (**the left hand**). Christian ministry is viewed as a battle that requires offense against opponents and defense against the attacks of the enemy.

6:8a. Paul's character was consistent regardless of his circumstances, whether receiving **glory** in the sense of recognition or **good report** from followers or **dishonor** in the sense of disregard or **evil report** from opponents.

6:8b-10. Paul's opponents had their own assessment of Paul. Seven statements contrast their worldly assessment with a godly assessment. (1) Though **regarded as** a deceiver, Paul was truthful; (2) though regarded as a counterfeit apostle by the opponents, he was regarded as genuine by God and true Christians; (3) though often at the point of death, he was still alive; (4) though disciplined by hardships, he was not put to death (cf. Ps 118:17-18 for an echo of the last two points); (5) though **sorrowful, yet** Paul was **always rejoicing**; (6) though materially **poor** by choice, he made **many rich** through the gospel; (7) though **having nothing** comparatively in this world, he possessed **all things** eternal.

6:11-13. After commending his ministry to the Corinthians, Paul concluded with a frank statement. The contrast between a **heart** that is **opened wide** versus one that is **restrained** or restricted is related to the intensity of affection in the life of Paul and the Corinthians, respectively. Paul's immense affection for them should now have been evident, but their **affections** for Paul were lacking. In return for what Paul had done for them, he exhorted them as his dear children to return affection to him.

6. Separation from Unbelievers (6:14–7:1)

6:14a. This classic discussion on separation shows how the Corinthians can open their hearts to Paul: by **not** being **bound together with unbelievers**. The **unbelievers** in the Corinthian correspondence are always non-Christians outside the church (1Co 6:6; 7:12-15; 10:27; 14:22-24; 2Co 4:4). Paul was not advocating separation from all unbelievers (1Co 5:9-11; 7:12-15), nor was he referring to his opponents in Corinth. The vocabulary of this paragraph argues that his concern was specific: the Corinthians should not join with unbelievers to eat a meal in a pagan temple (1Co 8–10; see the comments by Paul Barnett, *The Second Epistle to the Corinthians* [NICNT], Grand Rapids, MI: Eerdmans, 1997, 341–43). The primary application of this passage is not that of believers marrying only believers or Christians going into business partnerships with unbelievers. Avoiding idolatry and its crippling effects upon the Corinthians' affection for Paul are the main points.

6:14b-16a. Five parallel statements communicate the first reason for Paul's command. Believers should separate from pagans in this situation because there is a drastic division between their value systems. There are (1) no shared values (**partnership**, lit., an affiliation involving common goals and actions) between those who practice **righteousness** and those who practice wickedness, (2) no intimate **fellowship** (warm, affectionate relations) between those who belong to the realm of **light** and those who belong to the realm of **darkness**, (3) no **harmony** of working together between the members of **Christ** and the members of Satan (**Belial**), (4) no shared commitment between those who believe in Christ and those who do not, and (5) no common ground between worship in the church (believers are now collectively the **temple of** the **living God**) and worship in pagan temples.

6:16b-18. The second reason for Paul's command was scriptural. (1) God had a special relationship with Israel when they fled idolatry (Lv 26:1-2, 11-12). (2) Those who carried the Lord's vessels from Babylon were to **separate** from idolatry and **not touch** the **unclean** idols (Is 52:11). (3) When Israel rejected idols, they enjoyed a special family relationship with God (2Sm 7:14; cf. Dt 32:15-21). If the Corinthians avoided idolatry, their relationship with Paul would be much warmer.

7:1. These OT **promises** are the basis for Paul's exhortation concerning cleansing from the external and internal (**flesh and spirit**) defilement of idol worship. This act of **perfecting holiness** reflects a deep reverence for God.

7. Paul's Renewed Appeal (7:2-4)

7:2-3. By cleansing themselves, the Corinthians would expand their love for Paul (cf. 6:11-13). They should do this because Paul had not **wronged** them spiritually or financially. Paul said this not **to condemn** the Corinthians by implying that they all had wronged him (the comments were likely directed toward his opponents). They knew this because Paul had told them **before** that they have a place in his heart both now in life and later in death.

7:4. As the climactic conclusion of the "great digression" that discussed the superior nature of his new covenant ministry and provided a defense of Paul's ministry (2:14–7:4), Paul rehearsed four ministry themes: (1) frank communication with the Corinthians, (2) boasting about the Corinthians to others, (3) comfort from God in suffering, and (4) joy in suffering.

D. Paul's Joy over Corinthian Repentance (7:5-16)

7:5. Here Paul continued his travel narrative that ended abruptly in 2:13. **Even when** he traveled from Troas **to Macedonia**, he still did not have **rest**. His physical illness combined with external struggles with unbelievers and internal fears concerning the Corinthian situation robbed him of all respite. The pressures of ministry deeply affect a compassionate minister.

7:6-7. But Paul's depression turned to joy by means of (1) the arrival of **Titus** from Corinth, (2) the comfort Titus had received from the Corinthians, and (3) Titus's report that the Corinthians were yearning for him, grieving over the way they had treated him, and had a **zeal** to make things right. God works in people's lives to orchestrate comfort in the midst of suffering.

7:8-10. As Paul listened to Titus's report, he realized that the Corinthians had been grieved by his severe letter (**Corinthians C**, no longer extant; see the Introduction: Background). It hurt Paul to hear this, but he did **not regret** sending the letter because the godly sorrow it produced led to their repentance. They did **not suffer loss** (v. 9) means that they were not harmed by the letter in any way. The benefit of suffering comes from the reaction to it (v. 10): godly sorrow leads to change and the spiritual benefit of **salvation**, but worldly sorrow produces spiritual harm. Ministers should point out sin with the hope that the resulting grief will lead to change; those receiving rebuke from godly leaders should repent.

7:11. Seven character qualities flowed out of their **godly sorrow**: (1) **earnestness** to follow Paul's commands, (2) desire to clear themselves of charges brought against them by Paul, (3) **indignation** toward the person who had wronged Paul, (4) renewed respect for apostolic authority, (5) **longing** for Paul's return, (6) **zeal** to fulfill Paul's wishes, and (7) desire to punish the wrongdoer. Genuine repentance results in action.

7:12-13a. Paul had a threefold purpose when he **wrote** the severe letter. Initially, his aim was (1) to demand punishment of the **offender** who had personally attacked him, and (2) to seek restoration toward the **offended**—toward Paul himself. In retrospect, however, his main goal was (3) to have them demonstrate their devotion to him. The accomplishment of this purpose was a great comfort to Paul.

7:13b-14. The attention now shifts from the response of Paul to the response of Titus toward the Corinthian repentance. The Corinthians had **refreshed** him after his ministry to them. This gave Paul even more reason for rejoicing. Paul had assured Titus that the Corinthians would respond favorably, and they did. Paul **was not put to shame** because the truth of the gospel that Paul proclaimed to them matched the truth of his comments concerning Titus.

7:15-16. The **affection** of Titus toward the Corinthians was even greater when **he** remembered their **obedience** and reported it to Paul. Their **obedience** was manifested in the God-fearing way they treated Titus during his visit. Paul concluded this section by returning to the recurring theme of rejoicing over his renewed confidence in the Corinthians after their positive response to Titus and his severe letter.

II. Present Ministry in Corinth (8:1–9:15)

A. Complete the Collection (8:1-15)

8:1-2. Paul's concern to defend his apostleship in light of past events shifted to his concern for a monetary collection to benefit the poor Jewish believers in Jerusalem (cf. comments at Rm 15:26-27). He urged the Corinthians to complete the collection by informing them of the **grace** that God gave to the Macedonian churches. This grace is the spiritual work of God that enabled the Macedonians to give (for the connection between "saving grace" and "serving grace," see 1Co 15:10). The Greek word *charis* (grace) is used 10 times in 2Co 8–9 and has several different nuances (Harris, *Second Corinthians*, 559–560): (1) the enablement to give (8:1; 9:8, 14), (2) the **favor** or opportunity to give (8:4), (3) the **gracious work** of the collection itself (8:6, 7, 19), (4) the gracious character of the Lord (8:9), and (5) an expression of thanks to God (8:16; 9:15). Their motivation for giving was not external pressure but internal grace. The Macedonians (including at least the **churches** of Philippi, Thessalonica, and Berea, Ac 20:1-6) had great **joy** even though they were suffering, and they gave beyond their financial ability even though they were in **deep poverty**.

8:3-5. Three circumstances accompanied Macedonian giving. Paul testified that (1) they gave sacrificially on **their own**; (2) they intently pleaded with Paul for the opportunity to participate in the relief work (**participation** refers to an active fellowship with the Jewish believers, v. 4); and (3) their giving was the result of a prior rededication to the Lord and a commitment to Paul's spiritual leadership (v. 5). It was the **will of God** for them to submit to Paul's authority. If the poverty-stricken Macedonians could give like this, surely the comparatively wealthy Corinthians could give as well. The attitudes of the Macedonians should also challenge believers to give today regardless of economic status.

8:6. Based on the unexpected generosity of the Macedonians, Paul exhorted **Titus** to return to Corinth to finish the collection that he began before the arrival of the opponents. Titus eagerly accepted Paul's **appeal** (8:16-17).

8:7. The Corinthians were gifted in many areas (1Co 1:5), including an **earnestness** (or zeal) and love, which Paul cultivated. Now the Corinthians should exercise these virtues by giving to the collection. Those who have experienced an abundance of grace from God should abound in giving as well.

8:8-9. Paul did not force them to give. His intent was that the collection would prove the genuineness of their love for him as he compared their zeal with the zeal of the Macedonians. But the ultimate reason for giving is the example of Christ. Though he enjoyed all the riches of heaven, he voluntarily **became poor** in the incarnation. Through this giving, Christians enjoy spiritual riches. Giving to the collection is a response to the **grace** of Christ.

8:10-12. The Corinthians had a unique history with the collection. They responded to Paul's instructions and the presence of Titus a **year** earlier to become the **first** not only to **desire** to give but also to actually give. Because of this, it was fitting for Paul to speak his mind on the issue. Their desire never ceased, but the collection did. Now they should act on their desire once again and resume the collection (v. 11). They should do this according to their **ability** (**what a person has**, even though the Macedonians went beyond their ability, 8:3). This is what Craig Blomberg (*1 Corinthians*, NIVAC [Grand Rapids, MI: Zondervan, 1995], 85) calls a "graduated giving." The percent of giving should increase in proportion to resources. Paul does not restrict giving to 10 percent of one's income.

8:13-14. Paul's desire is not for the Corinthians to become poor like the Macedonians while the Jerusalem Jewish believers become rich. Nor should they spread their wealth to generate an economic equality where everyone has the same amount of money. Instead, they should give **by way of equality**—on the basis of the spiritual equality that already exists between Jews and Gentiles in the church. In **the present** Church Age, the Corinthians had material abundance, and the Jerusalem Jewish believers were poor. Yet they shared their spiritual (Rm 15:27) blessings with Gentiles. When everyone shares, the goal of equality is achieved. Christians should give materially to those who support them spiritually.

8:15. A quotation from the manna passage in Ex 16 supports Paul's exhortation to give. The experience in the wilderness taught Israel that God supplies for those who trust Him and that selfish hoarding should be rejected (Richard Hays, *Echoes of Scripture in the Letters of Paul* [New Haven: Yale University Press, 1989], 88–91). In the wilderness, equality was miraculously enforced (all had one omer regardless of how much they gathered); in the church, equality is realized through the action of the believers. Giving does not devastate because God supplies.

B. Administer the Funds (8:16–9:5)

8:16-17. After urging the Corinthians to resume their giving to the collection, Paul turned his attention to administrative issues. He offered a letter of recommendation for Titus and two other brothers who would help with the gathering and transportation of the funds. Paul praised God because He worked in the life of Titus to give him the same desire for the collection that Paul had. As evidence of Titus's desire, Paul pointed out that (1) he embraced Paul's exhortation to return, and (2) he did so not under compulsion but because he was **very earnest**.

8:18-19. Titus would return with an unnamed brother whose identity remains a mystery. Titus would introduce him. This fellow believer was commended because (1) he was highly respected among the Macedonian **churches** for his service in the **gospel** ministry and (2) he was **appointed** by the Macedonian **churches** to travel with Paul from Corinth to deliver the collection to Jerusalem. The collection itself was administered with a dual purpose: (1) primarily to promote praise to God and (2) secondarily to confirm Paul's **readiness** or eagerness to support Jewish Christians.

8:20-21. Paul anticipated the collection of a large sum of money, and he desired to be financially accountable. The brothers were traveling with Paul as a **precaution** against the accusation that Paul intended to embezzle some funds for himself. They would ensure that Paul was above reproach. The way we handle church funds should be an open book before the **Lord** and especially before church members.

8:22. A second unidentified messenger would assist Titus with the collection in Corinth. Paul commended him to the church as a fellow believer (a spiritual **brother**) whose zeal for the ministry had been tested by Paul on numerous occasions in numerous ways. His zeal had increased after hearing about the Corinthian situation.

8:23. Paul anticipated questions about the delegation. If they ask about Titus: he shares Paul's commitment to the Corinthians and works with him for the collection. If they ask about the other brothers: they are **messengers** (or "apostles" in a nontechnical sense) from the Macedonian churches to ensure the integrity of the collection, and they honor Christ in their lives.

8:24. Paul concluded this letter of recommendation by exhorting the Corinthians to demonstrate to the delegates and their sending **churches** (1) their love and (2) the genuineness of Paul's claim concerning them. They would do this by receiving the delegates and contributing to the collection.

9:1-2. This paragraph continues that thought of 8:16-24 by explaining why Paul was sending the brothers to complete the collection before his arrival in Corinth. Because Paul knew about the Corinthian intention to give, this portion of the letter may seem unnecessary. Paul kept boasting to the Macedonians that **Achaia** (the province that included Corinth) had been ready to give since Titus initiated the endeavor a year earlier. And this Corinthian zeal had motivated the Macedonians to give.

9:3-4. But good intentions do not always produce the desired results, and the Corinthians needed encouragement to translate their zeal into action. Therefore, Titus and the two brothers were being sent to Corinth with a threefold purpose: (1) to insure that Paul's **boasting** about the Corinthians' intention would **not be made empty** by a failure to complete the action, (2) to confirm that the collection was complete (as Paul kept telling the delegation that it would be), and (3) to avoid the **shame** that would come to everyone when the **Macedonians** arrived in Corinth with Paul to find the collection incomplete.

9:5. The intent of the three-man delegation, therefore, was to motivate the Corinthians to fulfill their promise by completing the collection before Paul's arrival. This would demonstrate that their generous and voluntary gift reflected their desire to bless the Jewish believers—rather than being seen as a stingy, last-minute gift coerced by Paul.

C. Reap the Benefits (9:6-15)

9:6. Paul's final reflection on giving builds on his previous distinction between generous and stingy gifts by identifying the benefits of generous giving. Using an agricultural principle that connects the amount of harvest in direct proportion to the amount of sowing, Paul began a new theme: generous giving produces a generous harvest. This is the first benefit of giving.

9:7. Every person should reflect personally on an amount for the collection. Attitudes of inward reluctance and outward **compulsion** must be replaced by a cheerfulness that seeks God's love. **God loves a cheerful giver** because a cheerful giver gives just as God gives—cheerfully—and thus manifests to the world His graciousness in a way that cannot be duplicated by one who gives grudgingly.

9:8-9. The principle of 9:6 is now explained. Christians who give generously should know that **God is able** to provide generously for them in return. Because giving Christians constantly receive divine resources, they are delivered from hoarding and able to give even more. The giver (**HE SCATTERED . . . HE GAVE** in v. 9 refers to the human giver rather than God) becomes like the righteous person who gives to the poor in Ps 112:9. This righteous act will be remembered **FOREVER**. This passage, however, does not support the claim that God is required to make Christians wealthy when they give. The rewards for giving in the NT are future-oriented (e.g., "store up for yourselves treasures in heaven," Mt 6:20) and focus on having an abundance for **every good deed** (9:8) and **righteousness** (9:9, 10) rather than hoarded material prosperity.

9:10-11a. God **supplies** the funds necessary for giving and the **bread for food** that results. As the giver's **righteousness** produces a **harvest** of giving, God increases the benefits to those in need. The principle is clear: God provides material benefits to believers who give to those in need. He enriches those who give **in everything** (materially and spiritually) so that they can give more generously (not so that they can become wealthy).

9:11b-12. Two additional benefits result from generous giving: the financial needs of the recipients are met and thanksgiving is directed toward God.

9:13. Paul was anticipating a time when the Jewish believers of Jerusalem would glorify God **because** the contribution was **proof** of Gentile conversion. Specifically, Jewish followers of Jesus would glorify God for (1) Gentile **obedience** that flowed out of a **confession of the gospel** and (2) for Gentile generosity both **to them** (Jewish believers) and **to all** those in need (cf. Gl 6:10). This anticipation became a reality when Paul arrived in Jerusalem (Ac 21:17, 20a).

9:14-15. In addition to thanking God, the Jerusalem recipients would pray for the Corinthians and yearn to meet them because God's grace had moved them to give generously. All of these benefits are possible because of the person and work of Christ—God's **indescribable gift**. And for this everyone should thank God.

III. Future Visit to Corinth (10:1–13:14)

A. Paul Defends His Authority (10:1-18)

10:1. In anticipation of his next visit and with an increased awareness of problems with opponents at Corinth, Paul finished this epistle with a passionate defense of his apostolic authority. The unity of the letter (see comments in the introduction) is established by the continuing themes of Paul's defense of his ministry and his exhortation to the Corinthians (cf. the continuing reflection on commendation in 3:1; 4:2; 5:12; 6:4; 10:12, 18; and 12:11). He appealed to the church as one who followed the pattern of Christ in **meekness** and forbearance, but he rejected the accusations of the opponents that he was twofaced: servile while with them (failing to deal with the wrongdoer) but demanding (in the severe letter) **when absent** (cf. 10:10).

10:2a. Paul was willing to exercise discipline in person **with the confidence** that he has the authority to do so, but appealed that he would **not** need to act this way. There was still time to repent and obey.

10:2b-4. Paul's opponents, and those who were siding with them, argued that Paul was walking **according to the flesh**, i.e., that his actions were devoid of supernatural power. Paul conceded that he lived a physical existence (**in the flesh**, v. 3), but the war he was about to wage against his opponents would be an evidence of divine power (**not . . . according to the flesh**). He would use **weapons** (not identified, but cf. Eph 6:13-17) that would destroy the **fortress**, the opposing arguments, of his opponents.

10:5-6. His battle plan was threefold: (1) demolish the **fortresses**, defined as false reasoning and arrogant argumentation that keep people from a true knowledge of God; (2) take **captive** wrong thinking with the goal of conforming that thinking to the gospel; and, after some obey Paul's appeal, (3) **punish** those who remain disobedient when Paul visits.

10:7. Paul commanded the Corinthians to **look at** (see the NASB footnote) the facts concerning his ministry. The leader of the opposition (**anyone . . . himself . . . he . . . him**) claimed to have a special relationship with Christ (it was his own claim **in himself**—a claim that Paul later rejected, cf. 2Co 11:13-15), but Paul too could claim this.

10:8. Although Paul boasted even more concerning the authority Jesus gave to him at his conversion, he will have no shame in the final judgment because his boast was in the Lord. The primary purpose of his ministry was to build up the church, not to tear it down.

10:9-11. The opponents accused Paul of tearing down the church through his forceful letters (in contrast to a ministry in Corinth that was unimpressive in appearance and oratory, v. 10). But Paul's mission to build up should be applied to his severe writing as well—it too was for their benefit, not to terrify them for the purpose of destruction. His opponents should have realized that his mission of building up would be accomplished both through his deeds when present as well as his letters while absent (v. 11). The strong words in letters would match his strong deeds in presence. Firm rebuke is sometimes needed to build up the church.

10:12. Verses 12-18 compare the negative boasting of the opponents to the positive boasting of Paul. They foolishly **commend themselves** by comparing **themselves** with others in their cultural subgroup apart from a biblical standard; Paul, with irony, claimed that he was **not bold** enough to do that!

10:13-15a. The biblical standard for Paul's **boast** was God's assignment (**measure**) to go into Gentile territory (the **sphere** of Corinth) to plant churches—an assignment recognized by the Jerusalem leaders (Gl 2:7-9). As proof that Corinth was part of his assignment, Paul reminded the Corinthians that he was the **first to come** to them with the **gospel** about **Christ** (v. 14). In contrast to the opponents who came later and tried to reap what Paul had planted, Paul as a church planter did not build on the **labors** of others.

10:15b-16a. Paul was confident that he would plant churches westward **to the regions beyond** Corinth (to Rome and Spain; see the comments on Rm 15:22-29). This enlargement would happen (1) as the Corinthians grew in their **faith** in God, (2) **within** the **sphere** of his divine assignment to the Gentiles, (3) **even more** than it had already, and (4) **by** the financial support of the Corinthians.

10:16b-18. Paul refused **to boast** in the work started by others (as his opponents were doing in Corinth). His boast was in the Lord Jesus, who gave him the assignment and granted success in Gentile territory (Jr 9:24). The mark of an approved minister is the Lord's commendation, not self-commendation (as the opponents were doing).

B. Paul Is Forced to Boast (11:1–12:13)

11:1. After denouncing all self-commendation, Paul reluctantly engaged in the very thing he condemned. The situation demanded it. If he did boast, he was a fool like the opponents; but if he did not boast, the opponents appeared to have the victory. He engaged in foolish boasting both to win back the straying Corinthians and to show the foolishness of the endeavor. Verses 1-21a prepare the Corinthians for Paul's foolish boast in 11:21b-23a. Paul both wished and commanded (v. 11:1b is best translated as an imperative: "bear with me," not **you are bearing with me**) the Corinthians to put up with this **little** display of foolish boasting.

11:2-6. Verses 2-6 give three reasons for Paul's foolish boasting. (1) The Corinthians are a **virgin** pledged to Christ, and Paul as their spiritual father had a **godly jealousy** (which characterizes God and every faithful minister, cf. Ex 34:14) to keep them **pure**—exclusively devoted—to their **one husband** until the consummation of their relationship at the rapture. Paul had to boast to alleviate his fear that the crafty opponents might influence the Corinthians' thinking, drive them from this pure devotion, and, in so doing, repeat the satanic attack on Eve. (2) Paul was compelled to boast because the Corinthians were already receiving the opponents' message about a different **Jesus**, a **different spirit** (a reference to an erroneous depiction of the Holy Spirit), and a **different gospel** from what Paul proclaimed at their conversion. The content of this different gospel probably reflected a legalism that elevated works as necessary for salvation. If they embraced the foolishness of the intruders, they could surely embrace the foolish boasting of the founder of the church. (3) The **most eminent apostles** could refer to the twelve Jerusalem apostles to whom the opponents claimed allegiance and Paul claimed no inferiority, but the context of the foolish boasting argues that Paul was referring sarcastically to his opponents who claimed to be "super apostles" (NIV). Whichever view one adopts, the point is the same whether the **most eminent apostles** are the legitimate Jerusalem apostles or Paul's insurgent opponents: Paul was, at the very least, their equal. The Corinthians should listen to Paul because the true apostle is certainly not **inferior** to those who exalt themselves. Paul conceded that he was **unskilled** in the showy oratory that the opponents demanded. His focus, however, was on the content of the gospel, a fact that the Corinthians had observed in many different circumstances (see the comments on 1Co 2:1-5). Content was more important than rhetorical embellishments.

11:7-12. Before giving his foolish boast, Paul revealed his fourfold intent for refusing financial support from the Corinthians (11:7-12). During his ministry in Corinth, Paul humbled himself by doing manual labor (1) **so that** the Corinthians **might be exalted** as they embraced the gospel. This followed the pattern of Christ (2Co 8:9) and true ministers who deny themselves for the benefit of others. Ironically, however, the Corinthians, influenced by the opponents who demanded payment, saw this as a **sin**! (2) Paul's goal was **to serve** the Corinthians without compensation during his ministry with them (vv. 8-9). To accomplish this goal, he initially **robbed other churches**—a figurative and ironic way to refer to receiving financial support from them. When his tentmaking resources dried up, he continued to receive support from churches when the brothers (perhaps Silas and Timothy, cf. Ac 18:5) arrived from Macedonia. His goal was (3) not to **burden** any of the Corinthians financially during his ministry to them (v. 9). In vv. 10-11, Paul pointed out that truth from **Christ** had so permeated his life that he refused to abandon his **boasting**, namely, his appropriate sense of Christian satisfaction in offering the gospel free of charge throughout **Achaia** (the larger region that included Corinth). Paul had a consistent missionary strategy: rejecting funds from churches while ministering to them, but accepting funds from churches when moving to other fields (Harris, *Second Corinthians*, 765–66). To counter his opponents who argued that Paul's refusal to receive support was an indication that he did not love them, Paul revealed the final reason for his refusal: (4) he loved them (v. 11), as **God** well **knows**. The opponents wanted Paul to lower himself to their level by accepting financial support from the Corinthians (v. 12). This would give them an **opportunity** to **boast** that they were equal with Paul. Paul refused to play this foolish game.

11:13-15. Paul explained why his opponents could boast of equality with him. Although they claimed to be Christians (2Co 10:7; 11:23), their mission in Corinth was both **false** and deceptive. Like **Satan**, they appeared righteous and true, but it was only a masquerade (v. 14). They were not Christians at all; they were servants of Satan (v. 15). In the final judgment, their masks will be removed and their works will be identified as evil. An authentic minister wears no mask.

11:16. The opponents had prevailed over some Corinthians through foolish boasting, and Paul was about to engage in the same activity to win back the straying Corinthians. Before the actual boast, however, Paul **again** emphasized the foolishness of it (11:16-21a; cf. 11:1). They should not view him as **foolish**, but, if they did, they should give him the same hearing that they gave his foolish braggart opponents.

11:17-19. Paul's upcoming excursus into **boasting**, which begins in v. 21b, was indeed **foolishness** and did not come from the prompting of **the Lord**. The Corinthians forced him to boast, but the impulse did not come from the Lord. The opponents (the **many** who are **foolish**, v. 18) defended their ministry **according to the flesh**—according to outward criterion only, and the Corinthians in their "wisdom" ironically embraced them **gladly** (v. 19). Both actions were foolishness, but Paul followed the lead of the opponents because the Corinthians would listen to it.

11:20-21a. Paul concluded this section by contrasting the "strong" behavior of his opponents with his "weakness." In their strength they had enslaved the Corinthians by devouring them financially, taking their money, exalting themselves, and figuratively striking them in the face. Ironically, they put up with this display of strong domination while rejecting the weak servanthood of Paul.

11:21b-23a. Still recognizing it as **foolishness** and insanity to focus on externals, Paul finally presented his foolish boasting by focusing on his ancestry. Both Paul and the opponents were (1) **Hebrews**, connected with the language and culture of pure-blooded Jews; (2) **Israelites**, belonging to the chosen people of God; and (3) **descendants of Abraham**, heirs to the Abrahamic promises. This boast in Jewish ancestry led the Corinthians to identify the opponents as **servants of Christ**—a title that Paul refused to apply to them (cf. 11:13).

11:23b-27. After a brief, foolish speech, Paul revealed an extensive list of his sufferings—the very things that, in contrast to the opponents, identified him as a true apostle. True ministers boast not about their accomplishments but about the Lord's comfort in suffering. This was genuine boasting for Paul: abundant **labors** in the ministry; several **imprisonments**; countless beatings; several encounters with **death** (v. 23b) as illustrated by the maximum halachic (Jewish law) punishment of **thirty-nine lashes** (reduced from forty lest the amount prescribed in Dt 25:2-3 be exceeded, v. 24); being **beaten with rods** by Roman authorities (Ac 16:22); **stoned** (Ac 14:19-20); **shipwrecked**, including one time when he was drifting on the open sea for 24 hours (v. 25); **dangers** experienced during travel: from river currents and bandits, from Jews (Ac 9:23) and Gentiles (Ac 16:16-24, 19:21-20:1) in every place on the surface of the earth: **city**, desert, and **sea**; and **false** brothers (like those who had infiltrated Corinth, v. 26). The **labor** and toil that Paul experienced as a missionary and tentmaker resulted in **many sleepless nights**, as well as **hunger**, **thirst**, going **without food**, **cold**, **and exposure** (v. 27).

11:28-29. Paul's external sufferings were climactically matched by his internal **concern for all the churches**, especially the ones he founded. The opponents made the Corinthians spiritually **weak**, and this affected Paul as well. When the Corinthians were **led into sin**, Paul burned with anger toward the opponents. Paul's external suffering and internal concern should challenge ministers who suffer little for the gospel and have minimal concern for their people.

11:30-31. Since the opponents believed it was necessary **to boast**, Paul too would continue to **boast** in order to win back the Corinthians. But instead of boasting in strengths, Paul would boast only in weaknesses. The God whom Paul blesses **knows** that his subsequent boast about extraordinary events in Damascus and the third heaven was **not** a lie.

11:32-33. Because of Paul's evangelistic ministry to Gentiles in Arabia (Gl 1:16-17), King **Aretas** instructed his **ethnarch in Damascus to seize** Paul, but Paul escaped through a window in a basket (Ac 9:23-25). This should be perceived not as an example of strength but as an example of weakness. The flamboyant persecutor of the church became persecuted and humbly retreated in a basket.

12:1. Because the opponents claimed that **boasting** concerning ongoing revelation **is necessary** to confirm apostleship, Paul moved **on** from the Damascus account to disclose that he too had received a major revelation from the Lord. In so doing, he showed that there is nothing gained by boasting. With the surpassing revelation came a humbling weakness.

12:2-4. To downplay his revelation, Paul recorded his experience in the third person (though he reverted to the first person in vv. 7-8): God suddenly caught up a follower of Christ **to the third heaven** or **Paradise**—the place where believers are **at home with the Lord** (2Co 5:8). Only God knows whether Paul ascended with his physical body or in a visionary state without the body (2Co 5:1-3). Mere words were not sufficient to articulate the content of the revelation (**inexpressible words** probably refers either to words "that humankind is incapable of expressing" or to words "that should not be expressed because they are so holy"; cf. BDAG, 134). Paul probably saw such amazing things in this vision that he was incapable of conveying them adequately to others. The date of this vision 14 years before the writing of 2 Corinthians makes it impossible to connect this experience with any vision recorded previously in Acts or Paul's epistles (see Harris, *Second Corinthians*, 835–36).

12:5-6. Paul's exceptional revelation was genuine (in contrast to the lies of the opponents) and the type of thing that people could **boast** about. But Paul refused to boast, choosing rather to boast in the **weaknesses** that resulted from the revelation. The reason for this reversal is the proper evaluation of a minister: genuineness in ministry is not found in exceptional experiences but in what one **sees** in the behavior of the minister and **hears** in his teaching.

12:7. Paul elaborated on four aspects of the revelation. (1) After the experience, God gave Paul **a thorn** in his **flesh** (best understood as a chronic physical ailment; see the comments on 1:8) as a consequence of the revelation. (2) The reason for the thorn was the extraordinary revelations Paul received in the experience. (3) God's purpose in the thorn was to benefit Paul by keeping him from being euphoric over the experience. (4) At the same time, Satan sent his demon to torment Paul through the thorn. A spiritual battle had been raging for 14 years.

12:8-9a. During **three** periods of an intense flare-up of the thorn, Paul prayed to Jesus for its removal (Harris, *Second Corinthians*, 164–182). Paul's request was denied, but God made an even greater provision. The thorn drove Paul to acknowledge his weakness, and in weakness he found Christ's **grace** (divine enablement) and strength to continue ministry with the thorn. It is the very confession of weakness that generates strength to endure.

12:9b-10. The experience gave Paul a new perspective: he **gladly** acknowledged and delighted in his **weaknesses** (plural, including multiple cases of verbal **insults**, calamities, **persecutions**, and great **difficulties** that come from serving Christ) in order that the power of Christ might surround him.

12:11-13. Being enamored by the "super **apostles**" (cf. the comment on 11:5) who had infiltrated the church, certain Corinthians had turned their backs on Paul. This compelled Paul to show that as an apostle he was not **inferior** to his opponents even though he was nothing apart from Christ (1Co 15:8-10). His apostleship was indeed authenticated by miraculous **signs** that were a mark of divine power (12:12), but this happened while he persevered through suffering. Apostles in the early church received the unique ability to perform miracles, which both authenticated them as true apostles and testified to the veracity of their message. Miraculous abilities were not the privilege of every believer then or now. The only area where he treated the Corinthians differently was his continued refusal to receive financial support from them (12:13; cf. 11:7-11). Ironically, Paul asked for forgiveness of **this "wrong."**

C. Paul Expresses Concern for the Corinthians (12:14-21)

12:14-15. As Paul prepared for his **third** visit to Corinth, he gave two reasons for continuing to refuse funds and not be a financial burden to them. (1) He was concerned with their spiritual condition, not their money, and (2) young **children** should not **save up** money for their parents. This does not mean that ministers should never exercise their right to be supported by their congregation (1Co 9:3-14; 2Co 11:8-9) or that children should not care for their aging parents (1Tm 5:8). As their spiritual father, Paul expressed his unconditional commitment to the spiritual lives of his infant congregation, even if his **love** was not reciprocated. The commitment of a true minister **gladly** increases even when the response of the congregation decreases.

12:16-18. Although Paul had not been a financial **burden** to them in the past, some thought that Paul had a devious plan to collect money for himself through his associates. The collection money would go to him. But this deception is flatly denied in v. 17. The Corinthians could not find any evidence for it. Indeed (v. 18), Paul **sent Titus** and **the brother** to promote the collection, but they shared the same mindset and behaved in the same manner as Paul—and the Corinthians knew it.

12:19. If the Corinthians thought that Paul's main concern was the defense of his fragile self-image, they were wrong. His concern was their edification, which Paul hoped to achieve through his defense.

12:20-21. Paul expressed his concern in three fears about his upcoming visit. The Corinthians would have: (1) the ongoing issues listed in vv. 20b-21 (**not what I wish**) and Paul would need to come with harshness (13:1-2, **not what you wish**), (2) continuing issues related to discord with the opponents (v. 20b), and (3) issues related to those continuing in their immoral lifestyle (v. 21). A genuine minister is humbled and mourns over the sinfulness of spiritual children.

D. Paul Gives a Final Warning (13:1-10)

13:1-3a. During his imminent **third** visit to Corinth, Paul would follow the concern for justice expressed in Dt 19:15. There were plenty of witnesses to the Corinthians' sin (Timothy, Titus, other repentant believers). Paul had warned Corinthian sinners during his **second** visit, and he warned them (12:20-21) and the rest of the church again in this letter (v. 2). But the time of warning was ending; the time for punishment was near (**if** in this context should not imply doubt about his coming). The display of stern punishment would be the dramatic **proof** of apostolic authority that the opponents had been demanding (but in a way that they least expected, v. 3a).

13:3b-4. Paul's experience of weakness (suffering and warning the Corinthians by letter) followed by strength (anticipated apostolic discipline, v. 3b) paralleled the model of Christ who was **crucified** under the condition of **weakness** but was resurrected as a demonstration of the **power of God**. Ministry is always a tension between weakness in suffering and strength in resurrection power.

13:5-6. Instead of examining Paul, the Corinthians were to **examine** themselves to see if their conduct was in harmony with the content of their faith. Paul expected this **test** would reveal that **Jesus Christ is in** them—that they were genuine believers—although he entertained the possibility that the actions of some might indicate that they were not true Christians. Paul insisted that Christian profession must be evidenced by Christian conduct. When they passed the test, they would **realize** that Paul, their Christian father, passed the test as well. Their true conversion testified to the truth of Paul's apostleship.

13:7-8. Lest the Corinthians think that Paul's only concern was his own vindication, his prayer was only that they might reject the **wrong** and do the **right** (i.e., that they might repent and reject the false teachers)—even if they continued to reject him as an apostle. Ministry is about other people, not our own status. Paul's concern was with the **truth** of the gospel message (v. 8). His actions—whether stern discipline or rejoicing over repentance—would be in harmony with this truth.

13:9-10. Paul would **rejoice** during his arrival in Corinth even if he was viewed as **weak** by not exercising discipline. He would **rejoice** because the Corinthians were **strong** in the Christian life by means of repentance. This would be an answer to his prayer and their **complete** restoration to Paul. The **reason** for writing this section was to challenge the Corinthians to repent. If this happened, Paul would not need to exercise his apostolic authority in severe discipline. Instead, he would exercise his primary function to build them up.

E. Conclusion (13:11-14)

13:11. Five terse commands summarize the message of the book: (1) **rejoice** in spite of difficulties, (2) make full restoration with everyone, (3) **be comforted** in suffering, (4) live with the same attitude toward the truth, and (5) promote **peace**. To accomplish this, they would have the help of God who is characterized by **love** and **peace**.

13:12-13. The final greeting focuses on community. The Corinthians should be able to **greet one another** with the cultural form of a **kiss**

that is **holy** because it reflected the reconciliation that comes from Christ. The churches in Macedonia likewise showed their Christian fellowship by sending a greeting. There should be no barriers that hinder the uniqueness of Christian fellowship.

13:14. The benediction is Trinitarian. Paul's prayer was that **all** true believers might continue to experience the **grace** that comes from **Christ**, the **love** that flows from **God**, and their **fellowship** with one another that is produced by the **Holy Spirit**.

BIBLIOGRAPHY

Barnett, Paul. *The Second Epistle to the Corinthians*. New International Commentary on the New Testament. Grand Rapids, MI: Eerdmans, 1997.

Barrett, C. K. *The Second Epistle to the Corinthians*. New York: Harper & Row, 1973.

Blomberg, Craig. *1 Corinthians*. NIV Application Commentary. Grand Rapids, MI: Zondervan, 1995.

Bruce, F. F. *1 and 2 Corinthians*. Grand Rapids, MI: Eerdmans, 1971.

Carson, D. A. *From Triumphalism to Maturity*. Grand Rapids, MI: Baker, 1984.

Furnish, Victor Paul. *II Corinthians*. Anchor Bible Commentaries. New York: Doubleday, 1984.

Garland, David E. *2 Corinthians*. New American Commentary. Nashville: Broadman & Holman, 1999.

Hafemann, Scott J. *2 Corinthians*. NIV Application Commentary. Grand Rapids, MI: Zondervan, 2000.

Harris, Murray J. *The Second Epistle to the Corinthians*. New International Greek Testament Commentary. Grand Rapids, MI: Eerdmans, 2005.

Hays, Richard. *Echoes of Scripture in the Letters of Paul*. New Haven: Yale University Press, 1989.

Hughes, R. Kent. *2 Corinthians*. Wheaton: Crossway Books, 2006.

Martin, Ralph. *2 Corinthians*. Word Biblical Commentary. Nashville: Thomas Nelson, 1986.

Scott, James M. *2 Corinthians*. Peabody, MA: Hendrickson Publishers, 1998.

GALATIANS

GERALD PETERMAN

INTRODUCTION

The Roman province of Galatia was located in central Asia Minor (current day Turkey). Acts mentions that during Paul's second missionary journey (Ac 13:13–14:28, c. AD 48) he did forceful—and also controversial—ministry in Antioch of Pisidia, with the result that "the word of the Lord was being spread through the whole region" (Ac 13:49). Because Paul later traveled through Galatia strengthening the disciples (Ac 18:23), Paul's second missionary journey probably included evangelism and church planting there. Galatian churches likely were made up of believers from the cities of Derbe, Lystra, Iconium, and Pisidian Antioch.

Author. The letter twice refers to Paul as its author (1:1; 5:2). As happens in a few of his letters, the closing refers to a postscript in his own hand (6:11; cf. 1Co 16:21; 2Th 3:17; Phm 19).

Date. Dating involves an intricate problem based on geography, on the timeline of events that Paul described in Galatians, and on the mission narrated in Acts. Probably the letter should be dated to AD 49, for the following reasons: First, Gl 2:1-10 is Paul's telling of the famine-relief visit (Ac 11:30). That is, what Paul described in Gl 2:1-10 is not the Jerusalem Council of Ac 15. Second, the churches addressed were in South Galatia (see below), founded during the first missionary journey (Ac 13:13–14:28), which happened in approximately AD 48. Since Paul was shocked that their temptation to abandon the gospel came so quickly (1:6), the time of writing can be placed at around AD 49. Third, Paul came to Christ probably around AD 35, and the events described in Gl 2:1-10 must have occurred before the letter was written. Therefore, the reference to "fourteen years" (2:1) must be all-inclusive—that is, the "three years" previously mentioned (1:18) plus 11 more. This yields AD 49 (35 + 14).

Recipients. There is disagreement regarding the recipients of the epistles. The preferred view is that Paul wrote to churches he planted in South Galatia, though some scholars hold the view that the recipients were in North Galatia. The reasons for holding to the North Galatia theory, and the problems with those reasons, are as follows:

First, Paul referred to preaching to the Galatians "the first time" (Gl 4:13). The comment implies that Paul wrote after he visited them a second time and the second visit could only be to North Galatia (Ac 16:6; 18:23). But the term better could be translated "at first" and be taken as a reference to his church-planting visit. It would then be contrasted with proclamation of the gospel that happens in the letter. Second, Paul passed through North Galatia during the second missionary journey according to Ac 16:6 and 18:23. This is true, but there is no indication that churches were planted. Third, "Galatian" is properly a term for an ethnic group in the north, not south. Paul, however, could have used "Galatian" to refer to the Roman province rather than the ethnic group. Fourth, Gl 2:1-10 and Ac 15 are so similar that they must describe the same event (the issues of Gentiles, Jerusalem, gospel, and circumcision). If so, Gl 2 was written after Ac 15, and the churches written to would have been established during the second missionary journal into North Galatia. But the events of Ac 15 were public, and the confrontation in Gl 2 was private. Thus they are two different meetings not one. Fifth, in Ac 13–14 Luke did not use the term "Galatian" to describe the churches planted. This is an argument from silence. In addition, Paul and Luke could have used different terminology. In further support of the South Galatian position, Paul mentioned Barnabas in the letter (Gl 2:1, 9, 13), implying that the recipients knew him. Barnabas was with Paul in South Galatia (Ac 13–14), but not in the North (Ac 15:36-40).

Purpose. As with Colossians (see Introduction to Colossians, "Themes"), Paul wrote to combat false teaching (cf. Gl 1:6-9; 3:1-5; 5:7-12). Somehow the apostle got news of the trouble (Galatians does not tell how), and he wrote to call the churches back to the true gospel that he had originally delivered. Unlike in Colossians, however, he founded the churches in Galatia himself and was particularly attached to them.

Since Paul was not speaking to the opponents but to the Galatians about the opponents, the source of this false teaching is never fully clarified. We know only one partner in the conversation. But the opinions of the false teachers are hinted at in a few places in the letter. First, some had come to the Galatians offering a distorted gospel (1:7). They probably challenged Paul's authority or perhaps even his apostleship (1:10-24). They required the Galatian believers to take on certain aspects of OT law, including at least circumcision (5:2-3) and festival days (4:10). They did these things with selfish motivations (6:12a, 13) and to avoid getting themselves persecuted for the cross of Christ (6:12b).

It follows that the false teachers could be called "Christian Jewish legalists." First, they could be called "Christian," not in the sense of being truly disciples of Christ (Ac 11:26), but in the sense that they had some degree of acceptance of Jesus. They could not be persecuted for the cross if they rejected Him. Second, they could be called "Jewish" in that they followed the law of Moses. Third, they were "legalists" because they required the Gentile converts to keep the law.

Themes. Several themes appear in the book of Galatians:

(1) *The True Gospel and Paul's Encounter with It.* Apart from Acts, Galatians provides the most information about Paul's life before the first missionary journey. He excelled in Judaism (1:13-14), was zealous for the law (1:14; cf. Ac 22), and had impeccable credentials (Php 3:4b-6). But his life was drastically transformed (1:15-24).

(2) *Gospel, Law, and God's Salvation Plan.* Indicators from the letter show that the Galatians had previously embraced Paul's gospel but were being threatened by Christian Jewish legalists who insisted that they adopt OT practices (3:2-4), including at least circumcision (5:2-3) and certain festival days (4:10). Paul viewed the legalists' message as another—that is, a false—gospel (1:6-9). Thus there is in Galatians, as there is in Romans, Paul's instruction on the role of the law in God's plan, on the gospel as God's grace, and on how the gospel of grace and justification by faith is consistent with God's previous revelation in the OT.

(3) *Jews and Gentiles.* Closely related to the above, in his explanation of gospel and law Paul had to touch on the relations between Jews and Gentiles in God's plan. Though this topic is more fully treated in Ephesians and Romans, nevertheless one sees in Galatians that even though Jesus is a thoroughly Jewish Messiah (4:4-5), He brings blessing to Gentile believers as well as Jewish believers (e.g., the Holy Spirit, adoption as sons). Indeed, it is *because* Messiah Jesus serves Jewish believers, bringing them blessing, that blessing can come to Gentile believers as well (Rm 15:8-9; Gl 4:4-7).

(4) *The Holy Spirit and Christian Life.* Paul reminded the Galatians that one proof of salvation by faith was reception of the Holy Spirit (3:1-5). As was predicted in the OT, He is a promised blessing of the new covenant (Ac 2:33; Gl 3:14; Eph 1:13). Unique to Galatians is the command to walk by the Spirit (5:16; cf. Rm 8:4), and the teaching on the fruit of the Spirit (5:22-23). In common with Romans is the close connection between adoption as children of God and the reception of the Spirit (Gl 4:6; Rm 8:14-17). Paul gave some instruction on what walking by the Spirit would look like in 6:1-10.

OUTLINE

I. Greeting (1:1-5)
II. Introduction: The Statement of the One True Gospel (1:6-9)
III. The Biographical Defense of the One True Gospel (1:10–2:21)
  A. Paul's Motivation and Origin of This Gospel (1:10-12)
  B. Before the Gospel—Paul's Former Life (1:13-14)
  C. The Gospel Broke Into and Transformed Paul's Life (1:15-20)
  D. Paul Preached the Gospel in Syria and Cilicia (1:21-24)

E. Paul and the Jerusalem Pillars Had the Same Gospel (2:1-10)
F. Confrontation in Antioch (2:11-14)
G. Justification, Law, Jews, and Gentiles (2:15-21)
IV. The Biblical Defense of the One True Gospel (3:1–5:12)
A. The Galatians' Experience of the One Gospel (3:1-5)
B. Faith and Children of Abraham (3:6-9)
C. Law, Works, Curse, and Christ (3:10-14)
D. Covenant Promise and the Children of Abraham (3:15-18)
E. The Purpose of the Law (3:19-22)
F. The Coming of Faith (3:23–4:11)
G. Personal Appeal (4:12-20)
H. Analogy—Hagar and Sarah (4:21–5:1)
I. Summary—The Freedom of the Gospel (5:2-12)
V. The Practical Defense of the One True Gospel (5:13–6:10)
A. Not Legalism Nor License but Liberty (5:13-15)
B. The Spirit vs. the Flesh (5:16-18)
C. Works of the Flesh (5:19-21)
D. Walking by the Spirit (5:22-26)
E. Fulfilling the Law of Christ (6:1-10)
VI. The Conclusion: Summary and Farewell (6:11-18)
A. Big Letters in Paul's Hand (6:11)
B. The Legalists' Motives (6:12-13)
C. The Meaning of the Cross (6:14-15)
D. Blessing (6:16)
E. Final Appeal and Benediction (6:17-18)

COMMENTARY ON GALATIANS

I. Greeting (1:1-5)

1:1. An **apostle** is one **sent** or commissioned as a representative of a church (Php 2:25; 2Co 8:23) or of God Himself (as here; cf. Rm 1:1; 1Co 12:28). Paul asserted that his apostleship—and therefore his gospel, see below vv. 6-9—was divine. It did not have a human source (**not . . . from men**) nor did it come via the **agency** of a merely human intermediary. Instead the commission came from **Christ** the Son and **God the Father**. Even here Paul forecasted one of the major concerns of the early part of this epistle: to defend himself against the charge of concocting the gospel message he preached. It was not a novelty he invented; he got it from God. Paul digressed briefly on the Father. As in Rm 4:24, He is said to have brought about the resurrection, which is a crucial element of the gospel (cf. 1Co 15:4).

1:2. Uniquely here, Paul's letter is addressed to several **churches** (on Galatia, see Introduction: Recipients, above). So it is a circular letter.

1:3-5. After Paul's frequent wish for **grace** and **peace** (see comments on 1Co 1:1-3), Paul digressed on the atonement of **Christ**, mentioning two elements. First, Christ's death was as a sacrifice on behalf of His people (**our sins**), and second, it was to **rescue us**, not only from future wrath—although it certainly does that (Rm 5:9; 1Th 1:10)—but also from this **present evil age** (cf. Rm 12:2; Eph 5:16).

As the next verses go on to warn against a false gospel, vv. 1-5 have summarized some key elements of the true gospel: **sins**, **grace**, atonement (**gave Himself**), resurrection, **rescue**, and **peace**. Furthermore, there are the beginnings of Trinitarianism in these verses, for they show both the combined and the unique work of the Father and the Son (e.g., the Father's **will**, the Son's atonement, the Father's work in raising the Son, **grace** and **peace** coming from both).

II. Introduction: The Statement of the One True Gospel (1:6-9)

1:6-7. Although the shift is to a thing (the **different gospel**), it is away from a person: God is the one who **called** the Galatians. In Paul's writings, the call is often seen as God's work of effectively drawing people to Himself (cf. Rm 8:30). But the Galatians were being influenced to move to a **different gospel**. The term **different gospel** appears elsewhere only in 2Co 11:4, where Paul called those who teach it servants of Satan (2Co 11:14-15). For Paul, a different gospel is not a Christian adjustment to be taken lightly, but a satanic distortion to be rejected. Paul's reaction is not as in Php 1:12-18, where the true gospel is preached, although with false motives. Here it is **another** gospel, a completely different kind of gospel—that is, it does not really qualify as gospel; it does not work as the real one.

Although the legalists surely would claim they were not **disturbing** anyone, Paul knew better. The term **some** implies that Paul could not identify the opponents by name. "Disturb" reflects Paul's theological perspective. **Distort** (*metastrepho*) appears only here and in Ac 2:20 in the NT and means "to cause a change of state, with emphasis upon the difference in the resulting state—'to change to, to turn into, to cause to be different from, to transform'" (L&N, 1:155; see also the variant reading for Jms 4:9).

1:8-9. Truth and power rest with the true gospel itself, not with particular people or beings. The language is hypothetical. Though it is impossible, even if Paul or a holy angel were to preach a different gospel, it could not save. Only the true gospel can save. Different gospels cause people to think they are saved when in fact they are still lost. Thus the seriousness of the issue caused Paul to call those who preach a contrary gospel **accursed** (Gk. *anathema*, which in the NT is a thing devoted to destruction; cf. Rm 9:3; 1Co 16:22; compare the verb form in Ac 23:14; Mk 14:71).

III. The Biographical Defense of the One True Gospel (1:10–2:21)

Since the gospel Paul previously delivered to the Galatians was under challenge, he was compelled to defend the gospel and also himself, because he was the one from whom they received it. This defense stresses the gospel's divine origin, its power in Paul's life, and Paul's knowledge of the gospel obtained independently of other apostles. Even though he gained his knowledge independently, he and the other apostles all agreed on it. These points were crucial for Paul to reestablish his credibility with the Galatian believers.

A. Paul's Motivation and the Origin of the Gospel (1:10-12)

Paul asked two rhetorical questions in v. 10a that together essentially convey, "I do not seek to please men but God." Probably a charge brought against him by the legalists was that, to please people, he preached a law-free gospel. As Jesus said, one cannot serve two masters, so Paul said that pleasing people precludes one from serving Christ. Verse 11 gives Paul's primary point: his gospel is divine, supernatural, and revealed. The next few verses support the point that the gospel is not of human origin.

The gospel came when Jesus Christ was revealed (objective genitive, "the revelation about Jesus Christ") to Paul. That is, Christ is the content of the revelation (this is common language for Paul: "preach him," v. 16; "preach Christ," Php 1:15-17), clarified by the encounter on the Damascus road and the three days of fasting thereafter.

B. Before the Gospel—Paul's Former Life (1:13-14)

Since Paul was intimately familiar with Judaism and also fully committed and successful in it (**advancing**), he had no reason to give it up. He held no sympathy for the message of Christians, for he **used to persecute** them, then the gospel changed everything for him. Paul reminded them that he was above others in zeal for tradition; cf. Ac 7:58; 9:1-30.

C. The Gospel Broke Into and Transformed Paul's Life (1:15-20)

We find four parts in Paul's continued biographical discussion: the situation surrounding his coming to faith in Christ (vv. 15-16a), a denial that he received his message from others (vv. 16b-17), a brief history related to his relationship with the other apostles (vv. 18-19), and a solemn affirmation that he was telling the truth on the origin of his gospel (v. 20). The denial is primary.

First, Paul presented the situation surrounding his coming to faith in Christ (vv. 15-16a). He was set apart in God's timing (cf. Jr 1:5; Is 49:1-6). God revealed His Son to Paul (cf. 1:12b; 2Co 4.6), so Paul saw Jesus in his revelatory experience on the road to Damascus (1Co 9:1). God selected Paul to preach Him among Gentiles, and the implications of Paul's focus for the Gentile mission were closely attached to this revelation (v. 16; cf. Ac 9:15). His ministry, of course, would be grounded in preaching a law-free gospel.

Second, Paul denied that he received the gospel from men or devised it himself (vv. 16b-17). His primary statement on this second point was that he did not **consult** (*prosanatithemi*, used twice in the NT [here and in 2:6], means "to take up a matter with" someone). What Paul was asserting was his independence from apostolic input as to the content of the gospel. Paul had received a divine revelation, and he did not need consultation with others to clarify the truth. Paul added detail to the account in Ac 9:19-20. Instead of consulting Jerusalem, Paul did ministry in **Arabia**, and then served for three years in **Damascus** (on the edge of Arabia). He had to flee Damascus due to persecution (2Co 11:32-33).

Third, Paul presented a brief history (vv. 18-19) that contains information not found elsewhere about his post-conversion, but pre-missionary journey life. He visited Jerusalem three years after the Damascus road experience. Paul paid a respectful visit to the other apostles, but his primary point was to argue for his independence from them, at least in terms of his reception of the message he preached. This visit lasted only 15 days, and its purpose was not to learn the gospel but to get to know **Cephas** (Peter). Paul did not interact with any other apostles **except James** (cf. 1Co 15:1-7 where only Peter and James are mentioned). James—the first among Jesus' brothers (Mk 6:3)—was an apostle but not on the order of the Twelve (cf. 1Co 15:7). In the broadest, least technical sense, "apostle" referred to recognized workers of local churches (Php 2:25; 2Co 8:23). But the Twelve and Paul were commissioned as witnesses to the resurrection and had unique, unrepeatable authority and power (2Co 12:12).

Fourth, Paul insisted that he was **not lying** (v. 20; see 1Th 2:5; 2Co 11:31). He needed to assert this because he was almost certainly being accused of the opposite by his opponents who, judging from what Paul said in these opening verses, claimed that Paul fabricated the gospel message and lied by claiming he got it from God.

D. Paul Preached the Gospel in Syria and Cilicia (1:21-24)

Paul's departure to **Syria and Cilicia** (modern southeast Turkey and Lebanon) provided further proof of his independent knowledge of the true gospel. He was far away and had no interaction with the other apostles and believers in **Judea**. As a result, he remained **unknown by sight** to them. But they had heard reports about Paul—the one who had been persecuting Judean believers and those in other regions was now **preaching the faith**. This word **faith** (*pistis*) is used by Paul with several different meanings in his letters. It can mean "an individual's trust or reliance upon Christ for salvation" (Rm 3:28; Eph 2:8), "faithfulness" (Rm 3:5), or, as it is used here, "that which is believed," i.e., the content of the gospel or Christian doctrine that one believes (cf. Gl 3:23; Php 1:27). The emphasis here is on the content of faith, while the action of faith (believing) is not excluded. Since churches in Judea were **glorifying God because of** Paul's transformation, it was clear that his gospel was implicitly affirmed.

E. Paul and the Jerusalem Pillars Had the Same Gospel (2:1-10)

2:1-5. Paul began to develop further his relationship with the church and apostles in Judea. **Fourteen years** (v. 1) is the total time between Paul's conversion and his second visit to **Jerusalem** (see Galatians Introduction: Date). The **revelation** (v. 2a) is probably the prophecy of famine given by Agabus in Ac 11:28 for several reasons: First, Ac 11:30 specifically states that Agabus's prophecy led to the sending of Barnabas and Saul (Paul). Second, the economic obligation of Gentiles to Jews was of unique importance to Paul (e.g., Rm 15:26-27; 2Co 8–9). Third, it best fits the timing of events to equate the visit of Gl 2 with the trip mentioned in Ac 11:27-30. As that passage tells, Paul's trip to Jerusalem was designed to supply economic aid to the Jerusalem church. Although Paul never doubted the truth of the gospel that he preached, he **submitted** his **gospel to them** (the church leadership) to learn if there was division between the Gentile and Jewish churches. Unity among believers was so important to him that such a division would make his work **in vain**. The issue could not be agreement on the *content* of the gospel. If it were, and he had found that there was disagreement, that would mean Paul had preached a false gospel for 14 years (that is, his work had been **in vain**).

Paul's gospel was affirmed—that is recognized as genuine (see 2:7-9). The syntax of vv. 3-4a is broken, but the thought should read, "Even though some **false brethren** tried to compel Titus **to be circumcised**, he was not." Titus was a Gentile, and Paul saw no need for him to be circumcised, though it was appropriate for him to circumcise Timothy, who was Jewish (through his mother), as a sign of the Abrahamic covenant and to avoid offending Jews on their missionary journeys (cf. Ac 16:3).

2:6-10. Paul argued that the fundamental difference between him and the Jerusalem apostles was not in the content of the gospel but in the focus of their respective ministries. As Paul said in 1:6-9, the truth of the gospel does not rest with human clout or **reputation**. Nevertheless, even those of **high reputation** did not need to correct or add to Paul's gospel. Both he and they were **entrusted** with the same gospel (cf. 1Th 2:4). But there was a difference: for Peter (v. 7)—as a representative of Jerusalem—the primary audience was Jews (**the circumcised**). For Paul, it was **Gentiles** (v. 8; cf. Rm 11:13). Paul's ministry was not so much approved as it was recognized as God's work (his ministry was the **grace . . . given** to Paul, v. 9a; cf. Eph 3:8). Furthermore, this division of labor was not made begrudgingly, but with peace (they extended to Paul the **right hand of fellowship**, v. 9b). The only request the Jewish leaders made of Paul—something that Paul had already been **eager to do**—was continuing to help the **poor** (an ancient nickname for the Jewish believers of the Jerusalem church; cf. Rm 15:26-27).

F. Confrontation in Antioch (2:11-14)

Paul further demonstrated his independence by his rebuke of **Cephas** (Peter) in **Antioch**. Defining the main characters helps to clarify the situation (though these points are debated among Pauline scholars): **Men from James** were probably Jewish Christians from Jerusalem. **Gentiles** were Gentile Christians. The **rest of the Jews** were probably Jewish believers from Antioch. **The party of the circumcision** was probably a group of non-Christian Jews of Jerusalem whom Peter did not want to alienate. Paul confronted Peter in person (**to his face**, v. 11) on his inconsistent actions because Peter was having table fellowship with Gentiles until "some from James," (vv. 12b-13) arrived. The Jewish people were taught, on the basis of the kosher laws in Lv 11, not to eat with Gentiles for fear of consuming unclean food (see *Jubilees* 22:16, written around 150 BC; 4Q394-399 B.I.1-3, from the Dead Sea Scrolls, c. 125 BC; and Josephus, *Ant.*, 13.245 [13.8.3], which notes that a common criticism of Gentiles against the Jewish people was their insistence on living separate lives, segregating themselves from Gentiles).

On this episode, Michael Bird writes, "Peter's separation signified a denial of the equal status of Gentiles in the messianic community and represented a demand (implied or verbalised) that Gentiles would have to judaize (i.e., undergo circumcision) in order to attain that status. Paul's rebuff to Peter concerns the sufficiency of faith in Christ for the entrance and inclusion of Gentiles as Gentiles in God's saving action" (*The Saving Righteousness of God: Studies on Paul, Justification, and the New Perspective* [Eugene, Oregon: Wipf & Stock, 2007], 131-132). This inconsistency in Peter spread to others and even included Paul's missionary partner **Barnabas**. For Paul this was about Peter not being motivated by his convictions (see in 2:1-10) but by fear (thus, **hypocrisy**).

Paul rebuked Peter because he saw his actions as denying **the truth of the gospel** (Jews and Gentiles together receiving the covenant promises offered by faith in Christ; cf. Eph 2). His rhetorical question acted like a statement: Your previous table fellowship with Gentiles (living like a Gentile) means your present attempts to get them to adopt Jewish practices is going to be fruitless.

G. Justification, Law, Jews, and Gentiles (2:15-21)

This section summarizes all that came before and makes the main points for what comes next. The law of Moses produces neither justification nor sanctification. Furthermore, justification does come to both Jews and Gentiles on the same basis: faith in Jesus Christ.

2:15-16. These verses continue the record of Paul's dispute with Peter. In contrast with **Jews**, here **sinners** refers to those without the law of Moses (**Gentiles**). But neither having the **Law** nor doing the **Law** (**works**) can justify. This word "justify" is so important for understanding Galatians (2:17; 3:8, 11, 24; 5:4).

Sometimes the verb "to justify" means "to show to be right" (e.g., Lk 7:29; Rm 3:4; Jms 2:24). Mostly, however, Paul used "to justify" in a legal sense meaning "to put in a right/just position before a judge," or "to declare to be innocent" (e.g., Rm 3:28; 4:5; 8:30; 1Co 6:11). For Paul the judge is God. So "to be **justified**" is to be put in a right relationship with God, to be innocent before Him. "Justification" is the noun that labels this event. When one is in a right relationship with God one has justification.

Justification comes only by **faith**. Therefore, even though Paul and Peter were in the privileged position of being **Jews**, they (**we**) **believed** in Jesus; and so should every person (**no flesh** has to do with all humanity regardless of ethnicity; cf. Ps 143:2). For emphasis Paul repeated this faith-works contrast three times.

Some translations of v. 16 say "through the faithfulness of Christ" (*pistis Christou*; NET, TNIV margin; cf. KJV). Against this understanding it should be pointed out, first, that what Paul meant by the noun "faith" (*pistis*) is partially explained by the verb "believe" (*pisteuo*; cf. 3:6-7; Rm 4:3, 9); second, if Paul had wanted to mention Christ's faithfulness as the grounds for one's salvation, there were clearer ways to say it, such as asserting that reconciliation or justification is based on the faith or faithfulness that Jesus Himself had, something Paul nowhere explicitly states ("Jesus Christ" is never found as the subject of the verb "to believe/be faithful," and it is never modified by a "faith" word). And third, this expression (*pistis Christou*) is contrasted with the phrase **works of the Law**. Since works of law entail human action, the contrast leads readers to expect that **faith** in 2:16 also entails human action (that is, it is a person's faith directed to Christ) rather than the action of Jesus Christ.

In accordance with the first use of this word in Galatians (*pistis*; see comments on 1:23), 2:16 is better translated "man is justified . . . through what is believed about Christ Jesus." This belief has an intellectual element but must be more than merely intellectual assent. It must be personal trust in Jesus for forgiveness (Ac 10:43) and reconciliation to God (Rm 5:11). The content of this belief has been summarized in 1:3-5 (**sins**, **grace**, atonement, resurrection, **rescue**, and **peace**; cf. 1Co 15:1-3). But it is simpler to read "faith in Christ" and realize that this faith has cognitive content.

2:17-18. Trusting Christ for justification puts one under the new covenant; the commands of OT law are no longer covenant requirements. Therefore conversion can be said to make one free from the requirements of the law, and from a Jewish perspective one who does not keep the law's demands is a **sinner** in the narrow sense of v. 16 (**sinner** = without law). But this does not mean that Christ encourages **sin** (by a broader definition). Instead, and ironically, the **transgressor** (a technical term for one who disobeys the law) is the one who considers the law still obligatory. For in Paul's view it cannot be obeyed, but leads to transgression (Rm 3:20; 4:15; Gl 6:13). Peter at first **destroyed** the law (abandoned its food laws and so could eat with Gentiles), but then later adopted the law again (**rebuilt** it).

2:19-21. Christians are no longer obligated to the commands of OT law because, through their union with Christ in His death (**crucified with**; cf. the comments on Rm 6:3; Col 3:3) they have **died to the Law** (death implies separation—in this case, separation from the law; cf. the comments on Rm 6:10; 7:1-4). Paul's death with Christ was **through the Law** since its curse demanded death (3:10-13). Jesus took this penalty demanded by (through) law; since we died with Him our death happens through law as well.

Paradoxically this death produces real life (**live to God**; cf. the comments on Rm 7:1-6), for under the new covenant what **lives in** the believer is not law but **Christ**. We live a human life (**in the flesh**) but it is lived **by faith**. As in Jn 3:16, the Son **loved** and **gave**; Paul took this love personally (**me**), as should every believer (Eph 3:14-19). Verse 21 implies that Peter's actions (shunning fellowship with Gentiles) have **nullified grace**, because they communicated that **righteousness** (what is needed for one to be right before God; cf. Rm 3:21-22; 1Co 1:30) **comes through** obedience to **the Law**.

IV. The Biblical Defense of the One True Gospel (3:1–5:12)

Paul moved to address the Galatians directly. The verbal link to the preceding is the crucifixion (mentioned in 2:21 and 3:1). Both the Galatians' own experience of the gospel and the OT prove that the different gospel that threatens them is worthless.

A. The Galatians' Experience of the One Gospel (3:1-5)

This first paragraph functions as an introduction to the biblical exposition that follows. The Galatians' own experience began so well—being in full accord with the true gospel and the Scriptures. Hence Paul expressed his dismay at their potential departure from biblical teaching and then exposited OT Scripture to demonstrate that justification by faith is in full conformity to it.

3:1. Showing deep concern for the Galatians, Paul rebuked them sharply (cf. 1Co 3:1). His words (**foolish**, v. 3; 1Tm 6:9; **bewitched**, only here in the NT) imply they were in danger of seriously misunderstanding the gospel. They needed to see **Christ crucified** again, for if righteousness were through obedience to the law, then He was crucified "needlessly" (2:21).

3:2-5. Paul next asked a series of rhetorical questions that drive at one (**only**) all-important **thing**: the Holy **Spirit**. He is a promised blessing of the new covenant (Ezk 36:27; Jl 3:1; cf. Jr

31:31-34) and is not **received** by obedience to **Law** but only **by hearing** the gospel and believing (**faith**; cf. 3:14). Paul said earlier that faith and law are mutually exclusive (2:15-16). Parallel to those two, **Spirit** and **flesh** (divine empowerment vs. mere human strength or effort) are likewise mutually exclusive. Since law and **flesh** are powerless (Rm 7:5; 8:3), attempting to grow in spiritual maturity (be **perfected**) by them is fruitless (**vain**). The Galatians' situation was dangerous, but with the words **if indeed** (v. 4), Paul held out the possibility that the Galatians' suffering would not be **in vain**.

B. Faith and Children of Abraham (3:6-9)

The link with 3:1-5 is the question, "How does one receive God's blessing?" By faith the Galatians received the Spirit (3:2b), a promised blessing of the OT. Likewise, and more important, Abraham received blessing—that is, **righteousness**—by faith.

Probably Paul's legalistic opponents claimed that the blessing of being in Abraham's family comes by way of law. For Paul, on the other hand, those characterized by trust (**those who are of faith**) are Abraham's children. To demonstrate that blessing comes by **faith**, not by works, Paul went to Gn 15:6. It is the first passage in the OT that links faith and righteousness. Furthermore, in Gn 12:1-3 God promised blessing to **ALL . . . NATIONS** through Abraham's family. Since being **BLESSED** like this is available to **ALL** (even **Gentiles**), it cannot come by the Mosaic law, for that had been given to Israel, not the Gentiles. Blessing comes to those who trust God, as Abraham did, not to those who rely on works.

C. Law, Works, Curse, and Christ (3:10-14)

This section helps explain why blessing is not by works. Paul cited key verses of the OT that he treated as basic principles of operation. The point is that, in contrast to the blessing that came to believing Abraham, the law does not yield blessing but a curse (cf. Dt 30:15-20; 2Co 3:7-9). The logic of vv. 10-14 runs this way:

1. The blessing of the **Law** is promised to those who obey it (v. 12, quoting Lv 18:5).

2. What Paul left unstated is that the blessing is never actually received. Instead, those who rely on **works** are not able to do **ALL** that is **WRITTEN IN** the law (cf. Rm 3:20; 4:15; 5:20; 6:14).

3. Thus, all who rely on law are **CURSED** (v. 10, quoting Dt 27:26).

4. The truth of statement 3 above is confirmed. Since Hab 2:4 says that blessing comes by faith (cf. Rm 1:16-17), it cannot come by obedience to law.

5. Through His crucifixion, **Christ redeemed** (*exagorazo* refers to buying someone or something out of a dangerous position; cf. 4:5) believers from the penalty of the **Law** (the **curse**; v. 13 quoting Dt 21:23).

6. Thus the **blessing** that was promised to **Abraham**—including the Holy **Spirit** (cf. 3:2)—comes to all those who have **faith**, even **Gentiles** (v. 14).

D. Covenant Promise and the Children of Abraham (3:15-18)

The flow of thought has to do with promise (cf. 3:14). Paul just said that the blessing promised to Abraham comes by faith. Here we see that the promises associated with the Abrahamic covenant take precedence over the Mosaic covenant (law) because they are qualitatively superior to and temporally prior to it.

Paul used an illustration from normal **human** life: a validated contract (**covenant**, v. 15) is legally binding. It can neither be ignored nor modified. Similarly, the law cannot **add conditions** to receiving the **inheritance** (v. 18; e.g., family, great name, land). The law could not provide these things for two reasons. First, the promise was graciously **granted** by **God** Himself (cf. Gn 12:1-3; 15:18-21). Second, it was made **four hundred and thirty years** before the law came (vv. 17-18; cf. Ex 12:40). For Paul, law and promise could not mix (v. 18a). If the inheritance were **based on** obedience to law, that would **nullify** God's promise.

God made a promise to Abraham and to his **seed**—that is, his family (Gn 13:15; 17:8). **Seed** in the Old and New Testaments is a collective singular. Use of the plural would imply different kinds of seeds (e.g., Mk 4:31). But there is only **one** family of God. Abraham's seed (singular) is Christ (v. 16), and all those "in Him" are part of Abraham's seed (v. 29).

E. The Purpose of the Law (3:19-22)

The Mosaic law may have unintentionally appeared in such a bad light in 3:15-18 that Paul came to discuss its function in the following passage. He gave two questions about law (vv. 19-20, vv. 21-22) and then a statement about its temporary nature (vv. 23-25).

Before getting to the details, Paul's presentation can be summarized in this way. Paul's opponents inappropriately prioritized the Mosaic covenant (the law). This misled the Galatians on the gravity and purpose of the Abrahamic covenant. To correct this, Paul compared these two covenants to a legal will—no small matter because in Paul's world, one's "last will and testament" was binding. The Abrahamic covenant came first (v. 17) and should have the greater weight regarding the means of salvation. But if Paul's opponents were right, then the law virtually cancelled out the Abrahamic covenant. Paul showed that the Abrahamic covenant was not set aside with the coming of the law (3:15-18). God's purpose in giving the law was never that it should save; it was to serve as a "chaperone" (traditionally translated as "pedagogue" or "tutor"; NIV 1984, "put in charge to lead us," 3:24), a male slave who accompanied the sons in affluent families, and who protected them by restricting their behavior until they matured ("held prisoners . . . locked up," 3:23, NIV 1984). The purpose of the law was never to save. It was to enable Israel to know how to avoid sin and thus God's temporal judgment as a corporate people, so that she could begin to fulfill her role in representing Him in the world. Salvation for the Jewish people was always through having a faith similar to Abraham's, not through keeping the law. That faith, following the cross, is explicitly in the atoning death of Jesus Christ. Now that this grace has come, believers are no longer under the chaperone, the law (3:23–4:7).

3:19-20. The law came as a mere addendum (**added**) to the promise in order to bring consciousness of sin (**transgressions**, cf. Rm 3:20; 7:7). Law's role was temporary—**until the seed**, that is Christ, arrived (cf. 3:23). Although the OT makes no explicit reference to **angels** having **ordained** the law, it is the NT view (cf. Ac 7:53; Heb 2:2). The OT speaks of the law being written by "the finger of God" (Ex 31:18; Dt 9:10). It is possible that this is a figurative way of speaking of a mediator. In Ex 8:19, the magicians marveled at the plague of gnats God caused through Moses, who functioned as "God's finger." In addition, in Lk 11:20 Jesus cast out demons by the "finger of God," which in Mt 12:28 is said to be the Holy Spirit. The "finger of God" may be an expression for God acting through a mediator. If this is the case, then it is possible that "the finger of God"—the mediator(s)—involved in the giving of the law represents angels, as the NT writers profess. But Moses is explicitly called the law's **mediator** in v. 19c (see also Ex 20:19; Dt 5:5). A mediator communicated the intentions of each **party**: God and Israel. Thus the law was a bilateral agreement. The words **God is only one** imply that the promise made to Abraham, unlike the giving of the law, was unilateral. In addition, if the law was written down by angels and mediated by Moses, then it is doubly removed from being the direct action of God toward His people, unlike the promises of the Abrahamic covenant.

3:21-22. Law was not **able to**—nor was it intended to—fulfill the promise, that is, to **impart** righteousness (**life**). Instead its role was painful but valuable. Law and all **Scripture** reveal that people are sinful; indeed, they may be described as caught or imprisoned by sin (**shut up**; cf. Rm 11:32). The goal is to demonstrate that there is no hope of escape from sin by means of works, and so to ensure that **the promise** comes only **by faith.**

F. The Coming of Faith (3:23–4:11)

3:23-25. Paul explained further the law's temporary function. **We** (v. 23) refers to Jews. They were **under the law** in that their lives were regulated by it (cf. 1Co 9:20). Here **faith** (v. 23 twice, v. 25) cannot be mere human trust in God, for Paul demonstrated that Abraham already had such faith (3:6-9; cf. Rm 4:3). Rather, as in 1:23, **faith** is the virtual equivalent of gospel. The coming of the gospel ended the rule of law.

The **tutor** (better "guardian" ESV, or even "chaperone"; *paidagogos* is only here and in 1Co 4:15) supervised minors. A child's coming of age ended the guardian's role (v. 25; 4:1-2). Thus, just as a guardian's role was temporary, so was the law's. The middle of v. 24 does not give a purpose statement (NASB: "to lead us" is not found in the original text) but a temporal expression and is better translated by the ESV: "our guardian until Christ came."

3:26-29. In 3:15-18 Paul implied that the legalists brought up the question of who was in Abraham's—and thus God's—family ("seed," v. 16; see also v. 29). Now in the age of the gospel not only Jews are God's children (**sons**; cf. Ex 4:22; Dt 14:1; Hs 11:1). Instead, **all** (that is, even Gentiles) can become children by **faith**. Just as all can become children, so **all** can **belong to Christ** (v. 29a).

Paul used baptism as shorthand for conversion, since when being **baptized** one gave evidence of inner faith by public confession of Christ (cf. Rm 10:9-10; 1Co 12:3), and only those receiving Christian baptism were already believers. As he did elsewhere (Eph 4:24; Col 3:10), Paul's metaphor of changing clothes (v. 27: **clothed . . . with**) illustrates that conversion entails becoming a new person. Verse 28 puts all on the same footing (**one in Christ**); all are equally welcome to come to Christ. Not all are simply equivalent, however. If **Jews**, **Greeks**, **slaves**, **free**, **male** and **female** no longer existed, Paul could not make such comments as "to the Jew first" (Rm 2:9-10), "slaves obey your masters" (Eph 6:5), and "wives, submit to your own husbands" (Eph 5:22). Likewise, if in church ministry there is no difference in role between men and women, Paul could not say that elders are men (1Tm 3:1-2) and that women are excluded from teaching leadership (1Tm 2:12).

Since becoming Abraham's family happens **according to promise**, it does not happen by law. It is God's act of grace received by faith.

4:1-7. Using the illustration of the **heir** as a minor (**child**), Paul further explained that the law's role was for a time when God's people were minors; that time was over. A child, as a person undeveloped, must learn basics first. In this context, the basics learned (**elemental things**, v. 3) were the OT laws as regulators of all life and as revealers of sin. They were further called **guardians** and **managers** (v. 2; Paul used the terms synonymously). Naturally, a time comes when basics are left behind.

The phrase **When the fullness of time came** (v. 4) does not speak of human events that constrained God. Rather, the Father **set** the **time** in advance. The time's completion (**fullness**, v. 4) was brought about by the coming of the **Son**. His coming is the center of history. The **Son** is fully prepared to **redeem** (v. 5; see comments on 3:13) because He is fully human (**born**) and fully Jewish (**under the Law** is the position of a Jewish person, Rm 2:12; 1Co 9:20-21).

Both expressions **those . . . under the Law** and **we** refer to Jews. **Adoption** into God's family was originally a uniquely Jewish blessing (Rm 9:4), which now has also come to Gentiles (**you**, v. 6; the pronoun is pl.). Closely related to adoption is receiving the Spirit (cf. Rm 8:14-17). The **Spirit** imparts assurance of being God's children (**sons**) and enables believers to recognize and confess their new intimate relationship with God (**Abba**). Making this truth personal to each reader, there is a shift from the plural (**you** pl.; **our**) in v. 6 to the singular in v. 7: **you** (sg.) **are no longer a slave**. Paul switched easily from **child** (vv. 1, 3) to **son** (vv. 6-7) since in this context the terms are not gender specific (cf. 3:28; Rm 8:14-16).

4:8-11. Coming to **know God** is the language of conversion (Jn 17:3); **did not know God** is said of the unconverted or pagans (Jr 5:4; 1Th 4:5). Before Christ (**at that time**) the Galatians were **slaves** to what they wrongly thought were gods (**no gods**; cf. 1Co 8:5). All that changed. Paul did not correct himself in v 9; instead of **rather**, it is better to read "more importantly." That is, the Galatians' change from ignorance to knowing comes at God's initiative.

Although the two situations are different in many ways, Paul drew a parallel between the Jewish infancy under law (cf. 4:1-7) and the Galatians' previous lives in paganism. He called both states slavery. Both were under **elemental things** (v. 9; see 4:3), and both were unable to bring salvation (**weak**). For the Galatians to return to observing the law was like returning to paganism **again**. The terms of v. 10 (e.g., **days**, **months**) probably refer generally to requirements of the Jewish religious calendar (e.g., Sabbaths, festivals).

In v. 11 Paul did not hint at loss of salvation. The question is whether his initial work (**labor**) resulted in their coming to true saving faith at all.

G. Personal Appeal (4:12-20)

The section is intensely personal, appealing to Paul's past relationship with the Galatians so as to move them back to the true gospel. As such he could assume knowledge of events he and they knew well, but about which we know nothing (e.g., **illness**, v. 13; **sense of blessing**, v. 15).

4:12a. Become is the first imperative of the letter. In keeping with his practice (1Co 9:19-23), Paul became like they were: free from the law. He exhorted them to **become** like he is: dead to the law and alive in Christ (cf. 2:19-21; see also the comments on Rm 7:1-6).

4:12b-16. The first time (v. 13) is better translated "at first" (ESV) and is to be contrasted with proclamation of **the gospel** that happens in the letter. Though impossible to know with certainty, Paul's **illness** could have been ophthalmia, an inflammation of the eyes that could be caused by a variety of medical conditions (cf. v. 15; 6:11). Whatever it was, it caused Paul to stop intermittently in the Galatian region and thus produced opportunities for preaching. Even though his suffering was potentially offensive to the Galatians (**trial**, v. 14a), contrary to expectation, they did **no wrong** (v. 12b) to Paul by despising his **condition** (v. 14a) and shunning him. Instead, they welcomed him with honor (**as an angel** . . . **as Christ**, v. 14b). His presence with them was a joy (**sense of blessing**, v. 15a). They even would have made great sacrifices for him (**plucked out** . . . **eyes**, v. 15b).

The recounting of this very positive history (vv. 12-15) makes v. 16 more pointed. It is not a question, but an ironic, biting statement: "So then, because I preached to you the truth, I have become your enemy!" (author's translation). Paul's strong words were intended to grab attention, show the Galatians the absurdity of what they were toying with, and bring them back to their senses.

4:17-18. Paul contrasted his motivations with those of the legalists. They sought the Galatians falsely, to cut them off (**shut . . . out**) from Paul and his gospel. Paul **sought** the Galatians for their good (in a **commendable** way) both in this letter and when he was **present with** them (v. 18).

4:19-20. Paul displayed directness, emotional transparency, and deep affection. As their spiritual parent (**my children**), he agonized over them as a woman in **labor** (cf. 1Co 4:14-15; 1Th 2:7). For v. 20 the ESV translation ("I wish I could be present") is better. Being **present with** them would grant first-hand information and more time; he could speak *with them* and not just *to them.*

H. Analogy—Hagar and Sarah (4:21–5:1)

4:21-23. On the phrase **under law** see 3:22 and 4:4. Paul could use "law" to mean the entire OT (e.g., Rm 3:19; 1Co 14:21); thus his references here are to Gn 16–21 and Is 54:1. Paul reminded readers of basic facts from Genesis: Hagar was a slave; Sarah was **free**. Ishmael was born through normal human action (**flesh**); but Isaac was born by God's action (**promise**). On Paul's previous contrast between flesh and promise see 3:3, 17-18.

4:24-27. Next, Paul moved to apply the facts from Genesis by way of an analogy (a better translation and meaning of the word than **allegorically**; the word is only here in the NT). Paul was not endorsing allegorical interpretation nor was he denying the historicity of the Genesis narrative of Hagar and Sarah. Rather, he was illustrating his point. What he said earlier by way of logic and exegesis (3:6-18; 4:1-7), he verified by way of a story. For Paul, the two mothers of Genesis—Sarah and Hagar—could easily be compared to two covenants, two Jerusalems, and two types of parentage. First, regarding covenants, Paul already implied that the new is superior to the old; so was Isaac's birth compared to Ishmael's. Second, there is a **present** rebellious **Jerusalem** (cf. Mt 23:37). The city is used to stand for the nation; the nation rejected God and murdered prophets (Lk 13:34-35). Likewise, there is a future righteous Jerusalem (**Jerusalem above**; cf. Heb 11:10; 12:18-24; Rv 21:2). Isaiah 66:7-11 depicts a redeemed Jerusalem as a mother to God's people. Third, there is a natural parentage that leads to **slavery**, to sin; there is a spiritual parentage that leads to freedom. This spiritual parentage happens by God's supernatural work (just as Isaac's birth did), and is as unexpected and joyful as the **BARREN** having **NUMEROUS . . . CHILDREN** (Is 54:1).

4:28-30. Born of **flesh** vs. born of **Spirit** is in keeping with Paul's earlier contrasts. Probably the persecution is to be found in Ishmael's laughter in Gn 21:9 . Those to be **CAST OUT** are the legalists. Paul implied that there is a disjunction between law and freedom.

4:31–5:1. In conclusion, first, Paul reiterated that believers have **freedom** because of their rebirth (parentage from the **free woman**). This rebirth comes about through their Savior's work (**Christ**). Second, he warned the Galatians not to take on the law as a means to acceptance before God. To do so would be to forfeit freedom (**slavery**).

I. Summary—The Freedom of the Gospel (5:2-12)

5:2-4. One **benefit** Christ gives (5:2) is freedom from law (chap. 4). Apparently the legalists did not tell the Galatians that accepting **circumcision** meant **obligation** to obey **the whole Law**. In that case, of course, one has no freedom from the law. Similarly, those who have professed faith in the gospel but **are seeking to be justified by law** have implicitly shown that they consider Christ inadequate; thus, they have turned **from grace** to legalism (v. 4). **Severed** is too strong; better is "alienated" (NIV). Paul was not describing loss of salvation. Rather, he asserted that if they sought justification by law, they were not and could not be saved by grace. They would then be **fallen**, in the sense of leaving behind grace as a means of salvation, so that they would not be saved.

5:5-6. Contrary to the false approach described in vv. 2-4, Paul gave the proper approach. First, salvation does not require obedience to law; it is by the **Spirit** (cf. 3:2-3). It is not by works; it is by **faith** (cf. 2:16). Further, in Paul's letters, first, **righteousness** is often a state of acceptance with God (e.g., Rm 3:22; 4:13; 10:5). Second, **hope**

is often objective; that is, not a feeling but a thing hoped for (Ac 28:20; 2Co 3:12; Eph 1:18). Thus v. 5b can be rendered "we are waiting for the future hope that our present righteousness will grant us." Furthermore, Christian living does not require obedience to law. Thus **circumcision** as part of conversion to Judaism does not matter. What matters is **faith**—ongoing trust in Christ—expressed though **love**. While the NT often views love as an attitude or motivation (Rm 5:7-8; 1Co 4:21; 13:3), here Paul has in mind the other side of love: godly action (1Jn 3:18). Joseph Fitzmyer, in his comments on 1Co 13:1-3, defines love as "a spontaneous inward affection of one person for another that manifests itself in an outgoing concern for the other and impels one to self-giving" (*First Corinthians*, The Anchor Yale Bible Commentaries, [New Haven, CT: Yale University Press, 2008], 489).

5:7. Paul made an appeal as in 3:1-5. While with them, the Galatians were following the proper course. Contrary to NASB, v. 7b does not necessarily speak of successful action by the legalists. Thus v. 7 could be better rendered, "While you were running well, who cut in on you so as to keep you from obeying the truth?"

5:8-10. The word **persuasion**, found only here in the NT, is not a neutral term and is better rendered "false rhetoric." Paul used the metaphor of **leaven** (v. 9; cf. 1Co 5:6) to refer to spreading error: If the legalist's false teaching was left unchecked, it could permeate and harm the **whole** church. Although Paul had fears about the Galatians (3:1-5), he was sure that those who trusted the gospel would come to **adopt** his **view**. In Paul's letters it is not uncommon to find serious concern and also confidence (cf. 2Co 7:16 vs. 11:3). Paul was unsure of the legalists' identity (**whoever**), but sure of their **judgment** (v. 10).

5:11-12. As the legalists we**re disturbing** the Galatians (v. 10), so also they were misrepresenting Paul. Apparently they asserted that, both before and after coming to Christ, Paul preached that **circumcision** was required. In fact, however, as a Christian, he preached only the **cross**. Proof of this is that he was **persecuted** by those who found the **cross** offensive (**stumbling block**).

Finally, Paul sarcastically dismissed the legalists as troublers. As with Jesus' command in Mk 9:43-45, Paul's words calling for legalists to **mutilate themselves** were not to be fulfilled literally. Rather they were meant to stir the Galatians to cut off relations with the legalists.

V. The Practical Defense of the One True Gospel (5:13–6:10)

In this section Paul defended the gospel from the charge of lawlessness by correcting a possible misunderstanding: freedom from the law would lead to an ethical free-for-all. Paul maintained just the opposite: freedom from law (vv. 2-12) allows the Holy Spirit to provide both ethical guidance and power for godly living (vv. 13-21). This lifestyle is characterized by love and service (see 5:6). Paul said that freedom obligated them to **serve one another**, **through love** (v. 13). But where does *love* originate? It is produced as a fruit by the Holy Spirit; something the law could not do (5:6, 16-22; see 6:1-10 for specific expressions of love). Non-Christians cannot replicate such love because they lack the Spirit, are dominated by the sinful nature, and receive no help from the law. Instead, destructive conduct characterizes their relationships (5:17-21). Paul's point was to underscore the futility of living by the law. The law could not save, nor could it lead one to growth in love and holiness.

A. Not Legalism Nor License but Liberty (5:13-15)

Christians have ethical obligations; as Paul said elsewhere (cf. Rm 6:1-15), freedom from law does not mean an opportunity for the "sinful nature" (so NIV; better than NASB **flesh**; cf. Rm 7:5; 8:3-8). **Flesh** refers to a conglomeration of human traits that contribute to one's disposition to sin (cf. the comments on Rm 7:5), the old sin nature. Even the believer still has the flesh (see Rm 8:12-13; 13:14), though he is no longer "in the flesh" (Rm 7:5). That is, he is no longer in the unsaved state under the absolute domination of the flesh as an unbeliever is)—just as he has a body descended from Adam though he is no longer "in Adam" (see the emphases on being "in" and "with" Christ in Rm 6:1-10). Rather than **freedom** underwriting licentiousness, properly used, it results in service to others. If one worries about respect for **Law**, one needs to hear that Christians are never said to "do" or "practice" the **Law**. Instead, when they **love**, they accomplish its real purpose (fulfilling it; cf. Rm 13:8-10), through the Spirit's energizing work.

The comment in v. 15 reveals Paul's assumption that the Galatians had strife. Therefore he warned them that, not only is service required, but also the lack thereof—selfishly harming others—is self-destructive.

B. The Spirit vs. the Flesh (5:16-18)

5:16-17. Paul explained further: since God's **Spirit** and the sinful nature (**flesh**) are opposed, following (walking by) the **Spirit** will ensure that one avoids sinful **desire**, however imperfect that avoidance might be. As in Gl 3:3, there is not a third option. Thus, 5:17c parallels Mt 6:24: one cannot serve two masters. Paul often used the verb **walk**, similar to OT idiom (e.g., Gn 5:24; 2Kg 20:3; Ps 1:1), to refer to a lifestyle (Rm 8:4; 1Co 3:3; Col 2:6; 1Th 2:12). **Walk by the Spirit** is an imperative with a promise. If one walks by the Spirit, then what logically follows from this is that one is not fulfilling the desires of the flesh. The imperative **walk by the Spirit** is based on the fact that "those who are led by the Spirit of God are sons of God" (Rm 8:14, NIV 1984) and "if you are led by the Spirit, you are not under the Law" (Gl 5:18). Believers can walk in the Spirit and not fulfill the lusts of the flesh precisely because of the fact that they have the Spirit. **You will not carry out** is actually an aorist-tense verb, and would be better translated "you are not ever going to carry out" **the desire of the flesh**. The verb indicates that Paul does not expect the child of God to be characterized by the **flesh** as an unbeliever is, because the Spirit is present and working in the believer's life.

There are many spiritual realities that are "now and not yet" for the believer. We are adopted as God's children (Rm 8:15) but await adoption as God's children (Rm 8:23). We are dead to sin (Rm 6:2, 7) but must reckon that it is so (Rm 6:11). Likewise, Christians are led by and walk in the Spirit so that they are not typified by carrying out the desires of the flesh, but neither are they sinlessly perfect since they await the "not yet" of their full and future redemption and the "present evil age" is still exerting its influence. So, indeed, one could say the past (aorist) **you will not carry out** indicates that the believer's life will not be typified, in any kind of a complete, undefined, global way, by fulfilling the lusts of the flesh.

Flesh in 5:17-24 refers to a conglomeration of human traits that contribute to one's disposition to sin, also known as "the old sin nature," traits that even a believer still has as a result of one's descent from Adam, including culpable weakness and also rebellion. For the unbeliever, living according to the flesh is the only option. Both believers and unbelievers have the flesh, and both believers and unbelievers can do the kinds of things in 5:19-21. But if Paul does not expect the child of God to be characterized persistently by the flesh because the Spirit is present and is leading him, then there is a difference between a Christian *sometimes doing* these acts and an unbeliever *practicing* them (see v. 21b).

For (v. 17) provides the basis for Paul's command in v. 16. There is an eschatological battle between the flesh and the Spirit. The believer must take sides on a daily basis ("walk by the Spirit," v. 16). One cannot serve two masters. And these two—the flesh and the Spirit—battle with this purpose in mind: **so that you may not do the things that you please**. That is, if the believer wants to walk in and be led by the Spirit, the flesh battles against this wish. If the believer wants to follow the flesh, the Spirit battles against this wish. But Paul makes it clear in this passage that the fight does not come to a draw. The Spirit does produce His fruit in believers.

5:18. But signals that there is hope in the midst of the conflict between the Spirit and the flesh. If believers are now part of the new covenant—and they are since they have the Spirit—then they are not under the enslaving, unhelpful law (see the comments on Rm 7:7-25, which deals with the powerlessness of the law to help an unbeliever defeat the power of sin). Since believers have divine resources available to them that the law did not provide, they can enter this conflict with considerable optimism. They walk in the Spirit, not under the law, so the flesh is at a disadvantage. And the Spirit leads, i.e., He takes the initiative in empowering and equipping the believer (**you are led by the Spirit**).

Verse 18 does not mean that following the **Spirit** will, at some point, result in being free from all law. Paul has made it clear that Christians are not under the law of Moses (see Rm 7:1-4; Gl 3:23–4:3). However, the NT believer is under the "law of Christ" (1Co 9:21; Gl 6:2; see comment on 6:1-2). Here **law** and **Spirit** denote the two covenantal options under which one might live and be governed, either the Mosaic **Law** or the new covenant grounded in the **Spirit**. The leading of the Spirit is an objective entailment of being converted, as is having one's flesh crucified in 5:24 and being made alive by the Spirit in 5:25. The subjective side of this is the believer following the Spirit's leading away from sin (5:18) and walking in the power of the Spirit (5:16). The law cannot provide such power and motivation for godly living.

C. Works of the Flesh (5:19-21)

5:19-21a. Now (v. 19) introduces practical considerations to assist the believer in fulfilling the command of 5:16. Paul was saying, "Let's be clear: To fulfill this command, you need good theological, ethical, objective input. Walking by the Spirit means avoiding certain things, things that characterize the flesh. In case you wonder what they are, here is a representative list." The list contains matters bearing upon sexual morality (e.g., **impurity**: the defilement brought on by sexual sin; **sensuality**: unrestrained passion); spirituality (**idolatry**, **sorcery** [Gk. *pharmakeia*]: using magic in an attempt to manipulate people, demonic beings, perhaps even God, or drugs to induce euphoric religious experiences); relationships (e.g., **enmities**: various types of hostility; **strife**: contentiousness that causes divisions); and social sins (i.e., **drunkenness, carousing**: being on the prowl for sinful pleasure). **Immorality** (Gk. *porneia*) is a general term for any aberrant sexual activity including adultery, fornication, bestiality, and homosexuality (cf. Mt 5:32; Ac 15:20; 1Co 6:18). For other vice lists see Rm 1:29-31; 1Co 6:9-10. Paul's inclusion of the phrase, **and things like these**, indicates he likely intended the list to be representative, not exhaustive.

5:21b. Paul repeated a solemn forewarning that he previously gave while with them: Those with a persistently ungodly lifestyle (**practice**) demonstrate that they are not currently in the present mystery form of the **kingdom** (Col 1:13; see the comments on Mt 13:10-17) and so will not **inherit** the future **kingdom**—that is, a place in the millennial kingdom and afterward eternal life (cf. 1Co 6:9-10; 15:50; Eph 5:5).

D. Walking by the Spirit (5:22-26)

5:22-23a. The **fruit** image often refers to good works (Pr 8:19; Is 5:1-7; Jn 15:1-8), and does not imply passivity. Virtues can and should be actively pursued (e.g., 1Co 14:1; 2Tm 2:22; 1Pt 3:11). Paul used fruit imagery, however, to emphasize the Spirit's role in the production of these virtues in a believer's life. As we are active in following the Spirit, He, not the law, produces these and other virtues.

Paul's list stresses character (e.g., **patience**: bearing with difficult people or situations while still maintaining one's composure; **self-control**: being restrained, holding oneself back from acting on evil desires) and relationships (e.g., **kindness**: being gracious or generous; **gentleness**: using the least amount of force or power needed when dealing with people). As with 5:19-21, Paul likely intended the list to be representative, not exhaustive (cf. Col 3:12-15). Paul is not espousing works salvation here. These fruit(s) are expressed, however imperfectly, by every believer who has the Spirit indwelling him, and as such testify that the believer in question is destined for the kingdom.

5:23b. This phrase is rhetorical. As Paul said elsewhere (1Tm 1:8-9), law is needed to regulate the ungodly life. The virtuous—those described by vv. 22-23—go above requirements of **law**, and so are not obligated to live by it.

5:24. Flesh (see the comments on 5:16-18) belongs to the believer's past (3:3, 5:17; cf. also Rm 7:5-6; 8:9-13). Although Paul often spoke of being crucified (passive) with Christ (e.g., Rm 6:6; 8:13; Gl 2:19; Col 3:5), the active verb here implies that the phrase **crucified the flesh** is a reference to repentance by a believer—i.e., forsaking the old life. Crucifying the flesh happens at conversion. Jesus was crucified, and believers are crucified with Him (see the comments on Rm 6:2-10). Therefore, in a sense, they have crucified the flesh. Though conversion is a one-time event, there is still the daily need for God's people to consider themselves dead to sin (Rm 6:11). If there is a tension here—and there is—then it is similar to Rm 6. We have died with Christ (Rm 6:2) (a statement of fact) *and* we are to consider ourselves dead (Rm 6:11, a command). The crucifixion of the flesh in Gl 5 is the theological equivalent of dying to sin in Rm 6. The flesh was crucified (that is, we died to sin) when we were converted. Paul used the active verb **have crucified** because he wanted the readers to see that this was a real part of their salvation, that their faith in Christ resulted in this crucifixion. The absolute power of the flesh was broken when they trusted Christ for salvation. This should provide great encouragement in the conflict against the flesh.

5:25-26. To **live by the Spirit** is to have new life—the equivalent of salvation. We could paraphrase 25a this way: "Since the Spirit has made us alive . . . ." It naturally follows that if the Spirit gave life, we should follow (**walk by**) Him. To follow Him entails forsaking fleshly habits (e.g., being **boastful**, **envying**).

E. Fulfilling the Law of Christ (6:1-10)

This section gives more guidance as to what walking by the Spirit looks like. There is movement back and forth between responsibility for oneself (e.g., vv. 1b, 3, 7-8) and responsibility for others (vv. 1a, 2, 6).

6:1-2. All are susceptible to temptation. Thus gentle and circumspect restoration is the proper response when, through weakness, someone falls into sin (**trespass**). At times life's hardships (**burdens**: a heavy weight, whether literal or figurative; Gk: *bare*; cf. Mt 20:12; Ac 15:28; Rv 2:24) are too hard to endure alone. The gospel involves self-sacrifice for the benefit of those who are weak (Rm 5:6; cf. Ac 20:35). Thus for Christians to imitate such behavior, they follow the **law of Christ** (cf. 1Co 9:21). This phrase could refer to the principle by which Jesus Himself lived, to the love command as summary of all law (Lv 19:18; Mt 22:39; Rm 13:8-10), or to the teachings of Jesus as a new Torah that replaces the law of Moses. These three overlap, so one need not make sharp distinctions. The last view seems more likely, however, since Paul knew Jesus' teaching well, and he set up the law of Christ as a contrast to the law of Moses.

6:3. A great hindrance to the love portrayed in v. 2 is a conceit in which one falsely **thinks** he is superior to others in their weaknesses.

6:4-5. To help prevent the conceit warned of in v. 3, one should **examine** (*dokimazo*, test, prove; cf. 1Co 11:28; 2Co 8:8; Php 1:10; 1Tm 3:10) oneself, but only for the sake of self-evaluation, and not to compare oneself to **another**. This self-reflection is called for since each person is responsible for oneself (his or her own **load**, Gk. *phortion*; cf. Mt 11:30; 23:4; Ac 27:10).

6:6. As Paul said elsewhere (1Co 9:3-14; 1Tm 5:17-18; cf. Mt 10:10), the one who **teaches** has the right to economic support. Supporting teachers of God's **word** is a way to help bear their "burdens" (v. 2). Paul often used the **share** word group (*koinoneo, koinonia*) to refer to economic partnership (Rm 12:13; 15:27; 2Co 9:13; Php 4:15; 1Tm 6:18). The people of God have an obligation to provide adequate remuneration for those who dedicate their lives to the ministry of the Word of God.

6:7-8. The proverb about sowing and reaping (cf. Ps 126:5; Pr 22:8; Hs 10:12-13; 2Co 9:6; Jms 3:18) reminds us that actions have causes and consequences. To ignore this cause-effect relationship is to **mock** God. As with 5:17, there are only two paths: flesh/corruption, Spirit/eternal life. The word **corruption** (*phthora*) can refer to literal decay (1Co 15:42; Col 2:22), to moral evils like lust (2Pt 1:4), or in this case to the eternal destruction of hell (2Pt 2:12). Sowing to one's **own flesh** includes such things as attempting salvation by works (3:2a) including circumcision (5:2), the evil deeds of the flesh (5:19-21), envy (5:26), and conceit (6:3) to name a few. Sowing **to the Spirit** includes such things as faith (3:2b), standing in freedom (5:1), the fruit of Spirit (5:22-23), bearing burdens (6:2), and providing economic support for those who teach the word in the church (6:6). If believers sow to the flesh, they will, in this life, reap the kind of moral decay Paul described, though their eternal destiny will remain intact.

6:9-10. Only God's timing determines when the fruit will come from our labor. On the human side there is need for perseverance (to **not lose heart**). While **good** should be done to **all**, Paul placed a higher priority on generously meeting the needs of other believers (the **household of faith**; cf. 1Co 3:9-17; Eph 2:19-22; 1Tm 3:15). While social justice causes are important, the priority must be given to caring for those in the body of Christ.

VI. The Conclusion: Summary and Farewell (6:11-18)

A. Big Letters in Paul's Hand (6:11)

Paul typically used a scribe to write for him (cf. Rm 16:22), but often appended greetings in his **own** handwriting (e.g., 1Co 16:21; 2Th 3:17). While **large letters** may be an indirect reference to a vision problem (cf. 4:15; 2Co 12:7), it is more likely that they draw attention to this closing.

B. The Legalists' Motives (6:12-13)

Those misleading the Galatians had motives that were merely external (**in the flesh**), prideful (**boast**), and selfish (avoiding being **persecuted**). On the one hand, they had some belief in Jesus as Messiah and they welcomed Gentiles to trust Him. On the other hand, they required circumcision and fell short in their own obedience to **the Law** (cf. Rm 2:17-24; 3:23; 8:3). It appears, then, that they wanted to **boast** about gaining the Galatians as converts to Judaism and so avoid persecution from Jews who rejected the concept of a crucified Messiah.

C. The Meaning of the Cross (6:14-15)

Here is sharp contrast. As in Php 3:4-6, Paul asserted that mere externals—**circumcision** or the lack thereof—mean nothing. Instead, for Paul the **cross**—a shameful means of torture and execution—was a cause for boasting. It brought two things: a decisive break from worldly perspectives (**world . . . crucified to me**) and real spiritual life (**new creation**; cf. 2Co 5:17).

D. Blessing (6:16)

The **rule** is the truth of v. 15 and to **walk by** it is the equivalent of walking by the Spirit (5:16). The phrase **the Israel of God** is found only here in the NT (but see Ps 125:5) and probably refers to those ethnic Israelites who will come to believe in Messiah throughout the Church Age. The phrase is almost universally viewed as proving that the Church replaces Israel in God's program, or that the Church is the New Israel. But the statement is brief enough that it is unlikely to be able to bear this much theological freight. On this issue, Robert L. Saucy writes,

> If we see the message of Galatians as a defense not only of justification by faith alone, but also of Paul's ministry of salvation to Gentiles as Gentiles, it becomes extremely unlikely that Paul would conclude his argument by calling Gentiles "the Israel of God." It is much more probable, in view of his strong condemnation of the Judaizers who sought to enslave the Gentile converts, that Paul sought to recognize also the validity of a true Israel. Thus, whether the reference is to Jews in the church who were presently walking according to Paul's rule or to the "all Israel" destined for eschatological salvation (Rm 11:26), it is more in line with the apostle's language, his overall theology, and the message of Galatians to view "the Israel of God" as a reference to Jewish people (*The Case for Progressive Dispensationalism: The Interface Between Dispensational and Non-Dispensational Theology* [Grand Rapids, MI: Zondervan, 1993], 201).

In addition, several other factors suggest that the **Israel of God** refers to believing Jews. First, taking this as a special blessing for messianic Jews fits the normal syntax of the Greek copulative *kai* as a continuative or conjunctive usage (a simple "and" or "and also"). Paul would be blessing those "who follow this standard *and* the Israel of God." This is the most normal way to translate the conjunction. To see this as referring to the Church requires an unusual use of *kai*, translating the word as an explicative ("even"). Then the translation would be a blessing upon those "who follow this standard, *even* the Israel of God." S. Lewis Johnson correctly notes, "We should avoid the rarer grammatical usages when the common ones make good sense" ("Paul and the Israel of God" in *Essays in Honor of J. Dwight Pentecost*, ed. Stanley D. Toussaint and Charles H. Dyer [Chicago: Moody, 1986], 187).

A second argument is based on the meaning and referent of the word "Israel." Of the 73 usages, this would be the only one that would *not* refer to physical descendants of Abraham, Isaac, and Jacob. It is unlikely that Paul decided to use the word in a "spiritual" sense when every other time he used it as literally referring to the people of Israel. It is sometimes argued that "Israel" in Rm 9:6 or 11:26 refers to the Church as the spiritual Israel, but see the comments there.

Third, understanding the "Israel of God" to refer to the faithful Jewish remnant would fit the context in a far better way. At the end of the epistle, having rebuked those who were demanding circumcision in addition to faith as a requirement for justification before God, Paul certainly wanted to bless everyone in Galatia who supported his teaching. Since some might have viewed Paul's sharp rebuke as attacking all Jewish believers, Paul added a specific blessing. This one was not just for those who accepted his teaching, but also for the Jewish believers who agreed with him. They were "the Israel of God," the loyal Jewish remnant of Israel (Johnson, "Paul and the Israel of God," 192).

E. Final Appeal and Benediction (6:17-18)

As an appeal to his authority and dedicated service, Paul called the scars he acquired from ministry (cf. 2Co 11:23-30) **marks** (Gk. *stigma*; only here in NT) that show he was owned by **Jesus**. Throughout the letter **grace** and legalism are starkly contrasted (e.g., 1:6-9, 14-16; 2:15-16; 3:1-5). Just as Paul began with the letter with a prayer for **grace** (1:3), so here he ended likewise (cf. 1Co 16:23; 2Co 13:14; Php 4:23).

BIBLIOGRAPHY

Anders, Max. *Galatians, Ephesians, Philippians, Colossians.* The Holman New Testament Commentary. Nashville: Holman Reference, 1999.

Fitzmyer, Joseph. *First Corinthians.* The Anchor Yale Bible. New Haven, CT: Yale University Press, 2008.

Fung, Ronald R. K. *The Epistle to the Galatians.* Grand Rapids, MI: Eerdmans, 1988.

George, Timothy. *Galatians.* The New American Commentary. Nashville: Broadman & Holman, 1994.

Johnson, S. Lewis, Jr. "Paul and the Israel of God." In *Essays in Honor of J. Dwight Pentecost,* edited by Stanley D. Toussaint and Charles H. Dyer. Chicago: Moody, 1986.

MacArthur, John. *Galatians.* The MacArthur New Testament Commentary. Chicago: Moody, 1987.

McKnight, Scot. *Galatians.* The NIV Application Commentary. Grand Rapids, MI: Zondervan, 1995.

Schreiner, Thomas R. *Galatians.* Zondervan Exegetical Commentary on the New Testament. Grand Rapids, MI: Zondervan, 2010.

Witherington III, Ben. *Grace in Galatia: A Commentary on Paul's Letter to the Galatians.* Grand Rapids, MI: Eerdmans, 1998.

EPHESIANS

GERALD PETERMAN

INTRODUCTION

Author. The writer of Ephesians identifies himself as Paul, an apostle of Christ Jesus by the will of God (see 1Co 1:1; Col 1:1). Apostle is his preferred title (Rm 1:1; 2Co 1:1; 1–2Tm), although in some letters he refers to himself as a slave (Php 1:1) and in others simply as Paul (1–2Th).

Date. The letter to the Ephesians is called a Prison Epistle (along with Philippians, Colossians, and Philemon) because it refers to Paul's chains (6:20; cf. Php 1:13; Col 4:3; Phm 9, 13), and to his being the Lord's prisoner (3:1; 4:1). Unlike other letters (e.g., Col 4:10), however, in Ephesians he mentions no fellow prisoners. Thus, Paul was incarcerated at the time. He could have written during his two-year Caesarean imprisonment (Ac 23:23-33; 24:47). Yet, Paul probably wrote while under house arrest in Rome (Ac 28:30). First, there are many similarities of content and wording between Ephesians and Colossians, suggesting that they were written near the same time, and Colossians was most likely written from Rome (see Introduction to Colossians). Furthermore, Tychicus delivers both letters (Eph 6:21-22; Col 4:7-9). Rome fits well with the large number of coworkers mentioned in Col 4:10-14, as compared to Caesarea's relative smallness. If written from Rome, Paul penned the letter around AD 60–62.

Recipients. Is this letter sent to Ephesus, where according to Acts (20:31) Paul spent three years doing ministry? If so, it appears rather general and impersonal, differing significantly from Paul's other letters, which are filled with references to specific needs or issues in the congregation (e.g., 1Co 7:1; 2Th 3:11-13). In addition, first, Eph 3:1-7 seems to assume that the readers are not familiar with Paul's calling and ministry. Second, as the marginal notes of most Bibles show, many ancient manuscripts of the letter do not contain the words "at Ephesus" (1:1). As a result, it is probably best to view Ephesians as a letter intended for all Christians in Asia Minor, with Ephesus being the primary or first recipient.

As for Ephesus itself, it was a port city in western Asia Minor, made the capital of the region by Emperor Augustus in 27 BC. With a population probably above 250,000, it was the most important city in the region. Thus it was a natural choice for Paul's church-planting ministry. Acts 19:10 reports that Paul's work there was so effective that after two years all who lived in Asia heard the word of the Lord, both Jews and Greeks. Paul's time in Ephesus spanned approximately AD 52–55.

Themes.

(1) *Unity of the Church.* All believers have a God-given unity, which they should recognize and seek to maintain (4:1-6). Their position as members of one another means laying aside falsehood and speaking truth with each other (4:25). Among Paul's letters, Ephesians is second only to Romans in its attention to Gentiles. Because of amazing grace, they share in blessings once enjoyed only by Israel (2:11-22).

(2) *Exaltation of Christ Rather Than His Suffering.* Although Paul referred to Christ's cross and blood (1:7; 2:13, 16), in Ephesians he does not use the verb meaning "crucify" (cf. 1Co 1:23; 2Co 13:4; Gl 3:1) or words for Christ's afflictions (cf. 2Co 1:5; Col 1:24; Ac 3:18). Instead Paul emphasizes Christ's exalted state: resurrected, glorified, and seated at God's right hand (Eph 1:20-23). All things have been subjected to this exalted Savior (1:22).

(3) *Community Life and Ethics.* Nearly half the letter treats how believers should live together and before the world. Very important is the address to wives and husbands (5:22-33), unique in the NT for its length and its treatment of marriage as a picture of Christ and the Church. Also there appear exhortations to community

love and harmony (4:25-32), to purity of lifestyle (5:1-14), and to the proper relationship between slaves and masters (6:5-9). "Be filled with the Spirit" (5:18) is a command unique to Ephesians.

(4) *Realized (vs. Future) Eschatology.* In the NT we find reference both to blessings already gained or realized and to those still future. For example, believers have peace with God (Rm 5:1) and are His children (8:16) now. But we also await adoption and groan as we wait (8:23). In Ephesians, although Paul made reference to future fulfillments (1:14; 2:7; 4:30; 5:5; 6:13), he emphasized realized eschatology. As further examples, believers already have every spiritual blessing (1:3), have already been raised up with Christ and seated with Him (2:6), are already united as one body (4:4), and are already light in the Lord (5:8).

(5) *Life as Spiritual Warfare.* This last theme is closely connected to the others. Although other letters warn about the enemy's work (e.g., 2Co 11:14; 1Pt 5:8), only Ephesians spends so much time on the defeat of evil forces. Christ has already been exalted far above all rule and authority and power and dominion (1:21). Believers are already God's light in a dark world (5:6-11). Significantly, Paul gave 11 verses (6:10-20) telling believers how to prepare themselves for spiritual conflict. In doing so, he gave a unique passage on the armor of God (cf. Is 59:17; 1Th 5:18).

OUTLINE

I. Greeting (1:1-2)
II. The Praise for God's Purposes (1:3-23)
  A. Blessings in Christ (1:3-14)
  B. Prayer and Digression on God's Power (1:15-23)
III. The Proclamation of God's Purposes (2:1–3:21)
  A. Regeneration—From Death to Life (2:1-10)
  B. Reconciliation—Jews and Gentiles as One (2:11-22)
  C. Revelation—Paul's Stewardship of God's Message (3:1-13)
  D. Reverence—Prayer and Doxology (3:14-21)
IV. The Application of God's Purposes (4:1–6:20)
  A. Applying God's Purposes in the Church (4:1–5:14)
    1. Unity of the Church (4:1-6)
    2. Diverse Gifts for the Church (4:7-16)
    3. New Life of the Church (4:17-24)
    4. Ethical Teaching for the Church (4:25–5:2)
    5. The Church as Light in the Darkness (5:3-14)
  B. Applying God's Purposes in Relationships (5:15–6:9)
    1. General Statement—Walking by the Spirit (5:15-21)
    2. Specific Commands—Household Relationships (5:22–6:9)
      a. Marriage (5:22-33)
        (1) Wives (5:22-24)
        (2) Husbands (5:25-30)
        (3) Marriage as Mystery (5:31-33)
      b. Children and Parents (6:1-4)
        (1) Children (6:1-3)
        (2) Fathers (6:4)
      c. Slaves and Masters (6:5-9)
        (1) Slaves (6:5-8)
        (2) Masters (6:9)
  C. Accomplishing God's Purposes in Spiritual Conflict (6:10-20)
    1. Be Strong (6:10-13)
    2. Stand Firm (6:14-17)
    3. Pray (6:18-20)
V. Conclusion, Final Greetings, Benediction (6:21-24)

COMMENTARY ON EPHESIANS

I. Greeting (1:1-2)

Paul identifies himself as the letter's sender and furthermore as one sent (apostle) by Jesus Christ. He writes to the faithful saints (one group) in Ephesus, giving a wish for grace and peace (cf. Rm 1:7; Php 1:2).

II. The Praise for God's Purposes (1:3-23)

At the outset of the epistle, Paul presents the great wealth that God gives to His people as followers of Jesus the Messiah (1:3-14) and then responds to his own statement with a prayer (1:15-23) that his readers would comprehend **the riches of** their glorious **inheritance** in Christ (1:18).

A. Blessings in Christ (1:3-14)

These verses of praise recount all that God has done for His people in Christ. God is to be blessed (praised) for the blessings He has given (cf. Ps 103). Some themes include:

God's Sovereignty. God, before the world began (v. 4), predestined and elected His own (vv. 4-5, 11). He chooses to reveal His plans (v. 9); He works all things according to His will (v. 11).

The Trinity. The blessings of this section have to do with God's Spirit (v. 3; cf. 1Co 12:1, 7)—and believers are sealed with the Spirit Himself (v. 13). God the Father gives every blessing, and He gives them in the Son. Thus the phrase in Christ (v. 3) or in Him (v. 4) appears 11 times in the paragraph. The Father, Son, and Spirit always work in harmony.

Manifold Grace. Christians are blessed with *every* spiritual blessing (v. 3). Paul's catalog includes election, adoption, blamelessness, forgiveness, knowledge of God's will, salvation, and the Spirit—all gracious gifts (v. 7).

1:3-6. The section starts with a call to praise God (v. 3a) and immediately gives a broad reason: believers have received every spiritual blessing that belongs to the spiritual world (heavenly places, v. 3b; see 1:20; 2:6; 3:10; 6:18). Then v. 4 mentions specific blessings, starting with election. Election is an astonishing blessing, for it has to do with God's loving choice of certain individuals to be His own. It is not dependent on human faith or deeds (Rm 9:10-13), since election happens **before the foundation of the world** (cf. Jn 17:24; 1Pt 1:20; Rv 13:8).

Election has as its goal blamelessness (v. 4b), which is not a human responsibility that flows from election. Rather, blamelessness is God's certain work. From eternity God chose us to be blameless and in history actually makes us so by the death of Christ (5:27; Col 2:22; Jd 24).

A further blessing is predestination: that action of God in which He decides from eternity what will happen (Rm 8:29-30; 1Co 2:7; Ac 4:28). Saying **He predestined us** (v. 5) is nearly the same as saying He chose us. From eternity, predestination's goal was that we would be adopted as sons (Rm 8:29; Gl 3:26) when we believe (cf. 1Jn 3:1).

Furthermore, all these blessings are freely bestowed **grace** (v. 6; cf. vv. 7b-8a). They all come in and through Christ (vv. 3, 5, 6). And it is God's will that His bestowal of grace should lead to worship (**praise**, **glory**).

1:7-10. Predestination is from eternity, but these verses treat blessings that happen in time. First, **redemption** and **redeem** have to do with liberation from bondage or danger (e.g., Israel from Egypt, Ex 15:13; David from oppression, Ps 119:134). All people, however, need **redemption** from sin, for it enslaves us (Jn 8:34; Rm 6:6, 17) and makes us liable to wrath (2:3; Rm 1:18). This kind of **redemption** comes only through Jesus Christ. The NT commonly uses **blood** to refer to Christ's death (see Ac 20:28; Rm 3:25; Col 1:20).

The second blessing is **forgiveness** of sins. Elsewhere in the NT forgiveness is seen as the content of salvation (4:32; Ac 2:38; 10:43; Rm 4:7-8). Forgiveness, received by God's grace, means no longer having to pay for one's own sins.

The third blessing is knowledge of His will. **Mystery** refers to some aspect of God's plan that was previously hidden but that has now been made known. In the NT the word appears most in Ephesians (3:3, 4, 9; 5:32; 6:19; cf. Rm 11:25; 1Co 1:26-27). His will pertains to His plan (**administration**) for all history (**the fullness of the times**, v. 10a). He makes Jesus Messiah the focus of all history and the One in and through whom God restores harmony to all creation.

1:11-12. There is a strong connection between **we** in v. 11 and **we** in v. 12. In v. 12 **we** is defined as those who **were the first to hope in Christ**, meaning Jewish believers. The Gospels and Acts show that Jewish Christians were the first to believe the gospel and receive the Spirit (cf. Ac 13:46). The phrase **we have obtained an inheritance** (v. 11; NASB) translates one word. Because of the word's OT background and because it is passive, it is better translated "we were made His inheritance" (HCSB). That is, believing Israel has begun to fulfill its OT role and has received the spiritual blessing of being claimed as God's portion or inheritance (Ex 15:17; Dt 9:29).

God's goal in choosing Israel as His inheritance was for them to glorify Him. This purpose was hinted at in the OT (Is 43:7; 44:23) but because of disobedience was never fully accomplished. Now this purpose has been fulfilled in the gospel because He is sovereign—that is, He **works all things** according to **the counsel of His will** (v. 11).

1:13-14. But God's inheritance is not limited to Israel. Here **you also** refers to Gentiles, the primary audience of the letter (2:11; 3:1). Because they heard and believed (cf. Rm 10:14), they also have received the blessing of the Holy Spirit. Concerning the Spirit, first, He seals. In the ancient world a seal both protected and announced ownership (cf. Ezk 9:4-6). Thus, God's own are fully secure and will most certainly receive eternal life (the **inheritance**). Second, He is the Spirit **of promise** because the OT promised He would be given (Ezk 36:25-27; Jl 2:28-29). Third, the Spirit is called a **pledge** (cf. 2Co 1:22; 5:5). He is a good faith deposit that guarantees future completion, that is, the redemption of God's possession (Mal 3:17; 1Pt 2:9). Finally, just as with Jews, so also Gentiles are **to the praise of His glory**.

B. Prayer and Digression on God's Power (1:15-23)

The primary idea of this paragraph concerns believers understanding what God has provided for them in Christ (see previous paragraph). This section has three parts: First, an introductory thanksgiving and reason for prayer (vv. 15-16); second, a report on the content of the prayer (vv. 17-19); third, a digression on God's power (vv. 20-23).

1:15-16. For this reason refers to the earlier praise section (1:3-14). Thus two things spur Paul's prayer: God's great past and present work (vv. 3-14), and the Ephesians' current faith and love (v. 15). But Paul still saw their faith and love as God's work, for he gave thanks for it.

1:17-19. Basically, Paul's request was that the believers would comprehend what God had already done (described in vv. 3-14). **Father of glory** does not quote a particular verse but uses OT language (e.g., Ps 29:3; 24:7). **Spirit of wisdom** refers to the Holy Spirit (cf. Is 11:2; 1Co 2:6-16). Having the **Spirit of wisdom** and **revelation** has to do with knowing God and grasping spiritual truth. Although believers are already indwelt by the Spirit (1:13; Rm 8:9-11), they continually need His work in them to understand the things of God (1Co 2:12). What Paul meant by knowledge and insight is conditioned by the OT (1Ch 28:9; Jr 24:7; Hs 2:20). It is not mere cognition but right thinking with right relationship.

There are three things that believers should comprehend: First is the **hope** to which He called them (v. 18; cf. Col 1:5). **Hope** has to do with future certainties such as salvation (1Th 5:8), resurrection (1Co 15:52-55), and eternal life (Ti 3:7). Second, they should know **the glory of His inheritance**. This refers not to what believers receive (that is, what God bestows), but to what God receives: His own people. Thus, Paul's prayer was for believers to know the astonishingly great value God places on them. Third, they should know God's **power** (v. 19). It is incomparable and able to bring believers to glory. This reference to power leads to Paul's digression (vv. 20-23).

1:20-23. God's greatest power is demonstrated in the resurrection and glorification of Christ. This event is eternally and cosmically significant, for it demonstrates both Christ's victory over death and His ongoing authority over all. Christ's position at God's **right hand** (v. 20) is one of favor, honor, and power (e.g., 1Kg 2:19; Jr 22:24; Ps 44:3), and His presence there determines the believer's present and future (see 2:4-7; Heb 7:25).

Christ's position of authority is described four ways (v. 21): (1) above all other thrones or powers (evil forces; cf. Col 1:16); (2) over every other name (cf. Php 2:9-11); (3) all things are under His feet (see Ps 8:6; 1Co 15:27; Heb 2:6-9); (4) He is head, that is, ruling authority, over all things for the benefit of the Church (HCSB), His body (v. 22; cf. 1Co 12:12-27). The second part of v. 23, which says the Church is Christ's **fullness**, probably refers to divine power and glory (see Col 1:19; 2:9) and here is passive. That is, the Church is what He fills with His glory and power.

III. The Proclamation of God's Purposes (2:1–3:21)

By His great power (1:20-23), first, God has spiritually regenerated sinners, transforming them from death to life (2:1-10). Second, He reconciled Jews and Gentiles, moving them from alienation to oneness (2:11-18). Third, He revealed the mystery of the Church to Paul, the apostle of the Gentiles, made him a steward of that message, and authorized him to proclaim it to the Gentiles (3:1-13).

A. Regeneration—From Death to Life (2:1-10)

2:1-3. The first of God's purposes is to transform those who are spiritually dead to become alive in Christ. At the outset, Paul gives the bad news. Life without Christ is separation from God (death) caused by sins. This sinful life is called a way of walking and is in keeping with the influence of three things. First, the **world** (v. 2) has to do with society's ungodly attitudes and practices. Second, the **prince** (v. 2) is Satan, the evil one (6:16) who works in those who disobey God (v. 2). The **air** is another way of talking about "heavenly places"—the unseen spiritual world (see 1:3, 20; 3:10; 6:12). Third, the **flesh** (v. 3) refers to self-centered human nature that craves (lusts for) wrong things (cf. 1Jn 2:16, and the comments on Rm 7:5-6). Each person **dead** in sin (v. 5) is heading for God's holy anger against and punishment of sin.

2:4-7. In contrast to the above, here is the good news. God has *both* holy anger against sin *and also* merciful **love** for sinners (v. 4). Sinners' conversion, described here, contrasts massively with vv. 1-3. Salvation is transfer from death in sin to life in Christ. Note that, first, new life happens purely by God's **grace** (v. 5) and entails rescue from wrath. Second, all happens because of Christ's prior work and exaltation and because God unites believers to Christ (v. 6). Thus, vv. 4-7 look back to 1:20-23. As Christ was raised and seated, so the believer gains a wholly new position of approval and security. Third, as there was a future to sin (wrath), so there is a future to saving grace—yet more grace **in the ages to come** (v. 7).

2:8-10. This section harks back to v. 5, reiterating and expanding on salvation by grace (cf. Rm 3:24). The phrase **and that not of yourselves** (v. 8) refers to the whole preceding statement: a grace-by-faith salvation does not originate with people; it is God's **gift**. Since it is by **faith**, it is not by human effort (**works**, v. 9; cf. Rm 3:20; Gl 2:16). God's goal is to eliminate human boasting (cf. Rm 3:27).

In contrast, while works do not produce salvation, salvation does produce good works (v. 10; cf. Php 1:11). Believers are God's creation (**workmanship**, *poiema*, means "something that is made" and appears elsewhere in Rm 1:20), being created for this purpose: that we do (lit., **walk in**) good works. Without Christ we walked in sin (v. 1); with Him we walk in good works that God predestined (**prepared beforehand**; cf. Rm 9:23).

B. Reconciliation—Jews and Gentiles as One (2:11-22)

In presenting God's purposes for Jews and Gentiles, Paul moves from describing Gentile *alienation* from both God and the Jewish people (2:11-12), to their *reconciliation* to the Lord and the Jewish people (2:13-18). Ultimately, he reveals the *unification* of believing Jews and Gentiles in a new body, namely the Church.

2:11-12. Before Christ's incarnation, Gentiles suffered a terrible plight. First, since they were pagans without any covenant standing before God, Jewish people disparaged them as the **Uncircumcision** (circumcision being the outward sign of the God's covenant with Abraham and all the Jewish people [Gn 17:1-27]). Second, they were alienated in various ways: from Christ (for they had no hope of a Messiah); from the people with whom God was working (Israel); from covenants that spoke of God's future blessing. Third, any hopes or gods they had were false. Paul reminds Gentile believers of this past plight so they might better understand their present blessings.

2:13-18. As happened in 2:4, so here is great contrast. Gentile believers, formerly alienated (far off), have been brought near to God by Christ's death (**blood**, v. 13; cf. 1:7), having now peace with God (Rm 5:1).

Furthermore, the law of Moses created a social and theological **barrier** (v. 14) and **enmity** (vv. 15-16) between Jew and Gentile. Christ's death, by being the one atoning sacrifice for the new covenant, rendered the old covenant (i.e. the law of Moses) inoperative (**abolishing**, v. 15). Christ's goal was not to bring Gentiles into Israel but to create from the two ethnic groups one new humanity (**man**, v. 15), establishing peace between them. Thus Christ, as Peacemaker, is called **our peace** citing Mc 5:5.

NEAR and **FAR** (v. 17) derive from Is 57:19 and in Ephesians refer to Jew and Gentile respectively. Since Jesus' earthly ministry targeted almost exclusively Jews, reference to His coming and preaching **TO YOU WHO WERE FAR AWAY** probably has to do with the apostles as His ambassadors continuing His ministry after Pentecost. As in Rm 5:1-2, peace with God entails also being welcomed into His presence (**access**). But neither Jew nor Gentile now comes by way of law with its sacrifices; both come to the Father by way of the Holy Spirit (cf. Rm 8:15-16; Gl 4:6).

2:19-22. Here four images stress Gentile and Jewish unification in the Church—the one new man—and they start out political: Gentiles are no longer **aliens** (v. 19), but as followers of Christ become **fellow citizens** with Jewish believers in Jesus. This does not mean that the Gentiles become part of the "commonwealth of Israel" (cf. 2:12) but rather that Jews and Gentiles now share a heavenly citizenship in the Church (Php 3:20). Likewise they are members of God's one family (**household**). From talk of a household, Paul moves to a construction (**building**) image (cf. 1Co 3:9-17; 1Pt 2:4-5). Verse 20 could be taken to mean the **foundation** laid down by **the apostles and prophets**, or could mean that **the apostles and prophets** are themselves **the foundation**. The latter is more likely (cf. Mt 16:18), for they were the first proclaimers of the gospel. Although some see the **prophets** as referring to those of the OT, this is unlikely. If Paul had meant OT prophets he would have reversed the order of words (prophets and apostles). Also, he describes "the mystery of Christ" having "now been revealed to His holy apostles and prophets" (3:4-5) indicating that he is speaking of prophets of the Church. Finally, when listing the gifts God gives the church, he mentions both "apostles" and "prophets" (4:11). This is significant in that Gentiles are now being placed into the "one new man" (2:15), the Church, not incorporated into Israel. Christ as cornerstone (cf. Is 28:16) is the absolute standard that determines the arrangement of all the other stones in the building (vv. 21-22).

From the construction image Paul moved naturally to a temple: the place where God dwells and is worshiped. God already dwells in this temple—His universal Church—even though construction is still ongoing (**are being built**, v. 22). Thus Gentile alienation is overcome by joining them to this new creation, the Church, in which Jewish and Gentile followers of Messiah are reconciled together.

C. Revelation—Paul's Stewardship of God's Message (3:1-13)

3:1. Apparently Paul started a prayer but broke it off at v. 2 to digress on God's commission to him on the Gentiles' behalf. (His prayer resumes in v. 14).

3:2-7. This section begins and ends referring to grace given Paul—grace intended to benefit Gentiles. Specifically, this grace came as a **stewardship** (v. 2) and in Paul's letters this word never has to do with money. Here it refers to Paul's ministerial commission (cf. 1Co 4:1-2; 9:17; Col 1:25), which will be spoken of later (vv. 8-12). The mystery (v. 3)—also called the **mystery of Christ** (v. 4)—was revealed to Paul on the Damascus road (Ac 9:1-9; Gl 1:12). **Mystery** refers to some aspect of God's plan that was previously hidden (cf. 1:10) and in this context is virtually equivalent to a particular truth found in the gospel (i.e., Gentile inclusion). Even though the gospel of Christ was not made known to earlier generations, it is no innovation; it was foreseen in the OT (Rm 1:2; Gl 3:8). On the other hand, only in the gospel age is the unification of Jews and Gentiles as equals now revealed.

Paul had told the Ephesians about the mystery **before in brief** (v. 3), probably referring to 1:9-10 and/or 2:11-22. As seen there, specifics of the mystery deal with Gentiles sharing, within the Church, privileges previously reserved for Israel alone: inheritance, family (**members of the body**, v. 6), and promises (e.g., forgiveness, Holy Spirit).

Paul stressed that he did not take this honor to himself, but became a servant of this gospel by God's grace and power (v. 7; cf. 1:19; 3:16). Thus 3:1-8 contains seven instances of the words **gift**, **give**, or **grace** (cf. vv. 2, 7, 8).

3:8-12. Paul probably called himself **the very least** (cf. 1Co 15:9; 1Ti 1:15) because of his pre-Christian history as a persecutor (Gl 1:13). Nevertheless, God gave him grace, which involved a two-pronged task. The first was Paul's preaching to Gentiles (v. 8). He did not preach an abstraction but a person—the Lord Jesus—a person with immeasurable wealth (2Co 8:9). Second, Paul was called to **bring to light** how God had chosen to work His plan. Here, God's plan is called **the administration of the mystery** (v. 9). It refers to the way God manages the Church, called a **mystery** because the complete unity of Jews and Gentiles was **hidden** in ages past but has now been revealed. Thus, the second aspect of Paul's task probably involved communicating the reconciliation of Jews and Gentiles as described in 2:11-18.

Furthermore, this task had a goal: making known God's richly diverse wisdom. Certainly God's **manifold wisdom** (v. 10) is at least seen in the catalog of spiritual blessings found in 1:3-14. The surprising thing in v. 10 is not what is made known, but how and to whom. First, God's wisdom is made known through the very existence of a multi-ethnic Church. Second, evil spiritual forces (**rulers and the authorities**, cf. 1:21) come to see that God is overturning their work of sowing hatred and division. As always, this **eternal purpose** is accomplished through Christ (v. 11).

3:13. For Paul, his commission meant suffering (1Co 4:9-13; 2Co 11:23-33). He suffered for others (**my tribulations**) to bring them the gospel (cf. Col 1:24), which promises eternal **glory** (Rm 8:17, 30; 1Th 2:12).

D. Reverence—Prayer and Doxology (3:14-21)

3:14-15. For this reason looks back to the reconciliation of Jews and Gentiles in Christ (2:11-22). Since in the ancient world a **name** revealed one's character and nature, Paul's prayer is directed to a Father who begets, intimately knows, names, and exercises sovereignty over all people groups.

3:16-19. The prayer contains two basic requests: strength (vv. 16-17) and knowledge (vv. 18-19). God has more than sufficient resources (**riches**) to grant these requests (cf. v. 20).

First, concerning strength: The "inner being" (NIV; cf. Rm 7:22; 2Co 4:16) is parallel to **heart** in v. 17 and refers to the location of the self (intellect, emotions, will). Contrary to NASB, v. 17 is not a goal of v. 16 but an explanation of it. That is, spiritual power is the indwelling Christ. Certainly Jesus inhabits every Christian (Rm 8:9-10). That indwelling is a blessing of conversion. The **dwelling** of 3:17, however, has to do with sanctification. It is Jesus taking up residence in us, making Himself "at home" in us. This happens **through faith**. As we trust Him, He makes us His home.

Second, concerning knowledge: Verses 18 and 19 are parallel. Thus **breadth . . . depth** (v. 18) is a spatial and poetic way of referring to Christ's immense love (v. 18; cf. Rm 8:35-39). Knowledge of His love is *both* intellectual *and* personal (cf. Php 2:1-2), *both* individual *and* corporate. The goal of this knowledge is **fullness**—being all that God wants us to be (cf. 4:13).

3:20-21. The closing doxology encourages readers and praises God. First, with language reminiscent of 1:19 they are reminded that He has the **power** to grant such bold requests and more still. Second, **glory** is given to Him, who alone deserves it (cf. Rm 16:25-27; Rv 4:11).

IV. The Application of God's Purposes (4:1–6:20)

Basically Eph 1–3 treats doctrinal truth. In contrast, Eph 4–6 treats application. The letter moves from what God has done to what Christians should do. The latter is always based on the former (cf. Rm 12:1-2). Paul exhorts believers to apply God's purposes in the Church (4:1–5:21), in their relationships (5:22–6:9), and in spiritual conflict (6:10-20).

A. Applying God's Purposes in the Church (4:1–5:14)

1. Unity of the Church (4:1-6)

Chapters 1–3 described the wealth of God's blessings (1:3-14), calling (1:19), and amazing works of regeneration and reconciliation (2:11-22). Now 4:1 introduces all that follows: in response to God's blessings Christians are to **walk in a manner worthy of** their **calling, or to** live worthy lives. As a word to describe conduct, "walk" is a favorite of Paul that appears repeatedly in this section (4:1, 17; 5:2, 8, 15).

4:2-3. These verses describe a **worthy** life, emphasizing relational terms (patience, tolerance). God, by the Spirit, has already given unity (cf. 2:11-22). Harmony in Christ's body is God's purpose. Thus Christians should live according to God's purpose and strive to maintain this unity.

4:4-6. Unity presupposes basic Christian truths. Christ's body can be only **one body**; each congregation is a local manifestation of it. Likewise God's Spirit is one, by whom all are baptized into one body (1Co 12:13). There is one saving message (the **gospel**), which holds out **one hope**: eternal life.

In the world are many false lords (1Co 8:5). But Jesus is the **one Lord** above all. Since there is **one Lord**, two results follow: First, there is **one faith**—the common belief confessed by all. Second, there is **one baptism**, which unites believers to Christ (Rm 6:2-4; Gl 3:27-28).

Since there is **one God** (Dt 6:4; 1Tm 2:5), He must be the God and Father of both Jews and Gentiles (**all**) in the Church. Thus, He rules over both and works in and through them.

2. Diverse Gifts for the Church (4:7-16)

Here the letter moves from the call to unity and the basis for it, to diverse gifts that each member has for building this unity. The goal of their use of gifts is **to attain to the unity of the faith** (v. 13).

4:7. Within this unity **each one** performs service that is enabled by Christ's **grace**. He gives grace—that is, grants spiritual giftedness—just as He wills (cf. 1Co 12:11).

4:8-10. Paul cited Ps 68 (at 4:8) because Jesus' victory and exaltation is another example of God's triumph, similar to the one in the psalm. Probably also, his use of the psalm is informed by Nm 18:6-14, where God gave Levites and priests as servants to His people.

Some traditions take v. 9 as referring to a descent into hell (based on a misunderstanding of 1Pt 3:19) but more likely it refers to the incarnation. Jesus ascended (was exalted after resurrection); before that He descended; that is, He became flesh (Jn 1:14). The **lower parts of the earth** refer to earth itself (like saying "the city *of* Chicago," where "the city" is "Chicago").

The result of Christ's exaltation (cf. Php 2:9-11) is that He **might fill all things** (v. 10). The filling is not spatial, but in light of 1:23 and Php 2:9-11 refers to exercising sovereignty.

4:11-13. While exercising this sovereignty, Christ distributes gifts. Spiritual gift lists appear in Rm 12:6-8; 1Co 12:8-10, 28-30; and 1Pt 4:10-11. Each list is representative, not exhaustive. Uniquely, v. 11 mentions **pastors** (lit., "shepherds" cf. Jr 23:1-2; 1Pt 5:2). Unlike 1Co 12, gifts in Ephesians are people who qualify (NASB **equipping**, v. 12) God's people to perform service that builds the Church (**body**, v. 12). This building has three overlapping goals: first, a two-aspect unity (**faith** and **knowledge**, v. 13); second, maturity (v. 14); and third, Christlikeness (vv. 15-16; cf. "fullness" in 3:19). Verse 13 gives a temporal limit, not to certain gifts, but to the building process itself. The process goes on until, at the return of Christ, the whole Church reaches unity.

4:14-16. Maturity is described two ways. First, in light of v. 14, it is stable in the vital realm of doctrinal truth. Second, in contrast to the malicious motives of false teaching, maturity is motivated by **love** (v. 15) and proclaims truth (better than **speaking the truth**, v. 15; cf. Gl 4:16). By proclaiming truth believers grow in Christlikeness (growing into Him; cf. 2Th 1:3; Col 1:10). This is not simply individualistic; the goal is the growth of the whole **body** (v. 16c).

3. New Life of the Church (4:17-24)

These verses further call readers to a worthy life (cf. 4:1-3), asserting that it is not like the old life (v. 22)—it is new life (vv. 23-24). The redundant expression **say, and affirm** (v. 17a) stresses the call's importance.

4:17-19. First, there is a description of what a worthy life is not: the readers *are* Gentiles but must not *live like* pagans (lit., Gentiles). Their former life included mental and spiritual error (**darkened** . . . **ignorance**), alienation from God (cf. 2:12; Col 1:21), stubborn rejection of truth (**hardness** . . . **callous**), and moral corruption (**impurity**). Ignorance of God leads to various sorts of immoral practice.

4:20-24. Second, there is a description of what a worthy life is: it is personal since it involves a responsibility to **learn Christ** (only here in NT). To learn Him entails receiving Him (cf. Col 2:6), listening to Him, and welcoming His **truth** (cf. Jn 14:6), and developing a whole new way of thinking (**mind**; cf. Rm 12:2). Though followers of Christ are already made new (2Co 5:17), they are commanded to **put on the new self** (v. 24; cf. Col 3:10). That is, they must apply His teaching to their lives. Elsewhere in Paul a similar tension exists between fact and command. Believers already died with Christ (Rm 6:8; Col 3:3); but they must consider themselves dead (Rm 6:11; cf. Col 3:5). They have salvation, but must put this salvation to work (Php 2:12-13).

Conversely, if the new self is put on, the old corrupted self must be laid aside.

4. Ethical Teaching for the Church (4:25–5:2)

Whereas the earlier paragraph spoke of the old and new life generally, this one tells what new habits should replace old ones. The two paragraphs are linked by the word **truth** (v. 24, v. 25) and the phrase **lay aside** (v. 22, v. 25). Comments on vv. 25-32 will be arranged according to the two primary themes of the paragraph: speech and anger.

4:25-32. First, regarding speech, Paul cited Zch 8:16 (**SPEAK TRUTH**), while urging that lying be replaced by truth. Truth is especially called for since other believers are not strangers nor our enemies but one body (cf. 1Co 12). **Unwholesome** speech (lit., rotten v. 29a; cf. Mt 7:17-18) both harms believers and grieves God's Spirit (v. 30). The Spirit seals us (cf. 1:13-14) and makes us one (1Co 12:12-13). Rotten speech should be replaced by that which builds up and passes on God's grace (v. 29b).

Second, and closely related, is anger. Anger is dangerous (e.g., Pr 29:22; Mt 5:22). Nevertheless, as Ps 4:4 demonstrates, not all anger is sin. But festering or uncontrolled anger (**bitterness** . . . **wrath** . . . **and slander**, v. 31) gives Satan an opportunity to work, for it divides the body of Christ and hinders the gospel.

Paul gave three directives about anger: (1) Anger should be dealt with quickly (v. 26). (2) Anger should be replaced by kindness (v. 32). Kindness is shown in a life transformed from taking (**steal**), to working (**labor**), to giving (v. 28). (3) Rather than bitterness or verbal abuse, we should offer forgiveness.

5:1-2. Receiving grace leads to giving it; so those receiving God's forgiveness should imitate Him (a common theme in Paul: 1Co 4:16; 11:1; 1Th 2:14; 2Th 3:7-9). Here imitation is implicitly defined as loving others. Christ's death, the supreme example of love, is described with words reminiscent of OT sacrifice (Ex 29:18; Lv 2:2; cf. Php 4:18).

5. The Church as Light in the Darkness (5:3-14)

While 4:17–5:2 contrasted the old and new life, this section also gives behavioral teaching that contrasts believers with nonbelievers. The difference is like night and day.

5:3-7. Sexual **immorality** (v. 3; see 1Co 5:1; 1Th 4:3), **impurity** (cf. Rm 1:24; Gl 5:19), and **greed** (Rm 1:29) all involve inappropriate longings. Not only must they be avoided, they must not be talked about approvingly (**named**). Likewise what suits God's people is thanksgiving (v. 20; Col 3:15; 1Th 5:18), while **filthiness**, **silly talk**, and **coarse jesting** (v. 4) do not.

The **immoral**, **impure**, or **covetous** person (v. 5) is not the believer who sometimes falls into these sins, but is the unbeliever given over to such a lifestyle. He is outside the **kingdom** (cf. 1Co 6:9-11), for he is an **idolater** (cf. Col 3:5). The unique phrase **the kingdom of Christ and God** is probably trans-temporal: the habitual sinner is not part of Christ's present kingdom (Col 1:13) and, without repentance, will not partake in God's coming kingdom (cf. 1Co 15:24). The one attempting to deceive the Ephesians with worthless arguments (**empty words**, v. 6) is probably an outsider who blindly fails to see that such sins bring wrath (cf. Rm 1:18; Col 3:6). Avoiding wrath is reasonable motivation for Paul's command: do not partake with them.

5:8-12. Before conversion, believers did not merely *live in* darkness (cf. Jn 12:46; 1Jn 2:9); they *were* **darkness** (v. 8). Now, since they are **Light** (cf. Mt 5:14), their lives should change accordingly. Living as **children of Light** will display godly fruit (cf. Gl 5:22-23), namely, **goodness**, **righteousness**, and **truth** (v. 9). Although these three overlap, the first (*agathosune*, cf. Rm 15:14, Gl 5:22) has to do with interest in the welfare of others, the second (*dikaiosune*, cf. Rm 6:13; Php 1:11) with conformity to God's standards, and the third (*aletheia*, cf. 1:13, 4:15) with following divine reality as opposed to human falsehood.

Verses 10-11 describe three further aspects of such a life. First, living as light means discerning (HCSB) those daily choices that please God (v. 10; cf. Rm 12:2; Php 1:10). Second, it means avoiding sin (v. 11a), for such deeds are fruitless. Third, although at times the verb **expose** can have people as its object (e.g., Jn 16:8; 1Tm 5:20), here it refers to **evil deeds**. Thus, living as light means exposing sin for the evil it is (v. 11b).

5:13-14. In these verses the topic probably is still transformation from being darkness to being light (v. 8a), but with a shift to evangelistic concerns. As believers expose evil, some nonbelievers repent and are transformed from darkness to light. This change—indeed, conversion—is further described as awaking from sleep and rising from the dead (v. 14; cf. 2:1-4; 1Th 5:6). In v. 14 Paul probably brought together a paraphrase of two passages from Isaiah (26:19; 60:1-2).

B. Applying God's Purposes in Relationships (5:15–6:9)

Since 4:1 Paul has treated behavior in the church, but now he discusses personal relationships. First, he treats the topic generally (5:15-21), and then specifically: spouses (5:22-33), children/parents (6:1-4), masters/slaves (6:5-9).

1. General Statement—Walking by the Spirit (5:15-21)

5:15-18. Believers are commanded to live wisely. Wise living is described in three ways: First, it makes good use of **time** in an evil age that is passing away (v. 16; cf. 1Co 7:31; Gl 1:4). Second, it seeks to learn God's **will** (v. 17; cf. v. 10). God's will deals primarily with morality rather than with matters of guidance about personal choices. Third, Paul's wording in v. 18 is unique in the NT, speaking not about what the believers are to be filled with, but about whom they are to be filled by ("be filled by the Spirit," NET). The wise are not controlled by alcohol, but are guided by the Spirit (v. 18).

5:19-21. Here are four subordinate clauses telling how the Spirit's filling manifests itself. First, this filling means instructing and encouraging each other in song (v. 19a; cf. Col 3:16). Second, it means genuine praise (with the **heart**) directed to Jesus (v. 19b). Third, those guided by the Spirit are known for thankfulness (v. 20; Col 3:17). Fourth, the Spirit leads believers to properly recognize and respect (**be subject to**) those above them in authority (v. 21), as shown in the examples that follow. Since not every believer is an authority, v. 21 does not teach that every Christian must be submissive to every other Christian.

Next are three examples of relationships properly characterized by submission and authority (wives/husbands; parents/children; masters/slaves).

2. Specific Commands—Household Relationships (5:22–6:9)

a. Marriage (5:22-33)

The first set of commands pertains to the marriage relationship. Paul addresses both wives and husbands, as well as the mystery of marriage itself.

(1) Wives (5:22-24)

Wives should **be subject** to their own husbands since the husband is an authority (v. 23). **Head** has this sense in 1:22 and 4:15 (cf. 1Co 11:3; Col 1:18; cf. the comments on 1Co 11:2-9). Such subjection, or submission, entails recognizing one's position under someone else in leadership (cf. Rm 13:1). Submission does not imply inferiority, since Christ Himself is submissive to the Father (1Co 15:28). Though Jesus is head, He is also Savior (v. 23b), implying that His leadership is characterized by sacrificial service (as is to be the husband's, vv. 25-28). Both husbands (vv. 25-27) and wives (v. 24) take as their model Christ and the Church (v. 24). Thus, the wife's perspective should be characterized (**in everything**) by such deference.

(2) Husbands (5:25-30)

Although wives are to submit, husbands are not commanded to lead but to love. This love has two bases: Christ's example (vv. 25b-27), and the one-flesh relationship (vv. 28-30).

5:25-27. Christ's love is beyond comprehension (3:19); as He seeks the good of the Church (vv. 25b-27), so husbands must love by joyfully pursuing the best for their wives, even if it entails sacrifice. Christ died to set the Church apart (**sanctify**, v. 26a) as His own. This sanctification is positional, not progressive (cf. 1Co 6:11), and happened by means of cleansing—that is, forgiving sin. The gospel message (**word**) does this spiritual cleansing. Christ's goal is a Church that is morally and spiritually beautiful (**in all her glory**, lit., glorious) at His second coming (cf. 2Co 11:2).

5:28-30. Generally, people naturally care for themselves. Therefore, since the husband and wife are one flesh (see in v. 31 Paul's later citation of Gn 2:24), the husband must love his wife in the same way that he cares for himself. Her good is his good (v. 28b). The same intimacy and care exists between Christ and His body, the Church (vv. 29b-30).

(3) Marriage as Mystery (5:31-33)

Gn 2:24, cited in v. 31, both undergirds 5:28-30 and also reveals a profound mystery (**great**, v. 32). As mentioned at 1:10, **mystery** refers to some aspect of God's plan that was previously hidden but which now, in the gospel, has been made known. While some OT passages mentioned God as husband to His people (e.g., Is 54:5-8; Hs 1–3; Jr 31:31-32), v. 32 makes clear that the **mystery** is the unexpected union between Christ and His Church—being His body—which is pictured in a Christian marriage.

The commands of 5:22-32 are summarized in v. 33. Husbands and wives have distinctive responsibilities: **love** and respect.

b. Children and Parents (6:1-4)

(1) Children (6:1-3)

Honoring parents is crucial (e.g., Pr 6:20; Mt 15:4), and thus Paul called for obedience to them, grounding the call in its correctness (v. 1b) and in the OT (v. 2). The NT does not give a specific age at which this command ceases to apply, but in this context the implication is that those still under parental training (v. 4) are the ones who obey. Probably "in the Lord" should attach to the verb "obey." The sense is "obey as part of your life in Christ."

Although other Mosaic commands gave promises (e.g., Dt 12:28; 28:1-3) this is the first command of the Decalogue that does so. As with similar statements in Proverbs (e.g., 3:1-2), Eph 6:3 does not guarantee health and prosperity but teaches that following a parent's wise counsel helps a child thrive and avoid pitfalls.

(2) Fathers (6:4)

Earlier Paul spoke about parents (v. 1: *goneis*); here he changed the word used in order to specifically address fathers (v. 4: *pateres*). In the ancient world, fathers were responsible for the children's education. Negatively, fathers should avoid things that hurt children and thus cause them **anger** (e.g., humiliation, abuse, tyranny). Positively they should train (**discipline**) them and verbally guide (**instruction**) them in distinctively Christian ways.

c. Slaves and Masters (6:5-9)

In the Greco-Roman world, slaves were considered part of the household. Hence, Paul addresses the relationship between believing slaves and masters as part of his household instructions.

(1) Slaves (6:5-8)

Regarding slavery, it should be said, first, that the practice in Paul's day was much like indentured servanthood: it was temporary and not based on race (Hoehner, *Ephesians*, 801). Second, Paul's commands do not mandate slavery but only regulate it.

With these caveats in mind, Paul put things negatively and positively. Negatively, slaves should avoid wrong motivations such as insincerity or pleasing only people (v. 6). Positively, they should show respect (v. 5), good will (v. 7a), and see their service as directed to God (vv. 5c, 6b, 7b). These commands are based on God's impartial reward and judgment (v. 8).

(2) Masters (6:9)

Just as slaves had obligations toward masters, so also did masters toward slaves. **The same things** refers to the kinds of Christian attitudes seen in vv. 5-8. Masters must not indulge in abusive, tyrannical, or manipulative treatment (v. 9b).

C. Accomplishing God's Purposes in Spiritual Conflict (6:10-20)

The Christian's behavior has cosmic significance. For we interact, not only with people, but also with an unseen spiritual world. Although other passages in the NT mention spiritual conflict (e.g., 2Co 10:3-5; Jms 4:7; 1Pt 5:8), this section is unique in its length and detail.

1. Be Strong (6:10-13)

Living a life worthy of our calling (4:1) means living in God's strength (cf. 1Sm 30:6; Zch 10:12), not ours. Paul mentioned strength/power in his two prayers (1:19; 3:16). Now believers are commanded to live by God's strength, using the armor that God supplies (full armor is only in this paragraph and Lk 11:22).

Regarding the armor, first, God's armor is needed because we **struggle** (v. 12; only here in the NT, *pale* refers to battle or hand-to-hand combat) against evil spiritual forces. The NT informs us that their **schemes** (v. 11; cf. 4:14) can include at least the following: tempting to immorality (1Co 7:5), attempting to deceive (2Co 2:11; 11:13-14), taking advantage of bitterness (Eph 4:27), hindering ministry (1Th 2:18).

Second, steadfast allegiance to the gospel is the goal of having the armor. With it we **stand firm** (vv. 11, 13) and **resist** (v. 13). Both verbs imply attack from the enemy and imply what Paul explicitly stated earlier: believers have already been given victory and every blessing (see 1:3-13 and 2:4-10).

2. Stand Firm (6:14-17)

Paul was probably under house arrest when writing this letter (see 3:1 and the comments on Ac 28:16), and so he used the Roman soldier's equipment to illustrate God's gracious provision for believers. The OT basis for God's **armor**, however, is drawn from Is 11:4-5 and 59:17.

In the ancient world girding oneself (v. 14) is done in preparation for strenuous activity (Pr 31:17; 1Pt 1:13). Thus, in an errant world, it is foundational to be girded with God's **TRUTH**—that Word that He has proclaimed (cf. 1:13; 4:21). Second, **RIGHTEOUSNESS** here is probably positional. **RIGHTEOUSNESS** based on our works is worthless (cf. Php 3:8-9). God offers us the **RIGHTEOUSNESS** of Christ (cf. 1Co 1:30; 2Co 5.21). Third, relying on Is 52:7, Paul commanded that we live ready to proclaim a **GOSPEL** that brings **PEACE** (v. 15). Fourth, **faith** itself is our **shield** (*thureon*, v. 16, refers to a large shield that covered the whole person). When the enemy attacks, our trust in God protects us. Fifth, our **HELMET** is **SALVATION** (v. 17). Confidence in daily battles comes from knowing that rescue from future judgment has already been given to us freely from God (Rm 6:23). Lastly, God's **word** is our offensive weapon, supplied by the **Spirit** (cf. Heb 4:12). Thus Scripture rightly understood and correctly proclaimed turns back evil, destroys strongholds (2Co 10:4), and rescues people from darkness (Ac 6:7).

Although prayer is important for the process described above (vv. 10-17), believers do not "pray" the armor onto themselves. Putting on the armor has to do with our moral choices—our lifestyle—that provide protection against the temptations of the world and the devil.

3. Pray (6:18-20)

In spiritual conflict **prayer** is vital. First, we must pray with **perseverance** (cf. Lk 18:1; Rm 12:12; Ac 2:42). Second, praying **in the Spirit** entails praying by His guidance and according to God's will (cf. Rm 8:26-27), and is probably not a reference to praying in tongues. Third, it is easy to lose focus. We must remain **alert**. Fourth, we should pray not only for ourselves but also for all God's people (**saints**). Fifth, heaven rejoices at the repentance of sinners. Thus, we must pray that the gospel be proclaimed with **boldness** and clarity (vv. 19-20).

V. Conclusion, Final Greetings, Benediction (6:21-24)

Tychicus, one of Paul's coworkers (Ac 20:4; 2Tm 4:12), delivered this letter and so could give personal encouragement and a verbal report (vv. 21-22). Paul closed with a benediction that is longer than most, but that has elements common to them (cf. Rm 16:25-27; 2Co 13:13). It calls on God to bless the readers of the letter with **peace**, **love**, **faith**, and **grace** (vv. 23-24).

BIBLIOGRAPHY

Anders, Max. *The Holman New Testament Commentary: Galatians, Ephesians, Philippians, Colossians.* Nashville: Holman Reference, 1999.

Boice, James M. *Ephesians: An Expositional Commentary.* Grand Rapids, MI: Baker, 2006.

Bruce, F. F. *The Epistles to the Colossians, to Philemon, and to the Ephesians.* Grand Rapids, MI: Eerdmans, 1984.

Hoehner, Harold J. *Ephesians: An Exegetical Commentary.* Grand Rapids, MI: Baker, 2002.

Klein, William W. "Ephesians." Vol. 12. of the The Expositor's Bible Commentary, edited by T. Longman, III, and D. E. Garland. Grand Rapids, MI: Zondervan, 2005.

MacArthur, John. *Ephesians: New Testament Commentary.* Chicago: Moody, 1986.

O'Brien, Peter T. *The Letter to the Ephesians.* Grand Rapids, MI: Eerdmans, 1999.

Stott, John R. W. *The Message of Ephesians.* Downers Grove, IL: InterVarsity, 1979.

PHILIPPIANS

GERALD PETERMAN

INTRODUCTION

Author. Pauline authorship of this letter has not been seriously doubted. Paul refers to himself as the author in 1:1.

Date. The letter makes reference to Paul's imprisonment (1:13), indicating that Paul was a Roman prisoner at the time. The question is: Where was he in chains? Although Caesarea is a possibility (Ac 23:23), the most likely place is Rome, for these reasons: First, Php 1:13 refers to "the whole praetorian guard"; most likely this was the emperor's private bodyguard. Second, the Christians "from Caesar's household" send greetings to the Philippians (4:22); most probably, Caesar's household was in Rome. Third, the incarceration mentioned in Ac 23:35 does not seem serious enough to call forth the martyrdom language seen in Php 1:19-26. If this is correct, then Philippians would have been written between AD 60 and 62.

Themes. While this letter is, in many ways, more positive than others (e.g., Galatians), and although Paul seems to have had a close and positive relationship with them (see below), the congregation was facing significant challenges. Their situation presents several principles and examples that Christians can apply in their lives today:

(1) *Paul's relationship with the Philippians.* In the NT there is evidence of only one congregation supporting Paul financially—the Philippians (see 4:15). Other unique ways he talks about them are that he and they have a partnership in the gospel (1:5), that he has them in his heart (1:7), and that they are his crown (4:1).

(2) *The Christ Hymn.* As Colossians (1:15-20) so Philippians (see 2:5-11) contains a hymnic description of Jesus' preincarnate glory, His taking on humanity, and His humility and death. There is much here for Christology. Paul's application, however, is ethical—Jesus is a model of godly humility, love, and obedience.

(3) *Suffering, a Joyful Mind-Set, and Unity.* Many readers are familiar with Philippians as a joyful letter (the "joy" word group appears 14 times in the letter). But closely related to these words are two others. First, the letter is filled with words relating to one's mind-set or Christian way of thinking. So the believers are exhorted to strive with one mind for the gospel (1:27); to have one mind (2:2; this word, *froneo,* appears 10 times); to have the mind of Christ (2:5); to beware of those with an earthly mind-set (3:19); and to set their minds on virtuous things (4:8). Second, such exhortations to joy and the mind of Christ are called for because the Philippians are encountering some type of suffering (1:28-30) and internal strife (4:2).

(4) *Christian Contentment.* Although contentment is mentioned elsewhere in the NT, here it receives its fullest treatment (4:10-13). Paul taught that contentment was learned, had to do only with our attitude toward finances, and could only be achieved through Christ's strength. Likewise when the subject is mentioned other places in NT (Lk 3:14; 1Tm 6:6-8; Heb 13:5; 2Co 9:8), contentment always has to do with wages, money, food, and clothing.

Background. According to Ac 16:12, Philippi was "a leading city of the district of Macedonia [modern Greece], a Roman colony." It was the first stop for Paul's missionary band after responding to the "Macedonian call" (16:9-10; c. AD 49–52) and Paul's first church planting in Europe. Its population—approximately 10,000—had a large number of Roman citizens, for Emperor Augustus added a significant number of retired soldiers to the city's population in 31 BC. Philippi was proud of its status, being governed by and patterned after

Rome itself. Hints of this appear in at least four places: First, the narrative in Acts implies that Philippi had a very small Jewish population and thus no synagogue (Ac 16:13). Second, some people in Philippi objected that the demands of the gospel were anti-Roman (16:20-21). Third, Paul's reference to his Roman citizenship gained him immediate respect (16:37-39). Fourth, Philippians is the only letter in which Paul used the "citizen" word group ("conduct yourselves" or "live as citizens" in Php 1:27; "citizenship" in 3:20).

OUTLINE

- I. Personal Matters: Paul, the Philippians, and His Own Circumstances (1:1-26)
  - A. Paul's Personal Greeting to the Philippians (1:1-2)
  - B. Paul's Personal Relationship with the Philippians (1:3-11)
    - 1. Paul's Thankfulness for the Philippians (1:3-8)
    - 2. Paul's Prayer for the Philippians (1:9-11)
  - C. Paul's Personal Evaluation of His Circumstances (1:12-26)
    - 1. Joy That the Gospel Was Proclaimed (1:12-18a)
    - 2. Joy That Christ Would Be Exalted (1:18b-26)
- II. Instructional Matters: Paul's Main Teaching concerning the Believer's Life (1:27–2:30)
  - A. Called to a Worthy Life (1:27-30)
  - B. Called to Unity through Humility (2:1-11)
    - 1. The Exhortation to Unity through Humility (2:1-4)
    - 2. The Example of Christ's Humility (2:5-11)
  - C. Called to an Obedient Life (2:12-30)
    - 1. The Exhortation to Continued Obedience (2:12-18)
    - 2. The Examples of Continued Obedience (2:19-30)
      - a. Timothy (2:19-24)
      - b. Epaphroditus (2:25-30)
- III. Exhortational Matters: Paul's Warning and Correction about Legalism (3:1–4:1)
  - A. The Warning about False Teachers (3:1-3)
  - B. The Example from Paul's Life (3:4–4:1)
    - 1. Paul's Previous Life as a Pharisee (3:4-6)
    - 2. Paul's New Life in Messiah (3:7-11)
    - 3. Paul's Ultimate Goal of Eternal Life (3:12-16)
    - 4. Paul's Call to Imitate the Best Models (3:17–4:1)
- IV. Applicational Matters: Paul's Practical Advice to the Philippians (4:2-9)
  - A. Live in Harmony (4:2-3)
  - B. Develop a Christian Mind-Set (4:4-9)
- V. Concluding Matters: Paul's Thankfulness for the Philippians' Partnership (4:10-23)
  - A. Personal Reflections (4:10-13)
  - B. Moral Commendation (4:14-17)
  - C. Theological Interpretation (4:18-20)
  - D. Final Farewell (4:21-23)

COMMENTARY ON PHILIPPIANS

I. Personal Matters: Paul, the Philippians, and His Own Circumstances (1:1-26)

A. Paul's Personal Greeting to the Philippians (1:1-2)

Paul's introduction is typical: the letter comes from Christ's bond-servants (Paul and Timothy), to the saints (= believers) in Philippi, wishing them grace and peace **from God our Father and the Lord Jesus Christ**. Paul's unique inclusion of both **overseers and deacons** (not mentioned in any other letter opening), probably is meant to address both leadership groups and include them in the solution to the disunity of this congregation (see 4:2-3).

B. Paul's Personal Relationship with the Philippians (1:3-11)

1. Paul's Thankfulness for the Philippians (1:3-8)

The first aspect of Paul's relationship with the church at Philippi was his gratitude for them. The bases for his thanks begin at v. 3. Although many translations render v. 3 temporally ("every time I remember you," NIV), the Greek preposition *epi* with the dative case is better rendered causally: "I thank my God for your every remembrance of me." Thus Paul's introductory thanks were related to the Philippians' recent financial support, which Paul later called "concern" (4:10). The second reason for Paul's joyful thanks was the Philippians' **participation in the gospel** (v. 5). This phrase is unique in Paul's letters. They not only believed the gospel but also were working with Paul to advance it.

Since this partnership of a congregation with Paul in the advance of the gospel was uncommon, Paul had unique affection for the Philippians. Having just received their support of him, he expressed his affection for them.

2. Paul's Prayer for the Philippians (1:9-11)

A second aspect of Paul's relationship with the Philippians was his praying for them. Paul's prayers have common themes: love (1Th 3:12), growth (Col 1:10), wisdom and knowledge (Eph 1:17), and good works (Col 1:10). Here Paul prayed that the believers would have a wise **love.** The goal was that they be able to **approve** (or better discern) **the things that are excellent**. That is, a wise love yields discernment. Such discernment, since it enables one to make **excellent** choices, will produce a **sincere and blameless** life (vv. 10-11). The goal, as always, was God's glory. This theme reappears in 1:20 and 2:11.

C. Paul's Personal Evaluation of His Circumstances (1:12-26)

In this personal section, Paul transitions from his own heart for the Philippians to a reflection on his own circumstances. Even though Paul referred to his imprisonment and possible danger, this section is void of complaint. Rather, it sets his life and suffering against the backdrop of the gospel.

1. Joy That the Gospel Was Proclaimed (1:12-18a)

1:12-14. Contrary to expectation, Paul's chains actually worked for the **greater progress of the gospel**. Paul saw this progress in two things: First, **the whole praetorian guard** (the emperor's bodyguard stationed in Rome) and **everyone else** learned that his **imprisonment** was **in the cause of Christ**. These two groups could have included hundreds, perhaps thousands, of unbelievers. Second, many other Christians were stirred up to proclaim the gospel. In Paul's view, the mere proclamation of the gospel must mean that it advances.

1:15-18a. But not all **proclaimed** the gospel with proper motives. Some **were preaching Christ even from envy and strife** (v. 15), hoping they could **cause** Paul **distress in** his **imprisonment**. It is not clear exactly how they intended to cause Paul distress. Perhaps they hoped to create in Paul a sense of frustration and discontent in his restricted circumstances: They were free to minister and thus considered themselves superior to Paul, while he was restricted and therefore they deemed him inferior to them. But for Paul it only mattered that Christ was proclaimed. When he heard of the proclamation, he found great joy.

2. Joy That Christ Would Be Exalted (1:18b-26)

Paul's reflections turned more general or philosophical. Even though as a prisoner he could face execution, all that mattered was that **Christ . . . be exalted** by life or by death.

1:18b-20. From the temporal joy of seeing Christ proclaimed in Rome (1:15-18a) Paul moved on to assert his fixed position of joy that rested in assurance of final **deliverance**. Probably Paul did not have in mind release from chains but, as with Job in the passage to which Paul alluded (Jb 13:16), he looked forward to deliverance before the only court that mattered: God's. This vindication would happen whether he lived or died and fit well with his eager expectation and hope: that **Christ will . . . , as always, be exalted in my body, whether by life or by death**.

1:21-24. Paul summarized and then applied to himself the teaching about his hope in spite of his circumstances. He examined life and death in light of Christ and made the great theological statement: **For to me, to live is Christ and to die is gain** (v. 21). He then unpacked how this is true. First, living is Christ because Paul's life was spent in joyful and **fruitful labor** for Christ's gospel (v. 22a). Thus, he was certain that **to remain on in the flesh**, his continued life, would be a blessing to the Philippians (v. 24). Second, dying was gain because it meant being **with Christ** (v. 23; cf. 1Th 4:17), which is **very much better** than this current human life (v. 23b). Verse 23 indicates that upon death the soul does not sleep until resurrection but rather goes directly into the presence of God.

Paul's statement, **and I do not know which to choose. But I am hard-pressed from both** (vv. 22b-23a), is difficult. Apparently, he was torn by a win-win situation: the divine commission to preach (1Co 9:16) and the desire to be at home with the Lord (2Co 5:8). By saying **I do not know**, he probably meant that he had no specific divine revelation from the Lord regarding these two options.

1:25-26. Nevertheless, exercising his own wise love (1:9), Paul became **convinced** that he would **continue with** the Philippians, and his goal was their growth in Christ. The verses are transitional, anticipating 1:27-30. Paul brought his affairs (1:12-26) and the Philippians' affairs (1:27-30) into the same story.

II. Instructional Matters: Paul's Main Teaching concerning the Believer's Life (1:27–2:30)

Here begins the heart of the letter (1:27–2:18). Contained in 1:27–2:18 are the themes of suffering (1:29; 2:8, 17), joy (2:8, 18), mind-set/thinking (1:27; 2:2, 5), and obedience/work (1:27–2:8, 12).

A. Called to a Worthy Life (1:27-30)

1:27-28. A worthy life is a major theme in Paul (Eph 4:1; 1Th 2:12; 2Th 1:11). His own worthy life was just glimpsed (1:12-26). In 1:27 he calls the Philippians to a similar life.

Even though Paul became **convinced** that he would "continue with" the Philippians, at times he might see them, at other times not (v. 27b; see Rm 1:13; 1Th 2:18). In either case, Paul gave an all-important exhortation: **conduct yourselves in a manner worthy of the gospel of Christ** (v. 27a). This worthy manner is then described in three ways: First, worthy living is not abandoning faith but **standing firm**. Second, it is **striving together for the faith of the gospel**. Such striving must be marked by unity (**one mind**). Here **faith** means that which is believed as in the phrase "the Christian faith" (cf. Gl 1:23; 3:23). Third, a worthy life is seen in not being **alarmed** in any way by **opponents** of the gospel. Paul added that this stark difference of response to the gospel is a **sign** (or "evidence") of the opponents' destruction, but of the Philippians' deliverance—and all this is from God.

1:29-30. Mention of opponents to the gospel brings up the subject of suffering. The struggle the Philippians faced was not a sign of God's displeasure. Rather, just as by God's sovereign mercy the Philippians came **to believe in** Christ, so **also** God granted that they **suffer for His sake** (Ac 5:41; Rm 8:17). Paul could view suffering as a gift because, first, it yields proven character and hope (Rm 5:4); second, it yields future glory (Rm 8:17); and third, those who suffer for the gospel reflect Jesus' life since they are following the path that He took (the sufferings of Christ, Col 1:24; 2Co 1:8-11).

Further, Paul identified with them saying that he and they experienced **the same conflict** (v. 30). They **saw** him experience it before (Ac 16:19-40), and they **now hear** about it by his letter.

B. Called to Unity through Humility (2:1-11)

Paul's next instruction focuses on the need for the Philippians to complete his joy by becoming unified through the only means possible—with humility. Beginning with an exhortation to unity (2:1-4) Paul then gave the ultimate example of humility, the Lord Jesus Himself.

1. The Exhortation to Unity through Humility (2:1-4)

Following on from the call to a worthy life in 1:27-30, Paul called the congregation away from **selfishness** and **empty conceit** (v. 3) and to unity (**same mind . . . same love . . . united in spirit . . . one purpose**, v. 2). This call is obtainable only through **humility** (v. 3) and grounded in the **encouragement**, **love**, and **fellowship** they experienced **in Christ** (v. 1).

2:1-2a. Here a series of conditional clauses ("if" statements) appeal to standard Christian experience: **encouragement**, **love**, **fellowship**, and **compassion**. That is, those who have come to enjoy encouragement, love, and fellowship with Christ and with the Spirit should live in harmony with one another. This unity is described in vv. 2b-4. Paul said **make my joy complete**, since the one thing that would have kept him from perfect joy concerning them would be their disunity.

2:2b-4. Unity has positive and negative aspects. Positively, it is **being of the same mind**, having **one purpose**, in humility passing on the **same love** received. Negatively, it is not **selfishness**, nor **conceit**, nor looking out merely for one's **personal interests**.

2. The Example of Christ's Humility (2:5-11)

To aid the Philippians in obeying his teaching, Paul gave them examples of love and humility (cf. 2:19-30). The greatest example is Christ Himself. Even though these verses primarily set forth Jesus as a model, they also give rich teaching on the deity and humanity of Christ. In a sense, Paul's illustration of Christ is far more exalted and overshadows the point he was illustrating.

2:5. Following Christ means adopting a certain **attitude** or mind-set. The English word **attitude** translates the Greek term *phroneo*, a theme-word in the book, appearing ten times (1:7; 2:2 [twice]; 3:15 [twice], 19; 4:2, 10 [twice]). Usually the word means "to employ one's faculty for thoughtful planning, with emphasis upon the underlying disposition or attitude."

2:6-8. The Son—the second person of the Trinity—existed from eternity in **the form of God** (v. 6a). **Form** sometimes means "the nature or character of something," and does not imply mere appearance; rather, the use of this word later (v. 7) and the parallel with the phrase **equality with God**, show that being in God's form means that Jesus is in very nature God (NIV).

Rather than considering this equality with God **a thing to be grasped** (v. 6b), He **emptied Himself** (v. 7a). The phrase **a thing to be grasped** poorly translates the Greek *harpagmos* (only here in the NT), for it implies one of two false things: (1) that Jesus had no equality with God but could have considered it something to grasp after (to gain it), or (2) that Jesus had equality with God but did not regard it as something to be grasped in order to keep it. Neither alternative is acceptable. Better is the HCSB, which translates *harpagmos* with "something to be used for His own advantage." That is, Jesus does not exploit His equality with God for selfish ends.

When emptying Himself the Son did not cease to be God nor did He give up His deity. He did not temporarily surrender the independent exercise of His divine attributes (as if, with the Trinity, such a thing could happen). Indeed the verse does not say He gave up anything. Instead, One so glorious and powerful did the unexpected: He took on **the form of a bond-servant** (v. 7b). That is, *emptying* happens by *taking on* a new role. He was able to become a bond-servant because of His incarnation (**in the likeness of men**, v. 7c). He further humbled Himself to the point of a most horrible death—**death on a cross** (v. 8).

2:9-11. Those who humble themselves will be exalted (Mt 23:12; Jms 4:10). So Jesus, who humbled Himself to the point of execution, was **highly exalted** by His Father. The Son is granted **the name which is above every name**, which could be the title "Lord" (*kurios*) or more likely "Jesus" (v. 10a; Eph 1:20-22). Alluding to Is 45:23, Paul says that on the last day, either willingly or unwillingly, at the name of Jesus **EVERY KNEE WILL BOW** and **every tongue will confess** His lordship.

C. Called to an Obedient Life (2:12-30)

Just as Christ obeyed, even to death (2:8), so the Philippians were to obey. This paragraph completes the instructional section that started in 1:27. Just as in the previous section, Paul moved from exhortation to example, so he does here. Paul addressed the uncertainty of his being present with them, and so exhorts them to obedience (2:12-18) and then gives living examples of people who live obediently.

1. The Exhortation to Continued Obedience (2:12-18)

2:12-13. Since the Philippians proved themselves—they **always obeyed**—Paul called them to **work out** their **salvation.** This is not working to gain salvation. Rather, as in the expression, "The farmer works the soil," so they were to take what they freely received (**salvation**) and make it bear fruit (cf. 1:11). Though the Philippians are commanded to work, *they* can only do this work because *God* is at work in them (v. 13), bringing about both desire (**will**) and accomplishment (**work**). Thus Paul affirmed two theological truths. First, even though humans make their own choices for which they can be held responsible, God is sovereignly in control. The Bible regularly sets these side by side (e.g., Gn 50:20; Lv 20:7-8; Is 10:5-15; Ac 4:27-28). One does not cancel the other. Second, God works in us to change our affections (cf. 2Co 7:11, 8:16; Gl 5:22).

2:14-16. Obeying and pleasing God will mean that the Philippians avoid **grumbling and disputing**. Paul's goal was for them to prove to be in practice what they already are by grace: **blameless and innocent children**. Such pure character will allow them to shine and hold out (better than NASB **holding fast**) the **word of life**. Compare Paul's commands here to Israel's failure in the wilderness where grumbling among the people was so common (e.g., Ex 15:24; 16:2; Dt 32:5).

Perseverance is necessary (Mt 24:13; 1Co 9:24-27; Heb 6:11-12; 10:36). Thus Paul set his command against the backdrop of Christ's return (cf. 1:6; 1Co 1:8), a **day** (v. 16) when secrets will be revealed (Rm 2:16). Philippian perseverance until that time will cause him joy (**glory**) and demonstrate that his work among them was not **in vain**.

2:17-18. Paul ended the heart of the letter as it began: with reference to his joyful suffering. As he had labored with them in the past (v. 16), so he rejoiced even if his death was considered a minor detail, like a **drink offering** which completes a **sacrifice** (see 2Tm 4:6). The phrase **the sacrifice and service of your faith** could be understood as Paul's **service** for the benefit of their **faith**. More probably in light of 2:30, it is the Philippians' **service** arising from their **faith**.

2. The Examples of Continued Obedience (2:19-30)

This paragraph cites Timothy and Epaphroditus as examples of fulfilling Paul's exhortation to live obedient lives, worthy of being imitated. As earlier, Paul gave Jesus as an example (2:6-11) and later called the Philippians to imitate his example (3:17). So here appear two honorable servants of Christ (v. 29) whose examples should be followed. Additionally, this paragraph resumes Paul's report from 1:12-26.

a. Timothy (2:19-24)

Paul commended Timothy in three respects: First, he and Paul were **of kindred spirit** (v. 20a). They had the same mind-set: the advance of the gospel is what really mattered to both of them. Second, Timothy was **genuinely . . . concerned for** the Philippians (v. 20b; cf. 2:1-4). Third, Timothy's **proven worth** (or better "character" [*dokime*]; Rm 5:3-5) was seen in his humble service with Paul **in the furtherance of the gospel** (v. 22). Timothy was contrasted with others (see those in 1:17) who **seek after their own interests** (v. 21a).

b. Epaphroditus (2:25-30)

Paul hoped to send Timothy to Philippi soon, but in the meantime sent **Epaphroditus**, whom the Philippians had sent to Paul as **a messenger and minister to** Paul's **need** (v. 25b; cf. 4:18). Paul commended Epaphroditus in three respects: First, he called him **my brother and fellow worker and fellow soldier**. Paul considered him a full partner in the work of the gospel (see Php 4:3; Rm 16:3; 1Th 3:2). Second, Epaphroditus had attitudes and emotions appropriate to his work. He had a **longing** for all the Philippians, and had **distress**, not concerning his own illness, but because the Philippians **heard that he was sick**. Thus, he was an example of not seeking merely his own interests, but those of others. Third, **he came close to death for the work of Christ, risking his life**. In this respect he was very much like Paul (2:17), willing to die in service to his Savior.

III. Exhortational Matters: Paul's Warning and Correction about Legalism (3:1–4:1)

Earlier Paul presented positive examples: Christ, Timothy, and Epaphroditus. But not all who claim to know Christ are worthy of imitation. Chapter 3 warns the Philippians against legalistic false teachers: those who claimed to know Christ but taught contrary doctrine, saying that Gentiles must be circumcised before they could be saved.

A. The Warning about False Teachers (3:1-3)

3:1. Since 3:1 is not the conclusion of the letter but its halfway point, **finally** is better translated as further (TNIV). Although the command to **rejoice** appears in 2:18 (see 1:4; 2:17, 28), this is the first time Paul added **in the Lord** (see 4:4). **The same things** probably refer to Paul's previous warnings to them concerning Judaizers (see 3:18).

3:2-3. Paul's three warnings are intense and ironic. First, contrary to common Jewish expression, it is not Gentiles who are **dogs** (contrast Mt 15:26) but these legalistic Jewish false teachers. Second, Paul's circumcision-free gospel did not make him an evil worker; the false teachers themselves were **evil workers**. That is because they turned circumcision—a matter of indifference for the new covenant (Ac 16:3; 1Co 7:19)—into a requirement for Gentiles (cf. Ac 15:1-5; Gl 5:2-6). Third, although false teachers promoted circumcision, Paul said they actually mutilate the flesh (HCSB; better than NASB, **false circumcision**). In contrast, believers are the true circumcision—that is, they experience the long-awaited promise of a circumcised heart (Dt 10:16; 30:6; Jr 4:4; 6:10; 9:26; 31:31-34).

Three more phrases define believers: First, since they live under the new covenant, they **worship in the Spirit of God** (see Jn 4:23; Ezk 36:27). Second, they do not take pride in religious works or heritage but **glory in Christ Jesus**. Third, in accordance with the very nature of saving faith, they put **no confidence in the flesh**—that is, in their physical circumcision or in any human ability to achieve salvation. This is in significant contrast to Pharisaic Judaism, which saw circumcision as a condition for salvation.

B. The Example from Paul's Life (3:4–4:1)

Paul uses his own transformation to dependence on Christ as a lesson for the Philippians.

1. Paul's Previous Life as a Pharisee (3:4-6)

In contrast to believers who put **no confidence in the flesh**, before meeting Christ Paul had reasons for confidence. These reasons included being **circumcised** (v. 5a) in accordance with Mosaic law (**eighth day**; Lv 12:3), a pure Jewish pedigree (**Israel**, **Benjamin**, **Hebrew**, v. 5b-d), being a **Pharisee** (v. 5e), exemplary **zeal** for God (v. 6a; see Rm 10:4), and outstanding achievements (**blameless**, v. 6b). **Blameless** does not mean "sinless." Rather, in accordance with Pharisaic interpretation of the OT, all his contemporaries could have seen his lifestyle and verified that he was a righteous man (cf. Lk 1:5-6).

From 3:4-6 it appears that before meeting Christ, Saul the Pharisee, even though he was persecuting the Church, served God with a clear conscience (cf. Jn 16:2). After the Damascus road experience (Ac 9:1-22), Paul could see that his previous clear conscience was actually blindness and rebellion (Ac 22:3-5; 1Tm 1:15-16; Ti 3:3).

2. Paul's New Life in Messiah (3:7-11)

Upon meeting Christ, however, Paul's perspective was transformed. He counted his previous confidence and pedigree as **loss** (rejected) and **rubbish** (utterly inferior; *skubala*, only here in the NT, refers to dung, chaff, or useless garbage). In comparison, knowing Christ had **surpassing value** (v. 8). Paul abandoned (lost) his previous confidence in order to gain Christ. Gaining Christ is described three ways: first, it is being **found in Him**—that is, being united with Him; second, it is not having one's own **righteousness**—a position of being morally acceptable to God because of human effort. Such righteousness is worthless before God. Third, it is having **the righteousness which comes** through **faith** in Christ (v. 9; Rm 1:17; 3:22).

From the phrase **that I may** (v. 10a), it is clear that there are two further goals of gaining Christ: first, the ongoing intimacy of knowing Christ, His **resurrection** and His **sufferings**. This is a life-long process of dying to self (**being conformed to His death**, v. 10). Second, as in Rm 8:17, suffering with Christ leads to being glorified with Him, so here glorification—that is, **resurrection** of the body (v. 11)—is the final goal of gaining Christ (Rm 8:23).

3. Paul's Ultimate Goal of Eternal Life (3:12-16)

Paul's radical transformation might leave the impression that he reached the goal. Verses 12-16 counter this wrong conclusion.

3:12-14. These verses fall into two sections. First, Paul gave disclaimers. Against his legalistic opponents who claimed perfection, Paul denied that he had **already become perfect** (v. 12) or **laid hold of** the prize (v. 13). Second, Paul gave positive statements. Paul described his current perspective as continuing to **press on** (v. 12), and **forgetting** the past (v. 13a). The past refers not to past failures and sins but to his own legalistic, but very successful, religion. Furthermore he was **reaching forward** (v. 13b) to gain the **prize** (1Co 9:24). All this happened **because** (v. 12, HCSB) he was apprehended by Christ.

The **prize of the upward call** is eternal life—that gift promised by God's call in the gospel. This prize is given to every believer who perseveres. Reflection on this truth and on the tension between divine sovereignty and human responsibility yields two conclusions. First, although by the grace of God the condition of salvation is simple trust (e.g., Ac 16:31), the NT repeatedly affirms that all those who believe (note the present tense), and only those who believe, are saved (Jn 3:16-18; 5:22-24; Rm 10:9-10; 1Jn 5:10). There is no indication that a person without belief is saved. Second, there is no indication in the NT that the requirement for perseverance is a cause for anxiety. Instead, vv. 12-14 and 1Co 9:24-27 give every indication that Paul was sure of his own perseverance.

3:15-16. The mature (NASB, **perfect**; cf. 1Co 2:6) should have the **attitude** Paul described. But some in the congregation may **have a different attitude**; if so, God will **reveal** it, either to the erring themselves or to those who correct them. In any case, the Philippians should **keep living** in accordance with the truth (**standard**) they have received.

4. Paul's Call to Imitate the Best Models (3:17–4:1)

3:17-19. Paul urged the believers to imitate him, just as many others (such as Timothy and Epaphroditus) were already doing. These three, and many others, gave not many patterns to follow but one **pattern** (*typos*, v. 17; see Rm 5:14; 1Co 10:6; 2Th 3:9). In contrast there were many—probably those who were Christian in name only—who did not imitate Paul but were in fact **enemies of the cross of Christ** (v. 18). As a result, their final destiny was **destruction**. **Destruction** means "the utter ruin and devastation of objects or (as here) people," but is not a reference to annihilation. It is a common NT word for eternal judgment (see Mt 7:13; Rm 9:22; Php 1:28; 2Pt 3:7; Rv 17:8). Paul further characterized these enemies three ways: First, instead of the Lord, their **appetite** (lit., "belly") was their god; they worshiped self. Second, rather than glorifying God, they took pride in shameful practices. Third, rather than dwelling on what is true and honorable (4:8), they set **their minds on earthly things**.

3:20–4:1. The Christian's primary allegiance is to no particular country or government, and there is no place for nationalistic arrogance since **our citizenship is in heaven**. Citizenship implies kingdom. Throughout the biblical narrative, the Lord's kingdom was partly present, partly contested (1Ch 28:5; Ps 2; 103:19; Ac 4:25-26). With the first coming of Christ, the kingdom is present in a unique way—the King who will fulfill the promise of 2Sm 7:12-16 is known by name—and Paul can even say believers have been transferred to the Son's kingdom (Col 1:13). Believers are citizens of heaven in that they live under the King's rule. But the final, uncontested, kingdom is still awaited (e.g., Mt 25:31-34; 2Tm 4:18; Rv 5:9-10).

Thus the Christian life involves waiting (1Th 1:10) for a Savior. At His return He will transform **the body of our humble state**—physical bodies subject to pain, disease and death—**into conformity with** His glorified body (see 2Co 5:1-5).

IV. Applicational Matters: Paul's Practical Advice to the Philippians (4:2-9)

In this section, Paul addresses two practical matters upon which the Philippians must act.

A. Live in Harmony (4:2-3)

Paul made other calls to unity (1:27-30; 2:1-4) and gave himself as an example of one focused on the gospel (3:17-19) and not on unnecessary distractions (1:12-18). Thus the groundwork has been done to address a particular conflict between **Euodia** and **Syntyche**. They should **live in harmony** (lit., "think the same;" see 2:5). These women shared Paul's **struggle in the . . . gospel** and were two of his **fellow workers**. Even though to resolve their conflict they needed help from an unnamed **true companion** in the congregation, they were genuine. Their names, along with all of God's elect, were in the book of life (see Ps 69:28; Lk 10:20; Rv 3:5).

B. Develop a Christian Mind-Set (4:4-9)

4:4-7. Christian joy, and along with it lack of anxiety, must be grounded in four things. First, **in the Lord** Himself—in who He is and what He has done (v. 4; Ps 33:1; 35:9). He **is near** (v. 5; probably meaning "ready to help"; but perhaps "coming soon"). Second, a constant inward focus only increases anxiety. Instead, believers should look outside themselves and demonstrate graciousness (HCSB; better than NASB **gentle spirit**) to all they come in contact with (v. 5). Third, anxiety is relieved by taking all things to God in **prayer**, for in it we commit all our needs and worries to a caring and capable God (1Pt 5:7; Eph 3:20). Anxiety is reduced through **thanksgiving** (v. 6; Col 3:15) as well, for in it we recall God's past faithfulness. Fourth, the **peace of God** is at work in believers to guard them. This peace (like the love of Christ, Eph 3:19) is beyond **comprehension**, able to **guard** even in great trial (v. 7).

4:8-9. Since habits, attitudes, and lifestyle follow from the mind, believers should set their minds on virtuous things (contrast 3:19). Paul gave a partial list of such things—**honorable**, **right**, **lovely**—but the list is only representative, not exhaustive. Thus he included ***anything* worthy of praise** (italics added). These worthy things the Philippians **learned** from watching Paul; now they should put them into **practice** in their own lives, imitating him (v. 9; see 3:17).

V. Concluding Matters: Paul's Thankfulness for the Philippians' Partnership (4:10-23)

Earlier Paul mentioned this church's **partnership** with him in the gospel (1:5). Here appears one particular way they partnered: in financial support. Paul responded to their gift in three ways.

A. Personal Reflections (4:10-13)

Paul's first response to their gift was to be overjoyed because of the Philippians' show of **concern** (v. 10). They had sent help other times (v. 16), but had recently **lacked opportunity**. The lack was probably their own deep poverty (2Co 8:1-2). But Paul's joy was not caused by feelings of relief, as if anxiety over his situation had finally been assuaged with a gift. Instead, he had **learned to be content** (v. 11; see Lk 3:14; 1 Tm 6:6-8; Heb 13:5) in all sorts of financial **circumstances**. These circumstances included **humble means**, **prosperity**, **abundance** and **need**

(v. 12). The inclusion of **prosperity** shows that believers need to strive for contentment, not only in times of need, but in times of **abundance** as well, for riches can be deceptive (Mt 13:22). Real contentment, first, is not automatic; it must be **learned** over time. Second, it is not human—not natural; it is supernatural, coming **through Him who strengthens** us (v. 13).

B. Moral Commendation (4:14-17)

Paul's second response to the Philippians' gift was to commend them for it: **you have done well** (v. 14). It was more than a mere offering; it was a demonstration of solidarity with Paul in his **affliction** (lit., "co-fellowshipping with affliction"). He further commended them by reminding them that they were unique (v. 15): **no** other **church shared with** him in **giving and receiving** (a unique expression in the NT, but see Ac 20:35). The relationship was reciprocal: He *gave* the gospel and *received* financial support; they *received* pastoral care and *gave* for his material **needs** (v. 16). The congregation sent help while Paul was in **Thessalonica**, the next stop in his mission (Ac 17:1).

In v. 17 Paul corrected a possible misunderstanding. It was not **the gift** that he sought; rather his heart was set on the spiritual gains (**profit** increasing to their **account** or fruit, HCSB) the Philippians would make because of their obedience and generosity (see Pr 19:17).

C. Theological Interpretation (4:18-20)

Paul acknowledged that all they sent through **Epaphroditus** had arrived (**in full**, v. 18). He then described their gift in terms reminiscent of OT sacrifice: **fragrant aroma**, **acceptable sacrifice** (see Lv 1:9; 2:2; 19:5; Nm 15:3-7; Eph 5:2). Their gift, even though sent to a poor imprisoned missionary, was worship **well-pleasing to God** (cf. Heb 13:16). Since they supplied his needs, Paul reminded them of the promise that **God** would **supply** their **needs** (v. 19; see Mt 6:33). Both Christian obedience in giving and God's rich supply are to His **glory** (v. 20).

D. Final Farewell (4:21-23)

Paul exchanged greetings between those with him and those in Philippi. The reference to **Caesar's household** indicates that Paul was probably in Rome when he wrote. The letter ends with the prayer that **grace**—the most precious gift from God, which comes through his Son the **Lord Jesus Christ**—would be with them all (**your** is pl.).

BIBLIOGRAPHY

Bruce, F. F. *Philippians.* Peabody: Hendrickson Publishers, 1989.

Carson, D. A. *Basics for Believers: An Exposition of Philippians.* Grand Rapids, MI: Baker, 1996.

Fee, Gordon D. *Paul's Letter to the Philippians.* Grand Rapids, MI: Eerdmans, 1995.

Fowl, Stephen E. *Philippians.* Grand Rapids, MI: Eerdmans, 2005.

Hansen, G. Walter. *The Letter to the Philippians.* Grand Rapids, MI: Eerdmans, 2009.

Hughes, R. Kent. *Philippians: The Fellowship of the Gospel.* Wheaton: Crossway, 2007.

MacArthur, John. *Philippians.* Nashville: Thomas Nelson, 2007.

O'Brien, Peter T. *The Epistle to the Philippians.* Grand Rapids, MI: Eerdmans, 1991.

Silva, Moisés. *Philippians*, 2nd ed. Grand Rapids, MI: Baker, 2005.

Thielman, Frank. *Philippians.* Grand Rapids, MI: Zondervan, 1995.

COLOSSIANS

GERALD PETERMAN

INTRODUCTION

Author. From the letter it appears that the primary Christian worker at Colossae was Epaphras, who told Paul of the church (1:7). Probably at the request of Epaphras, Paul wrote to encourage the congregation and to combat false teaching starting to take root there (see Themes).

Recipients. Little is known of Colossae itself. The city was in Asia Minor (modern-day Turkey) in the Lycus River Valley, on the major trade route between Ephesus and the Euphrates. In the first century it was less prominent than its neighbors, Laodicea and Hierapolis.

Although the book of Acts does not record any evangelistic work being done there, Ac 19:10 does mention that Paul's work in Ephesus (some 100 miles west of Colossae) was so effective that after two years "all who lived in Asia heard the word of the Lord, both Jews and Greeks." Probably at or near this time (AD 52–55) churches were planted in Colossae as well as in Laodicea and Hierapolis (4:13).

Date. The letter refers to Paul's bonds (1:13) and to his fellow prisoner Aristarchus (4:10), indicating that Paul was incarcerated at the time. He could have written during his two-year Caesarean imprisonment (Ac 23:23-33; 24:47). Yet, for the following reasons, Paul probably wrote while under house arrest in Rome (Ac 28:30). First, cosmopolitan Rome fits well with the large number of coworkers mentioned in the letter (4:10-14), as compared to Caesarea's relative smallness. Second, the letter to Philemon, written at the same time as Colossians, mentions Paul's hope to be released and find lodging with Philemon (v. 22). This hope is much more likely while he awaits trial in Rome than while incarcerated in Caesarea, for the length and outcome of the stay in Caesarea was always very uncertain. Recall that there was, from nearby Jerusalem, a Jewish mob set on killing him (Ac 23:13-33). If written from Rome, Paul penned the letter around AD 60–62.

Themes. On the one hand, Paul's statement that he rejoiced to see the Colossians' good discipline and the stability of their faith in Christ (2:5) shows that the church was basically sound. On the other hand, we find at least two statements that indicate problems. First a warning: "See to it that no one takes you captive through philosophy and empty deception" (2:8). Second we find a question: "Why, as if you were living in the world, do you submit yourself to decrees?" (2:20). These verses indicate that there was a threat in Colossae. Portions of the letter (especially 2:6-23) were written to preempt any problem.

The teaching threatening the church appears to have been a mixed religion that contained elements of Judaism (e.g., concern for Sabbaths) and elements of proto-Gnosticism (asceticism; attention to the elemental forces). Elements of the false teaching included attention to philosophy and traditions of men (2:8); circumcision (2:11-13); feasts, new moons and Sabbaths (2:16); and harsh treatment of the body (2:23).

The overall theme of the epistle is the supremacy of Christ, and it is developed in a variety of ways. First, we find a hymn about Christ that explains His exalted position in relation to the universe and to the Church (1:15-20). He is Creator of all and Head of the body. Second, Paul emphasizes the supremacy of Christ over the Church. This is in contrast to 1 Corinthians where the Church is the body of Christ and the individuals are members of each other. Here in Colossians, to emphasize the authority of the Lord Jesus, Paul puts forth Christ as the Head of the Church. In contrast, the Church is His body. Third, to emphasize Christ's supremacy over the lives of believers, there is a marked emphasis on realized eschatology: that is, rather than emphasizing what we are yet to receive, Paul puts the stress on what Christ has already accomplished for us. So, for example, believers have been made complete in Christ (2:10); they have been raised up with Christ to new life (3:1); and their life is hidden with Christ in God (3:3). There is no reference in Colossians to the rapture, to future resurrection of the dead, or to coming judgment. Paul's emphasis on realized eschatology is meant to show the readers that, since they have already been transformed by the Lord of all, they need pay no heed to the false teaching. Fourth, there is emphasis on wisdom (1:9, 28; 2:3, 23; 3:16; 4:5), knowledge (1:9-10; 2:2-3; 3:10), and mystery (1:26-27; 2:2; 4:3). Again this emphasis is expected in contrast to the false teaching, which brought its form of wisdom and knowledge; believers, however, already have in Christ all the treasures of wisdom and knowledge (2:3). Truth found in Him is far superior. In common with Paul's other letters, this one included practical aspects of following this superior Christ, such as prayer (1:9-11), teaching about vice (3:5-11) and virtue (3:12-17), and practical exhortations on proper relations within the household (3:18–4:1).

Striking similarities exist between Colossians and Ephesians. These include (1) reference to imprisonment (4:18; cf. Eph 6:20), (2) emphasis on realized eschatology (e.g., 2:10; cf. Eph 2:5-7), (3) personal reflections on Paul's ministry and suffering (1:24–2:5; cf. Eph 3:1-13), (4) specific treatment of household relations (2:18-25; cf. Eph 5:21–6:9), (5) shared phrases that are identical or nearly so (1:4; cf. Eph 1:15; Col 3:16; cf. Eph 5:19; Col 3:22; cf. Eph 6:6), (6) ten words that are found only in Colossians and Ephesians in the NT ("to reconcile," "alienated," "to root," "to make alive with," "to raise with," "growth," "ligament," "external service," "man-pleaser," and "hymn"), and (7) Tychicus as the bearer of both letters (Col 4:7-8; Eph 6:21). From this evidence it is probable that the letters belong to the same time and situation.

OUTLINE

I. Introduction (1:1-14)
   A. Greeting (1:1-2)
   B. Thanksgiving (1:3-8)
   C. Prayer and Digression (1:9-14)
II. Doctrinal: The Supremacy of Christ Declared (1:15–2:3)
   A. Christ's Supremacy over the Creation (1:15-17)
   B. Christ's Supremacy over the Church (1:18–2:3)
      1. Christ as Head of the Church (1:18-20)
      2. Christ as Reconciler of the Church (1:21-23)
      3. Christ as the Source of Paul's Ministry (1:24–2:3)
III. Polemical: The Supremacy of Christ Defended (2:4-23)
   A. Christ's Supremacy over Persuasive Argument (2:4-7)
   B. Christ's Supremacy over Vain Philosophy (2:8-15)
   C. Christ's Supremacy over Legalistic Religion (2:16-23)
IV. Practical: The Supremacy of Christ Applied (3:1–4:6)
   A. Christ's Supremacy Should Transform Authentic Followers of Christ (3:1-17)
      1. Seeking Things Above (3:1-4)
      2. Turning from Past Sins (3:5-11)
      3. Putting on Christ-Like Virtue (3:12-17)
   B. Christ's Supremacy Should Guide Household Relations (3:18–4:1)
   C. Christ's Supremacy Should Motivate Prayer (4:2-4)
   D. Christ's Supremacy Should Affect Conduct before Outsiders (4:5-6)
V. Conclusion (4:7-18)
   A. Tychicus Is Commended (4:7-9)
   B. Paul's Associates Send Greetings (4:10-14)
   C. Paul Gives Last Directions (4:15-17)
   D. Paul Says Farewell (4:18)

COMMENTARY ON COLOSSIANS

I. Introduction (1:1-14)

As was common in the letters of the Greco-Roman world and in the Pauline epistles, this letter begins with personal and introductory matters. These include a greeting identifying both the writer and the addressees, a statement of thanksgiving, and a prayer for the readers.

A. Greeting (1:1-2)

1:1-2. The letter comes from Paul, who by the **will of God** was an **apostle**—he was sent out with the commission to preach the gospel—and from Timothy, Paul's fellow worker and **brother**. The letter goes to the **saints and faithful brethren** (not two groups but one) at Colossae.

B. Thanksgiving (1:3-8)

1:3-8. The founder of the church in Colossae was **Epaphras** (v. 7; see 4:12; Phm 23), Paul's **beloved fellow bond-servant** (see v. 7; Rv 6:11). He **informed** Paul of the church's existence and of its **faith** and **love** (v. 8). Thus, in prayer Paul and Timothy gave thanks for the Colossians, not having seen them in person but having **heard** of their faith and love. Verse 5 should be closely attached to v. 4 rather than separated by punctuation: their **faith** and **love** are grounded in the **hope** stored **up** for them **in heaven** (cf. **faith, hope** and **love** in 1Co 13; Gl 5:5-6; 1Th 1:3). Thus hope is not subjective (feeling or longing), but objective—the thing hoped for: eternal life.

This **hope** was heard about in a message (**word**) characterized by its truth. It is good news (gospel). To begin to combat the false teaching that is troubling the Colossians (2:8, 16-19), Paul reminded them that this **gospel** is not unique to them; it was spreading through **all the world**, even reaching as far as them. Their reception (their **faith**) is further described as understanding God's **grace**.

C. Prayer and Digression (1:9-14)

1:9-14. Having heard of the Colossian church's faith led to Paul's unceasing prayer for them. Common in Paul's prayers are the themes of **knowledge** or **wisdom** (Eph 1:18-19) and this **understanding** should yield a lifestyle that is **worthy of the Lord** or worthy of the gospel (v. 10; see Php 1:9-10). A worthy life is described four ways:

First, the worthy life bears **fruit** (Mt 7:17; Jn 15:8); that is, it does **good work**. Second, it grows in **knowledge**, coming to know God and His will ever better (Eph 1:17). Third, it is **strengthened** with God's **power** (Eph 3:16), not for the purpose of show but for attaining **steadfastness** and **patience** (v. 11). Fourth, a worthy life **joyously** gives **thanks** for the blessing of sharing eternal life (**inheritance**) with **the saints in** God's kingdom, called a place of **Light** (v. 12).

At this point (v. 13), Paul digressed from prayer to describe what it means to share the inheritance. When we believe the gospel, God rescues us from the **domain of darkness**. Along with rescue, we are transferred **to the kingdom** that belongs to **His beloved Son**. On the one hand, there is no middle ground; one is either in darkness or in the Son's kingdom. On the other hand, there is a tension between the "now" and the "not yet," since for Paul, the kingdom was both present (Rm 14:17; 1Co 4:20) and yet to come (1Th 2:12; 2Tm 4:18). The Church, therefore, which lives under the rule of King Jesus, is not to be wholly equated with the kingdom since God's final, uncontested, kingdom is still awaited (e.g., Mt 25:31-34; 1Co 15:25-28; 2Tm 4:18; Rv 5:9-10; for the concept of the kingdom of God, see the comments on Mt 3:1-4; 13:10-17).

Finally, this transfer brings **redemption** (see Rm 3:24; 1Co 1:30), which is release from bondage, and further defined as **forgiveness of sins** (Eph 1:7).

II. Doctrinal: The Supremacy of Christ Declared (1:15–2:3)

Reference to the redemption found in Christ leads to a glorious description of this Christ. This Christ-hymn would be profitably compared to Php 2:6-11.

A. Christ's Supremacy over the Creation (1:15-17)

1:15-17. God is **invisible**, but He can be seen in His Son (Jn 14:9), who is the **image** (an *eikon*—a word used of paintings and statues—is something that represents an original; cf. Mk 12:16; Rm 8:29; Heb 10:1) of God (see 2Co 4:4). That is, as said later in 1:19 and 2:9, the Son exactly represents and displays who God is (see Heb 1:3). The Son is the "firstborn over all creation" (HCSB), not meaning that there was a time when He came into existence but rather that He has the role of the **firstborn**: He is the ruler over all creation (cf. Ex 4:22; Jr 31:9; Heb 1:6; Rv 1:5). His rule over creation naturally follows from **all things** being **created** by His plan and power (**through Him**) **and for** His glory (v. 16; Jn 1:3). Included in **all things** are **visible** things—people and animals—and **invisible** things—spirits and angels. Spirit beings are further described as **thrones**, **dominions**, **rulers**, and **authorities**. This was probably put here to show that the angels the Colossians were being tempted to worship (see 2:18) did not deserve and should not receive such honor since they are all under the authority of Jesus.

This unit of thought closes with the sweeping comment about Christ's past and present work. He was **before all things** in time when He created the universe. Now He is still active in creation holding **all things** . . . **together** (Heb 1:3).

B. Christ's Supremacy over the Church (1:18–2:3)

1. Christ as Head of the Church (1:18-20)

1:18-20. As Christ rules the universe, so also He has all authority (is **head**, *kephale*, a term used metaphorically of leaders, e.g., Is 9:14-15; Ps 17:44; 1Co 11:3; Eph 5:23) over the church and is its originating cause (**beginning**). Unlike Lazarus (Jn 11), who was raised from the dead only to die again, Jesus was the first to be raised in a glorified body, making Him **the firstborn from the dead**—that is, the one with authority to give resurrection life.

Christ has **first place** in both original creation and in new creation because the **Father** was pleased for full and complete deity (**the fullness**) to take up residence (**dwell**) **in Him**. Thus, as God-Man, Christ is uniquely suited, by means of His bloody death on the **cross**, to **reconcile all things** to God. The reconciliation of all things is best taken to mean He restores proper order and lordship to the universe, not that each and every being (**whether** . . . **on earth or** . . . **in heaven**) is restored to a proper relationship with God.

2. Christ as Reconciler of the Church (1:21-23)

1:21-23. From the topic of reconciliation above, Paul moved to remind the church of Colossae of its own reconciliation to God. There are four aspects to Christ's reconciliation of the Church. First, without Christ all people are **alienated**, **hostile**, and **engaged in evil**. This alienation is a result of the fall (Gn 3; Eph 2:1-7). Second, Christ's **death**, and our trust in Him, bring reconciliation to God (being properly related to Him). Third, God's goal is that those who are reconciled to Him in Christ would be **holy and blameless and beyond reproach**. Fourth, reconciliation requires **faith**. Two aspects of the structure of vv. 21-23 demonstrate that faith by its very nature is **steadfast**; it continues to cling to **the hope of the gospel** (see v. 5): (1) Paul said God **reconciled** (past tense) them, if they **continue** (present tense) in faith. Since the present cannot change the past, it is past reconciliation that produces, and is seen in, present faith (cf. Jn 8:31-32; Heb 3:14). (2) The conditional (if . . . then syntax) Paul uses implies confidence that the readers will persevere (see also comment on Php 3:12-14).

3. Christ as the Source of Paul's Ministry (1:24–2:3)

The supremacy of Christ is evident not only in the creation and the church, but also in His call of the apostle Paul's ministry of suffering, proclamation, and encouragement.

1:24-27. In discussing his own ministry, Paul rejoiced in his sufferings for the church in that they **fill**[ed] **up what** [was] **lacking in Christ's afflictions** (v. 24). Though exalted, **Christ** continued to endure **afflictions** through His persecuted followers (Ac 9:4). So, in one sense **Christ's afflictions** are not over (they are **lacking**), although these afflictions are not atoning. Thus, Paul's work as a minister (vv. 23, 25) has meant **sufferings**, which he gladly endures on behalf of the **church**. He endures his **share** since God gave him the task (**stewardship**) of **preaching the word of God**. Here the **word** is called the **mystery**: some aspect of God's plan that was previously hidden but that has now been made known (2:3; Rm 11:25; Eph 3:3). The **mystery** is further explained this way: Christ takes up residence in believers (**in you**, v. 27), even among **Gentiles**, those previously excluded from the people of God (Eph 2:11-13).

1:28-29. We refers to workers such as Paul and Epaphras. He described their work as proclaiming Him. There are five aspects to this proclamation: First, Christ is the center of their message. Second, one feature of the proclamation was **admonishing** every man—correcting wrong beliefs and practice. A third facet was **teaching**—guiding into correct beliefs and practice. Fourth, the goal of the proclamation was to **present** every man **complete in Christ**. Fifth, all this activity involved not merely human energy but **labor** and **striving according to His power**.

2:1-3. Paul was not emotionally detached in his work. He suffered and was not ashamed to tell of his **struggle** even to **those who** had **not personally seen** his face. He related the struggle, not to boast, but so that others **may be encouraged**. This encouragement stems from being "instructed **in love**" as this word is used in 1Co 2:16 (better than **knit together** of NASB). Instruction yields deeper understanding (**full assurance**) and has as its further goal knowledge, not just of facts, but also of a person: **God's mystery, that is, Christ Himself**. Spiritual **wisdom and knowledge**, which are treasures (Is 33:6), should be sought nowhere else, for they are found in Him.

III. Polemical: The Supremacy of Christ Defended (2:4-23)

Having declared the supremacy of Christ over all, Paul turned his attention to the problems threatening the Colossian church. There were false teachings threatening Christ's preeminence and so Paul needed to address them.

A. Christ's Supremacy over Persuasive Argument (2:4-7)

2:4-5. Here for the first time Paul directly asserted that his teaching about Christ (1:15-20; 2:1-3) addressed the church's problem: false teaching that attempts to **delude** them **with persuasive argument**. Even though the congregation was troubled, Paul's **rejoicing** shows that it is basically sound, having **good discipline** and **stability**.

2:6-7. In light of the warning not to be fooled by persuasive but false arguments, Paul exhorts the Colossians to apply what they know to be true. For Paul, there was no gap between believing and behaving. All those who **receive Christ Jesus**—that is, confess Him as their **Lord** (Rm 10:9; 1Co 12:3)—should live (**walk**) under His lordship (**in Him**). This life is described with four phrases: **firmly rooted**, **being built up**, being **established**, and **overflowing**. The first three refer to deep, well-informed attachment to Christ, the foundation; the last to continuous **gratitude** (1:3; 3:15-17; 4:2) for His work.

B. Christ's Supremacy over Vain Philosophy (2:8-15)

2:8-10. Paul reminded readers that being rooted in Christ means being on guard against false teachings (**philosophy and empty deception**), which are in accord with the **elementary principles of the world**. The HCSB translation is preferable, "the elemental forces of the world." For the following reasons it is best to view these **forces** (*stoicheia*) as evil spiritual beings that seek to control and destroy people's lives. First, here and in Gl 4:3-9 the *stoicheia* are personified as forces that enslave. Second, in this context the *stoicheia* are probably "the rulers and authorities" that Christ publicly shames (v. 15). Third, the NT regularly links heretical Christian teaching with the demonic (e.g., Mt 24:24; 2Co 11:14-15; 1Jn 4:1-3; cf. 1Co 10:19-20).

The false teachings the Colossians faced were based on mere human **tradition**, rather than on Christ (v. 8). The Colossians, and all believers, **have been made complete in Him** (v. 10) in that they have (among other blessings) forgiveness (1:14), reconciliation (1:22), and new life (2:13). They need no other source of spiritual wealth, since **the fullness of Deity dwells in** Him (see 1:19). So, as fully God and fully man, **He is the head over all**, including the elemental forces.

2:11-15. Paul mentioned four benefits of being in Christ. First, genuine **circumcision**—that is, a new heart. It is not literal (not performed by **hands**), but spiritual, being performed by the Holy Spirit (see Dt 10:16; Jr 9:26; Ezk 36.27; Rm 2:25-29; Php 3:3). Under the old covenant Israel was an ethnic community. So circumcision was performed on every unwilling male infant. The Church is a confessional community. The Holy Spirit (and thus the new heart) is a gift to only those who believe (e.g., Ac 2:38; 5:32; 10:44-45; Rm 8:9). Thus vv. 11-12 give no evidence that infant baptism should replace infant circumcision. Second, being **buried with** and **raised up with** Christ is a way of saying we have passed from old life to new life (Rm 6:1-4). Paul used "baptism" as a label to refer to the point of conversion. Both the local church and the new believer could look back on it as the time when Christ was confessed as Lord (cf. 1Co 12:3b) and when this faith in Him was demonstrated in action (submission to water baptism). Thus, although baptism is important, it does not make alive (v. 13) or cause salvation. Third, believers have new life (are **made . . . alive**) **with** Christ (v. 13). New life is given not because of our merit, but rather it comes to us while we are in the helpless state of being **dead in . . . transgressions and** being **uncircumcised** (a reference to literal lack of circumcision as a symbol of spiritual alienation). The fourth benefit is forgiveness of **transgressions** (v. 13). Transgression is the specific word for breaking commandments; thus v. 14 mentions the OT law, calling it a **certificate of debt consisting of decrees against us**. A **debt** is owed because of disobedience; but this debt is **canceled out** by the **cross**. On this cross Christ not only saved His people but also was victorious over **the rulers and authorities** (evil spiritual forces), making **a public display of them** (v. 15).

C. Christ's Supremacy over Legalistic Religion (2:16-23)

These verses provide all that is known about the false teaching that threatened the church. First are warnings (vv. 16-19), then a rhetorical question that acts as a command (vv. 20-22), and finally a short response (v. 23).

2:16-19. First, the Colossians are to be on guard against someone who requires that they obey OT law (e.g., food, drink, Sabbath). The whole law, as a **mere shadow**, looked forward to Christ and to **what** was **to come** (Heb 10:1). He is the **substance**—the real thing that casts the shadow (v. 17). We look to Him; He alone is our Judge. Second, the Colossians should guard against anyone who "condemns" (NLT) them by requiring an ascetic religion known for **self-abasement and the worship of the angels** (v. 18). Three errors characterize this false teacher: (1) false **visions**, (2) human arrogance (**inflated**, **fleshly mind**), and (3) departure from Christ, the **head** (v. 19). In contrast, real **growth** in godliness requires **holding fast** to Christ.

2:20-22. Paul appealed to the readers' experience of Christ: they **died with Christ** and so have been freed from "the elemental forces" (HCSB; see comments on 2:8-10). The forces require legalistic religion that follows the **commandments** of mere **men** (v. 22). Since the Colossians were thus joined with Christ (cf. 2:12-13), they should not **submit . . . to decrees** (v. 20). These decrees probably required abstaining (**Do not handle!**) from certain **food** and **drink** (2:16).

2:23. Paul admitted that from a human perspective such an ascetic **self-made religion** gives the **appearance of wisdom**. But the appearance is deceptive. Abstaining from certain **things** (food, drink, 2:16) and giving **severe treatment** to **the body** in fact are useless in a person's fight **against fleshly indulgence**. What actions *are* useful in such a fight? They appear next.

IV. Practical: The Supremacy of Christ Applied (3:1–4:6)

Having given a pointed critique of the false religion that threatened the Colossians, Paul moved to explain the only alternative: Christ's supremacy taking hold of them, transforming their lives, relationships, and public conduct.

A. Christ's Supremacy Should Transform Authentic Followers of Christ (3:1-17)

Paul begins by describing a transformed Christian life. As opposed to living by ascetic rules, they ought to live with new vitality because they are "in Christ." Paul's description of the genuine Christian life contains three elements:

1. Seeking Things Above (3:1-4)

3:1-4. The word "**if**" does not suggest uncertainty. Rather, the force is that *since* the Colossians have indeed **died** with Christ and been **raised up with** Him (see 2:12), their focus should not be on earthly **things** (v. 2). Their focus should be on honorable, right, and excellent things (Php 4:8) and supremely on Christ who is exalted—at God's **right hand**—above all others (Php 2:9-11). Their **life** is not drawn from, nor controlled by, forces from below; it is **hidden**—and therefore secure—**with Christ in God** (v. 3). He is **life** (Jn 14:6). At His return (see 2Th 1:7-10) Christ Jesus will be **revealed**, not in humility and suffering, but with **glory**. Because believers are so intimately joined with Christ, His future glory means their glory **also** (Rm 8:17, 30).

2. Turning from Past Sins (3:5-11)

Christian life is characterized by repentance from **things** in which we **once walked** (v. 7). Thus Paul moved from glorious things to be sought (3:1-4) to shameful things to be put away (3:5-11).

3:5-8. The battle against sin starts in the mind. Believers should **consider** themselves decisively separated from (**dead to**) **immorality**, **impurity**, and the like (Rm 6:11). Paul's lists of sins in vv. 5 and 8 are representative, not exhaustive (cf. Gl 5:19-21). The lists emphasize lustful sins (**evil desire**) and relational sins (**anger**, **abusive speech**), pointing out that such deeds deserve **wrath** (v. 6). Particularly rich is Paul's statement that **greed . . . amounts to idolatry** (v. 5; see Eph 5:5). No one can serve two masters (Mt 6:24). Lust, or power, or money can capture our heart and become an idol.

3:9-11. As a basis for his commands (**since**), Paul appealed to the readers' conversion to Christ, using a metaphor comparing their salvation experience with putting on clothes: On the human side, the Colossians have gone from trusting themselves to trusting the gospel (1:5-6). That is, they have **laid aside the old self** and **put on the new self** (vv. 9-10). Because God is at work in the gospel, this same faith can be described from the divine side, stressing the supernatural and transforming results of faith (**being renewed**, v. 10). The **old self** is the whole person as ruled by sin (see the comments on Rm 6:5-7); the **new** is the whole person reborn in Christ.

The first is known for lies. The latter is known for truth and is being constantly **renewed** (Rm 8:29; 2Co 3:18). Two things should be said: First, even though this old-to-new conversion is once-for-all and decisive, ongoing moral effort is still required. Thus Paul commanded: **do not lie** (v. 9). Second, we find here not just **new** individuals but also a new community consisting even of those once bitterly divided by social prejudice (e.g., **Greek**, **Jew**). For Christ **is all** that matters and He works **in all** kinds of people.

3. Putting on Christ-Like Virtue (3:12-17)

3:12-14. One should not merely avoid sin (3:5-11); one must also take the initiative to **put on** virtue, actively replacing bad behavior with behaviors that befit people who are **chosen** and loved by **God**. If believers are **beloved** by the Father, they should love those whom He loves (vv. 12-17). Again, the list is not exhaustive, but includes common relational attributes (**patience**, **forgiving**; cf. Gl 5:22-23). Above all is **love** (see the comments on 1Co 13:1-3, 13) for it is, literally, the "binding together that produces maturity" (NASB **perfect bond of unity**).

3:15-17. The shift continues, started in v. 14, from mostly individual concerns to mostly group concerns, for we see a reference to the **body** (v. 15) and **one another** (v. 16). Four things should be said. First, the **peace** brought by Christ's gospel should **rule** ("to serve as umpire") in the congregation (**body**). Second, corporate **thankfulness**—too often neglected!—is extremely important, appearing three times in as many verses. Third, the gospel (the **word** about **Christ**) dwells **richly** among believers when it is wisely taught, lovingly cherished, joyfully sung, and rightly applied (**teaching**, **singing**, **admonishing**). Fourth, all is done **in the name of** . . . **Jesus**—through Him as mediator and under His authority as **Lord**.

B. Christ's Supremacy Should Guide Household Relations (3:18–4:1)

From broad guidelines regarding virtue (3:12-17), Paul moved to address the responsibilities of specific relationships.

3:18-19. First, living for Christ should guide marital relationships. For wives to **be subject** does not imply inferiority or servility. Rather, it is right (**fitting**) that they give respect (Eph 5:33) to husbands as leaders. See the comments on Eph 5:22-24. Husbands must be known for **love** (v. 19), not persistent anger (bitterness). Elsewhere, Paul made clear that such love must follow Christ's example (Eph 5:25).

3:20-21. Second, living under Christ's supremacy should affect child-parent relationships. In keeping with OT law (Dt 5:16), children should obey their own parents (v. 20). **Fathers** should avoid a common tendency: to **exasperate** their **children** (v. 21) by being overly critical of their efforts. Such harsh treatment will hinder the child from developing perseverance.

3:22–4:1. Third, Christ should also be preeminent in slave-master relationships. (See the comments about slavery in NT times in the introduction to Philemon.) The two commands in vv. 22-25 given to slaves are not surprising: **obey** (v. 22) and **work** (v. 23). But the motivation for these commands is distinctively Christian, turning attention away from human masters to the one Master of all. Obedience should be sincere, motivated by fear of the **Lord**. Similarly, **work**, since it is done for **Christ** (v. 24), should be performed from the soul (**heartily**). What enhances this motivation is **knowing that** . . . **the Lord**, not any human master, is the impartial Judge. On the one hand, slaves have no earthly inheritance; but believers receive a heavenly one: the **reward** of eternal life in the Lord's presence (v. 24). On the other hand, there are consequences for disobedience (v. 25). We should affirm the truths of both v. 24 and v. 25. The NT regularly teaches that salvation is wholly by grace (Rm 3:24; Eph 2:8-9), yet believers will be evaluated for future rewards (not for their eternal destiny) based on their works (Rm 14:10-12; 2Co 5:10).

As the slave's motivation is changed by the gospel, so is the master's. The slave owner must consider his behavior in light of the **Master in heaven**. **Justice and fairness** exclude any kind of abuse or oppression. Although Paul's teaching was directed to literal slaves and masters, by way of secondary application it can be brought to bear on contemporary employee/employer relationships. The former should give eager, honest work with respect and proper motivations. The later should avoid oppression and facilitate a just and fair workplace.

C. Christ's Supremacy Should Motivate Prayer (4:2-4)

Paul moved from treatment of specific relationships back to the ways Christ's supremacy should affect the congregation as a whole. They fall into two more sections: prayer (vv. 2-4) and relationships with outsiders (vv. 5-6).

4:2-4. Paul's teaching addresses three common challenges to effective prayer: lack of dedication (**Devote yourselves**!), a sluggish approach to prayer (keep **alert**!), and prayers filled with requests but devoid of **thanksgiving**. He requests prayer for his preaching ministry (v. 3), first, for good opportunities (**door**; cf. 1Co 16:9, 2Co 2:12). Perhaps opportunities had been curtailed by his imprisonment (v. 3, the first reference to his incarceration in the letter; see 4:10, 18). Second, even such an experienced missionary as Paul asked for prayer that he might be enabled by God to make clear **the mystery of Christ** (see 1:27; 2:2).

D. Christ's Supremacy Should Affect Conduct before Outsiders (4:5-6)

4:5-6. Since witness to the gospel is so important, behavior toward nonbelievers (**outsiders**) must be characterized by **wisdom** and seized **opportunity** (Eph 5:15-16). The word for **respond** is used only here in Paul, probably implying that there were curious outsiders asking about Christianity (1Pt 3:15). Paul asserted that the answer to them should not be harsh or boring but rather should be a delicate blend of tact (**grace**) and wit or spice (**seasoned**), crafted for **each** individual **person**.

V. Conclusion (4:7-18)

A. Tychicus Is Commended (4:7-9)

4:7-9. Even when imprisoned (v. 10), Paul preferred not to write in a letter the details of his circumstances (cf. Philippians and Ephesians). Instead, Paul's **whole situation** (v. 9) would be explained in person by **Tychicus** (Ac 20:4; Eph 6:21; 2Tm 4:12), who carried the letter to the church, and by **Onesimus**, who accompanied Tychicus and was slave to Philemon (Phm 10, 15-16).

B. Paul's Associates Send Greetings (4:10-14)

4:10-14. Paul had six **fellow workers** who passed on greetings. The first three are indentified as Jewish Christians (**from the circumcision**): **Aristarchus**, a Macedonian of Thessalonica who traveled with Paul according to Ac 19:29, 20:40, and 27:2; **Mark**, who had years earlier assisted Paul and Barnabas on the first missionary journey (Ac 12:25; 13:13; 15:37; see also 2Tm 4:11); and **Jesus/Justus**, who is known only by this reference. The second group of three contains **Epaphras**, **Luke**, and **Demas**. **Epaphras** is commended for his ministry, as he was earlier (1:7). Paul's comment lets us know what hard work effective prayer is, since **Epaphras** was regularly **laboring** in it on the Colossian's behalf (v. 12). **Luke** appears as a companion to Paul elsewhere (Phm 24; 2Tm 4:10), but only here in the NT is he called a **physician** (v. 14). By tradition and assorted internal evidence (see the introductions to Luke and Acts) Luke is the author of the gospel that bears his name and the book of Acts. As such, he would be the only known Gentile to have authored any biblical books. **Demas** is otherwise unknown except for 2Tm 4:10 and Phm 24.

C. Paul Gives Last Directions (4:15-17)

4:15-17. Paul asked the Colossians to give greetings to believers in **Laodicea** (a town 10 miles west of Colossae). Apparently he wrote a letter to the church there (v. 16), but it has been lost. He greeted also **Nympha**, who is otherwise unknown. **House** churches were common, however, and are mentioned a few times in the NT (Ac 16:15; Rm 16:5; 1Co 16:19; Phm 2). Paul also directed the Colossians to read the Laodicean letter and the Laodiceans to read this letter to the Colossians, demonstrating the circular nature of NT epistles.

Finally, Paul asked them to pass on his exhortation to **Archippus**, a member of the church that met in Philemon's home (Phm 2). Apparently, he needed encouragement in the **ministry** task he had **received**. Unfortunately, there is no other evidence in the NT to tell what the task was or why it had gone unfulfilled.

D. Paul Says Farewell (4:18)

4:18. To verify authenticity, as was typical (1Co 16:21; Gl 6:11; 2Th 3:17), Paul added a hand-written **greeting**. To **remember** probably means to remember in prayer. The **grace** benediction is common in Paul (Rm 16:24; 1Co 16:23; Gl 6:18) and summarizes the all-important aspect of the gospel (1:6).

BIBLIOGRAPHY

Anders, Max. *Galatians, Ephesians, Philippians, Colossians*. The Holman New Testament Commentary. Nashville: Holman Reference, 1999.

Bruce, F. F. *The Epistles to the Colossians, to Philemon, and to the Ephesians*, 2nd ed. Grand Rapids, MI: Eerdmans, 1984.

Garland, David E. *Colossians, Philemon*. Grand Rapids, MI: Zondervan, 1998.

Hughes, R. Kent. *Colossians and Philemon: The Supremacy of Christ*. Wheaton: Crossway, 1989.

Lightfoot, J. B. *Colossians and Philemon*. Edited by Alister McGrath and J. I. Packer. Wheaton: Crossway, 1997.

MacArthur, John. *Colossians and Philemon: New Testament Commentary*. Chicago: Moody, 1992.

Moo, Douglas J. *The Letters to the Colossians and to Philemon*. Grand Rapids, MI: Eerdmans, 2008.

O'Brien, Peter T. *Colossians–Philemon*. Nashville: Thomas Nelson, 1982.

Still, Todd D. "Colossians." Vol. 12 of the The Expositor's Bible Commentary, edited by T. Longman, III, and D. E. Garland. Grand Rapids, MI: Zondervan, 2005.

1 THESSALONIANS

KEVIN D. ZUBER

INTRODUCTION

Author and Date. Paul lists two of his companions, but it is clear the apostle Paul is the primary author (compare "we" and "our" in 1Th 1:2, 5; 2:1, 6; 3:1; 4:1; 5:12 and "I" in 1Th 2:18; 3:5; 5:27; 2Th 3:17). Concerning the date, Luke recorded in Ac 18:12 that during Paul's stay in Corinth "Gallio was proconsul of Achaia" (the region of Southern Greece; for more on Gallio, see the comments on Ac 18:12-13). Ancient inscriptions place his tenure in office from July AD 51 to June AD 52. Paul probably arrived before Gallio began his tenure in AD 50. He probably wrote 1 Thessalonians in early AD 51 and 2 Thessalonians later that same year. Although these two letters are among the earliest of Paul's "canonical correspondence" (only Galatians is earlier), the themes and issues reflect a mature faith and a consistency of doctrine. At the time of writing these letters Paul had been a Christian for a decade and a half and a missionary preacher for nearly 10 years—he was no novice. "His theology was fully developed in his mind and tested in his ministry before he wrote these letters" (Charles C. Ryrie, *First & Second Thessalonians*, EBC [Chicago: Moody, 2001], 7).

Themes and Purpose. Paul wrote his letters in response to information he received from Timothy (see 1Th 3:6), and perhaps in other ways, about the faith and faithfulness of the Thessalonian believers. He had been quite concerned about them, given the vitriolic persecution he had faced there, but was relieved to find that in the main they were doing well, hence his repeated thanksgiving on their behalf (cf. 1Th 1:2-3; 2:13; 3:9; 2Th 2:13). However, some issues did need to be addressed. Persecution, along with the fact that some of their number had died, caused some confusion about matters related to the rapture of the church, the tribulation period, and the second coming of the Lord. Had they missed the rapture (1Th 4:13)? Had the tribulation begun (1Th 5:1-11; 2Th 2:1-12)? Others were still engaging in inappropriate behavior (e.g., 1Th 4:1-8), and still others had (for various reasons) lapsed into idleness along with its attendant evils (e.g. 1Th 4:9-12; 2Th 3:6-15). Therefore Paul wrote these letters to comfort, teach, and exhort.

Background. The city of Thessalonica (modern Solonika) was in a strategic location. Situated at the northwest corner of the Aegean Sea at the Thermaic Gulf, it was originally named Therma. In 315 BC Cassander, one of Alexander's generals, resettled the city and renamed it Thessalonica after his wife (Alexander's half-sister). During the Roman era it was a "free city," ruled by "politarchs" ("city authorities" Ac 17:6, 8)—representatives of the free citizens of the city (not by a Roman governor), and it was the capital of the Roman Province of Macedonia. It was given political favors by the Roman Empire. The city was at a crucial crossroads of land and sea trade. The most important Roman east-west highway, the Egnatian Way, ran right through the town. The sea trade from the south (North Africa, Egypt, Palestine) would come through the seaport of Thessalonica before heading into the interior of Macedonia. The city had a population of about 200,000 in the first century and (unlike Philippi) had a thriving Jewish community. Unfortunately, it was also a typical pagan city with numerous cults (and Paul made oblique references to them in the letters, e.g. 1Th 1:9—"turned to God from idols"; 5:5—"we are not of night nor of the darkness," a possible reference to the cult of Serapis, which involved nighttime initiations and had occult associations).

The story of Paul's mission in Thessalonica appears in Ac 17:1-10 (see the comments there).

The work began well, but opposition forced Paul and his companions to leave the city abruptly. The account in Acts noted that Paul was in the city "for three Sabbaths" (17:2b). From that, some have suggested that Paul was there for only three weeks, more or less. However, the letters indicate that Paul had taught them quite a bit and that they were fairly well grounded (see the several references to what they knew and had been taught, 1Th 1:5; 2:5; 4:1; 5:1-2; 2Th 2:5 and to their outstanding testimony of conversion, 1Th 1:6-9; 2:13-14; 3:7-8; 4:10). Moreover, he stayed there long enough to find work and supported himself (1Th 2:9). The two letters also indicate that he had a ministry among the Gentiles (leading them away from idolatry) outside the synagogue (cf. 1Th 1:9), and that he had grown emotionally "attached" to them (1Th 2:8, 19). Their relationship was strong enough that they could take some rather "stern" instruction from him (2Th 3:6). Also, in Philippians Paul noted that he received gifts from the Philippians while he was ministering in Thessalonica (Php 4:16), indicating a stay of more than a few weeks. So it is likely that his stay in Thessalonica should be calculated in months rather than weeks.

OUTLINE

- I. Paul's Greeting to the Thessalonians (1:1)
- II. Paul's Thanksgiving for the Thessalonians (1:2-10)
  - A. Thankfulness in Prayer and Remembrance (1:2-3a)
  - B. Thankfulness in Knowledge (1:3b-10)
    - 1. Knowledge of God's Choice of the Thessalonians (1:3b-5)
    - 2. Knowledge of the Thessalonians' Imitation of Paul (1:6-7)
    - 3. Knowledge of the Thessalonians' Spread of the Gospel (1:8-9)
    - 4. Knowledge of the Thessalonians' Waiting for Jesus (1:10)
- III. Paul's Ministry among the Thessalonians (2:1-16)
  - A. Purity in Paul's Motives (2:1-6)
    - 1. Boldness in the Midst of Opposition (2:1-2)
    - 2. Purity in the Midst of Ministry (2:3-6)
  - B. Purity in Paul's Emotions: Gentleness and Affection (2:7-8)
  - C. Purity in Paul's Life (2:9-12)
    - 1. Paul Worked Hard Not to Burden Them (2:9-10)
    - 2. Paul Taught Clearly in Order to Help Them (2:11-12)
  - D. Purity in Paul's Teaching (2:13-16)
    - 1. The Word Shaped These Believers (2:13)
    - 2. The Word Condemns Unbelievers (2:14-16)
- IV. Paul's Concern for the Thessalonians (2:17–3:13)
  - A. Paul's Separation from Them (2:17-20)
  - B. Paul's Sacrifice for Them: Sending Timothy (3:1-5)
  - C. Paul's Delight Over Them (3:6-10)
  - D. Paul's Instructions to Them (3:11-13)
- V. Paul's Firm Exhortations to the Thessalonians (4:1-12)
  - A. Introduction to the Exhortations (4:1-2)
  - B. Content of the Exhortations (4:3-12)
    - 1. Be Pure in Sexual Practices (4:3-8)
    - 2. Be Tender in Serving Others (4:9-10)
    - 3. Be Diligent in Personal Affairs (4:11-12)
- VI. Paul's Encouragement for the Thessalonians in Eschatology (4:13–5:11)
  - A. Be Encouraged about Deceased Believers (4:13-18)
    - 1. Promise of the Resurrection at the Rapture of the Church (4:13-14)
    - 2. Order of the Resurrection at the Rapture of the Church (4:15-17)
    - 3. Comfort from the Resurrection at the Rapture of the Church (4:18)
  - B. Be Encouraged about Escaping the Day of the Lord (5:1-11)
- VII. Paul's Exhortations for Sensible, Spiritual Living (5:12-22)

A. Their Relationships with Church Leaders (5:12-13)
B. Their Relationships with Christian Friends (5:14-15)
C. Their Attitudes toward Those Who Persecute (5:16-18)
D. Their Relationship with the Holy Spirit: Do Not Quench the Spirit (5:19-22)
VIII. Paul's Closing Words to the Thessalonians (5:23-28)
A. A Prayer for the Thessalonians (5:23-24)
B. Instructions to the Thessalonians (5:25-28)

COMMENTARY ON 1 THESSALONIANS

I. Paul's Greeting to the Thessalonians (1:1)

1:1. Some typically Pauline elements do not appear in this introduction. First and Second Thessalonians "are the only two letters in which Paul did not add some elaboration to his name and/or to the names of his co-senders" (Michael D. Martin, *1, 2 Thessalonians*, NAC [Nashville: Broadman & Holman, 1995], 47). There is no mention of his "apostolic" office (cf. Gl 1:1; Eph 1:1; Col 1:1) or of being a "servant" ("slave") (cf. Rm 1:1; Php 1:1) or his "authority." Silvanus (or Silas, cf. Ac 15:40; cf. 2Pt 5:12) and Timothy (Paul's "true child in the faith," cf. 1Tm 1:2; 2Tm 1:2) were Paul's companions on his second missionary journey (cf. the comments on Ac 16:1-3). Paul noted that the church was **in God the Father and the Lord Jesus Christ** (v. 1b). This was a congregation of some who had come out of the synagogue (Jews) and some who had "turned to God from idols" (Gentiles).

Paul's greeting combined elements of a Greek greeting and a Hebrew greeting. Paul combined the distinctively Christian term *charis* (**grace**) in place of the typical Greek *charein* ("Greetings!") and the term **peace,** the common Jewish greeting shalom (For Paul's combining of Greek and Hebrew greetings, see 1Co 1:1-3).

II. Paul's Thanksgiving for the Thessalonians (1:2-10)

A. Thankfulness in Prayer and Remembrance (1:2-3a)

1:2-3a. Paul was thankful to God (as the source of all blessings). He prayed regularly, corporately (**we give thanks . . . in our prayers**), and constantly (**always . . . constantly**, best understood as applying to the prayer of v. 1), and he was "other focused" (**for all of you**).

B. Thankfulness in Knowledge (1:3b-10)

1. Knowledge of God's Choice of the Thessalonians (1:3b-5)

1:3b-5. Paul noted his reasons and grounds for thanksgiving. He gave thanks for their virtues and qualities. The three virtues of "faith, love, hope" are a favorite triad of the apostle Paul (see 5:8; 1Co 13:13; cf. Col 1:4, 5). "*Faith, love, hope,* are here named in their logical order. 'Faith rests on the past; love works in the present; hope looks to the future'" (D. Edmond Hiebert, *The Thessalonian Epistles* [Chicago: Moody, 1971], 47; Hiebert cites J. B. Lightfoot, *St. Paul's Epistles to the Colossians and to Philemon* [Grand Rapids, MI: Zondervan, 1959 reprint of 1879 ed.], 134). Faith looks back to Christ on the cross; love looks up to Christ at the Father's right hand; hope looks forward to the coming of Christ for His own! Here the emphasis is on the "qualities" affixed to the virtues, thus **work** that flows from **faith**, **labor** that is motivated by **love**, and **steadfastness** that is grounded in **hope**. "Paul's stress is not on these virtues alone but rather on what [qualities] they produce" (Hiebert, *Thessalonian Epistles*, 47).

The concluding clauses **in our Lord Jesus Christ . . . in the presence of our God and Father** indicate "where" the virtues and qualities are to be lived out. By faith, love, and hope the Thessalonians were in union with Christ, and out of that relationship they demonstrated the appropriate work, labor, and steadfastness in the presence of the Father.

Paul also gave thanks for their election, which was grounded in God's love (**brethren beloved by God**; see Eph 2:4) and by His sovereignty (**His choice**; see 2Pt 1:10, "His calling and choosing you"). Their election was obvious based on the Thessalonians' positive response to the gospel (**for** 1Th 1:5a, or better "because": "I know you are among the elect *because* . . . "). It was evident in their reception of the gospel as the Word of God (1:5a, 6; cf. 1:13) and in their reception of the preachers of the gospel (1:5c). This **gospel** had been preached *with* words (cf. Rm 10:17), yet not merely *by* words (v. 5b) but with **power** (cf. 1Co 2:4-5), the inherent, supernatural power of the gospel as energized by the **Holy Spirit** (1Co 2:10-13). Paul and his companions preached this gospel with **full conviction**, and it produced **full conviction** in the Thessalonians.

2. Knowledge of the Thessalonians' Imitation of Paul (1:6-7)

1:6-7. Next, Paul gave thanks for their imitation of Paul, especially of his evangelistic efforts to the world. When the Thessalonians **received the word**—they accepted it as true. They immediately became **imitators** (*mimetai*; the English word "mimic" is derived from this word) of the apostles and **of the Lord** (as the apostles had "imitated" Christ; cf. 1Co 11:1). They received this Word **in much tribulation** (*thlipsis*, "intense pressure"), indicating severe persecution. But they endured (cf. 1Th 1:3; 3:8) and their testimony had spread to the surrounding regions—**Macedonia** to the north (Philippi) and **Achaia** to the south (Athens). They became **an example** (*typon* "type," the "mark" or "imprint" left by a die that strikes metal to make a coin, or a seal that leaves an imprint on wax) to other believers.

3. Knowledge of the Thessalonians' Spread of the Gospel (1:8-9)

1:8-9. Their imitation of Paul and their own exemplary conversion and ministry had **sounded forth** (*exechetai*; only here in the NT) from them. The term has the idea of a "trumpet blast" or even the echo of thunder, "like sound going forth in all directions" (Charles A. Wanamaker, *The Epistles to the Thessalonians, NIGTC* [Grand Rapids, MI: Eerdmans, 1990], 83). "The verb 'hath sounded forth' (*exechetai*) denoted the resounding reverberations of a loud noise." "The perfect tense indicates the abiding effect of the blast: 'the blast hangs on the air'" (Hiebert, *Thessalonians*, 63), though Paul may also have used the perfect tense to draw attention to the extraordinary nature of the impact of the gospel upon the Thessalonians.

Finally, Paul gave thanks for their unmistakable conversion to God. Verse 9 is the quintessential verse on *conversion*. "**Turned** is from the verb *epistrepho*, which is used in the NT to indicate that in the sinner's conversion there is a turning in the absolute opposite direction" (John MacArthur, *First & Second Thessalonians*, MNTC [Chicago: Moody, 2002], 27). The term "marks the radical change that has come into the lives of the Thessalonians" (Hiebert, *Thessalonians*, 67) and means "to change one's mind or course of action" (BDAG, 382). Because of their genuine conversion the Thessalonians began to **serve a living and true God**, in contrast to serving the dead and false idols of Greek pagan religion. "The word Paul chose for **serve** (*douleuein*) means to serve as a [slave], which is the most demanding form of servitude" (MacArthur, *Thessalonians*, 27). "The present infinitive (*douleuein*) denotes that it is a life of continuous, complete, and wholehearted service to God" (Hiebert, *Thessalonians*, 69).

4. Knowledge of the Thessalonians' Waiting for Jesus (1:10)

1:10. Another point Paul knew about the Thessalonians that caused him to be thankful to the Lord was their sensitivity to the imminent return of the Lord. They began to **wait for His Son. Wait for** means "to remain in a place and/or state, with expectancy concerning a future event" (L&N, 1:729). Warren Wiersbe writes, "The word translated 'wait' (found only here in the NT) in 1:10 means 'to await someone with patience and confidence, expectantly.' Waiting involves activity and endurance" (Warren Wiersbe, *Be Ready,* BSC [Colorado Springs: David C. Cook, 2010], 32).

Paul gave a note of assurance (anticipating his teaching later in the letter): because Jesus is the One who was "raised from the dead" (cf. 1Co 15:20-28) the Thessalonians can be assured that they too will be raised (cf. 1Th 4:16-17). His coming will rescue believers **from the wrath to come** (they will not have to experience the tribulation, cf. the comments on 1Th 5:9-10). Despite the potentially dangerous and stressful situation in which the Thessalonians found themselves, they responded ideally, and for these reasons Paul was thankful.

III. Paul's Ministry among the Thessalonians (2:1-16)

Part of Paul's purpose in writing this letter was to secure his good relationship with the Thessalonians and to distinguish himself and his coworkers from the often insincere and immoral itinerant philosophers who floated from city to city in those days. So Paul provided a brief apologetic about his purity in relationship to the Thessalonians. In this section, Paul's philosophy of ministry becomes evident, as demonstrated in the apostle's ministry in Thessalonica.

A. Purity in Paul's Motives (2:1-6)

1. Boldness in the Midst of Opposition (2:1-2)

2:1-2. First, his boldness, and that of his companions, was impressive in light of the harsh treatment they received in Philippi prior to coming to Thessalonica (see the comments on Ac 16:19). He noted the effect of his ministry in 2:1a. The coming of Paul and his companions was **not in vain** because the Thessalonians had become followers of Christ (cf. 1:9-10). Then he noted the conditions of his ministry. Paul and his companions began the work in Thessalonica after persecution. They had been forced out of **Philippi** (cf. Ac 16:19-24, 37) where they had been beaten (**suffered**) and imprisoned (**mistreated**). Still, they were bold, even though they continued to face **opposition**. Paul was reminding the Thessalonians that his was no self-serving, ease-seeking ministry. It is impressive to consider that Paul and Silas probably still had the scabs and sores on their backs from their beating in Philippi (Ac 16:22-23) when they walked into Thessalonica and nevertheless began to proclaim the good news again.

2. Purity in the Midst of Ministry (2:3-6)

2:3-6. Next Paul recalled the pure motives for their ministry stemming from his accountability to God. He was truthful in what he taught (**not from error**), chaste (i.e., not motivated by **impurity**), authentic (no **deceit**), authorized by God (**approved by God**, v. 4a; **God is witness**, v. 5), and not self-seeking or man-pleasing. Paul specified six characteristics of false teachers that were not true of himself or his ministry. First, he was not a "man-pleaser" ("to act in a fawning manner, *win favor, please, flatter*," BDAG, 129; cf. Gl 1:6-9). Second, he was not a "flatterer" ("praise as a means of gratifying someone's vanity—'flattering talk, flattery,'" L&N, 1:430; one who compliments others to win favor, to influence them, to gain power over them. He did not tailor the truth to fit popular opinion; cf. Martin, *1, 2 Thessalonians,* 74). Third, he was not greedy (self-seeking for monetary gain). Fourth, he used no **pretext** (*prophasis*, "a cloak," that is, something used to conceal or hide someone or something). Fifth, he was not a glory seeker ("glory seeking" has the idea of the pursuit of prestige, honor, esteem of others. Such persons "live for the applause"). And sixth, he was not a "taker." Here Paul is (subtly) saying, "You know I could have insisted that you show me (and the others) respect and demanded that you (tangibly) demonstrate it" (ESV on v. 6b, "we could have made demands").

Paul also made three affirmations about what was true of his life and work. First, he was a "God-pleaser," not pleasing people **but God**. Second, he knew that God **examines . . . hearts** (cf. 1Co 4:1-5). The man who knows that God knows, examines, and judges the heart (cf. Jr 17:10) is a man others can trust to serve with integrity (the heart is the inner man, "the real person, where thought, feeling, will, and motive converge." MacArthur, *Thessalonians,* 40). Third, he knew **God** was a **witness** to his ministry (cf. Rm 1:9).

B. Purity in Paul's Emotions: Gentleness and Affection (2:7-8)

2:7-8. Paul reminded them that his was a tender ministry, evoking images of maternal care and affection. Paul and his companions were **gentle** (v. 7, *epioi*, "mild, kindhearted, caring"). A textual variation has the similar word "babes" (*nepioi*; see the NET; NLT; TNIV). Manuscript evidence is uncertain; "babes" has good manuscript support, but "gentle" fits better with the overall metaphor. "The term **gentle** is at the heart of the verse. It means to be kind to someone and encompasses a host of other virtues: acceptance, respect, compassion, tolerance of imperfections, patience, tenderheartedness, and loyalty" (MacArthur, *Thessalonians,* 45). **Tenderly cares** (*thalpe*) has the idea of "warming" as a mother "warms" her child with a hug, or a hen covers her chicks with her wings, an image that the Lord Jesus used of his care for Israel (cf. Mt 23:37). The second image is that of the self-sacrifice of mothers (v. 8). This verse opens and ends with an expression of affection. The term **having so fond an affection** (*homeiromenoi*, only here in the NT) describes the feeling of a parent for a small child, "longing for a child," perhaps for a child that has died. **Very dear** (*agapetoi*) "signifies that the Thessalonians were the objects of a high, persistent love which desired only their true welfare (cf. 1:3)" (Hiebert, *Thessalonians,* 96). Paul demonstrated his affection and love by sharing his life with them—they had shared **also** their **own lives**. These are astounding words coming from one who was such a staunch ambassador for the Savior!

C. Purity in Paul's Life (2:9-12)

1. Paul Worked Hard Not to Burden Them (2:9-10)

2:9-10. Paul also recalled the conduct of his ministry, noting five qualities of his conduct, life, and ministry among them. He was hard-working, self-supporting (v. 9), well-behaved (v. 10), encouraging (v. 11), and purposeful (so that he might prove effective in his ministry,

v. 12). Paul worked hard, not just at preaching and teaching but also at his trade of tent-making to support himself. Paul behaved **devoutly** (*hosios*, "scrupulousness in one's relationship with and service to God") and **uprightly** (*dikaios*, "righteously," with an eye to the general idea of "living right") and was therefore blameless.

2. Paul Taught Clearly in Order to Help Them (2:11-12)

Paul also encouraged them as a father would (v. 11). He was **exhorting** (*parakaleo*, "to call alongside"; the word has the idea of instructing or applying instruction), **encouraging** (*paramutheomai*, "to encourage through comfort and consolation"), and **imploring** (*marturomai*, from which the English word "martyr" is derived, means "witness," and has the idea of adding a serious, heartfelt appeal) the Thessalonians. Paul wanted the Thessalonians to **walk... worthy**, that is live their lives in a noble, upright, God-honoring way—in a way commensurate with their "calling" (**who calls you** signals the concept of election yet again), in a way that spoke of their hope of heavenly **glory** (to live like one destined for heaven).

D. Purity in Paul's Teaching (2:13-16)

1. The Word Shaped These Believers (2:13)

2:13. Again Paul offered thanks to God for the Thessalonians' reception of the gospel. The Thessalonians had **heard** a word (verbally and audibly) preached by Paul and his companions (**from us**), a word from human agents (**the word of men**), but they heard it as something much more. It was **the word of God** that Paul preached when he preached the gospel (cf. 2:2, 8, 9; cf. Ac 8:14; 1Co 15:1-3), indicating that he viewed at least some of his teaching as inspired by God. And so it was the **word of God** the Thessalonians **received** (*paralabontes*, objectively perceived), **accepted** (*edexasthe*, inwardly welcomed, took to heart), and believed. This was not because of their own wisdom or powers of perception. The self-authenticating Word of God had performed its work of convicting and convincing them of the truth of Paul's message (cf. 1Co 2:4-5; Col 1:6). "The verb rendered **performs its work** means to work effectively, efficiently, and productively on a supernatural (divine) level (cf. 1 Cor. 12:6; Php 2:13" (MacArthur, *Thessalonians*, 58).

2. The Word Condemns Unbelievers (2:14-16)

2:14-16. But the same message that had transformed the Thessalonians was opposed by the world, and Paul noted that the Thessalonians had also experienced opposition. Again (cf. 1:6) they had become **imitators** of the original Jewish churches in Judea in how they had been persecuted. Just as Jewish believers of Judea had experienced opposition from their own people, the Jewish religious leadership, the Thessalonians had been opposed by their **own countrymen**. However, unlike the **Lord Jesus and the prophets**, they had not yet suffered martyrdom.

Some have alleged that Paul here holds "an unacceptable anti-Semitic position" (Ernest Best, *A Commentary on the 1st and 2nd Epistles to the Thessalonians*, HNTC [New York: Harper and Row, 1987], 122). In light of Paul's love and concern for his own people (Rm 9:1-3), that is unlikely. Rather, Paul's reference to **the Jews** does not refer to the entire nation but rather to the religious leadership of the Jewish people. That is because, first, Paul referred to an intra-ethnic conflict, with the Jewish leaders opposing Jewish believers in Judea as Gentiles opposed the Thessalonians. As such, Paul could not be referring to all Jews. Second, the sins Paul said the Jews committed are limited in the Gospels to those of the Jewish leaders, not the entire nation. For example, the Jewish leaders plotted Jesus' death (Jn 11:47–53), accused him before Pilate (Lk 23:2) and Herod (v. 10), and incited the crowd (Mt 27:20; Mk 15:11). Third, here Paul was describing the same sins found in the parable of the vine-growers (Mt 21:33-46) at the end of which the Jewish leaders acknowledged that Jesus was speaking of them and not the entire nation. (For a full discussion, see "Was Paul Anti-Semitic? Revisiting 1 Thessalonians 2:14-16," *Bibliotheca Sacra* 165 [January–March 2008]: 75-84). Paul noted that the Jewish leaders were **not pleasing to God**, that they were **hostile to all men**, that they were **hindering** the preaching of the gospel of salvation, and that they were in danger of the **wrath** of judgment for their sins. The reason for pointing this out to the Thessalonians was that this was also true of the Gentile leaders who persecuted them.

IV. Paul's Personal Concern for the Thessalonians (2:17–3:13)

A. Paul's Separation from Them (2:17-20)

2:17-18. Paul expressed a personal desire to see the Thessalonians (**I, Paul**) with a sense of urgency and sincerity. His forced and physical separation (**taken away**) only increased his **great desire** to be with them in more than **spirit**. He wanted to see them "face to face." This desire had been frustrated, in some manner not indicated, by **Satan**. **Hindered** is a military term and indicates the placing of an obstacle or impediment to an army's movement. The subtle alert to the real spiritual opposition Christians face is not to be missed.

2:19-20. Paul expressed his affection for the Thessalonians with an eschatological twist as he elaborated on why he was so affectionate toward them. It was because they were a cause of his future **hope**, the ultimate source of his present **joy**, and the basis for his expectation of reward—his **crown** (a victor's wreath, cf. 1Co 9:25). All of this will be fully realized **in the presence** of the **Lord Jesus** at the time of **His coming** when believers will be reunited and rewards distributed (at the "judgment seat" of Christ, cf. 2Co 5:10; for more on rewards, see Mt 6:1; 24:45-47; 25:19-23). **Coming** (*parousia*, "to be present") is a term used to refer to specific aspects of the Lord's return (cf. 1Th 4:15) or to the broader, multifaceted event associated with the beginning of the day of the Lord (cf. Mt 24:37; Rv 19:11–20:6). "In addition to the present verse, this epistle uses *parousia* three other times to denote the Rapture (1Th 3:13; 4:15; 5:23)" (MacArthur, *Thessalonians*, 74). On the referent for the word **coming**, Robert L. Thomas writes, "The complexity of the term *parousia* demands that it include an extended visit as well as the arrival initiating that visit. This is provided for adequately in the rarer meaning of *parousia*, 'presence' (cf. 1Co 16:17; 2Co 10:10; Php 2:12). Included in this visit is an evaluation of the saints (cf. 1Th 2:19; 5:23), which is the aspect in view here in 1Th 3:13 . . . This judgment cannot be completely dissociated from Christ's coming in the air (4:15-17), because this advent marks its initiation. Yet it must be conceived of as a session in heaven in some measure separate from the arrival itself" (Robert L. Thomas, "1 Thessalonians," in EBC, ed. Frank E. Gaebelein [Grand Rapids, MI: Zondervan, 1978], 269).

B. Paul's Sacrifice for Them: Sending Timothy (3:1-5)

3:1-5. Paul's concern for the Thessalonians made the separation intolerable. He **could endure it no longer**, and this led to Timothy's mission (**we sent Timothy**) to **strengthen** and **encourage** them in their faith. This mission was self-sacrificial, as Paul was **left behind at Athens alone** (3:1b). It indicated again Paul's deep affection for the Thessalonians, and it showed that he was willing to be inconvenienced for others. The mission also indicated that Timothy, Paul's **brother and God's fellow worker** (a unique title), was just the sort of fellow who was willing to be sent and serve, according to Php 2:19-24. This mission was undertaken because Paul knew that persecution could be disturbing and potentially destructive, even as it was inevitable. He had already prepared them **in advance**. Paul was not suggesting that they could lose their salvation when he feared that his **labor would be in vain** ("empty," "void," "to no purpose"), nor did he think that God's Word would prove to be "in vain" (cf. Is 55:11). He was concerned that some who had made a profession would be proven to be "false brethren," and that they would give up their professed faith because of persecution.

C. Paul's Delight Over Them (3:6-10)

3:6. Paul's joy over the Thessalonians and Timothy's positive report are the topics of vv. 6-10. The substance of the report was, overall, **good news**. Their **faith and love** were strong, they still had a favorable view of Paul (and his companions), and they too longed to see Paul. It may be significant that "hope" is not mentioned here (cf. 1:3). Timothy's report had revealed that some were worried that loved ones who had died had missed the rapture (cf. 4:13-18) and others were thinking that they had entered the tribulation ("Day of the Lord," 5:1-11). Perhaps they were not now doing as well in the matter of "hope" as they were in the matters of "faith and love."

3:7-10. The effect of the report on Paul and his companions was that they were relieved (**comforted**) and had greater confidence in the faith of the Thessalonians (**we really live**). The Thessalonians did **stand firm** (*stekete*, v. 8) and were not retreating. For this Paul offered still more thanksgiving, experienced still more and more joy, offered more prayer, and expressed yet again his renewed desire for fellowship. When Paul noted that he wanted to **complete what was lacking in** their **faith** he was not suggesting that their faith was defective but rather that there was more for them to know, to apply, to see lived out. "Not that the faith which they had was defective, but it still needed completing and rounding out" (Hiebert, *Thessalonians*, 152).

D. Paul's Instructions to Them (3:11-13)

3:11-13. Paul's prayer for the Thessalonians followed his response to Timothy's report. He prayed to return to Thessalonica, which he still desired even though his concerns were allayed.

He also prayed for an increase in their love, a theme he would repeat (cf. 4:9-10), and for them to be grounded in **holiness**, which is always an important goal for believers (cf. 4:1-8). He prayed all this with a view to the reality of Christ's return, a major theme yet to be developed. What he "prayed for" he "taught to" the Thessalonians.

V. Paul's Firm Exhortations to the Thessalonians (4:1-12)

A. Introduction to the Exhortations (4:1-2)

4:1-2. One of the means whereby the Thessalonians would experience the love and blamelessness for which Paul prayed for them in 3:11-13 would be through their own commitment to live pure lives. In 4:1-12, and actually running through the remainder of the book, Paul's exhortations related to purity. Beginning in vv. 1-2, Paul's instructions on purity were offered with three underlying ideas: One, this was instruction they had already been given: **as you received from us** . . . **for you know what . . . we gave you**; **just as we told you before** (vv. 1, 2, 6). Two, this instruction was needed and urgent: **we request and exhort** (v. 1). Note that Paul started with a request before giving the exhortation. "It is best not to equate the two words, but to understand the former as a gentle, friendly request and the latter as an authoritative apostolic plea" (Thomas, "1 Thessalonians," 11:270). The phrase **just as we . . . solemnly warned you** (v. 6) indicated that the matters with which Paul was dealing were not inconsequential or trivial. Three, this instruction was given by the authority of Jesus Christ: **exhort you in** [behalf of, or in the name of] **the Lord Jesus** ["that is with His authority"] (MacArthur, *Thessalonians*, 97); **what commandments** . . . **by the authority of the Lord Jesus** (v. 2). "Paul's directives did not originate from some arbitrary human sanction or some remote ecclesiastical authority (cf. Gl 1:1, 15-16; 2Pt 1:20-21). Instead they come from the authority of the Lord Jesus, and obedience to them was mandatory (cf. Mt. 7:21; Jn 15:14-17; 1 Jn 2:3-5)" (MacArthur, *Thessalonians*, 98).

B. Content of the Exhortations (4:3-12)

1. Be Pure in Sexual Practices (4:3-8)

4:3-8. The major concept or theme in these verses is **sanctification**. The term occurs three times, in 4:3, 4, and 7. This **sanctification** (*hagiosmos*) "is to be understood as the process of being separated from sin and set apart to God's holiness . . . God wants believers to separate from all that is evil, fleshly and impure" (MacArthur, *Thessalonians*, 103-04). **Your sanctification** further defines **this**, which is itself further defined as **the will of God** (v. 3).

Paul noted three aspects of sanctification. First, he gave a general idea related to sanctification. To **walk** is a well-known metaphor for "living the Christian life." It is the verb *peripateo*, which literally means to "walk around" (Mt 9:5; 11:5; Jn 6:66; Rv 2:1), used figuratively of the way believers or anyone behaves or conducts daily life (Mk 7:5; Gl 5:16, 25; Eph 2:2; 4:1; cf. 2Co 5:7) (cf. Mounce, *Expository Dictionary*, 772). Second, he gave a negative idea about sanctification. They must **abstain from sexual immorality**, v. 3. The term **abstain** means "do not practice or engage in at all." "[I]n this case [it means] staying completely away from any thought or behavior that violates the principles of God's Word and results in any form of illicit sexual behavior (Jn 8:41; Ac 15:20, 29; 21:25; 1Co 5:1; 6:13, 18; 2Co 12:21; Gl 5:19; Eph 5:3; Col 3:5; Rv 2:21; 9:21). "Total abstinence from sexual sin is a duty of then utmost importance for all believers . . ." (MacArthur, *Thessalonians*, 104, 105). Third, regarding sanctification, Paul gave a positive idea. Each person was to **possess his own vessel** (v. 4). This is an individual responsibility (**each of you**). This may refer to a man's (or woman's) own body (cf. MacArthur, *Thessalonians*, 106) or it may refer to a man's wife (cf. Thomas, "1 Thessalonians," 11:271). In the NT, **possess** (*ktaomai*) is always translated with the word "to acquire" or its equivalent (Mt 10:9; Lk 18:12; 21:19; Ac 1:18; 8:20; 22:28). In addition, **vessel** (*skeuos*) is used in 1Pt 3:7 for one's wife, and the sense is probably "to acquire one's own vessel, that is, wife." Paul is encouraging the Thessalonians who were experiencing severe temptation to immorality to get married as a way to forestall sexual sin.

Four characteristics should accompany the process of finding a spouse. It should be conducted, first, **in sanctification and honor** (v. 4; both nouns are governed by the same preposition **in** and should be viewed as a complex whole). **Sanctification** means "the process of becoming sanctified, holy, consecrated to God," here through abstaining from sexual immorality. **Honor** indicates "respect" for the process of acquiring a spouse and the person one is pursuing. There is a right way and a wrong way to seek a marriage partner.

Second, acquiring a spouse should be pursued without **lustful passion** (v. 5), that is, "Christians must not lower themselves to a level of pagan sexual behavior determined merely by unthinking passions and uncontrolled fleshly urges" (MacArthur, *Thessalonians*, 109). Third, the process must not parallel that of **the Gentiles who do not know God** (v. 5). Fourth, a mate should be pursued with integrity, not sinning against (**transgress**, v. 6) our brothers and sisters in Christ in the process. **Defraud** means "to take advantage of someone, usually as the result of a motivation of greed" (L&N, 1:757). One would defraud another by using him or her for one's own perverted sexual gratification. Such an act would not only be despicable but would also serve to invite disciplinary action from God.

Paul also explained in theses verses why sanctification (*hagiosmos*, "set apart from sin, set apart to holiness") was so important: (1) being set apart is pleasing to God (v. 1); (2) being set apart from sexual sin is God's will (v. 3); (3) being set apart is the proof that believers know God and therefore know better than the unbelievers (**Gentiles**) who do not **know God** (v. 5) why they should be set apart (cf. 1Pt 1:15-16); (4) being set apart is the only way to avoid the Lord's judgment since **the Lord is the avenger in all these things** (v. 6b) (cf. Mt 18:6-7); and (5) being set apart is the position to which God has called us—**God has not called us** to **impurity** (v. 7)—which is to say He has called believers to "purity"! Paul concluded by noting the gift of **His Holy Spirit to you** (v. 8b). Here he implicitly indicated the "how" of sanctification—"Walk by the Spirit and you will not carry out the desire [lust, KJV] of the flesh" (Gl 5:16).

2. Be Tender in Serving Others (4:9-10)

4:9-10. From the stark instruction on sexual morality Paul turned to an exhortation on brotherly love, reiterating an earlier theme of this letter (cf. 1:3; 3:12). Whereas sexual immorality is selfish and self-serving, brotherly love is other-interested, other-concerned, other-serving. "**Love of the brethren** (*philadelphia*) originally referred to affection for blood relatives but is always used in the NT in reference to Christian affection (Rm 12:10; Heb 13:1; 1Pt 1:22; 2Pt 1:7)" (MacArthur, *Thessalonians*, 117). The Thessalonians needed to recall what they knew about love, to remember that they had been **taught by God** about love, preeminently in the incarnation and sacrificial death of Christ (cf. Jn 3:16), to keep practicing that love, and even to **excel still more**.

3. Be Diligent in Personal Affairs (4:11-12)

4:11-12. Paul's exhortation on a proper and productive life was likely a response to some concerns raised by Timothy's report (cf. 3:6). Perhaps some had so embraced the promise of the Lord's return that they had stopped working and had begun to interfere with the everyday life of the other church members. Paul's antidote to such a lackadaisical outlook and disruptive behavior was fourfold; they were to: (1) **lead a quiet life**—avoid unnecessary conflict; (2) **attend to** their **own business** (cf. 5:13)—not be busybodies (cf. 2Th 3:11); (3) **work with** their own **hands** (v. 11c)—be self-supporting not eating another's bread (cf. 2Th 3:8) so as to **not be in any need** (v. 12b); and (4) **behave properly** (v. 12a)—maintain a good testimony with unbelievers (**outsiders**).

VI. Paul's Encouragement for the Thessalonians in Eschatology (4:13–5:11)

A. Be Encouraged about Deceased Believers (4:13-18)

1. Promise of the Resurrection at the Rapture of the Church (4:13-14)

4:13-14. During his ministry with the Thessalonians Paul had taught them about the end-time events and the coming of the Lord Jesus Christ. In the interim between that ministry and Timothy's visit (cf. 3:2, 5) some of the believers had died and the church was enduring persecution. The first of these circumstances caused some to think their loved ones had missed the Lord's return for His bride, the Church (cf. Jn 14:1-3; Eph 5:27). The second circumstance caused others to think that they had already entered the time of tribulation known as "the day of the Lord" (cf. Jl 2:30-32; Zch 14:1; Mal 4:1, 5; see the comments there). Paul dealt with those misunderstandings in the next two sections. These two questions would arise only if Paul had taught the Thessalonians that the coming of the Lord was "imminent"—that it could happen at any moment.

4:13-18. Paul first instructed them about the gathering of the saints—the supernatural event of the "catching away" of the church. The death of loved ones had prompted the question: "Had those believers missed that glorious event?" Paul's purpose here was pastoral (not polemical). It was to inform and comfort the **brethren** so that they **will not grieve** the loss of loved ones as the world grieves. They were to have **hope** (v. 13). The ground of this hope is the death (securing atonement; cf. 1Pt 2:21-25; Is 53) and resurrection (confirming that justification of Jesus; cf. Rm 4:25) of Jesus. Paul assured them that those loved ones were only **asleep** (used three times as a euphemism for death that gives the promise of an awakening). Those believers who are **asleep in Jesus** (v. 13) are not lost and gone forever, but they are "with the Lord" (cf. 2Co 5:8). It is clear that Paul thought of the state of believers who had died as both "asleep" (this pertains to their bodies) and as conscious (in His presence). This view denies any thought of "soul sleep" and helps to explain how these deceased ones can both return with Him (v. 14) and also **rise first** (v. 16). Their immaterial nature (soul; spirit) that is currently with Him will accompany Him to be rejoined to their bodies, which will be resurrected and transformed at the rapture.

2. Order of the Resurrection at the Rapture of the Church (4:15-17)

4:15-17. Paul explained how the event of the "catching away" was to unfold. There will be a series of distinctive steps, listed in vv. 15-17. He introduced the details of the sequence by affirming that his teaching was grounded in the teaching of Christ (see the comments on Mt 24:36ff.). The Thessalonians could be confident of what Paul taught since this was **by the word of the Lord.** (This may indicate some traditional teaching of Jesus not preserved in the gospel record or some direct revelation to Paul, but more likely is based on Jesus' teaching in Mt 24:36ff.). Paul then delivered the clearest teaching on the "rapture" of the Church to be found in the NT. He dealt with the persons involved, the plan of the event, and the point of his teaching. The word "rapture" is based on the Latin translation of this passage, which uses a form of the Latin verb *rapio* ("to seize," "to carry off violently") (cf. Alan Hultberg, "Introduction," in *Three Views on the Rapture*, 2nd ed. [Grand Rapids: Zondervan, 2010], 11) which is used to translate the Greek term *harpazo*, the verb Paul used, in verse 17.

The persons involved are all those who are **asleep in Jesus** (v. 14), also identified as **the dead in Christ** (v. 16), that is, deceased believers, as well as living believers who are identified twice as **we who are alive and remain** (vv. 15, 17). Paul had in mind those NT believers **in Christ** (v. 16), i.e., Christians, members of the Church, both deceased and living. Paul was keen to make the point that the living Church members would not be given preferential treatment over the deceased. Indeed, Christ will bring the living souls of those who died in Him to be reunited with their resurrected bodies (cf. 1Co 15:51-58). Paul included himself with those who were alive and remained (**we**). This indicates that Paul believed that the rapture could occur in his lifetime—indeed, that it could occur at any time. For him it was an imminent possibility. Paul identified the Lord as Jesus, **Christ**, and **the Lord Himself** as the agent performing this work. This contrasts with the event described in Mt 24:31 where, at the second coming, the angels will "gather together His elect." Thus, there are two distinct events associated with the *parousia*—the rapture and the second coming (or "revelation") of Christ. See the comments on Mt 24:3-35.

The sequence of events associated with the rapture of believers will begin when **the Lord Himself** descends (v. 16; cf. the comments on Ac 1:11; Jn 14:1-3) **from heaven**. Then there will occur three distinct sounds: first **a shout** (like a military "command"), second, **the voice of the archangel** (the only archangel named in the Bible is Michael, cf. Dn 12:1-3; Jd 9), and third, **the trumpet of God** (v. 16; cf. also the comments on 1Co 15:52). The exact nature of these sounds is unclear, but apparently the purpose is to summon believers and signal that the blessed hope (cf. Ti 2:13) is about to be realized. Next, the souls of the **dead in Christ** are reunited with their resurrected bodies. At death, the believer's immaterial nature (his soul) goes into the presence of the Lord consciously and enjoys that presence (see Php 1:21, 23).

But the Bible does not teach the immortality of the soul alone. It teaches the immortality *of the entire person*, body and soul. At the rapture of the Church, the soul of the believer will be joined once again to his resurrected body, and the believer will experience eternity in this mode. Then, living believers will be **caught up** (v. 17) along with those resurrected saints. The nature of the event is indicated by the term *harpazo*, which means "to grab or seize suddenly so as to remove or gain control, *snatch* . . . [or] *take away*" (BDAG, 134). It describes "a strong, irresistible, even violent act" (MacArthur, *Thessalonians*, 136). *Harpazo* is used to describe a "taking by force," or "snatching away" (cf. Mt 11:12; Jn 10:12; Ac 8:39). The location of the event is described as **in the clouds** and **in the air** (4:17b; cf. Ac 1:9).

It has often been suggested, without much warrant, that the term *apantesis* (**to meet**, v. 17) has a technical meaning pertaining to a specific type of meeting—that of a delegation from a city with a visiting dignitary. At such a meeting, it is suggested, a delegation proceeds out of the city to greet a dignitary outside the city's walls and then escorts the dignitary back into the city. Those who appeal to this meaning are many (see, e.g., Best, *The First and Second Epistles to the Thessalonians*, 199; Martin, *1, 2 Thessalonians*, 153 n. 86; Gene L. Green, *The Letters to the Thessalonians*, Pillar [Grand Rapids, MI: Eerdmans, 2002], 226; Anthony A. Hoekema, "Amillennialism," *The Meaning of the Millennium: Four Views*, ed. Robert G. Clouse [Downers Grove, Illinois: InterVarsity, 1977], 183, 216 n. 19; Wanamaker, *The Epistles to the Thessalonians*, 175; and many others). Actually, this view is based on a single work by Erik Peterson written in 1929–30 (Erik Peterson, "Die Einholung Des Kyrios", *Zeitschrift für systematische Theologie* 7, 1929–30 [682–702]). Through simple multiplication of citation it has achieved the status of "common knowledge" that the term here in 1Th 4 refers to this technical meaning. However, a study of Peterson's work and an analysis of the use of the term "to meet" in ancient Greek literature demonstrates that such a technical meaning is false.

Michael R. Crosby notes, "A computer search of the literature written during the several centuries surrounding Paul's era using the *Thesaurus Linguae Graecae* (*TLG*) produced 91 pages of citations of passages that employ forms of [*apantesis* and related forms], and only a minority of the uses of these terms describes formal receptions. For example, Philo Judaeus uses these words 27 times, but not once to describe the meeting of a dignitary. Similarly, Josephus employs them 92 times but only ten times in descriptions of formal receptions. In the LXX the noun [form of *apantesis* often] . . . designates the hostile meeting of armies, although it also describes virtually any kind of meeting" (Michael R. Crosby, "Hellenistic Formal Receptions and Paul's Use of *APANTHSIS* in 1 Thessalonians 4:17," *Bulletin for Biblical Research* 4:1994, 19 [15-34]). Furthermore, in neither of the uses of this term in the NT in Mt 25:6, 10 in the Parable of the Ten Virgins and in Ac 28:15 describing Paul's reception by the Christians in Rome does the term fit with its supposed "technical meaning." Indeed, neither the meeting in Ac 28:15 nor that of the bridesmaids and bridegroom in Mt 25 has any of the "formal features" of the Hellenistic formal reception of a visiting dignitary.

Here, in effect, is a case of choosing between two metaphors to describe the event. Either this is something like the "visiting dignitary" view in which a group of city officials and such go out to greet an honored guest or conquering hero and then return to the city, or else like a Bridegroom, coming to retrieve His bride in fulfillment of His promise in Jn 14:1-3 to take her to His Father's house, where the wedding feast will complete the formal union of marriage (cf. Rv 19:7-9). The first view imports a metaphor that is not found anywhere else to describe Christ's relationship with His Church. In fact the text does not indicate that the Lord and the raptured saints return to "the city," which is the earth in the metaphor. It just says they are with Him **always**. The second view incorporates several other key texts and provides a richer explanation of the event, using a recognized metaphor—Bride/Church and Bridegroom/Christ—from several other passages.

The arguments that this event comes before the tribulation are: (1) Paul has already promised the Thessalonians that Jesus "rescues us from the wrath to come" (1:10). This is "wrath" that the believer will miss and the unbeliever will face (cf. 2:16). It is best understood as the "wrath of the Lamb" (Rv 6:16)—the eschatological wrath that will come at the tribulation; (2) The tribulation is the 70th week of Daniel (cf. Dn 9:24-27)—the time concerning Daniel's people and Jerusalem (9:24a), the "time of Jacobs trouble" (Jr 30:7)—a time with a distinctly "Jewish character" (cf. Leon Wood, *The Bible and Future Events* [Grand Rapids: Zondervan, 1973], 76) as Jesus describes it in Mt 24—a time of judgment on "the nations" of the earth and the "nation" of Israel, hence, the Church's presence is "not in keeping with the purpose of the tribulation" (cf. Wood, *Future Events*, 76); and (3) As noted above, here in 1Th 4 and in other passages in the NT (e.g. Rm 13:11-12; Ti 2:13; cf. Jms 5:7, 8) it is clear that that the apostle believed that he might be among those "caught up." He placed himself among the **we who are alive and remain**. He believed the return of the Lord was "imminent"—it could happen at any time. Obviously, the signs, the "birth pangs" (cf. Mt 24:8) that announce the beginning of the tribulation, cannot come before the rapture if the rapture can happen "at any moment"; (4) The event described in Mt 24:29-31, the second coming (proper), is not the same event as the one described here. Here it is the Lord Himself who comes to take His own to Himself, but in Mt 24:31 this is the task of elect angels. Also, based on other texts that describe the second coming (proper) (cf. Jl 2:12-16; Zch 14:1-5; Rv 19:11-21), there are significant differences between the two events: here He comes **in the air** but then He comes to the Mount of Olives; here the prospect is comfort and fellowship with the Lord, then the prospect is judgment (cf. Mt 24:36-41; see the comments there and on 1Co 15:51-58).

The outcome of the event is a blessed promise—**so we shall always be with the Lord.**

3. Comfort from the Resurrection at the Rapture of the Church (4:18)

Paul concluded with the point of this teaching: this was a message of **comfort**, intended to give peace and hope to the church (v. 18).

B. Be Encouraged about Escaping the Day of the Lord (5:1-11)

5:1-11. Paul then instructed them about the day of the Lord (see the comments on Jl 2:30-32; Zch 14:1; Mal 4:1, 5; Mt 24:4-41). That he is turning to a new topic is indicated by his use of *peri de*—**Now as to** (cf. 4:9; cf. 1Co 7:1; 8:1; for the use of the phrase in another eschatological passage describing the surprise commencement of the day of the Lord, see the comments on Mt 24:36-41). The intense persecution they were experiencing caused some in Thessalonica to think they were already in the tribulation (cf. the comments on Mt 24:3-35; Rv 5, 6). Although they were well taught and knew **full well**, Paul offered a word of correction about **the times** (the simple chronology) **and the epochs** (the eras or seasons) of the end times.

Paul noted that indeed **the day of the Lord** will come unexpectedly—like **a thief in the night**, at a time when everyone was talking about **Peace and safety** v. 2b, 3a. To suggest, as some do, that **they** (the people alive at the time) will be saying "peace and safety" argues strongly that this is before the onset of the tribulation, not during the tribulation. It would be unlikely that any would be saying this during the tribulation. Furthermore, this day will come suddenly (as with labor pains) and bring devastating **destruction** (for the same points, which originated with Jesus, see the comments on Mt 24:36-51). No one caught in it will **escape**. However, in answer to the Thessalonians' concern, Paul noted this will not **overtake** the Thessalonians or any believers in the Church age. Believers are **not of darkness** or **of night**, but are **sons of light** and **day**. Indeed, believers will not even be there in that day because He promised that we—His Church—would be delivered from wrath (having been raptured, cf. 4:13-18) for **God has not destined us for wrath** (v. 9; cf. 1:10; 2Th 2:13). Besides, Jesus had already taken the ultimate wrath when He **died for us**, v. 10a.

Some might suggest the promise that believers will not have to endure wrath should or would also apply to those believers in the tribulation. This view is hard to reconcile with the clear indications that believers in the tribulation will be martyred (cf. Mt 24:9; Rv 6:9)—part of the worldwide devastation, death, and destruction that will come on the world (the seal judgments of Rv 6) because of the "wrath of the Lamb" (Rv 6:16). In other words, while believers are never the direct recipients of divine wrath, tribulation believers will suffer as a result of that wrath. The difference between "church age" saints and tribulation saints is simply in the promises: the church is promised deliverance *from* wrath, those saints will be delivered *through* wrath (cf. Rv 6:11).

Douglas J. Moo, who takes a posttribulational view, opines that the language here suggests the Thessalonians will be present when the day of the Lord arrives (Douglas J. Moo, *Three Views on the Rapture*, rev. ed., [Grand Rapids, MI: Zondervan, 1996], 204-05). Why warn them that that day will come like a thief? Why encourage them be watchful? Actually, Paul's point is not so much to "warn them" as to contrast their present experience and standing with that of those who *will* be overtaken by the day of the Lord. Again, they were concerned that the persecution they were experiencing meant they were already in that day. Paul was saying, "No, you cannot already be in that day because when it comes it will be sudden (like a thief), and that has not happened; it will be devastating (**destruction**) 'such as has not occurred since the beginning of the world until now, nor ever will' (Mt 24:21), and that has not happened; it will be like a woman in labor (recalling Jesus' description in Mt 24:6-8—those pangs include wars, famines, earthquakes) leading inexorably to all the judgments of that day, and that has not happened." In vv. 4 and 5 Paul was not so much talking to the Thessalonians about being "watchful" as he was saying they needed to be "consistent" with their calling and status. They were to remain **alert and sober** (v. 6), not to be ready to enter the day of the Lord, but simply because this is the quality of life for those who are **sons of light and sons of day** (v. 5).

Finally, the Thessalonians were to be confident because they will see the completion of their **salvation** and **will live together with Him** (vv. 9, 10). This word from Paul was meant to **encourage** and edify (**build up**) the Thessalonians. The application for them was not merely an eschatological promise to hold but their present life to live.

VII. Paul's Exhortations for Sensible, Spiritual Living (5:12-22)

A. Their Relationships with Church Leaders (5:12-13)

5:12-13. As Paul was concluding his letter he made a series of brief admonitions sandwiched between instruction related to eschatological events (4:13–5:11; 5:23), suggesting that 5:12-22 forms important instruction about Christians' relationships in light of these imminent prophetic events. He instructed the Thessalonians to be submissive to and appreciative of their leaders (5:12-13). **Appreciate** is literally "to know" these leaders, but the connotation is that of sincere gratitude because of their **work** ("labor to the point of exhaustion") on behalf of the church members.

B. Their Relationships with Christian Friends (5:14-15)

5:14-15. Paul also admonished them about conduct toward others depending on their need. **Unruly** means "to be out of step" with biblical Christian practice by living a disorderly and sinful life. It is the responsibility of *all* the **brethren**, not just the church leadership, to lovingly and gently confront believers who might be out of line in how they live.

C. Their Attitudes toward Those Who Persecute (5:16-18)

5:16-18. These verses probably have more relevance to the Thessalonians' historical situation than often thought. They were facing the prospect of insufferable persecution, yet Paul commanded (note the imperative mood of these verbs) them to **rejoice**, **pray**, and **give thanks**. "Uttered without any connecting particles, these crisp injunctions ring out with arresting terseness, delineating the attitude that must characterize their inner life" (Heibert, *Thessalonian Epistles*, 239). To **rejoice always** (*pantote*) has the idea of rejoicing in all circumstances—even those not naturally conducive to joyfulness. To **pray without ceasing** (*adialeiptos*) has the idea of prayer—not as an uninterrupted vigil but "constantly recurring" as well as with faithful consistency. "In the Christian life the act of prayer is intermittent but the spirit of prayer should be incessant" (Heibert, *Thessalonian Epistles*, 241). To **give thanks, in everything** is not to say "give thanks *for* everything" but to look past circumstances and know that "all things work together for good" (Rm 8:28). Jesus gave similar instruction for those facing similar hardships (**rejoice** and **give thanks** find a parallel in rejoicing and being glad in Mt 5:12; "**pray** for those who persecute you" is what the Lord taught in Mt 5:44).

D. Their Relationship with the Holy Spirit: Do Not Quench the Spirit (5:19-22)

5:19-22. It is impossible to say with certainty what prompted Paul to write these verses, but apparently there was a problem in Thessalonica opposite to that in Corinth. While the Corinthians were uncontrollably exuberant in their exercise of the gifts of the Spirit, some in Thessalonica were inappropriately wary. They were quenching ("to cause something or someone to cease functioning"; "to stifle, smother, suppress") the Spirit (v. 19). Verse 20 explains what this means: Some despised **prophetic utterances**, possibly because they could be counterfeited by the devil. Hence the need for discernment, which is the point of vv. 21-22. Prophetic utterances were to be evaluated by other prophets in the Church (see the "Excursus on Prophecy and Speaking In Tongues" that introduces the comments on 1Co 14:1-3; and the comments on 1Co 14:29-33a). In addition, regarding prophetic messages, church members should **hold fast to that which is good**, given from the Lord, but **abstain from every form of evil** prophetic messages. It is unlikely that 1Th 5:22 relates to actions in general (i.e., that every Christian should curtail all activities that anyone might consider inappropriate). Rather, the context indicates the refusal to embrace or apply prophetic utterances deemed as not originating from God. The application of these verses is that people should be allowed to discover and use their spiritual gifts in the local body, and only for good reasons should they not be permitted to do so (immaturity; disruptiveness). Regarding the gift of prophecy no longer being present with the church, see the comments on 1Co 13:8-13.

VIII. Paul's Closing Words to the Thessalonians (5:23-28)

A. A Prayer for the Thessalonians (5:23-24)

5:23-24. Paul offered his final prayer with the eschatological theme in mind. His desire for them was their complete sanctification (cf. 4:1-8), their full preservation—**spirit and soul and body**, and their final vindication (**without blame**) at the coming (*parousia*) of the **Lord Jesus Christ**. The culmination, final fullness, of this work is assured because **faithful is He** and **He also will** accomplish all that is necessary.

B. Instructions to the Thessalonians (5:25-28)

5:25-28. Paul's final requests included prayer for himself, and that the intimate gesture of the **holy kiss** be shared with all (cf. Rm 16:16; 1Pt 5:14). This "kiss" was a common gesture of fellowship meant to convey affection and unity. While it might still be an appropriate gesture in some cultures today, in others more culturally acceptable gestures would adequately fulfill the apostle's intent. Paul also asked that the letter be read to all so that its contents would be heard and known by the whole church, that all may be admonished and encouraged—and that the grace of the Lord be the basis of their fellowship.

BIBLIOGRAPHY FOR 1 AND 2 THESSALONIANS

Fee, Gordon D. *The First and Second Letters to the Thessalonians.* New International Commentary on the New Testament. Grand Rapids, MI: Eerdmans, 2009.

Green, Gene L. *The Letters to the Thessalonians.* Pillar New Testament Commentary. Grand Rapids, MI: Eerdmans, 2002.

Heibert, D. Edmond. *The Thessalonian Epistles.* Chicago: Moody, 1971.

Hendriksen, William. *I and II Thessalonians.* New Testament Commentary. Grand Rapids, MI: Baker, 1955.

MacArthur, John. *1 & 2 Thessalonians.* MacArthur New Testament Commentary. Chicago: Moody, 2002.

Martin, D. Michael. *1, 2 Thessalonians.* New American Commentary. Nashville: Broadman & Holman, 1995.

Morris, Leon. *The First and Second Letters to the Thessalonians.* New International Commentary on the New Testament. Grand Rapids, MI: Eerdmans, 1959.

Ryrie, Charles C. *First & Second Thessalonians.* Everyman's Bible Commentary. Chicago: Moody, 2001.

Thomas, Robert L. "1 Thessalonians." In *Expositor's Bible Commentary*, vol. 11, edited by Frank E. Gaebelein, 227–298. Grand Rapids, MI: Zondervan, 1978.

———. "2 Thessalonians." In *Expositor's Bible Commentary*, vol. 11, edited by Frank E. Gaebelein, 299–337. Grand Rapids, MI: Zondervan, 1978.

Walvoord, John F., and Mark Hitchcock, *1 & 2 Thessalonians.* Chicago: Moody, 2012.

● ● ● ●

2 THESSALONIANS

KEVIN D. ZUBER

INTRODUCTION

For introductory matters on 2 Thessalonians, see Introduction to 1 Thessalonians, pp. 1877–1878.

OUTLINE

I. Paul's Responses to Their Present Circumstances (1:1-12)
  A. Paul Responded with Kindness (1:1-2)
  B. Paul Responded with Thankfulness (1:3-10)
  C. Paul Responded with Prayer (1:11-12)
II. Paul's Warnings about the Future (2:1-17)
  A. There Will Be an Apostasy (2:1-3a)
  B. There Will Be an Antichrist (2:3b-10)
  C. There Will Be a Delusion (2:11-12)
  D. Believers Are Destined for Salvation (2:13-14)
  E. Believers Are Encouraged by Sound Teaching (2:15)
  F. Believers Are Comforted by God (2:16-17)
III. Paul's Exhortations about Present Responsibilities (3:1-15)
  A. Christians Must Pray Consistently (3:1-5)
    1. Pray for Protection (3:1-3)
    2. Pray about Commitment (3:4-5)
  B. Christians Must Discipline Lovingly (3:6-15)
IV. Conclusion: Paul's Wish and Benediction (3:16-18)

COMMENTARY ON 2 THESSALONIANS

I. Paul's Responses to Their Present Circumstances (1:1-12)

A. Paul Responded with Kindness (1:1-2)

1:1-2. Paul's greeting in this second letter followed the pattern of the greeting in the first letter (cf. commentary on 1Th 1:1).

B. Paul Responded with Thankfulness (1:3-10)

1:3-4. Paul expressed his **thanks to God** and mentioned his "speaking proudly," i.e., a godly boasting, in behalf of the Thessalonians to other churches. Paul was, on the whole, proud of them. Though some issues concerning the Thessalonians still needed to be addressed further, they had apparently responded well to the teaching, exhortation, and instruction of the first letter. Paul acknowledged his appreciation for the Thessalonians' **faith**, which was **greatly enlarged** (he had been concerned about that according to 1Th 3:3), for their mutual and growing **love** they had for **one another** (he had written about that, 1Th 4:9-10), and for their unwavering **perseverance and faith** in the face of persecution (yet another theme that had occupied him in the first letter).

1:5-10. Paul continued his encouragement of the Thessalonians by assuring them that they will be vindicated and will be **considered worthy**. "The passive infinitive rendered 'be counted worthy' is a judicial term and means, not 'to make worthy' . . . or 'to be worthy' but 'to reckon worthy, to be considered deserving'" (Heibert,

Thessalonian Epistles, 285). This is not salvation based upon works. Their "perseverance and faith" amidst their hardships due to persecution provided the evidence (**plain indication**) that, in God's defensible opinion (translated **righteous judgment**), they are counted **worthy** of the future **kingdom**. In other words, the maintenance of their faith amidst enormous challenges was proof that God destined them for the kingdom. In Paul's day, who else but truly saved believers would have suffered like this? In the future day of **the kingdom of God** (1:5), in the day He executes judgment (1:7-8) they will find **relief** from **affliction** (persecution) and justice (1:7, 6). Paul was indicating here that these believers were destined for the future kingdom, and also that the Church cannot be equated with that kingdom. It is the current manifestation of it without being the full realization of it, which awaits a climactic arrival. Those who cause the **suffering** ... **those who afflict**, those who **do not know God** and who **do not obey the gospel** ... will **pay the penalty of eternal destruction**. This is not annihilation (cf. Mt 25:46. The term **eternal** points to something enduring as with "eternal life"), but they will be separated from **the presence of the Lord** forever, all an outcome of the **righteous judgment** of God. It is the just recompense of God **to repay with affliction** those who persecute and **afflict** believers. The judgment will occur when **the Lord Jesus** is **revealed** and that time when the Lord exacts **retribution** on His enemies. When Jesus returns as the Judge at the end of the tribulation period (cf. Mt 13:24-30; 24:29-51; Rv 19:11-15), all of the **saints** will witness this event and **all who have believed** will marvel at it.

One of the main problems for the pretribulation rapture position (see comments at 1Th 4:13–5:11) relates to the "relief" that is promised Christians in 2Th 1:7 that comes "when the Lord Jesus will be revealed from heaven with His mighty angels in flaming fire." This rest for believers (1:7) and judgment of unbelievers (1:6, 9) is seen by many as taking place at the posttribulational second coming of Christ which, in their thinking, also includes the posttribulational rapture of the Church. But there is a preferable way to understand the passage that accords with a pretribulational rapture approach. The main thrust of the passage and therefore the time indicated is the time of the *final* destruction of the wicked, which is probably later than the time of the second coming. In 1:9, judgment involves literally "suffering the penalty—namely, eternal destruction." While living unbelievers will face judgment at the second coming, the *eternal* punishment of unbelievers appears to be associated less with the second coming than with the "great white throne judgment" in Rv 20:11-15. Many of the same elements of 2Th 2:7-8 (fire, the presence of angels, eternal punishment for the enemies of Christ, final rest for His people) are found also in Rv 14:10-11; 20:11-15. Only at this point will all conflict be gone and full rest with Him will arrive (see Rv 21:1-8). Those martyred during the tribulation are told to rest (Rv 6:9-11), but they will experience tension as well, awaiting God's vengeance against their persecutors. And even during the millennial kingdom there is rebellion and sin (see Rv 20:7-10), so that full rest does not come until the start of the eternal state. If the final rest of believers, and the final, eternal punishment of unbelievers is sealed at that point according to the book of Revelation, then it is likely that Paul envisioned the same sequence in 2Th 1.

C. Paul Responded with Prayer (1:11-12)

1:11-12. Paul's prayer for the Thessalonians in the light of this coming day was that God would continue His work in them, making them **worthy** of their election, growing in their sanctification (**goodness**) and in their faith. The aim is, as always, the glory of the **Lord Jesus**.

II. Paul's Warnings about the Future (2:1-17)

A. There Will Be an Apostasy (2:1-3a)

2:1-3a. Paul noted some false teaching that had affected the Thessalonians. This teaching perhaps came from one claiming to have a divine word, a **spirit** of prophecy, an authoritative **message**, or a supposedly authorized **letter** from some apostolic source. Spurious epistles using the names of recognized authorities were common in that era. This false teaching apparently affirmed that the rapture had occurred and the day of the Lord had begun. The false teaching had disturbed and threatened to deceive the Thessalonians. Neither of these events had started. Paul noted key elements of the day of the Lord to counter this false teaching and to prove that the day (the tribulation) had not yet come. He noted that when that day comes there will first be the rise of apostasy—not merely an increase in falling away from the faith but something of a major movement—an unprecedented increase of apostasy.

B. There Will Be an Antichrist (2:3b-10)

2:3b-10. Then there will be the appearance of the **man of lawlessness** (v. 3b). Paul recalled his previous teaching to reinforce this corrective instruction (2:5). Next, Paul noted that at that time **he who now restrains** will be removed—that is, there will be a removal of God's power of restraint of sin and rebellion (2:6, 7). Many suggestions have been offered as to the identity of the force or person **who now restrains** the coming and appearance of this **man of lawlessness**. Since this "lawless one" and his power derive from Satan, it seems reasonable to suppose that only One powerful enough to restrain Satan is the One in view. Since the work of such restraint is attributed elsewhere to the Holy Spirit (cf. Gn 6:3), it seems reasonable to suppose that He is the restrainer Paul had in mind here.

Paul also noted that the end of this deceiver, the **lawless one**, would come by the Lord's word, the **breath of His mouth**, and by the **appearance of His coming** (v. 8). This **lawless one** is the same individual identified in Dn 7:8 as "the little horn," in Dn 9:26 as "the prince who is to come," and in Rv 13:1-10, 18 as "the beast." He is the antichrist—a real person who will make his nefarious appearance in the tribulation period following the rapture of the church. He will offer himself for worship—a blatant claim to deity (he will be *anti*, in the sense of "instead of" with the idea of the "false Messiah" or "counterfeit Christ"), and he will take **his seat in the temple**, thus fulfilling the prophecies of both Daniel and Jesus (v. 4; cf. Dn 9:27; Mt 24:15; cf. Rv 13:1-8).

But Paul's main point is that that lawless one had not yet appeared. To drive home the point, Paul noted that this individual's power will be derived from Satan and manifested in false **signs and false wonders**. Those manifestations will result in deception and destruction, so those who accept them as genuine will **perish**. As a further warning, Paul noted that those who will be deceived by Satan will already have been handicapped because they **did not receive** a divinely granted **love of the truth**. The Thessalonians are to be warned but not worried.

Evidence from 2Th 2:1-10 is scanty for any view on the timing of the rapture, but pretribulational rapturists look to several features of the text to support their view. First, in 2:2, Paul urged them not to be shaken about teaching they had received regarding the arrival of the day of the Lord. If Paul had taught them that the Church would experience the woes of the day of the Lord (*aka* the great tribulation) and only after those woes experience the rapture, then it is unlikely that the Thessalonians would have been frightened by this teaching that maintained that the day of the Lord had arrived. But they *were* frightened, suggesting that Paul had taught them that they would not be present on earth during the day of the Lord because of escaping it through the rapture of the church.

A second point in the text supports a pretribulational understanding of the passage. Paul reassured the Thessalonians that they were not in the midst of the day of the Lord. He did it by referring to the absence of two key events that would signal the presence of the day of the Lord. One gets the impression from v. 3 that *before* the beginning of the day of the Lord, the "apostasy" and "revealing of the man of lawlessness" must take place, and *only then* will the day of the Lord commence (this is the common impression from the NASB, ASV, KJV, NKJV, NIV, RSV, NRSV, ESV, for example). But the syntax indicates a more likely interpretation. Verse 3 is an incomplete "if . . . then" sentence. It has only the "if" part, not the "then" part, which needs to be provided. The best understanding is to supply the "then" part from v. 2, the most likely candidate being "the day of the Lord has [not] come." Verse 3 should then be read this way: "Let no one in any way deceive you, for unless, first, the apostasy comes, and [second] the man of lawlessness is revealed, *the day of the Lord has not come* . . . ."

Rather than suggesting that the apostasy and revelation of the man of lawlessness must transpire *first*, prior to the beginning of the day of the Lord, the construction seems to suggest that, of the two events, the apostasy comes first, *then* the man of lawlessness is revealed, and only when both of these events have transpired will it be known that the day of the Lord has arrived. The Thessalonians could know that the day of the Lord had not yet started because two events within the day of the Lord that would signal its presence – the apostasy and the revealing of the man of lawlessness – had not taken place. The point is not that these two events happen *before* the day of the Lord, but happen *during* it, signaling its presence.

C. There Will Be a Delusion (2:11-12)

2:11-12. Because the unbelieving world will reject the truth of God (v. 10) and will be easily deceived, God will also judge them by sending a **deluding influence** (v. 11) with the purpose (**so that**) they **believe what is false**. Those who choose sin and lies over truth and take **pleasure in wickedness** are incapable of discernment about spiritual things (cf. 1Co 2:14) and will be ready victims of satanic deception.

D. Believers Are Destined for Salvation (2:13-14)

2:13-14. Paul offered several personal remarks,

in light *of the reality of apostasy and opposition, that r*eveal several matters of his concern. His **thanks to God** for them would have reminded them of their calling (cf. 1Th 1:4) and encouraged them to pursue sanctification (cf. 1Th 4:1-8) and to remain firm in their faith (cf. 1Th 3:7-8).

E. Believers Are Encouraged by Sound Teaching (2:15)

2:15. The hope-filled prospect of future salvation and current sanctification (2:14) would be accomplished as the Thessalonians heeded his admonition to **stand firm** (v. 15). Paul also included a word as to the means to accomplish that—they were to **hold** on **to the traditions** (the "rule of faith"; the truth about Jesus Christ). He **taught** them these traditions when he was first there in person or by his previous **letter** (cf. Ac 17:1-10).

F. Believers Are Comforted by God (2:16-17)

2:16-17. His prayer to **our Lord Jesus Christ and** to **God Our Father** (explicitly Trinitarian) would have reminded them of their security (in God's love and grace), would have given comfort (in their time of persecution and personal loss), and would serve to **strengthen** their **hearts** for the work and life and witness they were to continue in until the Lord's coming.

III. Paul's Exhortations about Present Responsibilities (3:1-15)

A. Christians Must Pray Consistently (3:1-5)

1. Pray for Protection (3:1-3)

3:1-3. Not only did the great apostle pray for the comfort and strength the Thessalonian believers needed. He himself also needed prayer. His request for prayer (**pray for us**) indicated what Paul valued most—the rapid spread and success of the preaching of the Word. It also indicated what Paul feared most—the opposition of **perverse and evil men**.

2. Pray about Commitment (3:4-5)

3:4-5. His **confidence in the Lord** (v. 4) and in them indicated his trust in them. They were loyal and responsive to his exhortations (**command**). However, his real confidence and assurance was in the faithfulness and protection of the Lord to produce the Christian commitment, specifically, **love of God** and the **steadfastness of Christ**, that would result in their standing firm (cf. 2:15) and ultimate sanctification (cf. 1Th 5:23-24).

B. Christians Must Discipline Lovingly (3:6-15)

3:6-15. Paul gave to the main group three pointed commands about the indolent: 1. They are to **keep away from** and not **associate with** them (vv. 6, 14), that is, they are not to offer the usual collegiality and fellowship of believers to the **unruly** ones (v. 6), meaning those who caused disorder in the church by their undisciplined life (see the comments on 1Co 5:9-13). 2. They are to **take special note** of such persons (v. 14), that is, make a public notice that such a person is under discipline. The objective of this action is to cause the persons being disciplined **shame** (v. 14) and regret that will lead them to repentance (cf. Mt 18:15-20). 3. They are to **admonish** that one (v. 15), not as if he or she were **an enemy**, but to bring about restoration of a brother or sister in the Lord.

Paul gave his own example of personal discipline and self-sufficiency as the pattern the unruly ought to follow and as the standard by which the group should judge the unruly. Paul was disciplined, self-sufficient, and conscientious—a model of diligence and hard work (vv. 7-9). Furthermore, he gave a direct command to the indolent. First, he noted the problem. Some were not working to support themselves (v. 11). Perhaps that was because they believed the imminent return of the Lord made such work unnecessary. Second, he suggested a solution in a proverbial-sounding phrase to the effect that if one does not work he should not eat (v. 10). That is, if one is lazy and indolent the rest of the group should not feed him or enable him to continue in his indolence. Finally, he gave the **command** that regardless of the imminency of the Lord's return believers are to stay busy and **not grow weary** in His service (v. 13).

IV. Conclusion: Paul's Wish and Benediction (3:16-18)

3:16-18. Paul's final words to the Thessalonians included a prayer for peace, which is what the Thessalonians needed in light of the persecution they were enduring, a personal word of authentication. This would have served to reinforce the instructions and admonitions of this letter, and a benediction for grace, which is what the Thessalonians needed to depend upon as they lived expectantly for the coming of the Lord (cf. 2:16).

BIBLIOGRAPHY

For the bibliography on 2 Thessalonians, see Bibliography for 1 Thessalonians on p. 1890.

1 TIMOTHY

JOHN KOESSLER

INTRODUCTION

Author and Date. Despite the clear statement of 1Tm 1:1 ascribing this letter to Paul, a number of critical scholars have assigned a second-century date to this letter (as well as to 2 Timothy and Titus). They base their position primarily on unique vocabulary in these letters, their concern for church structure, the apparent absence of themes common in other letters by the apostle, and the difficulty in fitting the events described in it into the chronology outlined in the book of Acts. New Testament scholar Donald Guthrie (*New Testament Introduction* [Downers Grove, IL: InterVarsity, 1970], 584–622) has answered these objections by pointing out:

(1) The uniqueness of the vocabulary can be explained by differences in circumstances and subject matter. Although Paul used many of these terms only in the Pastoral Epistles, they are not unique to the second century. While many of the doctrinal issues addressed in these letters are consistent with second-century Gnosticism, it is now widely recognized that these ideas were incipient in the first century.

(2) There is evidence of a leadership structure in the early church in the book of Acts. Paul appointed elders, and he mentioned church officers in his letter to the Philippians (Ac 14:23; Php 1:1). Those who see a leadership structure that reflects the second-century model, where each city had a single bishop, are making assumptions. There is nothing in the language of the text that requires such a conclusion.

(3) The content of the Pastoral Epistles is governed by the circumstances these letters were intended to address. It is not reasonable to expect every theological theme included in Paul's other letters to appear here. Some of the "missing" themes are implied in the language.

(4) The fact that the book of Acts ends with Paul's release from imprisonment and contains no record of his martyrdom is proof that Luke's coverage of the apostle's ministry was not exhaustive. It seems likely that those events that do not fit the framework of the missionary journeys described in the book of Acts took place after the two-year period of "house arrest" described at the end of the book. Guthrie posits that subsequent to his release, Paul visited Troas, Miletus, and Crete but concentrated his ministry in Macedonia and Greece. He visited the Lycus Valley, the cities of Philippi and Nicopolis, and then was probably re–arrested in Macedonia (Guthrie, New Testament Introduction, 598–599). In view of this, most conservative scholars estimate that this letter was written somewhere between AD 63 and 66.

Purpose and Theme. The apostle Paul wrote to Timothy to instruct him about conduct in the household of God (1Tm 3:14-16). The epistle also describes the organizational structure and ministry of the church.

In this letter Paul provided guidelines for Timothy, who remained in Ephesus while the apostle traveled on to Macedonia. Timothy's primary charge was to refute those who were teaching false doctrine (1Tm 1:3-4). In addition, Paul addressed matters of conduct in the assembly and the appointment of church leaders (1Tm 2:19-15; 3:1-13). These concerns are rounded out by a number of relational issues and ethical directives. The overall picture of Timothy's responsibilities does not seem to be that of a single pastor assigned to an individual congregation but of someone with broader authority. Acting on Paul's behalf, Timothy served as a leader to leaders. In all likelihood, this was Timothy's first sustained solo church assignment, acting in Paul's absence as a supervisor for the house churches in Ephesus.

Background. Timothy met Paul during his second missionary journey when "he was well spoken of by the brethren who were in Lystra and Iconium" (Ac 16:2). Although Timothy's father was a Gentile and presumably not a believer, his grandmother and mother were devout believers (2Tm 1:5). Some think Timothy was naturally timid and given to stomach problems (2Tm 1:7; 1Tm 5:23). Nevertheless, Paul described him as one who was unequalled in his capacity to care for others (Php 2:20). Paul felt confident enough in his young protégé's ministry ability to send him into troubled churches (1Co 4:17; 16:10). Because of his young age, Timothy had to be reminded to assert his authority (1Tm 4:12).

Like his mentor Paul, Timothy was imprisoned for a period of time and released (Heb 13:23). The church historian Eusebius (c. AD 265–c. 239) stated that Timothy became the first bishop of Ephesus. He seems to have drawn this conclusion from the nature of the tasks assigned to Timothy in this letter.

OUTLINE

- I. Paul's Charge to Timothy (1:1-20)
  - A. Paul's Greeting to Timothy (1:1-2)
  - B. Danger of False Doctrine (1:3-11)
  - C. Paul's Experience of Grace (1:12-17)
  - D. Timothy's Marching Orders (1:18-20)
- II. Regulations for the Assembly (2:1-15)
  - A. Guidelines for Prayer in the Assembly (2:1-8)
  - B. Guidelines for Women in the Assembly (2:9-15)
- III. Guidelines for Appointing Leaders in the Assembly (3:1-16)
  - A. Qualifications for the Office of Overseer (3:1-7)
  - B. Qualifications for the Office of Deacon (3:8-13)
  - C. Nature and Mission of the Church (3:14-16)
- IV. Threats Facing the Church and Defenses against Them (4:1-16)
  - A. Threats from Doctrinal Defection and Asceticism (4:1-5)
  - B. Timothy's Response to False Teaching (4:6-10)
  - C. Timothy's Responsibilities as a Minister (4:11-16)
- V. Guidelines for Relationships in the Assembly (5:1–6:2)
  - A. Treatment of Various Age Groups (5:1-16)
  - B. Treatment of the Elders (5:17-25)
  - C. Relationships between Slaves and Masters (6:1-2)
- VI. The Priority of Godliness (6:3-16)
  - A. Ungodly Character of False Teachers (6:3-5)
  - B. Value of Godliness and Contentment (6:6-10)
  - C. Pursuit of Godliness (6:11-16)
- VII. Final Commands (6:17-21)
  - A. Charge to the Rich (6:17-19)
  - B. Charge to Timothy (6:20-21)

COMMENTARY ON 1 TIMOTHY

I. Paul's Charge to Timothy (1:1-20)

A. Paul's Greeting to Timothy (1:1-2)

1:1-2. A typical letter in Paul's day began by identifying the sender and the recipients. Paul modified this format in a way that underscored his authority. He identified himself as **an apostle**, emphasizing his function as an authorized messenger and also the role of both the Father and the Son in the believer's salvation. Timothy was the apostle's **true child** (v. 2), not by birth but **in the faith**. This language reflects the deep affection each felt for the other.

B. Danger of False Doctrine (1:3-11)

1:3-11. Despite the bond of affection that existed between them, Paul **urged** Timothy to **remain on at Ephesus** (v. 3) instead of traveling with him to Macedonia. Paul's tone reflects the urgency of the situation in Ephesus posed by **strange** (false) **doctrines**. The false teachers emphasized **myths and endless genealogies** (v. 4). Religious fables, fictionalized accounts of many OT characters, and the theological speculations that accompanied them were common in the literature of Early Judaism and were features of the gnostic heresy in the second century as well. Paul's **instruction** (v. 5) provided the standard of comparison by which Timothy could judge the false teachers. The goal of sound teaching is **love**. As a result, it will affect the **heart** and **conscience** and produce a capacity for **sincere faith**. Many of the fabricated stories about OT notables emphasized works salvation, and preoccupation with them would distract from God's **administration** of His relationships with people, which is grounded in **faith** in Christ (e.g., *2 Apoc. Bar.* 14:12-14, early second century; *4 Ezra* 14:27-36, late first century). The false teachers aimed for other goals, and missed the mark by **straying from** the truth (v. 6) and concentrating on **fruitless discussion**. Their words were theologically defective and morally ineffective.

False teaching at Ephesus was legalistic. Paul noted that its proponents wanted to be **teachers of the Law** (v. 7). They emphasized the necessity of circumcision for salvation and dietary regulations (cf. 1Tm 4:3). Paul did not reject the validity of the law itself. The law is **good** (v. 8) but only if used legitimately. Walter Liefeld suggests, "one legitimate use of the law is to point out sin in whatever form it may take in a given culture" (Walter L. Liefeld, 1 & 2 Timothy and Titus, NIVAC [Grand Rapids, MI: Zondervan, 1999], 67.) When they required believers in Christ to obey the Mosaic law, false teachers distorted the law's true purpose. Some think **law** in v. 9 refers to the principle of law rather than the Mosaic code. The context (most notably, their desire to be teachers of the law and their interest in OT genealogies, features characteristic of Jewish teaching; cf. Ti 1:10, 14; 3:9) suggests that Paul was clarifying the proper use of God's law, which included giving people knowledge of what sin is (Rm 3:20). The condemned behaviors listed in v. 10 and preceding verses reflect the moral judgment of the law. The doctrine of false teachers was not able to make anyone truly righteous. The moral standard of the gospel is the same as that of the law. Both condemn the behavior described in vv. 10-11. The gospel has a power the law does not have (cf. the comments on Rm 7:7-12; Gl 5:1-6, 13-23). Believers are no longer obligated to keep the commands contained in the law of Moses, but now live under the new covenant law of Christ (1Co 9:20-21; see the comments on Rm 6:14; 7:1-4; 10:4).

C. Paul's Experience of Grace (1:12–17)

1:12-17. Paul had been called not only to preach Christ Jesus, but also to experience His power (v. 12). He differed from the false teachers both in authority and in doctrinal fidelity. These two are related. Paul's appointment came as a result of God's assessment that he would be **faithful**. The apostle also traced his ministry to the grace of God (v. 13). Christ showed mercy to him because he **acted ignorantly**. Though his ignorance did not absolve him of guilt, it did not close the door on the possibility of his being forgiven (cf. the OT concept of sins committed in ignorance vs. sins committed defiantly with full knowledge, Lv 5:15-19; Nm 15:27-31; and Lk 23:34). This distinguished him from the false teachers (cf. Ac 20:20). Paul did not deserve his calling. God's grace, faith, and love were extravagantly poured out upon him (**more than abundant**, v. 14).

Paul traced his own transformation to **grace** on the basis of **faith**, but such a radical change in life is not connected to keeping the law, as the false teachers maintained. Paul's experience was proof that the gospel is for sinners (v. 15). The doctrine of the false teachers assumed a capacity to act righteously apart from God's grace. Paul saw himself as a test case. Far from seeing himself as more deserving of God's mercy, Paul considered himself to be **the foremost** of sinners (v. 16). Paul's experience exhibited the power of the gospel vis-à-vis the law. God offers the grace to **believe** in Christ and receive **eternal life**. The **King** referred to in this doxology (v. 17) may refer specifically to God the Father, in view of the apostle's description of Him as **invisible**. Some have suggested that Paul is drawing from a familiar liturgical source.

D. Timothy's Marching Orders (1:18-20)

1:18-20. Although Paul did not provide details about the precise content of these **prophecies**, it is clear that they pertained to Timothy's commission (v. 18). They probably provided revelation regarding the precise nature of Timothy's gifts and the ministry in which they were to be discharged (cf. Ac 13:1-3). The **faith** spoken of in v. 19 is Timothy's reliance upon Christ both for salvation and for fighting **the good fight**. Subjective faith produces righteous practice as evidenced by a **good conscience**. Ignoring these responsibilities leads to spiritual shipwreck. It seems likely that the phrase **handed over to Satan** (v. 20) alludes to consequences that come as a result of church discipline. Elsewhere Paul talked about the spiritual implications of excommunication (see the comments on 1Co 5:3-5).

II. Regulations for the Assembly (2:1-15)

A. Guidelines for Prayer in the Assembly (2:1-8)

2:1-8. The apostle turned from his personal charge to Timothy to directives for church practice. First on his list of congregational responsibilities is a call to prayer. The outcome of the church's intercessory prayer is both environmental and personal. The church prays for its secular leaders so that those leaders will not harass the church, leaving its members free to live a **tranquil and quiet life** (v. 2), and so that the believers' lives may be marked by **godliness and dignity**. The title **God our Savior** (v. 3) is unique to the Pastoral Epistles (1Tm 1:1; 4:10; Ti 1:3; 2:10; 3:4). Elsewhere Paul also referred to Christ as Savior (Eph 5:23; Php 3:20; 2Tm 1:10; Ti 1:4; 2:13; 3:6). God's desire is that the gospel invitation be extended to all people (v. 4). While the atoning death of Jesus is provisional, potential, and sufficient to save every person, it is experiential, actual, and efficient only for believers. A stable government that viewed the church favorably would allow the church to spread the gospel.

The gospel is inclusive in the scope of its offer but exclusive with respect to its means. The effects of the gospel come only through Jesus Christ, who is the **one mediator . . . between God and men** (v. 5). Paul further described the Savior's mediatory work as a **ransom** ("a price paid to release a person from slavery"), indicating that it is redemptive and substitutionary in nature (v. 6). Paul described the nature of his ministry with three terms (v. 7). **Preacher** emphasizes his role as a herald of the gospel. **Apostle** underscores his doctrinal and ecclesiastical authority. **Teacher of the Gentiles** highlights his missionary responsibility. The phrase **men in every place** (v. 8) could include both men and women. However, the mention of women in the next verse suggests that Paul had males in particular in view here. It was customary to lift hands during prayer (Ps 63:4; 134:2; 141:2), which may have symbolized both reverence for God and a life as open to God as an upraised open hand was.

B. Guidelines for Women in the Assembly (2:9-15)

2:9-11. The context for the teaching in vv. 9-15 continues to be the public and corporate gathering of the church, even if it is in smaller home gatherings. Women who pray in the assembly must dress **modestly** ("an attitude of revulsion against what is base and unseemly") **and discreetly** ("habitual self-control of all passions and appetites"). Peter echoed Paul's emphasis on **good works** as a means of adornment (1Pt 3:3). These admonitions address extravagances of dress and hairstyle that were typical among wealthy women. The command to learn **quietly** is mirrored elsewhere in contexts that include men and address problems of disruptive behavior (2Th 3:12; cf. 1Co 14:28; 1Th 4:11).

2:12-15. Paul further explained the call to submission in v. 11 by forbidding a woman **to teach or exercise authority over a man** (v. 12). Both the syntax and the broader context suggest that Paul was prohibiting women not from all teaching but rather from the authoritative teaching of the Scriptures that is associated particularly with the office of overseer or elder (cf. 1Tm 3:1-7).

Paul gave two reasons for his prohibition, both indicating that it is not merely a cultural concern. First, he linked this prohibition with the order of creation of man and woman, indicating that male leadership was God's original creative design for men and women. The second reason for Paul's prohibition refers to the first woman being deceived (v. 14). This is not to suggest that women are inherently more gullible and prone to doctrinal error. Rather it is to show the destructive consequences that the original breakdown in roles caused. Although the Greek text literally says that women will be "saved" through the bearing of children (v. 15), **preserved** (as in the NASB) is the better sense. This does not mean that a godly woman will never have difficulties in childbearing. The idea is that she will be **preserved** from the influences of false teaching as she focuses on her wifely duties (see the role of a woman in 5:14-15, including the encouragement for **bearing of children**, as a means to remain faithful to the Lord and committed in her Christian life, much like 1Tm 2:15). In addition, there is a close connection between salvation and works in the Pastoral Epistles (see 1Tm 4:16; 5:8-10, 16, 24-25; 6:3, 12-14, 17-19; 2Tm 2:11-13; 3:6; 4:8; Ti 2:11-14; 3:6-8), though these works are an evidence and fruit of salvation, not its cause. A woman could not only protect herself from false teaching by concentrating on serving her family, but would also experience greater amounts of her future salvation in this life as well.

III. Guidelines for Appointing Leaders in the Assembly (3:1-16)

A. Qualifications for the Office of Overseer (3:1-7)

3:1-7. If women were not to teach and exercise authority over men, then the men had better do it, and that responsibility falls primarily to the overseers. The word **overseer** (*episkopos*, v. 1) is synonymous with the word "elder" (*presbyteros*) (see the use of these terms for the same office in Ac 20:17, 28; Ti 1:5, 7; 1Pt 5:1, and the verbs for "pastoring" or "shepherding" and "overseeing" in Ac 20:28 and 1Pt 5:2), so that a pastor, elder, and overseer are the same office. In other contexts the indefinite pronoun **any** might refer collectively to both men and women. Here the further description of this person as a husband in v. 2 indicates that Paul specifically had only men in view, so that the office of an **overseer** is restricted to men. **Above reproach** (v. 2) is the overarching qualification, further spelled out by what follows. **Husband of one wife** indicates that an elder cannot be involved in extramarital relationships, something common in the first-century Greco-Roman world. The phrase does not, however, automatically disqualify a divorced man since Scripture allows for divorce (and remarriage) under certain circumstances without God considering it sin (see the comments on Mt 19:1-9; 1Co 7:12-16). **Temperate** ("clear-headed in one's judgments") and **prudent** ("self-controlled," "serious" about his life and ministry) show how the candidate relates to himself, **respectable** ("well ordered") and **hospitable** toward others. **Able to teach** indicates his competence with the Word of God and provides one of the only hints in this passage about an overseer's function. A candidate for office of overseer must demonstrate a pattern of moderation in the use of alcohol and the expression of anger (v. 3). False teachers in Ephesus were divisive and motivated by avarice. In addition to the practical reason given in the next verse, this qualification may take aim at false teachers who forbade marriage (cf. 4:3), though Paul gave the reason for it in v. 5. Inability to **manage** ("to lead, preside over"; cf. the same word in 5:17, "rule") his children or household disqualifies him from serving as an elder. This parenthetic statement demonstrates that congregational management involves nurture. **Take care** is the same word used to describe the assistance offered by the Good Samaritan on the road to Jericho (Lk 10:34-35). Church leadership requires spiritual maturity. The word translated **new convert** (v. 6) was often used in contemporary Greek writings to refer to something newly planted. Spiritual neophytes should not be appointed to church office because they are especially vulnerable to spiritual conceit. **Reputation** is literally "testimony." It is not enough for a church leader to be well thought of by those within the assembly. Unlike the previous verse, which pointed to Satan as a cautionary example, the **snare of the devil** refers to a trap laid by the devil for the leader, as the devil tempts him to become proud about his position of importance in the church. God is opposed to those who are proud (Jms 4:6), and people will not hold them in high regard (Jms 4:10).

B. Qualifications for the Office of Deacon (3:8-13)

3:8-13. Paul listed the qualifications for deacons (v. 8) but did not give details about the nature of this office (cf. Php 1:1). However, the very title implies a practical, service-oriented labor for those in the church. Some find its origin in the appointment of the seven (cf. esp. Ac 6:2), but this cannot be pressed. Deacons do not necessarily need to possess teaching ability, but must have a firm grasp on the church's doctrine (v. 9). **Mystery** refers to that which was hidden but which God has revealed, and **the faith** is the content of what has been revealed. A **clear conscience** indicates that the deacon practices these truths. Deacons must prove themselves first (v. 10). Paul does not describe the process in detail but the language indicates that it involves an evaluation made by someone else, perhaps the overseers or the entire church body. **Women** (v. 11) may refer either to deacons' wives or to women who served as deacons, but **likewise** suggests that Paul is speaking of "female deacons" or what we might call "deaconesses." It would be unusual to give the requirements of deacons' wives, but not elders'. Some think Phoebe functioned as a female deacon in this capacity in the church of Rome (Rm 16:1). Deacons must meet the same standard of moral purity and family leadership as overseers (v. 12; see vv. 2 and 4). Although the deacon's role is a humble one, those who serve capably gain **high standing and great confidence** (v. 13). This echoes Jesus' admonition to His disciples that the highest rank in the kingdom belongs to the one who serves (Mt 23:11; Lk 22:26-27).

C. Nature and Mission of the Church (3:14-16)

3:14-16. Paul hoped to visit Ephesus again (v. 14) after his trip to Macedonia. However, after leaving Macedonia he wintered in Nicopolis (Ti 3:12). It is uncertain whether he was able to follow through on his plans. He may have returned to Ephesus prior to traveling to Nicopolis. In v. 15, Paul indicated the purpose for this letter. He was writing to instruct Timothy concerning the **conduct** of the local church, explaining the many guidelines for church government given in this epistle. The importance of the church is also explained. It is the **household of God** (v. 15) stressing the church's family aspect (cf. vv. 4 and 5). It is also the **pillar and support of the truth**, emphasizing its responsibility to preserve and proclaim the truth, and as the church fulfilled the directions Paul gave them through Timothy, they would be stronger at upholding the **truth** in Ephesus. The confessional statement in v. 16 summarizes the truth mentioned in v. 15. Many think these words, which summarize the theology of the incarnation, came from one of the church's early hymns. Unbelievers rejected the work of Jesus accomplished in His incarnation (**flesh**), so God **vindicated** Him by raising Him through the power of the **Spirit** (cf. Rm 1:4). While angels saw Him both before and after the resurrection and ascension, the Church does not preach to them but to **the nations**. And while people on the earth put their faith in Him, He no longer resides on earth but **in glory**, though He will some day return to the earth to establish His kingdom.

IV. Threats Facing the Church and Defenses against Them (4:1-16)

A. Threats from Doctrinal Defection and Asceticism (4:1-5)

4:1-5. Paul described a great falling away yet to come. This apostasy will be doctrinal in nature and demonic in origin (v. 1). He characterized the agents behind this apostasy as hypocritical liars who lack a moral compass. They are **seared** (lit., "cauterized") in **conscience** and self deceived (v. 2). His use of the perfect passive participle indicates that he sees this apostasy as having already begun. The apostates' teaching mixed an unhealthy disdain of marriage with Jewish dietary restrictions (v. 3). Paul considered a lifestyle of permanent celibacy appropriate only for those who possessed the gift to be "virgins" for Christ (cf. Mt 19:11). In 1 Co 7:7 Paul described both marriage and singlehood as a "gift." This is not a spiritual gift per se but a station in life for which God empowers the believer. Verse 4 could apply to marriage as well as foods. However, it seems particularly aimed at dietary restrictions. Sanctification **by means of the word of God** (v. 5) may refer to explicit statements of Scripture that what God created was good and that all foods are clean (cf. Gn 1:25, 31; Mk 7:19). **Prayer** probably refers to the common practice of giving thanks before meals (Mk 8:6).

B. Timothy's Response to False Teaching (4:6-10)

4:6-10. Timothy was responsible to know these things and to point them out to the church (v. 6). This was as essential to Timothy's own spiritual well-being. Doctrine is not the enemy of spiritual vitality. Many use v. 7 to support the practice of spiritual disciplines like fasting or solitude. However, the context has to do with doctrine. Timothy was to **discipline** himself to be godly by attending to the truths that nourish faith and avoiding the speculative fables that were popular among the false teachers (see the comments on 1:4-5). The Greek terms translated **discipline** (v. 8) in this and in the preceding verse both come from the root that is the basis for the word "gymnasium." Compared to bodily exercise, godliness provides the greater benefit. This is the third occurrence of **it is a trustworthy statement** (v. 9), which also appears in Paul's second letter to Timothy and the letter to Titus (1Tm 1:15; 3:1; 2Tm 2:11; Ti 3:8), and signals that what follows withstands the fiery test of experience and can be completely trusted. God is the **Savior of all men** (v. 10) in that He protects and provides for them (see this sense for "savior" in the LXX: Jdg 3:9; 2Kg 13:5; Neh 9:27), and in this sense He is the **Savior of all men.** Paul did not write, "God is potentially the savior of all" or "of all kinds of people" or "of everyone without exception." **Especially** means "to the fullest extent," "to an unusual degree" (see 5:17; 2Tm 4:13; Ti 1:10). However, God **especially**, to the fullest degree, provides and protects believers by providing for them eternal salvation. Those who have experienced the grace of Christ should especially hope in His goodness.

C. Timothy's Responsibilities as a Minister (4:11-16)

4:11-16. Paul concluded the chapter with a series of directives related to Timothy's ministry. Rather than being two distinct activities, **prescribe** and **teach** (v. 11) are both aspects of the same ministry of the Word. Age might have caused some to call Timothy's authority into question (v. 12). Consequently, Paul identified five foundational areas (**speech**, **conduct**, **love**, **faith**, **purity**) upon which Timothy must build his leadership credibility. The authority to lead may come with the office, but leadership credibility is a function of lifestyle. Paul emphasized three key elements of the public ministry of God's Word (v. 13): reading of Scripture, application (or **exhortation**) to the listener, and instruction. These are all facets of preaching.

In view of v. 13, the **spiritual gift** (v. 14) is probably related to Timothy's ministry of exhortation and teaching. This gift was given "through" a prophetic utterance, which was accompanied by the laying on of hands. The practice of laying on hands by the elders signified that Timothy was both commissioned and imbued by the Spirit for this ministry. The indwelling Spirit is bestowed upon believers at the time of salvation, and it is likely (though by no means certain) that the believer is given his spiritual gifts at that time, not unlike how a newborn possesses genetically all that he needs to become, let's say, an outstanding cyclist. But like the newborn who will later become a cyclist, spiritual gifts may be manifest only after years of growth in Christ. Some gifts, like preaching or teaching, can be improved by training. The OT ministry of Bezalel is a good example of this. Filled with the Spirit of God with skill, ability, and knowledge in all kinds of crafts, he and Oholiab taught others the same skills (Ex 35:30-34). This passage, however, cannot be cited in support of some miraculous gifts being received in connection with a "second blessing," or a post-conversion baptism of the Spirit (see the comments on Ac 2, 8, 10, and 19). Spiritual gifts bring with them a measure of human responsibility (1Tm 4:15). Those who possess spiritual gifts can improve the exercise of these God-given skills by diligent practice. Timothy must pay as much attention to himself as he does to his doctrine (v. 16). Lifestyle plays a confirmatory role in Paul's understanding of salvation. An inconsistent life contradicts the gospel and poses a stumbling block to others.

V. Guidelines for Relationships in the Assembly (5:1–6:2)

A. Treatment of Various Age Groups (5:1-16)

5:1-2. The word translated **rebuke** in this verse appears in contemporary sources in contexts that refer to a severe rebuke that seeks to punish rather than correct. Elsewhere Paul spoke of the appropriate rebuke that is the obligation of those who minister God's Word (2Tm 4:2). Family relationships provide the pattern for relating to the various age groups mentioned in these verses (v. 2). The apostle highlighted areas where a young leader might be especially vulnerable.

5:3-8. Honor (v. 3) refers to an attitude of holding someone in the highest regard. But the chapter's context indicates that this respect was shown through generous financial support (cf. v. 17, "double honor"). A true widow in the biblical sense is marked by both genuine need and godly character. Responsibility for support of the church's widows falls first on their **children or grandchildren** (v. 4). This is both an expression of reverent devotion to God and an obligation. Paul described this financial support as something owed. A widow must meet certain requirements before receiving support from the church (v. 5). Her life must demonstrate a pattern of hope in God and prayer. Paul's language stresses constancy in these things. The opposite of the true widow is one **who gives herself to wanton pleasure** (v. 6). Elsewhere the verbal form of this noun refers to those who live an opulent and self-indulgent lifestyle (Jms 5:5). These directives (primarily vv. 5 and 6) do not pertain merely to widows. Timothy must **prescribe** or command (cf. 1Tm 1:3; 4:11; 6:13; 6:17) the whole church to make it their aim to be **above reproach** (cf. 1Tm 3:2) (v. 7). Paul's summary principle (v. 8) condemns what might be described as apostasy of practice. In Roman culture, one's **household** could include extended family and slaves. The context here suggests that Paul was using the term more narrowly to refer to the immediate family.

5:9-16. Approved widows were eligible for support from the church (v. 9), similar perhaps to the practice described in Acts (Ac 6:1). The qualifications of marital fidelity and hospitality echo those demanded of overseers and deacons (1Tm 3:2, 12). Some think v. 10 points to an order of widows who served in the church (cf. v. 12). However, it is also possible that this ministry was informal. Walter Liefeld suggests that the presence of a "list" (v. 9) indicates that this was probably a formally and "openly recognized group qualified to receive financial assistance" (Liefeld, *1 & 2 Timothy, Titus*, 181). It was not a church office. Washing of **feet** could be literal, but is also emblematic of a variety of avenues of service.

Younger widows (v. 11) were those young enough for remarriage to be a viable option. The word translated **sensual desires** combines a Greek word for strong feelings with a preposition that means "against." These are desires that conflict with their commitment to Christ, either because they act upon them outside of marriage or because they "set aside their previous pledge." The **condemnation** or judgment mentioned here (v. 12) is not because remarriage is sinful but because of violation of a **previous pledge**. The exact nature of this commitment is unclear but probably involved a vow to serve Christ without the distractions of marriage (cf. 1Co 7:32-34). There were practical reasons for excluding younger widows from the list (v. 13). Some claim that Paul's characterization of young widows in this verse betrays a low view of women. However, the problem seems to be more a result of life situation than gender (cf. 2Th 3:6-12). Paul expressed his preference in this matter (1Ti 5:14) but stopped short of commanding it. If the younger widows married and concentrated on their wifely duties, they would avoid the enticements of false teachers (vv. 14-15; see the comments on 2:15).

Turned aside is the same term Paul used earlier to refer to the false teachers who had turned aside to fruitless discussion (1Tm 1:6). Although the home is the primary sphere of service for many, it is not the only context where God calls women to serve Him (1Co 7:34). The obligation (v. 16) to care for widows in one's family does not fall exclusively upon the women of the church who have the means to provide significantly for their widowed relatives (as indicated by Ac 6:1-5). Women are singled out because they would have greater sensitivity to a widow's needs.

B. Treatment of the Elders (5:17-25)

5:17-22. Elders are synonymous with the overseers mentioned in 3:1 (cf. Ac 20:17, 28; 1Pt 5:1-2). All elders **rule** (i.e., lead or govern) but not all **work hard at preaching and teaching** (v. 17). This verse supports the concept that it is **elders** (not deacons) who have the authoritative oversight of the church. Those who work hardest in teaching the Word should be accorded **double honor**, a reference to ample remuneration (1Tm 5:3), in contrast to the elders whose primary role does not involve teaching. Elsewhere, Paul described this as a right (1Co 9:4) and here appealed to OT law to support his assertion that those who preach and teach ought to receive a generous honorarium (v. 18; see Dt 25:4). Paul used the aphorism from Dt 25:4 to argue from the lesser to the greater. If the ox that serves the farmer deserves to eat, how much more must this be true of the elder who directs the affairs of the church? He also quoted Christ's words from Luke as Scripture (Lk 10:7; cf. also Mt 10:10), indicating that Luke's gospel was already in existence and considered Scripture. Any **accusation** against the church's leaders (v. 19) must be substantiated by **two or three witnesses** who can give firsthand evidence of the sin, this standard coming from the Mosaic law (Nm 35:30; Dt 17:6; 19:15). Jesus reiterated this requirement when He described the process for addressing sin in the church (Mt 18:16). Because of the elder's role as an example, church leaders who **continue in sin** after being confronted are subject to a public **rebuke** (v. 20). The present active participle conveys the idea of persistence in sin. **The rest** probably refers to the other elders. These directives must be followed **without . . . partiality** (v. 21), a standard drawn from Mosaic law (Dt 1:17; 10:17). Paul's reference to **the presence of God** is a reminder that God is witness to such proceedings. Some think **lay hands upon** (v. 22) signifies appointment to church office or a commission to ministry (1Tm 4:14; cf. Ac 6:6). Others take it as a reference to absolution or restoration following repentance. Doing either in haste may cause damage to the church. There is no evidence in Scripture of a ritual of restoration to ministry that involved the laying on of hands. Paul is probably warning Timothy against appointing those to church office who have not yet proven their character and spiritual maturity over time.

5:23-25. Paul urged Timothy to drink wine in moderation for the sake of his stomach (v. 23). Drinking wine is not inherently wrong since Jesus apparently drank wine in social situations (Lk 7:33-34). The Bible condemns the immoderate use of wine (Pr 20:1; 23:31-32). Verses 24-25 seem unrelated to the previous verse. Possibly they are loosely connected to v. 22. They offer assurance that God is aware of what is unseen by others. Hidden sins will be exposed on the day of judgment. Likewise, **deeds that are good** (v. 25) precede us to judgment. The phrase **those which are otherwise** could apply equally to good or evil deeds. Good deeds done in secret will one day be revealed. All hidden sin will eventually be exposed.

C. Relationships between Slaves and Masters (6:1-2)

6:1-2. The command that slaves must treat their masters with **honor** should not be taken as an endorsement of slavery. Elsewhere Paul said that those who have the opportunity to become free should do so (1Co 7:21-22). He urged slaves to submit to their masters for the sake of the gospel. Slaves and masters worshiped side by side in the early church. Believing slaves might be part of a household church (cf. Rm 16:5; 1Co 16:19; Col 4:15; Phm 2). Equality in Christ tempted some to show less respect for their masters than was appropriate (Gl 3:28).

VI. The Priority of Godliness (6:3-16)

A. Ungodly Character of False Teachers (6:3-5)

6:3-5. Paul returned to the theme that began this letter by contrasting the character of those who teach false doctrine with the character of those who teach doctrine that promotes spiritual health and godliness (v. 3). Throughout this letter the true nature of doctrine is measured by its moral affect as much as by its theological content. The marks of the false teacher are conceit, contentiousness, and an inability to grasp sound doctrine (v. 4). False teachers are drawn to obscure questions that only promote controversy. The false teacher's words and disposition betray his true motives. **Deprived of the truth** (v. 5) indicates that the false teachers are themselves deceived. They are driven primarily by greed. One implication of this is that the actions of false teachers expose their motives. Sound teaching has the church's best interest at heart, whereas false teachers are self-serving.

B. Value of Godliness and Contentment (6:6-10)

6:6-10. Paul could be speaking of the advantages of the life to come in v. 6. However, nothing in the context demands this interpretation. It seems more likely that he was contrasting the contentment that comes with godliness with the insatiable avarice of the false teachers. Although not a direct quote, v. 7 is comparable to others found in the OT (Jb 1:21; Ps 49:17; Ec 5:15). The Greek historian Plutarch paralleled this sentiment. It points to God's ownership of all things and our dependency upon Him. A standard of living limited to food and clothing (v. 8) hardly seems sufficient in the present age (at least for those in developed countries). Paul was not saying that it is wrong to have more, only that we cannot demand more than this. He gave the assurance that God will supply all that is truly needful. Many believers **want to get rich** (v. 9) and become so fixated upon that goal that it ultimately plunges them **into ruin and destruction** (not a reference to eternal condemnation). Paul did not write, "Money is the root of all evil" (v. 10). He actually said that it is the *love* of money that is the problem. It is the longing for riches, and the inappropriate obsession to obtain riches through any and all means, that has caused many to stray from the truth.

C. Pursuit of Godliness (6:11-16)

6:11-16. Even Timothy was not immune from such temptations. Paul offered a twofold strategy for dealing with this threat (v. 11). Timothy must **flee** from avarice and pursue the greater riches of **righteousness**, **godliness**, **faith**, **love**, **perseverance**, and **gentleness**. The juxtaposition of these two commands portrays the man of God as someone who is pursued by temptation and in pursuit of holiness. All these are freely given by the Holy Spirit (Gl 5:22-23). Yet Paul's use of the imperative implies a measure of responsibility. These qualities are freely given by God but are not automatic. They require the effort of obedience. In his response to the false teachers Timothy must **fight** for the faith (v. 12). Here Paul urged him to wage a battle of personal faith. The language of this verse makes it clear that the spiritual life involves a measure of struggle.

Timothy did not serve independently. He had been commissioned by God and would be held accountable to Him (v. 13). Paul's language is a reminder that we serve in the full sight of God. The reference to the trial of Jesus links Timothy's **good confession** with Christ's. Some think **the commandment** (v. 14) stands for all that Paul had charged Timothy to do in this letter. Others link it with Timothy's initial call to ministry or with some general command of Christ (e.g., Jn 13:34). More likely the better understanding is that **the commandment** should be drawn from the immediate context, namely the solemn commands in vv. 11-12, all stressing the single concept of the need for moral purity. The return of Christ mentioned in v. 14 serves as the primary motive for fulfilling this command. Paul's emphasis on the timing in this verse is consistent with Jesus' statement that only the Father knows the day and the hour (Mt 24:36). The **proper time** is God's own time. In this doxology of praise (v. 16) Paul stressed three divine attributes. God is immortal, invisible, and unapproachable. These last two are related, according to Ex 33:20. God is invisible because He is unapproachable by sinful humanity. It is Christ alone who enables us to approach and see the invisible Father (Heb 4:16, Jn 14:9).

VII. Final Commands (6:17-21)

A. Charge to the Rich (6:17-19)

6:17-19. If the desire to get rich leads some astray (cf. 6:9-10), the possession of wealth brings its own temptations (v. 17). Chief among them are the potential for arrogance and the temptation to hope in one's own wealth. The remedy in either case is to acknowledge our dependence upon God. It is possible for those who are materially wealthy to be poor toward God. Although Paul commanded the rich **to be generous and ready to share** (v. 18), giving is not a substitute for obedience. They must also **do good**. Every believer exercises a divine stewardship over his or her life and possessions. Instead of rejecting wealth, Paul urged the rich to rearrange their priorities (v. 19). True riches are eternal, possessed by those who are **storing up for themselves the treasure of a good foundation for the future**. True riches are the rewards that come with eternal life.

B. Final Charge to Timothy (6:20-21)

6:20-21. Timothy must guard the teaching that **has been entrusted** to him (v. 20). This is the language of stewardship. Truth has been deposited with Timothy in much the same way as one might entrust one's savings to the bank. He must give attention to the truth and ignore the speculations of the false teachers, labeled by Paul as **empty chatter**. In particular, Timothy must be on guard against the kind of message that comes from those who have **gone astray** (lit., missed the mark) **from the faith** (v. 21). They possess a false knowledge and therefore profess a false gospel.

BIBLIOGRAPHY

For All the Pastoral Epistles

Barclay, William. *The Letters to Timothy, Titus, and Philemon*. Philadelphia: Westminster, 1960.

Calvin, John. *The Second Epistle of Paul to the Corinthians and the Epistles of Paul to Timothy, Titus, and Philemon*, trans. T. A. Smail. Grand Rapids, MI: Eerdmans, 1979.

Elicott, Charles J. *The Pastoral Epistles of St. Paul*. London: Longman, Greens, Reader, and Dyer, 1864.

Fee, Gordon D. *1 and 2 Timothy, Titus*. New International Bible Commentary. Peabody, MA: Hendrickson, 1988.

Guthrie, Donald. *The Pastoral Epistles*. Tyndale New Testament Commentaries. Grand Rapids, MI: Eerdmans, 1990.

Hendriksen, William. *Thessalonians, Timothy, and Titus*. New Testament Commentary. Grand Rapids, MI: Baker, 1984.

Kent, Homer. *The Pastoral Epistles*. Winona Lake, IN: BMH Books, 1995.

Köstenberger, Andreas J. "The Pastoral Epistles." Vol. 12, rev. ed. of The Expositor's Bible Commentary, edited by Tremper Longman III and David Garland, 489–625. Grand Rapids, MI: Zondervan, 2006.

Lea, Thomas D. and Hayne P. Griffin, Jr. *1, 2 Timothy, Titus*. New American Commentary. Nashville: Broadman, 1992.

Liefeld, Walter L. *1 & 2 Timothy and Titus*. NIV Application Commentary. Grand Rapids, MI: Zondervan, 1999.

Oden, Thomas C. *First and Second Timothy and Titus*. Louisville: John Knox, 1989.

Wilson, Geoffrey B. *The Pastoral Epistles*. Carlisle, PA: Banner of Truth, 1982.

For 1 Timothy

Hiebert, D. Edmond. *First Timothy*. The Expositor's Bible Commentary. Chicago: Moody, 2001.

Stott, John R. W. *The Message of 1 Timothy and Titus*. The Bible Speaks Today. Downers Grove, IL: InterVarsity, 2001.

For 2 Timothy

Hiebert, D. Edmond. *Second Timothy*. The Expositor's Bible Commentary. Chicago: Moody, 2001.

Moule, H. C. G. *The Second Epistle to Timothy*. Grand Rapids, MI: Baker, 1952.

Stott, John R. W. *The Message of 2 Timothy*. The Bible Speaks Today. Downers Grove, IL: InterVarsity, 1984.

Warfield, Benjamin Breckinridge. *The Inspiration and Authority of the Bible*. Phillipsburg, NJ: Presbyterian and Reformed, 1948.

For Titus

Hiebert, D. Edmond. *Titus and Philemon*. The Expositor's Bible Commentary. Chicago: Moody, 1957.

Stott, John R. W. *The Message of 1 Timothy and Titus*. The Bible Speaks Today. Downers Grove, IL: InterVarsity, 2001.

● ● ● ●

2 TIMOTHY

JOHN KOESSLER

INTRODUCTION

Author and Date. Paul wrote the second letter to Timothy expecting to be put to death before long (2Tm 4:6-8). He must have penned it shortly before he was beheaded in Rome in AD 67. The letter is ascribed to Paul, but critical scholars argue that its language does not reflect the vocabulary and themes of the apostle's other writings. They also argue that the letter's emphasis on the importance of preserving apostolic tradition better suits a later stage in the church's life (cf. 2Tm 1:13; 2:2, 11-13).

Some of these differences can be explained by the nature of the problems addressed in the letter (see the introduction to 1 Timothy). They might also be traced to Paul's use of an amanuensis (scribe) to record this letter. According to 2Tm 4:11, Luke had remained with him during these final days of imprisonment. Polycarp (c. AD 70–160) and Clement of Rome (c. AD 90–100) seem to have been familiar with the Pastoral Epistles, and Irenaeus (writing between c. AD 175 and 195) explicitly identified Paul as their author.

This letter reveals a few additional details about Timothy. We know from Acts that he was "the son of a Jewish woman who was a believer" (Ac 16:1). In 2Tm 1:5 we learn the name of his mother and grandmother and discover that they were both women of "sincere faith."

Themes. Paul's second letter to Timothy gives us a view of the apostle's concerns as he neared the end of his ministry. One of the distinctive features of 2 Timothy is its personal nature. Many of the themes that appear in 1 Timothy and Titus are repeated here, but in this letter they appear through the lens of Paul's suffering. There is no record of Paul's execution in the book of Acts, which ends with his confinement in Rome some five years earlier (AD 60–62). This letter is the closest record of an account of Paul's last days. The tone of 2 Timothy is somber, but not despairing. Most of Paul's companions have gone, some because they have deserted him, others for the sake of ministry. Winter is approaching, and the apostle has asked Timothy to pick up a few personal items and bring his former colleague John Mark to him as soon as possible (2Tm 4:9-13). Paul's tone expressed urgency because he wanted Timothy to reach him in time, not because he was concerned for his own comfort, though the cloak he requested probably would have been used to keep him warm in his cell.

The apostle reflected upon the circumstances that led to his arrest. Alexander the coppersmith, who may be the same one who was "handed over to Satan" in 1Tm 1:20, did Paul "much harm" (2Tm 4:14). Although the apostle gave no further details, the language could suggest that Alexander was the one who delivered him over to the authorities. He warned Timothy to be on his guard against this man.

Paul also looked into the future and saw the threat of apostasy on the horizon. The things Paul experienced and the dangers Timothy would face were only a foretaste of the "difficult times" yet to come (2Tm 3:1). Of special concern was the growing influence of false teachers on the church (2Tm 3:6). No doubt Timothy was already well aware of this danger, coming from Ephesus. Paul had warned the church leaders at Ephesus that after his departure "savage wolves" would infiltrate the church "not sparing the flock" (Ac 20:29).

Background. One important feature of 2 Timothy is the clear indication it provides of the early church's view of Scripture. Some have criticized the doctrine of verbal inspiration, claiming that it was an innovation developed in the context of 19th-century doctrinal disputes.

However, 2Tm 3:16 declares all Scripture to be "inspired" (lit., God-breathed), one of the Bible's most important statements about the nature of the Scriptures.

Theologian B. B. Warfield was correct when he noted that such language indicates that the Scriptures are a "divine product" (B. B. Warfield, *The Inspiration and Authority of the Bible* [Phillipsburg: Presbyterian and Reformed, 1948], 153). Their power does not stem from God stirring the hearts of the writers to pen meaningful but fallible words. Nor should we think of them as mere human words that God somehow elevates in the act of preaching. The words of Scripture are God's Word, the words breathed out by God.

This does not necessarily mean they were given by means of dictation (cf. Lk 1:3), but that all Scripture should be regarded as God's truth. As such, it is true in fact as well as in principle. All that Scripture says happened did happen just as the text declares. This, in itself, has important implications for the question of authorship. If the biblical text asserts that Paul wrote this letter to Timothy, when in reality he did not, then it cannot be God's Word.

OUTLINE

- I. Paul's Appreciation for Timothy (1:1-7)
  - A. Paul Greets Timothy (1:1-2)
  - B. Timothy's Heritage of Faith (1:3-7)
- II. Paul's Experience of Suffering (1:8-18)
  - A. Suffering for the Gospel (1:8-14)
  - B. Suffering in Prison (1:15-18)
- III. Strengthened in Grace (2:1-10)
  - A. Strengthened through Grace and Instruction (2:1-2)
  - B. Strengthened through Hardship (2:3-4)
  - C. Strengthened through Endurance (2:5-10)
- IV. God's Solid Foundation (2:11-26)
  - A. A Foundation of Faithfulness (2:11-13)
  - B. A Foundation of Truth (2:14-19)
  - C. A Foundation of Purity (2:20-26)
- V. The Character of the Last Days (3:1–4:5)
  - A. The Threat of Apostasy (3:1-9)
  - B. The Antidote of Scripture (3:10-17)
  - C. A Sacred Charge (4:1-5)
- VI. Paul's Final Departure (4:6-22)
  - A. The Offering of Paul's Life (4:6-8)
  - B. A Prisoner's Appeal (4:9-18)
  - C. A Final Farewell (4:19-22)

COMMENTARY ON 2 TIMOTHY

I. Paul's Appreciation for Timothy (1:1-7)

A. Paul Greets Timothy (1:1-2)

1:1-2. Paul identified himself as an authorized messenger of Christ. This was not an elected office, but an appointment that came **by the will of God**. Paul was a messenger of **life in Christ Jesus**. Elsewhere Paul described Timothy as a fellow worker, brother, and servant (Rm 16:21; 2Co 1:1; Php 1:1; 1Th 3:2). Here he called him his dearly loved **son** (lit., "child") (v. 2).

B. Timothy's Heritage of Faith (1:3-7)

1:3-7. Paul characterized his devotion to God as service (cf. Ac 24:14). This heritage of worship was passed down to Paul by his **forefathers**. Paul's devotion to Christ was consistent with the true faith of his ancestors. Verse 4 may shed some light on the content of the petitions mentioned in the previous verse. They expressed Paul's longing for renewed fellowship with Timothy. Perhaps Paul prayed for his own release from prison or for a visit from Timothy. Timothy's spiritual heritage resulted in a **sincere faith** (v. 5) that Paul described as an indwelling faith. Similar language is used to speak of the Holy Spirit in v. 14 and of "the word of Christ" in Col 3:16. The **gift** (v. 6) probably refers to Timothy's ministry (cf. 1Tm 4:14). The Holy Spirit's presence does not relieve us of responsibility to be diligent in the exercise of our gifts. Timothy struggled with a natural **timidity** (v. 7). Yet the dynamic of the Holy Spirit was more than enough to compensate. The Spirit supplies the **power** to **love** God and others as well as the strength to control ourselves.

II. Paul's Experience of Suffering (1:8-18)

A. Suffering for the Gospel (1:8-14)

1:8-14. Paul's imprisonment contributed to Timothy's reluctance, sparking fear of retaliation. **The testimony of our Lord** (v. 8) is the gospel. To be ashamed of the gospel is to be ashamed of Christ. Those who come to Christ do so because the Father has called them. This **holy calling** (v. 9) is based upon God's **own purpose** and **grace**. Jesus Christ is the ultimate manifestation of divine grace (v. 10). **Immortality** is one facet of the **life** that comes to those who are in Christ. Elsewhere Paul identifies immortality as a characteristic of resurrection life (1Co 15:42, 50, 53, 54). **Preacher**, **apostle**, and **teacher** (v. 11) are related but not identical terms. While not all who preached and taught were apostles, the ministry of the Word was an essential aspect of the apostolic role (Ac 6:2; cf. 1Co 12:29). Commentators differ over the nature of what Paul mentioned he had entrusted to God (v. 12). Some think this refers to Paul's salvation. Others see it as a reference to the gospel or to Paul's ministry. But what is entrusted in this verse belongs to Paul rather than God, indicating that it refers to his life or ministry. The apostle's teaching set the standard for Timothy both in terms of its content and communication (v. 13). The same is true for all who teach. Apostolic doctrine provides the outline, Jesus Christ supplies the ethos. Possession of the truth is a sacred trust. God's servant must rely on the help of **the Holy Spirit who dwells in us** (v. 14). Indwelling indicates control.

B. Suffering in Prison (1:15-18)

1:15-18. It is unclear when these events took place. Paul's troubles in Asia Minor are mentioned in Ac 19 and 2Co 1:8. Ephesus was the most prominent city in this region. Phygelus and Hermogenes are not mentioned elsewhere in Scripture. **Onesiphorus** (v. 16) had become acquainted with Paul in Ephesus. He supported the apostle's ministry by providing hospitality. The reference to **the house of Onesiphorus** many indicate that he was a person of means with many servants. Onesiphorus showed kindness to Paul by searching for him in Rome (v. 17). This is in marked contrast with those who abandoned the apostle in Asia (v. 15). The apostle prays that Onesiphorus will be rewarded for the kindness he showed in Ephesus (v. 18). The use of **that day** here and in v. 12 indicates its futurity. Because it refers to a time when the church is delivered from all threats (v. 12) and rewards for faithfulness are handed out by the Lord (v. 18), the best understanding is that it refers to the time immediately following the rapture of the Church.

III. Strengthened in Grace (2:1-10)

A. Strengthened through Grace and Instruction (2:1-2)

2:1-2. God's grace is a source of power to those who have experienced it. Grace will enable Timothy to fulfill his ministry. Paul's use of the imperative implies human responsibility. This is not the grace of salvation but of God's enabling power (cf. 2Co 12:9). Timothy exercised a stewardship of the truth he had received. Paul's emphasis on the public nature of his instruction may be a deliberate contrast with those false teachers who claimed to possess secret knowledge.

B. Strengthened through Hardship (2:3-4)

2:3-4. Timothy was called to suffer as well as to teach. This is a reiteration of the command in 2Tm 1:8. The military analogy was a favorite of the apostle's (1Co 9:7; Php 2:25; Phm 2). Military service restricts one's personal liberty. Similarly, the primary interest of those who minister for Christ must not be everyday affairs (lit., "the concerns of this life").

C. Strengthened through Endurance (2:5-10)

2:5-10. Paul also compared serving Christ to the rigor of an athletic competition (v. 5). Both Christ's servant and the athlete must abide by the rules. Labor for Christ is like the effort of

the hard-working farmer (v. 6) who expects to reap a harvest. This metaphor emphasizes the expectation of those who serve. These analogies provide the motivation to do as Paul commanded. Paul promised that Jesus Himself will supply insight (v. 7). This very brief summary of the gospel (v. 8) highlights the deity of Christ when it describes Him as **risen from the dead**. His royal office as the Messiah of Israel is implied in the description **descendant of David** (lit., "of the seed of David"). Paul saw a joyful irony in his personal circumstances (v. 9). His confinement did not hinder the liberty of the gospel (cf. Eph 6:20; Php 1:13). Paul used the language of election to refer to groups and individuals (Rm 8:33; Eph 1:4; Col 3:12; 1Th 1:4; Rm 16:13). Those who fall into this category receive salvation and glory through Christ. Paul had the appropriate balance in his view of God's sovereignty and his evangelistic endeavors. He realized that even those predestined for salvation nevertheless had to hear the gospel to be saved, and God ordains that the witness of believers is the means for unbelievers to hear and believe.

IV. God's Solid Foundation (2:11-26)

A. A Foundation of Faithfulness (2:11-13)

2:11-13. This **trustworthy statement** (v. 11), which may come from an early hymn or confessional statement, emphasizes the believer's union with Christ. Union with Christ is a motive for enduring suffering and even death. Verse 12 echoes the words of Christ, who promised a throne to His disciples (Mt 19:28; Lk 22:30). He warned that He would deny those who deny Him. God will be true to His word. He will fulfill all His promises and make good His threats. Paul's primary emphasis is on God's faithfulness to save, but God also will be faithful to judge the unbelievers who deny Him (see the comments on Mt 10:32-33).

B. A Foundation of Truth (2:14-19)

2:14-19. The basic command of this verse is to **remind** the church of these things (v. 14). In particular, Timothy must warn the church of the danger of obscure disputes about words (cf. the comments on 1Tm 1:3-11; 4:7). Paul emphasized the accountability of the laborer. He described the nature of the work as **handling the word of truth** (v. 15). This language conveys the idea of sound exposition or orthodoxy. The apostle's warning in v. 14 pertains to profane and empty words (v. 16). The only advances to be made by these false teachers will be in the realm of ungodliness. False teaching has a corrosive affect, spreading through the church once it has been introduced. Hymenaeus (v. 17) is mentioned in 1Tm 1:20 as having been excommunicated along with Alexander. Philetus is mentioned only here. Their error involved the doctrine of the resurrection (v. 18). By saying that the resurrection had already taken place, they denied a future bodily resurrection. They may also have denied Christ's bodily resurrection (cf. 1Co 15:12-19). The solid **foundation** of God's truth (2Tm 2:19) is contrasted with that laid by the false teaching of Hymenaeus and Philetus. This inscription emphasizes the security and the responsibility of those who belong to Christ.

C. A Foundation of Purity (2:20-26)

2:20-26. Vessels of wood and earthenware (v. 20) were used for common purposes. These vessels provided Paul with an analogy for the false teachers and those who embrace their doctrine (cf. Rm 9:21). Those who turn away from false doctrine correspond to vessels of honor (v. 21). By framing this as a condition (if anyone cleanses himself), Paul implied that it may be possible for some who have been taken in by false teaching to consecrate themselves to the truth. Sexual temptation (v. 22) is only one dimension of youthful lusts. The alternatives (**righteousness, faith, love and peace**) are not automatic. They must be continuously pursued if they are to be attained.

The doctrine of false teachers was not only speculative; it was also combative (v. 23). Timothy must avoid **foolish and ignorant** debates with his opponents. In Ti 3:9 "foolish controversies" are linked with genealogies and disputes about the law. Such disputes give the appearance of knowledge but are ignorant (lit., "stupid" or "uneducated"). As the Lord's bond-servant (v. 24) Timothy must reflect God's kindness and patience when responding to those who reject him. **Able to teach** emphasizes disposition as much as it does skill (cf. 1Tm 3:3; Ti 1:7). It is possible to teach the right things in the wrong way (2Tm 2:25). Repentance, however, is not the result of human persuasion. It is a gift from God. These two images, one who has temporarily lost his senses, and someone who has been ensnared in a trap (v. 26), capture the cognitive and spiritual challenges posed by false teaching. The mind must be addressed, but the root problem is spiritual.

V. The Character of the Last Days (3:1–4:5)

A. The Threat of Apostasy (3:1-9)

3:1-9. The advance of false doctrine is a mark of **the last days** (v. 1), a period of time that began at Christ's first coming and culminates with His return. None of the vices in this list (v. 2) is unique to the end times, but these vices increase in scope and intensity as the final days draw near (cf. Rm 1:29-31). **Unloving** (v. 3) refers especially to a lack of affection in the context of family. **Irreconcilable** refers to those who will not make a treaty. **Malicious gossips** slandered like the devil (lit., "devilish"). Those who are **brutal** savage others like animals. Paul traced the downward spiral of humanity into sin to a rejection of God (v. 4; cf. Rm 1:23-25). Those Paul described in v. 5 have repudiated the source of true holiness. **Power** is synonymous with "reality" (cf. 1Co 4:19-20). The Holy Spirit is the key to such power (Ac 1:8; Rm 15:13; Eph 3:16), and the religion espoused and practiced by the false teachers was wanting in respect to the transforming power of the Spirit that is available through the true gospel.

The false teachers described were spiritual predators who targeted susceptible women (v. 6). The Greek term translated **weak women** may refer particularly to those who were wealthy and at leisure. False teachers hoped to enrich themselves off their support, and these women, beset by their sins, would grasp at any teaching that offered an escape from their bondage, even if it was false teaching. Those victimized by these teachers (v. 7) were devoted students who never came to the knowledge of the truth. Their root problem was spiritual. Jannes and Jambres (v. 8) were the names Jewish tradition (cf. CD 5:17-19) assigned to the magicians in Pharaoh's court (Ex 7:11). Paul describes the false teachers as depraved rebels who have been rejected by God. Despite the inroads false teaching had made in the church, its advances were temporary (2Ti 3:9). The false teachers are compared to Jannes and Jambres, suggesting that they share the same folly of preaching a weak and ineffective message.

B. The Antidote of Scripture (3:10-17)

3:10-17. Followed in v. 10 can mean to "investigate," "follow closely," and even "imitate." Timothy had done all these and was the antithesis of the false teachers. During his first missionary journey (v. 11) Paul fled from Iconium and was left for dead at Lystra. After he returned to Antioch, false teachers came from Jerusalem and taught that circumcision was necessary for salvation (Ac 14–15). The emphasis in v. 12 echoes the theme of Paul's exhortation to the churches in Lystra, Iconium, and Antioch (Ac 14:22). **Evil men and impostors** (v. 13) are probably not two separate categories, but two descriptions of the same people. The term **impostor** is used only here in the NT, but in Classical Greek it referred to a magician or wizard. This fits the reference to Jannes and Jambres in v. 8. Both traits were characteristics of the false teachers. There is an ironic parallel to v. 9 in this verse. Paul's command in v. 14 is based on the character of Timothy's teachers and the reliability of Scripture. That he began with the relational dimension of Timothy's experience is significant. Timothy's training started in the home (cf. 1:5). **From childhood** (v. 15) is literally "from infancy" and can describe a child of nursing age. Who first introduced Timothy to Christ is unknown, but his mother and grandmother introduced him to the Scriptures, which became the gateway to Christ.

The Scriptures are **inspired** (lit., "God-breathed") and as such are God's Word. This implies inerrancy in both historical fact and in doctrine. Charles Ryrie defines biblical inspiration this way: "God carried men along so that they wrote His message in the Bible" (Charles Ryrie, *Basic Theology* [Wheaton: Victor, 1987], 71). God superintended the writing of Scripture by his Spirit without blotting out the human author's personality, style, or vocabulary. Yet the result was the Word of God. For evidence that the verse should not be translated "Every inspired Scripture is also profitable" (NEB; see Daniel B. Wallace, *The Basics of New Testament Syntax* [Grand Rapids, MI: Zondervan, 2000], 139). Scripture can be used to instruct those who believe, reprove those who do not, and correct those who have been led astray. **Teaching** refers to the doctrinal dimension of the ministry of instruction. The three words that follow this term focus on the practical application of Scripture. **Reproof** is one of a group of words that are related to refutation or conviction. It is complemented by **correction** and **training** which refer to the positive alternative. **Correction** implies restoration of the fallen to a previous wholesome state. **Training** is more proactive and involves instructing all believers in righteousness. Scripture is more than adequate to prepare Timothy to face the challenge posed by false teachers. It will also equip him for life, enabling Timothy to be proficient in good works. The root of the Greek term that is translated **equipped** refers to making something become useful, suitable, or appropriate. Scripture supplies the believer with all the information needed to live the life God expects from those who belong to Him.

C. A Sacred Charge (4:1-5)

4:1-5. Possession of God's Word comes with accountability. The encouragement of the preceding verses prompted Paul to remind Timothy of the stewardship that comes with such a gift. The description of Christ as **judge** (v. 1) and references to **His appearing and His kingdom** remind Timothy that he will be accountable for this charge. The primary command of v. 2 is to **preach the word**. Reproof, rebuke, exhortation, instruction, and the declaration of the gospel (see v. 5) are all aspects of this work. Paul's earlier promise that the false teachers would not prevail (vv. 9 and 13) does not leave room for complacency (v. 3). The apostle foresees a time when sound (lit., "healthy") doctrine will not be tolerated. Preachers are accountable to God for what they teach; the church is accountable for how it hears. Those who only want to **have their ears tickled** are complicit in the work of false teachers. The verb that is translated **be sober** (v. 5) originally meant "to abstain from wine," but has a broader reference here. Timothy must keep his head, brace himself for hardship, and proclaim Christ.

VI. Paul's Final Departure (4:6-22)

A. The Offering of Paul's Life (4:6-8)

4:6-7. Paul's death was imminent, but the sacrifice had already begun. Drink offerings were a common feature of Jewish and pagan sacrifices (cf. Nm 15:5; 28:7, 14), while **departure** was a familiar euphemism for death. Paul changed his metaphor to underscore the struggle and reward that accompany ministry (v. 7). It was a **good fight**, not because of the goal, but because of the manner in which it had been executed (cf. 2:5; 1Co 9:27). Righteousness is the crown given by **the righteous Judge** (v. 8), and is the hope of all who look forward to Christ's appearing.

B. A Prisoner's Appeal (4:9-18)

4:9-15. The apostle's final letter concludes with a poignant appeal to Timothy to come **soon** (v. 9). This note of urgency is explained by Paul's impending execution and his sudden separation from his companions in ministry. **Demas** (v. 10) was a deserter and may have been the same person referred to in Col 4:14 and Phm 24. **Crescens** and **Titus** left for more noble reasons. Nevertheless, Paul was not completely isolated—**Luke** had remained (v. 11). The request that Timothy bring **Mark** is significant in light of the context. **Mark** had abandoned Paul and Barnabas in Pamphylia on the first missionary journey (Ac 13:13), an action that eventually led to a major split between Paul and Barnabas (Ac 15:38-39). **Tychicus** (v. 12) was one of Paul's trusted emissaries and may have been the bearer of this letter (Ac 20:4; Eph 6:21; Ti 3:12). Paul considered him "our beloved brother and faithful servant and fellow bond-servant in the Lord" (Col 4:7). The **cloak** (v. 13) would have been for personal comfort (cf. v. 21) while the **books** were for study. He expected Timothy to have enough time to make the trip. The apostle sensed his impending death but knew it would not come immediately. An **Alexander** (v. 14) is mentioned in connection with the riot in Ephesus (Ac 19:33), but it does not seem likely that he is the same one mentioned here. Paul did specify the **harm** Alexander did but expected God to redress the wrong. Paul's grievance against Alexander was ministry-related rather than personal. He **vigorously opposed** (v. 15) the apostle's message. Some suggest that Alexander was responsible for Paul's arrest, but this is not certain. Whatever he did, Alexander was powerful enough to be a threat to Timothy.

4:16-18. Scholars are divided about when this **defense** took place (v. 16). In view of the context, it seems best to connect it with his imprisonment at the time this letter was written, and **first** refers to the initial, investigative part of a two-part trial. In praying that **it not be counted against** those who deserted him at the trial, Paul echoed the gracious sentiment expressed by Stephen, whose martyrdom the apostle witnessed (Ac 7:59–8:1). The contents of v. 17 also resemble the experience of Stephen (Ac 7:55-56). However, Paul's reference to deliverance **out of the lion's mouth** is metaphorical for deliverance from those who would have harmed him (it is impossible to identify who they might be in this connection), and suggests that it is an allusion to Dn 6:7-24. Paul expected God to deliver him, even in death (v. 18). This is not an expectation of release from prison but of preservation through final suffering. It is significant that Paul did not yet see himself as having entered the **heavenly kingdom**.

C. A Final Farewell (4:19-22)

4:19-22. The apostle concluded this letter, as he did several others, with a list of personal greetings. Prisca and Aquila were partners in labor as well as in ministry with him in Corinth (Ac 18:2-3; cf. their presence in Rome, Rm 16:3). **Onesiphorus** brought aid to Paul during his imprisonment (1:17). **Erastus** (v. 20) accompanied Timothy to Macedonia while Paul remained in Asia during Paul's third missionary journey (Ac 19:22). **Trophimus** was from Ephesus and was the inadvertent cause of the riot there (Ac 21:29). This list of greetings (v. 21) is puzzling, in view of Paul's earlier statement that all had deserted him and that only Luke was with him (vv. 11 and 16). Perhaps Paul was referring to his missionary companions in v. 11, but to local believers here. Paul's last recorded words, appropriately enough, are a benediction (v. 22). The assurance of God's presence and the promise of His grace mark the themes of Paul's life and his preaching. The apostle's final thought was not for himself but for others.

BIBLIOGRAPHY

See Bibliographies for Pastoral Epistles on p. 1904.

●●●●

TITUS

JOHN KOESSLER

INTRODUCTION

Author and Date. Paul's letter to Titus is considered one of the Pastoral Epistles, along with the two letters to Timothy. It has much in common with 1 Timothy, especially in its guidelines for the appointment of church leaders, warnings about false teaching, and its emphasis on ethics. Like the other pastorals, the letter to Titus is addressed to an individual rather than a church. Many of its directives, however, are aimed at congregational life. Critical scholars have questioned Pauline authorship of Titus because of its vocabulary, guidelines for the appointment of church leaders, and emphasis on ethics (see the introduction to 1 Timothy). In view of its similarity to 1 Timothy, the letter was probably written between AD 63 and 66.

We know little about Titus. Paul described him as his "true child" in the faith (Ti 1:4). This may imply that he introduced Titus to faith in Christ. However, the apostle used similar language to refer to Timothy, who did not seem to have been converted by Paul (1Tm 1:2; cf. 2Tm 1:5). Titus is not mentioned in the book of Acts, but we do know that he accompanied Paul and Barnabas to the Jerusalem conference that settled the issue of circumcision (Gl 2:1; cf. Ac 15:1-29). Paul noted that the leadership did not compel Titus, who was a Greek and possibly from Antioch, to be circumcised during that visit (Gl 2:3). This was important evidence for his assertion that he preached the same gospel as the other apostles.

Paul sent Titus into difficult circumstances. When he became concerned about the condition of the troubled Corinthian church during his third missionary journey, the apostle sent Titus to follow up on his letter of rebuke (2Co 7:6-8). In 2Co 8:23 Paul referred to Titus as a partner, fellow worker, and a messenger, using the Greek term for apostle to indicate his authority to act on Paul's behalf. Titus seems to have possessed strong relational skills. The Corinthian church responded to him in a way that they did not to Paul. Titus felt a genuine affection for the church (2Co 7:15; 8:16-17).

Purpose and Theme. Paul's letter to Titus provided directions for his mission to Crete. The church had been planted, but leaders had not yet been appointed. Titus was sent to "set in order" (Ti 1:5) what remained. The church did not consist in its leaders, but it was not fully functional without them. The church in Crete was also wrestling with predatory false teachers (Ti 1:10). Paul's charge to exhort and speak against these men indicates that preaching was an important aspect of Titus's responsibilities in Crete.

In addition to the problems caused by false teachers, the culture itself posed a problem in Crete. The apostle's harsh depiction of Cretan values in Ti 1:12 reveals a culture that was prone to deceit, brutality, and excess. Paul's letter to Titus reflects many of the same concerns as his letters to Timothy. He emphasized the importance of appointing godly leaders and teaching sound doctrine and godly living.

The book of Titus corroborates the organizational structure of the church that is described in 1 Timothy. It links the church's doctrine with its lifestyle and provides a model for a well-ordered church.

OUTLINE

- I. Paul Reminds Titus of His Mission (1:1-16)
  - A. Paul Greets Titus (1:1-4)
  - B. Titus Must Appoint Elders (1:5-9)
  - C. Titus Must Silence False Teachers (1:10-16)
- II. Marks of Sound Doctrine (2:1-15)
  - A. Respect and Reverence in Relationships (2:1-10)
  - B. Righteousness and Godliness in Life (2:11-15)
- III. Marks of Christian Community (3:1-11)
  - A. Humility toward All (3:1-2)
  - B. Devotion to Doing Good (3:3-8)
  - C. Unity in the Congregation (3:9-11)
- IV. Final Greetings (3:12-15)
  - A. Plans and Directives (3:12-14)
  - B. Closing Benediction (3:15)

COMMENTARY ON TITUS

I. Paul Reminds Titus of His Mission (1:1-16)

A. Paul Greets Titus (1:1-4)

1:1-4. Paul was under authority as a **bond-servant of God** (v. 1). He exercised authority as an **apostle of Jesus Christ**. This calling bound him both to the church and to the truth, which has godliness as its goal. The phrase **in the hope of eternal life** (v. 2) probably refers to the faith and knowledge that lead to godliness. The hope of eternal life is embraced by faith and motivates godly living. Paul emphasized God's timing in revealing the message of the gospel (v. 3; cf. Gl 4:4; Heb 1:1). The gospel re-articulates the ancient promise of eternal life with fresh clarity. Titus was Paul's **true child in** the **faith** (v. 4; cf. 2Tm 1:2). This language could indicate that Paul introduced Titus to faith in Christ. Titus may have been converted when Paul turned his focus to the Gentiles in Antioch (Ac 13:46).

B. Titus Must Appoint Elders (1:5-9)

1:5-9. The establishment of the church in Crete was unfinished until Titus appointed elders in every city (v. 5). The Greek word translated **set in order** was used of setting and straightening broken limbs. For the identity of **elders** and their relationship to "pastors" and "overseers," see the comments on 1Tm 3:1. Paul's list of qualifications (Ti 1:6) is similar to 1Tm 3:2-7. Blamelessness is emphasized in this verse and the next, evidenced by moral purity and self-control. For **husband of one wife**, see the comments on 1Tm 3:2. Those who lead in the church must prove their capability in the home first (cf. 1Tm 3:5). Elders are also called overseers (Ti 1:7). These leaders function as God's stewards. Verse 8 introduces the positive alternatives to the negative traits listed above. The qualified leader is righteous in God's sight and devout in the eyes of others. Church leaders must continue **holding fast** to the truth even when others oppose it (v. 9). **The faithful word** describes the character of this truth and **the teaching** indicates a body of doctrine delivered to the church.

C. Titus Must Silence False Teachers (1:10-16)

1:10-16. Paul condemned those who taught that circumcision was necessary for salvation (v. 10). Driven by rebellion and greed, they proclaimed a deceptive and empty message. The Greek word translated **silenced** (v. 11) literally means "to stop the mouth." Titus must take steps to muzzle these teachers. False teachers upset **whole families**, perhaps with doctrine that was antithetical to family life or because they preyed on vulnerable households (cf. 2Tm 3:6). In v. 12, Paul quoted Epimenides of Crete (sixth or fifth century BC) as **a prophet of their own**, meaning that he was a spokesman for Crete, not that he spoke for God. His sentiment that **Cretans are always liars** was so widespread that the Greek verb "to Cretize" (*kretizo*) meant "to lie and cheat." Cultural values that conflict with biblical standards must be challenged (v. 13). The church's leaders must not be quick tempered (v. 7), but there are times when a sharp rebuke is necessary. The exact nature of these **Jewish myths** (v. 14) is uncertain, but see the comments on 1Tm 1:5-7. **Commandments of men** implies a form of legalism. Purity would have been a major concern for those who tried to bind the church to the law of Moses (v. 15). Paul's statement echoes Christ's teaching and emphasizes the priority of faith (Mk 7:19). Jewish legalism had no moral power (v. 16) as was evident in the character of those who championed such teaching.

II. Marks of Sound Doctrine (2:1-15)

A. Respect and Reverence in Relationships (2:1-10)

2:1-10. Doctrine (v. 1) is simply teaching that includes moral as well as theological content. Paul's directions to **older men** (v. 2) focus on the importance of self-control and dignity. They must live in a way that warrants the respect that is their due. Likewise, **older women** (v. 3) must take the lead in modeling reverence. Older women are charged with the important task of **teaching what is good**. Older women serve as mentors to **young women** (v. 4) in the art of being wives and mothers. Generally, the NT directive to women is to respect their husbands (Eph 5:33; 1Pt 3:2), but here older woman are charged with teaching young wives **to love their husbands**. The church must not treat women's mentoring roles as if they were demeaning. While Paul restricted women from teaching or exercising authority over men (1Tm 2:12), they could and should instruct other women. Titus 2:4-5 provides a curriculum for older women to follow as they set the standards for family life within the church. Paul characterized married women as homemakers, a responsibility that demands many of the same qualities required of those who hold church office. Even if a woman works outside the home (a rarity in Paul's day), she is still to maintain her familial duties at home.

The apostle's directive to young men (v. 6) is less detailed, focusing on a single area. To be **sensible** means "to keep one's head," with particular emphasis on moral virtue. Titus must lead the way in these areas (v. 7). His actions, doctrine, and manner of life provide the pattern. The phrase **sound in speech** (v. 8) probably refers to Titus's teaching more than it does to his personal conversation. These verses call for congruence between what the church teaches and the way its members live. Both shape Paul's concept of what constitutes sound doctrine. Slaves (v. 9) were a familiar feature of the Roman household. Freedom in Christ made some resentful toward their unbelieving masters. Others were tempted to take advantage of believing masters (cf. 1Tm 6:1; Eph 6:5; Col 3:32). Paul's rationale for asking slaves to submit to their masters with respect (v. 10) was redemptive rather than cultural. The aim was not to maintain the cultural status quo but to further the gospel.

B. Righteousness and Godliness in Life (2:11-15)

2:11-15. The assertion of v. 11 is especially poignant in light of the previous two verses. The voluntary submission of Christian slaves was radical proof that the grace of God was intended for every segment of society. The Greek word translated **instructing** (v. 12) in this verse conveyed the idea of training. Grace not only tells us what to do or not to do, it shows us how to comply. The deity of Christ is clearly affirmed in v. 13. He is both **God** (possessing all the divine attributes of God the Father, but a distinct Person from the Father; cf. Jn 1:1-18) **and Savior**. Paul calls Christ's return for the Church at the rapture **the blessed hope**, and with it comes accountability, providing the primary motivation for godly living in the current age. Jesus' death (v. 14) was a redemptive offering that purifies us from the guilt and power of sin. This verse emphasizes the comprehensive result of Christ's work. He redeems us from all wickedness and makes us eager to obey. Titus's teaching ministry in Crete included both encouragement and rebuke. The command not to let anyone **disregard** him (v. 15) may have been addressing Titus's demeanor, but it also had implications for his lifestyle.

III. Marks of Christian Community (3:1-11)

A. Humility toward All (3:1-2)

3:1-2. The command to submit to rulers and authorities (v. 1) provides the context for Paul's call to obedience and good works in this verse. The church's speech toward **all men** (v. 2) should be free from insult or slander, our relations marked by peace, and our deportment characterized by gentleness. Gentleness and kindness were characteristic of Jesus' ministry (Mt 11:29; 2Co 10:1).

B. Devotion to Doing Good (3:3-8)

3:3-8. Unbelievers are what believers once were: foolish rebels who were deceived, enslaved, and filled with malice (v. 3). Believers lose patience with the lost when they forget their own past. Kindness describes God's benevolent disposition toward sinful humanity (v. 4; cf. Rm 11:22; Eph 2:7). The Greek word translated **love for mankind** was used in secular Greek to describe the magnanimity of rulers. Paul had repeatedly emphasized the importance of godly behavior but was emphatic in denying that such works are the basis for our salvation. **Washing of regeneration** and **renewing by the Holy Spirit** (v. 5) describe how **His mercy** is demonstrated. Regeneration is new birth that comes as a result of the work of Christ and is imparted by the Holy Spirit. It is further described as "renewal," the same word used by Paul in Rm 12:2 when he speaks of the "renewing of your mind." Regeneration and renewal are both symbolized by the ordinance of baptism. God's Spirit is the agent of our regeneration and renewal (v. 6), and is given through Jesus Christ (cf. Jn 15:25; 16:7). The Holy Spirit is also described as dwelling within us (1Tm 1:14, cf. Rm 8:11; 1Co 3:16; 6:19; Gl 4:6; Eph 2:22). He is the possession of all who have been **justified** by the grace of Christ (v. 7). His presence guarantees our inheritance of **eternal life** (2Co 1:22). **This is a trustworthy statement** (v. 8) probably refers to the previous verses. The certainty of eternal life offers a powerful motive **to engage in good deeds** (for the connection between Christian ethics and immortal life, see the comments on 1Co 15:29-34). Faith and works are fully compatible as long as faith has precedence.

C. Unity in the Congregation (3:9-11)

3:9-11. Foolish controversies, genealogies, and **disputes about the Law** (v. 9) were all characteristics of the false teachers (1:10-16; cf. 1Tm 1:4; 6:4; 2Tm 2:16-17, 23; see the comments on 1Tm 1:3-5). Instead of building up the church, they create discord. The **factious man** (v. 10) is not always one who adheres to false teaching. It can also describe someone who is a member of a divisive party in the church (cf. 1Co 1:12; 11:18-19). A first and second warning implies that a process of confrontation and rebuke has been carried out (see the comments on Mt 18:15-18). The factious person's obstinacy after repeated warnings is proof of twisted thinking (v. 11). His or her persistence in divisiveness constitutes sin and demonstrates guilt.

IV. Final Greetings (3:12-15)

A. Plans and Directives (3:12-14)

3:12-14. Paul's language suggests he was at liberty when he wrote this letter (v. 12). He may have intended **Artemas** or **Tychicus** to take Titus's post. **Nicopolis** was on the west coast of Greece and was a Roman colony. **Zenas** (v. 13) is mentioned only here. **Apollos** was a native of Alexandria who became known for his rhetorical skill while in Ephesus. Priscilla and Aquila helped him understand the gospel better (Ac 18:24-28). Helping **Zenas** and **Apollos** (v. 13) meant providing funds or basic necessities required for their journey (v. 14). Paul expected the believers at Crete to contribute to this task.

B. Closing Benediction (3:15)

3:15. The phrase **all who are with me** may refer to Paul's traveling companions. Despite the hard things he had said about Crete, there were some in the church who regarded him with affection. To them (and to us) he offered a benediction of grace.

BIBLIOGRAPHY

See Bibliographies for Pastoral Epistles on p. 1904.

PHILEMON

GERALD PETERMAN

INTRODUCTION

Author. Without doubt, this letter comes from the apostle Paul, who wrote at least a portion with his own hand (19; i.e., not using a scribe). There is debate, however, regarding the occasion. It is at least clear that Philemon was a slave owner, living in Colossae. He owned Onesimus, who had wronged Philemon in some way (see the commentary on 18). Beyond this, one of two situations seems possible. Perhaps Onesimus ran away from Colossae and met Paul in Rome accidentally. With this letter in hand, Paul sent the slave back. Alternatively, perhaps the slave was estranged from his master and sought out Paul to act as a mediator.

Recipients. Uniquely in Philemon, Paul alternated between the second-person singular (e.g., 2, 4-8, 10, 12-14) and the second-person plural (3, 22 twice, 25). Further, although the letter is addressed to Philemon, it is also addressed to his church (2). Thus, the letter is both personal and public. This is not surprising in light of Philemon's probable position as a leader in the congregation. As a leader, his relationships were a matter of public importance (cf. 1Ti 3:1-7).

This letter is closely related to Colossians. Most of the people mentioned in its greeting (Col 4:10-14) also appear in Philemon (23-24).

Date. Traditionally, since the letter mentions Paul's imprisonment (v. 10), the letter to Philemon has been understood as written from Rome while Paul was under house arrest (Ac 28:16). If so, then the letter was probably written around AD 60–62. For alternative location(s), see the Introduction to Colossians.

Contribution. Philemon makes three closely related contributions to the NT. First, although other letters refer to tension or estrangement between members of a congregation (e.g., Php 4:2-3), this one spends the most time attempting to bring about reconciliation. Paul does not, however, command specific action. He leaves it to Philemon, the congregation, and the Spirit to decide the best course of action. Much practical application can be found here. Second, the gospel has power to change people and society. Onesimus—formerly useless but now useful (11)—goes from being a mere slave to being a brother in Christ. His new status entails being welcomed (17). This is radical social change. Third, the letter gives us a model of tact and compassion as we see Paul using all the respect he has earned in order to give it to one who is helpless.

Background. Slavery was a basic and accepted element of first-century society. While the practice strikes many of us as perverse and barbaric, we should keep in mind that ancient Greco-Roman slavery was different from American slavery in at least four ways: First, it was not associated with ethnicity. Slaves could come from any nation and race. Second, slavery was rarely permanent; many gained freedom within a decade. Some were able to save money and buy their own freedom. Others even gained Roman citizenship when freed. Third, for many, slavery acted as bankruptcy. If unable to pay debts, selling oneself as a slave ended obligations to creditors (in a sense gaining oneself a kind of freedom). Fourth, many slaves, whether owned by the government or by the wealthy, lived much more comfortably than freemen who were poor.

OUTLINE

I. Paul's Greeting: "From Paul to Philemon" (1-3)
II. Paul's Thanksgiving: "I Thank God for Your Love and Faith" (4-7)
III. Paul's Plea: "Do Not Punish Onesimus" (8-16)
IV. Paul's Request: "Let Me Cover Your Losses" (17-20)
V. Paul's Conclusion and Farewell: "I Am Confident in Your Obedience" (21-25)

COMMENTARY ON PHILEMON

I. Paul's Greeting: "From Paul to Philemon" (1-3)

1. Unlike in other letters, Paul did not refer to himself as an apostle (1Co 1:1; Rm 1:1) nor as a slave of Christ (Php 1:1). He is a **prisoner**—one socially weak and dependent just as the slave Onesimus. Further, although **Timothy** is mentioned in this greeting, he is not a co-author; Paul used the first person singular throughout.

2-3. Although Philemon is the primary recipient, **Apphia** (perhaps Philemon's wife), **Archippus** (otherwise unknown), and the church that met in Philemon's house (cf. Rm 16:3, 5; 1Co 16:19; Ac 16:15) were also greeted. **Philemon** was not Paul's assistant. As coworkers, he and Paul both served God (see Rm 16:3; 2Co 1:24; Php 2:25; Col 4:11).

II. Paul's Thanksgiving: "I Thank God for Your Love and Faith" (4-7)

4-5. Thanksgiving and prayer are common in Paul (cf. Eph 1:15-16; Php 1:3-4), with the thanks grounded in some work of God in people. Here thanks result from Philemon's love and faith (5). Verse 5 might seem odd until we realize that it is chiastic—that is, it has an *a-b-b'-a'* pattern. Love (*a*) is directed to the saints (*a'*); faith (*b*) is directed toward Jesus (*b'*).

6. Against the NIV ("active in sharing your faith"), this verse is not about evangelism. The challenges in 6 entail defining the word *koinonia* (**fellowship** in NASB; cf. 2Co 8:4; Php 1:5; Heb 13:16), discerning the relation between *koinonia* and **faith**, and defining *energes*, an adjective that has to do with accomplishing work (**effective** in NASB; "put into action" in NLT; elsewhere only at 1Co 16:9; Heb 4:12). In the NT both **fellowship** and **faith** are active. Thus the NLT probably comes closest: "And I am praying that you will put into action the generosity that comes from your faith as you understand and experience all the good things we have in Christ."

7. Philemon's love and faith (6) and his previous good works (7) grounded the request coming in 8 and following. As he refreshed others (7), so he should refresh Paul (20) by welcoming Onesimus (see 17).

III. Paul's Plea: "Do Not Punish Onesimus" (8-16)

8-12. Paul rarely commanded; rather, as in 7-8a, he reasoned with believers and appealed to the best in them (here the appeal is to Philemon's love). Next, Paul described the situation. Three features stand out: First, reference to his age and imprisonment should draw out Philemon's respect and compassion, respectively (9). Second, he mentioned Onesimus's conversion (**whom I have begotten**, 10). This detail becomes important later (16). Paul elsewhere talked about "fathering" his converts (1Co 4:15). With a play on words (**useless** to **useful**, 11), Paul clarified that this conversion was transformative. Third, over probably a brief period, Paul developed a strong godly affection for Onesimus (cf. 1Th 2:8); such affection made it painful to send the slave away (12).

13-14. Serving prisoners is a Christian virtue (Mt 25:36). On imprisonment for the gospel see Php 1:13 and 2Tm 2:8-9. Further, since a slave serves as a master's representative, Paul viewed Onesimus's work as Philemon's work. As elsewhere in Paul (cf. 2Co 9:7; Rm 12:8b), he did not command good works (here **your goodness** means "your act of goodness") to be done out of duty (**compulsion**); rather they should be done eagerly and freely.

15-16. Betraying his strong view of God's sovereignty, Paul proposed that divine providence was the reason for Onesimus's flight and then gave two sharp contrasts. First, the slave's short absence should not matter since it hardly compares with having him back eternally (that is, with eternal life). Second, in all spheres of life (**in the flesh and in the Lord**, 16), Onesimus is now not primarily a slave but a **beloved brother** (the same title given Philemon, 7).

IV. Paul's Request: "Let Me Cover Your Losses" (17-20)

17. Although Paul mentioned his request in v. 10, the specifics finally appear here—namely, whatever respect and reception Philemon would give to Paul, he should give to Onesimus when he arrives. The request is based on partnership. **Partner** is the equivalent of co-worker (v. 1)—one who both receives and also spreads the gospel.

18-20. Paul's wording assumes that, for the sake of discussion, Onesimus wronged his master. How he did so, however, cannot be determined. In any case, by drawing attention to his own handwriting (cf. 1Co 16:21), Paul solemnly promised to make good (18b-19a). But it is a debt Paul should not need to pay because he led Philemon to Christ. Therefore, Philemon already owed Paul a larger debt: redemption of his very life. Because these three are family in Christ (20), brotherly love shown to Onesimus not only refreshes the slave but Paul as well (cf. 7; 1Co 12:26).

V. Paul's Conclusion and Farewell: "I Am Confident in Your Obedience" (21-25)

21-22. Since Philemon's track record has shown obedience to God (e.g., 5-7), Paul made his request with confidence. Perhaps when Paul says that Philemon will obey **even more than what I say** (21) it is a veiled reference to Philemon freeing Onesimus the slave; but it is uncertain. The words might refer, instead, to Paul's desire to have Philemon return the slave to him to serve with him once again. As an itinerant church planter, Paul was dependent on Christian hospitality (22a). He was confident that Philemon's congregation (**your**, 22, is plural) was praying for him.

23-25. On the greetings here, see Col 4:10-14. Paul closed with his prayer that the greatest treasure—Christ's **grace**—would remain with them (**your** is plural; cf. Gl 6:18).

BIBLIOGRAPHY

Bruce, F. F. *The Epistles to the Colossians, to Philemon, and to the Ephesians*. 2nd ed. Grand Rapids, MI: Eerdmans, 1984.

Garland, David E. *Colossians, Philemon.* Grand Rapids, MI: Zondervan, 1998.

Hughes, R. Kent. *Colossians and Philemon: The Supremacy of Christ.* Wheaton: Crossway, 1989.

Lightfoot, J. B. *Colossians and Philemon.* Edited by Alister McGrath and J. I. Packer. Wheaton: Crossway, 1997.

MacArthur, John. *Colossians and Philemon.* New Testament Commentary. Chicago: Moody, 1992.

Moo, Douglas J. *The Letters to the Colossians and to Philemon.* Grand Rapids, MI: Eerdmans, 2008.

O'Brien, Peter T. *Colossians–Philemon.* Nashville: Thomas Nelson, 1982.

Still, Todd D. "Colossians." Vol. 12 of The Expositor's Bible Commentary, edited by T. Longman III and D. E. Garland. Grand Rapids, MI: Zondervan, 2005.

● ● ● ●

HEBREWS

RONALD SAUER

INTRODUCTION

Author. His identity remains unknown. But he was a Hellenistic Jewish Christian of exceptional literary ability; his Greek is the most scholarly of all the NT documents. The writer had previously been among the readers (13:19), knows them well, is acquainted with their history, including past and current leaders, has the liberty to speak his mind (5:13), and displays a pastor's heart (6:1, 9) for them. The style and vocabulary differ so significantly from Paul's that it is highly unlikely he was the author. Other guesses include Luke, Barnabas, Apollos, or other associates of Paul, and even Priscilla (perhaps with Aquila) or Mary, though the masculine singular participle "tell" in 11:32 is fatal for this understanding. No one today knows who wrote Hebrews, but the first recipients did.

Date. That the epistle was probably written prior to AD 70 is inferred from two hints. First, Jerusalem's temple was destroyed in AD 70. From the letter's recurring use of the present tense, the Levitical ritual, which was suddenly stopped by the temple's demise, seems to be in operation at the time of writing. For instance, Israel's high priest still is being appointed (5:1). And on earth priests are offering "the gifts according to the Law" (8:4). The high priest continually enters the Holy Place (9:7, 25). Consequently, "they offer continually year by year . . . the same sacrifices" (10:1), as they serve in the tabernacle (13:10). Second, since the author seeks to demonstrate the superiority of the Jewish Messiah over the Jewish religion, it is most unlikely that if writing after AD 70 he would have been indifferent to the catastrophe of that year and failed to have mentioned it. From his knowledge of the OT, the writer is convinced that the first covenant, with its Levitical ritual, "is becoming obsolete and growing old" and "ready to disappear" (8:13). The temple's destruction could have well served as conclusive proof to his maintaining that the old covenant and Levitical sacrifices were about to end, as demonstrated in God's allowing them to cease.

In 13:24 the author says to his recipients, "those from Italy greet you." This is frustratingly ambiguous. The author could have been in Italy and sent this greeting on behalf of his Italian acquaintances (in which case the author was in Italy but the destination of the letter is not specified), or he could have been in another region with Italian expatriates (in which case the author's location is not known but the letter was sent to Italy). It is impossible to be certain, but because there is so much emphasis on Jewish religious practices it seems feasible that the writer was in Italy and was writing to those in Judea.

Recipients. Regarding their ethnic identity, that they were Jewish is based on the following clues. (1) The expressions "the fathers" (1:1) and "the descendant of Abraham" (2:16) imply a Jewish descent, as do (2) Jewish antecedents in 6:1-2 and 9:15's remark that "a death has taken place for the redemption of the transgressions that were committed under the first covenant." (3) The letter's argument rests upon the OT as the incontestable authority, viewed as the Word of the Holy Spirit (3:7). (4) The minutest knowledge of the Jewish Scriptures on the part of the recipients is presupposed. And (5) the epistle's arguing for the superiority of the new covenant to the old is better explained if designed for Jews tempted to leave their faith in Jesus and return to Judaism without Him.

Regarding their past spiritual condition, fine progress had been made. They had been believers for some years (5:12), commendably weathered severe persecution (10:32-34), had been well taught by exceptional leadership (13:7), and had displayed loving service to other believers (6:10). But they eventually came under Jewish persecution for their faith and were doubting whether Jesus was indeed the Messiah. They also sensed another and worse wave of persecution on the horizon and had "become dull of hearing" [slow to understand] (5:11). They were discouraged (12:12-13), and regressing, and contemplating abandoning their faith in Jesus as the Jewish Messiah for Judaism. Regarding their location, this missive was not penned for all Jewish believers everywhere. They were a particular community. For they had a unique history (6:10; 10:32-34) not experienced by all Christians. Their congregation appeared to be homogenous and was well known by the writer, who was planning to visit them again (13:19). Possibly, they lived in Italy and their previous address was Rome. In AD 49 Jews in Rome underwent a bloodless persecution and were exiled from the city. The readers had "not yet resisted to the point of shedding [their] blood" (12:4), but did suffer "the seizure of [their] property" (10:34), and seemed to have been forced to leave their home city (13:14). On the other hand, their familiarity with the temple and its liturgy seems to indicate that they lived in Judea or even Jerusalem. Thus, the author might have written from Italy to Jewish believers in Israel.

Purpose. The immediate danger threatening the readers was neither apathy, nor mere backsliding, nor paganism, nor Gnosticism. Rather, the imminent peril was apostasy (3:12). Apostasy is the deliberate (10:26) and permanent rejection of Messiah Jesus (6:6) and, in the readers' case, a return to, or a remaining within, the Jewish faith without Jesus. The author's purpose was to exhort his readers to hold fast to their faith in Jesus as the Messiah (4:14) because the Jewish Messiah is superior even to the biblically revealed Jewish religion. It is clear that he was not disparaging the Jewish religion but rather demonstrating that it was designed to point to the coming Messiah. He was exhorting them not to return to the shadow of the good things to come (10:1) once they had experienced the reality to which it pointed.

The five warning passages in the book (2:1-4; 3:7–4:16; 5:11–6:20; 10:26-31; 12:18-29; see the outline below) warn those among the readers who considered abandoning Messiah Jesus to fully embrace Him as the One who brings covenantal perfection and completion, or to use Paul's term, salvation. As the interpretation of those passages will show, some among the audience of this epistle were still fixated upon angels as servants of God (1:5-7, 13-14), the OT priesthood (5:1-4), the law of Moses, which was the old covenant (7:11, 19; 8:13; 9:9), and the earthly tabernacle (9:24). It was necessary for them to embrace Jesus as their Messiah since He is the Son of God (4:14) and King of Israel, the quintessential high priest (5:10; 7:14) who makes one covenantally and salvationally perfect (10:12-14), who established the new covenant (8:6), and who entered into and serves in the heavenly tabernacle (9:11-15). The warning passages indicate that some had not yet gone all the way to the covenantal perfection found only in Jesus, and if they failed to do so, they would be excluded from the covenant He founded (i.e., they would not be saved).

The letter's intent is twofold: (1) Theologically, to demonstrate that the Messiahship of Jesus is the final and climactic word from God, superior to the Old Testament faith that merely pointed to Him. Jesus has "a more excellent ministry" inaugurated by "a better covenant" (8:6) than the old one of Moses (8:13). (2) Practically, not only to prevent the readers from turning away from their Messiah and returning to temple worship alone, but also to encourage them to "hold fast" to their "confession" (4:14) and thus persevere in the Christian faith and to "press on to maturity" (6:1). The heart of the letter is 5:1–10:18, which concerns the high priestly ministry of Jesus. He is in "heaven itself . . . in the presence of God (9:24) to make intercession for" us (7:25). According to 13:22, the writer calls his letter a "word of exhortation." Accordingly, the Greek hortatory subjunctive ("let us . . .") occurs 11 times, by which he urges his readers to join him in various endeavors.

Theme. A key word, "better," occurs 13 times. Messiah Jesus is better, for example, than "the angels" (1:4) and than all the leading figures of the Hebrew Bible. As priest He has offered up a better sacrifice (9:23) than those offered by Israel's other priests; consequently, His blood speaks of better things (12:24), such as our better eternal possession (10:34). Jesus is mediator of a better covenant (7:22) based on "better promises" (8:6) and offers us "a better hope" (7:19), because God has "provided something better for us" (11:40), which, in part, is "a better resurrection" (11:35). The writer's aim in using this word is that the Jewish Messiah Jesus is even better than the Jewish religion that pointed to Him.

OUTLINE

I. A Superior Person (1:1–7:28)
  A. Jesus Is Better Than the Prophets (1:1-4)
  B. Jesus Is Better Than the Angels (1:5–2:18)
    1. Better Than Angels in His Deity (1:5-14)
    • First Parenthetical Warning: The Danger of Drifting from the Gospel (2:1-4)
    2. Better Than Angels in His Humanity (2:5-18)
  C. Jesus Is Better Than Moses (3:1-6)
    • Second Parenthetical Warning: The Danger of Disbelieving the Gospel (3:7–4:16)
  D. Jesus Is Better Than Aaron (5:1–7:28)
    1. He Is a Fully Qualified High Priest (5:1-10)
    • Third Parenthetical Warning: The Danger of Defecting from the Gospel (5:11–6:20)
    2. He Is an Eternal High Priest (7:1-28)
II. A Superior Ministry (8:1–10:18)
  A. A Better Covenant (8:1-13)
  B. A Better Sanctuary (9:1-12)
  C. A Better Sacrifice (9:13–10:18)
III. A Superior Life (10:19–13:25)
  A. Exhortation to Fellowship (10:19-25)
    • Fourth Parenthetical Warning: The Danger of Disparaging the Gospel (10:26-31)
  B. Exhortation to Perseverance (10:32–12:13)
  C. Exhortation to Sanctification (12:14-17)
    • Fifth Parenthetical Warning: The Danger of Declining the Gospel (12:18-29)
  D. Exhortation to Service (13:1-21)
  E. Final Greetings (13:22-25)

COMMENTARY ON HEBREWS

I. A Superior Person (1:1–7:28)

A. Jesus Is Better Than the Prophets (1:1-4)

1:1-4. On the premise that a superior messenger brings a weightier message, this section indirectly shows Jesus' preeminence over the OT prophets. This comparison points to the superiority of His revelation to theirs. **Long ago** God disclosed truth **to the** Jewish **fathers**. This disclosure was given piecemeal **in many portions** ("at different times," HCSB) and was conveyed **in** a variety of different **ways** (1:1). More recently God **has** again **spoken**. However, this time His revelation was given **to us**; and this time it was not delivered through mere human seers, but by a divine spokesman, **His Son** (1:2a). His superiority over the Jewish prophets is seen in seven ways. (1) He, not they, was divinely **appointed heir of all things.** (2) It was **through** the Son that God **made the world**, whereas the OT seers are but a part of creation. (3) Jesus radiates the divine **glory** and possesses **the exact** same **nature** as does God. Moreover, (4) the Son **upholds** and preserves the material universe, (5) has **made purification** for humanity's **sins** (including the prophets' transgressions), and then (6) He did what no prophet could or would dare to do—**He sat down at the right hand of** God, in heaven (1:3). Finally (7), the Son is greater **than the angels,** just as His name is **more excellent** than **theirs** (1:4). None of these statements could ever be attributed to prophets. The Son is greater than they, and His message weightier than theirs.

B. Jesus Is Better Than the Angels (1:5–2:18)

This section proves Jesus' superiority over the angels, since He is both God and human. The author's argument is separated by a warning against the danger of spiritual drifting.

1. Better Than Angels in His Deity (1:5-14)

1:5-14. This paragraph justifies the claim in 1:4 of Jesus' preeminence over the angels. Justification comes by citing seven OT texts; two deal with His name (who He is) and five with His person (what He has done). Verse 5 quotes two messianic texts identifying the (1) superior name, Ps 2:7 and 2Sm 7:14. In both God calls Jesus—and none of the angels—**My Son**. An intimate, filial relationship exists between the first two members of the Trinity. (2) **When** (better translated "whenever"), for the second time, the Father **brings** this Son **into the world** (v. 6), Dt 32:43 directs **all the angels of God** to **worship Him**. **Again** is not a mere connective (i.e., not "Once again—here is another OT citation to support my argument"; cf. KJV; RSV). When it is used in this connective way (see Heb 1:5; 2:13 twice; 4:5; 10:30), it is followed immediately by the OT citation. But here it appears to be closely connected to the verb **brings** and is followed by other material before the citation, and when **again** is followed closely by a verb in Hebrews, it modifies the verb (see 4:7; 5:12; 6:1, 6). These points, along with the subjunctive mood of **brings** ("whenever He brings"), which the author used to project and consider the entrance of the Son, suggests that the author was not looking at Messiah's first coming, but toward His second coming. When that happens, God will command (**let all the angels . . . worship Him**) the angelic hosts to erupt in praise for Messiah. The point is that He who is worshiped by angels is greater than those angels who will render the homage. (3) According to Ps 104:4, the Father **makes His angels** like **winds, and His ministers** as **a flame of fire**. The angels may change their appearance according to God's wishes for them (**winds**; **fire**), in contrast to the Son who "is the same yesterday and today and forever" (Heb 13:8), and they are **ministers** ("those who engage in special administrative service"). But the **Son** is no servant. He is the King (v. 8). They who serve have an inferior status to the One who is over all. (4) While the angels are mere servants, Ps 45:6 (quoted in 1:8) addresses the Son as **O God** and presents Him as a ruler, whose **throne** is **forever and ever**. Unlike so many unjust human rulers, His reign (**scepter**) is **righteous**. Quoted in 1:9, Ps 45:7 guarantees that the Son's rule will be just, by stating that He has **loved righteousness and hated lawlessness**. With this high esteem of morality, such a One could treat His subjects only in perfect fairness. This is why (**Therefore**) **God . . . anointed** (the verb from which the Hb. title "Messiah" and the Gk. "*Christos*" is derived) Jesus to rule, **above** His angelic **companions**. (5) According to Ps 102:25, **the earth** and **the heavens are the works of** the Son's **hands** (Heb 1:10). That is, He created everything, angels included. Admittedly, angels do incredible deeds. But He who creates the universe and angels does greater works. (6) Angelic beings have only an eternal future; they exist forever into the future only from the time of their creation. But the Son is absolutely eternal. His existence stretches out of eternity past and into and beyond eternity to come. Ps 102:26-27 says to the Son, **You remain** (v. 11) . . . **You are the same**, and **Your years will not come to an end** (Heb 1:12). Finally, (7) according to Ps 110:1, the honor of sitting **at** God's **right hand** (Heb 1:13) was extended to no angel, but only to the Son. According to Leupold, God designated this position for His Son, "making Him coequal in rank and authority with Himself, and so virtually declaring His divine character" (H. C. Leupold, *Exposition of the Psalms* [Grand Rapids, MI: Baker, 1969], 771). Verse 14 concludes by describing the dignity of angels to be that of mere servants, **sent out to render service**, but the dignity of the Son is the dignity of God Himself.

• First Parenthetical Warning: The Danger of Drifting from the Gospel (2:1-4)

2:1-4. These verses comprise the first of five warning passages (in 2:1-4; 3:7–4:16; 5:11–6:20; 10:26-31; 12:18-29; and see the outline in the introduction). As the writer argues his case, he periodically takes temporary leave of the argument proper to strongly urge his audience to pay attention to what is being said, lest they suffer dire consequences for noncompliance. For an explanation of those for whom the warning passages are intended and their spiritual condition, also see the comments on 5:11–6:8. Apparently a significant number of the recipients had been exposed to and impressed by all that Jesus offered, but they had not as yet embraced the blessings found only in Him and the new covenant He inaugurated. If they failed to do this (if they neglected "so great a salvation," v. 3), they would not escape God's judgment. Rather than describing people who had trusted Christ but who might lose their salvation, this warning passage, and all the warning passages, address unbelievers who faced judgment if they did not come all the way to Jesus.

Looking back to the Son's superiority to the OT prophets and angels as demonstrated in chapter one, **For this reason** draws a conclusion expressed in the form of a duty: **we must pay much closer attention** to truth spoken by Jesus, which **we have heard**. The purpose for such attentiveness is **so that we do not drift away** (2:1).

To drift from divine truth is to drift from God. The word **for** that begins v. 2 furnishes a reason for greater attentiveness to Jesus' message.

The divine **word** delivered in the OT era **through angels proved unalterable. Every** intentional **transgression and** unintentional **disobedience** of that revelation was justly and thoroughly punished. That being the case, we **will** definitely not **escape** divine judgment **if we neglect so great a salvation.** Jesus' greater message brings greater blessings if accepted, but greater punishment if rejected (2:3). If judgment came upon those who disregarded the **word** as brought by angels, the consequences for rejecting the gospel brought by the Son are even more serious.

Several factors indicate just how **great** this **salvation** is: **it was** initially **spoken through the Lord** Jesus; then its authenticity **was confirmed to us**; and lastly, **God also** jointly testified to the gospel's veracity **by signs and wonders and by various miracles, and by gifts of the Holy Spirit** (2:4). Most likely this refers to the miracles that confirmed the apostolic message in the apostolic age (cf. 2Co 12:12; Ac 2:43; 5:12), not that God would consistently provide signs and wonders to confirm the gospel throughout this age. The essence of this initial warning text is the necessity of our giving constant, greater attention to Jesus' message.

2. Better Than Angels in His Humanity (2:5-18)

This paragraph finishes the discussion of Jesus' supremacy over the angels. In 1:5-14 the writer presented Him as superior to the angels in His deity. In 2:5-18 he presents Jesus even in His humanity as greater than these celestial beings, in four roles: as world ruler (2:5-9), as savior (2:10), as our brother (2:11-13), and as high priest (2:14-18).

2:5-9. For (2:5) justifies 1:8-9 depicting Jesus as a ruler (Your throne, the scepter of His kingdom, God anointed You). Part of the justification is that God did not **subject to angels the world to come.** Verses 6-8 quote Ps 8, which identifies the divinely appointed ruler of the world. That ruler is **MAN** (2:6) whom God **MADE . . . FOR A LITTLE WHILE LOWER THAN THE ANGELS**, yet **CROWNED HIM** (2:7), and **PUT ALL THINGS IN SUBJECTION UNDER HIS FEET** (2:8a). God appointed Adam and subsequent mankind to rule earth. But because of man's sin, creation revolted against its ruler. Currently **we do not yet see all things subjected to him** (2:8b). **But . . . Jesus . . . by the grace of God** did **taste death for everyone** (2:9). By doing so He regained for man what man had lost by sin and death, namely the dominion of the world. As a result, Jesus is divinely **crowned**, so that man may once again rule.

2:10-13. By His atoning death, Jesus assumed another role; He became **the author of** humanity's **salvation** (2:10). Those saved by His death are God's **many sons.** Jesus was perfected **through sufferings**, which were the appointed means for His qualifying and functioning as the perfect high priest. **To perfect** is used in 5:9 and 7:28 not for moral development in Christ but for His becoming the perfect mediator through His sufferings and death (see the comments on Mt 26:36-46). Because they and Jesus are **all from one Father** and have the same heavenly **Father . . . He is not ashamed to call them** His **brethren** (Heb 2:11). He who enjoys the intimacy of an older brother with God's children is greater in dignity than the angels (2:12-13), whose relation to believers is that of servants (see 1:14).

2:14-18. In His humanity Jesus occupies still one more role in relation to men. **Since** heaven's **children share in flesh and blood**, Jesus partook of **the same** elements. He did this so **that through death He might render powerless** the grip that **the devil** has on people (2:14). In doing so Jesus set **free those who through fear of death were subject** to various kinds of moral **slavery** (2:15). Those to whom **He** now gives **help** are not **angels, but . . . descendant[s] of Abraham** (2:16), a reference to the Jewish believers to whom this epistle was written. By being **like His** brothers **in all things**, Jesus became their **high priest . . . to make propitiation for the sins of the people** (2:17). Now He **is able to come to the aid of those who are tempted** (2:18). Inasmuch as angels could never assist humans in these ways, only He who can is greater than they.

C. Jesus Is Better Than Moses (3:1-6)

3:1-4. The Lord's superiority to the great lawgiver is presented here. The two are compared for four reasons. (1) Moses was viewed by Jewish people as the greatest man in the OT and most superior teacher of God's truth. (2) He was an effective spokesman for God, the Pentateuch coming from his pen. (3) Though not an official priest, on several occasions he was one of Israel's most effective intercessors (e.g., Ex 32:10-14). And (4) the failure of his followers in the wilderness prepares for the discussion of Jesus' followers. The readers are summoned to **consider Jesus, the Apostle** (i.e., messenger, like Moses) **and High**

Priest (again, like Moses the great intercessor) **of** their **confession** (Heb 3:1). What they are to consider about Jesus is that **He was faithful** to God in all duties assigned Him (3:2a). Analogous to the Lord's fidelity was that of **Moses**, who **also was** faithful **in all His house** (people) (3:2b). Though both were faithful to heaven, Jesus is **counted worthy of more glory than Moses**. The former's greater esteem is similar to a **builder** having **more honor than the house** he erects. People admire a beautiful house, but the real admiration goes to its constructor (3:3).

Verse 4 adduces the first reason for Jesus' greater honor. No **house** grows out of the ground, but **is built by someone**. In like manner, **the builder of all things is God**. Christ is the divine agent of creation (1:2, 10), of which Moses is but a part. The Creator enjoys more glory than His creature.

3:5-6. The second reason for Jesus' preeminence is that Moses served as a faithful servant **in all His house** (3:5), but Christ is **a Son over His house** (3:6a). In a family a son is prized more highly than a servant. And the author claims he and his readers **are** members of God's family, **if we hold fast our confidence** and **hope** (3:6b). Their current membership in the divine household will be demonstrated by their continuing in the faith. The "if" clause in v. 6 (**if we hold fast our confidence and the boast of our hope firm until the end**) provides the evidence for and the result of the "then" part of the verse (then [understood from the conditional statement] **we are** His **house**). This is called an "evidence-to-inference" condition. The "if" part of the verse provides the evidence and includes the result of the "then" clause, which chronologically comes before the "if" part. For this conditional construction see also, e.g., Jn 5:31; 8:31; 15:14; Rm 2:25; 1Co 13:1; Jms 2:17; Heb 12:8; and 1Jn 2:15. In Heb 3:6, their perseverance provides the evidence indicating that they are part of "His house." Failure to cling to Messiah Jesus indicates they are not. They are "His house," a fact that both precedes and ensures their holding fast their confidence to the end. For a thorough discussion of this construction and its relevance for 3:6, 14, see Fanning, "A Classical Reformed View," 209–18, in Herbert W. Bateman, ed., *Four Views on the Warning Passages in Hebrews* (Grand Rapids, MI: Kregel, 2007). The same observations apply to the conditional statement in 3:14 ("For we have become partakers of Christ, if we hold fast the beginning of our assurance firm until the end").

• Second Parenthetical Warning: The Danger of Disbelieving the Gospel (3:7–4:16)

3:7-19. This paragraph is half—and the negative part—of the next warning passage. This warning passage has the same overall theme as the others: Hold fast to and have faith in (cf. 3:12, 19) Jesus as the Messiah and the covenantal perfection He brings. For an explanation of the nature of these warnings and the spiritual condition of those for whom they are intended, see the comments on 2:1-4; 5:11–6:8. The warning proper, given here, is followed by an exhortation in the other half (4:1-16). Together both sections urge the recipients to hold fast to the gospel until the end. And their heavenly high priest stands ready to dispense grace to them (4:14-16), enabling them to endure.

The warning begins with **therefore** in 3:7. Looking back to 3:6b, which affirms membership in God's family by perseverance, this conjunction introduces the warning by quoting Ps 95 in Heb 3:7b-11. This psalm reviews the failure of Moses' generation in the wilderness. The epistle's readers are instructed, **IF** they **HEAR HIS VOICE** (3:7b) in the gospel, not to **HARDEN** their **HEARTS . . . AS IN THE DAY OF TRIAL IN THE WILDERNESS** (3:8). To "harden the heart" is to continually resist the divine will so that eventually neither the Word nor Spirit of God any longer exerts any influence upon that person. It was **IN THE WILDERNESS**, where Moses' generation **TRIED** God (3:9). To try God is to intentionally act contrary to His will, and see how far one can go in disobedience before being punished as He warned. As a result, the Lord **WAS ANGRY WITH** that **GENERATION** (3:10), and **SWORE** that **THEY** would **NOT ENTER** the promised land of Canaan (v. 11). In 3:12 the writer applies Ps 95 to his audience. They are to learn from Israel's failure, **that there not be in any one of you an evil, unbelieving heart that falls away from . . . God**.

As noted in the introduction and in the comments on Heb 2:1-4 and 5:11–6:8, this warning passage, as well as the others, was intended for those who were impressed with the teachings about Jesus as the Messiah and the new covenant He established, but were considering abandoning Him in favor of the old covenant alone. If they continued to have an **unbelieving heart** in relation to faith in Jesus for forgiveness, they placed themselves in peril of being excluded from God's eternal rest. Instead they are to **encourage one another day after day, as long as** they still have spiritual opportunity, and thus avoid being **hardened by the deceitfulness of sin** (3:13). Verse 14 justifies this summons to perseverance. **For** one's decision to follow Christ in times past will be proven to have been genuine by one's perseverance in years to come (see the comments on the similar conditional statement in 3:6). Failure to persevere proves that a person never truly believed. The words **evil, unbelieving heart** would never be used of a genuine follower of Christ.

In 3:16-18, the author confirms the need to hear God's voice and not harden one's heart. This confirmation comes as the author asks five questions in which he reviews Israel's desert failure. (1) Who **heard** the promise of a wonderful life in an incredible land flowing with milk and honey, and yet still **provoked Him**? The answer, those least expected to have rebelled, is given in 3:16's next question. (2) Was it not **all those who came out of Egypt** under Moses' capable leadership? (3) **With whom was** God **angry**? The question in verse 17 gives the answer: (4) **Was it not with those who sinned, whose bodies fell in the wilderness?** The final question (5) is raised and answered in 3:18: **To whom did He swear that they would not enter** Canaan, but to **those who were disobedient?** The conclusion drawn is that Israel's failure to enter Canaan was **because of unbelief** (3:19). This section of the second warning passage calls into question the possession of saving faith of some of the recipients of the letter.

4:1-16. This is the other half—the positive part—of the letter's second warning passage. This section turns from Israel's failure to enter Canaan's rest (3:11-19) to the readers' possible, similar failure. Moses redeemed Israelites out of physical Egyptian bondage and led them across the wilderness toward Canaan; but because of unbelief, they forfeited that delightful promised land. In like manner, the epistle's recipients claim to have been redeemed by Christ from moral bondage; they are now passing through their own wilderness of this sinful world, headed toward heavenly Canaan rest. Will they fail to enter it? In summary the paragraph maintains that since the promise of entering divine rest is still valid, they were (and we are) urged to seize it. The key word is "rest," occurring eight times (vv. 1, 3 [twice], 4, 5, 8, 10, 11). It carries two diverse meanings, one literal, and the other figurative. The former concerns physical life in the actual land of Canaan: entrance into it brings a cessation or resting from wilderness wanderings. The latter is spiritual, concerning new life in Christ: entrance into it brings cessation of sin's dominion and one's own efforts to secure divine favor. Emphasis can fall on the commencement of this rest of a new life upon turning to Christ, on experiencing it throughout one's earthly spiritual life, or on its climaxing in heaven's eternal rest.

Therefore, which introduces 4:1, applies Israel's desert failure to the readers. The divine **promise** is still valid for **entering His rest**. This being the case, the writer summons his readers to join him in a healthy **fear**. The purpose for this apprehension is so that none of them may **come short of** this salvation rest. This is no paralyzing fear, but a call from presumptuous complacency that heaven shall automatically be theirs. **For** (4:2) provides a reason for the desired fear. The author and readers **have had good news preached** to them, **just as** Moses' generation heard wonderful reports of a land flowing with milk and honey. **But** this optimistic **word . . . did not profit them**, since they had no **faith** in it. Many of the recipients also, on the basis of the parallel with the wilderness generation, did not have saving **faith**. In v. 3, **for** establishes, in a positive and negative manner, the principle that for a divine promise to benefit, it must be believed. Positively, **we who have believed** upon following Jesus now begin to **enter** this **rest** associated with the spiritual life. Negatively, for those who refused to believe, God **SWORE . . . THEY** would **NOT ENTER** Canaan's **REST**. Belief gains entrance into rest, unbelief bars access. Israel's failure to enter was not due to rest being unavailable; it had been available **from the foundation of the world** (4:3).

Divine rest, then, is more than life in Canaan; that literal rest is but a type of its spiritual counterpart. God's rest is therefore an issue not just for the past, but for the present and future as well. The citation of Gn 2:2 indicates divine rest was offered to mankind in the garden of Eden **ON THE SEVENTH DAY** of creation (Heb 4:4). Similarly the quotation of Ps 95:11 shows this rest was available centuries later to the original readers of that Psalm (Heb 4:5). Verse 6 summarizes the chapter's initial five verses: earlier generations **who** heard the **good news** of enjoying divine rest **failed to enter because of disobedience**. But that same promise now **remains** on the table for some to enter it (see 4:9). This being so, God **again fixes a certain day**;

i.e., He renews the promise and offers another opportunity. And that chance is **Today**—now, at the present time. So people are admonished **NOT** to **HARDEN** their **HEARTS** (4:7).

Moses' generation failed to enter Canaan, but Joshua led his generation into it. However, that rest did not exhaust the promise; otherwise God **would not have spoken** later about **another day** of opportunity for subsequent generations (4:8). From the previous three verses, **so** in 4:9 concludes that **there remains a Sabbath rest for the people of God**—i.e., a final, complete, and heavenly rest. Verse 10 elaborates on this Sabbath rest. **The one who has entered** this eternal and heavenly **rest has himself also rested from his** earthly **works, as God** ceased from His creating activity on day seven. The word **therefore** in 4:11 draws an inference from 4:9-10 expressed as an exhortation: **let us be diligent to enter that rest**. This is a call for the readers to do several things: first, examine themselves to see if they are genuine followers of the Messiah Jesus; second, put forth the effort to experience divine **rest** (God's peace, joy, power, fruitfulness, contentment) now; and third, lay hold of heaven's grace, which will enable them to persevere. Complying with this exhortation **will** avert a **fall** into **the same example of** Israel's **disobedience**. The **for** in v. 12 reinforces the call for diligence in 4:11. This confirmation comes by **the word of God** which, contextually, refers specifically to Ps 95, cited in 4:3, 5, 7. This divine **word**, pledging rest but warning of a hardened heart, is likened to a double-edged sword in that it will either bring a person into rest or bar him from it; it will either usher a person into salvation or into condemnation.

The word of God could have one of two referents. It could refer either to Scripture or to Jesus Christ as God's Word. The latter understanding fits the context of judgment in v. 11, as Jesus, the **[W]ord**, is living, active, sharp, piercing, and thus will **judge the thoughts and intentions of the heart** (v. 12). **No creature** is **hidden from His** [the Word's] **sight**, but He knows all that resides in the heart of each person, and each person is accountable to Him (**with whom we have to do**, v. 13). On the other hand, if **word** refers to Scripture, it is described in four ways. (1) It is **living**—i.e., valid; the promise of rest is still good, and the warning of failure is still in effect. (2) It is **active**. Scripture accomplishes its objectives of either conferring divine blessing or punishment. (3) It is **sharper than any two-edged sword**. A literal sword can penetrate the material makeup of a human being, his **joints and marrow**. But Scripture can penetrate both the material and immaterial (**soul** and **spirit**) of a person. Consequently (4) God's word is **able to judge the thoughts and intentions of the heart**. Nothing is more inaccessible to others than the **thoughts** and motives concealed in a person's heart. But the divine **word** penetrates to these inner ideas, assesses them all, and reveals a man's heart to himself. As never before, now in the light of **the word of God**, a sinner sees himself as he actually is.

In light of the theme of judgment in vv. 11, 12d, and 13, and in light of the likelihood of **His** (v. 13) having **[W]ord** as its antecedent, it may be best to understand **the [W]ord of God** as a reference to Jesus, though v. 12 is applicable to Scripture as well. **No creature is hidden from His** [the Word's—Jesus'] **sight**. We all stand **open and laid bare**—completely transparent—**to** His **eyes**. And it is this omniscient judge to whom we are accountable (**with whom we have to do**) to exercise diligence to enter into God's offered rest. A professing believer may be able to deceive others about his sincerity over this issue, but he cannot deceive God.

This second warning passage is a call to endure in their faith in Jesus. As 4:14-16 draws the warning to a close, it reiterates this summons to stay the course, that is, to **hold fast our confession** (v. 14, a synonym in Hebrews for having and persevering in faith). But it cannot be done solely by one's own efforts. Followers of Jesus need divine grace, and their heavenly high priest eagerly offers it to them. Looking back to the promise of entering rest as still valid but with failure possible, **therefore** in 4:14 issues the challenge, **let us hold fast our confession** of the Christian faith. Perseverance is possible because our **great high priest** intercedes for us from heaven and because He can **sympathize with our weaknesses** (4:15). Believers must then **draw near . . . to the throne of grace** in prayer, **so that we may receive . . . grace to help in time of need** (4:16). Believers can persevere, awaiting the promised land—and His gracious help, faithfully dispensed when needed, makes it possible.

D. Jesus Is Better Than Aaron (5:1–7:28)

In this section, Jesus is presented as a better high priest than Israel's first to hold this office, Aaron, as well as all his successors. This argument falls in two parts: first, Jesus is a better-qualified high priest, 5:1-10; and second, Jesus, like Melchizedek, is an eternal high priest, 7:1-28. Thrice previously Jesus has been called a "high priest" (2:17; 3:1; 4:15).

1. He Is a Fully Qualified High Priest (5:1-10)

5:1-4. The **for** commencing 5:1 expounds on His priesthood. Two qualifications are set forth that a man must satisfy to hold the high priestly office. He must (1) be a sympathetic human being, 5:1-3, and (2) he must be divinely appointed to this position, 5:4. Regarding the former, **every high priest** is **taken from among men**. Angels do not qualify for the post, and this is one reason for the Lord's incarnation. But being human is inadequate; the high priest must be humane, as well. He has to be able to **deal gently with** sinners (5:2), mindful that **he himself** is plagued with moral **weakness**. Owing to his own moral frailty, **he is obligated to offer sacrifices for sins**, first **for himself** and then **for the people** (5:3). Regarding the latter prerequisite, no man can appoint **himself** to the priesthood, **but receives it when he is called by God, even as Aaron was** (5:4).

5:5-10. Now that two qualifications for the priesthood have been identified, 5:5-8 demonstrates, in reverse order, that Jesus not merely measures up to them, but exceeds Aaron's ability in satisfying these requirements. Concerning divine appointment, Christ **did not** make **Himself . . . a high priest** (5:5). The identity of the One who appointed Jesus comes by the citation of two OT texts: The first is Ps 2:7, a messianic psalm that describes God's future enthronement of God's Son as king (Heb 5:5). This Psalm emphasizes that the sovereignty of God will be established over the nations when the divine and royal Son takes His throne. It identifies the Messiah with two different titles: the Anointed one (Ps 2:2) and the Son (2:12). The second text, Ps 110:4, is from a messianic psalm in which God announced the royal Messiah was also **A PRIEST FOREVER** (Heb 5:6), uniting both the royal and priestly offices. The Hebrew of Ps 110:3 is virtually unintelligible, leading many to prefer the LXX reading: "from the womb of the dawn, I have *begotten* you." (See Michael Rydelnik, *The Messianic Hope* [Nashville: B&H, 2010], 174-75.) This reading would certainly explain the linkage of these psalms in Heb 5—Ps 2 emphasizing the begotten Son and then Ps 110, using similar terminology in v. 3, and then calling Him the eternal priest in v. 4. Admittedly Aaron was a legitimate high priest, but only a high priest. Jesus was both high priest and king.

Concerning the second requirement, Jesus undoubtedly possessed a compassionate human disposition. What follows is a lesson from one specific incident during the Lord's earthly life (lit., **in the days of His flesh**), when His **prayers** were **offered . . . with loud crying and tears** to God, who could have saved **Him from death**, but refused to do so (Heb 5:7). This refers to Jesus' weeping in the garden of Gethsemane before His arrest and crucifixion (Mt 26:36-46; Mk 13:32-42; Lk 22:39-46). At that time, His divine Sonship did not exempt Him from adversity. Rather, **He learned** to be even more compassionate as He obeyed the Father's will and **suffered** (Heb 5:8). This does not mean that He did not know what obedience was before the cross, nor does it mean that He disobeyed before He suffered. Through His incarnation, in His human nature, which included suffering and death, Jesus learned experientially the meaning of obedience as a human being in a fallen world (see the comments on Mt 26:36-46). Such extreme suffering cultivated intense sympathy in His soul for others that surely exceeded that of Aaron's compassion. Through this adversity Jesus was **made perfect**—i.e., divinely prepared and made vocationally competent for His earthly work. A large part of that earthly task was to become **the source of eternal salvation** for mankind (Heb 5:9) and to be **designated by God as a high priest** (5:10; see also the comments on 2:10).

• Third Parenthetical Warning: The Danger of Defecting from the Gospel (5:11–6:20)

5:11. The third parenthetical warning begins with a rebuke. At this point the writer has just broached the letter's major theological theme, namely Jesus' high priestly ministry. But he surprisingly takes temporary leave of this argument to enter the third warning, running from 5:11–6:20, and its gist is, "Let us press on to the perfection Jesus the Messiah offers." In 5:11, the author informs the readers that he has **much to say** about Jesus as high priest. But he concedes that the topic is **hard to explain**. The problem is that they had **become dull of hearing**.

5:12. The **for** introducing v. 12 provides a ground for this accusation that they have spiritually regressed: **by this time you ought to be teachers** of others; yet they desired a refresher course in **the elementary principles** [lit., "the elementary principles of the beginning"] **of the oracles of God** ("of the beginning" is repeated in

6:1). These **elementary principles** do not refer to the basic facts of their faith in Christ or the author would not urge them to leave them behind (6:1). Rather they refer to the teachings of the OT, which as Jews, they should have already known. Further evidence of seeing these as OT foundations is in their description in 6:1-2. The various elements there could possibly refer either to OT foundations or NT foundations, but are more likely to refer to OT phenomena (see the discussion on 6:1-6 below). Thus, the writer is proposing that the Hebrews needed to move from an OT faith to a NT one, not from elementary Christian truths to a more mature spirituality. The **milk**, in connection with the beginning **elementary principles of the oracles of God** and babes, describes the previous obsolete covenant and those who continued to partake of it. It is inconceivable that one would return to the elementary principles (the milk) when the teachings and reality of the perfect new covenant and the Messiah were available.

5:13-14. Apparently these babes felt they needed more milk, but the author knows that rehashing old truths about the old covenant was not what they needed. If it were, he surely would have provided it. Instead, he proceeds to give them what they really needed (**solid food**), the truth about the superiority of Jesus the Messiah. **Not accustomed** means "to lack the capacity or knowledge to do something," in this case probably to grasp **the word of righteousness**, which in this context probably refers to the message about the perfections found in Messiah Jesus.

The author used **infant** (5:13) as a figurative expression in reference to the possibility that some of the readers were not genuine believers but merely trusting in the OT foundations of faith rather than fully trusting in Jesus as their Messiah. They are contrasted with the **mature** (that is, "an adult"; v. 14), a figurative expression for those who had received all the blessings of the new covenant in Christ. The word **mature** (*teleion*) occurs only in Hebrews here and in 9:11, where it cannot mean "spiritual maturity." Other related words (*teleiotes*, 6:1; *teleioo*, 2:10; 5:9; 7:19, 28; 9:9; 10:1, 14; 11:40; 12:23; *teleiotes*, 12:2; *teleiosis*, 7:11) in Hebrews refer explicitly to the final, perfect, and superior spiritual benefits of the new covenant, including the people and elements associated with it, and the perfect One who instituted it. The "perfection" words provide an implicit contrast with the *incomplete nature* of the old covenant, those who operated within it (e.g., the priests), and those still rooted in it (some of the readers of Hebrews).

The author's concern is not to encourage believers to become spiritually mature, but to encourage those who were still "incomplete in their faith" as adherents of the Mosaic covenant to embrace the perfect and complete "covenantal contents" of the new covenant, including salvation, through the perfect high priest, Christ. Those who possess the new covenant blessings found in the Messiah can digest **solid food**. That is, they comprehend the validity of the superiority of the new covenant over the Old (**because of practice** they **have their senses trained to discern good and evil** teaching) as specified in the contents of the book of Hebrews.

Since "milk," "infants," and "solid food" also occur in 1Co 3:1-4, it might appear that Heb 5:11-14 is speaking of the need for believers to go from carnality to greater spiritual maturity. But sometimes Paul uses "babes" (*nepios*) in reference to unbelievers (Rm 2:20; Gl 4:3), which is the most likely sense here, and those in Corinth *were* acting like unbelievers (1Co 3:1, 3, 4). Paul nevertheless called them "babes *in Christ*" (1Co 3:1) indicating that he recognized they were in fact believers. But such a label is neither found nor warranted in Heb 5. (Credit for some of the above interpretation on 5:11-14 goes to Craig A. Hill's unpublished paper, "The Use of Perfection Language in Hebrews 5:14 and 6:1 and the Contextual Interpretation of 5:11–6:3.")

6:1-3. Hebrews 6:1-8 is notoriously difficult. There are three major interpretations. First, some suggest that those described here are true believers who would lose their salvation if they apostatized. Against this understanding, however, is the impossibility of them being saved again, something that the proponents of this view would not concede. Moreover, Jesus promised that of all that the Father gave Him, He would not lose one of them (Jn 6:37-40). Second, others propose that the warning in Heb 6:1-8 is purely hypothetical. However, if the writer and readers knew that the passage was merely hypothetical, then much of the power of this warning would be eliminated. Moreover, if the writer knew that the warning was hypothetical but his readers believed it to be real, then the writer's integrity would be questionable. A third and preferred view is that the people described in vv. 1-8 are those who have been exposed in significant ways to the truth of Jesus as Messiah, but who are being tempted to turn away from Him perhaps because of persecution (cf. 10:32-36), and return to the community and practices connected to the old covenant. In other words, 6:1-8 describes unbelievers who were well taught, perhaps having even made some sort of profession of faith, but who were on the cusp of abandoning their association with this community of Jewish believers and returning to Judaism without Jesus. See both the arguments above under 5:11-14 and below.

Therefore (6:1) suggests that there were among the Hebrews those who were too long in the state of incomplete faith, close to believing in Jesus but not fully decided. Thus, they were considering leaving their superficial faith, now that they were experiencing persecution. What follows is the teaching they needed to motivate them to full faith in Jesus as the Messiah. They are directed to leave the **elementary teaching about the Christ**, better translated as "the beginning doctrines about the Messiah," as found in the Old Testament. They were to **press on to maturity** (better "perfection" or "completeness"); see the comments on 5:14. **Press on** is a true passive verb ("let us be borne along" to spiritual wholeness or completion by God's influence). This exhortation is directed to readers who were considering abandoning the messianic community and returning to temple worship. They are called to move from the OT foundations of faith to the complete or perfect faith in the Messiah Jesus.

The writer describes six foundational elements his readers were to leave behind. A case can be made that these describe foundations of Christian faith, not the incomplete OT faith. However, this is not true for all of them. Although it is possible that five of the six could refer either to OT foundations or NT teachings, in 6:2 the phrase "instruction about washings" as it is used in Hebrews can only refer to the ritual washings of the OT (cf. 9:10) and not Christian baptism. Moreover, if these were NT teachings, the writer would not have encouraged them to leave them behind (6:1). Therefore, the entire list should be understood as referring to OT practices and beliefs. Thus, the writer is challenging these Jewish people to move from an OT faith to a NT one, not from foundations of NT faith to spiritual maturity. Their understanding of the OT laid a foundation for faith, but they needed to build on it and believe fully in the One who was perfect and who brought completion.

The first of the six elements they were to leave is **repentance from dead works**. Judging from the occurrence of "dead works" in 9:14, this is probably a reference to disobedience to the Torah (with the idea that these are "works that bring death" [cf. Dt 30:15-20] and thereby defile the conscience). These Hebrews had already learned from the OT to turn away (the sense of **repentance**) from dead works (cf. Ezk 14:6; Hs 14:1-2). They understood repentance as turning away from sin but had not yet decided to put their faith fully in Messiah Jesus. The second foundation, **faith toward God**, is not "faith in Christ" for salvation in a NT sense. This is a reference to "faithfulness" or "steadfastness" in awaiting God's fulfillment of His promises, enjoined so often in the OT (cf. Hab 2:4 and the meaning of "faith" there). But God had already sent Jesus the Messiah. There was no longer any need to wait faithfully for God's promised deliverer to come.

The third foundation is **instruction about washings** (see 9:10 for the same word **washings**, where, as here, it refers to various Levitical ritual washings, not NT baptism). The fourth is **laying on of hands**, referring to the placing of one's hands upon an animal that is sacrificed as a symbolic act of identifying with that animal as prescribed in the law (e.g., Lv 4:1; 16:21). The fifth foundational element is belief in the **resurrection of the dead**, a promise taught in the OT (cf. Dn 12:2; Is 26:19). The sixth and final foundation of OT faith is **eternal judgment**, a common teaching rooted in the OT (cf. Gn 18:25; Ex 34:6-7; Is 33:22; Dn 7:9-14).

There are some circumstances under which **God** would not permit some of these readers to "be borne along to perfection" (Heb 6:1). Those circumstances are specified in 6:4-6.

6:4-6. For introduces an explanation of the circumstances under which God would not permit one to come to all the perfections found in Jesus the Messiah. Verses 4-6 are frequently interpreted as a reference to the experience of those who are truly saved. Although possible it is not a necessary understanding, and in light of the meaning of the *tel-* words in Hebrews ("perfect" or "complete"; see the explanation under 5:14 above), it is preferable to see these verses as describing blessings which nevertheless come short of actual salvation.

If a person is characterized by the five participles in vv. 4-6 (**enlightened**, **tasted** the heavenly gift, **been made** partakers, **tasted** the word, and

have fallen away), and still chooses to turn away, then God will not permit this person to be borne toward the spiritual completeness found only in the Messiah. All five of these participles are governed by the same article in v. 4, denoting individuals for whom all five characteristics are true and not conditional or hypothetical. **Enlightened** is the same word used in Jn 1:9 for the spiritual enlightenment brought to every person through the incarnate Word, though clearly not every person responds correctly to it. Neither there nor here does it require a full salvific sense. Nor does **tasted of the heavenly gift** require that those who are described by this phrase are saved. **Tasted** (*geuomai*) is used in Heb 2:9 for Jesus "tasting" death, but the word probably has the more superficial sense of its use in Mt 24:34 for Jesus "tasting" the wine laced with gall but not drinking it. Some of the readers of Hebrews had a good taste of the messianic faith, and yet were considering abandoning it.

To be **made partakers of the Holy Spirit** sounds as if everyone in this community was indwelt by the Spirit and saved. But **partaker** (*metochos*) was also used in Lk 5:7 for those fishermen who associated with each other while they worked, and in Heb 1:9 where angels are called the "companions" of the Son (for this point, see John MacArthur, Jr., *Hebrews: An Expository Commentary.* MacArthur New Testament Commentary [Chicago: Moody, 1983], 144). It does not denote one who is "indwelt" by or who "has" the Spirit, any more than the Son being indwelt by angels. But it suggests that the recipients targeted by this warning section had been present when the Holy Spirit manifested Himself in this messianic community. These also **tasted the good word of God** (6:5; for "tasted," see the comments on 6:4), a reference to their experiencing the ministry of the Word in this community of faith. They also experienced the **powers of the age to come** (a reference to various miracles present in the community [see 2:4] which will become commonplace during the millennial kingdom, the meaning of **age to come**). None of the six blessings indicate that those described are actually saved—only that they had come very close.

Another characteristic is true of the ones whom "God will not permit to be borne along to spiritual completion" (6:1, 3): those who have **fallen away**. This participle describes those who "fail to follow through on a commitment, fall away, commit apostasy" (BDAG, 770). In this context, it refers to unbelievers who forsake this group of believers in favor of a return to Judaism without Messiah Jesus. The writer says of them, **it is impossible to renew them again to repentance**. Those who were considering apostasy by returning to OT faith without Messiah had previously (at least superficially) turned to Jesus. If they were to turn away now it would be impossible to bring them back to that point of **repentance** once again (here the word **repentance** refers to turning to Jesus the Messiah with full faith and is used differently from the phrase **repentance from dead works** in 6:1; see the comments there). They could not be renewed later because **they again crucify** [better, "because they crucify"] **to themselves the Son of God and put Him to open shame** (i.e., they align themselves with those who participated in crucifying and shaming Jesus). **Crucify** is an adverbial participle, almost universally interpreted causally ("because they crucify"). It could, however, be a temporal participle ("while they crucify" they cannot be renewed to repentance), but the word **impossible**, combined with the depth of exposure to the Messiah *and* the repudiation of Him in spite of that full light, seems to support the causal sense. If they apostatize, they will never again be brought back to the point of **repentance**.

Nevertheless, God alone knows the point of no return, and believers should never consider anyone beyond His reach. They should continue to call upon all people to turn to the Messiah Jesus, even those who seemed to have apostatized. But at this point in the text, the writer is exhorting those on the point of turning away to put their trust in Messiah Jesus, the perfect high priest who makes all those who come to Him perfect. Hebrews 6:4-6 also seems to find a parallel in the experience of Esau in 12:16-17. For the contrast between Heb 6 and the unpardonable sin, see the comments on Mt 12:31-32.

6:7-8. Having warned his readers, the author now gives an explanation, introduced by **for**, and an illustration from agriculture. The **ground** represents a person. The **rain** symbolizes the opportunities he has to hear the gospel. The **vegetation** represents the proper response to the gospel and the blessings from God that result from it. But the ground that yields **thorns and thistles** stands for one who hears the gospel but does not respond properly. Like infested ground that was often **burned** to clear it for greater productivity, so the unbeliever exposed to the truth will eventually be judged.

6:9-12. Despite the rebuke, exhortation, warning, and fearful illustration, the writer now gives a word of encouragement. This section marks a vast contrast to the apostates of 6:4-8. Even **though** the writer is **speaking in this** ominous **way**, in the readers' case he is **convinced of better things concerning** them (6:9) than being "cursed" and "burned" like the thorns and thistles of 6:8. The **better things** that he is certain to see in his readers are the virtues **that accompany salvation**. He is hopeful of most of them being genuinely saved and optimistic about those who were dull (5:11) or sluggish (6:12) coming to Christ by faith. The **for** beginning 6:10 furnishes the basis for this optimism. **God** will not **forget** the readers' **work and the love** shown when they **ministered . . . to the saints** (true believers) **and** were **still ministering to** them (6:10). Brotherly love is an unquestioned token of possessing spiritual life (1Jn 3:14). He clearly sees this in most of them. Saved though they are, the writer is not satisfied with their spiritual growth. He wants **each one** of them to **show the same diligence** that they have already shown in loving service to others, **so as to** obtain a full assurance of their **hope** (Heb 6:11). They are to exert necessary moral effort so as to increase in the certainty of someday possessing all that is divinely pledged to them. The design of this growth in assurance of salvation is **so that** they **will not be sluggish** in discharging their spiritual duties. Rather he wants them to become **imitators of those who through faith and patience inherit the promises** (6:12). But some of the readers of Hebrews did not have faith and were in danger of not resting in Christ.

6:13-20. The basis of the writer's above encouragement is his assurance that God is faithful to His promises. This paragraph confirms the claim of 6:12 that only a persevering faith eventually secures divinely promised blessings. This confirmation comes through the example of Abraham, the father of Jewish people. He is the classic biblical example of a person who believed God's promises. **For when God made the promise to Abraham** (v. 13) in Gn 12:2 that someday he would father numerous offspring, He guaranteed this promise by adding an oath to it. The oath was sworn by God in Gn 22:17, assuring Abraham that the Lord would **SURELY MULTIPLY** his children (Heb 6:14). The effect of this divine oath on the patriarch was that it encouraged him to **patiently** wait, and eventually he **obtained the** promised progeny (6:15).

For (6:16) explains the significance in antiquity that an oath had on its recipient. A person customarily swore in the presence of an authority, such as a ruler, king, etc. Such an authority could use his power to punish him, should he fail to live up to his sworn oath. Consequently a sworn oath verified by appropriate authority would end **every dispute** and remove all doubt from the recipient. Because God wanted **to show . . . the unchangeableness of His purpose** to bless Abraham **even more** than His promise could, He **interposed** the promise **with an oath** (6:17). God's objective in all this was that **by** the **two unchangeable things**, guarantees of the divine promise and oath, Abraham and his heirs would **have strong encouragement to** persist in **the hope set before** them (6:18). **This hope** is sure—a joyful certainty of someday possessing all benefits divinely pledged them. Such a **hope** is also an **anchor of the soul**. An anchor is thrown overboard, and though a sailor does not see it, it plunges to, and takes hold in, the sea's bottom, securing the ship and holding it in place during a storm. Similarly, a believer's hope **enters within** the heavenly sanctuary behind the **veil** (6:19) and rests on God; here **Jesus has entered . . . for us** (6:20). Inasmuch as divine promises rest on God's character and are confirmed by His oath, they are absolutely certain of fulfillment. Jesus has entered heaven, preceding us **as a forerunner**. The gospel has pledged that we, too, will someday enter there. It is absolutely certain to happen. This hope, this certainty, the believer can confidently maintain.

2. He Is an Eternal High Priest (7:1-28)

A discussion of Jesus' high priestly ministry began in 5:1-10. But the third warning passage of 5:11–6:20 temporarily delayed its continuance. The concluding words of 5:10 about "a high priest according to the order of Melchizedek" are repeated in the closing words of 6:20, indicating that warning three is finished. In 7:1, the writer resumes discussion of this priestly theme. Chapter 7 presents Jesus as an eternal priest, as is Melchizedek. This text falls into three subsections.

7:1-10. The first section elaborates on the person of Jesus. The opening **for** explains how Jesus has become "a high priest [forever] according to the order of Melchizedek" (5:10; 6:20). The first three verses (7:1-3) form but one sentence in Greek. Its grammatical subject is **Melchizedek** (7:1), and its main predicate is **remains a priest perpetually** (7:3). As such, Melchizedek is presented as one **made like the Son of God** (7:3)—both are eternal priests. To show this resemblance, the writer turns to the OT. From Gn 14, he presents five historical facts about Melchizedek in Heb 7:1-2a; then he interprets most of these in 7:2b-10. These five historical details are: (1) **Melchizedek** was the **king of Salem** (ancient Jerusalem) (7:1, 2) and (2) **priest of the Most High God** (7:1). He occupied both royal and priestly positions. (3) He **met Abraham** (7:1) following the patriarch's victory over Mesopotamian kings (Gn 14:17-24). (4) **And** Melchizedek **blessed him** (Heb 7:1). Lastly, (5) **Abraham** gave Melchizedek **a tenth** of the spoils of war (7:2a). Now the initial two details are interpreted. (1) **First of all, by the translation of his name, king of righteousness**, Melchizedek was identified as a morally and politically just king ruling over the city of Salem. Jesus, too, has been divinely appointed king (1:8-9; 2:7). (2) **Then also** Melchizedek's name means **king of Salem** ("peace"). In the capacity of priest, both he and Jesus can reconcile sinners to God, thus helping them obtain peace with heaven.

Briefly suspending the interpretation of the remaining historical facts, 7:3 touches on the significance of what is not said about Melchizedek. In the pages of Genesis, he appears **without father, without mother, without genealogy, having neither beginning of days nor end of life** (7:3). The writer sees as much significance in what Genesis does not reveal about Melchizedek as in what it does disclose about him. Genesis is a book of genealogies. It records the father and birth and death of its leading characters. The omission of this information about Melchizedek is seen to be a providentially intended type. A type is a divinely purposed historical illustration, which prefigures its corresponding reality that is yet future. What is true in type of Melchizedek is true in reality of **the Son of God**. In His humanity, Jesus had a mother (Mary) and a genealogy, but in His deity, He had neither **father**, **mother**, nor **genealogy**. What is true of Melchizedek in figure is true of Jesus in fact from His divine nature, namely He has **neither beginning of days nor end of life**. Since Melchizedek's death was never mentioned in Genesis, then, so to speak, **he remains a priest perpetually**. But in actuality this is the case with Jesus.

Picking up with the fifth historical note about Melchizedek with the word **now** (7:4), the author resumes interpreting the information about him. Regarding (5) above, his dignity is seen in that **Abraham apportioned a tenth part of all the spoils** to him (7:2). It was custom in antiquity to tithe to political and religious superiors. In giving a tithe to Melchizedek, Abraham recognized his preeminence. Accordingly, the author calls on the readers to **observe how great** Melchizedek **was** (7:4), extending his supremacy from the Jewish patriarch Abraham to those who descended from him, and specifically to the priestly tribe of Levi. Levitical priests too receive tithes, so are they on a par with Melchizedek? No. They have legal authorization **to collect a tenth from** their Jewish brethren. But needing no such legal authorization, Melchizedek's dignity is such that he **collected a tenth from Abraham** himself, the source of Levitical priests (7:6).

Verse 7 now interprets the fourth historical fact gleaned from Genesis about Melchizedek: **The lesser is blessed by the greater**. That Melchizedek is greater than Abraham is the point the writer has been constructing all along. His superiority extends also to all Levitical priests who derive from the patriarch. True, they, like Melchizedek, **receive tithes**; but they, unlike him, are mere **mortal men** (7:8). By its silence on Melchizedek's death, **it is witnessed** by Scripture **that he** typically or figuratively **lives on** (7:8). And their inferiority is seen again from another angle of the fifth historical fact. **So to speak, through Abraham even Levi** the grandson **paid tithes** to Melchizedek (7:9). **For**, in 7:10, argues from solidarity (the close relation here, between progenitor and offspring). **He was still in the loins of his father** when Abraham gave a tithe to Melchizedek. Levi did not literally participate with Abraham in this act (note the **so to speak**, which indicates the writer did not mean this literally but figuratively). But if Abraham is the fountainhead of the Jewish people, then there is a sense in which all are inferior to him, including Levi, and Melchizedek is the superior of all of them.

Melchizedek is sometimes seen as a Christophany, a preincarnate appearance of Christ. But this is highly unlikely, for several reasons. First, Melchizedek is **made like the Son of God** (v. 3), which is a peculiar statement if he *was* the Son of God before the incarnation. Second, Melchizedek is called a **man** in 7:4, an unlikely label if this were a reference to Jesus. Third, Melchizedek had a **genealogy** (7:6, though it is not presented anywhere in Scripture). Fourth, Melchizedek was a long-time resident of Salem, and king over it (7:1-2), while most

Christophanies were brief. Fifth, Ps 110 *compares* Christ with Melchizedek, indicating that they were not the same people (for these arguments, see Kent, *Hebrews*, 126–127).

7:11-25. Having discussed His person, the writer, with the word **now** (7:11), turns to the priesthood of Jesus. In 7:4, the author summoned the readers to "observe how great this" king-priest Melchizedek "was." Part of Melchizedek's greatness was seen in his superiority over the Levitical priests (7:5-10). This preeminence will now be seen in Jesus, who is in **the order of Melchizedek** (5:10; 6:20; 7:11) but even greater. With His priesthood, Jesus can bring **perfection**, the bringing of a sinner into an ideal relationship with God. This did not come **through the Levitical priesthood. The Law**, which perfected nothing (7:19), authorized this inadequate priesthood. Both its authorizing warrant and its constituted priesthood failed to properly reconcile people with God. So there was **need . . . for another priest to arise**, one like Melchizedek and not like Aaron (Levi). **For** of 7:12 extends this need further. **When the priesthood is changed**, there must be also **a change of law** that gives warrant to the new priesthood. The word **for** in 7:13 verifies the need for a fresh warrant. The new priest **belongs to another tribe, from which no one has officiated at the altar** as priest. Jesus **was descended from Judah** (7:14), and the Mosaic law never authorized any from that tribe to function as priest. The need for a new authority, which establishes the priesthood, **is clearer still** (7:15), since **another priest . . . according to the likeness of Melchizedek** has already taken office. At this point the author begins unpacking how the new priest Jesus is like Melchizedek; in doing so, the author shows the superiority of the Lord's priesthood over Levi's in four ways. First, Jesus' priesthood rests on a firmer basis. He did not **become** a priest **on the basis of a law of physical requirement** (7:16). This probably refers both to someone with a physical defect being prohibited from serving as a priest, and the need for one's father to be from the tribe of Levi. Rather, the warrant for Jesus' priesthood is **the power of an indestructible life** (7:16). Second, the Lord's priesthood is more effective than its Levitical counterpart. The latter's legal warrant **is set aside . . . because of its weakness and uselessness** (7:18). But Jesus' priestly ministry is **a better hope**, enabling sinners to actually **draw near to God** (7:19). Third, the Levites became priests **without an oath** (7:21), **but** Jesus became a priest **with an oath through the One who said to Him, . . . "YOU ARE A PRIEST FOREVER"** (Ps 110:4). A divine oath puts it in cement, and God **WILL NOT CHANGE HIS MIND** (Heb 7:21). And fourth, Christ's priesthood is without successor. Levitical priests are **prevented by death from continuing** in office (7:23). **But** Jesus **holds His priesthood permanently** (7:24), **since He always lives** (7:25).

7:26-28. This concluding section reveals the preeminence of Jesus, presenting Him as the exemplary priest—He is precisely what sinful mankind needs. **Such a high priest** is **holy**—i.e., in relation to God, reverent and pleasing to Him; **innocent**—i.e., in relation with people, He never injured any nor was a bad influence to them; **undefiled**—i.e., in relation to Himself, morally untainted from contact with mankind; **separated from sinners**—i.e., different from them in that He was removed from sin in heart and life; **and exalted above the heavens**—i.e., regarding His position, intimate with God and sharing His authority, there being nothing between them. He **does not need daily . . . to offer up sacrifices, first for His own sins** (7:27; cf. Lv 9:7). The reason no sacrifice is necessary for Him lies in His being One **made** the **perfect** high priest **forever** (Heb 7:28) on the basis of His self-sacrifice. Verse 28 summarizes vv. 26-27. Every high priest was a sinful man and thus needed to offer sacrifices for himself and for all the people. But this new high priest is sinless, holy, blameless, set apart, and also has the power of an endless life, not a temporary appointment. Since He is **exalted above the heavens** (v. 26), His intercession comes from the highest realm, all of which makes Him the **perfect** high priest **forever**.

II. A Superior Ministry (8:1–10:18)

What follows is the next main section of Hebrews. With the word **now** (8:1) the writer turns from the presentation of Jesus' superiority over the OT's leading personalities (chaps. 1–7) to the presentation of His having **obtained a more excellent ministry** (8:6). The premise is a better worker can produce a better product.

A. A Better Covenant (8:1-13)

8:1-6. These verses form the preamble to the second major section of Hebrews. This preamble introduces the three priestly themes of sacrifices (8:3), sanctuary (8:4-5), and covenant (8:6), around which a priest's ministry revolves. These will then be discussed in detail, but in inverted order of their introduction: covenant (8:7-13), sanctuary (9:1-12), and sacrifices (9:13–10:18). Before proceeding, the writer sums up and gives **the main point** of the first seven chapters: **we have such** an incredibly great **high priest** just depicted in those chapters. His greatness is such that He **has taken His seat at** God's **right hand . . . in the heavens**. Although Jesus is seated, He is certainly not idle (8:2). He serves as **a minister** interceding for believers in Him. One of the major responsibilities of a priest was to offer sacrifices (8:3). In fulfillment of His high priestly duties, Jesus did **have something to offer**. He offered Himself as a sacrifice once when He died on the cross.

Next the writer turns from sacrifices to the place of priestly service, the sanctuary (8:4). This verse concedes to Jesus not being **on earth**. In that case, He would not be a priest, **since there are** Levitical priests functioning in the earthly sanctuary. But that sanctuary is a mere **copy** or PATTERN (8:5) of the heavenly one, where Jesus serves as priest. Finally, the writer mentions the third major element of priestly service, covenant (8:6). Christ's ministry is **more excellent** since He is **the mediator of a better covenant**.

8:7-13. For justifies the claim in 8:6 of Jesus functioning on the basis of "a better covenant." This justification comes by comparing the old and new covenants. **That first** Mosaic **covenant** was not **faultless**. Had it been, there **would have been** no need **for a second** one to replace it. In contrast to the idea of the earlier covenant being faultless, **for** in 8:8 argues otherwise. The problem with the Mosaic covenant was not in itself, since it was "holy and righteous and good" (Rm 7:12). Rather, God found **fault with** His people who failed to keep it. A subtle shift is made from blaming the covenant to blaming the people with whom it was made, the reason for this shift appearing in Heb 8:9. Commencing in 8:8 and continuing through 8:12, Jr 31:31-34 is quoted. By that prophet God announced that He would establish A NEW and better COVENANT with the Jewish people. Hebrews 8:9 declares that this new one will NOT be LIKE THE COVENANT . . . MADE WITH THEIR FATHERS following the exodus. The reason for its dissimilar nature lies in the people's failure to obey that first COVENANT. Verse 10 now tells what this new covenant will be like. It will largely rest upon divine undertaking to achieve certain objectives. The determination to accomplish these objectives is expressed in God's resolve: I WILL do such and such; this expression I WILL occurs seven times in 8:8-12. By listing some of its promises, this divine responsibility, along with the nature of the new covenant, is spelled out. (1) Putting His LAWS INTO THEIR MINDS, AND writing THEM ON THEIR HEARTS, God will give His people both an understanding and resolve to obey them (8:10). (2) The Lord WILL BE THEIR GOD, AND THEY SHALL BE MY PEOPLE. This will be no one-sided relationship, but a mutually committed and an affectionate one, from both parties. (3) ALL the followers of Messiah WILL be enabled to KNOW the Lord, FROM THE LEAST TO THE GREATEST OF THEM (8:11). The cause of this greater intimacy lies in God's being MERCIFUL TO THEIR INIQUITIES and in the fact that He will REMEMBER THEIR SINS NO MORE (8:12). The significance of Jeremiah's prediction of **a new covenant** means that **the first** is **obsolete**. It served its purpose but is now obsolete and **is ready to disappear** (8:13).

On the basis of the mention of THE HOUSE OF ISRAEL and THE HOUSE OF JUDAH in 8:8, 10, some interpreters claim that the terms "house of Israel and Judah" refer to the Church, indicating that the Church has replaced Israel in God's thought. Yet, the passage nowhere affirms this replacement theology. More likely these verses refer to God's inauguration of the new covenant with the faithful remnant of Israel, of which the Jewish recipients of this letter are a part. Only the spiritual promises of the new covenant are available now. The national promises are yet to be fulfilled in the future millennial kingdom. Nevertheless, as a result of the Lord inaugurating this covenant, Gentile believers today receive the spiritual benefits of the new covenant by their being grafted into the spiritual benefits of the Abrahamic promises (Rm 11:17-24; 2Co 3:6).

B. A Better Sanctuary (9:1-12)

9:1-12. This section's initial word **now** turns from a comparison of covenants to a comparison of sanctuaries. The reason for the shift is that the sanctuary was the place where priests carried out their work. This comparison further reveals the inferiority of the Levitical priesthood. These priests served in an earthly sanctuary (9:1-10), but Jesus in the heavenly one (9:11). In 9:1, the author concedes that, inferior though it was, **the first covenant** provided for a priestly ministry and a place where it would be carried out, in **the earthly sanctuary**.

Although the sanctuary as a whole is mentioned in 9:1, in 9:2 the writer begins to describe some of its parts. The sanctuary proper is the **tabernacle**, which was divided in half. The initial half is **the outer** room; **this is called the holy place**. The phrase **behind the second veil** (9:3) describes the tabernacle's other half, **called the Holy of Holies**, while the next verse (9:4) lists its furniture. Israel's **priests** have daily access to enter **the outer tabernacle** repeatedly, carrying out their work (9:6). The word **but** (9:7) marks a sharp contrast with **the second** room. Into it **the high priest** alone enters, and only **once a year**. This annual entrance is for offering up a sacrifice **for himself and for the sins of the people**. This physical sanctuary, with its priestly service, was a teaching device. The lesson that **the Holy Spirit** was **signifying** through it was clear: **the way into** God's presence was limited (9:8). Israelites could enter the sanctuary's courtyard, but could not enter the holy place. Priests enjoyed daily access into the holy place, but could go no further. While the high priest was authorized to enter the holy of holies, that privilege was restricted to just once yearly.

In 9:9, the author cites the typical significance of this earthly structure: it was **a symbol** illustrating restricted access to God **for** that era. Additionally, all the **gifts and sacrifices . . . offered** in it were also illustrations of the real sacrifice to be subsequently offered at Calvary. Consequently, they could not **make the worshiper perfect in conscience**. The reason that gifts and sacrifices could not cleanse a sinner is that they related to **regulations for the body**, concerned with items of diet and external washings. All these were imposed **until a time of reformation** (9:10), i.e., the time when the Messiah would come and set things morally right by bringing a sinner into an ideal relationship with a holy God. Israel's earthly sanctuary and priesthood foreshadowed good things to come. But when **Christ appeared as a high priest**, He brought these predicted **good things** to His followers. Moreover, in appearing as **high priest**, He too entered a sanctuary, but **not** the earthly one **made with hands**; instead, Jesus went into **the greater and more perfect tabernacle . . . that is to say, not of this creation**, into the heavenly sanctuary (9:11). The Pentateuch states that Moses was shown the pattern of the true tabernacle in heaven, God's throne room, as a pattern for the building of the earthly tabernacle (Ex 25:9, 40). The basis of Messiah's entrance into the heavenly tabernacle was not animal blood, but rather **His own blood**. As a result, He has **obtained eternal redemption** (Heb 9:12).

C. A Better Sacrifice (9:13–10:18)

9:13-28. The climax of the doctrinal portion of Hebrews occurs here. It compares the innumerable Levitical sacrifices with the single sacrifice of Christ. The former failed to expunge sin, but the latter did. In 9:12, the last word was "redemption." Jewish people were familiar with this concept. But the redemption they knew was annual. So the word **for** (9:13) introduces a substantiation of the claim in the previous verse that Jesus has indeed obtained eternal—not annual or yearly—redemption. Verses 13-28 list five accomplishments of Jesus' sole sacrifice, any one of which points to the reality of eternal redemption. But add all five together, and it is certain that such everlasting moral deliverance has been secured for humanity.

Admittedly Levitical sacrifices, consisting in animal **blood** with their **ashes**, when sprinkled on **those** ceremonially **defiled**, did remove this ritual defilement from the **flesh** (one's body) (9:13). Specifically, being cleansed by water mixed with the ashes of the red heifer would ceremonially cleanse one's physical body if he had contacted a corpse (see Nm 19:13, 20). Otherwise the physical filth remained, one was excluded from the company of his fellow Jews, and its corrupting effect continued. But this was an external, physical cleansing only. In contrast, **the blood of Christ** was, first, **much more** effective than the involuntary sacrifice of a heifer. Jesus' sacrifice cleanses the **conscience from dead works** (Heb 9:14) in contrast to the external decontamination of the red heifer sacrifice. Second, His atoning **death** put into effect the **new covenant** (9:15). This was essential **for the redemption of the transgressions that were committed under the first covenant**. As a person's **death** makes **valid** his last will and testament (i.e., his "covenant") (9:16-17), similarly the divine **first covenant** and the subsequent new one were both **inaugurated** with **blood** (9:18). This **shedding of blood** was necessary, for **without** it, according to the principle established by God, **there is no forgiveness** (9:22). Third, while animal sacrifices were sufficient to purify the earthly sanctuary, Jesus' **better** sacrifice brought about the purification of **the heavenly** sanctuary (so 9:23, the **heavenly things** likely referring to the priestly office of the Messiah and the need for a sacrifice that would remove sin). Fourth, the Lord's death effected a more potent sacrifice, enabling Him to enter not just the **holy place made with hands** (9:24), **but into heaven itself**.

Animal blood was sufficient only to admit Israel's high priest into the earthly holy of holies. With His sacrifice offered on the cross, He appeared **in the presence of God for us**. Fifth, His sacrifice, in contrast to OT sacrifices, accomplished the removal of **sin** (9:26). When, therefore, Jesus appears **a second time** on earth, it will not be to **bear the sins of many**, but to bring **salvation** to us (9:28). In bringing chap. 9 to an end, the transitional expression **once**, occurring three times in 9:26-28, leads to similar expressions in chap. 10, "having once been cleansed" (10:2), "sanctified . . . once for all "(10:10), "one sacrifice" (10:12), and "by one offering He has perfected for all time" (10:14). All these expressions prepare for 10:1-18, arguing that Jesus' one sacrifice for sin is eternally effective, never needing repetition.

10:1-18. This section contrasts Christ's sacrifice with the numerous Levitical sacrifices, which were ineffective for internal cleansing from sin (10:1-4). The Mosaic **Law** only predicted **good things to come** (10:1), but it could not provide these blessings. Owing to this, it could never bring **worshipers** (10:2) into an ideal relation with God **by the same sacrifices which they offer continually** (10:1). The repetition itself is proof of their ineffectiveness. Confirming this, the author argues that had these sacrifices been able to effect that desired relationship (10:2), they would **have ceased to be offered**. This is because **the worshipers, having once been cleansed, would no longer have had consciousness of sins**. Instead these yearly offerings reminded people of their sins (10:3). The reason for their limited effectiveness lies in the impossibility of **the blood of bulls and goats** to remove the guilt of **sins** (10:4). The red heifer sacrifice in Nm 19, mentioned in Heb 9:13-14 above (see the comments), did provide an external sanitization, but here the author's concern is internal cleansing from the spiritual corruption caused by sinful acts.

There is no real link between animal blood and humanity's moral failures. Animals are not of the same nature as the offender (human), nor of the offended (divine). OT sacrifices served a typological role, but not a salvific role. Offering animals also did not save the individual, no matter how sincere, since the ceremonial aspects of the law saved no one (see Rm 3:20). But when one trusted in the God of Israel as Abraham did, that believer was counted righteous. Offering sacrifices flowed from the life of one rightly related to God by faith, but was not the means of the right relationship. God said that *He* would cleanse the believing offerer from his sin when he brought the required sacrifices, and without the heart attitude of trust and repentance (see "humbling one's soul"—or better "*afflicting* one's soul"—in Lv 16:29, 31), the sacrifices meant nothing at best, and at worst were repugnant to God (see Ps 40:6-10; 51:10-18; Is 1:11-15; Mc 6:6-8). The one who offered the sacrifice did not thereby earn God's favor. But the OT believer needed cleansing from sin, just as a NT believer does, and God determined in the OT that the means for this cleansing was through the believer making animal sacrifices. Those offered by one who believed resulted in forgiveness by God (see Lv 1:4; 4:26-31; 16:20-22; 17:11; Ps 25, 32, 51, 103, 130; Is 1:18; Ezk 18:22; Heb 9:13).

The offering of sacrifices by one who was righteous by faith was an important part of a believer's response to God's moral will, and these sacrifices functioned in somewhat the same way a credit card functions in the purchase of an item. As far as the store management is concerned, when a purchase is made with a credit card, the item is sold and the deal is done. For the OT believer in God, animal sacrifices sufficed to pay for sin. The trusting person who offered the sacrifice had assurance that God forgave him and restored the relationship with him. But since the blood of bulls and goats cannot atone for a human's moral failures, *God knew* that the price of paying for sin would ultimately be paid by the death of His Son (for this approach, see John S. Feinberg, "Salvation in the Old Testament," in *Tradition and Testament: Essays in Honor of Charles Lee Feinberg*, edited by John S. Feinberg and Paul D. Feinberg [Chicago: Moody, 1981], 70–72).

Being therefore ineffective for bringing about salvation, the Levitical sacrifices were superseded by the offering of Jesus. At His first advent, Jesus acknowledged that the Father did not derive complete **PLEASURE** in these Levitical offerings (10:6). Since animal blood has limited effectiveness, Christ also realized that God did not indefinitely want these sacrifices, **BUT** had **A BODY . . . PREPARED FOR** Him (10:5). Perceiving His divine mission, the Messiah made a commitment, **I HAVE COME . . . TO DO YOUR WILL, O GOD** (10:7, 9). And what God willed for Jesus was to take **away the first** covenant and **to establish the second** (10:9).

These last few verses (10:5-9) constitute a commentary on Ps 40:6-8. In that Psalm, David remembers what was written about the future messianic Redeemer IN THE SCROLL OF THE BOOK. Writing in the first person, in the voice of the Redeemer, he refers to the book of the law (Torah). The message of the Torah was not to emphasize its many sacrifices but that God actually desired Israel's service, as seen in the slave who had his own ear pierced to demonstrate his willing service to his master (Ex 21:6). Thus, the Hebrew text says, "ears you have dug out for me." In the commentary in Hebrews, the author cites this verse but substitutes a synecdoche (whole for the part), the ear representing the whole body of the Messianic Servant of the Lord, who hears and obeys His Master.

The outcome of Jesus' carrying out His Father's will is given in Heb 10:10: **By this will we have been sanctified through the offering of the body of Jesus Christ once for all**. These last three words are expanded in 10:11-18, which argues for the eternal effectiveness of Jesus' one sacrifice. The Jewish priest **stands daily ministering and offering** repeatedly **the same sacrifices**, though they **can never** remove **sins** (10:11). Unlike the standing priest, **but** (10:12) points to Jesus' different posture of sitting DOWN at God's RIGHT HAND, following the offering of His one sacrifice. **For** (10:14) tells why Jesus sat down. **By one offering He has** brought believers forever into a right relationship with God. The Levitical priest stands remaining on duty, offering over and over what can never remove sins. Jesus sits, because His task as an offering priest is over. Now He can give attention to intercessory prayer. But is God satisfied with the sacrifice of Christ? The Spirit's testimony about this (10:15) answers the query by quoting God in Jr 31:34, AND THEIR SINS . . . I WILL REMEMBER NO MORE (Heb 10:17). From this divine pledge of eternal forgiveness, 10:18 concludes **there is no longer any offering for sin**. Animal sacrifices, which never could remove sin, need not be offered anymore in this age, nor does Jesus need ever to make another sacrifice. It does appear that sacrifices will be restored in the millennial temple, where they will be offered as a memorial for the death of Christ (cf. comments at Ezk 40:38-43).

III. A Superior Life (10:19–13:25)

Since Jesus possesses a superior ministry (8:1–10:18), He can offer Christians a better life. This is the letter's final section. It revolves around four major exhortations related to fellowship (10:19-25), to perseverance (10:32–12:13), to sanctification (12:14-17), and to service (13:1-25). These four build on, and lead to, one another. By faithfully fellowshipping with God and their spiritual family, believers are empowered to persevere, which cultivates holiness, and this in turn enriches service to others. Interspersed among these four exhortations are the last two parenthetical warning passages.

A. Exhortation to Fellowship (10:19-25)

10:19-25. Relating back to God's pledge never to recall believers' sins (10:17), **therefore** (10:19) draws an inference expressed as three subordinate exhortations: **let us draw near** (10:22), **let us hold fast** (10:23), and **let us consider** (10:24). This threefold exhortation is reinforced by two reasons—our having both access to God (10:19) and a high priest over the family of God (10:21). In prayer believers possess **confidence to enter the** heavenly **holy place** (10:19). This access is secured not by the believer's performance in the spiritual life, but by something much more sure, the atonement, obtained by the sacrifice (**blood**) **of Jesus**. Further described in 10:20, this access is **a new** (i.e., previously unavailable) **and living** (i.e., effective—it really works) **way** (i.e., a method of doing something, specifically here, of appearing before God). This access Jesus **inaugurated for us through . . . His flesh** (i.e., the offering of His body in sacrifice). As such He is now our **great priest over** the community of God's people (10:21).

All this being so, in 10:22 the writer urges his readers to join him in drawing **near** heaven's throne in prayer. The twofold manner in which prayer is to occur is (1) **with a sincere heart**, i.e., in sincerity, and (2) **in full assurance of faith**, i.e., certain of having the divine ear. Their periodically approaching God may be done after becoming followers of Christ when their **hearts** were **sprinkled clean** and their **bodies** were **washed with pure water**. This last phrase most likely does not refer to baptism, which is only symbolic of cleansing. Rather, it is a figurative expression that refers to the spiritual cleansing that Messiah's sacrifice made possible (cf. 1Jn 1:9). A similar figurative expression is used in Ezk 36:25 to refer to the cleansing brought by the new covenant. Fidelity in prayer enables one to comply with the next summons, **let us hold fast . . . our hope** (Heb 10:23). The wavering Jewish believers are being exhorted to embrace faith in the divine promises as true. Hope patiently waits until one possesses the blessings vouchsafed in those promises. The believer's waiting will not be in vain, **for He who promised is faithful** to deliver all pledged benefits. A follower of Christ is not to live in isolation, but is part of a new community. So 10:24 speaks to the social obligation of being concerned about one another. The intent is **to stimulate . . . love and good deeds** in this community. Mutual consideration cannot be expressed by **forsaking** their **assembling together**, **but** it can happen only by **encouraging** each other (10:25).

- **Fourth Parenthetical Warning: The Danger of Disparaging the Gospel (10:26-31)**

10:26-31. In assigning a reason not to abandon congregational meetings, **for** (10:26) introduces the epistle's fourth warning passage. Some who had once been associated with the recipients of this letter were in the habit of avoiding their spiritual community. This can lead one to deliberately sin **after receiving the knowledge of** the gospel (10:26). The intentional moral failure in view here is neither wrongdoing in general nor a particular serious sin such as murder, adultery, or stealing. Instead it is contextually described as departing from association with those who make up the community of the Messiah. This abandonment is motivated by the refusal to have faith in Jesus as Messiah by someone who had never genuinely come to know Him. (For an explanation of the spiritual condition of those who are the addressees of the warning passages, see the comments on 2:1-4, and especially 5:11–6:8.) For one who persists in spurning the Messiah's sacrifice, **there no longer remains a sacrifice for** his **sins** because of his refusal to avail himself of the benefits of Jesus' sacrifice. The Levitical priesthood cannot, and the heavenly high priest will not, make an offering to atone for this willful sin. **But** instead what awaits those who turn away from Christ is awful divine **judgment and . . . FIRE** that will **CONSUME** them (10:27). An infraction of the Mosaic law often resulted in the execution of the guilty (10:28). But **much severer punishment** remains for the spiritual turncoat. His apostasy is described as trampling **under foot the Son of God**, no longer regarding **the blood of the covenant** as efficacious but now as ordinary, and insulting **the Spirit of grace**. Only eternal death is worse than physical death. The writer verifies this punishment to be worse and shows how certain it is (10:30). **For** the church knows the identity and the resolve of **Him who** warned, **VENGEANCE IS MINE, I WILL REPAY**, and **THE LORD WILL JUDGE HIS PEOPLE** (Dt 32:35-36). This divine avenger means what He says and will carry out His threats. God will repay those who mistreat His genuine followers, and He will punish the abusive professing believers among His people. The author concludes this warning by giving his own evaluation on this worse punishment (Heb 10:31). It is **terrifying**, coming as it does from the **hands of the living God**. On the identity of these deniers of the faith, see the comments on 6:6.

B. Exhortation to Perseverance (10:32–12:13)

The readers were urged again to endure adversity as they had done successfully, earlier in their walk with Christ. If they did it once, they can indeed do it again. For many OT believers weathered life's ills and persisted in their relationship with God. And these believers before the coming of the Messiah had far fewer spiritual resources than those after He had come, because God has provided something better for Jesus' followers (11:40). So believers are to run with endurance the race that lies before them (12:1), mindful of adversity being one of heaven's tools to mold character and forge conduct into what God desires (12:3-11). So the discouraged must strengthen tired hands and weakened knees while they return to and remain on the spiritual path following their Messiah (12:12-13).

10:32-39. Beginning in this section, the recipients are summoned to recall **the former days** following their decision to follow Jesus as their Messiah, **when** they **endured a great conflict of sufferings** (10:32). During this difficult time, they often were verbally taunted and suffered physical afflictions (**tribulations**, 10:33). Moreover, they ministered to **prisoners** and joyfully **accepted . . . the seizure** of their **property** (10:34). In view of their track record of persevering and their knowledge of how to persevere, 10:35 prohibits throwing **away** their **confidence**—i.e., that frame of mind enabling them to bear suffering with determination. The reason it must be retained is its yielding **a great reward**, which consists of their being peacefully sustained and subsequently being divinely recompensed.

For the current time they need **endurance**. The reason for this **need** is **so that when** they **have done the will of God**, they will **receive** all that God has **promised** (10:36). God's intention for them is to remain loyal to Christ and stay the course. How long must they persevere? Only for **A VERY LITTLE WHILE**, and then Jesus **WILL COME** (10:37), and all such need for enduring is over.

How does one persevere? The **RIGHTEOUS ONE SHALL LIVE BY FAITH** (10:38)—i.e., by constantly relying on the Son of God to enable him in all Christian duties, like perseverance. A failure to stay the course means the professing believer **SHRINKS BACK** in apostasy. Vastly understated, God then **HAS NO PLEASURE IN HIM**. The author is confident that he and his readership belong to that group **who have** genuine **faith** and will at Jesus' return obtain eternal life (the sense of **preserving . . . the soul**) (10:39).

11:1-40. The recipients were informed of their need to persevere (10:36) and of faith as the means of doing so (10:38). But what is faith? To ensure that both writer and readers are on the same page, 11:1 defines it. To prove this definition is not mere theory, the writer illustrated faith by telling stories of OT believers. They did what the readers need to do, namely persevered by faith. The common denominator for the OT characters in Heb 11 was that all of them had good reasons for not persevering and for returning to the life they had before their encounter with God, but none of them did (see 11:15). The key phrase, then, is **by faith**, occurring 19 times.

11:1-2. *Prologue.* **Faith** is not formally defined here, but what is given is a description of what **faith** does. There are two parts to the description. First, **faith** gives an **assurance of things hoped for**; i.e., the certainty of things future, such as the second coming of Christ, resurrection and glorification of the dead, being taken to heaven, etc. Second, faith provides **the conviction of things not seen**; i.e., the persuasion of things invisible, such as the forgiveness of sins, the Holy Spirit living within believers, Christ as intercessor, and our access to God in prayer. These characteristics are not impractical. **For by** the possession and exercise of faith in daily life, our ancestors received divine **approval** on their lives.

11:3-12. *First "By Faith" Series.* To show that the characteristics of faith in 11:1 are not alien to any of his readership, in 11:3 the writer starts with Gn 1: **By faith we understand that the worlds were prepared by the word of God**. There were no human eyewitnesses to the making of the material universe. Scripture attributes it to divine activity, and we believe it. From Heb 11:3 onward, individuals who displayed faith are mentioned. From Gn 4, **by faith** in the divine revelation that heaven requires bloody sacrifices, **Abel offered to God a better sacrifice than Cain** (Heb 11:4), and **Cain** became enraged at God's acceptance of his brother's sacrifice (see the comments on Gn 4:5-7). From Gn 5, **by faith Enoch . . . was pleasing to God** (Heb 11:5). This expression **by faith** means that he believed the disclosure of all the divine truth revealed to him was factual, that he conformed his character and conduct to it, and that he lived in dependency on God. With such faith, it is possible for anyone to thus please God (11:6). From Gn 6–9, **Noah** took to heart the warning about a flood that was **not yet seen** (Heb 11:7). But his faith was seen in building **an ark** that delivered **his household**. From Gn 12, convinced **by faith** about a **place** he would someday **receive**, Abraham left home before knowing the location of that place (Heb 11:8). After arriving in it, **by faith** he **lived** for decades **in the land of promise**, waiting for the Lord to give the land to him (11:9). From Gn 21, **by faith** in divine fidelity, his wife **Sarah**, though barren, **received ability to conceive** (Heb 11:11). Consequently, from this elderly, impotent couple came offspring as numerous **AS THE STARS OF HEAVEN** (11:12).

11:13-16. *Editorial Commentary.* In this brief aside, the author gives his own perspective on the OT people of faith mentioned thus far. They all **died in faith, without receiving** all blessings divinely promised (11:13). **But** they gradually saw these promises **from a distance**—i.e., they would be fulfilled on the other side of the grave. As their life drew to a close, these believers **welcomed** the promises or joyfully anticipated them in the next life, confessing to being temporary residents **on the earth** (11:13). True, they were **seeking** a homeland (11:14), but **a heavenly** (11:16) and not an earthly one (11:15). No doubt Abraham expected an ultimate literal fulfillment of the land promises of the Abrahamic covenant in the future millennial kingdom. Nevertheless, upon his death, he was looking for a heavenly homeland, beyond this life.

11:17-31. *Second "By Faith" Series.* Resumed here are accounts of other individuals selected from the OT, who demonstrated in life and action the faith defined in 11:1. It is not clear the extent to which Abraham believed in the doctrine of the resurrection, but his faith in God encompassed the possibility that God could restore life. God promised Abraham that Isaac, not some other son, would be the one through whom the promises of a great progeny would be fulfilled (Gn 21:12, cited in Heb 11:18). Yet Abraham set out to sacrifice Isaac at God's command (Gn 22:2-4). His belief in God's ability to raise one from the dead is reflected in his words in Gn 22:5, "We will worship and [*we will*] return to you." **When he was dying** (Heb 11:22), Joseph **made mention of the** still future **exodus** of Israel, and **gave orders concerning his bones** to be buried in Canaan (Gn 50). Joseph's faith persuaded him that departure from Egypt would come and his people would possess the promised land. Owing to the conviction that he would be the deliverer of the Jewish people (Ex 2), Moses chose **to endure ill-treatment** with the Hebrew slaves rather **than to enjoy** the prestigious but temporary luxuries of the Egyptian royal court (Heb 11:25). His attention was on future **reward**, confident that suffering in the will of God would bring **greater riches** than could **the treasures of Egypt** outside of that will (11:26). As such, Moses chose to identify with the people through whom the future Messiah would come and the reproach that came with it, rather than the life of ease of an Egyptian prince. Israel's 40 years in the wilderness were spent in unbelief, so no examples from that period are mentioned. The writer moves on to Jos 6, where **the walls of Jericho fell down after they had been encircled**. Nothing seems more pointless and unrelated to reality than walking around walls **for seven days** blowing horns. But those walls were leveled **by faith** in the power of God. Because of her **faith**, **Rahab the harlot**, though morally stained, was cleansed and **did not perish along with** her countrymen (Heb 11:31). God had power over her heart, as He did over the walls of her city.

11:32-38. *Rapid "By Faith" Survey.* At this point the author realizes that he cannot keep going in detail. So he announces his intention to abbreviate by referring to believers in groups rather than as isolated individuals. Accordingly, in 11:32 he cites examples of the judges (**Gideon**, **Samson**, etc.), the monarchy (**David**), and the prophets (**Samuel**). It was **by** their **faith** that God accomplished amazing things through them. They **conquered kingdoms** as Gideon with a handful of soldiers (Jdg 7); **performed acts of righteousness** as David and Solomon; **obtained promises** as did the Patriarchs (Gn 12, 15, 17); **shut the mouths of lions** (Heb 11:33) as Daniel (Dn 6); **quenched the power of fire** as Shadrach, Meshach, and Abednego (Dn 3); **escaped the edge of the sword** as did Elijah from Jezebel (1Kg 19) and Elisha from Jehoram (2Kg 6:30-33); **from weakness were made strong** as Samson (Jdg 16:28-30); **became mighty in war** as David facing Goliath (1Sm 17); **put foreign armies to flight** (Heb 11:34) like Abraham routing Chedorlaomer (Gn 14); **women received back their dead by resurrection** as did the widow of Zarephath (1Kg 17:17-24) and the Shunammite woman (2Kg 4:14-17). All those belong to the victorious category.

While not victorious, but just as important, are the believers mentioned in Heb 11:35-38. Citing people mentioned both in Scripture and in the intertestamental literature, the writer refers to people of faith who did not always have great victories. In the story of Hannah and her sons (2Macc 7) they **were tortured**, refusing to renounce God to obtain **release** from captors, convinced **they** would **obtain a better** release, namely a **resurrection** wrought by God from the grave. **And others** in Heb 11:36 introduces the tragic but perhaps most noble category. These faithful believers **experienced mockings and scourgings** as did Jeremiah at the hands of Pashhur (Jr 20:2, 7). Jeremiah was also **stoned** in Egypt according to Jewish tradition. According to other traditions, Isaiah was **sawn in two**, Uriah the prophet was **put to death with the sword** (Jr 26:23), while others from the Maccabean period **went about in sheepskins . . . destitute, afflicted**, and **ill-treated** (Heb 11:37). All these accepted by faith these unfavorable vicissitudes to be the divine lot assigned them, and by faith maintained a hope in the brightest future.

11:39-40. *Epilogue.* **All** the OT believers mentioned above received divine commendation **through their faith**. Still, they **did not receive** everything **promised** to be given through the coming of Messiah (11:39). The reason for this is that **God had provided something better for us**—a better hope, better covenant, better promises, better high priest, better access to God, better sacrifice, better possession, and a better resurrection. Heaven planned that only in company with us would they enter into these incredible benefits. Eventually the Messiah, whom OT believers anticipated, did come. Now together, both followers of Jesus the Messiah, during their earthly sojourn, and OT believers, in their heavenly city, enjoy these blessings.

12:1-13. Begun at 10:32, the exhortation to persevere is finished here, by assigning seven reasons to endure. Looking back to the presentation in chap. 11 of the OT believers who endured, **therefore** indicates the writer is saying to his readers we also must similarly endure in faith. The main thought in 12:1 is **let us . . . run with endurance the race that is set before us**. The author likens living the Christian life to running a race, due to the similarities between them: in both endeavors there is a start and finish, both require effort and the runner's path marked out by others, both require discipline, and each has a reward at the end. This moral **race** is to be **run with endurance** ("the capacity to continue to bear up under difficult circumstances"), under a summons to persevere. This phrase indicates the believer's spiritual life is to be no short one-hundred-meter dash, but a marathon, and one encompassed with difficulties.

The first reason to persevere is that **we have so great a cloud of witnesses surrounding us**. This refers not to angelic observers of earthly behavior but rather to the OT believers (chap. 11) whose lives of faith continue to witness or testify of its value. Believers today must follow their example of faith by keeping on keeping on. If only one believer from the past had endured, that would be sufficient to show that it can be done; but there are countless faithful people whose lives are **witnesses** in the sense that their lives demonstrate that perseverance is doable.

In persevering it is essential to **lay aside every encumbrance**, or moral hindrance, that makes endurance harder, and especially to be discarded is **the sin** of unbelief, **which so easily entangles us**. Believers **run** by **fixing our eyes on Jesus** (12:2), i.e. by relying on Him to enable them to persevere. Christ is the appropriate object of trust, since He is **the author**, from whom our **faith** derives, and the **perfecter**, who deepens and matures it. Moreover, He did what believers must now do, that is He **endured**, and He is currently **at the right hand of the throne of God** to assist His followers by intercession. A second reason to persevere is that Jesus, as well as many others, **endured** much greater **hostility by sinners against Himself** (12:3) than have the readers. This perspective ought to prevent the addressees from growing **weary and** losing **heart**. A third motive to stay the course is that the letter's recipients can endure more than they have to date. They **have not yet resisted** the forces of evil **to the point of shedding** their **blood** (12:4). A fourth reason to endure is divine discipline, evidence that God is our Father, and we His sons (12:5-6). His **DISCIPLINE** ("to punish for the purpose of improving behavior") is not to be taken **LIGHTLY** (12:5). Much of the modern church has neglected the truth that sometimes God, as a loving parent, must correct His children so they learn to obey Him more often and please Him more consistently. This punishment is always instructional and developmental and is never condemnatory as it relates to eternal destiny. God **DISCIPLINES** those He **LOVES** (12:6). Discipline is divine instruction, training, correction, chastisement, and guidance—all designed to produce proper character and conduct in God's children.

Still another reason to remain loyal to Christ is the duty to **endure** trials and difficulties **as** divine **discipline** (12:7). Heaven uses all forms of adversity as effective tools to accomplish in the believer's life what needs to be done. A sixth reason to persevere is that we accepted the discipline of our **earthly fathers**, flawed though it sometimes was. **We** should **be subject** even more to the perfect discipline of our heavenly **Father** (12:9), who implements it always **for our good** (12:10). A final motive to endure is that divine discipline accepted enables us to **share His holiness** (12:10) and to **live** in the fullest extent (12:9). Admittedly current **discipline . . . seems not to be joyful, but sorrowful** (12:11). **Afterwards** it eventually produces the desirable **fruit** or effect of righteous character and conduct. Sadly, however, divine discipline does not benefit all believers. Profiting are only **those who have been trained by it**—i.e., embraced it as from God and endured it, allowing heaven to do in them all that was necessary. Owing to the beneficial nature of trials used in God's hand as discipline, **therefore** in 12:12 summons the **weak and . . . feeble** believers to **strengthen** themselves and to get back in the race, serving their Lord. In making **straight paths for** their **feet**, they are to live as the gospel prescribes (12:13). This is so those who are spiritually **lame may not** deteriorate further and become **put out of joint** or defect from their faith in the Messiah, **but rather** be spiritually **healed**.

C. Exhortation to Sanctification (12:14-17)

12:14-17. The yield of moral "righteousness" (12:11) leads easily to the summons of the pursuit of holiness. But the writer begins urging his readership to **pursue peace with** the help of **all men** and women. The **peace** in view is less harmony and concord among believers, and more tranquility of heart, freeing one of anxiety caused by the trials and discipline in 12:3-13. But the addressees are especially to **pursue . . . sanctification**. This growing virtue is essential, for **without** it **no one will see** in heaven and throughout eternity **the Lord**.

In their corporate pursuit of peace and holiness, the readers are to **see to it** that three dangerous circumstances are avoided: First they must **see to it that no one** in their congregation **comes short of the** saving **grace of God** (12:15); it is inadequate to profess faith in Christ. They are to do everything possible to ensure that each actually possesses it. Second, they must prevent any **root of bitterness** from springing up. This is not an attitude of resentment; rather, this expression is an allusion to Dt 29:18, "that there will not be among you a root bearing poisonous fruit and wormwood"—an Israelite who spurns the Lord for false gods. Accordingly, in Heb 12:15 it figuratively refers to an apostate forsaking Christ. In the body of Christ such an individual can cause trouble and defile **many**. And third, the congregation must ensure none of their members become **like Esau, who sold his own birthright for a single meal** (12:16). He illustrates an apostate who forfeits his spiritual **birthright** bequeathed by the Messiah for something far less, namely mere outward ritual or the temporal safety that denying their faith might bring. As Esau later tried to regain his lost **blessing** but **was rejected**, finding no opportunity **for repentance** (12:17), so it will be for the defector from the faith.

- **Fifth Parenthetical Warning: The Danger of Declining the Gospel (12:18-29)**

12:18-24. Having urged his readers not to be like Esau, the writer turns to his fifth parenthetical warning. To solidify this warning to these Jewish believers, in 12:18-19 the writer depicts old covenant faith in a sevenfold portrayal in contrast to a sevenfold portrayal of new covenant faith in 12:22-24. The comparison shows that the glorious nature of the Sinai covenant was surpassed by the even more glorious new covenant. To spurn the superior for the lesser glory is to make an Esau-like barter. The comparison begins by the writer saying **you have not come to**... (12:18). This means that most of the Jewish readers had indeed moved on from a mere old covenant faith and were not on the brink of apostasy. In the midst of the comparison the opposite is affirmed: **you have come to Mount Zion** (12:22) meaning they were inducted recently into a new covenant faith in the promised Messiah.

The sevenfold portrayal of the two faiths is: (1) both are likened to mountains, which were often places of worship. The old covenant is represented by what **can be touched** (12:18). This refers to Mount Sinai, as in 12:20—**IF EVEN A BEAST TOUCHES THE MOUNTAIN, IT WILL BE STONED.** The depictions of the old covenant are derived from the terrifying but glorious giving of the law on Mount Sinai (cf. Ex 19:18-20; 20:18). New covenant faith, on the other hand, is called **Mount Zion** (Heb 12:22), which is further identified as **the city of the living God, the heavenly Jerusalem**. (2) The old covenant is likened **to a blazing fire** (12:18), a reference to the awe-inspiring Shechinah glory that descended on Mount Sinai (Ex 19:18). On the other hand, the second representation of the new covenant is **myriads of angels** (HCSB rightly provides the nuance, "in festive gathering"), rejoicing over the readers joining their celestial company. (3) The old covenant is called **darkness** (Heb 12:18), a reminder of the glorious but terrifying smoke that descended on Mt. Sinai with the giving of the old covenant (Ex 19:18). The new covenant faith is called **the general assembly** of elect people, **enrolled** as citizens **in heaven** (Heb 12:23). (4) Old covenant faith is linked to **gloom** (12:18), an image of the dread that filled Israel when the Sinai covenant was given (Ex 20:18). The effect of new covenant faith is just the opposite, bringing a relationship with **God, the Judge of all** (Heb 12:23), who is now our Father. (5) The first covenant is described by **whirlwind** (i.e., a storm, 12:18), an OT depiction of God's glorious but fear-inducing nature (Ex 19:18-20; 20:18; Is 29:6; 30:30; Ezk 13:10-16; 38:22). Set over against this is the new covenant's leading sinners **to the spirits of the righteous made perfect** (Heb 12:23)—i.e., to join deceased OT and NT believers now in ideal relationship with God. (6) The old covenant is compared to **the blast of a trumpet** (12:19; Ex 20:18) that signaled God's approach from a distance. In contrast the messianic faith of the new covenant is associated with **Jesus** (Heb 12:24), who approached sinners so closely that He became human and willingly offered Himself as a sacrifice for their sins. Lastly (7), according to Dt 4:10-12, Moses and the people of Israel heard a terrifyingly loud trumpet (Ex 19:19) and the frightening sound of God's voice (Dt 4:10-12, here called **the sound of words**, Heb 12:19). The author uses a "lesser to greater argument." If there was sheer panic at Mt. Sinai when God communicated with the Jewish people, even more frightful is the prospect of refusing **Him who is speaking** (v. 25) from the heavenly realities (seen in vv. 22-24) only reflected by the earthly events. But this new covenant faith is depicted in terms of the spirituality, glory, confidence, access, privileges, and of the eternal. Should the readers forsake the latter for the former, they, too, will forfeit the greater for the lesser. It was essential for these Jewish believers to maintain their faith in the promised Messiah who had established the greater and more glorious new covenant. As glorious as the Sinai covenant was, it paled in comparison with the greater glory of the messianic faith.

12:25-29. This section contains the epistle's conclusion to the last warning text. The readers are admonished **not** to **refuse Him who is speaking** and who provides the better disclosure of truth and better blessings of the Messiah (12:25). Israel **did not escape** punishment **when they refused him** [Moses] **who warned them** at Mount Sinai. **Much less will we** avoid divine penalty should we **turn away from Him who warns from heaven**. The words **much less** (12:25) are justified by the prediction of the divine voice **ONCE MORE** shaking **NOT ONLY THE EARTH**, as at Mount Sinai, but **ALSO THE HEAVEN** (12:26). This future shaking is explained as a final judgment, which will be a **removing of** the temporal, so that the eternal **may remain** (12:27). In view of believers being in process of receiving citizenship in an eternal **kingdom**, they are to **show gratitude** by which they can **offer to God an acceptable service**. Such service is to be performed **with reverence** ["being cautious to revere and fear God fully"] **and awe** ("an emotion of profound respect for one who is divine," 12:28). That reverent attitude is well merited, **for our God is a consuming fire** (12:29), who will punish and consume the irreverent who reject Him.

D. Exhortation to Service (13:1-21)

At the close of chap. 12, the readers were reminded of their duty to serve God acceptably (12:28). The question, then, is what constitutes acceptable service? This section answers that query by offering concrete guidelines for performing approved ministry.

13:1-6. The first aspect of service relates to duties of love. Earlier in 6:10, the writer acknowledged that his readers "continue to serve" their fellow believers. In 13:1, he urges them to **let love of the brethren continue**. They are doing a commendable job of demonstrating godly affection toward one another, and they must not allow it to stop. In 13:2, the author turns to love of strangers. The letter's recipients are not doing as well here; they must stop neglecting **to show hospitality**—i.e., love to strangers. The believer is to love not just those inside, but also those outside the community of faith—to show concern not only for those whom he knows, but also for those whom he does not know. The reason for doing this is that **some have** unknowingly **entertained angels** as guests. One such incident is Gn 19, where Lot extended hospitality to two angelic visitors, who later saved his life. The point is that greater blessings are often received by those giving hospitality than by those receiving it. In 13:3, the author focuses on suffering love. The readers are instructed to **remember** to minister to **the prisoners . . . and those who are ill-treated**. They are to carry out their ministry sympathetically by viewing themselves in the unfortunate situation of the victims. In 13:4, the writer deals with married love. **Marriage is to be held in honor among all**. One way to esteem this relationship is by keeping the sexual commitment between husband and wife **undefiled**, abstaining from sex before, and outside of, marriage. For **God will judge** the sexually immoral. In 13:5, the writer speaks about love of money. The believer's lifestyle should be **free from the love of money**, and he must be **content with what** is materially divinely provided him. Such a standard is justified, because God has personally pledged to **NEVER DESERT . . . NOR . . . FORSAKE** His people—i.e., to leave them in the lurch financially. This section ends in 13:6 with love of the Savior. Based on God's commitment not to abandon us, each believer can say, **THE LORD IS MY HELPER**, and **WHAT WILL MAN DO TO ME?** Our affection ought gladly be given such a faithful and helpful divine companion.

13:7-17. The second aspect of acceptable service pertains to certain congregational duties. The readers are to **remember** their past leaders and **imitate their faith** (13:7). This is reasonable, for the object of their leaders' faith was **Jesus Christ**, who is the object of the readers' faith. He **is the same yesterday** when their leaders leaned on Him, and He remains **the same . . . today** when the readers need to confide in Him (13:8). What Jesus did for their leaders He will do for them. A second duty of the faith community is not to **be carried away by . . . strange teachings** (13:9), such as those advocating certain dietary restrictions. **For** justifies this responsibility: the believer's moral life is **to be strengthened by grace, not by foods**. This essential divine grace is obtained from our **altar** (13:10)—i.e., Jesus' sacrifice. Those Jewish priests who are not believers in Jesus **have no right to** partake of this sacrifice. The reason they cannot is explained by analogy: taking **the bodies of those animals** sacrificed in the temple, priests discard them **outside** of Jerusalem's wall (13:11); similarly, they also rejected

Jesus, so that He **suffered outside the** city's **gate** (13:12). The point is that those who reject Jesus as Messiah are unable to partake of His sacrifice and the divine grace coming through it. Jesus being crucified outside of Jerusalem leads to a third duty, and that is to **go out to Him outside the camp** of religious acceptance. The readers are exhorted to leave the Levitical system and make full, public identification with their Messiah, the fulfillment of the Hebrew Bible's sacrificial system. Moreover, they needed to be willing to bear any ensuing **reproach** for doing so (13:13). Their determination to accept the same reproach given to Jesus might force them from home like refugees. Painful though it would be, it would be all right, **for here we do not have** a permanent **city** or place to live; we are headed toward the heavenly **city which is to come** (13:14; cf. also 11:13-16). A fourth duty is to offer to God the **sacrifice of praise** (13:15), especially when persecuted and disgraced, and the sacrifices of **doing good** and sharing some of our resources with the needy (13:16). A final responsibility concerns their current **leaders**, whom the readers must **obey** ("sincere cooperation in following those who lead a community") and to whom they are to **submit** ("to yield to and follow the authority of those who are in charge"; 13:17). This will enable the leaders to **watch over** their spiritual lives **with joy and not with grief**, the latter being to the readers' disadvantage. Leading a congregation is enormously challenging, and it is the responsibility of the community to work in a productive and cheerful way with those who provide leadership. Failure to do so will result in strife and in impeding the progress of the church. Assuming that the leaders are not outright false teachers or moral miscreants, the congregational constituency *must* follow their lead.

13:18-21. The third aspect of acceptable service concerns prayer duties. The godly, scholarly author humbly requests his struggling audience to **pray** for him (13:18), that he may be providentially allowed to visit them (**be restored** to them) **sooner** (13:19). Turning from their praying for him, in 13:20-21 he prays for them, petitioning **the God of peace** to **equip** them **in every good thing** so they may **do His will**, especially by persevering to the end. God would provide for them as **the great Shepherd of the sheep** and through the **blood** of the Messiah, offered as an **eternal covenant**, a reference to Messiah's death that established the new covenant (Jr 31:31-34; Mt 26:28).

E. Final Greetings (13:22-25)

13:22-25. The congregation is urged to take to heart the writer's brief **word of exhortation** (13:22). They are informed of Timothy's recent release from jail and possibly accompanying the author to visit them (13:23). Mutual greetings are exchanged in 13:24, and the letter ends with heaven requested to bestow **grace** on **all** of the readers (13:25).

BIBLIOGRAPHY

Allen, David L. *Hebrews*. New American Commentary. Nashville: Broadman & Holman, 2010.

Bateman, Herbert W., ed. *Four Views on the Warning Passages in Hebrews*. Grand Rapids, MI: Kregel, 2007. See the fine introductory article by Herbert W. Bateman IV ("Introducing the Warning Passages in Hebrews: A Contextual Orientation"), and the articles and responses by Grant R. Osborne ("A Classical Arminian View"), Buist M. Fanning ("A Classical Reformed View"), Gareth Lee Cockerill ("A Wesleyan Arminian View"), Randall C. Gleason ("A Moderate Reformed View"), and George H. Guthrie ("Conclusion").

Bruce, F. F. *The Epistle to the Hebrews*. New International Commentary on the New Testament. Grand Rapids, MI: Eerdmans, 1990.

Feinberg, John S. "Salvation in the Old Testament." In *Tradition and Testament: Essays in Honor of Charles Lee Feinberg*. Edited by John S. Feinberg and Paul D. Feinberg. Chicago: Moody, 1981, 39–77.

Guthrie, Donald. *Hebrews*. Tyndale Old Testament Commentaries. Downers Grove, IL: InterVarsity, 2009.

Guthrie, George H. *Hebrews*. NIV Application Commentary. Grand Rapids, MI: Zondervan, 1998.

Hill, Craig A. "The Use of Perfection Language in Hebrews 5:14 and 6:1 and the Contextual Interpretation of 5:11–6:3." Unpublished paper.

Hughes, Philip Edgcumbe. *A Commentary on the Epistle to the Hebrews*. Grand Rapids, MI: Eerdmans, 1987.

Kent, Homer A. Jr. *The Epistle to the Hebrews: A Commentary*. Grand Rapids, MI: Baker, 1972.

MacArthur, John, Jr. *Hebrews: An Expository Commentary*. MacArthur New Testament Commentary. Chicago: Moody, 1983.

Newell, William R. *Hebrews: Verse-by-Verse: A Classic Evangelical Commentary*. Grand Rapids, MI: Kregel, 2005.

O'Brien, P. T. *The Letter to the Hebrews*. Pillar. Grand Rapids, MI: Eerdmans, 2010.

JAMES

JOHN F. HART

INTRODUCTION

This short epistle has become famous for its supposed conflict with Paul's teaching of justification by faith. In light of its themes on wealth and worldliness, James may be the most relevant NT book for the church of the 21st century, especially the Western church.

Author. The author says nothing of himself other than that he is "James [lit., "Jacob," *Iakobos*; "James" is an anglicized form of the name], a bond-servant of God and of the Lord Jesus Christ." Only two men had sufficient prominence to have commanded the authority necessary for writing the epistle. (1) The apostle James, son of Zebedee and brother of the apostle John (Mt 4:21; 10:2; Ac 1:13a), can be considered only if the book was written before his death in AD 44. (2) The book is usually attributed to James, the Lord's half-brother (Mk 6:3), since he gained distinction as the leader of the church in Jerusalem (Ac 12:17; 15:13; 21:18). Early church leaders largely support this opinion (e.g., Eusebius, Origen).

James appears to be the oldest of four half-brothers born to Mary and Joseph (Mt 13:55; Mk 6:3). He did not believe in Jesus as the Christ until after the resurrection (Ac 1:14). Some hold that he is the James to whom the Lord made a special resurrection appearance (1Co 15:7).

Date. If the Lord's half-brother wrote the book, it must have been written before his death in AD 62 (the date given by Josephus, *Ant.* XX.9.1). An early date is supported by the lack of any mention of a Jewish/Gentile controversy as found in Acts (Ac 15) or the Epistles (e.g., Galatians). If the book was written before the Jerusalem Council (AD 49), the date of writing could be as early as AD 45–48 (most evangelicals). If the dispersion in 1:1 refers to the scattering of Jewish believers in Ac 8:1, dated at about AD 34, the book could have been written as early as AD 35–36. James is probably the first NT book written.

James, like a few other lesser-known letters (2 Peter, 2–3 John, Jude), was not widely accepted as Scripture until late in the fourth century. This was because the early church focused first on the Gospels and the letters of Paul. Since James did not have apostolic authorship, it remained less widely received at first.

Recipients. Numerous details best fit a Mediterranean location for the readers (3:12; 5:7). Both Syrian Antioch (cf. Gl 2:12) and the land of Israel have been suggested. These Jewish believers had been displaced from their homes as the result of persecution (1:1). Some of the readers were being mistreated for their faith (2:7; 5:1-4). Financial difficulties tempted them to focus on wealth (4:13), envy the rich (2:2), and become worldly (4:4).

The author is sufficiently aware of his specific Jewish-Christian readers (see commentary at 1:1) to understand their life situation. While the readers perceived themselves as having wisdom, they actually lacked it. Anyone lacking wisdom could receive it through prayer since God is a generous giver (1:4). But the readers suffered from prayerlessness (4:2). They thought of God as miserly (1:16-17) and unmerciful (5:11). As a result, they became unmerciful like the God they envisioned (2:6, 15-16). Since they were financially tight, their trials deceived them into thinking God was tempting them (1:13, 16). Because they responded wrongly to their trials, the outcome was a divisive and judgmental spirit (4:1, 11; 5:9), arrogance (4:6, 16), and hypocrisy (1:26; 3:17).

James corrected these errors by showing that perseverance in trials is essential so that one might be mature (Gk. *teleios*) and complete (1:4). Abraham added works to his faith, and his faith was made complete (i.e., matured; Gk. *teleioo*, 2:22). Anyone who controls his tongue is a perfect or mature (*teleios*, 3:2) person. The Christians who will rule in the world to come will be those who are "rich in faith" (2:5).

The author never questioned the sincerity of the readers' faith. He addressed the readers as "brothers," "beloved brothers," or "my beloved brothers," a total of 19 times. The dominating themes of maturity and "rich faith" help define the readers' "faith" as an immature (but genuine) faith (see commentary at 2:17). The readers needed to become mature Christians, combining faith and works.

Themes. Major subjects include the believer's response to trials, temptation, and suffering; the need for works to be added to faith for spiritual growth; the value of controlling the tongue; a biblical perspective on wealth, worldly possessions, and the poor; the significance of faith in prayer; and a biblical understanding of wisdom. The book is united around the themes of trials and prayer that begin and end the book like literary "brackets" (1:2-12; 5:10-17). Eschatology (prophecy) contributes to James's theme as well (1:12; 2:5; 5:1-3, 7-9). Simply stated, James teaches that a joyful endurance of trials can mature faith so that believers may be rewarded by Christ at His return.

Imperatives permeate the epistle. The letter alludes frequently to the teachings of Jesus. Numerous parallels exist, especially with the Sermon on the Mount (see sidebar). Familiar Jewish heroes are cited, such as Abraham, Job, and Elijah.

Parallels between James and the Sermon on the Mount

James	Matthew
1:2	5:11-12
1:4	5:48
1:5	7:7
1:17	7:11
1:20	5:22
1:22	7:24
1:23	7:26
2:5	5:3, 5
2:10	5:19
2:11	5:21-22
2:13	5:7
2:15	6:25
3:12	7:16
3:18	5:9
4:2	7:7
4:3	7:7-8
4:4	6:24
4:8	6:22
4:11-12	7:1
4:13-14	6:34
5:2	6:19-20
5:9	5:22; 7:1
5:10	5:11-12
5:12	5:34-37

OUTLINE

I. Salutation (1:1)
II. Prologue of the Letter: Testing of Faith (1:2-18)
  A. Perfect Design for Testing (1:2-8)
  B. Proper Perspective in Testing (1:9-11)
  C. Generous God behind Testing (1:12-18)
III. Maxim: Quick to Obey, Slow to Speak, Slow to Anger (1:19-20)
IV. Body of the Letter: Godly Responses in Trials (1:21–5:6)
  A. Quick to Obey in Trials (1:21–2:26)
    1. Nature of True Obedience (1:21-27)
    2. Sin of Partiality (2:1-13)
    3. Value of Good Works (2:14-26)
  B. Slow to Speak in Trials (3:1-18)
    1. Power of the Tongue (3:1-12)
    2. Nature of True Wisdom (3:13-18)

C. Slow to Get Angry in Trials (4:1–5:6)
1. Worldliness: The Source of Anger (4:1-6)
2. Humility: The Solution to Worldliness (4:7-10)
3. Slander: The By-Product of Anger (4:11-12)
4. Pride: The Accompaniment to Worldliness (4:13-17)
5. Judgment: The Outcome of Worldliness (5:1-6)

V. Epilogue: Final Applications Regarding Trials (5:7-18)
1. Recall for Endurance in Suffering (5:7-11)
2. Solution to Hopelessness in Suffering (5:12-18)

VI. Conclusion: Restoring the Disobedient (5:19-20)

COMMENTARY ON JAMES

I. Salutation (1:1)

1:1. James (see Introduction: Author) is God's **bond-servant** (*doulos,* "slave"), a term used of Christ's willing submission to the Father (Php 2:7). He wrote to Jewish Christians (**twelve tribes**; cf. Lk 22:30) who were **dispersed abroad**, a likely reference to the scattering of Ac 8:1. **Greetings** (*chairo*) also means "rejoice" (cf. v. 2).

II. Prologue of the Letter: Testing of Faith (1:2-18)

A. Perfect Design for Testing (1:2-8)

1:2-3. The readers are to **consider** their trials with **all** (not some) **joy**. Trials are unpredictable (**encounter** means "fall into") and not all the same (**various**). **The testing of . . . faith** is designed to reveal the quality of one's faith and to produce stamina. **Testing** could also be translated "the approved part" of one's faith. It is not just the *tested* faith that produces endurance; it is the *approved* or *genuine* part of one's faith that produces maturity.

1:4-8. Believers must cooperate with God and **let endurance have its** beneficial outcome. The words **perfect** [two times, *teleios*] and **complete** introduce the theme of maturity (see Introduction). In maturity, believers are **lacking in nothing** spiritually (cf. 1Co 2:15; Heb 5:14). In trials the believer often **lacks wisdom**, or "skill for living" (v. 5). "Wisdom" is not primarily knowledge, but godly behavior in difficult situations (cf. 3:15). The solution is to **ask . . . God** for it. The readers may have viewed God as miserly and critical, but God **gives to all generously and without reproach**. The prayer for skill for dealing with trials is answered liberally and willingly. Requests must be offered **in faith without any doubting** (v. 6), since in the NT doubting is usually treated as sin and that which opposes faith (cf. Mt 14:31; Rm 14:23). The imagery of **the surf of the sea** that is **tossed by the wind** depicts the instability of the immature. The **man** who doubts **ought not to expect that he will receive anything** of wisdom **from the Lord** (v. 7), since he is **double-minded** (cf. 4:8). Caught between following Christ and the world (1:27; 4:4), the doubter becomes **unstable in all his ways**.

B. Proper Perspective in Testing (1:9-11)

1:9-11. Joy is dependent on how believers "consider" (v. 2) their circumstances. The follower of Christ who is poor (**brother of humble circumstances**) needs **to glory** or boast in his trials because God is lovingly developing his character through trials. This is a **high position**. **The rich man** (v. 10) is to glory in **his humiliation**, i.e., his mortality. The rich are no different from beautiful, but temporary, **flowering grass**. James probably had in mind physical death for the rich person, which might come suddenly, even **in the midst of** one's **pursuits**. At that time, wealth is of no advantage.

C. Generous God behind Testing (1:12-18)

1:12. Blessed means "to be richly rewarded by God" both in this world (referring esp. to the development of character through trials, 1:4) and in the next (Mt 5:11-12). The believer who **perseveres under trial** and is finally **approved** at the final evaluation before God receives the **crown of life**. The **crown of life** is a future reward given to faithful Christians (cf. Rv 2:10), i.e., **those who love Him** (cf. 2:5). This reward is an enriched and enhanced eternal life, bestowed upon those who have persevered, following either death or the rapture. "While heaven is entirely a gift of grace, it admits of degrees of felicity, and that these are dependent upon how faithfully we have built a structure of character and service upon the foundation of Christ" (Michael Green, *The Second Epistle of Peter and the Epistle of Jude*, TNTC [Grand Rapids, MI: Eerdmans, 1968], 76.)

1:13. The phrase **let no one say** subtly introduces the theme of the tongue (see 3:1-12). **God cannot be tempted by evil** can be translated, "God must not be put to the test by evil people." Jewish Christians would recall how Israel was judged for putting God to the test (Nm 14:22; Ps 78:18).

1:14-15. Satan tempts all believers. But **each one is** ultimately **tempted when he is . . . enticed by his own lust**. A temptation is not sin unless it is **conceived** and **gives birth**. That **sin is accomplished** means sin has become "full-grown" (NIV, ESV). Any sin by an unbeliever brings eternal death (hell). But "full-grown" sin brings early physical **death** (Pr 10:27; Eph 6:2-3).

1:16-17. Temptation is not from God but **every perfect gift** is. God is **the Father** or creator **of lights** such as the sun (Gn 1:14-16; Ps 136:7). Stars may have **variation or shifting shadow**, but God does not (Heb 13:8). He *never* solicits anyone to sin.

1:18. The most perfect of all gifts (v. 16; Rm 6:23) is new birth (**He brought us forth**). It begins sovereignly with **the exercise of His will**. As the **first fruits**, Christians are the initial harvest that anticipates creation's redemption (Rm 8:20-21).

III. Maxim: Quick to Obey, Slow to Speak, Slow to Anger (1:19-20)

1:19-20. The maxim lists the three essential character qualities in trials and summarizes the body of the epistle (see Introduction). **Quick to hear** (see 1:22–2:26) counteracts sluggishness to obey God; **slow to speak** (see 3:1-18) corrects sins of the tongue; and **slow to anger** (see 4:1–5:12) evades outbursts in trials. Human anger, customarily sinful (Mt 5:22), **does not achieve** God's **righteousness** (cf. 3:18; 5:6, 16), either in oneself or in others.

IV. Body of the Letter: Godly Responses in Trials (1:21–5:6)

A. Quick to Obey in Trials (1:21–2:26)

1. Nature of True Obedience (1:21-27)

1:21. Verse 21 begins the body of the letter. Holiness ("righteousness," v. 20) is developed by **putting aside all . . . wickedness**. The goal of sanctification is to **save your souls** (cf. 5:20), better translated "save your life (lives)." In the OT (LXX), the phrase means deliverance from physical death (e.g., Gn 19:17; 1Sm 19:11). Jesus used this sense (Mk 3:4; Lk 6:9) but added a spiritual meaning: by submission to Christ, the believer delivers his life from worldliness (see the comments on Rm 6:15-23), enables him to experience the abundant Christian life, and preserves it for eternal reward (Mt 16:24-27; Mk 8:34-38). James uses both concepts: sanctification can save believers' lives from early physical death (vv. 10-11, 14-15) and bring future reward (v. 12; 2:12-13).

1:22-25. To "receive the word" (v. 21) is now clarified as **prove yourselves doers of the word**. Believers who are **merely hearers** of biblical truth are self-deceived (cf. v. 7; Gl 6:3; 1Jn 1:8). A believer who does not act on truth is like **a man who looks at his natural face in a mirror** (v. 23). James has just referred to our spiritual birth (v. 18) and will allude to our new self in the "law of liberty (v. 25). So **natural face**, which is literally "the face of one's birth," corresponds to the believer's spiritual birth. The Christian looks in the mirror of God's Word (2Co 3:18 NASB) at his new self, transformed by new birth (v. 18). But the Christian who has **gone away** from the mirror (v. 24) has tragically **forgotten what kind of person he** is in Christ (v. 24; cf. 2Pt 1:9). The **law of liberty** (v. 25) is the "law" or "principle" by which God frees believers from sin (Gl 2:4; 5:1, 13; 1Pt 2:16), namely, the gospel, creating in them new selves (2Co 5:17; Eph 4:24; Col 3:10). For **blessed**, see v. 12.

1:26-27. Pious devotion is **worthless** or empty if it does not curb a person's tongue or meet practical needs. **To visit orphans and widows** (v. 27; cf. Dt 10:18; Ps 146:9) means to "look after" them (NIV). Providing for the unfortunate is linked to the command to **keep oneself unstained by the world**. Our hearts follow our treasures (Mt 6:21). So the one who gives financially to help others guards her or his heart from the blemish of worldly, monetary values.

2. Sin of Partiality (2:1-13)

2:1-4. The maxim in 1:19 contains the injunction to be "quick to hear." In this passage, being "quick to hear" God's Word means, among other things, refusing to show favoritism to the rich. James pointed out that true religion consists in showing kindness to the disadvantaged (1:27), and the related idea is that of refusing to cater to the rich (2:1-13). These readers would be especially susceptible to such partiality in light of their oppressive circumstances (cf. 1:1-12)—that is, they might be tempted to show partiality to the rich in the hope of gaining financial assistance from them. Discrimination is one of the worldly stains to avoid (1:27). Showing **favoritism** or honor to anyone other than Christ disregards the exclusive glory that belongs to Him (**our glorious Lord**). James illustrates partiality with a rich man who **comes into** the reader's **assembly** or church meeting (vv. 2-4; cf. 1Co 14:23-25) and is given **special attention**. Money, prestige, or the need for financial security may have driven their **evil motives**, an understandable but unacceptable impulse even during hard times.

2:5. The rich rely on their money (Mt 19:23), but the **poor of this world** become wealthy or **rich in faith**. To be **heirs of the kingdom** may be equivalent to entering and enjoying the kingdom at the end of the age. Others understand the phrase to mean that faithful believers will receive a position of authority in the future world (Lk 12:43-44; Ac 20:32; Col 3:24; Rv 2:26). For **those who love Him**, see 1:12.

2:6-7. James asked how the readers could have **dishonored the poor** since (1) God Himself honors the poor (1:6), (2) the rich force believers **into court** with false charges, and (3) the rich **blaspheme the fair name** of Jesus (1:1; 2:1) held so dear by Christians.

2:8-9. Jesus made **LOVE YOUR NEIGHBOR** (Lv 19:18, 34) a foremost command (Mt 22:39; Mk 12:31). This is **the royal law** because of its preeminence and because it was sanctioned by the King, the Lord Jesus. The OT command to love one's neighbor (v. 8; Lv 19:18) prohibited **partiality** (v. 9), particularly against the poor (Lv 19:15).

2:10-13. The Mosaic law is an indivisible unit. Breaking one command incurs the same penalty for breaking **the whole law**. Please note that although the law is a unit, this does not mean that all commandments are equal. Jesus referred to both the greatest commandments (Mt 22:36-40) and the "weightier provisions" of the law (Mt 23:23). The word **guilty** does not refer to feelings of blame but to God's judicial indictment. God is "one" (cf. Jms 2:19) and spoke against both **ADULTERY** and **MURDER** (v. 11). To violate either one makes a person **a transgressor of the law**. The sin of partiality is elevated to the sins of adultery and murder. Christians must **speak** and **act** (v. 12) out of the forgiveness they have received. For **the law of liberty**, see the commentary at 1:25. The evaluation or **judgment** (v. 13) of Christians who have **shown no mercy** will be exacting (cf. 3:1). For those who treat others with mercy, mercy **triumphs** (wins out) **over** a stern evaluation (cf. Mt 5:7, 12). This judgment is limited to believers since the verse forms an inclusio with 3:1, where the judgment is on James and all Christian teachers. For God's evaluation of Christians in the future, see the comments on Rm 14:10-12; 1Co 3:10-17.

3. Value of Good Works (2:14-26)

2:14. For James, being "quick to hear" (1:19) meant to be prompt to obey God's command to do good deeds that benefit others. But the readers had neglected good works, content to claim their justification before God by faith alone. James agreed that justification before God was by faith alone. But believers must add works to their faith to develop maturity. Then they will be justified (called righteous) by their works in the eyes of other people (cf. Mt 5:16). A person who **says he has faith** finds it easy to talk his faith while lacking useful deeds. Bible teachers may be in mind (cf. 3:1-12). The question **Can** [**"that"** is not in Gk.] **faith save him?** demands a negative answer in Greek ("Faith cannot save him, can it?") and appears to contradict justification by faith alone (Rm 3:27-28; 4:4-5; Gl 2:16; Eph 2:8-9). But James's use of the Greek verb "save" (*soizo*) is flexible. This is evident in 5:15, where James uses the word in a way that does not mean "delivered from eternal judgment." Contextually, "save" in v. 14 is equivalent to the believer's triumph over a stern evaluation ("judgment") by God mentioned in 2:13 and 3:1 (an inclusio). (Also see comments on "save" at 1:21.) So the phrase, "Can faith [alone] save him?" asks if a believer without acts of mercy will be able to escape a strict evaluation at the believer's final performance review.

2:15-16. What if a Christian **brother or sister** has life-threatening conditions such as lack of **clothing** and **need of daily food**? Well-wishing words cannot provide any meaningful assistance for them. So it is if one has genuine faith, but does not activate it during times of trial. **What use is that?** suggests especially that when saving faith is connected with action, there is great benefit *in this life*.

2:17. The conclusion (**even so**) is that **faith**, without **works**, **is dead**. Faith is all **by itself** and lacks vibrancy. A "dead faith" is a weak, lethargic (immature, but nevertheless present) faith (cf. "sin is dead," Rm 7:8; also see "Introduction: Recipients"). James's point appears to be that if one has true faith in Christ, it does one no practical good in this life of trials if it is not put into action. Neither does a "dead faith" "save one's life" (see the comments on 1:21).

2:18-19. The words **someone may** . . . **say** introduce an imaginary opponent ("well" is not in the

Gk. text). In two other NT passages introducing an imaginary objector, the response of the inspired author begins with a remark of his opponent's foolishness (cf. Rm 9:19-20; 1Co 15:35-36). This makes it likely that the objector's words to James continue through v. 19 (cf. Richard Francis Weymouth, *The New Testament in Modern Speech*, ed. Ernest Hampden-Cook (Boston: Pilgrim Press), 1903) and James's response begins in v. 20 with "you foolish fellow." The opponent challenges: **Show me your faith** by [some Gk. texts read **without**] your **works, and I will show you** by my works **my faith** [the order of the Gk. words is given]. The opponent insists that faith cannot be seen through works. One may start by naming a doctrine and then try to show the work that will always come from that belief ("show me your faith by your works"). Or one could do the reverse. He could name a good work and try to demonstrate the doctrine that must be behind it ("and I will show you by my works my faith"). The opponent thinks both are impossible. Suppose James starts with a doctrine: "I believe God is a God of love (doctrine). So I treat others with sacrificial love (a good work)." The objector would answer, "Ha! I know lots of people who love others sacrificially and don't even believe in God. So works don't show what you believe!" The objector is so confident in his argument that he answers for James: "James, **you believe that God is one** [a doctrine], and **you do well**, i.e., you do good works. But **the demons also believe** God is one [a doctrine], but do no good works. They just **shudder** in fear of judgment." With this argument, the objector rests his case.

2:20. James's response now begins (vv. 18-19 are the objector's thoughts). The opponent's words are **foolish** and lack wisdom (1:5; 3:13-17). Often Christian teachers (3:1) have an unteachable spirit. Likewise, James questions if his opponent is **willing to recognize** the truth: **faith without works** secures eternal life but **is useless** to meet the practical needs of others, to experience blessings for one's self in this life, or to gain eternal rewards.

2:21-23. Abraham initially believed God and was justified before God by faith alone (Gn 15:6; Rm 4:1-5, 9-12; Gl 3:1-6). His faith was in a God who could resurrect the dead (Rm 4:17-21). In Gn 22, 30 years after his initial faith for which God counted him righteous, Abraham **offered up Isaac his son on the altar** (Gn 22:1; Heb 11:19). **You see** (second person singular) corrects the objector's contention that faith cannot be seen in works. Abraham's faith is unmistakably visible. Being **justified by works** is not before God (Rm 3:20; Gl 3:11) but before people (cf. Mt 5:16).

In addition, **justified** sometimes means "to demonstrate that one is in the right" (cf. Lk 7:29, 35; Rm 3:4; 1Tm 3:16) and does not always have the Pauline sense of "God's declaration that one is innocent of the charge that he is a sinner" and is given eternal life. Abraham's **faith was** cooperating or **working with his works**, so that faith might be **perfected** (*teleioo*), i.e., matured. Abraham's works brought added depth in a practical sense to the faith he possessed inasmuch as it enabled him to experience the blessings of a fresh encounter with God (cf. Gn 22:15-19), and he gained an extraordinary reputation among men (**he was called the friend of God**, v. 23; cf. 2Ch 20:7; Is 41:8). A believer combines faith with good works, not so that he can attain heaven, but so that he may gain spiritual blessings in this life and honor from the Father in the world to come.

2:24. You see (second person *plural*) now addresses the readers. The word **alone** (*monon*) modifies the verb **justified,** not the words **by faith**: "You see that a man is justified [i.e., demonstrates to others that he is righteous or holy; see the comments on "justified" for v. 21 above] by works, and not *only* [*monon*] by faith." James was calling attention to two ways of justification: by faith before God, and by works before people. While one is justified (declared righteous) before God by faith alone, one is justified (demonstrates his godliness) before people by his or her works.

2:25. By faith (Heb 11:31) **Rahab the harlot** received the Jewish spies and hid them in her house (Jos 2:1-24). She could have betrayed the spies, but she **sent them out by another way**, adding works to her new faith. Rahab had faith in the God of Israel (Jos 2:11), yet if she had not acted on that faith, she would have perished when Jericho was destroyed (see comment on 1:21 on "save your souls"). Instead, she activated the faith she had, hid the spies, was spared, and experienced God's blessings among the Jewish people.

2:26. For a **body** to be active and alive, it must have a **spirit**. So also **faith** in Christ must have **works** added to it since works give vitality and energy to faith. On **dead** faith, see 2:17.

B. Slow to Speak in Trials (3:1-18)

1. Power of the Tongue (3:1-12)

3:1. Chapter 3 introduces James's second division of the body of his epistle (see 1:19). In trials, the tongue can veer out of control, evidencing pride, anger, and false wisdom. The tongue has positive (vv. 2-5b) and negative qualities (vv. 5b-12). **Many of** the Jewish Christian readers longed to **become** Bible **teachers**. James was a Bible teacher and knew that he, along with all teachers, would **incur a stricter judgment** at the judgment seat of Christ (see commentary on 1:12, 20; 2:12-13).

3:2. We (James includes himself) **all stumble** or sin **in many ways** (Pr 10:19). To be a **perfect** person (*teleios*) means to be "mature." If one can **bridle** the tongue (1:26), the most insubordinate body part, he will be able to control the rest of his **body as well**.

3:3-4. Small things can control much larger objects, like **bits** in horses' **mouths** or **a very small rudder** in a large ship. **Inclination** (Gk. *horme*) carries the nuance of "impulse." Like the whim of a ship's pilot, impulsive words can shipwreck one's life.

3:5-6. The tongue **boasts of great** beneficial **things**, such as encouraging others (Pr 10:21; 12:18). Negatively, the power of the tongue is like **a small fire** that has **set aflame** and destroyed an immense **forest**. One rumor can destroy numerous churches. Since most sins are initiated by speech, the tongue is the **very world of iniquity** (v. 6). It **sets on fire the course of our life**, such as provoking a broken marriage.

3:7-8. From earth to heaven, **every species of beasts and birds** has been tamed. From the ground to the sea, every variety of **reptiles and creatures of the sea** has been subdued **by the human race**. James is surely speaking hyperbolically. There may be some species not yet tamed. His main point is that, in contrast to domesticating the animal kingdom, **no one can tame the tongue**. It can be caged (controlled), yet it is always **restless**. Believers dare not let the tongue out of the cage.

3:9-10. With the tongue **we bless our Lord and Father** in church or private prayer. Moments later believers may **curse** people, all of whom **have been made in the likeness of God** (Gn 1:26-27; 9:6). This is hypocritical and radically illogical. God is blessed, but one with God's image is cursed. This passage teaches that sin has not destroyed the image of God in people, including the unbeliever. Therefore, every person is to be treated with respect.

3:11-12. Nature itself demonstrates the absurdity of a forked tongue. A **fig tree** and a **vine** produce just one kind of fruit. God determined that productivity would be after its kind (Gn 1:11-12, 24-25). Just as there is consistency in nature about what trees, plants, or springs produce, so God's people must learn to speak with consistent goodness.

2. Nature of True Wisdom (3:13-18)

3:13-14. James continued his warning about the tongue and described how true godly wisdom ("skill for living and applying God's Word") will help curtail its destructiveness in the context of a church. Wisdom is best expressed in actions (vv. 13-18), not speech (3:1-12). A person who is **wise** will **show** this wisdom **by his good behavior**. **Gentleness** (*prautes*, "being kindhearted in attitude and behavior without any harshness") recalls Christ's character (*praus*, Mt 11:29). Sins like **bitter jealousy** (**jealousy** is "powerful feelings of antagonism and hostility") and **selfish ambition** ("antipathy flowing from harsh rivalry") (v. 14) can be covered up hypocritically so as to **lie against the truth**.

3:15-16. The "wisdom" of selfish ambition (v. 14) is (1) **earthly**, limited by human understanding; (2) **natural** or "soulish" (*psychikos*), a term emphasizing both strictly human values and characteristics, and the absence of the Spirit (1Co 2:14; Jd 19); and (3) **demonic** (the work of Satan).

3:17-18. Heavenly wisdom is **first pure** ("free from moral defect or stain"; in this context, promoting harmony and countering hypocrisy), **then peaceable, gentle, reasonable** (necessary for unity; cf. 4:1). James illustrates the growth of righteousness in the church with the sowing of seed in a field. If the **fruit** desired is **righteousness** (v. 18), the seed must be **sown** under the proper conditions, i.e., in **peace**. Anger cannot "grow" God's righteousness (cf. 1:20). Therefore, the ones who sow the seed must be **peacemakers**.

C. Slow to Get Angry in Trials (4:1–5:6)

1. Worldliness: The Source of Anger (4:1-6)

4:1. Chapter 4 addresses "slow to get angry," the complement to seeking peace (3:18). This is the last of the three qualities ("quick to obey," "slow to speak") for handling trials given in James's maxim (see 1:19). The **source of . . . conflicts among** these believers was the worldly **pleasures that wage war in** their **members**, i.e., parts of the physical body (Rm 6:13, 19; 7:23).

4:2-3. The readers' **lust** or coveting was for material things. Since hatred is tantamount to **murder** (Mt 5:21-22; 1Jn 3:15), "murder" need not be literal. Believers can destroy each other with their words. Nevertheless it is possible for believers to kill someone because of covetousness. If believers **cannot obtain** their desires, they should not **fight and quarrel** for them but pray for them. Unfulfilled desires may result from prayerlessness or prayers with **wrong motives** (v. 3).

4:4. The readers were spiritual adulterers (cf. Jr 3:8-9; Hs 1:2), i.e., they were being unfaithful to God and having a "spiritual affair" with the world as they sought to satisfy their own cravings at the expense of church harmony. **Whoever wishes** [*boulomai*, "the wish to possess or experience something, and planning to gain it"] **to be a friend of the world** cannot be God's friend (cf. 2:23). A Christian's worldliness **makes** him **an enemy of God** in the sense that he loses spiritual intimacy (friendship) with Christ (Jn 15:1-8) and shifts his loyalty to the world away from the Father.

4:5. The readers thought that **Scripture speaks** without a **purpose** and that God would not discipline their disobedience. James paraphrases Ex 20:5. The last clause is better translated, "the Spirit He has caused to live in us [by regeneration] yearns jealously [for our fidelity to God]."

4:6-10. But (v. 6) introduces how self-centered believers can change. Whatever pleasures the world offers (vv. 1-3), God's **greater grace** provides the power to resist them. "Grace" means "the practical bestowment of good will by God," here manifested as the capacity from Him to live godly lives (cf. Eph 4:29). God is **OPPOSED TO** and may even punish **THE PROUD**. But divine favor and personal motivation (**GRACE**) are given **TO THE HUMBLE** (Pr 3:34).

2. Humility: The Solution to Worldliness (4:7-10)

4:7-10. Worldly Christians need to **submit** themselves **to God** by determining to be faithful and obedient only to Him. Then they can **resist the devil** (cf. 1Pt 5:9) **and he will** eventually **flee from** them (Lk 4:13). The solution to worldliness and its disruptive effects in the church is to **draw near to God** (v. 8). **He will** reciprocate and **draw near** to believers. **Cleanse your hands** points to believers ridding themselves of selfish and sinful acts (Is 1:16), and **purify your hearts** denotes the cleansing of impure, self-seeking motives (Ps 73:13). For **double-minded**, see 1:8. Brokenness over sin should cause Christ followers to **mourn and weep** (v. 9; cf. Mt 5:4). Worldly **laughter** and **joy** that come when one "gets his way" at the expense of others are inappropriate in a Christian setting, and one should instead **mourn and weep** over such tendencies. To grieve over sin, believers must **humble** themselves (v. 10) before **the Lord**. God promises that He **will exalt** the humble (v. 10), in this life and/or the next (cf. 1Pt 5:6). When a believer humbly sets aside his own quest to satisfy his cravings at the expense of others, and determines to serve others (the sense of being **humble**), God will cause him to be valued in the body of Christ.

3. Slander: The By-Product of Anger (4:11-12)

4:11-12. James continued his warning about the need to control one's anger in trials and its destructiveness in the body of Christ. If a Christian **judges his** Christian **brother**, he indirectly **speaks against the** royal **law** of love (Lv 19:16-18; Mt 22:39), love being the essence of the "law of Christ" (cf. Gl 6:2; for the royal law, see 2:8, 9). He also **judges the law** of Christ (1Co 9:21; Gl 6:2), supposing Christ's commands to love are below him, or that he has sufficient authority to set aside "the royal law" (Jms 2:8). Only one has such power (4:12). As **Judge**, God **is able to save and to destroy**, i.e., to preserve one's physical life or to take it in death (Mk 3:4; Lk 6:9) as a discipline. Part of the humility that promotes accord in the church is the willingness to submit to and obey the royal law.

4. Pride: The Accompaniment to Worldliness (4:13-17)

4:13-17. James had been discussing how selfish and worldly desires caused disruption in the church, especially through words. But such carnal preoccupations can also manifest themselves through presumptuous business practices as well, and James turns to that topic in these verses. The self-assured plan to **go to** a foreign **city**, to **engage in business**, and **make a profit** (v. 13) was a presumptuous and world-like plan. A Christian's wages are for more than selfish pleasures (Eph 4:28). To project the future confidently but not know what **life will be like tomorrow** (v. 14) is foolish (Lk 12:16-21). Life is brief, like a fleeting **vapor**. By saying **If the Lord wills** (v. 15; Ac 18:21; 1Co 16:7), one recognizes and depends upon God's sovereignty, and thereby avoids the world's way for doing business. Entrepreneurial plans that exclude God (vv. 13-15) make believers **boast in** their **arrogance** (v. 16), as if they have the ability to make themselves profitable. People may boast in the Lord (1:9; Gl 6:13-14), but **all such boasting** about themselves **is evil**. If a person **knows the right thing to do** (v. 17; such as saying, "If the Lord wills," v. 15) and yet **does not do it, to him it is sin**. This failure is often called the "sin of omission."

5. Judgment: The Outcome of Worldliness (5:1-6)

5:1-3. James addressed worldliness and selfishness in the church. But in 5:1-6 he described the fate of the unbelieving rich who are likewise worldly. As believers listen in on the judgment to come on the unbelieving rich, worldly desires that have fueled their anger toward others will be transformed and anger will subside. While believers are addressed in chap. 4 (note the uses of "brethren/brother" (4:11) and the assumption that they comprehend God's sovereignty, 4:15), here there is no clear indication James is addressing rich believers—though some of the actions of the rich in this passage could be true of more worldly believers (esp. 5:4). With **come now**, James takes on the character of an OT prophet. As a group, the unbelieving **rich** live unrighteously and carry out social injustices. Great **miseries** will come on these unjust rich unbelievers in the future day of the Lord (cf. Is 13:6; Ezk 30:2-3). **Consume your flesh like fire** (v. 3) alludes to the judgments immediately preceding and following the second coming of Christ (Rv 17:16; 18:3-19). The term **last days** (pl.) involves the entire Church Age leading up to Christ's return (2Tm 3:1; 2Pt 3:3).

5:4-6. Sabaoth (v. 4) is a transliterated Hebrew word for "armies." The unbelieving rich are like animals that have **fattened** their **hearts** (through materialism), awaiting the slaughter. Armageddon will be **a day of slaughter** when Christ and His heavenly armies destroy the wicked (Rv 19:11-21). The rich may have **condemned and put to death** (v. 6) poor believers by withholding their wages or by using the legal systems to falsely accuse the **righteous** believer, leading to his execution.

V. Epilogue: Final Applications Regarding Trials (5:7-18)

1. Recall for Endurance in Suffering (5:7-11)

5:7-8. With v. 7, James began his conclusion and returned to his central theme of endurance in trials. **Brethren** addresses the Christian readers again to encourage those who might be facing abuse from the unrighteous rich. In Israel, the **early** autumn and **late** spring **rains** were needed for a successful harvest. God's harvest of people (**the precious produce of the soil**) is not yet complete. But James's point here seems to be that the steadfastness of these believers in the midst of hardship will result in great rewards (on rewards, see the comments on 1Co 3:14).

5:9-11. Believers must **not complain** (v. 9) or grumble **against** another brother lest they be judged (Rm 14:10-12; see commentary on 1:12; 2:12). **The Judge is standing right at the door** symbolizes the imminent return of Christ in the rapture (see commentary on 1Th 4:13–5:11). Believers need **an example** of how to endure **suffering and** how to respond in **patience** (v. 10). Most of the OT **prophets** (Heb 11:32-38) suffered patiently as they **spoke** God's message. For **blessed** (v. 11) see commentary on 1:12. **The outcome of the Lord's dealings** with Job was that his suffering was removed and his family and possessions were restored (Jb 42:10-17).

2. Solution to Hopelessness in Suffering (5:12-18)

5:12. In trials, one might rashly take an oath, or swear by lesser things such as **by heaven or by earth** to disguise the truth. Words by themselves must be truthful (**your yes is to be yes**). On the one hand, oaths themselves are not prohibited; on the other, a believer should not be forced to take an oath in order to tell the truth. Unrepentant deception will cause the believer to **fall under** God's **judgment** (discipline) now, and bring disapproval at the judgment seat of Christ (see 2:12, 13).

5:13-16. Along with thinking about future rewards for steadfastness in hard times (v. 11), James presented another practice to help believers bear up when suffering (cf. the theme of suffering in vv. 10-11), namely, asking the elders to pray for them. Anyone **suffering** should **pray** in faith (cf. 1:6). Anyone free from suffering can be **cheerful** and **sing praises** (cf. Eph 5:18-19). **Sick** (*astheneo*) can mean "physically sick" (see, e.g., Jn 5:3; 2Tm 4:20), but it sometimes refers to spiritual, ethical, emotional, or moral weakness (e.g., see Rm 4:19; 1Co 8:11-12; 2Co 11:29; 1Th 5:14), and that is probably the better sense in this passage for reasons that will be argued below (cf. Daniel R. Hayden, "Calling the Elders to Pray," *Bib Sac* 139 (1982): 258–66). The spiritually weak believer should **call for the elders of the church** to **pray over him** (cf. Ac 20:35). **Anointing** with oil was sometimes used in calling God to heal one physically (Mk 6:13), but it also symbolized joy, was used for celebrative purposes, and provided refreshment (Ps 23:5; Lk 7:38, 46; Jn 12:3). The latter sense is preferred here. A simple **prayer offered in faith** (v. 15; cf. 1:5-7) by the elders **will restore** [lit., *soizo,* "save" or perhaps better "rescue, deliver"] **the one who is** spiritually or emotionally **sick** (*kamno,* used in Heb 12:3 for "growing weary," not for physical disease). **The Lord will raise him up** was offered by James with no qualification (such as, "If it is the Lord's will" or "If he has enough faith," etc.), likely indicating a reference to *spiritual* and *moral* restoration for those who have suffered rather than for the physical healing of disease. The prayer of faith by the elders may not always be answered absolutely in the strengthening of the discouraged believer, however. Perhaps the person has sinned and even though he calls for the elders of the church and they pray in faith, he does not respond to the Lord following their prayer. If the passage deals with a spiritual healing rather than a physical healing, it seems like the faith of the "weak" believer has some role in his deliverance. So there could be exceptions in which the weakened believer is not "delivered." This may be a "general promise" like those in the book of Proverbs. For example, *usually* "a gentle answer turns away wrath" (Pr 15:1), and much in James is similar to Proverbs.

5:15-16. If one's spiritual weakness was due to the commission of **sins**, those sins **will be forgiven him** (v. 15) as he seeks the spiritual restoration through the elders' prayers. This does not indicate that all physical illness is caused by sin, but the mention of the forgiveness of sins here does support the understanding that James is discussing spiritual, emotional, or moral restoration. To **confess your sins to one another** (v. 16) is not necessarily done in public (Mt 5:23-24), but here it does seem to be a part of the restoration process involving the elders. **Healed** (*iaomai*) is sometimes used for physical healing (e.g., Lk 5:17; Jn 4:47; Ac 9:34), but it is also used metaphorically for spiritual restoration (Mt 13:15; Jn 12:40; Ac 28:27; Heb 12:13; 1Pt 2:24), the metaphorical sense being preferred in light of James's apparent emphasis on spiritual strengthening.

5:17-18. Elijah was a prophet (v. 10) but had **a nature like ours** (Gk. *homoiopathes* is literally "of similar suffering"). The prayers of Elijah about the **rain** were to restore Israel from idolatry (1Kg 18:37; cf. Jms 4:4-5). Once again, the reference to *this* episode suggests that James's point is about the power of prayer by church leaders to help restore one who is morally weak due to suffering. If this passage were about physical healing, James might have noted the raising of the widow of Zarephath's son back to life (1Kg 17:17-24) as a supreme example of physical healing (Hayden, "Calling the Elders to Pray," 265). Instead he focused on the power of Elijah's prayer to bring about great good, and thereby drew the parallel with the effectiveness of the prayer of elders to help restore one who is weak.

VI. Conclusion: Restoring the Disobedient (5:19-20)

5:19-20. The letter ends with a call for mercy (2:13; 3:17). **Any among you** shows that James is concerned about restoring a wayward believer. **One turns him back** indicates one believer lovingly confronting another who has strayed into sin, so as to help restore him spiritually. **Save his soul from death** (see commentary on 1:21) refers to physical, not eternal, death. **Death** may also include the idea of moral corruption, hardship, and the lack of the abundant Christian life that come upon a believer as consequences of sin (see the comments on Rm 6:15-23). **Will cover a multitude of sins** alludes to Pr 10:12 (cf. 1Pt 4:8), where love brings God's forgiveness.

BIBLIOGRAPHY

Blue, J. Ronald. "James." The Bible Knowledge Commentary: New Testament, edited by John F. Walvoord and Roy B. Zuck. Wheaton: Victor, 1983.

Davids, Peter H. "James." *New Bible Commentary: 21st Century Edition*, edited by D. A Carson et al. Downers Grove, IL: InterVarsity, 1994.

Guthrie, George H., and Douglas J. Moo. *Hebrew–James: Zondervan Illustrated Bible Backgrounds Commentary*. Edited by Clinton E. Arnold. Grand Rapids, MI: Zondervan, 2007.

Hiebert, D. Edmond. *The Epistle of James*. Chicago: Moody, 1979.

Hodges, Zane C. *The Epistle of James. Proven Character through Testing*. Dallas: Grace Evangelical Society, 1994.

Nystrom, David P. *James*. NIV Application Commentary. Grand Rapids, MI: Zondervan, 1997.

1 PETER

LOUIS BARBIERI

INTRODUCTION

Author. There is no New Testament letter that has any earlier or stronger external attestation to its authorship than 1 Peter. An early testimony comes from Irenaeus who relates the work to Peter. Internally, the author states his name at the beginning (1:1) and he makes several allusions to Jesus Christ. The command to elders in 5:2 to "shepherd the flock of God among you" is reminiscent of Jesus' command to Peter in Jn 21:15, 17. The expression in 1Pt 5:5, "clothe yourself with humility," recalls the Lord's clothing Himself with a towel when He washed the disciples' feet (Jn 13:3-5). The admonition in 1Pt 5:7, "casting all your anxiety on Him," reflects the teaching of Jesus in Mt 11:30. Many similarities in language and grammatical structures can also be found between 1 Peter and the recorded messages of Peter in the book of Acts. The authorship of this letter by Simon Peter, the disciple of Jesus Christ, is not questioned by conservative scholarship, though many liberal scholars question Petrine authorship.

Date. Two important factors must be considered when the dating of 1 Peter is discussed. First, according to church tradition Peter died around AD 67 or 68. Second, the emperor Nero is thought to have begun his persecutions of Christianity in AD 64. Since the persecutions mentioned in the letter do not seem to be well organized, an acceptable date for 1 Peter would be around AD 65.

Recipients. Peter sent his letter to regenerated individuals who were scattered throughout five Roman provinces of modern-day Turkey: Pontus, Galatia, Cappadocia, Asia, and Bithynia. Some believe his readers were primarily Jewish because Peter is referred to as having an "apostleship to the circumcised" (Gl 2:7-8). His many uses of Old Testament texts as well as the fact that he says his readers are part of the "diaspora" (1Pt 1:1) might lead one to that conclusion. However, that he says his readers were in a time of "ignorance" (1:14) and that they were involved in "abominable idolatries" (4:3-5) might cause one to reconsider. These are expressions usually not used in describing Jews. If Gentiles were part of Peter's audience, perhaps he was thinking of them as being dispersed in a world where they were "aliens and strangers" (2:11). The five Roman provinces probably had larger Gentile populations, but Jews would have been found in all of these areas. Although Paul's primary ministry was directed toward Gentiles, he began his ministry in every city by going to the synagogue. Peter's primary ministry was directed toward Jews, but surely he had some ministry among Gentiles. It is probably best to conclude that the recipients of 1 Peter were a combination of both Jews and Gentiles, with Jews being the primary audience. Though both groups are addressed in the book, certain passages appear primarily directed to a Jewish context (e.g., 2:9-12).

Purpose. It was becoming clearer that the followers of Jesus Christ, "Christians" as they were called (Ac 11:26), were developing beliefs that distinguished them from Judaism. Romans tolerated the practice of Judaism, but if Christianity was unique, it was no longer an approved state "religion." Consequently, followers of Jesus were coming under official persecution. It was the increase in this persecution that prompted Peter to write this letter. The impression one receives from the letter (cf. 1:6; 3:13-14; 4:12) is that the persecutions were sporadic and local rather than well organized and widespread. Peter's purpose for writing is clearly stated in 5:12. He wrote to give an exhortation and testimony to the true grace of God.

Background. It is clear from 5:13 that Peter was in "Babylon" at the time of the writing of his first letter. The location of "Babylon" has been debated throughout church history. Three possibilities have emerged:

(1) "Babylon" was a city in Egypt. The Babylon that was in Egypt was a small military base for Roman soldiers and it is doubtful that Peter and those mentioned in this letter ever visited that site. It is only the Coptic (North African) Church that has held this view.

(2) "Babylon" was located on the Euphrates River in modern-day Iraq. The best argument for this possibility is that it is in keeping with a normal (literal) understanding of the text. In addition there does not seem to be any evidence historically that Babylon was ever used symbolically before John wrote the book of Revelation. There is, however, no evidence that Peter and those associated with him ever visited ancient Babylon.

(3) "Babylon" was the city of Rome. There is good church tradition that Peter did reach the city of Rome where he ministered and ultimately was martyred. If persecutions were increasing, Peter may have used "Babylon" symbolically to conceal his true location in the imperial city. Christians were beginning to equate the wickedness and persecution of Rome with that of the ancient oppressor of Israel. If Peter's letter fell into the wrong hands, the symbolic use of "Babylon" could potentially keep his location a secret. Surrounding statements in the verse may support the symbolic interpretation, for Peter refers to Mark (probably John Mark) as his "son." No mention is made in Scripture of Peter having any children.

Some of the outstanding characteristics of 1 Peter are:

(1) There are a number of similarities to the writings of Paul, especially to the book of Ephesians.

(2) Peter's exposition in 3:18-22 is one of the most difficult portions of the NT to interpret.

(3) There is an emphasis on the sufferings of the believer, but also an emphasis on the sufferings of Jesus Christ. The sufferings of Jesus are mentioned in every chapter (cf. 1:11, 19-21; 2:21-24; 3:18; 4:13; 5:1).

(4) There is an emphasis on the return of the Lord (cf. 1:3, 13, 21; 3:15).

(5) There are a number of Old Testament quotes and allusions.

OUTLINE*

- I. Introduction (1:1-2)
  - A. The Author (1:1a)
  - B. The Addressees (1:1b-2)
- II. Canticle of Praise (1:3-12)
  - A. The New Birth (1:3a)
  - B. The Living Hope (1:3b)
  - C. The Glorious Inheritance (1:4)
  - D. The Omnipotent Protector (1:5-12)
- III. Conduct Before God (1:13–2:12)
  - A. Holiness (1:13-16)
  - B. Love (1:17-25)
  - C. Growth (2:1-8)
  - D. Praise (2:9-12)
- IV. Conduct Before Men (2:13–4:19)
  - A. The Christian and Government (2:13-17)
  - B. The Christian and Business (2:18-25)
  - C. The Christian and Family (3:1-7)
  - D. The Christian and Society (3:8-22)
  - E. The Christian's Example (4:1-19)
- V. Conduct of the Church (5:1-11)
  - A. Conduct of the Pastor (5:1-4)
  - B. Conduct of the People (5:5-11)
- VI. Conclusion (5:12-14)

*Outline adapted from Elvis E.Cochrane, *The Epistles of Peter* (Grand Rapids, MI: Baker, 1965).

COMMENTARY ON 1 PETER

I. Introduction (1:1-2)

A. The Author (1:1a)

1:1a. Peter, a nickname bestowed by Jesus (cf. Jn 1:42), was reaffirmed after confessed Christ's person (cf. Mt 16:18). He denied Jesus, but his rock-like character emerged in the church. He was **an apostle**, sent out to serve and proclaim Jesus, a commission giving him authority to write.

B. The Addressees (1:1b-2)

1:1b. The addressees are **chosen**, indicating their election by God, and **aliens** of the dispersion, emphasizing their position in the world. The true home of believers is heaven. As long as one lives on earth, he is "dispersed." Specifically, Peter wrote to people in five provinces in modern-day Turkey.

1:2. Peter clarifies "chosen" with three phrases. Election originates in **the foreknowledge of God the Father**, part of His plan, accomplished through the Spirit's sanctifying work, and based on Jesus' **blood**, applied for salvation and continual cleansing. A final salutation requests that believers will have **grace** and **peace** multiplied in their lives.

II. Canticle of Praise (1:3-12)

A. The New Birth (1:3a)

1:3a. Peter blesses the **Father of our Lord Jesus Christ**, presenting Jesus as God and Messiah. In **mercy** God has caused us **to be born again**. In mercy God withholds what is deserved (cf. 1:23). Jesus spoke with Nicodemus (Jn 3) of being "born from above." Both comments reflect a change of status and participation in a God-given life called regeneration or the new birth wherein God takes a spiritually dead person and grants new spiritual life. Peter begins his song of praise where eternal life begins.

B. The Living Hope (1:3b)

1:3b. The first result of the new birth and the first characteristic of the Christian life is **hope**. This hope is **living** because it is based on a resurrected Savior.

C. The Glorious Inheritance (1:4)

1:4. The believer anticipates a glorious **inheritance**. Three negative modifiers, **imperishable**, **undefiled**, and **will not fade away** (one Gk. word), show that the inheritance is not earthly. The inheritance cannot perish, waste away, does not have internal defects, and is unchangeable. It is **reserved**, awaiting His arrival when full possession will be realized.

D. The Omnipotent Protector (1:5-12)

1:5. The believer has not entered this glory, but lives as a sojourner. Nevertheless God's protection surrounds him. Peter combines **the power of God** and the **faith** of the believer. Both continue until final **salvation** is **revealed**. Until then the believer rests in God's powerful protection.

1:6-9. This brings rejoicing to the believer, even though life brings **various trials** producing **the proof of** [our] **faith** (v. 6; cf. Jms 1:3). Men use fire to purify gold; God uses trials to distinguish between genuine and superficial faith. Men consider gold valuable, yet it is perishing. Faith is of greater value for it will endure longer than creation. The testing of faith will **result in praise and glory and honor** (v. 7) when Jesus returns. Peter had seen Jesus; his readers had not (v. 8). Nevertheless, through God's working, his readers loved Him. Through faith in the risen Christ, they rejoiced with **joy inexpressible and full of glory**, experiencing a taste of heaven on earth. Trials are normal on earth; one day promised **salvation** will be realized (v. 9).

1:10-12. Peter lingers over the word **salvation** and the OT **prophets** who marveled over God's **grace** (v. 10). The prophets **made careful searches and inquiries** because they did not understand who would fulfill the predictions or when He would come (**what person or time**). Yet they did understand that, through the Holy Spirit's superintendence, they were writing predictions about the future Messiah's **sufferings . . . and the glories to follow** (v. 11). Sufferings had to come before glory. The prophets also understood they were not writing these things for themselves (v. 12), but for those who would follow many years later. **The gospel** was declared, accompanied by the Spirit's work (cf. 1:2). This **salvation** is something the **angels long to look** into. Unfallen angels do not need salvation; fallen angels (demons) are confirmed in wickedness. They learn about salvation by observing earthly believers.

III. Conduct Before God (1:13–2:12)

A. Holiness (1:13-16)

1:13-16. Peter's message has been brief, but he turns to application (v. 13). In light of what

God has done, how does this affect relationships? He first comments on relationships of believers and God. **Prepare** (lit., "gird") **your minds for action** pictures serious reflection. Men anticipating strenuous actions would take the bottom of their long-flowing robes and tuck them into their belts. "Let's roll up our sleeves," might be equivalent today. The believer must be **sober in spirit**, or morally alert. Furthermore he must **fix [his] hope completely on the grace** coming with Jesus, a sure hope. A Hebraism, **obedient children** (v. 14), admonishes readers to be "children of obedience," not **conformed** (cf. Rm 12:2) to their former lusts that sprang from ignorance. But, like **the Holy One who called [them]** (v. 15), they should be holy. Peter appeals to Scriptures: **YOU SHALL BE HOLY, FOR I AM HOLY** (v. 16; cf. Lv 11:44; 19:2; 20:7). True devotion to God is expressed in holy living.

B. Love (1:17-25)

1:17-21. In this new relationship with God, their father and judge, believers must **conduct [themselves] with fear** (v. 17), a healthy reverence. There was great cost in salvation, having nothing to do with **perishable** ("the ability to decay" or "rot") **things like silver or gold** (v. 18). The cost was the **precious** (suggesting something of great value, something highly esteemed) **blood** of Jesus, like a **lamb unblemished and spotless** (v. 19), an allusion to the Passover lamb (Ex 12:1-13). This was God's plan **before the foundation of the world** (v. 20), which demonstrates that mankind has nothing to do with the plan God has chosen to put into effect. If this plan was conceived in the mind of God before the foundation of the world, God would have no one to consult with except Himself. However, this plan—including salvation for mankind—was not effected until Jesus appeared. He died but God raised Him from the dead, returning Him to heaven, where the believer's hope is fixed (v. 21).

1:22-25. Since Peter's readers have responded in saving faith, a change has occurred in their lives. Peter pictures their souls as having been **purified** ("to be set apart," "to consecrate" is the sense). One result of this consecration must be unqualified **love** (v. 22). By loving surrounding individuals, that quality is best demonstrated. This love must be **sincere**, not pretended, and fervent, used of competing athletes straining every muscle. The readers had been **born again** (v. 23; cf. 1:3) through an **imperishable** seed, **the living and enduring word of God**. Isaiah 40:6-8 was written originally to encourage the Jewish people that God would enable them to return to their land after the Babylonian exile, and that His promise would be fulfilled. The promise made through Isaiah would be equally encouraging for Peter's audience who were also in exile (see 1Pt 1:1), and that as persecuted Jewish believers, they were promised not only that their salvation was certain, but that they too would some day be restored to their land. This would surely take place because **THE WORD OF THE LORD ENDURES FOREVER. WORD** (v. 25) is the Greek *rhema*, an uttered word, which had been **preached** to Peter's readers.

C. Growth (2:1-8)

2:1-3. Believers do not live in isolation. If they are to love those around them (cf. 1:22), some behaviors must be put aside. **Putting aside** (v. 1) pictures the removal of a coat, the tense (aorist) implying a definite act. Qualities to be removed include **all malice**, a word implying all kinds of evil conduct. **All** (every form of) **deceit and hypocrisy and envy** must be shed. **Deceit** is a fishing term, "to bait the hook"; not surprising considering Peter's profession. **Hypocrisy and envy** are forms of deceit. **Hypocrisy** originated in the theatre where actors spoke behind masks. Audiences never saw the actor's actual face, only the face on the mask that was required for the show. **All slander** must be removed. One obsessed with envy often slanders the one he envies. Instead Peter exhorts, **like newborn babies, long for the pure milk of the word, so that . . . you may grow in respect to salvation** (v. 2). This does not necessarily mean Peter's readers were recent converts. All believers' desire for continued growth should be like that of a newborn. **Long for** is used of the deer "panting" for water brooks (LXX Ps 41:1 [English translations 42:1]; see also Rm 15:23; 2Co 7:7). The believer has **tasted the kindness of the Lord** (v. 3; cf. Ps 34:8) through responding to the gospel; he matures by feeding on the word.

2:4-8. Peter continues his allusion to Ps 34, which calls for the faithful to draw near to the Lord to enjoy fellowship, so Peter emphasizes the importance of **coming to Him** (Jesus) (v. 4). Christ is **a living stone** because He was raised from the dead. Not all accept Him, but in God's sight He is **precious** (highly esteemed). Those who recognize Jesus are united in a **spiritual house** becoming **a holy priesthood** (v. 5). Jesus said He would build (same verb as v. 5) His church (cf. the comments on Mt 16:18): not an earthly building, but the worldwide invisible body with Him as head (cf. 1Co 12:12-13; Eph 4:4; Col 1:18). Everyone in that body functions as a priest. **Spiritual sacrifices** are offered **through Jesus Christ** by this priesthood, which will be accepted. This was foreseen and ordained by God. Peter cites several passages using the stone metaphor (vv. 6-8; cf. Is 8:14, 28:16, and Ps 118:22). Those believing in Jesus hold Him in highest honor (**precious value**). Those who refuse to believe find this stone to be an instrument of judgment. Since they did not believe, God ordained they would experience His appointed judgment (cf. Mt 21:42-46 where Jesus quoted this same psalm and applied it to the chief priests and Pharisees who were rejecting Him). See the comments on Rm 9:14-23 for the possibility that God predestines those who are condemned.

D. Praise (2:9-12)

2:9-12. Unlike those who are rejected by God (see 2:8), Peter's readers are **A CHOSEN RACE** (v. 9), probably referring to Jewish believers; a **royal PRIESTHOOD**, a function no longer related to one tribe. They are a **HOLY NATION**, a set apart group, a **PEOPLE FOR God's OWN POSSESSION**. Many scholars claim that this verse indicates that the Church replaces Israel in God's program, that the Church is the "New Israel," and that ethnic Israel has significance in God's plans only as it is incorporated into the Church that replaces Israel. But Peter is writing primarily to Jewish believers, and these terms are perfectly suitable for the present remnant of Israel, for Jewish believers during the current Church Age. This terminology pertains to redeemed ethnic Israel, not to Gentiles becoming part of Israel by virtue of being in the Church, and cannot be used to support replacement theology. Some things have value because of their owner. God's purpose is for believers to **proclaim the excellencies of Him who has called you out of darkness into His marvelous light**. God's **excellencies** are His virtues, His eminent qualities, which are to be reflected through believers. They were alienated from God, but through mercy (cf. 1:3) they are members of His family (v. 10). As **aliens and strangers**, these Jewish believers who were dispersed should live to bring praise to God. This will occur as readers **abstain** (hold back) from **fleshly lusts** (v. 11), a term referring to desires from man's corrupt nature, desires that fight against man's soul. Positively, Peter urges these Jewish believers to keep their **behavior excellent among the** pagan **Gentiles** (v. 12). **Excellent** implies being "good" or "honest." A good paraphrase would be "winsome." Even a winsome believer might be slandered as an evildoer. But a final accounting is coming, a **day of visitation**, when evildoers will acknowledge the truthful character of believers they have maligned.

IV. Conduct Before Men (2:13–4:19)

A. The Christian and Government (2:13-17)

2:13-17. In light of all God has done (cf. 1:3-12), there are practical implications affecting believers' earthly relationships. First, Peter mentions civil authority. The biblical principle is believers must **submit** to ("rank oneself under") **every human institution** (v. 13). This is done **for the Lord's sake**. Peter could be remembering Jesus' example. As man He always submitted to authority. One also submits to authority because it has been ordained by God (see the comments on Rm 13:1-7). **The punishment of evildoers and the praise of those who do right** (v. 14) is government's God-ordained task. Because of evil, governments do not carry out these mandates perfectly. By submitting to authority the believer **may silence the ignorance of foolish men** (v. 15). There will be no fuel for their fiery criticisms. When believers act responsibly toward civil authority, they are acting freely, remembering they are God's bondslave (v. 16). Nevertheless, the exception to this principle is found in Ac 5:29: When the authorities require disobedience to God, the believer has no alternative but to "obey God rather than men." Verse 17 is a fitting motto: all people should be honored, brothers in Christ should be loved with God's love, God is to be reverenced, and the land's highest ruler honored for his position.

B. The Christian and Business (2:18-25)

2:18-20. Peter addresses **servants** (*oiketes*), meaning "a domestic slave," one involved in the most degrading, galling kind of service. His instruction is to **be submissive . . . with all respect** (v. 18). This attitude is demanded toward masters who are **good and gentle** as well as those who are **unreasonable**, or difficult. To demonstrate this attitude finds favor with God and man (v. 19). Responding patiently when wrongly treated is impossible unless one has been changed internally (v. 20).

2:21-25. The best illustration of one treated unjustly is Jesus (v. 21). His example inspires any believer who is being unfairly treated. Jesus

COMMITED NO SIN, NOR WAS ANY DECEIT FOUND IN HIS MOUTH (v. 22). It is interesting that although Peter had walked with Jesus for approximately three years, when it came to describing His unjust treatment, Peter thought of the passage from Isaiah (the suffering Servant from Is 52:13–53:12). He did not use his own words to describe Jesus' treatment, but resorted to quoting the prophet. Jesus did not retaliate when He was mistreated, and those who have been saved by His death should do the same. He did not respond to those falsely accusing Him. He entrusted His case to the One **who judges righteously**, the Father (v. 23). Jesus' sufferings did not result from His own sin; He **bore our sins in His body on the cross** (v. 24). His death resulted in the removal of sin from believers because He stood in the believer's place (on dying **to sin and** living **to righteousness**, see the comments on Rm 6:1-14). The gain for His followers came through His suffering and death. Followers of Jesus are now united under a shepherd who cares and guards them as His sheep.

C. The Christian and Family (3:1-7)

3:1-6. The submission of the servant (cf. 2:18-25) is commanded of wives toward believing and unbelieving husbands. Peter emphasizes unbelieving husbands, for he says they might be **disobedient to the word** (v. 1). This individual may be won to the Lord through the wife's godly living (v. 2), rather than her words. The wife is encouraged to avoid inappropriate preoccupation with appearance, like **braiding the hair, and wearing gold jewelry, or putting on** [gaudy or extravagant] **dresses** (v. 3). The emphasis should rest on less superficial things, such as **the hidden person of the heart** (v. 4). The former qualities fail; the latter never diminish and are precious to God. Peter cites **Sarah** from Genesis as one who followed this principle (vv. 5-6). Abraham was not the greatest husband, twice creating lies about his relationship with Sarah. But she demonstrated her hope in God by showing respect for her husband's authority. To follow Sarah's example puts one in her train.

3:7. Peter admonishes husbands to **live with [their] wives in an understanding way.** There is no indication the wife might be an unbeliever. Peter encourages husbands to work hard at understanding their wives, an admonition requiring time and energy. A wife should never be viewed merely as a sexual object, but there must be broader understanding. A godly husband will seek to understand his wife's moods, feelings, needs, fears, and hopes. He will listen to her with his heart, demonstrate love, and stimulate joy. The phrase **weaker** vessel is interpreted in different ways, but perhaps Peter was reminding husbands that wives are (usually) physically weaker than their husbands and should be assisted by them when needed, but also that some wives can be broken by the pressures and responsibilities of life (although this happens to some men also). Most likely, he is calling on husbands to be understanding of their wives weaker position as the ones called to submit to them. Moreover, husbands must give their wives greater honor as **fellow heir[s] of the grace of life** (cf. Gl 3:28). This means men are to recognize the spiritual equality of their wives. Husbands who fail to honor their wives will find their prayers being hindered. Since they are failing to honor their wives properly, perhaps the sense of guilt keeps them from praying as they should, or possibly God will not answer the prayers of men who disobey Him by not caring for their wives.

D. The Christian and Society (3:8-22)

3:8-12. Peter continues with general exhortations, loosely based on the theme of submission in 2:13–3:7. Believers should be sympathetic toward fellow believers (v. 8). Sympathy and selfishness cannot coexist. Love that exists among family members should be the practice of the church. Being tenderhearted and humble in spirit keeps relationships strong, leaving no place for evil or insult (v. 9). Blessings should be paramount. To emphasize these qualities, Peter quotes Ps 34:12-16 (vv. 10-12), describing a person who wishes to live a life he can love and find worthwhile. This person must guard his speech, turn from evil, and do what is good by zealously seeking peace. The Lord delights in such a person, but He also sees and judges those who are evil.

3:13-17. Believers will not be free from opposition and hardship. If one suffers **for the sake of righteousness, [he is] blessed** (vv. 13-14). This paradoxical statement reflects the words of Jesus (cf. Mt 5:10-12). **Blessed** does not mean one "feels delighted." It means "to be highly privileged," because one is the object of divine favor (see the comments on Mt 5:1-6). What man can truly harm the believer? Instead of being afraid, the believer should **sanctify Christ as Lord in [his] heart** (v. 15). To "sanctify" (*hagiazo*) means "to consecrate" or "set something apart," but here has the sense "to revere something or someone as holy." When the believer experiences suffering, he must continue to speak boldly on behalf of Christ, out of reverence for Him, rather than be intimidated or TROUBLED by those who persecute believers. He must be more concerned about pleasing Christ than about what men might do. Although this acknowledgement is in the heart, the believer must be ready to speak a word of **defense** (the word *apologia*, a "formal defense," from which is derived the English word "apologetics"). However, the words **always** and **to everyone who asks** make the reference general and comprehensive. It should be remembered that there are direct as well as implied questions. Peter failed when asked for a testimony (cf. Jn 18:17, 25-27). Testimonies must always be given **with gentleness** ("a mildness of attitude and action," its opposite being "harshness") **and reverence** (*phobos*, here meaning "deep respect"). The spirit of a defense may be more important than the words spoken. If the Christian's conduct is consistently good, accusers will often be silenced. But sometimes it is God's will for suffering to occur when one is acting properly (vv. 16-17).

3:18-22. No better illustration of unjust suffering exists than Jesus (v. 18), who suffered concerning **sins once for all** that were not His. He is **the just** One who died for **the unjust** to bring people to God. That He was **put to death in the flesh** suggests violence, but He was **made alive in the spirit**, possibly implying that the Holy Spirit played a part in the resurrection (see the comments on Rm 1:4; 8:11), or the reference might be to Jesus' human spirit. Although both views are possible, the reference is probably to the role of the Holy Spirit in the resurrection of Jesus (Jesus' spirit did not die and thus did not have to be **made alive**). The cooperation of the three persons of the Godhead in all of Jesus' works is thus emphasized. Here Peter begins a long digression, possibly the most difficult NT passage to interpret. Through the agency of the Spirit, Jesus went and made **proclamation to the spirits now in prison**, who are explained in verse 20. They were people who were alive during the 100 years it took Noah to build the ark (cf. Gn 5:32; 7:6). Jesus, with the cooperation of the Holy Spirit, was preaching through Noah, but the testimony was rejected and those people drowned. Now they are **spirits** (disembodied souls) imprisoned awaiting final judgment. The deliverance of Noah's family is seen as a figure of the gospel. Those entering the ark by faith experienced deliverance. Those who today enter Christ by faith find salvation (see 1Pt 1:5, 9). The phrase **Corresponding to that** is often overlooked by those who insist wrongly that baptism is necessary for salvation. Noah and his family correspond to the believers to whom Peter is writing. The waters of the flood in Noah's day manifested God's judgment. They correspond to the waters of baptism, but just as the flood waters saved no one, neither do the waters of baptism (Noah was **brought safely through the water**, v. 20, but was not saved by it). Baptism is a profound figure of escaping God's judgment by being united with Christ in His death and resurrection (see the comments on Rm 6:1-10). By faith Noah entered the ark and the ark rose above the waters of judgment. Peter's believing audience are in Christ by faith (cf. 1:5, 9) and are saved because of His **resurrection** (cf. the mention of resurrection in 1:3, in context with faith in 1:5, 9). Just as Noah was saved by being in the ark, so believers are saved by being *in Christ*, not by baptismal waters. Peter indicates more directly that baptism does not save. The means of salvation is not **the removal of dirt from the flesh** at the moment of baptism, **but an appeal to God for a good conscience**. The **appeal** meant "a pledge," probably the testimony one gives before he is baptized in water. But baptism also pictures resurrection, for the believer in Christ has been raised (cf. Rm 6:4). Peter continues Jesus' history beyond resurrection to His return to heaven. The God-man now sits at the right hand of God, where **angels and authorities** are subject to His control.

E. The Christians' Example (4:1-19)

4:1-6. The lesson from the previous section is Christ suffered **in the flesh** (v. 1). The believer should have the mind of Christ toward suffering. Individuals who stand true to Christ under persecution have not done evil. They saw God's hand performing His will in their lives. Formerly they lived in sinful desires (v. 2), including **sensuality, lusts, drunkenness, carousing, drinking parties, and abominable idolatries** (v. 3). Because they have gone in a new direction, old friends will not appreciate the changes, so the unbelievers malign their former, now saved, friends (v. 4). God will judge both those who are alive and those who are dead (v. 5), though not at the same time. The difference in judgment is the response to the gospel. In v. 6, **for** introduces an expansion of the dead being judged, mentioned in v. 5. The gospel was **preached** in order to save people. To be **judged in the flesh**

as men probably means to suffer physical death as a result of sin in this life, though it may refer to believers who are condemned by unbelievers "according to human estimation or standards" (**as**—lit., "according to"—**men**) for their faith. Those who believed the gospel and subsequently died will nevertheless **live in the spirit** (probably a reference to the Holy Spirit who gives eternal life; cf. the comments on Rm 8:10-11) **according to the will of God**.

4:7-11. The mention of judgment reminded Peter that **the end of all things is near** (v. 7), the expression used by John the Baptist announcing the kingdom (cf. Mt 3:2). Nothing hinders the Lord's return; therefore, believers must be **of sound judgment**, purposeful in **prayer**, and especially **fervent in** [their] **love for one another**. **Fervent** (v. 8) means "unceasing and intense activity," and was sometimes used of athletes straining every muscle to win. Love **covers a multitude of sins**; it stands ready to forgive repeatedly and expresses itself in **hospitality** . . . **without complaint** (v. 9). When some came to faith, family ties were broken. Traveling missionaries needed housing. The use of spiritual gifts (v. 10) is also critical since little time remains. Peter suggests two categories of gifts: speaking gifts and serving gifts. Gifts received (cf. 1Co 12:18-31) should be exercised realizing one is a **steward** [one entrusted with the oversight of the affairs and possessions of another] **of the manifold grace of God**. God has entrusted spiritual gifts to all His people, who must utilize them on His behalf. Speaking gifts must be based upon **the utterances of God** (v. 11), the Scriptures. Serving gifts are performed **by the strength which God supplies**. Regardless of the gifts, the end result is the same: **that in all things God may be glorified. Glory and dominion** belong to Him. If God is not being glorified, ulterior motives must be exposed and removed.

4:12-19. Believers should never be surprised by trials in this world (v. 12). They come to purify believers and are a reflection of **the sufferings of Christ** (v. 13). If the Savior suffered, should believers expect less? When one is **reviled for the name of Christ**, a paradoxical truth emerges—one is **blessed** (v. 14; cf. Mt 5:11) because **the Spirit of glory and of God rests on** [him]. As Jesus was sealed by the Spirit, the people of God suffering for His name are owned as His by a special anointing of the Spirit. As shekinah glory rested on Israel's tabernacle and temple, the Spirit resides in the believer today (cf. 1Co 6:19-20). The believer's suffering must not happen for wrong reasons: **as a murderer, or thief, or evildoer, or a troublesome meddler** (v. 15). One suffering as **a Christian** need not feel ashamed, but should recognize suffering as an opportunity to glorify God (v. 16). This is only one of three times that the term "Christian" occurs in the NT (cf. Ac 11:26; 26:28). Being identified as a "Christian" marks one out as a bearer of the blessings of salvation, for it identifies one as belonging to Jesus Christ. It was probably used by unbelievers in the first century as an insult. Peter believed God's judgment was imminent beginning with His own household, the Church (v. 17). Peter cited Pr 11:31 (v. 18), which indicates that salvation comes with a cost. Judgment for the believer in Jesus Christ speaks of a time following the rapture when regenerated believers will stand before the judgment seat of Jesus Christ (cf. 2Co 5:10; Rm 14:10; possibly 1Co 3:10-17). The purpose of this judgment is to evaluate the works the believer has performed in his life following his conversion to determine possible rewards (cf. 1Co 3:11-15). Any rewards received, such as the crowns mentioned in various passages (cf. 1 Co 9:25; 1Th 2:19; 2Tm 4:7-8; Jms 1:12; 1Pt 5:4), will some day be laid at the Savior's feet (cf. Rv 4:10). If the death of Jesus was expended for the righteous, the final estate of one who rejects God's way and stands under God's judgment can never be expressed adequately. The believer's sufferings are according to the will of God. But he has **entrust[ed]** (a banking term, to deposit funds) his soul to **a faithful Creator** who will do what is right (v. 19). This does not lead to resentment but to confidence.

V. Conduct of the Church (5:1-11)

A. Conduct of the Pastor (5:1-4)

5:1-3. Peter's exhortation is addressed to **elders** (v. 1, *presbyteros*; see the comments on 1Ti 3:1), signifying one who had the spiritual and chronological maturity to lead the church. Peter's admonition comes as a **fellow elder** who witnessed the **sufferings of Christ**. Witnesses are not merely spectators but those who give testimonies. Peter will share with them **the glory that is to be revealed**, a reference to the glory of Jesus that will be manifested to the Church at the time of the rapture. His exhortation is to **shepherd the flock of God among you** (v. 2), tend the flock entrusted to your care. Jesus told Peter three times to care for the flock (cf.

Jn 21:15-17). Such oversight should not be **under compulsion** (feelings of being compelled to do something out of a sense of duty or obligation), **but voluntarily** (a willingness to do something without being compelled to do it) **according to the will of God**. This is the way God acts toward people. His servants must follow His example when leading the church. The elder must always willingly serve, for that is his calling. He must not carry out his responsibilities fearing that if he does not do the job, it will not get done. God has many ways of accomplishing His purposes. Nor should it be **for sordid gain** [shameful, unrestrained greed] **but with eagerness**. The elder must love the sheep, not be interested in monetary profit. Those to whom he ministers have a responsibility as well. They need to remember Paul's words to Timothy (cf. 1Tm 5:17-18; also 1Co 9:9), for the elder should receive a fair wage in light of the responsibilities he is carrying. He must not put himself in the Lord's place, but be one who proves himself an **example to the flock** (v. 3). Sheep must be led, not driven.

5:4. When the Chief Shepherd appears, the elder-shepherd will give an account of his ministry, and this should motivate him to discharge his tasks with joy and enthusiasm. In the ancient world, crowns were given as rewards for victorious achievement. The elder-shepherd who faithfully serves his entrusted flock will be rewarded with **the unfading crown of glory**, a reward coming not from the sheep, but from the Lord Himself (for the concept of rewards, see the comments on Mt 25:21, 23; 1Co 3:10-15; 4:5).

B. Conduct of the People (5:5-11)

5:5. Younger men, probably younger in physical age, are encouraged to **be subject to** [their] **elders**. It is often difficult for younger people to be patient, but respect for age and for a Christian leader is always appropriate. All are admonished to be clothed **with humility toward one another**. "Clothed" is used of Jesus when he girded a towel around His waist and washed the disciples' feet (cf. Jn 13:3-10). One demonstrates humility when he does not think of himself at all. The reason such action is necessary is biblical: **GOD IS OPPOSED TO THE PROUD, BUT GIVES GRACE TO THE HUMBLE** (Pr 3:34; see the comments on Jms 4:10). Pride was the first sin (cf. 1 Tim 3:6) and always prevents humility.

5:6-10. Peter presents several practical exhortations. **Humble yourselves . . . that He may exalt you at the proper time** (v. 6). Deliberate self-subjection should be the believer's practice, realizing God is the sovereign Lord who will exalt the believer in His time (cf. Lk 14:11). This may occur before the people of God in this life, but possibly not until entering eternity. Regardless, God will never lift anyone up if they lack humility. Is it not possible that such humility will cause anxiety as personal rights are surrendered and others are served? In keeping with Ps 55:22, Peter admonishes believers to cast arising anxieties on the Lord (v. 7), for they know He cares for them. In most religions, worshippers must gain the favor of their gods. The believer knows God loves him and promises to care for him.

Sobriety is warranted, however, for an **adversary** (lit., "an opponent in a lawsuit"), **the devil** (lit., "a slanderer" or "accuser"), prowls about **like a roaring lion seeking someone to devour** (v. 8). Satan's purpose is to ruin people, but he may be resisted by one **firm in [his] faith** (v. 9). Jesus resisted the devil using Scripture. Since Peter recognizes that Satan is active today, it seems obvious that the church has not yet entered the full messianic kingdom when Satan will be bound for a thousand years (cf. Rv 20:2-3).

Believers worldwide will suffer; it is not unique to any person. But after suffering, the God of all grace who calls believers will accomplish His purposes (v. 10), including His perfecting, confirming, strengthening, and establishing His children (see the comments on Rm 8:28-30). To **perfect** means "to make something adequate or sufficient for something"; to **confirm** means "to cause someone to become stronger and more steady"; to **strengthen** means "to cause one to become more capable, less weak"; and to **establish** means "to provide a strong base for practice or belief." The promise is that God will strengthen believers while they suffer at the hands of the world and the devil, and in the end He will make all things right in **His eternal glory in Christ**.

5:11. In a concluding doxology (possibly a prayer) Peter says, **To Him be dominion forever and ever. Amen**. The term **dominion** is only used of God in the NT and describes the ability to keep under control, to acquire and retain mastery. Such power belongs to God now and for eternity.

VI. Conclusion (5:12-14)

5:12. Peter refers to **Sylvanus** (possibly Silas), a **faithful brother**, who wrote the manuscript. Whether vv. 12-14 were written by Peter's hand cannot be known. His brief exhortation was written to confirm his readers' faith and hope in God, so they would stand firm in His grace.

5:13. He mentions two individuals with him: **she** and **Mark**, usually thought to be his wife and John Mark, author of the second gospel. **Babylon** probably represents a figure understood by Christians but unknown among unbelievers should this letter fall into the wrong hands. Church tradition says Peter died in Rome. John may have used this figure for Rome (but see the comments on Rv 14:6-20). Perhaps before Peter's death Rome had become known by that symbol of a luxurious city given over to pagan idol worship.

5:14. With a final admonition of love, **a kiss**, Peter encourages believers to express their affection and good will toward others within the body. The kiss was a sign of unity and love. **Peace be to you all who are in Christ** reflects a Hebrew benediction. True peace is only possible for those in Christ. Apart from Him no one enjoys the blessing Peter describes in this epistle.

BIBLIOGRAPHY

Blum, Edwin H. "1 Peter." In *The Expositors Bible Commentary*, Vol. 12, edited by Frank E. Gaebelein. Grand Rapids, MI: Zondervan, 1981.

Clowney, Edmund P. *The Message of 1 Peter.* Bible Speaks Today. Downers Grove, IL: InterVarsity, 1989.

Davids, Peter H. *The First Epistle of Peter.* New International Commentary on the New Testament. Grand Rapids, MI: Eerdmans, 1990.

Goppelt, Leonhard. *A Commentary on 1 Peter*. Grand Rapids, MI: Eerdmans, 1993.

Grudem, Wayne A. *The First Epistle of Peter.* Tyndale New Testament Commentaries. Grand Rapids, MI: Eerdmans, 1988.

Hiebert, D. Edmond. *1 Peter*. Winona Lake, IN: Brethren Missionary Herald, 2002.

Kelly, J. N. D. *Commentary on the Epistles of Peter and Jude.* Harper's New Testament Commentaries. Peabody, MA: Hendrickson, 1969.

MacArthur, John. *1 Peter.* MacArthur New Testament Commentary. Chicago: Moody, 2004.

Marshall, I. Howard. *1 Peter.* InterVarsity Press New Testament Commentary. Downers Grove, IL: InterVarsity, 1990.

McKnight, Scot. *1 Peter.* NIV Application Commentary. Grand Rapids, MI: Zondervan, 1996.

Schreiner, Thomas. *1 Peter.* New American Commentary. Nashville: Broadman & Holman, 2003.

● ● ● ●

2 PETER

LOUIS BARBIERI

INTRODUCTION

Author. While no NT book has any stronger external attestation for authorship than 1 Peter, 2 Peter probably has the weakest in the entire NT canon. There are early allusions to the book by church fathers such as Justin Martyr, Irenaeus, Ignatius, and Clement of Rome. The first person to connect Peter's name with this letter is Origen (c. 250), and he says it is disputed. However external evidence for authorship was often weak on shorter epistles.

Internally a number of things point to Peter as the best candidate for authorship. Certainly no forger would deviate from the known greeting of a recognized Petrine letter (1 Peter), but at the beginning of this letter the author refers to himself as "Simon Peter." The author knows many facts about Peter's life (cf. 1:16-18) that are confirmed by gospel accounts (cf. Mk 9:2-8; Mt 17:1-8; and Lk 9:28-36). The author also is anticipating his imminent death (1:13-15) as he said was prophesied (cf. Jn 21:18-19). The writer seems familiar with the writings of the apostle Paul and with Paul himself (3:15-16). The reference to a first epistle (3:1) and the similarity with 1 Peter in subject matter (issues like eschatology, the flood, and Christian liberty) all lead to the conclusion that the same individual wrote both epistles.

Why do some object to the Petrine authorship of 2 Peter? Some believe that the similarity to the book of Jude demonstrates that a forger simply borrowed his material from Jude. It seems clear however that 2 Peter precedes Jude. 2 Peter says false teachers will be coming into the church (2:1) but Jude says they are in the church (Jd 3-4). Others believe the author "slipped" in 3:2 and failed to include himself in the apostolic circle when he referred to "your apostles." But the author's wording does not demand that interpretation; furthermore he calls himself an "apostle of Jesus Christ" in 1:1.

The differences in writing style between the two epistles cannot be denied. However mention is made of an amanuensis, Sylvanus, who assisted Peter with writing the first letter (cf. 1Pt 5:12). No mention of assistance is found in the second letter. Perhaps the second letter is more characteristic of Peter's true Galilean Greek.

Finally, some critics say the author is too eager to connect himself to Peter the apostle because of his many references to Jesus Christ. However, how many references are too many? If the writer had never mentioned Jesus or only mentioned Him a few times, critics would have rejected the authorship because of the few references. Despite the objections the best conclusion on authorship is that the same individual, Simon Peter, wrote both of the letters that commonly bear his name in the NT.

Date. Several factors must be kept in mind when a date for the writing of 2 Peter is suggested. If indeed the apostle Peter wrote this book, he stated that he believed his death was imminent (2Pt 1:13-15). The reference to this being the second letter he was writing to the same group (3:1) and his familiarity with the apostle Paul and his letters (3:15-16) would imply the passing of time. In light of all this, a date in either AD 67 or 68 would be acceptable.

Recipients. Because of the mention of a second letter in 3:1, it is generally concluded that this letter was sent to the same group of people who received Peter's First Epistle. Therefore this letter was sent primarily to Jewish believers in the Dispersion (the Diaspora), scattered throughout what we know as modern-day Turkey.

Purpose. The statement in 2Pt 3:17-18 leads to the conclusion that his purpose in this letter is twofold: first to warn against false teachers and second to encourage spiritual growth.

OUTLINE

I. Introduction (1:1-2)
 A. The Author (1:1a)
 B. The Addressees (1:1b)
 C. The Greeting (1:2)
II. Characteristics of the Christian Life (1:3-21)
 A. The Initiation (1:3-4)
 B. The Continuation (1:5-11)
 C. The Proclamation (1:12-21)
III. Caution in the Christian Life (2:1-22)
 A. The Features of the False Teachers (2:1-3)
 B. Old Testament Figures Applied to the False Teachers (2:4-9)
 C. The Future of the False Teachers (2:10-22)
IV. Confidence in the Christian Life (3:1-16)
 A. Peter's Aim (3:1-2)
 B. Peter's Admonition (3:3-7)
 C. Peter's Assurance (3:8-16)
V. Conclusion (3:17-18)

COMMENTARY ON 2 PETER

I. Introduction (1:1-2)

A. The Author (1:1a)

1:1a. The unique signature, **Simon Peter**, argues for authenticity. No forger would alter the known introduction of 1 Peter. Peter could have begun any way he chose. He called himself **a bond-servant** (Gk. *doulos*) **and apostle**, demonstrating humility and showing the authority to write this letter.

B. The Addressees (1:1b)

1:1b. This letter is written to believers who have a **faith** that comes about through **the righteousness of our God and Savior, Jesus Christ**, including the first letter's recipients (cf. 3:1). **Faith** in this verse is without an article implying it might be the content of faith (cf. Jd 3) or the believer's saving faith in Jesus Christ. The latter is preferable since Peter was talking about faith that comes through our God and Savior, one person, not two, Jesus Christ.

C. The Greeting (1:2)

1:2. This greeting is identical with 1 Peter. Inserting **knowledge** is significant, for Peter was writing to people who claimed real knowledge. Experiencing God's grace and peace is dependent on **the knowledge** about **God**. As the believer gains knowledge, grace and peace are multiplied in his life.

II. Characteristics of the Christian Life (1:3-21)

A. The Initiation (1:3-4)

1:3-4. The writer presents an appeal for holy living based on the readers' calling. **Divine power** has been given, not earned, and it supplies all that is needed for godliness. This comes through the calling of Jesus Christ, who is God's **glory and excellence**. The person of Jesus attracts; His power produces response. **Precious . . . promises** have been given to believers, including the promise of becoming partakers of **the divine nature**. Believers do not become God, but they possess the righteousness that comes from God (see the comments on Rm 1:17; 3:21-26) and share fellowship with the godhead, enabling them to escape the world's **corruption** caused **by lust**.

B. The Continuation (1:5-11)

1:5-7. Having begun a new life in Christ, Peter admonished his readers to equip themselves with specific virtues of the Christian life that started with **faith** (v. 5) and continues with faithful daily dependence on God. The grace of God demands **diligence** ("doing one's best") as believers grow. It leads to **moral excellence** (cf. 1:3), a Greek word used of that which fulfilled its designated purpose. But the Christian life is more than faith and practical goodness. There is also **knowledge**, which Christians need not fear, for truth will lead to understanding. Next is **self-control**, a Greek word meaning "to control the passions," which follows when believers submit to the control of the indwelling Spirit. From self-control springs **perseverance**, the ability to endure difficult things. To perseverance is added **godliness** or reverence toward God and fellow men. This leads to **brotherly kindness**, the outworking of the previous quality (cf. 1 Jn 4:20). The crowning Christian progress is **love** (Gk. *agape*), a deliberate desire for the highest good in the one loved (see the comments on 1Co 13:1-3).

1:8-11. The believer with true knowledge of Christ should possess these fruitful qualities. One who refuses to grow is blind, having purposefully forgotten his forgiveness. In a call for zeal, Peter encouraged his readers to pursue their calling, a beautiful blending of God's sovereign call and the believer's responsibility. Christian calling and Christian living go together. As one's calling is confirmed, two results follow. First he **will never stumble** (v. 10), a metaphor picturing a horse's surefootedness. Since Peter denied his Lord, and yet he was restored (cf. Jn 21:15-17), perhaps he means the believer will never fall in such a way as to lose his salvation. Instead the believer will finally achieve his lifelong goal, entrance into the Savior's **eternal kingdom** (v. 11). While salvation is never by works, the believer who pursues the course Peter outlined (cf. vv. 5-6) anticipates an especially glorious meeting with his Savior in heaven (cf. 2Tm 4:7-8, 18; Ac 7:56).

C. The Proclamation (1:12-21)

1:12-15. To produce growth, believers need information. Peter sensed a responsibility to **remind** his readers of things he had learned, truths they knew but had not recently considered. Christians **established in the truth** (v. 12) can lapse into serious sin and error. That is why Peter wanted to **stir . . . up** their memory. This was his solemn duty, though he knew his death was **imminent** (v. 14) as revealed by the Lord (cf. Jn 21). Peter was working so that after his **departure** his knowledge would be available. That Peter preached in many cities including Rome is well documented. His public ministry was greatly appreciated. But there is also testimony from church history that he spent time in the last years of his life working with John Mark (see Introduction on Mark). He could possibly here be referring especially to Mark, who ministered with him (cf. 1Pt 5:13), but without excluding what he was writing to his readers as well. The second gospel (Mark's) is often called "The Gospel According to Peter." Peter was filling Mark with his recollections of Jesus. The process of writing that gospel may have already started, but certainly following Peter's death, there would have been a clamor within the church to make sure Peter's remembrances of Jesus Christ and his teachings were written down.

1:16-21. These truths needed to be preserved because they were not fables. Peter was an **eyewitness** of Jesus' **majesty** at the transfiguration (cf. the comments on Mt 16:28–17:8) when His glory was revealed and God spoke: **This is My beloved Son with whom I am well pleased** (v. 17). That Peter did not give the complete spoken statement is another argument for authenticity. No forger would have changed the complete statement known from the gospels. Through this **the prophetic word** (v. 19) was confirmed, or brought into clearer focus. For the disciples, Scriptures never originated as the product of human will (the likely meaning of **one's own interpretation** [v. 20; i.e., the visions did not originate with, nor derive their meanings from, the prophets; cf. the NIV, NET, TNIV). Instead, men **spoke** God's revelation as they were **moved** ("carried along," "driven in a certain direction") **by the Holy Spirit**. Paul said Scripture was "breathed out" by God (see the comments on 2Tm 3:16). In the process, the writers were directed by the Spirit so that the choice of their words formed exactly the message that God wanted communicated. A Christian's faith is not based upon **cleverly devised tales** (v. 16) but on revelation from the Spirit conveyed through the prophets (vv. 20-21) and eventually recorded in Scripture.

III. Caution in the Christian Life (2:1-22)

A. The Features of the False Teachers (2:1-3)

2:1-3. With a drastic change of tone, Peter gave stern warnings against heretical teachings entering the church. That **false teachers** would come is not surprising, as they had arisen **among the people** of Israel in the past (v. 1). **Destructive heresies** come, the worst being denial of the Lord who accomplished redemption. The results are that they bring **swift destruction upon themselves** (v. 1), lead others away, and discredit the Christian cause (v. 2). In their **greed** they exploit **many**. But God's judgment will fall. While these false teachers arise **among the people** and **among you**, God is able to distinguish between genuine and counterfeit teachers, as well as genuine and counterfeit believers—an important point in determining the identity of those in 2:20-22 who apostatize. They are not genuine believers. Since they were not believers, their denial of the Lord **who bought them** indicates that the Messiah's redemptive death made provision not just for the elect but even for the lost. The fact that Jesus' death has "bought" all men does not mean all men will be regenerated. It is not until an individual places his faith in Christ's provision on the cross on his behalf that the accomplishment of Christ's work is applied in him.

B. Old Testament Figures Applied to the False Teachers (2:4-9)

2:4-9. Genesis is cited, demonstrating while God's certain judgment punishes sin, He remembers His own. One illustration is the **angels** who sinned, possibly when they followed Lucifer (cf. Is 14; Ezk 28; Rv 12:4). However these angels have been **cast . . . into hell** (the verb *tartaroo*), from which they never escape, indicating that this verse cannot describe the origin of demons, for none of these angels ever leaves Tartarus. Peter was probably thinking of Gn 6 when the sons of God cohabited with the daughters of men (see the comments on Gn 6:1-4). The point is clear: God punishes sin. A second illustration is **the ancient world** in the days of **Noah**. God delivered eight people but destroyed everything else. Judgment is certain, but He cared for His own. Finally **Sodom and Gomorrah** are mentioned with the rescue of **Lot** (vv. 7-8), who was **oppressed by the sensual conduct of unprincipled men**. Second Peter presents facts not found elsewhere. Lot was **tormented** by his surroundings, yet he remained in Sodom. Peter may have been implying that Lot was God's witness to that city, and that Lot was distinct from those who lived in the wicked city. Just as God **rescued . . . Lot**, distinguishing him from the unrighteous with whom he lived, so God will rescue His people and distinguish them from the false teachers whose end is unenviable (cf. the comments on 2:17-22). His conclusion is **the Lord knows how to rescue the godly** (illustrated by His deliverance of Noah's family and Lot) **from temptation**, and **to keep the unrighteous under punishment for the day of judgment** (as in the case of the demons, the wicked world, and Sodom and Gomorrah).

C. The Future of the False Teachers (2:10-22)

2:10-13a. False teachers are under God's providential control. They **indulge the flesh** (see Peter's development of this characteristic in vv. 13b-16) and **despise authority** (developed in vv. 10b-13a). One of the ways their scorn for **authority** is observed is by their disdain for **angelic majesties** (lit., "glories" or "glorious ones," a reference to evil angelic beings that are fallen but still give evidence of God's creative power). Not even the good **angels** (v. 11), who are superior to the evil angels, denounce the fallen angels. This serves to indicate the extraordinary arrogance of the false teachers. They are like brute beasts following their passions (v. 12). They will be destroyed. Their lives will rob them, not pay them a reward. They receive a reward, but not the expected one (v. 13a). They sow unrighteousness; they will reap the same.

2:13b-16. Here Peter developed the theme of the false teachers' indulgence of the flesh introduced in 2:10a. Going against societal norms, false teachers practice reveling in daylight hours (v. 13b). They are **stains and blemishes** on the world viewing individuals as sexual objects (v. 14). Their lusts are never satisfied; they are slaves to sin. They have trained themselves in unbridled desires seeking more things. They are viewed as **accursed children**, a Hebraism meaning "children whose mother was a curse." Peter was not being vindictive but descriptive. They have come under God's curse, deliberately forsaking the right way, following **the way of Balaam** (v. 15), the Gentile prophet hired to curse Israel. He loved the wages of unrighteousness. His primary concern was his pay (cf. 1 Pt 5:2), but his counsel was godless. He encouraged the Moabites to enter into physical relationships with the Israelites, thus bringing immorality into the Jewish nation. False teachers were guilty of the same, for their preoccupation with things sexual was continuing to bring ruin to their followers (cf. v 13).

2:17-22. While vv. 10-16 describe the characteristics of false teachers, Peter began to describe their destructive influence upon others in vv. 17-22. They are **springs without water and mists driven by a storm** (v. 17), pictures of empty profession and parched lives. What good is a spring without water, or a promising storm producing no rain? False teachers promise **freedom** from moral restraints (v. 19) to new converts who have **barely escape[d]** their pagan backgrounds (v. 18) and do not know any better. Ironically, the false teachers themselves are **enslaved** by **corruption**. Their words are deceptive. The pronoun **they** in v. 20 has its closest antecedent in the false teachers in v. 19, not the victims of their deception. Because false teachers have some **knowledge of the Lord**, they have **escaped the defilements of the world** much as Christians have (see the similar terms in 1:3-4 for true believers). While they are similar in many ways to true believers, Peter noted that they are distinct from them (see the comments on 2:1, 4-9 above), and that God knows the difference between the two. He will rescue the truly righteous (see 2:7-9) but judge those who are false. Their "religious" associations have given them an air of spirituality, producing an escape from some of the corrupting influences of the world. However, consistent lifelong growth (cf. 1:5-11) is absent. Instead the false teachers become entangled again in the world's defilements, resulting in a worse state (both greater moral corruption and eschatological judgment, 2:4-10; and cf. Jesus' words, Mt 12:45ff.). Ignorance of the way of righteousness is preferable to apostasy from it. Christianity became known as **the way** (v. 21). Knowing **the way** but turning from it brings serious consequences. Scriptures suggest there will be degrees of punishment for the wicked. While all will be separated from God, those with rejected knowledge will suffer greater condemnation. Two "proverbs" (cf. Pr 26:11) describe false teachers, showing they will be given over to their chosen lot (v. 22). The **DOG** has removed internal corruption only to return to it. The pig has been washed, but returns to the **mire**. Peter devoted many words to false teachers. He was clearly concerned about those masquerading in religious garb who were leading astray new converts.

IV. Confidence in the Christian Life (3:1-16)

A. Peter's Aim (3:1-2)

3:1-2. Peter returned to the **beloved**, saying this is his **second letter**. He was writing reminding them of things heard from **the holy prophets** and Jesus' words communicated through the **apostles.**

B. Peter's Admonition (3:3-7)

3:3-6. Mockers will come (v. 3) denying the Lord's return (v. 4). These individuals live self-indulgent lives asking, **Where is the promise of His coming?** They believe the universe is unchanging, so Christ's return is impossible. Peter's answer is they have willingly forgotten a cataclysmic event, when **the world at that time was destroyed, being flooded with water** (v. 6, cf. Gn 6–8). The "unchanging" world was radically changed.

3:7. Present creation has been preserved, awaiting a different judgment. The world was destroyed by the word of God through water. Another judgment will occur **by His word** through fire, the destruction of the universe (cf. 3:12).

C. Peter's Assurance (3:8-16)

3:8-10. The delay in the Lord's coming is a problem only from the human perspective. God and men look at time differently. The phrases **one day is like a thousand years, and a thousand years like one day** (v. 8) reflect Ps 90:4. God views time with a perspective humans lack. For people time sometimes flies, and sometimes it drags. While it appears God is working slowly, God is never **slow about His promise** (v. 9). His delay should be viewed as an illustration of patience. God takes no pleasure in the death of the wicked, but in mercy He gives **you** time to repent. In the context, **you** refers not to people in general but to believers (see the occurrences of second person plural verbs and pronouns, as a reference to believers, in 3:1, 2, 8), providing sufficient time for those chosen for salvation to come to faith before they die or before His coming. The sense of v. 9 is thus: God is "patient toward you, not wishing for any *of you* (God's chosen) to perish but for all *of you* to come to repentance."

But like the unexpected arrival of the destroying water, the day of the Lord **will come like a thief** (see the comments on Mt 24:36-41; 1Th 5:1-4). As that day proceeds, the earth and its works will be consumed **with intense heat** (cf. 3:7). Some scholars contend that the day of the Lord will cause the burning of this earth, which will then be replaced by the new heavens and new earth. They also note that there is no mention of a millennial kingdom and claim that this passage refutes the notion. In response, it is true that Peter excludes any explicit mention of the millennial kingdom, but it is an argument from silence to say that there is no such thing. The following argues in favor of a future millennial kingdom: (1) Peter's omission of the unambiguous mention of the millennial kingdom was a result of his conflating the end-time events, presenting a simple panorama of the end without every detail included. The prophets commonly compressed events in this way. (2) The millennial kingdom is implicit in this text by use of the phrase **the day of the Lord**. This **day** brings this world to a close and, according to the OT, contains the idea of a messianic kingdom within it (see the references below). There are two parts to **the day of the Lord**: It has an evening, which is the time of judgment, known prophetically as the great tribulation period (cf. Jl 2:1-2; Am 5:18-20; Zph 1:14-15; 1Th 5:1-11), and it has a day that follows it, a time of profound worldwide blessing (Jl 3:17-21; Zch 14:6-9), which is the one-thousand-year reign of Messiah Jesus on this earth that follows the tribulation. When **the day of the Lord** is complete, i.e., when the millennial kingdom is complete, this world will be destroyed by fire. (3) Peter has presented a simple, panoramic, end-time scenario, without explicit mention of the millennium because his emphasis has been on what has lasting value. The millennium will come to a close (see the comments on 1Co 15:20-28), but the new heavens and the new earth will last forever.

3:11-16. Peter's application demonstrates a link between what one believes and how one lives. What effect should these events have on believers? These should not lead to apathy or despair, but to an expectant hope of the Lord's coming. When that day arrives, there will be a new beginning, as promised (cf. 1:4; Is 65:17ff.; 66:22). The present heavens and earth will be destroyed with **intense heat** so that the **new heavens** and **earth** can appear (v. 12; see the comments on Rv 21:1ff.). There righteousness will dwell. Since only righteousness will survive, believers are encouraged to live righteously and be found by God in **peace, spotless and blameless** (v. 14). These are characteristics a true believer should demonstrate and that will mark him in clear contrast to unbelievers who live ungodly lives. The delay in the Lord's coming is His way of giving men time to come to **salvation** (v. 15). These ideas were also presented in Paul's letters. That Peter called Paul **our beloved brother** demonstrated his love for Paul. They did not always agree (cf. the comments on Gl 2:11-14), but Peter recognized in Paul's writings scriptural authority. Some of Paul's writings were **hard to understand** (v. 16), a sentiment shared by every NT student and scholar today. Untaught, unstable individuals were twisting Paul's teachings, as they did also **the rest of the Scriptures, to their own destruction**. Clearly Peter acknowledged Paul's words as "Scripture."

V. Conclusion (3:17-18)

3:17. The recipients of this letter have been warned about false teaching by Peter and by Paul in his many epistles, some of which the readers were probably aware. They are responsible to **guard** themselves against the arguments of wicked individuals. Error has many attractive faces, and even experienced believers can be deceived, falling into error.

3:18. Peter concluded as he began—with growth. **Grow**, a present tense imperative verb, could be translated, "make it your habit to always be growing." If one is not growing, he is stagnant. Growth must always be in the **grace and knowledge of our Lord and Savior Jesus Christ**. The more one knows of Christ, the more His grace is invoked. Knowledge of Christ becomes the safeguard against error. Growth is always in direct relationship with time spent in Scripture. A fitting closing is a reminder that glory belongs to Christ. False teachers were seeking glory for themselves, but glory is truly His **both now and to the day of eternity. Amen**.

BIBLIOGRAPHY

Blum, Edwin A. "2 Peter." In Vol. 12 of The Expositor's Bible Commentary, edited by Frank E. Gaebelein, 257–293. Grand Rapids, MI: Zondervan, 1981.

Green, Michael. *The Second Epistle General of Peter and the General Epistle of Jude.* Tyndale New Testament Commentaries. Grand Rapids, MI: Eerdmans, 1968.

Hillyer, Norman. *1 and 2 Peter, Jude.* New International Bible Commentary. Peabody, MA: Hendrickson, 1992.

Kelly, J. N. D. *Commentary on the Epistles of Peter and Jude.* Harper's New Testament Commentaries. Peabody, MA: Hendrickson, 1969.

Kistemaker, Simon. *Exposition of the Epistles of Peter and the Epistle of Jude.* New Testament Commentary. Grand Rapids, MI: Baker, 1987.

Lloyd-Jones, D. Martyn. *Expository Sermons on 2 Peter.* London: Banner of Truth, 1983.

MacArthur, John. *Second Peter and Jude.* MacArthur New Testament Commentary Series. Chicago: Moody, 2005.

Moo, Douglas J. *2 Peter and Jude.* The NIV Application Commentary. Grand Rapids, MI: Zondervan, 1996.

1 JOHN

RONALD SAUER

INTRODUCTION

Author. Although the writer never identified himself by name, he apparently was the apostle John, a view supported by several factors: (1) Tradition—A number of early church leaders attributed this missive to him. (2) Epistolary hints—The writer described himself not merely as one of many eyewitnesses observing Jesus from a distance, but as one who was quite intimate and privileged by unique experiences with Him. He not only heard and observed Jesus, but even touched the Lord with his hands (1:1). (3) Literary style—The limited vocabulary, simple grammar, and theological thought all resemble that found in John's other writings. This apostle's fingerprints are all over 1 John.

Date. First John was likely composed in the city of Ephesus around AD 90–95. According to early church tradition, as an old man John served the church in the city of Ephesus.

Recipients. The letter's last words are "guard yourselves from idols" (5:21). This warning suggests that 1Jn was sent not to Jews but to Gentiles, who resided not in Israel but on heathen soil, such as Ephesus. But it is unlikely this missive was sent only to the church in that city, because it lacks the usual epistolary introduction identifying the author, addressees, and their geographical location. Further, 1Jn ends without the customary request to convey greetings to specified individuals. Besides the name of Jesus Christ, the only other name mentioned is that of Cain (3:12). All this intimates 1Jn to have been a circular letter; that is, it was sent to the church in, and to the churches around, Ephesus—with all of whom the writer enjoyed personal acquaintance.

In 2:26, John informed his readership what prompted him to take pen in hand and record this letter: "These things I have written to you concerning those who are trying to deceive you." He was speaking probably about incipient Gnosticism. Its basic premise saw a sharp dualism between spirit and matter: The spiritual was regarded as divine and good, while the materialistic was deemed created (though not by God) and evil. This fundamental Gnostic premise adversely touched two areas of Christianity: orthodoxy (correct doctrine) and orthopraxis (correct conduct).

Regarding the former, Gnosticism denied the incarnation, for a pure spirit like God could have nothing to do with evil matter, such as a human body. So Gnosticism offered two possible solutions to this problem. Docetic Gnostics denied Jesus' humanity. He only "seemed" to be a human being. This was an attempt to preserve Christ's deity at the expense of His humanity. The other solution was Cerinthian Gnosticism. It maintained the earthly Jesus was nothing more than a human being, upon whom the heavenly "Christ" or "Logos" descended at His baptism but then left Him prior to the cross. This was an attempt to preserve Jesus' humanity at the expense of His deity. With respect to orthopraxis, the Gnostic heresy had an inadequate sense of both sin and moral behavior. Some Gnostics claimed, "we have not sinned" (1:10), and others, "we have no sin" nature (1:8). According to them sin was a matter of the evil flesh, from which they had supposedly been liberated; sin was not a matter affecting the noble spirit, into which their knowledge had allegedly brought them. So moral conduct was an unnecessary issue to discuss.

Purpose. The writer mentioned five objectives for his letter: First, he sought to refute the doctrine and practice of "those who are trying to deceive you" (2:26). Second, because the readers were being influenced by heresy, John said he was writing so his readers might not go on sinning (2:1). Third, to reaffirm apostolic truth, the author intended to proclaim "what we have seen and heard so that you too may have fellowship with us" (1:3). Fourth, by writing these things, he conceded a personal objective, namely, "so that [his] joy may be made complete" (1:4). Fifth and chiefly, he wrote to reassure them of their salvation—"so that you may know that you have eternal life" (5:13).

The genuineness of one's profession (claim) of salvation can be proven or disproven by three tests: (1) The moral test: obeying God's commands. "By this we know that we have come to know Him, if we keep His commandments" (2:3). (2) The social test: loving the brethren. "We know that we have passed out of death into life, because we love the brethren" (3:13). (3) The theological test: accepting the doctrine of the incarnation. "Whoever believes that Jesus is the Christ is born of God" (5:1). Those who had withdrawn from this Christian community (see 2:19) did not embrace any of these three features, indicating that they were not right with God. However, John reassured his recipients that if these things were true of them, *they* were in the right, not the secessionists.

Theme. The theme of 1Jn is the assurance of salvation. John said that he wrote his gospel "so that you may believe that Jesus is the Christ, the Son of God; and that believing you may have life in His name" (Jn 20:31). The purpose of John's gospel was evangelistic—to bring people to saving faith in Christ. In contrast, the major purpose of 1Jn is to provide reassurance to his readers of their salvation—how believers in Christ may know that they, and not the heretics who withdrew from them (see 2:19), have eternal life (5:13). First John is a letter of certainty. Accordingly, the key word is "know," occurring 37 times.

OUTLINE

I. Prologue (1:1-4)
  A. The Contents of John's Message (1:1-2)
  B. The Purpose of John's Letter (1:3-4)
II. Unorthodox Claims Tested by the Thesis of Jesus' Message (1:5–2:2)
  A. The Thesis of Jesus' Message (1:5)
  B. First Unorthodox Claim: Knowing Christ but Living in Sin (1:6-7)
  C. Second Unorthodox Claim: Having No Sinful Nature (1:8-9)
  D. Third Unorthodox Claim: Committing No Sins (1:10–2:2)
III. Three Assurances of Salvation Discussed (2:3-29)
  A. The Moral Assurance: Obeying Indicates One's Spiritual Status (2:3-6)
    1. Obedience Indicates Salvation (2:3)
    2. Disobedience Indicates Lack of Salvation (2:4)
    3. Obedience Leads to Love for God (2:5)
    4. Obedience Leads to Christlikeness (2:6)
  B. The Social Assurance: Love for Christians Indicates Salvation (2:7-17)
    1. Love Indicates One Is in the Light of the New Era (2:7-11)
    2. Those in the New Era Overcome the Sinful Era (2:12-17)
  C. The Theological Assurance: Belief in the Doctrine of the Incarnation (2:18-29)
    1. Heretics Abandoned Belief in the Incarnation (2:18-19)
    2. True Believers Embrace the Truth of the Incarnation (2:20-21)
    3. Heretics Reject the Incarnation (2:21)
    4. Heretics Do Not Have God (2:22-23)
    5. True Believers Must Abide in the Truth (2:24-29)
IV. Three Assurances of Salvation Expanded (3:1–4:6)
  A. The Moral Assurance: Obedience and the Righteous Life (3:1-10)
    1. God's Love and the New Birth (3:1)
    2. Moral Purity and the New Birth (3:2-3)
    3. Moral Impurity and Lawlessness (3:4)
    4. Moral Impurity and Jesus' Work (3:5-10)

a. Believers Have Righteous Behavior (3:5-7)
b. Believers Do Not Sin Like the Devil (3:8)
c. Believers Have God's Seed (3:9-10)
B. The Social Assurance: Loving the Brethren (3:11-24)
1. Believers Love Other Believers (3:11-14)
2. Unbelievers Will Hate Believers (3:15)
3. Believers Sacrifice for Other Believers (3:16-18)
4. Believers Receive Assurance through Love for Other Believers (3:19-24)
C. The Theological Assurance: Holding to the Doctrine of the Incarnation (4:1-6)
1. The Need for Discernment (4:1-4)
2. The Source of Heresy (4:5-6)
V. The Three Assurances of Salvation Integrated (4:7–5:12)
A. The Social Assurance: Loving the Brethren (4:7-21)
1. The Command for Loving Believers (4:7-8)
2. The Example of Loving Believers (4:9-12)
3. The Divine Empowerment for Loving Believers (4:13-16)
4. The Spiritual Development from Loving Believers (4:17-18)
5. The Impetus for Loving Believers (4:19-21)
B. The Moral Assurance: Obeying Commands (5:1-5)
1. The Theological, Social, and Moral Assurances Are Integrated (5:1-3)
a. Those Who Believe in the Incarnation Are Reborn (5:1a)
b. Those Who Believe in the Incarnation Love Other Believers as an Act of Obedience to God (5:1b-3)
2. The Theological, Social, and Moral Assurances Provide Victory (5:4-5)
C. The Theological Assurance: Holding to the Doctrine of the Incarnation (5:6-12)
1. Believers Possess Credible Evidence for the Incarnation (5:6-11)
2. Believers Possess Assurance of their Salvation (5:12)
VI. Epilogue: Reassurance of Five Certainties (5:13-21)
A. Certainty #1: Assurance of Salvation (5:13)
B. Certainty #2: God Meets Needs through Prayer (5:14-15)
C. Certainty #3: God Helps Others through Prayer (5:16-17)
D. Certainty #4: Deliverance from the Evil One (5:18-19)
E. Certainty #5: Our Knowledge of Him Is True (5:20-21)

COMMENTARY ON 1 JOHN

I. Prologue (1:1-4)

A. The Contents of John's Message (1:1-2)

1:1-2. These verses accomplish three objectives: (1) They announce the writer's theme to be the eternal, living **Word** of God, Jesus. (2) They state the writer's apostolic authority as one who was closely involved with Christ. (3) They identify two purposes for the letter.

Christ is **what** has existed **from the beginning** of eternity past. During Jesus' earthly ministry, according to the writer, **we** apostles **heard** His teachings, **have seen with our eyes** His service to the needy, carefully beheld His actions, and even **touched [Him] with our hands**. John wrote about God's **Word** incarnate in Jesus who brings eternal **life** (v. 1). How were the apostles, mere mortals, able to experience that audible, visual, and tangible access to the divine Christ? They were able because Christ, though an intimate relationship **with the Father** in eternity past, **was manifested to us** (v. 2).

B. The Purpose of John's Letter (1:3-4)

1:3. The immediate purpose for wanting to **proclaim** his experience of seeing and hearing Jesus is so his readers **may have** horizontal **fellowship** with the saints and vertical **fellowship with the Father, and . . . His Son**.

1:4. A second purpose for writing **these things** is **so** John's **joy may be made complete**. These purposes are important to the author.

The unorthodox teachings to which his readers are exposed can erode their confidence in the truth, thus injuring their relationship both with God and the Christian community. Such injured relationships will impair their joy. John will set forth apostolic truth, which, if they hold fast to it, maintains their horizontal and vertical relationships and increases their joy.

II. Unorthodox Claims Tested by the Thesis of Jesus' Message (1:5–2:2)

A. The Thesis of Jesus' Message (1:5)

1:5. A summary of **the message**, which John **heard from** Jesus, consists in two parts. Positively, **God is Light** or absolutely holy. Negatively, **in Him there is no darkness** or sin **at all** (v. 5). This summary or thesis now assesses three false claims in 1:6–2:2. Each heretical assertion is followed by John's denial of it, and then the antidote or the truth of the matter.

B. First Unorthodox Claim: Knowing Christ but Living in Sin (1:6-7)

1:6-7. The initial Gnostic claim (**if we say**) is that they **have fellowship** or a relationship **with** God. While they assert this, false teachers nevertheless **walk** (live) **in** moral **darkness** and sin. Their claim is thus denied: they **lie** and are not living according to **the** gospel's **truth** (v. 6).

The proper perspective is to **walk in the light**. This means believers conduct themselves according to Christian truth, so as to live a holy life. In doing this, two things follow: (1) **we have fellowship** (relationship) **with one another**—with God and believers; and (2) **the blood of Jesus... cleanses** from any inadvertent **sin** (v. 7). Neither of these facts was true of the Gnostics.

C. Second Unorthodox Claim: Having No Sinful Nature (1:8-9)

1:8. The next heretical assertion is to **have no sin** nature. This means either that the false teachers believed their sinful nature was eradicated, or they had morally progressed beyond their innate sinful condition, and so were no longer capable of sinning. Either way, they were **deceiving** themselves.

1:9. To **confess our** acts of sin is to admit a sinful disposition. In response to confession, God is found **faithful** (reliable) **and righteous** (justly capable) **to forgive** and purge us from **all** defiling effects of **our sins**. Verse 9 is frequently seen as reflecting a believer's admission of specific acts of sin so that sanctification can continue to occur. This is not an objectionable view of the verse. But it can also be interpreted as one of the components of John's anti-Gnostic intent. The Gnostics did not believe they sinned or had a sin nature, and so did not confess ("to admit that something is factual or true," and especially in the context of this passage, to admit one has done wrong) any sin at all. As a result, they would not be saved (**forgive us our sins and ... cleanse us from all unrighteousness**). Verse 9 could, then, be a "salvation" verse, explaining that one must acknowledge and admit to personal sinfulness in order to be forgiven of it, rather than a "sanctification" verse.

D. Third Unorthodox Claim: Committing No Sins (1:10–2:2)

1:10. The final heretical assertion is to **have not sinned** and never been guilty of committing an act of wrongdoing. Divine dealings with humankind are based on the premise that they have sinned. To deny this is to **make Him a liar** (v. 10).

2:1-2. The proper perspective on this third assertion avoids two moral extremes: (1) Leniency. Confessing sin (1:9) does not imply sin in a Christian's life to be the norm. John wrote **so** his readers **may not sin** at all. (2) Severity. **If anyone sins**, his case is not hopeless; **Christ** is his **Advocate with the Father** (v. 1). Jesus does not plead our innocence; that is, He does not claim that we are free of wrongdoing. Nor does He plead our merits; that is, Jesus does not maintain that our virtues and good deeds are sufficient to obtain and maintain divine favor. Rather, **He Himself is the propitiation for our sins**. His atonement satisfies God's just demands regarding our moral failures, thus securing forgiveness (v. 2).

III. Three Assurances of Salvation Discussed (2:3-29)

A. The Moral Assurance: Obeying Indicates One's Spiritual Status (2:3-6)

1. Obedience Indicates Salvation (2:3)

2:3. To **have come to know Him** means to have come to faith in Christ. The way **we know that** this has occurred in our life is **if we keep** (obey) **His commandments**. Obedience is not the means but a fruit, evidence, or result of regeneration.

2. Disobedience Indicates Lack of Salvation (2:4)

2:4. The person who claims to **have come to know** Christ, yet **does not keep his commandments** is wrong. **The truth is** neither **in him** nor affects him. John should not be understood to refer to the recurring sins of truly saved individuals. He made it clear in 2:1-2 that believers do sin, but that the blood of Jesus also covers them on those occasions. But if an individual professes to be right with God, yet lives in consistent disobedience, denies the reality of sin, is repulsed by believers, and does not believe in the incarnation, all these factors together indicate that one has not embraced the Savior in any saving way.

3. Obedience Leads to Love for God (2:5)

2:5. On the contrary, **in** an obedient believer **the love** for **God** is **perfected** (i.e., matures). Obeying and loving God, even imperfectly, is how **we know that we are in** a true and right relationship with **Him**. Love for God expresses itself in obeying His commands.

4. Obedience Leads to Christlikeness (2:6)

2:6. Obedience, in turn, results in imitating Jesus. One professing that **he abides in** a relationship with **Him** must conduct himself **as He walked**. The genuineness of one's relationship with an invisible God is seen in a person's visible behavior.

B. The Social Assurance: Love for Christians Indicates Salvation (2:7-17)

1. Love Indicates One Is in the Light of the New Era (2:7-11)

In 2:7-11, John began to explore the importance of love for other believers in light of the passing away of the current era (see the eschatological theme in 2:18). Love for other believers is one of the more important—if not the *most* important—component of the Christian life during this present time, in which there is an inauguration of fullness of future messianic days. Such love's presence becomes a prime marker that one is in a right relationship with the Father.

2:7-8. The author gives his audience not **a new commandment** . . . **but an old** one that, **from the beginning** of their exposure to the gospel, they had repeatedly **heard** (v. 7). This admits that the **old commandment** described in v. 7 is **new** in a sense. Jesus raised the OT's injunction to "love your neighbor as yourself" (Lev. 19:18) to a higher level: "love one another, even as I have loved you" (John 13:34). Such love is **true** or being expressed **in** the readers' lives, **because** their moral **darkness** is being removed and **the true Light** of holiness is increasing (v. 8). One of the primary indicators that they are in the **Light** of the Messianic Age is through their love for other Christians.

2:9-10. Verse 9 indicates that the "command" of vv. 7-8 is the divine summons to love especially other believers. The one claiming to be saved but who **hates his** Christian **brother**, as the Gnostics did, remains **in the darkness** of his unregenerate life (v. 9). But **one who loves** a fellow Christian **abides in the Light**: He has embraced the gospel, is saved, and is characterized by progress in living a holy life. **In him** is no moral **cause for** his **stumbling** into sin (v. 10). If one continually remains in Christian fellowship and love for other believers, this will enable him to avoid stumbling into the sin of apostasy, something of which the Gnostics were guilty.

2:11. The writer affirms three facts about the Gnostic heretic, here described as **one who hates his** Christian **brother**: (1) he **is in** . . . **darkness**, i.e., unsaved; (2) **walks** or lives **in** accord with **the darkness** of sin; and (3) **does not know where** he is **going**—i.e., fails to perceive his eternal destination. The reason for this sad condition is **the** sinful **darkness** . . . **blinded** the heretic's moral judgment (2:10).

2. Those in the New Era Overcome the Sinful Era (2:12-17)

2:12-15. God's family, like most human families, has members at different levels of maturity. The initial group addressed is **little children**. These are new converts or immature believers. John assures them they **have been forgiven** on account of Jesus' atonement (v. 12). The next group addressed is **fathers**. These are believers advanced in years and spiritually mature. They **know** Christ intimately, He who has existed **from the beginning** of eternity. The last group is the spiritual adolescents, **young men**. They **have overcome** the Devil (v. 13). Here John repeated basically the same remarks to each group. This was his way of saying, "What **I have written** in v. 13 about your being saved I meant, and will not retract it (v. 14). It is also possible that John used the present tense of the verb "to write" in 2:12-13 to emphasize the essence of his message and its result, but in 2:14 used the aorist form of the verb to unpack the implications of vv. 12-13. Before 2:12, John used the verb *grapho* ("I write") exclusively in the present tense (see 1:4; 2:1, 7, 8), perhaps to place in the foreground and emphasize the primary points of his letter. But after 2:13, he exclusively used the aorist form of the verb (see 2:14, 21, 26; 5:13). Perhaps he did so to exemplify the practical ramifications of his instruction or to expand on his foundational points, which received emphasis with the present tense. John presented the main themes of his letter in 1:1–2:11 (a correct understanding of Jesus' incarnation, 1:1-2, developed in 2:18-23; obedience to God, 1:6-8; 2:4-5, developed in 3:1-10; love for Christians, 2:7-11, developed in 3:11-24). Christians are prohibited from loving **the world** or **the things** in it. The **world** represents values and ways of thinking and living opposed to God. **If anyone loves the** sinful **world**, he has no **love** for **the Father** (v. 15).

2:16-17. Since no form of worldliness **is . . . from the Father**, it is contrary to His will, and He does not sanction it. Examples of worldliness are: (1) **the lust of the flesh**, evil desires from within oneself; (2) **the lust of the eyes**, coming from without, greed aroused by what is seen; (3) **the boastful pride of life**, arrogance in one's possessions, accomplishments, or social position (2:16). The sinful **world** with one's **lusts** for it **is passing away**—i.e., is transient. It therefore makes little sense for the believer to crave worldly things since they will not endure. Since the believer doing **the will of God lives forever**, only what is eternal is divinely approved as a legitimate object for his or her affection (v. 17). (On "doing the will of God," see the comments on Mt 7:21.)

C. The Theological Assurance: Belief in the Doctrine of the Incarnation (2:18-29)

Previously, John presented two "tests" whereby one could be reassured of his right standing with God. The first was a moral test. Those who claim to know God demonstrate it by seeking to live in obedience to Him. The second was a social test. Those who claim to know God love what He loves, namely other believers. For those who display these characteristics, John reassured them that they are right with God. But he provided a third test, this one theological. It relates to a proper understanding of the doctrine of Christ's incarnation.

1. Heretics Abandoned Belief in the Incarnation (2:18-19)

2:18-19. The **antichrist** (2:18) *par excellence* is the "man of lawlessness" (Mk 13:14; 2Th 2:1-12; see comments there). Scripture teaches that his appearance signals **the last hour** of this age. **Now many antichrists have appeared.** John was indicating that there were forerunners of the **antichrist**. These were professing Christians who rejected orthodox Christianity's teaching on the identity of Jesus Christ. The **antichrists** of v. 18 are identified here as those who **went out from us**—i.e., they abandoned the church. Their defection has **shown** they never shared the church's heavenly birth (v. 19).

2. True Believers Embrace the Truth of the Incarnation (2:20-21)

2:20-21. They can recognize the secessionists' spurious nature by their defection, as well as by their erroneous doctrine, because they **have an anointing from the Holy One** (v. 20), that is, they had received the Holy Spirit from the Lord Jesus Christ (cf. Jn 14:26; 15:26). This gift of the Spirit, and His teaching ministry (cf. v. 27), enabled them to actually **know** the truth (v. 20). In other words, this gift of the Spirit includes the illuminating work of the Spirit. This illumination gave these believers insight about the truth—an appreciation for it, an application of it—that those without the Spirit lacked. But it provided more: The anointing granted to them genuine knowledge of the truth, cognitive content of the truth, and an intellectual grasp of the information and facts of the truth, that those who did not have this illumination simply did not possess (cf. 1 Co 2:6-12). Thus, he went on to explain, he was not writing fruitlessly to persons who did **not know the truth**, but he was writing to those who **do know it**. John's readers had the "cognitive content," "the intellectual information" that the ones who had departed (cf. 2:19) lacked.

3. Heretics Reject the Incarnation (2:21)

2:21. The writer reminded his readers that they **know the truth** of the gospel. And **because no** theological **lie** comes from this **truth**, they possessed the necessary criterion to recognize the secessionists' faulty doctrine.

4. Heretics Do Not Have God (2:22-23)

2:22-23. Verse 22 identifies the "antichrists" in v. 18 with the secessionists of v. 19. Both groups are one and the same: they deny that the historical, earthly **Jesus** is identical with the heavenly, divine **Christ**. These heretics reject the divinity of both **the Father and the Son**. The person who denies that Jesus is **the Son** of God **does not have** a relationship with **the Father**. Conversely, to confess **the Son** is to acknowledge who he is, and this provides the evidence that one enjoys a right relationship both with Jesus and **the Father also** (v. 23).

5. True Believers Must Abide in the Truth (2:24-29)

2:24-26. To protect their relationship with God, the readers have an objective (v. 24) and subjective (2:27) safeguard. The former is to **abide in** the truth of the incarnation, which they **heard from the beginning** of their exposure to the gospel (v. 24). The next verse offers a reason for retaining the truth. It is to realize **the promise** (of **eternal life**) **which** God **Himself made to** those in relation with Him (v. 25). John provided these exhortations for the faithful because of the attempt of the false teachers to deceive them (**those who are trying to deceive** his Christian readership). The antichrists (2:18) and defectors (2:19) have spurned the truth and can adversely influence the readers to do so.

2:27-29. The subjective safeguard is **the anointing** or Holy Spirit **received** at conversion. The Spirit **has taught** and enables the readers to retain the truth and relation with God (v. 27). Yet another motive is furnished here to **abide in** the truth and in relationship with **Him**. Negatively, it is **not** to **shrink away from Him in shame at His coming** in the rapture of the Church, and positively to **have confidence** on that day (v. 28). The Lord's return should be a happy occasion for believers, and it will be if their character and conduct "in this world" has paralleled that of Christ's (4:17). Every true believer is destined for eternal life. And every true believer will likely experience some **shame at His coming** because no believer has lived as righteously as he should. Those true believers, however, who have lived carelessly will **shrink away from Him in shame**, though they are saved. A result of retaining the truth and maintaining one's relationship with the Lord is living righteously. Membership in God's family can be recognized by family resemblance. God **is righteous**. Consequently, **everyone** living righteously **is born of Him** (v. 29).

IV. Three Assurances of Salvation Expanded (3:1–4:6)

A. The Moral Assurance: Obedience and the Righteous Life (3:1-10)

Chapter 2 ended by affirming that every person who lives a consistently righteous life gives evidence thereby that he is born of God (2:29). Chapter 3's initial paragraph resumes and develops this idea of rebirth leading to right conduct. And more to the point, right living is proof of membership in God's family. The opposite is just as true: sinful living as a lifestyle is evidence of being in Satan's family—i.e., under demonic influence and dominion. Family likeness is indicative of family membership.

1. God's Love and the New Birth (3:1)

3:1. Rebirth is the result of that **great . . . love**, which the **Father has bestowed upon us**. That affection causes believers to be **called** God's **children**.

2. Moral Purity and the New Birth (3:2-3)

3:2-3. Although believers do not appear to the world **now** as **children of God**, **what we will be** in future glorification **has not appeared as yet**. Upon seeing Jesus at His return, **we will be like Him** (v. 2). This does not mean that believers become divine as He is divine, but similar to Him in the glorified resurrection body, as well as purity. At the rapture of the Church, believers will be fully and perfectly sanctified, completely free from the sin nature and the sinful deeds that flow from it. It is at this point that the transforming work of the triune God will be completed in the believer who then becomes **like Him. Everyone who has this hope** of seeing Jesus at His return and becoming like Him, progressively though imperfectly, **purifies himself** now (v. 3).

3. Moral Impurity and Lawlessness (3:4)

3:4. Unlike believers who are becoming pure like Jesus (v. 3), this verse speaks of those committing sin. **Sin is lawlessness** or the breaking of God's moral law. Those who make a practice of sin disregard the divine standard and resort to their own measuring stick.

4. Moral Impurity and Jesus' Work (3:5-10)

a. Believers Have Righteous Behavior (3:5-7)

3:5-7. The purpose of Jesus' incarnation was that He might take away our sins. Only because **in Him there is no sin** could He remove ours (v. 5). Consequently, no person who abides in a relationship with Him persists in sin. For this theme, see the comments below on 3:8. To claim to have a relationship with the sinless One and yet deliberately, consistently, commit sin is a contradiction in terms (3:6). The readers must let no one deceive them about morality. The truth is only he who does what is right is righteous, like Jesus (v. 7).

b. Believers Do Not Sin Like the Devil (3:8)

3:8. The devil started sinning **from the beginning** and continues to sin now. Similarly, **the one who** persists in **sin is of the devil**—i.e., influenced and dominated by him. Jesus came to **destroy the** influence **of the devil** (v. 8). The one "born of God" (v. 9) does not persist in sin; that is, there is a difference between the believer's old, unregenerate life, and his new life in Christ. The Christian now sins periodically, but no longer incessantly as the devil does.

c. Believers Have God's Seed (3:9-10)

3:9-10. There is a reason believers no longer sin incessantly as the devil does. It is **because**

His seed—the divine principle of life in the Holy Spirit—**abides in him**. The new birth produces a radical change (v. 9). But whoever does not do what is right as a lifestyle **is not of God**. This is particularly true of one lacking **love** for **his** Christian **brother** (v. 10).

B. The Social Assurance: Loving the Brethren (3:11-24)

John shifted abruptly from his exploration of righteousness as an indicator that his recipients (not the secessionists) were in a right relationship with God to the love of fellow Christians as another indicator. On the connection, Donald Burdick writes, "The two concepts [righteousness and love] are not unrelated. In fact, they may be viewed as two ways of referring to the same thing. The relationship of righteousness... and love is explicitly stated by both Jesus (Matt. 22:34-40) and Paul (Rom. 13:8-10)" (Donald W. Burdick, *The Letters of John the Apostle* [Chicago: Moody, 1985], 259). In 2:9-11, the one who does not love other believers is in moral darkness (ignorant of divine things and as a result lives in sin and error). In 3:11-24, John intensified the characteristics of those antagonistic to believers. They were like Cain (v. 12), abided in the spiritual state of death (v. 14), and did not have eternal life (v. 15). These were the traits of the secessionists who stood condemned before God.

1. Believers Love Other Believers (3:11-14)

3:11-14. The essence of the Christian **message** is **we should love one another** (v. 11). Christians must **not** be like **Cain**. He was under the influence **of the evil one**, at whose instigation he **slew his brother** (v. 12). The term **brother** stems from the Cain-Abel story of v. 12, but now is applied to spiritual family. As Cain hated Abel, much of **the world** will hate believers (v. 13). Believers are vastly different. When Christians love their brethren, they have evidence that that they have **passed out of** spiritual **death into** spiritual **life**. John's point is not so much, "If you do not love your brothers then you are not saved!" but "Because you love fellow Christians, this is one of the reassurances that you are saved." The person **who does not love** other believers **abides in** spiritual **death**—i.e., is still unsaved (v. 14).

2. Unbelievers Will Hate Believers (3:15)

3:15. A lack of love for the children of God is evidence of spiritual death. **Everyone who hates**—whether an active display of hostility or a passive withholding of affection—is likened to **a murderer** who cannot have **eternal life abiding in him**.

3. Believers Sacrifice for Other Believers (3:16-18)

3:16-19. Jesus **laid down His life for us**. So **we** too **ought to lay down our lives for the brethren** (v. 16). A common way of demonstrating affection is assisting the needy materially. The professing believer with **the world's goods**, who refuses to help, lacks **the love of God**... **in** himself (v. 17). Believers must **not love** only **with word or with tongue**—just talk—**but in deed** (action) **and truth** (reality, v. 18). Loving others in reality (v. 18b) is how **we**... **know**... **that we are of the truth** (i.e., we know that we are true believers).

4. Believers Receive Assurance through Love for Other Believers (3:19-24)

3:19-24. Love expressed in action, especially in action that demonstrates love for other Christians, **will assure our heart** of being saved (v. 19) since those who withdrew from the community John addressed had no love for Christians. A true believer might have an overly sensitive conscience (**heart**) that periodically might lead to thoughts of self-condemnation (v. 20). But John noted that **God is greater** in pronouncing a more authoritative verdict on our salvation **than our heart** (our conscience), which is fallible and often errs. God **knows all things** about us and takes everything into consideration. A conscience disarmed of any sinful accusations and that **does not condemn** enables us to **have confidence** about our being saved and living in a manner pleasing **before God** (v. 21). Another result of a clear conscience is answered prayer. **Whatever** obedient believers **ask** in accord with God's will they **receive from Him**. Jesus' atonement is the ground for prayer, but obedience is the condition for answered prayer (v. 22). God's commands are summed up in the chief command, consisting of two parts: to **believe in**... **Jesus Christ, and love one another** (v. 23). Complying with divine **commandments** is evidence one **abides in** a relationship with God. Evidence that Jesus **abides** in relationship with a believer comes **by the Spirit** who is living and working in the believer's life. This evidence consists in the Spirit empowering believers "to practice righteousness" (2:29), persuading them to **believe in**... **Jesus Christ** (v. 23), encouraging them to keep **His commandments** (v. 24), and leading them to "love the brethren" (3:14).

C. The Theological Assurance: Holding to the Doctrine of the Incarnation (4:1-6)

Some of the ideas in 3:23-24 are further developed in chap. 4. For example, the command in

3:23 "that we believe" is balanced in 4:1, where the readers are warned about what not to believe. And 3:24 affirms that the Spirit assures Christians of their relationship with Jesus. But that implies a caution, for **the spirits** of 4:1 have a profound influence on **false prophets**. There is a **spirit of truth** and a **spirit of error** (4:6). Both spirits influence teachers. To distinguish the two, readers are offered two criteria by which they can **test the spirits** (4:1), so as to discern which teachers are from God and those who are not. The first criterion is confession—i.e., does a teacher ascribe to the doctrine of the incarnation? The second criterion is congregation—i.e., do the people of God recognize the voice of God when teachers speak? Last, the command in 3:23 to "love one another" will be further developed in 4:7-21.

1. The Need for Discernment (4:1-4)

4:1. The apostle prohibited his audience from believing **every spirit**. This expression refers to a supernatural spiritual being who influences human teachers. The teachers' doctrine must be assessed by other church leaders and teachers who are acknowledged to be fully orthodox. It is their responsibility **to see whether they** [those who teach] **are from God**. Such testing is essential **because many false prophets** are currently disseminating heresy.

4:2-3. This gives one criterion, though not the *only* one, by which the church can recognize a divinely inspired teacher: He publicly acknowledges that the divine, heavenly **Christ** came **in the flesh** in the person of the earthly, human **Jesus** (v. 2). But **every spirit** leading a teacher who **does not** preach **Jesus** to be the heavenly incarnate Messiah **is not** sent **from God**. A teacher's denial of the doctrine of the incarnation is a sufficient enough test to know that he is not divinely inspired and does not preach the truth of God. Worse, **this is the** very **spirit** who will animate the future, personal antichrist. That spirit **now** is **already in the world** inspiring spurious teachers (v. 3). There is at work in the world a satanic parody of Jesus and the Holy Spirit. Jesus was present in body prior to His ascension, and then He sent the Holy Spirit. But the **spirit of the antichrist** is in the world now, to be followed by the physical presence of the antichrist later.

4:4. A true prophet, with true teaching, also can be identified by the audience that listens to him. John's readers are **from God**—i.e., are genuine Christians. They have intellectually **overcome** false teachers by refusing to embrace their heresy, **because** the Holy Spirit, **who is in** them, is **greater** than Satan **who is in the world**.

2. The Source of Heresy (4:5-6)

4:5-6. Heretics **are** a part of, and influenced by, **the** unbelieving **world**. So what **they speak** and teach is derived not from God but **from the world**. And these spurious prophets can be identified by the unregenerate people of the **world** who **listen to them** (v. 5). Orthodox teachers **are from God**. John and those like him are dispatched by heaven. Anyone **who knows God listens to us** (i.e., to orthodox teachers). That audience **not from God does not listen to us**. That is, unbelievers do not want to hear the truth of God preached, and they refuse to accept and live by it.

V. The Three Assurances of Salvation Integrated (4:7–5:12)

A. The Social Assurance: Loving the Brethren (4:7-21)

The flow of the argument in this section connects with the theme mentioned in 3:23. That verse contained a twofold divine commandment to "believe in . . . Jesus" and to "love one another." The readers' complying with that command is traced to "the Spirit" (3:24), who inspires faith and love. The "Spirit" reappears in 4:13. From Him comes the readers' love for others and their conviction in the veracity of the incarnation (4:14-15). This letter sets forth three tests by which a professing Christian can know that he or she is saved. But to the writer, these tests are not to exist in isolation from one another; rather, they are to work together to reassure believers. So 4:7–5:12 will integrate or blend together these three tests in a manner John had not previously formulated.

1. The Command for Loving Believers (4:7-8)

4:7-8. The writer urged his readers to **love one another** and gave three reasons why they should: (1) **Love** has as its ultimate source **God**. That a believer loves others suggests that he or she has a relationship with God. If one loves God, he will love what God loves, and in this context that is especially other believers. This is implicit in the second reason why Christians should love. (2) **Everyone who loves is born of God**. Loving others is not the cause but an effect of the new birth. As a member of the heavenly family, the believer reflects that family trait of love. (3) The one who **knows God** is acquainted with Him as a divine Person who lavishly expresses and demonstrates love. It follows, then, that the believer should also be a loving person (4:7). But **the one who does not love** never was converted. That **God is love** justifies this claim. It is impossible to be a recipient of God's love and to come into relationship with Him without subsequently showing that same love to others, especially, but not exclusively, to other Christians (v. 8).

2. The Example of Loving Believers (4:9-12)

4:9-12. The love of God was manifested in this way: by incarnation God **sent His** unique **Son into the** sinful **world** through the incarnation. The purpose of this mission is **so that** sinners **might live through Him** (4:9). The epitome of **love** consists not in our loving God but in His taking the initiative to love us. Because of that love **He . . . sent His Son to be** the payment **for our sins** (4:10, see also comment on 2:2). **God loved us** in the following way: not waiting for us to love Him, He first loved us. Since God gave the best He had (His Son) for us, then believers **ought to love one another** (v. 11). When believers love **one another**, it shows (1) that **God abides in us**—i.e., it is evidence of our relationship with an invisible God; (2) that **His love is perfected in us**—i.e., we display divine affection toward others. The Greek word rendered **perfected** is *teleioo*. It refers to something that has reached its goal, and by so doing replaces an imperfect state by a better one. The goal of God's love is for a sinner to accept it, and then display that same affection toward his fellow man; his imperfect condition of failing to love others is now being replaced by that moral condition whereby he grows in love for others. And a display of love for others also shows that (3) though **no one has** ever **seen God**, they do perceive Him through mutual Christian affection (v. 12).

3. The Divine Empowerment for Loving Believers (4:13-16)

4:13-16. One way **we know that we abide in** a relationship with God is by **His Spirit**, whom **He has given us**. The Spirit fosters affection in us toward the brethren (v. 13). The Spirit stimulates our accepting by faith the apostolic testimony of the incarnation (v. 15). John and his apostolic associates **have seen** and testify **that the Father has sent the Son** as **Savior of the world** (v. 14). Given John's historical context in his battle against the Gnostic heretics, if someone denied that Jesus of Nazareth was God's Son, he was not saved. Conversely, anyone who **confesses that** the historical, earthly **Jesus is the** heavenly **Son of God** shows that **God abides in** relationship with **him, and he** is **in** a relationship with **God** (v. 15). By accepting the doctrine of the incarnation, John and other like-minded people **have come to know and have believed the love which God has for** them. Three evidences of being saved are mentioned here: (1) knowledge of the truth, (2) believing it, and (3) remaining **in** or displaying **love** to others (v. 16).

4. The Spiritual Development from Loving Believers (4:17-18)

4:17-18. A Christian's love should be **perfected** ("to overcome or supplant an imperfect state of things by one that is free [from] objection," BDAG, 996) (v. 17), i.e. gradually grow and show itself more and more toward others. A fully developing love gives reassurance to a believer that he or she is right with God, and will enable him to have confidence on the day of judgment. The believer does not dreadfully anticipate it. Nor will that day hold any terrors for him regarding his eternal destiny (though shame is an expectation for those believers who do not strive to abide in Christ. See the comments on 2:28). This confidence arises because of the believer being a loving person in this world as Jesus is Himself loving (v. 17). Such growing affection displayed toward other believers harbors no fear of divine judgment. In fact, a maturing **love casts out** and refuses to tolerate **fear**. The disciple **who fears** coming judgment has not matured **in** his **love** (v. 18).

5. The Impetus for Loving Believers (4:19-21)

4:19-21. This section affirms that **we love** Him and other believers. The cause of our affection is **because He first loved us**. Our love is a response to His (v. 19). The professing believer who claims to love God but **hates his brother . . . is a liar**. If one cannot do the easier (**love his brother whom he has seen**), he cannot do the harder (**love God whom he has not seen**, v. 20). Another reason that Christians should love is the **commandment . . . from Him** to do so. The disciple is to show affection for both **God** and **his brother** (v. 21).

B. The Moral Assurance: Obeying Commands (5:1-5)

John continues to integrate the letter's three tests of salvation. In this section the social and moral tests are linked, with emphasis falling on the latter. The catalyst for this section is the "commandment" in 4:21 that the believer "who loves God should love his brother also."

Is this mere theory? No, it is a divinely established law borne out in Christian experience. In these verses the author argues that God's commands are "not burdensome" (v. 3), and the believer's rebirth enables him to obey them (5:4). Complying with the divine commands is evidence of affection for God (5:3). An obedient believer, then, does not disregard the command to love his brethren. If he is obeying God, he is therefore obeying His command to love other believers.

1. The Theological, Social, and Moral Assurances Are Integrated (5:1-3)

a. Those Who Believe in the Incarnation are Reborn (5:1a)

5:1a. Whoever believes that Jesus of Nazareth **is the Christ** of heaven **is born of God**. It is expected that a believer will love his heavenly Father, just as a child loves his earthly parents. And in a family, it is typical and expected that the children of the same parents will love their siblings. So the child of God should love the Father's other children. Here the new birth joins together faith (**believes**) and love.

b. Those Who Believe in the Incarnation Love Other Believers as an Act of Obedience to God (5:1b-3)

5:1b-3. The following litmus test enables believers to **know** whether they **love the children of God**. It is **when** they **love God**. And they recognize affection for Him when obeying **His commandments** (v. 2). When one is obeying God's commands, one cannot remain in a relationship with others that lacks affection for them. In 4:20 John taught that love for one's Christian brother is evidence of love for God. In 5:2 he gives the corollary or the other side of this truth: love for God proves love for the brother. Love for God and love for man are so inseparable that the presence of either is evidence of the other. And the opposite is just as true: if either is found alone, it is not genuine love. If love to the brethren proves the reality of one's love to God, then love to God proves the worth of one's love to men. Loving others finds its strongest motive in loving God. One way a Christian manifests his love for God is by obeying His commandments. If obedient, a Christian cannot withhold love from fellow believers, for one of the commandments is to love them (1Jn 4:21). **For** in v. 3 justifies equating love for God with obedience, as in the previous verse. **This is** our **love** for **God, that we keep His commandments. His commandments are not burdensome** but are reasonable precisely because He provides the power to obey the commandments He has given.

2. The Theological, Social, and Moral Assurances Provide Victory (5:4-5)

5:4-5. The individual **born of God overcomes the** wicked **world**. The divinely implanted nature and new life within enable one to gradually and more successfully overcome sin. While the believer increases in victory over sin, in this life he or she will never be completely (perfectly) free of it. Hence what is said in 2:1, "if anyone sins." The immediate means of **victory** is **faith**—relying on Him who became flesh to assist us to live correctly in our flesh (v. 4). Victory in the Christian life is a virtue that is like all other virtues—it is progressive in nature. As the believer matures, he or she increases more and more in victorious living. The overcomer of v. 4 is more precisely identified here, as is the content of his faith. **The one who overcomes the world** is only **he who believes** in the incarnation (v. 5).

C. The Theological Assurance: Holding to the Doctrine of the Incarnation (5:6-12)

Belief in the incarnation—that a divine person became human—seems ludicrous. An intelligent faith depends on reliable witnesses and the credible testimony they furnish. So this paragraph identifies three objective witnesses (vv. 5-8) and a subjective one (v. 11) to the incarnation. John provided the ultimate and divine source of these four witnesses (v. 9), the importance of the acceptance or rejection of all this evidence (v. 10), and a conclusion (v. 12).

1. Believers Possess Credible Evidence for the Incarnation (5:6-11)

5:6-7. That **Jesus Christ . . . came** refers to His appearing on earth for 33 years. That He **came by water and blood** . . . represents the two terminal points of Jesus' earthly ministry, **water** referring to His baptism inaugurating His public ministry, and **blood** to His death, which concluded it. These events point to the first piece of evidence concerning the incarnation, divinely furnished on these two occasions. At Christ's baptism, the Spirit descended upon Him from heaven, and the Father spoke, calling Jesus "My beloved Son" (Mt 3:17). At the crucifixion, there were a supernatural eclipse of the sun (Mt 27:45), an earthquake (Mt 27:51), a temple veil rent in two (Mt 27:51), a partial resurrection of saints (Mt 27:52-53), and an unusual witness, a Roman soldier (Mt 27:54) crucifying Jesus, who acknowledged Him to be the Son of God.

5:7-8. A second piece of evidence John cited for the incarnation relates to the work of the Spirit. **The Spirit** also testifies, employing all the evidence in v. 6 to persuade people of the reality of the incarnation. Only one witness, the Spirit, was explicitly identified in v. 6. So John, in vv. 7-8, reiterated all three pieces of evidence to lend more weight to their otherwise independent testimony. **There are three that testify: the Spirit and the water and the blood**, mentioned previously in v. 6. Each of these **three are in agreement**, and each furnishes evidence that confirms the incarnation.

A textual variant exists in vv. 7-8 of the AV. Following the authentic words "For there are three that testify" in v. 8a are added the words *"in heaven, the Father, the Word, and the Holy Spirit."* Then following the authentic words of the AV in v. 8c, "and the three are in agreement," are added, *"on earth."* Four factors point to these variants as scribal additions that were not actually penned by John. First, they are found only in four late, inferior Greek mss. Second, they are quoted by no Greek Church fathers, who would have likely used them in their Trinitarian debates with heretics. Third, they are absent from most ancient versions (copies of the NT in languages other than the Gk. it was written in; e.g., Syriac, Coptic, Armenian, Ethiopic, Arabic). And fourth, if genuine, there is no good reason for their omission.

5:9-11. The water, the blood, and the Spirit provide potent evidence for the incarnation. The fourth piece of evidence is **the testimony of God** Himself. Divine testimony **is greater** than **the testimony of men** because it is more authoritative, more accurate, more trustworthy, more important, and more deserving of acceptance. The object of this divine testimony concerns the fact that He has borne evidence **concerning His Son** (v. 9). **The one who believes** and accepts the evidence about **the Son of God** now **has the testimony in himself** (v. 10). The divine witness is no longer merely something the believer heard about. This new, spiritual, **eternal** life (v. 11) has come to reality in his or her own life, beginning at regeneration; it is then that this believer starts to experience heaven's peace, joy, and power. But the ones spurning it, as the Gnostics did, **made** God **a liar**, attributing falsehood to the divine witness **given concerning His Son** (v. 10). **The** internal **testimony is this, that God has given us eternal life.** The believing sinner's changed life is weighty proof of the reality of the incarnation. It confirms heaven's giving of its **Son**, in whom **this** new **life** is found (v. 11).

2. Believers Possess Assurance of their Salvation (5:12)

5:12. He who has a relationship with **the Son has** that eternal **life** mentioned in v. 11. But **he who does not have** such a relationship with **the Son of God does not have** that **life**. John's encouragement here, as throughout the epistle, must be read against the background of those who had withdrawn from the community he was addressing. Those secessionists did not have the Son and had no stake in eternal life. Regardless of what the apostates might have said about these believers, regardless of how they might have accused them of being wrong about spiritual things, John reassured the believers they were right and possessed all the blessings promised in Christ, especially eternal life.

VI. Epilogue: Reassurance of Five Certainties (5:13-21)

First John is a letter of assurance. So it appropriately ends on a note of assurance, with the author mentioning five realities of which believers can be certain.

A. Certainty #1: Assurance of Salvation (5:13)

5:13. John's epistle was **written . . . to you who believe in . . . the Son of God . . . that** its readers **may know that** they **have eternal life**. The first of five realities of which believers can be sure is possessing their own salvation.

B. Certainty #2: God Meets Needs through Prayer (5:14-15)

5:14-15. Another certainty is the wonderful **confidence** of answered prayer. **If we ask anything according to His will, He hears** and responds to **us** (v. 14). A believer's prayer is in harmony with the divine will when it is in harmony with Scripture or is prompted by the Spirit. Since **we know that He hears** and honors requests in accord with His will, **we know that we** will be granted such **requests** offered to Him in prayer (v. 15).

C. Certainty #3: God Helps Others through Prayer (5:16-17)

5:16-17. A third certainty is about praying for others (v. 16). The **brother** is a professing but not a genuine Christian, and he is observed persisting in some **sin not leading to** eternal **death** (i.e., hell). By this John probably means that any sin, except the sin leading to eternal death, can be forgiven and eternal death escaped. The

sin leading to death is that mentioned in 2:19, namely, apostasy—defecting from the church and repudiating the gospel, after a previous profession of faith in it. In the context of 1 John, the sin leading to death includes a persistent, willful rejection of orthodoxy as it relates to the incarnation, sinless life, and atoning death of Jesus Christ. The secessionists were guilty of such a sin.

Regarding the category of sin that could be forgiven (i.e., **not leading to death**), the Christian **shall ask** in prayer, and it is expected that **God will . . . give** spiritual (eternal) **life** (i.e., salvation) to that sinner. The verb **will give** is a gnomic future, which means that, while there may be some exceptions, usually its action will be realized. **I do not say that he should make request for this** indicates that John is not absolutely forbidding prayer for one engaged in apostasy. The language of the phrase indicates simply that he cannot guarantee that prayer offered for any of the secessionists who had apostatized will have the effect typical of believing prayer promised in vv. 15 and 16a. Nevertheless, John does seem to parallel what Jesus said regarding casting pearls before swine (Mt 7:6). The ongoing attempt to minister to those who are recalcitrant, whether by witnessing to them, teaching them the Word, or (as here) praying for them, seems to be without much purpose. Even if prayer for one confirmed in his rejection of Christianity ceases, the believer can hold on to the hope that God might still work in the heart of such a one to turn to Him.

Verse 16 is often explained as referring to a real Christian persisting in some serious sin that results in his premature, physical death. While possible, this view is unlikely for the following reasons. First, this letter presents the genuine believer as incapable of persistent sin (3:6, 9-10; 5:18). Second, in response to the intercessor's prayer God **will give** the persistent sinner **life** (Gk. *zoe* meaning the new, spiritual life divinely imparted to the unbeliever at conversion). If the **brother** is a Christian, he already has this **life**; it cannot be given to him again. And third, the **death** in view is best interpreted by its opposite, namely **life**; if this **life** is eternal life, then the **death** must in like manner be eternal death, not physical death. **All unrighteousness is sin**, even if not every sin leads inevitably and only to eternal death. No sin puts a person beyond the parameters of God's grace. Faith in Christ for the forgiveness of sins will lead to escaping eternal death. But persisting in the refusal to embrace Christ as the sinless and crucified Son of God incarnate will lead to eternal death. So the church has abundant matters to pray about (v. 17).

D. Certainty #4: Deliverance from the Evil One (5:18-19)

5:18-19. The fourth certainty concerns security of membership in the divine family. No one **who is born of God** continually **sins** (see comments on 3:8). The reason for this lies in the unique Son of God, who **keeps**, or morally protects, the believer. Consequently, the Devil (**the evil one**) is unable to **touch** or get a grip on **him**, i.e. unable to injure his relationship with God so as to place his salvation in jeopardy. The author and his readers **are of God**—i.e., they belong to Him. While Satan cannot "touch" them (v. 18), **the whole** unbelieving **world lies** under the influence and dominion **of the evil one** (v. 19).

E. Certainty #5: Our Knowledge of Him Is True (5:20-21)

5:20-21. The author maintains that Jesus appeared **and has given us understanding**. This means that during the incarnation Jesus revealed spiritual truth—and even God Himself—to humankind (Jn 1:18). Its objective is so **we may** be able to recognize the **true** God and have a relationship with Him. And **we are in** a relationship with the **true** (genuine) God, and this relationship has been put in effect by **His Son Jesus Christ** (v. 20). Since the Lord is "the true One" (v. 20), the readers must **guard** themselves **from idols** and false gods. In v. 18 the Son of God protects believers, but they, too, have responsibility, and it is to remain loyal to "the true One" by abstaining from idolatry.

To sum up, the purpose of this letter is to provide professing Christians with three assurances by which they may know for certain, and find reassurance, that they are genuine children of God. These three are the moral assurances (obeying the commands of Christ), the social assurances (loving fellow Christians), and the doctrinal assurances (believing in the incarnation). The letter is relevant for today. Not only are there heretics who erroneously claim salvation, there are also not a few people in the church who erroneously think that they are saved. And it is a common experience for some genuine Christians to doubt their salvation. All three groups—heretics, professing unbelievers, and real believers—can profit from John's first epistle by applying his tests of salvation to themselves.

BIBLIOGRAPHY

Akin, Daniel L. *1, 2, 3 John*. The New American Commentary. Nashville: Broadman & Holman, 2001.

Bruce, F. F. *The Epistles of John*. London: Pickering & Inglis, 1970.

Burdick, Donald W. *The Letters of John the Apostle: An In-depth Commentary*. Chicago: Moody, 1985.

Law, R. L. *The Test of Life: A Study of the First Epistle of St. John*. Edinburgh: T & T Clark, 1909.

MacArthur, John. *1–3 John*. The MacArthur New Testament Commentary. Chicago: Moody, 2007.

Marshall, I. H. *The Epistles of John*. The New International Commentary on the New Testament. Grand Rapids, MI: Eerdmans, 1964.

Stott, John R. W. *The Epistles of John: An Introduction and Commentary*. Tyndale New Testament Commentaries. Grand Rapids, MI: Eerdmans, 1964.

Yarbrough, R. W. *1–3 John*. Baker Exegetical Commentary on the New Testament. Grand Rapids, MI: Baker Book House, 2008.

2 JOHN

RONALD SAUER

INTRODUCTION

Author. From a literary point of view, it is obvious that the author of 1 John is the same person who penned 2 John, for the vocabulary, grammar, style, and theology are the same in both letters. The apostle John's fingerprints are all over 1 and 2 John.

Date. John was writing from Ephesus about AD 95, in part concerning hosting traveling Christians visiting a city on business or ministry. The comforts of the modern hotel were unknown in the ancient world. Inns were infamously dirty, flea-infested places of ill repute, and innkeepers were notoriously rapacious. Consequently, in their travels Christians were customarily hosted by members of local churches. Paul, for example, was extended hospitality by Lydia in Philippi (Ac 16:15), by Jason in Thessalonica (Ac 17:7), by Gaius in Corinth (Rm 16:23), and by Philip in Caesarea (Ac 21:8). But such hospitality could easily be abused. Should traveling false teachers, who posed as Christian missionaries, be offered hospitality? The author issued instructions concerning whom to host and whom to refuse, and why.

Recipients. Accordingly, the letter's recipient has been understood to be either a local church or a certain woman in a local church. The following reasons have been argued in favor of both views: (1) The addressee is called "the chosen lady" who is loved by "all who know the truth" (1). Christians everywhere would more likely know of this particular church than an individual in it. But a prominent woman of means could be widely known. And the expression "all who know the truth" could be intended to mean, not that she was known by "all" believers everywhere, but just all those in her particular church. (2) The second-person plural in 6, 8, 10, and 12 seems to favor a church, referring to a plurality of recipients, not an individual. But the letter is addressed to a group of people—"the chosen lady and her children"—which in itself is sufficient to account for the second-person plural. (3) The letter's warning against false teachers applies more to a church than to a family. But if this family had been accustomed to extending hospitality to traveling heretics, the warning is just as applicable to them as to a local assembly. (4) The command to "love one another" (5) better suits a church than a family. Yet acrimony can plague a family as well as a church. Furthermore, the writer may be stressing the proper use of love prior to addressing the family's misuse of it by hosting false teachers. (6) The NT elsewhere personifies the church as a woman (1Pt 5:13), and as the wife (Eph 5:22-33) or the betrothed (2Co 11:1) of Christ. If "the chosen lady" here is in like manner a local church, then who would her "chosen sister" of 13 be, a sister church? Furthermore, the switch in 6 from-second person singular ("I ask you, lady") to first-person plural ("we love one another") is more likely said to a woman and her children than to a church and its members. The most natural reading of the text, then, identifies the recipient as an individual woman with her children.

Purpose. Recently the writer had crossed paths with this lady's children. To his delight he found them living exemplary Christian lives and was writing to inform her of it. But the children had informed John of their mother's sincere but misguided hospitality to traveling heretical teachers. So he penned this letter to encourage this lady to keep displaying Christian love to all but, on the other hand, to cease assisting heterodox deceivers in their ministry. The key words are "truth" (1, 2, 3, 4) and "love" (1, 3, 5, 6). The latter comes from obeying the former. Following the truth leads to loving God and humanity.

OUTLINE

I. Prologue (1-3)
II. The Christian's Path (4-6)
III. The Christian's Peril (7-11)
IV. Epilogue (12-13)

COMMENTARY ON 2 JOHN

I. Prologue (1-3)

1-3. Writing to an individual, the author deemed it unnecessary to identify himself as an apostle, and instead used the term **the elder**. This speaks of age, office, and dignity, depicting him as speaking in a loving, fatherly role. He addressed **the chosen lady**, a woman divinely selected for salvation, **and her children**. The cause of the apostle's brotherly love for this family is **the truth**. To embrace the gospel's **truth** is to experience God's love, fostering an affection in the believer for others. The author wrote elsewhere (1Jn 5:1) that one born of God loves both the Father and those born of Him. Furthermore, the revelation of the truth contains the command to love one another (1Jn 4:21; 2Jn 5). **Truth** currently **abides in us and will be with us forever** (2). Responding to **truth** also brings **grace**, **mercy**, and **peace** to **be with us**, all **from God**.

II. The Christian's Path (4-6)

4-6. John informed this lady of his delight in having earlier found **some of** her **children** living (**walking**) in accord with Christian **truth** (4). The apostle urged her to continue complying with the **commandment** to **love one another** (5). This **love** is equated with living **according to** God's **commandments** and sums up all **commandments** (6). This apostle was convinced that Christian love is demonstrated by obeying the Lord's commands (Jn 14:15, 21; 1Jn 5:2).

III. The Christian's Peril (7-11)

7-9. This section begins with the causal conjunction **for**. This word substantiates 5-6. The fresh summons there to obedience and love was due to false teachers; they were tampering with the truth, and their false teaching could mar Christian love and obedience. The letter's recipient is reminded of her duty to love because **many deceivers** were spreading false teaching in her community. Their error was denying the **coming** of Christ **in the flesh** as **Jesus** of Nazareth. Such deception can seduce the saints from the truth and thus from brotherly love (7).

The NT warns that false teaching breeds arguments among believers (2Tm 2:14), leads to ungodliness (2Tm 2:16) and can upset believers' faith (2Tm 2:18). In view of these many heretics, a caution is given: **watch yourselves**. This caution's intention is twofold: to avoid losing the joy, peace, etc., that **we have accomplished**; and that you **may receive a full reward** on judgment day (8). This **reward** includes, in part, hearing the Lord's "well done, good and faithful servant," as well as everlasting honor and recompense for having lived as divinely prescribed. Any teacher not remaining **in the teaching** of the incarnation of **Christ, does not have** a relationship with **God**. He **goes too far**—he advocates things beyond orthodox Christian doctrine. **The one who abides in the teaching** that God became flesh **has** a relationship with **both the Father and the Son** (9).

10-11. John gave two instructions on how to deal with false teachers not ascribing to **this teaching**. First, **do not receive him into your house**; that is, withhold hospitality of providing room and board. This instruction does not prohibit inviting false teachers into one's home for a discussion about the truth; but it does forbid offering them a place to stay during their itinerant mission. Second, **do not** say, "Welcome," or encourage him by **greeting** him (10). To greet a traveling heretical evangelist by providing him lodging and food approves of and shares **in his evil deeds** of spreading heresy. Similarly, for a Christian today to financially contribute to a religious cult or unorthodox church or to a false teacher is to encourage and assist in the spreading of their false doctrines and practices.

IV. Epilogue (12-13)

12-13. John had **many** other **things** to discuss with this lady, but decided not to do it in writing. In a future visit they could **speak face to face**, increasing their **joy** (12). **The children of your . . . sister** (or the nieces and nephews of the addressee) sent their greetings to her. It would be difficult to see both **children** and **sister** as representing a church. But should these refer to a church, who would her **sister** be? So this **sister** is taken literally. Perhaps the reason this **sister** herself did not ask to be remembered is that she lived elsewhere, was dead, was absent, or for some reason failed to meet with the writer.

BIBLIOGRAPHY

See Bibliography for John's Epistles on p. 1986.

● ● ● ●

3 JOHN

RONALD SAUER

INTRODUCTION

Author. That this letter is from the same hand that penned 1 and 2 John seems certain, for all three missives are written in the same Greek style and grammar, employing the same basic vocabulary. The same themes, such as truth and love, appear in them.

Recipient. This letter's addressee is Gaius, a congregant in a Johannine church. In that assembly he has a thriving ministry of extending hospitality to traveling missionaries. But these missionaries reported to John that Gaius is being hindered by the prominent church leader, Diotrephes. In the NT, he is mentioned only in 3 John, and secular history fails to mention him. Diotrephes was forbidding assistance be given to itinerate evangelists, so as to prevent any external influence. This practice better enabled him to control his church.

Purpose and Theme. The key word is "truth" (1, 3, 4, 8, 12). And the "truth" advocates Christians supporting Christian causes. So, arguing that believers have the duty and privilege to support the gospel's mission work, John wrote to encourage Gaius to continue his hospitable service to the saints. This focus establishes the missive's theme as that of Christian hospitality. Though Diotrephes rejected John's authority, the apostle would appropriately deal with him in a coming visit.

OUTLINE

I. Introduction (1-2)
II. Commendation of Gaius (3-8)
III. Condemnation of Diotrephes (9-10)
IV. Confirmation of Demetrius (11-12)
V. Conclusion (13-14)

COMMENTARY ON 3 JOHN

I. Introduction (1-2)

1-2. John **the elder** wrote to his **beloved Gaius**. (Gaius was a common name in the Roman world, so it is unsurprising that there was a Gaius of Corinth [Rm 16:23] and a Gaius of Derbe [Ac 19:29]. Probably the Gaius of 3Jn is different from those two.) As in 2Jn 1, so here the author called himself **the elder**. This term speaks of age, dignity, and office, and it pictures John giving instructions like a loving father. Unlike Diotrephes, the author did **love** Gaius **in** the realm of **truth**, meaning in light of Christian revelation: "we love, because He first loved us" (1Jn 4:19). Accordingly, in 2 Gaius is addressed as **beloved**. This term assured him that he was the recipient of God's love, and of John's as well. Gaius was prospering spiritually, but John prayed that he **may prosper . . . in all respects**, especially **in**

good physical **health**, a sterling example of godly well-wishing and prayer for a friend.

II. Commendation of Gaius (3-8)

3-4. The initial verse in this section furnishes the basis for the writer's conviction in 2 that his recipient is prospering. That basis lay in John's having received reports from **brethren** returning from mission work. They informed John of the recipient's good state. He **was very glad** that Gaius's behavior sprang from his faithfulness to **the truth**, and specifically his spiritual lifestyle (**walking in the truth**). John's greatest gladness came from hearing that his spiritual **children** were **walking in the truth**, meaning they were conforming their character and conduct to Christian **truth** (4). **My children** is a typical expression of John for those over whom he had supervision and fatherly care (1Jn 2:1).

5-8. Likely because Gaius had been criticized (by Diotrephes?), John now encouraged him by noting that he was **acting faithfully** in services rendered for the brethren and even for **strangers**, who were itinerant missionaries (5). Others **testified** speaking highly **before the church** of his **love**. Gaius showed brotherly affection for these strangers in practical, hospitable ways by serving them. John encouraged Gaius to continue helping these traveling evangelists. The clause **send them on their** way likely was a technical term for early missions, including with it financial support (cf. Ac 15:3; Rm 15:24; 1Co 16:6; 16:11; Ti 3:13). These missionaries **went out** on mission trips **for the sake of** spreading **the Name** of Jesus, never asking for and rarely receiving material support **from the Gentiles** (7). **Therefore** (because these missionaries are appropriately selective regarding those from whom they receive support) John concluded **we** believers **ought to support such** who leave home to preach. The purpose of supporting missionaries today is the same as then: to do so is to **be fellow workers with** them in spreading **the truth**.

III. Condemnation of Diotrephes (9-10)

Having commended Gaius for his generosity in receiving the traveling missionaries, John next cited Diotrephes, in contrast, as one who rejected the apostle and as such, rejected those sent by him.

9. Saying that he **wrote** to Gaius's **church** previously, John was not referring to the present letter since Diotrephes had already rejected it. Neither was this a reference to 1 or 2 John, since the issue in those letters was doctrinal error. Likely this referred to a lost letter urging them to assist traveling evangelists; that letter had been rejected and suppressed by Diotrephes. Thus, John could say that Diotrephes did not accept him. The reason that Diotrophes rejected John was not a doctrinal error but an inflated ego. Rather than Christ having first place among them, Diotrephes **love[d] to be first** himself. Therefore he did **not accept** the apostle's authority.

10. In 9 John dealt with the problem of Diotrephes' character (pride), but here he would address his actions. John would certainly make a future visit (not as in the NASB "If I come," indicating a hypothetical circumstance, but rather "when I come"; the Gk. word *ean* can be translated "whenever," the only uncertainty being the time of the visit, not its eventuality; cf. 4). Then he would expose Diotrephes' **deeds**, consisting of (1) **accusing** (or babbling about) John **with wicked words**; (2) being inhospitable to traveling **brethren**, thereby challenging John's authority; (3) hindering those in the church **who desire** to display hospitality, even to the point of casting them **out of the church**.

Diotrephes' offense appears to have entailed several things. He prohibited the church from complying with John's earlier correspondence, in which the apostle urged the congregation to support traveling missionaries. And he was a self-promoted demagogue rather than an elder or pastor. Diotrephes sought to isolate the assembly from outside influences, like John's, so he could better control church affairs and ministry. Last, he allowed no teaching and leadership but his own. Periodically the modern church will encounter such people in its ranks. Beware of those who usurp authority and try to make disciples of self rather than disciples of Christ.

IV. Confirmation of Demetrius (11-12)

11-12. Gaius was **not** to **imitate** Diotrephes' **evil** example of rebelliousness and inhospitality, **but** rather the **good** one of Demetrius. The reason for this exhortation is that he who habitually **does good** gives evidence being a child **of God**. The opposite is true as well: he who persists in doing **evil has not seen** God, i.e., been saved (see 1Jn 3:5, 9-10; 5:18). In this verse, the participles (the one who does good or does evil) refer to customary or characteristic behavior, indicating that those who consistently do good identify themselves as true believers who have experienced salvation, while those who consistently practice evil show themselves to be unregenerate, never having experienced God in their lives.

In 11 John made a general request to receive traveling missionaries, but in 12 he specified Demetrius as the one to be received and commended to Gaius for three reasons: (1) He enjoyed **a good testimony from everyone**. (2) **The truth** commended him; **truth** being personified, meaning that if the truth could speak, it too would testify that Demetrius' life was in accord with its own standards. (3) John personally attested to his good character.

V. Conclusion (13-14)

13. John had **many** other **things to** mention, but too numerous to do so **with pen and ink** (a similar phrase to "paper and ink" in 2Jn 12).

14. He planned to **see** Gaius **shortly**, when the apostle would rebuke Diotrephes (see 10) but also **speak face to face** with Gaius about those items he chose not to disclose in this letter (13). John bid Gaius farewell with the Hebraism **peace be to you**, a phrase Jesus used with His disciples (Jn 20:19). **Friends** with John send Gaius their greetings, thereby associating themselves with John's request to Gaius. And he wanted Gaius to **greet** his **friends by name**, showing that there were in that church people who supported John, despite Diotrephes' opposition.

This brief and personal letter is a great reminder today for the continuing need to support and show hospitality to missionaries who bring the gospel around the world, as a trait of true Christian virtue.

BIBLIOGRAPHY

See Bibliography for John's Epistles on p. 1986.

●●●●

JUDE

Louis Barbieri

INTRODUCTION

Author. The writer of this brief letter claims to be a brother of James (1), but does not classify himself as an apostle (17). The style of writing is similar to the Letter of James. External evidence pointing to Jude as author is surprisingly early and strong, giving no indication of canonical rejection. The Gospels indicate that Jesus had brothers named James and Judas (Mt 13:55; Mk 6:3). Therefore there is no reason to doubt the authenticity of this book as written by Jude, the brother of James and the half-brother of Jesus Christ.

Date. It appears that some of Jude's readers had been fortunate enough to have heard the apostles (17-18). Although similar in many ways to 2 Peter, Jude was probably written after that letter. Second Peter warns that false teachers will come (2Pt 2:1-2), while Jude states that they are present already (4). Since Jude's name appears at the end of the lists of Jesus' brothers, it may be assumed that he was the youngest member of the family. Although Jude does not directly mention the destruction of Jerusalem, that historical incident would have had no bearing on his admonitions. A date in the decade of AD 80 would be acceptable for the writing of this book.

There are a considerable number of verbal parallels between Jude and 2 Peter (cf. for example Jd 4 with 2Pt 2:3; Jd 7 with 2Pt 2:6; Jd 12 with 2Pt 2:17), leading many to propose that there was literary dependence between the two letters, which is likely. It is impossible to be certain which writer borrowed from or shared with the other, but literary dependence need not undermine the inspiration of either of these epistles. The key to inspiration is not the process through which the letters were created, but the end product itself. For a concise but helpful discussion of the literary dependence, see D. A. Carson and Douglas J. Moo, *An Introduction to the New Testament* (Grand Rapids, MI: Zondervan, 2005), 655–657.

Recipients. Jude makes many allusions to incidents from Jewish history and assumes his readers have a basic knowledge of intertestamental and apocalyptic literature. In light of this, it is best to conclude that Jude was sent to Jewish brethren, probably residents of the land of Israel, who were gathered into local fellowships.

Purpose. Jude's original intent was to write to believers in Christ concerning their common salvation (3), but false teachers had silently crept in among the faithful and were perverting the truth. In light of this development, Jude wrote his letter to urge believers to contend earnestly for the faith they had received.

Themes. There are a number of outstanding characteristics of the book.

(1) There are sharp contrasts in attitude toward the saints and the false teachers.

(2) Jude is very similar to James in that both are to the point, picturesque, and emphasize practice.

(3) Jude makes great use of triplets: 1—called, beloved, kept; 2—mercy, peace, love; 5-7—Israel, angels who sinned, Sodom and Gomorrah; 11—Cain, Balaam, Korah.

(4) Jude makes use of apocalyptic literature. The reference in 9 may come from *The Assumption of Moses*, and 14 and 15 from *The Book of Enoch*. This does not mean that those books are inspired Scripture. Non-canonical writings do contain things that are true. That Jude may quote from these nonbiblical sources simply means that the facts he brings into the inspired text are true.

OUTLINE

I. Introduction and Benediction (1-2)
   A. The Writer and the Recipients (1)
   B. The Benediction (2)
II. The Reason for Jude's Theme (3-4)
   A. His Intention and God's Direction (3)
   B. The Reason for the Lord's Leading (4)
III. The Historical Examples of Judgment for Apostasy (5-7)
   A. Unbelieving Israel (5)
   B. Certain Angels (6)
   C. Sodom and Gomorrah (7)
IV. The Present False Teachers (8-19)
   A. Their Evil Nature and Deeds (8-10)
   B. Their "Old" Doctrines (11)
   C. Figures of Their Character (12-13)
   D. Prophetic Judgment Pronounced on Them (14-15)
   E. Their Characteristics (16)
   F. Warning from the Apostles (17-19)
V. The Program for the Faithful (20-23)
   A. Bible Study (20a)
   B. Prayer (20b)
   C. Abiding in His Love (21a)
   D. Looking for His Coming (21b)
   E. Soul Winning with Discretion (22-23)
VI. The Doxology (24-25)
   A. His Grace to Us (24)
   B. Our Worship for Him (25)

COMMENTARY ON JUDE

I. Introduction and Benediction (1-2)

A. The Writer and the Recipients (1)

1. Jude identified himself as a **bond-servant** (lit., "slave," Gk. *doulos*) **of Jesus Christ** and a **brother of James** (cf. Mt 13:55-56). He once did not believe in Jesus' deity (cf. Jn 7:2-5), but became a devoted follower. His older brother, James, was the leader of the church in Jerusalem (cf. Ac 12:17; 15:13). His readers are identified as regenerated individuals: **called** by God the Father and **kept** by and for Jesus Christ.

B. The Benediction (2)

2. Jude prayed that three qualities, **mercy**, **peace**, and **love** would overflow in his readers' lives. **Mercy** is the idea of showing compassion to one who was suffering and is used of both God and man. **Peace** speaks of tranquility, quiet, and rest. **Love** is a strong feeling of affection between those who are closely associated. If these qualities were truly present in every regenerated individual, what would the world be like?

II. The Reason for Jude's Theme (3-4)

A. His Intention and God's Direction (3)

3. Jude planned to write a letter concerning **our common salvation**. Instead he wrote urging his readers to **contend earnestly** ("to expend enormous effort on behalf of something"), but not angrily, **for the faith** (1Tm 4:1). Since Jude says this **faith** was **once for all** (or completely, wholly) handed down, he is implying there was a body of truth that had been communicated from the apostles. Jesus had promised the apostles in the Upper Room that the Spirit would teach them all things and guide them into the truth (cf. Jn 14:26; 16:12-15). Even in the church's early days there was a recognized content of accepted belief.

B. The Reason for the Lord's Leading (4)

4. False teachers had crept into the church. It had been predicted (cf. 2Pt 2:1-2) that **ungodly persons** who **deny our only Master and Lord** would come. These individuals viewed God's grace as an excuse for open sin.

III. The Historical Examples of Judgment for Apostasy (5-7)

A. Unbelieving Israel (5)

5. Although ungodly individuals occasionally appear to have the advantage, Jude cited three illustrations from biblical history to demonstrate what awaited the disobedient false teachers: First, Israel, following her deliverance from Egypt, failed to **believe** that God would grant them victory over the Canaanites (cf. Nm 14, especially v. 11) and as a result, that generation died in the wilderness.

B. Certain Angels (6)

6. Second, angels who fell—possibly referring to the sin of the angels who followed Satan in his rebellion against God (Ezk 28:11-19; Rv 12:3-4) or, preferably, to Gn 6 when the sons of God cohabited with the daughters of men—have been **kept in eternal bonds** while awaiting final **judgment** (cf. the comments on 2Pt 2:4).

C. Sodom and Gomorrah (7)

7. Third, **Sodom and Gomorrah** are the biblical archetypes for wicked **immorality** (Gn 19), and God judged them with destruction by fire and brimstone (Gn 19:23-29). God's judgment on all three OT rebellions provides **an example** for false teachers to heed.

IV. The Present False Teachers (8-19)

A. Their Evil Nature and Deeds (8-10)

8-10. As did false teachers in the past, the present false teachers **reject authority**, speaking against **things which they do not understand** (10). Not even angelic beings act this way (8, see the comments on 2Pt 2:10-11), as in Michael's contest with the devil over Moses' body (9). While this idea may come from *The Assumption of Moses*, that Jude cited it means the story is true. Jude's point was that Michael's rebuke was God-directed, not personal (10).

B. Their "Old" Doctrines (11)

11. Further OT illustrations indicated these false teachers' actions were not new. They followed the path of **Cain**, who sinned because of jealousy (Gn 4:8), **Balaam**, who sinned because of avarice (Nm 31:16; cf. 25:1-9), and **Korah**, who sinned by rebellion (Nm 16). Each of these examples was self-directed and unwilling to submit to God's established authority and order.

C. Figures of Their Character (12-13)

12-13. Jude described the character of false teachers. Their concern was only for themselves. They promised blessings like **clouds, autumn trees, waves of the sea**, but there was no rain, no fruit, and only scum littering the beach. They were like **wandering stars**, which could refer to the angels that sinned (cf. 6), doomed to black darkness forever.

D. Prophetic Judgment Pronounced on Them (14-15)

14-15. Jude quoted a prophecy from the intertestamental book *1 Enoch* 1:9 (a work compiled from several sources gathered between the third century BC and perhaps the first century AD). Although this book was not canonical, Jude believed its words clearly applied to the false teachers. Enoch was placed in **the seventh generation** from Adam (counting inclusively as the Jewish people of that time did—Adam, Seth, Enosh, Kenan, Mahalalel, Jared, and Enoch; Gn 5:1-24), although that designation is not found in Genesis. In Jewish thinking, the number seven emphasized perfection. Enoch, a man who walked with God, was held in that light. His prophecy clearly stated that the **Lord** was coming with **many thousands of His holy ones** to execute judgment on the **ungodly**. False teachers will give an account for their **ungodly deeds** when the Lord returns.

E. Their Characteristics (16)

16. False teachers' characteristics were noted: **grumblers, finding fault**, governed by their own **lusts**, whose **flattering** speech boosted the egos of those who could help them. These characteristics demonstrate that false teachers do not serve God's people but are always self-serving in their motives.

F. Warning from the Apostles (17-19)

17-19. In the first imperative in the book, Jude reminded his readers **to remember**. The influx of false teachers was predicted by the **apostles of our Lord Jesus Christ** (Ac 20:29-30; 1Tm 4:1; 2Tm 3:1-5; 4:3-4). These **mockers** who **cause divisions** were clearly unbelievers. They were **devoid of the Spirit**. Possession of the Spirit in one's life is a clear indication of regeneration. Failure to possess the Spirit means one is unregenerate and still unforgiven of sin (cf. Rm 8:9).

V. The Program for the Faithful (20-23)

A. Bible Study (20a)

20a. In contrast to unbelieving false teachers, believers were encouraged to build themselves up **on** [their] **most holy faith**. Previously, Jude admonished his readers to contend for the faith (3), which is revealed through Scripture and demands one's constant attention, while here he encouraged them to grow in their faith.

B. Prayer (20b)

20b. Jude also encouraged his readers to be **praying in the Holy Spirit**. This is not a reference to speaking in tongues, but to prayer that is under the authority of the Holy Spirit in accordance with God's Word and so guided and energized by the Holy Spirit (Eph 6:18).

C. Abiding in His Love (21a)

21a. Believers were further admonished to keep themselves **in the love of God**. Believers do this by focusing on prayer that is energized by the Holy Spirit and by continually being built up in the faith (cf. 20). God's love that first drew the believer (1) should be demonstrated to others (2). Jesus' words from Jn 15:19 apply here: "I chose you out of the world."

D. Looking for His Coming (21b)

21b. Furthermore believers must be looking for the coming of our Lord Jesus **to eternal life**. At Christ's return the promised eternal state will be realized.

E. Soul Winning with Discretion (22-23)

22-23. Until that day, the believer is to continually share the mercy he has received with others. Some are **doubting**, needing to be won to Christ through love. Some need to be arrested from their normal course of life, for they figuratively are snatched from the fire. Their garments may be **polluted by the flesh**. While the believer detests the unbeliever's sin, he loves the sinner and seeks to reach him with the truth.

VI. The Doxology (24-25)

A. His Grace to Us (24)

24. Jude concluded with the One who is able **to keep** [us] **from stumbling**. He furthermore can **make** [us] **stand in the presence of His glory blameless.** Christ is able to take sinful people and make them fit for heaven, and keep them secure until they are in His presence. This is the assurance that brings **great joy**.

B. Our Worship for Him (25)

25. To such a one truly belong the **glory, majesty, dominion and authority**, which can only be accomplished **through Jesus Christ**. A final statement asserts that these qualities always rightfully belong to God. **Amen.** So let it be!

BIBLIOGRAPHY

For the bibliography on Jude, see the bibliographies for 1 and 2 Peter on pp. 1966 and 1972.

● ● ● ●

REVELATION

DANIEL GREEN

INTRODUCTION

Author. The writer of this epistle identifies himself as John (1:1, 4), and the early church was nearly unanimous in its understanding that this refers to the apostle. This identification is strengthened by John's name appearing without explanation or defense. In addition, the author has a good understanding of the OT and is likely Jewish. He also was intimately acquainted with the seven churches to which the epistle is written and unapologetically exercises authority over them. Critics of Johannine authorship have offered no convincing alternatives.

John wrote from the island of Patmos, 37 miles from Miletus, in the Ikarian Sea. This Roman penal colony was a place of exile for political enemies of the state. Its stark landscape consisted of hills and rocky ground formed by volcanoes. Early church tradition says that John was forced to work in its mines.

Date. Two dates have been proposed for the time of writing. The early one is AD 54–68, during the reign of Nero. The text's heavy emphasis on persecution and its failure to mention the AD 70 destruction of the temple and Jerusalem support this position, as does the external testimony of the Muratorian Fragment (AD 170–190), which states that John wrote Revelation during the reign of Nero. The consensus view, however, points to a later date during the reign of Domitian (AD 95). This is supported by the testimony of the Church father Irenaeus (AD 185) and the belief that the serious spiritual degeneration evident in the seven churches would increase in likelihood as more time passed. This view sees no need for a mention of the localized judgment on Jerusalem in a book describing worldwide retribution.

Recipients. John wrote to seven historic churches in Asia Minor, now known as Turkey (see map). The members of these churches are addressed in a clockwise order in chaps. 2:1–3:22: Ephesus, Smyrna, Pergamum, Thyatira, Sardis, Philadelphia, and Laodicea. This is the likely order in which they were visited by the courier who delivered the letter to them. While these fellowships may have been chosen only because of a burden on the apostle's heart, some suppose that the choice was motivated by their relatively easy accessibility along main thoroughfares.

These believers were probably a mixture of Jews and Gentiles. They likely hailed from different socioeconomic backgrounds, including business owners, artisans, public officials, homemakers, and slaves. They lived among pagans who engaged in gross immorality and idolatry. The superpowers of Greece and Rome had dominated their cities for several centuries, taxing them heavily and setting up military garrisons within them.

Purpose. The purpose of the book is to comfort persecuted Christians, while exhorting them to persevere in faith, in light of Christ's ultimate victory over the satanically motivated people of the earth. This thesis is supported by the prevalence of the overcomer (victor, conqueror) theme. Each of the seven churches is encouraged to seek the reward of those who overcome the temptation to apostatize under persecution (2:7, 11, 17, 26; 3:5, 12, 21). In addition, the Lamb Himself overcomes (5:5; 17:14), as do those who resist Satan (12:11) and the beast (15:2) during the last days. Overcomers will inherit eternal life (21:7). Understanding this emphasis is essential for a proper interpretation of the book. While Revelation provides much insight into events yet to transpire

Seven Churches of Asia

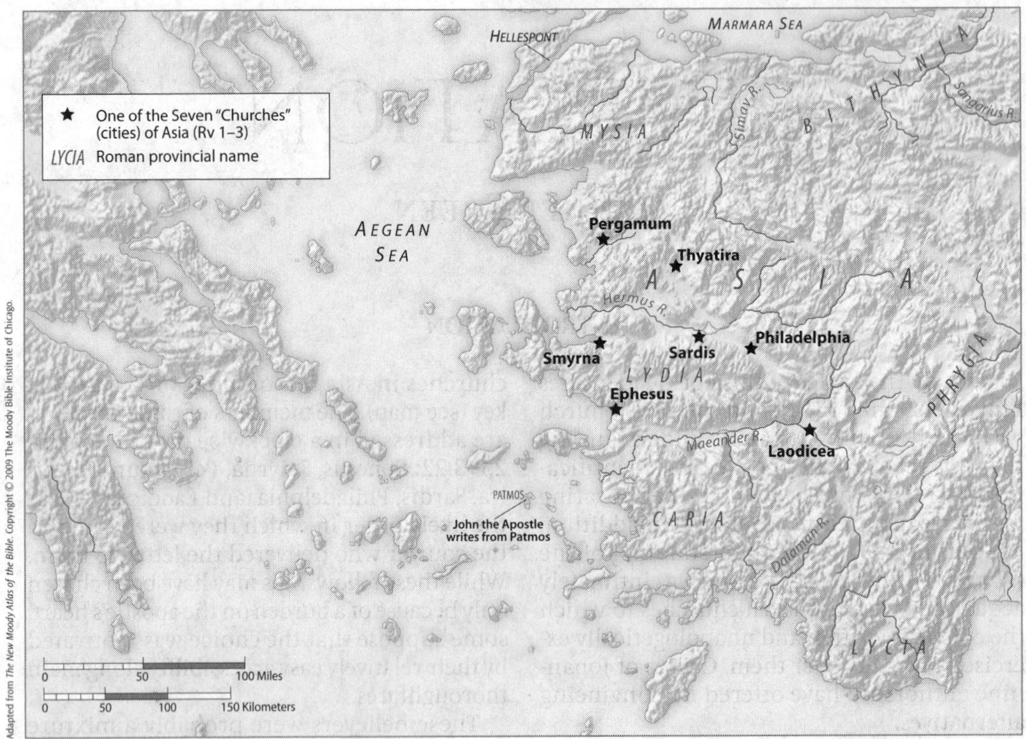

on earth, it was originally written to people in desperate need of faith and encouragement. All prophetic information is given in support of the main theme. In the end, the original readers would be vindicated if they remained in the faith, resisting idolatrous worship of the Roman emperor. Those who rightly understand that Revelation is essentially about the end of days need to be careful not to lose track of this emphasis in their justifiable interest in the details of events yet to come.

Themes. While Revelation is written out of pastoral concern, it is also theologically rich. Its *Christology* pictures Christ as the ruler of heaven and earth (1:5, 14-20; 5:7-14; 11:15-16; 14:1; 15:2-4; 19:11-16; 20:1-6; 21:14; 22:3), the wrathful Lamb who destroys His enemies (6:1-8, 15-17) but saves those of faith (6:9-10; 7:10; 21:27; 22:17), and the kind shepherd and central focus of His people (7:17; 21:22-23; 22:3-5). The *wrath of God* the Father is also prominent (11:13, 19; 15:2, 7-8; 16:5-20; 18:4-8, 20; 20:11-15). The terror of the *Great Tribulation* (6:1–18:24) and *the physical nature and spiritual activities of heaven* (4:1–5:14; 7:9-17; 14:1-5; 19:1-10; 21:1–22:5) are spoken of more in this book than anywhere else in Scripture. There are also implications for *social and economic justice* (17:1–18:24). Abuses of power and economic advantage will be judged. Continuity with John's gospel and epistles is also evident in such shared themes as the shepherd (Jn 10:10-11; Rv 7:17), the dangers and ultimate destruction of the world system (Jn 16:33; 1Jn 2:15-17; Rv 17:1–18:24), the demise of Satan (Jn 12:31; Rv 12:7-9), and the tabernacle of God among men (Jn 1:14; Rv 21:3).

The letter has certain characteristics of apocalyptic literature, such as symbolism and predictions concerning a cataclysmic end to the world. However, the author is identified, which is uncommon in such writings. More important is John's own identification of the material as prophecy (22:7, 19). It is clearly not purely symbolic. It should be understood as prophetic narrative, which includes apocalyptic and epistolary elements.

There is no scholarly consensus as to the structure of the material. Plausible suggestions can be found in Blaising (cf. Craig A. Blaising, et al., *Three Views of the Millennium and Beyond*

[Grand Rapids, MI, Zondervan, 1999], 206; Alan Johnson, *Revelation*, vol. 7, EBC, ed. Frank E. Gaebelein [Grand Rapids, MI: Zondervan, 1981], 414–15; and Mark Wilson *Charts on the Book of Revelation: Literary, Historical and Theological Perspectives* [Grand Rapids, MI: Kregel, 2007], 31). This commentary will follow the outline implied by 1:19.

There are five enduring grids for interpreting the book:

The *exclusively preterist* view is that many of the events described in the book took place during John's lifetime, and thus provided a contemporary description of events that the churches were facing. Typically, its adherents hold to an early date of writing and thus see the events described as coming to pass during the turbulent reign of Nero, although some see fulfillment still taking place as late as the fifth century. Thus, the images related to the enemies of God's people, such as the beast (chap. 13) and the seven hills (chap. 17), are aligned with Rome and its pagan worship. Some extreme adherents believe that Christ came for the second time when Titus invaded Jerusalem in AD 70. This view was developed in the early seventeenth century and has enjoyed a resurgence of popularity in recent years.

The *historicist* view sees the events described in the book as a panorama of history from the time of John until the present. A form of this approach understands the seven churches of chaps. 2 and 3 as descriptive of the devolution of the fervent NT church (Ephesus, Smyrna) into the apostasy of the present day (Laodicea). A significant weakness of this position is its Eurocentric view of Church history as well as the constant need to reinterpret data in light of new developments.

The *idealist* view takes the details of the book as a general description of the battle between good and evil as it continues into the present Church Age. There is little attempt to associate the details of the book with any specific events of the past or future. This spiritualizing approach simply focuses on the ultimate triumph of Christ over the forces that oppose Him and His kingdom.

The *preterist/futurist* view (also known as the "eclectic" view) interprets Revelation as being especially pertinent to John and his readers while at the same time showing how their first-century setting has parallels with the future. One of the difficulties with this approach is the need for seeing multiple referents in virtually every part of Revelation after chap. 4 (a first-century fulfillment and a future, eschatological fulfillment). If this is John's approach, he gives few clues to indicate he expected his readers to look for multiple temporal and referential layers in his book. This approach also tends to confuse the book's meaning and its significance (the relevance of Revelation for John's original readers and the Church in any generation).

The *futurist* view, while focusing on the purpose of the book for the original audience, still holds that chaps. 6–22 will be fulfilled literally in the future. Thus, the details of these chapters will be worked out in real events yet to come. It is the view adopted in this commentary.

For a survey of some contemporary approaches see C. Marvin Pate, et al., *Four Views on the Book of Revelation*, Grand Rapids, MI: Zondervan, 1998, 17–34.

OUTLINE

I. The Things That Were (1:1-20)
   A. The Greeting to the Seven Churches (1:1-8)
   B. John's Vision from Patmos (1:9-20)
II. The Things That Are (2:1–3:22)
   A. The Message to Ephesus (2:1-7)
   B. The Message to Smyrna (2:8-11)
   C. The Message to Pergamum (2:12-17)
   D. The Message to Thyatira (2:18-29)
   E. The Message to Sardis (3:1-6)
   F. The Message to Philadelphia (3:7-13)
   G. The Message to Laodicea (3:14-22)
III. The Things That Will Be (4:1–22:21)

- A. The Father and the Lamb in Heaven (4:1–5:14)
  - 1. The Vision of the Throne (4:1-11)
  - 2. The Vision of the Lamb (5:1-14)
- B. The Seal Judgments (6:1–8:5)
  - 1. The First Six Seal Judgments (6:1-17)
    - a. The First Seal—Conquest (6:1-2)
    - b. The Second Seal—War (6:3-4)
    - c. The Third Seal—Inflation and Famine (6:5-6)
    - d. The Fourth Seal—Death (6:7-8)
    - e. The Fifth Seal—Martyrdom (6:9-11)
    - f. The Sixth Seal—Cosmic Upheaval (6:12-17)
  - 2. The Interlude about the Faithful of the Tribulation (7:1-17)
    - a. The 144,000 Jewish Believers Serving on the Earth (7:1-8)
    - b. The Nations Worshiping in Heaven (7:9-17)
  - 3. The Seventh Seal Judgment (8:1-5)
- C. The Trumpet Judgments (8:6–11:19)
  - 1. The First Six Trumpets (8:7–9:21)
    - a. The First Trumpet—Earthly Destruction (8:7)
    - b. The Second Trumpet—Aquatic Destruction (8:8-9)
    - c. The Third Trumpet—Water Pollution (8:10-11)
    - d. The Fourth Trumpet—Light Destroyed (8:12)
    - e. The Fifth Trumpet—Demonic Affliction (8:13–9:12)
    - f. The Sixth Trumpet—Death (9:13-21)
  - 2. The Digression about the Little Book and the Two Witnesses (10:1–11:14)
    - a. The Little Book (10:1-11)
    - b. The Two Witnesses (11:1-14)
  - 3. The Seventh Trumpet (11:15-19)
- D. The Seven Signs (12:1–14:20)
  - 1. The First Sign—The Woman (12:1-6)
  - 2. The Second Sign—War in Heaven (12:7-12)
  - 3. The Third Sign—Israel Attacked and Preserved (12:13–13:1a)
  - 4. The Fourth Sign—The Beast from the Sea (13:1b-10)
  - 5. The Fifth Sign—The Beast from the Earth (13:11-18)
  - 6. The Sixth Sign—The Lamb on Mount Zion (14:1-5)
  - 7. The Seventh Sign—Judgment against the Rebellious (14:6-20)
- E. The Interlude in Heaven (15:1-8)
- F. The Seven Bowl Judgments (16:1-21)
  - 1. The First Bowl—Painful Sores (16:1-2)
  - 2. The Second Bowl—The Sea Turned to Blood (16:3)
  - 3. The Third Bowl—Fresh Water Turned to Blood (16:4-7)
  - 4. The Fourth Bowl—A Scorched Earth (16:8-9)
  - 5. The Fifth Bowl—Darkness (16:10-11)
  - 6. The Sixth Bowl—Demonic Assault (16:12-16)
  - 7. The Seventh Bowl—Worldwide Devastation (16:17-21)
- G. The Destruction of Babylon the Great (17:1–18:24)
  - 1. The Destruction Detailed (17:1-18)
  - 2. The Destruction Mourned (18:1-24)
- H. The Second Coming of Christ (19:1-21)
  - 1. The Celebrations of God's Servants (19:1-10)
  - 2. The Return of Christ (19:11-21)
- I. The Millennium (20:1-15)
- J. The New Heaven and New Earth (21:1–22:5)
- K. The Concluding Message (22:6-21)

COMMENTARY ON REVELATION

I. The Things That Were (1:1-20)

A. The Greeting to the Seven Churches (1:1-8)

1:1-3. The content of the book was revealed by **Jesus Christ** (v. 1). The transmission of the material began with God the Father and was given progressively to Jesus, an angel, the apostle himself, and finally the seven churches of Asia Minor. Blessings were promised for the one who would read the prophetic scroll to the various congregations, as well as to those who would hear and obey its teachings. **For the time is near** (v. 3) gives the motivation for living in obedience: Christ may return at any time and when He does, He will hold men accountable for the lives that they have lived. There are no events that must transpire before the rapture of the Church, which introduces the last phase of earth's history.

1:4-8. John issued a greeting to the churches in the name of the triune God. The words **from Him who is and who was and who is to come** (v. 4) describe the eternality of the Father. He is everlastingly existent, unbounded by time. The phrase **the seven Spirits** may refer to angels, but it more likely describes His spiritual perfection, or perhaps that of the Holy Spirit. The number seven appears 54 times in the book and has to do with what is flawless or complete. Some take this as an allusion to Is 11:2, but only six attributes are present there. It more likely refers to His intense interest in, and ministry through the Holy Spirit to the seven churches. Jesus is said to be **the faithful witness, the firstborn of the dead, and the ruler of the kings of the earth** (v. 5). He can be trusted as He reveals the things to come. The second phrase refers to the priority of His resurrection (1Co 15:23), which anticipates that of all Christians in the rapture (1Th 4:13-18). That He presently rules over the world from heaven may have been a comfort to the first-century church, which was so mistreated by Domitian and other Roman officials. He had not lost control. He had freed them from their sins by shedding His blood on the cross (a description of redemption). He had also made them **a kingdom, priests to His God** (v. 6). Although the Church and Israel are distinct peoples of God, there are yet similarities. OT Israel was a physical people of God, a kingdom of priests (Ex 19:5-6), whereas the Church is a spiritual kingdom of believer-priests who offer spiritual sacrifices to God. Perhaps their notable status in God's eyes encouraged early believers surrounded by pagan worship and false priests. It certainly elicited praise from John, who pens a mini-doxology to the One who reigns forever. **Behold, He is coming** (v. 7) begins a quotation that combines elements of Dn 7:13-14 and Zch 12:10. This cannot, as some claim, be narrowed to the Roman invasion of Jerusalem in AD 70, as John conceives of the "tribes" in a universal sense (5:9; 7:9; 11:9; 13:7). When Jesus the Messiah returns, He will cause great consternation for both Jews and Gentiles who have rebelled against Him. This paragraph ends as it began with God's statement of His own greatness. **The Alpha and the Omega** are the first and last letters in the Greek alphabet and emphasize both His sovereignty (Is 44:6-7) and eternality.

B. John's Vision from Patmos (1:9-20)

1:9-11. John comforted the churches by recognizing them as fellow sufferers. Like them, he had paid a price for speaking the truth about Jesus (v. 9). Writing from the stark environs of Patmos (see introduction) he was **in the Spirit** (v. 10), referring to the divinely induced state of the prophet as he received his vision from Jesus. The phrase **the Lord's day** is commonly understood to mean Sunday. More likely here it refers to John being carried by vision to see "the day of the Lord" or perhaps, since the word for Lord is an adjective, it may refer to a "Lordly day" or a day characterized by being filled with the Lord's presence. Nevertheless, the vision came with instructions to record it in writing for delivery to the seven churches.

1:12-16. John's vision next focused on supreme majesty. Jesus Christ appeared in His heavenly splendor. He stood in the midst of the **seven golden lampstands** (v. 12), the seven churches who were to be light to their world (v. 20). The apostle recorded numerous aspects of His appearance. He was dressed in a manner worthy of royalty and priesthood as He tended the living lamps. As Messiah, He has now been glorified with the Father (Jn 17:4-5). **White hair** (v. 14) signifies His wisdom and commands respect, and blazing eyes suggest purity and judgment. His **bronze feet** (v. 15) were ready to trample His enemies should they not be devoured by the sword in His mouth (Is 11:4).

The description of the exalted Jesus here is similar to the description of the Ancient of Days in Dn 7. Perhaps the Son is described as possessing the Father's glory here because He has been glorified in answer to His own prayer in Jn 17:4-5: "Glorify Me together with Yourself, with the glory which I had with You before the world was." His face shone with the glory of His perfections, and He spoke with overwhelming power. Different parts of this description are reiterated in the letters to the churches (e.g., for His flaming eyes, cf. 2:18), probably to encourage them with a different aspect of His authority and power based upon the church's needs. Most comforting was the picture of the **seven stars** (v. 16) in His hand. These stars were "angels" as seen in v. 20. Another permissible translation here could be "messengers." This is preferred as the word most likely refers to responsible human leaders of these churches as held in the hand of God during perilous times (Dn 12:3), rather than to spirits. These messengers appeared to have responsibility for the spiritual oversight of the church, making it unlikely that these are angels, and it is equally unlikely that God would use a human agent (John) to communicate with angelic beings. In addition, the imagery may be a polemic against the seven stars of the Imperial cult, which appeared on Domitian's coins.

1:17-18. John was momentarily paralyzed before the majestic presence. However, Christ assured him with a touch. Referring to His eternal resurrection life, He asserted His sovereignty over death and destinies.

1:19-20. Jesus gave John the outline of what He was about to reveal, along with a general interpretation of the symbols of vv. 12 through 16.

II. The Things That Are (2:1–3:22)

The seven churches are addressed here. They have a common structure that includes: (1) a greeting, (2) commendations, (3) corrections, (4) an exhortation to repent, and (5) a promise of reward for those who **overcome**. Most are also encouraged by some aspect of Christ's character from 1:4-20.

A. The Message to Ephesus (2:1-7)

2:1-7. The church at **Ephesus** had a rich spiritual heritage, as a host of people had repented of occult practices at the time of their conversion under the preaching of the apostle Paul (Ac 19–21). The city itself was past its prime, its once bustling harbor having become filled with silt as a result of deforestation. To compensate for the lost business, the city had turned to religious tourism that involved fertility rituals and cult prostitution at the temple of the goddess Artemis. Jesus commended this church for its enduring service in such an environment. In 1:16 Jesus was described as holding the seven stars in His right hand and walking among the seven lampstands, a description reiterated here. This description implies His intimacy with the Ephesian church, an intimacy that they, however, had abandoned (v. 4). They had maintained doctrinal integrity, refusing to tolerate false teachers whom they put to the test with Scripture. They had also rejected **the deeds of the Nicolaitans** (v. 6). This may refer to an early clerical hierarchy, but should more likely be understood as a group that promoted sexual promiscuity. Church fathers such as Irenaeus and Tertullian equated them with antinomian gnostics. Despite maintaining doctrinal purity the church had lost its heartfelt love for the Lord. If this coldness did not change, they faced the potential end of ministry usefulness. A wonderful future in heaven, **the Paradise of God** (v. 7), awaited those who would **overcome** temptation to leave the faith.

B. The Message to Smyrna (2:8-11)

2:8-11. Smyrna was a beautiful and important seaport boasting a population of about 200,000, quite large for its time. It was a center for science and medicine, and the birthplace of the noted author Homer. It was also a regional center for emperor worship in the first century, whose citizens were expected to burn incense to Zeus once a year. As the one who conquered death (the description of Jesus in 1:17-18 is reiterated here), Christ would enable them to conquer death that might come to them through persecution and receive **the crown of life** (eternal life, v. 10). The church itself was commended for its deep spirituality (**you are rich**) (v. 9) in the context of persecution and financial loss. Perhaps they had lost opportunities for income because of their faith. Antagonistic Jews, **the synagogue of Satan**, had made life difficult for them, and the Devil had instigated the imprisonment of some. This church is the only one of the seven not to receive correction. **Be faithful until death** (v. 10) indicates the extent to which the believers were expected to persevere. Under no circumstances could apostasy be excused. This should be a sobering lesson for modern believers tempted to leave the faith. The Smyrnans who persevered in their professions of faith would receive eternal life, symbolized by **the crown of life**. Such **overcomers** would not experience **the second death** (v. 11), that is, hell.

C. The Message to Pergamum (2:12-17)

2:12-17. Pergamum was an important buffer state for Rome, and had thus contributed to the Roman victory at the battle of Magnesia several centuries earlier. The people worshiped Caesar and the spirit of Rome, earning the distinction from Jesus as a place **where Satan dwells** (v. 13). As the **One who has the sharp two-edged sword** (see this description in 1:16), Jesus Christ will judge those who killed His people (v. 13; cf. the sword by which He judges His enemies in 19:15), a point that would encourage these believers. The church in the city received a commendation for ultimate bravery in the face of potential martyrdom, following the model of Antipas's endurance during the days of persecution under Domitian (AD 89–96). According to Christian tradition, John ordained Antipas as bishop of Pergamum, after which Antipas was burned to death on a pagan altar in AD 92. Yet they had compromised significantly by allowing false teaching and immorality among them. On **Balaam** (v. 14), see the comments on Nm 22:1–25:16; 31:15-16. John parallels this instruction with the perverted doctrine of the Nicolaitans among the Pergamese. Jesus commanded the believers to repent of sexual immorality and idolatry (for Christian involvement in idolatry, see the comments on 1Co 8 and 10), which were bound together in pagan rites, lest He come against them with a **sword** (v. 16). Overcomers would receive **hidden manna** (v. 17), that is, spiritual blessing. The parallel with the wilderness account continues here. As the people of Moses' generation received food from heaven, which sustained them, so Christians receive spiritual sustenance from on high. Those who persevered were promised a **white stone**, which is perhaps an invitation to a banquet in heaven, and **a new name**, known only to God and themselves. The modern church should consider why its orthodoxy has not resulted in more consistent sexual ethics among its members. Followers of Christ should live in the fear of God and in anticipation of a glorious future.

D. The Message to Thyatira (2:18-29)

2:18-29. Thyatira was an important communication center that had been founded after the death of Alexander the Great by one of his generals, Seleucus. Macedonian military garrisons were subsequently stationed there, leading to the worship of a local patron warrior by the populace. Its vigorous commerce was founded on bronze and a valuable purple dye culled from plant roots. A devout businesswoman, Lydia, was from this city, and had been instrumental in the founding of the church (Ac 16:11-15, 40). The description of Jesus in 1:14-15 is recapped here, with the **eyes like a flame of fire** (emphasizing His ability to search **the minds and hearts** [v. 23] of all and to see the secret immoral deeds of **Jezebel** and those she misled) and **feet . . . like burnished bronze** (which may suggest both His strength and purity—like refined metal—whereby He judges His enemies). This description would motivate the believers in Thyatira to reconsider their sinful actions. He commended them for their overall spiritual growth and mentioned several fine attributes that they possessed. His attention turned quickly to their unacceptable toleration of **Jezebel** (v. 20), a false prophetess who had led them into sins similar to those being committed at Pergamum. This false teacher is named symbolically after the notorious Sidonian princess who incited Israel to worship Baal and Asherah after her marriage to King Ahab of Israel (1Kg 16:30-33; 21:25-26). The Lord threatened a **bed of sickness** and **great tribulation** for her and her followers should they not repent (v. 22). God knows all and promised to be gracious to those who did not partake of **the deep things of Satan** (v. 24). Those not dabbling in the occult would **overcome** and receive authority over nations (vv. 26-27). This reference to Ps 2 revealed an exhilarating truth. Believers who persevered in faith would be co-rulers with Christ in the millennial kingdom. They would also know Jesus intimately, the **morning star** (Rv 22:16). He is the brightest star in the entire galaxy (cf. the comments on Nm 24:17) and will cause His faithful followers to shine brightly in the messianic kingdom as in Dn 12:3 (Robert L. Thomas, *Revelation 1–7: An Exegetical Commentary* [Chicago:Moody, 1992], 2:510, 1:235). Neither ancient Rome, nor any other power would have ultimate victory over the people of God.

E. The Message to Sardis (3:1-6)

3:1-6. Mints for gold and silver provided significant revenue for **Sardis**, a city otherwise past its commercial prime. Rebuke characterized the address to this church. Its spiritual reputation exceeded reality, as its members were showing no sign of spiritual life (v. 1). As possessor of the **seven Spirits** (1:4), probably a reference to His spiritual completeness, Jesus is displeased with their spiritual **deeds**, which had not been **completed** (v. 2). Should they not repent, Jesus would come upon them suddenly (v. 3), as had Cyrus the Persian who conquered the city in 549 BC by scaling its rear wall. Some believers were commended, though, for not polluting themselves (v. 4), presumably a reference to their maintenance of moral and doctrinal integrity. Overcomers (v. 5) were promised fellowship with Jesus and white garments, visible rewards for faithfulness. **The book of life** is best understood figuratively. Genuine believers are known to the mind of God. This figure should not be pressed to suggest that every person starts out in a positive relationship with God, losing such status only in the event of heinous sin. Rather, it emphasizes the security of the faithful, with whom Jesus will gladly identify before the Father and the heavenly host.

F. The Message to Philadelphia (3:7-13)

3:7-13. Attalus II Philadelphus founded **Philadelphia** in 159 BC during his reign as the king of Pergamum. The citizenry changed the name for a short time to Neocaesarea after Rome sent financial aid following an earthquake in 17 BC. It was considered the cultural gateway to Asia. Jesus uses this gateway status, referring to Himself as the One **who opens and no one will shut, and who shuts and no one opens** (v. 7). He is sovereign over who is admitted to His kingdom. He holds the **key of David**, an allusion to Is 22:22. The OT context records God's assurance to faithful Eliakim that Shebna would not be able to usurp his place in Israel. Similarly, the **synagogue of Satan** (v. 9) would not be able to frustrate God's intended blessing of this church. It is difficult to identify the **synagogue of Satan**. It may be a harsh reference to unbelieving Jews who, by their opposition to the gospel, had become unknowing servants of Satan. But they may have been Gentiles who had been circumcised (**who say that they are Jews and are not**) and now are trying to force this teaching on other Gentiles. It is important to read this without the grid of 2,000 years of the Church's anti-Semitism. The writer himself was Jewish and sees a glorious future for his fellow Jews. Whatever their precise identity might be, the phrase **who say that they are Jews and are not** refers to their failure to be spiritually fulfilled in Messiah (Rm 2:28-29). Tragically, their only connection to Jesus was a shared bloodline.

At some future point all who reject Christ, Jew and Gentile, will bow at the feet of God's children and acknowledge the believers' victory. This may be at the judgment of the sheep and goats prior to inauguration of the millennial kingdom (Mt 25:31-46). The faithful Philadelphian church had followed Scripture and refused to deny Christ. **I also will keep you from the hour of testing** (v. 10) is His promise to them. The meaning of this phrase has been extensively debated, giving rise to three major interpretations: (1) This is a promise specific to the Philadelphians and thus has no broad future application, a view rendered unlikely by the presence of the phrase **the whole world**. (2) It assures believers that they will be preserved while going through the great tribulation, a view supported by parallel grammar in Jn 17:15. Then (it is argued by posttribulationists) believers remain in the world but are kept from the evil one, just as believers remain on earth during the tribulation but are kept from, or will not be the objects of, God's wrath. While Jn 17:15a does indicate that believers are not "removed from ["out of," *ek*] the world" after Christ's ascension, they are however "kept [i.e., "preserved"] from ["out of," *ek*] the evil one" (Jn 17:15b). John 17:15 indicates that believers are "in Christ" but never "in the evil one." Judging from the similar wording in Rv 3:10, Christians will likewise not be "in **the hour of testing**," i.e., they will not be present on earth during the future tribulation. (3) It provides assurance that no Christian will be present during the future tribulation. This is the most natural interpretation and the simplest translation of the word *ek*, although it requires that there be a different set of new converts during said tribulation. There was no rebuke for this faithful church, which was encouraged to persevere and receive the **crown** as a reward (v. 11). Each would also become a **pillar in the temple** (v. 12), a phrase suggestive of eternal life with God. Pillars were often the last part of a temple left standing during the frequent earthquakes in the city. **The new Jerusalem**, a literal heavenly city, would be their ultimate destiny.

G. The Message to Laodicea (3:14-22)

3:14-22. Laodicea was on the south bank of the Lychus River, 100 feet above the water. It had a weigh station related to extensive Roman shipping to Syro-Palestine, and was also known for the production of eye medicine and wool. There was a significant Jewish population among the Greeks, as 2,000 families had been settled there centuries earlier following deportation from Babylon. The One who was a **faithful and true**

Witness (1:5) wanted to see more followers like Himself in the city. Jesus spoke to the congregation as **the Beginning of the creation of God** (v. 14). While false teachers through the centuries have taken this as proof of a beginning point for the existence of the Second Person of the Trinity, such understanding is ruled out by the assertion of His eternality in 1:8 and 1:18. The phrase means that Jesus is preeminent. **Beginning** (Gk. *arche*) means "originator," "initiator" (cf. Rv 22:13; Col 1:27), and refers to one who constitutes an initial cause and thus is preeminent. He is the Lord of all creation. No commendations were given to this church. Instead, they were censured for being **lukewarm** (v. 16). Christ wanted them to be either **cold or hot**. Both words are positive in context. Like the healing hot springs near Hieropolis, and the refreshing cool springs in Colossae, their testimony was to demonstrate positive attributes. Their spiritual apathy instead mirrored the tepid water of their city. Verse 17 is an ironic rebuke to those whose confidence in money and medicine had left them bankrupt and blind spiritually. They did not recognize their deepest needs. This should be a correction to contemporary ministries that focus only on the surface needs of people and not their deeper spiritual needs as well. The Laodiceans were encouraged to return to the Lord, who would direct them into keen insight and works worthy of reward. They needed to see Jesus' rebukes as an act of loving concern. **If anyone hears My voice and opens the door** (v. 20) is not best understood as an evangelistic invitation. The Laodicean congregation, like all the churches addressed, consisted of Christians. Only intimates shared meals in the ancient culture, so the appeal was for deeper spiritual fellowship. An amazing promise was given to the one **who overcomes**. Like the faithful in Thyatira, he would be given co-regency with the Son in the messianic kingdom (v. 21). Rather than being dominated by Roman rulers, persevering believers would enjoy royal status.

III. The Things That Will Be (4:1–22:21)

A. The Father and the Lamb in Heaven (4:1–5:14)

These chapters look to the future for the first time in the book and contain John's initial description of heaven. He was caught up in a vision where he saw the Father and the Son in the midst of a host of angels. The Father received praise for His creation of the world, and the Son for His redeeming work on the cross. The original readers would have been comforted by understanding that, while their world was most uncertain, heaven was properly focused and stable.

1. The Vision of the Throne (4:1-11)

4:1. Some see **Come up here** as a reference to a pretribulational rapture of the Church. It is better understood as God's call to John to behold the next vision (see 6:1, 3, 5, 7). He was invited to look through a door in heaven to see events that were yet future.

4:2-3. While **in the Spirit** (see 1:10), he saw a throne. Seated there was a theophany, a veiled appearance of God the Father. John describes His beauty and majesty without ever mentioning His name. He likens His appearance to jasper (a translucent, diamond-like stone) and a carnelian (a fiery red stone). The emerald rainbow (Gn 9) may suggest that God will not depart from His faithfulness to Israel in the coming tribulation.

4:4-11. Twelves, or multiples thereof, in Scripture (e.g., elders, tribes of Israel, and disciples of Jesus) often indicate order or administration. These **twenty-four** beings (v. 4) recognized God's sovereignty. Some scholars have understood them to be representatives of the Church in heaven, as the term **elders** is often used of church leaders who may also receive crowns for service (1Pt 5:1-4). In addition, saints may be rewarded with white garments for the same (Rv 19:8). Others see the beings as angels, a position supported from Johannine literature, which describes angels in white garments (Jn 20:12), and angels (albeit evil), who wear crowns (9:7). The second interpretation is supported by the parallel between the explanatory work of an elder in 7:13-14 and that of angels elsewhere (e.g., 10:8-11; 17:1), John calling an elder "my lord" in 7:14 (making it likely that this is a supernatural being, not a redeemed human), and the apparent distinction between the elders and the bride of Christ (the Church) in 19:4-10. These elders are probably angelic beings.

Terrifying sounds (lightning, thunder, and rumbling, v. 5) coexisted with the complete tranquility suggested by a crystal sea (v. 6). About the throne of God appeared angels of the cherubic order (v. 6; see Ezk 1:4-24; 10:10-22). They each had four different faces, six wings, and eyes all around, perhaps signifying their unceasing attention to the throne. **In the center** suggests that these angels surrounded it, front and back.

Praise was on their lips as they spoke the familiar refrain, acknowledging God's eternality (1:8), while also praising His holiness. They called Him **Almighty** (v. 8). This name of God appears only nine times in the NT, eight in Revelation (1:8; 4:8; 11:17; 15:3; 16:7; 16:14; 19:15; 21:22; and 2Co 6:18). These various kinds of angels shared a most expressive adoration for their Maker. Having praised Him with their lips, they fell before the throne of the Eternal One, yielding their sovereignty to His in the casting of their crowns (v. 10). Their focus was on one particular work of God, His creation. They recognized that because God had made everything in the universe, it was rightfully His. Because all creation existed via the exercise of His will, God was hailed as **worthy** of the honor due eternal majesty (v. 11). He was constantly praised. Believers are created beings that have no right to act independently but should rather humbly submit themselves to their Maker.

2. The Vision of the Lamb (5:1-14)

5:1. The new chapter moves from the focus on John's vision of the enthroned Father to his vision of the Lamb. Here, the Father held an opisthograph, a document with writing on both sides. Its **seven seals** may communicate authority and importance. Seals were normally lines of clay or wax that secured a scroll at certain places, and warned those without authority not to access the contents. The wills of both Augustus Caesar and Vespasian were marked in such fashion according to Roman law.

5:2-4. A mighty angel called attention to a problem. It would take a special person to open the document. He would need to be **worthy** (v. 2), bearing the requisite authority. The reference to opening continues the theme of 4:1. God was revealing the secrets of the inner sanctum: Himself, His dwelling place, and His plans. However, it appeared at first that no one in all creation could open the scroll (v. 3), which caused the apostle to weep profusely (v. 4). His deep desire for insight was frustrated by the inability of anyone to unseal, much less decipher, the letter.

5:5-6. John was soon comforted by one of the angelic elders who pointed him to a heroic figure, One who **has overcome** (v. 5), having earned the right to break the seals. This One, the second person of the Godhead, was described under the metaphors of **Lion . . . from the tribe of Judah**, and **Root of David**. The first term pictures Him as a Hebrew and the fiercest of a fierce and royal tribe (Gn 49:9-10). The second reiterates this physical and royal descent while connecting Him with David, himself a royal offspring of Judah, and recipient of a covenant ultimately fulfilled by the **Root** who now appeared (2Sm 7:12-16). His victory connected Him with His followers among the seven churches who had been charged to overcome in the midst of great difficulty. John's attention was riveted on the one who appeared as a slaughtered lamb. The form of the word **Lamb** (v. 6) used here suggests smallness, but does not imply cuteness, a concept foreign to the Greek mind. Perhaps it is employed to inspire awe in Christ who is at once both immensely powerful and uncommonly gentle. The presence of horns on the lamb may have suggested messianic character, since horns often describe dominion (cf. the comments on Dn 7:7-24). But reference to the Paschal Lamb may also be implied (Jn 1:29; 19:14, 31-46; 1Co 5:7). **Seven eyes** indicate omniscience, by which He kept track of all events transpiring on earth, and read the attitudes of the human heart.

5:7-10. These verses constitute the structural center of the chapter. They stress the Lamb's authority, demonstrated as He came from the midst of the angelic throng to receive the scroll from the Father's hand (v. 7). The angels, having fallen prostrate in worship, each possessed a **harp and golden bowls full of incense** (v. 8). The former suggests their inclination to musical worship. This is affirmed by the number **twenty-four**, which parallels the orders of worshiping Levites in 1Ch 25:6-31. The **bowls** likely held not general prayers, but cries for justice from the mouths of brutally martyred saints (6:9-11). In time they would be emptied, as God's righteous wrath was expressed against their tormentors. The redemption of which the host sang implies a purchase made, in this case at the cost of the Lamb's blood shed on the cross. **Every tribe** (v. 9) does not guarantee universal salvation, but does imply that a vast spectrum of people will benefit eternally from the work of the cross. These will represent the Lamb as a **kingdom** and as **priests** (v. 10). The words **reign upon the earth** make an important point. Believers will reign for and with the Lamb not only in heaven, but also on earth during the millennial kingdom (3:21; 20:4; 21:1-3).

5:11-14. Since a myriad is equal to ten thousand, it was literally millions of angels who proclaimed the worthiness of the Lamb to receive boundless praise (v. 11). **Every created thing** (v.

13) indicates that even the lost will be compelled to praise the Lord (Php 2:9-11). The focus is shared by the Creator Father and the Redeemer Son. Modern believers should understand that the doctrines of creation and salvation are inseparably connected. It is theologically inconsistent to embrace the latter while failing to fully embrace the biblical teaching on the former as well. The God who created all things in a perfect and mature state (Gn 1:25, 31) is the same One who provides for the redemption of that creation after the fall (see the comments on Rm 5:12-21; 1Co 15:45-49).

B. The Seal Judgments (6:1–8:5)

These chapters are part of a larger section (6:1–18:24) that describes the tribulation, during which God will exercise His wrath toward rebellious sinners, and work to bring Israel to repentance. This section assured first-century believers that persecutors of God's people would not ultimately escape justice. **Seals**, **trumpets**, and **bowls** are labels John used to describe the judgments of this time period.

Their sequence is debated. Some scholars hold to a recapitulation, or reiteration, theory, that is, that there is one set of judgments, which is described three different ways. Others believe that there are three separate and consecutive sets of judgments. Insofar as the seventh seal contains the trumpets (8:1-6), and the seventh trumpet anticipates the bowls (11:15-19; 16:1), there is *some* reiteration. Yet, for the most part, the plagues unfold in a consecutive manner and intensify as they progress (see the reference to one-fourth of the population dying in 6:8, while the fraction is one-third in 9:15). This understanding of the arrangement parallels OT judgments (e.g., Ex 7–11). This chronological progression is interrupted, however, by a number of interludes that describe events without reference to time (7:1-17; 10:1–11:14; 12:1–14:8). John's description of the seal judgments appears to parallel the teaching of Jesus in the Olivet Discourse (Mt 24:4-31).

1. The First Six Seal Judgments (6:1-17)

a. The First Seal—Conquest (6:1-2)

6:1-2. The Lamb now exerted His authority in opening the first seal. Some see **a white horse, and he who sat on it** (v. 2) as a reference to the conquering Christ, which is consistent with the overcomer theme. Nevertheless, given the negativity associated with all of the other riders, this one is best understood as the conquering beast, the evil ruler of the tribulation period (Dn 9:26-27) who is a wicked parody of Jesus. He would establish sovereignty by force.

b. The Second Seal—War (6:3-4)

6:3-4. The opening of the second seal revealed a **red horse** (v. 4), suggesting the bloodshed of war. The people of the world turned on one another as peace was removed. The size of the sword suggests great human loss.

c. The Third Seal—Inflation and Famine (6:5-6)

6:5-6. The **black horse** is emblematic of death. The **scales** could represent either judgment in general, or the instrument used to weigh the terribly scarce food. The second view is rendered likely by the voice from among the angels that announced vastly inflated prices. Although estimating such inflation across millennia is difficult, it is probably at least 1,000 percent. **Barley** was filler, mixed with other foods by the poor. Common staples such as **oil** and **wine** are pictured as far beyond the financial reach of most people. A universal famine would come upon the earth.

d. The Fourth Seal—Death (6:7-8)

6:7-8. Death is personified as a rider upon the fourth horse. **Hades** was on his heels. These terms are often coupled in Revelation (1:18; 6:8; 20:13-14). While the latter is sometimes used in Scripture for the place of the dead in general, its use elsewhere in the book suggests eternal loss (for this, see the comments on 20:13-15). The **ashen** color of the steed suggests putrefaction of human flesh. It could be that the horrific magnitude of human loss, one quarter of the earth's population, will render timely burial impossible. **Sword**, **famine**, and **pestilence** summarize the second, third, and fourth plagues. The destruction caused by **wild beasts** may point to the complete upheaval of creation order that will characterize the time period.

e. The Fifth Seal—Martyrdom (6:9-11)

6:9-11. The fifth seal calls for special attention because its focus is not on judgment but on martyrs. These had been **slain** (see 5:6) for their faithfulness to God and His Word (v. 9). Their imprecatory prayer (v. 10), a cry to God for vengeance against their adversaries, is strategic to John's theme, and the book indicates that one of the reasons for God's judgment against the world during the tribulation is the murder of tribulation saints (see 8:3-5; 16:7; 18:20). While God delayed in the execution of judgment, it would come in due time. Those who remained faithful until death would receive **white**

garments in heaven as a reward (v. 11), and their prayers would be answered. These verses must have been a great comfort to the churches of the first century who suffered under Roman tyranny.

f. The Sixth Seal—Cosmic Upheaval (6:12-17)

6:12-17. The sixth seal anticipates cosmic upheaval. Exhaustive metaphors describe the disturbance of the heavenly bodies (vv. 12-14). The rebels of the earth, small and great, would be terrified by these events, which the prophets foretold (v. 15; see Is 2:19-21; Jl 2:30-31). There would be nowhere to hide from the righteous Father and the wrathful Lamb. The prayers of the martyrs would indeed be answered. Pre-wrath rapture proponents find the rapture here, just before the manifestation of God's wrath in 6:17. This is unlikely for a number of reasons: (1) The Church is said to be altogether exempt from the time period (see the comments on 3:10). (2) A fine distinction between the impact of God in the earlier and later seals cannot be sustained since Christ is the author of all of them (6:1, 3, 5, 7, 9, 12). The whole period is a period of God's wrath. (3) It is very unlikely that the broad language of v. 15 allows for the exclusion of all believers. (4) The chronology of the seal judgments appears to place them in the first half of the tribulation, thus indicating that the entire tribulation contains God's wrath, not simply the latter portions of it as required by the midtribulational, pre-wrath, and posttribulational approaches. While John often emphasized love in his writings, he did not hesitate to mention the severity of God toward the rebellious. Many modern believers should develop a more balanced view of their Lord.

2. The Interlude about the Faithful of the Tribulation (7:1-17)

The first interlude of the book develops the contrast between the peril of the godless inhabitants of the earth and God's faithful. The former would experience desperation and destruction, while the latter would enjoy protection on earth and exhilarating worship in heaven.

a. The 144,000 Jewish Believers Serving on the Earth (7:1-8)

7:1-3. Four angels were commissioned to delay the winds of judgment until God's bond-servants could be sealed for protection. The **seal** indicates God's ownership and thus protection by God. No more judgment would be exacted against the earth until their safety was assured. They seem to be the answer to the critical question posed in 6:17. *These* can withstand the wrath of the Lamb because they are rightly related to the Father and bear His seal upon their foreheads. They appear in stark contrast to those who are later seen as identifying with the beast by accepting his mark (13:16).

7:4-8. The number of the bond-servants was 144,000, representing 12,000 persons from each of the twelve tribes of Israel (v. 4). There are notable differences in this tribal list when compared to 18 others found in Scripture. Judah is placed first, perhaps because the Messiah is descended from it. Dan and Ephraim, present in Gn 49, are omitted. **Levi**, absent from some later lists, is included. It may be that Dan and Ephraim are excluded for having participated in idolatry (Dt 29:18-21; Jdg 18:30-31), while **Levi** is included since its inheritance has always been to minister before the Lord. Attempts to interpret the numbers in this paragraph as symbolic of the Church are unjustifiably arbitrary. For example, one approach is to view the 144,000 as derived from the numbers 12 x 12 x 10 x 10 x 10, expressing the completeness of salvation and thus, of necessity, referring to the Church (see Christopher R. Smith, "The Tribes of Revelation 7 and the Literary Competence of John," *Journal of the Evangelical Theological Society* 38 [1995]: 215). But this fails to draw the clues from the text of Rv 7 itself regarding the constituency of the 144,000. A more natural reading is that literal Israel is in view (John *does* specify 12 tribes x 12,000 from each tribe—tribes that he explicitly names), in literal numbers, even as Dan, Ephraim, and Levi are assumed to be literal.

b. The Nations Worshiping in Heaven (7:9-17)

7:9-12. The meaning of **after these things** (v. 9) is not clear. It may connect the innumerable persons gathered before the Father with the bond-servants above. Were the 144,000 evangelists who had witnessed to the great throng? Perhaps it is better to take the words as simply shifting the focus to a new scene in heaven. Their **white robes** may indicate martyrdom (6:11). **Palm branches** were often instruments of praise (see the comments on Mt 21:4-9). Their song blessed and thanked God for His perfections.

7:13-17. A rhetorical question leads to the identification of the multitude (v. 13). Their white garments identify them as beneficiaries of redemption through the shed blood of the Lamb (v. 14). Assuming that the rapture of the Church occurs before the **tribulation** (see 3:10), these must be converted after its onset. Their sudden appearance in heaven suggests that they are martyrs. They would never suffer again. Rather, they would enjoy eternity with the One **who sits on the throne** (v. 15). Every physical and spiritual need would be met by God the Father who will shelter them. The very center of their existence would be the **Lamb**, their **shepherd** (v. 17). He would tenderly lead them to ultimate refreshment (Ps 23:1-2; Jn 10:1-8) and **wipe every tear from their eyes**, bringing relief from the terrors that they had suffered for Him on the earth. The persecuted believers of the seven churches no doubt took great comfort from this passage. Should they suffer at the hand of Domitian, they too would one day experience ultimate blessing with the Lamb. Until then, they would have to persevere. Modern believers should take note that suffering in this life, be it physical, emotional, or spiritual, will one day yield to unfathomable bliss. What an encouragement!

3. The Seventh Seal Judgment (8:1-5)

8:1. This verse connects the first two series of judgments. The silence in heaven is striking, considering the extraordinary activity and noise in the previous heavenly scenes. Silence in Scripture indicates respect, submission, and anticipation (Hab 2:20; Zch 2:13; 1Co 14:34). Here it is, according to Alan Johnson, "silence before the great storm of God's wrath" (*Revelation*, 488). The seventh seal has no content of its own. Rather, it contains and serves to introduce the trumpet judgments.

8:2-5. Seven angels were given trumpets to announce the outpouring of God's anger. The prayers of the saints were mixed with incense before the throne of God (vv. 3-4; see Ex 30:1-5). These were prayers for vindication before their enemies (6:10), used to stoke the wrath of the First Person. God responded with a fearsome display of anger, through lightning and an earthquake (v. 5).

C. The Trumpet Judgments (8:6–11:19)

8:6. The seven angels now **prepared . . . to sound them**, each indicating another set of judgments, each with increasing intensity. These judgments take place after the seal judgments (Rv 6–7), probably in the last half of the tribulation. The events associated with the trumpets strongly parallel those of the exodus, albeit on a vastly wider scale.

1. The First Six Trumpets (8:7–9:21)

a. The First Trumpet—Earthly Destruction (8:7)

8:7. The first trumpet (Ex 9:17-26) consisted of a horrifying mixture of elements that were cast upon the earth. These destroyed one-third of the remaining vegetation, intensifying the famine.

b. The Second Trumpet—Aquatic Destruction (8:8-9)

8:8-9. The sea was struck next (Ex 7:20-25), wrecking havoc with marine life and human commerce. **A great mountain burning with fire** likely describes a colossal meteor hurled into the sea by God. Fully one-third of all life in the sea would be lost, and a region bearing one-third of the world's saltwater bodies would be affected. The extinction of aquatic life would be so extensive as to taint the sea red with its blood. A major food source would vanish, and untold numbers of ships would perish along with their crews. The latter may have borne particular significance to early believers dominated by a great naval power like Rome.

c. The Third Trumpet—Water Pollution (8:10-11)

8:10-11. The third trumpet announced the pollution of earth's fresh water supply by **the** star **Wormwood**. Like the embittering tree bearing its name, it would foul the taste and purity of the world's most essential resource. Many fatalities would follow.

d. The Fourth Trumpet—Light Destroyed (8:12)

8:12. As an angel blew the fourth trumpet, John saw cataclysmic damage taking place among the heavenly bodies. The natural result of such an occurrence would be unprecedented darkness day and night, as well as unbearable cold. The believers in the seven churches may have thought of the ancient Egyptians who suffered greatly for resisting God's command to free His people Israel (Ex 10:21-29).

e. The Fifth Trumpet—Demonic Affliction (8:13–9:12)

8:13. A soaring **eagle** then pronounced triple woe upon the earth, an anticipation of the last three trumpet blasts. The **eagle** may symbolize an angel (4:7; 14:6, where an angel is said to be **flying in midheaven**), the comparison coming perhaps from flight and from eagles hunting their prey (as this angel may participate in judgment against the world). This added emphasis, along with pregnant statements in 9:12 and

11:14, signaled that the worst of the judgments were yet to come. The parallel wording of 8:13 and 3:10 may be meant to contrast the fortunes of God's friends and enemies as judgment visits the planet.

9:1-12. The apostle next turned his attention to a **star from heaven . . . fallen to the earth** (v. 1), a probable reference to an angel (Jb 38:7) cast out of God's presence. This wicked angel was allowed to release the inhabitants of an abyss who are identified as **locusts** (v. 3). This is but a figurative description of the innumerable swarm of demons that rose from the smoky pit, destroying everything in their midst. Some scholars have associated them with the rebellious angels of 2Pt 2:4-6. They did not target a crop, but instead those humans who did not identify themselves with Christ. Their grotesque appearance was terrifying. For five horrible months they would subject the rebels to torturous bites, a figurative description of physical and psychological torment worse than death. God would give them over to the satanic hordes. The ruler of the fiendish horde bore two names, one in each of the two primary languages of Scripture: the Hebrew **Abaddon** (v. 11), and the Greek **Apollyon**, both suggesting destruction. God the Father will use the evil spirit world for His glory in the destruction of the rebellious humanity so adamantly opposed to His will. Such rebels persecute God's twenty-first-century people in many regions of the world, just as they did in the first century AD. What assurance it is for modern Christians to know that God has not forgotten their suffering. He will one day exercise fierce vengeance on the persecutors of His people. The words **two woes are still coming** (v. 12) anticipate the remaining trumpet judgments.

f. The Sixth Trumpet—Death (9:13-21)

9:13-21. The sixth judgment describes the worst destruction yet in John's vision. A voice sounded from the altar (v. 13), a place of worship in heaven. Perhaps it is intended to call to mind the former pleas of the martyrs (6:9-10; 8:3). An unidentified source commanded the angel to release four other angels for more mayhem (v. 14). These will likely be demons cast from God's presence to incite the actions that followed. The remaining activity originated from the Euphrates River. Verse 15 identifies the terrific scope of this judgment: one third of remaining humanity would die. The army of **two hundred million** in the next verse has occasioned much discussion, principally around two questions: (1) Are the riders on the horses men or demons? (2) Should their numbers be understood figuratively or literally? Those who believe that a human army is meant cite the numerous times in Scripture when God uses such units as instruments of His chastening. Walvoord, while not holding the position himself, cites the size of the modern Chinese army as evidence for the plausibility of the numbers (John Walvoord, *The Revelation of Jesus Christ* [Chicago: Moody, 1966], 166 n. 13). If this most literal interpretation is maintained, then vv. 17-19 represent John's best attempt to describe modern, mechanical warfare given the experience and vocabulary at his disposal. Those who see demons as the principals cite that it is actually the horses and not the riders who inflict the harm, suggesting a more figurative approach (Robert L. Thomas, *Revelation 8–22: An Exegetical Commentary* [Chicago: Moody, 1995], 46). This view has in its favor the connection between the locust-like demons in 9:2-10 and the **two hundred million** in 9:16-19 (both groups resembling horses, having breastplates, pain-inflicting tails, the features of lions). If the two groups are not identical, they are closely related, supporting the demonic identity of the **two hundred million** in 9:16. Others question whether the number is intended literally (Gregory Beale, *The Book of Revelation* [Grand Rapids, MI: Eerdmans, 1999], 509), or if such a massive corps, if literal, could be mobilized. These latter objections are no impediment to the second, preferred view, as such numbers of angels are present earlier in the book (5:11). Innumerable hordes of demons would torment the rebels. The chapter closes with yet another indictment of humankind's hard-heartedness. Rather than being moved to repentance by the ghastly events taking place, the inhabitants of earth would persist in multifaceted idolatry. Modern Christ-followers should gain an appreciation for the ingrained rebelliousness of the human race and the righteousness of their God in addressing it.

2. The Digression about the Little Book and the Two Witnesses (10:1–11:14)

These verses belong to a section (10:1–11:14) that does not advance the narrative chronologically but rather enhances it with more detail. John also switches scenes back and forth between heaven and earth. This literary device, called alternation, is meant to intensify reader (or listener) interest.

a. The Little Book (10:1-11)

10:1-3. I saw calls attention to a new movement in the book. A messenger in the vision came from God bearing **a little book**. Some believe this to be Christ, as his appearance in the clouds is reminiscent of the Son of Man (Dn 7:13-14), and he exercises dominion. However, such a descent seems most unlikely before the second coming. In addition there are no other Christophanies in Scripture after the incarnation. Finally, the wording of the passage suggests that this is another angel of the same kind (cf. **angel** in vv. 5, 8, 11), presumably, as the one mentioned in 9:1. The book that was open in the angel's hand was different from the scroll of 5:1-2, and its content was not yet revealed. Instead, God spoke through **seven peals of thunder**.

10:4-7. John was commanded to stop writing and to keep what he had heard in the thunder to himself (v. 4). This secret revelation may have been another series of judgments or some other aspect of prophecy that John was not allowed to reveal for reasons known only to God (Jn 21:25; 2Co 12:1-4). The angel swore an oath to God by raising his right hand (vv. 5-6; see Dn 12:7), acknowledging His sovereignty (Neh 9:6). The phrase at the beginning of v. 7 is best rendered "but that in the days of the trumpet call to be sounded" (ESV). The end would not come before the trumpet sounded, but in association with it. Such a future cataclysm was revealed by God to the prophets of old (Is 24–27).

10:8-11. Finally, John was allowed to deal with **the little book** (v. 9). The voice from heaven (v. 4) commanded him to take it from the angel who, in turn, instructed him to eat it. The results paralleled the bittersweet experience of the aforementioned prophets (Jr 15:15-18; Ezk 2:8–3:3). The joy of representing God and His Word would be accompanied by the overwhelming shock and sorrow related to the coming judgments. As modern believers study God's Word, they should at once rejoice in God's righteousness, while not neglecting to meditate upon its terrible consequences for rebellious humanity.

b. The Two Witnesses (11:1-14)

The interpretation of these verses is disputed. Many commentators take the description of the temple to be symbolic for the Church, but the details of the text preclude this view. The specifics mentioned in connection with **the temple**, **the altar**, **the court which is outside the temple**, **the holy city**, and the oppression from the Gentile **nations** (note that the **nations** here are not worshiping, which would likely be the case if John were symbolically describing the Church), make it unlikely that the Church is in view.

11:1-2. The building of the tribulational temple will be one of the signs of the last days and may be the same one that Ezekiel places in the millennium (Ezk 40–48). The apostle was given a hollow reed, indigenous to southern Israel, by which to measure the building. Only the Holy Place and Holy of Holies were included, not the court of the Gentiles who would be dominating Israel during the last three and one-half years of the tribulation. The measuring of the human populace is enigmatic, but may refer to a spiritual checkup (Ezk 43:10). If it is related to the measuring of Zch 2:1-13, chastening will be due Israel before unprecedented blessing.

11:3-4. John saw two witnesses, ministering for 42 months. This will probably take place during the second half of the tribulation since witnessing is presumably unopposed in the first half. Their sackcloth symbolizes their mourning for the sins of the rebellious world. They are called **olive trees** and **lampstands**. This imagery brings to mind Zch 4:9, 13-14 where two other anointed witnesses (Zerubbabel and Joshua; cf. the comments on Zch 4:11) are associated with another literal rebuilding of the temple in Jerusalem after the Babylonian captivity. Olive oil was a common source of fuel, and lamps shed light. Perhaps these two will spread the light of God's Word in the power of the Spirit. They will be at the beck and call of their Lord.

11:5-6. The staying power of these individuals was due to their extraordinary ability to protect themselves. If anyone tried to harm them, he was destroyed with flames issuing from their mouths! Like Elijah and Moses before them, they, with God's enablement, controlled the forces of nature (1Kg 17:1; Ex 7:20).

11:7-8. The words **when they have finished their testimony** are crucial to this chapter. These faithful witnesses would be kept untouched by God until their service for Him was complete. Sinners would hear from God one more time. Only then would the beast have his way with them. The use of the word **overcome** in association with his victory is most significant. In all but two places in Revelation the word is reserved for the victory of the Lamb or the perseverance of His followers. But at this point in the vision, the outlook seemed dismal for the faithful. As John looked on, he saw the witnesses lying dead on the streets of Jerusalem, the same place that Jesus had been executed by crucifixion. The figurative references to the city as **Sodom** and **Egypt** depict the utter depravity into which this once faithful city had sunk. Once again, prophets of God were martyred.

11:9-10. People of every ethnicity gave approval to this horrible act (see 5:9 for parallel wording describing the followers of the Lamb in heaven). This mass of God-haters further desecrated the bodies of the prophets by denying them even the decent burial accorded criminals (Dt 21:22-23). It is sheer irony that here the only earthly celebration of the entire tribulation breaks out. The whole world would rejoice that the prophets who stung them with relentless rebukes were out of the way.

11:11-14. What John saw next would be a source of rejoicing for the righteous. God breathed life into the dead prophets, striking fear into their killers (v. 11). The prophets were snatched away into heaven (v. 12). Although the words **come up here** are reminiscent of 4:1, these representatives of the Lord would be taken physically into His presence rather than beholding a vision. God would avenge their mistreatment by causing an earthquake that would kill 7,000 people (v. 13). The remainder would give **glory to the God of heaven**. This most likely refers to a legitimate, although localized, conversion of people who were previously antagonistic to Christ (see 16:9 for the contrary response).

The vision of the witnesses is instructive to modern believers as it was to their first-century counterparts. First, no believer will be taken from the earth before God's purpose for him is complete. This is true not only in outreach ministry, but in any sphere of influence to which one has been called. Second, those who suffer will be satisfied with God's righteous punishment of their tormentors. Third, God's mercy is so great as to break through to some of the most hardened sinners.

3. The Seventh Trumpet (11:15-19)

11:15. From this verse on, John is brought to the cusp of the second coming. For the first time plural voices are heard, announcing the transition of power. The visible rule of earth would soon take place through the co-regency of the Father and His Anointed One, the Lord Jesus. The seventh trumpet contains the bowl judgments, and it, along with them, terminates at the second coming (see the comments on 12:1-6). Some midtribulationists place the rapture of the Church here based on the assumptions that the ascension of the two witnesses (v. 12) is representative of the rapture of the Church, and that the blowing of the last trumpet is to be associated with the trumpet of 1Th 4:16. Yet it is difficult to view Moses and Elijah as symbolic for a much larger group (the Church) since they appear to be presented as actual individuals throughout this chapter. Neither is the simple presence of trumpets in two passages sufficient reason for equating them (see also the comments on 1Co 15:51-58). And the conditions following the seventh trumpet fit better with the second coming of Jesus to the earth than with the rapture of the Church (note the reign of Christ over the world in 11:15-17, and the rage of the nations in 11:18).

11:16-17. The angelic host in heaven again broke into praise (4:4), acknowledging the eternality and omnipotence of the new rulers.

11:18. This verse provides an overview of the events yet to come. While some see a chronological progression here, it is best understood as a broad summary set in triplets: the enemies of God were wrathful, God was wrathful, the enemies of God were judged and destroyed; the prophets were rewarded, the saints were rewarded, those who feared the name of God were rewarded. Johnson (*Revelation*, 509) points out the strong emphasis on faithful prophets throughout the book (16:6; 18:20, 24; 22:6, 9).

11:19. The open heavenly temple indicates that faithful Jewish believers will have access to God despite the adverse circumstances of the tribulation period. The ark, a symbol of forgiveness, will assure them of their redemption. First-century believers may have taken similar comfort from the vision (Heb 10:19-22). The lightning and thunder signified the presence of God as in 4:5.

D. The Seven Signs (12:1–14:20)

These signs are not explicitly associated with either the trumpet judgments or the bowl judgments. Since the bowl judgments are near the end of the tribulation and are associated with the return of Messiah, so these seven signs are evident during the time of the trumpet judgments, probably during the second half of the tribulation (the 1,260 days of 11:3; 12:6). They are roughly concurrent with the trumpet judgments, and seem to provide a survey of the last half of the tribulation (Thomas, *Revelation*, 2:115).

1. The First Sign—The Woman (12:1-6)

12:1-6. The first sign is that of **a woman clothed with the sun, and the moon** and the **stars** (v. 1). Some have understood her to be the Virgin Mary, but a symbolic meaning, as is clearly intended with the harlot of chap. 17, is more likely. Others think that the Church is in view, but it did not, in any sense, bring forth Jesus. The best understanding is that these luminaries identify the woman as symbolic of Israel. This interpretation fits well with the symbols in Joseph's dream in Gn 37:9-10. The **sun and the moon** stood for Joseph's parents, Jacob and Rachel (Gn 37:10), and the eleven **stars** (Joseph was the twelfth) were Joseph's brothers, here representing the 12 tribes of Israel. The more likely understanding of the **woman** is that she symbolizes Israel. The **child** she bore is Jesus the Messiah (v. 2), who is of Jewish descent (Rm 9:5). While she was in labor, a great dragon (Satan) appeared to destroy her child (v. 4). The **seven heads** most likely symbolize the seven consecutive world empires of Rv 17:10 (see the comments on 17:3-4), with the **ten horns** resting on the seventh head and representing a rebellious confederacy aligned with the Devil and the antichrist (13:2; and see the comments on Dn 7:7-8, 24). The **diadems** refer to his political clout. The **stars of heaven** that were **swept away** (v. 4) probably represent fallen angels choosing to follow Satan (see the mention of angels being cast out of heaven in 12:7-8, and "star" used in reference to an angel in 9:1), and not martyred Jewish believers. One **third** of the Jewish tribes did not cease to exist. The imagery depicts the seductive power and influence of the **dragon**. Verse 5 overviews various features of the Messiah's kingdom (birth, rule, ascension) although the events are not in order. Finally, it was revealed that Satan would pursue Israel into the wilderness, where God would give her special protection for the final three-and-one-half years (**one thousand two hundred and sixty days**) of the tribulation period (v. 6).

2. The Second Sign—War in Heaven (12:7-12)

12:7-12. The second sign is a **war in heaven**, further accentuating the age-old battle that would continue through the tribulation period. This pitched conflict featured **Michael** (the leader of God's faithful angels) versus Satan (the leader of the demonic foes) (v. 7), with Michael's followers prevailing (v. 8). Apparently, Satan will have access to heaven until this time. John's overall handling of this conflict may be understood in the following sequence. (1) Satan has many human followers on the earth (Jn 8:42-44) over which he now rules with God's permission (1Jn 5:19). (2) His ultimate defeat is assured by Christ's death on the cross (Jn 12:31-32). (3) During the great tribulation he will be cast out of heaven (Rv 12:8) to earth where he will seduce the world (13:4). (4) After the tribulation, he will be bound by God and unable to oppose believers until near the end of the millennium (Rv 20:2). (5) Then he will be released to foster one final rebellion (Rv 20:7-8). (6) After that he is cast finally into the lake of fire where he will experience eternal torment (Rv 20:10). The vision describes this fiend as **the serpent** (v. 9; see Gn 3:1), **the devil** ("the slanderer"), and **Satan** ("the adversary"). During his vision the apostle heard a loud voice praise God for His sovereign deliverance of His people from **the accuser of our brethren** (v. 10). No railing slander against a believer would ever again be heard in heaven. As this portion of the vision concluded, John heard testimony that these believers in the tribulation had overcome the accuser (v. 11). Although Satan would do serious damage to God's people, they would prevail in the end. The verses above may well be the theological center of the book as they emphasize the certainty of Satan's defeat, and the perseverance of the saints. While the vision assured ultimate victory, it was still distant. The Devil would pour out his wrath during the short time he had left (v. 12). The defeated rebel would destroy as long as he was allowed to operate.

First-century believers suffering under Roman rule would have been greatly heartened by such good news. If future generations of believers could make it through the tribulation, they could faithfully endure as well. Present-day believers may also rejoice that ultimate victory has been assured through Christ's work on the cross and that no accusation of Satan will ever be received against them!

3. The Third Sign—Israel Attacked and Preserved (12:13–13:1a)

12:13–13:1a. In the third sign, the dragon turned his wrath against the woman Israel. The nation, however, was supernaturally preserved by God who granted it sanctuary in a wilderness location. **A time and times and half a time** (v. 14) (Dn 7:25) is a reference to a three-and-one-half-year period during the great tribulation in which God will meet all of Israel's needs. **Wings of the great eagle** is a metaphor of deliverance that was used regarding Israel's exodus from Egypt (Ex 19:4-6). Perhaps it is employed here to suggest that Israel will once again be delivered from oppression. God would frustrate

Satan's attempt to destroy Israel with a flood by opening a crevice in the earth that drinks in the water (vv. 15-16). While the possibility of a literal flood cannot be disproved, the term is more likely a metaphor for enemies of Israel (Ps 144:7-8; Dn 11:40) whose efforts God will thwart. **The earth** (v. 16) is also probably a metaphor for supernatural deliverance by God. In Ex 15:12, Moses said, "The earth swallowed them [the Egyptians at the exodus]," when in reality it was the sea—or more precisely, "the right hand" and "lovingkindness" of God (Ex 15:11, 13). **The rest of her children**, whom the Devil hotly pursued, is best understood as a believing remnant of Jewish people who come to faith in Messiah Jesus during the tribulation period. **And the dragon stood** translates the most trustworthy Greek manuscripts, and refers to Satan who summoned the foul character that followed.

4. The Fourth Sign—The Beast from the Sea (13:1b-10)

13:1b-10. The fourth sign depicted **a beast coming up out of the sea** (v. 1b). The symbolic use of **beast** represents the cruel nature of the human being who will rule the world by the power of Satan. This **beast** is distinct from the dragon in chap. 12, also called a beast, though the beast of chap. 13 is closely connected to the dragon and derives his authority from the dragon (13:2). Johannine writings use the familiar term "antichrist" to refer to any individual or attitude that is contrary to apostolic doctrine (1Jn 2:18, 22; 4:3), but reserve the term **beast** for this individual, or the group that he leads. The **sea** is often used in Scripture as a symbol for opposition to God (Ps 74:13-14; Is 57:20-21). Sea monsters (Jb 26:12-13) in the OT consistently stand for nations that persecute God's people (Beale, *Revelation*, 683). The beast, therefore, will be the epitome of the enemies of God. **Ten horns** are emblematic for countries, or rulers, that will follow him in a confederacy (Dn 7:7-8). Since Daniel identified this beast as arising from the world's fourth great empire (Rome), this is understood by many to refer to a revived Roman empire (see the comments on Dn 7). **Seven heads** represent a number of past Gentile dynasties, and **diadems** (crowns) stand for his political power. He and his final evil empire are both a continuation, and the apex, of this line of rebellious kingdoms. He had **blasphemies** against the God of heaven boldly displayed. John no doubt recognized him as the "little horn" of Daniel's prophecy (Dn 7:7-8, 20-25), and the worst of a long line of Gentile sovereigns who had oppressed Israel. **His fatal wound was healed** (Rv 13:3) describes his feigned death and resurrection, a counterfeit of Christ's, which would will result in worldwide worship of both him and Satan (v. 4; 2Th 2:3-12). The zenith of his power would last **forty-two months** (v. 5; cf. Dn 9:27; Rv 11:2), the second half of the tribulation, and would issue in the domination of God's people. Verse 7 says that he would **overcome** them for a while, only the second time the word is used of the forces of evil in Revelation (see also 11:7). Perhaps John uses it here to heighten the tension of the narrative. Who would win in the end? The victory of the beast would appear so complete that the whole world would worship him, **everyone whose name has not been written . . . in the book of life** (v. 8). No unbeliever's name can remain in God's record book (Ex 32:32; Ps 69:28). The word order of the Greek text may seem to favor associating **from the foundation of the world** with the death of Christ, but the parallel construction of 17:8 warrants a connection with the names written in the book. The world would turn to wholesale idolatry. None of this had escaped the providence of God, however, and He would expect His saints to persevere. This aspect of the vision no doubt encouraged first-century believers in the midst of Domitian's aggression. Faithfulness was expected of them too.

5. The Fifth Sign—The Beast from the Earth (13:11-18)

13:11-18. Another beast (of a similar sort) describes the assistant to the beast in chap. 13, a false prophet who will share the antichrist's evil attributes. He was **out of the earth** (or land) (v. 11), in contrast to the beast who was out of the sea. The greater contrast, however, is with the heavenly lamb (5:6). This one was earthly, worldly, and unholy. The phrase is symbolic. Therefore, the theory that this person is from the land of Israel, and thus Jewish, finds no support here. He is described as having **two horns like a lamb**, indicating his superficial gentleness. But he **spoke as a dragon** (v. 11), describing his intimidating threats. **He exercises all the authority of the first beast**, while in the **presence** of the first beast (v. 12), demonstrating his subordination to the first. This false prophet would perform many miracles by the power of Satan (2Th 2:9-11) and enforce worship of a talking idol of the first beast through universal economic leverage. Those who did not have a mark on their bodies showing such allegiance would be denied food or, in some cases, be killed (vv. 13-17). The first beast would be known by his number **six hundred and sixty-six** (v. 18). Some have associated this number with the base six numerical system of Babylon (implied in Dn 3:1), concluding that this individual is the perfect representation of humanism. In the ancient world, letters of an alphabet were sometimes assigned numerical coefficients so that a specific person came to be associated with a number equal to the value of his name. No conclusive identification of an individual has ever been made for the number 666, and attempts to do so based on modern alphabets are far-fetched and impossible. It may be best to accept the general sense of the number as suggested above. Believers should not fixate on minor prophetic details, but should instead concentrate on consistent faithfulness to God during perilous times.

6. The Sixth Sign—The Lamb on Mount Zion (14:1-5)

14:1-5. The sixth sign featured the **Lamb . . . standing on Mount Zion**, a reference to a prophetic vision of the ultimate triumph of the Lamb following His second coming, when He joins the 144,000 on literal Mount Zion at the beginning of His millennial reign. In support of this understanding, the 144,000 were guaranteed preservation throughout the tribulation (7:3-4) with that preservation demonstrated here. **Zion** is typically understood as earthly Jerusalem, even in the NT (cf. Mt 21:5; Jn 12:15; Rm 9:33; 11:26; 1Pt 2:6). Hebrews 12:22 is the lone exception, but Heb 12:23 gives a clear indication of "Zion" there being *heavenly* Zion; see the comments there. Finally, the Lamb standing on Mount Zion (v. 1) parallels the actions of some other major players in Revelation (the dragon, 13:1; the beast out of the sea, 13:1; and the second beast out of the earth, 13:11). These are presumably the same group mentioned in 7:1-8. God's own mighty and melodic voice was heard. Along with various orders of angels (5:8), they sang a **new song** to God (v. 3) that only they were able to learn. These, who bore the brunt of the horrors of the tribulation, would be the special focus of His attention. They would enjoy special fellowship with Him. The most likely meaning of not being **defiled with** women and keeping chaste is that they have not engaged in false worship. In the OT, frequently Israel's idolatry was described as spiritual adultery (Ex 34:11-17; Nm 25:1-9; Hs 1:2; 2:2). The unflagging attention of these faithful servants was on the Lamb, whom they constantly followed around heaven. Their witness for Christ showed that they were also truth tellers, unlike some in the early church (2:9; 3:9). As **first fruits** (v. 4), their presence anticipated a great influx of Israelites into God's family during the great tribulation.

7. The Seventh Sign—Judgment against the Rebellious (14:6-20)

14:6-11. The last sign associated with the trumpets featured both the temporal and eternal judgment of those who rebelled against the God of heaven. The content of the **eternal gospel** (better "good news," *euangelion*, v. 6) centers on judgment, and probably does not denote here the positive message of Christ's death on the cross. The "good news" here relates to the impending judgment of God purging the world of all evil. While doom is threatened for those who stay fixed against God, mercy will be extended to those who repent, even during the tribulation period. A reverent response to such grace will be expected. Unbelieving humankind was commanded to **fear God** and **give Him glory** (v. 7). The fear of God may be defined as a wholesome dread of displeasing Him. Giving Him glory means to see Him as utterly significant. Their time would be short, as **Babylon the great** (v. 8) would soon meet its doom.

A definitive interpretation of **Babylon** has proven elusive. Attempts have generally followed one of four lines. (1) It is a cryptic reference to Rome used by the early church to keep certain truths secret from its persecutors (1 Pt 5:13). A variation of this view is that it stands for Rome, either in John's day or in the future, as the center of worldwide apostasy. This view has enjoyed acceptance in some form by a broad spectrum of scholars ranging from preterists to premillennial dispensationalists. It handles many details well. (2) It refers to Jerusalem as a city set against God and the object of judgment. But Scripture generally aligns Jerusalem with God and Babylon against Him. (3) It stands figuratively for the entire world system set against God, including major cities like Rome, Babylon, or Sodom. This view understands option 2 as too narrow. (4) The term stands for a literally rebuilt city of Babylon on the banks of the Euphrates River. This position has the advantage of a more consistently literal approach. Opponents of this view insist that prophecies of its final destruction (Is 13:19-22; Jr 51:24-26) were fulfilled during the sixth century BC, thus precluding a rebuilt city. Proponents respond that the *details* of these prophecies have never been fulfilled, and thus still look forward to the future (Charles Dyer, "The Identity of Babylon in Revelation 17–18," *BibSac* 144 [July–September 1987] 305–316; and [October–December 1987] 433–449). In addition, Zch 5:5-11, written about 20 years after the fall of Belshazzar's Babylon (539 BC), looks for a future building of an idolatrous shrine in Shinar, which is Babylon (Gn 10:10). The late twentieth-century building project of Saddam Hussein on the very foundations of the ancient city is not the fulfillment, but demonstrates the plausibility of a literal rebuilding of the city. If this approach is correct, then there was a judgment in Gn 11:1-9, a second under Belshazzar, with the final destruction to take place during the great tribulation (Is 14:1-4, 7). This is the best choice. Babylon will be rebuilt and destroyed again.

The words, **fallen, fallen** (Rv 14:8) are proleptic, anticipating the details of the destruction in 17:1–18:24. A third angel proclaimed a different message, one of doom, for all who worshiped the beast (vv. 9-10). God would sentence anyone who took his mark (13:16) to eternal damnation. John piles up terms to accentuate the terrors of hell. It is a place where the **wrath of God** and **the cup of His anger** (v. 10) are fully expressed toward unrelenting rebels who turn from Him to idolatry. God's wrath is never capricious, but is always a response to the violation of His justice. Hell is a place where **fire and brimstone** (Gn 19:24) will rain down on hopelessly lost sinners. The **Lamb** of God and the **holy angels** will be present and will approve of such punishment. The apostle uses the phrases **forever and ever**, and **no rest day and night**, to remove even the faintest hope of escape or relief. This verse also indicates that their torment is eternal in duration. They will not be "annihilated" at some time in the future (**forever and ever** is used for the length of God's life [15:7], and for the reign of God's bond-servants with Him [22:5]).

14:12-13. People in the tribulation will be faced with an exceedingly difficult but abundantly clear option: persevere through faith in the Lord Jesus, even unto death, or take the mark of the beast and be sentenced to unfathomable suffering at the hand of the Father and the Lamb. Those martyred by the beast for refusing his mark will be taken to heaven to **rest from their labors** (on earth) (v. 13). Such is the testimony of the Holy Spirit Himself. The early church would have been encouraged to continue in faith by such a passage. They would have seen their own need to stay the course with Christ rather than apostatizing in emperor worship. Modern believers should take heed as well. Perseverance is essential. Those who claim Christ should demonstrate such allegiance with steady faith. They should also unquestionably embrace the doctrine of hell and its eternal punishment. To deny such is to deny the very gospel itself.

14:14-20. The vision of a **sharp sickle** followed (v. 14). The view that the reaping in vv. 14-16 describes the midtribulational rapture ignores the context of the following verses, which is one of gathering for judgment (14:19-20), not a joyful gathering as the rapture would be, and should be rejected. John saw the **son of man** (Dn 7:13-14) ready to judge the nations (Jl 3:13). As an angel cried out his agreement, the judgment began, assisted by the angelic host. The **great wine press** (v. 19) describes the destructive fury of God the Father, as administered through His Messiah-Son. Here the vision took an unexpected turn. The judgment would take place **outside the city** of Jerusalem (v. 20) as rebellious armies were destroyed (19:15-19). The phrase **up to the horses' bridles** describes the extent of splashing, as military steeds ran over the blood-saturated region. The first-century church could rejoice in the midst of its trials, for the forces of evil would ultimately be ruined. Modern believers may also have their understanding of Christ enhanced. He is not only a savior, but also a destroyer of His enemies.

E. The Interlude in Heaven (15:1-8)

15:1. This verse forms a superscription for chaps. 15 and 16 (Johnson, *Revelation,* 546), introducing the final phase of retribution. The seal and trumpet judgments had now passed. The bowl judgments remained and were called **the seven [last] plagues**. The wrath of God would be quickly consummated in these.

15:2-4. Many would die for refusing to take the mark of the beast. By such faithfulness, they would glorify God and be **victorious** (v. 2). The **sea of glass** depicts the holiness and splendor of God. **The beast**, **his image**, and **the number of his name**, are all included to emphatically demonstrate the victory of the saints. The martyrs sang the **song of Moses** (v. 3; Ex 15:1-18), which the Israelites sang after they were delivered from Egypt and passed through the Red Sea. It is composed from various lines of the Psalms and Prophets, extolling God for His attributes. John continues to develop his overcomer (victor) theme here. He wants his readers to be very clear that to persevere is to win. If they should die for resisting Domitian, they would join the throng singing the victory song. Believers' perspectives on this present life should be molded by their anticipation of a future with the Lord.

15:5-8. In the second part of this scene, John saw the heavenly **tabernacle of testimony** opened, out of which came angels (v. 6). Their **linen** garments and **golden sashes** represent the righteousness of God and, perhaps, His glory (v. 6). Their full **bowls** (5:8; 8:1-5) stand for God's intent to vent His righteous wrath. These vessels may be intended to bring to mind those in the OT tabernacle (1Kg 7:50). No one in the vision could stand to be in the presence of the omnipotent and glorious First Person whose anger was fierce, and ready to be expressed again.

F. The Seven Bowl Judgments (16:1-21)

While the bowl judgments bear similarities to the trumpet judgments there are also significant differences in scope and detail. The trumpet judgments, for instance, impact one-third of the affected entities (8:7-8) while the effect of the bowl judgments is universal (16:3-4, 18). In addition, the response to the bowl judgments is more venomous—blaspheming and satanic opposition are present (16:9, 13-14). An air of finality is also unique to the bowls (16:17). Thus, they are best seen as two separate groups of retributions. They also bear some resemblance to the plagues of the book of Exodus. The brief description of the first six bowls may be intended to accentuate the nearness of the end of time, or the importance of the seventh bowl.

1. The First Bowl—Painful Sores (16:1-2)

16:1-2. This series of punishments was initiated by a command from heaven. These were divinely planned and orchestrated events, not natural disasters or haphazard environmental catastrophes. The pouring out of the first vessel resulted in ulcerated sores (Ex 9:9-11) breaking out on the idolaters who had taken the beast's mark (v. 2). Such identification with His enemies was intolerable to the God of heaven.

2. The Second Bowl—The Sea Turned to Blood (16:3)

16:3. The second bowl resulted in the obliteration of all sea animals (Ex 7:17-21). The substance poured out by the angel turned the seas into thick, semicoagulated blood, resulting in the death of all marine life (the second trumpet in 8:8-9 saw only one-third die).

3. The Third Bowl—Fresh Water Turned to Blood (16:4-7)

16:4-7. The next bowl affected freshwater life (Ex 7:17-21), with a result similar to what happened with the sea. However, John heard impressive words associated with this bowl. God was praised as eternal (**who are and who were**), **holy**, and **righteous** (v. 7). This last attribute was directly related to His decision to judge the persecutors of His people. They had **poured out the blood of saints and prophets** (v. 6) (Eph 4:11-12) and would thus be destroyed. The penalty would be blood for blood. John also returns to the themes of **the altar** (6:9-10) and an **Almighty** God (see 4:4-11) who takes vengeance on the enemies of His loved ones. The phrase **they deserve it** (v. 6) suggests an important literary and theological point. The perspective of Revelation toward those who resist and rebel against the Lord is not at all sympathetic. They are seldom pictured as the beneficiaries of evangelism, and never of prayer, apparently because their longstanding resistance to God has hardened them to the gospel. Rather, they are consistently presented as rejecting God, and destroying His people. They will therefore be destroyed themselves, and rightly so.

4. The Fourth Bowl—A Scorched Earth (16:8-9)

16:8-9. The fourth bowl made the sun burn with inordinate heat and scorch the earth. The rebels **did not repent**, that is, they did not change their heart in any way toward God. **Blaspheme** means "to ruin one's reputation by speaking slanderously about him." **Repent** means "to have a significant change of mind, and as a result, of life, due to comprehending the debilitating consequences of sin."

5. The Fifth Bowl—Darkness (16:10-11)

16:10-11. The next bowl afflicted the **throne of the beast** (2:13), thus darkening **his kingdom**. The beast had been granted some temporary authority over the earth (see 2Co 4:4; Col 1:13 on Satan), which was now removed. John saw God assaulting this domain with darkness. Exactly how this would cause pain is not evident. At the least, it would increase anxiety and fear. Combined with the sores from the previous plague, it would make life miserable.

6. The Sixth Bowl—Demonic Assault (16:12-16)

16:12-16. The sixth bowl caused the Euphrates River to dry up, facilitating the movement of a massive, eastern army. John saw **demons**, in the form of **frogs**, coming from the members of the satanic trinity (16:13). Frogs were symbolically related to the Egyptian goddess Heqt during the bondage, and may be used here to recall those dark days of oppression. These seducing spirits led military units from around the world to rally at a place called, in Hebrew, Armageddon (Dn 11:40-45). This "mount" and its accompanying plain are an extension of the Great Plain of Esdraelon, an enormous, largely flat fertile area southwest of the Sea of Galilee. The plain encompasses Megiddo and extends from the coast north of Mt. Carmel southeast to the Jordan River. It is the perfect location for staging the armies that will participate in the campaign of Armageddon. Verse 15 is a parenthetical digression that reinforces the argument of the book. Addressed to the seven churches of 2:1–3:22, it urged steadfast perseverance in the face of persecution. If they stayed pure in their devotion to Christ, they would be rewarded.

7. The Seventh Bowl—Worldwide Devastation (16:17-21)

16:17-21. The words **it is done** (v. 17), associated with the seventh bowl, indicate that there would be no more judgments once this one was complete, and the coming of the kingdom was near. An **earthquake** of unparalleled magnitude shook **the great city** (vv. 18-19). Some understand this to be Babylon, and the words **the great** may seem to support this view. A better view is to see it as Jerusalem. This fits the exact word order used to describe it in 11:8, as well as the topographical changes described in Zch 14:4. The significance of the division of the city into three parts is not clear. The words **Babylon the great was remembered** signal a transition to the consideration of that literal city's judgment. God would keep track of her sins and punish them. God never acts capriciously. His wrath is exercised when His justice is offended. The phrases **every island fled away** and **the mountains were not found** (v. 20) are hyperboles for the absolute chaos brought to the city itself, as well as everything associated with it. God would use the forces of nature against the city by hurling down inordinately large hailstones. These phenomena would have no positive effect at all on the rebels who would continue to curse their Maker.

G. The Destruction of Babylon the Great 17:1–18:24

This part of John's vision described the end for the city of Babylon on the Euphrates, and the world of people that followed her ways. It highlighted the truth of the apostle's earlier writing (1Jn 2:15-17). All who loved the power, idolatry, and riches of the world so exemplified by the city would see their dreams destroyed before their eyes. This section does not describe more judgments beyond the seals, trumpets, and bowls but highlights certain aspects of them.

1. The Destruction Detailed (17:1-18)

17:1-2. John was invited to witness the future destruction of the literal, rebuilt, city of Babylon (v. 1) (see the comments at 14:6-20). Its moral destitution is depicted by the symbol of a **harlot** (Is 1:21) and its despicable character juxtaposed with the lovely holiness of the new Jerusalem (21:1–22:5). Although the historic city was literally on many waters (Jr 51:13), John's meaning is made clear in v. 15. **Many waters** stands for people groups from around the world that are influenced or dominated by the city. Exactly what the **harlot** represents in this chapter is debated. Many interpret the symbol as a reference to idolatry in the form of false religion (Hs 2:5-8; Jr 3:8-9). For them, the harlot represents a worldwide religious system that will hold sway over the beast for a period of time. They also see major distinctions between chaps. 17 (religious Babylon) and 18 (commercial Babylon). Others believe that the **harlot** consistently represents commercial idolatry in both chapters. Structural features favor such an understanding. In both, the city is named (17:5; 18:2), indicted (17:6; 18:3), linked with godless kings (17:12; 18:9), and sentenced to doom (17:14-16; 18:8-9). Since the term **harlot** can also be used figuratively of commercial idolatry (Is 23:7-8, 17), and chap. 18 clearly describes commercial enterprise, it stands to reason that the symbol represents a commercial entity in chap. 17 as well (see Thomas R. Edgar, "Babylon: Ecclesiastical, Political, or What?" *JETS* 25:3 [September 1982] 333–341). If this view is correct, the idolatry of Babylon is commercial and not that of a strictly religious nature. There is an idolatrous spirituality of bold independence from God associated with it, but not in the sense of organized religion.

17:3-4. John saw the harlot sitting on a **beast** that had **seven heads** (v. 3; see 13:1-10), whose **scarlet** color stood for sin (Is 1:18). She was in the Babylonian wilderness (Is 21:1), filthy rich and besotted with immorality. The figure of the woman on the scarlet beast suggests the strong influence of Babylon. Although the beast will have military and economic power (13:1-7, 16-17) the harlot city will still possess significant economic leverage for a time. The meaning of the **seven heads** and **ten horns** is uncertain. One suggestion is that the heads stand for six successive Gentile empires (Egypt, Assyria, Babylon, Medo-Persia, Greece, Rome), with the seventh being the **ten horns** that constitute a final, yet unknown, cooperative of rulers taking their cues from the restored city.

17:5-6. The word **mystery** describes the city. It is not "mysterious," suggesting a symbolic interpretation, but rather is something that was not known previously. **MOTHER OF HARLOTS** indicates that restored Babylon would be the worst of all unfaithful cities in history, and the spiritual progenitor of others. She would be a wanton murderer of faithful believers who refused to participate in her deeds.

17:7-8. The beast would successfully deceive the nations into believing his feigned resurrection from the dead (13:3, 14) but his doom would come swiftly. **Is not** means that he was defeated in the plan of God, though he would be allowed to act freely for a time. The phrase **was, and is not** is also a parody of the One "who is and who was and who is to come" (1:8), indicating the intention of the antichrist to project himself as one who is divine.

17:9-10. These verses are critical to the theory that the harlot is some form of the Roman Empire, either past or revived. It posits that the **seven mountains** are those outside of the city of Rome, and the **kings** refer to seven successive Roman emperors. Roman coins, literature, and official documents from the time period do refer to such hills. But since the hills in the vision belong to the beast and not the woman, and the hills are both geographical and political, this interpretation breaks down. Others suggest that the hills are references to the Rome of John's day, but that the city represents only one of seven successive empires. The stronger explanation is that the seven hills stand for the Gentile leaders of seven successive kingdoms (see vv. 3-4). John uses the word "king" in Revelation to speak of a king representatively for his kingdom. This appears to be the case in Rv 16:12, 14, where the "kings from the east" gather for war, which suggests that more than just a handful of royals is in view. In Rv 18:3, the kings who have been involved in the spiritual immorality with the harlot are paralleled with the nations who have done the same. This suggests that "king" in some cases in Revelation is used by metonymy for their empires, supporting the interpretation that sees the **seven kings** in 17:10 as seven successive world empires. In addition, the phrase **they are seven kings** (v. 10) is not likely to refer to the emperors of Rome, for there were 11 of them from Augustus to Domitian, not ten (even Galba, AD 68, Otho, AD 69, and Vitellius, AD 69, were accorded full emperor status). The first five empires had already fallen. **One is** refers to the Roman Empire of John's readers. **When he comes** (v. 10) refers to the advent of the future beast.

17:11-13. The beast would be like the other world rulers, similar to them in his character and influence. Thus he has continuity with the previous seven empires and their leaders (he is **one of the seven**, v. 11) before his supposed death (see the comments on 13:3). He would also be the head of the **eighth** empire, after his feigned resurrection. The **ten kings** would be contemporaneous rulers appointed by the beast who would use their influence to promote his agenda.

17:14-18. The beast and the ten kings would wage an ultimately unsuccessful war against the Lamb and His faithful followers (v. 14; 16:14-16; 19:19-21). Toward the end of the tribulation they would violently break with Babylon, shaking off its influence and destroying its authority. Their **common purpose** (v. 17) would be carried out according to the decree of God (Ps 75:6-7). He would use their selfish intent to execute judgment against idolatry. Verse 18 emphasizes this turning of the tables. This lesson was no doubt a comfort to the early church. God, who is always in ultimate control, would destroy the harlot whose idolatrous mind-set was shared by their persecutors. Believers should take heart that God causes even human evil to be used for His glory (Gn 50:20).

2. The Destruction Mourned (18:1-24)

18:1-3. The **glory** (v. 1) emanating from God's avenging angel contrasts with the fate of the once vibrant city. **Fallen, fallen** (v. 2) points to the fulfillment of the ruination anticipated earlier (14:8). **Demons** and detestably **unclean . . . birds** would make a home there. To describe the dwelling of the birds as a **prison** does not make sense here. It is better to see it as their "haunt," or "watch." They hovered over it. Verse 3 explains why. The city had engaged in so much covetous and idolatrous behavior, that no semblance of decency remained. Evil had taken over completely.

18:4-8. These verses contain clear allusions to ancient Babylon. The voice that spoke called to mind words formerly used to exhort Israelites to remain pure after their exile there was completed (Is 52:11). They had been expected to leave the moral filth of that country far behind. Such would also be expected of future believers in and around the harlot city. They were to separate themselves from its values and activities as well. The city of John's vision was then likened to ancient Shinar, whose inhabitants had pridefully constructed a ziggurat. Brick after brick had been laid in wholesale rebellion against God (Gn 11:4-5). As in the ancient account, God would also come down to judge the city that John saw. **I SIT AS A QUEEN** (v. 7; cf. Is 47:7-9) are the words that the angel tauntingly put in her mouth. Her doom was certain, as God would mix double strength in His cup the retribution due her. **One day** (v. 8) describes the suddenness with which the city and its system would come crashing down. God will judge the boastful pride of life (1Jn 2:16), and His people are to avoid it at all cost.

18:9-10. Specific stakeholders would suffer loss. The first group consisted of **kings** (v. 9). Perhaps they will gain political influence in association with the harlot. These rulers are not the same as the ten horns who had attacked her (17:10), and will no doubt exercise less political leverage. Their remorse was shown through the phrases **woe, woe**, **one hour**, and they stood **at a distance** (vv. 10, cf. 15-16, 17, 19). These are recurrent structural markers that distinguish the kings (vv. 9-10) from the land merchants (vv. 11-17a) and sea merchants (vv. 17b-19) who follow. None of them would be able to handle emotionally what they saw.

18:11-17a. John saw land merchants who were shaken by their loss of customers. **Cargoes** (vv. 11, 12) usually describes products carried on the sea and is a good word choice here. The merchants were middlemen who sold a vast array of goods from around the world: expensive gems, materials for the finest clothing, furniture made of exquisite marble and wood, coveted spices, expensive food stuffs, animals, and chariots. The final terms, **slaves** and **human lives** (v. 13), describe the same entity, human beings in bondage, to be sold in the marketplace. In the ancient world, slaves were regarded as animals or implements. Some staffed the large households of the rich, while others filled their brothels and provided fodder for the beasts at the amphitheater (Henry B. Swete, *The Apocalypse of St. John* [Grand Rapids, MI: Eerdmans, n.d.], 234). These merchants had exercised no conscience whatever. Anything had been permissible for a profit. Their cry of distress (v. 16) was a bit different from that of the kings (v. 10), emphasizing not loss of power, but loss of sales. Many first-century Christians were among the slave population and would have taken great comfort in the ultimate ruin of all such despicable people. Babylon represents the corruption of human trafficking and idolatrous materialism—both of which will be judged.

18:17b-19. The sea merchants were universally devastated. Their response was different only in emphasizing their losses on the water.

18:20. This verse is a parenthetical encouragement to the original audience (see 16:15). They were called to wholesale celebration over the demise of the harlot. No sympathy whatever was extended. The judgment would be not only for God Himself, but for the satisfaction of His suffering saints as well (cf. 6:9-11; 8:3-5; 16:7).

18:21-24. A **millstone** (v. 21) was a part of the ancient mechanism used for grinding grain, and could weigh thousands of pounds. These allude to Jeremiah's prophecy, which is fulfilled in this chapter (Jr 51:63-64). The stone would crush the city and everything associated with it. Family relationships, business, and the enjoyment of the arts would all cease (Rv 18:22). The merchants were conceited in their success and taken in by the harlot's **sorcery** (v. 23). This term may mean that she had bewitched or seduced them. She had also spilled the blood of the saints. First-century AD believers could certainly relate to the circumstances in future Babylon. They were immersed in a Roman culture characterized by riches and saturated with false gods. They would have been greatly satisfied to know that perpetrators of such idolatry would ultimately meet their demise.

H. The Second Coming of Christ (19:1-21)

1. The Celebrations of God's Servants (19:1-10)

Chapter 19 begins the description of the return of Christ. The first 10 verses refer to the celebrations taking place just prior to Christ's return, and vv. 11-21 describe the details of the Messiah's second advent in power.

19:1-5. After these things (v. 1) marks a return to time sequence in the vision and points to the celebrations that will take place after the destruction of Babylon and preceding the return of Christ. There are two celebrations—one for the destruction of Babylon (19:1-5) and one for the marriage supper of the Lamb (19:6-10) The fourfold use of **hallelujah (**vv. 1, 3, 4, 6) punctuates human and angelic celebration over the demise of the harlot. The word means "Praise Yah" (the contracted form of Yahweh, a name of God associated with His promise-keeping). He would be faithful to avenge cruelty toward His people (Dt 32:43). The Lord was praised for His attributes of grace, power, and glory.

19:6-10. The celebration would reach its apex as the **Lamb** prepared to take a pure bride in marriage (vv. 6-7). The Lamb was the focus of attention, but the bride was radiant in her beautiful dress. Its **fine** white **linen**, often used as a symbol for spiritual cleansing (Zch 3:1-5), stands for the faithful works of believers (v. 8). Although it is possible that the white garments represent imputed righteousness, they are more likely related to works flowing out of such righteousness. The bride **has made herself ready** for this day (v. 7). The exact identity of the bride, as well as the time and location of this event, is debated. It may be best to see the bride as the Church, with celebration initiated in heaven, but extending through the millennium on earth. Raptured believers will be joined later by converts from the tribulation and the millennial period. Believers should look forward with great anticipation to this celebration, and should be full of good works befitting their faith (Eph 2:8-10; Ti 2:11-14).

2. The Return of Christ (19:11-21)

The second coming is an essential Christian doctrine and the subject of extensive revelation (e.g., Ps 2:1-12; Is 34:1-9; Dn 7:13-14; Zch 14:1-8; Mt 25:31-46; 1Th 5:1-11).

19:11-12. John saw Jesus Christ seated on a **white horse** (v. 11) indicative of coming judgment. He wore a ruler's crown and had eyes ablaze with purity. There is no ground for certainty regarding His **name** that is written (v. 12).

19:13-16. While it is possible to understand Christ's bloody garments as looking back at His crucifixion, the context does not support the view. Instead, the stained garments look ahead to the bloodying of His clothes in the slaughter of these enemies (v. 13; cf. Is 63:1-6). His name, **The Word of God**, indicates that He is the ultimate revealer of God's will (Jn 1:1, 14). The army that accompanies Him is probably His redeemed. The **called and chosen and faithful** (17:14) are with the Lamb when He wages war. They have clothes similar to His bride (cf. 19:8 and 14), and they are mounted on **white horses** like their Leader (19:14), suggesting that they are not angelic beings. These are raptured believers who were raptured prior to the tribulation, who subsequently return with Him to earth. The **sword** in His mouth (v. 15) symbolizes the spoken word by which He defeats His enemies. His fierce wrath would be expressed in fulfillment of Ps 2, and He would be proclaimed king of all. His title, **KING OF KINGS, AND LORD OF LORDS**, is placed on His thigh, where the sword was usually strapped (Ps 45:3). Mention of His **thigh** may be literal and intended to accentuate His great strength, as the quadriceps are one of the most powerful muscles in the body. But it is perhaps more likely that it appeared on the part of the garment that covered the thigh, thus making it highly visible. No Roman emperor or world dictator would be able to stand against Him. Believers in the early church were no doubt gratified when they heard these words read.

19:17-18. The **supper of God** (v. 17) forms a grotesque contrast with that of the supper of the Lamb (v. 9). **Birds** were summoned as a cleanup crew in anticipation of human carnage. Rebels from all walks of life would be judged (v. 18).

19:19-21. These verses summarize the campaign of Armageddon and its results (16:16). The vision pictured the beast and his allies, numbering ten (cf. 17:12-14), waiting to battle the descending King of Kings. Note that while they planned the battle of Armageddon, it will never actually transpire because Jesus' second coming interrupts it. Their resistance will be to no avail. The beast and the false prophet will be thrown into the lake of fire (see 14:6-20). Their allies will be slaughtered next, and sent to their eternal doom as well (14:9-11). The terseness of the account may be intended to convey the effortlessness of the Messiah's victory.

I. The Millennium (20:1-15)

The nature of the millennium is widely debated. Premillennialists believe that there will be a literal 1,000-year rule of Christ on the earth, *following* His second coming. Amillennialists believe that the millennium is figurative of the spiritual reign of Christ through the Church *leading up to* His second coming. Three claims amillennialists use in support of their position are: (1) The number 1,000 is used symbolically in the OT to signify completion (1Ch 16:15; Ps 50:10; 84:10). (2) The period of 1,000 years is mentioned only here in the entire NT.

(3) Chapter 20 does not follow 19 sequentially, but is a recapitulation of it. Premillennialists reply that: (1) These symbolic uses do not preclude literal interpretation elsewhere. (2) There are numerous passages in the OT that point to a future, literal kingdom on earth (e.g., Ps 2:1-12; 72:8-11; Is 2:1-4; 9:6-7; 11:1-9; 35:1-10; Jr 23:5-6; Mc 4:1-8; Zch 14:9-11), so the mention of its specific length only at the end of Revelation demonstrates progressive revelation. (3) There are numerous structural clues in Rv 19–20 that suggest sequential progression. The imprisonment of Satan, and the millennial reign of Christ, for instance, both occur logically after the return of Christ to subject His enemies (cf. Blaising, *Three Views*, 212–227). The best interpretation of the data leads to the conclusion that there will be a literal kingdom on the earth, following the second coming and preceding the eternal state. Its length is mentioned six times in this chapter (vv. 2, 3, 4, 5, 6, 7).

20:1-3. The **abyss** is a place of confinement for certain demons prior to their eternal torment in the lake of fire. Satan would be **bound** there for **a thousand years** to keep him from deceiving the nations during the reign of Christ. The amillennialist claim that Satan is bound during a present, spiritual millennium is strained (Lk 8:12; 1Pt 5:8). The reference to the **serpent of old** is reminiscent of the ruin that he brought to Eden (Gn 3:1-19).

20:4-6. Verses 4a-b refer to Church saints resurrected at the rapture, who rule and reign with Jesus (**thrones . . . they sat on them**; cf. 3:21). After this, John saw the resurrection of another group, the tribulation saints, those who **had been beheaded** (martyred) during the tribulation for resisting idolatry. **They came to life** means that their bodies had now been joined, through resurrection, to their souls that were already in heaven (Php 1:21). They also **reigned with Christ**. This calls attention to the believer's co-regency with Christ during the kingdom. The phrase **this is the first resurrection** (v. 5b) summarizes the experience of all believers, including those martyred in the tribulation (cf. v. 4). The first part of v. 5 is parenthetical, anticipating the resurrection of the wicked dead in v. 12 (the second resurrection). The believers spoken of here had overcome by not giving in to the demands of the harlot. The meaning of their service to God as **priests** (v. 6) is that they would minister before Him for the rest of eternity, commencing with the millennium. They would be free from fear of the **second death** (v. 12). First-century believers, under pressure to engage in emperor worship, must have been encouraged. If they had to give their lives for Christ, their reward awaited them. Believers of every generation can take courage as well. Whatever cost Christ calls His people to bear will be worth it in eternity.

20:7-10. Near the end of the millennium, God will release Satan to lead some of the inhabitants of earth in one final rebellion. The term **Gog and Magog** (v. 8) is symbolic for the nations from around the world that will gather, one last time, against the saints and Jerusalem. It is probably used here to remind readers of the terrible slaughter of God's enemies in Ezk 38–39 (see the comments on those chapters), but the details vary too much to be the same event. There will be no need, in the millennial kingdom, for Christ to come to be known by Gentiles (Ezk 38:23) or Israel (Ezk 39:7) after reigning for close to 1,000 years. Nor does it make sense for there to be a seven-year cleanup on the threshold of eternity (Ezk 39:7). Here, as with the earlier militants, God will destroy these last rebels with fire. Not even experiencing the wonderful leadership of Christ and the ideal environment of the millennium will convince these insurgents to obey. After this, **the devil** (v. 10) will be cast into the **lake of fire** to join the **beast** and the **false prophet**. The worst enemies of God's people in the history of the world will be tormented forever and ever. God's faithful will overcome! The early Christians could look forward to reigning in a kingdom many times greater than that of their Roman persecutors.

Concerning the time of the rapture, posttribulationists maintain that all people saved during the tribulation will be raptured at the end of the great tribulation at the second coming of Christ. If unbelievers are subsequently judged following the second coming, who will be left in natural bodies to populate the millennial kingdom? Posttribulationists maintain that God will lift the hardening of Israel immediately following the rapture of tribulation believers, that Jesus will preach the gospel to the Jewish people while He is coming in the air, and they will trust Him, escape the judgment against the unbelieving world, and be alive in natural bodies to populate the kingdom (so says Robert Gundry, *The Church and the Tribulation* [Grand Rapids, MI: Zondervan, 1973], 82–83, 136, 169). The problem is that this does not fit the eschatological time table, which indicates that Israel is saved *before* the second coming, serving as a prerequisite for it (cf. the comments on Mt 23:37-39; Ac 3:19-21; Rm 11:25-27), nor does it adequately account for the presence of Gentile nations in the millennial kingdom. These factors make the posttribulational understanding of Israel's salvation problematic. Israel will embrace Jesus as Messiah and Deliverer near the end tribulation period but prior to the second coming. Pretribulationists, on the other hand, posit that a vast number of Jewish people and Gentiles will be saved during the tribulation. Many of these will be alive in their natural bodies when Christ returns to earth, and they will be spared the judgment the rest of the Christ-rejecting world experiences at that time. They will enter and populate the millennial kingdom in their natural bodies, and unfortunately they will even produce some rebellious offspring (20:7-10).

20:11-15. John saw a figure from whom **earth and heaven fled away** (v. 11). This hyperbole communicates abject terror. The one from whom men will desperately wish to escape is Christ (Jn 5:22-23). The **great white throne** upon which He sat is one from which sentences of eternal separation from God will be issued. Every person ever born who sinned and had not trusted in God's revelation to them was there. Whereas their spirits will go to hell immediately upon death, they will on this day stand before their Creator in resurrected bodies. He will judge them by His infinitely perfect knowledge **according to their deeds** (v. 12; cf. also Rm 2:6-11, 15-16). This should not be understood as teaching salvation by works. Rather, it means that one's deeds indicate one's spiritual state (1Jn 3:7-10). This **second death** (v. 14) indicates a lasting loss far beyond the extinction of life in this world. Christians should trust God to righteously address all evil done to them (Rm 12:17-21). The great white throne should not be confused with the judgment seat of Christ, where believers will have their service considered for reward (Rm 14:10-12; 1Co 3:10-16; 2Co 5:10).

J. The New Heaven and New Earth (21:1–22:5)

This section provides information not revealed in the other visions of heaven. The eternal state is pictured as a physical place. It includes land, buildings, trees, and water. Believers will interact with one another and engage in meaningful service for God. This corrects some long-held misconceptions. Heaven is not a place of passive rest, or endless, blissful contemplation of God.

21:1-2. John saw an eternal state in which a beautiful **city** was descending from **heaven** (v. 2). Some interpreters understand it to be suspended above the earth, while others say that its sturdy foundation argues for it being grounded. This is more likely. Each entity is described as **new**. The emphasis is not on time, but on freshness or better quality. This place superseded everything that had ever come before it. The city brings to mind Eden, and is set in contrast to Babylon (17:1–18:24). The absence of a **sea** indicates safety from enemies (12:18; 13:1; 17:2). It will bear the name **Jerusalem** (v. 2). Like the earthly one, it will be loved by God. Unlike its namesake, it will never rebel. It is the place that Jesus has prepared for His followers (Jn 14:2-3).

21:3-4. John's tabernacle theme (Jn 1:1, 14) reaches its apex here. God will live in intimate, uninterrupted fellowship with His people, who will be completely free of emotional pain forever. What perspective this must have been for believers in the seven churches who had multiplied sorrows due to persecution. All believers should look forward to relief from various sorrows of life.

21:5-8. It is done (v. 6) indicates the end of all things temporal. Everything related to the old heaven and earth had run its course. God would bring about new conditions. **The Alpha and the Omega** again brings to mind the eternality of the Son who gave His life for sinners (1:18; 22:13). The apostle uses the offer of water symbolically as an invitation to salvation (Jn 4:10-14; 7:37-39). God wanted him to communicate this good news to the original audience before it was too late. The one who overcomes, who perseveres in faith, will receive the privileges due beloved sons. By contrast, all unbelievers, typified by the behaviors in v. 8, will be excluded from the new Jerusalem.

21:9-11. John was carried to a high mountain rather than the harlot's wilderness (17:1). **Wife of the Lamb** (v. 9) indicates the faithful city, new Jerusalem, in contrast to the harlot (17:3). It reflected the **glory of God** (v. 11). God's glory is intrinsic divine light that emanates from His person. Her **brilliance** (lit., shining star) was like top-grade jasper.

21:12-21. The **high wall** (v. 12) signifies its unchallenged safety. The names of **the twelve tribes of . . . Israel** on the **gates** bring to mind Ezekiel's millennial temple (Ezk 48:30-35). Another parallel is drawn by the reference to the **twelve apostles**, whose names are on the **foundation stones** (v. 14). Some equate the twelve tribes with the Church, which is represented by the apostles, but it is better to see the apostles not only as the foundation stones of the Church (Eph 2:20), but also as distinct representatives of Israel and the leaders of the faithful remnant of Israel (Mt 19:28; Lk 22:30; Rm 11:1-6). It appears, therefore, that Israel and the Church maintain distinct identities throughout eternity, though together they comprise a unified people of God. Whether or not this suggests different functions for the two in heaven is not clear. Although some have envisioned the city as a pyramid, it will probably be a cube, extending **1,500 miles** in each dimension (v. 16). **Seventy-two yards** (v. 17) is more likely the thickness of its wall than its height. Apparently **angelic measurements** are similar to those used by humans. The material of the wall was "like" a costly stone, and "as" **jasper**, which has been compared to clear quartz. The material was not jasper, but similar to the earthly stone with which John was familiar. Other materials listed in the passage should be probably be understood in a similar fashion. The street was "like" gold and the gates "like" pearls, and so on. The interior buildings were as **pure gold** (v. 18). The colors of the stones covering the wall spanned the spectrum of a rainbow, from yellow and green to fiery red, purple, and blue. Each gate consisted of a **single pearl** (v. 21). The **street of gold** was so free of impurities as to be clear.

21:22-27. The most glorious feature of the city was not, however, its beautiful architecture. Far more impressive were its rulers, the **Lord God the Almighty and the Lamb** (v. 22). The glory radiating from the two would provide all necessary light. The presence of **light** (v. 24) and absence of **night** are literal here, but still reminiscent of Johannine theology of purity and sin (Jn 1:4-5; 1Jn 1:5-7; 2:8-9). The Godhead dispels all negative influence. The **nations** were Gentiles who had persevered in resisting the beast and Babylon, finding their joy in serving the Lamb in the new city. The words **nothing unclean** (v. 27) introduce another set of exclusions (21:6). Unbelievers who lived in habitual sin while on earth would have no part in the new Jerusalem. What should most excite believers about heaven is not its admittedly astounding beauty and bliss. Instead, they should look forward to being with the wonderful Father and the Lamb forever, without sin or physical distance to limit fellowship.

22:1-5. Water is sometimes used figuratively for God, who brings peace from chaos (Is 8:6; 33:21-24), but that is not likely here. More to the point is a continuing parallel with Eden (Gn 2:10-17; 3:22-24). Paradise will be regained. It may be that the river will flow under a dual throne that straddles it. The presence of a **healing** tree (v. 2) has led some to place this paragraph back in the millennium, but this would ruin the clear sequence of the text. Better is the view that it symbolizes God's work in maintaining the invulnerable state of the redeemed. Verses 3-5 reveal some of heaven's wonderful blessings: absence of death through the removal of the Edenic curse (v. 3; see Gn 3:1-24), opportunity to **serve** God, and the privilege of ruling as had been intended originally (v. 5; see Gn 1:28). Believers in the new Jerusalem would be servant-kings, ever praising and serving God, yet reigning themselves for eternity.

K. The Concluding Message (22:6-21)

22:6-9. The referent of the words in v. 6 is not immediately clear. It could be that the phrase **these words are faithful and true** are spoken by the angel and what follows by John. Or the whole verse could be spoken by the angel. The former is more likely based on its parallel with 1:1. The words translated **soon** (v. 6) and **quickly** (v. 7) suggest imminence. The rapture of the Church would come suddenly and without preceding signs. Those who heeded **the prophecy of this book** (vv. 7, 10) would receive one of the seven blessings offered in the book (1:3; 14:13; 16:15; 19:9; 20:6; 22:7; 22:14). The angel rebuked the apostle's inappropriate worship, identifying himself as a **fellow servant** (v. 9), and recognizing John's own prophetic function (19:10). Believers should go beyond being curious about this book and obey its teachings. They should also reserve awe for God alone.

22:10-12. John was to share what he had seen with others so that they could heed God's commandments (v. 10). There was no time to waste. When Jesus returns, eternal destinies will be finalized. The words of v. 11 are ironic. Of course, it is always best for sinful people to repent. But if not, the verse implies, so be it. **Reward** (v. 12) of one kind or another will be given at that time (see 20:11-15).

22:13-15. The Son of God's final reference to His eternality introduced another encouragement to persevere. **Those who wash their**

robes (v. 14) refers to first-century believers who would demonstrate saving faith by resisting the idolatry around them. They would experience the blessings of the tree of life (22:2) in the new Jerusalem. John again mentions those excluded from eternal life (21:8, 27). **Dogs** (v. 15) denotes those who refuse to repent and turn to Christ in faith. **Sorcerers** and liars are also targets of John elsewhere (1Jn 2:22-23; 5:21). They would miss the pleasures of the city from above.

22:16-17. The book nears its conclusion with various directives. The first sentence of v. 17 indicates the longing of the Holy Spirit and the Church as a whole for the return of Christ. The second invites agreement from the seven churches. The verse's final two sentences offer salvation to anyone in the seven churches who may not yet have trusted in Christ when it was read. Jesus identifies Himself as the source of the message that the angels had mediated. Reference to Him as **the root and the descendant of David** (v. 16; see Is 11:2) marks Him both as an Israelite and the successor to His forefather's throne. **Bright morning star** identifies Jesus as the One who would introduce the new day, that is the rule of Messiah. Verse 17 echoes the messianic thrust of Is 55:1-7. In both, the recipients are invited to drink freely of life-giving water and be in a lasting relationship with God through a connection with David. The openness of the invitation is emphasized by the threefold use of **come**. It was issued by the **Spirit** and the **bride**, that is, the Holy Spirit and the Church. There was to be no hesitation. All who wished to accept the offer were welcome. No payment would be required. Jesus offered everyone hearing the message of the book an opportunity to make sure of his salvation. Perhaps some among the seven churches were not yet believers. What motivation these verses provide for modern followers of Christ! They should look forward to the return of Christ and hold forth the gospel to whoever will listen. Salvation is a free gift of God's grace. The wrath of God is coming against all who rebel against Him. Those who drink of the water of life will reign with masses of the redeemed in the millennial kingdom and, finally, in all eternity (5:8-9; 22:5).

22:18-19. John warned the recipients of the book not to add to what God had said. While such a warning could well pertain to Scripture as a whole, here it refers more narrowly to the book of Revelation. Some scholars take this to mean that the text of the book itself should not be tampered with in any fashion. Others see a somewhat different warning. If the present text is parallel to Dt 4:2 and 29:19-21, then the prohibition is against false prophecy that contradicted what John has said (Beale, *Revelation*, 1150–1151). This makes good sense in the context of the seven churches that were assaulted with idolatrous religious thought. Two severe penalties were attached to disobedience in this matter. First, the very **plagues** of the book itself would be sent against any violator (v. 18). False prophets would not be delivered from the great tribulation, but would instead be left to experience its full fury. Second, such persons would miss the blessings of salvation associated with the **tree of life** (v. 19; see 22:2). Each of the major so-called Christian cults has abused the text of the Bible, twisting its meaning to support their false doctrines. Their founders have also written works that their followers consider to be on par with Scripture. These false prophets and their disciples will experience eternal damnation. Believers should not associate with them in any way.

22:20-21. The letter ends on a positive note. The One whom the seven churches longed for would come and vindicate them (v. 20). The **amen** (v. 21) is a hearty invitation from John. Believers wait for the coming of Jesus, who will put an end to all of their troubles and bring them to their eternal home. The final words are a characteristic Christian benediction expressing the hope that the churches would continue to experience the favor of Jesus Christ in their lives until His blessed return.

BIBLIOGRAPHY

Alcorn, Randy. *Heaven*. Wheaton: Tyndale, 2004.

Archer, Gleason L., Paul D. Feinberg, Douglas J. Moo, and Richard R. Reiter. *Three Views on the Rapture: Pre-, Mid-, or Post-Tribulational?* rev. ed. Grand Rapids, MI: Zondervan, 1996.

Beale, Gregory. *The Book of Revelation*. Grand Rapids, MI: Eerdmans, 1999.

Blaising, Craig A., Kenneth L. Gentry Jr., and Robert B. Strimple. *Three Views of the Millennium and Beyond*. Grand Rapids, MI: Zondervan, 1999.

Constable, Thomas. *Notes on Revelation*. 2008 edition. www.soniclight.com/constable/notes.htm.

Dyer, Charles. "The Identity of Babylon in Revelation 17–18." 2 parts. *Bibliotheca Sacra* 144 (July–September 1987): 305–316; (October–December 1987): 433–449.

Edgar, Thomas R. "Babylon: Ecclesiastical, Political, or What?" *Journal of the Evangelical Theological Society* 25:3 (September 1982): 333–341.

Johnson, Alan. "Revelation." In vol. 7 of The Expositor's Bible Commentary. Edited by Frank E. Gaebelein, et al. 399–603. Grand Rapids, MI: Zondervan, 1981.

MacArthur, John. *Revelation*. 2 vols. MacArthur New Testament Commentary. Chicago: Moody, 2000.

Michaels, J. Ramsey. *Revelation*. Downers Grove, IL: Tyndale, 1999.

Pate, C. Marvin, Kenneth L. Gentry, Sam Hamstra Jr., and Robert L. Thomas. *Four Views on the Book of Revelation*. Grand Rapids, MI: Zondervan, 1998.

Seiss, Joseph A. *The Apocalypse*. Grand Rapids, MI: Zondervan, 1957.

Swete, Henry B. *The Apocalypse of St. John*. Grand Rapids, MI: Eerdmans, n.d.

Thomas, Robert. *Revelation 1–7: An Exegetical Commentary*. Chicago: Moody, 1992.

———. *Revelation 8–22: An Exegetical Commentary*. Chicago: Moody, 1995.

Walvoord, John. *The Revelation of Jesus Christ*. Chicago: Moody, 1966.

Wilson, Mark. *Charts on the Book of Revelation: Literary, Historical and Theological Perspectives*. Grand Rapids, MI: Kregel, 2007.

● ● ● ●

SCRIPTURE INDEX

GENESIS

EXODUS

LEVITICUS

NUMBERS

DEUTERONOMY

JOSHUA

JUDGES

2 SAMUEL

1 KINGS

2 KINGS

1 CHRONICLES

2 CHRONICLES

EZRA

NEHEMIAH

ESTHER

JOB

PSALMS

PROVERBS

ECCLESIASTES

SONG OF SOLOMON

ISAIAH

JEREMIAH

LAMENTATIONS

EZEKIEL

DANIEL

HOSEA

AMOS

OBADIAH

JONAH

MICAH

NAHUM

HABAKKUK

ZEPHANIAH

HAGGAI

ZECHARIAH

MALACHI

MATTHEW

MARK

LUKE

JOHN

ACTS

ROMANS

2 CORINTHIANS

GALATIANS

EPHESIANS

PHILIPPIANS

COLOSSIANS

1 THESSALONIANS

2 THESSALONIANS

1 TIMOTHY

2 TIMOTHY

TITUS

PHILEMON

HEBREWS

JAMES

1 PETER

2 PETER

1 JOHN

2 JOHN

JUDE

REVELATION

SUBJECT INDEX

A *c* after a page number indicates a chart, an *s* a sketch, and an *m* a map.

A

B

C

D

E

F

G

H

I

J

K

L

M

N

O

P

Q

R

S

U

V

W

Y

Z

INDEX
OF MAPS, CHARTS & SKETCHES

MAPS

CHARTS

SKETCHES